THE COMPENDIUM OF AMERICAN GENEALOGY

The Standard Genealogical Encyclopedia of

THE FIRST FAMILIES OF AMERICA

THE COMPENDIUM OF AMERICAN GENEALOGY

The Standard Genealogical Encyclopedia of
THE FIRST FAMILIES OF AMERICA

EDITED BY
FREDERICK ADAMS VIRKUS, F. I. A. G.

Executive Director, The Institute of American Genealogy; Editor-in-chief, The Magazine of American Genealogy, and the Lineage Record Book. Member The British Record Society (London), Deutscher Roland, Verein für deutschvolkische Sippenkunde (Berlin), Zentralstelle für Deutsche Personen und Familiengeschichte (Leipzig), Oesterreichische Gesellschaft Adler für Familien und Wappen Kunde (Vienna), Het Genealogisch-Heraldisch Genootschap "de Nederlandsche Leeuw" (The Hague), Schweizer Archiv für Heraldik (Lausanne), Istituto Araldico Romano (Rome), Genealogiska Samfundet I Finland (Helsingfors), Dansk Genealogisk Institut (Copenhagen), Real Sociedad Hispano-Americana de Genealogia y Heraldica (Mexico City), American Eugenics Society, numerous American Genealogical and Historical societies.

VOLUME IV
1930

Baltimore
GENEALOGICAL PUBLISHING COMPANY
1968

Originally Published
Chicago, 1930

Reprinted
Genealogical Publishing Company
Baltimore, 1968

Library of Congress Catalog Card Number 68-27449

PREFACE

The publication of this volume of THE COMPENDIUM OF AMERICAN GENEALOGY marks the fourth milestone toward the completion of the Genealogical History of the American Nation in this Standard Genealogical Encyclopedia of The First Families of America.

A work of such large proportions will require many volumes of the size of this one, and will probably cover the span of two generations, but the progress achieved within the comparatively short period since the World War, out of which this work originated as a war measure, already gives it the distinction of having compiled and published a larger number of lineages than all the other general genealogical compilations combined during the first three hundred years of American history.

With more than 8,000 lineages in this volume added to the number published in Volumes I, II and III, a total of more than 29,000 lineages, and with the combined indexes listing upward of a quarter of a million names of ancestors, it is unquestionably the first reference and research source in American genealogy.

To those familiar with the earlier volumes the gradual change in the treatment of the subject matter from the rigid abridgment in the first volume to fuller and fuller data in each succeeding volume, will be apparent. While the broad scope and the reference character of the work place an arbitrary limitation upon the nature and volume of the data comprising each record and lineage, which limitation must be observed, nevertheless the change has become so marked in the present volume that the work is no longer the abridgment originally planned. Therefore, the strictly qualifying term "Abridged" has been eliminated from its title, and this volume is issued under its more nearly correct title, THE COMPENDIUM OF AMERICAN GENEALOGY.

For the benefit of those not familiar with the history of this work it may be stated that it had its inception in 1917 as a war measure. Participation in the World War by the United States made necessary a source of information for furnishing the lineages, with their inter-marriages, of large numbers of men and women who were engaged, or desired to participate, in the various war activities. The necessity for such information demonstrated the real need for an authoritative genealogical work of national character, one which could be accepted as the standard for the nation. Thus, this work was born of necessity to meet a crisis, and the names, files and voluminous data compiled during the war are the foundation upon which it is based.

The honor, and it is an honor, of formulating so great a national project, was assumed by the editors of this work, although the honor of formulating the project is overshadowed by the conviction that a national service is being rendered, and it is in this spirit that the work is being carried out.

A conception of the monumental task involved in this compilation may be had when it is realized that it required nearly seven years (1917-24) of most painstaking labor to complete Volume I, published in December, 1924. It contains over 5,000 records and upward of 10,000 lineages, comprising 1,148 pages.

Volume II, published in December, 1926, contains over 1,600 records and upward of 5,000 lineages, comprising 628 pages. In this volume effort was directed toward completeness of lineages rather than toward including a larger number of records, with the result that, in Volume I the records average 2 lineages, whereas in Volume II the records average about 3½ lineages.

Volume III, published in December, 1928, contains over 2,000 records and upward of 6,000 lineages, comprising 810 pages.

Volume IV, published in December, 1930, contains over 2,000 records and upward of 8,000 lineages, comprising 912 pages.

Additional volumes, each complete and independent in itself, will be issued annually. Suggestions of names, and data pertaining to them, will be thankfully received and accorded every consideration for inclusion in this work. However, the editors reserve the right to accept for publication or reject any data submitted to them at their discretion. The records in this work are included with only one view, to increase the usefulness of the work; no space has been paid for, nor can it be.

ACKNOWLEDGMENTS

Sincere thanks are due to the many persons who have kindly loaned books and manuscripts which have assisted greatly in the production of this work, and also to many who have offered suggestions that materially aided in the solution of knotty problems. Especially are thanks due to officers and members of the hereditary-patriotic, genealogical and historical societies. Their hearty co-operation has been a constant source of encouragement, so that it may truly be said that courtesies received from them have contributed in a larger degree toward the completion of this volume than any other extraneous source.

CONTENTS

INDEX TO ILLUSTRATIONS

ARMORIAL BEARINGS:

(See also Vols. 2 and 3)

HOMESTEADS:

(See also Vols. 2 and 3)

PORTRAITS:

MISCELLANEOUS:

EXPLANATION AND ANALYSIS OF RECORDS

While every person acquainted with genealogical usages and terms will readily understand the lineage records as they appear in this volume, an explanation is here given for the information of those not familiar with the subject.

Since no standardized system for recording American genealogies had been formulated at the time this work was projected it was found necessary to develop a style to conform to American genealogical usages and at the same time be clearly understandable by the lay researcher. It is gratifying to find that the system adopted for this work has met with general approval for its simplicity of style and clarity of presentation.

In numbering the generations in America it was found necessary to represent the subject of the record as number 1, and his parents as number 2, since under this system the lineages of both father and mother, not often equal in the number of generations, always conjoin in their common number 2. Thus, the subject is represented as number 1; his parents are always numbered 2; his grandparents in both lines of descent are always numbered 3; his great grandparents in both lines of descent are always numbered 4; and so on, to the earliest known ancestor in America, who is given the highest number, which shows the number of generations in America in each line of descent.

Confusion was also avoided under this method of numbering by eliminating the designation "10th from," or "5th from," as the case may be; the numbers, as given in the records, show clearly the number of generations in America and that the subject is a descendant OF the ancestors named; of course, he is also descended FROM the ancestors, but in a generation one number lower than that given the ancestors in the record.

Records are divided into sections or paragraphs, each one ending with a period, as follows: Name of the subject with place and date of birth. Paternal lineage of the father's surname (the main stem, or trunk line), from the earliest known ancestor in America down to the father (numbered 2). Collateral paternal lineage (if any), from the earliest known ancestor in America down to the generation in which it connects by intermarriage with the main stem. Maternal lineage of the mother's surname (the main stem, or trunk line), followed by collateral maternal lineage similar to the paternal. The names of the parents of the subject conjoined in their common number 2, followed by the names of their children numbered consecutively in the order of birth, and to whom married. Data of marriage of the subject (numbered 1), the children of this marriage, also numbered consecutively in the order of birth, with data of education, military service and marriage. Biography of the subject (numbered 1), ending with the present residence address.

It will be noted that the surname of the earliest ancestor, in each lineage, appears in **Bold Face** type; this is to emphasize that the following generations, whose Christian names only are given, are all of the same surname as the name in the **Bold Face** type unless, or until, the surname is changed by the marriage of a daughter, in which case her husband's name appears also in **Bold Face** type to emphasize the change in surname. In some records it will be noted that the surname changes frequently and every change is emphasized by **Bold Face** type.

Where the cross-reference (qv) appears after the name of an immigrant ancestor it is intended to refer the reader to the list of Immigrant Ancestors on pages 727-777 of this volume, where data pertaining to him will be found. This method was adopted in order to avoid frequent repetition of the identical data, and it permits the compilation of a comprehensive list of immigrant ancestors to all the colonies which, in itself, is a valuable genealogical and biographical contribution.

The double dates which will be found throughout the work in the earlier generations in the records are made necessary by the change from the Old Style to the New Style of reckoning of the beginning of the year. In 1563, France adopted January 1st as the beginning of the year. Scotland adopted January 1st in 1600, but it was not until 1752 that England adopted the same date. Before 1752 (when the year began March 25th), in the records of the colonies that followed the English custom, dates between January 1st and March 24th, inclusive, were often indicated by two consecutive years (1700/01), to be interpreted at the option of the reader, as conforming to the New, or to the Old Style. For example: February 22, 1700/01, meant February 22, 1700, if the year was considered in the Old Style, ending March 24; if considered in the New Style, ending December 31, it would be 1701. The last year of a double date corresponds to our present system of reckoning.

Hyphenated double dates, as 1700-01, indicate that the exact time of the event to which these years refer is not definitely known, but that it did occur during either of the years. When a period of years is hyphenated, as 1700-05, it indicates that the event referred to occurred between those years.

The latest volume of this series should always be consulted first because it contains corrections and amendments of lineages in the earlier volumes. However, the earlier volumes contain many thousands of lineages not reprinted in this volume and should be consulted for names not found in the index to this volume.

ABBREVIATIONS

A

A.A.A.S...........American Association for the Advancement of Science.
A.-A.-G...........Assistant adjutant-general.
A.A.U.W..........American Association of University Women.
A. and H.A. Co...Ancient and Honorable Artillery Company.
A. and M..........Agricultural and Mechanical.
A.B.C.F.M.........American Board of Commissioners for Foreign Missions (Congregational).
A.B. (also **B.A.**)..Bachelor of Arts.
A.C................Army Corps.
Acad..............Academy, academic.
A.C.P.............American College of Physicians.
A.C.S.............American College of Surgeons.
Actg..............Acting.
A.-D.-C...........Aide-de-camp.
Adj................Adjutant, adjunct.
Adj.Gen...........Adjutant General.
Adv...............Advocate.
A.E.F.............American Expeditionary Forces.
A.E. and P.......Ambassador Extraordinary and Plenipotentiary.
æt................Ætatis (of the age).
A.F. and A.M.....Ancient Free and Accepted Masons.
Agr.............Agriculture.
Agrl.............Agricultural.
Agt...............Agent.
A.I.A.............American Institute of Architects.
A.L...............American Legion.
Ala...............Alabama.
A.L.A.............American Library Association.
Am................American.
A.M. (also **M.A.**).Master of Arts.
A.M.A.............American Medical Association.
Am. Soc. C.E......American Society of Civil Engineers.
Am. Soc. E.E......American Society of Electrical Engineers.
Am. Soc. M.E......American Society of Mechanical Engineers.
A.N.A.............Associate National Academician.
Ante............Before.
Anthrop..........Anthropological.
Antiq............Antiquarian.
A.N.U.............Army and Navy Union.
A.O.A.............Army Ordnance Association.
Appmt...........Appointment.
Apptd............Appointed.
Apts..............Apartments.
A.P.V.A...........Assn. for the Preservation of Virginia Antiquities.
A.-Q.-M..........Assistant quartermaster.
A.R.C.............American Red Cross.
Archæol.........Archæological.
Ariz.............Arizona.
Ark..............Arkansas.
Arty.............Artillery.
A.S...............Air Service.
A.S.S.C...........Air Service Signal Corps.
Assn.............Association.
Asso.............Associate, associated.
Asst.............Assistant.
Astron..........Astronomical.
Astrophys.......Astrophysical.
Atty.............Attorney.
Aug..............August.
Av...............Avenue.

B

b................Born.
B.A. (also **A.B**)...Bachelor of Arts.
B.Agr.............Bachelor of Agriculture.
Bap..............Baptized.
Bapt.............Baptist.
B.Arch...........Bachelor of Architecture.
Batln.,Batt.orBn...Battalion.
B.C...............British Columbia.
B.C.E.............Bachelor of Civil Engineering.
B.Chir............Bachelor of Surgery.
Bd................Board.
B.D...............Bachelor of Divinity.
B.E...............Bachelor of Education.
B.E.F.............British Expeditionary Forces.
Bet...............Between.
B.F.A............Bachelor of Fine Arts.
Bibl..............Biblical.
Bibliog...........Bibliographical.
Biog..............Biographical.
Biol...............Biological.
Bks...............Barracks.
B.L. (or **Litt.B.**)..Bachelor of Letters.
Bldg.............Building.
Blk...............Block.
B.L.S.............Bachelor of Library Science.
B.M.E.............Bachelor of Mining Engineering.
Bn...............Battalion.
B.O...............Bachelor of Oratory.
B.O.R.............Baronial Order of Runnemede.
Bot..............Botanical.
Boul.............Boulevard.
B.Pd. (or **Pd.B.**)..Bachelor of Pedagogy.
Br...............Branch.
Brig.............Brigadier, Brigade.
Brig.Gen..........Brigadier General.
Brit..............British, Britannica.
Bro..............Brother.
B.S. (also **S.B.** or **Sc.B.**).........Bachelor of Science.
B.Th..............Bachelor of Theology.
Bur..............Bureau.
Bvt..............Brevet.
Bvtd.............Brevetted.
B.W.I.............British West Indies.

C

Ca...............Circa (about).
C.A...............Central America.
C.A.C.............Coast Artillery Corps.
Calif.............California.
Can..............Canada.
Capt.............Captain.
Cav..............Cavalry.
C.D...............Colonial Dame.
C.D.A.............Colonial Dames of America.
C.D. 17th C.......Colonial Daughters of the 17th Century.
Cdr..............Commander.
C.E...............Civil Engineer.
C.E.F.............Canadian Expeditionary Forces.
Ch...............Church.
Ch.D.............Doctor of Chemistry.
Chem.............Chemical.
Chem.E...........Chemical Engineer.
Chirurg...........Chirurgical.
Chmn.............Chairman.
C.-I.-C...........Commander in Chief.
Circa.............About, approximately.
Civ..............Civil.
Climatol.........Climatological.
Clin.............Clinical.
Clk..............Clerk.
C.L.M.A...........Colonial Lords of Manors in America.
Co...............Company, county.

C.O. .... Commanding Officer.
Col .... Colonel.
Coll .... College.
Colo .... Colorado.
Com .... Committee.
Comd .... Commanded.
Comdg .... Commanding.
Comdt .... Commandant.
Commd .... Commissioned.
Commn .... Commission.
Commr .... Commissioner.
Com. Sub .... Commissary of Subsistence.
Conf .... Conference.
Confed .... Confederate.
Congl .... Congregational.
Conglist .... Congregationalist.
Conn .... Connecticut.
Cons .... Consulting.
Consol .... Consolidated.
Constl .... Constitutional.
Constn .... Constitution.
Constrn .... Construction.
Contbr .... Contributor.
Conv .... Convention.
Corpl .... Corporal.
Corpn .... Corporation.
Corr .... Correspondent, corresponding.
Cos .... Companies, counties.
C.O.T.S. .... Central Officers' Training School.
C.P.A. .... Certified Public Accountant.
C.S. .... Christian Science.
C.S.A. (or **C.S. Army**) .... Confederate States Army.
C.S.B. .... Bachelor of Christian Science.
C.S.N. (or **C.S. Navy**) .... Confederate States Navy.
Ct .... Court.
C.W.S. .... Chemical Warfare Service.
Cyclo .... Cyclopedia.

D

d .... Died.
D.A.C. .... Daughters of the American Colonists.
D.Agr. .... Doctor of Agriculture.
D.A.R. .... Daughters of the American Revolution.
Dau .... Daughter.
D.B.R. .... Daughters of the Barons of Runnemede.
D.C .... Daughters of the Cincinnati; also District of Columbia.
D.C.G .... Descendants of Colonial Governors.
D.C.L .... Doctor of Civil Law.
D.C.W .... Daughters of Colonial Wars.
D.D. .... Doctor of Divinity.
D.D.S .... Doctor of Dental Surgery.
Dec .... December.
Del .... Delaware, delegate.
Dem .... Democratic.
D.Eng. (also **Dr. Engring.**, or **E.D.**) .... Doctor of Engineering.
Dep .... Deputy.
Dept .... Department.
Desc .... Descendant.
D.F.P.A .... Daughters of Founders and Patriots of America.
D.H.D .... Daughters of Holland Dames.
Dir .... Director.
Disch .... Discharged.
Dist .... District.
Div .... Division, divinity.
D.K.E .... Delta Kappa Epsilon.
D.Litt. (also **L.H.D.**) Doctor of Literature.
D.P.H. (also **Dr.P.H.**) .... Diploma in Public Health, or Doctor of Public Health, or Doctor of Public Hygiene.
Dr .... Doctor.
D.R. .... Daughters of the Revolution.
D.Sc. (or **Sc.D.**) .. Doctor of Science.
D.S.C .... Distinguished Service Cross.
D.S.D.I. .... Descendants of the Signers of the Declaration of Independence.
D.S.M .... Distinguished Service Medal.
D.S.T .... Doctor of Sacred Theology.
D.T.M .... Doctor of Tropical Medicine.
D.V.M .... Doctor of Veterinary Medicine.
D.V.S .... Doctor of Veterinary Surgery.

E

E .... East.
Ecol .... Ecological.
Econ .... Economic.
Ed .... Educated.
E.D. (also **D.Eng.**, or **Dr.Engring.**) Doctor of Engineering.
Ed.B .... Bachelor of Education.
Ed.D .... Doctor of Education.
Edn .... Education.
Ednl .... Educational.
E.E. .... Electrical Engineer.
E.E. and M.P. ..... Envoy Extraordinary and Minister Plenipotentiary.
Elec .... Electrical.
Electrochem ..... Electrochemical.
Electrophys ...... Electrophysical.
E.M. .... Engineer of Mines.
Ency .... Encyclopædia.
Eng .... England.
Engr .... Engineer.
Engring .... Engineering.
Engr. O.R.C ...... Engineer Officers' Reserve Corps.
Engr. R.C .... Engineer Reserve Corps.
Engrs .... Engineers.
Entomol .... Entomological.
e.s .... Eldest son.
Ethnol .... Ethnological.
et seq .... Et sequentes (and those that follow).
Evang .... Evangelical.
Exec .... Executive.
Exhbn .... Exhibition.
Expdn .... Expedition.
Expn .... Exposition.
Expt .... Experiment.

F

F.A .... Field Artillery.
F.A.C.P .... Fellow American College of Physicians.
F.A.C.S .... Fellow American College of Surgeons.
F.E .... Forest Engineer.
Feb .... February.
Fed .... Federation.
F.F.V .... First Families of Virginia.
Fgn .... Foreign.
Fla .... Florida.
Frat .... Fraternity.
F.R.C.P .... Fellow Royal College of Physicians (England).
F.R.C.P.E .... Fellow Royal College of Physicians of Edinburgh.
F.R.C.S .... Fellow Royal College of Surgeons (England).
F.R.S.E .... Fellow Royal Society of Edinburgh.
Frt .... Freight.
Ft .... Fort.

G

G-1 (or other number) .... General Staff Officer No. ....
Ga .... Georgia.
G.A.R .... Grand Army of the Republic.
g.dau .... Granddaughter.
Gen .... General.
Geneal .... Genealogical.
Geod .... Geodetic.
Geog .... Geographical.
Geol .... Geological.
Ger .... Germany.
g.g.dau .... Great granddaughter.
g.g.son .... Great grandson.
G.H.Q .... General Headquarters.
Gov .... Governor.
Govt .... Government.
Grad .... Graduated, graduate.
g.son .... Grandson.
Gt .... Great.
Gynecol .... Gynecological.

H

Hdqrs...Headquarters.
H.G...Home Guard.
H.I...Hawaiian Islands.
H.Ty. (or **H.T.**)...Hawaiian Territory.
Hist...Historical, Historic.
Homœ...Homœpathic.
Hon...Honorary, honorable, honorably.
Ho. of Rep...House of Representatives.
Hort...Horticultural.
Hosp...Hospital.
H.S...Holland Society.
H.S.A...Huguenot Society of America.
H.S.S.C...Huguenot Society of South Carolina.
Hts...Heights.

I

Ia...Iowa.
I.A.G...Institute of American Genealogy.
Ibid...Same.
Ida...Idaho.
Ill...Illinois.
Inc...Incorporated, Inclusive.
Ind...Indiana.
Ind.Ty...Indian Territory.
Inf...Infantry.
Ins...Insurance.
Insp...Inspector.
Insp.Gen...Inspector General.
Inst...Institute.
Instn...Institution.
Instr...Instructor.
Instrn...Instruction.
Internat...International.

J

J.A.G...Judge Advocate General.
Jan...January.
J.D...Doctor of Jurisprudence.
J.g. (or **Jr.g.**)...Junior Grade.
Jour...Journal.
Jr...Junior.
Jud...Judicial.
J.U.D...*Juris Utriusque Doctor* Doctor of (Both Canon and Civil) Laws.

K

Kan...Kansas.
K.C...Knight of Columbus.
K.P...Knight of Pythias.
K.T...Knight Templar.
Ky...Kentucky.

L

La...Louisiana.
Lab...Laboratory.
Lang...Language.
L.A.P.W....League of American Pen Women.
Laryngol...Laryngological.
Lbr...Lumber.
L.H.D...Doctor of Literature (also D. Litt.).
L.I...Long Island.
Lit...Literary, literature.
Litt.B. (or **B.L.**)...Bachelor of Letters.
Litt.D...Doctor of Letters.
LL.B...Bachelor of Laws.
LL.D...Doctor of Laws.
LL.M. (or **M.L.**)...Master of Laws.
Lt. (or **Lieut.**)...Lieutenant.
Lt.Col...Lieutenant Colonel.
Lt.Gen...Lieutenant General.
Lt.Gov...Lieutenant Governor.
Ltd...Limited.
Luth...Lutheran.

M

m...Married.
M.A. (or **A.M.**)...Master of Arts.
Mag...Magazine.
M.Agr...Master of Agriculture.
Maj...Major.
Maj.Gen...Major General.
Mar...March.
Mass...Massachusetts.
Math...Mathematical.
M.B...Bachelor of Medicine.
M.C...Member of Congress, Medical Corps.
Mcht...Merchant.
Md...Maryland.
M.D...Doctor of Medicine.
M.Di...Master of Didactics.
Me...Maine.
M.E...Mechanical Engineer; Methodist Episcopal.
Mech...Mechanical.
M.E.Ch...Methodist Episcopal Church.
Med...Medical.
Med. O.R.C...Medical Officers' Reserve Corps.
Med. R.C. (or **M.R.C)**...Medical Reserve Corps.
Mem...Member.
Met...Metropolitan.
Metall...Metallurgical.
Meteorol...Meteorological.
Meth...Methodist.
M.F...Master of Forestry.
Mfg...Manufacturing.
Mfr...Manufacture, manufacturer.
Mfrs...Manufacturers.
M.G...Machine Gun.
Mgr...Manager.
M.I...Military Intelligence.
Mich...Michigan.
Micros...Microscopical.
Mil...Military.
Minn...Minnesota.
Miss...Mississippi.
M.I.T...Massachusetts Institute of Technology.
M.L. (or **LL.M.**)...Master of Laws.
M.Litt...Master of Literature.
Mlle...Madamoiselle (Miss).
Mme...Madame.
Mng...Managing.
Mo...Missouri.
M.O.F.W...Military Order of Foreign Wars of the United States.
M.O.L.L...Military Order of the Loyal Legion of the United States.
Mont...Montana.
M.O.W.W...Military Order of the World War.
M.R.C. or **Med. R.C.**...Medical Reserve Corps.
M.R.C.P...Member Royal College of Physicians.
M.R.C.S...Member Royal Coll. Surgeons.
M.S. (or **M.Sc.**)...Master of Science.
Mt...Mount.
M.T.C...Motor Transport Corps.
Mtn...Mountain.
Mus...Museum, musical.
Mus.B...Bachelor of Music.
Mus.D. or **Mus.Doc.)**...Doctor of Music.
Mut...Mutual.
M.V.M...Massachusetts Volunteer Militia.

N

N...North.
N.A...National Academician; North America; National Army.
N.A.D...National Academy of Design.
Nat...National.
N.B...New Brunswick.
N.C...North Carolina.
N.D...North Dakota.
N.E...Northeast, also New England.
N.E.A...National Education Association.
Neb...Nebraska.
N.E.H.G.S...New England Historic Genealogical Society.
N.E.S...New England Society.
Nev...Nevada.
N.G...National Guard.
N.G.N.Y...National Guard of New York.
N.H...New Hampshire.
N.J....New Jersey.
N.M...New Mexico.
N.M.O.S.A.W...Naval and Military Order of Spanish-American War.

N.O.U.S..........Naval Order of the United States.
Nov..............November.
Nr...............Near.
N.S..............Nova Scotia.
N.T..............New Testament.
Numis............Numismatic.
N.W..............Northwest.
N.Y..............New York (state).
N.Y.G.B.S........New York Genealogical and Biographical Society.

O

O................Ohio.
Obstet...........Obstetrical.
O.C..............Order of the Crown.
O.C.G............Order of Colonial Governors.
Oct..............October.
O.F.P.A..........Order of Founders and Patriots of America.
Okla.............Oklahoma.
Ont..............Ontario.
Ophthal..........Ophthalmological.
O.R..............Organized Reserves.
O.R.C............Officers' Reserve Corps.
Ore..............Oregon.
Orgn.............Organization.
Ornithol.........Ornithological.
O.T..............Old Testament.
O.T.C............Officers' Training Camp.
O.T.S............Officers' Training School.
O.W..............Order of Washington.

P

p................Page.
Pa...............Pennsylvania.
Pass.............Passenger.
Path.............Pathological.
P.B.K............Phi Beta Kappa.
Pd.B. (or **B.Pd.**)..Bachelor of Pedagogy.
Pd.D.............Doctor of Pedagogy.
Pd.M.............Master of Pedagogy.
P.E..............Protestant Episcopal.
Pharm............Pharmaceutical.
Pharm.D..........Doctor of Pharmacy.
Pharm.M..........Master of Pharmacy.
Ph.B.............Bachelor of Philosophy.
Ph.C.............Pharmaceutical Chemist.
Ph.D.............Doctor of Philosophy.
Ph.G.............Graduate in Pharmacy.
Phila............Philadelphia.
Philol...........Philiological.
Philos...........Philosophical.
Phys.............Physician, Physical.
Phys. and Surg...Physicians and Surgeons.
Physiol..........Physiological.
P.I..............Philippine Islands.
Pl...............Place.
P.-M.............Paymaster.
Polit............Political.
Poly.............Polytechnic.
Post.............After.
P.Q..............Province of Quebec.
P.R..............Porto Rico.
Prep.............Preparatory.
Pres.............President.
Presbyn..........Presbyterian.
Presdl...........Presidential.
Prin.............Principal.
Prof.............Professor.
Prog.............Progressive.
Propr............Proprietor.
Pros.Atty........Prosecuting Attorney.
Pro Tem..........Pro tempore (for the time being).
Psi U............Psi Upsilon.
Psychol..........Psychological.
Pt...............Port or Point.
Pub..............Public, publisher, publishing, published.
Pvt..............Private.

Q

Q.-M.............Quartermaster.
Q.M.C............Quartermaster Corps.
Q.M.Gen..........Quartermaster General.
Q.M.O.R.C........Quartermaster Officers' Reserve Corps.
Q.M.R.C..........Quartermaster Reserve Corps.
Que..............Quebec (province).
qv...............*quod vide* (which see).

R

R.A.M............Royal Arch Mason,
R.C..............Roman Catholic; Reserve Corps.
R.C.S............Revenue Cutter Service.
Rd...............Road.
R.D..............Rural Delivery.
R.E..............Reformed Episcopal.
Rec..............Recording.
Ref..............Reformed.
R.F..............Reserve Force.
R.F.D............Rural Free Delivery.
Regt.............Regiment.
Regtl............Regimental.
Rep..............Republican, representative.
Rev..............Reverend, Revolution.
R.I..............Rhode Island.
R.O.T.C..........Reserve Officers' Training Corps.
R.R..............Railroad.
R.T.C............Reserve Training Camp.
Ry...............Railway.

S

s................Son.
S................South.
S.A..............South America.
S.A.M.E..........Society of American Military Engineers.
S.A.R............Sons of the Am. Revolution.
S.A.T.C..........Students' Army Training Corps.
Savs.............Savings.
S.A.W............Society of American Wars of the United States.
S.A.W.V..........Spanish-American War Veterans.
S.B. (also **B.S.** or **Sc.B**)..........Bachelor of Science.
S.C..............Society of the Cincinnati; also South Carolina; also Sanitary Corps.
Sc.D (or **D.Sc.**)...Doctor of Science.
S.C.D............Doctor of Commercial Science.
Sch..............School.
S.C.V............Sons of Confederate Veterans.
S.C.W............Society of Colonial Wars.
S.D..............South Dakota.
S.D.P............Sons and Daughters of the Pilgrims.
S.E..............Southeast.
Sec..............Secretary.
Sect.............Section.
Sem..............Seminary.
Sept.............September.
Sgt..............Sergeant.
S.I..............Staten Island; also Sulgrave Institution.
S.J..............Society of Jesus (Jesuit).
S.J.D............Doctor Juristic Science.
S.M..............Master of Science.
S.M.D............Society of Mayflower Descendants.
S.N.S............St. Nicholas Society.
Soc..............Society.
Sociol...........Sociological.
S.O.R.C..........Signal Officers' Reserve Corps.
S.O.S............Service of Supply.
Spl..............Special.
Sq...............Square.
Sr...............Senior.
S.R..............Sons of the Revolution.
S.R.C............Signal Reserve Corps.
S.S..............Southern Society; also Sunday school.
St...............Saint; street
Sta..............Station.
Statis...........Statistical.
S.T.B............Bachelor of Sacred Theology.
S.T.D............Doctor of Sacred Theology.
Supt.............Superintendent.
Surg.............Surgical.
S.V..............Sons of Veterans.
S.W..............Southwest.
S.W. 1812........Society of the War of 1812

T

T. and S.........Trust and Savings.
Tech.............Technical, technology.
Technol..........Technological.

Temp............Temporary.
Tenn............Tennessee.
Ter. (or **Ty.**).....Territory.
Tex.............Texas.
T.H. (or **H.T.**)....Territory of Hawaii.
Th.D............Doctor of Theology.
Th.M............Master of Theology.
Theol...........Theological.
Topog...........Topographical.
Tp. (or **Twp.**)....Township.
Trans...........Transferred.
Treas...........Treasurer, treasury.
Twp. (or **Tp.**)....Township.
Ty. (or **Ter.**).....Territory.

U

U...............University.
U.B.............United Brethren in Christ.
U.C.V...........United Confederate Veterans.
U.D.C...........United Daughters of the Confederacy.
Univ............University.
U.P.............United Presbyterian; Union Pacific.
Urol............Urological.
U.S.............United States.
U.S.A...........United States Army.
U.S.C.G.........United States Coast Guard.
U.S.C.T.........U.S. Colored Troops.
U.S.C.W.........Union Society of the Civil War.
U.S.D. 1812......United States Daughters of 1812.
U.S.M.A.........United States Military Academy.
U.S.M.C.........United States Marine Corps.
U.S.M.H.S........United States Marine Hospital Service.
U.S.N...........United States Navy.
U.S.N.A.........United States Naval Academy.
U.S.N.G.........United States National Guard.
U.S.N.R.F........United States Naval Reserve Force.
U.S.P.H.S........United States Public Health Service.
U.S.R...........United States Reserves.
U.S.R.C.S........U. S. Revenue Cutter Service.
U.S.V...........United States Volunteers.
U.S.W.V.........United Spanish-War Veterans.

V

Va..............Virginia.
Vet.............Veteran, veterinary.
V.M.I...........Virginia Military Institute.
V.F.W...........Veterans of Foreign Wars.
Vol.............Volunteer; volume.
Vols............Volunteers.
V.p.............Vice president.
Vs..............Versus (against).
Vt..............Vermont.

W

W...............West.
Wash............Washington (state).
W.C.T.U.........Women's Christian Temperance Union.
W.I.............West Indies.
Wis.............Wisconsin.
W.Va............West Virginia.
Wyo.............Wyoming.

Y

Yale-S...........Sheffield Scientific School of Yale University.
Y.M.C.A.........Young Men's Christian Assn.
Yrs.............Years.
Y.W.C.A.........Young Women's Christian Association.

Z

Zoöl............Zoölogical.

THE COMPENDIUM of American Genealogy

Lineage Records

1–**HOOVER, Herbert Clark,** *b* West Branch, Iowa, August 10, 1874.
8–Hans Heinrich **Huber,** of Oberkulm, Canton Aargau, Switzerland, descended from medieval Huber family of Canton Bern;
7–Gregor Jonas (*b* July 6, 1668-*d* Apr. 13, 1741, at Ellerstadt, district of Dürkheim, the Palatinate), *m* Anna Maria Kreutzer, or Hartmann? (*b* 1675-6-*d* Apr. 12, 1756);
6–Andrew (*b* Jan. 29, 1723, at Ellerstadt-*d* 1794, in Randolph Co., N.C.), who first used name **Hoover,** arrived at Phila. on ship "Two Sisters," Sept. 9, 1738, and lived with elder brother in Lancaster Co., Pa., until *m* 1745, Margaret Catherine Pfautz (John Michael[7], *m* Catherine–, of Swiss origin, who arrived at Philadelphia from Palatinate on ship "William and Sarah," Sept. 18, 1727, and settled in Lancaster Co.); settled near Uniontown, Carroll Co., Md., moved to N.C. ca. 1779;
5–John (*b* Md., 1760-*d* Ohio, Nov. 18, 1831), *m* in N.C., 1784, Sarah Burket (Sept. 20, 1767-Dec. 29, 1843; Christian Burkhart[6], of Swiss origin, who first settled in Elizabeth Tp., Lancaster Co., later moved to Md., and was in Randolph Co., N.C., 1790; Emmanuel[7]); moved late 1801 north to nr. West Milton, Miami Co., O.;
4–Jesse (*b* in N.C., 1800-*d* in Ia., Nov. 1856), *m* in Ohio, Apr. 18, 1819, Rebecca Yount (*b* Feb. 11, 1801, in Ky., en route north to Ohio), moved 1854, to West Branch, Ia.;
3–Eli (July 16, 1820-July 24, 1892), *m* 1840, in Ohio, Mary Davis (below); *m* 2d, Aug. 17, 1854, in Iowa, Hannah Leonard;
2–Jesse Clark (2 below).
7–John Rudolph **Waymire** (*b* in Hanover, Germany, ca. 1725-*d* in N.C., 1801), *m* 2d, Elizabeth Tank (or Louck?);
6–Rosannah (1751-Aug. 16, 1814), *m* George (Jundt) **Yount** (1740-Apr. 23, 1810);
5–John (Sept. 23, 1768-Dec. 1, 1822), moved from N.C. to Ky., thence to Ohio, 1801,02; *m* Mary Löw (Mar. 28, 1771-July 22, 1842),
4–Rebecca (1801-96), *m* Jesse **Hoover** (4 above).
9–Edward **Pole,** *m* Mary–;
8–Ann (*d* 1729), *m* Marmaduke **Coate** (*d* 1728), came to America, 1715;
7–William (1702-42), *m* 1727, Rebecca Sharp (*b* 1703; Hugh[8] [1668-1742], judge, Burlington Co., N.J., *m* Rachael, dau. of Thomas French);
6–Marmaduke (1738-1822), settled in Miami Co., O., 1806; *m* Mary Coppock;
5–Henry (*b* Aug. 18, 1770), *m* in S.C., Feb. 1793, Mary Haskett (Isaac[6], *m* Lydia–);
4–Lydia (Oct. 23, 1793-Aug. 12, 1826), *m* John **Davis** (May 2, 1781-Mar. 5, 1852 or 53; Abiather[5]);
3–Mary (Oct. 26, 1820-Mar. 3, 1853), *m* Eli **Hoover** (3 above);
2–Jesse Clark (*b* in Miami Co., O., Sept. 2, 1846-*d* W. Branch, Ia., Dec. 13, 1880), of West Branch, Ia.; *m* Mar. 12, 1870, Huldah Randall Minthorn (May 4, 1848-Feb. 22, 1883); issue: I–Theodore Jesse (qv for maternal lineages); II–Herbert Clark (1 above); III–Mary (*b* Sept. 1, 1876; *m* Mar. 8, 1899, Van Ness Leavitt).
1–*m* Feb. 10, 1899, Lou Henry, dau. of Charles D. Henry, of Monterey, Calif.; issue: 1–Herbert Clark, Jr., *b* London, Eng., Aug. 4, 1903; grad. Stanford, '25, *m* June 26, 1925, Margaret E., dau. of Douglas S. Watson, of San Francisco (issue: Herbert Clark, 3d; Peggy; a dau., *b* Apr. 12, 1930); 2–Allan H., *b* London, July 17, 1907; grad. Stanford, '29; Harvard School of Business Administration.
1–A.B. in engring., Stanford, '95; hon. degrees from universities of Pa., Harvard, Yale, Columbia, Brown, Princeton, Johns Hopkins, George Washington, Dartmouth, Rutgers, Ala., Oberlin, Liege, Brussels, Warsaw, Cracow, Oxford, Rensselaer, Tufts, Swarthmore, Williams, Manchester, Prague, Ghent, Lemberg, and Cornell Coll.; awarded gold medals by Civil Forum, Nat. Inst. Social Sciences, Nat. Acad. Sciences, Am. Inst. Mining and Metall. Engrs., Western Soc. Engrs., City of Lille, City of Warsaw; Audiffret prize, French Acad.; elected freeman of Belgian, Polish and Esthonian cities. Engaged in mining, railway and metallurgical work in U.S., Mexico, Can., Australia, Italy, Great Britain, South Africa, India, China, Russia, etc., 1895-1913. Represented Panama-Pacific Internat. Expn. in Europe, 1913-14; chmn. Am. Relief Com., London, 1914-15; chmn. of Commn. for Relief in Belgium, 1915-19; U.S. food administrator, June 1917-July 1, 1919; chmn. Am. Relief Administration, engaged in children's relief in Europe, 1919-28; chmn. European Relief Council, 1920-28; Sec. of Commerce in Cabinets of Presidents Harding and Coolidge, 1921-29; elected 31st President of the U.S. for term 1929-33. Home: Stanford University, Calif. Official residence: The White House, Washington, D.C.

1–**HOOVER, Theodore Jesse,** *b* West Branch, Ia., Jan. 28, 1871.
7–William **Minthorn,** sailed from Eng. ca. 1725, *d* on board ship leaving wife and 4 sons who landed in Conn.;
6–William (*b* 1716);
5–William, *m* — Lewis, a widow;
4–John (*b* nr. Hartford, Conn., Nov. 4, 1768-*d* ca. 1859), *m* Lucindy Sherwood;
3–Theodore (*b* Oct. 11, 1817-*d* at West Branch, Ia., Oct. 1866), moved to Iowa, 1859; *m* in Can., Jan. 4, 1842, Mary Wasley;
2–Huldah Randall (2 below).
5–Francis **Wasley** (1751-1831, aet. 80), *m* in Toronto, Can., Hannah Scott (1762?-1835, aet. 73), a widow with 2 children (Henry[6], *m* Mary–; John?[7]);
4–Henry (*b* in Bucks Co., Pa., Apr. 19, 1793-*d* Sept. 21, 1864), moved to Toronto, Can.; *m* Ann Tool (Nov. 14, 1790-Sept. 14, 1872; Aaron[5], moved from Bucks Co., Pa., to Can., 1799, *m* Rachael Haworth, *b* in Eng.);
3–Mary (*b* Sept. 1, 1818-*d* in Ore., June 11, 1903), *m* Theodore **Minthorn** (3 above);
2–Huldah Randall (May 4, 1848-Feb. 22, 1883), *m* Mar. 12, 1870, Jesse Clark **Hoover** (*b* in Miami Co., O., Sept. 2, 1846-*d* W. Branch, Ia., Dec. 13, 1880), of West Branch, Ia. (for issue and Hoover lineages see Herbert Clark Hoover).
1–*m* June 6, 1899, Mildred Crew Brooke (see Vol. III, p. 254); issue: 1–Mildred Brooke, *b* Palo Alto, Calif., May 13, 1901; *m* Aug. 27, 1922, Cornelius Grinnell Willis, son of Dr. Bailey Willis, *m* Margaret Baker (issue: Theodore Hoover; David); 2–Hulda Brooke, *b* Palo Alto,

Aug. 19, 1906; A.B., Stanford U., '27; *m* Dec. 5, 1925, Charles Alexander McLean, Jr., of Boise, Ida.; 3–Louise Brooke, *b* London, Eng., Mar. 29, 1908; *m* June 21, 1925, Earnet Albert Dunbar, son of Everett Dunbar, of Alameda, Calif., *m* Adela Kruger (issue: Della Lou; Vivian Dawn).

1–A.B., Stanford U., '01. Assayer and surveyor, 1901-02; mgr. of mines, Mono Co., Calif., 1903-06; mgr. of mines in Mexico, and consulting engr., Mexico, and London, Eng., 1906-10; consulting engr., London and San Francisco, 1910-16, San Francisco, 1916-19; prof. of mining and metallurgy, Stanford U., 1919-30, dean of engring., since 1925. Author (see Who's Who in America). Mem. S.R., S.A.R. Republican. Club: University. Winter place: 627 Salvatierra, Stanford University, Calif. Residence: Rancho del Oso, Swanton, Calif.

1–**ABBE, Cleveland, Jr.,** *b* Washington, D.C., Mar. 25, 1872.
9–John **Abbe** (qv);
8–Samuel (1646-1697/98), of Wenham, Mass., later at Windham, Conn., 1697; *m* 1672, Mary Knowlton (*b* 1649 or 53; William[9], of Hingham and Ipswich, Mass., freeman, 1641/42, *m* Elizabeth–);
7–Ebenezer (1683-1758), of Salem, Mass., and Windham, Conn.; *m* 1707, Mary Allen (*d* 1766; Joshua[8], of Mansfield, Conn., *m* Mary–);
6–Joshua (1710/11-1807), called "King Abbe;" large landowner at N. Windham, Conn.; *m* 1736, Mary Ripley (1716-69; Joshua[7], of Willimantic, Conn., *m* Mary Backus; Joshua[8]; John[9]; William[10], qv);
5–Phineas (1746-1800), of Windham Center, Conn.; *m* 2d, 1778, Susanna Brown (1750-1804; Gen. Thomas[6], served in Am. Rev., *m* Sarah Bishop);
4–Moses Cleveland (1785-1871), of Windham; *m* 1809, Talitha Waldo (*b* 1789; Zaccheus[5], of Waldo Pl., Windham, Conn., *m* Esther Stevens);
3–George Waldo (1811-79), of New York City; *m* 1837, Charlotte Colgate (1817-85; Bowles[4], a founder of Colgate Soap Co., *m* Lourina Townsend; Robert[5], from Eng.);
2–Cleveland (1838-1916), B.S., Harvard; LL.D., Glasgow; distinguished meteorologist; founder of telegraphic daily weather reports and forecasts of Cincinnati Observatory; founder U.S. Weather Bur. (see Vol. IX, Who's Who in America); mem. Nat. Acad. Sciences (Marcellus Hartley medallist; Symons medallist); *m* 1870, Frances Martha Neal (1838-1908); *m* 2d, 1909, Margaret Augusta Percival (*b* 1865); issue (1st marriage): I–Cleveland, Jr. (1 above); II–Truman (see Vol. I, p. 39, for other lineages); III–William (1877-1928; *m* Louisa Hart Howson, *b* 1880).
1–*m* Apr. 12, 1903, Frieda Dauer, *b* Braunschweig, Germany, Nov. 10, 1878; dau. of Conrad Dauer, of Wolfenbüttel-Braunschweig, Germany; issue: 1–Ernst Cleveland, *b* Washington, D.C., Aug. 21, 1905; B.S., Cornell, '28; 2–Elfriede Martha, *b* Washington, Feb. 6, 1919.
1–A.B., Harvard, '94, A.M., 1896; Ph.D., Johns Hopkins, 1898; studied geography, Imperial U., Vienna, 1901-03. Asst. editor and editor, Monthly Weather Review, 1910-18; asst. prof. economic geography, Coll. City of New York, 1921-25; extension asst., dept. forestry, N.Y. State Coll. of Agr., 1925-26; now in private editorial work for Cornell U., dept. of chemistry (see Who's Who in America). Fellow Geol. Soc. America, Am. Geog. Soc.; mem. Gesellschaft für Erdkunde (Berlin); Philos. Soc. of Washington, I.A.G. Residence: 123 N. Quarry St., Ithaca, N.Y.

1–**ABEEL, John Howard, III,** *b* Montreal, Wis., Feb. 15, 1893.
9–Stoffel Janse **Abeel** (*b* ca. 1622-will proved, Oct. 14, 1681), from Holland, 1647, settled at Albany, N.Y.; carpenter, firemaster, magistrate, commissary; *m* 1660, Neeltie Janse Croon (Kroon);
8–Johannes (1667-1711/12), 2d mayor of Albany, 1694, 1709; alderman; justice; *m* 1694, Catalina Schuyler (David[9], *m* Catalina Verplank);
7–David (1705-71), of Albany; capt. Co. I, comd. by Joseph Robinson, 1755; *m* 1726, Mary Duyckinck (1702-80; Garret[8]);
6–Garret (1734-99), of New York, N.Y.; ens. co. I, comd. by Joseph Robinson, 1755; capt. Co. I, comd. by Leonard Lespenard, 1772; 1st maj., 2d Regt. Militia, 1775; *m* 1760, Mary Byvanck (1742-95);
5–Garret Byvanck (1768-1829), of New York; *m* 1794, Catherine Marschalk (1775-1832);
4–John Howard (1815-96), of New York; *m* 1838, Catherine Emeline Strobel (1808-90);
3–George (1839-1918), of New York; *m* 1861, Julia Emelia Guenther (1841-94);
2–George Howard (2 below).
5–Samuel **Coutant** (1764-1833), *m* Margaret Hutchens (1770-1830);
4–John (1804-88), *m* 1825, Catherine Jenkins (1808-1903);
3–Hulda Maria (1832-1920), *m* 1854, as his 2d wife, Zephaniah Sutton **Birdsall** (1802-72), of Cleveland, O.;
2–Ella Frances (*b* 1866), *m* 1885, George Howard **Abeel** (1862-1915), of Ironwood, Mich.; issue: I–Howard Francis (*b* and *d* 1886); II–George Howard (*b* 1887; *m* Martha Mary Wiggins); III–Mildred (*b* 1888; *m* Thomas Harbine Monroe); IV–John Howard (1 above).
1–*m* Oct. 17, 1922, Mary Stella (Greene) Brockman (Sept. 29, 1893-Aug. 23, 1927), dau. of William Egbert Greene, *m* Margaret Cecelia Holland; issue: 1–Mary Elizabeth, *b* Los Angeles, Calif., July 8, 1923; 2–John Howard, *b* Los Angeles, Jan. 17, 1925.
1–M.E., Mich. Coll. of Mines. Jr. civil engr. with City of Los Angeles, Calif., 1927-28; genealogical researcher of Abeel and kindred families. Pvt., Hdqrs. Co., 364th Inf., 182d Brig., 91st Div., World War. Mem. I.A.G., Wash. State Hist. Soc. Episcopalian. Republican. Residence: 815 N. G St., Tacoma, Wash.

1–**ABELL, Horace Avery,** *b* Schenectady Co., N.Y., Sept. 21, 1883.
10–Robert **Abell** (qv);
9–Sgt. Caleb (1646-1731), of Norwich, Conn.; sgt. of Norwich Train Band, 1701; selectman, 1682; constable 1684, 1706; *m* 1669, Margaret Post (1653-1700; John[10], *m* Hester, dau. of William Hyde);
8–Caleb (1677-post 1746), of Lebanon, Conn.; constable, 1719-20, 1727-32; *m* 1704/05, Abigail Sluman (1678/79-1748; Thomas[9], *m* Sarah, of Norwich, Conn., dau. of Thomas Bliss);
7–Daniel (1705/06-1794), of Lebanon; *m* 1727, Sarah Crane (1707-post 1787; Jonathan[8], *m* Mary, dau. of Robert Hibbard, of Windham; Lt. Jonathan[9]);
6–Jonathan (1733-1802), of Lebanon; served in Col. Eleazer Fitch's first Co., 3d Regt., in French and Indian War, and in Col. James Barrett's Regt. during Am. Rev.; *m* 1754, Lydia Bliss (1736-post 1802; Henry[7], *m* Bethia, dau. of Thomas Spofford; Nathaniel[8]; John[9]; Thomas[10]; Thomas[11]);
5–Jonathan (1767-post 1830), of Lebanon, Conn., and Schenectady Co., N.Y.; *m* 1790, Lucy Treadway (1769-post 1830; probably dau. of William, of Lebanon, Conn.);
4–William Bliss (1795-1853), of Schenectady Co., N.Y., constable, 1832-33; *m* 1816, Mary McCarthy (1798-1843; William[5], *m* Martha Reed);
3–Stephen Holland (1825-1912), of Schenectady Co.; *m* 1846, Margaret A. Wing;
2–Walter Wing (2 below).
10–John **Wood** (*d* 1655), of Portsmouth, R.I.; mem. Portsmouth Town Council, 1648; *m* Elizabeth–;
9–John (1620-1704), of Newport, R.I.; dep. Gen. Assembly; *m* Mary Peabody (John[10], *m* Dorothy Tooley, *m* 2d, Mary Rogers);
8–Thomas (1666-1729), of Little Compton, R.I., *m* 1690, Content–;
7–William (1700-78), of Little Compton, R.I., and Dartmouth, Mass.; *m* 1st, 1718, Hannah Shaw (1699-1734; Isreal[8], *m* a dau. of Peter Tallman; Anthony[9], *m* Alice, dau. of John Stonard);
6–Content (1726-54), *m* Edward **Wing** (*b* 1727), of Dartmouth, Mass., and Glens Falls, N.Y. (Edward[7], *m* Sarah Tucker; Daniel[8]; Daniel[9], qv);
5–Russell (*b* 1754), of Quaker Hill and Glens Falls, N.Y.; *m* 1787, Nancy Field;
4–William Russell (1791-1879), of Dutchess and Schenectady cos., N.Y.; *m* 1825, Jane Clark Bolton;
3–Margaret A. (1828-1913), *m* Stephen H. **Abell** (3 above).

7–Dr. Hugh **Bolton** (1687-1772), from Ireland ca. 1730, settled at Londonderry, N.H., later at Peterboro, N.H., at Colerain, Mass., 1741; *m* Elizabeth Patterson (*d* 1755);
6–Dr. Matthew (1732-74), of Colerain, Mass.; *m* 1762, Mary McClanathan (Dea. Thomas[7], *m* Jean–); *m* 2d, Hannah McClanathan, sister of 1st wife;
5–Dr. Thomas (1774-1834), of Colerain, Mass., and Columbia Co., N.Y., *m* Fanny Clark;
4–Jane C. (1801-57), *m* William R. **Wing** (4 above).
8–Lt. John **Clark** (ca. 1660-ca. 1750), from Ireland to Boston, 1718; later settled at Colerain, Mass.; *m* Agnes Adams;
7–Matthew (ca. 1700-1746), of Colerain; *m* Jennett Bothwell (1703-89; Alexander[8], *m* Jane Doneca);
6–Matthew (1744-1813), of Colerain; sgt. in Col. Ephraim Doolittle's 24th regt.; marched from Colerain to Bennington on an alarm; *m* Jane Workman (1759-1813; John[7], *m* Phebe, dau. of James Stewart, *m* Jane–);
5–Fanny (1779-1848), *m* Dr. Thomas **Bolton** (5 above).
6–Peter **Otten** (*d* 1775), from Germany; *m* Catherine Wolff (*d* 1788);
5–Adam (1757-1820), *m* Agnes Brevers;
4–John Adam (1792-post 1859), *m* Marie Catherine Heusgen (John Theodore[5]);
3–John Carl (1822-63), *m* 1847, Marie Theresa Koenen (Constantin[4]);
2–Katherine (*b* 1855), *m* 1874, Walter Wing **Abell** (1851-1904), of Schenectady, N.Y.; prof. of music and composer; issue: I–Bliss (*b* 1875; *m* Louise Barrup); II–Theressa (*b* 1878; *m* George Washington Tilden); III–Horace Avery (1 above).
1–*m* Aug. 11, 1906, Rita Hunting (qv for genealogy); issue: 1–Doris Hunting, *b* Schenectady, N.Y., Jan. 2, 1914.
1–Union Classical Inst., Schenectady, N.Y. Head draughtsman and chief of field parties, Schenectady Ry. and United Traction Co., 1909-15; asst. engr. maint. of way, Schenectady Ry., 1915-17; engr. of way and structures, N.Y. State Rys., Rochester, 1917-30. Served with 2d Regt., N.Y. State, 1901-07. Mem. S.A.R., The Gov. and Co. of Mass. Bay in N.E., I.A.G., N.E.H.G.S., Soc. of the Genesee, Soc. Am. Military Engrs., Am. Soc. C.E. Republican. Clubs: Rochester, Brook-Lea Country, Chamber of Commerce. Summer place: Windsor Beach, Summerville, N.Y. Address: New York State Railways, 267 State St., Rochester, N.Y.

1–**ABELL, Rita Hunting (Mrs. Horace A.),** *b* Gallupville, N.Y., Aug. 4, 1885.
9–John **Hunting** (1597-1689), came to Dedham, Mass., 1638; ruling elder at Dedham; *m* ca. 1617, Hester Seaborne (*d* 1676);
8–John (ca. 1628-1718), of Dedham, Mass.; *m* 1671, Elizabeth Payne (*b* 1648; Thomas[9], qv);
7–Nathaniel (1675-1753), Harvard, 1693; of East Hampton, N.Y.; *m* 1701, Mary Green (1679-1733; John[8]; Percival[9]);
6–Capt. Nathaniel (1702-70), of East Hampton; *m* 1728, Mary Hedges (bap. 1710; William[7], *m* Abiah Mulford; Daniel[8]; Stephen[9]; William[10]);
5–Joseph (1740-71), of East Hampton; *m* Sarah Hedges (*d* 1818; Daniel[6]; William[7]; Daniel[8]; Stephen[9]; William [10]);
4–Joseph (1766-1845), removed from L.I., 1785, and settled in Schoharie Co., N.Y., *m* 1791, Catherine Hess;
3–Ira (1803-74), of Gallupville, N.Y.; *m* 1825, Ruth McDonald;
2–Charles Albert (2 below).
5–Philip **Knight** (1773-1856), *m* Eunice–;
4–William (1806-39), *m* Sarah O'Briant (John[5], *m* Martha Gordiner);
3–John C. (1834-1907), *m* Catherine Young (Matthew[4], *m* Nancy McMillen);
2–Ella (*b* 1862), *m* 1882, Charles Albert **Hunting** (1846-1917), of Schenectady, N.Y., issue: I–Louis Matthew (*b* 1884); II–Rita (1 above); III–Jessie L. (*b* 1889; *m* 1919, Carl Arzt).
1–*m* Aug. 11, 1906, Horace Avery Abell (qv for genealogy and issue).
Residence: 966 Culver Rd., Rochester, N.Y.

1–**ABELL, Lewis Parker,** *b* St. Catharines, Ont., Apr. 29, 1873.
8–Robert **Abell** (qv);
7–Benjamin (*d* 1699), of Norwich; *m* 1678, Hannah (*d* post 1717), probably dau. of John Baldwin, Sr.;
6–Benjamin (ca. 1687-1769), of Norwich; *m* 1714, Lydia Hazen (*b* 1694; Lt. Thomas[7], *m* Mary Howlett);
5–Elijah (1729-99), of Chatham, Conn., and Lempster, N.H.; *m* 1754, Anne Lathrop (1731-64; John[6], *m* Elizabeth Abell);
4–Abel (1757-1841), of Middle Haddam (Chatham), Conn.; lt. and paymaster in Am. Rev.; recorded in a list of men confined on the prison ship "Old Jersey"; *m* 1783, Lucy Hubbard (*d* ca. 1800);
3–Robert (1791-1857), of Vernon, N.Y., and St. Johns, Ont., Can.; *m* 1828, Julia Anna Tucker (1806-89; William[4], *m* Maria, dau. of Robert Hilton);
2–Chandler McKelsey (2 below).
7–William **Hilton** (*d* Bethlehem, Albany Co., N.Y., 1749), from Leeds, Yorkshire, Eng., 1686, settled in Albany Co., N.Y.; served in Colonial wars; *m* 1693, Anna Berkhoven;
6–Jacobus (James) (*b* 1705), *m* 1733, Judith Martin;
5–Robert (1749-1829), served in Albany militia as comrade with his uncle Richard Hilton, 1767; served in Am. Rev.; established the Homestead; *m* 1774, Elizabeth Burgess;
4–John Burges (1783-1832), served War 1812; *m* Hannah Ostrander (Andrew[5], *m* Jane Davis);
3–James B. J. (1812-96), *m* Hannah Sayre Richards (g.dau. Ephraim Sayre, of Madison, N.J., soldier Am. Rev.);
2–Rachael Josephine (1841-83), *m* 1862, Chandler McKelsey **Abell** (1835-82), of St. Catharines, Ont., Can.; issue: I–James Sayre (1864-71); II–Julia Anna (*b* 1866; *m* 1895, Jesse Albright); III–Rebecca Josephine (1868-73); IV–Asahel Hubbard (*b* 1871); V–Lewis P. (1 above); VI–Charles Richards (1875-1878); VII–Franklin Theodore (1877-1919); VIII–Chandler McKelsey, Jr. (*b* and *d* 1880).
1–*m* June 5, 1907, Edna Brooks Lafferty, *b* Abillene, Kan., Sept. 12, 1880; dau. of William S. Lafferty, *m* Alma V. Short; issue: 1–Herbert Lewis (*b* and *d* May, 1909); 2–Alma Louise, *b* Los Angeles, Calif., July 21, 1911.
1–On staff of Electrical World, 1897-1899, New York; with General Electric Co.'s dist. office, Denver, 1901-06; U.S. Reclamation Service, 1909; engring. dept., Los Angeles, Calif., 1910-1918; with U.S. Geol. Survey, Washington, D.C., 1918-19; with engring. dept., City of Los Angeles, since 1919. Mem. S.R. Residence: 1500 N. Western Av., Glendale, Calif.

1–**ADAMS, Charles Nathan,** *b* Norwalk, Conn., Jan. 3, 1866.
9–Edward **Adams** (*d* 1671), from Eng., 1640; settled New Haven, Conn.; at Milford, Conn., 1646; Fairfield, 1650; *m* Margaret Savage, or Mary–(*b* 1687; she *m* 2nd, Anthony Beery);
8–Nathan (*b* post 1656–will dated 1748, proved 1748/49), of Fairfield, Conn.; *m* 1st, ca. 1687, Mary James (Joseph[9], *m* Mary–);
7–Nathan (bap. 1694-1724), *m* ca. 1714, Rebecca Clapham (she *m* 2d, 1724/25, Joshua Jennings);
6–Nathan, *m* Mary Burr (Daniel[7], *m* Mary–);
5–Nathan (1745-1812), *m* Rhoda Scribner (1747-1812);
4–Moses S. (1784-1851), of S. Salem, N.Y.; *m* 1st, 1808, Mary Abbott (1789-1836);
3–Abijah Abbott (1809-73), of Wilton, Conn.; *m* 1833, Anna Warren (1807-73; Shubal[4], of Ridgefield, Conn., *m* Salome–);
2–George Warren (2 below).
8–Matthew **Marvin** (qv);
7–Matthew (bap. 1626-*d* Norwalk, Conn., 1712), town clk., 1661, 62; selectman, 1660, 79; *m* ca. 1650, Mary–(*d* ca. 1709);
6–Sgt. John (1678-1774), of Norwalk and Sharon, Conn.; apptd. collector, 1708, surveyor of highways, 1711; selectman, 1703-13, 19; constable; rep. in Legislature, 1734, 38; *m* 1st, 1704, Mary Beers (ca. 1685-1720; James[7], of Fairfield, Conn.);
5–Seth (1709-84), of Norwalk, Conn., and Brookhaven, L.I.; *m* Phebe Lees (Lt. William[6], of Norwalk, *m* Mehitable Ruscoe);
4–Seth (1751 or 52-1836), of Brookhaven, L.I., and Norwalk, Conn.; vol. in Capt. Griffin's Co., 3d N.Y. Regt.; enlisted later in 2d N.Y. Line, Cont. Army, and was sgt.; according to tradition was incarcerated in N.Y. Sugar House;

m 1788, Hannah Gregory (1761-1846; Abraham[5], *m* Elizabeth Betts);
3–Charlotte (1805-73), of Norwalk; *m* 1833, as his 2d wife, George **Homan** (1802-66), *b* Phila., Pa. (Joseph[4]);
2–Emma Elizabeth (1836-1912), of Brooklyn, N.Y., and Norwalk, Conn.; *m* 1864, George Warren **Adams** (1839-1910), of Norwalk, Conn.; farmer; issue: I–Charles Nathan (1 above); II–Bertha Louise (*b* 1871; *m* George F. Canfield).
1–*m* Sept. 26, 1899, Frances Caroline Riggs (Oct. 26, 1875-Feb. 2, 1925), dau. of Nathan Clark Riggs, of Oxford, Conn.; issue: 1–Howard Sherman, *b* Norwalk, Conn., July 28, 1900; ed. Kimball Union Acad., '19; *m* Dec. 15, 1928, Jean Linton, dau. of James D. Coltman, of Black Rock, Bridgeport, Conn.; 2–Ernest Marvin, *b* Norwalk, Feb. 7, 1902; B.S., Middlebury, '25.
1–Florist, Bridgeport, Conn., 1903-1926; started Seir Hill Gardens, 1926. Congregationalist. Republican. Residence: Seir Hill Gardens, Belden Hill Av., Norwalk, Conn.

1–**ADAMS, Frank Manning**, *b* Upper Lisle, N.Y., Apr. 15, 1866-*d* Glendora, Calif., June 8, 1930.
7–William **Adams** (*d* 1655) settled at Hartford, Conn., 1640; removed to Farmington; *m* Elizabeth (Hancock) Heacock (*d* 1655);
6–Benjamin (1649-1713), of Wethersfield, Conn.; soldier in King Philip's War, under Capt. Edwards; *m* 1690, Elizabeth Dickinson (1668-1725; Thomas[7]; Nathaniel[8], went to Conn. with Hooker, from Wethersfield to Hadley, Mass., and founder of same);
5–Amasa (1708-90), of Wethersfield; *m* 1731, Hannah Camp (*d* 1798; Joseph[6], of Hartford);
4–Amasa (1753-1819), of Wethersfield and Bristol, Conn.; served in three commands in Am. Rev.; *m* 1st, 1783, Sarah (Deming) Griswold (*d* 1794);
3–Horace (1787-1878), of Bristol, Conn., and Triangle, N.Y.; served in War 1812; *m* 1812, Lois Wilcox;
2–Perry (2 below).
8–John (Willcocks) **Wilcox**, "John of Hartford" (qv);
7–John (*d* 1676), of Hartford and Middletown, Conn.; *m* 4th, 1671, Esther Cornwall;
6–Ephriam (1672-1713), of Middletown, Conn.; *m* 1698, Silence Hand;
5–John (1712-91), of Guilford, Conn.; *m* 1740, Martha Coe (1713-1795; John[6], of Stratford, Conn.);
4–Benjamin (1743-1807), of Middletown and Bristol, Conn.; town official of Bristol; served in Am. Rev.; *m* Lois–(1748-82); *m* 2d, Philena Rowe (1759-1821);
3–Lois (1792-1877), of Bristol, Conn., and Triangle, N.Y.; *m* Horace **Adams** (3 above);
2–Perry (1827-1902), of Whitney Point, N.Y.; cooper; m 1854, Diana Matilda Manning (1832-1911); issue: I–Martin (*b* 1856; *m* May Latimer); II–Lizzie (*b* 1859; *m* Elbert James Moore); III–Frank M. (1 above).
1–*m* June 5, 1901, Mary Ellen Chamberlin, (qv for genealogy); issue: 1–Horace Chamberlin, *b* Pasadena, Calif., Dec. 23, 1903; B.S., Calif. Inst. Tech., '25; 2–Eleanor Wilbur, *b* Pasadena, May 18, 1907; A.B., U. of Calif., '29.
1–Orange grower. Dry goods salesman and buyer, 12 yrs.; editor St. Louis Drygoodsman, 4 yrs.; writer for trade journals, 14 yrs.

1–**ADAMS, Mary Ellen Chamberlin (Mrs. Frank M.)**, *b* E. Bridgewater, nr. Montrose, Pa., May 15, 1871.
9–Henry **Chamberlin** (ca. 1598-1674), from Eng. in the "Diligent," settled at Hingham, Mass., 1638; *m* Jane–;
8–William (ca. 1620-1678), of Hull, Mass.; *m* Sarah Jones;
7–Joseph (1665-1752), from Hull, Mass., to Colchester, Conn.; *m* 1688, Mercy Dickinson (1668-1735; John D.[8]; Nathaniel [9], founder of Hadley, Mass.);
6–William (1688-1756), from Hadley, Mass., to Colchester, Conn; *m* 1710, Sarah Day (1691-1768; Thomas D[7]);
5–Peleg (1713-post 1766), from Colchester to Kent, Conn.; sgt., capt. 13th Regt. Militia; *m* 2d, 1752, Jane Higgins (*d* post 1766);
4–William (1754-1833), of Jewett, N.Y.; served in Am. Rev.; *m* 1777, Mary Wilcox (1756-1822);
3–Abraham (1794-1855), from Kent, Conn., to E. Bridgewater, Pa.; *m* 1819, Almira Sweet (1797-1869);
2–Lewis Ephraim (2 below).
5–Zephaniah **Knapp** (1736-1816), from Wales, setled in Columbia Co., N.Y.; removed to Luzerne Co., Pa., 1796; *m* 1760, Milla Roe (*d* 1806);
4–Joseph (1763-1833), of Moosic, Luzerne Co., Pa.; removed to Pittston, Pa., 1798; served in Am. Rev.; *m* 1784, Margret Dickson (1765-1852);
3–James (1807-83), of S. Montrose, Pa.; *m* 2d, 1841, Mary Fiske Wilbur (*b* 1818);
2–Verta Alice (1846-1923), of S. Montrose, Pa.; *m* 1869, Lewis Ephraim **Chamberlin** (1828-88), of E. Bridgewater, Pa., and Binghamton, N.Y.
1–*m* June 5, 1901, Frank Manning Adams (1866-1930; qv for genealogy and issue).
1–Mem. Chamberlain Assn., Glendora Woman's Club. Republican. Residence: Glendora, Calif.

1–**ADAMS, Giles Ernest William**, *b* Middletown, Tex., Dec. 20, 1874.
5–Nathan **Adams**, *b* in Va.;
4–Joel (1771-1864), *m* Janey Pane;
3–Giles Jackson (1816-1909), *m* Martha Ann Denham (1815-71);
2–James Franklin (1845-1909), vocal music teacher; served in Mo. cav. in Civil War; *m* 1867, Jessie Anne Jacobs (1848-80); *m* 2d, 1881, Nancy Jane Cooper; issue (1st marriage): I–John Carson (1868-1919; *m* Lyda Massey, see their son, Ralph R., Vol. III, p. 21); II–Ira Eugene (*b* 1870; *m* Cora Higgins); III–Clara Etta (*b* 1872; *m* Thomas J. Norrell); IV–Giles E. W. (1 above); V–Albert Elmo (*b* 1878; *m* Grace Autry; *m* 2d, Rosa Hopp); VI–Lucy Ann (*b* 1881; *m* Lon Neighbors; *m* 2d, Sol Heath); VII–James Virgil (*b* 1886; *m* Helen Rauch).
1–*m* July 31, 1898, Maggie Bailey (Dec. 31, 1877-June 25, 1902); dau. of Frank Bailey, of Eolian, Tex.; issue: 1–Ruth Vivian, *b* Cisco, Tex., Aug. 23, 1900; *m* Mar. 30, 1920, Lt. James Weston Hammond.
1–*m* 2d, Dec. 20, 1904, Emma Dorothy Bergmann, *b* Bow Valley, Cedar Co., Neb., Aug. 26, 1883; dau. of Frank Bergmann; issue: 1–Jack Ernest, *b* Dallas, Tex., June 13, 1906.
1–Studied San Marcos Teacher Normal, and Baylor U., med. dept., 2 yrs. Commissary agent, dining car dept. S.P.Ry., since 1910. Mason. Christian. Republican. Residence: 101 Rigsby Av., San Antonio, Tex.

1–**ADAMS, Annette Talbot Belcher (Mrs. Henry N.)**, *b* New London, Conn., Oct. 3, 1876.
9–Gregory **Belcher** (1606-74), from Eng., 1632; a founder of Braintree, Mass., 1634; *m* Catherine–;
8–Samuel (1637-79), of Braintree; *m* 1663, Mary Billings (bap. 1645; Roger[9], of Dorchester, *m* Hannah–);
7–Moses (1672-1728), settled at Dorchester, Conn.; *m* 1694, Hannah Lyon (*b* 1673; George[8], of Milton, Mass., *m* Hannah Tolman);
6–William (1701-32), of Preston, Conn.; *m* 1730, Mehitable Stearns (*b* 1712; Nathaniel[7]; Nathaniel[8], *m* Mary–; Martin[9], *m* Jane Green);
5–Capt. William (1731-1801), of Preston; served as Capt. in Conn. troops, 1775-77; in battles of White Plains, Brandywine, Germantown and at Valley Forge; *m* 1752, Desire Morgan;
4–William (1772-1851), of Preston; later at Granby, Mass.; *m* 2d, 1808, Sally Wilson (1789-1831);
3–Nathan (1813-91), of New London, Conn.; *m* 1841, Ann P. Wilson;
2–William (2 below).
9–James **Morgan** (qv);
8–John (1645-1712), came with his father; settled at Preston, Conn., ca. 1692; Capt. of Train Band; commr. to Pequot Indians; dep. Gen. Ct., 1690, 1693-94; *m* 1st, 1665, Rachel Deming or Dymond (*b* 1640; John[9], qv);
7–James (1680-1721), of Preston; *m* ca. 1704, Bridget–;
6–Capt. Daniel (1712-73), of Preston; *m* 1730, Elizabeth Gates (1713-93; Joseph[7], *m* Elizabeth Hungerford; George[8] *m* Sarah, dau. Nicholas Olmstead, *m* Sarah, dau. Joseph Loomis, qv);
5–Desire (1736-1801), *m* Capt. William **Belcher** (5 above).
11–William **Brewster**, Mayflower Pilgrim (qv);
10–Jonathan (1593-1659), *m* Lucretia Oldham;
9–Mary (*b* 1627), *m* John **Turner** (*d* ca. 1697; Humphrey[10], qv);
8–Ezekiel (1650-1703/04), of New London, Conn.; *m* 1678, Susanna Keeney (*b* 1662; John[9], *m* Sarah, dau. William Douglas; William[10], of New London, *m* Agnes or Annie–);

7–Ezekiel, *m* 1729, Borodell Denison (*b* 1712);
6–Prudence (*b* Groton, Conn., 1732-*d* Salem, Conn., 1823), *m* Samuel **Fox** (*b* Preston, Conn., 1724-*d* New London, Conn., 1809);
5–Ezekiel (*b* Groton, Conn., 1756-*d* New London, Conn., 1844), *m* 1791, Susan Child;
4–Rachel W. (*b* Plainfield, Conn., 1793-*d* New London, Conn.), *m* 1810, Increase **Wilson** (*b* Preston, Conn.-*d* New London, Conn.);
3–Ann P. (*b* New London, Conn., 1816-*d* New London, 1872), *m* Nathan **Belcher** (3 above);
2–William (1845-1928), of New London; *m* 1871, Anne Pimer (*b* 1848); issue: I–Gregory (*b* 1872); II–Louise (*d* infancy); III–Annette T. (1 above); IV–Norman; V–Rachel (*d* infancy); VI–Nathan; VII–Hugh Dugdale (*d* infancy); VIII–Duncan; IX–Roger Billings (*d* infancy).
1–*m* July 9, 1902, Henry Nicholas Adams, *b* Bethlehem, Pa., Nov. 2, 1873; capt. in Spanish-Am. War; maj. in World War; son of Samuel Adams, of Allentown, Pa.; *m* Susie Weaver; issue: 1–Anita Belcher, *b* New London, Conn., Jan. 9, 1906; *m* Jan. 21, 1928, William Gibson Buttfield, of Plainfield, N.J., (issue: Henry Adams, *b* Jan. 15, 1929); 2–Barbara Weaver (*b* Sept. 4, 1911-*d* July 3, 1928).
1–Ed. Williams Memorial Sch., New London, Conn., and Burnham Sch., Northampton, Mass. Mem. D.F.P.A. Club: Plainfield Country. Residence: 934 Park Av., Plainfield, N.J.

1–**ADAMS, Eleanor Pierrepont Edwards (Mrs. Howard),** *b* Newark, N.J., Dec. 22, 1875.
9–Thomas **Edwards,** *m* Rachel Day;
8–William;
7–Thomas, *m* Camilla Brown;
6–Henry;
5–William;
4–Henry, *m* Elizabeth–;
3–Charles, *m* Harriet Smith;
2–Arthur Mead (2 below).
9–John **Ward** (1620-94), *m* Sarah Lyman;
8–Nathaniel (1656-1732), *m* Christiana Swain;
7–Nathaniel (1691-1783), *m* Mercy Ward;
6–Nathaniel (1712-54), *m* Martha Harrington;
5–Abraham (*d* 1802), *m* 1776, Hannah Biggs (*b* 1752);
4–Caleb Smith (*b* 1780), *m* Abigail Nichols (1779-1846);
3–Caleb Smith (1818-91), *m* Diadamia Bowles (1823-95);
2–Emma Cornelia (1847-96), *m* 1871, Arthur Mead **Edwards,** M.D.; issue: I–Harriet Smith (*b* 1873; *m* 1900, Harry Walter Foster); II–Eleanor P. (1 above).
1–*m* Apr. 14, 1903, Howard Adams, *b* Howard Co., Md., Dec. 8, 1871; son of Orson Adams, of Howard Co.; issue: 1–Howard, Jr., *b* Baltimore, Md., June 30, 1904; *m* June 29, 1928, Robins Miller, dau. of Edward Rich, of Catonsville, Md. (issue: Mary Eleanor); 2–Pierrepont, *b* Baltimore, Apr. 24, 1913.
1–Mem. O.C., B.O.R., C.D.A., D.F.P.A., D.A.R., Order of the King. Episcopalian. Republican. Club: Gibson Island. Summer Place: Gibson Island, Md. Residence: 100 Overhill Rd., Baltimore, Md.

1–**ADAMS, James Taylor,** *b* Colly, Letcher Co., Ky., Feb. 3, 1892.
4–William G. **Adams** (1789-1865), *b* N.C.; from Tenn. to nr. Whitesburg, Ky., ca. 1825; *m* Polly Adams (1785-1839; John[5], of Wilkes Co., N.C., *m* Letty Simpson);
3–Spencer (1825-1905), *m* Celia Church (dau. of Mrs. Peggy Adams Church, sister of William G., 4 above);
2–Rev. Joseph (2 below).
6–William **Short** (*b* prob. Eng.-*d* Va.);
5–William, from Va. to Tenn.;
4–William Granville, from Tenn. to Va.; *m* Patience Ann Brooks;
3–William Alfred, *m* Elizabeth Davis (Thomas[4]);
2–Mary Jane (1854-1929), *m* 1875, Rev. Joseph **Adams** (1855-1900), Bapt. minister; issue: I–Celia Ann (*b* 1877; *m* Solomon Banks); II–Joseph (*d* infancy); III–James Taylor (1 above).
1–*m* Dec. 16, 1908, Dicy Roberts, *b* Lipps, Va., Nov. 10, 1892; dau. of Shadrick R. Roberts, served in Mexican War, *m* Letty, dau. of Spencer Adams, (3 above); issue: 1–James Taylor, *b* Hilliard, Ky., Nov. 14, 1910; 2–Naomi Mary, *b* Mountain Home, Ark., Sept. 18, 1914; 3–Virginia Cecile, *b* Boonville, Mo., Nov. 21, 1918; 4–Lenore Corene, *b* "Wanderers Rest," Big Flat, Ark., Dec. 27, 1921; 5–Eva Fair, *b* Trammell, Va., Mar. 28, 1925; 6–Spencer Greenfield, *b* Wise, Va., Aug. 26, 1928.
1–Publisher, Gazette, Wise, Va., News, Cumberland Gap, Tenn., News, Neon, Ky., Times, Coeburn, Va. (country weeklies); The Vagabond Gazette (monthly); The Liberal (weekly), Wise, Va.; Adams Family Records (quarterly). Engaged in collecting material for a history of the Adams Family. Residence: Wise, Va.

1–**ADKINS, Samuel B.,** *b* Town Hill, Pa., Oct. 13, 1858.
7–Thomas **Adkins** (*d* 1694), from Eng., 1630, settled at Hartford, Conn.;
6–Benoni (*b* 1690), *m* 1715, Esther Hall;
5–Thomas (*b* 1716), *m* 1738/39, Mary Aspinwal (Eleazar[8]);
4–Isaiah (1756-1842), of Meepoopany, Pa.; pvt. in Am. Rev.; *m* Rhoda Carey;
3–Samuel (1794-1847), of Meepoopany; served in War 1812; *m* Hannah Hix;
2–Andrew Jackson (1828-1905), merchant, Shickshinny, Pa.; *m* 1855, Martha Jane Kocher (*b* 1835); issue: I–Samuel B. (1 above); II–Harriet Adele (*d*; *m* L. W. Deubler, *d*); III–Jennie (*m* W. H. Thomas, *d*); IV–Mason H. (*b* 1872; *m* Maud Kelly).
1–*m* Jan. 12, 1893, Elsie A. Allegar, *b* Shickshinny, June 17, 1871; dau. of N. B. Allegar (John[3]; John[4], soldier in Am. Rev.).
1–Druggist prior to 1916; editor 1916-30. Mem. I.A.G. Mason. Methodist. Democrat. Residence: Shickshinny, Pa.

1–**AINSWORTH, Josephine,** *b* West Union, Ia., Sept. 21, 1900.
8–Edward **Ainsworth** (1652-1740), from Eng., ca. 1687; settled at Roxbury, Conn.; *m* 1687, Joanna Hemmingway or Hemenway (1670-1748);
7–Nathan (1715-76), of Woodstock, Conn.; *m* 1736, Huldah Peake (1718-49);
6–Nathan (1740-1776 or 77), of Woodstock; soldier in Am. Rev.; *d* a prisoner in the hands of the British; *m* 1764, Phebe Kinsley (*d* post 1777);
5–Abial (1777-1866), of Woodstock; *m* 1806, Artemesia Stowell (1784-1853);
4–Parmenus (1808-1901), of New Woodstock, N.Y.; *m* 1831, Kezia Webber (*d* 1847);
3–Lucian Lester (1831-1902), of Cazenovia, N.Y., and West Union, Ia.; served in Civil War as capt. of 6th Ia. Cav., 1862-65; mem. Ia. Legislature, 1859-62 and 1871-72; mem. Congress, 3d Ia. Dist., 1875-76; *m* 1859, Margaret McCool (1833-1921);
2–Willard Joseph (1870-1926), lawyer, West Union, Ia.; *m* 1899, Mabel Thorne (*b* 1872); issue: I–Josephine (1 above); II–Philip Thorne (1905-06); III–Sallie Belle (*b* 1909).
1–B.A., State U. of Ia., '23, J.D. 1926 (Kappa Beta Pi). Practiced law, West Union, Ia., 1926-27; general sec., Beadle County Y.W.C.A., 1927–. Mem. D.F.P.A., D.A.R., A.A.U.W. Club: Altrusa. Methodist. Democrat. Address: C/o Y.W.C.A., Huron, S.D.

1–**AKERS, Lewis Robeson,** *b* Asheville, N.C., Aug. 25, 1881.
4–Moses **Akers,** of Montgomery Co., Va.; *m* Catherine Altizer;
3–Amos, of Pulaski Co., Va.; *m* Missouri Kelly;
2–Rev. William David (*b* 1855), prof. Asbury Theol. Sem.; *m* 1878, Mary Istalena Robeson (1856-1924); issue: I–Lewis R. (1 above); II–Dwight Cumming (*b* 1884; *m* Florence Turner); III–Helen Constance (*b* 1887; *m* Harry Clyde Maitland); IV–William David, Jr. (see Vol. III, p. 24, for Robeson lineage).
1–*m* July 6, 1905, Nellie Dyer, *b* Delaware Co., O., Nov. 4, 1880; dau. of Rev. Rolla Dyer, of Tryon, N.C.; issue: 1–William Gerald, *b* Mt. Vernon, O., June 26, 1906; Asbury Coll., '27; 2–Lewis Robeson, Jr., *b* Nevada, O., Dec. 19, 1907; Asbury Coll., '28; 3–Dorothy Dyer, *b* Nevada, Mar. 26, 1909; Asbury Coll., '31; 4–Richard Lawrence, *b* Cleveland, O., Oct. 30, 1919.
1–B.S., Asbury Coll., '03, A.B., A.M., 1904 (D.D., 1916); studied Harvard Div. Sch., 1909; in Europe, 1922; B.D., Ashland Sem., 1924; M.A., U. Ky., 1927; LL.D., O. Northern U., 1927; L.H.D., Birmingham Southern Coll., 1929; Litt.D., McMurry Coll., 1929. Ordained M.E.

ministry, 1904; pastor in Ohio, 1904-24; v.p., 1924-25, pres., 1925–, Asbury Coll. (see Who's Who in America). Mem. S.A.R. Summer place: "Wildflower Cottage," Lakeside, O. Residence: Wilmore, Ky.

JAMES ALEXANDER, of Kishacoquillas, Pa. (b on Spring River, Nov. 27, 1801-d at "The Willows," Sept. 28, 1886).

1–**ALEXANDER, Robert Ard,** *b* Kishacoquillas, Pa., Feb. 15, 1852.
5–John **Alexander** (*b* 1700), from Scotland, 1736, settled at W. Nottingham, Chester Co., Pa.; *m* 1722, Margaret Glasson (Ronald[6], of Scotland);
4–James (1726-91), of Chambersburg, Pa.; removed to Kishacoquillas Valley, Pa., 1755; served in Capt. Alexander Peoples' Co., 1st Bn., Cumberland Co. Militia, 1777, for which service he received 1600 acres of land located in Clearfield Co., Pa.; *m* Rosy Reed (*d* 1792; Robert[5]);
3–James (1772-1847), of Kishacoquillas Valley; *m* 1792, Jane Adams (1776-1834; William[4], *m* Mary–);
2–James (2 below).
5–John **Alexander** (same as 5 above);
4–James (same as 4 above);
3–Robert (1766-1843), *m* 1790, Elizabeth McClure (1768-1832);
2–Celia (1810-90), *m* 1834, James **Alexander** (1801-86), see portrait; issue: I–Jane Elisabeth (1836-1910; *m* Rev. L. L. Haughwout); II–James Porterfield (1838-1912; *m* 1874, Annie A. Halsey); III–Celia Ann (1841-1918); IV–Missouri Mary (*b* 1843); V–Napoleon Bonaparte (1845-1846); VI–Matilda Virginia (1847-55); VII–Lucy Josephine (1850-71); VIII–Robert Ard(1 above); IX–Emma Rosalind (1854-1927; *m* Hugh W. Brown).
1–*m* Feb. 25, 1885, Margaret E. Maclay (1858-May 10, 1897); dau. of Capt. Charles Maclay, *m* Nancy Owens; issue: 1–Lucy Maclay, *b* Kishacoquillas, Pa., Mar. 5, 1888; A.B., Vassar, '12; 2–Robert Plunkett, *b* Belleville, Ill., Mar. 1, 1891; ed. U. Ill., and Washington and Jefferson Coll.; *m* Sept. 6, 1927, Margaret Cole, dau. of George Alexander Maxwell, of Cambridge, N.Y. (issue: James Ard, *b* Oct. 29, 1928); 3–Nora Margaret, *b* Belleville, Feb. 18, 1895; grad. Ill. Woman's Coll., '16; *m* June 22, 1926, Lt. F. A. Ingalls, U.S.M.A., '24; son of William B. Ingalls, of Desota, Mo. (issue: Robert Alexander, *b* July 21, 1928).
1–*m* 2d, Jan. 1, 1902, Jessie L. Alexander, *b* Charlotte, N.C., 1868; A.B., Wilson Coll., '87; dau. of Rev. Dr. Samuel C. Alexander, of Millerstown, Pa., A.B., Jefferson, '58, *m* 1862, Nancy Price; issue: 1–Mary Graham, *b* Belleville, Ill., Oct. 5, 1905; A.B., Wilson Coll., '28.
1–A.B., Washington and Jefferson Coll., '76. Retired farmer. Presbyterian. Democrat. Residence: 615 S. Jackson St., Belleville, Ill.

SHESHBAZZER BENTLEY (1802-75), "Was one of the best known men of his day, large hearted and generous to a degree, and gained considerable prominence in politics, being elected county commissioner in 1835, and sheriff in 1840, being the last sheriff from the river district of the county and was, as well, prominent in local affairs. He owned a large tract of land below Monongahela City, part of which is now West Monongahela. He died at Washington, Pa., March 20, 1875" (Some Pioneer Families of Washington County, Pa.)

1–**ALEXANDER, Jennie Stuart Wilson (Mrs. William Herron),** *b* Monongahela, Pa., Aug. 29, 1865.
8–John (Bentlea) **Bentley** (*d* 1748), from Eng., settled in Chadd's Ford, Delaware Co., Pa., as early as 1700; land surveyor under William Penn, 1701; settled at Radnor, Pa., 1701; moved to White Clay Creek, New Castle Co., Del., 1703; received grant of 100 acres at Phila., 1704; mem. first Baptist Ch. which met at his home, 1704; deacon; after his death the meetings were held at the house of his son, Jeffrey; removed to Birmingham Tp., Chester (now Delaware) Co., Pa., ca. 1722, where he set up "an ordinary for the succour and support of travailers"; removed to Newlin Tp., 1732, where he purchased 385 acres; *m* Mary Mills (*d* ca. 1760; Richard or Samuel[9], Welsh Tract purchasers, and lived nr. Radnor, Pa., 1701);
7–Jeffrey (1700-79), gave a lot of ground and built a meeting house, with small help from others, 1752; succeeded his father as deacon; *m* Eleanor Banner;
6–George, 1st lt. in Capt. John Miller's co. of Associators for Chester Co., 1747-48; fitted out a wagon for General Forbes' expdn., ca. 1758; removed to Jacob's Creek, Westmoreland Co., Pa., about the time of Am. Rev.; later settled on west bank of Monongahela River, Washington Co., *m* Jane Charter or Chartier;
5–Sheshbazzer (1747-1800), millwright and farmer; purchased 1050 acres at Pigeon Creek, later purchased 297 acres at mouth of Mingo Creek; mem. Com. Corr., 1792; *m* 1775, Hannah (House) Baldwin;
4–House (1775-1842), of Bentleyville, Pa., which town was laid out by his brother, Sheshbazzer, in 1816, and named for the Bentley family; inherited large holdings on the west

bank of the Monongahela River; *m* 1799, Frances Wallace;
3-Sheshbazzer (1802-75), of Monongahela, Pa. (see portrait); *m* 1825, Elizabeth Shouse (1804-72; John[4]);
2-Sarah Jane (2 below).
7-James **Wallace** (will dated 1774), from Scotland, settled in Frederick Co., Md.; *m* Mary Douglass, a widow;
6-Eleanor, *m* John **Hopkins**, soldier in Am. Rev.;
5-Elizabeth, *m* 1779, Col. William **Wallace**, pvt. in Am. Rev.; ens. militia, 4th Co., Capt. Marquis' 3d Bn., 1784; col. ca. 1791 or 92; sheriff of Washington Co., 1792; justice of the peace and the Ct. of Common Pleas; asso. judge;
4-Frances (1782-1865), of Somerset Tp.; *m* 1799, House **Bentley** (4 above);
3-Sheshbazzer, *m* Elizabeth Shouse (3 above);
2-Sarah Jane (*b* 1832), *m* 1860, William Hugh **Wilson** (1833-1921); issue: I-Margaret Elizabeth (*b* 1861; *m* 1888, William Courtney Hodill); II-William Wallace Bentley (1863-65); III-Jennie S. (1 above); IV-Maude (*b* 1869; *m* 1900, John Nesbit Jenkins); V-Roxanna Bentley (*b* and *d* 1871); VI-Eliza Logan (qv for Wilson and Clarke lineages).
1-*m* June 14, 1888, William Herron Alexander, *b* Dayton, O., May 26, 1864, banker, with Alexander & Co.; son of James Sansom Alexander, of Monongahela, Pa.; issue: 1-Jean Alexander, *b* Monongahela, Pa., June 6, 1891; B.A., Smith, '15; M.A., Chicago, 1918; *m* Oct. 6, 1920, John Hamilton McMahon (issue: John Alexander; William Wallace).
1-Ed. South Western State Normal Sch. Mem. C.D.A., D.A.R. (chapter regent, now state v.regent), Woman's Home and Foreign Missionary Socs. (pres.), Monongahela City Pub. Library Bd. Clubs: Friday Conversational (pres.), Chautauqua Woman's (v.p.), Twentieth Century (Pittsburgh), Woman's Auxiliary Y.M.C.A. (pres. and state v.p.). Presbyterian. Republican. Summer place: Chautauqua, N.Y. Residence: 500 Meade St., Monongahela, Pa.

1-**WILSON, Eliza Logan,** *b* Monongahela, Pa., June 17, 1873.
4-Hugh **Wilson** (Apr. 18, 1758-Sept. 3, 1827), from Ireland, supposedly from Ballygallon, in Coleraine, where his brother Joseph lived; his nephew, John Willson, of Augusta, Ga., in his will, mentions "his honored and beloved father Joseph, of Ballygallon in the Parish of Ballyackrin within the liberties of Coleraine." He makes a bequest also to his "beloved Aunt Sibbey Willson, wife of his Uncle Hugh, of Carlisle, Pa." Hugh Willson located first in Carlisle, but came to Williamsport (now Monongahela), 1816, and established a trading and general merchandising store; he was one of the first ruling elders in the Presbyn. Ch. there; among his many religious books were a book of prayers published in 1710, and a rare old Bible of great size, which came from Ireland and contains carefully preserved records of the Willson family; *m* June 8, 1786, Sibbey Holmes (Feb. 16, 1766-Aug. 21, 1846, her mother was Hetty Holmes, *d* Jan. 11, 1804), she attended the ball given in Phila. in honor of the signing of the Declaration of Independence, and the grey satin gown she wore on that occasion is a valued heirloom of the family; issue: Jane, Joseph, Hetty Holmes, William, Abraham Holmes, Mary, Eliza Holmes, John;
3-Joseph (Oct. 19, 1789-July 9, 1875), followed in his father's footsteps both in business and church affairs; began and completed in 1826-27 several scrap books, one of 174 pages in long hand; *m* Feb. 16, 1830, Margaret Galbraith Clarke (Aug. 28, 1793-June 17, 1836), some of her paintings and needlework are heirlooms in the family;
2-William Hugh (2 below).
5-Thomas (Clark) **Clarke,** from Ireland 1771, settled on a farm at Chadd's Ford on the Brandywine; served in Am. Rev., taken prisoner by the British; entertained General Lafayette and other famous war leaders at his home; *m* Martha Stuart Dunlop, of the Protestant Stuarts who fled from Lanarkshire, Scotland, persecuted by the Papist Stuarts, she was cousin to the Earl of Bute, and Charles the Pretender; issue: Mary, Samuel, William, John, Robert, Thomas, Elizabeth, Francis (probably);
4-Samuel, preceded the others to the West—to Washington Co., where he became a prothonotary, then Va., and founded the town of Clarksville in what is now Greene Co., Pa.; the brick house with circular staircase in which they lived is still standing; *m* Dorcas Cooke, a cousin of Elizabeth Patterson, who *m* Jerome Bonaparte; issue: Maria, Matilda, Elizabeth, Jennette, Dorcas, Annabelle, Margaret Galbraith, Emeline;
3-Margaret Galbraith (1793-1836), *m* 1830, Joseph **Wilson** (3 above);
2-William Hugh (1833-1921), first asso. with his father in merchandising, then for many yrs., identified with river transportation; Presbyterian; Republican; *m* Nov. 15, 1860, Sarah Jane Bentley (*b* 1832); for issue and other lineages see Mrs. William H. Alexander.
1-Became bookkeeper of Chill W. Hazzard Co., 1903, and 3 yrs. later became mgr. of "The Daily Republican" of Monongahela, with which she was continuously identified for 21 yrs., establishing and keeping the paper and company on a sound financial basis until 1924, when the plant was sold; city treas., 1925, the only woman treas. in the state, in this capacity she collected the largest amount of city taxes in the city's history and had no exemptions. Mem. D.A.R., etc. Presbyterian. Republican. Club: Monongahela Valley Country. Residence: Stanton St., Monongahela, Pa.

1-**ALLAN, Corlynn Ann Visscher (Mrs. Donald Budington),** *b* Gouveneur, N.Y., Dec. 24, 1868.
7-Harmen **Visscher** (1619-92), from Hoorn, Holland, 1640; settled at Rennsselaerwyck, N.Y., *m* Hester Tjerkse;
6-Frederick, *m* 1st, 1692, Margarita Hansen (*d* 1701);
5-Harmon (*b* 1701), *m* 1739, Cathrina Brouwer;
4-Frederick (1741-1809), of Caughnawaga, N.Y.; col. in Am. Rev.; mem. Legislature, 1782; judge Ct. of Common Pleas, Montgomery Co., N.Y., 1787-1801; *m* 1768, Gazena De Graff;
3-William Brouwer (1776-1847), *m* 1810, Ann Easton (1791-1872);
2-William Charles (1815-92), *m* 1843, Elizabeth Moultener (*d* 1864); *m* 2d, 1867, Catherine Amelia Booth (1848-74); issue (1st marriage): I-Helen Rogretta (1844-1916; *m* Charles Dillenbeck); issue (2d marriage): I-Corlynn Ann (1 above); II-Glenn Howard (1871-97).
1-*m* Mar. 19, 1895, Donald Budington Allan, *b* Omaha, Neb., Aug. 27, 1866; son of James Thomas Allan, of Omaha; issue (all *b* Omaha, Neb.): 1-Carlisle Visscher, *b* Jan. 23, 1896; U. Ill., 1915-17; U.S.M.A., 1917; A.B., Columbia U., '22, B.S., 1924; *m* Nov. 8, 1921, Margaret Scovill, dau. Clarence Aikin Aspinwall, of Washington, D.C. (issue: Donald Aspinwall); 2-James Porter, *b* Sept. 12, 1897; 3-Katharine Booth, *b* May 15, 1906; Sullins Coll. (Va.), 1924-25; A.B., U. Neb. '27.
1-Mem. D.F.P.A., D.A.R., Episcopalian. Republican. Club: Woman's. Residence: 817 S. 37th St., Omaha, Neb.

1-**ALLEN, Lee Rogers,** *b* Carlisle, Pa., Sept. 25, 1892.
9-William **Allen** (qv);
8-Samuel (1632-1700), Salem, Mass.; *m* 1660, Sarah Tuck;
7-Joseph (1672-1711), Manchester, Mass.; *m* 1696, Catharine Leach (*b* 1680);
6-Samuel (1698-99-1775), Manchester and Billerica, Mass.; *m* 1740-41, Hannah Marsters (*b* 1720);
5-Capt. Jeremiah (1752-53-1837), Manchester and Billerica; *m* 1776, Abigal Putnam Rogers;
4-Capt. Americus (1787-1864), of Billerica, Mass., and Shippensburg, Pa.; *m* 1813, Rachel Swaggot (1796-1872);
3-Capt. William Henry (1834-1906), Shippensburg; *m* 1859, Ann Gatchell Clark;
2-Americus Rogers (2 below).
10-John **Rogers** (1594-1674), Watertown, Mass.;
9-John (1611-1685-86), freeman, Watertown, 1637, later of Billerica, Mass.; *m* 1640, Percilla Dawes (*d* 1663);
8-John (1641-95), Billerica, Mass.; *m* 1667, Mary Shed (1648-88);
7-John (1680-1736), Billerica; *m* Abigal Putnam (1681-1754);

6–Samuel (1722-23-1788), *m* 1751, Rebecca Farmer;
5–Abigal P. (1756-1835), *m* Jeremiah **Allen** (5 above).
9–John **Farmer** (*b* and *d* in Eng.) *m* Isabella Muston (*d* 1686), Billerica, Mass.;
8–Edward (*d* 1727), Billerica, Mass.; *m* Mary Brown (1642-1719);
7–Oliver (1685-86-1761), *m* 1716-17, Abigal Johnson (1697-1773; Ebenezer[8]; Hon. Maj. William[9]; Capt. Edward[10], qv);
6–Rebecca (1726-1809), *m* Samuel **Rogers** (6 above).
10–William **Coale** (qv);
9–Capt. William (1623-78), from Bristol Parish, Va., to West River, Anne Arundel Co., Md.; capt. provincial troops, 1674; *m* Elizabeth Harrison Thomas (*d* 1726; Philip[10], qv);
8–Philip (*b* 1673), *m* 1697, Lady Cassandra Skipwith (*b* 1678; Sir Grey[9], qv);
7–Capt. Skipwith (*d* ante 1759), on Lord Baltimore's staff; gentleman justice, Md.; *m* 1732, Margaret Holland;
6–Philip (1739-94), of Harford Co., Md.; iron master; *m* Ann Dallam;
5–Samuel (1752-1839), to Cecil Co., Md.; iron master; *m* Ann Gatchell;
4–Emelia Jane (1807-76), from Elkton, Md., to Cumberland Co., Pa.; *m* 1830, James **Clark** (1805-68), of Cumberland Co., Pa. (William[5], *d* Cumberland Co., Pa.);
3–Ann Gatchell (1839-1919), *m* Capt. William H. **Allen** (3 above).
8–Elisha **Gatchell** (*b* Eng.-*d* 1753-54), to America ante 1716, settled Chester Co., Pa.; *m* Rachel– (*d* 1760);
7–Elisha, Jr., from Eng., *d* Chester Co., Pa.; *m* 1733, Marey Worley;
6–Jeremiah (1734-1802), of Chester Co.; *m* 1753, Hannah Brown (*d* 1874);
5–Ann (1775-1854), *m* Samuel **Coale** (5 above).
9–Samuel **Lincoln** (qv);
8–Mordecai (1657-1727), Hingham, Mass.; *m* 1st, 1685, Sarah Jones (Abraham[9], *m* Sarah, dau. of John Whitman, qv; Thomas[10], from Eng., 1638, *m* Ann–);
7–Mordecai (1686-1736), Hingham, Mass., and Amity, Pa.; *m* 1729, Mary Robeson (1705-83; Andrew[8], qv);
6–Abraham (1736-1806), of Exeter, Pa.; co. commr., 1772-78; mem. Gen. Assembly, 1782-86; Pa. del. to ratify Federal Constn., 1787; mem. constl. conv., 1789-90; del. to deliver address of welcome to Washington at close of Am. Rev.; *m* 1760, Ann Boone (1737-1807; James[7] [1709-85], Exeter, Pa., *m* 1735, Mary [1714-56], dau. of Hugh, son of Edward Foulke, qv; George[8], qv);
5–Ann (1774-1824), *m* 1807, George Michael **Brobst** (1771-1826);
4–Catharine (1810-69), *m* 1833, Benjamin **Stahle** (1794-1859);
3–Mary Margaret (1839-1916), *m* 1864, Franklin **Bitting** (1820-1901);
2–Catharine Delilah (*b* 1865), *m* 1889, Americus Rogers **Allen** (1861-1917), M.D., fellow Am. Coll. of Surgeons; surgeon.
1–*m* May 11, 1918, Julia Westcott David, *b* Bridgeport, Pa., Feb. 15, 1890; dau. of William P. David.
1–Ed. Conway Hall; Dickinson Coll., ex-'14 (Beta Theta Pi). Asst. sec., Fire Ins. Co., Phila. Mem. B.O.R., O.F.P.A., I.A.G., Boone Family Assn. Summer place: 10 E. Drive, Margate, N.J. Residence: 5240 Schuyler St., Germantown, Phila., Pa.

1–**ALLEN, Robert Webster,** *b* Chicago, Ill., May 20, 1906.
5–Zadok (Allyn) **Allen,** of Westfield, Mass.; *m* 1780, Lucy Herrick (Jonathan[6], of Montgomery, Mass., *m* Elizabeth–);
4–Winthrop (1781-82-1854), *m* 1814, Mercy Hall;
3–William H. (1825-1903), of Rose, Wayne Co., N.Y.; *m* Mary Barnes (1826-88; John[4], *m* Mary Cowan);
2–Elmer J. (2 below).
9–Edward **Doty,** Mayflower Pilgrim (qv);
8–Isaac (*b* 1648-49), Plymouth, Mass.; *m* Elizabeth England;
7–Samuel (*b* 1695), of Oyster Bay, N.Y.; *m* Charity Mudge;
6–Elias (1732-1806), of Clinton, N.Y.; *m* 1755, Amy Dean (1735-82; Nicholas[7]);
5–Amy (1766-1829), *m* 1786, Thomas **Hall** (1764-1843);
4–Mercy (1796-1853), *m* Winthrop **Allen** (4 above).
11–John **Webster** (qv);
10–Robert (1627-76), of Hartford, Conn.; *m* 1652, Susannah Treat (1629-1705; Richard[11], qv);
9–Jonathan (1656-1735), of Hartford; *m* 1681, Dorcas Hopkins (*d* 1769; Stephen[10], *m* Dorcas, dau. of John Bronson; John[11], *m* Jane–);
8–Jonathan (1682-1758), of Hartford; *m* 1704, Esther Judd (1686-1782; Benjamin[9], *m* Mary Lewis);
7–Jonathan (1705-81), of Glastonbury, Conn.; *m* 1730, Mabel Risley (*d* 1781; John[8], *m* Mary Arnold);
6–Elizur (1743-91), of Whitehall, N.Y.; *m* Ruth Densmore (1747-1829);
5–Elizur (1767-1854), of Warsaw, N.Y.; *m* 1791, Elizabeth Warren (1774-1848; Col. Gideon[6], officer at Ticonderoga during Am. Rev., *m* Unice Chipman);
4–William H. H. (1813-92), of Coldwater, Mich.; *m* 1840, Mary E. Dickson (1819-97; John[5], *m* Asenath Adams);
3–Clarissa A. (1841-1916), of Coldwater; *m* 1866, William Adams **Coombs** (1840-98);
2–Susan Snow (1872-1911), *m* 1904, Elmer J. **Allen** (1865-1917), telegrapher.
1–Not married. Mem. S.M.D., S.A.R., I.A.G., N.E.H.G.S. Vestryman and treas. St. Mark's Ch. (Episcopal). Republican. Clubs: Bon Ami Social, Coldwater Country. Residence: 199 W. Pearl St., Coldwater, Mich.

1–**ALLEN, Sara Jane Wilson (Mrs. William Porter),** *b* Newark, N.J., Sept. 17, 1878.
7–Hendrick **Wilson** (ca. 1680-1750; said to have been son of Henry, of Bristol, Eng.), of L.I.; ca. 1720-30 bought the southern part of Volkerse's tract, which lay north of the New Amwell road and bet. the Millstone River and Royce Brook;
6–Myndert (1716-1800), perhaps of Millstone, N.J.;
5–Myndert (1747-1830), of Millstone, N.J.; served in Am. Rev.; *m* 1780, Jannette Van Arsdalen (1756-1836; Hendrick[6], *m* Jane Ditmars);
4–William Minard (1790-1886), of Roycefield, N.J.; served in War 1812; *m* 1817, Jane Bergen (1797-1872; James[5], *m* Annette Van Voorhees);
3–Myndert W. (1818-71), of Brooklyn, N.Y.; prof. of music; *m* 1841, Elizabeth White (1822-74; John[4], *m* Miriam Harrington; Samuel[5], *m* Mary Brinkle);
2–Minard Alexander (2 below).
10–Obadiah **Bruen** (1606-1680/81; son of John [1560-1625], of Bruen Stapleford, Co. Cheshire, Eng., *m* 2d, Anne Fox, and desc. Henry II, King of England); came from Eng., settled at Plymouth, Mass., 1640-41; recorder and selectman, Gloucester, Mass., and New London, Conn., 1641-66; founder of Newark, N.J., 1666; *m* 1632 or 33, Sarah–(living 1679);
9–Hannah (1643-ante 1686), *m* 1663, John **Baldwin** (*b* 1640);
8–John (*b* ca. 1670-living 1743);
7–David (living 1778);
6–Patience (*b* ca. 1746), *m* Nathaniel **Dickinson** (1744-95), of Springfield, N.J.;
5–Elizabeth, *m* Nathaniel **Bond** (*b* 1759), served in Am. Rev.;
4–John (1789-1824), *m* 1813, Mary Parcel Hand (1798-1870; Col. Aaron[5], served in Am. Rev.; William[6]; Jonathan[7]);
3–Emily Woodruff (1814-80), *m* 1839, William H. **Chatterton** (1807-75);
2–Cornelia Jane Hand (1845-1929), *m* 1877, Minard Alexander **Wilson** (1853-1922), of Irvington, N.J.; musician and printer; issue: I–Sara Jane (1 above); II–Frederic Minard (*b* 1880; *m* Jessie Davis Brown); III–Elizabeth Bond (*b* 1882; *m* Howard C. Shay, 1878-1929); IV–Paul Alexander (*b* 1888; *m* Mary Turton).
1–*m* Jan. 10, 1923, William Porter Allen, *b* New York, N.Y., Jan. 13, 1858; son of John Terhune Allen, of New York, *m* Harriet Smith.
1–Mem. D.A.C., Nat. Soc. Magna Charta Dames, Huguenot Soc. of N.J., D.A.R., U.S.D. 1812, Rev. Memorial Soc. of N.J., I.A.G., N.J. Hist. Soc., Géneal. Soc. N.J., N.Y.G.B.S., Kenmore Assn. Methodist. Republican. Residence: 36 Orange Av., Irvington, N.J.

1–**ALLIBONE, Lawrence Washington,** *b* Phila., Pa., Apr. 2, 1857.
7–John **Marshall** (*d* 1729), *m* 1688, Sarah Smith (*d* 1749);
6–Thomas (1694-1740), *m* 1718, Hannah Mendenhall (b 1696);

5-Thomas (1727-1759-60), *m* 1st, 1752, Edith Newlin (Nathaniel[6] [*d* 1766], *m* 1733, Esther, dau. of Thomas Metcalf, of Sadsbury, *m* Jane-); see Vol. III, p. 505, for Newlin lineage;
4-Esther, *m* 1774, Thomas **Allibone** (1752-1809; Benjamin[5]);
3-William, Jr. (1781-1821), of Phila.; *m* 1801, Sarah Smith (1784-1839); see Vol. III, p. 505;
2-Thomas (2 below).
8-Richard **Smith** (bap. 1593-*d* 1647; son of William, of Eng.);
7-Richard (bap. 1626-1688), *m* 1653, Anne, dau. of William Yates, of Eng.;
6-Hon. Manuel (1670-1720), warden St. Mary's Ch., Burlington, N.J.; *m* Mary Willis (B. Willis[7] [*d* 1713], also warden St. Mary's, Burlington, N.J.);
5-Mary, *m* 1729, George **Eyre** (1700-61); see Vol. I, p. 526, for Eyre lineage;
4-Samuel (1734-88), of Burlington, N.J.; *m* Elizabeth Folwell;
3-Nathan (1767-1819), of Haddonfield, N.J., and Phila., Pa.; *m* 2d, Elizabeth Kay;
2-Emma Louisa (2 below).
7-William **Folwell** (*d* 1710), of Salem, Salem Co., N.J.; *m* Hope-;
6-Nathan (*d* 1731), of Mansfield Tp., Burlington Co., N.J.; *m* Sarah-;
5-Nathan (*d* 1760) of Springfield Tp., Burlington Co.; *m* 1724, Elizabeth Bullock (*d* 1760; John[6]);
4-Elizabeth, *m* Samuel **Eyre** (4 above).
7-Garves **Kay,** of Kirk Burton, Yorkshire, Eng.;
6-John (1656-1741/42), of Waterford Tp., Gloucester Co., N.J.; *m* 1684, Elizabeth Fearne (*d* 1713; Josiah[7], *m* Elizabeth-);
5-Isaac (1704-1756-57), of Waterford Tp.; *m* 1738, Mary Ann Gregory (Joseph[6], of Salem Co., N.J.);
4-Joseph (*d* 1806), of Waterford Tp.; *m* in Christ Ch., Phila., Pa., 1767, Judith Lippincott;
3-Elizabeth (1780-1852), *m* Nathan **Eyre** (3 above);
2-Emma Louisa (1812-78), *m* 1833, Thomas **Allibone** (1809-76), mcht., Phila., Pa.; for issue see Vol. III, p. 505.
1-*m* Apr. 19, 1899, Anna Jaffray Phillips, *b* Bristol, Pa.; dau. Symington Phillips, of Bristol (Rev. William W.[8], of New York).
1-Princeton, '79 (hon. C.E. 1893). Retired supt. of Sunbury (Pa.) div. of Pa. R.R. Co. Residence: 207 Ludlow Av., Spring Lake, N.J.

1-**ALSTON, Thomas Lynch,** *b* Charleston, S.C., Nov. 17, 1856-*d* Mar. 18, 1927.
7-John (Allston) **Alston** (1666-1719; son of William), exile for participation in the Monmouth Rebellion; settled at St. John's, Berkley, S.C.; mem. Carolina Commons; House of Assembly, 1695; *m* 1695, Elizabeth (Sanders) Harris; "Colonial records";
6-William (1695-97-1744), *m* 1721, Estha La Bruce (1702-81; Joseph, M.D.[7], *m* Estha Robins, their 4th dau. Elizabeth, *m* Thomas Lynch, a "signer");
5-Joseph (1733-82), of "The Oaks," Georgetown, S.C.; soldier in Am. Rev.; mem. House of Commons in S.C., 1768; mem. Provincial Congress, Charleston, S.C., 1775; mem. Com. of Safety, 1775; *m* Charlotte Rathmahler (1736-84; John[6], "Colonial records");
4-Col. William (1756-1839), began to write name Alston; of "Clifton," Georgetown, S.C.; soldier in Am. Rev.; capt. of Waccamaw Co., Georgetown, S.C., Col. Harvey's regt., 1781; mem. S.C. Senate; *m* 1st, 1777, Mary Ashe (their son, Joseph [1779-1816], was gov. of S.C., 1812, *m* Theodosia, dau. of Aaron Burr); *m* 2d, 1791, Mary Motte;
3-William Algernon (1782-1860), of "Rose Hill," Georgetown, S.C.; *m* his cousin, Mary (Young) Allston;
2-Col. John Ashe (2 below).
6-John **Alston,** 7 above;
5-John (*d* 1750 or 55), *m* Deborah; *m* 2d, Sarah Belin (*b* 1717; James[6], *m* Sarah Terkitt);
4-Capt. William, Jr. (1738-81), began to write name Allston, of Brook Green, Georgetown, S.C.; capt., Marion's Brigade in Am. Rev.; *m* 2d, 1775, Rachel Moore (1757-1841; John[5] [1726-88], *m* Elizabeth [1737-90], dau. of John Vander Horst, *m* Mary Elizabeth, dau. of Elias Foisson; John[6], *m* Rachel Villie Ponteux); their son, Washington Allston (1779-1843), was noted artist both in Europe and America, *m* Mary Young;
3-Mary (1778-1841), wrote name Allston; as Widow Young, *m* 2d, her cousin, William A. **Alston** (3 above).
9-Richard **Buford** (*b* 1617), from Eng. in the "Elizabeth," 1635, settled in Lancaster Co., Va.; *m* 1640, a dau. of John Vause;
8-John (1642-1722), of Christ Ch. Parish, Lancaster Co., Va.; *m* 1662, Elizabeth Parrotte (*b* 1645; Richard[9] [*d* 1686], vestryman Christ Ch., Va., high sheriff, 1657, sr. justice, Middlesex Co. Ct., 1673, *m* Margaret-, *d* 1687);
7-Thomas, Sr. (1663-1716), *m* Mary- (*d* 1720);
6-Henry, Sr. (1684-1720), Lancaster Co., Va.; *m* 1707, Mary Osborne (Henry[7], *m* 1684, Mary Simpson, *m* 2d, 1688, Alice George);
5-William, Sr. (*b* 1708), *m* 1729, Elizabeth Owen;
4-Maj. William, Jr. (*b* 1747), of Middlesex Co., Va.; Am. Rev.; ens. of 1st troup, N.C. Dragoons, 1774-79; settled nr. Gourdine Station, Williamsburg Co., S.C., on the Santee River among the Huguenots; *m* Frances June (*d* 1836);
3-Frances June (*d* 1836), *m* as his 3d wife, 1805, Rev. Hugh **Fraser** (1763-1838), rector of All Sts. Parish Waccamaw, Georgetown, S.C.;
2-Fanny Buford (1820-97), *m* 1838, Col. John Ashe **Alston** (1818-58), ed. U.Va.; mem. State Legislature; artist; issue: I-Hugh Fraser (*b* 1839); II-Theodosius (1840-79; "M.D.", in C.S.A.); III-John Ashe, Jr., M.D. (1842-82; *m* Emma Sanders); IV-Washington (1844-62); V-Helen (1845-1918); VI-Fanny (1851-1919); VII-Rowland, M.D. (1853-1920); VIII-Thomas Lynch (1 above); IX-Algernon (1857-64); X-Algernon, 2d (*b* 1864).
1-*m* Feb. 7, 1884, Helen LeRoy Sanders, *b* Edgefield, S.C., Dec. 30, 1860; ed. private schs., Greenville Female Coll., Greenville, S.C.; Episcopalian; dau. of William Alston Sanders, M.D.; issue: 1-William LeRoy (qv); 2-Helen (qv).
1-Ed. Charleston High Sch. and Porter Mil. Acad., Charleston, S.C. Vestryman and lay reader of the Ch. of Resurrection, Greenwood, S.C.; propr. Anderson Foundry and Machine Works, Anderson, S.C., retired from business, 1900. Mem. Soc. Cincinnati. Mason.

1-**ALSTON, William LeRoy,** *b* Ninety-Six, Abbeville, S.C., Feb. 12, 1885.
8-William **Sanders,** first settler of what is now Sumter Co., S.C., first grant, dated May 29, 1734; justice of peace, 1734-35; *m* Felicia Ferguson;
7-William, "Oakland Plantation," Sumter Co., S.C., *m* Martha Cantey;
6-William (1748-1810), *m* 1771, Sarah Ragan (William[7], of Clarendon Co.);
5-William (*d* 1818), soldier Am. Rev.; *m* 1799, Eunice Garner (Richard[6], of Richland Co., S.C. *m* Philadelphia-);
4-Marion (1806-73), *m* Salley Norflett Alston, of Halifax Co., N.C.;
3-William Alston, M.D. (1837-1915), *m* 1859, Mary Elizabeth Frazier (*b* 1841; Col. Marshall[4] [1806-70], *m* 1840, Sarah Anne Harris, 1820-48);
2-Helen LeRoy (2 below).
10-John **Alston** (qv);
9-John (*d* 1704), *m* Anne Wallis (*b* 1645);
8-Col. John (1673-1758), from Eng.; first Am. record 1711, Chowan Co., N.C.; extensive land owner, Chowan Co.; justice ct. of Oyer and Terminer; revenue collector for the King; sheriff; vestryman, St. Paul's Parish; col. of N.C. militia; *m* Mary Clark (John[9] [*d* 1689]; g.dau. of John Palin, chief justice of N.C., 1731); "Colonial records";
7-Joseph John (1700-81), "Colonial records"; of Halifax, N. C.; *m* Eupham Wilson (Willis[8], "Colonial records," of Norfolk Co., Va., mem. House of Burgesses, 1720-50, *m* Mary, dau. of Jeremiah Simons);
6-Col. Willis (1750-1837), Am. Rev.; col. of Halifax Dist., N.C.; mem. Assembly, 1776; mem. Constl. Conv., 1776; *m* Elizabeth Wright;
5-Gen. Joseph John, "General Jack" (*d* 1831), *m* Margaret B. Thomas (*d* 1866);
4-Salley Norflett (1823-73), *m* Marion **Sanders** (4 above);
3-William A., *m* Mary E. Frazier (3 above);
2-Helen LeRoy (*b* 1860), *m* 1884, Thomas Lynch **Alston** (qv).
1-Not married. B.Sc. in E. and M.E., Ala. Poly. Inst., 1904 (Alpha Tau Omega). Mgr., Gen. Electric Co., Charleston, W.Va. Mem. N.C. Soc. Cincinnati. Residence: 628 Edgefield Av., Greenwood, S.C. Address: Charleston, W.Va.

ALSTON

John Alston, from England to North Carolina.
Arms: Azure, ten estoiles of six points, four, three, two, one, or.
Crest: A crescent argent, charged with an estoile or.
Motto: Immotus.

1–**ALSTON, Helen,** *b* Ninety Six, Abbeville Co., S.C., Jan. 3, 1888.
8–Samuel **Ashe,** "Colonial records";
7–John Baptista of N.Carolina; "Colonial records"; eminent lawyer; speaker of Assembly, 1727; mem. His Majesty's Council of N.C., 1733; mem. House of Commons, 1786; Senator, 1789-95; mem. N.C. Cont. Congress, 1789; *m* 1719, Elizabeth Swann (1699-1729; Col. Samuel[8] [1653-1707], colonial wars, collector of customs, 1693; speaker House of Burgesses, only Crown officer in the Colony apptd. by the King; *m* 2d, 1698, Elizabeth, dau. of Maj. Alexander Lillington [1643-97], Colonial officer, gov. of N.C., judge of Precinct Ct., 1690, Legislator, 1678, *m* Sarah James, dau. of Thomas James, "Colonial Records," son of John Lillington, *m* Sarah Porter; Col. Thomas[9]; William[10]);
6–Maj. Gen. John (1721-81), Am. Rev.; of New Hanover Co., N.C.; Ashe Co. and Asheville, N.C., were named for him; brig.gen., 1778; elected to Lower House of Assembly; speaker; mem. Com. of Safety, Wilmington, N.C.; *m* Rebecca Moore (Col. Maurice[7] [1670-1740], speaker of Assembly, 1726, *m* Margaret, dau. of Col. Benjamin Berringer of Barbados, *m* Margaret Foster; Gov. James[8] [1641-1704], colonial gov. of S.C., 1700); their sons, Maj. Gen. John Ashe, Jr., N.C. mem. Soc. Cincinnati, and Maj. Sam, original mem. Soc. Cincinnati, N.C.;
5–Mary, *m* Col. William **Alston** (1756-1839);
4–William Algernon (1782-1860), of "Rose Hill," Georgetown, S.C.; *m* his cousin, Mary (Young) Allston;
3–Col. John Ashe (1818-58), *m* 1838, Fanny Buford Fraser (1820-97);
2–Thomas Lynch (qv), *m* 1884, Helen LeRoy Sanders.
1–Ed. private and graded schs., Charleston, S.C., and Anderson, S.C.; St. Mary's Sch., Raleigh, N.C.; Converse Coll., Spartanburg, S.C. Mem. C.D.A., D.C.G., D.A.R., U.D.C. Residence: 628 Edgefield Av., Greenwood, S.C.

1–**ALVORD, Dorothy Maria,** *b* Kent, Wash., Apr., 6, 1895.
10–Alexander **Alvord** (qv);
9–Thomas (1653-88), of Windsor, Conn., and Northampton, Mass.; soldier in the Falls Fight, 1676; *m* 1681, Joanna Taylor (1655-1737/38; John[10], *m* Thankful Woodward);
8–Thomas (1683-1768), of Northampton, Mass.; received land grant at Fallstown (now Bernardston), from Gen. Ct. of Mass., 1734, for his father's services in Falls Fight; garrison soldier in Meadows Fight at Deerfield, 1703-04; *m* 2d, Mary Strong (*b* 1690; Thomas[9], *m* Mary Stebbins);
7–Asahel (1720-61), of Northampton, Mass., and Colchester, Conn.; *m* 1741, Rachel Gould (*b* 1720; Thomas[8], *m* Mary Crittenden);
6–Thomas Gould (1742-1810), of Durham, Conn., and Homer, N.Y.; served in French and Indian War; cannonier in Col. Lamb's Regt., during Am. Rev.; *m* 1st, 1762, Keziah Orvis (1743-95; Ebenezer[7], *m* Elizabeth Root);
5–Ebenezer (1767-1844), Farmington, Conn., and Homer, N.Y.; *m* Rachel Crampton (1770-1843; Miles[6], *m* Rhoda Keyes);
4–Sylvester (1796-1863), of Homer, N.Y.; *m* 1825, Lucy Hall (1800-82; Moody[5], *m* Lois Huntington);
3–Thomas Moody (1832-1919), of Pialschie, later called Thomas, Wash.; pioneer from New York to Wash., 1853, to Calif., 1859; *m* 1859, Maria Julia Smith (1832-1911; Horace[4], *m* Harriet Otis);
2–Irving Thomas (2 below).
4–Jarvis **Jones,** from Wales before Am. Rev.;
3–Rev. Charles Pinkney, *m* Sarah McLaughlin, of Fayetteville, N.C.; *m* 2d, Juliette Packer, of Coldwater, Mich.;
2–Eudora Mary Caroline (*b* 1865), *m* 1891, Irving Thomas **Alvord** (*b* 1865), farmer, Centralia, Wash.; issue: I–Eugene Irving (*b* 1892; *m* Helen Timmerman, *d* 1923; *m* 2d, 1925, Margaret Simmons); II–Dorothy Maria (1 above).
1–A.B., Wash. State Coll., '19 (Alpha Chi Omega, Mu Phi Epsilon); Columbia U., 1919-20; U. Calif., 1926-27. Teacher English, Centralia High School, 1921-23, 1924-26; asst. librarian, Ellensburg Normal School, 1927-28; librarian Olympia Public Library, since 1928. Mem. D.A.R., A.A.U.W. Methodist. Residence 109 E. 19th St., Olympia, Wash.

1–**AMBLER, Alfred Seger, II,** *b* Danbury, Conn., Feb. 17, 1868.
8–John **Ruggles** from Nasing, Co. Essex, Eng., to Roxbury, Mass., 1634; *m* Barbarie–;
7–John (*b* 1632), of Roxbury, Mass.;
6–Rev. Benjamin (1676-1708), of Suffield, ordained 1698; *m* Mercy–;
5–Capt. Joseph (1701-91), of New Milford, Conn.; *m* 1722, Rachel Tolls;
4–Elizabeth, *m* Eli **Seger;**
3–Polly (1784-1844), *m* 1806, Dea. Benjamin **Ambler** (1787-1867), of Danbury, Conn.; see Vol. III, p. 505, for Ambler lineage;
2–Alfred Seger (2 below).
9–Rear Admiral Thomas **Graves** (1605-1653), of Charlestown, Mass.; *m* Katharine Gray (Thomas[10], *m* Katharine Myles);
8–Joseph (*b* 1645), *m* 1666, Elizabeth Maynard (John[9], *m* Mary Axtell);
7–Richard (*b* 1672), *m* Joanna–;
6–Lebbens (*b* 1705), *m* 1730, Amity Whitney;
5–Amity (*b* 1734), *m* 1762, Francis Dawson **Swords** (1731-1800), enl. 1775 at Stamford, Conn. Vols., Am. Rev.;
4–Lovia Drusilla (1771-1831), *m* 1791, Nathan **Banks** (1770-1850), of Fairfield, Conn.;
3–Betsey (1801-86), *m* as his 2d wife, 1825, Ezra **Taylor** (1785-1867), of New Fairfield, Conn. (Zalmon[4] [1759-1815], in 5th Conn. Regt., Am. Rev., settled at Ridgefield, *m* Hannah [1757-1810], dau. of Theophilus Benedict [1738-1810], ens., 16th Conn. Regt., Am. Rev.); see Vol. III, p. 505, for Taylor lineage;
2–Drusilla (2 below).
10–John **Whitney** (qv);
9–John (*b* Eng., 1620 or 21), *m* 1642, Ruth Reynolds (Robert[10], *m* Mary–);
8–Nathaniel (*b* 1646), *m* 1673, Sarah Hagar;
7–William (1683-1721), *m* 1706, Martha Pearce (Joseph[8]);
6–Amity (*b* 1712), *m* Lebbens **Graves** (6 above).
2–Alfred Seger **Ambler** (1824-67), of Danbury; hat-box mfr.; *m* 1846, Martha Phillips Holmes (1823-61); *m* 2d, 1863, Drusilla Taylor (1832-88), see Vol. III, p. 505, for issue.
1–*m* Aug. 27, 1889, Fannie Gertrude Bishop (see Vol. III, p. 505 for genealogy); issue: 1–Gertrude Beatrice, *b* Beatrice, Neb., July 25, 1890; mem. D.A.R.; *m* July 23, 1910, Frederick Gwynne Weston, of Waterloo, Ia. (issue: Ruth, *b* Dec. 29, 1916), *m* 2d, Aug. 1, 1923, Joseph Hamilton Lukens, of Kansas City, Mo.
1–Loan agt., Northwestern Mutual Life Ins. Co. of Milwaukee, Wis., Residence: 3136 Cottage Grove Av., Des Moines, Ia.

1–**ANDERSON, Alice Simms (Mrs. James Blythe),** *b* Harrodsburg, Ky., Nov. 3, 1868.
9–Richard **Taylor** (*b* 1612), will proved in Norfolk Co., Va., May 21, 1679; *m* Margaret Hodges (will proved in Norfolk Co., Aug. 15, 1679);

8–Thomas (*b* 1679, posthumous son), will proved in Norfolk Co., Mar. 19, 1746/47; *m* Mary–;
7–Richard, on Jan. 30, 1741, patented 400 acres and on Aug. 20, 1745, patented 1200 acres in Goochland Co., Va., "on mill branch of Willis River";
6–Samuel (*d* 1791, in Cumberland Co., Va.), *m* Sophia Creed;
5–Samuel (*d* 1812), of Cumberland Co.; served as 2d lt. in Am. Rev.; went to Ky., 1779 (quoting from Grimes heirs vs. Morgan heirs, Fayette Co., Ky., Circuit Court: "Isaac Clinkenbeard deposeth and saith that in the latter part of the year 1779 I came to this Lick in company with John Taylor, Sam'l Taylor, John Hart, John McIntire and Wm. Clinkenbeard and John Taylor informed us it was called Bramblets Lick"); entered 3,300 acres, Dec. 1781; entered on The Waters of Shawnee Run 1900 acres, Mar. 1785 (from Lincoln Co., Ky., entry book); mem. 1st and 2d constl. convs. and Ky. Senate; mem. Va. Legislature from Mercer Co., 1788-89; built on the Shawnee Run entry in 1790 the first stone house in Mercer Co. which bears the date and inscription: "Look to your laws rather than to your progenitors for inheritance"; *m* Elizabeth Hughes (William[6], of Cumberland Co.);
4–Dr. John (1767-1841), *m* 2d, bond Aug. 18, 1821, Polly (Denny) McCormick (1786-1859), widow of Andrew S. McCormick;
3–Ann Elizabeth (1824-1913), *m* 1842, John Haldon **Grimes** (see Vol. II, p. 20, for Grimes, Broaddus and Tyler lineages; Robert Tyler, the immigrant, of Daptford, Kent, Eng., *m* Joanne Ravens, June 29, 1663);
2–Lucy E. (2 below).
7–Marmaduke (Semmes) **Simms** (will proved 1692/93), of St. Mary's Co., Md.; moved to Md. ca. 1660; door keeper, Upper House Md. Assembly, 1662; *m* 1668, Fortune Mitford (now Medford, will proved 1701), widow of Bulmer Mitford;
6–Marmaduke (will proved 1717), of Newport, Charles Co., Md.; *m* Elizabeth Clarkson (William[7], *m* Ruth, widow of Edward Gaile);
5–Francis (*b* ca. 1700-will proved 1771), of Charles Co., Md.; *m* 1733, Lucretia Chapman;
4–Ignatus (*b* 1745-*d* in Patrick Co., Va., 1819), began to write name Simms; served in Am. Rev.; *m* 1st, Sabra– (*d* 1788);
3–William Marmaduke (1788-1844), War 1812; went to Ky., 1809; *m* 2d, Catharine Jacqueline Carter Porter;
2–James Edward (2 below).
9–Lady Diana Skipwith, *m* Maj. Edward **Dale** (see Vol. II, p. 370, No. 9 under Landis);
8–Katherine, *m* Capt. Thomas **Carter** (see Vol. II, p. 370, No. 8 under Landis);
7–Thomas (1672-1733), commr. of Lancaster Co., Va., 1705-29; commd. by Gov. Spotswood capt. of Lancaster Co. militia, Apr. 7, 1711; *m* Aug. 22, 1695, Arabella Williamson (William[8]; James[9] [*d* 1656], commr. Isle of Wight Co., Va., 1646, and commr. Lancaster Co., 1652, *m* Ann Underwood);
6–Joseph (1696-1751), tobacco inspector at the Port of Corotoman, 1724-25 until 1738; commd. lt., 1742; used seal, Jan. 2, 1739, showing a crest of the Bedfordshire Carters—a demi Talbot out of a mural crown and below the crest the initials T.C.; *m* 1719, Catharine Stevens (James[7], of King and Queen Co., Va.);
5–Capt. John (1725-ca. 1793), *m* Susannah Winslow;
4–Mary Catharine (1770-1819), *m* Capt. John **Porter,** Corpl. 2d Va. Regt., subsequently asst. dep. wagon-master-gen. in Am. Rev. (see Vol. II, p. 20, for Porter lineage);
3–Catharine Jacqueline Carter (1809-79), *m* William Marmaduke **Simms** (3 above).
8–Maj. Robert **Beverley** (*d* 1686), of Middlesex Co., Va.; justice, 1673; elected clk. House of Burgesses, 1670; apptd. cdr. of Berkley's forces, 1676; *m* Mary Keeble, widow (1639-78);
7–Capt. Harry (*d* 1730), of "Newlands," Spotsylvania Co, Va.; justice, Middlesex, 1700; surveyor, King and Queen and King William cos., 1702-14; presiding justice, Spotsylvania; cdr. of the sloop "Virgin," 1716, sent by Gov. Spotswood in quest of pirates, captured by a Spanish man-of-war nr. the Bahamas and taken to Vera Cruz where he escaped, arriving in Va., ca. Aug. 1717; *m* ca. 1700, Elizabeth Smith (Robert[8]; Maj. Gen. Robert[9] [*d* 1687], of "Brandon," Middlesex Co., Va., long a mem. of the Council);
6–Susannah (*b* 1706), *m* 1726, Benjamin **Winslow** (*d* 1751; Thomas[7] [*d* 1726], of Essex Co., Va.);
5–Susannah (*d* ca. 1792), *m* Capt. John **Carter** (5 above).
2–James Edward **Simms** (1844-1908), served in Co. A, 9th Ky. Cav., C.S.A.; *m* 1867, Lucy Elizabeth Grimes (1847-81).
1–*m* June 16, 1898, James Blythe Anderson (see Vol. I, p. 420); issue: 1–Joseph Caldwell, *b* Lexington, Ky., May 30, 1899; 2–Elizabeth Blythe (Jan. 4, 1903-Apr. 27, 1924).
1–Ed. Ky. Female Orphan School, Peabody Normal, and Nashville U. Teacher. Regent for Ky., Nat. Soc. Magna Charta Dames; v.p. Soc. Mareen Duval Descendants; mem. U.D.C., Woman's Club. Residence: "Glengarry," R.F.D. 7, Lexington, Ky.

1–**ANDREWS, Elizabeth Lenoir Key (Mrs. Garnett),** *b* Chattanooga, Tenn., Mar. 30, 1876.
4–David **Key,** of Greeneville, Tenn.;
3–Rev. John, settled in Tenn.; *m* Margaret Armitage;
2–David McKendree, LL.D. (2 below).
7–Prob. John **Lenoir,** Huguenot; came to America, after revocation of Edict of Nantes, 1685; sea capt. and merchant; lost at sea in his own ship;
6–Thomas (*d* 1765), Brunswick Co., Va.; removed to Tarborotown, N.C., 1759; *m* Mourning–(b 1709);
5–William (1751-1830), *m* 1771, Anne Ballard;
4–William Ballard (1775-1852), *m* 1802, Betsey Avery;
3–Albert S. (1803-61), *m* 1837, Catherine Freeling Welcker;
2–Elizabeth (*b* 1838), *m* 1857, David McKendree **Key,** LL.D. (1824-1900), 1st grad. Hiwassee Coll., 1850; lt. col. C.S.A.; U.S. senator, 1875-77; Postmaster Gen., 1877-80; U.S. dist. judge; issue: I–Emma (1858-86); II–Albert Lenoir (see Vol. I, p. 225); III–Katharine (*m* S. R. Read); IV–Sarah (*m* Zeboin Cartter Patten); V–Margaret (*b* 1866); VI–John S. (1868-1921); VII–David McKendree, Jr. (1871-88); VIII–Henry Lenoir (*b* 1874); IX–Elizabeth Lenoir 1 above).
1–*m* Oct. 30, 1895, Garnett Andrews (qv for genealogy).
Residence: Rossville, Ga., Route 1, LaFayette Rd., adjoining Chickamauga Nat. Park.

1–**ANDREWS, Garnett,** *b* Washington, Wilkes Co., Ga., Sept. 15, 1870.
8–James **Andrews,** from Eng., ca. 1670; bought 133 acres of land on the south side of the Rappahannock River, land which is now St. Anne's Parish, in northern part of Essex Co., which was formed from Rappahannock, 1692; in 1674, with Nicholas Copeland, received a grant of 567 acres for transporting 12 persons into the colony; *m* Elizabeth–;
7–John (1680-1754), *b* Essex Co., Va.; *m* 1st, Ann Stockdale (Philip[8]);
6–John (ca. 1712-1771);
5–James (ca. 1736-1767), probably *m* Miss Garnett (James[6]; John[7]);
4–John (1762-1816), with his brother Alexander and other relatives, removed from Va. to Ga., bet. 1785-97; settled in what is now Oglethorp Co.; aet. 19, served in Cont. Army, present at siege of Yorktown; *m* 1789, Nancy Goode;
3–James Garnett (1798-1873), planter; judge Superior Ct. of Ga. nearly 24 yrs.; *m* Annulet Ball;
2–Col. Garnett (2 below).
8–John **Goode** (1620 or 30-1709; son of Richard, of Cornwall, Eng.), went to the Barbados, 1643-50; came to Va. ante 1660; *m* ca. 1650 Frances Mackarness;
7–Samuel (1655-58-post 1734), *b* Barbados; *m* Martha Jones;
6–William (1700-60), of Henrico Co., Va.; *m* Phebe Goode;
5–John (*b* bet. 1720-50), *m* Frances Hunter;
4–Nancy (1770-1828), *m* John **Andrews** (4 above);
3–James G. (1798-1873), *m* Annulet Ball (3 above);
2–Col. Garnett (1837-1903), lt.col., C.S.A.; law partner of Senator John Sharp Williams, Yazoo City, Miss.; mayor of Chattanooga, Tenn., 1891; *m* 1867, Rosalie Champe Beirne (1841-1927); issue: I–Garnett (1 above); II–Champe Seabury (*b* 1876); III–Andrew Beirne

(qv for maternal lineages); IV–Oliver Burnside (*b* 1882).
1–*m* Oct. 30, 1895, Elizabeth Lenoir Key (qv); for issue, see Vol. I, p. 224.
1–Grad. V.M.I., '90; Worcester Poly. Inst., 1892. Identified with mfg. business since 1896; pres. Richmond Hosiery Mills, etc. (see Who's Who in America). Served as capt. Tenn. N.G., 1890; mem. War Industries Bd., employment service, Dept. of Labor, etc. Mem. S.A.R., I.A.G. Clubs: Mountain City, Chattanooga Golf and Country, Calumet (New York). Residence: Chickamauga, Ga. Address: Route 2, via Chattanooga, Tenn.

1–**ANDREWS, A(ndrew) Beirne,** *b* Yazoo City, Miss., Jan. 10, 1878.
8–Edward **Ball** (*b* ca. 1642), from Eng. to Branford, Conn., 1664; a founder of Newark, N.J., 1665; high sheriff of Essex Co., N.J., 1683; *m* ca. 1664, Abigail Blatchley (*b* 1650; Thomas[9], dep. Conn. Gen. Assembly, *m* Susanna Ball);
7–Thomas (1687/88-1744), constable, Newark, N.J., 1715-16; *m* ca. 1710, Sarah David (*d* 1778, aet 88);
6–Ezekiel (*d* 1804, aet 83), built "Tuscan Hall," nr. Newark, N.J., ca. 1772; *m* Mary Jones (*d* 1810, aet 84), of Sag Harbor, L.I.;
5–Dr. Stephen (1749-83), ed. Coll. of N.J.; surgeon Am. Rev.; *m* Sarah Ross;
4–Frederick (1771-1820), *d* Savannah, Ga.; *m* 1803, Eliza Toxey;
3–Annulet (1810-72), *m* Garnett **Andrews** (1798-1873).
4–Col. Andrew (O'Beirne) **Beirne** (1771-1845), from Roscommon Co., Ireland, 1793; settled in Monroe Co., W. Va., 1800; mem. 25th and 26th Congresses; comd. a co. at Battle of Norfolk, 1814; *m* Ellen Keenan (Edward[5] [1742-1826], *m* Nancy Donnally [1755-1810]; Patrick[6]);
3–Andrew (ca. 1797-1872), *m* Ellen Gray;
2–Rosalie Champe (2 below).
9–John **Carter** (qv);
8–Robert (1663-1723), of "Corotoman"; burgess; speaker; pres. of Council; treas. of Colony; actg.gov.; *m* 1688, Judith Armistead (John[9], "The Councillor," lt.col. of Horse, 1680, mem. Council, 1688; *m* Judith–; William[10], qv);
7–John, sec. Va.; *m* ca. 1732, Elizabeth Hill (Col. Edward, Jr.[8], of "Shirley");
6–Edward, of "Blenheim," *m* Sarah Champe (Col. John[7], of Fredericksburg, Va.);
5–Jane, *m* Gen. William **Bradford,** officer in Brit. Army;
4–Jane, *m* Dr. Landon Carter **Gray,** prof. U. Va.;
3–Ellen (*d* 1845), *m* Andrew **Beirne** (3 above);
2–Rosalie Champe (Feb. 28, 1841-Aug. 12, 1927), *m* 1867, Col. Garnett **Andrews** (1837-1903), lt. col., C.S.A.; law partner of Senator John Sharp Williams, Yazoo City, Miss.; mayor of Chattanooga, Tenn., 1891 (for issue and paternal lineages see Garnett Andrews).
1–*m* Dec. 28, 1912, Narcissa McGuirk (qv for genealogy and issue).
1–C.E., Ala. Poly. Inst., '96. Manufacturer; mgr. Dayton Hosiery Mills. Mem. I.A.G. Clubs: Mountain City (Chattanooga, Tenn.). Residence: Dayton, Tenn.

1–**ANDREWS, Narcissa McGuirk (Mrs. A. Beirne),** *b* Florence, Ala., Nov. 26, 1891.
4–James or Felix **McGuirk,** editor of a paper in Ireland, from Co. Armagh, to Brooklyn, N.Y., ca. 1817 (*m* Rosa Lee?);
3–Col. John (*b* Ireland, 1827-*d* 1871), served in Mexican War, 1847-48, and in C.S.A.; *m* 1855, Louise Virginia Mahaffey;
2–John Autry (2 below).
5–Lt. George **Tucker,** *m* Elizabeth Jackson;
4–Minerva, *m* James E. **Mahaffey,** merchant and planter, La Grange, Tenn.;
3–Louise V. (1834-72), *m* John **McGuirk** (3 above).
11–William **Presley,** from Eng.; burgess, 1647; will proved 1650;
10–Col. Peter (*d* 1693), burgess, 1657; *m* 1660, Elizabeth Thompson (Richard[11] [*d* 1649], *m* Ursula Bysche);
9–Elizabeth, *m* 1st, Ebenezer **Saunders** (1661-93), atty. and land owner;
8–Edward (1686-living 1744), vestryman St. Stephen's Parish, 1720; *m* 1717, Winifred (Kent ?);
7–William (1718-79), *m* 1738, Elizabeth Hubbard (1721-89; Thomas[8], regimental q.m., 1st Va., 1777-78);
6–Thomas (1739-ante 1808), served in Am. Rev.; *m* 1764, Ann Turner;
5–Rev. Turner (1782-1853), minister; educator; engr.; cut the first canal at Muscle Shoals under contract with U.S. Govt.; *m* 1799, Frances Dunn (1779-1824; Ishmael[6], of Brunswick Co., Va., *m* Mildred Dudley);
4–Louisa Turner (1803-79), *m* 1819, Judge Robert Coleman **Foster** (1796-1871), of Nashville, Tenn.;
3–Narcissa (1826-79), became an invalid from nursing Union and Confed. soldiers; *m* 1852, John Wightman **MacAlester** (1810-88), from Ireland, aet. 18; grad. Trinity Coll.; merchant; banker, scholar;
2–Elizabeth (*b* 1862), *m* 1889, John Autry **McGuirk** (1862-1919), of Holly Springs, Miss.; issue: I–John Autry (*b* 1890); II–Narcissa (1 above); III–Robert Charles (*b* 1895; *m* 1927, Martha Taylor).
1–*m* Dec. 28, 1912, Andrew Beirne Andrews (qv for genealogy); issue: 1–Andrew Beirne, Jr., *b* Dayton, Tenn., Jan. 6, 1916; 2–Rosalie Champe, *b* Dayton, Aug. 5, 1925.
1–Ed. Anniston High Sch., Noble Inst., and pvt. instruction. Mem. U.D.C. (chapter pres.). Residence: Dayton, Tenn.

1–**ANGELLOTTI, Marion Polk,** *b* San Rafael, Calif.
9–Silvester **Stover** (*b* in Eng.-*d* ca. 1688), of York, Me.; received a grant of land with 3 others at Cap Neddick, 1649, but bought out interest of other two; added other lands by purchase and built and fortified a home there; signed the submission, 1652; *d* after beginning of Indian War of 1688; will proved 1689/90; his widow held the fort, and was paid by Gen. Ct. for "provisions furnished to soldiers on the march and otherwise" in the war; was finally compelled to abandon "the best fort in the Eastern part" which was "within a week seized by the enemy and burnt"; her will was made at Scituate, and proved at Plymouth, 1722; her petition for pay is in Gen. Ct. papers; *m* ante 1660, Elizabeth Norton (*d* 1722; Henry[10], of York, gave bonds in Gen. Ct. at Boston, 1634/35, provost marshal 1652,55, took oath of allegiance 1652, returned to Eng., 1657, but inventory of estate filed at York, 1678, *m* Margaret–);
8–George (ca. 1668-1750), of York and Gloucester, moved to Gloucester at outbreak of Indian War, 1688; selectman; returned to York, 1712; *m* 1692, Abigail Elwell;
7–Isaac (1697-ca. 1788), of York; *m* 1st, 1724, his first cousin, Mary Stover;
6–Isaac (1745-1823), of York; signed deeds at York, 1783,84; removed to Penobscot and was deeded land there, 1788; *m* 1769, Martha Stover (1744-post 1784), called Polly in some old records;
5–Jeremiah (1770-1824), of Penobscot and Blue Hill; farmer, and owned "Stover Farm" on the Sedgwick rd.; *m* 1792, Abigail Devereux, of Penobscot;
4–Lois Hibbert (1794-1837), of Blue Hill; *m* 1821, Isaac Smith **Osgood** (see Vol. II, p. 70, for Osgood lineage);
3–Lois Frances (1836-1913), *m* 1860, Giuseppe **Angellotti** (1824-83), left Italy after the fall of the Roman Republic, 1848, for which he had fought with the youth of Rome in the 3 weeks fighting; escaped the Austrians and went to Monte Video; hearing of the discovery of gold in Calif., he went there in sailing vessel around the Horn; settled in Marin Co., Calif., where the first land he bought, was recorded 5 Oct., 1852, in Book 1 of Deeds in San Rafael C.H., it being an alcalde deed; naturalized 1865; a public spirited citizen he donated land for school site, and for church cemetery; mcht. and hotel owner; died of yellow fever in Guaymas, Mexico, and buried there;
2–Frank Marion (2 below).
10–Thomas (Millett) **Millet** (1605-76), from Eng. in the "Elizabeth," with his wife and son Thomas, 1635, settled at Dorchester; bought of William Perkins, teaching elder of the ch. at Gloucester, all the property he owned in the town, and succeeded him in the church work there, 1655; engaged in ministry work at Gloucester; removed to Brookfield shortly before his death; *m* Mary Greenoway (*d* 1682; John[11]);

9–Mehitable (1641-99), of Gloucester; *m* Isaac **Elwell** (1641-1715; Robert[10], of Gloucester, *d* there 1683, mem. Salem Ch., 1643, freeman 1640, bought land at Gloucester, 1642, selectman, there 14 yrs., *m* Joane–, *d* 1675);
8–Abigail (1676-1740), *m* George **Stover** (8 above).
11–Francis (Mathes) **Matthews** (*d* ante 1653), came over with Mason, 1631; at Durham Point, 1631; Oyster river, 1633; signed the combination, 1639; removed to Dover prob. 1647; *m* as early as 1630, Thomasine Channon (*d* ca. 1700);
10–Walter (*d* 1678), of York and Isle of Shoals; constable, 1658; original homestead still in possession of descs.; *m* Mary–(*d* post 1678);
9–Susanna, *m* Dea. Rowland **Young,** of York (Rowland[10] [*b* in Scotland], of York, 1637, *m* Joanna [*d* 1698], dau. of Robert Knight [ca. 1585-1676], mcht. of York, there before 1643, took oath of allegiance, 1652);
8–Mary, *m* 1701, Dependence **Stover,** (*d* 1723), of York (Silvester[9], above);
7–Mary (1702-post 1747), *m* 1st, 1724, her 1st cousin, Isaac **Stover** (7 above).
9–John **Devereux** (qv);
8–Robert (*d* ca. 1740), of Marblehead; inherited from his father "two-thirds of all my land within the Stone wall now lying in Marblehead being three hundred acres more or less with my now dwelling house and barn," which the father had purchased in 1659 from the agent of Rev. Hugh Peters, attainted of treason; but this property was by the crown restored to the heir of the Rev. Peters, after it had been in the possession of the Devereux family for nearly half a century, and Robert Devereux was obliged to repurchase it from the heir; *m* Hannah Blaney (1667-ca. 1740; John[9] [*b* in Eng., 1627], of Lynn, *m* 1660, Hannah, dau. of Daniel King, of Lynn);
7–Ralph (bap. "at adult age" 1727-ante 1784), of Marblehead; *m* 1729, Ruth Potter, of Lynn;
6–Ralph (1739-1824), of Marblehead and Penobscot; moved to Penobscot just before Am. Rev. and took up land extending one mile back from the river; part of this land is still in the name of Devereux, and the son of Mark C., still lives in the farm house which his g.g.g.father built; *m* 1765, Lois Ingerson Hibbert;
5–Abigail (1770-1854), of Penobscot; *m* 1792, Jeremiah **Stover** (5 above).
10–Nicholas **Potter** (*b* Eng.-*d* 1677), of Lynn, Mass.; interested in iron works; removed to Salem, 1660; received lands at Lynn, 1638; freeman, 1638; *m* 1st, ante 1630, Emma–(*d* ante 1658);
9–Capt. Robert (1630-1709), selectman, Lynn; one of 7 who purchased of the Indians, for £16, all the tract of land which included the towns of Lynn and Reading; capt. King Philip's War; *m* 2d, 1659, Ruth Driver (ca. 1637-1704; Robert[10] [ca. 1592-1680], from Eng., settled at Lynn, 1630, freeman 1634/35, appraiser, *m* Phebe–);
8–Capt. Benjamin (1680-1745), of Lynn; received the grant of land at Narragansett No. 3 given for his father's service as capt. in King Philip's War; *m* 1705, Ruth Burrill;
7–Ruth (1710-1809), *m* 1729, Ralph **Devereux** (7 above).
10–George **Burrill** (ca. 1591-1653), from Eng., settled at Lynn, Mass., 1630; freeman, 1630; received 200 acres, 1638; founder at Lynn of the Burrill family long known there as the "Royal Family of Lynn" because of the long and distinguished service to the town and colony of its earlier members; *m* in Boston, Eng., 1626, Mary Cooper (1606-53);
9–Lt. John (1631-1703), one of the "7 Prudential men" of Lynn; selectman; rep. Gen. Ct., 1691, 97; lt. Lynn militia; *m* 1656, Lois Ivory (1640-1720; Thomas[10], of Lynn, 1638, *m* Ann South); their sons, "the beloved Speaker" John, and Capt. Theopholis, capt. of Lynn Co. in Pt. Royall Expdn., left severally in their wills to the First Church of Christ at Lynn, funds for the "furnishing of the Lord's Table," with which silver was purchased now considered among the most historic communion plate in America; several of the pieces bear the Burrill Coat of Arms;
8–Ruth (1682-1771), *m* Capt. Benjamin **Potter** (8 above).
10–Robert (Hebert) **Hibbert** (qv);
9–Joseph (bap. 1648-1701), of Beverly; *m* Elizabeth– (*d* post 1701);
8–Jeremiah (1693-1743), of Beverly, Gloucester and Manchester, *m* 2d, 1719, Hannah Leach, of Gloucester;
7–Capt. Joseph (1723-1801), of Gloucester, Manchester, Marblehead and Castine; sea capt.; brought to N.E. the first news of the great Lisbon Earthquake, 1755; removed to Castine, 1771; comd. the cartel "Lavinia," in Am. Rev., and carried prisoners of war; *m* 1744, Lois Ingersol;
6–Lois I. (1749-*d* at Penobscot), of Marblehead; *m* 1765, Ralph **Devereux** (6 above).
11–Richard (Ingerson) **Ingersol** (qv):
10–Lt. George (1618-94), of Gloucester, Falmouth and Salem; received land grant at Wenham, 1642, Gloucester, 1646; selectman, 1646; bought land in Falmouth, 1658; rep. Gen. Ct. from Falmouth, 1658,83,85; lt. co. raised for defense against the Indians at Falmouth in King Philip's War; officer of York Bn.; removed to Salem, 1694 and *d* there; *m* ante 1642, Elizabeth– (*d* post 1694);
9–Samuel (ca. 1652-1734), of Falmouth, Charlestown and Gloucester; received the land at Narragansett No. 3 for his own and his father's services in King Philip's War; removed to Charlestown where he and his wife and children were bap.; removed to Gloucester, 1700; *m* Judith Madiver (ca. 1660-1721; Michael[10] [*d* ca. 1670], planter, Richmond Island, 1641-42, settled at Black Point, took oath of allegiance at Spurwink, 1658);
8–Josiah (ca. 1687-ca. 1768), of Gloucester; *m* 1712, Mary Stevens;
7–Lois (*b* 1725-*d* Castine), *m* 1744, Capt. Joseph **Hibbert** (7 above).
11–William **Stevens** (*d* ante 1680), from Eng. to Mass., ante 1632; received by order of the Gen. Ct. £10 for seeing to the erection of a movable fort, Boston, 1634, Salem, 1636, Gloucester, 1642; freeman, 1640; one of best shipbuilders of Colonial N.E.; selectman, Gloucester; rep. Gen. Ct., 4 yrs.; *m* Philippa– (*d* 1681);
10–Dea. James (bap. 1641-1697), of Gloucester; dea.; selectman, 1669, 1674-91; rep. Gen. Ct. 10 yrs.; lt. military co. of Gloucester; *m* 1st, 1656, Susanna Eveleth (Silvester[11] [*d* 1689], from Eng. to Boston, 1642, land recorded to him at Gloucester, 1648, selectman, 1648, 51; rep. Gen. Ct., 1673; freeman, 1652; became possessor of large tracts of land west of the Annesquam; wrote name Eversleigh, *m* 1st, Susanna–, *d* 1659);
9–Samuel (1665-1756), mcht.; rep. Gen. Ct., 6 yrs.; of Gloucester; *m* 1693, Mary Ellery (1677-1759; William[10] [1643-96], from Eng. to Mass., settled at Gloucester, 1663, selectman, freeman, 1672, rep. Gen. Ct., 1689, *m* 2d, 1676, Mary [1655-living 1741], dau. of John Coit[11] [*d* ante 1667], *m* 1652, Mary [bap. 1639-*d* 1692], dau. of William Stevens [11 above], son of John Coit[12] [*d* ante 1659], of Gloucester, from Wales to N.E., Salem, 1638, freeman 1647, selectman, 1648, removed to New London, 1651, *m* Mary Jenners, 1596-1676);
8–Mary (1694-1789), of Gloucester; *m* 1712, Josiah **Ingersol** (8 above).
2–Frank Marion **Angellotti** (*b* 1861), of San Rafael and San Francisco; LL.B., Hastings Coll. of Law, U.Calif., 1882; dist. atty., Marin Co., Calif., 1885-91; judge Superior Ct., Marin Co., 1891-1903; asso. justice Supreme Ct. of Calif., 1903-15; chief justice Supreme Ct. of Calif., 1915-21; resigned to enter private practice; chief counsel Western Pacific R.R., 1921; charter pres. Mt. Tamalpais Parlor, Native Sons of Golden West, Marin Co., 1884; Mason (Grand Master, Calif., 1898-99); gov., S.C.W. (Calif.), 1918-24; life trustee Hastings Coll. of Law, U.Calif., 1924; *m* 1884, Emma Cornelia Cearley (*b* 1860; see Vol. II, p. 70, for Cearley and Polk lineages).
1–Ed. private schools. Vol. R.C. canteen worker in World War, served at St. Germain-des-Fosses; Chalons-sur-Marne; Chaligny with Evacuation Hosp. 13 in the St. Mihiel offensive; with the Army of Occupation at Treves (German, Trier), wounded in line of duty near Toul, France, Sept. 1918. Author (see Who's Who in America). Address: Care Judge Frank M. Angellotti, Mills Bldg., San Francisco, Calif.

1–**ANGLE, Edward John,** *b* Cedarville, Ill., Apr. 1, 1864.

5–Henry (Engel) **Angle** (1740-1810; his parents came from Switzerland, were among the early Swiss Quakers or Mennonites emigrating to America), lived in Strasburg Tp., Lancaster Co., Pa., until 1779; pvt. Lancaster Co. militia, 1777; moved to Washington Co., Md., 1779; owner of a large plantation; *m* Elizabeth–;
4–John (1766-1826), *m* Susanna Miller;
3–Daniel (1790-1835), *m* Elizabeth Bouslough (see Vol. III, p. 594, for Bouslough lineage);
2–John Bouslough (2 below).
6–Richard **Swan,** from North of Ireland early in the 18th Century, and settled in Paxtang Tp.;
5–James (*b* 1711), settled at Hanover; *m* Mary–;
4–Sarah (1758-1815), *m* Robert **Bell** (1747-96), pvt. Lancaster Co. militia (Walter[5] [1700-47], from Ireland, 1730, settled in East Hanover Tp., Lebanon Co., Pa., *m* Elizabeth–);
3–James (1772-1841), mem. Pa. Legislature from Dauphin Co.; *m* Catherine Young;
2–Jane (2 below).
6–Thomas **Rutherford** (*b* Parish of Derry-Lousan, Co. Tyrone, Ireland, 1707-*d* 1777), from Ireland bet. 1720 and 1730; settled at Paxtang, Pa.; *m* 1730, Jean (*b* Parish of Gorty-Lowery, Co. Tyrone, Ireland, 1712-*d* 1789), dau. of John Mordah, *m* Agnes–;
5–Eleanor (1733-99), *m* William **Wilson** (1714-59), of Paxtang (Hugh[6] [ca. 1673-1738], from Ireland, 1726, settled in Derry Tp., Pa., *m* Mary–);
4–Martha (1759-ca. 1830), *m* 1781, William **Young** (ca. 1749-1796), of Hanover (see Vol. III, p. 594, for Young lineage);
3–Catherine, (1782-1826), *m* James **Bell** (3 above);
2–Jane (1817-1908), *m* 1840, John Bouslough **Angle** (1820-92); for issue see Vol. I, p. 423.
1–*m* June 6, 1889, Agnes Lillian Wolf, *b* Freeport, Ill., Aug. 8, 1863; dau. of Judge George Wolf, of Freeport; issue: 1–Sarah Jane (Mar. 15, 1890-Aug. 1, 1903); 2–Florence, *b* LaSalle, Ill., Nov. 28, 1893; U.Neb., '16; *m* Nov. 11, 1916, Guy E. Reed (issue: Robert Angle; Barbara); 3–Edward Everett Dupuytren (see Vol. III, p. 594); 4–Barbara Josephine (Mar. 30, 1898-Mar. 23, 1905); 5–Agnes Evelyn, *b* Lincoln, Sept. 16, 1904; U.Neb. 1927; *m* Jan. 15, 1927, Harry E. Stevens (issue: Patricia Anne).
1–B.Sc., U.Wis., '86 (Alpha Tau Omega, Sigma Xi, Pi Gamma Mu); M.D., U.Cincinnati, 1887; M.D., U.Pa., 1895, A.M., U.Neb., 1898. Physician; formerly prof. skin and genito-urinary diseases, Neb. Coll. of Medicine. Mem. S.C. W., S.A.R. Clubs: Rotary, Knife and Fork, Country, University. Summer place: "Interlaken," Nevis, Minn. Residence: 2219 S St., Lincoln, Neb.

1–**ANTHONY, Alfred Williams,** *b* Providence, R.I., Jan. 13, 1860.
9–John **Anthony** (qv);
8–Abraham (1650-1727), of Portsmouth, R.I.; freeman, 1672; dep., 1703-11; speaker House of Deps., 1709-10; *m* 1671, Alice Woodell (1650-1734; William[9], *m* Mary–);
7–William (1675-1744), of Portsmouth, R.I., and Swansea, Mass.; *m* 1694, Mary Coggeshall (1675-post 1739; John[8], *m* Elizabeth Timberlake; desc. John Coggeshall, qv);
6–James (1712-48), Swansea, Mass.; *m* 1734, Alice Chace (1717-48; Eber[7], *m* Mary Knowles [William[8]; Henry[9]]; William[8]; William[9]; William[10]; qv);
5–Daniel (1740-1824), removed to Providence, R.I.; surveyor; laid out the Providence turnpike; mem. Soc. of Friends; *m* Mary Bowen (*b* 1742; Richard[6], *m* Remember Goodspeed);
4–Richard (*b* 1767), cotton mfr., Anthony, R.I., and North Providence; *m* 1791, Abigail Eddy (Capt. Barnard[5], capt. Am. Rev., desc. Samuel Eddy, qv; *m* Patience–);
3–James (1795-1836), cotton mfr., North Providence; built and owned villages of Greystone and Centredale, R.I.; *m* 1818, Sarah Porter Williams (*b* 1792; Rev. Nehemiah[4], desc. Robert Williams, qv);
2–Lewis Williams (2 below).
9–Richard **Waterman** (ca. 1590-1673), from Eng., 1629, settled at Salem, Mass., at Providence, 1638; one of seven to whom Roger Williams deeded land at Providence; an original mem. 1st Bapt. ch. in America, 1639; freeman, 1655; commr., juryman, warden; col. of militia; *m* Bethia– (*d* 1680);
8–Resolved (1638-70), dep. Gen. Ct., 1667; *m* 1659, Mercy Williams (1640-1705; Roger[9], qv);
7–Ens. Resolved (1667-1719), settled at Greenville, R.I., 1689; rep. Smithfield in Gen. Assembly, 1715; ens. militia; *m* 1st, Anne Harris (*b* 1673; Andrew[8]; William[9]);
6–Resolved (1703-46), rep. Smithfield in Gen. Assembly, 1739,40,41; built Greenville Tavern, 1733; *m* 1722, Lydia Mathewson (*b* 1701);
5–Capt. John (ca. 1728-1777), shipmaster and sea capt. and "went on China voyages"; an early mfr. in N.E.; erected one of the first paper mills in America and was called "Paper-Mill John"; engaged in printing and publishing, 1769; *m* 1750, Mary Olney (1731-63; Capt. Jonathan[6], founder of Olneyville, R.I., *m* Elizabeth, dau. of Christopher Smith; James[7], *m* Hellelujah, dau. of Daniel, son of Chad Brown);
4–John Olney (1758-96), *m* Sally Franklin (1762-1842; Capt. Asa[5], capt. French and Indian War, *m* Sarah Paine);
3–George (1793-1850), *m* 2d, 1823, Britannia Franklin Baxter;
2–Britannia Franklin (2 below).
10–John **Howland,** Mayflower Pilgrim (qv);
9–Desire, *m* Capt. John **Gorham** (qv);
8–Temperance, *m* Thomas **Baxter** (qv);
7–John, *m* Desire Gorham;
6–Isaac (*b* 1717), *m* Abigail Taylor;
5–David (*b* 1745), served in Cont. Army 3 yrs.; *m* Winifred Baxter (*b* 1750);
4–Franklin, served in U.S.N., 30 yrs.; q.m. many yrs.; *m* Susan Phinney;
3–Britannia F. (1807-95), *m* George **Waterman** (3 above).
2–Lewis Williams **Anthony** (*b* 1825), partner, Greene & Anthony, wholesale boots and shoes, 1851, eventually becoming sr. mem. of Greene, Anthony & Co.; dea., Roger Williams Free Bapt. Ch.; pres. Free Bapt. Home Mission Soc.; mem. bd. Free Bapt. Printing Establishment of Boston; pres. Traders' Nat. Bank, Providence; dir. Nicholson File Co., Providence, Great Western File Co., Beaver Falls, Pa., Smith & Anthony Co., mfrs. of heating apparatus, Boston, Central Real Estate Co., Providence and Free Bapt. Pub. House, Boston; mem. bd. of fellows of Bates Coll., Lewiston, Me.; pres. bd. trustees of Storer Coll., Harper's Ferry, W.Va.; v.p., bd. trustees Y.W.C.A. of Providence, and prominent in other financial and benevolent enterprises; *m* 1847, Britannia Franklin Waterman (1825-92); *m* 2d, 1894, Emily Frances (Waterman) Tozer (*d* 1898; sister of 1st wife); *m* 3d 1899, Lucinda Williams, dau. of Jonathan Preble; issue (1st marriage): I–Edgar Waterman (1848-1916; *m* 1878, Clara Dickenson Wilder); II–Sarah Britannia (1851-65); III–Kate Jackson (*b* 1852); IV–Mary Chace (1854-55); V–Charles Lewis (1856-59); VI–Abbie Leslie (1858-65); VII–Alfred Williams (1 above); VIII–George Waterman (*b* and *d* 1863).
1–*m* Sept. 15, 1885, Harriet Wyatt Angell, *b* Providence, R.I., Mar. 18, 1857; dau. of John Wilmarth Angell (desc. of Thomas Angell, an original settler of Providence), *m* Elizabeth Herman Stillwell (desc. Nicholas Stillwell, early settler of New York); issue: 1–Elisabeth Williams, *b* Bangor, Me., Apr. 7, 1887; A.B., Bates, '08; A.M., Columbia, 1911; Ph.D., Clark, 1923; prof. history, Skidmore Coll., Saratoga Springs, N.Y., 1923-27; tutor of history, Radcliffe Coll., 1927-28; author : "Colonial Women of Affairs"; co-author: "The Making of the Nation"; *m* June 12, 1914, Robert Cloutman Dexter, A.B., Brown U., '12; Ph.D., Clark, 1923; gen. sec. Asso. Charities of Montreal; served Am. Red Cross, during World War; prof. sociology, Skidmore Coll., 1923-27; sec. dept. of social relations of Am. Unitarian Assn.; author: "Social Adjustment"; son of William Dexter, of Woodstock, Vt. (issue: Lewis Anthony, *b* Nov. 1915; Harriet Angell, *b* June 1917); 2–Margaretha (*b* Berlin, Germany, Mar. 17-*d* Mar. 20, 1889); 3–Lewis Wilmarth (Aug. 11, 1891-Dec. 20, 1898); 4–Alfred Williams, Jr., *b* Lewiston, Me., June 1, 1894; Ph.B., Brown '15; chief machinist's mate, U.S.N., 6th Naval Dist., Charleston, S.C., commnd. ens., U.S.N.R. F. (engring.), Apr. 15, 1918; ordered to U.S.N.A. for spl. officers' training course; commnd. ens. (temp.) U.S.N. (engring), Sept. 18, 1918; resigned Jan. 13, 1919; now with **Arthur D.**

Little, Inc., Cambridge, Mass.; *m* Apr. 14, 1917, Kathryn Frances (*b* Sept. 30, 1890), dau. of John Ryan (issue: Elisabeth Willson, *b* Dec. 22, 1917; John Williams, *b* Nov. 25, 1920).
1-*m* 2d, Feb. 26, 1903, Gertrude Brown Libbey, *b* Lewiston, Me., June 16, 1879; dau. of Winfield Scott Libbey, mfr. of Lewiston (Asa M.[8]; Peter[4]; Stephen[5]; Nathaniel[6]; Mathew[7]; John[8], from Eng. ca. 1635), *m* Annie E. Shaw; issue (all *b* Lewiston, Me.): 1-Richard Lewis, *b* Dec. 24, 1903; Yale, 1925; *m* Apr. 18, 1925, Wilhelmina, dau. of William Groomes, of New Haven, Conn. (issue: Barbara Jane, *b* June 15, 1926); 2-Warren Shaw, *b* July 12, 1906; Yale 1927; *m* Oct. 13, 1928, Kathrine, dau. of Charles A. Hitchcock, of Brooklyn, N.Y., *m* Gertrude Volck; 3-Charles Sheldon, *b* May 21, 1912.
1-A.B., Brown, 1883, A.M., 1886; Cobb Div. Sch., 1883-85; U. of Berlin, Germany, 1888-90; (D.D., Bates, 1902, Brown, 1908; LL.D., Colby, 1914, Bates, 1920). Ordained Free Bapt. ministry, 1885; pastor, 1885-88; prof. N.T. exegesis, Cobb Div. Sch., 1890-1908; prof. Christian lit. and ethics, Bates Coll., 1908-11; corr. sec., treas., etc., various Baptist organizations. Author (see Who's Who in America). Mem. I.A.G. Clubs: Clergy, National Arts, Quill, Authors, Delta Upsilon, Martindale Country. Winter place: 105 E. 22d St., New York, N.Y. Legal residence: Lewiston, Me.

1-**ARCHER, Gleason Leonard,** *b* Great Pond, Me., Oct. 29, 1880.
11-Thomas **Rogers,** Mayflower Pilgrim (qv);
10-John, lived at Plymouth, Mass., 1631, Duxbury, Mass., 1634; rep. Gen. Ct.; *m* 1639, Ann Churchman;
9-Anna (*d* post 1704), *m* 1st, 1664, John **Tisdale,** Jr. (*d* 1675), dep. Gen. Ct., Taunton, Plymouth Colony; killed by Indians;
8-Abigail, *m* 1685, William **Makepeace;**
7-Abigail (1686-1724), *m* Immanuel **Williams;**
6-John (*b* 1704), *m* Elizabeth Caswell;
5-Joshua (ca. 1747-ca. 1833), *m* 1771, Bethiah Clark (*b* 1751);
4-Simeon (1782-1858), *m* 1812, Harriet Kenney (1798-1877);
3-Simeon (1830-88), *m* 1857, Marilla M. Spooner (1837-93);
2-Frances Martha (1857-1905), *m* 1875, John Sewall **Archer** (*b* 1851), blacksmith and lumberman; issue: I-Clifford S. (1876-1924; *m* Susie B. Humphrey); II-Hiram J. (*b* 1878; *m* Helen M. Stinchfield); III-Gleason Leonard (1 above); IV-Perley C. (1883-1903); V-Ella M. (*b* and *d* 1885); VI-Maurice C. (1886-99); VII-infant (*d*); VIII-Maude M. (*b* 1889; *m* Roger Gordon); IX-Harold N. (*b* 1891; *m* Lottie M. Nickerson); X-Claude M. (1892-1910).
1-*m* Oct. 6, 1906, Elizabeth Glenn Snyder, *b* New Haven, Conn., Apr. 24, 1884; dau. of Rev. Henry S. Snyder, B.D., Yale, 1885; Congl. minister, *m* 1883, Maria Louise Bradley; issue: 1-Allan Frost, *b* Boston, Mass., Jan. 22, 1908; 2-Marian Glenn, *b* Woburn, Mass., Nov. 14, 1910; 3-Norman Bradley (Sept. 22, 1912-Dec. 22, 1912); 4-Gleason L., Jr., *b* Norwell, Mass., May 22, 1916.
1-Student Boston U., 1902-04, LL.B., same, 1906; (LL.D., Atlanta Law Sch., 1926). Admitted to Mass. bar, 1906, founded the Suffolk Law Sch. same yr. and since dean and treas. same, also trustee. Author (see Who's Who in America). Trustee First M.E. Ch. of Boston. Democrat. Mem. S.M.D., S.A.R., Am. Bar Assn. Residence: 20 Derne St., Boston, Mass.

1-**ARCHIBALD, Cora Hume (Mrs. Byron J.),** *b* Columbia, Mo.
6-George **Hume** (qv);
5-George (1729-1802), Culpeper, Va.; surveyor; sgt. 1st Va. Regt. in Am. Rev.; *m* Jane Stanton (Thomas[6], of Culpeper, will in Madison C.H., Va., Nov. 13, 1790);
4-Reuben (1772-1831), Culpeper, Va.; planter; *m* Anna Finks (1773-1839), in Culpeper (Finks family Bible in possession of Sallie Hume Douglas);
3-Lewis (1803-70), farmer nr. Columbia, Mo.; *m* nr. Richmond, Ky., 1823, Henrietta Monroe McBain (1804-1905), of Annapolis, Md. (marriage certificate in possession of Mrs. B. J. Archibald);
2-James Robert (2 below).
5-Thomas **Carrick** (*b* 1755), pvt. N.J.Cont. Line, 1775-76; *m* Henrietta Monroe, of Annapolis, Md.;
4-Elizabeth (1787-1878), of Annapolis, Md., and Richmond, Ky.; *m* Ignatius **McBain;**
3-Henrietta Monroe (1804-1905), of Annapolis, Md.; *m* nr. Richmond, Ky., Lewis **Hume** (3 above).
4-David **Booth** (*b* Eng., 1752-1850), of Beaufort, N.C., New York, Richmond, Va., Cynthiana, Ky., and Mo.; *m* Margaret Kirkman, nr. Richmond, Va.;
3-Elijah, *m* Sallie Wood, of Cyanthiana, Ky.;
2-Sallie Wood (*d* 1915), *m* James Robert **Hume** (1829-81), *b* Columbia, Mo.; mcht. and landowner; issue: I-William (*d* infancy); II-Henrietta (*d* 1921; *m* Dr. J. B. Pettijohn, issue: Cora Hume; *m* 2d, Arthur P. Buck, issue: Carrick Hume); III-Cora (1 above); IV-Mary (*d* 1889; *m* N. E. Peterson); V-Carrie (*d* 1918; *m* A. B. Lewis, issue, Carrie Lewis Coey); VI-Sallie (Mrs. Alan E. Douglas, see Vol. II, p. 123).
1-*m* Dr. Edwin P. Talley (*b* Talley Hall, on Dardenne Prairie, nr. Wentzville, Mo.-*d* Mora, N.M., Apr. 6, 1889), son of Dr. John Archer Talley, *m* Paulina Preston; issue: 1-Paulina Cabell, *b* Columbia, Mo., *m* Charles N. Petteys (issue: Edwin Talley); 2-John Archer, *b* Wentzville, Mo., *m* Charlotte New (issue: John Raymond; Edwin Archer).
1-*m* 2d, Byron J. Archibald, *b* Portland, Me.; son of Judson Archibald, *m* Agusta Ayer; issue: 1-Mary Irene, *b* Las Vegas, N.M., *m* Rupert B. Turnbull, of Los Angeles, Calif. (issue: Loretta Yale; Rupert, Jr.; Raymond; Byron George); 2-Henry Caldwell, *b* Las Vegas, N.M., grad. U.S.N.A., '22; *m* at Honolulu, T.H., Hazel Denison.
1-Ed. Christian Coll., and Mo. State U. Mem. D.A.R., Am. Lit. League. Prominent in civic organizations. Episcopalian. Residence: 811 Jackson Av., East Las Vegas, N.M.

1-**ARDERY, William Breckenridge,** *b* Bourbon Co., Ky., Aug. 11, 1887.
5-John (Audley) **Ardery** (ca. 1760-1830), from Ireland, settled in Cumberland Co., Pa.; removed to Bourbon Co., Ky., 1787, with brothers James and William; soldier Am. Rev.; *m* 1780, Mary Watt;
4-John (1790-1852), of Bourbon Co., Ky.; *m* 1818, Elizabeth McConnell (1785-1834; William[5] [*d* 1823], soldier Am. Rev., from Lancaster Co., Pa., took up 2,000 acres in Bourbon Co., *m* 1768, Rosannah Kennedy; Alexander[6], of Lancaster Co., Pa.);
3-Lafayette (1827-92), of Bourbon Co.; *m* 1852, Ann Elizabeth Breckenridge;
2-William Porter (2 below).
7-Alexander **Breckenridge** (*d* 1744), a Scottish Covenanter, from Scotland, via Ireland, 1728, to Phila., Pa.; settled in Orange Co., Va.; *m* Jane Preston (Archibald[8], of Derry, Ireland);
6-George (*d* 1790), patriot in Am. Rev.; *m* ca. 1740, Ann Doak;
5-Alexander (1743-1813), from Washington Co., Va., to Bourbon Co., Ky.; soldier Am. Rev.; *m* 1st, Magdolen Gamble (1746-ante 1806);
4-John (1785-1854), of Bourbon Co.; *m* 1820, Ann Weir Brooks;
3-Ann Elizabeth (1832-94), *m* Lafayette **Ardery** (3 above).
9-Thomas **Brooks** (qv);
8-Caleb (1632-96), at town meeting, Medford, Mass., 1693; chosen to superintend building of 1st ch.; *m* 2d, 1669, Hannah Atkinson (1632-1702; Thomas[9]);
7-Ebenezer (1670-1742), rep. Gen. Ct., from Medford, 1704; *m* 1692/93, Abigail Boyleston (1674-1756; Thomas[8] [1644-95], *m* Mary [1648-1722], dau. of Thomas Gardner, son of Thomas, qv; Thomas[9] [ca. 1615-ca. 1653], *m* Sarah- [*d* 1704]; Thomas[10] [*d* 1648]; Henry[11], *b* 1575);
6-Samuel (1710-66), was voted keeper of town ammunition, Medford, 1746; *m* Abigail Hastings;
5-Abijah (1759-1812), soldier Am. Rev.; removed from Boston, Mass., to Clark Co., Ky.; 1st cousin of Gov. John Brooks, gov. of Mass., 7 yrs.; *m* ca. 1791, Nancy Strode (1770-1855; Capt. John[6] [1736-1805], soldier Am. Rev., founder of Strode's Station, Clark Co., Ky., *m* 1758, Mary Boyles [1739-89]; Edward[7] [*d* 1716 aet. 108], whose parents *d.* on the "Paysay" en route to America);

4–Ann Weir (1798-1888), *m* John **Breckenridge** (4 above).
9–Thomas **Hastings** (qv);
8–John (1653/54-1718), *m* 1679, Abigail Hammond (*d* 1718);
7–Samuel, *m* 1719, Bethea Holloway;
6–Abigail (*d* 1776), *m* Samuel **Brooks** (6 above).
4–Richard **Adair** (1788-1866), from Snow Hill, Md., to Bourbon, Ky.; later removed to Nicholas Co., Ky.; *m* 1811, Mary Tarr (1796-post 1866; Charles[5] [*b* 1761], of Md., Ky., and Ill., *m* Mary Richardson, *b* 1772);
3–Robert Ferris (1833-1907), of Bourbon Co.; *m* 1854, Sarah Isabella Dodson;
2–Mary Ella (2 below).
7–John **Dodson,** of Calvert and Charles cos., Md.; *m* Bathsheba Hurley;
6–John Hurley, of Charles Co., 1775-78; soldier Am. Rev.; *m* Mary Ann Smoot, of Charles Co.;
5–Henry (*b* 1785), of Washington, D.C.; *m* Rebecca Darnall (James[6], of Lower Marlboro, Prince George Co., Md., soldier Am. Rev., *m* Ann Meekins);
4–George (1808-90), *m* 1835, Parmelia Ellen Curtis;
3–Sarah Isabella (1839-1920), *m* Robert Ferris **Adair** (3 above).
7–John **Curtis** (*d* post 1813), prob. of Loudoun Co., Va.;
6–John (*d* 1813), soldier Am. Rev.; received Ky. land grants; established Curtis' Station, Mason Co., Ky.; trustee town of Washington, Ky.; *m* Nancy Edwards (*d* post 1813);
5–James (1770-1833), *m* 1796, Sarah Emily Edwards;
4–Parmelia Ellen (1817-69), *m* George **Dodson** (4 above).
7–James **Edwards** (*b*–Aberdeen, Scotland-*d* 1804), Rev. patriot, of Va.; to Ky., 1786; located at Kenton Station; later removed to Ohio; founded the town of Aberdeen; *m* Sarah Everitt;
6–Jacob (1753-92), from Fairfax Co., Va., with his parents, to Mason Co., Ky.; a trustee of Washington, Ky.; soldier Am. Rev.; *m* 1779, Elizabeth Marshall (*d* post 1792), of Va.;
5–Sarah Emily (1780-1826), *m* James **Curtis** (5 above).
2–Mary Ella Adair (1855-1918), *m* 1880, William Porter **Ardery** (1855-1916), of "Rocclicgan," Bourbon Co., Ky.; pres. Peoples' Deposit Bank, v.p. Nat. Bank, Paris, Ky.
1–*m* Apr. 14, 1910, Julia Hoge Spencer (qv for genealogy); issue: 1–William Spencer, *b* Lexington, Ky., Mar. 1, 1911; 2–Winston Breckenridge, *b* Paris, Ky., Dec. 7, 1912; 3–Phil Pendleton, *b* Lexington, Mar. 7, 1914.
1–Ed. privately and Centre Coll. (Phi Delta Theta). Editor and owner, Paris Democrat. Dem. state campaign chmn. Lawyer, farmer; rep. from Bourbon Co. in Gen. Assembly of Ky., 1924,26,28. Mem. S.A.R. (pres. Bourbon Co. Chapter), Isaac Walton League of Bourbon Co. (pres.). Mem. Disciples of Christ. Democrat. Residence: "Rocclicgan," Paris, Ky.

1–**ARDERY, Julia Hoge Spencer, (Mrs. William B.),** *b* Richmond, Va., Sept. 16, 1889.
8–Samuel **Spencer** (ca. 1672-1705), from Eng., via Barbados, to Phila. (now Montgomery) Co., Pa., ca. 1700; *m* ca. 1697, Elizabeth Whitton (1676-1702; Robert[9], of Eng., who took up land in Pa., 1686);
7–Samuel (1699-1777), of Upper Dublin, Phila. Co., Pa.; *m* 1723, Mary Dawes (1701-76; Abraham[8] [*d* 1731], Quaker, of Whitemarsh, Phila. Co., from London to Pa., ante 1713);
6–Nathan (1734-1806), removed to Loudoun Co., Va., 1761; patriot in Am. Rev.; *m* 1756, Hannah Lofborough (*d* 1779; Nathaniel[7], of Phila. Co., *m* Margaret–);
5–John (1763-1816), from Loudoun Co., Va., to Belmont Co., O.; served in Am. Rev.; *m* 1780, Lydia Phillips (1762-1820; Edmund[6], of Pa. and Loudoun Co., Va.);
4–Joseph (1786-1821), *m* Sarah White;
3–George (1816-63), of Belmont Co., O.; *m* 1838, Elizabeth Hoge;
2–Isaac J. (2 below).
8–William **Smith** (1669-1743), Quaker, of Eng.; to America, 1684; landed at New Castle, Del.; purchased land of John Chapman, he and Chapman being the only two white men living in what is now Wrightstown Tp., Bucks Co., Pa.; *m* 1690, Mary Croasdale (1669-1716; Thomas[9], from Eng., 1682, received large land grants from William Penn);
7–Thomas (*d* 1750), of "Windy Bush," Bucks Co., Pa.; *m* Elizabeth Sanders (*b* 1706; Robert[8], *m* Rebecca Linton);
6–William (*b* 1731 or 32), removed from Bucks Co. to Loudoun Co., Va., and later to Ohio; Am. Rev. patriot; *m* 1754, Ann Williamson;
5–Jane (1773-1853), *m* Isaac **White** (1765-1853), of Loudoun Co., Va., and Belmont Co., O., (Thomas[6], patriot in Am. Rev., from Pa. to Loudoun Co., Va., later to Ohio;
4–Sarah (1793-1837), *m* Joseph **Spencer** (4 above);
8–William **Hoge** (qv);
7–William (ca. 1708-89), patriot in Am. Rev.; *m* Anne– (*d* ante 1789), Quakeress;
6–Soloman (1729-1811), of Loudoun Co., Va.; *m* 1st, Anne Rollings (*d* ca. 1771);
5–Isaac (1763-1838), of Loudoun Co., and Belmont Co., O.; *m* 1784, Elizabeth Nichols;
4–Soloman (1789-1866), of Belmont Co.; *m* 1813, Sarah Seaman;
3–Elizabeth (1815-1914), *m* George **Spencer** (3 above).
9–George **Chandler** (1633-87), *d* at sea en route to America; *m* Jane–, who settled in Chester Co., Pa.;
8–Swithin (*b* 1674), of Del.; *m* Ann–;
7–Charity (1707-ante 1751), *m* as his 1st wife, 1728, John **Nichols** (*d* 1767), of Chester Co., Pa. (Thomas[8], from Eng. to Del. ca. 1716);
6–James (1734-91), from Chester Co., Pa., to Loudoun Co., Va.; patriot in Am. Rev.; *m* 1754, Elizabeth Sharp (*b* 1732; John[7], of Chester Co., *m* 2d, Anne Bryan);
5–Elizabeth (1767-1836), *m* Isaac **Hoge** (5 above).
10–Capt. John **Seaman** (*d* 1695), from Essex, Eng., to Hempstead, L.I., ca. 1645; propr. of Hempstead; magistrate under Dutch rule; officer in restoration of rule; landholder under first English patent of Hempstead, 1651; *m* 1st, Elizabeth Strickland (Capt. John[11], from Eng., was at Charlestown, Mass., 1629);
9–Jonathan, *m* Jane–;
8–Jonathan (*d* 1755), removed to Kakiat, Rockland Co., N.Y., post 1711; in Orange Co. militia, 1715; *d* Orange Co., N.Y.; *m* Elizabeth Denton (Samuel[9], of Hempstead, L.I., *m* Mary, dau. of John "Rock" Smith, of Hempstead; Rev. Richard[10], qv);
7–Jonathan (*d* 1743), moved to Frederick Co., Va.; *m* Elizabeth–(*d* post 1753);
6–Jonathan (1721-85), of Berkeley Co., Va.; officer Va. Colonial militia, 1758; Am. Rev. patriot; *m* 1741, Elizabeth Baldwin (*d* ante 1785; Thomas[7], *m* Elizabeth–; George[8], *m* Mary Ellison; George[9], from Eng., to Warwick, R.I., 1644, removed with family to Gravesend, L.I., 1656, propr. of "Baldwin's Neck," L.I., removed to Hempstead with Capt. John Strickland);
5–Jonah (1751-1811), served in Am. Rev. as issuing commissary at Ft. Henry, Wheeling, W. Va.; *m* 3d, 1794, Elizabeth Harris (1774-post 1811; Daniel[6], served in Am. Rev., *m* Sarah–);
4–Sarah (1795-1860), *m* Soloman **Hoge** (4 above).
8–Philip **Pendleton** (qv);
7–Henry (1683-1721), *m* 1701, Mary Taylor (1688-1770; James[8], qv); among their sons, Edmund was judge Va. Supreme Ct. Appeals; del. Cont. Congress 1774-75; wrote resolutions offered to Congress which led to adoption of Declaration of Independence;
6–John (1719-99), clk. of Va. House of Burgesses during Am. Rev.; *m* 2d, ca. 1760, Sarah Madison (prob. dau. Thomas[7]), cousin Pres. James Madison;
5–Capt. Henry (1762-1822), served in Am. Rev.; removed to Louisa Co., Va., from Hanover Co.; *m* 1st, 1785, Alcey Ann Winston;
4–Col. Edmund (1786-1838), *m* 1808, Unity Yancey Kimbrough;
3–Dr. Philip Barbour (1819-1907), *m* 1847, Jane Kimbrough Holladay;
2–Sally Louise (2 below).
13–Sir John **Barne** (*b* Eng. 1568-1619), mem. Va. Co. of London; an incorporator of 2d Va. Charter, 1609; *m* Ann Sandys (Edwin[14], archbishop of York);
12–Ann (*d* 1633), *m* Sir William **Lovelace** (bap. 1583/84-1628), of Woolwich; knighted 1609; mem. Va. Co. of London and an incorporator of 2d Va. Charter (Sir William[13], of Lovelace Place, knighted 1599, mem. Va. Co. of London and

incorporator of the 3d Va. Charter, 1614, mem. Parliament, 1624, *m* ca. 1580, Elizabeth, dau. of Edward Aucher, ca. 1539-1568);
11–Anne, *m* Rev. John **Gorsuch** (*d* 1647);
10–Anne (*b* 1638/39), *m* Capt. Thomas **Todd** (qv);
9–Thomas (1660-1724), justice of the peace, Gloucester Co.; *m* Elizabeth Bernard (Col. William[10], qv);
8–Philip (1681 or 88-ante 1740), of King and Queen Co., Va.; *m* post 1705, Ann Day (Edward[9], *m* Jane [Coppinhall] Walker);
7–Mary (ca. 1712 or 17-post 1740), *m* Maj. John **Bickerton** (ca. 1700-70), in Va. 1732; justice of the peace, Hanover Co., 1740; vestryman St. Paul's Parish 1743-65; capt., 1743; maj., 1747; had large land patents;
6–Alice (1730-75), *m* 1746, John **Winston** (*b* 1724), of Hanover Co.; vestryman, St. Paul's Parish; ch. warden (James[7], *m* Barbara, dau. of William Overton [*b* 1638], from Eng., 1680);
5–Alcey Ann (1769-1813), *m* Capt. Henry **Pendleton** (5 above).
8–John **Kimbrough** (*d* ante 1716), of St. Paul's Parish; patented land in New Kent Co., Va., 1687; *m* Margaret–(*d* post 1716);
7–John (*d* between 1750-65), of New Kent, Hanover and Louisa cos., Va.; *m* Elizabeth–(*d* post 1765);
6–William (*d* 1765), *m* Sarah Field (*d* 1800; John[7], patriot of Am. Rev., of Hanover and Louisa cos.);
5–Capt. Joseph (ca. 1760-1804), Am. Rev.; *m* 1785, Elizabeth Yancey;
4–Unity Yancey (1787-1866), *m* Col. Edmund **Pendleton** (4 above).
8–John **Yancey,** of Wales; one of several brothers, Huguenots, who settled in Va. on the Rappahannock River, ca. 1642; *m* Abigail Hicks;
7–Charles, officer in Colonial wars, and in French and Indian War; *m* Mlle. Dumas;
6–Capt. Charles (*b* 1741), Am. Rev.; *m* 1762, Mary Crawford;
5–Elizabeth (1765-1804), *m* Capt. Joseph **Kimbrough** (5 above).
10–John **Crawford** (*b* 1600; son of Earl Crawford), from Scotland, to Va.; said to have been killed in Bacon's Rebellion, 1676;
9–David (*b* 1625);
8–Capt. David (1662-1762), of Va.; burgess, 1692; *m* 1695, Elizabeth Smith;
7–David (1697-1766), of Hanover Co., Va.; *m* Anne Anderson (1708-1803; John[8], *m* Sarah, dau. of Samuel Waddy, of New Kent Co.; Robert[9]; Robert[10]; Richard[11]);
6–Mary (1741-1841), patriot Am. Rev.; *m* Capt. Charles **Yancey** (6 above).
10–Capt. Thomas **Holladay,** from Eng. to Va., 1650; was living at Jamestown, Va., 1660;
9–Anthony (*d* 1718), settled in Isle of Wight Co., Va.; lawyer; mem. House of Burgesses; sheriff, 1698; justice of the peace; *m* widow of Col. John Brewer, of Isle of Wight Co.;
8–Joseph (1669-1712/13), *m* Charity–;
7–Capt. John (*d* 1742), capt. of rangers; justice; magistrate of Spotsylvania Co., Va.; *m* Elizabeth–;
6–Joseph (1726-95), Rev. patriot; succeeded his brother, John, as inspector of tobacco, Fredericksburg, 1761; reappointed by Gov. Fauquier; reappointed with his brother Benjamin, by Patrick Henry, 1777; *m* Elizabeth Lewis (Henry[7], patriot Am. Rev., *m* Martha–);
5–Thomas (1765-1823), of Louisa Co., Va.; *m* Ann Overton Harris (Lt. Frederick[6], Am. Rev., *m* ca. 1771, Eliza, dau. of Richmond Terrill [Richmond[8]; William[9]; William[10]]; Frederick[7]; Col. William[8]; Maj. Robert[9]);
4–Waller (1802-56), *m* 1st, 1821, Sarah Smith Kimbrough (1800-40; John[5], *m* Jane Smith; Barnett[6]; William[7]);
3–Jane Kimbrough (1827-1915), *m* Dr. Philip B. **Pendleton** (3 above);
2–Sally Louise (*b* 1853), *m* 1878, Isaac J. **Spencer** (1851-1922), D.D., LL.D.; ed. Hillsdale, Mich., and Bethany Coll.; held pastorates at Bellair, O., Baltimore, Md., Augusta, Ga., Clarksville, Tenn., Louisville and Winchester, Ky.; edited Missionary Weekly, 10 yrs.; minister of Central Christian Ch., Lexington, Ky., 27 yrs.; curator, Transylvania U., and Hamilton Coll.; issue: I–Jessie; II–Howard Gale (*m* Mary Curtis); III–Evelyn Holladay; IV–Julia H. (1 above).
1–*m* Apr. 14, 1910, William Breckenridge Ardery (qv for genealogy and issue).
1–Ed. Transylvania U. (Delta Delta Delta), Hamilton, Sayre, and Bourbon colls. Mem. D.B.R., F.F.V., D.F.P.A., D.A.R. (state historian, 1925-26; regent, Jemima Johnson Chapter; nat. vice chmn. hist. research com., 4 yrs.; mem. state bd., 6 yrs.), C.A.R. (organizing pres. Martin's Fort Soc.), Nat. Geneal. Soc., Ky. and Va. hist. socs., Taylor Assn., Filson Club. Compiled and pub. Ky. Court and other records. Residence: "Rocclicgan," Paris, Ky.

1–**ARMSTRONG, Laura Lee (Mrs. Charles H.),** *b* Bridgeport, Conn., June 15, 1864.
9–John **Howland** (qv);
8–Desire (1623-83), *m* 1643, Capt. John **Gorham** (qv);
7–Jabez (1656-1725), *m* Hannah (Sturgis) Gray (*d* 1736; Edward Sturgis[8]);
6–Lt. Joseph (1692-1762), *m* 1725 or '26, Deborah Barlow (1705-73; Lt. John[7], *m* Ruth [Sherwood] Drake, dau. of Thomas Sherwood, Jr.);
5–Isaac (1730-98), of Redding, Conn.; soldier Am. Rev.; *m* 1752, Ann Wakeman (1730-1808);
4–Isaac (1761-1813), of Redding; soldier Am. Rev.; *m* 1780, Sarah Morgan (1763-1836);
3–Col. Joseph (1788-1866), *m* 1812, Eliza Goodrich (1791-1879);
2–Caroline Eulina (1829-1916), *m* 1854, Gurdon Bartram **Lee** (1832-1903), of Redding and Bridgeport, Conn.; issue: I–Ella (June 25, 1858-Feb. 27, 1883); II–Laura (1 above).
1–*m* Nov. 26, 1885, Charles Henry Armstrong (Jan. 28, 1860-Jan. 1, 1921); son of Frank Armstrong, of Bridgeport, Conn., *m* Elizabeth–; issue (all *b* Bridgeport, Conn.): 1–Frank Lee, *b* Dec. 24, 1886; 2–Gurdon Chapman (Mar. 26, 1888-Nov. 22, 1893); 3–Charles H., Jr., *b* Dec. 19, 1899; 4–Lorraine Lee (Mrs. Walter H. Rubsamen, qv for other lineages).
1–Mem. S.M.D., D.F.P.A., D.A.R., U.S.D. 1812, Pilgrim John Howland Soc. Episcopalian. Residence: 20 Brooklawn Av., Bridgeport, Conn.

1–**RUBSAMEN, Lorraine Lee Armstrong (Mrs. Walter H.),** Bridgeport, Conn., Oct. 12, 1901.
9–Walter **Lee** (*d* 1717 or 1718), from Eng.; settled at Windsor, Conn., 1654, where he became a freeman; removed to Northampton, Mass., 1656; to Westfield, Mass., 1664; *m* 1st, Mary–(*d* 1696);
8–Nathaniel (1663-1745), of Westfield; *m* Abigail Warner, of Farmington;
7–Nathaniel (1700-36), of Westfield; *m* 1732, Dorothy Taylor (*b* 1710);
6–Daniel (1732-92), of Westfield and Southwick, Mass.; *m* 1762, Agnes Campbell;
5–Daniel (1762-1841), of Westfield; soldier Am. Rev., 1776-82; *m* 1785, Jerusha Page (1768-1813);
4–Milo (1805-77), of Redding, Conn.; *m* 1830, Lucy Ann Bartram (1806-1905);
3–Gurdon Bartram (1832-1903), of Redding and Bridgeport, Conn.; *m* 1854, Caroline Eulina Gorham (1829-1916);
2–Laura (qv for Howland lineage), *m* 1885, Charles H. **Armstrong** (1860-1921).
1–*m* Jan. 19, 1924, Walter H. Rubsamen, *b* Summit, N.J., June 28, 1898; son of Louis C. Rubsamen, of Murray Hill, N.J., *m* Irma Shultz; issue: 1–Barbara Lee, *b* Nov. 13, 1924; 2–Walter Sanford, *b* Feb. 22, 1926.
1–Mem. D.F.P.A., D.A.R., Junior League. Episcopalian. Residence: 20 Brooklawn Av., Bridgeport, Conn.

1–**ARMSTRONG, Edward Cooke,** *b* Winchester, Va., Aug. 24, 1871.
6–James **Armstrong** (1700-70), Scotch-Irish, resided in New York;
5–John (1745-96), *m* Hannah Lamb;
4–William (1781-1839), *m* 1806, Phoebe Mead (1784-1862; Joseph[5], *m* Amelia–);
3–James Lamb (1807-95), moved to Alexandria, Va., thence to Baltimore, Md.; *m* 1829, Mary Jane Smith (see Vol. III, p. 35, for Smith lineage);
2–James Edward (2 below).
8–Harrick **Lent**;
7–Hercules;
6–Rachel, *m* Capt. James **Lamb** (1701-94);
5–Hannah or Rachel, *m* John **Armstrong** (5 above).

7–William **Hickman** (*d* 1697), of "Old Plantation," Calvert Co., Md., perhaps son of Nathaniel, 2d, of Md., and g.son of Nathaniel (*d* ca. 1656), of Northumberland Co., Va.; *m* ca. 1686, Mary Hinton (Thomas[8]);
6–William (ca. 1689-1737), *m* Margaret Wilson (Francis[7]);
5–William (ca. 1725-1791), removed to Frederick Co., Va., *m* ca. 1756, Jane–(Edward Talbott[6]?);
4–John (1759-1806), col. of Militia in Am. Rev., settled at Alexandria, Va.; removed to Front Royal, Va., of which he was one of founders; *m* 1785, Mary Harris (Benjamin[5], *m* Rebecca Birckhead, of Calvert Co., Md.);
3–John Thomas (1795-1884), War 1812; *m* 1817, Rebecca Trout (see Vol. III, p. 35, for Trout lineage);
2–Margaret (1832-1920), *m* 1855, James Edward **Armstrong**, D.D. (1830-1908); issue: I–Joseph Lamb (1856-1919); II–Charles Martin (*b* 1857); III–Emma Kate (1862-1918); IV–Frances Stuart (*b* 1867); V–Edward Cooke (1 above).
1–*m* June 8, 1905, Emerline Mason Holbrook (see Vol. III, p. 35, for genealogy); issue: 1–Percy Holbrook, *b* Baltimore, Md., Apr. 7, 1906.
1–A.B., Randolph-Macon Coll., '90, A.M., 1894; Ph.D., Johns Hopkins, 1897; (LL.D., Randolph-Macon, 1917; L.H.D., Oberlin, 1927). Prof. French language, Princeton, 1917–. Author (see Who's Who in America). Nat. dir. of French instrn. in the training camps, 1918, World War. Chevalier de la Legion d'Honneur. Residence: 26 Edgehill St., Princeton, N.J.

1–**ARMSTRONG, William Clinton, Jr.**, *b* New Brunswick, N.J., Apr. 21, 1897.
10–Rev. Joseph **Hull** (qv);
9–Capt. Benjamin, *m* Rachel York (Richard[10]);
8–Ens. Benjamin (1680-1732), *m* 1705, Sarah Drake;
7–Judge Joseph (1706-68), *d* Newton, N.J.; apptd. judge Ct. of Common Pleas, Sussex Co., 1761; *m* 1730, at Piscataway, N.J., Susannah Stelle;
6–Mercy, *m* Richard **Hunt** (1720-1819), served in Am. Rev.;
5–Sarah (1763-1830), *m* George **Armstrong** (1749-1829), *b* Blairstown, N.J. (Nathan[6] [1717-77], *m* Effie Wright, 1724-1811);
4–John (1788-1873), of Frelinghuysen Tp.; *m* Lydia Kirkpatrick (1794-1832; Capt. John[5], *m* Lydia Lewis);
3–Richard Turner (1823-1902), *m* Dec. 21, 1853, Esther Ann Lundy (1836-1917; see Vol. III, p. 36, for genealogy);
2–William Clinton (2 below).
10–Capt. Francis **Drake** (*d* Sept. 24, 1687), at Greenland, Portsmouth, N.H., as early as 1654, but after 1668, at Piscataway, N.J.; capt. militia, July 15, 1675; *m* Mary (prob.) Walker;
9–Rev. John (*d* 1741), dep. Gen. Assembly, 1683; overseer of highways; founder, 1689, and first pastor of Bapt. ch. at Piscataway; *m* July 7, 1677, Rebecca Trotter (William[10], from Newbury, Mass., to Elizabethtown, N.J., 1666, *m* Catherine Gibbs);
8–Sarah (1686-1749), *m* 1st, Ens. Benjamin **Hull** (8 above).
9–Poncet **Stelle,** Sieur des Loriers, France (*b* ca. 1650), came to America ca. 1676; licensed to keep tavern at Shrewsbury, Monmouth Co., N.J., 1693; *m* Eugenia Legereau, Huguenot refugee;
8–Rev. Benjamin (1684-1759), many yrs., pastor Bapt. ch. at Piscataway; *m* 1st, ca. 1708, Mercy (Hull) Piatt;
7–Susannah (*b* Aug. 3, 1710), *m* Judge Joseph **Hull** (7 above).
11–John **Manning** (*b* ca. 1615), to America, 1635; *m* Abigail–;
10–Jeffrey (*d* 1693), of Piscataway; *m* 1676, Hepzibah Andrews (Joseph[11], of Hingham, Mass.; Sir Thomas[12], Lord Mayor of London);
9–Mary, *m* Nov. 16, 1677, Samuel **Hull** (14th child of Rev. Joseph, 10 above, qv);
8–Mercy (Jan. 22, 1684-Dec. 21, 1746), as widow of Thomas Piatt, *m* Rev. Benjamin **Stelle** (8 above).
2–William Clinton **Armstrong** (*b* nr. Blairstown, N.J., May 6, 1855), ed. Princeton U., '77; genealogist and local historian; mem. I.A.G., *m* Dec. 19, 1888, Stella Virginia Lenher (for issue see Vol. II., p. 76).
1–*m* Oct. 23, 1929, at St. James Reformed Ch., Allentown, Pa., Rev. Joseph S. Peters, officiating, Herminia Genevieve Hoover, *b* Hackettstown, N.J., Nov. 14, 1902; dau. of Henry Ellsworth Hoover, *m* Anna Caroline Kelly.
1–Flying cadet in aviation at Princeton, N.J.; Camp Dick, Tex. and Scott Field, Ill.; enlisted Jan. 17, 1918-honorably disch., Dec. 1, 1919. Residence: Blairstown, N.J.

1–**ARTHUR, Chester Alan,** *b* New York, N.Y., July 25, 1864.
8–Hugh **Stone,** of Andover, Mass.; *m* Hannah Foster;
7–Hugh (*b* 1682), *m* Dorothy–;
6–Benjamin (*b* 1713), of Haverhill, Mass.; *m* Mary Nichols;
5–Uriah (*b* 1744), of Piermont, N.H.; *m* Hepzibah Hadley;
4–George Washington (1777-1854), ed. Dartmouth Coll.; *m* Judith Stevens (*d* 1854, aet. 84);
3–Malvina, *m* Rev. William **Arthur** (1797-1875), see Vol. II, p. 18, for Arthur lineage;
2–Chester Alan (2 below).
9–Col. Edward **Digges** (1621-75), from Eng. to Va., 1650; gov. of Va., 1655; auditor gen., 1670-75; receiver gen., 1672-75; mem. Council, 1674; *m* Mary Elizabeth Braye;
8–Catherine, *m* William **Herndon** (qv);
7–Edward (1678-1743), *m* 1698, Mary Waller;
6–Edward (1704-59), sheriff Spotsylvania Co., Va.; vestryman St. George's Parish; *m* Mary Brock;
5–Joseph (1737-1810), of "Mattapony," Spotsylvania Co., Va.; vestryman of St. George's; signer of Fredericksburg Resolutions; mem. Com. Safety; *m* 2d, 1765, Mary Ann Minor (1741-1822; John[6], *m* Sarah–);
4–Dabney (1783-1824), *m* Elizabeth Hull (*d* 1824);
3–Commodore William Lewis, U.S.N. (1814-57), *m* Elizabeth Frances Hansbrough (Col. Joseph[4], of Culpeper C.H., Va., *m* Sarah Parker);
2–Ellen Lewis (1837-80), *m* 1859, Gen. Chester Alan **Arthur** (1830-86), 21st President of the U.S., Sept. 20, 1881-Mar. 4, 1885; issue: I–Chester Alan (1 above); II–Ellen Herndon (1871-1915; *m* Charles Pinkerton).
1–*m* May 8, 1900, Myra Townsend (Fithian) Andrews, *b* New York, N.Y., Jan. 1, 1870; dau. of Joel A. Fithian, of Bridgeton, N.J., *m* Fannie Barrett Conolly; issue: 1–Chester Alan, Jr., *b* Colorado Springs, Colo., Mar. 21, 1901; *m* in London, Eng., June 29, 1922, Charlotte (*b* Aug. 16, 1897), dau. of Charles S. Wilson, of Los Angeles, Calif.
1–A.B., Princeton, '85. Clubs: Knickerbocker, Union, Racquet and Tennis, The Brook, Turf and Field (New York), Travellers (Paris). Residences: 25 Champs Elysees, Paris; Hobgoblin Hall, Colorado Springs, Colo., U.S.A.

1–**ARTHUR, Joseph Charles,** *b* Lowville, N.Y., Jan. 11, 1850.
5–Bartholomew **Arthur** (*b* Eng. ca. 1725), settled Groton, Conn.; served in Am. Rev.; ship carpenter;
4–Richard (1749-90), of Westfield, Mass.; *b* Preston, Conn.; pvt. 8th Regt. Conn. Militia, Am. Rev., 1776-78; *m* Hannah Bradford;
3–Joseph (1786-1872), of Martinsburgh, N.Y.; *m* 1809, Sibyl Shaler Bush (1784-1861; Jonathan[4]; Moses[5]; Jonathan[6]; Jonathan[7]; John[8], from Eng., to Salem, Mass., 1635);
2–Charles (2 below).
8–Gov. William **Bradford,** Mayflower Pilgrim (qv);
7–Maj. William (1624-1704), dep. gov. Plymouth Colony, 1692; *m* Alice Richards;
6–Israel (1678-1760), of Kingston, Mass.; *m* 1701, Sarah Bartlett;
5–Abner (1707-84), of Kingston; *m* Susannah Porter;
4–Hannah (1751-1831), *m* Richard **Arthur** (4 above).
4–Christopher **Allen** (*d* ante 1815), of Barkhampsted, Conn.; *m* Experience Slade (*b* 1754);
3–Charles Woodworth (1797-1894), of Fletcher, Vt.; *m* 1823, Phebe Manning (1807-97);
2–Ann ((1823-1915), *m* 1847, Charles **Arthur** (1819-1902); issue: I–Joseph Charles (1 above); II–Mary Florence (*b* 1855; *m* Charles Maxon Tradewell); III–Luella Sibyl (1858-62).
1–*m* June 12, 1901, Emily Stiles Potter, *b* Lafayette, Ind., July 1, 1861; dau. of William S. Potter.
1–B.S., Ia. State Coll., '72, M.D., 1877, student Johns Hopkins, 1879, Harvard, 1879, Sc.D.,

Cornell, 1886 (Sigma Xi), student U. of Bonn, 1896; (LL.D., State U. of Ia., 1916; Sc.D., Ia. State Coll., 1920, Phi Kappa Phi). Prof. emeritus, botany, Purdue U. Author (see Who's Who in America). Mem. Bot. Soc. America (twice pres.), Deutsche Bot. Gesellschaft, Am. Philos. Soc., Am. Acad. Arts and Sciences, Phila. Acad. Sciences, Ind. Acad. Sciences (pres.), I.A.G. Address: 915 Columbia St., Lafayette, Ind.

1–**ATKINSON, Henry Morrell,** *b* Brookline, Mass., Nov. 13, 1862.
7–John **Atkinson** (qv);
6–John (*b* 1667), *m* 1st, Sara Woodman;
5–Dea. Ichabod (*b* 1714), *m* 1733, Priscilla Bailey;
4–Lt. Amos (*b* 1754), minute man at Concord and Lexington; *m* 2d, Anna Knowlton;
3–Amos (*b* 1792), *m* 1818, Anna Greenleaf Sawyer;
2–George (1822-1915), Boston; *m* 1852, Elizabeth Staigg (*b* Yorkshire, Eng., 1825-*d* 1904); issue: I–Mary (1853-56); II–George (1854-56); III–Richard S.; IV–Elizabeth (*m* George O. G. Coale, see Vol. I, p. 430); V–Marian (1858-74); VI–James Sawyer (1860-83); VII-Henry Morrell (1 above).
1–*m* Apr. 5, 1888, May Peters (qv); issue: 1–May Peters, *b* Atlanta, Ga., Oct. 15, 1889; *m* Oct. 10, 1916, Jackson Porter Dick; 2–Henry M., Jr. (Feb. 23, 1892-Nov. 2, 1918); Harvard, '15; 2d lt., 1st lt., and capt., attached to Bty. C, 71st Arty., C.A.C., and in France, July 1918; died at Angers, France, of pneumonia contracted from exposure and overwork caring for fellow officers and men during the influenza epidemic.
1–Harvard, '84, A.B., conferred 1908; LL.D. (hon.), Oglethorpe U., 1926. Chmn. bd. Ga. Power Co. (see Who's Who in America). Mem. I.A.G. Clubs: The Brook, The Links, Harvard (New York), Nat. Golf Links of America (L.I.), Piedmont Driving (pres.), Capital City, Atlanta Athletic, Druid Hills Golf (Atlanta). Summer place: "The Burches," North Hatley, P.Q., Can. Winter home: "Atlanta-by-the-Sea," Tucker's Town, Bermuda. Residence: Mayfair House, Atlanta, Ga.

1–**ATKINSON, May Peters (Mrs. Henry M.),** *b* Atlanta, Ga., Mar. 16, 1868.
5–William **Peters** (1702-89), from Eng. to Pa., ca. 1735, where he erected Belmont Mansion (still standing in Fairmount Park, Phila.) was register of the admiralty; judge of common pleas, quarter sessions and orphans cts., Phila.; mem. Assembly; sec. of the Land Office; *m* 1741, Mary Brientnall, of Pa. (John[6]);
4–Richard (1744-1828), sec. Cont. Bd. of War in Am. Rev.; del. Cont. Congress; U.S. dist. judge; *m* 1776, Sarah Robinson (*d* 1804; Thomas[5]);
3–Ralph (1777-1842), *m* 1806, Catharine, dau. David Hayfield Conyngham, from Ireland to Phila.;
2–Col. Richard (1810-89), pioneer of Atlanta, Ga., 1844; prominent civil engr.; ry. builder and financier; *m* 1848, Mary Jane Thompson (1830-1911; Joseph[3]); issue: I–Richard (1848-1921; *m* 1874, Harriet Parker Felton); II–Mary Ellen (1851-1919; *m* as his 2d wife, 1877, George Robison Black); III–Ralph (1853-1923; *m* Eleanor H. Goodman); IV–Edward (*m* Helen Wimberly); V–May (1 above).
1–*m* Apr. 5, 1888, Henry Morrell Atkinson (qv for genealogy and issue). Residence: Mayfair House, Atlanta, Ga.

1–**ATWOOD, Mary Louise,** *b* Madison, Wis., Jan. 25, 1855.
10–Richard **Warren** (qv);
9–Mary, *m* 1628, Robert **Bartlett** (1603-76);
8–Mary, *m* Jonathan **Morey;**
7–Mary, *m* Nathaniel (Wood) **Atwood** (1651-1724; Dea. John[8], propr. Plymouth, Mass., 1636, *m* Sarah Masterson);
6–John (*b* 1684), began to write name Atwood; *m* Sarah Leavitt;
5–Isaac (*b* 1719), *m* Lydia Wait;
4–Isaac (1747-1836), *m* Hannah Chubbuck (1750-98);
3–David (1779-1869), *m* Mary Bell (g.dau. John Bell, Am. Rev.);
2–David (2 below).
10–Richard **Warren** (qv);
9–Mary, *m* 1628, Robert **Bartlett** (1603-76);
8–Joseph (1639-1711), *m* Hannah Pope (1637-1709);
7–Mary (1673-ante 1738), *m* John **Barnes** (1669-1745);
6–Mary (*b* 1701), *m* Richard **Wait** (*b* 1693);
5–Lydia (*b* 1725), *m* Isaac **Atwood** (5 above).
2–David **Atwood** (1815-89), editor and pub. State Journal, Madison, Wis.; mayor of Madison, 1868; mem. 41st Congress, 1870-71; *m* Aug. 23, 1849, Mary Sweeney (1819-1906; Connor Murray[3]; John[4], from Ireland, 1784); issue: I–Charles D. (1850-78; *m* Elizabeth Ward); II–Harrie F. (1852-1906); III–Mary Louise (1 above); IV–Elizabeth Gordon (Mrs. Edward P. Vilas, see Vol. I, p. 432).
1–Vassar, '76. Mem. S.M.D., C.D.A., D.F.P.A., C.D. 17th C., D.A.R. Residence: 235 W. 102d St., New York, N.Y.

1–**AVERY, Eliza Warren,** *b* East Lyme, Conn., Sept. 21, 1871.
9–Christopher **Avery** (qv);
8–Capt. James (1620-1700), of Gloucester, and New London, Conn.; freeman, 1645; grand juror at Gloucester; selectman, 23 yrs.; ens., lt., and capt. of New London Co. troops; dep. Gen. Ct., 24 times; commr. and asst. judge of Co. Ct.; soldier in wars of 1657, and 1675; *m* 1643, Joanna Greenslade (1622-94);
7–Capt. Thomas (1651-1736), of New London, Conn.; noted Indian interpreter; dep. Gen. Ct.; soldier in King Philip's War, 1675; lt., Winthrop's expdn., 1690; capt., 1693; *m* 1677, Hannah Minor (1655-92; Lt. Thomas[8], qv);
6–Abraham (1691/92-1761), of New London, Conn.; *m* 1727, Jane Hill (1701 or 02-1744; Jonathan[7], *m* Mary Sherwood; Charles[8], *m* Ruth [Brewster] Picket);
5–Jonathan (1737-1805), of Lyme, Conn.; grand juror, 1775-76; surveyor of highways, 1778; tithing man, 1781; *m* 1760, Preserved Smith (1737-1833; Simon[6], *m* Dorothy Beckwith; Samuel[7]; Nehemiah[8]; Nehemiah[9]);
4–Abraham (1763-1834), of Lyme, Conn.; pvt. 4th Co., 3d Regt., Conn. militia, 1779-89; *m* 1785, Elizabeth Noyes;
3–Thomas (1798-1869), of E. Lyme, Conn.; *m* 1845, Elizabeth Brace Griswold;
2–William Andrew (2 below).
8–Rev. James **Noyes** (qv);
7–Rev. Moses (1643-1729), of Lyme, Conn.; grad. Harvard, 1659; 1st pastor at Lyme; preached there 60 yrs.; *m* Ruth Pickett (1654-90; John[8], merchant of New London, Conn., *m* 1651, Ruth, g.dau. Elder William Brewster, Mayflower Pilgrim, qv);
6–Moses (1678-1743), of Lyme; *m* 1713, Mary Ely (1691-1767; Judge William[7] [1647-1717], co. ct., New London, Conn., *m* 1681, Elizabeth Smith; Simon[8], *m* Elizabeth–);
5–Moses (1714-86), of Lyme; *m* 1748, Hannah Selden (*b* 1727; Joseph[6] [*b* 1682], of Hadley and Lyme, Conn., *m* Anne Chapman; Joseph[7] [ca. 1651-1725], *m* Rebekah Church; Thomas[8] qv);
4–Elizabeth (1765-1837), of Lyme; *m* Abraham **Avery** (4 above).
8–Matthew **Griswold** (qv);
7–Matthew (1653-1715 or 16), of Lyme, Conn.; dep. and commr.; *m* 1683, Phebe Hyde (1663-1704; Samuel[8], *m* Jane Lee; William[9]);
6–Rev. George (1692-1761), of Lyme, Conn.; B.A., Yale, 1717; 1st pastor Lyme 2d Soc. Ch., 1719-61; *m* 2d, 1736, Elizabeth Lee (1701-58; Ens. Thomas[7] *m* Elizabeth Graham; Thomas[8]; Thomas[9]);
5–Andrew (1745-1813), of Lyme; justice of peace; lt. 4th co., 3d Regt., Conn. Militia, 1779; ens. and leader of the "Flying Guards," 1781; active in civilian work in Am. Rev.; *m* 1768, Eunice Prince (1751-1844; William[6], *m* Mary Holland; Joseph[7]; Robert[8]);
4–Andrew (1787-1847), of Lyme; *m* 1816, Lucinda Johnson (1795-1851; Reynolds[5], *m* Phebe Smith; Caleb John[6]; John[7]);
3–Elizabeth Brace (1823-52), of Lyme; *m* Thomas **Avery** (3 above).
9–Samuel **Gorton** (qv);
8–John (*d* 1714), of Warwick, R.I.; mariner; soldier in King Philip's War; *m* 1665, Margaret Weeden;
7–Capt. John, ship capt.; of Warwick, Cranston, E. Greenwich, and Westerly; dep. from Westerly, 1705; *m* 1700, Patience Hopkins (Thomas[8], *m* Sarah–);
6–William (*d* 1761), of Cranston, R.I., and New London, Conn.; *m* 1736, Lydia Collins (1714-1809; John[7], *m* Susanna Daggert);
5–Benjamin (1737-1825), of Waterford, Conn.; *m*

1769, Mehitable Douglas (1747-1837; Robert[6], *m* Sarah Edgecomb);
4-Robert (1776-1885), of E. Lyme, Conn.; *m* 1806, Esther Ann Gardiner (1781-1831; Benajah[5]);
3-William Gardiner (1809-85), of E. Lyme; *m* 1830, Eliza Raymond Warren (1805-66; Moses[4], *m* Mehitable Raymond; Capt. Moses[5]; Joshua[6]; Joshua[7]; Daniel[8]; John[9], qv);
2-Lockie Payne (1843-1926), of E. Lyme and Norwich, Conn.; *m* 1869, William Andrew **Avery** (1847-77), farmer and salesman; issue: I-Eliza Warren (1 above); II-Ellen Lockie (*b* 1875); III-Williemiene Griswold (1876-87).
1-Ed. Peddie Inst., 1890, Conn. State Normal, 1893. Genealogist. Sch. teacher 7 yrs.; newspaper correspondent, 14 yrs. Mem. S.M.D., D.A.R. (sec.), N.E.H.G.S., Avery Memorial Assn. Club: Mayflower (sec.). Conglist. (treas. ch. parish house assn.; sec. Foreign Missionary Soc.). Republican. Residence: 28 Perkins Av., Norwich, Conn.

1-**AVERY, Russ,** *b* Olympia, Wash., Aug. 23, 1872.
9-Christopher **Avery** (qv);
8-Capt. James (1620-1700), settled at New London, Conn.; acquired large tracts of land at Groton, and built the homestead called the "Hive of the Averys"; selectman, 1660-80; commr., 1663-78; lt. Train Band, 1665; ens., lt., and capt. in King Philip's War; cdr. of soldiers from Stonington, New London and Lyme thruout the war; rep. Gen. Ct., 1656-80; asst. judge Prerogative Ct.; *m* 1st, 1643, Joanna Greenslade (1622-bet. 1693-98);
7-Samuel (1664-1723), of Groton, Conn.; *m* 1686, Susanna Palmer (1665-1747);
6-Humphrey (1699-1788), removed to Wyoming Valley, Pa.; *m* 1st, 1724, Jerusha Morgan (1704-63);
5-Solomon (1726-98), of Tunkhannock, Pa.; pvt. Am. Rev.; *m* 1751, Hannah Punderson (1733-75);
4-Cyrus (1771-1833), of Tunkhannock; *m* 1791, Lydia Marcy (1772-1817);
3-Cyrus Henry (1803-77), of Garden Prairie, Ill.: *m* 1825, Clarinda Kasson (1806-86);
2-William Hartly (1836-1912), of Los Angeles, Calif.; lawyer, banker; *m* 1868, Nellie Townsend Fox (1847-1921); issue: I-Xora (*b* 1870; *m* Perry T. Tompkins); II-Russ (1 above); III-Kasson (*b* 1883); IV-Yerva (*b* 1886).
1-*m* Aug. 22, 1917, May Smith, *b* Salem, Ind.; dau. of Robert Smith, of Salem, *m* Mary Holstein.
1-Litt.B., U. Calif., '94 (Phi Delta Theta); LL.B., Harvard, 1897. Practised law, 1897-1917; judge, Superior Ct., Los Angeles Co., Calif., 1917-25. Clubs: University, Wilshire Country, Athletic, Casa del Mar, Harvard, Lincoln, Sierra. Mason. Residence: 214 N. Rossmore Av., Los Angeles, Calif.

1-**AYER, Thomas Parker,** *b* Merrimack, N.H., Apr. 3, 1886.
9-John **Ayer** (qv);
8-Peter (1633-99), cornet, Haverhill Co.; dep., Colony of Mass. Bay, 1680; *m* 1659, Hannah Allen;
7-Samuel (1669-1743), Haverhill, Mass.; *m* 1693, Elizabeth Tuttle;
6-Peter (*b* 1696), *m* 1st, Lydia Peaslee; *m* 1751, Elizabeth Carleton;
5-Richard (1726-81), *m* 1753, Martha Mitchell (*d* 1767);
4-Peter (1756-1825), *m* 1787, Abigail Eaton;
3-Robert (1791-1875), *m* 1st, Louisa Sanborn; *m* 2d, 1845, Elizabeth Paige (*d* 1894);
2-Joseph Warren (2 below).
5-Jonathan **Philbrick** (1749-1818);
4-William (1777-1815), *m* Jane McCrillis;
3-Caleb (1815-84), *m* Eliza Day;
2-Harriet Lizzie (*b* 1852), *m* 1871, Joseph Warren **Ayer** (1847-1924); merchant; issue: I-Mary L. (*b* 1872); II-Frances P. (*b* 1875); III-Josephine (*b* 1878); IV-George Warren (*b* 1884; *m* Anne E. Mitchell); V-Thomas Parker (1 above).
1-*m* Sept. 4, 1920, Leta Frances Tucker, *b* Waco, Tex., Aug. 27, 1893; dau. of Earl M. Tucker, Waco, Tex.
1-A.B., Brown U., 1909; U. of Ill. Library Sch., 1913-14. Librarian, Richmond (Va.) Pub. Library, since June 1924 (see Who's Who in America). Mem. Phi Kappa Psi. Mason. Address: Public Library, Richmond, Va.

1-**BACKUS, Frances Belden (Mrs. Herbert),** *b* Dayton, O., Jan. 26, 1868.
9-Lt. Samuel **Smith** (qv);
8-Lt. Philip (1633-80), *m* Rebecca Foote (Nathaniel[9], qv);
7-Jonathan (1663-1737), *m* Abigail Kellogg (*b* 1671);
6-Elisha (1705-84), *m* Sarah Field (1707-95);
5-Gad (1749-1827), mem. Mass. militia in Am. Rev.; *m* Irene Waite;
4-Paulina (*b* 1786), *m* 1801, Samuel (Belding) **Belden** (1775-ante 1868);
3-Alonzo (1810-97), *m* 1831, Cynthia Potter (1811-62);
2-Dexter Alonzo (2 below).
10-Hugh **Wells** (son of Thomas), from Colchester, Essex Co., Eng., to Wethersfield, Conn., 1635; *m* in Eng., Frances Belcher;
9-John (1628-92), of Stratford, Conn., and Hatfield, Mass.; *m* Sarah- (*d* 1743);
8-John (1670-1720), of Hatfield, Mass.; *m* ca. 1699, Rachel Marsh (*b* 1674), see Vol. II, p. 96;
7-John (1700-67), *m* Martha Allis (1703-64; Ichabod[8]; John[9]; Lt. William[10], qv);
6-Martha (1731-1817), *m* 1748-49, Elisha **Waite** (1725-1816), soldier Am. Rev.;
5-Irene (1752-1842), *m* Gad **Smith** (5 above).
2-Dexter Alonzo **Belden** (1833-1912), *m* 1860, Caroline Kiler (1836-1923); issue: I-Harry Kiler (1861-68); II-Hettie Kiler (1865-1924, *m* 1892, Harry Albert McGinnis); III-Frances (1 above).
1-*m* July 26, 1898, Herbert Backus, *b* Columbus, O., July 24, 1852, son of Lafayette Backus, *m* Harriet Denig, of Columbus, O.; issue: 1-Georgea Alden, *b* Columbus, O., Oct. 13, 1900; O. State U., '22; *m* May 27, 1924, Edwin Harold Morse.
1-Mem. D.A.C., D.A.R. (state regent 1926-29, v.p. gen. Nat. Soc., 1929-30), U.S.D., 1812, Cincinnati chapter N.E. Women. Residence: 1789 Oak St., Columbus, O.

1-**BACON, John Baptiste Ford,** *b* Jacksonville, Fla., Aug. 24, 1891.
7-John **Bacon** (*d* 1678), of Charlestown, Mass.; *m* Susanna Draper (*d* 1678);
6-Ephraim (1675-1713), *m* Elizabeth Griggs;
5-Ephraim (ca. 1713-ca. 1773), settled in Woodstock, Mass. (now Conn.); *m* Sarah Fairbanks;
4-Ebenezer (1761-1838), soldier Am. Rev.; led colony from Conn. and settled in Otsego Co., N.Y.; *m* 2d, Eunice Hough;
3-Milton Hough (1803-89), settled at Phillipstown, Ill., as pioneer physician in that locality; *m* Sarah Berthier Reeves (1822-1916; Jeheil H.[4] [1799-1881], laid out town of Burnt Prairie, Ill., *m* Mary Pickering [*d* 1860], of Phila., Pa.);
2-Mark Reeves (2 below).
6-Jean **Baptiste,** from Lyons, France, to Danville, Ky.; introduced grape cultivation in Ky.; *m* 1790, Hannah Shuck;
5-Margaret (*d* 1840), *m* 1807, Jonathan **Ford;**
4-John Baptiste (1811-1903), of New Albany, Ind., and Creighton, Pa.; founder of plate glass industry in America; *m* Mary Bower (1806-97);
3-Edward (1843-1920), *m* Evelyn Carter Penn;
2-Mary (2 below).
7-Col. William **Floyd** (*b* ca. 1720) from Amherst Co., Va., to become one of the founders of the City of Louisville, Ky.; *m* Abigail Davis;
6-Col. John (1750-83), one of the original trustees of Louisville; *m* 2d, Jane Buchanan;
5-Maj. George Rogers Clark (1781-1821), comd. a regt. at Battle of Tippecanoe; *m* 2d, Sara Fontaine;
4-Jane Buchanan, of Louisville, *m* James Steptoe **Penn** (1817-54), of Bedford Co., Va. (Robert C.[5] [1789-1856], *m* Lucinda [1795-1878], dau. of James Steptoe [1750-1826], clk. of Bedford Co., 54 yrs., *m* Frances, dau. of Col. James Calloway, soldier Am. Rev.; Gabriel[6]);
3-Evelyn Carter (1844-70), *m* Edward **Ford** (3 above).
2-Mark Reeves **Bacon** (*b* 1852), mem. 65th Congress; *m* Elizabeth I. Cooper (*d* 1882); *m* 2d, 1889, Mary Ford (*b* 1864); issue (1st marriage): I-Elizabeth (*b* 1882; *m* George A. Ford); issue (2d marriage): II-John B. F. (1 above); III-Milton Edward (*b* 1895; *m* Dorothy Spence).
1-*m* Oct. 24, 1925, Heloise Carnahan Lysle (qv for genealogy); issue: 1-Heloise Bacon, *b*

Pasadena, Calif., May 7, 1927; 2–John B. F., Jr., *b* Pasadena, May 30, 1929.
1–Ph.B., Yale, '15. Instructor, U.S. Army Sch. of Aeronautics, Berkeley, Calif., 1918-19. Mem. S.A.R. Clubs: Yale (New York), Detroit Athletic (Detroit, Mich.), Annandale Golf (Pasadena, Calif.). Residence: 2613 Biddle Av., Wyandotte, Mich.

1–**BACON, Heloise Carnahan Lysle (Mrs. John B. F.),** *b* Fillmore, Calif., June 29, 1896.
5–James **Lysle,** soldier Am. Rev.; *m* Mary Wilson (1763-1849);
4–George (1800-77), *m* Margaret McIlvaine (1804-80);
3–Addison (1834-1908), coal operator and banker, Pittsburgh; later removed to Los Angeles; *m* 3d, Maria B. Hayes (1846-1920);
2–Addison Hayes (1873-1913), of Los Angeles, Calif.; *m* Florinda Carnahan (*b* 1874; Robert[3] [1832-95], *m* Sarah Nandino, *b* 1843); she *m* 2d, Edward F. Sherman, of Pasadena, Calif; issue: I–Heloise C. (1 above); II–Marjorie (*b* 1898; *m* O. D. Knight).
1–*m* Oct. 24, 1925, John B. F. Bacon (qv for genealogy and issue).
1–A.B., Leland Stanford, Jr. U., '19 (Kappa Alpha Theta), M.A., Columbia U., 1920. Residence: Wyandotte, Mich.

1–**ROBBINS, Alice Lyman Manley (Mrs. Clifton Z.)** *b* Washington, Mass., Sept. 6, 1874.
10–Gov. William **Bradford,** Mayflower Pilgrim (qv);
9–Maj. William (1624-1704), dep. gov. Plymouth Colony, 1682; *m* Alice Richards (*d* 1671); *m* 2d, Widow Mary Wiswall;
8–Joseph (1674-1747), of Plymouth, and Montville, Conn.; *m* 1698, Anne Fitch (1675-1715);
7–Anne (*b* 1699), *m* 1723, Timothy **Dimmock** (*b* 1698; John[8]; Shubal[9]; Thomas[10]);
6–Timothy (1726-95), of Mansfield, Conn.; Am. Rev.; *m* 1749 or 50, Desire Dimmock (1732 or 33-1802);
5–Eunice (1753-1801), *m* 2d, Asa **Manley** (1735/36-1788);
4–Daniel (1780-1854), of Coventry, Conn.; *m* 1805, Matilda White (ca. 1780-1872; Abner[5], *m* Jerusha Thompson);
3–Frederick White (1810-71), see portrait; *m* 1844, Mary Louise Hale (1819-64; see their dau., Mrs. John W. Bailey for other lineages);
2–John Adams (2 below).
9–Richard **Lyman** (qv);
8–Richard (*d* 1662), of Northampton, Mass.; *m* Hepzibah Ford (Thomas[9]);
7–Thomas, *m* Widow Ruth Holton;
6–Enoch, *m* Diana Smith;
5–Samuel, *m* 1757, Sarah Bartlett;
4–Samuel, soldier Am. Rev.; *m* 1778, Ruhamah Allen;
3–Clark Thaddeus, *m* 1842, Lydia R. Mack.
2–John Adams **Manley** (1850-1928), *m* 1st, 1873, Sarah Jane Lyman (1848-1918); *m* 2d, Stella Alice Micott; issue (1st marriage): I–Alice L. (1 above); II–Frederick John (*b* 1879; *m* Alma Metcalf).
1–*m* Jan. 3, 1899, Clifton Zebulon Robbins, *b* Bloomsburg, Pa., Apr. 29, 1873; son of John M. Robbins, of Bloomsburg; issue (all *b* Shenandoah, Pa.): 1–Rhoda, *b* Jan. 24, 1901; *m* Dec. 20, 1926, Edward S. Shedd (issue: Nancy Alice); 2–John Manley, *b* Jan. 15, 1903; *m* July 25, 1925, Adeline Rogers; 3–Rachel Lavere, *b* Apr. 2, 1917.
1–Residence: 229 Market St., Bloomsburg, Pa.

1–**BAKER, Harold Dean,** *b* Providence, R.I., June 22, 1872.
5–Samuel **Baker** (1754-1838), of Rehoboth, Mass.; *m* 1777, Bethany Mason (1756-1838);
4–Samuel (1787-1872), of Rehoboth; *m* 1810, Patience Pierce;
3–Nelson Orrin (1816-1910), of Rehoboth; *m* 1836, Lydia Pierce (1817-1913);
2–Edwin Granville (2 below).
10–Capt. Michael **Pierce** (1615-76), from Eng., 1645, settled in Hingham, Mass.; later removed to Scituate; *m* 1st, ante 1646, Persis Eames (1621-62; Anthony[11], qv);
9–Capt. Ephraim (ca. 1648-1719), of Warwick, R.I., and Weymouth, Mass.; *m* Hannah Holbrook (*d* 1719; Capt. John[10]; Thomas[11]);
8–Ephraim (*b* 1674), of Rehoboth and Swansea, Mass.; *married* Mary Low (John[9], *m* Mary Rhodes; Anthony[10]; John[11]);
7–Dea. Mial (1692-1786), of Rehoboth and Swansea; *m* Judith Ellis (1686-1744);
6–Rev. Nathan (1716-93), of Rehoboth and Swansea; preached in the Hornbine or Pierce Bapt. Ch., at Rehoboth (still standing); *m* 1736, Lydia Martin (1718-98; Ephraim[7], *m* Thankful, dau. of Samuel Bullock; John[8], from Eng., *m* 1671, Johanna, dau. of Thomas Esten; Richard[9], from Eng., ca., 1663);
5–Rev. Preserved (1758-1828), of Rehoboth and Swansea; *m* 1st, 1784, Sarah Lewis (1765-1823);
4–Patience (1792-1889), of Rehoboth; *m* Samuel **Baker** (4 above);
3–Nelson O., *m* Lydia Pierce (3 above);
2–Edwin Granville (1839-1921), of Rehoboth, and Providence, R.I.; dealer in hides and furs; *m* 1861, Margaret Dean (1840-1919); issue: I–George M. (*b* 1862; *m* Gertrude Hopkins); II–Blanche M. (1863-65); III–Frank N. (*b* 1865; *m* Elizabeth Dent); IV–Mabel S. (1867-72); V–Edwin Granville (*b* 1870; *m* Esther Boyden); VI–Harold D. (1 above); VII–Walter S. (*b* 1874; *m* Lillian Robinson); VIII–Grace E. (*b* 1877; *m* Walter P. Peirce); IX–Ernest C. (*b* 1879; *m* Rosalind Freeman); X–Bessie F. (*b* 1885).
1–*m* Apr. 9, 1901, Nancy Clarke Packer (qv for genealogy and issue).
1–Gold, silver and platinum refiner. Clubs: Highland Country, Touisset Tennis. Conglist. Republican. Summer place: Touisset Point, Warren, R.I. Residence: 148 County St., Attleboro, Mass.

FREDERICK WHITE MANLEY (1810-71).

1–**BAILEY, Emma Agnes Manley (Mrs. John William),** *b* Washington, Mass., Feb. 24, 1859.
6–Lazarus **Manley** (*d* 1748), of Charlestown, Mass., and Coventry, Conn.; *m* 1700/01, Sarah Hartshorn (Thomas[7]);
5–George (*d* 1795), of Coventry, Conn.; *m* 1733, Elizabeth Turner (*d* 1793; Dr. Robert[6], of Wethersfield, Conn.);
4–Asa (1735/36-1788), of Coventry; *m* 2d, 1780, Eunice (Dimmock) Gurley;
3–Daniel (1780-1854), of Coventry, Conn., and Washington, Mass.; *m* 1805, Matilda White (1780-1872; Abner[4], *m* Jerusha Thompson);
2–Frederick White (2 below).
10–John **Howland,** Mayflower Pilgrim (qv);
9–Desire, *m* John **Gorham** (qv);
8–Temperance, *m* Edward **Sturgis,** Jr.;
7–Desire, *m* Capt. Thomas **Dimmock** (Shubal[8], *m* Johanna Bursley; Thomas[9], *m* Ann Hammond);
6–Ens. Thomas, *m* Ann Mason;
5–Desire (1732 or 33-1802), *m* 1749 or 1750, Timothy **Dimmock** (1726-95), Am. Rev.;

4–Eunice (1753-1801), *m* 2d, Asa **Manley** (4 above).
8–Lt. John (Heald) **Hale,** of Hadley, Mass.;
7–Thomas (1650-1725), of Enfield, Conn.; *m* 1675, Priscilla Markham (William[8] [1621-90], one of the first settlers of Hadley, Mass., *m* Priscella [*d* 1688], dau. of George Grave, at Hartford, Conn., 1636-73, dea., dep., 1646, 1657-58, *m* Sarah–);
6–William (1687-post 1738), of Enfield, Conn.; *m* 1710, Mary (Cault) Colt (1696-1734; Abraham[7], *m* Hannah Loomis);
5–Dea. William (1724-1807), of Enfield, Conn., and Tyringham, Mass.; soldier French and Indian War; *m* Hannah Brewer (1729-1817; Capt. John[6], *m* Anne–);
4–John (1752-1803), of Tyringham, Mass.; pvt., Am. Rev.; *m* Abigail Hall (1754-1833; Ebenezer[5], sgt. Cont. Army, *m* Anne Pease);
3–Eli (1791-1864), of Tyringham; *m* 1813, Lucy Crittenden (1793-1869; William Sumner[4], Am. Rev., served in navy, taken psr., *m* Mary Brayman);
2–Mary Louise (1819-64), *m* 1844, Frederick White **Manley** (1810-71), farmer, sch. master, agent for Western R.R., 1844-71 (see portrait); issue: I–Harriet Lucy (1846-1903; *m* James Allen Youngs); II–Frances Louise (1848-1918; *m* Abram Craver); III–John Adams (see his daughter, Mrs. Clifton Z. Robbins for other lineages); IV–Gilbert Eli (*b* 1853; *m* 1882, Esther Howe Merrick); V–Alice Irene (1855-58); VI–Emma A. (1 above); VII–Mary Hale (*b* 1862; *m* Dwight B. Gardner).
1–*m* Oct. 18, 1882, John William Bailey, *b* Middletown, Conn. (Nov. 26, 1854-Apr. 21, 1928); son of John S. Bailey, of Middletown, *m* Betsey S. Peters.
1–Ed. Oread Collegiate Inst. (pres. Oread Collegiate Assn., 1915-16), Worcester, Mass. Mgr. W.U. Tel. Co., Windsor and Middletown, Conn. Lectured, 1910-15, "The Passion Play of 1900 and 1910," "Education, Manners, and Customs of Early N.E.," "Jonathan Trumbull in the War of the Revolution." Mem. S.M.D. (mem. state bd. assts., 18 yrs.), S.D.P., D.A.C. (chaplain), D.F.P.A., D.A.R. (regent, 1906-08), U.S.D. 1812, I.A.G., Soc. N.E. Women. Conglist. Republican. Residence: 114 High St., Middletown, Conn.

1–**BAKER, Nancy Clarke Packer (Mrs. Harold Dean),** *b* Providence, R.I., June 28, 1876.
9–John **Packer** (1626-89), from Eng., 1655; settled at Groton, Conn.; *m* 1676, Rebecca Wells Latham (*b* 1651; Ens. Hugh[10]; Hugh[11]);
8–Capt. James (1681-1765), of Groton; *m* 1706, Abigail Avery (Capt. John[9]; James [10]; Christopher[11], qv);
7–James (1710-65), *m* Zerviah Eldredge (1715-95; Daniel[8]; Daniel[9]; Sgt. Samuel[10]);
6–Dea. James (1734-1803), removed from Groton, Conn., to Guilford, Vt.; *m* Rebecca Walworth (1736-1814);
5–Rev. Jeremy (*b* 1762), *m* Rebekah– (1760-1803);
4–John (1788-1857), removed from Guilford, Vt., to Clayton Co., Ia.; *m* 1810, Sarah Wilder;
3–Henry Harrison (1818-99), of Guilford, Vt., and Hanson, Mass.; *m* 1844, Jane Robson (1825-1909), of N.S.;
2–James Clough (2 below).
9–Thomas **Wilder** (qv);
8–Lt. Nathaniel (1650-1704), killed by Indians; *m* 1673, Mary Sawyer (*b* 1652; Thomas[9], qv);
7–Capt. Nathaniel (1686-1775), of Lancaster, Mass.; *m* 1707, Demaris Whitcomb (1686-1772; John[8]);
6–Aaron (1723-90), removed to Townshend, Vt.; *m* 1744, Priscilla Clark (*d* 1784; Joseph[7]);
5–Dea. Aaron (*b* 1754), removed to Petersham, Mass.; *m* 1775, Abigail Younglove (*d* 1843; John[6]; John[7]; John[8]; Rev. John[9]; Samuel[10]);
4–Sarah (1791-1893), removed to Guilford, Vt.; *m* John **Packer** (4 above);
3–Henry, *m* Jane Robson, (3 above);
2–James Clough (*b* 1851), musician, Cambridge, Mass.; *m* 1875, Sarah Jane McLaughlin (*b* 1858), of N.S.
1–*m* Apr. 9, 1901, Harold Dean Baker (qv for genealogy); issue (all *b* Attleboro, Mass.): 1–Harold Dean, *b* May 3, 1902; B.S., Dartmouth Coll., '23 (P.B.K.); *m* May 9, 1924, Lucy, dau. Arthur Alexander McRae, of Attleboro, Mass. (issue: Penelope Dean; Patience); 2–Royal Packer, *b* Oct. 8, 1904; ed. Dartmouth Coll., U.Va.; 3–Bradford Granville (Mar. 5-Sept. 28, 1906); 4–Jean Lucille (Aug. 21, 1919-June 7, 1920).
1–Mem. D.F.P.A., S.D.P., D.A.C., D.C.W., D.A.R. (state treas., Mass.), Daus. of Union, N.E. H.G.S., Attleboro Museum of Art, (treas.); trustee Attleboro Community Chest, District Nurses Assn., Anti-Tuberculosis Soc., Boy's Health Camp. Conglist. Republican. Clubs: North Purchase (pres.), Chaminade, Women's, Attleboro Art, Highland Country, Touisset Tennis, etc. Summer place: Touisset Point, Warren, R.I. Residence: 148 County St., Attleboro, Mass.

1–**BAKER, H(enry) Warren,** *b* Heuvelton, N.Y., Apr. 7, 1877.
8–Robert **Austin** (1634-87), from Eng., 1638; settled in Mass.; later at King's Town, R.I.;
7–Jeremiah (1665-1754), of King's Town and Exeter, R.I.; *m* 1695, Elizabeth–(*d* 1754);
6–Pasko (1698-1774), of Exeter; *m* 1725, Margaret Sunderland (1703-73; Daniel[7], of King's Town, *m* Elizabeth Sheldon);
5–Isaac (1737-1824), of Argyle, N.Y.; soldier Am. Rev.; *m* 1760, Rhodinah Vaughan (1740-1810; David[6], soldier Am. Rev.);
4–Daniel (1782-1831), of De Peyster, N.Y.; soldier War 1812; *m* 1803, Mary Elizabeth Davis (1782-1860; Gardner[5]);
3–Daniel (1806-88), of De Peyster; *m* 1833, Amanda Hurlbut (1813-80; Philo[4], *m* Julia Sweet);
2–Martha Louise (1848-95), *m* 1870, James Augusta **Baker** (1845-93), of Halett & Davis Piano Co., Boston, Mass.; issue: I–John Ferguson (*b* 1871; *m* Gertrude Thompson); II–Louise Warena (*b* 1873; *m* James B. Schmidt); III–Henry Warren (1 above); IV–Carrie Maude (*b* 1879; *m* William R. Todd); V–Mary Irene (1882-1924; *m* Herbert Raven); VI–James Austin (1887-1900).
1–*m* Dec. 20, 1905, Maude S. Conrad (qv); issue: 1–Warren Emmet, *b* E. Orange, N.J., Dec. 16, 1909.
1–Mgr. Windham Silk Co., New York, since 1910. Mem. bd. of mgrs., Silk Travelers' Assn. Enlisted in Mass. Vol. Militia, 1897-1900; mem. Dean St. Signal Corps, N.Y., and state vol. militia. Trustee Free Pub. Library; deacon Presbyn. Ch. of Munn Av., E. Orange. Mem. S.A.R. (pres. Orange Chapter), N.E. Soc., St. Lawrence Soc. Republican. Clubs: E. Orange Golf, etc. Mason. Residence: 65 Carnegie Av., E. Orange, N.J.

1–**BAKER, Maude S. Conrad (Mrs. Henry Warren),** *b* London, Eng., Dec. 1, 1878.
9–Rev. Hans **Herr** (qv);
8–Rev. Christian (1680-1749), of Willow St., Pa.; *m* 1704, Anna– (*d* 1755);
7–Christian (1717-63), of Willow Street; *m* 1742, Barbara–;
6–Barbara (1745-1806), *m* 1767, Capt. Henry **Kendig** (1742-1809), capt. in Am. Rev. (Jacob[7], *m* Alice Wade);
5–Alice (*b* 1775), of Lampeter, Pa.; *m* 1794, Capt. John **Martin** (1772-1844), of Lampeter; lt. and capt. in War 1812 (Christian[6], *m* Mary Barr);
4–Mattie (1797-1838), of Lampeter; *m* 1820, Henry **Mehaffey** (1795-1885; John[5], *m* Mary Monderback);
3–Martha (1821-1901), of Lampeter; *m* 1841, Benjamin **Conrad** (1817-55); of New Danville, Pa. (Daniel[4], *m* Mary Erisman);
2–Daniel (1842-1911), of Lancaster, Pa.; *m* 1874, Sophy F. Bentzen (1841-1922); issue: I–Martha Matilda (*b* and *d* 1875); II–Benjamin Bentzen (*b* Montreal, Can., 1876; *m* 1905, Hilda P. Ellis, of Manchester, Eng.); III–Maude S. (1 above).
1–*m* Dec. 20, 1905, Henry Warren Baker (qv for genealogy and issue).
1–Ed. private schs., Girls' High Sch., Brooklyn, N.Y.; grad. Miss Whitcomb's Sem., Brooklyn Heights; studied languages and music abroad 4 yrs. Mem. D.A.C., D.A.R. (regent Orange Mt. Chapter), U.S.D. 1812. Clubs: Woman's. Presbyn. Republican. Residence: 65 Carnegie Av., E. Orange, N.J.

1–**BAKER, Mary Ellen,** *b* Macon Co., Ill., Aug. 17, 1874.
5–Michael **Baker** (probably son of Jacob [*b* 1709], and g.son of George Peter [*b* 1680]); settled in N.C.; *m* Margaret Davis (*d* 1815);
4–Nathan (1771-1824), farmer; settled in Beaufort Co., N.C., 1790; *m* 1792, Elizabeth Aston (1768-1844; James[5], *m* Mary McDowell);

3–William Davis (1800-83), of Decatur, Ill.; farmer; moved to Ill., 1828; *m* 1823, Marilla Martin (1799-1893; Josiah[4], soldier Am. Rev., *m* Mary McCleary; John[5], of Mecklenburg Co., N.C., served in French and Indian War, *m* Mary McDowell);
2–Nathan Martin (2 below).
5–J. Henry **Price** (*d* 1796), came from the Palatinate ca. 1749, settled at New River (now Montgomery Co.), Va.; *m* Mary–;
4–Adam (1760-1828), of Rockingham Co., Va.; *m* Catharine Miller (Henry[5], *m* Mary Elizabeth Koger; desc. Adam Miller, founder of Massamutten Colony, Va.);
3–John (1799-1849), of Seven Mile, Butler Co., O.; *m* 1822, Elizabeth Rhinehart;
2–Sarah Elizabeth (2 below).
6–Jacob **Runkle** (*d* ca. 1791), *m* Anna Marie–(*d* 1813);
5–Peter (*d* ca. 1821), *m* Margaret–; *m* 2d, Rebecca–;
4–Barbara, *m* Jacob **Rhinehart** (Lewis[5]);
3–Elizabeth (1805-84), *m* John **Price** (3 above);
2–Sarah Elizabeth (1841-1912), *m* 1864, Nathan Martin **Baker** (1837-1922), Presbyn. minister; chaplain 116th Ill. Vol. Inf., 1862-64; issue: I–Florence Floatie (*b* 1870; *m* William Thomas Burrill); II–Mary Ellen (1 above); III–Emma Lavena (*b* 1876); IV–Clara Martin (*b* 1883).
1–A.B., Lincoln (Ill.) U., '00; B.L.S., N.Y. State Library Sch., 1908. Instructor Latin, Mo. Valley Coll., Marshall, Mo., 1901-05, librarian, 1905-06; head cataloger Bryn Mawr Coll., 1908-12; head cataloger Mo. State U. Library, 1912-19, Carnegie Library, Pittsburgh, Pa., 1920-23; librarian U. of Tenn., 1923–. Mem. D.A.R., East Tenn. Hist. Assn., Mo. Library Assn. (pres. 1917-19), Tenn. Library Assn. (pres. 1928-30). Presbyterian. Club: Faculty Women's. Address: University of Tennessee Library, Knoxville, Tenn.

1–**BALDWIN, Ralph Lyman,** *b* Easthampton, Mass., Mar. 27, 1872.
8–Joseph **Baldwin** (qv);
7–Jonathan (1649-1739), *m* Thankful Strong (*b* 1663; John[8], qv);
6–Ezra (*b* 1706), *m* 1728, Ruth Curtis (*b* 1708; James[7] [1686-1766]; Benjamin[8] [1652-1733]; John[9], 1611-1707);
5–Ezra (1737-1824), *m* 1764, Elizabeth Lyman;
4–Lyman (*b* 1768), *m* Phoebe Hull (*b* 1769);
3–Ezra C. (1797-1866), *m* 1831, Amelia Ann Squire;
2–Lyman Norwood (2 below).
10–Richard **Lyman** (qv);
9–Richard (*d* Northampton, Mass., 1662), from Eng. with his father, 1631; moved to Hartford, Conn., later to Windsor; original settler of Northampton, 1654; 1st recorder of deeds there; *m* Hepzibah Ford (Thomas[10]);
8–Thomas (*b* Windsor, ca. 1649-*d* 1725), removed to Durham, 1708/09; dea.; rep. Gen. Ct.; *m* 1677, Ruth (Holton) Baker (William Holton[9]), widow of Joseph Baker;
7–Thomas (*b* 1678), *m* 1706, Elizabeth Parsons (*b* 1684; Samuel[8] [1652-1734], *m* Elizabeth, dau. of Capt. Aaron Cook; Cornet Joseph[9], qv);
6–Thomas (bap. 1714/15-1761), *m* Ann– (*d* 1772);
5–Elizabeth (1743-1808), *m* Ezra **Baldwin** (5 above).
9–George **Squire** (*d* 1691), from Eng.; at Concord, Mass., 1640; removed to Fairfield, Conn., 1644; sgt.; *m* Ann–;
8–George (*b* Concord, Mass., 1642/43), freeman, Fairfield, Conn., 1672; *m* Ellen, prob. dau. of Ephraim Wheeler;
7–George (ca. 1674-post 1724), from Fairfield to Durham, Conn.; *m* Jane (Edwards?);
6–Samuel (ca. 1711-1751-52), *m* 1st, Abigail–(*d* ca. 1750);
5–David (bap. 1738/39-1804), *m* 1761, Huldah Bishop (1742-ca. 1783; William[6] [*b* 1714]; John[7] [1655-1731]; John[8], *m* Susanna Goldham; John[9] [*d* 1676], to America, 1639);
4–Thaddeus (1764-1820), *m* Anna Talcott (1770-1806); *m* 2d, Amelia Hayden;
3–Amelia Ann (1812-92), *m* Ezra C. **Baldwin** (3 above).
9–William **Hayden** (qv);
8–Daniel (1640-1712/13), selectman; lt. Train Band, 1697; troop of horse 1698; one of 17 troopers in King Philip's War, 1675; *m* 1664, Hannah Wilcockson (*d* 1722; William[9], *m* Margaret–);
7–Samuel (1677/78-1742), *m* Anna Holcomb (*d* 1756, aet. 81; Sgt. Benajah[8], *m* Sarah Eno);
6–Samuel (*b* 1707), from Windsor to Torringford, Conn., 1765; *m* 1737, Abigail Hall, of Somers;
5–Augustin (1740-1823), in French and Indian War, 1758; his diary is still extant; moved to Torringford, 1765; *m* 1769, Cynthia Filer (*b* 1747; Jeremiah[6], *m* Jerusha Kelsey; Jerubabel[7] [*b* 1674]; Jerubabel[8] [*b* 1644]; Walter[9] [*d* 1690], a first settler of Windsor);
4–Amelia (1784-1823), *m* Thaddeus **Squire** (4 above).
9–Thomas **Miner** (qv);
8–Ephraim (*b* 1642), *m* 1666, Hannah Avery (*b* 1644; James[9] [1620-1700]; Christopher[10], qv);
7–James (1682-1726), *m* 1705, Abigail Eldredge (*b* 1688; Daniel[8] [1650-1726]; Samuel[9], from Eng.);
6–Charles (*b* 1709), *m* 1741, Mrs. Mary Wheeler (*b* 1720; widow of Isaac Wheeler, and dau. of Thomas Wheeler[7] [1700-55]; Isaac[8] [1676-1737]; Isaac[9] [1646-1712]; Thomas[10], 1602-86);
5–Thomas (*b* 1743), Am. Rev.; *m* 1st, 1765, Mary Page (*b* 1749; John[6] [*b* 1720], *m* Mary Hewitt; Joseph[7] [*b* 1679/80], *m* Mary Miner; John[8]; John[9], qv);
4–Adam (1774-1847), *m* Betsey Frink (1778-1850), see Vol. III, p. 50, for Frink lineage;
3–Elisha Frink (1807-61), rep. Mass. Legislature; *m* 1837, Adaline Jane Spelman;
2–Harriet Parsons (2 below).
11–Richard **Warren** (qv);
10–Elizabeth, *m* 1635/36, Richard **Church** (qv);
9–Caleb (1642-1722), *m* 1667, Joanna Sprague (1644-78; William[10], qv);
8–Rebecca (1678-1757), *m* 1695/96, Joshua **Warren** (1668-1760; Daniel[9] [1628-1716]; John[10], qv);
7–Elizabeth (1704-29), *m* 1726, Peter **Gibbons** (ca. 1700-*d* of smallpox, 1729), of Boston;
6–Peter (1730-1822), *m* Sarah Greene (*b* 1731);
5–Timothy (1762-1847), Am. Rev.; *m* Elizabeth Hayes (1762-1832);
4–Affa (1793-1821), *m* 1810, Samuel **Spelman** (1788-1870), see Vol. III, p. 50, for Spelman lineage;
3–Adaline Jane (1811-88), *m* Elisha F. **Miner** (3 above).
2–Harriet Parsons, (1838-1905), *m* 1858, Lyman Norwood **Baldwin** (1837-1907), mcht.; town assessor; for issue see Vol. III, p. 50.
1–*m* May 27, 1896, Mary Pierce Hosford (*b* Haydenville, Mass., Oct. 28, 1871-*d* Oct. 22, 1928); dau. of Charles L. Hosford, *m* Harriet Isabelle Pierce; issue: 1–Dorothy Spelman, *b* Northampton, Mass., Jan. 4, 1900; *m* June 23, 1923, Thomas C. McCray (issue: Alden C., *b* June 10, 1924; Kent Baldwin, *b* June 7, 1928); 2–Robert Miner, *b* Northampton, Mass., Feb. 6, 1902; 3–Howard Hosford, *b* Haydenville, Mass., Sept. 17, 1904; 4–Barbara Pierce, *b* Hartford, Conn., May 19, 1907; 5–Elizabeth Spencer, *b* Haydenville, Mass., Sept. 25, 1908; 6–Marion Lyman, *b* Haydenville, Mass., Oct. 23, 1910.
1–Grad. Williston Sem., Easthampton, 1890; (hon. Mus. B., Trinity, 1925). Music under private teachers, Boston. Dir. pub. sch. music; organist; composer; author (see Who's Who in America). Mem. I.A.G. Summer place: Haydenville, Mass. Residence: 8 Forest Rd., West Hartford, Conn.

1–**BALDWIN, S(amuel) Prentiss,** *b* Cleveland, O., Oct. 26, 1868.
7–Richard **Baldwin** (qv);
6–Barnabas (1665-1741), *m* Sarah Buckingham;
5–Sylvanus (1706-85), of Woodbridge, Conn.; *m* Mary French;
4–Charles (1751-1818), of Meriden, Conn.; *m* Susannah Hine;
3–Seymour Wesley (*b* 1807), *m* 1st, Mary E. Candee;
2–Judge Charles Candee (2 below).
8–Zaccheus **Candee** (1640-1720), of New Haven, Conn.;
7–Samuel (1678-1748), of West Haven, Conn.;
6–Caleb (1722-77);
5–David (1747-1841), of Oxford, Conn.;
4–David (*d* Oxford, 1851);
3–Mary E. (1813-36), *m* Seymour W. **Baldwin** (3 above).
10–Capt. Thomas **Prentiss** (qv);
9–Thomas (1649-85), *m* Sarah Stanton; *m* 2d, Ann Lord;
8–Samuel (ca. 1680-1728), *m* Esther Hammond;
7–Jonas (1710-66), *m* Lucy Denison;
6–Col. Samuel (1736-1807), officer Am. Rev.; *m* Phebe Billings;
5–Samuel (1759-1818), surgeon Am. Rev.; *m* Lucretia Holmes;

4–Samuel (1782-1857), chief justice of Vt.; U.S. senator and U.S. dist. judge; *m* Lucretia Houghton;
3–Charles William (*b* 1812), *m* Caroline Kellogg;
2–Caroline Sophia (1842-1916), *m* Judge Charles Candee **Baldwin** (1834-1895), judge Circuit Ct., Cleveland, O.; issue: I–Mary Candee (*b* 1864; *m* John Pascal Sawyer, see Vol. I, p. 818, and Vol. III, p. 410); II–S(amuel) Prentiss (1 above); III–Seymour David (1875-78).
1–*m* Feb. 15, 1898, Lilian Converse Hanna (qv).
1–A.B., Dartmouth, '92, A.M., 1894, LL.B., Western Reserve, 1894. Atty. at Law and scientist; dir. Baldwin Bird Research Lab.; research asso. in Biology, Western Reserve U. Mem. M.O.L.L. Clubs: Union, Chagrin Valley Hunt. Summer Place: "Hillcrest Farm," Gates Mills, O. Residence: 11025 E. Boulevard, Cleveland, O.

1–**BALDWIN, Lilian Converse Hanna (Mrs. S. Prentiss),** *b* Cleveland, O.
5–Thomas **Hanna**, came from the North of Ireland to southern Va., 1763;
4–Robert (1753-1837), settled in Columbiana Co., O., 1801; *m* 1776, Catharine Jones (1753-1835);
3–Benjamin (1779-1853), of Columbiana Co.; *m* 1803, Rachel Dixon;
2–Dr. Leonard (2 below).
7–William **Dixon** (*b* ca. 1662-1708), from Ireland to New Castle Co., Del.; *m* ca. 1690, Ann, dau. of William Gregg;
6–Henry (ca. 1695-ca. 1742), of New Castle Co.; *m* 1715, Ruth Jones (*d* ca. 1758);
5–John (1717-67), of New Castle Co., Del., and Chester Co., Pa.; *m* 1742, Rebecca Cox (*d* ca. 1787);
4–Joshua (1750-1831), of Chester Co., Pa., and Columbiana Co., O.; *m* 2d, 1783, Dinah Battin (1760-1833);
3–Rachel (1785-1851), *m* Benjamin **Hanna** (3 above).
9–Edward (Convers) **Converse** (qv);
8–James (1620-1715), from Eng. to Woburn, Mass.; *m* 1643, Ann Long (*d* 1691; Robert[9], *m* Elizabeth–);
7–Maj. James (1645-1706), of Woburn; *m* Hannah Carter (1650-91; John[8], *m* Elizabeth Kendall);
6–Capt. Josiah (*d* 1771), of Woburn, *m* 1706, Hannah Sawyer (1689-1747; Joshua[7], *m* Sarah Wright);
5–Lieut. Josiah (1710-75), of Woburn, Mass., and Stafford, Conn.; *m* 1732, Eleanor Richardson (1714-85; Nathaniel[6], *m* Abigail Reed);
4–Col. Israel (1743-1806), of Randolph, Vt., and Stafford, Conn.; *m* 2d, 1771, Hannah Walbridge (1752-1830; Maj. Amos[5], *m* Margaret—);
3–Porter (1778-1870), of Stafford, Conn., and Unionville, O.; *m* 1810, Rhoda Howard (1785-1873);
2–Samantha Maria (1813-97), *m* 1835, Dr. Leonard **Hanna** (1806-62), physician, later commission merchant and shipping, Cleveland, O.; issue: I–Helen Gertrude (*b* 1836; *m* 1862, Henry S. Hubbell); II–Marcus A. (1837-1905; U.S. Senator from Ohio; *m* 1864, Charlotte Augusta, dau. of Daniel P. Rhodes, of Cleveland); III–Howard Melville (1840-1921; *m* 1863, Kate Smith); IV–Salome Marie (*b* 1844; *m* 1868, George W. Chapin; *m* 2d, J. Wyman Jones); V–Seville Samantha (*b* 1846; *m* 1887, James Pickands; *m* 2d, Jay C. Morse); VI–Leonard Colton (*b* 1850; *m* 1876, Fanny Mann; *m* 2d, Coralie Walker); VII–Lilian Converse (1 above).
1–*m* Feb. 15, 1898, S. Prentiss Baldwin (qv). Residence: 11025 E. Boulevard, Cleveland, O.

1–**FULLINWEIDER, Ruth Ballard (Mrs. George C.),** *b* Estherville Ia., Sept. 30, 1872.
10–Francis **Cooke** (qv);
9–Jane (ca. 1614-1666), *m* 1627/28, Experience **Mitchell** (1609-89), from Eng. in the "Ann," 1623;
8–Hannah, of Plymouth, Mass.; *m* Dea. Joseph **Hayward** (1643-ca. 1718; Thomas[9], *m* Agnes Beaumon, of Wales);
7–Hannah (1691-1761), of Bridgewater, Mass.; removed to Morris Co., N.J.; *m* 1714, Maj. Ebenezer **Byram** (1692-1753), rep. Gen. Ct. Mass., 1738,49; maj. militia; judge co. ct.; built the famous "Black Horse Inn", 1745, still being used, Mendham, N.J.;
6–Abigail (1730-1817), as Widow Thompson, *m* 2d, 1751, Benjamin **Pitney** (ca. 1728-1798; James[7], *m* Susanna Smith);
5–Elizabeth (1760-1850), of Mendham, N.J.; *m* 1775, Caleb **Baldwin** (1752-1810), gunsmith; served in Am. Rev., detached to mfr. and repair fire arms for the govt. (Caleb[6], of Newark, N.J., *m* Hannah Beach);
4–Phoebe (1781-1841), of Washington Co., Pa.; *m* 1797, Thomas **Kirkpatrick** (1769-1856; Andrew[5], *m* Elizabeth–);
3–Baldwin (1808-77), of Youngstown, O.; *m* 1835, Meribah Condit (1816-97; Rev. Ira[4], *m* Mary Miller, of Morristown, N.J.);
2–Amanda (1844-91), *m* 1869, Dr. Ezra Harding **Ballard** (1837-1900), M.D., U.Mich., '68; physician and surgeon; co. officer, treas. and co. supt. of schools; issue: I–Ruth Ballard (1 above); II–Dr. Carl Harding (qv. for paternal lineage).
1–*m* May 16, 1894, George Clay Fullinweider, Alton, Ind., Nov. 11, 1872; son of Henry Clay Fullinweider, of Alton, Ind.
1–School teacher, Estherville, Ia., 1891-94. Mem. Magna Charta Dames, S.M.D., D.A.R. (chapter v. regent). Presbyterian. Republican. Clubs: Huron Country, Junior Bridge. Residence: Huron, S.D.

1–**BALLARD, Carl Harding,** *b* Estherville, Ia., Feb. 5, 1877.
10–Dea. Gregory **Stone** (qv);
9–Elder John (bap. 1618-1683), dep. Mass. Gen. Ct.; ruling elder Cambridge Ch.; *m* 1639, Anne Treadway;
8–David (1646-1737), Framingham, Mass.; in King Philip's War; *m* 1675, Susanna–(living 1721);
7–Samuel (1685-1750), Framingham; *m* 1707, Bathsheba–;
6–Samuel (1714-1786-87), Framingham; in Am. Rev.; *m* 1737, Rebecca Clark (*b* 1716; Capt. Isaac[7], *m* Sarah Stow);
5–Jason (1737-1809), of Fitzwilliam, N.H.; *m* 1762, Deborah Goodnow (1742-1813; Elijah[6], *m* Deborah Swain);
4–Deborah (1765-1813), Fitzwilliam; *m* 1789, Joseph **Ormsby** or Ormsbee (1764-1851), in Am. Rev.;
3–Ruth (1797-1844), *m* 1818, Ezra **Ballard** (ca. 1796-1871), of Helena, N.Y.;
2–Ezra Harding (2 below).
2–Dr. Ezra Harding **Ballard** (1837-1900), M.D., U.Mich., 1868; physician and surgeon; co. officer, treas. and co. supt. of schs.; *m* 1869, Amanda Kirkpatrick (1844-91); issue: I–Ruth Ballard (Mrs. George Clay Fullinweider, qv for maternal lineage); II–Carl Harding (1 above).
1–*m* Apr. 29, 1903, Ora May Babcock (qv for genealogy and issue).
1–M.D., U.Mich., '00 (Phi Chi); interned at Blodgett Memorial Hosp., Grand Rapids, Mich., 1901-02; post grad. work, Vienna, Austria. 1927. Eye, ear, nose and throat specialist; prof. Roentgenology, U. of Neb., 1920-26. Mem. S.M.D., S.A.R., A.M.A., etc. Presbyn. Republican. Residence: 421-16th St., Santa Monica, Calif.

1–**BALLARD, Ora May Babcock (Mrs. Carl Harding),** *b* Lansing, Mich., May 1, 1878.
9–Thomas **Blodgett** (qv);
8–Samuel (1633-87), *m* 1655, Ruth Eggleston;
7–Samuel (1658-1743), *m* Huldah Simonds;
6–Joshua (*b* 1694), *m* Dinah Morse;
5–Joshua (1722-1816), was first white child *b* Stafford, Conn.; served in Am. Rev.; *m* 1749, Hannah Alden;
4–Ezra (1773-1868), served in War of 1812; *m* Clarissa Kibbe (1779-1838);
3–Ruth Butler (1823-1910), *m* 1840, Darius Ambrose **Babcock** (1820-1906), of St. Joseph Co., Mich.;
2–Darius Ambrose (2 below).
9–John **Alden** (qv);
8–Joseph (1624-97), removed to W. Bridgewater, Mass.; freeman, 1659; *m* Mary Simmons (Moses[9], qv);
7–Joseph (1667-1747), of Bridgewater, *m* 1690, Hannah Dunham (1670-1748; Daniel[8], *m* Mehitabel Hayward);
6–Daniel (1691-1767), removed to Stafford, Conn.; *m* 1717, Abigail Shaw (ca. 1695-1755; Joseph[7]);
5–Hannah (1727-94), *m* Joshua **Blodgett** (5 above).
2–Darius Ambrose **Babcock** (*b* 1847), of Three Rivers, Mich.; *m* 1870, Olive S. Avery (1854-1917); issue: I–Dallas (1873-74); II–Frank Clayton (1875-1923); III–Ora M. (1 above); IV–Olive Marie (*b* 1880); V–Josephine Hestaline (*b* 1884); VI–Grace Vivian (*b* 1887).

1–*m* Apr. 29, 1903, Dr. Carl Harding Ballard (qv); issue (all *b* Omaha, Neb.): 1–(adopted) Barbara Janet, *b* Mar. 13, 1909; 2–Clay Harding, *b* Dec. 31, 1911; 3–Ruth Babette, *b* Oct. 17, 1917; 4–Bonnie Nadine, *b* Jan. 9, 1919.
1–Taught sch., Fabius, Mich., 1894-98. Dep. co. treas., St. Joseph Co., Mich., 1898-99. Grad. nursing course, Union Benevolent Assn. Hosp. (now Blodgett Memorial), Grand Rapids, Mich., 1902; asst. supt., same, until 1903. Mem. S.M.D.; Alden Kindred; O.E.S. Residence: 421-16th St., Santa Monica, Calif.

1–**BALLARD, James Clinton,** *b* St. Helena, La., Jan. 17, 1866.
5–Capt. Kedar **Ballard** (1747-1834), served thruout Am. Rev. with Gen. Nathanael Greene's Army; *m* 1783, Theresa Sumner;
4–Edwin (*b* 1785), *m* 1807, Mary Wright;
3–Kedar, *m* 1836, Susan Hines;
2–William Edwin (2 below).
4–Church (or Henry Church) **Clinton** (*d* 1793);
3–Rev. Thomas (1792-1875), Meth. preacher; *m* 1828, Anne L. Hanna (Hon. Henry[4], from S.C. to Miss., 1791, mem. legislature, his name appears on first constn. of Miss., *m* Leoticia Knox);
2–Sarah E. (1840-1919), *m* 1864, William Edwin **Ballard** (1837-95), Methodist minister; issue: I–James Clinton (1 above); II–W. H. (1867-97; *m* 1893, Josie Ray); III–George C. (*b* 1870).
1–*m* Sept. 17, 1903, Luda B. Bowman, *b* Ouachita Parish, La., May 4, 1877; dau. of Francis E. Bowman, *m* 1870, Pauline Chapman; issue: 1–Francis Edwin, *b* Natchez, Miss., Aug. 6, 1905; A.B., Millsaps Coll., '24; M.A., Vanderbilt U., 1926; *m* Nov. 26, 1929, Janet, dau. of Clarence W. Morris, of Dallas, Tex.; 2–Jean Clinton, *b* Natchez, Oct. 2, 1912.
1–A.B., Southern Normal Sch.; M.D., Vanderbilt U., 1891. Apptd. actg. asst. surgeon Public Health Service, 1899; co. health officer, 1893-99. Commd. 1st lt. Med. Reserve Corps, Sept. 25, 1908, served until 1913, including 2 yrs. in the Philippine Islands; capt., Apr. 2, 1917, maj., Nov. 17, 1917; lt. col. Reserve, May 2, 1919. Mem. S.A.R. (registrar Ark. State Soc.), Soc. Cincinnati, S.C.V., A.L., I.A.G., K.P., Odd Fellow. Residence: Biloxi, Miss. Address: 1121 W. 33d St., Little Rock, Ark.

1–**BALLARD, Smith Sabin,** *b* Georgia, Vt., Apr. 3, 1861.
8–William **Ballard** (qv);
7–Joseph (1667-1722), of Andover, Mass.; ens. in colonial wars; *m* 2d, 1692, Rebecca (Rea-Stevens) Horn or Orne;
6–Jeremiah (1697-1761), cdr. Mass. troops, 1746-47; capt. in colonial wars; *m* 1721, Mary Dane (Lt. Francis[7]; Rev. Francis[8]; John[9], propr. at Ipswich, 1635);
5–Daniel (1728-1808), soldier Am. Rev.; *m* 1754, Ruth Houlton (1735-1817; Joseph[6]; James[7]; Joseph[8], qv);
4–Henry (1768-1826), *m* Anna Sabin (Ichabod[5] [*b* 1726]; Timothy[6]; Benjamin[7]; William[8], a founder of Rehoboth);
3–Benjamin Sabin (1803-75), *m* 1828, Lepha Rogers (Thomas[4]; Thomas[5]; Thomas[6]);
2–Henry Thomas (2 below).
9–Henry **Whitney** (bap. 1620);
8–John (*b* ante 1649), *m* 1675, Elizabeth Smith (Richard[9]);
7–Henry (*b* 1680), *m* 1710, Elizabeth Olmstead; (Lt. John[8], *m* Mary, dau. of Thomas Benedict, qv; Richard[9], qv);
6–Richard (1722-72), *m* 1745, Esther Clark (*b* 1719; Noah[7], *m* Sarah, dau. of Michael Taintnor II, *m* Widow Mabel Olmstead Butler; Daniel[8]);
5–Jerusha (*b* 1755), *m* David **Gates**;
4–Betsey, *m* Adonijah **Brooks** (1778-1815; Adonijah[5] [1738-1809], *m* Olive Harrington, 1740-1828);
3–Smith Adonijah (1810-94);
2–Judy Harrington (1839-79), *m* 1858, Henry Thomas **Ballard** (1830-1907); he *m* 2d, 1882, Augusta L. Montey (*b* 1858); issue (1st marriage); I–Smith Sabin (1 above); II–Charles Whittemore (1863-64).
1–*m* June 23, 1886, Alice Burton Griswold (qv for genealogy and issue).
1–With Central Vt. R.R., 1888; in insurance business since 1893. Mayor of Montpelier, 1911. Mason (32°), K.P., I.O.O.F., B.P.O.E., Knights of Khorassan; past potentate, Mt. Sinai Temple A.A.O.N.M.S. Mem. Automobile Club, of Vt., Miami Advertising, Exchange, Aero, etc. Residence: 985 N.W. 5th St., Miami, Fla.

1–**BALLARD, Alice Burton Griswold (Mrs. Smith Sabin),** *b* Cambridge, Vt., Sept. 11, 1865.
8–Edward **Griswold** (qv);
7–John (1652-1717), of Eng., and Windsor, Conn.; *m* 1672, Mary Bemis (*d* 1679); *m* 2d, 1680, Bathsheba North (1654-1736; Thomas[8], *m* Mary, dau. of Walter Price);
6–Joseph (1690-1771), of Windsor; *m* 1714, Temperance Lay;
5–John (1726-76), of Windsor and Killingworth, Conn.; soldier Am. Rev.; *m* 1749, Mary Ward (Peletiah[6], *m* Jerusha Kelsey);
4–John (*b* 1749), removed to Johnson, Vt., where he was one of the first settlers; soldier Am. Rev., 1777-84; *m* 2d, 1780, Abigail Williams (Benoni[5], *m* Abigail, dau. of John Smith; Joseph[6]; Daniel[7]; Rev. Roger[8], qv);
3–Willard (1798-1876), merchant, Cambridge, Vt.; town clk., and treas.; *m* 1821, Almira Chadwick;
2–David Chadwick (2 below).
9–Thomas **Stanton** (qv);
8–Thomas (1638-1718), of Stonington, Conn.; rep. Gen. Assembly, 1683-89; *m* 1659, Sarah Denison (1642-1701; Capt. George[9], of Stonington, *m* 1st, Bridget Thompson; William[10]);
7–Mary (*b* 1660), *m* 1679, Robert **Lay** (1655-1742), of Saybrook, Conn. (Robert[8]);
6–Temperance (1691-1773), *m* Joseph **Griswold** (6 above).
9–Daniel **Thurston** (*d* 1693), *m* 1655, Ann Pell (Joseph[10], of Boston, *m* Elizabeth–);
8–James (*b* 1670), *m* 1693, Mary Pierson (*b* 1671; Samuel[9], *m* Mary, dau. of John Poor, qv; Dea. John[10], *m* Dorcas–);
7–Abner (*b* 1699);
6–Moses (1721-1800), *m* Hannah Sewell; *m* 2d, Catherine Emerson;
5–Moses (1746-1809), *m* 1768, Esther Bigelow (1744-1831; Elizur[6], *m* Mary, dau. of William Fiske; Joshua[7], *m* Elizabeth, dau. of Thomas Flagg; Bartholomew[8]; John[9]);
4–Mary (1775-1845), *m* 1794, David **Chadwick** (1773-1850);
3–Almira (1800-77), *m* Willard **Griswold** (3 above).
5–William **Chadwick** (*b* 1731), *m* Eunice Goss;
4–Peter (1776-1846), *m* 1797, Hannah Thurston (1777-1857; Moses, 5 above);
3–Elias (1800-84), *m* Maria Melvin;
2–Mary Anne (2 below).
7–John **Melvin** (1656-1726), *m* Hannah Lewis (1655-96; John[8], *m* Mary, dau. of Abraham Brown);
6–Jonathan (1688-1737), *m* 1714, Sarah Hartwell (*b* 1694; Ebenezer[7], *m* Sara Smedley; John[8]; William[9]);
5–Nathan (1730-1807), *m* Anna–(1739-1818);
4–Theodore (1771-1836), *m* 1798, Bethiah Ellis (*b* 1780; Judah[5], *m* Chloe Lockwood);
3–Maria (1808-70), *m* Elias **Chadwick** (3 above);
2–Mary Anne (1838-94), *m* 1857, David Chadwick **Griswold** (1826-1910), mfr.; issue: I–Willard Lucius (1860-1926); II–George Dyer (*b* 1861); III–Alice Burton (1 above); IV–Harriet (*b* 1873).
1–*m* June 23, 1886, Smith Sabin Ballard, (qv); issue: 1–Edward Griswold, *b* Jeffersonville, Vt., May 12, 1889; ed. Norwich U.; *m* May 15, 1914, Beatrice Edward (*b* 1893), dau. of Ernest Hamilton, of New York (issue: Alice Hamilton, *b* 1915); 2–Richard Henry, *b* Barre, Vt., Oct. 19, 1891; B.S., U. of Vt., '15; capt. U.S. Air Service; *m* Aug. 28, 1915, Amy Dorothy (*b* 1893), dau. of Hartwell B. Farrar, of Enosburg, Vt.
1–Ed. Johnson Normal Sch. Taught sch., 1881-84. Appointed by Gov. Meade to represent Vt. at Child Welfare Congress, Washington, 1910. Mem. I.A.G., D.A.R., D.F.P.A., U.S.D. 1812, Woman's Club (Montpelier, Vt., pres. 1911), Miami Woman's Club, League of Am. Penwomen, O.E.S., etc. Residence: 985 N.W. 5th St., Miami, Fla.

1–**BALLOU, Oscar Brown,** *b* Uxbridge, Mass., Sept. 19, 1853.
7–Maturin **Ballou** (qv);
6–James (*b* 1652), of Providence; *m* 1683, Susanna Whitman (1658-1725; Valentine[7], *m* Mary–);
5–Obadiah (1689-1768), of Providence; *m* 1717, Damaris Bartlett (John[6], *m* Sarah Aldrich); *m* 2d, Sarah (Whipple) Salsbury;

4–Obadiah (*b* 1730), of Cumberland, R. I.; *m* 1753, Martha Smith; *m* 2d, Mary Ann Fairfield;
3–William (*b* 1789), of Burrillville, R.I.; *m* Philadelphia Ross (*b* 1789; Isaac[4]);
2–William Ross (1816-1906), of Burrillville, R.I.; contractor and builder; *m* 1852, Alice Brown (1823-54; James[3] [1788-1859], *m* Nancy Cooper, 1780-1849).
1–*m* May 9, 1899, Nellie Willey (*b* Kennebunkport, Me., 1864-*d* July 5, 1914).
1–*m* 2d, Oct. 13, 1916, Emma Cooper Kellogg, *b* Westmorland, Kan., Dec. 20, 1872; dau. of William Cooper, of N.Y.
1–Pres. Ballou & Wright. Republican. Mem. Ballou Family Assn., I.A.G. Clubs: Mazamas, Oregon Motor, Portland Chamber of Commerce. Residence: 1085 Westover Rd., Portland, Ore.

1–**BANCROFT, Wilder Dwight,** *b* Middletown, R.I., Oct. 1, 1867.
8–Thomas **Bancroft** (qv);
7–Thomas (1649-1718), capt. King Philip's War; *m* Sarah Poole;
6–Samuel (1693-1772), *m* Sarah Lampson;
5–Samuel (1715-82), *m* Lydia Parker;
4–Rev. Aaron (1755-1839), A.B., Harvard, 1778; minute man at Lexington and Bunker Hill; pres. Am. Unitarian Assn., etc.; *m* Lucretia Chandler;
3–George LL.D. (1800-91), A.B., Harvard, 1817; distinguished historian; Sec. of the Navy; minister to England and to Germany; *m* Sarah Dwight;
2–John Chandler (1835-1901), A.B., Harvard, '54; *m* Louisa Mills Denny (*d* ca. 1873); *m* 2d, 1876, Harriet Burfort, dau. George James, of Fredericksburg, Va., and Zanesville, O.; issue (1st marriage): I–Wilder Dwight (1 above); II–Pauline (Mrs. Carl G. Flach, see Vol. I, p. 80, for Chandler lineage); (2d marriage): I–Hester (Mrs. Rodolph L. Adlercron, see Vol. I, p. 80).
1–*m* June 19, 1895, Katharine Meech Bott, dau. Arthur Bott, Albany, N.Y. (*b* in Germany), *m* Mary, dau. of Joseph Warner, *m* Jane Meech, Middlebury, Vt.; issue (all *b* Ithaca, N.Y.: 1–Mary Warner, *b* Sept. 12, 1896; Cornell, 1918; 2–Hester, *b* May 2, 1899; Cornell, '25; 3–John Chandler, *b* Apr. 7, 1902; Harvard, '23; 4–George, *b* Jan. 29, 1905; Harvard, '27; 5–Jean Gordon, *b* July 11, 1909; Cornell, '30.
1–A.B., Harvard, '88 (D.K.E.); Strassburg, Leipzig (Ph.D., 1892), Berlin, Amsterdam; (hon. D.Sc., Lafayette, 1918; hon. Sc.D., Cambridge, 1923; LL.D., U. Southern Calif., 1930). Prof. physical chemistry, Cornell. Past pres. Am. Chem. Soc., Am. Electrochem. Soc.; hon. mem. English Chem. Soc., French Chem. Soc., Am. Electrochem. Soc., Polish Chem. Soc. Lt. col., act. chief of research div., Jan. 1-July 1, 1919, C.W.S., World War (see Who's Who in America). Clubs: Tavern (Boston), Harvard, University, Chemists (New York), Cosmos (Washington). Summer place: "The Bluff," Newport, R.I. Residence: 7 East Av., Ithaca, N.Y.

1–**BANNISTER, John Conkey,** *b* Evanston, Ill., Nov. 15, 1860.
7–Christopher (Banister) **Bannister,** of Marlboro, Mass.; *m* Jane Goodenow (Thomas[8], of Sudbury, Mass., *m* Jane–);
6–Joseph (*b* 1679), of Marlboro; *m* Sarah–;
5–Joseph (*b* 1711), of Brookfield, Goshen and Conway, Mass.; *m* 1734, Mary Hinds (1716-99; John[6], *m* Hannah [1691- 1764], dau. of John Corliss; John[7]; James[8]);
4–Capt. John (1744-1832), began to write name Bannister; capt. Am. Rev.; *m* 1778, Sarah (Adams) Stow (1745-1824; Benjamin Adams[5], *m* Persis, dau. of Ephraim Potter; Thomas[6]; Nathaniel[7]; William[8]; William[9]);
3–Amos (1789-1815), of Conway, Mass., and Canton, N. Y.; *m* 1807, Mary Nash (*b* 1784; Tubal[4], of Greenfield, Mass., *m* Mary, dau. of Gad Corse; Daniel[5]; Daniel[6]; Lt. Timothy[7]; Thomas[8], qv);
2–Henry (2 below).
8–Richard **Kimball** (qv);
7–Richard (1623-76), from Eng. with parents; propr., Ipswich, 1648; of Topsfield and Wenham, Mass., 1652; largest tax-payer; selectman; *m* in Eng., Mary–;
6–Ens. Samuel (1651-1716), of Wenham, Mass.; ens. militia; served King Philip's War; selectman and freeman, 1682; surveyor, 1676; constable, 1677; *m* 1676, Mary Witt (John[7], of Lynn, Mass., *m* Sarah–);
5–Ebenezer (1690-1760), of Wenham, Mass.; yeoman and mason; removed to Beverly, Mass., and to Hopkinton, 1740; *m* 1712, Elizabeth Carr (Richard[6], of Salisbury, Mass.);
4–Boyce (1731-1802), from Wenham to Shutesbury, Mass.; *m* 1755, Rebecca (Howard) Hayward (*d* 1790);
3–Rev. Ruel (1778-1847), Presbyn. minister; from Marlboro, Vt., to Leroy, N.Y., 1805, and to Leyden, N.Y., 1816; *m* 1799, Hannah Mather;
2–Lucy (2 below).
9–Rev. Richard **Mather** (qv);
8–Timothy (1628-84), *m* 1650, Elizabeth (or Catherine) Atherton (Maj. Gen. Humphrey[9], qv);
7–Atherton (1663-1734), *m* 1st, Rebecca Stoughton (1673-1704; Thomas[8]);
6–William (1698-1747), *m* 1721, Silence Buttolph (*b* 1701/02; Sgt. Daniel[7]; Lt. John[8]; Thomas[9]);
5–Timothy (1722-1802), *m* 1748, Hannah Fuller (1722-57; Joseph[6]; Sgt. Joseph[7]; John[8]; William[9]);
4–Timothy (1757-1818), *m* 1779, Hannah Church (1761-1827; Dea. John[5]; Capt. Benjamin[6]; Samuel[7]; Richard[8]);
3–Hannah (1781-1860), *m* Ruel **Kimball** (3 above);
2–Lucy (1815-86), *m* 1840, Henry **Bannister** (1812-83), of Conway, Mass., Canton, N.Y., Evanston, Ill., issue: I–John C. (1 above); II–Mary (*d*; *m* Oliver A. Willard); III–Henry Martyn (*d*; *m* Delia C. Ladd); IV–Charles Kimball (*d*; *m* Emily White); V–Ellen (*d*; *m* Orlando H. Merwin); VI–Lucy (*d*; *m* Irving Queal).
1–*m* Dec. 25, 1886, Frances E. Bryant (qv for genealogy and issue).
1–A.B., Northwestern U., '83. Teacher, Princeton (Ill.) High Sch., 1883-90. Mfr., Kewanee, Ill., and Boston, Mass.; v.p., Walworth Co., 1891-1925; retired. Clubs: University (Chicago), Glenview, Rotary, Franklin Inst. Mason. Residence: 24 W. Palm Lane, Phoenix, Ariz.

1–**BANNISTER, Frances Bryant (Mrs. John C.),** *b* Princeton, Ill., May 17, 1866.
8–Stephen **Bryant** (qv);
7–Stephen (*b* 1657/58), of Middleboro, Mass.; *m* Mehitable– (*b* 1659);
6–Ichabod (1699-1759), of Middleboro and N. Bridgewater, Mass.; *m* Ruth Staples (1702-77; John[7], of Raynham, Mass., *m* Hannah Leach [*d* 1757]; Joseph[8]; John[9]);
5–Dr. Philip (1732-1812), of N. Bridgewater; *m* 1757, Silence Howard (1738-77; Dr. Abiel[6], *m* Silence, dau. of Capt. Nehemiah Washburn; Maj. Jonathan[7]; Capt. John[8]; John[9]);
4–Dr. Peter (1767-1820), of Bridgewater and Cummington, Mass.; *m* 1792, Sarah Snell (1768-1847; Ebenezer[5], of Bridgewater and Cummington, Mass.; Zachariah[6]; Josiah[7], *m* Anna, dau. of Jonathan and g.dau. of John Alden, Mayflower Pilgrim, qv; Thomas[8]); among their sons was William Cullen Bryant, famous poet;
3–John Howard (1807-1902), of Cummington, Mass., and Princeton, Ill.; *m* 1833, Harriet E. Wiswall (1808-88), of Jacksonville, Ill. (Elijah[4], *m* Hannah, dau. of Edmund Hodges, *m* Mercy, g.g.g. dau. of Francis Cooke and Stephen Hopkins, qv; Noah[5]; Ebenezer[6]; Enoch[7]; Elder Thomas[8]);
2–Elijah Wiswall (2 below).
8–Lt. Samuel **Smith** (qv);
7–Chileab (ca. 1635-1731), *m* Hannah Hitchcock (1645-1733);
6–Chileab (1685-1746), *m* Mercy Golding (1686-1756);
5–Phineas (1717-87), of Granby, Mass.; capt. of a co. in Col. Porter's regt., 1775; served as delegate to the Provincial Congress; mem. Gen. Ct., 1777-81; *m* 2d, Elizabeth Smith (*b* 1728);
4–Levi (*b* 1752), Lexington Alarm; *m* 2d, Lucy Stebbins (1765-1837);
3–Sidney (1806-88), *m* Laura Lusetta Doolittle (1813-92; Asher[4]; Joel[5]; Samuel[6]; Jonathan[7]; Samuel[8]; Sgt. Abraham[9], qv);
2–Laura (1846-1913), *m* 1865, Elijah Wiswall **Bryant** (1836-92); issue: I–Frances (1 above); II–Kate (*b* 1869; *m* 1899, William Edward McVay); III–John Howard (1870-72); IV–Will-

iam Cullen (*b* 1871; *m* 1893, Lydia Warfield); V–Laura Sue (*b* 1875; *m* 1898, Albert H. Ferris); VI–Dr. John Howard (*b* 1876; *m* 1903, Lillian R. Warfield).
1–*m* Dec. 25, 1886, John Conkey Bannister (qv); issue: 1–Bryant, *b* Princeton, Ill., Oct. 24, 1887; U.Ill., '11, Boston Tech.; *m* Oct. 24, 1914, Zulemma, dau. of Regin L. De Bolt (adopted dau.: Mary Eleanor, *b* May 17, 1920); 2–Kimball, *b* Princeton, July 4, 1889; M.D., U.Ill. '11; Med. Sch., Northwestern U., 1914; *m* Sept. 23, 1916, Elizabeth C., dau. of John Scott Davis, D.D. (issue; all *b* Phoenix, Ariz.: Kimball, *b* July 11, 1917; John Clayton, *b* Oct. 16, 1919; Mary Elizabeth, *b* Oct. 2, 1922; Bryant, *b* Dec. 2, 1926); 3–Elizabeth, *b* Kewanee, Ill., July 26, 1891; Northwestern U., 1914; *m* Apr. 3, 1915, Walter H., son of Frederick Weber (issue: Janet Elizabeth, *b* Kewanee, Ill., Jan. 11, 1918; Frances Bryant, *b* Boston, Mass., May 9, 1923); 4–Laura Smith, *b* Kewanee, July 29, 1893; Northwestern U., 1916; *m* Aug. 8, 1925, Clifton Henry, son of Melville Merry, *m* Emma Mead (issue: Clifton Henry, Jr., *b* Chicago, Ill., Aug. 9, 1926; Anne Mead, *b* Chicago, Nov. 26, 1928); 5–John Howard, *b* Kewanee, July 23, 1895; U.Ill.; *m* Sept. 15, 1921, Katherine, dau. of Judge William Holland, of Houston, Tex. (issue: John, *b* Houston, Sept. 24, 1922); 6–Frances Sue, *b* Kewanee, Aug. 5, 1897; ed. Ferry Hall (Birmingham, Pa.) and Boston Conservatory Music; *m* Nov. 21, 1917, Dr. Reuben L., son of Rev. G. A. Larson (issue: Kimball Bannister, *b* Evanston, Ill., Nov. 18, 1918; Mary Frances, *b* Miami, Ariz., July 7, 1922); 7–Mary Willard (Aug. 13, 1902-June 7, 1912).
1–Ed. Princeton (Ill.) High Sch. Mem. D.F.P.A., S.M.D., D.C.W., D.A.R. Residence: 24 W. Palm Lane, Phoenix, Ariz.

1–**BARDIN, Donna Cordell (Mrs. J. Carter),** *b* Richmond, Va., July 6, 1883.
7–Hon. John **Campbell** (1705-88), from Ireland to Va.; speaker of N.C. House, 1754-57; del. Provincial Congress, 1776; *m* Mary Elizabeth Hill (*d* post 1753);
6–James (*d* 1800), *m* Mary Kinchen (*d* ante 1800; William[7], *m* Mary, dau. of Col. John Dawson; William[8], magistrate N.C., 1729, sheriff, Northampton, 1745);
5–Mary or Polly (1760-1850), *m* Richard **Cordell** (1760-1840), soldier Am. Rev.;
4–Rev. Campbell (1790-living 1850), *m* ca. 1818, Polly Penny (1797-living 1850);
3–Henry Lewis (1821-73), served C.S.A.; *m* Sarah Elizabeth Avery;
2–Robert Rivers (2 below).
10–Christopher **Avery** (qv);
9–Capt. James (1620-1700), founder of clan called "The Groton Averys"; moved from Gloucester to New London, Conn., then Pequot; built and occupied "The Hive of the Averys," Groton, which burned 1894; noted Indian fighter in command of Pequot allies at Narragansett Fort when they defeated the Mohicans; dep. Gen. Ct., New London; *m* 1643, Joanna Greenslade (*b* 1622);
8–James (1646-1728), dep. Gen. Ct., New London, 6 terms; commr. of peace; lt. and capt. of Train Band; advisor and councillor of the Pequot tribe; *m* 1694, Deborah Stallyon (1651-1729; Edward[9]);
7–Benjamin (1696-1772), *m* 1734, Thankful Avery (1718-1813);
6–Jacob (*b* 1737-living 1790), served Am. Rev.; *m* 1764, Ann Fales;
5–Jacob (1766-1846), *m* Elizabeth Hardy (living 1790; John[6], *m* Rebecca, dau. of John Byrd, N.C., justice of peace, *m* Rebecca, dau. of Nathaniel Sutton);
4–Hardy (1789-1810), *m* Mary (Polly) Rivers;
3–Sarah Elizabeth (1833-67), *m* Henry Lewis **Cordell** (3 above).
9–Solomon **Pool** (*d* 1739), *m* Grace-(living 1739);
8–Richard (*d* 1734), *m* Joanna DuVal (*b* 1680; Maureen[9], Huguenot in Md., *m* 2d, Susanna–, *d* 1692);
7–Joseph (1705-living 1757), *m* Miriam Jackson (*d* 1757; Samuel[8], *m* Elizabeth Hoskins; William[9] [*d* 1697], *m* Elizabeth–);
6–William (1748-post 1820), soldier in Am. Rev.; *m* Clarky Morris;
5–Elizabeth (1770-post 1836), *m* William **Rivers** (1767-post 1815), soldier in War 1812 (Richard[6], justice peace; Halifax Conv., 1776; mem. N.C. House of Commons, 1794; Richard[7]; Robert[8]; Pierre[9], a Huguenot);
4–Mary, called Polly (1790-1865), *m* Hardy **Avery** (4 above).
11–John **Biggs** (*d* post 1641), *m* 1st, Mary Dassett (*d* 1650; John[12], *d* 1677);
10–Timothy (1630-83), comptroller and surveyor general of customs, N.C., 1679; *m* Mary– (*d* 1689);
9–Mary (*d* post 1739), *m* John **Morris** (*d* 1739);
8–Aaron (ante 1739-living 1785), commr., N.C., 1758; *m* Miriam Robinson;
7–Joshua (*d* 1777), *m* Rebecca Early (living 1777; John[8], *m* Ann–; John[9], *m* Mary, dau. of William Bush, *m* Martha–);
6–Clarky (living 1777), *m* William **Pool** (6 above).
12–John **Robinson** (*d* 1699);
11–Thomas (*d* 1718), *m* Sarah Symons (living 1718; Jeremiah[10], burgess, N.C., 1680-1703, *m* Rebecca–; Matthew[11], *m* Ann, dau. of Gov. Robert Daniels, landgrave, 1691, dep. gov., 1716-17);
10–Joseph (*d* post 1718), *m* Jane Clare (1686-post 1742; Timothy[11], *m* Mary, dau. of William Bundy; William[12], *m* Mary–);
9–John (*d* 1764), *m* Mary Moore (*b* 1731; John[10], *m* Mary, dau. of Richard Ratcliffe, *m* Damaris, dau. of Zachariah Nixon);
8–Miriam (living 1785), *m* Aaron **Morris** (8 above).
8–Col. William **Byrd** (qv);
7–Col. William (1674-1744), burgess, 1702; receiver-general, and councillor, 1705; co. lt., 1715; a founder of Richmond, Va.; *m* 2d, 1724, Maria Taylor (Sir Thomas[8], of Eng.);
6–Maria, *m* as his 2d wife, Col. Landon **Carter** (1711-post 1776), of "Sabine Hall," Richmond, Va.; burgess, 1748-64 (Robert[7], known as "King" because of his vast possessions, *m* 2d, Elizabeth, dau. of Sir Thomas Landon, of London; Hon. John[8], qv);
5–Martha Jackson (1765-post 1839), *m* 1782, James **Elkins** (1755-1836), soldier Am. Rev. (James[6]; Richard[7]; Ralph[8]);
4–James (1801-post 1835), *m* 1822, Mittie Carter;
3–Alfred Carter (1835-94), *m* Emeline Reeves (1838-88; James[4]);
2–Nancy Ann Elizabeth (*b* 1864), *m* 1880, Robert Rivers **Cordell** (1860-91); issue: I–Donna (1 above); II–Henry Lewis (*b* 1885),
1–*m* 1899; issue: 1–Eileen Louise, *b* Austin, Tex., Feb. 14, 1900; *m* at El Paso, Tex., July 16, 1918, Capt. F. W. Koester, U.S.A., of Ft. Riley, Kan., son of Fred Koester (*d* 1921), of Atchison, Kan. (issue: William Stanley, *b* Nov. 14, 1919).
1–*m* 2d, May 10, 1924, John Carter Bardin, *b* La Grange, Tex., Feb. 18, 1875; son of David Wasdin Crockett Bardin (1837-1918; William[3]; William[4]; William[5]; William[6]; John[7]), *m* 1865, Lorinda Loden (1840-1913).
1–Ed. pub. schs.; studied criminal law. Genealogist. Mem. C.D.A. (state pres.), N.H.S., Founders of Manakin (nat. pres.), D.A.R., U.S.D. 1812 (past state registrar, state treas.), U.D.C. (past state rec. sec., past chapter registrar, chapter pres.), O.E.S. (past worthy matron), Rebekah Lodge (noble grand), Clan Campbell Memorial Com. (nat. vice chmn.), League Am. Pen Women, 8 et 40 (past state parliamentarian). Residence: 429 Centre St., Dallas, Tex.

1–**BARNES, Harriet Southworth Lewis (Mrs. Albert M.),** *b* Phila., Pa., Apr. 21, 1860.
9–William **Lewis** (qv);
8–William (*b* 1620), Farmington, Conn.; *m* Mary Hopkins (William[9]);
7–William (bap. 1656-1737), Farmington; *m* Sarah Moore (Isaac[8]);
6–Capt. Jonathan (1697-prob. 1769), Kensington and New Britain, Conn.; *m* Elizabeth Newell (Thomas[7]);
5–Adonijah (1722-1799) New Britain; soldier French and Indian War; *m* Mary Bronson (James[6]);
4–Seth (1772-1849), New Britain, Conn., and Phila., Pa.; *m* 1795, Lydia Wright (Thomas[5]);
3–William Goodwin (1806-66), Phila.; *m* Eliza Lucy Southworth (Samuel[4]);
2–Henry Martyn (2 below).
8–Thomas **Wright** (1610-70), from Eng. with wife and child, settled at Wethersfield, Conn.;

7–Samuel (prob. 1644-1690), of Wethersfield; *m* 1659, Mary Butler (Dea. Richard[8]);
6–David (1678-1752), of Newington, Conn.; *m* 1710, Mary Belden (1687-1769; Lt. Jonathan[7]);
5–Thomas (*b* 1721), of Newington; *m* 1756, Esther Andrews (*b* 1740; Caleb[6]);
4–Lydia (1772-1858), of Phila., Pa.; *m* Seth **Lewis** (4 above).
10–John **Howland,** Mayflower Pilgrim (qv);
9–Hope (1629-83), *m* Elder John **Chipman** (qv);
8–Hope (*b* 1652), *m* John **Huckins** (Thomas[9]);
7–Elizabeth (1671-1741), *m* Dea. John **Lewis**;
6–Gershom (1704-66), *m* Mary Maltby;
5–Mary (1742-1823), *m* Jacob **Smith,** Jr. (1738-1807);
4–Lemuel (1774-1852), *m* Nancy Jones (1778-1861; Joseph[5]);
3–George W. (1811-40), *m* Harriet Humphreville (1812-96; Lemuel[4]);
2–Frances Amelia (1836-1900), *m* 1856, Henry Martyn **Lewis** (1831-1906), pres. S.S. White Co., Phila., Pa.; issue: I–Frederick Humphreville (*b* 1858; *m* Alice M. Law); II–Harriet S. (1 above); III–Nellie (Mrs. Edward C. Cutler, see Vol. II, p. 253, for Smith lineage); IV–Henry Bertram (see Vol. I, p. 687, for Lewis lineage).
1–*m* Apr. 14, 1887, Albert Mortimer Barnes (Feb. 11, 1845-Mar. 28, 1916); son of Merrick Barnes, of Worcester, Mass.
1–Mem. Pa. Soc. of N.E. Women, Woman's Club of Germantown. Presbyterian. Residence: The Fairfax, Germantown, Philadelphia, Pa.

1–**BARNES, Milford Edwin,** *b* Columbus Junction, Ia., Nov. 28, 1883.
5–John (Barns) **Barnes** (1735-1804), from Ireland, ca. 1760; settled New Perth, Charlotte (now Washington) Co., N.Y.; capt. co. of rangers in Am. Rev.; 2d lt. Cont. Army, 1775-76; *m* Elizabeth Hamilton;
4–Thomas (1763-1817), of Greene Co., O.; served as teamster in War 1812; *m* 1786, Jane McClain (1764-1841);
3–Thomas (1799-1885), of Idaville, Ind.; *m* 2d, 1846, Mary Hammill (1815-55);
2–John Albert, D.D. (*b* 1847), of Monmouth, Ill.; began to write name Barnes; pvt. Co. H, 142d Ind. Vol. Inf.; *m* 1868, Mary Emaline Sharp (1847-1925); issue: I–Ella Margaret (*b* 1869); II–Infant (*b* and *d* 1871); III–Thomas Harvey (*b* 1873; *m* Luella White); IV–Samuel Charles (1875-78); V–Andrew Wallace (*b* 1878; *m* Leila Hope Andrew); VI–Wilda Hutchison (*b* 1881); VII–Milford Edwin (1 above); VIII–Anna Beatrice (*b* 1886; *m* William Percy McAtee); IX–Clara Mae (*b* 1890); X–Clarence Albert Barnes, M.D. (*b* 1893; *m* Mildred May Morgan).
1–*m* Feb. 24, 1916, Mary Emma Robinson (qv for issue).
1–A.B., Monmouth Coll., '05, S.B., U.Chicago, 1912; M.D., Rush Med. Coll., 1914; grad. London Sch. Tropical Medicine, 1919; Dr.P.H., Johns Hopkins Sch. of Hygiene and Public Health, 1925 (Delta Omega). Prof. preventive medicine and hygiene, U. of Ia., 1930-. Senior state dir. for internat. health div. of Rockefeller Foundation, 1916-30. Mem. S.A.R., I.A.G. Republican. Presbyn. Residence: 201 Ferson Av., Iowa City, Ia.

1–**BARNES, Mary Emma Robinson (Mrs. Milford E.),** *b* Newton, Ia., Sept. 30, 1881.
9–Robert **Coe** (qv);
8–Benjamin (1629-94), *b* Eng.; at Stamford, Conn., 1633; *m* 1660, Abigail Carman (John[9], *m* Florence Fordham, came to Jamaica, 1631);
7–Joseph (1665-1743), of Jamaica, L.I., and Newark, N.J.; *m* Judith–;
6–Benjamin (1709-76), of Jamaica; he and 5 sons served in Am. Rev.; removed to Redstone Presbytery, Westmoreland Co., Pa.; founded Tarentum on the Allegheny River; *m* 2d, 1742, Rachel Pruden;
5–Lt. Benjamin (1748-1833), of Morristown, N.J.; served with Westmoreland Co. Rangers, 1778-83, and with Washington Co. Rangers;
4–Elder Benjamin (1795-1873);
3–Eliza J. (1825-1910), *m* 1846, Robert **Hunter** (1818-1904);
2–Mary Agnes (*b* 1852), of Los Angeles, Calif.; *m* 1872, William Harvey **Robinson** (1848-1929); issue: I–Grace Elizabeth (*b* 1874; *m* 1897, Andrew Hans [1868-1907]; *m* 2d, 1917, John Buck, *b* 1872); II–Anna May (1876-99; *m* 1899, Albert Wilson); III–John William (*b* 1878; *m* 1911, Hazel McCloud); IV–Mary Emma (*b* 1881); V–Florence Belle (*b* 1883); VI–Robert Hunter (*b* 1890; *m* 1921, Myra Withers).
1–*m* Feb. 24, 1916, Milford E. Barnes (qv); issue: 1–Milford Edwin, Jr., *b* Cheingmai, Siam Apr. 24, 1918; 2–Mary Margaret, *b* Bangkok, Siam, Dec. 6, 1921.
1–A.B., Monmouth Coll., '05. Mem. D.A.R. Residence: 201 Ferson Av., Iowa City, Ia.

1–**BARNES, Samuel Denham,** *b* Morley, Mo., Nov. 7, 1869.
9–John (Dunham) **Denham** (qv);
8–Rev. Jonathan (1632-1717), missionary to Indians, Saco, Me.; *m* 1655, Mary de Lannoye or Delano (*d* 1656; Philip[9] [*b* 1602], French Huguenot from Holland in the "Fortune," 1621, settled Duxbury, Mass., in Pequot War, *m* 1634, Hester Dewsbury);
7–Daniel (1656-1742), *m* Rebecca Norton (*d* 1783);
6–Daniel (1711-97), *m* 1739, Sarah Huxford (1723-1788);
5–Cornelius (1748-1816), began to write name Denham; Am. Rev.; *m* 1769, Sarah Butler (1746-76);
4–Samuel (*b* 1773), *m* 1803, Matilda Goodale (1780-1850);
3–Olivia (1807-87), *m* 1831, Romulus **Barnes** (see Vol. III, p. 53, for Barnes, Webster, Bradford lineages);
2–Charles M. (2 below).
9–Richard **Kimball** (qv);
8–Benjamin (1637-75), *m* 1661, Mary Hazeltine (1642-1707);
7–Samuel (1682-1738), *m* Eunice Chadwick;
6–Mary (*b* 1719), *m* 1740, Thomas **Hale** (see Vol. III, p. 53, for Hale lineage);
5–Mary (1745-1827), *m* 1766, Solomon **Goodale** (see Vol. III, p. 53, for Goodale lineage);
4–Matilda (1780-1850), *m* 1803, Samuel **Denham** (4 above);
3–Olivia, *m* 1831, Romulus **Barnes** (3 above);
2–Charles Montgomery **Barnes** (1833-1907), chaplain (capt.) 93d Ill. Vol. Inf. in Civil War; publisher; *m* 1860, Ellen Moore (1837-1923); for issue see Vol. III, p. 53.
1–*m* Mar. 27, 1905, Martha Anne Williams (see Vol. III, p. 54, for genealogy).
1–B.S., U.Chicago, '94; M.D., Dunham Med. Coll., 1901. Physician. Served as 1st lt., M.R.C., with 21st Inf., U.S.A., on duty Calif. border, 1898. Mem. S.M.D., S.A.R. (pres. Hawaiian Soc., 1914-16, pres. Los Angeles chapter, 1926-28). Associated Patriotic Agencies (pres. 1928). Mem. council Inst. Am. Geneal. Clubs: University, Sunset Canyon Country. Residence: 7416 Rosewood Av., Los Angeles, Calif.

1–**BARNEY, Russell Harrison,** *b* Odessa, Neb., Oct. 18, 1888.
9–Jacob (Berney) **Barney** (qv);
8–Jacob (ante 1634-1693), *m* Hannah Johnson (*d* 1659); *m* 2d, 1660, Ann Witt (1637-1701);
7–John (1665-1728), *m* Mary Throop (*b* 1667);
6–Jonathan (1703-85), *m* Anna Deane (1709/10-62);
5–Abiel (1731-93), *m* ca. 1771, Mary Brooks (1752-1843);
4–Hiriam (1785-1842), *m* Azuba Tarbell (1786-1858; Dea. Reuben[5]. of Chester, Vt.);
3–Hiriam (*d* 1902), *m* Clarrissa Marshall (1814-1892);
2–Reuben Edgar (*b* 1843), from Olney, Ill., to Riverside, Calif.; *m* 1879, Mary Bell Wilson (*b* 1856); issue: I–Robert Edgar (*b* 1881; *m* 1905, Clara Pearl Chaplin; *m* 2d, Laura–); II–Clarissa Mabel (*b* 1882; *m* 1909, Sigurd Christian Oien); III–Mary Eleanor (*b* 1886; *m* 1908, Lloyd Truman Folsom); IV–Russell H. (1 above); V–Grace Margaret (*b* 1890; *m* 1914, William H. Johnston); VI–Harold Wilfred (*b* 1892; *m* 1921, Mima Randall Graham); VII–James Stewart (*b* 1895; *m* 1918, Grace–); VIII–Frances Belle (*b* 1898; *m* 1916, Roy Stinger; *m* 2d, Ernest L. Vehlow).
1–*m* June 20, 1914, Helen Mollie Roberts (qv for issue).
1–Ed. Neb. Agrl. Coll. Homesteaded in northern Montana. Residence: 3313 W. Grandview Boul., Spokane, Wash.

1–**BARNEY, Helen Mollie Roberts (Mrs. Russell Harrison),** *b* Rockford, Minn., Sept. 27, 1891.

8–John **Bull** (1674-1736), lived Providence Tp., Phila. Co., Pa.; *m* Elizabeth– (1676-1736);
7–Richard (1714-99), of Chester Co., Pa., removed to Racoon Valley, Cumberland Co., Pa.; *m* Elizabeth Pawling (*b* 1719; Henry[8], of Padsbury, Eng., mem. Duke of York's expdn.);
6–Henry (1749-1816), of Chester Co., Pa.; built stone grist and saw mill of stone, and a dwelling which is still standing; mem. 3d Co., 5th Bn., Cumberland Co. Militia, under Lt. Col. Mitchell; *m* 1769, Grace Brown (*d* 1838);
5–Jemima (1787-1830), of Mexico, Pa.; *m* 1810, Francis **Jordon** (1787-1845);
4–Samuel (1815-75), of Mexico, Pa.; minister; *m* Rebecca Ann Jones (1811-80);
3–Sarah (1841-1914), settled at St. Anthony's Falls (now Minneapolis), Minn.; *m* 1861, Daniel H. **Buckwalter** (1840-1915), flour miller, Minneapolis;
2–Bessie A. (1862-1927), of N. Hollywood, Calif., and Havre, Mont.; *m* 1882, Orlando Chester **Roberts** (*b* 1861); issue: I–Earl Victor (1882-1883); II–Marvin Chester (*b* 1884; *m* Anna Anderson); III–Hazelle Marie (*b* 1891; *m* Raymond V. Love), and IV–Helen Mollie, twins (1 above); V–Newell Bruce (1893-1910).
1–*m* June 20, 1914, Russell Harrison Barney (qv); issue: 1–Marian Adelyne, *b* Havre, Mont., Oct. 20, 1916; 2–Hazelle Belle, *b* Havre, Jan. 18, 1920; 3–Elizabeth Irene, *b* Spokane, Wash., June 30, 1922; 4–Richard Earle (adopted), *b* Tacoma, Wash., May 19, 1929.
1–Ed. Mont. State Coll. Sponsors home for orphans until placed in adoption. Mem. D.A.R. Residence: 3313 W. Grandview Boul., Spokane, Wash.

1–**BARR, Emma D. Williams (Mrs. James Henry),** *b* Clermont Co., O., Oct. 15, 18–.
6–Levi **Bayliff,** from Eng.; settled in Va., nr. Jamestown;
5– —, of Jamestown, Va.; *m* Lucy Flower (desc. Sir William, of Eng.);
4–Daniel (1775-1837), of Jamestown; *m* 1796, Martha Ferguson (1773-1834);
3–Emma (1810-81), of Clermont Co., O.; *m* 1826, James **Fagan** (1804-95; Joseph[4] [1774-1855], *m* 1802, Rachel [1784-1844], dau. of Archibald Gray [*b* 1750], of Pa. and Clermont Co., O., *m* Miss Brown; Patrick[4], of Co. Tyrone, Ireland; son of John O'Hagan, baron of Tullaghog);
2–Martha Ann (1833-1917), of Clermont Co., and Cincinnati, O.; *m* 1862, James Henry **Williams** (ca. 1833-85); issue: I–Stella Grace (*m* Maj. Augustus Mortimer Van Dyke); II–Emma D. (1 above); III–Florence Bayliff.
1–*m* Oct. 7, 1889, James Henry Barr (June 12, 1853-Dec. 21, 1912); son of Henry Barr, of Cincinnati, O., and Ludlow, Ky.; issue: 1–Ingle (see Vol. III, p. 54); 2–Catherine Hibbard, *m* 1917, David S. Gaston.
1–Mem. Inst. Am. Gen., N.E.G.H.S., Twentieth Century Club, Woman's Nat. Farm and Garden Assn. Residence: 5392 Wilkins Av., Squirrel Hill, Pittsburgh, Pa.

1–**BARRETT, Jesse Marshall,** *b* Maxwell, Ind., Sept. 16, 1872.
5–Edward **Barrett** (1740-1829), from Ireland, 1750; settled in Cabell Co., W. Va.; pvt. in Am. Rev.; *m* Esther Wallace Burnsides (1763-1838);
4–James (1783-1863), of Cabell Co.; *m* 1801, Sarah Hatfield (1783-1863);
3–William (1811-59), of Hancock Co., Ind.; *m* 1836, Rebecca Hayzlette (1818-88);
2–Templeton Theodore (1848-1903), farmer and stockman; *m* 1869, Artemecia Cooper (1849-91); issue: I–Ellison Sanford (*m* Eva Belle Curry); II–Jesse Marshall (1 above).
1–*m* Apr. 7, 1897, Bertha Black (qv for issue).
1–B.S., Purdue U., '94, A.C., 1895. Farmer and stockman. Analytical chemist, 1894-1903. Presbyn. Residence: R.R. 2, Napton, Mo.

1–**BARRETT, Bertha Black (Mrs. Jesse M.),** *b* LaFayette, Ind., Jan. 10, 1878.
5–Samuel **Black** (*b* 1727-*d* Beverly Manor, Augusta Co., Va., 1782); 2d lt., Am. Rev.; *m* 1755, Jane Porter (*d* 1814);
4–Samuel (1782-1830), soldier War 1812; *m* 1806, Louisa Ferguson (1782-1832);
3–Samuel (1828-1853), Dayton, Ind.; *m* 1849, Sarah Alexander;
2–Samuel Alexander (2 below).
8–James **Alexander,** from Scotland, 1659; settled in Va.;
7–William;
6–James (1762-1818), *m* his cousin, Mary Alexander (1763-86);
5–Jesse (*b* Mecklenburg Co., N.C., 1782 or 90-1844), corp. War 1812; buried Motterville, Ill.; *m* 1801, Rebecca Jane Ferguson (1781-1857; John[6] [1763-1818], served in Am. Rev., *m* ca. 1780, Elizabeth–, 1763-1809);
4–James (1805-72), Nicholas Co., Ky.; *m* 1825, Mary Ann Grimes (1806-77);
3–Sarah (1827-79), *m* Samuel **Black** (3 above).
6–Aaron **Jennings** (1730-1807), served in Am. Rev., pensioned; mem. war com., Fairfield, Conn.; *m* Eunice Taylor;
5–Asaael, *m* Polly Waters;
4–Polly (1804-69), *m* William **Northcutt** (1801-61);
3–Willis (1827-75), *m* 1848, Melinda Dunlap;
2–Allie Eliza (2 below).
6–Elijah **Mitchell** (*b* Va., 1761-1847), N.C. militia in Am. Rev., pensioned Preble Co., O.; buried at Warren, Ind.; *m* Sarah Ireland;
5–Zerna (1803-42), *m* 1824, Robert **Dunlap** (1799-1843);
3–Melinda (1833-85), *m* 1848, Willis **Northcutt** (3 above);
2–Allie Eliza (1850-86), *m* 1872, Samuel Alexander **Black** (1850-1911), lumberman; issue: I–Samuel Freddie (1874-75); II–Bertha (1 above); III–Myrtlemae; IV–Lina (1884-93).
1–*m* Apr. 7, 1897, Jesse Marshall Barrett (qv); issue: 1–Jesse Marshall, *b* Cedar Rapids, Ia., June 9, 1900; ed. Mo. U., 1922; Harvard, 1925; *m* June 27, 1922, Alma, dau. of Lycurgus Finley, of Charleston, Mo., *m* Rachel Logan (issue: Rachel Alice); 2–Frank B. (*b* and *d* 1907); 3–Alice Halline, *b* Napton, Mo., Sept. 27, 1910; ed. Northwestern U.
1–Mem. D.A.R., U.S.D. 1812, Mo. Hist. Soc., Ky. Hist. Soc. Residence: R.R. 2, Napton, Mo.

1–**BARRETT, Stephen Melvil,** *b* Nebraska City, Neb., Mar. 3, 1865.
4–Thomas **Barrett** (ca. 1785-1856), *d* Hawkins Co., Tenn.;
3–John (1802-93), *m* Priscilla Wright; removed to Jackson Co., Mo., ca. 1836;
2–Robert Wright (1825-79), *m* 1853, Julia Ellen Perry, of Jackson Co., Mo.; issue: I–John W. (1856-1923); II–Mary (*b* 1858; *m* 1884, John Deboard); III–William Perry (*b* 1860); IV–Robert (*d* 1862); V–Stephen M. (1 above); VI–Charles (1868-70); VII–Nora (1873-74); VIII–Thomas (1875-1903).
1–*m* Dec. 24, 1889, Dolly Susan Cassell, *b* Jackson Co., Mo., Feb. 27, 1871; dau. of George Cassell, of Jackson Co.; issue: 1–Edith Mary, *b* Greenwood, Mo., May 28, 1891; *m* May 28, 1912, Howard Henry McKnight (issue: Lowis Betty, *b* 1916; Dorris Geene, *b* 1925); 2–Bertha, *b* Blue Springs, Mo., Jan. 11, 1895; *m* Aug. 19, 1914, Carl M. Britt (issue: Glenn, *b* 1918); 3–Mabel, *b* Independence, Mo., Feb. 22, 1897; 4–Stephen Melvil, Jr., *b* Independence, Sept. 30, 1899; *m* Oct. 12, 1922, Annie May Humphry (issue: Gordon Melvil, *b* 1924; Stephen H., *b* 1926); 5–George William, *b* Rich Hill, Mo., Sept. 15, 1903; *m* Jan. 24, 1925, Neva Meredith (issue: Janice Meredith, *b* 1926); 6–Jessie D., *b* Lawton, Okla., Apr. 15, 1907; *m* June 17, 1925, J. Frank Davis; 7–Dorothy Ellen, *b* Edmond, Okla., Mar. 25, 1909; 8–Samuel Cassell, *b* Norman, Okla., Feb. 5, 1911; 9–Jack Pershing, *b* Claremore, Okla., Nov. 23, 1916.
1–B.S., Drury Coll., Springfield, Mo., '04 (A.M., 1909). Instr. and supt. schs. in Mo., 1895-1904; prof. edn., U.Okla., 1909-14; pres. Univ. Prep. Sch., Clarence, Okla., 1914-17; sec. and dir. Okla. State Bd. of Vocational Edn., 1917-19; pres. Okla. Mil. Acad., 1919-24; supervisor of publications, public schools of Kansas City, 1925–. Author (see Who's Who in America). Elected mem. Academie Latine of Arts, Science and Belles Lettres (Paris). Residence: 715 S. Park Av., Independence, Mo.

1–**BARRETT, Wilbert Hamilton,** *b* Shiloh, N. J., Feb. 26, 1858.
9–William **Davis,** from Wales to Boston, 1660; *m* Mary Johnson;
8–Rev. Jonathan, *m* Mary–;
7–Elnathan (*b* 1680), *m* 1705, —Barrett (*d* 1759);
6–Samuel (1713-73), *m* Anna Davis (1713-85);
5–Samuel (*b* 1741), *m* Hannah Dutton;

4–Zebediah (1780-1854), *m* 1799, Sarah Ayars (1775-1820);
3–Lois (1805-92), *m* 1826, Abel Sheppard **Tomlinson** (see Vol. II, p. 97, for Tomlinson lineages);
2–Lucinda Maxson (1832-59), *m* 1856, Reuben Tittsworth **Barrett** (1832-85), served in 3d N.J. Vol. Inf. in Civil War, wounded at Gettysburg.
1–*m* May 18, 1881, Elizabeth Benner (see Vol. II, p. 97, for genealogy and issue).
1–Ed. Union Acad. and South Jersey Inst. Manufacturer (retired); dir. in bank and mfg. corpns. Mem. S.C.W., S.A.R. (pres. Mich. Soc. and pres. gen. Nat. Soc., 1926-27), I.A.G. Clubs: Union League (Chicago), Adrian, Lenawee Country. Residence: 225 Toledo St., Adrian, Mich.

1–**BARRICKMAN, Wilhoite Carpenter,** *b* Bullitt Co., Ky., Mar. 7, 1871.
6–Michael (Willheit) **Wilhoite** (*d* Orange Co., Va., 1746), a "German Protestant," with wife and sons, Tobias, John, and Adam, arrived at "Germanna," Va., 1719, "immediately from England," prob. sent over by the King as skilled workers in Gov. Spotswood's iron mines; patented land in Spotsylvania Co., 1728; *m* Margaret–;
5–Tobias (*d* Culpeper Co., Va., 1762), began to write name Wilhoite; *m* Catherine–;
4–William (*b* Culpeper Co., Va.-*d* Oldham Co., Ky.), to Ky., ca. 1800; *m* Elizabeth Shirley (James[5], see below).
3–Anne, *m* 1813, Jonathan **Barrickman,** Ky. pioneer;
2–William (2 below).
8–Christopher (Zimmerman) **Carpenter** (*b* Germany or Switzerland-*d* Va., 1748), with the "Colony of 1717," settled at "Germanna," Spotsylvania Co., Va., 1717; lt. Va. militia, 1740, 42; owned over 1000 acres of land; will probated Orange Co., Va.; *m* Elizabeth–;
7–John (*d* 1782), with parents to Va.; began to write name Carpenter; will probated Culpeper Co., Va.; *m* Barbara Kercher (Andrew[8], 1st treas. and ch. warden, Hebron Lutheran Ch., Spotsylvania Co., Va., *m* Margarita–);
6–John (1725-1804), will probated Madison Co., Va.; *m* Ursula Blankenbaker (Nicholas[7], *m* Apolonia–, members "Germanna" Colony of 1717);
5–Michael (1758-1818), lt. Va. troops, Am. Rev.; from Va. to Ky., 1805; *m* Rebecca Delph;
4–Joel (1782-1822), *m* Rhoda Anne Wilhoite;
3–Wilhoite (1817-98), lawyer; judge Bullitt Co. Ct., Ky.; mem. Ky. Senate; *m* 1842, Letitia Magruder;
2–Sarah Elizabeth (2 below).
8–Michael **Wilhoite** (same as 6 above);
7–Tobias (5 above);
6–Michael;
5–Tobias (*b* Culpeper Co., Va., 1750-*d* Mercer Co., Ky., 1839), to Ky., ca. 1795; became members Soc. of Shakers, 1808; *m* 1773, Mary Shirley (1755-1844; James[6] [*d* Madison Co., Va., 1803], ranger Berkley Co., Va., French and Indian War, pvt., 10th Va. Regt., Am. Rev., received large mil. grants of land in Ky., *m* 1754, Judith, dau. of Moses Garriott, one of the "Culpeper Minute Men," in Am. Rev.);
4–Rhoda Anne (1783-1849), *m* Joel **Carpenter** (4 above).
9–Alexander (McGregor) **Magruder** (qv);
8–Samuel (1654-1711), of "Good Luck," Prince George Co., Md.; civil and military officer in Md., 1676-1705; mem. Md. Assembly, 1704-07; *m* Sarah Beall (1669-1743; Col. Ninian[9], qv);
7–Ninian (1686-1751), vestryman St. Paul's, Prince George Parish, Md.; *m* Elizabeth Brewer (*b* 1690; John[8], burgess, *m* Sarah, dau. of Col. Henry Ridgeley, qv; John[9], *m* Elizabeth Howard);
6–John (1709-82), *m* Jane– (*d* 1787);
5–Archibald (1751-1842), soldier Am. Rev. from Montgomery Co., Md.; *m* Cassandra Offutt (1760-1835);
4–Levi (1796-1868), *m* 1st, Elizabeth Aud (1797-1839);
3–Letitia (1819-1902), *m* Wilhoite **Carpenter** (3 above);
2–Sarah Elizabeth (1843-1923), *m* 1870, William **Barrickman** (1824-1901), farmer; landowner; stockbreeder; issue: I–Wilhoite C. (1 above); II–Lillian (*d* 1928); III–Mary (*b* 1875; *m* J. H. Ewing); IV–Samuel DeHaven (*d* infancy); V–Jane (*b* 1878; *m* Robert Sheets); VI–William M. (*b* 1882; *m* Mary Wickstead).
1–*m* Feb. 20, 1897, Harriet Love Theobald (qv for genealogy); issue: 1–Elizabeth, *b* Jefferson Co., Ky., Jan. 8, 1900; U.Tex., '23; *m* 1925, Herbert Ash (issue: Barbara); 2–Harriet, *b* Jefferson Co., Mar. 20, 1901; U.Tex., '23; *m* 1923, L. G. Blackstock (issue: Mathis W.).
1–Grad. law dept., U.Louisville, 1899. Sec. and mgr., Crime Suppression League of Dallas; dep. Federal Food Administrator for Tex., 1917-18. Mem. S.A.R., Am. Clan Gregor Soc., I.A.G. Mason (32° K.C.C.H., Shriner). Residence: 112 N. Montclair Av., Dallas, Tex.

1–**BARRICKMAN, Harriet Love Theobald (Mrs. Wilhoite C.),** *b* Vicksburg, Miss., Mar. 11, 1870.
8–Clement **Theobald** (qv);
7–John (1666-1713), Charles Co., Md.; *m* Mary Fendall (1673-1751; Capt. Josias[8], Provincial Gov. of Md., 1658-60);
6–John (*b* 1699), Charles Co.; *m* 1729, Elizabeth (Mason) Jenifer (Robert Mason[7] [*d* 1701], from Va. to St. Mary's Co., Md., ca. 1677 alderman St. Mary's Co., 1689, burgess, 1692, high sheriff, 1692-93, commd. justice Md. Provincial Ct., 1691; *m* Susanna–);
5–Samuel (1740-1830), went to Ky., 1785; *m* 1st, Elizabeth Smith;
4–William (1766-1834), Bourbon Co., Ky.; *m* 1789, Mary Brown (1770-1837; James[5] [1740-1825], lt. in Am. Rev., *m* 1764, Ann Davis);
3–Henry B., *m* 1827, Lucy Crump Bacon;
2–Nathaniel Bacon (2 below).
9–William **Bacon** (*b* in Eng.-*d* Northumberland Co., Va., 1660); *m* Margaret–;
8–Edmund (1641-1705), from Eng. to Va., settled in New Kent Co., Va.; capt. Va. Militia; *m* Anne Lyddall (George[9], col. Va. Militia);
7–John, sheriff New Kent Co., Va.; *m* Sarah Law (*d* 1709); *m* 2d, Susannah Parks (John[8]);
6–Lyddall (1719-75), Mecklenburg Co., Va.; *m* 1740, Mary Allen (*d* 1816);
5–Lyddall (*b* 1755), capt. Va. troops, Am. Rev.; *m* Anne Apperson; *m* 2d, –Crump;
4–Elizabeth, *m* John C. **Bacon** (Burwell[5], soldier Am. Rev., *m* –Christian);
3–Lucy Crump (1811-44), *m* Henry B. **Theobald** (3 above);
2–Nathaniel Bacon (1842-72), sgt., Co. F., 5th Mo. Inf., C.S.A.; *m* 1865, Lucy Anne Edney Jones (1845-70; Samuel[3], *m* Anne Wallace).
1–*m* Feb. 20, 1897, Wilhoite Carpenter Barrickman (qv for issue).
1–Mem. D.A.R. Residence: 112 N. Montclair Av., Dallas, Tex.

1–**BARTOW, Virginia,** *b* Rochester, N.H., Dec. 30, 1896.
8–Rev. John **Bartow** (qv);
7–Theophilus (*b* 1710), *m* Bathsheba Pell (Thomas[8] [1675-1739], 3d lord of the manor, *m* Anne, dau. of the reigning Indian chief of Westchester Co.; John[9], qv);
6–John (1740-1816), *m* 1761, Mary Ryder (Barnardus[7]);
5–Augustus (1762-1810), *m* 1786, Clarinna Bartow (1763-1839);
4–William Augustus (1794-1869), *m* 1826, Jane Hasbrouck;
3–Charles Edward (1833-1911), *m* 1865, Sarah Jane Scofield (1839-1910), see Vol. III, p. 55, for Scofield lineage;
2–Edward (2 below).
6–John **Abbott**;
5–John, *m* –Twombly;
4–John, *m* Betsy Dixon;
3–John James, *m* Mary Augusta Hall;
2–Alice (*b* N. Berwick, Me., Sept. 23, 1864), *m* Sept. 3, 1895, Edward **Bartow** (see Vol. III, p. 55).
1–A.B., Vassar, '18, M.S., 1921; Ph.D., U.Ill., 1923. Residence: 304 Brown St., Iowa City, Ia.

1–**BASS, Robert Perkins,** *b* Chicago, Ill., Sept. 1, 1873.
9–Samuel **Bass** (qv);
8–Thomas, of Braintree, Mass.; dea.; *m* 1660, Sarah Wood (Nicholas[9]);
7–John (1675-1753), of Braintree; *m* 1695, Elizabeth Neale (*b* 1675; Henry[8], *m* Hannah Pray);
6–Henry (1704-83), of Braintree; *m* 1735, Elizabeth Church;

5–Ebenezer (1746-1814), of Windham, Conn.; served on the Galley Trumbull, Lake Champlain, 1776; *m* 1769, Ruth Waldo (1748-1834; Zaccheus[6], *m* 1746 or 47, Tabitha–);
4–Joel (1774-1871), of Windham; sgt. Battle of Plattsburg, 1814; *m* 1796, Polly Martin (*b* 1777; Aaron[5], *m* 1766, Eunice–);
3–Joel M. (1798-1855), of Williamstown, Vt.; *m* 1825, Katherine Wright Burnham (1805-90; Dr. Walter[4], *m* 1795, Submit Smith);
2–Perkins (2 below).
9–John **Foster** (*d* 1687), from Eng., settled at Salem, Mass.; *m* ca. 1649, Martha Tompkins (*b* ca. 1630);
8–Samuel (*b* 1652), *m* 1st, 1676, Sarah Stewart;
7–Samuel (1680-1762), *m* 1701, Sarah Roberts (Abraham[8], *m* Sarah–);
6–Jonathan (*b* 1712), *m* 1733, Dorothy Merrow;
5–Jonathan (*b* 1737), *m* 1761, Sarah Townsend;
4–Aaron (*b* 1769), *m* 1793, Mehitable Nichols;
3–Dr. John H. (*b* 1796), *m* 1840, Nancy Smith;
2–Clara, *m* Perkins **Bass** (1827-99), lawyer; U.S. dist. atty. for Ill.; issue: I–Gertrude (*m* 2d, Murray Warner); II–John Foster (*b* 1866; *m* Abigail Bailey; III–Robert Perkins (1 above).
1–*m* Jan. 1912, Edith Harlan Bird, *b* E. Walpole, Mass., May 27, 1887; dau. of Charles Sumner Bird, of E. Walpole; issue: 1–Perkins, *b* East Walpole, N.H., Oct. 6, 1912; 2–Edith, *b* Peterboro, N.H., Oct. 12, 1913; 3–Joanne, *b* Peterboro, July 12, 1915.
1–A.B., Harvard, '96; (A.M., Dartmouth). Mem. N.H.Ho. of Rep., 1905-09, Senate, 1909-10; gov. of N.H., 1911-13. Was dir. marine labor of U.S. Shipping Bd., chmn. Nat. Adjustment Commn., and mem. War Labor Policy Bd., during World War. Counselor in industrial relations (see Who's Who in America). Clubs: Tavern (Boston), Harvard (New York), University (Chicago). Residence: Peterboro, N.H.

1–**BATCHELDER, Mark Daniel,** *b* Lincoln, Vt., Oct. 2, 1868.
10–Rev. Stephen **Batchelder** (qv);
9–Nathaniel (*b* 1590), *m* Hester Mercer;
8–Nathaniel (ca. 1630-1710), mem. N.H. Gen. Ct., 1694-95; *m* 1676, Mary (Carter) Wyman;
7–Thomas (1685-1764), *m* 1718, Sarah Tuck (1689-1764);
6–Capt. Nathaniel (1722-84), *m* 1743, Hannah Butler;
5–Joseph (1750-1827), from Hampton, N.H., to Plainfield, Vt.; pvt., Capt. Peter Clark's Co. from Lyndeborough, N.H., Am. Rev.; *m* 1769, Sarah Ferrin (*b* 1751);
4–Nathaniel, *m* Martha Dunklee (1770-1863);
3–Mark (1805-64), *m* 1839, Mary Martin (1815-1906);
2–Hon. James H. (2 below).
10–John **Gove** (1604-48), from Eng. to Charlestown, Mass., 1638; *m* probably 2d, Mary Sale (*d* 1681, aet. 80; Edward[9], *m* Elizabeth Gifford);
9–Edward (1630-91), Salisbury, Mass.; dep. Gen. Ct.; freeman; rep. N.H. Assembly, 1680; *m* 1660, Hannah Partridge (*d* 1691; William[10]);
8–John (1661-1737), lived at Hampton Falls, now Seabrook, N.H.; entered as a soldier from Hampton, 1708, called ens., 1709; *m* 1686, Sarah, widow of William Russell, of Hampton Falls;
7–John, *m* Ruth Johnson;
6–Daniel, *m* Elizabeth Hunt;
5–Daniel, *m* Miriam Cartland;
4–Moses, *m* Hannah Chase;
3–Daniel, *m* Sarah Taber (desc. Francis Cooke, qv);
2–Phoebe H. (*b* 1841), *m* 1864, James Henry **Batchelder** (*b* 1844).
1–*m* Mar. 20, 1888, Mary A. Williams, *b* at Bridport, Vt., Apr. 11, 1868; dau. of Joseph Swift Williams; issue: 1–Ella Lucille (*m* D. N. Crawford); 2–Joseph H. (*m* Isabelle Coffey); 3–May Belle (*d* young); 4–Corinne (*m* Lt. Col. Whitman R. Conolly, U.S.A.).
1–Pioneer in street railway advertising. Mem. S.M.D., O.F.P.A. (Ill. State councillor, 1922), S.C.W., I.A.G., N.E.H.G.S. Clubs: Midland (Chicago), Creve Coeur, Peoria Country. Residence: 312 Parkside Drive, Peoria, Ill.

1–**BATES, Arthur Laban,** *b* Meadville, Pa., June 6, 1859.
9–John **Tower** (qv);
8–Ibrook, *m* Margaret Hardin;
7–Rachel, *m* Joshua **Bates** (Joseph[8]; Clement[9], qv);
6–Isaac, *m* Martha Clark;
5–Laban (1748-1832), sgt. in Am. Rev.; mem. Mass. Legislature; *m* Olive Wheelock;
4–Nahum, *m* Perley Ballow;
3–Capt. Laban, *m* 1824, Mary Blake Thayer;
2–Samuel Penniman (2 below).
10–Thomas **Thayer** (*d* 1665), from Eng., ca. 1636; original propr. Braintree, Mass.; *m* 1618, Margerie Wheeler (*d* 1672);
9–Ferdinand (bap. 1625-1713), *m* 1652, Huldah Haywood (*d* 1680; William[10]);
8–Isaac (*b* 1668), *m* 1691, Mercy Ward;
7–Ebenezer (*b* 1694), *m* 1719, Mary Wheelock;
6–Capt. Ebenezer, served in Am. Rev.; *m* Hannah Green;
5–Lt. Elias (1742-1806), Am. Rev.; *m* 1763, Hannah Ellis;
4–Capt. Elias (*b* 1773), *m* 1797, Ruth Stapels;
3–Mary (*b* 1802), *m* Laban **Bates** (3 above).
8–Thomas **Fisher** (*d* 1638), from Eng., settled at Dedham, Mass., *m* Elizabeth– (*d* 1652);
7–Dea. Samuel (*d* 1704), Wrentham, Mass.; *m* Mehitible Snow (*d* 1693);
6–Ebenezer (1669-1726), Wrentham; *m* Sarah Guild (John[7], *m* Sarah, dau. of Anthony Fisher, qv; John[8], qv);
5–Thomas (1699-1760), *m* Sarah Blake (*b* 1705);
4–Abijah (1750-1821), *m* 2d, 1810, Rosanna Fairbanks;
3–Sarah Prince, *m* John **Bates** (see Vol. 1, p. 217, for Bates lineage);
2–Sarah Josephine (2 below).
9–Jonathan **Fairbanks** (qv);
8–George (*d* 1683), from Eng., to Dedham, Mass.; *m* Mary Adams;
7–Dr. Jonathan (*b* 1662), of Medway; *m* 1st Sarah–;
6–Dr. Jonathan (*b* 1689), *m* ca. 1726, Hannah Cooledge;
5–Lt. Joshua (1727-81), served in Am. Rev.; *m* Lydia Ellis;
4–Rosanna, *m* Abijah **Fisher** (4 above).
9–John (Coolidge) **Cooledge** (qv);
8–John (1628-90), of Watertown; ens. King Philip's War, 1676; *m* Hannah Livermore (*b* 1639; John[9], qv);
7–John (1662-1713 or 24), King Philip's War; *m* 1699, Mary–;
6–Hannah, *m* Jonathan **Fairbanks** (6 above).
2–Sarah Josephine Bates (1836-1907), *m* 1856, Samuel Penniman **Bates,** LL.D. (1827-1902), A.B., Brown, '51; educator; state historian of Pa.; issue: I–Edward Thayer (1857-89); II–Arthur Laban (1 above); III–Gertrude L.; IV–Josephine M. (*m* Curtis L. Webb); V–Alfred J. (see Vol. I, p. 217); VI–Walter Irving (see Vol. I, p. 217); VII–Florence L. (*m* Floyd Reynolds Stewart).
1–*m* Oct. 20, 1909, Emily Wells Rusling (qv); issue: 1–Josephine Rusling, *b* Meadville, Pa., Sept. 1, 1913; 2–Arthur Rusling, *b* Meadville, Mar. 14, 1917.
1–A.B., Allegheny, '80, A.M., '83 (LL.D., 1920); Oxford U., Eng., 1884. Lawyer, bank director, Meadville, Pa. Mem. Congress 6 terms, 1901-13 (see Who's Who in America). Clubs: Meadville Country, University, Iroquois. Residence: Meadville, Pa.

1–**BATES, Emily Wells Rusling (Mrs. Arthur L.),** *b* Trenton, N.J., Oct. 18, 1884.
9–John **Simcock,** charter mem. William Penn's Council, 1682; Pres. Council 1687; chief justice, Pa. Supreme Ct., 1696; *m* Elizabeth Budd;
8–Mary, *m* John **Cook,** an original propr. of N.J.; speaker of Assembly; chief justice of Pa. (Arthur[9] [*d* 1699 or 1700], of Phila., original propr. of N.J., first chief justice and governing councillor of Pa., *m* Margaret–);
7–Arthur, *m* Elizabeth–;
6–Hannah, *m* 1757 or 58, Capt. Benjamin **McCullough** (1736-89), came to N.J. ante 1750; served in Am. Rev.;
5–Col. William (1759-1840), of Asbury, N.J.; wagonmaster in Am. Rev.; mem. N.J. Assembly and Council; co. judge 35 yrs.; *m* Keturah Hunt (*d* 1788);
4–Mary (1782-1805), *m* 1800, Maj. Henry **Hankinson** (see Vol. III, p. 57, for Hankinson lineage);
3–Eliza Budd (1803-88), *m* 1825, Gershom **Rusling** (1796-1881; James[4] [1762-1826], from Eng. to New York, 1795; settled nr. Hackettstown, N.J., *m* 1st, 1787, Mary [1766-1809], dau. of Joseph Fowler, of Eng., *m* Hannah [Frazier] Rose);

2–Gen. James Fowler (2 below).
13–Thomas **Rogers,** Mayflower Pilgrim (qv);
12–Joseph (*d* 1678), came with his father; lt., 1647; removed to Eastham, 1664; mem. Council of War, 1658; *m* Hannah–;
11–Elizabeth (*d* 1681), *m* John **Drake** (qv);
10–John (*d* 1689), of Simsbury, Conn.; *m* Hannah Moore (*d* 1686; Thomas[11]);
9–Elizabeth (*d* 1726), *m* as his 2d wife, 1653, William **Gaylord** (*d* 1656; Dea. William[10], qv);
8–Nathaniel (*b* 1656), *m* 1st, 1678, Abigail Bissell;
7–Josiah, *m* 1713, Naomi Burnham;
6–Sarah, *m* 1738, Capt. Ammi **Trumbull** (1712-66);
5–Sarah (1747-1839), *m* 1770, Capt. Hezekiah **Wells** (1736-1817), soldier Am. Rev. (Lampson[6], *m* Mabel, dau. of Jeremiah Bissell);
4–Dea. Ira (1783-1857), *m* 1814, Persis Pease;
3–Emily Hannah (1822-91), *m* 1842, Isaac **Wood** (1815-89);
2–Emily Elizabeth (2 below).
10–Robert **Pease** (qv);
9–John (1630-89), obtained a land grant at Springfield; *m* Margaret Goodell (*d* 1681);
8–Capt. John (*d* 1689), dep. Gen. Ct.; capt. A. and H.A. Co.; *m* Mary–;
7–Jonathan (1668-93), *m* Elizabeth Booth (1668-1722);
6–Peletiah, *m* Jemima Booth;
5–Dea. Samuel (1746-1815), soldier in Am. Rev.; *m* 1786, Elizabeth Secton (Dea. Joseph[6], *m* Rebecca Chapin [Jonathan[7]; Japhet[8]; Dea. Samuel[9], qv]);
4–Persis (1789-1863), *m* Dea. Ira **Wells** (4 above).
2–Gen. James Fowler **Rusling,** LL.D. (1834-1918), A.B., Dickinson, '54; lawyer; served 1st lt. to col., U.S.V., 1861-67; bvtd. brig. gen. U.S.V.; *m* 2d, 1870, Emily Elizabeth Wood (1848-1927; see Vol. I, p. 897).
1–*m* Oct. 20, 1909, Arthur Laban Bates (qv for genealogy and issue).
1–Mem. Magna Charta Dames, C.D.A., D.A.R. Clubs: Women's Literary, Country. Residence: 636 Highland Av., Meadville, Pa.

WISE

John Wise of Sydenham, 1400 (recorded by Sir Henry St. George, in his "Visitation of Devonshire," 1620).
Arms: Sable, three chevronels ermine.

1–**BATTLE, Lula A. Wise (Mrs. George F.),** *b* Liberty Co., Ga., Oct. 6, 1876.
9–John **Wise** (*d* 1695), from Eng. in the "Transport," 1635; settled at "Clifton," Accomac Co., Va.; party to Northampton protest, 1652; justice, Accomac Ct., 1663; signed Accomac memorial, 1677; *m* Hannah Scarborough (Col. Edmund[10]; Capt. Edmund[11], qv);
8–John (*d* 1717), justice; burgess, 1705-06; *m* his 1st cousin, Matilda West (Col. John[9], of Accomac, *m* Matilda, dau. Col. Edmund Scarborough);
7–John (*d* 1767), presiding justice, Accomac; *m* Scarborough Robinson (Col. Tully[8], *m* Sarah West);
6–John (1723-70), king's lt. Accomac and Norfolk; maj. Accomac militia; *m* 2d, 1753, Margaret Douglas (Col. George[7], *m* Tabitha, dau. of Hill Drummond);
5–William (1755-1816), served in Am. Rev.; removed to Ga.; *m* 1786, Sarah Margaret–;
4–John (1790-1834), *m* 1816, Rachel Jones (1791-1871; Bridger[5], [*b* 1759], *m* Rachel–, *b* 1762);
3–John Bridger (1820-64), *m* 1840, Katie McElveen (1822-93; William[4], *m* Susan Harvey; William[5], S.C., Am. Rev.; *m* Margaret–);
2–Henry William (2 below).
5–John **Neville** (1750-1803 or 04), will probated, July 30, 1804, Bulloch Co., Ga.; Am. Rev.; *m* 1768, Frances Ann Nixon (1752-1815);
4–Jacob (1769-1864), *m* 1798, Nicey Henderson (1780-1889; Capt. Micheal[5], *m* June Green);
3–Jacob (1812-80), served C.S.A.; *m* 1833, Elvira Kirkland (1812-83; g.dau. Richard Kirkland, Am. Rev.);
2–Susan (1844-1907), *m* 1864, Henry William **Wise** (1841-1907), pvt. Co. F, 22d Bn., Ga. Heavy Arty., C.S.A.; buried at Brunswick, Ga.; issue: I–Sallie J. (*b* 1867; *m* Alex Calder); II–Carry B. (1869-70); III–Julia A. (1870-71); IV–Kate C. (*b* 1873; *m* Henry Hooker; *m* 2d, C. P. Tyler); V–Lula A. (1 above); VI–Della D. (1878-1913; *m* Edgar E. Wilchar); VII–Rufus L. (1879-1913); VIII–Maggie G. (*b* 1882); IX–Henry (1884-86).
1–*m* May 8, 1898, George Franklin Battle, *b* Montgomery Co., Ga., Oct. 4, 1876; son of John Robinson Battle; issue: 1–Margaret Frances, *b* Decatur Co., Ga., Sept. 8, 1910; Wesleyan U., '32; 2–George Franklin, Jr., *b* Decatur Co., Feb. 1, 1913.
1–Served with Ga. Red Cross, during World War. Mem. D.A.R., U.D.C. Residence: Shotwell St., Bainbridge, Ga.

1–**BATES, Lindell Theodore,** *b* Tacoma, Wash., Feb. 13, 1890.
9–Nathaniel (Bats, Badts) **Bates,** came to America ante 1638; mentioned in official records of New Amsterdam, 1663;
8–Thomas (*d* 1694), resided nr. New Amsterdam ante 1665; *m* 1669, Mary Butcher; *m* 2d, Elizabeth Stwiel;
7–William (ca. 1675-1720), of New York, N.Y.; *m* Widow Esther Hance Fell;
6–William (*b* 1715), of New York; *m* Phebe–; *m* 2d Anna Maria–;
5–Thomas (1754-1856), went from N.Y. to Can. and was given a grant of land nr. Halifax; *m* 2d, Mary Freeman (*d* 1808);
4–Stephen Freeman (*b* 1802), returned to U.S., 1839; *m* 1826, Elizabeth Wallace;
3–William Wallace (1827-1911), shipbuilder; capt. 56th Ill. and 19th Wis. vols. in Civil War; U.S. commr. of Navigation; authority on Am. Merchant marine; *m* 1855, Marie Cole (1824-98; Welcome[4], of Marshfield, Vt.);
2–Lindon Wallace (1858-1924), eminent civil engr.; *m* 1881, Josephine White (Georges E.[8], of Can.); issue: I–Hon. Lindon Wallace, Jr. (1883-*d* on S.S. Lusitania, May 7, 1915; twice mem. Assembly; nominee for Congress); II–Lindell T. (1 above).
1–Not married. Ph.B., Yale-S., '10, LL.B., J.D., N.Y.U., LL.M., N.Y. Law Sch., LL.D., U.Paris and U.Madrid. Lawyer. Rep. nominee for Congress, 1916. Cdr. 1st class, Order of Isabella (Spain). Mem. Holland Soc., S.C.W., S.R. Clubs: Union League, Lenox, Lawyers, Assn. of the Bar. Residence: 55 E. 65th St., New York, N.Y.

1–**BATTEY, Herbert Verner,** *b* Mineral, Ill., Feb. 27, 1862.
9–Caleb **Carr** (qv);
8–Nicholas (1654-1709), *m* Rebecca Nicholson (1656-1703; Joseph[9] [*b* Bootle, Eng.-*d* 1693], *m* Jane– [*d* 1691], both were victims of religious persecution, 1661-64, imprisoned at Boston, banished from Salem, to Barbados, 1664, to Portsmouth, R.I., 1669);
7–Margaret (1684-post 1767), *m* 1707, John **Battey** (1688-1767; Samson[8] [*d* post 1716], from Eng. to Conanicut Island, R.I.; settled at Jamestown, R.I., ante 1677; *m* Dinah–, *d* 1698);
6–Samson (1709-44), *m* 1743, Ethelanna Westcott;
5–Josiah (1744-1817), *m* 1767, Anne Brown (1746-1817);
4–Sampson (1779-1841), *m* 2d, 1814, Abigail Phillips (1792-1873);
3–Silas (1815-95), *m* 1833, Mercy Bennett (1814-1905);

2–George (2 below).
10–Stukeley **Westcott** (qv);
9–Jeremiah (*d* 1686), *m* 1665, Eleanor England (*d* 1686; William[10], *m* Elizabeth–);
8–Stukeley (1672-1750), *m* 1693, Priscilla Bennett (*d* 1754; Samuel[9], *m* Anna–);
7–Josiah (*b* 1694);
6–Ethelanna (*b* 1726), *m* Samson **Battey** (6 above).
10–Simon **Cooper** (*d* ca. 1618), of Dedham, Eng.; *m* Lydia– (*d* 1674); she *m* 2d, Gregory Stone (qv);
9–John (*b* Eng., 1617/18-*d* Cambridge, Mass., 1691), freeman, town clk., selectman; dea., First Parish Ch., now Shephard Memorial, at Harvard Square; grave is in old cemetery at Harvard Square; *m* ca. 1642, Anne Sparhawk (*d* 1717/18);
8–Samuel (1653-1717/18), owned and prob. built the "Cooper-Austin" House; *m* 1682, Hannah Hasting (1655/56-1732);
7–Samuel (1688-1748), dea.; *m* 1720, Sarah Kidder (*b* 1690);
6–Nathaniel (1720-93), to Uxbridge, Mass., 1763; to Croydon, N.H., 1768; *m* 1746, Elizabeth Axtell, of Grafton;
5–Nathaniel, Jr. (1748-1821) of Uxbridge, Mass., Bapt. minister; *m* 1765, Mary Aldrich (1748-90);
4–Calvin (1779-1846), Bapt. minister, Chestnut Hill, Conn., over 20 yrs.; *m* 3 times; *m* 1800, Ruth Cooper (1779-1816);
3–Calvin (1810-87), *m* 1833, Harriet Kies (1812-89; Wilson[4], *m* Betsey Hulet);
2–Louisa Fisher (1841-1915), *m* 1861, George **Battey** (1837-1915); issue: I–Herbert V. (1 above); II–Frank Silas (*b* 1867; *m* Lizzie M. Rasmussan); III–Ray Calvin (*b* 1879; *m* Edith V. Russell); IV–George (*b* 1881; *m* Olive A. Lawrence).
1–*m* Sept. 17, 1884, Lena Louisa Betterman, *b* Ottawa, Ill., Aug. 1, 1866; dau. of Carl H. Betterman, of Seneca, Ill., *m* Magdalena Hearn; issue: 1–Carl Verner, *b* Portsmouth, Ia., June 23, 1885; *m* Oct. 16, 1909, Minnie E. Hetzel, of Avoca, Ia. (issue: Charlene V.; Jean M.); 2–George Earl, *b* Walnut, Ia., Feb. 5, 1887; sgt., U.S.A., World War, served in France; *m* Jan. 19, 1924, Alice I. Heldridge (issue: Ruth A.; George E.); 3–Percy Betterman, *b* Walnut, July 19, 1888; M.D., Creighton U.; capt., M.C., U.S.A., World War; asst. supt., State Instn., defective delinquents, Napanoch, N.Y.; *m* Nov. 16, 1925, Laura M. Ryan, of Hartford, Conn.; 4–Lena Louise, *b* Walnut, Apr. 23, 1891; 5–Bess Beatrice, *b* Harlan, Ia., Aug. 14, 1896; 6–Herbert Virgil, *b* Avoca, Ia., Oct. 12, 1898; *m* Oct. 8, 1921, Frances Jensen (issue: Norma Jane).
1–Atty. Clk. Municipal Ct. of Council Bluffs, 1924. Served on legal advisory bd. during World War. Mason (Shriner). Mem. S.A.R., I.A.G. Residence: 107 Glen Av., Council Bluffs, Ia.

1–**BAXTER, Donald Erskine,** *b* Warren, O., Aug. 26, 1882.
12–Hon. John **Carver,** Mayflower Pilgrim (qv);
11–Catherine, *m* John Tilley, Mayflower Pilgrim (qv);
10–Elizabeth (1607-87), *m* ante 1624, Hon. John **Howland,** Mayflower Pilgrim (qv);
9–Desire (ante 1627-83), *m* 1643, Capt. John **Gorham** (qv);
8–Temperance, *m* Thomas **Baxter** (qv);
7–Thomas, of Yarmouth, Mass., settled at Wethersfield; *m* 1705, Mary Lattimer;
6–Timothy (*b* 1706), of Wethersfield; *m* 1726, Sarah (Goodrich) Kilbourne (*b* 1702);
5–John (1727-1814), of Wethersfield; *m* Ruth–;
4–Moses (1764-1806), of Sandisfield; *m* 1789, Esther– (*d* 1823);
3–Otis (1805-86), of Sandisfield; *m* 1834, Phoebe White (1814-75);
2–Erskine (2 below).
9–Henry **Adams** (qv);
8–Ens. Edward (1630-1716), *m* Lydia Becknell Rockwood;
7–Henry (1663-1749), of Medfield; *m* 1691, Patience Ellis;
6–Ebenezer (1704-50), of Providence; *m* 1744, Elizabeth Sears;
5–Corpl. Ebenezer (1746-98), of Canterbury, Conn.; Am. Rev.; *m* 1770, Mary Carpenter (1752-1825);
4–Mary (*b* 1790), of Beckett, Mass.; *m* Isaac **Mills** (1781-1824);
3–Isaac (1811-89), of Nelson, O.; *m* 1838, Angeline King (1821-98; James Sterling[4]);
2–Martha Glenn (1845-1927), *m* 1863, Erskine **Baxter** (1834-1920); issue: I–Bryson Spurgeon (*b* 1863; *m* Grace H. Bennett); II–Mabel Agnes (1865-1928; *m* Isaac W. Troxel); III–Angeline Phoebe (*b* 1869); IV–Edwin Otis (*b* 1869, *m* Elma Haughton); V–Donald Erskine (1 above).
1–*m* Oct. 5, 1909, Frances (Welker) Tarbell, (divorced), *b* Manchester, Tenn., Aug. 24, 1882; issue: 1–Jane Stuart, *b* New York, N.Y., Sept. 6, 1919; 2–Donald Bruce, *b* Los Angeles, Calif., June 17, 1921.
1–*m* 2d, Jan. 27, 1930, Delia Myra Dantzler, *b* Billings, Mont., Aug. 14, 1892; dau. of Charles French Beardsley.
1–Ed. Hiram Coll., '02; M.D., Baltimore Med. Coll., 1908 (Phi Chi); U. of Louisville, 1909. Asst. supt. Minneapolis municipal hosps., 1912-14; dir. Infantile Paralysis Commn. of N.Y. City, 1916; supt. Peking Med. Coll., 1918-21; private practice, Los Angeles, since 1921. Pres. Certified Laboratory Products, Don Baxter Inc., Stanford Table Co. Author. Chief of the bureau of tuberculosis with rank of maj., in France; decorated by Serbian govt. Mem. B.O.R., S.M.D., S.C.W., Sons Revolution, A.M.A., Assn. Mil. Surgeons, etc. Mason. Christian. Democrat. Clubs: Los Angeles Athletic, Breakfast, Casa Del Mar, Santa Monica Swimming, Hollywood Athletic, Pacific Coast, Rivera Country. Residence: 2000 N. Edgmont St., Los Angeles, Calif.

1–**BAYMAN, Nettie Shreve (Mrs. James Fremont),** *b* Shreve, O., Apr. 23, 1868.
4–Richard **Shreve** (1760-1822), of Burlington Co., N.J.; *d* Crawford Co., Pa.; capt. troop of Light Horse from Burlington Co., N.J., 1782; *m* 1783, Margaret Newbold (1766-1852);
3–Thomas (1787-1857), *m* Mary Wigle;
2–Thomas Newbold (1839-1921), farmer; *m* 1863, Rebecca Hinkle (1842-1920); issue: I–Emma T. (1865-91; *m* Francis M. Barnhart); II–Nettie (1 above); III–Gertrude M. (*b* 1871); IV–Harvey M. (*b* 1873; *m* Sallie Sollenberger).
1–*m* June 28, 1905, James Fremont Bayman, *b* Pierceton, Ind., Jan. 19, 1869; son of Alexander Bayman, of Pierceton.
1–Grad. Ohio Normal Training, and Leland Powers Sch., Boston, Mass. Public reader on Chautauqua and Lyceum bureaus, teacher and lecturer, 20 yrs. Mem. D.A.R. (past regent, Fort Industry Chapter, Toledo, O.; chmn. nat. defense, State of Wash.). Clubs: Dramatic, of Toledo (pres.), Woman's Edn. Residence: 2503 33d Av. S., Seattle, Wash.

1–**BEAL, Junius Emery,** *b* Fort Huron, Mich., Feb. 23, 1860.
8–Zechariah **Field** (qv);
7–Sgt. Samuel (1651-97), *m* 1676, Sarah Gilbert (1655-1712);
6–Thomas (1680-1747), *m* 1713, Abigail Dickinson (1690-1775);
5–Dr. Simeon (*b* 1731), *m* 1763, Margaret Reynolds (1742-96);
4–Dr. Edward (1777-1840), *m* 1807, Sarah (Leavenworth) Baldwin;
3–Dr. Junius L. (1808-67), *m* 1831, Maria (Briggs) Packard;
2–James Edward (2 below).
9–John **Beal** (qv);
8–Caleb (1636-1716), *m* 1664, Elizabeth Hewitt (*b* 1644);
7–Josiah (1677-1743), styled sgt.; *m* 1701, Rachel Hersey or Hershey (*d* 1743);
6–Seth (1710-86), Am. Rev.; *m* 1731, Abigail Clarke;
5–Seth (1736-83), at Bunker Hill; *m* 1761, Leah Nash;
4–Bernard (1773-1850), *m* 1796, Deborah Lapham;
3–Emery (1797-1861), *m* 1822, Sophronia Rice;
2–Loretta (1837-61), *m* 1858, James Edward **Field** (1832-94), an adopted child of his uncle, Rice Aner Beal (1823-83), *m* Phoebe Beers (1825-1900), and assumed the name **Beal.**
1–*m* Nov. 29, 1889, Ella Travis, *b* Cooper, Mich., Feb. 1, 1862; dau. of Daniel D. Travis, of Cooper; issue: 1–Travis Field (Sept. 3, 1894-July 27, 1923), B.L., U.Mich., '17; ens., U.S.N., 1918-19; 2–Loretta F., *b* Ann Arbor, Mich.,

Apr. 16, 1897; B.A., U.Mich., '23; *m* 1927, Albert C. Jacobs (issue: Loretta, *b* Oct. 1928).
1-B.L., U.Mich., '82. Editor and pub. Ann Arbor Courier (weekly), Times (daily), 1882-1904 (see Who's Who in America). Regent U. of Mich. Mem. S.C.W., S.A.R., Washtenaw Co. Pioneer and Hist. Soc. (pres.). Clubs: Rotary, University, Ann Arbor Golf, Huron Hills Golf, Barton Hills Golf (Ann Arbor), University (Detroit). Residence: 343 S. 5th Av., Ann Arbor, Mich.

1-**BEALL, Grace Gorsuch (Mrs. Magruder),** *b* Vashon, Wash., Nov. 5, 1893.
8-John **Fay** (qv);
7-Capt. John (1668-1747), dea. Congl. Ch., Westboro, 1727; 1st town clk.; selectman many terms; town treas., 1722; assessor; magistrate; *m* 1690, Elizabeth Wellington (1673-1729; Benjamin[8], *m* Elizabeth Sweetman);
6-Capt. Benjamin (1712-77), of Westboro; town treas., 1742-43, 66-68; selectman 5 terms; comd. a co. during French and Indian War; *m* 2d, 1765, Elizabeth (Hapgood) Stow (1725-84; Capt. Thomas Hapgood[7], of Shrewsbury, Mass.);
5-Col. Joel (1769-1830), *m* 1803, Hannah Rice Wood;
4-Capt. Joel Wood (1807-57), *m* 1828, Lucy Dutton;
3-Martha Willard (1839-1912), *m* 1862, Edward Salt **Atkinson**;
2-Sarah Caroline (2 below).
10-Simon **Willard** (qv);
9-Benjamin (1664-1732), *m* Sarah Lakin;
8-Joseph (1693-1774), *m* 1715, Martha Clark;
7-Joseph (1720-99), *m* 1747, Hannah Rice;—
6-Martha (1760-83), *m* 1777, Joseph **Wood**;
5-Hannah Rice (1783-1860), *m* Joel **Fay** (5 above);
4-Capt. Joel W., *m* Lucy Dutton (4 above);
3-Martha Willard, *m* Edward S. **Atkinson** (3 above);
2-Sarah Caroline (*b* 1867), *m* 1891, Frank William **Gorsuch** (1861-1920); issue: I-Edward John (*b* 1892; *m* Margaret Harmeling); II-Grace (1 above); III-Helen (*b* 1895); IV-Carroll Fay (1899-1927); V-Jeanne (*b* 1903; *m* Vern Kelley).
1-*m* Oct. 25, 1912, Magruder Beall (1885-1923); son of Lewis C. Beall; issue (all *b* Vashon, Wash.): 1-Fielder Magruder, *b* Aug. 15, 1913; 2-Kenneth Gorsuch, *b* Sept. 23, 1915; 3-Robert Allan, *b* Mar. 15, 1920.
1-Residence: Vashon, Wash.

1-**BEATTY, Mary Mays,** *b* Doylestown, Pa., May 10, 1867.
5-Rev. Charles **Beatty** (1712-73; John[6], officer British Army, *m* Christiana Clinton, desc. William the Conqueror, Edward, 9th Baron Clinton, Adam de Poynings of Sussex temp. Henry III, Robert Hickman, of Bloxham Co., Oxon, Llewellyn ap Ivor, Lord of St. Clere, Botolph Stourton, of Stourton, Wilts, Richard Talbot, John de Fynes, Hubert de Vaux, Robert de Stafford, Walter Diencourt, William de Braose, Humphrey de Bohun, William de Saye, Hugh de Beauchamp); *m* Ann Reading (1724-68); see Vol. III, p. 60;
4-Reading, M.D. (1757-1831), *m* 1786, Christina Wynkoop (see Joseph M. Beatty, Vol. III, p. 60, for Wynkoop lineage);
3-John (1800-94), *m* 1833, Mary Assheton Henry (see Vol. III, p. 60, for Henry-Penn lineage);
2-Joseph Henry (2 below).
8-Rev. William **Mays,** came to America, 1611;
7-John, *m* — Newcomb;
6-Henry;
5-Thomas (1753-1830), of S.C.; Am. Rev.; *m* 1782, Mary Hamilton (1765-post 1842);
4-Thomas Washington (1784-1873), War 1812; *m* 1809, Henrietta Myers (see Vol. III, p. 60, for Myers lineage);
3-Mary (1810-64), *m* 1826, Abraham **Kearns** (see Vol. I, p. 231, for Kearns lineage);
2-Olive McConnelly Kearns (*b* 1842), *m* 1865, Joseph Henry **Beatty** (1840-1920); see Vol. III, p. 60, for issue.
1-Ed. Doylestown, Pa., Public School, and Doylestown Classical and Literary Sem., '87. Instr. geography and English, Pa. Inst. for the Deaf, Mt. Airy. Mem. D.A.R., U.S.D. 1812, Pa. Hist. Soc., Bucks Co. Hist. Soc., Germantown Hist. Soc., Geneal. Soc. of Pa., Inst. Am. Genealogy. Residence: 172 Maplewood Av., Germantown, Pa.

1-**BEAUMONT, André Alden,** *b* San Antonio, Tex., Aug. 4, 1870.
8-William **Beaumont** (1607/08-1699), from Eng., 1635; settled at Saybrook, Conn., 1640; *m* 1643, Lydia Danforth (1624-86; Nicholas[9], of Cambridge, Mass.);
7-Samuel (1657-1748), of Saybrook; *m* 1687, Hester Buckingham (1668-1709; Rev. Thomas[8], *m* Hester Hosmer);
6-Samuel, of Saybrook; *m* 1716, Abigail Denison (John[7], of Wethersfield, Conn., *m* Ann Mason);
5-William (1725-1812), of Lebanon, Conn.; *m* 1747, Sarah Everett (1721-1813), of Windham, Conn.;
4-Isaiah (1757-1837), of Lebanon; served in Am. Rev., and was present at siege of Boston, and present at attack on Trenton, and in battle of Princeton, where he was wounded; subsequently discharged at Morristown, N.J., 1777; *m* 1780, Fear Alden (1755-1836; Andrew[5], of Lebanon, *m* Rebecca Stanford);
3-Andrew (1790-1853), postmaster of Wilkes-Barre, Pa.; held many co. offices; mem. Pa. Legislature; mem. Congress, 1833-37; *m* 1813, Julia Ann Colt (1793-1872; Arnold[4], *m* Lucinda Yarrington);
2-Eugene Beauharnais (1837-1916), grad. U.S.M.A., '61; col. U.S.A.; served through Civil War; aide to Gen. John Sedgewick until the latter's death, then as aide to Gen. James H. Wilson; served in Tex., 1866-75; at U.S.M.A., 1875-79; in Kan., Colo., N.M., Ariz. and Tex., 1879-92; brevetted five times for gallantry, and awarded Congressional Medal of Honor; *m* 1861, Margaret Jane Rutter (1837-79; Nathaniel[3], of Wilkes-Barre, Pa., *m* Mary Ann Cist); *m* 2d, 1883, Maria Lindsley Orton (1837-1901), of Lawrenceville, Pa.; *m* 3d, 1905, Stella Orton Rusling (1839-1914); issue (1st marriage): I-Natalie Sedgwick (1861-1924; *m* Gen. George Alexander Forsyth, U.S.A., 1837-1915); II-Hortense Darling (*b* 1866; *m* Maj. Charles Pinckney Elliott, U.S.A.); III-Eugene Beauharnais (*b* 1868; *m* Josephine Fay White); IV-André Alden (1 above).
1-*m* Apr. 20, 1899, Elsie Peironnet Butler (1870-1920); dau. of Edmund G. Butler, of Wilkes-Barre; issue: 1-André Alden, Jr. (qv for Butler lineage); 2-Edmund Butler, *b* Harvey's Lake, Luzerne Co., Pa., Aug. 17, 1907; B.A., Yale, '28; 3-Elsie Peironnet, *b* Wilkes-Barre, May 25, 1909; Vassar, '30.
1-B.A., Yale, '94. Auditor, royalty accts., Lehigh & Wilkes-Barre Coal Co., since 1896. Mem. I.A.G., Wyo. Hist. and Geological Soc., Concordia Soc. Republican. Episcopalian. Residence: 112 Yeager Av., Forty Fort, Wilkes-Barre, Pa.

1-**BEAUMONT, André Alden, Jr.,** *b* Wilkes-Barre, Pa., Apr. 3, 1900.
8-John **Butler** (1653-1733), from Eng.; settled New London, Conn., 1682; *m* Catherine Houghton;
7-John, *b* Eng.; *m* Hannah Perkins;
6-Zebulon (1731-95), of Lyme, Conn., and Wilkes-Barre, Pa.; capt. of provincial co., of Conn., 1761; mem. expdn. against Havana, Cuba, 1762; emigrated to Wyoming Valley, Pa., 1769; lt. col. in Conn. Line, 1778, Col. Charles Webb's Regt; in command of forces which fought British and Indians at battle of Wyoming, July 3, 1778; served throughout Am. Rev.; *m* 1760, Anne Lord;
5-Lord (*b* 1770), of Wilkes-Barre; gen. of militia in Pa.; first high sheriff of Luzerne Co.; prothonotary, clk. of cts., registrar of wills, recorder; *m* Mary Pierce;
4-Lord (1806-61), civil engr., Wilkes-Barre; *m* 1830, Abi Slocum (1808-87);
3-Edmund G. (1845-1925), lawyer, Wilkes-Barre; *m* 1869, Clara Theresa Cox (1849-1916; Henry W.[4], *m* Caroline Peironnet);
2-Elsie Peironnet (1870-1920), *m* 1899, André Alden **Beaumont** (qv for Beaumont lineage).
1-*m* June 25, 1929, Cecelia Mary Casserly, *b* San Francisco, Calif., Jan. 31, 1899; dau. of John B. Casserly, of San Mateo, Calif.
1-B.A., Yale, '21; A.M., Princeton, 1922, Ph.D., 1925. Instructor history, N.Y.U., 1923-24, 25-26, asst. prof., 1927-29, asso. prof., 1929—. Mem. Am. Hist. Assn. Residence: 25 E. 9th St., New York, N.Y.

1-**BECKER, Christopher Henry,** *b* St. Louis, Mo., Oct. 9, 1851.

5–Henry **Becker** (1680-1751), from Germany to Northampton Co., Pa., 1710; *m* Anna Margret Hartmann (1685-1749);
4–Henry (1730-1804), col. Pa. troops in Am. Rev.; *m* Elizabeth Drumond (1733-1807; Donald[5], *m* a Cherokee Indian princess);
3–Henry (1760-1842), *m* Catherine Baldwin (1764-1844);
2–Carl Cornelius (1820-64), mining engr.; removed from Germantown, Pa., to St. Louis, Mo.; enlisted in Co. C, 3d Mo. Vols.; *m* at Corondelet, Mo., Elizabeth Munier (*b* Jamestown, Va., 1825-*d* San Francisco, Calif., 1881; g.dau. of Leon de Lesdernier, lt. in Am. Rev.; from Jamestown, Va.); issue: I–Christopher Henry (1 above); II–Elisa (*m* Mr. Diehl); III–Catherine (*m* Mr. Kauffmann).
1–*m* Nov. 14, 1875, Anna Margaretta Schindel (Mar. 12, 1852-1915); dau. of Philipp Schindel, of Hoch-Weisel, Hessen, Germany; issue: 1–John Otto, *b* San Francisco, Calif., Oct. 14, 1876; *m* Nov. 2, 1912, Anna Elisabeth Parker, dau. of Oskar Frederich, of Portland, Ore.; 2–Catherine A., *b* Alameda, Calif., Nov. 20, 1877; *m* July 2, 1904, Ira Earnest Noyes (issue: Anna Laura, grad. U.Calif., '28; Raymond B.); 3–Phil Sheriden, *b* Alameda, Mar. 24, 1880; *m* Mar. 25, 1909, Meta Coon Becker.
1–Received a degree in forestry from U. at Giessen, Germany (Pi Tau Sigma). Retired. Mem. S.A.R., Sons of Union Vets. of the Civil War. Residence: 52 Princess St., Sausalito, Calif.

1–**BECKETT, Mary Maltby (Mrs. Harry A.)** *b* Saybrook, O., May 17, 1875.
7–Judge William (Maltbie) **Maltby** (1645-1710), from Eng. ante 1663; to New Haven Co., Conn., 1666; to Branford, Conn., 1672; cornet of New Haven Co. troopers, 1673; sheriff, 1674 and 1679-80; collector, 1674 and 77-78; auditor, 1679-80; surveyor, 1676-82; justice, 1689-1706; admitted freeman, 1682; mem. Gen. Ct., 1686; rep., 1685-1706; commr., 1687-97; ens., Branford Train Band, 1690; owned 3 ships; 1st wife unknown; *m* 2d, post 1674, Hannah (Hosmer) Willard (living in 1689; Thomas Hosmer[8], will dated 1685); *m* 3d, 1692, Abigail Bishop;
6–Daniel (1679-1731), *m* 1702, Esther Moss (*b* 1678; John[7], of New Haven, Conn., *m* 1677, Mary Lathrop; John[8], to America, 1639);
5–Capt. Daniel (1715-76), col. in Am. Rev.; *m* 1736, Mary Harrison (*b* 1718);
4–Benjamin (1750-1847), Am. Rev.; *m* 1771, Abigail Munger (1750-1816);
3–Daniel (1793-1884), *m* 1818, Esther Gilbert Topping (1796-1873);
2–Harrison (2 below);
10–Rev. Richard **Mather** (qv);
9–Timothy (1628-84), came with father to Boston, 1635; only son to become a farmer; *m* 1st, 1650, Catherine or Elizabeth Atherton (Maj. Gen. Humphrey[10], qv);
8–Richard (1653-88), *m* 1680, Catherine Wise;
7–Lt. Joseph (1686-1749) of Lyme, Conn.; lt. in colonial army; *m* Phoebe–;
6–Joseph (1715-97), of Lyme; *m* Anna Booth;
5–Abner (1751-1838), soldier Am. Rev.; *m* 1st, 1775, Lucy Mary Lord;
4–Lucy (1781-1861), *m* 1799, Capt. Edward Wells **Hinman,** organized a co. bearing his name in War of 1812;
3–Eunice (1807-75), *m* 1830, Thomas **Hough** (Bezaliel[4]; Thomas[5]; Daniel[6]; James[7]; Samuel[8]; William[9]);
2–Emily Adelia (*b* Atwater, O., 1839-*d* Long Beach, Calif., 1922), *m* 1860, Harrison **Maltby** (*b* Southington, O., 1830-*d* Long Beach, Calif., 1914); issue: I–Minda (*b* 1862; *m* Thomas J. Osborne); II–Albert Sylvester (*b* 1865; *m* Eliza Leahy); III–Helen (1870-93; *m* Rev. Franklin Lewis); IV–Stella (*b* 1873; *m* Louis C. Hinman, *d*); V–Mary (1 above); VI–Benjamin, D.D.S. (*b* 1879; *m* Caroline Almy); VII–Ruth (*b* 1885; *m* Harrison Moore).
1–*m* Aug. 27, 1904, Harry Andrew Beckett, *b* Butler Co., Pa., Mar. 12, 1874; S.A.R.; atty. at law; son of William Beckett, of Cleveland, O., *m* Mary Reinhart McCaslin; issue: 1–Herbert Maltby, *b* Cleveland, O., June 9, 1905; Ed. Dartmouth, and U.Mich., '28; *m* June 19, 1926, Aurel Grace, dau. of Robert Fowler, of Cleveland; 2–Dorothea, *b* Lakewood, O., May 18, 1909; Ohio Wesleyan, '31; 3–Margaret, and 4–Donald Harrison (twins), *b* Lakewood, May 10, 1912 (Donald H., *d* Mar. 11, 1915).
1–Grad. Grand River Inst., '94; normal course, Berea (Ky.) Coll., 1896. Mem. D.F.P.A., Women Descendants A. and H.A.Co., D.A.C. (state registrar for Ohio, 1925-27), D.A.R. (regent Western Reserve Chapter, 1926-28), U.S.D. 1812, Soc. New Eng. Women. Residence: 1307 Manor Park, Lakewood, O.

1–**BECKWITH, Constance Dickinson,** *b* Chicago, Ill., Apr. 6, 1871.
9–Richard **Seymour** (qv);
8–John (1641-1713), freeman at Hartford, 1667; *m* Mary Watson (John[9], *m* Margaret–);
7–John (1666-1748), *m* 1693, Elizabeth Webster (*d* 1754; Robert[8], *m* Susanna, dau. of Richard Treat, qv; Gov. John[9], qv);
6–John (*b* 1694), *m* 2d, 1733, Hannah Ensign (*b* 1712; David[7]; David[8]; James[9]);
5–Elias (*b* 1738), served in Am. Rev.; *m* ca. 1767, Tryphena Hurlbut (*b* 1745; Dr. Josiah[6]; Jonathan[7]; Samuel[8]; Thomas[9]);
4–Josiah Hurlbut (1769-1829), *m* ca. 1796, Fanny Bradley;
3–Harriet Angeline (1807-1910), *m* 1834, Asahel Lane **Beckwith** (see Vol. II, p. 265, for Beckwith lineage);
2–Albert Clayton (2 below).
8–Stephen **Bradley** (1642-1702), *m* 1st, 1663, Hannah Smith (George[9], of New Haven);
7–Stephen (1668-1701/02), *m* Sarah Ward (*b* 1674; Andrew[8], *m* Tryal Meigs; Andrew[9], *m* Esther Sherman);
6–Stephen (1696-1782), *m* 1718, Jemima Cornwall, of L.I.;
5–Timothy (1735-1806), *m* ca. 1765, Esther Shipman;
4–Fanny (1775-1841), *m* Josiah H. **Seymour** (4 above).
9–Edward **Shipman** (qv);
8–John (1664-1705?), *m* 1686, Martha Humphrey (*b* 1663; Michael[9], qv);
7–John (1687-1742), of Saybrook, Conn.; *m* 1715, Elizabeth Kirtland (1688-1778; Lt. John[8]; Nathaniel[9]; Philip[10]);
6–Samuel (*b* 1726), *m* 1st, 1745, Sarah Doty;
5–Esther (1746-1826), *m* Timothy **Bradley** (5 above).
10–William **Carpenter** (qv);
9–Joseph (1633-75), *m* 1655, Margaret Sutton (John[10]);
8–Benjamin (1658-1727), *m* Renew Weeks (1660-1703; William[9]; George[10]);
7–Jotham (1682-1760), *m* 1st, 1707, Desire Martin (1684/85-1727; John[8], *m* Mercy Billington [Francis[9]; John[10], Mayflower Pilgrim, qv]; Richard[9]);
6–Desire (*b* 1716), *m* 1738, Hezekiah **Hicks** (son of James or John Hicks[7], sons of Ephraim[8], *m* 2d, Hannah Wells; Daniel[9]);
5–Dea. Gideon (*b* 1752), of Taunton, Mass., and E. Calais, Vt.; *m* 1774, Selah Williams;
4–Eleanor (*d* 1845), *m* 1805, John **Dickinson** (see Vol. III, p. 511, for Dickinson lineage);
3–Nathaniel (1810-83), mem. Wis. Constl. Conv., 1846; capt. 4th Wis. militia; *m* 1841, Phila Foster;
2–Isadore Adelaide (2 below).
10–Richard **Williams;**
9–Samuel, *m* Mary Gilbert;
8–Seth (1676-1761), Taunton, Mass.; *m* Mary Dean (John[9]; John[10]);
7–James (1703-79), Taunton; *m* 1722, Sarah Barney (*b* 1705-living at Bristol, R.I., 1738; Dep. John[8], *m* Mary, dau. of Dea. William Throop; Jacob[9]; Jacob[10]);
6–Joshua (ca. 1732-1760), Taunton; *m* Ruth Reed;
5–Selah, *m* Gideon **Hicks** (5 above).
9–William **Reed** (qv);
8–John (*d* 1721, aet. 72), *m* Bethia Fry (*d* 1730; George[9]);
7–George (*d* 1765), *m* Sarah Whitmarsh (*b* 1701; Samuel[8] [1665-1718], *m* Hannah Pratt; Nicholas[9], *m* Hannah, dau. of William Reed, qv);
6–Ruth (1727-70), *m* Joshua **Williams** (6 above).
10–Rev. Thomas **Foster,** from Eng.; *m* Abigail Wimes (Matthew[11]);
9–Sgt. Thomas (ca. 1600-1682), came in 1634; *m* ca. 1638, Elizabeth– (*d* 1694/95);
8–Dea. John (1642-82), *m* 1st, 1663, Mary Chillingsworth (*d* 1702; Thomas[9], at Lynn, Mass., 1637, rep. Gen. Ct., *m* Joanna–);
7–Dea. Chillingsworth (1680-1764), *m* 2d, Susannah (Gray) Sears (*d* 1730; John Gray[8]);
6–Nathaniel (*b* 1725), Am. Rev.; *m* 1st, 1746, Phebe Wing (*b* 1726/27; John[7] [1680-1758], *m* 3d, Widow

Rebecca Freeman Vickerie [*b* 1694; Dea. Thomas Freeman[8]; Maj. John[9]; Edmund[10], qv]; John[8]; John[9]; John[10], qv);
5–Sgt. Thomas, of Kent, Conn.; *m* 2d, Hannah Bliss, both of Kent, Conn.;
4–Artemas (1781-1854), *m* Priscilla Titus (see Vol. III, p. 511, for Titus lineage);
3–Phila (1815-73), *m* Nathaniel **Dickinson** (3 above);
2–Isadore Adelaide (1844-1915), *m* 1870, Albert Clayton **Beckwith** (1836-1915), settled at Elkhorn, Wis., 1856; pvt. and corpl., 1st Ia. Baty., 1861-63; postmaster; editor and genealogist of Beckwith Genealogy; issue: I–Constance (1 above); II–Mabel Foster (*b* 1876).
Dickinson (1 above); II–Mabel Foster (*b* 1876).
1–Ed. Whitewater (Wis.) State Normal School. Public school teacher. Mem. D.A.R., I.A.G. Residence: 301 Randall Pl., Elkhorn, Wis.

1–**BEEBE, Louise Tice Palmer (Mrs. Clyde Albert),** *b* Pittsford, Mich., Mar. 27, 1883.
9–Walter **Palmer** (qv);
8–Dea. Gershom (*d* 1718), of Stonington; *m* 1667, Ann Denison (1649-94; Capt. George[9]);
7–Capt. Ichabod (1677-1752), of Stonington; *m* 1697, his cousin, Hanna Palmer (*b* 1680; Nehemiah[8], *m* Hannah, dau. Thomas Stanton; Walter, 9 above);
6–Lt. Ichabod (1702-49), of Stonington; *m* 1728, Elizabeth Noyes (1706-60; Capt. Thomas[7], *m* Elizabeth, dau. Gov. Peleg Sanford; Rev. James[8], a founder of Yale Coll.; James[9], qv);
5–Col. Elias Sanford (1742-1821), of Stonington; officer in 4th Co., 4th Bn., Cont. Army; served on L.I. in Am. Rev.; *m* 1761, his cousin, Phebe Palmer (1742-93; Dr. Joseph[6]);
4–Noyes (1771-1853), of Stonington; *m* 2d, 1813, Hanna Babcock;
3–James Monroe (1817-95), of Lyndonville, N.Y.; *m* 1841, Louisa Tice (1819-82);
2–Charles Bingham (2 below).
9–Edward (Elmer) **Elmore** (1625-76; son of Samuel, high sheriff, Suffolk Co., Eng.; g.son of John, Bishop of London); came from Eng. in the "Lion," to Cambridge, Mass., 1632; owned Harvard Sq.; a founder of Hartford, Conn., 1636; killed in King Philip's War; *m* Elizabeth–;
8–Samuel (1649-91);
7–Jonathan (1686-1758);
6–David (1736-89), began to write name Elmore; *m* Jemima Curtis (*d* 1784);
5–Eliakin (1764-1834), of LeRoy, N.Y.;
4–Jonathan J. (1805-92), of Bergen, N.Y.;
3–Montraville Hulburt (1828-1904), of Sanborn, N.Y.; *m* 1849, Geraldine Alma Smith (*d* 1891);
2–Esmeralda Viola (1850-1886), *m* 1880, Charles Bingham **Palmer** (1848-1913), carriage maker; issue: I–Louise T. (1 above); II–Burr Hurlbut (*d* infancy).
1–*m* Dec. 23, 1903, Clyde Albert Beebe, *b* Mendon, Mich., June 8, 1883; son of Albert Beebe, of Mendon; issue: 1–Palmer E., *b* Mendon, Mich., Jan. 19, 1907; Culver Mil. Acad., 1924; Mich. State Coll., 1927-28; *m* Apr. 20, 1929, Elizabeth Hiler, of Benton Harbor, Mich.; 2–Neva Louise, *b* Mendon, Mich., May 17, 1909; Olivet Coll.; Acad. Fine Arts, Chicago, Ill., 1 yr.
1–Taught dist. sch., 2 yrs. Mem. D.F.P.A., D.A.R. (chapter regent), Y.W.C.A. (trustee 4 yrs.). Conglist. Republican. Clubs: Ossoli, Fed. Women's (dir.), Eleanor (trustee). Residence: 617 Pipestone St., Benton Harbor, Mich.

1–**BEEBE, Ethelyn Church Mason (Mrs. Frederick),** *b* Logansport, Ind., Dec. 15, 1874.
8–Arthur **Mason** (*b* 1631), from Eng., 1639; settled at Boston, Mass.; "biscake baker"; constable; *m* 1655, Joanna Parker (1635-1708; Nicholas[9], *m* Ann–);
7–Arthur (1674-ante 1725), mariner or baker, Boston; *m* 1701, Mary Stoddard (*d* 1746; Sampson[8]; Anthony[9], qv, *m* Mary, dau. Emand Downing, *m* 1638, Lucy, sister of Gov. Winthrop);
6–Sampson (1705-ante 1746), glazier, Boston; *m* 1731, Mary Brightman, widow;
5–Sampson (ca. 1733-ca. 1795), boatbuilder, Boston; matross in Am. Rev., Capt. Jonathan Stoddard's Co., Col. Thomas Craft's (arty.) Regt.; *m* 1759, Abigail Stone (William[6]);
4–Sampson Alden (*d* ca. 1807), boatbuilder, Boston; buried Copps Hill Burying Ground; *m* 2d, 1804, Elizabeth (Douglas) Hunt;
3–Sampson (1805-78), of Boston; *m* 1833, Mary White Church;
2–Sampson Douglas (2 below).
10–William **White** (qv);
8–Peregrine (*b* 1660), of Middleborough, Mass.; *m* Susanne–, of Weymouth;
7–Mark (1689-1758), of Middleborough, Charlestown, Concord and Westford, Mass.; *m* 1712, Susannah–;
6–Dea. Mark (1716-98), of Acton, Mass.; *m* 1st, 1742, Anna Chamberlain (1720-55);
5–Marah (1755-94), of Acton; *m* 1779, Ebenezer **Heald** (1754-1814), served in Acton Co. of Minute Men in Am. Rev., responding to Alarm of Apr. 19, 1775 (John[6], Am. Rev.);
4–Elizabeth, of Hubbardston, Mass.; *m* 1803, Benjamin **Church** (1776-1806; Asa[5], sgt., q.m. sgt. under Capt. Thomas Eustis, in Am. Rev.);
3–Mary White (1804-76), of Concord; *m* Sampson **Mason** (3 above).
5–Daniel **Wunderlich** (1737-99), from Würtemberg, Germany, 1753; settled in Pa.; *m* 1763, Eva Barbara Sienchele (1744-1821);
4–John David (1775-1840), of Pa.; *m* 1802, Mary Magdalene Titzel (1778-1864);
3–Simon (1821-69), of Ind.; *m* 1st, Sarah Grable (1831-59);
2–Emma Jane (1854-87), *m* 1873, Sampson Douglas **Mason** (1849-1923), of Ft. Worden, Wash.; issue: I–Ethelyn Church (1 above); II–Sherman Hurd (*b* 1880; *m* 1910, Francesca Pauline Weaver); III–Marian Jane (*b* 1884); IV–Roy Skinner (*b* 1886; *m* 1910, Ethel Coblentz).
1–*m* June 23, 1896, Frederick Beebe (Mar. 14, 1866-Nov. 11, 1927); son of Gaylord DeWitt Beebe, of Chicago, Ill.; no issue; adopted dau. Faith Eleanor, *b* Kent, Wash., Mar. 5, 1913.
1–Ed. Annie Wright Sem., Tacoma, Wash. Mem. D.A.R. Club: Athena. Presbyterian. Republican. Residence: 2120 N. Anderson St., Tacoma, Wash.

1–**BEEBE, Hiram Ernest,** *b* Ipswich, S.D., Feb. 7, 1886.
11–John **Beebe** (*d* 1650), *d* on shipboard from Eng.; *m* Rebecca–;
10–John (*b* 1628), lt. in Indian wars; *m* Abigal York (*b* 1638), of Stonington, Conn.;
9–John (1661-96);
8–Joseph (*b* 1684), *m* 1706, Elizabeth Graves;
7–Lt. Jonathan (1709-59), *m* Hannah Lewis;
6–Ira (1735-92), lt. Am. Rev.; *m* Jemima Hicock;
5–Eli (*b* 1759), *m* 1776, Elizabeth Baldwin;
4–Charles (1788-1874), *m* 1811, Elizabeth Train (1795-1881);
3–Hiram (1812-85), *m* 1834, Lucretia Jackson (1815-65);
2–Marcus Plin (1854-1914), of Sandusky, N.Y.; *m* 1875, Leota Frances Fuller (*b* 1865; George Alonzo[3] N.Y. to Ia.; served in Civil War, buried in Soldier's Cemetery, Cairo, Ill., *m* Emily Beede, of Eagle, N.Y.); issue: I–Inez E. (*m* Elwood C. Perisho); II–Gertrude L. (*m* Norman T. Mears); III–M. Plin (*m* Alice C. Conklin); IV–Hiram E. (1 above); V–Marjorie L. (*m* A. Lyman Beardsley).
1–*m* July 9, 1913, Lucy Valentine, *b* White, S.D., May 27, 1889; dau. of W. A. Valentine, of White, S.D.; issue: 1–Beatrice May, *b* Ipswich, S.D., May 17, 1921; 2–Edward Richard, *b* Ipswich, Sept. 30, 1923.
1–B.S. (M.E.), U. of S.D., '07 (Phi Delta Theta); B.S. (E.E.), M.I.T., 1910, A.B., 1911. V.p., Bank of Ipswich, S.D. Adj. State University Cadet Corps; co. chmn. Liberty Loan campaigns. Club: Hamilton (Chicago). Residence: Ipswich, S.D.

1–**BEERY, Joseph E.,** *b* Lancaster, O., Aug. 21, 1861.
5–Abraham **Beery** (1718-99), from Switzerland to Phila., Pa., 1736; *m* Mary Cochenour (*d* 1800);
4–John (1767-1834), *m* 1792, Barbara Kagay (1768-1865);
3–Daniel (1798-1873), *m* 1820, Anna Huffman (1794-1855);
2–Frederick (1822-69), farmer; *m* 1843, Elizabeth Warner (1825-1904; Joseph[3] [1794-1875], *m* Susanna Stoneburner); issue: I–Susan (1845-1917; *m* John W. McLaughlin, *d*); II–Mary Ann (*b* 1849; *m* John Kanode, *d*); III–Dr. L. W. (*b* 1852; *m* Ann Reber); IV–Maria (*b* 1853); V–D. F. (1856-1910; *m* Mary Graham, *d*); VI–

Joseph E. (1 above); VII–Ida E. (*b* 1864; *m* Isaac N. Miesse, *d*); VIII–James A. (*b* 1866; *m* Martha Strople).
1–*m* June 22, 1887, Frankie Blair, *b* Mantua, O., Sept. 6, 1863; dau. of Chauncy Blair, of Mantua, O.; issue: 1–Florence, *b* Columbus, O., Apr. 5, 1888; *m* Dec. 27, 1923, Dr. Edward H. Eldridge (issue: Joseph B.); 2–Jean Ingelo, *b* Columbus, Nov. 4, 1895; *m* Jan. 21, 1920, Howard Cole Ginn, 2d lt, 329th Inf., 83d Div., Camp Sherman, O., and Ft. Sill, Okla., Aug. 15, 1917-May 15, 1918, promoted to 1st lt., Mar. 1919; served with A.E.F. in France, May 16, 1918-Aug. 1st, 1919 (issue: Adelaide).
1–M.D., U.Cincinnati, '86. Physician. Mem. I.A.G., etc. Residence: 802 W. Broad St., Columbus, O.

1–**BELL, Clara M. Greer (Mrs. Edgar Lee),** *b* Ft. Wayne, Ind., Sept. 24, 1870.
10–Thomas **Rogers,** Mayflower Pilgrim (qv);
9–John (*d* 1691), lived at Plymouth, Mass., 1631, at Duxbury, 1634; rep. Gen. Ct.; *m* 1639, Ann Churchman;
8–Abigail (1641-1727), *m* John **Richmond** (ca. 1627-1715; John[9], qv);
7–Edward (1665-1741), King Philip's War; dep. R.I. Assembly; *m* 1st, Mercy–;
6–Nathaniel (ca. 1700-1763), killed in Louisburg Expdn.; *m* 1732, Alice Hackett (*b* 1715; John[7], *m* Elizabeth Elliott);
5–Gideon (*d* 1801), served in Am. Rev.; *m* 1760, Hannah Richmond;
4–Rev. Edmund (1780-1861), Bapt. minister, 1808; preached at Milford, N.Y., 20 yrs.; removed to Rome, O., 1829, where a ch. was built for him; *m* 1st, 1801, Ruth Leaming (1780-1838; Judah[5], *m* Thankful Tuttle);
3–Ruth Lovina (1812-89), *m* 1829, Chauncey Collins **Walkley** (1810-92), of Greene, Noble Co., Ind.; justice of the peace, 1847-57; (David[4]);
2–Ruth Lovina (2 below).
9–Richard **Williams** (*b* 1606), *b* in Wales; came to Salem, Mass., 1633; *m* Frances Dighton;
8–Elizabeth (1647-1724), *m* John **Bird** (1642-1732; Thomas[9]);
7–Dighton, *m* Isaac (Myrick, Merrick) **Mirick;**
6–Dighton, *m* John **Richmond;**
5–Hannah (*d* 1780), *m* Gideon **Richmond** (5 above).
2–Ruth Lovina Walkley (*b* 1850), *m* 1869, John W. **Greer** (1845-1912).
1–*m* June 28, 1904, Edgar Lee Bell, *b* Coshocton Co., O., July 5, 1867; son of Rev. Thomas Hamilton Dunn Bell, Methodist Minister, Coshocton Co., O.; issue: 1–Richmond T., *b* Milwaukee, Wis., Oct. 9, 1905; B.S. in Chemistry, U. Wis., '27 (Pi Kappa Alpha, Alpha Chi Sigma); Ph.D. in Chemistry, U.Va. (Sigma Xi); mem. faculty U.Va.; lt., Field Arty., U.S.A.; Mason; Episcopalian; mem. S.M.D., S.A.R., Scabbard and Blade.
1–Mem. bd. dirs., Industrial Sch. for Girls, and A.R.C., Milwaukee. Chmn. of a group of 50 rep. women war workers of Milwaukee during the World War. Mem. S.M.D., D.A.R. (organizer and charter mem. Mary Penrose Wayne Chapter, Ft. Wayne, Ind.; rec. sec., Milwaukee Chapter, 6 yrs.), I.A.G. V.p. Christian Endeavor Soc. of Tabernacle Bapt. Ch. Club: Social Economics (advisory chmn.). Residence: 254 24th St., Milwaukee, Wis.

1–**BELL, Clara Carlton Preston (Mrs. William B.),** *b* Elkader, Ia., Aug. 21, 1880.
10–Edward (Carleton) **Carlton** (qv);
9–Lt. John (1630-68), *m* Hannah Jewett (1640-post 1695; Joseph[10], qv);
8–Edward (1664-1711), *m* Elizabeth Kimball (1670-1716; Benjamin[9], *m* Mercie, dau. of Robert Hazelton; Richard[10]);
7–Edward (*b* 1690), *m* Hannah Kimball (1691-1732; Richard[8]; Thomas[9]; Richard[10], qv);
6–Richard (1713-58), began to write name Carlton; *m* 1738, Hannah Hutchins (*b* 1717; Samuel[7], *m* Hannah Marrill);
5–Caleb (1757-1823), *m* 1779, Margaret Day;
4–Peter (1787-1861), served in War 1812; *m* 1810, Clarissa Ladd (1789-1882; Daniel[5], Am. Rev.);
3–Caleb Day (1815-67), *m* 1st, 1839, Julia Hine;
2–Julia Lucinda (2 below).
10–Robert **Day** (qv);
9–John (*d* ca. 1730), *m* Sarah Maynard, of Hartford;
8–John (1677-1752), *m* 1st, 1696, Grace Spencer (1674-1714; Samuel[9], *m* 1st, Hannah [Willey] Hungerford Beachford, dau. of Isaac Willey; Ens. Gerard[10], qv);
7–Benjamin (1704-77), *m* 1729, Margaret Foote;
6–Adonijah (1733-99), *m* Sarah Loomis;
5–Margaret (1758-1810), *m* Caleb **Carlton** (5 above).
11–Nathaniel **Foote** (qv);
10–Nathaniel (1620-55), *m* 1646, Elizabeth Smith (Lt. Samuel[11], of Wethersfield, Conn.);
9–Nathaniel (1647-1703), soldier in King Philip's War; *m* 1672, Margaret Bliss (Nathaniel[10]; Thomas[11], qv);
8–Ephraim (1685-1765), *m* 1708, Sarah Chamberlain;
7–Margaret (1711-1801), *m* Benjamin **Day** (7 above).
10–Joseph **Loomis** (qv);
9–Nathaniel (ca. 1626-1688), freeman, 1654, admitted to the ch., 1663; mem. Windsor Troop of Horse in King Philip's War; *m* in 1653, Elizabeth Moore (*b* 1638; Dea. John[10], *m* Abigail Moore);
8–Josiah (1660-61-1735), removed to E. Windsor, Conn., 1700; *m* 1683, Mary Rockwell (1662/63-1738; Samuel[9], *m* Mary Norton);
7–Lt. Caleb (1693-1784), *m* 1728, Joannah Skinner (Dea. John[8], *m* Sarah–);
6–Sarah (1734-1802), *m* 1753, Adonijah **Day** (6 above).
8–Thomas **Hine** (*d* 1696), at Milford, Conn., 1640;
7–John (1656-1739), *m* Elizabeth–;
6–John (1686-post 1740), *m* 2d, Mehitable Waters;
5–Abraham (1728-1811), *m* Sarah Bristol;
4–Aaron (1777-1854), *m* Bethia or Thyra Hitchcock;
3–Julia (1815-54), *m* Caleb D. **Carlton** (3 above).
9–Matthias **Hitchcock** (qv);
8–Nathaniel, *m* 1670, Elizabeth Moss (1652-1706; John[9]);
7–Ebenezer (1689-estate administered 1726), *m* Anna Perkins;
6–Ebenezer (1717-estate administered 1764), *m* Rebecca Thomas;
5–Timothy (1748-1820), *m* Abigail Clark;
4–Bethia (1784-1841), *m* Aaron **Hine** (4 above);
3–Julia, *m* Caleb D. **Carlton** (3 above);
2–Julia Lucinda (*b* 1848), *m* 1870, William Alexander **Preston** (1839-1920; James Isaac[3], of Prairie de Rouche, Ill., fought in Black Hawk War); issue: I–Mary Elizabeth (1871-1919; *m* 1896, Dr. Willis LeRoy Stearns); II–Donna (1872-95); III–Clara C. (1 above).
1–*m* Sept. 5, 1906, William Bonar Bell, *b* Milton, Ia., June 2, 1877; son of Robert Pollock Bell, *m* Isabell Bonar, of Milton, Ia., formerly of Mansfield, O.; issue: 1–Julia Carlton, *b* Fargo, N.D., Jan. 7, 1911; 2–David Bonar, *b* Fargo, Nov. 16, 1913.
1–Ph.B., U. Ia., '04. Mem. D.F.P.A., D.A.C., D.A.R., Summer place: McGregor Heights, Ia. Residence: 803 Rittenhouse St., Washington, D.C.

1–**BENEDICT, Walter Lewis,** *b* Brooklyn, N.Y., July 30, 1878.
10–Thomas **Benedict** (qv);
9–John (1640-post 1727), of Southold, L.I.; selectman; dea.; rep. to Gen. Ct.; *m* 1670, Phoebe Gregory;
8–Benjamin (*d* 1773); removed to Ridgefield, thence to Stamford, Conn.; selectman; 3d dea.; *m* Mary– (*d* 1771);
7–Amos (1722-1809), removed from Norwalk to S. Salem; *m* Martha Sturtevant;
6–Solomon (1776-1803), of Ridgefield, Conn.; *m* Abigail Rundell (*d* 1798);
5–Solomon, *m* Hannah Benedict (Joseph[6]; Col. Joseph[7], served as maj. and lt. col. during Am. Rev.);
4–Jesse (*b* 1797), *m* 1818, Esther Keeler (*b* 1799);
3–Lewis (1826-97), *m* 1847, Mary Esther Avery (1829-67), of N.Y.;
2–Lewis Hanford (1849-1927), of Brooklyn, N.Y.; removed to Minneapolis, Minn.; *m* 1870, Emma Lewis Kellogg (1849-1928), of S. Salem, Conn.; issue: I–Clarence Kellogg (1872-77); II–Edith May (1874-82); III–Walter L. (1 above); IV–Robert Kellogg (*b* and *d* 1882); V–May Emma (*b* 1888; *m* Charles Harrison).
1–*m* Sept. 17, 1902, Mary Daniel (**qv for genealogy and issue**).
1–B.S., U. Minn., '99 (Sigma Chi). **Traffic mgr.** of Washburn Crosby Co. Mason (32°), Conglist. Republican. Clubs: **Automobile, Traffic.** Residence: 4657 Aldrich Av. S., Minneapolis, Minn.

1–**BENEDICT, Mary Daniel (Mrs. Walter Lewis),** *b* Portland, Me., Oct. 2, 1876.
10–William **Crocker** (qv);
9–? William (1634-92);
8–? Eleazer (*b* 1651), *m* 1682, Ruth Chipman (1663-98; John[9], qv);
7–Abel (*b* 1695), *m* 1718, Mary Isum;
6–Daniel (*b* 1723), *m* — Morton;
5–Roland (1757-1839), served in Mass. line, Am. Rev., corp. marines, in Penobscot Expdn.; signed assn. test; *m* 1780, Mehitable Merrill;
4–Thomas (1788-1872), lt., War 1812; *m* 1816, Clarissa Stowell;
3–Mary (1822-1909), *m* 1845, Jessie Phillips **Daniel** (1825-67);
2–Thomas William (2 below).
10–Nathaniel **Merrill** (qv);
9–Nathaniel (*b* 1638), *m* 1661, Joanna Ninian (Ninney);
8–John (*b* 1663); *m* 1st, Lucy Webster (1664-1718; John[9], *m* Ann Batt);
7–John (1696-1773), settled at Haverhill, Mass.; dea., 1730; kept first ferry across the Merrimack River; *m* 1723, Lydia Haines;
6–Thomas (1724-88), lt., French and Indian War, 1756; signed assn. test; *m* Mehitable Harriman;
5–Mehitable (1766-1856), *m* Roland **Crocker** (5 above).
9–Rev. John **Spofford** (1612-78), *m* Elizabeth Scott (*b* 1625), of Ipswich, Mass.;
8–Samuel (1653-1749), of Rowley, Mass.; *m* 1676, Sarah Birkee (*d* 1729);
7–Mehitable (*b* 1678), *m* 1720, Nathaniel **Harriman;**
6–Mehitable (*b* 1727), *m* Thomas **Merrill** (6 above).
9–Samuel **Stowell** (qv);
8–David (1660-1724), of Watertown, Mass.; *m* 2d, 1692, Mary Stedman (1678-1724);
7–John (1709-62), *m* 1722, Sarah Ford;
6–Benjamin (1730-1802), selectman, Worcester, 1776; served in Am. Rev.; *m* Elizabeth Parker (1733-1821);
5–William (1756-1829), served in Am. Rev.; *m* 1781, Kate Nixon (1758-1842), of Framingham, Mass.;
4–Clarissa (1794-1843), *m* Thomas **Crocker** (4 above).
12–Richard **Warren** (qv);
11–Mary (1612-76), *m* Robert **Bartlett** (qv);
10–Rebecca (1633-57), *m* 1649, William **Harlow** (1624-91), Selectman and Deputy from Plymouth to Gen. Court of Colony of Plymouth, Mass.;
9–Samuel (1652-1734), *m* 1685, Hannah– (*d* same day as husband, 1734);
8–John (1685-1771), *m* 1706, Martha Delano (1680-1794; Philip[9], qv);
7–John (1707-80), *m* 1731, Mary Rider (1716-79);
6–Sylvanus (1738-99), capt. during Am. Rev.; town treas. for many years; *m* 1758, Desire Sampson (1738-96);
5–Desire (1767-1800), *m* 1790, Capt. Samuel **Stephens** (*b* 1767; Edward[6], *m* Phoebe Harlow);
4–Desire (1798-1869), *m* 1819, Artemus **Felt** (1800-85), of Woodstock, Me.;
3–Samuel Stephens (1832-1901), of Greenwood, Me.; *m* 1850, Martha Clark (1829-92);
2–Helen Medora (qv for genealogy), *m* 1874, Thomas William **Daniel** (*b* 1850).
1–*m* Sept. 17, 1902, Walter Lewis Benedict (qv for genealogy); issue: 1–Alice May, *b* Minneapolis, Minn., June 13, 1906; *m* Aug. 19, 1925, Walter Vernon Brown, *b* Oct. 10, 1899, son of George Andrew Brown, of Minneapolis (issue: Jean Marie, *b* Nov. 5, 1928).
1–B.A., U.Minn., '99 (Delta Delta Delta). Mem. D.F.P.A., S.M.D., D.A.C., D.A.R., U.S.D. 1812, Minn. Hist. Soc. Conglist. Republican. Clubs: Woman's (Minneapolis), Ladies' Thursday Musical. Residence: 4657 Aldrich Av. S., Minneapolis, Minn.

1–**DANIEL, Helen Medora Felt (Mrs. Thomas William),** *b* Portland, Me., Mar. 4, 1854.
8–George **Felt** (1601-82), from Eng. with John Endicott, 1628; settled at Salem; home destroyed 3 times by Indians; a founder of Charlestown, Mass., and an early settler of Boston, *m* Elizabeth Wilkinson (1601-94; Widow Prudence[9]);
7–Moses (*b* 1651), *m* Hannah Maine;
6–Aaron Felt (1715-69), of Lynn, Mass; *m* 1739, Mercy Waite (1717-60);
5–Sgt. Peter Felt (1745-1817), Temple, N.H.; Am. Rev.; *m* 1769, Lucy Andrews (1748-1805), of Ipswich;
4–Joshua (1773-1812), Woodstock, Me.; *m* 1794, Lucy Spofford;
3–Artemus (1800-85), *m* 1819, Desire Stephens;
2–Samuel Stephens (2 below).
9–Rev. John **Spoffard** (1612-78), Vicar of Silkestone, from Yorkshire, Eng.; settled in Newbury and Ipswich, Mass.; 1st settler of Georgetown, Mass.; *m* Elizabeth Scott (*b* 1625), of Ipswich;
8–John (1648-96), *m* 1675, Sarah Wheeler (*d* 1732);
7–Jonathan (1684-1772), *m* Jemima Freethe, of York, Me.;
6–David (*b* 1710), Am. Rev.; mem. Com. Correspondence and Safety; *m* 1735, Hannah Cheney (*d* 1755), of Rowley, Mass.;
5–Sgt. Eldad (1745-1809), Am. Rev.; *m* 1768, Lucy Spaulding (*d* 1837);
4–Lucy (1777-1841), *m* Joshua **Felt** (4 above).
11–James **Chilton** (qv);
10–Mary (1608-79), came with father; *m* 1627, John **Winslow** (qv);
9–Mary (1630-78), *m* 1650, Edward **Gray** (*d* 1663), to America, 1621;
8–Desire (1651-90), *m* Capt. Nathaniel **Southworth** (1648-1710; Constant[9], qv);
7–Mary (*b* 1676-1757), *m* 1706, Joseph **Rider** (1671-1766);
6–Jemima (*b* 1712), *m* 1733, Noah **Sampson** (1704-40?; Nathaniel[7], *m* Keturah Chandler; Abraham[8], *m* Lorah, dau. Alexander Standish, *m* Sarah, dau. John Alden, qv; g.dau. Capt. Myles Standish, qv);
5–Desire (1738-96), *m* 1758, Sylvanus **Harlow** (1738-99), Am. Rev.;
4–Desire (1767-1800), *m* 1790, Capt. Samuel **Stephens** (*b* 1767), War 1812;
3–Desire (1798-1869), *m* Artemus **Felt** (3 above).
9–Edward **Small,** came with Ferdinando Gorges, ca. 1632; settled at Piscataqua; magistrate, 1645; removed to Dover, N.H.;
8–Francis (1620-1713), lived in Falmouth, Me., 1657; bought land from Indian chief, Scitterygusset; at Kittery, Me., 1668, had house and trading camp where Cornish now stands; Indians sold him entire Ossipee tract of land to make good their debt to him, 1668; *m* Elizabeth Leighton;
7–Samuel (1666-1738), *m* 1694, Elizabeth Heard Chadbourn;
6–Dea. Samuel (1700-92), 3d and last owner of the famous Ossipee lands; 1st dea. Congl. Ch., Scarboro, Me., 1728; clk., Scarboro, 1727-, served 52 yrs.; selectman; moderator, 1786; mem. Com. of Correspondence, Inspection and Safety, aet. 78; mem. conv. at Cambridge, to form a state govt., aet. 79; *m* 1717, Anna Hatch (*b* 1700);
5–Joshua (1725-1803), *m* 1744, Susanna Kinnard, of Kittery, Me.;
4–Lucy (1763-1827), *m* 1785, Ephraim **Clark** (1756-1847), seaman, privateer "Dolton," Am. Rev.; prisoner, 1776-79; served 1779-81; prisoner again, 1781-82; at Kittery, Me., 1784; settled in Limington, Me.;
3–Nathaniel (1786-1850), of Kittery, Me.; War 1812; *m* Mary Adams (1795-1869);
2–Martha (1829-92), of Limington, Me.; *m* 1850, Samuel Stephens **Felt** (1832-1901), removed to Greenwood, Me.; issue: I–George (1852-1920); II–Frederick (*b* and *d* 1853); III–Helen Medora (1 above); IV–Estella (1856-95); V–Alice May (1864-1923; *m* George Cross, *d* 1924); VI–Elizabeth (*b* 1867; *m* Henry Cummings).
1–*m* Oct. 29, 1874, Thomas William Daniel, *b* Auburn, Miss., July 16, 1850; son of Jessie Phillips Daniel, of Lafayette, Ala.; issue: 1–Thomas Lester, *b* Aug. 12, 1875; grad. U.Minn., '01 (Sigma Chi); mech. engr.; 2–Mary (Mrs. Walter Lewis Benedict, qv for other lineages).
1–Mem. S.M.D., D.F.P.A., D.A.R., U.S.D. 1812. Residence: 4657 Aldrich Av. S., Minneapolis, Minn.

1–**BENNETT, Russell White,** *b* Buffalo, N.Y., Apr. 9, 1871.
10–William **Pynchon** (qv);
9–Maj. John (1626-1703), "most worshipful maj."; lt. Springfield Co., 1653; capt. Hampshire Co. Troop of Horse, 1663; capt. expdn. against the Dutch, 1664; maj. Hampshire Regt., 1671; dep. Gen. Ct., 1659, 1662-64; asst., 1665-86 and 1693-

1702/03; commr. to Mohawks, 1680; magistrate, 1652-55; councillor, 1686-89; judge Ct. Common Pleas; judge Probate Ct.; *m* 1645, Amy Wyllys (1625-99; Gov. George[10], qv);
8–Col. John (1647-1721), capt. Hampshire Troop; maj. King Philip's War; rep. Gen. Ct., 1709-14; councillor, 1715-16; judge Ct. of Common Pleas, 1710-21; *m* Margaret Hubbard (*d* 1716; Rev. William[9], historian of Ipswich, Mass.);
7–Col. John (1674-1742), *m* 1702, Bathshua Taylor (1683-1710; Rev. Edward[8], qv);
6–William (1703-83), of Springfield; *m* 1738, Sarah Bliss;
5–John (1742-1826), Springfield; *m* 1768, Lucy Horton;
4–Sally (1783-1828), *m* 1809, Hon. Samuel **Eastman** (1783-1864), grad. Dartmouth Coll., 1802; atty., Hardwick, Mass.; selectman, 1813-16; senator, 1819-20 (Ebenezer[5]; Joseph[6]; Joseph[7]; Joseph[8]; Roger[9], qv);
3–Henry Lyman (1812-40), removed to Savannah, Ga.; lt. Ga. militia; *m* 1833, Hannah Cooper White;
2–Georgia Ann (2 below).
9–Thomas **Bliss** (qv);
8–Lawrence (*d* 1676), came with his father, 1635; early settler at Springfield, Mass.; constable, 1660; selectman, 1665 and 69; *m* 1654, Lydia Wright (*d* 1699; Dea. Samuel[9], *m* Margaret–);
7–Peletiah (*b* 1674), lt.; *m* 1698, Elizabeth Hitchcock (Luke[8]; Luke[9], qv);
6–Sarah (1712-96), *m* William **Pynchon** (6 above).
9–Thomas **Horton** (qv);
8–Jeremy, Springfield; *m* 2d, 1664, Mary Gilbert (*d* 1708);
7–Jeremiah (1665-1713), Springfield; *m* 1690, Mary Terry (1667-1731; Sgt. Samuel[8], qv);
6–Capt. John (1702-will proved 1789), Springfield; *m* 1727, Mary Chapin (*b* 1705; Samuel[7], *m* Hannah Sheldon; Japhet[8], *m* 1st, Abelenah Cooley; Samuel[9], qv);
5–Lucy, *m* John **Pynchon** (5 above).
9–John **White** (qv);
8–Capt. Nathaniel (ca. 1629-1711), removed to Hartford, then to Middletown; dep. Gen. Ct., 85 times; lt. and capt. Middletown Train Band, 1690; owned about 1500 acres; *m* Elizabeth– (*d* 1690, aet. 65);
7–Joseph (1667-1725), Middletown Upper Houses; constable, 1698-1721; *m* 1693, Mary Mould (1665-1730; Hugh[8], shipbuilder, New London, 1660, *m* Martha Coit);
6–Ebenezer (1707-56), large landowner, Middletown, Conn.; *m* 1731, Ann Hollister (1707-87; Joseph[7]; John[8]; Lt. John[9], qv);
5–Elizur (1750-1823), mcht.; removed to Canaan, Conn.; later at Granville, Washington Co., N.Y.; *m* 1769, Hannah Cooper (*d* 1828, aet. 79; Lamberton[6]; Thomas[7]; Thomas[8]; Thomas[9], came in the "Christian," 1635, at Windsor and Springfield, *m* Mary Slye);
4–Capt. Ebenezer (1781-1810), capt. of brig and lost at sea; *m* 1806, Elizabeth Sage (1785-1859; Capt. Epaphras[5], *m* Elizabeth W. Ranney; Timothy[6]; Timothy[7]; David[8], qv);
3–Hannah Cooper (1809-85), of Cromwell, Buffalo, N.Y., and Fla.; *m* Henry L. **Eastman** (3 above);
2–Georgia Ann (1839-1921), *m* 1870, William Morris **Bennett** (1844-1926), mcht.; legislator; mem. Fla. Constl. Conv. (John[3], from Eng. to Toronto, Can.); issue: I–Russell White (1 above); II–Henry Eastman (see Vol. III, p. 513, for Eastman and other lineages); III–Helena Emma (1876-1905; *m* John M. Hewitt); IV–Alice Morris (*b* 1877; *m* Lewis A. Morris).
1–*m* Nov. 28, 1894, Laura Marsh, *b* Indianapolis, Ind., May 2, 1870; dau. of Dr. Henry Bird Marsh, of Indianapolis; issue: 1–Dorothy Dean, *b* Jacksonville, Fla., July 19, 1897; *m* Frank T. Scarborough (issue: Theodore Raymond; Marjory Campbell); 2–Morris Willson, *b* Okahumpka, Fla., Aug. 22, 1898; *m* Elise Carroll; 3–Donald Eastman, *b* Dowling Pk., Fla., May 23, 1907; 4–Russell Hardy, *b* Jacksonville, Fla., Jan. 26, 1911.
1–C.P.A. and sec.-mgr., Assn. Standard Container Mfrs.; sec.-treas., Fla. Forestry Assn. Served as field auditor, U.S. War Dept., 1917-18; asst. dist. auditor, Emergency Fleet Corpn., U.S. Shipping Bd., 1918-19. Mem. Am. and Fla. Insts. of Accountants, N.E.H.G.S., Conn. Hist. Soc., I.A.G. Residence: 108 W. 17th St., Jacksonville, Fla.

1–**BENTON, Frederick Henry,** *b* Plainville, Conn., May 17, 1858.
9–Edward **Benton** (ca. 1615-1680), from Eng. 1639, settled at Guilford, Conn.; original mem. Puritan Ch.; freeman, 1650; *m* Anne– (*d* 1671):
8–Dea. Daniel (1637-72), of Guilford; *m* 1658, Rachall Guttridge (*d* 1685; Richard[9], freeman, 1650);
7–Ebenezer (1663-1758), of Guilford; soldier in Colonial wars, and drew bounty land; ens. militia, resigned 1727; *m* 1694, Abigail Graves (1670-1733; John[8], of Guilford, capt. Indian war, dep. for Guilford, dea.; Dea. George[9] [*d* 1692] of Hartford, an original settler);
6–Ebenezer (1700-76), of N. Guilford; *m* Esther Crittenden (1700-78; Thomas[7], of Guilford; Abraham[8]; Abraham[9], Guilford, 1639);
5–Josiah (1736-99), of Goshen, Conn.; *m* 1765, Mehitable Smith (*d* 1812);
4–Jesse (1766-1827), of Goshen, Conn., and New Marlboro, Mass.; *m* 1793, Susannah Rogers;
3–Frederick (1805-63), of New Marlboro, Mass., Farmington and Derby, Conn.; *m* 1827, Gratia T. Brooks (1809-86);
2–David Rogers (2 below).
9–William **Rogers** (qv);
8–Noah;
7–Ens. Josiah (1679-1757), settled at Branford, Farmington, Conn., and Chicopee, Mass.; *m* 1701, Ruth Wheeler, of Milford; *m* 2d, 1713, Lydia Goodsell (Thomas[8]):
6–Mary (bap. 1725), *m* David **Booth**;
5–Mahitabel (1749-1829), *m* Jason **Rogers** (1748-1833), of Underhill, Vt. (Joseph[6]; John[7]; Noah, 8 above):
4–Susannah (1772-1812), *m* Jesse **Benton** (4 above);
3–Frederick, *m* Gratia T. Brooks (3 above);
2–David Rogers (1828-91), of New Haven, Conn.; first in the country to be engaged in steam heating; *m* 1851, Eunice Talitha Hills (1826-1913; Eleazar[3]); issue: I–Lewis David (*b* 1854; *m* Susan Wirth); II–Frederick Henry (1 above).
1–*m* Dec. 4, 1882, Lillian Idlewild Armstrong (*d* 1912); dau. of Philando Armstrong, of New Haven; issue: 1–Roger Armstrong, *b* New Haven, Conn., Jan. 9, 1890; B.A., Yale, '14; *m* Sept. 16, 1914, Virginia Walker, Vassar, 1912, dau. of Charles M. Walker, of New Haven (issue: Mary Elizabeth, *b* Nov. 28, 1916; Roger Armstrong, *b* Dec. 24, 1917; Nancy, *b* July 11, 1921).
1–*m* 2d, Apr. 4, 1917, Alice Hubbard (Breed) Foster (qv).
1–Retired manufacturer. Clubs: Union League, Union League Farmers, Waltonian (New Haven), Ft. Lauderdale (Fla.) Golf and Country. Summer place: "Twin Brook Farm," Wallingford, Conn. Residence: Cá di Fiore, Old Venice, Ft. Lauderdale, Fla.

1–**BENTON, Alice Hubbard Breed (Mrs. Frederick H.),** *b* Salem, Mass., Mar. 23, 1872.
10–Allen **Breed** (qv):
9–Allen (*d* 1707), of Lynn; *m* ante 1660, Mary– (*d* 1671);
8–Allen (1660-1730), of Lynn; soldier in King Philip's War; *m* 1684, Elizabeth Ballard (*d* 1743), of Lynn (William[9]; William[10], came in the "James," 1635, mem. A. and H.A. co.);
7–John (*b* 1689), of Lynn; *m* 1717, Lydia Gott (1699-1789), of Wenham (John[8]; Lt. Charles[9]; Charles[10], came in the "Abigail," 1628);
6–Josiah (1731-90), of Lynn; taken prisoner at Concord Bridge and was one of first 5 prisoners of Am. Rev. exchanged for Lt. Gould, British Army; *m* 1755, Mary Breed (1733-67; Joseph[7], *m* Susannah Newhall [Joseph[8]; Thomas[9]; Thomas[9]]; Ens. Joseph[8]; Allen[9]; Allen[10]);
5–Allen (1759-1842), of New Ipswich, N.H.: served in Am. Rev.; fought at Battles of Bunker Hill and Bennington; *m* 1781, Lucy Taylor (1762-1825; Capt. Reuben[6], served in Am. Rev.; Samuel[7]; Abraham[8]; Abraham[9]; William[10]);
4-Josiah (1782-1855), of Nelson, N.H.; *m* 1806, Sarah Ann Baker;
3–Capt. Lucius Hubbard (1809-45), shipmaster of Salem, Mass.; *m* 1839, Rebecca Stacey;
2–Hubbard (2 below).
11–Abraham **Temple** (*d* post 1639), from Eng., settled at Salem, 1636; *m* Abigail–; *m* 2d, Margaret–;

10-Richard (1623-89), at Charlestown, 1644, Concord, 1654; *m* ca. 1645, Joanna– (*d* 1688);
9-Abraham (1652-1738), of Concord, Mass.; served in Colonial War; *m* 1673, Deborah Hadlock (*d* 1743; John^{10});
8-Isaac (1678-1765), of Concord; served in Colonial War; *m* 1699, Martha Joslyn (*d* 1768; Nathaniel^{9});
7-Abraham (*b* 1708), of Shrewsbury; served in Colonial War; *m* 1732, Elizabeth Stratton (Joseph^{8}, of Marlboro);
6-Jonathan (1735-1813), *m* 1760, Dorothy Morse (*b* 1739; Joseph^{7}, *m* Abigail Barns; Joseph^{8}; Joseph^{9}; Joseph^{10}, qv);
5-Sarah (*b* 1762), *m* 1781, Thomas **Baker** (1756-1842), served in Am. Rev. (Robert^{6} [*b* 1713], *m* Lydia–; Joseph^{7} [*d* 1755], *m* Elizabeth–);
4-Sarah Ann (1785-1865), *m* Josiah **Breed** (4 above).
9-George **Varnum** (1594-ca. 1649), settled at Ipswich, ca. 1635; *m* Hannah–;
8-Samuel (1619-post 1702), served in King Philip's War; *m* 1645, Sara Langton (Roger^{9}, of Ipswich);
7-Thomas (1662-1739), *m* 1697, Joanna Jewett (1677-1753; Nehemiah^{8}, of Ipswich; Joseph^{9}, qv);
6-Samuel (1704-48), *m* Mary Goodhue (1716-51; Ebenezer^{7}, of Dracut; Joseph^{8}; William^{9}, qv);
5-Deborah (1744-1804), *m* 1762, William **Stacey,** Am. Rev.;
4-Samuel (1776-1815), *m* 1800, Hannah Vinton;
3-Rebecca (1810-84), *m* Capt. Lucius H. **Breed** (3 above).
9-Jonas **Eaton** (*d* 1673), propr. Reading, Mass., 1647; freeman, 1653; selectman, 1645; *m* Grace–;
8-Joshua (1653-1717), *m* 1st, 1678, Rebecca Kendall (Francis^{9}, qv);
7-Capt. Thomas (1685-1774), *m* 1708, Lydia Pierce, of Watertown (Benjamin^{8}; Anthony^{9}; John^{10}, qv);
6-Ruth (1716-99), *m* 1734, John **Nichols** (1712-75; Dea. Thomas^{7}; Capt. Thomas^{8}, *m* Rebecca Eaton [John^{9}; Jonas^{10}]; Richard^{9});
5-Lydia (1739-98), *m* 1759, John **Vinton** (1732-1801; John^{6}, *m* Mary Parker [Ebenezer^{7}; Nathaniel^{8}; Thomas^{9}]; John^{7}; John^{8}; John^{9});
4-Hannah (1777-1864), *m* Samuel **Stacey** (4 above).
8-Richard **Goldsmith** (*d* 1673), from Eng., settled at Wenham, Mass.; received land grant, 1644;
7-Zaccheus (1662-1747), of Wenham, Mass.; freeman, 1685; selectman; *m* Martha Hutton (1661-1744; Richard^{8}, selectman and constable, Wenham, served King Phillip's War);
6-Zaccheus (*b* 1701), of Wenham and Ipswich; *m* 1729, Mehitabel Kimball (1707-77; Caleb^{7}; Richard^{8}; Richard^{9});
5-John (1736-post 1812), of Moultonboro, N.H.; soldier in Am. Rev.; *m* 1762, Martha Lamson (*b* 1741; Thomas^{6}; Thomas^{7}; John^{8}; William^{9});
4-Nathaniel (1780-1845), of Salem, Mass.; served in War 1812; *m* 1811, Nancy Taylor;
3-Elizabeth (1818-90), of Salem, Mass., *m* 1839, Capt. William Henry **Clough** (1815-70; Andrus G.^{4} [1782-1852], *m* 1808, Lydia [1786-1850], dau. of Robert Phippen, *m* Lydia Valpy; Peter^{5}, *m* 1777, Sarah [Gray] Pease, a widow [John Gray^{6}; John^{7}; Robert^{8}; Robert^{9}]; Peter^{6}; Samuel^{7}; Samuel^{8}; John^{9});
2-Ada Elizabeth (2 below).
10-Samuel **Corning** (ca. 1603-1693), from Eng. to Beverly, ca. 1638; freeman, 1641; ens. Mass. Bay Colony, 1677; selectman, 1682-87; founder 1st ch. at Beverly; *m* Elizabeth– (1603-88);
9-Samuel (1641-1718), *m* Hannah Bachellor, of Wenham (Joseph^{10}, from Eng., freeman Salem, 1638, later at Wenham, rep. Gen. Ct.);
8-Samuel (1670-1760), *m* 1690, Susannah Knowlton (John^{9}; John^{10} [1610-54], freeman, Ipswich, 1641, *m* Marjery Wilson; William^{11}, *d* on voyage and buried Annapolis, Md.);
7-David (1705-52), *m* 1726, Priscilla Thissel (1707-90; Richard^{8}; Richard^{9}; Jeffrey^{10});
6-Anna (1739-1835), *m* 1760, Benjamin **Corning** (1738-ca. 1780), served in Am. Rev.; *d* on prison ship (Benjamin^{7}, *m* Susannah–; John^{8} [1676-1760], *m* Elizabeth–; Samuel^{9}, 9 above);
5-Anna (1763-1855), *m* 1784, Capt. James **Taylor** (1763-1811; William^{6}; James^{7}; James^{8});
4-Nancy (1790-1857), *m* Nathaniel **Goldsmith** (4 above);
3-Elizabeth, *m* Capt. William H. **Clough** (3 above);
2-Ada Elizabeth (1849-1909), *m* 1871, Hubbard **Breed** (1844-96), 1st treas., Edison Electric Ill. Co., Boston, issue: I-Alice Hubbard (1 above); II-Dr. Nathaniel Perkins (*b* 1877; *m* Elizabeth Lucas Whatley); III-Vinton Corning (1889-1910).
1-*m* Oct. 3, 1899, Henry Chase Foster (1871-1905).
1-*m* 2d, Apr. 4, 1917, Frederick Henry Benton (qv).
1-Mem. D.F.P.A., D.A.R. (chapter regent), Breed Family Assn. Unitarian. Republican. Clubs: Fort Lauderdale Golf, Fort Lauderdale Woman's. Summer place: "Twin Brook Farm," Wallingford, Conn. Residence: Cá di Fiore, Fort Lauderdale, Fla.

1-**BENTON, Hale Powers,** *b* Ludlow, Ky., Nov. 27, 1871.
8-Andrew **Benton** (qv);
7-Samuel (1658-1746), surveyor of highways, Hartford, 1713-14; selectman, 1715; 1st propr. Tolland, Conn., 1716; *m* 1679, Sarah Chatterton (*b* 1661; William^{8}, of New Haven, *m* Sarah–);
6-Caleb (1694-1775), *m* 1718 or 19, Hannah Ensign (Thomas^{7}, of Hartford; David^{8});
5-Abraham (1725-1807), of Hartford; *m* 1759, Martha Cook; theirs was first marriage at Sandisfield, Mass.;
4-Elijah (1770-1854), *m* 1795, Wealthy Ann Edgecomb (1778-1814);
3-Corydon Philemon (1810-81), of Home City, O., and Coldwater, Mich.; editor and publisher; *m* 1831, Phebe Ann Baldwin;
2-Dwight (2 below).
8-Joseph **Baldwin** (qv);
7-Jonathan (1649-1739), *m* Thankful Strong;
6-Ezra (*b* 1706), *m* Ruth Curtis;
5-Abiel (1730-1802), *m* Mehitable Johnson;
4-Seth (1775-1832), *m* Rhoda Hall (Timothy^{5}, *m* Dorothy Hull);
3-Phebe Ann (1813-56), *m* Corydon Philemon **Benton** (3 above).
9-William **Bowne** (qv);
8-Judge James (1636-95), an original grantee of Monmouth Patent, 1665; dep. Gen. Assembly; mem. of Assembly of Patentees and Deputies, Shrewsbury, 1667, and Portland Point, 1669; mem. N.J. Assembly, 1670,79,80; dep. to meet Gov. and Council at Woodbridge, 1675, and at Elizabeth Town, 1677; recorder of Monmouth Co., 1680; minister of justice for Province of East Jersey, 1685; *m* 1665, Mary Stout (Richard^{9}, qv);
7-Andrew, *m* Anna (Seabrook) Bray;
6-Peter, *m* Deliverance Holmes (Jonathan^{7});
5-David, *m* Mary Nicholls (Benjamin^{6}; William^{7}, *m* Mary, Countess of Mulford);
4-Sarah, *m* 1814, George **McAroy,** M.D. (*d* 1825), to Franklin, O.; grad. Princeton; surgeon War 1812 (William^{5}, Indian mcht., from Belfast to N.J., *m* —Gordon, of Freehold, N.J.);
3-Mary Anne Bowne (1816-88), *m* 1837, John Pearl **Haggott,** M.D. (1805-61), surgeon 57th Ohio Vol. Inf., died in service with rank of major;
2-Sarah Elizabeth (2 below).
11-William **Lawrence,** settled at Middletown, N.J., 1667; dep. Gen. Ct., Portland Point, 1669-70; mem. Gen. Assembly, 1672;
10-Hannah, *m* Joseph **Grover** (Lt. James^{11}, to Gravesend, L.I., 1648; asso. in Monmouth Patent, justice, dep., assemblyman, etc., *m* Mary–);
9-Hannah, *m* James **Seabrook;**
8-Thomas, *m* Mary–;
7-Anne, as Widow Bray, *m* 2d, Andrew **Bowne** (7 above).
9-Rev. Obadiah **Holmes** (qv);
8-Capt. Jonathan (1637-1713), mem. N.J. Assembly, 1668,70,72; asso. in Monmouth Patent, 1672; *m* 1665, Sarah Borden (Richard^{9}, qv);
7-Jonathan, *m* Deliverance Ashton (Rev. James^{8}, *m* Deliverance, dau. of John Throckmorton; James^{9}, dep. Colony of R.I., 1652-65);
6-Deliverance, *m* Peter **Bowne** (6 above).
2-Sarah Elizabeth Bowne Haggott (1840-1913), *m* 1866, Dwight **Benton** (1834-1903), studied in Italy 3 yrs.; served in U.S.V. in Civil War, taken prisoner, escaped; settled at Cincinnati as a professional landscape and portrait painter; taught in the Art Acad. of Cincinnati; art critic; corr., writer and botanist, settled in Rome, Italy, 1880-1903; Hawaiian consul general in Italy, 1895-99; editor The Roman World, 1898-1903; issue: I-Corydon

Pearl (*d* 1871, aet. 3); II–Dwight, Jr. (*b* 1869); III–Hale Powers (1 above); IV–Corydon Pearl (*b* 1873; *m* Romea Arioli); V–Imogen (*b* 1881; *m* Prof. Ralph Benton).
1–*m* Sept. 21, 1914, Lilian Marie Babcock, *b* Minneapolis, Minn., Mar. 26, 1886; dau. of Courtlandt Babcock, (Robert[3], banker, Kalamazoo, Mich.), *m* Marie Sleight; issue: 1–Hale Powers, Jr., *b* Rome, Italy, July 31, 1915; 2–Gordon Gray (Mar. 27, 1919-May 9, 1920); 3–Lilian Marie, *b* Rome, Oct. 1, 1921; 4–Beatrice Elizabeth, *b* Moena, Italy, July 25, 1924.
1–Ed. abroad. Asst. to the dir. of Am. Acad. in Rome. Apptd. Hawaiian vice and dep. consul gen. in Italy, 1895-99. Vol. foreign service of A.R.C., Dept. Mil. Affairs, with rank of capt., 1917-19. Commd. capt. by Sec. of War, Mar. 12, 1919. War recognitions: European campaign, Italian campaign, 1918, Chevalier Ordre Léopold, II, Belgian, 1919. Club: Royal Aniene Rowing. Residence: Via Nicola Fabrizi, No. 8, Rome, Italy.

1–**POMEROY, Christina King (Mrs. C. K.),** *b* Chicago, Ill.
9–John **King** (qv);
8–William (1660-1728), *m* Elizabeth Denslow;
7–William (1687-1769), *m* Esther–;
6–Reuben (1718-47), *m* Sarah Mosely;
5–Bohan, *m* Thankful Taylor;
4–William (1774-1836), *m* Pamela Phelps;
3–William, *m* Christina Rockwell;
2–Henry William (2 below).
6–Adam **Martin** (1739-1818), officer Am. Rev.; *m* Abigail Cheney;
5–Walter, officer War 1812; *m* Sarah Turner;
4–Abigail, *m* Philo **Rockwell**;
3–Christina, *m* William **King** (3 above);
2–Henry William **King** (1828-98), mcht., Chicago; *m* Aurelia Roxana Case (1834-1900); I–Henry W. (*d* 1888); II–Christina (1 above); III–Francis (see Vol. I, p. 177); IV–Elizabeth (Mrs. Cyrus Bentley, qv for Bradford lineage).
1–*m* May 30, 1883, S. Harris Pomeroy, *b* Chicago, Feb. 21, 1861; son of Theodore Pomeroy, of Pittsfield; issue: 1–Theodore; 2–Roxana.
1–Mem. Colonial Dames, etc. Residence: Hotel Ambassador, Chicago, Ill.

1–**BENTLEY, Elizabeth King (Mrs. Cyrus),** *b* Chicago, Ill., Sept. 27, 1865.
10–Gov. William **Bradford,** Mayflower Pilgrim (qv);
9–Maj. William (1624-1703/04), *m* Alice Richards (1627-71);
8–Alice (1662-1745), *m* 1680, Rev. William **Adams** (1650-85);
7–Alice (1682-1735), *m* 1701, Nathaniel **Collins** (1677-1756; Rev. Nathaniel[8], of Middletown; Edward[9], qv);
6–Ann (1702-78), *m* 1723, Ephraim **Terry** (1701-83; Samuel[7]; Sgt. Samuel[8], qv);
5–Ephraim (1728-1807), *m* 1756, Martha Olmsted (1737-1814);
4–Anne (1768-1852), *m* 1799, William **Norton** (1767-1841);
3–Roxanna (1801-42), *m* 1831, John Randolph **Case** (1804-77);
2–Aurelia Roxana (1834-1900), *m* Henry William **King** (1828-98), mcht., Chicago; (for issue and King lineages see Mrs. C. K. Pomeroy).
1–*m* Jan. 8, 1889, Cyrus Bentley, *b* Chicago, Ill., Sept. 5, 1861; B.A., Yale, '82; LL.B., Union Coll. of Law (Northwestern U.), 1884; lawyer; son of Cyrus Bentley, *m* Anna Riley; issue: 1–Margaret, *b* Elmhurst, Ill., Aug. 28, 1892; *m* Dec. 6, 1919, David Osborne Hamilton; 2–Richard, *b* Elmhurst, June 5, 1894; Yale, '17; 2d lt., 1st lt. and capt. in World War; *m* Dec. 9, 1922, Phoebe Wrenn Norcross.
1–Mem. S.M.D., D.A.R., Residence: 1505 Astor St., Chicago, Ill.

1–**BETTS, Mary Atkinson Monie (Mrs. Joseph Shawen),** *b* Raleigh, N.C., Feb. 27, 1876.
8–Henry **Towles** (*b* 1652), from Eng.; settled first in Accomac Co., Va.; leased 1000 acres land there; on tax lists, 1680-87; deed on file, 1689, for 800 acres bought by Henry Towles; removed to Middlesex Co., Va.; *m* ca. 1668, Ann Stokely (Francis[9]);
7–Henry (1670-1734), of Towles Point, Lancaster Co., Va.; built "Old House," still owned by family; *m* 1709, Hannah Therriotte (William[8]; Dominick[9], Huguenot refugee, granted large tracts of land by crown in Lancaster Co., Va.; naturalized, 1673);
6–Stokely (1711-65), of Towles Point, Va.; *m* 1736, Elizabeth Martin (Thomas[7], of Corotoman, Va., *m* Catherine–);
5–Henry (1738-99), served as col. of Militia during Am. Rev.; atty. at law; mem. House of Delegates, 1783; del. from Lancaster Co., Va. to Phila. convention to ratify U.S. Constitution, 1787-89; clk of ct., 1794-99; *m* 1760, Judith Haynes (*d* 1804);
4–Thomas (1784 or 85-1822), removed to Northumberland Co., Va.; *m* 1807, Margaret Delany Moore;
3–James Moore (1808-78), removed to Raleigh, N.C.; *m* 1838, Mary Ann Callum (1815-1901; Robert[4], *m* Hannah, dau. John Smith, *m* Mercy Eldredge);
2–Margaret Delany (2 below).
8–Isaac **Sharpe** (*d* 1735; son of Anthony Sharpe from Eng. to Ireland, founded "Roundwood," estate nr. Dublin); from Ireland, 1702/03; settled in Salem Co., N.J.; landed propr.; mem. Salem Co. Assembly; judge of Salem Ct., 1709-25; returned to Ireland ca. 1726, where he died; *m* 1704, Margaret Braithwaite, of Salem, N.J.;
7–Sarah, widow of Thomas Mason, *m* 2d, Thomas **Robinson** (*d* 1766);
6–Margaret, *m* ca. 1765, Sharpe **Delany** (1739-99), from Ireland; settled in Phila., 1761; served as col., 2d Bn., Pa. militia, Am. Rev.; first collector Port of Phila., apptd. by President Washington, 1789;
5–Sarah (1767-1814), *m* 1787, James **Moore** (1757-1813), served as col. 1st Pa. regt. militia and on Gen. Washington's staff at Valley Forge during Am. Rev.; served in Wyoming Valley, 1784; charter mem. of Phila. Soc. of Cincinnati (Judge James[6] [1730-1802], apptd. judge of Supreme Ct., Pa., 1791, *m* 1752, Elizabeth Creswell [*b* 1732], dau. of Judge James Whitehill, to Lancaster Co., Pa., 1723);
4–Margaret Delany (*b* 1789), *m* Thomas **Towles** (4 above);
3–James, *m* Mary Ann Callum (3 above);
2–Margaret Delany (1844-78), *m* 1872, John Miller **Monie** (1840-1920; John[3], *m* Margaret Miller), from Scotland, 1859; settled in Newbern, N.C.; later of Raleigh; served with Co. H, 1st N.C. Cav., 9th Regt., C.S.A.; lt., 1865; wounded; issue: I–Mary A. (1 above); II–John Miller (*b* 1881; *m* Evelyn Burruss).
1–*m* Feb. 15, 1905, Dr. Joseph Shawen Betts, *b* Scotts Hill, N.C., Sept. 5, 1867; son of Rev. Alexander Davis Betts, D.D., of Greensboro, N.C.; issue: 1–John Monie, *b* Raleigh, N.C., July 4, 1906; ed. U. of N.C.; 2–Margaret Delany, *b* Greensboro, N.C., May 5, 1910; 3–Henry Alexander, *b* Greensboro, Mar. 29, 1912.
1–Ed. Peace Inst. (Raleigh, N.C.) Mem. D.A.C., D.F.P.A., D.A.R. (mem. bd. of govs.; past-regent), U.D.C., N.C. Hist. Soc.; mem. bd. Greensboro Hist. Museum Soc.; exec. com. Greensboro chapter Red Cross. Methodist. Club: Woman's. Residence: 424 N. Elm St., Greensboro, N.C.

1–**BETTS, Philander,** 3d, *b* Nyack, N.Y., May 28, 1868.
8–Thomas **Betts** (1618-88), from Eng.; a founder of Guilford, Conn., 1639; *m* ante 1639, Mary Raymond (ca. 1624-ca. 1724), sister of John Raymond, of Salem, Mass.;
7–James (1663-1753), *m* ca. 1704, Hannah Boughton (1675-1748; John[8], of Norwalk);
6–Benjamin (1710-80), *m* 1729, Rebecca Taylor (1704-1805; Lt. John[7]; Capt. John[8], of Northampton, Mass., both served in Pequot Indian Wars);
5–Elijah (1746-1800), Am. Rev.; *m* 1768, Adah Taylor (1730-1831, aet. 100; Reuben[6]; Lt. John[7], above);
4–James (1781-1858), *m* Esther Benedict (*d* 1859);
3–Philander (1812-94), *m* 1835, Jane Elizabeth Wilcox (1816-85; Augustus[4], *m* Fanny Benedict; John[5] [1760-1812], Am. Rev., *m* Margaret Kelsey, 1760-1804);
2–Philander (2 below).
9–David (des Marest) **Demarest** (1620-93), from Picardy to New Amsterdam, 1663; founded a French colony on the Hackensack River, N.J., 1677; *m* Marie Sohier;

8–David (1652-91), *m* 1675, Rachel Cresson (Pierre[9]);
7–Jacobus (*b* 1681), *m* 2d, 1719, Margreitje Cozine (Herring);
6–Johannes (1720-83), *m* Rachel Zabriskie;
5–James J. (1749-1825), *m* 1774 Rachel Smitt;
4–Cornelius J. (1785-1863), served in War 1812; *m* Catherine Holdrum (1788-1852);
3–John C. (1811-80), *m* Isabella Tallman;
2–Sarah Tallman (1846-1901), *m* 1867, Philander **Betts** (1841-1919), sanitary engr.; issue: I–Philander, 3d (1 above); II–Eugene (*b* 1870; *m* Anna Louise Eldridge); III–Frances (*b* 1872; *m* John Aljoe Hubbard); IV–Percy De M. (*b* 1874); V–Guy (*b* 1875; *m* Grace M. Ackerman); VI–Irving Wilcox (*b* 1880; *m* Bessie Harris Boardman).
1–*m* Nov. 19, 1896, Nancy Bell Hammer, *b* Pittsburgh, Pa., Aug. 29, 1870; dau. of Jacob Brickley Hammer, of Pittsburgh, *m* Martha Ann Shirk; issue: I–Philander Hammer, *b* Washington, D.C., Nov. 17, 1897; grad. Rutgers, '22; served U.S.N. for 2 yrs. as an expert radio operator in various vessels in and out of New York Harbor, including investigation of radio telephone, and temp. service in Customs Service which included the inspection and test of all radio apparatus on civilian ships entering New York Harbor.
1–B.S., Rutgers, 1891, M.S., 1895 (Beta Theta Pi, Theta Nu Epsilon); E.E., Columbian (now George Washington) U., 1903 (Ph.D., 1914). Chief engr. N.J. State Bd. of Public Utility Commrs., since 1910; compiler and editor of the hist. records in connection with all War Dept. construction in this country. Maj. Engr. R.C., July 14, 1917; lt. col. Q.M. Corps, Mar. 18, 1918; active duty, War Dept., Washington; hon. discharged, May 31, 1919; col. Engr. R.C., comdr. 373d Engrs. Mem. S.A.R. (pres. Monmouth Co., N.J.), M.O.W.W. (sr. past comdr., N.J. Chapter), N.J. State Reserve Officers' Assn. (gen. staff), A.L., I.A.G., etc. Mason (33°). Reformed Church. Residence: 100 Tenth Av., Belmar, N.J.

BIGELOW

Arms: Or, three lozenges azure.
Crest: A ram's head erased azure.

1–**BIGELOW, Carle Muzzy,** *b* Woonsocket, R.I., Dec. 22, 1889.
9–John **Bigelow** (qv);
8–Samuel (1653-1720), *m* 1674, Mary Flagg (1658-1720);
7–Samuel (*b* 1679), *m* 1716, Mary Gleason (1682-1752);
6–Dea. Amariah (1722-80), *m* 1752, Sarah Eveleth;
5–Abel (1755-1821), *m* 1778, Martha Bigelow (1753-1848);
4–Capt. Asa (1794-1876), *m* 1817, Lois Harthan (1793-1839);
3–Merrill Harthan (1828-57), *m* 1849, Charlotte E. Willard (1831-99);
2–Ervin Elliott (*b* 1855), mech. engr.; *m* 1878, Mary Melissa Willis (1859-1919; Clark C.[3] [1839-1922], *m* Melissa Crumb, 1844-69).
1–*m* June 4, 1914, Olive Nicholson, *b* Pawtucket, R.I., Nov. 30, 1889; dau. of Squire Senior Nicholson, of Leeds, Eng., now of Pawtucket, R.I.; issue: 1–Rosalind Emma, *b* Saylesville, R.I., Mar. 29, 1915; 2–Ervin Senior, *b* Newton, Mass., Mar. 11, 1919; 3–Olivia Marea, *b* Newton, July 18, 1923.
1–B.S., R.I. State Coll., 1912, M.E., 1921 (Theta Chi, Tau Kappa Alpha). Pres. Bigelow Kent, Willard & Co., consulting engrs. and accountants; also pres. Waste Eliminators, Laundry Management Service, Victory Fertilizer Co. Mem. advisory bd., R.I. State Coll.; Soc. of Industrial Engrs. (dir.); Inst. of Management (fellow). Clubs: Theta Chi (New York), Engineers, University. Summer place: "Gray Shingles," Duxbury, Mass. Residence: 227 Temple St., West Newton, Mass.

1–**BEVAN, Ralph Hervey,** *b* Providence, R.I., July 21, 1881.
11–Roger **Williams** (qv);
10–Mercy (1640-1725), *m* 1659, Resolved **Waterman** (1638-70; Richard[11]);
9–Waite (1668-1711), *m* 1685, John **Rhodes** (1658-1716; Zachariah[10] [1603-65], the immigrant);
8–Maj. John (1691-1776), dep. Gen. Assembly; maj. colonial militia, 1714; *m* Catherine Holden (*d* 1731; Charles[9]);
7–Capt. Charles (1719-77), of Warwick, Mass.; *m* 1739; Deborah Greene;
6–Capt. Peter (1741-1823), of Pawtuxet; *m* 1761, Hester Arnold (Simon[7] of Warwick, *m* Lydia Green; Israel[8]; Stephen[9]; William[10]);
5–Phebe, *m* 1790, Josiah **Medbery** (1766-1844; Ebenezer[6]);
4–Rosanna S. (1804-45), *m* 1824, Capt. Hervey **Mason;**
3–Hervey (1829-1912), *m* 1851, Betsy B. Medbery;
2–Emma Rosanna (2 below).
11–John ("Surgeon John") **Greene** (qv);
10–Maj. John (1620-1708), dep. gov. of R.I.; *m* Anne Almy;
9–Capt. Peter (1654-1723), *m* Elizabeth Arnold;
8–Maj. Peter (1682-1767), *m* Keziah Davis;
7–Deborah, *m* 1739, Capt. Charles **Rhodes** (7 above).
8–John (Medbury) **Medbery,** from Wales to Swansea; *m* 1680, Sarah–;
7–Thomas (1686-1774), *m* ca. 1714, Bethia Very;
6–John (1714-79), *m* 1740, Anna Camp (Nicholas[7]);
5–John (1754-1825), lt. Am. Rev.; *m* 1779, Abigail Viall (Samuel[6], Am. Rev.);
4–Jesse (1787-1842), of Rehoboth, Mass.; *m* 1810, Elizabeth Viall;
3–Betsy B. (1829-73), *m* Hervey **Mason** (3 above).
11–John **Tilley,** 16th signer of the Mayflower Compact (qv);
10–Elizabeth (*d* 1687), of Swansea, Mass.; *m* John **Howland,** 13th signer of the Mayflower Compact (qv);
9–Hannah, *m* 1661, Jonathan **Bosworth;**
8–Jabez (1673-1747), *m* 1701, Susannah–;
7–Patience (1717-47), *m* 1740, John **Bullock** (1715-1788; John[8]; Richard[9]);
6–Elizabeth (*d* 1786), *m* 1767, Josiah **Kent** (1741-1799), Am. Rev. (Josiah[7]; Samuel[8]);
5–Patience (1768-1798), *m* 1789, Thomas **Viall** (1763-1796; Lt. Samuel[6], killed by explosion in the "Spitfire," 1777);
4–Elizabeth (1789-1878), *m* 1810, Jesse **Medbery** (4 above).
2–Emma Rosanna Mason (*b* 1856), *m* 1880, Alexander **Bevan** (1850-1922); issue: I–Ralph Hervey (1 above); II–Meril E. (*b* 1884; *m* Frank W. Fletcher); III–Ernest E. (*b* 1887).
1–Not married. A.B., Brown U., 1904; Rhodes scholar from R.I. at Oxford U., 1904-07; B.C.L. (Roman and English law), 1906 (Delta Upsilon, P.B.K.). Publicist or student of scientific measures for progress. Contbr. to Jour. of N.E.A., Outlook, Forum, Advocate of Peace, American Educational Digest, First World Conf. on Edn., etc. Mem. commn. (of World Fed. of Edn. Assns.) on a World University, 1924-25 (see Who's Who among N. American Authors, Who's Who in the East, or Who's Who in America). Residence: Providence, R.I.

1–**BIDWELL, Grace Mary Stockton (Mrs. Harry D.),** *b* Mosiertown, Pa., Oct. 10, 1875.
7–Robert **Stockton** (1688-1747), from the North of Ireland, settled in Nottingham Tp., Chester Co., Pa., ca. 1732; *m* Isabel– (*d* 1747);
6–Thomas (1709-95), *m* Margaret Fleming;
5–David, capt. Am. Rev.; *m* Ann– (*d* 1810);

4–Robert, col. War of 1812; *m* — McAmy;
3–John McAmy (1805-72), *m* Eliza Logan (1814-93);
2–Cyrus Jerome (1845-1925), farmer; pvt. U.S.V. in Civil War; *m* 1874, Lucina Anna Boles (1859-1905); issue: I–Grace Mary (1 above); II–Frederick Everett (*b* 1877; *m* Lucy Swisher); III–Herbert John (*m* Maude Demmler); IV–Iva Blanche (*m* G. Ralph Clark); V–Frank Tenny (*b* 1886; *m* Harriet Margaret Stansbury).
1–*m* Jan. 1, 1906, Harry Dupont Bidwell, *b* Pittsburgh, Pa., Dec. 13, 1872; son of DeWitt Clinton Bidwell, of Pittsburgh.
1–Residence: 500 E. Beach St., Gulfport, Miss.

LEETE

Arms: Argent, a fesse gules between two rolls of fuses sable, fired proper, a martlet of the field.
Crest: On a ducal coronet an antique lamp or, fired proper.

1–**BILDERBACK, Carolyn Leete (Mrs. J. B.),** *b* Santa Barbara, Calif., Oct. 5, 1881-*d* Portland, Ore., Aug. 9, 1929.
10–Gov. William **Leete** (qv);
9–John (1639-92), of Guilford; *m* ca. 1670, Mary Chittenden;
8–Dea. Pelatiah (1681-1768), of Guilford; *m* 1705, Abigail Fowler;
7–Dea. Pelatiah (1713-86), of Leete's Island; *m* 1740, Lydia Cruttenden;
6–Pelatiah (1744-1806), of Leete's Island; *m* 1767, Bethiah Norton;
5–Noah (1770-1827), of Leete's Island and Verona, N.Y.; *m* 1792, Huldah Ward;
4–Rev. Charles Ward (1799-1858), of Verona, N.Y.; *m* 1822, Adeline Loomis;
3–Allen Norton (1825-1913), of Verona; *m* 1851, Abigail Button;
2–Charles Norton (1852-1925), of Verona; *m* 1874, Caroline Roxanna Nelson (1856-1917); issue: I–Harley Marion (*b* 1874; *m* 1903, Lucy Ware Williams); II–Nelson Allen (1878-1912); III–Carolyn (1 above); IV–Mary Mather (*b* 1891); V–Helen (*b* 1893; *m* 1921, Samuel Thaxter Farquhar).
1–*m* Nov. 18, 1911, Dr. Joseph Brown Bilderback, *b* Jenkintown, Pa., Nov. 21, 1869; son of William Henry Bilderback, *m* Margaret Palmer; issue: 1–Jane, *b* Portland, Ore., 1912; 2–Caroline, *b* Portland, Ore., 1915.
1–B.A., U.Calif., '04. Mem. C.D.A.

1–**BIRD, Annie Dudley Bedford (Mrs. Joseph E.),** *b* Paris, Ky., Dec. 12, 1861.
9–Edward **Brock,** lived in Calvert Co., Md., ante 1672;
8–Mary (*d* 1748), *m* William **Offutt** (*d* 1734), from Eng. ante 1696, settled in Calvert Co., Md.;
7–Judge James (*d* 1750), justice of peace 1777,80; mem. 1st co. ct., Montgomery Co., Md.; *m* 1725, Rachel Beall (Col. Ninian[8], qv);
6–Elizabeth, *m* 1746, Lt. Stephen **Lewis,** in Lee's Legion, Am. Rev.;
5–Lt. Thomas (1749-1809), Am. Rev.; *m* 1773, Elizabeth Payne;
4–Nancy (1774-1835), *m* 1793, Gen. James **Garrard** (1773-1838), brig. gen. War 1812; mem. Ky. House and Senate; see Vol. II, p. 209, for Garrard lineage;
3–Elizabeth Lewis (1806-73), *m* 1825, Augustine Volney **Bedford** (1802-63), see Vol. II, p. 209, for Bedford lineage;
2–Jeptha Dudley (2 below).
8–Sir John **Payne** (qv);
7–William (1672-1776), sheriff Fairfax Co., Va.; justice of peace of oyer and terminer; vestryman, 1750-65, and ch. warden, 1751-52, 57-58, Truro Parish; mem. Fairfax Co. Com. of Safety; *m* 1712, Alicia Jones (*d* 1760; Edward[8], *m* Richmond Co., Va., 1679, Alicia Lunn); *m* 2d, Ann Jennings;
6–Col. Edward (*b* Stafford Co., Va., 1726-*d* Fayette Co., Ky., 1806), mem. Fairfax Co., Va., Com. of Safety; sheriff; justice of peace of oyer and terminer; vestryman, 1765-74, and ch. warden, 1765-66, 70-71, 73-74, Truro Parish; mem. conv. held at Danville, Ky., May 23, 1785; elector of Senate for 1792, from Fayette Co., Ky.; *m* 1750, Anne Holland Conyers (*b* 1728; Henry[7], of Stafford Co., Va.);
5–Elizabeth (1757-1827), *m* Thomas **Lewis** (5 above).
2–Jeptha Dudley **Bedford** (1837-93), *m* 1860, Annie Eliza Hall (1842-70); *m* 2d, 1875, Armilda Toland; issue (1st marriage); I–Annie Dudley (1 above); II–James Franklin (*b* 1865); issue (2d marriage): I–Frances Elizabeth (*b* 1877).
1–*m* Feb. 25, 1885, Joseph Elmer Bird, *b* Patriot, O., June 21, 1861; son of George Bird, of Ohio, *m* Mary Brown Briggs; issue: 1–Elmer Bedford, *b* Mansfield, Ill., Dec. 2, 1886; *m* May 16, 1913, Verdie Steiner (issue: Barbara Eleanor; Marjorie Elizabeth); 2–Annie Laurie, *b* Billings, Mo., Aug. 21, 1893.
1–Librarian gen. N.S.C.D. XVII C., 1927-30, and Ida. state pres., 1925-32; Ida. state historian D.A.C.; Ida. state regent D.A.R., 1929-31. Residence: Route 1, Nampa, Ida.

CAPT. CLARENCE EUGENE BISSELL

1–**BISSELL, Clarence Eugene,** *b* Manchester, Conn., Sept. 7, 1893.

11–John **Bissell** (qv);
10–Samuel (1630-98), to Windsor, Conn.; *m* 1658, Abigail Holcombe (*d* Aug. 17, 1688; Thomas[11]);
9–John (1659-1740), to Lebanon, Conn.; *m* Sarah Fowler (*d* Aug. 25, 1751);
8–John (1683-Mar. 8, 1771), *m* Hannah Denslow (Nov. 14, 1690-Jan. 13, 1752);
7–Ozias, Sr. (May 13, 1731-Mar. 16, 1822), Bolton, Conn., to Vernon; soldier French and Indian War; capt., 1775, 2d Co., Col. Hinman's Regt., at siege of Boston; capt., Col. Huntington's Regt. and taken prisoner at Battle of Long Island; capt. 1st Bn. of Conn. Line, 1778; capt. Foot Co., Col. Wells' Regt., 1781; *m* 1st, Mabel Roberts (*d* Oct. 31, 1803);
6–Ozias, Jr. (1752-1826), at Lexington Alarm; *m* Elizabeth Kilborn;
5–Ozias, III (1779-1853), *m* Sarah Bidwell (*d* July 25, 1831);
4–Lewis Glover (1801-92), *m* Parmelia Beckwith (June 29, 1802-Jan. 16, 1872);
3–Lewis (July 6, 1829-Sept. 1, 1900), *m* 1st, Cornelia Palmer (*d* Aug. 7, 1892);
2–Robert Palmer (July 9, 1856-Sept. 6, 1923), *m* Clara Bunnell (*d* 1891); *m* 2d, 1892, Henrietta Brough (*b* May 23, 1873); issue (1st marriage): I–Mabelle A. (*d* 1918; *m* –LaPlace); (2d marriage): I–Clarence Eugene (1 above).
1–*m* May 5, 1917, Alzina Heatley, *b* Fall River, Mass., Aug. 12, 1895; dau. of David Heatley, of Wellesley, Mass.
1–*m* 2d, Oct. 7, 1922, Margaret, dau. of William Henry Maines, of Ridgewood, N.J.; issue: 1–Robert Dale, *b* S. Manchester, Conn., June 16, 1924; 2–Margaret Ann, *b* Larchmont, N.Y., June 2, 1927; 3–William Maines, *b* Providence, R.I., Dec. 31, 1929.
1–Ed. Tilton (N.H.) Sch., ex '11. With the Pawtucket Mills of The U.S. Finishing Co. Second lt. cav., U.S.A., Aug. 12, 1917; 1st lt., May, 1919; capt., Aug. 1922. With Co. C, 104th Inf., 26th Div., A.E.F., Oct. 1917-Mar. 12, 1919, on duty as c.o. casual depot, Winchester, Eng. Cited for exceptionally meritorious service. Mem. O.F.P.A., S.A.R., M.O.F.W., A.L. Clubs: Larchmont Men's, Sojourners. Summer place: Oak Bluff, Martha's Vineyard Island, Mass. Residence: 263 Olney St., Providence, R.I.

REV. JOHNSON OATMAN, JR. (1856-1924); attended Bordentown (N.J.) Collegiate Institute (now Military Academy); studied privately for Methodist Episcopal ministry; devoted his talents to the writing of sacred songs, of which he published several thousand, including "No, Not One"; "Higher Ground"; and "Count Your Blessings."

1–**BLACHLY, Miriam Eulalie Oatman (Mrs. Frederick F.),** *b* Lumberton, N.J., Dec. 2, 1887.
5–David **Oatman,** *m* Hannah Johnson;
4–William, *m* Eleanor Chamélier;
3–Johnson (*b* 1822), of N.J.; *m* 1847, Rachel Ann Cline;
2–Rev. Johnson (2 below).
10–James **Rogers,** from Eng., in the "Increase"; settled at New London, Conn.; *m* Elizabeth, dau. of Samuel Rowland;
9–Samuel, *m* Mary Stanton; *m* 2d, Joanna Williams;
8–Daniel, *m* Grace Williams;
7–Nathaniel;
6–Nathaniel, *m* 1782, Sarah Tubbs (Alpheus[7]);
5–William (*b* 1784?), of Pa.; capt. in War 1812; *m* 1804?, Lydia–;
4–Hannah ? (*b* ca. 1805), *m* Amos **Cline;**
3–Rachel Ann (*b* 1826), *m* Johnson **Oatman** (3 above).
4–Matthias **Ried,** from Germany; *m* Magdalen–;
3–Charles or Karl Matthias (1827-62), served with Union Army during Civil War; killed in Seven Days Battle before Richmond; *m* 1849, Wilhelmina Bischoff (*b* 1826; Michael[4], *m* Theresa–);
2–Wilhelmina (*b* 1857), *m* 1878, Rev. Johnson **Oatman,** Jr. (1856-1924), attended Bordentown (N.J.) Collegiate Inst. (now Mil. Acad.); studied privately for M.E. ministry; devoted his talents to the writing of sacred songs, of which he published several thousand, including "No, Not One," "Higher Ground," and "Count your Blessings" (see portrait); issue: I–Charles Percival (*b* 1879; *m* Helen Githens Frymier); II–Bertha Cline (1880-81); III–Miriam Eulalie (1 above); IV–Rachel Mila (*b* 1890; *m* Philip Van Arsdale; *m* 2d, Horace Meyer Kallen).
1–*m* Nov. 29, 1914, Frederick Frank Blachly, Ph.D. (qv); issue: 1–Frederick Johnson, *b* Oklahoma City, Okla., Sept. 21, 1917; 2–Charles Howard, *b* Oklahoma City, Dec. 2, 1919.
1–A.B., Oberlin Coll., '12 (Phi Beta Kappa), A.M., Columbia U., 1924; Ph.D., Brookings Instn., 1930. Author and research worker in political science and comparative government and administration. Mem. Nat. Woman's Party, League for Independent Political Action. Residence: 4323 Cathedral Av. N.W., Washington, D.C.

1–**BLACHLY, Frederick Frank,** *b* Salida, Colo., Aug. 20, 1880.
9–Thomas **Blachly** (*d* 1674), from Eng. in the "Speedwell," to Mass., 1635; at Hartford, Conn., 1641; removed to Branford, Conn., 1645; signed agreement with those who migrated to settle Newark, but did not go with them;
8–Aaron (1644-99), *m* Mary Dodd; *m* 2d, Hannah or Sarah Foote;
7–Dr. Ebenezer (*b* 1677);
6–Ebenezer (*b* 1709), *m* Annie Miller; *m* 2d, Mary Miller; *m* 3d, Mrs. Franciss; *m* 4th, Mrs. Estis; *m* 5th, Mrs. Nichols;
5–Dr. Miller (1738-1815), surgeon 4th Pa. line, Am. Rev.; *m* Eleanor Boyd (William[6]);
4–Miller (1773-1850), *m* 1795, Phoebe Bell (Onesimus[5]); *m* 2d, Eleanor–;
3–Dr. Eben (1800-77), *m* Minerva Seely; *m* 2d, ante 1847, Jane Trew;
2–Andrew Trew (2 below).
9–William **Bradley** (qv);
8–Abraham (1650-1718), deacon First Ch., New Haven, 1696-1718; dep. Gen. Assembly 12 terms; justice of the peace and quorum for New Haven Co. 9 terms; *m* 1673, Hannah Thompson (*d* 1718; John[9], from Eng. with Gov. Eaton, 1637);
7–Dea. Daniel (1679-1723), of New Haven; *m* 1702, Sarah Bassett (*b* 1682; John[8] [1652-1717], of New Haven, propr. 1685, rep. 1704-10);
6–Dea. Daniel (1706-73), of Hamden, Conn.; *m* 1727, Abigail (Punchard?) Burchard (1708-74; William[7], *m* Hannah Brown);
5–Jabez (1733-93), of Hamden; *m* 1754, Esther Beach (1731-94; Moses[6]; desc. Richard Beach, a signer of orig. compact);
4–Rev. and Judge Dan (1767-1838), of Marcellus, N.Y.; B.A., Yale, 1789; ordained, 1790; *m* 1st, 1790, Eunice Beach (1766-1804);
3–Rev. Dr. Dan Beach (1804-73), M.D.; missionary in Siam, 38 yrs.; introduced medicine, surgery, and vaccination to natives; taught art of cutting and pounding Siamese type; *m* 1st, Emilie Royce; *m* 2d, 1848, Sarah Blachly (*b* 1817);
2–Mary Adele (1854-1926), *m* 1877, her cousin, Andrew Trew **Blachly** (1847-94), banker, Delta, Colo.; issue: I–Arthur Trew, M.D. (*b* 1878; *m* Marian–; *m* 2d Mary Cole; *m* 3d, Winifred–);

II–Frederick Frank (1 above); III–Clarence Dan, Ph.D. (*b* 1881; *m* Margaret Gray Bacon); IV–Howard Dwight (*b* 1883; *m* Mary–); V–William Harold (1885-1906); VI–Ralph R. (*b* 1887); VII–Louis Dwight (*b* 1890; *m* Natalie Norton); VIII–Edward Hugh (*b* 1892).
1–*m* Nov. 29, 1914, Miriam Eulalie Oatman (qv for issue).
1–A.B., Oberlin, '11; Ph.D., Columbia, 1916. Prof. govt., U. of Okla., 1916-25; pvt. research in Europe on comparative governmental administration, 1924-25; mem. sr. staff, Inst. for Govt. Research, since 1925. Author (see Who's Who in America). Mem. Am. and Southwestern Polit. Science assns.; sec. Okla. Municipal League; dir. Okla. Bur. Municipal Research. Summer place: Granite Ledge, Brightwater, Bath, Me. Residence: White Oaks, 4323 Cathedral Av. N.W., Washington, D.C.

1–**BLACK, J(ohn) Edwin,** *b* Lawrence Co., Ill., Mar. 10, 1843.
9–William George **Lake,** from Eng., 1638, settled nr. Boston; removed to Conn., 1662; *m* Mary Gardner;
8–Elijah, *m* 1679, Rebecca Ellerton;
7–Constant E., settled on Eastern Shore of Md., 1703; *m* 1705, Miss Janness (*d* 1706); *m* 2d, 1709, Eliza Willins;
6–Constant, *m* 1732, Mildred La Mont, of Annapolis, Md.;
5–Constant, *m* 1756, Anna Weir;
4–Constant or Jonathan, both in Md. State troops, during Am. Rev.; Jonathan, *m* Mary–;
3–Constant (*b* 1776), settled in Shenandoah Valley, Va.; removed to Trumbull Co., O., 1808; to nr. Jeromesville, Ashland Co., O., 1812; *m* 1797, Ann Straughn, of Penns Neck, N.J.;
2–Mary (1798-1884), *m* 1821, William **Black** (1796-1888), farmer; of N.C.; removed to Lawrence Co., Ill., 1838.
1–*m* June 20, 1868, Maggie E. Finley (1842-70) dau. of J. M. Finley.
1–*m* 2d, Jan. 20, 1872, Ellen J. Finley (Jan. 20, 1851-May 15, 1910); dau. of J. M. Finley, of Bridgeport, Ill.; issue (all *b* Bridgeport, Ill.): 1–Amabel, *b* Nov. 19, 1872; *m* Dec. 20, 1894, T. D. Bryson, son of T. D. Bryson, of Bryson City, N.C. (issue: Edith; Thot Dillord, Jr.; C. Edwin; Marion; Kathleen); 2–Stanley Warren, *b* Jan. 20, 1876; *m* Mar. 1901, Mariana Fischer (issue: Ellen E.; Louise B.; Stanley W.; Fischer S.); 3–Floyd Henson, *b* Feb. 2, 1888; *m* June, 1914, Zarafinka Kirova, of Constantinople, Turkey (issue; K. Edwin).
1–Retired farmer. Mem. Ill. Legislature, 1888, 92. Baptist. Democrat. Residence: Huntingdon, Carroll Co., Tenn.

1–**BLACKFORD, Byron Haverly,** *b* Bellefonte, Pa., Apr. 29, 1904.
5–James **Miller** (1780-1857), of Beech Creek, Pa., *m* Ellen– (1785-1860);
4–Samuel (1812-92), *m* Eliza Huff (1818-99);
3–Elizabeth Ellen (1849-1920), *m* 1869, George Irvin **Blackford** (1849-99; Samuel^{4}, *m* Elizabeth, dau. of Solomon Lohr, resided Centre Co., since 1825);
2–Clyde Irvin (2 below).
6–Ens. Francis **Steel** (1741-1817), from North of Ireland, settled nr. Warrick Furnace, Chester Co., Pa., 1774; ens., 4th Bn., Pa. Militia from Chester Co., Am. Rev.; participated in Battle of Brandywine; *m* 1771, Margaret Crow (1752-1849), from Derry Co., Ireland;
5–Francis (1776-1852), of Bellefonte, Pa.; *m* 1802, Elizabeth Cary (1787-1869);
4–Eliza (1809-52), *m* 1832, Christopher (Everly, Heverly) **Haverly** (1810-54; Christian^{5} [*d* 1848], of Oxford, Chester Co., Pa., *m* 1798, Hannah–, *d* 1856);
3–Francis Steel (1833-1916), *m* 1st, Hannah Poorman, dau. of Michael Poorman; *m* 2d, 1878, Mary Anne Scanlon (1858-92; Patrick^{4} [1825-1909], *m* 1853, Bridget [1837-1915], dau. of Christopher Nolan, *m* Mary McNevin, both *d* Co. Mayo, Ireland, ante 1840);
2–Carolyn Inez (1879-1921), *m* 1903, Clyde Irvin **Blackford** (1871-1928).
1–Not married. Ed. Bloomsburg, Calif., and Lock Haven Teacher's Coll., 1923-25; Pa. State Coll., 1926-28. Merchant. Residence: 6-8 E. Bishop St., Bellefonte, Pa.

1–**BLACKMAN, William Waldo,** *b* Bridgewater, N.Y., May 25, 1856.
8–Adam **Blackman,** from Eng. to Stratford, Conn., 1640; first minister there; *m* Jane–;
7–John (*d* 1662), *m* ca. 1653, Dorothy Smith (Rev. Henry^{8}, of Wethersfield, Conn.);
6–Ebenezer, *m* 2d, 1694, Abigail Curtiss (Jonathan^{7});
5–Ebenezer, *m* Mehitable–;
4–Peter (*b* 1735), *m* Mary McEwen (Gersham^{5}; desc. Robert McEwen, from Scotland, landed at Perth Amboy, N.J., 1682);
3–Gersham, *m* 1806, Marcy Howland;
2–William Wise (2 below).
9–Cornelius **Waldo** (qv);
8–John, soldier King Philip's War; *m* ca. 1676, Rebecca Adams (Samuel^{9});
7–Edward (1684-1767), *m* 1706, Thankful Dimmock (Shuabel^{8});
6–Shuabel (1707-76), *m* 1730, Abigail Allen (Samuel^{7});
5–Jesse (*b* 1736), lt. Am. Rev.; *m* 1760, Bridget Thompson (Samuel^{6});
4–Ephraim (1764-1812), Commissary War 1812; *m* Eunice Dimmock;
3–Ephraim (1786-1873), *m* Sally Delight Converse (William^{4});
2–Sarah Angeline (1822-97), *m* 1841, William Wise **Blackman** (1819-85), dentist, Waterville, N.Y.; issue: I–Emily M. (*d* 1918; *m* George W. Bailey); II–William W. (1 above).
1–*m* Sept. 14, 1887, Lora Coates Jackson, *b* West Grove, Pa., Sept. 30, 1855; dau. of late Isaac Jackson, of West Grove; issue (all *b* Brooklyn, N.Y.): 1–Kenneth (*b* and *d* 1889); 2–Elinor, *b* Mar. 23, 1892; Vassar, '14; 3–William Jackson, *b* May 25, 1893; Cornell, '17; entered Aviation Service U.S.A., Apr. 20, 1917; commd. 1st lt., Dec. 28, 1917; in France 9 months; aboard the "Tuscania" when it was sunk; both legs broken by fall off airplane, Issoudun, France; *m* Aug. 20, 1924, Catherine Robinson (issue: Jackson Farr, *b* Oct. 6, 1925).
1–M.D., New York Homeopathic Med. Coll., 1877. Physician, Brooklyn, N.Y. Trustee and pres. New York Homeo. Med. Coll. and Flower Hosp. Mem. S.M.D. Club: University. Summer place: "Breeze Lodge," Douglas Hill, Me. Residence: 519 Clinton Av., Brooklyn, N.Y.

1–**BLAKE, Frances Greenough (Mrs. Arthur W.),** *b* Boston, Mass., Apr. 18, 1843.
7–William **Greenough** (qv);
6–Capt. John (1672-1732), ens., capt., A. and H.A.Co.; *m* 1693, Elizabeth Gross (*b* 1673);
5–Thomas (1710-85), dea. New Brick Ch., Boston, 1755; mem. Com. of Safety in Am. Rev.; *m* 1st, 1734, Martha Clark (*d* Sept. 5, 1749, aet. 37);
4–John (1742-81), freeman, 1774; house on Copps Hill was confiscated during Am. Rev.; removed to Wellfleet, taught sch.; *m* 1766, Mehitabel Dillingham (*d* 1798), of Marlborough, Mass.;
3–David (1774-1836), mcht., dealer real estate, Boston; *m* 1799, Elizabeth Bender (1776-1866), of Marlborough;
2–Henry (1807-83), hon. A.M., Harvard, 1852; importer, architect, Boston; *m* 1837, Frances Boott (1809-97); issue: I–Francis Boott, M.D. (1837-1904); II–Frances (1 above); III–Henry, Jr. (1849-80); IV–Florence (*b* 1852; *m* John Larkin Thorndike, see their dau. Mrs. Nathaniel Simpkins, Vol. I, p. 218).
1–*m* Apr. 25, 1878, Arthur Welland Blake (Nov. 5, 1840-Feb. 28, 1893), Harvard, '61; mem. firm Blake Bros., Boston and N.Y.; son of George Baty Blake, of Boston; issue: 1–Anne, *b* Brookline, Mass., Feb. 11, 1879; *m* June 18, 1902, Frederic L. W. Richardson (issue: Margery; Arthur; Frederic; Francis; Joseph; David; Julian); 2–Beatrice, *b* Brookline, June 23, 1883; *m* Sept. 5, 1906, William Gifford Nickerson (July 15, 1879-Oct. 7, 1914); son of Albert Nickerson, of Boston (issue: William G.; Henry G.).
1–Mem. C.D.A. Club: Chilton. Residence: "Kernwode," Brookline, Mass.

1–**BLANCHARD, Arthur Alphonzo,** *b* Boston, Mass., May 4, 1876.
8–Thomas **Blanchard** (qv);
7–Samuel (1629-1707), came with his father; con-

stable, Charlestown, 1657; later at Andover; *m* 1673, Hannah Dagget (1648-1725; Thomas[8], *m* Elizabeth Humphrey Fry);
6–John (1677-1750), of Charlestown and Billerica; *m* 1701, Mary Crosby (1680-1748; Simon[7], of Billerica, *m* Rachel Brackett; Simon[8], *m* Anne Brigham; Thomas[9], qv);
5–Simon (1725/26-1796), of Billerica; *m* 1746, Rebecca Sheldon (1727-1814; Samuel[6], *m* Sarah Hutchinson);
4–Joseph (1776-1828), of Billerica; *m* 1798, Sarah Brown (1774-1826; Col. Jonathan[5], of Tewksbury, Am. Rev., *m* Mary French);
3–Joseph (1805-56), of Billerica; *m* 1840, Rhoda Worcester;
2–Adolphus Joseph (2 below).
9–Rev. William **Worcester** (qv);
8–Samuel (*d* 1681), *m* 1659, Elizabeth Parrott;
7–William (1661-1706), *m* 1690, Martha Cheney;
6–Moses (*b* 1691), *m* Mercie–;
5–Eldad (1732-79), *m* 1761, Rebecca Osgood;
4–Eldad (1763-1853), Am. Rev.; *m* Esther Brown;
3–Rhoda (1815-68), of Tewksbury; *m* Joseph **Blanchard** (3 above);
2–Adolphus Joseph (1850-1912), of Billerica; *m* 1875, Louise B. Rand (1854-80; Alphonzo L.[3], of Portsmouth, *m* Louisa Jane Dodge); *m* 2d, 1904, Fannie H. Moorehead.
1-*m* Aug. 8, 1905, Eugenia M. Lord, *b* Somersworth, N.H., July 22, 1877; dau. of Christie L. Lord, of Worcester, Mass., *m* 1873, Helen A. Dow, of Somersworth; issue (all *b* Newton, Mass.): 1–Shirley Louise, *b* June 20, 1906; 2–Helen Lord, *b* Oct. 29, 1909; 3–Malcolm Adolphus, *b* Oct. 13, 1913; 4–Joseph, *b* Apr. 21, 1916.
1–S.B., M.I.T., '98; Ph.D., U.Leipsic, 1902. Asst. prof. chemistry, M.I.T., 1908-14, asso. prof. since 1914. Author (see Who's Who in America). Mem. Am. Chem. Soc., A.A.A.S., Am. Acad. Arts and Sciences, N.E.Assn. Chem. Teachers, etc. Republican. Unitarian. Clubs: Appalachian Mountain, Unitarian Laymen's League, Univ. (Boston); Rexhame Country, Marshfield Country. Residence: 25 Evans Rd., Brookline, Mass.

1–**BLAUVELT, Martin Emerson,** *b* Yonkers, N.Y., Mar. 19, 1883.
9–Gerrit Hendricksen **Blauvelt** (1620-83), from Holland to Rensselaerwyck, N.Y., 1637; settled at New Amsterdam, 1646; *m* 1646, Marritje Moll (ante 1625-ante 1679; Lambert Huybertsen[10], of Bushwick, L.I., *m* Hendrickse Cornelis);
8–Hendrick Gerritsen (bap. 1648), of New Amsterdam; *m* 1673, Marritje Josephs Waldron (*b* 1652; Joseph[9], *m* Annetje Daniels);
7–Joseph Hendricks (*b* 1687), of Tappan, N.Y.; *m* 1711, Elizabeth Van Dalsen (Jan[8], *m* Annetje Van Raltsvelt);
6–Johannes Joseph (*b* 1714), of Tappan; maj. Am. Rev.; *m* Margrietje Smidt (*b* 1720; Cornelius[7], *m* Vrowtje Van Houten);
5–Joseph (1740-89), served under his father, Am. Rev.; *m* 1769, Johanna Demarest (1749-1817; Nicholas[6], *m* Elsje–; David D.[7], *m* Marritje Lozier);
4–Johannes Joseph (1770-1855), of Clarkstown, N.Y.; *m* 1791, Rachel Van Orden (*b* 1774; Jacobus[5], of New Hempstead, N.Y., *m* Maria Blauvelt);
3–John J. (1804-60), of Clarkstown; *m* 1840, Ann Berry (1814-80; William[4], *m* Anna Blauvelt);
2–Martin (1846-1915), of Paterson, N.J.; *m* at Brooklyn, N.Y., 1881, Caroline Millicent Orchard (*b* Paterson, N.J., 1851; John Yoe[3], of Eng., *m* Mary Herbert Holgate, *b* Eng.); issue: I–Son (*d* infancy); II–Martin E. (1 above).
1–*m* Apr. 10, 1926, Alliene Shugard Righter (qv for issue).
1–A.B., Columbia, '05, A.M., 1912. Studied law, 1905-08. Admitted N.Y. Bar, 1908; practiced law, 1908-29, at Yonkers, N.Y. Mem. H.S. (treas., Westchester Co., N.Y., branch), S.A.R., Westchester Co. (N.Y.) Hist. Soc.; Assn. of Blauvelt Descendants (ex-pres.). Reformed. Residence: 3 Robins Pl., Yonkers, N.Y.

1–**BLAUVELT, Alliene Shugard Righter (Mrs. Martin E.),** *b* Parsippany, N.J., Apr. 17, 1888.
7–Isaac **Stiles** (*d* 1714), *m* Hannah–;
6–"Long" Jonathan (1688-1768), *m* Rebecca Canfield;
5–Capt. John (1709-77), *m* Rachel–;
4–Dea. John (1753-1830), q.m., Morris Co. militia, N.J., in Am. Rev.; at Pequannock, N.J.; *m* 1776, Mary Sandford (1755-1843);
3–Locky (1786-1882), *m* 1806, John **Righter** (1786-1857), of Parsippany, N.J.;
2–George Edgar (1829-1913), of Parsippany, N.J.; *m* at Newark, N.J., 1882, Hester Maria Cadmus Baldwin (*b* Belleville, N.J., 1852-1891); issue: I–Augusta (*m* Mr. Smith); II–Chester Newell; III–Edward (*d* young); IV–Alliene S. (1 above).
1–*m* Apr. 10, 1926, Martin Emerson Blauvelt (qv); issue: 1–Martin Emerson, Jr., *b* Oct. 17, 1928.
1–Ed. Newark City Hosp. Training Sch. for Nurses. Mem. U.S.A. Nurses Corps, 1916-19; served overseas 9 months, 1918-19. Supt. Grace Hosp., Richmond, Va., 1919-23. Mem. D.A.R., Westchester Co. (N.Y.) Hist. Soc. Reformed Church. Residence: 3 Robins Pl., Yonkers, N.Y.

1–**BLISS, Elizabeth Bancroft,** *b* Berlin, Germany, Nov. 6, 1868.
11–Elder William **Brewster** (qv);
10–Love (*d* 1650), *m* 1634, Sarah Collier (1615-91; William[11], *m* Jane–);
9–Sarah (*b* 163–), *m* 1656, Benjamin **Bartlett** (1632-91; Robert[10], qv, *m* Mary, dau. of Richard Warren, qv);
8–Rebecca, *m* 1679, William **Bradford** (William[9], William[10], qv);
7–Alice (1680-1775), *m* William **Barnes**;
6–Mercy (1708-91), as widow of Samuel Cole, *m* 2d, 1733, Barnabas **Hedge** (John[7]; Elisha[8]; William[9]);
5–Mercy (1734-79), *m* 1753, Thomas **Davis** (*b* 1722), to Plymouth, Mass., from N.C., 1737 (Thomas[6], from Eng., to Albany, N.Y., thence to N.C.);
4–William (1758-1826), *m* 1781, Rebecca Morton;
3–Elizabeth (1803-86), *m* Alexander **Bliss** (1792-1827);
2–Bvt. Lt. Col. Alexander (2 below).
10–George **Morton** (qv);
9–Sec. Nathaniel (1613-85), from Eng. with father; *m* 1635, Lydia Cooper (Ephraim[10], *m* 2d, Mary Harlow);
8–Remember (*b* 1637), *m* 1657, Abraham **Jackson** (*d* 1709?);
7–Nathaniel (*b* 1665?), *m* 1686, Ruth Jenny (Samuel[8]);
6–Nathaniel, *m* 2d, Rebecca Poor;
5–Rebecca, *m* 1753, Nathaniel **Morton** (*b* 1731; Nathaniel[6] [*b* 1706], *m* 1730, Meriah Clarke; Nathaniel[7] [1660-1709], *m* 1706, Mary Faunce; Ephraim[8] [1623-93]; George[9], same as 10 above, qv);
4–Rebecca (1762-1847), *m* William **Davis** (4 above);
3–Elizabeth, *m* Alexander **Bliss** (3 above);
2–Bvt. Lt. Col. Alexander, U.S.A. (1827-96), first sec. Am. Legation and mil. attache at Berlin; first asst. q.m. gen. U.S.A.; *m* Eleanor Taylor Albert (1842-74; William Julian[3], congressman, *m* Emily Jones); issue: I–William Julian Albert (see Vol. II, p. 272); II–Elizabeth B. (1 above).
1–Mem. C.D.A. Club: Colonial Dames (Washington). Summer place: Juniper Hill, York Harbor, Me. Residence: 1621 21st St., Washington, D.C.

1–**BLISS, Harry Alfred,** *b* Cleveland, O., Aug. 3, 1867.
9–Thomas **Bliss** (qv);
8–Ens. Lawrence (*d* 1676), came with his father, 1635; early settler at Springfield, Mass.; constable, 1660; selectman, 1665 and 69; *m* 1654, Lydia Wright (*d* 1699; Dea. Samuel[9], *m* Margaret–);
7–Pelatiah (*b* 1674), lt.; *m* 1698, Elizabeth Hitchcock (Luke[8]; Luke[9], qv);
6–Pelatiah (1701-64), of East Windsor, Conn.; *m* 1722, Ann Stoughton (*d* 1736);
5–Reuben (1726-1806), of Springfield, Mass.; *m* 1753, Elizabeth Hitchcock (1732-1812);
4–Stoughton (1758-1836), of E. Windsor, Conn.; *m* 1780, Zerviah White (1758-1832), of Springfield, Mass.;
3–William (1790-1828), of Cleveland, O.; *m* 1813, Cynthia Wolcott (1789-1848);
2–Lt. William Samuel (1827-81), *m* 1865, Anna Maria Johnston (*b* 1840), of Strongsville, O.;

issue: I–Harry A. (1 above); II–Maria Louise (*m* Charles P. Horr).
1–*m* Aug. 31, 1910, Blanche L. Fisher, *b* Cleveland, O., Aug. 11, 1879; dau. of Capt. Newton D. D. Fisher; issue: 1–Wolcott (*d* infancy); 2–Imogene Fisher, *b* Nov. 29, 1917.
1–Wholesale hardware mfr. agt. Pres. and gen. mgr. Bliss Supply Co., Cleveland. Treas. Grafton Stone Co. Sec. and treas. U.S. Power Squadron; mem. Cleveland Naval Reserve, Cleveland Gatling Gun Battery, Veteran Troop "A," Cleveland. Mem. S.V., I.A.G., Soc. Desc. of Henry Wolcott (pres. 1924; chmn. Henry Wolcott Foundation Fund), N.E. Soc. of Cleveland and the Western Reserve (treas., chmn. entertainment com.), Conn. Hist. Soc. Clubs: Cleveland Yacht (dir., chmn. house com.), Hermit (charter mem.). Summer residence: Clifton Park Lagoon, Lakewood, O. Residence: 1827 Idlewood Av., Cleveland, O.

BOARDMAN

Arms: *Argent, on a bend azure, three boars' heads sable.*
Crest: *A bull's head tenné.*
Motto: *Semper fidelis.*

ARTHUR EDWIN BOARDMAN

1–**BOARDMAN, Arthur Edwin,** *b* Macon, Ga., Mar. 20, 1850.
8–Thomas (Boreman) **Boardman** (bap. 1601-1673), from Claydon, Eng., 1634; settled at Ipswich, Mass.; *m* in Eng., Margaret– (*d* 1679);
7–Thomas (1643-1719), of Ipswich; began to write name Boardman; *m* 1668, Elizabeth Perkins (1650-1718; Sgt. Jacob[8]);
6–Offin (1676-1750), of Salisbury, Mass.; *m* 1698, Sarah Heard;
5–Offin (1698-1735), of Newbury, Mass.; *m* Sarah Woodman (*d* 1752);
4–Jonathan (*b* 1735), of Newbury; *m* 1761, Rebecca Moody;
3–Jonathan (bap. 1780), of Newburyport, Mass.; *m* 1804, Sarah Horton;

JOSEPH M. BOARDMAN (1808-93), at 80 years.

2–Joseph M. (1808-93), Macon, Ga. (see portrait); *m* 1840, Maria Therese Lord (1805-47); *m* 2d, 1848, Caroline Augusta Pierpont (1823-81; Rev. John[3], of Hollis St. Ch., Boston); *m* 3d, 1882, Elodia Billings Trapp (1829-91); issue (2d marriage); I–Arthur Edwin (1 above); II–Juliet Morgan (1853-1928; *m* Harney Twiggs Powell, 1847-1923); III–John Lewis (1863-1905; *m* Mary Ellen Spence, 1872-1925); IV–Elodia Russell (1866-1905; *m* William Roland Chandler Smith, *d* 1902).
1–*m* Oct. 20, 1875, Rebecca Warner Tallman (Oct. 15, 1852-Nov. 21, 1923); dau. of George Clinton Tallman, of Utica, N.Y.
1–C.E., Rensselaer Poly. Inst., '70 (Theta Xi). Retired. Built water works at Macon, Americus, Brunswick, Cartersville, Ga., at Florence and Tuscaloosa, Ala., Fernandina, Ocala, Tampa, Fla., Richmond, Ky., Johnson City, Tenn.; built filter plants at Columbus, Ga., Charlotte and Raleigh, N.C.; built gas works at Macon and Brunswick, Ga., Richmond, Ky.; electric works at Macon and Brunswick. Consulting engr. Mem. Macon Vols. 1872-90. Mem. bd. of directors of above mentioned works, and pres., Macon and Tampa. Mem. Christ Episcopal Ch. Independent Democrat. Residence: Macon, Ga.

1–**BODMAN, Alice Maconda Pratt (Mrs. Joseph Day),** *b* Norwich, Conn., Sept. 29, 1860.
9–Matthew **Pratt** (qv);
8–Joseph (1639-1722), *m* Sarah Judkins;
7–John (*b* 1668), *m* Mercy or Mary Newcomb;
6–John (1696-1769), *m* Jael Beals;
5–Ezra (1740-1807), *m* Abigail Clark;
4–Bela (1777-1843), *m* Sophia W. Lyon;
3–Bela (1810-44), of E. Weymouth, Mass.; *m* Nabby Bates Tirrell (*d* 1883);
2–George (2 below).
9–Christopher **Avery** (qv);
8–Capt. James (1620-1700), *b* Eng., *d* New London, Conn.; soldier in King Philip's War; dep. Gen. Assembly, of Hartford and New Haven,

20 times; *m* 1643, Joanna Greenslade (*b* 1622), of Boston, Mass.;
7–James (1646-1748), New London, Conn.; *m* 1669, Deborah Sterling or Stallion (1649-1729);
6–Hannah (*b* 1683), Groton, Conn.; *m* Samuel **Morgan** (1669-1729/30);
5–Timothy (ca. 1723-95), Stonington, Conn.; *m* Deborah–;
4–Theophilus (1759-1828), Salem or Stonington, Conn.; Am. Rev.; *m* 1795, Mary Hinckley (1767-1825);
3–Charlotte Maconda (1805-65), of Salem, Conn.; *m* 1826, Orramel **Whittlesey** (1801-76);
2–Sarah Victoria (1831-1923), of Norwich, Conn., and Kansas City, Mo.; *m* 1858, George **Pratt** (1832-75), grad. Yale, 1857 (class poet; Skull and Bones), lawyer; rep. Conn. Legislature many yrs. from Norwich, Conn.; issue: I–Alice Maconda (1 above); II–Orramel W. (1862-1926; *m* Bertha Pepper); III–Gertrude (1864-1918); IV–Bela Lyon (1867-1917; *m* Helen L. Pray); V–Susie Warren (1870-73); VI–Minot Tully (1872-1908; *m* Lillian Nelson).
1–*m* Apr. 20, 1882, Joseph Day Bodman, *b* Williamsburg, Mass., Apr. 20, 1860; son of Lewis Bodman, of Williamsburg; issue: 1–George Pratt, *b* Bement, Ill., July 10, 1883; *m* Aug. 21, 1907, Clara Luella, dau. of Sydney McCracken, of Overbrook, Kan. (issue: John Morgan; Mary Pratt; George Minot; Clara Luella; Joseph Day; Alice Maconda; Thomas Allyn; Orramel Whittlesey; Karolyn Whittlesey); 2–Emily Nash, *b* Bement, Apr. 22, 1885; B.S., Simmons Coll., '08; *m* June 1912, William M. Leiserson (issue: Avery; Lee; Sarah; Ruth; Charles Frederick; Mark; Philip Day); 3–John Whittlesey, *b* Knoxville, Tenn., Oct. 4, 1888; B.S., U. of Mo., '10; *m* June 1912, Ida S. Garrett, of Cambridge, Mass. (issue: Priscilla; Winston); 4–Charlotte Maconda, *b* Kansas City, Mo., Nov. 17, 1893; A.B., U. of Wis., '16; *m* Oct. 4, 1916, Charles B., son of Charles T. Neal, of Kansas City (issue: Alice; Margaret; Virginia).
1–Mem. D.C.W., D.A.R., etc. Clubs: Woman's City (Chicago). Life mem. Chicago Art Inst. Episcopalian. Republican. Residence: 433 W. 61st Terrace, Kansas City, Mo.

1–**BOHN, Elizabeth Prince (Mrs. Charles F.),** *b* St. Paul, Minn., May 1, 1875.
10–William **Brewster,** Mayflower Pilgrim (qv);
9–Jonathan (1593-1659), *m* 1624, Lucretia Oldham;
8–Mary (1627-91), *m* 1645, John **Turner**;
7–Ruth (*b* 1663), of Duxbury, Mass.; *m* 1695, Capt. Thomas **Prince** (1658-1704; Elder John[8], qv);
6–Job (1695-1731), *b* Scituate, Mass., *d* Jamaica, W.I.; *m* 1722, Abigail Kimball (1703-80), of Boston and Kingston, Mass.;
5–Kimball (1726-1814), of Kingston, Mass.; Am. Rev.; *m* 1749, Deborah Fuller (1729-1826; Jabez[6] [*b* 1692]; John[7] [*d* 1697]; Rev. Samuel[8] [*d* 1695]; Dr. Samuel[9], Mayflower Pilgrim, qv);
4–Job (1765-1831), of Kingston; removed to Turner, Me., post 1790; *m* 1790, Hannah Bryant;
3–Rufus (1801-81), of Buckfield and Bangor, Me.; merchant; *m* 1828, Sophia Brewster;
2–Thomas Brewster (2 below).
8–Elder William **Brewster** (qv);
7–Love (*d* 1650), of Plymouth and Duxbury, Mass.; Pequot War; *m* 1634, Sarah Collier (1615-91), of Duxbury;
6–Wrestling (*d* 1696/97), of Duxbury; *m* Mary–(1661-1742);
5–Wrestling (1695-1767), of Kingston; *m* 1722, Hannah Thomas;
4–Thomas (1729-1815), of Pembroke and Kingston, Mass.; his homestead called "Woodside"; *m* 1794, Mary Hall (1767-1861), of Cape Cod;
3–Sophia (1804-64), of Kingston; *m* Rufus **Prince** (3 above).
9–Richard **Warren,** Mayflower Pilgrim (qv);
8–Ann, *m* 1633, Thomas **Little** (qv);
7–Hannah (*d* 1710), *m* 1662, Stephen **Tilden** (bap. 1629-1711; Nathaniel[8], qv);
6–Mary (1668-1718), *m* 1692/93, James **Thomas**;
5–Hannah (1698-1788), *m* Wrestling **Brewster** (5 above).
2–Thomas B. **Prince** (1838-1921), of Bangor, Me., and St. Paul, Minn.; contractor; *m* 1861, Fannie Mary French (1840-79; Henry[3], of Orrington, Me.); *m* 2d, 1883, Mrs. Esther Thompson; issue (1st marriage): I–Frances Evelyn (1862-1922; *m* George Clinton Cahoon); II–Thomas Harold (*b* 1867; *m* Emma Murray); III–Samuel (1868-72); IV–Lillian S. (*b* 1873; *m* Charles K. Stucker); V–Elizabeth (1 above); VI–Charles Eugene (*b* 1878; *m* Rose Painter).
1–*m* Dec. 26, 1900, Charles Frederic Bohn, *b* Milwaukee, Wis., Apr. 15, 1874; son of William Bohn, of Yakima, Wash.; issue: 1–Carolyn Winnifred (Oct. 26, 1901-Sept. 28, 1916); 2–Karl Kenneth, *b* Yakima, Wash., Oct. 12, 1903; B.A., Coll. of Puget Sound; 3–Muriel Elizabeth Maxine, *b* Yakima, Aug. 19, 1910; ed. Coll. of Puget Sound; 4–Donald Douglas Frederic, *b* Tacoma, Wash., Jan. 9, 1913.
1–Ed. Wis. State Normal Coll. Mem. S.M.D., D.A.R. Congregationalist. Residence: 3610 N. Stevens St., Tacoma, Wash.

1–**BOLLES, Mabel Beardsley (Mrs. P. Dexter),** *b* in Neb., July 2, 1888.
9–William **Beardsley** (qv);
8–Joseph (1634-1712), of Stratford, Conn.; *m* 1665, Abigail Dayton, of L.I.;
7–Josiah (*b* 1681), of Stratford; *m* 1712, Mary Whitmore, of Middletown, Conn.;
6–Ens. Benjamin (1727-1802), of Stratford; *m* 1st, Thankful Beardsley (1727-87);
5–Benjamin (1752-1837), of Genoa, Cayuga Co., N.Y.; served in Am. Rev. under Gen. Washington; *m* 1785, Amelia Stevens;
4–James (1786-1867), of Hartford, Conn., and Malone, N.Y.; *m* Elizabeth Darby, of Vt.;
3–Oliver Augustus (1823-76), of Malone, N.Y.; *m* Mary Eliza Miller, of Can.;
2–Truman Charles (*b* Malone, N.Y. 1863), jeweler and optician, Seattle, Wash.; *m* 1884, Elise Von Maurer (*b* 1865); issue: I–Mabel (1 above); II–Everett James (*b* 1891; *m* Irene Walsh); III–Ethel May (*b* 1895; D.A.R.; *m* David Arnold Webbertt); IV–Walter Haywood (*b* 1898; S.A.R.; *m* Marjory Van Pelt).
1–*m* Nov. 27, 1907, Perley Dexter Bolles, *b* Fairdale, Pa., June 16, 1882; son of Anson Bolles, of Scranton, Pa., *m* Eliza Marshall.
1–Mem. D.A.R. Residence: East Seattle, Mercer Island, Wash.

1–**BOND, Catharine Alcorn Wales (Mrs. T. Allen),** *b* Norfolk, Va.
10–Nathaniel **Wales** (qv);
9–Nathaniel (*d* 1662), *m* Isabel Atherton (Humphrey[10], *m* Mary, dau. of John Wales, of Eng.);
8–Nathaniel (*d* 1708), *m* Joanna Faxon (*b* 1661; Thomas[9], *m* 1653, Deborah [*d* 1662], dau. of Richard Thayer [bap. 1601-1668]; Thomas[10] [1601-80], ruling elder of Braintree, *m* Joan–);
7–Capt. Elkanna (1685-1763), of Braintree, Mass.; served in Colonial War; *m* 1708, Elizabeth Holbrook (*d* 1763; Samuel[8] [*b* ca. 1654], *m* Lydia–; Capt. John[9] [*b* 1618/19], *m* Elizabeth Stern; Thomas[10] [*b* 1601], *m* Jane–);
6–Nathaniel (1717-90), ens. and capt. Colonial Army; mem. Com. of Public Affairs, 1774, Com. of Safety, 1779; *m* 2d, 1754, Ann (Waldo) Fitch (1719-1801);
5–Benjamin (1759-1837), pvt. in Am. Rev.; *m* 1787, Susanna Ludden (1768-96; Joseph[6] [*b* 1716], *m* Elizabeth Wild; Benjamin[7] [1680-1752], *m* Sarah–; Benjamin[8] [1650-90], *m* Eunice, dau. of Capt. John Holbrook; James[9] [1611-93], *m* Alice–);
4–Asaph (1790-1864), pvt. in War 1812; *m* 1815, Eliza Osborne Butler;
3–William Henry (1824-97), cashier Merchants & Mechanics Savings Bank, Norfolk, Va., 1855-97 (oldest bank in Va.; succeeded by son, John Edgar; son William Henry, Jr. [1865-1914], became pres.), gave up four keys of this bank to provost marshal, during War between the States; capt. Home Guards, War between the States; *m* 1855, Anna Babcock Haff;
2–Charles (2 below).
10–Nicholas **Butler,** from Eng. in the "Hercules," ante 1637; settled at Dorchester, Mass.; moved to Martha's Vineyard, 1651; *m* Joyce–;
9–John (bap. 1624-1658), *m* Mary Lynde (*b* 1628/29; Thomas[10], of Charlestown);
8–John (1649/50-will dated 1733), gentlemen and capt.; coroner for the co.; sgt. Militia Co., 1691; lived on Great Neck;
7–Nicholas (1678-1772), of Edgertown; *m* 1730, Thankful Marchant (1717-62);
6–Matthew (*b* 1736), wrecked at Gray Head, buried at sea; lived in Martha's Vineyard; *m* Elizabeth Osborne (1736-72);

5–Henry (ca. 1762-1812), Master Marine; lost at sea on a voyage from Lisbon, Portugal, to Norfolk, Va.; *m* 1792, Charlotte Norton;
4–Eliza (1799-1865), a beautiful dancer; danced for Marquis de Lafayette, who had the floor cleared, while she danced the Fishers Hornpipe, 1824; *m* Asaph **Wales** (4 above).
8–Louis **Haff,** *m* Connerto–;
7–Jacob, of Crum Elbow, Dutchess Co., N.Y.;
6–Jacob (will dated 1757), *m* Margaret–;
5–Capt. Jacob, settled in N.Y.; life mem. "Sailors Snug Harbor," N.Y.City; moved to Evansville, Ind., and lived there until after 1849, returned to N.Y., buried in Sailors Snug Harbor; piloted the first steamboat up the Hudson River; *m* Elizabeth Watkeys (1785-1849);
4–John (1808-49), *m* 1834, Elizabeth Babcock;
3–Anna Babcock (1835-1913), *m* 1855, William Henry **Wales** (3 above).
11–Elder William **Brewster,** Mayflower Pilgrim (qv);
10–Jonathan (1593-1659), came in the "Fortune," 1622; dep. gov.; *m* 1624, Lucretia Oldham;
9–Rev. Nathaniel (*d* 1690), grad. in 1st class of Harvard, 1642; *m* Sarah Ludlow;
8–Timothy, *m* Mary Hawkins (Zachariah[9]);
7–Mary, *m* her cousin Daniel **Brewster** (*b* 1687);
6–Mary (*b* 1754), *m* 1778, Nehemiah **Heart**;
5–Anna (1783-1832), *m* 1804, Oliver **Babcock** (Rev. Oliver[6]; Elder Stephen[7]; Capt. John[8]; John[9]; James[10], qv);
4–Elizabeth, *m* John **Haff** (4 above);
3–Anna Babcock, *m* William Henry **Wales** (3 above);
2–Charles (*b* 1868), *m* Marie Stewart Glover; issue: I–Catharine A. (1 above); II–Walton Glover (*m* Katharine Booker).
1–*m* Dec. 9, 1922, T(homas) Allen Bond, *b* Petersburg, Va.; son of Thomas Baker Bond; issue: 1–Marie Glover, *b* Norfolk, Va., Feb. 10, 1924; 2–Thomas Allen, II, *b* Richmond, Va., Nov. 17, 1926.
Residence: Lochaven, Norfolk, Va.

1–**BOSWELL, Jesse Virgil,** *b* Farmington, Mo., Apr. 26, 1876.
5–John **Boswell** (*d* 1765), planter of Charles Co., Md.; *m* Elizabeth—;
4–Peter (1754-1807), of Prince George Co.; *m* 1783, Ann Bayne Finley;
3–William Finley (*b* Fairfax, Va., 1806-*d* 1856), of Statesville, Tenn.; *m* 1830, Mallissa Eddings (1814-1902; William[4], soldier Am. Rev.);
2–Robert French Osborne (2 below).
9–Roger **Fowke** (son of John, *m* Dorothy, dau. of John Cupper), from Eng., 1651, settled in Westmoreland Co., Va.; *m* Mary Bailey (William[10]);
8–Gerard (*d* 1669), from Eng. with his parents, 1651, settled at Westmoreland Co.; removed to Charles Co., Md., 1664; lt. of Troops, Westmoreland Co., 1660, col., 1662; burgess for Westmoreland, 1663; for Charles Co., 1665; justice, 1667; *m* 1661, Ann (Thoroughgood) Chandler (Adam[9] Thoroughgood);
7–Gerard (1662-1734), of Charles Co., Md.; *m* 1st, Miss Lomax; *m* 2d, Sarah Burdett;
6–Catherine, of Charles Co.; *m* Ebsworth **Bayne**;
5–Martha Hawkins, of Prince George Co., Md.; *m* 1750, Charles **Finley** (1722-87; Charles[6], *m* Elizabeth Harris; Col. Robert[7], *m* Jane Johnson);
4–Ann Bayne (1757-1807), of Prince George Co.; *m* 1783, Peter **Boswell** (4 above);
3–William Finley, *m* Mallissa Eddings (3 above);
2–Robert French Osborne (1846-79), of LaFayette, Ky.; dentist; *m* Mary I. Armour (*d* 1873); *m* 2d, Emma Helber (*b* 1854); issue (1st marriage): I–son (*d* infancy); issue 2d marriage): I–Jesse Virgil (1 above); II–Robert Leslie (*m* Alma Krekel; *m* 2d, Lena Alma Revoir).
1–*m* Dec. 7, 1903, Anite Bain Campbell (qv); issue: 1–Mary Kathryn, *b* Springfield, Mo., Apr. 29, 1905; A.B., Drury Coll., '26; M.A., Peabody Coll., 1930.
1–Attended Carleton Coll. 2 yrs. D.D.S., Vanderbilt U., Nashville, Tenn., '01. Practiced at Fulton, Ky., 1901-02; moved to Greenville, Miss.; removed to Springfield, Mo., 1904, engaged in practice of dentistry since then. Pres. Springfield Dist. Dental Soc. Methodist. Republican. Clubs: Springfield University (sec. 1917, 18, 29; pres. 1930), Art Museum Assn. Residence: Springfield, Mo.

1–**BOSWELL, Anite Bain Campbell (Mrs. Jesse V.),** *b* Lake Providence, La., Jan. 15, 1880.
10–John **Slaughter,** said to have settled in Va., ante 1620; received a land grant on Knight's Creek, Essex Co., 1635;
9–Francis (1630-56), capt. militia; justice, Rappahannock Co., Va.; *m* 1652 (?), Elizabeth Underwood (Col. William[10], *m* Margaret–);
8–Francis (1653-1718), planter, Richmond Co., Va.; *m* 1679, Margaret Hudson;
7–Robert (1680-1726), Essex Co.; *m* 1700, Frances Anne Jones (Lt. Col. Cadwallader[8], *m* Katherine–, of Stafford Co.; Richard[9], *m* Anne Townsend);
6–Robert (ca. 1702-1769), capt. 1729; justice of Orange Co., 1745; burgess, 1742; vestryman, St. Mark's Parish, 1731; *m* 1723, Mary Smith (Augustine[7] [*d* 1736], a founder of Fredericksburg, *m* Susannah Darnell; Maj. Lawrence[8]);
5–Martha, of Culpeper, Va.; *m* 2d, William **Broadus** (1755-1830), sgt. and 2d lt., Capt. Hamilton's co. and Capt. Ewell's co., 1st Regt. from Va., 1776-80; was in the battles of Monmouth and Barren Hill Ch.; pay-master at Harper's Ferry;
4–Catharine W. (1790-1819), of Culpeper, Va.; *m* 1808, William Mills **Thompson** (1775-1837; William[5], *m* Frances Mills);
3–Martha Frances (1814-69), of Culpeper and Loudoun cos., Va.; *m* 1835, Samuel **Campbell** (1797-1882), of Leesburg, Va.;
2–Robert Gray (2 below).
11–Col. Richard **Ewen** (qv);
10–Elizabeth, *m* 1656, Richard **Talbott** (qv);
9–Elizabeth (1656-1719), *m* 1676, Benjamin **Lawrence** (qv);
8–Benjamin (*d* 1719), of "Benjamin Fortune," Anne Arundel Co., Md.; *m* 1710, Rachel Mariarti (Edward[9]);
7–Levin (1712-56), lived at Elk Ridge, Md., and later "Dorsey's Grove;" *m* Susannah Dorsey;
6–John (1743-82), of "Valley Farm," Linganore Hills, Md.; mem. Com. Observation, Frederick Co., Md., 1775; justice, 1777; soldier Am. Rev.; *m* Martha West (Stephen[7], *m* Martha Hall);
5–Ann West (*d* 1840, aet. 77 yrs.), *m* Thomas **Mansell;**
4–Louise Lawrence (*d* 1818), *m* 1810, William Ellis **Bain** (*d* 1863; William[5], soldier Am. Rev., *m* Elizabeth Montgomery Bell);
3–Ann Louise (1816-1901), of Lexington, Ky.; *m* 1834, John H. **Robb** (*d* 1855);
2–Patti (2 below).
10–Maj. Edward **Dorsey** (qv);
9–Maj. Edward (1645-1705), of Annapolis, Md.; capt. militia, Anne Arundel Co., 1686, maj. 1687; recommd. maj., 1689 and 1694; judge High Court of Chancery, Md., 1695; mem. Md. Assembly, 1694-97, 1701-05; justice, Anne Arundel Co.; *m* Sarah Wyatt (Col. Nicholas[10]);
8–John (*d* 1764), *m* Honor Elder (John[9], of Md.);
7–Susannah (*b* 1717), *m* Levin **Lawrence** (7 above);
2–Robert Gray **Campbell** (1846-95), lawyer, Louisville, Ky., and Providence, La.; *m* 1872, Nannie A. Browder (Col. B. M.[3]); *m* 2d, 1876, Patti Robb (1850-1919); issue (2d marriage): I–Anite Bain (1 above); II–Robert Granville (*b* 1882; *m* Frank Huckstep).
1–*m* Dec. 7, 1903, Jesse Virgil Boswell (qv for issue).
1–Mem. D.A.R., U.D.C., Springfield Art Museum Assn. Episcopalian. Clubs: The Hopewells, Tri Psi Sorority. Residence: Springfield, Mo.

1–**BOUTON, S(tephen) Miles,** *b* Blockville, N.Y., Sept. 24, 1876.
8–Jean (John) **Bouton** (qv);
7–John, Jr. (*b* 1657), *m* Sarah Greggorie, of Norwalk, Conn.;
6–Nathaniel (*b* 1691), *m* 2d, Mary–;
5–Nathaniel, Jr. (*b* 1726), *m* Lydia Penoyer; *m* 2d, Rachel Kellogg, of Norwalk, Conn.;
4–Enos (*b* 1770), *m* Prudence Hayes;
3–Stephen (1795-1877), *m* 2d, Electa Spaulding, of Groton, N.Y.;
2–Harry Bowker (*b* 1852), of Blockville, N.Y.; *m* 1874, Almina M. Lewis (1857-1925); issue: I–S. Miles (1 above); II–Harry B., Jr. (*b* 1878; *m* Belle Campbell).
1–*m* Nov. 11, 1903, Frieda Dorothea Kleinsang, *b* Altona, Germany, Oct. 7, 1882; dau. of Heinrich Kleinsang, of Pinneberg, Germany; issue: 1–S(tephen) Miles, Jr., *b* Buffalo, N.Y.,

Nov. 18, 1907; ed. Oberrealschule, Berlin, and U.Berlin; 2–Noel Lewis, *b* New York, N.Y., Apr. 28, 1910; ed. Oberrealschule, Berlin.

1–LL.B., Albany Law Sch., '99; spl. studies in polit. history, U. of Berlin, 1911-12, 1925-26-27. Spl. newspaper correspondent for Baltimore Sun and Brooklyn Daily Eagle. With German armies on various fronts as war corr., 1914-16; in charge Asso. Press Bur., Stockholm, Sweden, 1916-19; in Petrograd, summer, 1917; 1st enemy corr. to enter Germany after armistice. Author (see Who's Who in America). Mem. Foreign Correspondents Assn., Berlin. Unitarian. Residence: Luitpoldstrasse 30, Berlin W 30, Germany.

1–**BOUTON, Mildred Thomas Vaughan (Mrs. William P.),** *b* Tippah Co., Miss., Nov. 1, 1867.

7–Gilley **Gromarrin** (*d* 1716), of Henrico Co., Va.;

6–Gilley (Marion) (*d* 1747), *m* Mary–;

5–Mary, *m* 1765, Caldwell **Pettipool** (P'Pool), of Richmond, Henrico Co., Va.; pvt. 6th Va. Regt. during Am. Rev. (son of Seth or William Pettipool);

4–Wiltshire Gromarrin (1770-1852), *m* 1792, Martha Ingram (1773-1847; Pines[5], *m* Lucy Hamlette);

3–Samuel (1798-1880), carpenter; *m* 1824, Elizabeth (Betsey) Morgan (1804-79; John[4], *m* Sarah Neblett).

2–George Washington **Vaughan** (1816-71; Lemuel[3], *m* 1st, Mildred Thomas), of New Market, Ala.; removed to Tippah Co., Miss.; mcht. at Selmer, McNairy Co., Tenn.; maj. in C.S.A.; *m* Matilda Wheeler; *m* 2d, 1847, Mary Marion Pettipool (1827-90); issue (2d marriage); I–Samuel Pettipool (1847-49); II–Elizabeth Catherine (1849-1914; *m* 1868, Francis Marion Treadwell); III–William Lewis (1851-53); IV–Laura Mildred (1853-74; *m* 1872, Bradley Thomas Kimbrough); V–Mary Marion (1855-1923; *m* 1871, Lucius Eugene Lipford); VI–George Washington (1857-62); VII–Virginia (1859-61); VIII–John Wiltshire (1861-1913; *m* 1885, Willa Aileen Ayres); IX–Caldwell Pines (1864-1924; *m* 1895, Blanche Leta Porterfield); X–Mildred Thomas (1 above); XI–Lemuel George (1869-1925; *m* 1889, Clara Elinor Winborn).

1–*m* Dec. 18, 1884, William Paisley Bouton (Nov. 26, 1848-Sept. 3, 1917); son of Ralph Leonard Bouton (Jared[3]; Daniel[4]; Nathaniel[5]; John[6]; John[7]), *m* Annie Jane Gibson (Moses[3]; Andrew[4]); issue (all *b* Benton Co., Miss.): 1–Ethel Vaughan, *b* Mar. 21, 1886; B.M., Cumberland U., '10, *m* Mar. 10, 1915, Walter Jackson, son of James Franklin Baird, *m* America Emeline Swain (issue: Edward Bouton, *b* Mar. 3, 1918); 2–George Ralph, b Sept. 27, 1887; B.S., Castle Heights Prep. School, '06, A.B., Cumberland U., '10; *m* May 4, 1917, Margaret Wharton, dau. of James Lewis Chambers, *m* Caroline Louise Wharton (issue: Mildred Louise, *b* Apr. 10, 1927; William Paisley, *b* Dec. 13, 1929); 3–Frank Donnell, *b* May 17, 1889.

1–LL.B., Cumberland U., '06. Mem. D.A.R., I.A.G., etc. Presbyterian. Residence: 139 Hatton Av., Lebanon, Tenn.

National Society
The Sons and Daughters of the Pilgrims
Organized December 24th 1908
Incorporated December 20th 1909
This is to certify that
Harold King Bowen
is entitled to membership in the Society
as Governor General

1–**BOWEN, Harold King,** *b* Whittemore, Ia., Dec. 31, 1896.

11–Richard **Kimball** (qv);

10–Henry (1615-76), came in the "Elizabeth," 1634; *m* Mary Wyatt (*d* 1672), also came in the "Elizabeth," with her parents (John[11], *m* Mary–);

9–Sarah (1654-92), *m* Daniel **Gage** (1639-1705; John[10] [1609-72], Colonial wars, from Eng. to Ipswich, Mass., *m* Amee–);

8–Daniel (1676-1747), mem. No. Regt., Essex, and Capt. Haseltine's Bradford Co., 1710; *m* Martha Burbank (Caleb[9], *m* 1669, Martha, dau. of Hugh Smith, from Eng., 1642; John[10], from Eng. to Boston, 1640, *m* Joanna–);

7–Abigail (*b* 1724), *m* Stephen **Russell,** capt. in Am. Rev. (see Vol. III, p. 79, for Russell lineage);

6–Lydia, *m* Ephraim **Hall,** Jr., served in Am. Rev. (see Vol. II, p. 273, for Hall lineage);

5–Stephen Russell (1766-1839), *m* Hannah Wilson (1768-1859; see Vol. II, p. 273, for Wilson lineage);

4–Phineas, *m* Lydia Huntley (see Vol. II, p. 273, for Huntley lineage);

3–Lydia Ann, *m* David Wood **King** (see Vol. III, p. 79, for King lineage);

2–Lydia May (2 below).

8–Daniel **Gage** (1676-1747), Colonial wars; *m* Martha Burbank 8 above;

7–Martha, *m* James **Wilson**;

6–Jesse (*b* 1739), served in Am. Rev.; *m* 1st, Ruth Merrill;

5–Hannah (1768-1859), *m* Stephen R. **Hall** (5 above).

2–William Walker **Bowen** (*b* 1869), charter fellow, Am. Coll. of Surgeons; med. mem. Northern Ia. State Exemption Bd., 1917-19 (see Vol. II, p. 273, for Bowen lineage); *m* Lydia May King (*b* 1871); issue: I–Harold King (1 above); II–Lydia Margaret (*b* 1905; *m* 1929, Walter Robinson Ingram, Ph.D.).

1–*m* July 25, 1929, Alta Ruth Brown (qv).

1–Inspector in charge, U.S. Immigration Service. Mem. S.D.P. (gov. gen. nat. soc.), S.M.D. (Past gov. Ia. Soc.), S.C.W., S.A.R. (past pres. Ia. Soc.), S.A.W., A.L., Legion of America (cdr.-in-chief), S.R., 40 Hommes et 8 Chevaux, I.A.G. Mason. (K.T.). Republican. Presbyterian. Residence: 628 S. 12th St., Fort Dodge, Ia. Address: New City Hall, Gary, Ind.

MRS. HAROLD KING BOWEN

1–**BOWEN, Alta Ruth Brown (Mrs. Harold King),** *b* Meadville, Mo., July 25, 1905.

10–Rev. Chad (Browne) **Brown** (qv);

9–Daniel (1645-1710), Smithfield and Providence, R.I.; *m* 1669, Alice Hearndon (Benjamin[10] [*d* 1694], *m* Elizabeth, dau. of William White, *m* Elizabeth–);

8–Jeremiah, *m* 1715, Sarah Tucker;

7–Jeremiah, *m* Sarah–;
6–Abraham, *m* 1765, Zilpha Eddy;
5–Luke (*b* 1766), Gloucester, R.I.; *m* 1788, Mary Butler;
4–Luke E. (*b* 1808), *m* 1824, Ann Gleason (*b* 1805);
3–Nathan B. (*b* 1842), Union Vet. of Civil War; *m* 1869, Catherine Elizabeth Stevenson;
2–Luke Eddy (2 below).
10–Samuel **Eddy** (qv);
9–Zachariah (1639-1718), *m* 1663, Alice Paddock (1640-92; Robert[10], qv);
8–Zachariah (1664-1737), *m* 2d, Ann Phillis;
7–Joseph (*b* 1713), *m* Barsheba Smith;
6–Zilpha, *m* Abraham **Brown** (6 above).
6–Nathaniel **Stevenson,** Sr. (1751-1839), Am. Rev.; *m* 1779, Mary Allen (*d* aet. 100 yrs. and 6 mos.);
5–Nathaniel, Jr. (1795-1886), *m* 1818, Jane Bryson (1796-1872);
4–Alexander Bryson (1825-1911), *m* 1849, Catherine Dunn (1826-72);
3–Catherine Elizabeth (1850-1928), *m* Nathan B. **Brown** (3 above).
5–James **Herbert** (*d* 1849, aet. 75, lacking 4 days), *m* Barbara Truax (*d* 1856);
4–Jesse, *m* Patsy Hoffman;
3–William Chauncey, *m* Nancy Ann Miller;
2–Ella (*b* 1880), *m* 1901, Luke Eddy **Brown** (*b* 1877), Spanish-Am. War vet.; issue: I–Harold Herbert (*b* 1902); II–Alta Ruth (1 above); III–Melba Catherine (*b* 1908).
1–*m* July 25, 1929, Harold King Bowen (qv).
1–Mem. S.D.P. (dep.gov.gen. Nat.Soc., 1929-31), A.L.Auxiliary, P.E.O. Presbyterian. Residence: 628 S. 12th St., Fort Dodge, Iowa.

1–**BOYD, Harry Otto,** *b* Oct. 4, 1875-*d* Dec. 13, 1908.
6–James **Fulkerson** (1737-99), capt. in Am. Rev.; justice, 1780; *m* 1764, Mary Van Hook (1747-1830);
5–Hannah DeBough (1769-1844), *m* 1786, Benjamin **Sharp** (1762-1844);
4–Altossa Pinkney (1797-1840), *m* John **Wyatt** (1788-1865);
3–Sarah Hanna (1820-1906), *m* 1843, Alexander Sterling **Hughes** (1818-97);
2–Joanna (*d* 1924), *m* 1864, James Alexander **Boyd** (1830-93).
1–*m* Nov. 22, 1896, Lilian Floy Bigelow (qv for issue).

1–**BOYD, Lilian Floy Bigelow (Mrs. Harry O.),** *b* Seattle, Wash., Aug. 18, 1874.
9–Abraham (Toppan) **Tappan** (qv);
8–Isaac (*b* 1653), of Woodbridge, Middlesex Co., N.J.; *m* 1st, 1669, Hanna Kent;
7–Isaac (*b* 1673), *m* Nancy Wilkinson, of Woodbridge, N.J.;
6–James (1750-1809), pvt. in Am. Rev.; of Westfield, N.J.; *m* Nancy Dunham (1751-1826);
5–Jane (1785-1820), *m* 1801, Henry **Rogers** (1776-1837);
4–Catherine (1815-82), *m* 1833, Daniel Mulford **Crane** (1810-87; John[5] [1764-1843], *m* 1792, Elizabeth or Betsy [1775-1822], dau. of Jonathan Mulford [1748-92], pvt., minute man, N.J. State troops, Am. Rev., *m* 1771, Debora Ludlow, 1744-1801);
3–Sarah Elizabeth (1836-1907), of Ind.; *m* 1853, Walter Buel **Hall** (1833-1919);
2–Emma K. (1853-1922), *m* 1873, Harry or Henry A. **Bigelow** (1849-1907), served with Co. M, 9th Ill. Cav., Army of the Tenn., Civil War; issue: I–Lilian F. (1 above); II–Clair V. (1880-1927; *m* Jeanette McKenzie); III–Daniel Earl (*b* 1886; *m* Winifred King).
1–*m* Nov. 22, 1896, Harry Otto Boyd (qv); issue: 1–Harold Warren, *b* Everett, Wash., Dec. 14, 1897; *m* May 1919, Dorothy Thorpe (issue: Harold; Donn); 2–Lora Fern, *b* Sumas, Wash., Jan. 23, 1901; *m* Dec. 23, 1920, William Russell MacTaggart.
1–Mem. D.R., Daus. of Pioneers of Washington, A.L.Auxiliary, Daus. of the Nile, O.E.S. Residence: Auburn, Wash.

1–**BOYLES, Katherine,** *b* Chicago, Ill., Oct. 28, 1868.
6–Joseph **Barnes,** surgeon;
5–Joseph (1754-1826), lived at Litchfield, N.H.; *m* Sarah Hills (1757-1850);
4–Joseph (1784-1864), *m* 1st, 1810, Elizabeth Putnam (1786-1831);
3–Mary Louisa (1811-93), *m* 1829, Samuel **Boyles** (1806-71), of Milford, N.H.;
2–Charles Carroll (2 below).
4–Samuel **Dickinson** (*b* Hawley, Mass., ca. 1784-*d* 1840), *m* 1808, Jemina Hardin (1787-1826);
3–Albert Franklin (*d* 1881), *m* Ann Eliza Anthony (1814-86).
2–Charles Carroll **Boyles** (1833-1916), dry goods merchant, Chicago, Ill.; *m* 1858, Martha Elizabeth Shoup (*d* 1861); *m* 2d, 1864, Hannah Dickinson (1838-1920); issue (1st marriage): I–Margaret L. (*b* 1860; *m* Alfred J. Barnes, divorced); issue (2d marriage): I–Charles Dickinson (*b* 1865; *m* Edith May Johnson); II–Jessie (1867-69); III–Katherine (1 above); IV–Thomas D. (1870-1901; *m* Rachel Yates).
1–Dir. Fla. State W.C.T.U. Mem. D.A.R., I.A.G., etc. Corr. sec. Cemetery Assn. Episcopalian. Residence: Orange City, Fla.

1–**BOYNTON, Mary Louise,** *b* Waverly, Ill., Mar. 20, 1881.
9–John **Boynton** (1614-1671), from Eng. in the "John," 1638; a founder of Rowley, Mass., 1639; *m* 1643/44, Ellen Pell;
8–Capt. Joseph (1645-1730), town clk.; dep. Gen. Ct.; capt. Rowley mil. co.; *m* 1669, Sarah Swan (1647-1718; Richard[9], dep. Gen. Ct.);
7–Dea. Joseph (1670-1755), *m* 1693, Bridget Harris (1673-1757; Nathaniel[8]);
6–Ephraim (*b* 1707), *m* 1732, Sarah Stewart;
5–John (1736-1825), lt. and capt. in Am. Rev.; selectman at Winchendon, Mass., and Weathersfield, Vt.; *m* 2d, 1763, Elizabeth Beman;
4–Capt. Cyrus (1780-1844), mem. Vt. Legislature, 1831; *m* 1804 Hannah Graves (1788-1844);
3–David Jewett (1823-1900), realtor, Chicago, Ill., and Los Angeles, Calif.; *m* 1848, Martha S. Challen (1828-72);
2–Horace Rollin (2 below).
8–William **Homes** (1663-1746), *b* Scotland; went to Ireland, thence to America, 1686, but returned to Ireland, 1689, where he was ordained Presbyn. minister, 1693; came to America again, and was pastor at Chilmark (Martha's Vineyard), Mass., 1714-46; *m* 1693, Katherine Craighead (Rev. Robert[9], of Ireland);
7–Robert (1694-1727), shipowner and capt.; lost at sea; *m* 1716, Mary Franklin (1694-1731; Josiah[8], *m* Abiah, dau. of Peter Folger; their son was Benjamin Franklin, noted American patriot);
6–William (1717-1785), of Boston; mem. Provincial Congress of Mass.; *m* 1740, Rebecca Dawes (1718-88; Thomas[7], *m* Sarah Story);
5–William (1742-1825), Boston; *m* 1764, Elizabeth Whitwell (William[6], of Boston);
4–Henry (1776-1845), Boston; *m* 2d, 1814, Isabella Porter;
3–William (1820-69), clergyman; lawyer; editorial writer, St. Louis, Mo.; *m* 1843, Julia Rebecca Salter (1819-96; Cleveland Jarman[4], of Waverly, Ill.);
2–Mary Louise (2 below).
10–John **Porter** (ca. 1596-1676), from Eng.; settled at Hingham, Mass., 1637; later at Salem Village (Danvers); deacon; dep. Gen. Ct.; selectman, 1649-76; *m* Mary–;
9–Samuel (1636-60), *m* Hannah Dodge (1642-88; William[10]);
8–John (1658-1753), moderator, Wenham, Mass.; dep. Gen. Ct.; *m* Lydia Herrick (Henry[9], of Beverly, *m* Lydia–);
7–Benjamin (1692-1778), settled at Boxford, Mass., 1716; selectman; *m* 1716, Sarah Tyler (Moses[8], *m* Ruth Perley);
6–Moses (bap. 1719), selectman, Boxford; *m* 1741, Mary Chadwick (*b* 1720);
5–Aaron (1752-1837), physician, Portland, Me.; *m* Paulina King (Capt. Richard[6], *m* 1st, Isabella Bragdon, their son, Rufus King, was the distinguished statesman; John[7], from Eng. to Watertown, Mass., ca. 1710);
4–Isabella (*d* 1860), *m* Henry **Homes** (4 above);
3–William, *m* Julia Rebecca Salter (3 above);
2–Mary Louise (*b* 1857), *m* 1879, Horace Rollin **Boynton** (1854-1910), issue: I–Mary Louise (1 above); II–Julia Salter (*b* 1883; *m* 1911, George Wishart Edmond); III–Elizabeth Ives (*b* 1884); IV–Horace Rollin (*b* 1888; *m* 1923, Marjorie Moor); V–Frederic King (*b* 1889; *m* 1917, Regine Roehse; *m* 2d, 1924, Jewel–); VI–Henry Homes (*b* 1891; *m* 1918, Marguerite Rhodes).
1–Ed. high schs., Oakland and Los Angeles, Calif., Yale Sch. of Fine Arts, and Los Angeles Library Sch. Librarian, Deane Hobbes Blanchard Memorial Library, Santa Paula, Calif. Residence: Santa Paula, Calif.

BRADFORD

Arms: Argent, on a fess sable, three stags' heads erased or.
Crest: A stag's head erased or.

1–**BRADFORD, Samuel Webster,** *b* Baltimore, Md., Jan. 31, 1856.
6–John **Bradford,** of London (bro. to Samuel Bradford, Bishop of Rochester and dean Westminster); *m* Mary Skinner (Mathew[7], M.D.; Robert[8], Bishop of Bristol and Worcester);
5–William (*d* 1757), from Eng., ca. 1700; settled Baltimore Co., Md., nr. what is now Abingdon, Harford Co.; was sent by Bishop of London to be teacher upon the plantations; 1st registrar, St. John's Episcopal Ch., Baltimore Co., Md., and one of its vestry; *m* in Eng., Elizabeth Lightbody;
4–William (1740-94), of Harford Co.; mem. Harford Com. during Am. Rev.; signer Harford Dec. of Independence, Mar. 22, 1775; capt. Co. 13, Harford Co., during Am. Rev.; *m* 1764, Sarah McComas;
3–Samuel (1774-1849), of Harford Co.; *m* Jane Bond;
2–Augustus Williamson (1806-81), of Bel Air, Md.; lawyer; gov. of Md. during Civil War (see portrait); *m* 1835, Elizabeth Kell (1812-94; Judge Thomas[3], of Baltimore, Md.); issue: I–Mary Matilda (*b* 1836; *d* infancy); II–William Kell (1838-71); III–Emmeline Kell (*b* 1840); IV–Jane Bond (*d* 1904); V–Augustus Williamson (*d* 1920); VI–Elizabeth (*d* 1914; *m* Thomas McElderry); VII–Charles Hubert (*d* 1916); VIII–Thomas Kell (*d* infancy); IX–Infant (*d* infancy); X–Thomas Kell (*d* 1911; *m* Jennie Mayer); XI–Ida (*b* and *d* 1855); XII–Samuel Webster (1 above).
1–*m* Aug. 1, 1881, Cornelia Norris, *b* Baltimore, Nov. 5, 1858; dau. of John Charles Norris, of Harford Co., Md.; issue (all *b* Bel Air, Md.): 1–Augustus Williamson (Apr. 29, 1882-Apr. 4, 1912); 2–Smith Norris, *b* Dec. 22, 1884; 3–Elizabeth Kell, *b* Feb. 3, 1888; 4–Samuel, *b* Sept. 21, 1890; *m* Jan. 22, 1927, Eleanor Roberts (issue: Eleanor McDonald, *b* Feb. 8, 1928); 5–Alexander Norris (Dec. 18, 1893-June 2, 1894).
1–B.A., Princeton, '75, M.A., 1909 (Phi Kappa Sigma). Atty.-at-law; chief clk. of Circuit Ct., Harford Co., Md. Mem. S.A.R., Md. Hist. Soc., I.A.G. Club: University (Baltimore). Mason (past master). Residence: Bel Air, Md.

AUGUSTUS WILLIAMSON BRADFORD (b Bel Air, Harford Co., Md., Jan. 9, 1806-d Baltimore, Mar. 1, 1881); grad. St. Mary's Coll., Baltimore, 1824; admitted to the bar, 1827; presidential elector on the Clay ticket, 1844; member of the "Peace Conference," Washington, 1861; 35th governor of Md., 1862-66; surveyor, Port of Baltimore, 1867-69.

1–**BRADLEY, Harold Cornelius,** *b* Oakland, Calif., Nov. 25, 1878.
9–William **Bradley** (qv);
8–Abraham (1650-1718), deacon First Ch., New Haven, 1696-1718; dep. Gen. Assembly, 12 terms; justice of the peace and quorum for New Haven Co., 9 terms; *m* 1673, Hannah Thompson (*d* 1718; John[9], from Eng. with Gov. Eaton, 1637);
7–Capt. Daniel (1679-1723), of New Haven; *m* 1702, Sarah Bassett (*b* 1682; John[8] [1652-1717], of New Haven, propr. 1685, rep. 1704-10);
6–Dea. Daniel (1706-73), of Hamden, Conn.; *m* 1727, Abigail Burchard (1708-74; William[7], *m* Hannah Brown);
5–Jabez (1733-93), of Hamden; *m* 1754, Esther Beach (1731-94; Moses[6]);
4–Rev. and Judge Dan (1767-1838), of Marcellus, N.Y.; B.A., Yale, 1789; ordained, 1790; *m* 1st, 1790, Eunice Beach (1766-1804);
3–Rev. Dan Beach (1804-73), M.D.; missionary in Siam, 38 yrs.; introduced medicine, surgery and vaccination to natives; taught art of cutting and pounding Siamese type; *m* 1st, 1834, Emelie Royce (1811-45);
2–Cornelius Beach, LL.D. (see Vol. III, p. 84), *m* 1871, Mary S. Comings (1844-1921).
1–*m* 1908, Josephine Crane, *b* Chicago, Ill.; issue: 1–Mary Cornelia (*d*); 2–Charles Crane; 3–Harold C.; 4–David John; 5–Stephen Crane; 6–Joseph Crane; 7–Richard; 8–William.
1–A.B., U.Calif., 1900 (Delta Upsilon, Sigma Xi); Ph.D., Yale, 1905. Prof. physiol. chemistry, U.Wis., since 1919; research dir. Woods Hole Marine Biol. Lab., since 1910. Author (see Who's Who in America). Mem. Am. Chem. Soc., A.A.A.S., Am. Physiol. Soc., Am. Soc. Biol. Chemists, etc. Clubs: Sierra, Am. Alpine. Residence: College Hills, Madison, Wis.

1–**BREESE, Zona Gale (Mrs. William L.),** *b* Portage, Wis., Aug. 26, 1874.
9–Richard (Gael) **Gale** (*d* 1678 or 79), from Eng. to Watertown, Mass., 1640; bought East half of Dummer Farm, 240 acres, on Charles River, Watertown, 1661; *m* 1640, Mary Castle;
8–Abraham (1643-1718), freeman, 1682, selectman at Watertown; *m* 1673, Sarah Fiske (1656-1728; Nathan[9], selectman, Watertown, *m* Susanna–);
7–Abraham (1674-1788?), selectman, Watertown; *m* 1699, Rachael Parkhurst (1678-1767; John[8] [*d* 1725], *m* Abigail Garfield [1646-1724]; George[9]);

6–Josiah (*b* 1722), moved from Waltham to Sutton; made the campaign to Sheffield for the relief of Ft. William Henry; *m* Elizabeth–;
5–Henry (1750 or 52-1836), pvt. in Lexington Alarm; soldier Am. Rev.; capt. in "Shay's Rebellion"; lived at Princeton, Aubury and Lynn, Mass., Barre, Vt., and Pittsford, N.Y., where he was buried; *m* 1772, Elizabeth Drury (1751-1820);
4–Henry (1781-1829), removed from Brattleboro, Vt. to Pittsford, N.Y., 1814; *m* Sallie Neal (1776-1853);
3–Franklin (1804-48), removed to Galetown, Green Creek Tp., Sandusky Co., O.; *m* 1828, Sallie Ray (1807-49; Israel[4], 1775-1860);
2–Charles Franklin (2 below).
4–Edward **Beers** (*d* 1859), from Eng. to Pittsford, N.Y., 1804; *m* Ellen Billinghurst (Rev. Thomas[5], from Eng., 1798, settled at Pittsford, N.Y., first Bapt. pastor in Monroe Co., N.Y., *m* Ellen Brown);
3–Thomas Cook (1815-ca. 1858), of Cuba, N.Y.; *m* Harriet Taylor (1816-ca. 1858; Joseph[4], from Eng. to Middleton Junction, Wis., 1832, *m* Constance Hoath);
2–Eliza (1846-1923), came to Wis., 1858, to Middleton Junction and Portage; *m* 1872, Charles Franklin **Gale** (*b* 1842), of Portage, Wis.
1–*m* June 12, 1928, William Lleywelyn Breese, *b* Portage, Wis., June 29, 1864; pres. City Bank, Portage, Wis.; pres. Portage Hosiery Co.; pres. Consumers Lumber Co.; trustee Ripon (Wis.) Coll.; son of Lleywelyn Breese (*b* Wales), mem. Wis. Legislature and sec. of state, *m* Mary Ann Evans, of Milwaukee, Wis.
1–L.B., U.Wis., '95, M.L., 1899 (hon. Litt. D., 1929); P.B.K. (hon. Western Reserve U.), 1924. Author (see Who's Who in America). Regent, U.Wis.; chmn. Wis. Free Library Commn., 1923–. Residence: Portage, Wis.

1–**BRENDLINGER, Margaret Robinson,** *b* Port Perry, Pa., Sept. 22, 1873.
5–Joseph **Brendlinger** (1738-1825), from Württemberg, Germany, settled in Douglas Tp., Pa.; *m* Rosina Schober (1748-1800);
4–Jacob (1770-1852), *m* Anna Maria Kurtz (1775-1854);
3–Frederick (1809-81), *m* Maria Knabb Hill;
2–Peter Franklin (2 below).
6–Jacob **Hill,** paid quit rents to Penn ante 1734;
5–Jacob, capt. Am. Rev., under Col. Daniel Hunter, Oley, Berks Co., Pa.;
4–Peter (1776-1863), *m* Maria Knabb (1778-1854; Michael[5] [*b* 1717], from Bavaria);
3–Maria Knabb (1814-93), *m* Frederick **Brendlinger** (3 above).
8–John **Smith** (MacDonald), (*b* Co. Managhan, Ireland, ca. 1655), came to America;
7–John (1686-1765);
6–Sarah (*d* 1807), sister of Col. Robert Smith (1720-1803), Am. Rev.; *m* Samuel **Cunningham**;
5–Margaret (1776-1842), *m* William **Lewis**;
4–Hester (1803-80), *m* Dan **Kirkpatrick**;
3–Margaret (1827-89), *m* Charles Fahnestock **Brown** (1837-90; James[4] [1794-1877], *m* Mary Smith [1794-1865], dau. of Judith Stewart);
2–Hannah Emily (1852-1924), *m* 1872, Peter Franklin **Brendlinger** (*b* 1850), civil engr. (for issue see Vol. III, p. 86).
1–A.B., Vassar, '95 (P.B.K.); post-grad. work. Yale (winter), 1898-99; Vassar (winter), 1900-1901. Prin. and part owner, Hillside Sch., Norwalk, Conn. (see Who's Who in America). Pres. Norwalk Branch A.A.U.W.; pres. Conn. State Federation of Univ. Women. Mem. I.A.G., etc. Clubs: Woman's University (New York), College (ex-pres.), Vassar (ex-pres.), both of Phila., Woman's City (pres.). Residence: Hillside, Norwalk, Conn.

1–**BRENTON, Cranston,** *b* Jamaica, N.Y., Nov. 20, 1874.
8–Gov. William **Brenton** (*d* 1674), from Hammersmith, Eng., to Boston; admitted freeman, 1634; settled at Newport, R.I., ca. 1634; pres. Colony, 1660-61; dep. gov. R.I. and Providence Plantations, 1663-66; gov., 1666-69; mem. Troop of Horse, 1667; *m* Martha Burton;
7–William;
6–Jahleel (1691-1767), *m* 1715, Frances Cranston;
5–Benjamin (1737-1830), *m* Rachael Cook;
4–James, *m* Sarah Buckman;
3–James Jahleel, *m* Elizabeth Eldred;
2–Benjamin Jahleel (2 below).
9–Roger **Williams** (qv);
8–Freeborn (1635-1710), *m* Thomas **Hart** (*d* 1671);
7–Mary (1663-1710), *m* 1680, Samuel **Cranston** (1659-1727), maj. 1698; gov. of R.I., 1698-1727 (John[8], qv);
6–Frances (1698-1740), *m* Jahleel **Brenton** (6 above).
2–Benjamin Jahleel **Brenton** (1832-1911), mcht., accountant; *m* 1861, Orvetta Hall (1844-1928); issue: I–Theodora (1863-83; *m* Clement Edward Gardiner); II–Laura Case (1869-1923; *m* Eliot McCormick; *m* 2d, Charles Howard MacDonald); III–Mabel Favilla (1872-96; *m* Ellsworth Skidmore); IV–Cranston (1 above).
1–*m* June 19, 1901, Elizabeth Alden Curtis, of Hartford, Conn.; issue: 1–William, *b* Hartford, Aug. 22, 1906; Princeton, '27.
1–B.S., Trinity Coll., Conn., '99 (Delta Psi), M.S., 1902; grad. Berkeley Div. Sch., 1901. Prof. English lang. and lit., 1906-14, Trinity Coll. In charge of personnel, A.E.F., Y.M.C.A. in Eng. during World War. Ordained priest, P.E.Ch., 1902. Social service worker (see Who's Who in America). Mem. S.C.W. Address: Cathedral of St. John the Divine, New York, N.Y.

1–**BRINSMADE, John Chapin,** *b* Springfield, Mass., Apr. 24, 1852.
8–John **Brinsmade** (qv);
7–Lt. Daniel (1645-1702), of Stratford; *m* Sarah Kellogg (*b* 1664; Daniel[8], *m* Bridget Barton);
6–Daniel (1687-1731), of N. Stratford; *m* 1715, Mary Sherman or Jackson;
5–Daniel (1718-93), B.A., Yale, 1745, M.A.; *m* Rhoda Sherman, of New Haven;
4–Daniel Nathaniel (1751-1826), B.A., Yale, 1772, M.A.; mem. state conv., 1788, and ratified U.S. Constn.; judge co. ct., Woodbury, 1777; *m* 1779, Abigail Farrand;
3–Daniel B. (1782-1862), *m* 2d, 1814, Mary Gold;
2–William Bartlett (2 below).
8–Nathan **Gold** (qv);
7–Nathan (1663-1723), chief justice of Conn.; lt. gov., 1723; *m* Hannah Talcott (1663-96; Lt. Col. John[8], of Hartford);
6–Rev. Hezekiah (1694-1761), A.B., Harvard, 1719, A.M.; *m* Mary Ruggles (*d* 1750; Rev. Timothy[7], of Guilford, Conn.; Capt. Samuel[8]; Capt. Samuel[9]; Thomas[10]);
5–Rev. Hezekiah (1731-90), B.A., Yale, 1751; pvt. in Am. Rev.; *m* 1758, Sarah Sedgwick (*d* 1766; Benjamin[6]; Samuel[7]; William[8]; Robert[9], qv);
4–Benjamin (1762-1846), *m* 1784, Eleanor Johnson (1764-1858);
3–Mary (1794-1883), *m* Daniel B. **Brinsmade** (3 above).
8–Samuel **Chapin** (qv);
7–Henry (*d* 1718), of Springfield, Mass.; rep. Gen. Ct., 1689; *m* 1664, Bethia Cooley (1643/44-1711; Benjamin[8], said to belong to the family of the Duke of Wellington, *m* Sarah–, of Longmeadow);
6–Benjamin (1682-1756), *m* 1704, Hannah Colton (1688-1739; Isaac[7], *m* Mary, dau. Lt. Thomas Cooper, *m* Mary Slye; Q.M. George[8], from Eng. to Springfield, Mass., 1644, later at Longmeadow, q.m. Hampshire Co. troop, 1663, served in King Philip's War, *m* Deborah Gardner);
5–Capt. Ephraim (1729-1805), at Ticonderoga, 1777; *m* 1755, Jemima Chapin (1735-1804);
4–Col. Abel (1756-1831), in French and Indian War and Shay's Rebellion; *m* 1779, Dorcas Chapin (1754-1841);
3–Col. Harvey (1787-1877), postmaster at Springfield; state senator; *m* 1810, Hannah Chapin;
2–Charlotte Blake (2 below).
8–Dea. Samuel **Chapin,** as above;
7–Japhet (bap. 1642-1712), *m* 1st, Abilenah Cooley (1642-1710; Samuel[8], *m* Ann, dau. James Prudden, bro. famous Peter Prudden, from Eng. to Conn.);
6–John (1674-1759), *m* 1701, Sarah Bridgman (1681-1756; John[7] [1645-1712], *m* 1670, Mary, dau. Isaac Sheldon; James[8], from Eng. ante 1640, settled at Hartford, Conn., later at Springfield, an orig. settler at Northampton, 1654, *m* Sarah–);
5–Phineas (1715-88), *m* Bethia Chapin (1718-93);
4–Capt. Phineas, at Ticonderoga, 1777; *m* Sabrina Wright (1755-1813; George[5]; Henry[6]; Benjamin[7]; Lt. Abel[8], *m* Martha, dau. Samuel Kritchwell, of Hartford, Conn.);

3–Hannah (1790-1868), *m* Harvey **Chapin** (3 above);
2–Charlotte Blake (1824-1900), *m* 1848, William Bartlett **Brinsmade** (1819-80), B.A., Yale, 1840; civil engr., supt. Conn. River R.R.; issue: I–John Chapin (1 above); II–Anna Louise (1854-1919); III–William Gold (1858-1908; *m* 1885, Ada Gibson Colton).
1–*m* Oct. 4, 1876, Mary Gold Gunn, *b* Washington, Conn., Jan. 20, 1853; dau. of Frederick William Gunn, founder of The Gunnery Sch., Washington, Conn.; issue (all *b* Washington, Conn.): 1–Frederick Gunn, *b* Mar. 8, 1882; A.B., Harvard, '04; *m* Jan. 3, 1922, Josephine Hulburt, dau. Joseph Sutphin (issue: Cynthia; Philip Gunn; Richard Sutphin); 2–William Bartlett (Jan. 4, 1884-Aug. 1, 1894); 3–Chapin (Mar. 1, 1885-Aug. 7, 1928); A.B., Harvard, '07, LL.B., 1910; M.A., Yale, 1924, Ph.D., 1926; served as 2d lt., A.E.F.; *m* Aug. 7, 1924, Helen J., dau. Rev. Robert Carter, of Bridgeport, Conn. (issue: Mary Gunn, *b* Oct. 6, 1925; Chapin, *b* and *d* Apr. 1928); 4–Eleanor Gold, *b* Nov. 15, 1886; Vassar, '07; *m* June 27, 1914, Hunnewell Braman (issue: William Brinsmade; Hunnewell, Jr.; Grenville Chapin; Helen Hunnewell); 5–Mary, *b* Nov. 18, 1888; Vassar, '09; 6–John Chapin, Jr., *b* Sept. 28, 1891; A.B., Harvard, '14; *m* Aug. 11, 1924, Elen, dau. of Nels Martin; 7–Charlotte Blake, *b* Sept. 20, 1893; Vassar, '15; *m* June 26, 1920; Alfred Raymond Bellinger (issue: Peter Frederic; Rossiter Raymond; Hilda Chapin); 8–Abigail Irene (May 29, 1896-Oct. 1918); Vassar, '17.
1–A.B., Harvard, '74. Retired prin. of The Gunnery Sch., teacher and prin. for 48 yrs. Served as mem. Conn. Ho. of Rep., several terms; mem. Constl. Conv., 1902; state senator, 1911; pres. State Civil Service Commn.; mem. Conn. Council Edn. (see Who's Who in America). Mem. S.A.R.; Am. Acad. Polit. and Social Sciences; Conn. Civil Service Reform Assn. Clubs: Litchfield Co. University; Harvard (Conn.); Graduate (New Haven). Residence: Washington, Conn.

1–**BROCKMAN, William Everett,** *b* Louisa, Va., May 18, 1891.
9–Henry **Brockman** (*b* 1623), from Manor House, Beachborough, Kent Co., Eng., ca. 1670; prob. settled in Md.;
8–Samuel, of Orange Co., Va.; removed to Spotsylvania Co., Va., 1732; *m* Mary Henderson;
7–John (1700-75), of Orange Co., Va.; *m* Mary Collins (Lt. Joseph[8]);
6–John (1740-1825), of Orange Co., Va.; removed to Caswell Co., N.C.; thence to Greenville Dist., S.C.; officer Am. Rev.; *m* Amelia Martin (*d* 1825);
5–John (ca. 1757-1823), of Orange Co.; *m* Mary K–;
4–Asa, of Orange Co.; soldier War 1812; *m* Lucy Ellis Quisenberry;
3–John (*d* 1905), of Orange Co.; soldier C.S.A.; *m* 1855, Martha P. Estes;
2–William Joseph (2 below).
9–Thomas **Quisenberry** (*b* 1608), from Eng. to Va., 1624; returned to Canterbury, Eng. to marry; returned to Va. and settled Westmoreland Co.;
8–John (1627-1717), of Westmoreland Co.; *m* Anne Pope;
7–Humphrey;
6–Thomas (*d* 1795), *m* Joyce Dudley (Robert[7], of Spotsylvania Co., *m* Joyce–);
5–Aaron, *m* 2d, Sallie Ellis;
4–Lucy Ellis, *m* Asa **Brockman** (4 above).
7–George **Hume** (qv);
6–Charles (1739-1821), of Culpeper Co., Va.; *m* 1764, Hannah James (*b* 1745);
5–John (1766-1838), of Culpeper Co.; *m* Ann Elizabeth Clarke (1768-1832);
4–Mary or Polly, of Culpeper; *m* Rev. Isham **Tatum,** M.E. minister;
3–Rachel Ann (*d* 1903), of Orange Co., Va.; *m* 1853, William B. **Estes**;
2–Mary Hannah (1859-1924), of Green Co., Va.; *m* 1878, William Joseph **Brockman** (1858-1929); issue: I–Clarence Aubrey (*b* 1881; *m* Lucy Morton Watts); II–Roy Estes (*b* 1883; *m* Annie Hunt); III–Daisy Lee (*b* 1885; *m* William A. Elwood, *d*); IV–Josie Anna (*b* 1888; *m* Walter F. Burt); V–William Everett (1 above); VI–Eugene Cecil (1892-1919; *m* Marie Toepper); VII–Mary Ethel (*b* 1895; *m* Ellis R. Hall); VIII–John Bryan (*b* 1897; *m* Violet Edith Roberts).
1–*m* June 8, 1918, Marguerite Terrett, *b* St. Paul, Minn., Feb. 5, 1896; dau. of George Hunter Terrett, of St. Paul.
1–Ed. George Washington U., Washington, D.C. (Sigma Nu). Advertising mgr., Northwest Bancorporation and affiliated banks. Employed in govt. printing office, 8 yrs.; newspaper reporter. U.S.A. Air service, 1917-19; assigned at Kelly Field, Tex., Lovefield, Dallas, Tex.; air service hdqrs., Tours, France; pvt., sgt.; master signal electrician; 2d lt., Air Service Reserves. Author and compiler: "Hume, Kennedy and Brockman Families", 1916; "Early American History," 2 vols., 1926. Mem. A.L. Clubs: St. Paul Athletic, Town and Country. Mason (32°). Residence: 2808 West River Rd., Minneapolis, Minn.

1–**BROUN, Waller Mordecai,** *b* Mobile, Ala., Oct. 22, 1854.
5–Robert **Broun** (1714-57), physician; from Scotland to Charleston, S.C., 1735; *m* Elizabeth Thomas (Edward[6]; Rev. Samuel[7]);
4–Archibald (1752-97), capt. Am. Rev., wounded during siege of Savannah, Ga.; *m* 1780, Mary Deas (1762-1857; John[5], of "Thoroughgood," mem. Gen. Assembly, *m* Elizabeth Allen);
3–Archibald (1795-1863), removed to Mobile, Ala.; *m* 1818, Ann Harleston (1797-1860; Nicholas[4], of Bosis, nr. Charleston, *m* Ann Olney Somers);
2–Charles Deas (2 below).
5–Moses **Mordecai** (1707-81), *m* at Bonn, Germany, Esther Whitlock;
4–Jacob (1762-1838), *m* 1784, at Phila., Pa., Judith Myers;
3–Dr. Solomon (1792-1869), *m* Caroline Waller;
2–Mary Ellen (*b* 1830) *m* 1854, Charles Deas **Broun** (1824-91); issue: I–Waller M. (1 above); II–Elizabeth Harleston; III–Armantine.
1–*m* Oct. 16, 1883, Louise Helene Townsley (Apr. 13, 1862-Aug. 22, 1897); dau. of Oscar Townsley, *m* Elise Barclay; issue (all *b* Mobile, Ala.): 1–Edward Randolph, *b* July 28, 1884; *m* Savilla Hamilton; 2–Oscar Townsley, *b* Jan. 29, 1886; 3–Elise Barclay, *b* Jan. 14, 1888; A.B., H. Sophie Newcomb Memorial Coll., '09; mem. D.A.R.; 4–Helene Gertrude (June 24, 1890-Jan. 3, 1919); 5–Charles Deas, II, *b* Sept. 9, 1893; *m* Mar. 8, 1923, Agnes Ewald, of Wytheville, Va.; 6–Goronwy Owen, *b* July 31, 1895; *m* Apr. 29, 1927, Emily Nash Mullen, of St. Louis, Mo.
1–*m* 2d, 1899, Marie Coralie Townsley, *b* 1858.
1–Ed. private sch., and Washington and Lee U. Asst. Treas. Mobile & Ohio R.R. Co., Residence: Mobile, Ala.

1–**BROUSE, Charles Robert,** *b* Rockford, Ill., Apr. 26, 1892.
5–John Andrew **Brouse** (1728-1822), settled at Berkeley Springs, Va.; *m* 1768, Elizabeth Smith (1748-1822), moved to Highland Co., O., 1818;
4–Adam (1773-1839), served in War 1812; *m* 1800, Sarah Fenner (1780-1868);
3–John A. (1808-93), chaplain, 100th Ind. Vols. during Civil War; *m* 1839, Mary Catharine Downey;
2–Olin Robert (2 below).
6–Robert **Downey** settled in Va.; *m* Susannah–;
5–Joseph (1755-1801), col. in Brit. Army during Am. Rev.; *m* 1789(?), Catharine Jacoby (*b* nr. Middletown, Md., 1767-*d* 1826);
4–Robert (1790-1879), *m* 1812, Barbara Beeler (1794-1873);
3–Mary Catharine (1822-98), *m* John A. **Brouse** (3 above);
2–Olin Robert (1843-1921), served in 132d Ind. Vols. during Civil War; settled finally at Rockford, Ill.; *m* 1891, Lillian Armil Utter (*b* 1867); issue: I–Charles R. (1 above); II–Florence Lillian (*b* 1898).
1–Not married. Grad. Purdue Coll. (Beta Theta Pi). Served as 1st lt., Baty. E, 54th Regt., C.A.C., during World War. Residence: 845 N. Church St., Rockford, Ill.

1–**BROWN, Belle Gilman,** *b* Cambridge, Mass., June 9, 1868.
8–John **Brown** (*b* 1588/89), from Eng., in "The

Elizabeth," 1635; landed in Boston; removed to Salem, 1638; later to Hampton, N.H.; one of the largest land owners, and the third man in wealth on the oldest tax list, 1653; ship builder and stock-raiser; *m* Sarah Walker (1618-72);
7–Thomas (1657-1744), of Hampton; Indian wars; *m* 1685, Abial Shaw (1662-1739);
6–Joseph (1689-1759), of Hampton and Rye, N.H.; Colonial wars; *m* 1715, Elizabeth Moulton (1693-1760);
5–Dr. Samuel (1720-94), of Hampton and Chester; signed Assn. Test, 1776; *m* 1745, Susannah Knowles (*d* 1789);
4–Joseph (1758-1802), of Chester; Am. Rev.; *m* 1791, Lydia Hall (*b* 1765; Samuel[5]; Andrew[6]);
3–Joseph (1796-1876), of Chester; *m* 1822, Abiah How (1773-1847);
2–Joseph Andrew (*d* 1902), of Bradford and Boston, Mass.; sr. partner and founder of Brown, Durrell & Co.; *m* 1859, Maria Antoinette Rollins (1839-95); issue: I–Susie A. (*b* 1864); II–Bessie Stearns (*b* 1868; *m* Ernest Howard Krause), and III–Belle Gilman, twins (1 above).
1–Ed. Private schls. and abroad; Von Prieser Sch., Stuttgart, Germany; Miss Hersey's Sch., Boston. Mem. D.F.P.A., D.A.R. (corr. sec. Warren and Prescott Chapter; del. to nat. congress). Clubs: Women's Rep. (Boston), Bostonian Soc. (life mem.), Hersey Sch. Assn. Residence: Hotel Puritan, 373 Commonwealth Av., Boston, Mass.

1–**BROWN, Curtis,** *b* Lisle, Broome Co., N.Y., Oct. 30, 1866.
10–Elder William **Brewster,** Mayflower Pilgrim (qv);
9–Jonathan (1593-1659), mem. Miles Standish mil. co., 1643; settled at New London, Conn., 1649; rep. Mass. Gen. Ct.; dep. Conn. Gen. Ct.; cdr. in Pequot War; *m* 1624, Lucretia Oldham (*d* 1679);
8–Rev. Nathaniel (*d* 1690), grad. in first class of Harvard, 1642; 1st minister Brookhaven, L.I.; *m* 2d, 1655, Sarah Ludlow (Gov. Roger[9], qv);
7–Timothy (1658-1747), *m* 1685, Mary Hawkins (Zachariah[8]);
6–Joseph (1709-60), *m* 1734, Ruth Biscoe (1709-78);
5–Deborah (1741-1832), *m* 1762, Capt. Daniel **Roe** (1740-1820), lt. French and Indian War; capt. Am. Rev.;
4–Charlotte, *m* Daniel **Brown** (1765-1838; Joseph[5] [*b* 1731], from Edinburgh, Scotland, to N.Y., soldier Am. Rev., *m* Mehetable Vail);
3–Alfred Nathaniel (1813-88), *m* 1838, Mary Elizabeth Smith;
2–Lewis Henry (2 below).
9–Henry **Curtis** (1621-61), from Warwickshire, Eng., 1643; settled at Northampton, Mass., propr., 1653; original settler at Windsor, Conn.; said to be first person buried at Northampton; *m* 1645, Elizabeth Abeel or Abel;
8–Nathaniel (1657-95), of Windsor, Conn.; killed by Indians at Northfield, Mass.; *m* Prudence–;
7–Samuel (1685-1760), to Woodbury, Conn.; *m* 1710, Lois Wentworth;
6–Maj. Elnathan (1712-81), Am. Rev.; went to Stockbridge, Mass., 1763; *m* 1737, Rose Weller (1714-1808; Thomas[7]);
5–Abel (1740-1829), Am. Rev.; *m* 1765, Sarah Neal (1748-1831);
4–Iram (1773-1857), *m* Margaret Carpenter (1776-1848);
3–John Carpenter (1802-90), *m* Bethia Monroe (1803-65);
2–Ellen (1843-1914), *m* Lewis Henry **Brown** (1840-1917), 1st lt., 1st N.Y. Vet. Cav., 1864-65.
1–*m* Aug. 25, 1890, Caroline Louise Lord, *b* Lisle, Broome Co., N.Y., Apr. 3, 1871; dau. of late William Delafield Lord, of Lisle; issue: 1–Marshall Lord Curtis, *b* N.Y. City, May 23, 1895; Harrow Sch., Eng., '14; entered Cambridge U., 1914, but left to enter army; 2d lt., 1st lt., and capt., c.o. 14th, later 7th Bty., Motor M.G. Co.; gassed and invalided to Eng.; mentioned in despatches twice; *m* Oct. 18, 1917, Eva, dau. of Chevalier Carlo Albanesi, of London (issue: Ann Curtis; Carol Curtis); 2–Beatrice Curtis, *b* Richmond, Surrey, Eng., Aug. 24, 1901; St. Felix School, '19; 3–Spencer Curtis, *b* Jan. 20, 1905, London, Eng.; Harrow Sch., and Cambridge U.
1–Pres. Curtis Brown, Ltd., New York; mng. dir. Curtis Brown, Ltd., London, Internat. Pub. Bureau (see Who's Who in America). Club: Devonshire. Residence: 27 Cheyne Walk, London, Eng.

1–**BRUSH, William Whitlock,** *b* Orange, N.J., July 28, 1874.
10–Thomas **Brush** (qv);
9–Richard (ca. 1645-ca. 1711), *m* ca. 1669, Johanna (Hannah) Corey (John[10] [1611-80], freeman, 1662, whale commr., 1644, Quaker, *m* ca. 1638, Anne–);
8–Robert (1685-bet. 1766-78), trustee; *m* bet. 1705-13, Rebecca Rogers (David[9]; Jonathan[10]);
7–Jonathan (1713-1787), *m* 1736, Elizabeth Smith (1718-96; Josiah[8], of Long Swamp, Huntington, L.I., *m* Christina Petty; Samuel[9]; Nicholas[10]);
6–Joshua (1742-81), signed "Articles of Assn.," May, 1775; *m* 1764, Margaret Ireland (1744-1822; Joseph[7] [1713-93], Am. Rev., *m* ca. 1735, Elizabeth Losee; John[8] [*b* ca. 1687], *m* Sarah–; Thomas[9] [ca. 1650-1710/11], *m* Mary Abrahams; Thomas[10], an original settler of Hempstead, L.I., 1644, *m* Joan–);
5–Jonathan (1774-1837), *m* Rebecca– (1771-1855);
4–Joshua (1794-1864), *m* 1817, Sarah Rolph (1795-1873; Benjamin[5], *m* Sarah, dau. of Jacob Brush; Moses[6]; Benjamin[7]; John[8]; Henry[9]);
3–Jonathan Ethelbert (1818-89), from Smithtown, L.I., to New York, N.Y.; *m* 1841, Cornelia Turck (1819-81);
2–Clinton Ethelbert (2 below).
8–Thomas **Whitlock** (1620-1703), from Eng. to Mass., ca. 1650; from Gravesend, L.I., to Middletown, N.J., 1665; ens., 1673; constable at Westchester, 1679; *m* 1st, Susannah Stock;
7–John, *m* Mary–;
6–Thomas, *m* Margaret Crawford (Gideon[7], *m* Sarah, dau. of William Redford);
5–John (1733-77), lt. Am. Rev., killed in action at Atlantic Highlands, N.J.; *m* 1758, Lydia Bowne (1737-1832; Samuel[6]; James[7]; William[8]);
4–John (1772-1858), *m* 1st, 1799, Catherine Morrell (1773-1808); *m* 2d, 1810, Mary Schanck (1785-1857);
3–William S. (1812-1903), *m* 1837, Rebecca S. Fanshaw (1819-69; Daniel[4], to America, 1803, *m* Rebecca, dau. of William Ramage, *m* Mary Melvin);
2–Eliza Thomson (*b* 1846), *m* 1869, Clinton Ethelbert **Brush** (1844-1905), *b* New York, N.Y., *d* South Orange, N.J.; served Co. B, 71st N.G.N.Y., Civil War, 1863; mem. Lincoln Post No. 11, G.A.R., Newark, N.J.; issue: I–Rebecca Whitlock (*m* George Benjamin Toye); II–Grace Cornelia; III–William W. (1 above); IV–Grace Louise (qv for other lineages); V–Clinton Ethelbert, Jr. (*m* Ruby Ray Riley); VI–Eddie (*b* and *d* 1881).
1–*m* Apr. 28, 1897, Jean Evelyn Mitchell, *b* Port Hope, Ont., July 18, 1874; dau. of John Robert Mitchell (*d* May 9, 1918), *m* Lizzie Goggin Gill (*d* Oct. 7, 1915); issue: 1–John Mitchell, *b* Brooklyn, N.Y., Nov. 9, 1899; Princeton, '21, Coll. of Physicians and Surgeons, '25; *m* July 5, 1924, Josephine, dau. of Charles H. Marple, *m* Mora Balcombe.
1–B.S., New York U., '93 (Delta Phi), C.E., 1894, M.S., 1895. Chief engr., water supply, City of New York (see Who's Who in America). Mem. New Eng. Soc. of Brooklyn. Summer place: Harrison, N.Y. Residence: 385 Clinton Av., Brooklyn, N.Y.

1–**BRUSH, Grace Louise,** *b* Orange, N.J., Nov. 25, 1876.
10–Thomas **Brush** (qv);
9–Thomas (ca. 1640-1698/99), of Huntington, L.I., constable, 1689; trustee, 1694-95; *m* Sarah (Weekes, Wicks) Wickes (Thomas[10], to America, 1635, in the "Expedition," patentee of Huntington, L.I., one of original settlers of Stamford, Conn., *m* Isabella, dau. of Richard Harcutt);
8–Jacob (ca. 1660-1728), *m* Mary Rogers (Jonathan[9]);
7–Jacob (1688-1731), *m* Mary– (1694-1761);
6–Jacob (1727-1813), signed "Articles of Assn.," 1775; *m* 1749, Sarah Platt (1725-67; Obadiah[7], *m* 1722, Mary Smith; Jonas[8] *m* Sarah, dau. of Timothy Scudder; Isaac[9]; Richard[10]);
5–Sarah (1763-1855), *m* 1782, Benjamin **Rolph** (1752-1832), Am. Rev. (Moses[6] [1718-91], *m* 1744, Phebe Smith, *b* 1720);

4–Sarah (1795-1873), *m* 1817, Joshua **Brush** (1794-1864);
3–Jonathan Ethelbert (1818-89), *m* 1841, Cornelia Turck (1819-81; Jacob J.[4] [1795-1840], *m* Margaretha, dau. of William Rockefeller; Jacob A.[5]; Abraham[6]; Johannes[7]; Jacobus[8]; Lt. Paulus[9]);
2–Clinton Ethelbert (2 below).
8–Roelof Martense **Schenck** (qv);
7–Garrett R. (1671-1745), to Pleasant Valley, N.J., 1696; *m* ca. 1693, Neeltje Coerten van Voorhies (1676-1750; Coert S.[8], *m* 2d, Manetje G., dau. of Gerret W. van Couwenhoven; Steven C.[9]);
6–Garrett (1712-57), *m* 1737, Janetje W. van Couwenhoven (1714-92; William W.[7], *m* Annetje Van Voorhees; William G.[8]; Gerret[9]; Wolfert[10]);
5–John (1745-1834), wrote name Schanck; capt. militia of Monmouth Co., Am. Rev.; *m* 1767, Mary (Denice) Denise (1750-1829; Teunis[6] [1692-1797], *m* 2d, 1731, Francyntje Hendrickson; Dionys[7], *m* 1685, Helena Cortelyou; Teunis Nyssen[8], *m* 1640, Phabea Faelix);
4–Mary (1785-1857), *m* as his 2d wife, 1810, John **Whitlock** (1772-1858)
3–William S. (1812-1903), *m* 1837, Rebecca S. Fanshaw (1819-69);
2–Eliza Thomson (*b* 1846), of 385 Clinton Av., Brooklyn, N.Y.; *m* 1869, Clinton Ethelbert **Brush** (1844-1905), *b* New York, N.Y., *d* South Orange, N.J.; served Co. B, 71st N.G.N.Y., Civil War, 1863; mem. Lincoln Post No. 11, G.A.R., Newark, N.J.; for issue and other lineages see William Whitlock Brush.
1–Mem. D.A.R., Daughters of Defenders of the Republic, Inst. Am. Genealogy. Residence: 385 Clinton Av., Brooklyn, N.Y.

LEO CHARLES BROWNE

1–**BROWNE, Leo Charles,** *b* Gainesville, Fla., Apr. 28, 1878.
4–Thomas N. **Browne** (1775?-1848), of Williamsburg, Va.; *m* Susan Becket (1806-37; James[5]);
3–Col. James Becket (1820-96), of Columbia, S.C.; sgt. in Civil War (see portrait); *m* 1851, Anna Waring (1833-71), of Bossier Parish, La.;
2–John Morton (2 below).
6–Robert (Gillam) **Gilliam** (1720-95), of Granville Co., N.C., or Williamsburg, Va.; maj. in Am. Rev.; acting justice of peace, 1785 and sheriff, 1786-88, Newberry Dist.; *m* 1745, Mary Wallace (?);
5–Robert (1760-1813), of Granville Co.; capt. Am. Rev.; *m* 1784, Elizabeth Caldwell (1757-1851; William[6], *m* Rebecca Parks; John[7], *m* Margaret Philips);
4–James (1791-1878), of Newberry, S.C.; officer War 1812; *m* 1813, Sarah Carolina Satterwhite (1796-1849; John[5] [1761-1817], *m* 1789, Susan [1760-

HON. JAMES BECKET BROWNE (b Columbia, S.C., Jan. 16, 1820-d Gainesville, Fla., July 16, 1896); merchant, Palatka, Fla., until 1861, where he was postmaster several terms, and sheriff of Putnam Co., Fla., 2 terms; served as pvt., Co. B, 2d Fla. Cav., C.S.A., 1863-64, and as ordnance sgt., 1864-65; merchant and contractor, Gainesville, Fla., 1866-96; was member city council, and mayor of Gainesville, 1871, 85, 94.

1810], dau. of Capt. Michael McKie, of Va.; John[6] [1734-1808], *m* 1760, Frances–, *m* 2d, Mary–);
3–James Michael (1838-64), of Greenwood, S.C.; *m* 1859, Frances Deare Donnelly (1841-83; Rev. Samuel Thomas[4] [1801-78], from nr. Phila., *m* Mary Rebecca Becket [1803-92]; James[5]);
2–Annie Juliet (*b* 1860), *m* 1877, John Morton **Browne** (1854-1912), farmer, fruit grower.
1–*m* Aug. 4, 1904, Mrs. Julia Strader McCoy White, *b* Baltimore, Md., ca. 1879; dau. of Robert H. McCoy, *m* Annie Rutledge Ransom Wilson; issue: 1–Leo Charles, Jr., *b* Baltimore, Md., Apr. 12, 1909.
1–*m* 2d, Nov. 14, 1928, Evelyn Louise Barrow (qv).
1–M.A., St. Leo Mil. Coll., '94. Clerk, station agent's office, Plant System, 1895-96; pvt. sec. to gen. supt., B.&O.R.R., Pittsburgh, Pa., 1900-02; chief clk., gen. mgr.'s office, Mexican Ry., Mexico City, 1904-12; asst. gen. mgr., United Rys. of Yucatan, Mex., 1913-15; asst. sec., Pan-Am. Commn. Corpn., 1916-18; pres. Leo C. Browne & Co., Inc., investments, since 1919. Mem. La., Fla., Ga., S.C., Va. and Tenn. Hist. Socs., N.C. State Literary and Hist. Assn., I.A.G., Geneal. Soc. of N.J., N.E.H.G.S., N.Y. G.B.S., New Orleans Assn. of Commerce, Mexico Soc. of New Orleans. Clubs: Automobile Club of La., La. Motor Transport Assn., Motor League of La. Address: Pan-American Bank Bldg., P.O. Box 185, New Orleans, La.

1–**BARROW, Evelyn Louise (Mrs. Leo Charles Browne),** *b* New Orleans, La., May 25, 1907.
6–William **Barrow** (1725?-1787), of Tarboro or Halifax, N.C.; lived in S.C.; moved to N.C. before Am. Rev.; sheriff Tarboro County, N.C.; *m* 1760, Olivia Ruffin (*d* 1803), she moved to La., 1798 (William[7], of Va.);
5–Bennett (1777-1833), apptd. trustee Acad. of Tarborough, N.C., 1813; moved to La., 1816; *m* 1805, Martha Hill;
4–Robert James (1817-87), of La.; gen. C.S.A. in Civil War; *m* Mary Elinor Crabb (Henry[5] [1793-1827], judge Tenn. Supreme Ct., *m* Jane Ann, dau. of Willie Barrow, *m* Jane Green);
3–Robert James (1850-71), *m* 1869, Sarah Louise Barrow;

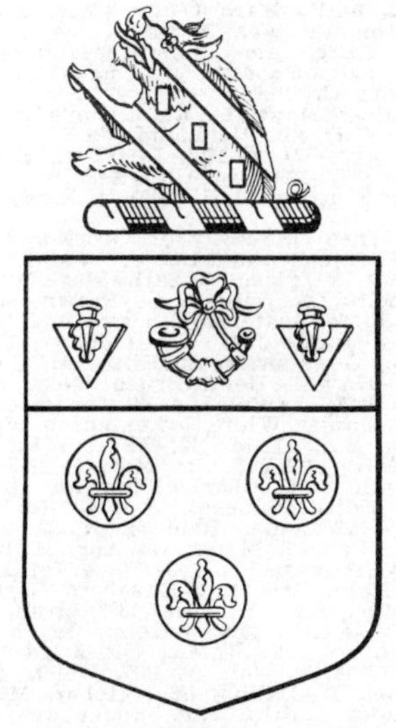

BARROW

Arms: *Argent, three torteaux each charged with a fleur-de-lis or, on a chief azure, a bugle-horn gold between two pheons of the field.*

Crest: *A demi-boar rampant or, charged with three billets between two bendlets sable.*

2–Robert James (2 below).
7–William **Barrow,** 6 above;
6–William (1765-1823), of N.C.; *m* 1792, Pheraby Hilliard (1775-1827);
5–Robert Hilliard (1795-1823), *m* Eliza Pirrie;
4–Robert Hilliard (1824-78), lt. col. 11th La. Inf., C.S.A. ("Rosale Guards"); *m* 1844, Mary Eliza Barrow;
3–Sarah Louise (1849-1913), *m* Robert James **Barrow** (3 above).
11–Rt. Hon. John **Alston** (qv);
10–John (*d* 1704), *m* Anne Wallis (*b* ca. 1645 in Eng.; John[11], pres. Oxford Coll.);
9–Maj. John (1673-1758), from Eng., 1694; justice Ct. of Oyer and Terminer, and Supreme Ct. of N.C., 1724; revenue collector for king; sheriff; vestryman of St. Paul's Parish; col. N.C. militia; *m* Mary Clark (John[10], *m* 2d, Mary, dau. Capt. John Palin, chief justice of N.C., 1731; Humphrey[11], *m* Jane–);
8–Solomon (*d* 1785), of Warren Co., N.C.; *m* ca. 1729, Sarah Ann Hinton;
7–John (1735-1802), *m* 1761, Elizabeth Hynes (*d* 1781);
6–Lucretia, *m* James **Pirrie,** a Scotsman;
5–Eliza, *m* Robert Hilliard **Barrow** (5 above).
7–William **Barrow,** 6 above;
6–Bartholomew (1766-1853), moved from N.C. to La., 1820; *m* 2d, Bethya Brantley;
5–David, *m* 2d, Sarah Hatch;
4–Mary Eliza (1825-1920), *m* Robert Hilliard **Barrow** (4 above).
4–Garrett **Bradley,** judge La. Supreme Ct.; *m* Susan Saunders;
3–Peter Warren (1841-1900); *m* 1870, Margaret Hughes, from Ireland, 1853;
2–Mary Eveline (2 below).
5–Peter **Hughes,** *b* and *d* in Ireland;
4–Patrick (*d* 1846), *m* Fannie Bann (*d* 1843); both *b* and *d* in Ireland;
3–Margaret (1841-1906), immigrant; *m* Peter W. **Bradley** (3 above);
2–Mary Eveline (*b* 1871), as Widow Campbell, *m* 2d, 1906, Robert James **Barrow** (1872-1917), Spanish War Vet.; issue: I–Evelyn Louise (1 above); II–Robert James IV (*b* 1908); III–Mary Robertine (*b* 1910).
1–*m* Nov. 14, 1928, Leo Charles Browne (qv).
Residence: New Orleans, La.

1–**BROWN, Fannibelle Leland (Mrs. Oswald),** *b* Albany, N.Y., May 3, 1882.
9–Henry **Leland** (1625-80), from Eng., 1652; settled at Dorchester, Mass.; later removed to Sherburne, Mass.; *m* in Eng., Margaret Badcock;
8–Hopestill (1655-1829), of Sherburne, Mass.; farmer; *m* Abigail Hill;
7–John (1689-1859), of Holliston, Mass.; farmer; *m* Abigail Badcock;
6–Samuel (1711-83), of Holliston; *m* Dinah White;
5–Asa (1738-1822), of Chester, Vt.; farmer; *m* Lois Marshall;
4–Simeon (1776-1847), merchant; Chester; established the Green Mountain Coffee House at Landgrove, Vt.; justice of peace; established line of stages in Vt. and carried first mail over Green Mountains, 1829; established first line of stages from Nashua, N.H., to Troy and Saratoga, and from Hartford, Conn., to Haverhill, N.H.; *m* Sylvia Pond;
3–Simeon (1816-47), of Chester, Vt.; later of N.Y. City; operated Clinton and Metropolitan hotels, New York, N.Y.; *m* 1848, Eleanor A. Moore (1831-89);
2–Simeon (2 below).
5–Benjamin **Radford** (1747-1820), of Burlington, Mass.; in Am. Rev. under Col. Glover, of Marblehead, 1775, and under Gen. Gates, 1777; *m* Mary Smith (1750-1801), of Burlington;
4–Jeremiah Smith (1792-1854), of Ipswich, Mass.; served in War 1812, disch., 1815, by Capt. Rufus McIntire, U.S. Arty.; *m* 1820, Lydia Field (1799-1870), of Quincy, Mass.;
3–William Henry (1823-90), of New York, N.Y.; *b* Dedham, Mass.; operated restaurants Mount St. Vincent and The Casino, Central Park, N.Y. City; *m* 1844, Eliza A. Edwards (1828-60), of Boston;
2–Fannie Belle (*b* 1854), of N.Y.; *m* 1879, Simeon **Leland** (1853-1913), of N.Y.; mgr. Hotel Wolcott and Prince George Hotel, N.Y.
1–*m* Apr. 27, 1911, Oswald Brown, *b* Aston Manor, Warwickshire, N.Y., Feb. 17, 1882; son of Joseph Brown, of Birmingham, Eng.
1–B.A., Barnard Coll., N.Y., '05 (Alpha Omicron Pi), M.A., Columbia, 1908. Mem. D.A.R. (Seattle chapter), Women's University Club (Seattle), A.A.U.W., Seattle Alumnae Chapter Alpha Omicron Pi. Residence: Bryn Mawr, Wash.

1–**BROWNE, Ella Haskell (Mrs. George),** *b* Gloucester, Mass., Jan. 13, 1849.
8–William **Haskell** (*b* 1617), from Eng.; landed at Salem, Mass., 1632; settled Gloucester, 1643; *m* Mary Tybbot (Walter[9]);
7–Joseph, *m* Mary Graves, of Andover;
6–Joseph, *m* Sarah Davis;
5–David, *m* Elizabeth Pope;
4–Aaron, *m* Sarah Burnham;
3–Abel, *m* Eunice Harlow;
2–Leonidas (2 below).
10–Tristram **Coffin** (qv);
9–Tristram (1632-1704), of Newbury; rep. Gen. Ct. of Mass., 1695-1701,02; lt. Newbury Co., 1683; *m* Judith (Greenleaf) Somerby (1625-1705);
8–Peter (1667-1746), of Newbury; *m* Apphia Dole (1668-1725);
7–Tristram (1696-1727), *m* Dorothy Tufts (Peter[8] [1648-1721], dep. from Medford to Gen. Ct., 1689, 92, 95, 97, 1700, 02, 15, capt., 1706);
6–Peter (1723-96), of Gloucester, Mass.; *m* 1743, Mary Currier (*b* 1722), of Amesbury, Mass.;
5–Peter (1750-1821), A.B., Harvard Coll., 1769; *m* Mary Forbes (1754-95; Rev. Eli[6], D.D.);
4–Mary Forbes (1775-1820), of Gloucester; *m* Henry **Phelps** (1766-1852);
3–Sarah Coffin (1804-88), *m* 1825, Henry **Haskell** (1800-81);
2–Sarah Elizabeth (*b* 1827), *m* Leonidas **Haskell** (1827-1918), maj. in Civil War; issue: I–Elizabeth Hayes (1847-1929; *m* Lt. George Asbury); II–Ella (1 above); III–Broderick; IV–Leon; V–Frank; VI–Ortega; VII–Henry (*d* 1928; *m* Olive–); VIII–Alice G.
1–*m* Aug. 6, 1873, George Browne (1840-1912), of Salem, Mass.; son of George Browne, of Salem; issue: 1–George Albert (see Vol. I, p. 505); 2–John White, *b* Staten Island, N.Y., July 7, 1877; ed. St. Marks Sch., Southboro, Mass.; officer, World War; *m* Fannie Browne, of Portland, Ore.; 3–Belmore, (see Vol. I, p. 504).
1–Mem. I.A.G. Residence: 1816 Garden St., Santa Barbara, Calif.

1–**BROWNLEE, Avis Gertrude Yates (Mrs. Milne H.),** *b* Holland, Mich.
7–Joseph Christopher **Yates** (1665-1730), from Eng., and settled at Albany, N.Y.; *m* Hubertje Marcellis (*d* 1736);
6–Christoffel (1684-1754), *m* 1706, Catelyntje Winne;
5–Peter (*b* 1727), col. 14th Albany Militia; *m* Sarah Van Alsteyn;
4–Christopher Peter (*b* 1750), maj. 2d N.Y. Cont. Line; *m* 3d, Rebecca Winne;
3–John Christopher (1799-1855), served in 2d N.Y. Militia in War 1812; *m* 3d, Mary Elizabeth Stevenson (1821-99);
2–Dr. Oscar Edgar (2 below).
10–Nicholas **Danforth** (qv);
9–Rev. Samuel (1626-74), grad. Harvard, 1643, and was fellow and tutor there; *m* Mary Wilson (1633-1731);
8–Rev. Samuel (1666-1727), *m* Hannah Allen (1668-1761);
7–Samuel (1697-1755), *m* 1736, Bethiah Crossman (1700-87);
6–John (*b* 1736), *m* 1761, Rhoda Deane (*b* 1740);
5–Polly (1763-1842), *m* 1786, Rev. Isaac **Briggs** (1762-1837);
4–Nancy (1793-1871), *m* 1812, Stephen **Fairbanks** (1788-1863);
3–Nancy (1825-1909), *m* 1840, Czar **Giddings** (1819-1905);
2–Gertrude Isabella (*b* 1847), *m* 1877, Dr. Oscar Edgar **Yates** (1845-1901), physician and surgeon; issue: I–Grace Winifred (*m* Rev. Albertus T. Broek, D.D.); II–Amy Metella (*m* Maj. Edward D. Kremers, M.C.U.S.A., retired); III–Avis Gertrude (1 above).
1–*m* May 21, 1921, Milne Hume Brownlee, *b* London, Eng., Apr. 6, 1886; machine gunner, 47th Canadian Inf., service in England, France and Belgium; participated in Regina Trench, Vimy Ridge, etc., wounded 2 days after Vimy Ridge in bombing raid, 1917; son of George Alexander Brownlee, of Scotland, *m* Hannah Skae Burn.
1–Mem. S.M.D. (state sec.), D.A.R., Calif. Geneal. Soc., Women's City Club, English-Speaking Union. Residence: 1300 Sacramento St., San Francisco, Calif.

1–**BROWNSON, James Irwin,** *b* Washington, Pa., Jan. 25, 1856.
8–Richard **Brownson,** came from Eng., living at Hartford, Conn., 1640;
7–Richard (*d* 1687); and thru his g.son;
5–Timothy (1701-1766 or 76), *m* Abigail Jewel (?);
4–Richard (*b* 1737), surgeon Am. Rev.; *m* Mary McDowell;
3–John (1768-1836), *m* Sarah Smith;
2–James Irwin, D.D. (2 below).
6–William **McDowell** (1680-1757), from Scotland to Ireland, thence to Chester Co., Pa., 1718; settled at the foot of "Parnells Knob," 10 miles west of Chambersburg, Pa., 1731; *m* Mary–;
5–John (1716-94), officer Am. Rev.; *m* Agnes Craig;
4–Mary, *m* Dr. Richard **Brownson** (4 above);
3–John, *m* Sarah Smith (3 above);
2–James Irwin. D.D., LL.D. (1817-99), A.B., Washington Coll., '36; pastor 1st Presbyn. Ch., Washington, Pa.; *m* 1843, Sarah Ellen Maclay (*d* 1853); *m* 2d, 1855, Eleanor McCullough Acheson (1826-1905; David[3] [1770-1851], from Ireland, *m* Mary, dau. of John Wilson); issue (1st marriage): I–Sarah Smith (*b* 1844; *m* Henry R. Whitehill); II–John Maclay (1845-1904); III–Elliott C. (1847-49); IV–Ellen Maclay (1849-1901); V–Mary R. (1852-53); issue (2d marriage): I–James Irwin (1 above); II–Mary Wilson (see Who's Who in America); III–Marcus Acheson (see Who's Who in America); IV–Margaret McKnight (*b* 1860; *m* Edwin Linton, see Vol. I, p. 506); V–Robert McKennan (*b* 1865; *m* Lillian Stroach); VI–Alexander Acheson (1867-77); VII–Lauretta Morgan (*b* 1871; *m* Andrew T. Taylor).
1–Not married. A.B., Washington and Jefferson, '75 (Phi Kappa Psi). Lawyer now pres. judge Ct. of Common Pleas, 27th jud. dist. of Pa. Pres. trustees Washington and Jefferson Coll.; trustee Pa. Training Sch. Clubs: Bassett, Nemacolin, Washington Co. Country. Residence: George Washington Hotel, Washington, Pa.

1–**BRUCE, Sallie Hare White (Mrs. Helm),** *b* Lexington, Va., Feb. 29, 1860.
7–Henry **White,** came from England and settled at Ellison's Mill, 1680; naval officer; *m* 1659, Mary Croshaw;
6–John (1695-1758), settled at Ellison's Mill (now Gaines Mill), nr. Richmond, Va.;
5–Barrett (1727-82), *m* 1754, Elizabeth Starke;
4–William (1773-1820), *m* Mildred Ellis;
3–William Spottswood (1800-73), *m* Jane Isabella Watt;
2–James Jones (1828-93), prof. Greek and acting pres. Washington and Lee U.; *m* Mary Louise Reid (1832-1901); issue: I–Sallie Hare (1 above); II–Isabelle (*m* William G. Brown, see Vol. III, p. 94, for maternal lineages); III–Agnes Reid (*m* Judge Joel W. Goldsby); IV–Reid (*m* Lucy Preston; *m* 2d, Elizabeth Corse).
1–*m* Dec. 17, 1884, Helm Bruce (Nov. 16, 1860-Aug. 10, 1927; see Vol. I, p. 334, for genealogy); issue: 1–James White, *b* Lexington, Va., Oct. 27, 1886; B.A., Yale, '12; M.D., U.Pa.; capt. M.C., U.S.A., A.E.F.; *m* Nov. 5, 1918, Edith Dumesnil, dau. Charles Duncan Campbell (issue: Edith Dumesnil; Louise Reid; Mary Ormsby); 2–Louise Reid (Sept. 27, 1888-Feb. 3, 1914); Pelham Manor; *m* Apr. 26, 1911, Dr. John Williamson Price, Jr. (see Vol. I, p. 334; issue: Helm Bruce); 3–Elizabeth Barbour, *b* Louisville, Ky., Mar. 15, 1890; grad. nurse, Presbyn. Hosp., 1916; 4–Helm, Jr., *b* Louisville, Jan. 6, 1895; U.Mo., 1914-15; 2d lt., 13th F.A., 1917-18; *m* Nov. 20, 1917, Helen, dau. of Frederick L. Ballou, of Natchez, Miss.
1–Grad. Ann Smith Acad., under pvt. tutors, and Mrs. Carrington's Sch., Richmond, Va. Was chmn. woman's com., Ky. div. of Council of Nat. Defense, and v. chmn. Louisville A.R.C. during World War. Pres. Woman's Club of Louisville; 1st v.p. C.D.A. of Ky. Residence: 1411 3d St., Louisville, Ky.

1–**BRUMBAUGH, Christian Hunt Syme (Mrs. C. Claude),** *b* Lewisburg, W. Va., Jan. 20, 1877.
5–John **Syme** (*b* 1729), of Hanover Co., Va.; lt., capt., and lt. col. during Am. Rev.; capt. 10th Va. Regt., 1776; col. Va. militia, 1778-81; captured by Tarlton; mem. House of Burgesses, 1752-55, Priory Council, 1759, first Va. Conv. from Hanover Co., 1776; *m* ca. 1750, Mildred Merriwether;
4–Nicholas, *m* Jane Johnson;
3–William Henry (1808-78), *m* 1832, Ann Mays (1814-85);
2–John Nicholas (*b* 1849), of San Mateo, Calif.; *m* 1868, Christian Hunt (1848-1917); issue: I–Mary Maxwell (*b* 1872; *m* Arthur Peyton); II–Christian Hunt (1 above); III–Johnson Reynolds (*b* 1879; *m* Zoe Kean); IV–Rhoten Hunt (*b* 1887; *m* Ethel Nordling).
1–*m* Jan. 17, 1901, C. Claude Brumbaugh, *b* Guthrie Center, Ia., Feb. 11, 1874; son of Daniel Brumbaugh, of Guthrie Center.
1–Residence: Granger, Wash.

1–**BRUMBAUGH, Catherin Elliott Brown (Mrs. Gaius Marcus),** *b* Mansfield, Pa., June 15, 1868.
9–Nicholas **Brown,** from Eng., 1630; settled at Lynn, Mass.; *m* Elizabeth–;
8–Thomas (1626-83), from Eng.; *m* 1652/53, Mary Newhall (1637-65; Thomas[9], qv);
7–Thomas (1654-1723), of Lynn, Mass., and Stonington, Conn.; *m* 1677, Hannah Collins (John[8], of Lynn);
6–Thomas (1692-1763), of Stonington; *m* 1715, Deborah Holdridge;
5–Thomas (1717-91), of Stonington, and Wyalusing, Pa.; *m* 2d, 1761, Patience Brockway;
4–Daniel (1771-1859), of Wyalusing; *m* 1st, 1793, Mary Wigton (1774-1835; Thomas[5], soldier Am. Rev., at Forty Fort);
3–Daniel Warren (1814-98), of Wyalusing; *m* 1836, Catherin Adeline King;
2–Charles W. (2 below).
11–Stephen **Hopkins,** Mayflower Pilgrim (qv);
10–Constance (*d* 1677), *m* 1623, Nicholas **Snow** (qv);
9–Stephen (*b* 1636), *m* 1663, Widow Susana (Dean) Rogers;
8–Bathsheba (*d* ante 1753), of Eastham, Mass.; *m* John **King (*d* 1753);**
7–Ebenezer (*b* 1700), *m* Mercy Myrick;
6–Barzilla (1736-post 1790), *m* 1758, Lydia Hinckley (*b* 1736);

5–Nathaniel (1760-85), soldier Am. Rev.; *m* Anna Mead (1762-1840);
4–Jeremiah (1784-1870), of Tompkins Co., N.Y.; *m* 1803, Sarah Campbell (1785-1846);
3–Catherin Adeline (1819-77), of Tompkins Co.; *m* Daniel Warren **Brown** (3 above);
2–Charles W. (1846-1918), of Mansfield, Pa., and Washington, D.C.; physician and surgeon; *m* 1866, Mary Eleanor Elliott (1849-1921), D.F.P.A.; issue: I–Catherin Elliott (1 above); II–Mabel Franc (1876-98).
1–*m* Oct. 1, 1889, Dr. Gaius Marcus Brumbaugh, *b* Huntingdon, Pa., May 7, 1862 (see Who's Who in America); son of Dr. Andrew B. Brumbaugh, *m* Maria Frank; issue (all *b* Washington, D.C.): 1–Charles Andrew, *b* May 13, 1897; A.B., Pa. State Coll., '21; lt. in World War; *m* June 28, 1923, Ann Eleanor, dau. of Henry LeVan Hoyer, *m* Jennie Seiders (issue: Eleanor Catherin, *b* 1924; Robert Marcus 1928-29); 2–Marcus Morton (1899-1900); 3–Elliott Frank, *b* Jan. 25, 1903; A.B., George Washington U., '28.
1–Ed. St. Ursula, and Elmira Coll. Mem. S.M.D. (historian), D.F.P.A. (nat. registrar, 1918-28), N.S.D.A.R. (registrar gen., 1911-15; state regent, 1916-18), treas. Nat. and pres. State Officers Clubs, D.A.R., C.A.R. (nat.-corr. sec. bd.; state org. sec. and editor C.A.R. magazine), U.S.D. 1812. Methodist. Republican. Summer place: Oshcalui Lodge, Wyalusing, Pa. Residence: 1954 Biltmore St. N.W., Washington, D.C.

1–**BRUNSON, Jessie Alma Mellichamp (Mrs. Peter C.),** *b* Orangeburg, S.C., Nov. 6, 1866.
6–William **Mellichamp,** a Huguenot, came from France by way of Switzerland and the British Isles, arrived at Charleston, S.C., ca. 1697; justice of the peace, 1726;
5–Thomas (*d* 1773), *m* Elizabeth Elliott (*d* 1761; Robert[6] [*d* 1727], *m* 1st, Elizabeth Screven [*d* 1725]; Humphrey[7] [*d* ante 1700], *m* 1685, Elizabeth Cutt; Robert[8] [1643-1724], dep. Gen. Ct., from Scarborough, 1685, councillor of N.H., 1692-1715, *m* a sister of Col. William Pepperell);
4–St. Lo (1757-1827), served Am. Rev.; *m* 1782, Rebecca Stiles (1764-1802; Benjamin[5] [*b* 1735], capt. militia. Am. Rev.; *m* 1759, Sarah Staples);
3–St. Lo (1789-1877) served in War 1812; *m* 2d 1822, Margaret Geddes Lorimore (1806-77);
2–Stiles Rivers (2 below).
9–Peter **Manigault** (qv);
8–Judith, *m* ca. 1721, James **Banbury;**
7–Mary (*d* 1757), *m* 1741, John **Bounetheau** (*d* 1757), Huguenot, settled at Charleston, S.C.;
6–Peter (1742-98), justice of the peace, Charleston, S.C., 1772-75; prisoner on "Torbay," prison ship, Charleston Harbor, 1787; lt. in bn. of arty., Charleston militia, Am. Rev.; clk. of ct. of Wardens, 1787; *m* 1st, 1764, Ann Anderson (*d* 1776);
5–Ann (*b* 1765), *m* 1782, John David **Miller;**
4–James Anderson (1785-1849), *m* 1812, Sarah Mills (Mackey) Crocker;
3–Frederick John David (1815-70), *m* 1836, Mary Catherine Recard (1815-50);
2–Sarah Carolina (2 below).
8–Robert **MacGregor** (*d* 1734), known as Rob Roy, of Scotland, who took his mother's name **Campbell** for the same reason that his g.son used the name of Mackey; *m* Helen Mary, dau. of MacGregor of Cromar;
7–James, adopted the name of **Drummond** (*d* France, 1752);
6–James (1737-93), soldier Am. Rev.; adopted name of **Mackey** because the political troubles of the time prevented his using the name MacGregor;
5–John (*b* 1766), *m* 1785, Abigail Mills (*b* 1765);
4–Sarah Mills Crocker (*b* 1788), *m* James A. **Miller** (4 above);
3–Frederick J. D. *m* Mary C. Recard (3 above);
2–Sarah Carolina (1839-1922), *m* 1866, Stiles Rivers **Mellichamp** (1841-1922), C.S.A.; issue: I–Jessie Alma (1 above); II–Edith Rivers (*b* 1868; *m* 1891, John James Andrews, *d* 1912); III–Lurline LeMontier (*b* 1870; *m* 1893, Albert Clarence Ligon, *d* 1926).
1–*m* July 8, 1885, Peter Craddock Brunson (qv); issue: 1–St. Lo Earle, *b* Orangeburg, S.C., July 11, 1890; ed. Queen's Coll., Charlotte, N.C., and Coll. for Women, Columbia, S.C.;

Mac GREGOR

Arms: *Argent, a fir tree growing out of a mount vert, surmounted of a sword bendways, supporting on its point in the dexter canton an imperial crown proper.*

Crest: *A naked cubit arm holding a sword enfiled with three crowns, all proper.*

Motto: *My might makes my right.*

m May 1922, John Battle Burch, 1st lt., M.T.C., son of Edward J. Burch, *m* Alice Mellichamp; 2–Stiles Mellichamp, *b* Orangeburg, Dec. 21, 1892; ed. Coll. of Charleston, S.C.; Davidson Coll.; volunteered in Am. Field Service, Apr. 1917, served in France; Aspirant in Foreign Legion, Dec. 30, 1918; 32d Regt. Arty., French Army; participated in battle of Chemin des Dames, France; Battle of the Piave, Italy; decorated with Fatiche di Guerro at Vincenza, Italy, Apr. 25, 1918, Italian War Cross, No. 445, at Treviso, Italy, July 14. 1918.
1–Mem. Magna Charta Dames, C.D.A., Huguenot Soc. of S.C., D.A.R., U.D.C., I.A.G. Residence: Orangeburg, S.C.

1–**BRUNSON, Peter Craddock,** *b* Beaufort Dist., S.C., Apr. 21, 1861.
4–Lazarus (Murdoch, Murdock) **Murdaugh,** to America after Am. Rev., with brothers Charles and William; landed at Beaufort, S.C.; settled in upper part of Colleton Co.; *m* —Wilson;
3–Josiah Putnam, *m* Ursula Varn, of German origin;
2–Susan (Apr. 22, 1826-Jan. 12, 1892), *m* Nov. 7, 1844, Isaac Nelson **Brunson** (Sept. 18, 1813-Nov. 26, 1864), of Beaufort and Colleton cos., S.C. (George W.[3] [1773-1852], *m* Edy Smith, *d* aet. 94); issue: I–Martha (*b* 1845; *m* William H. Perreyclear); II–George Washington (*b* 1847; *m* Sophia Stevens); III–Josiah Murdaugh (*b* 1848; *m* Sarah Elliott); IV–William Pembroke (*b* 1851; *m* Leonora Neuffer); V–Isaac Nelson (1853-1928); VI–Susan (1854-1927; *m* Christian D. Kortjohn); VII–Frederick Newton (*b* 1856-*d*; *m* Georgia Baum; *m* 2d, Maud Goldsmith); VIII–Charles Preston (*b* 1859-*d*; *m* Fanny Jenney); IX–Peter Craddock (1 above); X–Henry Hamilton (*b* 1864-*d*; *m* Harriet Carson).
1–*m* July 8, 1885, Jessie Alma Mellichamp (qv for issue).
Residence: Orangeburg, S.C.

1–**BRUNSON, Mary Litta Pelham (Mrs. William W.),** *b* Crookston, Minn., July 6, 1884.
12–John **Stow,** from Kent, Eng., 1634; returned to Eng., 1635, and back to America, 1636, bringing his four sons, Thomas, John, Samuel and Stephen; settled at Roxbury, Mass.; *m* —Biggs;
11–Rev. Samuel, of Roxbury; *m* Hope Fletcher;
10–John (1650-88), of Charlestown, Mass.; *m* 1668, Mary Wetmore;
9–John (1671/72-1759), of Charlestown; *m* 1698, Bethsheba Hubbard;
8–John (*b* 1699), of Charlestown; *m* 1722, Anna Hubbard;
7–John (*b* 1725), *m* 1742, Abiah Sage;
6–Jonathan (1747-77), *m* 1772, Abigail (or Abigial) Elles;
5–Jedidiah (*b* 1773), of Middletown, Conn.; *m* 1791, Dinah Eton Higbee (Noah[6] [*b* 1735], *d* N.Y., pvt. Col. Canfield's Regt., West Point, 1781, *m* 1763, Mary Cooper);
4–Samuel (1792-1883), of Cromwell, Conn.; *m* 1815, Lois Sage (*d* 1877);
3–Lemuel Sage (1824-99), of Middletown, Conn.; emigrated to Ashtabula, O., where family had shipyard on Lake Erie; removed to Wis. after storm wrecked shipyard; served as nurse in hosp. at Nashville, Tenn., and grad. Nashville Med. Coll., 1865; enlisted Co. I, 16th Wis. Inf.; chased out of Mo. by bushwhackers; enlisted in Lincoln's 2d call for men and served until end of war; practiced medicine till death, at Hawley, Minn.; *m* 1850, Cornelia C. Barrett;
2–Lois Cornelia (2 below).
9–Humphrey **Barrett** (1592-1662), from Kent, Eng., 1639; settled Concord, Mass.; *m* Mary– (*d* 1663);
8–Humphrey (1630-1716), *b* Eng.; of Concord, Mass.; dea.; dep., rep. Gen. ct., 1691; ens.; *m* 2d, 1674, Mary Potter (1656-1713; Luke[9] [1608-97], *m* 1644, Mary, dau. Walter Edmunds);
7–Benjamin (1681-1728), of Concord, Mass.; in Grafton, 1728; *m* 1705, Lydia Minott (*b* 1687);
6–Stephen (*b* 1720), of Concord, Mass.; *m* 1750, Elizabeth (Hubbard) How;
5–Benjamin (1759-1845), of Paxton, Mass.; pvt. Capt. Ralph Earll's Co., Col. Danforth's Regt., 1777-78; enlisted Mass. Militia, 1779; *m* 1786, Clarinda Barnes;
4–Stephen (1791-1877), of Paris, N.Y.; served N.Y. state militia, War 1812; *m* 1816, Lucia Smith;
3–Cornelia C. (1825-69), of Kingsville, O.; *m* Lemuel S. **Stow** (3 above).
10–George **Hubbard** (qv);
9–John (*d* 1702), of Wethersfield, Hadley, and Hatfield; *m* Mary Merriam;
8–Jonathan (1659-1747), *m* 1681, Hannah Rice (Samuel[9] [*d* 1684], *m* 1st, Elizabeth King; Dea. Edmund[10], qv);
7–Joseph (1688-1768), *m* 1713, Rebecca Bulkeley (1696-1772; Capt. Joseph[8] [*b* 1670], *m* 1691, Rebecca [Jones] Minott, dau. John Jones, from Eng. in the "Abigail," to Concord, 1650, *m* Dorcas– [*d* 1709]; Maj. Peter[9] [*b* 1643], *m* Rebecca [*b* 1645], dau. Capt. Joseph Wheeler, killed by Indians in King Philip's War, 1675, *m* 2d, Sarah, Widow Merriam; Rev. Peter[10], qv);
6–Elizabeth, as Widow How, *m* 2d, Stephen **Barrett** (6 above).
2–Lois Cornelia **Stow** (1852-1923), of Burr Oak, Wis.; *m* 1882, John Harrison **Pelham** (1846-1914), pvt. Co. A, 10th Ill. Cav., 1864-65; building contractor; issue: I–Mary Litta (1 above); II–Roscoe Barrett (*b* 1886).
1–*m* Nov. 27, 1907, William Wallace Brunson, *b* Corry, Pa., Nov. 6, 1874; son of Michel Brunson, (*d* 1917) of Seattle, Wash.; issue: 1–Perry Pelham, *b* Seattle, Wash., Aug. 6, 1909.
1–Ed. business coll. Saleswoman. Mem. exec. bd., 4th and 5th Liberty Loans, Seattle, Wash. Mem. D.A.R., D.U.V. Address: Suquamish, Wash.

1–**BRYANT, W(illiam) Sohier,** *b* Boston, Mass., May 15, 1861.
9–Thomas **Bryant** (*b* in Eng., 1611-*d* Barbados B.W.I., 1661), *m* Martha Chaplin;
8–Edmund (*d* 1662), *m* Eleanor–;
7–William (*b* Barbados B.W.I., 1645-*d* 1697), *m* 1681, Hannah Gillett (*d* Boston, Mass.);
6–John (1689-1742), *m* 1711/12, Katherine Noaks;
5–John (1717-1758), *m* 1741, Lois Browne;
4–Capt. John (1742-1816), *m* 2d, 1779, Hannah Mason;
3–John (1780-1865), maritime mcht., Boston; *m* 1807, Mary Cleveland Smith;
2–Henry, M.D. (1820-67), A.B., Harvard, '40, M.D., 1843; served in French Army in Algiers, and in 20th Mass. Inf.; head of hospitals at Washington during Civil War; naturalist; *m* 1848, Elizabeth Brimmer Sohier (1823-1916); for issue and other lineages. see Vol. I, p. 464.
1–*m* Sept. 1, 1887, Martha Lyman Cox (divorced, 1919); dau. late James S. Cox, Phila.; issue: 1–Mary Cleveland, *b* Boston, June 20, 1888; *m* Fessenden S. Blanchard; 2–Elizabeth Sohier, *b* Cohasset, Mass., July 13, 1890; 3–Alice de Vermandois, *b* Boston, May 15, 1892; A.B., Barnard, '17; *m* 1917, Lawrence Kelso Frank; 4–Julia Cox, *b* Cohasset, June 25, 1893; 5–Gladis de Peyster, *b* Boston, Dec. 16, 1894; 6–William Sohier, Jr. (Dec. 8, 1896-1912).
1–A.B., Harvard, '84 (D.K.E., Zeta Psi, Porcelian Club), A.M., M.D., 1888. Physician, specializing in ear, nose, and throat (see Who's Who in America). Served as 1st lt., asst. surgeon, 1st Regt. Mass. Arty., 1898; maj. and brig. surgeon, U.S.V., 1898-99; maj. and lt. col. M.C., World War; col., Med. O.R.C., June 1919. Decorated Officer of the Crown of Italy and Chevalier of the Legion of Honor. Mem. S.M.D., S.C., M.O.L.L., M.O.F.W., N.M.O.S.A.-W., M.O.W.W., A.L., etc. Club: Century. Residence: 30 E. 40th St., New York, N.Y.

1–**BRYNE, Clara Martina Coe (Mrs. A. Willis),** *b* Meriden, Conn., Apr. 28, 1866.
9–Robert **Coe** (qv);
8–Robert (1626-59), came with father, settled at Stratford, Conn.; *m* 1650, Hannah Mitchell (1631-1702; Matthew[9]);
7–Capt. John (1658-1741), mcht., miller, innkeeper, Stratford; dep. Gen. Assembly, 1701 and 15; ens. 1698; lt. 1706; capt. 1709; served in French and Indian War, 1708; *m* 1682, Mary Hawley (1663-1731; Lt. Joseph[8], *m* Catherine Birdseye);
6–Capt. Joseph (1686-1754), pioneer at Durham, Conn.; Rep. Gen. Assembly, 1728; ens. 1722; lt. 1725; capt. 1729; *m* 1708, Abagail Robinson (1690-1775; David[7], *m* Abigail Kirby);
5–Dea. Joseph (1713-84), of Durham, and Middlefield, Conn.; *m* 2d, 1739, Abigail Curtis (1719-76; John[6], *m* Hannah Johnson; Benjamin[7]; John[8]; John[9], of Stratford);
4–Joseph (1753-1828), of Middletown, Conn.; *m* 1779, Elizabeth Cornwell (1755-1838; Lt. Nathaniel[5], *m* Mary Cornwell; Joseph[6]; John[7]; William[8], of Middletown);
3–Calvin (1794-1886), of Meriden, Conn.; selectman; town treas.; *m* 1820, Harriet Rice;
2–Winfield Rice (2 below).
9–Robert (Royce) **Rice** (*d* 1676), from Eng. in the "Frances," to Stratford, Conn., 1650; removed to New London, 1657; constable, 1660; dep. Conn. Assembly, 1661; mem. City Council, 1663-67,68; Conglist.; *m* 1624, Mary Sims or Elizabeth–;
8–Samuel (*b* ca. 1642), removed to New London; to Wallingford; ens. militia; *m* 1st, 1667, Hannah Churchill (*d* ca. 1689; Josiah[9], *m* Elizabeth Foote);
7–Samuel (1672-1757), *m* 1693, Hannah Benedict;
6–Ezekiel (1699-1765), justice of the peace; served in French and Indian wars; commd. lt.; capt., 4th co., Wallingford, 1743; *m* Abigal Alling;
5–Ezekiel (1739-1805), *m* Lydia Hugh (1740-1813);
4–Hezekiah (1764-1852), of Middletown, Conn.; *m* Lydia Stow (1765-1864);
3–Harriet (1800-91), *m* 1820, Calvin **Coe** (3 above).
9–William **Andrews** (qv);
8–Ens. Samuel (*b* Eng., 1632-*d* Wallingford, Conn., 1704), took oath of fidelity, 1654; *m* Elizabeth Peck; had 16 children (Dea. William[9], of North Haven);
7–Samuel (Apr. 30, 1663-Jan. 31, 1727), *m* Aug. 27, 1685, Annah Hall;
6–Samuel (June 29, 1697-Aug. 5, 1784), *m* Abigail Tyler (Jan. 29, 1697-Feb. 13, 1786; John[7], Wallingford);
5–Nicholas (1725-86), *m* Lydia Hull;
4–Marvel (1765-1848), *m* 2d, Sally Bronson (*d* 1816, aet. 44); he *m* 4 times;
3–Amon (1804-85), *m* Clarissa Ruth Butler (1808-44);
2–Mary Elizabeth (*b* Meriden, Conn., Apr. 11,

1839-*d* Apr. 25, 1906), *m* 1860, *m* Winfield Rice **Coe** (1839-1914), farmer, Meriden, Conn.; issue: I–Augusta (1861-65); II–Clara Martina (1 above); III–Philip Andrews (*b* 1870; *m* Carrie Lines Davis); IV–Winfield Rice (*b* 1873; *m* Emma Higgins); V–Bessie (*m* John Akers); VI–Helen Adalaide.
1–*m* Nov. 11, 1921, Andrew Willis Bryne, *b* Truro, Cape Cod, Mass., Sept. 3, 1862; son of William Henry Bryne, of Wellfleet, Cape Cod, Mass.
1–Grad. Emerson Coll. of Oratory, Boston. Founder of Miss Coe's School of Oratory. Mem. D.A.C., D.F.P.A., S.D.P., D.A.R., Nat. Soc. N.E. Women (pres. gen. and pres. Hartford Colony). Clubs: Emerson College, Republican. Congregationalist. Residence: 79 Linnmoore St., Hartford, Conn.

1–**BUCKLEY, Monroe Leer,** *b* Bourbon Co., Ky., Feb. 2, 1905.
6–Simon **Nichols** (1724-1813), from Scotland, settled in Md.; *m* 1755, Ann–;
5–James (1777-1855), of Ky. and Mo.; *m* 1802, Nancy Whaley (*d* 1840);
4–Julia (1803-66), of Harrison Co., Ky.; *m* 1834, Lewis F. **Weimar** (1794-1867), from Germany (George Ludwig[5]);
3–Elizabeth (1845-1930), of Fayette Co., Ky.; *m* 1862, Thomas **Buckley** (1845-1915; Timothy[4], *m* Ellen Callahan);
2–Benjamin Franklin (2 below).
9–William **Turner** (*d* 1696), from Eng., settled in Va.; removed to N.C. ante 1663; *m* Katherine–;
8–William, of N.C.; *m* Miss Nixon;
7–Edward (*d* 1803), of N.C. and Ky.; took oath of allegiance for Rowan Co., N.C., 1778; *m* Ann Davies (James[8]);
6–John (1738-1813), of N.C., and Madison Co., Ky.; sgt. Am. Rev.; *m* 1st, Rebecca Smith (*d* 1774; Andrew[7]);
5–Thomas (1764-1847), allotted land by N.C. for services as pvt., Am. Rev. 1778; to Madison Co., Ky.; *m* 2d, 1814, Anne Berry (1785-1833; James[6], *m* Sarah Grubbs);
4–James Berry (1822-67), of Ky. and Mo.; *m* 1841, Mary Jane Tribble;
3–Amelia (1852-1915), of Ky.; *m* 1874, James Monroe **Leer** (1841-94);
2–Charlotte Corday (2 below).
11–William **Tandy,** of Va., 1650;
10–Henry, of Rappahannock Co., Va.;
9–Henry (*d* 1705), of Essex and King cos., Va.;
8–Henry (*d* 1741), of S. Farnham Parish, Essex Co., Va.; *m* Frances Crittenden ? (Henry[9]);
7–Frances, *m* Thomas **Burris** (1730-98);
6–Sallie (1753-1830), of Va.; *m* 1768, Andrew **Tribble** (1741-1822), of Va. and Ky.;
5–Dudley (*d* 1877), of Madison Co., Ky.; *m* 1819, Matilda Tevis;
4–Mary Jane (1822-59), of Ky.; *m* 1841, James Berry **Turner** (4 above);
3–Amelia, *m* James Monroe **Leer** (3 above);
2–Charlotte Corday (see Vol. III, p. 98), *m* 1896, Benjamin Franklin **Buckley** (*b* 1863), tobacco broker of Lexington, Ky.; issue: I–Benjamin Franklin, Jr. (qv for other lineages); II–Monroe Leer (1 above).
1–Not married. A.B., Transylvania Coll., '26 (Kappa Alpha, Phi Delta Phi), LL.B., Yale U., 1929. Lawyer. Mem. S.R. Mason. Christian. Republican. Clubs: Ashland Golf, Lexington Country, Pyramid. Residence: 152 Forest Av., Lexington, Ky.

1–**BUCKLEY, Benjamin Franklin, Jr.,** *b* Bourbon Co., Ky., May 12, 1901.
10–Matthaus **Weimer,** of Mittelstadt, Germany;
9–Jakobus, of Mittelstadt; *m* 1638, Anna, dau. of Martin Kramer;
8–Hans Jacob (*b* 1658), of Tübingen; *m* 1682, Argina Nuphinan;
7–Johann Adam (*b* 1688), of Tübingen; *m* 1710, Maria, dau. of Sebastian Lutz;
6–Johannis (*b* 1723), of Tübingen; *m* 1744, Eva Maria, dau. of Johann Jacob Zahn, of Kerrenberg, Germany;
5–George Ludwig (1756-1827), of Tübingen; *m* 1786, Christina Dorothy Vetter (1761-1848; Christopher[6]);
4–Lewis F. (1794-1867), came from Germany; *m* 1834, Julia Nichols (1803-66), of Harrison Co., Ky.;
3–Elizabeth (1845-1930), of Fayette Co., Ky.; *m* 1862, Thomas **Buckley** (1845-1915; Timothy[4], *m* Ellen Callahan);
2–Benjamin Franklin (2 below).
6–Henry **Leer** (1720-1802), Am. Rev.; *m* Ann–;
5–David (1769-1852), *m* Elizabeth Wright (1770-1844; William[6], Am. Rev.);
4–David (1803-85), *m* Corday Kenney (1809-97; James[5], Am. Rev.);
3–James Monroe (1841-94), stockman and farmer; *m* 1874, Amelia Turner;
2–Charlotte Corday (2 below).
8–Robert **Tevis,** French Huguenot; settled in Md.; *m* 1707, Susannah Davies;
7–Nathaniel (1710-98), Madison Co., Ky.;
6–Robert (*d* 1823), *m* 1798, Mary (Hobbs) Parker (Joseph Hobbs[7], 1st rep. from Nelson Co., Ky., 1792, *m* Ann, dau. of Thomas Maynard, Am. Rev.);
5–Matilda (1805-61), *m* 1819, Dudley **Tribble** (1797-1877);
4–Mary Jane (1822-59), of Ky.; *m* 1841, James Berry **Turner** (1822-67);
3–Amelia (1852-1915), of Ky., *m* James M. **Leer** (3 above);
2–Charlotte Corday (see Vol. III, p. 98), *m* 1896, Benjamin Franklin **Buckley** (*b* 1863), tobacco broker of Lexington, Ky.; issue: I–Benjamin Franklin, Jr. (1 above); II–Monroe Leer (qv for other lineages).
1–*m* Oct. 15, 1923, Beulah Mae Saunders, *b* Fleming Co., Ky., Mar. 27, 1900; dau. of M. C. Saunders, of Lexington, Ky.; issue: 1–Benjamin Franklin, III, *b* Lexington, Ky., Sept. 22, 1924.
1–Grad. U.Wis., '23 (Alpha Tau Omega). Pres. Lexington Bd. of Fire Underwriters, 1927-28; gen. agent for state of Ky. Sylvania Ins. Co.; v.p. Southern Bedding Co.; dir. Commonwealth Bank & Trust Co. Mason (K.T., Shriner), Odd Fellow. Christian. Democrat. Clubs: Ashland Golf, Lions, Pyramid. Residence: 152 Forest Av., Lexington, Ky.

1–**BUEL, Elizabeth Cynthia Barney (Mrs. John L.),** *b* New York, N.Y., Feb. 16, 1868.
10–Jacob **Barney** (qv);
9–Jacob (*b* 1634), came with his father; Bapt. minister; founded churches, Charlestown and Swansea, Mass.; one of founders of Boston Bapt. Ch., 1668; removed to Bristol, R.I., later at Rehoboth, Mass.; *m* 2d, 1660, Anne Witt (John[10], *m* Sarah–);
8–Joseph (1673-1730), lt., Rehoboth, Mass.; *m* 1692, Constance Davis (James[9], *m* Elizabeth Eaton);
7–John (1703-57), of Swansea and Taunton; *m* 1729, Hannah Clark (Aaron[8], *m* Sarah Lange);
6–John (1730-1807), a pioneer at Guilford, Vt.; supervisor of town, 1772-73; collector and highway commr., 1777; fence-viewer; overseer of poor; mem. com. to sell town land; mem. com. sent to Windsor Conv., 1777; capt. in French and Indian War; drilled men for service in Am. Rev.; *m* 1748, Rebecca Martin (*b* 1729, Edward[7], *m* Rebeckah Peck);
5–John (1753-93), of Guilford, Vt.; Am. Rev.; *m* 1st, Sarah– (1757-75);
4–John (1775-1863), removed to Waukeshau, Wis.; capt. and maj.; *m* 1799, Sarah Grow (Nathaniel[5], *m* Susanna Dow);
3–Danford Newton (1808-74), of Henderson, N.Y.; pres. Wells, Fargo & Co., express agts.; buried at Irvington-on-Hudson, N.Y.; *m* 1833, Cynthia M. Cushman;
2–Newcomb Cushman (2 below).
10–William **Bradford,** Mayflower Pilgrim (qv);
9–Maj. William (1624-1704), rep.; dep. gov. of Mass.; *m* 1651, Alice Richards (1627-71; Thomas[10], *m* Welthian Loring);
8–Thomas (1657-1708), *m* ca. 1681, Anne Smith (Nehemiah[9], *m* Anne Bourne);
7–Jerusha (1693-1739); *m* 1716, Hezekiah **Newcomb** (1693-1772; Simon[8], highway surveyor; Lt. Andrew[9], large landowner, selectman, lt. of militia, cdr. fortifications; Capt. Andrew[10], qv);
6–Peter (1718-79), served in French and Indian War; on expdn. to Can.; *m* 1740, Hannah or Mary English (1722-96; Richard[7], *m* Mary Hincksman);
5–Phebe (1741-85), *m* 1760, Nathanial **Cushman** (1738-1817);
4–Peter Newcomb (1780-1848), large landowner and farmer, Ty. of Wis.; pres. bd. trustees, Carroll Coll.; *m* 1804, Sarah Kellogg (1784-1844; Levi[5], Am. Rev., *m* Cynthia Wright);
3–Cynthia Maria (1807-43), *m* Danford N. **Barney** (3 above).

9-Edward **Sturgis** (qv);
8-Edward (bap. 1624), came with his father; settled at Yarmouth; *m* Elizabeth-;
7-Thomas (1659-1708), constable, Yarmouth, 1681; mem. Grand Inquest, 1684; surveyor, 1685; freeman, 1689; *m* 1680, Abigail Lathrop (Barnabas[8], *m* Susanna Clark);
6-Thomas (1686-1763), merchant, Barnstable; *m* 1717, Martha Russell (Rev. Jonathan[7], *m* Martha Moody);
5-Thomas (1722-85), of Barnstable; *m* Sarah Paine (William[6], *m* Sarah Bacon);
4-Thomas (1755-1821), *m* 1785 or 86, Elizabeth Jackson (Hezekiah[5], *m* Elizabeth Thacher);
3-William (1806-95), removed from Barnstable to N.Y. City; *m* 1831, Elizabeth Knight Hinckley (1809-48; Isaac[4], *m* Hannah Sturgis);
2-Elizabeth Jackson (*b* London, Eng., 1837-*d* 1905), *m* 1864, Newcomb Cushman **Barney** (1839-1916), banker and broker, New York; issue: I-Newcomb Sturgis (1865-66); II-Elizabeth C. (1 above); III-Sturgis (1870-72); IV-Danford Newton Sturgis (1876-97).
1-*m* May 28, 1895, John Laidlaw Buel, M.D., *b* Litchfield, Conn., Nov. 26, 1861; ed. Columbia, 1888; mem. S.C.W., etc.; son of Henry Wadhams Buel, M.D., of Litchfield; issue: 1-Katharine Barney, *b* Litchfield, Conn., Apr. 8, 1905; *m* Nov. 15, 1926, Stewart Weaver Tompkins, of Torrington, Conn. (issue: Henry Buel Sturgis).
1-B.A., Columbia Coll., '97. Mem. O.C., D.B.R., S.M.D., C.D.A., D.F.P.A. (nat. pres.), S.D.C.W., D.A.C., C.D. 17th C., D.A.R. (ex-v.p.gen., hon. state regent Conn.), Litchfield Hist. Soc. (v.p.). Served on com. nat. defense, Speakers' Bureau, Conn. Council of Defense, War Relief Service Com. (D.A.R.), chmn. Litchfield Liberty Loan Com., sec. Litchfield Chapter A.R.C. Clubs: Colonial Dames (Washington), Nat. Officers' and State Regents of D.A.R. Residence: "East Meadows," Litchfield, Conn.

1-**BULKLEY, Louis Carleton,** *b* Westchester Co., N.Y., Sept. 19, 1862.
8-Master Peter **Bulkeley** (qv);
7-Dr. Peter (1643-91), physician, Fairfield, Conn.;
6-Capt. Gershom (1679-1753), served in Conn. Troop of Horse, Fairfield Co.; *m* 2d, Rachel Talcott (*b* 1681/82; Lt. Col. John[7], chief mil. officer Conn., *m* 2d, 1676, Mary Cook; Hon. John[8], qv);
5-Peter (*b* 1715/16), *m* 1740, Anne Hill;
4-Gershom (1748-1820), removed to Sasco, Conn.; *m* 1st, 1773, Elizabeth Chapman;
3-William (1790-1860), of Rye and Brooklyn, N.Y.; *m* Mary Bartram Osborne;
2-Philemon Carpenter (2 below).
9-William **Hill,** son of James, of Eng.; came from Eng.;
8-William (*d* 1684), from Eng.; settled at Fairfield, Conn.; dep. Gen. Ct., 1651-55,58,59,61, 67-69,71; mem. war com. for Fairfield, 1653; commr., 1666-78; clk. of ct., 1666; *m* Elizabeth Jones (Rev. John[9], from Eng. to Boston and Concord, Mass., "preacher" of the church at Concord, thence to Fairfield, *m* Sarah-);
7-Eliphalet, *m* (Hester) Esther Ward (Dr. William[8], *m* 1657, Deborah Lockwood; Andrew[9], qv);
6-William, *m* Abigail Barlow;
5-Anne (bap. 1719-1795), *m* Peter **Bulkley** (5 above).
8-Capt. Robert **Chapman** (qv);
7-Nathaniel (1653-1726), of Saybrook, Conn.; had longest legislative service on record, 43 yrs.; *m* 1681, Mary Collins (1663-95; John[8] [1640-1704], *m* Mary Trowbridge);
6-Rev. Daniel (1689-1741), M.A., Yale, 1707; pastor, ch. at Green's Farms, Conn.; *m* 1710, Grizzel Dennie (bap. 1696/97-1754), of Fairfield (Albert[7], *m* Elizabeth, dau. of Rev. Samuel Wakeman);
5-Dennie (1730-93), fifer in Am. Rev.; *m* 1750, Desire Lovel or Lovewell (*d* 1810, aet. 85);
4-Elizabeth (1751-95), *m* Gershom **Bulkley** (4 above).
9-Jehu **Burr** (qv);
8-Maj. John (1633-will probated 1694), officer French and Indian War; asst. magistrate; sgt. maj., 1694; *m* Sarah Fitch (Capt. Thomas[9], qv);
7-John (1673-1705), *m* Elizabeth Hanford (Rev. Thomas[8], qv);
6-Col. Andrew (1696-1763), of Fairfield; col. in command Conn. forces in expdn. against Louisburg; *m* Sarah Sturgis (1701-45; Jonathan[7], *m* Sarah, dau. David Osborne, g.dau. Capt Richard Osborne, qv);
5-Elizabeth (1726-1815), *m* Daniel **Osborne,** Sr. (1725-1804; Samuel[6], *m* 1724, Hannah Couch; Capt. John[7]; Capt. Richard[8], qv);
4-Daniel, Jr. (1760-1801), *m* Mary Burr Bartram;
3-Mary Bartram (1790-1850), *m* William **Bulkeley** (3 above).
9-Hon. John **Wakeman** (qv);
8-Rev. Samuel (1636-92), *m* 1656, Hannah Goodyear (Stephen[9], qv);
7-Capt. Joseph (1670-1726), *m* 1697/98, Elizabeth Hawley (Ebenezer[8], *m* Esther, dau. of Andrew Ward, qv);
6-Catherine (bap. 1700-1753), *m* 1722, Capt. John **Burr** (1698-1752; Col. John[7] [1673-1750]; Nathaniel[8] [1640-1712]; Jehu[9], 9 above);
5-Mary (1732-1806), *m* Ebenezer **Bartram,** served on brig "Defence," Am. Rev.;
4-Mary Burr (1765-1843), *m* Daniel **Osborne** (4 above);
3-Mary Bartram, *m* William **Bulkley** (3 above);
2-Philemon Carpenter (1828-1904), lumberman; *m* 1855, Mary Jane Moody (*b* Eng., 1829-*d* St. Louis, Mo.; dau. of William Moody, *m* Jane Cross); issue: I-Mary Ezit (*b* 1856); II-William Moody (1858-99); III-Louis Carleton (1 above).
1-*m* Mar. 19, 1894, Caroline Rogers Kemper (see Vol. III, p. 99, for genealogy and issue).
1-Gen. sec. Shreveport Fed. of Community Work. Fellow Am. Pub. Health Assn. Mason (32°). Club: Rotary. Residence: 1044 Rutherford Av., Shreveport, La.

1-**BULLARD, Mary Blackmar (Mrs. William L.),** *b* Columbus, Ga., Nov. 13, 1860.
8-Caleb **Carr** (qv);
7-Nicholas (1654-1709), of R.I.; ens., 1680; lt., 1692; mem. Legislature, 1680,89,96,99;
6-Nicholas, *m* Margaret Battey;
5-Frances Battey (1751-1837), *m* Theophilus **Blackmar** (1750-1842), of Scituate, R.I.;
4-Charles (1778-1862), *m* Henrietta Burton (*b* 1779; Judge John[5], asso. justice Supreme Ct. of R.I., 20 yrs.);
3-Alfred Owen (1799-1865), *m* 1827, Betsy Brainerd Arnold;
2-Alfred Owen (2 below).
5-Col. Dan **Brainerd** (1756-99), comd. troop militia in N.H. alarm; served in Conn. troops in Am. Rev.; *m* Susannah Clark;
4-Betsy, *m* Capt. John **Arnold** (1770-1853);
3-Betsy Brainerd (1799-1831), *m* 1827, Alfred Owen **Blackmar** (3 above).
10-James **Blood** (*d* 1683), from Eng. to Concord, Mass., ca. 1638; *m* Ellen-;
9-Richard (ca. 1617-1683), one of original petitioners for Groton, Mass., and its largest propr.; *m* Isabel-;
8-Joseph (*d* ante 1692), of Mendon and Dedham, Mass.; *m* Hannah-;
7-Richard (ante 1687-1768), *m* Joannah- (*d* 1767);
6-Capt. Nathaniel (1716-1801), colonial service, 1758; *m* 1742, Ruth Hall (1720-1811);
5-Richard (1746-1820), corpl. and lt. at Lexington Alarm, and in Am. Rev., 1780; *m* Mary Blood (1749-1808);
4-Jacob (1771-1857), *m* Phoebe Eddy (1774-1841);
3-Dexter (1805-91), mem. Mass. Legislature; *m* 1828, Ann Gordon Dana (1805-85);
2-Mary Ann (*b* 1831), *m* 1851, Alfred Owen **Blackmar** (*b* 1830), banker Columbus, Ga.; issue: I-John (*b* 1853; *m* 1884, Susie Beatrice Wellborn); II-Savannah (*b* 1859; *m* 1882, Clarence Julian Edge); III-Mary (1 above); IV-Betsy Brainerd (*b* 1863); V-Dana (*b* 1866; *m* 1890, Nattie Ion Barden).
1-*m* Oct. 26, 1881, Dr. William Lewis Bullard; issue (all *b* Columbus, Ga.): 1-Mary Elmira (Mrs. William Hart, qv); 2-Louise, *b* Aug. 1, 1884, ed. Lucy Cobb Inst.; *m* Nov. 2, 1909, Leighton Wilson MacPherson (issue: Mira Elizabeth); 3-Ann Dana, *b* Nov. 1, 1886.
1-Mem. C.D.A., D.A.R. Summer place: Warm Springs, Ga. Residence: 1408 3d Av., Columbus, Ga.

1-**HART, Mary Elmira Bullard (Mrs. William),** *b* Columbus, Ga., Apr. 20, 1883.
4-Wiley **Bullard** (*b* Twiggs Co., Ga.-*d* Washington Co.), *m* Martha Daniels;

3–Lewis (*b* Twiggs Co., Oct. 8, 1808-*d* Washington Co., July 9, 1869), *m* Elmyra Peacock (*b* Apr. 21, 1827-Sept. 12, 1872);
2–Dr. William Lewis (*b* Tennville, Ga., Feb. 29, 1852-*d* May 18, 1925), grad. Emory U., 1877, and Med. Coll., Baltimore; studied in London and Vienna; grad. Royal London Opthalmic Hosp.; *m* 1881, Mary Blackmar (qv for genealogy).
1–*m* Jan. 20, 1909, William Hart, *b* Pulaski, Va., July 13, 1880; son of William Thomas Hart (1840-1902; James Brookes[3] [1812-70], *m* Maria Virginia Collier, of Tallahoosa Co., Ala.), *m* Lucy Gaines Bentley, of Pulaski Co., Va.; issue (all *b* Columbus, Ga.): 1–Ann Louise, *b* Jan. 26, 1911; 2–Mary, *b* July 28, 1914; 3–William, *b* Jan. 22, 1918.
1–Ed. Lucy Cobb Inst., Mt. Athens, Ga. Mem. C.D.A., D.A.R. Club: Woman's Reading. Summer place: Warm Springs, Ga. Residence: 1408 3d Av., Columbus, Ga.

1–**BURCH, Frank Persons,** *b* Westfield, N.Y., Nov. 20, 1881.
12–Richard **Rathbone** (*b* 1574), *m* Marian Whipple;
11–John (*b* 1610), *m* 1633;
10–John (1634-post 1683), *m* Margaret Dodge (Tristram[11]);
9–Thomas (1657-1734), *m* Mary Dickens (Nathaniel[10], *m* Joan Tyler);
8–Mary (*b* 1687), *m* 1706, Jonathan **Burch** (*b* ca. 1675), see Vol. III, p. 101, for Burch lineage;
7–Jonathan (*b* 1707), Stonington, Conn.; *m* 1735, Mary Rathbun, of Lyme, Conn.;
6–Jonathan (*b* 1740), founder of Hartford, Vt., 1772; Am. Rev.; *m* 1765, Eunice–;
5–Jonathan (1766-1838), War 1812; *m* 1786, Sally Hosford;
4–Oliver Wheeler (1801-83); *m* 1st, 1827, Mary Sprague Tower;
3–Horace (1827-94), *m* 1852, Mary Ann Dier (1832-1904);
2–Oliver B. (2 below).
10–William **Hosford,** at Dorchester, Mass., 1633; ruling elder, Windsor, Conn., 1637; returned to Eng., 1654; to America with 2d wife, 1655;
9–John (*d* 1683), *m* 1657, Phillipa Thrall;
8–Capt. Dr. Obadiah (1677-1740), *m* 1704, Mindwell Phelps (1682-1771);
7–Joseph (1715-61), *m* 1737, Eunice Beach;
6–Joseph (1743-1819), soldier Am. Rev.; *m* 1764, Mary Peters;
5–Sally (1766-1845), of Wells, Vt.; *m* Jonathan **Burch** (5 above).
7–Cornelius **Tower,** *m* Hannah Higgins;
6–Isaac (1744-1826), soldier Am. Rev.; *m* 1770, Mary Sprague (1752-1826), see Vol. III, p. 101, for Sprague lineage;
5–John (1780-1855), *m* 1804, Lucy Munson (1785-1838; Samuel[6], *m* Martha Barnes);
4–Mary S. (1808-51), *m* 1827, Oliver W. **Burch** (4 above);
3–Horace, *m* Mary A. Dier (3 above);
2–Oliver Burdette (*b* 1857), of Westfield, N.Y.; *m* 1880, Edith May Persons (*b* 1858); for issue see Vol. III, p. 101.
1–*m* Dec. 31, 1908, Myrtle Ross, *b* Clarendon, Pa.; dau. of Frankie Ross, of Titusville, Pa.; issue: 1–Frank Burdette, *b* Sept. 19, 1909; 2–Merril Glen, *b* Feb. 24, 1910; 3–Gladys Lillian, *b* Jan. 5, 1912.
1–*m* 2d, Sept. 5, 1923, Ottie V. Eby, *b* Taneytown, Md., Dec. 12, 1883; James L.[2] (1845-1921), *m* 1870, Susanna A., dau. of Jacob Spangler, *m* Elizabeth Detter; Christian[3], *m* Elizabeth Martin.
1–Pres. Chamber of Commerce; justice of peace. Served as pvt. Med. Corps, Spanish-Am. War and Philippine Insurrection; lt. 74th Inf., U.S.A., World War; instr. under Mil. Training Commn. Sec. Burch Genealogical Soc.; mem. S.M.D., S.A.R. (v.p. state soc.), U.S. W.V., A.L., I.A.G. Mason. Elk. Summer place: Washington Co., Md. Residence: De Soto City, Fla.

1–**BURDETTE, Frank Lee,** *b* Putnam Co., W.Va., Jan. 20, 1867.
5–Edward **Cornwell** (1735-1805), soldier Greenbrier Co. militia in Am. Rev.; *m* Frances–;
4–Sarah (1762-1816), *m* William **Burdette** (ca. 1761-1836), soldier in Monroe Co., Va., militia in War 1812;
3–Alexander (1802-63), of Monroe and Putnam cos., Va.; *m* 1823, Mary Lively Hill;
2–James Robinson (2 below).
5–James **Hill** (1758-1831), Va. soldier in Am. Rev.; served in southern campaign, 1780-81; *m* Anne–;
4–James, Jr. (1779-1842), *m* 1801, Elizabeth Lively;
3–Mary Lively (1804-72), *m* Alexander **Burdette** (3 above).
6–Joseph **Richeson** (1721-82), capt. Caroline Co., Va., militia; in Am. Rev., 1779-81; *m* Elizabeth–;
5–Jane, *m* ca. 1775, James **Lively** (*d* 1814), from Eng., settled in Amherst Co., Va.;
4–Elizabeth (1781-1857), *m* James **Hill,** Jr. (4 above).
9–Jasper **Lillard,** lived on the Loire River, France; Huguenot; *m* —Isaacs;
8–Moise (Moses), *m* Lilli (Lillian) Balssa, a great-aunt of Honoré de Balzac, the noted French author;
7–Jean (John) (ca. 1668-1788, later date traditional), from France with his brother Benjamin, ca. 1700; *m* 1700, Mildred Jones (*d* ca. 1720);
6–Benjamin (*b* ca. 1701), *m* 1724, Elizabeth Lightfoot (William[7], related to Lee family of Va.);
5–Thomas (1726-1814), of Culpeper Co., Va.; sgt. Am. Rev.; served at Yorktown; *m* Ann– (*d* ca. 1826);
4–John (1765-1834), pvt. Va. militia in Am. Rev., served at Petersburg and Yorktown; settled at Sperryville, Va.; *m* 1786, Rachel Garrett (1770-ca. 1830; John[5], Am. Rev., with George Rogers Clark Expdn. to Ill., *m* Nancy, dau. of Benjamin Lillard, 6 above), they were ancestors of William Jennings Bryan;
3–Elizabeth (1795-1882), of Culpeper Co., Va.; later in Cabell Co., W.Va., 1826; *m* 1813, William Pitt **Yates** (1786-1869), pvt. Va. militia in War 1812; crippled in service at Norfolk (Richard[4] [*d* 1816], pvt. Am. Rev., and War 1812, *m* Mary Pitt [*d* 1822], related to Sir William Pitt, Lord Chatham);
2–Elizabeth (1832-90), of Cabell Co., Va.; *m* 1859, James Robinson **Burdette** (1828-1909), landowner Monroe Co., later in Putnam and Cabell cos.; personal friend of Gov. James McDowell of Va. (for issue see Vol. III, p. 101).
1–*m* July 6, 1910, Laura Buckner (qv); issue: 1–Franklin Lillard, *b* Huntington, W.Va., Dec. 7, 1911.
1–Ed. Marshall Coll., State Normal Sch., '86; L.I., Peabody Normal Coll., Nashville, Tenn., 1891; A.B., U.Nashville, 1892, and George Peabody Coll., 1920; studied in Grad. Sch. of U. Chicago, 1901-02. Prin. Clarksville (Tenn.) High Sch., 1892-93; supt. Weston (W.Va.) pub. schs., 1893-97; supt. Clarksburg (W.Va.) pub. schs., 1897-1916; Supt. W.Va. Schs. for Deaf and Blind, 1917-20; teacher of history and Latin, Huntington city schs., since 1920. Author: First Counties and Settlers of West Virginia; Early Forts and Battlegrounds in West Virginia; History of the Ona Community of Cabell Co. Mem. W.Va. State Bd. Edn., 1915-17. Mem. S.A.R. (state sec., 1928-29), S.R. (state historian, 1913-16). Mason. Bapt. Summer place: Yatesmont, Ona, W.Va. Residence: 632 9th Av., Huntington, W.Va.

1–**BURDETTE, Laura Buckner (Mrs. Frank L.),** *b* Cabell Co. W.Va., Mar. 10, 1871.
5–Jonathan **Watkins** (1761-1854), of Valley Forge, Chester Co., Pa.; soldier Pa. militia, in Pa. Navy, and in Cont. Army, Am. Rev., pensioned; to Athens Co., O.; *m* 2d, Elizabeth Haney;
4–David (*d* 1821), of Athens Co., O.; *m* Elizabeth Hutchinson;
3–Martha (1813-1905), of Athens Co.; *m* David C. **Buckner** (*d* 1850);
2–Joseph A. (1835-1913), soldier Va. Cav., C.S.A., under Gen. Albert Gallatin Jenkins; *m* Olga Handley (1846-73; John[3] *m* Eleanor Summers).
1–*m* July 6, 1910, Frank Lee Burdette (qv).
Residence: 632 9th Av., Huntington, W.Va.

1–**BURDG, Ida M. Easton (Mrs. Oliver P.),** *b* Dexter, Mich., Aug. 22, 1863.
10–Hopestill (Layland) **Leland** (1580?-1655), from Eng., ca. 1624, to Weymouth, Mass., ca. 1638;
9–Henry (1625-80), of Dorchester and Sherborn, Mass.; *m* Margaret Babcock;
8–Ebenezer (1657-1742), of Medford, Mass.; *m* Deborah–;

7–Capt. James (1687-1768), *m* 1716, Hannah Learned (*b* 1690; Benoni[8] [*b* 1657], of Chelmsford, *m* 1680, Mary Fanning, *m* 2d, Sarah–; Isaac[9] [*b* Eng., bap. 1623/24], *m* 1646, Mary, dau. of Isaac Stearn; William[10], qv);
6–Moses (1717-97), pvt. Am. Rev.; *m* Mrs. Abigail Robins (*d* 1797), of Littleton;
5–Mary (1748-1828), of Sutton, Mass.; *m* 1765, Abraham **Taylor** (*b* 1743), served in Am. Rev. (Thomas[6] [*b* ante 1700], *m* 1st, 1741, Lydia, dau. Caleb Taylor, bro. of Thomas[6]);
4–Dea. James (1773-1826), *m* 1797, Lucy Goldthwaite;
3–Obed (1799-1853), of Dexter, Mich.; *m* 1827, Almira Meriam;
2–Olive O. (2 below).
9–Thomas **Goldthwaite** (ca. 1610-1683), from Eng. with Gov. Winthrop's fleet, 1630; *m* 1636, Elizabeth– (*d* ante 1671);
8–Samuel (bap. 1637-1718), *m* 1666, Elizabeth Cheever (1645-1726; Ezekiel[9], famous master Boston Latin Sch., *m* Mary–);
7–Ezekiel (1674-1761), *m* 1695, Esther Boyce (Joseph[8], *m* Elinor–);
6–Samuel (ca. 1703-1789), *m* Sarah Reed (Jacob[7], *m* Elizabeth Green);
5–Stephen (bap. 1734-1812), *m* Patience Very (Joseph[6], *m* Ruth Foster);
4–Lucy (1774-1826), *m* Dea. James **Taylor** (4 above).
10–William **Meriam** (*d* 1635), of Eng.;
9–Joseph (*b* ca. 1600), *m* Sarah Goldstone (John[10], *m* Frances–);
8–Joseph (ca. 1630-1677), *m* 1653, Sarah Stone (Dea. Gregory[9]);
7–John (1662-1727), *m* 1688, Mary Wheeler;
6–Ebenezer (1706-61), of Lexington; *m* Esther Gleason (*d* post 1734, Thomas[7]); *m* 2d, 1747, Elizabeth Locke (bap. 1720; Ebenezer[7], 6 below);
5–Ebenezer (1734-95), of Oxford; *m* 1753, Phebe Locke;
4–Joel (1775-1846), *m* 1st, 1800, his cousin, Sarah Meriam;
3–Almira (1804-73), of Oxford, Mass.; *m* Obed **Taylor** (3 above).
9–William **Locke** (*d* 1631), mariner, of Stephany Parish, London, Eng.; *m* Elizabeth–;
8–William (*b* Eng., 1628-*d* Woburn, Mass., 1720), to America in the "Planter"; large landowner; dea.; *m* 1655, Mary Clarke (William[9], *m* Margery–);
7–William (*b* 1659), *m* 1683, Sarah Whittmore (Francis[8], *m* Isabel Park);
6–Ebenezer, *m* Elizabeth Poulter (Jonathan[7], *m* Elizabeth–);
5–Phebe (*b* 1731), *m* Ebenezer **Meriam** (5 above).
9–Thomas **Burnap** (bap. 1630), *m* Mary, daughter of John Pearson, *m* Maudlin Ballard (or Bullard);
8–Thomas (1664-1726), *m* Sarah Walton (Samuel[9], *m* Sarah Maverich; desc. Rev. William Walton, qv);
7–Ebenezer (*b* 1697-1723), *m* 1719, Hannah Lilley (Samuel[8], *m* Hannah–);
6–Ebenezer, Jr. (1723-1804), Am. Rev.; *m* 1749, Mary Wyman (*d* 1793);
5–Sarah, *m* 1777, Jotham **Meriam** (1749-98), pvt. Am. Rev. (Ebenezer[6], 6 above);
4–Sarah (1778-1822), *m* Joel **Meriam** (4 above);
3–Almira, *m* Obed **Taylor** (3 above);
2–Olive O. (1835-1905), *m* 1859, Fernando **Easton** (1834-88), farmer; issue: I–Celesta (*b* 1860); II–Ida M. (1 above); III–Harry F. (*b* 1870); IV–Edith (*b* 1873; *m* 1914, Thomas Waltz).
1–*m* June 30, 1891, Oliver P. Burdg, *b* Butlerville, Ind., Dec. 23, 1861; son of Lewis Burdg (*d*), *m* Sarah Malmsbury.
1–Teacher 30 yrs.; financial sec., First M.E. Ch., Riverside, Calif., 11 yrs. Mem. D.A.R. Methodist. Republican. Club: Women's. Residence: 441 Lemon St., Riverside, Calif.

1–**BURNETT, Edgar Albert,** *b* Hartland, Mich., October 17, 1865.
8–Robert (Burnap) **Burnett** (*b* 1595) from Eng., ca. 1635; propr. at Roxbury, Mass., 1640; removed to Reading, 1642; large landowner and selectman; *m* Sarah–;
7–Robert (*d* 1695), propr. Reading; selectman and town officer; *m* Sarah Browne;
6–Benjamin (*b* 1667), farmer and landlord, Reading; sentinel on expdn. to Can., 1711; removed to Hopkinton, Mass., ca. 1724; dea., 1725; *m* 1700, Elizabeth Newhall (*b* 1678; Thomas[7] [1653-1728], lt. King Philip's War, weaver and selectman, Malden, 1700, *m* Rebecca, dau. Thomas Greene; Thomas[8] [1630-87], 1st white child *b* Lynn, *m* Elizabeth, dau. Thomas Potter; Thomas[9], qv);
5–Jonathan, removed to Hopkinton, 1724; sold property to Seth Morse; removed to Hampton, Conn.; *m* 2d, 1747, Elizabeth Averill;
4–James (1756-1840), began to write name Burnett; of Windham (later Hampton), Conn.; corpl., sgt., Conn. troops, Am. Rev., pensioned; *m* 1781, Chloe Martin;
3–Jonathan (1799-1881), removed to Green Oak, Mich.; *m* 1831, Sarah Clough (1808-84);
2–Ellsworth Solon (2 below).
8–George **Martin**;
7–George, *m* 1706, Anna Choate (John[8]; John[9]; John[10], qv);
6–George, *m* 1733, Grace Howard;
5–David, *m* Elizabeth Hendee (*b* 1733; Josiah[6], *m* 1729, Bathsheba, dau. Benoni Larned; Ens. Richard[7], *m* Elizabeth, dau. Lt. Exercise Conant; Richard[8] [1610-70], came in the "Hopewell," 1634, at Norwich and Killingsworth, Conn., *m* Hannah Elderkin);
4–Chloe, received pension Mar. 26, 1844; *m* James **Burnett** (4 above);
3–Jonathan, *m* Sarah Clough (3 above);
2–Ellsworth Solon (*b* Green Oak, Mich., 1837-*d* 1895), of Bancroft, Mich.; *m* 1863, Eliza M. Crane (1839-1916); issue: I–Carrie Amelia (*b* 1864; *m* Perry G. Holden); II–Edgar Albert (1 above); III–Sarah (1867-1915; *m* Charles E. Chalker); IV–Lyman Crane (*b* 1881; *m* E. Pearl Hensel).
1–*m* June 20, 1899, Nellie E. Folsom, *b* Hermon, N.Y., Oct. 11, 1861; dau. of Martin R. Folsom, of Hermon, *m* Cornelia–; issue: 1–Knox Folsom, *b* Lincoln, Neb., Aug. 19, 1903.
1–B.S., Mich. State Agrl. Coll. '87 D.Sc., 1917. Dean of Agrl. Coll., U.Neb., 1909-28; dir. Neb. Agrl. Expt. Station, 1901-27; acting chancellor U.Neb., from Jan., 1917; chancellor, Mar., 1928– (See Who's Who in America). Mem. Am. Ednl. Corps, A.E.F. Univ., Beaune, France. Residence: 3256 Holdrege St., Lincoln, Neb.

1–**BURR, Eben Erastus,** *b* Norfolk, Conn., Sept. 24, 1880.
9–Benjamin **Burr** (*d* 1681), original propr. Hartford, Conn., 1636; *m* Ann–;
8–Samuel (*d* 1682), of Hartford; *m* Mary Baysee (John[9], *m* Elizabeth–);
7–John (1670-1741), of Farmington, Conn.; *m* Sarah–;
6–Ebenezer (1712-94), of Norfolk, Conn.; *m* 1st, 1740, Hepsibah Brown (1712-72; Cornelius[7], *m* Abigail Barber);
5–Daniel (1747-1808), of Norfolk; *m* 1773, Betty Brown (*d* 1832; Titus[6], *m* Rachel Marshal; Cornelius, see above);
4–Ebenezer (1791-1855), of Norfolk; *m* 1817, Pamelia Benton (1794-1856; Jesse[5], *m* Susanne Rogers);
3–Erastus (1823-1908), of Norfolk; *m* 1847, Nancy Potter (Christopher[4], *m* Esther Smith);
2–Ralph Christopher (*b* 1854), of Norfolk; *m* 1879, Julia Warner Munson (1856-1929; John N.[3], *m* Mary Warner); issue: I–Eben Erastus (1 above); II–Charles Munson (*b* 1881; *m* 1919, Mabel L. Case); III–Ralph Sterling (*b* 1886).
1–*m* Apr. 14, 1909, Sarah Amanda Wilcox (qv).
1–Farmer and ice dealer. Retired. Congrlist. Granger. Address: Norfolk, Conn.

1–**BURR, Sarah Amanda Wilcox (Mrs. Eben E.),** *b* Sheffield, Mass., Oct. 18, 1889.
10–John **Wilcox** (qv);
9–John (*d* 1676), of Hartford and Middletown, Conn.; *m* 2d, 1650, Catharine Stoughton (Thomas[10], qv);
8–Samuel (1658-1714), of Middletown, Conn.; *m* 1683, Abigail Whitmore (1659-87; Francis[9], *m* Isabel Parke);
7–Samuel (1684-1725), of Middletown; *m* 1707, Esther Bushnell (1683-1762; William[8], *m* Rebecca–);
6–Elijah (1721-1809), of Middletown and Bristol, Conn.; *m* 2d, 1759, Mary Bushnell (William[7], *m* Mary Bates);
5–Solomon (*b* 1768), *m* 1790, Lydia Pardee (David[6], *m* Phebe Woodruff);
4–William Henry (1802-47), *m* 1825, Sarah Comstock;

3–William Oliver (1830-69), of Sheffield, Mass.; *m* 1851, Amanda Malvini Allen (Garner[4], *m* Sally Baker);
2–Willie Garner (1859-1926), of Sheffield, and Norfolk, Conn.; *m* 1886, Caroline Elizabeth Parrott (1862-1920; Henry[3], *m* Sarah C. Hinman); *m* 2d, 1921, Nellie Elizabeth Munson (*b* 1863); issue (1st marriage): I–Sarah Amanda (1 above); II–Levia Anna (*b* 1892; *m* 1920, Davis Ingraham Church); III–Henry Oliver (*b* 1899; *m* 1925, Ada May Kinney).
1–*m* Apr. 14, 1909, Eben Erastus Burr (qv).
1–Mem. Conn. Hist. Soc., Winchester Soc., I.A.G. O.E.S. Congrlist. Granger. Republican. Residence: Norfolk Conn.

1–**BURT, Benjamin Wise,** *b* Newhill, N.C., Feb. 13, 1862.
5–John **Burt** (*d* 1780);
4–John (1752-1826), served Am. Rev.; *m* Priscilla Senter (*b* 1760);
3–Alfred C. (1792-1859), *m* Elizabeth Simmons (1807-87);
2–John Henderson (1823-1900), *m* Nancy Ellen Rollins (1825-1921; Burwell[3], *m* Elizabeth Ragland, sister of Nancy, same as 3 in wife's record); issue: I–Joseph Judson (1856-1922: *m* Annie Rollins); II–Thomas Bascomb (1858-1922; *m* Etta Rollins; *m* 2d, Lulu Edwards); III–Augustus C. (1860-1905; *m* Susan Koonce); IV–Benjamin W. (1 above); V–Frederick J. (*b* 1869; *m* Dorothy Stone).
1–*m* Nov. 21, 1889, Ida McPheeters Rollins (Feb. 22, 1866-May, 1894); issue: 1–Zula Tracey, *b* New Hill, N.C., Mar. 11, 1891; ed. Littleton Female Coll., and Peace Inst., Raleigh, N.C.; *m* Sept. 24, 1914, John Harry Bright (issue: Doris, *b* Dec. 23, 1915; Rachel, *b* Dec. 14, 1918; Ruth, *b* Jan. 26, 1921; John Harry, *b* Feb. 24, 1926).
1–*m* 2d, Dec. 17, 1896, Lenna Williams Judd (qv for issue).
1–Coll. Physicians and Surgeons, Baltimore, Md., 1884,85,86, M.D. Mem. N.C. State and Wake Co. (N.C.) med. socs. Residence: Holly Springs, N.C.

1–**BURT, Lenna Williams Judd (Mrs. Benjamin W.),** *b* Chatham Co., N.C., Apr. 24, 1869.
5–John **Judd** (*d* 1805);
4–William (*d* 1839), *m* Elizabeth Solomon (William[5] [*d* 1814], served Am. Rev., *m* Dianah–; William[6], of Edgecombe Co., N.C.);
3–John W., *m* Melinda Dennis (Anderson[4] [*d* 1829], *m* Anna, dau. of William Pegram; Joseph[5] [*d* 1795], *m* Mary Shepherd);
2–John Thomas (2 below).
6–John **Ragland,** from Wales to Eng., thence to Va., bet. 1700-20; settled in Henrico Co., and took up lands in that and other cos.; his home "Ripping Hall," on the Chickahominy was burned, 1825; *m* Ann Beaufort, his kinswoman;
5–William (*d* 1789), settled on Cape Fear River in Chatham Co.; also of Northampton Co., N.C.; served Am. Rev.; *m* Sarah Avent;
4–Frederic (1766-1812), *m* 1795, Mary Barham (1775-1851);
3–Nancy (1803-84), *m* William H. **Cross** (Parish[4], *m* Elizabeth, dau. of Burwell Williams, served Am. Rev.);
2–Louise Frances (Sept. 22, 1841-Mar. 22, 1915), as widow of Benjamin Rush Avent, *m* 2d, 1866, John Thomas **Judd** (1843-1914), mem. N.C. Legislature, 1909-10; issue: I–Sarah Laurena (Mrs. Nathaniel G. Yarborough, see Vol. III, p. 281); II–Lenna W. (1 above); III–James Mahlon (see Vol. III, p. 279); IV–John Herbert (*b* 1873; *m* Essie Florence Rollins; *m* 2d, Catherine Lamb); V–William Arthur (1875-1929; *m* Mary Lee Burt); VI–Zebulon (see Vol. III, p. 279); VII–Eugene Clarence (*b* 1882; *m* Mary Eleanor Pritchard).
1–*m* Nov. 20, 1889, William Oscar Rollins, *b* Chatham Co., N.C. (Mar. 22, 1868-Feb. 24, 1894); son of Gaston, g.son of James Rollins; issue: I–Hal Judd, *b* Cokesbury, N.C., Mar. 11, 1892; Trinity Coll., '11, D.V.M., Kansas City Coll., 1913-16; 1st lt., U.S.A., Veterinary Corps, 1917-19; *m* Jan. 14, 1925, Jamie Hamer, dau. of Edmund C. Cole (issue: Betty Ann, *b* Rockingham, N.C., Apr. 28, 1926).
1–*m* 2d, Dec. 17, 1896, Dr. Benjamin Wise Burt (qv); issue: 1–Milton Stanley, *b* Newhill, N.C., Sept. 30, 1899; attended A. and E. State Coll. (N.C.), 1922-24, Ph.G., U. of N.C., 1925-28 (Kappa Psi, pharmaceutical fraternity); won Brabham prize for high scholarship; 2–Mary Lois, *b* Newhill, July 20, 1904; B.S.M., N.C. Coll. for Women, '25; *m* Aug. 1, 1929, Graham Jussely Burkheimer.
1–Residence: Holly Springs, N.C.

BURROUGHS

Arms: Argent, the stump of a laurel tree eradicated proper.
Crest: A lion passant.

1–**BURROUGHS, Mary Stewart,** *b* Germantown, Phila., Pa., Nov. 27, 1860.
9–Samuel **Hinckley** (qv);
8–Gov. Thomas (bap. 1619/20-1705), Barnstable, Mass.; commr. for United Colonies, 1678-92; dep. gov., 1680; gov. 1681-92; *m* 1641, Mary Richards (Thomas[9], of Weymouth, Mass.); *m* 2d, 1660, Mary (Smith) Glover, widow (1630-1703);
7–Abigail (1669-1725), *m* 1697/98, Joseph **Lord** (1672-1748), of Chatham, Mass.;
6–Alice (1714-92), *m* 1737, Benjamin **Kettell** (1711/12-1745/46);
5–Alice (1743-99), *m* 1764, Joseph **Whittemore** (1742-90), of Charlestown, Mass.;
4–Sarah (1767-98), *m* 1786, William **Burroughs** (1744-96), of Boston, Mass.;
3–John (1792-1841), *m* 1821, Margaret Proctor (1790-1859);
2–John (2 below).
9–Robert **Dingee,** was at Hempstead, L.I., 1683, *m* Rebecca–;
8–Christopher (*d* 1727/28), *m* Mary–;
7–Charles, *m* Hannah–;
6–Charles, *m* Mary Miers;
5–Daniel (*d* 1786), mem. State Senate, Sussex Co., Del., 1776; *m* Macada Hazzard;
4–Daniel (1776-1807), *m* Mary Fenner;
3–John Henry (1807-79), *m* Mary Stewart (1812-84);
2–Elizabeth Fenner (1835-1922), *m* 1858, John **Burroughs** (1827-71); issue: I–John Henry (1859-1919); II–Mary Stewart (1 above); III–Laura Margaret (1866-86).
1–Mem. C.D.A., D.F.P.A., O.C.G., D.A.R., Pa. Soc. of N.E. Women, Geog. Soc. (Phila.). Summer place: "Stockden," Buckingham, Pa. Residence: Hotel Clinton, Philadelphia, Pa.

1–**BURTON, Marion Helen Andrew (Mrs. Frank V.),** *b* Boston, Mass., Nov. 22, 1883.
10–William **Judson** (qv);
9–Lt. Joseph (1619-90), leading man in Conn.; *m* 1644, Sara Porter (*d* 1696; John[10], of Windsor, Conn.);
8–John (1647-1709), one of orig. signers of the "Fundamental Articles for Settlement of Woodbury," 1672; *m* 1673/74, Elizabeth Chapman; *m* 2d, Hannah–; *m* 3d, Mrs. Mary Orton;
7–Joseph (1679-1758);
6–Joshua (1732-76), served Am. Rev.; resided at Woodbury, Conn.; *m* 2d, Deborah Levenworth;
5–Joshua (*b* 1772), from Woodbury, Conn., to Arlington, Vt., ca. 1790 or 1800; *m* Lucretia Baker;
4–Sheldon (1797-1860), *m* 1826, Caroline Merrifield (1805-79; her mother, Sofia–, was a cousin of Ethan Allen);
3–Joshua Sheldon (1829-74), of Austin, Minn.; *m* 1855, Mary Ann Rankin Higgs (*b* 1837); of St. George's, **Bermuda;**

2–Harriet Louise (1857-87), *m* 1881, Thomas Winter **Andrew** (*b* 1857), from Shrewsbury, Eng., to Boston, Mass.; ret. banker, of Phila., Pa.; issue: I–Henry (*b* and *d* 1882); II–Marion Helen (1 above); III–Porter (1885-87).
1–*m* Oct. 9, 1909, Frank Vail Burton, *b* Albany, N.Y., June 3, 1874; son of Samuel Vail Burton, of Albany, N.Y.; issue: 1–Frances, *b* Bridgeport, Conn., Sept. 19, 1910; 2–Louise, *b* Bridgeport, Jan. 10, 1912; 3–Marion, *b* Bridgeport, Jan. 12, 1916; 4–Winter Andrew, *b* Bridgeport, Apr. 23, 1917; 5–Jane Vail, *b* Phila., Pa., Mar. 4, 1921.
1–Grad. Boston Normal Sch. of Gymnastics (now dept. phys. ed. and hygiene, Wellesley Coll.), 1904. Residence: Auburndale, Mass.

HON. CHARLES SIDNEY CHACE (b Swansea, Mass., Jan. 10, 1840), ed. Dighton Academy; moderator of annual town meetings, Dighton, Mass., 40 years; chairman Board of Selectmen 33 years; overseer of the poor 33 years; chairman Board of Health 33 years; has been member of the Mass. House of Representatives and Senate.

1–**BUTLER, Della Chace (Mrs. Edward),** *b* Dighton, Mass., Nov. 4, 1861.
9–William **Chace** (qv);
8–William, Jr. (1622-85);
7–Joseph (1652-1724), *m* 1694, Sarah Sherman;
6–Moses, *m* 1742, Alice Sherman (Samuel[7], *m* Martha Knowles);
5–Samuel, *m* 1772, Mary Earl;
4–Earl (1784-1877), *m* 1808, Lydia Sherman (1780-1873);
3–Daniel Sherman (1814-1900), *m* 1839, Belinda Pierce (1814-90);
2–Hon. Charles Sidney (2 below).
8–Richard (Haile) **Hale** (1640-1720), settled first at Newport, R.I., moved to Swansea, Mass., 1677; *m* Mary–;
7–John (1677-1718), *m* Hannah Tillinghast;
6–John (1703-31), *m* Elizabeth Mason;
5–Dea. John (1726-1810), *m* Bethiah Bosworth;
4–Daniel (1758-1830), began to write name Hale; served Am. Rev.; mem. Mass. Legislature 14 terms; mem. Constl. Conv.; *m* 1780, Cynthia Buffington;
3–Jonathan B. (1800-58), *m* 1830, Rosanna West;
2–Mary Mason (2 below).
10–Edward **Bosworth** (qv);
9–Jonathan (*b* ca. 1611), lived at Cambridge, Hingham, Rehoboth, and Swansea, Mass.; *m* Susanna–;
8–Jonathan (*d* 1687), Swansea and Rehoboth; *m* 1661, Hannah Howland (John[9], Mayflower Pilgrim, qv, *m* Elizabeth, dau. of John Tilley, Mayflower Pilgrim, qv);
7–Jonathan (*b* 1680), *m* 1703, Sarah Rounds;
6–Ichabod (1706-75), *m* 1727, Mary Bowen (*b* 1706);
5–Bethiah (1727-1813), *m* 1747, Dea. John **Haile** (5 above).
2–Mary Mason Hale (1843-June 23, 1914), *m* 1861, Hon. Charles Sidney **Chace** (*b* 1840), see portrait and biography; issue: I–Della (1 above); II–Charles Herbert (*b* 1870).
1–*m* Feb. 4, 1884, Edward Butler, *b* Wareham, Mass., Sept. 16, 1858; son of Jerome Butler, of Wareham.
1–Mem. S.M.D., D.F.P.A., D.A.R., U.S.D. 1812, George Washington Memorial Assn. Residence: Elm St., Dighton, Mass.

1–**BURTON, Lucina Carpenter Clement (Mrs. Frederick H.),** *b* Evansville, Ind., Sept. 10, 1861.
9–Robert (Clemens, Clements, Clemence) **Clement** (qv);
8–Robert (1624-1712), *m* 1652, Elizabeth Fawne (*d* 1715);
7–John (1653-92), of Haverhill, Mass.; *m* Elizabeth Ayer (1652-99);
6–Nathaniel (1689-1748), of Haverhill; *m* Sarah Merrill (1694-1748);
5–Samuel (1726-1801), of Haverhill; *m* Elizabeth Carleton (1728-99);
4–Richard (1760-1815), of Salem, N.H.; served Am. Rev.; *m* Mehetable Runnels (1764-1803; Lt. Thomas[5], *m* Phebe–);
3–Caleb (1797-1860), of Landaff, N.H.; *m* Ruth Adams Moore (1805-72; Dr. Isaac[4], *m* Mary dau. of Maj. Gen. Timothy Bedel, served Am. Rev.);
2–Converse (2 below).
10–William **Carpenter** (qv);
9–William (1631-1703), of Rehoboth, Mass.; *m* 1651, Priscilla Bennett (*d* 1663);
8–John (*b* 1652), of Rehoboth; *m* Rebecca Readaway;
7–Eliphalet (*b* 1679), of Rehoboth; *m* Rebecca–;
6–Eliphalet (*b* 1709), of Woodstock, Conn.; *m* 1730, Mary Bacon;
5–Ephraim (*b* 1735), of Woodstock; served Am. Rev.; *m* 1761, Tabitha Chaffee (1739-1824);
4–Willard (1767-1854), of Woodstock; *m* 1791, Polly Bacon (1769-1860);
3–Willard (1803-83), of Evansville, Ind.; *m* 1836, Lucina Burcalow (1816-84);
2–Louise (1843-1908), *m* 1860, Converse **Clement** (1839-1907), mcht.; issue: I–Lucina C. (1 above); II–Ruth Carpenter (*b* 1867; *m* Jacob Vandeer Litt; issue: John Carpenter, *b* Dec. 5, 1899, *m* June 17, 1924, Kathryn Jones, *b* Oct. 3, 1904 [issue: John Vandeer, *b* Nov. 18, 1928]; Willard David, *b* Dec. 15, 1900).
1–*m* Apr. 23, 1882, Frederick Herbert Burton, *b* London, Eng., Sept. 1, 1856; son of James Henry Burton, *m* Elizabeth Keller; issue: 1–Ralph White, *b* Evansville, Ind., July 18, 1883; *m* June 29, 1912, Marion Deane, dau. of Frank Bayliss Leonard, of Raynham, Mass., *m* Mary Washburn Deane; 2–Guy Herbert, *b* Evansville, Oct. 15, 1888; *m* Feb. 21, 1916, Katherine Mitchell, dau. of John Clement, *m* Kate Mitchell Bachop.
Residence: 177 Lenox Rd., Brooklyn, N.Y.

1–**BUSH, Clara Phebe,** *b* Hudson, Mich., June 23, 1865.
9–Henry **Wolcott** (qv);
8–Simon (1625-87), lived east side of river, Windsor, Conn.; mem. 1st Conn cav., 1658; served King Philip's War; capt. of foot, Simsbury; dep., 1673; *m* 2d, 1661, Martha Pitkin (1639-1719; sister of William Pitkin, atty. gen. and treas. of Conn.; Roger[9]); their son, Gen. Roger, was gov. of Conn., and was father of Oliver, also gov. of Conn. and a "signer";
7–Lt. Henry (1670-1745), of Windsor; lt. Windsor Train Band; an orig. propr. Tolland and Wellington, Conn.; *m* 1696, Jane Allyn (1670-1702; Capt. Thomas[8], *m* Abigail, dau. of Rev. John Warham, *m* Mrs. Jane Newberry; Hon. Matthew[9], of Windsor, *m* Margaret Wyatt, of royal descent);
6–Lt. Thomas (*b* 1702), of Windsor, and Taghanic, N.Y.; early settler of Tolland; *m* 2d 1738, Fanny Dubelorey;
5–Francis, of Taghanic; *m* Lydia Race;
4–Gideon (1776-1857), of Greene Co., N.Y.; *m* 1803, Caroline Decker (1784-1864; Lawrence[5], of Hillsdale, Columbia Co., N.Y., *m* Caroline Hallenbeck);

3–Lydia (1810-88), of Polo, Ill.; *m* 1833, Nicholas **Bush** (1803-90; John[4] [1761-1839], soldier Am. Rev., *m* Eve Smith);
2–Charles Smith (2 below).
8–Richard **Booth** (qv);
7–Joseph (1656-1703), of Stratford, Conn.; *m* 2d, Hannah Wilcoxin (1664-1701; John[8], of Stratford);
6–James (1688-1776), of Stratford; *m* 1733, Martha (Clark) Peck (1695-1747);
5–John (1736-1822), of Stratford; *m* 1763, Lucy Curtis (1741-1817; Henry[6], of Stratford, *m* Anne Thompson);
4–John (1764-1825), of Stratford; *m* 2d, 1786, Jerusha Lewis (1765-96; Eli[5], soldier Am. Rev., *m* Naomi, dau. of James Walker, *m* Jerusha Nichols);
3–Levi (1790-1871), removed to Grand Gorge, Delaware Co., N.Y., 1809; *m* 1809, Phebe Harley (1793-1860; Thomas[4] [1746-1814], of Shelter Island, N.Y., fled to Conn., during Am. Rev. when his buildings were burned, *m* Mary Paine, of Shelter Island);
2–Hephzibah Jane (1835-1906), *m* 1855, Charles Smith **Bush** (1834-1918), from Delaware Co., N.Y., to Polo, Ill., 1856; to Hillsdale Co., Mich., 1859-67; with Lake Shore and Mich. Southern R.R., 1867-74; returned to Polo; town clk., Eagle Point Tp., Ogle Co., 1883-1904; farmer; Mason (32°).
1–*m* Samuel Joseph Sprecher, *b* Polo, Ill., Jan. 16, 1868 (divorced, 1900); son of George Thomas Sprecher, of Hagerstown, Md., and Polo; issue: 1–Hephzibah Kathryn, *b* Creighton, Neb., Apr. 16, 1891; *m* Mar. 7, 1914, Frank C., son of Fred Goetker, of Hamilton, O. (issue: Frances K., *b* 1914; Frank C., Jr., *b* 1917); 2–Charles Harley, *b* Creighton, Sept. 17, 1892; *m* Dec. 20, 1916, Dora May, dau. of William Rohde of Milledgeville, Ill. (issue: William Joseph, *b* 1918; Donald Charles, *b* 1920; George Harry, *b* 1923; Ruth L., b 1927).
1–Chiropodist, since 1926; school teacher, 1904-16; chiropodist, Sterling, Ill., 1916-17; U.S. Govt. employ, 1917-26. Mem. Soc. of Descendants of Henry Wolcott, O.E.S. Methodist. Rep. Summer place: Milledgeville, Carroll Co., Ill. Residence: 546 Belden Av., Chicago, Ill.

1–**BUTZ, Charles Allabar,** *b* Alburtis, Pa., Mar. 14, 1874.
6–John **Butz** (*d* 1750), from Bavaria to Phila., Pa., 1738;
5–Peter (1718-80), *m* 1743, Barbara Carl (1718-95);
4–John (1747-1827), pvt., 2d Bn., Northampton Co., Pa., Militia in Am. Rev.; *m* Maria Elizabeth Miller (1747-1827);
3–Peter (1773-1847), *m* Elizabeth Schmoyer (1785-1866 Daniel[4], Am. Rev.);
2–William (1817-1883), carpenter, contractor, farmer; *m* 1869, Hannah Floranda Fegely (1836-1920); issue: I–William P. (*b* 1869; *m* Minnie Geiger); II–Charles A. (1 above).
1–*m* Apr. 28, 1904, Jennie Bertha Fritch, b Mertztown, Pa., Jan. 8, 1883; dau. of Levi Long Fritch, of Mertztown, *m* Sarah A. Miller; issue: 1–Geraldine Euroma, *b* Fredricksburg, Pa., Jan. 29, 1906; *m* Apr. 18, 1929, Earl A. Watson; 2–Althea Fritch, *b* Bethlehem, Pa., June 20, 1913; 3–Charles Albert, *b* Bethlehem, Oct. 13, 1920.
1–A.B., Ursinus, '99, A.M., 1905; Ph.D., Central U., 1919; grad. Ursinus Sch. of Theology, 1902. Clergyman, Reformed Church in U.S. Historical research work and writer, artist and poet; pres. Butz Family Assn., 1912–; mem. S.A.R. Residence: 1337 Montrose Av., Bethlehem, Pa.

1–**BYERS, Hester Ann Long (Mrs. George W.),** *b* Terre Haute, Ind., Dec. 23, 1859.
9–John **Sibley** (qv);
8–Joseph (1655-1711), of Salem, Mass.; *m* 1683, Susanna Follett (*b* 1662; Robert[9], pioneer of Mass., *m* Persis Black);
7–Joseph (1684-1754), of Lynn, Mass.; *m* 1707, Elizabeth Boutell (*b* 1682; John[8], Reading, Mass., soldier King Philip's War);
6–John (1711-78), of Sutton, Mass.; soldier Am. Rev.; *m* 1732, Hannah Marsh;
5–Elisha (*b* 1746), of Sutton; soldier Am. Rev.; *m* 1763, Lydia Carriell (*b* 1744; Daniel[6]);
4–Elisha (1764-1812), of Sutton; soldier Am. Rev.; War 1812; *m* Coziah Tiffany;

Arms: Per pale azure and gules, over all a griffin between three crescents argent.
Crest: Out of a ducal coronet a swan's head between spread wings.

3–Sylvester (1795-1879), of Terre Haute, Ind.; served in War 1812 (see portrait); *m* 1826, Catherine Rockwell (1804-55; Jonathan[4], of Elmira, N.Y.);

SYLVESTER SIBLEY (b Bennington, Vt., Oct. 1795-d Terre Haute, Ind., Oct. 1879) a pioneer of Terre Haute, 1818; served in the War of 1812.

2–Jane Emily (2 below).
10–Rev. Samuel **Skelton** (1584-1634), from Eng., 1629, settled at Salem, 1629; 1st minister of Salem; *m* 1613, Susanna Travis (*d* 1631);
9–Susannah (*b* 1613), of Salem, Mass.; *m* 1635, John **Marsh** (*d* 1674);
8–Zachary (1637-93), of Salem; *m* 1664, Mary Silsby (*d* 1695; Henry[9], of Lynn);
7–Elder Benjamin (1687-1775), of Salem and Sutton, Mass.; *m* 1709, Hannah King (*b* 1684; John[8], of Salem, soldier King Philip's War);
6–Hannah (1713-86), of Sutton; *m* Capt. John **Sibley** (6 above).
2–Jane Emily Sibley (1841-1925), *m* 1857, Thomas **Long** (1833-81), locomotive engr., 1850-81; 1st lt., Co. D, 11th Ind. Vol. Cav., 1861; issue: I–Hester Ann (1 above); II–George M. (1865-1919; *m* Hattie Hoke); III–Thomas Wade (*b* 1870; *m* 1897, Mary Hossey); IV–Sylvester Sibley (*b* 1872; *m* Lulu Price); V–Charles A. (1876-1919).

1–*m* Sept. 7, 1887, George William Byers, *b* Terre Haute, Ind., Dec. 2, 1859; son of George Byers (1840-1909), of Green Co., Ind.; Civil War Vet.; *m* Margaret Ferguson; issue: 1–Helen, *b* Mattoon, Ill., June 19, 1893; *m* July 21, 1921, Rodney B. Wyatt (issue: William Byers).
1–Mem. D.A.C., D.F.P.A., D.A.R., U.S.D. 1812, Ladies of the Grand Army. Summer place: "Elm Lawn Farm," Route 121, Tuscola, Ill. Winter place: 518 N. Central Av., Glendale, Calif. Legal residence: Inman Hotel, Champaign, Ill.

1–**BYROM, Seymour Butts,** *b* Byromville, Ga., June 26, 1880.
8–Henry **Byrom** (*d* ca. 1717), from Eng., 1697, settled nr. Tappahannock, now Essex Co., Va.; *m* Frances Mills;
7–James (*d* 1748), of Tappahannock, Va.; *m* Elizabeth–;
6–Henry (ca. 1705-ca. 1778), of King and Queen Co., Va.; *m* ca. 1724, Miss Scott;
5–William (ca. 1725-1815), of Amelia Co., Va., and Wilkes, Warren and Jasper cos., Ga.; *m* Mary Ann Fretwell (*d* ante 1815);
4–John, of Warren and Jasper cos., Ga.; *m* 1815, Cynthia Hardwick Fitzpatrick (1798-1882);
3–William Hardwick (1817-73), of Jasper Co., and Byromville, Dooly Co., Ga.; *m* 1848, Susan Maria Gunn (1829-1917);
2–John Seymour (2 below).
4–Elijah **Butts,** of Conn.; *m* Laura Fisk (1784-1862);
3–Elijah (1808-71), of Conn., and Ga.; *m* ca. 1830, Ann J. Tomlinson;
2–Eoline (1852-80), *m* Goodrich D. White; *m* 2d, John Seymour **Byrom** (1849-1911), of Byromville, Ga.; banker, merchant, and planter; issue (1st marriage): I–Annie (1873-75); issue (2d marriage): I–William Hardwick (*m* Emma Lou [Dudney] Brown); II–Seymour Butts (1 above).
1–*m* Sept. 29, 1900, Katharine Rodgers Clayton, *b* Macon, Ga., Nov. 10, 1879; dau. Edgar Hunter Clayton, of Memphis, Tenn.; issue: 1–John Seymour, *b* Byromville, Ga., July 1, 1901; *m* Dec. 12, 1922, Lena Elizabeth Cline, of Macon, Ga.; 2–Katharine Eoline, *b* Byromville, Nov. 22, 1902; ed. Mary Baldwin Sem., Staunton, Va., spl. course, Language and Music, 1919-20; *m* July 16, 1928, Ewald George Vockroth, of New York, N.Y. (issue: George Byrom).
1–Mem. firm J. S. Byrom & Sons, merchants, bankers, and planters, Byromville, Ga., 1901-11; pres. Byrom Corpn. and The Byrom Nat. Bank, Byromville, 1912-17; owner S. B. Byrom & Co., bankers and planters, 1918-27; owner S. B. Byrom & Co., and J. S. & S. B. Byrom, bankers, Byromville, Ga., since 1927. Trustee Byromville public schools, 1906-16. Mem. I.A.G. Democrat. Club: Capital City (Atlanta). Residence: Byromville, Ga.

1–**CADY, Helen Anna Prudden (Mrs. G. V. Lloyd),** *b* Chelsea, Mich., Feb. 9, 1870.
9–Rev. Peter **Prudden** (qv);
8–Samuel (1643-85), of Milford, Conn.; *m* Grace Judson (*d* 1686; Lt. Joseph[9], of Stratford, *m* Sarah, dau. of John Porter, of Wethersfield);
7–John (1680-1762), of Milford; *m* 1707, Mary Clark (*d* 1732);
6–John (1708-86), *m* Hannah Newton (g.dau. of Roger Newton, successor of Rev. Peter Prudden, as minister of Milford);
5–Col. Fletcher (1737-98), of Milford; moved to Bethlehem late in life; capt. of co. of vols. guarding coast of L.I. Sound during Am. Rev.; in service 7 yrs., as ens., capt., lt., maj. and col.; *m* 1760, Sarah Treat;
4–Fletcher Newton (1772-1843), of Milford and Enfield, Conn.; *m* 1804, Anne Parsons (1785-1825);
3–Nehemiah Fletcher (1818-76), of Enfield, Conn., and Ann Arbor, Mich.; *m* 1843, Juliet Davis (1822-48);
2–Arnold Fletcher (2 below).
9–Richard **Treat** (qv);
8–Robert (1624-1710), *m* Jane Tapp (*d* 1703);
7–Gov. Josiah (1662-1721), of Milford, Conn.; *m* 2d, Mrs. Elizabeth Merwin (*d* 1715);
6–Edmund (1710-1801), of Milford; *m* Alice Buckingham (1715-85);
5–Sarah (1745-1813), *m* Fletcher **Prudden** (5 above).
2–Arnold Fletcher **Prudden** (1844-1928), farmer and banker, Chelsea, Mich.; *m* 1866, Wilhelmina Mensing (1846-1925); issue: I–Helen (1 above); II–Adah Juliet (*b* 1872; *m* Richard Vernon Williams; *m* 2d, Frederick La Vigne).
1–*m* Dec. 26, 1924, Guy Victor Lloyd Cady, *b* Napoleon, Mich., Mar. 12, 1869; son of Porter Allen Cady, of Jackson Co., Napoleon, Mich.
1–Mich. State Normal Coll. (life certificate to teach). Mem. C.D.A., D.F.P.A., D.C.G., D.A.R. (chapter regent 1917-19; mem. state bd.). Clubs: Mosaic, Emerson, Garden of America. Conglist. Republican. Residence: 311 S. Wisner St., Jackson, Mich.

1–**CALEFF, George Oliver Francis,** *b* Rochester, N.Y., Dec. 28, 1882.
9–Robert (Calef, Califf) **Caleff** (ca. 1648-1719), from Eng., settled at Boston ante 1688, later at Roxbury; *m* ante 1671, Mary– (*d* 1720);
8–John (ca. 1675-1748), *m* 1702, Deborah King (bap. 1679-post 1748; William[9]);
7–William (1706-1784-85), *m* 2d, 1736, Lois Sawyer (1718-99);
6–William (1737-1812), *m* 1759, Anna Rowell (1736-1813);
5–William (1761-1843), *m* 1785, Hannah Eastman (1764-1823);
4–William (*b* 1786), *m* 1816, Polly Kimball;
3–Amos George (1823-63), *m* 1861, Olive (Kimball) Hall (1835-1909);
2–George Dana (1862-1926), wrote name Calef; *m* 1882, Claudia Estelle Francis (*b* 1866).
1–*m* Sept. 21, 1918, Christine (Dykes) Snelgrove, *b* Ayr, Scotland, Apr. 15, 1887; dau. of James Dykes, *m* Agnes Rogers, both of Ayr, Scotland.
1–Residence: 256 Gregory St., Rochester, N.Y.

1–**CALLENDER, Estelle Victoria Hudgins (Mrs. William Edward),** *b* Norfolk, Va., Apr. 27, 1872.
10–Gov. Samuel **Matthews** (*d* 1660), from Eng., 1620, settled in Warwick Co., Va., opposite Jamestown; owned a plantation of 2,944 acres, on which he built his home "Denbigh"; capt.-gen. and gov. of Va., 1622-60; *m* ante 1620, Francis Hinton, of Eng. (Sir Thomas[11]);
9–Francis (*d* 1675), of York Co., Va.;
8–Baldwin (1670-1737), justice of peace, York Co.;
7–Sarah, *m* Samuel **Timson**;
6–Mary, *m* Thomas **Buckner**;
5–William, of Gloucester Co.; *m* 1773, Elizabeth Smith;
4–Susan, *m* 1808, Robert **Hudgins** (1772-1821);
3–Robert King (1812-1903), of Mathews Co., Va.; *m* 1834, Sarah James White;
2–William Edward (2 below).
8–John **Buckner** (qv);
7–Thomas, of Gloucester Co.; burgess, Va., 1718; *m* 1698, Sarah Morgan (Capt. Francis[8], burgess, 1653);
6–Thomas (1702-56), *m* Mary Timson (6 above).
8–Col. Thomas **Pettus** (*d* 1698; son of Sir John Pettus, of Norwich, Eng.), of James City Co., Va.; mem. Gov.'s Council under Sir William Berkley, 16 yrs.; *m* Elizabeth Mouring;
7–Ann, *m* Capt. Philip **Hunley**;
6–Caleb;
5–Mary (1752-1843), *m* 1770, Capt. William **Davenport** (1746-87), served Am. Rev.; after the war he went to negotiate a treaty for the govt. with the Creek Indians of Ga. and Tenn. and was killed by them;
4–Elizabeth (*b* 1771), of Norfolk; *m* 1791, John **White** (1756-1834), of Mathews Co.; soldier Am. Rev.;
3–Sarah James (1816-91), *m* Robert K. **Hudgins** (3 above).
10–Gregory **Stone** (qv);
9–Elder John (1618-83), of Cambridge Ch., Cambridge, Mass.; *m* 1639, Anne Howe (Elder Edward[10]);
8–Nathaniel (1660-1732), of Framingham, Mass.; *m* 1684, Sarah Waite (*b* 1664; Capt. John[9], of Malden);
7–Capt. Hezekiah (1710-71); selectman of Oxford and Framingham; *m* 1735, Ruth Howe (1714-1809), of Sudbury, Mass.;
6–Capt. Jesse (1737-1803), of Ward, Mass.; capt. Am. Rev.; *m* 1759, Elizabeth Livermore (1735-1814);
5–Dea. Isaac (1769-1857), of Auburn, Mass.;

mem. Mass. Legislature, 1837; *m* 1789, Lucretia Drury (1773-1810);
4–Jeremy (1798-1837), of Auburn; *m* 1821, Ann Green Mitchell (1800-61), of Savannah, Ga.;
3–Capt. Edward Erastus (1826-92), U.S.N., served in Mexican and Civil wars with distinction; *m* 1848, Fannie Leonide de Montalant (1827-77);
2–Louise Victoria (1852-1915), of Norfolk; *m* 1870, Capt. William Edward **Hudgins** (1837-1920), harbor master and city collector, Norfolk, Va.; issue: I–Estelle V. (1 above); II–Louise de Musset (*b* 1874; *m* William J. Baxter); III–Lucile de Montalant (*b* 1876; *m* Dr. Stark Armistead Sutton); IV–William Edward, Jr. (*b* 1878); V–Charles Robert (*b* 1881); VI–Leonide de Montalant (*b* 1883; *m* Edward Huger Lucas); VII–Caroline Elizabeth (*b* 1886; *m* George T. Willis); VIII–Albert Mayo (*b* 1888); IX–Herbert Vermillion (*b* 1889); X–Louis Eugean Le Masurier (*b* 1893).
1–*m* Aug. 11, 1897, Rev. William Edward Callender, *b* Liverpool, Eng., Dec. 10, 1866; son of Robert Callender, *m* Marion Kerr, of Paisley, Scotland; issue: 1–Mabel O. (Apr. 2-June, 1899); 2–Virginia Ormustoun, *b* Charlotte, N.C., Mar. 4, 1901; ed. Gunston Hall (Washington, D.C.); *m* June 22, 1921, James Brooks Johnston, son of J.J. Johnston, of Norfolk (issue: J. B., Jr., *born* Mar. 31, 1922; Virginia Callender, *b* Dec. 29, 1923; Edward Callender, *b* June 28, 1925); 3–Louise de Montalant, *b* Mt. Pleasant, S.C., Apr. 16, 1904; ed. Chatham Hall, Va.; *m* July 29, 1927, Dr. James Brooks West, son of Harry West, of Hickrey, Norfolk Co., Va., *m* Sally Brooks (issue: James Brooks, Jr., *b* Aug. 4, 1928); 4–William Edward, Jr. (*b* and *d* 1907).
1–Ed. Notre Dame Convent, Baltimore. Mem. D.F.P.A. (pres. Va. Soc.), C.D.A. (1st rec. sec., Norfolk Chapter), D.C.G., D.A.R. (1st regent Falls Ch. chapter; genealogist Great Bridge chapter), Nat. Geneal. Soc., A.P.V.A. (v. chmn.), U.D.C., King's Daughters, Woman's Club, Norfolk Soc. of Arts. Residence: 15 Pelham Pl., Norfolk, Va.

1–**CAMPAU, Francis Dénis,** *b* Grand Rapids, Mich., Sept. 8, 1880.
9–Leonard (Campeau) **Campau,** from France to Montreal, Can., 1630; *m* Francoise Maugé;
8–Etiénne (*b* 1638), *m* 1662, Catherine Paulo;
7–Jacques (1667 or 77-1751), from Montreal, Can., to Detroit, Mich., 1708, as pvt. sec. to Antoine de la Mothe Cadillac, founder of Detroit; *m* 1699, Cécile Catin;
6–Jean Louis (1702-74), *m* 1725, Marie Louise Robert;
5–Jacques (1735-89), *m* 1st, 1760, Catherine Ménard;
4–Louis (1767-1834), *m* 1789, Thérèse Morand;
3–Antoine (1797-1874), began to write name Campau; *m* Sarah Cottrell (1801-79);
2–Andrew Sylvestre (1839-1920), fur trader, real estate dealer; *m* 1877, Mary Elizabeth Blackwell (1859-1916; Lewis M.[3], *m* Lovice Smith); issue: I–Antoine Blackwell (*b* 1878; *m* Kathryn A. Britton); II–Francis Dénis (1 above).
1–*m* Aug. 2, 1909, Ethel Laurens Dunn, *b* Jackson, Tenn., Apr. 4, 1884; dau. of William Clement Dunn, of Mt. Vernon, O.; issue: 1–Jacqueline Dénise, *b* Grand Rapids, Mich., Sept. 10, 1915.
1–Ph.B., U.Chicago, '03 (Psi Upsilon); LL.B., Harvard, 1905. Atty. Furniture Mfrs. Ass'n, and sec. Furniture Mut. Ins. Co. (see Who's Who in America). Mem. Grand Rapids Bar Assn. Republican. Catholic. Clubs: Kent Country, University, Harvard, Muskegon Country, National Arts (N.Y. City), Arts (Washington), Furniture. Summer place: Thornewood, Grandville, Mich. Residence: Pantlind Hotel, Grand Rapids, Mich.

1–**CLAPP, Helen Statira,** *b* Harlan Tp., Fayette Co., Ia., June 27, 1889.
10–Thomas **Clapp** (1597-1684), from Eng., 1634; settled at Dorchester, Mass.; removed to Weymouth, thence to Hingham, later at Scituate; dep. Gen. Ct., 1649; overseer of the poor, 1667; *m* Abigail–;
9–Samuel (1641-1711), *m* 1666, Hannah Gill (*d* 1722);
8–Stephen (1670-1756), *m* 1696, Temperance Ghoram or Gorham (1675-1764; John[9], *m* Mercy or Mary Otis; Capt. John[10], *m* Desire Howland);
7–John (1697-1767), *m* 1724, Mercy Otis (1700-61);
6–Samuel (1725-1808), *m* 1751, Lucy Dwella (bap. 1731);
5–Stephen (1752-1829), pvt. Am. Rev.; commd. lt., 1779; *m* Katy Wheeler (1762-1813; Ephraim[6]);
4–Constant (1784-1868), removed to Salem, N.Y.; *m* 1811, Statira Bartlett (1784-1856; Samuel[5]);
3–Alfred Freeman (1819-86), removed to Clapps' Mill, N.Y.; *m* 1851, Sarah Chamberlin (1819-69);
2–Andrew Chamberlin (1852-96), removed to Fayette Co., Ia.; *m* 1886, Anna Elizabeth Harvey (*b* 1858; William[3], from Scotland, *m* Magdalen MacFarlane); issue: I–Anna Madge (*b* 1887); II–Helen Statira (1 above); III–Alfred Harvey (1891-1918 in France with A.E.F., died of acute pulmonary tuberculosis); IV–Kitty Dorothy (*b* 1893; *m* 1917, Harry Wilbur King); V–Edith May (*b* 1895; *m* 1927, Hobart Campbell).
1–B.Sc., Des Moines Coll., '10. Pvt. sec. law firm of W. H. Antes, since 1917; staff West Union Argo-Gazette, 1911-14. Dep. co. supt. of schs., Fayette Co., Ia., 1914-17; treas. City of West Union, Ia., 1928-30; sec.-treas. bd. of West Union Public Library since 1927. Mem. D.F.P.A., D.A.R., West Union chapter Red Cross (dir.) Presbyn. Republican. Residence: West Union, Fayette Co., Ia.

CANNON

Arms: Gules, a two-handed sword in bend sinister, between three mullets argent.
Crest: Out of a crescent argent, a buckle azure.

1–**CANNON, Charles Albert,** *b* Concord, N.C., Nov. 29, 1892.
8–James **Cannon,** in Dorchester Co., Md., 1683; *m* Rose or Rosanna Pope (Robert[9], of Dorchester Co., will dated 1700, proved 1701, *m* Eliza–, will dated and probated 1716);
7–James (will dated 1711-proved 1711-12), planter Dorchester Co., Md.; *m* Mary–;
6–James (*b* ca. 1700), of Dorchester Co.; *m* 1724, in Harford Co., Md., Mary Bowen (or Boren);
5–James (1731-84), removed from Md. to N.C.; settled in Mecklenburg Co., N.C., 1768; tailor; purchased 124 acres in Rowan Co., 1769; *m* Margaret Alexander;
4–James (1762-1837), farmer and cabinet maker; removed from the Catawba River settlement to Poplar Tent, then in Mecklenburg Co. (now Cabarrus Co.); purchased 2 tracts of 150 and 105 acres in Mecklenburg Co.; claimed to have served Am. Rev.; *m* 1790, Ann Black (1771-1857; "Heroic pioneer" William[5]);
3–Joseph Allison (1808-87), farmer; *m* 1843, Eliza Caldwell Long (1821-1905; David[4] [*d* 1837, aet.

52], *m* 1813, Margaret [*b* 1793], dau. of William Andrews, *m* Barbara Caldwell);
2–James William (2 below).
8–Joseph **Alexander,** will probated in Cecil Co., Md., 1730;
7–James (*d* 1779), named among first purchasers of the Munster lands in Cecil Co., Md., 1714; acquired considerable land in Md. and N.C.; ruling elder of the New Castle Presbytery, 1725, and frequently after that in those of the Synod of Phila.; *m* 1st, Margaret McKnitt;
6–Theophilus (will dated and probated in 1768), of Cecil Co., Md.; *m* Catherine– (probably a dau. of Michael Wallace);
5–Margaret (*d* 1802), *m* James **Cannon** (5 above).
4–John H. **Bost** (*d* 1845), lived at Bost Mills, Cabarrus Co., N.C., where he owned several thousand acres of land, and a grist mill on Rocky River; *m* 1819, Catherine Boger (1790-1842);
3–Martin Luther (1826-1903), having inherited the ancestral homestead from his father, he continued to live on this place, supervising the work of its many acres as his father had done; *m* 1856, Rosetta Crowell;
2–Mary Ella (2 below).
10–Yelverton (Crowe) **Crowell** (*d* 1683), from Eng.; among the earliest settlers of Yarmouth; settled at Charlestown, Mass.; at West Yarmouth, 1640;
9–Edward (ca. 1644-1688), removed from Barnstable to Woodbridge, N.J., 1685; *m* 1673, Mary Lothrop;
8–Edward (1685-1756), town clk., Woodbridge, N.J., 1731-56; *m* 1st, 1707, Sarah Veal;
7–Edward (1715-will dated 1792), emigrated from N.J. to Halifax, N.C.; *m* Martha Rabun, aunt to Gov. William Rabun, of Ga.;
6–George (*b* ca. 1755), probably son of Edward; it is said he lived to be 107 years of age;
5–George, of Halifax Co., N.C.; *m* Sara Gillespie;
4–Jennings (*b* 1807), *m* 1827, Ann Reid (1808-59);
3–Rosetta (*b* 1834), *m* Martin Luther **Bost** (3 above);
2–Mary Ella (*b* 1857), *m* 1875, James William **Cannon** (1852-1921), issue: I–Joseph Franklin (*b* 1876; *m* Annie Ludlow); II–infant (*b* 1877); III–Adelaide Rosette (*b* 1878; *m* J. B. Douglass; *m* 2d, David H. Blair); IV–Margaret Louise (*b* 1880; *m* 1902, Julian S. Carr, Jr. [see Vol. I, p. 552]; *m* 2d, Clark Howell); V–James William, Jr. (*b* 1881; *m* Frances Anna Brown); VI–Mary Ella (*b* 1883; *m* Charles Hill); VII–Martin Luther (*b* 1885; *m* Ohla Brown); VIII–Eugene Thomas (*b* 1886; *m* Emma Finlayson); IX–Fred Wadsworth (*b* 1888); X–James Ross (*b* 1890; *m* Ashlyn Lowe); XI–Charles A. (1 above); XII–Laura McGill (*m* Charles Lambeth).
1–*m* June 5, 1912, Ruth Louise Coltrane (qv for issue).
1–Residence: Concord, N.C.

1–**CANNON, Ruth Louise Coltrane (Mrs. Charles A.),** *b* Concord, N.C., Oct. 15, 1891.
12–John **Robinson,** resided at Crostwick, Parish of Romaldkirk, North Riding of Yorkshire, Eng.; *m* —Savage;
11–John, *m* Ann Dent;
10–George (living 1634), *m* Frances Layton (*d* 1648);
9–John (*d* 1651), *m* Elizabeth Potter (*d* 1688);
8–Christopher (1645-93), from Eng. to Va., ca. 1666; settled on the Rappahannock River, in that part which was afterward Middlesex Co.; clk. Middlesex Co., 1675-88; mem. Va. Assembly, 1685-86,88; mem. Gov's Council, 1691; sec. of state for Va. Colony, 1692-93; vestryman Christ Ch. Parish, Middlesex Co.; *m* 1st, Agatha Obert (*d* 1685/86; Bertram[9]);
7–John (1683-1749), rep. Middlesex Co. in House of Burgesses, 1711,14; mem. Gov.'s Council, 1720-49; acting gov. of Va., 1749; lived for a time at Urbana, later at "Piscataqua," Essex Co.; *m* 1st, ca. 1701, Katherine Beverley (Maj. Robert[8], of Middlesex Co.);
6–William (1709-92), justice Spotsylvania Co., Va.; maj. militia, 1743; clergyman; col. Am. Rev.; *m* 1st, 1737, Agatha Beverley (Capt. Harry[7], of Spotsylvania Co.);
5–Katherine (1742-98), *m* 1757, her cousin, Beverley **Winslow** (1734-93), 1st lt., 1756; capt. militia French and Indian War, 1758; lt. Am. Rev., 1781; col. Spotsylvania militia; sheriff Spotsylvania Co., Berkeley Parish, 1764; owned land in Orange Co., Va., and Fayette Co., Ky.;
4–William (1766-1838), lived in Port William, Gallatin (now Carrollton, Carroll) Co., Ky.; lawyer; clk. Gallatin Circuit Ct., 1805-38; *m* 1791, Peggy Mills (1776-1816; William[5], soldier Am. Rev., *m* Margaret Swift);
3–William Beverley (1814-83), student Gallatin Acad., Ky.; lawyer; Democrat; *m* 2d, 1847, Martha Jane Woolfolk;
2–Mariam Smith (2 below).
9–Thomas **Owen,** the first of the family recorded in Va.; lived and died in Henrico Co., Va.; *m* Elizabeth Brookes;
8–Thomas;
7–John;
6–Bracket (1739-1802), of Prince Edward Co., Va.;
5–Col. Abram or Abraham (*b* 1769), emigrated from Va. to Ky., 1785; settled at Owen's Station nr. Shelbyville; served in Gen. Wilkinson's Wabash Campaign, 1791; lt. in Capt. Lemon's Company at St. Clair's Defeat, and was with Col. Hardin in the action near White River; comd. first military company raised in Shelby Co., Ky.; rendered valuable service in Wayne's expdn., 1794, rising in rank to maj. then col.; mem. State Legislature; mem. Constl. Conv., 1799; mem. State Senate; a.-d.-c to Gen. Harrison, 1811, when he led his troops against Tecumseh and his warriors in the Battle of Tippecanoe, in which battle he was killed; *m* Martha Dupuy;
4–Nancy Gwyn, *m* 1825, Hugh Turner **Woolfolk** (1800-48; Robert[5]);
3–Martha Jane (1826-1905), *m* William Beverley **Winslow** (3 above).
8–Bartholomew **Dupuy** (ca. 1660-1743; son of Jean, *m* Anne De St. Hyer); lt. Royal Guardsmen of his Majesty Louis XIV, of France; Huguenot, from France after the revocation of the Edict of Nantes, 1685; to Germany thence to Eng., 1699, to America 1700, settled in Manikintown, King William Parish, Va.; *m* 1685, Countess Susanne La Villon;
7–Capt. John James (*b* probably 1698-will dated and recorded 1775), of King William Parish, Cumberland Co., Va.; *m* 1728, Susanne Le Villain (John Peter[8]);
6–Bartholomew (will dated 1790), of Amelia Co., Va.; moved to Woodford Co., Ky.; *m* Mary Mottley;
5–Martha (*d* 1836), *m* Col. Abram **Owen** (5 above);
4–Nancy Gwynn, *m* Hugh T. **Woolfolk** (4 above);
3–Martha Jane, *m* William B. **Winslow** (3 above);
2–Mariam Smith (1859-1915), *m* as his 2d wife, 1884, Daniel Branson **Coltrane** (*b* 1842), banker and cotton mfr. (for issue and other lineages see Jenn Winslow Coltrane).
1–*m* June 5, 1912, Charles Albert Cannon (qv); issue: 1–William Coltrane, *b* June 29, 1913; 2–Marian Winslow, *b* Jan. 21, 1916; 3–Charles Albert, Jr., *b* Aug. 28, 1919; 4–Mary Ruth, *b* Jan. 9, 1922.
1–A.B., Greensboro (N.C.) Coll. for Women, '11. Mem. C.D.A., D.A.R., U.D.C. Summer place: Blowing Rock, N.C. Residence: Concord, N.C.

1–**JONES, Mariam Elizabeth Coltrane (Mrs. Robert E.),** *b* Concord, N.C., Oct. 2, 1894.
6–Col. John **McGee** (will dated 1773, proved 1774), supposedly the Am. immigrant, is said to have been a man of great wealth who lived on Sandy Creek, now a part of Randolph Co., N.C.; col. in British Army; served in the New York expdn., French and Indian War, 1755-56; recommended to be made captain of militia, Orange Co.;
5–Samuel (will dated 1808-probated 1810), ship owner, Phila.; removed to Asheboro, Randolph Co., N.C.; *m* — Busick;
4–Sophia (1783-1882), *m* Daniel **Coltrane** (*d* 1831), of Randolph Co.;
3–Kelly (1818-59), farmer, of Randolph Co.; *m* 1839, Mary Cossett (1819-91; Thomas[4] [1787-1858], *m* Sarah Williams, 1788-1871);
2–Daniel Branson (2 below).
9–John **Beverley,** of Eng., adhered to Charles I, and at the Restoration his name appears

in the list of those on whom it was intended to confer the Order of the Royal Oak;
8–Maj. Robert (*d* 1686), lawyer; settled in Lancaster Co., Va.; justice, 1673; clk. House of Burgesses, 1670; *m* 1st, Mary Koeble, widow (*d* 1678);
7–Capt. Harry (1669-1731), justice, Middlesex Co., 1700, surveyor King and Queen and King William cos., 1702-14; burgess, 1705-06; comd. the "Virgin," 1716, which was captured by the Spanish man-of-war, he escaped and came to Va., 1717; presiding justice Spotsylvania Co., ca. 1720; *m* ca. 1700, Elizabeth Smith;
6–Susannah (1706-78), *m* 1726, Benjamin **Winslow** (*b* 1700-will proved 1751);
5–Col. Beverley (1734-93), *m* 1757, Katherine Robinson (1742-98);
4–William (1766-1838), *m* 1791, Peggy Mills (1776-1816);
3–William Beverley (1814-83), *m* 2d, 1847, Martha Jane Woolfolk (1826-1905);
2–Mariam Smith (1859-1915), *m* as his 2d wife, 1884, Daniel Branson **Coltrane** (*b* 1842), banker and cotton mfr.; for issue and other lineages see Jenn Winslow Coltrane.
1–*m* June 5, 1923, Robert Eldredge Jones, *b* Franklin, Va., Nov. 16, 1894; son of John Paul Jones, of Franklin, *m* Odell Rawls; issue: 1–Robert E., Jr., *b* Concord, N.C., Aug. 15, 1924; 2–Branson Coltrane, *b* Concord, Aug. 15, 1927.
1–Grad. Greensboro Coll., '13. Mem. C.D.A., D.A.R., U.D.C., A.L. Auxiliary. Residence: 84 N. Union St., Concord, N.C.

1–**COLTRANE, Jenn Winslow,** *b* Marshall, Mo., July 15, 1887.
9–Patrick **Coltrane,** provost of Wigton, had seizin of the lands of Airlies, 2 miles from Wigton (Wigtown), 1663, in the parish of Kikrinner in Galloway, southwestern Scotland; also of Culmalzie;
8–William, provost of Wigton, and had seizin of Airlies, 1679; had seizin of Drummoral in the parish of Whithorn, 1689; commr. for the Burgh of Wigton in the last Scottish Parliament, which was opened, 1700; he is on record as "Provost-Cultraine," and had seizin, 1690, of Meikle Arrow;
7–Patrick, had seizin of the lands of Meikle Arrow, 1710; *m* Elizabeth, dau. of John Stewart, of Physgill;
6–David, came from Scotland and settled in N.C.; legatee of Benjamin Rawlings, Edgecombe Co., N.C., 1738; justice of the peace, Edgecombe Co., 1739,43; petitioned for a grant of 530 acres in Edgecombe Co., 1743; returned to Scotland and *d* there; *m* Mary Wallace;
5–William (*d* 1835), of Randolph Co., N.C.; messenger from Charles Bond to Governor Caswell, 1778, with a requisition for $40,000 for repairing and outfitting the vessel "Pennsylvania Farmer" for use in Am. Rev.; *m* Rachel Worthington;
4–Daniel (*d* 1831), of Randolph Co.; *m* Sophia McGee (1783-1882);
3–Kelly (1818-59), *m* 1839, Mary Cossett (1819-91);
2–Daniel Branson (2 below).
7–Thomas **Winslow** (*d* bet. 1725-26), lived in Sittenbourne Parish, Essex Co., Va., 1698, this being the earliest record found of him in this country, lived in St. Ann's Parish; *m* Ann Parker (Robert[8]);
6–Benjamin (*b* 1700-will proved 1751), surveyor, St. George Parish, Spotsylvania Co., 1733; justice, 1736; duties collector and inspector of Tappahannock warehouses, 1738; sheriff Essex Co., 1739; *m* 1726, Susannah Beverley;
5–Col. Beverley (1734-93), 1st lt., 1756; capt. militia French and Indian War, 1758; lt. Am. Rev., 1781; col. Spotsylvania Militia; sheriff Spotsylvania Co., Berkeley Parish, 1764; owned land in Orange Co., Va., and Fayette Co., Ky.; *m* 1757, Katherine Robinson (1742-98);
4–William (1766-1838), *m* 1791, Peggy Mills (1776-1816);
3–William Beverley (1814-83), *m* 2d, 1847, Martha Jane Woolfolk (1826-1905);
2–Mariam Smith (2 below).
9–Maj. Gen. Robert **Smith** (*d* 1687), from Eng. to Brandon, Middlesex Co., Va., 1622; mem. Council, 1663-87; maj. Va. troops in war bet. Eng. and Holland, 1666; *m* Elizabeth–, widow of Sir Thomas Lunsford, probably a dau. of Gov. Christopher Wormeley, *m* Mary Adams;

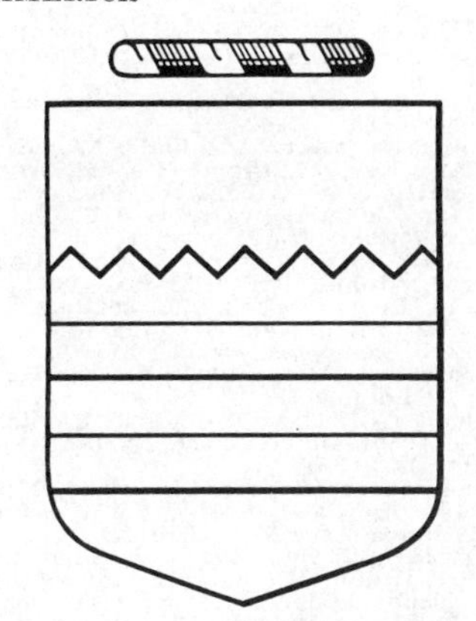

COLTRANE

Arms: Gules, two bars or, a chief indented of the last.

8–Robert (1658-1702), collector and receiver of Va. duties, 1699; *m* Elizabeth–;
7–Elizabeth, *m* ca. 1700, Capt. Harry **Beverley** (1669-1731), Spotsylvania Co., Va.; officer in colonial wars, 1716; justice Middlesex Co., 1700; surveyor King and Queen and King William cos., 1702-14; burgess, 1705-06; comd. the "Virgin," 1716, which was captured by a Spanish man-of-war, he escaped and came to Va., 1717; presiding justice Spotsylvania Co., ca. 1720;
6–Susannah (1706-78), *m* Benjamin **Winslow** (6 above).
2–Daniel Branson **Coltrane** (*b* 1842), enlisted in Co. I, 5th Cav. Troop, Guilford Co., during War between the States; entered actively into the struggle nr. Seven Springs, N.C., later, his troop was made a part of the command of Gen. J. E. B. Stuart, and from his first battle at Brandy Station, 1863, until the close of the war, he took part in every important engagement in which Gen. Stuart's troops were engaged; wounded three times; now sgt.; organizer Concord (N.C.) Nat. Bank, 1883; later became pres.; chmn. Concord sch. bd., 16 yrs.; trustee and treas. Stonewall Jackson Manual Training and Industrial Sch.; treas. State School; pres. governing bd. N.C. Christian Advocate of Greensboro, organ of the Southern Meth. Conf. of N.C., over 25 yrs.; *m* Ella Vanice (1844-82); *m* 2d, 1884, Mariam Smith Winslow (1859-1915), principal factor in the organizing of the Woman's Foreign Missionary Soc., 1888, pres., 1889-1911; issue (1st marriage): (2 died infancy); III–Lester Durrett (*m* Julia Gay); IV–Mary Juanita (*m* David A. Garrison); issue (2d marriage): I–Jenn Winslow (1 above); II–Ruth Louise (Mrs. Charles A. Cannon, qv for other lineages); III–Mariam Elizabeth (Mrs. Robert E. Jones, qv); IV–Mary Branson (*b* 1900; *m* Frank A. Dusch).
1–Ed. Randolph-Macon Woman's Coll., '06 (Kappa Delta, nat. treas. 3 yrs., nat. pres. 4 yrs.). Mem. D.A.C., C.D.A., D.C.W., Scions of Colonial Cavaliers, D.A.R. (historian gen. Nat. Soc.), U.S.D. 1812, U.D.C., Nat. Officers Club of D.A.R., Club of Colonial Dames (Washington), I.A.G.; charter mem. Southeastern Council. Residence: Concord, N.C.

1–**CAPERTON, Woods Archibald,** *b* Waco, Tex., July 21, 1879.
11–Thomas **Harris** (qv);
10–Maj. Robert (1635-1701), from Wales to Va., ca. 1651; of "The Forks"; *m* as her 2d husband, 1650, Mary (Claiborne) Rice (Col. William Claiborne[11], qv);
9–Col. William (1652-98), burgess, Henrico and Hanover cos., Va.; *m* 1679, Temperance Overton (*d* 1699; William[10], of Va., *m* Mary Waters; son of Gov. William Overton, of Hull, Eng.);

8–Maj. Robert (1697-1765), maj. Colonial wars; burgess from Hanover Co., Va.; *m* 1720, Mourning Glenn;
7–Lucy, *m* William **Shelton,** of Albemarle Co., Va.;
6–Mourning, *m* Capt. Archibald **Woods** (1749-1836), Am. Rev. (William[7] [1707-82], from Ireland, settled in Albemarle Co., Va., Am. Rev. and Colonial wars, *m* 1741, Susannah Wallace; Michael[8], qv);
5–Lucy (1772-1854), *m* 1790, William **Caperton** (1766-1846; John[6] [ca. 1732-post 1816], from Scotland, to New York, 1753, settled on New River, Va., nr. present dividing line of Monroe and Sumner cos., W.Va., at what is now called Crump's Bottoms, W.Va., *m* 1753, Mary [Polly] Thompson);
4–Archibald (*b* 1791), *m* 18–, Maria Haslip;
3–Woods Archibald (1828-62), *m* 1851, Amanda Colbert (1832-1903);
2–Joseph Colbert (1852-90), of Forest, Miss.; *m* 1878, Ada Eastland (1854-90); for issue and Woods lineage see Vol. II, p. 55.
1–*m* Dec. 18, 1902, Sue Evans, *b* Goshen, Tex., Feb. 9, 1881; dau. of George Evans, of Athens, Tex.; issue: 1–Helen Terry, *b* Waco, Tex., Mar. 17, 1904; *m* June 27, 1927, Henry Kenneth Metcalf, of London, Eng. (issue: Patricia Mary, *b* May 24, 1928); 2–Woods Archibald, Jr., *b* Indianapolis, Ind., Feb. 11, 1909; 3–Mary Evans, *b* Indianapolis, Aug. 29, 1912.
1–Ed. grade and 2 yrs. high schools and 2 yrs. at Strother's Private School of Mathematics and English, Waco, Tex. Pharmaceutical salesman in Tex., 4 yrs.; mgr. southern dept. of Eli Lilly & Co., 2 yrs.; asst. sales mgr. and sales mgr., Eli Lilly & Co., Indianapolis, Ind., since 1906. Clubs: Indianapolis Athletic, Woodstock, Columbia, Indianapolis Gun, Chamber of Commerce. Residence: 4830 N. Meridian St., Indianapolis, Ind.

1–**CARPENTER, Annie Isabelle,** *b* St. Paul, Minn.
10–William **Carpenter,** came in the "Bevis" (qv);
9–William (1605-59), settled at Rehoboth, Mass.; rep., 1641,43; dep., 1645; constable, 1641; propr. and town clk., 1643-49; commd. capt., 1642; *m* Abigail–;
8–William (1631/32-1703), town clk., Rehoboth, 1656; dep., 1668; *m* 1st, 1651, Priscilla Bennet (*d* 1663);
7–Benjamin (1663-1738), *m* 1691, Hannah Strong (1671-1762; Jedediah[8], *m* Freedom, dau. of Henry Woodward; Elder John[9], qv);
6–Ebenezer (1709-77), of Coventry, Conn.; *m* 1739, Eunice Thompson (1722-77; John[7], *m* Jerusha, dau. of Nehemiah Palmer; William[8], *m* Bridget Cheseborough; John[9], *m* Hannah Brewster);
5–James (1741-1813), of Coventry; served Am. Rev.; rep. Vt. Legislature, 1786-87; *m* 1761, Irene Ladd (1744-1817);
4–Cephas (1770-1859), *m* Anne Benton (1773-1845);
3–Ira (1798-1862), *m* Esther Annie Luce (1802-35);
2–Cephas Warner (1832-1902), *m* 1858, Cynthia Elizabeth West (1834-1906).
1–Mem. D.F.P.A. Residence: "The Angus," St. Paul, Minn.

1–**CARPENTER, Agnes Coe (Mrs. William James),** *b* Brady's Bend on Allegheny River, Pa., May 31, 1874.
9–Robert **Coe** (qv);
8–Benjamin (*b* 1629), *m* Abigail Carman (John[9], *m* Florence Fordham, of Jamaica, L.I., 1631);
7–Joseph (1665-1743), settled at Newark, N.J., 1710; *m* Judith–;
6–Benjamin (1708-93), settled at Morristown, N.J.; removed to Redstone Presbytery, Westmoreland Co., Pa., 1777; founded Tarentum on the Allegheny River; had 5 sons in Am. Rev.; *m* Abigail–; *m* 2d, 1742, Rachel Prudden;
5–Peter (1753-1836), lt. Am. Rev.; settled in Cross Creek Tp., Washington Co., Pa., 1777; *m* 1781, Mary (Shearer) Allen (1754-1832; William Shearer[6], Am. Rev., *m* Sarah–);
4–Benjamin (1783-1857), *m* 1803, Susannah McKibbin (1779-1858; Thomas[5] [1755-1823], Am. Rev., *m* Margaret Chambers; John[6] [*d* 1798], Am. Rev., *m* Sarah–);
3–Peter (1811-91), *m* 1835, Christina Le Vier (1808-81; Daniel[4], [1766-1844], *m* Rosanna Say [1778-1857]; James[5], of Mifflin Co., Am. Rev., *m* Mary Reed; James[6], of Cumberland Co., Am. Rev., *m* Christine Annabelle Harris);
2–Samuel W. (2 below).
9–Rev. Peter **Prudden** (1600-56), from Eng., 1637; pastor first Ch. Milford, Conn.; *m* Joanna Boyse;
8–Rev. John (1645-1725), grad. Harvard, 1668; pastor First Ch., Jamaica, L.I., 1676-92, Newark, N.J., 1692-99; *m* Abigail–;
7–Joseph (1692-1776), ruling elder, Morristown Presbyn. Ch.; *m* Joanna Lyon (Benjamin[8], *m* Bethia Condit; Henry[9], from Scotland with his two bros., *m* Mary Bateman);
6–Rachel (1718-76), *m* Benjamin **Coe** (6 above).
6–Leonard (Steffen) **Stephen,** from Germany to Washington Co., Md., 1740;
5–Leonard (*d* Huntingdon Co., Pa., 1795), *m* Margaret– (*d* 1814);
4–Leonard (1781-1858), *m* 1814, Margaret Shively (1794-1874; Jacob Sheibley[5], *m* Barbara, dau. Daniel Isenburg, from Germany to Md., 1740; Christian[6]; Uhli or Oley[7] [*b* 1726], in York Co., Pa., 1760; Christian Scheibleii[8], French Huguenot, from Switzerland, with wife and 7 children, settled in Lancaster Co., Pa., *m* Barbara Spitler);
3–Jacob (1815-81), *m* 1841, Agnes McBride (1819-90; John[4] [1790-1839], *m* 1812, Elizabeth Miller [Joseph[5], *m* Catherine–; John[6], of York Co., served Am. Rev.]; William[5], of Va., who with 7 bros. served Am. Rev.; William[6], of Va., 1735, who with three bros. was killed on Braddock's Field in the French and Indian War);
2–Margaret Elizabeth (*b* 1852), *m* 1871, Samuel Wallace **Coe** (1845-1918), helped develop first oil fields in Pa.; contractor and producer; resided in Parker, Armstrong Co., for 40 yrs., removed to Tulsa, Okla., 1911; issue: I–Cora (1873-74); II–Christina Agnes (1 above); III–Anne Elizabeth (*b* 1876; m Rev. Charles W. Kerr); IV–Edna Pearl (*b* 1879; *m* J. B. Keener); V–Wallace Ross (*b* 1881; *m* Eleanor Knaurr); VI–Claude Emmett (*b* 1884; *m* Elizabeth McAllister); VII–George Henry (*b* 1887; *m* Esther Harris); VIII–Margaret (*b* 1890; *m* Frank Baumgarner); IX–Jennie (*b* 1894-*d* infancy).
1–*m* Nov. 12, 1900, William James Carpenter, *b* in Eng., 1860; architect, mem. A.I.A.; son of William Carpenter, *m* Annie Gillett; issue: 1–Edward Coe, *b* Pittsburgh, Pa., Mar. 31, 1903; U.Fla. (Pi Kappa Phi); *m* 1926, Jacqueline Pursley (issue: John William, *b* Nov. 5, 1927); 2–Robert Coe, *b* Pittsburgh, Sept. 22, 1904; U. Fla. (Pi Kappa Phi); law student Stetson U.; 3–William Richard, and 4–James Clarence (twins), *b* Beaver, Pa., Nov. 29, 1909; Stetson U., 1931.
1–Ed. Edinboro and Clarion teachers training schools, 1892; Allegheny Coll. (Kappa Kappa Gamma); Meadville Conservatory of Music. Mem. D.A.R., St. Petersburg Woman's Club (pres.), Federation of Women's Clubs (state chmn. literature). Summer place: Camp Telufa-on-Lake Chautauqua, N.Y. Winter Residence: 737 N. Woodland Boul., DeLand, Fla.

1–**CARR, L(aura) Maude,** *b* Riverside, Ia., Dec. 28, 1882.
10–Caleb **Carr** (qv);
9–John (1664-1714), of Newport, R.I.; granted privilege of running ferry bet. Newport and Jamestown, franchise remained in family 170 yrs.; *m* Waite Easton (1668-1725; Peter[10]; Gov. Nicholas[11], qv);
8–Samuel (1694-1739), of Newport; gunsmith; *m* 1719, Mary Green (*d* 1745);
7–Capt. Caleb (1720-83), of Newport; *m* 1741, Elizabeth Phillips (1722-1805);
6–Caleb (1744-1818), of Newport, R.I., later at Pompey, N.Y.; was in Battle of Saratoga, 1777; *m* Margaret Adams (*d* 1831), of Milford, Mass.;
5–Col. James (1775-1832), of Pompey or Galway; comd. a regt. at Sackets Harbor, N.Y., in War 1812; *m* 1792, Hulda Collins (1773-1853);
4–Chauncey (1793-1873), of Saratoga Co., N.Y., moved to Riverside, Ia.; *m* 1816, Elizabeth Keene (1795-1879);
3–Chauncey (1817-1904), removed from Pompey, N.Y., to Ill., thence to nr. Riverside, Ia., where he owned a large farm, specialized in

apples; *m* 3d, 1847, Mary Mitchell Morgan (1820-73);
2–James Edward (2 below).
4–Robert **Craig**, from Ireland, to Pa.; *m* in Ireland, Catherine Johnston;
3–Robert (1816-1901), *m* Sarah Godlove (1826-1900);
2–Mary Jane (1855-1907), *m* 1874, James Edward **Carr** (1848-1907), teacher for 25 yrs.; issue: I–Iva Myrtle (*b* 1876; *m* William G. McCreedy); II–Bertha Mabel (*b* 1879; *m* John W. Tener); III–L. Maude (1 above); IV–Mary Edna (*b* 1888; *m* Chester C. Scott).
1–Summer work at Ia. Teachers' Coll., Cedar Falls, and other summer insts. Taught 6 yrs. in Ia. rural and grade schools and 1 yr. in Idaho; now in secretarial work. Mem. I.A.G. Methodist. Republican. Club: Business and Professional Women's, etc. Residence: 219 S. 25th St., Cedar Rapids, Ia.

1–**CARR, Lillian E. Hunt (Mrs. Lorin),** *b* Leesville, O., Aug. 24, 1853.
4–Caleb **Hunt**;
3–Horatio (1790-1875), pvt. War 1812; *m* Matilda Roby (1793-1852);
2–John Levi (1817-90), merchant; *m* 1841, Susan Catherine Gregory (1817-96); issue: I–Elizabeth E. M. (1842-54); II–John Edwin (1843-44); III–Caroline V. (1846-1917); IV–Sabella M. (1850-1927; *m* 1869, Merideth C. Price); V–Lillian E. (1 above).
1–*m* Nov. 9, 1875, Lorin Carr (Sept. 13, 1850-July 31, 1926), son of Amos Carr, of Leesville, O.; issue (all *b* Leesville, O.): 1–Don Merideth, *b* Oct. 3, 1876; mem. Ohio N.G.; sec. to Major Butler during Spanish-Am. War; spl. stenographer to the commr. in Gen. Land Office at Washington; pvt. sec. to Sec. Ballinger of the Interior Dept., then supt. of Yakima Indian Reservation in State of Wash., 12 yrs.; now engaged in abstract and insurance business; *m* Feb. 6, 1902, Agnes M., dau. of Judge George Beltzhoover; 2–Lynn Hunt (July 4, 1880-Feb. 4, 1917); 3–Irma, *b* May 9, 1882; *m* Mar. 22, 1928, Henry C., son of William H. Baker, of E. Orange, N.J.
1–Ed. Scio Coll. Mem. U.S.D. 1812. Methodist. Republican. Club: Woman's. Residence: 3046 Tuscarawas St. W., Canton, O.

1–**CARROLL, Mary Grace,** *b* "Evergreen," Hampden, Baltimore Co., Md., Mar. 21, 1870.
5–Charles **Carroll**;
4–Charles (1751-1836), of On Elkridge, nr. Guilford, Md.; *m* Elizabeth– (1769-1850);
3–David (1811-81), *b* on Elkridge, nr. Savage, Md.; *d* at Mt. Vernon Mills, Baltimore Co., Md.; *m* Anne Ayler (1818-87), of Chestertown, Md.;
2–James Albert Holland (2 below).
4–Thomas **Cockrill,** Gent. (1768-1815), refugee from Ireland; naturalized 1797; 1st lt. War 1812, decorated with sword for services; *m* Rebecca Veazey (Capt. John Ward[5], *m* Mary Wilmer, of Cecil Co., Md.);
3–Dr. James Jackson (1815-78), surgeon in Union Army, Civil War; *m* Mary Eveline Ford (Joseph Young[4], *m* Mary Evelyn, dau. of Archibald Shaw, of "Rose Hill," Md., *m* 2d, Mary, dau. of Thomas Clarkson).
2–James Albert Holland **Carroll** (1843-82), cotton duck mfr., Mt. Vernon, Md.; capt. Md. militia during Civil War; *m* Aggie Yocum; *m* 2d, Mollie Pearce Cockrill (1851-1920); issue (2d marriage): I–Mary Grace (1 above); II–Florence Elizabeth (*m* William Calvin Chesnut); III–Albert Hynson (1874-1926); IV–Walter Cockrill (*b* 1876; *m* Edith Gibbs).
1–Grad. art, Goucher Coll., '94. Mem. U.S.D. 1812, Md. Hist. Soc., I.A.G. Clubs: Baltimore Country, Nova Scotia Yacht. Summer place: "Spruce Top," Chester, N.S. Residence: 121 Roland Av., Roland Park, Baltimore, Md.

1–**CALLENDER, Mary Harriet (Minnie) Holton (Mrs. William F.),** *b* Northfield, Mass., June 16, 1855.
8–William (Houlton) **Holton** (qv);
7–John (*d* 1712), *m* Abigail Fisher;
6–William (1679-1755), of Northfield, Mass.; *m* 1706, Abigail Edwards (*b* 1680; Samuel[7]);
5–William (1709-ca. 1798), capt.; *m* Bethia– (*d* 1773);
4–Lemuel (1749-86), *m* Lydia Shattuck;

HOLTON HOMESTEAD, Northfield, Mass.

3–Luther (1777-1835), *m* 1801, Betsey Hodges (*b* Hanover, N.J.–*d* 1845);
2–Cyrus (1813-94), *m* at Northfield, 1843, Amanda Brown (1825-1918; John[3], of Northfield, Mass.); issue: I–Eleanor Maria (1848-92); II–Henry Cyrus (1853-1927; *m* Mary, dau. William D. Alexander, of Northfield, Mass.; issue: 2 sons); III–Mary Harriet (1 above).
1–*m* June 16, 1886, William Field Callender, *b* Cambridge, Mass., July 11, 1851; son of Joseph Callender, *m* Elizabeth Field.
1–Ed. private schs., Northfield, Mass.; Prospect Hill Boarding Sch., Greenfield, Mass.; Villa Maria Convent, Montreal, Can. Mem. Holton Family Assn. (sec., 1924–). Residence: Old Holton Homestead, Northfield, Mass.

1–**CARNES, William Watts,** *b* Somerville, Tenn., Sept. 18, 1841.
4–Alexander **Carnes,** served in Cont. Army in Va.; granted 400 acres in Caswell Co., N.C.; *m* Rachel–;
3–David B. (1788-1842), *m* 1812, Nancy Johnston Scott;
2–James Alexander (2 below).
8–Gilbert (Johnstone) **Johnston** (1700-75), took part in the rising of Scotland in the first Jacobite contest for the Stuart dynasty; on failure of that he fled to Ireland where he *m* 1724; in 1745, he joined the army of Prince Charlie, the young pretender, and after the defeat at Culloden, he again escaped to Ireland; came to N.C. 1746; *m* Caroline–;
7–Henry, began to write name Johnston; from Ireland to N.C. with parents; *m* Catherine Knox;
6–James (1752-1805), lt. col. in Am. Rev.; *m* Jane Ewart (Robert[7]);
5–Mary or Margery, *m* Abraham **Scott,** lived in Gaston Co.;
4–William, *m* 1790, Elizabeth Davis;
3–Nancy Johnston (1794-1826), *m* David B. **Carnes** (3 above).
8–George **Durant** (qv);
7–John (*b* 1662), *m* 1684, Sarah Yorke (Thomas[8], *m* Ann, dau. Sir Philip Yorke);
6–George (*b* 1685), *m* Hagar Crisp (Capt. Nicholas[7], *m*—Wilkins);
5–Sarah (*b* 1717), *m* Joseph **Blount** (1716-77), mem. Assembly, 1746-54,68 (John[6] [*b* 1669], mem. Assembly, 1711, justice of the peace, judge of ct., 1722, mem. Gov.'s Council, 1722-25, *m* 1695, Elizabeth, dau. of John Davis, *m* Mary–; Capt. James[7] [*d* 1685 or 86], from Eng. to Va., 1660, settled in Isle of Wight Co., moved to Chowan Dist., N.C., 1669, burgess, 1672, mem. Gov.'s Council and mem. Grand Council, *m* 1665, Ann Willis, of Ipswich, Mass.);
4–Sarah (*b* 1747), *m* 1771, William **Littlejohn** (*d* 1822), from Scotland ante 1760, settled in Chowan Co.;
3–Elizabeth Margaret (1779-1840), *m* 1822, William Watts **Jones** (1761-1840), lawyer; mem. Assembly from New Hanover Co. and Wilmington, 1808-16; had rice plantations at Belvidere Park on Cape Fear River, nr. Wilmington, and nr. Edenton, N.C. (Sir William[4] [*d* ca. 1763], a Welsh Baronet, from Eng., 1723, to N.C., *m* 1760, Susan Watts);
2–Elizabeth Margaret (1823-55), *m* 1840, James Alexander **Carnes** (1818-64), of Memphis, Tenn.; cotton planter, plantations in Coa-

homa and Tunica cos., Miss.; brig.gen., comdg. the western div. of the state; issue: I–William Watts (1 above); II–Robert Scott (1842-78; *m* Sarah Francis Payne); III–Lizzie Jones (*b* 1844; *m* Samuel Tate); IV–Mary Eliza (1846-1920; *m* P. C. Conley; *m* 2d, C. J. Hatch); V–Sallie Little (1848-86; *m* Isaac C. Meason; *m* 2d, Shepherd Spencer); VI–Samuel T. (*b* 1850; *m* Kate B. Kerr); VII–David B. (*d* aet. 7 mos.); VIII–James A. (1853-73).

1–*m* Apr. 4, 1866, Kate W. Payne (May 27, 1845-Feb. 17, 1872); dau. of George Payne, of Macon, Ga., *m* Emily H. Sims; issue (all *b* Macon, Ga.); 1–Charles Quintard, *b* Jan. 2, 1868; ed. U.Ala.; *m* Nov. 24, 1891, Anna B., dau. of Albert Tennille, of Macon, *m* Anna Paullin (issue: Katharine P.; Estelle T.); 2–Kate Payne, *b* Dec. 29, 1869; *m* Apr. 25, 1900, Robert Eames, son of Charles Stevens Faulkner, of Keene, N.H., *m* Eliza Eames; 3–Elizabeth J. (Feb. 5, 1872-Jan. 1, 1887).

1–*m* 2d, Mar. 31, 1875, Lila K. Payne (Oct. 18, 1850-Aug. 1911); sister of first wife; issue: 1–Lila P., *b* Macon, Ga., Jan. 2, 1876; *m* June 11, 1907, Watson E., son of Eliasaph Dorchester, of Geneva, N.Y., and Tampa, Fla., *m* Sarah Ann Bogart (issue: Clara E.; Lila P.; Phyllis C.); 2–James A. (Mar. 7, 1880-Aug. 27, 1883); 3–Mary Conley, *b* Macon, May 19, 1882; *m* Aug. 11, 1925, Charles Walker, son of Charles W. Ward, of Detroit, Mich., *m* Esther Bannister; 4–Robert Scott, *b* Macon, Mar. 6, 1884; ed. U. of South; *m* Aug. 21, 1907, Laura, dau. of Claude T. Deatrick, of Columbus, O., *m* Hattie E. Osborne (issue: Nell Elizabeth; Mary C.; William W.); 5–Samuel William (Oct. 3, 1885-Jan. 29, 1886); 6–Lois, *b* Macon, Apr. 29, 1888; *m* June 9, 1914, Ewing C. Lewis, of Memphis, Tenn., son of Thomas Fielding Lewis, of Jackson, Tenn., *m* D'Etta Jane Fisher (issue: Katherine); 7–Gladys, *b* Memphis, Tenn., Apr. 8, 1890; 8–Phyllis, *b* Memphis, Apr. 9, 1890; *m* June 7, 1916, Frank A. Winn, Jr., son of Frank A. Winn, of Tampa, Fla., *m* Mary Hall (issue: Frank A.; William Carnes; Mary E.).

1–U.S.N.A., 1857-61. Retired; gen. insurance agent for 5 states; sec. and treas. Memphis Light & Power Co., Memphis, Tenn.; later again gen. agent for 3 states; had orange grove in Manatee Co., Fla. and also engaged in insurance. Sheriff of Shelby Co., Tenn., 2 yrs. Drill master C.S.A.; 1st lt. field baty. under Capt. W. H. Jackson; became capt. of baty. till promoted chief of arty. of a div., Army of Tenn. after battle of Chickamauga; ordered on duty in C.S. Navy, 1864. Mason (K.T.). Mem. Confederate Hist. Assn. of Memphis. Episcopalian. Democrat. Residence: Bradenton, Fla.

1–**CARSON, Katherine Waller,** *b* Davidson, N.C., Oct. 25, 1881.

6–Thomas **Carson** (*d* 1783), from Ireland, ca. 1771, with his six sons, landed at Charleston, S.C.; settled in Wilkes Co., Ga., later at Abbeville, S.C.;

5–Thomas (ca. 1761-ante 1807), served Am. Rev.; moved to Washington Co., Ala.;

4–Col. Joseph (1785-1817), col. 8th Regt. Miss. Militia; col. Miss. vols. in Creek War; lawyer, St. Stephens (now), Ala.; *m* 1814, Caroline C. Green (1794-1830; Abner[5] [1762-1816], *m* Mary Hutchins [1768-1825], of Miss.; Col. Thomas Marston[6]; Thomas[7]; Thomas[8], *m* Martha, dau. of Maj. Henry Filmer, qv);

3–Dr. James Green (1815-63), M.D., U.Pa.; cotton planter in Adams Co., Miss., until 1845, and Carroll Parish, La., 1845-63; *m* 1835, Catharine Waller;

2–William Waller (2 below).

8–Col. John **Waller** (*b* 1617), from Eng., 1635, settled in Va.; received land grant in Gloucester Co., Va., 1667; *m* Mary Key or Kay;

7–Col. John (qv);

6–Edmund, Gent. (1713-71), capt. co. of foot; 2d clk. of Spotsylvania Co., Va., 1742-51; *m* 1740, Mary Pendleton (Philip[7]);

5–Rev. William Edmund (1747-1830), of Spotsylvania Co., Va., went to Ky., ca. 1783; Bapt. preacher; returned to Va., 1802; *m* Mildred Smith (Stephen[6], of Orange Co.);

4–William Smith (1785-1855), of Frankfort and Lexington, Ky.; cashier Bank of Ky., more than 40 yrs.; *m* 1810, Catharine Breckinridge (*d* 1864; Gen. James[5]);

3–Catharine (1815-88), of Ky.; *m* Dr. James G. **Carson** (3 above).

10–James **Taylor** (qv);

9–James, *m* Sarah–;

8–Col. James (1674-1729), of Orange Co., Va.; *m* 1700, Martha Thompson (1679-1762; Col. William[9], served in Royal Army; Sir Roger[10]);

7–Col. George (1711-92), mem. Com. Safety, 1774; del. Va. Conv., 1775; drilled co. of Orange Co. militia for service in Am. Rev.; burgess, 1748-58; *m* 1st, 1738, Rachel Gibson (1717-61); eleven sons served in Am. Rev., nine were officers;

6–Lt. Jonathan (1742-1804), of Orange Co., Va.; lt. of Va. militia; *m* 1764, Ann Berry (1745-1808);

5–Rachel (*b* 1769), *m* 1787, John Gibson **Finnie** (*d* 1811), of Botetourt Co., Va.;

4–John Gibson (*d* 1834), *m* 1824, Fannie Sehon Casey (1802-49; Peter[5], *m* Nancy, dau. of Maj. Andrew Waggener);

3–James Peter (1834-1912), of Caseyville, Ky.; mcht.; pres. Oliver-Finnie Grocer Co., Memphis, Tenn.; *m* 1857 Mary Emma Chamberlin (1840-1916; Perley[4], of Strafford, Vt., *m* Anne Read, of Baltimore; Warren[5]; Amasa[6]; William[7]; William[8]; Joseph[9]; William[10]; Henry[11], of Hingham, Mass.);

2–Rachel (*b* 1858), *m* 1880, William Waller **Carson** (*b* 1845; see Vol. III, p. 112); issue: I–Katherine Waller (1 above); II–James Finnie (1885-1903); III–Emma Finnie (*b* 1887; *m* 1925, Henry Whiting McIlwaine); IV–William Waller, Jr. (*b* 1889; *m* 1915, Eliza Hamilton Nelson).

1–A.B., U.Tenn., '02 (Chi Omega); A.B., Smith Coll., 1903. Served overseas with Y.W.C.A., Feb. 1919-May 1920. Mem. C.D.A., D.A.R., U.D.-C., I.A.G., A.A.U.W. Presbyterian. Democrat. Club: Cherokee Country. Residence: 1705 W. Clinch Av., Knoxville, Tenn.

1–**CARSON, Eliza Louisa Boone (Mrs. Roger T.),** *b* Mobile, Ala., Sept. 27, 1875.

7–George **Boone** (qv);

6–Squire (1696-1765), of Rowan Co., N.C.; removed to Holman's Ford, on the Yadkin River, N.C., 1748; *m* 1720, Sarah Morgan (parents of Daniel Boone);

5–George (1739-1820), of Rowan Co., N.C.; Am. Rev.; *m* 1764, Nancy Linville (1744-1814; William[6] [*d* 1766], *m* Ellender [*d* 1766], dau. of Morgan Bryan [1671-1763], *m* 1719, Martha Strode, *d* 1747);

4–William Linville (1768-1847), of Shelby Co., Ky.; lt. War 1812; *m* 1789, Nancy Grubbs;

3–Rev. Hampton L. (1802-51), of Fayette, Mo.; *m* 1822, Marie Louisa Roberts (1805-70);

2–Thomas A. (2 below).

11–John **Morgan,** of Caerleon, 2d son of Sir Thomas Morgan, called of Pencoyd, (*b* 1519); *m* 1st, Elizabeth, dau. of Lewis ap Richard Gwyn, of Van;

10–William (*d* 1592), created first Baronet of Llantarnam; purchased the grange of Ceven Vynoche and Llantarnam Abbey, 1553; sheriff, 1568; M.P. for County, 1571; *m* Lady Frances Somerset, of Llantarnam;

9–Sir Edward, 2d Baronet of Llantarnam (1562-1653), *m* 1st, Mary, dau. of Sir Francis Engelfield; *m* 2d, Frances (Morgan) Lewis;

8–Sir James, 4th Baron of Llantarnam; non juror as late as 1675; *m* 2d, Lady Alice Hopton, of Canon-Frome, cousin of 1st wife;

7–Edward, joined the Soc. of Friends of Haverford, Radnor and Merion monthly meetings and lived nr. Gwynedd, then in Phila. Co. (now Montgomery Co.), Pa.; *m* Margaret–;

6–Sarah (1700-77), *m* Squire **Boone** (6 above).

10–William **Claibourne** (qv);

9–Mary, as Widow Rice, *m* 2d, 1650, Maj. Robert **Harris** (1630-1700);

8–Col. William (1652-87), of Weyanoke, Va.; *m* Temperance Overton (William[9], *m* Mary Walters);

7–Maj. Robert (1689-1765), of Albemarle Co., Va.; *m* 1720, Mourning Glenn;

6–James (1722-92), of Albemarle Co.; *m* Mary Harris (1725-90);

5–Lucy, *m* Higgason **Grubbs** (*d* 1830; William[6]);

4–Nancy (1771-1835), *m* William L. **Boone** (4 above);

3–Hampton L., *m* Marie Louisa Roberts (3 above);
2–Thomas Allen (1841-94), lawyer, Mobile, Ala.; *m* 1866, Ophelia Ann Turner (*b* 1843); issue: I–Eliza Louisa (1 above); II–Florence Armide (*b* 1876; *m* Dr. B. T. Huston); III–Thomas Allen (*b* 1879; *m* Corinna Griffith, *d* 1923); IV–Henry Stockton (*b* 1881; *m* Mary Champion); V–Capt. B. B. (*b* 1883; *m* Dorethea Harris); VI–Corinne Evelina (*b* 1886; *m* Joseph B. Hollon).
1–*m* Jan. 20, 1910, Roger Taney Carson, *b* Fayette, Mo., Mar. 23, 1864; son of Maj. George Hampton Carson (*d* 1918), of Fayette, Mo.; issue: 1–Helen Boone, *b* Fayette, Mo., Feb. 27, 1911; ed. U.Ariz.; U.Southern Calif.; *m* Oct. 12, 1927, Willis C. Royall (issue: Willis Calhoun, Jr.); 2–Eloise Lanter, *b* Fayette, Oct. 11, 1915.
1–Mem. D.A.R., Boone Family Assn. (state dir.). Episcopalian. Democrat. Residence: 1014 E. 5th St., Tucson, Ariz.

1–**CARTER, Marion Williams Pierce (Mrs. Miles Leach),** *b* Attleboro, Mass., May 24, 1867.
9–Aquila **Chase** (qv);
8–Thomas (*b* 1654), oath of allegiance, Newbury, Mass., 1678; served in King Philip's War; *m* 1677, Rebecca Follansbee (*d* ante 1713; Thomas[9], *m* Mary–);
7–Mary (*b* 1694/95), of Newbury, Mass.; *m* 1719, John **Horton,** Jr. (*b* 1696; John[8], corpl. King William's War, *m* Mehitable Garnsey; Thomas[9], Thomas[10], qv);
6–Ruth (*b* 1720), of Rehoboth, Mass.; *m* 1738, George **Round** (1718-91), Am. Rev. (George[7], *m* Susanna Cole; John[8]);
5–Chase (1746-1821), dea. of Baptist Ch. of Rehoboth for 46 yrs.; *m* 1st, 1767, Mary Mason (1750-67);
4–Mary (1767-1849), *m* 1785, Barnard **Pierce** (1764-1842);
3–Jeremiah (1786-1837), *m* 1806, Candace Wheeler;
2–Alfred (2 below).
9–John **Wheeler** (*d* ca. 1669), from Eng. in the "Mary and John," to Salisbury, Mass., 1634; settled at Hampton, N.H., later at Essex, Mass.; *m* 1611, Anne Yeoman (*d* 1662);
8–Henry (ca. 1634-1696), *m* ca. 1658, Abigail Allen (William[9], of Salisbury, 1639, *m* Ann Goodale);
7–James (1667-1753), *m* ca. 1690, Grizel Squire (Philip[8], of Boston, *m* Rachel Ruggles);
6–Col. Philip (1698-1765), *m* ca. 1720, Martha Salisbury (William[7], of Swansea, *m* Hannah Cole);
5–Capt. Philip (1733-74), *m* 1750, Mary Ingalls (1734-78; Benjamin[6], *m* Mercy Jencks);
4–Corpl. Shubael (1757-1812), *m* 1781, Chloe Martin (1764-1850; Lt. Daniel[5], of Rehoboth, *m* Rebecca Horton);
3–Candace (1789-1882), *m* Jeremiah **Pierce** (3 above).
9–John **Brown** (qv);
8–Capt. John (ca. 1623-1662), also called lt.; mem. militia, Rehoboth, 1647; ens., 1653, 54; *m* 2d, Lydia Buckland (William[9], *m* Mary Bosworth);
7–Capt. Joseph (1658-1731), at Kingston, 1702; at Attleboro, 1709; rep., Attleboro, 1712,26,28; selectman, 1712,13,14,15,25; dep., 1718; *m* 1680, Hannah Fitch (1662-1739; John[8], *m* Mary–);
6–Benjamin (1694-1742), *m* 1719, Sarah Freeman (Ralph[7], of Attleboro, *m* Mary–);
5–Christopher (1734-1796), *m* 1756, Esther Perry;
4–Anne (*b* 1758), *m* 1778, John **Williams** (*b* 1753), drummer, Am. Rev. (Theophilus[5]; Thomas[6]; Thomas[7]);
3–Thomas (1791-1864), *m* 1816, Polly Richardson;
2–Martha Richardson (2 below).
8–Samuel **Richardson** (qv);
7–Stephen (1649-1717/18), *m* 2d, 1674/75, Abigail Wyman (ca. 1660-1720; Francis[8], qv);
6–William (*b* 1678), removed to Stoneham; *m* 1703, Rebecca Vinton (*b* 1683; John[7], *m* Hannah, dau. Thomas Green; John[8]);
5–William;
4–Abiathar, *m* Martha Faulkner;
3–Polly (1794-1881), *m* Thomas **Williams** (3 above);
2–Martha Richardson (1837-1909), *m* 1865, Alfred **Pierce** (1822-1919), contractor (see Vol. II, p. 71, for Pierce and other lineages).
1–*m* June 30, 1892, Miles Leach Carter (see Vol. II, p. 71); issue: 1–Bernadetta Richardson, *b* Attleboro, Mass., Dec. 6, 1904; grad. Gorham Normal, '29.
1–Ed. Abbott Acad.; Lasell Sem.; Cowles Art Sch. Art teacher, Danbury, Conn., 1894-99, Attleboro, Mass., 1899-1922. Mem. D.A.C., S.D.-P. (gov. R.I.), D.C.W., D.F.P.A., D.A.R. (regent), I.A.G. Clubs: North Purchase, Woman's, Alpha Whist, League for Girls and Women, Keramic (Providence, R.I.). Summer Home: Westport Point, Mass. Residence: 325 S. Main St., Attleboro, Mass.

JOHN HOPEWELL (b Greenfield, Mass., Feb. 2. 1845-d Washington, D.C., Mar. 28, 1916); entered employ of L. C. Chase & Co., manufacturers of saddlery and robes, Springfield, Mass., as a youth, became a partner in 1875, and the senior partner, 1885-1916; was also director Sanford (Me.) Mills, Reading Rubber Mfg. Co., First Nat. Bank of Boston, and pres. Electric Goods Mfg. Co., Canton, Mass.

1–**CASSELBERRY, Mabel Gertrude Hopewell (Mrs. Clarence Marmaduke),** *b* Cambridge, Mass., Oct. 14, 1878.
10–Gov. William **Bradford,** Mayflower Pilgrim (qv);
9–Maj. William (1624-1704), of Plymouth, Mass.; *m* 1652, Alice Richards (*d* 1671);
8–Alice (1662-1745), *m* 1680, Rev. William **Adams** (1650-85), of Ipswich, Mass.;
7–Alice (1682-1735), *m* 1701, Rev. Nathaniel **Collins** (1681-1758; Rev. Nathaniel[8], of Middletown; Edward[9], qv);
6–John (*b* 1704), removed to Enfield, Conn.; *m* 1728, Mary Meachen (*b* 1706);
5–Ariel (1737-1820), *m* 1762, Mary Stebbins (1739/40-1810);
4–Hannah (1777-1819), *m* 1800, Jonathan **Pease** (1778-1839), of Enfield, Conn.;
3–Betsey Collins (1813-46), *m* 1836, Charles **Blake** (1811-98), of Springfield, Mass.;
2–Sarah Warriner (1844-1919), *m* 1870, John **Hopewell** (1845-1916), of Springfield, Mass.; issue: I–Charles Frederick (*m* Vera Sarah Stiebel); II–Frank Blake (*m* Helen Clark); III–Mabel Gertrude (1 above); IV–Nellie Harriet (1881-1920; *m* Clarence Conant Colby); V–Henry Chase (*m* Hilda Prince).
1–*m* June 5, 1906, Dr. Clarence Marmaduke Casselberry, *b* Pottstown, Pa., Oct. 5, 1875; son of Marmaduke Burr Casselberry, of Pottstown.
1–Ed. priv. school. Mem. S.M.D., D.A.C., D.F.-P.A., D.C.W., D.A.R., N.E.H.G.S. Trustee Roxbury Home for Aged Women. Evangelical Lutheran. Republican. Clubs: Brae Burn Country, Mass. Republican, Community. Residence: 188 Franklin St., Newton, Mass.

1–**CARTER, Nellie Estes (Mrs. Jacob Monroe),** *b* Boston, Tex., Apr. 4, 1872.

4–Benjamin **Estes** (will recorded 1816), of Bedford Co., Va.; *m* 1791, Selah Thorpe;
3–William (*b* Bedford Co., Va., 1792), sgt., q.m., p.m. in War 1812; *m* Susan Shelton (Thomas[4], of Pittsylvania Co., Va.);
2–Benjamin Thomas (2 below).
4–Daniel **Hicks,** *m* Mary–;
3–Jesse Hair (1805-71), *m* 1827, Mary Wilson B. Dickins;
2–Jessie Annabella (1835-1910), *m* 1858, Benjamin Thomas **Estes** (1830-1902), judge 5th judicial dist., Tex.; issue: I–Jesse Hicks (1865-1910); II–Sue Dickins (1867-95); III–William Lee (*b* 1870; *m* Annie Poindexter Dunn); IV–Nellie (1 above); V–Benjamin Thomas, Jr. (*b* and *d* 1875).
1–*m* Jacob Monroe Carter, *b* Pike Co., Ark., Oct. 5, 1865; judge 5th Dist., Ark.; son of William Henry Carter, of Pike Co.; issue (all *b* Texarkana, Ark.): 1–Benjamin Estes, *b* Nov. 1, 1893; Harvard, '16, law sch., 1922; served as 2d lt. 5th F.A., U.S.A., on Mexican border, 1916; 1st lt., 1917, capt. 1918; with A.E.F. in France, 1918; participated in campaigns at Verdun, 2d Marne, St. Mihiel, Meuse-Argonne; adj. 12th F.A., on staff of chief of arty., 1st Army, etc.; *m* Sept. 26, 1923, Hilda, dau. of Frank O. Arnoldson, of Belmont, Mass. (issue: Lydia Carter); 2–Jacob Monroe, *b* Nov. 24, 1894; Harvard, '17; *m* Dec. 30, 1922, Pauline Almedia, dau. Paul Robert Booker (issue: Juliette Nelle); 3–Jesse Hicks, *b* Apr. 29, 1900; U.S.N.-A., 1921; lt. U.S.N.; *m* Dec. 11, 1920, Marie, dau. Clarence Duane Allen; 4–Nellie Maxey, *b* Feb. 17, 1906; U. of Tex., '29.
1–Ed. Augusta Female Sem., Staunton, Va. Served in canteen and hosp. supply dept., A.R.C., during World War. Mem. C.D.XIIC., D.A.R., U.S.D. 1812, U.D.C., A.L. Auxiliary, etc. Residence: 700 Hickory St., Texarkana, Ark.

1–**CASTLE, George Parmelee,** *b* Honolulu, Hawaii, Apr. 29, 1851.
37–Alpin, King of Scotland;
36–Kenneth, I, King of Scotland, A.D. 850-60;
35–Constantine, II, King of Scotland, A.D. 864-877;
34–Donald, VI, King of Scotland, A.D. 889-900;
33–Malcolm, I, King of Scotland, A.D. 942-54;
32–Kenneth, III, King of Scotland, A.D. 971-95;
31–Malcolm, II, King of Scotland, A.D. 1005-34;
30–Docha, *m* Finleg;
29–Macbeth, King of Scotland, slain by Malcolm, III;
28–Donald, VII, Bane, King of Scotland, 1093 (*d* 1098);
27–Bethoca;
26–Hexilda, *m* Sir William **Cummin,** Chamberlain of King William;
25–William;
24–Sir Richard, a great benefactor to the monks of Kelso, etc.;
23–Sir William, Earl of Buchan, *m* Margaret, dau. of Fergus, Earl of Buchan;
22–Alexander **Cumyn,** Earl of Buchan (*d* 1289), one of the six regents of Scotland, 1286; *m* Elizabeth de Quincey (desc. Charlemagne);
21–Agnes, *m* Sir Gilbert **d'Umfraville,** 8th Earl of Angus (*d* 1307-08);
20–Robert (*d* A.D. 1274-1326), 9th Earl of Angus, *m* Alianore;
19–Sir Thomas, of Harbottle Castle, Northumberland; *m* Joan, dau. of Adam Rodam;
18–Sir Thomas, lord of Riddlesdale and Kyme; *m* Agnes;
17–Lady Joan, *m* Sir William **Lambert,** of Owlton, Durham and Harbottle Castle, Northumberland;
16–Robert, of Owlton;
15–Henry (living A.D. 1447), of Ongar, Essex;
14–Elizabeth, *m* Thomas **Lyman,** of Navistoke, Essex, ca. 1488;
13–Henry, of Navistoke and High Ongar, Essex, A.D. 1517; *m* Alicia, dau. of Simon Hyde;
12–John (*d* 1587, Navistoke), of High Ongar; *m* Margaret, dau. of William Gerard;
11–Henry (*d* 1609), of High Ongar; *m* Phillis, dau. of John Scott, of Navistoke;
10–Richard (1580-1640), from Eng. in the "Lion," with his wife and children, to Boston, 1631; freeman, 1633; an original propr. of Hartford, Conn., 1636; *m* in Eng., Sarah, dau. Roger Osborne;
9–Richard (*d* June 3, 1662), of Northampton, Mass.; *m* Hepzibah Ford (Thomas[10]);
8–Sarah, *m* John **Marsh** (John[9], *m* Ann, dau. of Gov. John Webster);
7–Sarah, *m* Lt. John **Merrill** (1669-1748; Dea. John[8], *m* Sarah Watson, of Hartford; Nathaniel[9], of Newbury, Mass.);
6–Ebenezer;
5–Hannah, *m* Ebenezer **Griswold**;
4–Hannah (*b* Norwich, Conn., Aug. 23, 1754-*d* Sudbury, Vt., Feb. 20, 1833), *m* Jesse **Tenney** (*b* Norwich, Conn., Apr. 20, 1741-*d* Sudbury, Vt., Jan. 8, 1815), pvt. Am. Rev. 1780-81;
3–Dea. Levi (*b* Bennington, Vt., Feb. 22, 1781-*d* New Lisbon, N.Y., Aug. 9, 1869), lived at Plainfield and West Exeter, N.Y.; soldier War 1812; paymaster, 1817; q.m., 1818, 135th Regt., N.Y. Militia; ch. dea.; justice of the peace; *m* Mary Kingsbury (*b* Rindge, N.H., Mar. 21, 1783-*d* Plainfield, N.Y., May 17, 1853);

HON. SAMUEL NORTHRUP CASTLE (1808-94), and MARY (TENNEY) CASTLE (1819-1907).

2–Mary (1819-1907), *m* 1842, as his 2d wife, Hon. Samuel Northrup **Castle** (see Vol. II, p. 282, for issue and other lineages); see portrait.
1–*m* Oct. 17, 1879, Ida Mary Tenney, *b* Plainfield, N.Y., June 30, 1856; dau. of Lucian Pomeroy Tenney of Plainfield; issue: 1–Dorothy, *b* Honolulu, H.T., Dec. 28, 1882; 2–Margaret Tenney (Mrs. Alfred Marston Tozzer, see Vol. II, p. 282, for maternal Tenney lineage).
1–Ed. Punahou Sch., Honolulu, U.Mich., 1 yr., and Detroit Med. Sch. Capitalist, educationist, philanthropist. Mem. Advisory Council Rep. of Hawaii. Entered firm of Castle & Cooke, Honolulu, 1875, becoming a partner, 1882, v.p. 1894-1903, pres. 1903-16, and again v.p. from 1916; also dir. First Nat. Bank of Hawaii and First Am. Savings & Trust Co. Mem. S.A.R., etc. Address: P.O. Box 2990, Honolulu, H.T.
"Although the above record ends with one individual, George Parmelee Castle, it must be remembered that among the many others who can claim this descent also, are all of the descendants of Jesse Tenney, Dea. Levi Tenney, Samuel Northrup Castle and his first and second wives, Angeline and Mary Tenney Castle, and many others too numerous to mention."

1–**CASTLE, William Ernest,** *b* Alexandria, O., Oct. 25, 1867.
8–Henry **Castle** (1613-1697/98), from Eng. in the "Transport," to Va., 1635; settled finally at Woodbury, Conn., ca. 1673; *m* 1666, Abigail Fitch (*d* 1725; Daniel[9]; Abraham[10]);
7–Isaac (1672-1727), of Woodbury, Conn.; *m* Sarah Adams (*d* 1708; Samuel[8], Fairfield and Woodbury, *m* Mary Meeker); *m* 2d, 1715, Joanna (Richardson) Warner (*b* 1683; Sgt. Thomas

Richardson[8], *m* Mary Senior, widow of Daniel Warner);
6–Samuel (1704-81), of Roxbury, Conn.; in French and Indian War; *m* Martha–;
5–David (1725-1823), Jericho, Vt.; *m* 1747, Phebe Sanford (*d* 1820);
4–Abel (1749-1848), Essex, Vt.; served in Am. Rev.; *m* 3d, 1787, Sarah Woodworth (1754-95);
3–Augustus (1791-1880), Granville, O.; pvt. War 1812; *m* 1st, 1816, Almira Lane;
2–William Augustus (2 below).
4–Gen. Elias **Fassett** (1771-1822);
3–Harry, M.D. (1794-1872), from Cambridge, Vt., to Johnstown, O.; *m* Clarissa Peck (1803-90), of Johnstown;
2–Sarah (1835-1929), *m* 1854, William Augustus **Castle** (1824-1910), farmer, school teacher, township trustee; issue: I–Clarence Fassett (*b* 1856; *m* Mary Shirk); II–Albert Aubrey (1859-1903); III–Edward Howard (1865-1929); IV–William E. (1 above); V–Mary (*b* 1871); VI–Walter (*b* 1877; *m* Anna Patt).
1–*m* Aug. 18, 1896, Clara Sears Bosworth, *b* Wellsville, Kan., Oct. 3, 1870; dau. of Charles Bosworth, from Warren, O., to Wellsville, Kan., 1869, *m* Mary Sears of Warren, O.; issue (all *b* Cambridge, Mass.): 1–William Bosworth, *b* Oct. 21, 1897; Harvard, ex-'18, M.D., 1921; pvt. Medical R.C., Dec. 17, 1917-Dec. 1918; 2–Henry Fassett (July 23, 1900-Nov. 20, 1919); 3–Edward Sears, *b* Dec. 25, 1903; A.B., Harvard, '25, Ph.D., 1929.
1–A.B., Denison, '89; A.B., Harvard, '93, A.M., 1894, Ph.D., 1895, (LL.D., Denison, 1921; Sc.D., U.Wis., 1921). Instr. vertebrate anatomy, U.Wis., 1895-96; instr. biology, Knox, 1896-97; instr. zoology, Harvard, 1897-1903, asst. prof., ibid, 1903-08, prof., ibid, 1908–. Mem. Nat. Acad. Sciences, etc. Author (see Who's Who in America). Residence: 186 Payson Rd., Belmont, Mass.

1–**CATHCART, Arthur Warren,** *b* Washington, D.C., June 17, 1857.
3–James Leander **Cathcart** (1765-1843; son of Malcolm Hamilton, who came to America ca. 1768, and returned to Ireland 1771); came from Ireland 1771, settled at Philadelphia, Pa.; midshipman on the "Confederacy," 1779; in 1785 he was clk. on the schooner "Maria," Captain I. Stephens, of Boston bound for Cadiz when the vessel was captured by pirates and taken to Algiers, where he was sold as a slave; apptd. Christian sec. to the dey and regency of Algiers, 1792; released 1796; apptd. U.S. consul for Tripoli by President Adams, 1797; apptd. consul for Algiers, 1802; commd. consul for Madeira, 1806; apptd. consul for Cadiz, Spain, 1815; clk. 2d comptroller's office, U.S. Treasury, 1824-43; *m* 1798, Jane Bancker Woodside (1783-1844);
2–Thomas Jefferson (2 below).
4–Thomas **Barclay** (1756-1833), from Ireland to America, 1775, when he enlisted in Am. Rev. from Newcastle Co., Del.; lived in Del., Pa., Md., Va. and Washington, D.C.; clk. in the first auditor's office in the Treasury; *m* — (*d* 1826);
3–John Davidson (1790-1870), non-commd. officer in Capt. Davidson's Co., comd. by Brig. Gen. Smith, served in Battle of Bladensburg, discharged Sept. 21, 1814; sgt. Union Light Inf., Oct. 1814; assessor, 1815; sec. sch. bd., 1816; councilman, 1817; alderman, 1836,40; mem. Union Fire Co.; dir. Fireman's Ins. Co.; justice of the peace; trustee of public schs.; clk. in the treasury; apptd. chief clk. in the office of the commr. of customs, 1849; apptd. to act as commr. in the absence of the commissioner of customs by Presidents Filmore, Pierce, Buchanan and Lincoln, 1850-64; *m* 1814, Ann Atmore Woodside;
2–Annie Reynolds (2 below).
8–Gerrit **Bancker** (*d* 1691), from Holland ante 1655; settled at Albany, N.Y., 1657; prosperous Indian trader and mcht.; *m* 1658, Elizabeth Van Eps (Dirk[9], *m* Maritie Damiens);
7–Evert (1665-1734), rep. in 9th Colonial Assembly, 1702; mayor of Albany; *m* 1686, Elizabeth Abeel;
6–Adrianus or Adrian (1703-72), *m* 1729, Gertrude Elizabeth Van Tearling (*b* 1709; Floris[7], gov. of Dutch Guiana);
5–Jannetie (*b* 1735), *m* 1758, James **Duthie;**
4–Elizabeth (*b* 1759), *m* 1778, Capt. John **Woodside** (1749-1835), commd. lt. by Cont. Congress, 1776, served in 3d Pa. Regt., Cont. troops; taken prisoner by the British; exchanged, 1778, and annexed to the 9th Pa. Regt.; called into service in N.J., 1780, as "capt.-lt.," 1st Regt., Pa. Arty.; hon. discharged 1785; clk. U.S. Treas. Dept., Phila., 1785; served in comptroller's office, 1790 (John[5], of Phila., *m* Elizabeth–);
3–Ann Atmore (1790-1835), *m* John D. **Barclay** (3 above);
2–Annie Reynolds (1828-1915), *m* 1855, Thomas Jefferson **Cathcart** (1825-60), chief clk., 2d comptroller's U.S. Treasury; issue: I–Arthur Warren (1 above); II–Amelia Eliza (1859-1916); III–Edith H. (1860-63).
1–*m* Oct. 27, 1886, Mary Arline Corbett, *b* nr. Ballston, Va., Dec. 19, 1866; dau. of Virgil P. Corbett, of nr. Ballston; issue: 1–Ethel May (Sept. 14, 1887-Feb. 28, 1902); 2–Paul Hamilton, *b* Ballston, Va., July 9, 1893; A.B., George Washington, '20; *m* Nov. 2, 1926, Marion Hastings, dau. of Francis Marion Patterson, of Washington; 3–Robert Malcolm, *b* Ballston, Oct. 6, 1896; *m* June 16, 1928, Karren Elizabeth, dau. of Carl F. Nelson, of Kansas City, Mo.; 4–Ruth Arline, *b* Phila., Pa., Oct. 20, 1903; studied at Corcoran Art. Sch.; Beaver Coll., Jenkintown, Pa.
1–Spencerian Business Coll., 1876; Corcoran Scientific Sch. of Columbian Coll., 1886. Started as machinist with Monotype Machine Co., 1887, supt., 1898; v.p. Corbett Bros. Co., N.Y. City, 1907; started building and selling suburban houses on his land, 4 miles south-west of Washington, D.C., 1909, now retired. Treas. of ch. trustees. Mem. S.A.R. Presbyterian. Democrat. Residence: Ballston, Arlington Co., Va.

1–**CATTLE, Claudine Mercedes Brown (Mrs. Robert Turner),** *b* Kansas City, Mo., Dec. 31, 1889.
10–Adam (Thorogood, Thoroughgood) **Thorowgood** (qv);
9–Ann (*b* Stafford Co., Eng.-*d* Va., 1669), *m* Col. Gerard **Fowke** (1606-71), mem. Va. and Md. House of Burgesses, 1663, 1665; justice for Charles Co. Md., 1667; col. of co. militia, Westmoreland Co., Va.;
8–Col. Gerard (1662-1734), of Charles Co.; *m* 2d, Sarah Burdett, of Charles Co.;
7–Frances (1691-1744), of Charles Co.; *m* 1710, Dr. Gustavus **Brown** (1689-1762), from Scotland to Md., 1708; vestryman of Port Tobacco Parish and asso. judge of Charles Co. Ct., 1755;
6–Rev. Richard (1725-89), of Md., and Va.; rector of King and Queen Parish, St. Mary's Co., Md.; ed. Scotland; ordained by Lord Bishop of London, 1750; *m* ca. 1750, Helen Bailey;
5–John (1760-1816), of Md., and Va.; *m* Susan Pearson Alexander (1762-post 1845; John[6] [1711-63], *m* Susanna Pearson; Robert[7]; Robert[8]; Capt. John[9]; John[10]);
4–William Bailey Clark (1799-1879), of Va. and Ky.; removed to Lafayette Co., Mo., ca. 1845; *m* 1824, Matilda Fontaine;
3–Dr. James Terrell (1827-87), of Ky., and Independence, Mo.; pres. Brown, Hughes & Co. (now First Nat. Bank), of Independence; *m* 1856, Susan Hannah Biggerstaff (ca. 1840-87; John[4], *m* Hannah Oldhan);
2–William Bailey Clark (2 below).
7–Rev. Peter **Fontaine** (1691-1757), from Eng., to Va., 1715; rector of Westover Parish, Va., 40 yrs.; *m* 2d, Elisabeth Wade;
6–Aaron (1753-1823), of Va. and Ky.; *m* 1773, Barbara Overton Terrell (1756-ca. 1796; Richmond[7], *m* Ann Overton);
5–James Terrell (1776-1840), *m* 1799, Deborah Hobb (1776-1867; Joseph[6], of Md. and Ky., *m* Ann Maynard);
4–Matilda (1803-76), *m* William Bailey Clark **Brown** (4 above).
9–John **Nutting,** *m* Woburn, Mass., 1650, Sarah Eggleton (Eggleden, Iggleden);
8–Sarah (*b* 1663), *m* 1681, Matthias **Farnsworth,** Jr. (1649-ca. 1693);
7–Josiah (1687-1744), *m* 1719/20, Mary Pierce (*b* 1696);
6–James (*b* 1727), in Capt. Humphrey Hobb's Co. Rangers, Indian war, 1748; mem. Com. Safety, Charlestown, N.H.; lt., capt. Am.

Rev., from Charlestown; m Susanna– (1730-56);
5–Susanna (1756-post 1787), m at Unity, N.H., 1782, Joseph **Weed** (b Kingston, N.H., 1760-d post 1787);
4–James (1787-1850), m 1814, Hannah Currier;
3–Harriette Irene (1829-1903), of Kendall and Murray, N.Y., and Seward, Neb.; m 1859, Claudius **Jones** (1826-96), of Kendall, N.Y.; removed to Seward, Neb., 1872, where he was a pioneer banker; founded first bank in Seward Co.;
2–Anna Bell (2 below).
9–Aquila **Chase** (qv);
8–Moses (1663-1743), of W. Newbury; m 1684, Anne Follansbee (ca. 1668-1708);
7–Samuel (1690-ca. 1743), of Newbury; m 1713, Hannah Emery;
6–Francis (b 1715), m 1737, Sarah Pike (Hugh[7]);
5–Sarah (1749/50-1840), of Unity and Newton, N.H.; m ca. 1770, Abner **Currier** (1745-92), Am. Rev.; selectman and signer of assn. test, Unity, N.H.;
4–Hannah (1790-1891), m James **Weed** (4 above);
3–Harriette I., m Claudius **Jones** (3 above);
2–Anna Bell (1869-1918), of Chicago, Ill., Seward, Neb., and Kansas City, Mo.; m 1888, William Bailey Clark **Brown** (1861-1920), grad. Westminster Coll., Fulton, Mo.; studied law at Harvard; lawyer, Kansas City; judge ct. of bankruptcy; issue: I–Claudine Mercedes (1 above); II–Sue Irene (b 1891; m Robert Babson [d 1929], son of Charles Sumner Alling, m Annie P. Babson).
1–m June 19, 1912, Robert Turner Cattle, b Seward, Neb., July 5, 1889; son of Walter Cattle; issue (all b Seward, Neb.): 1–[illegible]bert Turner, Jr., b Jan. 21, 1914; 2–William [illegible]alter (Nov. 15, 1915-Dec. 23, 1917); 3–John [illegible]ed, b July 11, 1918; 4–Walter, b July 6, 1921; [illegible]-Sarah Fontaine, b Jan. 6, 1926; 6–Dorothy Anne, b Sept. 28, 1928.
1–Attended Mary Baldwin Sem., Staunton, Va. Mem. D.A.R., H.S.A. Episcopalian. Residence: Seward, Neb.

1–**CAVERT, Abba Lincoln Shepard (Mrs. Charles F.),** b Rainbow, O., Nov. 22, 1862.
9–Ralph **Shepard** (qv);
8–Thomas (1635-1719), m Hannah Ensign;
7–Thomas (1665-1726), m Hannah Blanchard;
6–Thomas (1692-1775), m Sarah Hotchkiss;
5–Jacob (1742-1813), m Patience Bradley;
4–Jacob (1773-1820), m Phoebe Pauline Kidder; m 2d, Sarah Wright;
3–Courtland (1800-83), m 1824, Hannah Lake;
2–Thomas Lake (2 below).
5–Archibald **Lake** (b in Eng.), m 1762, Mary Bird (1742-1802);
4–Andrew (1769-1849), m 1797, Elizabeth Goss (1778-1845);
3–Hannah (1807-83), m Courtland **Shepard** (3 above).
9–John **Woodruff** (qv);
8–John (1637-1703), m Sarah Ogden;
7–John (1665-1750), m Sarah Cooper;
6–David (1695-1749), m Eunice Ward;
5–Elias (1734-1802), m Mary Joline;
4–Abner (1764-1835), m Catherine Roll (1767-1837);
3–Elias (1793-1874), m Eleanor McGuire;
2–Elizabeth Jane (1831-97), m Thomas Lake **Shepard** (1827-1908), farmer; issue: I–Viola Celeste (1851-1911; m John Warren Reed, 1849-1912); II–Flora May (1853-81; m James Boyce); III–Harold Burton (1854-74); IV–Ida (1858-87); V–Salmon Chase (b 1861; m Florence Grace Racer); VI–Abba Lincoln (1 above); VII–Cortland Woodruff (b 1865; m Leah Alberta Adair); VIII–Eleanor (b 1867); IX–Edward Stanton (b 1869); X–Thomas (b and d 1871); XI–Preston Bird (b 1873; m Elizabeth LaMora King).
1–m Apr. 11, 1893, Charles Forward Cavert (1860-Oct. 6, 1914); son of James Cavert, m Ann Maria LeSeur; issue: 1–Esma Garnet, b Los Angeles, Calif., Aug 16, 1894; ed. Washburn Coll.; m Aug. 17, 1917, Earl J. Bush; 2–Shepard Lesseur (Jan. 29-Mar. 5, 1896); 3–Charles Darrell (Mar. 27-May 7, 1899).
1–Teacher, 1882-84; law student with Judge Horton of Kan., 1897; asst. registrar of deeds; genealogist. Mem. I.A.G. Unitarian. Republican. Residence: Chicago, Ill. Address: 245 Oak St., Columbus, O.

1–**CHACE, Arnold Buffum,** b Cumberland, R.I., Nov. 10, 1845.
8–William (Chase) **Chace** (qv);
7–William (1622-1684/85), a Quaker, from Eng. with his father, 1630; large landowner at Yarmouth, Mass.; m Mary–;
6–Joseph;
5–Job;
4–Jonathan;
3–Oliver (1769-1852), began to write name Chace; built the 2d cotton mill in America at Swansea, Mass., 1806; m Sarah Buffington;
2–Samuel Buffington (2 below).
8–Robert **Buffum** (qv);
7–Caleb (1650-1731), m 1672, Hannah Hope;
6–Benjamin (1686-1735), m Elizabeth Buxton;
5–Joseph (1717-96), m 1736, Margaret Osborne (b 1719; William[6]);
4–William (1741-1829), prominent anti-slavery advocate; m Lydia Arnold;
3–Arnold (1783-1859), abolitionist; 1st pres. Am. Anti-Slavery Soc.; m Rebecca Gould (desc. Daniel Gould, who was whipped on the Boston Common for being a Quaker);
2–Elizabeth (b 1806), m Samuel Buffington **Chace** (b 1800); issue: I–Arnold Buffum (1 above); II–Elizabeth (m —Wyman); III–Daughter.
1–m Oct. 24, 1871, Eliza Chace Greene, b Milton, Mass. (Mar. 2, 1851-Dec. 9, 1924); dau. of Christopher A. Greene, of Providence, R.I.; issue: 1–Arnold Buffum, Jr. (qv for maternal lineage); 2–Malcolm Greene, b Lincoln, R.I., Mar. 12, 1875; Ph.B., Yale-S., '96; m Apr. 15, 1903, Elizabeth, dau. of John Webley Edwards (issue: Malcolm G., Jr., b New York, N.Y., Jan. 13, 1904; Eliot, b Jan. 15, 1906, m July 6, 1929, James Cox Brady; Jane, b Providence, Aug. 27, 1909; Elizabeth, b Providence, Sept. 7, 1911; Arnold Buffum, b Hyannis, Mass., July 11, 1914); 3–Margaret Lillie, b Lincoln, R.I., Nov. 20, 1876; m Oct. 14, 1908, Russell Sturgis Rowland, M.D., of Detroit, Mich. (issue: Frances Lester, b Detroit, Mich., Oct. 22, 1909; Margaret Chace, b Detroit, Nov. 10, 1910; Sarah Greene, b Detroit, June 17, 1913; Arnold Chace, b Farmington, Mich., July 21, 1916); 4–Edward Gould, b Providence, R.I., Oct. 16, 1882; A.B., Williams, '05; m Oct. 17, 1906, Christine McLeod (issue: Christine, b Apr. 14, 1909; Eliza, b Jan. 21, 1913; Jessie, b Aug. 22, 1914).
1–A.B., Brown, '66, A.M., 1869 (Sc.D., 1892). Cotton mfr. Chancellor Brown U. (see Who's Who in America). Summer place: Albion, R.I. Residence: 99 Power St., Providence, R.I.

1–**CHADWICK, George Halcott,** b Catskill, N.Y., May 27, 1876.
7–Sgt. John **Chadwick** (1651-1707), of Malden, Boxford and Bradford, Mass.; m 1674, Mary Barlow (1652-1734; Edmund[8] [d 1674], of Cambridge, m Mary, dau. James Pemberton);
6–John (1677-1756), of W. Boxford, Mass.; m Mehitabel Hazeltine, or Hasseltine (1686-1748);
5–Dea. John (1720-97), Boxford; dea. 2d Congl. Ch., 1788-95; ens. 1762; m 1743, Susanna Peabody;
4–Dr. Edmund (1752-1826), ed. Oxford, Eng.; pvt. and surgeon Cont. Army, in battles of Ticonderoga, Saratoga and spent the winter at Valley Forge, 1777-78; settled at Deerfield, N.H., 1779; m 1779, Elizabeth Gookin;
3–Alexander Scammel (1789-1866), of Deerfield, N.H., later at Frankfort, 1816, and at Gardiner (now Farmingdale), Me., 1821; lt. in Battle of Ft. Erie, 1814; moderator, 1840-49; selectman, 1837-48; assessor; alderman; rep., 1832-35; m 1816, Hannah Kimball;
2–Nathaniel Kimball (2 below).
8–Lt. Francis **Peabody** (qv);
7–Capt. John (1642-1720), rep. Gen. Ct., from Boxford; m 1st, 1665, Hannah Andrews (Robert[8] [d 1668], m 1636, Grace–);
6–Ens. David (1678-1726), m Sarah Pope (1683-1756; Capt. Seth[7] [1648-1727], propr. Dartmouth, m Deborah [1654-1711], dau. Ezra Perry; Thomas[8], qv);
5–Susanna (1721-94), m John **Chadwick** (5 above).
8–Daniel **Gookin** (qv);
7–Rev. Nathaniel (1656-92), of Cambridge; m 1685, Hannah Savage (b 1667 or 77; Capt. Habijah[8] [d 1682], m 1661, Hannah [b 1640], dau. Maj. Gen. Edward Tyng [1600-81], m Mary Sears; Maj. Thomas[9], qv, m Faith, dau. William Hutchinson, qv);

6–Rev. Nathaniel (1687-1734), of Hampton, N.H., *m* 1711, Dorothy Cotton;
5–Rev. Nathaniel (1713-66), of N. Hampton, N.H.; *m* 1748, Love Wingate (*b* 1720; Col. Joshua[6] [1679-1769], of Newbury, *m* 1702, Mary Lunt [1682-1772; Henry[7] (*b* 1653), *m* Jane–; Henry[8] (*d* 1662), *m* Anne–]; John[7] [*d* 1687], *m* Mary, dau. Eld. Hatevil Nutter, 1604-75);
4–Elizabeth (1754-1816), of N. Hampton; *m* Dr. Edmund **Chadwick** (4 above).
10–Gov. Thomas **Dudley** (qv);
9–Ann (*d* 1672), the "First American poetess"; *m* 1628, Gov. Simon **Bradstreet** (qv);
8–Dorothy (1630-72), *m* 1654, Rev. Seaborn **Cotton** (1633-86; John[9], qv);
7–Rev. John (1658-1710), *m* 1686, Anne Lake (1663-1737; Capt. Thomas[8] [1615-75], killed by Indians, *m* Mary [*b* 1629], dau. Stephen Goodyear, qv);
6–Dorothy (1693-1748), *m* Rev. Nathaniel **Gookin** (6 above).
9–Edward **Colburn** (1618-1700), from Eng. in the "Defiance," 1635; *m* Hannah–;
8–Ezra (1658-1739), of Ipswich; *m* 1681, Hannah Varnum (*b* 1661; Samuel[9], *m* Sarah, dau. Roger Langton; George[10] [1594-1649], of Ipswich, *m* Hannah–);
7–Ezra (1685-ante 1716), *m* 1706, Lucy Nelson (*b* 1688/89; Capt. Philip[8] [1633-91], *m* 1666, Elizabeth Lowell [1648-1731; John[9] (1595-1647), *m* Elizabeth Goodale; Percival[10], qv]; Thomas[9] [*d* 1648], from Eng. 1638, freeman, Rowley, Mass., *m* Joan, daughter Thomas Dummer, of Badgeley Eng.);
6–Jeremiah (*b* 1710), Dracut, Mass.; *m* Sarah Jewett (Joseph[7] [*b* 1656]; Thomas[8]; Thomas[9]);
5–Sarah Elizabeth (1750-1821), *m* Maj. Henry (Hendrick Smidt) **Smith** (1738-1827), from Holland, 1747, settled at Pittston, Me., 1764; at Ticonderoga, and at Quebec under Gen. Wolfe in French War;
4–Sallie (1772-1811), *m* 1789, Nathaniel **Kimball**, from N.H.;
3–Hannah (1798-1862), of Pittston, Me.; *m* Alexander S. **Chadwick** (3 above).
11–William **Brown** (ca. 1600-1680), from Rusper, Sussex, Eng.;
10–Phebe (1622-64), as widow of Thomas Lee and Greenfield Larrabee, *m* 3d, "Mr." James **Cornish** (1612 or 15-1698?);
9–Dea. James (1663-1740), *m* 1693, Elizabeth Thrall (1667-1714; Timothy[10] [1641-97], *m* Deborah [1641-94], dau. of Thomas Gunn, of Dorchester, Mass.; William[11], qv);
8–Capt. James (1694-1784), *m* 1719, Amy Butler (*d* 1763; Thomas[9], of Hartford, Conn.);
7–Sgt. Elisha (1722-94), *m* 1740, Hepsibah Humphrey (1724-55; Charles[8]);
6–Capt. James (1744-1813), *m* 1766, Ruhama Bidwell (1743-1814);
5–Eber (1772-1849), *m* Elizabeth Lumice or Loomis (1772-1832), and removed to Lexington, Greene Co., N.Y.;
4–Eber, Jr. (1793-1867), soldier War 1812; *m* 1815, Ruth Vorse or Vorce (1795-1872; Charles[6] [1766-1856], drummer boy in Am. Rev., pensioned, *m* Lucretia– [ca. 1769-1844]; Corpl. Jesse[6] [1746-1818], Am. Rev., *m* 1766, Ruth Moss; Richard[7]; Mark[8]; Matthew Force[9], *m* 1667, Elizabeth Palmer);
3–Lucinda (1816-51), *m* 1838, George Washington **Halcott** (1817-83), of Lexington, N.Y., later removed to Catskill, N.Y. (Maj. John[4] [1758-*d* Halcott, N.Y., 1831], from Eng. during Am. Rev., served in Cont. Army, *m* 1790, Letitia Jenkins [*d* 1854, aet. 79] of Newburgh, N.Y.).
2–Nathaniel Kimball **Chadwick** (1822-1906), mcht. of Gardiner Me., Boston, Mass., and Catskill, N.Y.; *m* 1845, Martha Harris Chadwell (1825-70); *m* 2d, 1873, Celia Serena Halcott (*b* 1843); for issue see Vol. III, p. 523.
1–*m* Feb. 22, 1908, Bertha Elisabeth Ellwanger, *b* E. Henrietta, N.Y., June 24, 1875; dau. of William Gottlieb Ellwanger, of Rochester, N.Y.; issue: 1–Elizabeth Ellwanger, *b* Canton, N.Y., Feb. 5, 1909; 2–George Halcott, Jr., *b* Ogdensburg, N.Y., Aug. 1, 1913.
1–Ph.B., U.Rochester, '04 (Alpha Delta Phi; P.B.K.; Sigma Xi), M.S., 1907. Geologist; prof. St. Lawrence U., 1907-14, U.Rochester, 1914-1923; acting prof., Williams Coll., 1925-26, Vassar, 1929-30 (see Who's Who in America). Fellow Rochester Acad. Science (ex-pres.), A.A.A.S., Geol. Soc. America, Paleontol. Soc. America; pres. Greene Co. (N.Y.) Hist. and Geneal. Soc. Residence: 175 Bridge St., Catskill, N.Y.

1–**CHAFFEE, Mary Belle,** *b* Detroit, Mich., Jan. 13, 1875.
9–Thomas **Chaffee** (*d* 1683), from Eng.; was living at Hingham, Mass., 1635; *m* Dorothy–;
8–Joseph (1639-94), of Swansea, Mass.; *m* 1670, Annis Martin (*d* 1729/30; Richard[9], of Rehoboth, Mass., *d* 1695);
7–John (1673-1757), of Woodstock, Conn.; *m* 1700, Sarah Hills (*d* 1735; Gershom[8] [1631-bet. 1710 and 1721], *m* Elizabeth, dau. of John Chadwick, *m* Mary Barlow; Joseph[9], *m* Rose Clark; George[10], *m* Mary–);
6–Joseph (1701-02-1760), of S. Wilbraham, Mass.; *m* 1730, Hannah May (1704-87);
5–Comfort (1737-1811), of S. Wilbraham; Am. Rev.; *m* 1758, Mary Bliss;
4–Nathaniel Bliss (1772-1834), *m* 1795, Tabitha Chubbuck;
3–Joel (1806-40) of S. Wilbraham, and Rochester, N.Y.; *m* 1826, Melissa Sophronia Case;
2–Merrick Joel (2 below).
10–Thomas **Bliss** (qv);
9–Nathaniel (1621-54), of Springfield, Mass.; *m* 1646, Catherine Chapin (ante 1630-1712; Dea. Samuel[10], qv);
8–Samuel (1647-1749), of Longmeadow, Mass.; *m* 1671, Sarah Stebbins (1654-1721; Lt. Thomas[9], *m* Hannah Wright; Rowland[10], qv);
7–Nathaniel (1679-1751), of Wilbraham; *m* 1704, Mary Morgan (1686-1739; David[8], *m* Mary–);
6–Nathaniel (1704-71), of Wilbraham; *m* 1733, Priscilla Burt (1701-69; David[7] [1668-1735], *m* Martha Hale, dau. of Thomas Hale, *m* Priscilla Markham; Nathaniel[8], *m* Rebecca Sikes, dau. of Richard Sikes; Henry[9], qv);
5–Mary (1734-74), *m* Comfort **Chaffee** (5 above).
8–Thomas **Chubbuck** (*d* 1696), from Eng., and settled at Hingham, Mass.; living there in 1634;
7–John (*b* 1648), of Swansea, Mass.; selectman, 1679, and 1690; lt. in Phip's expdn.; *m* 1668, Martha Beal (Nathaniel[8], *m* Martha–);
6–Nathaniel (*b* 1686), of Wareham, Mass.; *m* 1707, Margaret Joy (*b* 1683; Joseph[7], *m* Mary Prince);
5–Ebenezer (1725-1810), of Wareham, and Ellington, Conn.; soldier French and Indian War; lt. in Am. Rev.; *m* —Burgess;
4–Tabitha (1775-1829), of Ellington, *m* Nathaniel Bliss **Chaffee** (4 above).
9–Dea. Samuel **Chapin** (qv);
8–Japhet (bap. 1642-1712), of Chicopee, Mass.; in Battle of Turner's Falls, 1676; dea. of ch. at Springfield, Mass.; *m* 1664, Abilenah Cooley (1642-1710; Samuel[9], qv);
7–Samuel (1665-1729), of Springfield; *m* 1690, Hannah Sheldon (1670-174–; Isaac[8], *m* Mary Woodford, of Northampton);
6–Samuel (1699-1779), of Ludlow, Mass.; *m* 1722/23, Anna Horton (*b* 1700; Jeremiah[7], *m* Mary Terry, of Springfield);
5–Jeremiah (1734-1814), of Granby, Mass., and Whitestown, N.Y.; Am. Rev.; *m* 1769, Caroline Fowler (1744-1811);
4–Paulina (1785-1869), of Granby, Mass.; *m* 1808, Seth **Case** (1785-1878), farmer and carpenter; War 1812;
3–Melissa Sophronia (1811-98), of Rochester, N.Y.; *m* 1826, Joel **Chaffee** (3 above);
2–Merrick Joel (1834-1907), chief clk., auditor's dept., Mich. Central R.R., Detroit; *m* 1857, Annie Love Clark (1838-1911); issue: I–George Otis (1860-64); II–William Frederick (*b* 1861; disappeared Oct. 1889); III–Merrick Joel, Jr. (1864-76); IV–Annie Maria (*b* 1866); V–Eugene Francis (1868-69); VI–Charles Herbert (*b* 1870; *m* Mary Cecelia Frauenfelder); VII–Ida Florence (*b* 1873; *m* Jonathan Chase); VIII–Mary Belle (1 above); IX–Grace Aurelia (1877-78).
1–Asst. in Detroit Public Library since 1901; asst. in Burton Hist. Collection of same since 1922. Mem. D.F.P.A. Baptist. Republican. Residence: 8904 Mackinaw Av., Detroit, Mich.

1–**CHAMBERLAIN, Orville Tryon,** *b* Leesburg, Ind., Sept. 1, 1841-*d* Prescott, Ariz., May 27, 1929.
8–Richard (Chamberlin) **Chamberlain** (*d* 1673), from Eng., first mentioned in N.E. in the "Register of Births and Burialls in Braintree from the yeare 1637 until the 1st month of

ORVILLE TRYON CHAMBERLAIN (1841-1929).

1644" wherein is recorded the birth of his son Richard, 1642; removed to Roxbury, where he is mentioned in the Roxbury land grant supposed to have been made ca. 1655; removed to Sudbury, 1667; *m* 2d, Sarah Bugbee (1630-bet. 1667-72; Edward[9], from Eng. in the "Francis," 1634);

7–Joseph (bap. 1655-1721), removed from Roxbury to Sudbury, 1667-68; enlisted in Capt. Jonathan Poole's co., which defended Hadley from an attack by Indians, 1675; served in Swamp Fight, 1675; served in "Falls Fight," 1676; returned to Sudbury, 1676; removed to Oxford, Mass., 1713; sr. mem. bd. selectmen, Oxford; *m* 1682, Hannah Gilbert:

6–Nathaniel (1689-1780), of Oxford; removed to Hatfield, 1722; served in Indian wars, 1725; at Arlington, N.H., 1743, Deerfield, 1744, Fall Town, 1755; served in French and Indian War; *m* 1st, 1714, Elizabeth Hunkins (bap. 1706-1737);

5–Moses (1716-96), of Northfield, Mass.; freeman, 1758; minute man in Am. Rev.; *m* ca. 1739, Jemima Wright (1717-1807; Remembrance[6], *m* Elizabeth–; Benjamin[7]; Sgt. Samuel[8]; Dea. Samuel[9]);

4–Wright (1758-1841), *b* Litchfield, Conn., *d* Gibson, Pa.; dea. Presbyn. Ch.; sgt., capt. Simon Stephen's Co., Newbury, Vt., under command of Col. Peter Olcott, 1779-81, Am. Rev.; *m* Hannah Heath (*d* 1797); *m* 2d, Sally Holdridge; *m* 3d, Mary (Polly) Billings; (Wright by his 3 marriages had 26 children, one of whom by 1st marriage was):

3–Milo (1785-ca. 1872), *d* Elkhart, Ind.; *m* 1st, 1807, Sally Cole (*b* 1791); *m* 2d, Widow Elizabeth Danforth (*d* Elkhart, Ind., ca. 1874); issue (2d marriage): I–Helena A. (*m* Dr. George H. Briggs); II–Eugenia A. (*m* —McWhorter, *d*); III–Maryetta (*d*; *m* David C. Payne); IV–Albert Napoleon (*d*; *m* Mary Sanders, *d*; issue: Albert, *d*; Laura [*d*; *m* George Evans, *d* and had issue: Russell and Wayne]; Garibaldi, *d*; Milo, *d*; Dean Swift, *d*; Mary [*d*, *m* Dr. John F. Werner and had issue: Dr. John Werner, Jr.]); V–Milo D.;

2–Dr. Joseph Wright (2 below).

9–Moses **Cleveland** (qv);

8–Samuel (1657-1735/36), sgt.; *m* 1680, Jane Keyes (1660-81); *m* 2d, 1682, Persis Hildreth (1660-98; Richard[9], *m* Elizabeth–);

7–Samuel (1685-1727), *m* 2d, 1719, Sarah Buswell (ca. 1699-post 1743; Robert[8], *m* Hannah Tyler);

6–David (*b* 1724), *m* 1744, Eunice Backus (1722-49); *m* 2d, 1750, Rebecca Tracy (*d* 1754), of Preston, Conn.;

5–Tracy (1751-1836), *m* 1773, Phebe Hyde (1748-1829; Jonathan[6], *m* Lucy Tracy);

4–Ruby (Arubah, Azubah), (1778-1845), *b* Canterbury, Conn., *d* Kirtland, O.; *m* 1st, at Pawlet, Vt., 1796, Zalmon **Castle,** a cabinet maker;

3–Minerva (1799-ca. 1870), *d* Michigan City, Ind.; *m* David **Tryon.**

DR. JOSEPH WRIGHT CHAMBERLAIN (1809-67), b at Gibson, Susquehanna Co., Pa.; was postmaster at Milford, Leesburg and Elkhart, Ind.; practiced medicine and surgery at Elkhart, 1843-67, and was an important factor in the development of that city.

2–Dr. Joseph Wright **Chamberlain** (1809-67) began to write name Chamberlain (see portrait and biography); *m* 1837, Caroline Tryon (1817-51), *b* Granville, N.Y.; *m* 2d, Oct. 31, 1853, Lydia A. Parmater (1818-79); issue (1st marriage): I–Orville T. (1 above); II–Sarah Minerva (Aug. 29, 1844-Jan. 5, 1917; *m* Oct. 17, 1865, Jacob S. Brown, *d* Oct. 27, 1906; issue: 1–Frederick J., *m* Mary Roy [issue: Sarah Margaret, *m* May 28, 1929, Warren Dart Reck; Jacob S.; William Roy; Barbara]; 2–Caroline Gertrude, *m* Harry B. Roberts, M.D.); III–Tully (ca. 1848-ca. 1872); IV–Helena Catherine (*b* Oct. 28, 1850; *m* May 3, 1870, Adrian D. Brown [Dec. 17, 1840-June 13, 1891; brother of Jacob S. Brown]; issue: 1–Guy C.; 2–Mabel C., *m* May 1898, J. C. Sipe, *d* [issue: Helena Rosa, Charles B., Carroll E.]; 3–Harold C., *m* Minnie–; 4–Thad C., *m* Mary– [issue: Dorothy, Charles]; 5–Carlotta C., *d*, *m* George Boesinger); issue (2d marriage): I–Caroline Emma (July 31, 1854-June 3, 1895; *m* 1874, John L. Bottorff, *d*; issue: 1–Joseph Livy Chamberlain, *m* Oct. 12, 1897, Inez I. Bentz [issue: Albert Joseph, *b* Dec 13, 1916]); II–Livy (Nov. 22, 1856-July 30, 1917; *m* Millicent Edwards).

1–*m* Sept. 1, 1869, Helen Maria Mead, *b* Lyons, Wayne Co., N.Y. (Aug. 28, 1843-May 31, 1911), dau. of Warren Washington Mead, *m* Susan Rogers Stearns; issue: 1–Edith, *b* Elkhart, Ind., Mar. 29, 1872; U.Mich.; *m* Oct. 12, 1897, Lt. Col. Louis Maltby, son of Rev. Franklin T. Simpson, D.D., *m* Lydia Ann Maltby.

1–U.Notre Dame, Ind., 1860-62 (hon. A.B., 1868). Enlisted as pvt. Co. G, 74th Ind. Vol. Inf., Aug. 6, 1862; hon. discharged as capt., June 9, 1865; awarded Congressional Medal of Honor. Lawyer, 1st city atty., Elkhart, Ind. Dist. Atty. (see Who's Who in America, Vol. 13). Mem. G.A.R., M.O.L.L., Legion of Valor. Address: 417 W. Franklin St., Elkhart, Ind.

1–**CHAMBERLAIN, William Henry,** *b* Kanona, N.Y., Aug. 15, 1866.

8–William **Chamberlain** (qv);

7–Jacob (1657/58-1712), *m* Experience (French?);

6–John (ca. 1694-1781), *m* Thankful Wilson (1693-1764);
5–Wilson (1724-91), soldier Am. Rev.; *m* 1748, Elizabeth Austin;
4–Joseph (1762-1800), soldier Am. Rev.; *m* 1786, Lucy Whitney;
3–Joseph (1790-1834), *m* 1813, Esther Wheeler;
2–Jesse Mark (2 below).
9–Richard **Austin** (qv);
8–Richard (1632-1703), *m* 1659, Abigail Bachelder (*d* 1693, aet. 57);
7–Joseph (1666-1739), *m* 1692 Elizabeth Pitts;
6–Joseph (1693-1756), *m* 1717, Joanna Call (*b* 1698; Thomas[7]; John[8]; Thomas[9]);
5–Elizabeth (1728-1776 or 77), *m* Wilson **Chamberlain** (5 above).
9–John **Whitney** (qv);
8–Benjamin (1643-1723), *m* Jane– (*d* 1690);
7–Jonathan (*b* 1680 or 81), *m* 1700, Susanna Fairbanks (*b* 1682; George[8]; George[9]; Jonathan[10]; qv);
6–Jonathan (1704-55), *m* 1726, Lydia Jones (1705-83; Elder John[7]; Abraham[8]; Thomas[9]);
5–Lt. Jesse (1730-1815), soldier Am. Rev.; *m* 1757, Mary Cheney;
4–Lucy (*b* 1765), *m* Joseph **Chamberlain** (4 above).
10–Richard **Thayer** (qv);
9–Richard (*d* 1705), *m* 1651, Dorothy Pray (*d* 1705; Quinton[10]);
8–Nathaniel (1658-1729), *m* 1679, Hannah Heydon;
7–Nathaniel (1680-1752), *m* 1704, Sarah Wales (Elder Nathaniel[8]);
6–Joanna (*b* 1706), *m* 1726, William **Cheney** (1704-56; William[7]; William[8]; William[9], qv);
5–Mary (*b* 1736), *m* Lt. Jesse **Whitney** (5 above).
9–Henry **Adams** (qv);
8–Peter (*b* 1622), *m* Rachael–;
7–John (*b* ca. 1651), *m* 1685, Michal **Bloice** (Richard[8], *m* Mychall Jennison);
6–Capt. Michael (1706/07-1776), *m* Sarah Shuttleworth (*d* 1747);
5–Mary (*b* 1732), *m* 1754, Joseph **Joslin** (*b* 1726; Capt. Israel[6], *m* Sarah Bailey; Nathaniel[7]; Nathaniel[8]; Thomas[9]);
4–Mary (*b* 1761) *m* 1783 or 84, Jeremiah **Wheeler**;
3–Esther (1794-1845), *m* Joseph **Chamberlain** (3 above);
2–Jesse Mark (1824-1911), farmer, mcht., miner; *m* 1860, Erville Ingham (1836-1923); issue: I–Joseph Redington (1861-1926; *m* Hope Summerell); II–William Henry (1 above); III–Lucy Cynthia (*b* 1868; *m* Asa George Baker).
1–*m* Oct. 26, 1898, Carrie Belle Stickney (Mar. 10, 1873-Oct. 1, 1907); dau. of Julius Stickney (Tyler[3]), *m* Eliza Aulls, of Wheeler, N.Y.; issue (all *b* Kanona, N.Y.): 1–Joseph Stickney, *b* Aug. 26, 1899; *m* Aug. 28, 1925, Dorothy, dau. of William F. Wood, of Marion, N.C.; 2–William Henry (Jan. 3, 1901-Mar. 5, 1903); 3–Julius Joslin, *b* May 31, 1903; *m* Oct. 1926, Gladys, dau. of J. E. Copeland, of Scotland Neck, N.C. (issue: Mary Ann); 4–Melissa Ervilla, *b* May 20, 1904; George Washington Hosp., Washington, D.C., 1926.
1–*m* 2d, Aug. 21, 1912, Minnie Spalding Carter, *b* Canisteo, Steuben Co., N.Y., Nov. 18, 1880; dau. of William Dwight Carter, *m* Fannie Chamberlain.
1–Cornell, '89 (Kappa Alpha). Retired farmer; mgr. State Industrial and Agrl. Sch., by appointment of Governor Whitman of New York; mem. New York Legislature. Mem. Chamberlain Assn. of America, Steuben Co. Agrl. Soc. (pres.). Mason. Club: Steuben. Residence: Kanona, Steuben Co., N.Y.

1–**CHAMPINE, Emojene Demarest (Mrs.),** *b* Newton, N.J., Aug. 4, 1866.
9–David **Demarest** (1620-93), from Picardy to New Amsterdam, 1663; del. to New Netherlands Provincial Assembly, 1664; magistrate, New Harlem, N.Y, 1672; "French Patent," Hackensack River, N.J., 1677; Huguenot; *m* 1643 Marie Sohier (1623-1689-93; Francois[10], from Nieppe);
8–David (1652-91), of "French Patent," Hackensack, N.J.; *m* 1675, as her 1st husband, Rachel Cresson (Pierre[9], French Huguenot);
7–David (1676-1768), of Hackensack, N.J.; *m* 1697, Sara Bertholf (bap. 1677; Rev. Guilliam[8]);
6–Jacobus (bap. 1703-ca. 1735), *m* 1726, Margaret De Groot;
5–Jacobus (bap. 1732-1803), removed to Warwick, N.Y.; pvt. Am. Rev.; *m* 1751, Tryntie Lozier or Le Seur (bap. 1734-1791; Jacobus[6]; Nicholas[7]; Francois[8], French Huguenot);
4–John (*b* 1764), of Warwick, N.Y.; *m* 1782, Anna Dill (*d* 1820; George[5], Am. Rev.);
3–Peter D. (1794-1848), *m* ca. 1815, Mary Weeden (1794-1873; Thomas[4]; Thomas Henry[5]);
2–Lorenzo D. (2 below).
10–Nicholas **Knapp** (ca. 1580-1670), from Eng. with Winthrop's fleet, to Watertown, Mass., 1630; propr. 1636-37; removed to Stamford, Conn., 1648; *m* 1st, 1630, Eleanor– (*d* 1658);
9–Caleb (1636-77), of Stamford; *m* ca. 1660, Hannah Smith (*d* post 1677; Henry[10], of Wethersfield and Stamford);
8–Capt. John (1664-1749), *m* 1st, 1692, Hannah Ferris (*d* ante 1727);
7–Lt. John (1697-1763), *m* 1st, 1723, Deborah Cross (1701/02-1735);
6–Nathaniel (1726-1812), removed to Goshen, N.Y.; *m* 1st, 1751, Jemima Ward;
5–Nathaniel, Jr. (1753-87), pvt. Am. Rev.; *m* Sarah Sutton (1748-1825);
4–Nathaniel (1769-1849), removed to Sugar Loaf, N.Y.; *m* 1792, Deborah Teed (1774-1854);
3–John (1797-1866), of Sugar Loaf; *m* 1821, Maria Holbert (1804-82; John[4]; John[5], Am. Rev.);
2–Amanda Maria (2 below).
11–William **Swain** (1585-1664), from Eng.; dep. Gen. Ct. of Mass. Bay, 1636; commr. to establish and govern Colony of Conn., 1636; asst., 1st. Gen. Ct., 1637; dep. Gen. Ct., New Haven, 1653-57;
10–Capt. Samuel (1610-82), came with father; lt. of Conn. Colonial forces, 1663; dep. Gen. Ct. Conn., 1663; removed to N.J.; lt. of Newark soldiers under Capt. Robert Treat, 1667-73; capt. of E. Jersey Provincial forces; dep. and "Third Man," Provincial Assembly of E. Jersey, 1673-76; *m* Johanna Ward (*d* 1689);
9–Elizabeth (1647-post 1706), *m* 1st, Josiah **Ward** (*d* post 1682);
8–Samuel (1669-1759);
7–Samuel, Jr. (1704-42), *m* ante 1732, Rebecca– (*d* post 1742);
6–Jemima (1732-ante 1782), *m* Nathaniel **Knapp** (6 above).
2–Lorenzo D. **Demarest** (1827-66), jeweler; *m* 1848, Amanda Maria Knapp (1829-1901); issue: I–Charles (1855-1917; *m* 1877, Elizabeth Knapp Rose); II–Ada (1859-61); III–Marie (*b* 1862); IV–Emojene (1 above).
1–married; issue: 1–Clifford Carleton Champine, *b* Fargo, N.D., June 15, 1885; LL.B., U.Minn., '08; *m* May 3, 1913, Marjorie Estabrook, dau. Harlan P. Roberts (issue: Margaret Roberts; Mary Elizabeth).
1–Genealogist. Mem. D.A.C. (state registrar, Minn. soc.), D.F.P.A., D.A.R. (state treas. Minn., 1917-25), Minn. Hist. Soc. Clubs: Woman's of Minneapolis, Tourist. Residence: 4129 Upton Av. So., Minneapolis, Minn.

1–**CHANDLER, Myrta Hice Kempf (Mrs. Clarence John),** *b* Chelsea, Mich., Dec. 31, 1869.
3–Johann Jacob (Kömpf) **Kempf** (1800-65), from Stammheim, Germany, 1830; settled first at Trumbauersville, Bucks Co., Pa.; moved to Ann Arbor, Mich., 1838; *m* 1827, Rosina Maier (1796-1857);
2–Charles Henry (2 below).
8–Hugue (Frere) **Freer** (will dated 1697), Huguenot, to America ca. 1677; patentee, New Paltz, N.Y.; *m* Marie Haye; *m* 2d, Janneke Wiban;
7–Hugo (1668-will dated 1706/07), *m* 1690, Maria Anna LeRoy;
6–Jonas (ca. 1701-1775), *m* 1727, Catharine Stokhard (*b* Germany-will dated 1781);
5–Elisha (*b* 1739), *m* Martha Everett (Robert[6], *m* Esther–);
4–Jonas E. (1789-1854), *m* 1810, Sarah Cooley (1793-1841);
3–Alva (1813-96), of Lima, Mich.; *m* 1833, Phoebe Ann Streeter (1815-93);
2–Mary Elizabeth (1838-1910), *m* 1855, Charles Henry **Kempf** (1831-1916), banker; issue: I–Charles Reuben (1857-59); II–George Henry (1860-1922; *m* Mary Carolinda Angevine); III–Wilbur Godfrey (1864-1917; *m* Katharine Cummings); IV–Myrta Hice (1 above).
1–*m* Jan. 1, 1896, Clarence John Chandler, *b* Canton, N.Y., Mar. 19, 1871; son of Harvey Gott Chandler, of Ogdensburg, N.Y.; issue: 1–Dorothy Elizabeth, *b* Chelsea, Mich., Jan. 4, 1897; ed. Lasell Sem., Auburndale, Mass.; 2–

Harold Kempf, *b* Detroit, Mich., Aug. 8, 1902; Amherst Coll., '25; *m* June 20, 1925, Elza Louise, dau. of August William Cornelius, of Asbury Park, N.J. (issue: Donald Geoffrey).
1–Temple Grove Sem. (Saratoga Springs, N.Y.), '88. Mem. D.F.P.A. (state chaplain), H.S.A., C.D.XVIIC., D.A.R. (dir. of chapter), U.S.D. 1812 (nat v.p., 1924-28; state pres., 1922-28; hon. state pres., 1928–), Mich. Hist. Soc., Detroit Hist. Soc., U.S. Flag Assn. Pres. Congl. Women's Missionary Soc. of Mich., 1927-29; mem. state bd. of trustees Congl. Ch. (pres. 1928, 29); mem. exec. com. Nat. Congl. Council, 1929-35. Republican. Clubs: Woman's City (Detroit), Theater Arts. Residence: Grosse Pointe, Mich.

1–**CHANEY, Lucian West,** *b* Heuvelton, N.Y., June 26, 1857.
8–John (Cheney) **Chaney** (qv);
7–Daniel (1633-1714), *m* 1665, Sarah Bayley (*b* 1644);
6–John (1676-1728), *m* Elizabeth Sarah Burrage (*b* 1691);
5–Moses (*b* 1715), began to write name Chaney; Am. Rev.; *m* 1738 Abigail Whittmore; *m* 2d, 1755 Hannah Woodard;
4–Moses (1764-1833); *m* 1782, Lucy Dexter (1762-1833);
3–Luther (1788-1848), *m* Sabra Allen (1788-1885);
2–Lucian West (1822-1900), clergyman; *m* 1854, Happy Temperance Kinney (*d* 1873); issue: I–Edwin (*d* infancy); II–Lucian West (1 above); III–Newcomb Kinney (*d* 1881).
1–*m* June 20, 1882, Mary Eudora Hill, *b* Red Wing, Minn., June 15, 1862; dau. of Daniel C. Hill, *m* Anna Hall; issue (all *b* Northfield, Minn.): 1–Newcomb Kinney (qv); 2–Gertrude, *b* July 31, 1884; Oberlin Coll., '08; *m* Rev. Dr. Watts Orson Pye, *d*; 3–Ralph Hill (qv); 4–Lucian West, 3d (1893-1905); 5–Edwin Hall, *b* June 28, 1897; ed. Oberlin Coll.; *m* Mary Snively (issue: Alan; Ruth Lee).
1–A.B., Carleton Coll., '78 (P.B.K.), B.S., 1879, M.S., 1882 (D.Sc., 1916). Statistician, U.S. Bureau of Labor Statistics. Author (see Who's Who in America). Club: Cosmos. Residence: 3350 18th St. N.W., Washington, D.C.

1–**CHANEY, Newcomb Kinney,** *b* Northfield, Minn., Apr. 27, 1883.
4–Reuben **Hill,** *m* Mary Chase (*b* 1804; desc. of a Chief Justice Chase, of Va.);
3–Daniel Chase (1830-1914), architect and builder; *m* 1858, Anna Hall (1838-81);
2–Mary Eudora, *m* June 20, 1882, Lucian West **Chaney** (qv).
1–*m* July 19, 1911, Elsie Elizabeth Webb, *b* Abingdon, Eng., Oct. 31, 1886; dau. of Edward Webb, of Oxford, Eng., *m* Elizabeth Harwood; issue: 1–Elizabeth Webb, *b* Cleveland, O., Oct. 29, 1912; 2–David Webb, *b* Cleveland, Dec. 19, 1915.
1–B.S., Carleton Coll. (Northfield, Minn.), '04 (P.B.K.); M.S., '05; Rhodes scholar, Balliol Coll., Oxford U., Eng., 1907-10; B.A. in chemistry, 1910; Harrison fellow in chemistry, U.Pa., 1910-11, Ph.D., 1911. Dir. chem. research, Nat. Carbon Co., since 1920 (see Who's Who in America). Mem. Am. Chem. Soc. (chmn. Cleveland Div.), Am. Phys. Soc.; fellow Am. Geog. Soc.; dir. Am. Inst. Chem. Engrs. Consulting chemist, C.W.S., U.S.A. Cooperating expert, Internat. Critical Tables. Clubs: Cosmos (Washington), Chemist's, Pennsylvania (New York), Dover Bay Country (Cleveland). Mason. Conglist. Residence: 2983 Yorkshire Rd., Cleveland Heights, O.

1–**CHANEY, Ralph Hill,** *b* Northfield, Minn., Dec. 4, 1886.
Son of Lucien West Chaney (qv for genealogy).
1–*m* Aug. 3, 1917, Alma Grace Effert, *b* White Plains, N.Y., June 12, 1893; dau. of Werner Effert, of White Plains; issue: 1–Lucian Werner, *b* Rochester, Minn., Jan. 21, 1921; 2–Rudolph Effert and 3–Ralph Hill, Jr. (twins), *b* Washington, D.C., June 4, 1922; 4–Viola Margaret, *b* Augusta, Ga., Aug. 27, 1924.
1–A.B., Oberlin, '09 (Alpha Omega Alpha, Pi Gamma Mu, Nu Sigma Nu), A.M., 1913; M.D., U.Pa., 1914; studied Mayo Foundation Grad. Sch., U.Minn., 1919-22. Prof. surgery, U.Ga., since 1922 (see Who's Who in America). Maj. M.C., U.S.A., with A.E.F., World War; lt. col., M.R.C., U.S.A. Fellow Am. Coll. Surgeons, A.M.A. Democrat. Conglist. Residence: 2571 Henry St., Augusta, Ga.

1–**CHASE, Alice Bradstreet,** *b* New York, N.Y., 1854.
8–Aquila **Chase** (qv);
7–Thomas (1654-1732), *m* 1677, Rebecca Follansbee (*d* 1711; Thomas[8]);
6–Thomas (1680-1756), *m* Sara Stevens (living 1732);
5–Rev. Josiah (1713-78), *m* 1743, Sarah Tufts;
4–Col. Josiah (1746-1824), q.m. in Am. Rev.; paymaster, 1780; *m* Hannah Grow (1748-1823);
3–Jotham Sewall (1790-1883), *m* 1814, Mary Gould (1792-1853);
2–Rufus (2 below).
10–Gov. Thomas **Dudley** (qv);
9–Anne (1612-72), *m* 1628, Gov. Simon **Bradstreet** (1603-97);
8–Dorothy, *m* 1654, Seaborn **Cotton** (1633-86);
7–Mercy (1666-1715), *m* 1684, Peter **Tufts** (*b* 1648);
6–Rev. John (1689-1750), *m* Sarah Bradstreet (*b* 1697);
5–Sarah (1725-99), *m* Rev. Josiah **Chase** (5 above).
2–Rufus **Chase** (1826-1919), of Brooklyn, N.Y.; *m* 1853, Julia Elizabeth Ritter (1831-1928); issue: I–Alice B. (1 above); II–Paul Dudley, (*b* 1857; *m* 1901, Annah Milledoler Fellowes); III–Lucy (Mrs. Osgood Putnam, qv for Ritter lineage); IV–Theodora (1860-84); V–Helen Christina (*b* 1868; *m* 1892, H. A. West).
1–Mem. C.D.A., D.C.G., H.S.S.C., D.F.P.A., D.A.R. Club: City. Residence: 3249 Pacific Av., San Francisco, Calif.

1–**PUTNAM, Lucy Chase (Mrs. Osgood),** *b* New York, N.Y., Jan. 9, 1859.
7–Daniel **Ritter** (*d* 1743), settled at Lunenburg, Mass.; *m* 1715, Lydia Bailey (*b* 1695);
6–Thomas (*b* 1716), *m* 1743, Mary Strong (1714-54);
5–John (1750-1802), *m* 1774, Hannah Brown (1745-1822);
4–David (1779-1842), *m* 1802, Anna Thompson (1780-1820);
3–Thomas (1806-76), *m* 1830, Delia Maria Ayers (1807-92);
2–Julia Elizabeth (1831-1928), *m* Rufus **Chase** (1826-1919), Brooklyn, N.Y. (for issue and Chase lineages see Alice Bradstreet Chase).
1–*m* Oct. 18, 1893, William Burger Boorum (*d* 1901).
1–*m* 2d, Oct. 14, 1908, Osgood Putnam (July 24, 1860-Jan. 11, 1919); A.B., Harvard, '83; son of Samuel Osgood Putnam, of Mass.
1–Ed. Packer Collegiate Inst., Brooklyn, '79; Bryn Mawr Coll., 1888-89. Mem. D.F.P.A., D.C.G., C.D.A. (past state pres.), Huguenot Soc. of S.C., D.A.R. (past regent Calif. Chapter). Clubs: Century, Town and Country, Bryn Mawr, City. Summer place: Camp Faraway, Glen Alpine, Lake Tahoe, Calif. Residence: 3249 Pacific Av., San Francisco, Calif.

1–**CHATFIELD-TAYLOR, Hobert Chatfield,** *b* Chicago, Ill., Mar. 24, 1865.
8–William **Taylor,** landowner, Marlboro, Mass., 1635;
7–William (*d* 1705), *m* 2d, 1699, Sarah Larkin;
6–Ebenezer (*b* 1701/02), of Shrewsbury, Mass.; *m* 1723, Mary Banister (*d* 1736, aet. 36);
5–Asa (*b* 1732/33), soldier Am. Rev.; *m* 1768, Sarah Williams;
4–Asa (*b* 1781), *m* 1804, Alma Otis;
3–John Otis (1806-98), settled at Chicago, Ill.; moved to Freeport, Ill., and later to San Diego, Calif.; *m* Harriet Eames;
2–Henry Hobart (2 below).
10–Robert **Williams** (qv);
9–Isaac (1638-1707), capt., deacon, Newton, Mass.; comdr. Troop of Foot; rep. Gen. Ct.; *m* 1st, Martha Parke (1642-74; Hon. William[10], mem. A. and H. A. Co., dep. Gen. Ct., 1655-67, *m* Martha Holgrave);
8–Isaac (1661-1739), *m* 1st, 1685, Elizabeth Hyde (1659-99; Jonathan[9], *m* Mary French);
7–Isaac (1686-1757), *m* 1708, Martha Whitney (*b* 1688);
6–Isaac (*b* 1725), *m* 1748, Sarah Stratton (*b* 1725; Ebenezer[7], *m* Lydia–, of Cambridge and Watertown, Mass.);
5–Sarah (*b* 1753), *m* Asa **Taylor** (5 above).
10–John **Otis** (qv);

9–John (1620-83), settled on "Otis Farm," Barnstable, Mass., 1678; took oath of fidelity at Hingham, 1661; moved to Scituate, 1661; *m* 2d, 1662, Mary Jacobs (*b* 1635; Nicholas[10]);
8–Judge Joseph (bap. 1666-1754), judge Ct. Common Pleas, Plymouth Colony, 1703-14; elected to the "Great and Gen. Ct.," 1710,13; removed to New London, 1721; *m* his cousin, Dorothy Thomas (Nathaniel[9], *m* Deborah Jacobs; William[10]);
7–James (1692/93-1754), *m* 1728 Sarah Tudor (*d* 1788);
6–John (1732-1817) *m* Lucy Darrow;
5–Judge John (1756-1843), *m* Nancy Angell (James[6]; William[7]; James[8]; John[9]; Thomas[10]);
4–Alma (1789-1831), *m* Asa **Taylor** (4 above).
9–Thomas **Eames** (qv);
8–John (1642-1733), selectman, Sherborn, 1672, Framingham, 1701; *m* 1682, Elizabeth Eames (1659-1727; Robert[9], *m* Elizabeth–);
7–John (1687-ante 1740), *m* 1712, Joanna Buckminster (*b* 1690; Col. Joseph[8], of Framingham, Mass., selectman, 17 yrs., rep., 12 yrs., comd. a co. of Grenadiers in Sir Charles Hobby's regt. in expdn. at Port Royal and subsequently at the comd. of a regt.);
6–Robert (1714-47), *m* 1740, Deborah Adams (*b* 1714);
5–John (1742-1806), lt. of Minute Men; *m* 1762, Ruth Stone (1743-1804; Capt. Hezekiah[6]; Nathaniel[7]; John[8]; Gregory[9]);
4–Asa (1780-1832), *m* Sally Butler (1781-1864; Capt. Eli[5], Am. Rev., *m* Rachel Stocking [Elisha[6]; Daniel[7]; Dea. Samuel[8]; George[9]]; Benjamin[6]; Joseph[7]; Richard[8]);
3–Harriet (1807-96), charter mem. St. Paul's Universalist Ch., Chicago, Ill.; *m* John O. **Taylor** (3 above).
8–George **Chatfield** (ca. 1624-1671; son of Henry[9], George[10], Francis[11], Richard[12], John[13], Thomas[14]); came from Eng. to Killingworth, Conn., 1663; *m* 2d, 1659, Isabel Nettleton (Samuel[9]);
7–John (*b* 1661), settled at Derby, Conn.; *m* 1684, Anna Harger (John[8]);
6–Lt. John (1697-1793), of Quaker Farms; ens. co. or train band, Oxford Parish, 1743; lt. 2d Co., Derby, 1750; *m* 1st, 1721, Elizabeth Johnson (*d* 1751);
5–Oliver (*b* 1730), enlisted in 3d Co., Conn. Regt., 1775, discharged 1775; enrolled as pvt. in Capt. Johnson's Co., 5th Bn. to reinforce Washington's Army in N.Y.; was in Battle of L.I., 1776; engaged in the retreat to N.Y., 1776; *m* Abiah–; *m* 2d, Zerviah–;
4–Oliver (*b* 1758), *m* 1782, Lucretia Strong;
3–Horace (1793-1851), *m* 1823, Catherine Bogue;
2–Adelaide (2 below).
9–Elder John **Strong** (qv);
8–Thomas (*d* 1689), trooper at Windsor, 1658; removed to Northampton, 1659; rep. Gen. Ct., 1667-69; *m* 2d, 1671, Rachel Holton (Dea. William[9]);
7–Hon. Adino (1676-1749), rep. Gen. Ct., 1726; removed to Woodbury, Conn., ca. 1700; *m* ca. 1702, Eunice– (1679-1763);
6–Ebenezer (1704-86), Woodbury, Conn.; *m* 2d, 1730, Mary Smith (1707-75);
5–Charles (bap. 1735-1812), *m* 1st, 1760, Betsey Hinman (1729-77; Hon. Andrew, Jr.[6], of Southbury, Conn.; Andrew[7]; Titus[8]; Edward[9]);
4–Lucretia (*b* 1762), *m* Oliver **Chatfield** (4 above).
6–John (Booge) **Bogue** (*d* 1748), from Scotland, ca. 1680, settled at East Haddam, Conn.; elder; rep. legislature, 1716; *m* 1st, 1692, Rebecca Walkley (1672-1733; Richard[7]);
5–Rev. Ebenezer (1716-67), apprentice; preacher of the Gospel; ordained at Farmington, Conn., 1751; taught many young men the Latin and Greek languages and prepared them for college; *m* 1750, Damaris Cook (*b* 1726; Capt. Samuel[6]; Samuel[7]; Samuel[8]; Henry[9]);
4–Publius Virgilius (1764-1836), grad. Yale, 1787; called to preach at Winchester, Conn., 1790; ordained, 1791, dismissed 1800; removed to Vernon, N.Y.; pvt. Am. Rev., pensioned; *m* 1791, Catherine Robinson (*b* 1766; Col. Timothy[5]; David[6]; David[7]; Thomas[8]);
3–Catherine (1801-63), *m* Horace **Chatfield** (3 above);
2–Adelaide (1843-83), *m* 1860, Henry Hobert **Taylor** (1835-75), mfr. of threshing machinery; dir. Commercial Nat. Bank, Elgin Nat. Watch Co., etc.
1–*m* June 19, 1890, Rose Farwell (Mar. 7, 1870-Apr. 5, 1918); dau. late Senator Charles B. Farwell, of Ill.; issue: 1–Adelaide, *b* London, Eng., Apr. 3, 1891; *m* Hendricks Hallett Chitman, Boston; 2–Wayne (see Vol. I, p. 545, for Farwell lineage); 3–Otis, *b* Lake Forest, Ill., May 6, 1897; Yale, '23; 4–Robert Farwell, *b* Chicago, Ill., Nov. 10, 1908.
1–*m* 2d, June 23, 1920, Estelle (Barbour) Stillman, dau. late George H. Barbour, of Grosse Pointe Farms, Mich.
1–B.S., Cornell U., '86 (Litt.D., Lake Forest, 1913). Author (see Who's Who in America). Chevalier Legion of Honor and Officier de l'Instruction Publique (French); Chevalier Order of SS. Maurice and Lazarus and Chevalier Order of the Crown (Italian); Chevalier Order of Isabella the Catholic (Spanish); Officer Order of the Crown (Belgian); Chevalier Order of St. James (Portuguese); Officer Order of the Bust of the Liberator (Venezuelan). Mem. S.C.W., S.C., S.R., S.A.R., I.A.G. Clubs, Chicago, University, Cliff Dwellers (Chicago), Union, Century (of New York), Metropolitan (Washington), etc. Residence: "Far Afield," Santa Barbara, Calif.

1–**CHATTERTON, Ray Webb,** *b* Belleville, Wis., July 23, 1877.
9–William **Chatterton** (*d* 1700), to New Haven, Conn., 1656; took oath of fidelity, 1657; *m* Mary Clark (*d* 1722);
8–Samuel (1671-1733), *m* 1st, Elizabeth Warner;
7–William (1704-58), *m* 1730, Elizabeth Ford;
6–Stephen (1731-97), *m* 1st, Sarah Payne;
5–Nathaniel (1755-1835), served as pvt. and matross in Am. Rev.; served under Capt. Henry Pauling, Col. Weissenfel's Regt., later with Capt. Joseph Thomas' Co., Col. Lamb's Regt. of Arty.; received 600 acres of land for services; *m* 1783, Mary (Manning) Storm;
4–John (1793-1875), *m* Hannah Stott;
3–Richard (1815-93), Co. B, 49th Wis. Vol. Inf. in Civil War; *m* Laura Lewis (1826-1902; Samuel[4] [*b* 1774], *m* 2d, Lucy Odell [1794-1872]; Morris[5] [1730-post 1790], mem. 4th Regt. Dutchess Co. Militia, entitled to land bounty rights under Capt. A. Badgley and Lt. E. Concklin, in Am. Rev., *m* 1753, Phebe Doughty, 1733-post 1790);
2–William Wallace (2 below).
8–John (Cunnabell, Conable) **Connabell** (1650-1724), from Eng. to Boston, 1674; in Falls Fight in King Philip's War; *m* 1688/89, Sarah Clayes (1666/67-ante 1700);
7–Samuel (1689/90-1746), *m* Abigail Treadway; *m* 2d, 1713, Mrs. Mary (Wilson) Diamond (1690-1759; William Wilson[8], *m* Mary Pierce; Dea. Edward[9], *m* Mary Hale);
6–Samuel (1717-96), mem. Capt. Agrippa Well's Co., Col. William's Regt. and served under Capt. Amasa Sheldon and Col. Elisha Porter, Am. Rev.; surveyor of highways, Bernardston, Mass.; *m* 1740, Mary English;
5–John (1749-1815), chmn. Com. Safety and Correspondence, 1779; served under Capt. Joseph Stebbins and Col. David Wells, Am. Rev.; *m* 2d, 1786, Sarah Dewey;
4–Elizabeth (1793-1844), *m* 1810, David **Coats** (1788-1815);
3–Elvira (1826-1905), *m* 1842, Thomas Clark **Webb** (1810-65);
2–Helen (2 below).
11–Thomas **Dewey** (qv);
10–Israel (1645-78), *m* 1668, Abigail Drake (1648-96);
9–Israel (1673-1730);
8–Jabez (1695-1753), *m* 1714, Deborah York (*b* 1696);
7–David (*b* 1721), *m* 1741, Deborah Tracy (Christopher[8]; Lt. Thomas[9], qv);
6–David (1746-1839), minute man under Capt. Oliver Smith; pvt. with Col. Samuel Prentiss' Conn Regt.; *m* 1768, Sarah Witter (1743-1804);
5–Sarah (1770-1806), *m* as his 2d wife, John **Connabell** (5 above).
2–Helen Webb (*b* 1852), *m* 1873, William Wallace **Chatterton** (1848-1922), agriculturist; enlisted aet. 16 in Co. H, 8th Wis. Vol. Inf., Civil War (see Vol. III, p. 591 for issue).
1–Not married. University agriculture course, 1906. Agriculturist. Mem. S.A.R., I.A.G. (life). Mason (32°). Residence: "The Elms," Belleville, Wis.

1–**CHESTER, Samuel Beach,** *b* Philadelphia, Pa., Nov. 15, 1880.
Is senior representative of the blood of the Chesters of Blaby, Leicestershire, Eng., and Wethersfield, Conn., William Chester (qv), of the male line, descending from a younger brother of the Rev. John Chester, whose eldest child, all daus., *m* the Rev. S. B. Jones, whose eldest *m* son was Capt. Paul Townsend Jones.
9–Leonard **Chester** (qv);
8–Capt. John (1635-98), *m* Sarah Welles (Gov. Thomas[9], of Conn.);
7–John (1656-1711), *m* 1686, Hannah Talcott (*d* 1741; Samuel[8]);
6–Col. John (1703-71), grad. Yale, 1722; col. 6th Conn. Regt.; mem. Com. of War; judge co. ct.; rep. Gen. Assembly; *m* 1747, Sarah Noyes (1722-97; Joseph[7]);
5–Col. John (1748-1809), capt. at Bunker Hill; col. in Am. Rev.; speaker Conn. House of Rep.; judge; founder Soc. Cicinnati; *m* 1773, Elizabeth Huntington (1757-1839; Gen. Jabez[6]);
4–John, D.D. (1785-1829), grad. Yale, 1804; *m* Rebecca Ralston (Robert[5], of Phila.);
3–Sarah Ralston (*b* 1819), *m* 1838, Samuel Beach **Jones,** D.D. (1811-83), B.A., Yale, 1831; head of Theol. Sem., Princeton; First Presbyn. Ch., Bridgeton, N.J.;
2–Paul Townsend (1840-83), capt. 2d Pa. Heavy Arty.; raised and comd. Jones' Independent afterwards Baty. "L", Pa. Arty.; dangerously wounded at Siege of Petersburg, Va.; *m* 1879, Grace Rogers (1853-1907); issue: I–Samuel Beach Jones, III, who assumed maiden name and arms of his paternal grandmother, Sarah Ralston Chester, co-heiress of the Rev. John Chester, 1901.
1–*m* Winifred de Mattos, dau. of G. W. C. de Mattos, a British subject; issue: 1–Winifred Pauline (*b* and *d* July, 1904); 2–Millicent Ralston, *b* June 20, 1905; *m* July 8, 1926, Robert, son of late Jules Petin, Chateau Naz de Velu, Aix-en-Provence, and La Germaine, nr. Hyeras, France (has issue); 3–John Leonard Paul Jones, *b* Hythe, Hampshire, Eng., Dec. 5, 1907; 4–Joan Mary, *b* nr. Maidenhead, Berkshire, Eng., Aug. 25, 1913.
1–Author of various works, including principal biography of Venizelos, 1921. Officer (Gold Cross) of the Order of the Redeemer of Greece, 1923. Address: c/o Duane, Morris & Heckscher, Land Title Bldg., Phila., Pa.

1–**CHEYLESMORE, Elizabeth Richardson French (Lady Cheylesmore).**
10–Edward **French** (qv);
9–Joseph, *m* Susanna–;
8–Joseph (1654-83), *m* Sarah Eastman;
7–Joseph (1679-1756), South Hampton, N.H.;
6–Daniel (1708-83), *m* Sarah Gould;
5–Gould (1741-1823), Am. Rev.; *m* Dorothy Whittier;
4–Daniel (1769-1840), atty. gen. of N.H.; *m* 1st, Mercy Brown (sister of Rev. Francis Brown, pres. Dartmouth Coll.);
3–Benjamin Brown (1800-70), lawyer, clk., U.S. Ho. of Rep.; commr. pub. bldgs. under Pres. Lincoln; pres. 1st telegraph co. operating bet. New York and Washington; *m* Elizabeth Richardson (William Merchant[4], chief justice of N.H.);
2–Francis Ormond (2 below).
9–Robert (Tucke) **Tuck** (qv);
8–Edward (*d* 1652), *m* Mary Philbrick;
7–John (1652-1742), dep.; *m* Bethia Hobbs;
6–Jonathan (1697-1781), dep.; *m* Tabitha Towle;
5–Jonathan (1736-80), *m* Huldah Moulton;
4–John (1780-1847), *m* Betsey Towle;
3–Amos (1810-79), mem. 31st and 32d Congresses, 1847-53; naval officer, Port of Boston under Pres. Lincoln; *m* Sarah Ann Nudd (see their son Edward, Vol. I, p. 365);
2–Ellen (1838-1915), *m* 1861, Francis Ormond **French** (1837-93), A.B., Harvard, '57, LL.B., 1859; prominent financier, New York; issue: I–Amos Tuck (see Vol. I, p. 366); II–Elizabeth R. (1 above); III–Ellen (Mrs. Paul Fitz Simons, see Vol. I, p. 366).
1–*m* July 14, 1892, Herbert Francis Eaton, 3d Baron Cheylesmore (*b* London, Jan. 25, 1848-*d* July 29, 1925), Cdr. and Knight Royal Victorian Order, Knight of Grace Order of St. John of Jerusalem, and Grand Cross, British Empire; maj. gen., Grenadier Guards; mayor of Westminster, 1904-05; chmn. London Co. Council, 2 yrs.; vice lord lt., London; chmn. Bisley Royal Rifle Assn.; issue: 1–Francis Ormond, 4th Baron Cheylesmore, *b* June 19, 1893; served Grenadier Guards, World war; received D.S.O. for bravery in action; residence; Happy Valley Ranch, Alix, Alberta, Can.; 2–Herbert Edward, *b* London, Eng., July 12, 1895; served in Grenadier Guards, World War, wounded 1917, pensioned; *m* Mar. 1921, Sheila Ashton Case, of Can.; residence: Queenswood, Eaglefield-Green, Surrey.
1–Residences: 16 Prince's Gate, London, S.W., Eng., and Cooper's Hill Park, Surrey.

1–**CHILDS, Frank Hall,** *b* Findlay, O., Feb. 16, 1859.
9–William (Child) **Childs,** from Eng. ca. 1630; freeman, Watertown, Mass., 1634;
8–John (*b* 1636), *m* 1668, Mary Warren;
7–Daniel (*b* 1677), *m* 1702, Beriah Bemis;
6–Daniel (*b* 1709), *m* 1729, Mary Bright;
5–Capt. Abijah (*b* 1734), selectman of Waltham, Mass., 1774-75; capt. 25th Regt., Cont. Army; *m* 1759, Beulah Harrington;
4–Daniel (1766-1829), served Am. Rev., 7 yrs.; *m* 1787, Phebe Parks (*d* 1826);
3–Nathaniel Phelps (1788-1842), moved to Providence, R.I., 1813, to nr. Tyrone, Steuben Co., N.Y., 1818; to nr. Attica, Seneca Co., O., 1837; *m* 1813, Eliza Betsey Emmes (1794-1890; Nathaniel[4], of Boston, 1790 Census, gunsmith in behalf of the provincial armies, served in Battle of Bunker Hill);
2–Nathaniel Emmes (2 below).
5–William **Hall** (ca. 1721-ca. 1806), Scipio, Cayuga Co., N.Y.; *m* Miss Frasier, of L.I., N.Y.;
4–William (1751-1820), of Sussex Co., N.J.; *m* Elizabeth Johnson (ca. 1758-1830), of Sussex Co. (William[5], had charge of batteaux which carried provisions from Ft. Stanwix to Ft. Oswego, during Am. Rev., *m* Susan Garner);
3–Henry Frasier (1789-1858), moved to Tompkins Co., N.Y.; deacon, 1832; moved to Seneca Co., O., 1835; *m* 1813, Susan Sellon;
2–Emily Amanda (2 below).
5–John **Sellon,** Bapt. minister; held an office under King of England; distant relative of Lord North; to Boston; *m* Elizabeth Fraiswell, a Highland lady;
4–Samuel (*b* Hardwick, Mass., 1764), wrote name Sellen; moved to Bennington, Vt., and to nr. Tyrone, Seneca (now Schuyler) Co., N.Y., 1814; *m* 1786, at Hardwick, Abigal Mosely (*b* Sutton, Mass., 1767; Joseph[5], *m* Sibbel Dudley);
3–Susan (1793-1871), *m* Henry F. **Hall** (3 above);
2–Emily Amanda (1818-91), *m* 1837, Nathaniel Emmes **Childs** (1814-80), see Vol. III, p. 119, for portrait, biography and issue.
1–*m* Feb. 18, 1886, Amy Hunt, *b* Chicago, Ill., Jan. 19, 1855; dau. of Edwin Hunt, from Eng., 1830, wholesale hardware mcht., Chicago, Ill., and niece of Alfred W. Hunt, artist of London, Eng.
1–LL.B., Kent Coll. of Law, Chicago, 1893. Began in govt. printing office, Washington, D.C., 1878, later in pension office and ry. mail service; began practice of law at Chicago, 1893; teacher in various schools. Author (see Who's Who in America). Mem. I.A.G. Residence: 15218 Friends St., Pacific Palisades, Calif.

1–**CHILDS, James Rives,** *b* Lynchburg, Va., Feb. 6, 1893.
8–Francis (Child) **Childs** (*d* 1699), patented land known as "The World's End" in Cecil Co., Md., 1665; *m* Grace–;
7–George (ca. 1670-1733/34), of Cecil Co.; *m* Margaret–;
6–John, prob. son of 7 (ca. 1695-1750), of "Orphan's Gift," Queen Ann Parish, Prince George Co., Md.; *m* Elizabeth–;
5–Lt. Gabriel D. (ca. 1735-1808), began to write name Childs; served in French and Indian War, and Am. Rev.; *m* Elizabeth–;
4–Rev. John (ca. 1770-1829), entered Meth. ministry, 1789; *m* Margaret Adams;
3–Rev. John Wesley (1800-50), Meth. minister, Va.; *m* 1834, Martha Binns Rives;
2–John William (2 below).
9–Thomas (Pierson) **Pearson,** of Wisbeach, in the Isle of Ely, Gent.; came to Va., 1639; *m*

Susannah Bland (sister of Theodoric Bland, qv);
8–Thomas;
7–Thomas;
6–Priscilla, *m* Gabriel **Adams** (ca. 1690-1750), vestryman, Truro Parish;
5–William (1723-1809), vestryman with George Washington, of Truro and Fairfax Parishes, Fairfax Co., Va.; justice of peace, Fairfax; *m* Ann Wrenn;
4–Margaret, *m* Rev. John **Childs** (4 above).
9–Dr. Thomas (Bunn) **Binns,** living at Jamestown, Va., with his wife and son Thomas and five servants, 1625; prob. an emigrant from Yorkshire, Eng.;
8–Thomas, prob. son of 9 (ca. 1622-1669), settled in Surry Co., Va.; *m* Martha–;
7–Thomas (ca. 1658-ca. 1699), of Surry Co.;
6–Charles (ca. 1699-1748), justice of peace; sheriff, Surry Co.; *m* Judith Eldridge (Thomas[7], *m* Judith, dau. of Richard Kennon, qv);
5–Martha (1748-78), *m* Timothy **Rives** (1743-1803; George[6] [ca. 1698-1746], of Surry Co., Va., *m* Frances, prob. dau. of Christopher Tatum, vestryman of Albemarle Parish, Surry Co.; Timothy[7] [ca. 1670-1716], of Surry Co.; *m* Judith–; William[8] [ca. 1636-post 1695], to Surry Co., Va., ca. 1653; Timothy[9] [ca. 1588-1643], Gent., of Oxford City);
4–Anthony (1776-1844), *m* Mary Browne Green;
3–Martha Binns (1812-1909), *m* Rev. John Wesley **Childs** (3 above).
8–Thomas **Green,** from Holland to Va.; *m* Martha–;
7–Thomas, "The Sea Gull," *m* Martha Filmer (Maj. Henry[9], qv);
6–Col. Abraham (1705-83), sheriff; justice of Peace, Amelia Co., Va.; *m* Elizabeth Cowles;
5–Abraham (ca. 1745-1810), col. Am. Rev.; *m* 1777, Elizabeth Browne;
4–Mary Browne (1779-1860), *m* Anthony **Rives** (4 above).
9–Col. William **Browne,** sheriff and justice of peace, Surry Co., Va.; burgess, 1676-77,79,81,82; *m* Mary Browne (Col. Henry[10], of "Four Mile Tree," Colonial Councillor, 1634-52, 1660-61, *m* Anne Fowler);
8–Capt. William (1671-1747), justice, Surry Co.; *m* Jane Meriwether (Nicholas[9] [1631-78], clk. and justice of Surry Co. and Va. Colonial Council);
7–Capt. William, of "Four Mile Tree"; *m* Mary Clements;
6–Maj. Henry, of "Pipsico"; sheriff and justice, Surry Co., Va.; burgess, 1762; *m* Hannah Edwards;
5–Elizabeth, *m* Abraham **Green** (5 above).
11–William **Edwards,** settled in James City Co., 1635; burgess, 1652,53; *m* Dorothy–;
10–William, clk. and justice, Surry Co., Va.; burgess, 1652-53; *m* 1678, Anne Harrison;
9–William, clk. of Surry Co., Gen. Ct., and Va. Colonial Council; *m* Ann Manfeild;
8–William, burgess, 1703-06; *m* Elizabeth Harrison (1690-1707; Benjamin[9] [1645-1712], of "Wakefield," Colonial Councillor, and original trustee of William and Mary Coll.; Benjamin[10], qv);
7–Col. Benjamin (1707-50), sheriff, Surry Co.;
6–Hannah, *m* Maj. Henry **Browne** (6 above).
6–Henry **Brown,** killed by the Indians nr. Salem, Va., ca. 1757;
5–Henry (ca. 1731-1799), of "Ivy Cliff," Bedford Co., Va.; *m* Alice Beard;
4–Col. Daniel (1770-1817), *m* Mary Hancock;
3–James Leftwich (1815-72), first pres. Franklin Literary Soc., Randolph-Macon Coll.; founder Hill City Masonic Lodge; tobacconist; *m* Mary Virginia Early;
2–Lucy Howard (2 below).
11–Capt. Thomas **Harris** (qv);
10–Mary (1625-ca. 1691), *m* ca. 1644, Col. Thomas **Lygon** (ca. 1620-1677), of Henrico Co., Va.; burgess, 1655-56;
9–Johan (1653-1726), *m* 1672, Robert **Hancock** (1650-1708), of Henrico Co. (Simon[10]);
8–Johan, *m* 1700, her 1st cousin, Samuel **Hancock** (*d* 1760; William[9]);
7–Samuel (ca. 1702-1760), *m* Elizabeth Jameston, of Henrico Co. (John[8]);
6–Simon, *m* Jane Flournoy (ca. 1735-1806; 6th from Laurent Flournoy, from France to Lyon after the massacre of Huguenots, 1652, and thence to Geneva after the massacre of St. Bartholomew);
5–Col. Samuel (1760-1837), served in Bedford Co. militia in Am. Rev.; *m* 1784, Mrs. Ann (Ammon) Moon (Christopher Ammon[6], of New Kent Co., *m* 1735, Mary Bristow, of Middlesex Co., Va.;
4–Mary (1784-1848), *m* Col. Daniel **Brown** (4 above).
10–Richard **Buford** (qv);
9–John (1642-1722), came with his father; *m* 1662, Elizabeth Parrott (*b* 1645; Richard[10], qv);
8–Thomas (1663-1716), *m* Mary– (*d* 1720);
7–Thomas (1682-1761), *m* Elizabeth– (*b* 1675);
6–Elizabeth (*b* 1709), *m* 1728, Lt. Col. Jeremiah **Early** (1705-87), of Middlesex, Augusta and Culpeper cos.; lt. col. French and Indian War; justice, Augusta Co. (Thomas[7] [1682-1761], *m* 1704, Elizabeth Johnson (*d* 1716?); John[8] [*d* Middlesex, 1694], from Ireland to Va., 1661, settled in York Co., *m* 1682, Margaret Loyall);
5–Joshua (1738-1812), *m* Mary Leftwich (1746-1818; Augustine[6]; 4th from Ralph Leftwich, from Eng. to Va.);
4–John (1786-1873), bishop, M. E. Church South; founder Randolph-Macon Coll., the 1st and for 44 yrs. pres. bd. of trustees; *m* 1822, Elizabeth Browne Rives (1805-57; Anthony[5], 1776-1844);
3–Mary Virginia, *m* James L. **Brown** (3 above);
2–Lucy Howard (*b* 1858), for 45 yrs. a teacher and prin. public schs., Lynchburg, Va., mem. C.D.A., D.A.R.; *m* 1890, John William **Childs** (*b* 1845), served in C.S.A., aet. 16; spl. messenger of Gen. Robert E. Lee, 1864-65; tobacconist, real estate and insurance agt.; issue: I–Martha (*b* and *d* 1891); II–James Rives (1 above); III–John Wesley (1894-1917).
1–*m* Aug. 13, 1922, Georgina de Brylkine, *b* St. Petersburg, Russia, Nov. 11, 1893; dau. of Paul Alexandrovitch de Brylkine (1861-1911), landowner of Pskov and Russian naval officer, *m* Mathilde Blan-Garen (*b* Paris, France, 1878).
1–Ed. V.M.I., 1909-11; A.B., Randolph-Macon Coll., '12; M.A., Harvard, 1915; Army War Coll., 1917. Principal, high sch. in Va., 1912-13; private tutor, 1915-16; asst. master, Lawrenceville Sch., 1916-17. Served in Am. Ambulance Corps in France, 1915; entered First O.T.C., Ft. Myer, Va., May 15, 1917; commd. 2d lt., inf., Aug. 1917 and apptd. a.-d.-c. C. O. 159th Brig., 80th Div.; detailed Mil. Int. Div., G.S., Oct. 1917, and in Feb. 1918 to G.H.Q., A.E.F., France, as chief of bureau of enemy ciphers, Radio Int. Section, G.S.; promoted 1st lt. and after Armistice detailed to Supreme War Council, Paris, and later to Am. Commn. to Negotiate Peace; demobilized in U.S. Oct. 1919, and became Asso. Press corr. at State Dept. and White House until 1921; on confidential mission to Europe for War Dept., 1921; entered Russia the same yr. with A.R. Administration, serving as asst. and later dist. supervisor, Kazan Dist., A.R. Administration until 1923; apptd. consul, Class VII, Oct. 6, 1923; detailed to Jerusalem, Nov. 20, 1923; to Bucharest, May 4, 1925; apptd. foreign service officer, class VIII, July 1, 1924, Class VII, May 23, 1929; mem. A.R. Administration. Capt. Mil. Int. Div., Gen. Staff, O.R.C. Fellow Royal Geog. Soc.; mem. Va. Hist. Soc. Residence: 911 Rivermont Av., Lynchburg, Va.

1–**CHILDS, Ruth Emerson,** *b* Crookston, Minn.
10–Samuel (Child) **Childs** (*d* 1675), from Eng., 1630, believed to have come to Plymouth Colony; soldier in Narragansett fight; killed by Indians;
9–Richard (*b* 1624), *m* 1649, Mary Linnett (Robert[10], of Barnstable, Mass.);
8–Richard (*b* 1653), *m* 1678, Elizabeth Crocker (1660-1716; John[9]);
7–Thomas (*b* 1682), *m* 1710, Mary–;
6–David (*b* 1711), of Barnstable, Mass.; *m* 1734, Hannah Cobb;
5–David (*b* 1735), of Barnstable; pvt. Am. Rev.; *m* 1758, Hannah Davis;
4–Josiah (1773-1814), began to write name Childs; *m* 1797, Beulah Fay;
3–Ellsworth (1802-64), of Westboro, Mass.; *m* 1838, Eliza A. Marshall (1809-96);

2–Ellsworth D. (2 below).
8–John **Fay** (qv);
7–John (1669-1747), dea. Congl. Ch., Westboro, 1727; 1st town clk.; selectman many terms; town treas., 1722; assessor; magistrate; *m* 1690, Elizabeth Wellington (1673-1729; Benjamin[8], *m* Elizabeth Sweetman);
6–Capt. Benjamin (1712-77), of Westboro; town treas., 1742-43, 1766-68; selectman 5 terms; comd. a co. during French and Indian War; *m* 1st, 1739, Martha Mills (1719-61); they were the g.parents of Eli Whitney, inventor of the cotton gin;
5–Benjamin (1744-1834), minute man and pvt. Am. Rev.; *m* 1772, Beulah Stow (1754-1834);
4–Beulah (1777-1869), *m* Josiah **Childs** (4 above);
3–Ellsworth, *m* Eliza Ann Marshall (3 above);
2–Ellsworth D. (1843-1927), pres. E. D. Childs Co., Westboro, Mass.; *m* 1866, Esther Hamblin (*d* 1868); *m* 2d, 1873, Eliza McLorinan (1846-1904); *m* 3d, 1911, Henrietta Stevens; issue (2d marriage): I–Jesse Carman (*b* 1875; *m* 1903, Blanche Kenyon); II–Ellsworth J. (1880-82); III–Ralph Downie (*b* 1883; *m* 1907, Jennie Barnes); IV–Ruth Emerson (1 above).
1–Grad. State Normal Sch., Mayville, N.D., 1906; grad. State Normal, Bellington, Wash., 1916. Teaching principal, Jefferson Sch., Yakima, Wash., Mem. D.A.R. Residence: 1613 Summit View, Yakima, Wash.

1–**CHISOLM, Benjamin Ogden,** *b* College Point, N.Y., June 1, 1865.
7–Alexander (Chisolm) **Chisholm,** from Scotland to Charles Town, S.C., 1717; *m* Janet, dau. of Alexander Fraser;
6–Alexander (*d* 1772), *m* 1742, Judith Radcliffe;
5–Christina (*b* 1745), *m* 1766, her cousin, Alexander **Chisolm,** Jr. (1738-1810), from Inverness-shire, Scotland, to S.C., 1747;
4–George (1772-1835), of "The Retreat," on Cooper River, S.C.; *m* 1796, Providence Hext Prioleau;
3–George (1796-1837), *m* 1823, Sarah Maynard Edings;
2–William Edings (2 below).
8–Rev. Elias **Prioleau** (1659-99; son of Rev. Samuel Prioleau, pastor of Huguenot Ch., Pons, France, 1650-83, *m* Jeanne Merlat; desc. ancient noble Venetian family of Priuli), from France to Charles Town, S.C., 1687, founder of Huguenot Ch., Charleston; *m* Jeanne Burgeaud;
7–Col. Samuel (1690-1752), mem. Royal Council; col. Royal Horse Guards; *m* 1713, Mary Magdalaine Gendron (Philippe[8], com. of Church Act, 1706);
6–Col. Samuel (1717-92), *m* 1739, Providence Hext;
5–Hext (1753-79), lt. Light Inf., 1776; *m* 1775, Margaret Williams (Robert[6], *m* Elizabeth, dau. of David Hext, 7 below);
4–Providence H. (1776-1860), *m* George **Chisolm** (4 above).
9–Paul **Grimball** (*d* 1711/12), from Eng. with his wife, 1681; sec. Province of S.C., 1686; receiver gen. and escheator, 1687; proprietor's dep., 1691; mem. Assembly, 1691; mem. Council, 1692;
8–Mary, *m* Capt. John **Hamilton** (*d* 1707), from Scotland to S.C. with Lord Cardross, 1680; dep. sec. of the Province, 1691, and later; mem. Assembly, 1697;
7–Ann, *m* David **Hext** (*d* 1754);
6–Providence (*d* 1775), *m* Samuel **Prioleau** (6 above).
8–William **Edings** (*d* 1712), received land grant on Edisto Island, S.C., May 1695; *m* Rachel–;
7–William, capt. English colonial troops; *m* Tabitha Bower (Henry[8], of Edisto Island);
6–William (*d* 1767), *m* 2d, Margaret Delagall (Philip[7]);
5–Benjamin (1742-84), *m* 1765, Mary Baynard (*d* 1792);
4–William (1766-1836), *m* 1785, Sarah Evans (John[5]);
3–Sarah M. (1802-35), *m* George **Chisolm** (3 above).
8–Jeremiah **Rogers** (1633-76), settled first in Dorchester, then Lancaster, Mass.;
7–Ichabod;
6–Ichabod (1684-1746), *m* Anna Nourse;
5–John (1717-58), *m* 1745, Mary Davenport (1725-92; James[6], *m* Sarah Franklin, sister of Benjamin Franklin);
4–John (1749-99), *m* 1785, Mary Pixton (George[5]);
3–John (1787-1841), *m* 1817, Mary Ann C. Muhlenberg;
2–Mary Ann (2 below).
8–John Conrad **Weiser** (1661-1746), from Germany to N.Y., 1710; settled at Livingston Manor, N.Y., later at Schoharie; *m* Anna Magdalena Ubele (*d* Germany, 1709);
7–Col. Conrad (1696-1760), settled in Berks Co., Pa., 1729; Indian interpreter and agt.; first pres. judge of Berks Co.; col. French and Indian War; *m* 1720, Ann Eve Feck (*d* 1781);
6–Anna Mary, *m* Rev. Heinrich Melchior **Muhlenberg** (1711-87), from Eimbeck, Hanover, Germany, arrived in America, Sept. 22, 1742; Patriarch of Lutheran Ch.;
5–Hon. Frederick Augustus (1750-1801), mem. Cont. Congress, 1779-80; mem. U.S. Congress, 1789-97 (first speaker 1789);
4–Henry William, *m* Mary Sheaffe (William[5], of Phila.);
3–Mary Ann C., *m* John **Rogers** (3 above);
2–Mary Ann (1827-1913), *m* 1848, William Edings **Chisolm** (1823-95), issue: I–Mary Fredericka (1851-1927; *m* Charles Miller Schieffelin); II–Jessie Edings (1854-55); III–John Rogers (1856-66); IV–George Edings (see Volume I, p. 546); V–William Augustus Muhlenberg (1862-66); VI–Margaret Willing (1863-1904; *m* James Hooker Hamersley, 1844-1901); VII–Benjamin O. (1 above).
1–*m* Nov. 12, 1888, Bessie Rhoades, *b* New York, N.Y., Nov. 9, 1867; dau. of John Harsen Rhoades, of New York; issue: 1–Nina Rhoades, *b* New York, N.Y., Sept. 8, 1889, *m* Feb. 4, 1913, Alvin Untermyer; 2–Barbara Muhlenberg (Sept. 17, 1891-May 24, 1900); 3–Winifred Wheelwright, *b* New York, N.Y., May 3, 1893; *m* June 5, 1917, Curtis Northrop Browne; 4–Dorothy Rogers (Aug. 27, 1895-Apr. 26, 1914); 5–Margaret Willing, *b* Orange, N.J., Nov. 1, 1897; 6–Elizabeth Harsen, *b* New York, N.Y., Nov. 17, 1900; *m* Oct. 10, 1925, Dr. Robert Ogden Du Bois (issue: Robert Ogden, *b* Oct. 30, 1926; Barbara Sievwright, *b* Dec. 31, 1927); 7–Priscilla Pixton, *b* New York Harbor, Me., July 22, 1905; *m* Feb. 24, 1927, Richard Neville Davis.
1–Ed. private school and Columbia Coll. Architect, banker. Apptd. commnr. for the U.S. on the Internat. Prison Commn., by President Coolidge, Dec. 18, 1923, resigned Mar. 8, 1929. Clubs: Union, Riding. Residence: Ridgefield, Conn. Address: 21 W. 10th St., New York, N.Y.

1–**CHRISTIAN, Elizabeth Sears Seabury (Mrs. Henry A.),** *b* Boston, Mass., Apr. 23, 1875.
10–John **Alden,** Mayflower Pilgrim (qv);
9–Elizabeth (1624/25-1717), *m* 1644, William (Peabody) **Pabodie** (1620-1707; John[10], *m* Isabel–);
8–Martha (*b* 1650), *m* Dr. Samuel **Seabury** (*b* 1640; John[9], qv);
7–Joseph (*b* 1678), *m* Phoebe Forbes Smith (1650-1715);
6–Sion (*b* 1713), *m* Anna Butts;
5–Philip (*b* 1740), *m* Sarah Pearse (*b* 1748);
4–Pierce (*b* 1773), *m* Elizabeth Hazzard (*b* 1772);
3–Franklin Perry (*b* 1807), originally named Sion; *m* Edith Howland (*b* 1811);
2–Charles William (2 below).
8–Richard **Sears** (qv);
7–Paul (1637-1707), *m* Deborah Willard (*d* 1721);
6–John (1677-1738), *m* Priscilla Freeman (1686-1764);
5–Willard (1714-65), *m* Susannah Howes (1720-63);
4–Ebenezer (1755-1835), *m* Hannah Gray (1768-1817);
3–Willard (1794-1878), *m* Ruth Cushman (1799-1885);
2–Elizabeth Willard (2 below).
9–John **Howland,** Mayflower Pilgrim (qv);
8–Hope (1630-83), *m* Elder John **Chipman** (qv);
7–Elizabeth (*b* 1647), *m* Hosea **Joyce** (ca. 1646-1712);
6–Lydia (*b* ca. 1682), *m* Ebenezer **Howes;**
5–Susannah (1720-63), *m* Willard **Sears** (5 above).
9–Robert **Cushman** (qv);
8–Thomas (1608-91), *m* Mary Allerton (1609-99), last survivor of Mayflower passengers (Isaac[9], Mayflower Pilgrim, qv);
7–Eleazer (*b* 1656), *m* Elizabeth Combes or Coombes;

6–James (*b* ca. 1700), *m* 1722, Sarah Hatch;
5–Ebenezer (1727-1813), *m* 1750, Zurviah Sherman (*b* 1730; Ichabod[6], *m* Mercy Ellis; Philip[7]; John[8]; Philip[9], qv);
4–Obed (1755-1833), *m* Ruth Barker (1761-1821);
3–Ruth (1799-1885), *m* Willard **Sears** (3 above);
2–Elizabeth Willard (1835-1912), *m* 1853, Charles William **Seabury** (1831-1901); issue: I–Frank (1854-1927; *m* Alice Barnard); II–William Hunt (*b* 1858); III–Elizabeth S. (1 above).
1–*m* June 30, 1921, Henry Asbury Christian (see Vol. I, p. 549, for genealogy).
1–Mem. S.M.D. Residence: 68 Monmouth St., Brookline, Mass.

1–**CHRISTIANCY, Carrie Estelle,** *b* Monroe, Mich., Nov. 30, 1868.
9–Jean **Godfrey** de Mauboeuf of Marboeuf, of Parish of St. Martin de Cantelan, a suburb of Rouen, diocese of Rouen, France; *m* Colette Danlerville;
8–Jacques (*b* France, 1653), to Canada; *m* at Three Rivers, 1683, Jeanne Brunet (*b* 1666; Pierre[9], *m* Marie Catherine Cottin);
7–Jacques (1684-1730), entered the fur trade at Detroit, 1710, and moved there, 1719 or 20; *m* ca. 1714, Marie St. Onge dit Chene (*b* Montreal, 1690-*d* 1738);
6–Jacques (1722-95), rendered valuable services as interpreter with the Indians; *m* 1758, Louise Clotilde Chapoton (1741-62; Jean[7], surgeon, French Army, *m* Marie Magdalene Esteve);
5–Gabriel Jacques (1758-1833), of Detroit; *m* 2d, 1794, Marie Therese Douaire de Bondy (1774-1814; Joseph[6], *m* Marie Joseph Gamelin);
4–Susanne (1795-1871), *m* Capt. James **McCloskey,** asst. q.m.gen., U.S.A., War 1812;
3–Elizabeth Leonora (1821-74), *m* 1839, Isaac Peckham **Christiancy** (1812-90), see Vol. III, p. 122, for portrait, biography, and Christiancy lineage;
2–Henry Clay (1841-1925), *m* 1863, Charlotte Elizabeth Brigham (1842-83), for biography, issue, and Brigham lineage, see Mrs. George E. Pickett, Vol. III, p. 122.
1–Teacher, Detroit public schools, retired. Mem. I.A.G. Club: Women's City. Residence: 395 Oakland Rd., Farmington, Mich.

JOHN LEONARD LOVERING (1809-62).

1–**CHRISTOPHER, Anna Tyler Lovering (Mrs. John G.),** *b* Hartford, Vt., Sept. 21, 1857.
8–John **Lovering** (*d* 1668), from Wales, 1654; settled at Ipswich, Mass., at Dover, N.H., 1657; *m* Esther (*d* 1675);
7–John (1663-1717), of Dover; *m* 1686, Hannah Kilham (1664-1710; Daniel[8], *m* Mary Safford);
6–Ebenezer (1693-1722), of Hampton, N.H.; *m* 1713, Esther Dearborn (1695-1783; Dea. John[7], *m* Abigail, dau. of Nathaniel Batchelder, of Hampton);
5–John (1715-78), of Hampton Falls, N.H.; *m* 1733, Anna Sanborn (1715-70; Dea. Reuben[6], *m* Sarah Sanborn);
4–Simeon (1752-1837), of Kinsington, N.H.; served in Am. Rev.; *m* 1773, Sarah Sanborn (1753-1837; Reuben[5], *m* Elizabeth Sleeper);
3–John (1781-1842), of Hartford, Vt.; *m* 1804, Hannah Porter Pease (1779-1842; Samuel[4], Am. Rev., *m* Sarah, dau. of Samuel Porter, *m* Sarah Caulkins);
2–John Leonard (2 below).
8–William **Tyler** (*d* 1692), *m* 1662, Abigail Terrell (*b* Eng.; Roger[9]);
7–John (1667-1741), *m* 1694, Abigail Hall (1674-1741; Thomas[8], *m* Grace Watson);
6–John (*b* 1710), *m* 1731, Phebe Beach (1710-40; Thomas[7], *m* Phebe Wilcoxen);
5–Col. Benjamin (1733-1814), *m* 1753, Mabel Andrews (1731-1823; Elisha[6], *m* Mabel–);
4–Ephraim (1759-1823), *m* 1781, Abigail Pardee;
3–Hon. Austin (1790-1844), of Claremont, N.H.; *m* 1814, Almira Kingsbury;
2–Ellen Almira (2 below).
8–Thomas **Yale** (qv);
7–Elizabeth (1667-1702), of New Haven, Conn.; *m* 1688, Joseph **Pardee** (1664-1742; George[8], qv);
6–Enos, of New Haven; *m* Abigail Holt (*b* 1686; Eleaser[7], *m* Tabitha, dau. of John Thomas, *m* Tabitha–);
5–Benjamin (1718-76), of New Haven; *m* 1746, Hannah Beecher (bap. 1727; Samuel[6], *m* Hannah, dau. of Nathaniel Farrington, *m* Sarah Whiting);
4–Abigail (1761-1814), *m* Ephraim **Tyler** (4 above).
9–Joseph **Kingsbury** (qv);
8–Nathaniel (1650-94), *m* Mary Bacon (John[9], *m* Rebecca Hall);
7–Daniel (1688-1754), *m* 1713, Elizabeth Stevens (*d* 1764);
6–Daniel (1715-83), Am. Rev.; *m* 1737, Beriah Mann (1717-55; Theodore[7], *m* Abigail Hawes);
5–Lt. Daniel (1742-1825), Am. Rev.; *m* 1766, Mary Thurston (1746-1828; Daniel[6], *m* Elizabeth Whiting);
4–Daniel (1767-1819), *m* 1797, Hannah Bailey (1778-1813; Ebenezer[5], *m* Hannah Trull);
3–Almira (1799-1867), *m* Hon. Austin **Tyler** (3 above);
2–Ellen Almira (1827-90), *m* 1854, John Leonard **Lovering** (1809-62), removed to Quechee, Vt., 1820, to Faribault, Minn., 1861; sch. teacher many yrs.; studied med. at Woodstock (Vt.) Med. Coll. (see portrait); issue: I–Leonard Austin (1854-1914; U.S.M.A., '76; col. U.S.A., see portrait); II–Ann Tyler (1 above).

COL. LEONARD AUSTIN LOVERING, U.S.A. (1854-1914).

1–*m* Apr. 14, 1887, Charles Watson Barrett (May 9, 1852-Oct. 20, 1907); son of Augustus Barrett (Peter[3], *m* Nancy Lynde), of Melrose, Mass., *m* Sarah J. Emerson; issue: 1–Leonard Lovering, *b* Claremont, N.H., Nov. 4, 1890; U.S.M.A., '12; Columbia Law Sch., 1926, admitted New York Bar, 1926; lt. col., U.S.A. (see portrait);

m Helen Dean, dau. of William T. Andrews, of Stamford, Conn. (issue: Eleanor Andrews; Mary Dean); 2–Tyler Emerson, *b* Claremont, Aug. 20, 1893.
1–*m* 2d, Nov. 20, 1922, John Garrison Christopher, *b* St. Louis, Mo., July 4, 1855; son of John Christopher, of Rochester, N.Y., *m* Mary Haywood.
1–Ed. Lasell Sem., Auburndale, Mass., '81. Mem. C.D.A., D.F.P.A., D.A.R. (N.H. state regent), U.S.D. 1812. Summer place: "Hillstead," Claremont, N.H. Residence: 1532 Riverside Av., Jacksonville, Fla.

LT. COL. LEONARD LOVERING BARRETT, U.S.A.

1–**CHUBB, Caroline Hinman Parker (Mrs. Thomas C.),** *b* Hartford, Conn., June 29, 1897.
10–Charles **Chauncy** (qv);
9–Sarah (*b* 1631), of Ware, Eng.; *m* 1659, Gershom **Bulkley** (1636-1713);
8–Rev. John (*b* 1661), of Colchester, Mass.; *m* 1701, Patience Prentiss;
7–Gershom (*b* 1704), of Wethersfield, Conn.; *m* 1733, Abigail Robbins (*b* 1714);
6–Rev. John (*b* 1738), *m* 1759, Judith Worthington (*b* 1742);
5–John (*d* 1788), *m* 1787, Theodosia Foote (1766-1802);
4–Roxana (1788-1869), of Colchester, Conn.; *m* 1809, James Mather **Goodwin** (1785-1870);
3–Henry Wheaton (1823-76), of Hartford, Conn.; *m* 1846, Caroline Althea Hinman (1827-74);
2–Caroline Anna (*b* 1859), of Hartford; *m* 1880, John Dwight **Parker** (1850-1919), asst. sec. Conn. Mut. Life Ins. Co., Hartford (for issue see Vol. I, p. 832).
1–*m* Nov. 19, 1916, Walton Hall Smith, *b* Kansas City, Mo., Feb. 18, 1898; Yale, '19 (divorced, Apr. 23, 1926).
1–*m* 2d, 1929, Thomas Caldecot Chubb, *b* East Orange, N.J., Nov. 1, 1899; see Who's Who in America; son of Hendon Chubb, *m* Alice Margaret Lee.
1–Ed. Nat. Cathedral Sch., Washington. Singer. Mem. S.M.D., D.F.P.A., C.D.A., C.D.XVII C., D.A.C., D.A.R., U.S.D. 1812, Mil. Soc. of the Frontier, Woman's Club (Paris, France), Woman's Club (Chicago), etc. Summer place: "Edgemere," Fenwick, Saybrook Point, Conn. Address: Morgan & Co., Paris, and Hartford Trust Co., Hartford, Conn.

1–**CHURCHILL, Arthur Howard,** *b* Brooklyn, N.Y., Apr. 14, 1862.
8–John **Churchill** (qv);
7–Eliezer (1652-1716), of Plymouth;
6–Elkanah (1691-1764), of Plymouth; *m* 1720, Susannah Manchester;
5–Amaziah (1721-1813), of Plymouth; *m* 1745, Elizabeth Sylvester (1722-1803);
4–Solomon (1762-1835), of Plymouth; Am. Rev.; *m* 1783 or 84, Elizabeth Bartlett;
3–William (1798-1861), of Plymouth and Boston, Mass.; and N.Y.; *m* 1824, Mary Myrick Haden;
2–William (2 below).
9–Edward **Doty,** Mayflower Pilgrim (qv);
8–Edward (*d* 1689), of Plymouth; *m* 1662, Sarah Faunce (*b* 1645/46, John[9], *m* Patience, dau. of George Morton, qv);
7–Martha (*b* 1671), of Plymouth; *m* 1696, Thomas **Morton** (1667-1748);
6–Sarah (1706-85), *m* 1727, Joseph **Bartlett** (1703-83);
5–Thomas (1742-1808), Am. Rev.; *m* 1765, Elizabeth Bartlett;
4–Elizabeth (1766-1811), *m* 1783 or 84, Solomon **Churchill** (4 above).
10–John **Alden,** Mayflower Pilgrim (qv);
9–Elizabeth (1624-1717), of Plymouth; *m* 1644, William **Pabody** (1620-1707);
8–Hannah (1662-1723), of Plymouth; *m* 1683, Samuel **Bartlett** (*d* 1714);
7–Elizabeth (ca. 1695-1773), of Plymouth; *m* 1716/17, Joseph **Bartlett** (1693-1756);
6–Sylvanus (1719-1811), of Plymouth; *m* 1743, Martha Wait (1726-1809);
5–Elizabeth (1749-79), of Plymouth; *m* 1765, Thomas **Bartlett** (5 above).
8–James (Mirick) **Myrick** (*b* 1612), from Wales, settled at Charlestown, Mass.; *m* 1652, Margaret– (*d* 1708);
7–Isaac (1665-1731), of Newbury, Mass.; Capt., Col. Church's Regt., Siege of Port Royal, 1704; *m* 1694, Mary Newell (*d* 1710);
6–Andrew (1705-77), of Charlestown and Nantucket, Mass.; *m* 1728/29, Jedidah Pinkham;
5–Andrew (1741-1816), of Nantucket; *m* Elizabeth Coffin;
4–Elizabeth (1781-1828), of Nantucket; *m* 1799, Zophar **Haden** (1775-1837);
3–Mary Myrick (1803-50), of Nantucket; *m* William **Churchill** (3 above).
10–Tristram **Coffin** (qv);
9–James (1640-1720), of Nantucket; *m* 1663, Mary Severance (*d* 1724);
8–Mary (1665-1741), *m* Richard **Pinkham** (*d* 1718);
7–Jonathan (*d* 1789), *m* Hannah Brown (1689-1730);
6–Jedidah (*d* 1789), *m* Andrew **Myrick** (6 above).
9–Tristram **Coffin** (qv);
8–John (1647-1711), of Haverhill, Mass.; *m* Deborah Austin (*d* 1718);
7–Peter (1671-1749), of Nantucket; *m* Hope Gardner (1683-1750; Joseph[8], *m* Bethia, dau. of Thomas Macy, qv);
6–Peter (*b* 1729), of Nantucket, Mass.; *m* Priscilla Coleman;
5–Elizabeth (1745-96), *m* Andrew **Myrick** (5 above).
10–Tristram **Coffin** (qv);
9–Mary (1645-1717), of Haverhill; *m* 1662, Nathaniel **Starbuck**;
8–Priscilla (1676-1762), of Nantucket; *m* John **Coleman** (1667-1762);
7–Elihu (1699-1789), *m* 1720, Jemima Barnard (1699-1779; John[8], *m* Mary Macy [John[9]; Thomas[10]]);
6–Priscilla (1731-70), *m* 1750, Peter **Coffin** (6 above).
8–Robert **Starkweather,** came from Wales, Scotland or Isle of Man, 1640, settled at Roxbury, Mass.; *m* Jennet Roberts (John[9], of Roxbury, Mass.);
7–John (*b* 1646), of Roxbury; *m* Ann– (*d* 1727);
6–John (1680-1750), of Ipswich; *m* 1708, Mary Herrick (1690-1786);
5–Robert (1728-1819), of Stonington, Conn.; *m* 1752, Sarah (Eveleth) Colby (1732-1824);
4–Charles (1767-1835), of Stonington; *m* 1785, Deborah Brown (1764-1843);
3–Rev. John (1800-65), of Worthington, Mass.; *m* 1830, Mercy (Hubbard) Hall;
2–Sarah Jane (2 below).
9–George **Hubbard** (1601-84), settled at Hartford, Conn.; *m* 1640, Elizabeth Watts (*d* 1702; Richard[10]);
8–Joseph (1643-86), of Middletown, Conn.; *m* 1670, Mary Porter (1650-1707);
7–John (1678-1726), of Middletown; *m* 1702/03, Mary Phillips (*d* 1736);
6–Joseph (1703-89), of Middletown; Am. Rev.; *m* 1728, Elizabeth Hollister (1710-85);

5–Manoah (1739-1801), of Middletown; Am. Rev.; *m* 1762, Hannah Woodward;
4–Joseph (1775-1823), of Middletown; War 1812; *m* 1796, Sarah Brooks (1775-1850);
3–Mercy (1800-87), of Middletown; *m* 2d, 1830, Rev. John **Starkweather** (3 above);
2–Sarah Jane (1835-1915), *m* as his 2d wife, 1858, William **Churchill** (1825-73), of Boston, Mass., and N.Y.; issue: I–William (1859-1920; *m* 1889, Llewella [Pierce] Clough); II–Arthur H. (1 above); III–Clarence (1865-1927).
1–*m* June 20, 1894, Cora Hatch, *b* Feb. 14, 1866; dau. of Thomas Jefferson Hatch (1834-73).
1–Ed. Montclair, N.J., pub. schs. Associated with Phelps Dodge Corpn., New York, for 49 yrs., cashier for more than 30 yrs. Mem. S.M.D. (dep.gov. and historian, N.J., Soc.) Huguenot Soc., S.A.R. (chapter pres.), I.A.G. Trustee Montclair Art Assn.; mem. Advisory bd. Montclair Community Chest. Residence: 6 Westover Rd., Montclair, N.J.

1–**CLAPP, Edward Fonda,** *b* Arkansas City, Kan., Feb. 25, 1893.
9–Thomas **Clapp** (1597-1684), from Eng. 1633, settled at Weymouth, Mass.; deacon at Scituate, 1640; dep. Gen. Ct., 1649; overseer of poor, 1667; *m* Abigail–;
8–Thomas (1639-91), housewright, Dedham, Mass.; *m* 1662, Mary Fisher (*b* 1644; Lt. Joshua[9] [*b* 1621], from Eng., 1637, *m* Mary, dau. of Dea. Nathaniel Aldis, of Dedham);
7–Samuel (1682-1772), farmer, Dedham; *m* 2d, Bethiah Dean (1697-1778; Dea. Samuel[8] [1666-1731], of Taunton; John[9], [1639-1716], first white child *b* in Taunton);
6–Jonathan (*b* 1714), farmer, Norton, Mass.; *m* —Hewes, of Wrentham;
5–David (1744-1823), of Norton; in old French war, 1759; went to Can., 1778; lt. under Gen. Sullivan; capt. of militia of Norton; mem. State Legislature, 1792-95; *m* 1767, Hannah King (1748-1839);
4–George, of Norton; painter, Dorchester; farmer, Norton; *m* Esther Lincoln, of Taunton;
3–Perez C. (*d* 1893), of Mass.; *m* 1848, Sarah I. Collins (*d* 1868);
2–Henry Beecher (2 below).
9–Jellis Douwese **Fonda** (1604-62; son of Douw [*b* 1580], of Amsterdam, Holland); came from Holland, 1642, settled at Rensselaerwyck (nr. Albany); settler at Beverwyck (Albany), 1654; *m* Hester Douwese Jans (1615-90), dau. of Douwe Janzoon de Vries VanArentsvelt (1580-1653), glazier, burgess of Leyden, 1615;
8–Douw Jellise (1640-1700), of Albany and Troy; mem. Dutch Reformed Ch., Albany, 1683; *m* 1666, Rebecca Conyn (Leander[9]);
7–Jellis (1670-1738), of Albany, 1697; Schenectady, 1700-20; gunsmith; *m* 1695, Rachel Winne (Peter[8]);
6–Douw (1696 or 1701-1780), of Schenectady, moved to Caughnawaga, 1751; *m* 1st, 1725, Maritje Vrooman (*d* 1756);
5–John (1739-1814), of Caughnawaga, N.Y.; maj. Tryon Co. bn. of minutemen; first tax collector Tryon Co.; pvt. Capt. Fonda's Co., Col. Fisher's Regt. Tryon Co. Militia; *m* 1768, Angelica Hansen (1750-1846; Capt. Henry[6]);
4–Giles (1789-1852), of Caughnawaga and Johnstown; moved to Hancock Co., Ill.; *m* 1811, Mariah Dockstader (1791-1845; Henry G.[5]);
3–John Giles (1822-1910), of Fonda, N.Y., and Fountain Green, Ill.; lt. Mexican War; col. Civil War; co. surveyor Ill. and Kan.; mayor of Warsaw, Ill.; *m* 1849, Mary McConnell (1825-76);
2–Nellie (*b* 1859), *m* 1884, Henry Beecher **Clapp** (1851-1924), Kan. pioneer; cattleman, freighter, grocer; issue: I–Fred Henry (*b* 1885; *m* Verna Margaret Evans); II–Omar (1888-89); III–Edward Fonda (1 above).
1–*m* Apr. 24, 1918, Mabel Florence Smith, *b* New York, N.Y., Sept. 26, 1902; dau. of Ernest C. Smith, of Eng., *m* Margaret Hummer, of Germany; issue: 1–Evelyn Nellie, *b* New York, N.Y., Jan. 20, 1919; 2–Edward Fonda, Jr., *b* New York, Apr. 26, 1921.
1–Asst. to chief draftsman, Warren & Wetmore, architects, New York, 1921-30. Life underwriter, Penn Mutual Life Ins. Co., 1930–. Served in U.S.N., Sept. 7, 1912-Dec. 20, 1920, last rating, chief pharmacist's mate. Mem. S.A.R., I.A.G., A.L. Congregational. Republican. Club: New York Architectural (pres. 1928-29). Residence: 242 Hart Boul., W.N.B., Staten Island, New York, N.Y.

1–**CLARK, Albert Benjamin,** *b* Sheffield, Mass., June 5, 1854.
8–Dea. George **Clark** (*b* Eng.-*d* Milford, Conn., 1690), called senior and carpenter; one of first settlers of Milford, 1639; *m* Sarah– (*d* 1689);
7–Thomas (1638-1719), largest landowner in Milford; *m* 1st, Hannah Gilbert (*d* 1703), of New Haven, Conn. (William[8]);
6–George (1673-1726), *m* 1705, Sarah (Beard) Buckingham (*b* 1675; Capt. John Beard[7], *m* ca. 1655, Hannah [Hawley] Ufford or Offit);
5–Thomas (1715-74), *m* Deborah Buckingham (1718-1808; Samuel[6], *m* Silence Clark);
4–Elisha (1758-1840), soldier Am. Rev., pensioned; *m* 1777, Sarah Beach (1760-1851; Landa[5], soldier Am. Rev., with Washington when he crossed the Delaware, *m* Abigail Baldwin);
3–Elisha (*b* 1778), from Milford, Conn., to Sheffield, Mass.; *m* Jane Baldwin (*d* 1853; Isaac[4], *m* Sarah Camp);
2–Orren Elisha (*b* Harwinton, Conn., 1815-*d* 1884), dairy farmer; *m* 1853, Esther Daniels (*b* Lopen, Eng., 1835-*d* New Haven, Conn., 1924; George[3], *m* Mary Prier); issue: I–Albert B. (1 above); II–Emma Augusta (*b* 1858; *m* Dwight W. Blakeslee); III–Ida Estelle (*b* 1865; *m* Fred W. Ford).
1–*m* Oct. 5, 1882, Lillian Amelia Burt (qv for issue).
1–Ed. S. Berkshire Inst. Mem. Mass. Bar, 1880–. Special justice Lee Ct.; mem. Mass. Legislature, 1897, 1912,13. Pres. Berkshire Bar Assn.; chmn. Rep. Town Com., 25 yrs. Federal Appeal Agt. for Div. 3 and Legal Advisory Bd. during World War. Mason. Residence: 83 Franklin St., Lee, Mass.

1–**CLARK, Lillian Amelia Burt (Mrs. Albert B.),** *b* New Milford, Conn., Oct. 5, 1862.
10–Henry **Burt** (qv);
9–Dea. Jonathan (*b* Eng.-*d* 1715), of Springfield, Mass.; dea.; actg. atty.; town clk.; made only record of the destruction of Springfield by the Indians, 1675, *m* at Boston, 1651, Elizabeth Lobdell (*d* 1684);
8–John (1658-1712), of Springfield, Mass.; *m* 1684, Sarah Day (1664-1716; Thomas[9], *m* Sarah Cooper);
7–Capt. John (1687-1770), *m* 1st, 1710, Abigail Rix (1689-1726; Thomas[8], *m* Abigail Ingersol);
6–John (1712-94), of Springfield; *m* 1733, Sarah Stebbins (1708-61; Joseph[7], *m* Rebecca Cotton);
5–Rix (1748-77), *m* 1772, Lucy Mun (*b* 1744; Samuel[6], *m* Sarah Van Horn);
4–Rix (1772-1841), *m* 1793, Miriam Wright (1774-1863; Stephen[5], *m* Rachel Wright);
3–Henry (1795-1855), *m* 1818, Sarah Brigham Pratt;
2–Andrew Sigourney (2 below).
8–Thomas **Brigham** (qv);
7–Capt. Samuel (1652-1713), of Marlboro, Mass.; his home was a garrison during Queen Ann's War; was rewarded by the govt. for his patriotism; treas., selectman, rep. Gen. Ct.; founder of the tanning industry and shoe trade in Marlboro; *m* 1684, Elizabeth Howe (1665-1739; Abraham[8], *m* Hannah Ward);
6–Charles (1700-81), of Grafton, Mass.; rep. Gen. Ct., magistrate, selectman; served in colonial wars and Am. Rev.; *m* Mary Peters (1716-97), of Newport, R.I.;
5–Sarah (1743-1813), of Grafton; *m* 2d, ante 1773, Col. John **Goulding** (1726-91), soldier Am. Rev. (Capt. Palmer[6], *m* Abigail Rice);
4–Martha, called Patty (*b* 1779), of Grafton; *m* 1796, Joseph **Pratt** (1774-1843; Seth[5], minute man in Am. Rev., *m* Margaret Stacy);
3–Sarah Brigham (*b* 1798), of Shrewsbury, Mass.; *m* Henry **Burt** (3 above).
8–Jeremiah **Meacham** (*d* 1695), from Eng. to Salem, Mass., bet. 1630 and 42; *m* 1st, 1640, Margaret– (*d* 1679);
7–Capt. Isaac (1643-1715), *m* at Topsfield, Conn., 1669, Widow Deborah (Browning) Perkins (1646-post 1704; Thomas Browning[8]);
6–Ebenezer (1678-1744), *m* 1720, Mary Adams (*b* 1699; John[7], *m* Esther–);
5–Barnabas (1731-1812), from Enfield to Windsor,

Conn.; Am. Rev.; *m* 1758, Margaret Owen (1742-1824; Samuel[6], *m* Margaret Griswold);
4–Barnabas (1759-post 1811), to Salisbury, Conn.; Am. Rev.; *m* Abigail Weldon (*b* 1757; Jesse[5], *m* Ruth–);
3–Hiram (1805-87), of Sheffield; *m* 1833, Saloma Gorham;
2–Ann Smith (2 below).
9–Capt. John **Gorham** (qv);
8–Jabez (1656-1725), of Bristol, R.I.; wounded in King Philip's War; *m* ante 1677, Hannah (Sturgis) Gray (*d* 1736; Edward[9], *m* Alice–);
7–Jabez (1684-1745), *m* 1st, Leah– (*d* Bristol, R.I., 1739);
6–Nathan (*b* 1725), *m* Susanna–;
5–George (1759-1848), Am. Rev., pensioned; *m* Mary Wells (1760-1824);
4–Elisha (1796-1848), *m* 1815, Pamelia Bosworth (1797-1825; Raymond[5], *m* Rachel Hinkson);
3–Saloma (1816-1881), *m* Hiram **Meacham** (3 above);
2–Ann Smith (1837-1915), of Sheffield, Mass.; *m* 1853, Andrew Sigourney Burt (1829-99), of Sheffield; (adopted in infancy by Elnathan and Electa Dewey, of Westfield, Mass.), and adopted their name **Dewey;** produce mcht.; issue (surname Dewey): I–Mae Inez (1855-1912; *m* Llewellyn E. Griswold); II–Ermina Alice (*b* 1861; *m* Frederick C. Pidsley); III–Lillian Amelia (1 above); IV–Hiram Eddie (1864-72).
1–*m* Oct. 5, 1882, Albert Benjamin Clark (qv); issue (all *b* Lee, Mass.): 1–Albert Benjamin (*b* and *d* 1886); 2–Albert, *b* Mar. 26, 1888; Trinity Coll., '11, LL.B. (cum laude), Boston U. Law Sch., 1914; *m* May 20, 1920, Lillian Evelyn, dau. of Elmer Lowry, *m* Grace Moore (issue: Albert Raymond); 3–Emma Augusta, *b* Feb. 1, 1891; Smith, '13; *m* Sept. 5, 1912, Dr. Sturges Bradford Shields, capt. World War; son of Dr. Nelson Turner Shields, *m* Eleanor Beers, of New York, N.Y. (issue: Sturges Bradford).
1–Mem. Mass. State Rep. Com., 2 yrs., Lee Rep. Town Com., 4 yrs. Mem. D.C.W., D.A.R. (organized two chapters, and mem. of Ex-Regents Club of Mass.), N.E.H.G.S., Bosworth Assn., Chapin Family Assn., Pilgrim John Howland Soc. Clubs: State Fed. of Women's, Founders, State Child Welfare. Residence: 83 Franklin St., Lee, Mass.

1–**CLARK, Elroy Newton,** *b* North Hero, Vt., July 22, 1860.
9–William **Hyde** (qv);
8–Samuel (*b* Hartford, Conn., ca. 1637), *m* Jane Lee;
7–Thomas (1672-1775), of Norwich, Conn.; *m* 1697, Mary Backus (1672-1753);
6–Capt. Jacob (1703-82), in Battle of Bennington, Am. Rev., 1777; *m* 1727, Hannah Kingsbury (*b* Haverill, Mass., 1709-*d* Bennington, Vt., 1770);
5–Jacob (1730-1815), to North Hero, Grand Isle Co., Vt.; *m* 1753, Hannah Hazen (*b* 1729-*d* Georgia, Chittendon Co., Vt.);
4–Jonathan (1767-1829), *m* 1793, Hannah Bronson (*b* New Milford, Conn., 1775);
3–Rueben (*b* 1794), *m* 1816, Rebecca Tobias (*b* 1799; James[4], *m* Mary Bloodgood);
2–Sarah Ann, *m* Ransom Loup **Clark** (Stephen[3], *d* Alburg, Grand Isle Co., Vt., 1825); issue: I–Clinton (*b* 1863); II–Mary Ann (*d* 1922); III–Warren (*d* 1928; m Josephine Evarts); IV–Alice (*d* 1897; *m* Frank Rowell); V–Martha (*d* 1920; *m* Charles Wiley); VI–Charles Hyde (*b* 1857; *m* Grayce E. Champion); VII–Elroy N. (1 above); VIII–Clayton Arthur (*b* 1862; *m* Flora Lane).
1–*m* July 1, 1901, Alice Babcock Calkins, *b* New York, N.Y., Sept. 23, 1870; dau. of Frank A. Calkins, of Denver, Colo.; issue: 1–Ruth Moulton, *b* Denver, Colo., Nov. 14, 1906; Pine Manor, Wellesley, Mass., '28.
1–A.B., U.Vt., '85 (Delta Psi, P.B.K.), LL.B., Georgetown U., 1892. Gen. atty. D.&R.G.W. R.R.Co. (see Who's Who in America). Clubs: Colorado Motor, University, Lakewood Country, Denver Athletic. Residence: 850 Lafayette St., Denver, Colo.

1–**CLARK, Hattie Loanza Benton (Mrs. John Sinclair),** *b* B'hamdun, Syria, June 20, 1861.
8–Andrew **Benton** (qv);
7–Samuel (1658 or 68-1746), of Hartford and Tolland, Conn.; *m* ca. 1679, Sarah Chatterton (*b* 1660; William[8], of New Haven, Conn.);
6–Daniel (*b* 1696), *m* 1722, Mary Skinner, of Hartford;
5–Daniel (*b* 1724), *m* 1746, Mary Wheeler, of Hartford;
4–Jacob (1760-1843), Am. Rev., from Tolland, Conn.; *m* 1782, Sarah Ladd (*d* post 1843);
3–Azariah (1790-1857), of Tolland; *m* Presenda Ladd;
2–Rev. William Austin (2 below).
4–Capt. Daniel **Howe,** only survivor of his family in the Deerfield (Mass.) massacre; Indians took him with them to the northern end of Lake Champlain, and he made his escape by skating down the length of the lake where their arrows failed to reach him;
3–Anna, *m* 1807, Joel **Goulding,** of Philipston, Mass.;
2–Loanza (1822-99), practiced medicine; *m* 1847, Rev. William Austin **Benton** (1818-1874), of Tolland, Conn.; missionary in Syria, 1847-69; issue: I–Charles William (1852-1913; *m* Elma Hixson); II–George Henry (1853-1901; *m* Jeannette Lyall); III–Edwin Austin (1856-1915); IV–Hattie Loanza (1 above); V–Mary Lathrop (*b* 1864).
1–*m* June 11, 1883, Prof. John Sinclair Clark (Feb. 25, 1849-Sept. 5, 1913); son of William Murray Clark, of Minneapolis, Minn.; issue (all *b* Minneapolis, Minn.): 1–Miriam Sinclair, *b* May 2, 1886; B.A., U.Minn., '09; author (see Who's Who in America); *m* Dec. 27, 1910, Zenas L., son of Alden H. Potter, of Minneapolis (issue: Jean Clark; Margaret Bliss; Constance Benton); 2–Margaret Benton, *b* Feb. 24, 1890; B.A., Smith, '11; *m* June 11, 1914, Howard D. Williams, son of Henry David Williams, of Springfield, Mass. (issue: David Benton; Annie Sinclair); 3–Beatrice E., *b* Feb. 22, 1896; B.A., Smith, '18; *m* Nov. 12, 1923, Percy Bourne, son of James Neave Brown, of Birmingham, Eng. (issue: Barbara Bourne; Neave Sinclair).
1–Ed. U. of Minn. Mem. Soc. N.E. Women. Congregationalist. Republican. Address: c/o Mrs. Z. L. Potter, 103 Lincoln Park Dr., Syracuse, N.Y.

1–**CLARKE, Grace Giddings Julian (Mrs. Charles Burns),** *b* Centreville, Ind., Sept. 11, 1865.
6–René (St. Julien) **Julian** (*b* ca. 1650), soldier under William of Orange in battle at the Boyne, 1690; from Paris, France, to Chesapeake Bay, Md., ca. 1692 or 93; *m* Margaret Bullock, of Bermuda;
5–Isaac, of Md., or Va.; *m* Barbara White (Dr. Robert[6], surgeon British Navy, *m* Margaret Hogue or Hoge);
4–Isaac (ca. 1750-1831), removed from N.C. to Ind.; *m* Sarah Long (John[5]; Edward[6], came with William Penn, 1682);
3–Isaac (1781-1823), from N.C. to Ind., 1808; mem. State Legislature, 1822; *m* 1809, Rebeckah Hoover (Andrew[4], *m* Elizabeth Waymire);
2–George Washington (2 below).
8–George **Giddings** (1608-76), from St. Albans, Herts., Eng., in the "Planter," 1635; settled at Ipswich, Mass.; dep. Gen. Ct.; *m* Jane Tuttle (1615-80);
7–John (1639-91), of Ipswich; lt. in militia; *m* Sarah Alcock;
6–Thomas (*b* 1683), *m* Sarah Butler;
5–Joshua (1719-1807), of Lyme, Conn.; *m* Jane Reed (1724-1803);
4–Joshua (1756-1833), of Lyme; Am. Rev.; town official of Hartford, Conn.; *m* Submit Jones, of Barkhamsted; *m* 2d, Elizabeth Pease, of Enfield, Conn. (1756-1827);
3–Joshua Reed (1795-1864), *b* Athens, Pa.; soldier War 1812; mem. Ohio Legislature, 1826; mem. U.S. Congress, 1838-59; *d* at Montreal, Can.; *m* Laura Waters.
2–George Washington **Julian** (1817-99), mem. Ind. Legislature, 1845; Free Soil candidate for V.P. of U.S., 1852; mem. U.S. Congress, 1849-51 and 1860-71; surveyor-gen. of N.M., 1885-89; author; *m* 1845, Anne E. Finch (1827-60); *m* 2d, 1863, Laura Ann Giddings (1839-84); issue (2d marriage); I–Grace G. (1 above); II–Paul (*b* 1867).
1–*m* Sept. 11, 1887, Charles Burns Clarke, *b* Irvington, Ind., Jan. 15, 1862; son of Thomas

Moore Clarke, of Shoals, Martin Co., Ind.
1-Ph.B., Butler U., '84, Ph.M., 1885. Mem. editorial staff, Indianapolis Star, since 1911. Pres. Ind. Fed. of Women's Clubs, 1909-11; dir. Gen. Fed., 1912-16. Author and editor. Clubs: Indianapolis Woman's, Irvington Woman's, Indianapolis Propylaeum, Soc. Ind. Pioneers, Ind. Hist. Soc. Residence: 115 S. Audubon Rd., Irvington, Indianapolis, Ind.

1-**CLARKE, Mary Emeline Bosworth (Mrs. James T.),** *b* Batavia, N.Y., July 3, 1850.
9-Edward **Bosworth** (qv);
8-Jonathan (1613-88), of Hingham and Rehoboth, Mass.; *m* Elizabeth- (1614-1705);
7-Jonathan (ca. 1636-ante 1717), of Swansea, Mass.; *m* 1661, Hannah Howland (John[8], Mayflower, qv);
6-John (1671-1719), of Barrington, R.I.; *m* 1702, Elizabeth Toogood (1682-ca. 1773);
5-David (1718-post 1786), of Lebanon, Conn.; *m* 1743, Mary Strong (1722-86);
4-Jabin (1752-ca. 1792), of Whitehall, N.Y.; *m* 1773, Luna West;
3-Stephen Strong (1785-1827), of Fairhaven, Vt., and Buffalo, N.Y.; *m* 1806, Mary Raymond (1789-1859);
2-William Raymond (2 below).
9-John **Alden,** Mayflower Pilgrim (qv);
8-Elizabeth, *m* William **Pabodie** (*b* 1620);
7-Mercy (*b* 1649), *m* John **Simmons**;
6-Martha (*b* 1677), *m* 2d, 1709, Samuel **West** (*b* 1672);
5-Moses (*b* 1716), *m* Jemima Eaton;
4-Luna (1754-1822), *m* Jabin **Bosworth** (4 above);
3-Stephen Strong, *m* Mary Raymond (3 above);
2-William Raymond (1810-99), of Batavia, N.Y.; farmer, deacon; *m* Juliet Sill; *m* 2d, 1843, Susan Sherman Wilcox (1817-98); issue (1st marriage): I-William Harvey (1839-1918; *m* 1867, Emma J. Starks, 1848-1927); II-Adelaide Juliet (1841-1925; *m* 1865, Marion Nichols); issue (2d marriage): I-Charles Milton (1846-1910; *m* 1874, Fannie L. Smith, 1851-1925); II-Mary Emeline (1 above); III-Franke Stephen (1853-80).
1-*m* Sept. 21, 1875, James Thomas Clarke (Dec. 11, 1854-Jan. 16, 1915); son of Thomas Clarke, of Batavia, N.Y.; issue (all *b* Rochester, N.Y.): 1-Walter Bosworth, *b* Aug. 8, 1876; ed. Rochester U.; *m* Apr. 1, 1899, Veronica, dau. of Joseph Frauel, of Rochester (issue: Bonita; James; Rosemary; Margaret); 2-Ernest James, *b* Nov. 17, 1877; *m* May 7, 1901, Hattie, dau. of George Hutchinson, of Brooklyn, N.Y. (issue: Verne; Lincoln; Walter); 3-Grace Lillian, *b* Jan. 2, 1881; *m* Sept. 7, 1909, James B., son of John Miller, of Coalport, Pa. (issue: Susan Sherman); 4-Katharine Bosworth, *b* Dec. 2, 1886; ed. Pratt Inst.; D.A.R.; 5-Pansy Bosworth (christened Frances Willard), *b* Aug. 24, 1888.
1-Ed. Mrs. Bryan's Young Ladies' Sem., Batavia, N.Y. Genealogist. Mem. S.M.D., W.C.T.U. (treas. Monroe Co., N.Y., del., to Nat. Conv. at Atlanta, Ga., 1890; del. to National and World's Conv., Chicago, 1893), California state supt. of work for young people. Historian of the Bosworth Assn. of America; compiler of the Bosworth Genealogy, and editor of Bosworth Bulletin. Residence: 3320 Randolph Av., Oakland, Calif.

1-**CLAY, Brutus Junius,** *b* Whitehall, Ky., Feb. 20, 1847.
7-Capt. John (Claye) **Clay** (qv);
6-Charles (1638-86), Henrico Co., Va.; in Bacon's Rebellion; *m* Hannah Wilson (John[7], of Henrico Co., Va.);
5-Henry (1672-1760), *m* 1708/09, Mary Mitchell (1693-1777; William[6], of Chesterfield Co., Va., *m* Elizabeth-);
4-Charles (1716-89), *m* Martha Green;
3-Maj. Gen. Green (1757-1828), settled in Ky.; represented Ky. district in Va. Legislature; mem. Va. Conv. that ratified the Federal Constn.; a framer of the Ky. Constn.; mem. Ky. House and Senate; led 3,000 Ky. vols. to relief of Ft. Meigs, 1813 (see portrait); *m* Sallie Lewis (*b* 1776; Col. Thomas[4], Am. Rev.);
2-Maj. Gen. Cassius Marcellus (2 below).
7-Maj. Henry **Filmer** (qv);
6-Martha, *m* Thomas **Greene,** "The Sea Gull" (Thomas[7], from Holland to Va., *m* Martha-);

HON. BRUTUS JUNIUS CLAY

5-Thomas (1665-1730), *m* Elizabeth Marston (1672-1759; Thomas[6], justice of Henrico, 1682, *m* Elizabeth Marvell);
4-Martha (1719-93), *m* Charles **Clay** (4 above);
3-Maj. Gen. Green, *m* Sallie Lewis (3 above);

MAJ. GEN. CASSIUS M. CLAY (1810-1903).

2-Maj. Gen. Cassius Marcellus (1810-1903), B.A., Yale, '32; served in Mexican War; maj. gen. U. S. V. in Civil War; Am. minister to Russia 1861-69, and negotiated the purchase of Alaska; founder of Berea Coll., Ky. (see portrait); *m* 1833, Mary Jane Warfield (1815-1900; Dr. Elisha[3]); issue: I-Warfield (1835-52); II-Green (1837-83); III-Mary Barr (1839-1924); IV-Sally Lewis (*b* 1841; *m* James Bennett); V-Brutus Junius (1 above); VI-Laura (*b* 1849); VII-Anne Warfield (Mrs. S. Dabney Crenshaw, see Vol. II, p. 108).
1-*m* Feb. 20, 1872, Pattie Amelia Field (1848-91), dau. of Col. Christopher Irvine Field, of Boliver Co., Miss.; issue (all *b* Richmond, Ky.): 1-Belle Lyman (Mrs. Harris Hancock, qv); 2-Christopher Field (qv); 3-Orville Martin, *b* May 7, 1879; M.D., Gross Med. Coll., 1902; *m* June 28, 1905, Elizabeth, dau. of Daniel Long Wise; 4-Mary Warfield, *b* Sept. 26, 1882; *m* Sept. 30, 1907, Edward Douglas Johnston; 5-Charlotte Elizabeth, *b* May 31, 1890; *m* Oct. 1, 1883, Victor Vernon.

1–*m* 2d, Jan. 15, 1895, Lalla Rook (Fish) Marsteller, *b* Florence, Ky., Mar. 26, 1862; dau. of T. S. Fish, *m* Nancy Poore, of Nicholasville, Ky. (Mrs. Clay has one son by former marriage, William F. Marsteller, atty. at law, Cleveland, O.).
1–C.E., U.Mich., '68 (Delta Phi), M.A., 1918. Diplomat, financier, planter, mfr. Was tendered position of Am. minister to Argentina, 1897, by President McKinley, but declined; apptd. by Pres. McKinley Am. commissioner to Paris Exposition, 1900; apptd. by Pres. Roosevelt E.E. and M.P. to Switzerland, 1905-10. Life mem. Institute of Geneva, Union Soc. of the Civil War (see Who's Who in America). Residence: Richmond, Ky.

MAJ. GEN. GREEN CLAY (1757-1828).

1–**CLAY, C(hristopher) Field,** *b* Richmond, Ky., Dec. 19, 1874.
7–Gen. Robert **Lewis,** from Eng. to Va., 1700;
6–Lt. Stephen, of Fairfax Co., Va.; lt. in Am. Rev.; *m* Elizabeth Offut (Judge James[7], *m* Rachael, dau. of Col. Ninian Beall, qv);
5–Col. Thomas (1749-1809), of Fayette Co., Ky.; col. in Am. Rev.; mem. 1st Ky. Constl. Conv.; 4th judge of Lexington (Ky.) Circuit; *m* 1773, Elizabeth Payne (*b* 1757; Col. Edward[6] [1726-1806], *m* Anne Holland Conyers, *b* 1728);
4–Sallie (1776-1867), *m* Maj. Gen. Green **Clay** (1757-1828); see portrait;
3–Maj. Gen. Cassius M. (1810-1903), see portrait; *m* Mary Jane Warfield;
2–Brutus Junius (2 below).
10–Henry **Field,** from Eng. in the "Expectation," 1635; settled at Jamestown, Va., where he died; and thru his grandson:
8–Abraham;
7–Abraham, will probated in Culpeper Co., Va., 1775;
6–John, educated in Eng.; burgess from Culpeper Co., Va., 1761-66, 1766-68; ensign in British Army in French and Indian War; was present at Braddock's defeat; col. in Am. Rev.; killed at Point Pleasant by the Indians under Cornstalk; his heirs were granted large tracts of land in what is now Bourbon Co., Ky.; *m* Anna Clark;
5–Ezekiel Henry (1750-82), killed in battle of Blue Licks; *m* Elizabeth Field (Henry[6], burgess, mem. Va. Constl. Conv.);
4–Ezekiel Henry (1782-1866), *m* 1810, Patsey Irvine (Col. William[5], Am. Rev., mem. Va. Legislature from Ky., *m* Elizabeth Hockaday);
3–Christopher Irvine (1813-73), of Bolivar Co., Miss.; *m* Charlotte E. Martin;
2–Pattie Amelia (2 below).
6–Maj. John **Martin** (1749-1837; 1st cousin of Gen. George Rogers Clark), sgt. and capt. of minute men in Am. Rev.; promoted maj. for bravery at siege of York, Pa.; first sheriff of Clark Co., Ky.; *m* 1775, Elizabeth Lewis (David, Sr.[7], of Albemarle Co., Va.);
5–John Lewis (*b* Albemarle Co., Va., 1779), of Louisville, Ky.; owned cotton plantations in Bolivar Co., Miss.; *m* 1st, Catherine Blanton;
4–Orville, *m* Sarah Sneed, of Frankfort, Ky.;
3–Charlotte E. (*d* 1850), *m* 1846, Christopher Irvine **Field** (3 above);
2–Pattie Amelia (1848-91), *m* 1872, as his 1st wife, Brutus Junius **Clay** (qv for Clay lineages); see portrait.
1–*m* June 14, 1899, Elinor Wise, *b* Evans, Colo., Feb. 8, 1877; dau. of Daniel Long Wise, of Boulder, Colo., *m* Sarah McCutcheon; issue: 1–Katherine Belle, *b* Denver, Colo., Oct. 20, 1901; *m* Sept. 3, 1924, William Covington Benton (issue: Field Clay, *b* Aug. 25, 1926; Elinor Katherine, *b* Feb. 28, 1929).
1–Ed. U.Colo. Attorney-at-Law, firm of Clay & Benton. Mem. S.R. Mason. Episcopalian. Residence: 2044 Bellaire St., Denver, Colo.

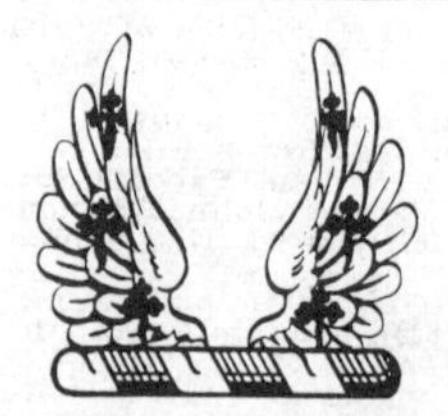

CLAY

Arms: Argent, a chevron engrailed between three trefoils slipped sable.
Crest: Two wings expanded argent, semes of trefoils slipped sable.

1–**HANCOCK, Belle Lyman Clay (Mrs. Harris),** *b* Richmond, Ky., Nov. 4, 1872.
8–Richard **Warfield** (qv);
7–John (1675-1718), *m* 1696, Ruth Gaither (John[8], *m* Ruth Morley);
6–Benjamin (1702-69), of Warfield's Range, Howard Co., Md.; *m* 1731, Rebeckah Ridgely (1693-1755; Judge Nicholas[7], *m* Sarah, dau. of Capt. George Worthington);
5–Elisha (1741-1818), mem. Com. Observation in Am. Rev.; went to Ky., 1791; *m* 2d, Ruth Burgess (Joseph[6], mem. Com. Safety, Anne Arundel Co., Md.; soldier Am. Rev., *m* Elizabeth Dorsey);
4–Dr. Elisha, *m* Maria Barr (Robert[5], of Phila.);
3–Mary Jane (1815-1900), *m* Maj. Gen. Cassius Marcellus **Clay;**
2–Brutus Junius (qv for Clay lineages), *m* 1st 1872, Pattie Amelia Field (1848-91).
1–*m* Sept. 30, 1907, Harris Hancock (qv); issue: 1–Thomasia Harris, *b* Cincinnati, O., Sept. 25, 1908; 2–Belle Clay, *b* Cincinnati, Jan. 15, 1912.
1–Mem. C.D.A., D.A.R., etc. Residence: 2367 Auburn Ave., Cincinnati, O.

1–**HANCOCK, Harris,** *b* "Ellerslie," Albemarle Co., Va., May 14, 1867.

HARRIS

Arms: Argent, a lion rampant sable, over all a chevron ermine.
Crest: A falcon with outstretched wings.

9–Capt. Thomas **Harris** (qv);
8–Maj. Robert, of "The Forks," Hanover Co., Va.; *m* ca. 1660, Mary (Claiborne) Rice (Col. William Claiborne[9], qv);
7–Capt. William, *m* ca. 1695, Temperance Overton (1679-1710; William[8], qv);
6–William (*b* 1707), *m* Henrietta–;
5–Anna Amelia, *m* William **Day** (John[6], *m* Miss Esom);
4–Lucy (1768-1845), *m* June 8, 1785, her cousin, John **Harris** (*b* Aug. 26, 1763; John[5]; John[6] [*b* 1703], *m* Ann–; William[7], 7 above);

CAPT. RICHARD JOHNSON HANCOCK (Mar. 22, 1838-Apr. 19, 1912); served in C.S.A., 1861-65; 3d lt., 2d lt., 1st lt. and capt. Co. D, 9th La. Regt., Hayes Brig.; thrice severely wounded (From a photograph taken while he was convalescing from a wound received at Gettysburg).

3–John Overton (*b* "Oxford," Caroline Co., Va., 1794-1878), of "Ellerslie," Albemarle Co., Va.; *m* Sept. 20, 1820, Barbara Winfield Terrell (1804-83);
2–Thomasia Overton (Aug. 27, 1845-Mar. 15, 1930), *m* Nov. 22, 1864, Richard Johnson **Hancock** (1838-1912), see portrait; issue: I–Harris (1 above); II–Thomas Hightower (qv for other lineages); III–Elizabeth Hazelwood (Sept. 10, 1871-Apr. 1915); IV–Richard Jordan (Mar. 21, 1873-Feb. 1920); V–Arthur Boyd (qv for other lineages); VI–Thomasia Overton (*b* July 1, 1877; *m* Schuyler Poitevent); VII–Charles Russell (*m* Mabel Bolton); VIII–Emma Lewis (Dec. 12, 1881-June 18, 1907); IX–Jane Crawford (*b* July 16, 1884; *m* James Woods Garth).
1–*m* Sept. 30, 1907, Belle Lyman Clay (qv for issue).
1–Grad. U.Va., '86, A.B., Johns Hopkins, 1888, Cambridge (Eng.), A.M., Ph.D., Berlin, 1894, D.Sc., Paris, 1901. Prof. mathematics, U. of Cincinnati, since 1900. Author (see Who's Who in America). Mem. various math. and scientific socs., U.S. and abroad; treas. Am. Assn. University Profs., 1917-21; fellow A.A.A.S. (v.p. sect. A, 1923). Residence: 2367 Auburn Av., Cincinnati, O.

TERRELL

Arms: Argent, two chevronels azure, a bordure engrailed gules.
Crest: A boar's head couped and erect argent, issuant out of the mouth a peacock tail proper.
Motto: Sans crainte.

1–**HANCOCK, Thomas Hightower,** *b* "Ellerslie," Albemarle Co., Va., Jan. 9, 1869.
9–Robert **Terrell,** of Reading, Eng.;
8–Timothy (*b* at All Hallows, Eng., 1656), *m* Dorothy Colland;
7–Timothy, Jr., from Eng., settled in New Kent Co., Va.; *m* Elizabeth Foster;
6–Joseph (*b* Nov. 16, 1699);
5–Joseph (Jan. 28, 1745-Apr. 9, 1787), *m* Sept. 29, 1767, Elizabeth Mills (Jan. 26, 1747-Nov. 22, 1833; Nicholas[6]);
4–Charles (July 3, 1768-Aug. 1839), *m* Ann Lewis;
3–Barbara Wingfield (1804-83), *m* 1820, John Overton **Harris** (1794-1878);
2–Thomasia Overton (2 below).
11–Nicholas **Martian** (qv);
10–Elizabeth, *m* Col. George **Reade** (qv);
9–Mildred, *m* Col. Augustine **Warner,** II (1642-1681), speaker Va. Ho. of Burgesses (their son John, *m* Frances Fielding, and their son Fielding *m* Betty, sister of George Washington);

8–Elizabeth, *m* her cousin, Col. John **Lewis** (1669-1725), mem. Royal Council, co. lt., judge Supreme Ct. (John[9] [*b* 1635], of "Warner Hall," *m* Isabella, dau. of Augustine Warner, I; Gen. Robert[10], qv);
7–Col. Robert (1704-66), of "Belvoir"; *m* Jane Meriwether (Nicholas[8], *m* Elizabeth Crawford);
6–Mildred, *m* John **Lewis** (1729-80), "the honest lawyer," of King and Queen Co., Va. (Zachary[7] [1702-69], *m* 1725, Mary [1699-1781], dau. of Col. John Waller, *m* Dorothy King; Jean[8], from Wales, 1692, King and Queen Co., Va.);
5–John Zachary (*d* Mar. 7, 1784), ens. Am. Rev.; *m* 1st, Elizabeth Woolfork or Woodfolk;
4–Ann (1768-1843), as widow of William Phillips, *m* 2d, Charles **Terrell** (4 above);
3–Barbara W., *m* John O. **Harris** (3 above);
2–Thomasia Overton (1845-1930), *m* 1864, Richard Johnson **Hancock** (1838-1912); for issue and other lineages see Harris Hancock.
1–*m* Sept. 26, 1894, Marie Louise Price, *b* Mobile, Ala., May 16, 1874; dau. of Thomas Henry Price, of Mobile, Ala.; issue (all *b* Atlanta, Ga.): 1–Elizabeth Erskine, *b* July 23, 1895; B.A., Smith Coll.; 2–Richard Harris, *b* July 13, 1899; B.L., Atlanta Law Sch.; 3–Emma Louise, *b* Aug. 12, 1908; Boston U., '31; 4–John Overton, *b* Aug. 9, 1914.
1–M.D., Coll. Phys. and Surg. (Columbia), '91 (Chi Phi). Practicing physician since 1893; founder, pres. and chief surgeon, Atlanta Hosp.; gen. surgeon, Ga. Power Co., Southern Ry. Co.; consulting surgeon S.A.L.Ry. (see Who's Who in America). Democrat. Episcopalian. Mason. Odd Fellow, K.P. Residence: 308 Crew St., Atlanta, Ga.

LEWIS

Arms: *Argent, a dragon's head and neck erased vert, holding in the mouth a bloody hand proper.*
Crest: *A dragon's head and neck erased vert.*
Motto: *Omne solum forti patria est.*

1–**HANCOCK, Arthur Boyd,** *b* "Ellerslie," Albemarle Co., Va., June 26, 1875.
8–William **Hancock,** from Eng., 1707; atty. for Lord Pollock and held a grant for large tract of land nr. New Bern, N.C.; commr. for New Bern, 1723; *m* Eliza–;
7–Hector (*d* 1751), of Cartaret Co., N.C.; *m* Ann–;
6–Nathaniel, of Onslow Co., N.C.; *m* Sarah Ward (Enoch[7], mem. Provincial Congress, Hillsborough, N.C., 1775);
5–Enoch, of Onslow Co.;
4–William (1773-1849), *m* 1st, Dorothy–;
3–Nathaniel (1802-54), *m* 1824, Elizabeth Hightower (1801-50; Jordan[4], of Lunenburg Co., Va., *m* Elizabeth Hazelwood);
2–Richard Johnson (1838-1912), capt. C.S.A., 1861-65; *m* 1864, Thomasia Overton Harris (1845-1930); for issue and other lineages see Harris Hancock.
1–*m* June 30, 1908, Nancy Tucker Clay (qv); issue: 1–Arthur Boyd, Jr., *b* Paris, Ky., Jan. 24, 1910; 2–Nancy Clay, *b* Cincinnati, O., Jan. 2, 1912.
1–Ed. Johns Hopkins U., 1891-93; A.B., U.Chicago, '95. Breeder of thoroughbred horses. Pres. Bourbon Lumber Co. (see Who's Who in America). Clubs: Rotary, Country. Residence: Paris, Ky.

HANCOCK

Arms: *Gules, on a chief argent, three cocks of the field.*
Crest: *A demi-griffin argent, armed or.*
Motto: *Redeem time.*

1–**HANCOCK, Nancy Tucker Clay (Mrs. Arthur B.),** *b* Paris, Ky., Feb. 6, 1877.
9–Capt. John (Claye) **Clay** (qv);
8–Charles (1638-86), of Henrico Co., Va.; in Bacon's Rebellion, 1676; *m* Hannah Wilson (John[9], of Henrico Co.);
7–Henry (1672-1760), *m* 1708/09, Mary Mitchell (1693-1777; William[8], *m* Elizabeth–);
6–Henry, of Cumberland Co., Va.; will probated, 1764; *m* 1735, Lucy Green (*b* 1717; Thomas[7] [*b* 1665], *m* Elizabeth [1672-1759], dau. of Thomas Marston, justice of Henrico Co., 1682, *m* Elizabeth Marwell; Thomas[8], the "sea Gull," *m* Martha, dau. of Maj. Henry Filmer, qv);
5–Dr. Henry (1736-1820), of Cumberland Co., Va., and Bourbon Co., Ky.; *m* 1754, Rachel Povall (*d* 1820 aet. 81 yrs.; sister of Francis Povall, mem. Congress);
4–Henry (1779-1863), of Bourbon Co.; 2d lt. in War 1812, under Gen. Harrison; *m* Peggy Helm (1779-1854);
3–Samuel (1815-88), of "Marchmont," Paris, Ky.; *m* 1836, Nancy T. Wornall (1816-99; Thomas[4], *m* Sally Ryan);
2–James E. (1850-1910), of "Marchmont"; *m* 1871, Elizabeth Alexander (1849-1910; Charlton[8], of Paris); issue: I–Belle Brent (*m* Nov. 15, 1893, Miller Ward, son of Judge Quincy Ward, *m* Mary E. Miller); II–Samuel (*m* Amelia Field,

dau. of Col. Ezekiel Field Clay, of "Runnymede," *m* Mary L., dau. of John T. Woodford, *m* Elizabeth Buckner, g.dau. of Col. Henry Clay, of Bourbon Co., Ky.); III–Nancy Tucker (1 above); IV–James; V–Charlton.
1–*m* June 30, 1908, Arthur Boyd Hancock (qv for issue).
1–Ed. privately and at Miss Armstrong's Sch., Cincinnati, O. Clubs: Paris Country, Lexington Country. Residence: Paris, Ky.

1–**CLEARY, Helen Clarke Jenks (Mrs. P. Roger),** *b* St. Clair, Mich., Aug. 3, 1865.
9–Joseph (Jenckes) **Jenks** (qv);
8–Joseph (1632-1717), from Eng. with his father; one of the founders of Pawtucket, R.I., and established first iron and steel foundry there; *m* Esther Ballard (*b* 1633), of Pawtucket;
7–Maj. Nathaniel (1662-1723), of Providence, R.I.; *m* Hannah Bosworth (1663-1723; Jonathan[8], *m* Hannah, dau. of John Howland, qv);
6–Jonathan (*b* 1688), of Pawtucket; *m* Mary Slack, of Scituate, Mass.;
5–Jonathan (1718-87), of Cumberland, R.I.; *m* 1736, Harriet Pullen, of Smithfield, R.I.;
4–Lt. Jeremiah (1739-1811), began to spell name Jencks; of Smithfield; 3d signer of the Assn. Test in Newport, N.H.; lt. Newport vols. which took part in capture of Ticonderoga; removed to Newport, 1776; *m* 1775, Lucy Whipple (1746-1819), of Cumberland, R.I.;
3–Jeremiah Whipple (1780-1852), began to spell name Jenks; of Newport, N.H.; *m* 1803, Hester Wright Lane (1784-1850), of Sutton, N.H.;
2–Robert Henry (2 below).
5–Capt. John **Clarke** (1731-1834), from London, Eng., 1774; settled Boston; removed to Waterville, Me., where he was a shipbuilder; was capt. of a company, 1781; is said to have been one of the Boston Tea Party; *m* 1768, Maria Theresa Lark (1751-98), of Vienna, Austria;
4–George (1775-1823), of Waterville; *m* 1796, Mary McDonald (1776-1856);
3–Capt. John (1797-1876), of Waterville, Me., and St. Clair, Mich.; *m* 1819, Mary Sherburne (1795-1871);
2–Mary Sherburne (1829-1910), of Hallowell, Me., and St. Clair; *m* 1854, Robert Henry **Jenks** (1827-98), farmer, banker; postmaster, 20 yrs., mayor, 4 terms, St. Clair; issue: I–Emeline Clarke (1857-1927; *m* Benjamin F. Crampton); II–Herbert Lind (1859-73); III–Lucy Arzelia (*m* John L. Rees); IV–Helen C. (1 above); V–John H. (*b* 1866; *m* Marie Davidson Cleveland; *m* 2d, Carrie M. Ballinger); VI–Benjamin Lane (*b* 1869; *m* Louise Davidson); VII–Owen T. (1872-1928).
1–*m* June 27, 1889, P. Roger Cleary, M.E., *b* Mota Estates, Ireland, Aug. 14, 1858; pres. Cleary Coll. (founded by him, 1883), Ypsilanti, Mich., affiliated with Mich. State Normal; author; son of Roger Cleary, of Mota Estates, Boris O'Kane, Tipperary Co., Ireland, *m* Julia Costello; issue (all *b* Ypsilanti, Mich.): 1–Charles Brooks, *b* Oct. 15, 1890; ed. Cleary Coll., 1910; A.B., U.Mich., '14; served in U.S.A. on Mexican Border, 1916-17; commd. 2d lt., at Ft. Sheridan, 1917; with A.E.F., 1918: attended Arty. Sch., Saumur, France; lt., 7th F.A., aide to Gen. Holbrook; *married* 1923, Althea May Weaver, of Nachitoches, La. (issue: Patricia May, *b* 1923; Thomas Weaver, *b* 1924); 2–Marjory Julia, *b* July 2, 1892; ed. Cleary Coll., '15, Normal Coll., 1915, U.Mich., 1918 (Pi Beta Phi); sec. War Industries Bd., Washington, 1918; *m* Dec. 31, 1919, Charles Arthur McKinny, served A.E.F., son of Pres. Charles McKinny, *m* Minnie Alderman (issue: Charles A., Jr., *b* 1920; 2–Owen Cleary, *b* 1924); 3–Ruth Marie, *b* July 11, 1894; ed. Cleary Coll., '16, Normal Coll., 1916, U.Mich., A.B., '21 (Pi Beta Phi); sec. War Industries Bd., Washington, 1918; 4–Owen Jenks, *b* Jan. 4, 1900; ed. Cleary Coll., '19, Normal Coll., 1922, A.B., U.Mich., '25; U. Detroit Law, 1931 (Phi Kappa Sigma, Delta Theta Phi); 2d lt., 1918; served at Ft. Sheridan and Camp Perry; with R.O.T.C., Mich. and Ohio State colls. to 1919; v.pres. Cleary Coll.
1–Ed. Somerville Coll., 1884-87. Completed record of soldiers in Great War from southern half of Washtenaw Co., Mich., under commission from Gov. Sleeper, and also record for Ypsilanti. Mem. D.F.P.A., D.A.R. (as chapter historian collected data which was afterward used by Rev. Harvey Colburn in centennial history of Ypsilanti, entitled, The Story of Ypsilanti; state librarian, 1920-23; mem. nat. and state committees), Ladies' Library Bd., 16 yrs. (sec. 12 yrs.; wrote Hist. of Ypsilanti Library Assn., 1918), A.L. Auxiliary (charter mem.), Ladies Lit. Club, Ypsilanti Fed. of Women's Clubs (sec.). Residence: 7 N. Normal St., Ypsilanti, Mich.

1–**CLEGHORN, Maude Egbert White (Mrs. Daniel Oliver),** *b* Farragut, Ia., May 18, 1882.
10–William **White,** Mayflower Pilgrim (qv);
9–Resolved (1614-80), came on Mayflower with his father; *b* Leyden, Holland; settled Salem, Mass.; *m* 1640, Judith Vassail (*d* 1670 or 74), *b* Scituate, Mass. (William[10] [*b* 1630], *m* Anne King; John[11], a founder of the Jamestown Colony, 1607);
8–Samuel (*b* 1646), of Rochester and Marshfield, Mass.; *m* Rebecca Green (1646-1711);
7–William (1690-will made 1780), *m* Elizabeth Cadman;
6–Abner (ca. 1725-1794), of Dartmouth, Mass.; *m* 1746, Ruth Brownell; they removed to Dutchess Co., N.Y.;
5–William A. (1756-1802), of Mabbettsville, N.Y.; served in Am. Rev., 7th Regt. Militia, under Maj. Adams, Dutchess Co., N.Y.; *m* Eunice White;
4–Isaac (1784-1867), of Mabbettsville; *m* ca. 1810, Mary Cline (1791-1883), *b* Clove, N.Y., *d* Dover Plains, N.Y. (Abraham[5] [1767-1850], *m* 1775, Eleanor, dau. of 2d lt. Daniel Uhl, served in Am. Rev., 5th Regt., Dutchess Co., Militia, with Capt. George Emigh's co. of minute men, g.dau. John Uhl, of Beekman, N.Y., *m* Margaret [1731-98], dau. of Frederick Streit, of Rhinebeck, N.Y., *m* Catherine Moul, from Bavaria; Henry[6]);
3–Egbert (1821-1901), of Beekman, N.Y.; moved to Kewanee, Ill.; drill capt., 134th Ill. Vol. Inf. in Civil War; buried Farragut, Ia.; *m* 1846, Mary Ann Wright;
2–John Halstead (2 below).
11–Richard **Warren,** Mayflower Pilgrim (qv);
10–Sarah (living 1696), *m* 1634, John **Cooke,** Mayflower Pilgrim (qv);
9–Sarah, *m* 1658, Arthur **Hathaway** (1631-1712), juror, selectman, magistrate, Dartmouth, 1671 (Arthur[10]);
8–Hannah (will proved 1749), *m* George **Cadman** (will proved 1719), juryman, surveyor, selectman, treasurer, overseer of poor (William[9], *m* Elizabeth–);
7–Elizabeth, *m* William **White** (7 above).
11–Thomas **Bradford** (qv);
10–Ann (*d* 1656), *m* in Eng., Samuel **Wilber** (*d* 1656), from Eng., 1633; settled Boston; removed to Aquednock, R.I., 1638;
9–William (*d* 1710), was in R.I. as early as 1630; *m* 1653, Martha–;
8–Samuel (1664-1740), *m* Mary Potter (g.dau. of Samuel[10], an original patentee of Portsmouth, R.I.);
7–Mary (*b* 1697), *m* 1717, Charles **Brownell** (1694-1774), of Little Compton, R.I.;
6–Ruth (1727-1806), of Little Compton, R.I.; *m* Abner **White** (6 above).
8–William **White** (1665-1750), of Salisbury, Conn. (originally Weatog);
7–Benjamin (will made 1763), of Washington Hollow, Dutchess Co.;
6–William (1732-will made 1811), of Dutchess Co.; *m* Ruth– (*b* 1729);
5–Eunice (1762-1816), *b* Washington Hollow, N.Y.; *m* William A. **White** (5 above).
5–Gershom **Halstead** (1750-1822), *b* Scotland; of New Windsor, N.Y.; in 2d Regt., Ulster Co. Militia in Am. Rev.; *m* 1773, Mary Smith (1753-1839), of New Windsor, N.Y.;
4–Phoebe (1791-1871), of Orange Co., N.Y.; *m* 1810, John **Wright** (1786-1838; David[5], in 2d Regt., Ulster Co. Militia, Am. Rev.);
3–Mary Ann (*b* Warwick, N.Y., 1827-*d* 1916), *m* Egbert **White** (3 above).
5–Lewis **Robbins,** *m* Phebe–;
4–Josiah (*b* 1805), of Rockland, Me.; *m* 1831, Mahala York (*b* 1813; Thomas[5], *m* Mary–);
3–Charles Warren (1835-1914), *b* Chenault, Ky.; *m* at Union Star, Ky., 1861, Mary Louisa Watlington;

2–Annie Maria (2 below).
6–James **Cox,** *m* Nellie Luckett, of Va.;
5–James (1793-1881), of Fauquier Co., Va.; *m* at Union Star, Ky., 1819, Mary Elizabeth Seaton (1804-76; William[6], farmer of Culpeper Co., Va., and Union Star, Ky., *m* Judith, dau. of Capt. Tolliver, of Va.);
4–Judith Tolliver (1824-1912), of Union Star, Ky.; *m* 1843, Nathaniel Read **Watlington** (1814-88), *b* Norfolk, Va. (Armstead[5], *m* Mary Louise Blake);
3–Mary Louisa (1844-1912), of Union Star, Ky.; *m* Charles Warren **Robbins** (3 above);
2–Annie Maria (*b* 1862), *m* 1880, John Halstead **White** (*b* 1858), ranchman, stock raiser and v.p. Chadron (Neb.) State Bank; issue: I–Maude Egbert (1 above); II–Edith Mary (*b* 1884; *m* Harry Ernst Reische); III–Charles Halstead (*b* 1886; *m* Martha Amanda Groves); IV–Edward Franklin (*b* 1887; *m* Blanche Katherine Sperling); V–Bernice Emma (*b* 1889; *m* James Rudolph Nylen).
1–*m* July 7, 1910, Daniel Oliver Cleghorn, *b* Ft. Scott, Kan., Oct. 24, 1869; son of Daniel Benjamin Cleghorn, of Rapid City, S.D.
1–Ed. Chadron (Congl.) Acad. Mem. S.M.D., D.F.P.A., D.A.R. Residence: 461 Shelton St., Chadron, Neb.

1–**CLEMANS, Pearl Anna Chase (Mrs. Earl Amos),** *b* Oshkosh, Wis., Aug. 17, 1876.
8–Aquila **Chase** (qv);
7–Thomas (1654-1733), of Newbury, Mass.; *m* 1677, Rebecca Follonsbe (*d* 1711);
6–Nathan (1704-84), of Newbury; *m* 1740, Joanna Cheney (*d* 1784);
5–Edmund (1748-1822), of Newbury; *m* 1769, Esther Merrill (*b* 1749);
4–Merrill (1773-1860), of Newbury; *m* 1796, Sally Tucker;
3–Edmund (1808-97), of Me.; *m* 1832, Anna Spofford;
2–Arthur Edmund (2 below).
9–John **Spofford** (1612-78), from Eng., 1638; settled at Rowley, Mass.; propr. ante 1643; *m* Elizabeth Scott (ca. 1625-91; Thomas[10], *m* Elizabeth–);
8–John (1648-97), of Rowley; *m* 1675, Sarah Wheeler (David[9], from Eng. in the "Confidence," 1638, *m* Sarah Wise, dau. Humphrey, *m* Susan–);
7–Jonathan (1684-1772), of Rowley; *m* Jemima Freethe (John[8], *m* Hannah Bray);
6–David (1710-72), *m* 1st, 1734, Hannah Cheney (1712-55; Eldad[7], *m* Mary Walker);
5–Eldad (1745-1809), of Townsend, Mass.; sgt. in Am. Rev.; in battles of Trenton and Princeton; *m* 1768, Lucy Spalding (1749-1837);
4–Isaac (*b* 1782), *m* 1804, Anna Fish;
3–Anna (1808-1901), *m* Edmund **Chase** (3 above);
2–Arthur Edmund (*b* 1853), bookkeeper, Oshkosh, Wis.; *m* 1874, Alida Eldora Little (*b* 1856); issue: I–Pearl Anna (1 above); II–Thomas Lynn (*b* 1886; *m* Eola Bunting); III–Ruby Fern (*b* 1890); IV–Arthur Morgan (*b* 1893; *m* Grace Lupient).
1–*m* July 10, 1901, Earl Amos Clemans, *b* Clemansville, Wis., Dec. 26, 1874; v.p. Oshkosh State Teacher's Coll., 1924–; son of George S. Clemans, of Clemansville; issue: 1–Charles Chase, *b* Bay City, Mich., Sept. 23, 1903; D.D.S., Marquette U., '27. 2–Donald Earl, *b* Oshkosh, Wis., Dec. 9, 1906; Oshkosh State Teachers' Coll.
1–Mem. D.F.P.A., D.A.R., etc. Conglist. Republican. Residence: Oshkosh, Wis.

1–**CLEVELAND, Estelle Gillet Iddings (Mrs. Francis D.),** *b* Baltimore, Md., Feb. 27, 1863.
7–Richard **Iddings** (*d* 1726), from Wales, settled in Chester Co., Pa.; *m* Sarah–;
6–William, *m* Mary–;
5–William, *m* Hannah Lewis;
4–James, had a Quaker school for boys in Del.; Quaker preacher; *m* Mary Peirce (Caleb[5] [1692-1797], *m* 2d, Ann, dau. Robert Mendenhall, *m* Phoebe Taylor; Caleb[6], *m* Mary Walter; George[7], qv);
3–Caleb Peirce (1788-1863), of Phila.; *m* 1812, Harriet Hill Jackson (1789-1876; Richard B.[4], *m* Deborah, dau. Mordecai Moore, *m* Elizabeth Coleman; Dr. John[5], *m* Mary, dau. Levin Hill; Dr. John[6], *m* Mary Blackburn; John[7]);
2–William Penn (2 below).
8–Jonathan **Gillet** (qv);
7–Josiah (bap. 1650-1736), of Windsor, Conn.; *m* 1676, Joanna Taintor (1651-1735);
6–Gen. Jonathan (1685-1759), *m* 1717, Sarah Ely (1685-1759);
5–Jonathan (1720-79), lt., 17th Cont. Inf. during Am. Rev., taken prisoner in battle of L.I., 1776; *m* 1747, Phoebe Marvin;
4–Joseph (1756-80), *m* 2d, 1780, Mary Miner;
3–Martin (1787-1837), *m* 1808, Eliza Edwards (1791-1858; William[4], *m* Mary Adams);
2–Almira (1826-96), *m* 1847, William Penn **Iddings** (1822-1906), mcht.; issue: I–Charles Fry (1848-1906; *m* Viola Hoxie); II–Joseph Paxson (1857-1920; Ph.B., Yale-S., '77, grad. student in chemistry and mineralogy, 1877-78; geologist, author, see Who's Who in America, Vol. VII); III–Lola Lammot (1858-1918; grad. Vassar, '89); IV–Estelle Gillet (1 above).
1–*m* Feb. 4, 1892, Francis Dixon Cleveland, *b* Jersey City, N.J., Mar. 25, 1867; son of Orestes Cleveland, of Jersey City; issue: 1–Arthur Iddings (Sept. 21, 1894-May 10, 1926); B.S., Yale-S., '16; 2–Francis Dixon, Jr., *b* Winchester, Mass., Oct. 10, 1900; B.S., Yale-S., '21.
1–Mem. D.F.P.A. Conglist. Republican. Club: Valley Hunt. Residence: 465 Calaveras St., Altadena, Calif.

1–**CLEVELAND, Paul Williams,** *b* Oak Park, Ill., Dec. 24, 1878.
9–Moses **Cleveland** (qv);
8–Isaac, *m* Elizabeth (Pierce) Curtis;
7–Curtice, *m* Remembrance Currier;
6–William (ca. 1752-ca. 1778), sgt. and 2d lt. Cont. Army; *m* Mary–;
5–William, *m* Nancy Ann Baker;
4–Josiah Douglas, *m* Lucy Brayn;
3–Festus Portius, *m* Mary Lyon;
2–Festus Waudby (1850-1926), railway official; *m* 1875, Edith Clementine Williams (1855-1925); for issue see Vol. III, p. 126.
1–*m* Dec. 4, 1910, Mary Louise Spring, *b* Beardstown, Ill., Nov. 18, 1879; dau. of Sylvester Omer Spring, of Peoria, now of Chicago, Ill., *m* Anna Frances–; issue: 1–Cynthia, *b* New York, N.Y., Mar. 20, 1919.
1–Grad. Northwestern U., '01, (Sigma Chi) LL.B., 1904 (Phi Delta Phi). V.p. John Burnham & Co., investment bankers, Chicago. Capt. Am. Protective League during World War. Mem. O.F.P.A., I.A.G., Bibliophile Soc. Clubs: Chicago, Racquet, Tavern, University, Midday, Indian Hill Country, Caxton. Residence: 1325 Astor St., Chicago, Ill.

1–**CLINE, Isaac Monroe,** *b* nr. Madisonville, Monroe Co., Tenn., Oct. 13, 1861.
3–John (Kline) **Cline** (*d* ca. 1864), of Dutch ancestors who settled in New Amsterdam, descendants moved to Pa., thence to Va.; *m* ca. 1826, Mary Hawk, of English ancestry and 2d cousin of President James Monroe; removed from Va. to Monroe Co., Tenn., 1836;
2–Jacob Leander (2 below).
3–George **Wilson** (*d* ca. 1845), of Ga., of Carolina and Ga. family; *m* ca. 1834, Rebecca Harris (*d* ca. 1908), whose father was a slaveowner and planter nr. Madisonville, Monroe Co., Tenn., of Scotch and Irish ancestry;
2–Mary Isabel (1843-1920), *m* 1860, Jacob Leander **Cline** (1833-1915), from Va., *d* Sweetwater, Tenn.; issue: I–Isaac Monroe (1 above); II–Jinnie Alice (*b* 1863; *m* Jim Summit, *d*; *m* 2d, Rennie Frank, *d*); III–Marget Clementine (1866-68); IV–George Washington (1868-1920; *m* Juretta Mangus, *d*); V–Joseph Leander (*b* 1870; *m* Ula Jackson); VI–Sarah Rebecka (*b* 1872; *m* Frank Airheart); VII–Thomas Alexander (*b* 1875; *m* Alice Cook); VIII–Cora Della (*b* 1876; *m* Arthur Brakebill).
1–*m* 1st, Mar. 17, 1887, Cora May Ballew, *b* Camden, Mo. (June 2, 1866-Sept. 8, 1900); dau. of Joseph Ballew, *m* Arraha Bossia Clemens; issue: 1–Allie May, *b* Abilene, Tex., Dec. 10, 1887; St. Simeon's Coll., New Orleans; *m* Jan. 29, 1915, Capt. Ernest E. B. Drake (issue: Miss Frances Cline); 2–Rosemary, *b* Galveston, Tex., Aug. 24, 1889; New Orleans Coll. of Oratory; *m* Sept. 9, 1912, Vora Williams (issue: Wesley Monroe; Vorus Ballew); 3–Esther Ballew, *b* Galveston, Tex., July 2, 1894; Newcomb School, New Orleans; *m* Mar. 27, 1917, Albert Allen Jones (issue: Allen Monroe Cline).

1–A.B., Hiwassee Coll., Tenn., 1882, A.M., 1885; M.D., U. of Ark., 1885; Ph.D., Texas Christian U., 1896 (Pi Gamma Mu). Sr. meteorologist. U.S. Weather Bureau in charge New Orleans Forecast Dist. (see Who's Who in America). Mem. I.A.G. Clubs: Arts (Washington), Nat. Arts (New York). Mason. Address: Weather Bureau Office, New Orleans, La.

1–**CLOPTON, Virginia Marshall (Mrs. Hoggatt),** *b* "Live Oaks," Ky.
10–John **Waller,** "An ancient planter of Va., on 30 Jan. 1606 pd. for land in Va. and on the 22 Nov. 1622 at a Court for Va. put in a request in Va., etc."; one of the early promoters of the Va. Colony but no record remains to show that he came to Va.; said to have desc. from Alluered de Waller who went to Eng. with William the Conqueror;
9–John, M.D. (*b* 1617), of Newport Pagnall, Bucks, Eng.; *m* Mary–;
8–Col. John (1673-1754, will prob. 1758), from Eng. to Va., ca. 1686, settled in King and Queen Co.; sheriff, 1702; justice, King William Co., 1705, burgess 1710-14, 1720-22; 1st. clk. of Spotsylvania Co., Aug. 7, 1722-Apr. 6, 1723; lt. col. militia of Spotsylvania Co.; vestryman St. George Parish; *m* Dorothy King (1675-1759), established his home "Newport" in Spotsylvania Co. Va.;
7–Mary (1699-1781), *b* in King and Queen Co.; *m* Jan. 9, 1725, Zachary **Lewis** (1702-65; Zachary[8], *b* in Wales, from there to Va., 1692, settled first in Middlesex Co., removed to King and Queen Co., 1693, where he had large grants; *m* ca. 1700, Mary Walker [Col. Thomas[9], Gloucester Co., burgess 1662; Col. Thomas[10], to Va. ca. 1620, settled in Gloucester Co., 1625]);
6–John (1729-80), called the "honest lawyer"; *m* ca. 1747, Anne Lewis (*b* ca. 1731; dau. Col. Robert[7], of "Belvoir"); see Vol. III, p. 616, for Lewis lineage;
5–Nicholas (*b* ca. 1748) soldier Am. Rev.; moved to Jefferson Co., Ky., 1784; *m* 1771 Mary Allen (Capt. James[6]; Capt. James[7]);
4–Hannah (*b* 1772), *m* 1787, Lewis **Field** (1763-1845), in Am. Rev. aet. 16; taken prisoner by Indians, saved from burning at the stake by adoption into the tribe, later captured by the British and taken prisoner to Quebec where he was held for 2 yrs. before being returned to Va.; the only Lewis Field who received a Rev. pension, the original claim now in the possession of Mrs. Virginia Marshall Clopton (1 above); see Vol. III, p. 616 for Field lineage;
3–Mildred Lewis (1792-1876), *m* Capt. John **Marshall** (3 below);
2–Lewis F. (2 below).
10–John **Crawford** (ca. 1595-ca. 1676), from Scotland to Va., ca. 1625, the yngst. son of an earl Crawford; a widower with one son, settled first in James City Co., afterwards in St. Peter's Parish, New Kent Co., Va.;
9–David (ca. 1620), of "Assaquin," New Kent Co., burgess, vestryman;
8–Elizabeth (ca. 1650), *m* 1671, Col. Nicholas **Meriwether** (1647-1744; son of Nicholas [*d* Dec. 19, 1678], *m* Elizabeth Wodenhouse of Wales); he obtained various grants of land amounting to 23,782 acres of land in Albemarle Co., and established "The Farm" and built "Old House";
7–Jane, *m* 1725, Col. Robert **Lewis,** "Belvoir," Fredericksville Parish, Albemarle Co., Va.;
6–Anne, *m* John **Lewis** (6 above).
9–John **Clark,** from Eng. to Jamestown, Va.; *m* ca. 1620, Hannah Wyatt, dau. of Sir Dudley Wyatt, Knt. (*d* post 1650, his will recorded 25 April, 1651, in secretary's office, James City, Va., in which he leaves legacy to dau. Mrs. Hannah Clark);
8–Jonathan or John Sr. (ca. 1625-post 1683), he and son John, Jr., listed in the U.S. Census, 1683, of Middlesex Co., he pat. land, 1662, in King and Queen Co., Va.; *m* Mary Bird ("red headed Scotch beauty");
7–John, Jr. (ca. 1660-post 1735), was granted land 20 Oct., 1691, in Drysdale Parish, King and Queen Co., "On the north side of the Mattapony River" where he established his home "Clarkson," near the present P.O. Station of Brisco; was granted land in Hanover and Caroline cos.; *m* ca. 1695, Elizabeth Lumpkin (Capt. Jacob[8], capt. in Indian wars from Lancaster and Middlesex cos.; he received land grant, 1682, in King and Queen Co., where he settled and established "Newington," *d* 1704, buried at Mattapony Church, which was built upon the "Newington" estate, on land donated by Capt. Lumpkin; was justice and burgess for King and Queen Co.; one of his daus. *m* Col. George Braxton and were the grandparents of Carter Braxton a "signer," who was born at "Newington");
6–Jonathan (1698-1734), Drysdale Parish, King and Queen Co., was granted land in Caroline Co., 30 Sept., 1730, and in Albemarle Co. he received a joint grant with his father, 1734, known as the "Clark's Tract," consisting of 3,277 acres, where he and his wife removed to shortly before his death; *m* ca. 1723, Elizabeth Ann ("Nancy") Wilson (6 below).
16–Sir John **Fitz Roger** (ca. 1386-1441), of "Bryanstone," Dorsetshire, Eng. (g.son of Aaron or John Fitz Roger [ca. 1260 in Rome] who fled with his father from Rome, ca. 1270 to London, Eng.; desc. Roger I, King of Sicily, 1093-1154); *m* 1406, Agnes de Mercaunt, both are buried in St. Martin's Church, "Bryanstone";
15–Thomas, Gent. (1408-71), *b* at "Ashington," Somersetshire, moved to "Bryanstone" with his father; *m* 1st, 1433;
14–Thomas, Esq. (1435-89), Sergeant-at-Law, under appmt. of the Crown, 1478, was created "Serviens ad Legem," a life office bestowed because of professional attainments and worth of character, and was granted special arms, which he asked for being the 2d son; *m* 1483, as his 2d wife, Catherine de Courtenay 1444-Jan. 12, 1515; desc. Alfred the Great, Emperor Charlemagne of France, Hugh Capet, King of the Franks, William the Conqueror, Malcolm I, King of Scotland, and 6 sureties of the Magna Charta);
13–John (1485-1530), of Deritend, "a chapelry near Birmingham, Warwickshire;" *m* ca. 1505, Margery, dau. of Sir Henry Wyatt of "Abingdon Castle," Kent Co.;
12–Rev. John, the Martyr (*b* 1507 at Deritend-burned at the stake Feb. 4, 1554, at Smithfield, Eng.), B.A., Cambridge, 1525; chosen to the Cardinals Coll., Oxford, took Holy Orders in the R.C. Church; rector Church of Holy Trinity the Less, 1532; called to Antwerp Brabant, 1534; while here he was converted to the Protestant faith, and translated the Bible in the English language, which he corrected, prepared and edited the publication of the whole Bible, the first complete edition of both Old and New Testament in English, culminating in the introduction of the folio Bible in Eng., 1537; returned from Saxony to Eng., 1548, and was made rector of St. Margaret Moyses, vicar of St. Sepulchre, and prebend of St. Pancras in the Cathedral of St. Paul, London;
11–Bernard (*b* 1543 in Wittenberg, Saxony, *d* 1583) *m* 1564, and settled in Scotland;
10–Thomas Matthew (*b* 1565 in Scotland-*d* 1610), *m* 1585, Miss MacMurdo (McMurdock);
9–John (*b* 1609 in Scotland-*d* ca. 1680), *m* ca. 1640, Lucy Iverson, settled in Edinburgh;
8–Giles (*b* 1653 in Edinburgh, *d* 1730 in King and Queen Co., Va.), ed. at Edinburgh, after maturity moved to Worcestershire, Eng., from there he emigrated to Va., where he patented land, Apr. 18, 1670; *m* 1672, Rachael Eastham (Esam), in Eng.; he returned to Va., 1680, arriving in his own ship and settled on his land grant, on Dragon Swamp, Stratton Major Parish, King and Queen Co.;
7–Lucy (*b* 1675 in Eng., *d* 1760 in Va.), *m* 1700, William **Wilson,** King and Queen Co.;
6–Elizabeth Ann (1701-*d* post 1759), *m* ca. 1723, Jonathan **Clark** (6 above);
5–Ann (*b* 1727, *d* ca. 1744 Essex Co., Va.), *m* ca. 1743 Torquil **Macleod** of Scotland, an officer of dragoons, settled in Essex Co., Va.;
4–Ann Clark (*b* ca. 1744, Essex Co., Va., *d* 1809), *m* 1767, in Caroline Co., Va., Capt. William **Marshall,** "Fairhope," Henry Co., Ky. (see Vol. III, p. 616, for Marshall lineage);
3–Capt. John (1784-1830), *m* 1813, Mildred Lewis Field (3 above);

2-Maj. Lewis Field (1825-77), served in the C.S.A. during the War between the States, was promoted Sept. 20, 1862, to the staff of Gen. Albert Rust, 2d. Div., 1st. Corps, Army West Miss. and East La., wounded and honorably discharged, 1863; *m* 1854, Mary Helen Mar Fore or Faure (1836-1911; Joshua Fore[3] [1800-ca. 1878], *m* ca. 1824, Narcissa Young, dau. of Capt. Masterson Ogden [*b* ca. 1700 in Baltimore, Md.], Capt. War 1812, said to have desc. from Robert Ogden [1687-1733], *m* Rebecca Rice of Lexington, Ky.).
1-*m* Jan. 1, 1888, R. Barton Seate (or Seitz) (for issue see Vol. III, p. 616).
1-*m* 2d, June 17, 1905, Col. Hoggatt Clopton (1831-1912); Heloise Marshall, third, only living ch., *m* Oct. 15, 1919, Lt. L. D. Webb, U.S.N.
1-Mem. D.B.R., D.A.R., A.P.V.A., Va. Hist. Soc., Sulgrave Instn., Lewis Assn. of Am., etc. Clubs: Los Angeles Woman's (organizing pres.), Carlton, Congressional Country (Washington). Residence: Wardman Park Hotel, Washington, D.C.

1-**CLOUD, Susan Caswell Vail (Mrs. Harrie B.),** *b* Coldspring, Wis., Apr. 1, 1871.
8-Jan Willemszen **Dutcher,** in Ulster Co., N.Y., 1686; took Eng. oath of allegiance; *m* post 1662, Grietje Cornelisse (Cornelis[9]);
7-Roelof (ca. 1677/78-1737), a founder of Salisbury, Conn., 1720; *m* 1700, Jannetje Bresie (Christopher[8], *m* Christine, dau. Nicholas Claeszen);
6-Johannes (bap. 1708-1777), Salisbury; *m* 1732, Christine Chisholm (1716-55; John Chisem[7], *m* 1713, Jannetje Buys; Robert[8], from Eng. to Kingston, N.Y., *m* Margaret Weldyn or Weldon);
5-Hannah (1749-1830), *m* 1771, Ezekiel **Fuller** (see Vol. III, p. 127, for Fuller lineage);
4-Matthew (1771-1863), *m* ante 1798, Elizabeth Weldon;
3-Augustus Eggleston (1801-68), *m* 1825, Lavina Ransford Hurlburt (1808-94);
2-Frances Dutcher (2 below).
9-Richard (Wescott) **Westcott** (ca. 1612-1651), from Eng. to Wethersfield, Conn., 1639; removed to Fairfield; *m* 1639, Joanna-(*d* 1682);
8-John (*b* 1646), from Stamford, Conn., to Bedford, N. Y., 1680; *m* 1667, Ruth Hyatt or Hoyt (*b* 1650; Thomas[9]);
7-Richard (*b* 1668), *m* 1693, Rachel Holmes (*b* 1670; John[8]);
6-Abram (1716-91), began to write name Westcott; served in 2d Regt., Westchester Co. Militia, Am. Rev.; *m* 1745, Elizabeth Kellum (*b* 1721/22; Theophilus[7], *m* Elizabeth Roger or Rodger);
5-Ruth (*b* 1756), *m* 1775, Elijah **Weldon** (*b* 1753), Am. Rev., Conn. line; living at Platte Kill, Ulster Co., N.Y., 1811, (John[6]; James[7]);
4-Elizabeth (*b* 1780), *m* Matthew **Fuller** (4 above);
3-Augustus E., *m* Lavina R. Hurlburt (3 above);
2-Frances Dutcher (1829-1905), *m* 1849, Ensign Butts; *m* 2d, 1868, De Loss White **Vail** (1817-99); issue (mother's 2d marriage): I-Alice May (1869-92); II-Susan Caswell (1 above).
1-*m* Aug. 13, 1904, Harrie Baylor Cloud, *b* Montgomery, Ala., Mar. 12, 1876; son of Dr. William Barton Cloud, *m* Mary Davis.
1-Mem. S.D.P., D.A.R., I.A.G. Episcopalian. Residence: 267 Prairie St., Elgin, Ill.

1-**CLUM, Cornelius Wilson,** *b* Claverack, N.Y., Sept. 6, 1860.
4-William **Clum** (1762-1837), of Claverack, N.Y.; buried at Philmont, N.Y.; *m* Elizabeth Fritts (1756-1854);
3-Philip (1786-1866), of Philmont; *m* Jane Shufelt (1790-1883);
2-William Henry (2 below).
8-Abraham Pietersen (Van Deursen) **Van Deusen** (*b* Haarlem, Holland, where bap. Nov. 11, 1607), to New Amsterdam, 1636; one of the "Twelve Men," 1641; *m* Dec. 9, 1629, Tryntje Melchiors;
7-Teuwis Abrahamsen (*b* 1631), at Albany, N.Y., 1653; at Claverack, N.Y., 1667; *m* Helena Robberts;
6-Robbert T. (*b* 1665), began to write name Van Deusen; of Claverack, N.Y.; *m* 1689, Cornelia Martense Van Buren;
5-Robbert (1700-77), of Livingston Manor, N.Y.; farmer; *m* 1724, Christina Roorbach;
4-Tobias R. (bap. May 21, 1748), innkeeper Hudson, N.Y.; *m* 1771, Hannah Spoor;
3-Johannes T. (John T.) (1777-1861), resided at Hudson and Claverack, N.Y.; *m* 2d, Esther Woodworth;
2-Elizabeth Ann (1821-1918), *m* 1841, William Henry **Clum** (1815-90), farmer; issue: I-Henry Woodworth (1842-62); II-Jane Elizabeth (1844-1922); III-Cornelia (*b* 1845); IV-Sarah Ellen (1847-63); V-George Adam (*b* 1849); VI-John Philip (*b* 1851; *m* Mary Denison Ware; *m* 2d, Belle Atwood; *m* 3d, Florence Baker); VII-Charles (*b* and *d* 1854); VIII-Robert Augustus (Sept. 27, 1855-Aug. 7, 1914; *m* Feb. 22, 1881, Mary Irene Shidy; issue: Clara Leland, *b* Jan. 9, 1882); IX-Cornelius W. (1 above); X-Alfred (*b* 1863; *m* Lizzie W. Bohrer).
1-*m* Oct. 20, 1886, Mary Greer Herring, *b* New York, N.Y., Aug. 29, 1866 (William Herring[2] [Jan. 21, 1833-July 10, 1912], asst. dist. atty., New York, N.Y., U.S. atty. for Ariz., and chancellor, U.Ariz., *m* Feb. 16, 1858, Mary E. [Mar. 19, 1834-May 15, 1903], dau. of Samuel Inslee [1806-76], *m* 1828, Phoebe Parker [1804-37]; Caleb[3] [1791-1878], *m* Mary Greer, *d* 1858); issue: 1-Dorothy Herring, *b* Denver, Colo., Mar. 13, 1889; *m* Jan. 16, 1923, Charles Henry Gibson; 2-Mary Elizabeth, *b* Washington, D.C., Aug. 22, 1891; 3-Helen Van Deusen, *b* Washington, June 2, 1894; 4-Marjorie Inslee, *b* Kensington, Md. (Nov. 20, 1897-Sept. 16, 1918); 5-Bertha, *b* Kensington, June 10, 1900; 6-John Philip, *b* Kensington, Aug. 30, 1910.
1-Editor and owner, The Montgomery Press, weekly newspaper, Montgomery Co., Md. Residence: Kensington, Md.

1-**CLUM, Harold Dunstan,** *b* Saugerties, N.Y., June 1, 1879.
6-Philip **Clum,** with two brothers, settled in the Hudson valley early in the 18th Century; mentioned in Columbia Co. ch. records, ca. 1725;
5-Philip (1749-98), of Cheviot (then East Camp), N.Y.; *m* Helene Ham (1752-1842; Peter[6], of Clermont, N.Y., *m* Marcibe Ieikman);
4-Philip P. (1782-1829), *m* 1804, Maria Hyser (1786-1853);
3-Alexander (1814-97), from Cheviot to Saugerties, N.Y.; capt. sailing vessels; *m* 1st, 1850, Jane Maria Freleigh (1832-55);
2-Charles (*b* 1850), of Saugerties, N.Y.; *m* 1876, Rachel Buffin Merchant (*b* 1851); issue: I-Harold Dunstan (1 above); II-Charles Alfred (*b* 1882; *m* Elsie Girton); III-Anna May (*b* 1885; *m* John Walter Maxwell).
1-*m* Nov. 8, 1910, Florence Brewster Corse, *b* Saugerties, N.Y., Feb. 8, 1880; dau. of Henry Corse.
1-A.B., St. Stephen's Coll., '01; M.A., Columbia, 1903. In U.S. consular service; Am. consul-gen. at Guayaquil, Ecuador, 1926-(see Who's Who in America). Home: 208 Burt St., Saugerties, N.Y. Address: Am. Consulate-General, Guayaquil, Ecuador.

1-**COCHRANE, Thomas Childs,** *b* Brooklyn, N.Y., Apr. 29, 1902.
6-Thomas **Cochran** (*b* 1703), from Ireland, ca. 1720; settled Colerain, Mass.; *m* Elizabeth Scott;
5-Samuel (1746-1810), of Guilford, Vt.; soldier N.Y. militia during Am. Rev.; *m* Martha Wilson;
4-Samuel (1785-1845), of Springville, N.Y.; *m* 1805, Catherine Gallup;
3-David Henry (1828-1907), pres. Brooklyn Poly Inst., 1864-1900; *m* 1851, Harriet Rawson;
2-Thomas (*b* 1861), retired educator, New York; *m* 1898, Ethel Childs (*b* 1874); issue: I-Thomas Childs (1 above); II-Harriet Pamelia (*b* 1912).
1-*m* June 5, 1924, Elizabeth Mercelis Paul, *b* Paterson, N.J., Feb. 4, 1902; dau. of John Searing Paul, of Paterson.
1-B.S., N.Y.U., '23 (Psi U.), M.A., 1925, Ph.D., U.Pa., 1930. Asst. instr., N.Y.U., 1923-25; fellow in history, U.Pa., 1826-27; instr. history, New York U., 1927-. Mem. N.Y. State Hist. Soc., I.A.G. Clubs: Heights Casino, Brooklyn, West Side Tennis, Forest Hills (L.I.). Residence: 43 Fifth Av., New York, N.Y.

1–**CODINGTON, Katherine Mabel Smith (Mrs. Joseph L.),** *b* Peru, Neb., Sept. 18, 1874.
10–Matthew **Smith,** from Eng., 1637; settled at Charlestown, Mass.; *m* Jane–;
9–Matthew (*b* Eng.-*d* post 1684), of Woburn, Mass.; *m* 1655, Alice Loader (*d* ante 1684); *m* 2d, Mary (Giles) Very Cutler;
8–Matthew (1659-90), of Woburn; *m* 1683/84, Mary Cutler (1663-1744; John[9]; John[10], of Eng.);
7–Matthew (1684-1751), of Lyme and E. Haddam, Conn.; lt. of south co. militia, 1732; made capt., 1734; licensed tanner, 1705-06; *m* 1706, Sarah Mack (1684-1755; John[8]; the immigrant);
6–Thomas (1710-97), of E. Haddam; minuteman in Am. Rev.; *m* 1st, 1737, Hannah Gates (1714-54; Samuel[7]; Capt. George[8]);
5–Thomas (1738-1821), of E. Haddam; corpl. in Conn. regt.; *m* 1760, Mary Greene (1736-1810; Warren[6]; William[7]; William[8]);
4–Diodate (1772-1834), of Conn. and Pa.; inspector for mail route from Pittston to Charlottesville, Va., 1812-14; established some of the first foundries in Lackawanna Valley, Pa.; *m* 1797, Rachel Alworth (1776-1848; William[5]; James[6]);
3–Benjamin (1798-1873), farmer, Pa.; *m* 1818, Lydia Gardiner (1802-32; Richard[4], Am. Rev.; John[5], Am. Rev., *m* Elizabeth Mumford; Peregrine[6]; Stephen[7]; Benoni[8]; George[9]; Rev. Michael[10], of Eng.);
2–Richard Byron (1830-1901), of Pa.; removed to Mo., 1858-62; mfr. farm implements, 1861-62; recruited and organized 18th and 24th Mo. regts.; removed to Neb., 1862; organized Peru Mfg. Co.; organized the first "Union League" in Neb., during the war; assisted in founding and building the State Teachers Coll. (then a Methodist Coll.); *m* 1856, Margaret Chapman (1834-1903; John[3]; William[4]); issue: I–Eldora Isabella (*b* 1857; *m* Robert Rudolph Baliman); II–Ida May (1859-80); III–Georgia Anne (1861-64); IV–Nelson Gaylord (1863-64); V–Charles Benjamin (*b* and *d* 1865); VI–Edward John (1866-1926; *m* Minnie Rowe); VII–Josephine Withy (*b* 1869; *m* 1893, Wiley Buchanan); VIII–Nelle Jean (*b* 1870; *m* 1893, Jacob Wambold); IX–Katherine Mabel (1 above); X–Margaret Ethel (*b* 1878; *m* 1899, John Elmer Larson).
1–*m* Apr. 3, 1902, Joseph Leeper Codington, *b* Tallula, Ill., May 30, 1866; son of William Alexander Codington, of Ill. and Neb., *m* Elizabeth Watkins.
1–Ed. pvt. schools, State Teachers' Coll. (Neb.), Midland Coll., and Omaha U. Supervisor of normal training, Bellevue Coll.; teacher manual arts, Omaha public schs., 8 yrs.; teacher elementary grades, 12 yrs. Mem. S.M.D., S.D.P., D.A.C. (state historian), D.F.P.A. (councilor, registrar, rec. sec., Neb. soc.), D.A.R. (state historian). Christian. Republican. Residence: Hotel Hamilton, Omaha, Neb.

1–**CODMAN, Richard, Jr.,** *b* Boston, Mass., Mar. 7, 1873.
8–Robert **Codman** (qv);
7–Stephen (1650-1706), *m* Elizabeth Randall;
6–Capt. John (1696-1755), *m* 1718, Parnell Foster (g.dau. of John Winslow, came in the "Fortune," 1621, *m* Mary Chilton, Mayflower Pilgrim);
5–John (1720-92), mem. "Boston Tea Party"; *m* Abigail Ashbury;
4–Hon. John (1755-1803), prominent merchant, Boston; *m* 1st, Margaret Russell (Hon. James[5], Charlestown, Mass.);
3–Charles Russell (1784-1852), mcht., Boston; *m* 2d, Sarah Ogden;
2–Richard (2 below).
7–William **Sargent,** settled in Gloucester, Mass., ca. 1678; *m* 1678, Mary Duncan (Peter[8], *m* Mary Epes, step-dau. of Samuel Symonds, dep.gov. Mass., *m* Martha [Reade] Epes);
6–Epes (1690-1762), justice of Essex Co., Mass.; maj. Essex Co. militia; rep. Gen. Court; he and his sons owned nearly all of East Gloucester; Sargent family museum at Gloucester contains many family heirlooms, Copley family portraits, etc.; *m* 1st, 1720, Esther Maccarty (1701-43);
5–Daniel (1731-1806), *m* 1763, Mary Turner (1743-1813);
4–John Turner (1769-1813), *m* Christiana Keadie (1778-1867);
3–Henry Jackson (1808-67), *m* Margaret Atwood Williams;
2–Susan Williams (1842-98), *m* 1865, Richard **Codman** (*b* 1842), A.B., Harvard, '64 (D.K.E.), A.M., 1870; issue: I–Lucy Sturgis (*b* 1869; *m* William Gibson Borland); II–Susan Sargent (*b* 1871; *m* John S. Codman, see Vol. I, p. 532); III–Richard, Jr. (1 above); IV–Alfred (*b* 1874; *m* Lydia Eliot); V–Margaret (*b* 1883).
1–*m* Jan. 4, 1917, Helen Winnifred Radke (qv for issue).
1–Harvard, ex-'96 (D.K.E.). Farmer. Residence: Fair Oaks, Sacramento Co., Calif.

1–**CODMAN, Helen Winnifred Radke (Mrs. Richard, Jr.),** *b* Marshalltown, Ia., May 3, 1894.
9–Michael (Dwinel, Dwinell) **Dunnell** (*d* 1713 or 17), from France, settled at Topsfield, Mass., ca. 1660; *m* Mary–;
8–Dr. Michaill (*b* 1670), "chirurgeion" and 1st physician of Topsfield; *m* 1st, Hannah–;
7–Michael (*b* 1707), recorded as died in War of 1755; *m* 1727, Lucy Towne;
6–Bartholomew (1728-1801), moved to Keene, N.H.; *m* Sarah Moulton (*d* 1822);
5–Bartholomew (1762-1813 or 14), minuteman in Am. Rev., fought in battles of Lexington and Concord, 1775; *m* Rebecca Towne (*d* 1830, aet. 64), of Rindge, N.H.;
4–John (1784-1853), moved from Brendon, Vt., to Canton, nr. Ogdensburg, St. Lawrence Co., N.Y., 1840, to Lockport, Niagara Co., N.Y., 1850, to Fairhaven Tp., Carroll Co., Ill.; *m* 1812, Prudence Atwood (*d* ca. 1852);
3–Martin Van Buren (1836-1925), wrote name **Dwinell;** moved from Carroll Co., Ill., to Marshall Co., Ia., 1865; *m* 1856, Adeline Simmons;
2–Leona Louise (2 below).
5–George **Brush,** *m* Margaret Simmons; *m* 2d, Maria–;
4–Eliza Jane (*b* 1813), *m* 1830, John **Simmons** (*b* 1806; Philip[5]);
3–Adeline (*d* 1909), *m* Martin Van Buren **Dwinell** (3 above);
2–Leona Louise (*b* 1860), *m* 1889, Joseph **Radke** (*b* 1864), ranchman; issue: I–Paul (*b* and *d* 1891); II–Helen W. (1 above); III–Hazel Doris (*b* and *d* 1897).
1–*m* Jan. 4, 1917, Richard Codman, Jr. (qv); issue: 1–Richard, III, *b* Sacramento, Calif., Oct. 29, 1917.
1–U.Calif., ex-'18. Mem. D.A.R. Summer place: Al Tahoe, Calif. Residence: Fair Oaks, Sacramento Co., Calif.

1–**COHN, Frances Marguerite Hinckley (Mrs. Sylvan),** *b* Cambridge, Mass., May 25, 1885.
10–Samuel **Hinckley** (qv);
9–Samuel (1642-1727), of Barnstable, Mass.; *m* 1664, Mary Goodspeed (1647-66; Roger[10], a founder Barnstable; *m* 1641, Alice Layton);
8–Benjamin (1666-post 1745), of Barnstable; *m* 1686, Sarah Cobb (*b* 1666; Henry[9], qv);
7–Benjamin (1694-1745), *m* 1716, Abigail Jenkins (*b* 1695; g.g.dau. of John Howland, Mayflower Pilgrim, qv);
6–Edmond (1719/20-1798), *m* 1744, Sarah Howland (1722-1802; Isaac[7]; g.g.g.dau. John Howland, qv);
5–Enoch (1751-1842), pvt. Am. Rev.; *m* Mercy Crocker (1757-1835);
4–Enoch (1793-1881), *m* 1820, Lucy Ellis (1802-62);
3–Enoch Russell (1823-89), *m* 1848, Frances Ellen Hill (1826-99);
2–Charles Russell (2 below).
9–Daniel **Thurston** (*d* 1693), from Cransbrook, Co. Kent, Eng., prob. 1635; at Newbury, Mass., 1638; *m* Anne Pell (Joseph[10], of Lynn, Mass.);
8–James (*b* Newbury, 1670), settled at Exeter, N.H.; *m* 1693, Mary Pearson, of Rowley, Mass.;
7–Abner (*b* 1699);
6–Peter (1739-1812), of S. Lancaster, Mass.; Am. Rev.; *m* Dorothy Gates (1739-1831; Hezekiah[7], settled at Hingham, Mass.);
5–Gates (1760-1816), *m* 1790, Elizabeth Pollard (1763-1849; John[6], of Bolton, Mass., Am. Rev.);
4–Henry (1790-1842), of Lancaster, Mass.; *m* 1815, Aurelia Warren (1794-1847; James[5], of Armenia, Dutchess Co., N.Y.; Stephen[6] [1735-1800], Am. Rev.);
3–William Pierce (1828-72), of Boston; *m* 1857, Elizabeth Harris Hooper (1831-1910; Henry Northey[4], of Boston);

2–Marguerite Aurelia (*b* 1859), *m* 1884, Charles Russell **Hinckley** (1849-1926), settled at Centralia, Wash.; issue: I–Frances M. (1 above); II–Thurston Russell (*b* 1889).
1–*m* 1903, Marion Jason Vaughan; issue: 1–Russell Hinckley, *b* 1904; *m* 1925, Esther Elouise, *b* 1904, dau. of Edouard and Helena Eben.
1–*m* 2d, July 8, 1912, Sylvan Cohn, *b* San Francisco, Calif., Nov. 12, 1883; son of Goodman Cohn of San Francisco, *m* Sarah Hyman.
1–Ed. privately. Mem. S.M.D., D.F.P.A., D.A.C., D.A.R., Order Lafayette, U.S.D. 1812, Hempstead Family Assn. (Conn.). Residence: Benson Hotel, Portland, Ore.

LT. COL. HERBERT CLAIBORNE COLE, M.C., U.S.A.

1–**COLE, Herbert Claiborne** (Dec. 14, 1881-Apr. 7, 1930).
10–William **Claiborne** (qv);
9–Lt. Col. Thomas (1649-83), killed by Indians; *m* Miss Dandridge;
8–Capt. Thomas (1680-1732), of "Sweet Hall," King William Co., Va.; *m* 3d, Anne Fox (1684-1733; Henry[9], of King William Co., *m* Anne, dau. of Col. John West, nephew of 3d Lord Delaware);
7–Col. Augustine (1721-87), of "Windsor," burgess; state senator; *m* Mary Herbert (Buller[8], *m* Mary Stith; Lord John[9], desc. first Earl of Pembroke); among their sons, Buller and Richard, were officers in Am. Rev.;
6–Lucy Herbert (*b* 1760), *m* 1775, Col. John **Cocke**; apptd. Surry Co. com., 1776;
5–Herbert;
4–Maria, *m* **—Childress**;
3–Herbert C., *m* Catherine Sloan Stuart;
2–Maria Stuart (2 below).
7–John **Harrison** (*b* 1715), *m* Sarah Daniel (John[8], Am. Rev., *m* Anne, dau. of John Williams, Welsh immigrants to Hanover Co., Va.);
6–James (1748-1815), lt. col. in Am. Rev.; mem. conv. which formed the first constitution of the U.S.; *m* Elizabeth Hampton (1758-99);
5–Richard (1786-1829), col. in War 1812, under Jackson at New Orleans; *m* Catherine Sloan (*d* 1859);
4–Mary Vivian, *m* Samuel **Stuart**;
3–Catherine Sloan (1833-57), *m* Herbert C. **Childress** (3 above).
11–William **Hampton** (qv);
10–Rev. Thomas (1623-post 1690), James City Co.;
9–Capt. John (1650-55-1718), to King William Co., Va.; *m* 1677, Mary Mann, at the home of her uncle John Mann, of "Timberneck," Gloucester Co., Va., ancestor of Page family of Va.;
8–John (1683-1748), of Fairfax Co., Va.; *m* 1712, Margaret Wade (1694-1773; James[9], of New Kent Co., Va.);
7–Anthony (1715/16-1776), killed by Indians; mem. N.C. Provincial Congress, 1773; *m* Elizabeth Preston, of Va. (their son Col. Wade, of Am. Rev. and general in War 1812, was the largest slaveowner in the south, and was the father of Gen. Wade Hampton, C.S.A.);
6–Elizabeth (1758-99), *m* James **Harrison** (6 above).
2–Maria Stuart Childress (1857-95), *m* 1879, John Thomas **Cole** (*d* July 2, 1919), of Monroe, La., issue: I–Sara (*d* 1926; *m* —Matthews; *m* 2d, R. O. Morrison); II–Herbert C. (1 above); III–Katherine Earl (*m* 1906, Edward Strange Pegram); IV–Jefferson Davis.
1–*m* June 16, 1908, Estelle Hynson (see Vol. III, p. 130).
1–Ed. La. State U., Tulane U., and med. schs.; post-grad. work Washington U., and N.Y. Med. Sch. Capt. Med. Corps, La. Inf., served on Mexican Border, 1916; Maj., Med. Corps, with 156th Inf., 39th Div., transferred to 79th Div., then to 5th Regular Army Div., promoted lt. col.; served in France, Aug., 1918-July 1919.

1–**COLBY, Lydia,** *b* Henry Co., Ill., Mar. 15, 1871.
9–Anthony **Colby** (1590-1661), from Beccles, Eng. to Boston, 1630; founder of Amesbury, Mass., 1632; *m* Susannah Haddon (*d* post 1684);
8–Isaac (1640-ante 1684), of Amesbury and Haverhill, Mass.; *m* Martha Jewett;
7–Anthony (*d* post 1734), of E. Haverhill; snowshoe man in war; *m* Mary Currier; *m* 2d, Elizabeth West;
6–Isaac (1712-62), *m* 1733, Sarah Davis; *m* 2d, 1757, Hanna Keath;
5–William Davis (1741 or 42-1812), of Hopkinton, N.H.; soldier in last French and Indian War; *m* Elizabeth Straw (1753-1840);
4–Timothy (1782-1866), of Hopkinton; *m* Lydia Herrick;
3–Jonathan (1808-85), of Petersburg, Ill.; *m* 1837, Lydia Ingalls;
2–William Davis (2 below).
9–Henry **Herrick** (qv);
8–John (1650-80), of Beverly, Mass.; *m* 1674, Mary Redington (Capt. John[9], *m* Mary Gould);
7–John (1675-1722), of Beverly; *m* 1696, Sarah Kimball (Ens. Samuel[8], *m* Sarah, dau. of John Witt; Richard[9]; Richard[10], qv);
6–Jonathan, *m* Mary Dodge (Jonathan[7], *m* Esther Friend; Edward[8]; Richard[9], qv);
5–Asa, *m* Annis Allen;
4–Lydia (1778-1866), *m* Timothy **Colby** (4 above).
9–William **Allen** (qv);
8–Samuel (1632-1700), Salem, Mass.; *m* 1660, Sarah Tuck;
7–Jonathan (1684-1762), *m* 1709, Mary Pierce;
6–John, *m* Lydia Osborne;
5–Annis, *m* Asa **Herrick** (5 above).
9–Edmund **Ingalls** (qv);
8–Henry (1627-1718-19), of Andover, Mass.; *m* 1st, Mary Osgood (*d* 1686); *m* 2d, Sarah Farnum Abbott;
7–James (1669-1735), of Andover; *m* Hannah Abbott (*d* 1753);
6–James (1695-1767), of Pomfret, Conn.; *m* Mary Stevens (1693-1773);
5–Ephriam (1725-1805), of Pomfret; *m* Mary Sharpe;
4–Ephriam (1764-1831), of Pomfret; *m* Lucy Goodell (1779-1829);
3–Lydia (1809-58), of Petersburg, Ill.; *m* Jonathan **Colby** (3 above).
10–William **White,** Mayflower Pilgrim (qv);
9–Resolved (1614-1690 or 94), *m* 1st, 1640, Judith Vassall (1619-70); *m* 2d, 1674, Mrs. Abigail Lord;
8–John (*b* 1644);
7–Abigail (1676-1753), *m* William **Sharpe** (1673-1751; Lt. John[8] [1643-76], *m* Martha Vose; Robert[9] [1615-53], from Eng., 1635, settled at Dorchester, Mass., removed to Muddy River, Mass., 1650, *m* Abigail–);
6–John (1703-79), *m* Dorcas Davis (*d* 1754);
5–Mary (1733-1809), *m* Ephriam **Ingalls** (5 above).
4–Francis **Dodds** (1740 or 50-1795; probably son of one of three brothers who came to Baltimore, 1730, following a religious uprising in Ireland); of Spartanburg, S.C.; *m* 2d, Margaret (Craig) Kirkpatrick (1749-1846);
3–Gilbert (1793-1872), of Petersburg, Ill.; Presbyn. Minister; *m* Mary Clinton (1800-66; James[4] [1761-1847], lt. Sumter's brig., Am. Rev., *m* Ann Armstrong);
2–Mary Elizabeth (1840-1909), *m* William Davis

Colby (1838-1913), farmer, Atkinson, Ill.; issue: I–Alfred Ingalls (1868-99; *m* Eva Blanche Vail; II–Lydia (1 above); III–Alice Dodds (*b* 1872; *m* William George Ramsay, D.D.); IV–Mary (*b* and *d* 1874); V–William Davis (*b* 1878; *m* Fannie Jane Vail).
1–Ed. Presbyn. Acad. (Geneseo Collegiate Inst.), 1890; Ill. State Normal U., 1899. Teacher in Henry Co. schs., and Kewanee, Ill.; critic teacher, Northern Ill. Normal Sch., DeKalb. Contributor to Ill. Hist. Journal; compiler and editor of Dodds Genealogy. Mem. D.A.R., Ladies of G.A.R. Conglist. Republican. Club: Columbian. Residence: 315 S. Henry St., Geneseo, Ill.

1–**COLBY, Franklin Green,** *b* Brooklyn or New York, N.Y., Aug. 10, 1858.
10–Anthony **Colby** (1590-1661), from Eng., 1630, settled at Salisbury, Mass., ca. 1639; *m* Susannah Haddon (*d* post 1684);
9–John (bap. 1633), *m* 1655/56, Frances Hoyt (John[10], *m* Frances–);
8–Anthony (*b* 1665);
7–Jacob (*b* 1688 or 90), *m* Hannah Hunt;
6–Zaccheus (*b* 1712);
5–Ephraim (1747-1823), of Ogden, N.Y.; Am. Rev.; *m* Mary (Merrill?), (1739-1806);
4–Dr. Zaccheus (*b* 1775), of Greece, N.Y.; War 1812; received land grant; *m* 2d, Mrs. Anna Webster;
3–Hall (1800-84), inventor latitude and longitude instrument, ca. 1870 or 75, basis of present instrument now in use; *m* Elizabeth Barrett;
2–Solomon or Salmon Barrett (1822-82), *m* 1848, Margaret Coffin Hill (*b* 1830; William[3], editor, 1825, New York Courier); issue: I–Eliza Hall (*b* 1849; *m* Frank J. Wyman); II–William Hall (*b* 1852; *m* Francis E. Kinyon); III–George Barrett (*b* 1854; *m* Helen Halsey); IV–Edward Barrett (*b* 1856; *m* Nellie Whitney); V–Franklin Green (1 above); VI–Benjamin Barrett (*b* 1860; *m* Alice Lee Scoby).
1–*m* July 19, 1882, Jessy Hornor (Sept. 15, 1858-Aug. 18, 1889); dau. of Judge Charles West Hornor, *m* Sarah E. Smith.
1–*m* 2d, Feb. 1, 1893, Josephine Wood, *b* New York, N.Y., Jan. 26, 1862; dau. of Walter R. Wood, of N.Y. City.
1–In international oil business outside and against the Standard Oil Co. of N.J. for about 20 yrs. Under Philippine Products Co. (pres.), developed new method of extracting cocoanut oil, Manila, P.I., 1905-07; pres. United Oil Co. which merged to Colby & Co., Liverpool and New York, overseas syndicate, for war purposes. Acted in New York for buying and dir. shipping line during World War. Life mem. N.Y. Hist. Soc., Sussex Co. (N.J.) Hist. Soc., I.A.G. Republican. Clubs: Nat. Arts (founder, trustee, now 2d v.p.), Lawyers. Residence: R.D. 1, "The Tamaracks," near Andover, N.J.

1–**COLE, Festus Clark,** *b* Iberia, O., Dec. 16, 1855.
6–John **Cole** (*b* 1670), from Eng., settled at Rehoboth (now Secunk), R.I.; *m* in Eng.;
5–John (*b* ca. 1705), came with his father; *m* a sister of Benjamin Franklin; *m* 2d, Mary Bowen;
4–Thomas (1735-1827), of Voluntown (Sterling), Conn.; *m* 1757, Miriam Kinne (1737-1827);
3–Amos (1759-1852), of Sterling; *m* 4th, 1816, Lucy Clark Burnham (1778-1846);
2–Henry Walcott (2 below).
8–Thomas **Gleason** (1607-86), from Sulgrave, Eng., 1636; took oath of fidelity, Watertown, Mass., 1652; *m* Susanna Page (*d* 1691), at Boston;
7–Sgt. Isaac (1654-98), *b* Watertown, Mass.; soldier from Enfield, Conn., in King Philip's War; in Falls Fight, 1676; *m* 1684, Hester Eggleston;
6–Isaac (1687-1761), of Enfield; *m* 1712, Mary Prior (*d* 1781);
5–Joseph B. (1721-1809), *m* 1744, Hannah Colton (*d* 1809);
4–Jonah B. (1766-1836), *m* Hannah Blodgett (*d* 1849);
3–Rossetter (1789-1870), removed from Enfield to Highland, Mich.; served as fifer War 1812; surveyor; teacher; *m* 1819, Mary Whitney Locke;
2–Mary Charlotte Osgood (Sept. 24, 1826-Sept. 30, 1906), removed from Georgetown, N.Y., to Iberia, O., thence to Highland, Mich., later to Ann Arbor, Mich., after death of her husband; ed. her six children there; *m* Belding, Mich., Sept. 24, 1850, Henry Walcott **Cole** (July 7, 1820-Apr. 6, 1872), of Sherburn, N.Y.; mcht., Iberia, O.; teacher music, Central Coll., Iberia; farmer, Clyde, Mich.; issue: I–Charles Henry (*b* 1853; *m* Carrie E. St. John); II–Festus Clark (1 above); III–Edwin Locke (*b* 1857); IV–Mary Emily (*b* 1859; *m* Mark J. Prall); V–Lucy Kate (*b* 1863); VI–Rossetter Gleason (*b* 1866; *m* Fannie Louise Gwinner).
1–*m* Oct. 25, 1894, Myrtle Alice Moon, *b* Fallassburg, Mich., July 26, 1865; dau. of Wilbur H. Moon, of Fallassburg; issue: 1–Harold Moon, *b* Jan. 18, 1896; *m* Mar. 15, 1925, Esther Anderson; 2–Lucy Ellura, *b* July 8, 1899; *m* May 19, 1925, Harry L. Grill.
1–Grad. U.Mich., '81. Supt. schools, Hinsdale, Ill., 1882-85; Instr. West Div. High School, Chicago, 1885-86. Lumber dealer, Iron Mountain, Mich., 1890–. Clubs: Pine Grove Country, Rotary. K.P. Residence: 212 W. E St., Iron Mountain, Mich.

1–**COLE, Redmond Selecman,** *b* Andrew Co., Mo., Aug. 22, 1881.
11–James **Cole** (*b* 1600), from Eng. to Saco. Me., 1632; settled at Plymouth, Mass., 1633; *m* 1624, Mary Lobel (Mathieu[12] [*b* 1538], French physician; Jean De Lobel[13], French lawyer);
10–Hugh (1627-99), of Swansea, Mass.; *m* 1st, 1654, Mary Foxwell (*b* 1635; Richard[11], *m* Ann Shelly);
9–Hugh (1658-1738), of Swansea, Mass.; *m* 1681, Deborah Buckland (1660-1724; Joseph[10], *m* Deborah Allen);
8–Hugh (1683-1753), of Mass.; *m* 1705, Martha Luther (1681-1765; Samuel[9], *m* Mary–);
7–Joseph (1716-85), of R.I., and settled in Washington Co., Va., post 1771; *m* 1738, Freelove Mason (*b* 1720; Joseph[8] [1687-1761], *m* 1714, Elizabeth [1693/94-1757], dau. of Joseph Barney, *m* Constance Davis; Joseph[9] [1662/63-1748], *m* 1686, Lydia [1666-1758], dau. of Obadiah Bowen, *m* Mary Clifton; Sampson[10], qv);
6–Joseph (1750-1826), of Washington Co., Va.; *m* a dau. of Israel Cole;
5–John (1771-1848), of Washington Co.; *m* 1790, Sarah Williams? (1766-1816);
4–Peleg (1795-1859), of Washington Co.; *m* 1821, Mary Todd (1802-31; James[5], *m* Jean–);
3–James Lowry (1827-84), of Washington Co.; *m* 1849, Eliza Patterson;
2–James Buchanan (2 below).
6–James **Wheeler** (will probated 1804), of Washington Co., Va.; *m* Abigail–;
5–Lydia (1770-1841), *m* Sampson **Cole** (1756-1833; Joseph[6], 7 above);
4–Elizabeth (ca. 1795-1880), *m* 1814, Rev. Andrew **Patterson** (1775-1862), capt. in War 1812; of Washington Co., Va.;
3–Eliza (1834-94), *m* James L. **Cole** (3 above).
7–Stephen **Bedford** (*d* 1758), co. capt., co. justice and co. sheriff of Cumberland Co., Va.; *m* Elizabeth Flippen;
6–Thomas (1730-85), co. justice; mem. Com. of Safety of Charlotte Co., Va.; *m* 1750, Mary Ligon Coleman;
5–John (1764-1841), of Nelson Co., Ky.; *m* 1788, Mary Ann Marshall (1765-1839);
4–John (1797-1838), of Meade Co., Ky.; *m* 1823, Elizabeth Burke Howard (1804-40; William[5], *m* Lucy–);
3–Alexander Marshall (1828-1912), *m* 1851, Mary Elizabeth Selecman;
2–Virginia Lee (2 below).
6–Henry **Selecman** (*d* 1815), from Germany to Va., 1765; settled in Prince William Co., Va.; *m* ca. 1765, Margaret Harmon (*d* ca. 1810);
5–George (1769-1839), of Prince William Co.; *m* ca. 1796, Jane Davis (*d* ca. 1815);
4–Henry Wisheart (1797-1871), of Andrew Co., Mo.; *m* ca. 1823, Mary Simpson (1797-1850; William[5] [1757-1820], of Fairfax Co., Va., *m* Jane Keen, 1760-1821);
3–Mary Elizabeth (1830-99), of Andrew Co., Mo.; *m* Alexander Marshall **Bedford** (3 above);
2–Virginia Lee (1860-1926), *m* 1880, James Buchanan **Cole** (*b* 1856), doctor of osteopathy; issue: I–Redmond S. (1 above); II–Mary Elizabeth (1883-1907); III–Frances Cleveland (1887-1928);

IV–James Alexander (*b* 1889; *m* Delpha Lawrence); V–Virgil Bedford (*b* 1897); VI–Virginia Lee (*b* 1902).
1–*m* June 11, 1910, Mary Thompson Cross (qv); issue: 1–Olivia Harris, *b* Pawnee, Okla., June 24, 1913; 2–Virginia Bedford, *b* Pawnee, Nov. 10, 1919.
1–Student Kirksville (Mo.) State Normal Sch., 1899-1901; A.B., U.Mo., '05, A.M., 1906; studied law same univ., 1907-09 (Delta Tau Delta, Delta Sigma Rho, Phi Alpha Delta). Admitted to bar, 1909; co. atty. Pawnee Co., Okla., 1910-15; registrar Pawnee Co., 1916-17; mayor of Pawnee, 1917; asst. U.S. dist. atty., western dist. of Okla., 1917-19; judge 21st Judicial Dist. of Okla., 1919-23; resumed practice at Tulsa. Mem. S.A.R., Wis., Kan., Okla., Ky., Va., Tenn. and Mo. state hist. socs., I.A.G. Mason. Methodist. Democrat. Residence: 1312 S. Owasso, Tulsa, Okla.

1–**COLE, Mary Thompson Cross (Mrs. Redmond S.)**, *b* Laddonia, Mo., Oct. 22, 1884.
6–William **Cross** (1733-98), settled in Botetourt Co., Va., ca. 1769; *m* Elizabeth–;
5–William (1766-1848), of Botetourt Co., Va., Madison Co., Ky., and Howard Co., Mo.; *m* Sarah McGowan (*d* 1851);
4–John (1793-1861), of Howard Co., Mo.; *m* 1817, Sarah Blythe;
3–William Blythe (1820-96), of Randolph Co., Mo.; *m* 1850, Mary Jane Shores;
2–John Newton (2 below).
8–Nicholas **Gentry**, immigrant to Hanover Co., Va., 1677-83; British soldier in Bacon's Rebellion;
7–Nicholas (1697-1779), *m* Jane–;
6–David (1724-1812), *m* 2d, Mary Estes;
5–Onie (ca. 1765-1823), *m* 2d, 1793, William **Blythe** (William[6], of N.C., *m* Mary Osborne);
4–Sarah (1797-1870), *m* John **Cross** (4 above).
5–Claiborn **Johnson** (ca. 1759-1840), enlisted in Am. Rev. aet. 18; placed on Mo. pension roll, 1834; *m* 1794, Betsey Simms;
4–Susan Rice (1800-72), *m* 1829, William **Shores** (1796-1872), Meth. preacher in Howard Co., Mo.;
3–Mary Jane (1830-98), *m* William Blythe **Cross** (3 above).
5–Colden **Williams** (1763-1832), served in 10th Regt., N.C. Cont. Line; settled in Howard Co., Mo.; *m* 1787, Mary Short (1767-1823);
4–Elizabeth (1802-65), of Howard Co.; *m* 1817, Nero Morgan **Thompson** (1794-1866);
3–Margaret Dun (1822-88), of Howard Co.; *m* 1845, Thomas Banks **Harris** (1818-1904);
2–Olivia McClure (1850-1928), *m* 1876, John Newton **Cross** (*b* 1850), farmer and teacher, Modesto, Calif.; issue: I–Lulu Harris (1877-1927; *m* Edwin H. Morris); II–Annie Helen (*b* 1878; *m* Charles Henry Caswell); III–Mary Thompson (1 above); IV–William Thomas (*b* 1887; *m* Dorothy Embry);
1–*m* June 11, 1910, Redmond S. Cole (qv for issue).
1–B.S. in edn., Mo. U., '08. Methodist. Democrat. Residence: 1312 S. Owasso, Tulsa, Okla.

1–**COLE, Robert Franklin**, *b* Kaufman, Tex., Dec. 16, 1883.
8–James **Dale** (1630-98), English family, sailed from Ireland to Phila., 1695; *d* in Md.;
7–John (1688-1778), *d* in Worcester Co., Md.;
6–Thomas (1744-1812), *d* in Tenn.; officer in Am. Rev.; capt. Md. Line; *m* Elizabeth Evans;
5–Adam (1768-1851), *d* in Ala.; joined a co. of vols., aet. 14; D.A.R. Chapter at Memphis, Tenn., named for him; *m* 1790, Mary Hall (Jordan[6], of Sussex Co., Del.);
4–Sophia Woodson (1805-84), *d* in Miss.; *m* 1818, aet. 13, Dr. Robert **Turner** (1794-1856), surgeon's mate, War 1812 (Berryman[5] [*b* 1757], ens. in Am. Rev., *m* Susan–);
3–Sarah Jane (1824-76), *d* in Tex.; *m* 1846, Capt. Armstead Beresford **Cole** (1822-73), *d* in Tex.; capt. Chippewa, Miss., state militia, 1858; 1st lt., Pontotoc, Miss., dragoons (army of Miss.), 1861; 1st lt., Pontotoc Minute Men (Miss. cav.), 1862; capt. Co. A, Harris Bn., Miss. troops, 1864; capt. Co. D, 35th Regt., Tex. militia, 1871, Civil War (Samuel[4] [1799-1865], recorded in Tuscaloosa, Ala. census of 1830, Pontotoc Co., Miss., 1840 and 50, Angelina Co., Tex., 1860, *m* 1819, Lucy–, of Ga. or S.C., *b* ca. 1803);
2–William Dale (2 below).
6–Ninion **Chamberlain**, came from Ireland, with his son John;
5–John (1740-95), Tenn.; enlisted in Picken's brig. which reinforced Gen. Daniel Morgan at Cowpens against Cornwallis; *m* ca. 1782, Hannah Lockey;
4–Jane, *m* 1813, William **Corley**, moved to Blount Co., Tenn., ca. 1800 (Austin[5], of Roanoke, Va.);
3–William Franklin (1823-92), *b* in Tenn., *d* in Ala.; enlisted soldier in 30th Ala. Regt., C.S.A.; surrendered at Appomattox; *m* ca. 1852, Martha Malvina Wilson (Hugh[4], *m* Mary Purcell);
2–Flora Tennie (1854-1919), *m* 1880, William Dale **Cole** (1847-91), mcht. and postmaster, Fairy, Tex.; issue: I–Mattie Josephine (*b* 1882; *m* 1904, Nonie A. Leeth); II–Robert Franklin (1 above); III–Leon Bertram (*b* 1885; *m* 1913, Mattie Lulu Johnson); IV–Myrtle Belle (*b* 1887; *m* ca. 1905, Charles Jones; *m* 2d, John Marks); V–Lucy Dee (*b* 1889; *m* 1910, Clyde Edward Crouch); VI–Willie Dale (*b* 1892; *m* 1913, Percy Herbert Mulcahy).
1–*m* July 18, 1914, Dorothy Vera Shatel, *b* New York, N.Y., July 16, 1895; dau. of Max Shatel, came from Russia ca. 1891, *m* Sarah Colton.
1–Labor commr., Nev., 1917-20; mem. Nev. Industrial Commn., 1917-20. Mem. Nev. dist. exemption bd., 1917-18; chief div. of administration, U.S. Bd. of Mediation, Washington. Genealogist Dale Genealogy. Mem. S.C.V. Clubs: Bannockburn Country, Texas. Residence: 2915 Conn. Av., Washington, D.C.

1–**COLTON, Ethan Theodore**, *b* Palmyra, Wis., Nov. 22, 1872.
8–George **Colton** (qv);
7–Capt. Thomas (1651-1728), ens., 1679, lt., capt., 1693, served in Indian wars; *m* 2d, 1691, Hannah Bliss (1665-1737);
6–Ebenezer (1696-1765), *m* 1733, Deborah Chandler (1709-69);
5–Henry (1738-87), Am. Rev.; *m* 1768, Mary Burt (1745-83);
4–Ethan (1780-1828), *m* 1804, Ruth Stebbins (1784-1814);
3–Theodore Sedgwick (1805-82), *m* 1832, Aurelia Smith (1810-89);
2–Harvey Theodore (1841-1912), farmer; pvt. 13th Wis. Vol. Inf. in Civil War; *m* 1866, Jane Congdon (1847-1919); issue: I–Jennie Aurelia (*b* 1868; *m* Benjamin Franklin Burr, 1858-1928); II–Ethan T. (1 above).
1–*m* Oct. 11, 1900, Caroline Cullen Quigg, *b* Chicago, Ill., Jan. 26, 1872; dau. of Thomas Quigg, *m* Caroline Graham; issue: 1–Ethan Theodore, Jr., *b* New York, N.Y., Oct. 31, 1904; Wesleyan U., Conn., '25; Harvard Med. Sch., 1929; *m* Aug. 25, 1928, Adeline, dau. of Randolph Miller; 2–Elizabeth Graham, *b* Upper Montclair, N.J. (Sept. 10, 1906-Dec. 20, 1926), ed. Northfield Sem., and pvt. sch., Weimar, Germany; 3–Marjorie Congdon, *b* Glen Ridge, N.J., Jan. 8, 1912; ed. The Baldwin Sch., Bryn Mawr, Pa.
1–B.A., Dakota Wesleyan U., '98 (LL.D., 1929); post-grad. work, U.Chicago and Columbia. Exec. sec., foreign com. Nat. Councils of Y.M.C.A. (see Who's Who in America). Organized and directed Y.M.C.A. wartime service in Russia and Siberia, 1918. Residence: 109 Haddon Pl., Upper Montclair, N.J.

1–**CONDON, Emma Louise Wathen (Mrs. Richard L.)**, *b* Marion Co., Ky., June 25, 1869.
8–John **Wathen** (ca. 1625-98), from Eng., 1646; settled St. Marie, province of Md.; large landowner; *m* ca. 1650, Mary Mullett (ca. 1630-post 1698);
7–John (ca. 1662-1705), of Calvert and Charles cos., Md.; *m* ca. 1684, Susannah or Ann Hudson(?);
6–Hudson (ca. 1694-1760), of Charles Co.; *m* 1715, Sarah Mudd (*d* post 1760);
5–Henry Hudson (1741-74), of Leanordstown, Md.; *m* 1763, Susannah or Ann– (*d* post 1774);
4–Henry Hudson (1766-1851), of St. Mary's Co., and Marion Co., Ky.; soldier Am. Rev.; founder of Wathen distilling business in Marion Co.; *m* 2d, 1798, Mary Spalding (1773-post 1851);
3–Richard (1815-80), of Marion Co.; *m* 1838, Mary Sophia Abell (1817-91);

2–John Bernard (1844-1919), of Marion Co. and Jefferson Co., Ky.; distiller and capitalist; *m* 1867, Margaret Adams (*b* 1844); issue: I–Emma Louise (1 above); II–Richard (*b* and *d* 1872); III–Eleanor (*b* 1873; *m* Howard J. Pullum, *d*); IV–Josephine (*b* 1875; *m* Charles Edwin Cooney); V–Richard Eugene (*b* 1877; *m* Ada Walsh, *d*); VI–Gertrude (*b* and *d* 1879); VII–John Bernard (*b* 1880; *m* Laura Effie Ewell); VIII–Otho Hill (*b* 1881; *m* Fay Duffy); IX–Margaret (*b* 1883; *m* James P. Edwards).

1–*m* June 24, 1905, Richard Lawrence Condon, *b* Yonkers, N.Y., Mar. 4, 1855; son of Lawrence Richard Condon (1820-1908), of Yonkers; issue: 1–Richard Wathen, *b* Louisville, Ky., May 20, 1908; ed. Newman Sch., Lakewood, N.J., Philips Acad., Yale.

1–Ed. Nazareth Coll., Bardstown, Ky., 1889. Mem. C.D.A., D.C.W., D.F.P.A., D.A.R., U.S.D. 1812, Soc. of Dames of Ct. of Honor, Soc. of the Ark and the Dove. Clubs: Filson, Louisville Country. Catholic. Republican. Residence: 418 W. Oak St., Louisville, Ky.

JOHN HOLMES CONVERSE

1–**CONVERSE, John Holmes,** *b* Racine, Wis., July 26, 1878.

9–Edward (Convers) **Converse** (qv);

8–Samuel (1637 or 38-69), sgt. Woburn Train Band; *m* 1660, Judith Carter (*d* 1677; Rev. Thomas[9], of Woburn, *m* Mary Parkhurst);

7–Samuel (1662-ca. 1732), founder of Thompson, Conn.; *m* ante 1694, Dorcas Pain;

6–Edward (1696-1784), ens. and constable, Thompson, Conn.; *m* 1717, Elizabeth Cooper (1700-76; John[7], *m* Elizabeth–);

5–Asa (*b* 1730), Am. Rev.; *m* 1755, Ruth Lee;

4–Solvin (1758-1814), *m* 1780, Sarah Holmes;

3–Freeman (1803-46), *m* 2d, 1836, Emily Miller (1813-96, sister of Judge Oliver Miller, of Md.);

2–John Holmes (2 below).

7–John **Holmes** (qv);

6–David (1692-1745), *m* 1720, Bathsheba Sanford (Thomas[7]; Robert[8]);

5–David (1721-79), capt. French and Indian War; surgeon in Am. Rev.; *m* Temperance Bishop (their son Abiel was the father of Oliver Wendell Holmes);

4–Sarah (1760-1844), *m* Solvin **Converse** (4 above).

9–Rev. John **Lothrop** (qv);

FREEMAN CONVERSE (1803-46).

8–Samuel (1622-1701), *m* Elizabeth Scudder;

7–Joseph;

6–Temperance (*b* 1704), *m* 1727, as his 2d wife, John **Bishop** (1685-1754), of Norwich, Conn. (Samuel[7]; Thomas[8]);

5–Temperance (*b* 1735), *m* David **Holmes** (5 above).

REV. JOHN HOLMES CONVERSE (1837-1904), and JANE BAKER (JONES) CONVERSE (1834-1925).

2–John Holmes **Converse** (1837-1904), Episcopal minister, and scholar; *m* 1868, Jane Baker Jones (1834-1925); issue: I–Agnes Howard (*b* 1871; *m* A. R. Van Meter); II–Arthur Freeman (1873-74); III–Eliza Baker (1874-1923); IV–Frederick Lyttleton (*b* 1876, *d* same day); V–John Holmes (1 above).

1–Not married. Dep. U.S. shipping commr. Mem. O.F.P.A., S.R., S.A.R. Clubs: Torresdale, Frankford Country. Residence: 3307 Race St., Phila., Pa.

1–**CONGER, Louis Herbert,** *b* Valparaiso, Ind., Aug. 2, 1882.

8–John **Conger** (*d* 1712), from Eng., 1667, with wife and eldest son; settled at Woodbridge, N.J.; participated in first distribution of land there, 1669; *m* Mary–;

7–Job (*b* 1694), *m* Mary Percy;

6–Job (*b* 1728), to Albany Co., N.Y.; *m* 1751, Mary Carrington (1732-1802);
5–Uzziah (1758-1841), Cayuga Co., N.Y.; served 7 yrs., Am. Rev., corp. 5th Albany Co., 3d Rensselaerwyck Regiment, N.Y.; *m* Mary Hungerford (1764-1847);
4–Rev. Enoch (1792-1872), chaplain, corp., Bloom's 19th Regt., N.Y., War 1812, wounded at Queenstown; circuit riding preacher in the Western Reserve; located in Ohio; *m* 1814, Esther West (1796-1882);
3–Seymour Beach (1825-64), a "Fortyniner"; Civil War, killed in action, bvtd. lt. col., 3d W.Va. Cav.; *m* 1846, Mary Abigail Barker (1828-1913; g.dau. of Jonathan Barker, War 1812, killed at Ft. Erie);
2–Clinton Barker (1847-1912), engr.; writer; *m* 1874, Cornelia Elvira Smith (*b* 1852); issue: I–Amy Florence (*b* 1874); II–Seymour Beach (*b* 1876; *m* 1910, Lucile Bailey, *b* 1882); III–Louis H. (1 above); IV–Ralph Gilbert (*b* 1891; *m* 1916, Julia Lathrop Henning).
1–*m* July 19, 1910, Hazel Lomison Snyder, *b* Three Rivers, Mich., Oct. 20, 1887; dau. of Ashbel Wilson Snyder (*b* 1841), q.m., 25th Mich. Inf., Civil War; *m* 1882, Elizabeth Lomison (*b* 1851); issue: 1–Louis Herbert, Jr., *b* Muskegon, Mich., Mar. 22, 1915; 2–Alan Douglas, *b* Muskegon, Mar. 23, 1917.
1–A.B., U.Mich., '05. Editor, Holland Sentinel, 1908-10; sec. Kalamazoo Commercial Club, 1911-12, Muskegon Chamber of Commerce, 1913-15, West Mich. Pike Assn., 1915-23; pres. wholesale and retail coal co. Pres. Rotary, 1921-22; trustee Bd. of Education. Mem. S.R. Summer place: Hack's Shack, nr. Muskegon. Residence: 560 W. Webster Av., Muskegon, Mich.

Stansbury

Arms: *Per pale argent and or, a lion rampant per fesse gules and sable.*
Crest: *A lion rampant.*
Motto: *Consequitur quodcunque petit.*

1–**CONWAY, Laetitia Yeamans Staige Stansbury (Mrs. Peter V.D.),** *b* Snowden, Spotsylvania Co., Va., May 7, 1858.
6–Tobias **Stansbury** (1662-1709), came to Md.; apptd. "ranger" by gov. of Md. to protect colonists against Indian attacks; *m* Sarah Raven;
5–Luke (1689-1742), large landowner; *m* Jane– (*d* 1759);
4–Capt. Tobias (1718-57), Md. militia, French and Indian War; *m* 1746, Mary Hammond;
3–Gen. Tobias Emerson (1757-1849), lt. cdr. Am. Rev.; brig. gen., Md. troops in War 1812; del. Md. Gen. Assembly, 1801-23, speaker 9 times; *m* 1811, Ann Dew (*d* 1822), of Baltimore Co., Md.;
2–John Lewis (2 below).
4–William **Smith** (son of William Samuel Smith, *m* Miss Yeamans, perhaps g.dau. of Sir John Yeamans, qv), from Bristol, Eng., settled at Hampton, Va., *m* Nancy Jennings;
3–Yeamans (1777-1849), owner of estate "Snowden," nr. Fredericksburg, Va.; *m* 1804, Anne Osborne Marye;
2–Mary Osborne (2 below).
5–James **Marye** (*b* 1767), from Rouen, France, to Eng., 1726; thence to Va., 1729; ed. for R.C. priesthood; joined Huguenots, was ordained minister Ch. of Eng.; settled at Manakin Town, Va.; rector St. George's Parish, at Fredericksburg, Va., Oct. 1735; *m* 1728, Laetitia Maria Anne Staige;
4–Rev. James, Jr. (1731-80), succeeded his father as rector of St. George's Parish; *m* Elizabeth (Osborne) Grayson (1737-1831; Capt. Osborne[5], English marine service);
3–Anne Osborne (1777-1860), *m* Yeamans **Smith** (3 above);
2–Mary Osborne (1820-1901), *m* 1851, John Lewis **Stansbury** (1816-88), Baltimore Co., Md.; issue: I–Annie Osborne (1852-64); II–Julia Belle (1853-1921; *m* William Fitzhugh Ficklen); III–Virginia Ward (1855-83; *m* Lindlay Hoffman Maitland); IV–Laetitia Yeamans (1 above); V–Carville Contee (1860-83).
1–*m* Mar. 6, 1895, as his 2d wife, Peter Vivian Daniel Conway (1842-1924; see Vol. II, p. 25 for genealogy and portrait).
1–Mem. C.D.A., H.S., Founders of Manakintown, D.A.R., U.S.D. 1812, U.D.C. Residence: 3528 28th St., San Diego, Calif.

1–**COOK, Ross Keelye,** *b* Phila., Pa., Aug. 24, 1885.
8–Richard **Ridgway** (ca. 1650-1722), Quaker, from Welford, Berkshire, Eng., 1679, in the "Jacob and Mary," to Burlington, N. J.; justice of peace, 1712-20; *m* 1673, Elizabeth Chamberlain (ca. 1655-92), of Berkshire, Eng.;
7–Thomas (1677-1724), Quaker, of Little Egg Harbor, N.J.; *m* 2d, 1712, Elizabeth Andrews (1695-1725), of Mansfield and Little Egg Harbor (Edward[8] [1677-1716]; Mary Wright[9], imprisoned at Boston by Gov. Endicott for preaching against the burning of witches and persecution of Quakers, 1660; Sgt. Peter Wright[10] of Sandwich, Cape Cod, founder of Oyster Bay, L.I., 1653);
6–Jacob (1723-99), Quaker, of Springfield Tp., Burlington Co.; in Battle of Trenton, and was disowned by Chesterfield Friends Meeting for "bearing arms"; *m* 1750, Isabella Schooley (1721-94);
5–Andrews (1762-1837), Quaker, of Woodbury, Gloucester Co., N.J.; *m* 1788, Lydia Clark (1769-1804; Judge Thomas[6] [1737-1809], v.p. Proprietor's Assn. of West Jersey, 1772, justice peace, 1772; mem. Com. of Correspondence, and Com. of Observation [Gloucester Co.], 1774, mem. both Provincial Congresses, 1775-76);
4–John Paul (1801-90), of Camden, N.J.; Quaker; *m* 1825, Elizabeth B. Steelman (1807-31; desc. Lt. Anders Larsson Dahlbo, who came from Sweden, 1638, and settled at Kingsessing [Phila.], Pa.; and Peter Gunnarson Rambo, qv);
3–Mary (1827-1911), of Greenwich Tp., and East Orange; Quaker; *m* 1853, Christian Henry **Cook** (1825-63), of Phila.;
2–Capt. and Q.-M. Richard Augustus (Jan. 24, 1860-Sept. 27, 1899), of Phila.; regtl. q.-m., 19th Inf., 1st Brig., Pa. N.G.; furniture salesman; *m* 1884, Amelia Kiesling (*b* 1859); issue: I–Ross K. (1 above); II–Arthur (1887-88); III–Earl Raymond (*b* 1892); IV–Edythe May (*b* 1894; *m* Philip Sheridan).
1–*m* Oct. 23, 1907, Anna Gertrude Campbell, *b* North East, Cecil Co., Md., Jan. 1, 1885; dau. of William Campbell, of Kirklyn, Del. Co., Pa., *m* Mary Adelaide Harlan (g.g. dau. of Lt. Roger Kirk); issue: 1–Ridgway Allison, *b* Phila., Pa., June 24, 1910.
1–Asst. sec. of a N.Y. corpn. Served in N.J. militia reserve, 1918-1920. Mem. N.J. Hist. Soc., Swedish Colonial Soc., S.C.W., S.A.R. (corr. sec.). Residence: 173 Renshaw Av., East Orange, N.J.

1–**COOKE, Robert George,** *b* Sturgis, Mich., Oct. 31, 1906.
10–Pierre Gibaut dit **Poitevin** (*b* 1610), *m* Renee Lorliere;
9–Gabriel (1641-1700), *m* Suzanne Durand (*b* 1653; Etienne[10], *m* Genevieve de la Mar);

8–Angelique (*b* 1677), *m* at Montreal, 1698, Jacques **De Lacelle** (*b* Paris, France, 1670), of Montreal (Gilles[9], *m* Anne Beauregard);
7–Angelique (*b* 1706), *m* 1727, Pierre Descompts dit **Labadie** (1702-82), from France, 1726, to Montreal, settled at Detroit, Mich., 1740 (son of Jean Baptiste Descompts, of LaRochelle, France, *m* Marie Anne Manceau; g.son of Alexander de Labadie, Chevalier and Seigneur de la Chausseliere, col. in the French Army);
6–Antoine Louis (1744-1806), obtained large grants of land from the Indians, who surnamed him "Badichon"; *m* 3d, 1784, Charlotte Barthe Reaume;
5–Louis (*b* 1788), *m* 1812, Victoire Berthiaume (1795-1881; Joseph[6], *m* Catherine Pilet);
4–Gregoire (1812-90), dropped surname Descompts; moved to Kalamazoo, Mich.: *m* 1836, Marie Binet, of Montreal (*d* 1890; Gabriel[5], *m* Marie Robert);
3–Marie Elizabeth (Eliza) (1837-1913), *m* George **Cooke** (1829-1919), came to America, 1843, with his mother, 4 bros. and sister, settled nr. Middleville, Mich., 1847 (Robert[4], of Dolington, Sussex, Eng., came to America ca. 1842, with his son Robert, settled in Monroe Co., N.Y., both were drowned, *m* 1815, Sophia Kemp)
2–Joseph Robert George (2 below).
11–Jacques **Frappierre** (Frapier) of LaRochelle, France; *m* Marie Rene;
10–Hilaire (*b* 1651), of Quebec; *m* 1668, Rose Petit (1646-1719; Jean[11], *m* Jeanne Gueribour);
9–Madeliene (1680-1759), *m* at Quebec, 1706, Pierre **Esteve** (*d* at Detroit, 1736; Antoine[10], *m* Marguerite Le Blond);
8–Marie Madeliene (1706-53), *m* 1720, Dr. Jean Baptiste **Chapoton** (1684-1760), surgeon-maj. in the French Army, to Can., 1705-06 (Andre[9], *m* Anne Cassaigne; Tendrez[10]);
7–Marie Charlotte (*b* 1737), *m* 1760, Dr. Pierre **Barthe,** of Montreal, surgeon in the French Army (Theophile[8] [*b* Gascony, France, 1695], to Can., "Gunsmith to the King," *m* 1721, Margaret, dau. of Charles Alavoine [*d* 1749], capt. militia, *m* Marie Therese Marchand, 1664-1728);
6–Charlotte (1763-1849), *m* 1st, Lt. Louis Reaume; *m* 2d 1784, Antoine Louis Descompts dit **Labadie** (6 above).
8–Henry **Walrath**;
7–Johannes Petrus, from Germany; among first settlers of Beul, N.Y., ca. 1760;
6–Jacob?;
5–William (1772-1858), to Mich. post 1839; *m* Margaret Irving (1776-1839; James?[6]);
4–Cornelius (1804-64), *m* Polly Goodal (1807-73);
3–Mary Alice (1834-1901), *m* George **Mitchell** (1836-83), Civil War (George[4] [1810-38], of Royalton, N.Y., *m* Rhoda Marvin [1816-65], of Rutland, Vt.);
2–Cora (*b* 1864), of Middleville, Mich.; *m* George Freeman; *m* 2d, 1886, Joseph Robert George **Cooke** (1858-1910); *m* 3d, Bishop Schriber, of St. Paul (*d* 1925); issue (1st marriage): I–Dr. Floyd Freeman (*b* 1883); (2d marriage): I–Basil (*b* and *d* 1888); II–Mildred (*b* 1893; *m* 1918, Wallace Jones, issue: Eloise, Lenore, Emory); III–Robert George (1 above).
1–Not married. Ed. U.Minn., 1926-27 (Phi Sigma Kappa); Minneapolis Sch. of Art, 1928-29. Club: Phi Alpha Chi (charter mem. and 1st pres.), Paletitte, Garden (sec. and treas.). Residence: 1856 Marshall Av., St. Paul, Minn.

1–**COOLIDGE, Harold Jefferson,** *b* Nice, France, Jan. 22, 1870.
9–John **Coolidge** (qv);
8–Jonathan (1646/47-1723/24), *m* Martha Rice (1662-95);
7–John (*b* 1690/91), *m* Hannah Ingram;
6–Joseph (1718/19-1771), *m* Marguerite Olivier (1726-1816);
5–Joseph (1747-1820), *m* Elizabeth Boyer (1754-86);
4–Joseph (1773-1840), *m* Elizabeth Bulfinch (1777-1837);
3–Joseph (1798-1879), A.B., Harvard, 1817; *m* Eleonora Wayles Randolph;
2–Joseph Randolph (2 below).
9–John **Jefferson,** from Wales with father; part-founder of Yorktown, Va.; burgess, 1619; and probably thru:
8–Thomas (*d* 1697), owned a plantation in Henrico Co., Va., 1677; *m* Martha Branch (William[9], of Henrico Co.; Christopher[10], qv);
7–Capt. Thomas (1679-1725), lived at "Osborne," on the James River, Chesterfield Co.; justice, 1706; *m* 1697, Mary Field (Peter[8], *m* Judith Seane);
6–Peter (1707/08-1757), of "Shadwell," adj. gen. of Va.; *m* 1739, Jane Randolph (Isham[7], of "Dungeness");
5–Thomas (1743-1826), author of the Declaration of Independence and 3d President of the U.S.; *m* 1772, Martha Wayles (1748-82);
4–Martha, *m* 1790, Thomas Mann **Randolph** (1768-1828; see Vol. I, p. 352 for Randolph lineage);
3–Eleonora W. (1796-1876), *m* Joseph **Coolidge** (3 above).
10–Thomas **Gardner** (qv);
9–Lt. George (ca. 1620-1679), from Eng. to Salem, Mass.; *m* ca. 1647, Elizabeth (Horne) Orne (*d* 1658);
8–Samuel (1648-1724), of Salem; rep. Mass. Gen. Ct.; mcht.; *m* Elizabeth Brown (1644-83; widow of Joseph Grafton);
7–Capt. John (1681-1721), at the defense of Haverhill against the Indians; capt. provincial militia; rep. Gen. Ct.; *m* Elizabeth Weld (*b* 1681);
6–John (1707-84), *m* Elizabeth Putnam (1700-64);
5–John (1731-1805), *m* 2d, Elizabeth Pickering (1737-1823);
4–Samuel Pickering (1767-1843), *m* Rebecca Russell/Lowell (1779-1853);
3–John Lowell (1804-84), *m* Catherine Elizabeth Peabody (1808-83);
2–Julia (1841-1921), *m* 1860, Joseph Randolph **Coolidge** (1828-1925), lawyer; issue: I–Joseph Randolph, Jr. (see Vol. I, p. 351); II–John Gardner (see Volume I, p. 351); III–Archibald Cary (see Vol. I, 351); IV–Harold J. (1 above); V–Julian Lowell (see Vol. I, p. 352).
1–*m* Feb. 19, 1903, Edith Lawrence (qv); issue (all *b* Boston, Mass.): 1–Harold Jefferson, Jr., *b* Jan. 15, 1904; 2–Lawrence, *b* Jan. 17, 1905; 3–Emily Fairfax, *b* Oct. 13, 1907.
1–A.B., Harvard, '92 (magna cum laude), LL.B., 1896. Lawyer, Boston (see Who's Who in America). Clubs: Harvard, Somerset, Harvard Travelers, Club of Odd Volumes, Tennis and Racquet (Boston); Country (Brookline); University, Harvard (New York); Westmoreland (Richmond, Va.). Republican. Episcopalian. Residence: 303 Berkeley St., Boston, Mass.

1–**COOLIDGE, Edith Lawrence (Mrs. Harold J.),** *b* Boston, Mass., Nov. 10, 1879.
9–John **Lawrence** (qv);
8–Nathaniel (1639-1724), ens. mil. co.; selectman; dea.; rep. Gen. Ct., 1692; from Watertown to Charlestown, 1694; *d* at Lexington; *m* 1661, Sarah Morse (John[9], of Dedham, *m* Hannah–);
7–John (1667-1747), from Groton, to Cambridge Farms, 1699; assessor, 1701; town constable, 1705; selectman; *m* 1687, Hannah (Anna) Tarbell (1670-1732; Thomas[8], *m* Hannah–);
6–Amos (1716-85), from Lexington to Groton, 1742; capt. militia; selectman, 1756-71; *m* 1749, Abigail Abbott (1721-84; Nehemiah[7], *m* Sarah Foster);
5–Samuel (1754-1827), maj. Am. Rev.; selectman, assessor, town clk., Groton; dea. over 40 yrs.; *m* 1777, Susanna Parker (*b* 1755; William[6], of Groton, Mass., *m* Sarah Richardson);
4–Amos (1786-1852), Boston mcht.; mem. Mass. House of Rep., 1821; *m* 1st, 1811, Sarah Richards (1790-1819; (Giles[5] [*b* 1754], *m* 1789, Sarah, dau. of Rev. Amos Adams of Roxbury; Abijah[6] [1718-73], *m* Hulda Hopkins; Thomas[7] [*d* 1726], *m* Hannah Upson; Thomas[8] [ca. 1600-ante 1639], an original settler of Hartford, Conn.);
3–Amos Adams (*b* 1814), *m* 1842, Sarah Elizabeth Appleton (1822-91; Hon. William[4] [1786-1862], *m* 1815, Mary Ann, dau. of James Cutler; Rev. Joseph[5], *m* Mary Hook; Isaac[6], *m* Elizabeth Sawyer; Isaac[7]; Col. Samuel[8]; Samuel[9], qv);
2–Amory Appleton (2 below).
9–Henry **Silsbee** (qv);
8–Nathaniel (ca. 1651-ca. 1717), carpenter; *m* 1st, 1671, Deborah Tompkins (*d* ante 1697; John[9], *m* Margaret–);
7–Nathaniel (1677-1769), *m* 2d, Martha–;
6–William (bap. 1715-ca. 1783), carpenter; *m* 1735, Joanna Fowle (Zachary[7], *m* Ruth Ingalles);

5–Capt. Nathaniel (1748-91), master-mariner, owner of several vessels engaged in trade with West Indies; *m* 1770, Sarah Becket (John[6], *m* Rebecca Beadle);
4–Zachariah Fowle (1783-1873), *m* 1810, Sarah Boardman;
3–John Boardman (1813-67), Harvard, '32; mcht.; *m* 1849, Martha Mansfield Shepard (Michael[4], *m* Harriet Fairfax Clark);
2–Emily Fairfax (June 7, 1850-Apr. 4, 1895), *m* as his 1st wife, June 1, 1871, Amory Appleton **Lawrence** (Apr. 22, 1848-July 8, 1912), Harvard, '70; Boston mcht.; issue: I–Amos Amory (*b* 1874); II–John Silsbee (*b* 1878; *m* 1907, Emma Atherton); III–Edith (1 above).
1–*m* Feb. 19, 1903, Harold Jefferson Coolidge (qv for issue).
1–Ed. pvt. schs., Boston. Club: Chilton. Summer place: Pride's Crossing, Mass. Residence: 303 Berkeley St., Boston, Mass.

1–**COOPER, Myers Young**, *b* St. Louisville, O., Nov. 25, 1873.
9–John **Cooper** (1594-1662), from Eng. in the "Hopewell," 1635; freeman, Boston, 1636; town officer; owner of 200 acres; land propr., 1638; settled at Southampton, L.I., 1639; *m* "Wibore" (*b* 1593);
8–John (1625-77), of N.J.; *m* 2d, Sarah– (*d* 1688);
7–James (*d* ca. 1722), of N.J.;
6–James (1700-ca. 1753), of N.J.; *m* 1st, Abigail– (*d* 1734);
5–Moses (1727-78), removed from N.J., started to Washington Co., Pa., but died in Fayette Co.; *m* 1751, Mary Doty (1733-1823);
4–Moses (1754-94), settled in Washington Co., Pa.; pvt. in Am. Rev.;
3–Moses (1794-1867), of Washington Co.: *m* 1811, Christianna Young (1794-1884; John[4] [1760-1829], *m* Loanna Myers, 1776-1863);
2–Lemuel (2 below).
5–Michael **Greenlee** (1700-88), from Eng. to Ireland thence to America, 1714, settled at Sussex (or Kent) Co., Del.; bought land in Kent Co., Del., 1754; *m* 2d, 1760, Esther Davis (1740-96; John[6]);
4–Samuel, of Del.; *m* 1777, Mary Jones (Thomas[5]);
3–Samuel (1787-1876), of Kent Co., Del., and Fayette Co., Pa.; *m* 1812, Nancy Gantz or Gans, (1790-1863; William[4]);
2–Anne (*d* 1908), of Zollarsville, Washington Co., Pa.; *m* 1854, Lemuel **Cooper** (1832-90), of Washington Co., Pa., went to Ohio, 1865; educator; issue: I–Agnes; II–Sanson Milligan (*b* 1858; *m* 1884, Ella I. Harvout); III–James; IV–Angie; V–Ella; VI–Samuel; VII–Dora; VIII–Myers Y. (1 above).
1–*m* Dec. 15, 1897, Martha Kinney (qv for issue).
1–Ed. Lebanon (O.) Normal U.; (LL.D., Lincoln Memorial U., 1923, Wilmington Coll., 1926, St. Xavier Coll., O. Wesleyan U., Bethany Coll., Muskingum Coll., Baldwin-Wallace Coll., 1929). In real estate business, Cincinnati, since 1896; built more than 2,000 homes, largely for people of modest means, and never had mortgage foreclosure (plan nationally copied); pres. Myers Y. Cooper Co., Raymond Realty Co., Hyde Park Lumber Co., Hyde Park Savings Bank, Norwood Nat. Bank. Gov. of Ohio, 1928—(see Who's Who in America). Mem. Christian (Disciples) Ch. Republican. Home: 3590 Mooney Av., Cincinnati, O. Address: Columbus, O.

1–**COOPER, Martha Kinney (Mrs. Myers Young)**, *b* Newport, Ky., Jan. 12, 1874.
8–Joel **Kinney**, from Ireland, 1660, settled at Hartford, Conn.; landed propr.;
7–Joel (1671-1755), of Hartford, Conn.;
6–Joel (1716-1811), of Hartford; *m* thrice;
5–Timothy (1741-1821), of Hartford; *m* 1765, Delight Kinney, of Vt.;
4–Joel (*b* 1768), of Hartford, Conn., and Lavonia, N.Y.; *m* Elizabeth Holmes, of Vt.;
3–Sylvanus (1807-97), of N.Y. and Mich.; *m* 1835, Hannah Crane (1810-49);
2–Joel Fernando (2 below).
9–Thomas **Axtell** (bap. 1619-1646), from Berkhamstead, Hertfordshire, Eng., to Sudbury, Mass., 1642; *m* Mary–;
8–Henry (bap. 1641-1676), came from Eng. with parents; settled at Marlborough, Mass.; one of the proprs.; drew land in first division, 1660; kld. by Indians in King Philip's War; *m* June 14, 1665, Hannah Merriam (George[9], of Concord, Mass.);
7–Daniel (ca. 1673-1735 or 36), of Marlborough; *m* 1702, Thankful Pratt (William[8], of Mass.);
6–William (*b* Apr. 13, 1713), settled at Berkley, Mass.; removed prob. to Taunton, Mass.; *m* Nov. 2, 1739, Hannah Spooner, of Middleboro, Mass.;
5–Joanna (1746-1846), of Berkley, Mass.; *m* 1763, Bernice **Crane** (1743-1828), soldier in Am. Rev.;
4–William (*b* 1781), of Berkley; *m* 1808, Hannah Briggs (1785-1813);
3–Hannah (1810-49), *m* 1835, Sylvanus **Kinney** (3 above);
2–Joel F. (1840-1917), atty. at law; *m* 1865, Sarah Ann Walker (1840-1910); issue: I–Frank Harvey (1868-1924; *m* Eda Koester; *m* 2d, Lenore Pfeifer); II–James William (1870-1907; *m* Terese Garner); III–Emma; IV–Martha (1 above).
1–*m* Dec. 15, 1897, Myers Young Cooper (qv); issue: 1–Raymond, *b* Cincinnati, O., May 8, 1899; *m* Dorothy Van Winkle Britmemy, *b* Nov. 8, 1899; dau. of Elmer E. Britmemy (issue: Dorothy Ann; Myers Young, II); 2–Martha Anne, *b* May 24, 1902; *m* Ferris Mills Judy (issue: Joan, *b* Feb. 3, 1926; Cooper, *b* May 25, 1928).
1–Mem. C.D.A. (sec. nat. soc.), D.A.C., D.A.R., I.A.G., Columbus Geneal. Soc. (trustee). Home: Cincinnati, O. Address: Governor's Mansion, Columbus, O.

1–**COOPER, William Ross**, *b* Buchanan Co., Ia., Feb. 7, 1869.
6–Archibald **Cooper** (1724-90), from Armagh Co., Ireland, 1754; settled Delta, York Co., Pa.; pvt. Pa. militia, 1779; *m* Nancy–;
5–William (1749-90), of Delta, Pa.; pvt. Pa. militia, 1778; *m* 1776, Margaret McVey;
4–Archibald (1783-1814), of Delta; killed in Battle of Ft. McHenry, Baltimore, 1814; *m* 1804 or 1805, Margaret Barrett (ca. 1785-1860);
3–William (1806-83), removed from Delta, to Jefferson Co., O., 1835; to Buchanan Co., Ia., 1850; farmer and stock raiser; *m* 1829, Elizabeth Ross (1810-70; Hugh[4]; Col. William[5]; Hugh[6] [*b* ca. 1695], settled in York Co., Pa., 1723);
2–James Niel (2 below).
6–Dr. Joseph **Jackson** (1690-ca. 1760; son of John, *m* Katherine McKinley), practiced at Carrickfergus, Ireland; thence moved to Limavady (Newtown), Derry Co., Ireland; *m* Elizabeth Vance (their son Andrew, Sr. [ca. 1735-1767], was father of Andrew Jackson, President of U.S.); *m* 2d, ca. 1745, Mary Carr, a widow, sister of Sir James Carr, of Londonderry, Ireland;
5–Margaret (1746-1839), *m* 1769, William **McCaughey** (1745-1827); from Derry Co., Ireland, 1773; settled at Upper Oxford Tp., Chester Co., Pa.; pvt. in Col. Anthony Wayne's regt.; pvt. Pa. militia at Battle of Trenton, 1776; also at Valley Forge;
4–Janet (1770-1847), of Chester Co., Pa.; *m* 1799, her 1st cousin, Joseph **McCaughey** (1775-1840), removed to Jefferson Co., O., later to Starke Co., O.; pvt. in War 1812, in service around Lake Erie;
3–William (1814-71), of Canal Fulton, Starke Co.; *m* 1836, Jane Richeson (1818-91); removed to Buchanan Co., Ia., 1854;
2–Janet (1841-1924), of Buchanan Co., *m* 1866, James Niel **Cooper** (1840-1923) removed from Buchanan Co. to Montgomery Co., Ia., 1900; farmer and stock raiser; issue: I–William R. (1 above); II–Dean Gordon (*b* 1870; D.V.M.; *m* Lucinda Jane Sutter); III–Zada Mary (*b* 1875; prof. U. of Ia.); IV–Jay Clark, M.D. (*b* 1877; *m* Mary P. Moore).
1–*m* June 1, 1898, Myrtle Allen, *b* Harrisonville, Mo., Apr. 1, 1869; dau. of Thomas Allen, of Harrisburg, Pa., Granville, Ill., and Mo., *m* Ruth Whiteaker; issue: 1–Helen Margaret, *b* Kansas City, Mo., July 7, 1900; B.S., K.C.U.; *m* June 26, 1926, James Stuart, son of B. F. Dunn, of Kansas City; 2–Louis Allen, *b* Kansas City, Mar. 13, 1906.
1–D.V.M., Ia. State Coll., '92. Apptd. vet. insp., Bureau of Animal Industry, U.S. Dept. of Agriculture, 1897; prof. breeds and breeding,

K.C. Vet. Coll., 12 yrs. (trustee). Mem. S.A.R., S.V. (Civil War), I.A.G. Mason (K.T., Shriner). Conglist. Republican. Residence: 5631 Locust St., Kansas City, Mo.

1–**COOVER, John Edgar,** *b* Remington, Ind., Mar. 16, 1872.
6–Dieterich (Kober, Cover) **Coover** (*b* ca. 1700), came from Rotterdam in "The Thistle," to Phila., 1730, settled in Cumberland Co., Pa.;
5–Ditrick (1745-1823), blacksmith, Upper Allen Twp., Cumberland Co., Pa.; *m* 1st, 1768, Marie Hauck;
4–Christian (ca. 1774-1837), in forge and distillery business, Cumberland Co., Pa.; *m* Sarah Houch (*d* 1860);
3–Adam (1810-82), farmer, Huntsdale, Cumberland Co., Pa.; *m* 1837, Elizabeth Hemminger (1819-88);
2–John Calvin (2 below).
7–Jacob **Keller** (1706-94), from Switzerland to Ephrata, Lancaster Co., Pa., ca. 1732; *m* —Imhoff;
6–Jacob (1733-1804), *m* —Landis;
5–Jacob (1761-1830), *m* —Hoover; *m* 2d, —Hoover;
4–John (1784-1875), *m* Sarah? Harshberger;
3–Daniel (1813-97), farmer and preacher, Dickinson, Pa.; *m* Katherine Kline (1813-98);
2–Elizabeth Hadessah (1846-1918), *m* John Calvin **Coover** (1842-1922), carpenter and farmer; issue: I–John Edgar (1 above); II–Alvah Burton (*b* 1875; *m* Hattie Bell Hartman; *m* 2d, Elizabeth Quakenbush); III–Charles William (*b* 1877; *m* Mary Elizabeth Ish; *m* 2d, Edith Davies McLeod); IV–Mabel Catherine (*b* 1879; *m* George E. Perley, *d*); V–Mary Hadessah (*b* 1883; *m* Jack C. Black).
1–*m* June 3, 1905, Margaret Evelyn Brooks, *b* nr. Knoxville, Tenn., Feb. 20, 1876; dau. of Fulton Clay Brooks (*b* 1844; Moses[3] [*b* ca. 1806], *m* Margaret King), of LaCrosse, Kan., later Larned, Kan., *m* Caroline Virginia Grammar (*b* 1854); issue: 1–Calvin Clay, *b* Palo Alto, Calif., Jan. 15, 1912.
1–Ped.B., Colo. State Normal Sch., '98 (P.B.K., Sigma Xi); A.B., Stanford, '04, A.M., 1905, Ph.D., 1912. Engaged in various lines of business, and as principal of schs. in Colo. and Calif. until 1910; asst. in dept. psychology, Stanford, 1910, asso. prof. since 1912. Author (see Who's Who in America). Capt. Sanitary Corps, U.S.A., 1918-19, at Med. Research Lab., Hazelhurst Field, Mineola, L.I. Mason. Unitarian. Club: Faculty. Residence: 535 Salvatierra St., Stanford University, Calif.

1–**CORBIN, Channing Moore,** *b* "Moss Neck," Va., July 28, 1857.
23–Robert (Corbyn) **Corbion**;
22–Robert, gave lands to the Abbey of Talesworth bet. 1154-61;
21–William;
20–Hamon;
19–William;
18–Thomas, living temp. Edward I; *m* Felicia, dau. of John Lulley;
17–William, of Birmingham; *m* Edith Frebody;
16–William, of Kingswinford, Co. Stafford; *m* Felicia, kinswoman of Sir John Sutton of Dudley, Knight;
15–Henry, *m* Margery, dau. of John Day;
14–William, *m* Margery Blunt, dau. of —Blunt, Knight;
13–Thomas, *m* Joan–;
12–Nicholas, of "Corbyn Hall," in Kingswinford, seized of "le Hall End," Co. Warwick (Jure uxorio); *m* Johanna, dau. and co-heiress of William Sturmy, *m* Eleanor–;
11–Richard, *m* Anne, dau. of Thomas Ramsey, of Hitcham, Co. Bucks;
10–Thomas, of "le Hall End" (*d* ca. 1584), in 1574, he used a seal displaying his shield "in chief three ravens," the earliest instance; *m* Anne (*d* 1606), dau. of William Reppington, of Anniston;
9–George, of "le Hall End" (1543-1636), buried in the chancel of Kingswinford; *m* Mary (*d* 1614), dau. of William Faunt, of Foston, Co. Leicester;
8–Thomas, of "le Hall End" (1594-1638), buried at Kingswinford; *m* 1620, Winifred Grosvenor (*b* 1605; Gawin[9] [1566-1626; desc. of Adam le Gravenor temp. Edward I], of Sutton, Co. Warwick, *m* Dorothy Pudsey, of Langley, Co. Warwick, who descended from Simon Pudsey, of Bolton-by-Bolland in right of his wife temp. Edward II, *m* Catherine, dau. of John de Bolton);
7–Henry **Corbin** (1629-Jan. 8, 1676), of London; draper; came to Md. in the "Charity," 1654; settled in Lancaster Co., Va.; established "Buckingham Lodge," on South side of Rappahannock River, also owned "Pickatone" in Westmoreland and "Corbin Hall," in Middlesex; justice of Lancaster Co., 1657; vestryman, Christ Ch., Middlesex; burgess Lancaster Co., 1658-60; mem. Council, 1663; justice Middlesex, 1673; *m* ca. 1655, Alice (*d* ca. 1684), widow of Rowland Burnham, and dau. of Richard Eltonhead, of "Eltonhead," Lancaster Co., Va. (desc. of Hugh le Norrys, called Hugh le Haigh, occurs in the Pipe Rolls 6, Richard I, when he paid fines for taking part in Rebellion; he had a grant from William, son of Iro of 4 oxgangs of land at Eltonhead in Sutton, Hugh enfeoffed William le Norrys his youngest son who took the name Eltonhead);
6–Gawin (*d* Jan. 1, 1744), of "Buckingham Lodge" and "Laneville," Va.; justice Middlesex, 1698; burgess, 1698-9-1701-2-3-5-1718-1722; collector and naval officer of the Rappahannock river dist.; *m* 2d, Jane (Lane) Wilson (*d* post 1715; Capt. John Lane[7], burgess, 1692-93, unseated on petition), widow of Willis Wilson;
5–Richard (1708-post 1783), of "Buckingham Lodge," "Laneville," "Moss Neck" and "Richland"; burgess Middlesex, 1748-49; mem. council, 1750, and through the colonial period; co. lt. of Essex 1752; receiver gen., 1754-76; a Loyalist, when Washington wrote him in 1754 before the campaign of Great Meadows for a commn. of lt. col. he sent this reply: "Dear George, I enclose you your commission. God prosper you with it. Your Friend—Richard Corbin"; *m* 1737, Elizabeth Tayloe (John[6] [1687-1744], of "Mt. Airy," burgess 1727-28,30, mem. Council 1732, *m* Elizabeth, widow of Stephen Lyde, and dau. of David Gwyn, of Richmond Co., Va., burgess, 1702-03, *m* Katherine, widow of William Fauntleroy, and dau. of Col. Samuel Griffin, justice of Northumberland Co., Va., 1692, *m* Sarah, widow of Thomas Griffin; William[7] [*d* 1710], of "Mt. Airy," Richmond Co., Va., sheriff Rappahannock Co., 1687, burgess Richmond Co., 1700,01,1702-06; justice, col. and cdr.-in-chief, militia, Richmond Co., 1704, subdued an attempted uprising of the Indians, *m* Anne [1664-94], dau. of Henry Corbin, 7 above);
4–John Tayloe (ca. 1746-post 1783), of "Laneville," burgess King and Queen Co., 1769-74, a Loyalist arrested 1776 and confined to that part of Caroline Co. bet. the Pamunkey and Mattoponi rivers under bond of £10,000, not to depart from thence until permitted by the Convention or the Com. of Safety; *m* Mary Waller (*b* 1752; Benjamin[5] [1716-86], settled in Williamsburg, Va., clk. of council, burgess James City Co., 1742-60, judge Gen. Ct., 1779-83, mem. Conv. 1775-76, *m* 1746, Martha [1728-80], dau. of Robert Hall, burgess; Col. John[6], qv);
3–Maj. Richard (1766-1814), of "Laneville," "Corbin Hall," "Moss Neck," "Farley Vale," and "Nestling Green Branch"; mem. House Dels. from Middlesex Co., 1796, from King and Queen Co., 1798-99, 1800; raised and equipped an arty. co. and served in War 1812, being promoted to maj.; *m* Rebecca Parke Farley;
2–James Parke (2 below).
6–John **Farley,** of Antigua, Leeward Islands; *m* 2d, 1717, Rebecca Christian;
5–Col. Francis (*d* 1779), with his bro., Simon, purchased 2600 acres in N.C. called Lura Town or the Land of Eden from Col. William Byrd (5 below); *m* Eleanor (Parke) Wallace, widow (James Parke[6], *m* Eleanor Watkins; nephew of Daniel Parke, II, gov. and capt. gen. of the Leeward Islands, distinguished himself at Blenheim as aid to Marlborough, elected to Parliament but was unseated for bribery, killed at Antigua; g.son of Daniel Parke, I [ca. 1628-1679], in Va., 1652, justice York Co., 1653, sheriff, 1659, burgess, 1666, mem. Council, 1670, sec. of State and Treas., 1678-79, *m* ca. 1658, Rebecca [*d* 1672], widow of Bartholomew Knipe, and dau. of

George Evelyn, prominent in Md., in James City Co., Va., 1649, son of Robert Evelyn, of Long Ditton and Godstone, Surry, Eng.);
4–James Parke (*d* ca. 1777), ed. William and Mary Coll.; served in Am. Rev.; *m* Elizabeth Hill Byrd;
3–Rebecca Parke (*d* 1822), *m* Maj. Richard **Corbin** (3 above).
7–William **Byrd** (1652-1704), from Eng., 1674; established "Westover," in Va.; burgess; mem. Council; auditor and receiver gen. of Va.; *m* Mary (1652-99), widow of Samuel Filmer and dau. of Col. Warham Horsmanden (*d* ca. 1683 in Eng.), of Charles City Co., Va.; burgess, 1657-59; mem. Council, 1657 (desc. of Daniel Horsmanden the loyalist, rector of Ulcombe, Kent and through her mother Ursula, dau. of Warham St. Leger, Mary Byrd desc. from one of the most eminent knightly families of Eng.);
6–Col. William (1674-1744), of "Westover"; author; receiver gen. and pres. of the Council; founder of Richmond, Va.; *m* 2d, Maria (1698-1771), dau. and co-heiress of Thomas Taylor, of Kinsington, Eng.;
5–William (1728-77), of Westover; mem. Council, 1754; importer of thoroughbreds; *m* 1748, Elizabeth Hill Carter;
4–Elizabeth Hill (1754-1819), *m* 1st, 1771, James Parke **Farley** (4 above).
8–John **Carter** (1620-69), from Eng. to Va., 1649; burgess; member Council; col. comdg. expdn. against Rappahannock Indians, 1654; *m* 1st, June Glyn; *m* 2d, Eleanor Brocus; *m* 3d, Anne Carter (Cleve); *m* 4th Sarah, dau. of Gabriel Ludlow;
7–Robert (1663-1732), of "Corotoman"; speaker House of Burgesses; treas. and pres. of the Council, and actg. gov.; *m* 1st, 1688, Judith Armistead (Col. John[8] [1635-98], of "Hesse," Gloucester Co., Va., justice, before 1675, high sheriff, 1675, burgess, 1685, lt. col. of Horse, 1680, col. and co. lt., 1685, apptd. to Council, 1687; refused to take the oaths after the accession of William and Mary, becoming a Jacobite, *m* Judith, dau. of Theophilus Hone (*d* post 1679; William[9] [bap. 1610-ante 1660], came to Va., 1635, *m* Anne–; Anthony[10], of Deighton Park in the West riding of Yorkshire, Eng., *m* 1608, Frances Thompson);
6–John (1690-1743), seized of "Shirley" (Jure uxorio); barrister of the Middle Temple; sec. of state 1722; mem. Council, 1724; *m* 1723, Elizabeth Hill;
5–Elizabeth Hill, *m* William **Byrd** (5 above).
10–Capt. Edward **Hill** (*d* 1624), of Elizabeth City Co., Va.;
9–Col. Edward (*d* 1663), of "Shirley"; speaker House of Burgesses, 1644-45,54, 1658-59; mem. council, 1651; burgess, 1639,42,44,45,47,49; chosen gov. of Md., 1646, by the insurrectory party; was taken prisoner by Gov. Calvert; cdr.-in-chief of Henrico and Charles City cos., Va., and in 1657, when in command of a force of colonists and friendly Indians he was defeated by the hostile Indians which gave the name of Bloody Run to a stream, now within the limits of the city of Richmond; disfranchised and fined for this defeat by the Assembly;
8–Col. Edward (1637-1700) of "Shirley"; atty. gen., 1679; speaker House of Burgesses, 1684; mem. council, 1688; treas., 1693-99; cdr.-in-chief of Charles City and Surry cos.; judge of the Admiralty Ct. for Va. and N.C. disfranchised by Bacon's House of Burgesses, 1676; *m* —Williams(?);
7–Gen. Edward (*d* 1748), of "Shirley"; collector James river, 1716; burgess, 1704-05; *m* 1696, Tabitha Scarburgh;
6–Elizabeth (*d* 1777), *m* John **Carter** (6 above).
9–Edmund (Scarborough) **Scarburgh** (qv);
8–Col. Edmund (ca. 1611-1671), of "Seaside," Accomac Co., Va.; vestryman North Hampton Parish, 1652; speaker House of Burgesses, 1645; surveyor gen., 1665-71; *m* Mary Charlton (Stephen[9], mem. council, 1644-45,52);
7–Tabitha, as widow of Maj. Gen. John Custis, *m* 2d, Gen. Edward **Hill** (7 above).
5–Maj. George **Hoomes**, granted land by the British Crown in Caroline Co., Va., 1670; built "The Mansion" which was first called Bowling Green, 1675;
4–Col. John Waller (*d* 1805), a great sportsman and importer of thoroughbreds; ed. at Donald Robertson's Sch.; treas. Caroline Co., Va., 1777; gave material aid to the cause of America in the Am. Rev.; entertained with a great banquet on the lawn of his estate, "The Mansion" General Washington and his army when returning from Yorktown in honor of Marquis de LaFayette; mem. House Dels., 1791-95; mem. Va. State Senate, 1796-1803; *m* Hannah Battaile;
3–Richard Hay (*d* 1884), 2d lt. in War 1812; *m* Eliza Lewis Taliaferro.
2–James Parke **Corbin** (1810-68), of "Laneville," "Corbin Hall," and "Nestling Green Branch"; *m* 1st, 1833, Jane Catherine Wellford (1808-55; Dr. John S.[8], of Fredericksburg, Va.); *m* 2d, 1856, Eliza Lewis Hoomes (1840-93); issue (1st marriage): I–Richard (1833–killed in battle, of "Moss Neck" 1863; mem. Co. B, 9th Va. Cav., C.S.A.; courier of "Stonewall" Jackson; *m* 1856, Roberta Carey); II–Spotswood Wellford (1835-97; lt., C.S.N.; *m* 1858, Diana Fontaine, dau. of Commodore Matthew Fontaine Maury); III–Frances Nelson (1838-1911; *m* 1857, William H. Dickenson); IV–Catharine (1839-1918; *m* 1st, 1862, Col. Alexander S. Pendleton, killed in battle, C.S.A., *m* 2d, 1871, Commodore John Mercer Brooke, U.S. and C.S.N., prof. V.M.I.); V–James Parke (1848-1908; ed. V.M.I.; served in C.S.A., participated in battle of New Market; *m* 1876, Edmonia Fitzhugh Ficklen); issue (2d marriage): I–Channing Moore (1 above); II–Elizabeth Farley (*b* 1859; *m* 1878, Joseph Swift Browne, *b* 1858); III–Tazewell Tayloe (*b* 1861); IV–Champe Carter (*b* 1863; m Sallie Gatchell); V–Sophia Hoomes (*b* 1867; *m* Eugene Bowie).
1–Not married. Ed. Ky. Agrl. and Mech. Coll. (Now Ky. U.). A Virginia gentleman with the traits and inclinations of his ancestors. Residence: Lexington, Ky.

1–**CORBIN, Walter Everett,** *b* Brimfield, Mass., Oct. 28, 1885.
8–Clement **Corbin** (qv);
7–James (1665-1736), of Woodstock, Conn.; held many public offices; *m* 1697, Hannah Eastman (1679-1752; Philip[8], *m* 1678, Mary Barnard *b* 1645);
6–Philip (*b* 1708), of Dudley, Mass.; *m* 1731, Dorothy Barstow;
5–Lemuel (1740-1825), of Dudley; capt. Am. Rev.; *m* 1763, Rebecca Davis (1736-1820; Samuel[6], *m* 1731, Mary Weld, 1695-1786);
4–Philip (1764-1845), of Dudley, Mass., and Union, Conn.; was selectman several yrs.; state rep., 1814-15; *m* 1789, Rhoby Healy (1768-1840; Capt. Samuel[5] [1738-1817] Am. Rev., *m* 1759, Phebe Curtis, 1737-97);
3–Healy (1799-1878), of Union, Conn.; state representative, 1851-52; *m* 1825, Nancy Coy (1803-78; David[4] [1773-1831], *m* 1797, Lucy Kinney [1774-1851]; Archibald[5] [1741-94], Am. Rev.; *m* 1760, Elizabeth Badger, 1740-1806);
2–Miner Healy (2 below).
10–Widow Christian **Brown** (qv);
9–Dea. Henry (1615-1701), of Salisbury, Mass.; *m* 1641, Abigail– (*d* 1702);
8–Henry (1659-1708), of Salisbury; *m* 1682, Hannah Putnam (1663-1731; John[9], *m* 1652, Rebecca Prince; John[10], qv);
7–John (1685-1738), of Salem, Mass.; *m* 1708, Mary Elsy (*d* 1731);
6–Jonathan (1716-99), of Brimfield, Mass.; sgt. in Indian wars; lt. in Am. Rev.; *m* 1741, Abigail Russell (1716-1803; John[7], *m* Rebecca [*b* 1689], dau. Thomas Blodgett [1661-1740], *m* 1685, Rebecca Tidd, *d* 1750);
5–Jonathan (1744-1803), of Brimfield; soldier in Am. Rev.; *m* 1779, Abigail (Dunbar) Sargent (*d* 1809);
4–Jonathan (1782-1865), of Brimfield; *m* 1810, Lucretia Bugbee (1787-1849; David[5], *m* 1772, Hannah [1748-1845], dau. William Thompson);
3–James Henry (1811-90), of Brimfield; *m* 1846, Anne Howard Holbrook (1812-97; Zenas[4] [1768-1857], *m* 1807, Sarah Billings Howard, 1772-1843).
2–Miner Healy **Corbin** (1840-1919), *m* 1st, 1868, Jane Betsey Dimmick (1849-80); *m* 2d, 1881, Sarah Billings Brown (1851-1926), of Brimfield; issue (1st marriage): I–Minnie Jane (1871-1924; *m* 1899, William Arthur Royce [*b* 1878]; *m* 2d, 1913, Burton Carlton Reynolds); II–Herbert Miner (1873-1928; *m* 1901, Chella

Blanche Davis); III–Arthur (*b* and *d* 1875); issue (2d marriage): I–Walter Everett (1 above); II–Erford Healy (*b* 1889; *m* 1913, Harriet Frances Eaton, *b* 1883).
1–*m* Sept. 14, 1910, Lottie Adelaide Squier (qv).
1–Ed. Hitchcock Free Acad., Brimfield, Mass., Pratt Inst., 1909. Commercial artist and photographer. With J. & R. Lamb, N.Y., 1909-10, Springfield Photo-Engraving Co., 1911-21. Conglist. Republican. Residence: 16 N. Maple St., Florence, Northampton, Mass.

1–**CORBIN, Lottie Adelaide Squier (Mrs. Walter Everett),** *b* Monson, Mass., Mar. 21, 1884.
9–Robert **Fuller** (*d* 1706), from Eng., 1638; settled at Salem, Mass.; *m* Sarah Bowen (*d* 1676);
8–Jonathan (1640-1709), of Rehoboth; *m* 1664, Elizabeth Wilmot (*b* 1647);
7–Daniel (*b* 1669), of Rehoboth, Mass., and Ashford, Conn.; *m* Mary–;
6–Elizabeth, *m* 1715, Philip **Squier** (Philip[7] [*b* 1655], of Boston and Newbury, Mass., *m* Mary Smith?);
5–John (1727-1805), of Ashford, Conn.; removed to Monson, Mass.; *m* 1751, Millicent Scott (*b* 1731);
4–Solomon (1766-1834), of Monson; *m* 1784, Sarah Moulton (1768-1851; Freeborn[5], *m* Jerusha Munger);
3–Rensselaer (1807-63), *m* 1832, Olive Skinner;
2–Edgar (2 below).
8–Sgt. Thomas **Skinner** (1617-1704), from Eng., ca. 1650; settled at Malden, Mass.; *m* Mary– (*d* 1671);
7–Abraham (bap. 1649-1694), of Eng., and Malden, Mass.; *m* Hannah (Lewis?);
6–Abraham (1681-1776), of Malden, Mass., and Woodstock, Conn.; *m* Tabitha Hills (1690-1771);
5–Benjamin (1727-74), of Woodstock, Conn.; *m* 1751, Elizabeth Lyon (*b* 1731);
4–Thomas (1767-1842), of Monson, Mass.; *m* 1790, Jemima Moulton (1770-1838);
3–Olive (1810-73), *m* Rensselaer **Squier** (3 above).
9–Dea. Simon **Peck** (*d* 1688), of Hingham, Mass.; *m* 1660, Prudence Clap (1637-87; Edward[10], *m* Prudence Clap);
8–John (1667-1725), removed to Mendon, Mass.; *m* Millicent–;
7–Simon (*b* 1694), of Mendon; *m* Sarah–;
6–John (1726-1805), removed to Ashford, Conn.; *m* 1755, Elizabeth Dennison (*d* 1767);
5–Joseph (1758-1855), removed to Monson, Mass.; Am. Rev.; *m* 1782, Eunice Jennings;
4–Ira (1788-1871), of Monson; *m* Mary Eastman Bullard (1787-1857; Luther[5], *m* Anna Eastman);
3–Ira (1817-82), removed to Wales, Mass.; *m* 1853, Charlotte Orcutt (1826-1913; Warren[4], *m* Selenda Johnson);
2–Mary Celenda (2 below).
8–Jonathan **Jennings** (1653?-1733), of Windham, Conn.; *m* Susanna– (*d* 1700);
7–Joseph (*b* 1685), of Windham, Conn.; *m* 1707, Sarah Geers;
6–Robert (*b* 1719), of Windham; *m* 1749, Sarah Badger (*b* 1730);
5–Eunice (1755-1832), *m* Joseph **Peck** (5 above).
2–Mary Celenda Peck (*b* 1859), *m* 1880, Edgar **Squier** (*b* 1853); issue: I–Homer Wilton (*b* 1881; *m* Doris Laura Sutcliffe); II–Lottie Adelaide (1 above).
1–*m* Sept. 14, 1910, Walter Everett Corbin (qv).
1–Grad. Monson Acad., '01. Taught in public schs., 1902-10. Mem. D.A.R., I.A.G., N.E.H.G.S. Universalist. Republican. Club: Woman's. Residence: 16 N. Maple St., Florence, Northampton, Mass.

1–**COREY, Robert Francis,** *b* Westboro, Mass., June 7, 1873.
9–James **Walker** (qv);
8–James (1645-1718), of Taunton, Mass.; *m* 1673, Bathsheba Brooks (1655-1738);
7–Lt. James (1674-1749), of Taunton; *m* 1699, Sarah Richmond (1670-1727);
6–Col. Elnathan (1706-75), of Taunton; *m* Hannah Crossman (1705-28);
5–Elnathan (1727 or 28-1815), of Dighton; *m* 1756, Hannah Bugbee (*d* 1810);
4–Matilda (1760-1835), of Woodstock, Conn.; *m* 1779, Dr. Jacob **Corey** (1756-1839), town clk. (John[5], of Sturbridge; John[6], one of the first settlers of Sturbridge);
3–George Vernon (1800-87), of Sturbridge; *m* 1837, Martha M. Griggs (1812-93);
2–Francis Edwin (2 below).
10–Thomas **Wight** (*d* 1674), from Isle of Wight, 1635, settled at Watertown, 1637, later at Dedham; was one of members from Dedham who voted to tax himself for first free school in Mass.; *m* 1st, 1635, Alice or Elsie– (*d* 1665);
9–Samuel (1639-1716), of Dedham; his home was burned by King Philip's Indians in 1676; *m* 1663, Hannah Albee (*d* 1723);
8–Jonathan (1682-1779), of Medfield; *m* 1704, Margaret Fairbanks (1685-1787);
7–Jonathan (1705-82), of Medfield; *m* 1732, Sarah Plimpton (1711-98);
6–David (1733-1822), of Medfield; *m* 1760, Catharine Morse (1737-1827);
5–David (1761-1813), of Sturbridge; town clk.; justice of the peace; *m* 1782, Susannah Harding (*d* 1829);
4–David (1786-1861), of Sturbridge; town clk., 13 yrs.; *m* 1810, Lucinda Marsh (1785-1860);
3–David (1811-76), civil engr.; capt. militia in Civil War; *m* 1836, Eunice F. Drake;
2–Mary Augusta (2 below).
9–Dr. Samuel **Fuller,** Mayflower Pilgrim (qv);
8–Rev. Samuel (1624-95), *m* 1654, Elizabeth Brewster (*d* 1713);
7–Dr. Isaac (1675-1727), *m* 1709, Mary Platt or Pratt;
6–Isaac (*b* 1712), of Bridgewater; *m* 1737, Sarah Packard (*b* 1719);
5–Lt. Isaac (1738-1803), officer Am. Rev.; *m* 1764, Mary Alden;
4–Eunice (1778-1858), of Bridgewater; *m* 1805, Simeon **Drake** (1780-1863);
3–Eunice F. (1811-75), *m* David **Wight** (3 above).
9–John **Alden,** Mayflower Pilgrim (qv);
8–Joseph (1624-97), farmer, Bridgewater; *m* 1659, Mary Simmons (Moses, Jr.[9]);
7–Dea. Joseph (1667-1747), Bridgewater; *m* 1690, Hannah Dunham (1669-1747/48; Daniel[8], of Plymouth);
6–Daniel (1691/92-1767), Bridgewater; *m* 1717, Abigail Shaw (1694-1755; Joseph[7]);
5–Mary (1743-1818), Bridgewater; *m* Isaac **Fuller** (5 above).
2–Mary Augusta Wight (*b* 1847), *m* 1870, Francis Edwin **Corey** (*b* 1846), physician State Sch. for Boys, Westboro, Mass.; health officer, Alhambra, Calif., 17 yrs.; issue: I–Robert Francis (1 above); II–Ethelind (1875-1916; *m* Charles Miller).
1–*m* June 7, 1913, Christine Kemp, *b* Ontario, Can., July 17, 1880; dau. of Melissa Ann Wrightman, of Silver Hill, Norfolk Co., Ont., Can.; issue: 1–Charlotte, *b* Alhambra, Calif., May 26, 1914; 2–Ethelind, *b* Alhambra, Oct. 5, 1917.
1–Jeweler in Mass., 1895-99; left for Calif., 1899; settled at Alhambra, 1903-10; orchardist, 1910-14; asst. mgr., winery at Wineville, 1914-19; surveyor for Los Angeles Co., 1919-29, now engaged in surveying private work. Mem. S.A.R., I.A.G. Trustee and sec. Presbyterian Ch. Republican. Clubs: Palos Verdes Golf, Cleveland Country, Aloha Beach. Summer place: Three Arch Beach, Laguna, Calif. Residence: 127 S. 2d St., Alhambra, Calif.

1–**COURSER, Fred William,** *b* Webster, N.H., Sept. 19, 1872.
7–John (Corser) **Courser** (ca. 1678-1776), from Scotland, first of the name at Boscawen, N.H.; signed Assn. List in Boscawen, N.H.; *m* 1716 or 17, Tabitha Kenney;
6–John (ca. 1718-ca. 1791), signed Assn. List, Boscawen, N.H.; *m* 1742, Jane Nichols;
5–Thomas (1743-1829), Am. Rev.; *m* Ann Dunlap;
4–Moses (1781-1830), War 1812; *m* 1804, Ruth Clough;
3–William Barnard (1814-90), *m* 1836, Nancy A. Morey;
2–Thomas Jefferson (2 below).
9–John **Clough** (ca. 1613-1691), from Eng. probably in the "Elizabeth," 1635; received land grant in the "first division," and again in 1640; took oath of fidelity, 1650; *m* 1st, Jane– (*d* 1679/80);
8–John (1649-1718), *m* 1674, Mercy Page (1655-1719; John[9]);
7–Joseph (1684-1732), *m* 1708, Mary Jenness (1688-1732);

6–Reuben (*b* 1724), Am. Rev.; *m* 1744, Love Sanborn (1726-67; Jonathan[7], *m* Theodate Sanborn [Dea. Benjamin[8]; Lt. John[9], qv]; Capt. Jonathan[8]; Lt. John[9], qv);
5–Reuben (1756-1817), Am. Rev.; *m* Hannah Sargent (1753-1831; David[6], signed Assn. List; Charles[7]; Philip[8]; William[9]; William[10]);
4–Ruth (ca. 1784-ca. 1816), *m* Moses **Courser** (4 above).
9–Capt. Robert (Seely) **Cilley** (qv);
8–Richard (ca. 1620-25-1686), *m* Martha– (*d* post 1692);
7–Benoni (ca. 1680-1746), *m* 1703, Eleanor Getchell (1684-1735 or 36; Samuel[8]; Samuel[9]);
6–Dorcas (1728-1806), *m* 1746, William **Morey** (ca. 1724-1804);
5–Col. William (1758-1838), Am. Rev.; *m* ca. 1780, Susanna Rowe (1762 or 63-1815; Nathan[6], *m* Lydia, dau. of Thomas Page; Robert[7], *m* Mehitable, dau. of William Swayne, *m* Mary, dau. of Thomas Webster);
4–Joseph (1786 or 87-1858), *m* 1813, Polly Woodbury (1782-1842; John[5], Am. Rev., *m* Elizabeth Sanborn [Joseph[6], signed Assn. Test in Wakefield, N.H.; Lt. Joseph[7]; Joseph[8]; Lt. John[9], qv]);
3–Nancy (1815-39), *m* William Barnard **Courser** (3 above).
6–Col. Andrew **Todd** (1697-1777; son of James, *m* Rachel Nelson, natives of Scotland, who removed to Ireland); came from Ireland to Londonderry, 1720; moderator; selectman, 14 yrs.; rep. of the town in the Provincial legislature; officer in French War, 1744; col. in war 1755; *m* Beatrix (*b* Ireland), dau. of John Moore, of Scotland;
5–Samuel (1726-65), *m* 1762, Ann Cochran (*b* 1733; Andrew[6], *m* 1723, Mary Rowan);
4–James (1764-1841), *m* 1785, Unity Page (1765 or 68-1808; William[5], Am. Rev., *m* Martha Page [Cornelius[6]; John[7]]);
3–Eli Page (1804-81), *m* 1833, Abigail Harriman Nelson;
2–Sarah Elizabeth (2 below).
9–Thomas **Nelson** (1619-48), from Eng. to Mass., settled at Rowley, 1639; mem. com. to settle the bounds bet. Hampton and Salisbury, then Colchester; freeman, 1639; dep. Gen. Ct., 1640; *m* 1st in Eng., name unknown;
8–Capt. Philip (ca. 1633 or 36-1691), grad. Harvard, 1654; justice of the peace; capt. of a co. which was attached to the command of Sir William Phipps on an expdn. against the French in Nova Scotia; *m* 2d, 1666, Elizabeth Lowell (1646-1731; John[9]; Percival[10], qv);
7–Joseph (1682-1743/44), *m* 1705/06, Hannah Brocklebank (*d* 1732; Capt. Samuel[8] [1627-76], killed by Indians in King Philip's War, capt. of Rowley Foot Co., 1673, ens., lt., capt. and dea., *m* Hannah–):
6–Jonathan (1723-1801), served in Am. Rev.; *m* 1752, Hannah Cheney;
5–Asa (1754-1837), served in Am. Rev.; *m* 1776, Abigail Harriman (1747-1814; Joshua[6]; Matthew[7]; Mathew[8] Leonard[9], from Eng., settled at Rowley, Mass., *m* Margaret–);
4–Asa (1787-1853), *m* 1811, Elizabeth Wadleigh (1790-1841; Thomas[5], Am. Rev., *m* Merriam, dau. John Atwood, Am. Rev.; Thomas[6], Am. Rev.; Capt. Jonathan[7], *m* Abigail Eastman [Peter[8]; Jonathan[9]; Thomas[10]; Roger[11]]; Robert[8]; John[9], qv);
3–Abigail Harriman (1814-76), *m* Eli Page **Todd** (3 above).
10–John **Cheney** (qv);
9–Daniel (1633-94), *m* 1665, Sarah Bayley (1644-1714; John[10], *m* Eleanor, dau. of John Emery; John[11], qv);
8–Daniel (1670-1755), *m* Hannah Dustin (*b* 1678; Thomas[9], *m* Hannah, dau. of Michael Emerson, qv);
7–Thomas (1703-will dated and proved 1767), *m* 1726, Hannah Stevens (*b* 1705; John[8], *m* Esther, dau. of Richard Barker; William[9], qv);
6–Hannah (1727-1802), *m* Jonathan **Nelson** (6 above).
2–Thomas Jefferson **Courser** (1837-1908), *m* 1866, Sarah Elizabeth Todd (1841-76); *m* 2d, 1876, Addie E. Marden (1848-1913); issue (1st marriage): I–Emma Jeannette (*b* 1867; *m* 1911, Harry H. Colby, *d* 1916); II–George Woodbury (1871-86); III–Fred William (1 above); IV–Sarah Abby (*b* 1876; *m* 1903, William D. Murray); **2d marriage**: I–Charles Henry (*b* 1878; *m* Maud May Robbins; *m* 2d, Lenora Davis).
1–*m* Apr. 30, 1901, Lora Edith Brown (qv for issue).
1–Engaged in farming, lumbering and cattle raising in N.H. Owns between 9,000 and 10,000 acres of land in N.H. and Me. V.p. Bath (Me.) Box Co. Residence: Warner, N.H.

1–**COURSER, Lora Edith Brown (Mrs. Fred W.),** *b* Bristol, N.H., May 29, 1868.
11–Richard **Bartlett** (qv);
10–Joanna, *m* as his 1st wife, ante 1640, William **Titcomb,** dep. Mass. Gen. Ct.;
9–Hannah (*b* 1642), *m* ca. 1660, Capt. Edward **Gove** (1639-91), from Eng., with his father John to Cambridge, Mass., 1640; removed to Hampton, N.H., 1655;
8–Mary (*b* 1666), *m* 1682, Joseph **Sanborn** (1659-bet. 1722-24; Lt. John[9], qv);
7–Abraham (1696-1757), *m* 1718, Dorothy Smith (1699-1788; John[8], *m* Rebecca, dau. of Capt. William Marston, *m* Rebecca, dau. of Robert Page; Robert[9], from Eng., *m* Susanna–);
6–Daniel (1728-1812), *m* 1748, Anna Tilton (1728/29-1759; Sherburne[7], *m* Anne Hilyard, 6 below);
5–Anna (1750-1840), *m* 1769, Jonathan **Brown** (1746-1825), called capt.; signed the Assn. Test in Candia;
4–Lt. Daniel (1771-1860), of Candia and Bridgewater, N.H.; selectman, 1805,11; lt. state militia; soldier War 1812; *m* 1790, Elizabeth French (1774-1831; Joshua[5] [1752-83], served in Am. Rev., *m* 1771, Elizabeth [1754-84], dau. of Jonathan Collins [*b* 1728], Am. Rev., *m* 1751, Elizabeth Prescott [*b* 1733; Jeremiah[7]; Jonathan[8]; James[9]]; Joshua[6], *m* Sarah–);
3–Richard French (1807-96), of Bridgewater, N.H.; called Capt. Dick Brown; *m* 1831, Mary Cynthia Mitchell;
2–Curtis (2 below).
9–Anthony **Morse** (qv);
8–Dea. Benjamin (1640/41-living 1707), of Newbury, Mass.; freeman, 1673; subscribed to oath of fidelity and allegiance, 1668,78; dea. 1st ch. at Newbury; *m* 1667, Ruth Sawyer (1648-living 1707; William[9] [1613-1702], from Eng., *m* Ruth Binford);
7–Dea. William (1673/74-1749), *m* 1696, Sarah Merrill (1677-living 1717; Daniel[8], *m* Sarah, dau. of John Clough, from Eng.; Nathaniel[9], qv);
6–Benjamin (1703-85), *m* 1726, Margaret Bartlett (*b* 1707; Daniel[7] [1682-1756]; Richard[8] [1649-1724]; Richard[9] [1621-98]; Richard[10], qv);
5–Capt. Daniel (1745-1826), served in French and Indian Wars and Am. Rev.; moderator, selectman, coroner and on sch. com., Bridgewater, N.H.; *m* 1766, Miriam Hoyt (1746-1812; Capt. John[6], Am. Rev.; Daniel[7]; John[8]; John[9]; John[10], qv);
4–Margaret (1775-1851), *m* 1797, Charles **Mitchell** (1770-1846; John[5] [1744-1816], Am. Rev., mem. Com. Safety, *m* Lydia Johnson, 1744-1807);
3–Mary Cynthia (1809-81), *m* Richard F. **Brown** (3 above).
9–William **Tilton** (qv);
8–Ens. Daniel (1645/46-1716), ens. King William's War; rep. Hampton in Colonial Assembly; speaker House of Rep.; *m* 1669, Mehitable Sanborn (William[9], qv);
7–Capt. Joseph (1677-1744), of Hampton, N.H.; *m* 1698, Margaret Sherburne (1679-1717; Capt. Samuel[8], *m* Love, dau. of John Hutchins; Henry[9], from Eng., settled at Portsmouth, N.H., *m* Rebecca, dau. of Ambrose Gibbons, dep.gov. N.H., 1630);
6–Sherburne (1699-1784), of Hampton, N.H.; signed Assn. Test, Kensington, N.H.; *m* 1726, Anne Hilyard (1708-65; Benjamin[7], *m* Elizabeth Chase [Joseph[8], *m* Rachel, dau. of William Partridge; Thomas[9]]; Timothy[8], *m* Apphia Philbrick [James[9]; Thomas[10], *m* Ann, dau. of Gov. Thomas Roberts, of Dover]; Emanuel[9], from Eng., settled at Hampton, *m* Elizabeth Parkhurst);
5–Sherburne (1735-1813), of Kensington, N.H.; was with Gen. Wolfe at the siege of Quebec; served in Am. Rev.; *m* Hulda Prescott (1738-1823; Hon. Benjamin[6]; John[7]; James[8], from Eng. to N.H.);
4–Jonathan (1779-1870), *m* Sally Clifford (1783-1833; Ebenezer[5] [1742-1833], Am. Rev., *m* Rhoda [*d* ca. 1840], dau. of John Elliot, Am. Rev., *m* **1743, Ruth Flanders [Jacob[7], *m* Ruth, dau.**

John Clough, and g.dau. John Clough; John[8]; Stephen[9]]);
3–Isaac Clifford (1808-85), of Wheelock, Vt., and Bridgewater, N.H.; *m* 1833, Lydia Jane Heath (1812-81; Samuel[4]; Samuel[5]; Daniel[6]; Samuel[7]; John[8]; John[9]; Bartholomew[10], from Eng. to Mass.);
2–Lucy Ann (1845-1923), *m* 1866, Curtis **Brown** (1847-71), of Bridgewater and Bristol, N.H.; issue: I–Lora Edith (1 above); II–Arthur Curtis (*b* 1870; *m* Eva J. Clark).
1–*m* Apr. 30, 1901, Fred William Courser (qv); issue: 1–Edith Jeannette, *b* Webster, N.H., July 1, 1904; N.H. Univ., ex-'27; *m* June 3, 1926, Benjamin Heald (issue: Emerson, *b* Oct. 22, 1927; Margaret Rose, *b* Oct. 25, 1928); 2–Infant (*b* and *d* Jan. 4, 1907); 3–Sarah Adaline, *b* Warner, N.H., May 7, 1908; 3 yr. course, Keene Normal Sch., 1930; 4–Margaret Nelson (Mar. 20, 1910-Aug. 9, 1923); 5–Fred William, Jr., *b* Bath, Me., Jan. 27, 1915.
1–Ed. N.H. Literary Instn. (valedictorian), 1888. Taught school 12 terms at New Hampton, N.H. Mem. D.A.R. (chapter sec., Bath, 1920-22, chapter historian, N.H., 1929–), I.A.G., A.B.C.F.M. (life), South Street (Bath, Me.) Parent Teachers Assn. (pres. 1921-22, treas. 1922-23), etc. Residence: Warner, N.H.

1–**COULTRAP, Mary Ball (Mrs. McKendree W.),** *b* Mt. Vernon, O., Feb. 5, 1874.
8–Alling **Ball,** from Eng., 1635, with brothers, Francis, John, Samuel, Richard and William, in the "Planter"; Alling settled in New Haven, Conn.; *m* Dorothy Fogal, of Eng.;
7–Edward (1644-1724), a founder of Newark, N.J.; high sheriff, Essex Co., 1693; committeeman on boundaries in matter of settlement with Lord proprs., Indians, etc.; *m* ca. 1664, Abigail Blatchley (Thomas[8], dep. Conn. General Assembly, in New Haven, 1643, Branford, 1645, *m* Susanna Ball);
6–Thomas (1687/88-1744), of Newark, N.J.; blacksmith; constable of Newark, 1715-16; removed to Vauxhall, 1718 or 1720, where he owned 400 acres of land; *m* 1710, Sarah Davis (*d* 1778 aet. 88; Thomas[7], *m* Mary Ward);
5–Timothy (1711-58), of Maplewood Sta., N.J.; farmer; cousin of Gen. Washington, who spent many nights in his home during Am. Rev.; the house, built 1743, is still standing on mountainside of Maplewood Station, nr. S. Orange, N.J.; *m* 1734, Esther Bruen (1715-1803; John[6], of royal descent, *m* Mary Tompkins);
4–John (1746-1838), of Boonton N.J.; dea. Morristown Bapt. ch., 64 yrs.; ens. Am. Rev.; *m* 2d, 1787, Martha Howell Fairchild (1756-1815);
3–Silas (1795-1864), of N.J.; removed to Knox Co., O. when a young man; farmer; justice of peace; *m* 1819, Mary Broadwell (1801-73; Stephen[4], *m* Elizabeth Allen);
2–Andrew J. (1832-1908), of Mt. Vernon, O.; farmer on farm which was purchased, 1799, by John for his son, Silas; *m* 1859, Rebecca McFadden (1831-1904); issue: I–Harry M. (1860-1925; *m* Lida Clark); II–Elmer (1861-62); III–William (1863-80); IV–Minnie B. (1865-92; *m* McKendree W. Coultrap); V–Charles (*b* and *d* 1867); VI–Ida May (*b* and *d* 1869); VII–Fred C. (*b* 1870; *m* Alice Yanger); VIII–Mary (1 above).
1–*m* Mar. 13, 1895, as his 2d wife, McKendree W. Coultrap, *b* Stella, Vinton Co., O., Mar. 29, 1859; son of William Coultrap, of McArthur, Vinton Co., O., *m* Rebecca Wilson.
1–Organized first Woman's Republican Club in DuPage Co., Ill. Received certificates in recognition of services during World War, from Red Cross, Council of Nat. Defense, and the U.S. Food Administration. Mem. bd. dir. Naperville Bd. of Health. Pres. Naperville Woman's Club (1915-17); pres. 11th Dist. Woman's Clubs (1920-22); treas. State Federation Women's Clubs. Mem. D.A.C. (state treas.), D.A.R. (organizing regent, Ft. Payne chapter), I.A.G., DuPage Co. Hist. Soc. (treas.). Residence: 409 E. Franklin Av., Naperville, Ill.

1–**CRAVEN, Charles Edmiston,** *b* Newark, N.J., Nov. 23, 1860.
5–Thomas **Craven** (1709-75; son of Thomas, *m* Anna–); from London, Eng., 1728, to Middletown, N.J.; schoolmaster; *m* 1736, Elizabeth (1714-77), dau. of Gershom Walling, *m* Miriam–;
4–John (1741-1829), Washington, D.C.; *m* 1794, Ann Richardson;
3–Elijah Richardson (1796-1823), M.D., Princeton, 1815; *m* 1823, Sarah Eccleston Landreth (1798-1885; John[4], *m* Margaret Nutter);
2–Elijah Richardson (2 below).
8–Clement **Weaver** (qv);
7–Elizabeth, *m* Rev. Thomas **Dungan** (*b* London, Eng., ca. 1632-1688), brought in childhood to Newport, R.I.; mem. Colonial Assembly, 1678-81; a patentee of E. Greenwich, R.I., sold his real estate there 1682; moved to Bucks Co., Pa., established 1st Bapt. Ch. in Pa.;
6–Jeremiah (ca. 1673-1761), *m* Deborah Drake (1686/87-ante 1726; Capt. George[7], *m* Mary Oliver);
5–Mary (*b* 1722), *m* Joseph **Richardson;**
4–Ann (1754-1840), *m* John **Craven** (4 above).
6–Thomas **Craven** (same as 5 above);
5–Gershom (1745-1819), M.D., Princeton, 1765; surgeon Am. Rev.; *m* 1774, Rebecca Quick (1755-1836; Tunis[6], *m* Catherine Phillips);
4–Tunis (1781-1866), naval officer of the Port of N.Y.; *m* 1803, Hannah Tingey (*d* 1835; Commodore Thomas[5], *m* Margaret Murdoch);
3–Margaretta (*d* 1828), *m* 1826, Lt. Francis **Sanderson,** U.S.N. (*d* 1831);
2–Hannah Tingey (1827-63), *m* as his 1st wife, Mar. 24, 1852, Elijah Richardson **Craven** (Mar. 28, 1824-Jan. 5, 1908), Presbyn. minister (see Who's Who in America, Vol. V); issue (1st marriage): I–Margaretta Tingey (*b* 1853); II–Francis Sanderson (1856-90; *m* Margaret J. Little, *d* 1925); III–John Eccleston (Nov. 24, 1858-Dec. 26, 1920; commodore, U.S.N.; *m* Emily H. Barnard); IV–Charles E. (1 above); issue (2d marriage): I–Evelina (*b* 1869).
1–*m* Dec. 28, 1886, Anna Schenck McDougall, *b* Brooklyn, N.Y., Apr. 19, 1863; dau. of Rev. James McDougall, Ph.D., Presbyn. minister, pres. York Collegiate Inst., *m* Virginia Coryell; issue: 1–Virginia Coryell, *b* Birmingham, Pa., Nov. 8, 1887; *m* Oct. 20, 1910, Robert Mather Lupton (issue: Anne Craven, *b* 1911; Virginia Coryell, *b* 1913; Margaret Tingey, *b* 1914; Millie Edwards, *b* 1915; John Mather, *b* 1917; Robert Mather, *b* 1918; Elizabeth, *b* 1921); 2–Sarah Landreth, *b* Downingtown, Pa., Oct. 18, 1889; *m* Mar. 30, 1925, Laurits Christian Eichner; 3–Julia McDougall, *b* Downingtown, Aug. 7, 1891; 4–James McDougall, *b* Downingtown, Mar. 17, 1894; *m* Jan. 1, 1921, Mabel Consuelo Pinna (issue: Kenneth, *b* 1922; Consuelo, *b* 1923; John Pinna, *b* 1924; Mabel, *b* 1926); 5–Charles Edmiston, Jr., *b* Mattituck, N.Y., Aug. 7, 1897; *m* Mar. 24, 1921, Charlotte Baber.
1–A.B. Princeton, '81, A.M., 1884; grad. Princeton Theol. Sem., 1886; (D.D., U.Pittsburgh, 1909). Ordained Presbyn. ministry, 1886; pastor South Presbyn. Ch., Montclair, N.J. (see Who's Who in America). Residence: 355 N. Fullerton Av., Upper Montclair, N.J.

1–**CRAVENS, Drusilla Lanier,** *b* Madison, Ind., Apr. 27, 1864.
6–Robert **Cravens** (*d* 1762; son of Joseph Cravens, on record in Del., 1709), on record in Va., 1743, where he was a landowner, 1745; justice or magistrate, Augusta Co.; commd. capt. of horse, 1743, Orange Co.; *m* Mary Harrison (sister of Daniel);
5–John (1722/23-1778), *m* Margaret (Hyatt) Dyer (John Hyatt[6]);
4–Joseph, M.D. (1769-1842), Madison, Ind.; *m* 1790, Polly Nichols (*d* 1842; John[5], will proved 1810);
3–Robert, M.D. (1796-1821), Madison, Ind.; *m* 1818, Sarah Paul (John[4], *m* Sarah Thornberry, of Germantown, Pa.);
2–Hon. John Robert (2 below).
8–John **Lanier** (ca. 1655-1719), from Eng., settled in Prince George Co., Va., as early as 1676; received land grant in Westover Parish, 1683, for importing 30 families into the colony of Va.; *m* Sarah–;
7–Sampson (1680-1743/44), Brunswick Co., Va.; *m* ante 1724, Elizabeth Washington;
6–Hon. James (post 1724-1786), rep. from Pitt Co. in Provincial Assembly, 1775; *m* 1748/49, Mary Cooke (Henry[7], of Brunswick Co., Va.);

5–James (1750-1806), Falmouth, Pendleton Co., Ky.; *m* 1774, Sarah Chalmers;
4–Alexander Chalmers (1778-1820), *m* 1797, Drusilla Cleaves Doughty (1778-1838; Elisha[5]);
3–James Franklin Doughty (1800-81), *m* 1st, 1819, Elizabeth Gardner (1798-1846; John[4], of Lexington, Ky.);
2–Drusilla (2 below).
9–John **Washington** (post 1622/23-ante 1678), of the Barbados and Surry Co., Va.; *m* 1658, Mary Flood (*d* ante 1678);
8–Richard (1660-will dated 1724), *m* ca. 1680, Elizabeth Jordan;
7–Elizabeth, *m* Sampson **Lanier** (7 above).
2–Drusilla Lanier (1824-1903), *m* Hon. John Robert **Cravens** (1819-99), *b* and *d* Madison, Ind.; lawyer; judge Circuit Ct., Jefferson Co., Ind.; issue: I–John Paul (1844-82; *m* Molly Reese); II–Robert (1847-1908); III–James (1849-1921; *m* Clara Duncan, *d*); IV–Alexander (1851-1911; *m* Leila Greenhow, *d* 1886); V–William Jackson (*b* 1853); VI–Elizabeth Gardner (1855-1927; *m* Dr. William R. Davidson, *d*); VII–Charles (b 1857); VIII–Joseph Marshall (*b* 1859); IX–Mary Louise (1861-1907; *m* John A. Sage); X–Drusilla Lanier (1 above); XI–Franklin (1865-96; *m* Rachel B. Miller); XII–Margaret (*b* and *d* 1867).
1–Mem. Magna Charta Dames (life), C.D.A., O.C., D.F.P.A., D.A.R., S.W. 1812. Residence: Madison, Ind.

1–**CRAWFORD, Adelaide Watts (Mrs. Byron H.)**, *b* Canton, Pa., July 4, 1871.
7–David **Watts** (*d* 1771), from Scotland, to Morristown, N.J.; *m* in Scotland, Martha Givens;
6–James (ca. 1730/33-1778), Turbitt Tp., Northumberland Co., Pa., killed by Indians in their attack upon Ft. Freeland; *m* Anne Walker (*d* post 1790);
5–Francis (1754-55-1808), 2d lt., Am. Rev. from Northumberland Co., Pa.; Presbyn.; *m* Jane Means (1758-1824; Samuel[6], killed in battle of Wyoming, Pa., *m* Elizabeth Clark, desc. William Clark, mem. Penn's 1st Council, 1682);
4–John (1787-1859), of Canton, Bradford Co., Pa.; *m* Mary Cowell;
3–William (1811-62), Towanda and Union tps., Tioga Co., Pa.; *m* Hannah Comfort (1813-80; Robert[4], Newburgh, Orange Co., N.Y., *m* Phoebe Thorn; Richard[5], of Wellsburg, Chemung Co., N.Y., Am. Rev., *m* Charity–);
2–Robert (2 below).
9–Jan Wouters Van der Bosch **Johnson** (ca. 1638-post 1695), from Holland, to Flatbush, N.Y.; at Branford, Conn., 1666-73; returned to S.I.; *m* Arentje Arents; *m* 2d, Wentje (Pieters, Peterson) Peters, of Amersfoort, N.Y.;
8–Jacobus Jansen (1672-1753), from Branford, Conn., to S.I.; *m* Sarah Benham (Joseph[9], of Wallingford, Conn., *m* Winifred King);
7–Cornelius (bap. 1703-will dated 1770), *m* 1st, Sarah (Membru or Mambrut) Membret (Jean[8], *m* Sara Guneau);
6–Sarah (bap. 1724), *m* Sgt. William **Coolbaugh** (1729-1801), *b* Amwell, N.J., to Kingwood, N.J.; Am. Rev.; *d* Smithfield Tp., Monroe Co., Pa. (William Colbroeck[7]);
5–Rachel (*b* 1765), of Kingwood, N.J.; *m* Christopher **Cowell** (1760-1825), from Amwell, N.J., to Wysox, Bradford Co., Pa., 1791; drowned (Christopher[6]);
4–Mary (Polly) (1789-1866), *m* John **Watts** (4 above).
9–William **Bonnell** (1617-69), from Cheshire, Eng. in the "James," to Mass., 1630; at New Haven, Conn., 1638; farmer, tanner; after death of wife returned to Eng.; *m* 1640, Anne Wilmot (Benjamin[10] [1585-1669], of New Haven, *m* Ann–);
8–Nathaniel (1644-post 1696), to L.I.; joined Elizabethtown Assn. of N.J., assisted in laying out 1st town, Elizabethtown, 1665; *m* 1665, Susannah Whitehead (*b* 1650; Isaac[9], from New Haven to N.J., judge, magistrate, capt. mil. co.; John[10]);
7–Isaac (ca. 1668-1712), "planter"; *m* Elizabeth– (*d* post 1712);
6–Abraham (1700-68), from Elizabethtown to Kingwood, Hunterdon Co.; propr. Old Bonnell Tavern, Clinton, N.J., where descendants live; *m* 1731, Mary Shinn;
5–Abraham (1732-97), lt. col. Am. Rev.; mem. Sons of Liberty; *m* Elizabeth Foster (1743-1822);
4–Clement du Mont (1766-1836), lived at Old Bonnell Tavern; judge, mem. Town council; *m* Rachel Woolverton;
3–Abraham Stockton (1795-1859), from Clinton, N.J., to Nesbit, nr. Williamsport, Lycoming Co., Pa., in lumber business; *m* Lydia Hull Beavers; *m* 2d, 1843, Sarah Lusk;
2–Jane Elizabeth (2 below).
8–John (Shene) **Shinn** (1623-1712), from Eng. to N.J.; owner of bolting mills; *m* in Eng., Jane–;
7–John (*d* 1737), from Eng. with parents; *m* 1st, 1686, Ellen Stayce (bap. 1666-*d* ante 1707; Robert[8] [1630-1701]; son of John of Yorkshire, Eng., from Eng., Aug., 1677 in the "Kent," to New Castle, Del., Quaker, his family came Nov., 1677, in the "Martha," mem. Assembly, 1682,84,85, council, 1684, commr. Lower House, judge Burlington Co., 1682, magistrate, removed to Phila., 1690; brother of Mahlon Stacy, qv);
6–Mary (*b* 1705), *m* Abraham **Bonnell** (6 above).
7–Judge Charles **Woolverton,** from Eng., Quaker; 1st judge, Hunterdon Co., N.J., 1721; purchased 1665 acres in Amwell Tp. on Delaware River, 1714; buried nr. George Fox in Rosemont cemetery, nr. Stockton, N.J.; *m* Mary, dau. of John Chadwick, *m* Elizabeth–;
6–Roger (1700-will dated 1747), of Hopewell, N.J.; tailor; *m* Mary–;
5–Charles (1741-1810), to Shamokin, Pa.; purchased land there, 1792; gave forage and teams in cause of Am. Rev.; *m* 1763, Mary Drake (Thomas[6] [1723-92], Am. Rev.; Benjamin[7]; Rev. John[8], of Piscataway, N.J.; Capt. Francis[9] [*d* 1687], from N.H. to N.J.);
4–Rachel, *m* Clement du Mont **Bonnell** (4 above).
11–George **Farley** (*d* 1693), from Kent Co., Eng.; in Roxbury, Mass., 1639; Woburn, 1645; to Billerica, 1654; selectman; soldier King Philip's War; *m* 1640, Christian Births (*d* 1702);
10–Caleb (1645-1712), *m* 1666, Rebecca Hill (*d* 1669; Ralph?[11]); *m* 2d, 1669, Lydia Moore (Golden[11]);
9–Caleb (*b* 1667), *m* 1686, Sarah Godfrey (*d* 1704), of Haverhill, Mass. (John[10] *m* Mary, dau. of Moses Cox, of Hampton, N.H., *m* Alice–; Dea. William[11]); *m* 2d, Lydia Hawse;
8–Caleb (*b* 1688/89), to N.J. with brother George; resided at Boundbrook, Somerset Co., N.J.; *m* Margrietje–;
7–Mindurt (Minard) (bap. 1720-1790), mem. Com. Safety, Hunterdon Co., N.J., during Am. Rev.; *m* Barbara Van Dieren (*d* 1808; Rev. —[8]);
6–Mary (*d* 1808), *m* Conrad **Apgar** (1755-1837), of Hunterdon Co., N.J.; hotel keeper, Cokesburg; soldier Am. Rev., pensioned (Johan Adam [Ebcher] Apgar[7], emigrant, settled in Hunterdon Co., 1749);
5–John (1778-ante 1840), to Lycoming Co., Pa., ca. 1800; *m* Mary Pickell (1779-1859; Baltus, Jr.[6] [1720-86], very wealthy, gave liberally to ch., loaned money to colonies during Am. Rev., *m* 1746, Sophia Van Horn [1726-64], *m* 2d, Anna–; Balthazar [Buechel[7]], [1686-1765], from Hartenburg, Germany, to Whitehouse, N.J., wealthy property owner, *m* 1718, Anna Gertrude Reitern, of N.Y.);
4–Catherine (1804-73), *m* as his 2d wife, James **Lusk** (*d* ca. 1843), of Bodines, Lycoming Co., Pa., justice (Sgt. Patrick[5], Am. Rev., *m* Eleanor, dau. of Robert Humes, of Lancaster Co., Pa., Am. Rev., *m* Anne–);
3–Sarah (1826-88), *m* Abraham S. **Bonnell** (3 above);
2–Jane Elizabeth (1851-1920), *m* July 4, 1869, Robert Thomas **Watts** (1849-1924), to Elmira, N.Y.; issue: I–Murray (*b* 1870; *m* Waitie Minard); II–Adelaide (1 above).
1–*m* July 4, 1888, Byron Hugh Crawford, *b* Pittsburgh, Pa., May 3, 1869; son of Hugh Crawford, *m* Lucy MacIntosh; issue: 1–Kathleen, *b* Canton, Pa., Apr. 21, 1889; mem. Mendelssohn and Beethoven Clubs, Canton; *m* Sept. 27, 1910, Norvin Clark, *b* May 14, 1886, son of Samuel Holmes, *m* Ella Clark (issue: Norvin, Jr., Rodman, Ella, Crawford, Franklin, Kenneth, Edwin); 2–Nellie (Feb. 9, 1890-Jan. 30, 1895).

1–Mem. D.F.P.A., C.D.A., H.S., D.A.R. Presbyn. Residence: Canton, Pa.

1–**CRAWFORD, Lydia Lefavour Benedict (Mrs. Wilmer H.),** *b* New Orleans, La., Dec. 16, 1881.
9–Thomas **Benedict** (qv);
8–John (1640-1727), of Huntington, L.I.; later selectman, Norwalk, Conn.; *m* 1670, Phoebe Gregory (John[9], *m* Sarah–);
7–James (1685-1762), of Ridgefield; *m* 1709, Mary Hyatt (1686-1767; Thomas[8], *m* Mary–);
6–John (1726-1814), Ridgefield; *m* 1749, Esther Stebbins (1724-1814; Joseph[7]);
5–Abijah (1755-1818), Ridgefield, moved to Pompey; *m* 1781, Amelia Buckley (1755-1837);
4–Bradley (1781-1853), of Cayuga; *m* 1806, Eliza Vernam (*d* 1821);
3–John Talcott (1814-53), of Texas; *m* 1840, Frances Sophronia Pierrepoint;
2–John Talcott (2 below).
10–Gov. William **Leete** (qv);
9–John (1639-92), of New Haven Colony; *m* 1670, Mary Chittenden (1640-1712; William[10], *m* Joanna Sheafe);
8–Anne (1671-1724), *m* 1691, John **Collins** (1665-1751), of New Haven;
7–Timothy (1699-1776), New Haven; *m* 1722, Elizabeth Hyde (*b* 1699);
6–Charles (*b* 1727), Litchfield; *m* 1752, Ann Huntington (*b* 1729);
5–Rhoda (1764-1855), *m* 1780, Evelyn **Pierrepoint** (1755-1808), of Litchfield, Conn.;
4–William (1797-1870), of Conn.; *m* 1818, Sophronia Frisbie (1797-1860);
3–Frances Sophronia (1821-1912), *m* John T. **Benedict** (3 above);
2–John Talcott (*b* 1850), pres. Benedict Mfg. Co., Shreveport, La.; *m* 1878, Lydia Carrie Lefavour (*b* 1860); issue: I–Lydia Lefavour (1 above); II–Alice Pearl (*m* William Mumford Dickinson); III–John Talcott, Jr. (1887-1921; *m* Auralia Kuhn); IV–Grover Cleveland; V–Margaret Frances (*m* Louis J. Shaner, *d*).
1–*m* Sept. 10, 1900, Wilmer Hayes Crawford, *b* New Orleans, La., Jan. 27, 1879; chemical business; son of Richard Hayes Crawford, *d*.
1–Mem. Dames of Court of Honor, D.F.P.A., Daus. of Am. Pioneers, Colonial Daus., C.D.XVIIC., D.A.R., I.A.G., Nat. Soc. N.E. Women, O.E.S., Inst. of Am. Govt. Presbyterian. Republican. Clubs: Cincinnati Woman's, Riverside Culture. Summer place: Biloxi, Miss. Residence: 2938 Vernon Pl., Cincinnati, O.

1–**CREVELING, Frances McDonald (Mrs. James G., Jr.),** *b* St. Louis Co., Mo., July 30, 1870.
5–Archibald **McDonald,** *m* Annie–;
4–Donald (1772-1805), *m* Sarah Critten (1781-1861);
3–Dennis (1802-71), of Berkeley Co., Va.; *m* 1829, Frances Virginia Orrick;
2–Donald (2 below).
8–Maj. Gen. John **Hammond** (qv);
7–Col. Thomas (*d* 1724), of Anne Arundel, Cecil and Baltimore cos., Md.; *m* Rebecca (Larkin) Lightfoot, Lady Lightfoot; *m* 2d, Mary Heath (*d* 1721);
6–Susannah, of Anne Arundel Co.; *m* 1719, John **Orrick** (1685-1749; James[7] [*d* 1690], from Scotland ca. 1650, settled in Md., received 510 lbs. of tobacco from Province of Md., 1681, for services he had rendered, *m* Mary–);
5–Capt. Nicholas (1725-81), of Baltimore Co., Md.; capt. Baltimore Co. troops in Am. Rev.; *m* 1st, Hannah Cromwell (1729-62);
4–Nicholas (1759-1822), of Berkeley and Morgan cos., W.Va.; justice and high sheriff of Berkeley Co.; *m* 1788, Mary Pendleton (1771-1838);
3–Frances Virginia (1811-82), of Berkeley Co.; *m* Dennis **McDonald** (3 above);
2–Donald (1830-89), of St. Charles Co., Mo.; physician; *m* 1859, Mary McDowell Baird (1834-99; William[3], of Lincoln Co., Mo., *m* Elizabeth Findley); issue: I–Edgar Baird (*b* 1861; *m* Mary Lou Banks); II–Elizabeth (*b* 1869); III–Frances (1 above); IV–Nora (*b* 1872).
1–*m* Oct. 11, 1899, James Gorman Creveling, Jr., *b* St. Louis, Mo., Oct. 14, 1869; son of James Gorman Creveling, of St. Louis, *m* Clemontina Jane Hanley; issue: 1–Donald McDonald, *b* Saw Luio Potosi, Mex., Oct. 15, 1901; B.S. in Mining, M.I.T., '24, M.S., 1925; 2–James Gordon, *b* Aguascalientes, Mex., Dec. 27, 1903; B.S., M.I.T., '25, M.S., 1926; 3–Mary Baird, *b* Aguascalientes, Aug. 30, 1905; Wellesley U.; *m* Nov. 8, 1928, Francis Russell Campbell.
1–Mem. C.D.A., D.A.R. Presbyn. Democrat. Clubs: Centennial, Belmont, Peabody. Residence: R.F.D. 3, Nashville, Tenn.

1–**CROSBY, Walter Wilson,** *b* Brooklyn, N.Y., Sept. 2, 1872.
9–Robert **Seaver** (*d* 1683, aet. 75), from Eng. ante June 1634; selectman, Rosbury, Mass., 1665; *m* 1634, Elizabeth Ballard;
8–Nathaniel (1645-76), *m* Sarah–;
7–John (*b* 1671), *m* Sarah–;
6–Nathanial (1697-1742), to Brookline; *m* Hannah White;
5–Abijah (1737-64), *m* Anne Winchester, of Brookline;
4–Joseph (1771-99), *m* Abigail Whitney;
3–William Whitney (*b* 1806), *m* Hannah Hewes Hunneman;
2–Hannah Adelaide (*b* Aug. 29, 1837-*d* Baltimore, Md., Aug. 1914), *m* Nov. 16, 1871, Wilson **Crosby** (1834-1904), grad. Rensselaer Poly. Inst., '57; lt., 14th Me. Inf., Civil War; engr. for 1st subway, New York, 1876; founder and sec. Me. Landowner's and Lumbermen's Assn.; for Crosby lineage see Vol. III, p. 141; issue: I–Walter Wilson (1 above); II–Hannah Gertrude (*b* 1874).
1–*m* Aug. 5, 1921, Florance Lapham Fletcher, *b* Washington, D.C., May 11, 1885; served with Y.M.C.A., 1918-19, in France, and with 32d Div. in Germany; dau. Frank A. Lapham, *m* Lydia Perry.
1–B.C.E., U.Me., 1893, C.E., 1896 (Beta Theta Pi, Phi Kappa Phi); D.Sc., U.Md., 1912; D.Eng., U.Me., 1926. Consulting engr., expert on highways, parks, traffic and transportation (see Who's Who in America). Maj. and asst. chief of staff 15th Div., U.S.A., 1916-17; maj. Engr. O.R.C., U.S.A., 1917; lt. col. 104th Engrs., 29th Div., A.E.F. Mem. S.R., S.A.R., M.O. F.W., M.O.W.W., A.L., etc. (see Who's Who in America, Who's Who in Engineering, Am. Men of Science, etc.). Addresses: 1040 Adella Av., Coronado, Calif.; Maryland Club, Baltimore, Md.

1–**CROSKEY, John Welsh,** *b* Philadelphia, Pa., Jan. 26, 1858.
7–John **Ashmead** (1648-88), from Eng. to Pa., 1682; *m* 1677, Mary Conner (or Courier; *d* 1688; William[8]);
6–John (1679-1742), *m* 1703, Sarah Sellers (*b* 1685; Samuel[7]);
5–John (1706-50), of Germantown, Pa.; *m* 1734, Ann Rush (1716-60 James[6]);
4–Capt. John (1738-1818), of Phila.; *m* ca. 1760, Mary Mifflin (ca. 1743-1814; Benjamin[5]);
3–Eliza (1788-1852), of Phila.; *m* 1808, George Duncan **Croskey** (*b* in Eng. 1778-*d* Phila. 1829);
2–Henry (1815-99), of Phila.; mcht.; *m* 1837, Ann Dunnohew (1819-92; Matthew[3], *m* Ann Robinson); issue: I–Henry (1838-40); II–Francis Ann (*b* 1840); III–Elisabeth (*b* 1843; *m* James Mackeown, 1839-83); IV–Alfred (1844-47); V–Harry (1848-1926; *m* 1867, Jane McCormick Quigley; *m* 2d, Nellie M. Shreves); VI–Albert (*b* and *d* 1850); VII–Ida (*b* 1851; *m* 1875, Thomas Mustin, *d* 1888; *m* 2d, 1893, W. S. Lloyd, 1860-1920); VIII–Knowles (*b* 1853; *m* 1877, Leilah Sloat; *m* 2d, Kate Charlotte Smith); IX–John W. (1 above); X–Mary Clay (1859-1901).
1–*m* Dec. 15, 1880, Elisabeth Estes Browning, *b* nr. Gloucester, N.J., Dec. 28, 1858; dau. of Cooper Browning, *m* Jane Mary Estes; issue: 1–Henry Browning, *b* Phila., Pa., Jan. 12, 1882; *m* July 24, 1920, Myrtle Emma Scott, *b* Mar. 3, 1892; 2–Mary Elisabeth, *b* Phila., June 11, 1883; *m* June 5, 1909, Lewis E. Bailey (issue: Elisabeth Browning, *b* July 21, 1912); 3–Marion Langley, *b* Swarthmore, Pa., Feb. 10, 1885; 4–John Welsh, Jr., (*b* Swarthmore, July 13, 1886-*d* Jan. 13, 1913).
1–M.D., Medico-Chirurg. Coll. of Phila., '89 (gold medalist); student at Swarthmore Coll., 1886-87; certificate of proficiency, Phila. Sch. of Anatomy, 1889. Chief asst. to surg. clinic, Medico-Chirurg. Coll., 1889, later lecturer on minor and operative surgery; asst. surgeon,

Wills Hosp., 1891-97; surgeon same, 1897-1902; apptd. ophthalmic surgeon to Phila. Gen. Hosp., 1901; ophthalmic surgeon, Samaritan Hosp., 1902-05; ophthalmologist, Home of the Merciful Savior for Crippled Children. Author (see Who's Who in America). Mem. S.R., Colonial Soc. of Pa., Hist. Soc. of Pa., Valley Forge Hist. Soc. Mason. Republican. Clubs: Paxon Hollow Golf, Overbrook Golf, Ocean City Golf, Kiwanis. Residence: 3325 Powelton Av., Philadelphia, Pa.

COL. WALTER ALEXANDER VAN RENSSELAER, M.D. (1836-79).

1–**CROWELL, Julia Schuyler Phelps Van Rensselaer (Mrs. Charles Harvey),** *b* Kingston, N.Y., Mar. 12, 1870.

9–Kiliaen **Van Rensselaer** (qv);

8–Col. Jeremias (qv), *m* 1662, Maria Van Cortlandt (1645-89; Oloff S.[9], qv);

7–Col. Hendrick (1674-1740), of Albany, N.Y.; active in Indian affairs, and "affairs of six nations"; mem. Colonial Assembly; *m* 1689, Catherine Van Burgh (*d* 1730; Johannes Pieterse[8], *m* Katrina [*b* 1605], dau. of Anneke Jans, and g.dau. William, Prince of Orange);

6–Col. Kiliaen (1717-81), of Albany; chmn. Com. of Safety; commd. col. 4th Regt. N.Y. Militia, Oct., 1775, and with his four sons served throughout Am. Rev.; wounded at Battle of Saratoga; mem. N.Y. Assembly, and Com. of Correspondence; *m* 1742, Ariantia Schuyler (1720-63; Dr. Nicholas[7], *m* 1714, Elsie Wendell);

5–Col. Philip (1747-98), of Albany; had charge of mil. stores of northern dept., during Am. Rev.; apptd. dep. commissary gen. of northern dept., by Gen. Schuyler, and confirmed by Congress, 1775; mem. Com. of Safety, Albany; *m* 1768, Maria Sanders (*b* 1749; Col. Robert[6], 2d mayor of Albany, served in Indian wars, *m* 1747, Elizabeth, dau. of Col. Peter Schuyler);

4–Robert Sanders (1773-1840), of Albany, N.Y., and London, Eng.; represented Am. merchants on London Exchange; *m* 1801, Catherine Nichols Bogart (1784-1859; Dr. Nicholas[5], lt. and surgeon-gen. in Am. Rev., *m* 1783, Elsie, dau. of Col. Harmanus Schuyler);

3–Schuyler (1812-74), of Albany; postmaster, Albany, 25 yrs.; *m* 1835, Cornelia Schuyler (1817-43; Alexander Hamilton[4], *m* Eleanor Giltner);

2–Col. Walter Alexander (2 below).

6–Rev. Eggo Tonkin **Van Hoevenberg** (*d* 1769; son of Rev. Rudolphus[7], *m* Antoinette Jansen Hamhuijs); from Holland, 1749, as missionary to the colonies; settled at Rhinebeck, N.Y.; preached in Dutch Ch.; ed. U. of Groningen and U. of Leyden; returned to Leyden, 1766, and *d* there; his three sons served in Am. Rev.; *m* 1751, Jannetje Radcliffe (*b* 1735; Joachim[7], *m* Hilletje Hoogerboom);

5–Lt. Henry (1758-1839), of Rhinebeck and Charlton, N.Y.; in Am. Rev. as q.m. under Maj. Nicholas Fish, 1776-77, and was apptd. q.m., Col. Graham's Regt., 1779; *m* 1782, Esther Dumond (1762-1840; Cornelius[6] [*b* 1733], Am. Rev., *m* 1760, Margaret, dau. of Herbert Hennes, of Harlem, N.Y.);

4–Lt. Henry (1790-1868), of Kingston, N.Y.; surgeon, War 1812; health officer, Port of N.Y., 1843-48; charter mem. Tammany Hall; charter mem. of the Acad. of Med.; *m* 1813, Jane Catherine Heermance (1792-1862; Gen. Martin[5], War 1812, *m* 1789, Sarah Kierstede);

3–Martin Henry (1815-1912), of New York, N.Y.; atty.-at-law; *m* 1842, Charlotte Read Phelps (1821-81; William[4], bank note engraver, *m* 1813, Chloe Read May);

2–Jane Catherine (1848-79), of Albany and Kingston, N.Y.; *m* 1866, Col. Walter Alexander **Van Rensselaer,** M.D. (1836-79), of Albany and Kingston; enlisted Apr. 28, 1861, as 1st Lt., Co. C, 20th N.Y. State Militia, 80th Vols., Union Army, Civil War; commd. capt., Co. B, 20th N.Y. State Militia, Oct., 1861, and maj. 80th Regt., N.Y. Vols., 1862; commd. lt. col., 20th Inf., 8th Brig., 5th Div., and later, col. of same; wounded at 2d Battle of Bull Run, 1862, returned to his regt., and was again wounded at Battle of Gettysburg, 1863, from the effects of which he died; in 1870, was brevetted for "distinguished services and gallant conduct at the Battle of Gettysburg, 80th Regiment"; honorably discharged, Nov., 1865, having taken part in eleven battles (see portrait); issue: I–Frances Cornelia (1867-68); II–Julia Schuyler Phelps (1 above); III–Schuyler (1871-75); IV–Walter Alexander (*m* Willma Brick Tompkins); V–Annette Maria (1877-1900); VI–Nicholas Bogart (*m* Minnie Catherine Burke).

1–*m* Aug. 9, 1892, Charles Harvey Crowell, *b* Windsor, Mass., Dec., 15, 1869; son of Harvey Stearns Crowell, of Pittsfield, Mass.; issue (all *b* Pittsfield, Mass.): 1–Harvey Van Rensselaer, *b* May 14, 1895; Ph.G., Mass. Coll. of Pharmacy, '21, Ph.C., 1922; *m* Dec. 8, 1917, Elizabeth, dau. Thomas Rutherford Trowbridge, of Litchfield, Conn. (issue: Schuyler Trowbridge, *b* 1921; Livingston Van Rensselaer, *b* 1922); 2–Schuyler Van Hoevenberg (Feb. 27-Aug. 24, 1897); 3–Merrithew Van Rensselaer, *b* Aug. 10, 1898; ed. B.S., Colgate U., '22; Columbia U., Sch. of Business Administration, '24; studied at Harvard; *m* June 25, 1925, Elizabeth Anne, dau. of William Fredrick Graeskě, of Fond du Lac, Wis.

1–Ed. Hill Side Acad., Montclair, N.J. Pres. Woman Suffrage Orgn., and hon. pres., New Citizen's Club, Pittsfield, Mass. Mem. Hoover's food com., during World War; organizing mem. Nat. Memorial Foundation, Washington; first woman in Mass. to serve as acting chmn. of a Rep. City Com., 1921. Mem. D.C.W., D.A.R. (regent, Peace Party Chapter, 1917-20), mem. D.A.R. exec. council; organized and directed a chapter of the Children of Am. Rev.; mem. A.L. Auxiliary, organized and directed auxiliary, Berkshire Co., 1921-24, v.p. A.L. Auxiliary, Dept. of Mass., 1925-27. Episcopalian. Republican. Residence: 88 Bradford St., Pittsfield, Mass.

1–**CROUL, Julia Josephine Toll (Mrs. Frank H.),** *b* Washington, D.C., Feb. 17, 1859.

7–Karl (Claas) Hansen **Toll** (1665-1738), from Sweden to Schenectady, N.Y., 1685; mem. Legislature, 1714-26; vessel owner and commander; *m* 1685, Elizabeth Rinckhout (Daniel[8], of Albany, N.Y.);

6–Capt. Daniel (1691-1748), killed in battle of Toll Farm; *m* Margaret Bradt (Samuel[7]);

5–John (1719-46), of Glenville, N.Y.; *m* 1742, Eva Van Patten;

4–Charles Hansen (1745-1832), adj., 14th N.Y. Regt.; *m* 1767, Elizabeth Ryley (1747-1839);

3–Capt. Philip Ryley (1773-1862), sgt., ens., capt., War 1812; to Mich., 1834; *m* 1817, Nancy DeGraaf;

2–Isaac DeGraff (2 below).

7–Claas Andres (Nicholas Andrew DeGraff) **DeGraaf** (*d* 1697), from Holland, settled at

Albany, N.Y., 1655; purchased farm "Claas Graven Hoek," nr. Schenectady, 1688; *m* Elisabeth Brouwer (*d* 1723; William[8], of Albany);
6–Jesse (*b* 1688), captured by French and Indians and taken to Canada but returned; *m* 1705, Aaltie (Alida Henion) Hennions;
5–Daniel (*b* 1708), *m* 1735, Gazena Beeckman Swits (*b* 1713; Simon[6]);
4–Judge Isaac (1757-1844), dep. commissary of issues in northern dept., N.Y., in Am. Rev.; *m* 1779, Susan Van Epps (*d* 1829; John B.[5]);
3–Nancy (1797-1898), real D.A.R.; *m* Philip R. **Toll** (3 above);
2–Isaac DeGraff (*b* Glenville, N.Y., Dec. 1, 1818-*d* Mar. 27, 1908), of Petoskey, Mich.; ed. Ovid (N.Y.) Acad.; supervisor, Fawn River, Mich., 15 yrs.; mem. Mich. Ho. of Rep., 1846, Senate, 1847; brig. and maj. gen., Mich. state troops; capt. Co. E, 15th U.S. Inf., Mar. 1846, served in Mexican War; examiner patents, Washington, 1854-61; comdt. Interior Guard; mem. Nat. Rifles, Washington, 1861; *m* Jan. 9, 1849, Julia Victoria Moran (*b* May 24, 1829-*d* Fawn River, Apr. 14, 1865), of Detroit, Mich. (Judge Charles[3], served War 1812, aet. 16 yrs., mem. Territorial Council and State Legislature, *m* Julia DeQuindre, sister of Maj. Antoine DeQuindre); issue: I–Anna J. (Nov. 1, 1849-Jan. 17, 1850); II–Charles Philip (1855-Mar. 21, 1920; *m* 1886, Irene Stella Hinchman); III–Julia J. (1 above).
1–*m* Apr. 27, 1881, Col. Frank Hobbs Croul, *b* Detroit, Mich., July 2, 1858; son of Jerome Alexander Croul, of Lyons, N.Y.; issue: 1–Frances Atwood, *b* Detroit, Mich., Apr. 11, 1889; *m* Oct. 2, 1911, John Alexander McPherson (issue: Frank Croul, *b* Mar. 15, 1914; John A., *b* Jan. 12, 1918).
1–Mem. C.D.A., D.A.R., U.S.D. 1812. Clubs: Colony, Women's City. Residence: 540 McDougall Av., Detroit, Mich.

1–**CRUIKSHANK, Barton,** *b* Albany, N.Y., Feb. 5, 1866.
6–Hugh **Cruikshank,** from Argyleshire, Scotland;
5–Hugh, *m* Elizabeth Pringle;
4–Alexander (1766-1833), *m* Jane Fleucker;
3–Hugh (*b* Dec. 18, 1792), *m* Sept. 1, 1817, Elizabeth Hughes;
2–James (2 below).
9–William **Hough** (1619-Aug. 10, 1683; son of Edward, of West Chester, Cheshire Co., Eng.), from Eng., ca. 1648, with co. led by Rev. Richard Blinman; settled at Greens Harbor, nr. Plymouth; to Gloucester on Cape Ann, 1642; selectman. Trynal Cove, 1651; to New London, Conn., 1651; *m* 1645, Sarah Caulkins;
8–Samuel (*b* 1653), of Saybrook, Conn.; *m* 1679, Susanna Wrotham (*d* 1684); *m* 2d, 1685, Mary Bate (James[9], of Haddam, Conn.);
7–James (1688-1740), of Wallingford, Conn.; *m* Hannah Clark (*d* 1718); *m* 2d, 1718, Sarah Mitchell;
6–Daniel (1721-68), *m* 1741/42, Mindwell Judd (*d* 1741/42); *m* 2d, 1743, Violet Benton;
5–Elijah (Jan. 23, 1748-Jan. 28, 1828), blacksmith; from Southwick, Mass., to Steuben, N.Y., thence to Gouverneur, N.Y.; Am. Rev., 1776-77, pensioned; *m* Apr. 27, 1769, Mary Ives (1746-1813);
4–Lemuel (Oct. 12, 1777-Jan. 22, 1866), sec. to Baron Steuben; ens. Oneida Co. militia; resided at Remsen, Boonville and Forest Port, N.Y.; justice of peace, 1820; mem. State Legislature, 1832; *m* May 16, 1802, Huldah Johnson;
3–Homer Johnson (Mar. 12, 1810-Jan. 27, 1877), lumberman and saw mill owner in western Adirondacks; *m* June 1834, Eleanor Richardson Green;
2–Chloe Rose (Apr. 19, 1836-Mar. 17, 1899), *m* June 9, 1857, James **Cruikshank,** LL.D. (Aug. 28, 1831-Jan. 1917), grad. Union Coll.; noted educator; issue: I–Elizabeth (1861-63); II–Barton (1 above); III–George Hough (*b* 1871; *m* Charlotte Jane Lloyd).
1–*m* Dec. 23, 1891, Edith Louise DuBois (qv for issue).
1–M.S., U.State of N.Y., '97; D.E., U.Santa Clara, 1903. Consulting engr., former offices in New York, San Diego and Los Angeles; now in charge engring. lab., U.Idaho. Pvt., corp., sgt., capt., Calif. N.G. Technical insp. munitions, War Dept., World War; maj. Engr. Reserves U.S.A. Residence: 136 S. Howard St., Moscow, Ida.

1–**CRUIKSHANK, Edith Louise DuBois (Mrs. Barton),** *b* Brooklyn, N.Y., Sept. 11, 1868.
8–Louis **DuBois** (qv);
7–Jacob (*b* 1661), of Kingston, Ulster Co., N.Y.; *m* 1689, Gerritje Gerritsen;
6–Gerrit (bap. 1704), of Kingston; *m* 1731, Margretje Elmendorff;
5–Conradt (*b* 1735), served in 3d Regt., Ulster Co. Militia in Am. Rev.; *m* 1763 or 64, Marie De Lamater;
4–Conrad (*b* 1777), *m* 1801, Sarah White;
3–Rev. Abram Contine (*b* 1802), *m* 1826, Mehitable Whitmore Sumner;
2–Ithamar (1830-1906), *m* 1852, Adeline Perrine Brink (1836-1912; Jacob[3], of Ulster Co., N.Y., wounded in War 1812, *m* Catherine, dau. of Peter Helm, *m* Elizabeth Perrine); issue: I–William Salmon (1854-88; *m* Irene Anderson); II–Viola Catherine (1856-1925; *m* 1876, Joseph Freeman Atwood, M.D.); III–Lillian Alice (*b* 1866; *m* 1887, Herbert Whiting Stickney); IV–Edith Louise (1 above).
1–*m* Dec. 23, 1891, Barton Cruikshank (qv); issue: 1–Helen DuBois, *b* Syracuse, N.Y., Jan. 3, 1909; 2–Douglas Barton, *b* Potsdam, N.Y., Jan. 26, 1911.
Residence: 136 S. Howard St., Moscow, Ida.

1–**CULVER, Edward Peck,** *b* Mt. Vernon, N.Y., Nov. 4, 1892.
8–Edward **Culver** (qv);
7–Gershom (1648-1717), *m* 1674, Mary Howell;
6–David (1680-1747), lived at Southampton, L.I.;
5–David (1738-1814), of Hebron, Conn.; Am. Rev.; *m* 1758, Mary Youngs;
4–David (1758-1848), Am. Rev.; *m* 1st, 1786, Abagail Eliza Mary Curtice (*d* 1797);
3–James (1796-1872), of Sandy Hill, N.Y.; *m* 1823, Kezia Lee;
2–Stephen Berry (2 below).
8–Thomas **Lee** (*b* Eng.-d 1641 on passage from Eng.), *m* Phebe Brown (Rev. Chad[9], qv);
7–Ens. Thomas, from Eng.; *m* 2d, 1676, Mary de Wolf (*b* ca. 1656; Balthazar[8], qv);
6–Col. Stephen (1698-1783), *m* 1719, Abigail Lord (1700-42; Richard[7] [1647-1727], settled at Lyme, Conn., 1680, lt. 1708, served in Crown Point Expdn., Queen Anne's War, *m* 1682, Elizabeth Hyde [1660-1736; Samuel[8] (1637-77), *m* 1659, Jane, dau. of Thomas Lee, 8 above; William[9], qv]);
5–Capt. Thomas (*b* 1734), *m* 2d, 1757, Mehitabel Peck (*b* 1738; Benjamin[6] [*b* 1711], *m* 1734, Sarah Champden; Samuel[7] [1678-1735], *m* 1699, Elizabeth Lee [*d* 1731]; Joseph[8] [1641-1718], *m* ca. 1662, Sarah– [*d* 1726]; William[9], see 9 below);
4–Stephen (1772-1856), *m* Mary Little (1787-1881);
3–Kezia (1803-86), *m* James **Culver** (3 above).
9–William **Peck** (1601-94), from Eng., in the "Hector," to Boston, 1637; a founder of the New Haven Colony, 1638; signed constn. for govt. of the colony; freeman, 1640; mcht.; trustee, treas., general business agt. of Colony Collegiate Sch.; *m* in London, 1622, Elizabeth– (*d* 1683); *m* 2d, Sarah, widow of William Holt;
8–Jeremiah (1623-99), from Eng., with father; preached and taught sch., Guilford, Conn., —1660; in charge Collegiate Sch., New Haven; succeeded Rev. James Fitch, as minister, at Saybrook, Conn.; to Guilford, 1666; to Newark, N.J.; 1st settled minister in Greenwich, Conn., 1678; *m* 1656, Johannah Kitchell (*d* 1711; Robert[9], of Guilford, Conn.);
7–Samuel (1659-1746), to Greenwich with father, 1678; wealthy and influential; justice of peace, ca. 50 yrs.; *m* 1686, Ruth Ferris (*d* 1745; Peter?[8]; Jeffrey?[9], of Stamford, Conn.);
6–Eliphalet (1699-ca. 1770), *m* 1732;
5–Samuel (1739-98), of Greenwich; *m* 1762, Hannah Sherwood (*d* 1811);
4–Jared (1773-1842), *m* Tamizon Adee;
3–Jared Hervey (1800-72), Rye to Port Chester, N.Y.; *m* 1839, Phebe C. Moseman;
2–Georgianna (*b* Port Chester, N.Y., 1851-1901), *m* 1887, Stephen Berry **Culver** (1841-1902), A.B., Union, '62; mining engr., Custom House, N.Y.; issue: I–Mary Richards (*b* 1889; *m* Roy Hunt); II–Edward P. (1 above).

1–Not married. B.E., Union, '15 (Psi U.). Asst. prof. engring., Princeton U., 1919—now prof. same. Served as 2d lt., Air Service, Mil. Aeronautics, World War. Mem. O.F.P.A. Summer place: Pilot Knob, Lake George, N.Y. Residence: Princeton, N.J.

1–**CULVER, Cora Louisa Whittier-Wait (Mrs. Fred W.),** *b* Traverse City, Mich., Oct. 26, 1867.
11–Thomas **Dudley** (qv);
10–Anne (1612/13-1672), of Andover and Salem, Mass.; *m* 1628, Gov. Simon **Bradstreet** (qv);
9–Dorothy (*d* 1671), of Andover, Mass., and Hampton, N.H.; *m* 1654, Seaborn **Cotton** (*b* at sea, 1633-*d* 1686);
8–Elizabeth (1665-98), of Hatfield, Mass.; *m* William **Williams** (1665-1741);
7–William (1688-1760), of Rutland, Mass.; *m* 1710, Hannah Stoddard (1688-1745);
6–Lucy (1721-60), of Weston, Mass.; *m* 1743, Rev. Joseph **Buckminster** (1719 or 1720-92);
5–Elizabeth (*b* 1758), of Framingham, Mass.; *m* 1785, Moses **Moody** (1765-1833), of Haverhill, Mass.;
4–Abigail Peaslee (1791-1875), of Hancock, Vt.; *m* 1807, Edmund **Whittier** (1787-1872), of Haverhill, Mass.;
3–John James (1809-95), of Haverhill, *m* 1833, Maryann Elizabeth Fox (1809-79), of Fairfield, Vt.;
2–Stephen Edwin (Whittier-Wait: 1834-1919), of Fairfield, Vt., and Traverse City, Mich.; druggist; *m* 1858, Maria Louisa Colburn (1835-68); issue: I–Ida Rowena (1859-76); II–Cora Louisa (1 above).
1–*m* Oct. 28, 1896, Fred William Culver, *b* Mt. Clemens, Mich., Jan. 3, 1869; son of Charles D. Culver; issue: 1–Lorraine Whittier, *b* Saginaw, Mich. (Nov. 13, 1897-June 1, 1918); 2–Donald Colburn, *b* Saginaw, Oct. 31, 1899; Ph.C., U.Mich., '22.
1–Ph.C., U.Mich., '90. Mem. C.D.A., C.D. 17th C., D.C.W., D.A.R., U.S.D. 1812, A.A.U.W. etc. Conglist. Residence: 421 N. Warren Av., Saginaw, Mich.

1–**CUMBOW, Caroline McIntire (Mrs. John H.),** *b* Red Wing, Minn., June 16, 1876.
10–Henry **Kingman** (1595-ca. 1667), from Eng. with his wife and 5 children, under the leadership of Rev. Joseph Hull; settled at Weymouth, Mass., ca. 1635; admitted freeman, 1636; licensed to keep a ferry, 1637; dep. 1638-52; mem. com. to lay out highways, 1649; grand juror; *m* Joanna– (*d* 1659);
9–John (1633-90), from Eng. with his parents; *m* Elizabeth– (*d* post 1685);
8–Samuel (1670-1709), of Weymouth; *m* 1696, Mary Mitchell (*d* post 1710; Jacob[9] [*d* 1675], of Bridgewater, *m* Susanna Pope; Experience[10], *m* Jane, dau. of Francis Cooke, Mayflower Pilgrim, qv);
7–Samuel (*b* 1710), *m* 1737, Phebe Washburn;
6–Mitchell (1744-1819), of Cincinnatus, N.Y.; Am. Rev.; *m* 1770, Keturah Latimer (1748-1835);
5–Col. John (1770-1859), of Cincinnatus, and Lenox, Mass.; *m* 1795, Miriam Isbell (*b* 1772);
4–Charles (1800-64), of Cincinnatus, and Mattoon, Ill.; *m* Nancy Root (1802-68);
3–Lyman Milford (1825-62), *d* in Battle of Fair Oaks; *m* 1850, Caroline Elizabeth Tidd (1828-1910);
2–Amelia Caroline (1852-1926), *m* Frederick Jesse **McIntire** (*b* 1852).
1–*m* June 26, 1895, Seymour Jerome Bigelow, *b* Minneapolis, Minn. (1863-1916); issue: 1–Caroline Kingman, *b* Duluth, Minn., Aug. 20, 1902; ed. U.Minn.; B.A., U. of S.D.; *m* Feb. 15, 1929, Nelson Whitford, son of Nelson Whitford Taylor, of Beaufort, N.C.
1–*m* 2d, Dec. 21, 1907, John Hendricks Cumbow, *b* Cumbow, Va., Sept. 14, 1868; son of Thomas Lilburn Cumbow, *m* Elizabeth McDonald; adopted, 1917, Caroline Kingman Bigelow (above), and changed surname to Cumbow.
1–Sec.-treas. Cumbow Lanning Oil Co. (Sioux Falls, S.D.). Mem. S.M.D., D.F.P.A., D.A.R. (chapter regent, sec., dir., and auditor), U.S.D. 1812 (state treas. and dir.), Woman's Alliance (sec. and dir.), Nat. Bd. Better Films. Clubs: Delphian, Business and Professional Women's, Altrusa (dir.), etc. Residence: 320 W. 27th St., Sioux Falls, S.D.

1–**CUMMINGS, Mary Augusta Marston (Mrs. Robert Fowler),** *b* New London, Conn., July 8, 1855.
9–Thomas **Marston** (1617-90), from Eng., 1634; settled at Salem, Mass.; later at Hampton, N.H.; *m* 1647, Mary Estow;
8–Ephraim (1654-1742), of Hampton; *m* 1677, Abiel Sanborn;
7–John (*b* 1680), of Hampton; *m* 1703, Bethia Tuck;
6–John (*b* 1713), of Hampton; *m* 1736, Susanna Blake;
5–Brackett (1747-81), of Falmouth, Me.; Am. Rev.; *m* 1770, Mary Geresh;
4–John (1773-1827), of Portland, Me.; *m* 1794, Peace Frye;
3–Ebenezer (1801-62), of Cumberland, Me.; *m* 1824, Sarah Rideout (1803-87);
2–Sanford Kingsley (1831-1904), ship builder, Augusta, Me.; later Ill. grain mcht.; *m* 1852, his 1st cousin, Sarah Marston Field (1831-1904), of Sidney, Me. (Benjamin[3], *m* Harriet Rideout, sister to Sarah, 3 above); issue: I–Benjamin Field (1853-55); II–Mary A. (1 above); III–Harriet Field (*m* Milton Doolittle).
1–*m* July 6, 1874, Robert Fowler Cummings, *b* North Oxford, Mass., June 17, 1848; son of Abel B. Cummings, of North Oxford, and Clifton, Ill.; issue: 1–Lenore, *b* Wenona, Ill., Mar. 24, 1875; ed. Onarga Sem.; *m* Mar. 16, 1922, Reinert August Jernberg; 2–Marion Marston, *b* Wenona, Jan. 1, 1876; ed. Ferry Hall, Lake Forest, Ill.; *m* Jan. 10, 1903, Ralph Cuyler, son of Edward D. Stevens, of Chicago, Ill. (issue: Ralph Cuyler; Sarah; Irene; Marion Marston; David Lincoln); 3–Austin Benjamin (Mar. 26, 1878-Feb. 11, 1881); 4–Florence, *b* Clifton, Ill., Apr. 11, 1883; ed. Ferry Hall, and U.Chicago; *m* Oct. 16, 1907, Thomas Johnston, son of Samuel Hair, of Chicago (issue: Thomas Johnston; Eleanor; Samuel Cummings); 5–Irene (Apr. 27, 1885-Dec. 30, 1903), victim of Iroquois Theatre Fire; 6–Marston, *b* Clifton, Feb. 10, 1892; ed. Todd Sem., Woodstock, Ill.; *m* Feb. 10, 1917, Dorothy Ann, dau. of George A. Dorsey, of Chicago (issue: Marcia Ann; John Marston).
1–Mem. D.F.P.A., D.A.R., Nat. Soc. N.E. Women (pres. gen., 1917-21). Clubs: Chicago Woman's, Hyde Park Travel (Chicago hon. pres.), Los Angeles Colony of N.E. Women (hon. pres.), Friday Morning (Los Angeles). Congregationalist. Republican. Residence: 5748 Kimbark Av., Chicago, Ill. Address: 833 S. Flower St., Los Angeles, Calif.

1–**CUMMINS, Albert Wilson,** *b* Smyrna, Del., Oct. 25, 1867.
5–Timothy **Cummins** (*b* ca. 1689; desc. of John Cummins, Lord of Badenoch, a regent of Scotland about the time of Edward I), from Scotland, settled at Oxford, Md., under the Lord Baltimore Patent; *m*–;
4–Daniel, dep. Del. Conv. that ratified the Constn. of the U.S.;
3–John (1777-1833), banker, mcht. and landowner; active in War 1812; speaker Del. Ho. of Rep., 1820; *m* Susan H. Wilson (1788-1842);
2–David J. (2 below).
7–Robert **Polk** (qv);
6–Ephraim, *m* Miss Williams;
5–Joseph, *m* Sarah Coverdale;
4–John, mem. Sussex (N.J.) Council of Safety, Am. Rev.; senator, Sussex Co., 1781; *m* 1776, Amelia Hurd; *m* 2d, 1811, Rachael Loper;
3–William (1781-1853), of Odessa, Del.; *m* 1809, Eliza Tatman (*d* 1816); *m* 2d, 1825, Margaret (Cochran) Pennington (*d* 1874);
2–Juliet (1832-94), *m* 1852, David J. **Cummins** (1824-98), bank pres., large land owner, Smyrna, Del.; issue: I–William Polk (1853-95); II–Margaret (*m* —Lea); III–Susan (*m* —McMichael); IV–Juliet Agnes; V–Edith (1861-1923; *m* —Davis); VI–Albert W. (1 above).
1–Not married. B.S., Lafayette Coll., '88 (Phi Kappa Psi; Pi Delta Epsilon), M.S., 1896. Editor Morning News, since 1912 (see Who's Who in America). Mem. S.A.R., I.A.G. Mason (32°). Episcopalian. Clubs: University (Phila.), Nat. Arts (New York), Torch. Residence: 2407 Delaware Av., Wilmington, Del.

1–**CUNNINGHAM, John Horatio,** *b* Centreville, Hickman Co., Tenn., June 27, 1877.
5–John **Cunningham,** Jr. (son of John [*b* ca 1730], of Scotland), came from Scotland to Ireland, with neighbors, the Wright family, to Charleston, S.C.; settled in Ky.;
4–Andrew (*b* Scotland-*d* Mobile, Ala., 1815, in War 1812), widow pensioned for War 1812 service; *m* in Fairfield Co., S.C., 1810, Ellen Wright (*b* Scotland), of the Wright family which came to America with John, 5 above;
3–John Robert, of Hickman Co., Tenn.; *m* Grace Kimmins (Joseph[4], *m* Margaret Cooper, of Va., reared by her uncles, Joel and Ned Cooper);
2–Armpstead (2 below).
8–Capt. Thomas **Clagett** (*b* 1635 or 40; son of Col. Edward Clagett, of London, Eng., *m* Margaret Adams), *b* Eng.; officer in Brit. Navy; had landed estates in Eng.; immigrated to Md., 1670; settled St. Leonardstown, Calvert Co.; one of his estates was "Weston"; *m* Sarah Pattison, of London;
7–Thomas (ca. 1675-1732), inherited "Weston," nr. upper Marlborough; *m* ca. 1700, Mary (prob.) Keene (*d* 1759);
6–John (*b* 1703 or 1705), *b* Prince George's Co., Md.; settled nr. Piscataway; *m* (prob.) Mary Meek;
5–William (*d* 1792), *m* Hariet Sothron;
4–Horatio (1779-1866), removed to Bedford Co., Tenn., 1809; *m* Rebecca Gantt (1786-1876; dau. of Elizabeth Gannt, widow, who removed to Bedford Co., Tenn., from Md.);
3–Horatio (1819-1912), of Hickman Co., Tenn.; *m* 1846, Elizabeth Jane Montgomery;
2–Laura Elizabeth (2 below).
7–Maj. William ("Boyne Water") **Montgomery** (son of Maj. William, killed in Battle of Boyne Water, 1690), wounded in Battle of Boyne Water; from Ireland, 1720, with wife, —Dunbar (William[9]);
6–Col. William (1736-1816), *b* Chester Co., Pa.; later removed to Danville, Pa.; censor of Pa., 1776; co. judge; mayor; gen. of militia, and large landowner; comd. a regt. of state militia, 1776, in Am. Rev.; mem. Pa. Legislature, and congressman; *m* Margaret Nivins;
5–William (1762-1838), served in Am. Rev. aet. 15, with his father, settled on Drake's Creek, Sumner Co., Tenn.; *m* ca. 1788, Jane McMillen;
4–John (*d* 1869), *b* Gallatin, Sumner Co., Tenn.; *m* 1825, Jane Dunn Strong Farrar (*d* 1891; Field[5], from S.C. to Charlotte, Dickson Co., Tenn., *m* Jane Dunn, dau. of Christopher Strong [1760-1850], from Ireland to Chester Dist., S.C., served in Capt. John Milen's Co., Col. Winn's Regt., S.C. troops, in battle of Rocky Mt., was defeated by Tarlton's dragoons nr. Rocky Creek, S.C.);
3–Elizabeth Jane (1828-1908), *m* Horatio **Clagett** (3 above);
2–Laura Elizabeth (*b* 1855), *m* 1876, Armpstead **Cunningham** (*d* 1903), of Centreville, Tenn.; issue: I–John Horatio (1 above); II–Sothron Spencer; III–James Robert (*m* Lucille Bondurant); IV–William Armpstead; V–Field Farrar; 3 others (*d* infancy or childhood).
1–*m* Mar. 27, 1902, Elva Clay Carter (qv for issue).
1–Atty. at law. Residence: 333 Burr Rd., San Antonio, Tex.

1–**CUNNINGHAM, Elva Carter (Mrs. John Horatio),** *b* Linden, Tenn.
9–Richard **Lane,** from Eng.; settled at Jamestown, Va.;
8–Joseph (*b* 1631), of Jamestown, Va., and Bertie Co., N.C.; vestryman in north west parish of Bertie Co., 1727;
7–Joseph (1665-1752 or 1758), *b* Jamestown; high sheriff Edgecombe Co., N.C.;
6–Joseph (1710-76), of Halifax Co., N.C.; *m* Patience McKinne (Barnabas[7], justice of Gen. Ct., mem. Colonial Assembly, vestryman, north west parish, Bertie Co., N.C., *m* Mary Exum);
5–Lt. Col. Joel (*d* 1795), of Bloomsbury and Raleigh, N.C.; Am.. Rev.; *m* 1772, Mary Hinton (*d* 1795; Col. John[6], *m* Grizelle Kimbrough);
4–Mary (*b* 1783), of Bloomsbury, N.C., and Edgecombe and Guilford cos., N.C.; *m* 1798, Isaac **Carter** (*d* 1812), g.son of Robert Carter, of Bertie Co., N.C.;
3–Thomas Lindley (1810-81), of Guilford Co., N.C., and Wayne Co., Tenn.; *m* 1st, 1839, Susan Swain Starbuck;
2–Henry Clay (2 below).
10–Edward **Starbuck** (1604-90), from Eng., 1635; settled Nantucket, Mass.; *m* Katherine Reynolds, of Wales;
9–Nathaniel (1635-1719), of Nantucket; *m* 1662, Mary Coffin (*d* 1717; Tristram[10], qv);
8–Nathaniel (1668-1753), of Nantucket; *m* 1690, Dinah Coffyn (James[9], *m* Mary–);
7–Paul (1694-1759), of Nantucket; *m* 1718, Ann Tebbitts;
6–Edward (1719-98), of Nantucket; *m* 1742, Damaris Worth (*d* 1780); William[7], *m* Mary–);
5–Matthew (*b* 1750), from Nantucket, Mass., to Guilford Co., N.C., 1795; disowned by the Quakers for taking part in Am. Rev.; was with John Paul Jones on the "Bon Homme Richard," and "The Ranger"; *m* 1776, Lydia Barney;
4–Seth (1779-1848), of Nantucket and Guilford Co., N.C.; *m* 1801, Ruth Swain (Reuben[5], *m* Hannah Macy);
3–Susan Swain (1820-58), of Guilford Co., N.C.; *m* Thomas Lindley **Carter** (3 above);
2–Henry Clay (1850-1917), of Waverly, Tenn.; atty. gen., 10th jud. dist.; *m* 1875, Sarah Caledonia Edwards (1853-1903; Thomas Wayne[3], of Linden, Perry Co., Tenn., *m* Virginia Watson); issue: I–Elva (1 above); II–Allena Edwards (*m* Charles David Hall); III–Roy Carter (*m* Andrena Ewin); IV–Mary Virginia (*m* Ralph H. Durkee).
1–*m* Mar. 27, 1902, John Horatio Cunningham (qv); issue: 1–John Horatio, Jr., *b* Nashville, Tenn., Feb. 4, 1903; A.B., U.Tex., '22; LL.B., 1925 (Kappa Sigma, Phi Delta Phi); *m* Oct. 10, 1926, Mary, dau. of Charles D. Long (issue: John Horatio, III, *b* 1927); 2–Clay Carter, *b* San Antonio, Tex., Feb. 6, 1907; LL.B., Cumberland U., '28; *m* Sept. 17, 1928, Lillian Hubly; 3–Sothron Clagett, *b* San Antonio, Tex., June 7, 1909; LL.B., Cumberland U., '29.
1–Mem. Inst. Am. Genealogy. Residence: 333 Burr Rd., San Antonio, Tex.

1–**CUNNINGHAM, Catherine Eloise Bain (Mrs. William Lee),** *b* Albany, N.Y., May 29, 1864.
9–Edward **Richards** (qv);
8–Nathaniel (1648-1726), *m* 1678, Mary Aldis (Dea. John[9]);
7–James (1683-1760), *m* Hannah Melcalf;
6–Samuel, *m* Hannah Melcalf;
5–Samuel (*b* 1757), *m* Mary White;
4–Henry White (*b* 1785), *m* Mehitabel Logan Minot;
3–Catherine Minot (1808-45), *m* Caspar **Bain** (Casparus[4], *m* Maria Clum);
2–Maj. Peter Clum (1837-1914), bvt. maj. for "conspicuous gallantry on field of battle"; chief of Bur. Engraving and Printing, Washington; *m* Sarah Abigail Hallenbeck; issue: I–James Thomas (*d* 1860, aet. 3); II–Alfred Casper (*d* 1860, aet. 1); III–Frank Howard (*d* 1864, aet. 2); IV–Catherine Eloise (1 above).
1–*m* Jan. 25, 1882, Charles Albert Jones (Apr. 15, 1860-1888); son of Charles Albert Jones, of Oneonta, N.Y.; issue: 1–Charles Albert, *b* Oneonta, N.Y., Oct. 26, 1882; *m* Nov. 25, 1911, Alice Engel (issue: Catherine Bain; William Frederick); 2–Pierre Chester, *b* Oneonta, Nov. 16, 1885; *m* Helen Smith (issue: Catherine Bain).
1–*m* 2d, Aug. 29, 1891, William Lee Cunningham, son of William Henry Cunningham, of Corning, N.Y., *m* Phoebe Jane Van Nostrand.
1–Mem. C.D.17thC., D.R. (corr. sec. gen., nat. soc., 1927). Address: "Belleair," Campbell Hall, Orange Co., N.Y.

1–**CURTIS, James Owen, Jr.,** *b* Portales, Roosevelt Co., N.M., Jan. 25, 1909.
11–Thomas (Blatchley) **Blakeslee** (*b* 1615-*d* Boston, ca. 1674, on a trading trip), came from Eng. to Boston, in the "Hopewell" with brother, Samuel (qv), 1635; resided Hartford, Conn., 1640; removed to New Haven, 1643; took oath of fidelity, 1644; removed to Branford, Conn., 1645; dep., 1667,71; freeman, 1669; signed New Plantation and Church Covenant of Branford, 1667; later resided at Guilford, Conn.; *m* Susanna Ball (Alling[12] [*b* Eng.], to Boston ante 1639, *m* Dorothy–); she *m* 2d, Richard Bristow;

10–Aaron (1644-99), signed fundamental agreement to found Newark, N.J., 1666; returned to Guilford, Conn., living there 1683; *m* 1st, 1665, Mary Dodd (*d* ante 1686; Daniel[11]);
9–Ebenezer (*b* 1677), from Guilford to Dix Hills, Huntington Tp., L.I.; pvt., Capt. Thomas Higbe's co. militia, from Huntington, 1715; *m*–;
8–Ebenezer (1709-post 1745), to Ponds, Milford Tp., nr. Pompton, Passaic Co., N.J.; *m* 1st, Hannah Miller; he *m* 5 times;
7–Mercy (Marcy or Mescy), (*b* 1745-*d* Tex., 1825), *m* in N.J., 1765, Daniel **McKinney** (*b* Scotland-*d* McKinney Station, Ky., ante 1824), resided N.J. until 1769 or 70; taken prisoner, 1779, kept in Canada until close of war; removed to Ky., built McKinney Station nr. Old Fort Crab Orchard, ca. 1783-84 (Daniel[8] [*d* 1809], from Scotland, to N.J., ca. 1750, *m* Margit Coffee, *b* Scotland-*d* N.J., 1808);
6–Daniel Younger (*b* N.J., 1769-*d* Tex., 1825), emigrated with his own family, his brother's family, and their aged mother, from (present) Lincoln Co., Ky., to Tex., 1824 (brother, Collin McKinney [1766-1861], famous in Texas history); *m* in Ky., 1794, Margaret McClure (*d* 1825);
5–Martha (Patsy) (*b* Ky., 1801-*d* Tex., 1887), *m* 1st, 1825, William **Collom** (*b* N.C. or Tenn., 1798-killed in Texas revolution, ante Mar. 27, 1838), served War 1812; emigrated to Lost Prairie, Ark., 1818; crossed river to Tex., 1819 (George[6]; Jonathan[7], served in N.C. during Am. Rev.);
4–Mary Ann (1828-57), *m* 1843, John Warren **Curtis** (*b* Tenn., 1819-*d* Mineral Wells, Tex., 1882), to Ark., ca. 1830; to Tex., 1840; 1st white landholder, Parker Co., Tex., was one of the founders of its co. seat, Weatherford; to Calif., in gold rush, returned with fortune; lt., frontier patrol, C.S.A. (Benjamin[5] [*b* N.C. or Tenn., 1801-*d* nr. Fayetteville, Ark., 1865], *m* in Tenn., Margaret Genety [*d* ante 1828]; James[6] killed in War 1812); he *m* 2d, 1858, Mary Ames (1840-1917);
3–William Riley (1846-1902), served C.S.A.; Tex. ranger; pioneer cattleman; *m* 2d, 1869, Alice Victoria Ghormley;
2–Col. James Owen (2 below).
9–Thomas **Tinsley** (*b* Yorkshire, Eng.-*d* Hanover Co., Va., 1700), came with his wife to Va., ante 1650, in which yr. there is a record of a land grant to him on Totopatomoys Creek, then in New Kent (now Hanover) Co., called "Totomoi"; this grant is still in the Tinsley family; *m* Elizabeth (Randolph?);
8–Thomas (*d* 1745), *m* Martha Ragland;
7–Thomas (*d* 1761), *m* Mary–;
6–William (1735-1800), of Hanover Co., Va.; pvt. Am. Rev., received land grant in Tenn. on the Cumberland River for services, which his sons developed, and which is known as Tinsley Bottoms to this day; *m* Jane Geese (1743-99);
5–John (1796-1853), *m* 1816, Alice Mulkey;
4–Elizabeth Jane (1827-92), *m* 1848, Rev. William Calvin **Ghormley** (1823-61), Christian minister; from Tinsley Bottoms, Tenn., to Tex., ca. 1859; *m* 2d, 1862, Dr. D. W. Stone (1822-80);
3–Alice Victoria (1852-1923), *m* William R. **Curtis** (3 above).
13–William **Dennison** (qv);
12–George (*b* Eng., 1618, bap. 1620-*d* Conn., 1694), from Eng. with father, 1631; served Pequot War, 1637; returned to Eng., fought under Cromwell, wounded at Naseby, nursed at home of John Borodell; returned to Conn.; served in King Philip's War as lt. and capt. New London troops; 2d in command in Great Swamp Fight, 1675, served on frontier; chosen with Maj. Mason to assist Pequot chiefs to govern their tribes; magistrate New London, Conn.; settled at Mystic, Conn.; dep. Gen. Ct., from Stonington, Conn., 1654-94; *m* 1640, Bridget Thompson (*d* 1643); *m* 2d, 1645, Ann Borodell (*d* 1712);
11–Ann (1649-94), *m* 1667, Dea. Gershom **Palmer** (1644-1718/19), lt. King Philip's War (Walter[12], qv);
10–Mercy (1668-1752), *m* John **Breed** (*b* 1662; Allen[11], *m* Mary–; Allen[12] qv);
9–Joseph (*b* 1708), from Conn. to N.C., S.C., and Tenn.; friend and asso. of Rev. Philip Mulkey, famous Bapt. minister; *m* 1738, Priscilla Avery;
8–Priscilla (1742-1808), *m* bet. 1755 and 59, Obediah **Howard**, served Am. Rev., in Broudon's Regt., S.C. troops;
7–Nancy, *m* 1772, Rev. Jonathan **Mulkey** (*b* 1752), Am. Rev.; see Vol. III, p. 81, for Mulkey and Helm lineages;
6–Rev. Philip (1775-1844), pioneer Christian minister in Tenn. and Ky.; *m* 1795, Ruth O'dle (1776-1840);
5–Alice (1797-1872), *m* John **Tinsley** (5 above).
13–Christopher **Avery** (qv);
12–Capt. James (1620-1700), founder of clan called "The Groton Averys"; moved to Gloucester to New London, Conn., then Pequot; built and occupied "The Hive of the Averys," Groton, which burned 1894; noted Indian fighter in command of Pequot allies at Narragansett Fort when they defeated the Mohicans; dep. Gen. Ct., New London; *m* 1643, Joanna Greenslade (*b* 1622);
11–James (1646-1728), dep. Gen. Ct., New London, 1696-1702; commr. of peace; lt. and capt. of Train Band; advisor and councillor of Pequot Tribe; *m* 1669, Deborah Stallyon (1651-1729; Edward[12] *m* Margaret–);
10–Capt. Christopher (1679-1753), *m* 1704, Abigail Parke (*d* 1713); *m* 2d, 1714, Prudence (Payson) Wheelock (*b* 1671; John Payson[11], of Roxbury, *m* Bathsheba, dau. of Thomas Tileston [1611-94], at Dorchester, 1636; set out elms in Meeting House Commons in 1676 which were used for gunstocks, 1776; Edward[12], qv);
9–Priscilla (*b* 1715), *m* Joseph **Breed** (9 above).
2–Col. James Owen **Curtis** (*b* 1870), *m* 1891, Carlie Higgins (1872-92); *m* 2d, 1897, Sadie Louise Eppler (*b* 1875); issue (1st marriage): 1–Carlie Fowler (*b* 1892; *m* Grover C. Mayne, 1885-1925); issue (2d marriage): I–Margaret Owen (Mrs. John K. Boyce, see Vol. III, p. 81); II–John William (1901-02); III–Sadie Claudia (*b* 1903; *m* John G. Ballard); IV–James O. (1 above); V–Richard Henry (*b* 1911).
1–U.S.M.A., '30; 2d lt., U.S.A.; with 2d Div. Cav., hdqrs. at Ft. Bliss, Tex. Residence: 1705 Polk St., Amarillo, Tex.

1–**CURTISS, Charles Franklin,** *b* Nora, Ill., Dec. 12, 1863.
9–John (Curtis) **Curtiss** (qv);
8–John, original patentee of Stratford, Conn.; freeman, 1658; ens. King Philip's War; *m* Elizabeth Welles (*d* 1682);
7–Joseph, "Most Worshipful" (*b* 1650), rep., 1671,86, 1689-94; magistrate, 1698, 1701-04; asst., 1698 and 22 successive yrs.; judge Co. Ct.; on com. to locate state boundary, 1700; *m* 1676, Bethia Booth (*b* 1658; Richard[8], qv);
6–Ephraim (1683-1775), *m* 1707, Elizabeth Stiles (1658-1775; Ephraim[7]; Francis[8]);
5–Elnathan (*b* 1726/27), *m* 1745, Sarah Ufford (1728-1814; desc. Thomas Ufford [*d* 1660], from Eng. 1632, to Stratford, Conn., *m* Phoebe Judson);
4–Stiles (1761-1827), of Huntington; *m* 1795, Betsey Hitchcock (1774-75-1816; Daniel[5] [*b* 1751], *m* 1773, Comfort Porter [*d* 1776]; Johnathan[6] [*b* 1701], *m* 1728, Miriam Mallory; Samuel[7]);
3–Morgan (1802-81), *m* 1833, Margaret Owen Curtiss;
2–Franklin (2 below).
7–Ephraim **Curtiss** (same as 6 above);
6–Stiles (*b* 1708), *m* 1730, Rebecca Judson;
5–John (1745-1825), *m* 1769, Mary Shelton (1747-1825);
4–Daniel (1781-1853), *m* 1810, Elizabeth ("Betsey") Pixlee;
3–Margaret Owen (1813-68), of Stratford and Shelton, Conn.; *m* Morgan **Curtiss** (3 above).
9–William (Pixley) **Pixlee** (*d* 1689), one of earliest settlers at Hadley, Mass.; *m* Sarah Lawrence (*d* 1713);
8–William (1669-1712), built ca. 1700, Old Pixley Homestead, Old Mill Green, Stratford, Conn.; *m* Grace Mitchell;
7–Peter (1702-88), *m* Mary Nichols (1707-99);
6–William (1734-1800), *m* 1756, Betty Judson (1737-76);
5–Peter (*b* 1764), *m* 1786, Elizabeth Curtiss;
4–Elizabeth ("Betsey") (1788-1864), *m* Daniel **Curtiss** (4 above);
3–Margaret O., *m* Morgan **Curtiss** (3 above);

2–Franklin (Dec. 6, 1835-Dec. 11, 1919), from Shelton, Conn.; farmer Nevada, Ia.; mem. Ia. Legislature; *m* Oct. 29, 1860, Margaret Schmitz (Nov. 22, 1838-Feb. 26, 1928); issue: I–Charles F. (1 above); II–Fannie (*b* 1867; *m* 1899, Louis B. Craig); III–Effie (*b* 1870; *m* 1900, Frank Howard Campbell); IV–Frederick M. (*b* 1872; *m* 1901, Marion Robb); V–Guy C. (*b* 1876; *m* 1920, Helen Weide); VI–Gertrude (*b* 1879; *m* 1905, Clayton Edward Paxton).
1–*m* Feb. 15, 1893, Olive Wilson, *b* Harper, Ia., Dec. 6, 1864; dau. of John Wilson; issue (all *b* Ames, Ia.): 1–Ruth, *b* May 12, 1894; Ia. State Coll., '17; *m* June 6, 1925, Cornelius John Murray; 2–Edith, *b* Jan. 6, 1896; Ia. State Coll., '18; *m* Apr. 26, 1919, John L. Shugart; 3–Helen, *b* Sept. 14, 1900; Ia. State Coll., '23; *m* Nov. 3, 1926, Gardner Cowles, Jr.
1–B.S., Ia. Agrl. Coll., '87, M.S. Agr., 1894; (hon. D.Sc., Mich. Agrl. Coll., 1907). Agriculturist; dir. Ia. Expt. Sta., and dean div. of agr., Ia. Agrl. Coll. (see Who's Who in America). Mem. Delta Tau Delta, Alpha Zeta, Sigma Xi, Sigma Delta Chi, Gamma Sigma Delta. Clubs: Des Moines, Grant (Des Moines, Ia.), Saddle and Sirloin (Chicago). Conglist. Residence: Ames, Ia.

1–**CURTISS, Lucy Ella,** *b* New Haven, Conn., July 25, 1868.
10–John (Curtis) **Curtiss** (qv);
9–John, of Stratford; *m* Elizabeth Welles (*d* 1682), supposed sister of Gov. Thomas Welles, of Conn.;
8–Capt. Joseph, "Most Worshipful" (*b* 1650, rep., 1671,86, 1689-94; magistrate, 1698, 1701-04; asst., 1698 and 22 successive yrs.; judge Co. Ct.; on com. to locate state boundary, 1700; *m* 1676, Bethia Booth (*b* 1658; Lt. Richard[9]);
7–Joseph (1687-1738/39), *m* 1711, Elizabeth Welles (John, Jr.[8]);
6–Joseph (1721-1801), *m* 1st, 1740, Martha Judson (*d* 1796; James[7], *m* Martha–, of Stratford);
5–Nehemiah (1740-1810), Am. Rev.; *m* 1st, Phebe Welles (*d* 1776, aet. 32; Joseph[6], *m* Martha–);
4–Judson (1768-1828), *m* 1st, Mary Lewis (*d* 1817; Benjamin[5], *m* Elizabeth–);
3–Agur (1811-89), *m* 1837, Mary Olive Hurd (1808-86);
2–Franklin A. (2 below).
9–William **Bunnell** (qv);
8–Benjamin, *m* Rebecca Mallory (Peter[9], *m* Mary Preston);
7–Benjamin (1679-1749), *m* Hannah Plumb;
6–Benjamin (*b* New Haven, Conn., 1704), *m* Mehitable Baldwin;
5–Isaac (1734-1822), pvt. Am. Rev.; *m* Ann Collins (1737-1822);
4–Philemon B. (*b* 1767);
3–Alva (1798-1883), *m* 2d, Widow Lucy (Perkins) Barns (1804-86; Peter Perkins[4], *m* Ascena Beecher);
2–Mary Elizabeth (1843-1911), *m* 1866, Franklin A. **Curtiss** (1842-1928), served in Co. B, 20th Conn. Vols., Civil War.
1–Grad. The Misses Bangs Pvt. Sch., New Haven, 1889. Mem. D.F.P.A., D.A.R. Clubs: Woman's, Garden. Residence: 258 Sherman Av., New Haven, Conn.

1–**CUSHING, Gertrude Waldo Wells (Mrs. William T.),** *b* Milwaukee, Wis., Aug. 18, 1859.
8–Dea. Thomas **Wells** (qv);
7–John (1638-77), of Wells, Me.; *m* 1664, Sarah Littlefield (*b* 1649);
6–Thomas (1672-1737), of Wells; *m* 1704, Lydia Ropes Gale (*b* 1672), a widow;
5–Nathaniel (*b* 1705), of Wells; *m* 1736, Dorothy Light (*b* 1709);
4–Robert (*b* 1743), of Wells; Am. Rev.; *m* 1769, Abigail Jefferds (*b* 1745);
3–Daniel (1774-1867), of Waterville, Me.; *m* 1797, Susanna Sweetser (1780-1820; Richard[4] [1749-1844], Am. Rev., *m* Sarah Matthews);
2–Charles Kimball (2 below).
7–Daniel (Hichens) **Hitchings** (1632-1723), from Eng., settled at Lynn, Mass.; *m* Eleanor– (*d* 1694);
6–Daniel (*d* 1735), Lynn; *m* 1708, Susanna Townsend;
5–Elkanah (1712-61), Lynn; *m* 1741, Phoebe Baldwin (*d* 1759);
4–William (1747-1833), of Lynn, Dorchester and Charlestown, Mass.; Am. Rev.; *m* 1773, Rebecca Davis;
3–Capt. Joseph (1785-1871), of Salem, Mass., and Waterville, Me.; War 1812; *m* 1813, Betsey Combs (1791-1840);
2–Sarah (1830-1904), Waterville, Me.; *m* 1853, Charles Kimball **Wells** (1817-92), grad., Yale, 1842; lawyer; issue: I–Gertrude Waldo (1 above); II–Charles William (1861-97; *m* Cate Gilbert); III–Mary E. (1864-87); IV–Susan P. (*b* 1866); V–Horace H. (1869-88).
1–*m* May 30, 1883, William Tileston Cushing, *b* Boston, Mass., Sept. 3, 1833; son of Tileston Cushing, Jr., of New York, *m* Hannah Dwight; issue: 1–Percy Marks, *b* New York, N.Y., Dec. 12, 1884; *m* Apr. 21, 1907, Josephine, dau. of Dr. Warren B. Chapin, of New York; 2–Mary Wells, *b* Bay Shore, L.I., N.Y., Apr. 11, 1892; Milwaukee Downer Sem.; *m* Nov. 10, 1915, R. S. Parr (issue: William T.); *m* 2d, Mar. 8, 1922, Dr. H. S. Sumerlin (issue: Gertrude W.).
1–Mem. O.C., C.D.A., D.F.P.A., D.A.R., Nat. Soc. of N.E. Women (sec.). Episcopalian. Republican. Clubs: Country (Coronado, Calif.), Social Economics (pres. 3 terms), Woman's (sec.). Legal residence: Milwaukee, Wis.

1–**CUTTER, Gladys Bond Gaston (Mrs. John S.),** *b* Glenwood, Ia., Mar. 22, 1890.
6–Alexander **Gaston** (1714-83; ancestors went from France at time of Huguenot persecutions, to Ireland), came from Ireland, with his brother, John, bet. 1720-24; settled at Richmond, Mass.; *m* Mary Wilson;
5–Alexander (1754-1823), of Berkshire Co., Mass. pvt. Am. Rev.; *m* 1786, Huldah Norton (1765-1832);
4–Heman (1786-1855), *m* 1812, Mary Wheeler (1793-1838);
3–James Kasson (1832-91), of Mills Co., Ia.; *m* 1857, Sarah Jane Cummings (1839-1906);
2–Willard Edgar (2 below).
11–William **Brewster,** Mayflower Pilgrim (qv);
10–Jonathan (1593-1659), mem. Miles Standish Mil. Enrollment, 1643; settled at New London, Conn., 1649; rep. Gen. Ct., Mass.; dep. Conn.; mil. cdr. Pequot War; *m* 1624, Lucretia Oldham (*d* 1678/79);
9–Benjamin (1633-1710), of Duxbury, Mass.; dep. Conn. Gen. Ct., 1689-97; lt. New London Troop, 1673; capt. mil. co., Norwich, 1693; *m* 1653, Ann (Addis) Darte (*d* 1709);
8–Jonathan (1664-1704), of Norwich, Conn.; *m* 1690, Judith Stevens (*b* 1670);
7–Joseph (1698-1770), apptd. lt. 5th Co. of Norwich, 1735; *m* 1723, Dorothy Witter;
6–Joseph (1726-75), commd. ens. 5th co., militia, 1764, Norwich, Conn.; *m* Deborah Avery;
5–Huldah (1767-1828), *m* 1790, Capt. Absolom **Pride** (1756-1844), pvt. Am. Rev., taken prisoner by British several times;
4–Cynthia (1795-1868), *m* 1816, Dr. Dan **King** (1791-1864), of Greenville, R.I.; War 1812;
3–Capt. Charles Phillip (1830-1900), served in Co. G, 8th Wis. Vol. Inf., Civil War; mcht. Glenwood, Ia., 35 yrs.; *m* 1866, Ellen Bethia Thompson (1843-91);
2–Mary Gleason (2 below).
11–Robert **Parke** (qv);
10–Thomas (ca. 1619-1709), from Eng., an incorporator of Preston, Conn.; an extensive landowner; *m* Dorothy Thompson (John[11], *m* Alice–);
9–Dorothy (1652-1704), *m* Lt. Joseph **Morgan** (1646-1704; James[10], qv);
8–Dorothy, *m* Ebenezer **Witter** (1668-1712), from Scotland;
7–Dorothy (1702-79), of Preston, Conn.; *m* Joseph **Brewster** (7 above).
2–Mary Gleason King (*b* Apr. 27, 1867), *m* Sept. 1. 1886, Willard Edgar **Gaston** (*b* Jan. 25, 1862); issue: I–Charles Kasson (June 28, 1887-May 24, 1902); II–Gladys B. (1 above); III–Vernon King (*b* May 30, 1892; *m* Oct. 21, 1915, Elna Green).
1–*m* Feb. 26, 1911, John Sydney Cutter, *b* nr. Coin, Ia., Apr. 30, 1889; son of Charles David Cutter; issue (both *b* Shenandoah, Ia.): 1–John Sydney, *b* Jan. 11, 1912; 2–Carolyn Laurabelle, *b* July 7, 1919.
1–Mem. S.M.D. (historian Ia. State Soc.), D.A.R.

(charter mem. Shen. Chapter), D.U.V., O.E.S., White Shrine of Jerusalem, Daus. of the Nile. Residence: 810 9th Av., Shenandoah, Ia.

1–**DAFFIN, Robert Linwood,** *b* Marianna, Fla., June 20, 1886.
8–John **Dickinson** (1627-1717), from Eng., 1654, settled in Talbot Co., Md.; brother of Walter, of "Croisadore"; *m* 1656, Mary Powell (Thomas[9], *m* Elizabeth Clements);
7–John, planter, landowner, Talbot Co., *m* 1692, Rebecca Wynne (Dr. Thomas[8], qv), widow of Solomon Thomas;
6–Charles (1695-1779), of Dorchester and Caroline cos., Md.; atty.-at-law; capt. militia, Am. Rev.; justice, 1737-53; sheriff, 1755-58; presiding justice 1st co. ct., Caroline Co.; chmn. Comm. of Observation and Inspection, Caroline Co.; judge of Orphans' Ct., 1776-79; *m* 1725, Sophia Richardson (Daniel[7], *m* Elizabeth, dau. of Maj. John Welsh; William[8], *m* Elizabeth, dau. of Col. Richard Ewen, qv, and widow of Richard Talbot, qv);
5–Henry (1740-89), of Caroline Co., Md.; lt., Col. East's Bn., Am. Rev.; signed "Period Proclamation Freemen of Md.," 1775; mem. Provincial Conv. of Caroline Co., 1775; mem. State Constl. Conv., 1776; apptd. treas. Eastern Shore, 1779; *m* 1776, Elizabeth Walker (Rev. Philip[6]); *m* 2d, 1787, Deborah Perry;
4–Rebecca, of Caroline Co., Md.; sister of Lt. Charles Dickinson, U.S.N., killed in duel with Andrew Jackson; *m* 1797, Thomas B. **Daffin,** of "Daffin House," built in 1783, on North Bank of Tuckahoe River;
3–William Richardson (1807-56), of Caroline Co.; with his sister, Charlotte Maria, 2d wife of Dr. Horace Ely (see 4 below), to St. Joseph, Fla., ca. 1837; mcht., St. Joseph, Fla., Eufaula, Ala., and Marianna, Fla., where he *d*; *m* 1840, Mary Jane (Ely) Findley;
2–Ernest Daffin (2 below).
10–Nathaniel **Ely** (qv);
9–Samuel (*d* 1692), of Springfield; *m* 1659, Mary Day (1641-1725; Robert[10]);
8–Dea. John (1678-1758), *m* 1703, Mercy Bliss (1680-1763; Samuel[9], *m* Mary Leonard);
7–Ens. John (1707-54), of W. Springfield; *m* 1733, Eunice Colton (1705-78; John[8], *m* Joanna–);
6–Col. John (1735-1815), of W. Springfield; Am. Rev.; *m* 1758, Dorcas Ely (1735-77; Joseph[7], *m* Margaret Leonard); *m* 2d, Abigail (Montague) Chapin;
5–Horace (1768-1809), of W. Springfield;
4–Dr. Horace (1787-89-1867), of Springfield, Mass., and Marianna, Fla.; M.D., Jefferson Med. Coll., '36; *m* 1811, Mary Jane Gregoire de Roulhac (1792-1835; Psalmet[5], *m* Anne Maule); *m* 2d Charlotte Maria Daffin (1798-1872; sister of William Richardson, 3 above);
3–Mary Jane (1816-82), of Plymouth, N.C., and Marianna, Fla.; *m* Benjamin Findley; *m* 2d, William Richardson **Daffin** (3 above);
2–Ernest Linwood (*b* 1856), merchant, Marianna; *m* 1878, Caroline Godfrey Justiss (1858-1920; John Baker[3], *m* Rhoda Martin); *m* 2d, Elizabeth (Wright) Stephens, widow of Dr. R. Rutledge Stephens (below); issue (1st marriage): I–Elizabeth Thomas (*b* 1879; *m* Joseph Fred Smith); II–Sarah Justiss (*b* 1881; *m* Rev. John W. Lafferty); III–Robert Linwood (1 above); IV–Charles Ernest (*b* 1889; *m* Myrtle Cates); V–John Baker (*b* 1895; *m* Martha Gray); VI–William Godfrey (1897-1904).
1–*m* Sept. 19, 1906, Frances Rutledge Stephens, *b* nr. Blackville, S.C., July 2, 1888; dau. of Dr. R. Rutledge Stephens, *m* Elizabeth Wright (above); issue: 1–Sarah Elizabeth (Sept. 19, 1907-Dec. 12, 1908); 2–Robert Linwood, Jr., *b* Marianna, Fla., Feb. 10, 1911; grad. U.Fla., class 1932 (Pi Kappa Alpha).
1–Broker. With J. W. Russ business and estate since 1900, sec. and Mgr. since 1903. Mem. State Realty Bd., City Council (twice elected). Vestryman St. Luke's Episcopal Church. Residence: Marianna, Jackson Co., Fla.

1–**DAHM, Cora Maud Guthier (Mrs. Thomas M.),** *b* Chicago, Ill., Sept. 29, 1888.
11–Gov. Thomas **Welles** (qv);
10–Thomas (1625-68), *m* 1654, Hannah Tuttle (1632/33-1683; William[11], qv), widow of John Pantry;
9–Rebecca (1655-1717), *m* 1680, James **Judson** (1650-1720/21; Lt. Joseph[10] [1619-90], *m* Sarah [1626-96], dau. of John Porter, qv; William[11], qv);
8–Sarah, *m* 1708, Nathaniel **Chauncey** (see Vol. III, p. 144, for Chauncey lineage);
7–Sarah (*b* 1711), *m* Israel **Burritt** (1687-1774);
6–Israel (1746-1833), capt. Am. Rev.; *m* Hester Holabird (1756-93);
5–Rachel (1788-1854), *m* 1810, Heman **Rowley** (see Vol. III, p. 144, for Rowley lineage);
4–William Burritt (1811-79), *m* 1833, Lura Curry (1813-88; Samuel P.[5] [1781-1869], *m* Anna Woodruff, 1786-1834);
3–Lucy L. (1843-1929), *m* 1864, Richard **Versema** (1843-1903);
2–Helen (1865-1927), *m* 1887, George **Guthier** (*b* 1863; Lorenz[3] [1828-1924], *m* Catherine Knecht, 1828-1905); issue: I–Cora M. (1 above); II–Roy E. (*b* 1890; *m* 1918, Clara Peterson); III–Herbert (*b* 1901).
1–*m* Sept. 1, 1920, Thomas Matthew Dahm, *b* McGregor, Ia., July 28, 1887; A.B., Northwestern, '08 (Phi Beta Kappa, Sigma Xi), A.M., 1909; Ph.D., U.Wis., 1926; 2d lt., C.A.C., World War; asst. prof. physics, 1922-27, asso. prof., acting head physics, U.Idaho, 1927–; issue: 1–Mary Ellen, *b* Madison, Wis., July 31, 1921; 2–Frances Anna, *b* Moscow, Ida., Oct. 13, 1922; 3–Margaret Constance, *b* Moscow, Jan. 6, 1924; 4–James Matthew, *b* Moscow, Sept. 6, 1925; 5–Virginia Josephine, *b* Moscow, Feb. 3, 1928.
1–A.B., Northwestern, '09 (Sigma Xi), A.M., 1910. Was statistician and auditor, Ordnance Dept., U.S.A., Washington, World War. Mem. S.M.D., D.A.R. Residence: Paso Robles, Calif.

1–**DALTON, Caroline Sparrow (Mrs. Robert F.),** *b* Washington, N.C., Jan. 19, 1867.
8–George **Sparrow,** from Eng. to Princess Ann Co., Va.;
7–Smith, of Craven Co., N.C.; *m* Mary Taylor;
6–George, *m* Martha Taylor;
5–Thomas, *m* Rehesa De la Mare;
4–Paul, *m* Ann Jennett;
3–Thomas (1783-1863), *m* Jane Jennette Sparrow (*b* 1788);
2–Thomas (2 below).
10–Thomas **Cornell** (qv);
9–Rebecca, *m* George **Woolsey** (1610-98);
8–Sarah (*b* 1650), *m* 1669, William **Hallett** (1648-1729);
7–Joseph (1678-1758), *m* 1st, 1702, Lydia Blackwell (*d* ante 1728);
6–Joseph (1704-31), *m* 1st, Lydia Alsop;
5–Lydia (*d* 1812), *m* 1755, Col. Jacob **Blackwell** (1732-80);
4–Samuel (1759-1832), *m* 2d, Mary Whitehead (*b* 1767);
3–John (1797-1869), *m* 1821, Ann Selby (*d* 1882);
2–Ann Maria (1822-1901), *m* 1844, Thomas **Sparrow** (1819-84); for issue see Vol. III, p. 351.
1–*m* Jan. 3, 1884, Robert Frank Dalton, *b* Mar. 26, 1857; son of Rev. Pleasant Hunter Dalton, of High Point, N.C.; issue: 1–Carter, *b* Greensboro, N.C., Nov. 9, 1884; ed. U. of N.C. and Harvard; lawyer; *m* Nov. 1916, Mary D. Land (issue: Mary Drew; Caroline Sparrow; Frank, Jr.); 2–Thomas Sparrow, *b* High Point, N.C., Sept. 5, 1887; ed. Bingham Sch. and U. of N.C.; pres. Southern Webbing Mills.
1–Mem. C.D.A., S.D.P., D.A.R., Magna Charta Dames, N.C. Hist. Soc., U.D.C. Residence: 203 Fisher Park Circle, Greensboro, N.C.

1–**DANA, Arnold Guyot,** *b* New Haven, Conn., Aug. 29, 1862.
7–Richard **Dana** (qv);
6–Daniel (1663 or 64-1749), *m* Naomi Croswell;
5–Caleb (1697-1769), *m* Phoebe Chandler;
4–George (1742 or 44-87), *m* Elizabeth Park;
3–James (1780-1860), *m* Harriet Dwight;
2–James Dwight (2 below).
7–Daniel **Silliman** (qv);
6–Robert (ca. 1666-1748), *m* Sarah Hull;
5–Ebenezer (1707-75), speaker Conn. House, 7 yrs., mem. Council, 28 yrs.; *m* 1728, Abigail Selleck (1707-72; Gold[6]; Jonathan[7]; Jonathan[8]; David[9]);
4–Gold Selleck (1732-90), B.A., Yale, 1752; brig. gen. Am. Rev.; *m* 2d, 1775, Mary (Fish) Noyes (1736-1818; Rev. Joseph Fish[5], *m* 1732, Rebecca,

dau. of William Peabody, g.dau. of William Peabody, *m* Elizabeth, dau. of John Alden, qv; Thomas[6]);
3–Benjamin, M.D., LL.D. (1779-1864), B.A., Yale, 1796; eminent chemist and geologist; prof. at Yale; *m* 1st, 1809, Harriet Trumbull;
2–Henrietta Frances (1823-1907), *m* 1844, James Dwight **Dana** (1813-95), B.A., Yale, '33; distinguished geologist; prof. at Yale; author; explorer (Wilkes Expdn.); recipient of the Wollaston and Copley medals; mem. highest learned bodies at London, Paris, Berlin, Vienna, Rome, Petrograd, pres. A.A.A.S.; etc.; issue: I–Frances H. (1846-1924; *m* George Douglas Coit); II–Edward Salisbury (See Vol. I, p. 576); III–Arnold Guyot (1 above); IV–Maria Trumbull (*b* 1867).
1–*m* Oct. 24, 1888, Grace Newton, *b* Brooklyn, N.Y., May 22, 1863; dau. of Albro J. Newton, of Brooklyn; issue: 1–Henrietta Silliman, *b* Sept. 15, 1889; Smith, '12; *m* Apr. 25, 1914, Thomas Denison Hewitt (issue: Katharine Dana, *b* July 5, 1918; Thomas Browning, *b* Sept. 1, 1921); 2–Katharine Trumbull, *b* July 20, 1896; Smith, '19; *m* June 18, 1921, Philip Henry English; 3–Albro Newton, *b* Brooklyn, N.Y., Dec. 4, 1898; Yale, '20; *m* Jan. 28, 1922, Katharine, dau. Judge Severyn Bruyn Sharpe (issue: Severyn Sharpe, *b* Nov. 30, 1923; Arnold Guyot II, *b* Sept. 24, 1926).
1–B.A., Yale, '83; with William B. Dana & Co., and sec., dir. of its successor, The William B. Dana Co., pubs., Commercial and Financial Chronicle, New York, 1887-1922; also on its editorial staff and editor of investment news dept. and mng. editor ry. and industrial sect.; in Europe, 1922-23; since engaged in financial research work. Author: American Responsibility for World Reconstruction, 1926; Porto Rico's Case, 1928; and in preparation, American "Prosperity" (so called) and its effects at home and abroad, embracing with other matter, a series of articles entitled, Is not Mass speculating a conspiracy making for sham prosperity?, which were pub. in the Chronicle, 1928-29. Club: Graduates. Residence: 21 Mansfield St., New Haven, Conn.

1–**DANIEL, John,** *b* Perry Co., Ala., July 6, 1862.
7–Capt. William **Daniel** (qv);
6–Robert (*d* 1720), justice of Middlesex, 1706; *m* 1687, Margaret Price (*b* 1670; Robert[7], *m* Jane–);
5–James (ca. 1709-60), bought land in Goochland (now Cumberland) Co., Va.; also land in Albemarle Co.; *m* 1725, Jane Hicks;
4–Abraham (*b* 1735), of Cumberland Co.; *m* Mary Smith;
3–Leonard (1765-1855), *m* Mary Spears (1770-1855; William[4] [*d* 1813], of Cumberland Co.);
2–John (2 below).
8–Christopher **Boroughs** (*b* 1612), from Eng., 1635; settled Norfolk Co., Va.; burgess from Princess Anne Co., Va.;
7–William, of Surry Co., Va.;
6–Zaccheus, of Brunswick Co., Va.; *m* —Dobson;
5–James, of Va.; *m* Anne Bryan; they removed to Orange Co., N.C.;
4–Bryan (1774-1850), of Moore Co., N.C.; *m* 1794, Sarah Waddell (1779-1851; Edmund[5] [1748-1815], of Chatham Co., N.C., Am. Rev., mem. Gen. Assembly, Commr., trustee, justice, *m* 1770, Lucy, dau. of John Birdsong [1725-89], of Chatham Co., N.C., Am. Rev., mem. Com. of Safety, Provincial Assembly, Constl. Conv.);
3–Mary (1794-1868), *m* 1818, Freeman **Winfield** (1791-1839);
2–Susan Lee (1819-1910), *m* 1838, John **Daniel** (1807-63); issue: I–Mary (1839-42); II–Julia (1843-72); III–Sue (*b* 1846; *m* Dr. J. F. Walker); IV–Sallie (*b* 1848; *m* Willis H. Edwards); V–Mattie (1849-1911); VI–Ellen (*b* 1851); VII–Maggie (*b* 1854); VIII–Freeman (1856-1913; *m* Tommie E. Bozeman); IX–Minnie (*b* 1859; *m* A. V. Mathis); X–John (1 above).
1–*m* Sept. 2, 1896, Grace Olive Knight, *b* Dalton, Ga., Feb. 15, 1875; dau. of Ray Knight, of Ill., Ga. and Ala.; issue: 1–Landon Garland, *b* Birmingham, Ala., July 26, 1897; 2–Ray Knight, *b* Nashville, Tenn., Oct. 20, 1899; 3–John, *b* Nashville, Jan. 19, 1903; 4–Harben Winfield, *b* Nashville, Aug. 6, 1906; 5–Robert Bradley (1909-14); 6–Grace Olive, *b* Nashville, Oct. 15, 1911.
1–A.B., U. of Ala., '84 (Phi Delta Theta, P.B.K.), A.M., 1885 (LL.D., 1914); studied Johns Hopkins U., 1886-88, U.Berlin, 1892. Prof. physics, Vanderbilt U., since 1894. Discovered depilatory effect of X-Ray (see Who's Who in America). Residence: 2500 Belair Av., Nashville, Tenn.

1–**DANIEL, Willie Smith Erwin (Mrs. William Madison),** *b* Cross Bridges, Tenn., Jan. 20, 1877.
6–Joseph **Erwin** (1729-73), of Pa.; removed to S.C.; *m* 1748, Agnes–;
5–Joseph (1759-1846), of N.C.; *m* 1782, Catherine Cowan;
4–Joseph (1794-1848), of La.; *m* 1816, Elizabeth Rogers;
3–Alexander Rogers, D.D. (1820-60), Methodist minister; *m* 1838, Louisa Boyd;
2–Joseph Boyd (2 below).
5–William **Edmiston** (1734-80), of Va.; soldier in French and Indian War and Am. Rev.; killed in battle of King's Mountain; *m* 1762, Elizabeth–;
4–Martha (1772-1859), of Va. and Tenn.; *m* 1794, William G. **Boyd** (1767-1839), assisted in laying off the old town of Franklin, Tenn.;
3–Louisa (1823-63), of Tenn.; *m* Alexander Rogers **Erwin** (3 above).
6–Henry **Foster** (1730-97), capt. S.C. Light Dragoons, in Am. Rev.; *m* 1754, Ann Dunlap, of Ashire, Scotland;
5–Anne (1769-1806), *m* 1784, William **White**;
4–Ruth (1784-1858), *m* 1799, Henry **Smith** (1780-1858), of N.C.; War 1812;
3–William Pryor (1818-1904), soldier C.S.A.; *m* 1844, Louisa Dean;
2–Frances Caldonia (2 below).
5–Joseph **Wilson** (*b* 1726), of Va.; in Va. line in Am. Rev.; *m* 1751, Martha Webster (*b* 1732);
4–Eleanor (1774-1858), of Va.; *m* Greenberry **Dean** (1775-1859; Richard[5], of Va., *m* Elizabeth Ferguson);
3–Louisa (1818-97), of Tenn.; *m* William Pryor **Smith** (3 above);
2–Frances Caldonia (*b* 1846), *b* Marshall Co., Tenn.; *m* 1868, Joseph Boyd **Erwin** (1846-1917), D.D.; Methodist minister; issue: I–Alexander Rogers (*b* 1870; *m* Mollie Matthews; *m* 2d, Mona Goodpasture); II–Louisa Eleanor (*b* 1874); III–Willie Smith (1 above); IV–Mary Josephine (*b* 1879; *m* McReynolds Hanner); V–Archie Rison, M.D. (*b* 188?; *m* Nellie Gee); VI–Porter M. (1885-1907; *m* Dr. M. J. Ferguson).
1–*m* Oct. 17, 1899, William Madison Daniel, *b* Clarksville, Tenn., Dec. 20, 1874; son of William Madison Daniel, of Clarksville; issue (all *b* Clarksville): 1–Frances Erwin (Feb. 3, 1902-July 6, 1902); 2–Eleanor Erwin, *b* June 15, 1903; ed. Randolph-Macon; *m* Apr. 15, 1926, Clarence W., son of Clarence Wellington Hussey, of Memphis, Tenn. (issue: Eleanor Erwin); 3–William Madison, *b* Feb. 23, 1916.
1–Ed. Nashville Coll. for Young Ladies. Mem. C.D.A., D.A.R., U.D.C., The King's Daughters (Tenn. state pres., 1925-30). Home service with A.R.C., and Council Nat. Defense, Army and Navy League, during World War. Trustee Madison St. M.E. Ch.; pres. bd. Clarksville Lib. Bd.; 1st v.p. Federation of Women's Clubs. Democrat. Residence: 316 Madison St., Clarksville, Tenn.

1–**DARBY, Milton Miller,** *b* Fairchance, Pa., July 29, 1891.
9–(probably) Ezra **Darby,** from Eng., 1620, settled probably in N.J.;
8–William, of Scotch Plains, N.J.; *m* Elizabeth–;
7–Dea. William (1693-1775) of Scotch Plains; *m* Mary– (1699-1761);
6–Samuel (1730-ante 1774), of Scotch Plains;
5–Samuel (1752-1850), of N.J. and Va.; pvt. in Am. Rev.; *m* Hannah Darby (1760-1850);
4–Samuel (1785-1848), of Pa.; *m* Elizabeth Benson (1790-1853; William O.[5], of Va., Am. Rev.);
3–Harrison Hagan (1832-1916), of Pa.; *m* Nancy Elizabeth Huntley (1830-1908; Robert[4]; Stoddard[5]; David[6]);
2–John Littleton (*b* 1867), poultryman, of Pa.; *m* 1890, Mary Alice Miller (*b* 1870); issue: I–

Milton Miller (1 above); II–Fred McKinley (*b* 1893); III–Helen May (*b* 1897); IV–Ralph (*b* and *d* 1904); V–Rixie Frances (*b* 1907); VI–John Littleton, Jr. (1909-17); VII–Robert Huntley (*b* 1914).
1–*m* Sept. 29, 1913, Mary Diana Smiley, *b* Fayette Co., Pa., Sept. 28, 1895; dau. of Jefferson Nixon Smiley, of Fairchance, Pa., *m* Mary Dunn; issue: 1–Mary Virginia, *b* Fairchance, Pa., June 26, 1916; 2–Frances Jane, *b* Fairchance, Aug. 8, 1923.
1–Retail lumber and building supplies and contracting, 1919-24; real estate and insurance, since 1924. Mem. I.A.G. Presbyterian. Republican. Residence: 86 Morgantown St., Fairchance, Pa.

1–**DARLING, Sarah Jane Andrews (Mrs. Dwight),** *b* Duxbury, Vt., Oct. 8, 1862.
9–John **Andrews** (*d* 1681), from Eng.; settled Tunxis (now Farmington), Conn., 1640; *m* Mary– (*d* 1694);
8–John (1645-1713), of Hartford, Conn.;
7–Stephen, of Glastonbury, Conn.; *m* 1705, Sarah Gillet;
6–Elisha (1706-50), of E. Glastonbury; *m* 1726, Ruth–;
5–Elisha (1730-1813), *m* Jerusha Keeney (ca. 1737 or 1738-1825), of Eastbury, Conn.;
4–Elijah (1758-1826), of Eastbury; Am. Rev.; *m* 1782, Mabel Fox (1762-1846);
3–Ira (1789-1863), capt. Vt. militia; *m* 1810, Abigail Black (1789-1864), of Berlin, Vt.;
2–Jacob Dutton (1826-94), farmer; *m* 1853, Rebecca Jane Freeman (1820-1904); issue: I–Abbie Lucretia (1859-1925; *m* 1st, Warren Palmer; *m* 2d, Fred F. Wilder); II–Sarah Jane (1 above); III–George J. D. (1868-1916).
1–*m* June 10, 1885, Dwight Darling (*b* Berlin, Vt., Apr. 19, 1859-*d* 1896); son of Andrew Jackson Darling, of Berlin, Vt.; issue: 1–Blanche Levina, *b* Chicago, Ill., July 4, 1892; grad. Smith, '14; *m* Oct. 31, 1917, Albert R., son of P. Bergesen, of Leland, Ill. (issue: Rebecca D., *b* Aug. 18, 1920; Dorothy D., *b* Oct. 7, 1926; Karen Louise, *b* May 29, 1929).
1–Mem. D.F.P.A., D.A.R. Residence: 65 E. State St. Montpelier, Vt.

1–**DARNEAL, Lulie Leigh Otey (Mrs. Hervey),** *b* Franklin Co., Va., June 17, 1852.
5–Col. John **Otey** (desc. chief high chamberlain, of James, II), served in Am. Rev.;
4–John Hopkins;
3–John Buford, *m* Angeline Middleton Browne;
2–James C. (2 below).
8–William **Claiborne** (qv); see Claiborne coat of arms, Vol. III, p. 152;
7–Lt. Col. Thomas (1647-83), of "Romancoke"; *m* Sarah Fenn (Capt. Sam[8]);
6–Capt. Thomas (1680-1732), of "Sweet Hall," King William Co.; *m* 3d, Ann Fox;
5–Col. Nathaniel, of "Sweet Hall"; *m* Jane Cole (William[6], of Warwick Co., Va.);
4–William (*d* 1809), of Manchester, Va.; *m* Mary Leigh (Ferdinand[5], of King William Co., Va.);
3–Nathaniel Herbert (1777-1859), of Franklin Co., Va.; mem. both branches of Va. Legislature; mem. Council during War of 1812; mem. Congress, 1825-37; *m* 1815, Elizabeth Archer Binford, of Goochland Co. Va.;
2–Elizabeth Herbert (2 below).
9–Col. John **West** (qv);
8–Hon. Col. John (1632-89), of "West Point," Va.; burgess, 1685; col. in Bacon's Rebellion; *m* Unity Croshaw (Maj. Joseph[9], of York Co., burgess, 1658);
7–Ann, *m* Henry **Fox,** of King William Co.;
6–Ann (1684-1733), *m* as his 3d wife, Capt. Thomas **Claiborne** (6 above).
2–James Coleman **Otey,** of Bedford Co., Va.; surveyor; *m* 1850, Elizabeth Herbert Claiborne (1829-55).
1–*m* Feb. 14, 1870, Hervey Darneal (Apr. 1840-Dec. 31, 1914); son of Dr. Walter Darneal, of Ky., *m* Susan Mary, dau. of William David Hubbell, of Columbia, Boone Co., Mo., *m* Eliza E., dau. of Capt. John Price, of Franklin Co., Ky.; issue: 1–Bettie Herbert (Mar. 11, 1871-July 29, 1877); 2–Hervey Kent (Dec. 4, 1873-July 22, 1877); 3–Susan Cole, *b* San Francisco, Calif., Jan. 23, 1878; *m* June 25, 1910, William Hayden Talbot; 4–Herbert Claiborne, *b* San Francisco, Jan. 17, 1880; 5–Hervey Otey, *b* Alameda, Calif., June 19, 1883; *m* Paris, France, Oct. 29, 1918, Marie Louise Germaine, dau. of Henri Roy, of Avallon, France; 6–Lulie Leigh (July 23, 1890-Feb. 17, 1892).
1–Mem. C.D.A., D.C.G., O.C., Magna Charta Dames, Huguenot Soc. of the Founders of Manakin in the Colony of Va., U.D.C., Inst. Am. Genealogy (life). Residence: 903 Grand St., Alameda, Calif.

1–**DAVENPORT, Lizzie Harley Able (Mrs. George D.),** *b* Rish's Store, Lexington Co., S.C., Jan. 10, 1878.
4–Jeremiah (Abell) **Able** (1746-1811; prob. desc. from Robert Abell, who came from Eng. prob. in Gov. Winthrop's Fleet to Mass.), his parents came to Va. ca. 1750; settled in Pendleton Dist., nr. Abbeville, S.C., ante 1790; *m* 2d, 1786, Elizabeth Roberts (*b* 1761);
3–Absalom Robert (1793-1859), *m* 2d, 1841, Matilda (Gibson) Murdock (1812-54; Moses Gibson[4] [*d* 1815], *m* 1811, Nancy Davenport, 1796-1844);
2–Dr. Absalom Robert (2 below).
5–Jacob **Long** (1742-99), he or his parents came from Holland and settled at Saxe Gothe Section, now known as Hollow Creek Section, Lexington Co., S.C.; served in Water's Regt. of militia of S.C. during Am. Rev.; was in Battle of King's Mountain and many battles in northern Va. and S.C.; *m* 1766, Mahala Elizabeth Minnich (1744-90);
4–Barbara (1772-1862), *m* 1805, John (Reich) **Rish** (1773-1846), of Hollow Creek Section (Adam[5], from Holland, Am. Rev.);
3–Levi (1815-75), Rish's Store P.O., Lexington Co.; served in Seminole War, 1835-42; home commr. officer and miller, War bet. the States, 1861-65; *m* 1838, Malissa (Abell) Able (1815-70; Asel R.[4] [1791-1827], *m* Elizabeth [*b* 1791], sister of John Rish, above; Jeremiah[5], above);
2–Elizabeth (1848-1918), *m* 1867, Dr. Absalom Robert **Able** (1850-1926), Edgefield Village, S.C.; M.D., U.Ga.; clk. of Lexington and Orangeburg Bapt. Assn.; organizer and sec. Bd. of Health, St. Matthews over 35 yrs.; sec. St. Matthews Dem. Club over 40 yrs.; past chancellor K.P.; Mason; issue: I–Lawrence Morse, M.D. (*m* Laura Pauline Spigener); II–Eugene Walter (*m* Cornelia Gunter); III–Lora Bertha (educator); IV–Lizzie Harley (1 above); V–Lucia Bee (educator); VI–Albert Seaman (officer U.S.N.R.C., fleet service, chief pay clk. and paymaster, 1917-1918, asst. supply and distributing officer, 6th Naval Dist. Hdqrs., Charleston, S.C., super cargo officer on merchant marine of a U.S. ship, 1919; *m* Elizabeth Eisenmann); VII–Robert Herman (*d* infancy).
1–*m* as his 2d wife, Oct. 21, 1928, George David Davenport (*b* 1869), of Johnston, S.C. (Moses Belton[2] [1848-1902], *m* 1866, Mikell Elliott Huiett [1848-1921]; Moses Belton[3] [*b* 1808], *m* —Galloway; William[4] [1784-1833], *m* Nancy Davenport Gibson, 1796-1844).
1–Registrar of vital statistics for S.C., St. Matthews and Amelia Dist., Calhoun Co. Red Cross service badge and certificate for service during World War; chmn. miscellaneous supplies for Calhoun Co. Mem. D.A.R. (past regent and treas. William Thomas Chapter, now state chmn. of geneal. research), U.D.C. (v.p., historian and registrar, St. Matthews Chapter), O.E.S. (past worthy matron); sec. and past pres. Women's Missionary Soc.; sec., treas. Ladies Aid Soc. of Bapt. Ch.; dir. West Eng. Cemetery Assn.; past sec. and treas., Calhoun Co. Public Library Assn. Residence: St. Matthews, S.C., and Johnston, S.C.

1–**DAVIDSON, Nettie May Adams (Mrs. William M.),** *b* Atlanta, Ill., Oct. 20, 1864.
6–Samuel **Adams,** with wife settled in what is now Fayette Co., Pa., as early as 1771; (were undoubtedly of Scotch-Irish descent); *m* Catharine–;
5–Robert (ca. 1743-1806), 2d maj., 3d bn., Westmoreland (now Fayette) Co. militia; *m* Elizabeth–;
4–Robert (ca. 1769-1817), early settler in Chillicothe, O.; *m* Patience Hull;

3–Dr. Elijah (1806-50), *m* Lydia Louisa Hunt;
2–Robert James (2 below).
10–Rev. Joseph **Hull** (qv);
9–Capt. Benjamin (1639-post 1707), of Hingham, Mass., and Piscataway, N.J.; *m* Rachel York (Richard[10]);
8–Ens. Benjamin (1680-1732), of Piscataway; *m* Sarah Drake (Rev. John[9]; Capt. Francis[10]);
7–Judge Joseph (1706-ante 1768), of Piscataway; *m* Susannah Stelle (Rev. Benjamin[8]; Poncet[9]);
6–Isaac (1731-post 1808), q.-m. in Am. Rev.; *m* Anne Dunham (John[7]; Benajah[8]; Edmond[9]; Benajah[10]; John[11]);
5–Isaac (1753-post 1808), Am. Rev.; to Mason Co., Ky., ca. 1789; *m* Massie Vaughan (William[6]);
4–Patience (1776-1852), *m* Robert **Adams** (4 above).
7–Robert **Hunt,** went to Cumberland Co., N.J., ca. 1700; *m* Rebecca Ayars (Isaac[8]; Robert[9]);
6–Bartholomew, *m* Mrs. Margaret (Booth) Wood;
5–John (*d* 1787), Am. Rev.; mem. Greenwich, N.J., "Tea Party"; *m* Anne Brewster (see Vol. III, p. 151, for Brewster lineage);
4–John (1787-1847), settled in Springfield, O., ca. 1812; *m* Sarah Foster;
3–Lydia Louisa (1814-50), *m* Elijah **Adams** (3 above).
10–Christopher **Foster** (1603-87), from Eng. in the "Abigail," 1635; settled in Lynn; removed to L.I., 1642; admitted a resident, Southampton, 1649; *m* in Eng., Frances–;
9–Nathaniel (1633-ante 1713), of Huntington, L.I.; *m* Sarah–;
8–Samuel (*d* ca. 1721), lived in Fairfield and Cape May, N. J.;
7–Jeremiah (1704-86), of Deerfield, N.J.; *m* Patience Sayre (Ephraim[8]; Daniel[9]; Thomas[10]);
6–Ezekiel (1729-88), maj. in Am. Rev.; *m* Martha Austin (Cornelius[7]; John[8]);
5–Ezekiel (1759-1821), Am. Rev.; *m* Hannah Preston (Col. Isaac[6]; Isaac[7]; Levi[8]; Roger[9]);
4–Sarah (1788-1832), *m* John **Hunt** (4 above).
10–Richard (Ormsbee) **Ormsby** (1608-44), "planter"; of Saco, Salisbury, Haverhill, and Rehoboth; *m* Sarah–;
9–John (1641-1718), of Rehoboth, Mass.; mem. Gallup's Co., in Phipps' Expdn. against Quebec, 1690; *m* Grace Martin (Richard[10]);
8–John (1667-1728), of Rehoboth, Mass., and Norwich, Conn.; *m* Susannah–;
7–John (1704-66), of Norwich and Canterbury, Conn.; *m* Mehitable Way (George[8]; George[9]);
6–Ezekiel (*b* 1738), Am. Rev.; *m* Sarah Coburn (Samuel[7]; Edward[8]; Robert[9]);
5–Jeremiah (1758-1826), of Hampton, Conn., and Pawlet, Vt.; *m* Lucy Lillie (Jonathan[6]; Elisha[7]; George[8]; George[9]);
4–John (1787-1847), of Hampton, Conn., and Windsor Co., Vt.; *m* Lora Amelia Flint (Mason[5] [1763-1808], *m* Mary Bingham, see Vol. III, p. 151, for Bingham, Bradford lineages; Bartholomew[6]; Joshua[7]; John[8]; Thomas[9]);
3–Charles Huntington (1809-82), to Springfield, Ill., 1833; *m* Cornelia Low;
2–Helen Lucretia (1836-82), *m* Robert James **Adams** (see Vol. III, p. 151, for portrait, biography, and issue).
1–*m* July 11, 1888, William Mehard Davidson, *b* Jamestown, Pa., May 8, 1863; (see Vol. III, p. 151, for genealogy); issue: 1–Helen Mehard, *b* Topeka, Kan., Sept. 14, 1890; Vassar, '14; Columbia; with A.E.F., World War.
1–Ed. pub. schs. and normal sch. Mem. S.M.D., C.D.A., H.S.A., D.A.R., I.A.G. Clubs: Twentieth Century, Woman's City. Residence: 6814 Thomas Boul., Pittsburgh, Pa.

1–**DAVIS, Harriet Woodward (Mrs. Caleb Forbes),** *b* Eau Claire, Wis., July 22, 1874.
9–Hon. Matthias **Nicoll** (qv);
8–William (1657-1723), from Islip, Northamptonshire, Eng., 1664; settled at N.Y.; patentee of Islip, 1683; clk. Queen's Co., 1683-88; mem. Council, 1691-98; speaker Colonial Assembly, 1702-18; atty. gen., 1687-90; *m* 1693, Anne Van Rensselaer (1663-1716; Col. Jeremias[9] [1629-74], 2d Patroon);
7–Benjamin (1694-1724), of Islip, L.I.; *m* 1714, his cousin, Charity Floyd (1692-1758; Col. Richard[8], *m* Margaret, dau. of Matthias Nicoll, 9 above);
6–Benjamin (1718-60), of Islip, grad. Yale, 1734; clk. Westchester Co., N.Y., 1746; incorporator, gov. and trustee, King's Coll., 1751-60; *m* 1746, Mary Magdalen Holland (1727-66; Edward[7], commr. Indian affairs, mem. Colonial Council; Capt. Henry[8], high sheriff, commr. Indian affairs);
5–Dr. Samuel (1754-96), U.Edinburgh, 1776; completed medical studies in Paris; received at court of Louis XVI; prof. chemistry, Columbia U.; *m* 1782, his 2d cousin, Anne Fargie (1764-92; Capt. Winter[6], *m* Eve Holland);
4–Frances Mary (1785-1861), of Stratford, Conn.; *m* 1809, George Bloom **Evertson** (1773-1829);
3–Frances Mary (1811-99), of Poughkeepsie, N.Y.; *m* 1828, William Amos **Woodward** (1801-83);
2–Francis William (2 below).
8–Robert **Livingston** (qv);
7–Philip (1686-1749), of New York; 2d Lord of Manor of Livingston; sec. Indian affairs, 1722; clk. Co. of Albany, 1721-49; mem. Provincial Council, 1724-49; *m* 1707, Catherine Van Brugh (*d* 1756; Peter[8]);
6–William (1723-90), grad. Yale, 1741, LL.D., 1788; apptd. brig. gen., 1775, and was made cdr.-in-chief of N.J. militia, 1776; first gov. of state of N.J., Aug. 31, 1776, and continued to hold office 14 yrs. till his death; *m* ca. 1745, Susanna French (bap. 1723-1789);
5–William (1755-1817), pvt. Union Co., N.J. Militia, Am. Rev.; admitted to bar, Union Co., N.J., 1780; *m* Mary Lenington;
4–Jane Anne (*b* 1783), *m* 1806, Joseph **Delaplaine** (*b* 1777);
3–George Patton (*b* 1814), of Philadelphia, Pa.; *m* Emeline Smith;
2–Ann Jay (1842-1917), of Madison, Wis.; *m* 1862, Francis William **Woodward** (*b* Ithaca, N.Y., 1830-1908), pub. horticultural magazine, New York (asso. with bro.); to Eau Claire, Wis., 1869; in lumber business; officer Bank of Eau Claire; owner, large wheat farm in Minn.; issue: I–Mary Delaplaine (Nov. 24, 1863-Feb. 17, 1893; *m* Charles G. Strong); II–Harriet (1 above).
1–*m* Oct. 18, 1899, Caleb Forbes Davis, Jr., *b* Keokuk, Ia., Apr. 15, 1871; son of Caleb Forbes Davis, of Keokuk; issue: 1–Caleb Forbes, III, *b* Keokuk, Ia., Aug. 24, 1901; grad. U.Washington, 1925, in elec. engring.; 2–Esther Woodward, *b* Keokuk, Dec. 15, 1904; B.A., Mills Coll., 1926.
1–Mem. C.D.A., D.A.R. Episcopalian. Republican. Residence: 3608 Schubert Pl., Seattle, Wash.

1–**DAVIS, James Madison (James M. F. Davis),** *b* Williamson Co., Ill., June 1, 1877.
7–Morgan **David** (ca. 1622/23-1694/95), *b* Lantwidvoyrde, Glamorganshire, S. Wales; Pembrokeshire, South Wales to Merion Tp., Pa., ca. 1684; *m* (late in life in Wales), Catherine–(*d* 1741), who *m* 2d, 1697, Evan Harry (*d* 1718/19), *m* 3d, James Thomas, and *d* a widow in Pencader Hundred, New Castle Co., Del.;
6–Evan, Sr. (1685/86-1748), *m* 1st, 1711/12, Jane–(*d* 1723); from Merion Tp., Pa., to New Castle Co., Del., ca. 1723; *m* 2d, 1724, Jane, dau. of Watkin Morgan and g.dau. of John Morgan;
5–David (1717-ca. 1793), began to write name **Davis;** from Merion Tp., Pa., with parents, ca. 1723, to New Castle Co., Del.; to Craven Co. (later Marion Dist.), S.C., 1739; served in Lyttleton's campaign, 1759-60, against the Cherokees in French and Indian War and in the S.C. militia 1775-80 against Tory and British raids in Am. Rev.; *d* Cheraw Dist. now Chesterfield Co., S.C.; *m* 1738, Jane Miles (bap. 1720-ante 1772);
4–James (Francis) (1743-ca. 1808-09), *b* Craven (now Marion) Co., S.C.; to Anson (later divided into Mecklenburg) Co., N.C., ca. 1762; thence to Tryon Co., N.C., ca. 1768-69, and again to Mecklenburg Co., N.C., ante 1784; to Ky., ca. 1791-92, and *d* in Lincoln Co.; pvt., Capt. Bowman's Co., 1st N.C. Cont. Line in Am. Rev.; *m* 1st, ante Oct. 1765, Margaret–(*d* ante 1779); *m* 2d, ante 1779, Jane (or Jean)–(ca. 1762-post 1840), who migrated from N.C. to Ky. and thence to Miss.;
3–William (1780-1860), *b* in Mecklenburg Co., N.C.; to Ky., with parents, ca. 1791-92; re-

sided in Lincoln Co., Ky., 1810, Madison Co., Ky., ante 1820-30, Obion Co., Tenn., 1830-ca. 1837, thence to Mo.; resided in Perry Co., Mo., 1850 and ante 1860 to Williamson Co., Ill. where he *d*; father of 20 children; pvt., Capt. Martin H. Wickliffe's Co., Col. Henry Remick's Regt., Ky. Mounted Vols. in War 1812, Aug. 24-Nov. 11, 1813; *m* 1st ca. 1808, Elizabeth Carter; he *m* 2d, Martha– (1810-post 1870), mother of 6 children;

2–Thomas Rush (2 below).

11–Sir William **Skipwith** (*d* 1610), for Skipwith ancestral lines see Vol. II, p. 370, under Landis; knighted by King James, Apr. 30, 1603; *m* 1st, Margaret (*d* 1594), dau. of Roger Cave, Esq., of Northampton, *m* Margaret, sister of William Cecil, lord high treas. of Eng.;

10–Sir Henry (*b* 1589), of Prestwould; knighted at Whitehall, July 19, 1609; created baronet, Dec. 20, 1622; *m* Amy, dau. of Sir Thomas Kempe, knight (*d* 1607), *m* Dorothie Thompson;

9–Lady Diana (*b* ca. 1625), to Va., 1649-50 with her husband, Maj. Edward **Dale** (qv);

8–Katherine (1652-1703), *m* ante 1670, as his 2d wife, Capt. Thomas **Carter,** Sr. (1630/31-1700), for Carter ancestral lines see Vol. II, p. 370, under Landis; he came from Eng. to Nansemond Co., Va., 1650; later of "Barford," Lancaster Co., Va.; purchased a large plantation on the Rappahannock River; commr. Lancaster Co. Ct., 1663; dep., 1663-65; burgess, 1667; vestryman Christ Ch. and St. Mary's; capt. Lancaster militia, 1667;

7–Capt. Thomas, Jr. (1672-1733), capt. Va. militia, Dec. 12, 1705-May 14, 1729; justice for Lancaster Co. continuously for 24 yrs.; *m* 1690, Arabella Williamson;

6–Peter, I (1706-89), *d* Fauquier Co., Va.; *m* 1730, Judith Norris (*d* 1785);

5–Peter, II (1743-91), of Amherst Co., Va.; pvt. Va. arty. militia in Am. Rev.; *m* 1763-64, Mary Ann Ellis (*b* 1747), removed from Amherst Co., Va., to Lincoln Co., Ky., with her children, 1796, and *d* there (Charles[6], *m* Susannah Harding);

4–Peter, III (1766-67-post 1837), of Amherst Co., Va.; *m* 1st, ante 1785, Delphia (*d* 1785-86), dau. of Larkin Sandridge, of Va.; *m* 2d, ca. 1787, Ann Martin (*d* ca. 1790); *m* 3d, ante 1793-94, Elizabeth Hamilton, of Va. who migrated with him ca. 1796 to Lincoln Co., Ky.;

3–Elizabeth (1793-94-ca. 1840), from Amherst Co., Va., with parents, ca. 1796, to Lincoln Co., Ky.; *m* William **Davis** (3 above);

2–Thomas Rush (1832-1917), from Obion Co., Tenn., with parents, ca. 1837 to Mo.; resided in Jackson Co., Ill., 1850, thence to Williamson Co., Ill., ca. 1855, where he *d*; served in Civil War, Co. E, 60th Ill. Vol. Inf., Jan. 15, 1862-Feb. 22, 1865; *m* 1st, 1855, Sinderella (Cinderilla) Young (1837-91), dau. of Rachel Young; *m* 2d, ca. 1893-94, a widow Brown (divorced her); *m* 3d, 1896, Nancy Catherine Franklin (a widow); issue (1st marriage): I–William Asbury (1856-75); II–Mary Elizabeth (*b* 1858; *m* 1876, Joseph Washington Stover, *b* 1857); III–John Ambrose (1859-73); IV–Samantha Rachel (1861-98; *m* 1881, John Hill Hearne, *b* 1863); V–George Carroll (1868-74); VI–Ella Margaret (1870-1900; *m* 1894, Robert Othmel Broadway, 1868-1925); VII–James Madison (1 above).

1–*m* ca. Apr. 10, 1899, at Jonesboro, Ill., Nettie Bonds (divorced at San Francisco, Mar. 10, 1902); dau. of John Bonds.

1–*m* 2d, Aug. 6, 1903, at Portland, Ore., Ellen F. Flynn, *b* nr. the Lakes of Killarny, Co. Kerry, Ireland (divorced by her at Portland, Ore., Aug. 16, 1907); issue: a son, still born 1904.

1–*m* 3d, Jan. 27, 1909, at Cheyenne, Wyo., Anna M. (Harmon) Rodgers (Sept. 2, 1872-Jan. 2, 1916), dau. of Robert E. Harmon, *m* Nancy M. Hackleman (divorced her at San Diego, Calif., final decree, Nov. 12, 1914); issue: 1–Helen, *b* Portland, Ore., Nov. 1, 1909.

1–*m* 4th, June 21, 1915, at Excelsior (nr. Minneapolis), Minn., Frances Martha Gould (*b* Frances Martha Stearns but raised under the name of Gould), *b* Readsboro, Bennington Co., Vt., Nov. 3, 1873; dau. of LeRoy N. Stearns (1843-75), *m* Martha Henrietta Alexander (1843-1921), who *m* 2d, 1876, Walter Henry Gould (1850-ca. 1912).

1–Retired. Interested in genealogical research; geneal. editor, publications of Mutual Aid Geneal. Soc., 1930–. Enlisted in U.S.A. under the name James M. F. Davis, July 29, 1895; served in Spanish-Am. War in Porto Rico, discharged and re-enlisted in Porto Rico, 1898, served in Philippines and U.S., total service 9 yrs., 2 mos. and 16 days, Spanish-Am. War, Porto Rican Occupation, and Philippine service medals. Mem. S.A.R., S.W. 1812, I.A.G. Address: P.O. Box 475, Johnson City, Tenn.

BEALE

Arms: *Sable, on a chevron between three griffins' heads erased argent, three estoiles gules.*
Crest: *A unicorn's head erased or, semee of estoiles gules.*

1–**DAVIS, John Williams,** *b* Petersburg, Va., Nov. 21, 1887.

8–Col. Thomas **Beale** (qv);

7–Thomas (1649-79), *m* Ann Gooch (Col. William[8] [1626-55], of Temple Farm, York Co., Va., burgess, mem. Council);

6–Capt. Thomas (1675-1728 or 29), comd. a co. of militia in service against Indians, 1704; *m* Elizabeth Tavener (1681-1720; Capt. John[7], *m* Elizabeth–);

5–William, *m* Ann Harwar;

4–Capt. Robert (1759-1843), ens. in Am. Rev., promoted to capt.; captured at Charlestown; *m* Martha Felicia Turberville;

3–Elizabeth Tayloe Corbin, *m* Williams Thomas **Davis**;

2–Richard Beale (1845-1917), B.A., Randolph Macon Coll.; B.L., U.Va.; served in Mahone's Brig., C.S.A., 1862-65; wounded at Seven Pines and the Battle of the Crater; fought in the battles of Chancellorsville, Manassas and Gettysburg; mem. Va. Gen. Assembly, 1875-77, 1901-03; mem. com. to revise the statute laws of Va.; trustee Randolph Macon Coll.; asst. atty. gen. of Va., 1911-14; mem. bd. of visitors to Mt. Vernon; hereditary mem. Soc. of the Cincinnati; *m* 1875, Nannie Warwick Hall (see Vol. I, p. 73, for Hall lineage); issue: I–Richard Beale (1876-77); II–Nannie Hall (*b* 1877); III–Carl Hall (*b* 1880; *m* 1907, Julia Wytche Budd); IV–Robert Beale (*b* 1884); V–John Williams (1 above); VI–Elizabeth Beale (Mrs. David Alexander Harrison, Jr., qv

for Lee lineage); VII–Rosina Leigh (1893-94).
1–*m* Oct. 22, 1921, Elizabeth Grimes Walker, *b* Washington, D.C., Nov. 30, 1897; dau. of James Wilson Grimes Walker (see Vol. I, p. 483), *m* Nina Chinn (qv); issue: 1–John Williams, Jr., *b* Washington, D.C., Oct. 28, 1926; 2–Elizabeth Walker, *b* Richmond, Va., Feb. 19, 1930.

CAPT. JOHN WILLIAMS DAVIS

1–Ed. Randolph Macon Coll., 1906; M.E., Cornell U., 1910; M.S., U.Ill., 1917 (Phi Kappa Sigma, Tau Beta Pi, Gamma Alpha, Eta Kappa Nu, Theta Tau, Sigma Xi). Asst. in elec. engring., Harvard, 1910-11; with Stone and Webster, Boston, 1911-12; instr. mathematics and physics, Vanderbilt U., 1912-13; instr. elec. engring., Leland Stanford U., 1913-14, U.Ill., 1914-17. Mem. commn. sent to Toronto, Can., by U.S. Govt., 1917, to establish schools of mil. aeronautics in the U.S.; assisted in establishing a school of mil. aeronautics at Champaign, Ill.; joint author of text book on mil. aeronautics used in that sch. and instr. wireless telegraphy. Enlisted as pvt. 1st class aviation section, S.E.R.C., at Chicago, June 26, 1917; commd. 1st lt., aviation section, S.C., U.S.R., Sept. 21, 1917; given flying status, June 11, 1918; adj., flying dept. Kelly Field, San Antonio, Tex., asst. to exec. officer U.S. Air Service, Washington, D.C.; responsible for helium and hydrogen supply of U.S. Air Service, 1918-19; disch. as capt., Air Service U.S.A., Apr. 5, 1919; design, construction and operation of helium plants, U.S. Bureau of mines, 1919-25; head of tech. dept. and consulting engr. Atmospheric Nitrogen Corpn. during design and construction of Hopewell, Va., synthetic nitrates plants, 1925–. Publications: Corona and Rectification in Hydrogen, by J. W. Davis and C. S. Breese (Proceedings of Am. Inst. of Elec. Engrs., 1917); A.C. and D.C. Corona in Hydrogen (physical Review, 1917); Helium, (Engring. and Mining Journal, 1920). Mem. Am. Inst. of E.E., Am. Phys. Soc., Am. Chem. Soc. Clubs: Cosmos (Washington), Country (Petersburg, Va.). Residence: 1801 S. Sycamore St., Petersburg, Va.

1–**HARRISON, Elizabeth Beale Davis (Mrs. David A., Jr.),** *b* Petersburg, Va., Sept. 18, 1889.
10–Richard **Lee** (qv);
9–Richard (1647-1711), councillor and burgess; *m* 1674, Laetitia Corbin (1657-1706; Henry[10], qv);
8–Richard (ca. 1678/79-1718), *m* Martha (Silk) Moore;
7–Martha (*b* 1716), *m* 1st, as his 3d wife, George **Turberville,** of Hickory Hill, Westmoreland Co. (John[8], burgess and sheriff);
6–John, *m* Martha Corbin;
5–George Lee, *m* Betty Tayloe Corbin;
4–Martha Felicia, *m* Capt. Robert **Beale** (1759-1843);
3–Elizabeth Tayloe Corbin, *m* Williams Thomas **Davis;**
2–Richard Beale (1845-1917), *m* 1875, Nannie Warwick Hall (for issue and other lineages see John Williams Davis).
1–*m* Oct. 10, 1914, David Alexander Harrison, Jr., *b* Prince George Co., Va., June 22, 1886; issue: 1–David A., 3d, *b* Petersburg, Va., August 30, 1916; 2–Ann Lee, *b* Hopewell, Va., Dec. 11, 1917; 3–Elizabeth Beale, *b* Hopewell, June 2, 1919; 4–Richard Davis, *b* Hopewell, Nov. 5, 1922; 5–James Grandison, *b* Richmond, Va., Oct. 30, 1925.
Residence: 313 Ramsay Av., Hopewell, Va.

DENISON

Arms: Argent, on a chevron engrailed gules, between three torteaux, an annulet or.
Crest: A dexter arm embowed, vested vert, the hand proper grasping a scimitar.
Motto: Domus grata.

1–**DENISON, John Hopkins,** *b* at Westfield, Mass., Oct. 14, 1870.
10–William **Denison** (qv);
9–Capt. George (1618-94), served under Cromwell, magistrate at New London, Conn., settled at Mystic, Conn., *m* Ann Borodell;
8–Capt. John (1646-98), Stonington, Conn., *m* Phebe Lay;
7–Robert (1673-1737), bought land in Mohegan of Owaneco, *m* Joanna Stanton;
6–John (1698-1776), Lyme, Conn., *m* Patience Griswold;
5–Samuel (1742-1836), of Lyme, Conn., and Bridgewater, Vt., *m* Mary Champlin;
4–Rev. John (1788-1812), of Jericho, Vt., *m* Lucretia Kellogg;
3–John Newton (1811-95), *m* Mary Frances Dean (1816-1900; Rev. Paul[4], *m* Mary Frances, dau. of Samuel Denison, 5 above);
2–John Henry (see Vol. I, p. 243), *m* Caroline Hopkins (1835-1920; see Vol. I, p. 243, for Hopkins lineage).
1–*m* Dec. 30, 1902, Pearl Livingston Underwood, dau. of Frank Livingston Underwood, of New York, and Litchfield, Conn.; issue: 1–Charis, *b* Boston, Jan. 18, 1905; 2–John H., Jr., *b* Litchfield, Conn., Aug. 18, 1907.
1–B.A., Williams, '90 (D.D., 1915). Clergyman; resigned as pastor Central Congl. Ch., Boston, 1910. With Y.M.C.A. in France, Aug. 1917-Aug. 1919 (see Who's Who in America). Clubs: Century, University (New York), Santa Barbara, Santa Barbara Country (Calif.). Summer place: Camerina, Williamstown, Mass. Winter place: Las Tunas, Santa Barbara, Calif. Address: 130 E. 67th St., New York, N.Y.

1–**DAVIS, Camilla Webb (Mrs. Joseph J.),** *b* College Hill, Miss., Jan. 23, 1869.
9–Giles **Webb,** burgess from Nansemond Co., Va., 1658-60; patented 681 acres on the Rappahannock River, 1667; *m* Judith, widow of Capt. Henry Randolph;
8–John, *m* Mary Samford;
7–James (1673-1716), of Essex Co., Va.; *m* Sarah–;

6–James (1705-71), of Essex Co.; *m* 1731, Mary Edmundson (Benjamin[7], *m* Margaret Underwood, of Essex Co.);
5–John (1747-1826), of Granville Co., N.C.; *m* 1772, Amy Booker (1752-1835; James[6], of Essex Co.);
4–Thomas (*b* 1776), of Person Co., N.C.; rep. his county in Legislature, 1816-17, 1821-29; *m* Mary Thomas, of Eastern Shore, Va.;
3–William (1804-32), of Person Co.; *m* 1827, Martha Thorp (1808-87; Benjamin Peterson[4] [*d* 1848], *m* 1800, Jane Taylor, 1776-1858);
2–William Presley (2 below).
5–James **Hayes,** from Ireland; *m* Miss Walker, of Eng.;
4–James (1785-1871), *m* 1805, Martha Green (William Wills[5], *m* —Archer);
3–James (1816-88), *m* 1843, Camilla Smith (1828-49), of Lunenburg Co., Va.
2–William Presley **Webb** (1829-1903), of Granville Co., N.C.; capt. Co. K, 55th Regt., A.P. Hill's Corps, Longstreet's Div.; also q.m.; banker, merchant; *m* 1st, 1850, his cousin, Martha Ann Webb (*d* 1860); *m* 2d, 1866, Emma Camilla Hayes (*b* 1844); issue (1st marriage): I–Lucy Thorp (1853-1927; *m* Thomas Anderson Feild); II–Benjamin Pomfret (1856-81); III–George Johnson (*d* infancy); issue: (2d marriage); I–Henry Percival (1867-89); II–Camilla (1 above); III–Annie L. (*b* 1870; *m* Wiley Perry Neal); IV–Susie McR. (*b* 1872; *m* John B. Yarborough); V–James L. (1874-97); VI–Emma C. (*b* 1877; *m* 1908, Stephen A. Martin); VII–William Presley (*b* 1878; *m* Dorothy C. Ransome, of Eng.).
1–*m* Aug. 13, 1890, Joseph Jonathan Davis, *b* Abram's Plains, Granville Co., N.C., Apr. 18, 1863; son of Isaac H. Davis, of Abram's Plains, *m* Anne Alexander Downey; issue: 1–Nettie Leland, *b* Abram's Plains, Granville Co., N.C., July 27, 1891; Statesville (N.C.) Female Coll., 1909; *m* Apr. 8, 1911, John Brooks Davis, son of William Luther Davis, of Ware Neck, Gloucester Co., Va., *m* Fannie Thornton (issue: William Luther, Jr., *b* 1912; Nettie Leland, Jr., *b* 1926); 2–Annie Webb, *b* Abram's Plains, Granville Co., May 14, 1893; A.B., Statesville Female Coll., '10; *m* June 30, 1920, Dr. Marion M. Sherman, son of Hiram Sherman, of Newport News, Va., *m* Margaret Wythe (issue: Margaret *b* 1922; Marion Moore, Jr., *b* 1928); 3–William Presley, *b* Louisburg, N.C., July 6, 1895; C. E., N.C. State Coll., Raleigh, N.C., '17; *m* Dec. 30, 1926, Hazel, dau. of Frank Cole, of Chester, Va., *m* Caroline (Nesper) Jones (issue: Joseph Jonathan, *b* 1929); 4–Sallie Slade, *b* Dinwiddie Co., Va., Feb. 18, 1898; Statesville Female Coll.; *m* June 12, 1915, Winfield Crichton Daniel, son of Capt. George Daniel, of "Tranquility," Granville Co., N.C., *m* Fannie Crichton (issue: Camilla Webb; Fannie Crichton; dau., Joseph J.; Emma Hayes; Winfield Crichton, Jr.); 5–Joseph Jonathan, *b* Abram's Plains, Granville Co., N.C., (Aug. 19, 1902-Nov. 24, 1929); Architectural Engring., N.C. State Coll., 1924; 6–Alexander Smith, *b* Stovall, N.C., May 28, 1905; Elec. Engr., State Coll., 1926.
1–Ed. Sunny Side Sem., Clarksville, Va.; Mary Baldwin Sem., Staunton, Va. Taught school many yrs.; genealogist. Presbyterian. Democrat. Residence: Stovall, N.C.

1–**DAVY, Mary Jane Aikenhead (Mrs. Burton H.),** *b* Rochester, N.Y., Oct. 16, 1867.
9–George **Felt** (1601-93), was of record at Charlestown, 1633; *m* Elizabeth Wilkinson (*d* 1694; Widow Prudence[10], *d* 1655);
8–George (1639-77), of Salem, Charlestown and Casco Bay; leader against Indians, 1677, when he was killed; *m* 1662, Phillippa Andrews (Samuel[9], *m* Jane–);
7–Samuel, *m* Elizabeth–;
6–Samuel (1698-1788), capt. French and Indian War; *m* Rachel Kibbee (*d* 1745);
5–Samuel (1735-1803), French and Indian War; ens. colonial army, 1773; 2d lt. 1775; constable and collector, 1775; 1st lt. Army of New Republic, 1776, later capt.; *m* 1761, Mehitabel Buell (1743-94);
4–Jehiel (1769-1842), capt. War 1812, wounded at Battle of Queenstown Heights; *m* 1793, Mehitabel Davis (*b* 1776);
3–Jehiel Ray (1818-1900), *m* 1843, Sarah Jane Moore (1824-1903);
2–Julia Pomp (1849-1922), *m* 1866, James McIntosh **Aikenhead** (1847-1918; John[3], from Scotland ca. 1840, *m* Mary McIntosh); for issue see Vol. III, p. 22.
1–*m* Jan. 5, 1892, Burton Hodges Davy (Apr. 29, 1862-Aug. 15, 1914); son of Judge John M. Davy, justice Supreme Ct., 20 yrs., Rochester, N.Y., *m* Elizabeth Hodges; issue: 1–Elizabeth Julia, *b* Rochester, N.Y., July 2, 1896; Wells, '18; *m* Mar. 26, 1919, Walter Joseph Salmon (issue: Burton Davy, Aug. 14, 1920); 2–James Burton, *b* Rochester, Nov. 16, 1897; Cornell, '20.
1–Ed. Genesee Wesleyan Sem., '88. Capt. of War Service Corps, Rochester, N.Y., and Red Cross instr. during World War. Mem. D.F.P.A. (pres. N.Y. Soc.), D.A.R., War Mothers of America, Women's Nat. Emergency Relief, Rochester Hist. Soc., Women's Nat. Rep. Club, Lyon Art Soc. (1st v.p. 1924-32), Harlem-New York Council of Women (pres. 1930), The Readers of N.Y. Address: 16 E. 69th St., New York, N.Y.

1–**DAWSON, Warrington,** *b* Charleston, S.C., Sept. 27, 1878.
8–William (Byles) **Biles** (*d* 1710), from Eng. in the "Eliza and Sarah," 1679; large landowner in Bucks Co. prior to the arrival of William Penn; he was established in 1679; an original settler on lands bought from Sir Edmund Andros; Quaker leader, and justice of the Uplands Ct., 1681; the first known meetings of Friends in Pa. were held at his house just below the Falls of Neshanny, 1683; *m* 2d (?), Jane or Joan, widow of Thomas Atkinson;
7–George, *m* Martha Kirkbridge or Kirkbride (Joseph[8], of Pa., *m* Phoebe, dau. of Randall Blackshaw, qv);
6–Joanna (*d* 1743), of Phila.; *m* Evan **Morgan** (*d* 1748; David[7], from Wales to America ca. 1700, *m* Mary–);
5–George (1743-1810), of "Prospect," nr. Princeton, N.J.; col. Cont. Army; explorer; *m* 1764, Mary Baynton;
4–Col. John (1770-1817), Morganza, Pa.; *m* 1795, Margaret Bunyan;
3–Judge Thomas Gibbes (1799-1861), *m* 2d, 1830, Sarah Hunt Fowler (Maj. Richard[4], *m* Elizabeth Waller; Col. Richard[5], *m* Sarah, dau. of Thomas Hunt of Hunt's Point);
2–Sarah Fowler (2 below).
9–Thomas **Budd,** from Eng., 1668; propr. in Province of Jersey, later in Pa., but was living in Jersey, 1690; Quaker; friend of William Penn;
8–John, treas. Province of West Jersey, 1683; *m* Rebecca Baynton;
7–Mary (*d* 1727), *m* as his 2d wife, Peter **Baynton** (drowned 1743-44), from Eng.; settled at Phila., Pa., ca. 1720;
6–John (1726-73), head of firm of Baynton, Wharton & Morgan; *m* 1747, Elizabeth Chevalier (*b* 1726; Peter[7], of Phila., *m* Elizabeth Wood);
5–Mary (*b* 1749), *m* Col. George **Morgan** (5 above).
10–Willem **deKay** (qv);
9–Jacobus Tunis (*d* 1691), *m* 1658, Hillegonda Theunisse (*d* 1707);
8–Jacobus (*b* 1672), *m* 1694, Sarah Willet (Col. Thomas[9]);
7–Col. Thomas (1697-1758), Orange Co., N.Y.: soldier French and Indian War; *m* 1723, Christiana (1707-84), dau. of Thomas Duncan, of Scotland;
6–Maj. George (1728-59), of New York; *m* 1754, Julianna Gale (*b* 1735);
5–Juliana, *m* 1772, James **Bunyan** (1748-1839), of N.Y. and Pittsburgh (James[6], qv);
4–Margaret (1775-1852), *m* John **Morgan** (4 above).
2–Francis Warrington **Dawson** (*born* London, Eng., 1840-*d* Charleston, S.C., 1889; see portrait, Vol. II, p. 38; oldest son of Joseph Austin and Mary Reeks of London, and elder brother of Rev. Joseph William Reeks, hon. canon of St. George's Cathedral, Southwark, and missionary rector of St. Peter's Ch., Wollwich; nephew of Capt. William A. Dawson, B.A., India Medal, killed in action

Sepoy Mutiny; desc. from Fisher Family in collateral line from Bishop John Fisher, martyr under Henry VIII), capt. army of Northern Va., C.S.A., chief ordnance officer of Gen. Fitzhugh Lee; founder and editor Charleston News and Courier; Knight of St. Gregory the Great; *m* 1874, Sarah Fowler Morgan (1842-1909), author "A Confederate Girl's Diary;" see portrait Vol. III, p. 598); issue: I–Ethel (*m* Herbert Barry, see Vol. I, p. 210); II–Warrington (1 above).

1–Not married. Ed. Ecole St. Thomas d'Aquin, Paris; University Sch. and Coll. of Charleston. Diplomat, author. Special newspaper correspondent in Spain, France, Russia, Belgium, Holland, Italy, Africa, England, 1898-1917. Confidential adviser to Am. ambassador 1917-19, sp. asst., since 1919. Hon. pres. Charleston, S.C., Council of Boy Scouts since 1924. Officer of the Legion of Honor. Author or editor of fifteen published works in French or in English, notably: The Scar; Adventure in the Night; The Green Moustache; Opportunity and Theodore Roosevelt; The Gift of Paul Clermont, etc. Gold medal of Paris Academie Francais, 1926. Life mem. I.A.G., etc. (see Who's Who in America). American address: c/o Council of Boy Scouts, West Wing Old Citadel, Charleston, S.C. Decorated Cdr. of the Legion of Honor of France, 1930. Official address: American Embassy, Paris, France. Residence: 19 rue du Marechal Joffre, Versailles, France.

1–**DAY, Frances Donizetti Stevens (Mrs. Loren True),** *b* New Haven, Conn., Jan. 15, 1863.
8–John **Stevens** (qv);
7–Dea. Timothy (1641-1708), Roxbury, Mass.; *m* 1665, Sarah Davis (Tobias[8], from Eng., to Roxbury and Andover, Mass., *m* Sarah Morrill);
6–Rev. Timothy (1666-1726), to Glastonbury, Conn.; 1st of the name Stevens to grad. Harvard Coll.; 1st minister, 1st Congl. Ch., S. Glastonbury; *m* 2d, 1701, Alice Cook (1679-1719), widow of Rev. John Whiting (Joseph Cook[7] [1643-90], *m* 1665, Martha, dau. of John Stedman [1601-93], *m* Alice-[1610-90]; Joseph[8] [*b* Eng.], lt. A. and H.A. Co., *m* in Eng., Elizabeth–);
5–Joseph (*b* 1711), *m* Jerusha Stow, of Upper House, Middletown, Conn.;
4–Elisha (1748-1813), of Glastonbury and Naugatuck, Conn.; Am. Rev., 7 yrs.; *m* Agnes Kimberly (Thomas[5], Am. Rev., of Newtown and Woodbury, Conn., *m* Lois Tuttle);
3–Hershall (1799-1870), *m* Clarissa Boughton (Jeremiah[4], of Ridgefield and Naugatuck, Conn., *m* Patty M. Perse);
2–Robert (2 below).
10–Rev. John **Youngs** (qv);
9–Col. John (bap. 1623-1697), *m* his step-sister, Mary Gardiner;
8–Zerrubable (1664-97), family tradition is he was lost at sea on return trip from Eng.; *m* Margaret–;
7–Judge Joshua (1684-1755), *m* Mary Mayhew (John[8], of New London, Conn.);
6–Judge Thomas (1719-93), grad. Yale, 1740; signed Assn. Test, 1775; chmn. Com. of Safety, Sag Harbor, L.I., 1776; subscribed $1,000 for the betterment of the Cont. Army, 1780; *m* Rhoda Budd;
5–Dea. Thomas (1748-1816), Suffolk Co., N.Y.; p.-m., Am. Army, 1786; *m* Lydia Tuthill (Lt. John[6], Am. Rev.);
4–Thomas (1777-1844), *m* Elmira Wheadon (desc. Thomas Wheadon, of Branford, Conn., *m* Hannah Sutcliff);
3–Thomas Hull (1806-35), *m* Harriet Levan Youngs;
2–Adelia Amanda (1831-1900), *m* 2d, 1856, Robert **Stevens** (*b* Naugatuck, Conn., 1823-*d* 1892); issue (all *b* New Haven, Conn.): I–Charles Creighton (1856-1928); II–Robertha Youngs (1858-1922; *m* 1st, Dr. Frank Lyman Forsyth; *m* 2d, Thomas C. Powell); III–Estella Irene (1859-60); IV–Clara Leontine (*b* 1861; *m* Isaac Frederick Baker); V–Frances D. (1 above); VI–Adelia Amanda (*b* 1864; *m* Rev. Allen C. Prescott; *m* 2d, Frederick C. Earle); VII–Herbert Hershall (1867-70); VIII–Harriet Eleanor Redell (*b* 1870; *m* Alonzo B. Hall; *m* 2d, Judson Mather Miner); IX–John Irving Inskip (1872-1902; *m* 1898, Belle Moulthrope).
1–*m* May 31, 1883, Loren True Day, *b* Bridgeport, Conn., Aug. 11, 1861; son of John L. Day, *m* Jane Ann Lewis; issue: 1–Dorothy, *b* Westport, Conn., May 7, 1894.
1–Mem. D.F.P.A., D.A.R. Address: P.O. Box 304, Westport, Conn.

1–**DEAN, Edwin Blanchard,** *b* Satara, India, July 21, 1866.
9–John (Deane) **Dean** (1600-60), to Taunton, Mass.; *m* Alice–;
8–Thomas (1639-1716), *m* Katherine Stephens (Thomas[9]);
7–Thomas (1673-1747), began to write name Dean; *m* Mary Kingsley (1676-1750; John[8]; Stephen[9]);
6–Ens. Elijah (1701-50), *m* Sophia Leonard (1717-62; Capt. Samuel[7]; Maj. Thomas[8]; James[9], qv);
5–Samuel (1748-1827), *m* Bethiah Robinson (1753-1835; Josiah[6]; Increase[7]; Increase[8]; William[9], qv);
4–Isaiah (1774-1801), *m* Lydia Randall (1767-1856; Capt. Benjamin[5]; Benjamin[6]; Joseph[7]; William[8]);
3–Dea. Josiah Robinson (1796-1871), *m* Betsy Wheaton Chase;
2–Rev. Samuel Chase (2 below).
9–William **Chase** (qv);
8–William (1622-85);
7–John, *m* Elizabeth Baker (Francis[8], qv);
6–John (1675-1755), *m* Sarah– (*d* 1757);
5–Elisha (*b* 1712), *m* Sarah Dean (*b* 1716; Seth[6]; Dea. Ezra[7]; Walter[8], qv);
4–Grindall (1757-1843), *m* Sarah Peck (*b* 1765; Samuel[5]; Samuel[6]; Samuel[7]; Joseph[8]; Joseph[9], qv);
3–Betsy Wheaton (1792-1852), *m* Dea. Josiah R. **Dean** (3 above).
9–George **Abbot,** of Rowley and Andover (qv);
8–Dea. John (1648-1721), *m* Sarah Barker (1647-1729; Richard[9]);
7–Dea. John (1674-1754), *m* Elizabeth Hardine (*d* 1756);
6–Capt. John (1704-93), *m* Phoebe Fiske (1712-1802; John[7]; Samuel[8]; William[9], qv);
5–Jeremiah (1743-1825), *m* Chloe Abbott (1737-1809; Zebediah[6]; Nehemiah[7]; George[8]; George[9]);
4–Jeremiah (1774-1857), *m* Eunice Blanchard (1778-1850; Joshua[5]; Josiah[6]; Thomas[7]; Samuel[8]; Thomas[9], qv);
3–Rev. Amos (1812-89), M.D.; began to write name Abbott; *m* Anstice Wilson;
2–Augusta Elizabeth (2 below).
9–William **Wilson** (*d* 1646), Salem, Mass.; *m* Patience–;
8–Joseph (1643-1718), *m* Sarah Lord (*d* 1727; Robert[9]);
7–John (*b* 1682), *m* Mercy Wright (John[8]; Walter[9]);
6–John (1720-74), *m* Hannah Frye (1726-1803; Ebenezer[7]; Lt. Samuel[8]; John[9], qv);
5–Dea. Joshua (1744-1823), *m* Dorothy Stevens (1751-1821; Abiel[6]; Abiel[7]; Lt. John[8]; John[9], qv);
4–Capt. David (1779-1875), *m* Elizabeth Barker (1784-1851; Isaac[5]; Ens. Richard[6]; Benjamin[7]; Lt. Richard[8]);
3–Anstice (1812-89), *m* Amos **Abbott** (3 above);
2–Augusta Elizabeth (*b* 1835), *m* Rev. Samuel Chase **Dean** (1823-90); issue: I–Horace Abbott (*b* 1857; *m* Elizabeth W. Wakeman); II–Carrie (*b* 1859); III–Walter Chase (1861-1927; *m* Martha Anna Pickering); IV–Frank Wilson (*b* 1863; *m* Sarah Ann Meston); V–George Robinson (1864-1919; *m* Emily Washburn); VI–Edwin B. (1 above); VII–Arthur Randall (*b* 1869; *m* Emma Quimby Fuller); VIII–Norman Peck (1871-1924; *m* Sophie Miller).
1–*m* July 8, 1896, Georgia De Cou, *b* West Union, Ia., Nov. 11, 1867; ed. Doane and Oberlin Colls. (George[2] [1826-92], *m* Mary Everett [1835-1926; Oliver[3]; Oliver[4]; Jeremiah[5]; Israel[6]; John[7]; Richard[8]]; Frederick[3]; Isaac[4]; Abner[5]; Jacob[6]; Jacob[7]; Isaac Decow[8]); issue: 1–Berta De Cou, *b* Clinton, Ia., Nov. 1, 1900; 2–Carol Chase, *b* Clinton, Oct. 9, 1902.
1–B.A., Doane Coll., Crete, Neb., 1888 (D.D., 1917); B.A., Amherst, 1889, M.A., 1904; B.D., Chicago Theol. Sem., 1893. Ordained Congl. ministry, 1893; pastor, 1893-1920; chmn. bd. of deans, and asst. to the pres., Carleton Coll., 1920-25; pres. Doane Coll., since 1925 (see Who's Who in America). Mem. war personnel bd., Nat. War Work Council of Y.M.C.A., New York, 1918; mem. same and hdqrs. chaplain, Y.M.C.A., Paris, 1919. Residence: Crete, Neb.

JOHN AMOS DEAN (b Aug. 8, 1848, on a farm near Griggsville, Ill., d Dec. 29, 1924, on his farm near Pittsfield, Ill.); attended public school at Walnut Grove; farmer; Methodist, supt. of Sunday school, etc.

1–**DEAN, Ella Rose,** *b* Harlan Co., Neb., Jan. 18, 1888.
11–Richard **Warren,** Mayflower Pilgrim (qv);
10–Ann (ca. 1612-75), *m* 1633, Thomas **Little** (*d* 1671), of Marshfield, Mass.;
9–Hannah (*d* 1710), of Plymouth and Marshfield, Mass.; *m* 1661/62, Stephen **Tilden** (1629-1711), of Marshfield;
8–Mary (1668-1724), of Scituate; *m* 1692/93, James **Thomas** (1663-ante 1728), of Duxbury;
7–Mary (1693-ante 1765), of Duxbury; *m* 172–, Joseph **Langerell** (*d* post 1777), of Duxbury;
6–Mary (*b* 1723), of Duxbury, Mass., and Lebanon, Conn.; *m* 1743, Samuel **Law** (*b* 1714), of Hebron, Conn.;
5–Mary (1747-1822), of Lebanon; *m* 1775, Elisha **Doubleday** (1713 or 1714-1806), of Lebanon;
4–Anna (1780-1854), of Lebanon and Litchfield, Conn.; *m* 1803, Amos **Dean** (1781-1857), of Lebanon and Litchfield, Conn., and Griggsville, Ill.;
3–Henry Elisha (1809-77), of Griggsville, Ill.; *m* 1842, Mary Lopp (Cohenour) Coughenour (1821-96), of Pa.;
2–John Amos (1848-1924), of Pittsfield, Ill. (see portrait); *m* 1883, Sarah Lervina Conkright (*b* 1863), of New Salem, Ill.; issue: I–Alvin Wesley (1883-1918; killed in World War); II–Harvey Edward (*b* 1885; *m* Ethel May Creech); III–Ella R. (1 above); IV–Julian Amos (*b* 1889; *m* Ruth Clayton); V–Daisy Pearl (*b* 1890; *m* Arthur Wesley Swedlund); VI–Earl Weaver (1892-1918; *d* Camp Taylor, Ky.; *m* Lena Locker); VII–Flossie Hazel (*b* 1894; *m* Charles Arthur Dean); VIII–Mary Lervina (*b* 1897; *m* Arthur Franklin Lipcamon); IX–Viola Belle (*b* 1899; *m* George Raymond Windmiller); X–Alice May (*b* 1902; *m* Claud William Hoos).
1–B. Ed., Ill. State Normal Sch., 1916 (Kappa Delta Pi), U. of Chicago, U. of Ill., U. of Wis. Taught country schs. of Pike Co., Ill., 1907-12, Harrisburg (Ill.) Tp. High School, 1916-21; Teacher chemistry, Olney (Ill.) Tp. High School, 1921–. Mem. S.M.D., I.A.G., N.E.H.G.S., Ill. State Acad. of Science. Methodist. Republican. Residence: 407 S. Elliot St., Olney, Ill.

1–**De COUDRES, Thomas Hart,** *b* Dryden, N.Y., Mar. 30, 1875.
4–Louis **de Coudres** (*b* 1745), enlisted in French army, 1765; came to America with French troops; discharged from American service in Am. Rev., 1783; *m* Catherine Bayonne;
3–Thomas (1791-1856), of Dryden, N.Y., and Newark, N.J.; *m* 2d, 1819, Mary Fox (1800-76; Curtis[4], a sea captain);
2–William Frederick (2 below).
8–John **Hart;**
7–Joseph, of Newton, L.I.;
6–Joseph (will dated 1776), of Hunterdon Co., N.J.;
5–Joseph (*d* 1794), of Hunterdon Co., N.J.; *m* 1764, Frances (Franky) Phillips (Theophilus[6], *m* Frances–; Theophilus[7]);
4–Amos (1776-1863), removed from Hopewell, N.J., to Groton, N.Y., thence to Dryden, N.Y.; *m* Ruth Stout (1780-1840; Andrew[5] [1728-1807], *m* 1753, Anne Stout, *m* 2d, 1777, Sarah [Stout] Morgan, sister of first wife; David[6] [*b* 1706], *m* Elizabeth Larrison; Jonathan[7], *m* 1685, Hannah Bullen; Richard[8], qv);
–John Phillips (1816-70), of Groton and McClean, N.Y.; *m* 1840, Eliza M. Boynton;
2–Mary Adeline (2 below).
9–Dolor **Davis** (qv);
8–Samuel (1639/40-ante 1720), Concord, Mass.; *m* 1666, Mary (Meddowes, Mead) Medow (*d* 1710);
7–Daniel (1673-1741), *m* 1698, Mary Hubbard (1682-1769);
6–Nathaniel (1715-1802), of Rutland, Me., and Rockingham, Vt.; *m* 1741, Susanna Lane (1720-95; John[7]; Col. John[8]; Job[9]);
5–Nathaniel (1754-1835), of Rockingham, Vt.; *m* 1780, Lydia Harwood (1761-1836 or 38; John[6] [*b* 1736], *m* Mary Pulsipher [1744-86; David[7]; Jonathan[8]; Benedict[9]]; John[7]; James[8]; Nicholas[9]; Andrew[10]);
4–Betsy (1795-1833), *m* John (Byington) **Boynton** (1798-1869), of Rockingham, Vt., and McClean, N.Y. (Abraham[5] [1773-1847], from Conn. to Rockingham, Vt., 1797; *m* Betsey Marsh, 1777-1824);
3–Eliza M. (1821-88), *m* John Phillips **Hart** (3 above);
2–Mary Adeline (1848-75), *m* 1870, as his 1st wife, William Frederick **de Coudres** (1837-1906).
1–*m* June 22, 1903, Minnie Mary Bosworth (qv for issue).
1–Grad. Cortland (N.Y.) State Normal Sch., '95; A.B., Brown U., '99. Submaster, Putnam (Conn.) High School, 1899-1902; same, Southbridge, Mass., 1902-05; supt. schools, East Hartford, Conn., 1905-12; same, Bristol, R.I., 1916-19. Mem. firm Bosworth Bros., Putnam, Conn., 1919–. Mem. S.A.R. Club: Putnam Country. Mason. Residence: 231 Woodstock Av., Putnam, Conn.

1–**De COUDRES, Minnie Mary Bosworth (Mrs. Thomas Hart),** *b* Hutchinson, Minn., July 31, 1875.
9–Edward **Bosworth** (qv);
8–Nathaniel (1617-90), built the first house at Bristol, R.I., 1680; *m* Bridget (Bellamy) Lobdell;
7–John (*d* 1725), *m* Sarah–(1656-1735);
6–John (*b* 1678), *m* 1707, Elizabeth Chamberlain (1683-1716; Henry[7]; John[8]);
5–John (*b* 1708), removed from Hull to Ashford, Conn.; *m* 1740, Mary Hayward (1719-78; Samuel[6] [*b* 1682], *m* Mary Paine; Jonathan[7]; William[8]);
4–Allen (1758-59-1830), of Ashford, Conn.; pvt. in Am. Rev.; *m* 2d, 1802, Sarah Harwood (bap. 1776-1859; Ezra[5] [*b* 1744], *m* 1769, Lydia, dau. of Nathan Hiscox; David[6]; Jonathan[7]; John[8]; Henry[9]);
3–Sanford (1813-70), removed to Woodstock, Conn.; *m* 2d, 1839, Mary Melissa Bugbee;
2–Chauncey Fenno (2 below).
7–Joseph **Healy,** *m* Prudence Goodfellow;
6–Thomas (*b* 1740), of Greenwich, R.I.; *m* 1775, Penelope Mott (Stephen[7], *m* 1732, Abigail Lawton);
5–Polly, *m* Joseph **Barrett** (1772-ca. 1813);
4–Phebe (1801-77), *m* 1817, Chester **Bugbee** (1789-1869; Willard[5] [1766-1844], Am. Rev., *m* 1788, Serepta Ainsworth; William[6]; Benjamin[7]; John[8]; John[9]; Richard[10]);
3–Mary Melissa (1820-96), *m* Sanford **Bosworth** (3 above).
9–James **Barber,** of Newport, R.I.;
8–Moses (1652-1732/33), of S. Kingston, R.I.; *m* 1692, Susanna Waite (*d*. 1758);
7–Daniel (1714-1813), removed to Exeter, R.I.; *m* Deliverance Tefft (1722-99; John[8] [*b* 1699], *m* 1721, Mary Reynolds);

6–Jonathan (1745-1839), Am. Rev.; *m* 1771, Sebra Stanton (1752-1822; John[7], *m* 2d, 1734, Susanna Lanphere; John[8]; Robert[9]);
5–Henry (1772-1810), *m* Anna Rathbun (1774-1857; Simeon[6]; Thomas[7]; John[8]; John[9]; John[10]; Richard[11]);
4–Dr. Smith (1799-1870), removed from Exeter to Voluntown; settled finally at Canterbury, Conn.; *m* 1823, Mary James;
3–Dr. Amenzer (1825-87), removed to Mecca, O., thence to Hutchinson, Minn.; *m* 1847, Mary Matilda Buck (1828-1909; Samuel[4], *m* 1824, Amity, dau. of Nathan Millington, *m* Amity Smith; Samuel[5], Am. Rev.);
2–Abbie Mary (2 below).
10–William **James**, freeman at Newport, R.I., 1655;
9–William, *m* 1677, Susanna Martin (*d* 1726; Joseph[10]);
8–William (will made 1743), of Charlestown, R.I.; *m* Mary–;
7–William (1708-73), of Newport and Hopkinton, R.I.; *m* 1738, Sarah Allen (Ebenezer[8]);
6–Ens. Allen (1743-1821), of W. Greenwich, R.I.; Am. Rev.; *m* 1765, Sarah (Concklin) Lewis (1743-1814; Thomas[7], *m* Martha, dau. of Nathaniel Potter);
5–Thomas (1778-1845), of W. Greenwich, R.I.; *m* 1798, Mary Gorton (1776-1817; Hezekiah[6]; Dr. Samuel[7]; Samuel[8]; Samuel[9]; Samuel[10]);
4–Mary (1805-83), *m* Dr. Smith **Barber** (4 above);
3–Dr. Amenzer, *m* Mary Matilda Buck;
2–Abbie Mary (*b* 1851), *m* 1872, Chauncey Fenno **Bosworth** (1843-1920), grain dealer of Putnam, Conn.; issue: I–Minnie Mary (1 above); II–Orra Fenno (1882-90).
1–*m* June 22, 1903, Thomas Hart de Coudres (qv); issue: 1–Rhea Maxine Bosworth, *b* E. Hartford, Conn., Nov. 5, 1906; Women's Coll. of Brown U., '27; R.I. Sch. of Design, 1931; 2–Ruth Helen, *b* E. Hartford, Apr. 9, 1908; R.I. Sch. of Design.
1–Mem. S.M.D., D.F.P.A., D.A.R., I.A.G., N.E.H.-G.S., R.I. Hist. Soc. Residence: 231 Woodstock Av., Putnam, Conn.

1–**De KOVEN, Annie Dean Larrabee (Mrs. John)**, *b* Chicago, Ill., Mar. 20, 1854.
9–Greenfield (Lareby) **Larrabee**, from Eng. ante 1648, settled at Lyme, Conn.; *m* Phoebe (Brown) Lee;
8–Greenfield (1648-1738/39), *m* 1673/74, Alice Park;
7–John (*b* 1677), of Windham;
6–John, *m* Hannah–;
5–John S. (1732-1818), *m* Mary Spaulding (*b* 1744);
4–William Henry (1770-1836), *m* Louisa Callender (1774-1844);
3–Lucius Callender (*b* 1799), *m* 1824, Calista W. Bugbee;
2–Charles Rollin (*b* Ticonderoga, N.Y., Feb. 17, 1825–*d* Chicago, Ill., June 3, 1899), hardware mcht., Chicago; *m* 1851, Mary Ann Wood (1827-1912; Peter[3] [1801-84], from Parish of St. Leonards, New Malton, Yorkshire, Eng., sailed from Liverpool July 20, 1832, arrived New York, Aug. 26, *d* Chicago, *m* 1824, Mary Ann Dean; Richard[4], *m* Ann–); issue: I–Rev. Edward Allan (1852-1924; A.M., Racine Coll., 1873; S.T.B., Gen. Theol. Sem., New York, 1876; D.D., Nashotah House [Wis.], 1909; rector Ch. of the Ascension, Chicago, 1884-1909; author; see Who's Who in America, Vol. 12); II–Annie Dean (1 above); III–Eleanor Louise (*b* 1856); IV–Mary Calista (1858-1925); V–Emily Wood (Mrs. John N. Tilton, qv); VI–Rosalind Garden (*b* 1860; *m* Charles A. Street. *d*); VII–Rollin North (1863-1902; *m* Berta Curtis, *d*); VIII–Caroline (*b* 1866).
1–*m* June 19, 1879, Cecil Barnes (*b* Portland, Me., 1852-*d* Chicago, 1880), A.B., Harvard, '72; school principal, Chicago; son of Judge Phinehas Barnes, grad. Bowdoin Coll.; *m* 1837, Ann Judson Butler; issue: 1–Cecil (see Vol. I, p. 207).
1–*m* 2d, Apr. 8, 1890, John de Koven (*b* Middletown, Conn., 1833-*d* Chicago, 1898); son of Henry Louis de Koven.
Residence: 1150 N. Dearborn St., Chicago, Ill.

1–**TILTON, Emily Wood Larrabee (Mrs. John N.)**, *b* Chicago, Ill., May 6, 1859.
Sister of Mrs. John de Koven (qv for lineage).
1–*m* Nov. 27, 1886, John Neal Tilton (Dec. 9, 1860-June 3, 1921); architect; son of John Rollin Tilton, artist, of London, N.H., later of Rome, Italy (desc. William Tilton, from Eng., ante 1640, settled at Lynn, Mass.), *m* Caroline Stebbins; issue: 1–Rollin Larrabee (qv); 2–John Neal, Jr., *b* Chicago, Ill., June 16, 1891; B.Arch., Cornell, '13, M.Arch., 1914; 3–Julian, *b* Chicago, June 16, 1891; 4–Edward Larrabee (Nov. 20, 1892-Oct. 7, 1905).
1–Organizer of local Red Cross work. Clubs: LaGrange Woman's, Woman's City. Residence: 123 S. Kensington Av., LaGrange, Ill.

1–**TILTON, Rollin Larrabee**, *b* Chicago, Ill., Feb. 22, 1888.
9–William **Tilton** (*d* ca. 1653), from Eng. to Lynn, Mass., ca. 1640; *m* Susanna–;
8–Ens. Daniel (1646-1715), rep. Hampton in Colonial Assembly; speaker, 1702-14; *m* 1669, Mehitable Sanborn (g. dau. of Stephen Batchelder);
7–Capt. Joseph (1677-1744), *m* 2d, 1717, Elizabeth (Hilliard) Shaw (*d* 1724);
6–Timothy (1718-85), of East Kingston; *m* 1746, Martha Boynton (1726-1822);
5–Nathan (1755-1804), served in N.H. militia during Burgoyne's invasion, and was present at the battle of Saratoga, Am. Rev.; *m* 1780, Susan Gale (1761-1841);
4–Maj. Daniel (1787-1841), drummer in War 1812; *m* 1st, 1816, Sallie Clough (1793-1831);
3–John Rollin Sargent Gale (1828-88), studied art at Rome, Italy; *m* 1858, Caroline Stebbins (*d* 1903);
2–John Neal (1860-1921), grad. Coll. of Architecture of Cornell, '80; of Chicago, later LaGrange, Ill.; pres. LaGrange Public Library Bd.; fellow A.I.A.; *m* 1886, Emily Wood Larrabee (qv).
1–*m* Apr. 25, 1914, Kathleen Glendower Cates, *b* St. Louis, Mo., Mar. 1, 1894; dau. of John Mullanphy Cates, of St. Louis, Mo., *m* Elizabeth Patterson LaMotte; issue: 1–Emily Neal, *b* Honolulu, Hawaii, Mar. 4, 1915; 2–Elizabeth LaMotte, *b* Ft. Wright, N.Y., May 23, 1917; 3–Ann deKoven, *b* Ft. McPherson, Ga., Dec. 15, 1927.
1–Racine (Wis.) Coll., 1907; Cornell U., 1911. Second lt., C.A.C., U.S.A., Sept. 25, 1909, 1st lt., 1911, Mexican Punitive Expedition and Border, 1916; capt., C.A.C., 1917, maj., 1920; Maj., Coast Arty., Nat. Army, May 10, 1918, lt. col., Sept. 26, 1918. Organized 3d Bn., 75th Arty. and 40th Arty.; service in Hawaii, 1913-16, France, 1919, Panama, 1920-1923; comd. harbor defenses of Pensacola, Fort Barrancas, Fla., 1923-24; Inspector General's Dept., 1924-28; Coast Arty. School, Fort Monroe, Va., 1928-29. Address: Care The Adjutant General, U.S.A., War Dept., Washington, D.C.

1–**DELAFIELD, Elizabeth Thomson Hanenkamp (Mrs. Wallace)**, *b* Glasgow, Mo., Aug. 22, 1849.
8–Peter **Jones** (1599-1662), from Wales, settled in Va., dep. clk. of Henrico Co., Va., 1623; *m* Margaret, dau. of Abram Wood; she *m* 2d, Thomas Cocke, son of Richard Cocke, qv;
7–Maj. Peter (1651-1726), founder of Petersburg, Va.; *m* Mary Wood;
6–John (*b* 1710), *m* Elizabeth Walker;
5–William (1745-81), Am. Rev., killed at Battle of Guilford C.H.; *m* 1771, Agnes Walker;
4–James (1772-1830), *m* Katherine Stith;
3–Richard Stith (1793-1853), *m* Lucy Gibson (1795-1870);
2–Agnes Catherine (2 below).
10–Lt. Col. Walter **Aston** (qv);
9–Mary, *m* ca. 1647, as his 2d wife, Lt. Col. Richard **Cocke** (qv);
8–Richard, "the Younger;" *m* ? Anne–;
7–Mary Ann, *m* 1706, Robert **Bolling**, Jr. (1682-1749; Col. Robert[8], qv, *m* Jane, dau. of Thomas Rolfe, g.dau. of John Rolfe, qv);
6–Anne, *m* John **Hall**;
5–Lucy (*b* 1736), *m* Richard **Stith** (1727-1802), see Vol. I, p. 238, for Stith lineage;
4–Katherine (1773-1858), *m* James **Jones** (4 above);
3–Richard S., *m* Lucy Gibson (3 above);
2–Agnes Catherine (1820-95), *m* 1848, as his 2d wife, Richard Pindell **Hanenkamp** (1815-99), wholesale sugar mcht., St. Louis; issue: I–Elizabeth T. (1 above); II–Lucy D. (*b* 1851; *m* Edward O'Fallon); III–Richard P. (1854-1920; *m* Elizabeth Gray).

1–*m* Apr. 23, 1874, Wallace Delafield (1840-1915), sr. mem. Delafield & Snow, underwriters; issue (all *b* St. Louis, Mo.): 1–Mary Sturges (July 27, 1875-June 26, 1876); 2–Agnes Hanenkamp (Mrs. Albert W. Niedringhaus, see Vol. I, p. 238); 3–Wallace, Jr. (May 25, 1878-Feb. 22, 1918; *m* Oct. 15, 1912, Amanda A. Offutt); 4–Edith; 5–Elizabeth; 6–Edna Simmons (*b* Feb. 5, 1893-*d* Nov. 9, 1925); *m* Feb. 9, 1916, Cyrus Burnham More (issue: Betty More, *b* Mar. 8, 1918).
1–Mem. D.F.P.A., O.C., C.D., D.C.G., D.A.R., U.S.D. 1812, F.F.V.; hon. mem. Spanish War Nurses. Summer place: Wequetonsing, Mich. Residence: 5026 Westminster Pl., St. Louis, Mo.

1–**DEMAREST, Benjamin Garrison,** *b* Passaic, N.J., June 26, 1867.
9–David (des Marest) **Demarest** (1620-97), from Picardy to New Amsterdam, 1663; founded a French colony on the Hackensack River, N.J., 1677; *m* Marie Sohier;
8–David (1652-91), *m* 1675, Rachel Cresson (Pierre[9]);
7–Daniel (1685-living 1753), dea. Schraalenburg Ch.; *m* 1707, Rebecca DeGroot (Pieter[8]);
6–Daniel (bap. 1728-will dated 1802), dea., Schraalenburg, N.J., 1784, elder, 1785; overseer, 1788; *m* 1st, 1752, Cornelia Lydecker (bap. 1724; Reyk[7], *m* Marytje Benson);
5–Gerrett or Garret (bap. 1757), *m* Angenietje Durie (David[6], *m* Margrietje Van Hoorn);
4–Daniel (*b* 1780), *m* Elizabeth Benson;
3–John (*b* 1810), *m* Anne Van Buskirk;
2–Daniel (*b* 1833), *m* Mary C. Garrison (*b* 1838); issue: I–Cornelius (1854-99; *m* Belle Christie); II–Lura Meta (*b* 1860; *m* George H. Ackerman); III–Benjamin G. (1 above); IV–George McLean (*b* 1874; *m* Ethel Husk).
1–*m* June 10, 1925, Eda Lord Murphy, *b* Blue Earth City, Minn., Mar. 20, 1881; dau. of Rev. Samuel Howell Murphy, *m* Sophia Lord.
1–LL.B., Columbia U., 1888; LL.M., N.Y.U., 1891, B.S., 1905, M.A., 1907, Ph.D., 1908. Lawyer. Mem. S.M.D., S.C.W., H.S.A., H.S. (N.Y.), S.R., S.W. 1812, N.J. Hist. Soc., Vet. Corps Arty. Residence: Montclair, N.J.

1–**DEMING, Horace Edward,** *b* Palmyra, N.Y., Mar. 31, 1850.
3–Jeremiah **Deming**, drowned very young, 1817: *m* 1816, Ruth Herrick (*b* 1799-1800), of Pittsfield, she *m* 2d a Sickles;
2–Dr. Jeremiah Pierce Herrick (2 below).
4–Joseph **Colt** (1727-87), *m* 1756, Desire Pratt (1729-1806);
3–Joseph (1766-1831), from Old Lyme, Conn., to Palmyra, N.Y.; *m* Betsey Cole (*b* 1775);
2–Mary (1810-81), as Widow Bortles, *m* 2d, 1842, Dr. Jeremiah Pierce Herrick **Deming** (1817-83), from Pittsfield, Mass., to Palmyra, N.Y., later to Shortsville, N.Y.; issue: I–Joseph Colt (1843-63, killed in Civil War); II–Mary Louise (1845-1912); III–Horace Edward (1 above); IV–Daniel Webster (1853-86).
1–*m* July 17, 1878, Caroline Springsteed, *b* Albany, N.Y., Feb. 13, 1845; mem. I.A.G.; dau. of Dr. David Springsteed, *m* Maria Louisa Spalding; issue: 1–Eleanor, *b* Brooklyn, N.Y., Aug. 2, 1879; A.B., Bryn Mawr, '03; 2–Ruth (Sept. 10, 1880-June 23, 1881); 3–Harold Simpson, *b* Brooklyn, Sept. 13, 1883; A.B., Harvard, '05; Harvard Law Sch., 1908; *m* Apr. 23, 1913, Katherine, dau. of William Nelson Barritt (issue: Warren; MacDonald; Barbara; Quentin; Angus); 4–Edith (May 8, 1885-Jan. 3, 1886); 5–Constance, *b* New York, N.Y., Apr. 29, 1886; A.B., Bryn Mawr, '10; *m* Mar. 4, 1914, Willard Lewis (issue: Willard Deming; Hildegarde; Guy Spalding); 6–Guy Spalding, *b* New York, May 9, 1888; A.B., Harvard, '10; Grad. Sch. of Applied Science, Harvard, 1910-12; 1st lt. (temp.), U.S.A., Oct. 14, 1917, capt. (temp.), Feb. 18, 1918, comdg. officer 12th Construction Co., Air Service U.S.A., Jan., 1918-May, 1919; in Eng., Aug. 18, 1918-Mar. 30, 1919; *m* Aug. 11, 1917, Elinor, dau. of Louis Frank Castle (issue: Jean; Ann); 7–Kenneth (Oct. 5, 1889-Oct. 11, 1889); 8–Agathe, *b* Woodstock, Conn., Oct. 15, 1891; A.B., Bryn Mawr, '13; B.S., Columbia, 1915.
1–A.B., Harvard, '71 (P.B.K.); travel in Europe and Orient, 1871-73; Harvard Grad. Sch., 1873-74, Law Sch., 1874-76. Attorney and counsellor at law. Author (see Who's Who in America). Mem. Am. Acad. Polit. and Social Science. Summer place: House of the Four Winds, Cragsmoor, N.Y. Residence: 924 West End Av., New York, N.Y.

1–**DENHAM, Thomas Samuel,** *b* Boone Co., Mo., May 13, 1887.
5–William **Denham,** settled in N.J.; removed to N.C.; thence to Lexington, Ky., 1785; *m* Elizabeth Parker;
4–John (1777-1842), of Madison Co., Ky.; *m* Elanor Freeman (1774-1845);
3–Samuel (1799-1872), from Ky. to Boone Co., Mo.; *m* 2d, Catherine Toalson (1819-51); he *m* 3 times;
2–George Washington (2 below).
4–Anthony **Drane,** *m* Mecie Lawless;
3–George Thomas, *m* Sarah Fenton;
2–Lina D. (*b* 1863), *m* as his 2d wife, Oct. 12, 1882, George Washington **Denham** (*b* nr. Rocheport, Boone Co., Mo., Nov. 11, 1848-*d* Columbia, Boone Co., Mo., Jan. 21, 1929), farmer; taught rural school; justice peace, Perche Tp., Boone Co., Mo., 1894-1900; officer Bapt. Ch., over 50 yrs.; sch. director, 30 yrs.; he *m* 1st, Oct. 13, 1872, Stevie Wilhite (*d* 1873); issue (1st marriage): I–son (*d* infancy); issue (2d marriage): I–Sallie Alice (*m* O. F. Hawkins); II–May Lina (*m* Cherlis Wilhite; *m* 2d, N. C. Murray); III–Thomas S. (1 above); IV–Emma M. (*d* infancy); V–Stella C. (*m* Porter Strawn); VI–John W.; VII–Rhoda L. (*m* Brown Roberts); VIII–Grace O. (*m* Grocer Owens); IX–Georgia (*m* William Blohn); X–Maude E. (*m* Ray V. Blanchard).
1–*m* June 1, 1919, Emma Pade, *b* McCook, Neb., Apr. 19, 1890; dau. of Henry Pade, *m* Amelia–; issue: 1–Dorothy Ruth, *b* Denver, Colo., Aug. 30, 1920; 2–Hazel Salina, *b* Greybull, Wyo., Oct. 2, 1921.
1–B.S. in Edn., U.Mo., '19. Supt. schools, Deep River, Ia., 5 yrs. Mem. I. A. G. Residence: Deep River, Ia.

1–**DENISE, Larimore Conover,** *b* Omaha, Neb., June 7, 1872.
7–Teunis (Nyssen, Denyse) **Denise,** from Holland to New Amsterdam, N.Y., 1638; *m* Femmetje Jans, (Phoebe Felix), widow of Hendrick the Boor;
6–Dyonis (Teunison) (bap. 1654), *m* 2d, Helena (Cortelyou) Van Brunt (Jacques Cortelyou[7]);
5–Tunis (1704-1797), wrote name, De Nyse and Denis; *m* 2d, 1731, Francintje Hendrickson (Daniel[6], *m* Catharine Van Dyke);
4–Maj. Denise (1745-prob. 1798), began to write name Denise; maj. Monmouth Co., N.J., in Am. Rev.; judge, Monmouth Co. Ct.; *m* Catharine Schenck (Garret[5], *m* Jane Nietje Cowenhouven);
3–Sidney (1784-1859), Montgomery Co., O.; *m* 1806, Ann Conover (1787-1847; Jacob[4], *m* Elinor Smock);
2–Jacob Conover (2 below).
5–Richard **Collier** (prob. Thomas[6] [*b* 1700]; Richard[7], *m* 1699, Mary Jarvis, of Boston; perhaps Thomas[8] [*d* in Mass., 1691]; Thomas[9], *b* in Eng., 1576-*d* Hingham, Mass., 1647), of Boston, Mass.; *m* 1759, Mary Green;
4–Thomas (*b* Boston, 1761-*d* Binghamton, N.Y., 1842), editor, Litchfield (Conn.) Monitor, 1784-1807; *m* Elizabeth Stockwell (1761-1829), of Norwich, Conn.;
3–Daniel Lewis (1796-1869), spent most of his life at Steubenville, O.; 2d postmaster Steubenville; lawyer; bank pres.; foster father of Sec. of War, Edwin M. Stanton in Cabinet of President Lincoln; *d* at Phila., Pa.; *m* 1823, Hetty Larimore (1804-98; David[4], 1st p.m., Steubenville, O., *m* Nancy Clark);
2–Mary Clara (*b* 1845), *m* 1870, Jacob Conover **Denise,** M.D. (1828-99), Jefferson Med. Coll., 1855; surgeon, 27th Ohio Vol. Inf., 1861-64; surgeon, Tripler Hosp., Columbus, O., 1864-65; eye, ear, nose and throat specialist, Omaha, Neb.; prof. and dean, Omaha Med. Coll. (U.Neb.); city and co. physician; issue: I–Larimore Conover (1 above); II–John R. Meredith (*d* infancy); III–Esther Collier (*b* 1878); IV–Francis William (*d* infancy); V–Daniel Lewis (*b* 1880; *m* 1910, Martha Hamer, *b* 1886).

1–*m* Oct. 28, 1902, Bernice Evans (Apr. 10, 1869-Mar. 28, 1917); dau. of Frank Evans, of Vinton, Ia., and Wichita, Kan., *m* Emma Wood; issue (all *b* New Kensington, Pa.): 1–Dorothy Bernice, *b* Nov. 13, 1903; *m* June 30, 1927, Harry Meredith Hagerman (issue: Elinor Bernice, *b* Apr. 21, 1928; Meredith Louise, *b* May 26, 1929); 2–Marguerite Meredith, *b* Nov. 1, 1907; Lindenwood, 1927; *m* Mar. 7, 1927, Henry Bouguard Betts (issue: Henry B., Jr., *b* May 25, 1928); 3–Paul Larimore, *b* Feb. 22, 1909.
1–*m* 2d, Apr. 23, 1919, Alma Dodds, *b* Valentia, Pa., May 16, 1887; dau. of Robert Cameron Dodds, of New Castle, Pa., *m* Sarah Ann McGowan.
1–A.B., Princeton, 1894; grad. Presbyn. Theol. Sem., Omaha, 1897; studied Western Theol. Sem., Pittsburgh, 1905; D.D., Bellevue (Neb.) Coll., 1916. Clergyman and educator; pastor, 1897-17; pres. Presbyn. Theol. Sem., Omaha, Neb., since 1924, (see Who's Who in America). Republican. Club: University. Summer place: Chautauqua, N.Y. Residence: 2020 Spencer St., Omaha, Neb.

1–**DENNISON, George Austin,** *b* New Boston, Ill., Nov. 20, 1873.
5–James (Denniston) **Dennison,** from Eng.; an early settler in Warrington Tp., York Co., Pa.; on assessment list of 1783; sgt., Capt. Clark's Co., 8th Regt., Pa. Line;
4–William (1760-1849), removed with his family across the Blue Mountains, 1801, settled near Lebanon, Warren Co., O., from here he removed to Connersville, Fayette Co., Ind., thence to Springfield, Ill., 1827, founded Dennison's Landing, afterward New Boston, Ill., 1828; *m* Rachael Johns (1776-1853), both buried at New Boston, Ill.;
3–Erastus Segustus (1809-49), began to write name Dennison; *m* Martha Jane Long (1820-1907);
2–Albert Erastus (*b* 1844), capitalist; *m* Elizabeth Hannah Roberts (*b* 1846); issue: I–Daisy (1866-1923; *m* 1887, William Banks Farver); II–Henry Franklin (1868-96); III–Josephine (*b* 1869; *m* Harvey Ira Prouty); IV–Viella (1871-79); V–George A. (1 above).
1–Not married. Ed. high sch.; spl. studies covering a number of yrs. under Leo Cooper, San Francisco, William T. Price, New York. Artist in sculptured enamels, pupil of Florence Koehler, London, Paris, Rome, and C. F. Ingerson, San Francisco. Asst. sec. Calif. State Bd. of Trade, San Francisco, 1895-1903; sec. Calif. Commn. to St. Louis Expdn., 1903-04, Lewis and Clark Expdn., Portland, Ore., 1904-06; sec. and mgr. Ocean Shore Land Co., San Francisco, 1906-08; sec. Calif. Commn. to Alaska-Yukon-Pacific Expdn., Seattle, 1908-10 (and sec. Fine Arts Jury, 1909); mgr. Cathedral Oaks Sch. of Art, Alma, Calif., 1910-12; chief Dept. of Horticulture, Panama-Pacific Internat. Expdn., San Francisco, 1913-15, and mem. superior jury of Internat. Jury Awards, 1915. With C. F. Ingerson, created, designed and constructed "The Samarkand," Santa Barbara, and the Ark of the Covenant for Temple Emanuel, San Francisco. Author (see Who's Who in America). Republican. Residence: Cathedral Oaks, Alma, Calif.

1–**DENT, Stanley Hubert,** *b* Eufaula, Ala., Aug. 16, 1869.
8–John **Dent** (ca. 1645-ca. 1712), from Eng. to Md. ca. 1662; *m* Mary Hatch;
7–John (ca. 1674-ca. 1732), *m* Katharine (probably) Turner;
6–John (1705-91); *m* wife's name unknown;
5–John (*b* ca. 1730), *m* Violetta Winnett;
4–Hatch (ca. 1759-ca. 1818), *m* Suzannah Edwards;
3–Stouten Warren (1806-83), *m* Mary Catherine Smoot (1817-94);
2–Stouten Hubert (1833-1917), capt. arty., C.S.A.; lawyer, banker, planter; mem. Constl. Conv. of Ala., 1901; *m* Anna Beall Young (1840-1902); issue: I–Edward Young (*b* 1861; *m* Annie McCormick); II–Nannie (*b* 1867; *m* J. E. Long; *m* 2d, W. W. Mangum); III–Stanley Hubert (1 above); IV–Henry A. (*b* 1872); V–Louise (*b* 1876; *m* George N. Hurt); VI–Caroline (*b* 1879; *m* Charles S. McDowell, Jr.).
1–*m* June 23, 1897, Etta Tinsley, *b* Louisville, Ky.; dau. of W. H. Tinsley, of Louisville, *m* Alice Cocke; issue: 1–William Tinsley, *b* Montgomery, Ala., Nov. 19, 1900; U.Va., 1922.
1–A.B., Southern U., '86; LL.B., U.Va., 1889. Lawyer. Pros. atty., Montgomery Co., Ala., 1902-09; mem. 61st to 66th Congresses, 1909-21 (chmn. Military Affairs Com. during World War). Democrat. Methodist. Residence: 432 Felder Av., Montgomery, Ala.

CAPT. BENJAMIN DENSMORE (1831-1913).

1–**DENSMORE, Frances Theresa,** *b* Red Wing, Minn., May 21, 1867.
8–Thomas **Dean** (*b* Kent Co., Eng., 1603-*d* Concord, Mass., 1675), to America in the "Elizabeth and Ann," 1635; *m* Elizabeth–; *m* 2d, Mildred–;
7–Joseph (1638-1717), of Concord, Mass.; *m* 1662, Elizabeth Fuller (Thomas[8], qv);
6–Hannah (*b* 1682), *m* Thomas (Dinsmoor, Dinsmore) **Densmore,** of Bedford, Mass.; weaver; living in Littleton, Mass., 1744; to Hollis, N.H., being 3d family in village; surveyor highways, 1746; of Scottish origin, supposed to have come to America from Ireland;
5–Eliphalet (*b* Bedford, Mass., 1734-*d* N.H., 1811), minuteman, Concord, Am. Rev.; lt., Bedford militia, which carried the "arm and hammer" flag (still preserved in Boston); capt., Col. William Prescott's Regt., in Battle of Bunker Hill; *m* Hannah Treadwell;
4–Daniel (1774-1829), to Phelps, N.Y., 1806; settled at Riga, N.Y., 1808; with his squirrel rifle, was among militia called out at the burning of Buffalo, N.Y., by the English in 1812; *m* 1st, at Amherst, Vt., 1798, Margaret Seaton Hartshorn;
3–Orrin (*b* Washington, N.H., 1805-*d* Red Wing, Minn., 1878), to New York, 1806; insp. schs., 1830,37; mem. co. bd. of supervisors; removed to Emerald Grove, Wis., 1845; thence to Red Wing, Minn., 1857; judge of probate, 1859-61; co. treas., 1861-64; city recorder, 1866; trustee State Insane Asylum (St. Peter, Minn.); dep. collector U.S. revenue, Goodhue Co.; mem. State Legislature, 1869-71 (chmn. com. on edn.); asst. U.S. marshal census 1870; with state dept. of pub. instrn., St. Paul, Minn., 1871-76; *m* 1828, Elizabeth Fowle (*b* Wheatland, N.Y., 1808-*d* Red Wing, Minn., 1891; Benjamin[4] [*b* Kent Co., Eng., 1772-*d* Emerald Grove, Wis., 1860], to N.Y., thence to Wis., *m* Martha Lea [*b* Birmingham, Eng.-*d* 1821], to N.Y.);
2–Benjamin (2 below).
9–Thomas (Tredwell) **Treadwell,** mentioned (by Felt) as being a settler in Ipswich, Mass., 1635; appears to have settled first in Dorchester, Mass.; freeman, 1638; *m* ? Mary Taylor (*d* Ipswich, Mass., 1686);
8–Thomas (*b* prob. Eng., ca. 1634-living 1712, may have *d* 1718), freeman, 1682; *m* 1664, Sarah Titcomb (*b* Newbury, Mass., 1640; William[9] [*b* Eng.-*d* Newbury, Mass., 1676], to America in the "Hercules," 1633; freeman, 1642, select-

man, 1646, rep. Gen. Ct., 1655, *m* Joanna, dau. of Richard Bartlett, qv);
7–Thomas (1665-1743), *m* Frances Sawyer (1670-1744; William[8], from Lancaster, Eng., to Salem, Mass., 1640, early settler at Reading, Mass., resided at Newbury, *m* Ruth–);
6–Thomas (*d* 1758), *m* Hepsibah Hobson (1700-65; John[7], *m* Dorcas–);
5–Hannah (*b* Ipswich, Mass., 1736), *m* Eliphalet **Densmore** (5 above).
7–John **Seaton** (*b* Scotland), from Ireland to Boxford, Mass., 1729;
6–John (*d* 1793), *m* Ismenia Seaton (*d* 1797), of Amherst and Washington, N.H. (Andrew[7] [*b* Scotland], uncle of John, from Ireland to Boxford, Mass., 1729);
5–Margaret (*b* 1752), *m* Timothy **Hartshorn**;
4–Margaret Seaton (*b* Amherst, N.H., 1776-*d* Riga, N.Y., 1823), *m* Daniel **Densmore** (4 above).
7–John (Ffillio, Fillow) **Philleo** (*b* southern France, 1667-*d* Fairfield, Conn., 1733), tradition says he was Huguenot refugee; bought land Norwalk, Conn., 1700; *m* Sarah– (*b* France);
6–Samuel (*b* prob. France-*d* ca. 1793), began to write name Philleo; *m* at Norwalk, Conn., 1731, Abigail Fountain;
5–Phineas (*b* Norwalk, Conn., 1749-*d* Dover, N.Y., ca. 1789), minute man, Dutchess Co., militia regt., Am. Rev.; *m* Silence Cummings (*d* 1798);
4–Elijah (*b* Conn., 1777-*d* 1823), War 1812; *m* Mary Ann (Moredock) Murdock (1799-1845);
3–Delia (*b* Bridgewater, N.Y., 1808-*d* Cazenovia, N.Y., 1844), *m* 1829, Joseph **Greenland** (*b* Eng., 1806-*d* Cazenovia, 1844), to America ante 1829;
2–Sarah Adelaide (*b* Cazenovia, N.Y., 1838-*d* Minneapolis, Minn., 1920), *m* 1866, Benjamin **Densmore** (*b* nr. Caledonia, N.Y., 1831-*d* Red Wing, Minn., 1913), see portrait; to Emerald Grove, Wis., 1846; ed. prep. sch., Beloit Coll. (Wis.), 1851-52; as civil engr., 1852-53, in charge of bldg. first section out of Chicago of the (subsequently) C.&N.W.R.R.; located at St. Paul, Minn., 1854; surveyor for railroads and town sites of Minn.; enl. 3d Minn. Inf., 1861; served Civil War; capt., Co. F, 2d Regt., U.S. Colored Heavy Arty.; issue: I–Frances T. (1 above); II–William Greenland (1869-72); III–Margaret Louise (*b* 1874).
1–Oberlin Conservatory of Music, 1884-86; hon. A.M., Oberlin Coll., 1924. Began studying music of the Am. Indians, 1893; has made spl. researches in Am. Indian music for Bureau of Am. Ethnology, Smithsonian Instn., since 1907 (see Who's Who in America). Collaborator, Bureau of Am. Ethnology. Mem. A.A.A.S., Washington Acad. of Sciences, Anthropological Soc. Washington (ex-sec.), Archaeol. Soc. Washington, 19th, 20th and 23d Internat. Congresses of Americanists, Soc. Women Geographers, Minn. Hist. Soc., Sigma Alpha Iota (hon. mem. Phi Chapter). Hon. mem. Thursday Musicale, Minneapolis, Minn. Author: Chippewa Music, Chippewa Music, II, Teton Sioux Music, Northern Ute Music, Mandan and Hidatsa Music, Chippewa Customs, Music of the Tule Indians of Panama, Handbook of the Collection of Musical Instruments in the U.S. Nat. Museum, The American Indians and their Music, Indian Action Songs, Poems from Sioux and Chippewa Songs. Residence: Red Wing, Minn.

1–**DENTON, Joey,** *b* Orleans Flat, Calif., Dec. 10, 1858.
8–Rev. Richard **Denton** (qv);
7–Daniel (1628-1703), of Jamaica, L.I.; town clk., Jamaica, 1656,57,61; magistrate; justice of the peace, 1665-66; returned to Eng. and in 1670 published a book giving a "brief description of New York"; copy has sold for $615.00; returned to America, moving to Springfield, Mass., then to Jamaica, L.I.; *m* 2d, 1676, Hannah Leonard (*b* 1659; John[8], *m* Sarah Heath);
6–Samuel (1679-1713), of Hempstead, L.I.; *m* ca. 1703, Deborah Wood, of Jamaica;
5–Daniel (ca. 1704-1750), Goshen, Orange Co., N.Y.; *m* 1725, Sarah Everett, of Jamaica;
4–Jonas (1743-86), of Goshen; *m* 1765, Eleanor Jackson (*b* ca. 1749; Michael[5], cornet of horse, 1738, judge of Ct. of Common Pleas, from Orange Co., N.Y., dep. to 1st conv. which formed the Provincial Congress in N.Y. City, 1775, mem. Provincial Congress of N.Y., 1775-77, pvt. 3d Orange Co. Militia in Am. Rev.);
3–Michael (1772-1824), of Chester, Orange Co., N.Y.; *m* 1803, Catherine Moffatt;
2–Edward Michael (2 below).
7–Samuel **Moffatt** (*b* nr. Ayrshire, Scotland-*d* prob. Woodbridge, N.J.);
6–William (*b* Ireland or Scotland-*d* Woodbridge, N.J.);
5–Samuel (*b* Ballylig, Co. Antrim, Ireland, 1704-*d* Blagg's Cove, Orange Co., N.Y., 1787), town officer, Cornwall, Orange Co., N.Y., 1765; signed with 5 sons, Assn. Test; *m* Ruth Burns (*d* 1734); *m* 2d, 1735, in Woodbridge, N.J., Anne Gregg (*b* Sluh Hull, Ireland, 1716-*d* Blagg's Cove, N.Y., 1794);
4–Maj. Thomas (1742-1805), of Blagg's Cove; capt., minutemen, 1775; maj. comdg. Orange Co. minutemen at Battle of Stony Point, Am. Rev.; hon. mem. S.C. (N.Y.); signed Assn. Test.; chmn. Com. Safety, 1774; magistrate and co. clk., 1778-94; *m* 1773, Susannah Howell;
3–Catherine (1782-1839), of Blagg's Cove, N.Y.; *m* Michael **Denton** (3 above).
8–Edward **Howell** (qv);
7–Richard (*b* Marsh Gibbon, Eng., 1629-*d* Southampton, L.I.), *m* 1st, Elizabeth Halsey (Thomas[8]);
6–Lt. Hezekiah (1677-1744), of Southampton, L.I.; *m* 1st, 1702, Phoebe Halsey (1671-1732);
5–Hezekiah (*b* Southampton, 1709-*d* Blooming Grove, Orange Co., N.Y., will proved 1784), *m* 1735, Susanna Sayre (*b* 1709; Job[7]);
4–Susannah (1743-1817), *m* Thomas **Moffatt** (4 above).
10–Thomas **Dudley** (qv);
9–Rev. Samuel (ca. 1610-1683), of Exeter, N.H.; lt., 1631; rep. for Salisbury, Mass., 1644; removed to N.H. and became pastor at Exeter; *m* 3d, Elizabeth– (living 1702);
8–Stephen (*d* 1735), of Exeter; served in Indian wars, 1695; *m* 1st, 1684, Sarah Gilman (1667-1713; Hon. Capt. John[9], of Exeter, *m* Elizabeth Treworgy);
7–Col. Stephen (1688-1734), of Exeter; *m* 1708, Sarah Davison (*b* 1682; Maj. Daniel[8], *m* Abigail Coffin);
6–Davison (1709-87), of Brentwood, N.H.; *m* Anna Ladd (*b* 1749; Dudley[7], *m* Alice Hurley, of Haverhill, Mass.);
5–Timothy (*d* 1778), of Brentwood; killed at Battle of Monmouth, N.J.; *m* 1769, Mary Leavitt (Timothy, Jr.[6], of Brentwood, *m* Elizabeth–);
4–Stephen (ca. 1770-1845), of Brentwood, and Barton, Vt.; *m* 1793, Deborah Elkins (1773-1825);
3–Mary Leavitt (1802-44), *m* 1830, Tullius **Strobridge** (1789-1866), of Claremont, N.H. (William[4], Am. Rev., of Middleboro, Mass., mem. Vt. Assembly and Land Tax Commn., *m* Hannah Tuttle);
2–Mary Mehitable (1832-1924), *m* 1856, Edward Michael **Denton** (1817-86), of Sacramento, and Nevada Co., Calif.; teacher, mcht., miner, farmer; *m* 2d, 1913, Frank C. Grant; issue (1st marriage, surname Denton): I–Mary Florence (*b* 1857); II–Joey (1 above); III–Edward Michael (*b* 1861; *m* Grace Austin-Robinson, *d*); IV–Kate Parker (*b* 1864; *m* George Leander Anderson, *d*); V–Emma Frances Hapgood (1867-99); VI–Carry Slater (*b* and *d* 1868); VII–Charles Hapgood (*b* 1869; *m* Alice Hardin-Lowry); VIII–Loney Sandford (*b* 1871; *m* Alice Lee).
1–Ed. State Normal Sch. (now Teachers' Coll.), San Jose, Calif. Taught school 34 yrs., retired. Mem. D.A.C., D.F.P.A. (chapter historian and registrar), D.A.R. (chapter regent, dir., historian and registrar), Native Daus. of the Golden West (pres.), etc. Christian. Republican. Residence: 1318 Lincoln Boul., Santa Monica, Calif.

1–**DEPEW, Ganson,** *b* Buffalo, N.Y., Mar. 6, 1866.
8–Francois (Dupuy, DePew) **Depew** (living 1702), came from Calais, France, to New Amsterdam; settled at Bushwick, Brooklyn, N.Y., 1661; mem. Dutch ch., Flatbush; had grant of 80-odd acres, Staten Island, 1680; removed to Rockland Co., N.Y., 1687; later to Westchester Co., 1702; *m* 1st, 1661, Geertje Willems Van Boerum (*d* ca. 1687; Willem Jacobs[9]);

7–Jan, Jean or John (bap. 1674-living 1722), of Tappan, N.Y.; *m* 1701, as her 2d husband, Jannetje Wiltse (bap. 1663; Hendrick^{8}, of Kingston, N.Y., soldier Esopus War, *m* Widow Margarita [Meyerings] Jansen); Jannetje had *m* 1st, Myndert Hendrickse (Hogencamp);
6–John (1705-83), began to write name DePew; Am. Rev.; prob. of Tappan, Rockland Co., N.Y.; removed to Cortlandtown, Westchester Co.; *m* ca. 1733, Elizabeth–;
5–Henry (1734-88), of Cortlandtown, N.Y.; *m* his cousin, 1756, Mary DePew;
4–Abraham (1762-1838), of Peekskill, N.Y.; *m* 2d 1787, Catherine Cranckheit;
3–Isaac (1800-69), began to write name Depew; resided at Peekskill, N.Y.; *m* 1832, Martha Minott Mitchell;
2–William Beverly (2 below).
8–Francois **Depew** (8 above);
7–William (*b* ca. 1663), of Verplank's Pt., N.Y.; *m* 1688, Lysbeth Weyt or White, from Barbados to Kitchawan, N.Y.;
6–Solomon (ca. 1702-1785), began to write name DePew; settled nr. Pue Pond, Cortlandtown, N.Y.; *m* ca. 1728, Sarah–;
5–Mary (1737-89), *m* 1756, her cousin, Henry **De Pew** (5 above).
8–Harck **Siboutszen** (ca. 1615-1681 or 84), from Languedoc, France, to New Amsterdam; removed to Newtown, L.I., 1650; received two grants of land, 1654 and 64; *m* at New York, 1642, Wyntie Teunis, from Holland;
7–Jan Herricksen (bap. 1657-living 1730), took surname **Cranckheyt;** removed to Manor of Cortlandt, Westchester Co., N.Y.; bought large tract of land (now Peekskill), N.Y.; *m* ca. 1695, Grietje, prob. Brouwer;
6–Jacobus (bap. 1708-1773), *m* 1st, ca. 1735, Geertje–;
5–James (bap. 1737-post 1804), merchant, Peekskill; supervisor, Rikes Patent, Westchester Co.; capt. colonial militia, 1775; capt. 3d Regt., Westchester Co. Militia, Am. Rev.; captured, but exchanged; *m* 1st, ca. 1763, Hester Lent (*b* ca. 1741; Lt. Hendrick^{6}, *m* Elizabeth Storm; Harck or Hercules^{7}, *m* Cornelia VanWert; Ryck A. VanLent^{8}, *m* Tryntie or Catrina, dau. Harck Siboutszen, 8 above; Abraham Rycken^{9}, of New Amsterdam);
4–Catherine (1765-1847), *m* Abraham **Depew** (4 above).
10–Matthew **Mitchell** (qv);
9–David (1619-85), large landowner, Stratford, Conn.; *m* Sarah Wheeler;
8–John (ca. 1654-1732), ens., Woodbury, Conn.; mem. Gen. Ct.; *m* Elizabeth Knell (1653-1730; Nicholas^{9}, *m* Elizabeth Newman);
7–John (bap. 1688/89-1748), lt., Woodbury; *m* 1st, Elizabeth Curtiss (bap. 1697-1738; Ens. John^{8}, *m* Johannah–);
6–Asahel (1723-97), pvt. Am. Rev.; *m* Olive Root (1726-1813; Joseph^{7}, *m* Susannah–);
5–Rev. Justus (bap. 1754-1806), pastor Ch. of Christ, New Canaan, Conn.; *m* 1779, Martha Sherman;
4–Chauncey Root (1786-1814 or 15), lawyer, Delhi, N.Y.; *m* ca. 1807, Anna MacArthur Johnston (1785-1864; Hon. Robert^{5}, *m* Elizabeth Ogden);
3–Martha Minott (1810-85), *m* Isaac **Depew** (3 above).
9–Capt. John **Sherman** (qv);
8–Joseph (1650-1731), *m* 1673, Elizabeth Winship (*b* 1652; Edward^{9}, *m* 2d, Elizabeth Parke);
7–William (1692-1741), *m* 2d, Mehitable Wellington (bap. 1687/88; Benjamin^{8}); among their sons was Roger, a "signer";
6–Rev. Josiah (1734-89), A.B., Princeton, '54; A.M., Harvard, 1758, and Yale, 1765; minister, writer and orator; chaplain 7th Conn. Regt. in Am. Rev.; *m* 1757, Martha Minott (*d* 1820; James^{7}, *m* Elizabeth Wilder);
5–Martha (1758-1829), *m* 1st, Justus **Mitchell** (5 above).
2–William Beverly **Depew** (1837-97), of Buffalo, N.Y.; *m* 1865, Helen S. Ganson (1840-1900); issue: I–Ganson (1 above); II–C. Mitchell (May 15, 1867-Apr. 21, 1927).
1–*m* Nov. 15, 1894, Grace Goodyear (Aug. 11, 1872-1914), dau. of Frank Henry Goodyear; issue: 1–Ganson Goodyear (Nov. 2, 1895-Mar. 31, 1924); 2–Lucia (Mrs. George E. Parkinson, qv).
1–*m* 2d, Sept. 30, 1915, Carrie Gorton **Ransom,** dau. of Henry W. Gorton, Buffalo, N.Y.
1–Ed. public grammar and high schools, Buffalo. Admitted to bar, 1890; mem. law firms of Greene, McMillan, Gluck & Pooley, attys. for N.Y.C.R.R. Co. and other corpns., and its successor, Pooley, Depew & Spratt, until 1902; associated with Frank H. Goodyear in lumber, coal and railroad business in Pa. until retirement, 1923; now dir. Buffalo & Susquehanna R.R. Co., Great Southern Lbr. Co., Millard Fillmore Hosp., Buffalo Fine Arts. Acad.; trustee Grosvenor and Buffalo Public libraries, 1910-14. Mem. Buffalo Lumber Exchange (ex-pres.), Chamber of Commerce, etc. Mem. H.S.A., H.S., S.C.W., S.A.R. (pres. Buffalo Chapter, 1925; pres. Empire State Soc., 1926-28; pres. gen. Nat. Soc., 1928-1929), I.A.G., etc. Clubs: Buffalo, Saturn, Park, Automobile (ex-pres.), Buffalo Country (ex-pres.), Wanakah, Transit, etc. Pres. Buffalo Dist. Golf Assn.; exec. com. U.S. Golf Assn. Mason (32°, Shrine). Residence: 165 Summer St., Buffalo, N.Y.

1–**PARKINSON, Lucia Depew (Mrs. George E.),** *b* Buffalo, N.Y., Jan. 22, 1900.
9–Dep. Gov. Stephen **Goodyear** (qv);
8–Lt. John (1650-1702), of New Haven, Conn.; *m* 1683, Abigail Gibbard (1660-1719; William^{9}, magistrate, New Haven, left estates in Eng., *m* Ann, dau. Edmund Tapp);
7–Andrew (*b* 1702), large landowner, Hamden, Conn.; *m* 2d, 1743, Esther Morris (1709-88; prob. dau. William^{8}; William^{9}, of Wethersfield, Conn., 1669);
6–Titus (1745-98), large landowner, New Haven (now Hamden), Conn.; *m* 1781, Abigail Atwater (1749-1836; Samuel^{7}, *m* Sarah, dau. Caleb Ball, who was g.s. Alling Ball, of New Haven, 1644; Daniel^{8}, *m* Abigail Tuttle; Samuel^{9}, *m* Sarah Alling; David^{10}, planter, New Haven);
5–John (1785-1826), of Genoa and Sempronius, N.Y.; removed to Barre, N.Y., 1825; *m* 1807, Julia Bradley; after death of parents, children were cared for by Henry Bradley, of Northville, N.Y.;
4–Bradley (1816-89), physician, Cortland, N.Y.; removed to western N.Y.; retired and resided at Buffalo; *m* 1845, Esther P. Kinne;
3–Frank Henry (*b* 1849), financier; lumber and coal operator; chmn. bd. dirs., Buffalo and Susquehanna R.R.; dir. U.S. Rubber, etc.; *m* 1871, Josephine Looney (*b* 1851; Robert^{4}, *m* Josephine Kidder);
2–Grace (2 below).
11–William **Bradley** (qv);
10–Abraham (1650-1718), *m* 1673, Ann Thompson;
9–Daniel (1679-1723), *m* Sarah Bassett;
8–Daniel (1706-73), *m* 1727, Abigail Punchard;
7–Jabez (1733-93), of New Haven, Conn.; *m* Esther Beach;
6–Judge Jabez (1765-1817), removed to Lee, Mass.; later to Northville (now King's Ferry), N.Y., 1794; *m* 1785, Esther Bradley (1765-1850; Ely^{7}, *m* Esther Goodyear [Theophilus^{8}; John^{9}, 8 above]; Joseph^{8}; Joseph^{9}; Joseph^{10}; William^{11}, qv);
5–Julia (1790-1826), *m* John **Goodyear** (5 above).
10–Henry (Kinney) **Kinne** (1642-1712), son of Sir Thomas, of Norfolk, Eng.; came from Holland; settled at Salem, Mass.; served King Philip's War; *m* Anna–;
9–Thomas (*d* 1687), of Salem; *m* 1677, Elizabeth Knight;
8–Thomas (1678-1756), began to write name Kinne; removed to Preston (now Griswold), Conn., 1715; founder of 1st Congl. Ch., Preston; *m* Martha Cox;
7–Moses (1710-98), of Preston and Voluntown, Conn.; *m* 1732, Abigail Read, of Norwich, Conn.;
6–Ira (*b* 1740), of Voluntown; *m* Miriam Goodell;
5–Moses (1768-1853), removed to and helped clear ground at Homer, N.Y.; settled finally at Cortland, N.Y.; *m* 2d, 1811, Polly Forbes (*d* 1838; dau. Alexander, of Aberdeen, Scotland);
4–Esther P. (*b* 1822), *m* Bradley **Goodyear** (4 above);
3–Frank Henry, *m* Josephine Looney (3 above);
2–Grace (1872-1914), *m* 1894, Ganson **Depew** (qv for issue).

1–*m* Nov. 29, 1920, Edward de Cernea, of New York, N.Y.
1–*m* 2d, Mar. 31, 1930, George E. Parkinson, *b* Toronto, Can., Oct. 14, 1901; son of Mathew Parkinson, of Toronto.
1–Ed. Private school and college. Address: 810 W. Ferry St., Buffalo, N.Y.

HENRY EUGENE De PUY (b Philadelphia, 1856-d 1920); educated public schools; when a young man started in employ of John B. Stetson, hat manufacturer, where he continued for 48 years, becoming secretary of the John B. Stetson Co., 1901, and when he died in 1920, was one of the principal directors of the great business he helped to create. In 1895 he was sent on a trip around the world, was the first to introduce Stetson hats in many foreign countries. He was a member of the Old York Country Club, Manufacturers Club and Philadelphia Chamber of Commerce. As councilman in Jenkintown, he devoted many long years to public service.

1–**De PUY, Clara,** *b* Ogontz, Pa., July 27, 1888.
11–Nicholas **De Puy,** from Paris to Holland, thence to America in the "Good Ship Pemberton Church," 1652; settled at New Amsterdam; *m* Catherine Renard, or De Vos, or De Vaux;
10–Moses, *b* Holland; settled Esopus, Ulster Co., N.Y.; *m* Maria Wyncoop;
9–Nicholas (*b* 1683), of Shawnee, Pa.; *m* 1707, Wyntie (Roosa);
8–Moses (1718-1802), *d* Rochester, N.Y.; justice of peace, Bucks Co., Pa.; *m* 1735, Anna Prye;
7–Moses;
6–John (1761-1831), of Yardley, Bucks Co., Pa.; *m* 1783, Elizabeth Strickland (*d* 1789);
5–John (1783-1876), of Phila., Pa.; *m* 1806, Elizabeth Van Horn (1789-1817);
4–John Stewart (1807-88), of Phila.; *m* 1833, Rebecca Watson (1807-36; Nathan[5], *m* Elizabeth Flowers);
3–Watson (1834-1915), of Phila.; *m* 1853, Eliza Johnson Harmon (1832-1908; Frederick Medsker[4] [1802-87], *m* 1831, Mary Ann [1808-33], dau. of Edward Johnson [son of Robert], from Lincolnshire, Eng., 1818, settled at Cato, Cayuga Co., N.Y., *m* Ann Clayton);
2–Henry Eugene (1856-1920), of Phila. (see portrait and biography); *m* 1884, Fannie Sheldon Noble (1859-1924); for issue and other lineages see Mrs. Herbert Aubrey Smith.
1–Ed. Sch. of Industrial Art, Phila., Pa. Chmn. League of Women Voters, Jenkintown; mem. bd. of dir. Jenkintown Day Nursey. Mem. S.M.D.; life mem. I.A.G. Clubs: Wyncote Woman's, Phila. City. Episcopalian. Republican. Residence: 312 Florence Av., Jenkintown, Pa.

1–**SMITH, Frances Marguerite De Puy (Mrs. Herbert Aubrey),** *b* Ogontz (now Elkins Park), Pa., Mar. 15, 1887.
9–Gov. William **Leete** (qv);
8–Anna (*b* 1661), of New Haven, Conn.; *m* 1682, John **Trowbridge** (1661-89);
7–Anna (1686-1721), of New Haven; *m* 1708, Rev. Samuel **Cook** (1687-1747);
6–Sarah (1712-1802), of New Haven; *m* 1733, James **Sherman** (1706-86);
5–Rebecca (1751-1833), of New Haven; *m* 1774, Benjamin **Brooks** (1746-1810; John[6] [1715-77], *m* 1738, Anne [1706-84], dau. of Lemuel Sherwood [1687-1732], of Stratford, *m* 2d, Experience Wheeler [1685-1721], and g.dau. of Matthew Sherwood, *m* Mary, dau. of Thomas Fitch, qv);
4–Benjamin (1778-1857), *m* 1810, Harriet Jones;
3–Harriet Jones (1818-1901), of Bridgeport; *m* 1839, William Henry **Noble** (1813-94);
2–Fannie Sheldon (2 below).
9–Theophilus **Eaton** (qv);
8–Hannah (1630-1704), of Eng.; *m* 1659, William **Jones** (*b* 1624), dep.gov. of New Haven;
7–Isaac (1671-1741), of Stratford, Conn.; *m* 2d, 1692, as her 2d husband, Deborah Clark (1672-1705);
6–Timothy (1696-1780), of New Haven; *m* 1737, Ann Goodrich (1712-83);
5–Isaac (1739-1812), of New Haven; *m* 3d, 1774, Sybil Benjamin (1755-1814);
4–Harriet (1790-1829), of New Haven; *m* Benjamin **Brooks** (4 above);
3–Harriet Jones, *m* William Henry **Noble** (3 above);
2–Fannie Sheldon (1859-1924), of Bridgeport; *m* 1884, Henry Eugene **De Puy** (1856-1920); issue: I–Frances Marguerite (1 above); II–Clara (qv for other lineages); III–Bertha Webb (Mrs. Robert William Davis, Jr., qv for other lineages).
1–*m* June 18, 1913, Herbert Aubrey Smith, *b* Jenkintown, Pa., Sept. 6, 1884; son of Andrew Jackson Smith, of Jenkintown; issue: 1–Henry De Puy, *b* Phila., Pa., May 8, 1914; ed. Valley Forge Mil. Acad.; 2–Marguerite Desiree, *b* Phila., Oct. 14, 1925.
1–Ed. Jenkintown High School and School of Industrial Art, Phila. Mem. Woman's Club. Residence: 147 Fernbrook Av., Wyncote, Pa.

1–**DAVIS, Bertha Webb De Puy (Mrs. Robert William, Jr.),** *b* Jenkintown, Pa., Nov. 28, 1890.
11–Gov. Thomas **Welles** (qv);
10–John (*d* 1659), of Eng.; *m* Elizabeth Bourne;
9–John (1648-1713), of Stratford, Conn.; *m* ca. 1670, Mary Hollister;
8–Comfort (ca. 1677-1717), of Newtown, Conn.; *m* 1704, Abel **Birdsey** (*d* 1679);
7–Elizabeth (*b* 1706), of Stratford; *m* 1727, Benjamin **Curtis** (1704-82);
6–Elizabeth (*b* 1733), of Newtown; *m* Capt. John **Glover** (1732-1802);
5–Elizabeth (1767-1837), of Newtown; *m* 1790, Sylvanus **Noble** (1756-1837);
4–Rev. Birdsey Glover (1791-1848), of New Milford, Conn.; *m* 1813, Charlotte Sanford (1792-1843);
3–William Henry (1813-94), of Bridgeport; *m* 1839, Harriet Jones Brooks;
2–Fannie Sheldon (2 below).
11–Gov. William **Bradford,** Mayflower Pilgrim (qv);
10–William (b 1624), *m* 1659, Alice Richards;
9–Alice (1659-1745), of Plymouth, Mass.; *m* 1680, Rev. William **Adams** (1650-85);
8–Elizabeth (1681-1767), of Dedham, Mass.; *m* 1697, Rev. Samuel **Whiting** (1670-1725);
7–Sybil (1708-55), of Windham, Conn.; *m* 1725, John **Backus,** Jr. (1698-1769);
6–Lucretia (1733-1803), of Windham; *m* 1753, Col. John **Benjamin** (1730-96);
5–Sybil (1755-1814), of Stratford; *m* 1774, Isaac **Jones** (1739-1812);
4–Harriet (1790-1829), of New Haven; *m* 1810, Benjamin **Brooks** (1778-1847);
3–Harriet Jones (1818-1901), of Bridgeport; *m* 1839, William Henry **Noble** (3 above);
2–Fannie Sheldon (1859-1924), *m* 1884, Henry Eu-

gene **De Puy** (1856-1920); for issue and other lineages see Mrs. Herbert Aubrey Smith.
1–*m* Apr. 18, 1911, Robert William Davis, *b* Phila., Pa., May 13, 1883; son of Robert William Davis, of England; issue: 1–Frances Elma, *b* Wyandotte, Mich., Feb. 11, 1912; ed. Hood Coll., Frederick, Md.; 2–Robert De Puy, and 3–Margaret Ann (twins), *b* Phila., Pa., Apr. 17, 1913.
Residence: Havre de Grace, Md.

1–**de ROPP, Elizabeth Annesley Morton (Baroness),** *b* Phila., Pa., Oct. 19, 1864.
9–Morton (Mortenson) **Morton** (*d* 1712), mem. of 10th Swedish expdn., 1654, sailed under Johan Classon Rising, 1st dir. of New Sweden; settled in Delaware Co., Pa.;
8–Morton (1675-1718);
7–John (*d* 1724, ante son's birth), *m* Mary Archer (she *m* 2d, John Sketchley);
6–Hon. John (1724-77), a "signer"; mem. Cont. Congress, his vote decided Pa.; *m* Anne Justus;
5–Sketchley (1750-95), maj. in Am. Rev.; *m* Rebecca Taylor (1757-1819);
4–John Sketchley (1780-1857), *m* 1803, Susan Crosby (1786-1857);
3–Sketchley (1810-78), *m* 1834, Elizabeth Ansley Newlin (1813-72);
2–John Sketchley (2 below);
7–Joseph **Baker** (*d* 1724), Rehoboth, Mass.; *m* Hannah–;
6–Joseph (1700-49), *m* 1722, Martha Sherman (1703-74);
5–Job (1723-82), *m* Mehitable Rice (1732-1800);
4–Job (1766-1805), *m* 1791, Rachel Weaver (1762-1850);
3–George Weaver (1792-1844), New Bedford, Mass.; *m* 1821, Ruth Howland Smith (1800-72);
2–Eleanor Smith (*b* 1840), *m* 1858, John Sketchley **Morton** (1835-1911), capitalist; issue: I–Elizabeth Annesley (1 above); II–Virginia (Mrs. Harry H. Webb, see Vol. III, p. 471).
1–*m* Oct. 6, 1892, Baron Alfred de Ropp, *b* Libau, Courland, Russia, May 1, 1858; son of Baron Theophil de Ropp, of Russia; issue (all *b* Oakland, Calif.): 1–Alfred, *b* July 8, 1893; Stanford U., '16; *m* 1919, Olivia, dau. of Horace D. Pillsbury, of San Francisco, Calif. (issue: Georgiana Olivia, *b* San Francisco, Calif., Oct. 9, 1923); divorced, 1924; *m* 2d, Aug., 1929, Zoe Belt, of New York, and Pine Neck, L.I.; 2–Vera Adele, *b* July 30, 1894; *m* 1918, Erick Fisher Wood, see Vol. II, p. 330 (issue: 1–Eric Fisher, Jr., *b* Los Angeles, Calif., Jan. 25, 1919; 2–Eleanor Morton, *b* Pittsburgh, Pa., May 19, 1921; 3–Peter de Ropp, *b* Pittsburgh, Nov. 9, 1922; 4–Alex Laughlin, *b* Pittsburgh, May 30, 1929); 3–Harold, *b* Oct. 19, 1895; Yale-S., '17; *m* 1919, Margaret Lloyd, dau. of Isaac Ridgway Trimble, of Baltimore, Md. (issue: 1–Margaret Elizabeth, *b* Los Angeles, Calif., Nov. 5, 1920; 2–Allison Arden, *b* Los Angeles, Oct. 19, 1928).
1–Mem. Americans of Armorial Descent, D.F.P.A., C.D.A., D.C.G., N.Y. Daus. of Revolution. Residence: Hotel Coronado, Coronado, Calif.

1–**DeVILBISS, Thomas Dills,** *b* Spencerville, Ind., May 12, 1860.
5–Casper C. (Devilbiss) **DeVilbiss** (1720-77), from Alsace to Frederick, Md., 1745; *m* Anne–;
4–George (1747-1813), *m* 1772, Elizabeth Ogie;
3–Alexander (1780-1831), *b* Frederick, Md., *d* Alexandria, O.; slave holder in Md.; to Licking Co., O., bet. 1818-21; platted town of Alexandria, 1830; mill owner; *m* 1808, Priscilla McClain, Bedford, Pa.;
2–Alexander (1816-61), from Frederick, Md., to Licking Co., O.; settled, 1843, in DeKalb Co., Ind., nr. Spencerville; carpenter, mfr. of fanning mills; *m* 1839, Lydia Clogston (1821-89; Samuel[3] [*d* 1860], from Scotland ante 1816, to Licking Co., O., *m* 1816, Hanna Carter [1800-80], *d* Rockford, Ill.); issue: I–Jason Asbury (1839-1848); II–Allen, M.D. (1841-1917; *m* 1868, Lydia A. Lipes); III–Laurinda (1843-1928; *m* 1863, Alexander Bowser, *d* 1922); IV–John Wesley (1846-79; *m* 1865, Mary Fisher); V–Alexander (1848-90; *m* 1875, Margaret Dilly); VI–William Fletcher (1851-1913; *m* 1881, Naomi Ridenour, *d* 1907; *m* 2d, Mrs. Emma Smith); VII–Alton Lovejoy (1855-1900; *m* 1879, Florence Kunkel); VIII–Thomas Dills (1 above).
1–*m* May 14, 1881, Adella Chapman (Jan. 11, 1857-Feb. 27, 1919), dau. Moses R. Chapman; issue: 1–Laurinda May, *b* Hoagland, Ind., Feb. 28, 1882; teacher, domestic science, North High Sch., Fort Wayne, Ind.; 2–Edwin Bowser, *b* Fort Wayne, Ind., Sept. 13, 1884; supt. motive power Pa. R.R., New York; *m* Sept. 6, 1911, Agnes McKay, *b* July 2, 1885 (issue: Robert Alexander, *b* July 29, 1912; Eleanor Adella, *b* Oct. 8, 1914; Janet McKay, *b* July 6, 1916); 3–Frank Allen, *b* Fort Wayne, Ind., Oct. 14, 1887, with Gen. Electric Co.; *m* June 18, 1910, Clair Stenger, *b* July 1, 1889 (issue: Frank [Sept. 22-27, 1918]; Thomas Allen, *b* Nov. 5, 1919; Bonnie Jean, *b* Feb. 23, 1922); 4–Bess Beatrice, *b* Fort Wayne, Ind., Dec. 7, 1890; *m* June 21, 1921, Louis Heber Dunten, *b* Aug. 3, 1889, lawyer (issue: George Louis, *b* July 4, 1922; Adella DeVilbiss, *b* Aug. 16, 1924; Louie Heber, Jr., *b* Jan. 6, 1929).
1–*m* 2d, July 24, 1920, Mrs. Inez Gray Seitz (*d* June 27, 1929), widow Albert Seitz, Kalida, O.
1–*m* 3d, Dec. 11, 1929, Mrs. Evelyn Dennis Griffith, widow John F. Griffith, of Vaughnsville, O.
1–Second salesman on the road, 1886, for Bowser Co., Fort Wayne, Ind., with this co. as traveling engr. until 1926; pres. Home Supply Co. since 1893; gen. mgr. Locust Oil Co., 1895-1913. Councilman, 1892; chmn. first Bd. of Pub. Works, 1894-96. An organizer of Anthony Boul. Presbyn. Ch., chmn. bd. of trustees. Published, 1927, History of the DeVilbiss Family in the U.S.A., 1727-1927. Mem. I.A.G. Residence: 2636 S. Anthony Boul., Fort Wayne, Ind.

1–**DICKERSON, Mahlon Alvendore,** *b* nr. Blooming Grove, O., Feb. 22, 1866.
4–Joshua **Dickerson** (*d* Washington Co., Pa., 1802-03), settled in Washington Co., ante 1790; *m* Abigail– (living 1810);
3–Joseph (1776-1837), *m* 1800, Abigail Hinds, of N.J. (Benjamin[4], *m* Mary, dau. of John Breese [1713-1803], of Eng., N.J. soldier in Am. Rev., *m* Dorothy Riggs [1713-1803], of Baskingridge, N.J.); their son Isaac Haines was g.father of President Harding;
2–William Bailey (2 below).
10–Richard **Harding** (1583-1657; son of John, *d* 1637, of Northampton, Eng.), from Eng., settled at Wessagusett, nr. Braintree, Mass., 1623;
9–Stephen (1623/24-1698), blacksmith; freeman, Providence, R.I., 1669; *m* Bridget Estance (Thomas[10]);
8–Abraham (1656-94), blacksmith, Providence; *m* Deborah–;
7–Stephen (1681-1750), sea capt., mariner, Warwick, R.I.; lived at Providence, R.I., and Waterford, Conn.;
6–Abraham (1720-1806), 2d lt., Am. Rev.; of Clifford, Pa.; *m* 1741, Anna Dolson (*d* 1802);
5–Abraham (1744-1815), settled in Wyoming Valley, Pa., 1774; *m* 1762, Huldah Tryon (1743-1812; Joseph[6] [1720-90], *m* Bridget Curtis (*b* 1720); James[7]; Joseph[8]; Abel[9]);
4–Amos (1764-1839), *m* 1784, Phoebe Tripp (1767-1844; William[5] [1736-1820], *m* 1756, Sarah [1738-1808], dau. of Joseph Slocum; Isaac[6]; Job[7]; Peleg[8]; John[9], qv);
3–Welthy (1797-1886), *m* 1814, Joseph **Baker** (1788-1834);
2–Emily Ann (1817-1900), *m* John R. Ross; *m* 2d, 1861, William Bailey **Dickerson** (1807-78); issue: I–Charles Jolley (*b* 1862); II–Mahlon A. (1 above).
1–*m* Jan. 21, 1894, Margaret Jane Hullt (Jan. 24, 1874-Jan. 4, 1923); dau. of Charles John Hullt; issue: 1–Clifton Harold, *b* Silverton, Ore., Mar. 25, 1895; served World War; *m* Leona Elizabeth Baumgartner; 2–Vadis Emma (Apr. 4, 1898-Apr. 20, 1903); 3–Fay Amelia, *b* nr. Silverton, Ore., Sept. 20, 1902; *m* Fay M. Bragg; 4–Helen Elizabeth, *b* nr. Medford, Ore., May 18, 1910.
1–Student, Willamette U., 1886-88. Mfr. of lumber and shingles; merchant; grower of fruit in Hood and Rogue River valleys; fruit insp.; dir. Fruit Growers Assn. Mem. I.A.G. Club: Country. Odd Fellow. Residence: 232 Coolidge St., Silverton, Ore.

DANIEL OLCOTT DICKINSON (1816-69).

1–**DICKINSON, Harriet Cory,** *b* Waukegan, Ill., July 14, 1853.
8–Nathaniel **Dickinson** (qv);
7–Nathaniel (*d* 1710), killed in battle with the Indians in Northfield, Mass., where a monument is erected to his memory; *m* 1660, Hannah Beardsley (William[8] [*b* in England], a Royal Patentee of Stratford, Conn., *m* Marie–);
6–John (1667-1761), rep. Gen. Assembly; *m* 1704 or 05, Hepzibah Wells (Col. Thomas[7], apptd. by Gov. Andros of Mass. military cdr. of Deerfield in French and Indian War, *m* Hepzibah Buell);
5–John (1706-99), col. 2d Mass. Regt. (Hampshire), Am. Rev.; mem. Mass. Gen. Assembly, 1746-56; chmn. coms. of safety, meeting at Hadley, Hatfield, Northampton, Springfield and Concord; pres. Provincial Congress, Boston; *m* 1734, Mary Coleman (Nathaniel[6], *m* Mary Ely; Dea. John[7], *m* Mehitable Johnson);
4–John (1744-1800), col. of militia in Am. Rev.; *m* 1766, Lois Bigelow (*d* 1813; Lt. John[5], *m* Tabitha, dau. of Noah Coleman[6] [Dea. John Coleman[7]]);
3–Leonard (1785-1858), *m* 1812, Mercy Hawley (Jehiel[4], *m* Amanda Cass, of Arlington, Vt.);
2–Daniel Olcott (2 below).
9–Joseph **Hawley** (qv);
8–Samuel (*b* 1647), recorded as the largest owner of lands or "commonage" in Conn., 1699; treas.; town clk.; recorder of Stratford, Conn., 16 yrs.; surveyor; adjusted the boundaries of several states; *m* Mary Thompson John[9], *m* Anne, dau. of Gov. Thomas Welles, of Conn.);
7–Ephraim (*b* 1692), a founder of Trumbull, Conn., and Arlington, Vt.; *m* 1711, Sarah Curtis (William[8]);
6–Jehiel (1712-88), founder of Arlington, Vt.; mem. Gen. Assembly; "reader" in the Episcopal Ch.; capt. of militia under Gen. Burgoyne; *m* 1731, Sarah Dunning, of New Milford, Conn.;
5–Andrew (*b* 1732), *m* 1752, Ann Hard (James[6]);
4–Jehiel (*b* 1765), *m* Amanda Cass;
3–Mercy (1796-1869), *m* 1812, Leonard **Dickinson** (3 above).
8–John **Cory** (*b* 1618), from Eng. bet. 1630-40, lived for a short time in Mass. then in New Haven, Conn.; *m* in Eng., Anne–;
7–John (1639-1685 or 86), town clk., recorder and arbitrator, Huntington, L.I.; *m* 1667, Mary Cornish;
6–John (1674-1720), *m* Prissilla Day (George[7], of Elizabeth, N.J.);
5–John (1703-68), founder of Westfield, N.J.; *m* 1738, Martha Denman (John[6], of Westfield, N.J.);
4–David (1750-1809), Am. Rev.; *m* 1769, Jemima Ross (1752-1825);
3–Eliakim (1772-1850), *m* 1791, Sarah Sayre (1774-1861; Benjamin[4], *m* Sarah Littell);
2–Susan Lucy (2 below).
8–Thomas **Sayre** (qv);
7–Daniel (1647-1708), *m* Hannah Foster (Christopher[8], *m* Frances–);
6–Samuel, founder of Elizabeth, N.J.;
5–Daniel (*d* 1760), *m* 1740, Rebecca Bond;
4–Benjamin (1743-1810), a founder of Westfield, N.J.; Am. Rev.; *m* 1768, Sarah Littell (*d* 1832; Benjamin[5], *m* Susan Tucker);
3–Sarah (*b* 1774), *m* 1791, Eliakim **Cory** (3 above).
2–Daniel Olcott **Dickinson** (1816-69), pioneer of Chicago, Ill., 1836; moved from Athens, Ill., to "Little Fort," now Waukegan, Ill., 1840, and was the first mayor and postmaster there for several yrs.; built a pier in Lake Michigan at Waukegan and owned 14 vessels to carry grain and merchandise to eastern ports, with warehouses at Buffalo, N.Y., Milwaukee, Wis., McHenry and Waukegan, Ill., before the day of rys.; prominent in ry., commercial and banking enterprises; at 20 he settled at "Fort Dearborn," Chicago; an organizer and charter mem. Chicago Bd. of Trade; grain mcht.; charter director Chicago & Milwaukee R.R. (later incorporated as the C.&N.W. R.R.); see portrait; *m* Dec. 11, 1839, Susan Lucy Cory (1817-55); *m* 2d, June 1856, Martha Cornelia Scott (*d* 1896; Rufus[8], *m* Martha Dickinson); issue (1st marriage): I–David Cory (1840-1901; served in 6th Ill. Cav. in Civil War; *m* 1862, Emma Monroe); II–Sarah Amanda (1842-90; *m* 1866, David Cory, issue: James Warren, *b* Nov. 10, 1866, Sarah Isabella, *b* Oct. 23, 1875, *m* 1902, Dr. Albert Corner, *m* 2d, 1912, Henry Peets); III–Mercy Adelia (1843-1923; *m* 1891, David A. Cory); IV–Daniel Olcott, Jr. (1845-1917; served in 2d Mass. Light Horse Baty. in Civil War; *m* 1888, Alida Bucken); V–Eliakim Cory (*d* infancy); VI–Fanny Cory (*d* infancy); VII–James Cory (1851-58); VIII–Harriet Cory (1 above); issue (2d marriage): I–Lucy Cornelia (*b* 1857; *m* 1883, Robert F. Greene, issue: Charles William, *b* 1884, *m* 1907, Margaret Odlin; Robert, *b* 1888; Margaret, 1894-1915; Katherine, *b* 1898, *m* 1924, J. Stevens Tolman, issue: Robert Greene, *b* 1927); II–Charles Scott (1859-1926; *m* 1888, Grace Sawyer, issue: Kenneth, *b* 1889, *m* Frances Pratt [issue: Kenneth, Jr., Frances]; Philetus, *b* 1891, *m* Ruth Allen [issue: Hugh, Anne, Ellen]); III–William Hibbard (*b* 1863; *m* 1890, Agusta Quaintance, issue: William Quaintance, *b* 1893); IV–Alice Martha (1865-1906); V–Emily Morton (1868-1925).
1–Author: "Some Chronicles of the Cory Family" and "Leaves from an Old New England Tree." Mem. D.A.R., I.A.G. Residence: 902 Madison Av., Helena, Mont.

1–**DICKSON, Donald Coty,** *b* Shreveport, La., Feb. 28, 1890.
10–John **Dickson** (1557-1625), mcht., Glasgow, Scotland;
9–David (1583-1662), minister; prof. divinity, U. Edinburgh;
8–Robert, to Northern Ireland after Battle of Pentland Hills, 1666; *m* 1670, Priscilla Kennedy;
7–Robert (*b* 1675), from Ireland to Pa.;
6–John (1703-61), of Antrim;
5–Gen. Joseph (1745-1825), of Chester Co., Pa.; removed to N.C.; mem. Com. of Safety, Rowan Co., 1775; capt. Colonial troops, same yr.; maj. of "Lincoln County Men" at Battle of King's Mountain; brig. gen. and state senator, 1788-95; founder and one of the first trustees U. of N.C.; mem. 6th Congress, 1799-1801; *m* 1763, Margaret McEwin (1741-1814; James[6] [ca. 1718-1777], from Scotland to Pa., later to Slatesville, N.C.; *m* 1740, Isabella [1720-1816], dau. of Sir Michel Miller, of Scotland, *m* Margaret McNaughton);
4–James (1766-1825), judge, Bedford Co., Tenn.; *m* 1786, Agnes Nancy Moore (1766-1847; William[5] [*d* 1799], apptd. in 1777, for Tryon Co., N.C., commissary regt. under Maj. Beatis in Am. Rev., mem. N.C. Gen. Assembly, 1769-73);
3–Maj. Bennet Smith (1808-85), maj., Tenn.

militia; *m* 1837, Sarah Ann Higginbotham;
2–George Bennet (2 below).
6–John **Higginbotham** (1690-1760), *m* Frances Riley;
5–Aaron (1715-87), capt., Amherst Co., Va., militia; *m* 1769, Clare Greene;
4–Maj. Green, in War 1812, under Andrew Jackson, wounded six times, made maj.; *m* Sarah Fortson, they removed to Green Co., Ala. (among their children, George and Benjamin served as capt. in C.S.A.);
3–Sarah Ann (1819-73), *m* Maj. Bennet Smith **Dickson** (3 above).
5–John Lucas **Coty,** the immigrant, arrived in Va.; lived in Halifax, Va.; *m* Drusilla Davenport;
4–John Lucas (ca. 1754-1834), Halifax, Va.; fifer in Am. Rev.; *m* Lucy Donahue;
3–Thomas Davenport (1834-1908), justice of the peace in De Soto Parish; "Knight of White Camelia" in reconstruction days, and during War Between the States; *m* 1858, Mary Jane McDonald;
2–Lucile (2 below).
6–Lord **Oldham,** *b* Oldham, England;
5–Richard, came to America with his wife, Mary O'Melan (*b* in Ireland);
4–Hannah (1815-75), *m* Mark **McDonald** (*d* ca. 1840), from Eng. to Paterson, N.J., later settled at Shreveport, La.;
3–Mary Jane (1837-1912), *m* Thomas Davenport **Coty** (3 above);
2–Lucile (*b* 1862), ed. at Keachie and Mansfield colleges; *m* 1884, George Bennet **Dickson** (1854-89), removed to "Pecan Point," La.; issue: I–George Bennet (*b* 1887; *m* Sallie Battle Tomkies); II–Grafton Coty (1888-1909); III–Donald Coty (1 above).
1–*m* Oct. 11, 1916, Adelaide Scanland Jeter (qv); issue (all *b* Shreveport, La.): 1–Donald Coty, Jr., *b* Nov. 17, 1917; 2–Warrick Jeter, *b* Dec. 13, 1920; 3–Adelaide Lucile, *b* Jan. 16, 1923; 4–Bennet Keth, *b* Jan. 1, 1927.
1–LL.B., Tulane U., 1914. Atty.-at-law, practicing in La., federal and dist. cts. Baptist. Democrat. Residence: 320 Egan St., Shreveport, La.

FREDERICK AUGUSTUS DICKS

1–**DICKS, Frederick Augustus,** *b* Natchez, Miss., Oct. 10, 1853.
5–Robert **Barber** (*d* Columbia, Pa., 1749; 2d son of John Barber, of Yorkshire, Eng.), came from Eng. to join his uncle, Robert Barber, of Chester, Pa., ca. 1699, as apprentice at shoemaking; inherited a considerable portion of his uncle's estate, 1708; mem. Chester Co. bd. assessors, 1724; 1st sheriff, Lancaster Co., Pa., 1729; *m* 1718, Hannah Tidmarsh (William[6]);
4–James (*d* nr. Columbia, Pa., 1786), capt., 1st co. of Hempfield Tp., 1775; capt., Col. Galbraith's Bn., 1776; comd. a co. in Battle of L.I., 1776; *m* Elizabeth Wright (*d* 1782; William[5]);

JOHN DICKS (b Dec. 1775, d Dayton, O., Nov. 1, 1859); was col. of the 75th Regt. Pa. Militia in the War of 1812; was commissioned by Gov. Snyder, in 1815, brigadier-general 2d Brig., 4th Div., Lancaster Co. Militia; was the first assistant burgess of Columbia Borough, under the first charter in 1814, and became chief burgess, 1815. In 1817 or 18, he moved with his family to the vicinity of Dayton, Ohio, where he passed the remainder of his life.

3–Mary (1774-1846), as widow Stake, *m* 2d, John **Dicks** (1775-1859), see portrait and biography;
2–George Jefferson (2 below).
8–John **Alden,** Mayflower Pilgrim (qv);
7–Ruth (*d* 1674), *m* 1657/58, John **Bass** (1632-1716);
6–Samuel (1660-1757), *m* 1696, Mary Adams (*d* 1706);

GEORGE JEFFERSON DICKS (1809-79), was Mayor of Natchez, Miss., and commander of The Natchez Fencibles, a noted military organization in war and peace for many years; was prominent in business life, greatly beloved by his friends, and highly esteemed by all who knew him.

BASS

Arms: *Sable, a bordure argent.*
Crest: *Out of a ducal coronet two wings proper.*

5–Samuel (1700-50), *m* Bethiah Bowditch;
4–Samuel (1743-93), pvt., Am. Rev., prisoner in Old Jersey prison ship, 1 yr.; *d* Boston, buried Boston Common; *m* Mercy North;
3–Daniel (1783-1840), to N.C.; to Woodville, Miss.; *m* in N.C., 1815, Martha Westbrook (1796-1833);
2–Martha Ann Eliza (1818-76), *m* 2d, as his 2d wife, 1845, George Jefferson **Dicks** (*b* Columbia, Pa., May 15, 1809-*d* Natchez, Miss., 1879), see portrait and biography; issue: I–Martha Virginia (1847-49); II–Alice Josephine (1849-54); III–Henry Bass (1852-83); IV–Frederick Augustus (1 above); V–Annie Rosalie (*b* 1855; *m* 1877, John Edward Gibbs, *d*); VI–Charles Barber (*b* 1857; *m* Margaret Douglas Fleming); VII–Robert Lee (1865-1926; *m* Ella Beaumont).
1–*m* Dec. 30, 1875, Lee James Guice, *b* Anoka Co., Minn., Oct. 7, 1857; D.A.R., U.S.D. 1812; dau. of Stephen Lee Guice, atty., Natchez, Miss., *m* Susan Reed; issue: 1–Annie Lee, *b* Natchez, Miss., Oct. 20, 1876; Nashville Female Coll., 1895; *m* Jan. 16, 1907, Hubert G. Todd (qv).
1–First registered druggist in Miss.; pres. F. A. Dicks & Co., Inc., Natchez, Miss., wholesale druggists, later becoming Finlay, Dicks & Co., Inc., of which he was pres., 28 yrs., retired; engaged in mfg. chemicals and medicines. Mem. Adams Light Inf., 1876-95. Mem. S.A.R., La. Hist. Soc., La. Phar. Assn., Miss. Phar. Assn. (charter and hon. mem.). Clubs: Round Table, Chess and Checkers, Paul Morphy. Summer place: "Dixie," Pass Christian, Miss. Residence: 203 Audubon Boul., New Orleans, La.

1–**TODD, Hubert Grey,** *b* St. Joseph Co., Mich., Sept. 1, 1872.
9–Christopher **Todd** (qv);
8–Samuel (1645-1714), owned mill and bakery; *m* 1668, Mary Bradley (1653-1724);
7–Samuel (1672-1741), *m* 1st, 1698, Susannah Tuttle (1679/80-1737; Joseph[8], *m* Hannah Munson; William[9], qv);
6–Stephen (1702-1772 or 73), of Wallingford, Conn.; *m* 1726, Lydia Ives (*b* 1709; Dea. Samuel[7], *m* Ruth, dau. Jonathan Atwater; Joseph[8], *m* Mary, dau. Thomas Yale, dep. Gen. Ct.; William[9], qv);
5–Caleb (1733-69), *m* Esther Johnson (*b* 1735; Dea. Isaac[6]);
4–Caleb (1765-1837), *m* 3d, 1799, Fannie Hatch (1775-1846);
3–Alfred (1799-1877), farmer and carpenter; *m* 1828, Mary Ann Hovey (see their son, Albert May Todd, Vol. II, p. 233, for Sayles lineage);
2–James Alfred (1838-1926), of Marcellus, N.Y.; removed to Mich.; served in Co. A, 11th Mich. Inf., 1861-63; *m* 1863, Marien Waterman Smith (1841-1915; Rev. Gabriel[3], *m* Sarah Burdick Grey); issue: I–Petrea Eugenia (1866-70); II–Raymond Smith (*b* 1869); III–Hubert Grey (1 above); IV–Dwight Imnah (*b* 1877; *m* Jessie V. Drake); V–Marien Almeda (*b* 1880; *m* Dr. Edwin D. Brooks).
1–*m* Jan. 16, 1907, Annie Lee Dicks, *b* Natchez, Miss., Oct. 20, 1876; dau. of Frederick Augustus Dicks (qv); issue: 1–Katherine Grey, *b* New Orleans, La., June 2, 1909.
1–Treas. F. A. Dicks & Co. Mem. S.A.R. Mason (K.T.). Residence: 2003 Audubon St., New Orleans, La.

1–**DICKSON, Adelaide Jeter (Mrs. Donald Coty),** *b* Bossier, La., Jan. 6, 1894.
5–Ambrose **Jeter** (*d* 1803), ens., Caroline militia, 1778; *m* 1st, 1760, Jane Stern;
4–John (1774-1823), capt. War 1812; *m* 1st, 1794, Jenny Chaffin (*b* 1776; Joshua[5]);
3–John Tinsley (*b* 1798), of Amelia Co., Va.; *m* Ann McAshan;
2–John Warrick (2 below).
12–Col. Walter **Aston** (qv);
11–Mary, *m* Richard **Cocke** (qv);
10–Capt. Thomas (1638-96), of Henrico Co., Va.; justice, 1678-80; sheriff, 1688; burgess; *m* Margaret Wood (widow of Peter Jones, mother of Maj. Peter Jones, II, founder of Petersburg, Va.; dau. Gen. Abram[11]);
9–James (1666-1721 or 25), of "Curles"; clk. of court; burgess, 1699; *m* 1691, Elizabeth Pleasants (*d* 1751; John[10], qv);
8–Elizabeth Pleasants, *m* 1742, Thomas **Poythress** (John[9], *m* Mary Batte; Maj. Francis[10]; Capt. Francis[11], qv);
7–Susanna, *m* William **Hall** (*b* ca. 1700), moved to N.C. (Robert[8], burgess, 1718; William[9], *m* Mary Tucker);
6–Dr. Robert (*d* 1780 or 86), surgeon, 3d N.C. Inf. Regt., 1774; *m* 1742, Anna Leary (Cornelius[7], *m* Elizabeth Haughton);
5–Sicily Ann, *m* John **Agee** (1749-1810), Am. Rev. (James[6] [1724-25-1821], Am. Rev., *m* 1747, Elizabeth Ford; Matthew[7], Huguenot from France, vestryman King William's Parish, granted 800 acres in Henrico Co., Va., 1725);
4–Elizabeth (1790-1874), *m* 1807, Nehemiah **McAshan,** Jr. (1784-1846; Nehemiah[6], *m* Miss Chambers);
3–Ann (1830-80), *m* 1850, John T. **Jeter** (3 above).
9–George **Young** (*d* Calvert Co., Md., will proved 1718), settled in Calvert Co., Md., middle of the 17th century; *d* at "Young's Attempt";
8–George, *m* Mary Parker;
7–Parker (*b* 1714/15), *m* 1746, Sara Miles;
6–George Parker, Am. Rev.; to Lexington, Ky.; *m* 1776, Mary Hellen (*b* 1757; Peter[7], *m* 1746, Penelope Patison; James[8] [*b* 1682]; David[9], *m* 1680, Sara–);
5–Priscilla (1779-1802), *m* ca. 1778, Nicholas **Bright** (*d* 1804) of N.Y.; Am. Rev. under Anthony Wayne;
4–Hon. George Young (1800-77), *m* 1822, Lodoiska de Maupassant (1804-82), came from France to America (Admiral Henri[5], of France, *m* Rose Massan de Angles [1735-1813], dau. of Veauve Francois Massan, *m* Elizabeth Doulon);
3–Rosa (1823-1912), *m* 1850, Dr. George W. **Dirmeyer** (*d* 1880), surgeon Bass Hosp., Mobile, Ala., during Civil War (Jacob[4], *m* Mary Bowman);
2–Marie Louise (1856-1917), *m* 1876, John Warrick **Jeter** (1850-1903).
1–*m* Oct. 11, 1916, Donald Coty Dickson, (qv for issue).
1–Mem. C.D.A., Founders of Manakin Town, D.A.C. (state sec.), D.A.R. (chapter regent), Parent-Teacher's Assn. (pres.). Residence: 320 Egan St., Shreveport, La.

1–**DICKSON, Margarette Adell Ball (Mrs.),** *b* Little Rock, Ia., June 4, 1879.
10–John **Ball** (*d* 1655), from Eng., settled at Concord, ante 1640; *m* Joanna King;
9–Nathaniel (1618-98), of Concord; *m* Mary Mousal (*d* 1669);
8–Nathaniel, *m* Mary Brooks;
7–Jeremiah (*b* 1701), of Townsend, Mass.; *m* Mary Stevens (1702-64);
6–Ebenezer (1729-97), of Pepperell, Mass.; in battle of Lexington; *m* Rebecca Butterfield (1729-1800), of Weston;
5–Abraham (1765-1840), a founder of Athens, Vt.; *m* Deliverance Perham (1765-1838);
4–Abraham (1786-1847), capt. of militia; *m* 1st, Hannah Edwards (1788-1839);
3–Abraham Edwards (1811-90), *m* Elvira Holden (Ephraim[4] [?], a founder of Athens);
2–Leroy Augustus (2 below).
5–Jesse **Jones** (1757-1826), in battle of Bennington, Vt.; a monument was erected to his memory as first settler at Hancock, N.H.; *m* 1785, Hannah– (1762-1840);
4–Mary Jane (1786-1865), *m* 1805, William **Grimes** (1781-1863), of Hancock, N.H.;
3–Mary Ann (1821-1904), *m* 1842, Franklin **Mansfield** (1814-72), of Alsted, N.H.;
2–Mary Adell (1845-1914), *m* 1868, Leroy Augustus **Ball** (1843-1920), served Co. K, 3d Vt. Vol. Inf., Civil War; teacher, merchant, farmer and banker (see portrait Vol. III, p. 46); issue: I–Mary Katherine (Mrs. James H. Chidester, see Vol. III, p. 46); II–Elmer Darwin (see Vol. III, p. 46); III–Carleton Roy (*b* 1873; *m* Bertha M. Steward); IV–Abbie Christine (*b* 1875; *m* Draper I. Younker); V–Margaret Adell (1 above); VI–Edward Graham (see Vol. III, p. 46); VII–Wilbur Mansfield (*b* 1888; *m* Ruth Bettes).
1–*m* June 1, 1904, George R. Dickson, *b* Plattsville, Wis., Feb. 22, 1882; son of Samuel T. Dickson, of Dell Rapids, S.D.; issue: 1–Margarette Adell (*b* Jan. 10, 1908-*d* infancy); 2–Gerald Ralph, *b* June 5, 1912; 3–Donald Dean, *b* Oct. 2, 1914; 4–Coral Christine, *b* Dec. 14, 1917.
1–B.A., Ia. Teachers Coll.; M.A., U. of S.D.; grad. work, U. of Ia., U. of Chicago. Prof. creative English, Valparaiso U. Poems included in many anthologies. Winner of several poetry prizes. Mem. D.A.R., Alpha Psi Omega, League of Am. Penwomen, British Poetry Soc., Am. Poetry Soc., poetry societies of S.D., Ind., and Chicago, Ill. Residence: 502 Freeman St., Valparaiso, Ind.

1–**DICKSON, Tracy Campbell,** *b* nr. Independence, Ia., Sept. 17, 1868.
5–William **Dickson** (1728-ca. 1794), from Ireland, settled at Cherry Valley, N.Y., 1741; farmer; served in Am. Rev.; *m* 1st, 1752, Elizabeth Campbell (1730– massacred by Indians, 1778; James[6] [1690-1770], in Londonderry, N.H., 1730, removed to Cherry Valley, N.Y., 1741, *m* Jane Humphrey, *m* 2d, Sarah [Simpson] Thompson, 1694-1773);
4–Robert (1763-1832), served in Am. Rev.; removed to Ripley, N.Y., 1809; farmer; first postmaster of Ripley; asso. judge Chautauqua Co.; *m* 1st, 1784, Olive Hungerford (1764-1812; Daniel[5]);
3–William (1790-1840), farmer and breeder of horses; *m* 1817, Elizabeth Dickson;
2–Capt. Campbell (2 below).
6–Matthew **Cannon** (*b* Ireland, 1717-*d* Cherry Valley, N.Y., 1792), from Ireland to New Castle, Del., ca. 1753; removed to Otsego Co., N.Y., ca. 1764; wounded and captured by Indians at massacre of Cherry Valley, Nov. 11, 1778; *m* Eleanor McKinley (massacred 1778);
5–Jane (1743-1836), *m* ca. 1767, Col. Samuel **Campbell** (1738-1824), ens., 1768, 2d lt., 1772, lt. col., 1775, col., 1778; wife and children taken as hostages and buildings burned by Brant and Butler at massacre of Cherry Valley, N.Y., Nov. 11, 1778; wife and children exchanged 1780; lived at West Troy, N.Y.; returned to Cherry Valley, 1784, where he entertained Gen. Washington; rep. N.Y. Assembly (James[6], same as 6 above);
4–Eleanor (1770-1844), *m* Samuel **Dickson** (1765-1822; William[5], same as 5 above);
3–Elizabeth (1797-1856), *m* William **Dickson** (3 above).
9–Lt. Thomas **Tracy** (qv); *m* 2d, Martha, dau. of Thomas Bourne (qv);
8–Capt. John (1642-1702), original propr. Norwich, Conn.; justice of the peace; rep. Gen. Ct.; *m* 1670, Mary Winslow (1646-1721; Josiah[9] [*b* Eng., 1606-*d* 1674], to America 1631, settled and *d* in Marshfield, Mass., freeman 1633, town clk. nearly 30 yrs., rep. Gen. Ct., selectman, *m* ca. 1636, Margaret [*d* 1683], dau. of Thomas Bourne, qv);
7–John (1673-1726), *m* 1697, Elizabeth Leffingwell (1676-1737; Ens. Thomas[8] [1649-1724], removed from Saybrook to Norwich, Conn., 1660, freeman, 1671, inn-keeper, mcht., landowner, rep. Gen. Ct., estate valued at £793, *m* 1672, Mary Bushnell [1655-1734; Richard[9], ca. 1620-1658, *m* 1648, Mary Marvin, 1629-1713]; Lt. Thomas[9], qv);
6–John (1700-1786), *m* 1724, Margaret Hyde (1702-89; John[7] [1667-1727], *m* 1698, Experience [1674-1763], dau. of Caleb Abel [1646-1731], *m* Margaret Post [1653-1700]; Samuel[8] [1637-77], settled in Norwich, 1660, *m* 1659, Jane, dau. of Thomas Lee, *m* Phebe Brown; William[9], qv);
5–Theophilus (1742-1813), *m* 1766, Sarah Gifford (1744-1824; Samuel[6] [1694-1753], *m* 1720, Experience Hyde [*b* 1700; sister to Margaret, 6 above]; Samuel[7] [1668-1714], *m* 1685, Mary Calkins [1669-1748; John[8], ca. 1634-1703, selectman Norwich, freeman, 1669, *m* Sarah (1634-1711), dau. of Robert Royce, in Boston 1632, disarmed 1639 for supporting Wheelwright and Ann Hutchinson, removed to Stratford, Conn., 1644, to New London, Conn., 1657, constable, rep. Gen. Ct.; *m* Elizabeth–; Hugh[9], qv]; Stephen[8] [1641-1724], original propr. Norwich, 1660, *m* 1667, Hannah [1645-71], dau. of John Gore [*d* 1657], *m* Rhoda Rose, *d* 1655);
4–Capt. Theophilus (1768-1842), removed from Preston, Conn., to Delphi, N.Y., 1797; *m* 1794, Thankful Draper (1771-1839; Nathan[5], *m* 1749, Johannah Roberts);
3–Riel Stephen (1811-62), farmer, justice of the peace; *m* 1st, 1838, Ardelia Robertson (*d* 1839); *m* 2d, Dolly Fairbank; *m* 3d, Lenora Tinsler (*d* 1869);
2–Lucy Ellen (2 below).
9–Jonathan **Fairbank** (qv);
8–Jonas (1624-killed by Indians, 1676), *m* 1658, Lydia Prescott (*b* 1641; John[9], qv);
7–Capt. Jabez (1670-1758), was in Lancaster garrison, 1704; cdr. of garrison, 1711; in Arcadian Expdn., 1707-10, and Lovewell's (Father Rasle's) War, 1722-26; lt., 1723; comd. a co., 1724; dep. Mass. Gen. Ct., *m* ca. 1695, Mary Wilder (1675-1718; Capt. Thomas[8] [1644-1716], lt., 1689, capt., 1704, selectman, justice of the peace, *m* 1668, Mary–; Thomas[9], qv); *m* 2d, 1719, Mary or Elizabeth Whitcomb;
6–Dea. Thomas (1707-91), soldier French and Indian War; *m* 1729, Dorothy Carter (bap. 1711-1784; Samuel[7] [1678-1738], *m* 1701, Dorothy Wilder [*b* 1686; Nathaniel[8], *b* 1650-killed by Indians, 1704, innkeeper, *m* 1673, Mary, *b* 1652, dau. of Thomas Sawyer, qv];
5–Dea. Joseph (1741-1813), *m* 1764, Ann Dole;
4–Thomas (1768-1857), *m* 1794, Dolly Nelson;
3–Dolly (1815-55), *m* Riel Stephen **Tracy** (3 above).
9–Richard **Dole** (qv);
8–Richard (1650-1723), *m* 1677, Sarah Greenleaf (1655-1718);
7–Richard (1678-1764), *m* 1st, 1706, Sarah Illsley (1689-1707; Joseph[8] [1649-1724]; William[9], ca. 1608 or 12-1681);
6–Dea. Enoch (*b* 1707), *m* 1729, Rachel Jewett (1709-92; Dea. Aquila[7] [1684-1760], *m* 1st, 1704, Ann Tenney [1683-1723; Thomas[8], 1648-1730, King Philip's War, *m* 1680, Margaret, *b* 1659, dau. of Andrew Hidden, ca. 1622-1702; Thomas[9], qv]; Ens. Joseph[8] [1654-1735], freeman 1684, King Philip's War, rep. Gen. Ct., *m* 1st, 1676, Rebecca [1655-1729], dau. of William Law [buried 1668], *m* Mary Cheney; Maximilian[9], qv);
5–Ann (1738-1821), *m* Joseph **Fairbank** (5 above).
9–Thomas **Nelson** (*d* Eng., 1648), to America in Rev. Mr. Roger's company, settled in Rowley, Mass.; freeman, 1639; rep. Gen. Ct.; 1st wife unknown;
8–Thomas (1635-1712), recorder Rowley, 1694-97; *m* 1659, Ann Lambert (*d* 1678; Francis[9] [*d* 1647], *m* Jane Barker, buried 1659);
7–Francis (*b* 1676), *m* 1702, Mary Ray;

6–Solomon (1703-81), *m* 1725, Mercy Chaplin (*b* 1705; Capt. Jeremiah[7] [1680-1765]; Joseph[8] [1646-1705]; Hugh[9], buried 1653);
5–David (*b* 1725), Am. Rev.; *m* 1757, Hannah Bailey;
4–Dolly (1772-1820), *m* Thomas **Fairbank** (4 above).
9–James **Bailey** (ca. 1612-1677), in Roxbury, ca. 1640; settled in Rowley, ca. 1642; held various town offices; large landowner; *m* Lydia– (*d* 1704);
8–John (1642-90), freeman 1669; soldier Gen. Phipp's expdn. against Canada, 1690: *m* 1668, Mary Mighill (1649-ca. 1693; Dea. Thomas[9] [buried 1654], *m* Ann Parrott);
7–Capt. Jonathan (1670-1733), selectman; *m* 1693, Hannah Walker (*d* 1702); *m* 2d, 1708, Sarah Jewett (1675-1730; Ezekil[8] [1643-1723], *m* 1663, Faith Parrot);
6–Shubael (*b* 1696), removed from Rowley to Lancaster, Mass., ca. 1722; *m* 1728, Ann Houghton (Joseph[7] [1678-1718], *m* Isabell Houghton [*b* 1687; Robert[8], 1659-1723, *m* 1680, Esther Lippenwell ?, 1658-1740]; John[8] [ca. 1650-1737], comd. garrison house, justice of peace, rep. Gen. Ct., magistrate, *m* 1st, 1671, Mary Farrar [1648-1724; Jacob[9] (*d* 1677), original propr. Lancaster]);
5–Hannah (*b* 1732), *m* David **Nelson** (5 above).
2–Lucy Ellen Tracy (1847-96), grad. State Normal Sch., Albany, N.Y.; *m* 1867, Capt. Campbell **Dickson** (1836-1911), in Mo., 1856, where he bought sheep which he drove to Tex., 1857, and remained there until beginning of Civil War; returned to Ripley, N.Y.; 2d lt., 9th N.Y. Cav., 1861, 1st lt., 1862, capt., 1863, hon. discharged for disability caused by three wounds, Nov. 21, 1863; drilled for oil in Pa., 1863-64, farmer and stock raiser, nr. Independence, Ia., 1865-77; mcht. and banker, Cleburne, Tex.; issue: I–Tracy C. (1 above); II–Howard (Aug. 7-Oct. 6, 1870); III–Frederick Dwight (*b* 1871; *m* 1901, Minnie Stevens, *d* 1903; *m* 2d, 1915, Nell Anderson); IV–Leonard Eugene (*b* 1873; *m* 1902, Sudie Davis); V–Evelyn (*b* 1876; *m* 1897, Robert Andrew); VI–Frances Anna (*b* 1883; *m* 1919, Alfred Howard Abernathy).
1–*m* Nov. 7, 1894, Isabella Kendrick Abbott (Oct. 21, 1874-Dec. 11, 1915); dau. of Col. Benjamin Franklin Abbott (1839-1911; Noah[3]; William[4]; William[5]; and if family tradition is correct, Capt. John[6]; John[7]; George[8], of Rowley, Mass.), *m* 1868, Mary Isabella Kendrick, see her sister, Mrs. Alexander W. Smith, for Kendrick lineage; issue: 1–Tracy Campbell, Jr., *b* The Armory, Springfield, Mass., Mar. 28, 1896; grad. U.S.M.A., 1917; capt. in regular army in France, during World War, resigned, Aug. 30, 1920; *m* Feb. 18, 1922, Elizabeth Morris (*b* Apr. 29, 1898), dau. of Edgar Webb Bassick, *m* Grace Elizabeth Morris (issue: Tracy Campbell, III, *b* Dec. 8, 1922; Grace Bassick, *b* Oct. 22, 1924; Isabella Abbott, *b* Oct. 26, 1927); 2–Benjamin Abbott, *b* The Armory, Springfield, Mass., Dec. 18, 1897; grad. U.S.M.A., 1918; 1st lt. and served in Siberia, resigned June, 1920; *m* June 18, 1924, Alice Baker (*b* Nov. 29, 1900), dau. of Jacquelin Smith Holliday, *m* Florence Baker (issue: Ariana Holliday, *b* Mar. 26, 1928).
1–Grad. U.S.M.A., '92. Apptd. 2d lt., 2d Arty., transferred June 19, 1894, to 1st lt. in Ordnance Dept. in which he has since served, except while on the retired list as a col., Aug. 16, 1915-Mar. 7, 1917; promoted through the grades to rank of col. on Mar. 4, 1920; brig. gen., Feb. 18, 1918-June 1, 1919; inspector of shops on the Panama Canal, 1910-14. Developed a rifle sight, detection of defects in metals by X-Rays, making of guns by cold-working, casting guns centrifugally. Commanded Watertown Arsenal, Mass., since Oct. 4, 1918. Mem. M.O.L.L., I.A.G. Clubs: Army and Navy (Washington), St. Botolph, Algonquin (Boston), Oakley Country. Address: Watertown Arsenal, Watertown, Mass.

1–**SMITH, Emily Eliza Kendrick (Mrs. Alexander W.),** *b* Americus, Ga., Dec. 21, 1858.
8–John **Kendrick** (1605-86), came to Boston, 1639; bought farm south of Muddy River (now Newton), Mass.; *m* Anne–;
7–Elijah (1645-80), *m* 1669, Hannah Jackson (1646-1737);
6–Ebenezer (1680-1761), *m* 1711, Hannah Stedman;
5–Nathaniel (1713-74), *m* 1738, Judith Ells (Ells or Eels);
4–Ebenezer (1740-86), *m* 1766, Ann Davenport;
3–Rev. Clark (1775-1824), *m* 1802, Esther Thompson;
2–Samuel Stillman (2 below).
8–Anthony **Thompson** (qv);
7–Capt. John (1632-1707), *m* 1656, Ann Vickers (or Vicaris);
6–Capt. Samuel (1669-1749), *m* 1695, Rebecca Bishop (*b* 1673; Dep.Gov. James[7]);
5–Dea. Gideon (1704-59), *m* 1729, Lydia Punderson;
4–David (1731-1807), *m* 1760, Hannah Griswold;
3–Esther (1777-1853), *m* Rev. Clark **Kendrick** (3 above).
4–John **Fryer** (1757-1818), of N.C.; minuteman and lt. of militia, in Am. Rev.; *m* Winnifred Fenn;
3–Zachariah Louis (1785-1861), *m* 1814, Sarah Matthews;
2–Emily Herbert (1822-78), *m* 1838, Samuel Stillman **Kendrick** (1812-81), of Poultney, Vt.; *d* at Atlanta, Ga.; issue: I–Mary Isabella (1842-93; *m* Benjamin Franklin Abbott; their dau. Isabella Kendrick Abbott, *m* Tracy Campbell Dickson, qv); II–John Ryland (*b* 1848; *m* Julia Lawton, D.A.R.); III–Edward S. K. (1850-1921; *m* Carrie Ackerman); IV–Helen F. (1856-1927); V–Emily Eliza (1 above); VI–Esther (*b* 1863; *m* William W. Gray, U.S.A.).
1–*m* Sept. 10, 1885, Alexander Wyly Smith (see Vol. I, p. 829), issue (all *b* Atlanta, Ga.): 1–Alexander Wyly, Jr. (see Vol. I, p. 829); 2–Esther Kendrick, *b* Dec. 27, 1894; ed. Miss Spence's Sch., New York; served at A.R.C. Canteen 9, Paris, Nov. 1918-July 1919; *m* Nov. 19, 1922, Edward M. Brown; 3–Theodore Hammond, *b* Jan. 15, 1896; B.S., U. of Ga., '16; Yale Law Sch.; served as 2d lt., U.S. Inf., Aug. 15, 1917; with Co. L, 327th Inf., 82d Div., and in France, Apr. 1918; captured on battlefield, Oct. 12, 1918, and prisoner of war until Nov. 29; resumed duty until disch., July 9, 1919; 4–Clarke Kendrick, *b* Feb. 6, 1898; U. of Ga., '18; 2d lt., inf., O.R.C. and hon. disch., Jan. 15, 1919.
1–Ed. pvt. schs. Mem. C.D.A., D.A.R. Residence: Pace's Ferry Rd., Atlanta, Ga.

1–**DIFFENBAUGH, Milton Hess,** *b* Greenland, Lancaster Co., Pa., June 25, 1870.
5–Adam (Dieffenbach) **Diffenbaugh** (*d* 1782), from Palatinate, Germany, in the "Bilander Townshead," 1737, settled at Phila., Pa., later in Lampeter Tp., Lancaster Co., Pa.; tanner and farmer; *m* Fraena (Fronica) Bare (John Bare[6], of Conestoga Tp., Lancaster Co., Pa.; Martin[7], Mennonite minister);
4–John (*d* 1811), of Lampeter Tp., Lancaster Co., Pa.; supplied forage in Am. Rev., 1778-79; *m* Maria Buckwalter;
3–Abraham (1782-1863), of Lampeter Tp.; *m* 1811, Barbara Kreider (1788-1842);
2–Abraham K. (1819-90), farmer; *m* Frances Charles Hess (1829-96); issue: I–Mary (*b* 1847; *m* Christian F. Andrews; *m* 2d, Aaron Denlinger); II–Benjamin H. (*b* 1849; *m* Hettie Leaman); III–Henry (*b* and *d* 1852); IV–Elizabeth (*b* 1853; *m* Benjamin Denlinger); V–Aaron H. (*b* 1855; *m* Lydia E. Leaman); VI–Lydia Ann (*b* and *d* 1857); VII–Franklin (1859-61); VIII–Frances (*b* 1860; *m* Aaron E. Hartman); IX–Amos H. (*b* 1862; *m* Clara High); X–Abraham L. (*b* 1865; *m* Emma High); XI–Infant (*b* dead); XII–Milton Hess (1 above); XIII–Infant (*b* dead).
1–*m* 1891, Mary E. Jones (Dec. 5, 1873-May 28, 1920); issue: 1–Earl Walton, *b* Lancaster, Pa., Feb. 15, 1892; Franklin and Marshall Coll.; Mason (K.T., 32°); *m* Elizabeth P., dau. of Samuel J. Pugh, of Lancaster (issue: Robert Pugh, *b* Dec. 23, 1915); 2–Ethel Fern (Oct. 24, 1897-July 29, 1898).
1–*m* 2d, May 5, 1902, Jeanette Ball Bushong, *b* New Holland, Pa., July 12, 1881; dau. of Dr. Israel Bushong, issue: 1–Clair Bushong, *b* Lancaster, Feb. 4, 1903; Franklin and Marshall Coll.; U.Pa.; *m* 1927, Elizabeth G., dau. of John O. Haas, of Lancaster (issue: Elaine

H., *b* July 26, 1928); 2–E. Frances, *b* Lancaster, May 27, 1907; B.A., Md. Coll. for Women, '29.
1–Millersville State Teachers Coll. Teacher in public schools; merchant, real estate and ins. broker. Mem. I.A.G., Lancaster County Hist. Soc. Mason (32°, K. T.), Elk. Presbyterian. Republican. Club: Hamilton. Residence: 1027 Woods Av., Lancaster, Pa.

1–**DINKINS, James,** *b* Madison Co., Miss., Apr. 18, 1845.
6–John **Kendrick** (1670-1715), of Gloucester Co., Va.;
5–William (*b* 1704), of King William Co., Va.; *m* 1726, Sarah Jones (*b* 1715), of Suffolk;
4–John (*b* 1735), *m* 1760, Amy Fox;
3–Lucy (1775-1849), *m* 1793, James **Dinkins** (*d* 1825; John[4], Am. Rev., *m* Fanny Henderson);
2–Alexander Hamilton (2 below).
8–Col. William **Ball** (qv);
7–Hannah, *m* Capt. David **Fox,** Jr.;
6–Henry, of King William Co.; *m* Anna West (Col. John[7] [1632-89], colonial gov. of Va., burgess, 1685, col. in Bacon's Rebellion, *m* Unity, dau. of Maj. Joseph Croshaw, of York Co., burgess, 1658; Sir Thomas[8], qv);
5–Col. Richard (will probated 1771), settled at Brunswick, Lunenburg Co.; *m* Hannah Williamson, of Surry Co., Va. (John[6], of Surry Co., Va., will probated 1731);
4–Amy (*b* 1740), *m* John **Kendrick** (4 above).
9–Gertrude (Springsteen) **Springs,** widow of Casper Springsteen (*d* in Holland), of Groeningen; with 3 sons and 1 dau., settled on Manhattan, ca. 1623 or 24;
8–Caspar, *m* Catharine Lothie (Abraham[9]);
7–Caspar Joosten (*d* 1729), began to write name Springs; moved to Newtown, L.I., 1700, to Kent Co., Del., 1729; *m* 1683, Maria Storm (Dereck[8]);
6–Frederick, mem. Capt. Nathaniel Hazard's co. militia, Queens Co., L.I.; *m* Abigail Betts (Thomas[7], *m* Mary Whitehead);
5–John, moved to Mecklenburg Co., 1766; *m* Sophia Gassoway;
4–Capt. John (1751-1818), capt. militia, prior to Am. Rev.; capt. in Am. Rev.; served in Indian wars; *m* 1776 or 80, Sarah Shelby Alexander;
3–William Polk (1790-1829), *m* 1812, his 1st cousin, Margaret Polk Springs (*b* 1796; Richard[4] [*b* 1754], capt. in Am. Rev., *m* 1781, Jean Baxter; John[5], above);
2–Cynthia (2 below).
7–William **Alexander,** belonged to the Scotch colony;
6–William, of Somerset Co., Md.; *m* his cousin, Agnes Alexander;
5–Col. Adam (1728-98), col. N.C. militia; signer Mecklenburg Declaration of Independence; *m* Mary Shelby (1735-1813; Evan[6], qv);
4–Sarah S., *m* Capt. John **Springs,** II (4 above);
3–William P., *m* Margaret P. Springs (3 above);
2–Cynthia (1822-72), *m* 1842, Alexander Hamilton **Dinkins** (1815 or 18-1872), cotton planter; issue: I–James (1 above); II–Margaret Springs (1846-79; *m* 1866, John Henderson); III–William Leonidas (*b* 1849; *m* 1874, Kate McWillie); IV–Sarah Tallulo (*b* 1852; *m* 1872, John B. Kemp); V–Blandina Baxter (1854-80; *m* 1878, E. A. Lindsley); VI–Hamilton Charles (1857-1927; *m* 1886, Willie Tunstall).
1–*m* Nov. 15, 1866 (golden anniversary celebrated 1916), Sue Hart, *b* S. Hampton Co., Va., Apr. 17, 1845; desc. John Hart, the "signer," and Col. Edward Riddick, of the Cont. Army; dau. of Capt. John D. Hart (1808-73), planter; issue: 1–Lynn Hamilton, *b* Canton, Miss.; Aug. 15, 1867; now pres. Interstate Trust & Banking Co., of New Orleans; mem. S.A.R., I.A.G.; 2–Miriam Cynthia, *b* Canton, Dec. 6, 1870; *m* Nov. 10, 1903, Cecil Guy Robinson (issue: Lynn Dinkins, *b* Sept. 22, 1905; James Dinkins, *b* Oct. 23, 1909); 3–Earl Jeffrey (Feb. 3, 1887-Feb. 3, 1891).
1–Banker (see Who's Who in America). Served 4 yrs. in C.S.A., 2 yrs. in 18th Miss. Inf., Army Northern Va., and 2 yrs. with Gen. Nathan Bedford Forrest as a.-d.-c. to Gen. Chalmers, and subsequently as capt. of his escort co.; was capt. of cav. at 19; participated in all the campaigns and battles of the Army of Northern Va. that Barksdale's Brigade engaged in, and in all Gen. Forrest campaigns. Mem. I.A.G. Clubs: New Orleans Country, Southern Yacht, Boston Club, Quartie Club. Summer place: Saluda, N.C., "The Land of the Sky." Residence: 6149 St. Charles Av., New Orleans, La.

1–**DIXON, Charles William,** *b* Douglas, Ark., July 27, 1879.
6–Henry **Dixon** (will proved 1795), of N.C.; had land grants in Caswell Co. for services rendered; *m* Elizabeth–;
5–Capt. Tilghman (1750-1816), of N.C. and Dixon Springs, Tenn.; capt., 1st N.C. Cont. Line; *m* 1789, Maria Don Carlos (1767-1806);
4–Dr. Don Carlos (1792-1841), of Dixon Springs; 1st lt., Tenn. Inf., 1812; paymaster, 1812-13; resigned July, 1813; *m* 2d, 1819, Elizabeth Harriet Bilbo (1800-25);
3–Dr. Charles William (1825-57), of Dixon Springs; 2d lt., Co. H, under Capt. William B. Walton, 1st Regt. Tenn. Vols., Mexican War; resigned Dec., 1846; *m* 1849, Eliza Virginia Bashaw (1833-53);
2–Charles Virginius (2 below).
4–George Lloyd **Baker** (1790-1836, whose mother Eleanora Lloyd from Wales), *m* in Great Britain, 1811, Elizabeth Josephine Warne (1794-1851; Joseph Bright[5]);
3–Anna Virginia (1826-64), *m* Dr. Samuel Henry **Pendleton** (see Vol. 1, p. 912, for Pendleton lineage);
2–Cornelia Emma (1855-1900), *m* 1878, Charles Virginius **Dixon** (1853-99), farmer, Douglas, Ark.; issue: I–Charles William (1 above); II–Samuel P.
1–*m* Apr. 3, 1907, Evelyn Traweek (qv); issue: 1–Tilghman Edmund, *b* Douglas, Ark., Dec. 31, 1908.
1–Ed. St. Mary's Coll., Marion Co., Ky.; M.D., U. of Louisville, 1904. Physician and surgeon. Mem. Med. R.C. and otherwise active during World War. Mem. I.A.G., A.M.A., Southern Med. Assn., S.E. Ark. Development Assn. (pres.), Soc. of Cincinnati; pres. Chamber of Commerce. Residence: Gould, Lincoln Co., Ark.

1–**DIXON, Evelyn Traweek (Mrs. Charles W.),** *b* Lincoln Co., Ark., Oct. 28, 1882.
5–Robert **Traweek,** from Wales to N.C.; served in N.C. militia in Am. Rev.;
4–Robert Lunsford (*d* ca. 1836), *m* Theresa Elizabeth Powell (Henry[5], *m* Elizabeth Pope);
3–Ripley Jefferson (1834-1910), *m* 1853, Mary Jane Armstrong (1836-1913);
2–William Thaddeus (2 below).
6–Philip (Busch) **Bush** (1733-1812), from Germany; was in Winchester, Va., 1749; one of the founders of Stephensburg, Va., 1758; capt. under Washington when he capitulated to the Indians and French at Great Meadows; *m* Catharine Slough;
5–John (*b* 1767), began to write name Bush; was with George Rogers Clark at Vincennes and Kaskaskia; with Harrison at Ft. Washington, and mem. of Gen. Harmer's expedition, 1789; *m* Jan. 11, 1792, Sally Craig (*b* 1772; Capt. John[6], *m* Sarah Page);
4–John Craig (1797-1884), *m* 1824, Mary Wright Gaines (1800-75);
3–Philip Edward (1831-1904), mem. 1st Arkansas Mounted Riflemen during War Between the States, 1860-65; *m* 1850, Virginia Lindsay Branson (1831-79);
2–Sally Craig (1860-1914), *m* 1880, William Thaddeus **Traweek** (*b* 1858); issue: I–Evelyn (1 above); II–William Thaddeus (*b* 1885; *m* Bera Butler; *m* 2d, Elizabeth De Pue); III–Arline (*b* 1902; *m* A. McC. Byrnes, Jr.).
1–*m* Apr. 3, 1907, Charles William Dixon (qv for issue).
1–Mem. S.D.P., D.A.R. (chapter regent, 1928-30), U.S.D. 1812 (state rec. sec., 1927-29), U.D.C., Ark. Pioneers. Residence: Gould, Lincoln Co., Ark.

1–**DOANE, Gilbert Harry,** *b* Fairfield, Vt., Jan. 28, 1897.
10–John **Doane** (qv);
9–John (1635-1708), of Eastham, Mass.; *m* 1662, Hannah Bangs (*b* 1644; Edward[10], qv);
8–Samuel (1673-1756), of Eastham; *m* 1696, Martha Hamblen or Hamlin (*b* 1673);
7–Simeon (1708-89), Eastham; *m* 1730, Apphia Higgins (*b* 1709; Elisha[8]);

6–Benjamin (1738-1824), of Eastham and N. Brookfield; *m* Ruth Smith (1739-78; John[7], of Eastham, *m* Phoebe Snow);
5–Benjamin (1772-1846), of Bakersfield, Conn.; *m* 1792, Azubah Doane (1772-1845);
4–James Harvey (1802-47), of Bakersfield; *m* 1829, Persis How (1807-73; John, Jr.[5]);
3–Bradley John (1846-1901), Bakersfield; *m* 1870, Ellen Harriet Randall (1850-1923);
2–Harry Harvey (2 below).
10–Thomas **Gilbert** (ca. 1592-1659), of Wethersfield; *m* Lydia–, who was condemned to be hung as a witch;
9–Obadiah (ca. 1630-1675), of Fairfield; *m* ca. 1660, Elizabeth Burr;
8–Obadiah (1662-ca. 1726), Fairfield; *m* Abigail–;
7–John (ca. 1696-ca. 1782), Fairfield; *m* Jemima Williams;
6–John (*b* 1736), settled at Fairfield, Vt.; *m* Lydia Merwin (*b* 1739; Thomas, Jr.[7]);
5–Nathan (1767-1804), Fairfield; *m* Lucy Sherwood ?;
4–Nathan (1804-84), Fairfield; *m* 1828, Cynthia Smith (1809-85; Joab[5]);
3–Capt. Hamilton S. (1829-1919), Fairfield; *m* Martha Barber Soule;
2–Maude Charlotte (2 below).
10–George **Soule**, Mayflower Pilgrim (qv);
9–George (ca. 1624-will dated 1697), *m* Deborah–;
8–Nathan (ca. 1680-1736), *m* 1704, Mary Gifford;
7–Timothy (1714-70), settled at Nine Partners, N.Y.; *m* 1736, Sarah Allen (Ebenezer[8]);
6–Joseph (1747-1820), Fairfield; *m* Eunice Hungerford (1751-1839; Samuel[7]);
5–Timothy (ca. 1767-1860), Fairfield; *m* Betsy Elliott (1770-1843; Benjamin[6]);
4–Harmon (1797-1877), Fairfield; *m* Polly Flint (1801-36; Edward[5]);
3–Martha B. (1834-1914), *m* Capt. Hamilton Smith **Gilbert** (3 above);
2–Maude Charlotte (*b* 1872), *m* 1896, Harry Harvey **Doane** (*b* 1873); issue: I–Gilbert Harry (1 above); II–Charles Bradley (*b* 1901; *m* 1927, Barbara Lindley Gill); III–Paul Soule (*b* 1905).
1–*m* June 23, 1923, Susan Howland Sherman (qv for issue).
1–B.A., Colgate, '18. Librarian, University of Nebraska, since 1925. Mem. B.O.R., S.M.D., Grolier Club (New York), First Edition Club (London). Residence: Lincoln, Neb.

1–**DOANE, Susan Howland Sherman (Mrs. Gilbert H.)**, *b* Newport, R.I., Sept. 16, 1895.
9–Philip **Sherman** (qv);
8–Peleg (*b* 1638), *m* Elizabeth Lawton (Thomas[9]);
7–Peleg (*b* 1666), *m* 1697, Alice Fish (*b* 1671);
6–Thomas (*b* 1699), *m* 1729, Sarah Sisson (1705-36);
5–Isaac (1736-1817), *m* 1768, Margaret Tabor (William[6]);
4–Perry (1771-1817), *m* 1795, Mary Clark (1770-1862);
3–Robert (1811-81), of Newport, R.I.; *m* 1839, Susan Baker Howland;
2–Benjamin Baker Howland (2 below).
9–John **Howland**, Mayflower Pilgrim (qv);
8–Jabez (1628-1712), mem. Rev. John Cotton's Ch.; constable; lt. King Philip's War; from Plymouth to Bristol, R.I., 1681; licensed to keep a hotel at Bristol, 1681; 1st town clk., 1681; assessor, selectman, dep. Gen. Ct.; ens., 1684; *m* ca. 1667/68, Bethiah Thatcher (*d* 1725; Anthony[9], qv);
7–Joseph (1692-1737), *m* Bathsheba Cary (David[8]);
6–Joseph (1717-75), *m* Sarah Barker (Jeremiah[7]);
5–Henry (1751-1843), *m* Susan Baker;
4–Benjamin Baker (1787-1877), *m* Phoebe C. Green;
3–Susan Baker (1818-93), *m* Robert **Sherman** (3 above);
2–Benjamin Baker Howland (1850-1906), of Newport, R.I.; *m* 1893, Charlotte Amelia Lawton (*b* 1860); issue: I–Charles Lawton (*b* 1894; *m* 1918, Dorothy Arnold); II–Susan Howland (1 above); III–Benjamin Howland (*b* 1897; *m* 1922, Katherine Ray Sheffield).
1–*m* June 23, 1923, Gilbert Harry Doane (qv); issue: 1–Cynthia Gilbert, *b* Newport, R.I., Aug. 2, 1924.
1–B.A., Wellesley, '17 (P.B.K.). Mem. S.M.D. Residence: Lincoln, Neb.

1–**DOBBS, Joseph Henry**, *b* Amherst, Va., Mar. 1, 1876.
6–Rev. Richard **Dobbs**, Middlesex Co., Va., bro. of Arthur Dobbs who was colonial gov. of N.C.;
5–Kedar (1749-1816), Lower Norfolk, Va.; *m* ca. 1781, —Willoughby;
4–Willoughby (*b* 1782), *m* 1805, Rachel Edmonds;
3–Joseph Edward (*b* ca. 1806), *m* 1840, Mrs. Leitha Scott;
2–Henry James (1841-1915), ed. McGuire Sch., Richmond, Va.; lt., Co. E, 18th Va., Pickett's Div., Army of Northern Va., 1861-65; wounded thrice; caught Gen. Armistead in arms as he fell at Gettysburg; Mason (33°), Elk; *m* 1873, Anne Daingerfield Quarles (1837-1916); issue: I–Nellie West (qv); II–Joseph Henry (1 above).
1–Not married. Ed. William and Mary Coll., '91. Sec. Tate Furniture Co., since 1902. Officer N.C. N.G. Mem. S.A.R. (chapter sec.). Clubs: High Point Country, Argentines, Sedgefield Country, Commercial (pres.). Mason, Elk. Residence: 320 Hamilton St., High Point, N.C.

1–**DOBBS, Nellie West**, *b* Cartersville, Ga., Aug. 19, 1874.
9–Col. John **Waller** (qv);
8–Thomas (ca. 1705 or 10-1757 or 64), King William Co., Va.; *m* ca. 1732, Elizabeth Dabney (1710-ca. 1760; Cornelius[9], of King William Co.);
7–Dorothy (*b* 1733), of King William Co.; *m* Aaron **Quarles** (*d* 1767), of King William and Essex cos.;
6–Col. James (*d* 1799), of King William Co.; *m* Anne–;
5–Capt. William Henry (*d* 1810), Essex Co., Va.; *m* 1768, Lucy Brockenbrough (*d* 1800);
4–Francis West (1769-1814), "Paradice," Westmoreland Co., Va.; *m* 1794, Lucy Daingerfield Smith;
3–Henry West (1795-1869), King William Co., Va., and Amherst, Va.; *m* 1833, Jane McDaniel (1816-71);
2–Anne Daingerfield (2 below).
8–Nicholas **Smith** (*d* post 1714), Gloucester Co., Va.;
7–Capt. Nicholas (*d* 1757), Essex Co., Va.; *m* Elizabeth Crawford;
6–Col. Francis (*d* 1762), Essex Co.; *m* 1729, Lucy Meriwether (*d* post 1740; Capt. Francis[7] [*b* ca. 1690], *m* Mary Bathurst; Nicholas[8], qv);
5–Col. Meriwether (1730-94), "Bathurst," Essex Co., Va.; *m* 1769, Elizabeth Daingerfield;
4–Lucy D. (1773-1820), Essex Co., Va.; *m* Francis West **Quarles** (4 above).
9–Col. John **Walker** (*d* 1671), Rappahannock Co., Va.;
8–Anne, of Warwick Co., Va.; as Widow Payne, *m* 2d, 1671, John **Daingerfield** (1640-1720), lived at "Greenfield," New Kent Co., Va.;
7–Col. William (1680-1735), *m* Elizabeth (Bathurst) Tomlin;
6–Col. William (1710-69), Richmond, Va.; *m* Katherine Fauntleroy;
5–Elizabeth (*d* 1796), *m* Col. Meriwether **Smith** (5 above).
9–Col. Samuel **Griffin** (1625-1702), Northumberland Co., Va.; *m* 1655, Sarah Griffin, widow of his bro. Thomas Griffin;
8–Katherine (1656-1728), Northumberland Co.; *m* 1683, William **Fauntleroy** (1649-86), Rappahannock Co., Va.; burgess, (Col. Moore[9], qv);
7–Griffin (1688-1750), Northumberland; *m* 2d, 1727, Ann Bushrod;
6–Katherine, *m* Col. William **Daingerfield** (6 above).
2–Anne Daingerfield Quarles (1837-1916), of Amherst Co., Va.; *m* 1873, Henry James **Dobbs** (1841-1915); issue: I–Nellie West (1 above; see Vol. III, p. 164, for McDaniel lineage); II–Joseph Henry (qv for Dobbs lineage).
1–Ed. Piedmont (Va.) Inst. and Albemarle Female Inst. Mem. D.A.R., U.D.C., High Point Country Club, Sedgefield Country Club. Baptist. Residence: High Point, N.C.

1–**DOOLEY, Laura Jane Sallee (Mrs. James H.)**, *b* Sheffield, Ill., Mar. 6, 1853.
5–William **Cleaver**;
4–Hannah (1771-1842), *m* 1790, Abraham **Hornbeck** (1758-1834), of Big Valley, Pa.; served in 8th Va. Regt. during Am. Rev.;

3–Mary (1793-1864), *m* 1809, James **Sallee** (1786-1852; Oliver[4]);
2–Stephen Brown (1827-*d* July 3, 1863), served 8th Ill. Inf., and 108th Ill. Inf., in Civil War; *m* 1850, Sarah Rebecca Bloom (1831-55; Peter[3], *m* Jane Hankins); issue: I–Loucina Acena (1851-52); II–Laura Jane (1 above); III–Lewis Franklin (1855-1921; *m* 1894, Carrie Alberta Loudon, 1867-97).
1–*m* Feb. 27, 1873, James Harvey Dooley, *b* Maple Park, Ill., Feb. 4, 1847; son of James Dooley (1811-73), of Maple Park, Ill., *m* in Ireland, Catherine Hogan (*d* 1848); issue: 1–Kate Rebecca, *b* York, Neb., Mar. 25, 1874, *m* May 17, 1897, John More Mills, son of John M. Mills, *m* Georgiana Sleigh (issue: 1–Laura Georgiana, *b* Mar. 19, 1898, *m* July 1921, Nathaniel Nicherson; issue, Georgiana, *b* May, 1922; 2–Marrion, *b* Apr. 17, 1900; 3–Ida Kathleen, *b* Dec. 28, 1902; 4–James Ira, *b* Apr. 18, 1905, *m* Sept. 1929, Mary Jane Mc Brian; 5–Helen, *b* Apr. 17, 1914; 6–Ethel, *b* Aug. 29, 1917); 2–Charles Franklin, *b* York, Neb., Sept. 9, 1877; served in Grigsby's Rough Riders, Spanish War; *m* May 2, 1906, Cecelia Juratch (*d* Sept. 1907); *m* 2d, Amelia Catherine Miriam Newham; 3–Ida Louesa, *b* Haddam, Kan., Feb. 5, 1879; *m* Feb. 27, 1908, Joseph J. Oliver (*b* Belle Plaine, Ia., Aug. 12, 1875), of Portland, Ore. (issue: Ralph Oliver, *b* Apr. 25, 1910; Edith Evelyn, *b* June 3, 1913); 4–James Ira, *b* Haddam, Oct. 29, 1880; *m* Nov. 8, 1915, Alma Matilda Meinig (*b* Sept. 2, 1887), dau. of Ernst F. Meinig, of Palouse, Wash. (issue: Mildred, *b* Jan. 3, 1923); 5–Annetta Irene, *b* Haddam, June 8, 1882; *m* Feb. 6, 1907, Christopher Nelson Darby, of Portland, Ore. (issue: Cecil Nelson, *b* Aug. 5, 1911); 6–Frederick Stephen (Oct. 8, 1885-July 16, 1894); 7–Cecil Herbert (Feb. 9, 1889-Oct. 5, 1918), mem. Co. M, 22d Engrs., A.E.F.; died in France; 8–Ralph Elwin, *b* Broken Bow, Neb., Apr. 21, 1893; *m* July 3, 1914, Avis Vienna Smith, dau. of James Loyd Smith, *m* Abbie Pearce, of Little Rock, Wash. (issue: 1–Katie Louise, *b* Jan. 17, 1915; 2–James Elwin, *b* Sept. 10, 1917; 3–Cecil Franklin, *b* July 14, 1919; 4–Loyd Ralph, *b* July 2, 1920; 5–Avis Elizabeth, *b* Feb. 24, 1924).
1–Taught school, 3 yrs. Mem. D.A.R., Legion Auxiliary, O.E.S., Rebecca. Methodist. Republican. Residence: Little Rock, Wash.

1–**DOUGLAS, George Perkins,** *b* Stowe, Vt., Oct. 7, 1865.
9–John **Coit** (qv);
8–Joseph (*d* 1704), dep. Gen. Ct., 1669; *m* 1667, Martha Harris (1648-1710; William[9], of Wethersfield, *m* Edith Bligh);
7–Solomon (*b* 1678), *m* 1706, Mary Stow;
6–Mary, *m* 1733, Ivory **Lucas**;
5–Mary (1737-1810), *m* William **Douglas** (see Vol. II, p. 293);
4–Ivory (1761-1825), *m* Phoebe Smith;
3–Henry (*b* 1802), *m* 1828, Ruby Cilley;
2–Christopher Fulton (2 below).
9–Nehemiah **Smith** (qv);
8–Nehemiah (1646-1727), town clk., Norwich; mem. Gen. Assembly, 1669, et seq.; *m* 1st, Lydia Winchester (1645-1723; Alexander[9], gent., from Eng., 1635, in the "Defense," rep. Braintree Gen. Ct., 1641, ens. Braintree Co., mem. A. and H.A.Co. of Boston, propr. Rehoboth);
7–Nehemiah (1673-1724), *m* 1696, Dorothy Wheeler (1679-1736; Isaac[8], *m* Martha, dau. of Thomas Parke; Thomas[9], at Lynn, 1635, removed to Stonington, Conn., 1669, rep. Gen. Ct., 1673, *m* Mary–);
6–Nathan (1702-84), *m* 1723, Mary Denison (1706-93; Dea. Daniel[7], *m* Mary, dau. of Robert Stanton, *m* Joanna, dau. Thomas Gardner; Capt. John Borodell[8], *m* Phebe Lay; Capt. George[9]; William[10], qv);
5–Nathan (1724-1810), *m* Betsey Denison (1726-1813; Robert[6], *m* Deborah, dau. of Matthew Griswold, 1653-1716);
4–Phoebe (1765 or 67-1853), *m* Ivory **Douglas** (4 above).
9–Capt. Robert **Cilley** (qv);
8–Richard (ca. 1620-25-1686), *m* Martha– (*d* post 1692);
7–Benoni (ca. 1680-1746), *m* 1703, Eleanor Getchell (1684-1735 or 36; Samuel[8]; Samuel[9]);
6–Benjamin;
5–John, *m* 1761, Abigail Clark, of Kingston, N.H. (John[6], *m* Elizabeth Clifford);
4–Ebenezer (1767-1848), *m* Polly Clement (William[5], *m* Molly [Polly] Hoyt);
3–Ruby (1802-68), *m* Henry **Douglas** (3 above).
9–John **Raymond** (1616-1703), *m* Rachel Scruggs (*d* 1666; Thomas[10]);
8–John (1650-1725);
7–John (*b* 1677), *m* 1699, Deborah Perry;
6–Barnabas (*b* 1710), *m* Alice Bent;
5–John (*b* 1742), *m* 1768, Elizabeth Norcot;
4–Barnabas (1773-1862), *m* 1799, Mary Mayo (see Vol. II, p. 293);
3–Augusta A. (*b* 1799), *m* 1824, Orren **Perkins**;
2–Louisa E. (1835-1903), *m* 1857, Christopher Fulton **Douglas** (1831-1911), dry goods mcht., capitalist; issue: I–Mary Ellen (*b* 1861; *m* 1882, Philip Gibson); II–George Perkins (1 above); III–a son (*b* and *d* 1872.)
1–*m* Oct. 18, 1899, Bessie Tabitha Pettit (qv for issue).
1–B.A., Yale, '89 (D.K.E., Wolf's Head); LL.B., U.Minn., 1890. Lawyer, and iron mining, Minneapolis. Mem. S.M.D. Clubs: Minneapolis, Lafayette, Minikahda, Woodhill, Athletic (Minneapolis), University, Yale (N.Y.), University (St. Paul). Residence: 2424 Park Av., Minneapolis, Minn.

1–**DOUGLAS, Bessie Tabitha Pettit (Mrs. George Perkins),** *b* Minneapolis, Minn., Oct. 22, 1870.
10–Thomas **Cornell** (qv);
9–Richard (ca. 1625-1694), *m* Elizabeth–;
8–Richard (ca. 1650-1726), *m* ante 1692, Sarah–;
7–Sarah, *m* 1715, Elnathan **Stevenson** (Edward[8]; Thomas[9]);
6–Charity (1723-80), *m* 1746/47, William **Pettit** (see Vol. I, p. 914);
5–William (1748-1804), moved to Sadsbury Tp., Chester Co., Pa., later to Catawissa, Pa., where he died; *m* 1770, Sarah Birdsall (1748-1804; Jacob[6], of Amwell, N.J.);
4–William (1773-1849), moved with his wife and several small children to Columbiana Co., O., 1810; a pioneer in that section; *m* 1799, Mary Phipps (1782-1843; Benjamin[5]; Robert[6]);
3–Joseph (1809-92), *m* Hannah Grubb Hussey;
2–Curtis Hussey (2 below).
9–Capt. Christopher **Hussey** (qv);
8–John (1635-*d* New Castle, Del., 1707), *m* 1659, Rebecca Perkins (Isaac[9], *m* Susannah–);
7–John (1676-1733), *m* Grace– (*d* 1700); *m* 2d, 1703, Ann Inskeep;
6–John (post 1703-1770), of Newberry; will probated York, Pa.; *m* 1733, Margaret (Record or Riccord ?);
5–Jedidiah (ca. 1740-1823), *m* Jane Penrose;
4–Christopher (1767-1851), *m* 1796, Lydia Grubb;
3–Hannah Grubb (1810-69), *m* 1832, Joseph **Pettit** (3 above).
8–John **Grubb** (1652-1708; son of John, g.son of Thomas, g.g.son of Thomas, g.g.g.son of Henry, M.P., 1571), from Eng. in the "Kent," to Burlington, West Jersey, 1677, settled at Grubb's Landing, Pa., 1682, later at Marcus Hook, Pa.; was justice of peace; mem. council of Del. and (twice) assembly of Pa.; *m* Frances Vane;
7–John (1684-1758), *m* Rachel Buckley (1690-1752; John[8], *m* Hannah Sanderson);
6–William (1713-75), *m* 1738/39, Lydia Hewes (1719-74; William[7], *m* Mary–);
5–John (*d* 1804), *m* 1769, Hannah Gilpin (1746-1823; Joseph[6] [1703/04-1792], *m* 1729, Mary Caldwell; Joseph[7], qv);
4–Lydia (1775-1846), *m* Christopher **Hussey** (4 above);
3–Hannah Grubb, *m* Joseph **Pettit** (3 above);
2–Curtis Hussey (1833-1914), capitalist; flour miller, Minneapolis; *m* 1857, Deborah McBride Williams (*b* 1833); issue: I–Irene Hussey (1858-77); II–Louis Williams (1862-84); III–Edward Curtis (1864-65); IV–Alice Mary (1868-69); V–Bessie Tabitha (1 above).
1–*m* Oct. 18, 1899, George Perkins Douglas (qv); issue (all *b* Minneapolis): 1–Deborah Louise, *b* Sept. 13, 1900; Vassar, '22; *m* 1924, Richard Lodge Tighe; Yale, '23; lawyer (issue: Deborah Douglas, *b* July 26, 1925; Douglas, *b* June 28, 1927; twin daughters, *b* Oct. 26, 1929); 2–Elizabeth Pettit, *b* Apr. 29, 1902; *m* 1926, Donald

Charles Cleveland (issue: Donald Stiles, *b* July 4, 1927; Eleanor Ann, *b* Dec. 21, 1929); 3–Eleanor George, *b* June 30, 1905; *m* 1927, Noyes Dorsey Robinson, of New York, N.Y.
1–Mem. I.A.G. Residence: 2424 Park Av., Minneapolis, Minn.

1–**DOUGLASS, William Angus,** *b* New York, N.Y., Aug. 16, 1852.
5–Walter **Dun** (1711-91), of Scotland; *m* Elizabeth Lenox (*b* 1728);
4–Rev. James (1751-1805), of Scotland; *m* 1781, Elizabeth Graham (1758-1840), of Auchinvale Castle;
3–Robert (1784-1835), from Scotland to U.S.; *m* at Chillicothe, O., 1818, Lucy Wortham Angus (1791-1851; John[4], *d* 1801);
2–Elizabeth (1819-54), *m* 1841, as his first wife, Benjamin **Douglass** (1816-1900), founder of the mercantile agency, now R. G. Dun & Co., New York (for issue and Douglass line see Robert Dun Douglass, Vol. I, p. 257).
1–*m* June 27, 1889, Eliza Kingman (May 9, 1862-Feb. 28, 1898); dau. of Abner Kingman, Boston; issue: 1–Elizabeth Dun, *b* Chicago, July 22, 1890; *m* May 24, 1919, Clyde E. Shorey (issue: William Douglass, *b* May 16, 1920; Clyde Everett, Jr., *b* June 9, 1922; Elizabeth Dun, *b* July 29, 1923); 2–Caro Anderson (June 8, 1892-Nov. 8, 1893); 3–William Angus, Jr. (Jan. 10, 1894-Nov. 15, 1909); 4–Abner Kingman, *b* Oak Park, Ill., Apr. 16, 1896; *m* Dec. 16, 1922, Helen Field James (issue: Kingman Douglass, *b* Sept. 29, 1923; Howard James, *b* May 21, 1925; William Angus, *b* May 30, 1929).
1–*m* 2d, Oct. 1900, Eva Beatta Markoe (Sept. 8, 1854-May 17, 1911); dau. of Hartman Markoe, New York.
1–*m* 3d, Mar. 6, 1913, Lillian (Pollock) McNutt, *b* Effingham, Ill., Nov. 12, 1873; issue: 1–Benjamin Pollock, *b* Oak Park, Ill., Apr. 20, 1916. Stepson: Donald E. McNutt, *b* Houston, Tex., Dec. 7, 1899; *m* June 26, 1928, Theresa Banks (issue: Nancy, *b* Dec. 7, 1929).
1–B.A., Lafayette, '72, M.A., 1876. Gen. mgr. Chicago district of R. G. Dun & Co. to Apr. 1, 1920, when retired. Mem. bd. mgrs. Presbyn. Hosp., Chicago. Clubs: Union League, Chicago, Oak Park, Oak Park Country. Residence: 317 N. Kenilworth Av., Oak Park, Ill.

1–**DRAKE, James Frank,** *b* Pittsfield, N.H., Sept. 1, 1880.
9–Robert **Drake** (1580-1668), from Eng. to Exeter, N.H., ca. 1638;
8–Abraham (*b* 1628), *m* Jane– (*d* 1676);
7–Abraham (1654-1714), *m* Sarah Hobbs;
6–Abraham (1688-1767), *m* 1711, Theodate Roby (1691-1783; Samuel[7]; Henry[8]);
5–Simon (1730-1801), pvt. Am. Rev.; *m* Judith Perkins (1736-1819; John[6]; Humphrey?[7]; Abraham[8]);
4–Maj. James (1755-1834), pvt. Am. Rev.; maj. N.H. militia; *m* 1781, Hannah Ward (1763-1848);
3–Col. James (1805-70), col. 18th Regt., N.H. Militia; *m* 1834, Betsey Seavey (1811-65);
2–Nathaniel Seavey (*b* 1851), shoe mfr.; *m* 1873, Mary Agnes Rogers Green (*b* 1857); issue: I–James F. (1 above); II–Agnes (*b* 1883; *m* Calvin Whitten Foss).
1–*m* July 25, 1907, Mildred Augusta Chase, *b* Plymouth, N.H., Apr. 30, 1883; dau. of Irving Hanson Chase, of Plymouth, *m* Minnie Elliott; issue: 1–Ruth Elliott, *b* Springfield, Mass., Apr. 6, 1910; Miss Porter's Sch., Farmington, Conn., 1928; 2–Virginia, *b* Plymouth, N.H., July 16, 1911; Miss Porter's Sch., 1929; 3–James Frank, Jr., *b* Springfield, Mass., June 26, 1913; 4–Constance Chase, *b* Springfield, Feb. 12, 1915.
1–A.B., Dartmouth, '02; Master Commercial Science, Amos Tuck Sch. (Dartmouth), 1903. Sec. Bd. of Trade, Springfield, Mass., 1903-08; sec. Phelps Pub. Co., Springfield, 1908-14, treas. and dir., 1914-18; asst. to pres. Gulf Oil Corpn., Pittsburgh, 1919-23; now pres. or dir. various corpns. (see Who's Who in America). Mem. Common Council, Springfield, 1908-12, pres. 1910-12. Commd. maj., Ordnance Dept., U.S.A., May 1918; served as comdg. officer finance div. Pittsburgh dist., lt. col., Mar. 25, 1919; hon. discharged, June 3, 1919. Mem. S.A.R., M.O.W.W., A.L. Clubs: Cosmos, University, Congressional Country (Washington), Rolling Rock (Ligonier, Pa.), University, Duquesne, Pittsburgh Golf, Fox Chapel Golf. Residence: 5210 Pembroke Pl., Pittsburgh, Pa.

1–**DRAPER, Martha Stark (Mrs. Charles A.).**
6–James **Stark** (1695-1754), in Stafford Co., Va., ante 1730; *m* Elizabeth Thornton;
5–John (*b* Scotland, 1717-*d* 1781), *m* 2d, Hannah Eaves;
4–James (1757-1818), of Stafford Co., Va., and Bourbon Co., Ky.; *m* 2d, 1786, Susanna Hart (1764-1803; Leonard[6], *m* Mary–; Valentine[6], will probated 1792, Rockbridge Co., Va., *m* Mary–);
3–James (1792-1874), to Pike Co., Mo., 1816; *m* 1815, Jane Watts;
2–Washington (2 below).
6–John Daniel **Jacoby** (will probated Culpeper Co., Va., 1768), *m* Anna Barbra– (*d* 1769);
5–John Francis Lucas (will probated Bourbon Co., Ky., 1788), *m* London, Eng., 1764, Frederica Loetspeig (1744-1832);
4–Elizabeth (1777-1847), *m* 1794, John **Watts** (1766-1839);
3–Jane (1797-1882), *m* James **Stark** (3 above).
8–Francis **Maybury** (will probated Surry Co., Va., 1712), *m* Elizabeth West Gilliam (John[9], *m* Margery–);
7–Hinchia (1697-1762);
6–Joel (will probated 1784, Greensville Co., Va.). *m* Winnifred Smith (William[7]);
5–Lewis (will probated 1798, Montgomery Co., Ky.), *m* in Brunswick Co., Va., 1773, Susanna Hamilton (John[6], *m* Ann Everard);
4–Mehetabel (1785-1859), *m* in Shelby Co., Ky., 1809, Lyna **Whitledge** (John[5], will probated Bourbon Co., Ky., 1783, *m* Alice–);
3–Thomas Benson (1810-44), *m* 2d, 1833, Christiana Jacoby;
2–Martha (2 below).
9–Peter **Bond** (will probated Baltimore Co., Md., 1705), moved from Va. to Md., 1660; *m* 2d, Else or Alice–;
8–William, *m* Mary (Westbury);
7–Alice (*b* 1708), *m* 1724, Thomas **Johnson** (will probated 1767), of Harford Co., Md.;
6–Mary (1725-post 1765), *m* 1742, James **Brice** (will probated 1765), of Harford Co.;
5–Samuel (1743-post 1812), *m* Rachel–;
4–Christiana (1778-1865), *m* 1809, Ralph Ladenberg **Jacoby** (1768-1822; John Francis Lucas[5], 5 above);
3–Christiana (1817-96), *m* 1833, Thomas Benson **Whitledge** (3 above);
2–Martha (1836-1923), *m* 1856, Washington **Stark** (1834-1914); issue: I–Augusta Belle (*m* Joseph Mackey Pepper); II–Cora Lee (*m* William A. Shelton); III–Lewis Whitledge; IV–Susan (*d* infancy); V–Martha Washington (1 above); VI–Christiana Jane (*m* Philip Hay Kilpatrick, *d* 1907); VII–Thomas Washington (*d* infancy).
1–*m* 1896, Dr. Charles A. Draper; issue: 1–Charles Stark, *b* Windsor, Mo., Oct. 2, 1901; A.B., Leland Stanford U., '22; S.B., M.I.T., 1926, M.S., 1928; 2–Ralph Clayton, *b* Windsor, Nov. 16, 1905; A.B., Leland Stanford U., '26; M.B.A., Harvard Grad. Sch. Business Administration, 1929.
1–Mem. I.A.G. Residence: 731 University Av., Palo Alto, Calif.

1–**DRAPER, Gideon Frank,** *b* Lakeville, Conn., July 20, 1858.
8–James **Draper** (qv);
7–James (1654-98), of Roxbury; *m* 1681, Abigail Whiting (1663-1721);
6–Gideon (*b* 1694), of Roxbury; *m* 1713, Abigail Aldis;
5–Gideon (1722-78), of Dover, N.Y.; *m* ca. 1742, Dolly Bassett;
4–John (*b* ca. 1750), *m* Miss Stewart;
3–Gideon (1780-1861), of Clifton Springs, N.Y., M.E. clergyman; *m* 1812, Elizabeth Cronise (1796-1861);
2–Gideon, D.D. (*b* Manchester, N.Y., June 22, 1828-*d* Yokohama, Japan, Dec. 8, 1889), ed. Genesee, Wesleyan Sem., Lima, N.Y., grad. Dartmouth Coll., 1849; admitted N.Y. bar; entered M.E. ministry, 1857; pastor English-speaking Union Ch., Geneva, Switzerland, 1873-74; held pastorates in U.S., 1857-72,75-85;

m 1857, Charlotte P. Brown (1832-*d* Hakodate, Japan, Apr., 1899), both buried Aoyama, Tokyo.
1-*m* Jan. 28, 1880, Mira Enid Haven, *b* Malden, Mass., May 6, 1859; dau. of Erastus Otis Haven, chancellor of Syracuse U., and M.E. bishop; issue (all *b* Yokohama, Japan): 1-Charlotte Enid, *b* Jan. 12, 1881; B.A., U. of Ill., '02; *m* Oct. 20, 1903, Percy Almerin, son of Eli Clark Smith, of Dixon, Ill. (issue: Francis Enid); 2-Winifred, *b* Apr. 12, 1889; B.A., Syracuse U., '11; 3-Gideon Haven, *b* June 22, 1890; B.A., Syracuse U., '12; *m* June 28, 1916, Mildred dau. of Chalkley W. Derr, of Mitchell, S.D. (issue: Dexter Derr); 4-Marion Romer, *b* Dec. 15, 1891; B.A., Syracuse U., '13; 5-Erastus Otis, *b* Jan. 2, 1901; B.A., Boston U., '24.
1-B.A., Syracuse U., '80 (D.K.,E. P.B.K., Phi Kappa Phi), S.T.D. Missionary of M.E. Ch. in Japan since 1880, except 4 yrs., 1882-86, spent in U.S. Mem. I.A.G., N.Y. State Hist. Assn., Am. Geog. Soc. Club: Business Men's. Residence: 222 B Bluff, Yokohama, Japan.

CARBERY

1-**DREFS, Clara Artemesia Newman (Mrs. Arthur G.),** *b* Washington, D.C., Feb. 19, 1895.
11-Benjamin **Gill** (*d* 1655), from Eng. in the "Ark," 1634; founded Anne Arundel Co., Md.: he signed first letter of Lord Calvert from Md. to Eng. describing voyage of the "Ark"; landed propr. 1,220 acres; "Gills Land" surveyed 1646;
10-Ann (*d* 1698), Anne Arundel Co.; lady in waiting to Queen Mary of Eng.; *m* Capt. James **Neal** (1615-84), to America, ante 1638; mem. Council of Md., 1643-44,61,62; commr. of treas., 1643; burgess for Charles Co., Md., 1665-66; capt. provincial forces of Md.; apptd. dep.-gov., 1660; lord of Woolaston Manor; 2,000 acres surveyed for him 1642;
9-Jane, of Charles Co., Md.; *m* Maj. William **Boarman** (1654-1720), burgess for St. Mary's Co., Md., 1671-75; high sheriff, 1679-81; commd. capt. of militia, St. Mary's Co., 1661, maj., 1676;
8-Ann, of St. Mary's Co.; *m* John **Guybert**;
7-Elizabeth, of Charles Co.; *m* John Baptist **Carbery,** of Md.; ed. in Eng.;
6-John Baptist (*d* 1777), of Charles Co.; *m* Mary Thompson;
5-Thomas (1745-1812), of Washington, D.C.; ed. Georgetown Coll.; *m* Mary Asoneth (*d* 1819);
4-Lewis (1794-1860), of Georgetown, D.C.; ed. Georgetown Coll.; civil engr. and surveyor of the county of Washington; *m* 1817, Artemesia Cloud (1800-36), ed. Georgetown Convent (Abner[5], Am. Rev.; purchased extensive property in Md. and Va. along the Potomac River, 1794; *m* 1800, Susannah Pimmet Smallwood);
3-Martha (1824-66), ed. Georgetown Convent; *m* 1855, Peirce **Shoemaker** (1816-91), estate included greater portion of Rock Creek Park which was sold to the govt., 1890; willed 3,500 acres of land in D.C., all of this property had been in the Peirce family over 125 yrs., original deeds in possession of present heirs; was third largest slave owner in D.C. (David[4], *b* D.C., War 1812, *m* Abigail, dau. of Isaac Peirce, *m* Elizabeth Cloud);
2-Clara Artemesia (2 below).
10-William **Bretton,** from Eng., to Md. ante 1649; landed propr., 500 acres surveyed for him, 1659, 300 acres, 1675; signed the act insuring religious toleration in Md., 1649; Bretton's Bay named for him; *m* Mary Nabb;
9-Mary, *m* William **Thompson**;
8-William, *m* Victoria Mathews (Dr. Thomas[9] [1600-76], to Md., 1633, Lord of St. Thomas Manor, 4,080 acres in Md. surveyed 1649; *m* Jane Cockshute, *b* 1610);
7-Thomas, *m* Jane Tait;
6-Mary (*d* 1793), *m* John B. **Carbery** (6 above).

MRS. CLARA ARTEMESIA (SHOEMAKER) NEWMAN (1865-1930).

2-Clara Artemesia Shoemaker (Nov. 11, 1865-Feb. 10, 1930), ed. Notre Dame Convent, Baltimore, Md. (see portrait); *m* 1886, Edwin Ameal **Newman** (1861-1927), engaged in real estate operations; founded Lakeland, Md.; edited the National Watchman, later purchased by Bryan and named the "Commoner"; inventor, among his inventions were several river and harbor dredge excavators, the thermostate, metal bee hives, etc.; pres. D.C. Dem. Assn.; mem. Dem. Nat. Com. (Enos[3], *m* Agusta, dau. of Maj. Mathis Walser, *m* Eva Werle); issue (all *b* D.C.): I-Lucian Cloud (*m* 1913, Ruth Grant Miller); II-Edwin Peirce Shoemaker (*m* 1925, Lucille O'Hara); III-Clara A. (1 above); IV-Helen Carbery (*b* 1899); V-Martha Louise (*b* 1901; *m* 1921, John Edmund Cammack); VI-Azadia Walser (*b* 1906; *m* 1928, William F. A. Herrmann).
1-*m* Mar. 19, 1921, Arthur George Drefs, *b* Buffalo, N.Y., Apr. 5, 18–; grad. U. of Pa., 1910; v.p. and treas. McQuay-Norris Mfg. Co., St. Louis; clubs: Detroit Athletic, Tam O Shanter Golf, Recess, Detroit and Algonquin Golf; son of Charles A. Drefs, of Buffalo, N.Y., *m* Elizabeth Zeigler.
1-Grad. St. Joseph's Coll., Emmitsburg, Md. Mem. D.A.R., Mo. Hist. Soc. Residence: 6643 Kingsbury Boul., St. Louis, Mo.

1-**DROLLINGER, Ziba Lloyd,** *b* Rolling Prairie, Ind., June 28, 1885.
4-Frederick **Drollinger** (*d* 1817), removed from Pa. to Guilford Co., N.C., where he *d*; ancestors came from Germany to Pa.; *m* ca. 1798, Barbara Wanick;
3-Gabriel (1810-88), removed with mother, brothers and sisters from Guilford Co., N.C., to nr. Easton, Preble Co., O., 1819; early settler in northern Ind., 1830; learned to speak Indian language; *m* 1834, Mary Elizabeth Chapman (1816-93; Samuel[4] [*b* Conn.-killed by a falling tree], from N.Y., to La Porte Co., Ind., ca. 1832, *m* Polly–, 1771-1848);
2-George Washington (2 below).
5-Ebenezer **Bailey,** of Hartford, Conn.; *m* Jemima–;
4-Ebenezer (1771-1815), of Hartford; to Cairo, N.Y., ca. 1805; to Hector, Tompkins Co., N.Y., ca. 1809; served War 1812, dying of epidemic contracted on the lines shortly after his re-

turn home; *m* ca. 1796, Lydia Bradley (1775-1821);
3–Ziba (1807-88), of Cairo, N.Y.; to La Porte Co., Ind., 1836; *m* 2d, 1846, Elizabeth Roberts (1821-99; William[4] [1771-1852], of Leaksville, N.C., Knoxville, Tenn., Shelby Co., Ind., and later of Kingsbury, Ind.; buried with wife in Winchell Cemetery, nr. Still Well, Ind., *m* Nancy Parish [1784-1849], dau. of —, *m* Mary–, 1754-1847);
2–Susan (*b* nr. La Porte, Ind., 1862), *m* 1883, George Washington **Drollinger** (*b* nr. Mill Creek, Ind., 1858), realtor and builder, Chicago, Ill.; issue: I–Ziba L. (1 above); II–Harley F. (*b* 1887; *m* 1912, Beatrice Busenbenz); III–Benjamin H. (*b* 1889; *m* 1922, Edna Corr); IV–George L. (*b* 1890; *m* 1913, Ossie Roysdon); V–Frank E. (*b* 1892; *m* 1924, Effie Chute); VI–Joseph Clyde (*b* 1895; *m* 1927, Mae Dunne); VII–Lottie A. (*b* 1898; *m* 1920, Palmer O. Spalding); VIII–Gabriel Owen (*b* 1905; *m* 1928, Dorothy Ashton).
1–*m* May 31, 1917, Valeria Le Conte Garrard, *b* Fortress Monroe, Va.; dau. of Col. Joseph Lees Garrard, U.S.A. (see Vol. I, p. 118, for genealogy).
1–Grad. La Porte (Ind.) H.S., 1904; U.S.M.A., 1911. Second lt., 16th Inf., June 13, 1911; 1st lt., July 1, 1916; capt., May 15, 1917; maj. Inf. N.A., June 13, 1911; lt. col. (temp.), Sept. 28, 1918-Mar. 24, 1920; maj., 35th Inf., July 1, 1920. Served in Alaska, 1911-12; at Presidio of San Francisco, 1912-14; on Mexican border, El Paso, Tex., 1914-16; on 1st Mexican Punitive Expdn., 1916-17; with 1st, 2d, and 3d divs., A.E.F., in France, 1917-18; awarded Croix de Guerre (Fr.). Served in Hawaii, 1919-23; prof. mil. science and tactics, Boston U., 1923-27; grad. Inf. Sch., Ft. Benning, Ga., 1928; grad. Command and Gen. Staff Sch., Ft. Leavenworth, Kan., 1930; assigned to 11th Inf., Ft. Benjamin Harrison, Ind., and joined June 21, 1930. Mem. I.A.G., M.O.W.W., U.S. Inf. Assn., Army Ordnance Assn., Assn. of Graduates U.S.M.A. Clubs: University, Army and Navy (Boston), Army, Navy and Marine Corps Country (Washington). Residence: Fort Benjamin Harrison, Ind.

1–**DROUGHT, Ethel Tunstall (Mrs. Henry P.)**, *b* San Antonio, Tex., Dec. 8, 1863.
6–Col. Richard **Tunstall** (*d* ante 1782), of King and Queen Co., Va., burgess, 1766-68; chmn. Com. Safety, 1774-75; *m* Annie Hall or Hill;
5–John, clk. King and Queen Co., Va., 1762; *m* Sarah Temple (Joseph[6] [*b* 1666], from Eng. to Va., of Presq'isle, King William Co., wealthy mcht., *m* Ann, only child of Benjamin Arnal);
4–Joseph (*b* 1758), *m* 1781, Jane Pearce (*b* 1760);
3–John Pearce (*b* 1782), *m* Jane Meriwether;
2–Warwick (2 below).
8–Nicholas **Meriwether** (*b* 1631), came from Wales to Va., 1678; clk. of the Council, 1655; *m* Elizabeth Woodhouse;
7–Nicholas (qv), *m* Elizabeth Crawford (Col. David[8] [*d* 1744], of New Kent Co., Va., burgess, vestryman);
6–Col. David (1690-1744), planter, Louisa Co., Va.; *m* Anne Holmes (*d* 1735/36; George[7], of King and Queen Co., Va.);
5–William (1730-90), to Jefferson Co., Ky.; *m* July 17, 1751, Martha Cocke Wood (1731-1801; Henry[6], of Goochland Co., Va., *m* Martha, dau. of William Aston);
4–David Wood (1756-95), *m* 1784, Mary Lewis (John[5], *m* Ann, dau. of Robert Lewis, of "Belvoir"; Zachary[6]; Zachary[7], to Va. ca. 1692);
3–Jane, *m* John P. **Tunstall** (3 above).
9–Thomas **Hall**, of Abington Parish, Gloucester Co., Va.; *m* post 1662, Margery–;
8–John (*b* 1664), *m* Elizabeth–;
7–John (*b* 1686), *m* twice;
6–John, *m* Sarah–;
5–Nathan, Episcopalian minister, of Henry or Patrick Co., Va.; Am. Rev.; *m* 1755 ?, Ann–;
4–Randolph (Randall) (1759-60-1821), Am. Rev.; from Henry Co., Va., to Garrard Co., Ky., 1783; Bapt. minister; probably first pastor of Forks of Dix River Ch.; *m* Sally–;
3–Rev. Nathan Huston, D.D. (1782-1858), from Va. to Ky., *d* Columbia, Mo.; Presbyn. minister; *m* 1807, Ann Crawford (1789-1822); *m* 2d, Mrs. Elizabeth (Pope) Trotter;
2–Florida Pope (2 below).
8–Nathaniel **Pope** (qv);
7–Col. Nathaniel (1640-ca. 1675), of Westmoreland Co., Va.; *m* Mary Sisson;
6–Nathaniel (1662-1719), atty. at law and king's Council for Westmoreland Co.; *m* 1690, Jane Brooks Brown (*d* 1719);
5–Worden (*b* ca. 1700-*d* 1748), of Westmoreland Co., Va.; *m* Hester Netherton;
4–Col. William (1746-1835), capt. Va. forces in Am. Rev.; sent by Va. Assembly to Louisville, Ky., and by its order mapped the town; original trustee of the town; high sheriff; justice of the peace; col. of militia, 1784, for punitive expdns. against Indians; *m* 1770, Penelope Edwards;
3–Elizabeth (*d* 1850 aet. 63), *m* 1st, Gen. George Trotter, of Lexington, Ky.; *m* 2d, Nathan Huston **Hall** (3 above).
8–John **Edwards**, from Wales to Md.; perhaps the following data is concerning him: Of Northumberland House, Northumberland Co., Va., received 1050 acres in Lancaster Co., Va., 1653, also 300 acres in Northumberland Co.;
7–William, *m* 1678, Ann Harrison;
6–William (*b* 1697), *m* a sister or daughter of William Haydon, of Lancaster Co., Va.;
5–Heydon or Hayden (1723-1803), from Northumberland Co., Va., to Bourbon Co., Ky.; *m* 1747, Penelope Sanford;
4–Penelope, of Fauquier Co., Va.; *m* William **Pope** (4 above);
3–Elizabeth, *m* 2d, Nathan Huston **Hall** (3 above);
2–Florida Pope (1825-1911), *m* Charles Boswell; *m* 2d, 1848, Warwick **Tunstall** (1814-93); issue (1st marriage): I–*d* infancy; issue (2d marriage): I–Florida (*m* Dr. Sharpe); II–Penelope (*d* infancy); III–Patty (*m* John E. Lockwood); IV–Fanny Lee (*d* infancy); V–Sallie French (*m* Walter Booth); VI–Virginia Lee (Gypsy); (*d* aet. 19); VII–Ethel (1 above).
1–*m* 1885, Henry Patrick Drought, *b* Scattery Island, Co. Clare, Ireland, 1858; son of Col. Thomas Drought; issue: 1–Robert (*d* infancy); 2–Harry P.; 3–Humphreys; 4–Frederick Gerald; 5–Francis Tunstall.
1–Ed. Miss Westcott's Sch., and St. Mary's Hall, San Antonio. Mem. C.D., D.A.R. Clubs: Art League, Woman's. Summer place: "Droughtfels," Comfort, Tex. Residence: 1215 N. St. Mary St., San Antonio, Tex.

1–**DuBOIS, Mary Constance,** *b* Philadelphia, Pa., Mar. 28, 1879.
8–Jacques **duBois** (1625-76), Huguenot refugee, from Holland to Wiltwyck, now Kingston, N.Y., 1675; *m* 1663, Pierronne Bentyn;
7–Pierre (1674-1737), from Kingston crossed Hudson; bought land which later became Fishkill; called founder of the churches at Fishkill and Poughkeepsie; *m* 1697, Jannetje (Jeannetta) Burhans, Brabant;
6–Jonathan (1704-87), *m* Ariantje Van Osterhout;
5–Peter (1734-73), *m* Mary Van Voorhees (1740-87; Coert[6], *m* Katrina Filkin or Fitkin);
4–Cornelius (1771-1846), came to New York aet. 15; patron of noted charities and public institutions, philanthropist, bank dir.; *m* 1803, Sarah Platt Ogden (1782-1836; Robert[5], *m* Sarah Platt; desc. Jonathan Ogden, settled at Elizabethtown, N.J., 1664);
3–George Washington, D.D. (1822-1909), Episcopal clergyman; noted missionary worker in Minn.; chaplain, 11th Ohio Regt., Civil War; *m* 1848, Maria Coxe McIlvaine (1831-1923; Charles Pettit[4], P.E. bishop of Ohio, *m* Emily, dau. of William Coxe);
2–Henry Ogden (*b* 1855), Episcopal minister; chief pastor Catholic Apostolic Ch., N.Y.C.; *m* 1878, Emily Stuart Meier Smith (1852-1924; Rev. Matson Meier[3], prof. Div. Sch. of the P.E. Ch., Phila., *m* Mary Stuart, dau. of Norman White, of New York, *m* a sister of William P. Dodge, distinguished mcht. and philanthropist).
1–Attended Rye (N.Y.) Sem., 1891-97, Columbia summer session, 1903, Columbia extension course, winter of 1903-04. Author (see Who's Who in America). Episcopalian. Residence: 380 Riverside Dr., New York, N.Y.

1–**DUDLEY, Etta Brown (Mrs. Frank A.),** *b* Niagara Falls, N.Y., Dec. 27, 1866.
5–David **Brown** (*d* 1830), of Hebron, Conn., and

Peru, Mass.; *m* 1761, Lydia Sweetland (1743-1814);
4–Solomon (1774-1856), of Hebron, Conn., and Peru, Mass.; *m* 1796, Sarah Gilbert (1776-1864);
3–Elijah (1798-1868), of Peru; *m* 1823, Harriet Payn;
2–Wesley Payn (2 below).
10–Elder William **Brewster,** Mayflower Pilgrim (qv);
9–Jonathan, *m* Lucretia Oldham;
8–Benjamin (1633-1710), of Norwich, Conn.; *m* 1659, Anne Darte (*d* 1709);
7–Benjamin (*b* 1673), of Norwich and Lebanon, Conn.; *m* 1696, Mary Smith (1672-1747);
6–Mary (1704-77), of Lebanon; *m* 1726, Benjamin **Payn** (1700-55);
5–Stephen (1735-1800), of Lebanon and Partridgefield; *m* 1756, Rebecca Bushnell (1737-1816);
4–Stephen (1774-1847), of Peru, Mass.; *m* 1798, Abigail Butts (*b* 1780);
3–Harriet (1800-70), *m* Elijah **Brown** (3 above);
2–Wesley Payn (1838-1927), of Niagara Falls, N.Y.; *m* 1863, Harriet Ann Sackett (1841-1927); issue: I–Lucy Marie (*b* 1864; *m* Harry Morrison Clark, *d* 1928); II–Jessie Marion (*b* 1865; *m* Edward Blake Wyman, *d* 1917); III–Etta (1 above); IV–Hattie May (*b* 1869); V–Edith Grace (*b* 1879; *m* Dr. Charles Soules Murrless).
1–*m* Dec. 17, 1890, Frank Alonzo Dudley, *b* Wilson, N.Y., Jan. 30, 1864; son of John Alexander Dudley, of Whitewater, Wis., *m* Henrietta Wright.
1–Mem. S.M.D., D.A.R. (state dir. N.Y. State N.S.D.A.R., 1925-27, 2d v.p. N.Y. State Officers Club, chapter regent and organizer of Niagara Falls Chapter), I.A.G., N.Y. State Hist. Soc., Niagara Falls Hist. Soc. Presbyterian. Republican. Residence: "Amigari," Lewiston Heights, Niagara Falls, N.Y.

1–**DUDLEY, Louise,** *b* Georgetown, Ky., Nov. 15, 1884.
10–Edward **Dudley,** from Eng. to Va., 1637, settled in York Co., later in Lancaster Co.; *m* Elizabeth Pritchard;
9–Col. Richard, high sheriff, Gloucester Co., Va., 1675; *m* a dau. of Henry Sewell;
8–James, *m* Anne Fleet (*d* 1722; William[9]);
7–William (*b* 1696), *m* 1721, Judith Johnson;
6–Robert (1726-66), *m* 1745, Joyce Gayle (Mathew[7], *m* Judith–);
5–Rev. Ambrose (1750-1825), capt. Am. Rev.; removed from Va. to Fayette Co., Ky.; *m* 1773, Ann Parker;
4–Gen. James (1777-1870), mem. conv. that framed 1st constitution of Ky., 1849; *m* 1802, Polly Ferguson (*d* 1823, Abram[5]);
3–Ambrose Ferguson (1803-40), *m* 1827, Nancy Moberley;
2–Richard Moberley (2 below).
10–Col. William **Claiborne** (qv);
9–Mary, as widow Rice, *m* 2d, 1650, Maj. Robert **Harris** (1635-1701), from Wales to Va., ca. 1651 (Capt. Thomas[10] [1576-1658], came from Wales, settled in, now Henrico Co., Va., 1611, *m* Adria, dau. of Thomas Osborne, who came to Va. with Harris);
8–Col. William (1652-87), burgess, Henrico and Hanover cos., Va.; *m* 1679, Temperance Overton (*d* 1699; William[9], of Va., *m* Mary Waters; son of Gov. William Overton, of Hull, Eng.);
7–Maj. Robert (*d* 1765), maj. Colonial wars; burgess from Hanover Co., Va.; *m* 1720, Mourning Glenn;
6–Lucy (*b* 1734), *m* William **Shelton** (*d* 1815; Thomas[7]);
5–Rev. Thomas (*d* 1793), killed by Indians; *m* Elizabeth Woods (Col. William[6] [*b* 1705], from Ireland, settled in Albemarle Co., Va., *m* Susannah Wallace; Michael[7] [1684-1762], of Ireland, *m* Mary Campbell; John[8], *m* Elizabeth Warship);
4–Betsy, *m* 1803, Richard **Moberley** (*b* 1778; John[5] [1755-1833], *m* 1st, 1777, Nancy Jenkins, 1761-1820);
3–Nancy (1806-44), *m* Ambrose F. **Dudley** (3 above).
5–William **Henton** (*d* 1780), of Rockcastle Co., Va.; *m* Mary–;
4–Thomas (*d* 1829), Am. Rev.; *m* Christine Brenen;
3–Thomas (1797-1869), *m* 1835, Nancy Darnaby;
2–Mary (2 below).
6–William **Darnaby** (*d* 1780), *m* Diana–;
5–Edward, came to Va. in "The Traveling Church," comd. by Capt. William Ellis; *m* 1758, Judith Gayle (Mathew[6] [*d* 1772], *m* Judith–);
4–Edward (1765-1845), *m* 1786, Mildred Ellis (1767-1823; Hezekiah[5], Spotsylvania Co., Va., *m* Mildred Burbridge);
3–Nancy (1808-82), *m* Thomas **Henton** (3 above).
2–Richard Moberley **Dudley** (1838-93), pres. Georgetown Coll.; *m* 1863, Elizabeth Thompson (*d* 1873), g.niece of Gov. Franklin of N.C.; *m* 2d, 1877, Mary Henton (1846-1915); issue (1st marriage): I–S. Frank (*b* 1864); II–Lizzie M. (1867-78); III–Myra (1868-93); IV–Thompson (1869-93); V–Pattie (*d* infancy); VI–Richard Moberley, Jr. (*d* infancy); issue (2d marriage): I–Anne Henton (*b* 1879; *m* W. O. Shewmaker); II–Mary Moberley (*b* 1880; *m* W. H. Pittman); III–June (*b* 1882; *m* R. E. Harvey); IV–Louise (1 above); V–Rose (*b* 1887; *m* R. D. Scearce).
1–A.B., Georgetown Coll., '05; Ph.D., Bryn Mawr, 1910; research student Bibliotheque Nationale, Paris, 1908-09, Oxford U., Michaelmas term, 1909. Prof. English, Stephens Coll., Columbia, Mo., since 1919. Author (see Who's Who in America). Residence: Sampson Apts., Columbia, Mo.

1–**DUERFELDT, Mary Edna Matthews (Mrs. Henry G.),** *b* Mankato, Minn., Sept. 23, 1874.
8–Caleb **Matthews** (1674-1755), from Eng., settled at Hartford, Conn.; *m* Elizabeth Frisbee;
7–Caleb (*b* 1706), *m* 1st, 1726, Hannah Hitchcock (*d* 1731);
6–Aaron (*b* 1727), Am. Rev.; *m* Huldah Frisbee;
5–Aaron (*b* 1745), of Camden, N.Y.; surveyor; went to N.Y., 1795; *m* Hannah Tuttle, the only white woman in Oneida Co., the winter of 1795;
4–Lyman (1782-1817), Camden; taught the first sch. in the county; *m* Polly Alcott (1785-1851);
3–Aaron (1808-76), Camden; *m* 1833, Sarah Ann Hibbard (1815-49);
2–Thaddeus LeGrand (1844-1915), Camden; enlisted at Mankato, Minn in Civil War, 1862, honorably discharged, 1865; *m* 1870, Kate Winifred Pryse (*b* 1853); issue: I–Wilfred LeGrand (1871-84); II–Mary Edna (1 above); III–John Aaron (*b* 1876; *m* Mabel Rollins); IV–James Lyman (1879-92); V–Francis Cadwell (1886-90).
1–*m* Apr. 21, 1897, Henry George Duerfeldt (July 16, 1871-June 18, 1922); son of Gust Duerfeldt, of Richardson Co., Neb.; issue: 1–Treacy Henry, *b* Helena, Mont., June 2, 1901; B.S., Coll. of Washington State, 1922, Ph.D., 1922; M.-S. in pathology, U.Chicago, 1927; M.D., Rush Med. Coll., 1928; *m* June 24, 1926, Florence Jane Barnhart (issue: Edna Clare); 2–Kathryn Louisa, *b* Detroit, Mich., Dec. 24, 1906; Cheney State Normal, 1927; *m* July 16, 1928, Russell S. Bock; 3–Theron Matthews, *b* Spokane, Wash., Oct. 13, 1912.
1–Mem. D.A.R. Baptist. Republican. Residence: 2215 Milford Pl., Spokane, Wash.

1–**DUNCAN, John Charles,** *b* nr. Knightstown, Ind., Feb. 8, 1882.
5–Thomas **Duncan,** from Scotland to Pa., ca. 1740;
4–James, *m* Mary Hogue;
3–Samuel (1810-94), miller; *m* 2d, 1844, Margaret Duffy (1818-93);
2–Daniel Davidson (2 below).
7–Thomas (Jessup) **Jessop,** landed at Newbern, N.C., 1772, with wife and one son, Thomas; settled in Perquimans Co.;
6–Thomas (*b* Leeds, Eng., ca. 1715-*d* 1783), lived at New Garden, N.C.;
5–Timothy (*b* 1742-*d* Morgan Co., Ind., 1831 or later), Quaker, manumitted his slaves, thereby reducing his fortune; migrated to Green Co., Ind.; *m* at New Garden, N.C., Hannah Pratt (*b* 1754);
4–Pratt (*b* N.C., 1772), to Ind.;
3–Tidamon (1800-66), from Greensboro, N.C., to Knightstown, Ind.; farmer, Quaker, abolitionist; *m* Lydia Morris (1810-75);
2–Naomi (1842-1906), *m* 1867, Daniel Davidson **Duncan** (1844-1911); miller; issue: I–Mary (*b* 1872; *m* 1913, George H. Jackson, *b* ca. 1854); II–John C. (1 above).

1–*m* Dec. 29, 1906, Katharine Armington Bullard, *b* Indianapolis, Ind., Aug. 21, 1879; dau. of Dr. William Mason Bullard; issue: 1–Eunice Naomi, *b* Berkeley, Calif., Dec. 16, 1907; U.Colo., '30.

1–A.B., Ind. U., '05 (Sigma Xi), A.M., 1906; Ph.D., U.Calif., 1909. Prof. astronomy, dir. Whitin Observatory, Wellesley Coll., since 1916 (see Who's Who in America). Residence. Observatory House, Wellesley, Mass.

1–**DURAND, E(dward) Dana,** *b* Romeo, Mich., Oct. 18, 1871.

5–Francis Joseph **Durand** (1740-1817; son of Charles, mem. Parliament of Besancou; son Charles Emanuel, of Besancou, France, of the nobility, provincial official, counselor at law), from France, settled at Norwalk, Conn., ca. 1757; removed to Charlotte, Vt., 1790-94; *m* 1762, Patience Weed, of New Canaan, Conn.;

4–Simeon (1768-1831), of Norwalk, Conn., Charlotte, Vt., and Elizabethtown, N.Y.; *m* 1791, Elizabeth Cable;

3–Edward (ca. 1799-1854), removed to Henrietta, O., 1817; *m* Tyrella Blair; *m* 2d, Marcia Porter Burrell, widow;

2–Cyrus Yale (2 below).

8–Robert **Day** (qv);

7–Thomas, of Springfield, Mass.; *m* Sarah Cooper;

6–John, of W. Springfield; *m* Mary Smith;

5–Capt. William, of Sheffield, Mass.; *m* 3d, Rhoda Hubbell;

4–John, of Sheffield, Mass., and Sheffield, O.; *m* Lydia Austin;

3–James, of Sheffield, O.; *m* Ann Eliza Austin;

2–Celia (*b* 1845), of Sheffield, O.; *m* 1867, Cyrus Yale **Durand** (1842-87); issue: I–G(eorge) Harrison (Harry) (*b* 1868; *m* Lillian Fisher); II–E. Dana (1 above); III–Walter Yale (1874-1926; *m* Sara Watson); IV–Albert Cyrus (*b* 1879; *m* Ruth Sawyer); V–Alice May (*b* 1884; *m* Henry W. Edgerton).

1–*m* July 15, 1903, Mary Elizabeth Bennett, *b* Nashville, Tenn., Sept. 26, 1871; dau. of Henry Stanley Bennett (*b* Brownsville, Pa., Apr. 16, 1838-*d* Oberlin, O., Aug. 5, 1895), *m* Lydia Sophia Herrick (*b* Austinburg, O., Dec. 4, 1835-*d* Nashville, Tenn., Mar. 16, 1889); issue: 1–Dana Bennett, *b* Washington, D.C., Aug. 22, 1904; *m* Sept. 8, 1926, Katherine Russell Hayes, of Swarthmore, Pa. (issue: Patience Woolman, *b* Oct. 7, 1928); 2–Bennett, *b* Washington, Nov. 5, 1906; 3–Mary Cecilia, *b* Blue Ridge Summit, Md., Aug. 8, 1910; 4–Eric, *b* Washington, D.C., Nov. 29, 1911.

1–A.B., Oberlin, '93, Ph.D., Cornell, 1896. Legislative librarian N.Y. State Library, 1895-97; asst. prof., Leland Stanford Jr. U., 1898-99; sec. U.S. Industrial Commn., 1900-02; dep. commr. U.S. Bur. of Corpns., 1906-09; dir. U.S. Census Bureau, 1909-13; prof. statistics and economics, U.Minn., 1913-17; U.S. Food Administration (served in Europe), 1917-19; advisor, ministry of food, of Poland, 1919-21; chief of Div. of Statis. Research, Dept. of Commerce, 1924-30; statis. asst. to Sec. of Commerce, 1930; author (see Who's Who in America). Residence: 3613 Norton Pl., Washington, D.C.

1–**EARL, Guy Chaffee,** *b* Red Bluff, Calif., May 7, 1860.

8–Prob. Ralph (Earle) **Earl** (qv);

7–Prob. Ralph (*d* 1716), *m* ante 1659, Dorcas Sprague (Francis[8], *m* Lydia–);

6–Prob. William, of R.I.; *m* 1695, Hepzibah Butts (*b* 1675; Thomas[7], *m* Elizabeth–);

5–Nathaniel (1705-90), known as "Capt. Nat"; of Great Barrington, Mass.; capt. in French and Indian War prior to 1750; moved to White Creek, Washington Co., N.Y.; *m* —Adams;

4–Daniel (1730-1817), owned foundry and went to N.S. to obtain coal to operate it; formed co. with sons Nathaniel and Robert and returned to White Creek, N.Y., 1776; made war materials; migrated to Onondaga Co., N.Y.;

3–Nehemiah (1771-1831), of N.S.; lived early life in Onondaga Co., N.Y., later removed to Zanesville, Sandusky, and Timochtee, O., and Tippecanoe Co., Ind.; *m* ca. 1793, Rebecca Danforth;

2–Josiah (2 below).

9–Nicholas **Danforth** (qv);

8–Jonathan (bap. 1627 or 28-*d* Billerica, 1712), known as "Capt. Jonathan"; *m* in Boston, 1654, Elizabeth Poulter (*b* Rayleigh, Eng.-*d* Billerica, Mass., 1689; John Poulter or Powter[9]);

7–Jonathan (1659-1711), known as "Ens. Jonathan"; *m* 1682, Rebecca Parker (Jacob[8], 1661-1754), she *m* 2d, as his 3d wife, Joseph Foster;

6–Samuel (1692-1749), soldier Narragansett wars; *m* 1714, Dorothy Shed (John[7]);

5–Thomas (*b* 1724), of Dunstable; corp. Am. Rev., 1776-81; *d* at Tyringham; *m* 1744, Sarah Butterfield, of Chelmsford;

4–Asa (1746-1836), of Dunstable; served as maj., 4th Mass. Regt., during Am. Rev., in battles of Bunker Hill, Saratoga, and present at surrender of Burgoyne; maj. gen. state militia; to Brookfield, Mass., thence to Mayfield, N.Y.; 1st settler in Onondaga Valley; bought and set up 1st sawmill, on Butternut Creek (now DeWitt Tp.), 1791; judge Ct. Common Pleas, 1st session held in his barn; state senator; supt. salt springs; *m* ca. 1767, Hannah Wheeler (ca. 1749-1837);

3–Rebecca (1777-1842), *m* Nehemiah **Earl** (3 above).

9–Thomas **Chaffee** (*d* 1683), from Eng.; of Nantasket (Hull), 1635; *m* Dorothy–;

8–Joseph (1639-46-1694), of Nantasket and Swansea, Mass.; *m* 1670, Annis Martin (*d* 1729/30; Richard[9]);

7–John (1673-1757), removed to Woodstock, Conn.; *m* 1st, 1700, Sarah Hills (*d* 1735; Gershom[8], *m* Elizabeth Chadwick; Joseph[9]; George[10]);

6–Joseph (1701/02-1760), *m* 1730, Hannah May (*b* 1704; Ephraim[7]);

5–Asa (1734-1810), Am. Rev.; *m* 1st, 1753, Mary Howlett (*d* 1783);

4–Molly (*b* 1756), *m* 1775, Darius **Chaffee** (probably brother of Asa, 5 above);

3–Joseph (1789-1849), of Stafford, Conn.; grad. Harvard Coll.; died of cholera en route to Calif.; *m* 1st, 1813, Elizabeth Tobias (1794-1829);

2–Adelia Tobias (1822-93), *m* at Tehana, Calif., 1857, Josiah **Earl** (1821-84), removed from Ind. to southern Calif.; from Red Bluff, Calif., to Virginia City, Nev., thence to Independence, Calif., finally at Oakland, Calif.; *d* in Sydney, Australia; issue: I–Edwin Tobias (1858-1920; *m* Emily Runyon, *m* 2d, Emily Jarvis); II–Guy Chaffee (1 above).

1–*m* Nov. 15, 1888, Ella Jane Ford (qv); issue (all *b* Oakland, Calif.): 1–Alice, *b* Sept. 23, 1889; U.Calif., '12; *m* Aug. 28, 1912, Beverly Burt, son of Charles J. Wilder (issue: Beverly Burt; Guy Earl; Anne; Alice; Earl, *d*; Eleanor; Marian); 2–Martha Ford, *b* May 11, 1891; U.Calif., '12; *m* May 17, 1913, Donald Houstan, son of Edward McDonald Graham (issue: Donald Houstan; Guy Earl, *d*; Chester; Martha Jane); 3–Elinore Hayes, *b* Jan. 18, 1894; U.Calif., ex. '16; *m* Apr. 10, 1917, Ransom, son of Tyler Henshaw (issue: Elinore Jane; Marjory); 4–Guy Chaffee, twin; A.B., U.Calif., '16; grad. work, Columbia U., 1916-17; pub. Los Angeles Express since 1925 (see Who's Who in America); served as 1st lt. Air service, U.S.A., and as pilot, with A.E.F., during World War, 1917-19; *m* Dec. 31, 1927, Eleanor dau. Dr. Granville MacGowan, of Los Angeles, Calif.

1–A.B., U.Calif., '83 (Beta Theta Pi). Admitted to bar, 1887; has practised law since 1889. Pres. and gen. counsel Great Western Power Co., Calif. Electric Generating Co. Regent U.Calif., 1902-34; state senator, 1893-98 (see Who's Who in America). Conglist. Republican. Clubs: Bohemian, Union League, Commonwealth, Claremont Country, Sequoyah Country, San Francisco Golf and Country. Residence: 2914 McClure St., Oakland, Calif.

1–**EARL, Ella Jane Ford (Mrs. Guy Chaffee),** *b* Mendocino, Calif., Mar. 20, 1860.

5–Daniel **Davison** (1737-1821), of Waterford, Vt., *m* Martha–;

4–Rev. Silas (1776-1842), of Waterford, Vt.; preacher; *m* Persis Rice (1771-1857);

3–Martha (1793-1831), *m* 1814, Robert **Ford** (1788-1835), stone mason, Grand Isles, Vt. (Robert[4] [*b* 1743], to Corinth, Vt., *m* Jemimah W., *b* 1755);

2–Jerome Bursley (2 below).
10–Robert **Dibble,** from Eng.;
9–Thomas, 3d on list of earliest settlers at Windsor, 1640;
8–Samuel;
7–Abigail (1666-post 1725), *m* George **Hayes** (qv);
6–Daniel (1686-1756), served in Queen Anne's War, 5½ yrs.; held captive by Indians in Can., sold to French priest who sold him to a Frenchman in Montreal, who set him up as a weaver and allowed him to earn his freedom, later ransom pd. by Conn. Colony to reimburse him; settled at Salmon Brook, Conn.; *m* 1st, 1716, Martha Holcombe;
5–Daniel (1716-86), of Salmon Brook; 1st Congl. Soc. organized at his house, 1739, met there until meeting house was built, 1743; on ch. covenant with wife, 1742; *m* Abigail Hayes (*b* 1723; Samuel[6], *m* Elizabeth Willcolkson; George[7], same as 7 above);
4–Obadiah (1754-1817), of Simsbury, Conn.; farmer; on ch. covenant with wife, 1793; commr., 1795; *m* Ahinoam Holcombe (1757-1844; Joshua[5], *m* Martha Griffin; Joshua[6]; Joshua[7]; Joshua[8]; Thomas[9]);
3–Chester (1792-1876), farmer, Granby, Conn.; teacher 30 yrs.; ch. covenant with wife, 1816; dea., 1842-58, when moved to Harwinton, Conn.; *m* Fidelia Holcombe (1795-1843; Nahum[4], *m* Rebecca Moore; Reuben[5], *m* Susanna Hayes, sister of Abigail, 5 above; David[6], *m* Mehetabel Buttolph; Nathaniel[7], same as 7 below);
2–Martha Pauline (2 below).
9–Thomas **Holcombe,** from Eng. to Dorchester, Mass., 1634; at Windsor, Conn., 1635;
8–Nathaniel (*b* 1648), of Windsor, then Springfield where he *d*; *m* 1670, Mary Bliss (Nathaniel[9], *m* Catharine, dau. of Dea. Samuel Chapin, qv; Thomas[10], qv);
7–Nathaniel (*b* Springfield, Conn., 1673-*d* Simsbury), *m* 1695, Martha Buell (Peter[8], of Windsor; *m* Martha, dau. of John Coggan, of Boston; William[9], from Wales, 1635);
6–Martha (*d* 1717), of Simsbury; *m* Daniel **Hayes** (6 above).
2–Martha Pauline Hayes (1831-90), *m* 1854, Jerome Bursley **Ford** (*b* Grand Isles, Vt., 1821-*d* 1889), moved to Granby, Conn.; to Calif., 1852; brought the 1st sawmill to Calif.; partner in Mendocino Lumber Co.; organizer of Presbyn. Ch. of Mendocino; brought 1st sch. teacher to Mendocino and had sch. in his home; later moved to Oakland; issue: I–Jerome Chester (*b* 1856; *m* 1900, Adeline Brayton, *d* 1916; *m* 2d, 1918, Minnie Belle Brainard); II–Catharine Pauline (*b* 1857; *m* 1920, Rev. John Read); III–Charles Denslow (1858-1915; *m* Nellie Lincoln, *d* 1927); IV–Ella J. (1 above); V–Susan Fidelia (*b* 1864; *m* Lawrence Haight Pierson, *d* 1918); VI–Persis Amanda (1866-67).
1–*m* Nov. 15, 1888, Guy Chaffee Earl (qv for issue).
1–Ed. Mendocino City and Oakland, Calif., schs., and Mark Hopkins Art Sch., San Francisco. Mem. Sorosis, Oakland Forum. Clubs: Ebell, Home, Claremont Country; Town and Country, and Women's City (San Francisco). Residence: 2914 McClure St., Oakland, Calif.

1–**EASTMAN, Clarence Willis,** *b* Concord, N.H., Jan. 3, 1873.
8–Roger **Eastman** (qv);
7–Samuel (1657-1725), of Kingston, N.H.; *m* 1st, 1686, Elizabeth Scriven;
6–Ebenezer (1701-46), Kingston; *m* 1729, Widow Mary Sleeper;
5–Edward (1732-1814), *m* 1758, Anna Judkins (1739-1817; Joel[6], *m* Mehitabel Elkins);
4–Benjamin (1759-1813), *m* 1787, Dolly Bean (1769-1853; Daniel[5], *m* Elizabeth–);
3–Edward (1788-1880), of Bristol, N.H.; *m* 1811, Susan Cheney;
2–Charles L. (2 below).
9–Edward **Gilman** (qv);
8–Hon. John (1624-1708), of Exeter, N.H.; *m* 1657, Elisabeth Trueworthy (1639-1719);
7–Lydia (*b* 1668), *m* Capt. John **White** (1664-1727), of Haverhill, Mass.;
6–Rev. Timothy (1700-65), of Haverhill and Nantucket; *m* 1728, Susanna Gardner;
5–Susanna (1731-68), *m* 1759, Enoch **Badger,** of Haverhill;
4–Susanna (*b* 1761), *m* 1790, Daniel **Cheney** (*b* 1761);
3–Susan (*b* 1793), *m* Edward **Eastman** (3 above).
9–Hon. Peter **Coffin** (1631-1715), of Nantucket, Mass., and Exeter, N.H.; *m* Abigail Starbuck;
8–Jethro (*d* 1726), of Nantucket and Mendon; *m* 1686, Mary Gardner (1670-1767);
7–Priscilla (1691-1772), *m* John **Gardner** (*d* 1759);
6–Susanna (1712-89), *m* Timothy **White** (6 above).
9–Edward **French** (qv);
8–Joseph (*d* 1710), of Salisbury, Mass.; *m* Susanna Stacy (*d* 1688);
7–Simon (1657-1732), of Salisbury; *m* 1st, Joanna–(*d* 1704);
6–James (*b* 1692), of Salisbury; *m* 1717, Phebe Gill;
5–Samuel (*b* 1723), of Salisbury; *m* 1749, Abigail Jackman (*d* 1759);
4–Moses (1755-1834), of Deerfield, N.H.; *m* Molly Smith (1761-93); *m* 2d, Eleanor Batchelder (1765-1830);
3–Smith (1798-1868), of Deerfield; *m* Anna True Philbrick (1801-55);
2–Sarah (1832-1908), *m* 1853, Charles Leonard **Eastman** (1826-1907), mech. engr.; issue: I–Fred W. (*b* 1869; *m* Florence Townsend); II–Clarence Willis (1 above). III–Florence Marion (*b* 1876; *m* 1905, Harry R. Sinclair).
1–*m* Aug. 29, 1906, Ann Hull Dey, *b* Iowa City, Ia., Sept. 20, 1875; dau. of Hon. Peter A. Dey, of Iowa City (desc. Col. Theunis Dey, of Bloomfield, N.J.; issue (all *b* Amherst, Mass.): 1–Anthony Dey, *b* July 8, 1908; Amherst, '30; 2–Philip Dey, *b* Nov. 25, 1909; Amherst, '32; 3–Karl Dey, *b* June 17, 1912.
1–B.S., Worcester Poly. Inst., '94; studied U. of Goettingen, 1895-96, U. of Leipzig, 1896-98, Ph.D., 1898; (A.M., Amherst, 1912). Prof. German, Amherst Coll., since 1909; moderator, Amherst, Mass. Author (see Who's Who in America). Mem. S.A.R. Episcopalian. Residence: Amherst, Mass.

1–**EASTMAN, Joseph Bartlett,** *b* Katonah, N.Y., June 26, 1882.
8–Roger **Eastman** (qv);
7–Samuel (1657-1725), Kingston, N.H.; *m* 1st, 1686, Elizabeth Scriven;
6–Ebenezer (1701-46), *m* 1729, Mary Sleeper;
5–Edward (1732-1814), *m* 1758, Anna Judkins;
4–Moses (1770-1848), *m* 1800, Susannah Bartlett;
3–Joseph Bartlett (1804-64), *m* 1837, Mary Huse;
2–John Huse (2 below).
10–Richard **Bartlett** (qv);
9–Richard (1621-98), removed from Oldtown in Newbury to Bartlett's Corner, nr. Deer Island at the Merrimac River; dep. Gen. Ct.; *m* Abigail– (*d* 1686);
8–Richard (1649-1724), *m* 1673, Hannah Emery (*b* 1654; John[9], qv);
7–Stephen (1691-1773), *m* Hannah Webster, of Salisbury, Mass.;
6–Joseph (1720-53), *m* Jane Colby (Ichabod[7], of Amesbury, Mass.);
5–Dr. Joseph (1751-1800), removed to Salisbury, 1773, where he was first physician; served in Am. Rev.; *m* 1773, Hannah Colcord (1754-1837; Samuel B.[6], *m* Mehitable Ladd);
4–Susannah (1779-1806), *m* Moses **Eastman** (4 above).
8–Abel **Huse** (1600-90), from Eng. to Newburyport, Mass., 1635; *m* 1663, Mary Sears;
7–Thomas (1666-1734), *m* ca. 1690, Hannah–;
6–Joseph (*b* 1712), *m* 1737, Mary Chase;
5–Carr;
4–John;
3–Mary, *m* Joseph B. **Eastman** (3 above);
2–John Huse, D.D. (1849-1917), clergyman; *m* 1879, Lucy King (1852-97); issue: I–Elizabeth (*b* 1880); II–Joseph Bartlett (1 above).
1–Not married. A.B., Amherst, '04 (Psi U., P.B.K.), LL.D., 1927. Mem. Interstate Commerce Commn. since 1919 (see Who's Who in America). Clubs: Boston City, Cosmos, Racquet. Residence: 2266 Cathedral Av. N.W., Washington, D.C.

1–**EASTMAN, Linda Anne,** *b* Oberlin, O., July 17, 1867.
8–Roger **Eastman** (qv);
7–John (1640-1720), *m* Hannah Heilie;
6–Roger (1682-1743), *m* Hannah Kimball;
5–Jonathan (1717-1807), *m* Elizabeth Wood (1730-1800);
4–Jonathan (1753-1816), *m* 2d, Ruth Dean;

3–William Dean (1797-1854), *m* 1823, Lois Harvey (1800-87; Moses[4], *m* Deborah Standish);
2–William Harvey (*b* 1836), retired; *m* Sarah Ann Redrup (1840-74); *m* 2d, Sarah Palmer (1848-1918); issue (1st marriage): I–Albert Harvey (*b* 1865; *m* Lottie Hohlfelder; *m* 2d, Ethel Reynolds); II–Linda Anne (1 above); III–Lois (*b* 1872; *m* William H. Ponting); 2d marriage: I–Frank Rollin (*b* 1877; *m* Stella Calhoon); II–Edith Leona (1881-1924); III–Mabel Melissa (*b* 1883); IV–William Joseph (*b* 1887).
1–Ed. Cleveland public schools, and private tutors; (M.A., Oberlin; LL.D., Western Reserve U.). Teacher pub. schs., W. Cleveland and Cleveland, 1885-92; prof., Library Sch. of Western Reserve U.; librarian, Cleveland Public Library, since 1918 (see Who's Who in America). Mem. A.L.A. (council since 1905, exec. bd. 1911, 1917-19, 2d v.p., 1917, commn. on library and adult edn., pres., 1928-29), charter mem. Ohio Library Assn. (pres., 1903-04), N.Y. Library Assn.; mem. Am. Library Inst., Bibliog. Soc. of America; charter mem. Women's City Club of Cleveland (1st v.p., 1920); mem. Cleveland Welfare Federation (2d v.p. 1921-23), etc. Residence: 1868 E. 82d St., Cleveland, O.

1–**EASTON, Edward** (Apr. 17, 1854-Feb. 13, 1920).
9–Andriese **DeGraaff,** from Holland, 1624/25; settled at New Amsterdam; *m* Anneken Webbert;
8–Claas Andries (ca. 1628-97), of Schenectady, N.Y.; *m* Elizabeth Brouwer (*d* 1725; William[9], of Albany, N.Y., *m* Elizabeth Drinckvelt);
7–Jesse (*b* 1688), *m* 1705, Altie (Alida) Hennion (*b* 1685; Nathaniel[8], *m* Anneken, dau. of David Ackerman, of Leyden, Holland);
6–Catherine (*b* 1719), *m* 1736, Adam **Conde** (1700-48), of Albany and Schenectady; killed in Indian war at Beukendael (parents *d* on passage to America from Holland, having gone there from France);
5–Jesse (1743-1818), of Charlton, Saratoga Co., N.Y.; *m* 1762, Parthenia Ogden (1744-1817; Jonathan[6], *m* Wilmot–; Jonathan[7] [*d* 1732], *m* Susannah Dunscomb, prob. of royal descent);
4–Alida (1763-1838), of Schenectady; *m* 1783, James **Boyd** (1762-1839), of Albany and Schenectady; pvt. in 3d Albany Co. Regt., Am. Rev., 1779-81 (John[5] [1725-99], from Kilmannock, Scotland, via Antrim, Ireland, to N.Y. State 1762, settled at Albany, later Johnstown, N.Y., *m* Ann [1739-1815], dau. of James Togan);
3–Jesse Conde (1803-91), of Albany, N.Y., and Chicago, Ill.; *m* 1824, Elcy Noble (1805-72; Edward[4], *m* Mary, dau. of William Leach, *m* Elcy Ward; David[5], of Johnsburg, N.Y., *m* 1768, Margaret, dau. of William Carruthers, of Hollywood, Ireland; Archibald[6] [*b* ca. 1700], of Ireland, *m* Eleanor Jamison);
2–Mary Jane (1827-1903), *m* 1847, Charles Patterson **Easton** (1824-85), issue: I–William (*b* Jan. 23, 1848; partner with father in lumber business, 1869; trustee 1st Reformed Dutch Ch.; K.T.; presidential elector, 1896; *m* Caroline Allen Newton, issue: Helen, *m* Dr. David Baker; Mary Boyd, *m* Westcott Burlingame); II–Edward (1 above); III–Alice (Mrs. Arthur W. Pray, qv for other lineages); IV–Frederick (Jan. 5, 1859-Apr. 3, 1920; lumber merchant; mem. Co. A., 10th Bn., N.G.S.N.Y., and Old Guard Albany Zouave Cadets, Mason, 32°, supt. public bldgs., State of N.Y., 1895-99, dep. co. clk., 1920; *m* Mary Sigourney Young, issue: Alice); V–Irving Boyd (*b* Nov. 22, 1868; Cornell, '91; lumber merchant, Albany, and New York; hon. mem. Royal Canadian Arty. Mess; mem. Alpha Delta Phi, Cornell Univ., Lumberman's clubs, New York, N.Y.; trustee 1st Presbyn. Ch., Yonkers; *m* 1912, Marion Burnett Ramsdell).
1–*m* Jan. 25, 1876, Sarah Frances Jones, *b* Albany, N.Y., May 24, 1854, dau. of Isaac Jones, of Albany, *m* Elizabeth Poinier; issue: 1–Edith, *b* Albany, July 5, 1878; *m* Oct. 15, 1902, Maj. Ernest Livingston Miller (1873-1927), maj. of cav., Army Reserve; capt. 83d F.A.; provost marshal at Ft. Russell, Wyo., 315th Cav.; with rank of maj., stationed at Camp Henry Knox, West Pt., Ky., until close of war; 2–Edward, Jr., *b* Albany, N.Y., Apr. 1, 1880; A.B. Yale, '02; LL.B., Albany Law Sch., 1904; resigned as judge of Recorder's Ct., City of Albany, to serve in U.S. Employment Bureau, Dept. of Làbor, during period of War; *m* June 8, 1904, Martha Van Antwerp (issue: Kate Van Antwerp, Edward, Jr., Mary Boyd, Elsy Noble, John Van Antwerp, Edith, Rufus Van Antwerp); 3–Mary Boyd, *b* Albany, Jan. 17, 1882; *m* Jan. 25, 1908, Andrew Thompson, of Buffalo and Niagara Falls, N.Y. (issue: David, Mary B., Andrew); 4–Roland Jones, *b* Albany, Aug. 26, 1884; 1st lt. 54th Brig., 27th Div., U.S.A., in France, May, 1918; cited for bravery while acting as aide to commanding gen., Feb. 19, 1919; engaged Somme offensive, Ypres-Lys, Dickebusch, Mont Kemmel sector, La Salle River; mem. V.F.W., A.L.; *m* July 2, 1909, Ellen M. May (issue: Ellen Elizabeth); 5–Arthur Boyd, *b* Loudonville, N.Y., Oct. 5, 1888; Dartmouth, '13; Mexican border, June 1916-17; 1st sgt., Co. D, Machine Gun Bn. 106, 27th Div., to France, May, 1918; engaged in Poperinghe line, Dickebusch, Belgian-Hindenburg line, Sept., Oct., 1918; mem. V.F.W., A.L.; 6–Robert Poinier, *b* Loudonville, June 23, 1890; corpl., U.S. Ordnance Corps, at Edgewood, Md.; apptd. master engr., sr. grade, chem. Warfare Service, U.S.A., Nov. 20, 1918; mem. A.L.; *m* 1921, Stella Sherwood (issue: Sally, Stella, Robert, Jr.); 7–William, *b* Loudonville, July 10, 1892; Yale, '16; ens., U.S.N.R.F., 1918; 4 yrs. service as naval aviator and instr. stationed at Cape May, Key West, Fla.; mem. A.L.; *m* June 28, 1926, Melba E. Gray (issue: Elizabeth, William); 8–Lillian Alice, *b* Loudonville, Mar. 15, 1894; served in records and files div. of the selective service hdqrs., Albany; 9–Conde Philip, *b* Loudonville, Dec. 5, 1896; Yale, '18; withdrew from Yale to enter service before he was of age; corpl. Co. C, 303d Engr. Corps, 78th Div., in France, May, 1918; engaged St. Mihiel offensive, Limey sector, Oct. 1918; mem. V.F.W., A.L.

1–**PRAY, Alice Easton (Mrs. Arthur W.),** *b* Albany, N.Y., Jan. 13, 1857.
4–Robert **Easton** (1775-1818; son of James, of Fifeshire, Scotland, *m* Margaret–), from Carnmonytown, Antrim, Ireland, 1818; settled in Montreal, Can.; *m* Eliza Craig (*d* 1818; Ephraim[5], *m* Jane–);
3–Ephraim (1803-79), of Albany, N.Y.; *m* 1824, Eliza (Patterson) Walker;
2–Charles Patterson (2 below).
4–William **Patterson** (*d* 1803; son of Mark, of Ireland), from Ireland; *m* Nancy Trimble (*d* 1812; James[5], Town of Manor Hamilton, Co. Leitram, Ireland, *m* Dorothy James);
3–Eliza (1796-1886), as widow of John Walker, *m* Ephraim **Easton** (3 above);
2–Charles Patterson (1824-85), *b* Albany, N.Y., *d* St. Augustine, Fla.; lumber mcht.; pres. Rep. Com., Albany Co., 1870; many times del. to Rep. state convs.; del. Rep. Nat. Conv., 1872, 1880; one of 306 who stood by Gen. Grant to the last ballot and received a bronze medal commemorating the struggle; pres. Young Men's Assn., 1860; pres. Albany Co. Bible Soc., 1870-73; a founder of Y.M.C.A.; trustee Albany Orphan Asylum; dir. Nat. Exchange Bank; mem. Bd. of Pub. Instrn., 1865-81 (pres. 7 yrs.); apptd. by Legislature, 1878, commr. to enlarge Clinton Prison, and 1880, apptd. mem. of commn. to erect City Hall in Albany; apptd. q.m. gen. with rank of brig. gen., by Gov. A. B. Cornell, Jan. 1880; *m* 1847, Mary Jane Boyd (1827-1903), of Albany (for issue and other lineages see Edward Easton).
1–*m* Feb. 4, 1880, Arthur Washington Pray (June 8, 1855-July 21, 1898); son of William Harmon Pray, of Boston, Braintree, and Walpole, Mass., *m* Elizabeth Sawin Bird.
1–Grad. Albany Acad. for Girls, 1875, Charter mem., 1888, and v.p., Y.W.C.A., Albany; trustee Albany Acad. for Girls. Mem. D.A.R. (charter mem. and present historian, Gansevoort Chapter; has been elected to every office in the chapter), Dutch Settler Soc., Albany Hist. and Art Soc. Residence: The Ten Broeck Apts., 399 State St., Albany, N.Y.

1–**EDGECOMB, Monnie May Hoagland (Mrs. James A.),** *b* Medical Lake, Wash., Sept. 1, 1880.
9–Dirck Jansen **Hoagland,** from Maersevun,

Province of Utrecht, Holland, 1657, settled in New Netherlands; *m* 1662, Annetje Hansen Bergen;
8–Jan Dircksen (*b* 1666), of Bedford, L.I.; *m* Jacoba Reyerse;
7–William (*b* 1692), of Flatbush, L.I.; *m* 1725, Lena Andriessen;
6–Derrick (*b* 1730), of Six Miles Run; *m* Martha–;
5–Derrick (*b* 1762), *m* 1780, Judah Van Fleet;
4–Derrick (1786-1874), of Hunterdon Co., N.J.; *m* Amy Stout;
3–Henry (1811-80), of Somerset Co., N.J.; *m* 1831, Sarah H. Anderson (*d* 1868);
2–Theodore (2 below).
9–William **Davis** (qv);
8–John (1643-1705), of Roxbury, Mass.; *m* 1667, Mary Devotion;
7–Samuel (1681-1760), of Roxbury; *m* 1st, Mary Chamberlin (*d* 1730);
6–Dea. Daniel (1719-86), of Roxbury; *m* 1st, 1741, Tamar Town (*d* 1761);
5–Capt. Daniel (1742-1807), of Oxford, Mass.; after the war he joined Co. of Ohio Associates, under Gen. Rufus Putnam; settled at Waterford, O., 1789; *m* 1762, Elizabeth Whittmore;
4–Hezekiah (1776-1816), of Killingly, Conn.; capt. of militia; *m* Betsy Coleman;
3–Ephraim (1807-62), settled at Windsor, O.; mcht. tailor; *m* 1836, Ann Baldenton;
2–Emily Harris (*b* 1848), of Moscow, Ida.; *m* 1868, Rev. Theodore **Hoagland** (*b* Hubbard tp., Trumbull Co., O., Nov. 22, 1832-*d* Moscow, Ida., Oct. 31, 1907), to New Bedford, Pa.; aet. 13 to Mercer Co., Ill.; teacher; to Neb.; Meth. minister, 1859–; served in Co. D, 7th Ia. Vol. Cav., 1863-66; issue: 3 eldest *d* young; IV–Harvey Hamer (*b* 1877); V–Monnie May (1 above).
1–*m* Dec. 11, 1897, James Arthur Edgecomb, *b* Renova, Pa., Sept. 21, 1874; son of E. F. Edgecomb, of Costello, Pa.; issue: 1–Alice Emily, *b* Moscow, Ida., May 14, 1899; grad. U.Ida., 1921 (Kappa Alpha Theta); *m* July 5, 1921, Dennis B., son of Elmer Brown, of Kellogg, Ida. (issue: Yvonne, *b* 1922; Bonnie Jean, *b* 1924; Darrell, *b* 1926; Joan, *b* 1929); 2–Theodora, *b* Moscow, May 19, 1900; *m* Oct. 10, 1925, Einar T., son of L. P. Larsen, of Tacoma, Wash.; 3–James Osgood (Apr. 11, 1904-July 20, 1916); 4–Roy Harvey, *b* Pullman, Wash., Dec. 24, 1906; served in U.S.N., Jan. 1926-Jan. 1930, Radio Div., U.S.S. New Mexico.
1–Attended prep. dept. of U.Ida. Mem. D.A.R. Methodist. Residence: 116 E. Fessenden St., Portland, Ore.

1–**EDWARDS, Ilda Eleanor Crumpton (Mrs. Charles V.),** *b* nr. Orrville, Dallas Co., Ala., Dec. 10, 1874.
4–Alexander **Crumpton,** of Va.; *m* Mary Griggs;
3–Henry Tally (1790-1879), of Walterboro, S.C.; moved to Pleasant Hill, Ala., 1832; *m* 1819, Matilda Smith Bryan (1798-1855; Rev. Richard[4] [1759-1826], Am. Rev., Meth. preacher);
2–Rev. Washington Bryan (2 below).
8–James **James,** Esq. (*d* 1769), from Wales, settled nr. Pennepec, Pa.; leader of the Welch settlers who came from Pa. to S.C. in 1735, and obtained the grant of land on each side of the Pedee River consisting of 173,840 acres known as the Welch Grant;
7–Philip (1701-53), of Pennepec, Pa.; moved to S.C., 1735; ordained at Welch Neck, 1743, and served as first pastor of Welch Neck Bapt. Ch.;
6–Ann, of Marlborough Dist., S.C.; *m* Peter **Kolb;**
5–Abel, of Marlborough Dist.; Am. Rev.; *m* Sarah James;
4–Ann, of Marlborough Dist.; *m* Maj. James **Pouncey** (William[5]; Anthony[6], granted land in S.C., 1749 and 51);
3–Eleanor Bainbridge, of Marlborough Dist.; *m* Claudius McRelas **Cochran** (1804-84; Thomas[4] [1746-1818], of Marlborough Dist., *m* Lucretia, dau. of Capt. Henry Council, of S.C., *m* 2d, Mrs. Griffin; *m* 3d, Elizabeth [House] Hunter).
2–Rev. Washington Bryan **Crumpton** (1842-1926), student Georgetown (Ky.) Coll., 2 yrs.; served with Co. H, 37th Miss. Inf., 3 yrs., as pvt., sgt. and lt.; wounded at Vicksburg, Atlanta and Nashville; ordained Bapt. ministry, 1870; pastorates in several country and village chs. in Ala. and First Ch., Meridian, Miss.; corr. sec. and treas., Ala. Bapt. Bd. of Missions; leader of prohibition; author (see Who's Who in America, Vol. 14); *m* 1872, Ellen Pouncey Cochran (1844-99); *m* 2d, 1910, Florence Harris, of Montgomery, Ala.; issue (1st marriage): I–William Cochran (1873-1915; *m* Mamie Carter); II–Ilda Eleanor (1 above); III–Martha Washington (*b* 1877; *m* Rev. James Madison Shelbourne); IV–Evangeline Claudia (*b* 1879); V–Washington Bryan (*b* 1882; *m* Ralphine Walker); VI–Henry Dansby (twin, 1882-1905); VII–Elizabeth Jane (1884-95); VIII–Dr. Robert Cochran (*b* 1886); IX–Marion Judson (1888-92).
1–*m* Nov. 20, 1900, Charles Vernon Edwards (qv); issue: 1–Charles Vernon, Jr., *b* New Orleans, La., Oct. 4, 1901; Tex. Agrl. and Mech. Coll.; *m* Jan. 25, 1921, Ruby Oran (issue: Charles Vernon, III; Bryan Crumpton; Netta Gwyn); 2–Martha Malvenia, *b* New Orleans, Oct. 6, 1903; A.B., Baylor Coll. for Women, Belton, Tex.; *m* June 1929, Hugh Orton Davis; 3–Ilda Eleanor, *b* Birmingham, Ala., Nov. 18, 1905; A.B., Baylor Coll. for Women; 4–Emma Kirtley, *b* New Orleans, La., Jan. 8, 1908; A.B., Baylor Coll. for Women; 5–Annie Crumpton, *b* Greenwood, Miss., Mar. 24, 1911; B.J., Baylor Coll. for Women; 6–Marion Dickins, *b* Greenwood, Dec. 4, 1912; 7–Ruth Hart, *b* Ft. Worth, Tex., Dec. 10, 1916.
1–A.B., Judson Coll., '93. Taught in Ala. grammar schs., 3 yrs., in Ky., 3 yrs. Mem. advisory bd. South-Western Bapt. Training Sch. for Young Women, Ft. Worth, Tex.; chmn. com. on christian edn., Woman's Missionary Union, Auxiliary to the Bapt. Gen. Conv. of Tex. Mem. I.A.G., D.A.R., U.D.C. Baptist. Democrat. Residence: 1401 Washington Av., Ft. Worth, Tex.

DANIEL MANN EDWARDS, JR. (Dec. 26, 1880-June 25, 1929).

1–**EDWARDS, Edith,** *b* Woonsocket, R.I. July 20, 1873.
10–John **Woodberry,** from Eng. ca. 1624/25; settled at Cape Ann; dep. Gen. Ct., 1635-38, from Beverly; removed to Salem, Mass.; *m* Agnes–;
9–Humphrey (1608-86), *m* Elizabeth–;
8–Isaac (1643-1725), of Salem; rep., 1703-05; *m* 1671, Mary Wilks (1651-1702);
7–Capt. Robert (1672-1746), rep. from Manchester to Gen. Ct., 1726,30; *m* 1693, Mary West (1676-1754; Thomas[8], rep.; John[9], rep. Gen. Ct. from Beverly);
6–Benjamin (*b* 1699), of Beverly, *m* Elizabeth–;
5–Hannah (1739-1800), *m* as his 2d wife, John **Edwards** (*b* 1734);

4–Azariah (*b* 1779), removed to Manchester, thence to Monroe, Me.; *m* Nabby Smith (*b* 1777; Andrew[5], *m* Nabby Woodberry);
3–Azariah (1802-70), removed to Lincoln, Me.; *m* Catherine Mann (Daniel[4], War 1812, *m* Elizabeth Hamblen);
2–Daniel Mann (2 below).
9–William **Arnold** (qv);
8–Stephen (1622-99), dep.gov. of R.I., 1664; gov.'s asst., 1667; *m* 1646, Sarah Smith (Edward[9], of Rehoboth, Mass.);
7–Elisha (1662-1710), *m* Susannah Carpenter (Ephraim[8]; William[9], qv, of Providence);
6–Catherine (*b* 1690), *m* 1712 (?), James **Ballou** (1684-1764; James[7], *m* Mary–; Maturin[8], qv);
5–Ariel (1715-96), *m* ca. 1740, Jerusha Slack (1722-96; Benjamin[6], *m* Jerusha Whiting; William[7]);
4–Dea. Ariel (1758-1839), *m* 2d, 1802, Edilda Tower (1771-1834; Levi[5], Am. Rev., *m* Mary Whipple);
3–Dr. Ariel (1805-87), *m* 1832, Hannah Horton (1803-73; Barnabas[4]);
2–Laura (1841-1918), *m* 1870, Dr. Daniel Mann **Edwards** (1844-1919); issue: I–Ariel Ballou (see Vol. II, p. 83, for Edwards lineage); II–Edith (1 above); III–Herbert (1874-75); IV–Percival (*b* and *d* 1878); V–Daniel Mann (see portrait).
1–Ed. private schs.; Lycee Racine, Paris; A.B., Bryn Mawr, '01. Mem. S.M.D., D.F.P.A., (pres. R.I. chapter, mem. nat. exec. bd.), D.A.C., D.C.W., D.A.R. (chapter sec., v.regent, and regent), U.S.D. 1812 (hon. state pres., hon. nat. v.p., pres. R.I. soc., mem. nat. exec. bd.), N.E.H.G.S., R.I. Hist. Soc., Bostonians, Monticellians. Episcopalian. Clubs: Providence Plantation (Providence), College, Women's Republican (Boston), Forum (London). Summer place: "Quisisana," Mendon Road, East Woonsocket, R.I. Residence: 97 Mount Vernon, Beacon Hill, Boston, Mass.

HORACE CHADWICK (1846-1927).

1–**EDWARDS, Ruth Edna Chadwick (Mrs. William P.),** *b* Chicago, Ill., Sept. 23, 1884.
5–William **Chadwick** (1730-97), settled at Deerfield, Mass., later at Lunenburg, Mass.; served in Am. Rev.; afterward called Capt.; *m* 1756, Eunice Goss (*d* aet. 91);
4–Peter (1776-1846), of Fletcher, Vt.; *m* Hannah Thurston;
3–Gilman Thurston (1811-97), of Ill. and Wis.; *m* 1836, Lois C. Gaylord (*d* 1857);
2–Horace (2 below).
9–Daniel **Thurston** (*b* Eng., 1636-*d* 1693), came to Newbury, Mass. as infant; *m* Mary Pell (Joseph[10], of Boston, *m* Elizabeth–);
8–James (*b* 1670), of Exeter, N.H.; *m* 1693, Mary Pearson (*b* 1671; Samuel[9], *m* Mary, dau. of John Poor, qv; Dea. John[10], *m* Dorcas–);
7–Abner (*b* 1699), of Exeter;
6–Moses (1721-1800), of Newbury; Am. Rev.; *m* 1st, Hannah Sewall (*b* 1721);
5–Moses (1746-1809), Am. Rev.; *m* 1768, Esther Bigelow (1744-1831; Elizur[6], *m* Mary, dau. of William Fiske; Joshua[7], *m* Elizabeth, dau. of Thomas Flagg; John[8], *m* Mary Warren);
4–Hannah (1777-1857), *m* Peter **Chadwick** (4 above).
8–William **Edwards** (*d* 1685), from Eng., ca. 1648, settled at East Hampton, L.I.; *m* Ann–;
7–John ? (*d* 1693), *m* Mary Stanborough;
6–John ? ;
5–Henry, probably son of John above (*b* 1726), of East Hampton, L.I.; *m* Esther–, later wife of Stephen Hodges;
4–Henry (*b* 1768), of East Hampton, later Saratoga Co., N.Y.; *m* 1791, Sarah Baker;
3–Daniel Shaw (1807-85), of Glenville, N.Y., later Adrian, Mich.; *m* 1836, Caroline Amanda Foskett;
2–Anna Wines (2 below).
8–Thomas **Baker** (qv);
7–Thomas (1654-1735), *m* 1695, Elizabeth Westover;
6–Nathaniel (1699-1772), *m* 1721, Sarah Ludlow (1704-68);
5–Samuel (1733-86), *m* 2d, 1764, Abigal Shaw (1739-1813);
4–Sarah (*b* 1769), *m* Henry **Edwards** (4 above).
8–John **Foskett** (1635-89), Charlestown, Mass.; soldier King Philip's War; *m* Elizabeth Leach (*d* 1682);
7–Robert (1672-post 1759), in French and Indian War from Lancaster Co., Mass.; *m* 2d, 1715, Susannah Whitney;
6–Ephriam (*b* post 1727);
5–Ephriam (1755-1835), of New Marlborough, Mass.; in Am. Rev. from Berkshire Co., pensioned, 1832; *m* Sebra Tuttle;
4–James (1782-1870), of New Marlborough; *m* 1806, Sarah McClurer (Joseph[5] [1747-1807], *m* Rebecca Densmore, 1742-1814);
3–Caroline A. (1807-50), of Pompey, N.Y.; *m* Daniel S. **Edwards** (3 above);

ANNA WINES (EDWARDS) CHADWICK (1847-1922).

2–Anna Wines (1847-1922), of Adrian, Mich.; ed. at Ypsilanti, Mich.; taught in Chicago public school for over 25 yrs. (see portrait); *m* 1878, Horace **Chadwick** (1846-1927), see portrait; served in Indian and Civil wars; issue: I–Alfred Edwards (*b* 1880; *m* Mary A. Chamberlain); II–Ruth Edna (1 above); III–Harold Horace (*b* 1888; *m* Marie Ellison).
1–*m* Oct. 23, 1906, William Pierrepont Edwards, *b* New Orleans, La., Nov. 30, 1867; judge 17th Judicial Dist. Ct. of La., 1904-16; mem. Constl. Conv., 1921; son of Wakeman Wakeman Edwards (1827-1921; Henry[3] [*b* 1802], *m* Betsy Rogers; Henry[4], above), *m* Martha Hollingsworth (1831-1908); issue (all *b* Abbeville, La.): 1–Anne Elizabeth, *b* Mar. 21, 1910; 2–Ruth Hollingsworth, *b* Dec. 25, 1912; 3–William Pierre-

pont, Jr., *b* Aug. 7, 1916; 4–Rogers Chadwick, *b* June 29, 1923.
1–Ed. Lewis Inst., Chicago, 1900-04; A.B., Mt. Holyoke Coll., '06. Residence: Abbeville. La.

1–**EDWARDS, Charles Vernon,** *b* Simpson Co., Ky., Apr. 1, 1870.
4–Evy or Eby **Edwards** (thought to be Ephraim), lived in Culpeper Co., Va.; *m* 1st;
3–Jeremiah (*d* 1826), of Culpeper Co.; *m* 1813, Martha Johnson;
2–John Washington (2 below).
4–William **Stark** (1763-1826), of Edgecombe Co., N.C.; with two bros. went to what is now Robertson Co., Tenn.; soldier in Am. Rev., wounded at Battle of King's Mountain; *m* 1785, Martha Morgan (1770-1821);
3–Ephraim, of Robertson Co.; *m* Rebecca Porter (*b* 1800; Benjamin[4], of N.C., *m* 1799, Mary Bridges);
2–Malvenia Eleanor (1825-84), *m* 1845, John Washington **Edwards** (1822-1912), of Franklin, Simpson Co., Ky.; issue: I–George Washington (1845-80; *m* Susan Dinning); II–Jeremiah (1851-52); III–John Tyler (1857-1924; *m* Emma Bradshaw; *m* 2d, Anna Holcomb); IV–Thomas Jefferson (1866-1927; *m* 1887, Drue Nettie Grainger); V–Charles Vernon (1 above).
1–*m* Nov. 20, 1900, Ilda Eleanor Crumpton (qv for issue).
1–A.B., A.M., Bethel Coll., Ky. (D.D.); studied 2 yrs. in Southern Bapt. Theol. Sem., Louisville, Ky. Pastor in Ky. and Tenn. 5 yrs.; 1st Bapt. Ch., New Orleans, La., 10 yrs.; greenwood, Miss., 4 yrs.; College Av. Bapt. Ch., Ft. Worth, Tex., 16 yrs. Mem. Phi Gamma Delta. Residence: 1401 Washington Av., Fort Worth, Tex.

1–**EDWARDS, Robert Seaver,** *b* Chicago, Ill., Jan. 27, 1876.
8–Thomas **Edwards** (*b* 1640), from Hereford, Eng., to Boston, Mass., ca. 1660; *m* 1661, Sarah–;
7–John (1666-1746?), goldsmith of Boston; mem. militia; 4th sgt. arty. co., 1704; tithing man, 1701,08,11; constable, 1715; assessor, 1720-27; *m* 1694, Sibella Newman;
6–John (1696-1725), *m* 1722, Mary Lewis (*b* 1703);
5–John (1725-75), bookseller; 2d sgt. arty. co., 1751; clk., arty. co., 1758-64; field town office, 1747-48; constable, 1752-54; *m* 1748, Abigail Webb (1727-64);
4–Thomas (1753-1806), B.A., Harvard, 1771, A.M.; judge advocate gen. Cont. Army, 1777-83, on staff of Gen. Washington and at Valley Forge, 1777-78, etc.; lawyer, Boston; rep.; commr. in bankruptcy; an original mem. Soc. Cincinnati (sec. 1787-1806); *m* 2d, 1802, Mary (Walker) Jewett (1768-1855);
3–John (1802-86), newspaper editor; owner Portland (Me.) Gazette; owner, Bangor Whig and Courier, 1837-41; returned to Portland, 1841; established "The Bulletin," 1841-70; *m* 1824, Sarah Merrill (1800-69; Othneil[4], *m* Ruth–); their son, Capt. John Edwards, 3d Arty., U.S.A., in Civil War, was brevetted lt. col. for gallant and meritorious services;
2–Henry Jewett (2 below).
10–Gov. John **Winthrop** (qv);
9–John (1606-76), gov. of Conn.; *m* 2d, 1635, Elizabeth Reade (*d* 1672; dau. Edmund of Eng.);
8–Elizabeth, *m* 1st, ca. 1653, Rev. Antipas **Newman,** minister of Wenham, later of Rehoboth;
7–Sibella (*b* 1670), *m* John **Edwards** (7 above).
8–Robert **Seaver** (1608-83), from Eng. in the "Mary and John" to Roxbury, Mass., ante 1634; *m* 1634, Elizabeth Ballard;
7–Joshua (1641-1730), of Boston; *m* 1677, Mary May Pepper;
6–Ebenezer (*b* 1687), Boston; *m* 1714, Margaret Heath;
5–Ebenezer (*b* 1721), Boston; *m* Tabitha Davenport;
4–Joshua (*b* 1779), Boston; *m* 1803, Nancy Sumner;
3–Robert (*b* 1812), Boston; *m* 1834, Abigail Fairbanks Patch;
2–Nancy Augusta (*b* 1834), of Boston; *m* 1870, Henry Jewett **Edwards** (1833-1910), of Portland, Me.; issue: I–Edith Augusta (*b* 1873); II–Robert Seaver (1 above).
1–*m* Sept. 1913, Teresa E. M. Pastene, *b* Boston, Mass., Oct. 7, 1886; dau. of Peter Pastene, of Boston; issue: 1–Esther Pastene, *b* Portland, Ore., Nov. 22, 1914; 2–Charles Pastene, and 3–Betty (twins), *b* Boston, Mass., June 24, 1919; 4–Jean Seaver, *b* Boston, June 10, 1924.
1–A.B., Bowdoin Coll., '00; chem. engr., M.I.T., 1902. Development and research engr., Rumford Chem. Works, since 1921. Consulting chem. engr. since 1906. Mem. S.C., Am. Inst. Chem. Engrs., Am. Soc. for Testing Materials, I.A.G. Residence: 202 Reedsdale Rd., Milton, Mass.

1–**EGGLESTON, William Green,** *b* Marble Hill, Prince Edward Co., Va., Oct. 15, 1859.
8–Richard **Eggleston,** from Eng. to Va., 1635; settled at "Powhatan," James City Co., Va.; was in Battle of Bloody Run, against Indians, 1656;
7–Richard;
6–Joseph (1678-1730), burgess; *m* 2d, Anne Pettus (1702-36; John[7]; Thomas[8], mem. Council; Col. Thomas[9], mem. Council);
5–Richard (*d* 1781), mem. Com. Safety, Cumberland Co., Va., 1775; *m* Rebecca Clough (*d* 1781; Richard[6], *m* 1718, Anne Poindexter);
4–Edmund (1773-1840), *m* 1795, Jane Segar Langhorne (*b* 1772);
3–Richard Beverley (1797-1853), col. Nottoway Co., Va. Militia; corpl. War 1812, aet. 15; *m* 2d, 1827, Elvira Du Puy (1805-78);
2–Joseph Du Puy, M.D. (2 below).
8–Edward **Booker,** from Eng.; living in York Co., Va. 1648; *m* a sister of Richard Glover;
7–Capt. Richard (ante 1652-post 1704), justice of ct.; mem. of Quorum; of Gloucester Co., Va.; apptd. capt. of militia, 1699; *m* 1st, Rebecca Leake (John[8], of York Co., Va.);
6–Edmund (1693-1758), burgess, Amelia Co., Va.; *m* Jane–(1689-1768);
5–William (1733-83), mem. Com. Safety, Prince Edward Co., 1775; mem. Constl. Conv. of Va., 1776; *m* 1755, Mary Flournoy (1734-1800);
4–John (1769-1825), mem. Va. House of Dels.; *m* Martha Jane Watkins (1771-1852);
3–John (1809-94), commission merchant; C.S.A.; *m* 1835, Lucilla Stanley Elliott (1817-53);
2–Anne Carrington (1836-98), *m* 1858, Joseph DuPuy **Eggleston,** M.D. (1831-1908), physician and planter; issue: I–William Green (1 above); II–Mary Cornelia (*m* R. A. Wailes; *m* 2d, Julian Taylor); III–Lucilla Margaret (1866-1912); IV–Joseph DuPuy (see Vol. I, p. 80, and Vol. II, p. 18); V–Nelia Purnell (1877-1906).
1–*m* June 17, 1896, Blanche Virginia Stokes, *b* Louisville, Ky., Sept. 27, 1873; dau. of Arthur Henry Stokes, of Louisville; issue: 1–William Stokes (qv for Segar, Daniel and Langhorne lineages); 2–Arthur Du Puy (qv for Martian, Du Puy and Trabue lineages); 3–Richard Beverley (qv for Buckner, Elliott and Stokes lineages).
1–Hampden-Sydney, 1877; U.Va., med. dept., 1878-79; M.D., Coll. of Phys. and Surgeons, Columbia U., 1881. Practiced medicine, Prince Edward Co., Va., 1881-83; active worker for the Australian ballot, 1883-91; asst. editor Am. Journal of Med. Sciences and Med. News, Phila., 1883-84; asst. editor Journal of the Am. Med. Assn., 1885-87; newspaper free lance, Chicago, 1888-89; editorial staff, Chicago Herald, 1889-90; editor Peoria (Ill.) Herald, 1891-94; spl. writer, 1895-96; editor Helena Independent, 1896-97, 1900-02, Helena Press, 1902-04, Great Falls (Mont.) Tribune, 1904-05; actively engaged in work for the short ballot, direct legislation, and prison and tax reform, 1905-20. Retired. Mem. Oakland Public Library Bd. Democrat. Residence: 5345 Manila Av., Oakland, Calif.

1–**EGGLESTON, William Stokes,** *b* Helena, Mont., May 20, 1897.
9–Capt. John **Langhorne** (qv);
8–John (*b* 1672/73), high sheriff, Warwick Co., 1728; *m* Anne Wade (*b* 1674; Armiger[9] [*d* 1708], *m* 2d, ca. 1673, Elizabeth–[*d* 1696]; Armiger [Armigall][10], [*d* 1676], justice of York Co., Va., burgess, 1656, *m* Dorothy [*d* 1667], dau. of Edward Moulson [*b* 1590]; desc. Armigall Wade, of Bellsize, nr. Hempstead, Eng.);
7–John (*b* ca. 1695), burgess, Warwick Co., 1748-49; presiding justice; *m* Mary (Rice?);

6–Maurice (ca. 1721-1791), mem. Com. of Safety, Cumberland Co., Va., 1775-76; officer in Am. Rev.; justice of Ct. Warwick Co., 1756-60 and of Cumberland Co., 1760-91; high sheriff, Cumberland Co., 1775-76; *m* ca. 1771, Mary Moulson;
5–Jane Segar or Segur (*b* 1772), *m* 1795, Edmund **Eggleston** (1773-1840);
4–Richard Beverley (1797-1853), *m* 2d, Elvira DuPuy;
3–Joseph DuPuy, M.D. (1831-1908), *m* 1858, Anne Carrington Booker (1836-98);
2–William Green (2 below).
10–Oliver **Segar** (*d* 1659), from Eng. to Lancaster Co., Va.; *m* Ellinor– (*d* 1678);
9–Randolph (*d* 1694), *m* 1st, Mary Jones (*d* 1690; Humphrey[10], *d* 1684);
8–Oliver (1684-1741), of Middlesex Co., Va.; high sheriff; justice of ct., and mem. of Quorum; *m* ca. 1720, Jane Daniel;
7–Mary (1726-post 1775), *m* 1745, William **Moulson** (1721-75; Richard[8] [*d* 1730], *m* Ann–, *d* 1721);
6–Mary (1748-93), *m* 2d, Maj. Maurice **Langhorne** (6 above).
10–William **Daniel** (*d* 1715), of Middlesex Co., Va.;
9–Robert (*d* 1720), *m* 1687, Margaret Price (*b* 1670; Robert[10] [*d* 1690], *m* Jane–, *d* 1687);
8–Jane (*b* ca. 1699), *m* Oliver **Segar** (8 above).
2–William Green **Eggleston** (qv for other lineages), *m* 1896, Blanche Virginia Stokes.
1–Not married. Grad. Oakland (Calif) Tech. High Sch., 1917; enlisted Aviation Service, Jan., 1918; grad. Aviation School, U.Calif., and School of Fire for F. A., 1918, and Aviation Sch., Carlstrom Field, Arcadia, Fla., 1919; 2d lt., aerial observer, reserve mil. aviator, Air Service, Signal R.C.; B.S., Coll. of Mines, U.Calif. (Pi Kappa Alpha). To Colo. as an asst. geologist, Union Oil Co. of Calif., 1926; to Venezuela as asst. geologist, Union Nat. Pet. Co. of Venezuela, 1927, petroleum engr. same, 1928; in Calif. as oil scout for Union Oil Co. of Calif., 1929; promoted to asst. petroleum engineer same, to petroleum engr., and 1930, to asst. chief petroleum engr. same. Mem. Am. Petroleum Inst. Club, University (Los Angeles). Residence: 5345 Manila Avenue, Oakland, Calif.

1–**EGGLESTON, Arthur Du Puy,** *b* Worsham, Va., Apr. 18, 1899.
8–Barthélémy **Du Puy** (1653-1743; 18th generation from Raphaël de Podio, Grand Chamberlain of the Empire, 1033, under Conrad le Salique, and Governor of the Royalties of Arles and de Bourgogne), *m* 1685, Contesse Susanne La Villian (*d* 1737), Huguenot to Va., 1700;
7–Pierre (1694-1777), *m* ca. 1723, Judith Le Fevre (*d* 1785; Isaac[8], *m* Madelenne–, from France to Va., 1700);
6–John Bartholomew (1723-91), *m* ca. 1753, Esther Guerrant;
5–Capt. James (1758-1823), capt. in Am. Rev.; mem. Va. State Legislature 20 yrs.; *m* 1782, Mary Purnell (1763-1828; William[6], of Md. and Va., *m* Anne Hall);
4–Elvira (1805-78), *m* 1827, Col. Richard Beverly **Eggleston** (1797-1853);
3–Joseph Du Puy, M.D. (1831-1908), *m* 1858, Anne Carrington Booker (1836-98);
2–William Green (2 below).
8–Sieur Antoine (Strabo) **Trabue** (1667-1724), Huguenot to Va., 1700; *m* 1699, Magdelaine Flournois (1671-1731; Jacob[9]; Jacques[10]; Jean[11]; Laurent de Flournois[12]);
7–Magdelaine, *m* Pierre **Guerrand** (Daniel[8], Huguenot to Va., 1700);
6–Esther (1735-1760-64), *m* John Bartholomew **Du Puy** (6 above).
10–Nicholas **Martian** (qv);
9–Elizabeth (*d* 1687), *m* Col. George **Reade** (qv);
8–Thomas, *m* ca. 1688, Lucy Gwynn (desc. of Hugh Gwynn, burgess; of Col. William Bernard, mem. of Council; of Capt. Robert Higginson, in charge of troops against Indians, Middle Plantation);
7–Clement (1707-63), col. French and Indian War, 1758; burgess; clk. Lunenburg Co., Va.; *m* 1730, Mary Hill (1711-86; Isaac[8], mem. Quorum, King and Queen Co., Va., 1702-14, *m* 1708 Margaret Jennings);
6–Nancy (*d* 1815), *m* 1st, 1768, William **Jameson** (*d* 1785), planter; capt. in Am. Rev.; mem. Com. of Safety, Charlotte Co., Va., 1775;
5–Margaret (Peggy) Jennings, *m* 1793, Thomas Colgate **Elliott** (*b* 1771), physician;
4–Lucilla Stanley (1817-53), *m* 1835, John **Booker** (1809-94);
3–Anne Carrington (1836-98), *m* Joseph Du Puy **Eggleston** (3 above);
2–William Green (qv for other lineages), *m* 1896, Blanche Virginia Stokes.
1–Not married. A.B., U.Calif., '23; asst. head worker, Palama Settlement, Honolulu, 1923-25; Oxford U., Eng., 1925-27. Newspaper man. Mem. Pi Kappa Alpha, Big "C" Soc., Order of the Golden Bear (U.Calif.), University Club (Honolulu). Residence: 5345 Manila Av., Oakland, Calif.

1–**EGGLESTON, Richard Beverly,** *b* Helena, Mont., Aug. 26, 1900.
9–John **Buckner** (1630-95; son of Thomas; g.son of Hugh, of Oxford, and g.g.son of Richard, of Cumnor, Eng.); came to Va., ca. 1667; burgess; brought first printing press into Va.; *m* 1661, Deborah Ferrers;
8–Elizabeth, *m* James **Williams,** from Wales to King and Queen Co., Va.;
7–Mary Elizabeth (1695-1740), *m* 1720, Jean Jacques (John James) **Flournoy** (1686-1740), Huguenot to Va., 1700 (Jean Jacques[7]; Jacques[8]; Jean[9]; Laurent[10]);
6–Mary (1734-1800), *m* 1755, William **Booker** (1733-83);
5–John (1769-1825), *m* 1791, Martha Jane Watkins (1771-1852; William[6] [*b* ca. 1731-post 1795], of Dinwiddie Co., Va., justice, mem. Va. Assembly, 1778-88, *m* Mary [*d* ante 1781], dau. of Edward Osborne; William[7] [*d* 1784], of Chesterfield and Charlotte cos., *m* Mildred–);
4–John (1809-94), *m* Lucilla Stanley Elliott;
3–Anne Carrington (1836-98), *m* 1858, Joseph Dupuy **Eggleston,** M.D. (1831-1908);
2–William Green (2 below).
7–George **Elliott,** from Eng. to Gloucester Co., Va.; *m* 1732, Patience (Colgate) Buckner, of Md.;
6–Col. George (*d* 1782), a.d.q.m. in Am. Rev.; *m* 1770, Mary Merritt or Marriott (John[7] [*d* ante 1764], *m* Mary [*d* 1789], dau. of Col. Henry Embry [*d* 1763], presiding justice Brunswick Co., Va., burgess, *m* Martha Patteson?, *d* 1772);
5–Thomas Colgate, M.D. (*b* 1771), *m* Margaret Jennings Jameson (dau. of Capt. William[6], *m* Nancy Read);
4–Lucilla Stanley (1817-53), *m* John **Booker** (4 above).
4–William Henry **Stokes** (1809-74), *m* 1833, Prudence Catherine Ward (*b* 1816; James D.[5], of N.S., *m* Prudence Von Meyer, of Baltimore, 1777-1849);
3–Arthur Henry (1843-79), *m* 1866, Blanche Virginia Mather (*b* 1850; James[4] [*b* in Eng., 1808-*d* 1900], brought to America in 1815, steamboat owner and capt. on Ohio and Miss. rivers, carried Federal troops and supplies on the rivers in Civil War, *m* Mary Lucinda Payne, 1811-82);
2–Blanche Virginia (*b* 1873), *m* 1896, William Green **Eggleston** (qv for other lineages).
1–*m* Aug. 11, 1927, Ella Ruth Harbine, *b* San Francisco, Calif., Dec. 25, 1900; dau. of Nathan William Harbine, of Sebastopol, Sonoma Co., Calif.
1–U.Calif., ex-'25 (Pi Kappa Alpha). Salesman, A. G. Spaulding & Bros., San Francisco store, 1923-27; mgr., of Oakland store, 1927–. Clubs: Sequoyah Country, Athens Athletic, Athenian Nile, Elks. Residence: 295 D, Perry St., Oakland, Calif.

1–**EHRENFELD, Charles Hatch,** *b* Shippensburg, Pa., Mar. 12, 1864.
7–Matthaeus Bernhard **Ehrenfeld** (1601-59), of Heilbronn, Germany;
6–Johann George (1638-1706), of Heilbronn; *m* Marie Barbara Werner;
5–George Nicolaus (1698-1773), of Heilbronn; *m* Anna Margaretha Brecht (1705-68);
4–George Frederick (1744-1809), came from Heilbronn, Germany, to Phila., Pa., 1783; *m* 1769, Sophie Friedericke Charlotte Bruckmann (1750-1824; Johann Clemens[5] [1726-76], of Heilbronn);

3–Dr. Augustus Clemens (1774-1839), of Phila., later in Mifflin Co., Pa.; both are buried in Salem Chyd., nr. Milroy, Pa.; *m* 1808, Charlotte Catherine Stitzer (1789-1868; Henry[4], of Phila., in Am. Rev., removed to Mifflin Co., Pa., also buried in Salem Chyd.);
2–Charles Lewis (2 below).
8–Thomas **Hatch** (1596-ante 1646; son of William Hatche, 1563-1627/28, of Tenterden, Kent Co., Eng.), of Wye, Kent Co., Eng.; to America, 1634; settled at Scituate, Plymouth Co., Mass.;
7–Thomas (*b* Wye, Kent Co., Eng., bap. 1628), with parents to Scituate; *m* 1662/63, Sarah Elmes (Rodolphus[8], *m* Catherine Whitcombe);
6–Rodolphus (1674-1743/44), *m* 1701, Elizabeth Tilden;
5–Asa (1716-45), *m* 1740, Mary Waite (1722/23-1765-66), of Scituate;
4–Asa (1741-1811), removed to Shaftsbury, Vt.; capt. in Am. Rev.; *m* 1766, Lydia Warner (1742-1811; Brig. Gen. Jonathan[5]);
3–Warner (1790-1874), of Shaftsbury; moved to Springfield, O., later to New Castle, Ind.; buried with wife at Springfield, O.; *m* 1829, Ann Maria Leese (1804-88; Jacob[4]);
2–Helen Margaret (1837-1912), of Springfield, O.; *m* 1860, Charles Lewis **Ehrenfeld** (1832-1914), A.B., Wittenberg Coll., 1856, A.M., 1859, Ph.D., 1878; Lutheran minister and prof. Latin and English, Wittenberg and Pa., Southwestern Normal Sch.; state librarian of Pa.; buried at Springfield, O. (see Vol. VII, Who's Who in America); issue: I–Anna Bell (1862-74); II–Charles Hatch (1 above); III–Augustus Clemens (1868-1915; *m* Leila Gebhart); IV–Frederick, Ph.D. (*b* 1872; *m* Alice Stockton Allen); V–Helen (Feb. 15-July 16, 1876).
1–*m* Apr. 16, 1891, Bertha Kate Spahr, *b* York, Pa., Mar. 30, 1860; dau. of Michael Brown Spahr, of York; issue: 1–Helen, *b* York, Pa., Jan. 29, 1897; Wells, '18; *m* Nov. 6, 1926, Lewis Crew Spencer, of Lancaster, Pa. (issue: Mary Levick); 2–Walter Spahr, *b* York, May 27, 1900; U.Pa., '22 (Phi Kappa Psi); S.A.T.C., 1918; *m* Apr. 14, 1925, Nina Fredericka Alvord, of Hamilton, N.Y., and York, Pa. (issue: Nina).
1–A.B., Wittenberg Coll., '86 (Phi Kappa Psi), A.M., 1889; Ph.D., U.Pa., 1894; (Sc.D., Wittenberg, 1916, Litt. D., Gettysburg Coll., 1925). Pres. York Collegiate Inst., 1916-28; chief chemist, York Mfg. Co. (refrigeration machinery), 1903-16; mgr. chemical and testing-materials dept., York Ice Machinery Corpn., since 1928 (see Who's Who in America). Pres. City Council, select branch, 1906-13; del. Pa. Rep. State Conv., 1910. Fellow A.A.A.S.; mem. S.R., Am. Chem. Soc., Am. Soc. Testing Materials, York Engring. Soc. (1st pres. 1910). Clubs: Outdoor, Rotary, York Country. Residence: 57 S. Beaver St., York, Pa.

1–**ELDRIDGE, Jay Glover,** *b* Janesville, Wis., Nov. 8, 1875.
9–William (Eldred, Eldredge) **Eldridge,** came to Yarmouth, Mass., ca. 1635; constable, 1657-62, 1674, 75, 77; surveyor of highways; *m* Ann Lumpkin (*d* 1676; William[10], from Eng., 1637, dep. Gen. Ct., *m* Tamasin–);
8–Elisha (1653-1739), name spelled "Eldredge" on tombstone; of Yarmouth, Eastham, and later, Wellfleet, Mass.;
7–Elisha (1690-1754), wrote name Eldredge; *d* Mansfield, Conn.; *m* Dorcas Mulford (1692-1755; Thomas[8], *m* 1690, Mary, dau. of Nathaniel Bassett [*b* 1621], of Yarmouth, and g. dau. William Bassett, came to America in the "Fortune," 1621, *m* 3d, Elizabeth Tilden; Thomas[9]);
6–Jesse (1715-94), *b* Eastham, Mass., *d* Willington, Conn.; *m* 1734, Abigail Smith;
5–Ebenezer (1745-73), of Mansfield and Tolland, Conn.; *m* 1764, Lydia Case (1747-73; Capt. William[6] [1716-76], *m* Lucy Tracy);
4–William Case (1765-1842), *b* Tolland, Conn., *d* Webster, N.Y.; enlisted 1781, in Light Dragoons; served with Gen. Washington; *m* 1786, in Willington, Conn., Zerviah Barker (1767-1835; Joseph[5], *m* Susanna–);
3–Elijah (1805-94), sch. master and farmer, N.Y., Mich., and Ill.; *m* Olive Experience Short (1811-84);
2–William Glover (2 below).
11–Elder William **Brewster,** Mayflower Pilgrim (qv);
10–Patience (*d* 1634), *m* Gov. Thomas **Prence** (qv);
9–Mary (1631-1711), *m* Maj John **Freeman** (1627-1718; Edmund[10], qv);
8–Nathaniel (1669-1760), *m* Mary Howland (1665-1743; Zoeth[9] [*d* 1676], *m* Mary Newland; Henry[10], qv);
7–Abigail (*b* 1693), *m* Samuel **Smith** (1691-will proved 1768; Samuel[8] [1668-92], *m* Bathsheba, dau. of Barnabas Lathrop; Samuel[9] [1641-96], *m* Mary, dau. of Gyles Hopkins, and g.dau. of Stephen Hopkins, Mayflower Pilgrim, qv; Ralph[10] [*d* 1685], from Eng., 1633);
6–Abigail (1718-93), *b* Eastham, Mass., *d* Willington, Conn.; *m* Jesse **Eldredge** (6 above).
2–William Glover (1842-1911), began to write name **Eldridge;** merchant; *m* 1866, Augusta Maria Van Wormer (1844-1921; Rev. Aaron[3], minister, circuit judge, of Ky. and Mo., *m* Mary, dau. of Rev. Hugh Wallis, *m* Susanna Upham); issue: I–Clara Adeline (*b* 1869; George W. Wolfe); II–Jay Glover (1 above).
1–*m* Sept. 20, 1900, Mary Evelyn Walker, *b* Pontiac, Mich., Jan. 12, 1875; dau. of Dr. Emory Judson Walker, of New Haven, Conn. (see Who's Who in America, 1918); issue (all *b* Moscow, Ida): 1–Robert Walker, *b* Jan. 24, 1903; B.S., U.Ida, '23; Ph.D., Yale, 1927; *m* Feb. 10, 1928, Dorothy, dau. of Maj. Royal B. Daggett, of White Plains, N.Y. (issue: Donald Francis, *b* Jan. 30, 1929); 2–Francis Glover (Dec. 4, 1905-Nov. 30, 1926); B.A., U.Ida., '27 (degree granted posthumously); 3–Grace Elizabeth, *b* Apr. 4, 1911; U.Ida., '33; 4–Hugh Wallace, *b* Nov. 9, 1913.
1–B.A., Yale, '96 (Beta Theta Pi, P.B.K.), M.A., 1899, Ph.D., 1906; studied in Germany, 1900; in France on leave, 1927. Prof. German lang. and lit. since 1901, U. of Idaho, dean of faculty since 1903, actg. dean., Coll. Letters and Science, 1927-29, actg. dean. of Grad. Sch., 1928-29 (see Who's Who in America). Served as Y.M.C.A. sec. with A.E.F. in France. Mason (K.T., 32°). Summer place: Camp Kenjockety, Moscow Mt. Residence: 822 Elm St., Moscow, Idaho.

1–**ELIOT, Charlotte Champe Stearns (Mrs. Henry W.),** *b* Baltimore, Md., Oct. 22, 1843.
8–Isaac (Sterne) **Stearns** (qv);
7–Isaac (1632-76), *m* 1660, Sarah Beers (1639-1723; Capt. Richard[8], qv);
6–Samuel (1667-1721), *m* Phoebe Wait;
5–Thomas (1710-84), *m* Abigail Reed (1717-49; Ebenezer[6] representative for 13 yrs., *m* Sarah Chapin, *b* 1699);
4–Josiah (1747-1822), officer Am. Rev., comd. co. from Lunenburg, Mass.; mem. Com. of Corr.; tax assessor; selectman; rep. Legislature, 1796-98; justice throughout commonwealth; senator from Worcester Co.; mem. Gov.'s Council, 1797-99; *m* 1769, Mary (King) Corey (1750-1828), among their sons was Asahel, LL.D., 1774-1839, mem. Congress, 1815-17, 1st prof. law, Harvard;
3–Maj. Thomas (1778-1826), *m* Priscilla Cushing (1779-1866); see Vol. I, p. 84 for Cushing lineage;
2–Thomas (2 below).
8–James **Blood** (*d* 1683), from Eng. to Concord, Mass., ca. 1638; *m* Ellen–;
7–Robert (*d* 1701), Concord, Mass.; with bro., John, owned "Blood's Farm," of 2000 acres; *m* 1653, Elizabeth Willard (*d* 1690; Maj Simon[8], qv);
6–Samuel, *m* Hannah Davis;
5–Oliver (*b* 1719), *m* Mary Foster (?);
4–Samuel (1751-1834), *m* Lucretia Heywood; both buried at Bolton, Mass.;
3–Thomas Heywood, *m* Mary Sawyer;
2–Charlotte (1818-93), *m* 1840, Thomas **Stearns** (1811-96), mcht., Lexington, Mass.; for issue see Vol. I, p. 84.
1–*m* Oct. 27, 1868, Henry Ware Eliot (1843-1919); son of William Greenleaf Eliot, D.D., of St. Louis, Mo.; for issue see Vol. I, p. 84.
1–Mem. C.D.A., O.C. Residence: 24 Concord Av., Cambridge, Mass.

1–**ELIOT, Willard Ayres,** *b* Sioux City, Ia., Jan. 24, 1871.
4–Andrew **Eliot** (1751-1813), pvt. 3d Tryon Co. Regt. Militia, during Am. Rev., *m* 1774, Jane (or Jennie) Ayres (1756-1824);

3–Elias (1793-1841), *m* 1813, Charity Warner (1795-1895; Charles[4], [1762-1837], pvt. Am. Rev.; *m* 1789, Sarah Stockwell, *b* 1768);
2–Warner Ayres (1833-96), *m* Loretta Spaids (1843-1918; Chauncey D.[3], of Chicago, Ill.); issue: I–Charles Warner (*b* 1862?; *m* Bessie Webb, *d* 1915); II–Raymond (*d* young); III–Chauncey Spaids (*b* 1867?; *m* Britomarte–); IV–Craig (1870-1885 or 86); V–Willard Ayres (1 above); VI–Kate (*b* 1872; *m* Charles Kenneth Grable, *d* 1916); VII–Florence (*b* 1877; *m* Irwin Van Ness Hitchcock).
1–*m* Dec. 29, 1896, Lillian Calista Post (qv for issue).
1–Attended Rollins Coll., Fla. Sent to France as Y.M.C.A. lecturer, Nov. 18, 1918; served under the Paris div. speaking with moving pictures and slides on birds, agriculture, and the Pacific Northwest in the hosps. and various camps in all parts of France until Aug. 1, 1919. Sec. of the advisory and employment dept. Y.M.C.A. of Portland. Pres. Ore. Audubon Soc. Author: Birds of the Pacific Coast. Residence: Portland, Ore.

1–**ELIOT, Lillian Calista Post (Mrs. Willard A.),** *b* Blair, Neb., Nov. 10, 1871.
9–Robert **Cushman** (qv);
8–Thomas (1607-91), ruling elder of the ch. at Plymouth; *m* 1635/36, Mary Allerton (Isaac[9], Mayflower Pilgrim, qv);
7–Eleazar (*b* 1656), *m* 1687, Elizabeth Combes (Francis[8]; John[9], *m* Sarah, dau. of Degory Priest, Mayflower Pilgrim, qv);
6–John (*b* 1690), *m* 1715, Joanna Pratt (John[7]; Daniel[8]; Joshua[9], came in the "Ann");
5–Charles (*d* 1791), soldier in Am. Rev.; *m* Mary Harvey, an Englishwoman;
4–Frederick (1758-1852), minute man in Am. Rev.; *m* 1784, Alice, probably dau. of Capt. Nathan Caswell, *m* Hannah Bingham;
3–Calista (1801-88), *m* 1820, Harlow **Post** (1798-1884; Capt. Jesse[4], capt. Vt. Militia, in War 1812);
2–Judson Harlow (2 below).
6–Michael (Huber) **Hoover,** built house 1728 at Swatara, Derry Tp., Dauphin Co., Pa., which is still standing, has inscription in gable, "Built in 1728 by Michael Huber;"
5–Michael (*b* Swatara, Pa., 1746-*d* 1818), *m* Maria–, or Mary Brickley (1741-1821);
4–George (1774-1826), buried at Swatara; blacksmith; *m* ca. 1798, Susanna Ryder;
3–Michael (1803-88), *m* 1826, Mary (Hershey) Eby;
2–Mary Catherine (2 below).
10–Jog (Jacob) (Hersche) **Hershey** (*b* 1535 at or nr. Appenzell, Innesholden, Switzerland);
9–Conrad, *m* 1621, Greth Lamere, at Appenzell;
8–Franziest, *m* 1662, Engle Darig, at Appenzell;
7–Hans, *m* 1692, Anna Geunder, at Appenzell;
6–Rev. Andrew (1702-92), came to America, 1719, with his father and brother Benjamin and settled in Lancaster Co., Pa.; chosen minister of the Mennonite Ch.;
5–Abraham (*b* 1747), lived nr. the Bingnagle Ch. which is located on the East bank of the big Swatara, five miles north of the village of Palmyra, Derry Tp., Dauphin Co., *m* Barbara Kreider (Rev. Martin Kreider or Krieder[6]);
4–Rev. Christian (1777-1853), United Brethren minister; led the Hoover, Hershey, Kurtz colony to Ia. and founded the town of Lisbon, Linn Co., 1847; *m* Elizabeth Yordy (Peter[5]);
3–Mary (1803-77), as Widow Eby, *m* 2d, Michael **Hoover** (3 above);
2–Mary Catherine (1844-1922), *m* 1865, Judson Harlow **Post** (1839-1910), druggist and jeweler; issue: I–Lillian Calista (1 above); II–Mabel Hoover (*m* Walter Willard Way).
1–*m* Dec. 29, 1896, Willard Ayres Eliot (qv); issue: 1–Calista Post, *b* Gainesville, Fla., Mar. 6, 1898; A.B., Reed, '20; Sc.D., Johns Hopkins, 1925; research asst. in bacteriology, 1925-27; instr. in bacteriology, 1927-29; asso. in bacteriology, Johns Hopkins, since 1929; 2–Mignon Hoover, *b* Jacksonville, Fla., July 10, 1899; A.B., Reed, '22; *m* Aug. 26, 1923, Theodore Sessinghaus Eliot, Ph.D. (issue: Theodore S., Jr.; Warner Ayres; Andrew Ely; Michael Hoover); 3–Craig Post, *b* Atlanta, Ga., Feb. 19, 1901; *m* Jan. 1, 1925, Jean Bess Pugsley (issue: Robert Fraser; Janet Post).
1–Ed. East Fla. Sem.; Fla. Normal, 1892. Mem. S.M.D. (dir. Ore. Soc., 1929-30), D.A.R. (corr. sec. Multnomah Chapter, 1928-29). Residence: Portland, Ore.

1–**ELLISON, Annie Corinne Colburn (Mrs. Frank Dexter),** *b* N. Stoughton, Mass., June 19, 1862.
4–Aaron (Colman) **Colburn** (1785-1810), of Boston; *m* 1808, Elizabeth Drake (1785-1855);
3–Aaron (1810-54), of Stoughton; *m* 1830, Eliza Erskine (1812-1900);
2–Charles Ellsworth (2 below).
9–John (Beal) **Beale** (qv);
8–Jacob (1642-1717), of Hingham, Mass.; *m* 1678/79, Mary Bisbee (1648-1717);
7–David (1684/85-1767); of Hingham; *m* 1st, 1709 or 1710, Rebecca Stodder (1675-1721);
6–Isaac (1717-93), of Hingham; *m* 1745, Sarah Cain (1722-92);
5–Elisha (1761-1830), of Hingham; in Am. Rev.; *m* 1780, Lydia Tower (1761-1833);
4–Charles (1792-1849), of Hingham; *m* 1816, Laurana Warren (1798-1888);
3–Elisha (1819-68), of Randolph; *m* 1841, Mary Ann Thayer (1825-48);
2–Mary Adelaide (1844-1926), *m* 1861, Charles Ellsworth **Colburn** (1839-1927), of Stoughton; issue: I–Annie C. (1 above); II–Mary Eliza (*b* 1864; *m* Evan W. D. Merrill); III–Alice Maria (1866-75).
1–*m* Apr. 15, 1926, Frank Dexter Ellison, *b* Belmont, Mass., Dec. 19, 1866; son of Henry M. Ellison, of Belmont.
1–Ed. Boston Normal Sch. Mem. D.F.P.A., D.A.C., D.C.W. (pres.), D.A.R. (ex-nat. officer). Unitarian. Republican. Summer place: Brant Rock. Residence: 20 Chapel St., Longwood Towers, Brookline, Mass.

1–**ELY, Warren Smedley,** *b* Bucks Co., Pa., Oct. 6, 1855.
7–Joshua **Ely** (1652-1703), from Eng., 1684; settled Trenton, N.J.; justice of peace, 1700-01; *m* 1673, Mary Senior (*d* 1698);
6–George (1682-1749), of Trenton; mem. first town council of Trenton; capt. of militia; *m* 1703, Jane Pettit;
5–Joshua (1704-83), of Solebury, Bucks Co., Pa.; *m* 1729, Elizabeth Bell;
4–George (1733-1815), of Bucks Co.; *b* Trenton, N.J.; mem. Pa. Assembly, 1760; *m* Sarah Magill;
3–Mark (1781-1835), of Bucks Co.; *m* 1815, Rachel Hambleton;
2–Isaac (2 below).
8–John **Simcock** (*b* 1630), judge Supreme Ct., 1686-93, chief justice, 1690-03; justice of co. cts., 1683; mem. Assembly, 1693-97; speaker, 1696, and one of five commrs. apptd. by William Penn to govern the provinces, 1688;
7–Jacob (1660-1726), coroner, Chester Co., Pa., 1691; *m* Alice Maris;
6–Jacob (1686-1716/17), *m* 1711, Sarah Waln (*b* 1692; Nicholas[7] [1650-1721], *b* Eng., came with William Penn on his first voyage to his Pa. province, in the "Welcome," and settled Bucks Co., 1682, removed to Phila. Co., 1696, mem. first Assembly, 1682-83, rep. Assembly, 1687,89,92,95, mem. first Grand Jury, 1683, *m* 1st, 1673, Jane Turner);
5–Sarah, *m* William **Magill**;
4–Sarah, *m* George **Ely** (4 above).
8–William **Biles** (qv);
7–Elizabeth (1670-1767), *m* 1688, Stephen **Beakes** (1668-99), mem. Assembly, 1697 (William[8], of Somersetshire, Eng., *m* Mary–);
6–Mary (1690-1756), of Falls Tp., Bucks Co., Pa., *m* James **Hambleton**;
5–Stephen (1729-1808), of Solebury, Bucks Co., Pa.; *m* 1752, Hannah Paxson (1732-1812; James[6], Margery Hodges);
4–James (1754-1833), of Solebury; *m* 1779, Elizabeth Paxson (1752-1832; Henry[5], *m* Elizabeth Lupton);
3–Rachel (1789-1878), of Solebury; *m* 1815, Mark **Ely** (3 above);
2–Isaac (1819-98), farmer, of Bucks Co., Pa.; *m* 1841, Mary Magill (1820-97; John[3], *m* Anne Ely); issue: I–Sarah Ellen (1842-76; *m* John S. Abbott); II–William M. (1844-1908; *m* Agnes S. Michener, *d* 1928); III–Anna M. (*b* 1845; *m* Frederick Smith); IV–Edgar C. (1846-57); V–

Rachel Anna (1850-51); VI–John H. (1851-1927; *m* Martha S. Gilbert); VII–Laura (*b* 1853; *m* Seth Walton); VIII–Warren S. (1 above); IX–Alice R. (*b* 1860; *m* Clarence T. Doty); X–Martha C. (*b* 1861; *m* Thomas B. Claxton).
1–*m* Mar. 29, 1882, Hanna S. Michener (1855-1902); dau. of Hugh B. Michener; issue: 1–Mary Florence, *b* Buckingham, Bucks Co., Pa., July 19, 1884; *m* Mar. 29, 1911, J. Carroll, son of Harry Molloy, of Pineville, Pa. (issue: Gerald Leedom, *b* Pineville, May 15, 1912; Kathleen Ely, *b* Pineville, July 1, 1913; H. Warren, *b* June 12, 1919-*d* Jan. 18, 1930).
1–*m* 2d, May 1, 1926, Josephine I. (Naugle) Burleigh (qv).
1–Librarian, Bucks Co. Hist. Soc., since 1900 (trustee). Farmer, 1882, real estate agent, 1882-85; miller, 1885-93; clk. Orphans' Ct., 1894-97; dep. clk., 1897-1912. Mem. I.A.G., Friends' Hist. Soc., Northampton Co. Hist. Soc. Club: Bucks Co. Country. Residence: 326 E. State St., Doylestown, Pa.

1–**ELY, Josephine I. Naugle (Mrs. Warren S.),** *b* New Castle, Pa., Sept. 18, 1881.
7–Donald **Cameron,** from Scotland, 1775, with sons Simon and John; settled Donegal Tp., Lancaster Co., Pa.;
6–Simon, took oath of allegiance before Justice James Bayley, Lancaster Co., 1778;
5–Charles (1771-1814), of Lewisburg, Pa.; warrantee 400 acres of land, Northumberland Co., Pa., Feb. 20, 1793; *m* 1793, Martha Pfoutz or Fouts (1771-1830; Conrad[6] [1734-98], from Zweibrucken, Germany, 1751, resided White Deer Tp., Northumberland Co., Pa., and was "one of the rangers, who with Sam. Brady and the Groves, were a terror to the Indians," was among the recruits enlisted by Capt. John Mather, Jr., 1759, for French and Indian War, *m* Elizabeth–, 1739-1827);
4–Daniel (1803-86), of Taylor Tp., Lawrence Co., Pa.; midshipman, apptd., Jan. 17, 1826, resigned, 1831; *m* 1822, Margery Copper (1803-89);
3–Isaphena (1830-1916), of Irish Ripple, Law Co., Pa.; *m* 1850, Samuel Aaron **Naugle** (1827-1907), of Law Co., Pa. (John[4], acquired a tract of 800 acres in Beaver [now Laurence], Co., Pa., 1806, *m* Elizabeth Hudson);
2–James Parker (*b* 1859), of Lakeland Highlands, Fla.; *m* 1881, Florence Belle Anderson (1860-95; Joseph[8], *m* Elizabeth Culbertson, of New Castle, Pa.); issue: I–Josephine I. (1 above); II–Vearle Allen (*b* 1883; *m* Lillian L. Dewar); III–Nina Georgia (1884-90); IV–Elizabeth Brown (*b* 1886; *m* Harold M. Gallager); V–Myrtle (1888-90); VI–Erma Walls (*b* 1895; *m* John M. Hover), and VII–Caroline (*b* 1895; *m* Stanley Matthews), twins.
1–*m* Walter Robert Burleigh (*b* 1875), son of Robert Hollister Burleigh, of Troy, Pa., *m* Ellen Strange.
1–*m* 2d, May 1, 1926, Warren Smedley Ely (qv).
1–Genealogist. Mem. D.A.R. (Bucks Co. chapter), Bucks Co. Hist. Soc. (chmn. com. of women). Residence: 326 E. State St., Doylestown, Pa.

1–**EMBRY, Ernest Francis (Miss),** *b* Texarkana, Ark., Oct. 17, 1901.
10–John **Buckner** (qv);
9–Richard (ca. 1678-1731), of "The Neck"; clk. House of Burgesses, 1714; justice Caroline Co., 1720; *m* Elizabeth Cooke;
8–Richard (*d* 1777), justice Caroline Co., 1732; sheriff, 1753; maj. militia, 1777; *m* Elizabeth Aylett;
7–Aylett (1745-1809), maj. Fauquier Co., militia; *m* 1776, Judith Presley Thornton;
6–Catherine Talliaferro (1779-1820), *m* Judge John Young **Taylor** (1765-1849);
5–Aylett Buckner, *m* Rebecca White Williamson;
4–Sallie McGee (1830-60), *m* Col. Ben Towler **Embry** (1820-92), served 2d Regt. Mounted Rifles, C.S.A.;
3–Aylett Taylor (1852-1924), *m* 1874, Elizabeth Francis Mourning (*d* 1882);
2–Ernest Finney (2 below).
11–Capt. John **Aylett,** from Eng., 1656, to Northern Neck of Va.; *m* Annie–;
10–Maj. William (*d* 1723), justice York Co.; vestryman, Bruton Parish; *m* Sybella Hubard;
9–Capt. William (ca. 1673-1735), *m* Anne, living 1749;
8–Elizabeth, *m* Richard **Buckner** (8 above).
12–Henry **Corbin** (qv);
11–Winifred (will proved 1711), *m* Col. LeRoy **Griffin** (*b* 1646), justice, Rappahannock Co., Va. (Thomas[12], of Va., 1651, *m* Sarah–);
10–Winifred (*b* 1682), *m* Peter **Presley,** II (*d* 1750; Peter[11], *m* Elizabeth Thompson);
9–Winifred, *m* Anthony **Thornton** (1695-1757), of St. Paul's Parish, Stafford Co., Va.; justice;
8–Anthony (died post 1778), of Ormesby, Caroline Co., Va.; lt. col. militia, 1777; burgess, sheriff, justice, mem. Caroline Co. Com. Safety, 1775; *m* 1st, Sarah Talliaferro (desc. Robert Talliaferro, Gentleman, 1635-1700, of Gloucester Co., Va., *m* Miss Goymes);
7–Judith Presley (1749-98), *m* Aylett **Buckner** (7 above).
2–Ernest Finney **Embry** (1875-1901), *m* 1899, Eva Dorothy Payne (now Mrs. Julian Wood Glass, see Vol. III, p. 179).
1–A.A., Lindenwood Coll., St. Charles, Mo., '21; B.L.I., Emerson Coll. of Oratory, Boston, '24 (Beta Sigma Omicron, Zeta Phi Eta). Teacher of expression. Actress. Residence: 118 W. Shawnee St., Nowata, Okla.

1–**ENDRESEN, Bessie Adaline Royce (Mrs. Einar Nicolai),** *b* Jeffersonville, Ind., Dec. 22, 1879.
8–William **Taylor** (qv);
7–Samuel (1651-1711), of Wethersfield, Conn.; *m* Sarah Cole Parsons;
6–John (1688-1761), of Wethersfield; removed to a farm in E. Middletown, Conn., which is still in family; *m* Elizabeth Bailey;
5–William (1722-79), of Middletown; *m* Ruth (Rich) Higgins;
4–Ozias (1760-1814), of New Hartford, Conn.; pvt. Am. Rev.; *m* Amelia Humphreys (*b* 1761);
3–Amanda (1800-59), of Canton, Conn.; *m* 1820, Daniel Wright **Royce** (1788-1875);
2–William Taylor (2 below).
10–William **Brewster,** Mayflower Pilgrim (qv);
9–Patience (*d* 1634), *m* 1624, Thomas **Prence** (qv);
8–Mercy (1631-1711), *m* 1649/50, Maj. John **Freeman** (1627-1719), asst. to Gov. Prence, 1666; maj. of militia;
7–Mercy (1659-1744), of Eastham, Mass.; *m* 1679, Samuel **Knowles** (1651-1737);
6–Mercy (*b* 1681), of Eastham; *m* 1702, Thomas **Rich;**
5–Ruth (1722-1813), as Widow Higgins, *m* William **Taylor** (5 above).
2–William Taylor **Royce** (1829-1908), of Columbus, O.; *m* 1877, Mary Virginia Perdue (*b* 1852); issue: I–Bessie Adaline (1 above); II–Jesse Danforth (*b* 1882; *m* Alma Raffelsen).
1–*m* Jan. 3, 1901, Rev. Harry Leonard Henderson (Oct. 1, 1867-Dec. 6, 1905); chaplain 27th Ind. Battery in Porto Rico, during Spanish American War; son of William Henderson, of St. Andrews, New Brunswick, Can.; issue: 1–Margaret Virginia, *b* Michigan City, Ind., Sept. 19, 1901; ed. U.Wash. (Kappa Delta); *m* June 8, 1929, James Dudley, son of Dr. Archibald Craig Fraser, of Lavagh House, Co. Leitrim, Ireland; 2–Helen Elizabeth Stewart, *b* Michigan City, June 1, 1903; ed. U.Wash. (Kappa Delta).
1–*m* 2d, Jan. 17, 1914, Einar Nicolai Endresen, *b* Christiansand, Norway, Oct. 22, 1882; son of Lars Christian Endresen.
1–Mem. D.A.R., O.E.S. Residence: 703 Fifth St., Hoquiam, Wash.

1–**EGGER, Mildred (Mittie) Letitia Dorsey (Mrs. Henry J.),** *b* Tuskegee, Ala., Nov. 10, 1867.
9–Edward **Dorsey** (qv);
8–Col. Edward (1645-1705), of "Major's Choice," Anne Arundel Co., Md.; asso. judge High Ct. of Chancery, 1695-96; burgess; maj. of troop of horse, 1689; col. 1702; *m* 1st, 1675, Sarah Wyatt (Nicholas[9]);
7–Capt. Joshua (1686-1747), justice, Baltimore Co., 1712-14; *m* 1711, Ann Ridgely (*d* 1771; Henry[8], *m* Catherine, dau. of Col. Nicholas Greenberry; Col. Henry[9]);
6–Henry (*b* 1712), *m* Elizabeth Worthington (Thomas[7], *m* Elizabeth Ridgely; Capt. John[8], qv);

5–Nicholas (1750-88), *m* 1773, Lucy Belt Sprigg (1752-1825; Col. Edward[6]);
4–John (1780-1870), *m* 1808, Mary Phillips (1791-1851);
3–Isham (1811-72), *m* 1833, Julia Lucas Murden (1816-1901);
2–John I. (*b* 1847), real estate owner; *m* 1866, Ophelia Florence Thornton (1849-82); issue: I–Mildred (1 above); II–Isham Jenkins (*b* 1869; *m* Nelie Smith); III–Annie Murden (*b* 1871; *m* Rinaldo M. Greene); IV–Florie Bell (*d* infancy); V–Katherine May (*d* infancy).
1–*m* Nov. 19, 1885, Sherwood W. Swanson (July 2, 1865-1901); son of M. B. Swanson; issue: 1–Sherwood Wilkinson, *b* Birmingham, Ala., Jan. 8, 1888; World War vet.; 2–Annie Dorsey, *b* Opelika, Ala., Apr. 12, 1892; *m* June 12, 1912, Halford S., son of Willis Wright (issue: Mildred; Agnes; Annie Katherine; Dorothy Sherwood; Halford, Jr.).
1–*m* 2d, 1896, Henry J. Egger (1865-1919); son of H. J. Egger; issue: 1–Agnes A., *b* Titusville, Fla., Sept. 11, 1897; *m* June 21, 1929, Arthur Beck, of Lebanon, Ind.
1–Mem. U.D.C., D.A.R., I.A.G., etc. Club: Miami Woman's. Residence: 2334 S. W. 22d Terrace, Miami, Fla.

1–**ENSIGN, Charles Trusdell,** *b* New Hartford, Ia., May 10, 1873.
8–James **Ensign** (*d* 1670), from Eng., 1630-34, settled at Newtown (Cambridge), Mass., 1635, later at Hartford, Conn.; freeman, Cambridge, 1634-35; an original settler and founder of Hartford; with his wife and 30 others formed the South or Second Congl. Ch., 1639; constable, surveyor, townsman; *m* Sarah Elson (*d* 1671);
7–David (1644-1727), of West Hartford; *m* 1663, Mehitable Gunn (divorced 1682); *m* 2d, post 1682, Sarah (Wilcox) Long (*d* 1717);
6–David (1688-1759), of West Hartford; *m* 1709, Hannah Smith (1688-1719);
5–Eliphalet (1718-92), of New Hartford, Conn.; in French and Indian War; freeman, New Hartford, 1752; *m* 1739, Dorcas Webster (*b* 1716; desc. John Webster, 5th gov. of Conn.);
4–Eliphalet (1748-1838), of New Hartford; in Am. Rev., pension, 1832; *m* 1777, Esther Dickinson (1757-1838);
3–Titus (1801-79), of New Hartford, Conn., Castile, N.Y., and New Hartford, Ia.; *m* 1829, Lucretia Belden;
2–Eliphalet William (2 below).
10–Richard **Belden** (1591-1655), from Eng., settled at Wethersfield, Conn., 1635;
9–William (1622-60), removed from Wethersfield to Norwalk, Conn.; freeman Watertown, 1657; left estate of £142, 7s, 8d; *m* 1646, Thomasine–;
8–Daniel (1648-1732), at Deerfield, Mass., 1686; taken prisoner in massacre of 1696, to Can. where he was sold to the French and finally released by Col. Schuyler; commr. to bear a copy of the Articles of Peace bet. Eng. and France; to Albany, later to Deerfield; served King Philip's War, mem. com. fortification; *m* 1670, Elizabeth Foote (1654-96), killed by Indians during King Philip's War (Nathaniel[9], *m* Elizabeth Smith; Nathaniel[10], qv);
7–William (1671-1759), sgt. Indian war, 1703-04; taken prisoner by Indians, 1696; *m* 1700, Margaret Arms (1683-1780; William[8], *m* Joanna Hawks; John[9]);
6–Daniel (*b* 1702), *m* 1727, Esther Smith;
5–William (*b* Deerfield, Mass., 1741-*d* 1822), served Am. Rev., Conn. line; *m* Priscilla Rider;
4–William (1772-1841), *m* Hannah Wescott;
3–Lucretia (1801-50), *m* Titus **Ensign** (3 above).
10–Nathaniel **Wright,** of London, Eng.;
9–Dea. Samuel (*d* 1665), dea., Springfield, Mass., 1639; *m* Margaret– (*d* 1681);
8–Lydia, *m* Lawrence **Bliss** (Thomas[9], qv);
7–Sarah, *m* Samuel **Smith** (Chiliab[8]; Lt. Samuel[9]);
6–Esther (1706-57), *m* Daniel **Belden** (6 above).
2–Eliphalet William **Ensign** (1844-1921), of New Hartford, Ia.; miller; served in 144th Ia. Inf. in Civil War; pensioner; *m* 1866, Martha Ann Raymond (*b* 1845); issue: I–Susan Laura (1867-1925; *m* 1892, Alva E. Smith); II–Jennie Louise (*b* 1869; *m* 1888, Elias S. Harmon; *m* 2d, 1926, Alva E. Smith); III–Florence Belle (*b* 1871; *m* 1902, George W. Whitnell); IV–Charles Trusdell (1 above); V–Nellie Lorraine (*b* 1875; *m* 1913, James Hendricks); VI–Harry Eliphalet (*b* 1877; *m* Winnifred Powell); VII–Martha May (1879-1906); VIII–Louis Belden (*b* 1881; *m* 1906, Lizzie Hart, *d* 1918); IX–Bessie Lucretia (*b* 1883; *m* 1918, James Pettijohn).
1–*m* Apr. 15, 1907, Irene Lovis Bazin, *b* Somerville, Mass., May 22, 1880; dau. of Savillian Etheridge Bazin, of Boston.
1–M.Di., Ia. State Teachers Coll., '99; B.A., Cornell, '02; S.T.B., Boston U. Sch. of Theology, 1907. Teacher 3 yrs.; clergyman 27 yrs. Mem. S.A.R., I.A.G., Gov. and Co. of the Mass. Bay in N.E. (Freeman). Methodist. Republican. Residence: Langdon, N.D.

1–**EUBANK, Earle Edward,** *b* Columbia, Mo., Mar. 20, 1887.
6–Richard **Eubank,** from Eng., settled in Bedford Co., Va., ca. 1725;
5–Achilles (1758-1844), served with Va. troops in Am. Rev., under George Washington; fought at Guilford C.H. and Yorktown, present at surrender of Cornwallis; removed to Clark Co., Ky., 1787, and was intimately associated with Daniel Boone in Indian fighting and early settlement; mem. Ky. Constl. Conv., also 1st Ky. Legislature; maj. Ky. militia; *m* 1st, 1778?, Polly Bush;
4–Ambrose (1780-1845), col. in Ky. militia; *m* 1801, Elizabeth Claiborne (*d* 1849);
3–Achilles (1823-70), *m* 1845, Mary Davis Kidd (1830-1902);
2–Peyton Adams (2 below).
4–Jesse **Houchens,** *m* Susanna Pierce;
3–Jesse Clements (1825-90), *m* 1848, Amanda Irene Kimbrough (1830-94);
2–Laura Boardman (*b* 1858), *m* 1882, Rev. Peyton Adams **Eubank** (*b* 1857-*d* Dec., 1914), of Ky.; to Eureka Springs, Ark.; missionary to Nigeria, W. Africa, under Southern Bapt. Conv.; issue: I–Earle Edward (1 above); II–Jessie May (1894-1913); III–Paul (1897-98); IV–Lilian (*b* 1902; *m* Theron William Morgan).
1–*m* Apr. 8, 1910, Eva Maude Stephens (*b* July 16, 1885, *d* June 17, 1923); dau. of Homer Bealey Stephens, of Stanton, Neb.; issue (all *b* Chicago, Ill.): 1–Evelyn Laile, *b* July 23, 1914; 2–Edward Earle (Sept. 8, 1915-June 16, 1923); 3–Lauriel Elsabeth, *b* Apr. 28, 1917; 4–Lois Lilian, *b* Dec. 15, 1919.
1–*m* 2d, June 5, 1928, Jessie Logan Burrall (qv).
1–A.B., William Jewell Coll., Liberty, Mo., 1908, A.M., 1913; Ph.D. cum laude, U.Chicago, 1916 (Phi Eta, Beta Epsilon, Kappa Delta Pi). Supervisor of schs., Bur. Edn., Philippine Islands, 1908-12; prof. sociology, head of dept. and dir. Sch. of Social Work, U.Cincinnati, since 1921. Acting dir. Bur. of Social Surveys, Chicago, 1916. Dir. Central Mil. Dept., Nat. War Work Council, Y.M.C.A., and dean Sch. of Assn. War Work, World War. Public speaker and author (see Who's Who in America). Clubs: Faculty, Torch. Summer place: "Burrallwood," Little Falls, Minn. Residence: 47 Lakewood Av., Burnet Woods, Cincinnati, O.

1–**EUBANK, Jessie Logan Burrall (Mrs. Earle E.),** *b* Hillsdale, Barron Co., Wis.
4–Henry **Burrall** (*b* 1768), of Conn.; *m* Hannah Randall (*b* Vt., 1775);
3–Henry (1805-91), of Meriden, N.Y.; *m* Marietta Merchant (*b* 1811);
2–Joel Henry (2 below).
4–Lemuel **Logan** (*b* Vt., 1797), *m* Elizabeth Hulburt (*b* Vt., 1800);
3–William Henry (*b* 1826), of Portland, N.Y., *m* Margaret Jackson Hyland (*b* Pittsburg, N.Y., 1830), of Colebrook, N.H.;
2–Lillie Jane (*b* 1857), *m* Joel Henry **Burrall** (1839-1923), of Herkimer Co., N.Y.; removed to Wis., issue: I–Fred Nelson (*b* 1877); II–Elizabeth Margaret (*b* 1879); III–Jessie L. (1 above).
1–*m* June 5, 1928, Earle Edward Eubank (qv).
1–Grad. State Teachers Coll., St. Cloud, Minn., '12; A.B. in Edn., U.Minn., '15. Lecturer; chief of sch. service, Nat. Geog. Soc., 1915-21; founder and teacher girls' S.S. class of 1,800 members, Washington, 1917-21; teacher univ. and coll. class of 1,300, Stephens Coll., since 1921. Author (see Who's Who in America). Mem. P.E.O., O.E.S. Residence: 47 Lakewood Ave., Cincinnati, O.

1–**EVERETT, Albert,** *b* Sutton, Mass., Mar. 25, 1840.
8–John **Johnson,** came with Gov. Winthrop's colony to Boston, 1630; first constable, Boston rep. from Roxbury to Gen. Ct., many yrs.; "surveyor general of all ye armies";
7–Elizabeth, *m* Robert **Pepper** (killed by Indians in Northampton);
6–Elizabeth (1645-1714), *m* Capt. John **Everett** (ca. 1635-1715), of Dedham; in expdn. to Can. and capture of Port Royal, 1690, comd. by Sir William Phipps; in defense of Mass. northern frontier, 1694 (Richard[7]); see Vol. III, p. 182, for Everett lineage;
5–Richard (1683-1746), selectman, Dedham; *m* Mary Fuller (1687-1782; Jonathan[6] [*b* ca. 1650], of Dedham);
4–Dea. Jonathan (1717-96), Attleboro; minute man Am. Rev.; *m* 1744, Jemmima Mann (*b* 1722);
3–Lt. Pelatiah (1750-1821), Westminster; commd. for gallant service on Saratoga battlefield, Oct. 7, 1777; dined with Washington at his invitation, 1783; an original mem. S.C.; *m* Mary Cutting; *m* 2d, 1802, Dorcas Fessenden (1779-1840);
2–Leonard Fessenden (1809-1905), *m* 1832, Frelove Darling (1818-53), see Vol. III, p. 182, for Darling lineage and issue; *m* 2d, Hannah Hopkins Mann.
1–*m* June 12, 1870, Fannie Reid (July 12, 1844-Apr. 6, 1922); dau. of Thomas Reid; issue: 1–Jennie Augusta (1871-74); 2–Frances Isabelle (1874-1921), *m* June 24, 1902, Frederick Hall Beals (Nov. 26, 1873-1915), A.B., Harvard, '00, A.M., 1903; prof. Occidental Coll., 1906 (issue: Frances Elizabeth, *b* Oct. 4, 1905; Edward Everett, *b* Nov. 6, 1908); 3–Albert Leonard (1884-85).
1–Ed. in the schools of his native place and at Appleton Acad.; enlisted in the Spring of 1861, was in many great battles of the Civil War in Va.; wounded at Ball's Bluff, wounded and promoted (warrant officer) at 2d Fredericksburg; severely wounded in repulse of Pickett's charge at Gettysburg; offered a commission by Gov. Andrew. Teacher in employ of the Freedman's Bureau in S.C., 2 yrs.; much of his life engaged in merchantile pursuits at Boston and Worcester. Mem. of many humanitarian organizations, reaching the head of three and entering the Grand Lodges of two. Engaged for many yrs. in study of historical matter concerning his native town, its military records and its soldiers since 1725; wrote a history of his regt., and family histories. Mem. Soc. Cincinnati, Post Ten, Mass. Dept., G.A.R., Residence: West Boylston, Mass.

1–**EVERETT, Elizabeth Hawley (Mrs. Francis D.),** *b* Pekin, Ill., Aug. 23, 1857.
9–Joseph **Hawley** (qv);
8–Ephraim (1659-90), New Stratford, Conn.; *m* 1683, Sarah Welles (1664-94; Capt. Samuel[9], *m* Elizabeth, dau. of Lt. John Hollister, *m* Joanna, dau. of Richard Treat, qv; Gov. Thomas[10], qv);
7–Gideon (1687-1730), Bridgeport, Conn.; *m* 1711, Anna Bennett (1691-1727);
6–Sgt. James (1713-46), *m* 1733, Eunice Jackson (1714-96);
5–Maj. Aaron (1739-1803), Bridgeport; brigade maj. Am. Rev.; *m* 1759, Elizabeth Hawley;
4–Capt. Gideon (1763-1813), Ferrisburgh, Vt.; capt. War 1812, died of wounds sustained in war; *m* 1784, Lavina Darrow (ca. 1765-1845);
3–Gideon (*b* Ferrisburgh, Vt., 1797-*d* 1852), to Ill., 1818; *m* 1820, Elizabeth Caldwell (*b* Ky., 1802-*d* 1883; John K.[4]);
2–William C. (2 below).
10–Gov. Thomas **Welles** (qv);
9–Ann (*b* ca. 1619), *m* 1646, Thomas **Thompson**;
8–Mary (1653-91), *m* 1673, Samuel **Hawley** (1647-1734; Joseph[9], qv);
7–Dea. Thomas (1678-1722), Bridgeport; *m* 1701, Joanna Booth (1678-1761; Ephraim[8] [1648-83] of Stratford, *m* ca. 1674, Mary Clark; Richard[9], qv, *m* 1640, Elizabeth, sister of Joseph Hawley, qv);
6–Capt. Ezra (1711-73), Bridgeport; *m* 1735, Abigail Hall (1715-86);
5–Elizabeth (1737-76), *m* 1759, Maj. Aaron **Hawley** (5 above).

HAWLEY

Arms: Vert, a saltire, engrailed, argent.
Crest: A dexter arm in armour proper, garnished or, holding in the hand a spear, in bend sinister, point downward, proper.

8–Ens. Richard **Nason** (*d* 1696), was at Pipe Stave Landing, Kittery, Me., 1639; *m* Sarah Baker (?);
7–Jonathan (*d* 1691), Kittery, Me.; *m* Sarah Jenkins (Reynold[8]);
6–Jonathan (*d* 1746), Kittery; *m* 1702, Adah Morrell (John[7], *m* Sarah Hodsdon);
5–Azariah (1716-87), Kittery; *m* Abigail Staples (*b* 1720; James[6] [1678-1725], *m* 1701, Mary (*b* 1684), dau. of William Tetherly, *m* Mary Roby; Peter[7], had land grants in Kittery, 1671 and 1699, *m* Elizabeth–);
4–John (1751-1827), Dover, N.H.; *m* 1777, Rebecca Perkins (1753-1848);
3–Rev. Reuben (1779-1835), preceptor of Gorham (Me.) Acad., 1806-10, 1815-34; *m* 1807, Apphia Thacher (1785-1808); *m* 2d, 1813, Martha Coffin;
2–Mary S. (2 below).
9–John **Heard** (will dated 1675, probated Feb., 1676), in Kittery, Me., 1640; *m* Isabel–;
8–James (*d* ante Mar. 3, 1675), *m* Shuah–;
7–Capt. John (*b* ca. 1667), of Kittery; on Sunday, July 4, 1697, Indians attacked Capt. John and his wife and others who were returning from "the meeting house in the Parish of Unity, in the Precinct of Berwick, where they had attended divine service," his wife was wounded and fell from her horse, she begged him to leave her and save the children at home, he was wounded but escaped; his wife, Maj. Charles Frost and Dennis Downing were killed; *m* Phoebe–;
6–Shuah (*b* 1694), *m* 1714, Capt. Nathan **Bartlett** (1691-1775), of Kittery, Me.; see Vol. III, p. 181, for Bartlett lineage;
5–Shuah (1716-1803), *m* 1732, Dr. Edmund **Coffin** (1708-89), on alarm list at Kittery, Me., 1758; see Vol. III, for Coffin lineage;
4–James (1745-1830), Saco, Me.; part owner of a privateer which captured several prizes during Am. Rev.; later captured and was prisoner at Halifax until 1778; *m* 1768, Martha McLellan;
3–Martha (1786-1871), *m* Rev. Reuben **Nason** (3 above).
6–Robert **Patterson** (1671-1769), *b* Ireland of Scotch parentage; to America, 1718; resided Saco, Me.;
5–Mary, *m* James **McLellan** (1712-85), *b* Ireland of Scotch parentage; to America, 1729; resided Saco, Me.;
4–Martha (1745-1825), *m* James **Coffin** (4 above);
3–Martha, *m* Rev. Reuben **Nason** (3 above);
2–Mary Shuah (1829-1909), *m* 1854, William Caldwell **Hawley** (1830-1918); issue: I–Martha Nason (*b* 1855; *m* H. R. Angelo); II–Elizabeth (1 above); III–William Norman (*b* 1859; *m* 1882, Elisabeth Cartlidge; *m* 2d, 1913, Ella [Daniel] Potter); IV–George Appleton (1861-1911; *m* Harriet Gable); V–Gideon Leonard (*b* 1865; *m* Belle Storer); VI–Nathaniel Nason (*b* 1870; *m* Ida May Reynolds).

1–*m* Sept. 13, 1881, James A., son of Joseph Bowen; issue: 1–George Hawley Bowen (July 26, 1882-Jan. 13, 1926), *m* March 18, 1919, Merlda Beatrice Orr (issue: Elizabeth Orr Bowen, *b* June 1, 1922).
1–*m* 2d, Mar. 2, 1899, Francis Denison Everett.
1–Mem. D.F.P.A., D.A.R., Chicago Woman's Club, Ossoli Club of Highland Park, Woman's Nat. Republican Club. Presbyterian. Residence: 314 Linden Park Pl., Highland Park, Ill.

DR. MONT ROYAL FARRAR (1872-1929), of Greensboro, N.C.; M.D., U. of N.C., 1905; practiced in Greensboro, N.C., and Nashville, Tenn.; inventor; 1st lt. Med. Corps, U.S.A., 1917, promoted to capt., Oct. 9, 1918, hon. discharged Sept. 13, 1920; on duty at Ft. Moultrie, S.C., with Coast Arty., Jackson Barracks, La., Camp Wadsworth, S.C., Camp Dix, N.J., and Fox Hills, N.Y.; went overseas with 57th Pioneer Inf., served 1 yr.; later assigned to duty with aviation co.; was asked to make out promotion papers for maj. for untiring services going over on the "Leviathan"; received a medal for War Service from France, also medal from state of N.C. for honorable World War service, and Cross of Honor from Guilford Chapter N.C., U.D.C. as S.C.V.; m 1905, Annie Lawrence Pleasants (b 1874; John Landis [3] [1826-79], served in 4th Ala. Regt., Co. B, in C.S.A., m 1862, Cornelia Lawrence, 1836-1900).

1–**FARRAR, Martha David,** *b* Greensboro, N.C., Feb. 19, 1907.
11–William **Farrar** (1594-1637; son of Nicholas [1546-1620], *m* Mary Woodenoth, *d* 1635); came from Eng., 1618, settled in Va.; mem. Council, 1623-33; *m* Cicely (*d* 1623), widow of Capt. Samuel Jordan, of "Jordan's Journey";
10–Col. William (*d* 1677/78), burgess, 1659-61, 1676; *m* Mary–;
9–Maj. William (1657-1721), of "Farrar's Island," Henrico Co., Va.; burgess, 1700-02; *m* 1st, 1682, Priscilla Baugh (William[10], *m* Jane, widow of William Branch, she *m* 3d, Abel Gower);
8–William, of "Farrar's Island"; *m* 1724, Judith Jefferson (Thomas[9] [*d* 1731], of Henrico Co., *m* Mary, dau. of Peter Field [*d* 1709], burgess for Henrico Co., *m* Judith, widow of Henry Randolph, and dau. of Henry Soane, speaker, burgess, 1660-61);
7–Peterfield (1730-1802 or 03), *m* 1754, Mary Magdelene Chastain (Dr. Stephen[8], one of the Huguenot immigrants to Manakintown, *m* Martha Dupuy), widow of James Cocke, of "Malvern Hill";
6–John (1754-1806), of Mecklenburg Co., Va.; in Am. Rev.; bought 1,900 acres of land, 1788; *m* 1775, Rebecca Warthen;
5–Edward, *m* 1805 (?), Mary Minter;
4–William Minter (1807-56), *m* 1833, Julia Amy Bingham (1808-71; Robert[5] [1775-1855], *m* Amey–);

MARY ANNIE (FARRAR) WATSON (1818-77), dau. of Powell Farrar.

3–William Bingham (1836-98), served in Co. D, 35th Regt., C.S.A.; inventor; *m* 1864, Martha David Watson (1848-1913; Dr. David[4] [1794-1847], *m* 1843, Mary Annie Farrar, see portrait [1818-77; Powell[5], *m* 1804, Phebe, dau. of Jacob Utley, lt. Am. Rev., Wake Co., N.C.; John[6], 6 above]);
2–Dr. Mont Royal (1872-1929), of Greensboro, N.C.; see portrait and biography; *m* 1905, Annie Lawrence Pleasants (*b* 1874), B.L., Woman's Coll., Richmond, Va.; mem. Guilford Chapter U.D.C. (John Landis[3] [1826-79], served Co. B, 4th Ala. Regt., C.S.A., *m* 1862, Cornelia Lawrence [1836-1900], see portrait); issue: I–

CORNELIA (LAWRENCE) PLEASANTS (Aug. 30, 1836-July 13, 1900), m Sept. 14, 1862, John Landis Pleasants.

Martha David (1 above); II–Cornelia Lawrence (qv for Lawrence lineage).
1–A.B., N.C. Coll. for Women, '28. Taught in high sch., 1928-29; taught English in grammar sch., 1929-30. Mem. U.D.C., Alethian Soc. Baptist. Democrat. Summer place: Ridgecrest, N.C. Residence: 510 Ora St., Daytona Beach, Fla.

1–**FARRAR, Cornelia Lawrence,** *b* Greensboro, N.C., Oct. 12, 1912.
7–William **Lawrence** (1734-66), received a grant of 1,900 acres in Granville Co., N.C., 1756; *m* 1756, Deabora– (1740-91); issue: William, in Am. Rev., Abraham, John, James, Mary;
6–Abraham (1759-1838), of Granville Co., N.C.; in Am. Rev.; *m* 1781, Leannah Jones (1763-1840); issue: William, Anna, Abraham;
5–William (1784-1832), of Granville Co.; *m* 1805, Liddie Pruitt (1789-1839; John[6], in Am. Rev., *m* Susanna Twittie); issue: John Pruitt, Lucy, Betsy, Martha, William Twittie, Turner, Charaty;
4–Turner (1811-81), of Granville Co.; *m* 1835, Priscilla Upchurch (1818-93); issue: Cornelia, John, Samuel, Sylvesta, William;
3–Cornelia (1836-1900), see portrait; *m* 1862, John Landis **Pleasants** (1826-79); issue: Ava, Mary, Alice Leslie, John Stephen, Annie Lawrence;
2–Annie Lawrence (*b* 1874), *m* 1905, Mont Royal **Farrar** (1872-1929), see portrait and biography; issuè: I–Martha David (qv for Farrar lineage); II–Cornelia Lawrence (1 above).
1–Mem. Children's Chapter U.D.C. Baptist. Residence: 510 Ora St., Daytona Beach, Fla.

1–**EWART, Frank Carman,** *b* Marietta, O., Sept. 4, 1871.
8–George (Geer) **Gear** (qv);
7–Jonathan (1662-1742), petitioned Gen. Ct. for new town of Preston, Conn.; *m* 1st, Mary– (*d* 1718);
6–Jonathan (1694-1750), of Preston; *m* 1st, 1721, Elizabeth Herrick (1702-44; Ephraim[7] [*b* 1664], removed to Preston, *m* Judith Woodbury; Ephraim[8] [1638-93], of Beverly, Mass., *m* Mary Cross, of Salem; Henry[9], qv);
5–Samuel (1731-65), *m* 1st, 1753, Esther Cornwall;
4–George (1760-1829), in Am. Rev.; settled at Middletown, Conn.; *m* 2d, 1799, Olive Arnold (1768-1844);
3–Hiram (1804-43), Bapt. minister of Middletown, later at Marietta, O.; *m* 1832, Jerusha Sage;
2–Jerusha Ann (2 below).
8–William **Cornwall** (*d* 1678), from Eng., settled at Middletown; *m* Joan–; *m* 2d, Mary–;
7–Samuel (1642-1728), of Middletown; *m* 1667, Rebecca Bull (*b* 1644; William[8], of Cambridge);
6–Samuel (bap. 1679-1730), *m* 1713, Phebe Hall (Samuel[7], of Middletown);
5–Esther (1726-ante 1761), *m* 2d, 1753, Samuel **Gear** (5 above).
8–David **Sage** (qv);
7–Timothy (1678-1725), *m* Margaret Holibert or Hurlbut (*b* 1684/85; Sgt. John[8], large landowner, Middletown, *m* 1670, Mary, dau. John Deming; Thomas[9], qv);
6–Amos (1722-59), *m* Rebecca Wilcox;
5–Elisha (1755-1801), of Upper Middletown (now Cromwell), Conn.; in Am. Rev.; *m* 1776, Martha Montague (their son, Elisha, was father of Russell Sage, financier);
4–Rufus (1777-1826), *m* Jerusha Butler;
3–Jerusha (*b* 1806), *m* Rev. Hiram **Gear** (3 above).
9–Richard **Montague** (qv);
8–John (ca. 1655-ca. 1732), of Wethersfield, Conn.; settled at Hadley, Mass.; *m* 1681, Hannah Smith (*b* 1662; Chileab[9] [*d* 1731, aet. 96], of Hadley, *m* Hannah [*d* 1733, aet. 88], dau. Luke Hitchcock, *m* Elizabeth Gibbons);
7–Richard (1684-1751), removed to Wethersfield; *m* 1715, Abigail Camp (*d* 1753, aet. 62);
6–John (*b* 1722), *m* 1750, Anna Belden (*d* 1815, aet. 94);
5–Martha (1754-1839), *m* Elisha **Sage** (5 above).
2–Jerusha Ann Gear (1833-1919), *m* 1855, Judge Thomas West **Ewart** (see Vol. III, p. 175, for Ewart lineage and issue).
1–*m* Aug. 22, 1894, Nettie Luella McVeigh, *b* Hooksburg, O., Apr. 15, 1872; dau. of George W. McVeigh, of McConnelsville, O.; issue: 1–Brainard Gilliam (Feb. 5, 1899-*d* in infancy); 2–Beatrice Marie, *b* Hamilton, N.Y., Oct. 15, 1903; Denison U., '27; 3–Donald McVeigh (Apr. 10, 1907-*d* in infancy).
1–A.B., Denison U., '92 (Kappa Delta Rho, Phi Beta Kappa), A.M., 1894 (L.H.D., 1919); studied at U. of Chicago, U. of Heidelberg (Germany), U. of Grenoble (France), U. of Havana (Cuba), Curso de Vacaciones (Madrid). Prof. Romance languages, Colgate U., since 1904. Author: Cuba y las Costumbres Cubanas, 1919. Annotated Rostand's L'Aiglon, 1904 (see Who's Who in America). Mem. I.A.G. Residence: Hamilton, N.Y.

1–**FARNHAM, Dwight Thompson,** *b* Candor, N.Y., Oct. 15, 1881.
11–Ralph (Farnum) **Farnham** (qv);
10–Ralph (*b* Eng., 1633), *m* 1650, Elizabeth Hall (Nicholas[11]);
9–Ralph (*b* Andover, Mass.), *m* Sarah Sterling (William[10], of Andover);
8–William (*b* Andover, 1693), to Windham, Conn.; *m* Anna Flint, of Salem, Mass.;
7–Zebediah (1721-1814), 1st lt., 6th Co., 8th Regt., from Windham and New London cos., Conn.; also 1st lt., 17th Regt. and of the marines in naval service on the "Providence," 1780; served in battle of L.I.; *m* Mary Fuller (*d* 1802; Stephen[8]); their son Levi also *d* on bd. prison ship;
6–Ebenezer (1750-*d* on bd. prison ship), in Am. Rev., 1778; served in R.I. 2 mos.; taken prisoner by British; *m* 1773, Joanna Benjamin (*d* 1836);
5–Joel (1774-1858), *m* 1797, Ruth Slosson (1777-1862);
4–Sylvester (1798-1873), *m* 1820, Patience Wood;
3–Enos Slosson (1825-95), of Owego, N.Y.; *m* 1849, Clarissa Venina Dwight (1822-97; Elijah[4] [*b* 1797]; Solomon[5]; Joseph, Jr.[6], of Great Barrington, Mass., *m* Mary Pynchon; Gen. Joseph[7]; Capt Henry[8], of Hatfield, Mass.);
2–LeRoy Dwight (2 below).
10–Myles **Standish,** Mayflower Pilgrim (qv);
9–Alexander (1627-1702), of Duxbury, Mass.; *m* Sarah Alden (1629-87; John[10], Mayflower Pilgrim, qv);
8–Ebenezer (1672-1734 or 55), of Plympton, Mass.; *m* 1697, Hannah Sturdivant (1679-1759);
7–Moses (1701-69), of Plympton; *m* 1723, Rachel Cobb (1702-69; John[8], *m* Rachel Soule, g.dau. George Soule, Mayflower Pilgrim, qv);
6–Sarah (1734-1821), *m* 1757, Ephraim **Tinkham** (1733-69);
5–Sarah Standish (1763-1821), *m* 1785, Peter **Wood** (*b* Middleborough, Mass., 1749-1829), settled at Owego, N.Y., 1847 (Edmond[6]; David[7]; David[8]; Henry[9], of Plymouth);
4–Patience (*b* 1791), *m* Sylvester **Farnham** (4 above).
9–Thomas **Thompson** (1617-55), from Eng. to Amercia, 1635; *m* Ann Welles (Thomas[10], of Conn.);
8–Thomas (1651-1705), *m* Elizabeth Smith;
7–Daniel, *m* 1727, Sarah Bronson;
6–Eleazer (*b* 1731), *m* Esther Hamilton;
5–Daniel (1758-99), *m* Lydia Mills (Peter[6], of Windsor, Conn.);
4–Austin (1794-1881), *m* Abigail Hallock;
3–Jerome (1822-92), *m* Miriam McCarty;
2–Coralyn (*b* 1851), *m* 1878, LeRoy Dwight **Farnham** (1850-1916), physician and surgeon.
1–*m* June 10, 1910, Mateel Howe, *b* Atchison, Kan., dau. of Edgar Watson Howe, of Atchison.
1–A.B.., Yale, '04. Cons. engr. in industrial and financial work in New York, since 1920. Author and lecturer (see Who's Who in America). Studied conditions in Europe, 1914; served as spl. engr. for Emergency Fleet Corpn. and Ordnance Dept., U.S.A., during World War, 1916-20; again studied conditions in Europe, 1920. Dir. Am. Management Assn.; mem. S.M.D., Am. Soc. M.E., Soc. Industrial Engrs., Am. Ceramic Soc., etc. Republican. Episcopalian. Clubs: Bankers, Nat. Arts, Yale, Westport Country, Fairfield Country Hunt. Summer place: Westport, Conn. Residence: 5 Gramercy Park, New York, N.Y.

1–**FARRAR, Thomas James,** *b* Oak Springs, Fluvanna Co., Virginia, Apr. 17, 1869.
9–Capt. William **Farrar** (*d* 1637), from Yorkshire, Eng., settled at Jamestown; distinguished mem. of the Va. Colony;
8–Col. William (*d* 1678), of Dutch Gap, and Henrico Co.; justice of the peace, burgess; *m* Mary–;

7–Thomas (1665-1742), of Dutch Gap, and Henrico Co.; m Katherine Perrin;
6–William (d 1744), m Sarah–;
5–Perrin, removed to Goochland, later to Louisa Co.;
4–Matthew, of Louisa Co.;
3–Garland (1801-81), of Fluvanna Co., Va.; m Mary L. Shepherd;
2–Thomas James (2 below).
10–John **Rolfe** (qv);
9–Thomas (b 1615), officer in Indian wars; maintained colonial forts for which he was honored with special grants and privileges by the colony; m Jane Poythress;
8–Jane (d 1676), m 1675, Col. Robert **Bolling** (qv);
7–Col. John (1676-1729), of Buckingham Co.; burgess; m 1697, Mary Kennon (Col. Richard[8], of Conjuror's Neck, Va., burgess, m Elizabeth Worsham);
6–Maj. John (1700-59), of Buckingham Co.; justice, burgess; head magistrate of Chesterfield Co.; m 2d, 1728, Elizabeth Blair (Dr. Archibald[7], from Scotland);
5–Col. Archibald (1750-1829), of Buckingham Co.; m 1774, Mary (or Jane) Randolph;
4–Sarah, m 1792, Joseph Cabell **Megginson** (1771-94), of Nelson Co.;
3–William Cabell (1794-1847), of Nelson Co.; m 1821, Amanda M. Bocock (b 1807; sister of Thomas S. Bocock, M.C., and speaker of Confed. House of Representatives);
2–Maria Louise (1836-1925), m 1868, Thomas James **Farrar** (1832-68), served in C.S.A.
1–m Dec. 28, 1899, Margaret Lynn Harris, b "Oakwood," Albemarle Co., Va., Mar. 25, 1870; dau. of William Henry Harris, of Covesville, Albemarle Co., Va., m Harriet Washington Towles.
1–A.B., Washington and Lee U., '95, M.A., 1897, Ph.D., 1901 (Delta Tau Delta, Pi Delta Epsilon); studied Goettingen, Ger., 1906, Paris, 1908. Grad. instructor, Washington and Lee, 1895-99; asst. principal, Donald Fraser Sch., Decatur, Ga., 1899-1901; principal, Presbyn. Inst., Blackshear, Ga., 1901-02; prof. English, Agnes Scott Coll., Decatur, Ga., 1902-05; prof. modern languages, Washington and Lee, 1905-10; prof. Germanic languages, ibid., since 1910. Author (See Who's Who in America). Mem. S.A.R., S.C.V. Clubs: University, Rotary. Presbyn. Democrat. Residence: Lexington, Va.

1–**FARROWS, Lucy Mills**, b Thompson, Conn., May 5, 1898.
6–John **Farrows**;
5–Ebenezer (1781-1858), of Scituate, Mass.; m Clarissa Paine (1777-1854);
4–Paine (1814-89), of Thompson, Conn.; m 1840, Mary Briggs (b 1816; John[6] [1786-1851], m Elizabeth, dau. of John Gallup; William[6]; Noah[7]; William[8]);
3–Albert (1841-1908), of W. Thompson, Conn.; m 1863, Lucy Alton Elliott;
2–Olin Dyer (2 below).
9–John **Nichols** (1640-1700), of Danvers, Mass.; m Lydia–;
8–Anna (or Abigail), m at Salem, Mass., 1686, Francis **Elliott**, mariner;
7–Thomas, m 1723, Lucy Flint (John[8] [b 1655], m ca. 1678, Elizabeth–; Thomas[9], qv);
6–Francis (b 1724), m 1749, Phebe Berry (b 1732);
5–John (b 1757), Am. Rev.;
4–Dyer Nichols (b 1797), m 1823, Eliza Greene;
3–Lucy Alton (1842-1921), m Albert **Farrows** (3 above).
10–Thomas **Greene** (qv);
9–Henry (1638-1717), of Malden; m 1671, Esther Hasse (1649-1747);
8–Henry (b 1672), of Malden and Charlestown; m 1695, Hannah Flagg (b 1675; Gershom[9], of Woburn, m Hannah Leffingwell);
7–Henry (b 1696), m 1721, Judith Guile (b 1700; Ephraim[8] [b 1662], of Amesbury, Mass., m Martha, dau. of Daniel Bradley; Samuel[9], m 1647, Judith, dau. of James Davis);
6–Capt. John (1736-1803), of Thompson, Conn.; m 1759, Abilene Guile (b 1734; Ephraim[7] [b 1705], m 1730, Abigail Converse);
5–Benjamin (1766-1846), m 2d, Esther Jewett;
4–Eliza (1802-84), m Dyer Nichols **Elliott** (4 above).
10–William **Jewett**;
9–John (b ca. 1643), m Elizabeth–;
8–Isaac, of Ipswich, Mass.; m 1695, Dorcas Hovey (John[9], m Dorcas Ivory; Daniel[10]);
7–David (bap. 1707/08), of Rowley, Mass., and Thompson, Conn.; m 1734, Sarah Stevens;
6–Lt. Joseph (1743-1802), m 1766, Rachel Nichols (1749-1839; Jonathan[7] [b 1703], m 1731, Mary Phelps; Thomas[8]; John[9]; William[10], b 1599);
5–Esther (b 1769), m Benjamin **Greene** (5 above).
10–John **Mills** (qv);
9–John (bap. 1632-1694), m 1653, Elizabeth Shaw or Shove;
8–John (1660-1722), of Braintree, Mass., and Woodstock, Conn.; m Hannah–;
7–Nathaniel (1710-87), m 1742, Sarah Holmes (1708-99; James[8] [1662-1743], m 1684, Jane–; David[9], of Eng., m 1658, Jane–);
6–Nathaniel (1743-1814), of Dudley, Mass.; soldier Am. Rev.; m 1762, Sally Corbin (1740-99; James[7] [b 1702], of Dudley, m 1739, Sarah Hele; James[8]; Clement[9]; John[10]);
5–John (1770-1861), m 1794, Lucina Whipple;
4–Rowland (1796-1874), m 1818, Mary Griggs (1798-1863; Benjamin[5] [1767-1831], m 1st, 1792, Sela, dau. of John Howe; Ens. Stephen[6]; Solomon[7]; Benjamin[8]; Joshua[9]; Thomas[10]);
3–Rowland (1827-1902), of Thompson, Conn.; m 1864, Angeline (Button) Pray (Hiram Button[4] [1807-62], m 1832, Catherine [1817-1900], dau. of Benjamin Weeks; Eli[5]);
2–Fannie (2 below).
9–Capt. John **Whipple** (qv);
8–Benjamin (1654-1704), m 1686, at Providence, R.I., Ruth Mathewson (James[9] [d 1682], m Hannah Field);
7–Benjamin (1688-1788), of Providence, R.I.; m 1734, Esther Miller (b 1683; Samuel[8], m 1682, Hester, dau. of Richard Bowen; John[9]);
6–Sgt. Jesse (1744-1824), of Providence; m 1770, Freelove Olney (1749-1807; James[7], m 1732, Hannah, dau. of Rev. Samuel Winsor; Epenetus[8]; Epenetus[9]; Thomas[10], qv);
5–Lucina (1774-1869), m John **Mills** (5 above).
2–Fannie Mills (b 1871), m 1893, Olin Dyer **Farrows** (b 1868), of Putnam, Conn.; issue: I–Ella (b 1894; m 1927, Joseph Powell); II–Lucy M. (1 above); III–Bertha (b 1899; m 1924, Clyde Miller, b 1901); IV–Albert E. (b 1903; m 1927, Bessie Mae Jarvis).
1–Grad. Putnam H.S. Teacher, Putnam, Conn., 14 yrs. Mem. D.A.R.; pres. P.T.A. Club: Sunnyside. Residence: 232 Woodstock Av., Putnam, Conn.

1–**FAUCETTE, William Dollison**, b Halifax, N.C., June 27, 1881.
3–William Douglas **Faucette** (d 1871), m 1847, Josephine Rebecca Wilkinson (b 1828; Richard[4], of Richmond, Va., m Amelia Bennett);
2–Charles William (2 below).
5–Bennet E. **Dickens**, of Md.; m Hannah Lovell;
4–Bennet E. (d 1872), m Nancy–;
3–Isaac Faulcon (1836-July 15, 1863), sgt., Co. K, 1st N.C. Inf., C.S.A.; killed in battle of Winchester, Va.; m 1858, Louisa Elizabeth Browning;
2–Florence Relinda (2 below).
6–Drewry **Gee** (ante 1748-1786), del. to Hillsboro Conv., 1775, to Halifax Conv., 1776; mem. Gen. Assembly, from Northampton Co., 1783; lt. col., Northampton troops in Am. Rev.; m Mary Atherton;
5–Boyce, m Jesse **Dupree** (d 1822), ens., Brunswick Co., Va., troops in Am. Rev., 1777;
4–Sallie Gee (1795-1867), m 1817, Elisha **Browning** (1785-1848; Levi[5], of Southampton Co., Va., in Am. Rev., m Margaret Purnell);
3–Louisa Elizabeth (b 1836), m Isaac Faulcon **Dickens** (3 above);
2–Florence Relinda (b 1859), m 1880, Charles William **Faucette** (1857-85); m 2d, 1904, Willis Alston Willcox (b 1861).
1–m Nov. 11, 1908, Belle Edwards Nash (qv); issue (all b Portsmouth, Va.): 1–Ellen Nash, b July 15, 1910; Randolph-Macon Coll., class of 1931; 2–Florence Willcox, b Mar. 21, 1913; 3–Belle Dollison, b Mar. 24, 1921.
1–B.E., N.C. State Coll., '01 (P.B.K.), C.E., 1910; (D.Sc., N.C. State Coll., 1929). Chief engr., Seaboard Air Line Ry. System since 1913 (see Who's Who in America). Mem. Am. Ry. Engring. Assn. (pres. 1928-29, Am. Soc. C.E., Am. Soc. Mil. Engrs., Am. Inst. Weights and

Measures, etc. Trustee N.C. State Coll. Mason. Democrat. Clubs: Oglethorpe, Rotary. Residence: 101 E. 34th St., Savannah, Ga.

1–**FAUCETTE, Belle Edwards Nash (Mrs. William D.),** *b* Portsmouth, Va., Oct. 28, 1883.
9–(?) Thomas **Nash,** from Wales with his wife and three children, to Norfolk, Va., 1661; settled on Western Branch; later on Southern Branch; and thru;
5–Cornelius (1776-1827), *m* Susan– (1771-1827);
4–John (1805-84), *m* 1st, Elizabeth Edwards (1810-39; Thomas[5], *m* Mary, dau. Thomas Watts);
3–Thomas Cornelius (1830-81), *m* 1853, Sophie Benson (1829-67; John[4], *m* Dolly Foster; Francis[5], *m* Sophie Butt);
2–Thomas Edwards (2 below).
5–Abraham **Watts** (1781-1830), of Portsmouth, Va.; *m* Mary Ann Smith (1783-1845);
4–George (1804-41), *m* 1st, Sarah Tucker Gaskins, of Princess Anne, Va.;
3–Abraham Smith (1832-1905), *m* Sarah Monrovia Bain;
2–Ellen Bain (2 below).
7–James **Bain,** from Scotland to Western Branch, Va.; *m* Anne Britton; and thru either:
6–William, Charles, or Robert;
5–James Britton (1772-1822), of Portsmouth, Va.; *m* 1792, Dikey Donevan (1775-1855; Timothy[6], of Ireland, *m* Phelia Hodges);
4–David Augustus Kay (1813-66), *m* 1st, Elizabeth Miles Chisman, of York Co., Va.;
3–Sarah Monrovia (1838-1914), *m* Abraham Smith **Watts** (3 above);
2–Ellen Bain (*b* 1859), *m* 1882, Thomas Edwards **Nash** (*b* 1859), of Portsmouth; issue: I–Belle Edwards (1 above); II–Thomas Lewis (*b* 1891; lt. cdr. U.S.N.; *m* Lucy Elizabeth Nelson), and III–Wilder Watts, twins (1891-92); IV–Sarah Elsie (*b* 1893).
1–*m* Nov. 11, 1908, William Dollison Faucette (qv for issue).
1–Mem. Froebel Circle, Telfair Art Acad., Mary McLean Soc. Residence: 101 E. 34th St., Savannah, Ga.

1–**FAULKNER, William Scott,** *b* Cobb Co., Ga., June 25, 1866-*d* Alameda, Calif., July 2, 1928.
5–Jeremiah **Robinson** (*b* 1745), in Am. Rev.;
4–Jane (*b* ca. 1790), *m* Samuel **Scott** (*d* 1847), from Scotland; settled at Powder Springs, Ga.; moved to Va., to Abbeville Dist., S.C., thence to Cobb Co., Ga.;
3–Jeremiah Robinson (1806-90), *m* 1830, Elizabeth Smith (1806-92; John[4], *m* Miss Anderson);
2–Elizabeth Jane (1836-1901), *m* Cobb Co., Ga., 1854, Thomas Peatry **Faulkner** (1834-1905), sgt., 2d Co. F, 1st Ga. Inf., C.S.A., enlisted 1862, and on muster roll until Aug., 1864, when he was taken prisoner at Chattanooga, Tenn.
1–*m* June 17, 1896, Anna Amelia Kirk (qv for issue).

1–**FAULKNER, Anna Amelia Kirk (Mrs. William S.),** *b* Jacksonville, Ala., Feb. 6, 1871-*d*.
6–Matthew **Edmiston** (ca. 1710-1795), from Scotland, settled in Augusta and Rockbridge cos., Va.; constable, Augusta Co., 1756; cornet, 1752, colonial militia; *m* Margaret–;
5–Agnes (ca. 1733-1765), of Augusta Co.; *m* 1750, as his 1st wife, James **Kirk** (1720-83);
4–Matthew (1760-1837), *m* 1787, Grace Johnston (1769-1858);
3–James Johnston (1794-1857), *m* 1820, Jane Walker;
2–Rev. William Robert (2 below).
5–Alexander **Walker** (*d* 1775), from Ireland, settled in Augusta Co.; *m* Elizabeth–;
4–Capt. Andrew (1756-1845), of Mecklenburg Co., N.C.; enlisted in Capt. William Hagen's Co., 1775, reenlisted in 1781, serving as q.m. under Gen. Davidson; commd. capt., 1781; *m* 1795, Elizabeth Moore;
3–Jane (ca. 1796-1835), *m* James Johnston **Kirk** (3 above).
6–Samuel **Freeman** (ca. 1715-1796), settled in N.C.; mem. Com. of Safety, Surry Co., N.C., 1775; *m* ca. 1740, Elizabeth Alexander (ca. 1720-post 1796);
5–Joshua (*b* ca. 1745), furnished supplies in Am. Rev.; served in War 1812, from Tenn.; *m* Lucy–;
4–Temperance (1776-post 1815), *m* ca. 1790, Reuben **Grant** (ca. 1750-1809), in Am. Rev., from Salisbury Dist.; ens., lt., 1776 (James[5] [1723-1805], mem. Com. of Safety, Salisbury Dist., Caswell Co., N.C., 1776, *m* ca. 1741, Ann–, ca. 1724-1808);
3–James Freeman (1808-78), *m* 1834, Elizabeth LeFevre Riley;
2–Margaret Leonora (2 below).
7–Isaac **LeFevre** (ca. 1667-ante 1720), French Huguenot; came to Manakin, Va., 1699; *m* Madeleine Parantos (*d* 1720);
6–Abram (ca. 1710-ca. 1797), *m* Catharine– (*d* ca. 1797);
5–Elizabeth (ca. 1765-post 1804), *m* John (?) **Orr** (ca. 1730-1804), of Washington Co., Va.;
4–Margaret (Peggy) (1794-1858), *m* 1816, Charles **Riley** (1793-1861), in War 1812;
3–Elizabeth LeFevre (1818-84), *m* James Freeman **Grant** (3 above);
2–Margaret Leonora (1838-1917), *m* 1866, William Robert **Kirk** (1834-93), Meth. ministry; issue: I–Anna Amelia (1 above); II–Ida (*b* 1874; *m* 1913, Clinton R. Bowen); III–Leonora Price (*b* 1877); IV–Grace Grant (*b* 1880; *m* 1912, Irwin D. McCray).
1–*m* June 17, 1896, William Scott Faulkner (qv); issue: 1–Emmet Kirk (1897-98); 2–Paul Pelham, *b* Americus, Ga., June 13, 1898; pvt., 16th Field Hosp., 2d Div., World War, July 1918-Aug. 1919; with Army of Occupation, July 1919; *m* Aug. 27, 1920, Helen Gertrude, dau. of Herbert A. Page, of Alameda, Calif., *m* Laura Peck (issue: Barbara Page, *b* May 28, 1921; Elizabeth Jane, *b* Sept. 14, 1922); 3–Annette, *b* Atlanta, Ga., Jan. 3, 1901; U.Calif.; 4–Jerome Keith, *b* Vincent, Ala., Dec. 3, 1902; U.Calif.; 5–Grace, *b* Birmingham, Ala., Aug. 24, 1904; U. Calif.; *m* July 21, 1928, Robert Ashley, son of Dr. J.D. Hill, of San Francisco; 6–William Cooke, *b* San Francisco, Calif., Mar. 24, 1906.
1–Mem. D.A.R. (chapter hist., 1922-24), U.D.C., U.S.D. 1812. S.C. Huguenot Soc., Huguenot Soc. Founders of Manakin in the Colony of Va. (nat. sec., 1922-27). Address: Mrs. Irwin D. McCray, 3549 Lakeshore Av., Oakland, Calif.

1–**FENGAR, Elsie Clay,** *b* New Bedford, Mass., July 3, 1887.
12–Elder William **Brewster,** Mayflower Pilgrim (qv);
11–Jonathan (1593-1659), of Plymouth, Duxbury, Mass., and New London, Conn.; rep. from Duxbury; mem. Miles Standish Mil. Co.; asst. to Gov. Winthrop, of Conn. Colony, 1657; *m* 1624, Lucretia Oldham (*d* 1678/79);
10–Ruth (1631-77), of New London, Conn.; *m* 1651, John **Picket** (*d* at sea, 1667), wealthy merchant of New London; sea capt.;
9–Mary (1660-1734), of New London; *m* 1672, Benjamin **Shapley** (1645-1706), mariner (Nicholas[10], of Charlestown, Mass.; Alexander[11], qv);
8–Mary (1677-1719), of New London; *m* 1701, Joseph **Truman** (Joseph[9]);
7–Elizabeth (1704-84), of New London; *m* 1725, John **Griffing** (1703-52; Sgt. Ebenezer[8], *m* Widow Mary Hubbell, dau. of Gabriel Harris);
6–John (1726-1801), of New London; marine in Am. Rev., on the "Oliver Cromwell"; *m* 1750, Mary Rogers (1728-99);
5–James (*b* 1751), of New London; *m* Hannah Strickland;
4–Frances (1797-1863), of New London; *m* 1817, Joseph **Miner** (1793-1845; Joseph[5], *m* Olive Prentis);
3–Olive Prentis (1830-87), of New London; *m* 1849, Richard **Fengar** (1824-99);
2–Cyrus B. (1863-1919), of New London; grad. Coast Guard Acad., '86; naval officer in World War; *m* 1886, Alice R. Clay (*b* 1867); issue: I–Elsie Clay (1 above); II–Marion F. (*b* 1891; *m* Duncan Belcher); III–Hazel F. (*b* 1894; *m* Harry Coyle); IV–Henry Clay (*b* 1897; *m* Gladys Thor).
1–Ed. Lasell Sem., Auburndale, Mass. Mem. S.M.D., D.A.R., I.A.G., Griswold Family Assn. Residence: 27 Post Hill Pl., New London, Conn.

1–**FERGUSSON, Alexander Cuthill,** *b* Philadelphia, Pa., May 31, 1874.
8–Anthony **Morris** (qv);
7–Anthony (1681-1763), came with his father; settled at Phila.; mem. Pa. Assembly, 2 yrs.;

alderman; mayor of Phila., 1738; asso. justice City Ct.; founder of Pa. Hosp.; his house on 2d St. still standing; *m* 1704, Phoebe Guest (George[8], from Eng. to Phila., 1681, lived in cave until house could be built, *m* Alice–);
6–John (*b* 1709), received "Spring Mill," or "Mt. Joy," from his father-in-law, 1739; mill still standing; *m* 1734, Mary Sutton (Richard[7], of Phila., *m* Mary–);
5–William (1735-66), mem. Colony in Schuylkill, 1761; mcht., Phila.; *m* 1758, Margaret Hill;
4–Richard Hill (1762-1841), justice; judge Ct. Common Pleas, Chester Co., 1786, also of Delaware Co., Pa., 1789; later at Burlington; *m* 1798, Mary Smith;
3–Edmund (1804-74), editor Bucks Co. Intelligencer, Doylestown, Pa.; removed to Phila.; editor of several journals and newspapers; started custom of selling newspapers on street; later editor at Trenton, 1855-56; founder of Beverly; corr. for N.Y. Tribune during Civil War; *m* 1827, Mary Palmer Jenks;
2–Mary Ann (2 below).
8–Richard **Hill,** sea capt.; in Md., 1673; received grant of 150 acres on Eastern Shore, from Lord Baltimore, 1673;
7–Henry, *m* Mary Denwood (Levin[8]);
6–Dr. Richard (*b* 1698), physician, South River; removed to Madeira; became interested in wine trade, 1739; returned to Phila., 1757; *m* 1721, Deborah Moore (1705-57; Dr. Mordecai[7], of Hill's Pt., Annapolis, Md., justice, *m* Deborah, dau. Thomas Lloyd, qv);
5–Margaret (1737-1816), wrote diary of Am. Rev. experiences; *m* William **Morris** (5 above).
9–Richard **Smith** (*d* 1688), propr. of N.J.; did not come to America; six of seven sons came to N.J.; Quaker, imprisoned in York Castle because of religious views; *m* Anne Yates (*d* 1688), also imprisoned in York Castle; estates confiscated by crown;
8–Samuel (1672-1817), had grant in N.J., 1702; Quaker; rep. Burlington Assembly, N.J., 1709,16; *m* 1st, 1698, Elizabeth Lovett (Edmond[9], of Chester, settled at Falls, Bucks Co., mem. Assembly);
7–Richard (1699-1751), of "Green Hill," country home still standing; mem. N.J. Assembly, 1732-51; trader and vessel owner, his wharf site now occupied by Burlington Club; *m* 1719, Abigail Rapier (Hon. Thomas[8], from Eng.);
6–Samuel (*b* 1720), historian; mem. and sec. King's Council, 1751-55; treas. Province of N.J.; *m* 1741, Jane Kirkbride (Joseph[7], justice of peace, 9 yrs., mem. Pa. Assembly, 13 yrs., *m* 3d, Mary, dau. Robert Fletcher, Quaker, Abington, N.J., widow of Enoch Yardley);
5–Richard S. (*b* 1752), mcht. of Phila.; summer residence, Moorestown; *m* 1775, Hannah Burling (1755-1840; Samuel[6], of New York, *m* Jane, dau. Ebenezer Large, Quaker, Burlington, *m* Dorothy, dau. Abraham Bickley);
4–Mary (1778-1848), *m* Richard Hill **Morris** (4 above).
6–Thomas **Jenks** (*d* 1799; son of Thomas, of Wales, *d* just prior to voyage to America, *m* Susan–); came with mother, 1723; settled at Wrightstown, Bucks Co., Pa.; Quaker; mill owner; *m* 1731, Mercy Wildman;
5–Joseph, miller, Bucks Co.; *m* 1763, Elizabeth Pearson (William[6], *m* Elizabeth–);
4–William, of Bridgetown; inherited estate with grist mill on Nechaminy Creek; *m* 1790, Mary Hutchinson (Michael[5], *m* Margery Palmer; John[6], *m* Phebe, dau. Joseph Kirkbride, 7 above, *m* 1st, Phebe Blackshire);
3–Mary Palmer (1804-75), *m* Edmund **Morris** (3 above):
2–Mary Ann (1840-1905), *m* 1863, Alexander Cuthill **Fergusson** (1839-1923), came from Ayr, Scotland, 1855; settled at Phila., Pa.; issue: I–Edmund Morris (*b* 1864; *m* 1898, Mary Fry Huber); II–Agnes McCall (*b* 1866; *m* 1893, Charles Edwin Noblit); III–Henry Alexander (1869-1911; *m* 1892, Jessie May Dysart); IV–Mary Morris (1871-76); V–Alexander C. (1 above); VI–Helen (*b* 1878; *m* 1908, George Albert Learned).
1–*m* Dec. 4, 1895, Linda Wilson Cook (Feb. 8, 1877-Sept. 25, 1911), dau. of William Henry Cook, of Phila., *m* Augusta Wilson; issue: 1–Augusta Margory (Sept. 11-30, 1896).
1–*m* 2d, Nov. 26, 1912, Mabel Marguerite Carter, *b* Phila., Mar. 28, 1883; dau. of Thomas H. Carter, of Phila.; issue (all *b* Edgewater Park, N.J.): 1–Angeline Carter, *b* June 23, 1914; 2–Margery Morris, *b* Aug. 24, 1917; 3–Alexander Carter, *b* Sept. 26, 1922.
1–Ed. Rittenhouse Acad., Phila. Entered Fergusson Bros., 1892 (chemical importing and jobbing business, continued as Alex. C. Fergusson Co., 1914–). Mem. Phila. Bd. of Trade. Mem. B.O.R. (surety). Clubs: St. Andrew Soc. (past pres.), Chemical (past pres.), Phila. Drug Exchange (dir.), Phila. Paint and Varnish, Mendian (past pres.), Union League, Riverton Country, Red Dragon Canoe. Kiwanis (past pres.). Residence: Edgewater Park, N.J.

1–**FERGUSSON, Sterling Price,** *b* Dixon's Springs, Tenn., Nov. 8, 1868.
4–Duncan **Fergusson** (1767-1808), from Scotland; settled nr. Waynesboro, N.C., 1793; *m* 1793(?), Isabella MacNabb (1767-1829);
3–Adam (1796-1862), *m* 1829, Hester Ann Hazard;
2–William Wallace (2 below).
4–Lot **Hazard** (1782-1862), of Carthage, Tenn.; *m* Tabitha Dixon Tunstall;
3–Hester Ann (1813-76), *m* Adam **Fergusson** (3 above);
2–William Wallace (1831-1922), atty.; served in engr. corps, C.S.A., on staff of Gen. W. B. Bate, 1861-65; *m* 1866, Medora Catherine Kerby (1846-1921; Frank[3], of Rome, Tenn.); issue: I–Sterling Price (1 above); II–Willard H. (*b* 1872; *m* 1900, Betty Temple); III–Frank K. (*b* 1874; *m* 1922, Ocie Hardesty Shepard); IV–Marina C. (*b* 1877; *m* A. J. McGaughey); V–Nina M. (*b* 1881); VI–Linton S. (*b* 1883; *m* Tabitha Dixon Martin); VII–Charles M. (*b* 1887; *m* 1915, Sadie Davis).
1–*m* Sept. 5, 1903, Carrie Milton Tucker, *b* Milton, Mass., July 5, 1875; dau. of Stephen A. Tucker, of Milton.
1–Ed. Haywood Acad., Riddleton, Tenn. Meteorologist, U.S. Weather Bureau since 1916. (See Who's Who in America). Fellow A.A.-A.S., Am. Meteorol. Soc.; mem. Boston Scientific Soc., Philos. Soc. of Washington, Appalachian Mtn. Club, Explorers Club. Mason. Unitarian. Democrat. Residence: 1329 Fairmont St. N.W., Washington, D.C.

1–**FERRIN, Augustin William,** *b* Little Valley, N.Y., Sept. 1, 1875.
7–Lt. Jonathan **Ferrin,** from Eng. to Amesbury, Mass., ca. 1699; in colonial wars; settled at Hebron, N.H.; *m* 1719, Sarah Wells (Titus[8]; Rev. Thomas[9], 1st settled minister at Amesbury, hon. B.A., Harvard U., 1703);
6–Enoch;
5–Enos (1749-1811), pvt. from Weare, N.H., in Am. Rev.; served at Cambridge, Mass., 1775; *m* Mary Currier;
4–Ebenezer (1777-1852), *m* Lydia Phelps (1782-1852);
3–Adna (1820-54), *m* Lucinda Sanders (1826-54);
2–Augustin William (2 below).
8–Francis **Van Hoesen,** from Amsterdam, Holland, to New Amsterdam, ca. 1670; and thru:
5–Garrett (1732-1817), Athens, N.Y.; soldier Am. Rev.;
4–Francis (1757-1837), Preble, N.Y.;
3–Mathias (1801-85), Preble;
2–Flavilla (1843-1910), *m* 1873, Augustin William **Ferrin** (1843-1903), entered U.S.A. aet. 19; disch. on account of illness contracted at siege of Port Hudson; newspaper man; founded Cataraugus Republican, 1868; issue: I–Augustin William (1 above); II–Susannah (*b* 1878; *m* 1905, Pliny Rogers).
1–Not married. B.A., Yale, '98 (P.B.K.). Pres. Moody Magazine and Book Co. Consul at Madrid, Spain, 1924-26, at Tabriz and Teheran, Persia, since 1928. Author (see Who's Who in America). Mem. S.A.R. Clubs: Yale (New York), University (Washington). Home: Hastings-on-Hudson, N.Y. Residence: Am. Consulate, Teheran, Persia.

1–**FERSON, Merton Leroy,** *b* Oxford, Ia., Mar. 2, 1876.
6–Paul (MacPherson) **Ferson,** from Argyleshire, Scotland, to Northern Ireland, thence to America, settled at New Boston, N.H., 1732;
5–James (1716-92), *m* Jennett Leslie (1718-1804);

4–James (1744-1821), *m* 1773, Mary MacNeill (1755-1834);
3–Paul (1785-1847), began to write name Ferson; *m* Eliza Roloson, or Anderson (*d* 1881);
2–Bradford (1842-1916), farmer, of Oxford, Ia.; *m* 1874, Amelia Weeks (1848-83; Henry[8]); issue: I–Merton Leroy (1 above); II–Henry Milo (*d* 1918).
1–*m* June 26, 1901, Ella Jane Wagner, *b* Frank Pierce, Ia., Sept. 4, 1878; dau. of John P. Wagner, of Kalona, Ia.; issue: 1–Kathryn Louise, *b* Iowa City, Ia., Oct. 6, 1913.
1–Ph.B., U.Ia., 1900 (Phi Kappa Psi, Phi Delta Phi, Delta Sigma Pi, Order of Coif), LL.B., 1901, A.M., 1905. Practiced law at Guthrie Center, 1901-02; law librarian, State U.Ia., 1903-10; prof. law, 1914-23; dean. Law Sch., 1917-23; prof. law and dean Law Sch., U. of N.C., 1924-28; dean. Coll. of Law, U.Cincinnati, since 1928 (see Who's Who in America). Mem. Am. Law Inst., Am. Bar Assn. Republican. Club: Cosmos (Washington). Mason (32°). Summer place: Iowa City, Ia. Residence: 312 Joselin Av., Cincinnati, O.

1–**FIELD, Walter Taylor,** *b* Galesburg, Ill., Feb. 21, 1861.
8–Robert **Field** (qv);
7–William (1650-1718), of Braintree, Mass.; *m* Rebecca–;
6–William (ca. 1691-ca. 1772), *m* Sarah–;
5–John (*b* 1718), Braintree; *m* 1748, Susanna Newcomb;
4–John (1752-1826), pvt. in Am. Rev.; settled at Peterboro, N.H., 1786; operated a large tannery; *m* 1776, Ruth Thayer;
3–Dea. John (1777-1856), tanner, Peterboro; *m* 1st, 1802, Beulah Reed (1778-1835), of Lempster;
2–Dea. Horatio Nelson (2 below).
8–Thomas **Thayer** (*d* 1665), from Eng. to Braintree, ca. 1636; *m* Margerie Wheeler;
7–Shadrach (1629-78), *m* 2d, Deliverance Priest;
6–Ephraim (1669-1757), *m* 1692, Sarah Bass (John[7], *m* 1657, Ruth, dau. John Alden, qv; Samuel[8], qv);
5–Christopher (1703-87), *m* Mary Morse, of Braintree;
4–Ruth (1752-1846), *m* John **Field** (4 above).
8–Thomas (Whitmore) **Wetmore** (*b* 1615; desc. John Whitmore, Lord of Whyttemore, lived during reigns of Henry, III, and Edward, I, at Whitmore Hall, Co. Stafford, Eng.); came from Eng., 1635; settled at Wethersfield, Conn., 1639; later removed to Hartford; *m* 1st, 1645, Sarah Hall (John[9]);
7–Izrahiah (1656/57-1742), magistrate, Middletown; *m* 1692, Rachel Stow (Rev. Samuel[8]);
6–Rev. James (1695-1760), began to write name Wetmore; B.A., Yale, 1714, M.A., 1717; pastor First Congl. Ch., New Haven, Conn.; later pastor Episcopal chs., N.Y. City and Rye, N.Y.; *m* Anna–;
5–James (1727-ca. 1797), removed from New York to nr. St. John's, N.B.; *m* Elizabeth Abrahams, of Westchester Co., N.Y.;
4–Charity (*b* 1760), *m* Daniel **Lamoreux,** a Huguenot, fled from France to N.Y. during persecutions;
3–Elizabeth (*b* 1781), *m* 2d, 1816, George Washington **Taylor,** of New York;
2–Charity Lamoreux (1821-1915), *m* 1839, Dea. Horatio Nelson **Field** (1813-1900), of Peterboro, N.H., later at Abington, Farmington, Galesburg and Chicago, Ill. (for issue see Vol. III, p. 187).
1–*m* Dec. 6, 1892, Sara Lounsberry Peck (qv for issue).
1–A.B., Amherst, '83 (Alpha Delta Phi), hon. A.M., 1918. With Chicago house of Ginn & Co., pubs., since 1890. Author, editor and contbr. to mags. (see Who's Who in America). Residence: 211 Park Av., Hinsdale, Ill.

1–**FIELD, Sara Lounsberry Peck (Mrs. Walter T.),** *b* Chicago, Ill., June 1, 1871.
4–Jacob **Peck,** of English descent; resided Cornwall, Addison Co., Vt.;
3–Sheldon (*b* Vt.), from Jordan, Onondaga Co., N.Y., to Lombard, Ill., 1837;
2–Charles (2 below).
8–Abraham **Shotwell** (*d* 1680), from Eng. after restoration of Charles, II; Quaker; settler at Elizabethtown, N.J., 1665; exiled from N.J., because of personal encounter with Gov. Carteret, regarding encroachment on property; obtained grant of land which was site of 1st Brooklyn bridge; in leather business;
7–Daniel, of Staten Island and Woodbridge, N.J., 1721; *m* Elizabeth–;
6–Joseph, Woodbridge; *m* 1716, Mary Manning;
5–Daniel (*b* 1725), Woodbridge; *m* 1753, Deborah Shotwell (*b* 1735; Abraham[6]; John[7]; Abraham, 8 above);
4–Daniel (1767-1838), of Rahway, N.J.; *m* ca. 1787, Keziah Terrill (*d* 1819);
3–Joseph (1800-62), removed to Rockford, Ill.; *m* Ann Ball (Dea. Aaron[4], of Scotch Plains, N.J., nr. relative of Mary Ball, mother of Gen. George Washington);
2–Harriet Louise (1835-1900), *m* Charles **Peck** (1828-1900), of Chicago, Ill.; corr. sec. of Chicago Acad. of Design (now Art Inst.); issue: I–Anna Harriet (*m* Henry C. Taylor); II–Laura Martha (*d*); III–Sara L. (1 above); IV–Charleta (*b* 1873; *m* Raymond M. Ashcraft).
1–*m* Dec. 6, 1892, Walter Taylor Field (qv); issue (all *b* Chicago, Ill.): 1–Walter Donald, *b* Aug. 8, 1895; Amherst, '19; *m* Jan. 17, 1918, Isobel, dau. Charles Edward Turgeon (*d* 1918), of Ottawa, Can.; 2–Ruth Alden (July 14, 1898-Dec. 8, 1915); 3–John Stanley, *b* July 23, 1904; Amherst, '28.
1–Ed. Kenwood Inst., Chicago, and Art Students League, New York. Residence: 211 Park Av., Hinsdale, Ill.

1–**FIELD, William DeYongh,** *b* Boston, Mass., Mar. 21, 1847.
8–Zechariah **Field** (qv);
7–Samuel (1651-97), killed by Indians in Falls Fight; *m* 1676, Sarah Gilbert (1655-1712);
6–Zechariah (1685-1746), *m* 1711, Sarah Mattoon (1687-1752), of Deerfield, one of the company captured by Indians and taken to Can. aet. 17;
5–Samuel (1719-89), served in war 1756; *m* 1745, Abigail Field, of Sunderland;
4–Samuel (1755-1837), adj. gen. in Am. Rev.; *m* 1776, Elizabeth Mattoon (1760-1838), of Deerfield;
3–Silas (1779-1862), *m* 1805, Ruth Bryant Faxon (1788-1880), of Halifax, Mass.;
2–Benjamin Faxon (2 below).
8–William **Towne** (*b* 1572), *m* Joanna Blessing;
7–Jacob (*d* 1704), *m* 1657, Catharine Symonds;
6–Jacob (1662-1741), *m* Phoebe Smith;
5–Elisha (1706-41), *m* 1738, Sarah Rhodes;
4–John (1740-1830), soldier Am. Rev., at Battle of Bunker Hill, also at laying of corner stone of Bunker Hill Monument; *m* 1763, Ann Cummings;
3–Capt. Solomon, *m* 1801, Lydia Goodale;
2–Elizabeth Safford (1814-95), *m* 1840, Benjamin Faxon **Field** (1806-93); issue: I–Benjamin F. Jr. (1841-*d*; *m* Laura Pomeroy, *d* 1922); II–Elizabeth (1843-54); III–Fanny (1845-1922); IV–William DeYongh (1 above).
1–*m* Oct. 25, 1876 (fourth in direct line to celebrate Golden Wedding), Bertha Farnham Williams (qv for issue).
1–Ed. Boston Latin-English H.S. With Tudor Co. Residence: Mattapoisett, Mass.

1–**FIELD, Bertha Farnham Williams (Mrs. William DeY.),** *b* Roxbury, Mass., Nov. 30, 1854.
8–Robert **Williams** (qv);
7–Capt. Stephen (1640-1720), capt. of the Red Troop of Horse, 1707-12, and in command of the frontier; *m* 1666, Sarah Wise (1647-1728; Joseph[8], *m* Mary Thompson);
6–Ens. Joseph (1682-1720), Roxbury; *m* 1706, Abigail Davis (1687-1771; John[7], *m* Mary Torrey);
5–Capt. John (1712-77), Roxbury; marched to Alarm, 1775; *m* 1st, 1737, Elizabeth Williams (1716-1747; John[6]; Samuel[7]; Samuel[8]; Robert[9]);
4–John Davis (1739-1807), mem. Provincial Congress, 1774; capt., 2d Co. Minute Men raised in Roxbury; at Battle of Bunker Hill; *m* 1768, Hannah Davis (1751-1844; Col. Aaron[5], rep. 1st, 2d, and 3d Provincial Congresses);
3–Aaron Davis (1787-1863), Roxbury; *m* 1814, Nancy Bugbee (1792-1868);
2–Aaron Davis, Jr. (2 below).
9–Ralph **Farnum** (qv);
8–Ralph (*b* Eng., 1633), *m* 1650, Elizabeth Hall (Nicholas[9]);
7–John, *m* Elizabeth Parker;

6–Dea. John, *m* Eva J. Barker;
5–John, *m* 1738, Sarah Frye;
4–James, *m* Rebecca Ingalls;
3–Putnam Ingalls, *m* 1816, Rebecca Ingalls;
2–Susan Burnap (1827-1919), *m* 1852, Aaron Davis **Williams**, Jr. (1821-99), of Roxbury; issue: I–Bertha Farnham (1 above); II–Marshall S. Perry (*b* 1857; *m* Edith M. Barrett); III–Emily Putnam (*b* 1865; *m* E.W. Dwight; *m* 2d, Percy T. Clulow).
1–*m* Oct. 25, 1876, William De Yongh Field (qv); issue: 1–Horace Farnham, *b* Roxbury, Mass., Aug. 13, 1877; Milton Acad.; mem. Mass. Legislature, 1915-16; *m* Oct. 1, 1908, Mary McGregor, dau. of William A. Means, of Boston, *m* Sophia P. Sword (issue: Horace F., Jr., Harvard, '32; John, ed. Amherst Agrl. Coll.; Geraldine, ed. Winsor Sch.); 2–Elizabeth Towne, *b* Weston, Mass., Oct. 3, 1879; *m* Oct. 18, 1905, James Hervey, son of Capt. O. A. Batcheller, U.S.N., of Charlestown, *m* Margaret Lyons (issue: William Field, *d* 1909; Edgar H.; Campbell Robinson; Oliver A.; James H., Jr.); 3–Gladys DeYongh, *b* Weston, June 11, 1886; Winsor Sch.; *m* Oct. 18, 1905, Edwards W. Herman, M.D., Harvard, '02, son of Joseph Edwards Herman, *m* Louise K. Mills (issue: Louise Field; Elizabeth Field; William Field; John Edwards).
1–Trustee Proctor Acad. Mem. D.A.C. (treas. Mass. Soc.), D.F.P.A., D.C.W., D.A.R. (chapter regent), Unitarian. Republican. Residence: Mattapoisett, Mass.

FISHER
Arms: Azure, in chief of ducal crown, in base a dolphin embowed.
Crest: An eagle rising.

1–**FISHER, Cassius Asa,** *b* Fremont, Neb., Feb. 15, 1872.
10–Anthony **Fisher** (qv);
9–Anthony (*d* 1670), surveyor, Dedham, 1652-54; selectman, 1664; *m* Joanna Faxon (Thomas[10], *m* Joane–);
8–Josiah (1654-1736), rep., 1699; selectman, 1697; *m* 1st, 1680, Meletiah Bullen (1655-93; Samuel[9], *m* Mary–);
7–Josiah (1683-1763), capt. militia; selectman, Dedham, 1736; *m* 1707, Elizabeth Avery (William[8], *m* Elizabeth–);
6–Joseph (1712-59), *m* 1738, Mary Metcalf (Nathaniel[7], *m* Mary–);
5–Ichabod (1747-1818), moved to Princeton, Mass., 1770, thence to Paris, Oneida Co., 1810, to Pomfret, N.Y., 1813; *m* 1770, Sibyl Everell (Benjamin[6], *m* Sarah–);
4–Joel (*b* 1784), from Princeton, Mass., to Oneida Co., 1808, thence to Pomfret, N.Y., 1809; in War 1812; *m* 1803, Lydia Matthies;
3–Ashabel (*d* 1858, aet. 54), moved to Oneida Co., thence to Pomfret, Chautauqua Co., N.Y.; *m* 1832, Fedelia Fisher (1813-92; Jabez[4], *m* Sally Fessenden);
2–Marcius Clay (*b* 1847), *m* 1868, Nellie LePrand (1849-1924); issue: I–Minnie Bell (*b* 1868; *m* 1888, John H. Clapham); II–Cassius Asa (1 above); III–Vernon C. (*b* 1882; *m* 1910, Carrie Holiway).
1–*m* Aug. 22, 1900, Evangeline Hazlewood, *b* Elkhart, Ind., Aug. 16, 1878; dau. of Robert Hazlewood, of Osceola, Neb., *m* Eleonora–; issue: 1–Eleonora H., *b* New Haven, Conn., May 5, 1903; 2–Maurice H., *b* Oconomowoc, Wis., June 19, 1905; B.Sc., Yale, '28; 3–Robert V., *b* Denver, Colo., Sept. 26, 1910.
1–Grad. Fremont (Neb.) Normal Sch., 1892; B.A., U.Neb., '98 (Sigma Xi, Kappa Sigma), M.A., 1900, Sc.D., 1927; post-grad. work Yale, 1902-03. Fellow in geology, U.Neb., 1898-1902; asst. instr. in geology, Yale, 1902-03; asst. geologist, 1896-1909, geologist, 1909-10, also asst. chief of fuel sect., U.S. Geol. Survey; consulting geologist and engr., splty. fuels, 1910–; mem. firm Fisher & Lowrie (see Who's Who in America). Clubs: Royal Societies (London), Cosmos (Washington), Denver. Residence: 314 Franklin St., Denver, Colo.

1–**FINCH, John Wellington,** *b* Lebanon, N.Y., Nov. 3, 1873.
8–Thomas **Lillibridge** (1662-1724), from Eng.; settled in R.I.; warden of Episcopal ch., Newport, 1699-1713; vestryman Narragansett Ch., 1718; *m* 1st, Mary Hobson; *m* 2d, Sarah Lewis, (*d* 1760);
7–Thomas (1703-57), *m* Mary Woodmansee;
6–Thomas (1729-1822), *m* Mary Hoxsie;
5–Champlain (*b* 1767), of Richmond, R.I.; *m* Hannah Wilcox;
4–Jireh (1795-1878), organized local militia for War 1812, and was its leader;
3–Wellington Jireh (1829-1901), of Lebanon, N.Y.; *m* Sarah Ann Allen;
2–Mary Ellen (1857-1917), *m* 1872, Delos **Finch** (1844-1914), served in Civil War; farmer; issue: I–John Wellington (1 above); II–Jerah Lillibridge (*b* 1875); III–Raymond D. (*b* 1877); IV–Clara Belle (*b* 1880; *m* Harry B. Fleming).
1–*m* Apr. 10, 1901, Ethel Ione Woods, *b* New London, Conn., Sept. 15, 1875; dau. of Byron A. Woods, D.D., (1851-97), *m* Ella Ione Towsley (1851-1909), of Phila., Pa.; issue: 1–Ione Lillibridge, *b* Victor, Colo., Nov. 6, 1902; ed. Emma Willard Sch., Smith Coll.; *m* June 25, 1924, George M., son of George L. Nye, of Denver, Colo. (issue: Nancy Clare; Susan Beatrice); 2–Nancy Allen, *b* Bologna, Italy, Apr. 6, 1908; ed. Emma Willard Sch., and U.Colo.
1–B.A., Colgate U., '97 (D.K.E., Sigma Gamma Epsilon), A.M., 1898, (hon. Sc.D., 1913); fellow, U.Chicago, 1898-99. Lecturer on geology, Colo. Sch. of Mines; instr. geology and physics, Colgate and U.Chicago, 1898-99; state geologist of Colo. 1901-02; consulting geologist and engr. (see Who's Who in America). Clubs: India House (N.Y.), Denver, Denver Country, Mile High, Am. Inst. of Mining and Metallurgical Engrs., Min. and Metall. Soc. of America, Soc. Econ. and Geologists, Am. Assn. Petroleum Geologists, A.A.A.S., etc. Residence: 668 Gilpin St., Denver, Colo.

1–**FISHBURN, Randolph Eugene (formerly Randolph Eugene Ticknor),** *b* Rockford, Ill., June 8, 1862.
8–William **Ticknor** (qv);
7–William (1664-1731), *m* 1696, Lydia Tilden (*b* 1666);
6–William (1700-60), *m* 1727, Abigail Heath (*b* 1703);
5–Daniel (*b* 1740), in French and Indian War; sgt. Am. Rev.; *m* 1764, Mehitable Tobey;
4–Elijah, *m* Zilpha (Tobey?);
3–Oran (1793-1875), War 1812; *m* 1817, Abigail Orton (1794-1876);
2–Aurora Orton (1828-97), farmer and mcht.; *m* Susan Wiggins Moore (*d* 1910), she *m* 2d, Eu-

gene Heald Fishburn; issue (1st marriage): I–Isabelle (1860-93; *m* Samuel S. Fowler); II–Randolph Eugene (1 above).
1–*m* Dec. 19, 1898, Louise Giffen, *b* New Orleans, La.; mem. C.D.A., D.A.R.; dau. of James Fortescue Giffen, of New Orleans; issue: 1–Isabelle, *b* Chicago, Ill., Dec. 6, 1899.
1–*m* 2d, June 12, 1913, Carmen Robles; issue: 1–Randolph E., *b* Tucson, Ariz., Feb. 4, 1919; 2–Mayhew Wainwright, *b* Tucson, Mar. 28, 1922.
1–Studied Columbia Sch. of Mines, 1880-84 (D. K.E.). Gen. engring. work, U.S., Australia, B.C., and Mexico; cons. engr. Internat. Boundary Commn., U.S. and Mex., since 1922 (see Who's Who in America). Served as 1st lt., 2d U.S. Engrs., Spanish-Am. War. Republican. Presbyn. Mason (32°, K.T., Shriner). Residence: Tucson, Ariz.

1–**FITCH, Clara Heaton (Mrs. Edward Wright),** *b* Jeffersonville, Clark Co., Ind., Jan. 6, 1848.
8–Nathaniel (Eaton) **Heaton** (*d* 1664), from Eng.; he and his wife were admitted to the first church at Boston; admitted freeman, 1636; *m* Elizabeth–;
7–Nathaniel (1639-1714), at Dedham, 1675, Wrentham, 1683; *m* Mary–;
6–Samuel (1681 or 82-ante 1752), of Wrentham, Mass.; went to Hebron, Conn., 1717; moved to N.J., 1734, and lived nr. Black River, 1741-42; *m* 1706, Sarah Hawes (*b* 1689);
5–Isaac (1731-1814), sgt., Phila. Bn. of the Flying Camp, in Am. Rev.; in battle of L.I.; removed from Hebron, Conn., to Frederick Co., Va.; settled finally at Jefferson, Pa.; *m* 2d, 1760, Hannah Bowen (1744-1827; Henry[6], Am. Rev.);
4–John (1760-1820), from Va. to Jefferson, Pa.; *m* Mrs. Sarah Morgan Robinson (*b* 1763);
3–John (1794-1842), of "Busseron Villa," Sullivan Co., Ind.; *m* 1819, Nancy Weaver;
2–Hiram Weaver (2 below).
8–William **Price** (*d* 1704), received land grant on Elk River, Cecil Co., Md., 1661; *m* Margaret–;
7–William (*d* 1721), of Elkton, Cecil Co.; *m* Mary Hyland;
6–John (*b* ca. 1711), on Elk River, Cecil Co.; later settled at E. Nottingham, Md.; *m* 1733, Abigail (Gatchell) Job (*d* ca. 1784), Quakeress and widow of Enoch Job (Elisha Gatchell[7], from Eng., ante 1716, settled in Chester Co., Pa., justice, 1745,49,52, Quaker, *m* Rachel, dau. Barnabas Willcox, from Eng., settled at Phila., mem. Gen. Assembly, 1685, justice, 1686,87,89, *m* Sarah–);
5–David (*d* 1773), of Octorara Hundred, Cecil Co., Md.; settled later at Redstone Settlement, Monongahela River, Pa.; *m* 1765, Ann Husband (William[6], of Cecil Co., Md.);
4–Abigail (1766-1813), *m* Isaac **Weaver** (1756-1830), of Jefferson, Green Co., Pa.; mem. Legislature;
3–Nancy (1797-1855), *m* John **Heaton** (3 above);
2–Hiram Weaver (1820-64), of Jeffersonville, Ind., and "Busseron Villa"; *m* 1844, Hulda Howard (1825-1917; Thomas Jefferson[3]); issue: I–Clara (1 above); II–Herman Howard (*b* 1850; *m* Julia Worthley); III–Bettie (*b* 1853; *m* Richard Meldrum Hartwell); IV–William Weaver (*b* 1856; *m* Mary Small); V–Hiram Ellis (*b* 1858; *m* Minnie Smart).
1–*m* Oct. 10, 1866, Edward Wright Fitch (July 5, 1843-July 10, 1910); mfr. chemist; sgt., 97th Ind. Vols. in Civil War; issue: 1–Jefferson Howard (see Vol. III, p. 190, for paternal lineage); 2–Benjamin Homans, *b* 1872; *m* 1906, Martha Sofia Jansson; 3–Allyn Chauncey, *b* 1875; *m* 1908, Mary F. Pierce; 4–Ellice Heaton (Mrs. Julian Craven Hall, Jr., see Vol. III, p. 190).
1–Mem. I.A.G. Residence: 2005 Forest Park Boul., Fort Worth, Tex.

1–**FITZGERALD, Francis Scott Key,** *b* St. Paul, Minn., Sept. 24, 1896.
11–Nathaniel **Tilden** (qv);
10–Marmaduke;
9–Marmaduke; *m* Rebecca Wilner;
8–Martha, *m* Col. Edward **Scott** (*b* 1685), mem. Colonial Legislature, Kent Co., Md. (John[9], from Eng. to Kent Co., 1635);
7–Edward (*b* 1706), *m* Hannah Smythe;
6–Dr. John (1728-90), innoculated soldiers of Cont. Army in Am. Rev.; charter mem. Washington and Lee Coll.; *m* Elizabeth Calder;
5–Hon. John (1768-1813), judge, state senator; *m* Elizabeth Goodwin Dorsey;
4–John (1805-40), Md. state senator; *m* Eliza McGruder Key (1801-69); niece of Francis Scott Key, author Star Spangled Banner (Philip Barton[5], Cont. Congress);
3–Cecilia Ashton (1833-1924), *m* 1852, Michael **Fitzgerald** (1812 or 14-1855), wholesale hardware mcht. Baltimore (son of Capt. Edward, of English army);
2–Edward (2 below).
7–John **Dorsey** (*b* 1660), mem. Lord Baltimore's Upper Ho. Provincial Assembly, Md.;
6–Caleb (1710-77), of Hockley-in-ye-Hole; forged guns for Washington in Am. Rev.;
5–Elizabeth Goodwin (*d* 1853), *m* Hon. John **Scott** (5 above).
4–Eliza McGruder (1801-69), *m* John **Scott** (4 above);
3–Cecilia Ashton, *m* Michael **Fitzgerald** (3 above);
2–Edward **Fitzgerald** (*b* 1854), broker and mfr., St. Paul, Minn.; *m* 1890, Mary McQuillan, (*b* 1862; Philip[3], of St. Paul, Minn.); issue: I–Francis Scott Key (1 above); II–Annabel (*b* 1901; *m* Lt. Clifton Sprague, U.S.N.).
1–*m* Apr. 3, 1920, Zelda Sayre, *b* Montgomery, Ala., July 24, 1900; dau. of Judge A. D. Sayre, of Ala. Supreme Ct., Montgomery; issue: 1–Frances Scott, *b* St. Paul, Minn., Nov. 21, 1921.
1–Ed. Princeton, 1913-17, left coll. to join army. Commd. 2d lt., 45th Inf., 1917; 1st lt., 67th Inf., 1918; served as a.-d.-c. to Brig. Gen. J. A. Ryan, 1918-19; hon. disch. 1919. Author (see Who's Who in America). Mem. C.A.R. Clubs: University, White Bear Yacht (St. Paul), Sound View (Great Neck, L.I.), Cottage (Princeton). Summer place: "Ellerslie" Edgemoor, Del. Address: c/o Guaranty Trust Co., 1 rue des Italiens, Paris, France.

REV. GEORGE WHITEFIELD FISHER (1831-84).

1–**FISHER, Irving,** *b* Saugerties, N.Y., Feb. 27, 1867.
9–Anthony **Fisher** (qv);
8–Capt. Daniel (1619-83), *m* 1641, Abigail Marriott (*d* 1683);
7–John (1656-1736), *m* 1681, Rebecca Ellis (1661-1740);
6–Jeremiah (*b* 1701), *m* 1725, Prudence Crosby (*b* 1705);
5–William (*b* 1739), soldier Am. Rev.; *m* Abisha–;
4–Zachariah (1767-1840), *m* Delight Norton;

3–John (1794-1861), *m* 1818, Almira King;
2–Rev. George Whitefield (2 below).
9–George **Norton,** of Salem, Mass., ca. 1629, with Rev. Higginson; rep. from Gloucester to Gen. Assembly, Boston, 1642-44;
8–George (1641-96), *m* 1st, Sarah Hart (*d* 1682);
7–George (1671/72-1742), *m* Hannah Younglove (*d* 1742);
6–George (1697-1721), *m* Agnes Austin;
5–George (*d* 1776), soldier Am. Rev.; *m* Patience–;
4–Delight (1770-1855), *m* Zachariah **Fisher** (4 above).
6–Hezekiah **King** (1690-1740), *m* Sarah Read (1694-1750);
5–John (1730-1808), officer Am. Rev.; *m* Elizabeth Fenner (1727-1808);
4–Hezekiah (1755-1823), *m* Mercy Thornton (1757-1824);
3–Almira (1795-1873), *m* John **Fisher** (3 above);
2–Rev. George Whitefield (1831-84), see portrait, B.A., Yale, '59, Congl. clergyman, Cambridge, N.Y.; *m* 1863, Ella Wescott (*b* 1846), see Vol. I, p. 818, for Wescott lineage and issue.
1–*m* June 24, 1893, Margaret Hazard, *b* Peace Dale, R.I.; dau. Rowland Hazard, and sister of Caroline Hazard, see Vol. I, p. 36, for lineage; issue: 1–Margaret (*b* Paris, France, Apr. 30, 1894-*d* Nov. 7, 1919); 2–Caroline, *b* New Haven, Conn., June 17, 1897; *m* June, 1921, Charles B., son of John Pascal Sawyer, see Vol. I, p. 818, and Vol. III, p. 410; 3–Irving Norton, *b* Santa Barbara, Calif., Nov. 8, 1900.
1–B.A., Yale, '88, Ph.D., 1891. Prof. of political economy, Yale. Author. Past pres. Am. Assn. for Labor Legislation, Nat. Inst. Social Sciences, Am. Economic Assn., etc. (see Who's Who in America). Clubs: Yale, Reform, Cobden (New York), Cosmos (Washington), Graduates (of New Haven), etc. Summer place: "Whimsy Cot," Narragansett Pier, R.I. Residence: 460 Prospect St., New Haven, Conn.

1–**FITZHUGH, William McPherson,** *b* Frederick Co., Md., July 27, 1853.
7–Col. William **Fitzhugh** (qv; see Vol. III, p. 191, for Fitzhugh arms);
6–George (*d* 1722), of Stafford Co., Va.; *m* Mary Mason (Col. George[7]);
5–William "Red Coat Billy" (1721-98), col. colonial army; *m* 1752, Anne Frisby (*d* 1793; Capt. Peregrine[6]);
4–Peregrine (1759-1811), capt. 3d Md. Dragoons; *m* 1781, Elizabeth Chew (1765-1854; Samuel[5]);
3–William (1782-1819), *m* Sophia Clagett (1792-1884), of Hagerstown, Md.;
2–Peregrine (1815-99), of Catoctin, Md.; *m* 1833, Sarah Margaretta Pottenger (1817-1900); issue: I–Mary Pottenger (1838-1911; *m* 1859, Dr. Maynard McPherson, 1836-1909); II–Sophia (1840-78; *m* 1859, Maj. Horatio McPherson, 1836-80; see son Fitzhugh); III–Isabella Hudson (1844-64; *m* 1862, Rev. Edward Griffith Perryman, 1836-88); IV–Sarah Margaretta (1846-76; *m* George Howard Thompson, 1844-1911); V–Katherine (*b* 1850; *m* 1870, William Hammond Hall, *b* 1846); VI–William McPherson (1 above); VII–Amy (1855-1900).
1–*m* Sept. 1, 1888, Mary Eccleston Marsh, *b* San Francisco, Calif.; C.D.A.; dau. of Elias Bowers Marsh (*b* 1823), of Phila., *m* Elizabeth Garwood; issue: 1–Lee (June 21, 1889-Jan. 19, 1891); 2–Marion Eccleston, *b* San Francisco; U.Calif., '17 (Kappa Alpha Theta), C.D.A.; reconstruction work at Anize Le Chateau, World War; 3–William McPherson, Jr., *b* Paris, France, June 15, 1901; Leland Stanford Jr. U., 1 yr.
1–U.Calif., '75 (Chi Phi). Consulting mining and civil engr. Dir. Academy of Sciences. Mem. Md. S.C. Clubs: Pacific Union, Bohemian, McCloud River, Menlo Country, San Francisco Golf. Summer places: Willow Creek Ranch Ah-Di-Na, on the McCloud River, Calif.; "Catoctin," Woodside, Calif. Residence: 2350 Broadway, San Francisco, Calif.

1–**MACPHERSON, Fitzhugh,** *b* San Francisco, Calif., Oct. 17, 1869.
8–Henry **Sewall** (1620-65), from Eng. to St. Mary's Co., Md., 1660; established "Mattapony"; gov. of Council, 1661; sec. of Md., 1661-65; *m* Jane Lowe (Vincent[9]);
7–Maj. Nicholas (1655-1737), of St. Mary's Co., Md.; mem. and sec. of Provincial Council of Md., 1686; dep.gov., 1689; *m* Susan Burgess (Col. William[8] [1622-86], *m* Ursula–);
6–Sophia, *m* John **Cooke,** of Prince George Co., Md.;
5–Ann (1749-1836), *m* Thomas **Buchanan** (1740-87), immigrant;
4–Judge Thomas (1768-1847), *m* Rebecca Maria H. Anderson; (James[6]);
3–Mary Sophia (*b* 1806), *m* Horatio **Mac Pherson** (*b* ca. 1788); see Vol. III, p. 191, for MacPherson lineage and arms;
2–Horatio (2 below).
9–Capt. James **Neale** (1615-84), favorite at Court of Queen Henrietta Maria; settled in Charles Co., Md., ante 1642; mem. Council, 1643-44; burgess, 1666; *m* Anne Gill;
8–Henrietta Maria, *m* 2d, Hon. Col. Philemon **Lloyd** (1647-85), of "Wye House" (Col. Edward[9] [1615-95], *m* Alice Crouch);
7–Gov. Edward (1670-1718), of "Wye House"; *m* a niece of Barbara Morgan, wife of Col. John Rousby;
6–Rebecca, *m* Capt. William **Anderson;**
5–James, banker, of London, later of Md.; *m* Melora Ogle (*b* 1750); see Vol. III, p. 191;
4–Rebecca Maria Harriet (1770-1840), *m* 1798, Judge Thomas **Buchanan** (4 above);
3–Mary Sophia, *m* Horatio **MacPherson** (3 above);
2–Horatio (1836-80), *m* 1859, Sophia Fitzhugh (1840-78), sister of William M. Fitzhugh (qv for Fitzhugh lineage); issue: I–Mary Buchanan (*b* 1862; *m* Commodore James Philips Parker); II–Harriet (1866-81); III–Louis (1868-70); IV–Fitzhugh (1 above).
1–Not married. Mem. B.O.R., Soc. Americans of Royal Descent, S.A.R. Residence: 417 Stockton St., San Francisco, Calif.

1–**FITZPATRICK, John Clement,** *b* Washington, D.C., Aug. 10, 1876.
6–William **Fitzpatrick;**
5–William, *m* 1780 or 81, —O'Brien, of Md.;
4–Nicholas (*b* 1782), *m* 1805-06, Henrietta Simms (*d* 1806-07);
3–John Clement (1806-62), capt. D.C. militia in the 1830's; financial clk. of U.S. Senate, 1832-60; alderman; *m* 1826, Mary Cecelia Hickey (1807-64; James F.[4], paymaster Md. Line);
2–James Nicholas (2 below).
9–William **Combs,** Gent., from Eng., with wife and servants, ca. 1640; settled at Medley's Neck, St. Mary's, Md.;
8–Ignatius (*b* 1635?);
7–Enoch (1690-1756);
6–William (1716-75);
5–William (*b* 1745);
4–William A. (1780-1833), *m* Elizabeth Manning (Robert[5] [1753-91], *m* 1771, Monica Fenwick);
3–Robert Manning (1815-70) *m* Catherine Crawford Forrest (1822-97; Andrew[4] [1791-1844], *m* Nancy Harris [1791-1861], dau. of Benjamin More [1758-1821], of Mass., after Am. Rev. removed to Greenleaf Point, Md., thence to Washington, D.C., where he owned and published the Washington Gazette, 1796-99, justice of the peace, Washington Co., 1802, *m* 1783, Rachel Homer);
2–Elizabeth Ann, *m* 1872, James Nicholas **Fitzpatrick** (1850-1916), asst. financial clk. of U.S. Senate, 1870-79; asst. chief, appointment div., U.S. Treas. Dept., 1880-1916.
1–*m* Feb. 18, 1922, Elizabeth Veronica Kelly, *b* Long Branch, N.J., June 30, 1887; dau. of John Kelly, of Trenton, N.J.; issue: 1–Elizabeth Lavery, *b* Phila., Pa., Apr. 4, 1924.
1–M.A., St. Mary's, 1918; L.H.D., George Washington U. Historian and archivist; with Library of Congress, since 1897, asst. chief manuscript div., since 1902. Author (see Who's Who in America). Club: Cosmos. Residence: 135 A St. N.E., Washington, D.C.

1–**FITZWATER, Perry Braxton,** *b* Hardy Co., W.Va., Sept. 8, 1871.
9–Thomas **Fitzwater** (*d* 1699), from Eng. in the "Welcome," with William Penn, 1682; settled in Bucks Co., Pa.; mem. Provincial Assembly; removed to Phila., 1690; *m* Mary– (*d* 1682); *m* 2d, 1684, Elizabeth Palmer;
8–Thomas (1665-1742), came in "Welcome," with his father; *m* 2d, 1732, Mary Potts Tyson;

7–Thomas (1700-61), *m* Rosannah–;
6–William (1725-1806?), soldier Am. Rev., from Augusta Co., Va.; called "Soldier Bill"; patented land Augusta Co., 1773; *m* Catherine–;
5–William (1750-1818), of Rockingham Co., Va.; soldier Am. Rev.; *m* Ann McCaslen;
4–William (1773-1863), pvt., Capt. Thomas Hopkins' Co., Rockingham Co., Va., Militia, "Flying Camp"; *m* 1804, Elizabeth Davis;
3–Philip Bramar (1815-1905), *m* Amelia Strawderman (1818?-1883?);
2–Cyprianus (1843-1927), surveyor; *m* 1861, Clerenda Delawder (1843-1911); issue: I–Seymour Welton (1863-1912; *m* Angeline Anderson); II–Almira Ellen (*b* 1865); III–Wilson Lorenzo (1866-96; *m* Annie Fitzwater); IV–Philip Carson (*b* 1867; *m* Mollie Whitmer); V–Amelia Jane (1868-1914); VI–Perry B. (1 above); VII–Francelia Angeline (1874-1904); VIII–Hiram Ward (1879-1905); IX–Laurinda Viola (*b* 1880); X–Elmer Sidney (*b* 1885).
1–*m* July 27, 1898, Addie Frances Kaylor, *b* Bellefontaine, O., July 17, 1871; dau. of Joseph Kaylor, of Logan Co., O.; issue: 1–Joseph Kaylor (*b* Elkhart, Ind., May 22, 1899-*d* Nov. 14, 1928); Muskingum Coll., '22; *m* Jan. 1, 1924, Beula Mae Grimes (issue: Suzanne); 2–James Perry, *b* Sidney, O., Aug. 23, 1900; Muskingum Coll., '23; 3–Timothy Titus, *b* Sidney, May 3, 1902; *m* Mar. 23, 1925, Eva Hanna.
1–Grad. teachers' course, Bridgewater Coll., '94; spl. study, same, 13 mos.; student Moody Bible Inst., 1898-99; grad. Xenia Theol. Sem., 1905; post-grad. work, Princeton Theol. Sem. and Princeton U., 1911-12; (D.D., Muskingum, 1909). Minister and mem. faculty, Moody Bible Inst. since 1913; dean, Evening Sch. of Inst., 1923-26; dean day and evening schools of Inst. since 1926. Author (see Who's Who in America). Residence: 1006 Brummel St., Evanston, Ill.

1–**ENGLAND, Esta Mary Fitzwater (Mrs. Charles E.),** *b* Lodge, Ill., Dec. 27, 1874.
9–Thomas **Fitzwater** (*d* 1699), from Eng. in the "Welcome," with William Penn, 1682; settled in Bucks Co., Pa.; mem. Provincial Assembly; removed to Phila., 1690; *m* Mary–(*d* 1682); *m* 2d, 1684, Elizabeth Palmer;
8–Thomas (1665-1742), came in "Welcome," with his father; *m* 2d, 1732, Mary Potts Tyson;
7–Thomas (1700-61), *m* Rosannah–;
6–William (1725-1806?), soldier Am. Rev., from Augusta Co., Va.; called "Soldier Bill"; patented land Augusta Co., 1773; *m* Catherine–;
5–William (1750-1818), of Rockingham Co., Va.; soldier Am. Rev.; *m* Ann McCaslen;
4–William (1773-1863), pvt., Capt. Thomas Hopkins' Co., Rockingham Co., Va., Militia, "Flying Camp"; *m* 1804, Elizabeth Davis;
3–Jesse (1813-99), settled at Washington Court House, O., Pratt Co., Ill., 1851; improved 300 acres land; *m* in Va., 1842, Mary E. McNett (1823-53; Samuel[4], *m* Mary E. Beaver);
2–James Harvey (*b* 1849), *m* 1873, Nancy Eleanor Barnes (*b* 1852; John[3], *m* Martha Philipps); issue: I–Arthur Little (*b* 1873); II–Esta Mary (1 above); III–Martha Daisy (1877-82); IV–James Roy (*b* 1878; *m* 1900, Myrtle McBride); V–Grant Barnes (*b* 1880; *m* 1906); VI–Harry (1884-87); VII–Bessie Eleanor (*b* 1886; *m* 1914 Dr. Ralph Bushee); VIII–Jean (*b* 1893; *m* 1918, Arthur Foster).
1–*m* Dec. 13, 1893, Charles Edward England (qv); issue (all *b* DeLand, Ill.): 1–Leland Stanford, *b* Mar. 28, 1895; *m* Mar. 30, 1917, Faye Marshall (issue: Leland Stanford, Jr., *b* Mar. 30, 1918; Marshall, *b* June 1, 1919); 2–Helen Beatrice, *b* July 2, 1897; *m* Nov. 17, 1917, Everet Brown Penhallegon (issue: Edward England, *b* Oct. 4, 1918); 3–Dorothy Jane, *b* July 23, 1900; *m* Feb. 8, 1921, Henry Burrage Curry (issue: Henry Burrage, Jr., *b* Mar. 9, 1923; Ann, *b* May 11, 1927); 4–Edward Herbert, *b* Jan. 21, 1902; *m* Apr. 19, 1924, Mildred Boruff (issue: Mary Adel, *b* Nov. 16, 1925; Edward Herbert, Jr., *b* Apr. 30, 1929).
Residence: College Hill, Decatur, Ill.

1–**ENGLAND, Charles Edward,** *b* DeLand, Ill., Apr. 9, 1866.
5–David **England,** of Bath (now Montgomery) Co., Ky.; *m* Lucy–;
4–Rev. Stephen (*b* Va., 1773-1825), moved from Bath Co., Ky., to Madison Co., O., 1813, to Madison Co., Ill., 1818, started 1st settlement in Sangamon Co., Ill., 1818; brought his family there 1819; Bapt. preacher in Ky. but established a Christian Ch. in his own home, 1819; organized a church, 1820, which was the beginning of what is now the Antioch Ch.; *m* in Va., 1791, Anna Harper (1772-1841);
3–Rev. John (1811-84), *m* Mary Smith;
2–Albert T. (1836-1917), enlisted in Co. F, 2d Ill. Cav., 1862, hon. discharged, June 1865; settled in Goose Creek Tp., Piatt Co., nr. DeLand, Ill.; *m* 1865, Harriet E. Plunk (1842-1916); issue: I–Charles Edward (1 above); II–George Thomas (1870-1900; *m* 1893, Lula Swartz); III–John A. (1872-74); IV–William Herbert (*b* 1877; *m* 1904, Nellie May Kirby).
1–*m* Dec. 13, 1893, Esta Mary Fitzwater (qv for issue).
1–Ed. Monticello H.S. and U.Ill. Farmer; pres. Builders Lumber Co.; dir. Nat. Bank of Decatur and Nat. Bank of DeLand. Residence: College Hill, Decatur, Ill.

1–**FLEMING, Emily White (Mrs. Vivian M.),** *b* Athens, Ga., Apr. 9, 1855.
8–Thomas **White** (qv);
7–John, from Lynn, Mass., to Southampton, L.I.; *m* Anna–;
6–James (*d* 1692), lived at Huntington, L.I., 1630; *m* Sarah–;
5–Jacob, *m* 1747, Abigail Lounsbury;
4–William, *m* 1778, Susannah Smith;
3–Anson, *m* 1818, Anna Fitch;
2–William N. (2 below).
9–Robert (Cilley) **Seeley** (qv);
8–Obadiah (*d* 1657), came with his father; settled at Stamford, Conn.; *m* 1647, Mary, widow of John Miller, from Eng. to Stamford;
7–Jonas (1657?-1703), *m* twice;
6–Eliphalet, *m* 1724, Sarah Holley;
5–Sylvanus, Am. Rev.; *m* Rebecca Tuttle;
4–Rebecca, *m* Caleb **Benedict;**
3–Caleb, *m* Deborah North;
2–Rebecca (2 below).
8–Matthew **Gilbert** (*d* 1680), came to New Haven, 1638; founded first Ch. of Christ; dea., elder; magistrate, 1658; dep.gov., 1661;
7–Samuel;
6–Ann, *m* Nathan **Tuttle;**
5–Rebecca, *m* Sylvanus **Seeley** (5 above).
9–Thomas **Benedict** (qv);
8–Thomas, *m* Mary Havemeyer;
7–Thomas, *m* Rachel Smith (Samuel[8], *m* Rachel, dau. of Judge Matthew Marvin, qv);
6–Thomas, *m* Deborah Waters;
5–Hannah, *m* Capt. John **Carter,** of Conn.;
4–Deborah, *m* Gabriel **North** (Benjamin[5], *m* Mary Freeman);
3–Deborah, *m* Caleb **Benedict** (3 above);
2–Rebecca (1820-85), *m* 1848, William N. **White** (1819-67), of Athens, Ga.; served in C.S.A.; issue: I–Anna Rebecca (*m* P. H. Mill); II–Emily (1 above); III–Mabel Elizabeth (*m* John Platt Moore).
1–*m* Dec. 19, 1876, Vivian Minor Fleming, *b* Chantilly, Hanover Co., Va., Apr. 19, 1844; soldier C.S.A.; son of George Frederick Fleming, *m* Mary Orrell Coleman; issue: 1–Annie, *b* 1864; *m* Horace Herbert Smith.
1–Ed. Lucy Cobb Inst., Athens, Ga. Mem. C.D.A., D.A.R., U.D.C., A.P.V.A., Kenmore Assn. (pres. since 1922), Mary Washington Monument Assn. Residence: Fredericksburg, Va.

1–**FLEMING, William Henry,** *b* Augusta, Ga., Oct. 18, 1856.
4–Robert **Fleming,** from North of Ireland or Scotland with his four bros.; landed prob. at Phila., ca. 1760-70; settled in Va.;
3–Robert, of Va., *m* Thurza Farrar;
2–Porter (2 below).
4–Pierre **Moragne,** Huguenot; came to Charleston, S.C., before the Am. Rev.; settled at New Bordeaux, S.C., 1764; served in Am. Rev.;
3–Isaac, as a child witnessed one of Tarleton's raids; *m* Margaret Blanton Caine;
2–Catherine Bathsheba (*b* 1823), *m* 1850, Porter **Fleming** (1808-91), farmer and mcht.; elder, Presbyn. Ch., Augusta, Ga.; issue: I–John M. (*d* 1870); II–Frank E. (*d* 1926); III–William H. (1 above); IV–Katherine L. (*m* Rev. W. S. Bean); V–Lauran L.; VI–Isaac Moragne (*d* 1926); VII–Mary Cecile (*d* 1923); VIII–Porter (*d* 1926).

1–*m* Aug. 22, 1900, Marie Celeste Ayer, *b* Rome, Ga., Dec. 3, 1877; dau. of Maj. W. F. Ayer, chief. q.m., Johnson's army at the surrender at Greensboro, N.C., 1865; issue: 1–William Cornelius, *b* Augusta, Ga., Sept. 12, 1901; A.B., U. of Ga.; LL.B., Yale Law Sch., 1926; 2–Virginia Ayer, *b* Augusta, Aug. 27, 1909; Converse Coll., '29.

1–C.E., U. of Ga., '75 (P.B.K.), A.M., 1890 (LL.D., 1920). Admitted to bar, 1880, and in practice at Augusta since 1880. Author (see Who's Who in America). Mem. Ga. Ho. of Rep., 1888-94 (speaker 1894); mem. 55th to 57th Congresses, from 10th Ga. Dist. Mem. Ga. State Bar Assn. (pres. 1894-95), Hayne Lit. Soc. (past pres.). Mason (grand cdr. K.T. of Ga., 1895). Democrat. Residence: 2631 Walton Way, Augusta, Ga.

FLINT

1–**FLINT, Thomas,** *b* San Juan Bautista, Calif., May 29, 1858.

9–Thomas **Flint** (*d* 1663), from Wales to Boston, ante 1650, settled nr. Salem, Mass.; *m* Ann Sutherick;

8–Capt. Thomas (1650-1721), of Salem; capt., King Philip's War, 1675; *m* 2d, 1674, Mary Dounton (William[9]);

7–Thomas (*b* 1678), Salem; *m* 1st, 1704, Lydia Putnam (*d* 1711);

6–Capt. Thomas (1705-75), Salem; *m* Priscilla Porter (*d* 1774, aet. 62);

5–Dr. Thomas (1733-ca. 1800), Salem; physician and surgeon in Am. Rev.; removed to Nobleborough, 1770; *m* 1st, 1762, Lydia Pope (*d* 1784);

4–Dr. Thomas (1767-1854), physician; removed to Me., settled on Sandy River, 1787; later at Farmington, Me.; *m* 1792, Sarah Bassett Norton;

3–Hon. William Reed (1796-1887), of New Vineyard, later at N. Anson; co. commr. 4 yrs.; mem. State Senate, 1847,48,55; surveyor, 20 yrs.; *m* 1823, Electa Weston (1802-85; Dea. Benjamin[4] [1765-1857], of Madison, *m* 1788, Anne Powers [1766-1831]; Joseph[5] [1732-75], pilot in Arnold's Expdn. up the Kennebeck River, *m* 1756, Eunice Farnsworth, 1735-1822);

2–Dr. Thomas (2 below).

11–John **Howland,** Mayflower Pilgrim (qv);

10–Hope (1629-83), *m* 1646, Elder John **Chipman** (qv);

9–Hope (1652-1728), *m* 1670, John **Huckens** (1649-78), of Barnstable, Mass.;

8–Mary (1673-1743), *m* ca. 1690, Nathan **Bassett** (ca. 1666-1743);

7–Samuel (1693-1770), *m* Martha–;

6–Sarah (1720-1804), *m* 1740, Maj. Peter **Norton** (1718-92), pvt. in Am. Rev.; maj. Cont. Army;

5–Ebenezer (1741-1804), *m* 1761, Elizabeth Smith (1743-1811);

4–Sarah B. (1767-1833), *m* Dr. Thomas **Flint** (4 above).

6–Rev. Daniel **Wilkins,** patriotic preacher during Am. Rev.; *m* Sarah Fuller;

5–Capt. Daniel (*d* 1776), capt., N.H. regt. in Am. Rev.; *m* Tabitha Weston (1748-1820);

4–Tabitha (1774-1848), *m* Thomas **Gilmore** (*d* 1814);

3–Mehitable Codman (1798-1869), *m* 1818, Joshua **Mitchell** (1796-1869);

2–Mary Ann (1837-1906), *m* 1857, Dr. Thomas **Flint** (1824-1904), of San Juan Bautista, Calif.; mem. Calif. Senate, 1876-80; issue: I–Thomas (1 above); II–Sarah (*d* 1894; *m* George Otis Mitchell, *d* 1913); III–Gertrude Williams (*d* 1868); IV–Richard Hall (*m* Elizabeth Agnes Smith).

1–*m* Dec. 2, 1896, Ada Mary Fisk, *b* St. Albans, W.Va., Apr. 1, 1872; dau. of Capt. Richard Henry Fisk, of Orange, N.J., *m* Ada Delia Anna Carr; issue (all *b* San Francisco, Calif.): 1–Dorothy, *b* Jan. 11, 1898; A.B., Mills Coll., '19; A.M., U.Calif., 1920; 2–Marjorie Chapman, *b* June 26, 1899; A.B., Mills, '20; 3–Thomas, *b* Apr. 20, 1903; A.B., Dartmouth, '24; M.D., U.Calif., 1928; 4–Harvey Fisk, *b* Oct. 2, 1904; U.Nev., '30; 5–Morton Mitchell, *b* Apr. 15, 1906; A.B. in C.E., Stanford, '29.

1–A.B., Dartmouth, '80 (Psi U.), A.M., 1883. Ranching, 1880-1925. Retired. Mem. Calif. Senate, 1888-1904 (pres. pro tem., 1894-1904); mem. San Benito Co. (Calif.) Bd. of Defense, 1917-18. Mem. S.M.D., S.A.R. Mason (32°), Elk. Episcopalian. Republican. Residence: 482 South St., Hollister, Calif.

1–**FLOWERS, Alan Estis,** *b* St. Louis, Mo., Oct. 4, 1876.

10–Aart Jacobsen (Van Wageninge) **Van Wagenen** (ca. 1610-1666), came from Holland, ca. 1650; *m* Annetje Gerrits;

9–Gerrit Aartsen (ca. 1650-1721), of N.Y.; *m* Clara or Claartje Pels (Evert[10], of Kingston, N.Y., *m* Jannetje Symens);

8–Aart Gerritse (ca. 1670-1699), of Kingston; *m* Aaltje Elting (Jan[9], *m* Jacomynte Slecht);

7–Gerrit (1697-1743), began to write name Van Wagenen; school-master; surveyor, Kingston; later at N.Y. City; *m* 1718, Teuntje Gerritsen Van Den Berg (Huybert Gerritsen[8], *m* Maria Lansing);

6–Jacob (1724-1803), *m* 2d, Mary Ewetse (Peter[7], *m* Catherine Bergen);

5–Peter (1775-1835), ins. broker, N.Y. City, *m* Sarah Plume (1773-1850; Isaac[6], *m* Sarah Crane);

4–Sarah Ann (1801-86), *m* 1826, Rev. James **Holmes,** D.D. (1801-73), Princeton; founder Presbyn. ch., Tipton Co., Tenn.;

3–Emma (1827-89), *m* 1843, Rev. David Hays **Cummins** (1813-73), of Covington, Tenn.;

2–Mary Emma (1851-1904), *m* 1871, William Pitts **Flowers** (1838-92), capt. and owner Miss. River steamboat (William L.[3], of Buckingham Co., Va., to Covington, Tenn., settled on plantation nr. Jackson, Tenn., *m* Mary A. White); issue: I–William Hayes (*m* Adelia Rawlings); II–Henry Cummins (*m* Caroline Louise Walker); III–Alan Estis (1 above); IV–Mary Greenwood (*b* 1879; *m* Dr. Joseph G. Wilson); V–Eunice White (*m* Arthur M. Loribond); VI–Eleanor Holmes (*m* Donald M. Gates).

1–*m* June 29, 1907, Ida Vander Grift Burns, *b* Pittsburgh, Nov. 15, 1880; dau. John Burns, of Pittsburgh and St. Louis; issue: 1–George Schluederberg, *b* Columbia, Mo., May 20, 1908; ed. Princeton, '31; 2–Nancy Holmes, *b* Columbus, O., Jan. 6, 1913; 3–Priscilla (Apr. 28-Nov. 23, 1920).

1–M.E. in E.E., Cornell U., '02 (Phi Mu Alpha, Lambda Phi Rho, Sigma Xi, Tau Beta Pi), M.M.E., 1914, Ph.D., 1915. Inventor and engr. in charge development DeLaval Separator Co. since 1923 (see Who's Who in America). Served as capt., Signal Corps, U.S.A., on duty in radio sect., Washington, 1918-19. Mem. Am. Inst. Elec. Engrs., Am. Soc. M.E., Am. Soc. for Testing Materials, Am. Phys. Soc., Am. Soc. Steel Treaters, Soc. Promotion Engring. Edn., A.A.U.P. Conglist. Clubs: Amrita, Chemists (N.Y.). Residence: 148 College Av., Poughkeepsie, N.Y.

1–**FONTAINE, Mary Ballard,** *b* Clifton Forge, Va., July 30, 1904.

10–John (de La) **Fontaine** (ca. 1500-1563), of France; Huguenot;

9–James (1549-1633), *m* twice;

8–Rev. James (1603-66), *m* 2d, 1641, Marie Chaillon (*d* aet. 63);

7–Rev. James (*b* 1658), from France to Eng., 1685; *m* 1686, Anne Elizabeth Boursiquot (*d* 1721);

6–Rev. Peter (1691-1757), from Eng. to Va., 1716; rector Westover Parish; chaplain of Va. Commn. which ran boundary line bet. Va. and N.C.; *m* 1714, Elizabeth Fourreau;
5–Abraham (*b* 1756), *m* Sarah Ballard;
4–Walter Lloyd (*d* 1860), col. in War 1812; *m* Margaret Nicholas;
3–Walter Scott (1825-83), *m* 2d, Mary Porter (1839-1913);
2–Berthier Maury (2 below).
8–George **Hankins**, from Eng. to Va., settled in Isle of Wight Co., 1640;
7–John, patented land in New Kent Co., Va., 1664; name in land books, Handkins;
6–Charles, owned 300 acres land in New Kent Co., 1704;
5–William;
4–William (1763-ca. 1825);
3–John Henry (1804-70), of Bacon's Castle, Surry Co., Va.;
2–Mary Dorcas (1863-1921), *m* 1901, Berthier Maury **Fontaine** (*b* 1862), city treas., Clifton Forge, Va.; issue: I–Virginia Hankins (*b* 1903; *m* Clarence Richard McPherson); II–Mary B. (1 above).
1–A.B., Hollins Coll., '26. Teacher. Residence: Clifton Forge, Va.

1–**FOOTE, Elizabeth Louisa,** *b* Rome, N.Y., Aug. 23, 1866.
9–Nathaniel **Foote** (qv);
8–Nathaniel (1620-55), Wethersfield; *m* 1646, Elizabeth Smith (*d* 1655; Lt. Samuel[9], of Wethersfield, rep. 13 yrs., asso. judge Co. Ct., 8 yrs.);
7–Daniel (*b* 1652), of Stratford, Conn.; *m* Sarah–; *m* 2d, Mary–;
6–Jehiel (1687-1740), *m* Susannah–;
5–George (1721-55), *d* at sea; *m* 1745, Hannah (Hard) Hurd;
4–John (1754-1826 or 46), removed from Stratford to Arlington, Vt.; *m* 1775, Ruth Searl (1756-1846);
3–Adoniram (1780-1866), *m* 2d, Emily Brainerd;
2–John Bartlit (2 below).
8–Daniel **Brainerd** (qv);
7–William (1673-post 1747), *m* 1698, Sarah Bidwell (*b* 1681);
6–Josiah (1711-92), of Middle Haddam, Conn.; served in Colonial wars and in Am. Rev.; *m* 2d, 1738, Hannah Spencer (1709-87);
5–Ezra (1744-1837), of Middle Haddam; deacon; justice; dep. Gen. Assembly; commd. during Am. Rev.; *m* 1st, Jerusha Smith (1743-1811; Lt. David[6], *m* Dorothy Brainerd);
4–Ezra (1769-1833), col. militia of E. Hartford, Conn.; *m* Mabel Porter (1770-1833; James[5], of E. Hartford);
3–Emily (1789-1854), *m* as his 2d wife, Adoniram **Foote** (3 above).
8–Rev. John **Young** (qv);
7–Benjamin (1640-97), *m* Elizabeth– (1643-1725);
6–Benjamin (1678/79-1768), *m* 1703, Mercy Landon (*d* 1782);
5–Seth (1711/12-1761), *m* Hannah Lawrence (1716-71);
4–John (1752-1834), in Am. Rev.; settled at Manlius (now Dewitt), N.Y., ca. 1788; *m* 1772, Elizabeth Parsons (1750-1825);
3–Rev. Seth (1784-1835), *m* 1809, Elizabeth Crossett (1787-1858).
2–Rev. John Bartlit **Foote,** D.D. (1826-1911), minister, M.E. Ch., retired 1895; resided at Syracuse, N.Y.; *m* 1851, Mary Stilphen (1826-59); *m* 2d, 1860, Louisa Young (1827-1919); issue (1st marriage): I–Osmon Cleander Baker (*d* 1870, aet. 18); II–Martha Emilie (1854-1924; *m* 1884, John M. Crow); III–John Stilphen (*d* infancy); issue (2d marriage): I–William Young (1863-1920; *m* 1900, Cecilia Von Schiller Heire; *m* 2d, 1906, Maie Sleight Becker); II–Mary Louise (*d* infancy); III–Elizabeth L. (1 above); IV–Mabelle Winifred (1869-1923; *m* 1912, Julius F. Eller).
1–A.B., Syracuse U., '88 (Alpha Phi), A.M., 1924; B.L.S., N.Y. State Library Sch., 1892. Librarian, N.Y. State Library, N.Y. Public Library, Drew Theol. Sem. (see Who's Who in America). Mem. A.L.A., N.Y. State Library Assn., Religious Edn. Assn., Internat. Council of Religious Edn., Poetry Soc. of America, A.A.U.W., etc. Residence: 905 University Av., Syracuse, N.Y.

1–**FOOTE, Edward Hibbard,** *b* Rome, N.Y., Dec. 31, 1858.
9–Nathaniel **Foote** (qv);
8–Nathaniel (1620-55), of Wethersfield; *m* 1646, Elizabeth Smith (*d* 1655; Lt. Samuel[9], of Wethersfield, rep. 13 yrs., asso. judge Co. Ct., 8 yrs.);
7–Daniel (*b* 1652), of Stratford, Conn.; *m* 1st, Sarah–; *m* 2d, Mary–;
6–Jehiel (1687-1740), *m* Susannah–;
5–George (1721-55), *d* at sea; *m* 1745, Hannah Hurd, of Stratford;
4–John (1754-1826), removed from Stratford to Arlington, Vt.; *m* 1775, Ruth Searl (1756-1846);
3–Capt. Adoniram (1780-1866), of Martinsburg and Turin, N.Y.; in War 1812; *m* 1804, Nancy Doty; *m* 2d, 1817, Emily Brainerd;
2–Norman Brainerd (2 below).
8–Peter (Van der Meulen) **Mills** (*b* 1622; was disowned by his father, Sir Peter Wouters Van der Meulen, of Amsterdam, because of religious differences); Puritan; from Amsterdam to America, 1650; studied for ministry at Leyden; *m* Dorcas Messinger (1650-88; Edward[9], in Bloomfield, 1652);
7–Peter (*d* 1754), of Wintonbury; began to use name Mills; *m* 1692, Joanna Porter (*b* 1671; John[8], *m* 1669, Joanna Gaylord; John[9], *m* Mary, dau. of Thomas Stanley, *m* Ann White; John[10]);
6–Rev. Jedidiah (*b* 1696/97), of Wintonbury; grad. Yale, 1722; *m* 1726, Abigail Treat (1704-75; Robert[7], *m* 1687, Abigail, dau. of Hon. Nicholas Camp, rep. to Gen. Ct., 1670, *m* widow Catherine Thompson; Gov. Robert[8], *m* Jane Tapp; Richard[9], qv);
5–Jedidiah (*b* 1727), grad. Yale, 1747; *m* 1756, Hannah Hawley (Obadiah[6], of Stratford; Samuel[7], *m* Bethiah, dau. of Ephraim Booth, *m* Mary Clark, g.dau. Richard Booth, qv; Samuel[8], *m* Mary Thompson; Joseph[9], qv);
4–Frederick (*b* 1759), of Derby, Conn.; *m* Rockoellano Storrs (*b* 1760);
3–Timothy (1789-1873), of Wintonbury, Conn.; *m* 1813, Catherine Taylor (1792-1874);
2–Maria (1823-1901), of Lowville, N.Y.; *m* 1848, Norman Brainerd **Foote** (1820-1900), wholesale merchant and mfr.; issue: I–Emily Mills (1849-1922); II–Frederick Norman (*b* 1852; *m* Nora F. Thompson); III–John Rogers (1854-1918; *m* Mary F. Kirkland); IV–Edward Hibbard (1 above); V–William Adams (*b* 1863; *m* Mary D. Smith); VI–Susan Cowan (1865-1913).
1–Not married. Sr. partner of The Foote System, financing philanthropies. A founder and organizing sec. Bedford Branch, Y.M.C.A., Brooklyn. Mgr. Am. Corpn. office, Shanghai, Manila, Singapore. Traveler, writer, speaker. A founder and chmn. Christian work com., Y.M.C.A., Manila; trustee Trinity Meth. Ch., Oswego, N.Y.; mem. bd. Central Meth. Ch., Manila; financial sec., Ch. of all Nations, New York. Mem. Foote Family Assn. Residence: 230 St. John's Pl., Brooklyn, N.Y.

1–**FOOTE, Francis Seeley,** *b* Brooklyn, N.Y., Mar. 31, 1883.
10–Nathaniel **Foote** (qv);
9–Nathaniel (*b* Eng., 1620-*d* 1655), Wethersfield, Conn.; *m* 1646, Elizabeth Smith (Lt. Samuel[10]);
8–Nathaniel (1647/48-1703), house carpenter; practiced law, Wethersfield; q.m., King Philip's War; *m* 1672, Margaret Bliss (1649-1745; Nathaniel[9], *m* 1646, Catharine, dau. Dea. Samuel Chapin, qv; Thomas[10], qv);
7–Ephriam (1685-1765), Colchester, Conn.; *m* 1708, Sarah Chamberlain (1693-1777; Joseph[8]; William[9]; Henry[10]);
6–Ephriam (1716-1800), Stockbridge, Mass.; *m* Margaret Smith; *m* 2d, Miss Lord; *m* 3d, Lucretia Lewis;
5–John (*d* 1833), Chatham, N.Y.; corpl., Am. Rev.; *m* 1784, Elizabeth Babcock (ca. 1760-1832);
4–Avery (1791-1867), *m* 1815, Joanna Osgood (1792-1846);
3–Warren (1821-1914), *m* 1843, Rhoda Reed;
2–Francis Seeley (2 below).
9–John **Reed** (*b* Cornwall, Eng., 1633-*d* 1730), from Eng., settled at Providence, R.I., 1660; removed to Norwalk, Conn., 1684; soldier and landowner; *m* 1655, Ann Derby, widow;
8–John (1670-1724), landowner, Norwalk; *m* 1687,

Elizabeth Tuttle (1666-1720; John[9], *m* Kattareen Dane, of New Haven, Conn.);
7–Daniel (1697-1775), of Norwalk; *m* 1719, Elizabeth Kellogg (1703-64; Joseph[8], of Norwalk, *m* Sarah Plume);
6–Daniel (1721-95), *m* Mary Bell (1723-1812);
5–Gershom (1749-1829), *m* Jerusha Castle (1751-1831);
4–Ezra (1790-1875), *m* Elizabeth Wilson (1796-1879);
3–Rhoda (1821-93), *m* Warren **Foote** (3 above).
7–Timothy **Gilbert** (*b* prob. Eng.), *m* Mary Fheith (1727-1811);
6–Timothy (1747-1825), *m* Martha Rogers;
5–Timothy (1772-1838), *m* 1794, Fear Shaw (1768-1852);
4–Timothy (1797-1865), founder of Tremont Temple in Boston, Mass.; *m* 1825, Mary Wetherbee (*d* 1843);
3–Mary Eunice (*b* Boston, 1827-*d* 1911?), *m* 1845, William Henry **Jameson** (1818-87), p.-m. with rank of maj., Union Army; bvtd. lt. col. "for faithful and meritorious services" (Henry[4], of Saco, Me., *m* Sarah–, *d* Boston, 1855);
2–Addie Sarah (*b* 1857), *m* 1882, Francis Seeley **Foote** (1848-1920); issue: I–Francis Seeley (1 above); II–Edna (*b* 1888; *m* 1910, Curtis Campaigne).
1–*m* July 15, 1913, Margaret Lucy Kingsbury, *b* Samadov, Bulgaria, Sept. 3, 1884; dau. of Frederick Lucas Kingsbury (*b* Jericho, Vt., Mar. 10, 1850-*d* Berkeley, Calif., Mar. 18, 1924; Joseph[8], *m* Eliza Whitcomb), grad. Dartmouth, 1875; attended med. sch., U.Vt., practiced medicine, Waterbury, Vt.; med. missionary, Samakov, Bulgaria, 1881-98; pastor Congl. Ch., Ventura, Calif., 1906-10; *m* Feb. 28, 1877, Luella Laughton Olds (*b* Norwich, Vt., Oct. 19, 1848-*d* Berkeley, Calif., Mar. 17, 1924); issue: 1–Elizabeth Luella, *b* Berkeley, Calif., Apr. 30, 1914; 2–Francis S., Jr., *b* Oakland, Calif., Dec. 10, 1916; 3–John Kingsbury, *b* Oakland, July 19, 1924.
1–E.M., Columbia Sch. of Mines, '05 (Delta Tau Delta, Tau Beta Pi, Sigma Xi). Civil engr. and prof. ry. engring., U.Calif., since 1917; dir. Surveying Camp since 1912 (see Who's Who in America). Asso. mem. Am. Soc. C.E.; mem. Am. Ry. Engring Assn. Clubs: Pacific Ry., Faculty. Residence: 2607 Shasta Rd., Berkeley, Calif.

1–**FORBES, Harriet Coleman (Mrs. Carroll R.),** *b* Logansport, Ind., Nov. 18, 1873.
8–Thomas **Coleman** (qv);
7–John (*b* 1635), *m* 1st, Hannah Porter (1642-77);
6–Dr. Noah (1671-1711), *m* Hannah Guernsey (*d* 1765);
5–Dr. Noah (1704-83), surgeon, Am. Rev., original mem. S.C.; *m* Mercy Wright (*b* 1709);
4–Dr. Asaph (1747-1820), admitted to practice of medicine by Conn. Med. Soc., 1774; surgeon Am. Rev.; rep. Gen. Assembly, 1803-04; *m* 1780, Eunice Hollister (*b* 1754; Dea. Elisha[5] [*b* 1722], capt. militia, Am. Rev.; mem. Com. of Correspondence, 1774; *m* 1st, Experience Robbins; Thomas[6]; John[7]; Lt. John[8], qv);
3–Dr. Asa (1788-1871), *m* 3d, Mary Keiffer (1800-72);
2–Dr. Asa (2 below).
9–Rev. James **Fitch** (qv);
8–Samuel (1655-1725), *m* Mary Brewster (Benjamin[9], *m* Anna Adis Dart; Elder William[10]);
7–Jabez (1695-1779), *m* Ann Knowlton;
6–Peletiah (1722-1803), *m* Elizabeth Burrows (1725-95);
5–Elisha (1756-1826), capt. Am. Rev.; *m* Elizabeth (Terry) Tyler (1758-1835);
4–Dr. Frederick (1784-1850), capt. War 1812; *m* 1st, Mary (Polly) Capen;
3–Hon. Graham (1809-93) col. Union Army, Civil War, U.S. Senator; *m* Harriet Satterlee (1809-81);
2–Emma (1838-95), *m* 1864, Dr. Asa **Coleman** (1832-1905), physician and surgeon; issue: I–Henry Fitch (*b* 1865; *m* 2d, Mary Fischer); II–Harriet (1 above); III–Charles Denby (1881-1919).
1–*m* June 21, 1917, Carroll Ralph Forbes, *b* Beatrice, Neb., Apr. 17, 1880; mining engr.; capt. and maj. engrs., U.S.A., World War; son of Wilson M. Forbes, of Topeka, Kan. Adopted son, John Carroll, *b* Denver, Colo., June 15, 1920.
1–Ed. U.Toronto, '90. Mem. S.M.D., D.F.P.A., D.C.W., D.A.R. Residence: 500 W. 8th St., Rolla, Mo.

1–**FORD, Charles Halsey Lindsley,** *b* Binghamton, N.Y., Dec. 10, 1887.
7–Oswald (Foord) **Ford** (*d* 1727), from Eng.; settled at Brookhaven, L.I., ca. 1660; *d* in Hunterdon Co., N.J.;
6–Charles (1699-1784), Woodbridge, N.J.; *m* ante 1770, Meribah Thornell;
5–Benjamin (1741-1811), removed from Woodbridge to Perth Amboy, N.J.; *m* 1769, Jemima Walker (1748-1810; Thomas[6]; Capt. Samuel[7] [*d* 1750], of Boston, Mass., and N.J.);
4–James (1783-1829), of Lawrenceville, Pa.; judge; mem. 21st and 22d Congresses, 1827-31; *m* 1806, Maria Lindsley;
3–Charles Halsey Lindsley (1808-83), Lawrenceville; *m* 1830, Eliza Madison Cruger (1809-84; Gen. Daniel[4], served with distinction in War 1812, mem. Assembly, 1813, mem. Congress from N.Y., 1816);
2–Charles Lindsley (2 below).
10–John (Linle) **Lindsley**, from Eng.; settled at Branford, Conn., ca. 1640;
9–Francis (*d* 1704), large landholder; a founder of Newark, N.J., 1666; *m* Susanna Culpepper;
8–John (1667-1749), *m* Elizabeth–;
7–Judge John (*b* 1694), judge of 1st ct. held in Morristown, 1740 et seq.; *m* Sarah–;
6–Eleazer (1737-94), lt. col. and col. Cont. Army; a.-d.-c. on staffs Gen. George Washington and Gen. Marquis de LaFayette; *m* (Wallace) Mary Miller (1738-1806);
5–Judge Eleazer (*d* 1825), *m* 1787, Eunice Halsey (1769-1857; Jeremiah[6], *m* Elizabeth Woodruff);
4–Maria (1788-1846), *m* Hon. James **Ford** (4 above).
10–Robert **Feake** (qv);
9–Elizabeth, *m* as his 2d wife, Capt. John **Underhill** (qv);
8–Deborah (*b* Oyster Bay, 1659), *m* Henry **Townsend** (Henry[9] [*d* 1695] settled at Oyster Bay, ante 1661);
7–Henry (*d* 1709), *m* Eliphal Wright;
6–Henry, *m* Elizabeth Titus (*b* 1699), "a beautiful Quakeress";
5–Absolom (1746-1817), *m* 1768, Helena DeKay (1746-1814);
4–Henry A. (1769-1837), *m* 1814, Elizabeth Hull;
3–Sarah Startin (1817-46), *m* 1839, Henry Rutgers **Miller** (g.son Capt. Anthony Rutgers, Am. Rev., del. 1st-3d Provincial Congresses of N.Y., mem. State Constl. Conv., *m* Gertrude, dau. Nicholas Gouverneur);
2–Sarah Townsend (1845-1919), *m* 1867, Charles Lindsley **Ford** (1841-1916), of Binghamton, N.Y.; issue: I–Henry Rutgers (1871-1917; *m* Katherine Stoneman Williams); II–Frances Cruger (*b* 1873); III–Elizabeth Townsend (*b* 1879); IV–Charles H. L. (1 above).
1–*m* Oct. 4, 1916, Frances Newkirk Alley, *b* Cortland, N.Y., June 19, 1893; served as R.C. dietitian at various hosps. during World War; dau. of Edward Alley, of Cortland.
1–B.A., St. Stephen's Coll., '10 (Kappa Gamma Chi); grad. Gen. Theol. Sem., 1913; studied Syracuse U., 1920-21. Ordained P.E. priest; chaplain St. John's Mil. Sch.; head jr. house and instr. history and Latin, Howe Sch.; prin. St. Faith's Sch., since 1923 (see Who's Who in America). Sr. Chaplain Coast Defenses, Boston, 1918; with 4th Anti-aircraft Sector, C.A.C., A.E.F., 1918-19. Now chaplain, O.R.C. and 105th Inf. N.Y.N.G. Trustee St. Stephen's Coll. Alumni Assn.; mem. A.L. (past cdr.), V.F.W. Republican. Mason (32°, K.T., Shriner), Odd Fellow. Club: Army and Navy (New York). Summer place: "The Little House," Gansevoort, N.Y. Residence: The Principal's House, St. Faith's Sch., Saratoga Springs, N.Y.

1–**FORTSON, Samuel Anthony,** *b* Lincoln Co., Ga., Sept. 2, 1876.
5–Thomas **Fortson** (1742-1824), *b* Orange Co., Va.; lt., 1780; removed from Orange Co., Va., to Wilkes Co. (now Elbert), Ga., ca. 1783, *m* 1st, in Va., Rachael Wynn;
4–Richard (1778-1836), *m* 1st, Lucy Arnold (1778-1847);
3–Benjamin Wynn (1808-84), cotton planter and slave holder; *m* 2d, 1841, Hannah Rebecca Ogilvie;

2–Samuel Anthony (2 below).
6–William **Ogilvie,** from Scotland with wife, settled in Fairfield Co., S.C.; *m* —Smith;
5–James (*b* Fairfield Co., S.C.), *m* Miss Parrott;
4–James (1777-1839), *m* 1797, Elizabeth Watson (1778-1870);
3–Hannah Rebecca (*b* Edgefield Co., S.C., 1815-*d* Wilkes Co., Ga., 1896), *m* Benjamin Wynn **Fortson** (3 above);
2–Samuel Anthony (1850-76), of Wilkes Co., Ga.; grad. Emory Coll., 1873 (Alpha Tau Omega); *m* as her 1st husband, 1875, Mary (Molly) Elizabeth Barksdale (1855-1901).
1–*m* Nov. 4, 1896, Alice Etta Lombard (qv for issue).
1–Ed. Emory U. (Alpha Tau Omega). Pres. Enterprise Mfg. Co., Augusta Factory, Sibley Mfg. Co.; dir. Ga. Railroad Bank and Lombard Iron Works. Clubs: Augusta Country. Residence: "Twin Cedars," 961 Meigs St., Augusta, Ga.

1–**FORTSON, Alice Etta Lombard (Mrs. Samuel A.),** *b* Augusta, Ga., Dec. 17, 1876.
10–Joseph **Loomis** (qv);
9–Joseph (ca. 1615-1687), of Windsor, Conn.; freeman, 1654; mem. Windsor Troop of Horse in King Philip's War, 1675-76; *m* 1646, Sarah Hill (bap. 1621-1653; William[10], *m* Phillis, dau. of Richard Lyman, qv);
8–Joseph (1649-will dated 1733), *m* 1st, 1681, Lydia Drake (1662-1702; John[9], *m* Hannah Moore);
7–Rachel (1693-1781), Windsor; *m* 1717, Ebenezer **Lombard** (1692-1780; David[8], *m* Margaret Philley; John[9]);
6–Joseph (1725-91), Springfield, Mass.; *m* 2d, 1765, Rachel Frost (1727-1807; Samuel[7], *m* Deliverence–);
5–Obed (1766-1840), Springfield; *m* 1790, Abigail Adlington (1768-1834);
4–Zelotus (1803-51), Springfield; *m* 1826, Ruby Sexton (1799-1889; Oliver Chapin[5], pvt. in Am. Rev., *m* Jerusha West; Samuel[6], *m* 1754, Sarah Chapin);
3–George Obed (1830-70), Springfield; *m* 1853, Frances Ellen Rowley;
2–George Rowley (2 below).
10–Edward **Fuller,** Mayflower Pilgrim (qv);
9–Samuel (ca. 1612-1683), *m* 1635, Jane Lathrop (bap. 1614; John[10], qv);
8–John (ca. 1656-1726), "Little John"; *m* ca. 1678, Mehitable Rowley (1660-ca. 1732; Moses[9], freeman, 1657, dep. Gen. Ct., 1692, *m* Elizabeth, dau. of Capt. Matthew Fuller, soldier and surgeon gen. Plymouth forces, and successor to Capt. Miles Standish);
7–Elizabeth (*b* ca. 1693), *m* her cousin, 1713, Dea. Samuel **Rowley** (ca. 1688-1767), settled at Hebron, Conn. (Moses[8], freeman 1690, *m* Mary Fletcher);
6–Samuel (1718-ca. 1774), of Hebron, Conn.; *m* 1744, Miriam Shailer (Abel[7], *m* Mary Parents);
5–Roswell (1761-1812-15), of Granville, Mass.; in Am. Rev.; *m* Lucinda Tinker (1762-1849; Phineas[6], *m* Charity Marshall);
4–Harmon (1807-93), *m* 1829, Dilecta Holcomb (1808-73; Dea. Bethnel[5], *m* Clarrissa Fuller; Capt. Nathaniel[6], Am. Rev.);
3–Frances Ellen (1837-76), *m* George O. **Lombard** (3 above);
2–George Rowley (1856-1929), *m* 1875, Alice Hephzibah Kendrick (1856-1916; Ely Simpson[3], *m* Frances Virginia Wilkinson); *m* 2d, 1917, Martha Swindell (*b* 1871); issue (1st marriage): I–Alice Etta (1 above); II–George Simpson (*b* 1879; *m* 1899, Alice May Clark, *b* 1880).
1–*m* Nov. 4, 1896, Samuel Anthony Fortson (qv); issue (all *b* Augusta, Ga.): 1–Samuel Donald, *b* Apr. 27, 1900; *m* Mar. 14, 1923, Edith Kathryn, *b* Jan. 20, 1900; dau. of David William Marks, *m* Catherine Pierce (issue: Catherine Barksdale, *b* 1924; Samuel Donald, Jr., *b* 1929); 2–Lombard, *b* June 5, 1902; *m* Feb. 16, 1929, Anne McKinne, *b* Dec. 2, 1904, dau. of Joseph Eve Campbell, *m* Nanette Verdery; 3–Howard Anthony, *b* Dec. 27, 1903; *m* in New York, N.Y., Nov. 16, 1929, Florence Burgess, *b* Aug. 2, 1908, dau. of William Henry Eckford, *m* Florence Franklin Burgess; 4–Martha, *b* July 29, 1905; *m* Apr. 26, 1927, Wiley James, *b* Jan. 5, 1907, son of John William Smith, *m* Etta Richards (issue: Barbara, *b* 1928); 5–Samuel Anthony, Jr., *b* June 14, 1908; 6–Charles Ogilvie, *b* Mar. 24, 1916.
1–Mem. D.A.R., I.A.G., Augusta Country Club, Woman's Club. Residence: 961 Meigs St., Augusta, Ga.

1–**FOSDICK, Florence Brown (Mrs. Lucian J.),** *b* Eminence, Ky., Dec. 27, 1858.
4–Swanson **Brown** (1728-1833), *b* in Scotland, *d* in Bracken Co., Ky., aet. 104; *m* Polly Woodsides (*d* aet. 102½);
3–William Woodsides (1779-1855), *m* ca. 1800, Sarah Staples (1780-1829);
2–Lawson Esom (2 below).
7–John **Craig** (*d* 1704, in Scotland), *m* Jane Taliaferro;
6–Capt. Toliver (1705-96), posthumous son; he and his wife were oldest defenders of Bryan's Station, nr. Lexington, Ky., 1782; *m* 1730, Mary (Polly) Hawkins (1716-1804; John[7], received land grant in King William Co., Va., 1731, *m* Mary Long?);
5–Sarah (*b* ca. 1747), *m* 1765, Manoah **Singleton** (*d* 1833), 2d lt. in Am. Rev.;
4–Elizabeth (Betsy) (1767-1852), *m* 1785, George **Neal** or O'Neal (1755-1836), in Am. Rev. (Hugh O'Neill[5], 3d son of the ancient house of O'Neall, of Shane's Castle, Antrim, Ireland, *m* Annie, dau. of Col. Cox, of Wilmington, Del.);
3–Mary (1794-1874), as Widow Hughes, *m* 2d, 1816, Benjamin Merrill **Forbes** (1793-1875).
2–Lawson Esom **Brown** (1818-91), dentist, Eminence, Ky.; *m* 1841, Mary Cracraft Watson (1824-47); *m* 2d, 1851, Caroline Owsley Forbes (1824-1911); issue (1st marriage): I–Sarah Jane (1843-1910; *m* 1860, Nestor B. Thompson); II–Lydia Ann (1845-97; *m* 1872, John W. Owen); III–Mary Esom (1847-1900; *m* 1867, Edwin Franklin King); issue (2d marriage): I–William Curtis (1851-1916; *m* 1892, Lucy Hocker); II–Florence (1 above).
1–*m* Jan. 13, 1881, Charles Stuart Woodruff (1841-88); son of Alexander S. Woodruff, of Newark, N.J., *m* Elizabeth Nock, of Halifax, N.S.
1–*m* 2d, Apr. 10, 1894, Tom Crutcher Helm (1845-1914); son of Judge Tom Helm, of Glasgow, Ky., *m* Mary Crutcher.
1–*m* 3d, Oct. 14, 1916, Lucian John Fosdick (1849-1927) of Mass.; son of Lucian Gardner Fosdick, of N.H., *m* Elmina Dexter, of Vt.
1–Ed. Eminence Bapt. Sem., 1876. Trustee N.E. Bapt. Hosp., Old Peoples Home, Bethel City Mission. Democrat. Mem. D.A.R., U.D.C., Boston Baptist Social Union, Brookline Woman's Club. Residence: 15 Garrison Rd., Brookline, Mass.

1–**FOSTER, Francis Apthorp,** *b* Cambridge, Mass., Sept. 21, 1872.
8–George **Willis** (*d* Cambridge, Mass., 1690), *m* Jane Palfrey (*d* ante 1690), a widow;
7–Thomas (1638-1725), to Medford, Mass.; *m* 1662/63, Grace Jay or Joy (1645-1712; William[8] [*d* ante Apr. 12, 1683], *m* 1644, Grace [*d* 1712], dau. of Abraham Newell, qv);
6–Stephen (*b* Billerica, Mass., 1679), *m* 1708, Martha Boardman (*b* 1683; Lt. Aaron[7] [ca. 1649-1702/03], of Cambridge, *m* Mary–, living 1717; William[8] [bap. Cambridge, Eng., 1615/16-*d* Cambridge, Mass., 1658; son of Andrew, of Cambridge, Eng., *d* 1616, *m* 1605, Rebecca Wright, *d* 1658], *m* Frances–, living Aug. 24, 1688);
5–Grace, *m* Nathan **Spear** (1728-96); see Vol. III, p. 195, for Spear lineage;
4–Grace (*d* 1811), *m* William **Foster**; see Vol. I, p. 609, for Foster lineage;
3–Leonard (1787-1855), *m* Lydia Gaubert;
2–Francis Charles (2 below).
8–John **Macomber** (*d* Taunton, Mass., ante 1690);
7–John (*d* ante Oct. 21, 1725), *m* Anna Evans (William[8] [*d* Taunton, ante Sept. 15, 1671], *m* Anna, dau. of William Hailstone, living 1675, Taunton);
6–John (1681-1747), *m* 1st, 1710, Elizabeth Williams;
5–Elijah, *m* Sarah Pitts;
4–Elizabeth (1756-1849), *m* 1785, Philip **Padelford** (1753-1815), see Vol. III, p. 195, for Padelford lineage;
3–Edward (1799-1870), *m* 1823, Elizabeth Louisa Farnum (1803-69; Zebediah[4] [1765-1834], *m* 1794, Elizabeth or Betsey [1772-1851], dau. of Benjamin Crapon; Zebediah[5], *m* 1763, Mary Hibbard);

2–Marion (2 below).
8–Richard **Williams** (bap. Wooton-under-Edge, Co. Gloucester, Eng., 1606-*d* Taunton, Mass., ante 1693; son of William Williams, buried Huntington, Co. Gloucester, 1618, *m* 2d, 1603, Jane Woodward, *d* Huntington, 1614), *m* at Whitcombe Magna, Co. Gloucester, 1632, Frances Dighton (bap. Gloucester, Eng., 1611), dau. of John Dighton (*d* Gloucester, Eng., 1640), *m* Jane Bassett (*d* Gloucester, 1631);
7–Nathaniel (bap. 1641-1692), of Taunton; *m* Elizabeth Rogers (John[8], of Duxbury, *m* at Plymouth, 1639, Ann Churchman; Thomas[9], Mayflower Pilgrim, qv);
6–Elizabeth (1686-1732), of Taunton; *m* John **Macomber** (6 above).
2–Marion Padelford (1833-1923), *m* 1857, Francis Charles **Foster** (1829-1915), A.B., Harvard, '50; lawyer, Boston; issue: I–Leonard (*d*); II–Caroline Padelford (*m* Christian Bors Isdahl); III–Francis A. (1 above).
1–Not married. Special student Lawrence Scientific Sch. (Harvard Univ.), 1895. Editor, county commissioner. Asst. sec. Gen. Soc. of the Cincinnati, and treas. of the Ga. Soc., 1904-26; mem. S.C.W., N.O.U.S., I.A.G., etc. (see Who's Who in America). Clubs: Boston City, Club of Odd Volumes (Boston). Residence: West Tisbury, Mass. Address: R.F.D. Box 31 A, Vineyard Haven, Mass.

Foster.

1–**FOSTER, Romulus Adams,** *b* Washington, D.C., Mar. 16, 1852.
8–John **Foster** (1626-87), from Eng., settled at Salem, Mass.; *m* 1649, Martha Tompkins (*b* 1630; Ralph[9], *m* Katharine Aborn);
7–Samuel (*b* 1652), of Salem, Mass.; *m* 1676, Sarah Stuard; *m* 2d, Margaret–;
6–Samuel (*b* 1680), of Reading, Mass.; *m* 1701, Sarah Roberts;
5–Lt. Benjamin (1715-91), of Reading; *m* Elizabeth Proctor;
4–Capt. James (*b* 1742), of Danvers, Mass.; in Am. Rev.; *m* 1765, Elizabeth Flint (*b* 1745);
3–James (1773-1843), of Providence, R.I.; *m* Cynthia Adams (1774-1840);
2–Adams (1794-1860), of Danvers; attorney; in War of 1812; *m* 1818, Mary Keith (1800-37); *m* 2d, 1850, Sarah Jane Burch (1827-1929, aet. 102); issue (1st marriage): I–Adeline (1819-24); II–Cynthia (*d* 1878; *m* Col. Claxton, a son of Commodore Alexander Claxon, U.S.N.); III–Jonathan Adams (1823-25); IV–Mary Adams (1826-1904; *m* Charles Clapp); V–Ellen (1829-58; *m* Dr. Henry Tabb); VI–Susan (1832-1907; *m* Isaac Vanderpool); VII–William Adams (*b* and *d* 1833); issue (2d marriage): I–Romulus Adams (1 above), and II–Remus Francis (twin, 1852-1908; *m* Ella E. Long); III–Jane Adams; IV–Elizabeth (*d* 1900).
1–Not married. Ed. med. dept., Columbian (now George Washington) U.; dept. arts and sciences, George Washington U., and a short course in law at the Nat. U. Physician; physician to Chinese Legation, 1888-90. Served 27 yrs. in Med. Corps, D.C. Nat. Guard, and retired with rank of maj.; decorated by comdg. gen., D.C. Militia, with "25 Years' Faithful Service" gold medal. Fellow A.M.A., Royal Soc. of Arts (London); mem. D.C. Med. Soc., A.A.A.S., Assn. Mil. Surgeons U.S., Mil. Service Legion, British Inst. of Philosophical Studies. Mem. S.A.R., S.W. 1812, I.A.G. Episcopalian. Residence: Tilden Gardens, 3000 Tilden St., Washington, D.C.

1–**FOSTER, Helen Rice (Mrs. Harry B.),** *b* Mendota, Ill., Aug. 8, 1882.
9–Edmund **Rice** (qv);
8–Joseph (bap. 1637-post 1684), of Sudbury; later at Watertown and Marlborough, Mass.; *m* 1677, Widow Sarah (Prescott) Wheeler (*b* 1637; John[9], *m* Mary Platts);
7–Jonathan (1679-1772), of Sudbury; dea.; *m* 1702, Ann Derby or Darby (1681-1773; Thomas[8]);
6–William (1708-80), Sudbury; *m* 1737, Mary Estabrook;
5–Capt. William (1737-1819), justice; rep. Gen. Ct.; in Am. Rev.; *m* 1772, Sarah Noyes (1746-1821; Joseph[6], *m* Elizabeth Gilbert; Joseph[7]; Joseph[8]; Rev. James[9]);
4–William (1782-1860), capt. of Sudbury militia; *m* 1810, Charlotte Whitman (1786-1857), of Westminster (Zachariah[6], veterinary; Zachariah[6]; John[7]; Zachariah[8]; John[9]);
3–Henry Marshall (1814-90), *m* 1847, Abigail F. Hastings (1822-1859);
2–Edward Hastings (1848-1911), settled at Mendota, Ill.; *m* 1879, Elizabeth Rachel Lee (1855-1920); issue: I–Arthur Henry (*m* Stella Kressinger; *m* 2d, Anne Tatham; *m* 3d, Hettie Wagoner); II–Helen (1 above).
1–*m* Oct. 8, 1903, Harry Bradford Foster, *b* Monmouth, Ill., Nov. 1, 1870; son of Thomas Calvin Foster, of Pawnee City, Neb.; issue: 1–Janet, *b* Mendota, Ill., Sept. 1, 1904; *m* George Mills McArthur; 2–Elizabeth Lee, *b* Keokuk, Ia., Mar. 15, 1906; 3–Harold Rice, *b* Keokuk, Sept. 13, 1907; 4–Martha Bowen, *b* Keokuk, Apr. 8, 1912.
1–Grad. Blackstone Sch., Mendota, Ill. Mem. D.F.P.A., D.A.R. Residence: Reedsburg, Wis.

1–**FOURT, David Leslie,** *b* Houston, Mo., May 20, 1895.
4–Andrew **Fourt,** removed from Green River region, Ky., to nr. St. Louis, Mo., 1811; later engaged in steamboat business; *m* —Wyatt;
3–John Tyler (1810-71), of nr. Marthasville, Warren Co., Mo., later moved to Houston, Mo.; mem. Mo. Legislature, 1861; *m* 1838, Serena Huffaker (1812-92), of McDonalds Co., Mo.;
2–Louis Andrew (2 below).
Desc. John **Jadwin,** who patented 650 acres land on south side of Rappahannock River, 1658; and thru:
5–Joseph, soldier N.C. Line, Am. Rev.;
4–Joseph, *m* Mary–;
3–Alexander (1815-94), removed from Knoxville, Tenn., to Mo., 1851-52; *m* 1845-46, Elizabeth North (1818-71);
2–Laura (1853-1910), *m* 1874, Louis Andrew **Fourt** (1847-1926); issue: I–Virda (*b* 1875; *m* 1901, R. E. Weimer); II–Albert Monroe (*b* 1879; *m* Katie Lyman, mem. D.A.R.); III–William Clay (*b* 1881; *m* Amea Angel Todd); IV–Ransome Wyatt (*b* 1884; *m* Goldie Todd); V–Louis Alexander (*b* 1890; *m* Alice Todd); VI–David L. (1 above).
1–*m* July 29, 1923, Ellen Elizabeth O'Donnell (qv for issue).
1–B.S. in Agr., U.Ida., '22. Dairy specialist, U. of Idaho. Mason. Mem. A.L. Residence: 1710 Franklin St., Boise, Ida.

1–**FOURT, Ellen Elizabeth O'Donnell (Mrs. David L.),** *b* Independence, Ore., Aug. 26, 1892.
9–James **Butler** (1630-81), from Ireland ante 1653, settled at Lancaster, now Nashua, Mass.; on tax list of Woburn, 1676-78; taxed at Billerica, 1679; *m* 1670, Mary– (*d* post 1698);
8–Dea. John (1677-1759), removed from Woburn to Dunstable; a first settler at Pelham, N.H.; town clk.; selectman; moderator; *m* 1702, Elizabeth Wilson (1684-post 1730; Samuel[9], of Woburn, *m* Elizabeth Pierce, desc. Thomas Pierce, *b* Eng., 1583-*d* Charlestown, Mass.);

7–Jacob (*b* 1718), rep. Pelham in Gen. Ct.; *m* 1746, Mary Eames (1723-65, Daniel[8], *m* Abigail Harnden; Samuel[9], *m* Mary–; Robert[10] [*d* 1712], to Salem, Mass., in company of Capt. Endicott; resided Charlestown, *m* Elizabeth–;
6–Daniel (1748-1831), of Pelham; soldier in Am. Rev.; *m* 1774, Molly Tenney;
5–Dole (1777-1862), of Pelham and New Boston, N.H., Galena, Ill., and Madison, Wis.; *m* 1798, Delilah Butler (1781-1847; Nehemiah[6], *m* Lydia Wood; Lt. Joseph[7], Am. Rev., *m* 2nd, Hannah Gragg; Dea. John[8], *m* Elizabeth Wilson; James[9], above);
4–Joseph Bradley Varnum (1809-79), of New Boston, N.H., Pittsfield, Ill., and Monmouth, Ore.; *m* 1839, Elizabeth Ingalls;
3–Orville (1840-1927), of Monmouth; *m* 1861, Nancy Ellen Murphy (1847-70);
2–Nancy Ellen (2 below).
11–Thomas **Tenney** (qv);
10–Dea. John (1640-1722), Bradford (now Groveland), Mass.; *m* 1st, 1663, Mercy Parrat (1646-67; Francis[11]);
9–Dea. Samuel (1667-1748), of Bradford; *m* 2d, 1690, Sarah Boynton (1671/72-1709; Capt. Joseph[10], *m* Sarah, dau. of Richard Swan, qv; John[11], *m* Ellen Pell);
8–Dea. Jonathan (1703-86), *m* Rebecca Hardy (1706-1738/39; Daniel[9], *m* Rebecca–);
7–Daniel (1732-1815), Am. Rev.; *m* Elizabeth Dole;
6–Molly (1758-1865), *m* Daniel **Butler** (6 above).
11–Edmund **Ingalls** (qv);
10–Henry (1627-1718), one of first settlers at Andover, Mass.; *m* 1st, Mary Osgood (John[11], of Andover, *m* Ann–);
9–Henry (1656-98), *m* Abigail Emery (1669-1756; John[10], *m* Mary Webster);
8–Henry (1689-1749), *m* Hannah Martin;
7–David (1726-1805), to Stoddard, N.H., thence to Londonderry; *m* Priscilla Howe (Israel[8]);
6–Israel (1760-1800), Am. Rev.; *m* Elizabeth French (*b* 1761; desc. William French, qv);
5–Israel (1793-1835), War 1812; *m* Mary Lord (1798-1871; desc. Roger Conant, qv);
4–Elizabeth (1821-1900), *m* Joseph B. V. **Butler** (4 above).
12–Francis **Cooke**, Mayflower Pilgrim (qv);
11–Jacob (*b* Holland, 1618-*d* 1663), to America, 1623; *m* 1646, Damaris Hopkins (Stephen[12], Mayflower Pilgrim, qv);
10–Jacob (1653-1747), *m* Lydia Miller;
9–William (*b* 1683), *m* Tabitha–;
8–Elisha (1717-94);
7–William (1737-1830), Am. Rev.; *m* Elizabeth Howe;
6–Rachel (1753-1832), *m* John **Murphy** (1752-1818);
5–John (*b* 1785), *m* Nancy Lamb;
4–William (1816-74), *m* Elizabeth Roundtree (1823-89; Turner[5], War 1812, *m* Mary, dau. of John Ferguson, Am. Rev., *m* —Henry);
3–Nancy Ellen (1847-70), *m* Orville **Butler** (3 above);
2–Nancy Ellen (*b* 1869), mem. D.F.P.A., U.S.D. 1812, D.A.R., Sons and Daus. of Ore. Pioneers; *m* 1889, John Franklin **O'Donnell** (*b* 1863), mcht.

1–*m* **July 29, 1923,** David Leslie Fourt (qv); issue: 1–John Edward Butler, *b* Boise, Ida., Apr. 18, **1924.**

1–Ed. Portland Acad., 1911; Ore. State Coll., 1912-13; Monmouth State Normal, 1916. Primary teacher, Corvallis, Ore., 1916-17, Ogden, Utah, 1918-21. Mem. D.F.P.A., D.A.R., U.S.D. 1812, Sons and Daus. of Ore. Pioneers, etc. Presbyterian. Republican. Summer place: 674 Multnomah St., Portland, Ore. Residence: 1710 Franklin St., Boise, Ida.

1–**FOWLER, Frank Ball,** *b* nr. Wenona, Ill., 1862.
9–William **Fowler** (qv);
8–Capt. William (*b* Eng.-*d* 1683), to Milford, Conn.; *m* 1st, 1645, Mary Tapp (Edmund[9] [*d* 1653], of New Haven, and Milford, *m* Ann–, *d* 1673);
7–Mark (1655-87), of New Haven, Conn.; *m*-(*d* 1688);
6–John (1680-1751), of Lebanon, Conn.; *m* 1707, Sarah Abbe (1686-1774; Samuel[7], of Wenham, Mass., *m* 1672, Mary Knowlton; John[8] qv);
5–Capt. Dijah (1717-1804), of Lebanon; *m* 1745, Abigail Bigelow (1723-96), see Vol. III, p. 195, for Bigelow lineage;
4–Mark (1756-1813), of Lebanon; *m* 1777, Miriam (Sterling) Warner;
3–Amos (1786-1863), of Litchfield, N.Y.; *m* 1810, Achsah Raymond;
2–Leroy Z. (2 below).
7–William **Sterling** (1637-1719), of Haverhill, Mass., and Lyme, Conn.; *m* 1659, Elizabeth– (*d* 1675);
6–Capt. Daniel (1673-1749), *m* 1699, Mary (Marvin) Ely (1666-1744), of Lyme (Reinold Marvin[7] [1634-76], of Lyme, *m* Sarah Clark; Reginald[8]);
5–John (1704-90), of Lyme, Conn., *m* 2d, 1731, Jane Ransom;
4–Miriam (1755-1843), of Lyme, Conn., and Litchfield, N.Y.; *m* 2d, Mark **Fowler** (4 above).
8–Robert **Ransom** (1636-97), of Plymouth, Mass.; *m* Susanna–;
7–Matthew (1661-86), of Sandwich, Mass., and Saybrook, Conn.; *m* 1682, Hannah Jones;
6–Joseph (*b* 1683), of Saybrook; *m* 1708, Jane–;
5–Jane (1714-1802), of Lyme, Conn.; *m* John **Sterling** (5 above).
8–Capt. William **Raymond** (1637-1709; son of George, of Eng.), from Eng. in early boyhood with his bro. John, to Beverly, Mass., 1651; dep. Gen. Ct., cdr. expdn. to Can., 1690; later at Salem, Mass.; *m* Hannah Bishop (1646-1738; Edward[9], *m* Sarah Raymond);
7–William (1666-1701), of Beverly; *m* Mary Kettle (John[8], of Gloucester and Salem, *m* 1642, Sarah Goodman);
6–William (*b* 1690), of Beverly, Rochester and Ware; *m* 1711, Deborah Balch (1693-1717; Benjamin[7], of Salem and Beverly, *m* 3d, Grace Mallet; John[8]);
5–Daniel (1717-63), of Rochester and Richmond, Mass., and Sharon, Conn.; *m* 1741, Elizabeth (Blackmer) Doty;
4–John (1750-1826), of Sharon and Stockbridge, Mass., and Litchfield, N.Y.; *m* 1780, Elizabeth Barrows;
3–Achsah (1788-1876), of New Canaan, Litchfield, and Utica, N.Y.; *m* Amos **Fowler** (3 above).
8–William **Blackmer** (1640-76), of Scituate, Mass.; *m* 1666, Elizabeth (Curtis) Banks;
7–Peter (1667-1717), of Scituate and Rochester, Mass.; *m* Elizabeth– (1673-1711);
6–John (*b* 1690), of Rochester; *m* 1711, Mary Brickett;
5–Elizabeth (*b* 1714), of Rochester and Richmond, Mass.; *m* Daniel **Raymond** (5 above).
9–John **Dunham** (qv);
8–John (1620-92), of Plymouth and Wellsfleet, Mass.; *m* 1643, Dorothy–;
7–Lydia (*b* 1666), of Plymouth, Mass.; *m* as his 2d wife, ante 1686, Robert **Barrows** (*d* 1707; John[8], qv);
6–Robert (1689-1779), of Plymouth, Mass., and Mansfield, Conn.; *m* 1711, Bethiah Ford (1690-1773; Michael[7], of Duxbury, and Scituate, Mass., *m* 2d, 1683, Bethia Hatch; William[8], qv);
5–Amos (1722-72), of Mansfield and Sharon, Conn.; *m* 1751, Mary Bailey;
4–Elizabeth, *m* John **Raymond** (4 above).
10–John **Bailey** (qv);
9–John (1613-91), of Salisbury and Newbury; *m* Eleanor Emery (*d* 1700; John[10], qv);
8–Rev. James (1650-1707), of Newbury and Roxbury, Mass., and Killingworth, Conn.; *m* 1672, Mary Carr (1652-94; George[9], qv);
7–Isaac (1681-1711), of Salem Village, Mass., Stonington and Lebanon, Conn., *m* 1702, Mercy Saxton (*b* 1686; Capt. Joseph[8], of Boston, Mass., and Stonington, Conn., *m* 1683, Hannah [Denison] Chesebrogh; Thomas[9]);
6–Joseph (1703-65), of Stonington and Lebanon, Conn., *m* 1724, Abigail Ingram;
5–Mary (*b* 1725), of Lebanon and Sharon, Conn.; *m* Amos **Barrows** (5 above).
9–Samuel **Gardner** (1615-96), of Wethersfield, Conn., and Hadley, Mass., *m* Elizabeth– (*d* 1676);
8–Elizabeth (*d* 1684), *m* 1664, John **Ingram** (1643-1722), of Hadley;
7–Nathaniel (*b* 1674), of Hadley; *m* 1696, Esther Smith (*b* 1674; Chileab[8] of Wethersfield, Conn., and Hadley, Mass., *m* 1660, Hannah, dau. of Luke Hitchcock, qv; Samuel[9], qv);
6–Abigail (*b* 1700), *m* Joseph **Bailey** (6 above).
9–Thomas **Brooks** (qv);
8–Caleb (1642-96), of Concord and Medford; *m*

1660, Susan Atkinson (1641-69; Thomas[9], of Concord, *m* Susannah-);
7-Mary (1663-1726), of Concord; *m* 1688, Nathaniel **Ball** (1663-1724); see Vol. III, p. 195, for Ball lineage;
6-Nathaniel (1692-1749), of Concord; *m* 1711, Sarah Baker (1693-1743; William[7], of Concord, *m* Elizabeth Dutton; Francis[8], qv);
5-Ebenezer (*b* 1721), of Hollis and Temple, N.H.; *m* 1746, Sarah Gookins;
4-Nathaniel (1751-1805), removed from Hollis to Litchfield, N.Y.; *m* 1775, Martha Boynton;
3-Joshua (1781-1846), of Temple, N.H., and Mexico, N.Y.; *m* 1824, Polly (Catlin) Wilcox (1788-1861);
2-Lucinda (2 below).
8-Daniel **Gookin** (qv);
7-Rev. Daniel (1650-1718), of Cambridge and Sherborn, Mass., *m* 1682, Elizabeth Quincy (1650-91; Col. Edmund[8], of Boston and Quincy, *m* 1648, Joana Hoar; Edmund[9], qv);
6-Rev. Edmund (1688-1740), of Sherborn, Mass., and Norwich, Conn.; *m* Sarah Tucker (*b* 1696; Benjamin[7], of Roxbury, *m* Elizabeth-; Benjamin[8]; Robert[9], qv);
5-Sarah (1725-81), *m* Ebenezer **Ball** (5 above).
8-William **Boynton** (1606-86), of Rowley, *m* Elizabeth Jackson;
7-Joshua (1646-1736), of Rowley and Newbury, *m* 1678, Hannah Barney (1661-1722; Jacob[8], of Charlestown, Salem, and Rehoboth, *m* 2d, 1660, Ann, dau. of Jonathan Witt; Jacob[9], qv);
6-Joshua (1679-1770), of Newbury, *m* 1708, Mary Dole (1688-1777; William[7], of Newbury, *m* 1684, Mary Brocklebank; Richard[8], qv);
5-Joshua (1717-63), of Rowley, Mass., and Hollis, N.H.; *m* 1743, Martha Stickney;
4-Martha (1745-1839), of Hollis, N.H., and Litchfield, N.Y.; *m* Nathaniel **Ball** (4 above).
8-William **Stickney** (*d* 1665), of Salem and Rowley, *m* Elizabeth-(1608-78);
7-Amos (1635-78), of Newbury and Rowley, *m* 1663, Sarah Morse (1641-1717; Anthony[8], qv);
6-Benjamin (1673-1756), of Newbury and Rowley; *m* 1701, Mary Palmer (1674-1747; Samuel[7], of Rowley, *m* Mary, dau. of Dea. John Pearson; Thomas[8]);
5-Martha (1714-78), *m* Joshua **Boynton** (5 above).
8-Capt. Thomas **Catlin** (1600-87), of Hartford, Conn.;
7-John (1640-1716), of Hartford; *m* 1665, Mary Marshall;
6-Samuel (1673-1754), of Hartford and Litchfield, *m* 1702, Elizabeth Norton (*d* 1724; John[7], of Branford and Farmington, Conn., *m* Ruth Moore; John[8]);
5-Thomas (1706-54), of Litchfield, Conn.; *m* 1732, Abigail Bissell (*b* 1712; Lt. Isaac[6], of Windsor and Litchfield, *m* Elizabeth Osborne; Thomas[7]; John[8], qv);
4-Roger (1742-1814), of Litchfield, Conn., and Winfield, N.Y.; *m* 1763, Elizabeth McNeil (*b* 1740; Adam[5], of Boston, Mass., and Litchfield, Conn., *m* Elizabeth Glen);
3-Polly (1788-1861), *m* 2d, Joshua **Ball** (3 above);
2-Lucinda (1825-1905), of Litchfield, N.Y., and Mexico, N.Y., Wenona, Ill., and Indianapolis, Ind.; *m* 1847, Leroy Z. **Fowler** (1817-71), of Litchfield, N.Y.; issue: I-Mary (*b* July 9, 1851-*d*; *m* Philip A. Crist); II-Frank B. (1 above).
1-*m* Oct. 16, 1907, Edith Keay (qv for genealogy); issue: 1-Constance, *b* Aug. 6, 1910; 2-Barbara, *b* June 1, 1913; 3-Richard K., *b* July 17, 1917.
1-Ed. Ill. Wesleyan U., 2 yrs. Pres. Fidelity Mutual Fire Ins. Co; sec. and mgr. Ind. Lumbermens Mut. Ins. Co. Mem. O.F.P.A., S.C.W., S.A.R., Inst. Am. Genealogy. Residence: 4007 Washington Boul., Indianapolis, Ind.

1-**FOWLER, Edith Keay (Mrs. Frank B.),** *b* Indianapolis, Ind., Sept. 15, 1877.
4-George **Farquahar** (*b* in Scotland-*d* Franklin, Ind.), *m* Dorothy Copeland;
3-Mary (*d* 1912), *m* William **Keay** (*b* Scotland, 1809-*d* Indianapolis, Ind., 1885);
2-William F. (2 below).
7-Christian **Webber** (1696-1778), Phila., 1727; *m* Appolonia- (1703-73);
6-Benjamin (1747-1816), *m* Mary Barbara- (1750-1815);
5-Catherine (1769-1849), of Montgomery Co., Pa.; *m* Frederick **Zearfoss** (1763-1844);
4-Catherine (1801-89), *m* 1821, George **Shellenberger** (1792-1889);
3-George (1827-64), *d* in Tenn. in Union Army; *m* 1853, Eliza Pool;
2-Laura (2 below).
5-Joseph **Pool** (1775-1863), *m* Hannah Hooker, N.C.;
4-Reuben, *m* Polly King;
3-Eliza (1834-63), *m* George **Shellenberger** (3 above);
2-Laura (1855-1916), *m* 1876, William F. **Keay** (1845-1915); issue: I-Edith (1 above); II-Elmer S. (*b* 1879; *m* 1917, Winnifred [Houghton] Brown).
1-*m* Oct. 16, 1907, Frank Ball Fowler (qv for issue).
1-Grad. Butler Coll., '99; U.Chicago, 1900. Residence: 4007 Washington Boul., Indianapolis, Ind.

HOAR

Arms: Sable, an eagle displayed with two heads, within a bordure engrailed of the first.
Crest: A deer's head erased.

1-**FOWLKES, Lucy Meriwether Fowlkes (Mrs. Francis V.),** *b* Nottoway Co., Va., Aug. 5, 1874.
7-William **Jennings** (1676-1775), from Eng., settled at Jennings, Nottaway Co., Va.; officer in Am. Rev.; *m* 1724, Mary Pulliam (1704-74);
6-Sarah (1730-82), Nottaway Co.; *m* 1746, John **Fowlkes** (1722-99);
5-John (1749-1824), Nottaway Co.; *m* 1769, Dicey Hall (*b* 1753), of Prince Edward Co., Va.;
4-John Hall (1777-1838), Lunenburg Co., Va.; *m* 1797, Elizabeth Dickinson Jennings (1779-1821);
3-Paschal Jennings (1813-82), Nottaway Co., *m* 1838, Martha Anne Hyde (1823-1919);
2-Martha Frances (2 below).
8-Leonard **Hoar** (1630-75; son of Charles, g.son of Charles); came from Eng. with his widowed mother, Joanna Hincksman, 2 bros. and 2 sisters, and settled at Braintree, Mass., 1639-40; M.D., Harvard, 1650; returned to Eng. and settled as a clergyman in Wenstead, Essex Co.; returned with his wife to Boston, Mass., 1672, and preached for a short time as asst. at South Ch.; pres. Harvard Coll., 1672-75; *m* Bridget Lisle (John[9], of Moyles Court, Co. Southampton, one of the judges who condemned Charles I, made to leave the country and was murdered at Lausanne, *m* Alice, dau. and co-heir of Sir White Beconsaw, Kent, she was beheaded by order of Judge Jeffries at Manchester, 1685);

7–Bridget Lisle of Boston; *m* 1689, Rev. Thomas **Cotton** (1657-1730);
6–Leonard Hoar (*b* 1690), of Mass., later moved to Va.; *m* Hannah–;
5–Dorothy (*b* 1726), of York Co., Va.; *m* 1750, William **Hyde**;
4–Richard (1772-1822), of Amelia Co., Va.; *m* 1819, Phoebe Stokes Mayes (*d* 1834);
3–Martha Anne (1823-1919), of Amelia Co.; *m* Paschal Jennings **Fowlkes** (3 above);
2–Martha Frances (1845-1923), *m* 1873, Henry Meriwether **Fowlkes** (1830-87); issue: I–Lucy Meriwether (1 above); II–William Hyde (*b* 1876; *m* Mary Katherine Hurt); III–Mattie Lavinia (*b* 1886; *m* Joseph Mason Anderson).
1–*m* Aug. 4, 1896, Francis Vaughan Fowlkes, *b* Amelia Co., Va., Oct. 15, 1867; son of Adrian Fowlkes (1839-1900), of Amelia Co.; issue: 1–Francis Meriwether, *b* Washington, D.C., Mar. 2, 1898; B.S., Hampden-Sydney, '22; M.S., U.Va., 1923; 2–Martha Hyde, and 3–Elizabeth Vaughan, twins, *b* Richmond, Va., Apr. 5, 1905; 4–Sarah Mayes (Aug. 15, 1908-July 10, 1909); 5–Paschal Dupuy, *b* Burkeville, Va., July 26, 1915.
1–Mem. I.A.G., etc. Baptist. Democrat. Residence: 3508 Seminary Av., Richmond, Va.

1–**FOX, Herbert Wright,** *b* Painted Post, N.Y., Feb. 7, 1873.
8–George **Gates** (qv);
7–Daniel (*b* 1680), *m* Rebecca Dutton;
6–David (1709-95), *m* Hannah Ackley;
5–Elizabeth (1733-79), *m* 1761, Daniel **Fox** (1722-1801; Isaac[6]; Samuel[7]; Thomas[8], qv);
4–Jehiel (1762-1823), *m* Jerusha Baldwin;
3–Norman (1792-1863), *m* 1831, Jane DeHart Freeman;
2–Charles James (2 below).
8–Richard **Baldwin** (qv);
7–Theophilus (1659-98), *m* 1683, Elizabeth Campfield;
6–Theophilus (ca. 1694-1745), *m* Jerusha Beecher (1705-90);
5–Capt. Hezekiah (1732-1822), from New Milford, Conn., to Chestertown, N.Y.; lt. French and Indian War; capt. in Am. Rev.; *m* 1759, Abigail Peet (*b* 1736; James[6]; Benjamin[7]; Benjamin[8]; John[9]);
4–Jerusha (1760-1819), *m* ca. 1786, Rev. Jehiel **Fox** (4 above).
9–Balthasar **DeHart** (*d* 1672), *m* Margaret Stuyvesant (sister of Gov. Peter Stuyvesant, qv);
8–Matthys (1667-1761), *m* 1695, Janetje Maurits;
7–Jacob (1699-1777), *m* 1723, Abigail Crane (ca. 1703-1770);
6–Matthias (1723-66), *m* 1746, Catherine Kingsland (1723-83);
5–Joanna, *m* William **Freeman** (*b* 1751); see Vol. I, p. 501 for Freeman lineage;
4–William (1781-1818), *m* 1805, Betsey Chesebrough;
3–Jane DeHart (1806-49), *m* Norman **Fox** (3 above).
9–William **Coddington** (qv);
8–Mary (1654-93), *m* 1674, Peleg **Sanford** (1639-1701; John[9] [*d* 1653], from Eng. to Boston, pres. R.I., 1653, *m* Bridget, dau. of William Hutchinson, qv);
7–Ann, *m* 1702, Dr. James **Noyes**, Jr. (1677-1718; James[8] [1640-1719], from Newbury, Mass., to Stonington, Conn., B.A., Harvard, 1659, minister Congl. Ch., a founder of Yale Coll., chaplain King Philip's War, *m* 1674, Dorothy Stanton; Rev. James[9], qv);
6–Bridget (1708-74), *m* 1727, Nathan **Chesebrough** (1707-69; see Vol. I, p. 501, for Chesebrough lineage);
5–Peleg (1736-1803), *m* 1772, Rebecca Barber;
4–Betsey (1777-1841), *m* William **Freeman** (4 above).
9–Thomas **Barber** (qv);
8–John (1642-1712), *m* 1663, Bathsheba Coggins (*d* 1688);
7–Thomas (1674-1714), *m* 1702, Sarah Ball (1685-1744);
6–Jonathan (1712-83), *m* 1740, Sarah Noyes (1712-61);
5–Rebecca (1752-1801), *m* Peleg **Chesebrough** (5 above).
5–John **Wright** (*d* 1804), of Granville, Mass.; capt. 4th Mass., Cont. Line, Am. Rev.; *m* 1767, —Robinson;
4–Calvin (1769-1843), *m* 1795, Sarah Treadway (1766-1839);
3–John Calvin (1801-62), A.B., Union Coll., 1820; state senator; judge Supreme Ct., New York State; *m* 1832, Louisa Marsh (1810-44; Silas[4], of Duanesburg, N.Y.);
2–Louisa Octavia (1843-1913), *m* 1865, Charles James **Fox** (1842-1903; brother of George Henry Fox, see Vol. I, p. 501, for Fox lineage), lumber mfr.; issue: I–Norman Wright (*b* 1866; *m* 1899, Stella Kerwin; *m* 2d, 1902, Fanny L. Hudson; *m* 3d, May Jean Mitchell); II–Caroline Wright (*b* 1870; *m* Frank L. Kershner); III–Herbert Wright (1 above); IV–Walter Wright (1878-1913; *m* Ethel McCormac); V–George Henry (*b* 1883; *m* Gertrude Olcutt).
1–*m* Feb. 7, 1906, Anna Moore, *b* Clayton, N.J., Jan. 19, 1878; dau. of D. Wilson Moore, of Clayton, *m* 1862 Anna Pierce; issue: 1–Herbert Moore, *b* Colorado Springs, Colo., Feb. 2, 1909; U.Del., '31.
1–A.B., Union Coll., '93 (Psi U.); B.S., U.Chicago, 1895. Chemical engineer. Clubs: Chemists (New York), University, Wilmington Country. Residence: 1216 Lovering Av., Wilmington, Del.

1–**FRAZIER, Harry,** *b* Rockbridge Co., Va., July 24, 1861.
4–John **Frazier** (1751-1832), from Ulster, Ireland, to Augusta Co., Va., 1795; *m* Margaret Anderson;
3–James Anderson (1780-1853), *m* Martha Rankin (1790-1869);
2–William (2 below).
6–John **Lewis** (1678-1762), from Ireland, 1728; founder of Augusta Co., Va., and city of Staunton; *m* Margaret Lynn (dau. Laird of Loch Lynn, Scotland);
5–Col. William (1724-1811), "Civilizer of the Border"; *m* Anne Montgomery (*d* 1808);
4–Alexander (1763-97), *m* Mary Fife;
3–James Alexander (1794-1860), *m* Prudentia Wilson (1799-1867);
2–Sue Massie (1828-1904), *m* William **Frazier** (1812-85), Yale, '32 (hon. M.A., 1879), LL.B., U.Va., 1834; lawyer, Staunton, Va. (for issue see Vol. III, p. 196).
1–*m* Sept. 20, 1882, Minnie Lurana Turpin (1862-1930), dau. of Dr. Walter Turpin, of Queen Anne Co., Md.; issue: 1–Gladys, *b* Louisville, Ky., Mar. 5, 1884; *m* Apr. 2, 1906, Alexander Erskine Milles; 2–Elizabeth, *b* Louisville, June 1, 1885, *m* Nov. 14, 1908, Lloyd R. Freeman; 3–Harry, Jr., *b* Hopkinsville, Ky., May 20, 1887; U. of Va., '06; *m* Oct. 12, 1927, Eleanor Lightner; 4–William, *b* Hopkinsville, Oct. 29, 1888; U.Va., '08; capt. Co. G, 2d Bn., 317th Inf., 80th Div., and in France, June 1918-July 1919; leg shattered by machine gun bullet, Oct. 6, 1918; in hosp. 2 yrs.
1–Ed. pvt. schs. and Staunton Mil. Acad. Consulting engr. for C.&O. and other rys. Mem. S.A.R. Clubs: New York (New York), Westmoreland, Commonwealth, Country (Richmond), etc. Summer place: "Thornwold," nr. Lewisburg, W.Va. Residence: 1826 Monument Av., Richmond, Va.

1–**FREEMAN, Ethel Bell Goodell (Mrs. William S.),** *b* West Chester, Pa., Jan. 12, 1865.
9–Robert (Goodale) **Goodell** (qv);
8–Zachariah (1640-post 1725), *m* 1666, Elizabeth (Beacham) Beauchamp (*b* 1648), they are the ancestors of President William Howard Taft (Edward[9], London mcht., with bro. from Eng., settled at Salem, 1637, *m* Mary–, *d* 1668);
7–John (1681-1752), of Marlborough, Mass., 1702, where he built the homestead which is still occupied by a descendant; *m* 1703, Elizabeth Witt (1676-1738; John[8], of Lynn, *m* 1676, Elizabeth Baker; John[9], of Lynn);
6–Nathan (1709-80), *m* Persis Whitney;
5–Nathan (1736-62), *m* Dinah Weeks;
4–William (1757-1843), in Am. Rev. under Gen. Gates; *m* 1787, Phoebe Newton (1768-1809; Micah[5]);
3–Rev. William, D.D. (1792-1867), see portrait and biography; *m* 1822, Abigail Perkins Davis;
2–William (2 below).
10–John **Whitney** (qv);
9–Thomas (1629-1719), freeman, 1690; *m* 1654, Mary Kedall or Kittall;

WILLIAM GOODELL, D.D. (Feb. 14, 1792-Feb. 18, 1867), grad. Phillips Andover Acad., 1813, Dartmouth Coll., 1817, and Andover Theol. Sem., 1820; first missionary to Turkey; founded several schools at Constantinople including the first school for girls there; translated the Scriptures into Armeno-Turkish.

8–Thomas (1656-1742), *m* 1678/79, Elizabeth Lawrence (1658-1742);
7–Lt. Benjamin (1687-1737), mem. Simon Mainard's garrison against the Indians; *m* 1st, Sarah Barrett (1692-1730; John[8] [1663-1715], *m* 1688, Deborah Howe [1667-1743]; John[9] [*d* 1711], *m* 1662, Mary Pond [*d* 1711]; Humphrey[10] [1592-1662], from Eng. to Concord, 1640);
6–Persis (1719-98), *m* Nathan **Goodell** (6 above).
9–George (Weekes) **Weeks** (qv);
8–Ammiel (1633-79), from Eng.; *m* Elizabeth Aspinwall (*d* 1723; William[9] *m* Elizabeth, dau. of Thomas Goodyear);
7–Supply (1671-1755), *m* 1st, 1699, Susannah Barnes (*d* 1712; Thomas[8], qv);
6–Col. John (1707-87), *m* 1731, Dinah Keyes;
5–Dinah (1737-1822), *m* Nathan **Goodell** (5 above).
9–John **Howe** (qv);
8–John (*d* 1680), *m* Elizabeth–;
7–Elizabeth (1675-1764), *m* Thomas **Keyes** (1674-1742; Elias[8]; Robert[9]);
6–Dinah (1710-84), *m* John **Weeks** (6 above).
8–Dolor **Davis** (qv);
7–Samuel (1639/40-ante 1720), Concord, Mass.; *m* 1660, Mary (Meads, Meddowes, Medow) Mead (*d* 1710);
6–Lt. Simon (1683-1763), *m* Dorothy Hale (1692-1776);
5–Rev. Joseph (1720-99), *m* 1743, Catherine Jones (1721-1815; Capt. James[6], of E. Sudbury, Mass., *m* Sarah Moore; Josiah[7]; Lewis[8], qv);
4–Lemuel (1765-1828), *m* 1788, Eunice Sherwin (1766-1818; Elnathan[5], *m* Eunice Brown);
3–Abigail P. (1800-71), *m* 1822, William **Goodell** (3 above);
2–William, M.D., LL.D. (Oct. 17, 1829-Oct. 27, 1894), grad. Williams Coll., 1851, Jefferson Med. Coll., 1854; practiced in Constantinople, 1855-61; first prof. gynecology U.Pa., 1874-93; *m* Sept. 4, 1857, Caroline Darlington Bell (Sept. 14, 1831-Dec. 31, 1896).
1–*m* Feb. 18, 1890, William Salter Freeman (see Vol. I, p. 612, for genealogy); issue (all *b* Phila., Pa.): 1–William Goodell, *b* Mar. 25, 1891; B.S., U.Pa., '13; served in 7th Inf. N.G.N.Y. on Mexican border 5 months, 1916; 1st lt., Ordnance R.C., Aug. 22, 1917; capt., ordnance, Sept. 27, 1918; hon. discharged, July 12, 1919; 2–Caroline Bell (Mrs. Abner Rutherford Renninger, qv for other lineages); 3–Morris de Camp, *b* Mar. 2, 1896; U.Pa., '18; enlisted in U.S. Marine Corps Reserve, Apr. 26, 1917; gunnery sgt., June 20, 1918; 2d lt., aviation, Oct. 28, 1918; on inactive list M.C.R., Feb. 1919.
1–Ed. Miss Agnes Irwin's Sch., Phila. Clubs: Sedgeley, Art Alliance. Mem. C.D.A., D.A.R., Pa. Soc. of N.E.Women. Residence: 2034 Chestnut St., Philadelphia, Pa.

1–**RENNINGER, Caroline Bell Freeman (Mrs. Abner R.),** *b* Phila., Pa., Feb. 10, 1893.
7–Alexander **Hemphill** (*d* 1768), of Scotch-Irish descent; Hemphill is the Irish form of Campbell; from Newtown-Limavady, Co. Londonderry, Ireland, to Thornbury, Chester (now Delaware) Co., Pa., ca. 1740;
6–James (*d* 1809), *m* 1750, Elizabeth Wills (*b* 1731; Thomas[7], of Middletown, Pa., *m* Ann, dau. of Peter Hunter, *m* Jane, dau. Richard Lee);
5–William (1776-1817), of Chester Co., Pa.; lawyer; prominent in councils of the Federal party; candidate for state senator, 1811; dep. atty. gen. Pa., 1803-08; *m* 1804, Ann McClellan;
4–Kezia Ann (1812-59), *m* 1830, Judge Thomas Sloan **Bell** (1800-61), of Phila.; dep. atty. gen. for Chester Co., 1823-28; mem. State Senate; mem. bd. of visitors of U.S.M.A.; pres. judge Chester and Delaware cos.; apptd. asso. justice Supreme Ct. of Pa., 1846 (William[5], *m* Jane Sloan);
3–Caroline Darlington (1831-96), *m* William **Goodell**;
2–Ethel Bell (2 below).
8–Robert **McClellan** (ca. 1698-1741; desc. Sir Thomas McClellan of the Campbell Clan, of Kirkcudbright Castle, who is buried in Dundrennan Abbey, Scotland), from the Province of Ulster, North Ireland, bet. 1720-25, with Scotch emigrants; settled in Middletown Tp., Chester (now Delaware) Co., Pa.; *m* 2d, Elizabeth (*d* 1759), dau. of James Ewing, from Hopewell Tp., Hunterdon Co., N.J., ca. 1727, to Chester Co., Pa., *m* Margaret–;
7–James (*d* 1793), *m* Martha Caldwell (*d* 1793; Henry[8], *d* 1758);
6–Col. Joseph (1747-1834), served in Gen. Wayne's Brigade, Am. Rev.; Soc. Cincinnati; mem. State Senate, 1797; first pres. Bank of Chester Co., 1814; *m* 1786, Kezia Parke;
5–Ann (1787-1860), *m* William **Hemphill** (5 above).
9–Arthur (Park) **Parke** (qv);
8–John (1706-87), *m* Elizabeth McKnight (1712-94);
7–Joseph (1737-1823), *m* 1st, Ann (Grubb) Sinclair, widow of George Sinclair (Nathaniel Grubb[8], *m* Ann Moore; John[9] [*d* 1708], *m* Frances–);
6–Kezia (1767-1842), *m* Joseph **McClellan** (6 above).
2–Ethel Bell Goodell (qv), *m* 1890, William Salter **Freeman**.
1–*m* June 9, 1917, Abner Rutherford Renninger, M.D., *b* Harrisburg, Pa., Sept. 2, 1875; son of Abraham C. Renninger, M.D.; issue: 1–Ann Rutherford, *b* Phila., June 21, 1921.
1–Ed. Chambersburg Acad., Pa. State Coll., U.Pa. Club: Penn Athletic. Residence: 254 S. 16th St., Phila., Pa.

1–**FRENCH, David Edwin,** *b* Curve, Giles Co., Va., July 26, 1871.
6–John **French** (ca. 1710-1750), from Westmoreland Co. to Frederick Co., Va., 1749; received land grant from Lord Fairfax, 1749; apptd. constable of Frederick Co., 1749; *m* ca. 1730, Martha–;
5–Matthew (1732-1814), of Giles Co., Va.; in battles of Guilford C.H. and Wetzell's Mills; *m* 1758, Sarah Payne (1740-1813), of Culpeper Co., Va.;
4–David (1772-1833), first clk. of Giles Co.; served 27 yrs.; capt. of co. militia; *m* 1797, Mary Dingess (1780-1828; Peter Dingess or Dinges[5] [1740-1809], from Holland in the "Brothers," 1751, in Am. Rev., *m* 1769, Mary Smith);
3–Guy Dingess (1798-1865), of Giles Co.; large land and slave owner; ed. Georgetown U.; *m* 1826, Araminta Chapman;
2–Henley Chapman (2 below).
6–Isaac **Chapman,** from Md. to Culpeper Co.; *m* Sarah Cole;
5–John (1740-1813), of Giles Co., Va.; ens. in

Am. Rev.; *m* Sarah Abbott (*d* post 1813; Richard[6], of Culpeper Co.);
4–Henley (1779-1864), lawyer; first commonwealth's atty. of Giles Co.; mem. Va. Senate, 1813-18; mem. Va. Constl. Conv., 1829; *m* 1803, Mary Alexander (1784-1837), of Monroe Co., W.Va. (James[5] [1750-1814], justice and soldier in Am. Rev., *m* 1772, Isabella [*d* 1834], dau. of Henry Erskine, *m* Jean Thompson; Andrew[6] [1708-88], from Ireland, Am. Rev., *m* 1735, Catherine [Thompson] Aiken);
3–Araminta (1808-76), *m* 1826, Guy D. **French** (3 above).
7–Robert **Easley** (*d* 1711), said to have come from Eng., ca. 1680; living in Henrico Co., Va., 1681;
6–Robert (probably);
5–Daniel (ca. 1725-1786), of Halifax Co.; Am. Rev.; *m* 2d, ca. 1756, Elizabeth Echols (living 1786);
4–Isaac (1761-1810), of Halifax Co., Va.; *m* 1782, his cousin, Judith Easley (1758-1852; William[5], Robert[6], above);
3–John S. (1790-1868), of Craig Co., Va.; War 1812; *m* 1820, Agnes Clark White;
2–Harriet Thomas (2 below).
5–Jeremiah **White** (*d* 1788), lt. of Militia, Pittsylvania Co., Va., 1780; *m* Jane, probably Hamilton;
4–Capt. John (*b* 1768), of Pittsylvania Co.; *m* 1794, Phoebe Howson Clark (*b* 1770; Thomas[5] [*d* 1792], of Halifax Co., *m* Phoebe Howson; Thomas[6] [*d* 1790], of Prince Edward Co., *m* Agnes, probably Worsham);
3–Agnes Clark (1797-1891), *m* John S. **Easley** (3 above);
2–Harriet Thomas (1833-94), *m* 1852, Henley Chapman **French** (1827-90), ed. Emory and Henry Coll., and U.S.M.A.; farmer and stockman; during the War Between the States he had charge of the saltpeter works on New River for the C.S.A.; issue: I–Guy D. (1853-1910; *m* Bettie E. Snidow); II–Mary Clark (*b* 1855; *m* Christian Snidow); III–William Wirt (1858-99; *m* Rose Baach); IV–Fannie Smoot (1860-90; *m* S. F. Day); V–Araminta Agnes (1862-1901); VI–Carrie Sue (1865-91); VII–Harriet Alverda (1867-1912; *m* W. S. Leake); VIII–John Easley (1869-1927; *m* Pricie Snidow); IX–David Edwin (1 above); X–Sarah Bernice (*b* 1875; *m* H. H. Holland).
1–*m* Nov. 15, 1899, Minnie Reid (qv for issue).
1–Studied law and was admitted to bar, 1895; organized Bank of Keystone, W.Va., 1905, and was pres. until 1923; pres. Bluefield Nat. Bank, since 1923; also pres. Bluefield Office Bldg. Co., Am. Finance Co.; trustee Bluefield Coll. City atty. of Bluefield, 8 yrs.; mem. W.Va. State Senate, 1910-14. Chmn. Bluefield and Mercer Co., W.Va., 4 minute men, World War; chmn. Mil. Training Camp Assn., Mercer Co., and mem. Legal Advisory Bd. for the co. Mem. co., state and Am. bar assns. Mem. S.A.R. (state pres., 1927-28, v.p. nat. soc., 1928-30). Mason (Shriner). Elk. Clubs: Bluefield Rotary (pres., 1927-28), Bluefield Country. Residence: 2126 Reid Av., Bluefield, W.Va.

1–**FRENCH, Minnie Reid (Mrs. David E.),** *b* Summers Co., W.Va., Nov. 21, 1875.
5–Jeremiah **Reid** (ca. 1755-1822), of Hampshire Co., Va., 1777; received land grant, 1777; *m* ca. 1775, Elizabeth McMahon (*d* 1828);
4–John (1780-1853), of Hampshire Co., now W.Va.; *m* ca. 1800, Nancy Orndorf;
3–John (1805-45), of Giles Co., Va.; *m* 1839, Mary Ann Wilson (1816-43; William[4] [*d* 1824], *m* Ann Reid [*d* 1843]; James[5] [d 1781], *m* Elizabeth–, *d* 1806);
2–William Albert (2 below).
7–John **French** (ca. 1710-50), removed from Westmoreland Co., to Frederick Co., Va.; received land grant from Lord Fairfax, 1749; apptd. constable of Frederick Co., 1749; *m* ca. 1730, as her first husband, Martha–;
6–Matthew (1732-1814), of Giles Co., Va.; present at battles of Guilford C.H., Wetzell's Mills; Matthew French Chapter, D.A.R., of Princeton, W.Va., named for him; *m* 1758, Sarah Payne (1740-1813), of Culpeper Co., Va.;
5–James (1763-1841), gentleman justice of Giles Co.; lt. of militia; *m* 1789, Susan Hughes (ca. 1763-1824), *b* N.C.;
4–Sarah (1798-1860), of Giles Co.; *m* 1818, William H. **Hare** (1800-54; Joseph[5] [1749-1853], of Huguenot descent, *b* N.C., *d* Giles Co., served in Am. Rev., *m* 1791, Phoebe Perdue);
3–Joseph (1819-1904), of Giles Co.; *m* 1842, Julia Ann Duncan (1823-1914; Rev. Landon[4] [1786-1867], pioneer minister and educator, of Giles Co., *m* Sarah, dau. of Thomas Kirk);
2–Phoebe Louise (1844-1912), of Athens, Mercer Co., W.Va.; *m* 1866, William Albert **Reid** (1841-78), ed. Emory and Henry Coll.; capt. C.S.A.; landowner; *m* 2d, 1880, Overton Caperton; issue (1st marriage): I–Walter Scott (1867-1907; *m* Katie Lee Hardy, *d*); II–Mary Maude (*b* 1871; *m* Hon. John D. Sweeney); III–Rupert Ray (1872-74); IV–Minnie (1 above).
1–*m* Nov. 15, 1899, David Edwin French (qv); issue: 1–David Edwin, Jr., *b* Keystone, W.Va., Oct. 19, 1900; ed. Washington and Lee U. and U. of W.Va.; *m* Sept. 7, 1927, Gladys Antoinette, dau. of Emmett L. Bailey, of Bluefield, W.Va.; 2–John Reid, *b* Keystone, Sept. 6, 1902; ed. Bluefield Coll.; 3–Harriet Louise, *b* Keystone, Oct. 3, 1904; A.B., U. of W.Va., '27, LL.B., 1930; 4–Frances Chapman, *b* Bluefield, W.Va., Nov. 6, 1906; ed. N.Y. Sch. of Fine and Applied Arts; 5–Elizabeth Wilson, *b* Bluefield, Jan. 24, 1912; ed. Bluefield Coll.
1–grad. Concord Normal Sch., Athens, W.Va. Writer since age 16. Mem. D.A.R. (vice regent and regent John Chapman Chapter, W.-Va. state chaplain), U.D.C., I.A.G., Va. Hist. Soc., League Am. Penwomen. Club: Bluefield Woman's (v.p.). Residence: 2126 Reid Av., Bluefield, W.Va.

1–**FRIES, Adelaide Lisetta,** *b* Salem, N.C., Nov. 12, 1871.
6–Philip Christoph **Vogler** (1725-90), from the Palatinate with his parents to Broadbay (now Waldoboro), Me., 1742; served on expdn. against Louisburg, 3 yrs.; removed to N.C., 1770; *m* 1746, Catharina Seitz (*d* 1770);
5–George Michael (1759-95); served N.C. militia, Am. Rev.; *m* 1781, Anna Maria Künzel (1761-92; John Frederick[6], *m* Salome Kasner);
4–John (1783-1881), *m* 1819, Christina Spach (1792-1863; John Gottlieb[5], *m* Martha Elisabeth Hege; Adam[6], came to America, ca. 1735);
3–Lisetta Maria (1820-1903), *m* 1838, Francis **Fries** (1812-63; John Christian William[4], [1775-1866; desc. of Sigismund Eberhard von Fries, col. and comdt., Höckst am Main, *m* Lady Julianna Anna Hamilton, of Scotland], from Germany to Salem, N.C., 1809, *m* 1811, Johanna Elisabeth, dau. of Toego Nissen, came to America 1770);
2–John William (2 below).
5–Rev. Hans Christian Alexander von **Schweinitz** (1740-1802; son of Hans Christian, desc. of Hancke von Swentze, counsellor at the Court of Ruprecht, Duke of Leignitz, titles confirmed 1350, *m* Fenne von Proedel); came from Silesia to Bethlehem, Pa., 1770; senior civilis of the Unitas Fratrum or Moravian Ch., *m* 1779, Anna Dorothea Elisabeth, Baroness von Watteville (1754-1813; John Michael[6], *b* Langguth, created Baron von Watteville, 1745, *m* Henrietta Benigna, dau. of Nicholas Lewis, Count von Zinzendorf, great leader of Moravian Church, *m* 1722, Erdmuth Dorothea, Countess Reuss);
4–Lewis David (1780-1834), changed "von" to "de"; hon. Ph.D., U. of Kiel, 1817; distinguished botanist; bequeathed his private herbarium, largest in America, to Acad. Nat. Sciences; author; mem. Acad. Nat. Sciences, Am. Philos. Soc.; corr. mem. Linnean (Paris), Soc. Nat. Sciences (Leipzig); *m* 1812, Louisa Amalia Le Doux (1791-1858; Jean or John[5] [1744-1823], of Huguenot family, which removed from nr. Bordeaux to Stettin, Brandenburg, 1691, *m* Elisabeth Malbranc);
3–Emil Adolphus de (1816-79), trustee and bishop of Southern Moravian Ch. (Unitas Fratrum), in Salem, N.C., 40 yrs.; *m* 1842, Sophia Amelia Herman;
2–Agnes Sophia (2 below).
6–Andreas **Schober** (*b* Moravia, 1710-*d* 1792), from Germany to Bethlehem, Pa., 1743; *m* 1743, Hedwig Regina Schuber (1721-1800);
5–Gottlieb (1756-1838), *m* Maria Magdalena Transou (Philip[6] [1724-93], came to America, 1762, *m* Magdalena Gander);
4–Anna Paulina, *m* Bishop John Gottlieb **Her-**

man (1789-1854), from Eng. to America, 1817 (son of Johann G. Herman, of Niesky, Germany, *m* Anna Regina Otto);
3–Sophia Amelia (1822-83), *m* Bishop Emil Adolphus de **Schweinitz** (3 above);
2–Agnes Sophia de (1849-1915), *m* 1870, John William **Fries** (1846-1927); issue: I–Adelaide Lisetta (1 above). II–Mary Eleanor (*b* 1873; *m* William Allen Blair).
1–Ed. Salem Acad. and Coll., '88, M.A., 1916. Archivist, Moravian Ch., 1911–. Has published History of Forsyth Co.; Hist. Sketch of Salem Female Acad.; The Moravians in Ga., 1735-40; Funeral Chorals of the Unitas Fratrum or Moravian Ch.; 3 vols. of Records of of the Moravians in N.C.; part author of a Brief History of the Moravian Ch.; The Moravian Ch. Yesterday and Today. Mem. Am. Hist. Assn., Moravian Hist. Soc. (v.p.), N.C. Lit. and Hist. Assn. (pres., 1922-23), Wachovia Hist. Soc. (corr. sec.), Nat. Geneal. Soc., N.E.H.G.S., I.A.G.; pres. N.C. Federation of Women's Clubs, 1913-15. Clubs: Winston-Salem Woman's, Salem Alumnae Assn. (pres.). Residence: 224 S. Cherry St., Winston-Salem, N.C.

1–**FULTON, Gertrude Lynn Tinker, (Mrs. J. Gault),** *b* Tolland, Mass., Apr. 9, 1868.
7–John **Tinker** (qv);
6–Amos (1657-1730), of Lyme, Conn.; *m* 1682, Sarah Durant;
5–Amos (1696/97-1760), *m* 1716, Lucy Lee (1699-1757; John[6], *m* Elizabeth Smith);
4–Martin (1739-1811), capt. in Am. Rev.; removed from Lyme, Conn., to Westfield, Mass.; *m* 1769, Mary Peck (1753-1827; John[5], *m* Catherine Lay);
3–Edward Lay (1791-1872), of Tolland, Mass.; *m* 1816, Laura Steele (1791-1865; Ebenezer[4], *m* Rachel Seymour);
2–Edward Lay (2 below).
9–Gov. William **Bradford** (qv);
8–Maj. William (1624-1704), of Plymouth, Mass.; removed to Kingston, Mass.; asst.; dep.gov.; mem. Gov. Andros' Council, 1687; chief mil. officer of Plymouth Colony; *m* 1st, Alice Richards (1627-71; Thomas[9], of Weymouth, *m* Wealtyan–);
7–Melatiah (*b* 1664), *m* John **Steele** (1660-1697/98);
6–Ebenezer (1695-1746), removed to Hartford, Conn.; *m* Susanna Merrills (*b* 1700; Daniel[7], *m* Susanna Pratt);
5–John (*d* 1785), *m* Christian– (*d* 1799);
4–Ebenezer (1753-1805), *m* 1778, Rachel Seymour (1755-1839; Allan[5], *m* Elizabeth Smith);
3–Laura (1791-1865), *m* Edward Lay **Tinker** (3 above).
9–John **Cowles** (qv);
8–Samuel (1639-91), of Farmington, Conn.; *m* 1660, Abigail Stanley (*d* 1734; Timothy[9], *m* Elizabeth–);
7–Joseph (1677-1760), removed to Meriden, Conn.; *m* 1st, 1699, Abigail Royce (1677-1714; Samuel[8], *m* Hannah Churchill or Churchwood);
6–Samuel (1712-98), removed to New Hartford, Conn.; *m* 1734, Martha Brooks (1714-78; Lt. Thomas[7], *m* Martha Hotchkiss);
5–Amasa (1744/45-1832), Am. Rev.; removed to Norfolk, Conn.; *m* 1766, Lucy North (1739-1826; Ebenezer[6], *m* Sybil Curtiss);
4–Ira (*b* 1768), *m* 1st, 1788, Sarah Lane;
3–Luman Lane (1797-1851), of Colebrook, Conn., and Lee, Mass.; *m* 1817, Menda Pinney;
2–Augusta Janette (2 below).
9–Humphrey **Pinney** (*d* 1683), from Eng. in the "Mary and John," 1630; settled at Dorchester, Mass.; *m* Mary Hall (*d* 1684);
8–Nathaniel (1641-76), *m* 1670, Sarah (Griswold) Phelps (1630-1715; Edward Griswold[9], qv);
7–Lt. Nathaniel (1671-1764), *m* 1693, Martha Thrall (*b* 1673; Timothy[8], *m* Deborah Gunn);
6–Capt. Abraham (1709-80), of Simsbury, Conn.; *m* Elizabeth Butler (1709-60; Jonathan[7], *m* Mary Easton);
5–Lt. Abraham (1735-1813), Am. Rev.; *m* 1761, Lucretia Barnard (1743-75; Francis[6], *m* Lucretia Pinney);
4–Israel (1767-1821), removed to Colebrook, Conn.; *m* 1787, Belinda Loomis (1762-1862; Timothy[5], *m* Mary Morton);
3–Menda (1793-1860), *m* Luman Lane **Cowles** (3 above).
2–Edward Lay **Tinker** (1819-98), *m* 1856, Emmeline Cross; *m* 2d, 1867, Augusta Janette Cowles (1828-85); issue (1st marriage): I–Edward Lay (1858-98; *m* 1882, Mary Hough, 1857-1926); II–Fred Cross (1862-76); issue (2d marriage): I–Gertrude Lynn (1 above); II–Irving Sterling (*b* 1870; *m* Harriet L. Hitchcock).
1–*m* Sept. 13, 1893, Joseph Gault Fulton (Sept. 6, 1868-May 5, 1927); son of George Fulton, of Louisville, Ky.; issue: 1–Edward Irving, *b* Anchorage, Ky., Jan. 4, 1895; A.B., Center Coll., '16; M.A., George Washington U., 1921; *m* June 27, 1922, Corinne, dau. John B. Brown, of Louisville, Ky.; 2–John Drake (Sept. 17, 1900-Sept. 16, 1927); *m* May 9, 1921, Martha, dau. Marvin Ellis, of Pewee Valley, Oldham Co., Ky. (issue: Mary Gertrude; Martha Ann).
1–A.B., Wellesley Coll., '88. Mem. D.F.P.A., S.M.D., D.A.R. Presbyn. Residence: Anchorage, Jefferson Co., Ky.

1–**GAGER, James Marvin,** *b* Sandusky, O., Mar. 19, 1880.
9–Dr. William **Gager** (*d* 1630), from Eng. with Gov. Winthrop, 1630; surgeon; reckoned of gov.'s household and was given salary from pub. treas.; deacon;
8–John (*d* 1703), of Charlestown, Mass., and Saybrook, Conn.; removed to New London, 1648, to Norwich, 1660; freeman, 1675; accompanied young Gov. Winthrop on Pequot conquest, 1645; *m* 1650, Elizabeth–;
7–Samuel (1654-1740), of Norwich; *m* 1695, Rebecca (Lay) Raymond;
6–John (*b* 1698), *m* 1734, Jerusha Barstow (Job[7], *m* Rebecca Bushnell);
5–Jason (1738-1809), *m* 1st, Zervia Roberts; *m* 2d, Lucy Peck (*b* 1747; Jonathan[6], *m* Bethiah Bingham; Benjamin[7], of Woodbridge, Conn., *m* Mary Sperry; Henry[8], qv);
4–Andrew (1773-1846), *m* 1796, Lois Webb;
3–Marvin (1804-99), of Tolland, Conn., and Woodstock, O.; *m* 1839, Lucretia (Ripley) Clark (1803-95), of London, O. (Hezekiah Augustus Ripley[4], *m* 1793, Hannah Marcy; Hezekiah[5], D.D., Yale, 1763, pastor Congl. Ch., Fairfield, Conn.; chaplain in Am. Rev.; David[6] [see 8 below], *m* Lydia Carey);
2–Byron (2 below).
11–William **Ripley** (qv);
10–John (*b* Eng.-*d* 1683), *m* Elizabeth Hobart (Rev. Peter[11] [*d* 1692], pastor at Hingham);
9–Joshua, *m* Hannah Bradford (1662-1758; Maj. William[10]; William[11], Mayflower Pilgrim, qv);
8–Hannah (sister of David Ripley, 6 above), *m* Samuel **Webb**;
7–Nathaniel, *m* Elizabeth Fitch;
6–John, *m* Anne Devotion (Ebenezer[7]);
5–John, Am. Rev., *m* Zipporah Robinson;
4–Lois (1772-1844), *m* Andrew **Gager** (4 above);
3–Marvin, *m* Lucretia (Ripley) Clark (3 above);
2–Byron (1845-1926), of Woodstock, O.; pres. Gager Lime & Mfg. Co.; *m* 1879, Bertha Alder (1855-1925; James[3], *m* Marie Rhoder; James[4], *m* Bertha Messner); issue: I–James Marvin (1 above); II–Charles Bouton (*b* 1883; *m* May Ward); III–Laura (*b* 1885; *m* Col. A. W. Gatewood); IV–Marie Alder (*b* 1888); V–Kathleen (*b* 1900; *m* William Carl Cartinhour).
1–*m* Nov. 5, 1908, Helen Bradley Steward (qv for issue).
1–Pres. Gager Lime Co.; dir. Hamilton Nat. Bank. Clubs: Chattanooga Golf and Country, Signal Mtn., Fairyland, Mtn. City. Congregationalist. Republican. Residence: 521 Battery Pl., Chattanooga, Tenn.

1–**GAGER, Helen Bradley Steward (Mrs. James Marvin),** *b* Cincinnati, O., Feb. 16, 1886.
4–Posey **Steward,** of Frederick, Md.; householder, 1790; *m* Sarah Beam, of Baltimore;
3–John Beam (*b* 1808), of Frederick; *m* Anna Mary Link (*b* 1809; Thomas[4], *m* Ann Mary Fouts);
2–Demetrius M. (2 below).
10–James **Bates** (qv);
9–James (1624-92), dep. Gen. Ct.; *m* Ann Withington;
8–Samuel (1648-99), of Saybrook, Conn.; *m* 1676, Mary Chapman (Robert[9], *m* Ann Blithe);
7–James (1683-1745), *m* Hannah Bull (*b* 1687);
6–Sara (1711-85), of Stamford and Ridgefield, Conn.; *m* William **Lee** (1710-85), of Norwalk, Conn.;

5–Daniel (1744-1833), *m* Esther Banks (1745-95; Nehemiah[6]; Joseph[7]; John[8]);
4–Mary Banks (1776-1873), of Dayton, O.; *m* Eli **Starr** (1779-1849);
3–George Bradley (1808-69), *m* 1828, Rebecca Pauling Schryver;
2–Harriet Elnora (2 below).
8–Albert Heymans **Roosa,** sailed from Gelderland with 8 children in "Spotted Cow," 1660; *m* Wyntje Ariens;
7–Neeltje, *m* Henry **Pauling**;
6–Henry, *m* 1713, Jacomyntie Kunst (Cornelius Barrentsen[7], *m* Jacomyntie, dau. of Cornelius Barrentsen Sleight, *m* Tryntje Tysse Boz; Jan Barrentsen[8], *m* Jacomyntie Cornelius);
5–Rebecca (bap. 1740-1832), *m* David **Schryver** (1748-1813; Peter[6]; Albertus[7], *m* Eva Lauerman);
4–Peter (*b* Rhinebeck, N.Y., 1784-*d* 1853), *m* Catherine Stout (David[6] [1734-1826], *m* Catherine Barcley);
3–Rebecca Pauling (1806-1889 or 90), *m* George B. **Starr** (3 above);
2–Harriet Elnora (*b* 1847), of Dayton, O., and Chattanooga, Tenn.; *m* 1865, Demetrius Minor **Steward** (1841-1922), pres. D. M. Steward Mfg. Co.; issue: I–George Clifford (1867-1902; *m* Caroline Watson Williams); II–Clarence Starr (*b* 1871; S.A.R.; *m* Anne Bisplinghoff); III–Marie Louise (Mrs. Frank Finley Hooper, qv for Starr lineage); IV–Robert Bruce (*b* 1879); V–Helen Bradley (1 above).
1–*m* Nov. 5, 1908, James Marvin Gager (qv); issue: 1–James Marvin, Jr., *b* Chattanooga, Tenn., Aug. 6, 1911.
1–Ed. Ohio Wesleyan U. Mem. D.F.P.A., D.A.R. Clubs: Signal Mtn. Garden, Junior League. Conglist. Republican. Summer place: Bluff Lodge, Signal Mtn., Tenn. Residence: 521 Battery Pl., Chattanooga, Tenn.

1–**HOOPER, Marie Louise Steward (Mrs. Frank Finley),** *b* May 28, 1877.
10–Dr. Comfort **Starr** (qv);
9–Dr. Thomas (1615-58), from Eng.; settled at Charlestown, Mass.; surgeon in Pequot War, 1637; *m* Rachel Harris;
8–Capt. Josiah (*b* 1657), *m* Rebecca– (*d* 1739);
7–Lt. Benjamin (*b* 1683), of Danbury, Conn.; *m* Eunice Taylor;
6–David (*b* 1724), *m* Abigail Beebe (1721-1806);
5–David (1755-1814), *m* 1778, Lucy Sanford (1759-1814; Elnathan[6], *m* Deborah White);
4–Eli (1779-1849), removed to Redding, Conn., thence to Middletown, O.; *m* 1800, Mary Banks Lee (1776-1873);
3–George Bradley (1808-69), removed to Dayton, O.; *m* 1828, Rebecca Pawling Schryver (1806-1889 or 90).
2–Harriet Elnora (*b* 1847), *m* 1865, Demetrius Minor **Steward** (1841-1922); for issue see Mrs. James M. Gager.
1–*m* June 25, 1907, Frank Finley Hooper, *b* Holly Springs, Miss., Nov. 23, 1877 (see Who's Who in America, Vol. 14).
1–Ed. U.Wis., U.Chattanooga. Mem. D.F.P.A., D.A.R., Art. Study Club, Chattanooga Art Assn. (charter mem.), Alliance Francaise, Chi Omega Alumnae Assn. Residence: 521 Battery Pl., Chattanooga, Tenn.

1–**GAIL, William Wallace,** *b* East Aurora, N.Y., June 29, 1880.
5–Isaac **Gail,** *m* Anna Lockwood;
4–Rev. Samuel (1790-1872), *m* Hannah Brown (1788-1872);
3–Rufus (*d* 1863), *m* Maria Storm (1810-71; desc. Dirck Storm, qv);
2–William Henry (2 below).
3–William **Wallace** (*d* 1887), from Scotland, aet. 19 or 20; incorporated two ry. cos., 1830 and 32, but project was abandoned account financial crisis, 1836-37; projected a ry. line from Buffalo to Olean, thence to Allegheny River, 1864, in Feb. 1865, the co. was organized, consolidated with Buffalo and Allegheny, took name of B.N.Y.N.P.; in the meantime he was building rys. out of Buffalo, in Can., Mich., etc.; when the ry. co. of which he was director failed, he reimbursed all stockholders from his private means as far as they would go; *m* Laura Marana Marsh (*d* 1882);
2–Julia (1844-90), *m* William Henry **Gail** (1840-1915), M.D., Albany Med. Sch.; served in 116th N.Y. Vols., and as asst. surgeon, 18th N.Y. Cav., Civil War; pres. Erie Co. Med. Soc.; issue: I–James Wallace (*b* and *d* 1867); II–Florence Marian (Mrs. James B. McCreary, qv); III–Clarence Wallace (*b* 1874; *m* Emily Trowbridge); IV–William Wallace (1 above).
1–*m* Mar. 25, 1905, Virginia Irene Gunderman, *b* Athens, Pa., Feb. 20, 1886; dau. of John Gunderman, of Athens, *m* Martha Estella Munn (g.dau. of Joseph P. Munn, of Conn.); issue: 1–William Henry (Nov. 27, 1906-Aug. 4, 1917); 2–William Morrison, *b* Cripple Creek, Colo., Nov. 8, 1908; 3–Robert Woodard, *b* Colorado Springs, Colo., Oct. 25, 1910.
1–A.B., Cornell, '05 (P.B.K.). Owner and mgr., Billings Advertising Co., also engaged in oil development and investment. Author (see Who's Who in America). Rotarian. Residence: R.F.D. No. 3, Billings, Mont.

1–**GALE, Hoyt Stoddard,** *b* Cleveland, O., Dec. 9, 1876.
10–Richard (Gael) **Gale** (*d* 1679), from Eng., settled at Watertown, Mass., 1679; *m* Mary–;
9–Abraham (1643-1718), freeman, 1682; selectman at Watertown; *m* 1673, Sarah Fiske (1656-1728; Nathan[10], of Watertown, *m* Susanna–);
8–Abraham (*b* 1674), selectman at Watertown; *m* 1699, Rachel Parkhurst (1678-1769; John[9] [*d* 1725], Watertown, *m* Abigail Garfield [1646-1724]; George[10]);
7–Abraham (1700-79), Weston, Mass.; *m* 1720, Esther Cunningham (*d* 1782; John[8], Watertown);
6–Daniel (1721-99), *m* Sarah Lamson (*b* 1721; John[7] [1686-1759], of Weston, *m* Sarah Rand, 1696-1759);
5–Daniel (1752-1809), *m* Esther Rice (1755-98; Comfort[6] [1720-1816], Worcester, Mass., *m* Martha Harris);
4–Daniel (1783-1867), *m* Elizabeth Holland (1787-1882; Luther[5] [1750-1820], *m* Elizabeth Spooner, 1750-1837);
3–Rodney (1811-85), *m* Marien Williams (1812-50; Thomas[4] [1787-1847], *m* Nancy Hawks);
2–George Rodney (2 below).
9–Thomas **Richardson** (qv);
8–Thomas (1645-will dated 1719), dep. Gen. Ct., 1703-04; *m* 1st, 1669/70, Mary Stimson (1645-90);
7–Nathaniel (1680-1758), *m* 1703, Mary Peacock (*d* 1756);
6–Hezekiah (1715-95), *m* Elizabeth Walker (1710-92);
5–Jacob (1742-1817), *m* Sarah Brown (*d* 1823);
4–Jacob (1769-1839), *m* Sarah Lewis;
3–Jacob (1794-1864), *m* Mary Brown (*b* 1805);
2–Helen Maria (1841-1924), *m* George Rodney **Gale** (1845-87), mfr.; issue: I–Hoyt Stoddard (1 above); II–Laurence Richardson (1879-1904); III–Arthur Hosmer (1883-1917).
1–*m* June 18, 1902, Almira Louise Miller, *b* New York, N.Y., Dec. 24, 1874; dau. of Benjamin R. Miller, of New York; issue: 1–Hoyt Rodney, *b* Boston, Mass., Aug. 1, 1904; A.B., Harvard, '26; Ph.D., Stanford, 1928.
1–A.B., Harvard, '00, S.B., 1902. Geologist; pres. The Pacific Eastern Production Co. (oil), subsidiary of Gulf Oil Corpn. Author (see Who's Who in America). Clubs: Cosmos (Washington), Jonathan (Los Angeles). Summer place: Greenfield, N.H., and "Hildrift," Jackson, N.H. Residence: 1775 Hill Drive, Eagle Rock, Los Angeles, Calif.

1–**GANDY, Charles Moore,** *b* Seaville (now Ocean View), N.J., Nov. 6, 1857.
7–Thomas **Gandy** (*d* 1748), settled at Cape May, N.J., ca. 1696, and purchased additional land from the West Jersey Co., 1710;
6–David (*d* ca. 1757), *m* Rebeckah–;
5–John (1740-1800), Am. Rev.; *m* 1774, Lydia Williams (1752-1828);
4–Thomas (1776-1867), *m* 1800, Elizabeth Springer (1781-1870);
3–John (1802-76), *m* 1827, Martha Corson (1820-75);
2–Lewis Corson (2 below).
6–Rev. Worthington **Smith,** from Eng. to N.J., or New England, thence to N.J.; *m* Mary Ann Tuthill;
5–Tuthill, owned land in Upper Tp., Cape May Co.; *m* 1748, Judith Gandy;
4–Uriah (1764-1843), served War 1812; *m* Sophia Corson (1770-1846);

3–Samuel G. (1792-1845), *m* 1815, Sarah Lee (1795-1875);
2–Eliza Ann (1827-1909), *m* 1847, Lewis Corson **Gandy** (1828-96), sea capt., mcht. marine.
1–*m* Nov. 6, 1884, Emma Rebecca Graham, *b* Phila., Pa., July 12, 1862; dau. of Robert Graham, of Phila., *m* Eliza Schloss; issue: 1–Lila Marguerite, *b* Ft. Concho, Tex., Mar. 15, 1887; 2–Charles Lewis, *b* Ft. Concho, Jan. 24, 1889; B.S., U.Mich., '10, M.D., 1912; honor grad. Army Med. Sch., 1914; 1st lt., M.C., U.S.A., May 6, 1914, capt. and maj., June 16, 1917, lt. col., Nov. 6, 1918-Feb. 20, 1920; served in P.I., 1914-17; with Army of Occupation in France and Germany, 1919-22; *m* June 29, 1916, Merry Alden, dau. of Maj. Gen. Charles Justin Bailey, of Jamestown, N.Y. (issue: Kate Alden; Charles L., Jr.; Elizabeth Corson).
1–M.D., Jefferson Med. Coll., 1879. Served from 1st lt. to col., Med. Corps, U.S.A.; participated in Sioux Indian, Spanish-Am., Philippine Insurrection and World wars, now retired (see Who's Who in America). Mem. I.A.G. Clubs: Army and Navy (Manila and Washington), Army and Navy of America (New York), West Point Army Mess, Governors Island. Residence: Ocean View, N.J.

1–**GANO, John Vallette,** *b* New York, N.Y., July 3, 1881.
8–Richard **Hubbell** (qv);
7–Richard (*b* Guilford, Conn., 1654-*d* Stratfield, Conn., 1738), known as lt.; to Fairfield Co. with parents aet. 8; wealthy planter; with father was one of the nine original members of the 1st Congl. Ch. of Stratfield Parish; *m* 2d, 1692, Hannah Silliman or Sillway, of Malden, Mass.;
6–Richard (*b* Fairfield, Conn., 1696-*d* 1787), mcht., engaged in trade with West Indies; business with son Amos under firm name, Richard Hubbell & Son, 1783-87; conducted coastwise trade with Boston; dea. Ch. of Christ, Stratfield Parish; served in Am. Rev.; *m* 1725, Penelope Fayerweather (1704-91);
5–Hezekiah (1728-84), *m* 1752, Anne Patterson (William[6]);
4–Ezra (*b* bet. 1757-61-lost at sea, Jan. 1805), sea captain; *m* 1795, Mary Alice Lewis (*d* 1805; David[5], of Stratford, Conn.);
3–Catharine Maria (1801-73), *m* in Georgetown, Ky., 1822, Dr. John Armstrong **Gano** (1800-44), physician, Cincinnati, O. (see Vol. I, p. 116, for Gano lineage; see Vol. III, p. 202, for Goforth and Meeks lineages);
2–John Armstrong (1826-98), financial editor and business mgr. Cincinnati Commercial; *m* 1880, Laura Vallette (1840-1919), see Vol. I, p. 116, for Vallette lineage; issue: I–John V. (1 above); II–Katharine V. (*b* 1884).
1–*m* June 13, 1928, Louise May Heinke, of Phila., Pa., dau. of Charles Albert Heinke, *d*.
1–A.B., Harvard, '04; A.M., 1905. Collection agent, The Nat. Collecting Co., and The Business Service Associates, Cincinnati. Residence: 291 Southern Av., Mt. Auburn, Cincinnati, O.

1–**GARDINER, Philip Stimson,** *b* Clinton, Ia., Feb. 23, 1872.
9–Lion **Gardiner** (qv);
8–David (1636-89), first child *b* of English parents in Conn.; *m* 1657, Mary Leringman, widow;
7–Lion (*d* 1723);
6–Lion (1688-1781), *m* 1720/21, Hannah Merry (*d* 1774; John[7]; Cornelius[8], from Ireland);
5–Jeremiah (1727/28-1815), *m* 1st, 1750, Mary Parsons;
4–Lion (1764-1858), *m* 2d, Sarah (Hodge) Schuyler (1789-1869; Reuben Hodge[6], of Canajoharie, N.Y., *m* Amy Haven);
3–Stimson Brockway (1819-1903), lumber mfr., Clinton, Ia.; *m* 1844, Nancy Bonney (1824-99; Jethro[4], of Penn Yan, N.Y., *m* Abigail, dau. of Cornelius Genung, Am. Rev.);
2–Silas Wright (2 below).
9–Thomas **Baker** (qv);
8–Thomas (1654-1735), *m* 1st, 1686, Ann Topping Thomas[9]; Capt. Thomas[10] [*d* 1687], of Southampton, L.I., from Eng. to Wethersfield, Conn., 1636; mem. Gov's Council, N.Y., rep. Conn. Gen. Ct., 1639);
7–Nathaniel (*b* 1699), *m* Catalyntje Schellinger (Jacobus[8], *m* Cornelia, dau. of Cornelis Melyn, qv);
6–Hannah, *m* Samuel **Parsons,** of E. Hampton, L.I. (Thomas[7]);
5–Mary (bap. 1729-1771), *m* Jeremiah **Gardiner** (5 above).
2–Silas Wright **Gardiner** (*b* Carroll Co., Ill., 1846-*d* 1907), reared at Penn Yan, N.Y.; lumber mfr., Clinton, Ia.; *m* 1870, Louisa Catherine Henkel (*b* 1850), lineal desc. Rev. Anthony Jacob Henkel, known in history as Rev. Gerhart Henkel, an exiled Lutheran clergyman who came from Germany to Pa., 1717, one of the founders of his ch. in America; issue: I–Philip S. (1 above); II–Elizabeth Louisa (*b* 1873; *m* Arthur John Cox); III–Mary Jeannette (Mrs. Frank G. Wisner, see Vol. III, p. 260); IV–Charlotte Margaret (Mrs. George D. Hulst, see Vol. III, p. 261).
1–*m* July 9, 1895, Margaret Eleanor Hench (qv); issue: 1–John Lyon, *b* Laurel, Miss., May 23, 1896; A.B., U.Mich., '19; 2d lt., 67th C.A.C., in France, World War; *m* May 24, 1918, Virginia Salsman (divorced, Oct. 1925; issue: John Lyon, Jr., *b* Dec. 13, 1920); *m* 2d, June 2, 1928, Ruth Cavanagh, of Lansing, Mich.; 2–Eleanor Hench, *b* Laurel, Oct. 28, 1898; C.D.A., D.A.R., *m* Dec. 2, 1922, Socrates Barozzi.
1–U.Mich., '93. Mech. engr. Lumberman. Pres. Southern Pine Assn., 1921-22. In Y.M.C.A. service, World War. Residence: Laurel, Miss.

1–**GARDINER, Margaret Eleanor Hench (Mrs. Philip S.),** *b* Center, Perry Co., Pa., Dec. 20, 1873.
9–Peter Gunnarson **Rambo** (qv);
8–Gunnar (1648/49-1723/24), *m* Annica (Ann) Cock (Peter Larsson[9], an original settler of New Sweden);
7–Peter (1679-will proven 1753);
6–Mary, *m* John (Copling) **Koplin,** justice of peace, 1757-62;
5–Ells (1747-68), *m* 1763, Michael **Ickes** (1741-78), from Upper Saxony to Perkiomen Creek, Montgomery Co., Pa.;
4–Nicholas (1764-1849), Am. Rev.; settled nr. Ickesburg, Perry Co., Pa., 1790; *m* 1st, 1785, Magdalena Christman (*d* 1797);
3–Elisabeth (1787-1859), *m* 1809, Peter **Hench** (1781-1814);
2–George (1810-92), tanning business; *m* 1863, Rebecca Ann Allison (1830-1907); issue: I–Martha B. (*b* 1864); II–George Allison (1866-99); III–Elizabeth C. (*b* 1869); IV–Margaret E. (1 above).
1–*m* July 9, 1895, Philip Stimson Gardiner (qv for issue).
1–U.Mich., '95 (Sorosis). Mem. C.D.A., D.A.R. Residence: Laurel, Miss.

1–**GARDNER, Edith Howard Bennet (Mrs. James Elias),** *b* Columbia, Mo.
10–Robert **Coe** (qv);
9–Robert (1627-59), came with his father; settled at Stratford, Conn.; *m* ca. 1650, Hannah Mitchell (bap. 1631-1702; Matthew[10], qv);
8–Capt. John (1658-1741), mcht., miller, innkeeper, Stratford; dep. Gen. Assembly, 1701 and 15; ens., 1698; lt., 1706; capt., 1709; in French and Indian War, 1708; *m* 1682, Mary Hawley (1663-1731; Joseph[9], qv);
7–Capt. Joseph (1686-1754), Stratford; pioneer at Durham, Conn.; rep. Gen. Assembly, 1728; ens., 1722; lt., 1725; capt., 1729; *m* 1708, Abigail Robinson (1690-1775; David[8], *m* Abigail Kirby);
6–Dea. Joseph (1713-84), of Durham, Conn.; *m* 2d, 1739, Abigail Curtiss;
5–Joel (1758-1846), of Middletown, Conn.; *m* 1781, Huldah Horton;
4–Huldah (1793-1886), of Morris Co., N.J.; *m* 1st, 1809, Walter **Bennet** (1786-1843), of Newtown, Conn. (Thomas[5] [1752-1836], *m* 1772, Molly Ford [1756-1814]; Ephriam[6] [1714-79], *m* 1745, Ann Baldwin);
3–Thomas Ford (1815-99), of Cayuga, N.Y., and Tarkio, Mo.; *m* 1836, Diana Howard (1814-55; Benjamin[4], *m* Mahitable Root);
2–Walter (2 below).
9–John **Curtiss** (1613-1707), from Eng., 1635, settled at Stratford, Conn.; *m* 1641, Elizabeth Welles (*d* 1681/82; sister of Gov. Thomas Welles);
8–Benjamin (1652-1733), of Stratford; *m* 1st, 1680, Esther Judson (1660-1713);

7–John (1681-1745), of Stratford; *m* 2d, 1715, Hannah Johnson (*b* 1680);
6–Abigail (1719-76), of Stratford; *m* Joseph **Coe** (6 above).
11–Barnabas **Horton** (1600-80), from Eng., 1638, settled at Hampton, Mass.; moved to New Haven, 1640, and to Southold, L.I., 1640, being a founder of that town; *m* 2d, 1638, Mary–;
10–Caleb (1640-1702), of Southold; *m* 1665, Abigail Hallock (1649-97; g.dau. Peter Hallock, the Pilgrim);
9–Barnabas (1666-1705), of Cutchogue, L.I.; *m* ca. 1686, Sarah Hines;
8–Caleb (1687-1772), of Southold; *m* 1714, Phebe Terry (1698-1776; Nathaniel[9]);
7–Nathaniel (1719-1804), of Roxbury, Morris Co., N.J.; *m* 1740, Mahitable Welles;
6–Nathaniel (1741-1824), of Morris Co.; *m* 1761, Rebecca Robinson (1742-1819);
5–Huldah (1762-1803), of Chester, N.J.; *m* Joel **Coe** (5 above).
4–Lt. Col. John **Grierson** (*d* 1837), fought under Wellington at Waterloo; later retired by Brit. Govt. on half-pay; *m* Margaretta H. Cross (*d* 1854);
3–Margaret (*b* Ireland), *m* 1830, Thomas C. **Philips** (*b* Ireland-*d* 1880);
2–Harriet Ann (*b* Columbia, Mo., 1840-*d* 1902), *m* 1867, Walter **Bennet** (1838-1913), lawyer, Cayuga, N.Y., and Tarkio, Mo.; issue: I–Margaret Grierson (*b* 1871; *m* 1887, Harry Rinehart); II–Edith Howard (1 above), and III–Kate Ford, twins (*b* 1883; *m* 1911, George Burril Stone, *b* 1883).
1–*m* Dec. 6, 1911, James Elias Gardner, *b* Athens, Tex., Feb. 8, 1882; son of James M. Gardner, of Santa Anna, Tex.
1–Mem. C.D.A. (state recorder), D.A.R. (chapter regent, now hon. regent), U.S.D. 1812 (state parliamentarian, now state curator), U.D.C., N.E.H.G.S. Residence: 1917 Ashland Av., Ft. Worth, Tex.

1–**GARLOCK, Nellie Terry (Mrs. William F.)**, *b* Port Gibson, N.Y., Aug. 12, 1868.
8–Richard **Terry** (1618-75), from Eng. in the "James," with bros. Thomas and Robert, 1635; settled Southold, L.I.; *m* Abigail–; and prob. thru:
6–Jonathan, *m* 1730, Jemimah Parshall;
5–Parshall (1734-1811), of New London, Conn., and E. Palmyra, N.Y.; *m* 1755, Deborah Clark;
4–Joshua (1764-1827), of E. Palmyra; *m* Elizabeth– (1765-1848);
3–Jesse (1800-90), buried at Port Gibson, N.Y.; *m* 1832, Lydia Marsh;
2–Charles Carroll (2 below).
9–John **Marsh** (*d* 1674), from Eng. in the "Mary and John," 1633; settled Salem, Mass.; *m* 1635, Susanna Skelton (*b* Eng., 1613; Rev. Samuel[10] [1584-1634], from Eng. to Salem, Mass., *m* Susanna Travis);
8–Zachary (bap. 1637-1693), of Peabody, Mass.; *m* 1664, Mary Silsbee (Henry[9], from Eng. to Lynn, Mass.);
7–Jonathan (*b* 1672), *m* 1st, 1697, Mary Very (Samuel[8]);
6–Jonathan (*b* 1699), of Salem, Mass.; *m* 1726, Esther Osborne (John[7]);
5–William (*b* 1732), of Guilford, Vt.; Am. Rev.; *m* 1756, Rachel Coates;
4–Hosea (1775-1859), of Phelps, N.Y.; *m* 2d, 1800, Lydia Beal;
3–Lydia (1814-1902), of Phelps; *m* Jesse **Terry** (3 above).
9–John **Beal** (qv);
8–Caleb (1636-1713), of Hingham, Mass.; constable, 1675; selectman, 1678; *m* 1664, Elizabeth Huet (1645-1721);
7–Josiah (1677-1743), of Conway, Mass.; *m* 1701, Rachel Hersey (1679-1743; James[8], of Hingham);
6–Seth (1710-86), in Am. Rev.; was at Boston and Dorchester; *m* 1731, Abigail Clark (*b* 1702);
5–John (1743-91), of Conway; *m* 1767, Lydia Horton (1743-1834; David[6], of Milton);
4–Lydia (1778-1862), of Phelps, N.Y.; *m* Hosea **Marsh** (4 above).
7–Andreas **Sharts**, from Holland ante 1700; settled in Livingston Manor, N.Y.; *m* Catharina Appolonia Groot;
6–Johannes (*b* Holland, ca. 1690), of Albany (now Columbia) Co., N.Y.; *m* Catharina Schmidt;
5–Johan Nicholas (1732-1828), of Hillsdale, N.Y.; pvt. Albany Co. militia, during Am. Rev.; *m* Mary Shuts (1736-1815; prob. Johannes[6], *m* Sarah Cole);
4–Andreas (1764-1835), of Hillsdale; *m* 1787, Cornelia White (1767-1848; prob. Johannes[5], *m* Jannetje Bresie);
3–Andrew A. (1794-1866), of Hillsdale; *m* 1815, Catharine Everts;
2–Lydia Jane (2 below).
7–Mathias (Ebbers) **Everts**, at Athens, N.Y., ante 1744;
6–Jan (*d* ca. 1794), *m* 1744, Anna Margreta Cartaret (Thomas[7], of Claverack, Columbia Co., N.Y.);
5–Matthias (bap. 1748-1825 or 26), of Lunenburg, N.Y.; began to write name Everts; *m* Eitje (Ichy Blass) Plass (*b* 1752; Johannes, Jr.[6], *m* 1749, Geesje Jannesen [b 1730], dau. of Jochim Jannsin, *m* Yaje [Van Hoesen?], g.dau. of Jan Albertson, *m* Lena?; Johannis[7]);
4–John (*b* Hillsdale, N.Y., 1770-*d* 1848, buried Newark, N.Y.); settled in Newark, N.Y., 1828, came through Erie Canal, *m* 1793, Sophia White (1771-1852; Peter[5], of Hillsdale, Colorado Co., N.Y., *m* Catharine Rohrback);
3–Catharine (1797-1869), *m* Andrew A. **Sharts** (3 above);
2–Lydia Jane (1837-1901), of Hillsdale, N.Y.; *m* 1859, Charles Carroll **Terry** (1838-1929), miller; issue: I–Carrie May; II–Alice Sophia (*m* Walter Scott Throop); III–Lois; IV–Nellie (1 above).
1–*m* Aug. 23, 1891, William F. Garlock, *b* Manchester Town, N.Y., Feb. 15, 1870; son of Cyrus Garlock, of Port Gibson, N.Y.; issue: 1–Laura Fern, *b* Port Gibson, N.Y., June 3, 1892; 2–Alice, *b* Port Gibson, Feb. 26, 1894; *m* Oct. 18, 1919, William A. Beal, Jr., of Macedon, Wayne Co., N.Y. (issue: Clarisa Fern, *b* Oct. 12, 1922; William, III, *b* Oct. 18, 1919); 3–Carroll Terry, *b* E. Palmyra, N.Y., July 20, 1895; enlisted U.S.A., World War, at Camp Dix, N.J., May 26-Aug. 24, 1918; served in France with 87th Div., Mar. 15, 1919; disch. Apr. 10, 1919, Camp Upton, L.I.; *m* Dec. 30, 1921, Dorothy Kampnick, of Newark, N.Y. (issue: Shirley Ann, *b* Jan. 19, 1923; Donald William, *b* May 20, 1925); 4–Emma Bernice, *b* Port Gibson, Feb. 2, 1898; 5–Walter Vincent, *b* Port Gibson, May 8, 1901; *m* Aug. 27, 1928, Catharine, dau. of Edward Hart, of Newark, N.Y.; 6–Lydia Sharts, *b* Port Gibson, Aug. 21, 1902; ed. Rochester Gen. Hosp., N.Y.; *m* Oct. 24, 1929, James Overend, Jr., of Brooklyn, N.Y.; 7–Everette Burt, *b* Port Gibson, Feb. 21, 1905; *m* Nov. 11, 1928, Olive, dau. of Allan Purdy, of Macedon, N.Y.; 8–Elbert William, *b* Port Gibson, July 6, 1907; *m* Aug. 7, 1929, Ethel Gourlay, dau. of Mark M. Gourlay, of Victor, N.Y.; 9–Dorothy Marguerite, *b* Port Gibson, Feb. 27, 1910.
1–Mem. D.A.R., U.S.D. 1812, I.A.G. Methodist. Republican. Residence: Port Gibson, Ontario Co., N.Y.

1–**GARRARD, Mabelle Moseley Smith (Mrs. William M.)**, *b* Benton, Miss., June 4, 18–.
9–Sir William **Moseley** (bap. 1608-1655; name appears in Domes Day Book under the form Meleslie), *b* in Eng.; came from Holland; commr. Lower Norfolk Co., Va., 1649; high sheriff and burgess (see portrait); *m* ca. 1626, Susannah Cockroft (*d* 1655);
8–Arthur (ca. 1630-1702), high sheriff and burgess; *m* —Hancock; *m* 2d, Anne Hargreaves;
7–Arthur (*d* 1730), *m* 1st, 1688/89, Sarah Hancock;
6–Robert (ca. 1700-1734), Henrico Co., Va.; in Indian wars; *m* ca. 1725, Sarah Taylor;
5–Robert (1732-1804), lt. in Am. Rev.; *m* 1758, Magdalene Guerrant;
4–Peter Guerrant (*b* 1776), capt. in War 1812; *m* 1st, Juliet Saunders;
3–Peter Guerrant (1805-67), served in Home Guard of C.S.A.; *m* 1846, Catherine Maria Starnes;
2–Mabelle Adeline (2 below).
10–Capt. Thomas **Harris** (qv);
9–Mary, *m* 1650, Col. Thomas **Ligon** (*b* ante 1625);
8–Johan, *m* Robert **Hancock;**
7–Sarah, *m* Arthur **Moseley** (7 above).
8–Jacob **Flournoy** (*b* 1663), *m* 3d, 1703, Madeline Prodham;

SIR WILLIAM MOSELEY

7-Magdalene (*d* 1731), *m* Anthony **Trabue** (1687-1724), from Eng. in the "Peter and Anthony";
6-Magdalene, *m* Peter **Guerrant** (Daniel[7], *m* Frances Torange; Daniel[8], French Huguenot, settled in Va., 1700);
5-Magdalene (bap. 1740-1826), *m* Robert **Moseley** (5 above).
9-Charles (Stearns) **Starnes** (*b* ca. 1625), from Eng. in the "Arabella," to Salem, Mass., 1630; freeman, Watertown, 1646; *m* 2d, 1654, Rebecca Gibson (John[10], *m* Rebecca-);
8-Shubael (1655-will probated 1734), settled at Lynn, Mass.; mem. Narragansett Expdn.; *m* ca. 1681/82, Mary Upton;
7-Shubael (*b* 1683), began to write name Starnes; town clk., Tolland, Conn.; *m* 1704, Rebecca Lariby (*b* 1684);
6-Peter (*b* 1710), *m* 1736, Hannah Stimson, of Tolland;
5-Ebenezer (*b* ca. 1738/39), *m* 2d, Elizabeth Young;
4-Dr. Samuel Scott (1781-1841), Williamson Co., Tenn.; *m* 1816, Nancy Matilda Wellborn;
3-Catherine Maria (1829-95), *m* Peter G. **Moseley** (3 above);
2-Mabelle Adeline (*b* 1858), *m* 1876, James David **Smith** (1856-1917), wholesale grocer and cotton mcht.; issue: I-Mabelle Moseley (1 above); II-George K. (*m* Ella Carter Faison); III-Rebecca Treadwell (*m* Gen. John Moseley Hairston); IV-Anne Agusta (*m* Ennis A. Tanner); V-Marion Moseley (*m* Dr. James Davidson Rives).
1-*m* June 14, 1908, William Mountjoy Garrard, IV, *b* Lawrenceville, Ill., Aug. 25, 18-; son of William Mountjoy Garrard, III (*b* Paris, Ky., July 4, 1850); issue: 1-William Mountjoy, V, *b* Indianola, Miss., Apr. 11, 1909; 2-James Moseley, *b* Indianola, Aug. 12, 1910; 3-Mabelle Smith, *b* Indianola, Mar. 13, 1913; 4-Mary Jayne, *b* Monteagle, Tenn., Aug. 13, 1915; 5-Robert Barrett, *b* Indianola, Miss., Dec. 13, 1919.
1-Attended Miss. State Coll. for Women. Mem. D.F.P.A., Huguenot Soc., D.A.R., U.S.D. 1812, F.F.V. Clubs: Country, Woman's, Delphian Soc., King's Daughters. Baptist. Democrat. Residence: Greenwood, Miss.

1-**GARRETSON, Austin Bruce,** *b* Winterset, Ia., Sept. 14, 1856.
7-John **Garretson** (*d* 1694), Christiana Hundred, Del.; *m* Ann-;
6-Casparius (1680-1726), from Eng.; settled at New Castle, Del., ca. 1700; overseer Quaker meeting, New Castle, 1726; *m* Ann-;
5-William (1716-92), *m* 1st, 1742, Mary Frazier;
4-William (*b* 1748), *m* 1774, Mary Wetherald;
3-Casparius (1776-1866), *m* 1802, Sarah Kirk;
2-Nathan (1809-86), lawyer; *m* 1829, Amelia Hutton; *m* 2d, 1851, Hannah Garretson Swaim (1820-84); issue (1st marriage): I-George Ernshaw (1833-1910; *m* Matilda Smith, *d*; *m* 2d, Amanda Smith); II-Albert Alonzo (1837-1907; *m* 1875, Mary T. Evans); III-Caroline (1839-1911; *m* 1859, Thomas Sturman); IV-Victoria Alexandrine (1841-88; *m* 1869, William Creighton); issue (2d marriage): I-Sarah Josephine (*b* 1852; *m* George Wilson); II-Austin Bruce (1 above).
1-*m* Sept. 2, 1879, Marie Ream (Apr. 23, 1857-Feb. 19, 1926); dau. of Levi Ream, of Osceola, Ia., and Somerset Co., Pa.; *m* Hily King; issue (all *b* Osceola, Ia.): 1-Ivan Ream, *b* Mar. 18, 1881; *m* Aug. 27, 1907, Nell Clark; 2-Aileen, *b* Apr. 5, 1883; *m* Nov. 20, 1906, Everett S. Seely (issue: Garretson, *b* 1908; Jan, *b* 1911; Elizabeth, 1915); 3-Vida, *b* Dec. 25, 1884.
1-Conductor rys., retired (see Who's Who in America). V.p., Order Ry. Conductors, 1897-1906, pres., 1906-19. Summer place: LaJolla, Calif. Residence: Cedar Rapids, Ia.

1-**GARRETT, Uarda Penelope Rosamond (Mrs. Rufus N.),** *b* Eurekaton, Tenn., Aug. 7, 1884.
7-Jacob (de Ferney) **Forney** (ca. 1721-1806; son of a French Huguenot, who fled from France and settled in Alsace); went from Alsace to Amsterdam, Holland, thence to America, 1739, settled in Pa.; returned to Germany to secure a legacy; returned to America and settled in "Ingleside," Lincoln Co., N.C.; iron mfr.; commd. capt. to fight Indians; co. commr.; mem. Com. of Safety; Forney Home used as Cornwallis hdqrs.; tablet to Jacob Forney in old Huguenot Ch., Charleston, S.C.; *m* 1754, Maria Bergner;
6-Catherine (1760-98), *m* 1782, Robert **Rosamond** (1754-87), soldier in Am. Rev.
5-Henry (1783-1828), of Lincoln Co., N.C.; *m* 1802, Ann Clarke (1785-1810);
4-John D. (1807-61), of Lincoln Co.; *m* 1829, Elizabeth Hefley (*b* 1809);
3-Henry Clarke (1829-55), of Madison Co., Tenn.; *m* 1851, Sarah Elizabeth Bradshaw (*b* 1826);
2-Henry Clarke (1854-1913), minister, Madison Co., Tenn.; *m* 1877, Theodocia Lavica Keirsey (*b* 1858); issue: I-Irby Frazier (1878-79); II-Dr. Eugene (*b* 1880; *m* Anna Trotter; *m* 2d, Inez Fennel); III-Uarda Penelope (1 above); IV-Esther Theodosia (Mrs. William Price Barton, qv); V-Dora Bell (*b* 1887; *m* Dr. Lawrence L. Purifoy).
1-*m* Mar. 1, 1910, Rufus Napoleon Garrett, *b* nr. Arkadelphia, Ark., Dec. 24, 1858; chmn. bd. First Nat. Bank, of El Dorado; v.p. El Dorado Foundry & Machine Co.; partner Cargile & Garrett Ranch, San Angelo, Tex. (see Who's Who in America); son of Mancil Garrett, of Arkadelphia, Ark., *m* Matilda Caroline Street; issue: 1-Uarda Rosamond, *b* El Dorado, Ark., June 1, 1911; 2-Rufus Napoleon, Jr., *b* El Dorado, Nov. 7, 1913.
1-Ed. Ouachita Coll., Arkadelphia, Ark., 1904; studied at U.Chicago. Mem. C.D.A., Huguenot Soc. of S.C., D.A.R. (state treas., state parliamentarian), U.D.C. (state treas.), I.A.G., Robert E. Lee Memorial Foundation (Ark. dir.), El Dorado Library Assn., El Dorado Y.W.C.A. Baptist. Democrat. Clubs: Ark. Federation of Music, (state pres.), El Dorado Golf and Country, Little Rock Garden, Little Rock Woman's City, etc. Summer place: Garrett Lodge, Ludington, Mich. Residence: Eight Oaks, El Dorado, Ark.

1-**BARTON, Esther Theodosia Rosamond (Mrs. William Price),** *b* Paris, Lamar Co., Tex., Oct. 19, 1885.
Sister of Mrs. Rufus N. Garrett, qv for genealogy.
1-*m* Sept. 9, 1914, William Price Barton, *b* Tuscumbia, Ala., Nov. 23, 1867; son of Clark Talbot Barton (1841-94), *m* Elizabeth Price (1849-1930); issue: 1-Esther Rosamond, *b* Jonesboro, Ark., Oct. 7, 1916.
1-A.B., and expression, Ouachita Coll., '05 (Alpha Kappa); post grad. work in languages, U.-Chicago, summer of 1910; expression and public speaking under Clarke; expression under Curry of Boston Sch. of Expression, summer term. Teacher mathematics and science, Paragould (Ark.) High Sch.; English and Latin, El Dorado (Ark.) High Sch.; expression and French and German, Junction City (Ark.) High Sch.; principal grade sch., El Dorado, Ark. Mem. D.A.R. (chapter regent), U.D.C. Baptist. Democrat. Clubs:

Treble Clef Music (pres.), Filo, Duplicate Bridge, Jonesboro Country, etc. Residence: 1238 Madison St., Jonesboro, Ark.

1–**GARRIGUES, Edmund,** *b* Salem, Columbiana Co., O., Oct. 31, 1856.
6–Matthew **Garrigues** (1679-1726; son of Jean, a French Huguenot, who went to Holland after Revocation of Edict of Nantes, 1685, *m* Marie de Franchmont, a widow), came from France via Holland, 1685, thence to Island of St. Christopher, W.I., ca. 1705, to Island of Martinique, thence to Phila., Pa., ca. 1712; kept the Prince Eugene Inn; *m* 1702, Suzanna Rochett, or Roche (*d* 1743);
5–Samuel (1719-83), Quaker; *m* 1740, Mary Ralph (1724-83; James[6], *m* Hannah–);
4–William (1746-1831), contractor and builder, Phila.; mem. Society of Friends; *m* 2d, 1787, Hannah Briggs (1758-1832; Samuel[5], *m* Mary Briggs);
3–William (1789-1870), contractor and builder, Phila.; later farmer, Lexington Tp., Stark Co., O.; *m* 1812, Margaret Humphreys (1790-1861; Richard[4], *m* Margaret Cruckshank);
2–Charles Humphreys (2 below).
6–Moses **Coates** (*b* Ireland, of English parentage), 1717, settled in Providence Tp., Montgomery Co., Pa.; *m* 1715, Susanna Weldon;
5–Samuel (1718-99), founder and first postmaster, Coatesville, Pa.; *m* 1743, Elizabeth Mendenhall (Aaron[6], *m* Rose Pearson);
4–Moses (1746-1816), *m* 2d, Mary Knight Vickers (1750-1824; Peter[5], *m* Ann–);
3–Aquilla (1791-1862), *m* 1823, Hannah S. Troth (1796-1871; Henry[4], *m* Hannah–);
2–Margaret Truman (1828-98), *m* 1849, Charles Humphreys **Garrigues** (1825-1909), farmer; carpenter; patternmaker; issue: I–Howard (*b* 1850; *m* Alice Hutton, *d* 1880; *m* 2d, Isabelle K. Willison, *d* 1921); II–Isabell (1851-1904; *m* 1876, William Haman Allman); III–Clarence (*b* 1854); IV–Edmund (1 above).
1–*m* Nov. 27, 1887, Augusta Charlotte Charleson (Mar. 28, 1864-June 27, 1924); dau. of Karl Jönson, of Sweden, *m* Helena Anderson; issue: 1–Walter M., *b* Massillon, O., Mar. 12, 1889; Cornell U., '11; *m* Nov. 30, 1916, Miriam (LeClair) Gardner, dau. of John LeClair (issue: Walter Don; Joan Charlotte; William Edmund); 2–a son (Oct. 10-Oct. 11, 1894).
1–Mech. engr.; with Russell & Co., 1893-1923, Massillon Foundry & Machine Co., 1923-26, Massillon Power Shovel Co., since 1927. Mem. Am. Soc. M.E. Residence: 51 S. 5th St. and Wellman Av., Massillon, O.

1–**GATES, Caleb Frank,** *b* Chicago, Ill., Oct. 8, 1857.
7–George **Gates** (qv);
6–Thomas (1665-1734), of E. Haddam, Conn.; town clk.; *m* 1692, Hannah Brainard (1667-1750);
5–Joshua (*b* 1708), *m* Lydia Brainard (1718-68);
4–Dea. Caleb (1749-1822), *m* 1775, Esther Foote (1748-99); *m* 2d, 1800, Elizabeth Percival;
3–Russell (1786-1834), *m* 1820, Mabel Kelsey, widow (1790-1863);
2–Caleb Foote (1824-90), mfr., Chicago Lead and Oil Works; *m* 1851, Mary Eliza Hutchins (1825-98); issue: I–Sarah Elizabeth (1852-98); II–Charles William (*b* 1853; *m* 1876, Alice Bennett); III–William Spaulding, M.D. (*b* 1855; *m* 1886, Lillian Warner Pillsbury); IV–Caleb Frank (1 above); V–Henry Barnes (*b* 1860; *m* 1882, Nellie Warner, *b* 1862); VI–Edward Hutchins (1861-78); VII–Adelaide L. (1864-65); VIII–Burnett Wright (*b* and *d* 1866); IX–Mary Foote (*b* and *d* 1867); X–Herbert Wright (*b* 1868; see Who's Who in America; *m* 1898, Harriet J. Kirk).
1–*m* May 31, 1883, Mary Ellen Moore, *b* Chicago, Ill., Oct. 5, 1861; dau. of Silas Milton Moore; issue: 1–Edward Caleb (July 2-Oct. 2, 1886); 2–Herbert Frank, *b* Mardin, Turkey, July 2, 1888; 3–Moore, *b* Mardin, Feb. 8, 1894; Princeton, '16; *m* Sept. 27, 1923, Harryette, dau. of Harris Reynolds, of Poughkeepsie, N.Y. (issue: Moore, Jr.; Harris Reynolds); 4–Elizabeth Davison, (Dec. 5, 1899-Mar. 31, 1900); 5–Caleb Frank, Jr., *b* Constantinople, Turkey, Dec. 24, 1903; Princeton, '26; *m* June 28, 1928, Elizabeth Farnum.
1–A.B., Beloit (Wis.) Coll., '77 (Beta Theta Pi, P.B.K., Pi Gamma Mu); grad. Chicago Theol. Sem., 1881; (D.D., Knox Coll., 1897; LL.D., Edinburgh U., 1899; Beloit, 1927). Ordained Congl. ministry, 1881; missionary A.B.C.F.M., Mardin, Turkey in Asia, 1881-94; pres. Robert Coll., Constantinople, since 1903. Author (see Who's Who in America). Club: Constantinople. Residence: Robert College, Constantinople, Turkey.

1–**GAY, Frederick Parker,** *b* Boston, Mass., July 22, 1874.
9–John **Gay** (qv);
8–Samuel (1639-1718), *m* 1661, Mary Bridge (*d* 1718);
7–Timothy (1674-1719), *m* Patience–;
6–Timothy (1703-93), *m* 1727, Azubah Thorp (*d* 1773);
5–Timothy (*b* 1733), *m* 1756, Amity Holmes;
4–Ichabod (1765-1824), *m* 1788, Ruth Billings (*d* 1831), of Stoughton;
3–Timothy (*b* 1795), *m* 1817, Mehitable Peabody;
2–George Frederick (2 below).
5–Nathaniel **Parker,** *m* 1746, Eunice Lakin;
4–Winslow (1755-1810), *m* Abagail Woods;
3–Nathaniel (1801-48), *m* 1829, Mary Parker;
2–Louisa Maria (1841-1910), *m* 1865, George Frederick **Gay** (1835-1904), mcht.
1–*m* Oct. 18, 1904, Catherine Mills Jones, *b* New Hartford, Conn., Dec. 17, 1878; dau. of Capt. Henry R. Jones, of New Hartford; issue: 1–Lucia Chapman, *b* Danvers, Mass., Oct. 3, 1906; Conn. Coll., 1928; 2–Louisa Parker, *b* Brussels, Belgium, Aug. 3, 1908; Conn. Coll., 1928; 3–William Coddington, *b* Berkeley, Calif., Apr. 4, 1920.
1–A.B., Harvard, '97 (Pi Eta, Sigma Xi); M.D., Johns Hopkins, 1901 (Nu Sigma Nu). Prof. bacteriology, Columbia, since 1923. Author (see Who's Who in America). Maj., M.C., U.S.A., 1918-19; mem. med. sect. Nat. Research Council, 1917-24, chmn., 1922-23, chmn. Med. Fellowship Bd., 1922-26. Fellow A.M.A., A.A.A.S. Comdr. Order of Crown of Belgium. Clubs: Century, Explorers. Summer place: Hillandale, New Hartford, Conn. Residence: 21 Claremont Av., New York, N.Y.

Arms: Azure, semee of cross crosslets and three cinquefoils argent.
Crest: On a chapeau gules, turned up ermine, a bull sable, armed or.
Motto: Un Dieu, un Roy.

1–**GEISSINGER, Anthony Wayne,** *b* Columbus, O., Nov. 27, 1884.
9–Maj. Edward **Dorsey** (qv);
8–Col. Edward (1645-1705), of "Long Reach," Md.; justice, 1679-89; asso. judge High Ct. of Chancery, 1695-96; burgess, 1694-97, 1701-05; capt., 1686; maj., 1687; maj. of troop of horse, 1689; col., 1702; *m* 1st, 1675, Sarah Wyatt (Nicholas[9] [*d* 1673], of Ann Arundel Co., *m* Damaris–);
7–John (1692-1764), *m* 1708, Honor Elder (John[8]);

6–Michael, of "Brothers Partnership," nr. Dayton, Md.; *m* 1733, Ruth Tood (*d* 1777; Capt. Lancelot,[7] *m* Elizabeth Rockhold; Thomas[8], a founder of Baltimore, *m* Ann Gorsuch, g.dau. Sir William Lovelace);
5–Ruth (1743-1805), *m* 1765, her cousin, Ely **Dorsey** (1744-1803), of Dorsey Hall; mem. Ann Arundel Co. Com. of Observation in Am. Rev. (Edward[6], *m* Sarah Todd, sister of Ruth, 6 above; Edward[7]; Hon. John[8]; Edward[9], 9 above);
4–Allen (1779-1849), of Poplar Springs, Md.; *m* 1802, Elizabeth Smith;
3–Alfred Warfield (1805-76), of Md.; removed to Mo.; served in C.S.A.; *m* 1840, Charlotte Heckrotten (1810-74); had 3 sons in C.S.A.;
2–Henrietta Alfredine (1843-1924), *m* 1865, James **Geissinger** (1844-1913), served in U.S.A. in Civil War; removed to Columbus, O.; issue: I–Alfred (1866-72); II–Henry Wilson, M.D. (1868-1923); III–Catherine (1871-72); IV–Rev. James Allen, D.D. (*b* 1873; *m* Effie Eugenia Bryan); V–John William (1876-1900); VI–Margaret Elzina (*b* 1881; *m* Orrin Wilson Jones); VII–Anthony Wayne (1 above).
1–*m* Aug. 5, 1909, Lulu Townsend Armstrong (qv); issue: 1–Wayne Townsend, *b* Columbus, O., Nov. 29, 1910; Ohio Wesleyan U., '32 (Sigma Chi).
1–LL.B., Ohio State U., '07. Atty. for Am. Surety Co. of N.Y. for middle Ohio; head of court and claim dept. of Equitable Surety Co. of St. Louis, 1911; head of surety underwriting dept. of Southwestern Surety Co. of Texas, 1913; state manager of Ohio for Nat. Surety Co. of N.Y., 1916. Commr. of securities of the State of Ohio, 1929-; sr. of Geissinger & Treadway, Inc., surety bonds; resident v.p. of Nat. Surety Co. since 1916. Mayor of Village of Upper Arlington; chmn. of Village Commn.; chmn. Village Planning Commn.; chmn. Zoning Commn. of Upper Arlington. Mem. O.F.P.A., S.C.W., S.A.R. (pres. chapter) Mason Trustee Broad St. M.E. Ch.; v.p. Federated Chs. of Franklin Co. Republican. Club: O.S.U. Faculty, Kiwanis. Residence: 1939 Edgemont Rd., Upper Arlington, Columbus, O.

1–**GEISSINGER, Lulu Townsend Armstrong (Mrs. Anthony Wayne),** *b* Audubon, Ia., Mar. 31, 1886.
8–Martin **Townsend** (1644-97), one of the founders of Watertown, Mass.; maj.; commr. sent by Mass. to treat with the Mohawks, 1694; *m* 1669, Abigail Train;
7–Rev. Jonathan (1687-1764), of Hebron, Conn.; B.A., Harvard, 1716, M.A., 1719; *m* Mary Sugars (Capt. Gregory[8], admiral of Sir William Phipps' flagship "Six Friends," in expdn. against Quebec, 1690; propr. Old Tyringham);
6–David (1725-1815), of Hebron, Conn.; mem. expdn. against Louisburg, 1745; minuteman, 1776; *m* 1751, Sarah Irene Loomis;
5–David (1753-1833), *m* 1784, Hannah Andrews Cone;
4–John (1785-1874), of Hebron, Conn.; *m* 1807, Isabella Chapman;
3–William Jarvis (1822-1901), of E. Haddam, Conn., and Zanesville, O.; *m* 1851, Elizabeth Burley (1833-1900; John[4], *m* Sophia, dau. of John Boyle; John[5]; John[6], Am. Rev.);
2–Clara Sophia (2 below).
10–Joseph **Loomis** (qv);
9–Nathaniel (1626-88), freeman, 1654; mem. 1st Conn. Cav., 1658; in King Philip's War; *m* 1653, Elizabeth Moore (Dea. John[10], dep. Gen. Ct., *m* Abigail–);
8–Jonathan (1664-1707), of Hartford; *m* 1688, Sarah Graves (*d* 1699; George[9], dep. Gen. Ct., Conn., *m* Elizabeth, dau. of Matthew Mitchell, soldier in Pequot War, dep. Gen. Ct.);
7–Dea. Nathaniel (1690-1769), *m* 1728, Mary Dyer, of Ashford, Conn;
6–Sarah Irene (1729-58), *m* David **Townsend** (6 above).
10–Gerard or Jared **Spencer** (1610-85), founder of Haddam, Conn.; commr., 1669; rep., 1674, et seq.; ens. Train Band, 1656; *m* 1634/35, Hannah–;
9–Mehitable (1642-91), of Lynn, Mass., and Haddam; *m* Daniel **Cone** (1626-1706), from Scotland; propr. E. Haddam, 1688;
8–Nathaniel (1674-1732), of E. Haddam; *m* 1695 or 1696, Sarah Hungerford (1679-1753), mem. 1st Congl. Ch., E. Haddam (Thomas[9], selectman of E. Haddam, 1704, *m* Mary Grey; Sir Thomas[10], qv);
7–James (1698-1774), lt. colonial troops, 1738; mem. Conn. Legislature, 1747-49; 1st clk, of Ecclesiastical Soc. of Millington (E. Haddam); *m* 1726, Grace Spencer (1704-67);
6–Sylvanus (1731-1812), mem. Ft. Edwards expdn., 1755; mem. Crown Pt. expdn., 1756; served in French and Indian War; minuteman Am. Rev.; was present at Battle of Bunker Hill; *m* 1755, Hannah Ackley (*d* 1790; Gideon[7]);
5–Hannah Andrews (1763-1843), *m* David **Townsend** (5 above).
9–Robert **Chapman** (qv);
8–Robert (1646-1711), of Saybrook, Conn.; surveyor; dep. Gen. Ct.; one of the founders of E. Haddam; *m* 1671, Sarah Griswold;
7–Robert (1675-1760), of E. Haddam; *m* twice;
6–Caleb (*b* ca. 1704), *m* 1731, Elizabeth Church;
5–Dr. Zechariah (1740-1835), grad. Yale, 1763; soldier Am. Rev.; *m* 1768, Isabella Stanton (1745-1816);
4–Isabella (1787-1854), *m* John **Townsend** (4 above).
11–William **Tracy** (*d* 1621; son of Sir John Tracy, of Toddington Castle, Gloucestershire, Eng., *m* Anne Throckmorton); from Eng. to Va., 1620 in the "Supply," with his wife, dau. Joyce, and son Thomas; councillor of state and gov. of Berkeley Hundred, 1620; active in promoting settlement of Va., and gave financial aid to the project;
10–Thomas (qv);
9–Mary, *m* Francis **Griswold** (*d* 1671), one of the 1st proprs. of Norwich; dep. Gen. Ct., 1661-71; mem. Ct. of Commrs., 1662 (Edward[10], qv);
8–Sarah (1653-92), *m* Robert **Chapman** (8 above).
2–Clara Sophia Townsend (*b* 1855), *m* 1883, Andrew Franklin **Armstrong** (*b* 1852; William[3], *m* 1834, Jane, dau. of Jacob Gibson, soldier War 1812); issue: I–Lulu Townsend (1 above); II–Helen Louise (*b* 1887; *m* E. E. Schwarztrauber).
1–*m* Aug. 5, 1909, Anthony Wayne Geissinger (qv for issue).
1–Ed. Lake Erie Coll., 1910. Former nat. vice chmn. Ellis Island Work, N.S.D.A.R. Mem. Descendants Barons of Runnemede; D.A.C. (dir.), D.F.P.A., D.A.R., U.S.D. 1812 (dir.), Isabella Creighton Missionary Soc. Clubs: Ohio State U. Faculty, Sorosis, Fidelis, Arlington Book, Norwester Women's, etc. Methodist. Residence: 1939 Edgemont Rd., Upper Arlington, Columbus, O.

1–**GAYLORD, Elizabeth Blake,** *b* Torringford, Conn., June 29, 1886.
10–William **Gaylord** (qv);
9–William (*b* Eng., ca. 1616-*d* 1656), of Windsor, Conn.; *m* 2d, 1653, Elizabeth Drake (John[10], qv, a descendant of King Alfred the Great);
8–Nathaniel (1656-1720), 2d settler of Pine Meadow (now Windsor Locks); *m* 1678, Abigail Bissell (1658-1723; g.dau. of John Bissell);
7–Josiah (*b* 1686), an original propr. of Torrington, Conn.; *m* 1713, Naomi Burnham (*b* 1688);
6–Dea. Nehemiah (1722-1801), of Torrington; dea. of ch. at Torrington, 45 yrs.; soldier in Am. Rev.; *m* 1748, Lucy Loomis (1727-1800; g.g.g.dau. of Joseph Loomis);
5–Joseph (1752-1821), patriot Am. Rev.; served on com. which secured food and clothing for soldiers; *m* 1771, Ruth Bissell (1750-1827);
4–Elijah (1778-1835), *m* 1800, Esther Loomis (1781-1812; desc. Joseph Loomis);
3–Giles Loomis (1807-93), *m* 1847, Sarah Blake (1813-81);
2–Hubert Giles (*b* 1852), farmer; of Torrington, Conn.; *m* 1879, Belle Annette Waterman (*b* 1855; desc. Joseph Loomis); issue: I–Charles Arthur (*d* in infancy); II–William Waterman (*b* 1884; *m* 1912, Mildred Chase Foye); III–Elizabeth Blake (1 above).
1–B.A., Mt. Holyoke, '09; B.S.C., Washington Sch. of Accountancy, 1922. Public accountant. Mem. D.A.R., I.A.G. Address: R.F.D. No. 3, Torrington, Conn.

1–**GERARD, Jessie Honor Bryant (Mrs. Franklin W.),** *b* Brooklyn, N.Y., Mar. 14, 1854-*d* Feb. 3, 1930.
7–Lt. John **Bryant** (*d* 1707-08), from Eng. to Plymouth, Mass., ante 1655; *m* 1665, Abigail Bryant

(*d* 1715; Stephen[8], *m* Abigail Shaw);
6–Samuel (1673-1750), of Plympton, Mass.; dea.; *m* 1st, Joanna– (1671 or 72-1736);
5–Nathaniel (1712-93), of Plympton; dea.; *m* 1733, Zerviah Curtis (1707-90);
4–Ezekiel (1746-75), of Plympton; *m* 1768, Lucy Bierce or Bearce (*b* 1747; Miall[5], *m* Elizabeth Sears);
3–Ezekiel (1772-1830), of Plympton; *m* 1798, Mercy Northrop (1776-1869; Enos[4], officer Am. Rev., *m* Anna Drake);
2–Ezekiel Drake (2 below).
7–William **Matthews** (*d* 1684), from Eng., admitted a planter at Guilford, Conn., 1674; *m* Jane–;
6–Caleb (1674-1755), of Cheshire, Conn.; *m* 1702, 1st, Elizabeth Hotchkiss (1684-1735 or 36; Daniel[7], *m* Esther Sperry);
5–Aaron (1721 or 22-1806), sgt. Am. Rev., 1775, ens., 1776; *m* 1742, Huldah Frisbie (1715 or 16-1797; John[6], *m* Susanna Henbury);
4–Samuel (1761-1812), of Plymouth, Conn.; admitted elector of Plymouth, 1818; *m* Mamre Catlin (*d* 1842, aet. 78);
3–Randall (1785-1862), *m* 1809, Amelia Atkins or Adkins (1790-1864);
2–Lucy Tyler (1822-85), *m* 1841, Ezekiel Drake **Bryant** (1815-88), clockmaker, Ansonia and Bristol, Conn.; issue: I–Watson (1842-47); II–Watson Dwight (1847-53); III–William Cullen (1849-1905; *m* Julia Mortimer Peters, *d* 1887; *m* 2d, Mary Whitney Peters, *d* 1904 sister of 1st wife); IV–Jessie Honor (1 above); V–Lucy Elmere (1856-1915).
1–*m* May 12, 1879, Franklin Ward Gerard, *b* Newburg, N.Y., Feb. 14, 1853; son of William H. Gerard, of Newburg, *m* Mary E. Chapman; issue: 1–Franklin Bryant, *b* New York, N.Y., Oct. 7, 1881; mem. Am. Soc. Mech. Engrs.; *m* Apr. 25, 1904, Lucy, dau. of Percy Milton Comstock, of Brooklyn, *m* Ella Amelia Kerr (issue: William Bryant, *b* Aug. 8, 1914); 2–Jessie Bryant, *b* New York, Aug. 20, 1884; New Haven Normal School, 1907; Simmons Coll., 1912-13; *m* Sept. 9, 1915, Robert Bartlett Butler (*d* Aug. 6, 1925), son of Elisaph Butler, of Guilford, Conn., *m* Fannie Robinson; 3–Margaret Bryant, *b* White Hills, Shelton, Conn., Aug. 30, 1887; New Haven Normal School, 1907; Simmons Coll., 1912-13; B.S., Teachers Coll., Columbia U., 1928; 4–Raymond Bryant, *b* New York, N.Y., June 1, 1889; Ph.B., Yale-S., 1911; C.E., Yale-S., 1915; *m* Feb. 5, 1921, Hilda, dau. of George Lewis Sargent, of New Haven, Conn., *m* Olive Bessie Forbes.
1–Instrumental in securing equal guardianship law in Conn., giving mother equal rights over child with the father; with Mrs. E. Foote Thompson, secured laurel as Conn. State flower; worked for migratory bird law; named "People's Forest" in Conn., started by Alain A. White and thru her efforts in D.A.R. and State Federation many acres were given—26 of clubs in Federation giving acres in her honor. Mem. D.F.P.A., D.A.R. (chapter historian, regent), etc. Residence: 158 Maple St., New Haven, Conn.

1–**GESTER, Kate Darling Howell (Mrs. William B.),** *b* Buffalo, N.Y., Apr. 21, 1860.
8–Edward **Howell** (qv);
7–Richard (1629-1700), of Southampton, L.I.; *m* 1st, Elizabeth Halsey (Thomas[8]);
6–Lt. Hezekiah (1677-1744), of Southampton; *m* 1st, 1702, Phoebe Halsey (1670-1732; Thomas[7]);
5–Hezekiah (1709-85), of Southampton; *m* 1735, Susannah Sayre (*b* 1709; Job[6], *m* Susannah Howell?; Job[7], *m* Sarah–; Thomas[8], qv);
4–Hezekiah (1741-1815), maj. in Cont. Army, Am. Rev.; removed to Orange Co., N.Y.; *m* 1767, Julianna Woodhull;
3–Nathaniel (1770-1851), of Canandaigua, N.Y.; *m* 1809, Fannie Coleman (1781-1842);
2–Augustus Porter (2 below).
7–Richard **Woodhull** (1620-90), from Eng. to L.I.; settled at Brookhaven, 1648; rep. Gen. Ct.; justice; magistrate; *m* Deborah Crewe;
6–Richard (1649-99), of Brookhaven, later at Southampton; *m* 1680, Temperance Fordham (Rev. Jonah[7], *m* Elizabeth Benning; Rev. Robert[8], *m* Elizabeth–);
5–Nathaniel (1693-1760), of Southampton; *m* Sarah Smith (Richard[6]);
4–Julianna (1736-1816), of Orange Co.; *m* Hezekiah **Howell** (4 above);
3–Nathaniel Woodhull, *m* Fannie Coleman (3 above);
2–Augustus Porter (1823-92), of Buffalo, N.Y.; *m* 1853, Caroline Matilda Reid (1834-96); issue: I–Sarah Eugenia (1855-1921; *m* George Turner Quinby, *d*); II–Thomas Morris (1858-1925; *m* Jane Leonard, *d*); III–Kate Darling (1 above); IV–Fanny Coleman (*b* 1869; *m* Joseph Ditto); V–Carl Lathrop (*b* 1873).
1–*m* Feb. 14, 1883, William Burr Gester, *b* Baltimore, Md., Mar. 14, 1854; son of Stephen Girard Gester, late of Phila., Pa.; issue: 1–George Clark, *b* Buffalo, N.Y., June 16, 1884; B.S., U.Calif., '08; *m* Apr. 24, 1913, Lillian McCauley, of Berkeley (issue: George C., Jr.; James William); 2–Stephen Howell, *b* Newcastle, Calif., Dec. 24, 1889; B.S., U.Calif., '12; *m* May 12, 1917, Violet, dau. Ernest H. Peters, of Napa, Calif. (issue: Howell Woodhull; Peter Warran; Stephen Clark).
1–Buffalo Sem., '79. Mem. D.F.P.A., C.D.A., D.A.R. Unitarian. Residence: 12 Brookside Av., Berkeley, Calif.

LOUIS GERMAIN (1836-1921), 1st lt., Co. D, 146th Ill. Vols., Civil War.

1–**GERMAIN, Mary Adaline Stone (Mrs. Louis),** *b* Noble Co., Ind., Oct. 11, 1841.
3–Richard **Stone,** from Eng., settled in Mifflin Co., Pa.; *m* 1791, Barbara Rupert (*b* 1772);
2–Richard (2 below).
5–David **McKinley,** "David the Weaver" (ca. 1705-1760), from Ireland, settled in York Co., Pa.; *m* in Ireland, ante 1728, Esther–;
4–John (1728-79), of Chanceford, York Co., Pa.; *m* Margaret– (*d* 1781);
3–Susanna (1772-1852), *m* Robert **Higgins** (*d* 1814);
2–Mary Ann (1810-65), *m* 1825, Richard **Stone** (1799-1874), of Mifflin Co., Pa.; a first settler of Noble Co., Ind., 1831; removed to Grundy Co., Ill., 1860; issue: I–Susan (*b* 1826; *m* Hamilton Smalley; *m* 2d, M. A. Scoville); II–Eliza (*b* 1828; *m* John Davis); III–William R. (*b* 1830); IV–Martha J. (1833-39); V–Richard R. (*b* 1835; *m* Nancy Frank); VI–Mary Ellen (1837-39); VII–Emily Angeline (*b* 1840; *m* Ambroze Lazenby); VIII–Mary Adaline (1 above); IX–Harriet (1844-47); X–Isabelle (*b* 1846; *m* Capt. A. W. Wilbern); XI–Arthur Franklin (*b* 1848; *m* Lydia Messer).
1–*m* Mar. 29, 1859, Louis Germain (Mar. 1836-Nov. 10, 1921); son of Pierre Silistine St. Germain (1791-1865), of Montreal, Canada, and Dannemora, Clinton Co., N.Y., *m* Julia Menard de Bellerose (1803-63); issue (all *b* Gardner, Ill.): 1–Carrie (July 7, 1860-Feb. 19, 1863); 2–Lottie (Oct. 3, 1862-Oct. 25, 1862); 3–Eva Stone, *b* July 24, 1864; *m* Jan. 15, 1885, George Leonard Wil-

kinson (issue: Dimmis; Louis Germain; Jean Laura); 4–Mabel Emily, *b* June 12, 1867; *m* June 12, 1890, Hiram Baker, son of Hiram Cash Goold, *m* Clementine L. Baker (issue: Grace; Lucile); 5–Grace Estella, *b* Mar. 31, 1873; *m* Mar. 4, 1899, Howard Bernard, son of Isaac Valentine Holmes, *m* Sarah Minerva Buzzell (issue: Laurence Germain; Hubert Germain; Virginia Germain); 6–Guy Louis, *b* Aug. 11, 1881; *m* 1905, Rhoda Davis (issue: Louis Ivan; Mabel Marie).
1–Mem. D.A.R. Residence: Gardner, Ill.

1–**GETMAN, Frederick Hutton,** *b* Oswego, N.Y., Feb. 9, 1877.
7–John Frederick (Kettemann) **Getman,** from Germany, settled at Stone Arabia, N.Y., 1730; *m* Johanna Bierman;
6–George, capt. French and Indian War; *m* Delia Schumacher;
5–George, served in Tryon Co. Rangers under his uncle, Christian Getman; *m* Elizabeth House;
4–George, served at Sacketts Harbor, 1812; *m* Elizabeth Empie;
3–Charles (1805-82), *m* Chloe Hutton (1815-84);
2–Charles Henry (1840-97), lumber mcht.; *m* 1870, Alice Peake (1843-1914; Aaron[3], *m* Elizabeth Foster).
1–*m* Nov. 26, 1906, Ellen M. Holbrook, *b* Worcester, Mass., Jan. 2, 1869; dau. of Eliphalet Holbrook, of Plymouth, Mass., *m* Harriet Rice.
1–Ed. Rensselaer Poly. Inst., Troy, N.Y., and Lehigh U.; grad. chem. dept., U.Va., 1896; Ph.D., Johns Hopkins, 1903 (P.B.K.). Asso. prof. chemistry, Bryn Mawr Coll., 1907-14; engaged in research in private lab., Stamford, Conn., 1914–. Trustee Ferguson Library, Stamford. Author and lecturer (see Who's Who in America). Clubs: Chemists (New York), Suburban, Woodway Country. Residence: 66 Glenbrook Rd., Stamford, Conn.

JUDGE SETH LEWIS

1–**GIBBS, Anné Nugent (Mrs. Wilbourn S.),** *b* Greenville, Miss., May 10, 18–.
6–John **Hardeman,** of Eng.; *m* in Va.; settled in Ga.; *m* Dorothy Edwards;
5–Col. Thomas (1750-98), mem. Capt. Bean's Co., engaged at King's Mountain; comd. a co. against Cherokee Indians in "Nicojack War," 1794, and acquired title of capt.; removed to Davidson Co., Tenn., 1786; mem. N.C. Legislature; *m* 1770, Mary Perkins (*b* 1754; Nicholas[6], *m* Bethenia Harden; Constantine[7] [*b* 1682], *m* Anne Pollard; Nicholas[8] [1641-1711], *m* in Henrico Co., Va., Sarah Childress);
4–Nancy (*b* 1774), *m* 1790, Seth **Lewis,** apptd. chief justice Miss. Ty., 1800, by Pres. John Adams, thru influence of Andrew Jackson; apptd. parish judge, La., 1810; apptd. dist. judge, La., 1813; judge 5th dist., 29 yrs. (see portrait);
3–Anne (1807-73), *m* 1827, John Pratt **Nugent** (1792-1873), from Ireland as a young man (James[4], *m* Aphra Pratt);

COL. WILLIAM LEWIS NUGENT (b East Baton Rouge Parish, La., Dec. 12, 1832-d 1897) grad. Centenary Coll., Jackson, La., '52; admitted to bar, 1856; apptd. inspector gen. of Miss., 1861, resigned 1862, to enter C.S.A., as pvt. Co. D, 18th Miss. Regt.; promoted to rank of capt. and assigned to adj. gen.'s dept., 1863-65; col., 12th Miss. Cav., to end of the war. Practiced law at Greenville, Miss.

2–William Lewis **Nugent** (1832-97), see portrait and biography; *m* 1860 Eleanor Smith (*d* 1865); *m* 2d, 1870, Aimee Webb (*b* 1850); issue (1st marriage): I–Eleanor (*m* Robert Somerville); issue (2d marriage): I–Cecile (1870-1921; *m* —Harris); II–Anné (1 above); III–William Lewis, Jr. (1874-1919); IV–Louis Coupery (1876-1918; *m* Mary Catchings Enochs); V–Bessie (Mrs. Harley R. Shands, qv).
1–*m* June 26, 1900, Wilbourn Smith Gibbs (1866-1921); son of Sandford Gibbs, of Huntsville, Tex., and brother of Mrs. Henry H. Hawley, qv; issue: 1–Wilbourn Sandford, *b* New Orleans, La., Feb. 28, 1909; ed. Huntsville Coll., Training Sch., Lawrenceville, N.J.; Princeton; U.Tex.
1–Ed. Whitworth Coll., Miss.; Mrs. Blake's Sch., New Orleans. Mem. D.A.R. (state librarian, Tex.) U.D.C., I.A.G. Club: Outlook. Methodist Episcopalian. Residence: 1125 11th St., Huntsville, Tex.

1–**SHANDS, Bessie Nugent (Mrs. Harley R.),** *b* Jackson, Miss.
7–Conrade **Webb**;
6–George, to Va., 1717; settled New Kent Co.; *m* 1728, Widow Lucy (Foster) Jones (Col. Joseph Foster[7]);
5–Foster (1735-95), paymaster-gen. Va. troops, Am. Rev.; *m* Sarah Shore (*d* 1808);
4–Maj. John Shore (1780-1840), *m* Elvira Clayton;
3–John Shore (*d* ca. 1853), *m* 1849, Julia Cecile Stollenwerck (1832-1916; Louis A.[4], of Phila., removed to Ala.);
2–Aimée (*b* 1850), *m* as his 2d wife, William Lewis **Nugent** (1833-97); for issue and Hardeman lineage, see Mrs. Wilbourn S. Gibbs.
1–*m* Dec. 9, 1908, Harley R. Shands, *b* Senatobia, Miss., Feb. 27, 1881; son of G. D. Shands; issue (all *b* Jackson, Miss.): 1–Aimée Cecile, *b* Dec. 7, 1909; ed. Sophie Newcomb Coll., New Orleans; 2–William Nugent, *b* Oct. 31, 1912; 3–Harley Cecil, *b* Sept. 10, 1916; 4–Wilbourn Coupery, *b* Mar. 17, 1923.
1–Ed. Belhaven Coll. and Goucher Coll., Baltimore. Mem. C.D.A., D.A.R., U.D.C., A.A.U.W. Methodist. Clubs: Chaminade, Shakespeare. Residence: 607 N. State St., Jackson, Miss.

1–**HAWLEY, Luteola Gibbs (Mrs. Henry H.),** *b* Huntsville, Tex., June 10, 1878.
5–Sgt. William **Rowntree** (*b* Va., 1747-*d* 1820), Am. Rev.; *m* 1768, Mary–;
4–Mary (1772-1851), *m* 1788, Maj. Elijah **Wilbourn** (*d* S.C., 1840), officer Am. Rev.;
3–Sabra Ann (*b* S.C., 1792-*d* Huntsville, Tex., 1864), *m* 1809, Hiram **Gibbs** (*d* Miss., 1844), his son Sandford St. John Gibbs divided the estate of his father among the six married children and their mother, in absence of a will or administrator (James[4]; John[5]);
2–Sandford St. John (2 below).
12–Thomas **Smith** (*b* Cropwell Boteler, Parish of Tithby, Eng.), moved to Nottingham and was known as Thomas Smith, of Nottingham and Gaddesby;
11–John (*d* 1602), of Cropwell, Eng.; his will recorded at Tithby;
10–John (bap. 1593-will proved 1642), purchased land of Sir Thomas Hutchinson, 1622; *m* 1630, Elizabeth, dau. of Thomas Garton; *m* 2d, Frances Wilcocke, of Cropwell;
9–Thomas (*b* 1631), became a mercer and later private banker; *m* Mary, dau. of John Hooper; *m* 2d, Fortune, dau. of Laurence Collin, who held Nottingham Castle against the forces of King Charles I;
8–Thomas (*d* 1727), inherited 1400 acres of land at Gaddesby and the bank at London; high sheriff of Nottingham Co., 1717-18;
7–Samuel (1684-1751), head of the banking house of Smith, Payne & Smith; *m* Elizabeth, dau. of John Cartlitch;
6–John (*b* 1719), came to America and located in N.C., now Wake Co., ca. 1730;
5–John (*b* 1740), of Anson Co., N.C.; soldier Am. Rev.; *m* Mary Flake (Samuel[6]);
4–James (1777-1852), of Anson Co.; *m* Mary Gathings (1787-1859);
3–Thomas Jefferson (*b* Anson Co., N.C., 1810-*d* Mexia, Tex., 1887), *m* 1832, Mary Washington Ledbetter;
2–Sallie E. (2 below).
8–Henry **Ledbetter**;
7–Richard, living in Brunswick Co., Va., ante 1734; *m* Hannah–;
6–Henry, *m* Edith–;
5–Charles (1740-1820), from Brunswick Co., Va., to Anson Co., N.C., 1772; *m* 1st, Mary Randall (1746-1800; Capt. Peter[6] [1723-86], officer Am. Rev., *m* 1742, Frances Barrett, 1725-70);
4–Rev. Henry (1771-1852), soldier War 1812; *m* 2d, 1806, Anne Prichard (1774-1813), widow of Mr. Dunn;
3–Mary Washington (*b* Montgomery Co., N.C., 1808-*d* Mexia, Tex., 1881), *m* Thomas Jefferson **Smith** (3 above);
2–Sallie E. (*b* Anson Co., N.C., 1844-*d* Huntsville, Tex., 1918), went by pvt. conveyance to Tex., 1859; returned to N.C. to complete her edn., valedictorian of her class; at close of Civil War, returned to Tex., by pvt. conveyance; *m* Jan. 1866, Sandford St. John **Gibbs** (*b* Union Dist., S.C., 1819-*d* Huntsville, Tex., 1886), pioneer mcht., pvt. banker, large land owner; capt. C.S.A.; moved to Tex., 1842; went to Miss., 1844; located permanently in Tex., 1846; asso. in business with his bro. Thomas, under firm name of T. & S. Gibbs; on death of Thomas, the name became S. Gibbs; pvt. bank was converted into a national, Gibbs Nat. Bank, 1890-1926, now First Nat. Bank; issue: I–Wilbourn S. (1866-1921; *m* Anné Nugent, qv); II–Mary Alla (*b* 1868; *m* Henderson Yoakum Robinson, 1864-1929); III–Thomas Clifton (1870-1926; *m* Jamesetta Hunt); IV–Sarah Sandford (*b* 1873; *m* Dr. Oscar L. Norsworthy); V–Dr. James Philip (*b* 1875; *m* Mary Brent McAshan); VI–Luteola (1 above).
1–*m* Nov. 18, 1903, Henry Houston Hawley, *b* Walla Walla, Wash., Jan. 6, 1868; pres. H. H. Hawley Co., wholesale watchmakers, jewelers and engravers supplies, Dallas and Houston, Tex., and Oklahoma City, Okla.; issue: 1–Henry Houston, Jr., *b* Huntsville, Tex., July 14, 1906; grad. Terrell Sch., Dallas; grad. Southern Methodist U., Dallas; student Pioneer Floating U., sec. H. H. Hawley Co.; 2–Sarah Alla, *b* Dallas, Tex., Mar. 30, 1918; grad. Mrs. H. B. Taylor's Sch.; student Miss Ella Hockaday Sch. for Girls, Dallas.
1–Mem. D.A.R. (chapter registrar), I.A.G., A.L. Auxiliary, Dallas Woman's Forum; Dallas Branch of the Needlework Guild of America (section pres. No. 7), Randolph-Macon Woman's Coll. Alumnae Assn., Cocke Sch. of Expression Alumni (hon.). Clubs: Dallas Woman's; Dallas Bankers Wives' (chmn. finance); Thursday Morning Study (treas.), Lakewood Country, Art Noon. Residence: 5701 Gaston Av., Dallas, Tex.

1–**GIBBONS, Brainard Frederick,** *b* Brooklyn, N.Y., Dec. 9, 1901.
10–Alexander **Baker** (*b* ca. 1607), from Eng. in the "Elizabeth," 1635, to Boston; mfr. of cordage; soon after landing at Boston he became interested in shipping and commercial business; *m* Elizabeth Farrar;
9–Joshua (1642-1717), of New London, Conn.; in 1700 received from Owaneco, Chief of the Mohegan Indians a deed for a large tract of land at Mohegan, Conn., on which his sons settled and where some of their descendants still live; *m* 1674, Hannah (Tonge) Minter (*b* 1654; George Tonge[10]);
8–John (1681-1750), of New London; *m* ca. 1701/02, Elizabeth Waterhouse (Jacob[9], from Eng. to Conn., ante 1639, *m* Hannah–);
7–John (1703-87), of Woodbury, Conn.; ens., 1741; lt., 1743 in Conn. troops in Pequot War; *m* Patience–;
6–Seth (*b* 1735), of Woodbury; enlisted in Capt. Joseph Hait's 4th Co., 7th Regt., Cont. Line, 1775; discharged, Dec. 23, 1775; also pvt. Conn. militia, 1777;
5–Thaddeus (*b* 1761), of Poultney, Vt., and Andover, N.Y.; *m* 1791, Ann Castle (*b* 1766; Reuben[6], *m* Eunice–; Samuel[7], *m* Martha–; Isaac[8], *m* Sarah–; Henry[9], *m* Hannah Squire; Henry[10], of Stratford, Conn.);
4–Thaddeus (1806-88), of Andover, N.Y.; physician; *m* 1835, Mary Storrs Spicer;
3–Dwight Brainard (1841-1922), of Andover; ed. Alfred (N.Y.) U.; partner firm of Baker & Young; formed the firm of Baker & Marks, and the Crescent Lumber Co.; founder and 1st pres., Republican Club at Suffern, N.Y.; postmaster; del. to Town, Co., State and Nat. convs.; *m* 1863, Henrietta Eliza Conklin (1844-1908);
2–Mabel Ettie (2 below).
11–William **Bradford,** Mayflower Pilgrim (qv);
10–William (1624-1704), of Plymouth; *m* 1652, Alice Richards (*d* 1671);
9–Hannah (1662-1738), of Kingston; *m* 1682, Joshua **Ripley** (1658-1739; John[10]; William[11], qv);
8–Joshua (1688-1773), of Hingham, Mass.; *m* 1712, Mary Backus (*b* 1692);
7–William (1734-1818), of Windham, Conn.; *m* 1757, Lydia Brewster;
6–Faith (1757-1824), of Windham; *m* 1779, Jabez **Spicer** (1753-1823);
5–Jabez (1788-1847), of Cornish, N.H.; *m* 1810, Mary Storrs Hovey (1788-1850);
4–Mary Storrs (1814-95), of Newbury, Vt.; *m* Thaddeus **Baker** (4 above).
12–William **Brewster,** Mayflower Pilgrim (qv);
11–Love (*d* 1650), of Plymouth; in Pequot War, 1637; mem. mil. co. of Miles Standish, 1643; grand juryman from Duxbury, 1645; a propr., 1645; *m* 1634, Sarah Collier (William[12]);
10–Wrestling (*d* 1697), of Duxbury, Mass.; *m* Mary– (1661-1742);
9–Jonathan (*d* 1753), of Windham, Conn.; *m* 1709, Mary Partridge (1693-1748);
8–James (1715-55), of Duxbury, Mass.; *m* 1738/39, Faith Ripley (1722-87);
7–Lydia (1739-1829), *m* William **Ripley** (7 above).
2–Frederick Howe **Gibbons** (*b* 1875), *m* 1895, Mabel Ettie Baker (*b* 1878).
1–*m* Dec. 9, 1922, Adele Marie Schmidt, *b* New York, N.Y., July 23, 1901; dau. of Adolphe Schmidt, of Pleasantville, N.Y., *m* Adele Marie Schmidt; issue: 1–Cynthia Jane, *b* Pleasantville, N.Y., Jan. 1, 1930.
1–B.S., New York U., '24 (Psi Up., Phi Delta Phi); J.D., 1926. Mem. law firm of **Yard & Gibbons.** Served with Squadron A, N.Y.N.G. Mem. S.M.D., S.A.R., I.A.G. Episcopalian. Republican. Clubs: Squadron A, Nannahagan Golf. Residence: "Shaggy Bark," Pleasantville, N.Y.

1–**GIBSON, Frederick,** *b* Ukiah, Calif., June 10, 1881.
4–George **Gibson,** of Salisbury Dist., of Rowan

Co., N.C.; served in Am. Rev.; *m* Margaret Lock;
3–Matthew Lock (*b* 1798 or 99), *m* Mary Jamison (John[4], soldier Am. Rev., prob. in expdn. to Canada);
2–Andrew Jackson (1822-1901), of Tenn.; farmer and stock raiser; *m* 1852, Ellen Montgomery (1841-1925); issue: I–Jefferson Davis (1861-1921; *m* Lena Acuff); II–Mary (*b* 1865; *m* Henry L. York); III–Taliatha (*b* 1867; *m* Marvin Patton James Petross); IV–Eliza Jane (*b* 1870; *m* Willis E. Seehorn); V–Melinda (*b* 1874; *m* John A. Rhodes); VI–Josephine (*b* 1877; *m* Frank S. Matthews); VII–Kate (*b* 1879; *m* Lafayette Grothe); VIII–Frederick (1 above); IX–Samuel (*b* 1883; *m* Mattie Gilbert); X–Charley (*d* infancy); XI–Mark (*d* infancy).
1–Mem. Order United American Mechanics (jr.), S.A.R., I.A.G. Enlisted, 1918, Ft. McDowell, San Francisco; served throughout World War, in Germany; disch., Ft. D. A. Russell, Cheyenne, Wyo., 1919. Mem. Christian Ch. Democrat. Address: Soldiers' Home, Sawtelle, Calif.

GILBERT

Arms: *Argent, on a chevron sable, three roses of the field.*
Crest: *A squirrel cracking a nut proper.*
Motto: *Mallem more quam mutare.*

1–**GILBERT, Pearl,** *b* Rossville, Ill., Nov. 13, 1876.
9–Capt. Thomas **Gilbert** (*d* 1666), from Eng., 1635, settled at Springfield, Mass.; *m* 1655, Cathrine (Chapin) Bliss (*d* 1712; Samuel Chapin[10], founder of Springfield);
8–Henry (1661-1740), built a fort at Brookfield, where he was an officer; *m* Elizabeth Belding (*d* 1735);
7–Samuel (*b* 1689), of Brookfield; *m* Lydia Barnes (*b* 1692; Thomas[8], *m* Mary How);
6–Samuel (*b* 1715), of Brookfield; *m* Ann–;
5–Elias (*b* 1748), of Worthington, Mass.; pvt. Am. Rev.; minute man; corpl. in Banister's Co. in expdn. on Ticonderoga, 1777; *m* Lydia Bowen;
4–Samuel (*b* Worthington, Mass., 1783-*d* 1855), of Danville, Ill.; *m* 1804, Polly (Mary) Morse; first settlers of Vermilion Co., Ill., 1826;
3–James (1817-61), of Rossville, Ill.; see portrait; *m* 2d, 1845, Sarah Mathers (1822-79);
2–Samuel Harvey (2 below).
10–Samuel **Morse** (qv);
9–Joseph (1615-76), *m* Esther Pierce (John[10], *m* Elizabeth–);

JAMES GILBERT (1817-61).

8–Joseph (1637-1718), of Sherborn, Mass., 1670; capt.; *m* 1671, Mehitabel Wood (1655-81; Nicolas[9], *m* Mary Pidge);
7–Joseph (*b* 1679 or 83), of Dedham; *m* 1702, Prudence Adams (1682/83-1772); Henry[8] [*b* 1657], *m* Prudence Tracy; Henry[9]; Henry[10], qv);
6–Joseph (1705-80), of Sherborn, Mass.; *m* 1735, Experience Morse (*b* 1710; Noah[7], *m* Mary Johnson);
5–Zebediah (1748-1817), of Windsor; pvt. Am. Rev.; *m* 1771, Mary Sabin (*b* 1751; Noah[6], *m* Mary Williams);
4–Mary or Polly (1789-1838), *m* Samuel **Gilbert** (4 above);
3–James, *m* Sarah Mathers (3 above);
2–Samuel Harvey (1854-84), farmer, Sedan, Kan.; *m* 1876, Fanny Bass (*b* 1856); issue: I–Pearl (1 above); II–Sarah Harriett (*b* 1879; *m* 1902, John W. Goodwine, *b* 1877); III–Charles Henry (*b* 1881; *m* Audrey Howard); IV–Samuel Harvey (*b* 1884; *m* Grace Pierson).
1–Ed. Ill. Teachers Coll. Mem. D.A.R., I.A.G., W.C.T.U. Methodist. Republican. Club: Twin Cities Woman's. Residence: 606 S. Goodwin, Urbana, Ill.

1–**GILDERSLEEVE, Virginia Crocheron,** *b* New York, N.Y., Oct. 3, 1877.
9–Richard **Gildersleeve** (qv);
8–Richard (1625-91), propr., Newtown, L.I., 1656, Hempstead, 1659; surveyor; town clk.; town drummer; *m* 1658, Dorcas– (*d* 1703);
7–Thomas (1661-1740), town clk., ch. warden; founder ch. of Eng., Hempstead, L.I., and St. George's Episcopal Ch.; surveyor; large landowner; *m* Mary–;
6–Thomas (1690-1748), Huntington, L.I.;
5–Henry (*b* 1724), from L.I. to Dutchess Co., N.Y., ca. 1770; *m* Mary Hall;
4–Henry (1765-1843), *m* Eunice Smith, of L.I.;
3–Smith James (1809-80), *m* Rachel Alger (1816-63);
2–Henry Alger (2 below).
9–John (Jean) **Crocheron** (will dated 1695, recorded 1696), probably a French Waldense from Holland; a planter of S.I., N.Y.; *m* Mary–;
8–Nicholas;
7–John;
6–Abraham (*d* 1778), *m* Elizabeth–;
5–Nicholas (*d* 1818), *m* Ann–;
4–John (1770-1820), S.I., N.Y.; *m* Catherine Ryerss

(1778-1828; g.dau. of Richard Connor, of S.I.);
3–Richard Connor (1812-67), S.I., N.Y.; *m* Anna Maria Geib (1821-49);
2–Virginia (1843-1923), *m* 1868, Henry Alger **Gildersleeve** (1840-1923), ed. College Hill, Poughkeepsie, N.Y., and Columbia U. Law Sch.; admitted to bar, 1866; served capt. and maj. during Civil War and was bvtd. lt. col. for gallant and meritorious services in Ga. and Carolina campaigns; judge Ct. of Gen. Sessions, 1876-89; judge Superior Ct., 1891-94; justice N.Y. Supreme Ct., 1894-1909, resigned; Democrat; mem. N.G.N.Y.; capt. of co. of Am. riflemen sent to Ireland, 1875; issue: I–Alger Crocheron (*b* 1869; *m* Josephine Milnor); II–Henry Alger, Jr. (1871-91); III–Virginia (*d* infancy); IV–a daughter (*d* infancy); V–Virginia Crocheron (1 above).
1–A.B., Barnard Coll. (Columbia U.), '99 (Kappa Kappa Gamma, P.B.K.); A.M., Columbia, 1900, Ph.D., 1908; LL.D., Rutgers Coll., 1916. Prof. and dean Barnard Coll. (Columbia U.), since Feb. 1911 (see Who's Who in America). Trustee Constantinople Woman's Coll., The Master's Sch., The Brearley Sch. Mem. Am. Nat. Com. on Internat. Intellectual Cooperation, administrative bd. of Inst. of Internat. Edn., bldg. com. of Am. Sch. of Classical Studies at Athens, division of ednl. relations of the Nat. Research Council, advisory bd. of the John Simon Guggenheim Memorial Foundation, Council of Internat. Fed. of Univ. Women (past pres.), Modern Lang. Assn. of America, Classical Assn. of the Atlantic States, Am. Council on Edn. (past chmn.). Pres. Reid Hall, Inc., Assn. to Aid Scientific Research by Women. Clubs: Women's Univ., Cosmopolitan, Women's City. Author: Govt. Regulation of the Elizabethan Drama. Episcopalian. Residence: 3007 Broadway, New York, N.Y.

1–**GILKEY, Herbert James,** *b* Montesano, Wash., Jan. 2, 1890.
12–Bernard **Capen** (qv);
11–John (*b* Eng., 1612/13-1692), to America with parents; freeman, 1634; dea., 1658, for 33 yrs.; selectman Dorchester, 16 yrs.; rep. Gen. Ct., 6 yrs.; mil. officer, 50 yrs.; capt. town militia; *m* 1st, Redegon Clapp (Nicholas[12], from Venn Ottery, Eng., to Dorchester, Mass.);
10–John (1639-1707), freeman, 1666; constable, 1674; *m* 1662, Susanna Barsham (William[11], *m* Annabella–);
9–Susanna (*b* 1664), *m* as his 1st wife, Andrew **Hall** (1665-1756), weaver, farmer; settled at Newton, Mass., 1695; bought 43 acres owned and occupied by his descendants ever since (Edward[10] [*b* Eng.-*d* 1670; son of Francis, of Henborough, Eng.], of Braintree, Duxbury and Taunton, Mass., 1640-41, served against Narragansetts, 1645, owned 50th part of Rehoboth, 1646-50, of Braintree, 1650-55, *m* Esther–);
8–Edward, *m* 1730, Mary Miller (*b* 1710; Samuel[9] [*b* 1678], *m* 1708, Elizabeth Child; Joseph[10], *m* Mary, dau. of Walter Pope);
7–Mary (1734-75), *m* David **Richardson** (1732-1825); see Vol. III, p. 546, for Richardson lineage;
6–Joseph, *m* Mary Carpenter;
5–Joseph, *m* Charlotte Thompson;
4–Mary (1811-97), *m* 1838, Elkanah **Walker** (1805-77), both went to Ore. as missionaries with Marcus Whitman, 1838;
3–Abigail Boutwell (1840-1918), *m* 1863, James Anderson **Karr** (1834-1914), founder Hogsiam, Wash.;
2–Mary Olive (2 below).
10–Robert **Ring** (*b* Eng., ca. 1640-1690), of Salisbury, Mass.; "cooper" and "planter"; received land in "first division"; took freeman's oath, 1640; carrying on a fishing business with headquarters on "Ring's Island," 1640; *m* Elizabeth–;
9–Jarvis (*b* prob. 1658), of Salisbury; took freeman's oath, 1690; witness in the trial of Susanna Martin for witchcraft, 1692; with wife signed petition in favor of Mrs. Bradbury who was accused of witchcraft, 1692; soldier Indian skirmishes, 1698, 1702; *m* 1682, Hannah Fowler (*d* 1743);
8–David (1693-1752), ens., capt.; *m* 2d, 1739, Mrs. Anna Gale (*d* 1746);
7–Anna (or Sarah) (*b* 1740), *m* 1762, Dr. John **Hay** (1737-1815), physician, of Woburn, Mass.; see Vol. III, p. 546, for Hay-Boutwell lineages;
6–Charlotte (*b* 1766), *m* Isaac Snow **Thompson** (1761-99), see Vol. III, p. 546, for Thompson lineage;
5–Charlotte (*b* 1786), *m* Joseph **Richardson** (5 above).
2–Mary Olive Karr (*b* 1865), *m* 1888, Herbert Luville **Gilkey** (*b* 1865); for issue see Vol. III, p. 546.
1–*m* Aug. 18, 1923, Mildred Virginia Talbot, *b* Urbana, Ill., Feb. 6, 1891; dau. of Arthur Newell Talbot, engineer, scientist, and educator (see Who's Who in America); issue: 1–Herbert Talbot, *b* Boulder, Colo., Nov. 27, 1924; 2–Arthur Karr, *b* Boulder, Sept. 25, 1926.
1–B.S., Ore. Agrl. Coll., 1911; B.S., M.I.T., 1916; B.S., Harvard, 1916; M.S., U.Ill., 1923. First lt. of engrs. mapping U.S. borders in N.M. and Va., Sept. 1917-July 1918; at Gen. Hdqrs., Chaumont, Hdqrs. 2d Army, Toul, 29th Engrs., G-2-C, France, July 1918-Feb. 1919; with Am. Relief Administration, with Herbert Hoover, Paris, Feb.-Aug. 1919; capt., Engr. R.C., 1920. Structural engr., with A. R. Lord, Chicago, 1919-21; teaching and concrete research, U.Ill., 1921-23; asst., asso. and prof. civil engring., U.Colo., 1923–. Mem. I.A.G., Am. Soc. C.E., Soc. Am. Mil. Engrs., Sigma Xi; fellow A.A.A.S., etc. (see Who's Who in Engineering, 1925). Residence: 838 14th St., Boulder, Colo.

DR. ALBERT FRANKLIN GILMAN

1–**GILMAN, Albert Franklin,** *b* Hallowell, Me., Sept. 9, 1871.
10–Edward **Gilman** (qv);
9–Hon. John (1624-1708), of Exeter; selectman, 1652; councillor for N.H., 1680-83; mem. House of Rep., speaker, 1693; *m* 1657, Elizabeth Treworgye (1639-1719; James[10] [*d* ante 1650], *m* Catherine, dau. of Alexander Shapleigh, an English merchant and shipowner and was interested in the early settlements of Me. and N.H., sending over from Eng. his goods in his own ships, agent for Sir Ferdinando Gorges and visited America before 1635);
8–Elizabeth (1661-ca. 1732), *m* 1678, Nathaniel **Ladd** (1651-91), mortally wounded by Indians in King William's War (Daniel[9], from Eng., 1634, lived at Ipswich and Salisbury, Mass., an original settler of Haverhill, Mass., *m* Anna–);
7–Mary (1682-post 1743), *m* 1704, Jacob **Gilman** (*d* 1743), from Eng.; a founder of Kingston, N.H., 1694; captured by Indians, taken to Canada, purchased his freedom by building a saw mill, and returned to Kingston;
6–John, of Kingston, N.H.; *m* 1735, Sarah Stevens;

5–Samuel Stevens (bap. 1750), removed to Washington Plantation (later Mt. Vernon), Me.; del. from Lincoln Co. to the conv. at Portland, 1787; *m* ca. 1770, Elizabeth Dudley;
4–Joseph (1781-1829), sgt. in War 1812; *m* 1802, Anna Stain (1778-1849; John[5] [1741-1822], from Germany to Boston, 1750, "thence to Kennebeck 2 yrs. before the Ft. Weston and Hallifax in 1756"; joined the marching co. and continued in services of the English until the conclusion of the war between France and England, 1759; mem. Com. Correspondence, Inspection and Safety, 1778 for the town of Winthrop; *m* 1775, Rebecca Emerson);
3–Albert Gallatin (1806-71), selectman of Mt. Vernon, Me., 1838-44; *m* 1838, Rachel Corfen White (1812-97), of Readfield, Me.;
2–William Franklin (2 below).
10–Gov. Thomas **Dudley** (qv);
9–Rev. Samuel (1606-83), pastor, Exeter, N.H., 1650-83; *m* 3d, Elizabeth– (*d* 1702);
8–Stephen (1656-1734), *m* 1684, Sarah Gilman (1667-1713; Hon. John[9], of Exeter, above);
7–Lt. James (1690-1746), one of the heroes of the famous Louisburg Expdn., 1745; an original propr. of Gilmanton, N.H.; *m* Mercy Folsom (*b* ca. 1691; Dea. John[8], of Exeter, N.H.; John[9] [*d* 1681], from Eng. in the "Diligent," *m* Mary Gilman);
6–Joseph (1728-92), moved to Raymond, N.H., where he built a saw mill; *m* ca. 1749, Susanna Lord (*d* 1802);
5–Elizabeth (*b* 1752), *m* Samuel Stevens **Gilman** (5 above).
2–William Franklin **Gilman** (1839-80), removed to Hallowell, thence to Chelsea, Me.; *m* 1866, Julia Ann Gordon (1842-1903), she *m* 2d, 1883, Alanson Perry; issue (1st marriage, surname Gilman): I–Minnie Agnes (*b* 1870; *m* Eugene Leroy Millett); II–Albert Franklin (1 above); III–Eugene Ellsworth (*b* 1875).
1–*m* Sept. 28, 1899, Agness Geneva McGlynn, *b* Meriden, Conn., Nov. 1, 1876; dau. Edward Thompson McGlynn, of Meriden, Conn.; issue: 1–Albert Franklin, Jr., *b* Meriden, Conn., July 28, 1900; served in World War 1918; Ph.B., U.Chicago, '25, A.M., 1926; 2–Gertrude Marcelle, *b* Maryville, Tenn., Dec. 5, 1904; Ph.B., U.Chicago, '25, A.M., 1927.

ALBERT FRANKLIN GILMAN, JR.

1–S.B., Amherst, '97 (Delta Tau Delta, Phi Lambda Upsilon), A.M., 1901; Ph.D., U.Denver, 1913. Prof. science, Dow Acad., Franconia, N.H., 1898-99; prof. chemistry and physics, Maryville (Tenn.) Coll., 1900-06; prof. chemistry, Ripon (Wis.) Coll., 1906-17, Huron (S.D.) Coll., 1917-18, Ill. Wesleyan U., 1918-20; Carroll (Wis.) Coll., 1920-21, Central Y.M.C.A., Coll. of Arts and Sciences, Chicago, since 1921. Author (see Who's Who in America). Fellow A.A.A.S., Mem. Am. Chem. Soc., Wis., S.D. and Ill. acads. of sciences. Episcopalian. Mason. Republican. Clubs: Lakeside Lawn Bowling, Chicago Lawn Bowling, Jackson Park Golf, Chicago Curling. Summer place: Mt. Vernon, Me. Winter place: St. Augustine, Fla. Residence: 5427 University Av., Chicago, Ill.

1–**GILLIGAN, Lillian Rich McLaughlin (Mrs. James J.),** *b* Boston, Mass., Apr. 20, 1866.
4–George **McLaughlin** (1735-1815), of Scotch parentage; brought from Ireland by sea capt., 1746; served with Mass. militia in French and Indian War; on expdn. to Crown Pt.; settled at Jones' Plantation (now China, Me.), Mass.; *m* 1763, Lois Sands (1743-1831; Thomas[5]; James[6]);
3–Charles (1771-1860), of Harlem, Mass. (now China, Me.); *m* 1797, Sarah (called Sally) Chadwick (1780-1858; James[4], *m* Rhoda–);
2–Oliver Wendall (2 below).
8–Richard **Williams** (qv);
7–Dea. Nathaniel (1639-92), of Taunton; *m* 1668, Elizabeth Rogers (*b* 1646; John[8], *m* Ann Churchman; Thomas[9], Mayflower Pilgrim, qv);
6–John (1675-1724), of Taunton; *m* Hannah Robinson (1670-1757; Increase[7]; William[8]);
5–Timothy (1714-70), of Taunton, Mass.; town clk., Easton, Mass., 1754-59; served in mil. co., 1757; settled finally at Woolwich (now Me.), Mass.; *m* 1736, Elizabeth Britton (*d* 1794; William[6]; William[7]; James[8]);
4–Elemuel (1751-1820), sgt. in Mass. troops, 1776, lt., 1777, maj., 1778, in Am. Rev.; at Valley Forge, 1777-78; 1st town clk., N. Anson, Me., 1778-1808; *m* 1777, Anna Hilton (1758-1850; Moses[5]; Ebenezer[6]);
3–William (1781-1839), of N. Anson, Me.; *m* 1807, Amy Gray (1788-1868);
2–Amy Hamilton Gray (1823-1902), of N. Anson, Boston and Malden, Mass.; *m* 1851, Oliver Wendall **McLaughlin** (1822-1906), merchant tailor, Boston, Mass.; issue: I–Fred Hamilton (1855-1911; *m* Mary Calista Hartshorn); II–Lillian Rich (1 above).
1–*m* Mar. 12, 1889, James Joseph Gilligan, *b* Jersey City, N.J., Oct. 1, 1861; son of Matthew Gilligan.
1–Grad. Petersilea Acad. Music and Languages, '84. Taught music 4 yrs. Mem. S.M.D., S.D.P. (registrar, N.H. chapter), D.F.P.A. (an organizer, N.H. chapter, corr. sec. 1927–), D.C.W., D.A.R., N.E.H.G.S., N.H. Hist. Soc., O.E.S. Club: Concord Woman's. Residence: 44 Rumford St., Concord, N.H.

1–**GILMAN, Alfred Alonzo,** *b* North Platte, Neb., Aug. 23, 1878.
10–Edward **Gilman** (qv);
9–Edward (1617?-53), came with father; *m* –Smith (Richard[10]);
8–Edward (1648-92), *m* Abigail Maverick;
7–Edward (*b* 1675);
6–Antipas (1705-93), *m* Lydia Thing;
5–Benjamin (1747-1804), *m* Elizabeth Ladd;
4–Benjamin, *m* Dorothy Jewel;
3–Rufus Alonzo (1801-86), *m* Ann Hannah Mooers;
2–Platt Jewel (2 below).
8–Edmund **Mooers** (*b* 1614), from Eng. in the "Confidence," to Boston, 1638; settled at Newbury, Mass., 1640; *m* Anna– (*d* 1670);
7–Jonathan (*b* 1646), *m* 1670, Constance Langhorn;
6–Jonathan (1694-1745), *m* 1714/15, Mary Poor (1692-1748);
5–Benjamin (1725-99), *m* 1749, Abigail Hazen (1728/29-1778);
4–Benjamin (1758-1838), officer during Am. Rev., mem. Washington's Life Guard; mem. Soc. Cin. maj. gen. militia, 1811; *m* 1791, Hannah Platt (1771-1809);
3–Ann Hannah (*b* 1808), *m* Rufus Alonzo **Gilman** (3 above);
2–Platt Jewel (*b* 1848), *m* 1875, Mary Eddy Hubbard (1846-1926); issue: I–Alfred Alonzo (1 above); II–Kate Miller (*b* 1880; *m* John Arthur Woolsey); III–Margaret Mooers (*b* 1882; *m* George Alpheus Saint); IV–Orilla Frances (*b* 1887; *m* Richmond Dillon Birge).
1–*m* Feb. 22, 1905, Gertrude Carter, *b* Babylon.

L.I., N.Y., May 10, 1874; dau. Frederick Brewerton Carter, of Brooklyn, N.Y.; issue: 1-Frederick Carter, *b* Kuling, China, July 5, 1907; grad. Stevens Inst., '29; 2-Louise Frances, *b* Changsha, China, Feb. 2, 1911; Wellesley Coll., 1932; 3-Edward Hubbard Platt, *b* Hankow, China, Nov. 14, 1913.

1-B.A., U.Neb., '98 (Delta Tau Delta, P.B.K.); grad. Phila. Div. Sch., 1901, S.T.D., 1918; dea. 1901, priest, 1902, P.E. Ch. Pres. Central China U. since 1924; suffragan bishop Dist. of Hankow since 1925 (see Who's Who in America). Decorated by Republic of China with 3d Order of the Growing Grain. Residence: 43 Tungting Rd., Hankow, China.

1-**GILMORE, Myron Tyrrel,** *b* Dedham, Me., Jan. 11, 1847.
7-John **Gilmore** (*b* Scotland, ca. 1660-1741), came from Ireland, ca. 1700, or later, with his wife and six children; settled at Raynham, Mass.; *m* Agnes– (*d* 1752);
6-James (*d* 1773, aet. 80), *m* Thankful Tyrrel (1705-89; William, Jr.[7], *m* Abigail–, of Abington, Mass.);
5-Tyrrel (1744-75), marched to Lexington Alarm, 1775; *m* Hannah Cook (*b* ca. 1745), of Foxboro, Mass.;
4-Samuel (1765-1845), Am. Rev.; one of the first settlers at Holden, Me.; *m* Reumah Hathorn (1767-1864);
3-David (1788-1868), *m* Sally Coombs;
2-Tyrrel (2 below).
8-Anthony **Coombs** (*b* prob. ca. 1650), French Huguenot, settled in Plymouth Co., Mass., later at Newburyport; *m* 1688, Dorcas Woodin;
7-Lt. Peter (bap. 1691-1768), New Meadows, Brunswick, Me.;
6-Peter, mem. First Church;
5-George, of New Meadows, Brunswick, Me.; *m* 1741, Abigail Berry;
4-Benjamin, of Poland, Me.; *m* Deborah Strout;
3-Sally (1794-1876), *m* David **Gilmore** (3 above).
6-John **Pearl** (1650-ca. 1720), from Eng. to Bradford, Mass., 1680; *m* 1680, Elizabeth Holmes (1660-1744), of Rowley, Mass.;
5-Richard (1702-93), *m* 1726, Sarah Stevens (1703-86), of Andover, Mass.;
4-John (1739-1825), served in Colonial wars and in Am. Rev.; marched to Lexington Alarm; *m* 1765, Eunice Kimball (1746-1830), of West Boxford, Mass.;
3-Peter (1791-1874), farmer and shoe maker; mem. West Parish Co. of Foot, 1812; *m* 1813, Rebecca Spofford;
2-Mary Wood (2 below).
8-John **Spofford** (*b* 1620), from Eng., 1638, settled at Rowley, removed to "Spofford Hill," Georgetown, Mass.; *m* Elizabeth Scott;
7-Samuel (*b* 1653), *m* 1676, Sarah Birkbee or Bisbee;
6-Samuel, *m* 1717, Sarah Stickney, of Bradford, Mass.;
5-Amos (*b* 1729), of West Boxford, Mass.; *m* 1754, Abigail Pearl;
4-Samuel (*b* 1764), *m* 1793, Deborah Robinson;
3-Rebecca (1794-1877), *m* Peter **Pearl** (3 above).
2-Tyrrel **Gilmore** (1815-90), farmer and school teacher; blacksmith, Dedham Village, 1860-70; *m* 1842, Lucinda M. Houston (*d* 1843); *m* 2d, 1844, Mary Wood Pearl (1815-88); issue: I-Pascal Pearl (*b* 1845; *m* 1881, Alma Maria Hart, *b* 1859); II-Myron Tyrrel (1 above); III-John Everett (*b* 1848; *m* 1878, Nellie Day, 1856-1923); IV-Francis Henry (1852-1912; *m* 1883, Hannah Lucétta Cole, 1864-1918); V-George Albert (1853-89); VI-Mary Adelaide (*b* 1862; *m* 1886, Willis F. Hart, M.D.).
1-*m* Apr. 1886, Mary (Parker) Spofford (*d* Jan. 10, 1918); dau. of John L. Parker, of Dedham, Me.
1-Ed. East Me. Conference Sem. Pres., San Diego (Calif.) Trust & Savings Bank, since 1908 (see Who's Who in America). Served as pvt., Co. B, 15th Regt., Me. Inf. Vols., Civil War, 1 yr. Past cdr., G.A.R. Conglist. Summer place: Pine Hills, Calif. Residence: 3004 6th St., San Diego, Calif.

1-**GILSON, Lulu Edna Purdy (Mrs. Franklin L.),** *b* Hutchinson, Kan., Oct. 28, 1880.
8-Francis **Purdy** (1610?-1658), from Eng. to Boston, 1633, thence to Fairfield, Conn., 1635; rector; *m* ante 1632, Mary Brundage (*b* ca. 1616; John Brundage or Brandegee[9] [ca. 1585-

WILSON PURDY (1839-1901); photograph taken at Newburgh, N.Y., April, 1863, while he was on a furlough.

1639], from Eng. ca. 1632, settled at Wethersfield, Conn., *m* Rachel–, *d* 1642);
7-Judge Joseph (ca. 1653-1709), early settler of Rye, N.Y.; supervisor, 1707-08; mem. Colonial Assembly; *m* 2d, Elizabeth Ogden (*d* 1742; John[8] [1600-83], *m* 2d, 1638, Judith, dau. of Lt. John Budd [*d* ca. 1670], *m* Katherine, dau. of Thomas Browne [*d* 1694], from Eng. to Concord, 1632, to Cambridge; Thomas[9]; Edward[10]);
6-Still John (1695-post 1770), land and mill owner, Northcastle, Westchester Co., 1753; *m* ca. 1726, Elizabeth– (*b* 1709);
5-Elisha (1740-1820), Episcopalian minister; served in 4th Regt. Ulster Co. Militia during Am. Rev.; *m* ca. 1761, Mehitable Smith;
4-Nathaniel (1786-1829), *m* 1809, Elizabeth Dickinson (1788-1853; Joseph[5] [1745-post 1792], served in Ulster Co. militia in Am. Rev., *m* Elizabeth–, 1749-1833);
3-John Smith (1812-63), of Balmville, Newburg, Orange Co., N.Y.; *m* 1834, Loretta Rhoades;
2-Wilson (2 below).
9-Rev. Thomas **Hooker** (qv);
8-Rev. Samuel (1633-97), B.A., Harvard, 1653, M.A., 1655; pastor, Plymouth, Mass., 1657-61, Farmington, Conn., 1661-97; *m* 1658, Mary Willett (1637-1712; Capt. Thomas[9], qv);
7-Hon. James (1664-1740/41), Farmington; speaker of Assembly; mem. Colonial Council and judge Supreme Ct. of the Colony; *m* 1691, Mary Leete (1671-1752; William[8] [1645-1687], *m* 1671, Mary, dau. Benjamin Fenn, *m* Sarah, dau. Sylvester Baldwin; Gov. William[9], qv);
6-Mehitable (1704-75), *m* 1724, Rev. and Dr. John **Smith** (1703-71), A.B., Yale, 1727, M.A., 1730; physician and Presbyn. minister, Rye and White Plains, N.Y. (Thomas[7], from Eng., 1715, founder Presbyn. Ch., N.Y. City, *m* Susannah Odell);
5-Mehitable (1744-1833), *m* Rev. Elisha **Purdy** (5 above).
6-Jeriah **Rhoades** (*d* 1812), of Marlborough, Ulster Co., N.Y.; served in Am. Rev.; *m* 1st, ca. 1758, Rebecca Lewis (*d* ca. 1780);
5-John (1759-1828), served in Am. Rev.; *m* Sarah– (1763-1833);
4-Zadock (*d* 1852), *m* 1st, Jane Raymond (1792-1837);
3-Loretta (1816-85), *m* John S. **Purdy** (3 above).
5-Jarvis **Smith** (*d* 1809), of Wilkes Co., N.C.; *m* Nancy Whittington;
4-Caleb (1783-1837), operated an iron bloomery, Elizabethton, Tenn.; *m* 1808, Elizabeth Doran (1785-1863; Alexander[5] [1760-1815], ens., King's Mountain, 1780, founder Duffield Acad., maj., War 1812, *m* 1780, Elizabeth [*b* 1758], dau. of John Lowry [*d* 1761], *m* Elizabeth–);
3-John Lowry (1810-67), *m* 1838, his cousin, Mary Malinda (Polly) Smith;

2–Lucinda Elizabeth (2 below).
5–Joseph **Wheatley,** of Wilkes Co., N.C.; *m* Mary (Polly) Poe;
4–Nancy (1784-1857), *m* 1807, Joshua **Smith** (*d* ante 1836; Jarvis[5], above);
3–Mary Malinda (1816-67), *m* her cousin, John L. **Smith** (3 above);
2–Lucinda Elizabeth (1847-90), *m* 1879, Wilson **Purdy** (1839-1901), vol. 1st N.Y. Mounted Rifles; pvt., Co. D, 1861, promoted through ranks to capt., Co. A, 1865; mustered out, 1865; bvt. maj., 1866; went to S.A., 1866, capt. of the river steamer "Edward Everett", 1867-73 (see portrait); issue: I–Lulu Edna (1 above); II–Ethel Wilson (*b* 1882).
1–*m* June 6, 1906, Franklin Leonard Gilson, *b* West Union, Ia., Mar. 21, 1875; son of George Monroe Gilson (Oliver[3]), *m* Ann Maria Clark; issue: 1–Marjorie Clifford, *b* Winfield, Kan., July 5, 1907; 2–Miriam Glenn, *b* Winfield, Nov. 1, 1909; 3–Teresa Elaine, *b* Winfield, May 19, 1911; 4–Gareth Franklin, and 5–Geoffrey Purdy, twins, *b* Emporia, Kan., Dec. 10, 1915; 6–Leonard Hooker, *b* Emporia, Nov. 20, 1920.
1–B.S. Southwestern Coll. (Winfield, Kan.), '13. Mem. D.A.C., Soc. Old Plymouth Colony Descendants, D.A.R. (chapter registrar, since 1924, state registrar, 1929), Daus. Union Vets., Literary League (pres. 1927-29). Residence: 801 W. 12th Av., Emporia, Kan.

1–**GITTINGS, Victoria,** *b* Baltimore, Md.
6–Thomas **Gittings** (1681-1760), settled in Kent Co., and later in "Long Green," Baltimore Co., Md., 1721-60; vestryman St. John's Parish, Baltimore Co.; had upwards of 2,000 acres of land including "Long Green"; *m* ca. 1734, 2d, Mary (Lee) Lynch (James Lee[7], *m* Margaret–);
5–Col. James (1735-1823), of "Long Green," Baltimore Co., Md.; justice of the peace, 1768-75; mem. com. Corr., 1774, and com. of Safety, 1775; capt. of co. militia, 1775; maj., 1776; later lt. col., styled "col." or "esq."; owned upwards of 3,000 acres and left a fortune valued at upwards of $300,000; *m* Elizabeth Buchanan (*b* 1742; Dr. George[6], burgess, Baltimore Co., 1745-50);
4–Richard (1763-1830), of "Berry Hill," Baltimore Co.; *m* 1788, Mary Sterett (1772-1847; John[5] [1750-87], *m* Deborah, dau. of Col. Charles Ridgely, of Baltimore Co.);
3–David Sterett, M.D. (1797-1887), of "Berry Hill," and "Rosslyn," Baltimore Co.; A.B., Dickinson Coll.; M.D., U.Md.; grad. work at Edinburgh U., 1818-20; *m* 1st, Juliana West Howard (Col. John Beale[4], of "Sherwood," Baltimore Co., *m* a dau. of Rev. William West, rector of St. Paul's P.E. Ch., Baltimore);
2–Richard James (2 below).
8–Richard **Smith** (*d* 1714; son of Richard, first atty. gen. of Md.), lord surveyor gen. of Md.; *m* 1696, Lady Mary Joanna Somerset (*d* 1697), from Eng., settled in Md. (Sir Charles[9], *m* Katherine Baskerville);
7–Charles Somerset (1697-1738), *m* Margaret–;
6–Elisabeth, *m* Young **Parran** (*d* 1772?);
5–John, *m* Ann Bourne;
4–Richard, *m* Mary Dare;
3–Ann, *m* Col. Alfred **Sellman** (Gen. Jonathan[4] [1753-1810], in Am. Rev., *m* Ann Elisabeth Harwood);
2–Victoria (1832-84), *m* 1855, Richard James **Gittings** (1830-82), received his education at Princeton and at Harvard; lawyer; jr. partner Machen and Gittings; state atty. Baltimore Co.; issue: I–Leila; II–David Sterett; III–Anna Sellman; IV–Louisa (*m* William Brogden); V–Mary Sterett; VI–Victoria (*d* young); VII–Alfred (*d* young); VIII–Richard (*d* young); IX–Victoria (1 above).
1–Mem. Md. Hist. Soc. I.A.G. Clubs: Woman's Literary, Woman's City. Summer place: Rosslyn Farm, Upper Falls P.O., Md. Residence: 231 W. Preston St., Baltimore, Md.

1–**GLASGOW, Arthur Graham,** *b* Buchanan, Va., May 30, 1865.
4–Arthur **Glasgow** (1750-1822), of Scottish descent, from cos. Down and Antrim, Northern Ireland, ca. 1766, settled on the plantation of "Green Forest" (or "Glas Gow," the greentree being the feature of the family arms), Rockbridge Co., Va., the towns of Buena Vista, Balcony Falls, and Glasgow are on this former plantation; *m* 1782, Rebekah McNutt (John[5]), widow of Ens. John McCorkle;
3–Robert (1790-1839), *m* his cousin, Catharine Anderson (her brothers were Col. John T. Anderson, of Mount Airy, Botetourt Co., Va.; Judge Francis Thomas Anderson, of Lexington, judge of the Supreme Ct. of Appeals of Va. and rector of Washington and Lee U.; and Gen. Joseph Reid Anderson, pres. of The Tredegar Co. of Richmond, Va.);
2–Francis Thomas (2 below).
5–Robert **Anderson** (ca. 1733-1825; son of Robert of Ireland, *m* Miss Graham); from Ireland to W.I., thence to Phila., 1755, to Botetourt Co., Va., 1764; *m* Margaret Neely (1738-1810);
4–Col. William (1764-1839), of Walnut Hill, Botetourt Co.; vol. in Am. Rev., aet. 16, fought in the Battle of Cowpens and Guilford C.H.; col. in War 1912; *m* Anne Thomas (Francis[5] [1743-1835], of "Montvue," nr. Frederick, Md.);
3–Catharine, *m* Robert **Glasgow** (3 above).
5–Thomas **Gholson,** from Eng.; planter, Mt. Hope Plantation, Brunswick Co., Va.; *m* Jane Perry;
4–Thomas (1783-1816), Gholsonville, Va.; mem. 10th to 14th Congresses; officer War 1812; *m* 1806, Anne Yates;
3–William Yates (1807-70), justice Supreme Ct. of Ohio; *m* 1827, Martha Ann Jane Taylor (Samuel[4]), niece and adopted dau. of Chancellor Creed Taylor, of Needham, Cumberland Co., Va.;
2–Anne Jane (2 below).
9–John **Yates,** settled in Elizabeth City Co., Va., 1636;
8–Rev. Robert, rector of Christ Ch., Middlesex Co., Va., 1699; returned to Eng., 1704;
7–Rev. Bartholomew (1677-1734), succeeded his father as rector Christ Ch., Middlesex Co., Va.; *m* 1704, Sally Mickleborough;
6–Rev. William (1720-64), rector Abingdon Parish, Gloucester Co., Va., 1758; pres. William and Mary Coll., 1762-64; rector Bruton Parish, Williamsburg, 1764; *m* Elizabeth Randolph (Edward[7]; Col. William[8], qv);
5–Col. William (1749-89), col. Am. Rev.; *m* Elizabeth Booth;
4–Anne, *m* 1806, Thomas **Gholson** (4 above).
8–Baron Christophe **de Graffenried** (qv);
7–Christopher (1691-1742), came in 1713, to succeed his father as head of the Swiss colony; *m* 1714, Barbara Needham (1688-1744; Sir Arthur[8], of Eng.);
6–Tscharner (*b* 1722), *m* 1742, Mary Baker (Henry[7], *m* Ruth Chauncey; Lawrence[8], burgess);
5–Mary (1753-1819), *m* Miller **Woodson** (1745-1823);
4–Martha Ann, *m* Samuel Creed **Taylor;**
3–Martha Ann Jane, *m* William Yates **Gholson** (3 above);
2–Anne Jane (1831-93), *m* 1853, Francis Thomas **Glasgow** (1829-1916), of "Green Forest," Rockbridge Co., and One Main St., Richmond, Va.; B.A., Washington Coll. (now Washington and Lee U.), 1847; read law at Richmond, 2 yrs., then joined his uncle Gen. Joseph R. Anderson, in The Tredegar Co., of which he was a mng. dir. for half a century; this Richmond Co. was the ordnance factory of the C.S.A. and supplied the Confederate Ironclad "Merrimac" with her armament; this ship in its first day's trial destroyed the U.S. fleet in Chesapeake Bay; the next day it fought a duel with the "Monitor," which had just arrived from Brooklyn, this being the first battle in history between armoured vessels; the "Merrimac," retreating to the support of Richmond, ran aground in the James River, and was blown up by its crew; during the Civil War Mr. Glasgow was responsible for the ore mines and blast furnaces of The Tredegar Co. in the Upper Valley of Va.; although this territory was frequently overrun by Federal troops, he kept the Tredegar Works in Richmond supplied with pigiron until the end; issue: I–Emily Taylor (*d* 1913; *m* Hubert Todd Houston); II–Anne Gholson (*d* 1917; *m* Francis Tarleton Clark); III–Joseph Reid (*d*); IV–Katherine Anderson (*d*); V–Cary Gholson (d 1911; *m* George Walter McCormack); VI–Arthur Graham (1 above); VII–Samuel Creed (*d* infancy); VIII–Francis Thomas (*d* 1908); IX–Ellen Anderson Gholson

(see Vol. III, p. 617); X–Rebe Gordon (Mrs. Carrington Cabell Tutwiler, see Vol. II, p. 111).

1–*m* Oct. 1, 1901, Margaret Elizabeth Branch, *b* Richmond, Va., Oct. 4, 1876; dau. of John Patteson Branch, of Richmond; issue: 1–Margaret (Marjorie) Gholson, *b* London, Eng., Nov. 8, 1902.

1–M.E., Stevens Inst. Tech., '85; E.D., 1928; Sc.D., Washington and Lee, 1929. Chartered civil engr. (Gt. Britain). United Gas Improvement Co., 1885-91; engr. and gen. mgr. Standard Gas Light Co. of City of N.Y., 1891; established Humphreys & Glasgow, Ltd., London, Eng., 1892, now chmn. bd.; chmn. Buildings Supplies Corpn. of Norfolk, Va. V.chmn. Red Cross Commn. to Roumania, 1917; U.S. War (munitions) Dept., Washington, France and Eng., 1918; fixed-nitrogen administrator, War Dept., 1919. Gold medalist Am. Gas Assn., 1910, and Franklin Inst., 1928. Author many patents and papers in gas technology. Life trustee Stevens Inst. Life mem. Am. Soc. M.E., Am. Soc. C.E., Inst. C.E. and Inst. Mech. Engrs. of Gt. Britain, etc. (see Who's Who in America). Clubs: Metropolitan, Chevy Chase (Washington), Westmoreland, Commonwealth (Richmond, Va.), University, Down Town (New York), Carlton, Wellington, Ranelagh (London). Domicile: New York. London residence: Moncorvo House, Ennismore Gardens, S.W. 7.

1–**GLAUSER, Emma Pearson Babb (Mrs. Edwin D.),** *b* Phila., Pa., Jan. 27, 1874.
7–Thomas **Babb,** settled nr. New Castle, Pa., now Del.; *m* ante 1700, Bethsheba Hussey (John[8], mem. Provincial Assembly, 1696; Christopher[9], qv);
6–Peter, *m* 1728, Mary Lewis (Evan[7], mem. Provincial Assembly);
5–Samson (*d* 1814), of Chester Co., and Tioga Co., Pa.; *m* 1767, Ann Way (1742-1834);
4–John (1773-1852), of West Chester, Pa.; *m* 1796, Lydia Clark;
3–John Way (1801-79), of West Chester; *m* 1830, Phoebe Harper Pearson;
2–Thomas Clark (2 below).
7–Henry **Hayes,** mem. Provincial Assembly, 1715,16,28,30; *m* Rachel–; *m* 2d, Isabella–;
6–James, *m* Mary Cox;
5–Hannah (1747-1814), *m* James **Clark** (1745-1808);
4–Lydia (1777-1854), *m* John **Babb** (4 above).
8–Randal **Vernon,** property surveyed 1701, patented 1711; mem. Provincial Assembly, 1689; *m* at Cheshire, Eng., 1670, Sarah Bradshaw, niece of James Bradshaw, head of Eng. Parliament at death of Charles I;
7–Jacob, *m* 1701, Ann Yearsley;
6–Jacob, *m* Elizabeth (Hickman) Cheyney (Benjamin Hickman[7], *m* 1701, Ann, dau. of Richard Buffington [*d* 1747], came to Upland ante 1677);
5–Phoebe, *m* Maj. John **Harper,** served under Anthony Wayne; charter mem. S.C.;
4–Mary (*b* 1766), *m* 1784, George **Pearson** (*d* 1814);
3–Phoebe Harper (1802-91), *m* John W. **Babb** (3 above).
7–Joseph **Gilpin** (qv);
6–Mary (*b* 1716), *m* 1736, Phillip **Taylor** (*d* 1762), mem. Provincial Assembly;
5–Mary (1753-1830), *m* George **Bradley** (1753-1832; Charles[6] [*d* 1757], *m* at Gloria Del Dei, Wilmington, Del., 1752, Mary Jeffries);
4–Joseph (1785-1854), *m* Hannah Carpenter (1768-1870; Capt. Thomas[5] [1739-1815], *m* 1763, Esther Trimble [1740-1813]; William[6] [1695-1748], from Eng. to New Garden, Chester Co., Pa., *m* Margaret [Richards] Wiley, *d* 1796);
3–William Carpenter (1813-87), *m* Harriet Amelia Thomas (1819-78; William[4], *m* Mary Johnson; Ezekiel[5], *m* Susannah Russell [Hughes?]);
2–Sarah Elizabeth (1841-98), *m* 1863, Thomas Clark **Babb** (1842-90), mfr. of shoes, West Chester, Pa.; issue: I–Lydia Clark (*b* 1864); II–Thomas Clark (*b* 1872; *m* Marie Corwin Smith); III–Emma Pearson (1 above); IV–Mary (*b* 1877; *m* George M. Hughes, M.D.).
1–*m* June 6, 1895, Edwin Dunlap Glauser (Nov. 5, 1867-Jan. 12, 1925); son of Stacy G. Glauser, of Newville, Cumberland Co., Pa., *m* Katherine Dunlap; issue: 1–Kathryn Dunlap, *b* Chester, Pa., Jan. 23, 1904; grad. Vassar, 1925; *m* Sept. 12, 1925, Herbert B. Spackman (issue: Kathryn Glauser, Jr.).
1–Regent Delaware County Chapter D.A.R.; mem. I.A.G. Residence: "Crestholme," Providence Rd., Chester, Pa.

1–**GLOVER, Fannie Virginia Jones (Mrs. Howard Clarke),** *b* Hogansville, Ga., May 4, 1876.
6–James **Trimble** (*d* 1766 or 67), from Ireland, bet. 1740-44; settled in Augusta Co., Va.; *m* Grace–;
5–Joseph (ca. 1740-ca. 1808), of Abbeville Dist., S.C.; pvt. militia in Am. Rev.; *m* Elizabeth–; *m* 2d, Widow Bowles;
4–John (1773-1850), from Morgan Co. to Troup Co., Ga., 1833; *m* Mary Harris (1779-1853);
3–Winifred (1812-84), of Hogansville, Troup Co., Ga.; *m* 1835, Thomas Johnston **Jones** (1814-55);
2–Thomas Jefferson (2 below).
10–John **Chew** (qv);
9–Joseph (1641-1716), *m* Miss Larkin;
8–Larkin (1686-1752), *m* Hannah Roy;
7–Ann (Nan), *m* 1723, Lord William **Johnston** (*b* 1697), to Spotsylvania Co., Va.;
6–Larkin (1727-1816), of Spotsylvania Co.; *m* 1745, Mary Rogers (1727-1800);
5–Littleton (1761-1842), of Granville Co., N.C.; sgt., Child's Co., 6th Regt., served 2½ yrs.; *m* 1781, Lucy Childs (1756-1826);
4–John (1793-1844), of Person Co., N.C.; *m* Patsy Mobley;
3–John Littleton (1832-77), of Jasper Co., Ga.; *m* 1853, Frances Asbury (Moreland) Livingston (1828-98);
2–Virginia Savannah (1854-85), of Hogansville, Ga.; *m* 1871, Dr. Thomas Jefferson **Jones** (1849-1916), physician; issue: I–Jesse Littleton (1872-73); II–Thomas Johnston (1874-75); III–Fannie Virginia (1 above); IV–John Littleton (*b* 1878); V–William Jefferson (1880-81); VI–Emmett (1882-85); VII–Ernest (*b* and *d* 1885).
1–*m* Aug. 11, 1898, Howard Clarke Glover, *b* Wilcox Co., Ala., Aug. 3, 1870; son of Nathaniel Banks Glover of Wilcox Co., Ala., and Newnan, Ga.; issue (all *b* Newnan, Ga.): 1–Virginia, *b* May 31, 1899; A.B., Hollins Coll., Va., '20; *m* Oct. 25, 1924, Edmund Francis, son of Ellison R. Cook, of West Point, Ga.; 2–Caroline Frances, *b* Sept. 9, 1901; ed. Hollins Coll., Va.; 3–Thomas Jones, *b* Feb. 24, 1904; A.B., Mercer U., Ga.; '25; 4–Mary Jones, *b* Mar. 6, 1906; A.B., Hollins Coll., '27; 5–Howard Clarke, Jr., *b* Dec. 17, 1908; ed. U.Va., and Mercer Coll.; 6–John Littleton, *b* Apr. 6, 1911; ed. Mercer U., and U.Va.; 7–Clifford Clarke, *b* May 15, 1913; 8–Winifred Trimble, *b* Nov. 7, 1917; 9–Nathaniel Banks, *b* Nov. 8, 1919.
1–Ed. Peabody Coll., Nashville, Tenn., '95. Mem. D.A.R., U.D.C., I.A.G. Residence: 45 College St., Newnan, Ga.

1–**GODDARD, Minnie May Doty (Mrs. Elmer F.),** *b* Greene Co., Tenn., June 15, 1883.
8–Edward **Doty** (qv);
7–Samuel (*b* 1643), of Plymouth, Mass.;
6–Isaac (*b* 1712), of Piscataway, N.J.;
5–Azariah (*b* 1745), of Piscataway;
4–Ephraim (*b* 1795), of Greene Co., Tenn.;
3–William Cooper (*b* 1816);
2–William Douglas Bruner (1853-1926), lawyer, of Greeneville, Tenn.; *m* Ruth Ann Kilday; issue: I–Minnie May (1 above); II–Roy Anderson (*b* 1885; *m* Ann Armstrong); III–Samuel Willard (*b* 1888; *m* Minnie Babb); IV–Monte (*b* 1897; *m* G. L. Lady, *d*); V–Hacker Douglas (*b* 1900; *m* Nannie Marion).
1–*m* June 7, 1905, Elmer Fernando Goddard, *b* Blount Co., Tenn., Oct. 4, 1872; son of W. A. Goddard, of Knoxville, Tenn.; issue: 1–Paul Douglas, *b* Sevierville, Tenn., Apr. 15, 1910; ed. U.Tenn.; 2–Herman Elmer, *b* Sevierville, Mar. 15, 1912; ed. U.Tenn.; 3–Helen Ruth, *b* Sevierville, Mar. 15, 1912; 4–Barbara Evelyn, *b* Dandridge, Tenn., Apr. 6, 1917.
1–Ed. U.Tenn. Editor and publisher the Dandridge Banner. Methodist. Residence: Dandridge, Tenn.

1–**GODING, Frederic Webster,** *b* Hyde Park, Mass., May 9, 1858.
9–Capt. Henry **Goding,** of Eng.; captain of the "Abigail," visited Mass., 1628;
8–Henry (1642-1720), settled in Watertown, Mass.; *m* 1663, Elizabeth Perry;

7–William (1669-1746), *m* 1701, Mary Pease;
6–William (1703-57), *m* 1st, 1731, Martha Spooner;
5–Jonathan Coolidge (1739-1825), *m* 1761, Hannah Larned;
4–Jonathan (1762-1836), *m* 1st, 1783, Ruth Sargent;
3–Jonas (1789-1865), *m* 1813, Patience Tolman;
2–Alphonso Landon (2 below).
10–William **Chandler** (qv);
9–Capt. Thomas (*b* Eng., 1630-d 1703), *m* Hannah Brewer;
8–Capt. John (1655-1721), *m* 1676, Hannah Abbot;
7–Ens. John (1680-1741), *m* 1701, Hannah Frye (*d* 1727);
6–Capt. John (1702-74), *m* 1727, Tabitha Abbot;
5–Joshua (1740-1816), *m* 1768, Irene Copp (*d* 1810);
4–Daniel (1768-1817), *m* 1794, Mehitable Arlin;
3–Jeremiah (1810-74), *m* 1829, Phidelia E. Chase (1815-34);
2–Lydia Mehitable (1830-1921), *m* Nov. 28, 1847, Alphonso Landon **Goding** (Apr. 12, 1828-June 16, 1909), contractor and builder; issue: I–Flora Catherine (*b* 1849; *m* John W. Wamsley); II–Alphonso Chandler (1851-1922); III–Octavia Josephine (1853-54); IV–Ella Medora (1855-93; *m* George L. Phelps); V–Horace Landon (1856-64); VI–Frederic W. (1 above); VII–Oscar Winfield (*b* 1860; *m* Belle W. Benton).
1–*m* June 8, 1880, Ella Blanche Phelps, *b* Kaneville, Ill., Nov. 13, 1858; dau. of Pliny M. Phelps; issue: 1–Hazel Vera, *b* Kaneville, Nov. 12, 1882; *m* Feb. 10, 1903, Herbert B. Ames (issue: Vivian Fredella, *b* Elburn, Ill., July 25, 1905; Lucille, *b* Elburn, Oct. 15, 1907; Esther, *b* Warrenville, Ill., Mar. 31, 1913; Leona, *b* Livermore, Me., July 19, 1915); 2–Frederic Landon, *b* Loudon, Tenn., Feb. 9, 1886; *m* May 24, 1916, Lucy Maudelle, dau. of Walter E. Twombly (issue: June Myrtelle, *b* July 18, 1917; Geraldine Jessifred, *b* Nov. 5, 1921; Vera Fay, *b* Sept. 23, 1923; Dorothy Imogene, *b* Mar. 31, 1925-*d* Apr. 10, 1925, and Frederic Eugene, twins, *b* Mar. 31, 1925-*d* Mar. 17, 1926; Ferne Joyce, *b* Mar. 19, 1927; Frederic Landon, Jr., *b* May 12, 1928).
1–*m* 2d, May 12, 1913, Jessie Eliza Ayre (*b* Montevideo, Uruguay, Jan. 22, 1880-*d* at Guayaquil, Ecuador, of yellow fever, June 7, 1918); dau. of Prof. Henry Castle Ayre, of U.Montevideo.
1–M.D., Northwestern U., 1882; Ph.D., Bethel Coll., Tenn., 1890. American consul-general, retired with pension (see Who's Who in America). Prof. science, Loudon Coll., Tenn., 1885-86. Mayor Rutland, Ill., 1888-98. Awarded Medal de Merito (Ecuador). Hon. mem. Med. and Surgical Soc. (Guayaquil, Ecuador). Fellow Royal Anthropol. Soc. of Australasia. Clubs: British (Montevideo), Metropolitano (Guayaquil). Author: Genealogy of the Goding Family, Ancestry of Lydia Mehitable Chandler. Address: Box 321, Livermore Falls, Me.

1–**GOETSCHIUS, Percy,** *b* Paterson, N. J., Aug. 30, 1853.
6–Johann Heinrich (Goetschi, Goetschiey) **Goetschius** (1675?-1739), from Switzerland, settled at New Gashenhoppen, nr. Phila., Pa., 1728; pastor German Reformed Ch., 1730;
5–Johann Heinrich (1714-74), the "Domine"; began to write name Goetschius; noted preacher, Hackensack, N.J., 1748-74;
4–Johann Mauritius (ca. 1751-ca. 1795), Am. Rev.; *m* 1773(?), Hannah Dater;
3–Jacob (1790-1848) *m* Hannah Banta (1799-1876);
2–John Henry (1831-1912), civil engr. and city surveyor; *m* 1849, Mary Ann Berry (*b* in Eng., 1831-*d* 1884); issue: I–Carmeen (1850-93; *m* 1869, William L. Bamber); II–Percy (1 above); III–Eula (*b* and *d* 1870).
1–*m* June 15, 1889, Marie C. C. Stephany, *b* Saarbrücken, Rhine-Province, Germany, June 14, 1858; dau. of Apollinar Stephany, of Rhine-Province, Germany; issue: 1–Percy Berry, *b* Syracuse, N.Y., June 2, 1890; M.D., Tufts Med. Coll., 1913; *m* Mar. 3, 1914, Pauline J., dau. of Albert J. Gaiser, of Brooklyn (issue: Marjorie Laura, *b* Sept. 23, 1915).
1–Grad. Stuttgart Conservatory of Music, 1876; title, Royal Württemberg Prof., conferred by King of Württemberg, Stuttgart, 1885; D. Mus., Syracuse U., 1892. Educator from 1876, retired, 1925. Author (see Who's Who in America). Summer place: Raymond, N.H. Residence: 274 Ray St., Manchester, N.H.

1–**GOLDSBY, Joel Walker,** *b* Selma, Ala., Nov. 24, 1862.
7–Isaac **Winston,** from Wales, ca. 1704; settled in Hanover Co., Va.; *m* 2d, Mary Dabney (their dau. Sarah, *m* 2d, Col. John Henry, and was the mother of Patrick Henry);
6–Anthony (*b* 1723), *m* 1747, Alice Taylor (*b* 1730; James[7], of Caroline Co., Va.);
5–Anthony (1750-1828), capt. Am. Rev.; *m* 1776, Keziah Jones (1760-1826);
4–William, *m* 1st, Mary Bacon Cooper (Edmund[5], of Brunswick Co., Va., *m* Martha Jackson);
3–John Anthony (1812-71), rep. from Sumter Co., 1840; pres. State Senate, 1845, two sessions; del.-at-large to Baltimore Conv., 1848; apptd. to Nashville Conv., 1849; gov. of Ala., 1853-57; elected U.S. senator, 1866, but was not seated; col. 8th Ala. Regt., C.S.A.; counties in Miss. and Ala. named after him; *m* Mary Agnes Jones (Joel[4], of Limestone Co., Ala.);
2–Mary Agnes (*d* 1916), *m* Thomas Jefferson **Goldsby,** of Randolph Co., Ala. (Col. Thornton Boykin[3], of Perry Co. and Summerfield, Ala.; planter, large landowner; purchased stock farm, 1839, and raised fine horses; dir. and pres. of Ala. & Tenn. R.R., *m* Sarah Warren [Smith] Ware, dau. of Maj. Thomas Smith, of Perry Co., Ala.).
1–*m* Oct. 7, 1885, Agnes Reid White (qv for genealogy); issue: 1–Mary Easley, *b* Mobile, Ala., Apr. 11, 1887; *m* Herbert Lee McConnell; 2–Louise, *b* Lexington, Va., Sept. 4, 1889; 3–Isabel, *b* Lexington, Feb. 14, 1893; 4–Winston, *b* Lexington, Sept. 11, 1896; 5–Reid White, *b* Lexington, Feb. 13, 1898; *m* Apr. 20, 1921, Virginia Hogg.
1–Ed. in Germany and Switzerland; U.Va. and Washington and Lee U. Admitted to bar, 1887, and practiced at Mobile. Mem. Ala. House of Rep., 1892-93; Ala. Senate, 1900-03 (pres. pro-tem., 1903); supervisor of census for southern dist. of Ala., 1910; chmn. Excise Commn. of Mobile, 1911-15; chmn. U.S. Exemption Bd. for southern dist. of Ala., 1917; judge 13th jud. circuit of Ala., since 1918. Residence: 452 Government St., Mobile, Ala.

1–**GOLDSBY, Agnes Reid White (Mrs. Joel W.),** *b* Lexington, Va., July 14, 1864.
7–Henry **White,** came from Eng. and settled at Ellison's Mill (now Gaines Mill), nr. Richmond, Va., 1680; naval officer; *m* 1659, Mary Crowshaw;
6–John (1695-1758), of Ellison's Mill;
5–Barrett (1727-82), *m* 1754, Elizabeth Starke;
4–William (1773-1820), *m* Mildred Ellis;
3–William Spottswood (1800-73), *m* Jane Isabella Watt;
2–James Jones (2 below).
6–Andrew **Reid** (*d* ca. 1751), of County Down, Ireland, to Pa.; settled Nelson Co., Va.;
5–Andrew (*d* 1765), "capt. of Rockfish"; *m* ca. 1740, his cousin, Sarah Reid (John[6], *m* Sarah Nisbet);
4–Andrew (1751-1837), one of the first justices of Rockbridge Co., Va.; co. clk.; *m* 1776, Magdalene McDowell;
3–Samuel McDowell (1790-1869), *m* Sallie Hare;
2–Mary Louisa (2 below).
7–Ephraim **McDowell** (qv);
6–John (1703-42), surveyor; capt. Augusta Co. militia; killed by Indians in battle at Balcony Falls, Va.; *m* 1734, Magdelen Woods (Michael[7], qv);
5–Col. Samuel (1735-1817), capt. in French and Indian War; served under Gen. Washington in Braddock's Campaign; col. in Am. Rev.; burgess; mem. Va. Conv., 1774-76; removed to Danville, Ky., 1783; pres. Ky. Constl. Conv., 1792; judge Circuit Ct.; *m* 1754, Mary McClung (William[6]; James[7]), among their sons was Ephraim, M.D., the "father of ovariotomy";
4–Magdalene, *m* Andrew **Reid** (4 above);
3–Samuel M., *m* Sallie Hare (3 above);
2–Mary Louisa (1832-1901), *m* 1858, James Jones **White** (1828-93), prof. Greek, Washington and Lee U., and acting pres.; issue: I–Sallie Hare (Mrs. Helm Bruce, see Vol. III, p. 94); II–Isabelle (Mrs. William G. Brown, see Vol. III, p. 94); III–McDowell Reid; IV–Agnes Reid (1 above); V–William Cabell; VI–Reid (*m* Lucy Preston; *m* 2d, Elizabeth Corse).

1–*m* Oct. 7, 1885, Joel Walker Goldsby (qv for issue).
Residence: 452 Government St., Mobile, Ala.

1–**GOLDSBY, Robert Echols,** *b* Fulton, Ky., Apr. 19, 1899.

6–Stephen **Goldsby** (*d* ca. 1782; believed Thomas[7]), of Amherst Co., Va.; family believed to have been among early settlers of Jamestown, Va.; *m* ca. 1750, Martha Stephens (Thomas[7] of St. Anne's Parish, Albemarle Co., Va.; John[8]); their son, Edward Thomas, *d* in Am. Rev., Feb. 3, 1778, mem. of Capt. William McKee's Co., 12th Va. Regt.;

5–James (1764-ca. 1845), emigrated to Green Co. (nr. Danville), Ky., ca. 1792-99, thence to Weakley Co., Tenn., ante 1836; *m* ca. 1782 Nancy– (1765-1845);

4–Edward Thomas (1796-1840), pvt. 10th Co., 15th Regt., Ky. Militia, War 1812; fought in Battle of New Orleans and witnessed the death of the British General, Pakenham; *m* 1816, Minerva Graham (ca. 1799- ca. 1872; Jeremiah[5], *b* 1779; William[6], *b* ca. 1750, went with his family from Va. to N.C., thence to Green Co., Ky., ca. 1792-95, *m* Elizabeth Lynn), sister of Mentor Graham, the school-teacher, who taught and befriended President Abraham Lincoln at New Salem, Ill.;

3–Elvin Anderson (1817-1900), of Union City, Tenn.; *m* 2nd 1847, Helena Weddington (1827-1902), of Franklin and Obion cos., Tenn. (Eli B.[4] [1792-1864], of Franklin Co., Tenn., *m* 1815, Margaret Palmer, 1798-1868);

2–Flavius Weddington (2 below).

9–Sir Charles **Anthony,** of Eng., who, for services rendered the crown, was knighted and given land in Va. (?);

8–Mark, early Va. settler, landed New Kent Co., afterwards moved to Wilkes Co., Ga.; *m* Isabella Hart;

7–John, lived at the Fall's Plantation (now Manchester) opposite Richmond, Va., and removing thence, built a fort on Walnut Hill, overlooking the Otter River in Bedford Co. (now Evington, in Campbell Co.), Va.; *m* Elizabeth Banks;

6–Rev. John (1746-1822), "one of the earliest and most devoted of the Virginia Baptist ministry" (see sketch in Taylor's "Virginia Baptist Ministers"); *m* Susan Austin, of Hanover, Va.;

5–John, *m* Miss Allen;

4–Sarah W., *m* 1830, Dr. Joel Hubbard **Echols** (4 below);

3–Joseph William (1833-1927), moved to Tate Co., Miss., 1849; enlisted in Co. D, 2d Regt., Miss. Cav. (also known as 4th Regt. and 45th Regt.), C.S.A., hon. discharged, 1862; ordained minister of Bapt. Ch.; *m* 1855, Minerva Susan Easley (3 below);

2–Mary Ellen (2 below).

9–John **Echols** (*b* ca. 1650), said to have emigrated from Scotland to Old Point Comfort, Va., and to have been in Bacon's Rebellion, ca. 1676;

8–Richard; (?)

7–Abram (either son or g.son of John, as above), *m* Sarah–;

6–Joseph (1735-89), of Halifax Co., Va.; *m* 1772, Elizabeth Street (1752-89);

5–David (1776-1859), of Chatham, Pittsylvania Co., Va.; *m* Dianah Tribble (Peter[6]) of Halifax Co., Va.;

4–Joel Hubbard (*d* ca. 1842), M.D.; ed. Lexington, Va.; of Chatham, Va.; *m* Sarah W. Anthony (4 above) of Pittsylvania Co.

5–Pyrant **Easley,** of Pittsylvania Co. (believed: Thomas[6]; William[7], *d* 1812, *m* Elizabeth–; William[8], *d* 1795, all of Pittsylvania Co.), *m* 1806, Mollie Ferguson;

4–Pyrant (1809-95), *m* 1829, Martha Ann Whitworth (ca. 1815-76) of Rockingham Co., N.C.;

3–Minerva Susan (1830-94), *m* 1855, Joseph William **Echols** (3 above);

2–Mary Ellen (1861-1930), *m* 1897, Flavius Weddington **Goldsby** (1864-99), grad. Bethel Coll. and Peabody Coll. (Tenn.).

1–*m* Apr. 16, 1925, Winifred Wailes (qv for genealogy); issue: 1–Robert Weddington, *b* Brooklyn, N.Y., Dec. 11, 1926 (see portrait).

1–B.S., Miss. Coll., '19; LL.B., Columbia, 1923 (Phi Delta Phi). Asst. in legislation, Columbia U., 1922-23; asst. to the dean of the law sch., 1923-24; admitted to the New York bar, 1924; asst. on staff of office of the legislative counsel, U.S. House of Rep., 1924-25; asst. to the solicitor, U.S. Dept. of State, 1925-26; with law firm of Sullivan & Cromwell, 48 Wall St., New York, since 1926. Mem. Assn. of the Bar of the City of N.Y. Commd. 2d lt. inf., U.S.A., Sept. 16, 1918 at Plattsburg, N.Y.; served as adj. and personnel officer, Oglethorpe U., Ga.; hon. discharged, Dec. 21, 1918. Baptist. Residence: 56 Winthrop St., Brooklyn, N.Y.

ROBERT WEDDINGTON GOLDSBY (At age of two years and nine months).

1–**GOLDSBY, Winifred Wailes (Mrs. Robert Echols),** *b* Memphis, Tenn., June 15, 1903.

7–Benjamin **Wailes** (*d* 1729), of Somerset Co., Md.; appointed by acts of assembly, 1711-12, commr. to lay out 3,000 acres of land for the Nanticoke Indians; mem. Lower House of Assembly from Somerset Co., 1717-23; moved to Prince George's Co., Md., 1721; *m* 2d, ante 1710, Elizabeth Covington (*d* 1729; Nehemiah[8] [*b* Eng.], emigrated to Somerset Co., 1662, with his parents, *m* 1679, Rebecca Denwood; Nehemiah[9], *m* Mary–);

6–Benjamin (*b* 1727), served in Am. Rev. from Prince George's Co., commd. capt. Oct. 20, 1777; *m* ca. 1751, Sarah Howard (William Stevens[7], *m* 2d, Sarah [Briscoe] Trueman, dau. of Philip Briscoe, *m* Susanna Swann; Edmund[8], Gent. [*b* Eng.; *d* Charles Co., Md., 1713], *m* 1681, Margaret, dau. of Thomas Dent [*b* Gisborough, Eng., ca. 1630, *d* St. Mary's Co., Md., 1676], *m* Rebecca Wilkinson), of Charles Co., Md.;

5–Levin (*b* 1768-*d* subsequent 1843), of Prince George's Co.; sent to Ga. 1792, by Robert Morris as his agent to survey and buy up lands in that new country, lived in Columbia, Richmond and Elbert cos., Ga.; moved to Miss., 1808, and was apptd. surveyor gen. of the Washington Dist., the territorial capital, later apptd. register of the land office of Miss.; 1st lt., Capt. George King's Opelousas Vol. Co., 16th (Thompson's) Regt., Va. Militia, War of 1812; *m* 1796, Eleanor Davies (ca. 1773-1841), of Prince George's Co. (their son, Benjamin Leonard Covington Wailes, commd. lt. col. state militia, 1824, rep. of Adams Co. in State Legislature, 1825-26, was state geologist and prof. of geology, U. of Miss., and author of "Report on the Agriculture and Geology of Miss.," 1854, "Memoir of Gen. Leonard Covington, U.S.A.," 1861, etc., termed by the historian, Claiborne, "in science, the foremost man in the State");

4–Edmund Howard (1799-1888), of Woodville, Miss.; *m* 1827, Jane Bell Newell (1811-69; George Bell[5], of Nashville, Tenn., *m* Lydia Howard, of Adams Co., Miss.); among their sons, Levin *d* in Cuba, and Col. George B.N.,

of Wilkinson Co., Miss., ed. Wesleyan U., Middleton, Conn., and was mem. La. Legislature 2 terms and speaker of the House;
3–Benjamin Howard (1835-1917), of Woodville, Miss., and Memphis, Tenn.; served in C.S.A. under Gen. Richard Taylor of La.; *m* Kate Anna Devenport (ca. 1843-1917; Charles[4] [1816-76], successively rep. of Iberville and St. Charles' parishes in La. Legislature and prominent planter, portrait in old Spanish Cabildo [City Museum] New Orleans, ed. St. Joseph's Coll., Bardstown, Ky., *m* 1840, Coralie, dau. of Gen. Joseph L. Bernard, 1799-1865, French surname, de Montjerey, dropped for convenience many years earlier, of New Orleans and East Baton Rouge, La., "filled worthily and zealously high places in the state government," *m* Anna, dau. of Isaac Holmes, *m* Frances Parham of Brunswick Co., Va.; John[5], from Va. to La. latter part 18th Century, apptd. alcade or judge of East Baton Rouge by Spanish govt., serving until transfer of province to the U.S., *m* Maria Magdalena, dau. of Philip Englehardt prominent planter, their son, John, Jr., though very young, was capt. under Gen. Andrew Jackson, War of 1812, and was apptd. gen. of La. troops by Gov. Johnson in 1826);
2–Charles Devenport (*b* 1872), of St. Charles' Parish, La., Woodville, Miss., and Memphis, Tenn., since age 14; *m* 1900, Hattie Boswell (2 below), of Memphis, Tenn.
15–John **Finley** of Forfarshire, Scotland (represented in rental book of the Cistercean Abbey of Cupar Angus as living in the township of Kethyk in 1457, having rented a twelfth part of the Abbey land);
14–John (rented one-sixth of Combrye land at Penticost, Scotland, in 1463), *m* Janet Rogers;
13–Andrew (rented one-fourth part of Auchinleyth in 1508 from Abbey of Cupar Angus), *m* Janet Hays;
12–James (*b* 1530) of Balchrystie, Newburn Parish, Fifeshire, Scotland, *m* ante 1567, Elizabeth Warrender (William[13]);
11–James (*b* 1583), rented lands in Newburn Parish up to 1652, *m* Mary–;
10–James (1614-1672) of Newburn Parish and Dundee, Scotland, *m* Margaret– (*d* 1677);
9–James (*b* 1641), of Fifeshire and Dundee, merchant; *m* 1660, Elizabeth Rixon or Rixton;
8–Col. Robert (1662-1716), saw military service in Ireland at age of 19; emigrated to America 1684; first settled in Charles Co., Md., moved to Annapolis; collector of port, 1698; apptd. col. for inspection of arms, Talbot Co., Md. 1708; clerk of court, Oxford, Md., 1707-11; entered grant of 2,500 acres of land, called King's Creek Plantation; *m* 1686, Jane Johnson (*d* 1725; Thomas[9], *m* Mary Baker, from Eng., 1660, to Calvert Co., Md.);
7–Charles (*b* 1689), *m* 1711, Elizabeth Harris;
6–Charles (1722-ca. 1787), *m* ca. 1750, Martha Hawkins Bayne (6 below);
14–Richard **Osborne** (Knt.), *m* Elizabeth Fyldane;
13–Richard, *m* Jane Broughton (John B.[14]);
12–Sir Edward, lord mayor of London, ca. 1592; *m* Ann Hewett;
11–Anne, *m* Robert **Offley** of London;
10–Sarah, *m* ca. 1627, Adam **Thoroughgood** (1602-1641; William[11], of Grimston, Norfolk Co., Eng., bishop of Norwich, *m* Anne Edwards [Frances E.[12]]; John[12]; John[13]; Thomas[14]; John[15], of Chalston Temple), came to America in 1631; capt. of Va. Council, Lower Norfolk Co.;
9–Ann, *m* ca. 1659-61, Col. Gerard **Fowke** (1606-1671; Roger[10], of Gunston Hall, Staffordshire, Eng., *m* Mary Bailey of Lea Hall), col. of horse under Charles I; fled to Va. 1651; owned land in Westmoreland Co.; mem. of Va. and Md. houses of burgesses; said to have been a descendant of Alfred the Great, Charlemagne, and William the Conqueror;
8–Col. Gerard (1662-1734), *m* 2d, Sarah Burdett;
7–Catherine, of Charles Co., Md.; *m* Ebsworth **Bayne** of Prince George's Co. Md. (will dated Apr. 9, 1792; John[8], capt. of Md. militia; in St. Mary's Co., 1683 or 84; mem. Md. Assembly; will dated and probated, Oct. 1700, *m* Ann Hawkins [*d* 1703]; Walter[9], came to America 1656; entered 5,000 acres of land on Port Tobacco creek, *m* Ellinor–, will dated Nov. 5, 1701);
6–Martha Hawkins, *m* ca. 1750, Charles **Finley** (6 above);
5–Ann Bayne (1757-1807), *m* 1783 (Broad Creek Church, Piscataway Parish, Prince George's Co., Md.), Peter **Boswell** (1754-ca. 1807), of Fairfax Co., Va. (John[6] [*d* 1765], of Charles Co., Md., *m* Elizabeth–; William or Michael [?][7]);
4–William Finley (1806-1856), *b* Fairfax Co., Va., *d* Weakley Co., Tenn.; *m* 1830, Malissa Eddings (1814-1902; William[5] [*b* 1758], of Culpeper Co., Am. Rev., *m* Mary E. [Polly] Johnson, of Wilkes or Caswell Co., N.C., *d* 1863, Dresden, Tenn.);
3–Leolin Eddings (*b* 1849, McCracken Co., Ky.) of Memphis, Tenn., *m* 1873, Annie Mary Porter (1853-1924; Josiah[4], of Pittsburgh, Pa. [*d* 1866]; *m* 1852, Margaret Josephine Armor [1826-1854]; Samuel[5] [*d* 1868], of Union Town, O., *m* 1825, Ann McKown, ca. 1797-1878);
2–Hattie (*b* 1875), *m* 1900, Charles Devenport **Wailes** (2 above); issue: I–Charles Devenport, Jr. (*b* 1901; *m* 1924, Virginia, dau. of George J. Hamner, *m* Florence Lantz, of Memphis; issue: Betty Ann, *b* 1925); II–Winifred (1 above); III–Leolin Boswell (*b* 1905); IV–Mary Evelyn (*b* 1907; *m* 1930, Howard Wesley Rash).
1–*m* Apr. 16, 1925, Robert Echols Goldsby (qv for genealogy and issue).
1–Ed. Central High School, Memphis, Tenn., Milligan Coll. (Tenn.) and William Woods Coll. (Mo.). Residence: 56 Winthrop St., Brooklyn, N.Y.

1–**GOLDTHWAITE, Nellie Esther,** *b* Jamestown, N.Y., Feb. 4, 1863.
9–Thomas **Goldthwaite** (1610-83), a cooper; from Yorkshire, Eng., 1630, settled in Salem, Mass.; *m* 1636, Elizabeth–; *m* 2d, 1671, Rachel Leach (Lawrence[10], *m* Elizabeth–);
8–Samuel (1637-1718), cooper and farmer; *m* 1666, Elizabeth Cheever (1645-post 1722; Ezekiel[9], *m* Mary–);
7–Ezekiel (1674-1761), farmer; *m* 1695, Esther Boyce (*b* 1680);
6–Samuel (1703-89), farmer, of Smithfield, R.I., and Northbridge, Mass.; *m* 1726, Sarah Reed (1703-87; Jacob[7], *m* Elizabeth Green);
5–Stephen (1734-1812), farmer; *m* 1756, Patience Very (1736-1826; Joseph[6], *m* Ruth Foster);
4–Dea. Thomas (1769-1846), farmer; *m* 1797, Mary Hardy (1773-1853);
3–Harvey (1804-83), *m* 1830, Lois Maria Stowe (1804-82), teacher (John[4] [1763-1837], *m* Sarah Healy, 1768-1852);
2–Lucian (1837-78), farmer, of Jamestown, N.Y.; *m* 1862, Octavia Churchill (1837-86; Silas[3], *m* Esther Parmelee, 1797-1844); issue: I–Nellie Esther (1 above); II–Lillie May (1866-67).
1–B.S., U.Mich., '94 (Sigma Xi, P.B.K., Omicron Nu, etc.); fellow in chemistry, U.Chicago, 1894-97, Ph.D., 1904. Teacher, 1886-91; head of chem. dept., Mt. Holyoke Coll., 1897-1905; research work, Rockefeller Inst., 1906-08 (see Who's Who in America). Mem. A.A.A.S., American Chem. Soc., American Home Economics Assn., A.A.U.W. Author. Residence: S. Hadley, Mass.

1–**GOODENOUGH, Caroline Louisa Leonard (Mrs. Herbert D.),** *b* Bridgewater, Mass., Dec. 31, 1856.
8–Solomon **Leonard** (1610-ante 1671), from Eng., 1630, settled at Duxbury, Mass.; one of the 54 original proprs. and first settlers of Bridgewater, 1656; *m* Mary–;
7–Jacob (1647-1717), of Duxbury and Bridgewater, *m* Phoebe Chandler (*d* 1678);
6–Joseph (1670-1749), Bridgewater; *m* 1695, Martha Orcutt (1671-1752; William[7], an original settler at Bridgewater);
5–Joseph (1696-1786), Bridgewater; *m* 1721, Mary Packard (1696-1770; Samuel[6], *m* Lydia, dau. of John Smith, *m* Lydia, dau. of Philip Eliot, qv);
4–David (1734-1813), Bridgewater; soldier Am. Rev.; *m* 1770, Mary Hall;
3–Caleb F. (1778-1840), Bridgewater; lt. in Mass. militia; *m* 1807, Nancy Thompson;
2–James Madison (2 below).
8–George **Hall,** from Eng.;

7-Joseph (1640-1705), Taunton; *m* Mary Bell (James[8], *m* Ester [1636-1721], dau. of John Lugg, from Eng. to Boston);
6-Capt. Joseph (1694-1763), *m* Elizabeth Leonard (James[7], *m* Lydia, dau. of Anthony Gulliver, came from Ireland);
5-Dea. Joseph (1720-1807), of Taunton; *m* Mary Andrews;
4-Mary (1750-1839), *m* David **Leonard** (4 above).
9-Thomas **Lincoln,** came to America 1638;
8-Thomas, lived in Hingham, Mass.;
7-Thomas, lived in **Taunton**;
6-Hannah, *m* Capt. Edmond **Andrews** (1692-1750; Capt. John[7] [*b* 1662]; John[8], from Wales);
5-Mary, *m* Joseph **Hall** (5 above).
8-Edward **Bangs** (qv);
7-Mercy, *m* Stephen **Merrick**;
6-Sarah, *m* Nathaniel **Crossman** (1680-1757; Robert[7]; Robert[8]; John[9], from Eng., 1639);
5-Abigail, *m* Caleb **Thompson** (Jacob[6], *m* Abigail, dau. of John Wadsworth, *m* Abigail, dau. of Joseph Andrews, from Eng., 1635, settled at Hingham and Duxbury, Mass.);
4-Nathaniel (1750-1833), *m* Hannah Thomas (Noah[5], *m* Mary Alden [John Alden[6]; Joseph[7]; John[8], Mayflower Pilgrim, qv]);
3-Nancy (1784-1863), *m* Caleb F. **Leonard** (3 above).
8-Peter **Brown,** Mayflower Pilgrim (qv);
7-Mary, *m* Ephraim **Tinkham**;
6-Mary, *m* Shubael **Thompson**;
5-John (1717-66), *m* Lydia Wood (Elnathan[6], *m* Mary Billington [Isaac Billington[7]; Francis[8]; John[9], Mayflower Pilgrim]);
4-Hon. Isaac (1746-1819);
3-Dea. Isaac (1781-1835), *m* 1808, Abiah Haskell;
2-Jane F. (2 below).
8-James **Leonard** (qv);
7-Judge Thomas (1641-1713), of Taunton, Mass.; *m* Mary Watson (1642-1723; George[8], *m* Phoebe, dau. of Robert Hicks, qv);
6-Elkanah (1677-1714), of Middleboro, Mass.; *m* Charity Hodges (1682-1739; Henry[7] [1652-1717], *m* Ester, dau. of John Gallup [son of Capt. John, qv], *m* Hannah, dau. of John Lake, from Ireland, 1631; William[8], qv);
5-Abiah (1707-91), of Middleboro; *m* 1740, Elder Mark **Haskell** (1709-85; Roger[6] [*b* 1680]; Mark[7] [1650-99], *m* Mary, dau. of John Smith, *m* Elizabeth, dau. of Robert Goodell, qv; Roger[8], qv);
4-Zebulon (1747-1820), of Middleboro; *m* Abigail Swift;
3-Abiah (1779-1853), of Middleboro; *m* Dea. Isaac **Thompson** (3 above).
10-Francis **Cooke,** Mayflower Pilgrim (qv);
9-John;
8-Sarah, *m* Arthur **Hathaway,** came to Plymouth, 1630;
7-Jonathan (1671-1727), *m* Susanna Pope (Capt. Seth[8]; Thomas[9], *m* Sarah, dau. of John Jenny, came from Eng., 1625);
6-Deborah, *m* Jireh **Swift**;
5-Jonathan (1730-63), *m* Elizabeth Bourne;
4-Abigail (1757-1811), *m* Zebulon **Haskell** (4 above).
12-Gov. John **Carver,** Mayflower Pilgrim (qv);
11-Katherine, *m* John **Tilley,** Mayflower Pilgrim (qv);
10-Elizabeth, *m* John **Howland,** Mayflower Pilgrim (qv);
9-Desire, *m* John **Gorham** (qv);
8-Col. John (1651-1716);
7-Mary, *m* Joseph **Hinckley** (1672-1753; Samuel[8], *m* Mary, dau. of Edward Fitzrandolph; Samuel[9], qv);
6-Mercy, *m* John **Bourne** (Hon. Melatiah[7], *m* Desire, dau. of John Chipman, *m* Hope, dau. of John Howland, Mayflower Pilgrim, qv; Shearjashub[8]; Richard[9], *m* Bathsheba, dau. of Andrew Hallet);
5-Elizabeth, *m* Jonathan **Swift** (5 above).
2-James Madison **Leonard** (1810-80), farmer, Bridgewater, Mass.; *m* 1842, Jane Thompson (1819-92); issue: I-Emma Frances (1844-1919); II-Elizabeth Morton (1846-1921; *m* Rev. Truman D. Childs); III-Mary Hall (1847-1921); IV-Clara Farnham (1849-1911; *m* Dr. Chester Irving Fisher); V-James Henry (1852-1917; *m* Mary C. Johnston); VI-Edith (*b* 1854); VII-Caroline Louisa (1 above); VIII-Jennie Thompson (1860-65).
1-*m* Aug. 22, 1878, Rev. Herbert Delos Goodenough (May 22, 1852-Aug. 24, 1927), A.M., Oberlin Coll.; missionary to the Zulus of South Africa, 31 yrs.; returned to America, 1922, and *d* at Rochester, Mass.; son of Darwin Goodenough, of Burton, Wis., *m* Malvina—; issue: 1-Leonard Delos, *b* Oberlin, O., June 7, 1879; A.B., Oberlin, '02; A.M., Cornell, 1911; *m* Aug. 29, 1905, Maude, dau. of William Williams, of E. Aurora, N.Y. (issue: Kenneth W.; William D.); 2-Herbert Harold, *b* Andover, Mass.; May 30, 1881; A.B., Oberlin, '05, A.M., 1912; *m* Aug. 19, 1908, Florence, dau. of Corice C. Pearl, of Norwalk, O. (issue: Eone; Aura; Flora Lois); 3-Aubrey Ward, *b* Adams Natal, South Africa, May 6, 1883; A.B., Oberlin, '06; A.M., Yale, 1907; Ph.D., Iowa U., 1920; *m* Aug. 27, 1906, Gertrude, dau. of Corice C. Pearl, of Norwalk, O. (issue: David Leonard; Herbert Maurice; Silvia); 4-Charles Douglas, *b* Adams Natal, South Africa, Nov. 13, 1884; U.Dublin, Ireland, 1914; was surgeon in British Army, France; enlisted in World War, 1915 and served with rank of capt.; *d* in influenza epidemic on Armistice Day, 1918; 5-Edith Dora, *b* Durban Natal, South Africa, 1888; A.B., Oberlin, '10; *m* 1920, Robert M. Metland (issue: Emma Isabel, *b* 1923); 6-Carolyn Lilian, *b* Umvote Natal, South Africa, Dec. 7, 1891; A.B., Ames (Ia.) Coll., '21; *m* Apr. 20, 1912, Elva Cornelius, son of Cornelius Andrews, of Burbank, S.D. (issue: Daniel Keith).
1-Grad. Oberlin Coll., 1877. Missionary of A.B.C.-F.M., went with husband to South Africa as missionary to the Zulus, 1881; left Africa for last time in 1913. Mem. I.A.G., Hist. Soc. of Old Bridgewater, Mass., John Howland Family Assn. Residence: Rochester, Mass.

JOHN KEMP GOODLOE (1823-92).

1-**GOODLOE, Abbie Carter,** *b* Versailles, Ky.
6-George **Goodloe** (1701-41), from Eng.; settled in Spotsylvania Co., Va.; justice of the Quorum, Caroline Co., 1735; *m* Diana Minor, of Va.;
5-Henry, soldier Am. Rev.; *m* Frances Diana Kemp;
4-Vivian, removed to Ky., and settled in Woodford Co.; *m* Dorothy Tompkins (sister of Judge Christopher Tompkins, lawyer and U.S. senator);
3-Kemp Minor, soldier War 1812; of Nathaniel Hart's famous co., in which every man was 6 feet tall or over; *m* 1822, Harriet Harris (desc. Elizabeth Washington [niece of Lawrence Washington], and g.dau. Col. John Logan, first treas. of Ky., and 3 times rep. of Ky. in Va. Legislature, before admission of Ky. to the Union);
2-John Kemp (1823-92), distinguished corporation lawyer of Ky.; soldier in Mexican War; fought in Battle of Buena Vista with young

Harry Clay; mem. state Legislature many yrs.; dist. atty. for La., apptd. by Pres. Lincoln; mem. law firm of Barr, Goodloe, and Humphrey; *m* 1852, Annie Locke; *m* 2d, 1864, Mary Lucretia Shouse (1843-1922; James[3], of Woodford Co., Ky., *m* Abbie, dau. of Goodloe Carter, of "Redlands," Charlottesville, Va., *m* his cousin, Diana Frances Goodloe); issue (1st marriage): I–James (*d* 1872); issue (2d marriage): I–Tevis (1865-1920; *m* Hallie Dudley); II–Caroline Tompkins (1869-1907; *m* George Warren Fuller); III–Harris (1876-99; *m* Philip Lightfoot Lee); IV–John Kemp (*b* 1881; *m* Mabel Mathews); V–Abbie Carter (1 above).

1–B.S., Wellesley. Author (see Who's Who in America). Clubs: Arts (Louisville, Ky.), Women's University (New York). Address: Women's University Club, 106 E. 52d St., New York, N.Y.

1–**GOODWIN, Esther Cory (Mrs. Otis P.),** *b* Pocahontas, Ark., July 25, 1875.

9–John **Cory** (1617 or 18-1685), from Eng. to Mass., 1635; a founder with Rev. John Young, of Southold, L.I.; whale commr., Southampton, L.I., 1644; received land grant, 1644; an early settler at Huntington, L.I.; town clk., 1644; *m* 1638, Ann–, or Hannah–;

8–John (1639-85), landowner; recorder; town clk.; arbitrator, Huntington; *m* 1667, Mary Cornish (1647-97; Thomas[9], of Newtown, L.I.; *m* Mary Stone);

7–John (1674-1720), a founder and landowner, Elizabethtown, N.J.; *m* 1700, Priscilla Tompkins or Day (1680-1722/23; George Tompkins[8]; Paul Tompkins[9]);

6–Elnathan (1701/02-1766), landowner Westfield, and Elizabethtown; *m* 2d, 1729, Sarah Simpson (1704-85);

5–Ebenezer (1730/31-1785), sgt., Am. Rev.; landowner, Elizabethtown; *m* 2d, 1755, Mary Mills, of Westfield, N.J.;

4–Job (1769-1824), of Sparta, N.J.; *m* 1790, Jane Morrow (1774-1830; James[5], from Ireland to Pa., and N.J., Am. Rev., *m* 1770, Jane Gardner);

3–David (1791-1870), War 1812; *m* 1812, Martha Wade (1794-1876; Samuel[4] [1773-1845], *m* ca. 1793, Nancy Van Kirk; Noadiah[5], capt. Am. Rev.; Samuel[6], of Mass.);

2–Dr. Charles Vance (2 below).

4–Benjamin **Jackson** (1778-1825), cousin to President Andrew Jackson; served in War 1812; *m* 1799, Sarah Morse (*b* 1780), related to Samuel F. B. Morse;

3–Amos M. (1817-55), of Luzerne Co., Pa.; removed to Ill.; *m* 1840, Esther McKnight (1814-69; Jesse[4], of Chester Co., Pa., *m* Mary McClure);

2–Adeline (1854-1925), *m* as his 2d wife, 1871, Dr. Charles Vance **Cory** (1821-81), of Sparta, N.J., and Ill.; issue: I–Lesbia Martha (1872-79); II–Esther (1 above).

1–*m* Oct. 14, 1894, Otis Pearl Goodwin, *b* Charleston, Ill., June 4, 1873; son of George Henry Goodwin, of Mass. and Ill.; issue (all *b* Charleston, Ill.): 1–Bennett Vance, *b* May 4, 1896; served with 1st Div., A.E.F. in World War; 2–Raymond E., *b* Sept. 21, 1900; *m* Jan. 1, 1928, Eva Cline Train; 3–Paul Henry, *b* Jan. 12, 1903; *m* Apr. 1, 1922, Bernice E. Bailes; 4–Inez Cory, *b* Dec. 2, 1907.

1–Mem. D.A.R. Methodist. Residence: 418 E. Harrison, Charleston, Ill.

1–**GORDON, Charles Henry,** *b* Caledonia, N.Y., May 10, 1857.

5–James **Gordon,** of Co. Badenoch, Scotland; *m* 1725, Janet McIntosh;

4–John (*b* 1728), *m* 1754, Ann McIntosh;

3–John (*b* nr. Newtonmore, Co. Badenoch, Scotland, 1767-*d* 1859), settled at Caledonia, Livingston Co., N.Y., 1809; *m* 1798, Elizabeth Cameron (1777-1843), of Ballintian, Co. Badenoch, Scotland (Angus[4], *m* Katherine McPherson);

2–John (1814-88), from Caledonia, N.Y., to Barry Co., Mich., 1859; *m* 1851, Jane Forrest; *m* 2d, 1854, Ann McKinnon (1833-1915; John[3] [1806-47; son of Donald, *m* Marian McDonald, of Island of Tyree, Scotland], sailed with his family for America, 1847, but *d* en route, *m* 1830, Isabel McArthur [1806-87], with her family settled in Ontario, Can., later removed to Mich.); issue: I–Isabel (1855-64); II–Charles H. (1 above); III–Jeannette (1859-64); IV–Nellie Ann (1865-1902; *m* Fred D. Havens).

1–*m* June 22, 1887, Mary Ett Hydorn (qv for issue).

1–B.S., Albion Coll., '86; M.S., 1890; Ph.D., U.-Chicago, 1895; U.Heidelberg, 1897-98 (Delta Tau Delta, Sigma Xi, Phi Kappa Phi). Supt. city schs., Beloit, Wis., 1895-97, at Lincoln, Neb., 1899-1903; mem. U.S. Geol. Survey, 1905-12; prof. geology, U.Tenn., since 1907 (see Who's Who in America). Treas. gen. Phi Kappa Phi, 1912-23, sec. gen. since 1923. Mason (32°). Club: Appalachian. Summer place: Elkmont, Tenn. Winter place: Anna Maria, Fla. Residence: 1616 W. Clinch Av., Knoxville, Tenn.

1–**GORDON, Mary Ett Hydorn (Mrs. Charles H.),** *b* Valley Center, Mich., Sept. 20, 1863.

4–Peter H. (Heydorn) **Hydorn** (1777-1843; ancestors from Flanders to Can.), settled at DePeyster, N.Y.; *m* —Morrison;

3–Peter James (1809-84), from DePeyster, N.Y., to Yarker, Can., later to Valley Center, Mich.; *m* 1st, Deborah Elizabeth Tryon;

2–John Henry (2 below).

10–(?) John **Alden,** Mayflower Pilgrim (qv);

9–(?) Joseph (ca. 1627-1697), of Bridgewater; freeman, 1659; *m* Mary Simmons (Moses[8], from Eng. in the "Fortune," settled at Duxbury, *m* Sarah–);

8–(?) Mercy, *m* 1688, John **Burrill** (1658-1731; John[7], at Weymouth, 1639, *m* Rebecca–; John[8], qv); and thru:

5–Ann (*b* 1743), *m* Samuel **Nevers** (*b* Dunstan [now Me.], Mass., 1737);

4–Lucy (*b* 1766), *m* 1784, James **York** (*b* R.I., 1760);

3–Stephen, *m* 1st, Sarah Nelson (1808-69), lived in Brownsville, Ontario, Can., where Sarah *d*; he moved to Valley Center, Mich. (William[4] [1760-1842], pvt. 5th Regt., N.Y. militia, Am. Rev., 1777-80, *m* 1791, Eunice Young [1772-1860], of White Plains, N.Y.; William[5], *m* Hannah–);

2–Ellen (1843-1922), *m* 1860, John Henry **Hydorn** (*b* DePeyster, N.Y., 1837-*d* 1911), settled at Valley Center, ca. 1859; issue: I–Sarah Melinda (1861-62); II–Mary Ett (1 above); III–William (*b* 1865; *m* 1889, Minerva Rice); IV–Harvey Stephen (*b* 1866; *m* 1893, Marian S. Pomeroy); V–Jennie (*b* and *d* 1873); VI–James Delford (1874-76); VII–Lewis Allison (*b* 1878; *m* 1898, Annie Tobin); VIII–Nellie Franc (*b* 1881).

1–*m* June 22, 1887, Charles Henry Gordon, Ph.D. (qv); issue: 1–Irene Hydorn, *b* Keokuk, Ia., May 4, 1889; U. of Tenn., '11; *m* May 30, 1911, Burton Ashton, son of Edwin C. Gaskill, of Mays Landing, N.J. (issue: Gordon Ashton, *b* 1913; Mary Hester, *b* 1916; Isabel, *b* 1918); 2–Helen Garnett, *b* Evanston, Ill., June 11, 1891; U. of Tenn., '11; *m* Oct. 10, 1913, Don Carlos Ellis (issue: Joan, *b* 1915; Mary Ellen, *b* 1918; Charles Gordon, *b* 1922); 3–Isabel, *b* Beloit, Wis., May 2, 1897; A.B., Albion Coll., '17; A.M., U.Tenn., 1920; Ph.D., Columbia, 1929; *m* June 22, 1925, Hugh Sevier Carter, *b* Apr. 5, 1895; A.M., Southwestern, 1916; Ph.D., Columbia, 1928; son of David Wendell Carter (*b* 1848), *m* 1884, Cornelia Stanley Keith; desc. of Col. John Carter (1737-81), founder of the family in Tenn.

1–Studied Albion Coll., 1880-81. Pres. Knoxville Y.W.C.A., 1928; pres. Ossoli Club, 1922-23. Residence: 1616 W. Clinch Av., Knoxville, Tenn.

1–**GORSSLINE, Raymond Myers,** *b* Bloomfield, Ont., Can., July 28, 1886.

9–Jacob (Gosselin) **Gorssline,** from Dieppe, Normandy, fled from religious persecution to Amsterdam, 1620; in London, Eng., 1645; *m* Martha Chauvel, Huguenot, of Dieppe;

8–Jacob (*b* Amsterdam, 1627), *m* in London, 1655, Sarah Gooris;

7–Jacob (1661-1722), *b* London, Eng.; to America bet. 1699-1701; settled at Newtown, L.I.; *m* ante 1684, Judith Liville or Lesveille;

6–Josse or Joseph (1701-72), of Newtown, L.I.; *m* 1st, 1723, Elizabeth Albertis or Albertus

(*d* 1757; Samuel[7]; John[8], *m* Elizabeth Scudder; Peter Caesar[9], of Venice, Italy, and Heeren Gracht, now Broad St., N.Y., *m* in New Amsterdam, 1642, Judith Jans Meynie, of Amsterdam, Holland);
5–Jacob, of Newtown, L.I.; began to write name Gorssline; *m* 1764, Sarah Hallett (*b* ca. 1740; John[6], *m* 1730, Sarah Blackwell; Samuel[7], early settler at Hell Gate, now Astoria, L.I., *m* Bridget Blackwell; Samuel[8]; from Eng. to Greenwich, Conn., then to Hell Gate, ca. 1652);
4–John (1769-1843), of Fish Lake, Prince Edward Co., Ont., Can.; *m* 2d, 1811, Sally Adams (*d* 1854);
3–Reuben Cronk (1813-95), of Bloomfield, Ont.; *m* 2d, 1855, Sarah Anne De Mille (1822-99), sis. of 1st wife (John I.[4], *m* Sarah Solmes; Isaac[5]; of French Huguenot descent, removed from Vt. to Can., 1792);
2–Rickerson Cronk (1860-1929), govt. civil service; of Bloomfield, Can.; *m* 1883, Helena Catherine Myers (*b* 1864; Adam Henry[3]; Rev. Frederick Augustus[4], Ch. of Eng. minister, Morrisburg, Ont., 1810); issue: I–Maude Antoinette (*b* 1885; *m* Albert Edward Shaw); II–Raymond Myers (1 above).
1–*m* Jan. 31, 1917, Baroness Genevieve De Bethune (1896-1917); dau. of Baron Charles De Bethune, of Alost, Belgium.
1–*m* 2d, June 2, 1923, Beatrice Marjorie Sparks, *b* Ottawa, Ont., Apr. 11, 1897; dau. of Nicholas C. Sparks, of Ottawa; issue: 1–John Ronald, *b* Ottawa, Ont., Feb. 7, 1925; 2–Marjorie Ruth, *b* Halifax, Nova Scotia, Dec. 31, 1927.
1–M.B., U.Toronto, '11, D.P.H., McGill U., 1921. Lt. Col. Royal Canadian Army Medical Corps, Canadian Regular Army, since 1911. House surgeon, Grace Hosp., Toronto, 1911. Served World War; D.S.O. Fellow Huguenot Soc. of London; mem. I.A.G., H.S.S.C. Club: Laurentian (Ottawa). Address: Care of Dept. of Nat. Defence, Ottawa, Ont., Can.

1–**GOSE, Mack F.,** *b* Sullivan Co., Mo., July 8, 1859.
5–Stephen **Gose,** from Germany, aet. 15; *m* Lizzie Spreker;
4–Christopher, farmer, Tazewell Co., Va.; *m* Mary Elizabeth Litz;
3–William, of Tazewell Co.; removed to Sullivan Co., Mo.; *m* 1822, Martha Knifong;
2–John Martin (*b* 1825), removed to Walla Walla, Wash. Ty., 1865; *m* 1853, Jane McQuown (Patrick[3]).
1–*m* Oct. 30, 1886, Lelah B. Seeley, *b* Rushville, Ill., Apr. 25, 1869; dau. of Charles H. Seeley, of Pomeroy, Wash.; issue: 1–Vyvien, *b* Pomeroy, Apr. 28, 1890.
1–Ed. Whitman Sem., Walla Walla, Wash. Began law practice, Pomeroy, Wash., 1883-1909; asso. justice, Supreme Ct. of Wash., 1909-15 (see Who's Who in America). Pres. Wash. State Bar Assn., 1915-16; mayor of Pomeroy, 1898-99; chmn. bd. overseers, Whitman Coll. Mason. K.P. Republican. Episcopalian. Residence: Pomeroy, Wash. Address: Olympia, Wash.

1–**GOULD, Janet Overall (Williams) Dean (Mrs. Chester M.),** *b* "The White Oaks," nr. Fayette, Mo., Sept. 27, 1878.
6–William **Williams** (*d* 1717), Prince George Co., Va.; settled below Petersburg on James River; moved to Nottaway;
5–Thomas (*d* 1798), Oak Hill, Nottaway Co., Va.; *m* Catherine Greenhill (David[6], Amelia Co., Va.);
4–Thomas Roper (*b* 1774), moved to Campbell Co., Va.; *m* Elizabeth Cross;
3–Francis Epps (1801-62), moved to Howard Co., Mo., 1835; *m* 1825, Martha Ann Talbot;
2–Robert Prewitt (2 below).
10–Walter **Talbot,** (g.son of Walter, *m* Jane Bolane), of Castle Talbot, Ireland;
9–Sir William, Baronet, principal sec., commd. judge of probate of wills and notary public of Md., 1670; returned to Eng. ca. June 15, 1671;
8–Lord Charles (killed on Salisbury Plains), *m* –Wallis;
7–Matthew (*b* Castle Talbot, Wexford, Ireland, 1699-*d* 1758), came from Eng., settled in Va.; apptd. by the Council to define the boundary line bet. Bedford Co. and Lunenburg; present at 1st ct. of Lunenburg Co., May 5, 1746; 1st ct. in Bedford Co. held in his home, May 1754; col. militia, Bedford Co., 1755; served in French and Indian War; vestryman 1755; sheriff 1757; *m* 1st, 1720, Mary Williston (1697-1736; James[8], of Queen Anne Co., Md., *m* –Belgrave);
6–Charles (1723-79), capt., 1757; sheriff, Bedford Co., 1755; justice 1776,77,78; in French and Indian War; mem. Commn. of the Peace till death; *m* 1749, Drusilla Gwynn (1727-79; David[7], of Lunenburg Co., *m* Mary–);
5–Williston (1750-1830), qualified as 1st lt., 1778; commd. co. commissary, Bedford Co., for Am. Rev. supplies; sheriff Campbell Co., 1793; *m* 1769, Elizabeth Cock (George[6], *m* Agnes–);
4–Charles Moyle (1771-*d* Campbell Co., Va., 1834), pvt. Va. militia, War 1812; *m* 1800, Martha Tomlinson Prewitt;
3–Martha Ann (1805-92), *m* Francis E. **Williams** (3 above).
8–Roger (Prouit, Pruit) **Prewitt,** French refugee; settled at Manakin, on the James River, Va., 1699; *m* Mary–;
7–Gen. George Byrd, French and Indian War; of Halifax Co., Va.;
6–Michael (1722-98), of Shelby Co., Ky.; *m* Elizabeth Simpkins (1724-89; dau. of Elizabeth Adams, cousin of John Quincy Adams);
5–Col. Joseph (1760-*d* Shelby Co., Ky., 1808), native of Va.; matross Am. Rev.; col. co. militia; *m* 1782, Leah Moss;
4–Martha Tomlinson (1783-1870), *d* at "The White Oaks," Howard Co., Mo.; *m* Capt. Charles M. **Talbot** (4 above).
10–Edward (Mosse) **Moss,** lived in York Co., Va.; wheelwright; *m* Eleanor–;
9–Edward (*d* 1716), justice York Co., 1687;
8–William (*d* York Co., Va., 1718), lived on the Roanoke River; *m* Elizabeth Goodwin (John[9], *m* Elizabeth, dau. of Augustine Moore, of Elizabeth City Co., Va.; Maj. James[10] [*d* 1678/-79; son of Peter, of London, Eng.], lived on Back Creek, justice, York Co., 1657-62, burgess, 1658, *m* Rachel [Porter?], 1630-66);
7–William, of Halifax Co.; *m* Rebecca Mason (Col. Charles[8], of Fairfax Co.);
6–Frederick (*b* 1735-*d* Jessamine Co., Ky., 1792), *m* ca. 1759, Sarah Tomlinson or Tompkins (1740-1828; Thomas[7], fought at Braddock's defeat);
5–Leah, of Halifax Co., Va.; *m* Joseph **Prewitt** (5 above).

ROBERT PREWITT WILLIAMS (1841-1910).

2–Robert Prewitt **Williams** (1841-1910), state treas. of Mo., 1901-05 (see portrait); *m* 1877, Anne Maughs Overall (1858-1907), ed. Science Hill Acad., Shelbyville, Ky.; issue: I–Janet Overall (1 above); II–Adele (*b* 1882; *m* Fred S. Brown); III–Berenice (*b* 1884); IV–Frances E. (Mrs. W. H. Belsher, qv for material lineages); V–Harriet (*b* 1889); VI–Dorothy (1892-1928; *m* Arthur B. Lane); VII–Susanne (*b* 1897; *m* John M. Geist).

1–*m* 1910, Walter Minturn Dean (Sept. 24, 1874-Oct. 12, 1918); son of Albert Flandrean Dean, of Evanston, Ill. (Minturn[3]); issue: 1–Walter Manley, *b* Riverside, Calif., June 5, 1911; 2–Elise Overall, *b* Riverside, Oct. 29, 1914.
1–*m* 2d, 1924, Chester Mason Gould, *b* Lowell, Mass., Feb. 20, 1882; son of Charles Gould, of Lowell, Mass.
1–A.M., Howard-Payne Coll., Fayette, Mo., '96; spl. work at Chicago U. and U.Calif. Author of Shakespeare Festival Pageant, produced, 1916, Lake Corinth, N.Y.; miracle play, "The Golden Rose," produced at Corona Woman's Club, 1919; Aylucha, hist. pageant, etc. Mem. D.A.R., Hist. Soc. of Southern Calif. Residence: El Encanto, Corona, Calif.

ASA NATHANIEL OVERALL (1828-70), at age 21.

1–**BELSHER, Frances E. Williams (Mrs. W. H.),** *b* Fayette, Mo., Aug. 3, 1886.
7–John **Overall** (will, Frederick Co., Va., 1742); came from Suffolk, Eng., to Prince William Co., Va.; settled in Frederick Co., 1740;
6–John, to Frederick Co., Va., 1748; justice of the quorum many yrs.; *m* 1753, Maria Christina Forman (*b* 1736);
5–Capt. William (*b* Frederick Co., 1754-killed by Indians, 1793), of Shenandoah Valley; capt. militia co., Am. Rev.; for services received 640 acres; with brothers moved to Watauga settlement, 1775, they settled the Bluff, now Nashville, Tenn., 1779; *m* 1783, Susannah Thomas (William[6]);
4–Maj. Wilson Lee (1792-1850), from Tenn., to St. Charles Parish, Mo., 1808; served 3d Co., 3d Regt., Capt. Music's Mo. Vols., War 1812; served Black Hawk War; granted land for services; mem. Mo. Legislature, 1826-30; mem. ry. conv. to promote rebuilding of the 1st ry. into Mo., 1836; probate judge, St. Charles; *m* 1811, Mary Griffith (Capt. Samuel[5] [*b* Oxford, Mass., 1766-1822], to Mo. 1797, War 1812, *m* in N.C., Sarah–; Daniel[6] [1726-*d* Laurens Co., N.Y., 1840], Mass. minuteman, 1775; Samuel[7], *m* Eleanor Esty);
3–Asa Nathaniel (1828-70), ed. St. Charles Coll. and Yale; mayor St. Charles, Mo.; gave substantial aid to the Confederacy (see portrait); *m* 1856, Mary T. Anderson;
2–Anne Maughs (2 below).
9–Joseph **Callaway,** from Eng. to Va.;
8–Joseph, lived in Caroline Co., Va.;
7–Col. William (1714-78), served French and Indian War; founded New London, in Bedford Co., Va., one of 1st trustees; a justice when court first met, 1754, justice 1754-75; colonial justice of peace under George III; burgess; mem. Assembly, 1754-64; 1st co. lt. in chief, Bedford Co.; *m* 2d, bet. 1743-54, Elizabeth or Ann Crawford, of Ky. (William[8], col. French and Indian War, 1755-61);
6–Mary, *m* Capt. Jacob **Anderson,** sgt. French and Indian War; capt. Am. Rev. (George[7] [1707-will 1778, Bedford Co., Va.], mem. Augusta Co. militia, 1742-58, served French and Indian War, *m* 1729, –);
5–William, pvt. Bedford Co. militia, Am. Rev.; sheriff Campbell Co., Va.; *m* 1783, Sarah Early;
4–Capt. James Callaway (1792-1864), soldier War 1812; made capt. by Pres. Monroe for patriotism in organizing a co. to defend the Capitol against British, 1812; from Bedford Co., Va., to Callaway Co., Mo.; mem. Mo. Legislature, 1834; *m* 1819, Jane Robinson Moorman;
3–Mary Tyre (1836-67), *m* Asa N. **Overall** (3 above).
11–Richard **Buford** (qv);
10–John (1642-1722), from Eng. with his father; *m* 1662, Elizabeth Parrott (*b* 1645; Richard[11] [*d* 1686], from Barbados, an early settler in Lancaster Co., Va., 1649, sr. justice, 1673-86, commr., 1655, high sheriff, 1657, *m* Margaret–, *d* 1687);
9–Thomas (1663-1716), *m* Mary– (*d* 1720);
8–Thomas (1682-1761), of Middlesex Co., Va.; *m* Elizabeth Johnson (*b* 1675);
7–Elizabeth (*b* 1709), *m* 1728, Lt. Col. Jeremiah **Early** (bap. 1705-1787), of Middlesex, Augusta and Culpeper cos.; served French and Indian War; justice, Augusta Co. (Thomas[8] [*b* 1682], *m* ca. 1704, Elizabeth– [*d* 1716?]; John[9], from Donegal, Ireland, to Va., 1661, settled in York Co.);
6–Col. Jeremiah (1730-79), lt. French and Indian War; trustee New London, Bedford Co., Va., 1761; capt. militia, 1758,63; col., 1778; high sheriff; justice of peace, Bedford Co., 1759-79; propr. Washington Iron Mines, Henry Co., Va., which became the property of his sons, John and Jubal Early; *m* 1st, 1750, Sarah Anderson (1732-70; George[7], *m* Mrs. Anna Cofer);
5–Sarah (*b* 1766), *m* William **Anderson** (5 above).
10–Zachariah **Moorman** (*b* Isle of Wight, Eng., 1620), joined English army aet. 19, capt. under Oliver Cromwell; did not sympathize with the Cromwell Govt., and emigrated to W.I.; sailed from Southampton, Eng., on the "Glasgow," for the Barbados, 1669; *m* — Chandler, of Ireland;
9–Thomas (*b* ante 1669), from Barbados, W.I., to S.C., settled nr. Charleston; later to Va.; *m* Elizabeth–;
8–Charles (*b* ante 1686), of Green Springs, Louisa Co., Va.; overseer Friends' Meeting House Camp Creek, Louisa Co.; *m* 1704, Elizabeth Reynolds (*b* 1688; Christopher[9]);
7–Achilles, *m* Elizabeth Adams (Robert[8], of New Kent Co., *m* Mourning–);
6–Andrew (*b* 1744), *m* 1771, Judith Clark (*b* 1749; Micajah[7] ens. Am. Rev., *m* 1736, Judith [*b* 1716], dau. of Robert Adams, *m* Mary Lewis; Christopher[8] [1681-1753], capt. militia, 1727, one of 1st justices of Louisa Co., *m* 1709, Penelope Bowling, perhaps Massie or Johnson);
5–James Clark (*b* 1779), *m* 1799, Janet Robinson (*b* 1779; John[6] [1736-1815], Am. Rev., *m* 1768, Janet Edgar [1739-1825]; Henry[7], from Ireland, of Lynchburg, Va.);
4–Jane Robinson (1806-96), *m* Capt. James C. **Anderson** (4 above);
3–Mary T. (1836-67), *m* Asa N. **Overall** (3 above);
2–Anne Maughs (1858-1907), *m* 1877, Robert Prewitt **Williams** (1841-1910), see portrait (for issue and Williams lineages, see sister, Mrs. Chester M. Gould).
1–*m* William Hardin Belsher; issue (all *b* Macon, Mo.): 1–Frances Susanne, *b* Jan. 8, 1907; *m* Mar. 16, 1929, Kendrick Porter; 2–Virginia Doris, *b* Nov. 4, 1909; 3–Elizabeth Ann, *b* Jan. 14, 1912.
1–Dep. recorder, Macon Co., Mo., 1923-24; clerk Probate Ct., 1925-27; dep. circuit clerk, 1927. Mem. C.D.A., D.A.R., U.S.D. 1812. Residence: Macon, Mo.

1–**GOURLEY, Joseph Harvey,** *b* Homer City, Pa., July 1, 1883.
5–John **Gourley,** from Scotland, 1773; settled at Greensburg, Pa.; farmer; *m* Jane Ralston;
4–John, *m* Margaret Stephenson;

3–Samuel Stephenson (1825-93), *m* Eliza Clements;
2–Rev. John (1850-1912), D.D.; *m* Elizabeth Anna Harvey (1853-1904); issue: I–Frank Britt (1879-1907); II–Mary Eliza (*b* 1880; *m* Walter D. Trager); III–Rebecca Grace; IV–Joseph Harvey (1 above); V–John Steele (*b* 1884); VI–Elizabeth; VII–Margaret Stephenson (*b* 1892; *m* Juneau Shinn).
1–*m* June 7, 1911, Lucy M. Kinney, *b* Wooster, O., Jan. 10, 1886; dau. of Isaac Kinney, of Wooster; issue: 1–Margaret Anita, *b* Dover, N.H., Sept. 19, 1913; 2–Lucy Elizabeth, *b* Wooster, O., Mar. 2, 1922.
1–B.S., Ohio State U., '08 (Alpha Zeta, Sigma Xi, Alpha Tau Omega), M.S., 1915. Chief dept. of horticulture, Ohio Agrl. Expt. Sta. and prof. horticulture, Ohio State U. Author (see Who's Who in America). Clubs: Wooster Century, Wooster Country, Rotary. Presbyn. Republican. Residence: 722 Quinby Av., Wooster, O.

1–**GRADY, Lily McAboy Wilcox (Mrs. William E.),** *b* Pittsburgh, Pa., Feb. 26, 1866.
10–John ("John of Hartford") **Wilcox** (qv);
9–John (*d* 1676), soldier Pequot War; *m* 2d, 1650, Katherine Stoughton (*d* ca. 1660; Thomas[10]);
8–Isreal (1656-89), *m* 1677/78, Sarah Savage (1657-1723/24; Sgt. John[9], *m* Elizabeth Dubbin);
7–Samuel (1685-1728), *m* 1714/15, Hannah Sage (John[8]);
6–Daniel (1715-89), *m* Sarah White (1718-1807; Daniel[7]);
5–Josiah (*b* 1750), *m* Eliza Treat; *m* 2d, Hilda Savage;
4–Lemuel (1780-1864), *m* 1801, Rhoda North;
3–Lemuel (1815-89), *m* Eliza Fleming;
2–Lemuel North (1841-1900), *m* 1864, Annie Christy McAboy (1842-1908); issue: I–Lily McAboy (1 above); II–Alice Fleming (1869-73); III–Frank Semple (*b* 1873); IV–Edwin Christy (*d* 1908); V–Norman Fleming (*b* and *d* 1884).
1–*m* Oct. 19, 1898, William Earle Grady, *b* Greenville, S.C., Sept. 9, 1871; son of William S. Grady, of Greenville; issue: 1–Lemuel Keith, *b* Tryon, N.C., Oct. 20, 1902; U. of N.C. '25; 2–Anna Elizabeth, *b* Tryon, Oct. 7, 1905.
Residence: Tryon, N.C.

1–**GRAHAM, Ephraim Foster,** *b* Pinewood, Tenn., Aug. 10, 1881.
6–James **Graham** (1695-1782), from Scotland to Rowan Co., N.C., 1744; ruling elder Old Presbyn. Ch.;
5–James, of Rowan Co.; leader of the "Regulators," Rowan Co., 1770-71; *m* Jean Foster;
4–John (1778-1828), settled nr. Third Creek, Rowan Co.; *m* 1804, Martha Anderson (1786-1819);
3–Samuel Lowry (1812-92), mfr. and farmer, Pinewood, Tenn.; *m* Frances Elizabeth Helm (*b* 1824);
2–John Meredith (1847-1907), of Franklin, Tenn.; mem. Tenn. Legislature, 3 terms; mfr. and farmer; *m* 1869, Anna Wright (1851-74); *m* 2d, 1878, Ellen Foster Cheatham (1851-1921); issue (1st marriage): I–Samuel Lowry (*m* Lila Berry); II–Anna Wright; III–John Meredith (*b* 1873; *m* 1902, Maybeth Sullivan, *b* 1881); issue: (2d marriage): I–Edgar Jones (*b* 1879; *m* Kate Nunnelly); II–Ephraim Foster (1 above); III–Frances Helm (*b* 1884; *m* Charles S. Caldwell); IV–Susan Cheatham (*b* 1885; *m* Edmund M. Ivens); V–Robert Cheatham (*b* 1888); VI–Richard Helm (1891-1918).
1–*m* Aug. 10, 1912, Fanny deRussy Hoyle, *b* Ft. Adams, R.I., Dec. 27, 1889; dau. of Gen. Eli Dubose Hoyle, U.S.A.; issue: 1–Ephraim Foster, *b* Fort Myer, Va., Sept. 9, 1913; 2–Fanny deRussy Hoyle, *b* Fort Bliss, Tex., Dec. 29, 1914; 3–Eli Hoyle, *b* Fort Oglethorpe, Ga., Feb. 23, 1917; 4–Helen Hoyle, *b* Columbia, Tenn., Sept. 10, 1919.
1–Grad. U.S.M.A., '03. Prof. mil. science and tactics, high schs., St. Joseph, Mo. Residence; St. Joseph, Mo.

1–**GRAHAM, James Clark,** *b* Aledo, Ill., Feb. 9, 1894.
5–Joseph **Graham** (1768-1847), from Scotland; served in War 1812; *m* Mary Ralston (*d* 1862);
4–Robert Joseph (1800-64), *m* 1825, Priscilla Bradman (*d* 1877);
3–James Ralston (1838-98), served in Civil War; *m* 1865, Margaret Cordelia Leslie (1846-1900);
2–Alvah Bradman (2 below).
11–William (Hosford) **Horsford** (*d* 1660), from Eng. to Dorchester, Mass., ante 1633; dep. Gen. Ct., Windsor, Conn., 1637;
10–John (*d* 1683), served in King Philip's War; *m* 1657, Phillipa Thrall, of Windsor, Conn.;
9–Timothy (1662-1741), *m* 1689, Hannah Palmer (*d* 1701);
8–Daniel (1695-1777), *m* 1721, Elizabeth Stewart (*d* 1781);
7–Daniel (1723-88), began to write name Horsford; a founder of Williamstown, Mass.; capt. Train Band, Conover, Conn.; *m* Martha Dibble;
6–Roger (1755-1818), to Charlotte, Vt.; *m* 1778, Mary Brown;
5–John (*b* 1784);
4–Ambrose (1805-97), *m* 1831, Acenath Conger;
3–Clark Ambrose (1835-1923), *m* 1872, Josephine Hoag (*d* 1906);
2–Marion Josephine (*b* 1873), *m* 1892, Alvah Bradman **Graham** (*b* 1868), D.D.S., practiced at Montezuma, Ia.
1–*m* Sept. 19, 1917, Dorothy Elizabeth Hall (qv); issue: 1–Marion Eloise, *b* Colfax, Ia., Aug. 21, 1918; 2–James Clark, *b* Fond du Lac, Wis., Oct. 28, 1919; 3–Marjorie Hall, *b* Fond du Lac, July 11, 1921; 4–Dorothy Jerene, *b* Madison, Wis., Oct. 11, 1923; 5–Shirley Joan, *b* Fond du Lac, Nov. 24, 1926.
1–A.B., Grinnell Coll., '16 (Pi Gamma Mu, P.B.K.); A.M., Columbia, 1920; grad. study, U.Wis., 1923-24. Mem. faculty Ripon Coll. (Wis.) since 1916, dean and prof. of English since 1924 (see Who's Who in America). Conglist. Mason. Residence: Ripon, Wis.

1–**GRAHAM, Dorothy Elizabeth Hall (Mrs. James Clark),** *b* Colfax, Ia., Mar. 10, 1894.
8–Anthony **Morris,** 2d (qv);
7–James (1688-1747), of Phila., Pa.; removed to Duck Creek, Del.; *m* 1709, Margaret Cook (1690-1766; John[8], of Del.);
6–James (1723-86), lived at Duck Creek, Del.; *m* 1750, Ann Tilton (1730-62; John[7], *m* Ann–);
5–Mary (1756-1835), *m* 1774, Isaac **Griffin** (1751-1827), in Am. Rev.; mem. Pa. Legislature 3 terms; mem. Congress 3 terms; moved to Fayette Co., Pa.;
4–Harriet (1782-1835), *m* 1799, Edward **Hall** (1776-1852), of Fayette Co., Pa.;
3–James Griffin (1808-73), removed to Columbus City, Ia.; *m* 1832, Celestia Miller;
2–Arthur Wright (2 below).
6–Thomas Kent **Young**;
5–Alexander (1783-1860), from Fleming Co., Ky., to Rush Co., Ind., later to Washington Co., Ia.; *m* Elizabeth Ricketts;
4–James Nelson (1816-98), *m* in Washington Co., Ia., 1837, Sallie Eyestone;
3–John Alex (1838-1921), of Washington Co., Ia.; capt. Civil War; *m* 1860, Elizabeth Runyon (1839-1925);
2–Ella Annette (*b* 1861), *m* 1882, Arthur Wright **Hall** (*b* 1852), of Columbus Junction, Ia.; issue: I–Fred Young (*b* 1884; *m* Gladys Squires); II–James Norman (*b* 1887; *m* Sarah Winchester); III–Harvey Wright (*b* 1890; *m* Arabella Macumber); IV–Dorothy Elizabeth (1 above); V–Marjorie Celeste Hall (*b* 1900; *m* Clair Forsythe).
1–*m* Sept. 19, 1917, James Clark Graham (qv for issue).
1–A.B., Grinnell Coll., '15. Mem. A.A.U.W., P.E.O. Conglist. Independent. Residence: Ripon, Wis.

1–**GRANT, Eugene Josias,** *b* St. Louis, Mo., Feb. 6, 1855.
9–Matthew **Grant** (qv);
8–Samuel (*b* 1631), *m* Mary Porter,
7–Josiah (1668-1732), *m* Rebecca Miner;
6–Oliver (1703-57), *m* Bridget Miner;
5–Oliver (1729-98), capt. Am. Rev.; *m* Anna Borodel Billings;
4–Miner (1756-1828), surgeon Am. Rev.; *m* Eunice Swift;
3–Denison (1789-1867), *m* Sally Byles;
2–Josias (2 below).
6–John **Northrop**;
5–William, drummer, pvt. and drum major Am. Rev.; *m* Ann Allen;

4-Remmington (*b* 1762), *m* Rhoda Knowles;
3-Harris (1793-1849), *m* Jane Ann Gray;
2-Mary Elizabeth (*b* 1831), *m* Josias **Grant** (1830-83); for issue see Vol. I, p. 301.
1-*m* Sept. 13, 1877, Jeannie Lovina Dailey (qv).
1-Poly. Inst. (Brooklyn, N.Y.), '68. Real estate operator and appraiser. Past pres. Brooklyn Real Estate Bd. Mem. O.F.P.A. (councillor, past dep.gov., past registrar N.Y. Soc.; past councillor gen., past registrar gen.), Nat. Soc. Colonial Descs. of America, S.C.W., S.R., I.A.G. (life), N.E. Soc. of Brooklyn (2d v.p.), Valley Forge Hist. Soc., Grant Family Assn. (pres.), Am. Flag Assn. Clubs: Westchester Country, Marine and Field (Brooklyn), Hempstead Country, Yorktown Country (Va). Residence: 379 Washington Av., Brooklyn, N.Y.

1-**GRANT, Jeannie Lovina Dailey (Mrs. Eugene J.)** *b* Great Barrington, Mass., Apr. 28, 1856.
9-Joseph **Bolles** (qv);
8-Thomas (1644-1727), moved to New London, Conn. (occupied present site of Woman's Coll.); *m* 1st, 1669, Zipporah Wheeler (*d* 1678);
7-John (1677-1767), of New London; *m* 1st, 1699, Sarah Edgecombe (*b* 1678);
6-Joseph (1701-85), of New London; *m* Martha-;
5-Joseph (*b* 1732), of New London; *m* Deborah Rogers (*b* 1736);
4-Jemima (1773-1813), *m* John C. **Kline** (1766-1829), of N. Egremont, Mass.;
3-Eliza (1800-80), *m* William **Dailey** (1793-1864);
2-Abram Hoagland (2 below).
8-Thomas **Tracy** (qv);
7-Jonathan (1648-1711), of Preston, Conn.; *m* Mary Griswold (1656-1711);
6-David (1687-1752), of Preston, Conn.; *m* Sarah Parrish (1692-1728), of Ipswich, Mass.;
5-David (1721-70), removed to Norwich, Conn.; *m* Abigail Cleveland (*b* 1720), of New Marlborough, Mass.;
4-David (1755-1814), of New Marlborough, Mass.; capt., adj. gen., Am. Rev.; *m* Electa Sheldon (1764-1834);
3-Silas Howe (1791-1878), capt. War 1812; removed to Hartsville, Mass.; *m* Emily Beach (1803-74);
2-Emily Sheldon (1830-79), *m* Abram Hoagland **Dailey** (1832-1907), atty.; surrogate, Kings Co., N.Y.; issue: I-Jeannie Lovina (1 above); II-Grace Emma (1860-61).
1-*m* Sept. 13, 1877, Eugene Josias Grant (qv).
1-Ed. Brooklyn Heights Sem., Convent of Sacred Heart. Musician, concert and oratorio singer, vocal teacher. Mem. D.F.P.A., C.D. 17th C., C.D.A., D.R. (1st v.p. gen.), Nat. Soc. N.E. Women (hon. pres. gen., hon. pres. Brooklyn Colony), Nat. Soc. Patriotic Women, Valley Forge Hist. Soc., Mass. Women in N.Y. (pres.), U.S. Flag Assn., Nat. Life Conservation Soc. Clubs: Woman's (Brooklyn), N.Y. City Fed. Women's (past pres.), N.Y. State Fed. Women's (past 1st v.p.), Chiropean (past pres.), Woman's Forum, The Priors, The Founders. Episcopalian. Residence: 379 Washington Av., Brooklyn, N.Y.

1-**GRANT, Frederick Clifton,** *b* Beloit, Wis., Feb. 2, 1891.
9-Matthew **Grant** (qv);
8-Samuel (1631-1718), of Windsor, Conn.; freeman, 1654; *m* 1658, Mary Porter (*b* 1638);
7-Josiah (1668-1732), removed to Stonington, Conn.; *m* 1696, Rebecca Miner (1672-1746; Ephraim[8], *m* Mary Avery);
6-Noah (1705-59), tythingman, lister, grand juror; capt. 4th co., 8th Regt., Train Band, 1757; *m* 1744, Hannah Miner;
5-John (1754-1824), removed to Middletown, N.Y.: draft for War 1812, held at his house or inn; *m* 1776, Thankful Lewis (1754-1836);
4-John (*b* Stonington, Conn., 1778-*d* 1856), removed to Wis.; served under Gen. Scott in War 1812; *m* Sarah Osgood (1786-1862);
3-Avery Christopher (*b* Attica, Genesee Co., N.Y., 1823-*d* 1901), of Ellington, Wis.; enlisted Co. I, 32d Wis. Vols., Aug. 19, 1862, assigned to 5th Brig., 1st Div., 16th A.C. of Sherman's command, hon. disch., Feb. 1863; *m* 1845, Ann Wickwire (*b* Horton, King's Co., N.S., 1825-*d* 1909);
2-Frank Augustus (*b* 1862), of Medina, Wis.; *m* 1888, Anna Lois Jack (*b* 1864); issue: I-Frederick Clifton (1 above); II-Mildred (1894-95); III-Wilbur Stanley (*b* 1898; *m* 1921, Josephine Loret; IV-Harland Edwin (*b* 1904; *m* 1927, Lucile Margaret Rupple).
1-*m* June 24, 1913, Helen McQueen Hardie, *b* Waukegan, Ill., Mar. 25, 1889; dau. George Fisher Hardie, of Evanston, Ill.; issue (both *b* Evanston): 1-Robert McQueen, *b* Nov. 25, 1917; 2-Eleanor Jean, *b* Nov. 6, 1921.
1-Ed. Lawrence Coll., Appleton, Wis.; Nashotah (Wis.) House; B.D., Gen. Theol. Sem., '13; S.T.D., Western Theol. Sem., 1922. Pres. and dean, Western Theol. Sem. since 1927. Author (see Who's Who in America). Residence: 2145 Orrington Ave., Evanston, Ill.

1-**GRANT, W(illiam) Henry,** *b* Phila., Pa., Dec. 17, 1858.
7-Edward **Grant** (ca. 1632-1682), shipwright, Boston; *m* ante 1656, Sarah Ware (1629-90; William[8], freeman, Dorchester, Mass., 1643, ruling elder, 1640, removed to Boston, ante 1653, *m* Eliza-);
6-Joseph (*b* 1660), *m* 1704, Mary Thacher (1671-ca. 1709 ?; Judah[7], *m* ca. 1666, Mary [ca. 1640-1708], to Yarmouth with father, buried Copp Hill, dau. of Thomas Thornton [*b* Yorkshire, Eng., 1609-*d* Boston, 1700/01], came to Yarmouth, Mass., 1662, non-conformist minister; Anthony[8], qv);
5-Samuel (1705-84), *m* 1729, Elizabeth Cookson (1708-78; John[6], *m* 1704, Rachel, dau. of Richard Proctor);
4-Moses (1744-1817), mem. Boston Com. of Inspection, Correspondence and Safety in Am. Rev.; *m* 2d, 1773, Sarah Pierce (1753-92; Capt. Joseph[5], *m* Sarah, dau. of Edward Cruft, *m* Abigail Foster [Capt. John[7] (1666-1723), *m* 1st, Sarah, dau. of John Richardson, g.dau. of Amos Richardson (*d* Stonington, Conn., 1683), Boston mcht. tailor, freeman Boston, 1665, rep. Stonington, 1676-77; William[8] (1618-98), mariner, captain of the "Dolphin," 1669, of Watertown, Mass., *m* Anne (1628-1714), dau. of William Brackenbury, *m* Alice-]);
3-George (1790-1849), *m* 1819, Sophia Bradford;
2-Charles Henry (2 below).
9-John **Woodson** (qv);
8-Robert, *m* ca. 1656, Elizabeth Ferris (Richard[9]);
7-Mary, *m* 1704, George **Payne**;
6-Josias (1705-85), *m* ca. 1732, Hannah or Anna Fleming;
5-Josias (1735-1804), *m* 1755, Elizabeth Fleming (Tarleton[6], *m* Hannah-);
4-Elizabeth Chichester (*b* 1769), first cousin to Dolly Madison (Dorothea Payne); *m* 1785, Henry **Bradford** (1757-1815; William[5], *m* 1754, Mary, dau. of Charles Morgan, *m* Ann-; John[6], *m* ca. 1716, Mary Marr);
3-Sophia (1801-82), *m* George **Grant** (3 above).
7-Richard **Collier,** *m* 1699, Mary Jarvis (John[8], *m* Mary Parkman);
6-Thomas (*b* ca. 1700);
5-Richard, mfr. of brass, Boston; removed to Norwich, Conn., ca. 1775, where he established a foundry; *m* 1759, Mary Green (Thomas[6], *m* Ann, dau. of Robert Calif, *m* Margaret Barton; John[7], *m* Bethia Messenger);
4-Thomas (1761-1842), *m* 1780, Elizabeth Stockwell (1761-1829);
3-Daniel Lewis (1796-1869), *m* 1823, Hetty Larimore (1804-98; David[4], *m* Nancy Clark [David[5], *m* Hannah C. Baird; James[6], *m* Nancy Reed]; Joseph[5], *m* Esther, dau. of David Wherry, *m* Isabella-);
2-Emma Clark (1827-1917), *m* 1848, Charles Henry **Grant** (1824-77), mcht. and mfr., Phila., Pa.; issue: I-George M. (1849-1927; *m* 1873, Ella Whittemore Schenck, 1852-1927); II-Daniel Lewis (1850-93; *m* 1875, Olga Rometch; *m* 2d, 1879, Marguerite Ghia); III-Charles Bradford (1852-1926; *m* 1879, Helen Marie Stevenson); IV-Hetty Collier (*b* 1854; *m* 1877, James Aull, 1845-1928); V-James Ralston (1856-1903; *m* 1882, Margie Bryan Kneass, *b* 1857); VI-Annie Meredith (*b* 1857; *m* 1887, William Torrey Baird, *b* 1855); VII-William Henry (1 above); VIII-Sophie Bradford (1860-87; *m* 1886, David McConaughy, Jr.); IX-Emma (1865-70).
1-Not married. Spl. student U.Pa., grad. with certificate of proficiency, 1878. Engaged in business, 1878-88; travelled in Asia and Eu-

rope visiting Christian missions, 1889-92, on return asso. with Bd. of Foreign Missions of Presbyn. Ch. of U.S.A., and in which he served as sec. for a time; sec. Foreign Missionary Conf. of N. America, 1893-1918, then elected hon. sec. for life; sec. trustees of the Canton Christian College, now the trustees of Lingnan Univ., since 1896, was also treas. about 25 yrs. Presbyterian. Republican. Club: National Arts. Residence: 15 Gramercy Park, New York, N.Y.

1-**GRANT, William Thomas, Jr.,** *b* Stevensville, Pa., June 27, 1876.
9-Matthew **Grant** (qv);
8-John (1642-84), *m* 1666, Mary Hull (1648-1720; Josiah[9]);
7-Josiah (1682-1762), *m* 1714, Sarah Cook (1690-1777; Nathaniel[8]);
6-Ebenezer (1723/24-1765), *m* 1747, Martha Hill (1724-64; Ebenezer[7]);
5-Isaac (1760-1841), *m* 1784, Hannah Tracy (1765-1841; Thomas, III[6]);
4-Charles, *m* Margaret Hines;
3-Elihu (1820-97), *m* Amanda M. Gifford;
2-William Thomas (1852-1928), *m* Amanda Lewis Bird (*b* 1854); issue: I-Elihu (*b* 1873; *m* 1899, Almy Chase, *b* 1872); II-William Thomas, Jr. (1 above); III-Olive (*b* 1886; *m* 1922, Henry Ramage Lilly, *b* 1878).
1-*m* Oct. 5, 1907, Lena Blanche Brownell, *b* Essex Junction, Vt., dau. of Hon. Samuel A. Brownell, of Essex Junction; issue: 1-Marian, *b* New York, N.Y.; 2-Helen Frances, *b* New York.
1-Founder, 1906, and chmn. bd. W. T. Grant Co., chain of dept. stores (see Who's Who in America). Mem. Mchts. Assn. of N.Y., Painters and Sculptors Assn., Boston Post Rd. Assn., Westchester Co. Chamber of Commerce, Home Rule Assn. (Westchester Co.), Am. Peace Soc., Am. Geog. Soc., Am. Museum of Natural History, N.E.H.G.S. Clubs: Athletic (New York), N.Y. Yacht, Knollwood, Pelham Country. Mason. Presbyterian. Residence: 145 W. 55th St., New York, N.Y.

1-**GRAVES, Waller Washington,** *b* Lafayette Co., Mo., Dec. 17, 1860-*d* June 17, 1928.
9-Capt. Thomas **Graves** (ca. 1575-1637), from Eng. in the "Mary and Margaret," with his wife and two sons, 1607/08; settled at Jamestown, Va.; rep. from Smythe's Hundred to 1st Assembly, 1619; cdr. Accomac, 1627; apptd. commr. to build fort at Old Point Comfort; commr. of cts., 1630-32; justice, 1631; *m* Katherine-;
8-John (*d* post 1639), settled in Elizabeth City Co., Va.; *m* Miss Perrin;
7-Ralph (*d* 1667), of New Kent Co., Va.; *m* Rachel Croshaw (Maj. Joseph[8], justice, York Co., Va., 1665, burgess, 1659-60);
6-Ralph (*d* 1794?), *m* Unity White;
5-Henry (ca. 1720-ante 1801), of Granville Co., N.C.; *m* Mary Williams (Lt. Col. John[6]);
4-David of Hanover Co., Va.; *m* Miss Wade;
3-Ralph Wade (1812-47), *m* 1st, 1832, Sarah Dorsey Larsh (*d* 1838);
2-Abram Larsh (2 below).
8-John **Waller** (*b* 1617), from Eng. to Va., 1635; settled in New Kent Co., Va., later at "Enfield," King William Co., Va.; *m* Mary Key, or Kay;
7-John (qv);
6-Col. John (ca. 1699-1776), of Spotsylvania Co.; *m* 1730, Agnes Carr (*d* 1777; Maj. Thomas[7], served in colonial wars, *m* Mary, dau. Cornelius Dabney, qv; Thomas[8]);
5-Thomas (1732-87), of Spotsylvania Co.; sgt. in Va. troops in Am. Rev.; *m* 1770, Sarah Dabney (John[6]);
4-Dabney (1772-1849), of Va.; *m* 1807, Elizabeth Minor (Thomas[5]);
3-Elizabeth Dabney (1808-81), of Spotsylvania; *m* 1830, Henry Smith Ellis **Pollard,** M.D. (1807-70), settled at Lexington, Ky.; removed to Mo.;
2-Martha Elizabeth (1837-1910), of Ky.; *m* 1857, Abram Larsh **Graves** (*b* 1834), of Palmyra, Mo.; issue: I-Henry Ralph (*b* 1858-*d* infancy); II-Waller Washington (1 above); III-Abram Larsh, Jr. (1862-1910; *m* Mrs. Ada [Miller] Ellis, *d*); IV-Sarah Elizabeth (*b* 1866; *m* C. Fred Fenton); V-Emma Jacintha (*b* 1875; *m* James Clemens, *d*).
1-*m* June 30, 1892, Alice Medora Ludwick (qv); issue (all *b* Butler, Mo.): 1-Ludwick, *b* July 8, 1893; ed. William Jewel Coll. and Kansas City Law Sch.; served as maj. U.S.A., with A.E.F. in France during World War; *m* Nov. 26, 1914, Elizabeth Ozelle, dau. of Irving Miller, of Junction City, Kan. (issue: Alice Mary, *b* Mar. 24, 1916; Elizabeth, *b* Aug. 7, 1922); 2-Waller Washington, Jr., *b* Jan. 25, 1898; ed. William Jewel Coll. and Kansas City Law Sch.; served as 2d lt., U.S.M.C., during World War; atty., Kansas City, Mo.; 3-John Lafayette, *b* Sept. 25, 1901; ed. William Jewel Coll., U. of Mo. and Cumberland U. (Tenn.); atty. at law, St. Louis, Mo.
1-Ed. Mo. State U. Admitted to Mo. bar, 1886. Became law partner of Judge John D. Parkinson. Apptd. co. sch. commr., 1886; city atty., 1891; judge 29th circuit, 1898-1904; judge Supreme Ct. of Mo., 1906; elected same, 1908-28 (see Who's Who in America).

1-**GRAVES, Alice Medora Ludwick (Mrs. Waller W.),** *b* Bates Co., Mo., Dec. 30, 1866.
6-Dr. David **Marchand** (1710-61; desc. of Huguenots who fled to Switzerland upon the revocation of the Edict of Nantes); physician at Sonvilier, Switzerland; came in the "Nancy," to Phila., Pa., 1754; settled nr. Hagerstown, Md.; *m* 1744, Judith Marie (Jacot) Gentle (*d* 1789), physician; practiced medicine with her husband;
5-Dr. David (1746-1809), came with his parents; settled at Sewickley Settlement, Pa.; surgeon with rank of capt., 3d Co., 2d Bn., Westmoreland Co., Pa., Militia in Am. Rev.; *m* 1766, Elizabeth Kaemerer (1744-1817; Ludwig[6]);
4-Judith (1772-1829), of Westmoreland Co.; *m* 1787, Henry (Loutzenheiser) **Lutsenheiser** (1761-1834);
3-Susan (1794-1857), of Bates Co., Mo.; *m* 1815, George Washington **Ludwick** (1786-1859), settled at Johnstown, Bates Co., Mo. (Jacob[4], from Germany to Alleghany Co., Pa., pvt. 6th Bn., Berks Co., Pa., Militia in Am. Rev., *m* Martha Madalen Baker?);
2-John Lafayette (2 below).
7-Gerrard **Menefee,** settled in Culpeper Co., Va.; received land grant from Lord Fairfax, 1763; *m* Agnes-;
6-Jonas (*d* 1782), of Culpeper Co.; *m* 1752, Elizabeth- (*d* post 1782);
5-Henry (1754-1844), of Culpeper Co.; Am. Rev.; settled finally in Rappahannock Co., Va.; *m* 1773, Sarah Dollins (1757-1825; Richard[6]);
4-Jonas (1782-1854), removed to Bates Co., Mo., 1846; *m* 1808, Polly Yancey (1787-1849; Philemon[5], Am. Rev.);
3-Philadelphia (1810-70), *m* 1833, James Patterson **Fletcher** (1808-45), of Culpeper, Va. (James[4], pvt. 3d Regt. Light Dragoons, 1777, *m* 1st, 1798, Edy [*d* 1825], dau. of Robert Bywaters);
2-Mary Elizabeth (1834-1909), *m* 1851, John Lafayette **Ludwick** (1829-1900), farmer and merchant; issue: I-John Franklin (*b* 1857; *m* Della McConnell); II-Andrew Bruce (*b* 1859; *m* Roberta Catron); III-Gustave Beuregarde (*b* 1861; *m* Estella McAfee); IV-Alice Medora (1 above); V-Arthur Lee (*b* 1871; *m* Margaret Galleher).
1-*m* June 30, 1892, Waller Washington Graves (qv for issue).
1-B.S., Butler Coll., '85. Mem. D.A.C., D.A.R., U.S.D. 1812, Va. Hist. Soc., Mo. Hist. Soc. Mem. Mo. Bd. Charities, 1920-24. Presbyn. Democrat. Residence: Jefferson City, Mo.

1-**GRAY, Charles Oliver,** *b* Heuvelton, N.Y., June 3, 1867.
7-John **Gray,** from north of Ireland; settled at Worcester, Mass., 1718;
6-John, Jr., *m* Isobel-;
5-Isaac, comd. a company in Battle of Bunker Hill; *m* Mary McLain;
4-Daniel C. (1766-1825), *m* Susanna Crawford (1773-1845);
3-Andrew M. (1801-68), *m* 1826, Sarah Hanna;
2-Walter Rutherford (1831-98), farmer; tp. supervisor; *m* 1861, Mary Jane Chambers (*b* 1838); issue: I-Sarah Jemima (*b* 1862; *m* Charles J. Fuller); II-Mary Lunetta (1864-1926); III-Charles Oliver (1 above); IV-Alfred Walter (*b* 1868; *m* Frances Newman); V-Justin Clarence (*b* 1872; *m* Eva Havens).
1-*m* June 6, 1893, Florence Irene Rollins, *b* Yon-

kers, N.Y., Nov. 5, 1863; dau. of Gustavus Adolphus Rollins, of Yonkers, N.Y.; issue: 1–Charles Oliver, Jr., *b* New York, N.Y., Mar. 25, 1894; A.B., Yale, '17, B. Mus., 1922; *m* June 5, 1927, Mary Wilson; 2–Edward Rutherford, *b* Smithtown, N.Y., July 26, 1896; B.A., Tusculum, '16, Yale, '17; M.A., Harvard, 1921; Ph.D., Yale, 1930; 3–Walter Rollins, *b* Smithtown, Aug. 17, 1900; A.B., Tusculum, '20; LL.B., Yale, 1924.
1–A.B., Hamilton Coll., '90 (D.K.E., P.B.K.), A.M., 1896; grad. Union Theol. Sem., 1894; post-grad. work Columbia and New York univs. (D.D., Hamilton, 1908; LL.D., Tusculum, 1920). Ordained Presbyn. ministry, 1893; held pastorates at Smithtown Branch, N.Y., Marshall, N.C.; pres. Tusculum Coll., 1908– (see Who's Who in America). Served with Y.M.C.A. at Camp Gordon during World War. Mem. S.A.R., Religious Edn. Assn., Southern Sociol. Congress. Residence: Greeneville, Tenn.

1–**GRAY, Carl Raymond,** *b* Princeton, Ark., Sept. 28, 1867.
8–Robert **Gray** (qv);
7–Robert (*d* 1718), *m* Miriam Lovejoy;
6–Robert (1706-67), *m* Lydia Peabody;
5–Robert (1729-1806), *m* Mrs. Abigail Chandler;
4–Rev. Robert (1761-1822), A.B., Harvard, 1786; Congl. minister; soldier Am. Rev.; *m* Lydia Tufts;
3–Dr. Peter Tufts (1790-1839), physician, Jefferson, Me.; *m* Elizabeth Kennedy;
2–Oliver Crosby (2 below).
9–Gov. William **Bradford,** Mayflower Pilgrim (qv);
8–Maj. William (1624-1704), *m* Mary (Atwood) Holmes;
7–Israel (1679-1760), *m* Sarah Bartlett (1681-1761);
6–Joshua (1710-58), *m* Hannah Bradford (1719-58);
5–Sarah, *m* Lt. John **Davis**;
4–Cornelius (1765-1845), *m* Hope Adams (1763-1853);
3–George (1798-1870), *m* Catherine Young (1804-49);
2–Virginia Lafayette (1834-86), *m* 1858, Oliver Crosby **Gray,** LL.D. (1831-1906), prof. U.Ark.; issue: I–Carl Raymond (1 above); II–Ethel (1871-1909; *m* LeRoy Kramer).
1–*m* Dec. 6, 1886, Harriette Flora (qv for genealogy and issue).
1–Prep. dept., U.Ark.; (LL.D., Md. State College Agr., 1916, U.Ark., 1929). President U.P. System, 1920— (see Who's Who in America). Mem. S.M.D., I.A.G., etc. Clubs: Metropolitan (New York), Army and Navy (Chicago), Omaha, Athletic, University, Omaha Country, Jonathan (Los Angeles). Summer place: Pleasant Point, Me. Residence: St. Regis Apts., Omaha, Neb.

1–**GRAY, Harriette Flora (Mrs. Carl R.),** *b* Liberty, Kan., Sept. 17, 1869.
8–Johannes (Ster, Starin, Staring) **Sterling** (*d* 1699), sailor; from Holland to New Amsterdam and became Indian trader; settled at Ft. Orange ca. 1670;
7–Nicholas (1663-1759), *m* Catharine–;
6–Adam (1688-1778);
5–Col. Heinrich (1730-1808), judge, Herkimer Co., N.Y., *m* Elizabeth Kash;
4–John, began to write name Sterling; *m* Phoebe Ann Aihme;
3–Harriette Catherine (1824-1905), *m* 1845, Elijah **Shults** (1824-60);
2–Mary Elizabeth (1851-74), *m* 1866, John Alexander **Flora** (*b* 1845).
1–*m* Dec. 6, 1886, Carl Raymond Gray (qv for genealogy); issue: 1–Carl Raymond, Jr. (see Vol. I, p. 303); 2–Russell Davis, *b* Wichita, Kan., Nov. 2, 1899; pvt. U.S. Marine Corps, World War; *m* Oct. 8, 1921, Eleanor, dau. of Herbert Pitt (issue: Eleanor Howard); 3–Howard Kramer, *b* St. Louis, Mo., Aug. 28, 1901; Princeton, '23; Harvard Med. School, 1927, *m* Sept. 2, 1925, DeWeena, dau. of J. H. Conrad.
Residence: St. Regis Apts., Omaha, Neb.

1–**GRAYSON, Clifford Mallet-Prevost,** *b* Philadelphia, Pa., July 14, 1857.
6–Benjamin **Grayson** (*d* 1757), from Scotland, settled at "Belle Air," Dumfries, Prince William Co., Va.; *m* Susannah Monroe (Andrew[7]; Andrew[8], qv); sister of Andrew Monroe, who was g.father of Pres. James Monroe;
5–Rev. Spence (1734-98), ed. Oxford U.; rector of Dettinger Parish, Prince William Co., Va.; chaplain of Grayson's additional Cont. Regt. in Am. Rev.; married Mary Elizabeth Waggener;
4–Benjamin (*b* 1761), of Bardstown, Ky.; *m* Caroline Taylor, of Eng.;
3–Capt. Alfred, U.S.M.C. (*d* 1823), *m* 1816, Elizabeth Coulter (1794-1858);
2–Frederick William Spence (2 below).
7–Henri (Mallet) **Mallet-Prevost** (1660-1728), *m* 1688, Louise Flournoy;
6–Jean Gabriel (1688-1752), *m* Jeanne Marguerite Masson;
5–Henri (1727-1811), *m* Jeanne Gabriella Prevost;
4–Paul Henri, called P. H. Mallet-Prevost (1750-1835), came to U.S. at time of French Rev.; was judge of Circuit Ct. of N.J.; founded Frenchtown, N.J.; *m* Jeanne Elisabeth Patry (*b* 1757);
3–Andre (1780-1850), *m* Hannah Coulter;
2–Mary (1822-1905), *m* 1852, Frederick William Spence **Grayson** (1818-1901), mem. Phila. bar; issue: I–Frederick William Spence, Jr. (1853-1910; *m* Kate Julius); II–Clifford Mallet-Prevost (1 above); III–Dr. Charles Mallet-Prevost (*b* 1859).
1–*m* Jan. 21, 1902, Anna Lewis Steel, *b* Phila., Pa., Nov. 23, 1867; dau. of Edward T. Steel, founder of Edward T. Steel & Co., mfrs., pres. Phila. Bd. of Public Edn. many yrs., mem. bd. of finance of Centennial Exposition, Phila., 1876; issue: 1–Helene Steel, *b* Germantown, Pa., Oct. 31, 1902; Bryn Mawr, '26; 2–Clifford Spence Monroe, *b* Germantown, Phila., Pa., Mar. 14, 1905; Harvard, '27; Harvard Law Sch., 1931.
1–Ed. U. of Pa.; Atelier Gerome, École des Beaux Arts, Paris, France. Artist (see Who's Who in America). Mem. S.R. Clubs: Century, Salmagundi, Art. Residence: Old Lyme, Conn.

1–**GREEN, Frederick William,** *b* Rock Island, Ill., Apr. 30, 1877.
10–Thomas **Davenport** (qv);
9–Charles (bap. 1652-1720), first town clk. of Leominster, Mass.; *m* Waitstill Smith (1669-1747);
8–Charles (*b* 1700), *m* 1722, Jemima Tolman (*d* 1735);
7–Charles (1730-1805), *m* 1755, Mary Hart (1734-1830);
6–Jemima (*b* 1759), *m* Joseph **Gilbert,** soldier Am. Rev.;
5–Mary, *m* Disbrow **Webb**;
4–Mary (1803-79), *m* 1822, Jesse **Johnson** (1798-1876);
3–Harriet (1828-87), *m* 1850, William C. **Green** (1822-96);
2–William Edward (*b* 1853), *m* 1876, Alvira Anne Davis (*b* 1855; John C.[3] [*b* N.Y.-*d* 1876?], *m* Jane Renfro, *b* 1834-living 1929).
1–*m* June 26, 1901, Jane Ryley Rhodes, *b* Wichita, Kan., Nov. 30, 1880; dau. of George Edwin Rhodes, of Harper, Kan., *m* Emma Myers Sharpless; issue: 1–William Edwin, *b* Sioux City, Ia., Nov. 24, 1902; Princeton, '25; *m* Feb. 23, 1928, Louise Elisabeth, dau. of Murray David Wimston, of Hamilton, O. (issue: Frederick William, II); 2–Theron Rhodes, *b* Little Rock, Ark., June 25, 1905; Princeton, '29; 3–Dorothy Louise, *b* Stamps, Ark., Nov. 19, 1907.
1–Vice pres. and dir. St. Louis Southwestern Ry. Lines, 1919— (see Who's Who in America). Commd. capt., 12th Engrs., U.S.A., May 7, 1917; maj., July 1, 1918. Served with 3d British Army in France; supt. Army Transport Service, Brest, and St. Nazaire, France; later cdr. 1st Grand Div. Transport Corps; hon. disch., Mar. 13, 1919. Awarded D.S.M. (U.S.); Officier Legion d'Honneur (France). Mem. S.R., M.O.W.W., A.L. Episcopalian. Clubs: Dallas (Tex.) Country, Bellerive Country, Noonday, Circle (St. Louis). Summer place: Alhaldie, Okoboji, Ia. Residence: 6203 Washington Av., St. Louis, Mo.

1–**GREEN, Olive Luella Banwell (Mrs. Walter H.),** *b* Vienna Cross Roads, O., Mar. 9, 1872.
10–Lt. Ralph **Sprague** (qv);
9–Ens. Phineas (1637-90), of Malden, Mass.; mem. Gen. Ct., 1689; in King Philip's War; *m* 1669, Sarah Hasey (1649-1718; Lt. William[10], officer in King Philip's War, *m* Sarah–);

8–William (1672-1704), of Andover, Mass.; *m* Hannah Spofford (Francis[9], a first settler, Rowley, Mass., *m* Mary Leighton; John[10], *m* Elizabeth Scott);
7–Edward (*d* 1730), of Andover; *m* 1721, Martha Look (Jonathan[8], *m* Mary Curtis, of Rowley);
6–Joseph (1730-56), of Andover and Methuen; *m* ca. 1751, Jemima Wilson (James[7], *m* Martha Gage, of Haverhill);
5–James (1753-1832), of Pelham, N.H.; Am. Rev.; *m* 1774, Persis Huse (Abel[6], *m* Mary Whittier, of Pelham);
4–James (1784-1844), of Barnston, Quebec, and Clark Co., O.; prominent farmer; *m* 1811, Mary Bailey (1791-1870; Timothy[5], ens. Am. Rev., *m* Zerviah Blodgett; Richard[6], Am. Rev.);
3–Darius (1816-82), of Harmony Twp., O.; prominent farmer and stock raiser; *m* 1837, Sarah Rice;
2–Lucina Elnora (2 below).
10–Dea. Edmund **Rice** (qv);
9–Thomas (1622-81), of Marlboro, Mass.; *m* Mary King;
8–Thomas (1654-1747), of Westboro, Mass.; *m* 1681, his cousin, Anna Rice (*b* 1661; Edward[9], *m* Agnes Bent);
7–Thomas (*b* 1683), of Westboro; *m* 1722, Mary (Holloway) Oakes (*b* 1681; Adam Holloway[8], *m* Hannah Hayward; Joseph[9]);
6–Asa (1726-78), of Northboro, Mass.; soldier French and Indian War; sgt. Am. Rev.; *m* Elizabeth Livermore (1725-75; Jonathan[7], *m* Abigail Ball);
5–Israel (*b* 1757), of Northboro; soldier Am. Rev.; *m* Sarah Maynard (Phineas[6], *m* Dorothy Rice);
4–Edward (1784-1843), prominent farmer and stock raiser; one of the first settlers of Clark Co., O.; *m* ca. 1808, Lucy Poole (1792-1877; William[5], Am. Rev., *m* Lois, dau. of Capt. Abijah Moore, Am. Rev.);
3–Sarah (1816-90), of Clark Co.; *m* Darius **Sprague** (3 above);
2–Lucina Elnora (1840-1907), of Clark Co., and Orleans, Neb.; *m* 1867, William Henry **Banwell** (1832-1912), physician and surgeon; lt. and capt. in Union Army throughout Civil War; later mem. U.S. secret service dept. (William Henry[3], *m* Hannah Castle); issue: I–Jessie Hannah (1868-1927; *m* Edgar Leland Means); II–Olive Luella (1 above); III–William Hayes (*b* 1876; *m* Myrtle McInroy).
1–*m* Dec. 18, 1890, Walter Henry Green, *b* nr. Elizabeth, Ill., Mar. 30, 1868; son of George H. Green, *m* Mary Tredinnick; issue: 1–Lucile, *b* Orleans, Neb., July 13, 1895; *m* Jan. 9, 1917, Joseph Charles Schaf, of Indianapolis, Ind. (issue: Martha Ann; Lucile Green).
1–Mem. D.F.P.A., D.A.R. Episcopalian. Republican. Residence: 3848 Washington Boul., Indianapolis, Ind.

1–**GREENE, Roger Sherman,** *b* Roxbury, Mass., Dec. 14, 1840.
5–William **Greene,** of Great Milton, Oxfordshire, Eng.; *m* Katherine Sloan, and as his widow, came to America;
4–William (*b* on passage to America, 1720?), port collector, Boston, Mass.;
3–Thomas (1757-1843), of Stoneham, Mass.; pvt. in Cont. Army; his 2 older brothers were capts., another a pvt. in Am. Rev.; *m* Anna Knight;
2–Rev. David (2 below).
8–John **Evarts** (1601-99), from Eng.; settled Guilford, Conn., 1650; *m* Elizabeth–;
7–James (1638-82), *m* Lydia Goodrich;
6–James (1667-1739), *m* Mary Carter;
5–Reuben (1719-96), *m* Honor Evarts;
4–James (1752-1824), *m* Sarah Todd, of Sunderland, Vt.;
3–Jeremiah (1781-1831), of Sunderland, Vt.; B.A., Yale; philanthropist, editor, 1802; *m* 1804, Mehetable Sherman (their son, William Maxwell [1818-1901], was atty. gen. of U.S., 1868-69, in cabinet of Pres. Johnson; sec. of state, 1877-81, in cabinet of pres. Hayes; U.S. Senator from N.Y., 1885-91);
2–Mary (2 below).
7–Capt. John **Sherman** (qv);
6–Joseph (1650-1731), *m* Elizabeth Winship (Edward[7]);
5–William (1692-1741), of Newton, Mass.; *m* Mehitable Wellington (Benjamin[6]);
4–Roger (1721-93), of Newton; a "signer"; U.S. senator from Conn.; *m* 2d, 1763, Rebecca Prescott;
3–Mehetable (1774-1851), *m* 2d, Jeremiah **Evarts** (3 above).

GREENE

Arms: Azure, three bucks trippant or, a mullet pierced or, for difference.
Crest: A buck's head erased draped ermine, a mullet pierced or.

8–John **Prescott** (qv);
7–Jonathan (1643-1721), of Watertown, Mass.; rep. Gen. Assembly, Concord, Mass., 9 yrs.; capt. state militia; *m* 1675, Elizabeth Hoar (*d* 1687; John[8], lawyer, Concord, Mass.; Joanna, widow of Charles Hoar[9], came to America);
6–Rev. Benjamin (1687-1777), of Salem; writer on pre-Revolutionary controversy; Harvard grad.; *m* 1715, Elizabeth Higginson (1696-1723; John[7]; Rev. Francis[8]);
5–Benjamin (1717-78), Harvard, 1736; of Salem, merchant and justice of peace; *m* 1741, Rebecca Minot (1720-61; James[6], *m* Martha Lane);
4–Rebecca (*b* 1742), of Salem; *m* Roger **Sherman** (4 above);
3–Mehetable, *m* Jeremiah **Evarts** (3 above);
2–Mary (1806-50), *m* 1829, Rev. David **Greene** (1797-1866), Yale, 1821, Andover, 1826; sec. A.B.C.F.M.; issue: I–David B. (1830-63; *m* Mary Augusta Green); II–Mary E. (1832-93); III–Anna (1833-1917; *m* Lewis H. Boutell); IV–Jeremiah Evarts (1834-1902; *m* Mary Bassett); V–Samuel (1835-1922; *m* Sarah E. Moore); VI–Sarah E. (1837-1922; *m* Samuel W. Boardman); VII–Martha S. (1838-1909; *m* Jeremiah Evarts Tracy); VIII–Roger Sherman (1 above); IX–Daniel C. (1843-1913; *m* Mary Jane Forbes); X–Jane H. (1845-1920; *m* Henry B. Loomis); XI–William J. (1847-64); XII–Henry H. (1849-1919; *m* Mary A.–).
1–*m* Aug. 17, 1866, Grace Wooster (May 2, 1833-Sept. 4, 1917); dau. of Jesse G. Wooster, of Naugatuck, Conn.; issue: 1–Agnes Margaret, *b* Chicago, Ill., Oct. 18, 1868; B.A., U.Wash., '85, B.A., U.Ore., 1891; *m* Oct. 18, 1898, Arthur L., son of Edmund Veazie, of Dallas, Ore. (issue: Grace E.; Emily A.; Harriet L.; Edmund A.); 2–Roger Sherman, Jr., *b* E. Berlin, Conn., Sept. 29, 1870; B.A., U.Wash., '94; *m* Sept. 6, 1907, Edith J., dau. of Halsey M. Jones, of Seattle, Wash. (issue: Roger Sherman, III; David Monroe); 3–Grace Evarts, *b* Olympia, Wash., Jan. 15, 1875; B.A., U.Wash., '02; *m* Sept. 25, 1906, George Kerr, son of William McConkey, of Hall's Prairie, B.C., Can.; 4–Mary Rhoda, *b* Olympia, July 27, 1876; B.A., U.Wash., '03; *m* Aug. 8, 1905, Cyrus A., son of Edmund P. Whipple, of Eugene, Ore. (issue: Cyrus Avery; Evarts Wooster).
1–*m* 2d, Aug. 4, 1918, May Collins (Kimball) Jones (Nov. 5, 1844-Jan. 15, 1929); dau. of Phillip Sargent Kimball, M.D., *m* Priscilla McIntyre, of Sutton, N.H.
1–A.B., Dartmouth, '59; (LL.D., U.Wash., 1887, D.D., South Chili Mission Corp., 1921). Retired judge and lawyer. Admitted to bar,

N.Y., 1862, Ill., 1866, Wash., 1887, U.S. Supreme Ct., 1869, Calif., 1919. Asso. justice Supreme Ct. of Wash., 1870-79, chief justice 1879-87; master in chancery, Seattle, 1905-17. Known as "Father of Lake Washington Canal." Apptd. by Gov. Magoffin, of Mo., 2d lt., 3d Mo. Vol. Inf., 1862; 1st lt., 1863; capt. Co. C, 51st U.S. Colored Regt., by Pres. Lincoln, 1863; hon. disch., 1865. Mem. S.A.R., G.A.R., M.O.L.L., Wash. State Hist. Soc., Dartmouth Assn. (see Who's Who in America). Baptist. Republican. Residence: 5219 22 Av., N.E., Seattle, Wash.

1–**GREENOUGH, Robert Battey,** *b* Cambridge, Mass., Nov. 9, 1871.
7–Robert **Greenough** (1654-1718), from Eng. to Rowley, Mass., ca. 1687; selectman, 1691; town clk.; *m* 1679, Martha Eppes (1654-86; David[8], *m* Elizabeth Symonds);
6–Daniel (1686-1764), *m* 1722, Hannah Balch;
5–James (1735-1815), Bradford, Mass.;
4–Parker (1775-1841), Bradford;
3–James (1802-85), Portland, Me.; *m* 1829, Catherine Greenough;
2–James Bradstreet (1833-1901), of Portland, Me.; prof. Latin, Harvard U., 1865-1900; *m* 1860, Mary Battey Ketchum (1835-93); issue: I–James Jay (1861-1913; *m* Katherine Nash Noble); II–Robert Battey (1 above).
1–*m* Oct. 16, 1900, Amelia Mackay Goodwin, *b* Cambridge, Mass., June 5, 1872; dau. of Hersey Bradford Goodwin, of Cambridge; issue: 1–Mary, *b* Boston, Sept. 11, 1901; Vassar, '23; *m* Oct. 15, 1927, Lloyd Bankson, son of James Means, of Manchester, Mass. (issue: Robert Greenough); 2–Ellen, *b* Boston, Jan. 31, 1903; *m* Jan. 19, 1924, Hardwick, son of Ernest Millmore Stires, of Garden City, L.I. (issue: Sarah Hardwick; Leslie); 3–Barbara, *b* Boston, Mar. 10, 1907; 4–Leslie, *b* Scituate, Mass., Aug. 26, 1910; Vassar, '32.
1–A.B., Harvard, '92, M.D., 1896. Visiting surgeon, Mass. Gen. Hosp., since 1915; asst. prof. surgery, Harvard Med. Sch., since 1909; surgeon in charge Collis P. Huntington Memorial Hosp. and dir. cancer commn. of Harvard U. (see Who's Who in America). Med. insp. (cdr.) U.S.N.R.F. Fellow Am. Coll. Surgeon, Am. Acad. Arts and Sciences, etc. Clubs: St. Botolph. Summer place: Osterville, Mass. Residence: 93 Ivy St., Brookline, Mass.

1–**GREENWOOD, Allen,** *b* Chelsea, Mass., Mar. 1, 1866.
7–Thomas **Greenwood** (1643-93; g.g.s. of John Greenwood, the separatist who started the Puritan faith, hung at Tyburn, London, for heresy, 1593); came from Eng., 1665; settled at Newton, Mass.; town clk.; *m* 1670, Hannah Ward (1651-86);
6–John (1673-1737), of Newton; selectman; *m* Hannah Trowbridge (1672-1728);
5–Josiah (*b* 1709), lt. Cont. Army; *m* 1731, Phebe Stearns (1711-63);
4–Moses (1748-1827), *m* 1772, Elizabeth Greenwood (1754-1827);
3–Moses (1776-1827), served in War 1812; *m* ca. 1796, Asenath Hill (1768-1851);
2–William Allen (1806-91), farmer, Waltham, Mass.; *m* 1835, Martha Green (1813-58); *m* 2d, 1860, Caroline Carleton (1825-1917); issue (1st marriage): I–William (1837-53); II–Mary (*b* 1838; *m* Dr. Charles M. Carleton); III–Arthur (1845-46); IV–Annie (*b* 1850; *m* Dr. George H. Jennings); issue (2d marriage): I–Maria (*b* and *d* 1862); II–Edward (*b* 1864; *m* Carrie Arras); III–Allen (1 above); IV–Grace (1868-1916), and V–Carrie (1868-69), twins; VI–Cora (*b* 1871).
1–*m* June 23, 1892, Bertha Underhill (1872-1915); dau. of Jesse Underhill, of Somerville, Mass.; issue: 1–Elizabeth (*b* and *d* 1899).
1–*m* 2d, Mar. 8, 1917, Hope Whipple (1894-1921); dau. of John Whipple, of Pawtucket, R.I.; issue: 1–Allen, *b* Washington, D.C., Dec. 17, 1917; 2–Carolyn, *b* Boston, Mass., Dec. 24, 1919.
1–*m* 3d, Aug. 16, 1924, Marion Tucker, *b* Dedham, Mass., July 4, 1893; dau. of Frederick M. Tucker, of Dedham; issue: 1–Grace, *b* Boston, Mass., Jan. 31, 1926.
1–M.D., Harvard, '89. Apptd. acting asst. surgeon, U.S.A., 1898, and assigned to 19th U.S. Inf., Ponce, P.R.; hon. lt. col. Royal Army Med. Corps, with British E.F. in France, summer, 1916; mem. sub. com. on ophthalmology, Gen. Med. Bd. of Council Nat. Defense, 1917; commd. maj. M.C. U.S.A., 1917, and on duty, surgeon gen.'s office, Washington; lt. col. M.C., sr. consultant in ophthalmology for A.E.F., 1918; col. M.R.C., U.S.A., 1919. Prof. ophthalmology, Tufts Med. Sch. (see Who's Who in America). Club: Harvard. Residence: Wellesley Hills, Mass.

1–**GREGG, Albert L.,** *b* Nevada, O., Feb. 13, 1866.
5–Robert **Gregg** (*d* 1789), sailed from Ireland for America, died on voyage;
4–Andrew (1770-1817), from Ireland, 1789; settled at Redstone, Washington Co., Pa., removed to Doublin, Jefferson Co., O.; *m* Jane Scott (1772-1851);
3–William (1802-78), removed to Crawford Co., O.; *m* Margaret Smith or Smyth (1804-55);
2–William Smith (1841-77), served in Civil War; *m* 1864, Louisa Jane Welty (*b* 1843); issue: I–Albert L. (1 above); II–Fred Marion (qv for maternal lineage).
1–*m* Dec. 24, 1893, Stella Hilborn Noblett, *b* Nevada, O., Nov. 16, 1869; dau. of Amos Hilborn Noblett, of Nevada.
1–Dentist, Cleveland, O. Mayor of Nevada, O., 1906-10. Mason, K.P. Residence: 6703 Bridge Av., Cleveland, O.

1–**GREGG, Fred Marion,** *b* Nevada, Ohio, Mar. 17, 1867.
5–Edward **Otis** (*b* Lyme, Conn., 1766), from Vt. to Ohio, 1810; *m* 1787, Mary Merrill;
4–Ezekiel (*b* Vt., 1790), soldier War 1812; *m* 1815, Mrs. Mary Miller Stansberry;
3–Marilla (*b* 1818), *m* —**Welty**;
2–Louisa Jane (*b* 1843), *m* 1864, William Smith **Gregg** (1841-77), served in Civil War; issue: I–Albert L. (qv for Gregg lineage); II–Fred Marion (1 above).
1–*m* June 30, 1898, Carrie Pettis Cockerill, *b* Lincoln, Mo., Dec. 18, 1869; dau. of Edward Estill Cockerill, of Fayette Co., O.; issue (all *b* Wayne, Neb.): 1–Genevieve Fana, *b* Aug. 21, 1899; Peru State Teachers Coll., '19; *m* 1928, Frank Hubbard; 2–Otis Cockerill, *b* Mar. 17, 1904; U.S.M.A., '27; 3–Helen Louise, *b* Apr. 19, 1905; Neb. Wesleyan U., '27.
1–A.B., Ohio Northern U., '94 (Phi Delta Kappa, Phi Kappa Phi, Phi Gamma Mu); A.M., U.-Chicago, 1915. Mem. Neb. Ho. of Rep., 1903-04; head dept. psychology, Neb. Wesleyan U., since 1919. Author (see Who's Who in America). Methodist. Republican. Residence: 5320 Leighton Av., Lincoln, Neb.

1–**GREGORY, Tappan,** *b* at Madison, Wis., Aug. 29, 1886.
8–Abraham **Tappan** (qv);
7–Samuel (*b* 1670), *m* 1702, Abigail Wigglesworth;
6–Benjamin (1720-90), *m* 1745, Elizabeth Marsh;
5–Benjamin (1747-1831), *m* 1770, Sarah Homes (1748-1826);
4–Arthur (1786-1865), *m* 1810, Frances Antill;
3–Benjamin Edward Antill (1813-62), *m* 1852, Rachel Bromby Staines;
2–Janet Macindoe (see Vol. I, p. 305, for Morris lineage), *m* 1880, Stephen Strong **Gregory** (1849-1920), brother of Charles Noble Gregory (see Vol. I, p. 305, for Gregory lineage).
1–Not married. B.A., Yale, '10 (Psi U.); LL.B., Northwestern, 1912 (Phi Delta Phi). Mem. law firm of Bayley, Merrick, Webster & Gregory, Chicago; asso. editor Am. Maritime Cases; has contributed a number of articles to Journal of Mammalogy; hon. curator of mammals, Chicago Acad. of Sciences. Author: Deer at Night in the North Woods. First lt., 313th F.A., Nov. 1917-June 1919; in France, May 1918-May 1919. Mem. Chicago Council on Foreign Relations, Am., Ill. State and Chicago bar assns., Am. Branch Internat. Law Assn., Chicago Law Inst., Am. Soc. Internat. Law, Field Mus. of Natural History, Am. Soc. Mammalogists, Mich. Acad. of Science, Arts and Letters, Geog. Soc. of Chicago, Chicago Hist. Soc., A.L., 80th Div. Vet.'s Assn., etc. Clubs: Press, Chicago, Camp Fire of Chicago, Yale, Northwestern University. Address: 19 S. La Salle St., Chicago, Ill.

1–**GREIG, Bessie Stearns (Mrs. Hugh Scott),** *b* Hampton, Ia., Oct. 19, 1871.
9–Charles **Stearns,** from Eng., 1646; settled at Watertown, Mass.; freeman, 1646; *m* 1654, Re-

becca Gibson (*b* 1635), of Cambridge;
8–John (1657-1722), of Cambridge; *m* 1681, Judith Lawrence (1660-1713);
7–George (1688-1790), of Watertown; *m* 1712, Hannah Sanderson (1689-1770);
6–Jonathan (1713-58), of Watertown; *m* 1736, Beulah Chadwick (1719-1804);
5–Capt. John (1751-1841), of Mendon, Mass.; soldier Am. Rev.; *m* 1779, Lucy Merril (1759-1835);
4–John (1783-1865), of Lee, Mass.; *m* 1808, Nancy Esleeck (*b* 1792);
3–John Esleeck (1810-73), of Castleton, N.Y.; *m* 1831, Elizabeth Proseus (1810-1906);
2–John Tyler (2 below).
11–Gov. William **Bradford,** Mayflower Pilgrim (qv);
10–Maj. William (1624-1703), *m* 1651, Alice Richards (1627-71);
9–Alice (*b* 1661), *m* 1680, Rev. William **Adams** (1650-85);
8–Alice (1682-1735), *m* 1701, Rev. Nathaniel **Collins** (1672-1756), of Enfield, Conn.;
7–Ann (*b* 1702), *m* 1723, Maj. Ephraim **Terry** (1701-83), of Enfield;
6–Mary (1724-83), of Enfield; *m* 1739, Ebenezer **Pease** (1719-84);
5–Ebenezer (*b* 1742), *m* 1771, Hulda Pease (*b* 1752);
4–George (1776-1845), *m* 1797, Esther Thompson (*b* 1777);
3–Jesse Thompson (1808-82), *m* 1833, Laura Ann Mallett (1815-1901);
2–Evelyn (*b* 1848), of Pringhar, Ia.; *m* 1869, John Tyler **Stearns** (1841-1907), atty.-at-law; issue: I–John Jesse (*d* infancy); II–Bessie (1 above); III–Glow Esleeck (*b* 1879; *m* William Brooks).
1–*m* Feb. 3, 1895, Hugh Scott Greig, *b* Toronto, Ont., Apr. 3, 1867; issue: 1–John Ebenezer, *b* Emery, S.D., Apr. 9, 1896; B.A., U.Minn., '17; *m* Nov. 10, 1921, Florence, dau. of Gail Morse, of Estherville, Ia.; 2–Mary Evelyn, *b* Emery (Jan. 9, 1899-Feb. 17, 1917).
1–Ed. All Saints Sch., Sioux Falls, S.D., and U. of S.D. Mem. D.F.P.A., D.A.R. (state treas.), P.E.O. Residence: Estherville, Ia.

1–**GRIER, Norman Mac Dowell,** *b* Pittsburgh, Pa., June 12, 1890.
5–James **Grier** (*b* 1746), from Ulster, Ireland; settled at Hagerstown, Md.; soldier Am. Rev.; *m* Fannie Grove;
4–Matthew (*b* 1806), dep. mayor, Pittsburgh, Pa.; *m* 1st, Nancy Caldwell; *m* 2d, Rebecca Coates Day;
3–Daniel Gillespie (1829-1926), *m* 1855, Margaret Conn (1831-87);
2–Rev. James Buchanan (1856-1923), minister Christian Ch.; *m* 1880, Marian Agnes Gibson (1859-1922); issue: I–Col. Harry Surgisson (*b* 1880; *m* Louise Strong); II–Jessie Gibson (*b* 1883; *m* John Calvin Webb); III–James Maurice (*b* 1887; *m* Fern Wilcox); IV–Norman MacDowell (1 above); V–Marion Lucas (*b* 1893; *m* Ruth Schiellein); VI–Dorothy Margaret (*b* 1900; *m* Howard Mitchell).
1–*m* Aug. 28, 1915, Margaretta Glover Gibson, *b* Avalon, Pa., Apr. 13, 1892; dau. of William G. Gibson, of Avalon, *m* Nancy Shafer; issue: 1–Elizabeth Frances, *b* St. Louis, Mo., July 8, 1917.
1–*m* 2d, Feb. 21, 1925, Christine Ruth (qv); issue: 1–John James, *b* Hanover, N.H., Feb. 17, 1926.
1–B.S., U.Pittsburgh, '11, A.M., 1912, Ph.D., 1919 (Phi Delta Theta, Phi Sigma, Pi Delta Epsilon, Pi Gamma Mu); studied Yale, 1912-14; U.Paris, 1919. Asst. prof. evolution, Dartmouth, 1923-26; prof. biology, Des Moines U., 1926-27; head dept. of science, State Teachers Coll., West Chester, Pa., 1927-28; prof. biology, Elizabethtown Coll., 1928–; assoc. prof. edn., Ala. Poly. Inst., 1928-29. Served in N.G. Pa., 1907-11; 2d lt., 14th Inf., N.G. Pa., 1911-12; 1st lt. C.W.S., U.S.A., and was gas officer, 5th A.C., 1918-19 (see Who's Who in America). Residence: Elizabethtown, Pa.

1–**GRIER, Christine Ruth (Mrs. Norman MacDowell),** *b* Lebanon, Pa., June 27, 1894.
7–Johannes **Bowman** (1725-85), from Switzerland; settled nr. Annville, Pa.; farmer; supplied grain to Cont. Army;
6–Abraham (*d* 1794), farmer; soldier Am. Rev.; *m* Christina–;
5–John (1773-1814), farmer; *m* Magdalena Ellenburger (1770-1850);
4–Joseph (1804-84), mcht.; *m* 1834, Frances Garman (1814-95);
3–Joseph Andrew (1838-1920), mcht.; *m* 1863, Lydia Ann Strickler (1840-1915);
2–Kate Emma (*b* 1868), *m* 1893, John **Ruth** (*b* 1868), chief reporter of Senate of Pa.; issue: I–Christine (1 above); II–Richard Bowman (*b* 1898; *m* Matilda Bowman).
1–*m* Feb. 21, 1925, Norman MacDowell Grier (qv for issue).
1–A.B., Smith Coll., '15. Mem. D.A.R. Lutheran. Republican. Residence: Elizabethtown, Pa.

JAMES FRANKLIN GRIFFIN (1834-1922), chief q.m. clk., Vt. brig., Army of the Potomac, 1862-65; banker, Topeka, Kan., 1871-87; treas., Washburn College, 1887-1911; retired, Los Angeles, Calif., 1911-22.

1–**GRIFFIN, Frank Loxley,** *b* Topeka, Kan., Aug. 19, 1881.
9–Joseph **Carter,** at Newbury, Mass., 1636;
8–Joseph, *m* Bethia–;
7–Susanna (*b* 1673), *m* 1698, Jonathan **Griffin** (*b* 1670; Matthew[8], qv);
6–Jonathan (1699-1769), *m* 1724, Sarah Hull (1701-91);
5–Sgt. Joseph (1736-1831), Am. Rev.; *m* 1766, Abigail Currier;
4–Jonathan (1769-1860), *m* 1793, Persis Flint;
3–Miles Flint (1802-68), *m* 1833, Cynthia Louisa Alden (1813-1901; desc. John Alden, Mayflower Pilgrim);
2–James Franklin (2 below).
9–Prob. Richard **Currier** (1616-87), Salisbury, Mass., 1640; *m* Anne–;
8–Prob. Samuel (1636-1713), *m* 1668, Mary Hardy (Thomas[9], lived nr. Haverhill, Mass.);
7–Samuel (*b* 1685), of Haverhill; *m* 1714, Abigail Kelly (1691-1734; John[8]; John[9], lived at Newbury, Mass.);
6–Jonathan (1715-76), *m* 1739, Esther Gage;
5–Abigail (1741-1837), *m* Joseph **Griffin** (5 above).
11–Henry **Scott** (desc. Egbert, first king of England), *m* Martha Whatlock, who came to America;
10–Ursula, of Rattlesden Parish, Eng., *m* Richard **Kimball** (qv);
9–Henry (1615-76), from Eng., 1634; *m* Mary Wyatt (John[10], came to America, 1634, *m* Mary–);
8–Sarah (1654-92), *m* 1675, Daniel **Gage** (1639-1705), of Ipswich (Sgt. John[9] [1604-73], from Eng. with Winthrop's fleet, 1630, *m* Amee [Wilford ?], *d* 1658);
7–Daniel (1676-1748), mem. Capt. Haseltine's Bradford Co., 1710; *m* 1697/98, Martha Burbank (1679/80-1745; Caleb[8] [1646-90], *m* 1669, Martha, dau. of Hugh Smith, from Eng., 1642; John[9]

[1600-83], from Eng., settled at Rowley, Mass., 1640, freeman 1640, *m* Jemima–, *d* 1693);
6–Esther (*b* 1716), *m* Jonathan **Currier** (6 above).
9–Thomas **Flint** (qv);
8–Capt. Thomas (1645-1721), *m* 2d, 1674, Mary Dunton (William[9]);
7–Ebenezer (1683-1767), *m* Gertrude Pope (Joseph[8]; Joseph[9]);
6–Ebenezer (*b* 1711), *m* 1737, Mary Putnam (Edward[7]; Edward[8]; Lt. Thomas[9]; John[10], qv);
5–Lt. Miles (1739-1831), 1st lt., Am. Rev.; *m* 1767, Susannah Pillsbury (*b* 1745; Capt. Caleb[6]; Caleb[7]; Moses[8]; William[9], qv);
4–Persis (1772-1860), *m* Jonathan **Griffin** (4 above);
3–Miles F., *m* Cynthia L. Alden (3 above);
2–James Franklin (1834-1922), see portrait and biography; *m* 1880, Hetty Rhees Parson (*b* 1858), see Vol. I, p. 923 for maternal lineage; issue: I–Frank L. (1 above); II–Lt. Col. John Alden (*b* 1883; engr., Los Angeles; *m* Violet Planner); III–James Birney (*b* 1884; *m* Ann Wyatt).
1–*m* Aug. 7, 1905, Mary Louisa Chambers (see Vol. I, p. 923 for genealogy); issue: 1–Helen Chambers, *b* Portland, Ore., Oct. 14, 1906; *m* May 2, 1928, Richard Latham, son of Dr. Charles H. Wollbert; 2–Ruth Hardy, *b* Williamstown, Mass., Mar. 13, 1908; 3–Frank Loxley, Jr., *b* Williamstown, Oct. 27, 1909; 4–Alice Rhees, *b* Portland, Ore., June 24, 1913.
1–S.B., 1903, S.M., 1904, Ph.D., 1906, U.Chicago (P.B.K., Sigma Xi). Prof. mathematics, Reed Coll., Portland, Ore. Author (see Who's Who in America). Mem. S.A.R. Club: University. Residence: 1444 E. 30th St., Portland, Ore.

COL. MICHAEL C. GARBER (1813-81), early Indiana journalist; editor Madison (Ind.) Courier, 1849-81; prominent in the organization of the Republican party and a delegate to its first National Convention, 1856. Because of his expert knowledge of transportation he was recommended for appointment as capt., Q.M. Dept. by Secretary Stanton, and served from Oct. 1861-July 1866; was col. and chief q.m. in the field on General Sherman's staff, 1865.

1–**GRIFFIN, Blanche Ada Garber (Mrs. Philip Van Rensselaer),** *b* Madison, Ind., Jan. 9, 1894.
6–Michael **Garber** (*b* 1707), from the Palatinate, sailed from Rotterdam in the "Hope," to Phila., 1734; *m* Anna– (*b* 1712);
5–Michael (1742-1824), York Co., Pa.; trustee, Staunton, Va., 1780; mayor; gentlemen-justice; *m* 1765, Magdalena Smoot (1744-1830);
4–Michael (1769-1845), Staunton, Va.; ens. 32d regt., colonial forces of Augusta Co., Va., 1795; capt., 1st Bn., 32d Regt.; mem. Augusta Co., Va., militia, "on duty"; *m* 1792, Margaret Smith (1775-1834; Thomas[6], *m* Agnes, dau. of John Cunningham, of Staunton, *m* Sarah–);
3–Michael Christian (1813-81), see portrait; noted editor, of Madison, Ind.; col. q.m. vols. and bvtd. maj., lt. col. and col. vols., Civil War; *m* 1837, Ellen Schell;
2–Michael Christian (2 below).
7–Michael **Schell** (1675-1770), came from the Palatinate, 1732; *m* 1st, Veronica–;
6–John (*b* 1729), of Goshenhoppen, Pa.; *m* 1753, Veronica Maurer (Jacob[7], *m* Sophia–);
5–John (1754-1825), of Schellsburg, Pa.; *m* Elizabeth Hillegas (1763-1842; George Peter[6], *m* Anne Barbara Hornecker; John Frederick[7], from Alsace in the "William and Sarah," 1685, *m* Elizabeth Barbara–);
4–Peter (1784-1862), Schellsburg; justice, 1812; mem. Pa. House of Rep., 1822; apptd. gov. and asso. judge of Bedford Co., 1831,42; burgess, 1832; *m* 1806, Eleanor Statler (1788-1859; Casper[5], *m* Rebecca Walter);
3–Ellen (1817-1908), *m* Michael C. **Garber** (3 above).
9–John **Goode** (1620-1709), from Eng. ante 1660, to Va.; settled at Whitby, Chesterfield Co., Va.; served in Bacon's Indian wars; *m* ca. 1650, Frances Mackarness;
8–Samuel (ante 1660-post 1734), of "Whitby," James River, Va.; *m* Martha Jones;
7–Samuel (1700-97), of Prince Edward Co., Va.; *m* Elizabeth Burwell (g.dau. of Col. Lewis Burwell, *m* Lucy Higginson);
6–Samuel (1749-will made 1796), pvt. in Charlotte Co. militia in Am. Rev.; *m* 1770, Mary Collier (1756-1804; John[7], *m* Elizabeth Meredith; John[8], from Eng. to Little York, Va.);
5–Philip (1771-1824), of Waynesville, O.; *m* 1793, Rebekah Hayes;
4–Samuel Mackarness (1795-1826), of Madison, Ind.; *m* 1824, Sarah Grover (Paul) Cravens;
3–Samuel Mackarness (1825-1909), of Madison; *m* 1846, Eliza Eggleston;
2–Blanche Eggleston (2 below).
9–Richard **Hayes,** from Ireland, ante 1646;
8–Richard, of Isle of Wight Co., Va.;
7–Richard;
6–Richard (*b* bet. 1710-20), provided men and horses and protection for the defenseless against the British; *m* Mary Venable (Abraham[7], qv);
5–Rebekah (1770-1855), of Amelia Co., Va.; *m* Philip **Goode** (5 above).
7–Peter **Paul** (*d* 1742), of Holland; on tax lists of Vincent and Coventry twps., Chester Co., Pa., 1729; *m* Mary–;
6–Michael (*d* 1801), *m* 1750, Ann Parker (1724-25-1813);
5–John (1758-1830), of Madison, Ind.; pvt. Am. Rev.; col. War 1812; *m* 1795, Sarah Thornberry Grover (1775-1866; Josiah[6], *m* Mary, dau. Benjamin Anderson, *m* Sarah Thornberry; William[7], *m* Eleanor–);
4–Sarah (1802-77), as Widow Cravens, *m* 2d, Dr. Samuel M. **Goode** (4 above).
9–Richard **Eggleston** came from England in 1635; settled at "Powhatan," James City Co., Va.; was in battle of Bloody Run against Indians, 1656;
8–Richard;
7–Joseph (1678-1730), of "Powhatan"; burgess; *m* 2d, Anne Pettus (John[8], *m* Anne, dau. Samuel Overton; Thomas[9]; Col. Thomas[10], *m* Mrs. Elizabeth Durant; Sir John[11], of Eng.);
6–William (1729-80), of "Locust Grove," Amelia Co., Va.; *m* 1757?, Judith Cary;
5–Matthew Jacquelin (1763-1839), Amelia Co.; *m* 1789, Anne Cary Eggleston (1771-1816; John[6], *m* Elizabeth Cary);
4–Miles Cary (*b* Va., 1791-*d* 1851), of Franklin and Jefferson cos., Ind.; lawyer, circuit judge; *m* 1822, Jane Elizabeth Sutherland (1795-1869; William[5], *m* Lydia Smith);
3–Eliza (1828-1915), Madison; *m* Dr. Samuel M. **Goode** (3 above).
9–Miles **Cary** (qv);
8–William (ca. 1657-1713), of Parish of Mulberry Island, Warwick Co., Va.; burgess, 1710; *m* Martha Scarbrook or Harwood (Col. John Scarbrook[9], of York Co., Va.);
7–William (*d* 1742), of Warwick Co.; *m* Judith Jones;
6–Judith, *m* William **Eggleston** (6 above).
2–Michael Christian **Garber** (*b* 1850), editor, Madison (Ind.) Courier; *m* 1874, Blanche Eggleston Goode (1852-1922); issue: I–Guilford Schell (1875-1904); II–Hugh Goode (*b*

1878); III–Michael **Eggleston** (*b* 1880; *m* Bessie Payne Hampton); IV–Samuel Mackarness (*b* 1882; *m* Elizabeth Jaques); V–Gladys Elizabeth (1889-91); VI–Blanche Ada (1 above).
1–*m* Nov. 3, 1925, Philip Van Rensselaer Griffin, *b* Evanston, Ill., Nov. 25, 1889; son of William Van Rensselaer Griffin, of Evanston, *m* Nellie Brown; issue: 1–Elizabeth Eggleston, *b* Tampa, Fla., Dec. 4, 1929.
1–Ed. Glendale Coll., Cincinnati; spl. student Coll. of Music, Cincinnati, and Hanover (Ind.) Coll.; certificate, Sch. of Library Science, Pratt Inst., Brooklyn, N.Y., 1920; reference librarian, Indianapolis Public Library, 1920-25; trustee Public Library, Winter Haven, Fla., 1926-27, librarian, 1927-29. Mem. D.F.P.A., A.L.A. Presbyterian. Republican. Summer place: Madison, Ind. Residence: 1004 Av. Z, N.W., Lake Hartridge Manor, Winter Haven, Fla.

1–**GRIFFITH, Frank Carlos,** *b* Dixfield, Me., Dec. 30, 1851.
7–William **Griffith** (*d* 1734), from Eng., ante 1700, settled at Carver, Mass. (?); *m* Lydia–;
6–Samuel (1700-70), *m* 1723, Eleanor Easty (1704-1756?);
5–Ephraim (1733-1823), *m* 1757, Mary Ellis (*b* 1739);
4–John (1763-1840), *m* Mary Boyden (1765-1846);
3–John (1787-1848), *m* 1805, Nancy Wormell (1788-1834);
2–Amos Wormell (2 below).
8–John **Stockbridge** (qv);
7–Charles (1634-83), *m* Abigail James (*b* 1636);
6–Thomas (1667-1717), *m* Sarah Reed (Thomas[7]; William[8]);
5–Micah (*b* 1714), *m* 1738, Mary Jones (*b* 1718; Isaac[6]; Isaac[7]; Edward[8]);
4–John (1757-1820), soldier Am. Rev.; *m* 1785, Mary Dillingham;
3–William (1788-1847), *m* 1816, Sarah Eustis;
2–Azubah Farwell (2 below).
9–Francis **Cooke,** Mayflower Pilgrim (qv);
8–Jacob (*b* in Holland 1618-*d* 1663), to America, 1623; *m* 1646, Damaris Hopkins (Stephen[9], Mayflower Pilgrim, qv);
7–Elizabeth (1648-92), *m* 1667, John **Doty** (*b* 1639; Edward[8], Mayflower Pilgrim, qv);
6–Samuel (1682-1740), *m* 1727, Mercy Cobb (Ebenezer[7]);
5–Marcy (1732-1812), *m* 1751, Edward **Dillingham** (Melatiah[6]; John[7]; Henry[8]; Edmund[9]);
4–Mary (1757-1841), *m* John **Stockbridge** (4 above).
10–Thomas **Buckminster** (*d* 1656), from Wales, ante 1640, settled at Brookline; *m* in Eng., Johanna– (*d* 1676);
9–Joseph (*d* 1668), *m* 1665, Elizabeth Clarke (Hugh[10], *m* Elizabeth–);
8–Col. Joseph (1666-1747), *m* 1686, Martha Sharpe (Lt. John[9], *m* Martha, dau. of Robert Vose; Robert[10], of Braintree, 1642);
7–Col. Joseph (1697-1780), capt. co. of grenadiers in the Port Royal Expdn.; removed to Framingham; *m* 1719, Sarah Lawson (John[8]);
6–Rev. Joseph (1720-92), *m* 1743, Lucy Williams;
5–Sarah (*b* 1747), *m* 1767, Chamberlain **Eustis** (Thomas[6]; William[7]; William[8]);
4–Thomas (1777-1813), *m* 1797, Hannah Graham (John[5]);
3–Sarah (1797-1891), *m* William **Stockbridge** (3 above).
11–Gov. Thomas **Dudley** (qv);
10–Anne (1612-72), the "First American poetess"; *m* 1628, Gov. Simon **Bradstreet** (qv);
9–Dorothy (1630-72), *m* 1654, Rev. Seaborn **Cotton** (1633-86; Rev. John[10], qv);
8–Elizabeth (1665-98), *m* 1686, Rev. William **Williams** (Isaac[9]);
7–Rev. William (*b* 1688), *m* Hannah Stoddard (Solomon[8]; Anthony[9], qv, *m* Mary, dau. of Emanuel Downing, *m* Lucy, dau. of Adam Winthrop);
6–Lucy (1719-1803), *m* Rev. Joseph **Buckminster** (6 above).
2–Amos Wormell **Griffith** (1821-1908), carriage maker; *m* 1844, Azubah Farwell Stockbridge (1826-1916); issue: I–Emma Frances (*m* William S. Carle; *m* 2d, William B. Merrill); II–Frank C. (1 above).
1–*m* May 8, 1884, Mary Catherine Lee, *b* Conesville, N.Y., June 28, 1855; dau. of John Allan Lee, of Catskill, N.Y.
1–Theatrical mgr., 1883-1923; dir. Poland Spring (Me.) Art Exhbn., 12 yrs.; organizer and librarian, Poland Spring Library; editor-in-chief, The Hilltop, 12 yrs. Author (see **Who's** Who in America). Mem. S.A.R., Actor's **Fund.** Propr. in Boston Athenaeum. Summer place: Poland Spring, S. Poland, Me. Residence: 71 Dale St., Roxbury, Mass.

1–**GRIFFITH, William,** *b* Memphis, Mo., Feb. 15, 1876.
5–Samuel **Griffith** (1736-86), from Wales to New York, 1765;
4–Capt. Samuel (1766-1815), soldier War 1812; pioneer to Mo., 1795; one of 1st white settlers, settled nr. St. Charles;
3–Asa (1796-1845), *m* 1841, Elizabeth Johnson;
2–Samuel Parker (2 below).
5–John (Downyng) **Downing** (*b* 1767), of Co. Derry, Ireland;
4–John, to Va., ca. 1819; planter;
3–William G. (1828-1902), from Fauquier Co., Va., to St. Louis, Mo.; *m* Mary Abagail Jones;
2–Minerva (*b* 1860), *m* 1875, Samuel Parker **Griffith** (1850-1907), banker, at Memphis, Mo.; issue: I–William (1 above); II–Marie Louise (*b* 1882).
1–*m* June 25, 1909, Florence Ianthe Vernon, *b* Brooklyn, N.Y., Sept. 28, 1874; dau. of Thomas Vernon (1818-93), of Appledore, Devonshire, Eng., settled at Brooklyn.
1–On staffs of various newspapers and mags., since 1901; editor of Current Opinion, William H. Wise & Co., and Forum Press publications, since 1925. Author (see Who's Who in America). Club: Authors. Summer place: "Appledore," Lime Rock, Conn., and Atlantic, Me. Residence: 15 Gay St. New York, N.Y.

1–**GRIFFITH, Fannie Bradley Lyford (Mrs. John W.),** *b* Detroit, Mich., Sept. 11, 1856.
7–Francis **Lyford** (qv);
6–Stephen (1683-1774), of Exeter, N.H.; *m* 1715, Sarah Leavitt (*d* 1781; Moses[7] [*b* 1650], *m* 1681, Dorothy, dau. of Rev. Samuel Dudley, son of Gov. Thomas Dudley, qv);
5–Moses (ante 1728-99), *m* 1748, Mehitable Smith (*d* 1803 or 06);
4–Oliver Smith (1753-88), Am. Rev.; *m* 1780, Elizabeth Johnson (*b* 1761);
3–Dudley (1781-1856), *m* Betsy Smith;
2–Oliver Smith (1823-1914), v.p. C.&E.I.R.R. Chicago; *m* 1852, Lavinia Amanda Norris (1825-1905); issue: I–Frank E. (*d* infancy); II–Fannie Bradley (1 above); III–Will Hartwell (see Vol. I, p. 306); IV–Harry Brooks (*b* 1861; *m* Josephine L. Goyette); V–Charles Warren (*d* infancy); VI–Oliver Smith (see Vol. I, p. 306).
1–*m* Feb. 5, 1878, John William Griffith, *b* Elizabeth, Ind., Jan. 16, 1849; son of Ephraim J. Griffith; issue: 1–Walter Lyford (see Vol. I, p. 307); *m* Mildred McRary Smith (qv).
1–Ed. Elmira (N.Y.) Coll. Mem. D.F.P.A., D.C.G., C.D.A., D.A.R. Residence: 3825 Cuming St., Omaha, Neb.

1–**GRIFFITH, Mildred McRary Smith (Mrs. Walter L.),** *b* Wilmington, N.C., Apr. 19, 1891.
8–Judge George **Walton** (son Lord Walton, of Eng.), *m* Elizabeth Rowe;
7–Catherine, *m* 1737, Nathaniel **Harris** (*b* 1716);
6–Elias (*b* 1747), *m* Alice Bell;
5–Mildred (*b* 1773), *m* Arthur **Wiggins** (*d* 1812);
4–Thomas Rowe Harris (*d* 1840), *m* 1833, Mary Josephine Arrington (*d* 1845);
3–Rozella Harris (1838-68), *m* 1856, George Alexander **Smith** (*b* 1835); see Vol. III, p. 215, for Smith lineage;
2–George Herbert (2 below).
5–James **Strange,** of Manchester, Va.; a founder, 1791, of a bank in Richmond, Va.;
4–Hon. Robert (*b* Manchester, Va., 1796-*d* "Myrtle Hill," 1854), ed. Hampden-Sydney Coll. (LL.D., Rutgers, 1840); rep. Fayetteville, N.C., in Ho. of Commons, 1821–; judge Superior Ct., 1826–; U.S. senator, 1836–; *m* 1817, Jane Ruffin Kirkland;
3–Col. Robert (*b* nr. Fayetteville, N.C., 1823-*d* 1877), of "Myrtle Hill"; grad. U. of N.C., aet. 17; lawyer; rep. New Hanover Co., N.C., 1852-53; state solicitor; *m* 2d, Elizabeth Maund Andrews;
2–Carolyn Wright (2 below).
6–Abner **Andrews** (*b* 1728), lived on Roanoke River, Bertie Co., N.C.; *m* ca. 1750, Mary Williams;

5–John (*b* 1752), sent to France on govt. service bet. 1781-85; to Edgecombe Co., N.C., ante 1798; *m* 1798, Elizabeth Maund Johnston (1772-1820; Col. Jonas[6]);
4–William Johnston (1800-55), *m* Virginia Hawkins (see Vol. III, p. 215, for Hawkins lineage);
3–Elizabeth Maund (1835-1915), hon. v.p. and charter mem. N.C. Soc. C.D.A.; *m* Col. Robert **Strange** (3 above);
2–Carolyn Wright (*b* 1872), *m* 1890, George Herbert **Smith** (*b* Scotland Neck, Halifax Co., N.C., 1857-*d* Wilmington, N.C., 1921), v.p. Acme Mfg. Co.; issue: I–Mildred McRary (1 above); II–Elizabeth Maund (*b* 1895; *m* Dana Burgess Van Dusen); III–Herbert (*d* infancy); IV–George Herbert, Jr. (*b* 1901).
1–*m* Dec. 23, 1914, Walter Lyford Griffith (see Vol. I, p. 307, for genealogy and issue).
1–Ed. St. Mary's Episcopal Sch., Raleigh, N.C.; Hollins (Va.) Inst.; Nat. Cathedral Sch., Washington, D.C. Mem. C.D.A. Club: Omaha Country. Residence: 3825 Cuming St., Omaha, Neb.

1–**GRIFFITH, Helen Sherman (Mrs. William O.)**, *b* Des Moines, Ia., Feb. 6, 1873.
8–Samuel **Sherman** (qv);
7–Dea. John (*b* 1651), clk., Woodbury, Conn., 1702-27; rep. Conn. Gen. Ct., 1699-1712; speaker, 1711-23; *m* Elizabeth–;
6–John (bap. 1687-1727), *m* 1714, Emma Preston (1688-1733; Hackaliah[7], *m* Emma, dau. of Thomas Fairchild; William[8]);
5–Hon. Daniel (bap. 1721-1799), dep. Gen. Ct., 1754-91; judge Probate Ct., 1758-95; justice of Quorum, 1761-86; Council of Safety, 1777-79; Gov.'s Council, 1777-81; judge Co. Ct., 1786-91; mem. Constl. Conv. of Conn., 1788, which met for the ratification of the Constn. of the U.S.; *m* 1744, Mindwell Taylor (1720-98; Nathan[6], *m* Hannah, dau. of Lt. Daniel Benedict);
4–Judge Taylor (1758-1815), *m* Elizabeth Stoddard (desc. Anthony Stoddard, Boston, 1639);
3–Charles R. (1788-1829), settled in O., 1812, justice Supreme Ct., of Ohio; *m* 1810, Mary Hoyt (*b* 1790), among their sons were John, Sec. of Treas. and Sec. of State in Cabinet of President McKinley, and William T., famous soldier;
2–Hoyt (1827-1904), of Lancaster, O.; pres. Equitable Life Ins. Co.; *m* 1855, Sarah Moulton (1837-87); issue: I–Frank Allen (1856-1902; *m* 1887, Ada Bacon, *d* 1900); II–Adeline M. (1859-1917; *m* Frank B. Wiborg, *d* 1930); III–Charles M. (1861-1911; *m* Bertha Bartlett); IV–Arthur Hoyt (*b* 1869; *m* 1904, Corsa Kintzley, *b* 1878); V–Helen (1 above).
1–*m* Oct. 28, 1896, William Oglesby Griffith *b* Cannes, France; son of John R. Griffith, of Eng.; issue: 1–Helen Sherman, Jr., *b* Washington, D.C.; *m* 1925, Dallas Lore, son of Dallas Lore Sharpe, *m* Grace Hastings, of Hingham, Mass. (issue: Helen Sherman; Grace Hastings); 2–Florence Oglesby, *b* Phila.; 3–Hoyt Sherman, *b* Phila.; attended M.I.T.; *m* 1925, Marie Louise, dau. W. W. Hepburn, *m* Jane Shaw, of Pa. (issue: Hoyt Sherman, Jr.); 4–John Ramsbottom, *b* Phila.
1–Ed. The Misses Vinton's School, Pomfret, Conn.; Univ. extension course under Prof. Dallas L. Sharp. Author (see Who's Who in America). Episcopalian. Republican. Clubs: Boston Authors, Acorn, Writers, Hollywood, Ia. Authors, Los Angeles Pen Women's. Residence: 500 E. Evergreen Av., Chestnut Hill, Philadelphia, Pa. Summer place: The Clearing, Saunderstown, R.I.

1–**GRISWOLD, Hervey DeWitt**, *b* Dryden, N.Y., May 24, 1860.
8–Edward **Griswold** (qv);
7–John (1652-1717), of Windsor and Killingworth, Conn.; dep. Gen. Ct. 12 yrs.; deacon; *m* 2d, post 1679, Bathsheba North (*d* 1736);
6–Daniel (1696-1737), of Killingworth; dep. Gen. Ct.; *m* 1721, Jerusha Stevens (*b* 1704; Dea. Josiah[7]; William[8], *m* Mary Meigs; John[9], from Eng.);
5–Daniel B. (*b* 1722), to Fairfield, N.Y.; 1st lt. in French and Indian War; *m* 1750, Mary Bushnell (Francis[6]; John[7]; John[8]; Francis[9]; Francis[10], qv);
4–Edward (1758-1843), pvt. in Am. Rev.; to Dryden, N.Y.; *m* 1783, Asenath Hurd;
3–Nathan (1798-1877), of Dryden; *m* 1821, Patience Lindsey (1802-66), their son, Nathan, killed in Civil War;
2–Benjamin (2 below).
9–Adam **Hurd**, one of 1st settlers at Stratford, Conn., bet. 1650-69; *m* Hannah Bartram;
8–John, *m* 1662, Ann (Porter) Judson (John Porter[9], of Windsor, 1639);
7–Ebenezer (*b* 1668), *m* Sarah Lane (*b* 1667; Robert[8], *m* Sarah Pickett);
6–Daniel (1696-1766), *m* 1st, 1719, Rachel Smith;
5–Abraham (*b* 1725), *m* 1753, Mrs. Mary Willcocks;
4–Asenath (1758-1852), *m* Edward **Griswold** (4 above).
8–William (Redfyn) **Redfield** (*d* 1662), came to America and settled at Boston, ca. 1639; *m* Rebecca–;
7–James (ca. 1646-1723), at Saybrook, Conn., 1683; had charge of a fort nr. the mouth of the Conn. River during King Philip's War; twice received grants of land on Pipe Stove's Pt.; removed to Fairfield, 1693; *m* Elizabeth How (*b* 1645);
6–Theophilus (1682-1759), *m* 1706, Priscilla Grenell or Grinnell;
5–Daniel (1707-58), of Killingworth, Conn.; *m* 1728, Elizabeth Graves;
4–Sylvester (*d* 1823), of Killingworth; *m* 1st, 1770, Martha Merrill (1752-1807);
3–Martha (1794-1881), to Dryden, N.Y.; *m* 1815, James Hervey **Hurd** (*b* 1791; Caleb Leete[4] [*b* 1753], *m* Mary Griswold; Daniel[5], same as 6 above, *m* 2d, Dorothy Leete [Caleb[6]; Andrew[7]; William[8], qv]);
2–Laura Eliza (2 below).
9–John **Alden**, Mayflower Pilgrim (qv);
8–Elizabeth (1623/24-1717), *m* 1644, William **Paybodie** (1619/20-1707; John[9], qv);
7–Lydia (1667-1748), *m* ca. 1683, Daniel **Grenell** (1668?-1740), of Portsmouth, R.I. (Daniel[8], *m* Mary, dau. William Wodell; Matthew[9], qv);
6–Priscilla (ca. 1690-1770), of Killingworth; *m* Theophilus **Redfield** (6 above).
2–Laura Eliza Hurd (1832-1917), of Dryden, N.Y.; *m* 1854, Benjamin **Griswold** (1822-1903), of Dryden; issue: I–Martha A. (1856-62); II–Hervey DeWitt (1 above); III–Frank (1865-1928, *m* 1898, Mary Hart); IV–Annie (*b* 1870; *m* 1897, Charles Grant Hotchkiss); V–Kate (*b* 1871; *m* 1892, Charles Gabriel Ballard).
1–*m* June 25, 1890, Frances Sheldon, *b* Dryden, N.Y., Aug. 11, 1863; dau. of Edward Sheldon, of Dryden; issue: 1–Laura Katherine, *b* Jhansi, India, Sept. 14, 1893; grad. nurse; *m* Aug. 7, 1926, Donald Emerson, son of James Mackenzie, of Boston (issue: Donald E., Jr., *b* Apr. 21, 1928); 2–Arthur Sheldon, *b* Lahore, Punjab, India, Mar. 15, 1896; B.A., Yale, '18, M.D., 1921; *m* June 23, 1923, Edith Estelle Hammond, dau. of Edward Olin Chapman, of North Haven, Conn. (issue: Richard Sheldon; Gordon Brewster); 3–Elizabeth, *b* Lahore, Punjab, India (May 17, 1898-Mar. 29, 1899); 4–Frances Louise, *b* Marathon, N.Y., May 29, 1900; B.Sc., Cornell, '22; *m* May 30, 1925, George Andrew, son of Robert Ballentine, of Jersey City, N.J. (issue: Patricia Joyce).
1–A.B., Union Coll., '85 (Phi Delta Theta, P.B.K.); grad. Union Theol. Sem., 1888; studied at univs. of Oxford, Eng., and Berlin, Germany, 1888-90; Ph.D., Cornell, 1900; (D.D., Union U., 1910). Missionary, Presbyn. Ch., in India, 1890-1926; prof. philosophy, Forman Christian Coll., Lahore, 1894-1913; mem. of Senate and Syndicate of Punjab U., several yrs.; sec. council, Am. Presbyn. Missions in India, 1913-18,22-25. Author (see Who's Who in America, Vol. XI). Mem. I.A.G., Punjab Hist. Soc., Am. Oriental Soc. Residence: 4611 Main St., Stratford, Conn.

1–**GRISWOLD, Thomas, Jr.**, *b* Ashtabula, O., Sept. 29, 1870.
8–Matthew **Griswold** (qv);
7–Matthew (1653-1715), soldier King Philip's War; *m* 2d, 1683, Phebe Hyde (*d* 1704);
6–Judge John (1690-1764), *m* 1713, Hannah Lee (*d* 1773);
5–Gov. Matthew (1714-1799), mem. Council of Safety, during Am. Rev.; justice of peace; gov. of Conn., 1784-86; *m* 1743, Ursula Wolcott (1724-88; Roger[6], gov. of Conn., justice Supreme Ct., Conn.);
4–Gov. Roger (1762-1812), 5th gov. of Conn.,

1811-12; justice Supreme Ct., Conn.; *m* 1788, Fanny Rogers (1766-1863; Col. Zabdial[5], of Conn., patriot Am. Rev.);
3–Roger Wolcott (1797-1878), *m* 2d, 1823, Juliet Griswold (1802-55);
2–Thomas (1842-1916), *m* 1866, Ruth Coleman Hubbard (1844-1920); issue: I–Mary Sabin (*b* 1868; *m* 1897, Thomas Dick Beach); II–Thomas, Jr. (1 above); III–Catherine Elizabeth (*b* 1872; *m* Robert Sheridan Fetch); IV–Amos Hubbard (*b* 1874; *m* 1897, Amelia Anne Isabelle Barry); V–John Boalt (*b* 1877; *m* Alice Webb); VI–Matthew Wolcott (*b* 1878-*d* infancy).
1–*m* Nov. 25, 1897, Helen Josephine Dow (Apr. 30, 1876-Apr. 18, 1918); dau. of Joseph Henry Dow of Cleveland, O.; issue: 1–Josephine, *b* Midland, Mich., Dec. 17, 1899; *m* Oct. 25, 1918, Louis H., son of George C. Ashmun, M.D. (see Who's Who in America), *m* Alice Ford (issue: Louis Heber); 2–Nelson Dow, *b* Midland, June 24, 1901; *m* Dec. 29, 1926, Marguerite Pomeroy, dau. of William Huntington Wells, of Brooklyn, N.Y., *m* Emma Louise Pomeroy; 3–Leila Ruth, *b* Midland, Aug. 27, 1913.
1–*m* 2d, Oct. 17, 1918, Vera Ann Hadsall, *b* Birch Run, Mich., May 21, 1896; dau. of Miles L. Hadsall, of Birch Run; issue: 1–Catherine, *b* Midland, Mich., Nov. 9, 1927.
1–B.S. in C.E., Case Sch. Applied Science, Cleveland, O., 1896, C.E., 1908 (Phi Delta Theta, Tau Beta Pi, Sigma Xi). Consulting engr., The Dow Chemical Co., Midland, Mich., since 1926. Patent attorney (see Who's Who in America). Episcopalian. K.P. Clubs: Saginaw, Saginaw Country, Saginaw Valley Torch (pres., 1929-30), Midland Country. Residence: 1016 Eastman Rd., Midland, Mich.

1–**GROSS, Christian (Channing),** *b* Chicago, Ill., Oct. 9, 1895.
7–Alfred **Gross**;
6–Conrad;
5–Alfred;
4–Christian (1823-1900), active in N.J. Republican politics, ca. 1855;
3–Dr. George, of N.Y., and N.J.; prof. U.Pa.; later at Buffalo, N.Y.;
2–Charles William (2 below).
9–Nicholas **Gilman**;
8–Seth;
7–Eunice, *m* ca. 1790, Joseph **Thayer**;
6–Eunice, *m* ca. 1812, James **Brown**;
5–Emma, *m* Caleb **Channing**, to Albany ca. 1830;
4–Natali, *m* in Ind., 1850, Newton **Prendergast**;
3–Winifred, *m* in Ill., ca. 1870, ——**Watkins**;
2–Natali (*b* 1871), *m* 1888, Charles William **Gross** (*b* 1865), of Chicago; issue: I–Charles Raymond (1893-1929); II–Christian (1 above).
1–*m* Jan. 28, 1922, Virginia Randolph Harrison (qv for issue).
1–B.S., U.Ill., '16 (Psi U.), U.Paris, U.Grenoble, etc. Diplomat; Am. charge d'affaires to Republic of Haiti, and dep. high commr. to Haiti, since 1926. Served with Ill. troops, in Mexican campaign; lt. inf., France and Siberia, World War. Decorated D.S.C., Brit. Mil. Cross, Croix de Guerre. Mem. I.A.G. Author (under name of Fairfax Channing): Siberia's Untouched Treasure and its Future Role in the World, 1923. Clubs: Chicago Athletic, Polo, Travellers, Fontainbleu, St. Cloud (all France). Address: Dept. of State, Washington, D.C.

1–**GROSS, Virginia Randolph Harrison (Mrs. Christian),** *b* New York, N.Y., Oct. 17, 1901.
4–John Randolph **Harrison,** *m* —Fairfax, of Va.;
3–Burton, *m* ca. 1873, Constance Cary, of Va.;
2–Frank (2 below).
5–William H. (Will) **Crocker,** to Calif., 1849;
4–George;
3–Fred, *m* in San Francisco, ca. 1860, —Eastman;
2–Mary (*b* 1881), of San Francisco; *m* 1900, Frank (changed name to Francis Burton, ca. 1893) **Harrison,** of Va.; issue: I–Virginia R. (1 above); II–Barbara (*b* 1903).
1–*m* Jan. 28, 1922, Hon. Christian (Channing) Gross (qv); issue: 1–Peter Christian Channing, *b* Washington, D.C., Jan. 30, 1923; 2–Barbara Virginia Crocker, *b* Paris, France, Oct. 28, 1924.
1–Ed. Foxcroft Sch., Va. Trained for operatic stage career, 1925–. Address c/o Hon. Christian Gross, Dept. of State, Washington, D.C.

1–**GROSVENOR, William Mason,** *b* St. Louis, Mo., Oct. 5, 1873.
7–John **Grosvenor** (ca. 1640-ca. 1691), from Eng., settled at Roxbury, Mass., 1670; *m* Esther Clark (1651-1738; Hugh[8]);
6–Sgt. Ebenezer (1684-1730), Pomfret, Conn.; *m* Anne Marcy (1687-1784);
5–Ebenezer (1713-93), Pomfret; *m* 1737, Lucy Cheney (1720-92);
4–Capt. and Rev. Nathan M. (1764-1814), Pomfret; *m* 1788, Lydia Adams;
3–Rev. Mason (1800-86), of Pomfret, Conn., Ashfield, Mass., Cincinnati, O., and Englewood, N.J.; *m* 1833, Esther Delia Scarborough (1812-46);
2–William Mason (2 below).
8–Henry **Adams** (qv);
7–Edward (1630-1716), of Medfield, Mass.; dep. Mass. Bay Colony; dep. Gen. Ct., 1689,92,1702; *m* 1652, Lydia Rockwood (*d* 1676; Richard[8], *m* Agnes Bicknell);
6–David (*d* 1753), *m* Katherine Adams (*d* 1749; Samuel[7]; Henry[8]);
5–Dr. David (*d* 1790);
4–Lydia, *m* Capt. and Reverend Nathan M. **Grosvenor** (4 above).
8–David **Sage** (qv);
7–John (1668-1751), *m* 1693, Hannah Starr (1673/-74-1753; Comfort[8]; Dr. Thomas[9]; Dr. Comfort[10]);
6–Benjamin (1703-34), *m* Mary Allen;
5–Benjamin (1725-1813), pvt. in Am. Rev.; *m* Abagail Blinn;
4–Selah (*b* 1767), *m* Zilpha Sly;
3–Hiram King (*b* 1806), *m* Cyrena Pilcher (*b* 1822; Louis[4], *m* Sallie Martin; James[5], of Ga.).
2–Col. William Mason **Grosvenor** (1835-1900), economics editor N.Y. Tribune, 1875-1900; editor "Dun's Weekly Review," 1883-1900; *m* 1859, Ellen M. Stone (1826-67); *m* 2d, 1870, Ellen (Sage) Martin (1846-1920); issue (1st marriage): I–Kate (*b* 1859; *m* Eldridge M. Fowler); issue (2d marriage): I–Willa (1871-72); II–William Mason (1 above); III–Richard (*b* and *d* 1879); IV–Donald (1881-84).
1–*m* Apr. 9, 1901, Marie Celine Dexter, *b* Waverly, N.Y., May 19, 1868; dau. of Stephen Chamberlin, of Starkey, N.Y., *m* Celia E. Comstock (she *m* 2d, Jeremiah Newton Dexter, jurist Salisbury, Conn., who adopted Marie Celine; issue: 1–Mary Dexter, *b* New York, N.Y., July 18, 1902; Vassar, '24; *m* Apr. 30, 1929, Ralph Oliver Ellsworth; 2–William Mason, Jr., *b* Buffalo, N.Y., Sept. 2, 1905; Columbia U.
1–B.S., Poly. Inst., '93; Ph.D., U.Pa., 1898. Consulting chemical engr. since 1907 (see Who's Who in America). Active mem. Textile Div., Council Nat. Defense, and adviser gas mask div., C.W.S. Mem. I.A.G. Clubs: Chemists, Lawrence Beach. Residence: 200 W. 58th St., New York, N.Y.

1–**GROVER, Edwin Osgood,** *b* Mantorville, Minn., June 4, 1870.
9–Thomas **Grover** (*d* 1661), from Eng., 1638; settled at Charlestown, Mass.; *m* Elizabeth–;
8–Thomas (*b* 1653), of Malden, Mass.; *m* Sarah Chadwick (John[9], of Watertown, freeman, 1656, removed to Malden, *m* Joan–);
7–Andrew (1673-1751), *m* ca. 1697, Mary–;
6–James (*b* 1699), lived in Norton, Mass.; *m* 1726, Sarah Austin;
5–Dea. James (1729-1805), moved to Peckersfield (now Nelson), N.H., ante 1774, settled ca. 1786, at Bethel, Me.; *m* 1754, Sarah Wellman, of Norton, Mass. (Samuel[6], *m* Hannah, dau. of John Hall, *m* Esther Bell; Isaac[7]; Thomas[8]);
4–Eli (1763-1837), of Bethel; *m* 1785, Mehitable Austin (1772-1853);
3–Andrew (1805-63), of Bethel; *m* 18–, Rachel E. Mason (1806-80 or 81; Walter[4]; Moses[5]; Daniel[6]; John[7]; Hugh[9], qv);
2–Nahum Wesley (2 below).
9–Christopher **Osgood** (qv);
8–Capt. Christopher (1643-1723), millwright, built Frye's Mill in Andover, Mass.; capt.; rep. from Andover, 1690; *m* 1663, Hannah Belknap (*d* 1697), of Lynn;
7–Ezekiel (1679-1741), of Andover; *m* 1710, Rebecca Wardwell (*b* 1691; Samuel[8] [*b* 1643], *m* Sarah Hooper Hawkes);

6–Ezekiel (1712-98), farmer, Blue Hill, Me.; *m* 1746, Mary Barker (1725-1810), of Pelham;
5–Ezekiel (1747-1816), *m* 1774, Mary Blaisdell (*b* Amesbury, Mass., 1751-*d* Blue Hill, Me., 1835; Enoch[6]; Jonathan[7]; Henry[8]; Ralph[9], qv);
4–David (1785-1865), to N. Bangor, Me., 1824; cabinet maker; *m* 1806 or 07, Abigail Herrick (1780-1853; John[5]; Samuel[6]; Samuel[7]; Henry[8]; Henry[9], qv);
3–Alvah (*b* 1808), *m* 1836, Lucinda Richardson (1806-1902; Marcus[4] [1780-1881]; Elisha[5]; Daniel[6]; Lt. Daniel[7] [1685-1748]; John[8]);
2–Frances Elizabeth (*b* 1840), *m* 1867, Nahum Wesley **Grover** (1835-1925), of Bethel; Congl. minister; issue: I–Frederick Orville (*b* 1868; *m* 1925, Ruth Havergal Creighton, *b* 1899); II–Edwin O. (1 above); III–Eulalie Osgood (*b* 1873; see Who's Who in America); IV–Anne Mason (*b* 1878).
1–*m* June 4, 1900, Mertie Graham, *b* Colebrook, N.H., Jan. 25, 1871; dau. of William A. Graham, of St. Johnsbury, Vt.; issue: 1–Frances, *b* Highland Park, Ill., July 30, 1903; Oberlin Coll., '25; 2–Hester, *b* Highland Park, Aug. 26, 1905; Oberlin, '27; 3–Graham, *b* Ridgewood, N.J., Oct. 31, 1914; Montverde Sch. (Fla.), '31.
1–B.L., Dartmouth, '94 (Phi Delta Theta); studied at Harvard, 1894; European travel, 1895; (Litt.D., U.Miami, 1929). Pres. The Prang Co., 1911-25, chmn. bd. since 1925. Prof. of books, 1926–, and dir. library, Rollins Coll., Winter Haven, Fla., 1928– (see Who's Who in America). Residence: Winter Park, Fla.

1–**GROVER, Nathan Clifford,** *b* Bethel, Me., Jan. 31, 1868.
9–Thomas **Grover** (*d* 1661), from Eng., 1638; settled at Charlestown, Mass., 1642; *m* Elizabeth–;
8–Thomas (*b* 1653), of Malden, Mass.; *m* Sarah Chadwick (John[9], of Watertown, freeman, 1656, removed to Malden, *m* Joan–);
7–Andrew (1673-ca. 1751), lived in the North Parish of Norton, Mass., later incorporated as Mansfield; *m* ca. 1697, Mary–;
6–James (*b* 1699), *m* 1726, Sarah Austin;
5–Dea. James (1729-1805), moved from Mansfield, Mass., to Peckersfield (now Nelson), N.H., and subsequently to Bethel, Me.; *m* 1754, Sarah Wellman, of Norton;
4–Elijah, *m* Hannah (Mason) Mills (*b* 1762);
3–Nathan (1797-1879), *m* Lucinda Barker (1796-1874; Daniel[4], of Waterford, Me.);
2–Daniel Barker (1831-97), farmer; *m* 1860, Martha Matilda Eames (1832-78); issue: I–Mary Lucinda (Mrs. George Albert Cheney, qv for the Abbott lineage); II–Nathan Eames (*b* 1864-*d* infancy); III–Sumner Abbott (*b* 1865; *m* Alberta Anderson); IV–Nathan Clifford (1 above); V–Arthur Curtis (qv for Eames lineage); VI–Oscar Llewellyn (*b* 1874; *m* Annie Louise Wilson).
1–*m* June 14, 1900, Anna Allen, *b* Corinth, Me., Dec. 10, 1874; dau. of Edward (?) Johnson, *m* Clara Hamilton; adopted by her aunt Arletta Hamilton Allen wife of Nathan Allen, of Portland, Me., following the death of her mother, and grew up under the name of Anna Allen; issue: 1–Dorothy Allen, *b* Orono, Me., July 8, 1901; Wellesley, '22; 2–Mary Hamilton, *b* Orono, Jan. 1, 1904; Wellesley, '26; *m* June 23, 1926, John Douglass, son of Douglass Fitch of Montclair, N.J., *m* Charlotte Waring (issue: Alan Douglass, *b* Feb. 5, 1928).
1–B.C.E., U.Me., '90 (Phi Kappa Phi, Tau Beta Pi, Beta Theta Pi), C.E., 1897; B.S., M.I.T., 1896. Chief hydraulic engr. in charge water resources branch, U.S. Geol. Survey, since 1913. Author (see Who's Who in America). Congregationalist. Club: Cosmos. Residence: 1442 Belmont St., Washington, D.C.

1–**GROVER, Arthur Curtis,** *b* Bethel, Me., Aug. 21, 1870.
7–Thomas **Eames** (qv);
6–Samuel (*b* 1664 or 65), *m* 2d, 1698, Patience Twitchell;
5–Samuel (*b* 1714), lived at Malden, Mass., and later at Dublin, N.H.; *m* 1738 or 39, Sybilla Haven;
4–Ebenezer (*b* 1756), moved from Dublin, N.H., to Bethel, Me.; *m* Elizabeth–;
3–Nathan (1797-1838), *m* 1825, Mary Abbott (1804-ca. 1870);
2–Martha Matilda (1832-78), *m* 1860, Daniel Barker **Grover** (1831-97), farmer (for issue and other lineages see Nathan C. Grover, qv).
1–*m* Sept. 9, 1895, Susan Colburn, *b* Orono, Me., Dec. 17, 1870; dau. of Charles Haley Colburn, of Orono; issue: 1–Newell Arthur, *b* Rutland, Vt., Dec. 12, 1899; *m* July 31, 1924, Isabel Elinor Mott; 2–Doris Elizabeth, *b* Rutland, Sept. 26, 1905.
1–Ed. Gould Acad. (Bethel, Me.), and U.Me. City engr., Rutland, 1897-1918. Mem. Vt. Soc. of Engrs., Boston Soc. of Civil Engrs. Mason (Shriner), K.P., Odd Fellow, etc. Residence: Rutland, Vt.

1–**CHENEY, Mary Lucinda Grover (Mrs. George A.),** *b* Bethel, Me., Apr. 13, 1861.
9–George **Abbott** (qv);
8–Benjamin (1661-1703), *m* 1685, Sarah Farnham;
7–Jonathan (1687-1770), *m* 1711, Zerviah Holt;
6–Jonathan (1714-94), *m* 1739, Martha Lovejoy;
5–Jonathan (1740-1821), *m* Mehitable Abbot (*d* 1777);
4–Jonathan (1776-1843), *m* 1799, Betsy Batchelder (*b* 1777);
3–Mary (1804-ca. 1870), *m* Nathan **Eames** (1797-1838);
2–Martha Matilda (1832-78), *m* 1860, Daniel Barker **Grover** (1831-97), farmer (for issue and other lineages see Nathan C. Grover).
1–*m* Aug. 24, 1881, George Albert Cheney, *b* Wells, Me., Feb. 23, 1856; son of Joseph Cheney, of Wells; issue: 1–Julian Oscar (1883-93); 2–Ethel Margaret, *b* Dec. 25, 1885; 3–Grover, *b* Sept. 30, 1888, *m* 1920, Alberta (*b* Tewkesbury, Mass.), dau. of Peter Annis, of Wells, Me. (issue: Mary Alberta, *b* Jan. 19, 1922; Madelene Margaret, *b* Mar. 25, 1929); 4–Sibyl Eames, *b* Dec. 23, 1897.
1–Residence: Wells, Me. P.O. address: North Berwick, Me.

1–**GUGGENHEIM, Caroline Morton (Mrs. Harry F.).**
11–George (Mourt) **Morton** (qv);
10–George (*b* 1615);
9–Richard (*b* 1640);
8–Abraham (*b* 1676);
7–Samuel (*b* 1709);
6–Abner (*b* 1735);
5–Abner (1774-1863), A.B., Dartmouth, 1799; lawyer, probate judge in Vt.; ed. Detroit Free Press, 1 yr.;
4–Julius Dewey, banker, Detroit, Mich.; *m* Emeline Sterling;
3–Julius Sterling (1832-1902), A.B., Union Coll. '54; Sec. of Agr., 1893-97, in Cabinet of Pres Cleveland; *m* 1854, Caroline Joy;
2–Paul (2 below).
10–Thomas **Joy** (qv);
9–Samuel (1639-71), mem. A. and H.A. Co.; *m* 1668, Ann Pitts (bap. 1644-1698; Edward[10], from Eng., 1639);
8–Samuel (1670-ca. 1746), of Salisbury, Mass.; *m* 1696, Marah Eastman (*d* 1728);
7–Ens. Benjamin (*b* 1712), of Salisbury; *m* 1st, 1735 or 1736, Sarah Sawyer;
6–Abijah (1740-83), of Salisbury;
5–Abijah (*b* 1780), of Raymond, N.H.;
4–Hiram (1810-68), of Winthrop, Me., and Chicago, Ill.;
3–Caroline (1834-81), *m* Julius S. **Morton** (3 above);
2–Paul (1857-1911), Sec. of the Navy, 1904-05; *m* Charlotte Goodridge (*b* 1858; Charles Lowell[3], *b* Lowell, Mass., *m* Charlotte Wheeler); issue: I–Caroline (1 above); II–Pauline (*m* J. Hopkins Smith; *m* 2d, Charles H. Sabin).
1–*m* Oct. 11, 1902, William C. Potter, *b* Chicago, Ill., Oct. 16, 1873; son of Edward Augustus Potter, *m* Harriet Berry; issue: 1–Jean Morton, *b* Chicago, Ill., Dec. 31, 1903; *m* Frederick Soldwedel; 2–Charlotte Morton, *b* Mexico City, Mex., 1906; *m* Reginald Minturn Lewis; 3–Pauline Morton, *b* New York, N.Y. (Mar. 11-May 11, 1918).
1–*m* 2d, as his 2d wife, Feb. 3, 1923, Harry F. Guggenheim, *b* West End., N.J., Aug. 23, 1890 (see Who's Who in America); son of Daniel Guggenheim, *m* Florence Schloss; issue: 1–Diane, *b* New York, N.Y., Apr. 23, 1924.
1–Residence: Port Washington, L.I., N.Y.

1–**GULLIVER, Julia Henrietta,** *b* Norwich, Conn., July 30, 1856.
8–Anthony **Gulliver** (1619-1706), from Eng., 1642;

settled at Milton, Mass.; *m* Lydia Kingsley;
7–Nathaniel (1675-1743), *m* Hannah Billings, of Dorchester, Mass.;
6–John (*b* 1690), *m* Margaret Hunt;
5–John (1727-1804), lt. Am. Rev.; *m* Sarah Trescott;
4–Gershom (1756-1840), capt. Am. Rev.; *m* Phebe Harvey;
3–John (1792-1879), served in War 1812; *m* Sarah Putnam;
2–John Putnam (2 below).
9–John **Putnam** (qv);
8–Nathaniel (1619-1700), judge; *m* Elizabeth Hutchinson;
7–Capt. Benjamin (1664-1715), capt.; surveyor of highways; *m* probably, Hannah Tarrant;
6–Rev. Daniel (1696-1759), A.B., Harvard, 1717; *m* Rebecca Putnam (John[7]);
5–Daniel (ca. 1717-1773), rep. to Gen. Ct.; *m* Hannah Ingalls;
4–Henry (1755-1806), officer in Am. Rev.; *m* Mary Hawkes;
3–Sarah (1790-1865), *m* John **Gulliver** (3 above).
8–Thomas **Curtis** (1598-1681), from Eng.; settled in Wethersfield, Conn., 1639; *m* Elizabeth–;
7–Joseph (1644-83), *m* 1674, Mercy–;
6–Thomas (1680-1752), in French and Indian War; *m* Mary Goodrich (John[7]; William[8]);
5–Zebulon (1711-98), *m* Lydia Cole;
4–Job (1745-1807), *m* Eunice Cowles;
3–Elizur (1782-1868), *m* Amanda Steele;
2–Frances Woodbury (2 below).
9–Gov. William **Bradford** (qv);
8–William, maj. Mass. Inf.; *m* Alice Richards;
7–Mercy (1660-1720), *m* 1680, Samuel **Steele** (1652-1710; John[8], came with father, *m* Mercy, dau. Andrew Warner, qv; John[9], qv);
6–Thomas (1681-1757), *m* 1709, Susanna Webster (*d* 1757);
5–William (1713-77), *m* Lydia– (1726-1801);
4–Isaac (*b* 1752), *m* 1777, Dorothy Pitkin;
3–Amanda (1783-ca. 1863), *m* Elizur **Curtis** (3 above);
2–Frances Woodbury (1823-92), *m* 1845, John Putnam **Gulliver,** D.D., LL.D. (1819-94), B.A., Yale, 1840; grad. Andover Theol. Sem., 1845; Congl. minister; pres. Knox Coll., 1868-72; prof. relations of Christianity and science, Andover Theol. Sem., 1879-94; issue: I–William Curtis (1847-1909; *m* Louisa, dau. Judge Ashbel Green, see Vol. I, p. 303); II–John Francis (1849-1923; *m* Adele M. McKean); III–Joseph Otis (*b* and *d* 1853); IV–Julia Henrietta (1 above); V–Mary (*b* 1860); VI–Herbert Putnam (1865-66).
1–A.B., Smith, '79 (P.B.K.); Ph.D., 1888; studied at Leipzig, Germany, 1892-93 (LL.D., 1910). Head of the dept. of philosophy and Bibl. lit., 1893-1902, pres., 1902-18, pres. emeritus, 1919–, Rockford (Ill.) Coll. Author. Mem. D.A.R. Officier d'Academie (see Who's Who in America). Residence: Eustis, Fla.

1–**GUNNETT, Dora Ethel Jack (Mrs. William E.),** *b* Edina, Mo., Apr. 19, 1862.
10–William **Hampton** (1586-post 1652), came to Va. in the "Bona Nova," 1620; settled first nr. old Point Comfort; established "Hampfield," Gloucester Co., Va.; *m* Joan– (*b* 1596), who came with their three children in the "Abigail," to Va.;
9–Rev. Thomas (1623-post 1690);
8–Capt. John (1650-55-1718), *m* 1677, Mary Mann, at the home of her uncle John Mann, of "Timberneck," Gloucester Co., Va.;
7–John (1683-1748), of Fairfax Co., Va.; *m* 1712, Margaret Wade (1694-1773; James[8], of New Kent Co., Va.);
6–Thomas (1728-96), Am. Rev.; *m* 1749, Sarah (Congers) Pattison, a widow;
5–Capt. Preston (*d* 1832), of Grant Co., Ky.; Am. Rev.; *m* 1779, Elizabeth– (*b* 1754), widow of Charles Conner;
4–Elizabeth (1780-1865), *m* 1800, John **Burch** (1770-1829; Benjamin[5], *m* 1756, Jane Crutchfield);
3–Sarah (1801-60), *m* 1819, William **Jack** (1790-1864; John[4] [1766-1822], *m* 1789, Mary Mason [1769-1853]; John[5] [1726-1806], *m* Eleanor Stevenson; James[6] [*b* 1705], capt. Am. Rev.; *m* Elizabeth McNulty; Patrick[7] [1678-1726], *m* 1699, Elizabeth Jervis);
2–Benjamin Burch (2 below).
10–Matthias **Corwin** (1590-1600-1656), came to Ipswich, Mass., 1633/34; a founder of Southold, L.I., 1640; *m* Margaret Morton (Thomas[11], of Eng.);
9–John (1630-1702), *m* 1658, Mary Glover (Lt. Charles[10] [1610-70], chief officer in command under arms at Southold, 1652-53);
8–Capt. John (1663-1729), served in Suffolk, N.Y., Regt., 1715; *m* ante 1698, Sarah–;
7–John (1705-55), *m* 2d, 1732, Elizabeth Goldsmith;
6–John (1735-1817), *m* 1755, Sarah Hubbard (1731-63; Capt. Isaac[7] [1694-1771], *m* 1721, Bethia [1698-1770], dau. of Thomas Goldsmith, *m* Bethia Terry);
5–Isaac (1759-1830), L.I. to Morris Co., N.J.; Am. Rev.; *m* Experience Reeves;
4–Deborah (1780-1846), *m* 1799, Amos **Leek** (1774-1857; Amos[5] [1747-1822], served in Morris Co., N.J., militia during Am. Rev., *m* Anna White);
3–Experience (1802-58), *m* 1820, William **Shangle** (1798-1874), of Chester, N.J. (Fredrick[4] [1770-1832], *m* 1793, Maria Patrey [1774-1834]; Heinrich[5], who came from nr. Strassburg to Phila. in the "Robert and Olliver," 1738, *m* 3d, Elizabeth Bercott, who was maid of honor to Queen Anne);
2–Sarah Corwin (2 below).
10–William **Purrier,** from Eng. in the "Hopewell," with wife and three children, settled at Ipswich, Mass., 1635; *m* Alice–;
9–Mary, *m* Thomas **Reeves;**
8–Joseph (1656-1736), *m* Abigail–;
7–Hezekiah (*d* 1770), *m* 1709, Jerusha Hallock;
6–Manasseh (*d* 1797), *m* 1st, 1734, Martha Curwin, of Southold, L.I.;
5–Experience (1759-1839), *m* Isaac **Corwin** (5 above).
10–Peter **Hallock,** "The Pilgrim," came from Eng. with Rev. Young and others, 1640; original purchaser of "Oyster Pond"; settled at Acqueboque, L.I.; *m* Widow Howell;
9–William (*d* 1684), *m* Margaret–;
8–William (*d* 1736), *m* Mary–;
7–Jerusha (*d* 1738), *m* Hezekiah **Reeves** (7 above).
2–Benjamin Burch **Jack** (1829-95), *m* 1857, Sarah Corwin Shangle (1836-1909); issue: I–John James (*b* 1860; *m* Della M. Funk); II–Dora Ethel (1 above); III–Ida Frances (*b* 1866; *m* John Louis Eckel); IV–Benjamin Franklin (*b* 1868; *m* Amanda Alice Russell); V–Edward Conn (*b* 1871; *m* Mary F. Lysaght); VI–Carrie May (*b* 1873; *m* Henry Williams); VII–Lillian Bell (1878-1920; *m* Dr. Walter Sherwood Taylor).
1–*m* Jan. 25, 1888, William Edgar Gunnett (Jan. 3, 1858-July 27, 1925); son of Joseph Gunnett (1825-1902), *m* Caroline Hartford (1832-1909); issue: 1–Gladys Dora, *b* Buffalo, Ill., Feb. 19, 1895; *m* Dec. 20, 1916, Russel Truesdale Evans, *b* Pasadena, Calif., Oct. 29, 1891 (issue: William Russel, *b* Oct. 13, 1920).
1–Mem. S.D.P., D.A.C., H.S.(Pa.), D.A.R. (chapter regent). Residence: 709 W. Commonwealth Av., Fullerton, Calif.

1–**GUTHRIE, David Vance,** *b* nr. Staunton, Va., Oct. 15, 1884.
6–John **Guthrie** (1708-90; son of John, *m* Jane Stuart), came from North of Ireland and settled in Chester Co., Pa., 1730; large landholder; elder Fagg's Manor Presbyn. Ch.; *m* Ann– (*b* 1715);
5–William (*b* Adams Co., Pa. 1736-*d* Henry Co., Ky., 1823), removed to Augusta Co., Va.; participated in battles of Brandywine, Paoli, Germantown and Monmouth; *m* Esther McClelland (*d* 1795);
4–John (1760-1845), of Augusta Co.; *m* 1794, Margaret Gilkeson (1773-1815; Hugh[5] [1746-1806], *m* Elizabeth [1746-1830], dau. of John Guthrie, above; William[6], below);
3–John Gilkeson (1815-91), of Augusta Co., Va.; served in C.S.A.; *m* 1846, Adeline Barclay Paxton;
2–Walter Craig (2 below).
7–Archibald **Stuart** (*b* Londonderry, Ireland, 1700-1759), fled from Eng. to Western Pa., 1725; family came, 1732; to Augusta Co., Va., ca. 1738; *m* Jane Brown;
6–Thomas (*b* Ireland-will recorded 1788), *m* Elizabeth Moore;
5–Elizabeth (1755-1826), *m* Capt. William **Paxton**

(1751-1817), uncle of Gen. Sam Houston, of Tex. (John[6] [*b* Ireland 1716-1787], to Lancaster Co., Pa., to Rockbridge Co., Va., 1750, *m* Martha Blair, 1726-1821);
4–James (1790-1858), of Rockbridge Co.; *m* 2d, Elizabeth Poage (1802-62; John[5] [1771-1853], *m* Rachel [1766-1855], dau. of Hugh Barclay);
3–Adeline B. (1830-1901), *m* John G. **Guthrie** (3 above).
6–William **Gilkeson** (*d* 1788), from North of Ireland to Pa., 1730; *m* Margaret Lynn (Hugh[7], of Phila.);
5–Hugh (1746-1806), *m* Elizabeth Guthrie (1746-1830);
4–William (1785-1864), *m* Sally Gilkeson (John[5] [1748-93], *m* Sarah Vance [1749-1810]; William[6], above);
3–David Vance (1826-71), *m* Mary E. Gamble;
2–Sally Lyle (2 below).
9–John **Rutherford** (*d* in Ireland), *m* Isabelle Alleine;
8–Katherine (*d* 1738), *m* 1702, John **Walker** (*d* 1734), from Scotland to Ireland, thence to Chester, Pa., 1726;
7–Jane (1712-93), *m* 1734, James **Moore** (1711-91);
6–Rachel (1736-1826), *m* William **McPheeters** (1729-1807);
5–Rebecca (1767-1830), *m* Capt. John **Gamble** (1757-1831), served in Am. Rev. (James[6] [1729-1781], *m* Agnes Bell; Robert[7], from Londonderry, Ireland, to Augusta Co., Va., 1735);
4–Rev. James (1788-1867), Presbyn. minister of S.C. and Ga.; *m* Sally Lyle Ramsey (1792-1856; James[5] [1753-1815], *m* Jane [*d* 1835], dau. of Samuel Lyle [1726-96], *m* Sarah McClung, *d* 1785);
3–Mary E. (1834-1906), *m* David V. **Gilkeson** (3 above).
2–Walter Craig **Guthrie** (1852-1928), principal Chamberlain-Hunt Acad., Port Gibson, Miss.; *m* 1882, Sally Lyle Gilkeson (1858-97); *m* 2d, Ruth Shreve (1864-1914); issue (1st marriage): I–David Vance (1 above); II–Frederick Preston (*b* 1891, *m* Lee Campbell Bowen); III–Edgar Paxton (*b* 1897); issue (2d marriage): I–William Shreve (*b* 1900; *m* Kate Herlitz), and II–Margaret Adeline (*b* 1900), twins.
1–*m* June 30, 1914, Hallie McPheeters See, *b* nr. Staunton, Va., May 31, 1885; dau. of Peter H. See (Charles Cameron[3], *m* Harriet Bosworth), *m* Mary R. Gamble (Dr. Robert[3] [1803-75], *m* Eliza Ann See; Capt. John[4], *m* Rebecca McPheeters, same as 5 above); issue: 1–Elizabeth See, *b* Baltimore, Md., Oct. 23, 1918; 2–David Vance, Jr., *b* Baton Rouge, La., June 20, 1926.
1–B.A., Washington and Lee U., '03, M.A., 1904; Ph.D., Johns Hopkins, 1908. Prof. physics and astronomy, La. State U., since 1912 (see Who's Who in America). Mem. I.A.G. Democrat. Presbyterian. Residence: Baton Rouge, La.

1–**GUYTON, Lucy Hall Milton (Mrs. Moses),** *b* Marianna, Fla., Feb. 23, 1872.
9–Ambrose (Cobbs) **Cobb** (*b* 1590), from Eng., to Va., ca. 1613; settled in York Co.;
8–Robert (*b* 1620);
7–Robert (*b* 1660), justice and sheriff;
6–John (*b* 1708), of Goochland Co., Va.; *m* Susannah Addison (Adm. John[7]);
5–John (*d* 1810), began to write name Cobb; of Richmond and Jefferson cos., Ga.; *m* 1769, Mildred Lewis;
4–Henry Willis (*d* ca. 1820), *m* Obedience Dutiful Bugg (see Vol. III, p. 333, for Bugg lineage);
3–Susan Amanda (1809-40), *m* John **Milton** (see Vol. I, p. 314, for Milton lineage);
2–Maj. William Henry (2 below).
10–Gen. Robert **Lewis** (qv.);
9–John (*b* 1635), of "Warner Hall," *m* Isabella Warner (Capt. Augustine[10], qv);
8–Col. John (1669-1725), burgess; mem. Council; judge Supreme Ct.; *m* his cousin, Elizabeth Warner (1672-1719; Col. Augustine, II[9], speaker Va. Ho. of Burgesses, *m* Mildred, dau. Col. George Reade, qv);
7–Col. Charles (1690 or 96-1779), of "The Byrd"; *m* 1717, Mary Howell of N.C. (John[8], of Va.);
6–Howell (1731-1814), of Granville Co., N.C.; *m* Isabella Willis (1733-1813; Col. Henry[7], burgess from Gloucester Co., 1715,18,23, founder of Fredericksburg);
5–Mildred, *m* John **Cobb** (5 above).
4–Michael **Hearn** (1780-1854), of Edgecombe Co., N.C.; *m* Martha Hall (1787-1848);
3–Lawrence Henry (1810-54), *m* 1836, Margaret Ann Bell (1821-ca. 1874);
2–Lucy Hall (1838-83), *m* 1857, Maj. William Henry **Milton** (1829-1900), pvt. to maj., C.S.A.; lawyer; planter, Marianna, Fla.; issue: I–Susan Amanda Cobb (*b* 1858; *m* Gov. William Yates Atkinson, *d*); II–Margaret Bell (*b* 1860; *m* Edward Jefferson Blackshear); III–William Hall (see Vol. I, p. 314, for Milton lineage and Vol. III, p. 333, for Bugg lineage); IV–Roberta Hearn (*b* 1868; *m* J. H. Carter); V–John (*b* 1870; *m* Floie L. Daniel; *m* 2d, Myrtle Merritt); VI–Lucy Hall (1 above).
1–*m* Jan. 29, 1902, Moses Guyton, *b* nr. Dublin, Laurens Co., Ga., Nov. 30, 1871; son of Moses Guyton; issue: 1–Charles Moses, *b* Marianna, Fla., Nov. 16, 1903; ed. U.Ga.; law degree, U.-Fla.; 2–William Milton (Feb. 28-Oct. 24, 1910).
1–Ed. Inst. at Columbia, Tenn. Mem. D.A.R., U.D.C. Residence: Marianna, Fla.

1–**HACKETT, Chauncey Craven,** *b* Washington, D.C., May 20, 1881.
9–William **Hackett** (qv);
8–Ebenezer (1687-1741), *m* Hannah Ring (Jarves[9]);
7–Ephraim (*b* 1711), *m* 1734, Dorothy Allen (Stillson[8]);
6–Jeremiah (*d* 1797), *m* Mary Robinson, of Canterbury, N.H.;
5–James (*d* 1802), ens. Am. Rev.;
4–Allen (1777-1848), *m* 1797, Mary Young (Joseph[5]);
3–William Henry (1800-78), lawyer; pres. N.H. Senate; *m* 1826, Olive Pickering (Joseph Warren[4], of Portsmouth, N.H.);
2–Frank Warren (1841-1926), lawyer; acting asst. p.m., U.S.N., during Civil War; asst. sec. navy, 1900-01 (see Who's Who in America, Vol. 14); *m* 1880, Ida Craven (see Vol. I, p. 962, for Craven lineage); issue: I–Chauncey Craven (1 above); II–William Henry Young (*b* 1886; *m* Louisa Low Haydock).
1–*m* May 23, 1914, Katharine Jennings, *b* New Almaden, Calif., July 6, 1887; dau. Hennen Jennings, of Washington, D.C.; issue: 1–Hennen Jennings, *b* Washington, D.C., Mar. 7, 1917; 2–Sylvia Joan, *b* Washington, May 30, 1918.
1–*m* 2d, Jan. 5, 1926, Mary Cleveland Moffett, *b* New York, N.Y., Apr. 10, 1906; dau. the late Cleveland Moffett; issue: 1–Mary Wendy Anne, *b* Washington, D.C., Feb. 20, 1927; 2–Thomas Truxtun, *b* Washington, July 24, 1928.
1–A.B., Harvard, '03, LL.B., 1906. Has practiced law in Washington, D.C., since admittance to bar of D.C., 1906; mem. firm Wilson & Hackett since 1921; gen. counsel Assn. Against Prohibition Amendment, 1923-26 (see Who's Who in America). Served as Capt. Air Service, U.S.A., with A.E.F., 1917-19, during World War. Clubs: Metropolitan, Chevy Chase (Washington), Cercle Interalliée (Paris). Residence: Metropolitan Club, Washington, D.C.

1–**HADLEY, Philip Bardwell,** *b* Shelburne Falls, Mass., Jan. 10, 1881.
7–Benjamin **Hadley**;
6–Thomas (*b* Watertown, Mass., 1712-*d* 1788), of Lexington, Mass.; stood on Lexington Common, Apr. 19, 1775, and his son, Samuel, was killed by fire of British; *m* 1741, Ruth Lawrence (1725-1819);
5–Ebenezer (*b* Lexington, 1751-*d* Peterboro, N.H., 1810), stood on Lexington Common, Apr. 19, 1775, with father and brother; served at Ticonderoga, 5 months; enlisted for 3 yrs., 1780; to Peterboro, 1804; brickmaker; *m* 1779, Phoebe, Winship (1755-1849);
4–Ethan (*b* Lexington, 1791-*d* Peterboro, N.H., 1872), brickmaker; *m* 2d, 1826, Betsey Persons (Bartholemew[5]);
3–Ethan (*b* Peterboro, 1828-*d* Chicopee Falls, Mass., 1914), mechanic, musician; served 102d N.H. Regt., Civil War; to Chicopee Falls, 1864; *m* 1850, Mary R. Youngman (1828-1910);
2–Edison Parker (2 below).
10–Jonathan **Fairbanks** (qv);
9–Jonas (*b* Eng.-*d* 1676), to Dedham with parents; to Lancaster, 1657, signed Covenant, 1659; killed with son Joshua by Indians dur-

ing raid on settlement, Feb. 10, 1676; *m* 1658, Lydia Prescott (*b* 1641);
8–Capt. Jabez (*b* Lancaster, Mass., 1670-*d* ca. 1758), officer French and Indian War; father and two brothers massacred by Indians; rep. Gen. Ct., 1714,21,22,23; *m* 1st, Mary Wilder (1675-1718);
7–Jonathan (1710-98), of Lancaster; *m* 1735, Thankful Sawyer (*d* 1782);
6–Lt. Jabez (1738-1822), lt., Lancaster Regt. militia, Am. Rev.; mem. Com. of Corr. and Safety, 1776; *m* 1758, Meriam Davis (1738-91), of Northboro;
5–Alpheus (1766-1832), *m* 1790, Polly (Mary) Willard, of Holden;
4–George Washington (*b* Sterling, 1799), *m* Joanna Flagg (*d* Shelburne Falls, Mass., 1861);
3–George Lyman (*b* West Boyleston, 1831), to Shelburne Falls; *m* Francelia E. Bardwell (1833-1923);
2–Elizabeth Emily (*b* Shelburne Falls, 1856-*d* 1915), *m* 1879, Edison Parker **Hadley** (*b* 1857), of Ann Arbor, Mich.; issue: I–Philip Bardwell (1 above); II–Dorothy Fairbanks (*b* 1893; *m* Charles Bardwell Hawks).
1–*m* May 16, 1908, Ruth Barbara Canedy (divorced), *b* Shelburne Falls, Mass., Nov. 17, 1879; dau. of Dr. Francis Joel Canedy, of Shelburne Falls; issue (all *b* Kingston, R.I.): 1–Jarvis Bardwell, *b* July 13, 1909; 2–Francis Canedy, *b* Feb. 26, 1912; 3–Barbara, *b* Mar. 21, 1916.
1–*m* 2d, Aug. 7, 1924, Faith Elizabeth Palmerlee, *b* Lapeer, Mich., June 21, 1898; dau. of Charles E. Palmerlee, of Lapeer.
1–Ph.B., Brown U., '03 (Delta U., Phi Kappa Phi, Sigma Xi), Ph.D., 1908. Chief, div. of biology, R.I. Agrl. Expt. Sta., 1908-20; prof. bacteriology, R.I. State Coll., 1912-20; asst. prof. bacteriology, U.Mich., 1920-27; asso. prof., since 1927 (see Who's Who in America). Summer place: Camp Beaver Tail, Scotty's Bay, P.O. Cedarville, Mich. Residence: Ann Arbor, Mich.

1–**HAEBERLE, Arminius Theophilus,** *b* St. Louis, Mo., Jan. 23, 1874.
7–James **Lemen,** to America, 1708; *m* 1714, Jane Burns;
6–Nicholas (1725-July 20, 1761);
5–James (1760-1823), *m* Catherine Ogle;
4–Josiah (1794-1867), *m* Rebeka Huff (1795-1858);
3–Catherine (1825-62), *m* Dr. Frederick B. **Bock** (1809-84);
2–Flora Lemen Bock (1841-1909), *m* Oct. 12, 1862, Louis **Haeberle,** D.D. (1838-1928); for issue and Ogle lineage see Frederick S. Haeberle.
1–*m* Aug. 22, 1904, Ida Wieneke, *b* California, Mo.; dau. of Christopher Wieneke, of California, Mo.
1–B.A., Washington U., St. Louis, Mo., '96. Instr. modern langs., St. Charles (Mo.) Coll.; prin. pub. schs., Hermann, Mo.; vice dir. Inst. Ingles, Santiago, Chile, 1898-1903; head of modern lang. dept., McKinley High Sch., St. Louis, 1904-07; Am. consul, Manzanillo, 1908-10, Tegucigalpa, Honduras, 1910-13, St. Michael's, Azores, 1913-15, Pernambuco, and Sao Paulo, Brazil, 1915-25; consul general, Dresden, Germany, 1925–. (see Who's Who in America). Mem. S.R. Home: 3206 Hebert St., St. Louis, Mo. Address: American Consular Service, Dept. of State, Washington, D.C.

1–**HAEBERLE, Frederick S.,** *b* St. Louis, Mo., Aug. 1, 1866.
10–John **Ogle,** from Eng., settled in New Castle Co., Del., 1664; *m* Elizabeth Wollaston;
9–John, *m* Elizabeth Graham;
8–John, *m* Elizabeth Robinson;
7–Thomas, *m* Catherine–;
6–Capt. Joseph (1741-1821), of Del.; removed to Va.; *m* Drusilla Briggs;
5–Catherine (1764-1840), *m* James **Lemen** (1760-1823);
4–Josiah (1794-1867), *m* Rebeka Huff (1795-1858);
3–Catherine (1825-62), *m* Dr. Frederick B. **Bock** (1809-84);
2–Flora Lemen (1841-1909), *m* Oct. 12, 1862, Louis **Haeberle,** D.D. (1838-1928), president, Eden Theol. Sem., St. Louis, Mo.; issue: I–Frederick S. (1 above); II–Selma (*b* 1867; *m* 1887, Theophilus Miller); III–Hulda (*b* 1870; *m* 1892, Eduard Bettex); IV–Arminius T. (qv).
1–*m* Dec. 17, 1902, Helen Carter (qv).
1–M.D., St. Louis Coll. Phys. and Surg., 1891; post-grad. work U.Berlin, Germany. Mem. St. Louis and Am. med. socs. Residence: Garrison and Hebert, St. Louis, Mo.

1–**HAEBERLE, Helen Carter (Mrs. Frederick S.),** *b* Nashville, Ill., Mar. 4, 1877.
5–Thomas **Livesay,** from Eng., ca. 1748, settled in Va.;
4–Alice (1759-1821), *m* 1784, Robert **Carter** (1761-1819), settled in Del.;
3–Livesay (1799-1875), *m* 1824, Mary Moore (1800-73; Thomas L.[4], soldier in Am. Rev., from King William Co., Va.);
2–William D. (2 below).
7–Anthony **Le Compte,** Huguenot from France, settled in St. Mary's Co., Le Compte's Bay, Md.; *m* Esther Doatloan;
6–Moses, *m* —Skinner;
5–Peter, *m* —Brannock;
4–Joseph, of Cambridge, Md.; *m* 1816, Leah Keene;
3–Thomas James (1817-74), lawyer and judge; *m* 1844, Harriet Stoker (1826-1901; desc. John Stoker, of Va., Am. Rev.);
2–Laura (2 below).
8–Edward **Keene** (*b* 1629; son of Henry, of Wadsworth, Eng.), came to Md., 1653;
7–John (1657-1725), capt. colonial militia 13 yrs.; *m* Mary Hopewell (Hugh[8], justice of Dorchester Co., Md.);
6–Edward (*d* 1754), *m* Anne–;
5–Ezekiel (*d* 1799);
4–Leah (1791-1861), *m* Joseph **Le Compte** (4 above);
3–Thomas James, *m* Harriet Stoker (3 above);
2–Laura (1848-83), *m* 1869, William D. **Carter,** M.D. (1837-1920), of Nashville, Ill.; surgeon 44th Vol. Civil War; surgeon of L. & N. R.R.; pres. Pension Bd. of Washington Co., 1890-1905; issue: I–John Paul (*b* 1876; *m* Nellie Zerweck); II–Helen (1 above).
1–*m* Dec. 17, 1902, Frederick S. Haeberle (qv).
1–Ed. Northwestern U., Am. Conservatory of Music. Mem. D.A.R., Ladies of the G.A.R., D.U.V., O.E.S., White Shrine, Woman's Relief Corps, etc. Summer place: Hotchkiss, Colo. Winter place: Ocean Grove, Miss. Residence: Garrison and Hebert, St. Louis, Mo.

HAFF.

Arms: Sable, on a mount vert, a lion or, holding a flagon argent.
Crest: The lion of the arms issuant.

1–**HAFF, Delbert James,** *b* Oakland Co., Mich., Feb. 19, 1859.
8–Lawrence Jurianse **Haff** (*b* 1649; son of Jurian Haff, native of Augsburg, Swabia, emigrated to Holland and was Dutch soldier in W.I. and Brazil), came from Dutch colony of Brazil with his mother, and settled at Breucklyn, New Amsterdam, 1654, *m* Knierte Pieters, dau. Pieter Jansen Meet, from Holland to New Amsterdam, in the "Rose Tree," 1662;
7–Jacob (bap. 1689), soldier French and Indian War, settled in Dutchess Co., N.Y.;
6–Lawrence (will dated 1753), *m* Hannah–;
5–Ellis, *m* Sarah Champion;
4–Joshua, *m* Sarah Green;

3–Jacob (ca. 1792-1862), educator, Troy, N.Y., *m* Susannah, dau. Benjamin Newton;
2–Ethan Clark (2 below).
8–Henry **Champion** (ca. 1610/11-1708/09), from Eng., settled at Saybrook, Conn., ca. 1647;
7–Henry (*b* 1654), *m* Susanna DeWolf (Balthazar[8], of Lyme, Conn.);
6–Joshua, *m* 2d, 1732, Sarah Griffin (*b* 1702); Jasper[7], *m* Ruth, dau. of Joseph Peck);
5–Sarah (1734-97), *m* Ellis **Haff** (5 above).
8–Hendrick Albertus (Bosch) **Bush** (will dated 1701), from Holland in the "Faith," to New Amsterdam, 1661, *m* 3d, ante 1672, Ebbertie Dircx (widow of Hugh Bruynsen);
7–Hendrick, *m* 1698, Maria Vanderbeck (Coenradus[8]);
6–Coenradus (bap. 1701), removed to Hackensack, *m* 1732, Marytgen Van Blarkum (Gysbert[7]);
5–Gysbert (*b* 1734), *m* Esther (or Ester) Rykeman;
4–Coenradus (1760-1832), large landowner, Parma, N.Y., *m* Caty Vischer (or Catharine Fisher; 1764-1851);
3–Hendrick, or Henry (1792-93-1877), *m* 1811, Rachel DeWitt (1795-1867);
2–Sarah Marilla (1827-1919), *m* Ethan Clark **Haff** (1825-65), Rensselaer Co., N.Y. (for issue see Vol. I, p. 927).
1–*m* Jan. 28, 1891, Grace Isabel Barse, *b* Detroit, Mich., Jan. 4, 1863; dau. late Maj. George Randolph Barse; issue: 1–Carroll Barse (see Vol. I, p. 927); 2–Madeline Barse, *b* Kansas City, Mo., June 7, 1894; A.B., Vassar, '15; 3–Gertrude Barse, *b* Kansas City, May 8, 1896; A.B., Vassar, '17.
1–A.B., U.Mich., '84, LL.B., 1886 (hon. A.M., 1909). Lawyer, senior mem. of Haff, Meservey, Michaels, Blackmar & Newkirk, Kansas City, Mo. Trustee Kansas City Chapter A.R.C.; trustee Kansas City Fine Arts Institute; mem. council I.A.G. (see Who's Who in America). Clubs: American (of Mexico City), Mexico City Country, University (Mexico), University, Congressional Country (of Washington), Kansas City, Blue Hills Country, Mission Hills Country, University (Kansas City). Summer place: Osterville, Cape Cod, Mass. Residence: 416 E. 36th St., Kansas City, Mo.

1–**HAFF, Willard,** *b* Jersey City, N.J., Sept. 24, 1869.
10–Richard **Jackson** (1582-1672), from Eng.; settled Cambridge, Mass., 1636; removed to L.I., 1640; later at Southold; *m* Isabelle Maltby (*d* 1661; John[11]);
9–Robert (1620-84), of Eng.; settled Stamford, Conn.; removed to Hempstead, L.I., 1640; magistrate many yrs.; dep., 1665; constable; overseer; Indian commr.; *m* ca. 1644, Agnes Washburn (ca. 1624-83; William[10]);
8–Col. John (1645-1725), patentee Hempstead, L.I.; commr., 1683; judge, 1685; high sheriff, 1691-1695; mem. Assembly; dep., 23 yrs.; col., 1699; *m* 1671, Elizabeth Seaman (Capt. John[9], *m* Elizabeth, dau. of John Strickland);
7–Samuel (1684-1725), of Hempstead; *m* 1st, Ruth Smith (*b* 1689);
6–Ruth (*b* 1709), *m* 1730, Abel **Smith** (1708-57), of Hempstead, L.I. (Abel[7]);
5–Sarah (*b* 1732), of Hempstead; *m* 1749, in Dutchess Co., N.Y., George **Peters** (1726-82);
4–Sarah (1769-1833), of Dutchess Co.; *m* Isaac **Germond** (1767-1833), of Washington, N.Y.;
3–Caroline (1804-72), of Dutchess Co.; *m* 1831, Stephen **Haff** (1801-70; Joseph E.[4]; Joseph[5]; Jacob[6]; Lawrence[7]; Jurian or George[8]);
2–Stephen (2 below).
10–Thomas **Lord** (qv);
9–Dorothy (*b* Eng., 1629-*d* 1656), of Hartford, Conn.; *m* 1651, John **Ingersoll** (1615-1684), from Eng.; one of seven "Foundation Men" who united to form ch. at Westfield, Mass., 1679;
8–Margery (*b* 1656), of Northampton, Mass.; *m* 1679, Jacob **Goff** (1649-97), of Wethersfield (Philip[9]);
7–Mary (1693-1769), of Farmington, Conn.; *m* 1712, John **Andrus** (1680-1740; John Andrews[8], of Wethersfield);
6–David (1718-98), of Kensington, Conn.; Am. Rev.; *m* 1747, Margaret– (*d* 1763);
5–Margaret (*b* 1752), of Litchfield and Waterbury, Conn.; *m* 1772, Stephen **Russell** (1743-1812), of Litchfield; Am. Rev.;
4–Ursula (1780-1868), of Litchfield; *m* 1804, Samuel **Van Duzer** (1772-1823), of Cornwall, Orange Co., N.Y. (Jacob[5], *m* Mary Ashley; Jacob[6]; Abraham[7]; Isaac[8]; Abraham[9]);
3–William (1807-84), of Cornwall; *m* 1833, Louisa Garland (1810-95), of N.Y.);
2–Katrina (1840-1917), of New York, N.Y.; *m* 1860, Stephen **Haff** (1834-92); mem. 7th N.Y. Regt., Civil War, 1861-65; for other lineages, see Vol. III, p. 219.
1–*m* June 17, 1896, Mary Christina Harris (qv for issue).
1–Ed. Leal's Acad. Credit mgr. Dir. Nat. Credit Men's Assn., 1920; v.p. and dir. Boston Credit Men's Assn.; mem. Boston City Club, Boston Chamber of Commerce, Arkwright Club, Huguenot Soc., S.C.W., S.A.R. Residence: 40 Columbus St., Newton Highlands, Mass.

1–**HAFF, Mary Christina Harris (Mrs. Willard),** *b* E. Haddam, Conn., Apr. 26, 1868.
8–Hon. Philip **Sherman** (qv);
7–Benjamin (1650-1719), of Portsmouth, R.I.; *m* 1674, Hannah Mowry (1656-1718; Roger[8]);
6–Amey (*b* 1681), of Portsmouth; *m* 1701, Stephen **Gardner** (1667-1743; Benoni[7] [1647-1731]; George[8]);
5–David (1720-98), of Montville Conn.; served in Am. Rev.; *m* 1744, Jemima Gustin (1720-98; John[6]; John[7]; Augustine Jean[8], Huguenot);
4–Amey (1745-1815), of Norwich, Conn.; *m* 1764, Dea. Nathaniel **Otis** (1742-1834; Joseph[5]; Judge Joseph[6]; John[7]; John[8]);
3–Anne (1789-1862), of Colchester, Conn.; *m* 1805, Samuel **Harris** (1780-1857; Capt. Nathaniel[4], in Am. Rev.; Jonathan[5]; Lt. James[6]; James[7]);
2–Dr. Nathaniel (2 below).
8–Maj. Simon **Willard** (qv);
7–Capt. Benjamin (1665-1732), of Lancaster, Mass.; *m* 1690, Sarah Lakin (1661-1740; Ens. John[8]);
6–Maj. Joseph (1693-1774), of Sudbury, Mass.; town officer; maj. Worcester Regt.; *m* 1715, Martha Clark (1694-1794; Capt. Isaac[7], *m* Sarah Stow; Lt. Thaddeus[8]);
5–Mary (1730-96), of Grafton, Mass.; *m* 1756, Lt. Daniel **Goddard** (1734-1807), of Shrewsbury, Mass.; lt. Am. Rev.;
4–Hezekiah (1771-1851), of Shrewsbury; q.m. gen. in War 1812; *m* 1795, Phoebe Halsey;
3–Paulina (1798-1856), of Preston, Conn.; *m* 1824, John **Mason** (1784-1856), pvt. in War 1812 (Sgt. Henry[4], served in Am. Rev., *m* Amey Williams; Hobart[5]; Nehemiah[6]; Lt. Daniel[7]; Maj. Gen. John[8]);
2–Juliet (2 below).
10–Thomas **Lord** (qv);
9–Anne (1621-88), of Eng., and Cambridge, Mass.; removed to Hartford, Conn.; *m* 1637, Thomas **Stanton** (qv);
8–Capt. John (1641-1713), capt. King Philip's War; of Stonington, Conn.; *m* 1664, Hannah Thompson (1645-1713; Anthony[9], qv);
7–Joseph (1668-1751), of Stonington; *m* 1696, Margaret Cheeseborough (Nathaniel[8]; William[9], qv);
6–Sarah (*b* 1707), of Stonington; *m* 1738, William **Halsey** (1703-83), of Southampton, L.I. (Jeremiah[7]; Thomas[8]; Thomas[9]);
5–Col. Jeremiah (1743-1829), of Stonington; *m* 1769, Esther Park (1753-1833; Silas[6], *m* Sarah Ayers; Hezekiah[7]; Robert[8]; Dea. Thomas[9]; Sir Robert[10], qv);
4–Phoebe (1772-1803) of Preston, Conn.; *m* Hezekiah **Goddard** (4 above);
3–Paulina, *m* John **Mason** (3 above);
2–Juliet (1832-75), of New London, Conn.; *m* 1855, Dr. Nathaniel Otis **Harris** (1823-1906); for other lineages, see Vol. III, p. 220.
1–*m* June 17, 1896, Willard Haff (qv); issue: 1–Marion Goddard, *b* New York, N.Y., July 18, 1898; N.Y. Sch. of Expression, 1917, A.B., Tufts Coll., '25, A.M., 1926; grad. work, Columbia, 1928-30; 2–Theodore Germond, *b* Arlington, N.J., Jan. 1, 1900; U.S.N.A., 1919; lt. U.S.N.; instructor, U.S.N.A.; *m* Dec. 26, 1922, Dorothy Edmonstone, dau. of Capt. Charles Conard, U.S.N., of Mare Island, Calif. (issue: Priscilla Alden Conard; Kathleen Conard Haff, *b* Mar. 1, 1930); 3–Alexander Otis, *b* Arlington, May 1, 1903; B.S., Tufts Coll., '25, M.D., Yale Med. Coll., 1929; 1st lt., M.C.R., Walter Reed Gen. Hosp., Washington, D.C.; 4–Kathleen Mason, *b* Arlington, Mar. 13, 1906; B.S., Tufts

Coll., '25, A.M., 1928; N.E. Conservatory of Music, 1926-27.
1-Mem. Magna Charta Dames, S.M.D., D.F.P.A., C.D. 17th C., Nat. Soc. Women Descs. of the A. and H.A. Co., D.C.W., H.S.A., D.A.R., U.S.D. 1812, etc. Residence: 40 Columbus St., Newton Highlands, Mass.

1-**HAINES, Thomas H(arvey),** *b* Moorestown, N.J., Nov. 4, 1871.
8-Richard **Haines** (qv);
7-Richard (*d* 1746), *m* 1699, Mary Carlile (*d* 1746);
6-Abram (*d* ca. 1757), *m* 1719, Grace Hollingshead (John[7], *m* Agnes Hackney);
5-Benjamin (1725-will dated 1800), *m* 3d, Sarah Butcher (John[6], *m* Mary-);
4-Clayton (1780-1816); *m* Rebecca Wills (*b* 1784; Zebedee[5], *m* Priscilla Moore);
3-Zebedee (1807-1860), *m* 1830, Elizabeth Hendrickson (1809-58; Joseph[4], *m* Elisabeth Forsythe);
2-Zebedee (2 below).
5-William **Harvey** (*d* 1779-80), killed by British at Valley Forge, Pa.; *m* Mary Streeper;
4-Samuel (1779-1863), *m* Esther Marshall (1780-1862; Thomas[4], *m* 1769, Anne Cock, *b* 1745);
3-Thomas Marshall (1820-86), *m* 1847, Deborah Philips (1820-53; Isaac[4], *m* Hannah Maule);
2-Anna Philips (1849-1924), *m* 1870, Zebedee **Haines** (1843-1923), educator, minister, farmer; issue: I-Thomas H. (1 above); II-Edgar T. (*b* 1873; *m* 1919, Flora McBane, *b* 1891); III-Alfred Sharpless (1875-1909; *m* 1901, Edith Hayes, *b* 1876); IV-Deborah Philips (1876-1914; *m* 1903, Evan B. Sharpless, *b* 1876); V-William Herbert (*b* 1881; *m* 1914, Hannah Cope, *b* 1888); VI-Mary Elizabeth (1886-1920).
1-*m* Dec. 27, 1901, Rachel A. Russell (1873-1903); dau. of Joseph Russell, of Colerain, O.
1-*m* 2d, Aug. 15, 1912, Helen Manley Hague, *b* Salem, O.; dau. of James Russell Hague, Columbus, O.
1-A.B., Haverford, '96; Ph.D., Harvard, 1901; M.D., Ohio State U., 1912. Dir. of surveys and dir. div. on mental deficiency, Nat. Com. for Mental Hygiene, 1917-25; psychiatrist (see Who's Who in America). Residence: 30 Oxford St., Montclair, N.J.

1-**HALE, (Charlotte) Elizabeth Prescott,** *b* New York, N.Y., Dec. 5, 1870.
10-Thomas **Hale** (qv);
9-Hon. Thomas (1633-88), selectman, Haverhill; King Philip's War; *m* 1657, Mary Hutchinson (1630-1716);
8-Capt. Thomas (1659-1730), selectman, Newbury; rep. Gen. Ct., 1713-14; justice; *m* 1682, Sarah Northend (1661-1732);
7-Capt. Thomas (1683-1747), selectman, Newbury; capt. militia; *m* 1704, Anna Short (1682-1770);
6-Capt. Thomas (1705-59), rep. Provincial Legislature; selectman and clk., Haverhill dist.; *m* 1728, Mary Smith (1711-70);
5-Lt. Benjamin (1735-81), Am. Rev.; town treas. and justice, Newbury; *m* 1762, Lydia White (1738-91);
4-Thomas (1773-1836), *m* 1797, Alice Little; *m* 2d, Mary Little, sister of 1st wife (*d* 1871);
3-Benjamin, D.D. (1797-1863), A.B., Bowdoin, 1818; P.E. priest; prof. physics and chemistry, Dartmouth Coll.; pres. Hobart Coll., 1836-58; started the first poly. inst. in the country in his sch. in Gardiner, Me.; elected pres. Columbia Coll., but declined; *m* 1823, Mary Caroline Alsop King (1799-1867);
2-Thomas (2 below).
9-George **Little** (qv):
8-Moses (1657-91), *m* 1679, Lydia Coffin (1662-1725);
7-Moses (1691-1780), *m* 1716, Sarah Jacques (1697-1763);
6-Moses (1724-98), capt. Lexington Alarm, 1775, col. 17th Mass. militia; commd. brig. gen., 1777, but declined on account of poor health; *m* 1743, Abigail Bailey (1724-1815);
5-Hon. Col. Josiah (1747-1830), rep. Gen. Ct., 25 yrs.; *m* Sarah Tappan (1748-1823);
4-Alice (1775-1819), *m* Thomas **Hale** (4 above).
4-Col. William **Searcy** (*d* 1846; Huguenot ancestors fled from France to the Carolinas upon revocation of the Edict of Nantes), planter at Murphreesboro, Tenn., plantation at Stoney Creek with over 300 slaves; *m* 1st, Elizabeth Green, of Charleston, S.C.;
3-Gen. Isham Green (1799-1841), maj. Seminole War; civil engr.; post-master, Tallahassee, Fla.; *m* Charlotte Pettes Prescott (1818-1907; Samuel[4], of Concord, Mass.);
2-Lucy Frederic (1840-1909), *m* 1870, Thomas **Hale** (1834-1919), B.A., Hobart, '53; pres. Pacific Marine Ins. Co., New York, N.Y.; 23d N.Y. Regt. Civil War; issue: I-Elizabeth Prescott (1 above); II-Thomas (*b* 1874; *m* 1901, Elizabeth Hall Henderson, *b* 1878).
1-Mem. D.F.P.A., D.C.G., C.D., D.A.R. Residence: 69 High St., Yonkers, N.Y.

1-**HALE, Prentis Cobb,** *b* South Haven, Mich., Dec. 12, 1858.
8-Thomas **Hale** (qv);
7-Thomas (1633-88), *m* Mary Hutchinson;
6-Joseph (1670-1761), *m* Mary Watson;
5-Ambrose (1699-1767), *m* Joanna Dodge;
4-Ambrose (1740-1811), *m* Mercy Daby;
3-Jacob (1769-1822), *m* Roccina Beebe;
2-Marshal (2 below).
8-Jan **Dyckman** (*d* 1715), from Holland, 1660, settled in New Amsterdam;
7-Jacobus (1692-1773);
6-William (1725-87);
5-William;
4-William (1761-1846), soldier Am. Rev.; *m* Maria Smith (1766-1845);
3-Evert Brown (1799-1881), *m* Harriet Hinckley (1801-38);
2-Prudence Tennant Dyckman (Cobb) (1828-1907), *m* 1854, Marshal **Hale** (1809-91), mcht., San Jose, Calif.; issue: I-Evert Wilben (1856-1914; *m* Birdenia Lee Hogan); II-Prentis Cobb (1 above); III-Della (1861-86; *m* Robert W. Burtis, *d*); IV-Jennie (*b* 1864; *m* Hiram B. Fisher); V-Marshal (see Vol. III, p. 220); VI-Reuben Brooks (see Vol. I, p. 130).
1-*m* Oct. 1, 1908, Linda (Bryan) Hoag (see Vol. II, p. 349); issue: 1-Prentis Cobb, Jr., *b* San Francisco, Calif., July 30, 1910.
1-Merchant and banker. Awarded Cross of Chevalier of Crown of Italy. Club: Pacific Union. Residence: 2430 Vallejo St., San Francisco, Calif.

1-**HALL, Arnold Bennett,** *b* Franklin, Ind., July 22, 1881.
9-Francis **Hall** (1606-08-1690; son of Gilbert, of Kent, Eng.); from Eng. with Rev. Henry Whitfield; settled at New Haven, Conn., 1639; removed to Fairfield, 1640; to Stratford, 1659; *m* 1627/28, Elizabeth- (*d* 1662);
8-Dr. Isaac (1629/30-1714), came with father; *m* 1666, Lydia Knapp (*b* 1644/45; Nicholas[9]);
7-John (1679-1749/50), of Stratford; *m* 1713, Abigail Grummond (*b* 1685; John[8]; John[9]);
6-Capt. Jabez (1724-76), *d* in service during Am. Rev.; *m* ca. 1746, Hannah Lyon (1726-1807; Capt. John[7]; Sgt. Samuel[8]; Richard[9]);
5-Lt. John (1751-1839), removed to Perrysburg, O.; *m* ca. 1780, Phebe Benedict (*b* 1760; Lt. John[6]; Capt. John[7]; Dea. James[8]; Lt. Thomas[9], founder Presbyn. ch. in America);
4-Dea. Horace (ca. 1787-1850), of Perrysburg, O.; War 1812; *m* 1808, Zylpha Mason (ca. 1787-1878;)
3-Nehin Columbus or Nelson (1820-89), of Chili, Ind.; *m* 1844, Letitia Griswold (1820-1903);
2-Columbus Horatio (1846-1926), A.B., A.M., B.D., D.D.; prof. of Greek and v.p. Franklin Coll.; *m* 1875, Theodosia Parks (1856-1919), M.S.; issue: I-Zoe Parks (1876-1907; *m* John Hall); II-Mary Griswold (*b* 1878; *m* 1905, Capt. George Messich Selby, M.D., 1879-1926); III-Arnold Bennett (1 above); IV-Theodore (1883-84); V-Letitia (*b* 1886; *m* Prof. Ralph Emerson Carter, A.M.); VI-Warren Short, Ph.B. (*b* 1889; *m* Jane Grace Dorsey); VII-Nelson Clarence, A.B., C.P.A. (*b* 1891; *m* 1923, Carol Evelyn Conlee, *b* 1897); VIII-Esther Marguerite, A.M., Ph.D. (*b* 1895; *m* Victor Lincoln Albjerg, Ph.-D.); IX-Florence Christine, A.B. (*b* 1903).
1-*m* June 15, 1911, Grace Stafford Carney, *b* Vernon, Ind., Mar. 23, 1884; dau. Henry Carney, of Franklin, Ind.; issue: 1-Grace Elizabeth, *b* Madison, Wis., July 23, 1922.
1-A.B., Franklin Coll., '04 (Phi Delta Theta, Phi Delta Phi, Delta Sigma Rho, P.B.K., Order of the Coif); J.D., cum laude, U.Chicago, 1907; post-grad. study, U.Chicago, 1907-09; (LL.D., Franklin Coll., 1924). Instr., Northwestern U., 1909-10; instr., asst. prof., asso. prof., and prof. polit. science, and asso. prof. law, U.Wis. 1910-26; pres. U. of Ore., 1926-.

Mem. Wis. War History Commn., 1919-1926; Social Science Research Council since 1924; dir. Hanover Conf. 1926,27; pres. Nat. Conf. on Science of Politics, 1924,25,26. Dir. Bank of Commonwealth, La Salle Extension U., State Library Bd. of Ore., Am. Branch of Inst. of Pacific Relation. Author (see Who's Who in America). Baptist. Independent Republican. Clubs: University (Portland, Ore.), Faculty, Eugene, Eugene Country. Residence: 1170 E. 13th Av., Eugene, Ore.

1-**HALL, Robert William,** *b* Cincinnati, O., Aug. 17, 1872.
6-Samuel **Nichols,** from Antrim, Ireland, 1753;
5-Thomas (*d* 1810), first settler at Antrim, N.H.; served Am. Rev.; hunter and trader with Indians; to Cattaraugus, N.Y., 1808; *m* 1777, Hannah Clarke, of Francestown;
4-Mary Ann, *m* Ephraim **Hall**;
3-William (*b* Sept. 20, 1808), with wife missionary among the Indians, 47 yrs.; *m* Oct. 22, 1834, Emeline Gaylord (*d* aet. 74);
2-Ephraim Gaylord (2 below).
10-Nathaniel **Fiske,** *m* Dorothy Symonds;
9-Nathan (1615-76), from Eng.; selectman, 1673; *m* Susanna-;
8-Lt. Nathan (1642-94), of Watertown, Mass.; served in colonial wars; selectman, 1684,88,91; *m* Elizabeth Fry (*d* 1696);
7-William (1678-1750), of Watertown, Mass., and Wallingford, Conn.; *m* Eunice Jennings (*b* 1686), of Framingham, Mass.;
6-Hannah, *m* Jeremiah **Powers**;
5-Aaron, *m* Olive Osborne;
4-Olive, *m* Richard **Crossette**;
3-Robert, *m* Dorothea Fisher;
2-Alice Cogswell (2 below).
10-Anthony **Fisher** (qv);
9-Anthony (*d* 1670), surveyor, Dedham, 1652-54; selectman, 1664; *m* Joanna Faxon (Thomas[10], *m* Joane-);
8-Josiah (1654-1736), rep., 1699; selectman, 1697; *m* 1st, 1680, Melethiah Bullen (1655-93; Samuel[9], *m* Mary, dau. of Samuel Morse, *m* Elizabeth-);
7-Josiah (1683-1763), capt. militia; selectman, Dedham, 1736; *m* 1707, Elizabeth Avery (Dea. William[8], *m* Elizabeth White; Dr. William[9]; Robert[10]);
6-Jonathan, *m* Mary Richards;
5-Jonathan, *m* Katherine Avery (William[6], *m* Bethiah Metcalf; Capt. William[7]; Dea. William[8]; Dr. William[9], above);
4-Jonathan, *m* Dolly Battelle;
3-Dorothea, *m* Robert **Crossette** (3 above).
10-John **Fairbanks**;
9-Mary, *m* Michael **Metcalf** (Michael[10], *m* Sarah Ellwyn);
8-Jonathan, *m* Hannah Kenrick;
7-Hannah, *m* James **Richards** (Nathaniel[8], *m* Mary, dau. of John Aldis, *m* Sarah, dau. of Philip Eliot, *m* Elizabeth-);
6-Mary, *m* Jonathan **Fisher** (6 above).
8-Thomas **Battelle** (1622-1706), from Eng., 1642; settled at Dedham, Mass., where he was selectman, 1677-85, town clk., 1687; *m* Mary Fisher;
7-John (1652-1712), *m* 1678, Hannah Holbrook;
6-Ebenezer (1691-1759), *m* 1718, Abigail Allen (Joseph[7], *m* Hannah Sabin; James[8]; Reginald[9]);
5-Ebenezer (1729-76), *m* 1751, Prudence Draper;
4-Dolly, *m* Jonathan **Fisher** (4 above).
9-John **Dwight** (qv);
8-Hannah, *m* Nathaniel **Whiting** (qv);
7-Abigail, *m* James **Draper**;
6-Ebenezer, *m* Dorothy Child (Joshua[7], *m* Elizabeth Morris; Benjamin[8]; Griffith[9]; Francis[10]);
5-Prudence, *m* Ebenezer **Battelle** (5 above).
2-Alice Cogswell Crossette (1839-1909), *m* 1869, Ephraim Gaylord **Hall** (1840-81), A.B., U.-Mich., 1861, M.A., 1866; capt. 11th Mich. Vols., Civil War; lawyer, asst. to pres. Erie R.R.; issue: I-Gaylord Crosette (*b* 1871); II-Robert William (1 above); III-Norman Fisher (1878-1906).
1-*m* Aug. 4, 1908, Mary Alice Bowers, *b* Saco, Me., Oct. 2, 1871; dau. of Hon. Roscoe L. Bowers, of Saco; issue (all *b* Bethlehem, Pa.): 1-Roberta Bowers, *b* Feb. 17, 1911; 2-Marjorie Crossette, *b* June 13, 1913; 3-Roscoe Bowers, *b* July 4, 1915.
1-Ph.B., Yale, '95 (Sigma Xi); A.B., Harvard, '97, M.A., 1898, Ph.D., 1901. Prof. biology, head of biol. dept., Lehigh U. (see Who's Who in America). Felow A.A.A.S.; dir. Pa. Forestry Assn. (life mem.), mem. N.E. Soc. of Pa., Fairbanks Fam. of America. Rotarian. Conglist. Republican. Clubs: Saucon Valley Country. Summer place: "Crossroad Cottage," West Baldwin, Me. Residence: 37 E. Church St., Bethlehem, Pa.

1-**HALL, Winfield Scott,** *b* Batavia, Ill., Jan. 5, 1861.
9-Nathaniel **Foote** (qv);
8-Nathaniel (1620-55), from Eng., with his father; *m* 1646, Elizabeth Smith (Lt. Samuel[9], of Wethersfield, Conn.);
7-Samuel (1649-89), of Hatfield, Mass.; *m* 1671, Mary Merrick (*d* 1690);
6-Daniel (1689-1740), *m* 1718, Mary Collyer (*d* 1769);
5-Joseph (1727-79), of Simsbury, Conn.; *m* 1757, Azubah Griswold (*d* 1829 aet. 93), of Windsor, Conn.;
4-Elisha (1764-1853), of Northampton, N.Y.; *m* 1783, Rebecca Clark Miller, of Avon, Conn.;
3-Joseph (*b* 1803), of Northampton, N.Y., and Neb. City, Neb.; *m* 1829, Angelina Spier (*d* 1839);
2-Sarah Adelia (1835-1918), of California, and La Crosse, Wis.; *m* 1858, Albert Nelson **Hall** (1834-1907), farmer, justice of peace, assemblyman; issue: I-Winfield Scott (1 above); II-Harvey Nelson (*b* 1866); III-Nettie Spier (*b* 1868); IV-Lottie (1871-75).
1-*m* Oct. 11, 1888, Jeannette Mary Winter, *b* Princeton, Ill., Dec. 15, 1860; dau. of William M. Winter, of Princeton, *m* Mary Ann Abbott; issue: 1-Albert Winter, *b* Zurich, Switzerland, Jan. 8, 1895; B.S., Haverford Coll., '17, M.D., Northwestern U., 1924, M.S., 1925; *m* June 28, 1924, Reba, dau. of Frank Haner, of Sun Prairie, Wis. (issue: Jeannette Fanny; have adopted 2 children, Mary and Frances, of deceased sister of Mrs. Reba Haner Hall); 2-Ethel Louise, *m* Lt. Paul Kingsley; 3-Reymond Ludwig, *m* Mary Case (issue: Winfield Philo; Richard Reymond; Norman); 4-Muriel Jeannette, *m* Ronald Appleton Scott (issue: Barbara).
1-B.S., Northwestern U., '87, M.D., 1888, M.S., 1889; M.D., U.Leipsic, 1894, Ph.D., 1895 (Phi Kappa Psi, P.B.K., Nu Sigma Nu, Alpha Omega Alpha, Sigma Xi, Pi Gamma Mu, Omicron Delta Kappa). Head dept. biology, Haverford (Pa.) Coll., 1889-93; U.Leipsic, 1893-95; prof. physiology, Northwestern U. Med. Sch., 1895-1919, prof. emeritus since 1919, and jr. dean med. faculty, 1901-13. Exchange prof. Universite Internationale (Brussels, Belgium), since 1921; dir. med. sociology, Bd. of Christian Edn., of the Presbyn. Ch., U.S.A., 1919-29 (see Who's Who in America). Ruling elder, Presbyn Ch. U.S.A. Republican. Summer place: "Wynnewood," Grand Haven, Mich. Residence: Irvington, Ala.

1-**HALLOCK, Gerard Benjamin Fleet,** *b* Holliday's Cove, W.Va., Jan. 28, 1856.
9-Peter **Hallock,** Pilgrim from Eng.; one of 13 Englishmen who landed at Hallock's Neck, L.I., 1626; returned to Eng. and in 1640, came to Southold, L.I.; settled finally at Aquebogue, nr. Mattituck; *m* Mrs. Howell, a widow;
8-William (1610-84), inherited the homestead; *m* Margaret Howell; had sons, Thomas, Peter, William, John;
7-Peter (*b* ca. 1665), settled at Southold, L.I.; had sons, Peter, William, Noah;
6-Noah (1696-1773), settled at Blue Point, L.I.; *m* 1721, Bethiah Youngs; had sons, Noah, William, Josiah;
5-William (1730-1815), soldier in Am. Rev.; *m* Alice Homan; both buried at Goshen, Mass.;
4-Rev. Moses (1758-1837), B.A., Yale, 1788; soldier in Am. Rev.; pastor, Plainfield, Mass., 45 yrs.; head of classical sch., 40 yrs.; *m* 1792, Margaret Allen (1760-1835), of Chilmark, Martha's Vineyard;
3-Homan (1803-94), type founder and missionary printer at Malta and Smyrna; co-inventor of Arabic type; printed 1st Arabic Bible; *m* 1828, Elizabeth (Fleet) Andrews (1799-1875);
2-Homan Benjamin (1830-95), printer, worked for Am. Bible Soc., New York; removed via

Erie Canal to Ohio, ca. 1852; settled as merchant at Steubenville; *m* 1854, Adelia Ann Farnsworth (1835-1928); issue: I–Gerard Benjamin Fleet (1 above); II–Robert Crawford, Ph.D., D.D. (*b* 1857; *m* 1885, Martha Wells); III–Effie Victorine (1859-1909; *m* 1886, Rev. William Paxton Braddock, *d* 1889); IV–Silas Farnsworth, M.D. (*b* 1861; *m* 1889, Sarah J. Cobb, *d* 1913); V–John Crawford, M.D. (*b* 1865; *m* Katherine Throck-Morton); VI–William Allen (*b* 1867; *m* 1899, Dorra M. Bigelow); VII–Henry G. C. (qv for maternal lineage); VIII–Charles C. Beattie (*b* 1871); IX–Mary Elizabeth (*b* 1874; *m* 1915, Rev. Dr. Albert B. Marshall); X–Frances Adelia, Ph.D. (*b* 1876); XI–Margaret Sutherland (*b* 1879; *m* 1906, Rev. Merlo K. W. Heicher, Ph.D.); XII–Homan Fitz Green (*b* 1883; *m* 1915, Elizabeth F. Wheeler).

1–*m* May 8, 1888, Anna Catherine Cobb, *b* Phila., Pa., 1858; dau. of Rev. Archibald P. Cobb, of Freehold, N.J.; issue: 1–Clarissa Cobb (Jan. 9, 1890-Jan. 20, 1893); 2–Archibald Cobb, *b* N.Y. City, June 13, 1893; Cornell U.; *m* Feb. 2, 1917, Elizabeth, dau. Hon. William H. Reid, of Tennent, N.J. (issue: Archibald C., Jr.; Richard R.); 3–Marianna Cobb, and 4–Adelia Cobb, twins; *b* New York, N.Y., May 11, 1897; A.B., Smith Coll., '21.

1–A.B., Princeton, '82; grad. Princeton Theol. Sem., 1885; (D.D., Richmond Coll., 1896; A.M., Princeton, 1901). Ordained Presbyn. ministry, 1885; pastor at Scottsville, N.Y., 1885-89; one of ministers at Brick Ch., Rochester, since 1890. Author of many books. Commr. Gen. Assembly Presbyn. Ch. U.S.A. 3 times. Trustee Elmira Coll. Life mem. Am. Bible Soc. Republican (see Who's Who in America). Residence: 10 Livingston Pk., Rochester, N.Y.

1–**HALLOCK, Henry Galloway Comingo,** *b* Holliday's Cove, W.Va., Mar. 31, 1870.
8–Matthias **Farnsworth** (qv);
7–Jothan;
6–Simeon;
5–Simeon, settled at Washington, N.H.; *m* Ellen or Esther Ellinwood;
4–Calvin (*b* 1776), removed to Pa.; *m* Lydia Biggsbee;
3–Silas (*b* 1804), of Washington, N.H.; *m* Mary Headington (Rev. Nicholas[4], Bapt. minister at Cross Creek, W.Va.);
2–Adelia Ann (1835-1928), *m* 1854, Homan Benjamin **Hallock** (1830-95), printer; worked for Am. Bible Soc., New York; removed via Erie Canal to Ohio, ca. 1852; settled as merchant at Steubenville (for issue and Hallock lineage see Gerard B. F. Hallock).
1–A.B., Princeton, '93; grad. Princeton Theol. Sem., 1896; Ph.D., Richmond Coll., 1896. Ordained Presbyn. ministry, 1896; apptd. missionary to China; became self-supporting missionary, 1905. Prof. homiletics and dean of Theol. Sch. of U.China, 1925-27. Author (see Who's Who in America). Address: Chinese P.O. Box 1234, Shanghai, China.

1–**HALLOCK, Lucius Henry,** *b* Suffolk Co., N.Y., Apr. 16, 1853.
9–Peter **Hallock** (*b* 1590), came to L.I., N.Y., 1626; returned to Eng. and in 1640, settled at Mattituck, L.I.; *m* 2d, Widow Howell;
8–William (1610-84), of Mattituck, L.I.; *m* 1640, Margaret Howell (*b* 1620; Widow Howell[9]);
7–Thomas (*b* 1660), *m* ca. 1680, Hope Youngs (*d* 1733);
6–Zerubabel (1696-1761), of Mattituck; *m* 1719, Esther Osman (1695-1773);
5–Zerubabel (1722-1800), of Mattituck; *m* 1743, Elizabeth Swezey (1722-1806);
4–Daniel (1755-1844), of Mattituck; aide-de-camp to General Putnam; *m* 1778, Mary Wells (1758-1829);
3–Ezra (1797-1882), *m* 1821, Lydia Emily Young (1802-98; Thomas[4]);
2–George Whitfield (1824-1903), farmer; *m* 1848, Hannah Jane Terry (1827-97); issue: I–James Horace (*b* and *d* 1850); II–Lucius Henry (1 above); III–Ezra Young (1854-74); IV–Evelyn Jessie (1856-1918; *m* 1878, Frank L. Young).
1–*m* Jan. 3, 1882, Mary Emma King, *b* Orient, L.I., N.Y., Oct. 3, 1855; dau. of Henry Y. King, of Orient; issue (all *b* Orient, N.Y.): 1–Ellis Henry, *b* Feb. 10, 1883; *m* Dec. 28, 1904, Edith M., dau. of Irving Coons, of Red Hook, N.Y.; 2–Grace Evelyn (May 2, 1884-Feb. 14, 1920); studied music and painting in oils at Boston U.; *m* Oct. 12, 1910, John L. Kahler; 3–Walter Royal (July 15, 1888-May 18, 1900); 4–George Whitfield, *b* Jan. 16, 1892; grad. Bliss Electrical Coll., Washington, D.C.; *m* Nov. 29, 1913, E. E. Jeannette, dau. of Benjamin L. Young, of Orient and Jamaica, L.I., N.Y. (issue: George Whitfield; Norman Everett).
1–Carpenter, 1870-73; partner firm of George W. Hallock & Son, farmers and produce dealers, 1873-1903, sr. partner, 1903-20, retired partner, since 1920. Trustee Orient Dist. Sch., 1890-1906, Southold Savings Bank, 1925; pres. bd. of trustees of the M.E. Ch., Orient, N.Y. Author: A Little Journey, 1925; Hallock Genealogy, 1928. Life mem. I.A.G. Republican. Residence: Orient, L.I., N.Y.

1–**HAMAKER, John Irvin,** *b* Elizabethtown, Pa., Nov. 29, 1869.
6–Johon (Hammaker) **Hamaker,** from Germany, 1740; settled in Lancaster Co., Pa.;
5–John (*b* 1740), *m* Maria Bolinger (1743-1821);
4–Abraham, *m* Elizabeth Hiestand (Peter[5]; Jacob[6], came to Lancaster Co., Pa., 1727);
3–John, began to write name Hamaker; *m* Elizabeth Bossler;
2–Jacob B. (2 below).
6–Mathias (Gisch) **Gish,** landed 1733;
5–Abraham (*d* 1789), *m* —Schrock;
4–John (1774-1871), *m* Elizabeth Engel (1775-1847; Johannes[5], founder of the Brethren in Christ);
3–John I. (1800-75), began to write name Gish; *m* Susanna Musser (1806-55);
2–Martha M. (1845-71), *m* 1868, Jacob B. **Hamaker** (1849-1907); issue: I–John Irvin (1 above); II–Jacob G. (*b* 1871; *m* Lillian Rugh); and III–Martha G. (twins; 1871-72).
1–*m* Aug. 12, 1914, Maud Ray Parker, *b* Madison, Mo., July 22, 1890; dau. of Richard Alexander Parker, of Shanghai, China; issue: 1–Madeline, *b* Washington, D.C., July 11, 1915; 2–Marjorie-Love, *b* Washington, Sept. 22, 1917; 3–Templin (July 16, 1919-Dec. 24, 1920); 4–Richard Franklin, *b* Lynchburg, Va., Jan. 10, 1924.
1–A.B., U.Kan., '93; Harvard U., 1893-97, A.M., 1895, Ph.D., 1897; studied U.Berlin, 1910-11. Prof. biology, Randolph-Macon Woman's Coll., since 1904. Author (see Who's Who in America). Methodist. Club: "Sphex." Residence: Lynchburg, Va.

1–**HAMILTON, Laurens Morgan,** *b* Tuxedo, N.Y., June 18, 1900.
10–Edward **Howell** (qv);
9–Maj. John (1625-96), his tombstone earliest in N.J., *m* Susannah– (ca. 1628-1711);
8–Susannah, *m* Col. Henry **Pierson** (1652-1701), of Southampton, L.I. (Henry[9], qv);
7–Josiah (1695-1776), he *m* 4 times; *m* Martha Halsey;
6–Benjamin (1741-96), *m* Sarah Gilbert;
5–Jeremiah (1766-1855), *m* Sarah Colt (Jabez[6]);
4–Henry Lewis (1807-93), *m* Helen Maria Pierson;
3–Helen Maria (1834-92), *m* William Gaston **Hamilton** (1832-1913), engr. and financier, New York;
2–William Pierson (2 below).
9–Daniel Janse **Van Antwerpen** (1635-1717), from Antwerp; was at Beverwyck (Albany), 1661, later at Schenectady; was dep. schout fiscal at Ft. Orange and at Altoona, on Delaware River; mem. Ct. of Justice and town supervisor; *m* Maria Simonse Groot (Simon S.[10]);
8–Rebecca (1692-1765), *m* Johannes **Fort** (1685-1746);
7–Johannes (1717-86), *m* Rebecca–;
6–Abraham (1760-1822), *m* Jane Monfoort (1757-1823);
5–Helen Maria (1781-1820), *m* Isaac **Pierson** (1770-1845);
4–Helen M. (1807-45), *m* Henry L. **Pierson** (4 above).
10–John **Taylor** (*b* 1610), from Eng.; settled at Cambridge; of Harvard Coll.; *m* Katherine Wilcox;
9–Rev. Joseph (1651-82), grad. Harvard, 1669; minister, Southampton, L.I.; *m* as her 2d husband, 1676, Mary Bryan (*b* ca. 1650; Richard[10]; Alexander[11]);
8–Joseph (1681-1718), *m* 1706, Mehitabel Halsey (*b* 1691; Isaac[9], *m* Abigail, dau. of John Howell[9] above; Thomas[10]; Thomas[11], qv);

7-Elizabeth (*d* 1807), *m* 1741, John **Spencer** (1696-1757), see Vol. III, p. 549 for Spencer lineage;
6-Samuel (1744-1818), of Middletown, Conn.; *m* 1771, Martha Eells (1743-1831);
5-Sally (1787-1859), *m* 1807, Joseph **Morgan** (1780-1847); see Vol. I, p. 640 for Morgan lineage;
4-Junius Spencer (1813-90), *m* 1836, Juliet Pierpont (1816-84); see Vol. III, p. 549 for Pierpont-Hooker lineage;
3-John Pierpont (1837-1913), famous financier; *m* 1865, Frances Louise Tracy (1842-1924), see Vol. I, p. 639 for Tracy lineage;
2-Juliet Pierpont (*b* 1870), *m* 1894, William Pierson **Hamilton** (see Vol. I, p. 640).
1-*m* Jan. 22, 1920, Gertrude (Malisch) Warren.
1-Ed. Groton (Mass.) School, and Mass. Inst. of Tech. Left M.I.T., 1918, to enter army; commd. 2d lt., inf., Sept. 1918; 2d lt., cav., 1919; resigned, Jan. 1920. Since 1920 engaged in business at Paris, France. Mem. S.R., S.A.R., etc. Clubs: St. Anthony (New York), Interallied, Golfers, St. Anthony (Paris). Residence: 1 bis Av. Foch, Paris, France.

1-**HAMILTON, Rosa Virginia,** *b* New Bern, N.C., June 21, 1873.
6-Thomas **Carr**, planter, Bedford Co., Va.; sgt. in Am. Rev., Cont. Line, lost leg in service;
5-Hezekiah, of Chesterfield Co., Va.; *m* 1790, Edith Parsons Ragland;
4-Elizabeth, of Chesterfield Co.; *m* her cousin, Richard **Carr**;
3-Mary Ann (1821-87), of Chesterfield Co.; *m* 1841, Bedell **Hamilton** (1810-95), from Newry, Ireland; pvt. Seminole War (son of Rev. William, Methodist missionary in Ireland, *m* Mary Ann Bradshaw);
2-James Wilky (2 below).
6-James **Fryer,** *m* Mary Grant, of Portsmouth, Va.;
5-Ann (1772-1821), of Portsmouth, Va.; *m* James **Waughop** (1769-1817), merchant marine;
4-Mary Ann (1800-84), of Portsmouth; *m* 1817, Amos **Edwards** (1794-1864), lt. War 1812, pvt. Mexican War (Oney[5], *m* Mollie Hancock);
3-Amos Wiseman (1831-91), pvt. Portsmouth Rifle Co. G. 9th Va. Regt., C.S.A.; *m* 1852, Mary Elizabeth Moore (1838-1916; John O.[4], *m* Ann Wyatt);
2-Sophia Ann (1855-1923), *m* 1871, James Wilky **Hamilton** (*b* 1845), pvt. C.S.A.; issue: I-Rosa Virginia (1 above); II-Mary Ann (*m* J. W. Nunnally; *m* 2d, Julian T. Jackson); III-James Walter (*d* infancy); IV-Isabel Alvira (*d* infancy); V-Annie Elizabeth (*m* W. B. Tucker); VI-William Edwards (*m* Eva Mary McGee; *m* 2d, Louise Lorain).
1-Teacher public school in N.C. Methodist. Democrat. Address: Warrenton, N.C. Home: Mathews Court House, Va.

1-**HAMILTON, Sally Parke Wellford (Mrs.),** *b* Atlanta, Ga., June 28, 1874.
4-Robert **Wellford** (1753-1823; son of William of Dare); physician and surgeon in British Army; came from Eng. with the mil. forces under Sir William Howe, and settled at Phila., Pa.; became a physician in Pa.; surgeon gen. of all the Va. forces which marched in 1794 to quell the Whiskey Rebellion in Pa.; *m* 1781, Catherine (Yates) Thornton (1760-1831; Rev. Robert Yates[5], *m* Mary Randolph);
3-Dr. Beverley Randolph (1797-1870), of Fredericksburg and Richmond, Va.; *m* 2d, Mary Alexander (1801-65); see Vol. III, p. 223;
2-Philip Alexander (2 below).
7-Anthony **Waddy,** *m* 2d, Ann Parke;
6-Harriet, *m* John **Street** (*b* 1700), came to Va. bet., 1720-30;
5-John (1735-1801), Hanover Co.; surveyed Parke property, 1752; q.m. in Am. Rev.; *m* Frances Parke;
4-Anthony (1773-1844), *m* Susan Goodall;
3-Parke, *m* Rebecca Williams (Thomas[4], of Richmond);
2-Mary Belle (2 below).
10-William **Parke,** from Eng. to Va., 1652; *m* Sarah-;
9-Daniel (1628-79), *m* Rebecca Evelyn (Capt. George[10], prominent in Md., settled in Va., 1649, *m* —Robins);
8-John (*d* 1710), of St. Peter's Parish;
7-Capt. John (*d* 1725), of New Kent Co., Va.;
6-John (*b* 1707), of St. Peter's Parish, 1747; *m* Susanne-;
5-Frances (*b* 1735), *m* bet. 1750-60, Capt. John **Street** (5 above).
2-Maj. Philip Alexander **Wellford** (1833-1909), Co. F, 21st Va. Inf., C.S.A.; *m* 1872, Mary Belle Street (*d* 1877); issue: I-Roberta (*b* 1873); II-Sally Parke (1 above); III-Thomas Spotswood (1876-1906; *m* Mary Byrd Dimmock).
1-*m* Nov. 27, 1895, Robert Patrick Hamilton, *b* Petersburg, Va., Dec. 23, 1872 (divorced, 1914); son of Robert P. Hamilton, of Petersburg; issue (all *b* Petersburg, Va.): 1-Robert Patrick, Jr., *b* Nov. 23, 1896; U.Va., '17; Columbia, 1924; Rhodes scholar at Oxford, Eng., 1921-23; enlisted U.S. Ambulance Service, June 1917; served with 66th Div., French Chasseurs Alpines, Jan. 1918-July 1919; participated in campaigns at Soissons-Noyon, Amiens, and the Hindenburg Line; awarded Croix de Guerre with silver star; *m* June 5, 1926, Portia, dau. of Charles Goulder, of Cleveland, O. (issue: Portia Virginia, *b* Jan. 3, 1930); 2-Philip Wellford, *b* Apr. 13, 1898; U.Va., '20; enlisted U.S.N., served at Newport, R.I., and on sea; *m* Oct. 2, 1924, Katherine Page, dau. of Alfred Willis Withers, of Gloucester Co., Va. (issue: Philip Wellford, Jr., *b* Aug. 29, 1927); 3-John Bland, *b* Nov. 8, 1902; U.Va., '22; *m* June 18, 1928, Jeanne Marie, dau. of Samuel Purcell Hatcher, *m* Grace Stewart.
1-Mem. C.D.A. Residence: 150 Chancellor St., University, Va.

1-**HAMLIN, Herbert William,** *b* Chicago, Ill., Dec. 3, 1870.
8-Capt. Giles **Hamlin** (qv);
7-William (1668-1733), *m* 1692, Susannah Collins (Nathaniel[8]);
6-Charles (1707-81), *m* 1st, 1735, Elizabeth Starr (Josiah[7]; Comfort[8]; Dr. Thomas[9]; Dr. Comfort[10], qv);
5-Charles (1736-1815), *m* 1761, Elizabeth Rogers;
4-Dea. Jabez (1780-1858), emigrated to the Western Reserve in a schooner-wagon; *m* 1st, ca. 1800, Charlotte Norton;
3-Rev. William Starr (1811-81), circuit riding M.E. minister; *m* 1st, 1836, Elizabeth Welsh (1813-41; James[4]);
2-John Austin (1837-1908), mfr.; original propr. Grand Opera House, Chicago; *m* 1860, Mary Ellen Donovan (*b* Ireland, 1837); for issue, see Vol. I, p. 137.
1-*m* June 26, 1908, Grace Ayer, *b* Montreal, Can., Feb. 1, 1884; dau. of Albert Azro Ayer, mfr. and exporter, of Montreal; issue: 1-Frederick Ayer (June 9, 1909-Feb. 5, 1917); 2-Mary Caroline, *b* Chicago, Mar. 10, 1911; 3-Robert Ayer, *b* Greenwich, Conn., Mar. 12, 1915.
1-Ph.B., Yale-S., '92, LL.B., 1894. Lawyer and writer. Clubs: University, Yale (N.Y.), Field (Greenwich, Conn.). Residence: Stanwich Rd., Greenwich, Conn.

1-**HAMMER, Edwin Wesley,** *b* Newark, N.J., Dec. 16, 1867.
11-John **Howland,** Mayflower Pilgrim (qv);
10-Hope (1629-83), *m* 1646, John **Chipman** (qv);
9-Lydia (1654-1730), Barnstable; *m* 1671, as his 3d wife, John **Sargent** (1639-1716), of Barnstable (William[10]);
8-Jonathan (1677-1754), Malden, Mass.; *m* 1st, 1699/1700, Mary Lynde (1678-1716);
7-Jonathan (1700/01-1777), *m* 1726, Deborah Richardson (1708-70);
6-Lucretia (1734-93), Leicester, Mass.; *m* 1750, Dr. Pliny **Lawton** (1732-61), of Suffield, Mass.;
5-Dr. William (1759-1802), original mem. S.C.; *m* 1784, Abigail Farrington (1763-1836), of Flushing, L.I.;
4-Charles (1787-1858), a founder and dir. U.S. Fire Insurance Co.; mcht.; coal operator, Schuylkill Co., Pa.; *m* 1809, Sophia Dobson Willson (1791-1844);
3-Alfred (1811-89), coal operator; inventor; *m* 1834, Mary Kean Nichols (1816-1902; g.g.dau. of Michael Hillegas, first treas. of the United States).
2-William Alexander **Hammer** (1827-95), mcht.; tax commr., Newark, N.J.; pres. State Tax Commn. of N.J.; prominent in affairs of Reformed Episcopal Ch.; *m* Martha Augusta Beck (1827-61); *m* 2d, 1862, Anna Maria Nichols Lawton (1840-1910); issue (1st marriage): I-Ella Augusta (*b* 1851; *m* John Hamilton Troutman, 1856-1918); II-Martha Virginia (1852-1926); III-John Beck (1856-80); IV-William Joseph

(*b* 1858; *m* 1906, Alice Maud White, 1863-1906); (2d marriage): I–Alfred L. (*d* young); II–Edwin Wesley (1 above); III–Mary Lawton (*b* 1874; *m* William Clarence Allen, 1877-1907; *m* 2d, Harold Francis, 1875-1926).
1–*m* May 28, 1890, Emily Augusta Thompson, *b* Fall River, Mass.; dau. of Richard Turner Thompson, of Fall River, *m* Sabrina Ann Sisson; issue: 1–Wesley Thompson, *b* Newark, N.J., Aug. 27, 1895; Litt.B., Princeton, '18.
1–Mgr. or engr. of various corpns., 1887-1911; consulting engr., since 1911; professional engr., State of N.Y. (see Who's Who in America). Consultant for U.S.N., 1917-18. Inventor and patentee; writer on technical subjects. Fellow Am. Inst. Elec. Engrs.; mem. Edison Pioneers, Am. Soc. Mech. Engrs., Franklin Inst. of Pa., N.Y. Patent Law Assn., S.R., S.C.W. Republican. Presbyterian. Clubs: Bankers, N.E. Soc. of the Oranges. Residence: 322 Tillou Rd., S. Orange, N.J.

1–**HAMMOND, Matthew Brown,** *b* South Bend, Ind., June 13, 1868.
7–John **Brown,** called "The Christian Carrier," of Priesthill, Scotland; martyred by John Graham, of Claverhouse, 1685;
6–John (*b* ca. 1684), came from Scotland, 1720; settled at Lancaster, Pa.;
5–Matthew (1732-77), mem. Com. of Safety, Northumberland Co., and Central Com. Corr. and Safety, Phila., 1776; rep. Pa. State Conv., 1776, that ratified Declaration of Independence and formed 1st Pa. State Constn.; served in Flying Camp, Cont. Army, contracted fever and died in service; *m* ca. 1760, Eleanor Lytle;
4–Mary (1764-1827), *m* 1787, James **Hammond** (1758-1831), of White Deer Valley, Pa.; served with Pa. militia, Am. Rev. (James[5], from Eng., ca. 1740, *m* Grace–);
3–Matthew Brown (1791-1867), removed to South Bend, Ind., 1833; *m* 1823, Susan McCormick;
2–Seth (2 below).
6–Hugh **McCormick** (*b* 1695; son of James, of Londonderry, Ireland), from Ireland, ca. 1735, settled in Lancaster Co., Pa.;
5–Hugh (1725-77), from Ireland; *m* Sarah Alcorn;
4–Seth (1756-1835), *m* Margaret Simmons;
3–Susan (1802-83), *m* Matthew B. **Hammond** (3 above).
4–John **Longley** (*d* 1851), of Somerset Co., Pa.; *m* Frances– (1781-1847);
3–Thomas (1807-92), removed to Elkhart, Ind., 1830; *m* ca. 1830, Mary Rupel;
2–Sarah (1842-1909), *m* 1863, Seth **Hammond** (1836-1927), of South Bend.; issue: I–Mary Fannie (*b* 1864; *m* Jesse Lester Drake); II–Matthew Brown (1 above); III–Lewis Wilbur (*b* 1873; *m* Georgianna Davis).
1–*m* July 2, 1902, Sunie Butler Denham, *b* Columbia, Mo., Sept. 11, 1873; dau. of the late John S. Denham, of Columbia; issue: 1–Marjorie McCormick, *b* Columbus, O., Feb. 14, 1905; A.B., Ohio State U., '27; 2–Seth, *b* Columbus, Jan. 5, 1915.
1–Ph.B., U.Mich., '91 (P.B.K., Beta Gamma Sigma); M.L., U.Wis., 1893; Ph.D., Columbia, 1898; studied at Tübingen, U.Berlin, 1893-94. Mem. faculty, Ohio State U., since 1904; prof. economics, since 1908; summers at U.Chicago and Columbia. Author (see Who's Who in America). Republican. Conglist. Clubs: Faculty (Columbus), Cosmos (Washington). Residence: 1159 Ashland Av., Columbus, O.

1–**HANDY, Harriet Godfrey Emery (Mrs. Thomas L.),** *b* Bay City, Mich., Oct. 5, 1870.
10–Anthony **Emery** (qv);
9–James (1630-1714), came with his father; settled at Kittery, Me.; selectman 8 terms; rep. Gen. Ct., 1693-95; grand juror; constable, 1670; *m* 1st, Elizabeth– (*d* post 1687);
8–Daniel (1667-1722), of Kittery; dea. Congl. Ch.; *m* 1695, Margaret Gowan (Smith?) (1678-1751);
7–Simon (1702-60), signer of Kittery Memorial, 1751; on alarm list, 1757; grand juror, 1744–; *m* 1725, Martha Lord (1713-60; Nathan[8]);
6–Stephen (*b* 1730), of Kittery; pvt. Am. Rev.; elder Freewill Bapt. Ch.; *m* 1753, Sarah Hodgdon (bap. 1741);
5–Stephen (1753-1830), of Gorham; soldier Am. Rev.; *m* 1st, 1775, Sarah Emery (*b* 1757; Daniel[6], *m* Sarah Shackley);
4–Hosea (1776-1836), of Monroe, Me.; *m* 1798, Hannah Bartlett (1780-1859);
3–Temple (1800-38), of Orono, Me.; *m* 1827, Diana Godfrey (1805-71);
2–Hiram Augustus (2 below).
11–Stephen **Hopkins,** Mayflower Pilgrim (qv);
10–Giles (ca. 1607-1690), *m* 1639, Catherine Wheldon;
9–Mary (1640-1700), of Eastham, Mass.; *m* 1665 or 67, Samuel **Smith** (1641-97), of Hingham, Mass., later at Eastham;
8–John (1673-1717), of Eastham; *m* 1694, Bethia Snow (1672-1734);
7–John (1703-67), of Chatham; *m* 1727, Elizabeth Brown (*d* 1762);
6–Mehitable (1735-1817), of Chatham; *m* 1754, Barnabas **Baker** (1734-97), of Yarmouth, Mass.;
5–Brown (1772-1842), of Carratunk, Me.; *m* 1793, Hannah Robinson (1772-1866);
4–Belinda (1796-1844), of Carratunk; *m* Benjamin **Goodrich** (1789-1868);
3–Elizabeth (1819-80), of Bingham, Me.; *m* ca. 1855, John **Anderson** (1812-ca. 1897);
2–Eunice Ward (1848-1913), of Peshtigo, Wis.; *m* 1869, Hiram Augustus **Emery** (1839-93), lumberman; issue: I–Harriet Godfrey (1 above); II–Hiram Augustus, Jr.; III–Elizabeth Marion (*m* Robert Horace Gaylord); IV–Ella (*m* Louis N. Merritt, divorced); V–Albert Nicholas (*d* 1891); VI–Diana (*d* 1911; *m* Adam Kolb).
1–*m* Apr. 20, 1892, Thomas Lincoln Handy (Feb. 4, 1866-Oct. 23, 1922); son of Thomas Handy, came from Newcastle, Eng., settled at Decatur, Ill.; issue (all *b* Bay City, Mich.): 1–Dorothy, *b* Mar. 23, 1893; ed. Briarcliff Manor; *m* Dec. 6, 1919, John Dolbeare White, of Utica, N.Y. (issue: Patricia Emery; Maureen Pierpont; John Dolbeare, Jr.); 2–Thomas Lincoln, Jr., *b* Mar. 1, 1896; *m* Nov. 4, 1918, Ruth Temple, dau. Henry A. Benson, of Flint, Mich. (issue: Virginia; Eunice E.; Thomas L., III); 3–Hiram Emery, *b* Apr. 29, 1900; Univ. Sch., Cleveland, O.; *m* June 3, 1924, Monica, dau. Herman G. Wendland, of Bay City (issue: Marylyn Mary; John Wendland); 4–Paul Augustus, *b* Apr. 6, 1906.
1–Ed. Kalamazoo Sem. and Alma Coll. Mem. S.M.D., D.F.P.A., D.A.R., U.S.D. 1812. Methodist. Republican. Residence: Bay City, Mich.

1–**HANKS, Stedman Shumway,** *b* Manchester, Mass., July 17, 1889.
8–Benjamin **Hanks,** from Eng. to Plymouth, Mass., 1699;
7–Benjamin, *m* Mary White;
6–Uriah, *m* Irene Case;
5–Benjamin (1755-1824), drummer in Am. Rev.; *m* Alice Hovey;
4–Horace (1780-1850), *m* Sophia Wright (*d* 1850);
3–Rev. Stedman Wright (1811-89), *m* Sarah Humphrey Hale (1827-1905);
2–Charles Stedman (1856-1908), A.B., Harvard, '79; lawyer and author; *m* 1888, Clarina Bartow Shumway (1857-1925); issue: I–Stedman S. (1 above); II–Clarina S. (*m* Herman Michelson).
1–*m* Feb. 11, 1919, Margery Hancock, dau. of Lewis Hancock, of Austin, Tex.
1–Groton Sch., '08; A.B., Harvard, '12. Sec. to Am. ambassador at Ct. of St. James, London, 1912; dept. state, 1913; agt. of Dept. State on confidential missions, 1913-14; asst. to pres. Am. Internat. Corpn., 1915-16. Pilot's certificate from Aero Club of America, 1916; maj., Aug. 15, 1917; was aide to Maj. Gen. George O. Squier, chief signal officer U.S.A., and as liaison officer with French, British and Italian aviation missions in U.S.; comdg. officer 18th Aero Squadron, San Diego, Calif., and 2d Wing, Concentration Brig.; mil. aviator, Jan. 11, 1918; later comd. Concentration Brig., A.S.; hon. disch., Jan. 7, 1919; lt. col. Air Corps Reserves, 1925. Pres. Stedman Hanks & Co., 1920–. Lecturer on airports etc. before scientific socs., at Harvard Engring. Sch., and Yale. Author: Honors, Courtesies and Ceremonies, 1914; International Airports, 1929. Mem. S.M.D., S.R. Clubs: Eastern Yacht, Early Birds, Harvard, Piping Rock (N.Y.); Harvard, Tennis and Racquet (Boston). Residence: Manchester, Mass.

1–**HANNA, Virginia Lee Phillips,** *b* Montclair, N.J.
9–Capt. Thomas **Morgan** (*d* Baltimore Co., Md., 1698), capt. colonial militia, Baltimore Co., 1693;
8–Jemima (*b* bet. 1665-70), *m* 1st, bet. 1685-87,

MURRAY

Arms: Azure, a crescent or, between three mullets argent.

James ("Morray") **Murray** (*d* 1704), of "Atholl," Baltimore Co., 1694; his will filed Baltimore Co., 1704, is sealed with coat of arms identical with that of Murray of Tullibardine and Strowan, and Murray of Muraythwaite;

7–Jabez (*b* 1699-living post 1755), of Baltimore Co.; *m* 1726, Mary Wheeler (bap. 1711; William[8] [1670-80-1738], *m* 1st prob. Susanna– [*d* 1703], *m* 2d, 1706, Martha West);

6–Keziah (*b* 1729), *m* 1756-62 (perhaps his 2d wife), Benjamin **Wheeler** (1720-25-1807), of Baltimore Co. (William[7] [ca. 1700-67], *m* 1st ca. 1720, Isabel [*d* ca. 1726], dau. Mordecai Price [1660-65-1715], *m* 1685-90, Mary (*d* 1718), dau. Thomas Parsons [*d* 1684], *m* Isabel [*d*

HANNA

Arms: Argent, three roebucks' heads couped azure, collared or, a bell pendent from each collar.
Crest: A cross crosslet fitchée issuing out of a crescent sable.
Motto: Per ardua ad alta (Through difficulties to Heaven).

1717], who *m* 2d, Benjamin Capel [*d* 1711]; William[8], same as 8 above);

5–Isabella (1765-1852), *m* 1782, Edward Spicer **Hall** (1760-1848), of Baltimore Co. (Joshua[6] [1708-15-1782], mem. colonial militia of Md., 1747, mem. Com. Observation, Baltimore Co., 1775, *m* Diana Spicer [*d* 1750], *m* 2d, Ann Spicer, both daus. of John Spicer [*d* 1739], *m* Juliatha [*b* 1689], dau. Augustine Hawkins [*b* 1663], *m* Susanna Carr; John[7] [1672-1756], *m* Jane Rawlins);

4–Edward (1795-1891), of Baltimore Co., Md., and Guernsey Co., O.; *m* 1827, at York Haven, Pa., Henrietta Catherine Roberts (1804-93; Francis Cateby[5], ship capt. of London and Baltimore, drowned at sea, 1804, *m* Elizabeth, dau. George Karg, *m* Catherine Snyder);

3–Henrietta Frances (*b* 1851), *m* 1874, Dr. Henry Hilbert **Harrison** (1839-1915; Hezekiah[4] [*b* Md., 1804-*d* 1877, Harrison Co., O.], *m* 1834, Lydia dau. of Peter Hilbert, *m* Elizabeth, dau. of Anthony Bricker; Peter [?][5], of Md., *m* ca. 1800, Luranna [*b* 1773], of Lower Potomac Hundred, Frederick Co., Md., dau. Jonathan Sparrow);

2–Elizabeth Fleming (*b* 1881), *m* 1905, Charles Augustus **Hanna** (*b* 1863); see Vol. I, p. 142, for Hanna lineage; issue: I–Elizabeth Harrison (see Vol. II, p. 136, for other lineages); II–Mary Eleanor (see Vol. III, p. 549); III–Virginia Lee Phillips (1 above).

1–Ed. Miss Porter's School, Farmington, Conn. Residence: 15 Rockledge Rd., Montclair, N.J.

1–**HANSON, Elizabeth Trimble Painter (Mrs. Henry W. A.),** *b* Salem, Va., Dec. 26, 1882.

7–George **Painter** (killed by Indians, Painter's Ft., nr. Edinburg, Shenandoah Co., Va., 1758);

6–John (ca. 1739-1807), mem. Frederick Co., Va., militia, 1756; served in Am. Rev.; *m* ca. 1760, Philbena Catherine–;

5–George (1772-1855), *m* 1795, Mary Lindamood (1777-1847);

4–John (1798-1870), *m* 1819, Catherine Speagle (1801-73);

3–Israel (1826-85), millwright, of Hampshire Co., Va.; *m* 1850, Juliana Wilson (1828-63);

2–Franklin Verzelius Newton (2 below).

5–James **Willson** (1757-1811), of Augusta Co., Va., received a grant of 200 acres for services in Am. Rev.; served 3 yrs.; *m* 1782, Mary–(1765-97);

4–Margaret (1783-1860), of Augusta Co.; *m* 1806, James B. **Trimble** (1785-1863);

3–Elizabeth (1816-84), of Augusta Co.; *m* 1850, Rev. Peter **Shickel** (1815-84);

2–Laura Trimble (*b* 1852), of Salem, Va., *m* 1875, Franklin Verzelius Newton **Painter,** D.D., Litt.D. (*b* 1852), prof. edn., Roanoke Coll., since 1906; established Va. Teachers' Reading Assn.; author (see Who's Who in America); issue: I–Julia Elizabeth (*b* 1876; *m* Archibald H. Throckmorton, LL.D., see Who's Who in America); II–Margaret V., M.D. (*b* 1880; *m* Thomas E. King); III–Elizabeth Trimble (1 above); IV–Laura Holland (*b* 1886; *m* Harold C. George, see Who's Who in America); V–Theophilus S., Ph.D. (*b* 1889; see Who's Who in America; *m* Anna Tyler Thomas); VI–Ruth Elaine (*b* 1892; *m* as his 2d wife, Dr. James Garfield Randall, see Who's Who in America).

1–*m* June 1, 1904, Henry W. A. Hanson, LL.D.; *b* Wilmington, N.C., Mar. 12, 1882; pres. Gettysburg Coll. (see Who's Who in America); issue: 1–Henry W. A., Jr., *b* Pittsburgh, Pa., Feb. 10, 1908; A.B., Gettysburg, '29; *m* Nov. 20, 1929, Mary D., dau. of M. P. Moller, of Hagerstown, Md.; 2–Theophilus Painter, *b* Harrisburg, Pa., Apr. 21, 1914; ed. Gettysburg Acad.; 3–Robert De Lolle, *b* Harrisburg, Dec. 13, 1917.

1–A.B., Roanoke Coll., '02 (P.B.K.), A.M., 1903. Dir. Woman's League of Gettysburg Coll. (pres. 1920-24), and Mother's Assistance Fund, Adams Co., Pa. Mem. D.A.R. Lutheran. Republican. Address: College Campus, Gettysburg, Pa.

1–**HANSON, Thomas Grafton,** *b* San Rafael, Calif., May 1, 1865.

7–John **Hanson** (1630-1715; son of Col. John Hanson, of the Swedish Army, killed at battle of Lutzen, 1632); with his three brothers, brought by Lt. Col. John Printz to Tinicum Island, 1642; removed to Kent Island, Delaware River, 1653; *m* Mary Hussey (Thomas[8]);

6–Col. Samuel (1685-1748), of Charles Co., Md.;

burgess, 1716,28; *m* 1706, Elizabeth Storey (1689-1764; Col. Walter[7], of Md.);
5–Col. Samuel (1716-94), of "Green Hill"; lt. col. Upper Bn., Charles Co., Md., Militia, 1776; *m* 1743, Anne Hawkins (1725-74; Hon. Thomas[6], of Charles Co., *m* Sarah–);
4–Capt. Thomas Hawkins (*d* 1802), of "Oxon Hill"; served with Md. Inf., Cont. Army, *m* 1778, Rebecca (Dulany) Addison (1750-1829; Hon. Walter Dulany[5], of Annapolis, Md., *m* Mary Grafton);
3–Thomas Hawkins (1792-1854), *m* 1819, Elizabeth Howard Beall (*d* 1837; Col. William Dent[4], 2d lt., 3d Md. Bn. Arty. in Am. Rev., later col. 3d U.S. Inf., mem. Soc. Cincinnati, *m* Sarah Brookes; John[5], of Prince George Co., Md., *m* Mary Dent);
2–Thomas Hawkins (1824-83), lawyer; removed to Calif., 1854; *m* 1860, Carlota Milewater (1841-91); issue: I–Emma (*b* 1862-*d* infancy); II–Thomas Grafton (1 above).
1–*m* Sept. 13, 1893, Pauline DeForest Pease, *b* Detroit, Mich., Sept. 13, 1869; dau. of Benjamin DeForest; issue: 1–Thomas Grafton, Jr., *b* Fort Wayne, Detroit, Mich., Feb. 19, 1895; 2d lt., 19th F.A., U.S.A., June 17, 1917; 1st lt., June 23, 1917; capt. (temp.), 1918; capt. Q.M.C., 1920; capt. U.S. Cav., 1927; *m* 1918, Lanette Stewart, of San Antonio, Tex.; 2–Elizabeth DeForest, *b* Fort Brady, Mich., Feb. 3, 1898; *m* 1916, Lt. Cdr. Boyd R. Alexander, U.S.N. (issue: Jane Hanson, *b* Sept. 8, 1921).
1–U.S.M.A., '87; Inf. and Cav. Sch., 1891. Commd. 2d lt., 19th Inf., June 12, 1887, and promoted thru the grades to brig. gen. N.A., Aug. 5, 1917-1919; retired at own request, Jan. 3, 1919. Served in Spanish-Am. War, in Philippine Insurrection, 1899-1901; comd. 178th Inf. Brig., 89th Div., Toul Sector, San Mihiel Salient, at Meuse Argonne during World War (see Who's Who in America). Episcopalian. Republican. Club: Union League. Residence: 975 Bush St., San Francisco, Calif.

1–**HARBISON, William Albert,** *b* Allegheny, Pa., Nov. 14, 1874.
14–Johanes (Harbieson) **Harbison** (*b* ca. 1442), *m* Belinda, dau. of James Sealy of Barleyfield, Co. Cork, Ireland;
13–Thomas (*d* 1535), had grant of lands in Shanroe, Co. Monaghan, Ireland, from his father-in-law, who had inherited it from his mother, a Carson, of same place; *m* Catherine Robinson;
12–Matthew, *m* 1537, Margaret, dau. of James Richardson, *m* Margaret Waggett, of Spittle, Co. Çork;
11–William, made executor of father's estate, 1564, consisting of 12 messuages of meadowland, etc., part of which he granted to his brother-in-law, John Foxe, as a compensation for loan received, 1573; *m* 1568, Jane, dau. of John Foxe, Sr.;
10–John (1569-ca. 1617), began to write name Harbison; bequeathed his land and house to his brother "William of Clogh, Co. Antrim," 1613; he and his wife remit and quitclaim to John Fosberry of Kilmore, Co. Monaghan, "taillour," a plot of ground in that town; *m* 1593, Catherine, dau. of George Scott, of Roagh, Co. Monaghan, who in a deed, 1597, made his son-in-lâw, John, executor "to have an estate and terms of yrs. in a house at Roagh, Co. Monaghan";
9–James (1596-ca. 1663), of Roagh; *m* 1621, Katherine, dau. of Thomas Polsagh;
8–Matthew (1635-ante 1680), *m* 1669, Eleanor (*d* ca. 1681), dau. of James Burton, of Dublin;
7–James (*b* 1670-will made 1738), *m* 1703, Mary, dau. of Archibald Burnside, *m* Mary–;
6–Matthew (1705-1771), made executor of his father's will; *m* 1739, Anne (*d* 1770), dau. of Walter Pawley, of Kilmore, Co. Monaghan;
5–Matthew (*b* 1740), from Ireland to Pa., bet. 1760-69, settled finally in Westmoreland Co.; *m* 1760, Margaret Carson (desc. of the old Carson family of Shanroe, Co. Monaghan);
4–James (1770-1843), a wheelwright in Westmoreland Co.; removed with James Hall, Abraham Fryer and William Hultz to Butler Co., 1793, settling there permanently, 1794; *m* 1797, Mary Brown (1777-1865; George[5], of Middlesex Tp.);
3–James (1804-83), of Butler Co.; *m* 1833, Martha Pollock;
2–Samuel Pollock (1840-1905), founder Harbison-Walker Refractories Co., Pittsburgh; philanthropist; *m* 1872, Emma Jane Boyd (see Vol. I, page 145); issue: I–Fanny (1873-87); II–William Albert (1 above); III–Ralph Warner (qv for Pollock lineage).
1–*m* Nov. 2, 1911, Harriet Virginia Euwer, *b* Allegheny (now N.S. Pittsburgh), Pa., Feb. 18, 1875; dau. late Anthony H. Euwer, of Ben Avon, Pa.; issue: 1–William Pollock (*b* and *d* 1913); 2–Cynthia Courtney, *b* Phila., May 31, 1913.
1–Princeton, '98. Mng. executor Estate of S. P. Harbison. Pres. Am. Commonwealth League, Agusan Coconut Co. (Manila), Men's Bible Class, White Plains Presbyn. Ch., Radium Emanation Corpn.; v.p. Ch. League, Czecho-Slovak Soc. of U.S.; treas. Bukidnon Assos. (trustee), Dr. Charles L. Goodell Radio Com., Presbyn. Pub. Co. (mem. of bd.), Travel Inst. of Bible Research; trustee Biblical Sem. in New York, Harbison Coll., Grove City Coll., N.Y. State Council of Religious Edn. (exec. com.); mem. Am. Bible Soc., Am. Tract Soc., Citizens Com. of One Thousand, Evangelistic Com. of N.Y. City (exec. com.), Federal Council of the Chs. of Christ in America, Greater New York Fed. of Chs., Hebrew-Christian Pub. Soc., Internat. Reform Fed. of Washington (mem. bd.), Internat. Daily Vacation Bible School Assn., Lord's Day Alliance of U.S., Met. Assn. of Daily Vacation Bible Schools, Moody Bible School (mem. bd.), Nat. Bible Inst., Poly. Inst. of P.R., South Eastern Europe Bible School, St. Andrae, Austria (sec. Am. council), Stony Brook Assembly and Stony Brook School for Boys, Winona Assembly and Winona School of Theol. (dir.), World's Sunday School Assn. (bd. mgrs.), World Alliance for Internat. Friendship thru the Chs., Philippine-Am. Chamber of Commerce, Nat. Municipal League, Nat. Conf. on State Parks, Am. Civic Reform Union, Chamber of Commerce of U.S., Internat. Narcotic Assn., Internat. Reform Fed., Nat. Assn. of Audubon Societies, Nat. Civil Service Reform League; Union League, Princeton, Princeton Alumni Assn., Transportation, Mid-York, Economic, Botanical Garden, Acad. of Polit. Science (New York), Am. Acad. of Polit. and Social Science, Hist. Soc. Pa., University, Duquesne, Acad. of Science and Art (Pittsburgh), Nat. Econ. League, I.A.G., Am. Civic Assn., Am. Fed. of Arts, Am. Forestry Assn. (Washington), University, City (White Plains), Westchester Hills Country, Westchester Biltmore Country, Saxonwood Hunt, and many others. Address: Graybar Bldg., New York, N.Y.

1–**HARBISON, Ralph Warner,** *b* Allegheny, Pa., Feb. 20, 1876.
5–Samuel **Pollock** (*b* Scotland-1812), pvt. Am. Rev., Lancaster Co., Pa., Militia; *m* in Scotland, Jean– (*d* 1824);
4–Samuel (1776-1853), pvt. War 1812; *m* Eleanor Young;
3–Martha (1809-97), *m* James **Harbison** (1804-83);
2–Samuel Pollock (1840-1905), founder Harbison-Walker Refractories Co., Pittsburgh; philanthropist; *m* 1872, Emma Jane Boyd (see Vol. I, page 145); issue: I–Fanny (1873-87); II–William Albert (qv for Harbison lineage); III–Ralph Warner (1 above).
1–*m* Apr. 24, 1905, Helen Mary Harris, *b* St. Thomas, Toronto, Can., Feb. 1, 1881; dau. of Elmore Harris, of Toronto; issue (all *b* Sewickley, Pa.): 1–Elmore Harris, *b* Apr. 28, 1907; 2–Samuel Pollock, *b* Mar. 15, 1909; 3–Frederick Harris, *b* Dec. 18, 1912; 4–Marjorie Moore (adopted).
1–A.B., Princeton, '98. Dir. Harbison-Walker Refractories Co., Pittsburgh; v.p. Radium Emanation Corpn., N.Y.; dir. Thews-Harbison-Thews, Inc., Phila. Mem. Presbyn. Assembly's com. on consolidation and reorganization of Ch. bds. and agencies, v.p. trustees Western Theol. Sem., pres. Presbyn. Hosp. Mem. nat. council Y.M.C. Assns.; pres. Pittsburgh Y.M.C.A.; mem. exec. com. War Work Council of Y.M.C.A. during World War, v.p. Pennsylvania Coll. for Women (Pittsburgh);

trustee American U. (Cairo) (see Who's Who in America). Clubs: Duquesne, University, Edgeworth Country, Allegheny Country. Residence: Pine and Woodland Rd., Sewickley, Pa.

1–**HARDESTY, Shortridge,** *b* Platte Co., Mo., Sept. 13, 1884.
4–George **Hardesty** (*d* ca. 1812), of Winchester, Va.; *m* Cordelia Dooley (1782-1873);
3–James William (1810-88), of Weston, Mo.; *m* 1839, Emily T. Wilhite (1821-91; Eleazer[4] [1800-80], of Weston, *m* Nancy Connell, *m* 2d, her sister, Agnes Connell, daughters of Jesse Connell, *m* Elizabeth C., dau. of Presley Gray [1764-1838], served in Fairfax Co., Va., Militia, Am. Rev., *m* Barbara Cotton);
2–John Henry (2 below).
8–William **Randolph** (qv);
7–Isham, of Goochland Co., Va.; *m* 1717, in London, Jane Rogers;
6–Elizabeth (1727-82), *m* 1752, John **Railey** (1721-83), of Stonehenge, Chesterfield Co., Va.; capt. Am. Rev.;
5–Martin (1764-1810), of Albemarle Co., Va.; *m* 1794, Elizabeth Mayo;
4–Daniel Mayo (1796-1858), of Weston, Mo.; *m* 1816, Lucy Jane Elizabeth Watson (1801-63; John[5] [*d* 1841], living in Milton, Va., 1790, *m* Jane Hord [*b* 1776], dau. Richard Price, of Milton);
3–Egbert Watson (1830-1920), of Weston; *m* 1854, Mary Elizabeth MacAdow;
2–Bertie Malin (2 below).
8–William **Mayo** (qv);
7–Daniel (1733-81), *m* Mary–;
6–Col. William (1754-1802), of Powhatan Co., Va.; col. Va. Line, Am. Rev.; *m* Catharine Swann (*d* 1806);
5–Elizabeth (1777-1856), *m* Martin **Railey** (5 above);
5–John (McAdow) **MacAdow,** of Ky.; *m* Mary Burns (*d* Platte Co., Mo.);
4–Samuel (*b* Ky. or Md., 1803-*d* 1850), of Platte Co., Mo.; *m* 1831, Julian Bean (1807-66; Benjamin[5] [*b* Md. 1780], from Va. to Platte Co., Mo., ca. 1838, *m* Farnetter Johnson, *b* Md. 1783);
3–Mary E. (1836-1927), *m* Egbert W. **Railey** (3 above);
2–Bertie Malin (*b* 1858), of Weston, Mo.; *m* 1881, John Henry **Hardesty** (1853-1926), farmer and banker, of Weston; issue: I–Egbert McAdow (*b* 1881; *m* Minnie Green Allison); II–Shortridge (1 above); III–Edward Mayo (*b* 1891; *m* Elizabeth Dean Allison); IV–John Henry (*b* 1896).
1–*m* Aug. 20, 1910, Adelia Valeria Ferrell (qv for issue).
1–A.B., Drake U., '05 (LL.D., 1928); C.E., Rensselaer Poly. Inst., 1908. Draftsman and designer, Waddell & Harrington, Kansas City, Mo., 1908-15; designing engr., Waddell & Son, 1916-17; mem. Waddell & Son, Inc., 1918-19; asso. engr. with J.A.L. Waddell, 1920-26, in charge of work on Newark Bay ry. bridges, Arthur Kill bridges, Mississippi River bridge (Cairo, Ill.), 17 standard highway bridge plans for Cuban Govt., Cooper River bridge (Charleston, S.C.); mem. Waddell and Hardesty, 1927– (see Who's Who in America). Mem. I.A.G., Am. Soc. C.E., Rensselaer Tech. Soc. Clubs: Winged Foot Golf, New Rochelle Tennis. Mem. Ch. Disciples of Christ. Democrat. Residence: 12 Cambridge Ct., Larchmont, N.Y.

1–**HARDESTY, Adelia Valeria Ferrell (Mrs. Shortridge),** *b* Faucett, Mo., Jan. 8, 1889.
4–Abram **Risk** (*d* 1854), of Ky.; *m* Malinda Davenport (*d* 1883), of Ky.; to Weston, Mo., 1837;
3–Sidney C. (1838-86), of Platte Co., Mo.; *m* 1862, Valera Thorp (1847-71), of Weston (David James[4] [*b* 1820], of Lexington, Mo., removed to Buchanan Co., Mo., 1838, and to Platte Co., 1848, *m* 1846, Sarah E. Linville; James[5] [*d* Lexington, Mo., 1836], of Va. and Ky., removed to Mo., 1812);
2–Dora (ca. 1868-ca. 1901), *m* ca. 1887, Ratliffe Floyd **Ferrell,** of Faucett, Mo.; issue: I–Adelia Valeria (1 above); II–James Sidney; III–Ratliffe Floyd, Jr.; IV–Jay E.; V–Logan Risk.
1–*m* Aug. 20, 1910, Shortridge Hardesty (qv); issue: 1–Julia McAdow, *b* Van Buren, Ark., June 16, 1911; ed. Smith Coll.; 2–Egbert Railey, *b* Kansas City, Mo., July 25, 1916.
Residence: 12 Cambridge Ct., Larchmont, N.Y.

1–**HARDING, Gena Russell,** *b* Warwick, R.I.
8–Abraham **Harding** (1615-55; son of John, of Boreham, Essex Co., *m* Agnes Greene, of Tarling, Eng.); from Eng., was at Dedham, Mass., 1638; settled at Braintree, 1642; an original grantee at Medfield, 1650; *m* Elizabeth–;
7–Abraham (1655-1734), *m* Mary Mason; *m* 2d, Sarah (Merrifield) Fairbank;
6–Samuel (1698-1780), *m* Mary Cutler;
5–Joseph (1728-76), *m* Mary Kingsbury;
4–Elisha (1748-1817), *m* Ruth Hewins;
3–Lewis (1786-1862), mem. Mass. Senate; *m* Irene Hartshorn;
2–George Warren (2 below).
9–William **Russell** (*d* Cambridge Farms, Mass., 1661-62), from Eng.; *m* Martha–;
8–John (1645-1733), *m* Elizabeth Fiske (David[9], *m* Lydia Cooper);
7–John (1671-1746), *m* Rebecca Blodgett (Thomas[8], *m* Rebecca Tidd);
6–Adonijah (1713-75), *m* Mary Sherman (Capt. John[7], *m* Abigail Stone);
5–Adonijah (1734-78), *m* Abigail Bond;
4–Titus (1769-1826), *m* Lucy (Danielson) Mighells (Nathaniel Danielson[5], *m* Mary Morgan);
3–Aaron Mighells (1796-1824), *m* Persis Haynes (Daniel[4], *m* Hannah Webber);
2–Harriet Mighells (1823-1906), *m* George Warren **Harding** (1818-87), wool mcht.; see Vol. I, p. 928, for issue.
1–A.B. Wells, '80; Radcliffe, 1881-83; George Washington U., 1889. Address: 2101 Connecticut Av., N.W., Washington, D.C.

1–**HARDY, H(arrison) Claude,** *b* Glenwood, Pa., Feb. 27, 1887.
9–Thomas **Hardy** (1605-77), from Eng., 1630, with Gov. Winthrop; one of first 12 to settle at Ipswich, Mass.; at Rowley, 1652; *d* at Bradford, Mass.; *m* in Eng., Lydia–;
8–William, of Bradford, Mass.; *m* Sarah–;
7–Thomas (*b* 1680), of Bradford; *m* 1721/22, Martha Hardy;
6–Reuben (1724-68), of Bradford and Tewksbury, Mass.; *m* 1743, Elizabeth Adams;
5–Moody (1751-ca. 1840), pvt. in Am. Rev.; of Tewksbury, Mass., and Goffstown, N.H.; *m* 1779, Hannah Wicom;
4–Israel (1784-1851), pvt. 1st regt. (Davis), N.H. Vols., War 1812; of Goffstown; *m* Polly Stevens (1789-1849);
3–Laurin M. (1811-88), of Goffstown, N.H., Barton, N.Y., Glenwood, Pa.; *m* Sarah J. Taylor (*d* 1861);
2–David Nelson (1845-1922), of Glenwood, Pa., and Barton, N.Y.; pvt., Co. A, 107th Pa. Vols., Civil War; *m* 1865, Hannah Elizabeth Potter (*b* 1846; Ralph[3], *m* Sarah Schoonover); issue: I–Minnie Isaacs (1866-1921; *m* 1889, Frederick M. Quick); II–Samuel Jerome (*b* 1870; *m* 1899, Clara B. Wells); III–Annah Grace (*b* 1873; *m* 1891, Jasper E. Gardner); IV–Lottie Hughes (*b* 1874; *m* 1898, Walter Davis); V–Bessie May (*b* 1876; *m* 1899, Frank H. Smith [*d* 1903]; *m* 2d, 1909, Jesse C. Morse); VI–John Sumner (*b* 1879; *m* 1903, Minnie Harrington); VII–James Garfield (1880-87); VIII–Harry Alonzo (*b* 1883; *m* 1915, Linda Bergen); IX–H. Claude (1 above), and X–Morton Clyde (twins, *b* 1887; *m* 1908, Pearl Johnson).
1–*m* June 26, 1912, Lula May Green (*b* Montrose, Pa., 1883-*d* Oct. 25, 1918); dau. of Jefferson Green, of Montrose, *m* Lydia–; issue: 1–Eloise (*b* and *d* Oct. 25, 1918).
1–*m* 2d, Nov. 19, 1919, Shirley Frances Newton, *b* Sidney, N.Y., Feb. 15, 1897; dau. of Horace D. Newton, of Sidney, N.Y.
1–B.A., Wesleyan U. (Conn.), '11 (Beta Theta Pi); M.A., U.Rochester, 1921; M.A., Syracuse, 1923; studied at U.Grenoble, France, 1914; candidate for Ph.D., New York U., 1931; (Phi Kappa Phi, Kappa Phi Kappa, Phi Delta Kappa, Pi Gamma Mu). Instr. modern languages, Wilbraham (Mass.) Acad., 1911-16; high school principal, Schenevus, N.Y., 1916-20; supt. schools, Fairport, N.Y., 1920-25, Oneida, N.Y., 1925-27, and at White Plains, N.Y., since 1927. Compiler: Hardys Past and Present. Mason (32°), Rotarian. Residence: 48 Park Av., White Plains, N.Y.

1–**HARDY, Ida Viola May (Mrs. William Harris),** *b* Warren Co., Miss., Nov. 2, 1866.
7–James **Lee,** from Eng. ca. 1607, settled at Jamestown, Va.;
6–Jesse, of Va. and N.C.; *m* Margaret Pitman;
5–Jesse (*b* 1740, Robeson Co., N.C.-*d* 1831, Sampson Co., N.C.), served in Am. Rev.; kinsman of "Light Horse Harry"; *m* Susannah Johnson;
4–James (1782-1843), *b* Sampson Co., N.C.; removed from N.C. to Miss.; *m* 1809, Mary Watson (1785-1843; William[5], of S.C.);
3–Eliza, *m* 1st, 1829, Benjamin Pulatki **May**;
2–James (2 below).
Desc. John **Hutchins,** from Eng., 1636, settled in Va.; and thru:
4–James (1781-1853), *m* 1806, Susannah Castleberry;
3–Telemachus (1808-51), *m* 1st, 1834, Mary Ann Ragsdale; *m* 2d, Emily Easterling;
2–Eliza (1835-75), *m* 1852, James **May,** planter; issue: I–Mary (1853-54); II–Ellen (1856-89; *m* Daniel Q. Weeks); III–Florence (1859-1922; *m* Harrison C. Miller); IV–Emily (*b* 1862; *m* William D. Berryhill); V–Nora (*d* infancy); VI–Ida Viola (1 above); VII–Eula Elizabeth (*b* 1870; *m* Robert G. Yates; *m* 2d, Henry E. Hilliard); VIII–Rosa Lee (*b* 1873; *m* Robert L. Wright).
1–*m* May 14, 1900, William Harris Hardy (Feb. 12, 1837– Feb. 15, 1917); son of Robert W. Hardy, of Collirene, Lowndes Co., Ala., *m* Temperance L. Toney; issue: 1–William Harris, Jr., *b* Hattiesburg, Miss., May 30, 1902; 2–Hamilton Lee, *b* Hattiesburg, June 25, 1904; 3–James Hutchins, *b* Pass Christian, Miss., Apr. 30, 1907; *m* Oct. 1927, Rose De Felice.
1–Asst. editor Texas Farmer, Dallas, 1894-95; owner editor and publisher the Southern Home Journal, 1896-99, Jackson, Miss. now engaged in writing negro dialect verses. Life long church worker; "Mother" of Mississippi's present "Age of Consent Law" and other advanced legislation. Mem. D.A.R., U.D.C.; charter mem. Southern Sociol. Congress. Episcopalian. Democrat. Residence: 4928 7th Av., Los Angeles, Calif.

1–**HARGIS, Gladys Marie Larey (Mrs. Henry Clinton),** *b* Mt. Pleasant, Kan., Oct. 11, 1865.
5–Michael **Larey,** *m* 1742, Regula Koch;
4–Michael (1752-94), of Orangeburg, S.C.; *m* 1774, Mary Cathrine Deramus (*b* 1755);
3–Daniel (1787-1870), of Orangeburg; *m* 1813, Marie Hall;
2–Jacob Angus (2 below).
4–William **Hall** (1760-1814), of Orangeburg, S.C.; soldier Am. Rev.; *m* 1785, Barbara Hawkins (1763-1825; Michael[5], from Eng. to Orangeburg; Sir William[6], *m* Mary Rolers or Rollo, dau. Sir Richard Rolers or Rollo, from Eng., settled on Royal land grants nr. Orangeburg);
3–Marie (1790-1852), of Orangeburg; *m* Daniel **Larey** (3 above);
2–Jacob Angus (1838-75), physician and surgeon, Platte Co., Mo.; *m* 1864, Anna Louise Hudson (1843-1929; Lemuel[3] [*b* 1813], *m* America Settle [*b* 1818], of Salvisa, Ky.); issue: I–Gladys Marie (1 above); II–Robert Ernest (*b* 1866; *m* Birdie Coleman; *m* 2d, Gertrude Ross); III–Marsdon Angus (*b* 1868; *m* Letitia McCrea); IV–Albert Eugene (*b* 1870; *m* Clara Rehbein).
1–*m* Oct. 7, 1891, Henry Clinton Hargis, *b* nr. Weatherby, Mo., Jan. 16, 1866; son of Fountain Fox Hargis (1817-87), *m* Margret Gilliland (1824-92); issue: 1–Byron Clinton (July 28, 1892-Aug. 12, 1896); 2–Gladys Elaine, *b* Winfield, Kan., Jan. 23, 1899; A.B., Oklahoma U., '21 (P.B.K.); *m* Oct. 17, 1923, Richard Henry, son of Dr. Robert Henderson, *m* Minnie J. Kincaid, of Milford, Ind. (issue: Barbara Hawkins, *b* 1929); 3–Vivienne Andree, *b* Winfield, Apr. 19, 1901; B.J., Mo. U., '22; journalism, New York.
1–Mem. D.A.R. (chapter regent, charter mem. chapter), D.U.V., White Shrine. Worthy Grand Matron Okla. O.E.S. (life mem.), 1920. Clubs: Civic, Art. Baptist. Democrat. Residence: 315 E. 8th St., Pawhuska, Okla.

1–**HARKNESS, Katherine Margaret Beebee (Mrs. Albert G.),** *b* Hamilton, N.Y.
10–Alexander **Beebee** (*d* 1624), of Great Addington, Eng., *m* Elizabeth–;
9–John (*d* 1638), of Great Addington; *m* Alice–;
8–John (1600-50), from Eng., died at sea, May 18, 1650; *m* Rebecca Ladd, of Broughton, Eng.;
7–Capt. James (1641-1728), in colonial wars; commr., justice, dep.; *m* Sarah Benedict (Thomas[8] [1617-90], in colonial wars);
6–Capt. James (1682-1750), in colonial wars; justice; *m* 1708, Abigail Sherman (Samuel[7], of Stratford, Conn., *m* Mary Wharton);
5–Joseph (1724-1803), of Danbury, Conn.; *m* Sarah Fargo (1721-93);
4–Samuel (1757-1812), of New York; *m* Mary MacWhorter (1759-97); see Vol. II, p. 143, for MacWhorter lineage;
3–Alexander MacWhorter, LL.D. (1783-1856), grad. Kings (now Columbia U.) College; *m* Mary Margaret Roorbach (1785-1830), see Vol. II, p. 143, for Roorbach and other lineages; *m* 2d, Mary Barnum, widow of David Picket Hoyt (see Vol. I, p. 388);
2–Alexander MacWhorter, D.D. (1820-97), prof. Colgate U. 47 yrs.; *m* Catherine Jane Hall (1822-1907); for genealogy and issue see Vol. II, p. 143.
1–*m* Sept. 3, 1884, Albert Granger Harkness, Litt.D. (Nov. 19, 1856-Jan. 23, 1923), A.B., Brown, '79; studied in Germany, 1879-83; prof. Brown U., 1889-1923; annual dir. Am. Sch. for Classical Studies, Rome, 1902-03; issue: 1–Albert (see Vol. II, p. 144, for genealogy and issue).
1–Mem. C.D.A., D.A.R., I.A.G. Residence: 7 Cooke St., Providence, R.I.

1–**HARNEY, William Randolph,** *b* Louisville, Ky., Jan. 24, 1869.
6–Thomas **Harney,** from Wales, ca. 1725, settled in Sussex Co., Del.; *m* Hannah Mills;
5–Jenathan or Genathan (*d* 1777), of Sussex Co.; lt. Am. Rev., wounded and captured, *d* in prison; *m* Isabella Mills;
4–Selby (1765-1814), of Nicholas Co., Ky.; *m* ca. 1800, Hannah Hopkins;
3–John Hopkins (1806-67), of Louisville, Ky.; editor Louisville Democrat; author of Harney's Algebra; *m* ca. 1828, Martha Wallace (Rev. William[4], *m* Jane Rankin);
2–Will Wallace (2 below).
8–Gerard **Hopkins** (qv);
7–Gerrard (*d* 1743), of Harford and Anne Arundel cos., Md.; *m* 1700, Margaret Johns (Richard[8] of Calvert Co., Md., *m* Elizabeth Kensey);
6–William (1717-87), *m* Rachel Orrick (John[7], of Md., *m* Susannah Hammond);
5–John (*d* 1814), of Md. and Ky.; Am. Rev.; *m* 2d, ca. 1768, Catharine Collier (John[6], of Todd Creek, Md.);
4–Hannah (1775-1814), *m* Selby **Harney** (4 above).
9–William **Randolph** (qv);
8–Thomas (1683-1730), of Goochland Co., Va., justice, 1728; lt., 1728; *m* 1710, Judith Fleming (Col. Charles[9], *m* Susanna Tarleton);
7–William (1712-45), of Tuckahoe, Va.; *m* 1735, Maria Judith Page (Mann[8], *m* Judith Wormley);
6–Thomas Mann (*b* 1741), of Tuckahoe; mem. Va. Conv., 1776; soldier Am. Rev.; burgess; *m* 1761, Anne Cary;
5–William (*b* 1769), of Chitower, Va.; *m* 1790, Lucy Bolling Randolph (Beverly[6], *m* Martha Cocke);
4–Col. Thomas Beverly, U.S.A. (1793-1867), *m* 1814, Maria Barbara Mayer;
3–William Mayer (1815-76), of New Orleans, La.; *m* 1842, Mary Eleanor Pitts (Maj. Thomas H.[4], *m* Frances Bernard Lambeth);
2–Mary St. Mayer (2 below).
10–Miles **Cary** (qv);
9–Henry (1650-1720), *m* Judith Lockey (Edward[10], of York Co.);
8–Henry (ca. 1675-1749), *m* Ann Edwards (John[9], of Surry Co., Va.);
7–Archibald (1721-1786-87), of Chesterfield Co.; *m* 1744, Mary Randolph (Richard[8], *m* Jane Bolling);
6–Ann (*b* ca. 1745), *m* Thomas Mann **Randolph** (6 above).
7–Christopher Bartholomew **Mayer** (1702-52; son of George Bartholomew), from Germany, 1752, settled at Fredericktown, Md.; *m* 1724, Eva Margaretta Scheifel (1704-65; Bartholomew[8], surgeon, *m* Anna Maria Bergfelder);
6–George Ludwig (1727-93), of Lancaster, Pa.; *m* 1st, ante 1755, Maria Barbara Diemer;
5–Christopher Bartholomew (1756-1815), Lancaster; *m* 1783, Susanna Burkhart;

4–Maria Barbara (1794-1867), *m* Thomas B. **Randolph** (4 above);
3–William M., *m* Mary E. Pitts (3 above);
2–Mary St. Mayer (1844-70), *m* 1868, Will Wallace **Harney** (1831-1912), of Orlando, Fla.; author of Southern poetry and prose; educator; newspaper editor.
1–*m* Oct. 10, 1900, Jane Bratton Montague (qv).
1–Ed. East Florida Sem. (now U.Fla.). Clerk, insurance, 1887-94; dep. collector of customs, 1896; broker and merchant, 1895-1910; treas. of corpn., 1910-20; v.p., 1921-24, pres., 1924-29. With Fla. State troops, 1890-92. Formerly v.p. Chase and Co.; pres., Harney Morrow Fruit Co.; dir. Bisbee Baldwin Co. Mem. I.A.G. Presbyterian. Democrat. Clubs: Seminole, Lions. Residence: 804 Oak St., Jacksonville, Fla.

1–**HARNEY, Jane Bratton Montague (Mrs. William R.),** *b* Orlando, Fla., Nov. 20, 1879.
9–Peter **Montague** (qv);
8–Peter (*b* 1634), of Middlesex Co., Va.; *m* 1663, Mary Doodes (*d* 1682; Minor[9], *m* Mary Garrett);
7–Peter (*b* 1666), of Middlesex Co.; *m* 1693, Elizabeth Morris;
6–Thomas (1694-1756), of Middlesex Co.; *m* 1716, Grace Nicholson (1688-1726; William[7], *m* Grace Lewis);
5–Thomas (1719-78), of Spotsylvania Co.; soldier Am. Rev.; *m* 1753, Jane Daniel (*b* 1733; Charles[6], *m* Jane Mickleborough);
4–William (1776-1865), of Cumberland Co., Va.; *m* 1799, Judith Street (Dudley[5], *m* Martha Miller);
3–James Madison (1806-79), of Alleghany Co., Va.; collector of Confed. taxes; *m* 1840, Jane Bratton (1800-44; Adam[4], *m* Elizabeth Feamster);
2–James Robert (2 below).
7–John **Preston** (qv);
6–Col. William (1729-83), of Augusta Co., Va.; col. Va. militia; burgess; col. in Indian wars and Am. Rev.; *m* 1761, Susanna Smith;
5–John (*d* 1827); of Richmond, Va.; mem. Va. Senate; state treas.; *m* Mary Radford (*d* 1810; William[6], *m* Rebecca Winston);
4–William Radford, of Lynchburg, Va.; moved to Mo.; *m* 1819, Elizabeth Cabell (Landon[5], *m* Judith Scott Rose);
3–Ouachita P. (1833-1904), of Orlando, Fla.; maj., Forrest's cav., C.S.A.; *m* 1853, Jane Eliza Pitts (1831-1904; Thomas H.[4], *m* Frances Bernard Lambeth);
2–Fanny Bernard (2 below).
9–Maj. Lawrence **Smith** (will dated 1700), came from Eng. ante 1675, settled in Gloucester Co., Va.; colonial officer; *m* Mary–;
8–William (*d* ca. 1734), of Spotsylvania Co.; capt. militia; *m* Elizabeth Ballard (Thomas[9], of York Co., *m* Katherine Hubard);
7–Francis (*d* post 1771), of Hanover Co., Va.; *m* ca. 1738, Elizabeth Waddy (Anthony[8], of Hanover Co., *m* Sara Parke);
6–Susanna (*b* 1739), *m* Col. William **Preston** (6 above).
2–Fanny Bernard Preston (1854-1908), *m* 1876, James Robert **Montague** (1842-1910); issue: I–Mary Elizabeth (*b* 1878; *m* Frank M. Warren); II–Jane Bratton (1 above); III–Frances Bernard (*b* 1884; *m* Albert R. Bogue); IV–Shirley Preston (*b* 1898; *m* Robert Morrow).
1–*m* Oct. 10, 1900, William Randolph Harney (qv for genealogy).
1–Mem. C.D.A., D.A.R., U.D.C. Presbyterian. Democrat. Residence: 804 Oak St., Jacksonville, Fla.

1–**HARPER, Cornelius Allen,** *b* Hazel Green, Wis., Feb. 20, 1864.
5–William **McMillan** (1717-92), from Ireland, 1742; settled Faggs Manor, Chester Co., Pa.; *m* ca. 1742, Margaret Rea (*d* 1768); *m* 2d, Mrs. Miller;
4–John (1752-1833), Presbyn. minister; founder of Jefferson Coll.; founded Acad. at Washington, Pa., the first coll. west of the Allegheny Mts.; *m* 1776, Catherine Brown (William[5], of Upper Brandywine, Chester Co., Pa.);
3–Jane (*b* 1777), *m* Rev. Morehead; *m* 2d, as his 2d wife, 1811, Samuel **Harper** (*b* 1754);
2–Moses Allen (1813-86), lawyer, of Clarksburg, W. Va.; *m* 1842, Hester Jane Lewis (1823-1904; Asher or Ashur[3], from Phila., prob. settled Clarksburg, W.Va., *m* prob. Miss White); issue: I–Charles Lewis (*b* 1846; *m* Clara Moore, *b* 1854); II–Salome (*b* 1849; *m* 1869, William Bates); III–Virginia (*m* Ellis Murdock); IV–Samuel Allen (1853-98); V–Catherine (*d* aet. 21); VI–Jefferson Crawford (*b* 1860; *m* B. Blanche Brigham, *d* 1929); VII–Caroline Alice (*b* 1862); VIII–Dr. Cornelius Allen (1 above); IX–Mildred Lindsay (*b* 1867).
1–*m* Apr. 23, 1901, Elisabeth Louise Bowman (qv for issue).
1–B.S., U.Wis., '89 (Phi Kappa Psi); grad. Columbian (now George Washington) U., Dept. Med., 1893. Practiced medicine in Madison since 1894. Mem. Wis. State Bd. of Health, 1904– (sec., exec. officer). Dean of state health officers now in service in U.S.A., has served 26 yrs. Mem. Wis. Legislature, 1911. Mem. Wis. Anti-tuberculosis Commn. which selected site for state sanatorium and superintended laying out of grounds and construction of bldgs. Mason. Presbyn. Residence: 520 N. Pinckney St., Madison, Wis.

1–**HARPER, Elisabeth Louise Bowman (Mrs. Cornelius Allen),** *b* Madison, Wis., Sept. 15, 1875.
4–John **Bowman,** *m* (prob.), Ann Drake;
3–John (*b* 1782), of Clarkson, Monroe Co., N.Y.; *m* 1812, Lovice McCarty (1792-1870; Capt. Clark[4] [*d* 1818], of Colchester, Conn., served Am. Rev., *m* 1788, Mabel Treadway, received pension for husband's Rev. services);
2–John McCarty (2 below).
8–Philip **Smith** (ca. 1633-1680), *b* Eng.; of Wethersfield, Conn.; lt.; dea.; and rep.; *m* 1657, Rebecca Foote (*b* ca. 1634), of Watertown, Mass.;
7–Jonathan (1663-1739), *b* Hadley, Mass.; of Hatfield, Mass.; *m* 2d, 1688, Abigail Kellogg (*b* 1671), her father and brothers, John and James, kept a ferry nr. Hadley for nearly a century;
6–Dea. Aaron (1715-98), *b* Hatfield, Mass.; prob. of Amherst; removed to Athol, Mass.; govt. agent; *m* 1734?, Abigail Scott (*b* ca. 1720);
5–Capt. Asa (1740-1815), *m* 1770, Lydia Lyndes (1745-1836), of Worcester, Mass.;
4–Luther (1784-1844), *b* Athol; *m* 1805, Abigail Raymond (1785-1874);
3–George (1810-44), of Athol; *m* 1833, Betsy Heywood Richardson;
2–Rosellah Mariah (2 below).
9–Thomas **Richardson** (qv);
8–Isaac (1643-89), of Woburn, Mass.; *m* 1667, Deborah Fuller (*b* 1650);
7–Benjamin (1674-1728), of Woburn; *m* 1699, Lydia (Draper) Whittemore;
6–Benjamin (1703-60), of Stoneham and Leicester, Mass.; *m* 1724, Patience Earle;
5–Benjamin (1732-1821), of Leicester, Mass.; *m* 2d, 1777, Mrs. Abagail (Whitcomb) French (*d* 1790); he *m* 4 times;
4–Gardner (1786-1827), of Worcester, Mass.; *m* 1810, Betsy Heywood (1787-1827);
3–Betsy Heywood (1814-81), *m* George **Smith** (3 above);
2–Rosellah Mariah (1834-1903), of Athol, Mass.; *m* 1854, Samuel Hunter Donnell (1823-60); *m* 2d, 1864, John McCarty **Bowman** (1817-92), *b* Henpeck, nr. Greece, N.Y.; attended Union Coll. (Psi U.); admitted to bar, and practiced law; assisted in mfr. of first horse mower; sold this through Wis., Mich., Ill., Ia., and Minn.; went from Janesville, Wis., to Madison; issue: I–John Henry (*b* 1866; *m* Margaret Van Vliet); II–Frank Favill, M.D. (*b* 1872; *m* Helen Louise Poole); III–Elisabeth Louise (1 above).
1–*m* Apr. 23, 1901, Dr. Cornelius Allen Harper (qv); issue: 1–Cornelius Allen, Jr. (Jan. 15, 1910-Feb. 13, 1912); 2–Samuel Bowman, *b* Madison, Wis., Sept. 9, 1912.
1–Ed. Granger Place Sch., Canandaigua, N.Y. Dir. Y.W.C.A. of Madison; pres. Madison Civic Chorus; head local French Relief, 1915-19; mem. Food Demonstration Bd., 1918-19. Mem. C.D.A., D.A.R. (regent John Bell Chapter, 1923; Wis. state historian, 3 yrs.), Wis. State Hist. Soc. (life mem.), I.A.G. Clubs: Civics, Woman's. Presbyterian. Republican. Residence: 520 N. Pinckney St., Madison, Wis.

1–**HARPER, Jesse Clair,** *b* Paw Paw, Ill., Dec. 10, 1883.
4–James **Harper** (*d* ca. 1860), from Ireland to

Argyle, N.Y., 1812; moved to Sterling, N.Y., ca. 1828; *m* Elizabeth Black;
3–William (1815-81), Ross Grove, Ill.; moved to DeKalb Co., Ill., 1844; *m* 1848, Sarah Irwin Kirk (1814-98; John[4], *b* in Scotland, *m* Jane Irwin);
2–James (2 below).
4–James **Congrave,** from Eng., to Naperville, Ill., ca. 1837; *m* Ann Price;
3–Mary (1823-89), *m* 1849, William Thomas **Patrick** (1823-99), from Eng., *d* at Paw Paw, Ill.;
2–Bertha (*b* 1858), *m* 1878, James **Harper** (*b* 1853); issue: I–Floyd Everett, LL.D. (*b* 1879; *m* 1908, Teckla Renz); II–Frank William (*b* 1880); III–Jesse Clair (1 above); IV–Florence May (*b* 1885; *m* 1910, Marc Clinton Clapp, *b* 1884).
1–*m* Feb. 5, 1912, Melville Helen Campbell (qv for issue).
1–Ph.B., Chicago U., '06. Athletic dir., Notre Dame U., 1913-18; cattle ranchman, firm of Campbell-Harper, Ranch, Sitka, Kan. Residence: 1103 N. Emporia Av., Wichita, Kan.

1–**HARPER, Melville Helen Campbell (Mrs. Jesse C.),** *b* Wichita, Kan., June 17, 1889.
7–Jonathan **Clark** (*d* Nottingham, Pa., 1725), said to have come from Eng. in 1715;
6–Henry (1713-97), moved York Co., Pa., 1748, Union Co., S.C., 1770; *m* 1741, Chester Co., Pa., Elizabeth Underhill (*d* 1783; John[7] [*d* 1760], Quaker, *m* 2d, 1736, Anne Brown Dutton);
5–Hester (1748-1818), *m* 1768, York Co., Pa., John **Campbell** (1742-1824), came from Eng., ca. 1756; moved to Padgett Creek, Union Co., S.C., ca. 1770;
4–Henry (1771-1838), *m* 1801, Margaret Darby (1779-1819);
3–James (1808-88), served in Co. H, 76th Ill. Vol. Inf., 1862-65; *m* 1836, Priscilla Patience Grover Mick (1819-86), Kankakee Co., Ill.;
2–Melville Clark (2 below).
6–William **Knight** (*b* 1721), *m* Sarah–;
5–James (*b* 1770), *m* 1790, Anne Williamson;
4–Elizabeth, *m* John **Mick** (John[5] [1772-1846], *m* 1795, Priscilla Grover; John[6], said to have come to America, ca. 1732, prob. settled in Md., served in Am. Rev.);
3–Priscilla P.G. (1819-86), *m* James **Campbell** (3 above).
6–Phillip (Schmidt) **Smith,** lt. in German Army; *m* Barbara Markey, from Cologne, Germany to Md., 1750;
5–Henry (*d* 1838), *m* Elizabeth Grovenstadt, Fayette Co., Pa.;
4–Henry (1791-1872), *m* Kezia Davis (*b* 1793);
3–James B. (1826-1909), *m* 1850, in Fayette Co., Pa., Mary Bryson (1828-96);
2–Sarah Ellen (2 below).
5–Andrew **Bryson** (1767-1842), from Londonderry, Ireland to Uniontown, Pa., ca. 1800; *m* 1791, Betty Kennedy (1770-1841);
4–William (1796-1872), *m* 1822, Anne Ayers (*b* 1800);
3–Mary (1828-96), *m* James Boliver **Smith** (3 above);
2–Sarah Ellen (*b* 1859), *m* 1876, Melville Clark **Campbell** (*b* 1849), pioneer cattle ranchman, Wichita, Kan.; issue: I–Jetta Grover (*b* 1879; *m* 1902, Claudius Chalmers Stanley); II–Melville Helen (1 above).
1–*m* Feb. 5, 1912, Jesse Clair Harper (qv); issue: 1–Katherine, *b* Crawfordsville, Ind., Nov. 19, 1912; 2–Melville Campbell, *b* South Bend, Ind., Mar. 5, 1914; 3–James Franklin, *b* Wichita, Kan., Dec. 4, 1918.
1–Wellesley Coll., ex-'12. Mem. D.A.R., I.A.G. Residence: 1103 N. Emporia Av. Wichita, Kan.

1–**HARRIS, Eva Ellsworth Gould (Mrs. Edward Lansing),** *b* Beaver Dam, Wis., June 4, 1855.
7–Christopher **Leaming** (1649-95), from Eng. to Boston, ca. 1670; settled at Southampton, L.I.; *m* 1674, Esther Burnet (*d* 1714), of Sag Harbor, L.I.;
6–Jeremiah (1689-1759), *m* 1716, Abigail Turner (1694-1764; Edward[7]);
5–Matthias (1719-89), of Conn.; *m* 1751, Philathea Gould (ca. 1732-1797);
4–Judah (1753-1829), of Bristol, Conn.; served in Am. Rev.; *m* 1774, Thankful Tuttle (1752-1826);
3–Daniel McIntosh (1794-1875), removed to Gilboa, N.Y., thence to La Porte, Ind.; served as corpl. War 1812; *m* 1818, Mary Tucker;
2–Anna (2 below).
9–John **Tucker,** from Eng. to Bermuda, 1636, thence to Hingham, Mass.;
8–Jabez (1646-1724), removed to Westerley (Charlestown), R.I.; *m* Rebecca–;
7–Moses (*b* 1675);
6–Simeon (*b* 1710), *m* 1737, Sarah Hall;
5–Silas (1740-77), served in Am. Rev., wounded at Hubbardton on retreat from Ft. Ticonderoga; *m* 1764, Mary Histed (*d* 1800);
4–Charles (1769-1853), *m* 1792, Charity Stevens (1770-1816; Colonel Gershom[5] [*d* 1826], served with Sir William Johnson on Crown Point Expdn., 1756, and on a pvteer. in War 1812, served Am. Rev., at battles of Bunker Hill and White Plains, apptd. overseer of the construction of the great iron chain which was stretched across the Hudson, served at Valley Forge, *m* 1764 or 65, Phoebe Henry [*b* 1737 or 44-*d* 1831]; Peter[6] [*b* 1710], *m* 1732, Abigail Cole);
3–Mary (1798-1876), of Gilboa, N.Y.; *m* Daniel McIntosh **Leaming** (3 above);
2–Anna (1819-61), of La Porte, Ind.; *m* 1835, Ingraham **Gould** (1811-71), of Me.; to Wis., 1853; Mason (32°); issue: I–Charles Henry Medbury (1837-1903; *m* 1860, Charlotte Ann Outhwaite, *b* 1841); II–Talcott Griffin (1842-95; *m* Kittie Link; *m* 2d, Laura Ingalls); III–Lucy Leaming (*b* 1849; *m* Charles M. Hambright); IV–Eva Ellsworth (1 above); V–Frances Anna (*m* Frederick George Castle, 1850-1923).
1–*m* Dec. 24, 1878, Edward Lansing Harris, *b* Delavan, Wis., Dec. 8, 1852; A.B., Syracuse U., '78 (D.K.E., P.B.K.), Ph.B.; son of David Franklin Harris; issue: 1–Fred Gould, *b* Port Jervis, N.Y., Sept. 28, 1879; B.A., Yale, '01 (D.K.E.); *m* Feb. 10, 1923, Rose Woods Kunde; 2–Roy Gould, *b* Cleveland, O., Mar. 18, 1883; Cornell, ex-'02 (D.K.E.); *m* Oct. 29, 1906, Harriet, dau. Alton H. Smith, of Cleveland (issue: Eva Lucile, *b* New York, N.Y., June 9, 1912); 3–Eva Lucile (1886-96).
1–B.S., Downer (now Milwaukee Downer) Coll., '75. Mem. D.F.P.A., D.A.C. (state regent, 1925-26), D.A.R. (war time state regent, 1917-20, v.p.gen. from Ohio, 1920-23), U.S.D. 1812, N.E. Women (Toledo Colony), I.A.G., Women's Club (organizer, 1st pres. 1911-15). Residence: 1818 Hastings Av., E. Cleveland, O.

1–**HARRIS, Elmo G.,** *b* Spartanburg, S.C., 1861.
8–Thomas **Harris** (qv);
7–Edward (will dated 1733), of Isle of Wight Co., Va.;
6–West (1715-95), of N.C.; soldier Am. Rev.; *m* Mary Turner;
5–Isham (*b* 1741);
4–James (1763-1804), *m* Priscilla Gilham (1766-1814);
3–William Washington (1788-1875), *m* Elizabeth Golightly (1785-1862);
2–David G. (1821-75), *m* Emily Liles; issue: I–Laura L. (1846-1922); II–Ella (*b* 1848; *m* K. Z. Ford); III–Mary (*b* 1850; *m* McCollier Pool); IV–William W. (*b* 1853; *m* Jennie Nivin); V–James G. (*b* 1856; *m* Charlee Lee); VI–J. West (*b* 1858; *m* Hattie Gentry); VII–Elmo G. (1 above).
1–*m* Apr. 24, 1890, Zoe Barrow, *b* Monticello, Ark., Mar. 16, 1867; dau. of Judge J. C. Barrow, of Little Rock, Ark.; issue: 1–Jean, *b* Little Rock, Ark., Sept. 3, 1891; *m* Aug. 26, 1915, George C. Wilson (issue: Zoe Minor, *b* Sept. 10, 1917; George C., III, *b* Oct. 17, 1921); 2–Zoe, *b* Rolla, Mo., Oct. 10, 1894; 3–Dixie, *b* Rolla, Aug. 2, 1897; *m* Dec. 27, 1928, Clarence H. Brorrage); 4–Emily, *b* Lansdown, Pa., Apr. 11, 1902; *m* Jan. 27, 1923, Glenn A. Dooley (issue: Jean, *b* 1924).
1–Civil Engr. Prof. civil engring., Mo. Sch. of Mines, 1891–. Mem. Am. Soc. C.E., Sigma Xi, Phi Kappa Phi. Mason (K.T.). Baptist. Democrat. Residence: 1101 State St., Rolla, Mo.

1–**HARRIS, Franklin Stewart,** *b* Benjamin, Utah Co., Utah, Aug. 29, 1884.
9–Thomas **Harris** (qv);
8–Thomas (post 1631-1711), *m* Elnathan Tew (1644-1711);
7–Richard (1668-1750), *m* —King;
6–Preserved (*b* Smithfield, R.I.), *m* Martha Mowry;
5–Nathan (*b* Providence, R.I., 1758-*d* 1835), *m* Rhoda Lapham;
4–Emer (1781-1869), farmer, Cambridge, N.Y., and Logan, Utah; *m* Deborah Lot;
3–Dennison Lot (1825-85), of Luzerne Co., Pa., and Monroe, Utah; farmer; *m* Sarah Wilson;

2–Dennison Emer (2 below).
6–Alexander **Stewart,** of Haddam, Conn.;
5–Samuel (*b* Williamstown, Mass., ca. 1750);
4–Philander Barret, *m* 1801, Sarah Scott;
3–Benjamin Franklin (1817-85), *m* 1837, Polly Richardson (*b* Ky., 1818-1897);
2–Eunice Polly (*b* 1860); *m* 1882, Dennison Emer **Harris** (1854-1912), sch. teacher, mcht. farmer, of Utah; issue: I–Dennison (*b* 1883; *m* Montez Thurber); II–Franklin S. (1 above); III–Leo Lot (*b* 1886; *m* Amy Hammer); IV–Milton Hyrum (*b* 1888; *m* Beatrice Dalton); V–Marion Luther (*b* 1893; *m* Marguerite Flamm); VI–Karl Harris (*b* 1894; *m* Zola Brown); VII–Ireta (*b* 1897; *m* Raymond Becraft); VIII–Sterling Richard (*b* 1899; *m* Viola Green).
1–*m* June 18, 1908, Estella Spilsbury, *b* Toquerville, Utah, Feb. 17, 1884; dau. of George Moroni Spilsbury, of Toquerville; issue: 1–Arlene, *b* Ithaca, N.Y., May 25, 1909; A.B., Brigham Young U., '29; 2–Franklin Stewart, Jr., *b* Logan, Utah, May 24, 1912; 3–Chauncy Dennison, *b* Logan, Jan. 31, 1914; 4–Helen, *b* Logan, Dec. 26, 1915; 5–Leah Dorothy, *b* Logan, Sept. 14, 1918; 6–Mildred, *b* Logan, Mar. 8, 1921.
1–B.S., Brigham Young U., '07; Ph.D., Cornell, 1911 (Sigma Xi, Gamma Sigma Delta, Phi Kappa Phi, Pi Gamma Mu, Alpha Kappa Psi). Prof. sciences, 1904-21, pres. since 1921, Brigham Young U. (see Who's Who in America). Mem. Ch. of Latter Day Saints. Republican. Residence: University Hill, Provo, Utah.

1–**HARRIS, John William,** *b* Dripping Springs, Tex., Jan. 12, 1876.
6–Samuel **Harris** (*d* at sea), buried on L.I., 1740;
5–Robert (1702-88), from Ireland, 1740, settled at Lancaster, Pa., later at Mecklenburg, N.C.; signer Mecklenburg Declaration of Independence, 1775; *m* 1727, Mary Ann Rogers;
4–William (*b* 1755), served in Am. Rev.;
3–Josiah (1805-76), *m* 1830, Maria Purvines (1810-1861);
2–William David (1831-1907), ranchman; served in C.S.A., 1861-65; *m* 1865, Annie Evelyn Buckow (*b* 1841); issue: I–Alice Evelyn (*b* 1866; *m* W. H. Jacobs); II–Joseph Newton (1868-1921; *m* Nettie Rowland); III–C. O. (*b* 1870; *m* Maymie Brown); IV–Annie E. (1873-75); V–John William (1 above); VI–David Edward (*b* 1879; *m* Lena Lowry); VII–Clarence (*b* 1882; *m* Mary Viera); VIII–Minnie (*b* 1884; *m* Howard Sackville).
1–*m* May 17, 1905, Eunice White, *b* Hiawatha, Kan., May 11, 1880; dau. of Cornelius J. White, II, of Hiawatha; issue: 1–Helen, *b* San German, P.R., Oct. 11, 1906; A.B., Trinity U., 1928; *m* Apr. 1929, F. Acevedo, of Rincon, P.R.; 2–William Donald, *b* Ensenado, P.R., Feb. 9, 1910; 3–Margaret Alice, *b* Mayaguez, P.R., Mar. 22, 1913; 4–Robert White, *b* Mayaguez, P.R., May 19, 1916; 5–Charles Cleland, *b* San Juan, P.R., Apr. 8, 1919.
1–B.A., Park Coll., '02 (LL.D., 1923); student Princeton Sem., 1902-05. Missionary to P.R. since 1906; founder, 1912, and pres., Poly. Inst. of Porto Rico, the only successful industrial co-educational coll. of liberal arts in Latin America (see Who's Who in America). Mason. Residence: San German, P.R.

1–**HARRIS, Laurence Van Doren,** *b* Manchester Center, Vt., Dec. 7, 1898.
9–Thomas **Harris** (1637-97), from Eng. to Boston, Mass.; *m* 2d, Rebeckah Josselyn (*d* 1712; Abraham[10], *m* Beatrice, dau. of Philip Hampson, of London);
8–Benjamin (1694-1722), of Boston; *m* Sarah Cary (1692-1735; John[9], *m* Sarah–; James[10]);
7–Cary (1721-50), of Boston; *m* 1743, Mehitable Crowell (1723-61; William[8] [1698-1750], *m* 1720, Mehitable [1698-1792], dau. of Robert Gould, of London; William[9], *m* 1691, Elizabeth Sargent);
6–William (1744-78), of Boston; capt. in colonial wars and died in service at Lancaster, Pa.; *m* 1767, Rebecca Mason (1738-1801; Thaddeus[7] [1706-1802], *m* 1736, Rebecca [1713-48], dau. Jonathan Williams; John[8]; John[9]; Hugh[10], qv);
5–Rev. Thaddeus Mason (1768-1842), of Charlestown and Dorchester, Mass.; librarian, Harvard U., 1791-93; Unitarian minister; 1793-1839; *m* 1795, Mary Dix;
4–Thaddeus William (1795-1856), physician, Cambridge; librarian, Harvard U., 1831-56; *m* 1824, Catherine Holbrook (1804-86; Dr. Amos[5], *m* Jerusha, dau. Col. Lemuel Robinson, q.m. gen. Am. forces at Cambridge; Luke[6]; John[7]; Peter[8]; Thomas[9]; Thomas[10], came to Mass., 1635);
3–Rev. Thomas Robinson (1842-1909), of Cambridge; served with Mass. Vols. in Civil War; pres. St. Stephen's Coll., Annandale, N.Y.; *m* 1867, Margaret Schenck Van Kleeck;
2–Rev. Robert Van Kleeck (2 below).
10–Edward **Dix** (*d* 1660), from Eng. to Taunton, Mass.; settled at Watertown; *m* Jane–;
9–John (1640-1714), of Watertown; *m* 1670, Elizabeth Barnard (John[10], qv);
8–John (1672-1726), of Watertown; *m* 1697, Martha Lawrence (George[9] [1637-1709], *m* 1657, Elizabeth Crispe [1637-81], dau. Benjamin Crispe);
7–James (1716-1801), of Watertown; *m* 1742, Sarah Bond (1725-64; William[8] [1695-1730], *m* 1717, Hannah Cunnable; William[9]; William[10], qv);
6–Elijah (1747-1809), of Worcester, Mass., *m* 1771, Dorothy Lynde (1746-1826; Joseph[7] [1703-88], *m* 1737, Mary Lemmon [1712-98]; Nicholas[8]; Joseph[9]; Thomas[10]);
5–Mary (1776-1852), *m* Thaddeus M. **Harris** (5 above).
9–Baltus Barents **Van Kleeck** (1644-1717), capt. militia of Dutchess and Ulster cos., N.Y., 1700; commr. of Post Rd., Dutchess Co., 1703; justice, 1712; rep. Gen. Assembly, 1715-17; *m* Tryntje Jans Buys (1657-1725);
8–Lauwrens (1690-1769), *m* Jacoba Lewis (*b* 1691);
7–Baltus (1723-85), *m* 1744, Sarah Varick (1722-71; Jacobus[8] [*d* ca. 1745], *m* Anna Maria, dau. of Andrias Bristeda; Jacobus[9]);
6–Lauwrens (1749-93), *m* 1769, Cornelia Livingston (1752-1920; James[7] [*b* 1728], *m* Judith Newcomb [1733-1808]; Gilbert[8]; Robert[9], qv);
5–Baltus Livingston, M.D. (1774-1843), *m* Agnes Boyd (1776-1838; Robert[6] [1734-1804], *m* Eleanor Cockle [1744-1815]; Robert[7], from Scotland and Ireland);
4–Rev. Robert Boyd (1810-80), minister at Fishkill, N.Y.; *m* Margaret Schenck Teller (1808-88);
3–Margaret Schenck (*b* 1847), *m* Thomas R. **Harris** (3 above).
9–Pieter (Van Doorn) **Van Doren** (*d* ca. 1658), from Gravezande, Holland; settled at Gowanus, N.Y.; *m* Catharine Stelting;
8–Jacob (ca. 1655-1720), of Gowanus, L.I., later at Hillsdale, N.J.; *m* 1690, Maria Bennet (*d* 1735; Aria[9] [*b* 1637], *m* Angenietje Jans Van Dyck);
7–Christian (1699-1781), began to write name Van Doren; of Middlebush, N.J.; *m* 1723, Alje Schenck (1705-1801), she had 352 descendants at time of her death (Jan Roelofse[8] [1670-1753], *m* 1691, Sarah Van Couwenhoven; Roelof Martense[9]; Martin[10], to America, 1650);
6–John (1726-1815), of Millstone, N.J.; *m* 1749, Martha Lott (1728-1805);
5–John (1757-1832), of Millstone, N.J.; *m* 1779, Catryntje Van Voorhees (1754-1814; Garret[6], *m* Meltje Nevius; Minne Lucasse[7]; Lucas Stevense[8]; Steven Coerte[9], qv);
4–Garret Voorhees, M.D. (1781-1858), of Millstone; *m* 1812, Jemima Dyckman (1797-1851; prob. Jacob[5], *m* Jemima Horn);
3–Charles Augustus (1826-86), served as q.m. gen. on staff of gov. of N.Y. in Civil War; *m* 1856, Anna Wood Smith;
2–Anna Charlotte (2 below).
8–Robert **Smith,** settled at Buckingham, Bucks Co., Pa., ante 1719; *m* 1719, Phebe Canby;
7–Timothy, of Buckingham, Pa.; *m* Sarah Kinsey;
6–Joseph (1753-1826), *m* 1774, Ann Smith (1754-1854; Samuel[7] [*b* 1730], *m* 1750, Jane Schofield [1726-1815]; Thomas[8]; William[10]);
5–Jonathan (1775-1822), *m* Elizabeth Parker (John[6], *m* Mary–);
4–Horace Binney (1808-82), *m* Mary H. Wright, of Phila., Pa.;
3–Anna Wood (1833-1908), *m* Charles A. **Van Doren** (3 above).
2–Anna Charlotte (1871-1926), *m* 1894, Rev. Robert Van Kleeck **Harris** (*b* 1868), rector, P.E. Ch., Winsted, Conn.; issue: I–Capt. Robert Van Kleeck, U.S.A. (*b* 1895); II–Laurence Van Doren (1 above); III–Margaret Anna (*b* 1903; *m* 1927, John William Moore, Jr.).

1–*m* June 20, 1922, Penelope Holmes Munsill (qv for issue).
1–Ed. Columbia U., 1916-17 (Phi Gamma Delta); grad. U.S.M.A., '21; B.S., M.I.T., 1922. Served as 2d lt., U.S.A.; commd. 2d lt., Nov. 1, 1918, 1st lt., 1919; served with 1st Engrs., with A.E.F. in Germany, 1919-20; retired from active service 1920. Now v.p. Kuhn, Smith & Harris, Inc., bldg. contractors. Mem. Am. Inst. of Mining and Metall. Engrs. Episcopalian. Republican. Club: Kew Gardens Country. Residence: 14 Greenway South, Forest Hills, N.Y.

1–**HARRIS, Penelope Holmes Munsill (Mrs. Laurence Van Doren),** *b* Hartford, Conn., May 28, 1900.
9–Thomas (Munsell) **Munsill** (ca. 1650-1712), from Eng. to New London, Conn., 1681; *m* Lydia–;
8–Jacob (*b* 1690), settled at Windsor; *m* 1st, Sarah Calkins (*d* 1710; John⁹, *m* Abigail–);
7–Calkins (*d* 1758), *m* Mary Booth (*b* 1721; Caleb⁸ [*b* 1695], *m* 1719, Mary Gleason; William⁹; Simeon¹⁰; Robert¹¹);
6–Zaccheus (*b* 1745), of Windsor; *m* 1768, Hannah Drake (*b* 1743; Noah⁷ [*b* 1714], *m* 1741, Hannah Skinner; Enoch⁸; Enoch⁹; John¹⁰; John¹¹, qv);
5–Levi (1775-1833), *m* 1799, Rachel Marshall (1781-1842), of Torrington, Conn. (Thomas⁶ [*b* 1726], *m* 1764, Desire Tuttle [1743-1808]; Thomas⁷; Thomas⁸, *m* Mary [1666-1728], dau. of John Drake, 10 above; Samuel⁹);
4–Marcus (1809-85), of Winchester, Conn.; *m* 1829, Charlotte Eno (1801-67; Daniel⁵ [1780-1860]; Samuel⁶; Samuel⁷; James⁸; James⁹);
3–Mills Samuel (1837-87), of Winchester; *m* 1859, Mary Jane Borden;
2–Gail Borden (2 below).
10–Richard **Borden** (qv);
9–John (1640-1716), *m* 1670, Mary Earle (1654-1734);
8–John (1675-1719), *m* Sarah–;
7–John (1710-61), *m* Mary Peters;
6–Gail (1745-77), of Gloucester, R.I.; *m* 1774, Mary Knowlton;
5–Gail (1777-1863), *m* 1800, Philadelphia Wheeler (1780-1828);
4–Gail (1801-74), of Galveston, Tex.; *m* 1828, Penelope Mercer (*d* 1844);
3–Mary Jane (1841-1912), *m* Mills Samuel **Munsill** (3 above);
2–Gail Borden (1864-1912), of Winchester and Hartford, Conn.; *m* 1895, Ruth Clarke Holmes (now Mrs. David Dillon Reidy, qv for other lineages).
1–*m* June 20, 1922, Laurence Van Doren Harris (qv); issue: 1–Laurence Van Doren, Jr., *b* Wallace, Ida., Oct. 26, 1923; 2–Richard Borden, *b* Winsted, Conn., Sept. 14, 1925.
1–Ed. Bennett Sch., Millbrook, N.Y., 1919. Mem. D.A.R. Summer place: Lake Placid, N.Y. Residence: 14 Greenway South, Forest Hills, N.Y.

1–**REIDY, Ruth Clarke (Holmes) Munsill (Mrs. David D.),** *b* Winsted, Conn., Nov. 22, 1873.
11–Francis **Holmes** (ca. 1600-will probated 1671), from Eng. to Fairfield, Conn.; settled finally at Stamford, Conn., ante 1648; *m* Anne–;
10–John (1635-1729), of Bedford, N.Y.; *m* 1659, Rachel Waterbury;
9–Stephen (1664-1710), of Greenwich, Conn.; *m* 1686, Mary Hobbe or Hobbs (*d* ca. 1741);
8–Jonathan (1687-1749), of Greenwich; *m* 1707, Sarah Seeley (1694?-1727; Jonas⁹; Obadiah¹⁰; Lt. Robert¹¹, qv);
7–Jonathan (*b* 1716), of Nine Partners' Tract, Dutchess Co., N.Y.; *m* 1739, Phebe Haight (Nicholas⁸ [ca. 1680-1730], of Flushing, L.I., *m* 1704, Patience, dau. Edward Titus [9 below]; Samuel⁹, 1647-1712);
6–Nicholas (1742-1763), of Dutchess Co.; *m* 1758, Phebe Titus (1739-92; Samuel⁷, *m* Mary, dau. John Jackson; Samuel⁸; Edward⁹; Robert¹⁰);
5–Joseph (1758-1826), of Winchester, Conn.; served in regt. of foot, Conn. troops in Am. Rev.; *m* 1778, Lydia Curtis (1751-1820; Zebulon⁶, of Wethersfield, *m* Lydia, dau. Nathaniel Cole; Capt. Thomas⁷; Joseph⁸; Thomas⁹; William¹⁰);
4–Rufus (1781-1855), of Winchester; *m* 1810, Esther Eno (1785-1831; Daniel⁵, of Windsor and Colebrook, Conn., *m* Esther Phelps; Capt. Samuel⁶; James⁷; James⁸);
3–Lucius Lorenzo (1811-54), of Winchester; *m* 1833, Mary Ann Seymour;
2–Charles Beecher (2 below).
9–Richard **Seymour** (qv);
8–John (*d* 1713), of Hartford and Farmington, Conn.; *m* ca. 1665, Mary Watson (John⁹ [*d* 1650], *m* Margaret Smith);
7–Zachariah (*b* 1684), *m* Hannah Olmstead (Joseph⁸, *m* Elizabeth Butler; Nicholas⁹; James¹⁰);
6–Joseph (*b* 1728), *m* Abigail Howard (Samuel⁷, *m* Alice Hooker; Nathaniel⁸; Rev. Samuel⁹; Rev. Thomas¹⁰, qv);
5–Stephen (*b* 1759), *m* Marietta Griswold;
4–Allen (1781-1870), *m* Mary Belden;
3–Mary Ann (1810-54), of Sandisfield, Mass.; *m* Lucius L. **Holmes** (3 above).
10–John (Pers) **Pierce** (qv);
9–Anthony (1609-78), of Watertown, Mass., later at Woburn; freeman, 1634; *m* 2d, 1633, Ann– (*d* 1682/83);
8–Daniel (1639/40-1723), of Watertown; *m* Elizabeth– (*b* 1642);
7–Daniel (1666-1723), of Groton, *m* Abigail–;
6–Isaac (*b* 1701), of Waltham; *m* 1725, Eunice Sanderson (1707-1803);
5–Isaac (*b* 1731), of Waltham and Sutton; *m* 1755, Martha Graves;
4–Jesse (1764-1820), of Millbury; served in 7th Mass. Regt. in Am. Rev., 1781-83; servant to Gen. Washington; *m* 1783, Lydia Gale (1764-1843; Josiah⁵, *m* Elizabeth–; Abraham⁶; Abraham⁷; Richard⁸, from Eng.);
3–Amos (1803-85), of Winsted, Conn.; *m* 1830, Helen Spencer;
2–Abigail Elvira (2 below).
9–Jared **Spencer** (qv);
8–Thomas (1646-99), *m* Elizabeth Bates (James⁹, *m* Ann Whittington);
7–Thomas, of Saybrook, Conn.; *m* 1702, Ann Douglas (1680-1723; William⁸, *m* Abiah Hough; William⁹);
6–Thomas, of Saybrook, Conn.; *m* Deborah–;
5–Thomas (1736-1807), of Winchester, Conn.; *m* 1760, Phebe Grinnell (1736-1812; George⁶, *m* Mary Post Bull; Daniel⁷, *m* Lydia, dau. William Peabody, *m* Elizabeth, dau. John Alden, Mayflower Pilgrim, qv; Daniel⁸);
4–Capt. Grinnell (1768-1843), settled at Winchester, Conn.; *m* 1795-96, Abigail Catlin (*d* 1811);
3–Helen (1805-69), *m* Amos **Pierce** (3 above);
2–Abigail (1848-1922), of Winsted; *m* 1867, Charles Beecher **Holmes** (1846-1900), banker, Winsted; issue: I–Russell Borden (1870-78); II–Ruth Clarke (1 above); III–Leila Strowbridge (*b* 1875; *m* Dudley Landon Vaill); IV–Helen Rockwell (*b* 1881; *m* Wing P. Joyner).
1–*m* Jan. 16, 1895, Gail Borden Munsill (Jan. 6, 1864-Feb. 21, 1912); issue: 1–Penelope Holmes (Mrs. Laurence Van Doren Harris, qv); 2–Gail Borden, *b* Hartford, Conn., Oct. 30, 1904; U.Va., '28.
1–*m* 2d, Sept. 19, 1922, Dr. David Dillon Reidy, b Winsted, Conn., Nov. 9, 1874; son of Patrick Reidy, of Winsted, *m* Ellen Dillon.
1–Mem. D.F.P.A., D.A.R. Clubs: Farmington Country, Green Woods Country. Residence: "Shadow Lawn," Winsted, Conn.

1–**HARRIS, Susanna Wilcox (Mrs. William T.),** *b* Waco, Tex., May 27, 1878.
9–John **Hopkins** (1613-54), from Eng., 1634, settled at Cambridge, Mass.; freeman, 1635; an original propr. of Hartford, Conn., 1636; *m* ante 1634, Jane Strong (*d* 1679);
8–Stephen (1634-89), *m* 1661, Dorcas Bronson (1642-97; John⁹, qv);
7–Lt. John (1665-1732), *m* 1683, Hannah Strong (1661-1730);
6–Capt. Timothy (1691-1748), *m* 1719, Mary Judd (1701-44; Thomas⁷; William⁸; Thomas⁹);
5–Rev. Samuel (1721-1803), of Salisbury, Conn., and Great Barrington, Mass.; noted theologian; pastor First Congl. Ch., Newport, R.I., 1770-1803; *m* 1748, Joanna Ingersoll (1725-93);
4–Maj. David (1753-1824), ed. Yale; of Great Barrington, Mass.; aet. 22 left Baltimore and enlisted at Cambridge under Col. Arnold for the Storming of Quebec; capt. 4th Cont. Dragoons, 1777; maj. 1st Cont. Dragoons; *m* 3d, 1801, Isabella Ford (1781-1805);
3–William Lux (1804-52), of Snow Hill, Md.; *m* 2d, 1836, Susanna Rebecca Warfield (1807-88);
2–Mary Louise (1850-1926), of Baltimore; *m* 1869,

Ephraim **Wilcox** (1843-1903), sgt. Civil War; wholesale grocer, Waco, Tex.; issue: I–Laura Belle (Mrs. A. C. Walker, qv); II–Harry F. (1875-1921; *m* Elma Lewis); III–Susanna (1 above); IV–Charlotte H. (*b* 1880); V–Olive Gates (*b* 1883; *m* Edward B. Hopkins, 1875-1929); VI–George H. (*b* 1887); VII–James C. (*b* 1889; *m* Ethel Gilbert Minor, *b* 1889).
1–*m* May 16, 1900, William Temple Harris, *b* Burnet, Tex., Nov. 12, 1877; son of Norvell Ward Harris, of Waco, *m* Sallie Curry; issue: 1–Helen King, *b* New Iberia, La., Mar. 4, 1902; B.A., U.Tex., '24; 2–Norvell Ward, *b* Texarkana, Ark., Sept. 21, 1906; B.A., Austin Coll., Sherman, Tex., '26.
1–Mem. S.D.P., D.F.P.A., D.A.R., U.S.D. 1812. I.A.G. Presbyterian. Democrat. Residence: Dallas, Tex.

1–**WALKER, Laura Belle Wilcox (Mrs. A. C.)**, *b* Baltimore, Md., Nov. 14, 1870.
Sister of Mrs. William T. Harris (qv for genealogy).
1–*m* Dec. 25, 1890, Alonzo Cornelius Walker, *b* Dayton, Ala., Apr. 7, 1857; son of James Alexander Walker, of Ala., *m* Amy Hudson, of Tenn.; issue: 1–Lottie May, *b* Wootan Wells, Tex., Oct. 8, 1891; 2–Howard Clayton, *b* Wootan Wells, Apr. 23, 1894; *m* June 14, 1917, Veneta Eoff, of Waco, Tex. (issue: Jane Belle, *b* May 30, 1919; Thelma, *b* Sept. 1, 1922; Howard Clayton, Jr., *b* July 29, 1927); 3–Mary Belle, *b* Bremond, Tex., Feb. 2, 1897; 4–Almon Cornelius, *b* Bremond, Feb. 12, 1899; *m* June 10, 1921, Mary H. Hearn, of Bremond (issue: Douglas Cornelius, *b* Mar. 11, 1922); 5–Dorothy Eaves, *b* Bremond, Feb. 25, 1902; 6–Thelma Leo (Oct. 3, 1907-Sept. 14, 1908); 7–Ryland Wilcox, *b* Bremond, Aug. 2, 1909.
1–Address: Box 117, Bremond, Tex.

1–**HARRISON, Marjorie (Mary) Butler (Mrs. H. Norris)**, *b* New York, N.Y., July 15, 1889.
8–John **Butler** (1653-1735), from Eng., was living at New London, Conn., 1689; *m* Katherine Haughton (1661-1728);
7–Jonathan (1700-60), *m* 1726, Temperance Buckingham (1708-61; Daniel[8]; Daniel[9], Puritan settler, *m* Sarah Lee);
6–Ezekiel (1734-81), of Saybrook, Conn.; *m* 1759, Mabel Jones;
5–Medad (1766-1847), of Kinderhook, N.Y.; *m* 1794, Hannah Tylee (*d* 1856);
4–Benjamin Franklin (1795-1858), of Albany, N.Y.; lawyer; mem. N.Y. Assembly; Sec. of War in Cabinet of President Martin Van Buren; *m* 1818, Harriet Allen;
3–Benjamin Franklin (1830-84), *m* 1855, Ellen Grenville Parker (*d* 1909; Willard[4], physician, New York);
2–Robert Gordon (2 below).
10–Theophilus **Eaton** (qv);
9–Hannah (1633-1707), *m* William **Jones** (Col. John[10], the regicide);
8–Isaac (1671-1741), of New Haven; *m* Deborah Clark;
7–Isaac (1703-59), *m* Deborah Parker;
6–Mabel (1736-1806), *m* Ezekiel **Butler** (6 above).
9–Christopher **Hussey** (qv);
8–Stephen (*b* Lynn, Mass., ca. 1632), to Nantucket; a Friend; *m* 1676, Martha Bunker;
7–George, *m* Elizabeth Starbuck;
6–Paul (*d* 1823?), from Nantucket to Hudson, N.Y.; *m* Margaret Barker (*d* 1823?);
5–Lydia (1768-1823), *m* Howard **Allen** (*b* 1772);
4–Harriet (1798-1853), *m* Benjamin F. **Butler** (4 above).
9–Henry **Leland** (*b* Eng., ca. 1625-*d* Sherborn, Mass., 1680), to America, 1652; *m* Margaret Badcock;
8–Hopestill (*b* Sherburne, 1655-*d* Dorchester, 1729), farmer; *m* Abigail Hill (John[9], of Sherburne);
7–William (1692-1743), *m* Mehitable Breck;
6–William (1724-62), *m* Jemima Daniels;
5–Oliver (1760-1838), to Holliston, Mass.; *m* Abigail Perry;
4–Charles (*b* Holliston, Mass., 1792), ed. as a physician, but became a mcht., Phila., *m* 1823, Charlotte Frost Godfrey (Benjamin[5] [1756-1822], *m* 1778, Bethiah Gibbs, 1762-1804);
3–Mary Sophia (1833-1901), *m* Albert Gallatin **Thorp** (ca. 1830-1902; John Howard[4] [*d* Rahway, N.J.], of Morristown, N.J., Am. Rev., tradition says he served as a spy for Washington at the Battle of Trenton, *m* Rachel, dau. of John Primrose, from Scotland, *m* Rachel–);
2–Mary Leland (*b* 1865), *m* 1888, Robert Gordon **Butler** (1860-1906), editor "Questions and Answers" New York Sun; librarian, New York Times; issue: I–Marjorie Mary (1 above); II–Hope (*m* Francis M. Huntingdon-Wilson); III–Eleanor Grenville (*m* Henri Louis Marindin).
1–*m* Oct. 12, 1912, Henry Norris Harrison (see Vol. I, p. 172); issue: 1–Robert Butler, *b* Jenkintown, Pa., Aug. 22, 1914; 2–Charles Leland, *b* Jenkintown, Feb. 2, 1917; 3–Christopher Norris, *b* Abington, Pa., Aug. 12, 1925.
1–Ed. Miss Beard's Sch., Orange, N.J.; La Prairie, Vevey, Switzerland; the Sorbonne, Paris; U.Grenoble, Dauphine. Mem. I.A.G. Residence: Wren House, Rydal, Pa.

1–**HARSHBARGER, Sarah Foster (Mrs. Oswald H.)**, *b* Reno, Nev., Feb. 23, 1874.
9–Reginald **Foster** (qv);
8–William (1636-1713), *m* 1661, Mary Jackson (1639-post 1713; William[9], of Rowley, *m* Joanna Foster);
7–William (1669-1755), mem. mil. co.; mem. Legislature; *m* 1690, Sarah Kimball (1669-1729; John[8], *m* Sarah–);
6–Asa (1710-87), *m* 1732, Elizabeth Abbot (1712-58; John[7]; John[8]; George[9], qv);
5–Asa (*b* 1733), *m* 1763, Hannah Symonds (*d* 1775);
4–Asa (1765-1861), of Canterbury, N.H.; pvt. in N.H. militia, Am. Rev., aet. 15; col. N.H. militia, War 1812; *m* 1794, Sarah Morrill;
3–Adam (1800-73), *m* 1832, Sarah Bradley Eastman (1805-73);
2–Asa Eastman (2 below).
10–John **Webster**, *m* Mary Shatswell;
9–Hannah, *m* Michael **Emerson** (qv);
8–Hannah, to whom 2 statues were erected at Haverhill, Mass., for her heroism in Indian wars; *m* 1677, Thomas **Dustin**;
7–Abigail (*b* 1690), *m* 1716, Samuel **Watts**;
6–Hannah (1718-76), *m* 1736, Benjamin **Emerson** (1716-94), patriot Am. Rev.;
5–Abigail (1737-63), *m* David **Morrill** (1733-79), lt. 9th Provincial N.H. Militia, 1774; lt., Am. Rev., at Ft. Edward, 1777;
4–Sarah (1772-1868), *m* Asa **Foster** (4 above);
3–Adam, *m* Sarah B. Eastman (3 above);
2–Asa Eastman (1841-77), settled at Reno, Nev.; *m* 1872, Sophia Steele (*b* 1854); issue: I–Sarah (1 above); II–Lucie Theone (*m* 1897, Samuel Calef; *m* 2d, 1908, W. W. Cross).
1–*m* Dec. 10, 1893, Oswald Horatio Harshbarger, *b* Cassville, Wis., May 10, 1861; son of S. Newton Harshbarger, of George Valley, Pa.; issue: 1–Asa Foster, *b* Klamath Falls, Ore., Sept. 21, 1894; *m* June 21, 1925, Helen Grace Davie; 2–Virginia, *b* Oakland, Calif., Oct. 7, 1899; *m* May 8, 1922, Edward LaForge (issue: Sally Virginia, *b* Paris, France, Apr. 10, 1927).
1–Grad. Bishop Whittaker's Sch. for Girls, Reno, Nev. Mem. C.D.A., D.A.R., National Officers Club (D.A.R.), O.E.S., etc. Residence: 269 Mather St., Oakland, Calif.

1–**HART, Irving Harlow**, *b* Grinnell, Ia., Sept. 3, 1877.
4–Alexander **Hart** (*d* post 1829), from Scotland, settled at Colerain, Mass.; *m* Betsey Rine Hart (1792-1863; Peter Rine[5], Hessian soldier, *m* Polly Gross);
3–Alexander (1817-1914), *m* 1843, Jane Maria Crane;
2–Alexis Crane (2 below).
9–John **Crane**, from Eng., settled at Muddy Brook, Mass., 1637; dep. Gen. Ct., 1649;
8–Benjamin (1630-91), settled at Wethersfield, Conn., ca. 1655; freeman, 1658; *m* 1655, Mary Backus (*d* 1717; William[9], qv);
7–Jonathan (1658-1737), dep. Gen. Ct., 1701-22; lt. in Indian war, 1704; *m* Deborah Griswold (1661-1704; Francis[8], *m* Mary, dau. of Thomas Tracy, qv; Edward[9], qv);
6–Joseph (1696-1781), *m* Mary Couch (1696-1766; Samuel[7] [*d* 1739], of Fairfield, Conn., *m* Edora–; Simon[8] [*d* 1688], from Eng. to Fairfield, ca. 1640, *m* Mary [*d* 1691], dau. Francis Andrews, *m* Anna, dau. Giles Smith);
5–Thaddeus (1728-1803), lt. col. Westchester Co. Regt., Am. Rev., wounded at battle of Ridgefield, Conn., 1777; mem. N.Y. Assembly, 1777-79, 1788-89; *m* 1st, Sarah Paddock;
4–James (1763-1829), pvt. Westchester Co. (N.-

Y.) militia, Am. Rev.; *m* 2d, 1808, Clarinda Hallock;
3–Jane Maria (1825-52), *m* Alexander **Hart** (3 above).
9–John **Hall** (1609-96), from Eng. to Mass., 1630; later settled at Yarmouth and Dennis; selectman, 1685; *m* Bethiah Farmer (John[10]);
8–John (1637-1710), *m* Priscilla Bearse (1644-1712; Austin[9] [1618-ante 1697], from Eng. to Mass., 1638, settled at Barnstable);
7–Bethiah (1667-1708), *m* Zachariah **Paddock** (1664-1718; Zachariah[8] [1640-1727], *m* Deborah, dau. of Richard Sears, qv; Robert[9], qv);
6–Peter (1697-1790), *m* 1720, Sarah Howes (1695-1776; Jonathan[7] [1669-1751], *m* Sarah–; Thomas[8] [*d* 1676], *m* 1656, Sarah [*d* 1683], dau. Edward Bangs, qv; Thomas[9] [1590-1665], from Eng., *m* Mary Burr, *d* 1682);
5–Sarah (*d* 1777), *m* Thaddeus **Crane** (5 above).
10–Peter **Hallock,** from Eng. to New Haven, Conn., 1640; early settler at Southold, L.I.; *m* Widow Howell;
9–William (*d* 1688-89), *m* Margaret–;
8–John (*d* 1737), *m* Abigail Swazey (*d* 1737), a Quakeress (John[9]; John[10]);
7–John (*d* 1765), Friends preacher; *m* Hannah–;
6–John (*d* 1757), of Northcastle, N.Y.; *m* Martha Quinby (*b* 1706; Josiah[7]; John[8]; William[9]);
5–John, of Stephentown (now Somers), N.Y.; *m* 1764, Hannah Dickenson;
4–Clarinda (1781-1859), *m* James **Crane** (4 above).
10–John **Howland,** Mayflower Pilgrim (qv);
9–Elizabeth (*d* 1690), of Plymouth; *m* 2d, 1651, John **Dickenson** (*d* 1680), of Oyster Bay, L.I.;
8–Joseph (1654-ca. 1721), of Oyster Bay; mem. Queen's Co., N.Y., militia; *m* 1680, Rose Townsend (*b* ca. 1657; Henry[9]);
7–Zebulon (1681-1751), of Oyster Bay; mem. Queen's Co., N.Y., militia; *m* 1st, Rose Townsend (John[8], *m* Rose, dau. of John Wright; Thomas[9]; John[10], qv);
6–Zebulon (*b* 1710), of Oyster Bay; supposed to have moved to Northcastle, N.Y.; *m* 1733, Joyce Hance (*b* 1710; John[7], *m* Joyce, dau. of Francis Borden; John[8]);
5–Hannah, of Northcastle; *m* John **Hallock** (5 above).
4–Thomas **Biggar,** from Scotland, settled at Montreal, Can.; *m* Annie Mitchell (1759-1843);
3–William (1800-76), Allison, Ia.; *m* Elizabeth Adams (1804-64; Archibald[4], *m* Margaret Armstrong, from Ireland, settled in Franklin Co., N.Y.);
2–Elizabeth Edith (1846-83), *m* 1875, Alexis Crane **Hart** (1846-1926), educator; pvt., corpl., Co. K, 46th Wis. Vol. Inf., Civil War, 1864-65.
1–*m* Dec. 22, 1902, Ida Fay Pew, *b* Hebron, Neb., Aug. 27, 1882; dau. of Ithamer Pew, of Hebron; issue: 1–Elizabeth Fay, *b* San Antonio, Tex., Sept. 9, 1903; primary diploma, Ia. State Teachers Coll., 1922; A.B., Grinnell, 1926; 2–Mary Leota, *b* Arlington, Tex., Dec. 17, 1905; B.A., Ia. State Teachers Coll., '23; M.S., Ia. State U., 1924; *m* Oct. 20, 1925, Franklin J., son of John Philip Zink, of Green Mountain, Ia., *m* Rosanna Maneval (issue: Mary Frances, *b* 1927; Elizabeth Jean, *b* 1929); 3–Irving Harlow, Jr., *b* Allison, Ia., Nov. 23, 1910; 4–Evan Alexis, *b* Allison, May 21, 1913.
1–A.B., Grinnell, '98 (P.B.K.); grad. work, State U. of Ia., 1900-01 (Phi Delta Kappa). Educator since 1898; dir. extension div., Ia. State Teachers Coll., since 1916 (see Who's Who in America). Pvt. and corpl., Co. K, 50th Ia. Vol. Inf., 1898, Spanish-Am. War. Mem. U.S.W.V., Ia. and Minn. state hist. societies. Summer place: Sandy Lake, McGregor, Minn. Residence: 2516 Walnut St., Cedar Falls, Ia.

1–**HART, Alice Ann Clark (Mrs. Jerome A.),** *b* San Francisco, Calif.
8–Richard **Clark** (*d* 1697), *m* Elizabeth–;
7–Thomas (*d* 1711), *m* Hannah–;
6–Thomas (1701-65), *m* Hannah Winans, and *m* 2d, Elizabeth–;
5–Abraham (1726-94), a "signer" (see portrait); *m* Sarah Hatfield (1728-1804);
4–Capt. Thomas (1753-89), *m* Elizabeth Clark;
3–Jonathan (1776-1849), *m* Catharine Jonas (1782-1854);
2–William Squire (1807-89), Calif. pioneer of 1846 (see portrait); *m* Alice Ann Duncan (1841-91; Lawrence[3], *m* Ann McRae, both from Scotland); issue: I–William Squire, Jr. (*d* 1898); II–Alice Ann (1 above).

ABRAHAM CLARK (1726-94), a Signer of the Declaration of Independence and a member of the Continental Congress, whose sons, Aaron and Captain Thomas Clark, served through the Revolutionary War.

1–*m* July 22, 1899, Jerome Alfred Hart, *b* at San Francisco, Sept. 6, 1854; editor and author (see Who's Who in America).
1–LL.B., U.Calif., 1895. Author: Abraham Clark, Signer of the Declaration of Independence, 1923. Mem. I.A.G. Residence: "Weyewolde," San Jose, Calif.

WILLIAM SQUIRE CLARK (1807-89). In 1847 he built the first wharf in San Francisco Bay and the first schoolhouse in San Francisco.

1–**HART, Thomas,** *b* Phila., Pa., Nov. 24, 1894.
7–Samuel **Hart** (ca. 1690-1750), from Ireland, ca. 1735; settled in Plumstead Tp., Bucks Co., Pa., 1737; *m* Elizabeth– (*d* 1750);
6–Lt. James (1717-66), lt., Asso. Regt. of **Bucks** Co. in the Austrian Succession, "**King** George's War"; *m* Jean Means (1726-99; **William**[7], *m* Mary–, of Plumstead Tp.);
5–James (1759-1826), pvt. Am. Rev.; shipping

mcht., Phila.; *m* 1785, Ann Hankinson (1765-1820; Thomas[6], *m* Jemima–, of Amwell, N.J.);
4–Thomas (1786-1852), Phila. mcht.; first counsellor at time of his death of the State in Schuylkill; *m* 1810, Mary McCalla (1789-1823; John[5], *m* Rebecca [Darrah] Bryan, dau. William Darrah [1725-1808], served in Benjamin Franklin's regt. on the Lehigh frontier, 1756-57; Capt. William[6], of Plumstead, capt. 7th Co., 2d Bn., Bucks Co. Associators during Am. Rev., chief of forage dept., commn. of purchase);
3–William Bryan (1813-64), grad. Princeton, 1831, A.M., 1834; *m* 1838, Sara Byerly (1817-86; John[4] [1785-1837], corpl., 2d Troop, Phila. City Cav., War 1812, *m* Anna Long [1796-1865]; Christopher[5] [1737-1823], *m* Elizabeth Clymer, 1749-1827);
2–Charles Byerly (2 below).
4–John **Hill** (1785-1854), from Eng. to Hulmeville, Bucks Co., ca. 1830; *m* Martha Smith;
3–George Washington (1831-1913), pres. 7th Nat. Bank and Am. Life Ins. Co., Phila.; *m* 1852, Sarah Jane White (1835-1916);
2–Ida Virginia (*b* 1856), *m* 1876, Charles Byerly **Hart** (1846-1918), ed. Friends Central Sch.; mfr., Phila. (for issue see Vol. I, p. 316).
1–*m* May 15, 1918, Margaret Newbold Smith, *b* Cape May, N.J., Aug. 31, 1899; dau. of Harry Hudson Smith (1869-1911), *m* Margaret Mesier Newbold (*b* 1876; now Mrs. Harry Clifton Adams); issue: 1–Margaret Newbold, *b* Phila., Mar. 17, 1919; 2–Thomas, Jr., *b* Phila., May 4, 1922.
1–A.B., U.Pa., '16 (Delta Psi). Dir. Houston Hall, U.Pa.; trustee Lankenau Hosp., Phila., Episcopal Acad., Overbrook, Pa.; mgr., Phila. City Inst. Library; sec. Phila. Charity Ball, Inc. Enlisted in 1st Troop Phila. City Cav., Apr. 30, 1917; 101st Cav. and 103d Trench Mortar Baty., 28th Div., at Camp Hancock, Augusta, Ga.; corpl. 103d Trench Mortar Baty., Jan. 1, 1918; transferred to Air Service, U.S.A., Apr. 25, 1918, as pvt.; cadet maj. of air service cadets at U.S. Sch. of Mil. Aeronautics, Princeton, N.J., Oct. 1, 1918, hon. discharged, Dec. 17, 1918. Mem. S.C.W. (sec. Pa. Soc., sec. gen. Gen. Soc.), S.R., S.W. 1812, Hist. Soc. Pa., Pa. Geneal. Soc. Clubs: Philadelphia, State in Schuylkill, Merion Cricket, St. Anthony (New York), Mask and Wig, Cape May Golf (gov.). Residences: 271 Hathaway Lane, Wynnewood, Pa., and cor. Madison and Stockton Avs., Cape May, N.J.

1–**HARTT, George Montgomery,** *b* New York, N.Y., Dec. 10, 1877.
8–Isaac **Hartt** (qv);
7–Samuel (1656-1730), of Lynnfield, Mass.; followed the sea and received a silver cup from the Grand Turk; *m* Sarah Endicott;
6–Jonathan (*b* 1710), of Lynn, Mass.; removed to Maugerville, Nova Scotia, (now N.B.), 1760, with his four sons in answer to the gov.'s pleas for settlers to take the place of the banished Acadians; remained Pro-Am., and one son fought with Am. forces against Cumberland, 1775; Jonathan *m* 1734, Mercy Hawks;
5–Samuel (*d* 1814), of Lynn, and Kingsclear, N.B.; *m* Mary Estabrooks;
4–Aaron (1788-1866), of Kingsclear; *m* Charlotte Estey;
3–Jarvis (1812-73), of St. Johns, N.B.; M.A.; *m* 183–, Prudence Boardman Brown;
2–George le Baron (2 below).
9–Nicholas (Browne) **Brown** (*d* 1673; son of Edward[10], *m* Jane Lide, of Eng.); early settler in Lynn, Mass.; *m* Elizabeth–;
8–Cornelius (*d* 1701), of Lynn; *m* 1664, Sarah Lamson (*d* 1683);
7–William (1681-1768), of Natick; *m* 1703, Widow Deborah Squire, of Cambridge;
6–Josiah (1706-61), of Cambridge; *m* 1731, Mary Seaver, of Brookline, Mass.;
5–Phineas (1742-1821), of Brighton, Mass.; soldier Am. Rev.; *m* 1775, Lydia Badcock, of Milton, Mass.;
4–Dea. William (*b* 1783), began to write name Brown; of Cambridge; *m* 1808, Martha Farrar;
3–Prudence Boardman (1816-73), *m* Jarvis **Hartt** (3 above).
9–Maj. Simon **Willard** (qv);
8–Elizabeth (*d* 1690), *m* Robert **Blood**;
7–James (*b* 1673), *m* Abigail Wheeler;
6–Martha (*b* 1712), *m* Capt. John **Nutting**;
5–Martha (*b* 1761), *m* Joseph **Farrar**;
4–Martha (*d* 1849), *m* Dea. William **Brown** (4 above).
8–Isaac **Hartt** (qv above);
7–Samuel;
6–Jonathan;
5–John;
4–George Whitfield (*d* 1819), of Fredericton, N.B.; *m* Mary Brown (*d* 1816);
3–Henry A. (1815-92), of New York, N.Y.; M.D.; founded the first hospital for incurable cases; *m* 1840, Jessie Addison Main (1809-95);
2–Margaret Florence Montgomery (1848-77), of N.Y.; *m* 1876, George le Baron **Hartt** (1849-1913), art editor N.Y. Daily Graphic many yrs.; he *m* 3d, 1895, Claudine M. Willington; issue (1st marriage): I–George Montgomery (1 above); (3d marriage): I–Constance Endicott, Ph.D. (*b* 1900).
1–*m* Aug. 29, 1913, Marie Russell (May 13, 1882-Oct. 6, 1928); dau. of George Russell, of Burlington, N.J.
1–Pres. and editor The Daily News, Passaic, N.J., 1901–. Reporter and writer since 1895 (see Who's Who in America). Gov. St. Mary's Hosp. Episcopalian. Clubs: Passaic City Yountakah Country, The Newspaper (N.Y.-C.), Pica (Paterson). Republican. Residence: 88 Boulevard, Passaic, N.J.

1–**HASKELL, Mary Gertrude Hanna (Mrs. Coburn),** *b* Cleveland, O., Dec. 7, 1866.
5–Robert **Hanna** (1753-1837; desc. Thomas Hanna, of Scotland), from the North of Ireland to southern Va., 1765, settled in Columbiana Co., O., 1801; *m* 1776, Catherine Jones (1754-1835);
4–Benjamin (1779-1851), of Columbiana Co.; *m* 1803, Rachel Dixon;
3–Dr. Leonard (1806-62), physician, later wholesale grocery merchant, Cleveland, O.; *m* Samantha Maria Converse;
2–Howard Melville (2 below).
8–William **Dixon** (ca. 1662-1708), from Ireland to New Castle Co., Del.; *m* ca. 1690, Ann Gregg (William[9]);
7–Henry (ca. 1695-ca. 1742), of New Castle Co.; *m* 1715, Ruth Jones (*d* ca. 1758);
6–John (1717-67), of New Castle Co., Del., and Chester Co., Pa.; *m* 1742, Rebecca Cox (*d* ca. 1787);
5–Joshua (1750-1831), of Chester Co., Pa., and Columbiana Co., O.; *m* 2d, 1783, Dinah Battin (1760-1833);
4–Rachel (1785-1851), *m* Benjamin **Hanna** (4 above);
3–Dr. Leonard (1806-62), *m* Samantha M. Converse (3 above);
2–Howard Melville (1840-1921), pres. Globe Iron Works Co., Cleveland, O.; *m* 1863, Kate Smith (1843-1919); issue: I–Helen (*b* and *d* 1864); II–Bessie (*b* and *d* 1865); III–Mary Gertrude (1 above); IV–Kate Benedict (Mrs. P. W. Harvey, qv for Converse lineage); V–Howard Melville, Jr. (*b* 1877; *m* 1907, Jean Claire Hanna); VI–Leonard (*b* and *d* 1881).
1–*m* June 4, 1895, Coburn Haskell, *b* Boston, Mass., Dec. 31, 1868; son of William A. Haskell, of Boston; issue: 1–Coburn Hanna, *b* Cleveland (June 28, 1898-May 27, 1899); 2–Melville Hanna, *b* Cleveland, O., July 7, 1901; *m* June 2, 1922, Katherine Adams, Newtonville, Mass.; 3–Katharine, *b* Thomasville, Ga., Mar. 19, 1903; *m* Oct. 12, 1926, Ralph Perkins; 4–Mary Coburn, *b* Cleveland, Sept. 9, 1905; *m* May 30, 1929, Jefferson Rukin Jelks; 5–Gertrude, *b* Cleveland, May 21, 1909.
Residence: 11719 Lake Shore Boul., Cleveland, O.

1–**HARVEY, Kate Benedict Hanna (Mrs. P. W.),** *b* Cleveland, O., Dec. 26, 1871.
10–Edward (Convers) **Converse** (qv);
9–James (1620-1715), from Eng. to Woburn, Mass.; *m* 1643, Ann Long (*d* 1691; Robert[10], *m* Elizabeth–);
8–Maj. James (1645-1706), of Woburn; *m* 1668, Hannah Carter (1650-91; John[9], *m* Elizabeth Kendall);
7–Capt. Josiah (1684-1771), of Woburn; *m* 1706, Hannah Sawyer (1689-1747; Joshua[8], *m* Sarah Wright);
6–Lt. Josiah (1710-75), of Woburn, Mass., and Stafford, Conn.; *m* 1732, Eleanor Richardson (1714-85; Nathaniel[7], *m* Abigail Reed);

5–Col. Israel (1743-1806), of Randolph, Vt., and Stafford, Conn.; *m* 2d, 1771, Hannah Walbridge (1752-1830; Maj. Amos[6], *m* Margaret–, Amos[7]; Henry[8]);
4–Porter (1778-1870), of Stafford, Conn., and Unionville, O.; *m* 1810, Rhoda Howard (1785-1873);
3–Samantha Maria (1813-97), *m* Dr. Leonard **Hanna** (1806-62);
2–Howard Melville (1840-1921), paymaster, U.S.N., 1862-65; engaged in lake shipping; pres. Globe Iron Works Co., Cleveland, O.; *m* 1863, Kate Smith (1843-1919); for issue and Hanna lineage see Mrs. Coburn Haskell.
1–*m* May 2, 1894, Robert Livingston Ireland; issue: 1–Robert Livingston, Jr., *b* Cleveland, O., Feb. 1, 1895; Yale-S., '18; *m* Feb. 9, 1918, Margaret Allen (issue: Louise, *b* 1918; Robert Livingston, 3d, *b* 1920; Melville Hanna, *b* 1922); 2–Elisabeth, *b* Cleveland, Oct. 31, 1897.
1–*m* 2d, Feb. 12, 1923, Perry Williams Harvey.
1–Mem. I.A.G. Residence: 11801 Lake Shore Boul., Cleveland, O.

1–**HARVEY, William Hope,** *b* Buffalo, Putnam Co., W.Va., Aug. 16, 1851.
5–William **Harvey** (1727-67), from Scotland with his brother Andrew; settled at Elkton, Cecil Co., Md., 1763; elder Seceden Ch.; *m* Rebecca Caruthers (1737-97; Robert[6]);
4–Robert (1756-1831), of Fincastle, Va.; had large iron works at Martha's Furnace, Va.; served in Am. Rev., and was with his brother, William, when he was killed in battle of Guilford C.H.; *m* 1st, 1777, Martha (Borden) Hawkins;
3–Henry Bowyer (1788-1837), settled at Buffalo, on the Kanawka River, Va., 1808; *m* 1809, Sarah Smith Hale;
2–Robert Trigg (2 below).
8–Richard **Borden** (qv);
7–John (1640-1716), removed to Va.; *m* 1670, Mary Earle (William[8], *m* Mary, dau. John Walker; Ralph[9], qv);
6–Benjamin (1692-1743), removed to Winchester, Va., 1737; agt. in purchase of Va. land for Lord Fairfax; owned "Borden's Tract" grant of 500,000 acres; *m* Zeruiah Winters (William[7], *m* Hannah, dau. James Grover, mem. 1st Assembly of N.J., 1668, *m* Rebecca–);
5–Benjamin (1715-58), *m* 1743, Magdalen (Woods) McDowell, widow of Capt. John McDowell;
4–Martha (1744-1822), *m* 2d, Robert **Harvey** (4 above).
7–Jeremiah **Bronaugh,** of Stafford Co., Va., 1700;
6–Jeremiah (1702-49), of King George Co., Va.; *m* Simpha Rosa Enfield Mason (1703-61; Col. George[7], *m* Mary Fowke; Col. George[8], qv);
5–William (1730-bet. 1796-1800), served in French and Indian War; in Am. Rev. with Gen. Washington; *m* 2d, 1762, Mrs. Mary Doniphan Cooke (1737-81);
4–Margaret (*b* 1770), *m* Joseph **Hale,** of Fauquier Co. (George[5]);
3–Sarah Smith (1793-1850), *m* Henry Bowyer **Harvey** (3 above).
6–Col. Joshua **Fry** (*d* 1754), ed. Oxford U., Eng.; to Va., ante 1710; prof. natural philosophy and mathematics, William and Mary Coll., 1732-37; magistrate, Essex Co.; presiding justice; surveyor; co-author with Peter Jefferson of map of Va., 1751; co. lt., Albemarle Co., 1745; commr. of boundaries bet. Va. and N.C.; burgess, 1745-54; mem. Council; col. and c.-i.-c. Va. forces in French and Indian War; comd. Ft. Cumberland, Va., had George Washington as lt. col.; *m* 1730, Mary (Micou) Hill (Paul, Micon[7], qv);
5–Henry (*b* 1738), *m* 1764, Susan Walker (Dr. Thomas[6], of Albemarle, Va.);
4–Reuben (1766-1805), *m* 1788, Anne Coleman Slaughter (Col. James[5] of Culpeper, Va.);
3–Anne Clayton, *m* 1820, William **Hope,** from Dublin, Ireland, to Owensville, Ky.;
2–Anna Maria de Limbrous (*b* 1821), *m* 1842, Robert Trigg **Harvey** (1814-96), of Buffalo and Huntington, Va.; commd. col. 181st Regt., 22d Brig., 5th Div., Va. Militia; served with C.S.A., taken prisoner; mem. Va. Legislature; issue: I–Thomas Hope (1844-1929; *m* 1874, Emma Florence McCullough); II–Fanny Lewis (*b* 1846; entered St. Joseph's Convent, Wheeling, W.Va., 1872); III–Clayton Hale (1847-1915); IV–Robert Smith (1849-94; *m* Josie Pickles); V–William Hope (1 above); VI–Henry Chapman (*b* 1854; *m* Imogene A. Hagen).
1–*m* June 26, 1876, Anna Ruth Halliday, *b* Gallipolis, O.; dau. of John T. Halliday, of Gallipolis; issue: 1–Mary Hope, *b* Gallipolis, O., May 14, 1877; *m* J. C. Hammond (issue: Mary; Richard); 2–Robert Halliday (June 7, 1879-1903); 3–Thomas William, *b* Chicago, Ill., Aug. 27, 1881; *m* Helen Brandebury (issue: Helen; Thomas, III; Ida); 4–Annette, *b* Gallipolis, O., Nov. 15, 1884.
1–*m* 2d, Apr. 21, 1929, Mrs. May Ellston Leake, *b* Cleveland, O., June 1867; dau. of W. T. Ellston, of Lincolnshire, Eng.
1–Studied at Marshall Coll.; admitted to W.Va. bar, 1870. Practiced law in Cabell Co., 5 yrs., Cleveland, O., 3 yrs.; removed to Chicago; estab. Coin Pub. Co.; removed to Colo.; real estate operator; removed to Ark., 1900; promoted Monte Ne as a resort, etc. Author (see Who's Who in America). Pres. The Pyramid Assn.; mem. World's Money Ednl: League (chief exec.). Promoted financing of the Mineral Palace in Colo.; promoted 6,000 miles of roads in the southwest. Residence: Monte Ne, Ark.

1–**HASKELL, Earl Stanley,** *b* Des Moines, Ia., Oct. 5, 1886.
5–Mordecai **Soper** (*b* Eng., 1746-*d* Vt., 1829), served in Vt. militia, 1780-81; *m* 1770;
4–Joseph (*d* 1850), capt. War 1812; *m* 1800, Electa Mansfield, niece of Ethan Allen, of Am. Rev. fame;
3–Harriet Eveline (1823-90), *m* 1843, Sylvester Smith **Haskell** (1823-1901; Abel Tandy[4], settled at North Stockholm, St. Lawrence Co., N.Y., *m* Cynthia Rockwell, niece of Gen. Israel Putnam, of Am. Rev. fame; William or Caleb[5], of Conn.);
2–Orville Calvin (2 below).
8–Thomas **Winslow** (prob. 1681-1744/45), proved his freedom, 1702, as apprentice to Timothy Clare; Quaker, of Perquimans Co., N.C.; *m* Elizabeth (Cleare) Clare (*b* 1686; Timothy[9], *m* Mary Bundy);
7–Joseph (*d* 1750), Quaker; *m* 1729, Pleasant Toms (1710-85; Francis[8], *m* Margaret Bogue);
6–Thomas (1738-83), *m* 1753, Elizabeth Phelps;
5–Henry (1771-1849), *m* 1794, Elizabeth Needham;
4–John (1800-76), *m* 1821, Elizabeth Henley (1803-41; Jesse[5], *m* Miriam Bundy);
3–Jesse Henley (1822-75), *m* 1849, Susannah Johnson (*d* 1871; John[4], *m* Lydia Faulkner);
2–Jane Lydia (*b* 1861), *m* 1884, Orville Calvin **Haskell** (1848-1905); issue: I–Burdette Winslow (1885-1913); II–Earl Stanley (1 above); III–Ruth (*b* 1889; *m* Ford Blakeslee, divorced; *m* 2d, Owen Person).
1–*m* Mar. 13, 1917, Eva Mabel Sanborn, *b* Pipestone, Minn., Jan. 20, 1890; dau. of Oliver E. Sanborn, of Pipestone, Minn., and Joplin, Mo.; issue: 1–Ruth Sanborn, *b* Washington, D.C., Mar. 27, 1918; 2–Robert Chester, *b* Washington, July 19, 1922.
1–Grad. Sch. of Agr., U. of Neb., 1904 (Delta Sigma Rho, Gamma Sigma Delta); B.S.A., Ia. State Coll. Agr. and Mechanic Arts, 1908, M.S.A., 1909. Investigator and agricultural economist (see Who's Who in America). Club: Cosmos. Mason (32°). Residence: 3622 T St. N.W., Washington, D.C.

1–**HASTINGS, Thomas Wood,** *b* St. Louis, Mo., Sept. 29, 1873.
9–John **Hastings** (*d* 1657; younger bro. of Henry, 5th Earl of Huntington; 2d son of George, 4th Earl who succeeded his elder bro. Henry, 3d Earl [1535-95], who *d* without issue); came from Eng., 1637 or 38; settled at Braintree, Mass., and was one of the 1st freeman, 1643; with three others, granted 1,000 acres of land for settlement and development; removed to Cambridge, 1654; *m* in Eng.; 2 sons with no record of coming to America; *m* 2d, Ann Meane, widow of John Meane (Thomas Hastings, qv, was either a younger bro. or a cousin of 9–John; almost certainly the former for cousinship is based upon one of them being a son of Henry, 3d, who records show *d* without issue);
8–John (*d* 1720), of Cambridge; *m* 2d, 1668, Lydia Champney (1643-90; Elder Richard[9]);

7-Daniel (1676-1755), of Cambridge and Hardwick, Mass.; *m* 1701, Abagail Cooksey;
6-Walter (1703-92), of Oxford and Hardwick; *m* 1733, Mary Thompson (1712-99); three of their sons served in Am. Rev.;
5-Daniel (1734-1820), with his younger bro., Jacob, served in French and Indian War; his bro., John, mem. Com. of Corr. inaugurated by Samuel Adams, 1772, del. to Mass. Constl. Conv., one of 5 reps. to Gen. Ct. of Mass., selectman, etc.; *m* Submit Jordan;
4-Theophilus (1764-1842), of Hardwick; aet. 18, sgt. in Am. Rev.; *m* 1785, Betsy Prince Ames (1768-1844);
3-Arba (*b* 1790), of Hardwick and Barre, Mass.; *m* 1818, Laura Hunt, of Barre;
2-Samuel Weston (2 below).
5-Preserve **Wood** (1756-1806), of Brookfield, Conn.; apptd. surgeon's mate, 1776; reentered Cont. service, 1777, and served Conn. Regt., in Cont. Line; served at White Plains, Trenton, and Princeton; *m* —Benedict;
4-Preserve (1784-1849), of Brookfield; *m* 1803, Eunice Merwin (1783-1845);
3-Thomas (1809-94), of Brookfield, Conn., and Macon, Ga.; *m* Rhoda Augusta Graves;
2-Frances Augusta (1846-1920), of Macon, Ga.; *m* 1868, Samuel Weston **Hastings** (1834-78), sutler in charge of army supplies in Civil War; cotton broker; merchant; issue: I-Arthur Lee (1869-1909); II-Samuel Weston (*b* 1871; *m* 1900, Elizabeth Thompson); III-Thomas Wood (1 above); IV-Franklyn Benjamin (*b* 1875; U.S.A.); V-Clarence Augustus (*b* 1877; *m* 1905, Nellie A. Wood).
1-*m* Oct. 9, 1909, Athenia Agnes Belknap, *b* Yonkers, N.Y., Sept. 7, 1876; dau. of Ethelbert Belknap, of Yonkers; issue: 1-Thomas Wood, Jr., *b* New York, N.Y., Dec. 1, 1910; 2-John Frazee, *b* New York, June 1, 1914.
1-A.B., Johns Hopkins, '94 (Phi Kappa Psi), M.D., 1898. Physician; instr. clin. pathology, 1901-06, prof., 1906-17, Cornell U. Med. Coll. Lt., Med. R.C., 1910-17; maj., M.C., U.S.A., June 17, 1917-July 20, 1918; maj. M.C., U.S.A., retired, 1928, for disability. Author (see Who's Who in America). Club: City (New York, N.Y.). Residence: Kinderhook, N.Y.

1-**HATFIELD, Catharine Calhoun Peckinpaugh (Mrs. Sidney J.),** *b* Alton, Crawford Co., Ind., Sept. 18, 1880.
5-George Peter **Peckinpaugh** (*d* 1785), from Germany, 1760; *d* Brownsville, Pa.;
4-John (1783-1867), of Cape Sandy, Ind.; *m* 1st, 1804, Christine Rice (*d* 1812; Nicholas[5], soldier Am. Rev., *m* Mary Ann Marilda Elizabeth Hickman);
3-Nicholas Rice (1810-59), of nr. Alton, Ind.; *m* 1832, Eleanor Sheckell (1815-89);
2-Abraham Nicholas (2 below).
9-John **Howland,** Mayflower Pilgrim (qv);
8-Desire, of Plymouth, Mass.; *m* John **Gorham** (qv);
7-Shubael (1667-ca. 1750), of Barnstable, Mass.; *m* 1695, Puella Hussey (*b* 1677);
6-Lydia (1701-63), of Barnstable; *m* 1720, Joseph **Worth** (ca. 1687-1790);
5-Joseph (*b* 1729), of Nantucket, Mass.; *m* 1753, Judith Starbuck;
4-Eunice (1756-1833), of Nantucket; *m* 1776, William **Wilson** (1751-1832);
3-Thomas Worth (1792-1863), of New Garden, N.C.; lawyer; apptd. commr. to Cherokee Indians, 1837; commn. signed by Pres. Van Buren; *m* 1827, Catharine Calhoun Caldwell;
2-Ruth Elizabeth (2 below).
7-Rev. David (Rhys, Rees) **Reese,** from Wales, 1700, settled in Pa.;
6-David (*d* 1808), of Charlotte, N.C., signed Mecklenburg Declaration of Independence; *m* Susan Ruth Polk;
5-Ruth Catharine (*b* 1744), of nr. Charlotte, N.C.; *m* William **Sharp** (1742-1818), mem. N.C. State Congress, 1775-76; a.-d.-c. to Gen. Rutherford against Indians, 1775, apptd. by Gen. Caswell with Avery, Winston and Lanier to form a treaty with them, 1777; mem. Cont. Congress at Phila., 1779-82;
4-Ruth (1770-1852), *m* 1789, Col Andrew **Caldwell** (1753-1828), officer Cont. Army; apptd. to administer oath of allegiance; mem. State Legislature; parents of Judge David F. Caldwell and Hon. Joseph P. Caldwell;
3-Catharine Calhoun (1810-74), of nr. Statesville, N.C.; *m* Thomas Worth **Wilson** (3 above).
2-Abraham Nicholas **Peckinpaugh** (1839-1912), of Alton, Ind.; lumberman; *m* 1860, Emma Williams (1842-65); *m* 2d, 1874, Ruth Elizabeth Wilson (1840-1927), of Morgantown, N.C.; issue (1st marriage): I-Son (1861-65); issue (2d marriage): I-Wenonah Ermine (*b* 1878; *m* Thomas Bayard Sonner, 1866-1923); II-Catharine Calhoun (1 above).
1-*m* Dec. 28, 1904, Sidney J. Hatfield, *b* Perry Co., Ind., July 11, 1880; son of William J. Hatfield (1856-93), of Perry Co.; issue: 1-Nicholas William, *b* Indianapolis, Ind., Jan. 26, 1910; ed. Butler Coll.; 2-Wenonah, *b* Indianapolis, Nov. 12, 1911; ed. U.Ind.
1-A.B., Oxford (O.) Coll., '02. Mem. S.M.D. (sec. Ind. soc., 1916-24, historian, 1924), D.A.R., Soc. of Ind. Pioneers. Residence: 3302 E. Fall Creek Boul., Indianapolis, Ind.

1-**HATHAWAY, Erwin Oren,** *b* Petersham, Mass., Nov. 8, 1867.
9-Nicholas **Hathaway,** from Eng. ca. 1630, settled at Taunton, Mass., a few years later;
8-John (1617-1704/05), of Taunton and Berkley, Mass.; constable at Taunton; served in King Philip's and King William's wars; *m* 1649, Martha Shepard (*d* 1683);
7-Isaac (1655-1722), of Berkley; *m* 1686, Mary Pitts (1650-1720);
6-Isaac (*b* 1688), of Berkley; *m* Damaris Babbitt (*b* 1691);
5-Abijah (*b* 1716), of Berkley; *m* 1748, Sarah Talbot;
4-Joel (1762-1838), of Berkley and Barre; served in Am. Rev.; *m* 1782, Sally Trafton (*d* 1841);
3-William (1803-78), of Barre and Petersham, Mass.; *m* 1836, Susan Forbes (1800-57);
2-Leander Thomas (2 below).
8-William **Spooner** (*d* 1684), from Eng., settled at Plymouth, Mass.; surveyor of highways, 1654; mem. Plymouth militia, 1643; *m* 1652, Hannah Pratt;
7-Samuel (1655-1739), of Dartmouth; constable; *m* Experienc Wing (*b* 1668);
6-Samuel (1693-1781), of Dartmouth; *m* 1717, Rebecca Weston (*d* 1729);
5-Amaziah (1726-98), of Hardwick, Mass.; *m* 1750, Lydia Fay (1730-1817);
4-Samuel (1763-1840), of Hardwick; served in Am. Rev.; *m* 1798, Hannah Williams;
3-Oren (1802-67), of Barre, Mass.; *m* 1829, Naomi Clark (1808-69);
2-Ellen Jane (2 below).
11-Thomas **Rogers,** Mayflower Pilgrim (qv);
10-John, lived at Plymouth, Mass., 1631, Duxbury, Mass., 1634; rep. Gen. Ct.; *m* 1639, Ann Churchman (Hugh[11]);
9-Anna (*d* post 1704), *m* 1st, 1664, John **Tisdale,** Jr. (*d* 1677), dep. Gen. Ct., Taunton, Plymouth Colony; killed by Indians;
8-Abigail (*b* 1667), of Duxbury and Taunton; *m* 1685, William **Makepeace** (*b* 1662/63);
7-Abigail (1686-1727), *m* 1703, Emmanuel **Williams** (*d* 1719);
6-John (1704-80), of Taunton; *m* Elizabeth Caswell;
5-Jacob (*d* 1810), of Middleborough, New Braintree, Barre, Taunton and Williamsburg, Mass.; *m* 1765, Sarah Dean (*b* 1743);
4-Hannah (1771-1830), of Hardwick; *m* Samuel **Spooner** (4 above);
3-Oren, *m* Naomi Clark (3 above);
2-Ellen Jane (1842-1921), *m* 1865, Leander Thomas **Hathaway** (1838-1908), corpl. Co. I, 25th Mass. Vols., Civil War, 3 yrs., severly wounded at Battle of Cold Harbor; issue: I-Gertrude Maria (*b* 1865; *m* John Newton, *d*; *m* 2d, Warren F. French); II-Erwin Oren (1 above); III-Fred Leander (*b* 1870; *m* May Celicia Phillips); IV-Frank Andrew (*b* 1873); V-Edith Ellen (1876-1927; *m* Eddie Oliver Russell); and VI-Marian Spooner, twins (1876-80); VII-Ruth Angelia (1878-79); VIII-Marjorie Susan (*b* 1882; *m* Benjamin Franklin White); IX-Alice Naomi (1884-86).
1-*m* June 23, 1892, Nina Vinetta Russell (qv); issue: 1-Leander Russell, *b* Springfield, Mass., Apr. 6, 1893; S.B. in C.E., Yale, '16; maj. U.S.A., served in World War; *m* June 16, 1917, Edith Fiske, dau. of James F. Bristol, of Guilford, Conn., *m* Elizabeth Dolph (issue: Elizabeth Fiske; Leander Russell, Jr.); 2-Chester Erwin, *b* Somerville, Mass., Mar. 5. 1896; Nor-

wich U.; left coll., ens. U.S.N. in World War; *m* Sept. 10, 1921, Ruth Houghton, dau. of Charles W. Jordan, of Yarmouth, Me., *m* Elsie Johnson (issue: Susan Elizabeth; Marjorie); 3–Herbert Frederick, *b* Nashua, N.H., June 14, 1907; S.B. in M.E., U.Minn., '28; 4–Pollyanna, *b* St. Paul, Minn., June 11, 1917; student U.Minn. High Sch.

1–S.B. in C.E., Worcester Poly. Inst., '89. Engaged in railway engring. in Mass. and N.Y., 1889-93, gen. engr., 1894-97; electric ry. engring., 1894-97; in general engring. practice thruout N.E., consisting largely of location and construction of electric rys., 1897-1913; dist. engr., U.S. Bureau of Public Rds., 1916– (dist. includes Minn., N.D., S.D., and Wis.). City engr., Nashua, N.H., 1908-13; mem. and clk. Bd. of Public Works, Nashua, 1908-13; v.p. Bd. of Trade; div. engr. N.H. State Highway Dept., 1902-13; sr. highway engr., U.S. Bureau of Public Roads, 1913-16. Baptist. Republican. Residence: 1295 Raymond Av., St. Paul, Minn.

1–**HATHAWAY, Nina Vinetta Russell (Mrs. Erwin Oren),** *b* Athol, Mass., Dec. 15, 1868.
9–William **Russell** (1605-62), from Eng. to Cambridge, Mass., ca. 1635; *m* Martha–;
8–Jason (1658-ca. 1736), of Menotomy (now Arlington), Mass.; *m* 1684, Mary Hubbard;
7–Hubbard (1687-1726), of Arlington; *m* 1710, Elizabeth Dickson;
6–Jason (1717-killed Apr. 19, 1775, by British in front of his home which is still standing), of Arlington; Am. Rev.; *m* Elizabeth Winship;
5–Jason (1742-1825), of Arlington, Mass., and Mason, N.H.; served in Am. Rev. from Mason; *m* 1762, Elizabeth Locke;
4–Jason (1763-1840), of Mason, N.H., and Madison, Me.; *m* 1787, Rebecca Looghton;
3–Dea. William (1796-1864), of Athens, Me.; Bapt.; *m* 1820, Achsah Kelley;
2–Warren (2 below).
8–John **Robbins** (*b* ante 1655), of Harwich, Mass.; *m* Sarah–;
7–Roger (*b* ante 1690), of Yarmouth, Mass.; *m* Mercy Blackman;
6–Richard (ca. 1712-1748), of Harwich and Yarmouth; *m* 1733, Hannah Berry;
5–William (1734-1814), of Harwich, Yarmouth, and Brewster; *m* 1757, Hannah Vincent;
4–William (*b* 1763), served in Am. Rev., from Harwich; *m* (intentions published, Dec. 23, 1784) Thankful Clark;
3–William (1802-61), *m* 1840, Susan P. Reynolds;
2–Sarah Ann (2 below).
11–Francis **Cooke,** Mayflower Pilgrim (qv);
10–Jane (*b* 1608), *m* Experience **Mitchel** (1609-89), from Eng. in the "Anne," 1623; lived in Plymouth, Duxbury and Bridgewater;
9–Sarah, *m* John **Hayward;**
8–Mary (1672-1712), of Bridgewater; *m* 1698, William **Ames** (1673-1712);
7–Bethiah (*b* 1706), of Bridgewater; *m* 1737, Timothy **Keith** (1711-40);
6–Levi (1738-1813), of Bridgewater; *m* 1759, Jemima Perkins (*b* 1738/39);
5–Bethia (1760-86), of Bridgewater; *m* 1777, Nathaniel **Reynolds** (1757-1828), served in Am. Rev.;
4–Luther (1777-1860), of Sidney, Me.; *m* 1801, Sarah Faught (1781-1869);
3–Susan P. (1815-60), of Sidney; *m* William **Robbins** (3 above);
2–Sarah Ann (1850-1927), *m* 1866, Warren **Russell** (1840-1908), of Petersham, Mass.; issue: I–Nina V. (1 above); II–Herbert Warren (*b* 1871; *m* Mary Clark); III–Eddie Oliver (*b* 1873; *m* Edith Ellen Hathaway, sister Erwin Oren Hathaway, qv).
1–*m* June 23, 1892, Erwin Oren Hathaway (qv for issue).
1–Ed. pub. schs., Petersham, Mass. Mem. W.C.T.U., League of Protestant Women. Baptist. Residence: 1295 Raymond Av., St. Paul, Minn.

1–**HAUXHURST, Stanley Cottrill,** *b* Milwaukee, Wis., Jan. 13, 1880-*d* Mar. 1, 1930.
6–Joseph (Hawxhurst) **Hauxhurst,** from Eng.;
5–Jacob (*b* ca. 1745), of Oyster Bay, L.I., N.Y.; *m* Mary Seaman;
4–James (1770-1844), of Oyster Bay; *m* Abigail Van Velzor (William[5], who came from the Netherlands);

STANLEY COTTRILL HAUXHURST (1880-1930).

3–Jacob Van Velzor (1817-1902), of Oyster Bay, and later of Spring Green, Wis.;
2–Sidney (2 below).
5–Patrick **Cottrill** (1774-1857), of Parsippany, N.J., later of Bridport, Vt.; *m* Jemima Wilson (1775-1829), bro. Richard, one of George Washington's Life Guards;
4–Mahlon (1797-1864), of Bridport and Montpelier, Vt.; *d* at St. Louis, Mo. (see photograph of homestead);
3–William Hutchins (1823-97), of Montpelier, Vt., later of Milwaukee, and Appleton, Wis.; *m* Frances Elizabeth Hall;
2–Julia Frances (2 below).

Home of Mahlon Cottrill (1797-1864), Montpelier, Vt.

9–John **Hall** (1600-ca. 1670), from Coventry, Eng., ca. 1630 to Charlestown and Yarmouth, Mass.; *m* ca. 1630, Bertha Lanard;
8–John (1633-ca. 1700), *m* Priscilla Bearse, of Barnstable;
7–Joseph (1660-ca. 1710), *m* Hannah Miller (Rev. John[8] [*b* 1631], *m* Margaret [*b* 1640], dau. of Josiah Winslow [1605-74], from Eng. in the "Good Angel," 1631, settled at Marshfield, *m* 1636, Margaret, dau. of Thomas Bourne, of Plymouth; Rev. John[9] [*d* 1663], "Most learned of N.E. ministers," first minister of Yarmouth, came from Eng., 1638);
6–David (1704-89), A.B., Harvard, 1724; D.D., Dartmouth, 1777; *m* 1731, Elizabeth Prescott;
5–Benjamin (1746-1833), of Sutton, Mass., later St. Albans, Vt.; pvt., Capt. Barthw. Woodbury's co., Col. Jonathan Holman's and Col. Jacob Davis' regts., 1776,80; *m* Elizabeth Mosely (ca. 1750-1822; Joseph[6], pvt. in Am. Rev., 1776-82, of Sutton, Mass.);
4–Charles, M.D. (1766-ca. 1836), of St. Albans, Vt.; *m* Charlotte Janes Hubbard;

3-Frances Elizabeth (1826-1901), of St. Albans; *m* William Hutchins **Cottrill** (3 above).
10-Rev. Peter **Bulkeley** (qv);
9-Rev. Edward (1614-1695/96), *m* Lucia-;
8-Hon. Col. Peter (1640-88), *m* Rebecca Wheeler (1645-1718);
7-Rebecca (1681-1747), *m* Maj. Dr. Jonathan **Prescott** (1677-1729);
6-Elizabeth (ca. 1713-1803), *m* David **Hall**, D.D. (6 above).
6-Jonathan **Janes** (1750-1823), of Brimfield, Mass., later St. Albans, Vt.; judge of Probate Ct.; pvt. on Lexington Alarm Roll in Capt. James Sherman's co., Col. Pynchon's regt., Apr. 19, 1775; also pvt. in Capt. Joseph Thompson's co., Col. Timothy Danielson's regt., 1775, and in Capt. Charles' co., Col. Bliss' regt., 1778;
5-Ruby (*d* 1841), *m* Ethan **Hubbard** (ca. 1774-1846);
4-Charlotte J. (ca. 1790-1860), *m* Charles **Hall** (4 above);
3-Frances E., *m* William H. **Cottrill** (3 above);
2-Julia Frances (1852-1922), of Montpelier, Vt., later of Milwaukee, Wis.; *m* 1878, Sidney **Hauxhurst** (1842-1902), of Oyster Bay, L.I., N.Y., later of Milwaukee, Wis. (see portrait and biography); issue: I-Stanley Cottrill (1 above); II-Grenville (*d* infancy); III-Sidney Peckham (*d* infancy).

SIDNEY HAUXHURST (1842-1902), Sgt., "Dillon's Buena Vista," 6th Wis. Baty., Light Arty., Quinby's Div., 17th A.C., 1861-64. Engagements: New Madrid, Island No. 10, Siege and Battle of Corinth, Port Gibson, Raymond, Jackson, Champion Hills, Vicksburg, Mission Ridge. G.A.R. Mem. firm Roundy, Peckham & Co., wholesale grocers.

1-*m* June 14, 1911, Louise Van Dyke (see Vol. II, p. 63, for genealogy and issue).
1-A.B., Williams, '02 (Delta Psi); LL.B., Harvard Law Sch., 1906. Mem. law firm of Van Dyke & Hauxhurst, Milwaukee. Mem. Am. Bar Assn. Capt. Q.M. Corps, U.S.A., assigned to Purchase, Storage and Traffic Div., General Staff, Washington, July 1918-Apr. 1919. Residence: 153 Prospect Av., Milwaukee, Wis.

1-**HAWES, George Edward**, *b* Fairhaven, O., Jan. 27, 1864.
7-Edward **Hawes** (*d* 1687), from Eng., settled at Dedham, Mass., 1635; *m* 1648, Eliony Lumber;
6-Joseph (1664-1756), of Needham; *m* Deborah Dewing (1668-1752; Andrew[7], *m* Ann-);
5-Jeremiah (*b* 1701-will dated, 1780); *m* 1733 or 34, Mary Patterson (*b* 1704; Joseph[6], *m* Mary Goodnow);
4-Joseph (1737-1811), of Needham and Natick, Mass.; soldier in French and Indian War and Am. Rev.; *m* 1st, 1764, Alacea Blake (1744-96);
3-Edward (1782-1821), *m* 1807, Martha Johnson (1785-1874; Ebenezer[4], *m* Elizabeth-);
2-Edward (1813-1901), of Framingham, Mass., and Fair Haven, O.; merchant; *m* 1845, Mary Jane Walden (1828-85; James[3], *m* Keturah Walden); issue: I-Sarah Elizabeth (1846-52); II-Elvira (1850-1924; *m* 1868, John Benjamin Cramer, *d* 1904); III-Laura (1854-1923); IV-George Edward (1 above); V-Martha Jane (1868-79).
1-*m* Oct. 15, 1890, Eva Cecelia McKean (Oct. 20, 1867-Jan. 23, 1920); dau. of William J. McKean, *m* Rebecca McBurney; issue: 1-Helen Rebekah, *b* Mercer, Pa., Dec. 28, 1894; B.A., Western Coll. for Women, Oxford, O., '14; *m* Aug. 2, 1921, Edwin B., son of Richard Hurrell, of Braddock, Pa. (issue: Barbara Cecelia, *b* Mar. 13, 1923; Margaret Anne, *b* Nov. 21, 1925); 2-Mary Walden, *b* Braddock, Pa., June 26, 1900; B.A., Western Coll. for Women, '20; 3-Edward McKean, *b* Braddock, Feb. 7, 1904; A.B., Washington and Jefferson U., '26, LL.B., U.Pittsburgh, 1929.
1-*m* 2d, July 21, 1922, Mrs. Ella Augusta (Stites) High, *b* Bridgeton, N.J., Oct. 23, 1869; dau. of Edmond A. Stites, of Bridgeton.
1-A.B., Washington and Jefferson, '85 (Phi Gamma Delta, Pi Gamma Mu), A.M., 1888, Pittsburgh Theol. Sem., 1888; (D.D., Erskine, 1908, Westminster, 1908, Washington and Jefferson, 1910). Pastor 2d Ch., Mercer, Pa., 1888-91, 1st Ch., Portland, Ore., 1892-98, 1st Ch., Braddock, Pa., 1898-1911, Bellefonte (Pa.), Presbyn. Ch., 1911-15, Market Square Ch., Harrisburg, Pa., 1915-26; pastor evangelist of Presbyn Ch., 1927-. Author (see Who's Who in America). Residence: 187 Maplewood Av., Phila., Pa.

1-**HAWES, Katharine Heath**, *b* Richmond, Va., Sept. 3, 1875.
9-Richard **Hawes** (*d* 1656), from Eng. in the "True Love," 1635, settled at Dorchester, Mass.; *m* Ann-;
8-Obadiah (1635-90), *m* Mary Humphrey (*d* 1676);
7-James (1663-1718), *m* Damaris Bird (*d* 1737);
6-Desire (1694-1742), of Dorchester, Mass.; *m* 1721, Jerusha Bird (*d* 1737);
5-Richard (*b* 1737), *m* Hannah Goff;
4-Jesse (1770-1808), *m* 1796, Anne Pierce;
3-Samuel Pierce (1799-1866), of Dorchester, Mass., and Richmond, Va.; *m* 1825, Judith Anna Smith;
2-Samuel Horace (2 below).
9-Robert **Pierce** (qv);
8-Thomas (1635-1706), *m* Mary Proctor (1642-1704);
7-John (1668-1744), *m* 1693, Abigail Thompson (1667-1747);
6-Samuel (1702-68), *m* 1732, Abigail Moseley (1711-66);
5-Col. Samuel (1739-1815), of Dorchester, Mass.; received commns. from British and Mass. militia on same day, accepted Mass. commn., served as col., Am. Rev.; *m* 1765, Elizabeth Howe (1744-97);
4-Anne (1778-1861), of Dorchester; *m* Jesse **Hawes** (4 above).
6-William **Smith**, from Eng. during latter part of 17th Century; settled at Gloucester, Va.; *m* Ann Sterling;
5-William (1720-90), removed to Henrico Co., Va.; *m* Mary-;
4-William Sterling (1758-1829), lt. 6th Regt., Cont. Line, 1777-81; *m* 1801, his cousin, Judith Smith (1769-1820);
3-Judith Anna (1806-74), of Va.; *m* Samuel Pierce **Hawes** (3 above);
2-Samuel Horace (1838-1922), of Richmond, Va.; lt. C.S.A.; mcht.; *m* 1867, Martha Crane Heath (1844-96; Stafford Robert Wilson[3], *m* Catherine C. Woodruff, of Newark, N.J.); issue: I-Horace Sterling (*b* 1868; *m* Mary Reid McCaw); II-Heath Woodruff (*d* 1873, aet. 5 mos.); III-Katharine Heath (1 above).
1-Mem. bd. trustees or dirs.: Richmond Urban League, Y.W.C.A., Assembly Training School for Lay Workers. Mem. A.P.V.A., Va. Hist. Soc., I.A.G. (life). Presbyterian. Democrat. Clubs: Woman's (Richmond and Ginter Park). Summer place: Green Cabin, Yorktown, Va. Residence: 3211 Chamberlayne Av., Richmond, Va.

1-**HAWKINS, Henry Gabriel**, *b* Choctaw Co., Ala., Oct. 5, 1865.
4-Joshua **Hawkins** (*d* 1832), wounded in Battle

of Brandywine while fighting like a lion, one wound was in leg, and British surgeon offered to cut off his leg, but he protested and the leg recovered; he received at same time a bullet (ounce ball) in the arm, which struck him after he had fallen in crouching position from leg wound, he carried the ball in his arm until his death;
3–Herbert, removed from Spartanburg Dist., S.C., to Pickens Co., Ala.; *m* Armind Foster;
2–Rev. Gabriel (*b* 1826), *m* Martha Elizabeth Lawrence (*b* 1836); issue: I–George Lawrence (*b* 1859); II–Henry Gabriel (1 above); III–W. Coke (1867-1918); IV–Rev. Ira F. (*b* 1869; *m* Katie Shackleford); V–Mary (*b* 1871; *m* Rev. J. J. Golden, *d*); VI–Lula (*b* 1873; *m* Rev. W. B. Jones); VII–Mattie (*b* 1877; *m* S. L. Heidelberg).
1–*m* Nov. 1895, Mary Aletha Terral (*d* Feb. 1898); dau. of Judge S.H. Terral, of Quitman, Miss. (at time of death was a justice Supreme Ct. of Miss.); issue: 1–Henry Terral (*d* infancy).
1–*m* 2d, Annie Betts Galloway, *b* Canton, Miss., Nov. 7, 1879; dau. of George Washington Galloway, of Canton; adopted dau. Stella Galloway.
1–A.B., U.Ala., '84 (Phi Delta Theta); 1 yr. postgrad. study, Vanderbilt U. Sch. of Religion and U. of Tenn. Educator, 1885-90, 1893-95; ordained minister M.E. Ch., S., 1896; pastor, 1896-1902, 1919-23; pres. various colleges, since 1902; pres. Whitworth Female Coll. since 1925. Author (see Who's Who in America). Democrat. Residence: Natchez, Miss.

1–**HAWLEY, Alan Ramsay,** *b* Perth Amboy, N.J., July 29, 1869.
8–Joseph **Hawley** (qv);
7–Samuel (1647-1734), rep. Colonial Assembly, 1690; *m* 2d, Patience (Nichols) Hubbell (*b* 1660; Sgt. Isaac Nichols[8]; Francis[9], qv);
6–Ephraim (1692-1771), of Stratford, Conn.; an original settler of Newtown, 1712; selectman, 1728; large landowner at Bridgewater; *m* 1711, Sarah Curtis (William[7]; William[8]);
5–Nathan (1717-66), of Bridgewater; *m* 1733, Kesiah Bunnell;
4–Jabez (1749-1808), of New Milford, Conn.; *m* Phebe Peet (1752-1807);
3–Rev. William (1784-1845), rector St. John's Ch., Washington, D.C., 3 yrs.; *m* Wilhelmina Douglas Pods (1783-1865);
2–Peter Radcliffe (2 below).
8–William **Bunnell,** an original propr. of New Haven, 1635; returned to Eng., 1654; *m* Ann Wilmot (Benjamin[9], *m* Ann–, of New Haven);
7–Benjamin (*d* 1696), *m* 1st, Rebecca Mallory (*b* 1649; Peter[8], came to New Haven, 1644, *m* 1648, Mary, dau. of William Preston, from Eng., signer of the New Haven Compact, 1635);
6–Sgt. Benjamin (1679-1749), was in Train Band, New Haven and Milford; one of the earliest settlers of New Milford, buying a "right" there, 1714; *m* 2d, 1717, Patience (Wheeler) Miles (*b* 1679; Joseph Wheeler[7], *m* 1678, Patience [*b* 1658], dau. of Richard Holbrook [*d* 1670], freeman Dorchester, Mass., 1648, of Milford, Conn., 1658, and of Huntington, L.I., where he took deed from Indians, 1653);
5–Kesiah (*b* 1718), *m* Nathan **Hawley** (5 above);
4–Jabez, *m* Phebe Peet (4 above);
3–Rev. William, *m* Wilhelmina D. Pods (3 above);
2–Peter Radcliffe (1829-86), of New York; *m* Isabella Merritt (1838-1904); issue: I–Jennie Merritt (*d* 1918; *m* Charles Leveé); II–Wilhelmina (*m* Bastin de Konign); III–William (*d* 1923); IV–Alan R. (1 above); V–Peter Radcliffe, Jr. (*d* 1873).
1–Ed. Trinity Sch. Retired stock broker. Mem. S.C.W. Clubs: N.Y. Athletic (life), Automobile of Am. (founder mem., chmn. house com.), Aero of Am. (founder mem., pres. 1913-19). Mason (32°). Trustee N.Y. P.E. Pub. Sch. (see Who's Who in America). Residence: 161 W. 75th St., New York, N.Y.

1–**HAWLEY, Selden,** *b* Brooklyn, N.Y., Mar. 7, 1883.
10–George **Mills** (1585-1674);
9–Samuel (1631-1726);
8–Timothy (1667-1751), *m* Sarah Longbotham;
7–Jonathan (1710-98), *m* Ruth Rudyard (1716-48);
6–Zophar (1740-1819), *m* 1767, Deliverance Miller (*b* 1747);
5–Nathaniel (1769-1832), *m* Huldah Reeve;
4–Sophia (1798-1842), *m* 1819, Truman **Hawley** (1796-1875), see Vol. III, p. 231, for Hawley lineage;
3–Oscar F. (1820-79), *m* 1st, 1845, Susannah Inslee (*d* 1857), see Vol. III, p. 231, for Inslee lineage;
2–Oscar F. (2 below).
9–Robert **Lockwood** (qv);
8–Gershom (1643-1718), *m* Lady Ann Millington;
7–Gershom, *m* Mary–;
6–James, *m* Sally Ferris;
5–Jacob, *m* 1765, Catherine Knapp (1744-71);
4–Charles (1766-1834), Am. Rev.; *m* 1789, Elizabeth Waterbury (1764-1854);
3–Jared (1810-93), *m* 1832, Rebecca Holmes (1811-1896).
2–Oscar F. **Hawley** (1846-98), lumber mcht.; *m* 1871, Sarah Miller (1847-78); *m* 2d, 1880, Julia Olive Lockwood (1853-1927), for issue see Vol. III, p. 231.
1–*m* Mar. 5, 1912, Marguerite Jeanne Mayordomo, *b* London, Eng., Dec. 17, 1882; dau. of Gabriel Mayordomo, of Madrid, Spain, *m* Marie Defer, of Chatenoix, France.
1–Mem. O.F.P.A., S.C.W., S.R., I.A.G. Served in 7th Regt., N.G.N.Y., 1908-11. Residence: Larchmont, N.Y.

1–**HAY, Anne Laurence Raynsford (Mrs. Charles Hammond),** *b* Providence, R.I., Mar. 13, 1878.
9–Edward **Raynsford** (1609-80), from Eng., 1630; settled at Boston; *m* 2d, 1633, Elizabeth Dillee or Dilloe (1607-88);
8–David (1644-91), of Boston; soldier in King Philip's War under Lt. Gillam and Maj. Savage, 1675-76; *m* 2d, 1682, Hannah–;
7–Edward (*b* 1683), of Boston, Mass., and Canterbury, Conn.; *m* 1705, Abigail Baulch (1683-1763);
6–Solomon (1715-63), of Canterbury; *m* 1734, Waitstill Adams (1717-91);
5–Thomas (1739-91), of Sheffield, Mass.; pvt. Am. Rev.; *m* 1783, Rhoda– (1732-1814);
4–Edmund (1784-1855), of Sheffield, Mass.; a founder of Scotland, N.Y.; *m* 1815, Barbara Ann Van Schaick (1795-1852);
3–Norton Thomas (1817-56), of Albany, N.Y.; *m* 1837, Lydia Ann Slingerland (1817-54);
2–Van Rensselaer Slingerland (1843-1925), of Albany; sgt. Co. C, N.Y. Vol. Inf., Civil War, stationed at Suffolk, Ft. Monroe, and Folly Island, S.C.; I.O.O.F. (mem. Friendly Union Lodge, #381, 50 yrs.; Past Grand); *m* 1872, Mary Egelsome MacCormack (1848-88).
1–*m* July 14, 1897, Charles Hammond Hay, *b* Slingerlands, N.Y., June 8, 1876; son of Charles David Hay, of Slingerlands: issue: 1–Mary Eleanore, *b* Slingerlands, Apr. 27, 1903; *m* Dec. 5, 1920, Patrick Joseph, son of James MacDonald, of Ireland (issue: John Crolly, *b* 1921; Mary Eleanore, *b* 1924; Edmund Raynsford, *b* 1925; Marsha Anne, *b* 1927; David Patrick, *b* 1929); 2–Herbert Marsham, *b* Slingerlands, Feb. 25, 1905; *m* Oct. 26, 1929, Agnes Marthe, dau. of James F. Connell, of Albany, N.Y.
1–Ed. Mme. Boutelle's Pvt. Sch. Mem. D.A.R. (Mohawk Chapter), Albany Colony N.E. Women, Dutch Settlers Soc. of Albany, N.Y. State Feder. of Women's Clubs. Mem. Dutch Reformed Ch. Residence: Slingerlands, N.Y.

1–**HAY, H(enry) Clinton,** *b* Portland, Me., Feb. 19, 1853.
8–James **Boutwell** (qv);
7–Sgt. James (1642-1716), Reading and Lynn, Mass., *m* 1665, Rebecca Kendall (1645-1713; Dea. Thomas[8], *m* Rebecca–);
6–Dea. Thomas (*b* 1669), *m* Abigail–;
5–Abigail (1696-1779), *m* Dr. William **Hay** (ca. 1684-1783), of Scottish family of Earl of Erroll; *b* in Scotland but came to America ante 1717; compelled to leave Scotland because of civil warfare over religious questions, he escaped by being smuggled on board ship in a whiskey keg; was subsequently disinherited by his family for marrying an American "commoner"; schoolmaster and later physician by profession; selectman, Reading, Mass., 1744;
4–John (1737-1815), physician, Reading and Woburn, Mass.; *m* 1762, Sarah Ring (*b* 1740; Capt. David[5], *m* 2d, Mrs. Anna Gale; Jarvis[6], was a witness in a witchcraft trial, Salisbury, 1692, *m* Hannah Fowler; Robert[7]);

3–Dr. Charles (1769-1831), *m* 1797, Chloe Smith (*b* 1774);
2–Henry Homer (1820-95), mcht., wholesale and retail drugs, and paints and oil, Portland, Me.; *m* Eleanor Seavey (*b* 1830); issue: I–Josephine Louisa (1849-1922; *m* Horatio Cook, *d*); II–Henry Clinton (1 above); III–Mary Adelaide (1856-1923; *m* Dr. William H. Flint *d*); IV–Charles Marcian (*b* 1859; *m* Elizabeth Campbell); V–William Benjamin (*b* 1861; *m* Lola Sherman); VI–Eleanor S. (*b* 1863); VII–Edward A. (*b* 1866; *m* Elizabeth Merrill).
1–*m* June 11, 1885, Sarah Alice Swazey, *b* Springfield, Mass., Mar. 23, 1852; dau. of Dr. George W. Swazey, of Springfield; issue: 1–George Swazey (May 19, 1886-*d* April 29, 1894); 2–Donald Worcester (July 6, 1888-April 29, 1894); 3–Clinton Allen (Dec. 13, 1891-May 2, 1894).
1–A.B., Harvard, '78; diploma, New Ch. Theol. Sch., 1885. Pastor Boston Soc., since 1902; asso. editor New Church Review, 1897, mng. editor, 1909-17, advisory editor, since 1917. Author (see who's Who in America). Residence: 156 School St., Belmont, Mass.

EDGAR EUGENE STRONG (1841-1923), merchant, Cleveland, O.; 1st lt., Conn. vol. inf. in Civil War; prisoner at Andersonville, 1864-65.

1–**HAYDEN, Elizabeth Strong (Mrs. Warren S.),** *b* Cleveland, O., June 20, 1880.
9–John **Strong** (qv);
8–John (1626-98), of Windsor, Conn.; *m* 2d, 1664, Elizabeth Warriner (*d* 1684);
7–John (1665-1749), of Windsor; *m* 1686, Hannah Trumbull (Dea. John[8]);
6–Dea. David (1704-1801), of Bolton, Conn.; *m* 1st, 1732, Thankful Loomis;
5–Ebenezer (1754-1824), of Bolton; *m* 1779, Lucy (Kilbourne) Lawrence (*d* 1793);
4–Eli (1789-1867), of Bolton; *m* 1812, Betsy Cowles (1794-1825);
3–William Cowles (1816-1890), of Talcottville, Conn.; *m* 1839, Lucy Maria Nichols (1820-91);
2–Edgar Eugene (2 below).
9–Joseph **Loomis** (qv);
8–Nathaniel (ca. 1626-1688), freeman, 1654; mem. Windsor Troop of Horse in King Philip's War; *m* 1653, Elizabeth Moore (1638-1728; Dea. John[9], *m* Abigail–);
7–Moses (1671-1754), removed to E. Windsor, Conn., 1700; *m* 1694, Joanna Gibbs (Samuel[8], *m* Hepsibah Dibble);
6–Thankful (1709-71), *m* Dea. David **Strong** (6 above).
8–George **Clarke** (1610-90), from Eng., 1637, settled at Boston, later at New Haven and Milford, Conn.; rep. from Milford to Gen. Ct. of New Haven and Conn.; *m* Sarah–;
7–Ens. George (1648-1734), of Milford, Conn.; rep. Gen. Ct. of Conn.; *m* 1st, ca. 1678, Abigail–;
6–Lt. George (1686-1762), of Milford; *m* 1722, Mary Coley (*b* 1685);
5–Hezekiah (1723-76), of Bethany, Conn.; served in Am. Rev.; *m* 1746, Mary Peck (*b* 1726);
4–Peck (1771-1854), of Northfield, Conn., and Conneaut, O.; served in War 1812; *m* 2d, 1805, Polly Kellogg (1782-1863);
3–Aaron (1811-81), of Northfield, Conn., and Conneaut and Cleveland, O.; *m* 2d, 1845, Caroline Elizabeth Bingham (1818-91);
2–Mary Ella (1846-1914), *m* 1869, Edgar Eugene **Strong** (1841-1923), see portrait; issue: I–Clinton Eugene (1869-94); II–Herbert William (*b* 1871; *m* Gladys Mosher); III–Edith (1876-79); IV–Elizabeth (1 above).
1–*m* Apr. 18, 1906, Warren Sherman Hayden (qv for issue).
1–B.L., Smith Coll., '03. Presbyterian. Republican. Club: Woman's City. Residence: 3035 Monmouth Rd., Cleveland Heights, O.

1–**HAYDEN, Warren Sherman,** *b* Danbury, Conn., Oct. 20, 1870.
8–John **Hayden** (qv);
7–Nehemiah (1647/48-1717/18), of Braintree, Mass.; *m* 1678/79, Hannah Neale (1658-1741);
6–Samuel, of Braintree; *m* Priscilla Webb (*b* 1697);
5–Christopher (1718/19-ca. 1805), of Braintree, Mass., and Morris Co., N.J.; *m* ante 1753, Elizabeth Sutton (ca. 1735-1817);
4–Samuel (1774-1840), of Morris Co., N.J., Rostraver Tp., Pa., and Smith Tp., O.; *m* 1798, Sophia Gray (1771-1841);
3–Daniel (1806-81), of Deerfield Tp., Portage Co., O.; *m* 1831, Abigail Heaton (1812-90);
2–Warren Luce (2 below).
8–Samuel **Sherman** (qv);
7–Benjamin (1662-1741), of Stratford, Conn.; *m* 1683, Rebecca Phippeny (1664-1739);
6–Enos (1699-1793), of Stratford and Bridgeport, Conn.; *m* 1725, Abigail Walker (*d* 1793);
5–Josiah (1729-1815), of Easton, Conn., and Sandgate, Vt.; *m* ante 1758, Miriam Gregory (1732-1825);
4–Isaac (1769-1842), of Sandgate; *m* 1796, Sarah Winton (1767-1857);
3–Grandison (1804-85), of Sandgate and W. Rupert, Vt.; *m* 1830, Emily Flower (1805-84);
2–Anna Flower (1835-92), *m* 1862, Warren Luce **Hayden** (1835-1918), minister, Disciples of Christ; issue: I–Flora (1866-1908); II–Stella (1868-69); III–Warren Sherman (1 above); IV–Emily (1873-79); V–infant son (*b* and *d* 1876).
1–*m* June 27, 1893, Blanche Rebecca Squire (Mar. 12, 1872-July 8, 1903); dau. of Frank Squire, of Hiram, O., *m* Delilah White; issue: 1–Margaret, *b* Hiram, O., Sept. 13, 1894; A.B., Wells, '16; *m* Sept. 8, 1922, Chester Arthur Thompson (issue: Warren Hayden; Joan); 2–Elizabeth, (Feb. 15-Mar. 29, 1903).
1–*m* 2d, Apr. 18, 1906, Elizabeth Strong (qv); issue: 1–Sherman Strong, *b* Cleveland, O., Feb. 9, 1908; A.B., Harvard, '30; 2–Eleanor Warren, *b* Cleveland, Dec. 27, 1912.
1–Ph.B., Hiram, '92. Rep., Lamprecht Bros. & Co., 1892-95; mgr. bond dept., 1895-1903; admitted to the bar, 1898, but never practiced; partner Hayden, Miller & Co., since 1903, investment bankers. Mem. Cleveland Met. Park Bd.; chmn. exec. com. Cleveland Community Fund; pres. Cleveland Chamber of Commerce, 1913-14, pres. Investment Bankers Assn. of America, 1917-18; trustee Western Reserve U., Hiram Coll., Lakeside Hosp., Cleveland Museum of Natural History, etc.; dir. Union Trust Co. of Cleveland, N.Y. Central R.R. Co., Mich. Central R.R. Co., C.C.&St.L.Ry. Co., White Motor Co., etc. Mem. S.A.R., I.A.G. (life). Republican. Clubs: Metropolitan, Bankers (New York), Union, University, Mayfield, Kirtland. Address: 1250 Union Trust Bldg., Cleveland, O.

1–**HAYES, Alfred,** *b* Lewisburg, Pa., Oct. 15, 1873.
6–John **Hayes** (ca. 1704-ca. 1789), from Londonderry, Ireland, with his wife and 4 children, to Chester Co., Pa., bet. 1730-40; kept a public house where Benjamin Franklin once spent a night; elder Presbyn. Ch.; had 4 sons in Am. Rev.; buried nr. Allentown, Pa.; *m* Jane Love (*d* ca. 1806, aet. 94);
5–Capt. Robert (1742-1819), capt. co. of associators in Am. Rev.; mem. Washington's Flying Camp, reporting for duty at 48 hrs. notice; moved to Northumberland Co., 1790,

lived nr. Warrior Run Ch. 9 yrs., then 7 yrs. at Derry; moved to Delaware Tp., nr. Dewarts, 1806; *m* Mary Allison (*d* aet. 80);
4–William (1776-1843), 2d postmaster, Lewisburg, Pa., apptd. during presidency of James Madison; leading mcht.; *m* 1803, Mary Wilson (1783-1827; William[5] [1743-1824], of Kelly Tp., *m* 1773, Elizabeth Robinson [1758-1815]; James[6] [1719-93], from Ireland aet. 7, settled Derry Tp., Dauphin Co., Pa., surveyor, *m* 1742, Martha Sterritt);
3–Thomas (1809-86), original incorporator, and trustee 1st Presbyn. Ch., active founder of U.Lewisburg (now Bucknell U.); mem. Pa. Assembly, 1858,60,61; moved to Phila., 1861; *m* 1834, Mary Hulme;
2–Alfred (2 below).
8–George **Hulme** (*d* 1714), from Cheshire, Eng., ca. 1700, purchased 300 acres, 1705, Middleton Tp., Bucks Co.; mem. Falls Meeting;
7–George (*b* Eng.-*d* 1729), *m* 1708, Naomi Palmer (*d* 1709); *m* 2d, 1710, Ruth Palmer (sister of 1st wife);
6–John, *m* 1st, Mary Pearson (Enoch[7], *m* Margaret Smith);
5–John (*d* 1818), mem. Pa. Assembly; acquired property in Milford, where he lived after 1796, name changed to Hulmeville, Pa.; justice of peace, 1789-96; *m* Rebecca Milnor (William[6], of Falls Tp., nr. Fallsington, Pa.);
4–Joseph, *m* (authorized by Middletown Monthly Meetings, Oct. 18, 1806), Beulah Canby (*b* 1784; Thomas[5], of Yardleyville, *m* Beulah, dau. of Samuel Carey, from Bristol, Eng., ca. 1731; settled in Newtown, Pa.);
3–Mary (1812-94), from Hulmeville, Pa., to Winona, Minn.; *m* Thomas **Hayes** (3 above).
5–Robert **Van Valzah** (*b* 1733), *m* Mary– (*b* 1739);
4–Dr. Robert (1764-1850), served in Am. Rev. aet. 16; located at Buffalo Cross Roads, ca. 1796; *m* Elizabeth Sutherland (1768-1840; Lt. Col. Thomas[5] [1732-1816], Am. Rev., *m* Jane–, *d* 1819, aet. 82);
3–William Ward (1809-57), farmer; *m* Sarah Louisa Forster;
2–Mary Miles (2 below).
7–Richard **Miles,** from Llandowery, Radnor, Wales, with William Penn, to Pa., 1682; settled on land purchased in Wales from Richard Davies; joined Great Valley Bapt. Ch., Apr. 22, 1711; *m* Sarah–;
6–James;
5–Richard, from Radnor Tp., Delaware Co., Pa., to Milesburg, Center Co., Pa., post 1790; *m* Mary Pugh, Quakeress, of Chester Co.;
4–Mary, *m* John (Forester) **Forster,** of Aaronsburg, Pa. (Capt. John[5], Am. Rev., *m* Jane Johnston);
3–Sarah Louisa (1817-62), *m* William W. **Van Valzah** (3 above);
2–Mary Miles (Aug. 11, 1840-June 19, 1919), Presbyn.; *m* Sept. 11, 1862, Alfred **Hayes** (1837-1912), A.B., Bucknell, '55, lawyer, Lewisburg, Pa., dist. atty., mem. Pa. Assembly 3 terms; issue: I–Charles Harold (1864-1914; U.S.N.A., '84; *m* 1892, Maud Smith, 1866-1916); II–William Van Valzah (*b* 1867; *m* 1903, Mary Coulbourn Conner, *b* 1876); III–Thomas (*b* and *d* 1872); IV–Alfred (1 above); V–Emma Beulah (*b* 1876; *m* 1908, Dr. James Douglas Nisbet, *b* 1861); VI–Matthew Cowden (*b* 1885; *m* Emma Alder Nesbit; *m* 2d, Winetta Mary Cerngross).
1–*m* June 15, 1905, Christine Grace Robertson (qv); issue: 1–Christine MacEwan, *b* New York, N.Y., June 30, 1906; 2–Alfred, Jr., *b* Ithaca, N.Y., July 4, 1910; 3–Miles Van Valzah, *b* Ithaca, Nov. 20, 1911.
1–Bucknell (Phi Kappa Psi); A.B., Princeton, '95 (P.B.K.), A.M., 1898; LL.B., Columbia, 1898; Cornell (Phi Delta Phi). Lawyer, admitted to practice before U.S. Supreme Court, 1903 (see Who's Who in America). Mem. S.R. Clubs: University (New York), Indian Harbor Yacht (Greenwich). Residence: Old Church Rd., Greenwich, Conn.

1–**HAYES, Christine Grace Robertson (Mrs. Alfred),** *b* Tiverton, nr. Rincaidine, Bruce Co., Ont., July 6, 1877.
5–John **Robertson,** from Inverness, Scotland, ca. 1793, to Pictou Co., N.S.; farmer; *m* Margaret McKay;
4–James (*b* Inverness, Scotland), *m* Nellie McDonald;
3–James, *m* Grace McMillan (William[4], *m* Ella McKenzie; Finlay[5], from Inverness, with John Robertson, 5 above);
2–Joseph (2 below).
4–Hugh **MacEwan,** lived at Ardlui, nr. Loch Tay, emigrated with Camerons from Perth, ca. 1828; farmer; *m* Kate Campbell, from Breadalbane, Perthshire; they followed their son John who came first as missionary from Perth;
3–Hugh, farmer, settled in Glengarry; *m* Christine Cameron, from Fortingale, Scotland (John[4], *m* Janet McGregor); 2 sons were distinguished Bapt. clergymen;
2–Susan (Aug. 14, 1841-June 12, 1913), *m* 1858, Joseph **Robertson** (Mar. 1, 1833-May 8, 1913), of Brucefield, London, Ont., Detroit, and Chicago; farmer, mcht.; dea. Bapt. ch., 1880-88; issue: I–James Finlay (*b* and *d* 1861); II–Hugh James (1862-66); III–William John (*b* 1864; *m* Jessie Sage); IV–Milton Henry (1867-1913; *m* Kate Russell); V–Peter Daniel (*b* 1870; *m* Kate Douglas, *d* 1900; *m* 2d, Margaret Cousin); VI–James Joseph (*b* 1873; *m* Dolly Hummel); VII–Edwin A. (1875-1911; *m* Frances Cummings); VIII–Christine G. (1 above); IX–Hugh Oswald (*b* 1880; *m* 1919, Maude Ella Allred).
1–*m* June 15, 1905, Alfred Hayes (qv for issue).
1–A.B., U.Mich., '00 (Pi Beta Phi). Prin., Lake Forest, Ill.; teacher Latin, Hinsdale, Ill., H.S., 1900-05; with Gad's Hill Social Settlement, Chicago, 1903-04. Sec. Tompkins Co., N.Y., Suffrage Orgn., 1915-16; mem. People's Council for Peace and Freedom, Woman's Peace Party, Woman's Internat. League for Peace and Freedom; organizer summer center, Greenwich Social Settlement, 1918-19. Residence: Old Church Rd., Greenwich, Conn.

1–**HAYES, Carlton Joseph Huntley,** *b* Afton, N.Y., May 16, 1882.
8–Nathaniel **Hayes** (1629?-1707), from Eng.; settled at Norwalk, Conn., 1651; an original purchaser of this site from the Indians; *m* 1664, Mary Kimberly (*b* 1643; Sgt. Thomas[9], *m* Alice–);
7–James (1672-1747), of Norwalk; *m* 1703, Mary Allen (Thomas[8], of Burlington, N.J.);
6–Nathaniel (1708-48), *m* 1738, Sarah Morehouse (*b* 1715?; Nathan[7], *m* Mary Lockwood);
5–Nathaniel (1744-1807), removed to Greene, N.Y.; served in Am. Rev.; *m* 1763, Elizabeth Holmes (1743-1818; Isaac[6], *m* Elizabeth Beecher);
4–Rev. Caleb (1771-1856), removed to Castle Creek, N.Y.; Bapt. clergyman; *m* 1793, Anna Cook (1776-1839);
3–Caleb Fairchild (1813-62), of Castle Creek, N.Y.; *m* Harriet West (1819-1905; William[4], *m* Mary Smith);
2–Philetus Arthur (2 below).
10–John **Huntley** (1623-76), from Eng. to the Barbados, 1648; resident of Boston, 1652; removed to Roxbury, 1659; an early settler of Lyme, Conn., 1661;
9–Aaron (1655-1745), of Lyme; *m* Mary Champion (1651-1732; Henry[10]);
8–John (1677-1750), of Lyme; *m* Elizabeth–;
7–Joseph (1707-58), of Lyme; *m* 1729, Ruth Williams (1712-39; Thomas[8], *m* Sarah Rogers);
6–John (1730-68), removed to Charlotte Precinct, N.Y.; *m* 1752, Lois Beckwith (*b* 1725; Matthew[7], *m* Elizabeth Raynor);
5–Williams (1755-1842), removed to Marathon, N.Y.; served in Am. Rev.; *m* 1778, Hannah– (1761-1827);
4–Joseph (1782-1847), removed to Coxsackie, N.Y.; minister; *m* 1809, Susan Eggleston (*b* 1782; Samuel[5], *m* Hester Buck);
3–Joseph (1820-71), of Marathon, N.Y.; musician, teacher of music; wrote several popular songs; *m* 1848, Catherine Adelia Simons (1825-1902; Timothy Cooper[4], of Cooperstown, *m* Permelia Smith);
2–Permelia Mary (1849-1922), Mus. B., Brown U., 1895; *m* 1869, Dr. Philetus Arthur **Hayes** (1848-1929), A.B., Hobart Coll., '68; M.D., Syracuse U., 1870; physician and surgeon, Afton, N.Y.; issue: I–Caleb Nathaniel, and II–Catherine, twins (*b* and *d* 1881); III–Carlton Joseph Huntley (1 above).
1–*m* Sept. 18, 1920, Mary Evelyn Carroll, *b* Oswego, N.Y., July 18, 1888; dau. James Carroll, of Oswego; issue: 1–Mary Elizabeth, *b* New

York, N.Y., Oct. 15, 1923; 2–Carroll Joseph, *b* New York, Oct. 16, 1925.
1–A.B., Columbia U., '04 (Alpha Chi Rho, P.B.K.), A.M., 1905, Ph.D., 1909; (LL.D., Notre Dame, 1921; L.H.D., Marquette, 1929). Asso. with Columbia U. since 1907, prof. history since 1919, and head dept. since 1922. Editor. Author (see Who's Who in America). Served as capt., U.S.A. Mil. Intelligence Div., Gen. Staff, during World War, 1918-19; maj., R.O.C. since 1928. Catholic. Democrat. Clubs: Columbia U., Men's Faculty, Canasawacta Country (Norwich, N.Y.). Summer place: Afton, N.Y. Residence: 427 W. 117th St., New York City, N.Y.

1–**HAYNES, Pierre Evan,** *b* Kirklin, Ind., July 28, 1885.
9–Thomas (Wheadon) **Whedon** (ca. 1635-1691), from Eng., 1653; an early settler of New Haven, Conn.; freeman, 1653; original propr. of Branford, Conn., 1667; *m* 1661, Ann Harvey;
8–Thomas (1663-1707), of Branford; *m* 2d, 1684, Elizabeth Ludington;
7–Thomas (*b* 1691), *m* Eunice Servaine; *m* 2d, Elizabeth–;
6–Thomas, *m* 1747, Mary Heath;
5–Mary (bap. 1756-1824), *m* 1777, Elisha (Aldridge) **Eldridge** (1756-1841), served in Am. Rev.;
4–Clark (1785 or 86-1856 or 58), *m* 1808 or 09, Chloe Jennison;
3–Maria Belle (1824 or 25-1900), *m* 1843, Eldridge Clark **Haynes** (1816-82; Henry[4] [1780 or 83-1862], removed from Saratoga Co., N.Y., to Holman, Ind., *m* 1808, Abigail, dau. Elisha Eldridge, 5 above);
2–George Eldridge (2 below).
9–Robert **Jennison** (*d* 1690), from Eng. with Gov. Winthrop to Charlestown, Mass., 1630; removed to Watertown, 1636; *m* Elizabeth–; *m* 2d, Grace– (*d* 1686);
8–Samuel (*b* 1645), *m* Judith Macomber (*d* 1722/-23);
7–Robert (*b* 1684), of Cambridge, Framingham and Sutton, Mass.; *m* Dorothy Rebecca (Maverick) Whittemore (Elias Maverick[8]; Rev. John[9]; Rev. Peter[10], of Eng.);
6–Joseph (1720-1818), of Cambridge; *m* 1745, Martha Twiss;
5–Peter (*b* 1750), served in Am. Rev.; *m* 1769, Mehitable Singletary;
4–Chloe (1792-1868), *m* Clark **Eldridge** (4 above).
9–Richard **Singletary** (*d* 1687), of Salem, 1637; freeman, Newbury, 1638; at Haverhill, 1652; *m* Susanne Cook (*d* 1682);
8–Nathaniel (*b* 1644), of Haverhill; *m* 1673, Sarah Belknap;
7–John (*b* 1675), removed to Sutton, Mass.; *m* Mary Greele;
6–Amos (1721-1806), removed to Topsfield, Mass.; mem. 1st Cont. Congress; *m* Mary Curtis;
5–Mehitable, *m* Peter **Jennison** (5 above).
5–Archibald (Gibson) **Gipson** (1763-1855), of Onslow or Wilkes Co., N.C.; removed to Ky., thence to Jamestown, Ind.; *m* ca. 1780, Veshta–(1763-1855);
4–Ezekiel (*d* ca. 1840), removed to Kirklin, Ind.; *m* ca. 1825, Rachel–;
3–Samuel Preston (1831-81), began to write name Gipson; *m* 1858, Mary C. Nicholson (*b* 1841; Capt. William[4], *m* Elisa Ann, dau. of John Ferguson, from Scotland, *m* Elizabeth–);
2–Eva Lorena (*b* 1865), *married*, George Eldridge **Haynes** (1851-1910), of Rochester, O., later at Kirklin, Ind.; *d* at Elwood, Ind.; sch. teacher, lawyer; issue: I–Pierre Evan (1 above); II–Paul Preston (1887-1923; *m* Hazel Garris); III–Parke Gipson (*b* 1891); IV–Hermon Paige (*b* 1892; *m* Ruth Evans); V–Mary Belle (*b* 1896; *m* Frank V. Osborne).
1–*m* June 9, 1917, Nellie Deborah Kidwell (qv).
1–Ed. Armour Inst. of Tech., 1903-04; Northwestern U., 1904-05, 1911-12. Consulting engr., specialist in low temperatures and rare gases, inventor of processes pertaining to same; pres. Dry Ice Co., Ltd., Can., 1927; pres. Haynes Process, Ltd., Can.; chemist, People's Gas, Light & Coke Co., Chicago, 1907-10; illuminating engr. for City of Chicago, 1910-14; chief chemist, Linde Air Products Co., 1914-21. Presbyn. Clubs: Chemists (New York), Buffalo Consistory. Residence: 351 Oakwood Av., East Aurora, N.Y.

1–**HAYNES, Nellie Deborah Kidwell (Mrs. Pierre Evan),** *b* Dallas Co., Ia., Dec. 1, 1883.
6–Matthew **Kidwell** (1761-post 1833), of Md.; removed to Monroe Co., Ky.; served in Am. Rev.; *m* 1781, Priscilla Moore;
5–Jonathan (*d* ca. 1845), removed to Philomath, Ind.; Universalist preacher; poet, author, publisher; *m* Rebecca– (1782-1857);
4–Starling Turner (*b* 1827), of Elwood, Ind.; *m* Mary Benefield (1804-87; Robert[5]);
3–Harvey Jackson (*d* 1860), *m* 1849, Mahala Quick (1830-60);
2–William Francis (1857-1913), asst. postmaster, Elwood, Ind.; *m* 1882, Mary Louisa Kidwell (*b* 1860; Leander Jerome[3], *m* Deborah Farlow; Hezekiah[4], *m* Jane Benefield, sister of Mary, 4 above; Jonathan, 5 above); issue: I–Nellie Deborah (1 above); II–Mahala Myrtle (*b* 1885); III–Edgar Irl (*b* 1888; *m* Matilda Elwood); IV–Ival Ernest (*b* 1891; *m* Faye Kyle); V–Helen Corinne (*b* 1901; *m* Frederick M. Hood).
1–*m* June 9, 1917, Pierre Evan Haynes (qv).
1–Ed. Elwood, Ind., H.S., De Pauw U. Club: Town (Buffalo). Residence: 351 Oakwood Av., East Aurora, N.Y.

1–**HAYNES, Rowland,** *b* Worcester, Mass., July 30, 1878.
10–Walter **Haynes** (qv);
9–John (1621-97), of Sudbury, Mass.; owner "Haynes Garrison House"; dea.; freeman, 1646; selectman, 1666; surveyor, 1672; *m* 1642, Dorothy Noyes (*d* 1715; Peter[10]);
8–James (1660/61-1732), one of the defenders of the garrison house, Sudbury, 1676; *m* 1689/90, Sarah Noyes (1669-1756; Joseph[9], *m* Mary Darvell or Darnell; James[10], qv);
7–James (1692-1755), *m* 2d, 1720, Mary Rugg (*d* 1777; John[8]);
6–James (*b* 1721), served in Am. Rev.; *m* 1st, 1741, Eleanor Lee (*d* 1759);
5–Joseph (1742-1822), removed from Sudbury to Princeton, Mass.; served in Am. Rev.; *m* 1763, Hannah Stratton, of Leicester, Mass.;
4–Samuel (1764-1844), removed to Guilford, N.Y.; *m* 1788, Louisa Brooks (*b* 1768; Charles[5], *m* Mary Hapgood);
3–Samuel (1789-1859), removed to Townsend, Mass.; *m* 2d, 1828, Eliza Spaulding (1804-63; Dr. Thaddeus[4]);
2–Charles Thaddeus (1835-1922), removed to Worcester, Mass.; *m* 1870, Sybel Wallace (1840-1917; Benjamin[3], *m* Susan Spaulding); issue: I–Herman Wallace (*b* 1873; *m* Gertrude Eames); II–Rowland (1 above).
1–*m* July 3, 1906, Wilhelmena Rigby Gill (qv for issue).
1–A.B., Williams Coll., '02 (P.B.K.); A.M., Clark U., 1905; grad. study, Union Theol. Sem. and Columbia U., 1902-04,05-06. Instr. philosophy, U.Chicago, 1906-07; instr. and asst. prof. psychology, U.Minn., 1907-11; field sec. Playground and Recreation Assn. of America, 1911-16; sec. on recreation, Bd. of Estimate and Apportionment, N.Y. City, 1916-17; dir. Recreation Council, Cleveland, O., 1920-22; dir. Welfare Fed., Cleveland, O., 1922-27; sec., U. of Chicago, 1927–. Author (see Who's Who in America). Trustee First Unitarian Ch., Univ. Settlement; mem. Chicago Hist. Soc. Republican. Clubs: Union League, University, Quadrangle, Rotary (trustee). Summer place: "Stonycroft," Mason's Island, Mystic, Conn. Residence: 5745 Blackstone Av., Chicago, Ill.

1–**HAYNES, Wilhelmena Rigby Gill (Mrs. Rowland),** *b* Poughkeepsie, N.Y., Feb. 9, 1867.
10–Allard **Anthony** (1610-85), from Holland to New Amsterdam; burgomaster, 1654; sheriff, 1664-73; *m* Hendrica Wessels;
9–Nicholas (1635-1712), sheriff Ulster Co.;
8–Allard (*b* 1660);
7–Nicholas (1685-1715);
6–Nicholas (1715-85), of New York; *m* 1733, Hester (Roome) Elsworth (1701-92; Peter Wilemse Roome[7] [*d* 1729], *m* 1684, Hester Van Gelder);
5–Theophilus (1735-1814), of New York; *m* 1759, Willimintjie Vredenburg;
4–Wilhelmena (1761-1800), *m* 1783, Robert **Gill** (1760-1836), from Eng., 1783; settled at Poughkeepsie, N.Y.;
3–Thomas (1785-1853), *m* Maria Conkrite (1780-1869);
2–John Rigby (1815-72), *m* 1861, Elizabeth Coit Ingersoll (1839-1912); issue: I–Sarah Coit (*b* and *d* 1863); II–Susie Maria (*b* 1864; *m* 1891,

Charles Van Winkle, *b* 1862); III–Wilhelmena R. (1 above); IV–Georgianna Boswell (*b* 1869); V–Elizabeth Ingersoll (*b* 1871).
1–*m* July 3, 1906, Rowland Haynes (qv); issue: 1–Thaddeus, *b* Kansas City, Mo., June 5, 1913; 2–John Anthony, and 3–Sybel (twins), *b* New York, N.Y., Nov. 2, 1915.
1–Mem. Nat. Soc. N.E. Women, Chicago Art Inst. Residence: 5745 Blackstone Av., Chicago, Ill.

1–**HAZARD, Mary Pierrepont Bushnell (Mrs. Rowland G.),** *b* Waterbury, Conn., Apr. 10, 1859.
9–James (Pierrepont) **Pierpont** (qv);
8–John (1617-82), Ipswich, 1640, Roxbury, 1656; *m* Thankful Stow (*d* 1668; John[9]);
7–Rev. James (1659/60-1714), A.B., Harvard, 1681; pastor First Congl. Ch., New Haven; a founder of Yale Coll.; *m* 3d, 1698, Mary Hooker (1673-1740; Samuel[8]; Rev. Thomas[9], qv);
6–Hezekiah (1712-41), *m* 1736/37, Lydia Hemingway (*d* 1779);
5–John (1740-1805), *m* 1767, Sarah Beers (1744-1835);
4–Mary (1778-1852), *m* 1st, 1796, Edward J. **O'Brien** (*d* 1799), of New Haven;
3–Maria Eliza (1799-1876), *m* 1822, Eli Whitney **Blake** (1795-1886);
2–Mary Elizabeth (1823-1916), *m* 1851, George **Bushnell,** D.D. (1818-98), B.A., Yale, '42; Congl. minister, Beloit, Wis. (for issue and other lines see George Ensign Bushnell, Vol. I, p. 37).
1–*m* Nov. 16, 1880, Rowland Gibson Hazard (1855-1918); brother of Caroline Hazard (see Vol. I, p. 36, for genealogy); issue (all *b* Peace Dale, R.I.): 1–Rowland (see Vol. I, p. 36, for Hazard line); 2–Elizabeth, *b* Apr. 27, 1884; *m* Jan. 1, 1908, Rush Sturges (issue: Benjamin Rush; Elizabeth Peace; John Pierrepont; Rowland; Alice Knight); 3–Margaret, *b* Jan. 25, 1885; *m* July 15, 1908, Robert H. I. Goddard (see Vol. I, p. 37); 4–Mary Bushnell, *b* Apr. 11, 1890; *m* Jan. 1, 1916, Wallace Campbell (issue: Wallace, Jr., *b* Aug. 3, 1917; Mary, Nov. 18, 1919-Oct. 16, 1922; Margaret Anne, *b* Mar. 3, 1923; Jane, *b* Oct. 7, 1924; Hugh David, *b* Feb. 20, 1930); 5–Thomas Pierrepont, *b* Oct. 26, 1892; B.A., Yale, '15; enlisted in 1st Cav., N.Y.N.G., Nov. 15, 1915; 2d lt. and 1st lt. regular army, Oct. 25, 1917; was personnel adjt. 14th Cav.; served at Del Rio, Tex., Aug. 28, 1917-April 1, 1918, Ft. Sam Houston, Tex., Apr. 2, 1918-Feb. 15, 1919, when discharged; *m* May 20, 1922, Anne Francis Cope (issue: Sophia Francis, *b* Mar. 10, 1923; Thomas P., Jr., *b* May 31, 1925; Mary Pierrepont, *b* Apr. 12, 1927; Anne Francis, *b* Dec. 5, 1929).
1–Mem. I.A.G. Winter place: "Dial House," Santa Barbara, Calif. Residence: "Holly House," Peace Dale, R.I.

1–**HEALD, Kenneth Conrad,** *b* Bennington, N.H., Mar. 14, 1888.
9–John **Heald** (*d* 1662), from Eng., settled at Concord, Mass., 1635; freeman, 1641; *m* Dorothy–;
8–John (*d* 1689), of Concord; *m* 1661, Sarah Dean (*d* 1689);
7–John (1666-1721), *m* 1690, Mary Chandler (1672-1759);
6–Samuel (*d* 1784), *m* Rebecca Fletcher (1717-1807);
5–Josiah (1744-1822), of Billerica, Mass.; *m* Tryphena Corey (1763-1813);
4–Josiah (1777-1843), of Lovell, Me.; *m* Lucy Corey (1778-1865);
3–Abel (1806-90), of Lovell; dea. Congl. Ch.; *m* 1834, Mary Andrews Stearns (1812-62; g.dau. of Abraham Andrews, soldier Am. Rev.);
2–Josiah Heald (2 below).
9–Maximilian **Jewett** (qv);
8–Joseph (1654-1735), of Rowley, Mass.; ens. in King Philip's War; *m* 1677, Rebecca Law (*d* 1729);
7–Aquila (1684-1760), of Rowley; *m* Martha Pearson;
6–Stephen (1727-1803), of Hollis, N.H.; dea.; *m* Hannah Cummings;
5–Noah (1758-1839), of Cornish, Me.; dea.; sgt. in Am. Rev.; *m* Lydia Boynton;
4–Mary (1799-1864), *m* 1826, Samuel Thurston **Pike** (1799-1875), dea. Congl. Ch., Hiram, Me.;
3–Ezra Barker (1833-1928), of Brentwood, N.H.; M.D., Bowdoin; ordained Congl. ministry, 1865, *m* 1856, Elizabeth Adams Mitchell (1836-1914; Isaac Lee[4], *m* Catherine Adams);
2–Mary Katharine (*b* 1859), *m* 1884, Josiah Heald **Heald** (*b* 1859); issue: I–Maj. Clarence Edward (*d* 1921; sec. and custodian Internat. Soc. of Genealogy and Eugenics; *m* Edith Hair); II–Elizabeth (*b* 1886; *m* Cleve Alpheus Purington, *d* 1928); III–Kenneth Conrad (1 above); IV–Josiah Eugene (*b* 1885).
1–*m* Dec. 26, 1914, Mary Marguerite Drach, *b* Newcastle, Colo., Oct. 4, 1888; dau. of Edward Drach, of Denver; issue: 1–Mary Katherine, *b* Washington, D.C., Apr. 11, 1917; 2–Kenneth Conrad, Jr., *b* Washington, Sept. 7, 1923.
1–U. of N.M., 1907-08; B.S. in Engring., Colo. Coll., 1912; studied Yale, 1912-14; (D.Sc., U.Pittsburgh, 1928). Geologist with Gulf Oil Co., Pittsburgh, Pa., since 1925. Author (see Who's Who in America). Capt. engrs., U.S.A., unattached, staff geologist, 1918. Congregational. Clubs: Cosmos, Mid-River (Washington), Polygon, Pittsburgh Athletic Assn., Graduate (New Haven, Conn.). Residence: 100 Gladstone Rd., Pittsburgh, Pa.

1–**HEATH, Frederic Faries,** *b* Milwaukee, Wis., Sept. 6, 1864.
8–Bartholomew **Heath** (1610-81), from Eng., 1635, settled at Newbury, Mass.; lived and *d* at Haverhill, Mass.; *m* 1642, Hannah Moyse (*d* 1677; Joseph[9]);
7–Josiah (1651-1717), of Haverhill, *m* 1st, 1671, Mary Davis (*b* 1647; John[8], of Dover and Haverhill);
6–John (*b* 1676), snowshoe man, Haverhill; to Norwich, Conn., 1713; *m* 1697, Hannah Haynes (Jonathan[7]);
5–Bartholomew (1710-89), original propr., Sharon, Conn., 1749; farmer, blacksmith; 1st lt., 9th N.Y. Regt. 2d Claverick Bn., Albany Co.; *m* 2d, 1741, Mehitable (Fuller) Crippen (*b* Colchester, Conn., 1722-*d* Sharon, 1797);
4–David (1766-1843), of Sharon; pupil of Noah Webster; Knight Templar; to Harpersfield and Slaterville, N.Y.; *m* 1st, 1786, Eunice Marchant (1768-1825; Amos[5], of Sharon);
3–Milo (1787-1874), of Sharon; later of Harpersfield, Slaterville and Seneca Falls, N.Y.; *d* Pewaukee, Wis.; *m* 1810, Sally Nash (1787-1843), of Harpersfield (Johnston[4]);
2–Ebin Cook (2 below).
9–Edward **Fuller,** Mayflower Pilgrim (qv);
8–Samuel (1617-83), *m* 1635, Jane Lathrop (*b* 1614; Rev. John[9], qv);
7–John (1656-1726), *m* Mehitabel Rowley (*b* 1660; Moses[8], of Barnstable);
6–Thankful (*b* 1689), *m* 1707, Jabez **Crippen** (1680-1785);
5–Mehitable (1722-97), *m* Bartholomew **Heath** (5 above).
2–Ebin Cook **Heath** (1829-96), jeweler, Milwaukee, Wis.; *m* 1860, Carrie Eliza Faries (1840-85; Dr. Robert J.[3], *m* Hannah Parmely); issue: I–Carrie Gertrude (1861-63); II–Frederic Faries (1 above); III–Jessie Fay (1867-1924; *m* William Thormaehlen).
1–*m* Dec. 16, 1893, Elizabeth Brown Dorethy, *b* Edinburgh, Scotland, Dec. 28, 1873; dau. of John Dorethy, *m* Elizabeth Brown; issue: 1–Stuart Eldridge, *b* Milwaukee, Wis., Oct. 30, 1895; 2–Dorothy, *b* Milwaukee, May 3, 1903.
1–Pres. Nat. Amateur Press Assn., 1884-85; staff artist Milwaukee Sentinel, 1888-1900; editor Social Democratic Herald, organ of Social Dem. (Socialist) party of America, 1902-14, the Commonwealth, 1918-20, New Day, 1921-23; mem. staff of Milwaukee Leader. Co-founder (with E.V. Debs) of the Nat. Social-Democratic (now Socialist) Party and 1st nat. chmn., 1900. Social-Dem. candidate for mayor of Milwaukee, 1900; alderman, 10th ward, 1904,06; sec. Nat. Socialist Conv., Chicago, 1908; mem. Milwaukee Sch. Bd., 1909-11; mem. Milwaukee Co. Bd. of Supervisors since 1910. Author (see Who's Who in America). Residence: 902 Locust St., Milwaukee, Wis.

1–**HEATH, Pamelia Dee Pray (Mrs. Homer H.),** *b* Whitehouse, O., Feb. 13, 1881.
10–Quinton **Pray** (1595-1677), settled at Lynn, Mass., ca. 1643; *m* Joanna–;
9–Richard (1630-93), *m* 2d, Elizabeth (White) Herenden (*d* 1701);
8–John (ca. 1665-1733), *m* 1678, Sarah Brown;
7–Hugh (ca. 1681-1761), *m* Abigail Blake (*d* 1761);
6–Jonathan (*b* 1724), *m* Phoebe Aldrich (*d* 1832);
5–Rev. John (1749-1830), officer Am. Rev.; *m* 1775, Deborah Wade (1755-1832);

4-John (1783-1872), *m* 1809, Lucy Dunham (1789-1874);
3-John Lansing (1812-38), *m* 1832, Lucina Cross (1814-92);
2-John Lansing (1839-1911), *m* 1866, Pamelia Catharine Hall (1841-81); *m* 2d, 1884, Mary E. Singer (1850-1914); issue (1st marriage): I-John Emmons (1867-1906); II-Mable (*b* 1869; *m* John Clark Greves); III-Pamelia Dee (1 above); issue (2d marriage): I-C. Louise (*b* 1886; *m* Clyde L. Dew); II-James Lansing (*b* 1888); III-Mary Irene (*b* 1891: *m* R. A. Welker); IV-Fanny E. (*b* 1896; *m* W. C. Timmons, D.D.).
1-*m* Mar. 1, 1905, Dr. Homer Harvey Heath, *b* Whitehouse, O., Aug. 14, 1877: son of Dr. Francis Marion Heath, of Whitehouse, *m* Abigail Kimber: issue: 1-Catharine Abigail, *b* Toledo, O., June 21, 1907; 2-Frank Lansing, *b* Toledo, June 10, 1911.
1-Mem. D.F.P.A., D.A.C., D.A.R., U.S.D. 1812. Residence: 923 Prospect Ave., Toledo, O.

1-**HEINL, Helen Margaret Corbin (Mrs. Robert D.)**, *b* New Harmony, Ind., Mar. 31, 1882.
6-John **Corbin**, of Va.;
5-Nathaniel (173--1803), called Nathan; lived at Gunpowder Falls, Md.; removed to Huntingdon Co., Pa.;
4-Shadrach (1766-1840), of Gunpowder Falls, Md., York and Huntingdon cos., Pa.; *m* 1794, Elizabeth Proudfoot, or Proudfit (1773-1812; David[5], of Hopewell Tp., York Co., Pa., Scotch Presbyn., mem. York co. militia, 1778; *m* Nancy Livingston);
3-John (1803-67), settled at New Harmony, Ind., 1836; removed to Newville, Calif, 1850; *m* 1st, 1828, Margaret Gibson (1810-43; William[4], of Pa.);
2-John (1840-1911), of New Harmony, Ind.: pres. Corbin Milling Co.; enrolled as pvt., 1861, as 2d lt., Co. G, 91st Ind. Inf., 1862: mustered in as 1st lt., 1864, and as capt., 1864; transferred to Co. G, 128th Ind. Inf., 1865; hon. disch., 1865; *m* 1869, Mary Ann Truscott (1849-1917), from Cornwall, Eng., 1860; issue: I-Laura Lee (*b* 1870: *m* H. W. Monical, *d* 1916); II-John (*b* 1871); III-Marcia Viets (*b* 1874; *m* Harry Cuyler Ford); IV-Helen Margaret (1 above); V-Courtland Gibson (*b* 1886; *m* Camilla Pauline Armstrong).
1-*m* Sept. 3, 1912, Robert Debs Heinl, *b* Terre Haute, Ind., Apr. 14, 1880 (see Who's Who in America); issue: 1-Robert Debs, *b* New York, N.Y., Aug. 12, 1916.
1-Grad. Coll. of Music, Cincinnati, 1899; received "Diploma of Distinction" and Springer gold medal, Packer Inst., Brooklyn, 1900,01; studied under Edward MacDowell, 1903-05, with Teresa Carreno, Berlin, 1906-07, with Harold Bauer, Paris, 1911. Concert pianist. Mem. D.A.R. Clubs: Mac Dowell (New York), Friday Morning (Washington). Arts, etc. Episcopalian. Republican. Residence: 2400 California St., Washington, D.C.

1-**HELMICK, Elizabeth Allen Clarke (Mrs. Eli A.)**, *b* Charleston, S.C., Mar. 9, 1866.
9-Joseph (Clark) **Clarke** (qv):
8-Joseph (1642-1726/27), *m* 1st, Bethiah Hubbard (1646-1707);
7-Thomas (1686-1767), *m* Elizabeth Babcock (*b* 1691; Capt. James[8], *m* Elizabeth-);
6-Joshua (1717-93), *m* Hannah Cottrell (1719-1803);
5-Thomas (1749-1832), *m* Olive Marsh (1756-1828);
4-Thomas (*b* 1778), *m* Wealthy Wright Chaffee (*b* 1780);
3-David Wright (1800-54), *m* Sarah Monroe (1807-95);
2-David Otis (2 below).
8-Joseph **Gardiner** (1601-79; son of Sir Thomas, Kt.); from Eng. to Newport, R.I., bet. 1635-40;
7-Benoni (1627-1731);
6-William (1671-1732), *m* Abigail Remington (1681-1763);
5-John (1696-1770), *m* Mary Taylor;
4-Benjamin (1750-1819), *m* Mary Howland (1766-1850);
3-John Howland (1805-73), *m* Hannah Dyer Allen (1804-37);
2-Mary Howland (1829-1919), *m* 1852, David Otis **Clarke** (1826-1918), educator; issue: I-Flora Matilda (*b* 1853; *m* Charles Edward Weeden); II-Elizabeth Allen (1 above).
1-*m* Nov. 20, 1889, Eli Alva Helmick, *b* Quaker Point, Ind., Sept. 27, 1863; U.S.M.A., '88; maj. gen., the insp. gen. U.S.A. (see Who's Who in America); issue: 1-Charles Gardiner, *b* Ft. Sherman, Ida., July 7, 1892; U.S. Naval Acad., '13; 2d lt. U.S.A., F.A., July 18, 1913; served on Mexican border; maj. and lt. col., F.A., World War; 3 citations; maj., F.A., July 1, 1920; *m* Sept. 1, 1919, Leah Louise, dau. of Alexander Stock, of Hillsdale, Mich. (issue: Judith Louise; Joyce; Charles Gardiner, Jr.); 2-Florence, *b* Ft. Reno, Okla., Oct. 27, 1898; U.Mich., '20; *m* Oct. 4, 1923, John Macaulay (issue: Florence Elizabeth, *b* Oct. 1, 1924; Margaret Moreen, *b* Nov. 1, 1925); 3-George, *b* Philippine Islands, July 18, 1903; U.Cincinnati, '26; 2d lt., 82d F.A., U.S.A., June 15, 1925.
1-Kan. State Agrl. Coll., ex-'85 (Pi Beta Phi). Mem. D.F.P.A., D.A.R. (registrar gen., 1926), League of Am. Pen Women, A.A.U.W., etc. Residence: 3506 Garfield St. N.W., Washington, D.C.

1-**HEMENWAY, Henry Bixby**, *b* Montpelier, Vt., Dec. 20, 1856.
8-Ralph **Hemenway** (qv);
7-Joshua (bap. 1643-1716), of Roxbury, Mass.; *m* 1st, 1667, Joanna Evans;
6-Joshua (*b* 1668), of Framingham, Mass.; *m* Rebeckah-;
5-Jonathan (*b* 1712), *m* 1744, Mary Foster;
4-Jonathan (1745-1818), of Barre, Mass.; *m* 1774, Martha Resign Wilder;
3-Jonathan Wilder (1784-1856), of Barre, Mass., and Chelsea, Vt.; *m* 1825, Sarah Hibbard or Hebard;
2-Francis Dana (2 below).
8-Robert (Hibbard, Hibbert, Heberd) **Hebard**, (qv);
7-Robert (bap. 1648-1710), of Wenham, Conn.; *m* Mary Walden;
6-Joseph (1678-1755), of Wenham; *m* Abigail Kendall;
5-Moses (1719-1813), of Lebanon, N.H.; *m* 1744, Hannah Murdock;
4-Roger (1757-1832), of Lebanon, N.H., and Brookfield, Vt.; was mem. of body-guard of Marquis de LaFayette; when they parted at close of war, the Marquis gave him his epaulet, which is still in the possession of the family; *m* Sarah Davidson (1775-1858);
3-Sarah (1791-1840), of Chelsea, Vt.; *m* Jonathan Wilder **Hemenway** (3 above).
8-Joseph **Bixby** (qv);
7-Benjamin (1650-1727), of Ipswich; *m* twice, both wives, Mary-;
6-Nathan (1694-1776), of Topsfield, Mass.; *m* 1718, Abigail Rogers, of Salem, Mass.;
5-Solomon (1732-1813), *d* Stafford, Conn.; *m* 1754, Abagail Newell (1730-1816);
4-Ichabod (1757-1824), of Chelsea, Vt.; *m* 1781, Lydia Orcutt (1756-1820; Daniel[5], *m* Lydia Cushman);
3-Ichabod (*b* Stafford, 1784-*d* Chelsea, Vt., 1852), *m* 1809, Susanna Lewis (1791-1874; James[4], *m* Grace Paddock);
2-Sarah Louisa (1828-90), of Evanston, Ill.; *m* 1854, Francis Dana **Hemenway** (1830-84), prof. exegisis, Garrett Biblical Inst., Evanston, Ill.; issue: I-Henry Bixby (1 above); II-William Butler (*b* and *d* 1858); III-Francis (*b* 1869; served in Spanish-Am. War).
1-*m* May 2, 1882, Lilla Maggie Bradley (Aug. 25, 1857-Mar. 29, 1883); dau. of Seth Eastman Bradley, of Evanston, Ill.; issue: 1-Ruth Lilian, *b* Kalamazoo, Mich., Mar. 23, 1883; ed. Northwestern U.; *m* James Henry Shaw.
1-*m* 2d, Oct. 13, 1885, Victoria Stevenson Taylor (Feb. 16, 1861-May 9, 1910); dau. of Andrew Taylor, of Kalamazoo, Mich., from Scotland; issue: 1-Hazel (Mar. 24-Mar. 28, 1887); 2-Margaret, *b* Kalamazoo, Dec. 15, 1888; A.B., U. of Calif.
1-*m* 3d, July 11, 1919, Garnet Ruth Roe (Aug. 25, 1888-Aug. 15, 1922); dau. of William A. Roe, of Chicago.
1-A.B., Northwestern U., '79 (Alpha Kappa Kappa), A.M., 1882; M.D., Chicago Medical Coll., 1881; licensed to practice, 1880. Medical asst., registrar of vital statistics. Practiced at Kalamazoo, 1881-90; health officer, Kalamazoo, 1884-85; sec. U.S. Bd. Examining Surgeons, 1887-90; instr., Rush Medical Coll., 1893-94; acting prof. pub. health, Coll. Physicians

and Surgeons, Chicago, 1900. Author (see Who's Who in America). Clubs: University (Evanston), Mid-Day Lunch. Residence: 620 S. Amos Av., Springfield, Ill.

1-**HEMENWAY, Herbert Daniel,** *b* Barre, Mass., Jan. 2, 1873.
8-Ralph **Hemenway** (qv);
7-Joshua (bap. 1643-1716), of Roxbury, Mass.; *m* 2d, 1678, Mary- (*d* 1703);
6-Ebenezer (1681-1755), of Framingham; *m* 1711, Hannah Winch (*d* 1737);
5-Daniel (1719-94), of Shrewsbury; *m* 1743, Ruth Bigelow (1719-94; Samuel[6], *m* Mary Gleason);
4-Daniel (*b* 1745), of Barre; *m* 1770, Mary (Smith) Carryl (*d* 1816; Ephraim Smith[5]);
3-Daniel (1791-1868), of Barre; *m* 1817, Persis Earle;
2-Chauncey Columbus (2 below).
9-Ralph **Earle** (qv);
8-William (*d* 1715), of Portsmouth, R.I.; freeman, Bristol, R.I., 1658; moved to Dartmouth, 1670; *m* 1st, Mary Walker (*d* 1660; John[9], *m* Katherine-);
7-Ralph (1660-1757), of Dartmouth and Leicester; town officer, Dartmouth; *m* Mary (Carr) Hicks (*d* 1757; Robert Carr[8]);
6-William (1690-1769), of Dartmouth, Leicester, Shrewsbury and Paxton; *m* Anna Howard, of Tiverton, R.I.;
5-William (1714-1805), of Leicester, Mass.; *m* 1739, Mary Cutting (1716-1808);
4-Joel (*b* 1759), of Leicester and Hubbardston; *m* 1st, 1782, Persis Witt (1763-1817; Oliver[5]);
3-Persis (1793-1871), of Hubbardston, Mass.; *m* Daniel **Hemenway** (3 above);
2-Chauncey Columbus **Hemenway,** farmer and veterinarian; *m* 1862, Sarah E. Parker (1843-1910); issue: I-Sarah Emma (Mrs. Edward M. Woodward, qv for Parker lineage); II-Mary Elizabeth (1866-1929; *m* George T. Whitten); III-Herbert Daniel (1 above); IV-Charles Parker (*b* 1875; *m* Carrie Macrillar); V-Francis Ellis (1877-1918; *m* 1908, Josephine Go-Benciong); VI-Alice Angeline (*b* 1879; *m* Arthur E. Gowetz).
1-*m* Nov. 24, 1903, Myrtle Luella Hawley, *b* Amherst, Mass., Sept. 21, 1881; dau. of Charles A. Hawley; issue: 1-Clyde Herbert, *b* Hartford, Conn., Sept. 11, 1904; *m* 1929, Angelina Louise Beland (issue: Clyde Herbert, Jr., *b* Apr. 1930); 2-Truth Mary, *b* Northampton, Mass., Apr. 7, 1907; Mass. Agrl. Coll., 2 yrs.; N. Adams Normal Sch., 2 yrs.; teacher Quincy; 3-Charles Daniel, *b* Carlisle, Pa., Apr. 24, 1915.
1-B.Sc., Mass. Agrl. Coll., '95; B.Sc., Boston U., 1895, post-grad. work, 1898. Expert, engaged in landscape community development work and food production gardens, since 1923; supt. grounds and their development, U.S. Vets'. Hosp. 89, Rutland, Mass. Author and lecturer (see Who's Who in America). Methodist. Clubs: Men's Union (pres.), Holden Civic (pres.), Civil Legion. Summer place: Crescent Beach, Conn. Residence: Holden, Mass.

1-**WOODWARD, Sarah Emma Hemenway (Mrs. Edward M.),** *b* Barre, Mass., June 17, 1864.
9-Thomas **Parker** (qv);
8-John (1640-99), of Reading, Mass.; *m* 1667, Hannah Kendall (1649-89);
7-John (1668-1740), of Reading; *m* 1691, Elizabeth- (*d* 1731);
6-John (1701-90), of Reading; *m* 1723, Sarah Lilly (*b* 1702; Samuel[7], *m* Hannah-);
5-Jacob (*b* 1726), of Reading; *m* 1748, Abigail Bancroft (*b* 1728; Thomas[6], *m* Lydia Deane);
4-Nehemiah (1760-1850), of Southboro and Princeton; *m* 2d, 1804, Anna Bragg (1772-1829);
3-Jonas (1805-49), of Boston and Brooklyn; officer in Mass. Militia, 1832-37; constable and collector, Brooklyn; *m* 2d, 1836, Mehitable Benson Silver (1814-1900);
2-Sarah Elizabeth (1843-1917), *m* 1862, Chauncey Columbus **Hemenway** (1830-1910), farmer and veterinarian (for issue and Hemenway lineage see Herbert D. Hemenway).
1-*m* Aug. 4, 1887, Edward Minton Woodward, *b* Paxton, Mass., Aug. 13, 1860; son of Albert Erastus Woodward, of Worcester; issue (all *b* Worcester, Mass.): 1-Harold Edward, *b* July 5, 1888; A.B., Amherst, '10; Ph.D., Columbia, 1912; *m* Oct. 15, 1912, Ethel, dau. of Inman L. Willcox, Ph.D., of Oxford, N.Y. (issue: David Willcox); 2-Ruth Lizzie, *b* July 14, 1890; A.B., Mt. Holyoke, '12; 3-Geraldine Mary, *b* Dec. 27, 1891; special course at Simmons, 1912; *m* Oct. 16, 1915, Frederick W., son of Charles Flint, of Paxton, Mass. (issue: Helen; Harold; Marjory; Charles); 4-Ethel Frances, *b* July 18, 1902; grad. Nissen Sch. of Phys. Edn., Boston, '24; 5-Albert Hemenway, *b* Sept. 8, 1904; A.B., Amherst, '26.
1-Mem. O.E.S. Baptist. Republican. Residence: 736 Pleasant St., Worcester, Mass.

1-**HENDEE, Jessie Mabel Hollister (Mrs. Lem E.),** *b* Milwaukee, Wis., Aug. 20, 1873.
11-William **Brewster,** Mayflower Pilgrim (qv);
10-Jonathan (1593-1661), of S. Duxbury, Mass.; town clk., New London, Conn.; dep. Gen. Ct., 1650; *m* 1624, Lucretia Oldham (*d* 1679);
9-Ruth (1631-77), *m* 1651, John **Pickett** (*d* at sea 1667), mcht., New London;
8-Mercy (1661-1725), *m* 2d, 1703, John **Arnold** (1652-1725);
7-Ruhama (1704-88), *m* 1st, 1736, as his 4th wife, Maj. Daniel **Ely** (1693-1776);
6-Lucretia (1742-43-1826), *m* 1761, Lt. Benjamin **Colt** (1738-81);
5-Benjamin (1762-1848), *m* 1785, Polly Hopkins (1766-1813);
4-Polly (1789-1852), *m* 1816, Benjamin **Bagley** (1778-1856);
3-Dudley Selden (1818-1906), *m* 1843, Martha Hopkins Allis (1816-67);
2-Helen Martha (*b* 1849), *m* 1866, Junius Wilson **Hollister** (1834-1909), 1st sgt., Co. F, 24th Wis. Vol. Inf., Civil War; issue: I-Alice Martha (*b* 1869; *m* Joseph F. Curtin); II-Jessie Mabel (1 above); III-Walter Junius (1877-1924; *m* Fannie Edith Fuller).
1-*m* Sept. 22, 1897, Lem Ellsworth Hendee, *b* Milwaukee, Wis., Dec. 19, 1872; son of Ceilan Abner Hendee, *m* Mary Louise Jones; issue: 1-John Hollister, *b* Milwaukee, Wis., Mar. 5, 1900; U.Wis.; *m* June 2, 1923, Caryl, dau. of Joshua Hayward Binney, of Milwaukee (issue: John Hollister; Thomas Richardson); 2-Virginia Hollister, *b* Milwaukee, Mar. 20, 1905; *m* Dec. 7, 1927, Carl E. Mueller.
1-Grad. Wis. State Coll. Taught kindergarten 3 yrs. Mem. S.M.D., D.A.R. Residence: 638 Summit Av., Milwaukee, Wis.

1-**HENDRIX, William Samuel,** *b* Ragland, Ala., May 27, 1887.
5-William **Griffin** (*d* 1837), *m* Martha Stovall (1758-1847);
4-Richard (1804-64), *m* 1825, Nancy Caian Whitworth (Buck[5], *m* Mrs. Sutherland, Irish);
3-Mary or Polly (1829-*d* Sylacauga, Ala., 1921), *m* 1846, Lewis **Hendrix** (1827-97), served with C.S.A. of the west (Hillary[4], *m* Sophia-);
2-William David (2 below).
4-William **Martin** (son of soldier, Am. Rev., who *d* aet. 107), *b* Asheville, N.C.;
3-William Alvin (*b* Barta Co., Ga., 1835), served C.S.A.; *m* Adeline Bathsheba Moore (1834-63);
2-Indiana Cornelia (1856-1927), *m* 1874, William David **Hendrix** (*b* 1849), retired capitalist; issue: I-Mollie Mary Emaline (Feb. 1, 1877-Oct. 25, 1923; *m* 1901, Casey Dunlap); II-William Samuel (1 above); III-Lena Myrtle (*b* 1892).
1-*m* June 25, 1913, Bertha Estella Bourdette (qv); issue: 1-Edith Bourdette, *b* St. Paul, Minn., Sept. 5, 1914; 2-William Edwin, *b* Austin, Tex., Oct. 29, 1916.
1-A.B., Howard Coll., Ala., '07 (Acacia), A.M., 1909; A.M., Cornell U., 1910; Ph.D., U.Chicago, 1922. Asst. in Romance languages, U.Ill., 1910-13; instr. same, U.Tex., 1913-16, adj. prof., 1916-20; chmn. Romance lang. dept., Ohio State U. Author (see Who's Who in America). Club: Faculty. Baptist. Democrat. Residence: 423 W. 9th Av., Columbus, O.

1-**HENDRIX, Bertha Estella Bourdette (Mrs. William Samuel),** *b* Miles City, Mont., Mar. 13, 1888.
4-Edward **Bourdette** (1804-83), *m* 1st, at Jamaica, N.Y., Mary A. Thomas (1808-48), of Brooklyn, N.Y.;
3-Clarence (1837-1919), *b* Brooklyn, N.Y., *d* Gunnison, Colo.; *m* 1858, Betsie M. Walker (1838-93), *b* Dewittville, Chautauqua Co., N.Y. (Shadrach Schofield[4] [*b* 1813], of N.Y., *m* Roxanna Wood, *b* 1812);
2-Henry Edwin (2 below).

5–Edward **Conroy,** of Va.;
4–Edward (1802-85), of Va., and Ohio; *m* 1835, Rebecca Scarff (1807-52; Nicholas[5], of Va., *m* Providence–);
3–George Washington (*b* 1839), of Green Tp., O.; *m* 1864, Amanda Maud Evans;
2–Cora Maud (2 below).
9–Francis **Hougham,** of London, Eng.; *m* Mary Plumb;
8–Jarvis (*b* 1708), *m* Eleanor–;
7–Jarvis (*b* 1729), to Md. as missionary, 1750 or 55; *m* and buried in Md.;
6–Aaron (1776-1856), to Ind.; *m* Catherine Shier Williams;
5–John, *m* Hannah Gordon (John[6], soldier Am. Rev., in Washington's army, his wife entertained the General);
4–Nancy (*b* 1819), *m* 1835, Samuel **Evans** (*b* nr. Chillicothe, O., 1807), of Lincoln, Ill.; known as the "cattle king of Ill."; made trip to Calif., '48 (Lemuel[5], served in War 1812);
3–Amand Maud (1844-1914), *m* George Washington **Conroy** (3 above);
2–Cora Maud (*b* Bloomington, Ill., 1870), *m* 1886, Henry Edwin **Bourdette** (*b* Henry Co., Ill., 1863), of Tumeremo, Venezuela, and Chicago, Ill.; issue: I–Bertha Estella (1 above); II–Edith Lucile (1889-90); III–Clarence Edwin (*b* 1891; *m* 1917, Edith Yvonne Wiggins); IV–Wilbur Earl (1893-1914); V–Evans Eugene (1896-97).
1–*m* June 25, 1913, William Samuel Hendrix (qv for issue).
1–B.A., U.Ill., '13. Mem. Univ. Woman's Club (Columbus), A.A.U.W., Central Ohio Symphony Club. Residence: 423 W. 9th Av., Columbus, O.

1–**HENRY, Frederick Augustus,** *b* Bainbridge, Geauga Co., Ohio, June 16, 1867.
7–William **Henry** (*d* post 1753), from N. of Ireland, ante 1735; settled Stow, Mass.; later removed to Lunenburg, Mass.;
6–Robert (ca. 1720-59), of Stow, Groton, and Shirley, Mass.; *m* 1742, Eleanor–;
5–John (1743-1819), of Stow and Shirley, Mass., Lebanon, Andover, Bolton and Enfield, Conn.; served in Am. Rev.; responded to Lexington Alarm; *m* 1766, Mary Gager (1744-1812; Rev. William[6], *m* Mary Allen, of Lebanon, Conn.);
4–Simon (1766-1854), of Enfield, Conn., Middlefield and Washington, Mass.; later removed to Bainbridge, Geauga Co., O.; *m* 1792, Rhoda Parsons (1774-1847; John[5], of Enfield, Conn., *m* Anne Osborne; John[6]);
3–John (1796-1869), of Washington, Mass., Bainbridge, Geauga Co., and Johnston, Trumbull Co., O.; served Jan.-Apr. 1814, in Lt. Matthew M. Jenkins' Baty., 4th Light Arty., War 1812; *m* 1819, Polly Jaqua (1800-81; Simon[4], of Salisbury, Conn., *m* Ruth Hanchett);
2–Charles Eugene (1835-1906), of Geauga Lake, and Cleveland, O.; 1st lt., brevet capt. and adj., 42d Ohio Vol. Inf., Civil War; U.S. Marshal of D.C.; farmer, post office inspector, ry. official, inspector Am. Surety Co.; *m* 1865, Sophia Marcia Williams (1840-1927); issue: I–Frederick Augustus (1 above); II–Marcia (*b* 1869); III–Mary A. (*b* 1871; *m* Abner G. Webb); IV–Don Pardee (1876-77); V–James G. (1880-1901).
1–*m* Jan. 25, 1893, Louise Adams, *b* E. Smithfield, Bradford Co., Pa., Oct. 23, 1868; dau. of Levi T. Adams, of E. Smithfield; issue: 1–Marcia Louise, *b* Geauga Lake, O., Oct. 19, 1893; A.B., Hiram Coll., '15; *m* June 12, 1919, Dr. Harry Clifford, son of Jacob Rosenberger, of Leipsic, O. (issue: Marcia Alice, *b* Mar. 2, 1922; James Henry, *b* June 3, 1925); 2–Charles Adams, *b* Cleveland, O., Mar. 29, 1896; A.B., Hiram, '20, B.S., Ohio State, 1920; *m* June 5, 1918, Blanche M., dau. of Frederick Hiram Hawley, of W. Rupert, Vt. (issue: Frederick Hawley, *b* Mar. 30, 1919; John Webster, *b* May 11, 1923; Charles Eugene, *b* Mar. 23, 1925); 3–Charlotte Sophia, *b* Cleveland, Apr. 27, 1900; A.B., Hiram Coll., '20, M. Soc. Sci., Smith, 1927; 4–Margaret Rhoda, *b* Cleveland, July 27, 1902; A.B., Hiram Coll., '24; *m* July 31, 1929, Elra Verne Messner; 5–Marian (Polly), *b* Cleveland, July 26, 1910; ed. Hiram Coll.
1–A.B., Hiram Coll., '88 (Phi Delta Phi); A.M., U.Mich., LL.B. Lawyer, judge. Admitted to bar, Ohio, 1891, and practiced in Cleveland, 1891-1905; judge Circuit Ct. 1905-12; prof. law, Western Reserve U., 1894-1911. Author (see Who's Who in America). Pres. bd. trustees, Hiram Coll.; v.p. Y.M.C.A., Cleveland; mem. Cleveland Chamber of Commerce (v.p., 1912-13). Mem. N.E.H.G.S., Western Reserve Hist. Soc., Philos. Club of Cleveland (pres. 1915-16), Loyal Legion, S.V. Clubs: Union, Tippecanoe. Disciples of Christ (first pres. internat. conv., 1913). Republican. Residence: Geauga Lake, Geauga Co., O.

1–**HENRY, Jane Byrd Ruffin (Mrs. Reginald B.),** *b* Norfolk, Va., July 22, 1897.
10–Lt. Francis **Mason** (*d* 1648), burgess; justice of Lower Norfolk Co., Va.; *m* Alice–;
9–Col. Lemuel, burgess; *m* Anne Seawell (Henry[10], of Seawell's or Sewell's Point, *m* Alice, dau. of Thomas Willoughby);
8–Alice, *m* Col. Samuel **Boush,** first mayor of Norfolk, Va.;
7–Maj. Samuel, burgess; vestryman of St. Paul's, Norfolk;
6–Samuel;
5–Elizabeth, *m* Col. Champion **Travis,** mem. convs., 1774-75; naval commr. (Col. Edward Champion[6], burgess, *m* Susannah Hutchings; Edward[7]);
4–Susan H., *m* Edmund **Ruffin** (1794-1865), mem. Va. Senate; pres. Va. Agrl. Soc.; fired the first gun at Fort Sumter, 1861;
3–Julian Calx (1822-64), *m* 1852, Charlotte Stockdell Meade;
2–Edmund Sumter (2 below).
11–John **Rolfe** (qv);
10–Lt. Thomas, *m* Jane Poythress (Capt. Francis[11]);
9–Jane, *m* 1675, Col. Robert **Bolling** (qv);
8–Maj. John (1676-1729), of "Cobbs," *m* 1697, Mary Kennon;
7–Jane (*d* 1766), *m* Col. Richard **Randolph,** of "Curles" (William[8], qv);
6–Richard (1715-86), *m* Anne Meade;
5–Elizabeth, *m* David **Meade** (Maj. Gen. Everard[6], *m* Mary Thornton; David[7], *m* Susannah, dau. of Sir Richard Everard, gov. of N.C., *m* Susannah, dau. of Rt. Rev. Richard Kidder);
4–John Everard (1792-1854), *m* Rebecca Wormeley Beverley;
3–Charlotte Stockdell (1833-1918), *m* 1852, Julian Calx **Ruffin** (3 above).
9–Theodorick **Bland** (qv);
8–Richard (1665-1720), of "Jordan's Point"; *m* Elizabeth Randolph (William[9], *m* Mary Isham);
7–Elizabeth (*b* 1706), *m* Col. William **Beverley,** of "Beverley Manor" (Robert[8], historian, *m* Ursula, dau. of William Byrd I, of "Westover"; Maj. Robert[9]);
6–Robert (1740-1800), of "Blandfield"; *m* 1763, Maria Carter (Col. Landon[7], of "Sabine Hall," *m* Maria, dau. of William Byrd II; Col. Robert[8], known as "King Carter," speaker of the House of Burgesses, pres. and c.-i.-c. of Va., *m* Betty Landon);
5–Carter (1774-1842), *m* 1795, Jane Wormeley (see Vol. III, p. 236, for Wormeley lineage);
4–Rebecca Wormeley, *m* 1830, John Everard **Meade** (4 above).
8–Thomas **Taylor,** of London;
7–Nathaniel, *m* Ann, dau. of William Cutlers of London;
6–Samuel (*d* 1805), from Eng. in the "Wellington," 1764, to York, Va.; *m* Anne (Vannah) Harrold;
5–Arthur (1770-1838), *m* 1789, Mary (*d* 1841), dau. of Abram Emmet, of Ireland, *m* Mary Earl, of Dorchester Co., Md.;
4–Carolina Virginia, *m* 1829, George James **Byrd** (see Vol. III, p. 236, for Byrd lineage);
3–Richard Willing (1832-78), *m* 1864, Jane Broadnax de Jarnette;
2–Cordelia Willing (2 below).
6–Joseph **de Jarnette,** of "Spring Grove," Va., of French Huguenot ancestry; *m* Mary Hampton;
5–Daniel, of "Spring Grove"; *m* Jane Coleman;
4–Robert Elliot, of "Clifton"; *m* Cordelia Fauntleroy Burke;
3–Jane Broadnax, *m* 1864, Richard Willing **Byrd** (3 above);
2–Cordelia Willing (see Vol. II, p. 143 for other lineages), *m* 1895, Edmund Sumter **Ruffin.**
1–*m* Apr. 30, 1918, Reginald Buchanan Henry,

M.D. (see Vol. II, p. 145); issue: 1–Evelyn Byrd, *b* Feb. 21, 1919; 2–Reginald Buchanan Willing, *b* July 18, 1926.
Residence: 511 Fairfax Av., Norfolk, Va.

1–**HENRY, Ryder,** *b* nr. Cambridge, Md., Jan. 15, 1867.
6–Rev. John **Henry,** Presbyn. minister; from Ireland to Rehoboth, Somerset Co., Md., 1700; *m* Mary (King) Jenkins, dau. Sir Robert King, Irish baronet;
5–Col. John, *m* Dorothy Rider (Col. John[6], of Md.);
4–John (1750-98), A.B., Princeton, 1769; del. Cont. Congress; 1st U.S. senator from Md., 1789-97; 9th gov. of Md., 1797-98; *m* Margaret Campbell (John[5], *m* Elizabeth Goldsborough);
3–John Campbell (1787-1857), *m* Mary Nevett Steele;
2–Ryder (1828-1900), gentleman farmer, Cambridge, Md.; *m* Octavia Murray Sulivane (1840-1906); for issue see Vol. III, p. 236.
1–*m* June 5, 1907, Louise Frelinghuysen Jackson (qv); issue: 1–Louise Frelinghuysen, *b* New York, N.Y., May 11, 1908; 2–John Campbell, *b* at New York, Sept. 29, 1912.
1–Retired merchant, farmer. Mem. I.A.G., Am. Geog. Soc. (N.Y.), N.Y. Chapter Colonial Order (treas.). Country place: Little Hornspoint, Cambridge, Md. Winter residence: 5 E. 93d St., New York, N.Y.

1–**HENRY, Louise Frelinghuysen Jackson (Mrs. Ryder),** *b* New York, N.Y.
6–William **Jackson,** from Edinburgh, 1685, to East Jersey, and to N.Y.; *m* 1694, Anna Wessels (Dr. Hartman[7]);
5–Patrick (bap. 1701), *m* 1727, Anna Van der Spiegel;
4–Rev. William (*d* 1813), of Bergen, N.Y.; *m* Anna Frelinghuysen (1738-1810);
3–Rev. John Frelinghuysen (1768-1836), *m* 1800, Hannah (Horn) Benson (1772-1854);
2–Dr. William H. (2 below).
4–Daniel **Robert** (*b* N.Y., 1746-*d* Mastic, N.Y., 1804), *m* Mary Taugier Smith, of St. George's Manor, L.I.;
3–Daniel (*b* Mastic, 1792-*d* 1878), *m* Jane Cowenhoven (1805-*d* New Utrecht, L.I., 1885);
2–Katherine (*b* New Utrecht, Nov. 20, 1833-*d* July 15, 1919), *m* at Bay Ridge, L.I., Dr. William H. **Jackson** (Apr. 7, 1811-Nov. 25, 1893), of New York; issue: I–Louise F. (1 above); II–Adelaide Robert (*m* Clement Henry); III–Anna Horn (*m* William Walton Rutherford); IV–Emily Serena; V–Margaret Augusta; VI–William Frelinghuysen (*d* childhood).
1–*m* June 5, 1907, Ryder Henry (qv for issue).
1–Residence: 5 E. 93d St., New York, N.Y.

1–**HERRICK, Glenn Washington,** *b* Otto, N.Y., Jan. 5, 1870.
9–Henry (Heyricke) **Herrick** (qv);
8–Ephraim (1638-93), of Beverly, Mass.; *m* 1661, Mary Cross;
7–Stephen (*b* 1670);
6–Edward (*b* 1695);
5–Ebenezer;
4–John;
3–Samuel B. (1789-1869), *m* Mary Vosselen (1794-1879);
2–Stephen Malum (2 below).
10–Henry **Botsford** (1610-85), from Leicestershire, Eng., 1638; settled at Milford, Conn., 1639; *m* Elizabeth– (bap. 1614-1692);
9–Elnathan (1636-91), from Eng. with father; *m* 2d, 1667, Hannah Baldwin (1644-1706; Timothy[10], *m* Mary Mepham);
8–Henry, *m* Christian Gunn;
7–Moses, *m* Sarah Leavenworth;
6–Theophilus, *m* Hannah Skeels;
5–Theophilus (1758-1841), *m* Dolly Bidwell;
4–Daniel (*b* 1782), *m* 1800, Polly Betsey Foote;
3–Luzon Alanson (*b* 1802);
2–Marion (Aug. 18, 1832-Nov. 10, 1875), *m* Dec. 9, 1852, Stephen Malum **Herrick**; issue: I–Edwin (1854-81); II–Emery (1857-1929); III–Marvin E. (1859-1928; *m* 1880, Lida Lamb); IV–George (1861-64); V–Willie E. (*b* 1863; *m* 1885, Mary Robinson); VI–Glenn W. (1 above).
1–*m* Aug. 17, 1898, Nannie Young Burke, *b* Mocksville, N.C., Nov. 19, 1869; dau. of Theodore Burke; issue: 1–Marvin Theodore, *b* Mocksville, N.C., July 3, 1899; A.B., Cornell U., '22; M.A., Harvard, 1923; Ph.D., Cornell, 1925; *m* Feb. 5, 1929, Nigel Hill, of Urbana, Ill.; 2–Stephen Marion, *b* Mocksville, July 18, 1904; A.B., Cornell, '26; M.A., U.Pittsburgh, 1928; 3–Anne Bertha, *b* Ithaca, N.Y., Nov. 15, 1909; ed. Vassar Coll.
1–B.S., Cornell, '96 (Alpha Gamma Rho, Pi Gamma Mu, Sigma Xi); grad. work, Harvard U., 1897. Prof. entomology, Cornell U., since 1912. Author. (see Who's Who in America). Clubs: University, Country. Episcopalian (clk. vestry, St. John's Ch., Ithaca). Republican. Residence: 219 Kelvin Pl., Ithaca, N.Y.

1–**HEWES, Henry Fox,** *b* Portland, Me., Aug. 27, 1867-*d* Boston, Mass., July 8, 1926.
4–Tracy **Hewes,** of Saco, Me.; *m* 1800, Sally Coolbroth;
3–Tracy (1813-88), Saco; *m* 1834, Elizabeth Rumery (1819-77);
2–James Tracy (2 below).
8–Joseph **Jewett** (qv);
7–Joseph (1656-94), King Philip's War; *m* Ruth Wood;
6–Jonathan (*b* 1679);
5–James (*b* ca. 1718), *m* Martha Scott, of Rowley, Mass.;
4–James (1758-1843), of Falmouth; *m* 2d, 1801, Ruby Bridges (*b* 1771; Moody[5]);
3–Jedediah (1807-64), mayor of Portland, Me., 1858-60; apptd. 1st Rep. collector of the Port of Portland by President Lincoln, 1861; *m* 1833, Elizabeth Fox;
2–Eleanor Bridges (2 below).
9–Thomas **Fox** (g.son of John Fox, of England, author of "The Book of Martyrs"); from Eng., settled at Cambridge, Mass., 1635; *m* Ellen Green;
8–Rev. Jabez, *m* Judith Rayner;
7–Rev. John, *m* Mary Tyng;
6–Hon. Jabez, *m* Ann Bradbury;
5–John, *m* Sarah Fox;
4–Charles, *m* Abigil McLellan;
3–Elizabeth, *m* Jedediah **Jewett** (3 above);
2–Eleanor Bridges (1840-1909), *m* 1865, Rev. James Tracy **Hewes** (1836-76), A. B., Bowdoin, '57; B.D., Harvard, 1861; Unitarian minister (for issue see Vol. I, p. 929).
1–*m* June 5, 1915, Margaret Gordon, dau. of H. Havelock Warman, of Moncton, N.B.; issue: 1–Henry Fox, *b* Boston, Apr. 9, 1917.
1–A.B., Harvard, '90, M.D., 1895. House officer, Mass. Gen. Hosp., 1895; practiced gen. medicine, Boston, 1896, asso. with Dr. E. G. Cutler; instr. clinical chemistry, Harvard Med. Sch., 1898-1906; instr. medicine, 1906-15; instr. Post-Grad. Sch., 1915-24; asst. visiting physician, physician-in-chief of out-patient dept., and consulting physician, Mass. Gen. Hosp.; consulting physician, Mass. Eye and Ear Infirmary, Boston; from 1910 practice confined to disease of the stomach and practice limited to consultations; was widely known as specialist in gastroenterology. Author: Text Book of Physiology and Hygiene, 1900.

HEYSHAM

Arms: *Gules, an anchor in pale or, on a chief of the last three torteaux.*

Crest: *A stag courant, pierced through the neck by an arrow.*

1–**HEYSHAM, Theodore,** *b* nr. Cold Point, Pa., Jan. 14, 1864.
5–William **Heysham** (1720-97), from Eng., ca. 1750, settled at Phila., Pa.; mcht. and shipowner; signer of the "Code of Honor" or

Non-Importation Resolution of Oct. 25, 1765; warden Port of Phila., 1778; commr. of salt, 1779; assisted in removing the bells from Christ Ch. on the entrance of General Howe and the British soldiers into the city; buried in Christ Church Burying Ground, Phila., nr. the tomb of Benjamin Franklin; *m* ca. 1755, Mary- (1723-91); seal of the coat of arms of Heysham Family brought from Eng. by Capt. William Heysham is in the possession of Theodore Heysham, the subject;
4-Robert (1758-1822), of Phila.; mcht.; vol. in Battle of Trenton, 1776; prisoner, 1777-78; commd. capt. co. of inf., Provisional Army of U.S., Phila., June 18, 1798, by Pres. John Adams, this commn. and the captain's sword are in the possession of Theodore Heysham, the subject; *m* ca. 1797;
3-Robert (1798-1867), of Phila.; connected with U.S. Naval Office, Phila., to 1846, and then with U.S. Custom House until 1853; retired to farm of son, Robert, in Plymouth Tp., Pa.; buried in Old St. David's Episcopal Ch. Burying Ground, Radnor, Pa.; *m* 1823, Anne Stewart (1803-38); marriage certificate signed by Bishop William White, 1st P.E. bishop of Pa., is in the possession of Theodore Heysham, the subject;
2-Robert (1824-92), of Norristown, Pa.; farmer Conshohocken Pike, nr. Cold Point, Montgomery Co., Pa., remained there from 1850 until 1869, when he retired moving to Norristown where he took up the study of law, but never sought to enter the profession; buried in Montgomery Cemetery, Norristown; *m* 1860, Sarah Elizabeth Hoopes (1840-1915); issue: I-Stewart (1862-84; *m* 1881, Lidie Adle); II-Theodore (1 above); III-Horace Besson (1873-1915).
1-*m* Oct. 24, 1900, Ella May Reese, *b* nr. Trooper, Montgomery Co., Pa., July 11, 1873; dau. of William Johnson Reese, of W. Norristown Tp., Montgomery Co., Pa., *m* Anna Rebecca Harding; issue (all *b* nr. Trooper, Montgomery Co., Pa.): 1-Anna Stewart, *b* July 30, 1901; A.B., Bucknell U., '24; *m* Oct. 24, 1925, Roy W. Schweiker (issue: Shirley Jeanne, *b* Aug. 23, 1927; Anne Heysham, *b* Sept. 28, 1929); 2-Theodore, Jr., *b* Jan. 9, 1904; A.B., Bucknell, '25; 3-Sara Reese, *b* June 12, 1906; A.B., Bucknell, '28.
1-Bucknell U., 1890-92; A.B., U.Pa., 1894 (Phi Gamma Delta, Phi Beta Kappa, Pi Gamma Mu), Ph.D., 1898; Crozer Theol. Sem. 1897. Ordained Bapt. minister, 1897; pastor, 1899-1906, 1911-23. Author and lecturer (see Who's Who in America). Mason (K.T.). Baptist. Republican. Residence: 225 Jacoby St., Norristown, Pa.

1-**HIBBARD, Mary Eastman Gale (Mrs. Charles Bell),** *b* Laconia, N.H., Aug. 19, 1860.
7-Bartholomew **Gale** (1648-168-), of Salem, Mass.; English shipwright; *m* 2d, Mary Bacon;
6-Daniel (*b* 1676);
5-Daniel, of Exeter, N.H. (5- and 6- may be same person);
4-Stephen (*d* 1813, aet. 74), to Gilmanton, N.H., 1780; served in French and Indian War; maj., alarm list, Am. Rev.; tradition says he was first man over the wall at Ticonderoga; *m* Susanna Flanders (1744-81; Thomas[5], of Exeter, N.H.);
3-Stephen (*d* 1864, aet. 86), from Gilmanton to Meredith (now Laconia), N.H.; *m* 1816, Polly Eastman;
2-Lucian (2 below).
7-Roger **Eastman** (qv);
6-Samuel (1657-1725), from Salisbury, Mass., to Kingston, N.H.; *m* 1686, Elizabeth Scriven, of Salisbury;
5-Samuel (1695-1753), *m* 1728, Mrs. Sarah (Brown) Clough;
4-Lt. Ebenezer (*b* Kingston, N.H., 1746-*d* Gilmanton, N.H., 1794), capt. at Battle of Bunker Hill; *m* 1773, Mary Butler (Stephen[5], of Brentwood, N.H., *m* 2d, Mary Gilman);
3-Polly (1789-1853), of Gilmanton; *m* Stephen **Gale** (3 above).
7-Sgt. John **Chadwick** (1651-1707), of Malden, Boxford and Bradford, Mass.; *m* 1674, Mary Barlow (1652-1734; Edmund[8], of Cambridge, *m* Mary, dau. James Pemberton);
6-John (1677-1756), of W. Boxford, Mass.; *m* Mehitable Hazeltine or Hasseltine (1686-1748);
5-Dea. John (1720-97), Boxford; dea. 2d Congl. Ch., 1788-95; ens. 1762; *m* 1743, Susanna Peabody (1721-94; Ens. David[6], *m* Sarah, dau. Capt. Seth Pope; Capt. John[7]; Lt. Francis[8], qv);
4-Dr. Edmund (1751-1826), ed. Oxford, Eng.; pvt. and surgeon Cont. Army, in battles of Ticonderoga, Saratoga and spent the winter at Valley Forge, 1777-78; settled at Deerfield, N.H., 1779; *m* 1779, Elizabeth Gookin;
3-Alexander Scammel (1789-1866), of Deerfield, N.H., later at Frankfort, 1816, and at Gardiner (now Farmingdale), Me., 1821; lt. in battle of Ft. Erie, 1814; moderator, 1840-49; selectman, 1837-48; assessor; alderman; rep. 1832-35; *m* 1816, Hannah Kimball;
2-Sarah Elizabeth (2 below).
10-Gov. Thomas **Dudley** (qv);
9-Ann (*d* 1672), the "First American Poetess"; *m* 1628, Gov. Simon **Bradstreet** (qv);
8-Dorothy (1630-72), *m* 1654, Rev. Seaborn **Cotton** (1633-86; John[9], qv);
7-Rev. John (1658-1710), *m* 1686, Anne Lake (1663-1737; Capt. Thomas[8], killed by Indians, *m* Mary, dau. Dep.Gov. Stephen Goodyear, qv);
6-Dorothy (1693-1748), *m* 1711, Rev. Nathaniel **Gookin** (1687-1734), of Hampton, N.H.;
5-Rev. Nathaniel (1713-66), of N. Hampton, N.H.; *m* 1748, Love Wingate (*b* 1720; Col. Joshua[6] [1679-1769], of Newbury; John[7], *m* Mary, dau. Hatevil Nutter);
4-Elizabeth (1754-1816), of N. Hampton; *m* Dr. Edmund **Chadwick** (4 above).
9-Edward **Colburn** (1618-1700), from Eng. in the "Defiance," 1635; *m* Hannah-;
8-Ezra (1658-1739), of Ipswich; *m* 1681, Hannah Varnum (*b* 1661; Samuel[9], *m* Hannah-; George[10] [1594-1649], of Ipswich);
7-Ezra (1685-ante 1716), *m* 1706, Lucy Nelson (*b* 1688/89; Capt. Philip[8], *m* Elizabeth Lowell; Thomas[9], from Eng., 1638, freeman, Rowley, Mass.);
6-Jeremiah (*b* 1710), Dracut, Mass.; *m* Sarah Jewett;
5-Sarah Elizabeth (1750-1821), *m* Maj. Henry (Hendrick Smidt) **Smith** (1738-1827), from Holland, with his father, 1747; settled at Pittston, Me., 1764; at Ticonderoga, and at Quebec under Gen. Wolfe in French War;
4-Sallie (1772-1811), *m* 1789, Nathaniel **Kimball,** from N.H.;
3-Hannah (1798-1862), of Pittston, Me.; *m* Alexander S. **Chadwick** (3 above);
2-Sarah Elizabeth (1819-73), *m* Feb. 9, 1853, Lucian **Gale** (May 25, 1818-Apr. 13, 1878), A.B., Dartmouth, 1844; lawyer, Meredith (now Laconia), N.H.
1-*m* Dec. 14, 1897, Charles Bell Hibbard, *b* Laconia, N.H. (Dec. 25, 1855-Feb. 20, 1927); son of Ellery Albee Hibbard, of Laconia; issue: 1-Ellery Gale (*b* Laconia -*d* 1900 in infancy); 2-Elizabeth Chadwick (*b* Laconia-*d* 1902 in infancy).
1-A.B., Swarthmore Coll., '82, A.M., 1891 (P.B.K.). Summer place: Camp, Meredith Neck, N.H. Residence: 176 Pleasant St., Laconia, N.H.

1-**HICKOK, Charles Nelson, II,** *b* Harrisburg, Pa., Aug. 1, 1879.
11-Edward (Hyccocks, Hickocks, Hickox) **Hickok** (*b* ca. 1562, of the "Landed Gentry," being addressed as Esquire; granted the right to "bear arms";
10-Thomas (ca. 1585-1611), *m* 1600, Elizabeth Sturley;
9-William (*b* 1609), wrote name Hickocks; from Eng. to New Haven, in the "Plaine Joan," 1635; removed to Farmington; after remaining in N.E. for some years, returned to his family estates in Warwickshire and spent the remainder of his days as a justice of the peace; *m* Elizabeth- (*d* 1655);
8-Sgt. Samuel (1638-94), wrote name Hickox; at Farmington, 1673; removed to Waterbury where he was one of original settlers; assignee of the first Indian deeds and is named in all fence divisions and proprs. lists; called sgt., 1686; townsman, 1682; *m* Hannah Upson (Thomas[9], *m* Elizabeth Fuller);
7-Ebenezer (1693-1774), at Danbury, 1722,36,41, thence to Norwalk; *m* 2d, 1729, Abigail Stephens (Samuel[8], of West Haven, Conn., *m* Abigail Clark; John[9]; John[10]; Sir Edward[11]);
6-John (1734-1810), began to write name Hickok;

went to Lake George in French War, 1757; pvt. and ens. in Am. Rev.; *m* 1757, Lydia Kellogg (1740-1828; Eliasaph[7], *m* Rachel Benedict; Daniel[8]; Daniel[9]; Martin[10]);
5-Jesse (1769-1826), Scipio, N.Y.; *m* 1791, Betsey Hoyt (1772-1852; John[6], *m* Keziah Wood; Ezra[7]; Daniel[8]; Zerubbable[9]; Walter[10]; Simon[11]);
4-John Hoyt (1792-1841), principal Bellefonte (Pa.) Acad., 2 yrs.; book publisher, teacher; *m* 1814, Mary (Polly) Lockwood;
3-William Orville (1815-91), in 1846, he opened a small shop for the manufacture of bookbindery specialties, which originated the present "Eagle Works," said to be the most complete of its kind in the world, incorporated as W.O. Hickok Mfg. Co., 1886, of which was 1st pres.; pres. Common Council, Harrisburg, Pa., 6 yrs.; apptd. col. on staff of the gov. of Pa.; Mason (Grand Master of Pa.); Presbyn.; *m* 1840, Caroline Louise Hutter;
2-William Orville (2 below).
10-Robert **Lockwood** (*d* 1658), from Eng. in the "Mary and John," to Salem, Mass., 1630; at Watertown, 1631; *d* at Fairfield, Conn.; sgt. Salem 1637; *m* as her 1st husband, Susannah Norman (*d* 1660; Richard[11]);
9-Ephraim (1641-1685/86), of Norwalk; freeman, 1667; *m* 1665, Mercy St. John (Matthias[10]);
8-Lt. James (1683-1769), rep. Gen. Assembly of Conn., 1721-51; justice, Norwalk, 1744-56; ens. 1729; lt. 2d Co., 1731; maj., 1746; later called col.; *m* 1707, Lidia Smith (Samuel[9], *m* Rachel Marvin; Thomas[10]);
7-Job (1718-61), removed to New Canaan; *m* Rachel St. John (ca. 1725-1761; Daniel[8], *m* Mary Benedict; James[9]; Matthias[10]; Matthias[11]);
6-Capt. James (1746-1833), *m* 1st, 1767, Phebe Lockwood (1748-73; Joseph[7]; Joseph[8]; Ephraim[9]; Robert[10]);
5-Job (1768-1843), *m* 1791, Sarah Hickok;
4-Mary (Polly) (1795-1868), *m* John Hoyt **Hickok** (4 above).
9-Sgt. Samuel **Hickok** (1638-94), 8 above;
8-Dea. Benjamin (1686-1745), *m* as her 2d husband, 1713, Sarah Lockwood (1678-1765; Lt. Jonathan[9], *m* Mary Ferris; Robert[10], above);
7-Silas (*b* 1714), *m* Ruth Clark (*b* 1716; Ephraim[8], *m* Hester Belden; James[9]; James[10]);
6-Nathan (*b* 1737), *m* 1759, Hannah Keeler (1737-69; David[7], *m* Mary St. John; John[8]; Ralph[9]);
5-Sarah (1766-1839), *m* Job **Lockwood** (5 above).
9-Philip Carl August (Von Vogel) **Fogel,** a dragoon of the Royal Prussian Cav., 1686;
8-Philip Gabriel, a native of Hanan, Chur Hesse, Germany; came in the "Samuel," 1731, landed at Phila., located in Bucks Co., Pa.; moved to Lynn Tp. (now Lehigh Co.), 1734, where he owned more than 500 acres;
7-Conrad, wrote name Vogel; of Lynn Tp.;
6-John (1753-1816), began to write name Fogel; moved to Upper Macungie Tp. nr. Fogelsville; in ranger service during Am. Rev., 1778-83; founder Fogelsville, Lehigh Co., Pa., ca. 1771; *m* Anna Rosina Schaed (1752-1812);
5-Margaret (1771-1857), *m* 1787, James **Wilson** (1751-1834), from Ireland, settled at Phila., then at Allentown, Pa.; mcht. and contractor; pvt. Am. Rev.; judge; state senator (John[6], of Scotch descent, came from Ireland, *m* Mary Motherwell);
4-Maria (1791-1878), *m* Charles Lewis **Hutter** (1792-1830; Col. Christian Jacob[5] [1771-post 1844], sent by Moravians of Zeist, Germany, to Bethlehem, Pa., at Lancaster, 1799, at Easton, Pa., 1808, lt. col. War 1812 in command of Northampton, Lehigh and Pike cos. militia, mem. Pa. Ho. of Rep., 1822-25; co. recorder of deeds, 1829, Mason [a founder and 1st Worshipful Master of Easton Lodge], *m* 1791, Maria Magdolene Huber [1769-1804]; Johann Ludwig[6] [1726-91], *m* Anna Maria Kuntz, 1729-1805);
3-Caroline Louisa (1817-1906), *m* 1840, William Orville **Hickok** (3 above).
9-George **Espy**;
8-Hugh, of Ireland;
7-Josiah (*d* nr. Harrisburg, Pa.), *m* in Ireland, Prissilla Mitchell;
6-George (1695-1761), from Ireland 1725; settled finally on the Swatara (then Derry Tp., Lancaster Co., Pa.); *m* 1714, Jean Taylor (1699-1781);
5-Col. David (1730-95), Bedford Co., Pa.; dep. Provincial Conf. held at Carpenter's Hall, Phila., 1775; mem. Council of Public Safety, 1776; col. Bn. of Associators, Bedford Co. Militia, 1776; prothonotary of Bedford Co., 1778; justice, 1778; under the Constn. of 1780-90; prothonotary, register, etc., 1790 to date of his death; original trustee Dickinson Coll.; mem. Gen. Assembly of Pa.; *m* 1775, Jane Woods (1755-1813; Col. George[6], *m* Jane, dau. Dr. William McDowell; George[7]);
4-Mary Elizabeth (1779-1815), *m* 1807, Dr. John **Anderson** (1770-1840; Thomas[5] [1734-1807], from Ireland 1755, *d* in Bedford Co., Pa., *m* ca. 1765, Anne Lyon; James[6]; Robert[7]);
3-Espy Lyon (1810-66), propr. Bedford Mineral Springs; *m* 1835, Louisa Harrison Watson;
2-Louisa Harrison (2 below).
6-Alexander **Watson,** *m* Sarah Neal (alias Glasgo);
5-John (1751-1821), to America, 1774; *m* 1776, Jane Wilson (1758-1803);
4-Dr. William (1778-1835), grad. Dickinson Coll., 1799; studied medicine with Dr. McCroskey of Carlisle, where he remained until June 1801, when he returned to Mifflintown, Pa.; removed to Bedford, Pa.; *m* 2d, 1811, Eliza Hartley (1786-1866; William[5], from France in the "Hyder Ali," 1783, *m* Susan Maria, dau. Capt. John Shaw, of East India Co.; John[6]);
3-Louisa Harrison (1817-84), *m* 1835, Espy Lyon **Anderson** (3 above);
2-Louisa Harrison (1850-1924), *m* 1873, William Orville **Hickok** (1849-81), gen. mgr. of the "Eagle Works" at Harrisburg; Mason; issue: I-William Orville, III (*b* 1874; *m* 1903, Avis Cochran); II-Ross Anderson (*b* 1876; *m* 1900, Helen Rankin Hastings); III-Louise Anderson (*b* 1878; *m* 1909, Arthur Brewster Emmons, II); IV-Charles Nelson, II (1 above).
1-Not married. Ed. Harrisburg (Pa.) Acad., 1890-94; St. Paul's Sch., Concord, N.H., 1894-97; Ph.B., Yale-S, '00. With The Latrobe Steel & Coupler Co., Chicago, 1900-03; Dayton (O.) Malleable Iron Co., 1903-05; The M.A. Hanna Co., Cleveland, O., since 1905 (dir., and v.p. various of its iron ore mining corpns.). Councilman Bratenahl Village; formerly treas. Cleveland Red Cross. Mem. Am. Iron and Steel Inst., Am. Inst. Mining and Metall. Engrs. Clubs: Tavern, Union, Kirtland, Pepper Pike Country (Cleveland), Chicago, University (Chicago), Duquesne (Pittsburgh), Kitchi Gammi (Duluth), Yale (N.Y. City). Life mem. I.A.G., N.E.H.G.S. Residence: 12505 Coit Rd., Bratenahl, Cleveland, O.

1-**HICKOK, Paul Robinson,** *b* Nebraska City, Neb., Apr. 6, 1877.
12-Edward (Hiccox, Hyccocks, Hickocks) **Hickok** (*b* ca. 1562), was of the "Landed Gentry," being addressed as Esquire; granted the right to bear arms;
11-Thomas (ca. 1585-1611), wrote name Hyccocks; *m* 1600, Elizabeth Sturley;
10-William (*b* 1609), wrote name Hickocks; from Eng. to New Haven, in the "Plaine Joan," 1635; removed to Farmington, after remaining in N.E. for some yrs. he returned to his family estates in Warwickshire and spent the remainder of his days as a justice of the peace; *m* Elizabeth-;
9-Sgt. Samuel (1638-94), wrote name Hickox; at Farmington, 1673; removed to Waterbury, where he was an original settler; one of the assignees of the first Indian deeds and is named in all fence divisions and proprs. lists; called sgt., 1686, townsman, 1682; *m* Hannah Upson (Thomas[10], *m* Elizabeth Fuller);
8-Dea. Benjamin (1686-1745), at Stamford, 1715; apptd. 1st dea. of Wilton Ch., 1732; mem. Hartford Gen. Assembly, 1728; *m* 1713/14, Sarah Lockwood (1678-1765; Jonathan[9], *m* Mary Ferris);
7-Ezra (1715/16-1794), joined ch. at Wilton, 1734; *m* 1733, Elizabeth St. John (*b* 1717/18; Matthias[8], *m* Rachel Bouton);
6-Carter (1746-ante 1773), *m* 1764, Leah Taylor (*b* 1749; Noah[7], *m* Elizabeth-);
5-Noah (1764-1831), *m* 1786, Betsy Hurlbut;
4-Carter (*b* 1788), *m* 1st, ca. 1807, Mary Hudson (*d* ca. 1833);
3-Goodyear Clark (1808-54), of Nelsonville, O.; *m* Sarah Jane Langdon (*b* 1814; John[4], *m* Mary Moorehouse);
2-Rev. Francis Marion, D.D. (2 below).

8-Thomas **Hurlbut** (1684-1753), settled at Woodbury, Conn.;
7-Daniel (*b* 1710), of Woodbury; *m* —Belden (*d* at Wilton);
6-Capt. Daniel (1740-1827), of Wilton; *m* 2d, Esther Patrick (*d* 1827);
5-Betsy (1769-1850), *m* Noah **Hickok** (5 above);
4-Carter, *m* Mary Hudson (4 above);
3-Goodyear Clark, *m* Sarah Jane Langdon (3 above);
2-Rev. Francis Marion, D.D. (1844-1916), Presbyn. minister; *m* 1873, Mary Matilda Robinson (*b* 1855; Rev. Nelson Cephas[8], *m* Mary Barr Kiddoo); issue: I-Paul Robinson (1 above); II-Rev. Ralph Kiddoo, D.D. (*b* 1880; *m* Grace Anderson); III-Mary Frances (*b* 1884; *m* Dr. Frederick Erdman).
1-*m* Sept. 6, 1900, Mary Elliott, *b* Rittman, O., Sept. 1, 1875; dau. of Rev. John Calvin Elliott, D.D., of Rittman.
1-B.A., Coll. of Wooster, '97 (Alpha Tau Omega); grad. Auburn Theol. Sem., 1900; (D.D., Hanover Coll., 1920). Pastor Forest Hill Presbyn. Ch., Newark, N.J., since 1928; mem. Presbyn. Bd. of Ch. Erection, since 1912; trustee Coll. of Wooster, 1915-22 (see Who's Who in America). Chaplain 5th Inf., Ohio N.G., 1900-09. Mem. S.A.R., S.V. Mason. Republican. Residence: 106 Heller Parkway, Newark, N.J.

1-**HIGBEE, Frederic Goodson,** *b* Fremont, O., Nov. 29, 1881.
9-Edward (Higby) **Higbee** (*b* 1615), from Eng. ca. 1630; settled in Mass.; landholder, New London, Conn., 1647; bought farm at Hartford from Indian sachem, 1664; freeman, 1667; *m* 1647, Jedidah Skidmore (*d* ca. 1660; Thomas[10], from Eng., settled in Cambridge, Mass., ca. 1640, later at L.I., *m* Ellen-);
8-John (1658-1688), of Middletown, Conn.; *m* 1679, Rebecca Treadwell (*d* 1707);
7-Edward (1684-1775), of Middletown; *m* 1706, Rebecca Wheeler (1687-1771);
6-Daniel (1711-62), of Sheffield, Mass.; *m* 1742, Mary Ives (*d* 1757);
5-Edward (1746-1800), of Berkshire Co., Mass.; began to write name Higbee; *m* 1770, Mary Wilson;
4-Stephen (1774-1813), of Oswego Co., N.Y.; *m* 1798, Christina McCollum (*b* 1778);
3-Joseph Benjamin (1813-1899), of Bellevue, O.; *m* 1843, Adeline D. M. Anderson (*d* 1891);
2-Jay Alvin (1845-1901) of Bellevue; corpl., Co. I, 169th Regt., O.V.I., Civil War; mill owner and grain mcht.; *m* 1868, Cora Lavina Goodson (*b* 1847); issue: I-Tryphene Adeline (*b* 1870); II-Jay Alvin (*b* 1879; *m* Katherine Scott); III-Frederic Goodson (1 above).
1-*m* June 10, 1912, Beth Mather, *b* Springdale, Ia., Jan. 1, 1891; dau. of Samuel Mather; issue: 1-Frederic Goodson, Jr., *b* Iowa City, Ia., Sept. 14, 1913; 2-Jay Anders, *b* Iowa City, June 18, 1919.
1-B.S., Case School of Applied Science, '03 (Zeta Psi, Triangle), M.E., 1908. Asst. engr., Osborn Engring. Co., 1903-04; instr. and asst. prof., 1904-08, Prof. and head dept. engring. drawing, U.Iowa, since 1908. Author (see Who's Who in America). Quaker. Republican. Club: Triangle. Residence: Iowa City, Ia.

1-**HIGBEE, Paul Dysart,** *b* Lancaster, Mo., May 4, 1888.
9-Edward **Higbee** (*d* 1699), from Eng. to Mass., ca. 1630; landholder New London, Conn., 1647; bought farm at Hartford from an Indian sachem, 1664; freeman, 1667; was at Huntington and Jamaica and Cold Spring Harbor, L.I.; *m* 1st, Jedidah Skidmore (Thomas[10]);
8-Edward (1652-1716), landholder Middletown, Conn., 1673, and Huntington, N.Y.; went to Middletown, Monmouth Co., N.J.; *m* ca. 1684, Abigail Adams (*b* 1660; John[9], *m* 1657, Abigail, dau. of Richard Smith, of Wethersfield; Jeremy[10], qv);
7-Edward (*b* Huntington, N.Y., 1685-*d* Suffolk Co., L.I.), to Monmouth Co., N.Y., 1710, and back to Burlington Co., N.J.;
6-Peter (*b* Trenton, N.J., 1710), of New Brunswick, N.J.; *m* 2d, —;
5-Obadiah (*b* New Brunswick, N.J., 1763-*d* 1808; buried 15 miles south of Pittsburgh, Pa., on Higbee farm), mem. N.J. militia, Am. Rev.; *m* 1st, Anna May Brower (1741-1812; Abraham[6] *m* 1725, Elizabeth Ackerman; Sybrant[7]; Jacobus[8]);
4-Obadiah (*b* Trenton, N.J., 1782), *m* 1807, Sarah Phillips (*b* 1786; Joseph[5], Am. Rev., *m* Mary Hale Laughlin);
3-Jesse (*b* Upper St. Clair, Allegheny Co., Pa., 1808-*d* Ashland, O., 1897), to Iowa City and Bloomfield, Ia.; member Christian Ch.; *m* Susan Newmyer (1826-83; David[4] [*d* 1865], *m* Jane Cunningham, *d* 1865);
2-Judge Edward (1847-1929), from Ashland Co., O., to Ia.; ed. U.Ia.; judge and later commr. Mo. Supreme Ct.; Mason (K.T., Shriner, Grand Master Mo., 1916), I.O.O.F.; mem. Christian Ch.; *m* Dec. 29, 1867, Mary Isabelle Birney (*b* 1848; Ebenezer[3] [1819-1902], *m* Elizabeth Lakin, 1821-1920); issue: I-George Birney (*b* 1868-*d* infancy); II-Helen Birney (*b* 1869; *m* 1892, William Adam Leyhe); III-Edna Belle (1873-1917; *m* 1895, John Eugene Markey); IV-Florence Dombey (*b* 1875; *m* 1908, Morgan Griffin Heap); V-Frances Elizabeth (*b* 1877; *m* 1904, Raymond Burkland); VI-Walter (*b* 1881; *m* 1907, Edna Reeves); VII-Paul D. (1 above); VIII-Zella Louise (*b* 1890; *m* 1916, Dr. Ralph Crumm).
1-*m* June 11, 1913, Eileen McGinnis (qv); issue (all *b* Kirksville, Mo.): 1-Laura Louise, *b* May 21, 1915; 2-Edward Laughlin, *b* Mar. 19, 1921; 3-Deborah Ross, *b* Jan. 29, 1923.
1-A.B., U.Mo., '09 (Delta Tau Delta), LL.B., 1911 (Phi Alpha Delta). Pros. atty., Adair Co., Mo., 1919-22; circuit judge, 1st judicial circuit of Mo., 1929. Mason (K.T., Shriner), I.O.O.F., Elk. Residence: 701 E. Normal Av., Kirksville, Mo.

1-**HIGBEE, Eileen McGinnis (Mrs. Paul D.),** *b* El Dorado, Kan., Oct. 18, 1893.
7-John **McGinnis,** from Co. Antrim, Ireland, to Pa., aet. 16; resided in Greenbrier, Frederick Co., Va.;
6-James (Allen), soldier Am. Rev., present at Lord Cornwallis' surrender; *m* Sarah Davis;
5-Edmund (1775-1838), to Cabell Co., Va., 1800; rep. Gen. Assembly at Richmond, Va.; *m* 1795, Sarah Bryan (1768-1846; Capt. Thomas[6] [*d* 1795], *m* Elizabeth-; Cornelius O'Bryan[7], *m* Rebecca-; Brian O'Brian[8], from Ireland to Berks Co., Pa., 1724);
4-Rev. Ira Edmund (1805-80), to Kan.; ordained M.E. ministry, 1838; *m* 1833, Malinda Kelso (1811-45);
3-Dr. James Allen (1836-1912), lt. Co. D, 79th U.S. Inf., Civil War; from Newport, Ind., to Butler Co., Kan.; *m* 1858, Sarah Ann Benedict;
2-Capt. Schyler Arthur (2 below).
7-Andrew **Simpson** (family Scotch-Irish Presbyterians and owned linen factories at Belfast and Edinburgh, which are yet extant), came from north of Ireland, bringing a company of 40 artisans, 1725, removed from Boston to Nottingham, N.H.; *m* Elizabeth (Betey) Patton (killed by Indians, 1753);
6-Andrew (ca. 1731-1799), signer Assn. Test; ensign, Am. Rev.; *m* Agnes Ayers (*d* 1807; William[7]);
5-Robert (1753-1835), *m* Lydia Longfellow (*b* 1784);
4-Marie Longfellow (1804-67), *m* Elisha H. **Benedict**;
3-Sarah Ann, *m* Dr. James A. **McGinnis** (3 above).
10-William **Thornton** (qv);
9-Francis (*b* 1651), settled in Stafford Co., Va., probably ante 1700; *m* 1st, Alice Savage (*b* 1651; Capt. Anthony Thomas[10], of Gloucester Co., Va., justice 1699, *m* Alicia Harmonion; Capt. John[11] [*b* 1624], burgess, 1666, *m* 2d, Mary Robins; Thomas[12], qv);
8-Anthony (1695-1757), St. Paul's Parish, Stafford Co., Va.; *m* Winifred Presley (Col. Peter[9], of Northumberland Co., Va.);
7-Judith P. (1734-57), *m* 1749, Thomas **Buckner** (*b* 1728);
6-Mary (*b* 1751), *m* Catesby **Woodford** (*b* 1738);
5-Elizabeth (*b* 1780), *m* Roger **Laughlin** (*b* 1771);
4-Simon (*b* 1811), *m* Rebecca J. Kemp (*b* 1817);
3-Rev. George Hamilton (1838-94), *m* 1862, Deborah Jane Ross;
2-Laura Rebecca (2 below).
7-James **Whitaker** (*b* Eng.), *m* a dau. of Joseph Musgrove;
6-Joseph (1755-1837), *m* Sara Op den Graeff (1759-1823);

5–Jane, left Phila., Pa., 1817, *m* 1807, Rev. William **Ross** (1785-1868);
4–Joseph (*b* 1816), from Tuscarawas, O., to Bureau Co., Ill.; buried Limerick, Ill.; *m* Mary Slutts (*b* 1819);
3–Deborah Jane (*b* 1842), *m* Rev. George H. **Laughlin** (1838-94);
2–Laura Rebecca (1868-1911), *m* 1890, Capt. Schyler Arthur **McGinnis** (1866-1917), atty.-at-law, geologist (for issue and other lineages see Harold H. McGinnis).
1–*m* June 11, 1913, Paul Dysart Higbee (qv for issue).
1–Ed. First Dist. State Teachers Coll., Kirksville, Mo. Mem. D.A.R., Alpha Sigma Alpha. Residence: 701 E. Normal Av., Kirksville, Mo.

1–**McGINNIS, Harold Hamilton,** *b* El Dorado, Kan., May 1, 1892.
9–Thomas **Benedict** (qv);
8–James (*b* 164–), *m* 1676, Sarah Gregory (*b* 1652);
7–Justice Thomas (1694-1776), *m* Abigal Hoyt (*b* 1694);
6–Capt. Elisha (1736-98), of Danbury, Conn.; served in 8th Co., N.Y. regt., Am. Rev.; *m* 2d, 1757, Mrs. Jerusha [Starr] Barnum (1727-98), widow of Thomas Barnum;
5–Felix (1767-1828), from N.Y. to Ohio; *m* 1787, Clarissa Hubbell (1767-1839; Jabez[6], of Conn., *m* Sarah–);
4–Elisha Hubbell (1795-1885), War of 1812, pensioned; from Rutland, O., to Kan.; *m* 1826, Marie Longfellow Simpson;
3–Sarah Ann (*b* Meigs Co., O., 1837-67), *m* 1858, Dr. James Allen **McGinnis** (1836-1912);
2–Capt. Schyler Arthur (2 below).
9–William **Longfellow** (1651-90; son of Edward, of Horseforth, Eng.), from Eng.; ens. Newbury Co., Essex Regt.; drowned in service in Gulf of St. Lawrence; *m* 1678, Anne Sewall, sister of Judge Smith Sewall, 1st gov. Mass., 1661;
8–Nathan (1690-1731), of Hampton Falls, *m* 1713, Mary Green;
7–Jonathan (1713-ante 1778), of Machias, Me.;
6–Nathan (1743-96), soldier Am. Rev., *m* 1765, Margaret Bigelow (1747-1842; Isaac[7], *m* 1734, Abigail Skinner; Sgt. Isaac[8]; Samuel[9]; John[10], qv);
5–Lydia (*b* 1784), *m* Robert **Simpson** (1753-1835);
4–Marie L. (1804-67), *m* Elisha H. **Benedict** (4 above).
8–Dr. William **Cocke** (*b* Sudbury, Suffolk, Eng., 1672-*d* 1720), physician, from Eng. to Williamsburg, Va., mem. Va. Colonial Council; sec. of state for colony under Gov. Spotswood; *m* Elizabeth Catesby (1681-1755), sister of Mark Catesby, naturalist (John[9], *m* May 16, 1670, Elizabeth Jekyll of the family that owned and occupied Castle Hedingham in Essex Co., Eng.);
7–Ann, of Caroline Co., Va.; *m* 1732, Maj. William **Woodford,** from Eng., to Caroline Co., Va.;
6–Catesby (June 19, 1738-1791), *m* Mary Buckner;
5–Elizabeth (*b* 1780), *m* Roger **Laughlin** (*b* 1771), of Roanoke, Va. (Thomas[6] [*b* Eng.-*d* Dec. 13, 1801], *m* 1755, Sarah Madison, 1st cousin of Pres. James Madison);
4–Simon (*b* 1811), of Mt. Sterling, Ky.; *m* 1835, Rebecca Jane Kemp (*b* 1817; Charles[5], of Cynthanna, Ky., *m* Martha, dau. of John Hamilton, Scotch immigrant boy who fought in Battle of Germantown, *m* Rebecca Davis; George or Reuben[6], *m* June Stuart);
3–Rev. George Hamilton (1838-1894), of Quincy, Ill.; classical scholar; pres. Hiram Coll. and Garfield U., 1889; minister of Christian Ch., Kirksville, Mo., 1891, et seq.; *m* 1862, Deborah Jane Ross;
2–Laura Rebecca (1868-1911), *m* 1890, Capt. Schyler Arthur **McGinnis** (1866-1917), atty.-at-law, geologist; capt. Troop I, "Rough Riders," Col. Roosevelt's Regt., Spanish-Am. War; issue: I–Harold Hamilton (1 above); II–Eileen (Mrs. Paul D. Higbee, qv for other lineages); III–Ward Allen (*b* 1895; *m* Harriet Hover, *b* 1899); IV–Grace (*b* 1897; *m* 1919 Maurice Lane Clark); V–Blanche (*b* 1900; *m* 1919, Dr. Fred Mix Still); VI–Arthur (*b* 1902; *m* 1927, Alice Jackson).
1–*m* Dec. 6, 1917, Minnie Frances Lee, *b* 1903, dau. of Thomas Lee; issue: 1–Arthur Allen, *b* 1925; 2–Ross Hamilton, *b* 1927.
Residence: Ruidoso, N.M.

1–**HIGGINS, Alvin McCaslin,** *b* Superior, Wis., Nov. 19, 1866.
8–William **Ilsley** (1608-81), from Eng. in the "Confidence," to Newbury, Mass., 1638; *m* 1633, Barbara–;
7–Isaac (*b* 1652), of Newbury; soldier King Philip's War; wounded 1675; granted bounty of land by Mass. in Buxton, Me.; *m* Abigail Poor;
6–Isaac (1698-1781), of Newbury; leader of militia companies against Penobscot uprisings; capt. in Louisburg Campaign, 1745; *m* 1721, Abigail Moody (1703-73);
5–Jonathan (1738-1809), of Portland, Me.; Lexington Alarm Call, 1775, and Am. Rev.; *m* 1764, Dorcas Ingersoll (1730-1810);
4–Clarissa (1767-1861), of Falmouth, Me.; *m* 1794, John **Higgins** (1772-1843), of Pittsterne, Me.;
3–Alvin M. (1803-85), of Yarmouth, Me.; capt. militia in Indian wars and uprisings in the West; treas. Cass Co., Ind., prior to Civil War; *m* 1837, Eliza Jane Reyburn (1817-59), sister of William Reyburn, comd. the Federal shore baty. at Hampton Rds., 1862, during the first battle of iron-clads;
2–William Reyburn (1838-95), Presbyn. clergyman, Logansport, Ind.; *m* 1864, Mary Elizabeth Condon (1836-1919).
1–*m* Apr. 12, 1899, Margaret Beatrice Keating, *b* Terre Haute, Ind., Nov. 27, 1876; dau. of Edward W. Keating, of Terre Haute.
1–Student Oberlin, 1884-88. Admitted to bar, 1888, and practiced at Terre Haute; 1st pres. Citizens Telephone Co., Terre Haute. Pres. Rep. League of Clubs for Ind., campaign of 1896, reelected, 1897; U.S. commr. for western Ind., 1897-1908; pres. Bd. of Public Safety, 1905. Enlisted in Vet. Corps Arty., N.G.N.Y., Mar. 1917; trans. to 9th Coast Arty., Oct. 9, 1917; chmn. Washington Heights Legal Advisory Bd., under Selective Service Act, World War. Author (see Who's Who in America). Mem. S.R. Club: Army and Navy of America. Residence: "Orchard Hill," Croton-on-Hudson, N.Y.

1–**HIGHLAND, Lucinda Earle Patton (Mrs. John Edgar),** *b* West Milford, then Va., now W.Va., Apr. 3, 1851-*d* West Milford, W.Va., Wednesday, May 29, 1929, at 9 a.m.; buried in a crypt in the Masonic Mausoleum, Clarksburg, W.Va., May 31, 1929.
5–Rev. Isaac **Morris** (*b* Berks Co., Pa., 1740-*d* Harrison Co., Va., 1830), *m* Apr. 11, 1766, Ruth Henton (*b* Va., 1750-*d* Harrison Co., Va., 1839); their son, Thomas (*b* Berks Co., Pa., Jan. 3, 1776-*d* Clermont Co., O., Dec. 7, 1844), emigrated from Harrison Co., Va., to ty., now O., 1795, atty., elected to O. Legislature, 1806, and served in Gen. Assembly 24 yrs., elected U.S. Senator from O., 1832, serving Dec. 1833-Mar. 4, 1839, nationally known for his debate Feb. 9, 1839, in Federal Senate on "Abolition of Slavery," with John C. Calhoun and Henry Clay, he *m* Nov. 19, 1797, Rachel Davis (1779-1853);
4–Hester (Esther), called "Hettie" (*b* Berks Co., Pa., Mon., May 27, 1771-*d* nr. New Hope, Brown Co., O., July 28, 1854), *m* 1797, James **Smith**;
3–Ruth (*b* Clermont Co., O., May 31, 1798-*d* nr. W. Milford, W.Va., Aug. 7, 1848), *m* as his 1st wife, at Clarksburg, Va., July 19, 1814, Col. Alexander Lewis **Patton** (*b* Lancaster Co., Pa., July 23, 1789-*d* nr. W. Milford, Va., May 21, 1866); see Vol. III, p. 244, for Smith, Lewis, Patton and other lineages;
2–Ebenezer Wilson (2 below).
4–Sanford **Carder** (*b* Culpeper Co., Va., Sept. 16, 1760, removed to Hampshire Co., and lastly to Fayette Co., O., where he *d* Aug. 7, 1845); *m* 1st, ca. 1789-90, Nancy Hoffman (*d* ante 1827; Conrad[5]), soldier Am. Rev.;
3–James (*b* 1791, Hampshire Co., Va., *d* 1859, Clarksburg, Va.), merchant; *m* 2d, Oct. 6, 1825, Randolph Co., Va., Lucinda Earle; issue, 10 children;
2–Sarah Ann (2 below).
9–Sir Richard **Earle** (qv);
8–Sir John (1614-60), from Eng. ca. 1649-52, with his wife and three children, Samuel, John and Mary, and for paying the passage of 34 persons received land grants aggregating

1,700 acres located on Earle's Creek and Yoecomico River, now Northumberland Co., Va., which, exclusive of other patents subsequently granted by the lords proprietors of the Northern Neck, descended in a single male representative for 100 yrs.; *m* 1st, ca. 1637, Mary Symons (1619-59);

7–Samuel (1639-97), Westmoreland Co., Va.; *m* 1st, Bridget Hale (relative Sir Mathew Hale, celebrated mathematician);

6–Samuel (1680-1746), surveyor of highways; *m* Phyllis Bennet (relative Gov. Richard Bennet, of Va.); issue: Samuel, Elizabeth, Hannah and Phyllis;

5–Maj. Samuel (*d* 1771), Justice County Ct. of Frederick Co., Va.; colleague of Lord Fairfax, 1743-52; high sheriff; church warden; maj. Col. George W. Fairfax's regt. of horse; burgess, 1742-47; collector of tobacco, 1748; surveyor of highways, 1747; justice Co. Ct. of Prince William Co., Va., 1738; educated at William and Mary Coll.; atty. at law; planter; *m* 1st, 1726, Anna Sorrell (1707-Dec. 30, 1748), dau. of Thomas Sorrell, *m* Elizabeth–, of Westmoreland Co., Va.; *m* 2d, post 1748, Elizabeth Holbrook (*b* 1728; Randolph[6], of Prince William Co., Va.; *m* Jeannette–); issue, 1st and 2d marriages, 13 children;

4–Maj. Esais (also written Ezaias, Ezias and Esias), (*b* ca. 1753-*d* Oct. 30, 1826), of Frederick Co., Va.; planter; capt. 51st Regt. Va. Militia; promoted to maj., 1795; *m* Frederick Co., Va., Dec. 15, 1785, Sarah (Sally) Brownley (1768-1840; John[5], of Frederick Co., Va.); issue, 8 children;

3–Lucinda (1801-77), *b* in that part of Frederick Co., now Clarke Co., Va.; *m* Oct. 6, 1825, Randolph Co., Va., James **Carder** (3 above);

2–Sarah (Sally) Ann (*b* Beverly, Va., July 12, 1826-*d* W. Milford, Harrison Co., Va., Nov. 12, 1854), *m* Clarksburg, Va., July 6, 1847, Ebenezer Wilson **Patton** (*b* Harrison Co., Va., May 12, 1822-*d* Clarksburg, W.Va., Oct. 28, 1879), presiding justice of the Harrison Co. Ct., 1857-58; civil engr.; constructed the W. Milford and New Salem turnpike, 1850-52; hotel propr.; mcht.; atty.; issue, 5 children.

1–*m* Jan. 25, 1867, Capt. John Edgar Highland, of Harrison Co., W.Va. (Oct. 19, 1832-May 4, 1903); Union Civil War vet.; capt. 21st Regt., 2d Brig., 1st Div., W.Va. Militia; school teacher, merchant; farmer; issue (all *b* Harrison Co., W.Va.): 1–Charles Bruce, *b* Oct. 31, 1868; merchant; *m* Oct. 7, 1902, Jessie, dau. of Edgar Amos, *m* Dorcas Clayton; 2–Virgil Lee (qv for Highland lineage); 3–Franklin Earle, *b* Apr. 29, 1872; merchant; *m* Dec. 16, 1896, Estelle, dau. of Prof. Rupert Roland Powell, *m* Elizabeth Brockman, of Va. (issue: Aileene Earle, *b* Dec. 6, 1899; Elizabeth Celeste, *b* Oct. 2, 1902); 4–Isophene, *b* Nov. 18, 1874, *m* Oct. 7, 1896, Emory Ellis, son of Marshall Tetrick, *m* Rose Shinn (issue: Irene Highland, *b* Mar. 24, 1902; Virginia Earle, *b* Jan. 29, 1912; Highland Marshall, *b* June 24, 1916); 5–Cecil Blaine, *b* Nov. 2, 1876; elected to State Senate, 1924, from 2d dist.; dir. Empire Nat. Bank; owner Wetzel Republican; *m* Feb. 10, 1909, Ella Cox, dau. of Josephus Clark, *m* Lina R. Cox (issue: Virginia Lee, *b* Feb. 25, 1910; Cecil Blaine, Jr., *b* Nov. 23, 1918); 6–Scotland G. (qv).

1–**HIGHLAND, Virgil Lee,** *b* Harrison Co., W. Va., Aug. 31, 1870, 3 o'clock p.m.

12–Richard **Highland,** of Waldron, Co. Sussex, Eng., the testator of 1591; issue, 6 children;

11–Peter, *m* in Eng. ante 1581; issue, several children;

10–Thomas (bap. Waldron, Co. Sussex, Eng., June 29, 1581, *d* Waldron, Feb. 10, 1629/30), *m* May 17, 1597, Agnes, dau. of John Woodman, of Mayfield; issue, 11 children;

9–Thomas (bap. Waldron, Co. Sussex, Apr. 23, 1604, *d* Scituate, Mass., bet. Feb. 14, 1682/83 and May 3, 1683, on which latter date his will was probated), came from Tenterden, Co. Kent, Eng., with wife and 8 children to Scituate, where he was a propr., 1637; took oath of allegiance and was a freeman at Scituate, Feb. 1, 1638/39; juryman and town officer; *m* 1626, Deborah Highland; he left his son Thomas lands in Waldron and a house in Tenterden; issue, 8 children; his son Samuel *d* a soldier in King Philip's War, 1676;

8–Thomas (bap. Tenterden, Co. Kent, Eng., Nov. 15, 1629, *d* post 1683, Scituate); *m* Jan. 1, 1660/61, Elizabeth Stockbridge (John[9], who before 1657 built the Stockbridge mansionhouse, at Scituate, used as a garrison in King Philip's War); issue, 5 children (son Thomas *d* in Sir William Phipp's Canada expdn., 1690);

7–John (*b* Scituate, Mass., Mar. 17, 1669/70, *d* post 1712), *m* Jan. 3, 1693/94, Elizabeth James (William[8], of Scituate); issue, 8 children;

6–John (*b* Scituate, *d* New Castle Co., Del., June 15, 1744), *m* Mary Garretson (also spelled Garrison; Henry[7], of New Castle Co., Del.); issue, 3 children;

5–Henry (*b* New Castle Co., Del., June 12, 1741, *d* there 1786), *m* in Del., Dec. 26, 1765, Mary Robinson (also spelled Robeson; Richard[6], of New Castle Co., Del.); issue, 6 children;

4–John (*b* Newport, Del., Aug. 21, 1770, *d* Clarksburg, Va., now W.Va., Dec. 1, 1814, where he and his family settled Oct. 1, 1806); *m* First Bapt. Ch., Phila., Dec. 26, 1799, Telitha Batten (1776-1854; Francis[5], *m* 1762, Deborah Hoffman; Francis[6], *m* 1730, Anne Cheeseman, of Gloucester Co., N.J.); issue, 4 children;

3–Jacob (*b* nr. Clarksburg, Va., now W.Va., Sept. 4, 1808, *d* nr. W. Milford, W.Va., Mar. 16, 1880), *m* Feb. 28, 1828, Nancy Jane Williams (*b* Aug. 7, 1808, *d* Nov. 21, 1890; Nathaniel[4], *m* Elizabeth, dau. of Capt. David Maxwell [*b* 1750, *d* Harrison Co., Va., 1820], capt. Am. Rev. from Del.); issue, 9 children;

2–John Edgar (Oct. 19, 1832-May 4, 1903), *m* 1867, Lucinda Earle Patton (1851-1929), (qv).

1–*m* Dec. 31, 1902, Gertrude Elizabeth Morgan, *b* Webster, Taylor Co., W.Va., Mar. 14, 1871; dau. of Dr. David Porter Morgan (Desc. Col. Morgan Morgan), *m* Annette R. Shinn; issue (all *b* Clarksburg, W.Va.): 1–Stephen Lee, *b* Apr. 30, 1905; 2–Anita, *b* Aug. 23, 1907; 3–Linda Marion, *b* July 17, 1912; 4–Florence Jean, *b* Jan. 19, 1916.

1–Ed. Scio (O.) Coll. and G. W. Michael's Sch., Delaware, O. Dir. Merchants Nat. Bank; pres. Empire Nat. Bank, Clarksburg, and Clarksburg Pub. Co., owner Clarksburg Daily Telegram (see Who's Who in America). Clk. Harrison Co. Ct., 1897-1902. Del. Rep. Nat. Conv., 1904; chmn. Rep. State Com. (W.Va.), 1908-16; mem. Rep. Nat. Com. from W.Va., 1916-28. Chmn. State Pub. Service Commn., 1913. Candidate, Aug. 6, 1918, primaries for U.S. senator, failing of nomination by narrow margin. Mason (32°), Odd Fellow, Elk (dir.). Clubs: Bankers, Nat. Rep. (N.Y.), Country, Rotary. Mem. S.C.W. (Mass.), S.R. (W.Va.), Sons of Union Civil War Veterans. Baptist. Made tour of England, Scotland, France, Italy, Switzerland, Austria and Germany, 1927. Residence: Clarksburg, W.Va.

1–**HIGHLAND, Scotland G.,** *b* Harrison Co., W.Va., Aug. 7, 1879.

12–Richard **Highland,** of Waldron, Co. Sussex, Eng., the testator of 1591; issue, 6 children;

11–Peter, *m* in Eng. ante 1581; issue, several children;

10–Thomas (bap. Waldron, Co. Sussex, Eng., June 29, 1581, *d* Waldron, Feb. 10, 1629/30), *m* May 17, 1597, Agnes, dau. of John Woodman, of Mayfield; issue, 11 children;

9–Thomas (bap. Waldron, Co. Sussex, Apr. 23, 1604, *d* Scituate, Mass., bet. Feb. 14, 1682/83 and May 3, 1683, on which latter date his will was probated), came from Tenterden, Co. Kent, Eng., with wife and 8 children to Scituate, where he was a propr., 1637; took oath of allegiance and was a freeman at Scituate, Feb. 1, 1638/39; juryman and town officer; *m* 1626, Deborah Highland; he left his son Thomas lands in Waldron and a house in Tenterden; issue, 8 children (his son Samuel *d* soldier in King Philip's War, 1676);

8–Thomas (bap. Tenterden, Co. Kent, Eng., Nov. 15, 1629 *d* post 1683, Scituate); *m* Jan. 1, 1660/61, Elizabeth Stockbridge (John[9], who before 1657 built the Stockbridge mansionhouse, at Scituate, used as a garrison in King Philip's War); issue, 5 children (son Thomas *d* in Sir William Phipp's Canada expdn., 1690);

7–John (*b* Scituate, Mass., Mar. 17, 1669/70, *d*

post 1712), *m* Jan. 3, 1693/94, Elizabeth James (William[8], of Scituate); issue, 8 children;
6–John (*b* Scituate, *d* New Castle Co., Del., June 15, 1744), *m* Mary Garretson (also spelled Garrison; Henry[7], of New Castle Co., Del.); issue, 3 children;
5–Henry (*b* New Castle Co., Del., June 12, 1741, *d* there 1786), *m* in Del., Dec., 26, 1765, Mary Robinson (also spelled Robeson; Richard[6], of New Castle Co., Del.); issue, 6 children;
4–John (*b* Newport, Del., Aug. 21, 1770, *d* Clarksburg, Va., now W.Va., Dec. 1, 1814, where he and his family settled Oct. 1, 1806); *m* First Bapt. Ch., Phila., Dec. 26, 1799, Telitha Batten (1776-1854; Francis[5], *m* 1762, Deborah Hoffman; Francis[6], *m* 1730, Anne Cheeseman, of Gloucester Co., N.J.); issue, 4 children;
3–Jacob (*b* nr. Clarksburg, Va., now W.Va., Sept. 4, 1808, *d* nr. W. Milford, W.Va., Mar. 16, 1880), *m* Feb. 28, 1828, Nancy Jane Williams (*b* Aug. 7, 1808, *d* Nov. 21, 1890; Nathaniel[4], *m* Elizabeth, dau. of Capt. David Maxwell [*b* 1750, *d* Harrison Co., Va., 1820], capt. Am. Rev. from Del.); issue, 9 children;
2–John Edgar (2 below).
8–John **Smith** (*b* 1655, Co. Monaghan, Ulster, Ireland); his dau. Mary, *m* William Fulton, g.father of Robert Fulton (1765-1815), the inventor;
7–John (*b* 1686, Co. Monaghan, *d* Dec. 19, 1765), *m* in Ireland, 1713, Susanna (*b* Ireland, 1691, *d* Chester Co., Pa., Dec. 24, 1767); came to America, 1720; settled in Chester Co., Pa., 1720; planter; stone dwelling built by him in Chester Co. is now (1930) standing; mem. Brandywine Manor Presbyn. Ch., Chester Co.; issue, 11 children;
6–Mary (*b* Chester Co., Pa., ca. 1735, *d* Weston, Harrison Co., Va., Aug. 11, 1799), *m* 1760, Alexander **Lewis** (*b* 1730, *d* Lost Creek, Harrison Co., Va., now W.Va., Dec. 13, 1814, where he had settled ca. 1799); merchant, Lewisburg, Pa., 1790-97; extensive landowner in Chester, Lancaster and Northumberland cos. Pa., 1765-97; erected stone dwelling house, Lewisburgh, Pa., 1790-91; issue, 8 children;
5–Susanna (*b* Chester Co., Pa., Nov. 5, 1761, *d* nr. West Milford, Harrison Co., Va., July 28, 1828), 2d cousin of Robert Fulton, the inventor; *m* 1786, William **Patton** (*b* Lancaster Co., Pa., Apr. 21, 1761, *d* nr. W. Milford, Harrison Co., Va., July 28, 1826), soldier Am. Rev., 1780-81, from Lancaster Co., Pa.; settled on Duck Creek, Harrison Co., Va., ca. 1799; farmer; stockman; issue, 9 children;
4–Col. Alexander Lewis (*b* Lancaster Co., Pa., July 23, 1789, *d* nr. W. Milford, W.Va., May 21, 1866), *m* 1st, Clarksburg, Va., July 19, 1814, Ruth Smith (*b* Clermont Co., O., May 31, 1798, *d* nr. W. Milford, Va., Aug. 7, 1848, dau. of James Smith, *m* (Esther), also called "Hettie," Hester, 1797, dau. Rev. Isaac Morris, *b* Berks Co., Pa., 1740, *d* Harrison Co., Va., 1830, *m* Ruth Henton, *b* Va., 1750, *d* Harrison Co., Va., 1839, parents of 12 children among whom were Hester Morris, above named (*b* Berks Co., Pa., Monday, May 27, 1771,-*d* nr. New Hope, Brown Co., O., July 28, 1854), of Clermont Co., O., emigrated from Harrison Co., Va., to ty., now Clermont Co., O., 1796, parent of 4 children; and Thomas Morris, *b* Berks Co., Pa., Jan. 3, 1776, *d* Clermont Co., O., Dec. 7, 1844, emigrated from Harrison Co., Va., to ty. now Ohio, 1795; *m* Nov. 19, 1797, Rachel Davis, 1779-1853; atty., elected Ohio legislature, 1806; served in general assembly 24 yrs.; elected U.S. senator from Ohio 1832, serving from Dec. 1833 to Mar. 4, 1839; nominee of Liberal party, Aug. 30, 1843, for v.p. of U.S. on ticket with J. G. Birney; "His memory should be kept freshly living among the lovers of liberty and progress," was the language of Hon. Salmon P. Chase, of Ohio, on hearing of the death of Sen. Morris; nationally known for his debate Feb. 9, 1839 in federal senate on abolition of slavery with Henry Clay and John C. Calhoun); Col. Alexander Lewis Patton, preceding, was promoted to rank of col. in the 11th regt. of Va. Militia, 1826 (succeeding Col. Jonathan Jackson, father of Gen. Thomas J. "Stonewall" Jackson); justice Harrison Co. Ct., 1834-35, and 1846-47; farmer; stockman; issue, 11 children;
3–Ebenezer Wilson (*b* Harrison Co., Va., May 12, 1822, *d* Clarksburg, W.Va., Oct. 28, 1879), presiding justice of the Harrison Co. Ct., 1857-58; civil engr.; constructed the W. Milford and New Salem turnpike, 1850-52; hotel propr.; mcht.; atty.; *m* 2d, Clarksburg, Va., July 6, 1847, Sarah (Sally) Ann Carder (*b* Beverly, Va., July 12, 1826, *d* W. Milford, Harrison Co., Va., Nov. 12, 1854);
2–Lucinda Earle (2 below).
5–Sanford **Carder** (*b* Culpeper Co., Va., Sept. 16, 1760, removed to Hampshire Co., and lastly to Fayette Co., O., where he *d* Aug. 7, 1845), *m* 1st, ca. 1789-90, Nancy Hoffman (*d* ante 1827; Conrad[6]), soldier Am. Rev.;
4–James (*b* 1791, Hampshire Co., Va., *d* 1859, Clarksburg, Va.), merchant; hotel propr.; *m* 2d, Oct. 6, 1825, Randolph Co., Va., Lucinda Earle; issue, 10 children;
3–Sarah (Sally) Ann (*b* Beverly, Va., July 12, 1826, *d* W. Milford, Harrison Co., Va., Nov. 12, 1854), *m* Clarksburg, Va., July 6, 1847, Ebenezer Wilson **Patton** (3 above).
10–Sir Richard **Earle,** of Dorset Co., Eng., desc. Henry de Erleigh from lordship of Erleigh; was Lord of Newton, and desc. Sir John Earle (1334-1410), known as the "White Knight," who *m* Margaret, dau. of Sir Guy de Brian; original ancestor went to Eng. with William the Conqueror;
9–Sir John (1614-60), from Eng. ca. 1649-52, with his wife and three children, Samuel, John and Mary, and for paying the passage of 34 persons received land grants aggregating 1,700 acres located on Earle's Creek and Yoecomico River, now Northumberland Co., Va., which, exclusive of other patents subsequently granted by the lords proprietors of the Northern Neck, descended in a single male representative for 100 yrs.; *m* 1st, ca. 1637, Mary Symons (1619-59);
8–Samuel (1639-97), Westmoreland Co., Va., *m* 1st, Bridget Hale (relative Sir Mathew Hale, celebrated mathematician);
7–Samuel (1680-1746), surveyor of highways; *m* Phyllis Bennet (relative Gov. Richard Bennet, of Va.); issue: Samuel, Elizabeth, Hannah, and Phyllis;
6–Maj. Samuel (*d* 1771), justice Co. Ct. of Frederick Co., Va.; colleague of Lord Fairfax, 1743-52; high sheriff; church warden; maj. Col. George W. Fairfax's regt. of Horse; burgess, 1742-47; collector of tobacco, 1748; surveyor of highways, 1747; justice Co. Ct. of Prince William Co., Va., 1738; ed. William and Mary Coll.; atty. at law; planter; *m* 1st, 1726, Anna Sorrell (1707-Dec. 30, 1748), dau. of Thomas Sorrell, *m* Elizabeth–, of Westmoreland Co., Va.; *m* 2d, post 1748, Elizabeth Holbrook (*b* 1728; Randolph[7], of Prince William Co., Va., *m* Jeannette–); issue, 1st and 2d marriages, 13 children;
5–Maj. Esaias (also written Ezaias, Ezias and Esias), *b* ca. 1753, *d* Oct. 30, 1826, of Frederick Co., Va.; planter; capt. 51st Regt. Va. Militia; promoted to maj., 1795; *m* Frederick Co., Va., Dec. 15, 1785, Sarah (Sally) Brownley (1768-1840; John[6], of Frederick Co., Va.); issue, 8 children;
4–Lucinda (1801-77), *b* in that part of Frederick Co., now Clarke Co., Va.; *m* Oct. 6, 1825, Randolph Co., Va., James **Carder** (4 above).
2–Lucinda Earle Patton (qv), *m* Jan. 25, 1867, Capt. John Edgar **Highland,** of Harrison Co., W.Va. (Oct. 19, 1832-May 4, 1903); Union Civil War vet.; capt. 21st Regt., 2d Brig., 1st Div., W.Va. Militia; school teacher; merchant; farmer.
1–Not married. Ed. public schools at W. Milford, W.Va. U., Iron City Coll., Pittsburgh, Pa., and G. W. Michael's School, Logansport, Ind. Gen. mgr. Clarksburg, W.Va., water plant and system since Feb. 1, 1906; author of standard sanitary plumbing code; Highland genealogy; contributes to newspapers and to the technical press. Mem. S.C.W., Lancaster Co. (Pa.) Hist. Soc., S.R., I.A.G., Am. Water Works Assn., N.E. Water Works Assn., Am. Soc. Municipal Improvements. Hydraulic engr.; authority on stream purification and sewage disposal; author of treatise on abolition of death penalty. Mem. Sons of Union Civil War Veterans. Mason. M.P. Church. Owns rare library. Residence: Clarksburg, W.Va.

DR. GEORGE ADDSION BAXTER (b Rockingham Co., Va., July 22, 1771-d April 14, 1841), one of the numerous preachers and teachers who studied under William Graham at Liberty Hall; licensed to preach, 1797, and became widely known among the Presbyterian clergy of Va. and Md.; became prof. mathematics and natural philosophy, Liberty Hall, 1798, and on the death of Mr. Graham, was chosen as principal of the academy, which in 1813 became Washington College and later Washington and Lee U.; continued as president until 1829, a period of 30 years, the longest administration of the presidents of that institution; during his presidency he continued as pastor of the Presbyterian Church in Lexington; prof. Theology, Union Theological Seminary, Hampden-Sidney, 1832-41.

1–**HILKEY, Charles Joseph,** *b* Greenfield, Mo., Aug. 12, 1880.
6–Lt. Jacob **Warwick,** from Eng., 1740; settled Augusta Co., Va.; *m* 1741, Elizabeth Dunlap, of Middlebrook, Va.;
5–Jacob (1743-1826), of Pocahontas Co., W.Va.; served on frontier as pvt. and lt. during Am. Rev.; Indian scout and did heroic work at Battle of Pt. Pleasant; commd. 1st lt., May 21, 1778; *m* 1765, Mary Vance (1743-1823), of Mountain Grove, Bath Co., Va. (Col. John[6], of N.C.);
4–Margaret (1773-1855), of Pocahontas Co.; *m* 1794, Adam **See** (1764-1850), of Randolph Co., W.Va.;
3–Jacob Warwick (1798-1862), of Randolph Co.; *m* 1825, Mary Anne Baxter;
2–Margaret Elizabeth (2 below).
5–William **Fleming** (1729-95), from Jedburgh, Scotland, 1755; settled Belmont, Botetourt Co., Va.; active in Indian campaigns in Va.; col. of regt. Va. militia, from Botetourt at Pt. Pleasant, under Gen. Lewis; severely wounded and reported killed; in frontier defense during Am. Rev.; co. lt., Botetourt Co., 1776; senator, 2 terms, under Va. Constn. of 1776; actg. gov. Va., June 1781, and called out militia to resist invasion of Lord Cornwallis, 1781; mem. Va. conv., 1788, and voted to ratify Federal Constn.; heir to earldom of Wighton; *m* 1763, Anne Christian (1743-1810; Capt. Israel[6], for whom Christiansburg, Va., was named);
4–Anne (1777-1846), of Belmont, Va.; *m* 1798, Dr. George Addison **Baxter** (1771-1841), see portrait and biography (Sidney S. Baxter, atty. gen. Va., 1834-52, was their son);
3–Mary Anne (1805-74), of Lexington, Va.; *m* 1825, Jacob Warwick **See** (3 above);
2–Margaret Elizabeth (1837-1918), of Tucker Co., W.Va.; *m* 1865, John Lyon **Hilkey** (1829-88), farmer; issue: I–Mary Jane (*b* 1866; *m* Josiah V. Carr); II–Lavinia (*d* infancy); III–John Christian (*b* 1871; *m* Louise Kinley); IV–Charles Joseph (1 above); V–James Edward (*b* 1882; *m* Grace Goodman).
1–Not married. A.B., Coll. of Emporia (Kan.), '05; A.M., U.Kan.; 1907; Ph.D., Columbia, 1910; J.D., U.Mich., 1915; S.J.D., Harvard, 1924. Instr. and prof. law, since 1910; dean, Lamar Sch. of Law, Emory U., since 1925. Author (see Who's Who in America). Mem. Am. Bar Assn., Am. Law Inst., Gamma Eta Gamma, Sigma Alpha Epsilon, Order of the Coif, S.A.R. Mason (32°). Club: Faculty. Presbyn. Republican. Address: Emory U., Atlanta, Ga.

1–**HILL, David Jayne,** *b* Plainfield, N.J., June 10, 1850.
7–John **Hill** (1624-85), from Eng. to Boston, 1640, later settled at Dover, N.H.; *m* 1656, Elizabeth Strong;
6–Joseph (1658-1713), *m* Susanna Beedle;
5–Samuel (1690-1775), *m* Hannah Allen;
4–Isaac (1724-1807), *m* Lydia Roberts;
3–Isaac (1759-1814), *m* Juliana Reeder (Capt. Jacob[4], master armorer Cont. Army; g.dau. Nathaniel Jayne, soldier Am. Rev.);
2–Rev. Daniel Trembly (2 below).
7–Rev. William **Thompson** (1597-1666);
6–John (*d* 1688), *m* Hannah Brewster;
5–William (*b* 1665), *m* Ruth Avery;
4–William (*b* 1710), *m* Mary Catlin;
3–William Catlin (1752-1832), *m* Tabitha Hunt;
2–Lydia Ann (1809-54), *m* Rev. Daniel Trembly **Hill** (1803-87); issue: I–Isaac Newton (1828-96; *m* Annie M. Andrews); II–Elizabeth Manning (1832-97; *m* Samuel T. Merritt); III–Lydia Ann (1840-95; *m* William L. Brown); IV–David Jayne (1 above).
1–*m* Aug. 25, 1874, Anna Liddell (May 7, 1852-Mar. 1880); dau. Walter James Forbes Liddell, Erie, Pa.; issue: 1–Walter Liddell, *b* Lewisburg, Pa., Aug. 7, 1875.
1–*m* 2d, June 6, 1886, Juliet Lewis Packer (Oct. 2, 1855-Jan. 16, 1923); dau. Judge Hezekiah Packer, Williamsport, Pa.; issue: 1–Catharine Josephine Packer and 2–David Jayne, Jr. (twins), *b* Rochester, N.Y., May 19, 1890.
1–A.B., Bucknell, '74, A.M., 1877; univs. of Berlin and Paris; (LL.D., Colgate, U.Pa., Union, Bowdoin; Docteur es Lettres, U.Geneva; D.C.L., Bucknell). Educator, historian, diplomat. Pres. Bucknell U., 1879-88, U.Rochester, 1888-96; asst. sec. of state, 1898-1903; E.E. and M.P. to Switzerland, 1903-05, to the Netherlands, 1905-07; A.E. and P. to Germany, 1908-11. Del. 2d Peace Conf., The Hague, 1907. Grand Cordon of the House of Orange, Grand Officer of the Legion of Honor. Mem. Am. Acad. Arts and Letters, etc. (see Who's Who in America). Clubs: Authors, Century, Republican, University (New York), Metropolitan, Cosmos (Washington), L'Union Interalliée (Paris). Residence: 1745 R.I. Av., Washington, D.C.

1–**HILL, Grace Annie,** *b* Richmond, Va., Apr. 4, 1878.
9–"Mr." William **Hill** (*d* 1649; son of James, mayor of Lyme Regis, Dorsetshire, Eng.); came from Eng. in the "William and Francis," 1632; settled at Dorchester, Mass.; selectman, 1636; rep. Gen. Ct., 1636; removed to Windsor, Conn., rep. in Gen. Ct. at Hartford, 1639,40,44; removed to Fairfield, 1644; auditor of public accounts, 1639; *m* 1619, Sarah Jourdain (*b* 1598/99; Ignatius[10] [1561-1640], mayor, 1617, dep. mayor, 1624, during plague, mem. of Parliament from Exeter, 1625,27,28, armiger, *m* 2d, 1593, Elizabeth [1576-1649], dau. of Thomas Baskerville, armiger; William[11], armiger);
8–"Mr." William (1629-84), town clk., 1650-84; rep. Conn. Gen. Ct., 1651-55,58,59,61, 1665-71; commissary for expdn. against the Dutch, 1653; registrar of deeds, 1654; asst. to Probate Ct., 1658; first Fairfield collector of customs, 1659; townsman, 1661; clk. of Fairfield Co. Ct., 1666; commr., 1666-70, 1672-78; commr. of United Colonies, 1675, Narragansett War; mem. standing council of War, 1676, King Philip's War; surveyor of towns and highways, 1667-68,70; town agent, 1669-70, to purchase land from Indians; nominated asst. judge of Gen. Ct., 1671; granted 150 acres of land, 1672; *m* Elizabeth Jones (1635-post 1684; Rev. John[9], from Eng. in the "Defence," to Boston, 1635, founder and pastor of Concord Ch., 1637; first min-

ister, 1644-65, of Fairfield, Conn., *m* in Eng., Sarah–, *b* 1601);
7–"Mr." William (1661-1739), dea. Congl. Ch., Fairfield; *m* 1st, 1691, Abigail Osborn (Capt. David[8] [*d* 1679], *m* 1669, Abigail, dau. of Col. Philip Pinckney; Capt. Richard[9], from Eng. in the "Hopewell," 1634);
6–"Mr." Joseph (1699-1797), of Fairfield and Greenfield, Conn.; dea. Congl. Ch., Greenfield Hill, Conn.; *m* 1731, Abigail Dimon (Capt. Moses[7], *m* Jane, dau. of Col. Philip Pinckney, qv; Moses[8], *m* Abigail, dau. of Gov. Andrew Ward, qv; Thomas[9]);
5–Maj. Jabez (1744-79), cornetist 2d Troop of Horse, 4th regt., Conn. Colony, 1769, Seven Years War; capt. 1774, 2d Troop of Horse, 4th Regt., Conn. Colony in Am. Rev.; promoted to maj. of 3d Conn. Regt. Light Horse Militia, 1776; *m* as her 1st husband, Sarah Read (1751-1809; Col. John[6], Am. Rev.; "Hon." John[7]; William[8]; William[9]);
4–Moses (ca. 1777-ante 1821), of Weston, Conn., and Huntington, L.I.; *m* ca. 1805, Phebe Robertson (1788-1837; Thomas[5], of Brookhaven and Huntington, L.I., *m* 2d, Elizabeth Soper);
3–Rev. William (1814-51), Presbyn. minister; Amherst Coll., 1833; principal Canterbury Acad., Orange Co., N.Y.; *m* 1836, Mary Benton Barnard;
2–Rowland (2 below).
9–Richard **Case** (*d* 1694), of Windsor and Hartford, Conn.; *m* 1663, Elizabeth Purchase (*d* post 1694; John[10]);
8–John (post 1669-1725), *m* Sarah Arnold (Henry[9], *m* Elizabeth, dau. of William Colfax, *d* 1660);
7–Mary (1711-54), *m* John **Barnard** (*d* 1771);
6–Samuel (bet. 1736-42-1805), French and Indian War and Am. Rev.; grand juror, 1779; *m* 1758, Abigail Gibbs (1742-1816; Henry[7], *m* Abigail Martin; Benjamin[8]; Samuel[9]; Giles[10]);
5–Samuel (1763-1828), War 1812; *m* 1784, Mary Benton (1763-86; Ebenezer[6], Am. Rev., *m* Amy Horsford; Ebenezer[7]; Ens. Ebenezer[8]; Daniel[9]; Edward[10]; Andrew[11]; Edward[12]);.
4–Benton (1786-1855), *m* 1811, Elizabeth Rea (1785-1853; William[5], Am. Rev., *m* Hannah Gibbs; John[6]; John[7]; John[8]; Joshua[9]; Daniel[10], of Suffolk, Eng., and Salem Village);
3–Mary Benton (1816-62), *m* Rev. William **Hill** (3 above).
10–Gov. John **Coggeshall** (qv);
9–Anne (1626-89), *m* 1643, Peter **Easton** (1622-94), from Eng. to Ipswich, 1634, Newbury, Mass., 1635, Hampton, N.H., 1638; Pocasset, R.I., 1638; a founder of Newport, 1639; sgt., 1644; freeman, 1655; commr., 1660-61; rep. Gen. Ct., 1661, 1671-75, 1680-81; gen. treas., 1672-77; atty. gen., 1674-76 (Gov. Nicholas[10], qv);
8–Waite (1668-1725), *m* John **Carr** (1664-1714), inherited home of his father at Newport, 1695 (Gov. Caleb[9], qv);
7–Patience (1709-1788), *m* 2d, 1730, Edward **Estes** (Richard[8], *m* Elizabeth Beck; Robert[9], of Eng.);
6–Waite (*b* 1733), *m* 1751, Lemuel **Jones,** Sr. (*b* 1730), Friend Minister (Thomas[7]);
5–Stephen (1766-1850), of Durham, Me.; Friend; *m* 1786, Eunice Hacker (1766-1853; Jeremiah[6], *m* 2d, Anne Southwick; Isaac[7]; George[8]);
4–Josiah (1792-1867), Friend; *m* 1825, Mary Austin (1798-1831; Jedediah[5], *m* Miriam Winslow; Benjamin[6]; Benjamin[7]; Thomas[8]; Joseph[9]);
3–Samuel Hopkins (1828-1904), Friend; educator, preacher; *m* 1851, Margaret Buffum Hawkes-Nichols (1829-73), adopted dau. of Caleb Nichols, and Eunice Hobby (Isaac Hawkes[4]; Lemuel[5]; Nathaniel[6]; Ebenezer[7]; Ebenezer[8]; John[9], *m* Sarah, dau. of Elder Thomas Cushman, *m* Mary, dau. of Isaac Allerton, Mayflower Pilgrim, qv);
2–Ann Maria (1852-1926), *m* 1871, Rowland **Hill** (1839-99), ed. Morris Acad. for Boys, Litchfield, Conn., and N.Y. City; merchandise broker, Richmond, Va.; mem. Common Council, 2 yrs.; mem. Bd. of Alderman, 4 yrs.; issue: I–Mary Barnard (*b* 1872; *m* 1903, Lindley Murray Binford, *b* 1864); II–Rowland, Jr. (1874-75); III–(Alferetta) Etta Margaret (*b* 1876; *m* 1906, Isaac Carrington Morton); IV–Grace Annie (1 above); V–Harriett Ross (*b* 1880); VI–William Rowland (*b* 1883; *m* 1812, Elizabeth Eugenia Lanier, *b* 1888, issue: Margaret Lanier, William R., Jr., Anne Bradstreet, Lewis Birchett, Lindley Binford, Elizabeth Anne).
1–Grad. City Normal Sch., 1895; thrice Peabody Medalist; pupil Harrisonburg, Va., State Normal four sessions, U.Va., summer sch. Teacher mathematics, Bellevue Junior High School. Mem. S.M.D., D.A.C., D.A.R., Am. Flag House and Betsy Ross Mem. Assn., Ams. of Royal Descent, life mem. Presbyn. League which owns and operates The Collegiate Sch. for Girls, Richmond, Va. Residence: The Shenandoah, Lee Circle, Richmond, Va.

1–**HILL, Fannie Ten Broeck Gillett (Mrs. James H.),** *b* Dawson, Ill., Mar. 22, 1863.
9–Jonathan **Gillett** (qv);
8–Joseph (bap. 1641-1675), one of the earliest settlers at Deerfield, Mass.; killed in King Philip's War; *m* 1664, Elizabeth Hawks (John[9]);
7–John (1671-1755), *m* 1700, Experience Dewey;
6–Ebenezer (1705-76), *m* 1730, Mary Ordway (1712-1791);
5–Lt. Israel (bap. 1738-1829), patriot Am. Rev.; *m* 2d, 1764, Susanna Durkee (*d* 1821);
4–Roger (1767-1819), *m* 1788, Mary Marsh (Capt. Abel[5], officer Am. Rev., desc. John Marsh, *m* Ann, dau. Gov. John Webster, qv);
3–Bezaleel (1789-1869), *m* 1830, Elizabeth Brewster Day (Samuel[4], desc. Robert Day, an original settler at Hartford, 1636; William Collier, asst. gov. Plymouth Colony; Elder William Brewster, qv);
2–Dr. Leslie Kemper (1836-Apr. 24, 1899), Beatrice, Neb., *m* Lucy Ann Cass (1836-1908); for issue see Vol. I, p. 342.
1–*m* Sept. 23, 1884, James Hamilton Hill, *b* N.Y. City, Mar. 29, 1858; son of Henry Hickson Hill, from Scotland, *m* Sarah Jane Hamilton, of Co. Monaghan, Ireland; issue: 1–Marian, *b* Lawrence, Kan., July 24, 1885; *m* 1907, Latham Marshall Higgins; 2–Gillette (see Vol. I, p. 343); 3–Beatrice Frances, *b* Beatrice, Neb., Dec. 4, 1897; *m* June 10, 1920, Earnest Bethune Erskine.
1–Ed. St. Mary's School, Knoxville, Ill., '81. Mem. C.D.A., D.A.R., I.A.G. Winter place: Galveston, Tex. Residence: 103 Franklin St., Denver, Colo.

1–**HILL, John Wilson,** *b* Ottawa, Ill., May 9, 1857.
8–Joseph (Hilles) **Hills** (1602-88; son of George Hilles); woolen draper in Eng.; came from Eng. in the "Susan and Ellen," 1638, to Boston, settled at Charlestown; selectman, 1644; rep. Charlestown in Gen. Ct., 1646,47, and was chosen speaker of its House of Deputies; capt. Train Band; dep., Malden; granted 500 acres on the Nassua River in N.H.; ruling elder; magistrate; compiler of Mass. laws, 1648; *m* 2d, 1651, Hannah Smith, widow of Edward Mellows;
7–Samuel (1652-1732), sgt. in King Philip's War, and was at the battles of Bloody Brook and Narragansett, 1675; *m* 1679, Abigail Wheeler (1655-1742; David[8] [*b* 1625], came to N.E. in the "Confidence," 1638, *m* 1650, Sarah Wise; John[9]);
6–Benjamin (1684-1762), *m* 1709, Rebecca Ordway (1690-1769; Hananiah[7], *m* Abigail–; James[8]);
5–Samuel (1710-62), *m* 2d, 1743, Elizabeth Swain (*d* 1793);
4–Reuben (1752-1828), served at Battle of Bunker Hill; settled at Hawke (now Danville), Rockingham Co., N. H.; removed to Warren, Knox Co., Me., ca. 1784, to Union, Me., ca. 1802; *m* 1779, Sarah Currier (1758-1825; Gideon[5], of Chester, N.H.);
3–Nathan (1784-1858), *m* 1807, Mary Ware (1787-1875);
2–Isaac (2 below).
4–Maj. Gen. George **Ulmer,** from Prussia with two brothers, 1755, and settled at Duck Trap, Me.; *m* 1780, Mary Tanner;
3–Mary, *m* John **Wilson** (1783-1848), from Eng.
2–Isaac **Hills** (1811-86), enlisted for Mexican War, but did not arrive at the front; raised a co. of soldiers early in the Civil War and was elected its capt.; taught school at Ottawa, Ill.; *m* 1833, Eliza Hall, of Cushing, Knox Co.; *m* 2d, 1844, Sarah Augusta Wilson (1822-94), of Belfast, Waldo Co., Me.; issue (1st marriage): I–Lysander (1834-1914; *m* 1864, Adelaide R. Cole, *d* 1897; *m* 2d, 1904, Edith Healy); II–Elizabeth Malcolm (1835-74; *m* John P. Pond; *m* 2d, Willard Gould); III–Sylvanus (1836-1910; *m* Viola Sanborn); IV–Ernestine (1842-92; *m* 1858, Charles P. Hinman, 1830-97); issue

(2d marriage): I–Nathan F. (1845-96; *m* 1867, Flora J. Reed, 1847-1900); II–Mary W. (1847-51); III–Isaac (1849-1926; *m* 1878, Ginevra Harper, 1849-1920); IV–Mary A. (1852-1915; *m* 1876, David A. Welsh, 1842-1900); V–John Wilson (1 above); VI–Charles Wilford (writes name Hills; *b* 1860; *m* 1887, Anna Corcoran, *b* 1864); VII–Henry Arthur (*b* 1863; *m* 1885, Anna Alice Little, 1861-1922; *m* 2d, 1924, Edith Curtis, *b* 1873); VIII–Burton Ulmer (*b* 1866; *m* 1889, Inez (Evans) Curtz, *b* 1869).

1–*m* Sept. 28, 1878, Ida E. Watson, *b* Clarkston, Mich., Nov. 9, 1858; dau. of Thomas Watson; issue: 1–Roy Wilson, *b* Frankfort, Mich., Jan. 12, 1881; B.S., Rose Polytechnic Inst., '04; LL.B., Northwestern U., 1907; lawyer; capt. Q.M.C., 1917-18; maj. engr. Reserve, U.S.A.; *m* Oct. 2, 1909, Rose A., dau. of William Loehde (issue: John W., II, *b* Nov. 12, 1913).

1–Patent and trade mark lawyer, Chicago, since 1891; now sr. mem. Hill and Hill. Mem. Ill. Legislature, 1904-08; chmn. com. investigating state charitable institutions, author of bill creating state bd. control for same. Mem. O.F.P.A., S.A.R. Mason (33°), Odd Fellow. Clubs: Chicago Athletic, Hamilton. Summer place: Frankfort, Mich. Residence: 1121 Columbia Av., Chicago, Ill.

1–**HILL, Joseph Adams,** *b* Portland, Ore., Aug. 19, 1880.

7–Dea. Joseph **Hill** (1699-1797), *m* 1731, Abigail Dimon (*d* 1774);

6–Capt. Ebenezer (1741-98), of 7th Regt., Conn. Line; *m* 1765, Mabel Sherwood (1745-1820);

5–Seth (1769-1821), squire; *m* 1793, Cynthia Banks (1772-1831);

4–Wakeman (1804-70), *m* 1827, Eunice Lyon (1806-70);

3–Joseph Wakeman (1832-64), of Westport, Conn.; *m* 1854, Ann Rebecca Wood (1835-1914);

2–Joseph Wood (2 below).

9–Edward **Adams** (*d* 1671), from Eng., 1640, to New Haven Colony; at Milford, Conn., 1646, Fairfield, 1650; *m* Margaret Savage;

8–Nathan, of Fairfield; *m* Mary James (Joseph[9], *m* Mary–);

7–Nathan (bap. 1694), *m* Rebecca Clapham (Peter[8]);

6–Nathan, lt. in Am. Rev.; *m* Mary Burr (Daniel[7], *m* Mary–);

5–Aaron, *m* 1st, 1784, Rhoda Hanford (Phineas[6]);

4–Jabez (*b* 1785), *m* Anna Bennett;

3–George S., *m* Polly Coley;

2–Jessie Katherine (1856-1901), *m* 1878, Joseph Wood **Hill** (*b* 1856), B.A., Yale, '78; M.D., Willamette U., 1881; in charge of Bishop Scott Acad., Portland, Ore., from 1878, now retired; issue: I–Joseph Adams (1 above); II–George Wakeman (1885-95); III–Benjamin Wood (*b* 1890; *m* 1929, Olive Gunderson).

1–*m* June 25, 1919, Edith Knight, *b* Colo., July 22, 1878; dau. of R. B. Knight, of Portland, Ore.

1–Ph.B., Yale-S., 1902; made hon. mem. class of '78, in which father was grad. With Am. Steel & Wire Co., Lake Erie Nail & Supply Co., and geol. dept. U.S. Govt. until 1906; mgr. East Side Fuel Co., Portland, 1906-07; elected v.p. Hill Mil. Acad., Portland, 1908, pres. and business mgr. since 1914. Active against compulsory edn. bill of Ore. (passed by popular vote Nov. 7, 1922), which aimed to close pvt. grade schools in Ore.; instituted suit vs. State of Ore. in Federal Ct. and won unanimous decision, 1925, against Ore. Compulsory Edn. Bill. Mem. S.A.R. Episcopalian. Republican. Clubs: University, Multnomah Amateur Athletic, Lions, East Side Commercial, Chamber of Commerce. Residence: 821 Marshall St., Portland, Ore.

1–**HILL, Mary Pelham,** *b* Phippsburg, Me., Dec. 18, 1865.

8–Peter **Hill** (qv);

7–Roger (1635-96), of Biddeford, Me.; selectman, 1685-86; "prudential man," 1660 and later; *m* 1658, Mary Cross (*d* 1696; John[8], *m* Frances–);

6–Dea. Ebenezer (1679-1748), settled at Biddeford, 1703, soon after was carried into captivity by several Indians who professed to be friendly, called in the usual manner and partook of food offered them, then decamped with their prisoners to Can., where they remained 3 years; dea. First Ch., Biddeford, 1730; *m* 1702/03, Abiel Snell (1677-1750; Capt. George[7], of Portsmouth, N.H.);

5–Jeremiah (1724-79), of Biddeford; rep. Gen. Ct.; served in Am. Rev.; mem. Provincial Congress; justice of peace, York Co., 1761-79; *m* 2d, 1768, Mary (Langdon) Storer (*d* 1806; John Langdon[6], of Portsmouth, N.H., *m* Mary Hall);

4–Hon. Mark Langdon (1772-1842), of Phippsburg, Me.; rep. to U.S. Congress, 1819-23; overseer Bowdoin Coll., trustee, 1821,42; collector of port at Bath, 1824; judge Ct. of Sessions; postmaster of Phippsburg; *m* 1797, Mary McCobb (1775-1817; James[5], of Phippsburg, *m* Mrs. Hannah [Nichols] Miller, formerly of Bristol, Me.);

3–Capt. John Langdon (1797-1847), of Phippsburg; *m* 1819, Silence Alexander Cushing (1799-1886; Christopher[4], *m* Eleanor, dau. Joshua Philbrook, *m* Elizabeth Alexander, of Bath, Me.);

2–Capt. George Langdon (2 below).

9–Tobias **Langdon** (*d* 1664), Portsmouth, N.H.; *m* 1656, Elizabeth Sherburn;

8–Capt. Tobias (1660-1725), *m* 1686, Mary Hubbard (Richard[9], *m* Martha Allen);

7–John (1708-80), *m* Mary Hall (Josiah[8], *m* Mary Woodbury);

6–John (1741-1819), four times gov. of N.H.; U.S. senator and pres. pro tem. of the Senate; *m* 1776, Elizabeth Sherburne (John[7]);

5–Mary (*d* 1806), as Widow Storer, *m* 2d, Jeremiah **Hill** (5 above).

7–Peter **Pelham** (ca. 1670-1756);

6–Peter (*d* 1751), *m* 2d, 1734, Margaret (Beath) Lowrey;

5–Thomas (*d* 1770), *m* Hannah (Cooper) Garrish (1730-ca. 1780; Edward Cooper[6], *m* 3d, 1729, Mrs. Mary [Southack] Fifield);

4–Mary (1766-1841), *m* 1785, Joseph **Beath** (1740-1828), naval officer in Am. Rev. (John[5], naval officer in Am. Rev.);

3–Hannah Cooper (1786-1873), *m* 1807, Robert **Larrabee** (1785-1863);

2–Anna Cummings (1826-88), *m* 1849, Capt. George Langdon **Hill** (1820-79), sea capt.; issue: I–George William (1850-1916; *m* 1871, Ella Florence Noyes); II–Mark Langdon (1851-96; *m* Hattie Dyer); III–Lillie (1854-65); IV–Annie Cummings (*b* 1856; *m* Rev. Frank Louis Bristol, *d* 1917); V–Emma Crosby (1860-61); VI–Charles Crosby (1864-65); VII–Mary Pelham (1 above); VIII–Hannah Larrabee (*b* 1866).

1–Published Vital Records of Topsham, Me., from the earliest date to 1892, also at work on the Vital Records of Phippsburg, Me., for same dates. Mem. D.A.R. (chapter pres., nat. v.chmn. geneal. research com., organized Topsham-Brunswick Chapter, organized Me. Soc. of Chapter Founders), U.S.D. 1812, Me. Hist. Soc., I.A.G. Congregational. Republican. Residence: 10 Elm St., Topsham, Me.

1–**HILLES, T(homas) Allen,** *b* Wilmington, Del., Jan. 21, 1852.

7–William **Evans**, from Wales, ca. 1698; settled 1st in Gwynedd Tp., later removed to Limerick, Phila. Co., Pa.; *m* Ann– (*b* Wales-will proved 1720);

6–William (*d* 1758), farmer; overseer Providence Meeting, 1745; *m* 1728/29, Rachel Roberts;

5–Ann (*d* ante 1761), *m* 1748, Hugh ("Ellis") **Hilles** (ca. 1715-will proved 1756), from Ireland ca. 1748, settled at Gwynned, Pa. (son of David, and probably desc. Richard Hilles [ca. 1514-1586 or 87], Master of Merchant Taylors' guild, prominent English reformer, mem. Corpn. of London and founder Merchant Taylors Sch., London, 1561); international traveler;

4–William (*b* 1752), removed to Westland, Washington Co., Pa., 1795; *m* 1776, Rebecca Pugh;

3–Samuel (1788-1873), of Wilmington, Del., teacher; *m* 1821, Margaret Hill Smith (1786-1882; John[4], of "Green Hill," Burlington, N.J. [desc. William Smith, of Bramham, *b* ca. 1570], *m* Gulielma Maria Morris [desc. Anthony Morris, qv]; desc. Thomas Lloyd, qv, and James Logan, qv);

2–William Samuel (1825-76), mfr., ry. treas., shipbuilder and owner; *m* 1849, Sarah Lancaster Allen (1819-97), see Vol. I, p. 929, for maternal lineage; issue: I–Susan Watson (*b* 1850; *m* 1871, Isaac H. Shearman); II–T. Allen (1 above); III–Samuel Eli (qv); IV–Margaret Smith (1856-1912).

1–*m* Sept. 25, 1878, Anna Edith Updegraff, *b*

Mount Pleasant, O., 1855; dau. of David B. Updegraff, of Mount Pleasant; issue: 1–Edith Hilles, *b* Chester, Pa., Dec. 1891; Vassar Coll., '14 (has adopted: Ann Taylor Hilles, *b* Jan. 24, 1929, and Allen Lancaster Hilles, *b* Apr. 14, 1929).
1–A.B., Haverford, '70. V.p. machinist-tool business; bank v.p. Residence: Glen Mills, Delaware Co., Pa.

1–**HILLES, Samuel Eli,** *b* Wilmington, Del., Mar. 7, 1854.
7–David **Price,** a Friend, from Brecknockshire, Wales, to Radnor Meeting, Pa., 1690, with wife and 6 children; *m* in Wales, ca. 1665, Joan Awbrey (ca. 1640-1699), dau. of Thomas Awbrey, desc. Welsh family of high antiquity;
6–Joan, *m* 1692, James **Pugh** (*d* 1724), from Wales, settled in the "Welsh Tract"; mem. Soc. of Friends; moved from Radnor to Chester Meeting, 1714; settled at Uwchlan, acquired a large landed property;
5–Hugh (1699-1748/49), *m* 1733, Mary Jones (*b* 1712/13; Cadwallader[6] [*b* 1687], from Bala, Merionethshire, Wales, to Pa., ca. 1697, *m* 1710, Elinor Evans);
4–Rebecca (*b* 1745), *m* William **Hilles,** (*b* 1752);
3–Samuel (1788-1873), *m* Margaret Hill Smith (1786-1882);
2–William Samuel (1825-76), mfr., ry. treas., shipbuilder and owner; *m* 1849, Sarah Lancaster Allen (1819-97); for issue and Hilles lineage see Thomas Allen Hilles.
1–*m* Oct. 28, 1880, Amy Yarnall Tatum (Aug. 5, 1852-Dec. 14, 1903), dau. of Samuel C. Tatum, of Cincinnati, O.; issue: 1–William Tatum, *b* Cincinnati, Apr. 1, 1883; A.B. Haverford, '04; A.M. Harvard, 1905; *m* Mary C., dau. Rev. David Allen Reed, of Springfield, Mass.
1–*m* 2d, Feb. 8, 1909, Mina B. Colburn, *b* Ellington, N.Y., May 19, 1868; dau. of Charles D. Colburn, of Jamestown, N.Y.; adopted dau. (July 6, 1922), Elizabeth Mary, *b* May 8, 1917.
1–A.B., Haverford, '74; LL.D., Tusculum Coll. (Greenville, Tenn.), 1930. Retired mfr., bank director. Summer place: Bemus Point, on Lake Chautauqua, N.Y. Winter place: Melbourne Beach, Fla. Residence: 911 Marion Av., Avondale, Cincinnati, O.

1–**HILLYER, Robert Silliman,** *b* E. Orange, N.J., June 3, 1895.
9–John **Hillyer** (qv);
8–James (1644-1720), of Simsbury, Conn.; *m* Mary (Wakefield) Dibble (*d* 1725), of Windsor, Conn.;
7–James (1683-1770), of Simsbury; *m* 1709, Joanna Hayes (1691-1780; George[8]),
6–Capt. James (1713-1808), mem. Conn. Assembly; capt. train bands; served in French and Indian War; *m* Mary Humphrey (1716-97);
5–James (1746-1825), of Granby, Conn.; *m* Ruth Holcomb, of Salmon Brook, Conn.;
4–Judge James (1776-1833), of Granby; removed to Henderson, Ky.; *m* 2d, 1827, Catherine Silliman (1801-36; Maj. William[5]; Gen. Gold S.[6], Am. Rev.);
3–Gen. William Silliman (1830-74), of St. Louis, Mo., and New York, requested by his friend, Ulysses S. Grant, to join his staff; rose from rank of capt. to col. and bvt. brig. gen.; aided Grant in his 1st presidential campaign, and later refused post as minister to Portugal; *m* Mary Shield Rankin (1832-96), of Newark, N.J.;
2–James Rankin (1860-1901), of E. Orange, N.J.; customs appraiser; *m* 1885, Lillian Stanley Smith (*b* 1863; Henry P.[3], of Phila., Pa.); issue: I–Henry Stanley (*b* 1887; *m* Margaretta Cadogan Wylie); II–Ethel Forde (*b* 1888; *m* Harold Raymond Medina); III–Lillian (*b* 1891; *m* Theodore McCurdy Marsh); IV–Robert S. (1 above).
1–*m* July 1, 1926, Dorothy Hancock Tilton, *b* Haverhill, Mass., Aug. 23, 1904; dau. of John Hancock Tilton, of Haverhill; issue: 1–Stanley Hancock, *b* Hartford, Conn., May 20, 1927.
1–A.B., Harvard, '17 (Delta Psi, P.B.K.); A.M. (hon.), Trinity Coll. Asst. Prof. English, Harvard Coll. Fellow Am.-Scandinavian Foundation, Copenhagen, 1920. Author (see Who's Who in America). Ambulance driver and lt., U.S.A., with A.E.F. in France, 1917-19. P.B.K. poet. Harvard, 1929. Mem. Cambridge Folk Lore Soc.; hon. curator of Modern literature, Widener Lib., Harvard Coll. Clubs: Harvard, Boston Authors, N.E. Poetry (pres. 1923-25), The Poets (N.Y.). Episcopalian. Democrat. Residence: Pomfret, Conn.

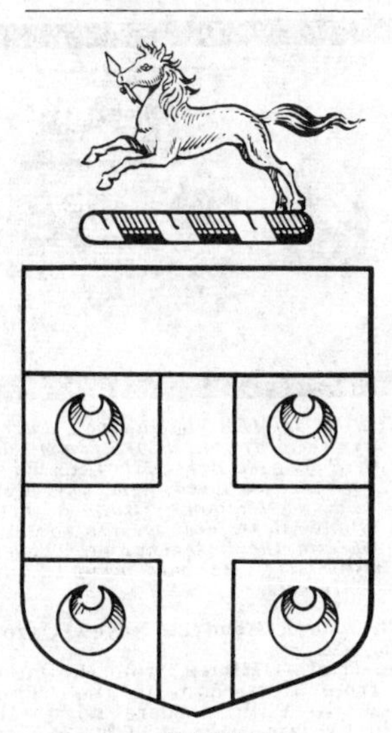

HILLS

Arms: Argent, a cross between four crescents azure, a chief of the last.
Crest: A horse courant gules, in the mouth a broken spearhead sable.

1–**HILLS, Elijah Clarence,** *b* Arlington, Ill., July 2, 1867.
9–William **Hills** (1608-83), from Eng., 1632; settled Hartford, Conn.; *m* Phyllis Lyman; *m* 2d, Widow Risley; *m* 3d, Widow Steele;
8–John (1648-92), of Hartford; *m* 1670, Jane Bushnell;
7–Samuel (1671-1753), of Saybrook, Conn.; *m* 1st, 1694, Phebe Leonard;
6–Samuel (1701-92), of Duxbury, Mass.; *m* 1722, Hannah Turner (1701-77);
5–Elijah (1736-1818), of New London, Conn.; *m* 1768, Grace Mariner (1737-1807);
4–Elijah (1772-1841), of Palmer, Mass.; *m* Olive Rider (1770-1841);
3–Cyrus (1796-1868), of Lamoille, Ill.; *m* 1st, 1821, Amanda Olds (1800-56);
2–Elijah Justin (1834-1913), mcht. Tampa, Fla.; *m* 1866, Mary Eleanor Larkin (*b* 1844); issue: I–Elijah Clarence (1 above); II–Justin Larkin (*b* 1871; *m* Mary Fay Jarvis).
1–*m* June 22, 1898, Metta Virgil Strough, *b* Orleans, N.Y., Apr. 1, 1873, dau. of George Henry Strough, of Clayton, N.Y.; issue: 1–Elijah Justin, *b* Winter Park, Fla., Apr. 24, 1899; A.B., Ind. U., '21; M.A., U.Calif., 1926; *m* June 24, 1924, Lucia B., dau. of Prof. Maro B. Jones, of Pomona Coll., Claremont, Calif. (issue: Lucia; Burt Larkin); 2–George Strough, *b* Winter Park, Nov. 1, 1900; A.B., Ind. U., '22; LL.B., Harvard, 1925; *m* Sept. 14, 1926, Alice Gertrude, dau. of Lee Shaw, of Rockford, Ill.; 3–Clarence Ballard, *b* Clayton, N.Y., Jan. 10, 1902; A.B., Ind. U., '23, M.D., 1926; *m* Sept. 14, 1929, Frances Desire, dau. of Dr. Robert E. Ramsay, of Pasadena, Calif.; 4–Ruth, *b* Colo. Springs, Colo., Feb. 2, 1904; A.B., U.Calif., '26.
1–A.B., Cornell, '92 (Beta Theta Pi, P.B.K.); studied U. of Paris; Ph.D., U.Colo., 1906, Litt. D., Rollins Coll., 1906. Prof. Romance philology, U.Calif., since 1922; editor D.C. Heath & Co., Boston, Mass., since 1916, dir. since 1922. Author (see Who's Who in America). Knight Cdr. of Royal Order of Queen Isabella (Spanish). Mem. Am. Acad. Arts and Sci-

ences, Royal Spanish Acad., Royal Spanish-Am. Acad. of Cadiz (Spain), Hispanic Soc., etc. Club: Nat. Arts (New York). Residence: 1570 Hawthorne Ter., Berkeley, Calif.

COL. GEORGE HIMES (b Hanover, Pa., Dec. 16, 1775-d New Oxford, Pa., 1850); commissioned lt. col., 124th Regt., 1st Brig., 5th Div., Pa. Militia, Dec. 28, 1803. Purchased, 1810, the first established and well-known "Dutch" Frederick's Tavern Stand at Oxford, on the route between Pittsburgh and the Susquehanna, which he conducted until 1828; afterward occupied with large business interests.

1-**HIMES, Joseph Hendrix,** *b* New Oxford, Pa., Aug. 15, 1885.
6-William (Heim) **Himes,** from the Palatinate; sailed from Rotterdam in the "Thistle of Glasgow" to Phila., where he qualified as required by law, Aug. 29, 1730; to Lancaster Co., Pa.;
5-Francis (1737-1811), began to write name Himes; *m* Catherine Christ (1739-1826);
4-George (1775-1850), of York Co., Pa.; *m* 1809, Helena C. Barnitz (1787-1857; Daniel[5] [1755-1827], *m* 1776, Susanna [1756-1806], dau. of Martin Eichleberger [1716-81], as justice of peace, 1774-75, assisted in establishing Am. independence, *m* 1738, Anna Maria–, both from the Palatinate);
3-Susan Catherine (1815-71), of York Co.; *m* 1835, Thomas **Himes** (1803-81);
2-George Thomas (1836-1917), of York Co.; merchant; *m* 1883, Martha Jane MacKnight (*b* 1847); issue: I-Joseph Hendrix (1 above); II-Susan Catharine (*b* 1887).
1-*m* May 6, 1915, Eilleen Canfield, *b* Los Angeles, Calif., May 27, 1893; dau. of Charles A. Canfield, of Los Angeles; issue: 1-Canfield MacKnight, *b* Canton, O., July 21, 1917; 2-Marillyn, *b* Canton, Mar. 15, 1921; 3-Katrina, *b* Thousand Islands, Can., July 17, 1926.
1-Pa. Coll., Gettysburg, 1900-04; Pa. State Coll., 1904-07. Spl. partner brokerage firm of E. A. Pierce & Co., New York, since 1924; dir. Munsey Trust Co., Washington, since 1925. Mem. 67th Congress, 16th Ohio Dist., 1921-23 (see Who's Who in America). Methodist. Republican. Mason (32°). Clubs: Alfalfa, Burning Tree, Capital Yacht, Congressional Country, Metropolitan, Riding and Hunt, Beach and Tennis, Catoctin Country, New York Produce Exchange Luncheon, Thousand Islands Country, Thousand Islands Yacht. Country homes: "Opawaka Lodge," Thousand Islands, N.Y., and "Prospect Hall," Frederick, Md. Residence: 1705 K St. N.W., Washington, D.C.

1-**HIMES, Leslie Roberts,** *b* S. Bethlehem Borough, Armstrong Co., Pa., June 7, 1892.
6-John **Space** (1757-1813), from Germany, settled at Hackettstown, N.J., later in Luzerne Co., Pa.; soldier N.J. Cont. Line at siege and surrender of Yorktown; *m* Abigail Mott;
5-Zephaniah (1789-1871), *m* Katie Armstrong (*d* 1868);
4-Sylvina (1814-98), *m* 1837, John **Himes** (1810-76);
3-Joseph C. (1846-1907), corpl., 78th Pa. Vols., 1862-65; *m* 1866, Margaret Rutherford (1848-1915; John[4] [*b* Ireland, Aug. 12, 1814-*d* Dec. 10, 1877; son of James], *m* June 18, 1847, Nancy [McIntosh] Tosh [*b* Ireland, Dec. 12, 1812-*d* June 14, 1894], both buried Leatherwood Cemetery, Porter Tp., Clarion Co., Pa.);
2-John R. (2 below).
4-John **Roberts** (*d* 1845), *m* Mary Ann Weckerly;
3-David Shannon (1845-1924), U.S.V. in Civil War; *m* Catharine Null (*b* 1841);
2-Mary Alverta (1870-96), *m* 1887, John Rutherford **Himes** (*b* 1868); for issue see Vol. III, p. 248.
1-*m* June 27, 1923, Helen Lytle (qv); issue: 1-Margery Lytle, *b* New Bethlehem, Pa., June 14, 1924.
1-L.L.B., U.Mich., '15. Admitted to bar, 1915, and since in practice at New Bethlehem, Pa. Ordnance sgt., 45th Arty., C.A.C., with A.E.F. in France. Mem. S.A.R. (chapter pres.), I.A.G., Sons of Union Vets., A.L. Residence: New Bethlehem, Pa.

1-**HIMES, Helen Lytle (Mrs. Leslie R.),** *b* Pittsburgh, Pa., May 10, 1894.
6-William **Lytle,** from Scotland to America;
5-John (1772-1858), *m* 1st, Ann Patton (*d* 1829), both buried at Crete Ch., Center Tp., Indiana Co., Pa.;
4-John (1798-1879), *m* Polly Robinson (1808-68);
3-Samuel (1838-95), served in Co. B, 67th Pa. Vol. Inf., 1865; to Shelocta, Pa.; *m* 1869, Amelia Cook (1848-1926);
2-Clark Cook (2 below).
6-John **Shields** (1759-1840), corpl. Cumberland Co., Pa. militia, Am. Rev.; *m* 1st, 1782, Mary Marshall (*d* 1816);
5-John, Jr. (1789-1872), *m* 1809, Elizabeth Speedy (1789-1860);
4-Andrew (1815-82), *m* Anna Catherine Craig (1817-1910);
3-Anna Elizabeth (1846-1928), *m* 1864, Henry L. **Kinter** (1837-95), musician Co. F, 74th Pa. Vol. Inf., 1862-65;
2-Margaret Ann (*b* July 9, 1871), *m* Dec. 13, 1892, Clark Cook **Lytle** (*b* Apr. 19, 1870).
1-*m* June 27, 1923, Leslie Roberts Himes (qv). Residence: New Bethlehem, Pa.

1-**HINCKLEY, George Walter,** *b* Guilford, Conn., July 27, 1853.
8-Samuel **Hinckley** (qv);
7-Ens. John (1644-1709), *m* 1668, Bethia Lathrop (1649-94; Thomas[8], *m* 1639, Sarah [Larned] Ewer, dau. William Larned; Rev. John[9], qv);
6-Gershom (1683-1774), of Lebanon, Conn.; *m* 1712, Mary Buell;
5-John (1730-1811), of E. Hampton, Conn.; *m* Azubah Smith (1738-1809);
4-Azariel (1768-1844), of Killingworth, Conn.; *m* Azubah Kelsey (1762-1841);
3-Abel Kelsey (1796-1854), of Guilford, Conn.; *m* Eliza Ann Parmalee (1798-1879);
2-Walter (2 below).
10-Joseph **Loomis** (qv);
9-Dea. John (1622-88), dep. Gen. Ct.; *m* 1648/49, Elizabeth Scott (1625-96; Thomas[10], from Eng. to Ipswich, Mass., 1634);
8-Dea. John (1649-1715), *m* 2d, 1696, Sarah (Boltwood) Warner (*d* 1726);
7-Mary (1672/73-1769), *m* 1695, Dr. and Dea. John **Buell** (1671/72-1746; Samuel[8], *m* Deborah Griswold; William[9], qv);
6-Mary (1696-1774), *m* Gershom **Hinckley** (6 above).
2-Walter **Hinckley** (1823-99), farmer; *m* Sally Eliza Lee (1825-78; Elon[3], of Guilford, Conn., *m* Grace Stone); issue: I-Edward Selden (*b* 1849; *m* Helen Steven); II-George Walter (1 above); III-Philetta Elizabeth (*b* 1855; *m* Leroy C. Evarts); IV-Jane Eliza (1861-1914); V-Grace Lee (*b* 1866; *m* 1888, David Webster Evarts, *b* 1863).
1-*m* Aug. 12, 1880, Harriet Elma Palmer, *b* S. Kingston, R.I., June 22, 1855; dau. of Benjamin R. Palmer, of Wakefield, R.I.; issue: 1-Alice Louise, *b* Windsor, Conn., Nov. 12, 1881; *m* Dec. 23, 1908, David R. Porter (issue: Esther; Hinckley; Jean; Robert); 2-Walter Palmer, *b* Bangor, Me., May 27, 1885; Bowdoin, 1909; *m* July 27, 1910, Nellie, dau. of Frederic Wagner, of Brooklyn, N.Y. (issue: Harriet); 3-Edward Benjamin, *b* Newport, Me., Nov. 16, 1887; ed. U. of Me. and Yale; *m* July 27, 1911, Marion, dau. of William Ireland, of Fairfield, Me. (issue: Louise; Faith); 4-Faith Jayne, *b* Oakland, Me., June 10, 1891; Oberlin 1 yr.; *m* Aug. 27, 1928, Lester Powley.

1–Ed. Guilford Inst. and Conn. State Normal Sch.; (hon. A.M., Colby, 1912; D.D., Bowdoin). Pastor, 1880-84; missionary Am. S.S. Union in Me. 3 yrs. and Me. state evangelist, 3 yrs.; founder, 1888, and since editor Good Will Record; founder and pres., 1889, Good Will Home Assn. and Sch., Hinckley, Me. Author. Baptist. Republican. Rotarian (hon. mem). Residence: Hinckley P.O., Fairfield, Me.

1–**HINMAN, Harold Jay,** *b* Albany, N.Y., Feb. 22, 1877.
8–Sgt. Edward **Hinman** (qv);
7–Capt. Titus (1655-1736), an original settler of Woodbury, Conn.; capt. Train Band; mem. Gen. Assembly 7 sessions bet. 1712-20; *m* 1703/-04, Mary Hawkins;
6–Eleazur (*b* 1704 or 05), of Woodbury; apptd. by Gen. Assembly with others to audit all colony accounts, 1776; mem. Legislature, 1749; *m* Hannah Scoville, of Waterbury, Conn.;
5–Peter (bap. 1742), of Woodbury; *m* 1753, Widow Mary Cunningham;
4–William Hawley (1768-1845), of Woodbury; *m* 1799, Lois Brown (1777-1833), of Albany Co., N.Y.;
3–Herman Hawley (1808-84), cabinet maker, New Baltimore, Greene Co., N.Y.; *m* 1843, Magdalen Slingerland (1816-78), of Clarksville, N.Y.;
2–Addison Josiah (1846-1920), of Albany, N.Y.; enlisted in Civil War aet. 18; 2d lt. of Cav.; later became a rancher; returned to Albany and became sec. of Commerce Insurance Co.; *m* 1871, Susan Mary DuBois Hotaling (*d* 1925); issue: I–Seymour Van Wyck (1872-73); II–Eugene Eunson (*b* 1875; *m* 1905, Nellie Edna Tallmadge); III–Harold Jay (1 above); IV–Addison Hotaling (*b* 1879; *m* 1906, Winifred LePage Gallien); V–Charles Parker (1881-82).
1–*m* June 7, 1906, Lucy E. Warner, *b* Warner's Lake, N.Y., July 21, 1882; dau. of Elias Warner, of Warner's Lake; issue: 1–Mildred Warner, *b* Albany, N.Y., Aug. 5, 1907; ed. Wellesley Coll.; 2–Martha Jean, *b* Albany, Oct. 26, 1909.
1–Ph.B., Union Coll., '99 (Alpha Delta Phi, P.B.-K.; hon. A.M., 1924); LL.B., Albany Law Sch., 1901. Practiced law, 1901-18; justice Supreme Ct. of N.Y., 3d Jud. Dist., since 1918; now asso. judge Appellate Div., third dept., State of N.Y. Mem. N.Y. Assembly, 1910-15 (chmn. judiciary com., 1912, minority leader, 1913, majority leader, 1914-1915); mem. Constl. Conv., 1915; dep. atty. gen., 1915-18; pres. bd. of trustees, Albany Law Sch.; v.p. bd. of trustees, Albany Acad. for Girls; life trustee, Young Men's Assn., etc. (see Who's Who in America). Clubs: University, Albany Country, Ft. Orange, Young Men's Rep., Capital City, Unconditional. Summer place: Warner's Lake, N.Y. Residence: 292 State St., Albany, N.Y.

1–**HOAG, Mary Esther Hotchkin (Mrs. William Harvey),** *b* Pulteney, N.Y., Jan. 30, 1887.
10–Samuel **Morse** (qv);
9–John (*b* Eng., 1611), did not come to America with parents; propr. Dedham, Mass., 1637; *m* in Dedham, Annas Chickering (*d* 1691);
8–Ezra (1643-97), *m* 1670, Joanna Hoare (*d* Braintree, Mass., 1691);
7–Seth (1686/87-1783), to Guilford, Conn.; *m* 2d, Elizabeth Barron (*d* 1782);
6–Hannah (1713-94), *m* 1741, Noah **Hotchkin** (Joseph[7], *m* Elizabeth Hills);
5–Rev. Beriah (1752-1829), soldier Am. Rev.; founder of 1st ch. of N.E. type west of the Hudson River at Greenville, N.Y.; *m* 1774, Thankful Dickinson (1752-1837);
4–Beriah (1783-1845), *m* 1804, Lucretia Daniels (1780-1864; prob. John[5], *m* at Lyme, Conn., by Rev. Stephen Johnson, Apr. 21, 1776, Lucretia Waterouse);
3–John Daniels (1817-94), *m* 1849, Esther Ann Wheaton;
2–Francis Granger (2 below).
9–John **Bellows** (*b* Eng., 1623-1683), from London, Apr. 1635, seeking the "Lavinian Shores"; *m* 1655, Mary Wood (*d* 1707);
8–Eleazer (*b* 1671), *m* 1692, Esther Barrett;
7–Eleazer (*b* 1696), *m* Sarah–;
6–Daniel (*b* Southboro, Mass., 1723-*d* Hebron, N.Y.), soldier Am. Rev.; *m* 1746, Deborah Rix;
5–Thomas (1753-1835), soldier Am. Rev.; *m* 1774, Deliverance Button (1754-1844), of Preston, Conn. (Matthias[6] [*b* 1730], soldier Am. Rev., *m* 1752, Mary Safford, *b* 1732); see Vol. III, p. 249, for Button lineage;
4–Susan (1794-1891), *m* 1820, John Marshall **Wheaton** (1794-1880);
3–Esther Ann (1829-97), *m* John D. **Hotchkin** (3 above).
9–Thomas **Rix** (*b* Eng., 1622; son of Robert, of Canninghall, Eng.), *m* 1st, Margaret– (*d* 1660), widow of Miles Ward;
8–James (*b* Salem, Mass.; bap. First Ch., Salem, Oct. 18, 1657), *m* Margaret–;
7–Thomas (*d* 1771), *m* 1718, Jerusha Tracy (1697-1785; Thomas[8] [1644-1721]; Thomas[9], qv);
6–Deborah (*b* Preston, Conn., 1720), *m* Daniel **Bellows** (6 above).
8–Samuel **Terry** (qv);
7–Samuel (1661-1730/31), *m* 1st, 1682, Hannah Morgan (*d* 1696/97; Isaac[8], *m* Abagail–);
6–Samuel (*b* 1690);
5–Samuel (1750-1813), soldier Am. Rev.; *m* Sarah Ogden (1748-1813; Joseph[6], *m* Mary Terry);
4–Mary (Polly) (1793-1865), *m* 1815, Dr. William Niles **Dean** (1795-1868); see Vol. III, p. 249, for Dean lineage;
3–Darius (1828-81), *m* 1859, Mary E. Stewart (1843-1919; John[4] [1796-1870], *m* 1840, Martha Haines, *b* Eng., 1820-*d* 1891); see Vol. III, p. 249, for Stewart lineage;
2–Laura May (*b* 1864), *m* 1886, Francis Granger **Hotchkin** (*b* 1858), teacher (for issue see Vol. III, p. 249).
1–*m* Dec. 3, 1913, William George Dean (Mar. 1, 1868-Mar. 4, 1917), bank pres.; son of George R. Dean, *m* Jane Godfrey.
1–*m* 2d, Aug. 30, 1922, William Harvey Hoag, *b* Millerton, Dutchess Co., N.Y., Feb. 25, 1887; student of medicine 1907-10; corpl., 9th Engrs. Train, 15th Cav. Div., U.S.A., service on Mexican border; hon. discharged, Sept. 30, 1919; son of Dr. Arthur F. Hoag, of Millerton, *m* Jessie Wheeler; issue: 1–Harvey (*b* Nov. 26, 1923-*d* infancy).
1–Grad. Geneseo State Normal Sch., 1906 (Alpha Delta). Mem. D.A.R. (past chapter regent; state recording sec.), N.Y. State Hist. Assn., O.E.S. Summer place: Lake Keuka, N.Y. Residence: Prattsburg, Steuben Co., N.Y.

1–**HOAN, Daniel Webster,** *b* Waukesha, Wis., Mar. 12, 1881.
7–Frederick **Streit** (1709-81), from Bavaria ca. 1725, settled at Rhinebeck, Dutchess Co., N.Y.; *m* Catherine Moul (1702-85);
6–Frederick (1742-1800), of Rhinebeck; *m* Catherine Bemer (Phillip Hendricksen[7], *m* Engel Dederick); *m* 2d, Elizabeth Rau; *m* 3d, Catherine Moore;
5–Catherine (*b* 1768), of Rhinebeck; *m* 1786, Nicholas **Moore** (1760-1833), served in Am. Rev. (Phillip Henry[6], mem. British Parliament from Province of Quebec, *m* Hannah More; Nicholas[7]);
4–Frederick (1787-1866), of Rhinebeck; *m* 2d, Margaret Row (*b* 1794);
3–Caroline (1816-91), of Waukesha, Wis.; *m* Hiram **Hood** (*d* 1851);
2–Margaret Augusta (1849-1927), of Waukesha; *m* 1869, Daniel Webster (*born* Horan) **Hoan** (1841-95), color sgt., Co. F, 193d N.Y. Vols., Civil War (John Horan[3], of Ireland, *m* Judith Delany, of Ireland); issue: I–William Henry (*m* Anna Kremer Senderhaup); II–George Francis; III–Gertrude J. (*m* Henry J. Josey); IV–Ella (*d* young); V–Daniel Webster (1 above).
1–*m* Oct. 5, 1909, Agnes Bernice Magner, *b* Morris, Ill., Jan. 22, 1883; dau. of Michael Magner, of Morris, *m* Bridget Walsh; issue: 1–Daniel Webster, *b* Milwaukee, Wis., July 22, 1910; 2–Agnes Bernice, *b* Milwaukee, Oct. 27, 1915.
1–B.A., U.Wis., 1905; student Chicago-Kent Coll. of Law, 1905-06. Practiced in Milwaukee from 1907; atty. for Wis. State Federation of Labor, 1908-10; directed fight which resulted in workmen's compensation act—the first of its kind in U.S.; city atty., Milwaukee, 1910-16; mayor of Milwaukee since 1916. Dir. Gt. Lakes Harbor Assn.; mem. bd. Milwaukee Auditorium. Author (see Who's Who in America). Methodist. K.P., Elk, Eagle. Club: South Side Community. Residence: 3322 Kilbourn Av., Milwaukee, Wis.

1–**HOBSON, Sarah Matilda,** *b* Island Pond, Vt., Sept. 25, 1861.
8–William **Hobson** (*d* 1659; son of Henry, of

Usflete, nr. Whitgift, southern part of West Riding); from Eng. ca. 1650, settled at Rowley, Mass.; *m* 1652, Ann Reynor (*d* 1693; Elder Humphrey[9], from Eng., 1639);
7–William (1659-1725), of Rowley; *m* 1692, Sarah Jewett (*b* 1673; Jeremiah[8] [1637-1714], of Ipswich, *m* Sarah Dickinson, 1644-1724);
6–Jeremiah (1697-1741), of Rowley; *m* 1729, Jane Dresser;
5–William (1730-1827), moved to Buxton, Me., ca. 1783; *m* 2d, 1759, Lydia Parsons (*d* 1783), of Gloucester, Mass.;
4–Samuel (1763-1839), of West Buxton, Me.; *m* 1788, Rachel Lane, of Rowley;
3–Samuel (1789-1858), of Hollis, Me.; *m* 1818, Hannah Sawyer (1799-1886; Jabez[4] [*d* 1847], *m* 1793, Elizabeth Hanson; Jabez[5] [*b* 1743], *m* 1765, Mary Pennell, 5 below);
2–Samuel Decatur (2 below).
9–John **Dresser** (*d* 1672), from Eng. to Salem, Mass., 1639; shoemaker, Rowley, Mass.; *m* Mary–;
8–Samuel (1643-1704), *m* 1668, Mary Leaver (1649-1714; Thomas[9], linen weaver, *m* 1643, Mary Bradley);
7–John (*b* 1680), *m* 1706, Elizabeth Kilborn (1685-1711; Isaac[8] [1660-1713], *m* Mary, dau. of John Cheney, of Newbury; George[9], at Rowley, 1643);
6–Jane (*b* 1707), *m* Jeremiah **Hobson** (6 above).
8–James **Sawyer** (*d* 1703), "a weaver at Ipswich, 1669"; first record in Gloucester, Mass., at birth of son, Nathaniel, 1677; *m* Martha–; *m* 2d, Sarah Bray, of Gloucester;
7–John (1676-1760), moved to Falmouth, Me., 1719; *m* 1701, Rebecca Stanford;
6–Joseph (1711-1800), of Cape Elizabeth, Me.; *m* Joanna Cobb (Ebenezer[7], *m* Mary–);
5–Jabez (1743-1816), of Buxton, Me., lived between "Old Corner and Duck Pond"; *m* 1765, Mary Pennell (*d* 1814), of Saco, Me.;
4–William (1779-1853), of Bar Mills, Me.; *m* Betsey Knight, of Buxton (Samuel[6], *m* Hannah–);
3–Eben (1807-53), of Hollis; *m* 1830, Sarah Haley (1813-95), of Biddeford Pool, Me.;
2–Mary Elizabeth (1831-86), of Hollis; *m* 1854, Samuel Decatur **Hobson** (1830-1911), lumber mfr.; issue: I–Howard Harry (*b* 1854; *m* Emma A. Mansur); II–Helen Melvina (*b* 1856; *m* Kimball B. Fletcher, Jr.); III–John Elmer (1858-68); IV–Eugene Faber (*b* 1859; *m* Nellie G. Lang [*d* 1916]; *m* 2d, Clara Buswell); V–Sarah Matilda (1 above); VI–Albion Wilbur (*b* 1865; *m* Florence Harris); VII–Mary Clemmer (*b* 1870; *m* Charles B. Tewksbury); VIII–Elsie Garland (*b* 1872).
1–Ph.B., Boston U., 1887, M.D., 1890 (Kappa Kappa Gamma). Teacher in Vt., 1879-83; medical practice, Chicago, since 1892; attending physician Chicago Home for Friendless, 1899-1904, consulting staff, since 1904; adjunct prof. pediatrics, Hahnemann Med. Coll., 1905-10; consulting staff, Algonquin Summer Camp, 1918-20, Daily News Sanitarium, 1920-29. Mem. A.M.A., Ill. Med. Soc., Chicago Med. Soc., Chicago Homeo. Med. Soc. (sec. 1909-10, pres., 1910-11), Am. Inst. Homeopathy (sec., 1914-15; editor of Journal, 1914-20), Chicago Council of Med. Women (v.p., 1926-28), Pres. Hyde Park Neighborhood Club, 1923-28. Congregational. Republican. Club: The Cordon. Residence: 5724 Kenwood Av., Chicago, Ill.

1–**HOCKER, William Adam,** *b* "Oak Grove," Buckingham Co., Va., Dec. 5, 1844-*d* Jacksonville, Fla., July 16, 1918 (see portrait).
4–Johann George **Höcker** (*b* Wurttemburg, Germany, Mar. 9, 1733-*d* "Erdenheim," Germantown, Pa., Oct. 4, 1820), refugee from religious persecutions in southern Germany, sailed from Rotterdam, Holland, in "ye good ship, Brothers, with Capt. William Muir, and landed in Pa., Sept. 16, 1751"; purchased a farm of 200 acres on Wissahickon Creek, nr. Germantown, Apr. 1763, built the house and named the place "Erdenheim" (see photograph); *m* Margaretta Mason (1739-July 5, 1816); both are buried in St. Michael's churchyard, Germantown, Pa.;
3–Johann Adam (called Adam), (*b* "Erdenheim," Dec. 19, 1763-*d* "Slate River Mills," Buckingham Co., Va., Feb. 4, 1847), mfg. miller, planter and large slave owner; pvt. Capt. Jacob

"ERDENHEIM," the home of JOHANN GEORGE HÖCKER (1733-1820), where ADAM HÖCKER (1763-1847), was born.

Buss' Co., 2d Bn., Northampton Co. (Pa.) militia, June 6, 1780, Am. Rev.; moved to Buckingham Co., Va., ca. 1790 (see portrait); *m* in Germantown, Pa., Mar. 4, 1797, Ann Dillet (*d* "Slate River Mills," June 22, 1825), a French Huguenot;
2–William (2 below).

ADAM HÖCKER (1763-1847), from a life-size portrait painted from life (artist unknown).

5–John **Lewis** (*d* 1799), planter, large slave owner, St. Ann's Parish, Albemarle Co., Va.; *m* Elizabeth–;
4–Owen (Sept. 12, 1750-1805, planter, large slave owner, Albemarle Co., Va.; *m* Sallie Perkins;
3–William (*b* Albemarle Co., Va., 1775-*d* White Sulphur Springs, W.Va., Sept. 1, 1837), resided at "Oak Grove," Buckingham Co., Va., planter, large slave owner; *m* 2d, Mrs. Ann (Tindall) Glover (*b* 1770-*d* "Oak Grove," May 27, 1838; Thomas Tindall[4], original owner of "Oak Grove," *m* Mary–);
2–Susan Mildred (2 below).
11–William **Parker** (2d bro. Thomas Parker Esq. of Browsholm), archdeacon and justice of Cornwall, Eng.;
10–James (eldest son), *m* Katherine Buller (eldest dau. Sir Richard[11], of Shillingham, Cornwall, Eng.);
9–Richard (9th son, 1620-80), "a Doctor of Phyzicke came to Virginy, married a Londoner and had issue six children. Liveth upon St. James River in ye uplands of Virginy and hath been High Sheriffe of ye said county"—from the English records of the

Parker family, entered under date Sept. 1, 1673, and now in possession of descendants; settled in Nansemond Co., Va., 1654, granted 1,500 acres of land; *m* Elizabeth Bailey (Capt. Richard[10], of London, Eng., and Accomac Co., Va.);
8–Mary, *m* Nicholas **Perkins,** landed propr., Bermuda Hundred and Henrico Co., Va., 1650 and later;
7–Nicholas (*died*-1711), will recorded in Henrico Co., Va.; landed propr.; *m* Sarah Childress (will proved Jan. 1722, Henrico Co.), a Quakeress;
6–Constantine (will probated Goochland Co., Va., May 18, 1761), landed propr., Goochland, Louisa, Henrico and Albemarle cos., Va.; *m* Ann Pollard, of Louisa Co., Va. (sister of Joseph Pollard, 1701-91, whose dau. *m* Edmund Pendleton, pres. Va. Conv. which ratified the Constn. of U.S.);
5–Harding (*d* ante 1821), planter, of Perkins Falls, Buckingham Co.; *m* Sara Price;
4–Sallie (will probated 1848, Albemarle Co., Va.), *m* Owen **Lewis** (4 above).
9–John **Price** (qv);
8–Matthew (*b* 1626), from Wales to Va., ca. 1630; "Son and heir, 1638"; *m* Miss Nelson;
7–John (1650-1711), of Henrico Co.; *m* Jane (Pew, Pughe) Pugh (Henry[8], *m* Jane–);
6–Daniel, lived in Henrico Co., 1767; *m* Sallie Coleman (Stephen[7]);
5–Sara (will recorded Fluvanna Co., Va., Feb. 26, 1821), *m* Harding **Perkins** (5 above).
2–Susan Mildred Lewis (*b* "Oak Grove," Buckingham Co., Nov. 27, 1811-*d* Lake Co., Fla., May 16, 1886), *m* Nov. 22, 1831, William **Hocker** (Feb. 3, 1808-June 9, 1870), will probated July 11, 1870, Buckingham Co.; planter, large slave owner; issue: I–William Adam (1 above); II–Nannie Lewis (1852-86; *m* Charles Fontaine Venable [1852-1913], see their dau. Elizabeth Marshall Venable, Vol. II, p. 243).

WILLIAM ADAM HOCKER (1844-1918).

1–*m* Nov. 17, 1868, Gertrude Alice Venable, *b* "Scott-Greene," Prince Edward Co., Va. (Nov. 24, 1848-Nov. 17, 1901); dau. of Thomas Frederick Venable (see his son, Matthew Walton Venable, Vol. II, p. 243); issue: 1–Mary Venable, *b* "Oak Grove," Buckingham Co., Va., Dec. 29, 1869; ed. Acad. of Art, Berlin, Germany; *m* Mar. 18, 1891, Gen. Charles Philip Lovell, served Spanish-Am. War and World War (issue: Charles P., Jr., Lt. Aviation Corps, World War; Gertrude Venable); 2–William, *b* "Oak Grove," June 3, 1871; U.Va.; *m* Dec. 18, 1901, Elizabeth Key Hansbrough, of Elizabethtown, Ky. (issue: Mary Elizabeth, Margaret); 3–Alice Walton, *b* "Kinderton," Lake Co., Fla., Mar. 20, 1883; Agnes Scott Coll.; *m* Dec. 3, 1902, Trusten Polk Drake, son of James E. Drake, of St. Louis, Mo., *m* Cornelia Polk (issue: Trusten Polk, Jr.; William Hocker); 4–Frederick Roché, *b* Leesburg, Fla., July 12, 1891; Washington and Lee, and U.Fla.; *m* Jan. 15, 1914, Mildred Ellen, dau. of Dr. James Clifton Montgomery, of Elizabethtown, Ky. (issue: Clifton Montgomery Hocker); *m* 2d, Aug. 29, 1925, Marie Amelia, dau. of Warren Wray.
1–*m* 2d, Dec. 1, 1909, his cousin, Mattie Norvell Glover (qv).
1–Ed. Hampden-Sidney Coll., and U.Va. Admitted to Va. bar, 1868; moved to Fla., 1874; mem. Fla. Legislature, 1877-91, Constl. Conv., 1885; state's atty. 5th Jud. Circuit of Fla., 1877-86 (resigned); judge same circuit, 1893-1901; mem. Supreme Ct. Commn. of Fla., 1901-03; justice Supreme Ct. of Fla., 1903-09, 1909-15 (resigned). Pvt. 2d Va. Cav., C.S.A., in battles of Five Forks, Apr. 1, 1863, Amelia Springs, High Bridge, and Farmville, until the surrender at Appomattox (see Who's Who in America, Vol. VIII).

1–**HOCKER, Mattie Norvell Glover (Mrs. William A.),** *b* Buckingham Co., Va., Jan. 10, 1870.
9–Ambrose (Cobbs) **Cobb** (*b* 1590), patented land on Appomattox River, Henrico Co., 1639; *m* Anne–;
8–Robert (1627-82), justice and high sheriff, York Co., Va.; first vestryman of Bruton Parish Ch., Williamsburg, Va.; *m* Elizabeth–(1634-84);
7–Robert (1660-1725), *m* Rebecca Pinkethman (*d* 1715; William[8], vestryman Bruton Parish Ch.); *m* 2d, Elizabeth Allen (Daniel[8]);
6–Capt. Thomas (*d* 1832), began to write name Cobb; of Columbia Co., Ga.; patriot and soldier from Va. in Am. Rev.;
5–Thomas, of Slate River, Buckingham Co., Va.; *m* Nancy Watson (*b* 1767; William[6] [*d* Albemarle Co., 1813], of Hanover Co., *m* 1767, Martha Pleasants, of Goochland Co.);
4–William, *m* Sallie Puryear (Reuben[5], *m* —Hendricks, of Buckingham Co.);
3–Dr. John Allen (1815-83), of Bedford City, Va.; *m* Amanda Marshall Williamson (John Marshall[4], of Prince Edward Co., Va., *m* Martha Johns Rudd);
2–Irene Amanda (*b* 1843), *m* 1860, Joseph Benning **Glover** (1826-1907); issue: I–John Alexander (*b* 1862); II–Mattie N. (1 above); III–Irene Cobb (1871-1925); IV–Joseph (*b* 1874).
1–*m* Dec. 1, 1909, Judge William Adam Hocker (qv).
Summer place: Rosalind Av., Roanoke, Va.
Winter place: 1769 S.W. 9th St., Miami, Fla.

1–**HOCKING, William Ernest,** *b* Cleveland, O., Aug. 10, 1873.
3–William **Hocking** (1804-77), from Eng., 1826; settled at Brantford, Ont.; *m* Grace Colemar (1808-93);
2–Dr. William Francis (2 below).
10–Degory **Priest,** Mayflower Pilgrim (qv);
9–Mary, *m* 1630, Phinehas **Pratt** (1590-1680; son of Henry, a non-conformist clergyman, imprisoned in Eng.); from Eng., 1621; settled at Plymouth, Mass.;
8–Aaron (ca. 1654-1735), of Charlestown, Cohasset and Hingham, Mass.; *m* Sarah Pratt (1664-1706), of Weymouth;
7–Henry (*b* ca. 1686), of Cohasset and Newton; *m* 1710, Hannah–;
6–Henry (*b* 1717), of Needham, Mass.; *m* 1743, Sarah Fuller;
5–Henry (1746-1801), of Newton and Southbridge; pvt., Lexington Alarm, sgt., 1776-77, Am. Rev.; *m* Elizabeth Murdock;
4–Freeman (1775-1855), of Southbridge; *m* Polly Lyon (1780-1852);
3–Abiel Lyon (1805-68), of Southbridge; *m* 1837, Hulda Griggs (1813-86), of Eastford, Conn.;
2–Julia Carpenter (*b* 1848), of Southbridge; *m* 1871, William Francis **Hocking,** M.D. (1836-1903), of Yonkers, N.Y., and Cleveland, O.; issue: I–William Ernest (1 above); II–Grace Louise (*b* 1875; *m* Prof. William H. Runyon); III–Mary Alantha (*b* 1877; *m* Frank E. Burgess); IV–Abiel (*b* and *d* 1879); V–Julia Clarissa (1880-1920; *m* George Ernest Trueman); VI–Gertrude Emily (*b* 1886; *m* Oliver Mark Richards).
1–*m* June 28, 1905, Agnes Boyle O'Reilly, *b* Charlestown, Mass., May 19, 1877; dau. of John

Boyle O'Reilly, editor, of Charlestown, and Boston; issue: 1–Richard Boyle O'Reilly, *b* Berkeley, Calif., Aug. 26, 1906; B.S., Harvard, '28; 2–Hester, *b* New Haven, Conn., Dec. 9, 1909; ed. Radcliffe Coll.; 3–Joan, *b* New Haven, Aug. 26, 1911.

1–Studied U. of Ia.; U. of Chicago; A.B., Harvard, '01, A.M., 1902, Ph.D., 1904; (L.H.D., Williams Coll., 1923); Harvard fellow univs. of Göttingen, Berlin, Heidelberg. Instr. philosophy and hist. of religion, Andover Theol. Sem., 1904-06, instr. and asst. prof. philosophy, U.Calif., 1906-08; asst. prof. and prof. philosophy, Yale U., 1908-14; prof. philosophy, Harvard, 1914–. Author (see Who's Who in America). Mem. Am. Philos. Assn., Am. Acad. Arts and Sciences, Naval Inst., Cambridge Shop, Old Cambridge Shakespeare Soc., etc. Residence: Madison, N.H. Address: 16 Quincy St., Cambridge, Mass.

1–**HODGDON, Charles Edward,** *b* Portsmouth, N.H., Oct. 27, 1848.

8–Nicholas (Hodsdon) **Hodgdon,** the town of Hingham, Mass., granted him a house and lot, 1635-36; freeman, 1636-37; received land grant at Kittery, Me., 1656,69,73; *m* 1st, ca. 1639, Esther Wines (*d* 1647);

7–Jeremiah (bap. 1643-ante 1716), went to Kittery; taxed in Dover, 1666; settled at Portsmouth, later at Newcastle; *m* 1666/67, Anne Thwaits (Alexander[8], from Eng. in the "Hopewell," 1635, *m* Anne–);

6–John (bap. 1680-1735/36), of Portsmouth or Newington; signed petition at Newington to settle a minister, 1713; *m* 1706, Mary Hoyt;

5–John (*b* 1708), of Newington, N.H.; *m* 1729, Mary Decker (*b* 1711; John[6], *m* Sarah–);

4–Benjamin (*b* 1750), pvt. in Am. Rev.; *m* 1778, Rosamond Coleman (*d* 1841; Phineas[5], *m* Abigail Huntress);

3–Ephraim (1779-1848), of Newington and Barnstead; *m* Abigail Thomas (*d* 1874; Stephen Jones[4], *m* Olive Bickford?);

2–Benjamin (2 below).

7–John **Frye** (1601-95), from Eng. in the "Bevis," to Boston, 1638; wheelwright and first settler at Newbury, Mass., moved to Andover; freeholder, 1645; selectman, 1670; *m* Ann or Annie– (1605-80);

6–Ens. Samuel (1649-1725), town propr. before 1681; corpl., 1692; ens., 1697; lt., 1698; capt., 1708; selectman, 1692, 1702-03; *m* 1671, Mary Aslebee or Aslett (Lt. John[7], *m* Mary–);

5–Col. Samuel (1694-1761), active in Andover and in colonial militia; farmer; saw, grist and filling mills were built for him in N. Andover, Mass.; *m* 1719, Sarah Osgood (Timothy[6], *m* Deborah–);

4–William (1724-98), pvt. in Am. Rev.; farmer, Andover; *m* 2d, 1768, Deborah Colburn (*d* 1823), of Dracut, Mass.;

3–Isaac (1769-1816), tanner, Portsmouth, N.H.; *m* 1802, Rachel Foster (1784-1859; David[4], *m* Rachel–);

2–Hannah Foster (1810-86), *m* 1832, Benjamin **Hodgdon** (1805-94), farmer; issue: I–Augustus Lord (1834-35); II–Hannah Elizabeth (1836-85; *m* James M. Garland); III–Lydia Frye (1840-1919; *m* Robert King); IV–Benjamin Franklin (1841-43); V–Henry Clay (1844-62); VI–Mary Abby (1847-48); VII–Charles Edward (1 above).

1–*m* Jan. 24, 1876, Martha Jane Locke (Jan. 24, 1855-Dec. 23, 1879).

1–*m* 2d, Nov. 30, 1882, Lillian Lewis Robertson (qv for issue).

1–Retired. Mem. Bd. of Edn., 1896-1921; councilman, 1877-78; alderman, 1895-96; assessor of taxes, 1905-20. Mem. S.A.R. Mason (32°), Odd Fellow. Residence: 1400 Woodbury Av., Portsmouth, N.H.

1–**HODGDON, Lillian Lewis Robertson (Mrs. Charles E.),** *b* Northfield, N.H., Oct. 11, 1856.

6–William (Robinson) **Robertson** (1703-90; of Scotch parentage), from North of Ireland to Londonderry, N.H., bought land Pembroke, N.H., 1748; *m* Margaret Woodend (1705-85), "a Hieland Lass";

5–John (*b* Londonderry, 1732-1816), pvt., Am. Rev.; signed test, 1776; selectman, Bow, N.H., 1768; ferrykeeper; constable, 1780; *m* 2d, 1766, Elizabeth Lovejoy (1738-1835; Caleb[5], pvt. Am. Rev., *m* Mehitable Chandler; Henry[6], *m* Sarah Farnum);

4–James (1767-1847), *m* 1792, Martha Parker (1773-1856; Samuel[5], fifer in Am. Rev., *m* Martha, dau. Rev. Daniel Mitchell [*b* North of Ireland, 1697-1776], licensed to preach by Boston Presbytery 1746, his 1st ch. was in Georgetown, Me., ordained Pembroke, 1760, 1st Presbyn. minister there, *m* Martha White);

3–James Parker (1802-71), *m* 1828, Mary Ann Hammond;

2–James Lewis (2 below).

10–William **Hammond** (ca. 1575-1652), from Eng., 1632, settled at Watertown, Mass.; *m* 1605, Elizabeth Paine (1587-1670; William[11], from Eng. in the "Francis," 1634);

9–Thomas (ca. 1618-1655), of Watertown; *m* 1654, Hannah Cross (1636-1656/57; John[10], from Eng. to N.E., 1634, *m* Hannah–);

8–Lt. Thomas (1656-1724/25), of Watertown and Ipswich; in King Philip's War, 1675-76; freeman, Watertown, 1690; selectman, 1694,96; *m* 2d, 1679, Sarah Pickard (1656/57-1712/13; John[9], *m* Jane–, of Rowley, Mass.);

7–David (1690-1765), farmer nr. boundary of Ipswich and Rowley; *m* 1719, Mary Platts (1684-1747; Samuel[8], *m* Philippa Felt);

6–David (1720-97), of Rowley; soldier French and Indian War, 1757, pvt., 1759-60; served in Am. Rev.; *m* 1743, Susanna Harris (*d* 1780);

5–Thomas (1747-1827), of Rowley and Dunbarton, N.H.; marched on Lexington Alarm, 1775; served in Am. Rev.; *m* 1773, Esther Dole (1756-1846; Nathan[6], *m* Phebe–; Dr. John[7], Am. Rev.);

4–Nathan (1781-1855), *m* 1805, Isabel Smith (1785-1812; William[5], *m* Peggy Allison?);

3–Mary Ann (1808-60), *m* James P. **Robertson** (3 above).

8–Thomas **Carter** (will dated 1676), from Eng., settled at Salisbury, Mass., 1639; shared in the 1st division of lots in Salisbury, 1639; commoner 1650; *m* Mary–;

7–John (1650-post 1718), of Salisbury; took oath of allegiance and fidelity 1677-78; soldier sent to defense of Marlboro, 1689; *m* Martha Brown (1654-1717/18; William Browne[8], *m* Elizabeth Murford);

6–Ephraim (*b* 1693), Concord, N.H.; garrison duty with son Ezra in French and Indian War, 1746-47; *m* 1717, Martha Stevens (*b* 1696; John[7], *m* Dorothy–);

5–Daniel (1719-1800), to Concord; mem. Com. Safety; signed test; pvt. Am. Rev.; *m* Hannah Fowler (*b* Salisbury, 1720-*d* Concord, 1802; Jacob[6], of Amesbury, Mass., *m* Mary Jones);

4–Col. John (1759-1847), of Concord, N.H.; pvt. Am. Rev., pensioned; lt. col., 1st Regt., N.H. Vols., War 1812; Democrat; *m* 2d, 1790, Widow Lucy Cavia Wells (1762-1842);

3–Nathaniel (1793-1842), grocer Bow, N.H.; Democrat; *m* 1820, Elizabeth Robertson (1798-1831; James[4], same as 4 above);

2–Elizabeth Susan (1829-71), *m* 1st, 1851, James Lewis **Robertson** (1828-56), farmer and carpenter; *m* 2d, Charles Hill Robertson (1835-88), teacher and farmer; issue (1st marriage); I–Lillian Lewis (1 above); issue (2d marriage): I–Frank C. (*b* 1860; *m* Belle Woodbury Gile); II–Hammond (1862-63); III–Sadie Hammond (*b* 1865; *m* Amos Rouse; *m* 2d, Frank Carter); IV–Mary Azelia (*b* 1868; *m* 1898, Clyde Ambrose Gile, *b* 1860).

1–*m* Nov. 30, 1882, as his 2d wife, Charles Edward Hodgdon (qv); issue (all *b* Portsmouth, N.H.): 1–Cora Eloise, *b* Apr. 16, 1884; *m* July 14, 1904, Albert F. Witham (issue: Edward; Pearl; John; Maurice; Norman; Phyllis); 2–Mildred, *b* Nov. 12, 1887; *m* Nov. 14, 1918, Howard K. Gratteau (issue: Kent; Ruth; Robert; Calvin); 3–Winifred, *b* Nov. 11, 1891; B.Sc., U. of N.H.; *m* May 12, 1923, Lewis Joseph Wadleigh (issue: John Nicholas, *b* Nov. 15, 1928); 4–Augusta (Aug. 5-Sept. 24, 1894).

1–Mem. King's Daus., Scotland Clan Donnachaidh, D.F.P.A., D.A.R., U.S.D. 1812, O.E.S., Rebekah. Baptist. Republican. Clubs: Graffort, Portsmouth City. Residence: 1400 Woodbury Av., Portsmouth, N.H.

1–**HODGES, Alice Elizabeth Smith (Mrs. Harley M.),** *b* Milford, Conn., Apr. 21, 1877.

10–William **Smith,** of Huntington, L.I.;

9–Benjamin (*d* ca. 1713), of Milford, Conn.; *m* 1660, Mary Baldwin (*d* 1680; Timothy[10], *m* Mary–);

8-Benjamin (*b* 1666), of Milford; *m* 1682, Sarah (Phippen) Houghter (Gamaliel[9]);
7-Ebenezer (1692-1763), of Milford; *m* 1719, Anna Fowler (William[8], *m* Anna Beard);
6-Ebenezer (1720-96), of Milford; *m* Jane Clark (1723-1810; Samuel[7], *m* Mary Clark; Dea. George[8]);
5-David (1756-1841), of Milford; sgt. Am. Rev.; *m* 1778, Mary Sanford (1755-1843; John[6], *m* Hannah Treat);
4-David (1780-1875), of Milford; mem. First Congl. Ch.; farmer; *m* 1st, 1803, Frances Baldwin (1785-1840; Edward[5], *m* Frances, dau. of Henry Summers);
3-Marcus (1813-95), of Milford and Orange, Conn.; farmer; mem. First Congl. Ch.; *m* 1844, Lucy Ann Garlick (1821-88; Capt. Samuel[4], *m* Huldah Gilbert; Dr. Samuel[5]);
2-Sereno Brace (2 below).
10-John **Bailey** (qv);
9-John (*b* 1613), from Eng. with father, 1635; *m* Eleanor Emery;
8-Rev. James (1650-1707), of Roxbury, Mass.; *m* 1672, Mary Carr (*d* 1688);
7-Isaac (1681-1711), of Danvers, Mass.; *m* Mercy Saxton (Capt. Joseph[8], *m* Hannah Dennison);
6-Joseph (1703-65), of Stonington, Conn.; *m* 1724, Abigail Ingraham (*b* 1700);
5-James (1735-1812), of Lebanon, Conn.; corpl. Am. Rev.; *m* 1762, Lucy Gay (1740-1833);
4-Hezekiah (1789-1863), of Lebanon; *m* 1814, Hannah Sherman (1790-1864; Daniel[5], *m* Eunice Stanton);
3-George Hezekiah (1832-1908), of New London, Conn.; *m* 1855, Sarah Elizabeth Rose (1836-72; Samuel[4], *m* Lucy Ann Whipple);
2-Jane Elizabeth (*b* 1857), of West Haven, Conn.; *m* 1876, Sereno Brace **Smith** (1845-1917), of Milford and West Haven, Conn.; merchant; teacher; mem. First Congl. Ch., of Milford, and later of West Haven; issue: I-Alice Elizabeth (1 above); II-Rena Judson (*b* 1884; *m* 1920, Robert Bates Hall).
1-*m* May 10, 1899, Harley Middleton Hodges, *b* England, Jan. 24, 1874; son of William Henry Hodges, *m* Sarah Drew, both of Eng.; issue: 1-Lois Elizabeth, *b* West Haven, Conn., Mar. 29, 1900; B.A., Smith Coll., '21; *m* June 30, 1923, Franklin Somers Clark, *b* New Haven, Conn., Mar. 26, 1897; son of Herbert Franklin Clark, of W. Haven (issue: William Hodges, *b* and *d* 1930).
1-State Normal Sch., New Haven, Conn., 1896. Taught in grade school, 1896-97; organist in First Congl. Ch. of West Haven; ardent ch. worker, holding many ch. offices. Mem. D.A.R., O.E.S. Republican. Residence: "Littledean," 654 Ocean Av., West Haven, Conn.

1-**HODGES, William Van Derveer,** *b* Westville, N.Y., July 6, 1877.
9-William **Hodges** (qv);
8-John (1650-1719), large real estate owner, Taunton; mem. coroner's jury, 1672; mem. 2d squadron, Taunton Mil. Co., 1682; constable, 1684; *m* 1672, Elizabeth Macey (*d* 1718/19; Capt. George[9], of Taunton, dep. Gen. Ct., magistrate, Plymouth co., *m* Susannah, dau. of Rev. Nicholas Street);
7-William (1682-1766), capt. 3d mil. co., Taunton; a founder of New Taunton, 1735; *m* 2d, 1719/20, Mary Clapp;
6-Job (1721-1808), settled at Norton (now Mansfield), Mass.; clk. 2d co. Norton militia, 1762; ens.; capt., West Co., 1771; mem. com. to build meeting house, 1765; mem. com. to keep river open for fishing, 1771; *m* Ruth Andrews (1723 or 1724-1808; Samuel[7], of Dighton, Mass., *m* Elizabeth Emerson);
5-Emerson (ca. 1764-1844), at Westmoreland, N.H., 1789; later removed to Londonderry, Vt.; constable; collector; selectman, 1801; prob. removed to N.Y.; *m* prob., 1792, Susan-;
4-James (1797-1867), removed to Henrietta, N.Y.; *m* Mary Campbell (*d* 1870; Isaac[5], of Lebanon, N.Y., *m* Elizabeth Edmond);
3-James Luther (*b* 1833), removed to Eyota, Minn.; later to Little Rock, Ark.; settled finally at Denver, Colo.; *m* 1st, 1855, Anna Withall (1832-75), from Eng.;
2-George Lincoln (*b* 1856), lawyer, Denver, Colo.; *m* Ella Van Derveer, of N.Y.; issue: I-William Van Derveer (1 above); II-Ella F. (*m* Norman Read); III-Irma C.
1-*m* Dec. 2, 1902, Mabel E. Gilluly (*d* Mar. 3, 1925); dau. of Joseph E. Gilluly, of Denver; issue: 1-Joseph Gilluly, *b* Denver, Apr. 30, 1909; A.B., Yale, '30; 2-William Van Derveer, Jr., *b* Denver, Sept. 18, 1911; A.B., Yale, '32.
1-*m* 2d, June 5, 1926, Catharine Stockton (Beasley) Lowndes.
1-LL.B., Columbia U., 1899 (Delta Psi). Lawyer since 1889. Treas. Rep. Nat. Com., 1924-28 (see Who's Who in America). Mem. Am. Law Inst. (council). Clubs: Denver, University, Denver Country, Cherry Hills Country, Denver Athletic, Mile High, St. Anthony; Metropolitan (Washington); Union League (New York). Residence: 300 High St., Denver, Colo.

1-**HODGSON, James (Levi) Goodwin,** *b* Burt, Ia., Apr. 22, 1892.
7-George **Hodgson** (*b* 1701), from Eng. to Ireland, thence to Pa., 1710; settled Pa.; at Greensboro, N.C., 1750; *m* Mary Thatcher;
6-John (*b* 1731), of Greensboro, N.C.; *m* Mary Mills;
5-Thomas (1756-95), of Greensboro; Quaker; *m* Patience Dillon (1762-1830; Daniel[6] [1713-1805], of Guilford Co., N.C., *m* Lydia- [1713-1800]; Luke[7], from Ireland to Nantucket, Mass., settled in Va., *m* Susan Garrett);
4-Amos (*b* 1782), of Pekin, Ill.; *m* Mary Barnett (1792-1845);
3-Levi (1826-94), of Burt, Ia.; *m* 1847, Anna Bennett (1830-1915; Michael[4]);
2-Elmer O. (2 below).
10-Daniel **Goodwin,** (*d* ca. 1712), in Kittery, Me., 1652; *m* 1st, Margaret Spencer (Thomas[11]);
9-James (*d* 1697), of Berwick, Me.; killed by Indians; *m* 1686, Sarah Thompson (Miles[10]);
8-Richard, of Somersworth and Rochester, N.H.;
7-Richard (*b* 1714), of Somersworth and Rochester; *m* Keziah Tibbetts, of Somersworth;
6-John, of Rochester, N.H.; selectman 1776,80; called capt. and col.; *m* Mehitable Locke (James[7]; Edward[8]; Capt. John[9]);
5-John (1789-1862), of Sandwich, N.H.; vet. War 1812; *m* Lydia Bickford (1800-80), of Somersworth;
4-James B. (1818-1902), of Rochester and Sandwich; *m* 2d, Elizabeth (Betsy) H. Stevens, of Farmington, N.H.;
3-Edwin Horace (1843-1928), of Worcester, Mass., and Burt, Ia.; *m* 1869, Eliza Daniels May (1848-1921; Oliver Wolcott[4]; William[5]; Oliver[6]; Col. Elisha[7]; Benjamin[8]; Elisha[9]; John[10]; John[11]);
2-Susie Aldrich (*b* 1871), *m* 1890, Elmer O. **Hodgson** (*b* 1864); *m* 2d, 1922, Will J. Easterly, of Neelin, Manitoba, Can.; issue (1st marriage): I-E. May (*b* 1891; *m* Edward Kelso); II-James Goodwin (1 above).
1-*m* Oct. 9, 1920, Gertrude Elizabeth Simms, *b* Chicago, Ill., Feb. 16, 1891; dau. of Richard Simms, *d*, of Richmond, Ind.; issue: 1-Marshall Goodwin, *b* Richmond, Ind., Apr. 11, 1922.
1-B.A., U. of Ia., '15; B.L.S., N.Y. State Library Sch., 1917; studied U.Ariz., 1922-24. Librarian, Internat. Inst. of Agr., Rome, Italy, 1925-29; supt., Business and Municipal Library, Queens Borough Pub. Lib., Jamaica, 1930- (see Who's Who in America). Served as corp. inf., A.E.F., 1918-19; cdr., Rome Post, A.L., 1927-28; adj. Dept. of Italy, A.L., 1927-28. V.p. 6th Section, Internat. Library Congress, Prague, 1926; official del., British Lib. Assn. to World Library Congress, Rome, 1929. Home: Lone Rock, Ia. Address: Queens Borough Public Library, Jamaica, N.Y.

1-**HOFFMAN, Irene Stoddard (Mrs. William M. V.),** *b* New York, N.Y., Mar. 6, 1867.
8-Anthony (Stodder) **Stoddard** (qv);
7-Rev. Solomon (1643-1729), A.B., Harvard, 1662; distinguished theologian; *m* Esther (Warham) Mather;
6-John (1682-1748), col. Mass. militia; *m* Prudence Chester (1690-1780);
5-Solomon (1736-1827), *m* Martha Partridge (1739-72);
4-Solomon (1771-1860), *m* Sarah Tappan (1771-1852);
3-Charles (*b* 1802), dea. of Old South Ch., Boston; *m* Mary Noble (Daniel[4], *m* Esther Belden Wolcott);
2-Charles Augustus, D.D. (2 below).
8-James **Prime** (*d* 1686), from Eng., was at New Haven, Conn., 1638, at Milford before 1644; *m* Mary-;

7–James (1633-1736), *m* Sarah–;
6–Rev. Ebenezer (1700-79), B.A., Yale, 1719; patriot preacher during Am. Rev.; *m* Experience Youngs;
5–Benjamin Youngs, M.A., M.D. (1733-91), B.A., Princeton, 1751; patriot in Am. Rev.; poet; *m* Mary (Wheelwright) Greaton;
4–Nathaniel Scudder, D.D. (1785-1856), B.A., Princeton, 1804; Presbyn. minister; educator; author; *m* 1808, Julia Ann Jermain (Maj. John[5], *m* Margaret Pierson);
3–Samuel Irenaeus, D.D. (1812-85), B.A., Williams, 1829; Presbyn. minister; editor New York Observer; author; *m* 2d, 1835, Eloisa Lemet Williams (Moses[4], of Ballston Spa, N.Y.);
2–Mary Elizabeth (1839-1917), *m* 1859, Charles Augustus **Stoddard,** D.D. (1833-1920), B.A., Williams, '54; Presbyn. minister; editor New York Observer; author (see Who's Who in America); issue: I–Ethel (*b* 1864; *m* 1894, Frederic J. Parsons, *b* 1860); II–Irene (1 above); III–Jermain Stoddard (*b* 1875; *m* 1900, Stuart Duncan, *b* 1869); IV–Marion (*m* Albert Gould Jennings).
1–*m* Apr. 21, 1887, William Mitchell Vail Hoffman (see Vol. I, p. 320, for genealogy); issue (all *b* New York): 1–C(harles) Gouverneur, *b* July 29, 1888; A.B., Harvard, '13; drove ambulance on French front, 1915-16; 2d lt., Air Service, Royal Flying Corps, Mar. 1917; 1st flight lt., May 1917; participated in Montdidier operations; 2–Stoddard, *b* Mar. 26, 1892; Columbia, '14; drove ambulance on French front, 1915-16; 2d lt., Air Service, Royal Flying Corps, Jan. 1917, 1st flight lt., Mar. 1917; participated in Verdun operations; 3–William M. V., Jr., *b* Apr. 20, 1898; Harvard, '20; enlisted and was in Mexican border service; promoted to sgt. and with A.E.F. in France.
1–Mem. C.D.A. Club: Colony. Residence: 35 W. 51st St., New York.

1–**HOGG, Clara Hyde Dewey (Mrs. Charles M.),** *b* Cadiz, O., Mar. 7, 1841.
8–Thomas **Dewey** (qv);
7–Josiah (bap. 1641-1732), of Windsor, Conn.; sgt. King Philip's War; *m* 1st, 1662, Hepzibah Lyman (1644-1732; Richard[8], *m* Hepzibah Ford);
6–Josiah (1666-ca. 1750), of Northampton, Mass.; *m* 1691, Mehitable Miller (*b* 1666; William[7], *m* Patience–);
5–John (1700-73), *m* 1726, Experience Woodward (1704-1801; John[6], *m* Experience Baldwin);
4–Daniel (1731-1816), of Lebanon, Conn.; comd. a co., 1775, for relief of Boston, Am. Rev.; served in R.I. campaign under Gen. Joseph Spencer; *m* 1753, Temperance Bailey;
3–Eliphalet (1762-1838), soldier Am. Rev.; *m* 2d, 1793, Rachel Ann Hyde (1761-1847);
2–Chauncey (2 below).
9–William **Denison** (qv);
8–Capt. George (bap. 1620-1694), served under Cromwell; settled at Mystic, Conn.; dep. Gen. Ct. from Stonington, Conn., 1654-94; capt. New London Co. troops in King Philip's War, 1675-76; *m* 1st, Bridget Thomson (1622-43);
7–Hannah (*b* 1643), *m* Capt. Joseph **Saxton** (*b* 1656);
6–Mercy (bap. 1686), *m* 1st, Isaac **Bailey** (Rev. James[7]);
5–Isaac (*b* 1707), *m* Abigail Hunt;
4–Temperance (1731-95), *m* Daniel **Dewey** (4 above).
9–Gov. John **Webster** (qv);
8–Mary, *m* John **Hunt**;
7–Jonathan (1637-91), *m* 1662, Clemence Hosmer (*d* 1698), of Northampton, Mass.;
6–Dea. Ebenezer (1676-1743), *m* 1698, Hannah Clarke (Capt. William[7], *m* Hannah Strond);
5–Abigail (*b* 1708), *m* 1730, Isaac **Bailey** (5 above).
4–Jesse **Pritchard** (*d* 1784), from Wales 1784, settled at Frederickstown, Md.; *m*– (*d* at sea);
3–John (*b* Wales 1750-1844), capt. in War 1812; *m* Sarah Beeson Brownfield;
2–Nancy (Oct. 27, 1804-1897), *m* 1823, Chauncey **Dewey** (1806-80), lawyer, judge, banker; issue: I–Eliphalet (1823-89; *m* Virginia Affic; *m* 2d, Sarah Knox); II–Orville C. (1833-1902); III–Mary (1836-69; *m* Fulton Moffett); IV–Clara Hyde (1 above); V–Charles P. (1843-1904; *m* Emma Scott); VI–Albert Brownfield (*b* 1846; *m* Louise Shufeldt).
1–*m* Nov. 28, 1860, Charles Mather Hogg (Jan. 29, 1839-Aug. 25, 1920); son of William Hogg, Co. Tyrone, Ireland; issue: 1–Anna, *b* Cadiz, O., Sept. 1861; *m* June 6, 1888; Hullihen Quarrier (issue: Charles Hogg, *d* at Straits of Gibraltar, 1919, while serving in World War); 2–Alberta, *b* Cadiz, Dec. 18, 1863; *m* Apr. 5, 1906, Jacob H. Lynn, son of Evans Lynn, of Phila., Pa.; 3–Chauncey Dewey (June 6, 1867-June 20, 1905).
1–Ed. Steubenville (O.) Sem. Mem. D.F.P.A., D.A.R., U.S.D. 1812. Residence: Cadiz, O.

1–**HOLBROOK, Evans,** *b* Onawa, Ia., Jan. 15, 1875.
9–Thomas **Holbrook** (1601-1674-76), from Eng., settled at Weymouth, Mass., 1634 or 35; *m* Joanna– (*d* ante 1677);
8–Thomas (ca. 1635-1697), of Braintree and Quincy; *m* Joanna–;
7–Peter (1655-1712), of Braintree and Mendon, Mass.; *m* 1st, Alice Godfrey (*d* 1705);
6–John (1679-1765), of Bellingham; *m* Hannah Chapin (1684-1770);
5–Josiah (1715-83), of Pompey, N.Y.; soldier in two French wars; *m* Peggy Ives; *m* 2d, Mary Moffitt;
4–David H. (1760-1832), physician, Lafayette, N.Y.; soldier Am. Rev., wounded at Battle of Bennington; *m* Mehitable Wells, of Goshen, N.Y.;
3–Henry Lawrence or Laurens (1799-1874), of Onawa, Ia.; *m* Mary Connelly;
2–Bernard David (1834-1910), lawyer and banker; *m* Mary Frances Oliver (1839-1920); issue: I–Olive B. (1863-64); II–Parker Kimball (*b* 1864; *m* Virginia Robinson); III–George Oliver (1866-1922); IV–Margaret Oliver (1867-74); V–David Oliver (1873-1919); VI–Evans (1 above); VII–Norah Kimmell (1877-89); VIII–Edith Oliver (*b* 1880; *m* Rex B. Kennedy); IX–Frank Lyon (*b* and *d* 1883).
1–*m* Oct. 4, 1902, Joanna Blessing Oliver (May 1, 1877-July 23, 1905); dau. of Addison Oliver, of Onawa, Ia., *m* Hannah Towne; issue: 1–Bernard David, *b* Chicago, Ill., Sept., 5, 1903; A.B., Stanford U., '24, A.M., 1925; 2–Joanna Oliver, *b* Chicago, July 14, 1905; A.B., Stanford, '25; *m* Nov. 1, 1926, Harvey Gladding Denham (issue: Mary Holbrook).
1–Student U.Mich., 1893-95; A.B., Stanford U., '97 (Alpha Delta Phi, Phi Delta Phi); Northwestern U., 1897-98; LL.B., U.Mich., 1900. Prof. law, U.Mich., since 1905. Author (see Who's Who in America). Episcopalian. Democrat. Club: University. Residence: Ann Arbor, Mich.

1–**HOLCH, Lillian Hubbard (Mrs. Henry G.),** *b* Providence, R.I., Nov. 5, 1875.
9–George **Hubbard** (qv);
8–John (1630-1702), of Wethersfield, Hadley and Hatfield; *m* Mary Merriam (William[9], *m* Sarah, dau. James Burges);
7–Dea. Isaac (1667-1750), Sunderland, Mass.; mem. council that installed Jonathan Edwards; *m* Anne Warner (1669-1750; Daniel[8]);
6–Rev. Jonathan (1703-65), of Sheffield, Mass.; *m* Rachel Ely (John[7], *m* Mary Bliss);
5–Moses (1747-1830), *m* 1st, Abigail Sheldon;
4–Elisha (*b* 1781), *m* 1811, Julia or Joanna Dibble (*d* 1815?), prob. of Killingworth, Conn.;
3–Henry (1815-1901), *m* 1839, Juliann Sizer (*b* Williamsport, Pa., 1818-*d* Wyoming, N.Y., 1884);
2–Hiram Wilbur (2 below).
11–William **Pynchon** (qv);
10–John (*d* 1703), *m* 1645, Amy Wyllys (*d* 1699; Gov. George[11], of Fenny Compton, Co. Warwick, *m* Mary–);
9–Mary (*b* 1650), *m* as his 1st wife, Joseph **Whiting,** mcht., Westfield, Mass., returned to Hartford, 1675 or 76; treas. of Conn., 1678–, for 39 yrs. (William[10], qv);
8–Mary (*b* 1672), *m* 1st, Joseph **Sheldon** (1668-1708), miller, Suffield, Mass.; rep. Mass. Gen. Ct. (Isaac[9], qv);
7–Benjamin (1705-52), soldier Father Rasle's War; settled in Suffield; *m* 1726, Abigail Kellogg (*b* Hadley, 1703; Nathaniel[8], m Sarah Boltwood);
6–William (1731-1816), *m* 1753, Hannah Noble (1735-1810), of Sheffield (Elisha[7], *m* Abigail, dau. Mark Warner, *m* Lydia Phelps);
5–Abigail (*b* 1757), *m* Moses **Hubbard** (5 above).
4–Abram **Ferguson,** of Broadalbin, N.Y.;

3–Calvin (*b* Broadalbin, N.Y., ca. Mar. 14, 1818-*d* Ilion, N.Y., Sept. 19, 1903), *m* Ann Tims (*b* Oxfordshire, Eng., Dec. 10, 1822-*d* Hinckley, N.Y., Sept. 24, 1899; Samuel[4], *m* Susan Griffin);
2–Josephine (*b* Broadalbin, Mar. 15, 1843-*d* Brooklyn, Oct. 12, 1917), *m* Hiram Wilbur **Hubbard** (*b* Bergen, N.Y., Oct. 19, 1842-*d* Bath, N.Y., Mar. 30, 1922); issue: I–Frederick Grant (1871-97; *m* Emily Phillips); II–Lillian (1 above).
1–*m* July 7, 1898, Henry George Holch, *b* Buffalo, N.Y., Feb. 23, 1869; son of Johann George Holch (1831-72), of Schwabish Hall, Germany, *m* Maria Schmidt; issue: 1–Edith, *b* Brooklyn, N.Y., Nov. 10, 1899; Adelphi and Pratt Inst.; *m* Mar. 23, 1923, William Rodney Fiske Adams, son of William Fiske Adams, *m* Ivy Bell Thompson (issue: Joan Fiske, *b* Jan. 20, 1926).
1–Packer Collegiate Inst., Brooklyn, N.Y. Mem. C.D.XVIIC., D.A.R., Soc. N.E. Women, Mass. Women in N.Y., L.I. Hist. Soc. of Brooklyn. Club: Rubenstein. Summer place: "Bayberry Lodge," Huguenot Park, S.I. Residence: 330 Clinton Av., Brooklyn, N.Y.

1–**HOLDEN, Ella Bancroft Jones (Mrs. William Henry),** *b* Belleville, Ont., Can., Sept. 2, 1861.
7–Hugh **Jones** (ca. 1637-1688), from Eng. to Salem, Mass., 1650-51; *m* 2d, 1672, Mary Foster (bap. 1649-1717; John[8], of Salem, *m* Martha Tompkins);
6–Hugh (1683-1770), Dracut, Mass.; *m* Hannah Wilson (*b* 1688; Samuel[7], *m* Elizabeth, dau. of Robert Pierce; John[8]);
5–Nathan (1721-99), signed Association Test, 1776; mem. "True Sons of Liberty"; patriot Am. Rev.; *m* 1743, Elizabeth Colburn (1724-ante 1799; Josiah[6], *m* Sarah, dau. Daniel Colburn; Thomas[7]; Edward[8]);
4–Nathan (1748-1813), signed Association Test, 1776; mem. "True Sons of Liberty"; removed to Mt. Vernon, N.H.; *m* Esther Butterfield;
3–Nathan (1787-1820), *d* Mt. Vernon, N.H.; *m* 1813, Sarah Bancroft;
2–Nathan, IV (2 below).
7–Thomas **Bancroft** (qv); *m* 2d, 1648, Elizabeth (1626-1711), dau. Michael Metcalf;
6–Capt. Ebenezer (1667-1717), removed to Lynn, Mass.; *m* 1692, Abigail Eaton (1677-1716; John[7], *m* Elizabeth, dau. of Thomas Kendall; William[8]);
5–Lt. Timothy (1709-72), removed to Dunstable (Tyngsborough), Mass.; *m* ca. 1733, Elizabeth Farwell (1715-54; Capt. Henry[6], *m* Susannah, dau. of Josiah Richardson; Joseph[7]; Henry[8]);
4–Jonathan (1750-1815), minuteman, at Lexington Alarm; later sgt., 2d lt., lt., Am. Rev.; *m* 1773, Martha Green (1749-1843; Isaac[5], *m* Martha, dau. of Jonathan Boyden; Eleazer[6]; William[7]);
3–Sarah (1789-1876), *m* Nathan **Jones** (3 above);
2–Nathan, IV (1816-92), removed to Belleville, Ont., Can.; merchant; *m* 1847, his cousin, Jane Clement (1825-95); issue: I–William Flint (1850-1915; *m* Helen Reese Price); II–Florence Howard (1852-1919; *m* Lewis Wallbridge Yeomans); III–George Augustus (*b* and *d* 1853); IV–Mary Alma (*b* 1855); V–Leila Jane (1856-1928; *m* Thomas Bleecker); VI–Philip Clement (1859-1922; *m* May Murrell); VII–Ella Bancroft (1 above).
1–*m* June 9, 1887, William Henry Holden (July 26, 1859-Jan. 31, 1925); son of John Henry Holden, of Merrickville and Belleville, Ont.; issue: 1–Howard Bancroft, *b* Belleville, Jan. 6, 1889; removed to Detroit, Mich.; *m* Mar. 4, 1914, Jessie Thomson, dau. of Hugh McLean of Vancouver, B.C. (issue: Marion Thomson; Jane Bancroft); 2–Marion Sawyer (*b* Detroit, Mich., June 21, 1891-June 7, 1903); 3–Alma Clement (Mrs. Frederick Adelbert Curtiss, qv for Holden lineages).
1–Mem. D.F.P.A., D.C.W., D.A.R., I.A.G. Club: Women's City. Residence: 947 Lakeside Dr., S.E., Grand Rapids, Mich.

1–**CURTISS, Alma Clement Holden (Mrs. Frederick Adelbert),** *b* Detroit, Mich., Sept. 9, 1894.
9–Richard **Holden** (qv);
8–Stephen (1658/59-1715), *m* ca. 1685, Hannah Lawrence (1664-ca. 1735; Ens. Nathaniel[9], *m* Sarah, dau. of Joseph Morse; John[10], qv);
7–Lt. John (ca. 1685-1753), *m* 1716, Sarah Davis (1694-1753; John[8], *m* Mehitable–; Samuel[9]; Barnabus[10]);
6–Caleb (1723/24-post 1795), Shelburne, Mass.; *m* 2d, 1766, Mary Farley;
5–Jonathan (1780-ante 1840), Hadley, Mass.; *m* 1803, Sally Owen (Elisha[6], *m* Lucretia, dau. of Dr. Moses Hayden);
4–Charles (1807-73), Merrickville, Ont., Can; *m* 1829, Tamar Sabrina Welton (1808-80; Harvey Bronson[5], *m* Lydia Harris; Aaron[6]; Eliakim[7]; Richard[8]; John[9]);
3–John Henry (1836-97), *m* 1856, his cousin, Mary Esther Sawyer (1836-89);
2–William Henry (2 below).
9–Thomas **Sawyer** (qv);
8–Nathaniel (1670-1756), *m* 2d, Elizabeth– (*d* 1768);
7–Capt. Nathaniel (1716-1805), *m* 1734/35, Mary Houghton (*b* 1715; Jonathan[8], *m* Thankful, dau. of Josiah White; John[9]; John[10], qv);
6–Capt. Nathaniel (*b* 1744), capt. Am. Rev.; *m* 1771, Catherine Ellis (*b* 1750; Abner[7], *m* Mary, dau. of Daniel Maccane; Joseph[8]; John[9]; John[10]);
5–Oliver (1772-1859), Heath, Mass.; *m* 1801, Mary (Polly) Wilder (1779-1853; Lt. Samuel[6], *m* Sarah, dau. of Josiah Ballard; David[7]; Ebenezer[8]; John[9]; Thomas[10], qv);
4–Merrick (1808-1900), Belleville, Ont.; *m* 1834, Esther Holden (1812-40; James[5], *m* 1st, Esther, dau. of Stephen Call; Caleb[6], same as 6 above);
3–Mary Esther, *m* John Henry **Holden** (3 above).
10–Robert **Clements** (qv);
9–Robert (ca. 1634-1714), *m* 1652, Elizabeth Fawne (*d* 1715; John[10], *m* Elizabeth–);
8–John (1653-92), *m* 1676, Elizabeth Ayer (1652-99; Robert[9], *m* Elizabeth, dau. of Henry Palmer; John[10]);
7–Lt. John (1686-1762), *m* ante 1708, Elizabeth Kimball (1683/84-1754; Henry[8], *m* Hannah, dau. of Onesiphorus Marsh; Henry[9]; Richard[10], qv);
6–Benjamin (1717/18-1786), Haverhill, Mass.; patriot Am. Rev., on alarm list, 1775; mem. Haverhill co.; *m* 1739, his cousin, Mary Bartlett (1720-1805; Christopher[7], *m* Mary, dau. of John Clement; Christopher[8]; Christopher[9]; Richard[10], qv);
5–Philip (1743/44-1817), pvt. Am. Rev.; Claremont, N.H.; *m* 1766, Phebe Sawyer (*b* 1747; John[6], *m* Abigail, dau. of Joshua Thompson; Joshua[7]; Joshua[8]; Thomas[9]);
4–Philip (1780-1834), removed to Brockville, Ont.; *m* 1803, Elizabeth Bancroft (1785-1851; Lt. Jonathan[5]);
3–Jane (1825-95), *m* 1847, her cousin, Nathan **Jones** (1816-92);
2–Ella Bancroft (qv for Bancroft lineages), *m* 1887, William Henry **Holden** (1859-1925), removed to Detroit, Mich.
1–*m* Oct. 10, 1916, Frederick Adelbert Curtiss, *b* Port Richmond, S.I., Mar. 7, 1895; son of Frederick Adelbert Curtiss, of La Canada, Calif.; issue: 1–Richard Holden, *b* Grand Rapids, Mich., June 13, 1927.
1–Mem. D.F.P.A.; D.A.R. Club: Women's City. Residence: 947 Lakeside Drive, S.E., Grand Rapids, Mich.

1–**HOLGATE, Stella Grace Sanford (Mrs. Isaac),** *b* Walcott, Rice Co., Minn., Apr. 8, 1865.
9–William **Wadsworth** (qv);
8–John (1638-1689), *m* 1662, Sarah Stanley (Thomas[9], *m* Benedicta–);
7–James (1677-1756), *m* Ruth Noyes;
6–James, *m* Abigail Penfield;
5–Gen. James (1752-1801 or 1821), Am. Rev.; *m* 1772, Mary Brace (Henry[6], *m* Elizabeth Cadwell);
4–Ariel Brace (*b* 1791), *m* Roxey Rouse Robinson (1783-1862; Capt. Jonathan[5], Am. Rev., *m* Roxey Rouse);
3–Susanna (1819-1903), *m* 1834, Abram **Sanford** (see Vol. III, p. 251, for Sanford lineage);
2–Carlton Washington (2 below).
8–George **Little** (qv);
7–Joseph (1653-1740), *m* 1677, Mary Coffin (1657-1725; Tristram[8], *m* Judith [Greenleaf] Somerby; Tristram[9], qv);
6–George (1682-1760), *m* 1710 or 11, Edna Hale (1684-1732; Thomas[7], *m* Sarah Northend; Thomas[8], *m* Mary Hutchinson; Thomas[9], qv);
5–Joseph (1727-1811), *married*, Elizabeth Ingalls (1725-64; Eldad[6], *m* Hannah Watts; Samuel[7], *m* Sarah Hendrick; Henry[8], *m* Mary Osgood; Edmund[9], qv);

4-Sarah (1762-1803), *m* Thomas Vickery **Vose** (see Vol. III, p. 251, for Vose and other lineages);
3-Gilman (1803-74), *m* 1828, Olive Nichols;
2-Sarah (1841-1917), *m* 1864, Carlton Washington **Sanford** (1835-1910); for issue see Vol. III, p. 251.
1-*m* Nov. 25, 1891, Rev. Isaac Holgate (Houlgate until May 15, 1913), *b* Toton, Nottinghamshire, Eng., Jan. 15, 1862; attended Doane Coll. abt. 3 yrs.; grad. Seabury Div. School, 1890; ordered deacon, 1890, ordained priest, 1891, P.E.Ch.; in active pastoral work until 1918, when retired; genealogist; son of Isaac Houlgate (immigrant 1872, with wife and 7 children; Joshua[3], of Eng., *m* Alice Ride; George[4], *m* Hannah–; Joshua Holdgate[5]), *m* Sarah Alton (George[3], of Eng., *m* Hannah Morrell).
Residence: 414 N. Monterey St., Alhambra, Calif.

1-**HOLLADAY, William Waller,** *b* Richmond, Va., Sept. 7, 1864.
7-John **Holladay** (qv);
6-Capt. Joseph (1726-95), inspector of tobacco; served in Am. Rev.; *m* Elizabeth Lewis (Henry or Harry[7]);
5-Lewis (1751-1820), lt. in Am. Rev.; justice, sheriff; *m* Elizabeth (Lewis) Littlepage (Zachary Lewis[6] [1702-65], of Spotsylvania Co., Va., burgess, 1757,58-61, *m* 1725, Mary [1699-1781], dau. of John Waller, qv; Zachary[7], to Va., ca. 1692, had land grant in King and Queen Co., 1694);
4-Waller (1776-1860), mem. Va. Conv. of 1829, and Va. Senate; *m* his cousin, Huldah Fontaine Lewis (Col. Zachary[5]);
3-Alexander Richmond (1811-77), lawyer, Richmond, Va.; mem. 31st and 32d Congresses; *m* Patsy Quarles Poindexter (Judge William G.[4]);
2-Alexander Quarles, LL.D. (1839-1909), 2d lt., 19th Va. Regt.; promoted col., 1861-65; lawyer; state senator; pres. Stonewall Jackson Inst. Abingdon, Va., and N.C. Coll. of Agr. and Mechanic Arts, and pres. and prof. English, Fla. Agrl. Coll.; *m* 1861, Mary Virginia Randolph Bolling (1841-99); for issue and other lineages see Vol. I, p. 362, 363, 364.
1-*m* Nov. 18, 1886, Maggie Murchison Williams (1865-89); dau. of George W. Williams, Wilmington, N.C.; issue: 1-Nannie Williams, *b* Wilmington, N.C., Sept. 9, 1887; Converse Coll., '05; *m* Emmet P. Crow (issue: Emmet; Fannie; Nancy; Marguerite); 2-Maggie Murchison, *b* Wilmington, Aug. 29, 1889; Converse Coll., '05; Miss Stuart's Sch., Washington; *m* Hal Venerable Worth, Raleigh, N.C. (issue: Hal; Thomas; Francis; George; William; Colvin; Marguerite).
1-*m* 2d, Oct. 18, 1896, Fannie Pritchard, *b* Raleigh, N.C., Oct. 12, 1878; dau. of Thomas Henderson Pritchard, D.D., Wilmington, N.C.; issue: 1-Miriam, *b* Wilmington, June 8, 1897; *m* Apr. 8, 1917, James Goodlett Thornton (issue: James; William; Frances); 2-Frances (1902-June 1903).
1-Rodman, city engr's. office, Richmond, 1880-81; transit man, James River improvement, Richmond, 1881-82; asst. to engr. maintenance of way, C.,C.&A.R.R., Columbia, S.C., 1882-85; in service of Atlantic Coast Line R.R. Co., 36 yrs., retired, Feb. 1, 1921. Residence: Wilmington, N.C.

1-**HOLLISTER, George Buell,** *b* Brooklyn, N.Y., Sept. 16, 1865.
9-John **Hollister** (qv);
8-John (1644-1711), *m* Sara Goodrich (*d* 1700; William[9], qv);
7-Thomas (1672-1741), *m* 1695, Dorothy Hills (1677-1741; Joseph[8], *m* Elizabeth–; William[9], *m* Mary Risley);
6-Lt. Gideon (1699-1785), *m* 1723, Rachel Talcott (1706-90; Nathaniel[7], *m* Elizabeth, dau. of Joshua Robbins, son of Gentleman John Robbins; Samuel[8], *m* Hannah Holyoke; John[9], *m* Dorothy Mott);
5-Nathaniel (1731-1810), Am. Rev.; *m* 1754, Mabel (Mehitabel Mathison) Matson (1739-1824), of East Hartford, Conn. (Thomas[6], *m* Rachel Fox; Thomas[7]; Thomas[8], *m* Mary Read; Thomas[9], *m* Amy Chambers);
4-Gideon (1776-1864), *m* Mary Olmstead (*d* 1827; Samuel[5], *m* Jerusha Pitkin; Nehemiah[7], *m* Clemence Hosmer; Joseph[8], *m* Elizabeth Butler; Nicholas[8], *m* Sarah Loomis; James[9], qv);
3-Edwin Madison (1800-70), dry goods mcht. and paper mfr.; *m* Gratia Taylor Buell (1801-88; Maj. John Hutchinson[4], officer Am. Rev., *m* Sarah [Taylor] Metcalf; Benjamin[5], *m* Mary Sprague; Benjamin[6], *m* Hannah Hutchinson; Samuel[7], *m* Deborah Griswold; William[8], *m* Mary–);
2-George (1832-1917), wholesale grain mcht.; *m* Phoebe Moore Conkling (1831-1917); issue: I-George B. (1 above); II-Mabel (*m* Arthur Amory Houghton).
1-*m* June 24, 1902, Marcia May McKinney (*b* Binghamton, N.Y.-*d* Feb. 12, 1909); dau. of Maj. Edward Phillips McKinney, of Binghamton.
1-*m* 2d, June 1, 1911, Hebe Barnes Canfield, *b* Watkins, N.Y., 1882; dau. of Robert Hamilton Canfield, of Corning, N.Y.; issue: 1-Buell, *b* Corning, Mar. 20, 1912; 2-Priscilla, *b* Corning, July 16, 1914.
1-Phillips Andover, '88; B.A., Yale, '92 (Scroll and Key). V.p. and dir. of sales, Corning Glass Works. Clubs: University, Yale (New York), City, Country (Corning), New Bedford (Mass.) Yacht, etc. Residence: 4 E. 5th St., Corning, N.Y.

1-**HOLT, Lucius Hudson,** *b* Atchison, Kan., Jan. 16, 1881.
9-William **Kelsey** (1600-75), original settler Hartford, Conn., propr., 1635;
8-Stephen (1647-1710), *m* Hannah Ingersoll;
7-Charles (1692-1777), *m* 1729, Hannah Larkham;
6-Charles (1733-73), *m* 1755, Sarah–;
5-Levi (1756-1806), *m* 1780, Sarah Fowler;
4-Betsy (1800-80), *m* 1823, Alvah **Holt** (for Holt lineage see Vol. III, p. 252);
3-Lucius Hancock (1825-1903), treas., **Billings** & Spencer Co., Hartford; *m* Sarah Ann Grinnell, from Eng.;
2-Fred Park (2 below).
10-Richard **Seymour** (qv);
9-John, *m* Mary Watson;
8-John, *m* 1693, Elizabeth Webster;
7-Zebulon, *m* 1733, Keziah Bull;
6-Margaret, *m* 1766, Barzillai **Hudson** (for Hudson lineage see Vol. III, p. 252);
5-William, *m* Mary Skinner;
4-William (1803-79), *m* Anna Miller;
3-William Miller, M.D. (1833-1901), B.A., Yale, '53; M.D., Jefferson Med. Coll., 1855; physician, Hartford; *m* Ellen Hieskell Bryan (for Bryan lineage see Vol. III, p. 252);
2-Regina Miller (*b* 1859), *m* 1880, Fred Park **Holt** (*b* 1860), pres. City Bank & Trust Co., Hartford, Conn.
1-*m* June 18, 1903, Katherine, dau. of Henry Augustin Beers (see Vol. I, p. 453); issue: 1-Guy Bryan, *b* New Haven, Conn., Dec. 16, 1904; *m* June 16, 1928, Helen Pennock; 2-Roger Clerc, *b* New Haven, June 29, 1906; *m* Jan. 22, 1930, Elizabeth Williams.
1-B.A., Yale, '02 (Phi Beta Kappa, Zeta Psi), M.A., 1904, Ph.D., 1905. Col., U.S.A.; prof. economics, govt. and history, U.S.M.A. Author (see Who's Who in America). Mem. I.A.G. Clubs: Elizabethan, Graduates (New Haven, Conn.), University, Yale, Zeta Psi (New York), Army and Navy. Residence: West Point, N.Y.

1-**HOLTON, Louis A.,** *b* Coatesville, Pa., May 1, 1869.
4-Thomas **Holton** (1742-1832), prob. from Eng.; settled Lower Oxford Tp., Chester Co., Pa.; *m* Mary Alexander (1758-1847);
3-Alexander (1801-77), of Oxford, Pa.; *m* 1824, Margaret McGinness (1801-89; Samuel[4], *m* 1799, Jane McCrea);
2-William Van Buren (2 below).
6-Rev. Francis **Alison,** D.D. (*b* Parish of Leck, Co. Donegal, Ireland, 1705-*d* Nov. 28, 1779), ed. U.Glasgow, Scotland; to America 1735; licensed Presbyn. minister, 1736, installed over ch. in New London, Chester Co., Pa., May 25, 1736, where he remained 15 yrs.; took charge of acad., Phila., 1752; became vice provost Coll. of Pa. (now U.Pa.), 1755; prof. moral philosophy; asst. pastor 1st Presbyn. Ch., Phila.; A.M., Yale, 1756; D.D., U.Glasgow, 1756 (1st clergyman in America to receive this degree); *m* Hannah Armitage (James[7], of New Castle, Del.; Benjamin[8], from Holm-

firth Parish, Yorkshire, Eng., to nr. Bristol, Pa., *m* Mary-);
5-Francis (1751-1813), *m* Mary Mackey (1757-1827; John[6], of nr. New London, Chester Co., mem. Constl. Conv., 1775, *m* Rachel Elder; Robert[7], of Chester Co., lt. provincial forces, 1747-48);
4-Sarah (1783-1843), *m* Alexander **Adams** (1768-1833);
3-Thomas (1810-50), of Londonderry, Chester Co.; *m* 1835, Ruth Anna (England) Carrington (1816-92);
2-Sarah Alison (1836-1929), *m* 1855, William Van Buren **Holton** (1836-1922), of Coatesville, Pa.; issue: I-Anna Margaret (*b* 1857; *m* Hon. Jacob Vandeyer Pennegar); II-Clark (*b* 1858); III-Mary (*b* 1860; *m* John Beebe Martin, *d*); IV-Jane (1862-1912; *m* Arthur Bertram Whittaker); V-Eva L. (*b* 1864; *m* George Washington Braidwood); VI-Louis Adams (1 above).
1-Retired mcht. Life mem. hist. societies of Pa. and Chester Co. Residence: 121 Strode Av., Coatesville, Pa.

1-**HOOBLER, Bert Raymond,** *b* Standish, Mich., May 5, 1872.
6-Seth **Worth,** Quaker; from Eng., settled at Nantucket Island, ca. 1700;
5-Jonathan, settled at Wading River, L.I., N.Y.;
4-Theodore R., settled at Redfield (Oswego Co.), N.Y.;
3-David, settled at Haskins, O.; *m* Mary Buffington, of nr. Trenton Falls;
2-Mary Roselia (1850-1922), *m* Hon. Samuel Reuben **Hoobler** (*d* 1918), farmer, teacher; mem. Mich. Legislature; issue: I-David Curtis (*b* 1868; *m* Stella Fletcher); II-Louise (1870-1828; *m* Melvin Morris; *m* 2d, John H. Hill); III-Bert Raymond (1 above); IV-Mabel Floy (*b* 1874; *m* William Mumford); V-Rolla Leo (*b* 1876; *m* Bessie Goodspeed); VI-Claudine (*b* 1882; *m* John Jones); VII-Halford Rex (*b* 1884; *m* Marion Blankinship).
1-*m* Oct. 15, 1906, Madge Genevieve Sibley (qv); issue: 1-Sibley Worth, *b* New York, N.Y., Apr. 30, 1911.
1-B.S., Wabash Coll., '01 (P.B.K., Sigma Xi, Phi Gamma Delta, Nu Sigma Nu), M.A., 1903; M.D., Cornell U., 1905; interned in Presbyn. Hosp., New York City; studied in Europe, 1914. Practiced at N.Y. City, 1905-14, also teaching in Cornell U.Med. Coll.; prof. diseases of children, Detroit Coll. of Medicine, 1914-; dir. pediatric teaching, Children's Hosp. of Mich. (see Who's Who in America). Presbyterian. Republican. Mason (K.T.). Residence: 805 Three Mile Drive, Grosse Pointe, Mich.

1-**HOOBLER, Madge Genevieve Sibley (Mrs. B. Raymond),** *b* Kalamazoo, Mich., July 4, 1876.
9-Roger **Clapp** (qv);
8-Preserved (1643-1720), of Dorchester, Mass.; capt. militia, dep., elder, Northampton, Mass.; *m* 1668, Sarah Newbury (1650-1716; Benjamin[9]; Thomas[10], qv);
7-Roger (1684-1762), of Northampton; *m* Elizabeth Bartlett;
6-Jonathan (1713-82), of Northampton; *m* Submit Strong;
5-Joseph (*b* 1736), of Easthampton; *m* Hannah Lyman;
4-Rufus, of Mich.; *m* —Ceeley (*d* 1847);
3-Edwin M. (*b* 1805), of Kalamazoo, Mich.; *m* Mary L. Steadman;
2-Mary Josephine (1846-1923), *m* Frederic Messenger **Sibley,** of Detroit; issue: I-Madge Genevieve (1 above); II-Frederick Merrill (*m* Mabel Bessenger).
1-*m* Oct. 15, 1906, Bert Raymond Hoobler (qv for issue).
1-A.B., U.Mich., '04 (Pi Beta Phi). Presbyterian. Republican. Clubs: Pi Beta Phi Alumnae, Women's City, College, U. of Mich. Women's Assn. Residence: 805 Three Mile Drive, Grosse Pointe, Mich.

1-**HOOD, Alice Howell (Mrs. Cornelius S.),** *b* Buffalo, N.Y., Aug. 14, 1848.
8-Edward **Howell** (qv);
7-Lt. Edward (bap. 1626-will made Apr. 29, 1699), from Eng. with father; *m* Mary Fordham (Rev. Robert[8], *m* Elizabeth-); 10 children; *m* 2d, post 1676, Mary (Bryan) Maltby (bap. 1637);
6-Jonah (*d* 1727), *m* Elizabeth-;
5-Samuel (1708-54), *m* Experience Hadley;
4-Jeremiah (1748-1846), of N.J.; officer in Am. Rev.;
3-Jared (1780-1855), of Parsippany, N.J.; *m* Masy Baker;
2-Lewis Baker (1818-96), *m* 1847, Georgianna Callander (1824-95), of Buffalo, N.Y.; issue: I-Alice (1 above); II-Louis James (*b* 1851; *m* Rebecca Williams); III-Mary E. (1859-82; *m* William Heath); IV-Harriet Stowe (1861-64).
1-*m* Cornelius Seaman Hood, *b* Seneca Falls, N.Y., Mar. 17, 1847; son of Cornelius Hood, of Seneca Falls; issue: 1-Louis Howell, *b* Seneca Falls, N.Y., Apr. 19, 1874; *m* 1901, Linda Coolidge, *d* 1901; *m* 2d, 1905, Clara Louise Dean.
1-Mem. D.F.P.A., D.A.R. Presbyn. Republican. Residence: 87 Cayuga St., Seneca Falls, N.Y.

1-**HOOD, George Ezekiel,** *b* Wayne Co., N.C., Jan. 25, 1875.
5-Nathaniel B. **Hood** (1737-1815), settled in Lenoir Co., N.C.;
4-Britton (1767-1848), of Wayne Co., N.C.;
3-John R. (1807-83) of Wayne Co.; *m* Dicy Grantham;
2-Edward Bass (1838-99), farmer, Wayne Co.; co. treas.; served with Co. F, 10th N.C. Heavy Arty., C.S.A.; *m* 1871, Edith Finlayson Bridgers (1850-1913); issue: I-Eunice; II-George E. (1 above); III-Sarah; IV-Daisy; V-Paul M. (*m* Annie Dargan); VI-Stella M. (*m* Louis B. Poole); VI-Robey Cleveland (*m* Clara Klute).
1-*m* Sept. 25, 1903, Julia Annie Flowers, *b* Mt. Olive, N.C., Sept. 23, 1877; dau. of Dr. Samuel B. Flowers, of Mt. Olive; issue (all *b* Goldsboro, N.C.): 1-Nannie Bridgers (Sept. 28, 1904-Nov. 8, 1921); 2-George Ezekiel, *b* July 15, 1910; ed. Davidson Coll.; 3-Frances Elizabeth, *b* Sept. 25, 1912.
1-Atty.-at-law. Former co. treas., mayor of Goldsboro, rep. N.C. Legislature, U.S. Congressman, presidential elector. Retired col. Nat. Guard. Author: The Origin of Man. Democrat. Methodist. Residence: 308 W. Mulberry St., Goldsboro, N.C.

1-**HOOD, Oscar Monroe,** *b* nr. Utica, Miss., Jan. 24, 1888.
4-James **Hood** (*b* nr. Belfast, Ireland, 1785-1830; of Scotch-Irish descent), from Ireland as a boy to Darlington, S.C.; later from Ga. to Knox Co., Tenn.; settled finally on a farm 9 miles east of Crystal Springs, Miss.; *m* 1st, 1813, Rachel Couzens (1797-1826; Jesse[5], *m* Mary Williamson);
3-Jesse Fox (1825-63), served with Co. A, 1st Miss. Inf., C.S.A.; *m* 1848, Elizabeth Strong;
2-Henry F. M. (2 below).
5-Nelson **Strong** (1760-1830), ancestors from England via Wales;
4-John (1800-50), from S.C. to Miss., 1820; *m* Delanie Adams (1802-85; John[5], ancestors from England via Wales);
3-Elizabeth (1833-1907), *m* Jesse Fox **Hood** (3 above).
4-Benjamin Patton **Bridges** (*b* nr. Princeton, Caldwell Co., Ky., Oct. 12, 1811-*d* nr. Carpenter, Copiah Co., Miss., Aug. 9, 1878), from Harlan, Ky., to Crystal Springs, Miss., ca. 1840; *m* 2d, Mrs. Mary Ray Spencer Loe;
3-Lorenzo Marcus (Bud), (1844-1906), served with Co. B, 3d Miss. Cav., C.S.A.;
2-Ella Nora Ophelia (1868-1923), *m* 1886, Henry Franklin Monroe ("Bunk") **Hood** (1849-1916), mcht. and farmer, Clarksdale, Miss.; issue: I-Oscar Monroe (1 above); II-Agnes Lorender (*b* 1889); III-Nona Elizabeth (*b* 1891; *m* 1917, John C. Kelley, Jr.); IV-Malcolm Henry (*b* 1893; World War vet.); V-Alice Ethel (*b* 1896; *m* Maj. Richard N. Ware, Jr., World War vet.).
1-*m* Dec. 4, 1916, Myrtle Mae Litchfield, *b* Vernon, Tex., June 26, 1888; dau. of James L. Litchfield, cattleman of Melrose, Curry Co., N.Mex.
1-Ed. Millsaps Coll., 1903-04. U.S. P.O. inspector, 1914-23; interested in real estate and ins.; co. auditor, 1925-29; re-entered postal service, June 11, 1930, at Durango, Colo. Served with Co. K, 2d Miss. N.G. on Yellow Fever quarantine along Miss. River, 1905. Mem. Kiwanis (sec.-treas.), Country Club. Mason (past patron O.E.S.), Elk. Residence: Durango, Colo.

1–**HOOKER, Frederic William,** *b* Centerville Tp., Que., Can., Feb. 4, 1878.
8–Rev. Thomas **Hooker** (qv);
7–Samuel (1633-97), minister at Farmington, Conn.; *m* 1658, Mary Willet (1637-1712), of Plymouth, Mass. (Capt. Thomas[8], qv);
6–Henry, *m* 1st, 1708, Elizabeth Hilliard (*d* 1754);
5–Gen. William (*b* 1716), *m* 2d, Abigail Evans:
4–Zibeon (1752-1840), maj. on Washington's staff in Am. Rev.; original mem. S.C.; Mason; buried with wife in St. Mary's Ch., Newton Lower Falls, Mass.;
3–Gustavus Adolphus (1784-1870), capt. militia many yrs., mem. Home Guards; Mason; *m* Pamelia McArthur (1791-1876);
2–George Barbour (1820-99), municipal councillor, assessor 3 times; pres. Co. Agrl. Soc., twice; *m* 1st, 1845, Sarah Jefferson; *m* 2d, 1873, Margaret Anne Hoare (1841-1901); issue (1st marriage): I–Sarah Pamelia (1846-1914; *m* Martin Burwash); II–Phebe Ann (*b* 1847; *m* Stephen Burwash); III–Jane (1849-1923; *m* Robert Watson); IV–Thomas (1852-1906; *m* Kate McDonald); V–George B. (1855-1926; *m* Jessie Watson); VI–Charlotte (1857-92; *m* William Watson); VII–Emma (1858-1918; *m* James McIntyre); VIII–Fannie (1860-1921; *m* Mathew Burwash); IX–Henry Gustavus (*b* 1865; *m* Annie Hoare); issue (2d marriage): I–Augusta Mary (1875-1919; *m* 1901, Thomas N. Burwash); II–Frederic William (1 above); III–Harriet Anne (*b* 1885; *m* 1903, Max Alaric Plumb, *b* 1871).
1–*m* Nov. 21, 1907, Polly Ann Bell, *b* Somis, Ventura Co., Calif., Nov. 2, 1879; dau. of Robert Bell (*b* 1843); issue: 1–Frances Margaret, *b* Somis, Calif., Dec. 7, 1908; 2–Robert Barbour, *b* Somis, May 15, 1910; 3–Eleanor Bell, *b* Somis, Feb. 14, 1912; 4–Alberta Ruth, *b* Holtville, Calif., Aug. 24, 1914; 5–Frederic William, Jr., *b* Fillmore, Calif., Oct. 29, 1916; 6–Thomas Henry, *b* Oxnard, Calif., Jan. 19, 1919; 7–Virginia Bell, *b* Santa Paula, Calif., Aug. 12, 1922.
1–Residence: 601 Etting Rd., Oxnard, Calif.

1–**HOOPER, Franklin Henry,** *b* Worcester, Mass., Jan. 28, 1862.
8–Robert **Hooper** (ca. 1606-ca. 1687), *m* Elizabeth Fletcher (*b* ca. 1605);
7–Henry (ca. 1665-1726), *m* Mary Collins (*b* 1669; John[8], *m* Abigail, dau. of Richard Johnson; Henry[9], qv);
6–Nathaniel (1710-60), *m* Hannah Chamblett (ca. 1706-47; Arthur[7], *m* Hannah–; Maurice Champney[8]; Henry[9]);
5–Robert (1741-1814), *m* Mary Ingalls (1740-1807; William[6], *m* Mary Lane; Eleazer[7]; Robert[8]; Edmund[9], qv; Robert[10]; Henry[11]);
4–Robert (1766-1843), *m* Mary Glover (1769-1850; Brig. Gen. John[5], *m* Hannah Gale; Jonathan[6]; Jonathan[7]; John[8]; Charles[9]);
3–William (1795-1828), Harvard, 1815; *m* Rebecca Hooper (1798-1830; William[4], *m* Mary, dau. of Benjamin Tyler Reed; Robert[5], 5 above);
2–William Robert **Hooper** (1819-91), editor, govt. employee; *m* 2d, 1851, Frances Nelson (1832-1904); issue: I–Martha Nelson (*b* 1853); II–Frances Nelson (1854-1922; *m* Jerome Dean Davis); III–Horace Everett (1859-1922; *m* Mary Alice Woodbury; *m* 2d, Harriet Meeker [Cox] Millard); IV–Franklin Henry (1 above); V–Louis Leverett (qv for maternal lineages).
1–*m* Oct. 19, 1887, Grace Martin Sessions, *b* Newtown, L.I., N.Y., July 6, 1858; dau. of John Sessions; issue: 1–Catharine Baker, *b* Brooklyn, May 26, 1889; 2–Leverett Franklin, *b* Brooklyn, Feb. 8, 1893.
1–A.B. (magna cum laude), Harvard, '83. With Ency. Britannica (except during war period) since 1899, as lit. adviser and Am. editor, now v.p. and sec. (see Who's Who in America). Episcopalian. Democrat. Clubs: Harvard (New York and New Jersey). Residence: 28 Clinton Av., Montclair, N.J.

1–**HOOPER, Louis Leverett,** *b* Worcester, Mass., May 18, 1867.
7–Matthew **Nelson** (*d* 1712), *m* Agnes Rackley (William[8]);
6–Matthew (*d* 1757), *m* Mary Cotton (Benjamin[7], *m* Elizabeth–; William[8]);
5–John (1719-73), *m* Sarah Folsom (*d* ca. 1800; Jonathan[6], *m* Anna [*b* 1691], dau. Nathaniel Ladd; John[7]; John[8], below);
4–Jonathan (1751-1830), *m* Martha Folsom;
3–John (1778-1838), Dartmouth, 1803; *m* Lois Burnham Leverett;
2–Frances (2 below).
13–Roger (Foulsham) **Folsom**;
12–William, *m* Agnes Smith;
11–Adam, *m* Emma–;
10–Adam (1560-1630), *m* Grace–;
9–Adam (*d* 1627), *m* Agnes–;
8–John (qv), wrote name Folsom; *m* Mary Gilman (1615-90; Edward[9], qv; Robert[10]; Edward[11]);
7–Peter (1649-1717), *m* Susanna–;
6–John (*d* 1757), *m* Sarah Lyford (Francis[7], *m* Rebecca, dau. Samuel Dudley),
5–Josiah (1725-1820), *m* Martha Eastman;
4–Martha (1756-1839), *m* Jonathan **Nelson** (4 above).
11–Roger **Eastman** (*d* 1604);
10–Nicholas;
9–Roger (qv);
8–John (1640-1720), *m* Mary Boynton (*b* 1648; William [9], *m* Elizabeth Jackson);
7–Zachariah (1679-1732), *m* Martha Thorne (*d* 1728; John[8]);
6–Jeremiah (*b* 1704), *m* Lydia Brown (Ephraim[7], *m* Lydia, dau. Nathaniel Eastman; Ephraim[8]; William[9]; Henry[10]);
5–Martha (1730-1804), *m* Josiah **Folsom** (5 above).
10–Thomas **Leverett** (ca. 1585-1650), *m* Anne Fitche (*d* 1656);
9–John (qv) *m* Hannah Hudson (ca. 1621-46; Ralph[10], *m* Marie, dau. John Twing);
8–Hudson (1640-94), *m* Sarah Payton (1643-79; Bazaleel[9], *m* Mary Greenough);
7–Thomas (1674-1706), *m* Rebecca Windsor (Joshua[8], *m* Sarah–; Robert[9]);
6–Knight (1702-53), *m* Abigail Buttolph (1704-74; Nicholas[7], *m* Mary, dau. Robert Gutteridge; Thomas[8]; Thomas[9]);
5–John (1737-77), *m* Mary Greenleaf;
4–John (1758-1829), *m* Lois Burnham;
3–Lois Burnham (1790-1859), *m* John **Nelson** (3 above).
10–John **Greenleaf**, *m* Margaret–;
9–Edmund (qv), *m* Sarah Dole (*d* 1663);
8–Enoch (*b* 1617), *m* Mary–;
7–Enoch (1647-1705), *m* Catherine Truesdale (1653-1712);
6–William (1693-1756), *m* Mary Shattuck (1690-1743; William[7], *m* Susanna, dau. Stephen Randall; William[8], qv);
5–Mary (*d* 1795), *m* John **Leverett** (5 above).
8–Thomas **Burnham** (qv);
7–Richard (1654-1731), *m* Sarah Humphrey (1659-1726; Michael[8], qv, *m* Priscilla, dau. Mathew Grant, qv; Samuel[9]);
6–Michael (1705-58), *m* Lois Wise (1703-49);
5–Ashbel (1738-1800), *m* Hannah Sage;
4–Lois (1764-91), *m* John **Leverett** (4 above).
8–David **Sage** (qv), *m* 1st, Elizabeth Kirby (1646-72; John[9], *m* Elizabeth Hinds; Humphrey[10]);
7–John (1668-1751), *m* Hannah Starr (1674-1753; Comfort[8] [1644-93], *m* Marah, dau. Joseph Weld [1595-1646], *m* Barbara Clapp [*d* 1655]; Thomas[9] [ca. 1616-58], *m* Rachel–; Comfort[10], qv; Thomas[11]);
6–Ebenezer (*b* 1709), *m* Hannah Coleman (1704-62; John[7], *m* Hannah, dau. James Wright; John[8]; Thomas[9], qv);
5–Hannah (1739-1814), *m* Ashbel **Burnham** (5 above);
4–Lois, *m* John **Leverett** (4 above);
3–Lois Burnham, *m* John **Nelson** (3 above);
2–Frances (1832-1904), *m* 1851, William Robert **Hooper** (1819-91); for issue and Hooper lineage see Franklin Henry Hooper.
1–*m* July 6, 1913, Gertrude Leonora Dunn, *b* Ticonderoga, N.Y., Nov. 3, 1885; dau. of George Jenkins Dunn, of Ticonderoga; issue: 1– Lois Leverett, *b* Washington, Oct. 12, 1917; 2–Robert William, *b* Washington, July 23, 1919.
1–A.B., Harvard, '89, A.M., 1898. Educator 1889-1911; disbursing agt., Columbia Instn. for the Deaf, since 1911 (see Who's Who in America, Vol. V). Clubs: Cosmos, Powhatan. Residence: Kendall Green, Washington, D.C.

1–**HOOPER, Mildred Walker Anderson (Mrs. James E.),** *b* Louisville, Ky., Sept. 21, 1898.
11–Abraham Isaacsen **Ver Planck** (qv);
10–Susannah, *m* John **Garland**;
9–Silvester (ca. 1670-1719), of Newcastle, Pa.; licensed by William Penn as Indian trader;
8–Suit, or Sudt (1694-1736), *m* 1713, Rev. James

Anderson (1678-1740), from Scotland; ordained Presbyn. minister, 1705; pastor First Donegal Presbyn. Ch., Susquehanna, Pa.;
7–Ann (*b* 1716), *m* 1735, John **Stuart** (1700?-1749?; George[8], justice, *m* Jean–);
6–Col. George (1736-87), co. commr., Lancaster Co., Pa.; on grand inquest of 1st Ct.; mem. Provincial Assembly, 1730-32; *m* 1758, Margaret Harris (1737-1815);
5–Anna (1764-1837), *m* 1786, Col. Dunning **McNair** (1762-1825), col. Pa. militia; built "Crows' Nest," nr. Wilkinsburg (formerly McNairstown), Pa.; later built "Dumplin Hall," which is said to have been hdqrs. for U.S.A. sent to put down the Whiskey Rebellion, 1794; mem. Pa. Legislature, 1800-01; mgr. Pittsburgh and Greensburg Turnpike;
4–Anna Maria (1804-47), *m* 1835, John Williams **Anderson** (1800-74), from Ireland with his father and bro.; in Newark, O., later at Louisville, Ky., 1830; mem. wholesale dry goods firm of Lawrence & Anderson; Presbyn. (James[5], from Ireland, *m* Sarah Bell);
3–Leven Lawrence (1840-98), ins. man; *m* 1st, 1862, Mildred Clark Lewis;
2–Lawrence Lewis (2 below).
10–Capt. Thomas **Walker,** from Staffordshire, Eng., ca. 1650; mem. Colonial Assembly from Gloucester Co., Va., 1663; maj., 1666; *m* Miss Baylor;
9–John, of York Co.; *m* Rachael Croshaw (Capt. Richard[10], of York Co.; Joseph[11], burgess);
8–Capt. Thomas, obtained a royal grant of land on the Mattaponi River, and removing to King and Queen Co. he founded the village of Walkerton; burgess; capt militia, 1707; *m* 1709, Susanna Peachy;
7–Dr. Thomas (1715-94), maj. under Gen. Braddock at Ft. Duquesne; adj. of frontier cos., 1754; burgess, Albemarle Co., 1768; next in rank to George Washington in arrangement of treaties with Indians; mem. Revolutionary Conv.; mem. Com. Safety of Va.; mem. Council, 1774; *m* 1741, Mildred Thornton (*b* ca. 1721; Col. Francis[8], [*b* 1682], justice, Caroline Co., 1723, burgess, *m* Mary, dau. of Col. John Taliaferro, of Snow Creek, Spotsylvania Co.; Francis[9], of Stafford Co., Va., *m* Alice, dau. Capt. Anthony Savage, justice of Gloucester Co.; William[10], Gent. of the "Hills," from Eng. to York Co., Va., ante 1646, settled in Petsworth Parish, Gloucester Co.);
6–Mary, *m* 1763, Capt. Nicholas **Lewis** (*b* 1742), dep. for Albemarle Co., 1775; capt. Albemarle Minute Men; comd. regt. against Cherokee Indians, 1776 (Col. Robert[7]; John[8]; Maj. John[9]; Robert[10], qv);
5–Robert Warner (*b* 1774), *m* Elizabeth Wood;
4–John Nicholas (1802-78), *m* Rachael Clark (1809-74);
3–Mildred Clark (1844-86), *m* Levan Lawrence **Anderson** (3 above).
6–James **Nourse** (1731-84), from Eng.; settled nr. Charlestown, W.Va.; built "Piedmont"; mem. Va. Legislature; one of 13 trustees of Berkshire Springs, claimed to be 1st town laid out after Declaration of Independence; commr. to settle Md. claims against U.S., 1781; removed to Annapolis; connected with U.S. Treas. Dept.; *m* 1753, Sarah Fonace (*d* 1784; dau. of Gabriel, of London, *m* Sarah, dau. of Joseph Burton);
5–James (1758-99), *m* 1789, Sarah Benois;
4–Charles Benois (1792-1864), *m* 1831, Rosa Logan (1805-95; Judge William[6] [1776-1822], judge Ky. Ct. of Appeals, U.S. senator, *m* Priscilla Christian, dau. Caleb Wallace; Gen. Benjamin[6] [1742-1802], with Col. Beauquette in expdn. against Indians of North, also in expdn. to N.W. Ohio and Ind., and with Daniel Boone in Ky., mem. Constl. Conv., Ky. 1792 and 99, *m* Anne, dau. William Montgomery, Am. Rev.; David[7], of Augusta Co., Va.);
3–Mary Priscilla (1843-1923), *m* 1867, Joseph Glass **Wilson** (1833-79);
2–Annie Jane (*b* 1867), of Louisville, Ky.; *m* 1891, Lawrence Lewis **Anderson** (*b* 1866), life ins. gen. agt.; Castlewood, Louisville; issue: I–Joseph Wilson (*b* 1892; *m* Lida McClarty); II–Lawrence Lewis, Jr. (*b* 1896); III–Mildred Walker (1 above); IV–Virgil Nourse (*b* 1900); V–Warwick McNair (*b* 1902; *m* Mary San Germano).
1–*m* June 18, 1919, James Edward Hooper (see Vol. III, p. 555, for genealogy); issue: 1–James Edward, Jr., *b* Ruxton, Md., Mar. 9, 1920; 2–Lawrence Lewis, *b* Ruxton, Nov. 26, 1924.
1–Mem. C.D.A., Junior League (Baltimore). Residence: Ruxton, Baltimore, Md.

1–**HOOPER, Marion Grant Baylies (Mrs. Robbert P.),** *b* Baltimore, Md., Jan. 27, 1872.
9–William **Phillips** (ca. 1584-1654), was one of 1st purchasers of and settlers at Taunton, Mass., 1637; *m* Elizabeth Parker;
8–Elizabeth (1619-78), *m* James **Walker** (qv);
7–Deborah (1664-1726), *m* 1685, George **Gooding** (1633-1712), from Eng.; settled at Dighton, Mass., 1677/78;
6–Joanna (1687-1765), *m* 1716, John **Godfrey** (1691-1758), capt. 5th Foot Co., Taunton, 1745 (Richard[7]; Richard[8], qv);
5–Brig. Gen. George (1720-93), Mass. militia, 1776-81, Am. Rev.; chmn. Com. Corr. and Safety, Bristol Co.; *m* 1744, Bethia Hodges;
4–Bethia (1749-96), *m* 1769, Thomas Sergeant **Baylies** (1748-1835);
3–Nicholas (1791-1859), *m* Dec. 21, 1820, Susan Stone;
2–William Thomas (2 below).
6–Robert **Porter,** *m* Mary Mercer;
5–Robert;
4–Rebecca, *m* 1798, Henry **Stone**;
3–Susan (1801-84), *m* Nicholas **Baylies** (3 above).
5–Enoch **Honeywell,** of Westchester, N.Y.; *m* Margaret Vail;
4–Sarah (*b* 1794), *m* 1813, Robert **Marshall** (1792-1831), from Eng. to Baltimore, Md.;
3–Jane Ann (1819-70), *m* 1839, Robert **Grant** (1809-68), officer in Mexican War; col. Civil War; inventor (see Vol. III, p. 554, for lineage);
2–Josephine Tilden (1851-1928), *m* 1871, William Thomas **Baylies** (1847-1924), for issue and other lineages see Vol. III, p. 554.
1–*m* Oct. 21, 1896, Robert Poole Hooper, *b* Baltimore, Md., July 15, 1872; son of James Edward Hooper, of Baltimore; issue: 1–James Edward (see Vol. III, p. 555); 2–Josephine Grant, *b* Phila., Pa., Sept. 7, 1899; *m* Sept. 24, 1927, William Spencer, son of Dr. Charles A. Service, of Bala, Pa.; 3–Robert Poole, Jr., *b* Phila., Mar. 5, 1901; Princeton, '22; *m* Oct. 1, 1924, Consuela I., dau. of Albert Lee, of San Juan, P.R. (issue: Virginia Lee, Robert Poole, III).
1–Spl. student, Goucher Coll. Mem. C.D.A., D.A.R.; mem. social service and woman's bd., Jefferson Hosp. Residence: "Wolverton," W. Mermaid Lane, St. Martin's Chestnut Hill, Pa.

1–**HOOVER, Harvey Daniel,** *b* New Oxford, Pa., June 17, 1880.
5–Ulrich **Hoover,** served with York Co. militia in Am. Rev.; *m* Eve–;
4–David (*d* 1860), *m* Catherine March (1803-68);
3–Daniel (1825-89), *m* Catherine Ditzler (1819-85);
2–Samuel Enoch (1854-1922), farmer; *m* 1878, Joanne Jane Gable (*b* 1862); issue: I–Harvey Daniel (1 above); II–Dillie Kate (*b* 1882; *m* Edward H. Diehl); III–Mary Grace (*b* 1899; *m* Paul Stock).
1–*m* June 17, 1902, Miriam Grace Stock, *b* New Oxford, Pa., Mar. 15, 1879; dau. of William D. Stock, of New Oxford; issue: 1–Dorcas Grace, *b* Pittsburgh, Pa., Oct. 20, 1904; Carthage Coll., '24; *m* June 17, 1924, Paul Harold Ensrud (issue: Norman Paul, *b* Apr. 25, 1925; Phyllis Jeanne, *b* May 7, 1927).
1–A.B., Susquehanna U., '99, A.M., B.D., 1902; Ph.D., Ill. Wesleyan U., 1907; (S.T.D., Pa. Coll., 1918; D.D., Wittenberg Coll., 1922). Pastorates at Friedens and East Pittsburgh, Pa., 1902-07; prof. sociology and philosophy, Susquehanna U., 1907-09; prof. philosophy and edn. and pres., Carthage (Ill.) Coll., 1909-26; prof. practical theology, Lutheran Theol. Sem., 1926– (see Who's Who in America). Mem. S.A.R. Clubs: University, Collegiate (Chicago), Kiwanis. Summer place: New Oxford, Pa. Residence: Gettysburg, Pa.

1–**HOPKINS Edwin Mortimer,** *b* Kent, N.Y., Sept. 16, 1862.
10–Stephen **Hopkins,** Mayflower Pilgrim (qv);
9–Gyles (ca. 1607-1690), *m* 1639, Katherine Wheldon (*d* ca. 1689);
8–Stephen (1642-1718), of Yarmouth, Mass.; *m* 1667, Mary Merrick (*b* 1650);

7-Joseph (1688-1771), of Harwich, Mass.; *m* 1712, Mary Mayo (1694-1771);
6-Joseph (1715-62), of Carmel, N.Y.; *m* 1736, Mary Berry (1717-98);
5-Capt. Solomon (1739-92), of Carmel; *m* Elizabeth Crosby (*d* 1804);
4-Maj. Jeremiah (1762-1829), *m* Thankful Stone (*d* 1833);
3-Enos (1789-1859), of Carmel; *m* 1809, Cynthia Cole (1788-1864);
2-William Ambrose (1818-86), farmer, Carmel, N.Y.; *m* 1845, Hannah Elizabeth Sunderlin (1822-1908); issue: I-Emma Louisa (1846-1908; *m* 1873, Theodore Yeomans); II-Franklin Augustus (1852-1926; *m* 1879, Emma Lois Drew; issue: Frank Louison, *b* 1885, *m* 1907, Maud E. Penrose, issue, Elizabeth Drew, *b* 1910, and Frank Penrose, *b* 1918); III-Henry Eugene, and IV-Henrietta Eugenia, twins (1856-60); V-Edwin Mortimer (1 above).
1-*m* June 17, 1890, Madeleine May Mundy, *b* N. Salem, N.Y., Nov. 2, 1863; dau. of Ezra F. Mundy (1833-1926), of Metuchen, N.J.
1-Student, N.Y. State Normal Coll., 1880-82; A.B., Princeton, '88 (P.B.K.), fellow, 1889, A.M., 1890, Ph.D., 1894; U.Oxford (on leave), 1901-02. Asst. prof. rhetoric and English language, 1889-92, asso. prof., 1892-93, prof. same since 1893, and head of the dept., 1902-09, U. of Kan. Author (see Who's Who in America). Mem. S.M.D. (gov. Kan. Soc., 1917), I.A.G., etc. Baptist-Episcopalian. Clubs: Fortnightly, University. Summer place: Woodland Park, Colo. Residence: 1234 Mississippi St., Lawrence, Kan.

ERNEST MARTIN HOPKINS

1-**HOPKINS, Ernest Martin,** *b* Dunbarton, N.H., Nov. 6, 1877.
6-Solomon **Hopkins** (*d* 1761), from Ireland ante 1735, settled at Newcastle, Lincoln Co., Me.;
5-David (1726-97), a petitioner for the incorporation of Sheepscott, 1750; pvt., Lt. Alexander Kelloch's Co., ordered to protect the eastern part of Lincoln Co., and stationed at Camden, 1779-80; *m* 1751, Jane Simpson (1729-1824), of Ireland;
4-Robert (1774-1820), *m* 1801, Priscilla Chapman (1780-1857);
3-Samuel C. (1817-88), *m* 1846, Philena S. Ford (1819-1903; Nathan[4], *m* Margaret Clark; Abner[5], *m* Lydia Trask);
2-Adoniram Judson (2 below).
9-George **Martin** (*d* 1686), of Salisbury and Amesbury, Mass.; *m* 1646, Susanna North (*d* 1692), executed as a witch;
8-George (1648-1734), of Ipswich; *m* Elizabeth-;
7-John (1686-1760), of Ipswich; *m* 1710, Jane Durkee;
6-Joshua (*b* 1717), of Ipswich and Lunenburg; *m* 1st, 1744/45, Sarah Story;
5-Ephraim (1745/46-1835), of Lunenburg, Mass., and Baltimore, Vt.; *m* 1769, Mary Burnham;
4-Ephraim Story (1783-1830), of Baltimore, Vt.; *m* 1805, Susanna Boynton (1783-1837);
3-Horace M. (1817-1903), *m* 1839, Lorinda B. Woodward (1818-85; Benjamin[4], *m* 1809, Mary [Polly] Angell; Rev. Nehemiah[5], Bapt. minister, Woodstock, Vt.);
2-Mary Cheney (2 below).
11-John **Perkins** (qv);
10-John (1614-86), q.m.; of Ipswich; *m* Elizabeth- (*d* 1684);
9-Corpl. Jacob (1646-1719), Ipswich; *m* 1667, Sarah Wainwright (*d* 1688; Francis[10], from Eng., settled at Ipswich, *m* 1647, Philippa, dau. of George Sewell);
8-Philippa (1670-1738), *m* 1685, Thomas **Emerson** (1661?-1738; Nathaniel[9], of Ipswich, *m* 1st, Sarah-; Thomas[10], qv);
7-Elizabeth (1693-1780), *m* 1715, as her 1st husband, Ephraim **Story** (1692-1731), of Ipswich (Samuel[8], *m* Elizabeth-);
6-Sarah (bap. 1726-ante 1752), *m* Joshua **Martin** (6 above).
9-John **Boynton** (1614-70), from Eng., 1638, settled at Rowley, Mass.; *m* Ellen Pell;
8-Capt. Joseph (1644-1730), of Rowley; town clk., capt. and dep., 1697-1714; *m* Sarah Swan (1646-1717/18; Richard[9], of Rowley, Mass., *m* Ann-, *d* 1658);
7-Jonathan (1684-1740), of Rowley; *m* 1711, as her 1st husband, Margaret Harriman (*b* 1686; Jonathan[8]; Leonard[9]);
6-Jonathan (*b* 1716/17), *m* 1739, Elizabeth Wood (*b* 1715; David[7], *m* 1714, Elizabeth Farrington);
5-Jonathan (1745-1814), of Rowley and Fitchburg; *m* ca. 1770, Elizabeth Divol (*d* 1792);
4-Susanna (1783-1837), *m* Ephraim S. **Martin** (4 above);
3-Horace M., *m* Lorinda B. Woodward (3 above);
2-Mary Cheney (*b* 1854), *m* 1877, Rev. Adoniram Judson **Hopkins** (1847-1924), A.B., Harvard, '74; Bapt. minister; supt. schs. and moderator town meetings, Dunbarton, N.H.; mem. bd. edn.; trustee Georgetown (Mass.) Pub. Library; pres. bd. trustees Uxbridge (Mass.) Free Pub. Library; mem. bd. edn., Perkinsville, Vt.; issue: I-Ernest Martin (1 above); II-Louis Bertram (*b* 1881; *m* 1907, Nora Lander, *b* 1885); III-Flora May (1889-90); IV-Robert Carl (*b* 1890; *m* Eleanor Adams); V-Marguerite Grace (1895-96).
1-*m* Feb. 2, 1911, Celia Stone, *b* Lebanon, N.H., Nov. 21, 1877; dau. of Charles W. Stone, of Hanover, N.H.; issue: 1-Dorothy Ann, *b* Boston, Mass., May 1, 1917.
1-A.B., Dartmouth, '01 (P.B.K., D.K.E.), A.M., 1908; (Litt. D., Amherst, 1916; LL.D., Colby, 1916, Rutgers, 1916, Brown, 1919, U.Pa., 1921, U. of N.H., 1922, McGill, Yale and Williams, 1925, Harvard, 1928). Pres. Dartmouth Coll. since 1916 (see Who's Who in America). Dir. B.&M. R.R. since 1920; pres. bd. trustees Woodrow Wilson Foundation, 1923; trustee Laura Spelman Rockefeller Memorial, 1924-29; mem. Rockefeller Foundation, 1928-; mem. Gen. Edn. Bd. 1930-; trustee Worcester (Mass.) Acad., Phillips Acad., Andover, Brookings Instn., trustee Industrial Relations Counselors; mem. N.H. division of the N.E. Council since 1929; mem. nat. advisory com. of Johns Hopkins Inst. of Law since 1929; councillor Nat. Industrial Conf. Bd. since 1930. Apptd. in charge industrial relations Q.M. Dept., U.S.A., Jan. 31, 1918; asst. to Sec. of War, in charge of industrial relations, June-Sept., 1918; rep. of War Dept. on War Labor Policies Bd., July-Sept., 1918. Mem. S.A.R. Baptist. Republican. Clubs: University (New York, Washington, Boston), Century, Town Hall (New York), Tavern (Boston). Summer place: Manset, Me. Residence: Hanover, N.H.

1-**HOPKINS, Lydia Climena,** *b* White Lake, Oakland Co., Mich., Apr. 9, 1846.
5-Consider **Hopkins,** of Hartford or New Haven;
4-Consider, of Hartford, Conn.;
3-Mark, farmer, Prattsburg, N.Y.; *m* Sarah Kellog (*d* 1852);
2-Erastus (1804-76), farmer, White Lake, Oakland Co., Mich.; *m* 1828, Lydia Ann Parker (*d*

1838); *m* 2d, 1839, Climena Clark (1810-64; Kunaz[3]); *m* 3d, 1867, Abigail Clark Dole (*d* 1884); issue (1st marriage): I–William Wadsworth (1828-71; *m* Harriet Crittenden); II–Lyman C. (1830-33); III–Ralph Willis (1832-1913; *m* Ann Rebecca Olmsted); IV–Mark Lyman (1834-35); V–Dan Gilbert (1836-62); issue (2d marriage): I–George Hiram (1842-1906); II–Lydia Climena (1 above); III–Charles Clark (1849-1916; *m* Clara Jane Potter).
1–Grad. Mich. State Normal, 1868. Teacher, Detroit, Mich., 1868-83; with Ill. Children's Home and Aid Soc., 1907-14. Mem. Woman's Relief Corps (chmn. exec. bd., 1891-92; pres. dept. Mich., 1902-03), D.A.R., I.A.G., Detroit Fed. of Women's Clubs (pres., 1897-98), Women's History Club (pres., 1889-95). Presbyterian. Republican. Residence: 538 Euclid Av. E., Detroit, Mich.

1–**HOPKINS, Mabel Florence Ford (Mrs. Walter),** *b* Baltimore, Md., Aug. 29, 1876.
10–Robert **Lockwood** (qv);
9–Joseph (*b* 1636), of Fairfield, Conn.; *m* a dau. of Robert Beecham;
8–Richard (*b* 1678), Worcester Co., Md., ca. 1700; *m* Mary Aydlott or Aydlock;
7–Armwell (1709-89), Kent Co., Del.; *m* Mary Holland, of Somerset Co., Md.;
6–Richard (1735-86), of Kent Co.; justice of peace, 1771,77, and was among the last to be apptd. by the Duke of York; mem. conv. which assembled at New Castle, Del., 1776, to reorganize the State of Del.; one of the small number of men present at the council held 1777; *m* Margaret Johnson (1737-1814);
5–Caleb (1777-1855), St. Louis, Mo., 1850; *m* 1802, Araminta Day (*d* 1839);
4–Mary Anne (1803-40), of St. Louis; *m* 1823, Edward Burke **Hardcastle** (1800-43; Aaron Burr[5]);
3–Addison Lockwood (1827-67), of St. Louis; *m* 1850, Octavia Alexander (1832-1919; Basil W.[4], of St. Louis);
2–Anna Alexander (1854-1921), *m* 1874, Charles Elias **Ford** (1852-1928), pres. The Ford Theatre Co. (John Thomas[3], of Baltimore); issue: I–Mabel Florence (1 above); II–Charles Elias, Jr. (1878-1906); III–Edith Octavia (*b* 1880; *m* 1906, Gordon Lippincott Reese, 1877-1924; *m* 2d, Walter Risteau Mitchell).
1–*m* Apr. 21, 1897, Perle Percy Dunan (Jan. 5, 1867-Feb. 25, 1901).
1–*m* 2d, Jan. 29, 1921, Walter Hopkins, *b* Baltimore, May 30, 1876; son of Robert Dixon Hopkins, of "Beechfield," Catonsville, Baltimore, Md.
1–Mem. bd. dirs. The Ford Theatre Co. Mem. Ch. Service League (dir.), D.A.R. (dir.), U.D.C., Md. Hist. Soc., Eastern Shore Soc., I.A.G. Episcopalian. Democrat. Clubs: Roland Park Garden, Baltimore Country, Beach and Tennis, Everglades, Embassy. Winter residence: The Breakers, Palm Beach, Fla. Residence: 4205 Somerset Pl., Baltimore, Md.

1–**HORN, Mary Louise Erwin (Mrs. Edwin C.),** *b* Athens, O., Apr. 3, 1871.
7–Joshua **Marsh** (*d* 1747), from Eng. to America, 1736; settled in Chester Co., Pa.; *m* 1675, Elizabeth Rogers;
6–Peter (*d* 1788-89), removed to Warrington Tp., York Co., Pa.; patriot; *m* 1743, Margaret–;
5–Deborah (*d* post 1820), *m* 1772, Joshua **Frazer** (*d* 1820), patroit Am. Rev.; resided in York Co., Pa. (James[6], *m* 1740, Rebecca Cox; Alexander[7], settled in York Co., Pa.);
4–Jane (1779-1868-69), *m* 1796, Robert **Erwin** (*d* 1854);
3–Robert (1812-86), *m* Rebecca Law (1817-44);
2–Dr. Robert Wesley (2 below).
10–William **Carpenter** (qv), came in the "Bevis";
9–William (1605-59), settled at Rehoboth, Mass.; rep., 1641,43; dep. 1645; constable, 1641; propr. and town clk., 1643-49; commd. capt. 1642; *m* Abigail–;
8–William (1631/32-1703), town clk., Rehoboth, 1656; dep. 1668; *m* 1st, 1651, Priscilla Bennet (*d* 1663);
7–Benjamin (1663-1738), *m* 1691, Hannah Strong (1671-1762; Jedediah[8], *m* Freedom, dau. Henry Woodward; Elder John[9], qv);
6–Ebenezer (1709-77), of Coventry, Conn.; *m* 1739, Eunice Thompson (1722-77; John[7], *m* Jerusha, dau. Nehemiah Palmer; William[8]; John[9]);
5–James (1741-1813), of Coventry; soldier Am. Rev.; rep. Vt. Legislature, 1786-87; *m* 1761, Irene Ladd (1744-1817);
4–Dr. Eber (1778-1841), Alstead, N.H.; *m* 1803, Judith Green (1780-1841; Ebenezer[5], *m* Mary Currier; John[6], Am. Rev.; Dea. Peter[7]; Peter[8]);
3–Dr. Eber Greene (1808-84), of Athens, O.; *m* 1833, Mary Kellogg Stanley;
2–Julia Eliza (2 below).
8–Capt. John **Stanley** (1624-1706; son of John who *d* enroute to Amercia, 1634); from Eng. to Hartford, Conn., 1634/35; settled finally at Farmington, Conn.; dep. Gen. Ct., 1659-96; capt. King Philip's War; *m* 1st, 1645, Sarah Scott (*d* 1661; Thomas[9], *m* Anna–);
7–Thomas (1649-1713), of Farmington; *m* 1690, Anna Peck (*d* 1718; Rev. Jeremiah[8], *m* Joanna, dau. Robert Kitchell, qv; Dea. William[9], of New Haven);
6–Thomas (1696-1755), of Farmington; *m* 1718, Esther Cowles (*b* 1697; Samuel[7], *m* Rachel, dau. Dea. Thomas Porter, of Farmington; Samuel[8]; John[9], qv);
5–Timothy (1727-1817), of New Britain; *m* 1757, Lydia Newell (*d* 1826; Capt. John[6], *m* Elizabeth, dau. Capt. Joseph Hawley);
4–Timothy (1771-1819), Marietta, O.; *m* 1795, Abigail Robbins;
3–Mary Kellogg (1814-96), of Marietta; *m* Dr. Eber G. **Carpenter** (3 above).
9–John **Robbins,** Gent. (*d* 1660), from Eng. to Newington, Conn.; dep. many yrs.; *m* Mary Willis (sister of Gov. Willis);
8–John (1649-89), of Conn.; *m* 1675, Mary Boreman, or Boardman (1644-1721);
7–Joshua (*b* 1678), *m* 1704, his cousin, Abigail Warner (*b* 1685; Lt. William[8], *m* Hannah, dau. Capt. Joshua Robbins; Daniel[9]; William[10]);
6–Ens. Thomas (1706-54), of Newington; *m* 1740/-41, Prudence Welles;
5–Ens. Unni (1741/42-1810), of Newington; *m* 1765, Mary Kellogg (Capt. Martin[6], *m* Mary Boardman; Capt. Martin[7], Am. Rev., *m* Dorothy, dau. Stephen Chester, g.dau. Capt. John Chester, *m* Sarah, dau. Gov. Thomas Welles, qv);
4–Abigail (1775-1823), *m* Timothy **Stanley** (4 above).
10–Gov. Thomas **Welles** (qv);
9–Judge John (1621-59), rep. from Stratford, Conn.; magistrate; judge Probate Ct.; *m* 1647, Elizabeth Bourne;
8–Capt. Robert (1648-1714), dep. from Stratford; *m* 1675, Elizabeth Goodrich (1658-98);
7–Joseph (1680-1744), of Hartford Co.; *m* 1709, Hannah Robbins;
6–Prudence (1712-64), *m* Ens. Thomas **Robbins** (6 above).
2–Julia Eliza Carpenter (1847-1902), of Athens, O.; *m* 1870, Robert Wesley **Erwin,** M.D. (1842-1909), physician; issue: I–Mary Louise (1 above); II–Roberta J. (*b* 1883; *m* Ernst E. Frank, *d*).
1–*m* Nov. 4, 1891, Edwin C. Horn, *b* Washington, Pa., Nov. 28, 1866; son of William Horn, of Washington, Pa.
1–Grad. Glendale Coll., '91. Mem. D.A.C., D.F.P.A., D.C.G., Desc. Plymouth Colonists, D.A.R., D.R., U.S.D. 1812, hist. socs. of Washington Co., Pa., and Bay Co., Mich. Presbyn. Clubs: Glendale Coll., Current Events, etc. Summer place: Bay City, Mich. Winter place: New Orleans, La. Residence: Washington, Pa.

1–**HORTON, Josephine Peckham Chase (Mrs. Charles H.),** *b* Amboy, Ill., Jan. 30, 1863.
9–William (Chace) **Chase** (qv);
8–William (1622-1684/85), a Quaker, from Eng. with his father, 1630; large landowner at Yarmouth, Mass.;
7–Samuel (ca. 1670-1758), Swansea, Mass.; *m* 1699, Sarah Sherman (*b* 1682; Samuel[8], *m* Martha, dau. of John Tripp, qv; Philip[9], qv);
6–Philip (*b* 1715), *m* 1735, Hannah Buffum;
5–Caleb (*b* 1738);
4–Caleb, *m* 1st, 1785, Rosamond Bullock (*d* 1834);
3–Simpson (1799-1855), *m* 1822, Rebecca Goff (1801-68);
2–Newton Simpson (1825-65), *m* 1857, Harriet Fish Peckham (1827-1916); issue: I–William Sheafe (*b* 1858; *m* 1887, Susan Gladdings Collins, 1866-

97); II–James Tanner (*b* 1861; *m* 1883, Alice Lake Root, *b* 1861); III–Josephine Peckham (1 above).
1–*m* Nov. 3, 1923, Charles Herbert Horton, *b* Rehoboth, Mass., Sept. 21, 1850; son of Otis Hiram Horton, *m* Elizabeth Barney Kingsley. Residence: 513 Main St., Woonsocket, R.I.

1–**HORTON, Thomas Corwin,** *b* Cincinnati, O., Aug. 3, 1848.
3–Jonathan K. **Horton,** 4th postmaster, of Union Village (now Greenwich), N.Y.; clk. of village, 1808-10; supt. of village, 1825-28, 1830-32; pres. of village, 1835-36; mem. Assembly, 1835; *m* Elizabeth Tice;
2–Henry Victor (2 below).
8–Cornet Joseph **Parsons** (qv);
7–Rev. Joseph (1647-1729), 1st justice; capt. train band, Northampton; rep., 1693-1724; *m* 1699, Elizabeth Strong (1648-1736; John[8], *m* Abigail Ford);
6–Joseph;
5–Aaron;
4–Col. Eli;
3–Sophia, *m* —**Daugherty**;
2–Sophia Mathilda Parsons (*b* 1811), *m* 1833, Henry Victor **Horton** (1805-71), jeweler; organizer "Sons of Temperance," Cincinnati, O.; mem. Know-Nothing Party; issue: I–Lewis V. (*b* 1835; *m* M. Clara Pomeroy); II–Elizabeth Tice (*b* 1836; *m* Col. James G. Baldwin, *d*); III–Alonzo C. (1838-1926; *m* Maria Bartlett); IV–Harry K. (*b* 1840); V–Angie (1842-1928; *m* Oscar Parsons, *d*); VI–Thomas Corwin (1 above); VII–Samuel C. (1856-1926); VIII–Ida M. (*b* 1857; *m* Lowell Cash, *d*).
1–*m* May 15, 1872, Anna L. Kingsbury (Aug. 28, 1852-Oct. 16, 1920); issue: 1–Ruth Pierson, *b* Phila., Pa., Dec. 25, 1886; *m* June 4, 1926, Clarence L., son of Clarence Wells, of Topeka, Kan.; 2–Helen, *b* St. Paul, Minn., Mar. 28, 1888; *m* Aug. 28, 1912, Paul E., son of Lucien Eli Walker, of Ft. Wayne, Ind. (issue: Margery Ruth; Juliana; Kenneth); 3–Margaret Kingsbury, *b* St. Paul, Mar. 15, 1890; *m* Feb. 20, 1915, Vernon, son of J.J. Morgan of Hollywood, Calif. (issue: Thomas Horton).
1–*m* 2d, Mar. 16, 1922, Harriet Louise Ransom (qv).
1–Ed. Farmers Coll.; (D.D., Los Angeles Bapt. Theol. Sem.). Supt. emeritus, Bible Inst. of Los Angeles, Calif. (founder of same, 1907); pastor since 1884 (see Who's Who in America). Pres. Internat. Fishermen's Club. Mem. bd. dirs. Bryan Memorial U., World's Christian Fundamentals Assn. Residence: 4150 Chestnut Av., Long Beach, Calif.

1–**HORTON, Harriet Louise Ransom (Mrs. Thomas C.),** *b* Odessa, N.Y., Jan. 13, 1876.
9–Robert **Ransom** (*d* 1697), from Eng. ante 1654, settled at Plymouth, Mass.; *m* 1660, Susanna–;
8–Joshua (1665-89), of Sandwich, Mass.; *m* 1st, 1686, Mary Gifford (*d* 1689);
7–Robert (1687-1777), of Colchester, Conn.; *m* 1707, Alice Newton (*b* 1686);
6–James (1713-73), of Colchester; *m* Sarah Treadway (*d* 1793);
5–James (1738-1823), of Colchester; lt., 8th Co., 2d Regt., Gen. Spencer's command, Am. Rev.; *m* 1757, Elizabeth Loomis;
4–Joel (1770-1820), of Colchester; *m* 1798, Charlotte Benham (*d* 1820);
3–Vincent (1802-76), of Colchester; *m* Adaline Cook (*d* 1876);
2–Joel H. (2 below).
9–Joseph **Loomis** (qv);
8–Dea. John (1622-88), admitted to Windsor Ch., 1640; resided at Farmington, 1652-60, returned to Windsor and was dea. of the ch.; dep. Gen. Ct., 1666-67, 1675-87; *m* 1648/49, Elizabeth Scott (1625-96; Thomas[9], *m* Ann–);
7–Dea. Samuel (1666-1754), *m* 1st, 1688, Elizabeth White (1667-1736; Lt. Daniel[8], *m* Sarah Crow);
6–Daniel (1709-84), *m* 1731, Hannah Withrell, or Wetherell;
5–Elizabeth (1738-1823), *m* James **Ransom** (5 above).
2–Joel H. **Ransom** (1838-1916), inventor, Odessa, N.Y.; *m* Maria Matthews (*d* 1879), from Eng. to Belleville, Can.; issue: I–Elizabeth (*b* 1866; *m* Charles E. Walker, *d*); II–William Vincent (*b* 1867; *m* Harriet Gano, *d*); III–Henrietta (*b* 1869; *m* Newell R. Rogers); IV–Miriam M. (1871-1914; *m* Lawrence J. Mattice); V–Frank (*b* 1873; *m* Mrs. Ada Barlemann); VI–Harriet Louise (1 above); VII–Elsie Lillian (*b* 1879; *m* 1902, Harry Gearing, *b* 1880).
1–*m* Mar. 16, 1922, Thomas Corwin Horton (qv).
1–Presbyterian. Republican. Residence: 4150 Chestnut Av., Long Beach, Calif.

1–**HOSMER, George Leonard,** *b* Lynn, Mass., Dec. 31, 1874.
9–James **Hosmer** (1605-85; son of Stephen, g.son of James), from Eng. in the "Elizabeth," to Concord, Mass., 1635; *m* 2d, Mary– (*d* 1641);
8–James (1637-76), killed in Sudbury Fight, King Philip's War; *m* 1658, Sarah White (John[9], *m* Joane–, *d* 1654);
7–Thomas (1672-1754), *m* 1696, Hannah Hartwell (1675-1755; Samuel[8] [*b* 1645], of Concord, *m* 1665, Ruth Wheeler, *d* 1713);
6–James (1709-60), *m* 1732, Elizabeth Davis (1714-1801);
5–Lt. Samuel (1734-96), soldier in Am. Rev.; *m* 1755, Ann Parlin (1732-1822);
4–Asahel (1775-1817), *m* 1800, Eunice Wright (1780-1872);
3–Franklin (1801-83), *m* 1844, Eliza Ann Stiles (1821-52);
2–George Franklin (2 below).
10–Thomas **Tracy** (qv);
9–Jonathan (1646-1711), *m* Mary Griswold;
8–Jonathan (1673 or 75-1704), *m* Anna Palmer;
7–Jonathan (*b* 1702), *m* Amee Palmer;
6–Samuel (*b* 1731), served Am. Rev.; *m* Anna Partridge;
5–Cyrus (*b* 1757), *m* Elizabeth Palmer;
4–Cyrus (1784-1860), *m* Hannah Mason Snow;
3–Cyrus Mason (*b* 1824), engr.; taught botany, Essex Inst., Salem, 1848-49; botany and materia medica, Mass. Coll. of Pharmacy, 1868-73; leading editor, "Lynn Transcript," 1869-79; clk. Common Council of Lynn, 1856-69; a founder, Free Public Forest, Lynn, 1881; *m* 1848, Caroline Mary Needham (George W.[4], *m* Caroline Rhodes);
2–Laura Caroline (*b* 1850), *m* 1874, George Franklin **Hosmer** (1849-1919), leather business; issue: I–George Leonard (1 above); II–Edith Tracy (*b* 1876); III–Louise (*b* 1880); IV–Laura (*b* 1882; *m* Arthur Palmer Ottaway).
1–*m* Aug. 28, 1901, Lucy Morse Harmon, *b* Winchester, N.H., Apr. 23, 1877; dau. of Rev. Elijah Harmon, *d* 1912; issue: 1–Chester Harmon, *b* Melrose, Mass., Jan. 13, 1903; grad. M.I.T., '25; *m* May 12, 1928, Marian Terry, dau. of Noble Earl Whitford, of Syracuse, N.Y.; 2–Miriam Jewell, *b* Wellesley, Mass., Dec. 13, 1906; U.Mich., '28; 3–Elizabeth Tracy, *b* Woburn, Mass., July 11, 1913; Cushing Acad., 1931.
1–M.I.T., 1897. Instr. geodesy, M.I.T., 1897, prof. geodesy, 1907–. Fellow A.A.A.S., Am. Geog. Soc.; mem. Am. Soc. C.E., Boston Soc. C.E., Soc. Am. Mil. Engrs., S.C.W., S.A.R., etc. Author textbooks in geodesy, astronomy and navigation. Author: Hosmer Genealogy. Summer place: East Machias, Me. Residence: Woburn, Mass.

1–**HOTCHKISS, Clarence Roland,** *b* Bradford Co., Pa., June 5, 1880.
10–Samuel **Hotchkiss** (qv);
9–Thomas (1654-1711), sgt. in the Colonial Wars; *m* Sarah Wilmot (1663-1731);
8–Samuel (1680-1730), served in Indian and border wars; *m* Sarah Bradley (*b* 1680);
7–Joseph, *m* Patience Collins (1719-54);
6–Samuel (1741-1804), in Am. Rev.; *m* Lydia Peck (*d* 1804);
5–Samuel, first clk. Cortland Co., N.Y.; *m* Milla Barnes?;
4–Ziba (1794-1877), pioneer of Bradford Co., Pa.; *m* Sally Ann Washburn (1793-1877);
3–Charles Barnes (1828-1900), Civil War vet.; contractor for carrying first U.S. mail in Bradford Co., Pa.; *m* Hanna Prince (1824-92);
2–Charles Frederick (1854-1914), farmer and contractor; *m* 1875, Melissa Taylor (1857-88); issue: I–Mary Theresa (1876-1907; *m* Hiram I. Pearl); II–Clarence Roland (1 above); III–Walter Horace (*b* 1888).
1–*m* July 2, 1908, Grace Evangeline North, *b* Olive Bridge, Ulster Co., N.Y., Jan. 31, 1880; dau. of George Sylvan North, *m* Delphine Winchell, of Kingston, N.Y.
1–B.B.A., Eastman, N.Y., '03 (Delta Theta Pi, Gamma Mu); LL.B., U.Ore., 1911. U.S. mar-

shal, Dist. of Ore., apptd., 1924, re-apptd., 1925. Served in Spanish-Am. War, Philippine Insurrection, Mexican border, World War, and has held ranks from pvt. to lt. col. Author (see Who's Who in America). Mem. U.S.W.V. (past dept. cdr., and nat. vice cdr.), M.O.W.W. (past chapter cdr., and mem. gen. staff), A.L., Scabbard and Blade, V.F.W., S.A.R., I.A.G. Mason, Odd Fellow. Clubs: Commercial, Mazama Mountaineering; Army and Navy (Washington). Residence: 834 E. Harrison St., Portland, Ore.

1-**HOTCHKISS, H(enry) Stuart**, *b* New Haven, Conn., Oct. 1, 1878.
8-John **Prescott** (qv);
7-Capt. Jonathan (1643-1721), *m* Elizabeth Hoar (*d* 1687);
6-Rev. Benjamin (1687-1777), Harvard, 1709; *m* Elizabeth Higginson (1696-1723);
5-Benjamin (1717-78), Harvard, 1736; *m* Rebecca Minot (1719-61);
4-Benjamin (1757-1839), *m* Hannah Blakeslie;
3-Elizabeth Daggett (1803-82), *m* Henry **Hotchkiss** (1801-71);
2-Henry Lucius (2 below).
10-John **Webster** (qv);
9-Robert (1627-76), *m* 1652, Susannah Treat (1629-1705);
8-John (1653-94), *m* Sarah Mygatt (Jacob[9], *m* Sarah, dau. of William Whiting, qv; Joseph[10]);
7-Capt. Daniel (1693-1766), *m* Mirriam (Cook) Kellogg (*b* 1690);
6-Noah (1722-1813), *m* 1749, Mercy Steele (*d* 1794);
5-Noah, LL.D. (1758-1843), of New Haven; Yale, 1778; famous lexicographer and author; *m* 1789, Rebecca Greenleaf (1766-1847);
4-Mary, *m* Horatio **Southgate**, of Portland, Me., lawyer;
3-Mary Webster (Southgate), (1819-60), of New Haven, Conn.; *m* 1838, Henry **Trowbridge** (1816-83);
2-Jane (1850-1902), *m* 1875, Henry Lucius **Hotchkiss** (*b* 1842), mfr. and banker, New Haven (for Hotchkiss and Trowbridge lineages and issue, see Vol. I, p. 375).
1-*m* Oct. 9, 1907, Elizabeth Wyndham Washington, *b* Washington, D.C.; dau. of Joseph E. Washington, of Wessyngton, Cedar Hill, Tenn.; issue (all *b* New Haven, Conn.): 1-Henry, *b* June 6, 1909; 2-Mary Bolling Washington, *b* July 21, 1911; 3-Stuart Trowbridge, *b* July 16, 1913; 4-Joseph Washington, *b* Nov. 22, 1919.
1-Ph.B., Yale-S., '00 (Delta Psi). Chmn. Bd. of General Rubber Co.; v.p. U.S. Rubber Co.; officer and dir. various other corpns. (see Who's Who in America). Capt., maj., lt. col., U.S.A., World War. Mem. S.C.W. Fellow Royal Geog. Soc., London. Clubs: University, Yale, St. Anthony, Lotos (New York), New Haven Lawn. Residence: 55 Hillhouse Av., New Haven, Conn.

1-**HOUGHTON, Harris Ayres**, *b* Elmira, N.Y., Feb. 25, 1874.
8-Ralph **Houghton** (qv);
7-James (ante 1652-1711), of Lancaster, Mass.; *m* Mary Sawyer (*b* 1653);
6-John (living 1770), of Lancaster (that part set off as Bolton, 1738); *m* 1st, 1718, Mehitable Wilson;
5-John (1727-1826), of Brattleboro, Vt.; road commr. under York govt. for purpose of opening a road from Brattleboro to Albany; *m* 2d, Susannah Dodge (?);
4-John (1774-1850), of Lincklaen, N.Y.; *m* 1801, Elizabeth Jackson (1784-1855), of Ballston Spa, N.Y.;
3-Royal (1802-81), itinerant Methodist clergyman of Carthage and Syracuse, N.Y., and thru central and northern N.Y.; *m* 3d, 1836, Cecilia Beverly (Stearns) Horr (1812-1900);
2-Oscar Allen, A.B., Ph.D., D.D. (1841-1908), Meth. clergyman, of Syracuse, Elmira, and central N.Y.; *m* 1869, Susan Harris Ayres, A.B., A.M., Ph.D. (1843-1900).
1-*m* Oct. 16, 1901, Virginia Boyd Dudley, *b* Pinnacle, nr. Bramwell, Mercer Co., W.Va., Dec. 8, 1876; dau. of Andrew Jackson Dudley, of Bramwell, W.Va.; issue: 1-Katherine, *b* New York, N.Y., Mar. 27, 1903; *m* May 27, 1927, George Howard, son of Jacob I. Fulton, of Taylorville, Ill. (issue: Edward Dudley, *b* New York, 1928); 2-Harris Dudley (Feb. 4, 1908-Jan. 4, 1914); 3-William Emmet, *b* Bayside, L.I., N.Y., Nov. 25, 1909; ed. Syracuse U.
1-A.B., Syracuse U., '95 (D.K.E., Theta Nu Epsilon), M.D., 1901. Physician, part time at Physicians Hosp., Plattsburgh, N.Y.; internist; specialist in diseases of metabolism. Practiced at Bayside, L.I., 1903-17, New York, 1919-29. First lt. M.R.C., 1911-17; capt. U.S.A., 1917-18. Apptd. mem. Queensborough Library Bd., by Mayor George B. McClellan, pres. one yr., in service 8 yrs. Mem. M.O.W.W., I.A.G., N.Y. Acad. Medicine, A.M.A. Methodist. Independent Republican. Residence: 2345 Broadway, New York, N.Y.

1-**HOUGHTON, Harry Ballentine**, *b* Norfolk, Va., Aug. 4, 1877.
10-John **Houghton** (qv);
9-John (1650-1737), magistrate; town clk., 1686-1725; rep. Gen. Ct., 1693-1714; dep., 1696-1717; on garrison duty, 1704-11; *m* 1st, 1671, Mary Farrar (1648-1724; Jacob[10] [*d* 1677], *m* ca. 1640, Ann-);
8-Jacob (1674-1752), town clk., Bolton, Mass.; *m* 1704, Rebecca Whitcomb (1671-1752; Josiah[9], *m* Rebecca Waters; John[10], to Dorchester, Mass., 1635, Scituate, 1640, Lancaster, Mass., 1654, *m* Frances-, *d* 1671);
7-Benjamin (bap. 1718-1774), Lancaster, Mass.; *m* 1720, Ruth Wheelock (bap. 1718; John[8]);
6-Abijah (1723-1802), Lancaster; *m* 1746, Alice Joslyn (1726-1808; Peter[7] [*b* 1686], *m* Alice Woods; Peter[8]; Nathaniel[9]; Thomas[10], qv);
5-Abijah (1749-1831), of Sterling, Mass.; capt., Benjamin Houghton's co. of minutemen, marched on Cambridge Alarm, 1775, sgt., trumpeter, Am. Rev.; wounded at Bunker Hill; *m* 1769, Mary Sawyer (*b* 1751; Abner[6]; Joseph[7]; Thomas[8]; Thomas[9], qv);
4-Abijah Otis (1792-1855), capt. arty., col., War 1812; published Orange Co. (N.Y.) Gazette, and Rahway (N.J.) Herald; early mayor of Brooklyn, N.Y.; *m* 1815, Eliza Farrand;
3-Carlos Palifax (1816-83), of Goshen, N.Y.; *m* 1836, Angelica Maria Taylor (1812-98; James[4]; Sgt. Moses[5]; Moses[6]);
2-Harry Sherman (2 below).
10-Nathaniel **Farrand**, from France to Eng., to Milford, Conn., 1639; named as one of 1st planters of Milford;
9-Nathaniel, *m* Mary Cobb;
8-Samuel (1681-1750), magistrate, Newark, N.J.; *m* Hannah Wheeler (1685-1748; Joseph[9], *m* Dorcas-);
7-Ebenezer (1707-77), *m* Rebecca Ward (1711-77; Bethuel[8]; Samuel[9]; John[10]; George[11]);
6-Bethuel (1741-94), lt., maj., Morris Co., N.J., served in state troops and militia; 1st maj., 3d Bn., Gloucester Co., N.J., resigned 1778; *m* 1763, Rhoda Smith (1747-1839; Samuel[7], *m* Hannah Allen; Richard[8], to N.J., ca. 1690);
5-Daniel (1764-1829), capt. and adj., 3d Regt., Morris Co., N.J., Militia, War 1812; *m* 1785, Phoebe Plum;
4-Eliza (1795-1869), *m* Abijah O. **Houghton** (4 above).
10-John (Plume) **Plum** (qv);
9-Samuel (1626-1703), of Branford, Conn., and Newark, N.J.; signer of "Fundamental Agreements," 1665, drawn up to govern people going to found Newark, N.J.;
8-John (1657-1710), *m* 1677, Hannah Crane;
7-John (1696-1785), *m* Joanna Tompkins (1708-60);
6-Robert (1729-69), *m* 1764, Deborah Farrand (1744-1806; Joseph[7] [brother of Ebenezer, 7 above], *m* Sarah Crissey, *d* 1815);
5-Phoebe (1766-1851), *m* Daniel **Farrand** (5 above).
11-Richard **Treat** (qv);
10-Gov. Robert (bap. 1624-1710), Milford, 1639; apptd. to survey and lay out town; capt. mil. forces, 1663; dep. N.J. Gen. Assembly; maj. in King Philip's War; in Great Swamp Fight; dep.gov.; 8th gov. of Conn., 1683; *m* Jane Tapp (*d* 1703, aet. 75; Edmund[11]);
9-Mary (*b* 1652), *m* Dea. Azariah **Crane** (1647-1730; Hon. Jasper[10], qv);
8-Hannah, *m* John **Plum** (8 above).
2-Harry Sherman **Houghton** (1848-1925), sec.-treas., Cranford Paving Co., Washington; *m* 1876, Alice Virginia Ballentine (*b* Portsmouth, Va.; Robert Samuel[3] [bap. 1824-*d* 1854 or 55 of yellow fever], *m* 1845, Elizabeth Ford.

1828-77); issue: I–Harry B. (1 above); II–Robert Otis (*b* 1878; *m* 1917, Myrtle A. Cranz); III–Elizabeth Ford (*b* 1879; *m* 1908, William Key Davidson); IV–Alice Virginia (*b* 1882); V–Alfred Macy (*b* 1885; *m* 1915, Mary V. Lowe); VI–Carlos Cranford (*b* 1887; *m* 1913, Lucy D. Lauck); VII–Vernon Taylor (*b* 1891; *m* 1919, Helen Todd); VIII–Woodson Plyer (*b* 1893).
1–*m* June 3, 1903, Edna Rosanna Wescott (qv for issue).
1–LL.B., Lake Forest U., 1901 (Phi Alpha Delta). With Marshall Field & Co., wholesale, 1898-1904; sales mgr., Turner & Seymour Mfg. Co., Torrington, Conn., Stamford Rolling Mills; pres., The Bridgeport Castings Co. Presbyterian. Republican. Clubs: Brooklawn Country, Algonquin, Rotary, Fairfield Beach, Contemporary. Residence: 600 Brooklawn Av., Bridgeport, Conn.

1–**HOUGHTON, Edna Rosanna Wescott (Mrs. Harry B.),** *b* Washington, D.C.
10–Robert **Ayers** (1650-1718/19), from Hopkinton, R.I., to Cohansey, N.J.; purchased of James Wass of London, Eng., by his agents, Nov. 20, 1705, 2,200 acres of south part of the Wass survey of 5,000 acres which James Wass purchased of John Fenwick of Salem, N.J., before he left Eng., 1675; *m* Ester Bowen (*b* 1675);
9–Isaac (1673-1761), of Salem, N.J.; *m* Hannah Barette (*d* 1793);
8–Caleb (1697-1771), *m* Patience Brooks (Timothy[9]; Rev. Timothy[10]; Henry[11]);
7–Nathan (1718-1811), *m* Elizabeth Bowen;
6–Rev. Nathan (1749-1811), *m* Amy–;
5–John, *m* Tamer–; *m* 2d, Lucinda Ines;
4–Nathan (1807-67), *m* Christiana Hires (1809-95; John[5]; Conrad[6]; Jacob[7]);
3–Mary (1828-1907), *m* 1845, Charles **Wescott** (1817-97), from Gloucester Co., N.J., to Camden, N.J. (Ochel, or Oshen[4] [ca. 1796-1870], of Woodbury, N.J. *m* 1816, Susanna Bigelow, of Phila.);
2–Edward Steward (2 below).
10–Henry **Pierson** (qv);
9–Joseph (*b* 1649), Southampton, L.I.; ens. and lt.; *m* 1675, Amy Barnes (*d* 1692; Charles[10] [*d* ca. 1663], 1st schoolmaster East Hampton, L.I., 1658, *m* Mary, dau. John Hand; William[11]; Edward[12]);
8–Henry, M.D. (*b* 1678), Southampton; *m* 1702, Abigail Ludlam (Henry[9], *m* Rachel–; William[10] from Mattock, Eng., 1653, to Southampton, L.I.);
7–Azel (1708-65), of L.I.; *m* 1735, Joanna Scudder (*d* ante 1762; Richard[8]; John[9]; John[10], of Newtown, L.I.);
6–Azel (1739-98), of Cedarville and Bridgeton, N.J.; capt. Am. Rev.; *m* 1760, Philothea Sayre (1741-94; g.dau. Thomas[8], *m* Mary–);
5–Azel, M.D. (1767-1815), of Bridgeton, N.J.; *m* 1789, Phoebe Clark (1767-1844; Daniel[6], *m* Rachel Holmes; Charles[7]; Daniel[8]; Thomas[9]; Richard[10]; Richard[11]);
4–Azel (1794-1824), Bridgeton; *m* 1816, Abigail Burt;
3–Lucius C. (1818-78), Bridgeton and Camden, N.J.; *m* 1841, Maria Rosanna Saurman;
2–Sara Minerva (2 below).
9–Henry **Burt** (qv);
8–David (1632-90), in Queen Ann's War he lost 2 sons and a dau., one son carried into captivity by French and Indians; contributed to founding of Harvard Coll.; town surveyor, Northampton; *m* 1655 (1st marriage recorded in Northampton), Mary Holton (*d* 1713; William[9], qv);
7–Benjamin (*b* 1680), of Deerfield; house burned in Indian Massacre of Feb. 29, 1704, family captured, taken to Montreal, Can., after three attempts, Lt. John Sheldon rescued them, left Quebec, May 30, 1706; returned to Norwalk, Conn.; purchased land, 1708, and propr. founder of Ridgefield; *m* 1702, Sarah Belden;
6–John (1711-98), musician, N.J. Cont. Line, Am. Rev.; to Salem, N.J.; *m* 1746,—Smith (*d* post 1798);
5–Moses (1771-1832), *m* 1792, Lovicy Westcott;
4–Abigail (1798-1883), *m* Azel **Pierson** (4 above).
10–Richard **Belden** (qv);
9–William (1622-60), removed from Wethersfield to Norwalk; *m* 1646, Thomasine–;
8–Daniel (*b* Hatfield, Conn., 1648-*d* 1731), to Deerfield, Mass., 1686; *m* 1670, Elizabeth Foot (1654-96), killed by Indians during King Philip's War (Nathaniel[9], *m* Elizabeth Smith);
7–Sarah (1682-1759), escaped death in 1696 by hiding in tobacco; *m* Benjamin **Burt** (7 above).
9–Richard **Westcott** (*d* 1649), came with Gov. Winthrop's colony to Salem, settled at Wethersfield, Conn., 1637, Fairfield, 1639; served in Pequot War; *m* Johanna– (*d* ca. 1682);
8–Daniel (*d* 1703/04), sgt. in Indian wars; rep. to Legislature, 1694; *m* Abigail Gaylord (*b* 1653; Samuel[9], *m* 1646, Elizabeth, dau. George Hull, qv; William[10], qv);
7–Ebenezer (*d* 1748), founder of settlements in Salem Co., N.J.; *m* Barbary–;
6–Samuel (*d* 1792), capt. 1st Regt., Cumberland Co. Milita, engagement at Haddonfield; served also in state troops; capt. of Fairfield, N.J., Foot Militia; resigned, 1779; *m* Hannah Shaw (Carll[7], *m* Hannah–; Edmund[8]);
5–Lovicy (1776-1863), *m* Moses **Burt** (5 above).
9–Stephen Coerte (Van Voorhees) **Voorhees** (qv);
8–Jan Stevense (*b* 1652), of Flatlands, L.I.; *m* 1680, Femmetje Aukes Van Nuyse (bap. 1662-will 1735; Auke Janse[9], *m* Madeline Peiterse);
7–Abraham Janse, Flatlands; *m* Styntje Vanderveer;
6–John Abrahamse (1734-1817), nr. New Brunswick, Somerset Co., N.J.; *m* Mary (Maria) Vanderbilt (*d* 1812);
5–Hendrick (*b* 1757), Bridgewater, Somerset Co., N.J.; in Am. Rev.; *m* Elizabeth Williams (*d* 1844);
4–Sarah Cockafore (1803-88), New Brunswick, N.J.; *m* 1820, Jacob **Saurman** (1793-1840);
3–Maria Rosanna (1823-1908), of Camden, N.J.; *m* Lucius C. **Pierson** (3 above);
2–Sarah Minerva (*b* 1847), *m* 1869, Edward Steward **Wescott** (1846-1919), pvt., Co. A, 1st N.J. Militia, Civil War; issue: I–Jeannette L. (*m* George G. Brown); II–Edna R. (1 above).
1–*m* June 3, 1903, Harry Ballentine Houghton (qv); issue: 1–Jeanne, *b* Washington, D.C., July 20, 1905; A.B., Smith, '27; 2–Wescott, *b* Chicago, Ill., July 14, 1911; Mercersburg (Pa.) Acad.
1–Ed. Goucher Coll.; George Washington U.; grad. Kindergarten Coll. of Washington, Sec., Associated Charities of Bridgeport, Conn. Mem. D.F.P.A., D.A.R. Presbyterian. Republican. Clubs: Brooklawn Country, Fairfield Beach, Contemporary, College (sec.). Residence: 600 Brooklawn Av., Bridgeport, Conn.

1–**HOUSE, Katharine Osborn Parsons (Mrs. William),** *b* Lock Haven, Pa., July 27, 1877.
8–Dea. Abel **Holbrook,** from Eng., 1673; *m* Hannah–;
7–John (1699-1752), Derby, Conn.; *m* 1723, Abigail Gun;
6–John (1726-1801), capt. 4th Co. Train Band, Derby, Conn., 1767; equipped a regt. at his own expense for Am. Rev.; *m* 1750, Esther Nichols (Adm. John[7], of the English Navy and brother of Gov. Nichols, of N.Y.);
5–Abigail (1764-1849), *m* 1789, Wilson **Hurd** (1763-1853);
4–Sarah (*d* 1853), of New Haven, Conn.; *m* 1815, Ezekiel **Gilbert,** of Seymour, Conn.;
3–Catherine (1821-99), of New Haven, Conn.; *m* 1841, Minott Augur **Osborn,** of New Haven;
2–Charlotte (*b* 1849), of New Haven; *m* 1872, William **Parsons** (*b* 1844), grad. Yale, 1868 (Wooden Spoon Soc., Wolf's Head); grad. Albany Law Sch.; lawyer; editor: History of Umatilla Co., Ore.; issue: I–William Osborn (*b* 1873; *m* Della Beagle); II–Minot Osborn (1875-90); III–Katharine Osborn (1 above); IV–Ethel Osborn (*b* 1884; *m* Charles Erwin Botden, *d*).
1–*m* Sept. 18, 1901, William House, M.D., *b* Ellenville, N.Y., Nov. 8, 1873; son of Jacob House, of Buffalo, N.Y., *m* Magdeline–; issue: 1–Janet Parsons, *b* Weston, Ore., June 20, 1903; *m* Dec. 26, 1926, Lt. Walter Pitman Ramsay, U.S.N.A., 1921, served on submarine patrol, World War; son of W. P. Ramsay, of Washington, D.C., *m* Susan Fite; 2–Priscilla Osborn, *b* Portland, Ore., Sept. 18, 1909; *m* Feb. 2, 1929, Frank Flint Dickson, enlisted C.A.C., Apr. 20, 1917, overseas

14 months, World War; son of John Ross Dickson, of Portland.
1–Mem. C.D.A., D.R. Residence: 452 Vista Av., Portland, Ore.

1–**HOUSTON, Samuel O'Grady,** *b* nr. Maryville, Blount Co., Tenn., Apr. 13, 1871.
7–Mrs. John **Houston** (1650-1747), from N. Ireland, 1735; settled in Pa.; later removed to Rockbridge Co., Va.;
6–John (1690-1754), of Rockbridge Co., Va.; *m* —Cunningham;
5–Samuel (1728-97), of Rockbridge Co.; *m* 1753, Elizabeth McCroskey;
4–Robert (1760-1835), of Rockbridge Co., Va., and Knox Co., Tenn.; *m* 1st, Elizabeth Lockhart, of Rockbridge Co.;
3–Robert (1802-65), of Knox and Blount cos., Tenn.; *m* ca. 1826, Dorothy Creswell;
2–Robert Lockhart (2 below).
6–William Henry **Creswell** (*d* 1776), of Abingdon, Va.;
5–Andrew (1757-1838), of Sevier Co., Tenn.; served Am. Rev.; *m* 1780, Dorothy Evins (1756-1833), of Abingdon, Va.;
4–William Evins (1784-1852), of Sevier and Blount cos., Tenn.; *m* Elizabeth McMurray (1781-1845);
3–Dorothy (1807-86), of Blount Co.; *m* Robert **Houston** (3 above);
2–Robert Lockhart (1844-1906), of Blount Co., Tenn.; farmer; mem. 2d Tenn. Cav., Federal Army, 4 yrs., present at Vicksburg, Chickamauga, and Murfreesboro (wounded in jaw); *m* 1868, Margaret Ann Nimon (1849-1927); issue: I–Frances (*b* 1868; *m* Dr. D. P. Love); II–Samuel O'Grady (1 above); III–Carl Thomas (1873-1903; *m* Mary Wade); IV–William Edgar (*b* 1875; *m* Alberta McDaniel); V–Robert Lockhart (*b* 1879; *m* Henrietta Muecke); VI–Joseph Oscar (*b* 1881; *m* Hattie McNelly); VII–Elizabeth (*b* 1886).
1–*m* June 26, 1901, Katherine McFarland Love, *b* nr. Knoxville, Tenn., Dec. 27, 1875; dau. of Ben S. B. Love, of Knox Co., Tenn.; issue (all *b* Knoxville, Tenn.): 1–Robert Benjamin, *b* Apr. 18, 1902; B. A., Maryville Coll., '23; M.A., U. of Tenn., 1925; *m* May 17, 1924, Belle Hedrick; 2–Carl Thomas, *b* Sept. 17, 1903; B.A., Maryville, '25; LL.B., U. of Tenn., 1928; 3–Max Lester, *b* Apr. 26, 1906; ed. Maryville Coll.
1–B.A., Maryville Coll., '98, LL.B., U. of Tenn., 1901. Began practice of law, Knoxville, Tenn., 1901; co. judge, Knox Co., Tenn., term 1926-34. Trustee Maryville Coll., dir. Farmers Mutual Fire Ins. Co.; v.p. South Knoxville Bank. Mem. S.A.R., etc. Residence: Knoxville, Tenn.

1–**HOVEY, Jessie Fluke (Mrs. Ford E.),** *b* Jefferson, Ia., Nov. 14, 1876.
6–William Temple **Coles** (*d* 1776 or 77), from Dublin, Ireland; *m* Sarah Jolly, of Salisbury, N.C.;
5–Henrietta Maria (*b* 1763), *m* 1782, Philip **Fishburn** (1758-1830);
4–Sarah (1784-1834), *m* 1804, Henry **Fluke** (*died* 1832);
3–Alexander (1809-82), *m* 1836, Julia McKenzie (1805-86);
2–Henry (1838-1916), *m* 1863, Elizabeth Tracy (1839-99); issue: I–Atta (*b* 1864; *m* 1882, Sol T. Upham); II–William Henry (1866-1927; *m* May Bonnell); III–Julia Mary (*b* 1868; *m* 1895, Stephen A. Boon); IV–Margaret Elizabeth (1871-90); V–Jessie (1 above); VI–Bessie (1876-1901).
1–*m* Apr. 30, 1901, Ford E. Hovey, *b* Henderson Harbor, N.Y., Sept. 3, 1876; son of Azel Hovey, of Henderson Harbor; issue: 1–Henry Azel, *b* Horton, Kan., June 3, 1903; ed. Ohio Wesleyan U.; *m* June 17, 1926, Evelyn O., dau. of Bishop Titus Lowe, of Singapore, Straits Settlements.
1–Mem. D.A.R. Trustee Fontenelle Boul. Home for Aged. Methodist. Republican. Residence: 117 N. Happy Hollow Boul., Omaha, Neb.

1–**HOWARD, Rossiter,** *b* Brooklyn, N.Y., June 18, 1878.
7–Abraham **Howard,** shipmaster, in Mediterranean trade; captured by Algerians and held a slave for some years, until released under a treaty bet. Eng. and Algiers; came to America ca. 1720, and settled at Marblehead, Mass., ca. 1722;
6–Joseph (*d* 1770), of Salem, Mass.; shipmaster and owner; *m* 1742, Elizabeth Pitts (*b* 1721; William[7], *m* Deborah Skinner);
5–John (1755-1848), of Salem; corpl. and drill sgt. in Col. Glover's regt., 1775; worked fitting out privateers at Salem and served under Capt. Samuel Tucker at sea; tent and sail maker; mem. Gen. Ct., 1817; *m* Jemimah Ashley Young;
4–Joseph (1780-1857), of Salem, Mass., and Brooklyn, N.Y.; ship owner and trader; mem. Gen. Ct., 1822; *m* 1806, Anstiss Smith;
3–John Tasker (1808-88), of Brooklyn, N.Y.; ship owner and trader; pioneer in shipping routes to Panama, Calif., Australia; founder of Plymouth Ch., Brooklyn; *m* 1831, Susan Taylor Raymond (1812-1906);
2–John Raymond (2 below).
8–John Kasper **Crowinshield** (qv);
7–John (1696-1761), *m* 1722, Anstiss Williams (1700-73; John[8]);
6–Anstiss (1727-68), *m* 1760, William **King** (*b* 1729; Samuel[7]);
5–Lydia (1764-1854), *m* 1785, George **Smith** (1762-1840; George[6]);
4–Anstiss (1785-1868), *m* Joseph **Howard** (4 above);
3–John T., *m* Susan T. Raymond (3 above);
2–John Raymond (1837-1926), of Montclair, N.J.; publisher and editor firm of Fords, Howard & Hulbert; pres. bd. edn., and of Montclair, Outlook and Tariff Reform clubs; capt. U.S.A., 1861-65; *m* 1871, Susan Raymond Merriam (*b* 1849); issue: I–Frank Ward (*b* 1872; *m* Louise Currier); II–George Merriam (*b* 1873; *m* Aline E. Herwig); III–Annie Howard (*b* 1875; *m* Thomas Christy Chapin, *d*); IV–Rossiter (1 above); V–Dr. Tasker (*b* 1879; *m* Mary Woodbury); VI–John Raymond, Jr. (*b* 1880; *m* Daisie Davis); VII–Edward Ford (1881-1903); VIII–Carrington (*b* 1883; *m* Cornelia F. Jefferson); IX–Rev. James M. (*b* 1885; *m* Gertrude L. Hunter).
1–*m* Oct. 19, 1905, Alice Woodbury, *b* Rockford, Ill.; dau. of Rev. Frank P. Woodbury, D.D., of Rockford, Ill., and Montclair, N.J., *m* Abbie Richards; issue: 1–Elizabeth Woodbury, *b* Paris, France, Oct. 26, 1907; Smith Coll., 2 yrs.; Antioch Coll., 1930; 2–John Tasker, *b* Paris, June 1911.
1–Grad. Phillips Acad., Andover, 1898; student, Harvard, 1901-02; studied singing and composition, New York and Boston, 6 yrs.; visited cities in Europe and studied art 10 yrs. Curator of ednl. work, Cleveland Museum of Art, since 1921, curator of classical art, since 1924, asst. dir. since 1925 (see Who's Who in America). Congregational. Republican. Club: Cleveland. Residence: 2459 Overlook Rd., Cleveland Heights, O.

1–**HOWE, George,** *b* Wilmington, N.C., Oct. 3, 1876.
9–Abraham **Howe** (*d* 1676), from Essex, Eng., ante 1640;
8–Isaac (1639-1714), *m* Hannah Robiohn (*d* 1728);
7–Isaac (1678-1760), *m* 1702, Submit Bird (1678-1760);
6–Thomas (1709-bet. 1788-95), *m* 1733, Sarah Searle (*d* 1795);
5–Thomas (1735-1816), *m* 1763, Hannah Leeds (1741-1807);
4–William (1770-1835), *m* 1797, Mary Gould (1772-1859);
3–George (1802-83), prof. S.C. Theol. Sem.; *m* 2d, 1836, Mrs. Sarah Ann (Walthour) McConnell (1803-85);
2–George (2 below).
4–James **Wilson,** from Scotland; *m* Mary Adams, of Phila., Pa.;
3–Joseph Ruggles, D.D. (1822-1903), A.B., Jefferson Coll., Pa., '44; B.D., Princeton, 1846; prof. theology; moderator Presbyn. Gen. Assembly, 1879; *m* 1849, Jessie Woodrow (their son, Woodrow, was 28th President of the U.S.);
2–Annie Josephine (1854-1916), *m* 1874, George **Howe** (1848-95), M.D.; issue: I–Joseph Wilson (*b* 1874; *m* Virginia Peyton Knight, *d*); II–George (1 above); III–Jessie Woodrow (1878-84); IV–Annie Josephine (*b* 1891; *m* Frank E. Compton).
1–*m* Oct. 27, 1903, Margaret Smyth Flinn, *b* Charleston, S.C., Mar. 30, 1878; dau. of John William Flinn, of Columbia, S.C., *m* Jane Adger Smyth, of Charleston.

1–A.B., Princeton, '97 (Zeta Psi, P.B.K.); Ph.D., U.Halle (Germany), 1903; studied Oxford U., Eng., Am. Classical Sch., Rome, 1912-13. Prof. Latin, U. of N.C., since 1903, dean. Coll. of Arts, 1919-22. Author (see Who's Who in America). Club: Chapel Hill Country. Residence: Chapel Hill, N.C.

1–**HOWE, Harriet Emma,** *b* Urbana, Ill., Dec. 10, 1881.
10–Edward **Howe** (qv);
9–Isaac (*b* Eng., 1628), *m* —Bowers;
8–Nathaniel (*b* prob. Lynn, Mass., 1650-*d* Greenwich, Conn., 1692);
7–Isaac (ca. 1675-*d* Greenwich, 1733), *m* 1701, Elizabeth Waterbury (*b* 1683);
6–David (*b* nr. Darien, Conn., 1720), *m* 1745, Rebecca Whiting;
5–Jacob (*b* 1746), *m* 1769, Sarah Bates;
4–Jacob (*b* 1773), *m* 1798, Elizabeth Seeley;
3–Henry (1813-68?), of Coshocton, O.; *m* Margaret Renfrew (1818?-1903; William[4] [*d* 1847], of Coshocton, *m* Sara, dau. of Lady Sara Vance Vail; James[5] [1767-1832], from Ireland, ca. 1810);
2–William Renfrew (2 below).
7–Daniel **Pocock**, from Eng., 1740, settled at Baltimore; removed to Harford Co., Md.; *m* 1745?, Sarah Pocock, teacher;
6–Salem (*b* 1747?), and thru his grandson;
4–Lloyd (*b* 1787?);
3–Joshua (1814-90), of Coshocton Co., O.; *m* 1833, Catherine Wilson (1812-92; John Potter[4], *m* Grace Vail, dau. of Lady Sara Vance Vail[5], and sister of Sara Vail, above);
2–Althea (1843-1928), of Coshocton Co.; *m* 1864, William Renfrew **Howe** (1843-1919), building contractor; issue: I–Sara Grace (*b* 1867; *m* Thomas J. Paisley); II–Mary Louise (*b* 1868, *m* Henry Heitsmith); III–Richard E. (*b* 1871; *m* Ida Ulitsch); IV–Harriet Emma (1 above).
1–B.L.S., U.Ill., '02; Ed. M., Harvard, 1928. Asso. prof., U.Chicago, since 1927. Mem. A.L.A. (council 1924-30), A.A.U.W., Spl. Libraries Assn. (pres. 1922-23), etc. Author (see Who's Who in America). Baptist. Republican. Residence: 5551 Kimbark Av., Chicago, Ill.

HOWE-HOW

Arms: *Gules, on a chevron argent, between three cross crosslets or, three wolfs' heads of the first.*
Crest: *On a wreath a wyvern parted, per pale or and vert, pierced through the mouth with an arrow.*

1–**HOWE, Joseph Homer,** *b* Bristol, Minn., Jan. 15, 1865.
9–John (How) **Howe** (qv);
8–Samuel (1642-1713), *m* 1st, 1663, Martha Bents (*d* 1680);
7–Samuel (1668-1731), *m* 1st, 1690, Abigail Mixer (1672-1703);
6–Lt. Samuel (*b* 1693), selectman, Framingham; *m* 1715, Ruth Death (*b* 1688);
5–Joseph (1724-94), *m* 1750, Sarah Stone (1732-97);
4–Joseph (*b* 1754), said to have hung lantern in tower in Lexington Alarm; pvt., sgt. and capt., Am. Rev., disch. by Gen. Washington; *m* 1780, Huldah Stacy;
3–Joseph (1786-1869), army blacksmith, pvt. War 1812; *m* 1808, Eunice Smith (1789-1868);
2–Joseph Pliny (1827-1903), 1st sgt. Vol. Co. at Sioux massacre, Minn., 1862; *m* 1853, Sabrena Sheldon Vosburgh (1830-1900; David J., M.D.[3] [1781-1875], surgeon on naval ship, Lake Erie, War 1812, *m* Doris Wright, 1800-59); issue: I–Hattie Ellen (*b* 1857); II–Edward Lincoln (1860-78); III–Florence Eliza (*b* 1862); IV–Joseph Homer (1 above); V–Cora Bell (1869-70).
1–*m* Nov. 17, 1897, May Miller Lewis, *b* Madison, Wis., July 19, 1868; dau. of Herbert A. Lewis, of Madison, *m* Sabra I. Warner; issue: 1–Joseph Warner, *b* Omaha, Neb., Jan. 19, 1902; B.E., Ia. State U., '24, M.A., 1925 (Tau Beta Pi, Sigma Xi); 2–Herbert Edward, *b* Omaha, Sept. 21, 1904; B.E., Ia. State U., 1926.
1–C.E., Ia. State U., '90 (Tau Beta Pi). Civil, municipal and railway engr.; engr. of construction, gen. foreman and supt., bridges and bldgs., U.P.R.R. Pres. Library Bd.; mem. Park Commn. of Cresco. Club: Cresco Country. Residence: 126 6th Av. E., Cresco, Ia.

1–**HOWE, Marshall Avery,** *b* Newfane, Vt., June 6, 1867.
8–John **Howe** (qv);
7–Josiah, of Sudbury, Mass.; *m* 1671, Mary Haynes (*b* ca. 1647; John[8], *m* Dorothy Noyes);
6–Capt. Daniel (1681-1768), Shrewsbury, Mass.; *m* 1725, Esther Cloyes (1702-59; James[7], *m* Mary–);
5–Jotham (1728-1809), of Shrewsbury; *m* 1753, Priscilla Rice (1731-1819; Luke[6], *m* Rachel Stow);
4–Gardner (1759-1854), Dover, Vt.; soldier in Am. Rev.; *m* 1789, Abigail Sherman;
3–Otis (1793-1872), of Wardsboro, Vt.; *m* 1819, Sally Marsh (1795-1877; Jesse[4], *m* Charity Stearns);
2–Marshall Otis (2 below).
9–John **Sherman** (qv);
8–Joseph (*b* 1650), of Watertown, Mass.; *m* 1673, Elizabeth Winship (*b* 1652; Edward[9], qv);
7–John (1674-1756), of Watertown; *m* 1698, Mary Bullen;
6–Joseph (1703-58), supposed to have been killed in battle with Indians nr. Ft. Edward, N.Y.; *m* 1728, Sarah (Perham?) Perrum (*d* 1772, aet. 69), of Sutton, Mass.;
5–Joseph, soldier Am. Rev.; *m* Abigail Muzzy;
4–Abigail (1771-1843), *m* Gardner **Howe** (4 above).
9–Thomas **Dexter** (qv);
8–William (*d* 1694 or 96), of Barnstable, Mass.; *m* 1653, Sarah Vincent;
7–John (1668-1744), of Rochester, Mass.; *m* 1702-03, Sarah Clark;
6–John (*b* 1727), of Rochester; *m* 1746, Sarah Handy;
5–David (1760-1854), Dover, Vt.; soldier in Am. Rev.; *m* 1780, Mary Butler;
4–Charles (1783-1852), Wardsboro, Vt.; *m* 1812, Lucinda Bascom (1788-1874; Joseph[5], *m* Esther Judd);
3–Avery Joseph (1818-93), of Wardsboro; *m* 1841, Mary White;
2–Gertrude Isabel (2 below).
11–Gov. Thomas **Mayhew** (qv);
10–Rev. Thomas (lost at sea 1657), *m* Jane Paine (Thomas[11]);
9–Rev. John (*d* 1688/89), *m* Elizabeth Hilliard;
8–John (*d* 1736), *m* Mehitable Higgins;
7–Keziah, *m* Daniel **Butler** (*d* 1735);
6–Rebecca, *m* Thomas **Butler** (1732-1816; David[7]; Thomas[8], *m* Jemimah, dau. of Thomas Daggett, *m* Hannah, dau. of Gov. Thomas Mayhew, above);
5–Mary (1755-1824), *m* David **Dexter** (5 above).
10–John **Putnam** (qv);
9–Lt. Thomas (1614-86), Lynn, Mass., 1640; *m* 1st, 1643, Ann Holyoke (*d* 1665; Edward[10], *m* Prudence Stockton);

8–Edward (1654-1747), of Salem Village (now Danvers), Mass.; *m* 1681, Mary Hale;
7–Isaac (1698-1757), Sutton, Mass.; *m* 1720, Anna Fuller;
6–Phineas (*b* 1722), *m* 1746, Lois Putnam (*b* 1724; Edward[7], *m* Sarah–);
5–Susanna (1755-1830), *m* 1778, Thomas **White** (1749-1831), of Uxbridge and Sutton, Mass., and Wardsboro, Vt.;
4–Daniel (1790-1872), *m* Mary Durant (1793-1874; William[5], *m* Mary Tyng);
3–Mary (1819-89), *m* Avery J. **Dexter** (3 above);
2–Gertrude Isabel (*b* 1845), Newfane, Vt.; *m* 1866, Marshall Otis **Howe** (1832-1919), farmer and agrl. writer; issue: I–Marshall Avery (1 above); II–Hermon Alline (*b* 1869; *m* 1903, Della Charlotte Landfear); III–Arthur Otis (*b* 1871); IV–Carlton Dexter (*b* 1874; *m* Alice Margaret Durfee); V–Clifton Durant (*b* 1874; *m* Elsie M. Newton).
1–*m* June 8, 1909, Edith Morton Packard (Nov. 19, 1873-Oct. 18, 1928); dau. of Rev. Edward Newman Packard, D.D., of Stratford, Conn., *m* Mary Elizabeth Ford; issue: 1–Gertrude Dexter, *b* New York, N.Y., Nov. 2, 1910; Mt. Holyoke, '32; 2–Prentiss Mellen, *b* Bridgeport, Conn., Aug. 20, 1912.
1–Ph.B., U.Vt., '90 (Phi Delta Theta, P.B.K., Sigma Xi; hon. Sc.D., 1919); Ph.D., Columbia, 1898. Asst. dir., New York Botanical Garden since 1923; editor, 1908-10, asso. editor 1911–, Bulletin of the Torrey Botanical Club. Author (see Who's Who in America). Unitarian. Residence: 214 Edgewood Av., Pleasantville, N.Y.

1–**HOWLAND, Fred Arthur,** *b* Franconia, N.H., Nov. 10, 1864.
10–Henry **Howland** (qv);
9–Zoeth (*d* 1676), of Dartmouth; *m* 1656, Abigail–;
8–Nicholas, of Dartmouth; tanner; large real estate holder; *m* 1697, Hannah Woodman (John[9], *m* Hannah Timberlake);
7–Samuel (*b* 1704), of Dartmouth; *m* 1st, 1723, Sarah Sowle (William[8]);
6–Samuel (*b* 1727), of Dartmouth; prob. also resided at Oblong, N.Y.; *m* 1748, Esther Brownell;
5–George (1751-1835), whaleman; moved to Lisbon, N.H., 1783, and settled at Sugar Hill, which place he named; *m* Mary Warner (1751-1845);
4–Jeremy (1778-1839), of Lisbon; comd. a co. of state militia; *m* Martha Jillson (1778-1847);
3–George (1803-35), of Lisbon; *m* Waity Aldrich (1805-46; Jethro[4], *m* Elsie Applebee);
2–Moses Nathan (2 below).
8–Edward **Shipman** (qv);
7–John (*b* 1664), *m* Martha Humphries (*b* 1663);
6–Abraham (*b* 1695), *m* Ruth Butler;
5–Abraham (*b* 1742), *m* Esther Hyatt (1750-1802);
4–John (1771-1871), *m* Lucy Hatch (1774-1857);
3–Rev. Isaiah Hatch (1810-72), *m* 1835, Charlotte R. Cook (Oliver[4], *m* Polly Bruce);
2–Sylvia Ann (1841-1901), *m* 1859, Moses Nathan **Howland** (1833-1906), dentist.
1–*m* Sept. 24, 1894, Rena Forbush (Jan. 13, 1874-Oct. 24, 1894).
1–*m* 2d, Feb. 1, 1899, Margaret Louise Dewey, *b* Montpelier, Vt., Apr. 2, 1875; dau. of Edward Dewey, of Montpelier, Vt., *m* Susan Griggs Lilley: issue (all *b* Montpelier, Vt.): 1–Louise Dewey, *b* June 25, 1900; Columbia U., 1930; 2–Sylvia Ann, *b* Feb. 28, 1902; *m* Dec. 1, 1928, Paul Starrett Sample of Pasadena, Calif.; son of Wilbur S. Sample, *m* Effie Madden; 3–Susan Griggs, *b* June 28, 1905; 4–Emily Shipman, *b* Mar. 16, 1907.
1–A.B., Dartmouth, '87 (Alpha Delta Phi); studied law with Hon. W. P. Dillingham, Waterbury, Vt.; admitted to Vt. bar, Oct. 1890. Pres. Nat. Life Ins. Co., since 1916; dir. Central Vt. R.R., Montpelier & Wells River R.R., Union Mut. Fire Ins. Co., Atlantic Nat. Bank of Boston; trustee Dartmouth Coll. Mem. Vt. State Bd. of Edn., 1920-23; commr. of Finance for Vt., 1927-29. Clk. Vt. Ho. of Rep., 1896; state's atty. for Washington Co., Vt., 1892-98; sec. of state, 1898-1902 (see Who's Who in America). Unitarian. Republican. Clubs: University (New York), St. Bernard Fish and Game (Canada). Residence: 120 State St., Montpelier, Vt.

1–**HOWLAND, William (Arthur),** *b* Worcester, Mass., May 1, 1871.
8–John **Howland,** Mayflower Pilgrim (qv);
7–John (*b* 1627), *m* 1661, Mary Lee (Robert[8]);
6–John (1674-1738), *m* 1719, Mary Crocker (1681-1759; Job[7]);
5–Job (1726-94), *m* 1753, Hannah Jenkins (1733-81; Benjamin[6]);
4–John (1757-1843), *m* 1786, Grace Avery (1755-1841);
3–John (1789-1878), *m* 1816, Nancy Morton (1795-1857);
2–Asa Allen (2 below).
8–Job **Lane** (qv);
7–John (1661-1714-15), *m* 1681, Susanna Whipple, of Ipswich;
6–John (1691-1763), commd. capt., 1711, later maj.; *m* 1st, 1714, Catherine Whiting;
5–John (1722-89), *m* Ruth Bowman (*d* 1759), of Lexington, Mass.;
4–John (1746-1808), *m* 1773, Ruhannah Reed (*d* 1817);
3–Roger (1796-1853), *m* Zelima Bacon (*d* 1856).
2–Dr. Asa Allen **Howland** (1820-1903), *m* 1847, Cornelia W. Collins (1823-69); *m* 2d, 1869, Emma Lane (1835-1907); issue (1st marriage): I–James Herbert (1848-1910; *m* 1880, Emily J. Smith); II–Edmund Collins (1850-84); III–Henry Allen (1855-57); IV–John Gordon (*b* 1857); V–George Brown (1859-65); VI–Grace Helen (*b* 1862; *m* 1890, Dr. George Buttler); VII–Frank Harris (*b* 1864; *m* Mabel Crawford); issue (2d marriage): I–William Arthur (1 above).
1–*m* June 24, 1896, Fredreka Barnard, *b* Davenport, Ia., Sept. 14, 1871; dau. of John F. Barnard, *m* Harriet Emma Shaw, both *d*; issue: 1–Barnard, *b* Worcester, Mass., May 12, 1898; Amherst, '21; 2–Dorothy Lane, *b* Ann Arbor, Mich., Nov. 25, 1900; *m* June 24, 1924, Robert M., son of Frederick O. Ball, of Detroit, Mich. (issue: Nancy Ann).
1–Grad. English High School, Worcester, Mass., '89; (hon. Mus. Doc., 1925). Professional musician, singer, teacher, director and composer (see Who's Who in America). Mem. S.M.D. (asst. genealogist nat. soc., mem. bd. Mich. Chapter), Pilgrim John Howland Soc. (pres. since 1924), Fine Arts Soc. Clubs: Detroit Athletic, Players, The Bohemians (first pres.), Pro Musica (dir.), Torch. Residence: 237 Frederick Av., Detroit, Mich.

1–**HOYT, Susan Upson (Mrs. Richard C.),** *b* Rockford, Ill., Sept. 27, 1855.
8–Thomas **Upson** (1600-55), from Eng. to Boston, 1637; a 1st settler at Hartford; an original propr. at Farmington; *m* 1647, Elizabeth Fuller (*d* post 1671);
7–Sgt. Stephen (1650-1730 or 35), propr. at Waterbury; soldier in Indian wars; dep. Gen. Ct. several terms; *m* 1682, Mary Lee (*d* 1716; John[8]);
6–Capt. Stephen (1686-1777), *m* Sarah Bronson (1691-1748; Isaac[7]);
5–Lt. Benjamin (1720-80), corpl. in Conn. militia in Am. Rev.; *m* 1743, Mary Blakeslee (*b* 1726/27; Moses[6]);
4–Ashbel (1762-1831), of Plymouth, Conn.; served in Am. Rev.; at West Point, 1777; *m* Mary Munson (1766-1857);
3–Lt. Munson (1797-1870), *m* Maria Preston (1800-79);
2–Lyman Davis (2 below).
7–Thomas **Miller** (ca. 1600-1680), of Middletown, Conn.; surveyor of highways, 1652; townsman, 1652; *m* 2d, 1666, Sarah Nettleton (*b* ca. 1641);
6–Joseph (1670-1717), *m* 1701, Rebecca Johnson (1681-1756);
5–Joseph (*b* 1702), *m* 1722, Thankful Hubbard (1698-1771);
4–Joseph (1723-85), of Granville, Mass.; served as pvt. in Hampshire Co. regt. in Am. Rev.; *m* 1752, Lydia Stowe (*b* 1733);
3–Luther (1771-1846), *m* 1808, Phoebe Wright (1790-1846);
2–Lucina J. (1829-64), *m* 1850, Lyman Davis **Upson** (1826-81); issue: I–Maria Phoebe; II–Lt. Miller (*d* 1928; *m* Minnie Cafferty); III–Susan (1 above); IV–Adelaide Patrick (*m* C. J. Hiatt); V–Lucina Jane (*m* Wilber Upson).
1–*m* June 4, 1884, Richard Cleveland Hoyt, *b* Holland Patent, N.Y., Aug. 19, 1855; son of William E. Hoyt, of Fayetteville, N.Y., *m* Mary Cleveland; issue: 1–Edward Lyman, *b* Aug. 31, 1887; *m* Marjory Katherine Smith, *b* July 8, 1891.
1–Ed. Rockford (Ill.) H.S. Mem. C.D.A., D.F.-P.A., D.A.R. Residence: Stratford Terrace Apts., Omaha, Neb.

1-**HUBBARD, Fred Clark,** *b* Urbana, Ill., May 24, 1876.
9-George **Hubbard** (qv);
8-John (1630-1702), *m* 1649, Mary Merriam (*d* 1693), of Concord, Mass. (William[9], of Eng., *m* Sarah-);
7-Isaac (1667-1750), of Sunderland, Mass.; dea. Congl. Ch.; mem. Council that installed Jonathan Edwards as preacher; *m* Anne Warner (*d* 1750; Daniel[8]);
6-Isaac (1695-1763), of Sunderland; *m* 1723, Christin Greene (Samuel[7], *m* Elizabeth Wyatt); *m* 2d, Abigail (Kellogg) Atherton;
5-Isaac (1730-1810), of Amherst, Mass.; *m* Summit Graves;
4-Chester (*b* 1770), of Wilmington, Vt.; *m* Dorothy Kellogg;
3-George Crocker (1815-98), of Wilmington; *m* 1840, Salome Dickinson Green;
2-Linus Green (2 below).
6-Timothy **Green** (1723-96), of Amherst, in French and Indian War; *m* Eunice Ellsworth (1717-92; Thomas[7], of Eng., later of Windsor, Conn.);
5-Timothy (*b* 1748), of Amherst; minuteman at Lexington Alarm; *m* 1st, 1770, Eunice Clark (1751-76; Simeon[6], *m* Rebecca Strong);
4-Clark (1776-1848), of Amherst; *m* 1798, Submit Hastings (1777-1863; Thomas[5], *m* Hannah Billings);
3-Salome Dickinson (1815-1904), *m* George Crocker **Hubbard** (3 above);
2-Linus Green (1844-1927), of Urbana, Ill., and Foley, Ala.; served in Civil War; farmer; Baptist; *m* 1870, Helen Lorena Stanard (1844-1914; David[3], of Lamoille, Illinois, *m* Hannah Haskins); issue: I-George David (*b* 1871; *m* 1901, Edna Almira Rugg, *b* 1878); II-Charles Linus (*b* 1873; *m* Grace Corwin); III-Clara May (1874-1910; *m* William Lee Bennett); IV-Fred Clark (1 above); V-Nelle Marilla (*b* 1880; *m* 1920, Martin Edward Robbins, *b* 1866); VI-Minnie Salome (*b* 1881).
1-*m* Aug. 17, 1904, Martha Caroline Koehn, *b* West Prussia, July 2, 1880; dau. of Otto Koehn; issue (all *b* Urbana, Ill.): 1-Robert Koehn, *b* Dec. 6, 1906; B.S. in Agr., U.Ill., '27; 2-Linus Otto, *b* Jan. 20, 1908; B.S., U.Ill., '29, M.S. in E.E., 1930; 3-Ralph C., *b* Dec. 28, 1909; B.S. in Agr., U.Ill., '31; 4-Beth Helen (Dec. 7, 1914-Jan. 7, 1915); 5-David Fred, *b* Dec. 7, 1914; 6-Joseph Everett, *b* Feb. 6, 1917.
1-Engaged in dairy business and real estate. Residence: 801 E. Oregon St., Urbana, Ill.

BENJAMIN HUDDLE (1803-60).

1-**HUDDLE, J(erome) Klahr,** *b* Bettsville, O., Mar. 25, 1891.
7-John (Hottel, Hotel) **Huddle** (ca. 1690-1760), from Rotterdam, 1732, in the "Pennsylvania" with his wife Margaret, and children, Charles, Henry, George, John, and Anna; settled Bucks or Lancaster Co., Pa.; removed to Shenandoah Co., Va., ca. 1745, where he purchased land;
6-Charles (ca. 1715-78), of Shenandoah Co., Va.; landowner; *m* Barbara- (*d* ante 1778);
5-Daniel (ca. 1758-1828), of Rockingham Co., Va.; prob. soldier Am. Rev.; pioneer settler Fairfield Co., O., 1814; *m* ca. 1785, Mary Beidler (*d* 1845);
4-Benjamin (1803-60), pioneer settler in Seneca and Crawford cos., O.; held various elective offices (see portrait); *m* 1823, Anna Seitz (1805-63; Lewis[5], *m* Anna Beery; Johannes[6], from Germany, ca. 1763, *m* Catherine Diehl);
3-Peter (1842-1909), of Tiffin, O.; *m* 1st, 1864, Amelia Elizabeth Klahr (1844-65; George H.[4] [1814-46], *m* Anna Catherine, dau. of Johann Conrath Geiger, from Germany, 1825, with his 2 yr. old dau.);
2-Elvin Klahr (2 below).
6-John **Newcomer** (1747-1824), prob. came from Switzerland; Mennonite; settled Washington Co., Md.;
5-Christian (1779-1850), of Washington Co.;
4-Peter (1805-90), of Medina Co., O.; *m* 1835, Mary Rohrer;
3-John (1836-1907), of Seneca Co., O.; *m* 1860, Susanna Muckley;
2-Emily Lora (2 below).
7-Martin (Funck) **Funk,** to America ca. 1750;
6-Martin (1755-1839), soldier Am. Rev.; of Bedford Co., Pa.;
5-Elizabeth (1779-1851), of Stark Co., O.; *m* Jacob **Troxel** (1774-1847), of Stark Co.; removed to Osnoburgh Tp., Stark Co., 1810;
4-Magdalena (1808-94), of Mahoning Co., O.; *m* 1833, George **Muckley** (1805-42), from Germany, 1810, to Stark Co., O.;
3-Susanna (1840-1903), of Seneca Co., O.; *m* John **Newcomer** (3 above);
2-Emily Lora (*b* 1864), of Seneca Co., O.; *m* 1890, Elvin Klahr **Huddle** (*b* 1865), pharmacist and chemist; issue: I-Jerome Klahr (1 above); II-Miriam West Newcomer (*b* 1900).
1-*m* Apr. 5, 1921, Carolena Heiby (qv for issue).
1-Ed. Heidelberg Coll., Tiffin, O., and George Washington U., Washington, D.C. High sch. principal, newspaper and commercial work in Ohio, until 1915; entered consular service, 1915, in Paris, Berlin, Warsaw, Hamburg, Cologne and State Dept. (see Who's Who in America). Mason. Mem. Reformed Ch. Address: c/o Dept. of State, Washington, D.C.

1-**HUDDLE, Carolena Heiby (Mrs. J. Klahr),** *b* Ft. Recovery, O., May 20, 1890.
4-Frederick **Heimligh,** of Alsatian origin; of Ohio; *m* Magdalene Engel;
3-Magdalene, *m* Valentine **Heiby** (*b* 1820);
2-John George (2 below).
4-George **Theurer,** of Alsatian origin; of Ind.; *m* Justiana Jetter;
3-Mathias (1829-1921), *m* Sarah Kurtz (Michael[4], *m* Rosina-);
2-Carolene Margaret (*b* 1858), *m* 1881, John George **Heiby** (*b* 1860), of Ft. Recovery, O.; issue: I-Theresa (*b* 1883; *m* 1904, Rev. William Benzin); II-Clarence Jacob (*b* 1885; *m* 1914, Ada Kieffer); III-Carl Mathias (*b* 1887; *m* 1924, Ann Girard); IV-Carolena (1 above).
1-*m* Apr. 5, 1921, Hon. Jerome Klahr Huddle (qv for genealogy); issue: 1-Carolyn Lora, *b* Hamburg, Germany, Mar. 10, 1922.
Address: c/o Hon. J. Klahr Huddle, Dept. of State, Washington, D.C.

1-**HUBBARD, Joseph Stiles,** *b* Atlanta, Ill., Apr. 26, 1867.
10-William **Hubbard** (qv);
9-Rev. William (1621/22-1704), A.B., Harvard, 1st class, 1642; historian, wrote "King Philip's War," and "History of New England"; Congl. minister, Ipswich; *m* 1646, Mary Rogers (1628-85; Rev. Nathaniel[10], *m* Martha Crane, of Ipswich);
8-John (1648-1709/10), Boston merchant; *m* 1671, Ann Leverett (1652-1717; Gov. John[9], *m* Sarah Sedgwick);
7-Rev. John (1677-1705), A.B., Harvard, 1695; pastor of Presbyn. ch., Jamaica, L.I.; *m* 1701, Mabel Russell (Daniel[8], *m* Mehitable Wyllys);
6-Dr. John (1703-73), judge Probate Ct., New Haven, and Ct. Common Pleas; rep. in Legislature; col. militia; *m* 1724, Elizabeth Stevens (1703-ante 1753; Ens. Samuel[7], *m* Melatiah Bradford Steele);

5–Rev. John, pastor 1st Congl. Ch., Meridian, Conn.; *m* 1750, Rebecca Dickerman (1726-ante 1786; Isaac[6], *m* Mary Atwater);
4–Dea. Isaac (1752-96), dea. Congl. ch., Wallingford, Conn.; *m* 1782, Jane Berry (1760-1841 or 42);
3–Ezra Stiles (1794-1861), of New Haven; *m* 1819, Eliza Church (1797-1867; Josiah[4], *m* Naomi Bradley);
2–George Boardman (1822-1900), minister of Congl. churches in Ill. and Wis. for 50 yrs.; *m* 1849, Jane Beardsley (Rev. William[3], *m* Bethiah Van Valkenburgh); issue: I–Rev. William Beardsley (*b* 1852; *m* Mary Ella Tuttle); II–Lillie Church (1857-1928; *m* Henry J. Bamford); III–Joseph Stiles (1 above); IV–Mary Bradley.
1–*m* Mar. 22, 1893, Carrie L. Stevens, *b* Albany, N.Y., Aug. 21, 1868; dau. of Isaac Stevens, of Albany, *m* Miriam Avann; issue: 1–Dana Stevens (Feb. 26, 1894-Feb. 22, 1898); 2–Miriam Beardsley, *b* Hawarden, Ia., Aug. 26, 1895; U.Wis., '18; *m* Aug. 21, 1920, John Currie Gibson, of Oshkosh, Wis. (issue: John Currie, Jr., and Richard Gordon); 3–Henry Stiles, *b* Beloit, Wis., Jan. 20, 1900; *m* June 19, 1921, Margaret Fuchs (issue: Henry Stiles, Jr.); 4–Caroline Lydia, *b* Beloit, Oct. 1, 1901; A.B., U.Wis., '25; *m* Sept. 13, 1925, Edward Numan Otis, of Madison, Wis.; 5–Fletcher Stevens, *b* Beloit, Sept. 18, 1905; A.B., U.Mo., '27; 6–Lillian Josephine, *b* Beloit, Jan. 24, 1910; U.Mo.
1–Ed. Beloit Coll. Acad., and Beloit Coll. Editor and pub. 30 yrs.; state mgr., 8 yrs.; official reporter Mo. Legislature. Mem. Mo. Press Assn. Congl. Republican. Residence: 1411 Bass Av., Columbia, Mo.

1–**HUGHES, Rupert,** *b* Lancaster, Mo., Jan. 31, 1872.
7–Rice **Hughes,** had land grant in Kent Co., Va., Apr. 1645;
6–Rice, had land grant in New Kent Co., Va., Oct. 6, 1698;
5–William, served in Capt. Mountjoy's co., 10th Va. Regt. during Am. Rev.;
4–William, *m* Judith Hughes (Josiah[5]; Orlando[6], from Wales ca. 1740, settled in Goochland Co., Va.);
3–Joshua William (1808-1901), *m* Martha Staton Askins (g.dau. Edward Askins, soldier Am. Rev.; desc. John Askins, from Scotland to Md. ca. 1650; and Edward Waters, sailed for America, 1609, was wrecked on the Bermudas and reached Va., 1622);
2–Felix Turner (2 below).
6–Jacob **Summerlin,** from Eng. to Va., 1710; settled in Isle of Wight Co., receiving land grants, 1717; and thru his g.son:
4–Winburn (1762-1842), pvt. Am. Rev., N.C. troops; *m* Milly Pearson;
3–Thomas (1797-1860), *m* Bathsheba RoBards (desc. William RoBards, lt. Goochland Co. militia, 1764);
2–Jean Amelia (*b* 1842), *m* Felix Turner **Hughes** (*b* 1838), ry. pres.; judge; for issue see Vol. III, p. 259.
1–*m* 1893, Agnes, dau. of Charles Hedge; issue: 1–Elspeth, *b* New York, May 23, 1897; *m* Mar. 10, 1922, Edward John Lapp; issue three daughters.
1–*m* 2d, 1908, Adelaide Mould (May 7, 1882-Dec. 13, 1923); dau. of Henry Scrivener Mould, Cleveland.
1–*m* 3d, Dec. 31, 1924, Elizabeth Patterson Dial, *b* Madison, Fla., May 19, 1902; dau. of William Dial, *m* Sarah Burton Whitner (desc. Gov. Spottiswoode, the DuVal and Mosby families of Va.; the Dials came from Wales ca. 1800).
1–B.A., Adelbert, '92 (Delta U., P.B.K.), M.A., Yale, 1899. Author (see Who's Who in America). Pvt. to capt., N.G.N.Y., 1897-1908; capt., 69th N.Y. Inf., Mexican border, 1916; capt. and maj., 1918-19, World War; lt. col. M.I.O.R.C. Mem. S.A.R., I.A.G. Clubs: Authors, The Players, The Lambs. Residence: 4751 Los Feliz Boul., Los Angeles, Calif.

1–**HUIDEKOPER, Frederic Louis,** *b* Meadville, Pa., Mar. 8, 1874.
4–Harm Jan **Huidekoper** (*b* Hoogeveen, Province of Drenthe, Holland, 1776– *d* Meadville, Pa., 1854; of an ancient family still noted in Holland; eldest son of Anne Huidekoper [1730-

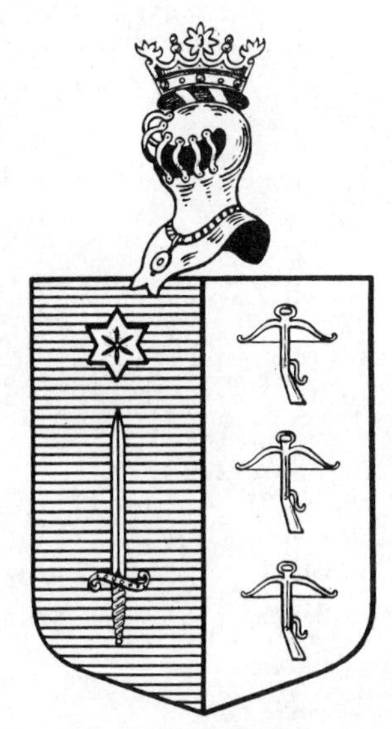

HUIDEKOPER

Arms: Party per pale, azure and argent. First, a sword, hilted, or, in pale, a mullet of six points in chief of the last. Second, three arbalets all proper.
Crest: A ridder's coronet (Friesland).

99], *m* 2d, 1775, Gesina Frederica Wolthers [1741-1813], and half-brother of Jan Huidekoper [1766-1835], Knight of the Netherlands Lion, who was the special and personal representative of the King of Holland in several important positions); came from the Helder, Holland, in the "Prudence," to New York, 1796; entered the employ of the Holland Land Co., at Oldenbarneveld (now Trenton Falls), N.Y., 1799; transferred to its main office at Phila., Pa., 1802; apptd. agt. gen. of its lands in Pa., 1804; removed to Meadville, Pa., Nov. 1804; assumed agency of its possessions east of Allegheny River, Jan. 1, 1805; built "Pomona Hall"; bought all the holdings of The Holland Land Co. in northwestern Pa., 1836; founded the Meadville Theol. School, Oct. 1, 1844; became a prominent figure in the state; *m* 1806, Rebecca Colhoon (1779-1839);
3–Edgar (1812-62), *m* 1838, Frances Shippen (3 below);
2–Capt. Frederic Wolters (2 below).
6–John (Colhoun) **Colhoon** (*d* 1757), descended from Unfridus de Kilpatrick and de Colquhoun (1190-1260), Scotland; came from Ireland and settled in Middleton Twp., Cumberland Co., Pa.; justice; judge; treas. Cumberland Co., 1757; *m* 1728, Rebecca– (1709-88);
5–Andrew (*d* 1794), began to write name Colhoon; 2d lt., Pa. troops, 1777-78; *m* 1777, Esther McDowell (5 below);
4–Rebecca (1779-1839), *m* 1806, Harm Jan **Huidekoper** (4 above).
7–Andrew **McDowell,** from Ireland to Phila., Pa., ca. 1725; settled in Chester Co., Pa.; justice, Chester Co., 1745; col. Associate regt. of Chester Co., 1747-48;
6–Andrew (*d* 1778), from Dublin, Ireland, accompanied by his brothers and sisters, in the "George and Ann," to Pa., 1729; capt., Associate regt. of Chester Co., Pa., 1747-48; capt., Pa. regt., 1758-59; owned iron works nr. Carlisle, Pa.; *m* 1729, Sarah Shanklin (*d* 1788);
5–Esther (1752-95), *m* 1777, Andrew **Colhoon** (5 above).
8–Edward **Shippen** (qv);
7–Joseph (1678/79-1741), Boston, Mass., and Phila., Pa.; mem. of The Junto, founded by Benjamin Franklin, 1727; *m* 1702, Abigail (1677-1716, dau. of Thomas Grosse[8], of Boston, Mass.); *m* 2d, Rose Budd, widow of Charles

Plumley and John McWilliams (7 below);
6–Edward (1703-81), founded Shippensburg, Pa.; mayor, Phila., 1744; one of the founders of The College of N.J. (now Princeton), and of U. of Pa., 1746-48; judge, Ct. Common Pleas, Phila., 1749-50; paymaster, British and Provincial forces, 1755; received public thanks for his services, 1760; mem. 1st Bd. of Trustees of The College of N.J., 1767-81; *m* 1725, Sarah Plumley (6 below);
5–Joseph (1732-1810), first grad. of Nassau Hall, now Princeton, 1753; col. Pa. colonial troops during French and Indian wars; served in Gen. Forbes' expdn. against Ft. Duquesne, 1758; sec. Provincial Council of Pa., 1762; judge Ct. Common Pleas, Lancaster, Pa., 1786; *m* 1768, Jane (or Jenney) Galloway (5 below);
4–Henry (1788-1839), capt. of co. of Jägers, Pa. militia, 1812, and participated in repulse of British at Baltimore, Md., 1814; judge 6th Judicial Dist. of Pa., 1825-39; *m* 1817, Elizabeth Wallis Evans (4 below);
3–Frances (1818-97), *m* 1838, Edgar **Huidekoper** (3 above).
8–Thomas **Budd** (qv);
7–Rose (*b* 1680), *m* Charles **Plumley** (*d* 1708); *m* 2d, John McWilliams; *m* 3d, Joseph Shippen (7 above);
6–Sarah (1706-35), *m* 1725, Edward **Shippen** (6 above).
8–Richard **Galloway,** from London, Eng. to Md., 1649; settled at West River, Anne Arundel Co., Md., *m* Hannah–;
7–Samuel (1659-1720), *m* 2d, London, Eng., 1689, Ann (Webb) Pardoe (*d* 1722/23; dau. of Borrington Webb[8], *d* 1720);
6–John (1693/94-1747), *m* 2d, Jane (Roberts) Fishbourne (*d* 1748; dau. of Edward Roberts[7] [1680-1741], mayor, Phila., Pa., 1739-40); and widow of William Fishbourne, mayor, Phila., 1719-21;
5–Jane (Jenney) (1745-1801), *m* 1768, Col. Joseph **Shippen** (5 above).
8–John **Evans** (1654-1740), from Radnorshire, Wales, to Phila., Pa., 1695; settled in New Castle Co., Del., 1711, and in Chester Co., Pa., 1725; *m* Lydia– (*d* 1735);
7–John (1700-38), mem. Assembly of Pa., 1734-37; justice, Chester Co., Pa., 1737; *m* 2d, 1722, Jane Howell (*d* 1788; Rev. Reynold[8]);
6–Evan (1732-94), mem. Supreme Exec. Council of Pa., 1770-80,85; mem. Chester Co., Pa., Associators and Com. of Observation, 1774; justice Common Pleas, 1774; del. to Provincial Congress, Phila., 1776; mem. of Conv. which framed first Constn. of Pa., 1776; col. of Elk (formerly 4th) Bn. and comd. militia of Chester Co. at Battle of the Brandywine, 1777; col. of 2d Bn., 1778; mem. Assembly of Pa., 1780-83; *m* 1755, Margaret Niven (Nivin) (William[7], *d* 1739);
5–Evan Rice (1763-1811), lawyer, Sunbury, Pa.; *m* 1797, Grace Wallis (5 below);
4–Elizabeth (1798-1875), *m* 1817, Henry **Shippen** (4 above).
8–Samuel **Wallis** (*d* 1718), settled at Patuxent, Calvert Co., Md.; *m* 1701, Frances Young (1683-1763; Arthur[9], *d* 1711);
7–Samuel (1705-54), removed to Deer Creek, Harford Co., Md., ca. 1731; *m* 2d, 1744, Grace Jacob (7 below);
6–Joseph Jacob (1745-95), surveyor of Northumberland Co., Pa., 1784; justice, 1787-94; *m* 1775, Elizabeth Lukens (6 below);
5–Grace (1777-1804), *m* 1797, Evan Rice **Evans** (5 above).
10–Valentine **Hollingsworth** (qv);
9–Catherine (1663-1746), *m* 1688/89, George **Robinson** (1666/67-1738); from Ireland, 1687, settled at Newark, New Castle Co., Del.;
8–Mary (1689-1730), *m* 1710, Thomas **Jacob** (1679-1753; John[9], of Cork, Ireland);
7–Grace (1718-80), *m* 1744, Samuel **Wallis** (7 above).
9–Jan **Lukens** (qv);
8–Peter (1696-1741), Horsham Twp., Montgomery Co., Pa.; *m* 1719, Gaynor Evans (1696-1786);
7–John (1720-89), apptd. one of surveyors to determine boundary between Pa. and Md., 1760; surveyor gen. of Pa., 1761-75, 1781-89; one of the founders of the Am. Philos. Soc., 1769; one of the commrs. to extend the Mason and Dixon Line westward to the Ohio River, 1781,-83; discovered comet subsequently known as "Lukens' comet," 1784; *m* 1741, Sarah Lukens (*d* 1786; William[8], 1687-1739/40);
6–Elizabeth (*d* 1793), *m* 1775, Joseph Jacob **Wallis** (6 above).
7–James **Christie** (1670-1768), mem. of a well-known family in Scotland; from Leith, Scotland, in the "Caledonia," to Isthmus of Darien, 1698; from Darien in the "Caledonia," to New York, 1699; settled at Schraalenburgh (later Bergen Fields, now Dumont), N.J., 1699; *m* 1703, Madeleine des Marets (7 below);
6–William (1720-1809), *m* 1743, Catherine Demarest (des Marets) (6 below);
5–James (1744-1817), capt. in N.J. militia, Am. Rev.; *m* 1772, Maria Banta (5 below);
4–Peter (1792-1853), surgeon's mate, U.S.N., 1810; grad. Med. Sch., Columbia Coll., N.Y., 1811; surgeon U.S.N., 1816; *m* 1817, Agnes Gillespie (1792-1846; John[5] [*d* 1813], who fled from Co. Donegal, Ireland, to Spain, went with his family to Nova Scotia, removed to Bangor, Me., and thence to Phila., Pa., arriving Nov. 28, 1799, and subsequently settled at Erie, Pa.);
3–Fitz-James (1818-48), Erie, Pa.; *m* 1841, Elizabeth Anna Johns (3 below);
2–Anna Virginia (2 below).
9–David des **Marets** (1620-93), mem. of an ancient and distinguished family in the Province of Picardy, France; descended from Baudouin, Seigneur des Marets, 1080; fled to Zeeland, Holland, 1640; removed to Mannheim, Germany; from Amsterdam, with his wife and 4 children, in the "Bonte Koe," to New Amsterdam, 1663; del. from Staten Island to the Gen. Assembly (Landtag) of the New Netherland and magistrate for S.I., 1664; one of the founders of New Haarlem (Harlem), 1665; overseer, 1667-68, 1671-72; "schepen" (alderman), 1673; magistrate, 1673,75; large landowner; *m* at Middleburg, Zeeland, Holland, 1643, Marie Sohier (1623-80; François[10]);
8–Jean (1645-1719), from Mannheim, and Amsterdam in the "Bonte Koe," to New Amsterdam, 1663; constable, 1670; lt. of militia, Bergen Co., East Jersey, 1683; mem. of Council and Com. of Safety of N.Y., 1689; settled at Nova Caesarea, New Barbadoes (now Hackensack), N.J.; *m* 1668, Jacomina de Ruyns (1648-91; Simon[9] [1615-78], a Huguenot, who fled from Landrecies—Cambresis, Province of Hainault, France, to Amsterdam, whence he came with his family in the "De Trouw" to New Amsterdam, 1659; settled at New Haarlem; corpl. in militia during Esopus War, 1663; removed to Flushing, L.I., 1666; *m* Landrecies, Hainault, France, 1639, Magdalena [*b* 1620], dau. of Lodowycks van der Straeten[10]);
7–Madeleine (1684-1749), *m* 1703, James **Christie** (7 above).
9–David des **Marets** (9 above);
8–Samuel (1656-1728), from Mannheim, and Amsterdam in the "Bonte Koe," to New Amsterdam, 1663; settled in Bergen Co., N.J.; *m* 1678, Maria de Ruyns (1662-ca. 1728; Simon[9], 1615-78);
7–Peter (1685-1772), began to write name **Demarest**; *m* 1717, Margritie Cornelius Haring (7 below);
6–Catherine (1722-1806), *m* 1743, William **Christie** (6 above).
10–Pieter **Haring,** from Hoorn, Holland, 1632; settled in New Amsterdam;
9–Jan Pietersen (1633-83), one of the "schepens" (aldermen) who governed the "outside people" on Manhattan Island, N.Y., 1673-74; removed to Tappan (now Rockland), Orange Co., N.Y.; *m* 1662/63, Margariet Cosyns (1641-1733), dau. of Cosyn Gerritsen[10]; generally known as "Grietie Cosyns," she was perhaps the most notable woman in the early days of New York, being celebrated for her great beauty and charm;
8–Cornelius (1672-1763), high sheriff, Orange Co., N.Y., 1709-18; mem. of the Assembly of N.Y., 1713-37; capt., militia of Orange Co., 1715; judge, 1727-33; *m* 1693, Catrina (*b* 1676), dau. of Matthys Servaes Vliereboom[9], of Albany, N.Y.;
7–Margritie Cornelius (bap. 1697), *m* 1717, Peter **Demarest** (7 above).
9–Epke Jacobs **Banta** (1620-90), Harlingen, Friesland, Holland; with his wife and five sons from Amsterdam, in the "De Trouw," to New Amsterdam, 1659; settled at Flushing, L.I., but removed before 1675 to Bergen (now

Jersey City), N.J.; judge, 1679; *m* in Holland, Sitska– (1624-ca. 1675);

8–Wiert Epke (1658-92), Minnertsga, Friesland; from Amsterdam in the "De Trouw," to New Amsterdam, 1659; *m* 1681, Gerretie de Mandeville (1663-ca. 1714; Giles Jansen[9] [*d* 1701], mem. of an ancient family in the Contentin, Normandy, France; fled to Garderen in the Veluwe, Guelderland, Holland; from Amsterdam, with his wife and five children, in the "De Trouw," to New Amsterdam, 1659; mem. of mil. co. of Capt. Pieter Stuyvesant, gov. gen. of New Netherland; *m* in Holland, ca. 1649, Elsie Hendricks, *b* ca. 1629);

7–Hendrick Wiert (1685-ca. 1750), *m* 1715, Catherine Lotts (7 below);

6–John Hendrick (1723-86), *m* 1747, Trientje Demarest (6 below);

5–Maria (1754-1815), *m* 1772, James **Christie** (5 above).

9–Paulus **Pietersen** (1632-1702), from Meerssen, Limburg, Holland, to New Amsterdam, 1655; mil. officer commd. by Gov. Pieter Stuyvesant and Council of the New Netherland to fortify Bergen (now Jersey City) against the Indians, 1663, and the Duke of York's expdn., 1664; took oath of allegiance, 1665; *m* 1658, Trientje Martens (ca. 1636-1702), a widow from Acken, Prussian Saxony, via Amsterdam in the "Guilded Beaver," to New Amsterdam, 1658;

8–Elena Pauluse (bap. 1661), *m* 1680, Lubbert Westervelt; *m* 2d, 1695, John **Lotts** (ca. 1670-1744), from Norwich, Eng.; settled at Hackensack, N.J.; purchased the present sites of Englewood and Passaic, N.J., 1695;

7–Catherine (1696-ca. 1754), *m* 1715, Hendrick Wiert **Banta** (7 above).

10–David des **Marets** (9 above);

9–David (1652-91), Mannheim, Germany; from Amsterdam in the "Bonte Koe," 1663; settled in Bergen Co., N.J., 1677; *m* 1675, Rachel Cresson (*b* ca. 1656; Pierre[10] [1610-82], mem. of an ancient family seated at Menil-le-Cresson, Picardy, France, and allied to the Cressons of Burgundy; fled to Sluis, Zeeland, Holland, ca. 1635; was living in Leyden, 1640; from Amsterdam in the "Bearer" to New Amstel on the Delaware River, 1657; made a trip to Holland, 1659; "schepen" [alderman] of New Haarlem, 1659-60; commd. co. New Haarlem militia in second Esopus War, 1663; removed to Staten Island, N.Y.; *m* Rachel Cloos, *d* 1692);

8–David, Sr. or III (1676-1760), began to write name **Demarest**; high sheriff, Bergen Co., N.J. 1714; justice, 1716; judge, 1738-49; mem. of Assembly of N.J., 1738-46; very large landowner in Essex and Bergen cos., N.J.; *m* 1697, Sara Bertholff (8 below);

7–David, Jr. or IV (1699-1768), *m* 1721, Marrija Lozier (7 below);

6–Trientje (1726-ca. 1768), *m* 1747, John Hendrick **Banta** (6 above).

9–Rev. Guilliaem **Bertholff** (1656-1725; son of Quirinus[10] [*b* 1620], g.son of Christoffel[11]); Sluis, Zeeland, Holland; with his wife and 3 daus. to New York, 1684; settled in Bergen (now Jersey City), N.J.; town clk. and reader, Harlem, 1690; went to Vlissingen (Flushing), Holland, for ordination, 1693-94; removed to Hackensack, N.J.; was the first, and for 15 yrs. the only, regularly ordained and established clergyman in N.J.; in 1717 his salary was £15 per annum; *m* at Sluis, Zeeland, Holland, 1676, Martyntje Hendrickse Vermuelen (*b* ca. 1660; William[10], of Vlissingen, Holland, *m* 1649, Martyntje Weymoers);

8–Sara (1677-ca. 1758), *m* 1697, David **Demarest,** Sr. or III (8 above).

9–François **Le Sueur** (ca. 1635-1671), from Challe-Mesnil, Terre de Caux, Normandy, France, to New Amsterdam, 1657; settled at Flatbush, L.I.; removed to Harlem and subsequently to Kingston, N.Y.; *m* 1659, Jannetie Pietersen (*b* at Amsterdam, Holland, ca. 1640; Hillebrandt[10]);

8–Nicholas (1668-1746), began to write name **Lozier**; settled in Bergen Co., N.J., ca. 1700; lt. in co. of Foot, New Hackensack precinct, N.J., 1715; *m* 1691, Tryntie Slott (8 below);

7–Marrija (1701-28), *m* 1721, David **Demarest,** Jr. or IV (7 above).

10–Jan Pietersen **Slott** (which became **Sloat**), Holstein, Denmark; from Amsterdam, with his family, to New Amsterdam, 1654; pres. of Bd. of Commrs. forming first Ct. at New Haarlem, 1660; commd. militia of New Haarlem in Esopus war, 1663; *m* Aeltie Jans;

9–Pieter Jansen (ca. 1640-1688), *b* at Amsterdam, Holland; from Amsterdam to New Amsterdam, 1654; settled at "Cromessne," Stuyvesant's Bouwerie, New Amsterdam; owned property nr. City Hall, New York; *m* 1663, Marritie van Winckel (ca. 1644-1700; Jacob Walighs[10] [1600-56], who came from Hoorn, Holland, in the "King David," to New Amsterdam, 1636; became one of the "Twelve Men" who governed the Province of N.J., 1641; "schepen" [alderman] of New Haarlem; settled nr. "Kill van Kull" [Newark Bay], N.J., ca. 1654; purchased from the Lords Proprietor lands in East Jersey embracing the present sites of Paterson and Passaic, N.J., *m* Catrina–);

8–Tryntie (1671-1708), *m* 1691, Nicholas **Lozier** (8 above).

7–Nicholas **Johns** (1688-1774), from Wales, with his wife, four sons and one dau., to Pa. before 1752; settled nr. Valley Forge, Chester Co., Pa.; *m* Jennette Godfrey (1687-1771);

6–John (1733-1805), from Wales to Pa. ante 1752; settled at Chambersburg, Pa.; *m* 1770, Hannah Davis (1748-92; Thomas[7] [1689-1751]);

5–Thomas (1770-1852), Elizabeth Town (now Hagerstown), Md., Chambersburg and Washington, Pa.; with John Shryock, built at Chambersburg, 1808, Hollywell paper mill which made bank notes for U.S. Government; *m* 1794, Elizabeth Shryock (5 below);

4–William (1799-1845), physician; removed from Chambersburg to Erie, Pa.; *m* 1820, Anne (or Nancy) Dunn (4 below);

3–Elizabeth Anna (1821-1902), *m* 1841, Fitz-James **Christie** (3 above).

7–Johannes **Shryock** (Schrayack, Shreyack, Shryok), (ca. 1705-88; son of Friedrich von Schrieck[8]); from Germany, via Rotterdam in the "Dragon," to Phila., Pa., 1732; settled in Manchester Twp., Lancaster (now York) Co., Pa., *m* 1736, Susanna Kern (1713-50); *m* 2d, Sabina–; *m* 3d, Anna Magdalena–;

6–Johannes Leonhardt (Leonard) (1738/39-1782), Elizabeth Town (now Hagerstown), Md.; soldier in French and Indian War, 1755-59, and participated in capture of Quebec, 1759; commd. 2d lt., 1777; *m* 1765, Maria Margaretha Streiter (*b* 1746; Rev. Johann Philipp[7], [*d* 1780], who came from Germany, via Rotterdam in the "Saint Andrew Galley," to Phila., Pa., 1737; settled in Bucks Co., Pa.; removed to Frederick and Elizabeth Town (now Hagerstown), Md., and, in 1755, nr. Harper's Ferry, Va.; *m* Anna Julianna [*b* 1717], dau. of Philipp Gottfried Wittmann[8]);

5–Elizabeth (1779-1854), *m* 1794, Thomas **Johns** (5 above).

5–Thomas Lindsay **Dunn** (1767-1816; eldest son of Samuel[6] [1738-1823], of Killyleagh, Co. Down, Ireland, *m* 1762, Catherine [1742-1804], dau. of Thomas Lindsay[7], of Co. Down, Ireland); from Ireland to Pa., 1786; owned Mt. Pleasant Iron Works, Path Valley (now Richmond), Franklin Co., Pa.; *m* 1790, Elizabeth Holliday (5 below);

4–Anne (or Nancy) (1802-36), *m* 1820, Dr. William **Johns** (4 above).

7–John (Holiday, Holyday) **Holliday** (ca. 1700-1770), from Ireland to Pa., ca. 1740; settled in Cumberland (now Franklin) Co., Pa., ca. 1742; his sons, Adam and William, founded Hollidaysburg, Pa., 1768; *m* ca. 1727, Jean– (*d* 1776);

6–John (ca. 1740-1806), Fannett Twp., Franklin Co., Pa.; *m* ca. 1760;

5–Elizabeth (ca. 1771-1825), *m* 1790, Thomas Lindsay **Dunn** (5 above).

2–Capt. Frederic Wolters **Huidekoper** (1840-1908), Meadville, Pa., and Washington, D.C.; A.B., Harvard, 1862, A.M., 1871; capt. 58th Pa. Militia in Civil War; pres. of many rys. and cos. (see Who's Who in America, Vols. III, IV and V); *m* 1867, Anna Virginia Christie (1843-1914); issue: I–Gracie (*b* and *d* 1872); II–Frederic Louis (1 above); III–Reginald Shippen (see Vol. I, p. 394).

1–*m* Sept. 14, 1916, Helena Katherine Elliott, *b* at New York, Jan. 4, 1895; dau. of John Stuart Elliott (1859-1913), *m* 1890, Helena Forsyth Ellis (1859-95); issue: 1–Stuart Elliott, *b* Wash-

ington, D.C., Dec. 20, 1917; 2–Frederic Fitz-James Christie, *b* Washington, D.C., Jan. 28, 1919.
1–A.B., Harvard, 1896; English literature and law, Christ Church, Oxford, 1896-98; Law School, Columbian (now George Washington) U., 1898-1900. Admitted to D.C. bar, 1900. Military writer and soldier (see Who's Who in America). Chevalier, Legion of Honor; awarded D.S.M. and Verdun Medal. Mem. Hereditary Order of the Descendants of Colonial Govs., Inst. Am. Genealogy, etc. Clubs: Metropolitan, Chevy Chase, Montgomery Country (Washington), University (New York), Bath (London). Former address: 1614 18th St., N.W., Washington, D.C. Addresses: 15 Chemin des Contamines, Geneva, Switzerland, and care of Morgan and Company, 14 Place Vendôme, Paris, France.

1–**HULBURT, David Willey,** *b* Westfield Town, Medina Co., O., July 26, 1853.
7–William **Hulburt** (qv);
6–William (*b* 1654), *m* Mary Howard, and had six sons;
5–Obadiah (*b* 1703), *m* Jane Parsons;
4–Obadiah (*b* 1738), *m* 1766, Jane Pease;
3–Obadiah, *m* 1805, Rachel Burr;
2–William (1810-75), farmer; *m* 1837, Sarah Pelton (*d* 1840); *m* 2d, Lucy Morley (*d* 1844); *m* 3d, 1845, Eleanore Brewster (*d* 1851); *m* 4th, 1852, Sarah Hart Willey (*d* 1876); issue (1st marriage): I–Sarah Priscilla (*b* 1840; *m* LeRoy Green); issue (3d marriage): I–Halsey Hally (*b* 1847; *m* Amy Foskett, *d*); II–Hiram Bruster (*b* 1849; *m* Mrs. Weltha Brooks); issue (4th marriage): I–David Willey (1 above); II–Moses Hart (1855-77).
1–*m* June 30, 1879, Ella Jones Farrar, *b* Cleveland, O., June 10, 1857; dau. of Andrew Jackson Farrar, *d*, of Cleveland; issue: 1–Arthur Spring (May 8, 1880-June 28, 1886); 2–Judson Farrar, *b* Burlington, Wis., Sept. 26, 1882; ed. U.Wis.; *m* June 30, 1909, Zada, dau. of Moses Black, of Meade, Kan. (issue: Virginia; Joy); 3–Mary Ella, *b* Circleville, O., Aug. 22, 1884; Ph.B., U.Chicago; 4–Willey Clement (Dec. 11, 1887-Aug. 7, 1888); 5–Clarence Hellings, *b* Milwaukee, Wis., July 28, 1889; S.B., U.Wis.; *m* Oct. 14, 1916, Alice McKinney, of Fonda, (issue: Hugh; Homer; Robert); 6–Lillian Isabelle, *b* Milwaukee, Sept. 25, 1892; ed. Milwaukee Normal; *m* July 12, 1924, Maurice Carl Sjoblom, of Grantsburg, Wis. (issue: Martha Ellen; Mary Ann).
1–Studied Oberlin Coll., 2 yrs.; A.M., Denison Coll., 1879 (D.D., 1905); B.D., Bapt. Theol. Sem., Morgan Park, Ill., 1882. Supt. Universal Sch. of Biblical Edn., since 1929. Preached first sermon, 1876; ordained Bapt. ministry, 1881; pastorates until 1896; state supt. for Wis., 1896-1921; exec. sec. City Missions in Wis., 1921-24; pastor Woodlawn, Wis., 1924–. Author (see Who's Who in America). Residence: Wauwatosa, Wis.

1–**HULING, Bruce Wyckoff,** *b* Cleveland, O., Dec. 7, 1876.
8–James **Huling** (1635-87), from Eng., ante 1680; settled at New York City, then Newport, R.I.; *m* ante 1658, Margaret– (1632-1707);
7–Capt. Alexander (1665-1725), of N. Kingston, R.I.; capt. R.I. militia; mem. Colonial Legislature; *m* ante 1700, Elizabeth Wightman (1664-1756; George[8], *m* Elizabeth Updike);
6–Alexander (1700-74), of N. Kingston; *m* 1st, Elizabeth Eunice Tarbox (*d* ante 1761);
5–Walton (1745-1823 or 24), Malta, N.Y.; high sheriff, Dutchess Co., during Am. Rev.; pvt. Dutchess Co. militia, 5th Regt., Am. Rev.; *m* ante 1776, Abiah Mosier (*d* 1828);
4–Alexander (1776-1828), Big Prairie, Wayne Co., O.; *m* 1800, Lydia Lane (1778-1823; Hezekiah[5], of Shaftsbury, Vt., *m* Deborah Thurston);
3–Nathan Lane (1803-56), of Big Prairie, *m* 1st, 1833, Eliza Wyckoff;
2–Bruce (2 below).
9–Pieter Claessen **Wyckoff** (qv);
8–Claes (Nicholas) Pieterse (*b* 1648), *m* Sarah Montfort (Peter[9]);
7–Peter (1675-ca. 1735), *m* Willemfstje Jansan Schenck; *m* 2d, Anne Elizabeth–;
6–Jacobus (James), *m* 1745, Catalyntje Gulick (Joachim[7]);
5–Joachim (1749-1841), served in Am. Rev.; *m* 1773, Hannah Yerkese (1755-1844);
4–Peter (1774-1841), *m* Elizabeth Bruce (1777-1849; James[5]);
3–Eliza (*b* Erie, Pa., 1809-*d* Big Spring Tp., O., 1853), *m* as his first wife, Nathan Lane **Huling** (3 above).
8–Edward **Shepard** (qv);
7–John (1627-1707), of Hartford, Conn.; *m* 1649, Rebecca Greenhill (*d* 1689); *m* 2d, 1691, Susannah, widow of William Goodwin, of Hartford; *m* 3d, 1698, Marthe, widow of John Henbury;
6–Edward or Thomas; and thru:
4–Edward (1783-1862), of Wethersfield, Conn.; *m* 1809, Mary Ayrault;
3–Charles Lewis (1812-72), of Cleveland, O.; *m* 1st, 1839, Elizabeth Hurst (*b* Eng., 1813-*d* 1851);
2–Mary Elizabeth (2 below).
7–Dr. Nicholas **Ayrault** (*d* 1706/07), Huguenot; from France with his brother, Dr. Pierre, after the revocation of the Edict of Nantes, both settled in R.I.; Dr. Nicholas removed to Wethersfield, Conn.; *m* in Providence, R.I., as her first husband, Mary Breton or Bretoun (1681-1741);
6–Capt. Nicholas (1705-75), of Wethersfield; *m* 1730, Jane Stocking (ante 1712-1775; Daniel[7], of Middletown, Conn., *m* Jane Mould);
5–Daniel (1735-1807), of Wethersfield; *m* 2d, 1784, Mary Balch (1752-1852; Ebenezer[6], of Wethersfield, *m* Sarah Belden);
4–Mary (1785-1854), of Wethersfield; *m* Edward **Shepard** (4 above);
3–Charles Lewis, *m* 1st, Elizabeth Hurst (3 above);
2–Mary Elizabeth (1841-1906), of Cleveland, O.; *m* 1870, Bruce **Huling** (1840-81), druggist, of Cleveland; pvt. Co. A, Regt. I, O.V.I., 1861; orderly sgt., corpl., Co. A, 21st Regt., O.V.I., 1861-63; issue: I–Charles Shepard (*b* 1870; *m* Addie A. Dart, *b* 1874); II–Daniel Ayrault (*b* 1875; *m* Teressa Marie Bertram; *m* 2d, Jean Collins); III–Bruce Wyckoff (1 above).
1–*m* Oct. 4, 1902, Cora Mabel Talcott (qv).
1–A.B., Western Reserve U., '00. Practiced law, 1900-06, Cleveland, O.; in bond and insurance business, 1906-10, Cleveland; div. sales mgr., B. F. Goodrich Rubber Co., Akron, O., 1910-30; mgr. B. F. Goodrich Rubber Co., Buenos Aires, 1930–. Clubs: University, Masonic, Anna Dean Country. Republican. Presbyterian. Address: c/o B. F. Goodrich Rubber Co., Buenos Aires, Argentina, S.A.

1–**HULING, Cora Mabel Talcott (Mrs. Bruce W.),** *b* Jefferson, Ashtabula Co., Ohio, Oct. 5, 1882.
10–John **Talcott** (qv);
9–Capt. Samuel (1635-91), of Wethersfield, Conn.; grad. Harvard, 1658; lt. Hartford Co. troop, 1679, capt., 1681, in King William's War; comd. a co. of dragoons at Deerfield, 1670; *m* 1661, Hannah Holyoke (1644-1677/78; Capt. Elizur[10], *m* Mary, dau. of Gov. William Pynchon);
8–Cornet Samuel (1662-98), Wethersfield; *m* 1679, Mary (Ellery?);
7–Ens. Samuel (1696-1739), Wethersfield; *m* 1723, Thankful Belding (1700 or 02-post 1747; Sgt. Ebenezer[8], *m* Abigail Graves);
6–Elizur (1728-post 1793), of Enfield, Conn.; *m* 1751, Mary King (post 1724-post 1793; Benjamin[7], *m* Remembrance Hall);
5–Elizur (1759-1835), Enfield; pvt. in Am. Rev.; *m* 1st, 1790, Sarah Baxter (1767-1853; Francis[8], *m* Abigail–);
4–Nelson (1804-56), of Nelson, O.; *m* 1832, Catherine Louisa Whiting (1813-1900; Elisha[5], *m* Sally Hulet);
3–Henry (1832-94), of Jefferson, O.; *m* 1855, Cordelia Jane Pritchard (1834-1922; John[4], *m* Polly Tillotson);
2–Albert Lewis (2 below).
8–Joel (Baily) **Bailey** (1658-1732; son of Daniel [bap. 1601-1674], from Eng., *m* Mary–), came from Eng. to Marlborough, Chester Co., Pa., ante 1685; *m* 1687, Ann Short, came from Eng. in the "Welcome," in 1648?;
7–Josiah (*d* 1791), wrote name Bailey; *m* 1734, Sarah Marsh (*d* 1791; William[8], *m* Sarah–);
6–Joel (1734/35-1825), West Marlborough; *m* 1st, 1757, Hannah Wickersham;
5–Gravenor (*b* post 1757), pvt., Capt. Joseph Luckey's 7th co., 1782, Newlin Tp., Chester Co., Pa., 1782; *m* post 1781;

4–Gravenor (1800-77), of Mecca, Trumbull Co., O.; *m* ante 1825, Elizabeth Headley (1799-1874; Joseph[5], *m* Sarah–);
3–William (1828-93), of Jefferson, O.; *m* 1854, Mary Ann Russell Tickner (1838-1919; John[4], *m* Rachel Durey, both of Co. Kent, Eng.);
2–Elizabeth Jane (*b* 1860), *m* 1881, Albert Lewis **Talcott** (*b* 1859), atty.; issue: I–Cora Mabel (1 above); II–John Albert (*b* 1886; *m* Harriet Imogene Phinney); III–Winifred Bailey (*b* 1892; *m* Herbert Gordon Hayes).
1–*m* Oct. 4, 1902, Bruce Wyckoff Huling (qv).
1–Western Reserve U. (Coll. for Women), Cleveland, O., 1903 (Gamma Delta Tau). Genealogist. Mem. C.D.A., D.F.P.A., Soc. Daus. Am. Pioneers, D.A.R., etc. Address: c/o B. F. Goodrich Rubber Co., Buenos Aires, Argentina, S.A.

1–**HULL, Alexander,** *b* Columbus, O., Sept. 15, 1887.
9–Joseph **Hull** (qv);
8–Benjamin (bap. 1639-1713), of Durham and Dover, N.H.; mem. Capt. Robert Mason's Troop of Horse, Indian wars; commd. capt.; tavern keeper; *m* 1668, Rachel York (Richard[9]; Richard[10]);
7–Benjamin (1680-1732), ens. Piscataway Mil. Co. No. 4, of Col. Thomas Farmer's regt. of N.J.; *m* 1704, Sarah Drake (1686-1758; Rev. John[8]);
6–Joseph (1706-68), of Newton, Sussex Co., N.J.; justice of peace, 1754-61, 1761-68; justice Ct. of Common Pleas, Sussex Co.; *m* 1730, Susanna Stelle (*b* 1710; Reverend Benjamin[7], *m* Mercy, dau. of Capt. George Drake; Poncet[8], Huguenot, from France, 1682, *m* Eugenie Legenau);
5–David (1746-1830), Steubenville, O.; saddler and hotel keeper;
4–James (1779-1838), *m* 1799, Achsah Curtis;
3–Robert Curtis (1819-78), of Steubenville and Columbus, O.; *m* 1847, Annie E. Edie;
2–James E. (1850-1900), of Columbus, O.; *m* 1886, Eva Jane Hummer (1861-1930; Samuel A.[3] [*d* 1879], *m* Elizabeth Starr, *d* 1868); issue: I–Alexander (1 above); II–Dorothy (*m* Claude M. Newlin).
1–*m* Aug. 11, 1920, Ruth Romig, *b* Big Rapids, Mich., Dec. 28, 1886; dau. of Edward Adams Romig, of Newberg, Ore.; issue: 1–Alexander, II, *b* Portland, Ore., July 17, 1928.
1–A.B., Muskingum Coll., '06; B.M., U.Pa., 1909; studied piano, violoncello, voice, composition and orchestration under pvt. teachers. Head dept. of music, Pacific Coll., Newberg, Ore., since 1908. Composer (see Who's Who in America). Mem. Portland Press Club, Authors League of America, etc. Residence: Newberg, Ore.

1–**HULL, Jep Rucker,** *b* Augusta, Ga., Oct. 8, 1888.
6–Hopewell **Hull** (desc. Rev. Joseph Hull [1594-1665], B.A., St. Mary's Hall, Oxford U., 1614, from Eng. with company of 106 persons to Boston, 1635, was founder of Barnstable, Mass.), came from Eng., 1755, settled in Somerset Co., Md.;
5–Hope (1763-1818) soldier Am. Rev.; pioneer Meth. preacher and educator in north Ga., organized Washington Acad.; *m* Ann Wingfield;
4–Asbury (1797-1866), lawyer, planter, banker, legislator and 47 yrs. treas. U.Ga.; mem. Secession Convention, 1861; *m* Lucy Harvie (John[5]);
3–James Merriwether (1838-1864), capt. C.S.A.; *m* Georgia Harris Rucker;
2–Asbury (2 below).
9–Peter **Rucker** (son of Ambrose), from Bavaria to Va., and had lands in Orange, Spotsylvania and Madison cos., Va.; *m* Elizabeth–;
8–Thomas; planter Bromfield Parish, Orange Co., Va.;
7–Cornelius, of Ruckersville, Va.; *m* Mary White;
6–John, *m* Elizabeth Tinsley;
5–Joseph, of Ruckersville, Ga.; *m* Margaret Speer (William[6]);
4–Tinsley White, *m* Sarah Harris;
3–Georgia Harris (1837-1908), *m* 1st, James Merriwether **Hull** (3 above).
10–John **Sibley** (qv);
9–Joseph (1655-1711), *m* 1684, Susannah Follet;
8–John (*b* 1687), *m* Zeruiah Gould (*b* 1694);
7–John (*b* 1714), *m* Abigail Towne (*b* 1715);
6–Stephen (1741-1828), soldier Am. Rev.; *m* Thankful Taft (1745-1837), sister of g.g.father of William Howard Taft;
5–Joel (1766-1839), *m* Lois Wood (1767-1832; Col. Ezekiel[6]);
4–Josiah (1808-88), settled at Augusta, Ga.; *m* 1st, Sarah Ann Sophia Crapon (1809-58; William[5], Providence, R.I.);
3–George Royal (1839-87), soldier C.S.A.; cotton mcht.; banker; *m* 1862, Emma Susan Hansel Tucker (1845-1911; Judge Daniel Reese[4]);
2–Alice Reese (see Vol. I, p. 396), *m* 1883, Asbury **Hull** (1860-1901), cotton factor; issue: I–Emma Georgia (1883-1929; *m* 1904, Andrew Claudius Perkins, issue: Alice Hull, Andrew C., Jr., 1908-28, Emma Sibley); II–Jep Rucker (1 above); III–Alice Sibley (*b* 1891; *m* 1916, Eugene Ellis Trader); IV–Asbury (1894-1902).
1–Not married. Richmond Mil. Acad., Augusta, Ga. Served in U.S.N. June 27, 1918-Oct. 26, 1920. Residence: 451 Greene St., Augusta, Ga.

1–**HULSIZER, Sarah Bond McClelland (Mrs. John),** *b* Cadiz, O., June 6, 1865.
4–Nicholas **Parrott** (1761-1854), of Hancock, Md.; patriot; *m* 1783, Elizabeth Moran (1764-1834; Edmond[5], sgt., 1776);
3–Charlotte (1802-63), *m* ca. 1823, John **McClelland** (1799-1881);
2–John Parrott (2 below).
4–James **Hutchison** (1763-1814), patriot; *m* Ann–(1763-1847);
3–William (1806-62), of Washington, Pa.; capt. Civil War; *m* 1828, Eliza Hornish (1806-78; Christian[4] [1763-1846], enlisted in Capt. Gear's militia in Am. Rev., *m* Elizabeth–, 1774-1847);
2–Catherine (1833-81), *m* 1851, John Parrott **McClelland** (1829-1913), of Washington, Pa., and Joliet, Ill.; mcht. tailor; issue: I–James Porter (1853-1924; *m* 1875, Mary Coffee); II–Mary Eliza (1855-1912); III–Charlotte Anne (*b* 1858); IV–George B. (*b* 1861; *m* Jean Davidson); V–Sarah Bond (1 above); VI–William Cortney (*b* 1868; *m* Agnes Raum); VII–Katherine (*b* 1872; *m* H. C. Francis); VIII–Frances (*b* 1876; *m* George Dennis, *d* 1904; *m* 2d, J. Elmo Smith).
1–*m* Jan. 5, 1910, John Hulsizer, *b* Finesville, N.J., Jan. 26, 1861; son of Richard Hulsizer, of Joliet, *m* Margaret Fraley.
1–Teacher pub. sch. at Cambridge, O., 1886-92, Joliet, 1892-1904, Chicago, since 1904. Mem. D.A.R., I.A.G. Presbyterian. Republican. Residence: 702 Morgan St., Joliet, Ill.

1–**HUME, Amber Verne Gossard (Mrs. Carleton Ross),** *b* Red Oak, O., Feb. 10, 1883.
10–John **Greene** (qv);
9–James (1626-98), Warwick and Kingston, R.I.; *m* Deliverance Potter (Robert[10], qv);
8–Sarah (1664-post 1716), N. Kingston, R.I.; *m* 1685, Henry **Reynolds** (1652-1716; James[9], qv);
7–John (1688-1774), N. Kingston, R.I.; *m* Hannah– (*d* ante 1753);
6–Elisha (1733-1810), N. Kingston; *m* 1758, Mary Dickinson (*b* 1734; Capt. John[7], *m* Mary Phillips);
5–Elisha (1763-1840), Am. Rev.; N. Kingston; *m* by 1788;
4–Thomas (1795-1864), in War 1812 as "Corpl. Thomas, Jr."; *m* 1814, Elsie Bell;
3–Miranda (*b* 1815), *m* 1848, Ashley **Wilson** (1815-1893);
2–Amelia Ann (2 below).
11–George **Soule,** Mayflower Pilgrim (qv);
10–George, settled at Dartmouth, Mass.; *m* Deborah–;
9–Mary, *m* Joseph **Deuel** (*d* 1726; Jonathan[10] [*d* 1709], *m* Hannah Audley; William[11] [*d* 1680], applied for land at Duxbury, 1640);
8–Joseph (1703-82), *m* 1st, ca. 1726, Margaret Potter (Stokes[9], *m* Elizabeth–; Nathaniel[10]; Nathaniel[11]);
7–Philip (ca. 1726-1812), of Oblong, Dutchess Co.; *m* 1749, Elizabeth Sherman (William[8], *m* Susanna–);
6–Michael (1750-1830), *m* 1769, Elsie Slocum;
5–Elizabeth, *m* William **Bell**;
4–Elsie (1797-1882), *m* Thomas **Reynolds** (4 above).
11–Anthony **Slocum,** *m* Deborah Almy;
10–Giles (*d* 1682), of Portsmouth; *m* Joan–;
9–Eleazar (1664-1727), Dartmouth, 1684; *m* Eliphel Fitzgerald;

8–Eleazar (1693/94-1738/39), *m* 1716, Deborah Smith (Deliverance[9]);
7–John (*b* 1717), *m* 1738, Deborah Almy (John[8], *m* Deborah–);
6–Elsie (1753-1808), *m* Michael **Deuel** (6 above).
2–Amelia Ann Wilson (1854-1923), *m* 1874, Rev. Thomas Madison **Gossard** (*b* 1847), retired Presbyn. minister; for issue see Vol. III, p. 261.
1–*m* Aug. 20, 1907, Carleton Ross Hume, *b* Tontogany, O., Apr. 30, 1878; A.B., U.Okla., '98, A.M., 1900; LL.B., U.Kan., 1904; Y.M.C.A. ednl. sec., Aug. 1918-July 1919; son of Charles Robinson Hume (see Vol. II, p. 178); issue (all *b* Anadarko, Okla.): 1–Ross Gossard, *b* June 9, 1908; A.B., U.Okla., '29; 2–Dorothy Anne, *b* Mar. 18, 1913; 3–Elizabeth Verne, *b* Mar. 7, 1915.
1–Hanover (Ind.) Coll. Mem. D.A.R., I.A.G. Residence: 503 W. Central Boul., Anadarko, Okla.

1–**HUMISTON, Wallace,** *b* Hamden, Conn., May 2, 1886.
9–Henry **Humiston** (*d* 1663), from Eng. to New Haven, Conn., ca. 1644; *m* 1651, Joane Walker;
8–Thomas (1655-1716), *m* 1694, Elizabeth Sanford (*b* 1671);
7–Ebenezer (1695-1769), *m* 1718, Grace Blakeslee (*b* 1694);
6–Ebenezer (*b* 1722), soldier French and Indian War; *m* 1740, Mary Butler (1723-83);
5–Ebenezer (1759-97), soldier Am. Rev.; *m* Hannah Humiston (1757-1846);
4–William (1785-1853), *m* 1807, Betsey Ann Talmadge;
3–Willis (1824-95), *m* 1850, Eunice Wooding (1830-1903);
2–Dwight Le Roy (2 below).
11–Peter **Bulkley** (qv);
10–Thomas (*b* 1617), *m* Sarah Jones (Rev. John[11]);
9–Sarah, *m* Eleazer **Brown**;
8–Elizabeth, *m* Michael **Todd** (1653-1744);
7–Eleazer (1707-71), *m* Thankful Heaton (1707-47);
6–Sybil (1735-1805), *m* Nathaniel **Heaton** (*b* 1732);
5–Thankful (1757-90), *m* 1776, Daniel **Talmadge** (1746-1831);
4–Betsey Ann (1789-1862), *m* William **Humiston** (4 above);
3–Willis, *m* Eunice Wooding (3 above);
2–Dwight LeRoy (1857-1920), mem. Conn. Legislature, 1897; *m* 1879, Katie Downs (*b* 1862); issue: I–Lillie H. (*b* 1881; *m* Wilfred J. Megin); II–Wallace (1 above); III–Rubie Amy (*b* 1891; *m* Alphonso Noble); IV–Leta Kathryn (*b* 1897; *m* William H. Bice).
1–Not married. Grad. Willimantic Normal Training Sch., '11; B.D., Yale, 1916. Ordained Congl. minister, (1917); pastor Northfield Congl. Ch., since 1918, also librarian Gilbert Lib., Northfield, since 1918. Residence, Northfield, Conn.

1–**HUMPHREY, Arthur Luther,** *b* nr. Holland, N.Y., June 12, 1860.
6–Arthur **Humphrey,** in New Roxbury (now Woodstock), Mass., 1686; dea.; selectman; constable; freeman; served in Indian wars; *m* Rachel–;
5–Ebenezer (1692-1784), French and Indian War; *m* 1732, Sarah Read;
4–Arthur (1735-1812), French and Indian War; freeman; marched on Lexington Alarm; *m* 1758, Mary Kingsbury (Josiah[5], of Oxford, Mass.);
3–Arthur (1770-1853), *b* Woodstock, lived on homestead nr. Holland, Erie Co., N.Y., and in Goshen, N.H.; *m* Alithea Morgan;
2–Arthur Kingsbury (2 below).
8–James **Morgan** (qv);
7–John (*b* 1645), Indian commr. and adviser; dep. Gen. Ct., 1690, from New London, 1693-94, from Preston; *m* 1st, 1665, Rachel Dymond;
6–Capt. John (1667-1746), lt. of Train Band, Groton, 1692, capt., 1714-30; *m* Ruth Shapley (Benjamin[7], of Groton, *m* Mary–);
5–John (1700-71), ens., lt. and capt., N. East Co. of Groton; *m* 1728, Sarah Cobb (*d* 1780);
4–Isaac (1750-1817), Hartland, Windsor Co., Vt., 1788; privateersman at burning of New London by Arnold; served in Am. Rev. and War 1812 with son Isaac; *m* Elizabeth Allyn (*d* 1833), of Groton;
3–Alithea (1778-1852), *m* Arthur **Humphrey** (3 above);
2–Arthur Kingsbury (1815-91), from Holland, Erie Co., N.Y., to Maquoketa, Ia.; *m* 1846, Huldah Orcutt (1822-70; Luther[8], *m* Amelia–); issue: I–Eliza Alithea (*b* 1847; *m* Michael Murphy); II–Evelyn Louise (1848-1921; *m* W. Scott Belden); III–Isaac Morgan (*b* 1850; *m* Bell Scott); IV–Charles H. (1853-63); V–Willis Lee (*b* 1855); VI–James Buchanan (*b* 1857; *m* 1884, Ruby Roberts; *m* 2d, 1917, Ida May Owen); VII–Edgar Kingsbury (1859-98); VIII–Arthur Luther (1 above); IX–Frankie D. (1862-63); X–Bertha Julia (*b* 1865; *m* Henry H. Baum).
1–*m* Jan. 16, 1890, Jennie Field, *b* June 16, 1869; dau. of Dexter Field; issue: 1–Arthur Field, *b* Colo. Springs, Colo., Feb. 18, 1891; *m* Oct. 7, 1916, Marguerite, dau. of Christian F. Fendrick (issue: Virginia S.; Arthur F., Jr.); 2–Frederick Dexter, *b* Denver, Colo., Apr. 1, 1902; grad. Lafayette Coll., Easton, Pa., '25; commd. 2d lt. A.O.R.C., 1925.
1–Pres. Westinghouse Air Brake Co., since 1919. Mem. Colo. Ho. of Rep., 2 terms (1893-95, speaker, 1895). Trustee U.Pittsburgh, St. Margaret Memorial Hosp. (see Who's Who in America). Mem. I.A.G. Clubs: Duquesne, Athletic, Longue Vue Country (Pittsburgh), Engineers, Bankers (New York), Union League (Chicago), Congressional Country (Washington). Residence: 361 Maple Av., Edgewood, Pittsburgh, Pa.

1–**HUNT, Arthur Billings,** *b* Fargo, N.D., Feb. 2, 1890.
10–Enoch **Hunt,** from Eng. with his son Ephraim; a first settler Weymouth, Mass.;
9–Capt. Ephraim (1610-87), of Weymouth; *m* Anna Richards (Thomas[10]);
8–Col. Ephraim (1650-1713), of Weymouth; capt. Canadian Expdn., 1690; col. expdn. against Groton Indians, 1706; *m* Joanna Alcock (1659/-60-1746; Dr. John[9], of Roxbury, *m* a dau. of Dr. Richard Palgrave, of Charlestown; George[10]);
7–Ephraim (1707-86), of Braintree; *m* 1729, Ruth Allen (*b* 1706);
6–Jonathan (*b* 1736), of Sherborn; *m* 1761, Sarah Vining;
5–John Vining (*b* 1776), of Goshen, Mass.; *m* Lydia Gloyd (1781-1846; Jacob[6], *m* Rachel–, of Plainfield, Mass.);
4–Jonathan (1801-54), of Goshen; *m* Lilley– (1805-75);
3–Frederick P. (1830-1912), of Goshen; *m* Sophia Billings;
2–Charles Joseph (1857-1922), *m* 1882, Mary Perkins (*b* 1863); issue: I–Edwin Perkins (*b* 1883; *m* Josephine Johnson); II–Helen Hunt (*b* 1888; *m* Rev. W. J. Bell); III–Arthur Billings (1 above).
1–Not married. B.A., Macalester Coll., '11; studied voice. Baritone; radio and concert singer. Musical dir. for Greater N.Y. Fed. of Churches, since 1923. Teacher, lecture-recitalist since 1922 (see Who's Who in America). Served 13 mos. overseas with Base Hosp. No. 37; citation and medal, Brit. Gen. Hosp., Glasgow, Scotland. Mason. Clubs: Athenaen, Bohemians, Town Hall. Residence: 96 Columbia Hts., Brooklyn, N.Y.

1–**HUNT, Ernest Leroi,** *b* Abington, Mass., Nov. 11, 1877.
10–Enoch **Hunt,** from Eng. with his son, Ephraim; a first settler at Weymouth, Mass.;
9–Capt. Ephraim (1610-87), of Weymouth; *m* Ann Richards (Thomas[10]);
8–Col. Ephraim (1650-1713), of Weymouth; *m* Joanna Alcock (1660-1746; Dr. John[9], of Roxbury, Mass.; George[10]);
7–Thomas;
6–Thomas (*b* 1696), of Weymouth;
5–Thomas (*b* 1721), of Weymouth;
4–Thomas (*b* 1746), of Abington, Mass.;
3–Noah (*b* 1778), of Abington;
2–Washington (1827-93), *m* Mary Nickerson (1835-1919); issue: I–Charles W. (1856-1908; *m* Helen Frances Gowell); II–Frank E. (*m* May Trow); III–Martha Ella (*m* Charles F. Harris, *d* ca. 1893; *m* 2d, William H. Smith); IV–Brenelle (*m* Hattie B. Sears); V–Ernest Leroi (1 above).
1–*m* June 4, 1907, Isabel Girling (Oct. 21, 1876-May 29, 1928); dau. of James Girling, of Worcester, Mass., *m* Eliza–; issue (all *b* Worcester,

Mass.): 1–Isabel, *b* Mar. 7, 1908; 2–Ethel Dorothy, *b* July 14, 1911; 3–Mildred Elizabeth, *b* Jan. 12, 1913.
1–*m* 2d, Sept. 21, 1929, Charlotte Stiles Alling, dau. of James Carey Alling (desc. Roger Alling and William Bradford).
1–Student, Mass. Coll. of Pharmacy, Boston, 1894-95; M.D., Harvard, 1902. Practiced in Worcester since 1903; interne, Worcester City Hosp., 1902-03, asst. pathologist since 1903, surgeon since 1919; asso. med. examiner, Worcester Co., Mass., since 1909, except period of military service (see Who's Who in America). Capt. M.C., U.S.A., active service, July 1918-Mar. 22, 1919; maj. med. sect. O.R.C., U.S.A. Mem. The Governor and Company of Mass. Bay in N.E., Worcester Hist. Soc., M.O.W.W., A.L.; chmn. Worcester chapter, A.R.C. Universalist. Republican. Clubs: Worcester, Economic, Worcester Country. Summer place: Greyrock, Saybrook, Conn. Residence: 20 Kenilworth Rd., Worcester, Mass.

1–**HUNT, George W.,** *b* Stoddard, N.H., Feb. 6, 1858.
9–William **Hunt** (qv);
8–Samuel (*b* 1635), of Concord, Mass.; *m* Elizabeth Redding (1634-1706; Joseph[9], of Ipswich, Mass., *m* Agnes–);
7–Samuel (1657-1742), removed to Tewksbury, Mass.; *m* 1678, Ruth Tod;
6–Peter (1692-1770), *m* 1715, Mary Sheldon (*b* 1692; John[7], of Billerica, Mass., *m* Deborah Hill);
5–Peter (1720-1814), *m* 1749, Mary Kimball (*b* 1730);
4–Tymothy (1756-1838), *m* 1781, Dolly Worcester (*b* 1761; Moses[5], of Bradford, Mass., *m* Mary Stickney);
3–Tymothy (1784-1860), *m* 1808, Mary Kendrick (*b* 1781; Daniel[4], of Hollis, N.H., *m* Mary Pool);
2–Timothy (1817-60), Stoddard, N.H.; *m* 1839, Tryphemia Fisher (1818-80; Dr. Harvey[3], *m* Charlotte Copeland).
1–*m* Dec. 5, 1886, Cora F. Baker (qv for issue).
1–I.O.O.F. Methodist. Republican. Residence: Summer St., Antrim, N.H.

1–**HUNT, Cora F. Baker (Mrs. George W.),** *b* Lempster, N.H., Mar. 20, 1864.
10–John **Baker,** from Eng., to Roxbury, Mass.; freeman at Charlestown, 1634;
9–Thomas (*d* 1683), came with father; loyal supporter of Rev. John Elliott; built the 1st tide mill at Boston Neck; *m* Elizabeth–;
8–John (1644-1722), of Roxbury;
7–Thomas (1678-1761), *m* 1702, Sarah Pike;
6–Capt. Joseph (1714-91), to Pembroke, N.H.; prominent in earlier wars; served in Am. Rev.; mem. Com. Safety, 1774; mem. 3d Provincial Cong. at Exeter, N.H., 1775; signed Assn. Test; *m* 1739, Hannah Lovewell (*b* 1721; Capt. John[7], noted Indian fighter, killed Paugus, Indian leader);
5–Capt. Lovewell (1743-1835), removed to Pembroke, N.H.; served in Am. Rev.; *m* 1766, Mary Worth;
4–John (1774-1858), Goshen, N.H.; *m* 1798, Sarah R. Lakeman (1778-1867);
3–Amos L. (1817-50), *m* 1842, Aurilia Maria Hall (1824-94);
2–Arvin G. (1843-1917), Marlow, N.H.; *m* 1863, Olive H. Huntley (*b* 1846); issue: I–Cora F. (1 above); II–Flora B. (*b* 1865; *m* Orison C. Huntley); III–Alice M. (1871-1911; *m* Lewis D. Hatch).
1–*m* Dec. 5, 1886, George W. Hunt (qv); issue: 1–Edith Belle, *b* Antrim, N.H., June 1, 1888; B.S., Simmons Coll., '11; *m* Sept. 29, 1923, Robert F., son of Benjamin Francis Folsom, of Springvale, Me. (issue: John Hunt).
1–Mem. S.M.D., D.F.P.A., H.S.A., D.A.R., N.E. Women, Odd Fellow (auxiliary), Rebekah Lodge. Club: Woman's (Antrim). Methodist. Republican. Residence: Summer St., Antrim, N.H.

1–**HUNTER, Dard,** *b* Steubenville, O., Nov. 29, 1883.
6–Thomas **Hunter** (*d* 1777), from Ireland, 1727, settled in York Co., Pa.; during French and Indian War organized and equipped a co. for the defence of the frontier; *m* Mary Canon;
5–James (1738-1810), of Westmoreland Co., Pa.; pvt., ens. and lt. in Am. Rev.; *m* Elizabeth McDonald;
4–James (1777-1829), of Westmoreland Co.; *m* Agnes Sloane (1777-1858);
3–Joseph R. (1804-86), of Westmoreland Co.; *m* 1835, Letitia Stafford McFadden (1815-86);
2–William Henry (*b* May 26, 1852-*d* June 3, 1906), of Chillicothe, O.; newspaper editor and author; *m* 1876, Harriett Rosemond Browne (1857-1925); issue: I–Philip Courtney (1881-1908); II–Dard (1 above).
1–*m* Mar. 24, 1908, Helen Edith Cornell (qv for genealogy and issue).
1–Student, Ohio State U.; grad Graphische Lehr und Versuchs-Anstalt, Vienna; also studied Kunstgewerbe Schule, Vienna, and at Royal Tech. Coll., London. Art dir., Roycroft Shop, E. Aurora, N.Y., 1903-10, Carlton Studio, London, Norfolk Studio, London, The Mill House Press, Marlborough, N.Y., 1913-18; v.p. News-Advertiser Co., Inc., Chillicothe, O.; pres. Mountain House Press, Chillicothe; v.p. Dard Hunter, Inc., Lime Rock, Conn.; settled on farm in N.Y. State, 1913; moved to Chillicothe, O., 1919. Makes the paper for limited editions of books issued by himself; designs, casts and sets the type, prints on hand press. Published: The Etching of Figures, 1915; The Etching of Contemporary Life, 1917 (both for the Chicago Soc. of Etchers—said to have been the first books in the history of printing produced entirely by the efforts of one man). Author (see Who's Who in America). Democrat. Hon. mem. Rowfant Club (Cleveland); mem. Am. Inst. of Graphic Arts (past v.p.). Residence: The Mountain House, Chillicothe, O.

1–**HUNTER, Helen Edith Cornell (Mrs. Dard),** *b* Williamsport, Pa., Mar. 24, 1885.
10–Thomas **Cornell** (qv);
9–Thomas (*d* 1673);
8–Stephen (*b* 1656), *m* Hannah Moshier;
7–William (*d* 1775), *m* Mehitable Fish (*b* 1684);
6–Daniel (1727-99), *m* 1744, Elizabeth Allen (1722-67);
5–James (1753-1828), of Washington Co., N.Y.; *m* 1775, Thankful Briggs (1751-99);
4–Stephen (1778-1855), of Washington Co.; *m* 1799, Deborah Pease (1783-1872);
3–Alonzo (1808-65), of Williamsport, Pa.; *m* 1839, Amanda Choate (1820-1906);
2–Edward Augustus (2 below).
5–William **Carpenter** (*b* nr. New York, 1710);
4–William (1761-1821), *m* Lois– (*d* 1814);
3–Charles (1800-91), of Kingsbury, Washington Co., N.Y.; *m* 1824, Nancy Burgess (1804-55);
2–Emma (1849-1916), *m* 1877, Edward Augustus **Cornell** (1840-1918).
1–*m* Mar. 24, 1908, Dard Hunter (qv for genealogy); issue: 1–Dard, Jr., *b* Marlborough, N.Y., May 15, 1917; 2–Cornell Choate, *b* Newburgh, N.Y., Feb. 3, 1919.
Residence: The Mountain House, Chillicothe, O.

1–**HUNTER, Lillian Acomb (Mrs. Livingston L.),** *b* Cuba, N.Y., Jan. 6, 1864.
8–Elder James **Humphrey** (1608-86), from Wendover, Eng.; settled at Dorchester, Mass.; bailiff, 1650; ruling elder many yrs.; *m* Mary– (*d* 1677);
7–Hopestill (1649-1730), of Dorchester; in the Narragansett Swamp Fight, 1675; selectman, 1708; *m* Elizabeth Baker (1660-1714);
6–Jonas (1696-1772), of Dorchester; *m* 1721, Susanna Payson (1703-1790);
5–Rev. James (*b* 1722), of Athol, Mass.; grad. Harvard, 1744; sch. teacher, Dorchester, 1748; ordained first minister of Athol, 1750, where he remained over 30 yrs.; *m* 1757, Esther Wiswall;
4–Lois Wiswall (1758-1848), of Athol; *m* 1780, Moses **Oliver** (1753-92), sgt. Am. Rev.;
3–Charles (1789-1866), of South Dansville, N.Y.; pvt. War 1812; justice of peace; *m* 1815, Phebe Willson (1795-1857);
2–Seraph (2 below).
9–Thomas **Wiswall** (1608-83), from Eng., 1635; lived in Cambridge, Dorchester and Newton, Mass.; elder; *m* 1632, Elizabeth–;
8–Enoch (1633-1706), of Dorchester; *m* 1657, Elizabeth Oliver (1637-1712; John[9], of Boston, freeman, 1634; Thomas[10], qv, from London in the "William and Francis," 1632);
7–John (*b* 1658), of Dorchester; *m* 1685, Hannah Baker (1662-90; Richard[8], from Eng., 1635, freeman, 1642, mem. A. and H.A. Co., 1658);
6–John (1688-1774), of Dorchester; *m* 1719, Sarah Pierce (*d* 1747);

5–Esther (1729-1822), of Dorchester; *m* Rev. James **Humphrey** (5 above).
2–Seraph Oliver (1821-1908), S. Dansville, N.Y.; ed. Alfred Sem., 1838; sch. teacher; studied at Rochester Med. Coll., and practiced in Cuba, N.Y., and Tidioute, Pa.; *m* 1852, James LaFayette **Acomb** (1828-1901), M.D.; issue: I–Seraph May (*m* Charles Mellon Knight); II–Lillian (1 above).
1–*m* Jan. 6, 1887, Livingston LeGrand Hunter (Jan. 10, 1861-Apr. 20, 1902); son of Jahu Hunter, of Tidioute, Pa.; issue (all *b* Tidioute): 1–James Livingston, *b* Oct. 31, 1890; ed. Kiskaminitus Sch., and U.Akron; *m* Aug. 24, 1918, Mae Kennebrook, of Buffalo, N.Y.; 2–Lela May, *b* Jan. 10, 1894; ed. Smith Coll., 1915, and U.Akron; *m* June 30, 1917, William Floyd, son of Herbert Clinger, of Nealtown, Pa. (issue: Dorothy; Elizabeth; William Floyd, Jr.); 3–Dorothy, *b* Sept. 5, 1896; ed. Smith Coll., 1918; *m* June 9, 1928, Marshall W., son of Charles Ulf, of Tidioute; 4–Jahu Acomb, *b* Aug. 5, 1901; ed. Harrisburg Acad., and Franklin and Marshall Coll.; *m* Aug. 26, 1926, Helen, dau. of John Jones, of Jamestown, N.Y. (issue: John Livingston).
1–B.S., U.Akron (Ohio), '85 (Kappa Kappa Gamma). Trustee L.L. Hunter Estate Trust; administrator, L.L. Hunter estate, 1902-18. Mem. D.A.C. (nat. pres. since 1928), D.C.W. (Mass. chapter), D.A.R. (Tidioute Chapter regent, 1911-20, treas. gen. nat. soc., 1920-23), U.S.D. 1812, I.A.G., Soc. N.E. Women, Mt. Vernon Assn., A.A.U.W. Clubs: Washington (Washington, D.C.), Woman's (Warren, Pa.), Women's (Tidioute, Pa.), Nat. Officers D.A.R., Conewango Country. Residence: Tidioute, Pa.

1–**HUNTINGTON, Frederick William,** *b* Brooklyn, N.Y., Sept. 19, 1892.
9–Simon **Huntington** (qv);
8–Christopher (1628-91), from Eng. to Saybrook, Conn., with his mother, Margaret Barret, 1633; granted 100 acres, 1668; was one of 12 patentees of Norwich, 1685; *m* 1652, Ruth Rockwell (William[9], qv);
7–John (1666-1703), of Norwich, Conn.; constable, 1691; *m* 1686, Abigail Lathrop (*b* 1667; Samuel[8], of Scituate, Mass., New London and Norwich, Conn.; Rev. John[9], qv);
6–John (1691-1737), ens. Tolland Train Band, 1722; lt., 1725; mem. com. to fix the place for the meeting-house, 1733; *m* 1723, Thankful Warner (1693-1739; Isaac[7], *m* Sarah, dau. of Robert Boltwood; Andrew[8]);
5–John (1726-74), of Tolland; *m* 1748, Mehetabel Steele (*b* 1733; Stephen[6]; James[7]; James[8]; George[9], qv);
4–Hezekiah (1759-1842), of Suffield, Conn.; soldier Am. Rev.; captured by British and confined on prison ship "Good Hope"; pensioned; studied law with Gideon Granger, of Suffield, and with John Trumbull; judge Superior Ct.; admitted to bar at Hartford, 1789, practiced at Suffield, 1790; dist. atty., 1806-29; rep. Gen. Assembly, Suffield; *m* 1788, Susan Kent (1768-1839; Maj. Elihu[5]; Samuel[6]; John[7]; Samuel[8]; Thomas[9], qv);
3–Francis Junius (1802-78), engaged in publishing of musical books at Hartford, Conn., and later at New York City; *m* 1833, Stella Bradley Bull (1810-87; Michael[4]);
2–Archibald Dunbar (1851-1929), affiliated with Am. Brass & Copper Co.; *m* 1891, Alvina Nissen (*b* 1871); issue: I–Frederick William (1 above); II–Margaret Kent (*b* 1895).
1–*m* June 2, 1917, Martha Elizabeth Locke, *b* Toledo, O., Mar. 22, 1897; dau. of Charles Locke, of Toledo and Piqua, O., *m* Florence Edgerton Nelson.
1–Served in U.S.N., Feb. 16, 1909-May 5, 1909; pvt. and corpl. C.A.C., U.S.A., May 14, 1914-Dec. 1, 1916; 2d lt. inf., Dec. 2, 1916; 1st lt., Dec. 2, 1916; capt., June 5, 1917; temp. maj., Oct. 4, 1918, permanent maj. of inf., Dec. 14, 1927; served overseas in World War with 18th Inf., 1st Div., June 14, 1917-July 5, 1919; comd. 2d Bn., 18th Inf. during St. Mihiel and Meuse-Argonne battles; awarded French Croix de Guerre, May 10, 1918. Mem. O.F.P.A., Soc. Founders of Norwich, Conn., S.A.R., Huntington Family Assn., I.A.G., Columbus Geneal. Soc. (sec.), Nat. Soc. of Scabbard and Blade (hon.), Soc. of the First Div. A.E.F., A.L. Mason. Episcopalian. Republican. Clubs: Army and Navy (Washington and Boston), Columbus Country, New England Chapter No. 12, National Sojourners. Address: 984 N. Nelson Rd., Columbus, O.

1–**HUNTON, Virginia Semmes Payne (Mrs. Eppa, Jr.),** *b* Warrenton, Va., Feb. 23, 1867.
8–John **Payne** (1612-73), from Eng. to Va., 1619, in the second supply of Gov. Yeardley; *m* Margaret–;
7–Richard (1633-96), of "Round Tree," Northumberland Co., Va.; *m* Millicent–;
6–John (1679-1760), of "The Elms," Lancaster Co., Va.; *m* Jeanne Monroe (kinswoman of James Monroe);
5–George (1716-1790 or 93), of "Red Hill," Westmoreland Co., Va.; *m* 1740, Frances (Fannie) Susannah Stone;
4–Capt. William (1755-1837), grad. Coll. of William and Mary; received a grant of 5,000 acres in Bowling Green, Ky.; cdr. of "Falmouth Blues," which he equipped at his own expense, served at Yorktown; *m* 1779, Susannah Richards; *m* 2d, 1801, Marion Andre Morson;
3–Arthur Alexander Morson (1804-68), *m* 1829, Mary Conway Mason Fitz Hugh;
2–William Henry Fitz Hugh (2 below).
9–Col. John **Washington** (qv);
8–Laurence (ca. 1661-1697), *m* 1690, Mildred Warner (Col. Augustine[9], qv);
7–Augustine (1694-1743), of "Wakefield," Westmoreland, Co.; *m* 1715, Jane Butler (1699-1728; Caleb[8]); *m* 2d, 1731, Mary Ball (1706-89; mother of Gen. George Washington);
6–Col. Augustine (*b* 1720), of "Wakefield"; *m* 1743, Anne Aylett (Col. William[7]);
5–Anne Aylett (*b* 1753), *m* Col. Burdette **Ashton**;
4–Sarah Washington, *m* Judge Nicholas **Fitz Hugh**;
3–Mary Conway Mason, *m* Arthur Alexander Morson **Payne** (3 above);
2–William Henry Fitz Hugh (1830-1904), of "Clifton," Fauquier Co., Va.; ed. U.Mo., V.M.I., and U.Va.; lawyer; brig. gen. C.S.A., wounded 3 times, taken prisoner 3 times; *m* Sept. 1, 1852, his cousin, Mary Elizabeth Winston Payne (1831-1920); for issue and maternal lineage see Vol. I, p. 404.
1–*m* Apr. 24, 1901, Eppa Hunton, Jr. (see Vol. I, p. 403, for genealogy); issue: 1–Mary Winter (*b* and *d* July 5, 1902); 2–Eppa Hunton, IV, *b* Richmond, Va., July 31, 1904; grad. Chamberlayne's Sch., Richmond, Va., 1920; B.A., U.Va., '25 (Phi Delta Phi, D.K.E.), B.L., 1927, admitted Va. bar, 1926.
1–Ed. Fauquier Inst., Hochelaga French Convent (Montreal). Mem. C.D.A., U.D.C., Country Club of Va. Life mem. I.A.G. Residence: 810 W. Franklin St., Richmond, Va.

1–**HUNTOON, Gardner Appleton,** *b* Atlantic, Ia., Oct. 6, 1874.
7–Philip **Huntoon** (*b* 1664; son of Rev. Philip of Eng., eminent divine and author, 1st prevost Durham Coll.); came from Eng. to Exeter, N.H.;
6–John (ca. 1696-1778), of Kingston, N.H.; corpl. in Capt. Ladd's co., 1724; selectman, Kingston, 1740; *m* Mary Rundelette;
5–Ens. Benjamin (*b* 1744), of Kingston; ens. in navy; his children were under James Tappan, sch. master, with Daniel Webster; *m* 1764, Deliverance Goss (*b* 1744);
4–Joseph (1767-1854), of Kingston; *m* Betsey Glidden;
3–Mason (*b* 1803), of Unity, N.H.; *m* 2d, Polly Chaffee;
2–Herman Mason (2 below).
8–Lawrence **Copeland** (*d* 1699 aet. 110), of Braintree, Mass.;
7–William (*b* 1656), of Braintree; *m* 1694, Mary (Webb) Bass (John[8], *m* 1657, Ruth, dau. of John Alden, Mayflower Pilgrim, qv);
6–Jonathan (*b* 1701-*d* aet. 90), *m* 1723, Betty Snell (Thomas[7]);
5–Dea. Joseph (*b* 1734), *m* 1760, Rebecca Hooper;
4–Winslow, settled in Acworth, N.H., 1804; *m* Hannah Slader;
3–Joseph, of Unity, N.H.; *m* Hannah Finlay (Robert[4], *m* Peggy Wallace; Samuel[5]; Joseph[6], from Ireland to Londonderry, N.H.; comd. vol. co. in Am. Rev., and in 1777, marched his co. to support of the Cont. Army at Saratoga);

2–Harriet (*b* 1855), *m* 1872, Herman Mason **Huntoon** (*b* 1852), of Des Moines, Ia.; with his brother Eli, built the first telegraph line thru Ia.; issue: I–Gardner Appleton (1 above); II–Gertrude Almeda (*m* 1898, Dr. Leslie M. Nourse); III–Edna May (*m* George Morris); IV–Mason (1884-1905); V–Harold Vincent (*b* 1895; *m* 1927, Helen McCall); VI–Raymond Copeland (*b* 1898; *m* 1922, Greta Howard).
1–*m* Sept. 2, 1896, Harriet Gesberg, *b* Iowa City, Ia., Feb. 23, 1874; dau. of Bernard Gesberg, from Germany to Iowa City; issue (all *b* Des Moines, Ia.): 1–Eloise, *b* Oct. 6, 1897; ed. Drake U.; *m* Dr. Clay Burkhardt, of Des Moines (issue: Royal); 2–Royal George, *b* Jan. 17, 1902; ed. Drake U.; *m* Patricia O'Bryan, of Lovilla, Ia. (issue: Georgann); 3–Genevieve, *b* May 26, 1912; ed. Drake U.
1–M.D., Ia. State U., '96, studied Berlin and Vienna. Physician since 1896 (see Who's Who in America). Clubs: Grant, Professional Men's (pres.), Des Moines Golf and Country. Christian. Republican. Residence: 1086 25th St., Des Moines, Ia.

1–**HUSTON, Charles Lukens**, *b* Coatesville, Pa., July 8, 1856.
3–Robert Mendenhall **Huston** (*b* Abingdon, Va., 1795-*d* Phila., 1864), dean, Jefferson Med. Coll., Phila., 1841-54; *m* Hannah West (g.niece Benjamin West 2d pres. of Royal Acadamy, historical painter to George IV);
2–Charles (2 below).
7–Jan (Lucken, Luckens) **Lukens** (qv);
6–William (1687/88-1739/40), *m* Elizabeth Tyson (1690-1765; Reynier[7], qv);
5–William (*d* 1803), *m* Elizabeth Pennington (*d* 1811);
4–David (1753-1831), mem. Phila. Co. militia, 1780; *m* Sarah Lloyd (1755-1834);
3–Dr. Charles (1786-1825), wrote name Lukens; manager Lukens Iron Works; *m* Rebecca Webb Pennock (1794-1854; Isaac[4], founder of the Brandywine [later Lukens] Iron Works);
2–Isabella Pennock (1822-89), *m* Dr. Charles **Huston** (1822-97), A.B., U.Pa., '40; M.D., Jefferson, 1843; pres. Lukens Iron & Steel Co. (for issue see Vol. I, p. 727).
1–*m* July 23, 1896, Annie Stewart (qv); issue (all *b* Coatesville, Pa.): 1–James Stewart, *b* May 9, 1898; Lehigh, '23; 1st class pvt., Am. Ambulance Service with 69th French Div., Sept. 1917-1919; Croix de Guerre (Ordre du Regiment) for special merit at Soissons, Aug. 1918; 2–Ruth, *b* Oct. 18, 1899; 3–Charles Lukens, Jr., *b* May 19, 1906.
1–A.B., Haverford, '75. V.p., works mgr. and chief engr. Lukens Steel Co. Mem. I.A.G. Summer place: Montrose, Pa. Residence: 64 S. 1st Av., Coatesville, Pa.

1–**HUSTON, Annie Stewart (Mrs. Charles L.)**, *b* Savannah, Ga.
6–Adam (Irick) **Eirich**, purchased a house in Savannah, Ga., 1763; described as "of Charlestown, in the Province of S.C., Planter"; obtained 1st of several crown grants of land in Ga., 1767;
5–Alexander, planter, Savannah; *m* Ruth Erwin (*b* 1754; Christopher[6], of Antrim Co., Ireland, *m* Ruth–), sister-in-law of Gov. Jared Irwin, of Ga.;
4–Ruth, *m* 1807, Francis Harvey **Welman**, cotton mcht., Savannah, Ga. (Capt. Samuel[5], of Warwick Parish, Bermuda, *m* Margaret Harvey), bro.-in-law of Dr. James Muir, chaplain George Washington's Masonic Lodge;
3–Ruth, *m* 1829, John Hope **Reid**, cotton mcht., Savannah (William[4], of Creich Parish, Fifeshire, Scotland, *m* Elizabeth Meldrum);
2–Elizabeth Meldrum, *m* 1860, James Turner **Stewart**, cotton mcht., Savannah; maj., Gen. H. W. Mercer's staff, C.S.A. (Andrew[3], mcht. ship owner, Greenock, Scotland, *m* Ann MacGregor, of the Glenglye family; Roger[4], of "Stewardfield" [now Ronachan], Kintyre, Scotland).
1–*m* July 23, 1896, Charles Lukens Huston (qv for issue).
Residence: 64 S. 1st Av., Coatesvile, Pa.

1–**IDOL, Pearl**, *b* Jamestown, N.C., Dec. 14, 1876.
5–Barnett **Idol** (ca. 1735-1786), from Germany in the "St. Andrew," 1752, settled in Bucks Co., Pa.; served in Am. Rev.; *m* ca. 1760, Elizabeth Meier (*d* 1798), from Switzerland to Pa. (Conrad[6]);
4–Barnett (1777-1861), of Rowan Co., N.C.; *m* 1802, Jerusha Shields (see Vol. III, p. 253);
3–Barnett Madison (1814-88), of Rowan Co.; *m* 1840, Rebecca Hussey;
2–William Hussey (2 below).
9–Christopher **Hussey** (qv);
8–John (1635-1711), *m* 1659, Rebecca Perkins (Isaac[9] [1611-95], of Ipswich, Mass., and Hampton, N.H., *m* Susannah–; John[10], qv);
7–John (1684-1770), of York Co., Pa.; *m* 1703, Ann Inskeep;
6–John (*d* 1781), to Orange Co. (now Guilford), N.C., 1759; *m* 1766, Mary Jessup (1740-1821; Thomas[7] [*d* 1783], *m* Sarah–, *d* 1757);
5–Stephen (1776-1843), of Guilford Co.; *m* Rebecca Brown (*d* 1867; William[6] [*d* 1794], Am. Rev., *m* Mary, dau. of William Gray [*d* 1794], Am. Rev.);
4–William (1801-55), Guilford Co.; *m* 1820, Beulah Hunt;
3–Rebecca (1821-1910), Guilford Co.; *m* Barnett M. **Idol** (3 above).
9–William **Woolman** (*d* 1682), from Eng. to Burlington, N.J., 1678;
8–John (1655-1718), came with his father; *m* 1684, Elizabeth Borton (*d* 1718; John[9], from Eng. to N.J., 1679, *m* Ann–);
7–Mary (*b* 1692), of Burlington Co., N.J.; *m* 1720, William **Hunt** (*d* 1745);
6–William (1733-72), Orange Co., N.C., 1752; minister Soc. of Friends; *d* in Eng. while there on a religious visit; *m* 1753, Sarah Mills;
5–Eleazor (1762-1840), of Guilford Co.; in Am. Rev.; *m* 1782, Lydia Worley (1759-1832; Henry[6], *m* Rachel–);
4–Beulah (1792-1857), of Guilford Co.; *m* William **Hussey** (4 above).
9–William **Clayton** (qv);
8–Mary, *m* 1682, John **Beals** (Thomas[9], *m* Sarah, dau. of John Edge);
7–Sarah (1713-1800), *m* John **Mills** (1712-94), Am. Rev.; from Frederick Co., Va., to Orange Co. (now Guilford), N.C. (John[8], from Eng.);
6–Sarah (*d* 1778), of Guilford Co.; *m* William **Hunt** (6 above).
5–William **Raper** (1725-95), from Eng., 1754; settled in Rowan Co., N.C., 1755; served in Am. Rev.; *m* 2d, 1770, Rebecca Simmons (William[6], *d* 1772);
4–William (1771-1859), of Guilford Co.; *m* Keziah Davis (1775-1851; William[5] [*d* 1799], Am. Rev., *m* Elizabeth– *d* 1818);
3–Austin (1810-76), Guilford Co.; *m* 1852, Martha Motsinger;
2–Louisa (2 below).
7–Jacob **Motsinger** (*b* 1700), from Germany, 1735, settled in Pa.;
6–Felix (1727-91), removed from Pa. to Rowan Co., N.C., 1776; served in Am. Rev.;
5–Daniel, *m* Dianna Winkler (Adam[6] [*d* 1799], *m* Catherine–);
4–Adam (1790-1864), of Rowan Co.; *m* 1814, Mary Idol;
3–Martha (1822-82), *m* Austin **Raper** (3 above).
6–Barnett **Idol**, 5 above;
5–Jacob (1761-1851), to Rowan Co., 1776; pvt. in Am. Rev.; *m* 1782, Chloe Johnson (1759-1859; Henry[6] [*d* 1809], from Va. to Stokes Co., N.C., 1778, in Am. Rev.);
4–Mary (1793-1873), of Stokes Co., N.C.; *m* Adam **Motsinger** (4 above);
3–Martha, *m* Austin **Raper** (3 above);
2–Louisa (*b* 1853), *m* 1875, William Hussey **Idol** (1847-May 20, 1930), of High Point, N.C.; issue: I–Pearl (1 above); II–William Chase (*b* 1879; *m* Ruth Siewers); III–Marvin Raper (1881-84); IV–John Blake (1884-87).
1–Mem. D.A.C., D.A.R. Baptist. Residence: 409 W. High St., High Point, N.C.

1–**INGHAM, Robert Maxwell**, *b* Phila., Pa., Dec. 13, 1881.
9–Edward **Howell** (qv);
8–Richard (bap. 1629-1700), *m* 1st, Elizabeth Halsey (Thomas[9]);
7–Hezekiah (1677-1744), *m* Phoebe Halsey (1671-1732);
6–Jedediah (1713-95), *m* Elizabeth Gould;
5–Dr. Ebenezer (1748-91), *m* Lydia Tuckness;
4–Mary Clarissa (1790-1822), *m* Col. John **Sinnickson** (1789-1862; Col. Andrew[6] [1749-1819], *m* Margaret [1756-92], dau. of Robert Johnson, 1727-96);

3–Harriet Howell (1814-77), *m* Jonathan **Ingham** (1814-83), see Vol. I, p. 139, for Ingham lineage;
2–William Henry (2 below).
6–John **Maxwell** (1701-86), from Ireland to Sussex (now Warren) Co., N.J., 1747, with his wife and children; *m* Ann– (1712-90), their son William was brig. gen. Cont. Army;
5–John (1739-1828), capt. Am. Rev.; *m* Mary Ann Clifford (1744-1804);
4–William (1785-1828), lawyer; *m* Sarah Dusenbery (1795-1866);
3–John (1816-1883 or 84), *m* Elizabeth Green Clark;
2–Mary Ellen (1844-1917), *m* William Henry **Ingham** (1844-1903), B.A., Yale, '67; coal mcht., Phila.; issue: I–Elizabeth Howell; II–Harriet Clifford; III–Howard Maxwell (1877-1922; *m* Augusta Pemberton Keller); IV–Robert M. (1 above).
1–*m* June 12, 1907, Mary Rosalia Bushnell, *b* Bradford, Pa., dau. Nathan Bushnell, New Haven, Conn.; issue: 1–Robert Maxwell, Jr., *b* Englewood, N.J., Oct. 12, 1908; 2–Rosalia Bushnell, *b* Englewood, Apr. 17, 1916.
1–Ph.B., Yale-S., '03. Civil engr. In service constrn. div., U.S.A., World War. Residence: 163 Sherwood Pl., Englewood, N.J.

1–**INGLES, Mary Frances Burris (Mrs. Thomas Smith),** *b* Havelock, Neb., May 6, 1894.
11–Gov. William **Bradford,** Mayflower Pilgrim (qv);
10–William (1624-1703), dep. gov. Mass.; *m* 1st, 1650, Alice Richards (1627-71);
9–Thomas (1657-1708), *m* Anna Smith (Nehemiah[10], *m* Elizabeth Bourne);
8–James (1689-1762), of Canterbury, Conn.; *m* Susanna Adams (1693-1753);
7–William (1718-86), *m* Mary Cleveland (1720-65);
6–John (1750-1827), *m* 1773, Elizabeth Bond (1755-1822);
5–Alice (1777-1812), *m* 1799, James **Adams** (1775-1857);
4–William B. (1808-73), *m* 1837, Mary Ann Knight (1809-71);
3–William K. (1841-1925), *m* 1866, Mary A. Bradley (*d* 1875);
2–Hattie Elizabeth (*b* 1870), *m* 1890, Erastus Booth **Burris** (1868-1911), r.r. master mech.; issue: I–William K. (*b* 1891; *m* Gertrude E. McCollough; *m* 2d, Esther E. Reck); II–Mary Frances (1 above).
1–*m* Feb. 28, 1916, Thomas Smith Ingles, *b* Decatur, Mich., Jan. 27, 1873; son of Robert G. Ingles, of Kansas City, Mo.; issue (all *b* Lincoln, Neb.): 1–Catharine Elizabeth, *b* Jan. 1, 1917; 2–Mary Frances, *b* May 25, 1918; 3–Thomas Burris, *b* Mar. 2, 1920; 4–William Shull, *b* Nov. 3, 1923; 5–Harriet Ann, *b* Feb. 14, 1925.
1–Residence: 2029 South St., Lincoln, Neb.

1–**ISHAM, Mary Keyt,** *b* Cincinnati, Ohio, Aug. 20, 1871.
7–John **Isham** (qv);
6–Isaac (*b* 1683), of Barnstable; *m* 1716, Thankful Limbert;
5–Daniel (*b* 1729), of Barnstable; *m* 1756, Katherine Foot;
4–Asa (*b* 1769), of Colchester, Conn., and Barnstable, Mass.; *m* 1794, Sarah Chapman, of E. Haddam, Conn.;
3–Chapman (1814-92), *m* 1838, Mary Ann Faulkner (1823-73);
2–Asa Brainerd (2 below).
7–Edward **Penn** (son of Adm. Penn, of Eng., and bro. of William, founder of Pa.), from Eng., settled nr. Harper's Ferry, Md., 1700; *m* —Taylor, of Quaker descent;
6–Benjamin (1739-1834), *m* Mary Sargent (1755-1817);
5–Rebecca (1783-1864), *m* 1801, William **Thrasher** (1776-1812);
4–Mary Ann, *m* Nathan **Keyt**;
3–Alonzo Thrasher, M.D. (1827-85), *m* Susannah Dorcas Hamlin;
2–Mary Hamlin (2 below).
10–James **Hamlin** (qv);
9–James (1636-1718), came to America prior 1642 with mother and sisters; *m* 1662, Mary Dunham (*b* 1642; John[10] [1613-92], of Middleborough, Mass.; *m* Mary–; Dea. John[11], qv);
8–Eleazer (1668-98), of Yarmouth, Mass.; *m* Lydia Sears (*b* 1666; Paul[9], *m* Deborah Willard);
7–Benjamin (*b* 1692), *m* 1716, Anne Mayo (Samuel[8]; Nathaniel[9], *m* Hannah Prence [Thomas[10], *m* Patience, dau. of William Brewster[11], qv]; Rev. John[10]);
6–Maj. Eleazer (1732-1807), in Am. Rev.; *m* 1st, Lydia Bonney (*d* 1769), of Pembroke, Mass.;
5–Europe (1759-1820), Hillsboro, N.H.; pvt. Am. Rev.; *m* 2d, Sarah Hale (*b* 1763);
4–Hannibal Gilman (1800-64), Cincinnati, O.; architect and builder; *m* 1825, Mary Tichnor Whitney;
3–Susannah Dorcas (1827-1904), *m* 1848, Alonzo Thrasher **Keyt**, M.D. (3 above).
11–John **Whitney** (qv);
10–Joshua (1635-1719), dea.; original propr. Groton, Mass.; in King Philip's War; selectman several times; *m* 3d, 1672, Abigail Tarbell;
9–William (1678-1754), to Plainfield, Conn., ca. 1700; *m* 1700, Lydia Perham (1673-1716);
8–William (*b* 1701), *m* 1723, Mary Whittemore;
7–William (*b* 1725), of Killingly, Conn.; *m* 1st, 1747, Arcoucher Dutcher (Christopher[8]);
6–Christopher (*b* 1751), received land grant, Solon, Cortland Co., N.Y.; soldier in Am. Rev.;
5–Ruluff (1777-1846), justice of peace, 1817; removed to Portsmouth, O., 1821; *m* 1800, Susanna Glenny (John[6], of Dryden, N.Y.);
4–Mary Tichnor (1803-80), *m* Hannibal Gilman **Hamlin** (4 above);
3–Susannah Dorcas, *m* Alonzo Thrasher **Keyt,** M.D. (3 above);
2–Mary Hamlin (1850-1929), *m* 1870, Asa Brainerd **Isham** (1844-1912), M.D., Med. College, of Ohio, 1869; (hon. A.M., Marietta Coll., 1889); enlisted pvt., 7th Mich. Cav., 1862; promoted sgt., Co. I.; severely wounded in action nr. Warrenton Junction, Va., May 14, 1863; promoted 1st lt., Mar. 21, 1864; slightly wounded and captured, Yellow Tavern, Va., May 11, 1864; prisoner 7 months; paroled for exchange, Dec. 11, 1864; hon. discharged on account of wound received in action Apr. 14, 1865; author (see Who's Who in America, Vol. VII); issue: I–Mary Keyt (1 above); II–Asa Chapman (*b* 1873; *m* Mary Elizabeth Swing); III–Susanna Hamlin (*b* 1875; *m* Richard Conkling Swing); IV–Alonzo Keyt (*b* 1877; *m* Lucy Grace Henderson); V–Frances (*b* 1880; *m* James Wilson Brown); VI–Helen (*b* 1882; *m* Edward Coburn Kirkpatrick); VII–Elinor Louise (*b* 1885; *m* Frank Pearce Atkins).
1–A.B., Wellesley, '94, M.A., U. of Cincinnati, 1898; U. of Chicago, 1898-99; Bryn Mawr, 1899-1900; M.D., Laura Memorial Med. Coll. (later absorbed into med. dept. U. of Cincinnati), 1903. Gave first course in psychology ever given at a med. coll., 1901-03; interne, Presbyn. Hosp., Cincinnati, 1903-04; gen. practice Cincinnati, 1904-09; mem. staff Columbus (O.) State Hosp., 1908-15; settled in N.Y. City, 1915; author (see Who's Who in America). Presbyterian. Republican. Mem. A.A.U.W. Clubs: Wellesley, Women's Univ. Residence: 34 The Clermont, 1406 E. McMillan St., Cincinnati, O.

1–**IVES, Sarah Noble,** *b* Grosse Ile, Mich., Mar. 10, 1864.
8–William **Ives** (qv);
7–John (1644-89), of Wallingford, Conn.; *m* Hannah Merriman (*b* 1653; Nathaniel[8], qv);
6–Gideon (1680-1767), *m* 1706, Mary Royce; *m* 2d, Elizabeth–;
5–Joel (1723-95), *m* Rebecca Merriman; *m* 2d, Experience Royce;
4–Joel (1760-1808), in Am. Rev., aet. 16;
3–Butler (1783-1846), Sheffield, Mass.; *m* 1807, Olive Hall Morse (*b* 1788);
2–William (2 below).
8–William **Hyde** (qv);
7–Samuel (1636-77), prob. Hartford, Conn.; *m* 1659, Jane Lee;
6–Samuel (ca. 1665-1742), of West Farms, Windham and Lebanon, Conn.; one of 1st town officers of Windham; *m* 1690, Elizabeth Calkins;
5–Elijah (*b* 1705), of Lebanon; *m* 1st, 1730, Ruth Tracy;
4–Moses (1751-1828), Livonia, N.Y.; *m* 1787, Sarah Dana (Anderson[6], massacred by Indians, in Wyoming Valley, Pa., 1778, his family escaped, returned through forest to Ashford, Conn.);
3–Milton (1797-1866), *m* 1821, Harriet Albina Edson;
2–Sarah Maria (2 below).

9–John **Alden,** Mayflower Pilgrim (qv);
8–Joseph (1627-97), of Duxbury, Mass.; *m* 1657, Mary Simmons, of Bridgewater, Mass.;
7–Joseph (1667-1749), *m* 1690, Hannah Dunham (*d* 1748);
6–Mary (1699-1782), of Bridgewater; *m* 1719, Timothy **Edson** (1694-1782; Joseph[7]; Samuel[8], qv);
5–Timothy (1722-67), of Stafford, Conn.; *m* Lydia Joy (1725-1806);
4–Sgt. Josiah (1758-1819), Randolph, Vt., 1781; in Am. Rev., 1777, corpl., 1778, sgt., 1779, hon. disch., 1780; *m* 1779, Sarah Pinney (1756-1805);
3–Harriet Albina (1797-1879), of Randolph, Vt.; *m* Milton **Hyde** (3 above).
2–William **Ives** (1817-74), of Sheffield, Mass.; first govt. surveying party, to lay base and meridian lines in Washington and Oregon territories, 1851-52; also first to survey Isle Royale, Mich.; *m* 1853, Sarah Maria Hyde (1828-64); *m* 2d, 1866, Lydia E. Hyde; issue (1st marriage): I–Mary Emma (1854-86; *m* 1881, John G. Cobb); II–Harriet Lavinia (*b* 1856; *m* 1881, Charles P. Gilchrist); III–Florence Lois (*b* 1861); IV–Sarah Noble (1 above); issue (2d marriage): I–Julia Margaret (*b* 1867); II–Zayde Louise (*b* 1872).
1–Grad. Detroit Training Sch. of Elocution and Eng. Lit.; studied art in New York 2 yrs., in Paris 3 yrs. Landscape painter; also contributor and illustrator, McClure Newspaper Syndicate, N.Y. Herald-Tribune; author (see Who's Who in America). Universalist. Republican. Clubs: Altadena Woman's, etc. Residence: 1094 E. Mariposa St., Altadena, Calif.

1–**MALUGE, Grace Elizabeth Ives (Mrs. William A.),** *b* Rubicon, Wis., Aug. 30, 1886.
9–George **Pardee** (qv);
8–George (1656-1723), of New Haven, Conn.; *m* 2d, 1686, Mercy Denison (1668-1757; James[9], *m* Bethia, dau. of Sgt. Jarvis Boykin);
7–George (bap. 1690-1763), *m* Sarah Bradley (*d* post 1763; Isaac[8] [post 1650-*d* East Haven, 1713], *m* Elizabeth–, post 1656-1713);
6–Jacob (1727-1807), of East Haven, Conn.; *m* Mary Hemingway;
5–Abijah (1753-1832), during Tryon's invasion, July 1779, Gen. Tryon made his house the British hdqrs., and burned it when he left; wounded in the arm by a ball from the British, while on guard duty, Am. Rev.; *m* 1777, Rosanna Moulthrop (1761-1844);
4–Isaac Holt (1781-1822), *m* 1806, Sally Hotchkiss (1781-1838);
3–Elizabeth M. (1820-1907), from East Haven, Conn., to Rubicon, Wis.; *m* William A. **Ives**;
2–George Washington (2 below).
10–Ralph **Hemingway** (qv);
9–Samuel (*b* Roxbury, Mass., 1636-1711), settled at East Haven, Conn., 1660; clk. town records; famous for his beautiful chirography; *m* 1662, Sarah Cooper (John[10], magistrate), their son Jacob was 1st student Yale, B.A., 1704;
8–John (1675-1737), *m* Mary Morris (1673-1743), g.parents of Pres. Rutherford B. Hayes;
7–Samuel (1713-77), *m* 1733, Mehitable Denison (1713-82);
6–Mary (1737-1802), *m* Jacob **Pardee** (7 above).
2–George Washington **Ives** (*b* 1860), *m* Oct. 10, 1883, Fannie Elizabeth Smith (Aug. 5, 1865-Dec. 31, 1901; Henry Westlake[3], sgt. U.S.V., Civil War, *m* Julia A. M. Warren [see Vol. II, p. 90, for Warren lineage]; Rowland C.[4] [1814-56], *m* 1836, Margaret Westlake [1815-96]; Capt. Nathaniel[5] [1788-1864], *m* 1812, Mary [1795-1901], dau. of Caleb Bentley, capt. Am. Rev.; Capt. William[6], *m* Mary Walker); issue: I–Prof. Frederick Walter (1884-1924; *m* Mary A. Parks); II–Grace E. (1 above); III–William Lovell (qv for other lineages); IV–Carrie Nell (*b* 1889; *m* William Carpenter); V–George Smith (*b* 1891; *m* Katherine Sherek); VI–Clifford Elihu (qv for other lineages); VII–Sarah Rosemond (*b* 1897; *m* Homer G. Spry); VIII–Irene Edna (*b* 1900; *m* Hillyer Estes).
1–*m* Apr. 7, 1904, William August Albert Maluge, *b* Wilton, Wis., Apr. 22, 1877; son of Carl Maluge, of Wilton, *m* Mary Ann Battalia; issue: 1–Charlotte Musetta, *b* Granton, Wis., July 30, 1906; 2–Ruth Eloise, *b* Marshfield, Wis., Mar. 1, 1913; 3–Grace Virginia, *b* Marshfield, Jan. 15, 1920.
1–Pupil School of Applied Art, Battle Creek, Mich., and Fireside Industries, Adrian, Mich. Compiling genealogy of Ives, Smith, Warren and Pardee families. Mem. S.M.D., I.A.G. Residence: 301 N. Peach St., Marshfield, Wis.

1–**IVES, William Lovell,** *b* Rubicon, Wis., Jan. 21, 1888.
10–"Mr." Nathaniel **Turner** (lost on "Phantom Ship," 1647), a founder of Colony of Mass. Bay, 1630; Pequot War, 1637; an original propr. of New Haven, 1639; dep. Gen. Ct.; capt. New Haven Colony troops; commr. United Colonies;
9–Mary, *m* "Mr." Thomas **Yale** (qv);
8–Mary (*b* 1650), *m* 1672, Joseph **Ives** (1648-94; William[9], qv);
7–Samuel (1677-1726), dea. North Haven Congl. Ch., 1718-26; *m* 1705, Ruth Atwater;
6–Samuel (1711-84), *m* 1744, Mary Gilbert (1717-post 1792; Joseph[7]; "Mr." Matthew[8]);
5–Dr. Levi (1750-1826), surgeon's mate in Am. Rev.; *m* 1772, Lydia Augur;
4–Elihu (1777-1849), *m* 1804, Lucy Whittemore (1781-1848);
3–William Augustus (1809-86), *m* 1842, Elizabeth Maria Pardee;
2–George Washington (2 below).
10–William **Peck** (ca. 1604-1694), from Eng., arrived Boston, 1637; a founder of New Haven Colony, 1638; merchant; *m* in London, ca. 1622, Elizabeth– (*d* 1683);
9–Rev. Jeremiah (1623-99), from Eng.; grad. Harvard; 1st rector Hopkins Grammar Sch., New Haven; 1st settled minister, Greenwich, Conn., 1678; *m* 1656, Joanna Kitchell (*d* 1711; Robert[10], qv);
8–Ruth (*b* 1661), *m* 1681, Jonathan **Atwater** (1656-1726; David[9], qv);
7–Ruth (1688-1758), *m* Samuel **Ives** (7 above).
8–Robert **Augur** (*b* in Eng.; son of John, *m* Ann–), of New Haven; *m* 1673, Mary Guilbert (1651-1731; Dep.Gov. Mathew[9], *m* Jane–);
7–John (1686-1726), shoemaker; *m* 1710, Elizabeth Bradley (Isaac[8] [*d* 1713], from Eng., 1st settled at East Haven, 1683, *m* 1674, Elizabeth–, *d* 1713).
6–Abraham (1724-98), *m* 1746, Elizabeth Bradley (1725-64);
5–Lydia (1753-1802), *m* Dr. Levi **Ives** (5 above).
2–George Washington **Ives** (*b* Oct. 2, 1860), *m* 1883, Fannie Elizabeth Smith (1865-1901); for issue and other lineages see Mrs. William A. Maluge.
1–*m* Apr. 15, 1914, Alma Beulow, *b* Jefferson, Wis., Oct. 9, 1893; dau. of Max Buelow; issue: 1–Fannie Emma Marie, *b* Jefferson, Wis., Feb. 12, 1921.
1–U.Wis., 1908-09; spl. course in sheet metal drafting, Nat. Sch. of Pattern Drafting, St. Louis, Mo. Sheet metal worker. Residence: Jefferson, Wis.

1–**IVES, Clifford Elihu,** *b* 1894.
10–Matthew **Moulthrop** (*b* Eng.-*d* 1668), at New Haven, 1639; admitted 1st Ch., New Haven, ante 1644; *m* in Eng., Jane– (*d* 1672);
9–Matthew (*b* Eng.-*d* 1691), at East Haven, 1638; in King Philip's War; *m* 1662, Hannah Thompson (*d* 1713; John[10], *m* Eleanor–);
8–Sgt. John (1668-1713), served in Indian wars; *m* 1692, Abigail Bradley (1671-1743; Joseph[9] [*b* 1646], *m* 1667, Silence, dau. of John Brockett [*b* Eng., 1610-*d* Wallingford, Conn., 1690], came with Davenport and Eaton to New Haven, surgeon, war bet. Holland and Eng., 1654, laid out Elizabethtown, N.J., 1664, a founder Wallingford, 1667-70, dep., commr., signed Covenant, 1639);
7–John (1696-1757), *m* Sarah Tuttle (1699-1734);
6–John (*d* ante 1785), *m* Abigail Holt (1736-1828);
5–Rosanna (1761-1844), *m* Abijah **Pardee** (1753-1832);
4–Isaac Holt (1781-1822), *m* 1806, Sally Hotchkiss;
3–Elizabeth M. (1820-1907), *m* William A. **Ives**;
2–George Washington (2 below).
9–Samuel **Hotchkiss** (qv);
8–Samuel (ca. 1645-1705), King Philip's War; *m* 1679, Sarah Talmadge (*b* 1652; Robert[9], *m* Sarah Nash);
7–Samuel (1683-1740), *m* Hannah Russell;
6–Joseph (1725-76), *m* Esther Russell (1729-88);
5–Isaac (1757-1812), *m* 1775, Lydia Fields;
4–Sally (1781-1838), *m* Isaac H. **Pardee** (4 above);
3–Elizabeth M., *m* William A. **Ives** (3 above);
2–George Washington (*b* 1860), *m* 1883, Fannie Elizabeth Smith (1865-1901), for issue and

other lineages see Mrs. William A. Maluge.
1–*m* Oct. 25, 1924, Leta Faye Albin, *b* Newman, Ill., July 18, 1892; dau. of Alfred Chapman Albin, of Newman; issue: 1–Virginia May, *b* Chicago, Ill., Aug. 1, 1925; 2–Robert Warren, *b* Wilmette, Ill. (May 13, 1927-Dec. 26, 1928).
1–M.E., U.Wis., '19. Pres. Ives Engring Co., Chicago, 1921-29; development engr., U.S. Gypsum Co., 1929–. Builder of special and automatic machinery. Club: Middlebrook Country. Residence: 1630 Washington Av., Wilmette, Ill.

Arms: Per pale argent and sable, a chevron and in base a crescent all counterchanged.
Crest: A bear sejant erect proper.

1–**IVY, Marie Etta Bartley (Mrs. George W.)**, *b* Greene Co., Tenn., July 29, 1870.
5–William **Alexander** (1739-1828; parents emigrated from Northern Ireland before early 1700's), was of Pa.; went to N.C. before Am. Rev.; lt. and capt. N.C. troops, Am. Rev.: to Greene Co., Tenn., 1796, settled on plantation on Nolichucky River; *m* 1761, Elizabeth King (1737-1817);

WILLIAM HENRY BARTLEY (b Greene Co., Tenn., May 12, 1845-d Sept. 13, 1914); corpl., Co. C, 2d N.C. Mounted Inf. Vols., 1863-65; injured in service and pensioned.

4–Stephen King (*b* Randolph Co., N.C., 1778-*d* 1862), of Greene Co., Tenn.; *m* 1803, Sarah Kennedy (1788-1870; Daniel[5] [1750-1802], of N.C., Tenn., Va., served under four forms of govt., 1783-1802, col. Am. Rev., with John Sevier, and Gen. Brown at King's Mountain, made brig. gen., *m* his cousin, 1774, Margaret Kennedy [Hughes], 1752-1802);
3–William (1812-66), of Greene Co.; *m* 1834, Isabel Johnson (1814-88);
2–Iva Adaline (1852-1922), *m* 1st, 1868, William Henry **Bartley** (1845-1914), mcht. (see portrait); *m* 2d, 1918, Frank M. Foster; issue (1st marriage): I–Marie Etta (1 above); II–Franklin Edgar (*b* 1872; *m* Lena B. Thornburg).
1–*m* Nov. 27, 1890, George W. Ivy, *b* Hamblin Co., Tenn., Oct. 15, 1857; son of William Manson Ivy, of Hamblin Co.
1–Ed. Prof. Joseph G. McFerren's Pvt. Sch. Mem. D.A.R., I.A.G. Club: Ladies Reading Circle. Methodist. Residence: 226 Montvue Av., Morristown, Tenn.

Arms: Argent, a chevron gules, between three crosses crosslet fitchee sable.
Crest: A dolphin naiant proper.

1–**JACKSON, Arthur Henry**, *b* New Haven, Conn., Aug. 25, 1863.
8–Henry **Jackson** (*d* 1686), settled at Fairfield, Conn.;
7–Joseph (*d* 1681), *m* Mary Goodwin (George[8]);
6–Joseph (*d* 1714), of Stratfield; *m* 1699, Elizabeth Sanford (*b* 1679; Ezekiel[7], *m* Rebecca Whelpley);
5–Ephriam (1704-68), *m* 1730, Martha Blackman (*b* 1707; John[6]);
4–David (*b* 1736), served in Am. Rev.; settled at Greens Farms, Conn.; *m* 2d, Esther Ward (*b* 1764);
3–Henry (1797-1842), of Redding, Conn.; *m* 1825, Frances Stephenson (1808-53);
2–Henry Edwin (2 below).
9–John **Taylor** (*d* 1647), from Eng. in the "Arabella," with Gov. Winthrop 1630; settled at Windsor, Conn., 1639; sailed for Eng. in the "Phantom Ship," 1647, was lost at sea; *m* 1640, Rhoda–, a widow;
8–Capt. John (1641-1704), *m* Thankful Woodward (Dr. Henry[9], *m* Elizabeth–);
7–Lt. John (1667-1744), of Norwalk, Conn.; *m* Wait Clapp (1670-1722; Preserved[8], *m* Sarah Newberry; Roger[9], qv);
6–Josiah (1701-81), *m* 1729, Thankful French (Samuel[7], *m* Abigail Hubbell);
5–Abijah (*b* 1740), *m* Isabella Wiley;
4–Samuel, of Westport, Conn.; *m* 1805, Betsey Sherwood (1788-1880; Solomon[5], *m* Phebe Shute);
3–Solomon G., of Westport; *m* 1832, Elizabeth Jarvis (1808-84; Nathan[4], *m* Betsey Sandford);
2–Rhoda Ann (1833-1910), of Westport and New Haven, Conn.; *m* 1859, Henry Edwin **Jackson** (1830-1904); issue: I–Frances Elizabeth (Aug. 9, 1860-Oct. 12, 1901); II–Arthur Henry (1 above).
1–*m* May 16, 1893, Mary Candee Torbet (qv).

1–Yale-S, ex-'83. With Decater & Hopkins Co., Boston. Founded Gamma Delta Psi, high sch. fraternity. Mem. O.F.P.A., S.A.R. Episcopalian. Republican. Residence: 249 Park St., New Haven, Conn.

1–**JACKSON, Mary Candee Torbet (Mrs. Arthur H.),** *b* New Haven, Conn., Aug. 12, 1869.
7–William **Tomlinson** (1643-1711), settled at Derby, Conn.;
6–John (1686-1756), *m* 1712, Elizabeth Wooster; *m* 2d, Hannah Merwin (John[7], *m* Hannah Platt);
5–Isaac (1749-1817), *m* 1775, Mary Hawkins (1744-1818; Capt. Zachariah[6], *m* Mary Tomlinson);
4–Silas (1776-1829), of Oxford, Conn.; *m* Mary (Polly) Hawkins (1777-1842; Elijah[5], *m* Anna Davis);
3–Burke (1807-42), of Quakers Farms, Conn.; *m* 1840, Juliette Candee;
2–Lucie Candee (2 below).
8–Zacheus **Candee** (1640-1720), of New Haven; propr., 1685; *m* 1670, Rebeka (Bristol) Bristow (1650-1739; Henry Bristol[9]);
7–Capt. Samuel (1678-1748/49), of W. Haven; *m* 1703, Abigail Pineon (1680-1743; Thomas[8], *m* Mary–);
6–Caleb (1722-77), Oxford, Conn.; *m* 1743, Lois Mallory (1721-90; Daniel[7], *m* Abigail Trowbridge);
5–Caleb (1743-1828), in Am. Rev.; *m* 1764, Anna Sperry (1741-1817; Moses[6], *m* Anna Blakeslee);
4–Levi (1774-1847), *m* 1808, Lucy (Beers) Peck (1783-1861);
3–Juliette (1811-53), of Quakers Farms, Conn.; *m* Burke **Tomlinson** (3 above);
2–Lucie Candee (1840-1913), of New Haven; *m* 1868, James Ewings **Torbet** (1838-1911), *b* Paterson, N.J.
1–*m* May 16, 1893, Arthur Henry Jackson (qv).
1–Mem. D.F.P.A. (registrar Conn. chapter), D.C.W., D.A.R., New Haven Colony Hist. Soc. Club: New Haven Woman's. Residence: 249 Park St, New Haven, Conn.

1–**JACKSON, Maria Clopton (Mrs. Charles Samuel),** *b* Richmond, Va., Sept. 20, 1862.
8–Robert **Booth** (*d* 1657), of York Co., Va.; clk. of York co., 1640 et seq.; burgess, 1653,54; *m* Frances–;
7–Ann (1647-1716), *m* William **Clopton** (qv);
6–William (*d* 1733), *m* 1718, Joyce Wilkinson;
5–William (*b* 1721), of Hanover Co., Va.; *m* Elizabeth Darrall Ford;
4–John (1756-1816), Am. Rev.; *m* Sarah Bacon;
3–John Bacon (1789-1860), of "Roselyn," New Kent Co., Va.; ed. Coll. of William and Mary; in War 1812; mem. State Senate, 1822-30; mem. of convention, 1829-30; judge of Peninsular Ct., 1851-60; *m* 1820, Maria Gaitskill Foster;
2–Francis Bacon (1830-65), *m* 1858, Mary Boyd (1834-1910; James[3]); issue: I–Maria (1 above); II–Frank Boyd (*d* 1904).
1–*m* Mar. 9, 1886, Charles Samuel Jackson, *b* Va., Sept. 15, 1860 (see Who's Who in America, Vol. XIII); issue: 1–Frances Clopton, *b* Oct. 19, 1887; *m* Lilian Eva–; 2–Dorothea, *d*; 3–Philip L., *b* Oct. 18, 1893.
1–Ed. St. Helen's Hall, Portland. Mem. C.D.A., D.F.P.A., H.S.S.C., D.A.R., U.S.D. 1812. Residence: 610 Salmon St., Portland, Ore.

1–**JACKSON, Eva,** *b* Methuen, Mass., Feb. 20, 1860.
8–Nicholas **Jackson** (*d* 1697), from Eng. to Rowley, Mass., ante 1646; *m* 1646, Sarah Riley (*d* 1655);
7–Caleb (1652-1718), *m* Elizabeth Howe (James[8], *m* Elizabeth,– executed as a witch, Salem, Mass., July 19, 1692; James[9]);
6–Caleb (*b* 1687), *m* 1719, Mary Averill (*b* 1697; William[7]; William[8]; Nicholas[9]);
5–Dr. James (1721-91), Rochester, N.H.; *m* 1748, Mary Scripture (1730-1808; John[6]; Samuel[7]; Samuel[8]);
4–Samuel (1765-1848), Madison, N.H.; *m* 1784, Jane Gentilhomme (1764-1855);
3–Ebenezer (1791-1872), *m* 1812, Anna Flanders (*b* 1788);
2–James Churchill (2 below).
8–Hugh **March** (qv);
7–Lt. James (*b* 1663), *m* Mary Walker;
6–Benjamin (*b* 1690), *m* Elizabeth Small (*b* 1695);
5–James (1728-85), *m* Marjery Jones (bap. 1735);
4–Col. John (1777-1831), served in War 1812; *m* Abigail W. Hodgdon;
3–Mittie Sherburne (1814-92), *m* Artemus **Harmon** (1802-82);
2–Caroline March (1838-67), *m* 1859, James Churchill **Jackson** (1826-89); for issue and other lineages see Vol. I, p. 431.
1–Mem. D.A.R. Residence: 2106 F St., N.W., Washington, D.C.

1–**JACKSON, George Pullen,** *b* Monson, Me., Aug. 20, 1874.
9–Abraham **Jackson** (*d* 1714), from Eng. in the "Ann," aet. 13, 1623; settled at Plymouth; *m* 1657, Remember Morton (1637-1707);
8–Nathaniel (*b* ca. 1665), *m* 1686, Ruth Jenney (*b* ca. 1661);
7–Nathaniel (*b* ca. 1694), *m* Abigail Chipman;
6–Nathaniel (1716-68), of Middleboro, Mass.; *m* 1734, in Plympton, Patience Cole;
5–Barnabas (*b* Plympton, Mass., 1754-*d* Somerset Co., Me., 1819), of Middleboro; pvt. Am. Rev.; *m* 1775, Lydia Oldham;
4–Barnabas (bap. Pembroke, Mass., 1778-*d* Abbott, Me., 1840), *m* Mary– (1777-1840);
3–Daniel (*b* Paris, Me., 1814-*d* Monson, Me., 1899), *m* Lucy Cobb Pool;
2–George Frederick (2 below).
11–James **Chilton,** Mayflower Pilgrim (qv);
10–Mary (*d* 1679), called the "Mayflower orphan"; *m* 1627, John **Winslow** (qv);
9–Susanna, *m* Robert **Latham** (*d* 1688), constable at Marshfield, Mass., 1643;
8–James, *m* Deliverance, Alger;
7–Joseph, *m* 1717, Sarah Hayward;
6–Thomas, *m* 1752, at Bridgewater, Abigail Hanmer;
5–Lucinda (*b* Bridgewater, Mass., 1767), *m* 1783, Joshua **Pool** (*b* 1762), pvt. Am. Rev.;
4–Thomas (*b* Bridgewater, 1787-*d* Monson, Me., 1883), *m* Lydia Cobb (*b* E. Carver, 1791-*d* Monson, 1870);
3–Lucy Cobb (*b* Norway, Me., 1814-*d* Abbott, Me., 1865), *m* Daniel **Jackson** (3 above).
7–Nicholas **Pullen,** *m* 1709, Mary Tucker;
6–James (*b* Rehoboth, Mass., 1720), *m* Lydia Woodcock;
5–James (1749-1829), pvt. Bunker Hill; *m* 1775, Phoebe Stanley;
4–Jonathan (*b* Attleboro, Mass., 1776-*d* Winthrop, Me., 1828), *m* 1800, Lucy Barrows;
3–Horace (*b* Winthrop, 1814-*d* Monson, Me., 1885), *m* 1841, Sophia Parker;
2–Ann Jane (*b* 1852), *m* 1872, George Frederick **Jackson** (*b* 1844), judge; retired mfr.; issue: I–Laura Ann (*b* 1873; *m* W. Irving Davids); II–George Pullen (1 above); III–Leta (1876-77); IV–Lena Sophia (*b* 1878; *m* 1909, Charles Fletcher Quillian, *b* 1883); V–Eloise M. (*b* 1880; *m* Charles H. Stoddard); VI–Leicester LeMont (*b* 1883; *m* Hazel Elliott); VII–Genevieve Lucy (*b* 1886; *m* Charles Spencer; *m* 2d, John Beckwith); VIII–Alpha June (*b* 1889; *m* Church Williams, *d* 1929); IX–Alberta Carol (*b* 1893; *m* Willis K. Ransom).
1–*m* Dec. 24, 1906, Inez Emeline Wright (Apr. 12, 1880-Dec. 23, 1918); dau. of Walter H. Wright (*d* 1928), of Wauwatosa, Wis.; issue: 1–Frances Helen, *b* Wauwatosa, Wis., Oct. 16, 1908; A.B., Birmingham-Southern Coll., '29; 2–George Irving, *b* Oberlin, O., Jan. 3, 1911.
1–*m* 2d, Dec. 18, 1926, Lois Diantha Barnes, *b* Nashville, Tenn., Nov. 15, 1891; dau. of Louis Corydon Mills, of Chattanooga, Tenn.
1–Student, Royal Conservatory of Music, Dresden, 1897-98; Vanderbilt U., 1900-01; Ph.B., U.-Chicago, 1904, Ph.D., 1911; post-grad. work U.Chicago, U.Munich, and U.Bonn. Prof. German, Vanderbilt U., since 1926. Pres. Univ. Philharmonic Soc., Grand Forks, N.D., 1913-18; founder 1920, and dir. (not conductor) and mgr. Nashville Symphony Orchestra; founder Nashville Choral Club. Author (see Who's Who in America). Clubs: Chicago Musicians', Fairyland Lookout Mountain, Fairyland Golf and Country (Chattanooga). Summer place: Lookout Mountain, Tenn. Address: Vanderbilt U., Nashville, Tenn.

1–**JACOB, Cary Franklin,** *b* Richmond, Va., Sept. 14, 1885.
10–William **Bradford,** Mayflower Pilgrim (qv);
9–Maj. William (1624-1704), *m* ca. 1652, Alice Richards;
8–Samuel (*b* 1668), lt.; *m* 1689, Hannah Rogers

(g.g.dau. Thomas Rogers, qv, and John Alden, qv);
7–Perez (*b* Duxbury, 1694-*d* 1746), *m* Abigail Belcher (*d* 1746), both buried in old burying ground in W. Attleboro;
6–Hannah (*b* 1723), *m* 1747, Jabez **Gay,** of Attleboro, soldier Am. Rev.;
5–Monica (*b* 1754), *m* 1776, Lt. Joseph **Baker,** of Dedham; soldier Am. Rev., as was his father;
4–Celia (1787-1854), of Dedham; *m* 1810, Ellis **Colburn,** of Dedham (g.son Jonathan Colburn, pensioner Am. Rev.);
3–Lucy Jane (*b* W. Dedham, Mass., 1824-*d* 1886), *m* Caleb **Jacob** (*b* Henrico Co., Va., 1822-*d* 1904); both buried Hollywood Cemetery, Richmond (John[4] [*b* 1790-*d* Henrico Co., 1863], *m* 1st, Virginia Mitchell, of Caroline Co., Va.);
2–John Franklin (2 below).
5–William **Sneed** (*d* 1836), of Albemarle Co., Va.; *m* Lucy Stevens;
4–Stapleton Crutchfield (1800-71), from Charlottesville to Bellevue, Nelson Co., Va.; *m* 1831, Elizabeth Nolan Craven (1811-73);
3–John Llewllyn (*b* Penn Park, nr. Charlottesville, 1837-*d* 1905), *m* Josephine Augustine Moore (1840-1906; Henry Carter[4], to Albemarle Co., *m* his cousin, Eliza Royster, dau. of Stephen Moore, *m* Mary Royster, of Charles City, Va.; Joseph[5], of "Poplar Grove," Orange Co., N.C. [brother Stephen, above]; maj. Am. Rev., *m* 2d, Elizabeth Sheppard, sister Augustin H. Sheppard, served over 20 yrs. in U.S. Congress);
2–Henrietta Moore (*b* Bellevue [Sneed plantation], nr. Arrington, Nelson Co., Va., 1863), *m* John Franklin **Jacob** (*b* Richmond, Va., 1852), retired commn. mcht.; issue: I–Cary F. (1 above); II–Lucy Jane (1886-90); III–Herbert Alwyn (*b* 1887; *m* Mary Shreckhise); IV–John Caleb (1890-94).
1–Not married. B.S., U.Va., '12 (Delta Phi, P.-B.K., Pi Gamma Mu, Theta Gamma, Phi Kappa Phi), M.S., 1916, Ph.D., 1917. Asso. prof. spoken English, Smith Coll., since 1927. Author and lecturer (see Who's Who in America). Democrat. Clubs: U. of Va. (New York), Farmington Country (Charlottesville, Va.). Residence: 10 West St., Northampton, Mass.

1–**JACOBS, Henry Eyster,** *b* Gettysburg, Pa., Nov. 10, 1844.
4–Martin (Jacob) **Jacobs** (1731-1803), from Alsace, 1753, settled in Frederick Co., Md.; removed to Washington Co. nr. Jacobs Church, so named from his gift of a tract of land for a church and school; *m* Barbara Musselman; *m* 2d, Anna B. Fehl;
3–Henry (1764-1821), began to write name Jacobs; of nr. Franklin Co., Pa.; *m* Anna Maria Miller (1770-1809; Henry[4] [1725-1817], of Washington Tp., Franklin Co., *m* Elizabeth [1742-1817], dau. of John Adam Heilman [1715-70], native of Germany);
2–Michael (2 below).
7–John Jacob **Eyster,** from Württemberg, Germany, 1717, settled at Oley, Berks Co., Pa.;
6–Christian, settled nr. York, Pa., 1739; *m* 1733, Margaretta Schmeiser;
5–Elias (1734-1829), of Oley, Pa.; *m* Maria Menken Lau (*d* 1811);
4–George (1757-1836), of York Co.; soldier Am. Rev., captured at Fort Washington, and one of the few survivors of the prison-ship "Jersey"; *m* 1780, Mary Magdalene Slagle (1763-1807);
3–Jacob (1782-1859), to Harrisburg, Pa.; sgt. and q.m., 93d Regt., Pa. Militia, 1800, col., 1811, brig. gen. 5th Div., 1814-21; state senator, 1818-22; *m* 1810, Mary Middlekauff (1792-1867);
2–Julianna M. (1811-92), *m* 1833, Michael **Jacobs** (1808-71), A.B., Jefferson, '28, of Gettysburg, Pa.; D.D., Jefferson Coll., and Wittenberg Coll., Springfield, O., 1858; a founder of Pa. Coll., Gettysburg, 1832; prof. mathematics, 1829-66, mathematics and natural science, 1832-65; issue: I–Henry Eyster (1 above); II–Mary Julia (*b* 1846; *m* John H. Harpster); III–Michael William (*b* 1850; *m* Romaine Merkel); IV–George Edward (*b* 1854; *m* Mary Arnold).
1–*m* July 3, 1872, Laura Hewes Downing, *b* Baltimore, Md., Nov. 21, 1852; dau. George F. Downing (William[3]; Richard[4] [1750-1826]; Richard[5] [1719-1804]; Thomas[6] [*b* Eng., 1691], after whom Downington, Pa., was named); issue: 1–Eugenia Anna (1873-77); 2–Charles Michael, *b* Gettysburg, Pa., Dec. 5, 1875; A.B., U.Pa., '95; grad. Lutheran Theol. Sem., Phila., 1899; studied U.Pa. and U.Leipzig; (D.D., Muhlenberg, 1913, LL.D., 1929; L.H.D., Augustana, 1929); pastor 1899-1913; prof. ch. history and dir. grad. sch., Lutheran Theol. Sem., since 1913, pres. since 1927 (see Who's Who in America); *m* Oct. 5, 1905, Abigail, dau. of Abel K. Shearer (issue: Margaret Abigail; Hilda Elinor; Charles Shearer); 3–Henry Downing, *b* Gettysburg, Dec. 29, 1877; A.B., U.Pa., '99; *m* Nov. 25, 1908, Leonebel Kays; 4–Laura Winifred, *b* Gettysburg, Sept. 3, 1883; *m* June 18, 1907, Luther K., son of Abel K. Shearer (issue: Helen Jacobs; Winifred; Elizabeth Downing); 5–Marguerite Eyster, *b* Phila., Pa., Oct. 8, 1897; *m* June 30, 1908, William M., son of Rev. Dr. Edward T. Horn (issue: Edward T.; Ruth M.; William M.; Henry E.; John C.; Robert T.; Marguerite E.; James G.).
1–A.B., Pa. Coll., '62 (Phi Gamma Delta, P.B.K.), A.M., 1865; grad. Lutheran Theol. Sem., Gettysburg, 1865 (D.D., 1877; L.L.D., Thiel Coll., 1892; S.T.D., Muhlenburg, 1907). Prof. systematic theology, Lutheran Theol. Sem., since 1883. Author (see Who's Who in America). Mem. Am. Hist. Assn., Pa. Hist. Soc. Republican. Residence: Mt. Airy, Philadelphia, Pa.

1–**JACOBY, Henry Sylvester,** *b* nr. Springtown, Pa., Apr. 8, 1857.
6–Peter (Jacobi) **Jacoby** (*d* 1761), from Germany, 1741, settled in Bucks Co., Pa., later in Haycock Tp.; *m* Maria Elizabeth Heuer (*d* 1790);
5–Conrad (1730-95), of Bucks Co., and Springfield, Durham and Bedminster Tps.; *m* 1755, Hannah Riegel (1729-1828; Matthias[6], came to America, 1732, *m* 1st, Maria–);
4–Peter (1759-1815), of Durham Tp., Bucks Co.; *m* 1780, Catherine Trauger (1763-1844; Christian[5] [1726-1811], from Germany, 1747, settled in Nockamixon Tp., Bucks Co., pvt. Nockamixon Co. of the associated bns. and militia, 1775, *m* Anna–, 1729-1821);
3–Benjamin (1786-1850), of N. Springtown, Pa.; pvt. War 1812; *m* 1st, 1809, Margaret Landis;
2–Peter Landis (2 below).
6–John **Landis** (*d* 1748), from nr. Mannheim, Germany, settled in Milford Tp., Bucks Co., Pa.; *m* Ann–;
5–Samuel (*d* 1771), of Milford Tp.; *m* Margaret–;
4–Samuel (1760-1839), *m* 1783, Susanna Newcomer;
3–Margaret (1788-1827), *m* Benjamin **Jacoby** (3 above).
5–Abraham (Schelle) **Shelly,** from Germany ca. 1730, settled in Milford Tp.; *m* Elizabeth–;
4–Jacob (1732-1812), *m* —Latshaw; *m* 2d, ante 1779, Barbara Landis (sister of Samuel, 4 above);
3–John (1779-1858), *m* 1st, Maria (Snyder) Bleam (1781-1833);
2–Barbara (1815-1904), *m* 1837, Peter Landis **Jacoby** (1812-76), farmer, N. Springtown, Bucks Co., Pa.; issue: I–Mary Ann (1838-61); II–Titus Shelly (1843-1916; *m* Emma Jane Bougher, *b* 1847); III–Amanda Shelly (1845-88; *m* Henry Unangst, 1843-1913); IV–Lewis Shelly (1848-1929; *m* Laura Roberta Broes, *b* 1851); V–John Shelly (*b* 1851; *m* Wiletta Loux, 1854-95; *m* 2d, Kate Ash, 1858-1926); VI–Henry Sylvester (1 above).
1–*m* May 18, 1880, Laura Louise Saylor, *b* Bethlehem, Pa., Apr. 1, 1857; dau. of Thomas Mill Saylor, of Bethlehem, *m* Emma Adeline Hillman; issue: 1–John Vincent, *b* Memphis, Tenn., July 25, 1884; B.S. in Agr., Cornell, '08; 2–Hurlbut Smith, *b* Memphis, Feb. 7, 1886; A.B., Cornell, '08, C.E., 1910; *m* July 26, 1912, Emma Betsey, dau. of Rev. Edson Joseph Farley, of Oneonta, N.Y., *m* Mary Jane Vaughn (issue: Hurlbut Saylor; Mary Vaughn; Betsey Ann); 3–Freeman Steel, *b* Bethlehem, Pa., Jan. 10, 1889; B.S. in Agr., Cornell, '10; *m* June 1, 1913, Ruth, dau. of Thomas McManamy, of Circleville, O., *m* Iva Jane Marburger (issue: Eleanor Ruth).
1–Ed. Excelsior Normal Inst., Carversville, Pa., and pvt. instrn.; C.E., Lehigh U., 1877 (Tau Beta Pi, Sigma Xi). Retired civil engr. Prof. emeritus bridge engring., Cornell U. Author (see Who's Who in America). Mem. Hist.

Soc. of Pa., Pa. German Soc., Nat. Geneal. Soc. (pres., 1930), Pa. Geneal. Soc., Hist. Soc. of Lehigh Co., Pa. Methodist. Republican. Clubs: University, Cosmos. Residence: Washington, D.C.

1-**JAEGER, Eva Elizabeth Sells (Mrs. Christian F.),** *b* Dublin, O., Nov. 30, 1872.
9-Samuel **Gorton** (qv);
8-Samuel (*b* Eng., 1630), to N.E. with parents, 1636; ct. interpreter bet. English and Indians; capt. mil. co., Warwick, R.I.; mem. Upper House of Assembly, 1676-83; asst. judge;
7-Samuel (1690-1784), *m* 1715, Freelove Mason (*d* post 1748);
6-Capt. Joseph (*b* 1729), *m* 1762, Mary Barton;
5-Rev. Hezekiah (*b* 1763), Broadalbin, N.Y., minister there 20 yrs.; *m* 1781, Susanna Potter (widow of Asa Bowdish);
4-Capt. Joseph (1786-1820), served War 1812; pioneer settler of Franklinton (now Columbus), O.; *m* 1809, Rachel Goetchius;
3-Nancy (1810-71), of Columbus, O.; *m* 1829, Fletcher **Sells** (1809-81), of Dublin, O.;
2-Cicero (2 below).
11-William **Arnold** (qv);
10-Joanna (1617-92), of Providence, R.I.; *m* 3d, 1646, Gov. Zachariah **Rhodes** (1603-65), immigrant; gov. R.I.; commr. from R.I.; dep., 1664-65; mem. Town Council;
9-Mary, of Warwick, R.I.; *m* 1675, John **Low,** of Warwick;
8-Rebecca (*d* 1723), of Warren, R.I.; *m* 1702, Andrew **Barton** (*d* 1723);
7-Benjamin (1703-93), of Warren; *m* 1727, Mary Haile (1708-74);
6-Mary (1740-72), *m* Joseph **Gorton** (6 above).
9-Roger **Williams** (qv);
8-Joseph (1643-1724), of Providence, R.I.; capt. King Philip's War; *m* 1669, Lydia Olney;
7-Joseph (1673-1752), of Providence; *m* Lydia Hearndon Horn (*d* Cranston, 1763);
6-Jemima (*d* 1796), *m* 1735, Benjamin **Potter** (*b* 1715);
5-Susanna (*b* 1762), *m* 2d, Hezekiah **Gorton** (5 above).
10-Jansen **Roeleff** (*d* 1637), from Holland, 1630; *m* Anneke Webber (1605-63), with her husband purchased land from Dutch W. I. Co.; dau. of Wolpert Webber, son of William The Silent King of Holland; she *m* 2d, Evaradus Bogardus (qv);
9-Sarah, of New Amsterdam; interpreter for the Indians, and received land grant for her services; *m* 1642, Dr. Hans **Kierschstede** (*d* 1667), came from Germany;
8-Catrina (*b* 1660), of New York; *m* 1681 or 82, Johannes **Kip** (De Kypt), Huguenot, (*b* 1655);
7-Sarah (*b* 1688), of N.Y. or R.I.; *m* 2d, Jans **Zabbrowsky** (g.son of Albrecht Zabrowskey, minister in Poland, came to America);
6-Rachel (*b* 1729), *m* Rev. Johannus Henrikus **Goetchius** (*d* 1772), from Switzerland to America, 1717; established the First Dutch Reform Ch. in America;
5-Rev. Stephen (*d* 1837), of Ulster Co., N.Y.; minister; served in Am. Rev.; established nine chs. in and nr. N.Y. State; *m* Elizabeth DuBois (*b* 1750);
4-Rachel (1785-1877), of Ulster Co.; *m* Capt. Joseph **Gorton** (4 above);
3-Nancy, *m* Fletcher **Sells** (3 above);
2-Cicero (1838-1901), of Dublin, O.; *m* 1862, Mary Johnson (1840-1904); issue: I-Harry (1863-92); II-Sherman (*b* 1865; *m* Nellie Hall); III-Nancy Gorton (*b* 1867; *m* Theodore Davis; *m* 2d, Jacob Hoffman); IV-Fletcher (1869-95); V-Eva (1 above); VI-Ida (*b* 1875; *m* 1904, Charles Steinbower).
1-*m* June 30, 1897, Christian Frederick Jaeger, *b* Dublin, Franklin Co., O., Nov. 30, 1872; issue: 1-Frederick Fletcher, *b* Columbus, O., May 30, 1899; M.E., Ohio State U., '21; *m* Nov. 29, 1920, Carrie Frances, dau. of Henderson Ward, of Columbus (issue: Frederick Fletcher; William Christian); 2-Bernard Christian, *b* Columbus, Jan. 24, 1902; Ohio State U., 1926; *m* 1925, Barbara Annette, dau. of Frank C. Sibbald (issue: Barbara Annette; Crevolin Cornelia).
1-Teacher for 6 yrs.; research work in genealogy, 20 yrs. (not professionally). Teacher in surgical dressings and bandages, A.R.C., during World War. Mem. C.D.A., D.A.C. (registrar, 1926-29), C.D.XVII Century, Dames of the Court of Honor (dir., v.p. for Ohio, 1929), D.A.R. (dir., v.chapter regent, historian, 6 yrs.), U.S.D. 1812, I.A.G., Archaeol. and Hist. Soc. (life), Kenmore Assn., McGuffey Soc., Pioneer Assn. of Franklin Co., O. Democrat. Summer place: 2249 Coventry Rd., Columbus, O. Residence: 52 W. Gay St., Columbus, O.

1-**JAMES, Darwin Rush,** *b* Brooklyn, N.Y., Jan. 10, 1873.
9-Philip **James,** from Eng. in the "Diligent," 1638, settled at Hingham, Mass.; *m* Jane Davenport? (*d* 1688);
8-Francis (1631-84), of Hingham; *m* ante 1660, Elizabeth Hyland (*d* post 1688; Thomas[9], of Eng. and Scituate, Mass., *m* Elizabeth-);
7-Thomas (1669-1724), of the "Mansion House," Hingham; *m* 1704, Patience (Tower) Farrow (1668/69-1751; Ibrook Tower[8], *m* Margaret Hardin);
6-John (1712-60), *m* 1743, Deborah (Bates) Stodder (*b* 1716; Joseph[7], *m* Deborah Clapp);
5-John (1744-1804), of Goshen, Mass.; *m* 1765, Lois Beal (1746-1810; Adam[6], *m* Jael Worrick);
4-Malachi (1767-1849), aide to Gen. Mattoon in Shay's Rebellion; *m* 1790, Elizabeth Lyman (1771-1856; Dea. Elias[5]; Elias[6], soldier Am. Rev.);
3-Lewis Lyman (1805-80), of Williamsburgh, Mass.; *m* 1832, Cerintha Wells (1807-65; Capt. John[4], *m* Sarah, dau. of Capt. Jonathan Warner, officer Am. Rev.);
2-Darwin Rush (2 below).
8-Thomas **Fairchild** (qv);
7-Samuel (1640-1704), of Stratford, Conn.; *m* Mary Wheeler;
6-Edward, *m* Elizabeth Blakeman;
5-Moses (*b* 1721), *m* Susanna Bosworth;
4-Daniel (1762-1831), of Sheffield, Mass.; *m* Mary Buckle;
3-Dea. Daniel (1804-81), of Curtisville, Mass.; *m* 1st, 1829, Octavia Briggs (1806-42);
2-Mary Ellen (1834-1912), *m* 1858, Hon. Darwin Rush **James** (1834-1908), mcht.; mem. 48th and 49th Congresses, 1883-87; chmn. Bd. of Indian Commrs., 1890; issue: I-Mary Isabel (1859-1926; *m* Horatio Mortier Adams); II-Alice (*b* 1862; *m* George Rossen); III-Grace Fairchild (*b* 1864; *m* William Crittenden Adams); IV-Gertrude (*b* 1867; *m* 1894, Warren Eveleth Derby, *b* 1858); V-Ida Eleanor (*b* 1870; *m* Harold Vernon); VI-Darwin R. (1 above); VII-Ethel (1877; *m* Edward Albert Quin).
1-*m* Dec. 23, 1896, Alice Burton Fonda, *b* Brooklyn, N.Y., July 10, 1874; dau. of John A. Fonda, of Poughkeepsie, N.Y. (James Henry[3]); issue: 1-Alice F., *b* Brooklyn, N.Y., Dec. 10, 1898; *m* Oct. 5, 1921, Norfleet E. Blaine (issue: Norfleet E., Jr.; Darwin James); 2-Darwin R., III, *b* Brooklyn, Sept. 6, 1901; Princeton, 1924; *m* Feb. 12, 1927, Gladys, dau. of John T. Underwood, of Brooklyn (issue: Carol).
1-Grad. Adelphi Acad., 1891; A.B., Princeton, '95. Pres. Van Duzer Extract Co., 1895-1912, Pyrene Mfg. Co., 1912-16, Am. Chicle Co., 1916-22, East River Savings Bank, since 1922; trustee Title Guarantee & Trust Co., East River Savings Bank, State Title & Mortgage Co., Nat. Am. Co., Aldar Realty Co., Gen. Surety Co., Fairchild Realty Co., Gen. Re-insurance Co., Met. Casualty Co., Brooklyn Bureau of Charities, Brooklyn Public Library. Mem. Municipal Civil Service Commn. (commr. during the term of Mayor John Purroy Mitchel); chmn. State Bd. of Housing since 1925. Presbyterian. Republican. Clubs: Princeton, City, Lakeville Golf and Country. Summer place: Bayhead, N.J. Residence: 301 Washington Av., Brooklyn, N.Y.

1-**JANNEY, Mahlon Hopkins,** *b* Alexandria, Va., Oct. 12, 1881.
8-Thomas **Janney** (qv);
7-Joseph (1675-1729), *m* 1703, Rebeckah Biles (*b* 1680; William[8], qv);
6-Abel (1712-74), removed to Loudoun Co., Va., 1748; *m* 1733, Sarah Baker (1712-post 1778; Samuel[7] [1676-ante 1760], *m* 1703, Rachel, dau. of Nicholas Warder; Henry[8], early settler Bucks Co., Pa., rep. Assembly, 6 sessions, justice, 1689, *m* in Eng., 1667, Margaret Hardman);
5-Joseph (will probated 1793), *m* 1764, Hannah Jones (*b* 1742; John[6], *m* Rebecca Head);
4-John (1765-1823), *m* 1795, Elizabeth Hopkins;

Janney

Arms: Ermine, a bend cotised gules.
Crest: On a wreath of the colors a hand in armor argent, thereon a falcon close proper, belled of the last.

3–Samuel Hopkins (1804-87), double 1st cousin of Johns Hopkins, philanthropist of Baltimore; *m* 1831, Elizabeth Mark;
2–Mahlon Hopkins (2 below).
9–William **Coale** (qv);
8–William (1667-1715), *m* 1689, Elizabeth Sparrow (Thomas[9], *m* Elizabeth Kensey, she *m* 2d, Richard Johns);
7–Eliza Jane (*b* 1692), *m* 1709, Richard **Snowden** (Richard[8], capt. provincial forces, buried May 20, 1711, *m* Mary–; Richard[9], qv);
6–Mary (1712-55), *m* 1730, Samuel **Thomas** (1702-80; Samuel[7] [1655-1743], *m* 1688, Mary Hutchins [*d* 1751]; Philip[8], qv);
5–Elizabeth (*b* 1736/37), *m* 1758, as his 3d wife, Johns **Hopkins** (*b* 1720), for Hopkins lineage see Vol. III, p. 271;
4–Elizabeth (*b* 1771), *m* John **Janney** (4 above).
9–Peter Gunnarsson **Rambo** (qv);
8–Gunner (1649-will proved 1724/25), *m* Ann Cock (Peter Larson[9], *d* 1724);
7–Peter (will proved 1753);
6–Ann, *m* 1733, Roger **North** (1704-85), lt. Pa. Provincial forces, 1748; had 8 sons in Am. Rev., accepted by D.A.R. as Rev. patriot altho too old for active service;
5–Lt. George, officer Am. Rev.; *m* 1st, 1787, Sarah Evans (*d* 1793; William[6], mcht., Phila.);
4–Ann Smith (1788-1870), *m* 1808, Samuel **Mark** (*d* 1831), moved to Alexandria, Va.; for Mark lineage see Vol. III, p. 271;
3–Elizabeth (1814-84), *m* Samuel H. **Janney** (3 above).
9–Francis **Triplett** (will proved 1701), patented land in Rappahannock Co., Va., 1666;
8–Thomas (*d* ante father);
7–Francis (will proved 1758), voter Fairfax Co., 1744; *m* Sarah Harrison (William[8] [*d* ca. 1748], *m* Sarah Hawley; Burr[9], burgess, ambassador to the Piscataway Indians, *m* Mrs. Mary Smith; Cuthbert[10]);
6–William (1730-1803), officer Am. Rev.; *m* Sarah Peake (William[7]; John[8], *m* Lucy–);
5–Penelope (1768-1854), *m* 1790, Robert Browne **Jamesson** (1770-1820), for Jamesson data see Vol. III, p. 271;
4–Commodore William, U.S.N. (1791-1873), *m* ca. 1819, Catherine Rose (1790-1864);
3–William Henry (ca. 1820-1845), *m* 1844, Cornelia Lee Turberville Taliaferro;
2–Williamina Henrietta (2 below).
10–Richard **Lee** (qv);
9–Richard (1647-1714), mem. King's Council, burgess; *m* ca. 1674, Laetitia Corbin (Henry[10], qv);
8–Richard (1678-1718), *m* Martha Silk, of London;
7–Martha (*b* 1716), *m* 1st, as his 3d wife, Maj. George **Turberville,** of Hickory Hill, Westmoreland Co., Va. (John[8], burgess and sheriff);
6–George Richard (*b* 1742), *m* 1769, Martha Corbin;
5–Gawin Corbin, of "Peckatone," Westmoreland Co., Va.; *m* 1792, Mary W. Daingerfield;
4–Mary Willis, *m* William Francis **Taliaferro** (1790-1836);
3–Cornelia Lee Turberville (1828-55), *m* William Henry **Jamesson** (3 above).
11–Maj. Lewis **Burwell** (qv);
10–Maj. Lewis (*d* 1710), of King's Creek, York Co., Va.; mem. King's Council; *m* 1st, Abigail Smith (1656-92; Anthony[11], *m* Martha Bacon, of Colchester, Eng.); niece and heiress of Nathaniel Bacon, the rebel; she was descended from 11 kings;
9–Joanna (1675-1727), *m* 1693, Capt. William **Bassett** (Capt. William[10], *m* 1670, Bridgett [*b* 1651], dau. of Miles Cary, qv);
8–Martha (1694-1738), *m* as his 3d wife, ca. 1719, Gawin **Corbin** (ca. 1650-1744), ed. Eng.; naval officer on the Rappahannock; burgess (Henry[9], qv);
7–Gawin (1725-ante 1760), vestryman of Stratton Major Parish; *m* his cousin, Hannah Lee;
6–Martha, *m* George R. **Turberville** (6 above).
11–Benjamin **Harrison** (qv);
10–Benjamin (1645-1712), burgess, justice, sheriff; *m* Hannah–;
9–Hannah (1678-1731), *m* 1692, Philip **Ludwell** (Philip[10], qv);
8–Hannah (1701-49), *m* 1722, Thomas **Lee** (1690-1750), built "Stratford"; pres. Council; gov. Va.; "President and Commander-in-chief of Colony" (Richard[9] same as 9 above; Richard[10], qv);
7–Hannah (*b* 1728), *m* Gawin **Corbin** (7 above).
10–Col. Moore **Fauntleroy** (qv);
9–William, justice, Rappahannock Co.; *m* 1680, Katherine Griffin (Col. Samuel[10], justice, Northumberland Co.);
8–Col. William (1684-1757), *m* Apphia Bushrod (John[9], *m* Hannah Keene);
7–Apphia, *m* 1705, Col. William **Daingerfield** (William[8], *m* Elizabeth [Bathrust] Tomlin; John[9], *m* Anne [Walker] Payne; William[10], qv);
6–Col. William, Am. Rev.; *m* Mary Willis;
5–Mary Willis, *m* Gawin Corbin **Turberville** (5 above).
10–James **Taylor** (qv);
9–James (1670-1729), *m* Martha Thompson (Col. William[10]; Sir Roger[11]; Sir William[12]);
8–Frances (ca. 1702-61), *m* 1721, Ambrose **Madison** (John[9], *m* Isabella Todd);
7–Elizabeth (1725-73) *m* 1st, John **Willis** (Col. Henry[8], founder of Fredericksburg, Va., *m* Anne Alexander, the widow Smith);
6–Mary, *m* Col. William **Daingerfield** (6 above).
2–Mahlon Hopkins **Janney** (1843-82), *m* 1868, Williamina Henrietta Jamesson (1845-82).
1–Not married. Grad. Potomac Acad., Alexandria, Va.; special work at U.Vt. Writer of special articles, stories, verse; genealogist. Civilian war work in office of chief of Ordnance, War Dept., during World War. Mem. Va. Hist. Soc., Taylor Family Assn., etc. Residence: 1812 K St., Washington, D.C.

1–**JEFFERSON, Mittie Shaw,** *b* Memphis, Tenn., Feb. 16, 1879.
9–John **Jefferson,** from Wales with father; part-founder of Yorktown, Va.; burgess, 1619; and probably thru:
8–Thomas (*d* 1697), owned a plantation in Henrico Co., Va., 1677; *m* Martha Branch (William[9], of Henrico Co.; Christopher[10], qv);
7–Capt. Thomas (1679-1725), lived at "Osborne," on the James River, Chesterfield Co.; justice, 1706; *m* 1697, Mary Field (Peter[8], *m* Judith Seane); their youngest son, Peter, was father of President Thomas Jefferson;
6–Field, inherited "Osborne"; *m* Mary Warren;
5–Warren, *m* Mary Killam;
4–Richard (*b* 1782), *m* Nancy Evans (*b* 1780);
3–Silas Warren (*b* 1814), *m* 1st, 1837, Jane White;
2–Joshua Taylor (1842-1919), *m* 1868, Mittie Shaw (1841-80); *m* 2d, 1886, Janie Glover (1864-1916); issue (1st mariage): I–William (*b* 1871); II–Janie Byrd (*b* 1874; III–Mittie S. (1 above); IV–Lona Walton (*b* 1880; *m* Eugene Howry; issue: Eugene LeRoy, Jr., *b* Sept. 20, 1910);

issue (2d marriage): I–Joshua Taylor, Jr. (*b* 1889; *m* 1921, Julia Jeannette De Fur); II–Edwin Walton (*b* 1892).
1–Ed. privately and European travel. Mem. Beethoven Club. Summer place: Fairmont. Residence: 440 Goodwyn Av., Memphis, Tenn.

1–**JEFFERYS, William Hamilton,** *b* Phila., Pa., July 3, 1871.
5–William **Miller,** from Scotland to Phila., Pa., 1757; *m* Kate Kennedy;
4–William, commr. of revenue under Presidents Adams and Jefferson; mem. First Troop, Phila. City Cav.; *m* Rachel Long;
3–Edward, chief engr. and one of the builders of Pa. R. R.; *m* Jessie Imbrie;
2–Elizabeth (1837-1908), *m* 1859, Charles Peter Beauchamp **Jefferys** (1831-1910), civil engr., Phila. (Hon. Lt. Col. Peter[3], colonial gov. Island of Nevis, B.W.I.; John Latysionere[4], gov. of same island); issue: I–Marie E. (*b* 1860; *m* Henry Lee Hobart); II–Louise (1861-63); III–Charles P. B., Jr. (1862-1901); IV–J. Margaretta (1863-1908); V–Edward Miller (see Vol. I, p. 656); VI–Harry L. (*b* 1869; *m* M. Celeste Klemm); VII–William H. (1 above); VIII–Maximilian (1876-98).
1–*m* June 10, 1897, Lucy Sturgis, dau. of John Parkinson Hubbard, of Boston; issue: 1–Anne, *b* Phila., July 27, 1898; *m* Algernon Robert Clapp; 2–Lucy Sturgis, *b* Shanghai, China, Mar. 18, 1904; *m* Ludwig Clifford Lewis; 3–Adelaide McCulloch, *b* Shanghai, Mar. 23, 1907; 4–William H., Jr., *b* Phila., May 27, 1913.
1–A.B., U.Pa., '94, M.A., 1897, M.D., 1898. Surgeon, St. Luke's Hosp. (Shanghai), 1901-17; prof. surgery, St. John's U., (Shanghai), 1905-17; supt. Phila. City Mission, since 1917. Author; editor (see Who's Who in America). Clubs: Shanghai, Shanghai Country (China), Authors (London), University, St. Elmo (Phila.). Residence: "Cosy Cottage," Rosemont, Phila., Pa.

1–**JENKS, George Sanford,** *b* St. Clair, Mich., Sept. 11, 1869.
9–Joseph **Jenks** (qv);
8–Joseph (1632-1717), founder of Pawtucket, R.I.; gov.'s asst.; *m* Esther Ballard (1633-1717):
7–Maj. Nathaniel (1662-1723), *m* 1686, Hannah Bosworth (1663-1723; Jonathan[8], *m* Hannah, dau. of John Howland, Mayflower Pilgrim, qv; Jonathan[9]; Edward[10]);
6–Jonathan (1688-1748), *m* 1707, Mary Slack;
5–Jonathan (1718-87), *m* 1736, Hannah Pullen:
4–Jeremiah (1739-1811), *m* 1776, Lucy Whipple (1746-1819);
3–Jeremiah Whipple (1780-1852), *m* 1803, Hester Lane (1784-1850; Jesse[4], pvt. Am. Rev.);
2–Bela Whipple (1824-97), realtor and farmer; *m* 1853, Sarah Carleton (1833-1907); for issue see Vol. III, p. 272.
1–*m* Aug. 24, 1901, Anna Catherine Fox, *b* Rondout, N.Y., Oct. 4, 1879; dau. of John H. Fox, *m* Sarah A. Mason.
1–Ed. Mich. State College. Associated with Spang Steel & Iron Co., 1889-93, Apollo Iron & Steel Co., 1893-1900, Am. Sheet & Tin Plate Co., 1900—. Mem. S.A.R., Am. Iron and Steel Inst. Mason. (Consistory, K.T.). Clubs: Duquesne, University, Oakmont Country. Residence: 5806 Howe St., Pittsburgh, Pa.

1–**JOHNSON, Ida Jennette Coe (Mrs. Franklin R.),** *b* Derby, Conn., Dec. 16, 1875.
10–Robert **Coe** (qv);
9–Robert (1626-59), *m* 1650, Hannah Mitchell (1631-1702);
8–Capt. John (1658-1741), dep. for Stratford in Conn. Assembly; ens., lt. and capt., 1709; served in Colonial and Indian wars; *m* 1682, Mary Hawley (1663-1731);
7–Capt. Ebenezer (1704-66), ens., lt. and capt., 1750; *m* 1728, Mary Blakeman (1705-73; g.g.dau. of Rev. Adam Blakeman, the first minister of Stratford, 1639);
6–John (1729-83), Stratford; took oath of fidelity at Derby, Conn., 1777; mem. Com. Inspection, etc., Derby; *m* 1755, Hannah Chatfield;
5–John (1764-1812), Derby; *m* 1785, Ruth Johnson (1765-1809; Isaac[6], Am. Rev.);
4–John Allen (1792-1849), Derby and Bethany; *m* 1812, Grace Smith (1797-1869);
3–John (1815-76), Bethany and Derby; *m* 1837, Mary Lewis Hoadley (1817-88);
2–Charles Hoadley (1849-1900), druggist, Derby, Conn.; *m* 1875, Ida Mary Fields (1850-1923); issue: I–Ida Jennette (1 above); II–Mary Alma (1884-1912; *m* Richard S. Tolman).
1–*m* Feb. 8, 1899, Franklin Russell Johnson, *b* Derby, Conn., Oct. 24, 1874; son of David Treat Johnson, of Derby and Ansonia, Conn.; issue: 1–Russell Hoadley, *b* Ansonia, Conn., Aug. 7, 1901; 2–Margaret Hoadley (*b* and *d* Sept. 17, 1908).
1–Mem. D.F.P.A., D.C.W., D.A.R., Women's Republican Club. Residence: 1101 Beacon St., Brookline, Mass.

1–**JOHNSON, Lucius Henry,** *b* Mt. Vernon, Ill., Feb. 9, 1863.
7–John **Johnson** (1675-1740), from Eng., settled in Md.;
6–Benjamin (1703-92), of Hanover C.H., Va.; *m* 1732, Mary Matlock;
5–John (1740-1784), of Louisa Co., Va.; *m* 1775, Betsy Foster (1743-1816);
4–James (1778-1860), of Jefferson Co., Ill.; *m* 1810, Clarissa Maxey (1780-1853);
3–John Nelson (1810-55), of Mt. Vernon, Ill.; *m* 1834, Sarah T. Hobbs (1815-93);
2–James David (2 below).
6–Joseph **Boswell** (1730-80), from Scotland, settled in southwestern Va.; *m* 1753, Elizabeth Elliott (1733-70);
5–James (1754-1800), of Va.;
4–William (1776-1858), of Va.; *m* 1800, Elizabeth Moore (1780-1850);
3–James Moore (1804-54), of Princeton, Ind.; *m* 1827, Nancy Foster (1810-52);
2–Martha (1843-71), of Mt. Vernon, Ill.; *m* 1860, James David **Johnson** (1838-1920), mcht.; issue: I–Lucius Henry (1 above); II–Sarah Agnes (*b* 1867; *m* James S. Courtney); III–Alva Wright Boswell (*b* 1871; *m* Caroline Wilson).
1–Not married. Spl. student Harvard, 1919-21. Widely known for many yrs. as mining editor and corr., mining camps of Colo.; Sunday editor and editorial writer, Denver Republican, then spl. writer Denver Post. Author (see Who's Who in America). Mem. S.A.R. Clubs: National Arts (New York), Denver Press, Denver Athletic. Residence: Denver Athletic Club, Denver, Colo.

1–**JOHNSON, Ludwell Harrison,** *b* Lexington, Va., Sept. 11, 1875.
5–Joseph **Johnson** (*d* Dec. 1791), moved to Sussex, Va., and after his death his widow settled at Bridgeport, Harrison Co. (now W.Va.), with her children; soldier Am. Rev.; *m* Abigail Wright (1753-1839; William[6], English Gent.);
4–William (Sept. 1791-1868), mcht.; farmer; mem. Legislature; *m* 1814, Olive Waldo;
3–Mortimer Howell (1815-89), served in C.S.A.; mcht.; lawyer; twice elected to State Senate; *m* 1835, Eliza Dulaney Kemble;
2–Porter (2 below).
9–Cornelius **Waldo** (qv);
8–John (*d* 1700), *m* ca. 1676, Rebecca Adams, of Charlestown, Mass.;
7–Edward (1684-1767), *m* 1706, Thankful Dimmock (*b* 1682);
6–John (1726-1814), *m* 1750, Jemima Abbott;
5–Jedediah (1772-1858), *m* 1794, Polly Porter (1776-1816; William[6]);
4–Olive (1798-1852), *m* William **Johnson** (4 above).
7–Thomas **Kemble,** from Eng., settled at Burlington, N.J.;
6–Samuel;
5–Thomas (1748-1806), *m* 1773, Priscilla Burr (*d* 1809; Henry[6]; John[7], from Ireland, settled nr. Burlington, N.Y.);
4–William (1800-68), *m* 1819, Margaret Dulaney (1801-74; William H.[5] [1763-1808], *m* Frances [*b* 1770], dau. of Joseph Shackleford, of Newton, Va.; William[6], *m* Mary, dau. of Benjamin Roberts, *m* —Abbott);
3–Eliza Dulaney (1821-79), *m* Mortimer Howell **Johnson** (3 above);
2–Porter (1845-1917), mcht., farmer; attended V.M.I.; served in Civil War; New Market Cadet; *m* 1867, Rose Mary Brown (1848-1913); issue: I–Fanny Kemble (Mrs. Vincent Costello, qv for Brown lineages); II–Richard Marmaduke (1871-1916); III–Waldo Porter (1873-1903); IV–Ludwell Harrison (1 above); V–Leake McClelland (*b* 1877; *m* Mona Bittle); VI–William Cabel (1879-1904); VII–Edmonia Preston (Mrs. Charles C. Beal, qv for other

lineages); VIII–Olive Waldo (*b* 1883; *m* 2d, Gustav A. Ludloff); IX–Alice Lee (*b* 1886; *m* Thomas J. Moreland); X–James Brown (*b* 1888; *m* Augusta Hermann).
1–*m* Sept. 12, 1900, Helen Costello, *b* Charleston, W.Va., Dec. 13, 1878; dau. of John Costello, *m* Margaret Aken; issue: 1–Helen Moore, *b* Richmond, Va., June 16, 1901; 2–Ludwell Harrison, Jr., *b* Charleston, W.Va., Aug. 16, 1902; *m* Apr. 17, 1926, Sarah Graham (issue: Ludwell Harrison, 3d); 3–Richard Costello (1909-11).
1–Ed. Churchland Acad., Va. Advertising mgr. for Thalhimer Bros., Richmond, Va., 1900-21. Residence: 415 N. Roseneath Rd., Richmond, Va.

1–**COSTELLO, Fanny Kemble Johnson (Mrs. Vincent),** *b* Brownsburg, Va., May 22, 1868.
6–John **Brown,** emigrated from Scotland to London; sent to America, 1750, as confidential sec. to Envoys Extraordinary Marshall and Pinckney;
5–John (1750-1810), clk. dist. gen ct. and Ct. of Appeals of Va.; *m* 1772, Anne Geddy (*d* ante 1802; James[6], *m* Elizabeth Waddill; James[7], from Scotland, 1735, banker and mem. Council, 1767, *m* Anne–);
4–James (1780-1859), mcht., later 2d auditor of Va. for 40 yrs. in Richmond; *m* 1802, Frances Goosely;
3–Ludwell Harrison (1818-59), civil engr. on many of the public works of Va. and W.Va.; *m* 1840, Margaret M. McClelland;
2–Rose Mary (2 below).
9–Col. Miles **Cary** (qv);
8–Capt. William (1657-1713), *m* 1683, Martha Scarsbrook (Maj. John[9], *m* Mary Martian);
7–William (*d* 1742), *m* Judith Jones;
6–Martha, *m* Ephriam **Goosely**;
5–William (1748-1809), *m* 1773, Ludwell Harrison (1754-1813; Benjamin[6], of Wakefield, *m* 1739, Susanna, dau. of Cole Diggs [1642-1744]; Nathaniel[7], *m* Mary Cary; Benjamin[8], of Surrey);
4–Frances (1783-1849), *m* James **Brown** (4 above);
3–Ludwell H. (1818-59), *m* Margaret M. McClelland (3 above);
2–Rose Mary (1848-1913), *m* 1867, Porter **Johnson** (1845-1917); for issue and other lineages see Ludwell Harrison Johnson.
1–*m* June 14, 1899, Vincent Costello, *b* Charleston, W.V., 1875; son of John Costello, of Charleston; issue: 1–Rose Margaret (Sept. 28, 1900-1928); *m* Apr. 12, 1921, Vernon Curtis Munson (*d* 1922; issue: Vernon Curtis); *m* 2d, 1924, David Cherry James; 2–Vincent Costello, *b* Charleston, W.Va., May 6, 1902; *m* June 5, 1926, Sylvia Rosamond, dau. of John T. Pierce, of Eng., *m* Anne McGreggor (issue: Vincent Desmond; Sylvia Daphne); 3–Ellen Moore, *b* Wheeling, W.Va., Aug. 18, 1909; *m* Mar. 12, 1928, Capt. Ian Fielding Pierce, son of John T. Pierce, *m* Anne McGreggor (issue: David Francis); 4–Fanny Kemble, *b* Wheeling, Aug. 4, 1911.
1–Author (see Who's Who in America). Residence: Station A, Charleston, W.Va.

1–**BEAL, Edmonia Preston Johnson (Mrs. Charles C.),** *b* Natural Bridge, Va., Feb. 28, 1881.
5–Thomas **McClelland** (1730-1800), removed from Scotland to Londonderry; came to America 1750; settled in Pa., removed from nr. Gettysburg to Cincinnati; *m* Mary Stanhope (*b* 1734);
4–Thomas Stanhope (1777-1835), lawyer, Nelson Co., Va.; *m* 1803, Margaret Cabell;
3–Margaret M. (1820-75), *m* Ludwell H. **Brown** (1818-59), of Va.;
2–Rose Mary (2 below).
10–Capt. Nicholas **Martian** (qv);
9–Elizabeth (*d* 1687), *m* Col. George **Reade** (qv);
8–Thomas, *m* 1688, Lucy Gwyn (Dr. Edward[9], of Ware Parish, Va.);
7–Col. Clement (1707-63), French and Indian War; *m* 1730, Mary Hill (1712-80);
6–Margaret (*d* 1766), *m* 1755, Judge Paul **Carrington** (1733-1818; Col. George[7], qv);
5–Anne (1760-1838), *m* 1780, Col. William **Cabell** (1759-1822; Col. William[6] [1730-98], *m* Margaret [*d* 1812], dau. Samuel Jordan, *m* Ruth Meridith; Dr. William[7], qv);
4–Margaret (1785-1863), *m* Thomas Stanhope **McClelland** (4 above);
3–Margaret M. (1820-75), *m* Ludwell H. **Brown** (3 above);
2–Rose Mary (1848-1913), *m* 1867, Porter **Johnson** (1845-1917); for issue and other lineages see Ludwell Harrison Johnson.
1–*m* Feb. 5, 1905, Charles Cleveland Beal (Jan. 2, 1881-Apr. 28, 1928); son of Burton A. Beal; issue: 1–Alice Lee Ludwell, *b* Newport News, Va., Nov. 27, 1905; *m* July 6, 1924, Stephen M. Pronko, Y.M.C.A. sec., Cebu, Cebu, P.I. (issue: Robert Carrington, *b* Youngstown, O., June 3, 1926; Leonard Cary, *b* Cebu, Cebu, P.I., Oct. 3, 1927); 2–Frances Coleman, *b* Norfolk, Va., Oct. 2, 1909; *m* July 1930, Meade McArdle; 3–Edmonia Cleveland, *b* Norfolk, Va., Aug. 16, 1911; 4–Ruth Tracy, *b* Norfolk, Feb. 20, 1914; 5–Margaret Murray, *b* Webster Groves, Mo., Mar. 7, 1923.
1–Ed. pvt. schs. Mem. D.A.R., U.D.C., Creative Reading Club. Residence: 229 Bompart Av., Webster Groves, Mo.

1–**JOHNSON, Nettie Eugenia Phelps (Mrs. William),** *b* Clayton, Mich., Oct. 12, 1850.
9–George **Phelps** (qv);
8–Jacob (1650-89), *m* Dorothy Ingersoll (1654-89; John[9], *m* Dorothy, dau. of Thomas Lord, qv);
7–Israel (*b* 1681), *m* 1704, Mary Pease (1681-1713; Lt. Robert[8], *m* 1678, Abigail Randall; Capt. John[9], *m* 1656, Mary, dau. of Robert Goodell or Goodale, from Eng., 1634);
6–Israel (*b* 1706), *m* Hannah Bennett (*d* 1737; William[7], William[8], *m* 1678, Susanna, dau. of Henry Bright; John[9], of Stonington, *d* 1691);
5–Israel (*b* 1733), *m* 1754, Priscilla Jones (*b* 1732; Capt. Ebenezer[6], killed at Crown Point, 1758, *m* Priscilla Smith; Benjamin[7], *m* Elizabeth Wilde; Thomas[8], *m* Mary, dau. of Richard North, 1608-87);
4–Israel (1757-1841), Am. Rev.; *m* 1779, Sarah Higby;
3–Israel (1784-1840), *m* Ruth Hawley;
2–Elias (2 below).
9–Edward **Higby** (*d* 1699), from Eng. to Mass., 1630; landholder at New London, Conn., 1647; bought land at Hartford from an Indian sachem 1664; freeman, 1667; was at Huntington and Jamaica, L.I.; *m* Jedidiah Skidmore (Thomas[10], *m* Ellen–);
8–John (1658-1688), of Middletown, Conn.; *m* 1679, Rebecca Treadwell (*d* 1707; Samuel[9]);
7–Edward (1684-1775), of Middletown; *m* 1706, Rebecca Wheeler (1687-1771; Joseph[8]);
6–John, *m* 1731, Sarah Cande (Candee) (Zaccheus[7], *m* Sarah–; John[8], Huguenot refugee, *m* Rebecca Bristow);
5–John (*b* 1732), Am. Rev.; *m* 1755, Mindwell Lewis;
4–Sarah (1760-1805), *m* Israel **Phelps** (4 above).
9–William **Lewis** (qv);
8–William (1620-90), capt. and 1st registrar of Farmington; *m* 1st, 1644, Mary Hopkins (William[9], *m* Mary–, who *m* 2d, Richard Whitehead);
7–Ebenezer (*d* 1709), settled at Wallingford, 1684; *m* 1685, Elizabeth Merriman (*b* 1669; Capt. Nathaniel[8], came 1649);
6–Malachi (*b* 1703), *m* 1728, Hannah (Sage) Wilcox (John Sage[7], *m* Hannah, dau. Dr. Comfort Starr; David[8], freeman, 1667, *m* Elizabeth Kirby, *d* 1670);
5–Mindwell, *m* John **Higby** (5 above).
9–Gov. Thomas **Welles** (qv);
8–Ann (*b* 1621), *m* William **Thompson**;
7–Mary, *m* Samuel **Hawley** (1647-1734; Joseph[8], qv);
6–Samuel (1674-1754), *m* Bethia Booth (Ephriam[7], *m* Mary Clark; Richard[8], qv; 19th in descent from Roger Bigod thru son Hugh, Earls of Norfolk of Royal Descent; 8th from Maude who *m* Sir Geoffrey de Say, descended from William de Say of France knighted by William the Conqueror, 1066, in line from William de Say who was a cup-bearer to Charlemagne in 751, and 4th from Geoffrey de Say, Magna Charta Baron; Katherine, 14th in line, *m* George Bothe *d* 1483, whose son, Edward, began to write the name Booth);
5–Obadiah (1708-51), *m* Sarah–;
4–Elias, *m* Ruth Lewis?;
3–Ruth (1783-1855), *m* 1810, Israel **Phelps** (3 above);
2–Elias (1817-92), *m* Harriet Curtis; *m* 2d, 1847, Clarinda Canfield (1819-86; Isaiah[3], *m* 1802, Mehitable Ells [Eells?], one of first women physicians; Isaiah[4] joined Colonial troops of

Westchester, N.Y., 1759, served in Am. Rev., *m* Rebecca–).

1–*m* May 12, 1875, William Johnson, *b* Durham, Blackwell Co., Eng., Oct. 7, 1842; issue: 1–William Harry, *b* Chicago, Ill., Mar. 2, 1876; *m* Margaret Davidson (issue: William David, *b* 1911; Martha Eugenia, *b* 1912; Ruth Elizabeth, *b* 1916); 2–Frank Phelps (*d*); *m* Ethel DeMoss; 3–Ruth Sophia, *b* Bedford, Ind., Oct. 3, 1884; *m* Harry B. Millikan (issue: Frank M., *m* Marion Link [issue: Joseph J. and John Robert]; William Johnson; Sarah Jane).

1–Mem. D.A.R., Women's Missionary Soc., Literary Club. Winter place: 220 E. Michigan Av., DeLand, Fla. Residence: 533 N. Washington St., Bloomington, Ind.

1–**JOHNSTON, (Bessie) Margaret Elizabeth Key (Mrs. James F.),** *b* Chattanooga, Tenn., Feb. 22, 1873.

7–Moses **Key** (1675-1748), from Scotland, 1700, settled in Chester and Delaware cos., Pa.; *m* 1701, Elizabeth Yearsley (*d* 1756; John[8], *m* Elizabeth–);

6–Moses (*d* 1746), of N.C.; mem. Pa. Assembly, 1723-24;

5–John (1735-94), of Green Co., Tenn.;

4–David (1765-1830), of Green Co.;

3–John (1798-1854), of Monroe Co., Tenn.; *m* Margaret Armitage (1804-82; Isaac[4], of Huntington Co., Pa., *m* Elizabeth Weston; Caleb[5] [*b* Germantown, 1737], moved to Huntington, *m* Mary Stryker);

2–Summerfield (2 below).

10–Jacob **Williams,** of Isle of Wight Co., Va.;

9–John, of Isle of Wight Co.;

8–George (*b* 1685), of Northampton Co., N.C.; *m* Sarah Mann (Thomas[9] [*d* 1735], Bertie Co., N.C., *m* Bridget Hooper; John[10] [*b* 1670], moved to Currituck Co., N.C., justice, assemblyman);

7–George (1710-48), *m* Priscilla–;

6–Samuel (1733-88), of Northampton Co., N.C.; capt. in Sevier's regt. in Battle of King's Mountain; rep. from Washington Co., N.C., in Franklin Legislature, 1782; killed in battle with Indians, at Nollychucky, Tenn., 1788; *m* Hannah Isbell (William[7]);

5–George (1787-1832), of Green Co., Tenn.; *m* Temple Kyle;

4–Samuel (1807-99), of Chattanooga, Tenn.; *m* 1827, Rebeca Davis (William[5]);

3–Elizabeth (1828-60), *m* John **Divine** (1818-92);

2–Mary (1846-1927), *m* 1871, Summerfield **Key** (1835-91), lawyer and judge; issue: I–(Bessie) Margaret Elizabeth (1 above); II–John Divine (1876-1921); III–Mary Summerfield (*m* Pearson Blythe Mayfield).

1–*m* Jan. 9, 1896, James Francis Johnston, *b* Cleveland, Tenn., Aug. 31, 1865; son of James Miller Johnson, *m* Sarah Tucker; issue: 1–Summerfield, *b* Chattanooga, Tenn., May 16, 1900; U.Va., 1922; Harvard Law Sch., 1925.

Residence: 505 Walnut St., Chattanooga, Tenn.

1–**JONES, Clifford Cloon,** *b* Covington, Ky., Jan. 26, 1879.

4–John Watson **Jones** (1785-1850), came from N.J. to Honey Grove, Tex.; served in War 1812, and was at Hull's Surrender, Detroit; *m* Tamezine Finley (1789-1853), of N.J.;

3–William Watson (1822-63), *d* at Paris, Tex.; *m* 1846, in Burlington, Ky., Mary Calvert;

2–Richard Bacon (2 below).

5–Christopher Columbus **Calvert,** and wife, early settlers of Fayette Co., Ky.;

4–Willis (*b* Va., 1794-1849), said to be 6th in descent from Lord Baltimore; of Fayette Co.; to Nashville, Tenn.; served War 1812, wounded in Battle of Raisin; *m* 1st, Elizabeth Ewing (*d* 1827), of Lexington, Ky.;

3–Mary (1823-95), *m* William W. **Jones** (3 above).

7–Hugh **McLellan** (1710-87), Scotch-Irish origin, from Ireland with wife, landed at Boston, 1733; settled at Gorham, Me.; land deed, 1739; colonial sentinel; scout; on Alarm List; soldier French and Indian War, 1754; mem. com. to purchase food for families of Am. Rev. soldiers, funds largely furnished by him; selectman, Gorham; elder Gorham Presbyn. Ch.; *m* Elizabeth McLellan (1708-1804), recognized Am. Rev. patriot; saved fort in 1750; both lineal descendants of Sir Hugh McLellan, Clan Argyl-Campbell, knighted 1515, in Scotland;

6–Lt. Cary (1745-1805), colonial constable; minuteman; ens.; selectman; made a daring and marvelous escape from prison ship "Jersey"; *m* 1st, 1767, Eunice Elder (1745-84; Samuel[7] [*d* 1753], Scotch-Irish origin, from Ireland to America, with wife, 1720, settled at Windham, Me., 1730, *m* Mary Huston);

5–Mary (1767-1832), *m* 1789, John **Clemons** (1763-1845), soldier Am. Rev., aet. 16; settled at Hiram, Me., 1790 (John[6] [*d* 1790], colonial soldier, 1755, founder of Hiram, Me., settled there 1780, *m* 1757, Abigail Southwick [1730-1834; desc. of Lawrence and Cassandra Southwick, landed at Salem, 1630, Quaker exiles who *d* at Shelter Island, 1660]; Isaac[7], aet. 9, landed at Salem, Mass., early in 1700, with bro. Jacob, aet. 7, "they became separated never to meet again, Jacob settled in Canada");

4–Cary (1790-1844), pioneer resident of Covington, Ky.; *m* 1813, Mary Merrill (*b* Cazenovia, N.Y., 1792-*d* 1882);

3–Martha (1831-88), *m* 1st, 1847, Samuel **Cloon** (1824-61), of Avondale, Cincinnati, O. (Samuel[4] [1799-1866], founder of Avondale, *m* in Marblehead, Mass., 1821, Sarah P. Smith, 1801-64);

2–Sallie Clifford (1853-1920), *m* Richard Bacon **Jones** (1849-1925), founder R. B. Jones & Sons, ins. agency, of Kansas City, 1889; issue: I–Richard Bryson (*b* 1872; *m* Alice Barse); II–Cary Watson (*b* 1875; *m* Bertha Mayer); III–Clifford Cloon (1 above); IV–Marguerite (*b* 1885; *m* John E. Clarke); V–Martha (*b* 1888; *m* Raymond G. Barnett); VI–Morton T. (*b* 1892; *m* Pauline Perry).

1–*m* Nov. 1, 1911, Elizabeth Smith, *b* Kansas City, Mo., May 29, 1885; dau. of William J. Smith, *m* Elizabeth Bussells; issue: 1–Clifford Cloon, 2d, *b* Kansas City, May 11, 1919.

1–Mem. firm R. B. Jones & Sons; chmn. bd. Kansas City Fire & Marine Ins. Co., dir. Commerce and Trust Co., Horner Conservatory of Music. Ex-pres. Nat. Assn. Ins. Agts.; pres. Kansas City Ins. Agts. Assn. Clubs: Kansas City, Chamber of Commerce, Cooperative, Kansas City Country, Mission Hills Country, Monterey Peninsula Country (Calif.). Mem. Christian Ch. Residence: 836 W. 57th St., Kansas City, Mo.

1–**JONES, Harry Stewart,** *b* Marion, O., Dec. 11, 1864.

6–Adam (deTurni) **Turney** (*b* 1725), Huguenot; from France, 1745; settled nr. Greensburg, Pa.: of Spanish-Judaic origin, and royal descent: *m* 1748;

5–John (1753-1824), pvt. Am. Rev.; served in Capt. George Knapingberger's Co., 2d Bn., Northampton Co. Militia; *m* 1773, Magdalena Grove;

4–Joseph (1792-1872), began to write name Turney; farmer, Columbus, O.; *m* 1812, Margaret Weber (*d* 1860);

3–Rachael, of Delaware, O.; *m* Mabah Dingy **Adams;**

2–Lenora Mabah (*d* 1892), of Marion, O.; *m* David Stewart **Jones** (1835-1911) contractor and builder; q.m. and sgt. Civil War; issue: I–Edith (*b* 1862; *m* George Donavin); II–Harry Stewart (1 above); III–Frank.

1–*m* Oct. 19, 1886, Henrietta Caroline Reiser, *b* Galion, O., Jan. 10, 1864; dau. of John Reiser; issue: 1–Lenore Ida, *b* Marion, O., Mar. 19, 1888; B.S., Columbia U., '22; M.A., 1923; 2–Lyman D., *b* Fostoria, O., Jan. 10, 1890; B.S., Purdue, '11; M.E., 1922; *m* 1911, Annetta Schumacher, of Lafayette, Ind.; 3–Henry Stewart, *b* Montgomery, Ala., June 24, 1901; B.S., Purdue, '22, M.E., 1927; *m* Apr. 16, 1929, Sara Frances, dau. of Hamilton Roddis, of Marshfield, Wis.

1–Ed. Ohio State U. Div. engr., city engr., gen. foreman, etc., C., R.I. & P. Ry., 1886-94; asst. chief engr., M. & O.R.R.; treas. and mgr. Montgomery (Ala.) Suburban St. Ry. Co., 1897-1901; chief engr., Mobile, Jackson & Kansas City R.R., 1901-03; valuation engr., G., M. & N.R.R., since 1926 (see Who's Who in America). Q.M. 14th Ohio Inf., 1896. Club: Gulf Hunting and Fishing. Episcopalian. Democrat. Residence: 1606 Monterey Pl., Mobile, Ala.

1–**JONES, Henry Llewellyn,** *b* Philadelphia, Pa., Feb. 11, 1870.
8–John **Borton** (*d* 1687), from Eng., 1679, settled at Burlington, N.J.; mem. N.J. Assembly, 1683-85; signer of First West Jersey Concession, 1676; *m* Ann–;
7–John, of Hillsdown, N.J.; *m* 2d, 1717, Ann Darnelly;
6–John (*d* 1759), *m* Elizabeth Lord (*d* 1759);
5–Elizabeth, *m* 1761, Joseph **Gaunt** (1740-1806), of Jobstown, N.J. (Hannaniah[6]; Peter[7]);
4–Sarah (*b* 1781), of Little Egg Harbour, N.J.; *m* 1799, Col. Reuben **Llewellyn** (1780-1838);
3–Elizabeth Gaunt, *m* William **Jones** (1813-51), of Gloucester Co., N.J. (William[4] [1776-1851], *m* 1802, Sarah [1776-1855], dau. of Lawrence Webster);
2–Reuben Llewellyn (2 below).
8–John **Bartram** (*d* 1697), from Eng. with William Penn, 1683, settled at Phila. (Darby), Pa.; mem. Pa. Assembly, 1689; *m* Elizabeth– (*d* 1723);
7–William (*d* 1712), mem. Pa. Assembly, 1708; *m* 1696, Elizabeth Hunt (*d* 1701; James[8]);
6–John (1699-1777), of Phila.; established a Botanical Garden at Darby; apptd. botanist to King George III; garden preserved as part of Phila. public park system; a founder of Philosophical Soc., 1743; *m* 1729, Ann Mendenhall (1703-89);
5–John (1743-1812), of Phila.; *m* 1771, Elizah Howell (1751-1784; Isaac[6]; Jacob[7]);
4–Dr. James Howell (1783-1818), of Phila.; *m* 1810, Mary Ann Joyce (1792-1876);
3–John William (1813-66), of Phila.; *m* 1834, Williamina Amelia Middleton (1813-86);
2–Mary Jones (1840-1910), of Phila.; *m* 1869, Reuben Llewellyn **Jones** (1842-92), farmer.
1–*m* Oct. 14, 1903, Ida Mae Hammond (Sept. 5, 1871-Oct. 2, 1908); dau. of William Hammond, of Norwich, Conn., and Keene, N.H., *m* Mary Byrnes; issue: 1–Kathryn Bartram, *b* Sydney, Australia, Oct. 23, 1904; grad. Miss Beard's Sch., Orange, N.J.; *m* John Carpenter Litt, son of Jacob Litt (von Jayder), of Patchogue, L.I., N.Y., *m* Ruth Carpenter (issue: John Carpenter Van deer Litt, *b* Nov. 18, 1928).
1–*m* 2d, Oct. 5, 1911, Louise Hunt Van der Veer (qv).
1–Topographical engr., Carnegie Steel Co., Pittsburgh; resident engr. N.J. Steel & Iron Co., Boston; later resident engr., Am. Bridge Co. (Sydney, Australia, and Shanghai, China); now with U.S. Steel Products Co. Am. vice consul at Sydney, Australia, 1903-08. Maj. engrs., U.S.A. during World War, now maj. 373d Engrs. Reserves. V.p. Argentine Am. Chamber of Commerce, Colombian Am. Chamber of Commerce. Mem. S.C.W., Colonial Soc. of Pa., Monmouth Co. Hist. Soc., Soc. Am. Mil. Engrs., A.L. Mason (32°), Elk. Clubs: Machinery, Circumnavigators, India House, Engineers. Winter place: 59 W. 46th St., New York, N.Y. Residence: 72 W. Main St., Freehold, N.J.

1–**JONES, Louise Hunt Van der Veer (Mrs. Henry Llewellyn),** *b* Freehold, N.J., May 17, 1865.
9–Janse **Van der Veer,** from Holland in the "Otter," 1659, settled at Flatlands, L.I.;
8–Cornelius Janse, magistrate, Flatbush, L.I., 1678-80; *m* 1672, Tryntje Yellis de Mandeville (*b* 1650);
7–Dominicus (1679-1755), of Flatbush, L.I.; capt. New Utrecht militia, 1715; sheriff Kings Co., L.I., 1736; *m* 1702, Jannetje Van Noortwyck;
6–Tunis (1704-75), of Freehold, N.J.; *m* 1723, Aeltje Schenck (*b* 1705; Gerrit Roelofse[7], *m* Neeltje Goerts Van Voorhees);
5–David (1748-1819), of Phila., Pa.; *m* 1765, Katharine Couvenhouven (1746-1811);
4–David (1778-1859), of Haddonfield, N.J.; *m* 1801, Elizabeth Morris (1785-1843);
3–Thomas (1807-80), of Freehold; *m* 1828, Margaret D. Smock (1810-57);
2–David Augustus (2 below).
8–John **Hunt** (*b* 1650), from Eng., 1708, settled at L.I., N.Y.; *m* 1675, Elizabeth Chudleigh (*d* 1708);
7–John (1685-1769), of Hopewell, N.J.; *m* Margaret Moore;
6–Wilson (1715-82), of Hopewell; *m* 1735, Susanna Price (1715-83);
5–James (1739-1832), of Hopewell; capt., 3d N.J. Co. in Am. Rev.; *m* 1760, Jemima Green (*b* 1742);
4–Wilson (1763-1823), of Hightstown, N.J.; *m* 1792, Mary Taylor (1769-1847);
3–George (1795-1875), of Freehold; *m* 1823, Ann Ely (1801-74);
2–Georgianna (1842-1915), *m* 1861, David Augustus **Van der Veer** (1833-1911), farmer; charter mem. Monmouth Co. Bd. of Agrl. Soc.; issue: I–Louise Hunt (1 above); II–Marianna Hunt (*b* 1870; *m* Edward Taylor); III–Ella Hunt (*b* 1875; *m* Bowel Bancroft Smith).
1–*m* Oct. 5, 1911, Henry Llewellyn Jones (qv).
1–Presbyterian. Republican. Club: Woman's (pres.). Residence: 72 W. Main St., Freehold, N.J.

1–**JONES, Livingston Erringer,** *b* Germantown, Pa., Mar. 30, 1878.
7–John Griffith **Jones,** came from Eng., 1698; settled at Phila., Pa.;
6–Griffith (*b* 1686), *m* 1709, Elizabeth Cunders;
5–Aquilla (1724-1800), *m* 1767, Elizabeth Cooper (1736-1808);
4–Isaac Cooper (1769-1865), *m* 1797, Hannah Firth (1778-1854);
3–Isaac Cooper (1814-95), *m* 1840, Sarah Whitall Woodruff (*b* 1820);
2–Thomas Firth (1844-1908), mcht., Phila.; *m* 1874, Cornelia Erringer (1851-1901); issue: I–Livingston Erringer (1 above); II–Arthur Woodruff (*b* 1879; *m* Dorothea Rehn).
1–*m* May 23, 1908, Edith Bolling (qv for issue).
1–B.S., Princeton, '99. Office boy and partner, Reeves, Parvin & Co., Phila., 1900-12; pres. Savings Fund Soc., Germantown, 1912-22; pres. First Nat. Bank, Phila., Pa. (see Who's Who in America). Clubs: University, Princeton, Germantown Cricket, Mid-Day, Sunnybrook Golf, Rhibault, Bras Coupe. Residence: "Chellowe," Chestnut Hill, Phila., Pa.

1–**JONES, Edith Bolling (Mrs. Livingston E.),** *b* Louisville, Ky., June 30, 1879.
8–Col. Robert **Bolling** (qv);
7–Robert (1682-1749), *m* 1706, Anne Cocke (*b* 1686);
6–Robert (1730-75), of "Bolling Brooke," Petersburg, Va.; burgess, 1774; home burned by Tories because of his principles; *m* 2d, 1758, Mary Marshall Tabb (1737-1814);
5–Thomas Tabb (1763-1810), *m* 1786, Seignora Peyton (1767-1837; Sir John[6], from Ireland to Va., 1700, served as capt. 3d Va. Regt. in Am. Rev.);
4–Thomas Redford (1797-1874), *m* 1818, Mary Pleasants Carter (1802-77);
3–James Carter (*d* 1863), *m* Mary Cecilia Raynal (*d* 1912);
2–Sanford Coley (1852-1930), *m* 1876, Ada Leonora Hart (1857-1927), of Hot Springs, Va.; issue: I–Raynal Cawthorne (1879-1918; killed in World War; *m* Anna Tucker Phillips, see Vol. I, p. 345); II–Edith (1 above); III–Robert Hart (*b* 1891; *m* Elizabeth Day Lanier).
1–*m* May 23, 1908, Livingston Erringer Jones (qv); issue (all *b* Germantown, Pa.): 1–Livingston Eric, *b* May 11, 1911; Princeton, '33; 2–Cornelia Livingston, *b* Mar. 30, 1913; 3–Peyton Bolling, *b* Sept. 22, 1915.
1–Mem. C.D.A. (Pa. Soc.). Episcopalian. Residence: "Chellowe," Chestnut Hill, Philadelphia, Pa.

1–**JONES, Lynds,** *b* Jefferson, O., Jan. 5, 1865.
8–Thomas **Jones** (1598-1671), from Eng., settled at Gloucester, Mass., 1642; freeman, 1653; *m* Mary North (*d* 1681; Richard[9], *m* Ursula–);
7–Benjamin (1649-1718), Enfield, Conn.; soldier King Philip's War; *m* 1678, Elizabeth Wild;
6–Thomas (1680-1763), *m* 1708, Mary Meacham (1685-1744; Capt. Isaac[7], of Enfield);
5–Capt. Israel (1716-98), Barkhamsted, Conn.; capt. local militia; constable; *m* 1744, Jemima Clark (1722-88);
4–Col. Israel (1753-1812), sgt., Cont. Army, 1775, ens., 1777, 2d lt., 1778, resigned, 1779; capt. 18th militia regt., 1778, and subsequently commd. a col.; *m* 1st, 1778, Rhoda Parsons (*d* 1796);
3–Lynds (1790-1851), of Jefferson, O.; *m* 1816, Phoebe Waters (1795-1858);
2–Publius Vergilius (2 below).
5–Israel **Burton**;
4–Jacob (*b* 1762);
3–William (1789-1858);
2–Lavinia (1827-91), as Widow Howard, *m* 2d, 1851, Publius Vergilius **Jones** (1819-92), mill-

wright and carpenter, Grinnell, Ia.; issue: I–Marcus Eugene (*b* 1852; *m* Anna E. Richardson); II–Charles Hughes (1854-1927); III–Carrie Louise (*b* 1856; *m* 1881, Franklin P. Morse, *d* 1913); IV–Edward Publius (*b* 1859; *m* 1888, Lulu Carson Bentley); V–Lucien Corydon (*b* 1861); VI–Lynds (1 above); VII–Burton Howard (*b* 1868); VIII–Arthur Julius (*b* 1871).

1–*m* Sept. 8, 1892, Clara Mabelle Tallmon, *b* Davenport, Ia., Oct. 3, 1868; dau. of George Washington Tallmon, of Grinnell, Ia., and Morgan Hill, Calif.; issue (all *b* Oberlin, O.): 1–Lynds Leo, *b* June 21, 1893; *m* Sept. 25, 1920, Lula Alma (Edwards) Johnston; 2–Theodore Burton (Apr. 16, 1896-Aug. 30, 1909); 3–George Tallmon, *b* Aug. 28, 1897; A.B., Oberlin, '20, A.M., 1921; *m* Aug. 28, 1924, Mary, dau. of George Burwell, of Benton Harbor, Mich. (issue: Frances; Margaret); 4–Beth, *b* Nov. 19, 1899; *m* Aug. 10, 1921, Max W. deLaurenfels (issue: Peter Max; Leroy Arthur; David John); 5–Harold Charles, *b* May 25, 1903; A.B., Oberlin, '28.

1–Student Ia. Coll., 1888-90; A.B., Oberlin, '92, Sc.M., 1895; Ph.D., U.Chicago, 1905. Prof. animal ecology, Oberlin Coll., since 1922, also curator Zool. Museum. Author (see Who's Who in America). Congregational. Republican. Residence: 352 W. College St., Oberlin, O.

1–**JONES, Samuel Fosdick,** *b* Cincinnati, O., Aug. 4, 1874.

Desc. David **Jones,** from Wales to Berks Co., Pa., ca. 1721; and thru:

Col. Jonathan, officer Am. Rev.;

3–John Davies, *m* Elizabeth Johnston (desc. of John Johnston, from North of Ireland to Phila., 1786);

2–Frank J. (2 below).

9–Stephen **Fosdick** (qv);

8–John (1626-1716), sgt. King Philip's War; *m* 1st, 1648, Ann Shapley;

7–Lt. Samuel (1655-1702), soldier King Philip's War; *m* Mercy Pickett;

6–Thomas, *m* Esther Updike;

5–Thomas U. (1725-76), surgeon's mate in Am. Rev.; *m* Anna Havens;

4–Richard, settled at Cincinnati, O., 1811; *m* Phebe L'Hommedieu;

3–Samuel (1801-81), cotton mfr., financier, Cincinnati; *m* Sarah Ann Wood;

2–Frances D. (2 below).

10–Elder William **Brewster** (qv);

9–Jonathan (1593-1661), *m* 1624, Lucretia Oldham;

8–Ruth (1631-1687?), *m* 1652, John **Pickett** (*d* 1667);

7–Mercy (1661-1725), *m* 1682, Lt. Samuel **Fosdick** (7 above).

2–Frank Johnston **Jones,** *m* 1866, Frances Dering Fosdick (1841-1917); for issue see Vol. I, p. 933.

1–*m* Dec. 3, 1910, Mary Catherine Cordes, *b* Denver, Colo., July 3, 1880; dau. Herman M. Cordes, of Denver.

1–M.I.T., '98 (Delta Psi); M.D., Columbia, 1902. Surgeon, specialty orthopedics; prof. emeritus orthopedic surgery, U. of Colo. First lt., M.C., U.S.A., Apr. 6, 1917; maj., Aug. 7, 1918; operating orthopedic surgeon A.E.F., Hospital 1, France, hon. discharged, Jan. 13, 1919. F.A.C.S., etc. Mem. S.M.D., S.R., M.O.L.L., M.O.F.W., A.L., I.A.G. Clubs: New York Yacht, St. Anthony (New York), Cosmos (Washington), Denver, University, Denver Country, Mile High, Cactus (Denver), California (Los Angeles). Residence: 1331 E. 7th Av., Denver, Colo.

1–**JONES, William Alfred,** *b* "Granite Hill," Manchester, Me., Mar. 4, 1862.

11–William **Carpenter** (1576-1660; qv);

10–William (1605-59), also came in the "Bevis," 1638; freeman of Weymouth, 1640; constable, 1641; rep. Gen. Ct., Plymouth, 1641,43,45, dep., 1656; removed to Rehoboth, 1645; town clk., 1645-49; town dir., 1647,55; contributed towards King Philip's War; *m* Abigail– (1606-1687/-88);

9–Joseph (ca. 1632/33-1675), also came in the "Bevis," 1638; moved to Swansea, 1661/62; founder first Bapt. ch. in Mass., 1663; founder of Attleboro, 1667; *m* 1655, Margaret Sutton (1635-1700; John[10], from Eng. in the "Diligent," 1638, settled at Hingham, *m* Elizabeth–);

8–Benjamin (*b* 1658), *m* Renew Weeks (1660 or 62-1703; William[9]; George[10], qv);

7–Elizabeth (*b* 1685/86), *m* as his 1st wife, James **Winslow** (1687-1773), of Assonet (Freetown), Mass., moved to Falmouth, Me., ca. 1728, "First Friend" at Falmouth (Lt. Job[8]; Kenelm[9], qv);

6–Nathan (1713-72), of Freetown, Mass., and that part of Falmouth, now Westbrook, Me.; *m* Charity Hall (Ebenezer[7]; Samuel[8]; George[9]);

5–Job (1745-1833), "Friend"; *m* 1772, Mary Robinson;

4–Miriam (1774-1816), *m* Jedediah **Austin** (1762-1838), of Pownal, Me.;

3–Mary (1798-1831), *m* as his 2d wife, Josiah **Jones** (1792-1867; Stephen[4]; Lemuel[5]; Thomas[6]);

2–Samuel Hopkins (2 below).

9–Gov. Thomas **Roberts** (will dated 1673; son of John), apprenticed, 1622, to Fishmongers Guild, of London; believed to have come from Eng. in the "Providence," with the Hiltons, and landed in Pomeroy's Cove, Hilton Point, 1623; pres. of the ct., 1638; 4th and last gov. of the Dover Colony, 1640-42; juror, 1646; Quaker sympathizer; *m* ca. 1627, Rebecca Hilton;

8–Sgt. John (1629-1694/95), of Dover Neck, N.H.; constable; selectman, 1665; marshal of N.H., 1679, and was called "Sergeant"; del. to N.H. Conv., 1689; *m* Abigail Nutter (living 1674; Elder Hatevil[9], 1603-75);

7–Mary, *m* ante 1692, Timothy **Robinson,** of Dover, N.H. (Timothy[8], *m* Mary, dau. of Robert Allen);

6–Timothy (1710-83), *m* 1730, Mary Allen (1712-94; Francis[7]; Robert[8]; John[9]);

5–Mary (1752-1824), *m* 1772, Job **Winslow** (5 above).

10–Robert **Cushman** (qv);

9–Elder Thomas (bap. 1607/08-1691), came with his father in the "Fortune," 1621; admitted to the ch. at Plymouth, 1633; juryman, 1635; received land grant at Kingston, 1637; ruling elder, 1649; *m* ca. 1635/36, Mary Allerton (1616-99; Isaac[10], Mayflower Pilgrim, qv);

8–Sarah (*d* post 1695), *m* as his 2d wife, Elder John **Hawkes** (1632/33-1694; Adam[9]);

7–Ebenezer (a minor of 17 and upward, 1694-*d* 1766), propr. or one of 60 grantees of New Marblehead, now Windham, Me., 1734; moderator, 1737; *m* 1701, Elizabeth Cogswell (1677-1718; John[8]; John[9]; John[10], qv);

6–Ebenezer (1702-59), propr. or one of 60 grantees of New Marblehead; *m* Anna Breed (*b* 1706; Samuel[7]; Allen[8], qv);

5–Nathaniel (*b* 1740), "Friend"; *m* 1771, Mercy Jones (*b* 1752; Lemuel[6]; Thomas[7]);

4–Lemuel (1774-1840), Friend minister, of Windham and China, Kennebec Co., Me.; *m* 1791, Abigail Winslow (1776-1851; Job[5], above);

3–Isaac (1802-90), "Friend"; *m* 1st, 1825, Esther Hobby (1804-32);

2–Margaret Buffum Hawkes Nichols (2 below).

15–Thomas **Stoughton,** of Stoughton, Surry, Eng.;

14–Gilbert, *m* Mary, dau. of Edward Bambesy;

13–Lawrence (will probated 1572), *m* Ann Comb, of Ford, Sussex;

12–Thomas (1521-76), *m* Elizabeth, dau. of Edmund Lewkenor;

11–Lawrence (1554-1615), *m* Rose, dau. of Richard Ive, of London;

10–Anthony (1598-1644), *m* Agnes, dau. Robert Pierce;

9–Rose (*b* 1629), came to N.E. with Capt. Israel Stoughton; 1643; *m* 1651, Richard **Otis** (killed by Indians, 1689), from Eng.; settled at Dover Neck (Stephen[10]; Richard[11]);

8–Mary, *m* Ebenezer **Varney** (Humphrey[9], *m* Esther, dau. of Elder Edward Starbuck, *m* Catherine Reynolds; William[10] (*d* 1654), *m* Bridget–, *d* 1672);

7–Nathaniel (1706-76), *m* 1727, Content Gaskill (*b* 1727; Samuel[8]; Samuel[9]; Edward[10]);

6–Lydia (*d* 1805), *m* 1751, Isaac **Rogers** (Jonathan[7]);

5–Hannah (1756-86), *m* 1773, as his 1st wife, John **Buffum** (*d* 1812; Joshua[6]; Caleb[7]; Caleb[8]; Robert[9], qv);

4–Margaret (1778-1848), *m* 1st, Remington **Hobby** (1774-1805; Remington[5]; Rev. William[6]; John[7]; William[8]);

3–Esther (1804-32), *m* Isaac **Hawkes** (3 above).

2–Samuel Hopkins **Jones** (1828-1904), educator;

m 1851, Margaret Buffum Hawkes Nichols (1829-73), adopted dau. of her Aunt Eunice Hobby, wife of Caleb Nichols; *m* 2d, 1874, Mary Thomas (1843-1925; Isaac[3] [*b* 1813], *m* Anna Ladd, *b* 1812); issue (1st marriage): I–Ann Maria (1852-1926; *m* 1871, Rowland Hill, 1839-99); II–Charles Nichols (1853-1913; *m* 1876, Lizzie Fowler, *b* 1849); III–Gwlia Elma (*b* 1857; *m* 1876, Thomas Winder Young, *b* 1854); IV–Marietta (*b* and *d* 1859); V–Gilbert (*b* and *d* 1860); VI–William Alfred (1 above); issue: (2d marriage): I–Isaac Thomas (*b* 1875); II–Cynthia Anna (1878-79); III–Olive Sutton (*b* 1881; *m* 1900, Freeman E. Klock, *b* 1875); IV–Mary Alice (*b* 1885; *m* 1904, Vernon William Bodette, *b* 1884).

1–*m* Nov. 17, 1886, Mary Ella Scripture, *b* Brooklyn, N.Y., Dec. 20, 1864; dau. of Sumner Scripture, *m* Josephine Robinson, both of Brooklyn, N.Y.; issue: 1–William Alfred, Jr. (Mar. 1-Dec. 11, 1888); 2–Lillian May, *b* Brooklyn, N.Y., Jan. 3, 1892; grad. Adelphi Acad., 1914; *m* June 15, 1916, James Salmond, Jr., of Arlington, N.J. (issue: James, III, *b* 1917; William Alfred, *b* 1924; Nancy Marian, *b* 1929); 3–Howard Scripture, *b* Brooklyn, Feb. 17, 1898; grad. structural engr., Pratt Inst., 1918; *m* 1923, Lillian Gladys, dau. of Frank Winne, *m* Lillian Gibson.

1–Buyer and sales mgr., 42 yrs., for Wm. H. Jackson & Co., mfg. tile mantles. Mem. S.M.D. Mason. Pres. bd. of trustees 1st Presbyn. Ch. Republican. Summer place: Asbury Park, N.J. Residence: 99 Seeley Av., Arlington, N.J.

1–**JONES, Alice Carey Ogburn (Mrs. William Clay)**, *b* Granville Co., N.C., Sept. 7, 1879.

8–Simon **Ogburn** (*d* 1669/70), *m* Gusie–, of Va.;
7–Nicholas (ca. 1653-1687), *m* Ann–, of Va.;
6–John (*b* ca. 1682);
5–John Henry (1719-74), Brunswick Co., Va.; *m* Tabitha Neblett, of Va.;
4–William (*b* 1748), *m* 1st, 1771, Hannah Warren;
3–Edmund Warren (1798-1856), planter, served in House of Commons, 1846, from Guilford Co., N.C.; mem. Constl. Conv., 1835; *m* Jane Lanier;
2–Thomas Jefferson (2 below).
9–John **Flood** (*d* 1661), came to Va. in the "Swann," 1610; rep. Gen. Assembly, 1630,32,42,-45; Charles City, 1638; capt.; Indian interpreter; lt. col., Surry Co.; in legislature, 1652-55; *m* ante 1625, Widow Margaret Finch;
8–Mary, *m* 3d, 1658, John **Washington**, from Eng. to Surry Co., Va.;
7–Richard (ca. 1660-1725), Surry Co.; *m* Elizabeth Jordan (*d* ca. 1735; Arthur[8], *m* Elizabeth Baron);
6–Elizabeth, *m* Sampson **Lanier** (1682-1742 or 43; John[7], qv);
5–James (post 1724-ante 1792), of Va. and N.C.; entered tract of land on Troubleson Creek, N.C., 1778, issued 1788; *m* ante 1750, Mary Cooke (Henry[6], *d* 1772);
4–Sampson (1764-1823), of Rockingham Co., N.C.; large planter, slaveholder; owner of grist mill; served in House of Commons, N.C., 1805,07; *m* ante 1790, Elizabeth Massey (1770-post 1834; Thomas[5], Am. Rev., *m* Mary Peeples);
3–Jane (1807-74), founder of Flat Rock Sunday Sch.; *m* 1824, Edmund W. **Ogburn** (3 above).
6–William **Gudger,** from Scotland to Md., 1730 or 33;
5–William (*d* 1833), to western N.C., ca. 1778; *m* Martha Young (*b* 1750); John[6], of Georgetown, Md., *m* a member of the House of Stuart);
4–Nancy (1777-1851), *m* John **Gash** (1769-1857; Martin Alley[5], *m* Ann–, 1732-1812);
3–Burditt Stuart (1816-91), *m* 1843, Elizabeth Foster Weaver;
2–Alice Cordelia (2 below).
6–Plikard Dederic **Siler** (1719-84), from Germany, 1741, settled finally in N.C., nr. what is now Siler City; planter, owner grist mill; patriot Am. Rev.; *m* 1744, Elizabeth Hartsoe (1727-1816), from Germany;
5–Weimer (1755-1831), of Macon Co., N.C.; *m* 1784, Margaret Rafferty (1767-1839), from Ireland;
4–Elizabeth (1788-1867), *m* 1811, Jacob **Weaver** (1786-1868), of Weaverville, N.C. (John W.[5], *m* Elizabeth Biffle);
3–Elizabeth F. (1817-88), of Buncombe Co., N.C.; *m* Burditt S. **Gash** (3 above);
2–Alice Cordelia (1856-81), *m* 1876, Thomas Jefferson **Ogburn,** D.D. (1849-1923), ed. New Garden Sch. (now Guilford Coll.); mem. N.C. Conference M.P. Ch., 48 yrs. (pres., 1885-88); sec. treas., Bd. Foreign Missions, 1895-1907; joined Western N.C. Conf. M.E. Ch., South; he *m* 2d, 1883, Nannie Ida Davidson, dau. of Littleberry Davidson, *m* Mary Avent Wilson; issue (1st marriage): I–William Lee (1877-98); II–Alice Carey (1 above); III–Mary Ellen (*b* 1881; *m* Luther Leonidas Gaskill); issue (2d marriage): I–Thomas Jefferson, Jr. (*b* 1885; *m* Virginia Gray Cudlipp); II–Herbert Hammond, M.D. (*b* 1886); III–Nannie Fletcher (1888-92); IV–Richard Davidson (1890-91); V–Bessie Bidwell (*b* 1892; *m* T. Bascom Whitaker); VI–Hilda Lanier (*b* 1895); VII–Roger Wendell, M.D. (1899-1927).

1–*m* Nov. 27, 1907, William Clay Jones, *b* High Point, N.C., July 6, 1871; son of Dr. William Oliver Jones, of High Point; issue (all *b* High Point, N.C.): 1–Elizabeth Lindsay, *b* Aug. 27, 1910; grad. Salem Acad., 1928; 2–William Clay, Jr., *b* June 18, 1914; 3–Thomas Ogburn, *b* Dec. 11, 1917.

1–Grad. N.C. Coll. for Women, '99. Teacher, 1899-1907. Mem. Bd. of Sch. Commrs. of High Point, 1919-20, 1920-25. Mem. D.A.R., U.D.C. Methodist. Democrat. Clubs: High Point Garden, Philomathean. Residence: 307 N. Main St., High Point, N.C.

1–**JOST, Ida Gertrude Johnson (Mrs. Albert),** *b* Plymouth, Ind., July 31, 1865.

8–Laurens Andriessen **Van Buskirk** (qv);
7–Thomas (1662-1748), officer King's Rangers; capt., maj. and col., colonial troops of N.J.; *m* 2d, 1720, Volkertie Collier;
6–Michael (*b* 1721), of Hunterdon Co., N.J.; ens., Md.; soldier French and Indian War; *m* ca. 1745, Mary Van Deventer (*b* 1726);
5–Isaac (1760-1843), of Monroe Co., Ind.; almost continuously engaged for several yrs. in Indian border warfare, in Va. militia in Am. Rev.; *m* Jerusha Littell (1756-1827);
4–Mary, of Monroe Co.; *m* John **Johnson** (*b* 1775 or 80);
3–James (1812-84), Meth. minister and presiding elder M.E. ch.; *m* 1836, Eliza Montgomery (*d* 1848);
2–Amasa (2 below).
5–Nehemiah **Smith** (1741-1827), pvt. in Am. Rev.; *m* Lydia Warrington;
4–Calista (1789-1884), *m* 1807, William **Sherman** (1784-1843), merchant;
3–Nehemiah, M.D. (1817-79), ed. Rush Med. Coll., physician and surgeon; *m* Caroline Catherine Dittrick (1822-89; Jacob[4], *m* Catherine Young);
2–Carrie Adelia (1848-1922), ed. Young Woman's Female Sem., *m* 1864, Amasa **Johnson** (1837-1901), capt. Co. D., 9th Ind. Vols., Civil War, 3 yrs.; lawyer; mayor Plymouth, Ind., 3 times; rep. for St. Joseph and Marshall cos. in Legislature, 1869; issue I–Ida Gertrude (1 above); II–Carrie (*b* 1869; *m* Claude F. Baker, 1870-1906); III–Edith Idell (*b* 1871; *m* Charles A. Seward); IV–Sherman Amasa (1878-1904).

1–*m* June 28, 1893, Albert Jost, *b* Francesville, Ind., Mar. 1865; son of Michael Jost, *m* Elizabeth Earl; issue: 1–Caroline Adelia, *b* Arkansas City, Kan., Oct. 16, 1896; attended Washington U.; *m* June 26, 1928, Harold G. Lampert.

1–Formerly public sch. instr. Mem. D.A.R. (chapter registrar), Daus. of Civil War Vets., Minute Women, O.E.S. Methodist. Republican. Club: Coterie (pres.). Residence: 1423 21st Av., Seattle, Wash.

1–**JUDD, Albert Francis, 2d,** *b* Honolulu, Hawaii, Dec. 20, 1874.

9–Dea. Thomas **Judd** (qv);
8–William (1636-90), *m* 1658, Mary Steele (*d* 1718; John[9], qv);
7–Thomas (1663-1747), *m* 1688, Sarah Freeman;
6–William (1689-1772), capt. militia; rep. Gen. Ct.; *m* 1713, Mary Root;
5–Elnathan (1724-77), *m* 1752, Miriam Richards;
4–Elnathan (1773-1845), *m* 1802, Betsey Hastings;
3–Dr. Gerrit Parmele (1803-73), surgeon under A.B.C.F.M. in Hawaii, 1828; adviser to the

king, organizer of govt., and premier; *m* 1827, Laura Fish (Elias[4], *m* Sybil, dau. Samuel Williams, lt. 6th Conn. Cont. Line in Am. Rev.);
2–Albert Francis (1838-1900), B.A., Yale, '62 (LL.D., 1894); LL.B., Harvard, 1864; justice 26 yrs. and chief justice 19 yrs. of Supreme Ct. of Hawaii; *m* 1872, Agnes Hall Boyd (*b* 1844; James Robert[3], *m* Elizabeth Camp); issue: I–Agnes Elizabeth (*b* 1873); II–Albert Francis, 2d, (1 above); III–James Robert (*b* 1876; *m* Alice Louise Marshall); IV–Allan Wilkes (*b* 1879; *m* Elizabeth McCarthy); V–Henry Pratt (*b* 1880; *m* Martha Case); VI–Charles Sheldon (*b* 1881; *m* Louise Luquiens); VII–Sophie Boyd (*b* 1883; *m* George Paul Cooke); VIII–Gerrit Parmele (*b* 1885; *m* Marguerite Foulke); IX–Lawrence McCully (*b* 1887; *m* Florence Hackett).
1–*m* July 21, 1899, Madeline Perry Hartwell, *b* Honolulu, May 26, 1875; dau. of Alfred Stedman Hartwell, of Honolulu; issue (all *b* Honolulu): 1–Son (*b* and *d* 1901); 2–Bernice, *b* Oct. 18, 1903; ed. Punahm Sch. and Dana Hall; 3–Dorothy, *b* Apr. 8, 1906; ed. Punahm Sch. and Pine Manor; *m* Aug. 28, 1929, William Alexander, son of Charles Winfred Jackson; 4–Albert Francis, 3d, *b* Mar. 15, 1909; ed. Punahm Sch. and Tamalpais Sch.
1–B.A., Yale, '97, LL.B., 1900. Lawyer; trustee Oahu Coll., of Bishop Estate and Bishop Museum, Charles R. Bishop Trust. Has been commr. of U.S. Dist. Ct. of Hawaii, and police magistrate at Honolulu; mem. Territorial Senate, 1911-13. Capt., Q.M. Corps, later supervisor of postal censors, during World War. Mem. S.A.R. Clubs: University (ex-pres.), Oahu Country. Residence: 622 Judd St., Honolulu, H.T.

1–**JUDD, Zebulon,** *b* Wake Co., N.C., Nov. 26, 1876.
6–John **Ragland,** from Wales to Eng., thence to Va. bet. 1700-20; settled in Henrico Co., and took up lands in that and other cos.; his home "Ripping Hall" on the Chickahominy was burned, 1825; *m* Ann Beaufort, his kinswoman;
5–William; settled on Cape Fear River in Chatham Co., N.C.; Am. Rev.; *m* Sarah Avent;
4–Frederic (1766-1812), *m* 1795, Mary Barham (1775-1851);
3–Nancy, *m* William H. **Cross** (Parish[4], *m* Elizabeth, dau. of Burwell Williams, Am. Rev.);
2–Louise Frances (1841-1915), as widow of B. R. Avent, *m* 2d, John Thomas **Judd** (1843-1914); for issue and Judd lineage see Vol. III, p. 279.
1–*m* Dec. 27, 1915, Edith Royster, *b* Columbia, S.C.; dau. of William Burt Royster, of Raleigh, N.C.
1–Ph.B., U. of N.C., '03; M.A., Columbia, 1914. Instr. French and English, U.Fla., 1903-05; supt. public instrn., Wake Co., N.C., 1905-14; prof. rural edn., U. of N.C., 1913-15; prof. psychology and edn. and dean, School of Edn., Ala. Poly. Inst., 1915– (see Who's Who in America). Mason (K.T., Shriner). M.E. Ch., S. Residence: Auburn, Ala.

1–**JUNKIN, George,** *b* Phila., Pa., June 25, 1891.
6–Joseph **Junkin** (*d* 1777), from Ireland, 1742; *m* Elizabeth Wallace (*d* 1796);
5–Capt. Joseph (1750-1825), 3 campaigns in Am. Rev., wounded at Battle of Brandywine; *m* Elenor Cochran (1750-1812);
4–Rev. George, D.D., LL.D. (1790-1868), founder and pres. Lafayette Coll., and Washington and Lee U.; *m* Julia Rush Miller (1797-1854);
3–George, LL.D. (1827-1902), lawyer; dir., prin., theologian; founder Real Estate Trust Co., Phila., Pa.; *m* Jeanie Wakeman de Forest;
2–Joseph De Forest (2 below).
14–Giles **De Forest** (*d* 1460), burgher and receiver of taxes for City and Perrage Avesnes, France;
13–Melchior (*d* 1530), Avesnes, France;
12–Melchior (1510-71), alderman of Avesnes, France; *m* Catherine Du Fosset (*d* 1579);
11–Jean (*b* 1543), first pres. of the Avesnes De Forest; *m* Anna Maillard (*d* 1640);
10–Jesse (1576-1624), headed expedition of Huguenot settlers to West Indies, 1623; *m* Marie Du Cloux;
9–Isaac (1616-74), from Holland in the "Rensselaerwick," to New Amsterdam, 1636; *m* Sarah Du Trieux (1625-92);
8–David (1669-1721), 17 of his g.sons served in Am. Rev., militia and Cont. Line; *m* Martha Blagg (1677-1740);
7–Samuel (1704-77), Am. Rev.; *m* Abigail Peat (1707-76);
6–Joseph (1731-77), *m* 1757, Susannah Mills;
5–Lt. Samuel (1758-1837), Am. Rev.; *m* Mary Curtis (*d* 1840);
4–William Carroll (1797-1844), *m* Zilphia Caroline Wakeman;
3–Jeanie Wakeman (1832-1909), *m* George **Junkin** (3 above).
11–Francis **Wakeman** (*d* 1626), *m* Ann Goode (*d* 1621);
10–John (1601-61), *m* Elizabeth Hopkins (1610-58);
9–Rev. Samuel (1635-92), *m* Hannah Goodyear (*d* 1721; Stephen[10], qv);
8–Capt. John (1659-1709), Colonial Wars; *m* Martha Hubbell;
7–Lt. Samuel (1693-1771), Colonial Wars; *m* Elizabeth– (1695-1759);
6–Capt. Samuel (1734-1809), Am. Rev.; *m* Mabel Burr;
5–Lloyd (1760-1825), *m* Sarah Redfield;
4–Zilphia Caroline (1801-43), *m* William Carroll **DeForest** (4 above).
11–Vincent **Meigs** (qv);
10–John (*b* 1612), *m* Thomasine Fry;
9–Elizabeth (*b* 1635), *m* Lt. Richard **Hubbell** (qv);
8–Martha (*d* 1710), *m* Capt. John **Wakeman** (8 above).
10–Jehu **Burr** (qv);
9–Daniel (*b* ca. 1642), *m* 1678, Abagail Glover;
8–Daniel, *m* Abagail–;
7–Timothy (*b* 1727), *m* Sarah Rowland;
6–Mabel (*d* 1818), *m* Capt. Samuel **Wakeman** (6 above).
10–John **Alden,** 7th signer of the Mayflower Compact (qv);
9–Elizabeth (1623/24-1717), *m* William **Pabodie** (1620-1707), bore arms in Capt. Standish's Duxbury Co., 1643;
8–Lydia (1667-1748), *m* Daniel **Grinnell** (1668-1740; g.son of Matthew Grinnell [qv], desc. Pierre Grinnell, 1480, Duchy of Bourgogne);
7–Pricalla (1689-1770), *m* Sgt. Theophis **Redfield** (1682-1739);
6–Capt. James (1735-88), Am. Rev.; *m* Sarah Grinnell (1738-93);
5–Sarah (1761-1821), *m* Lloyd **Wakeman** (5 above).
9–Chiefton James **McCord** (*d* 1689), Argyle, on the Isle of Skye; killed at Battle of Killecrankie Pass during Rev.;
8–John (*d* 1715), took part in wars with his father;
7–William (*b* 1680), from Ireland 1720; Indian wars; builder McCord's Fort;
6–John (*b* 1718), wife captured by Indians and held captive till re-captured, *m* Ann–;
5–William (1740-1806), served with 2d Pa. Bn., Am. Rev.; *m* Agnes McKinney (*d* 1783);
4–James (1783-1865), *m* Susan Davidson (1784-1818; Ens. John[5], Am. Rev.);
3–John Davidson (1808-1900), original incorporator Presbyn. Hosp. of Phila.; *m* Rosanna Blaine Robinson;
2–Mary Robinson (2 below).
8–Thomas **Robinson** (*d* 1740), from Ireland ante 1730;
7–Philip (1698-1770), Indian wars; builder Robertson Fort;
6–George (1727-1814), served in Indian and colonial wars and Am. Rev.; *m* Ann Wiley;
5–Thomas (1773-1830), *m* Mary McCord (1777-1843);
4–William Andrew (1795-1871), *m* Nancy Cochran (1797-1884);
3–Rosanna Blaine (1821-86), *m* John Davidson **McCord** (3 above);
2–Mary Robinson (*b* 1853), *m* Joseph De Forest **Junkin** (1855-1920), B.A., M.A., U.Pa., '74; noted corpn. lawyer, Phila. (for issue see Vol. III, p. 283).
1–*m* June 7, 1913, Martha Dorothy Johnson.
1–*m* 2d, June 12, 1929, Alice Gertrude Maslin, *b* St. Louis, Mo., Nov. 13, 1903, dau. of William Edward Maslin, *b* Oct. 28, 1870, Beardstown, Ill., *m* Alice Edell Bottomly, *b* Sept. 15, 1878, Cedar, Kan.
1–Pa. State, '13 (Theta Beta Sigma, Phi Delta

Theta). Farmer, actor, dramatic producer, radio director. Enlisted in U.S.N.R.F., May 20, 1918; ens., Dec. 24, 1918; instr. Naval Aviation, flying boats, Pensacola, Fla.; hon. discharged, Jan. 13, 1919. Residence: Hotel Mayfair, St. Louis, Mo.

1–**KAGEY, Charles Lemuel,** *b* New Market, Va., Dec. 22, 1876.
6–John Rudolph **Kagey** (ca. 1665-1748), from Switzerland to Lancaster Co., Pa., 1715, settled at Conestoga; *m* ca. 1720, Rebecca Patterson (1700-70; James[7], served in Cresap's War);
5–Henry (1728-83), of Shenandoah Co., Va., 1768; *m* 1756, Barbara Stoner (*d* 1781);
4–Abraham (1764-1831), of New Market, Va.; *m* 1803, Anna Neff (*d* 1831; Dr. Jacob[6]);
3–Henry Neff (1804-79), farmer, New Market; *m* 1839, Mary Neff (1808-49);
2–John Henry (1842-95), farmer, New Market; served in C.S.A. in Civil War; *m* 1874, Emma Frances Fultz (1854-1913; Walter[8], *m* Jane Stoner); issue: I–Harry W. (*m* Lulu Price); II–Charles Lemuel (1 above); III–Anna K.; IV–Thomas J., M.D. (*m* Eva Hinkel); V–Daniel F., D.D.S. (*m* Price Griffith).
1–*m* Mar. 4, 1901, Phebe Marie Wanzer, *b* Simpson, Kan., July 28, 1880; dau. of T. F. Wanzer, of Simpson; issue: 1–Lloyd M., *b* Beloit, Kan., Apr. 18, 1902; A.B., U.Kan.; LL.B., Washburn Coll.; *m* Oct. 20, 1928, Elizabeth, dau. of Ralph W. Dockstader, of Beloit.
1–Ed. Poly. Inst., New Market, Va.; studied law U.Va., awarded debater's medal, 1898. Lawyer, began practice at Hays City, Kan., 1898; co. atty., Logan Co., Kan., 1899-1900; moved to Beloit, Kan., 1900; E.E. and M.P. to Republic of Finland, by appmt. of Pres. Harding, Oct. 8, 1921-May 1, 1925. Resumed practice at Beloit (see Who's Who in America). Pres. Kan. State Hist. Soc., 1927-28. Clubs: Kansas City, Wichita. Mason (32°, K.T., Shriner). Republican. Episcopalian. Residence: Beloit, Kan.

1–**KAISER, Boynton Swift,** *b* Urbana, Ill., Feb. 23, 1913.
5–Martin **Kaiser,** from Switzerland, 1816, settled in Tuscarawas Co., O.; *m* Ursula Tschudy (1778-1836);
4–Martin (1807-97), came with father; *m* 1828, Mary Culver;
3–Peter Henry (1840-1929), *m* 2d, 1878, Beza Nancy Boynton;
2–John Boynton (2 below).
10–Edward **Culver** (qv);
9–Lt. Edward (1653-1732), soldier King Philip's War, 1675-76; mem. com. to establish the bounds of the "Volunteers Lands" in Windham Co., Conn., 1705; surveyor; lt. in command of Conn. scouts, 1712; founder and original propr. of Lebanon, Conn., 1698-99; original propr. of Litchfield, Conn., 1721; *m* 1682, Sarah Backus (*b* 1663; Lt. William[10] [1639-1721], propr. Norwich, *m* Elizabeth [1642-1730], dau. of Lt. William Pratt [*d* 1678], *m* Elizabeth, dau. of Hon. John Clark [1608-74], of Saybrook and Milford, who was one of the grantees named by King Charles II, of Eng., in the Conn. charter of 1662);
8–Ephraim (1683-1729), *m* 1707, Martha Hibbard;
7–Ephraim (1717-75), united with Moravians at Nazareth, Pa.;
6–Charles (1741-1817), *m* 1769, Anne Heil (1746-1818);
5–John (1775-1814), sent by Moravian Ch. to help build ch. at Goshen, Tuscarawas Co., O.; *m* 1807, Sarah Everett (1785-1813; Joseph[6], from Marietta to Gnadenhutten, O., *m* Sarah Davis; prob. John[7], *m* Mary Holder);
4–Mary (1808-81), *m* 1828, Martin **Kaiser** (4 above).
10–William **Boynton** (*b* 1606), *m* Elizabeth Jackson;
9–Caleb (1650-96), *m* Mary Moore (*b* 1648; Edmund[10], *m* Annie–);
8–Caleb (*b* 1685), moved to Wiscasset, Me., 1738; *m* Christian Parsons (John[9]);
7–John (*b* 1718), moved to Wiscasset, 1734; tomahawked by Indians while clearing land across the river; *m* Sarah Hilton;
6–John (1745-ca. 1785), *m* 1768, Hannah Taylor;
5–Capt. Joshua (1773-ca. 1852), sea. capt.; crossed ocean 60 times in his 18 yrs. service before the days of steam; *m* Beza Delano;
4–John Hancock (1816-99), *m* 1837, Huldah Heath (1815-94; John[5] [1787-1873], *m* Thedotha Castle);
3–Beza Nancy (*b* 1845), *m* 1878, Peter Henry **Kaiser** (3 above).
10–Philip **Delano** (qv);
9–Philip (ca. 1640-1708), *m* 1668, Elizabeth Clark (William[10], *m* Martha Nash);
8–Ebenezer (1675-1708), *m* 1699, Martha Simmons (John[9], *m* Mercy Pabodie);
7–Joshua (1700-51), *m* ca. 1721/22, Hopestill Peterson (Jonathan[8], *m* Lydia Thacher);
6–Hopestill (1735-1829), *m* 1758, Widow Abigail Prince (Ephriam[7], *m* Abigail Kimball);
5–Beza (1776-1850), *m* 1800, Joshua **Boynton** (5 above).
4–Daniel **Swift**;
3–Charles Judah (*b* Manhattan, Lucas Co., O., Oct. 25, 1841-*d* Corry, Pa., Feb. 13, 1886), *m* Alice Stilson (1852-1925);
2–Gertrude I., *m* 1910, John Boynton **Kaiser** (*b* 1887), librarian Oakland (Calif.) Free Library (see Who's Who in America).
1–Address: Care of Public Library, Oakland, Calif.

1–**KAY, Edgar Boyd,** *b* Warriors Mark, Huntingdon Co., Pa., Jan. 15, 1860.
7–John (Caius, Caye, Cay, Kaye, Key) **Kay** (*b* 1650?), from Eng. in the "Welcome," with William Penn, landed at "Penny-Pot" on the Delaware River, now Phila., Pa., 1682; *m* Margaret– (*b* 1652?);
6–John (1682-1767), *b* at "Penny-Pot"; William Penn gave him a patent covering a parcel of land, this patent is still in an excellent state of preservation and in on exhibition at the library of the Hist. Soc. of Pa., this patent was given in honor of his having been the "First Born" child in Phila. of English parentage; he *d* at Kenneth Square, Chester Co., Pa.;
5–John (1723-93), mfr. of fire arms; soldier Am. Rev.; commd. 2d col., 9th Pa. Regt. in active service; *d* at Ringold Manor, Md.;
4–William (1757-1844), *m* Rachel Boyd, of York Co., Pa.;
3–George Boyd (1791-1857), *m* Elizabeth Kline (1799-1893);
2–Isaac Franklin (1828-73), *m* 1857, Catharine Bell (1836-92; John[8], *m* Elizabeth–); issue: I–John Bell (*b* and *d* 1858); II–Edgar B. (1 above); III–Elizabeth Magella (1861-1929; *m* 1884, William A. Ford).
1–*m* Sept. 26, 1900, Florence Edna Means, *b* Wapakoneta, O., Dec. 21, 1878; dau. of Lyman North Means, *m* Elizabeth–.
1–C.E., Rensselaer Poly. Inst., Troy, N.Y., 1883 (Sigma Xi, D.K.E.). Educator, 1883-1912; consulting engr., Ala. R.R. Commn., 1903-15; chief engr., State Convict Bureau, Ala., and for several steam and hydro-electric power cos., and cities; has designed and built many water works, sewer and lighting systems, steam and electric rys.; pres. and engr. various cos. and water works; designer of municipal and U.S. Govt. incinerators (see Who's Who in America). Mason (32°, K.T., Shriner). Club: Washington City. Residence: 1840 Mintwood Pl. N.W., Washington, D.C.

1–**KEATOR, Alfred Decker,** *b* Accord, N.Y., June 9, 1886.
9–Melchert Claessen (Kater, Keter) **Keator,** came from Holland to N.Y.; Dutch soldier in New Amsterdam ante 1671; settled at Marbletown, N.Y., ca. 1674; *m* 1674, Susanna Richards, a widow;
8–Niclaes Melchertsen (*b* 1675), served in militia as early as 1691, taking part in the defense of Albany against the French; *m* 1699, Jannatje VanDerMark (*b* 1679; Thomas[9], *m* Jacomyntje Jacobs);
7–Thomas (*b* 1702), began to write name Keator; sgt. militia, 1738; signed Articles of Assn., 1775; served in 3d Regt. Ulster Co. Militia during Am. Rev.; *m* 1729, Lea Van Etten (*b* 1711; Jan[8], *m* Jannetje Roose);
6–Peter (1745-1804), associator, 1775; served in Ulster Co. militia, Cantine regt., Capt. John Hasbrouck's co.; *m* 1777, Geertje Roosa (*b* 1756; Jan[7], *m* Eva Klaarwater);
5–Moses (1780-1843), of Rosendale, N.Y.; *m* 1800, Mary Burger (1783-1864; Nicolas[6], *m* Maria Krom);
4–Thomas Garrison (1801-53), *m* Elizabeth Freer (1805-78; Ezekiel[5], *m* Elizabeth Sluiter);
3–Simon Peter (1828-99), served in Civil War;

m 1848, Hannah Coutant (1832-98; Isaac[4], *m* Katharine Clements);
2–Thomas Oliver (2 below).
9–Daniel **Brodhead,** from Eng., 1664, settled at Kingston, N.Y.; *m* Anne, dau. of Francis Tye, *m* Tellos Solomon;
8–Charles, of Marbletown, N.Y.; *m* 1693, Maria Ten Brook (1674-1717; Wessel[9], *m* Maria Ten Eyck);
7–Wessel Charles (*b* 1696), of New Paltz, N.Y.; *m* 1734, Catrina Dubois (*b* 1714; Louis[8], *m* Rachel Hasbrouck; Louis[9]);
6–Charles Wessel (1742-99), of Rochester, Ulster Co., N.Y.; *m* Sarah Hardenburg (*b* 1745; Abram[7], *m* Marritje Roosa);
5–Abram (*d* 1827), *m* 1792, Anne VanHorn (*b* 1773);
4–Abram VanHorn, *m* Helen Schoonmaker (*b* 1802; Joachim[5], *m* Elizabeth DePuy);
3–Elizabeth (1821-89), of Accord, N.Y.; *m* 1842, Marcus **Decker** (1820-1914; Joseph[4], of Blooming Grove, Orange Co., N.Y., *m* Phebe Helme);
2–Sarah Jane (1856-1914), *m* 1877, Thomas Oliver **Keator** (1854-1914), physician; issue: I–Frank (1879-1917; *m* Jessie Helen Laing); II–Alfred Decker (1 above).
1–*m* Feb. 5, 1915, Margaret Sievewright Dick, *b* Crete, Neb., Apr. 14, 1885; dau. of James Sievewright Dick, of Crete.
1–Studied State Normal Sch., New Paltz, 1902-06; B.A., Amherst, 1910; B.L.S., State Library Sch., Albany, 1913. Librarian, U. of N.D., 1918-28, also asso. prof. library science, 1921-28; librarian, Reading (Pa.) Public Library, 1928– (see Who's Who in America). Mem. S.A.R., Holland Soc. of New York, Hist. Soc. of Berks Co., Pa., I.A.G. Mason. Congregational. Republican. Club: Rotary. Residence: 636 N. 3d St., Reading, Pa.

1–**KEBABIAN, Edith Jennie Blakeslee (Mrs. John C.),** *b* Southington, Conn., Jan. 25, 1877.
10–Samuel (Blakesley) **Blakeslee** (qv);
9–Ebenezer (1664-1735), of New Haven; *m* Hannah Lupton (1665-1749; Thomas[10], *m* Hannah Morris);
8–Ebenezer (1685-1760), *m* 1706, Mary Ford (1684-1760; Mathew[9], *m* Mary Brooks);
7–Ebenezer (1711-71), began to write name Blakeslee; *m* 1731, Jemima Tuttle (1712/13-1760; William[8], *m* Mary Abernathy; Jonathan[9]);
6–Jotham (1736-92), patriot in Am. Rev.; clk. to Capt. Jonathan Dayton, also mem. Household Band; *m* 1st, 1758, Hannah Todd (1740-bet. 1771-75; Ithamar[7], *m* Hannah Blakeslee; Michael[8]; Christopher[9]);
5–Enos (1758-1812), of New Haven and Prospect; pvt. in Am. Rev.; *m* Hannah Sperry (Elihu[6], *m* Mary, dau. Japhet Mansfield);
4–Manning (bap. 1790-91-1832 or 33), of Prospect; *m* 1803, Sally Wilmot (*b* 1784; Amos[5], *m* Sarah Hine; Amos[6]; Asa[7]; Thomas[8]; William[9]);
3–Sherman (1815-91), of Prospect and Cheshire, Conn.; *m* 1838, Nancy Maria Mix (1818-1917; William[4], *m* Laura Hall; John[5]; Thomas[6]; Thomas[7]; Daniel[8]);
2–George W. (1844-1916), manufacturer, Southington, Conn.; *m* 1871, Helen Virginia Bristol (1845-1913); issue: I–Wilbur B. (*b* 1874; *m* Katherine Wills Walton); II–Edith Jennie (1 above).
1–*m* Oct. 8, 1902, John Couzu Kebabian, *b* Rodosto, Turkey, May 28, 1861; Yale, '88; son of George Kebabian, of Rodosto; issue: 1–George Aram, *b* New Haven, Conn., Apr. 17, 1907; Yale U., ex-'29, Yale School of Fine Arts, dept. of drama, 1928-30; 2–Helen Marie, *b* New Haven, Oct. 28, 1911; Smith Coll., '33; 3–Jack Seaver, *b* New Haven, Nov. 6, 1913; 4–Paul Blakeslee, *b* Watch Hill, R.I., July 24, 1917.
1–Mem. D.A.C., D.F.P.A., D.A.R., New Haven Colony N.E. Women, New Haven Colony Hist. Soc. Episcopalian. Summer place: Watch Hill, R.I. Residence: 682 Prospect St., New Haven, Conn.

1–**KEEFER, Horace Andrew,** *b* Schuylkill Haven, Pa., Sept. 8, 1856.
4–Frederick **Keefer** (1758-1834), of Gettysburg, Pa.; drummer and sgt. Am. Rev., 1775-81; govt. military contractor after war; *m* Ann Maria Krause (1769-1848);
3–Andrew (1803-76), merchant, Harrisburg, Pa.; postmaster, Schuylkill Haven, Pa.; noted Lutheran Sunday Sch. supt. and choir leader; *m* Catherine Brua (1810-36; sister of wife of Simon Cameron, U.S. senator from Pa., and Sec. of War);
2–John Brua (2 below).
4–Baron Joseph **Van der Schot,** from Austria to America on scientific exploration; *m* Mary Feather, of Reading, Pa.;
3–Otillia, *m* John **Royer,** of Reading, Pa.;
2–Caroline Rebecca (1834-1920), *m* 1854, Maj. John Brua **Keefer** (1832-1912), army officer; issue: I–Horace Andrew (1 above); II–Catherine Amelia (1857-1912; *m* Brig. Gen. Joseph Wilson Duncan, U.S.A., *d*); III–Edith Marian (*b* 1859; *m* Matthew Henry Paxton, *d*); IV–Mary Frances (*b* 1862; *m* Col. Frederick Steinman Foltz); V–Frank Royer (*b* 1865; *m* 1903, Mary Cornelia Terrell, *b* 1883); VI–Caroline Royer (*b* 1869).
1–*m* June 1884, Mary Katherine Fearons (Dec. 25, 1859-1929); dau. of Judge George Fearons, mayor of Newport, Ky.; issue: 1–Donald F., *b* Independence, Mo., 1887; 2–Katherine, *b* Kansas City, Mo., 1890; *m* Gordon Whyte (issue: Mary Jane; John).
1–Ed. Harrisburg Acad. Officer mgr., Paxton Furnaces, a McCormack and Cameron estate; supt. South Mt. Iron Co., nr. Gettysburg, Pa., a Jay Cooke and J. C. Fuller estate of Phila.; largely interested in cable constrn. in many western cities and two rys., 1883-1900; retired. Mem. Kan. Legislature, 1899-1901. Residence: Linglestown, Pa.

1–**KEENE, W(illiam) Faitoute,** *b* Newark, N.J., Sept. 15, 1870.
9–Joran (Kyn, Keen) **Keene** (qv);
8–Hans, *m* Willemka–;
7–Mathias (1667-1714), *m* Henricka Claasen;
6–John (1695-1758), *m* 1713, Susannah Steelman;
5–George, *m* 1755, Margaret Bristol;
4–Jonathan (1761-1837), *m* 1787, Elizabeth Ogden Nutman;
3–James (1800-67), began to write name Keene; *m* Margaret Ritchie Whitlock (1802-82);
2–Samuel Stryker (2 below).
9–Giles **Smith** (*d* 1669), of Hartford, Conn., 1639; an early settler of New London; of Fairfield, Conn., 1657, where he *d*;
8–Ebenezer (*d* 1717), named in records of Jamaica, L.I., 1703; *m* Clement Denton (Samuel[9]);
7–Robert, *m* 1724, Judith Fountain;
6–Abraham (1734-96), *m* Sarah French;
5–Abijah (1764-1826), Derby, Conn.; *m* 1784, Eunice Chatfield;
4–Sheldon (1791-1863), Bridgeport, Conn.; War 1812; *m* 1813, Polly Summers (*d* 1871);
3–Susan C. (1814-88), *m* William S. **Faitoute** (1808-70);
2–Ella Caroline (2 below).
10–William **French** (qv);
9–Francis (1624-91), Milford, Conn.; *m* Lydia Bunnell (*d* 1708; William[10], of New Haven);
8–Francis (1677-1751), *m* 1703, Anna Bowers (1669-1744; John[9]; George[10]);
7–Samuel (1704-83), *m* 1733, Martha Chapman (1714-80);
6–Sarah (1738-1805), *m* Abraham **Smith** (6 above).
9–George **Chatfield,** from Eng. with two bros. in Rev. Whitfield's company to Guilford, Conn., 1639; moved to Killingworth, 1663; *m* Sarah Bishop; *m* 2d, Isabel Nettleton;
8–John (1661-1737), *m* 1684, Anna Harger;
7–Ebenezer, *m* Abigail Pringle or Prindle;
6–Ebenezer (*b* 1729), *m* Rachel Umberfield;
5–Eunice (1765-1856), *m* 1784, Abijah **Smith** (5 above).
9–John (Umfreville) **Umberfield** (desc. Sir Robert de Umfreville, Lord of Tours and Vian, kinsman of William the Conqueror); came from Eng. to New Haven, Conn., ante 1664; began to write name Umberfield;
8–Samuel (1666-1748), *m* Experience Miller (1673-1724);
7–Thomas (1704-45), *m* 1731, Rachel Woolcott;
6–Rachel (*b* 1733), *m* Ebenezer **Chatfield** (6 above).
2–Samuel Stryker **Keene** (1846-75), broker on N.Y. Stock Exchange; *m* 1869, Ella Caroline Faitoute (*b* 1847); issue: I–William Faitoute (1 above); II–Marie Caroline (*b* 1874).
1–*m* Feb. 10, 1896, Lizzie Florence Olney (divorced 1906), dau. of Frank Fuller Olney, of Providence, R.I.

1-*m* 2d, Sept. 8, 1920, Mabel (Sweet) Burchard (qv).
1-S.B., C.E., M.I.T., '91 (Phi Gamma Delta). Retired. Was capt. and maj. R.I. militia. Mason (R.A.M.). Life mem. I.A.G. Clubs: Army and Navy of America, Cavendish, Automobile Club of America, Cragston Yacht and Country (New York); Graduates (New Haven), Woodway Country (Stamford), Shorehaven Golf (Norwalk), Tokeneke (Darien), Farmington Country (Charlottesville, Va.). Residences: Wilson's Point, S. Norwalk, Conn.; 1040 Park Av., New York, N.Y.

1-**KEENE, Mabel Sweet (Mrs. W. Faitoute),** *b* Wappingers Falls, N.Y., Sept. 27, 1874.
10-John **Sweet** (1579-1637; son of Robert, *m* Johanna-), from Eng. ca. 1630, with his wife and children (mentioned in Salem records, 1631); received land grant at Providence, 1637; *m* Mary-, returned to Salem, Dec. 1637, after death of husband;
9-John (1620-77), Warwick, R.I.; *m* ca. 1650, Elizabeth-;
8-Henry (*b* 1657), *m* Mary Griffin;
7-Benjamin (*b* E. Greenwich, R.I.), *m* 1717, Sussannah (Greene);
6-Francis (*b* 1726), moved to Hancock, Mass.;
5-Jesse (*b* Hancock, Mass.);
4-William (*b* Hancock, Mass.), *m* Sarah Dinsmore;
3-Eleazor Dinsmore (1808-60), *m* Jane A. Orr;
2-Clayton Emmett (1834-1908), *m* Charity Wilder Manning; issue: I-Clayton Manning (1867-98; *m* Amy Gunther); II-Lucy Dunham (1874-1928; *m* Liguori Alphonsus Doherty); III-Mabel (1 above).
1-*m* Oct. 27, 1904, Ross Burchard (Apr. 8, 1870-Nov. 14, 1918); son of Boardman Burchard; issue: 1-Mabel Manning, *b* Norwalk, Conn., Sept. 23, 1905.
1-*m* 2d, Sept. 8, 1920, W. Faitoute Keene (qv).
Residences: Wilson's Point, S. Norwalk, Conn.; 1040 Park Av., New York, N.Y.

1-**KELLAR Chambers,** *b* Memphis, Tenn, Mar. 4, 1867.
4-John (Koehler) **Kellar** (1755-1822), from Weisenburg, Alsace, then of France, as a soldier under LaFayette in Am. Rev.; captured by British nr. Newport, R.I., and carried to Eng. and remained prisoner until the treaty of peace, 1783; returned to America, 1803, and settled in Md.; soldier War 1812;
3-George Phillip (1800-43), *m* Sarah Conley, of Rockingham Co., Va. (Michael[4] [*d* 1815], from Ireland with his brother to Va., 1798, in the charge of Mr. Wise, the father of Gov. John Wise, of Va.; moved to Ky., 1810, and served in War 1812 as corpl. 1st Ky. Riflemen Regt., was in Battle of New Orleans and *d* on his way home, *m* Elizabeth or Betty Boyer);
2-Andrew Jackson (2 below).
5-Griffith **Rutherford** (*b* Rowan Co., N.C., 1725-1810; of Irish parents), lived west of Salisbury, N.C., in the Locke settlement; rep. Rowan Co. in conv. at Newbern, 1775; in 1776 led a force into the Cherokee country and assisted in destroying the cornfields and villages of the Indians; apptd. brig. gen. by Provincial Congress, 1776; comd. a brig. in battle nr. Camden, 1780, and was taken prisoner by the British; he was exchanged and was in command at Wilmington when that place was evacuated by the British at the close of the war; state senator, 1784, and soon afterward removed to Tenn. where he died; *m* Elizabeth Graham;
4-Margaret (1768-1828), of Rowan Co., N.C.; *m* Elijah Patton **Chambers** (1768-1834);
3-William Cathey (1802-83), of Sumner Co., Tenn., and Miss.; *m* 1830, Sarah Catherine Davidson;
2-Margaret Agnes (2 below).
6-John **Davidson** (*d* 1750), came to this country in early part of 18th Century with his bro. George, settled at Rockbridge Co., Va.; moved to Irdell Co., N.C., 1748; uncle of Gen. William Davidson, who was killed in Am. Rev.;
5-George (1728-1814), of Mass., and Irdell Co., N.C.; col. N.C. militia during Am. Rev., in which his four eldest sons fought with him; *m* Catherine Reece or Reese (1731-1814; William[6], *m* Penelope Groner);
4-Thomas (1770-1833), of N.C., and Tenn.; soldier in War 1812; *m* 1791, Agnes White (1772-1828), niece of Judge Hugh L. White;
3-Sarah Catherine (1811-95), of Irdell Co., N.C., and Miss.; *m* William Cathey **Chambers** (3 above);
2-Margaret Agnes (1841-1902), *m* 1865, Andrew Jackson **Kellar** (1835-1907), capt. Co. D, 4th Tenn. Inf., commd. lt. col., 1862, col., 1863; paroled, 1865; was a personal friend of Presidents Johnson, Hayes and Garfield; mem. S.D. Senate, 1897-98 (chmn. of judiciary com.); mem. Shiloh Park Commn.; issue: I-Chambers (1 above); II-Andrew Conley (*b* 1869); III-Werdna (*b* 1872); IV-Philip Rutherford (*b* 1876; *m* Dora Goodykoontz).
1-*m* Feb. 19, 1902, Florence Bullock, *b* Tecumseh, Mich., Oct. 3, 1878; dau. of Capt. Seth Bullock, of Deadwood, S.D.; issue: 1-Kenneth Chambers, *b* Lead, S.D., Jan. 6, 1906; A.B., U.Mich., '26; LL.B., Stanford, 1929.
1-B.S., Vanderbilt, '87 (Phi Delta Theta). Gen. counsel, Homestake Mining Co., since 1904; v.p., dir. and atty. First Nat. Bank, Lead, S.D.; v.p., dir. and atty. Hearst Mercantile Co.; dir. Northwest Bank Corpn., Minneapolis, Minn.; dir. Wyodak Coal & Mfg. Co.; dir. Hearst Free Kindergarten and Library Assn. (see Who's Who in America). Charter mem. and organizer of S.D. Soc. S.A.R. Mason (Shriner). Episcopalian. Republican. Club: Rocky Mountain (New York). Residence: Lead, S.D.

1-**KELLEY, Maria Louise Hamilton (Mrs. Robert Emmet),** *b* Washington, D.C., Jan. 2, 1860.
7-John **Hamilton** (*d* 1680), came to Charles Co., Md., 1674; dep. sheriff; *m* Elizabeth Burditt (*d* ante 1697; Thomas[8], *m* Verlinda Potter);
6-Alexander (ca. 1670-1730), planter and extensive landowner, Charles Co., Md.; *m* 1708, Elizabeth (Shercliffe) Green (*d* 1741; William[7]; John[8]);
5-Patrick (1717-90), of Charles Co.; subscribed to Patriot's Oath, 1778; *m* Anne Greene (*b* 1724; Francis[6], *m* Elizabeth Wheeler);
4-Edward (1759-1824), of Charles Co.; served in Am. Rev.; commd. lt., 2d Regt. Md. Militia, 1781; *m* 2d, 1796, Eleanor Hawkins (1778-1807; Capt. Josias[5], also col. 12th Bn., Charles Co. Militia, in Am. Rev.);
3-Edward Ignatius (1797-1841), of Charles Co., Md.; War 1812; *m* 2d, 1832, Ann Louise Spalding;
2-William Edward (2 below).
7-Thomas **Spalding,** from Eng., 1659; settled in St. Mary's Co., Md.; *m* 1674, Katharine-;
6-John (*d* 1724), *m* as her 3d husband, Priscilla (Field) Smith Harrison (*d* post 1726);
5-Basil (ca. 1718-1791), of Prince George's Co., Md.; *m* Catherine Edelen (*d* 1808; Thomas[6], *m* Comfort-);
4-George Hillairy (1770-1820), *m* 1799, Elizabeth M. Hargraves (1774-1834);
3-Ann Louise (1804-89), *m* 1832, Edward Ignatius **Hamilton** (3 above).
10-Robert **Brooke** (qv);
9-Baker (1628-79), surveyor gen. of the Province, 1671-79; mem. Md. Council; *m* 1664, Ann Calvert (1644-1714; Gov. Leonard[10], qv);
8-Baker (1666-98), of De La Brooke Manor; *m* 1690, Katherine Marsham (1672-1712);
7-Leonard (1692-1736), of Calvert Co., Md.; *m* 1722, Ann Darnall (ca. 1705-1779);
6-Capt. Leonard (1728-85), cdr. of "Horatio," that plied bet. the colony and London, Eng.; *m* 2d, at London, ca. 1753, Elizabeth Maxwell (1735-90);
5-Hester (1755-1835), of Prince George's Co., Md.; *m* 1781, Capt. Henry **Hill** (1750-1830), served in Am. Rev.; fitted out a co. at his own expense;
4-Mary Ann Hoskins (1795-1847), of Prince George's Co.; *m* 1st, 1814, James **Brooke** (1758-1822), of Kent Co.; *d* in Annapolis while mem. Legislature;
3-Henrietta Eleanor (1820-77), *m* 1837, Capt. George Hayward **Willson** (1810-73), of Kent Co.;
2-Anna Maria (1838-1915), *m* 1857, William Edward **Hamilton** (1835-1920), of Charles Co., Md.; issue: I-Maria Louisa (1 above); II-Edward Joseph (1861-1927; *m* 1889, Maude Young); III-James Brooke (*b* 1863; *m* 1902, Vera Pannewitz); IV-George Hayward (1866-

1926; *m* 1887, Rose Buchanan); V–William Edward, II (*b* 1868; *m* 1895, Annie Sydnor); VI–Clarence Spalding (*b* 1875; *m* 1906, Margaret Kennedy); VII–Bernard James (*b* 1876; *m* 1902, Adele Matthews; *m* 2d, 1921, Margaret House); VIII–Arthur Louis (*b* 1881; *m* 1906, Edith Paine).
1–*m* Dec. 2, 1886, Robert Emmet Kelley (Jan. 4, 1854-Dec. 12, 1900), from Richmond, Va., to Houston, Tex., 1883; issue: 1–Robert Hamilton, *b* Houston, Tex., July 25, 1888; A.B., Catholic U. (Washington), Georgetown U., U.Tex.; lawyer; *m* 1911, Mary Elizabeth, dau. of Dr. Charles B. Young, of Lynchburg, Va. (issue: Mary Ann; Mary Elizabeth; Frank Andrews).
1–Ed. Visitation Convent, Frederick, Md., and Sisters of Charity, Richmond, Va. Mem. C.D.A., D.A.R. Residence: The Plaza Apt. Hotel, Houston, Tex.

MARSHALL CHARLES KELLEY (1840-1918).

1–**KELLEY, Truman Lee,** *b* Whitehall, Muskegon Co., Mich., May 25, 1884.
9–John (Kelly) **Kelley** (*d* 1644), from Eng., 1635, settled at Newbury, Mass.;
8–John (1642-1718), *m* 1st, 1663, Sarah Knight (1648-1714; Dea. Richard[9], *m* Agnes Coffley);
7–John (1668-1735), *m* 1696, Elizabeth Emery (*b* 1680; Sgt. John[8], *m* Mary Webster);
6–Daniel (*b* 1716), of West Amesbury; *m* 1734, Mercy Smith, of Newbury;
5–Jacob (1751-1825), began to write name Kelley; settled at Gilmanton, N.H., ca. 1774; joiner; *m* Deborah Page (*d* 1831, aet. 82; David[6]);
4–Joseph S. (1793-1870 or 71), *m* Betsey E. Wingate;
3–William Wingate (*b* 1817), *m* 1839, Elizabeth Jane Osgood;
2–Marshall Charles (2 below).
10–Hatevil **Nutter,** elder and planter of Piscataqua;
9–Mary, *m* John **Wingate** (*d* 1687), to America as a young man;
8–John (*b* 1670), *m* Ann–;
7–John (*b* 1693), of Dover; *m* 1st, Dorothy Tebbets, of Dover (Samuel[8]);
6–Daniel (1722 or 23-1793), of Rochester; *m* Mary Frost (William[7], of Dover);
5–William (*b* 1750?), moved to Farmington, ante 1800; *m* Deborah Buzzell, of Farmington;
4–Betsey E. (1798-1842), *m* Joseph S. **Kelley** (4 above).
10–William **Osgood** (1609-1700), from Eng., settled at Salisbury, Mass.; *m* Elizabeth–;
9–John (1647-83), *m* Mary Stevens;
8–William (1673-1752), farmer; *m* Hannah Colby (*b* ante 1674-living 1746; John[9]; Anthony[10]);
7–Joseph (*b* 1698), *m* Aphia Pillsbury (1700-74; William, Jr.[8], of Newbury, *m* Mary Kenney);
6–Reuben (1726-95), Epping, N.H.; *m* 1st, 1748, Mary Brown (*d* 1753);
5–Samuel (1749-1834), Gilford, N.H.; *m* Betsey Sanborn (*d* 1824; Dea. John[6], of Gilmanton);
4–David S. (1790-1844), Meredith, N.H.; *m* Lydia Perkins (1794-1872), of Gilmanton;
3–Elizabeth Jane (1815-80), *m* William W. **Kelley** (3 above).
9–Dea. Stephen **Hart** (qv);
8–Mary (*d* 1710), *m* 1658, John **Lee** (ca. 1620-1689/90), from Eng. in the "Francis," 1634;
7–David (1674-1759), to Coventry, Conn., ca. 1709; *m* 1695, Lydia Strong (1675-1718; Jedediah[8], of Northampton, *m* Freedom, dau. of Henry Woodward, "pillar of the church" of Dorchester and Northampton; John[9], qv);
6–Rev. Jonathan (1718-88), B.A., Yale, 1742; *m* 1744, Elizabeth Metcalf;
5–Dea. Milo (1760-1829), *m* 1782, Ruth Camp (1760-1833; Hezekiah[6]);
4–Jonathan (1786-1866), grad. Yale, 1809; Andover Theol. Sem., 1832; ordained 1815; *m* 1st, 1817, Harriet Dewey Danforth;
3–Harriet Maria (1819-95), of Salisbury; *m* 1843, William James **Smith** (1813-90), Congl. minister (Richard[4], of Erie Co., Pa., miller and stout Presbyn., *m* Elizabeth Mack);
2–Maria Strong (2 below).
10–Gov. William **Bradford,** Mayflower Pilgrim (qv);
9–Dep. Gov. William (1624-1703), *m* Alice Richards (1629-71; Thomas[10]);
8–Alice (1661-1745), *m* 1st, 1680, Rev. William **Adams** (1650-85), B.A., Harvard, 1681 (William[9] William[10]);
7–Abiel (*b* 1685), *m* Rev. Joseph **Metcalf** (1682-1723), B.A., Harvard, 1703 (Dea. Jonathan[8]; Michael[9]; Michael[10], qv);
6–Elizabeth (*d* 1761 or 62), *m* Rev. Jonathan **Lee** (6 above).
10–Nicholas **Danforth** (qv);
9–Jonathan (*d* 1712), capt.; *m* Elizabeth Poulter (*b* 1633; John[10], *m* Mary–);
8–Ens. Jonathan (1658 or 59-1710 or 11), *m* 1682, Rebecca Parker (1661-1754; Jacob[9], of Chelmsford);
7–Samuel (1692-ca. 1749), soldier in Narragansett wars; *m* Dorothy Shed (*b* 1691 or 92; John[8], *m* Sarah Chamberlain);
6–Jonathan (1736-1802), soldier in Am. Rev.;
5–Col. Joshua (1759-1837), of Pittsfield, Mass.;
4–Harriet Dewey (1795-ca. 1824), *m* Jonathan **Lee** (4 above);
3–Harriet M., *m* William J. **Smith** (3 above);

MARIA STRONG (SMITH) KELLEY

2–Maria Strong (1851-living 1930), *m* 1878, Marshall Charles **Kelley** (1840-1918), lawyer; see

portraits; issue: I–William Ernest (*b* 1879; *m* Lucretia Kester); II–Grace Osgood (*b* 1881); III–Truman Lee (1 above); IV–Marshall Royal (1887-89); V–Arthur Caryl Wingate (*b* 1891; *m* Elizabeth Cameron); VI–Clarence Lincoln (*b* 1897).
1–*m* Aug. 26, 1911, Lura Osgood, *b* Mendon, Mich.; dau. of George Washington Osgood, *m* Louisa M. Rudd, both of Mendon.
1–Student U.Minn., 1902-03; A.B., U.Ill., 1909 (Gamma Alpha, Kappa Delta Pi [founder], Sigma Xi, Tau Psi Epsilon, Phi Delta Kappa), A.M., 1911; Ph.D., Columbia, 1914. Prof. edn. and psychology, Stanford U., 1926. Author (see Who's Who in America). Address: Harvard University, Lawrence Hall, Kirkland St., Cambridge, Mass.

1–**KELLOGG, Robert James,** *b* N. Fairfield, Ohio, July 7, 1869.
9–Samuel **Kellogg** (1630-1711; son of Martin and g.son of Phillippe); came from Eng., ca. 1664, settled at Hartford, Conn.; *m* 1st, 1664, Sarah (Day) Gunn (*d* 1677);
8–Samuel (1669-1708), of Colchester, Conn.; *m* ca. 1693, Hannah Dickinson (1666-1745);
7–Dea. Joseph (1696-1765), Hebron, Conn.; *m* 1717, Abigail Miller;
6–Joseph (*b* 1718), *m* 1739, Susanna King;
5–Corpl. Joseph (1746-1823), Newfield, N.Y.; *m* 1768, Mary Niles (1749-1841);
4–Solomon (1777-1873), *m* 1800, Martha Mack (1782-1857);
3–Moses Curtis (1801-71), *m* 1824, Elizabeth Swartout;
2–Theron Hotchkiss (2 below).
9–Roeloff (Swartwout) **Swartout** (*b* Amsterdam, 1634-*d* Hurley, N.Y., or Hackensack, N.J., 1715; son of Tomys; g.son of Rolef, of Groningen, Holland), *m* in Beverwyck, New Netherland, 1657, Eva Bratt de Hooges;
8–Barnardus (*b* Kingston, N.Y., 1673), *m* 1700, Rachel Schepmoes (*b* 1678);
7–Rudolphus (*b* Kingston, 1701), *m* in Poughkeepsie, 1725, Elsje Sanders (*b* 1703);
6–Barnardus (*b* Poughkeepsie, 1731-*d* 1794), *m* 1752, Maria van Steenberger (*b* 1730);
5–Barnardus (*b* New York, N.Y., 1761-*d* 1824), *m* 1778, Mary Brower (*b* 1761);
4–Robert (*b* Dutchess Co., N.Y., 1779-*d* 1840), *m* in Edenton, N.C., 1796, Sarah Richards (*b* N.C., 1780);
3–Elizabeth (1803-84), *m* Moses C. **Kellogg** (3 above).
8–Samuel **Penfield** (*b* Lynn, Mass., 1650), *m* 1675, Mary Lewis;
7–Samuel (*b* Lynn, 1676), *m* Hannaby–;
6–Peter (*b* Bristol, R.I., 1702), Fairfield, Conn.; *m* 1730, Mary Allen;
5–James (1732-94), *m* Ellen Burr (1733-1803);
4–Ephraim (*b* 1763), *m* 1795, Esther Turney (*d* 1854);
3–Samuel (1804-57), *m* 1832, Clara Ann Woodworth (1802-63);
2–Frances Ann Esther (1835-1908), *m* 1862, Theron Hotchkiss **Kellogg** (1832-1908), atty. at law; sometime pros. atty.; issue: I–Charles Romeyn (*b* 1863; *m* 1886, Edith Elliott); II–Clara Elizabeth (*b* 1865); III–Frederick William (*b* 1866; *m* 1890, Florence Scripps); IV–Robert James (1 above); V–Mary Frances (*b* 1872); VI–Theron Penfield (*b* 1875; *m* 1895, Carlossa Pond); VII–Edward Samuel (*b* 1878; *m* 1900, Daisy Evans, *m* 2d 1920, Cecil Newman).
1–*m* June 27, 1895, Georgianna Belle Houghton (qv for issue).
1–A.B., Cornell, '91 (P.B.K.), Ph.D., 1896; grad. work, Cornell, 1901-02; studied U.Berlin (not registered), 1914; research at Harvard (not registered), 1914-15; U.Chicago, 1917; Harrison Research Fellow in linguistic psychology, U. of Pa., 1922-23. Prof. modern languages and linguistics, Ottawa U., since 1925. Author (see Who's Who in America). Baptist. Republican. Residence: 415 S. Cedar St., Ottawa, Kan.

1–**KELLOGG, Georgianna Belle Houghton (Mrs. Robert J.),** *b* Norwalk, O., Jan. 22, 1869.
8–John **Houghton** (qv);
7–John (1650-1737), *m* Mary Farrar (1648-1724);
6–Jonathan (*b* 1685), of Lancaster, Mass.; *m* 1712, Thankful White (1689-1737; Josiah[7] [bap. 1643-1714], *m* 2d, 1678, Mary, dau. of Thomas Rice, *m* Mary King; John[8] [*d* 1673], from Eng. to Salem, 1638, *m* Joan–, *d* 1654);
5–Jonathan (*b* 1719), *m* 1740, Sarah Houghton;
4–Jonathan (*b* 1752), *m* 1774, Joanna Burgh (*b* 1755);
3–Asa (*b* 1795), of Westminster, Vt.; *m* 1822, Abigail Lowell;
2–George Burgh (2 below).
9–Percival **Lowell** (qv);
8–John (*b* Eng. 1595), *m* in Newbury, Mass., 1639, Elizabeth Goodell;
7–Benjamin (*b* 1642), *m* 1666, Ruth Woodman;
6–John (*b* 1683), *m* 1707, Mary Davis;
5–Moses (*b* 1726), of Putney, Vt.; *m* 1753, Sarah Bradbury;
4–Jacob (*b* Putney, 1762), *m* 1789, Sally Keyes;
3–Abigail (*b* 1796), *m* Asa **Houghton** (3 above);
2–George Burgh (1826-93), of Norwalk, O.; *m* 1859, Caroline Maria Eggleston (1839-1909; Jesse[3] [*b* 1805], *m* Sally, dau. of James Palmer, *m* Belinda, dau. of Samuel Goodrich, *m* Gerusha Buel); issue: I–Charles Eugene (1859-1915; *m* Mary Crohan); II–Rosa May (1863-65); III–Jesse Eggleston (1866-96; *m* Ada Eby); IV–Georgianna B. (1 above); V–Ralph Henry (1874-1920; *m* Lillie May Thayer); VI–Ella Delora (*b* 1881; *m* Daniel Webster Brown).
1–*m* June 27, 1895, Robert James Kellogg (qv); issue: 1–Carrie Frances, *b* Ithaca, N.Y., Mar. 11, 1902; *m* Mar. 4, 1922, (Oliver) Wesley Henderson (issue: Robert Wesley, *b* Jan. 24, 1923; William Thomas, *b* Sept. 28, 1924; Carolyn Elizabeth, *b* Dec. 22, 1926-*d* June 5, 1927; Donald Otis, *b* Sept. 26, 1928); 2–Delora Belle, *b* Decatur, Ill., Sept. 13, 1911; student Ottawa U.
1–Ed. Norwalk (O.) H.S., Sandusky Business Coll., and pvt. tutors in music. Residence: 415 S. Cedar St., Ottawa, Kan.

1–**KELLY, John Alexander,** *b* Chilhowie, Va., Sept. 2, 1889.
6–Benjamin **Kelly** (*d* ca. 1798), from Eng. to Pa.; settled in Frederick Co., Va., and finally, with wife and 8 children, in Botetourt Co., Va., 1792 or earlier; *m* Mary–;
5–Richard (1763-1853), *b* Frederick Co., Va.; soldier Am. Rev., 1780-81; settled in Carter Co., Tenn., 1810; *m* Catherine Howell;
4–Vincent (1787-1855), *m* 1815, Ann Simmons Alexander (1800-65; Alexander[5], of Mecklenburg Co., N.C., *m* Nancy Parsons);
3–John Alexander (1821-1900), A.M., Emory and Henry; mem. Va. Legislature, 1869-70; judge of 16th judicial circuit of Va., 1870-95; *m* 1843, Martha Matilda Peck;
2–Francis Alexander (2 below).
9–Richard **Borden** (qv);
8–John (1640-1716), *m* 1670, Mary Earle (William[9] [*d* 1715], *m* Mary, dau. of John Walker; Ralph[10], qv);
7–Benjamin (1692-1743), from Monmouth Co., N.J., to Va., 1733 or earlier, settling nr. present site of Winchester; one of the original justices of peace, Orange Co., Va., 1734; granted 91,200 acres in Rockbridge Co., Nov. 6, 1739, by George II; *m* Zeruiah Winter (William[8] [*d* 1733], *m* 1688, Hannah [Grover] Gardiner, dau. of James Grover, qv);
6–Lydia (ca. 1720-99), *m* 1743 or 44, Jacob **Peck** (originally Johann Jakob Beck; ca. 1700-1801), from Wurttemburg, Germany, to Pa.; settled in Va., 1740;
5–Benjamin (1746-1827), planter, surveyor; settled in Botetourt (now Craig) Co., Va., 1783 or earlier; *m* Margaret Carper;
4–John (1772-1848), one of the original justices of peace, Giles Co., 1806; high sheriff, Giles Co.; *m* 1801, Elizabeth Snidow;
3–Martha Matilda (1827-90), *m* 1843, John Alexander **Kelly** (3 above).
7–John (Schneido) **Snidow**, of Lancaster Co., Pa.; *m* Mary Elizabeth–;
6–John (*d* 1765), moved to the New River Section of Va., 1765; *m* Elizabeth Helm (*d* post 1794);
5–Christian (1760-1836), pvt. Am. Rev., 1776; lt., 1778; one of original justices of peace, Giles Co., 1806; mem. Va. Gen. Assembly, 1812, 1820-22; col. militia; *m* 1784, Mary Burke (1760-1825; Thomas[6] [1741-1808], capt. in Am. Rev., *m* Clara Frieze; William[7] [*d* 1754], of the "Long Meadow," nr. Staunton, Va.);
4–Elizabeth (1787-1860), *m* John **Peck** (4 above);

3–Martha Matilda, *m* John Alexander **Kelly** (3 above);
2–Francis Alexander (1855-1913), principal and supt. of high schools; *m* 1876, Elizabeth Strother Patton (1853-1925); for issue and other lineages, see Vol. III, p. 287.
1–Not married. B.A., Emory and Henry, '11 (Sigma Alpha Epsilon, P.B.K.), M.A., Columbia, 1916, Ph.D., 1920. Instructor in German, 1920-21, asst. prof., 1921-27, asso. prof. since 1927, Haverford Coll. Served with U.S.N.R.F., Apr.-Dec., 1918. Mem. I.A.G. Residence: Haverford, Pa.

1–**KELSEY, Horatio Nelson,** *b* St. Mary's, O., June 14, 1865.
8–William **Kelsey** (ca. 1600-1680), from Eng., ante 1632; settled at New Towne (Cambridge), Mass.; removed to Hartford, Conn., 1636, to Killingworth, 1663; *m* 1625-28, Bethia Hopkins (*b* ca. 1605-10);
7–Lt. John (ca. 1636-1709), of Killingworth; *m* 1668, Hannah Disborough (*d* 1718; Nicholas[8], *m* Mary Bronson);
6–Lt. Joseph (1673-1740), *m* 1st, 1699, Hannah Hayden (1680-1736; Nathaniel[7], *m* Sarah Parmelee);
5–Gideon (1718-64), *m* 1744, Esther Chatfield (1724-1817; George[6], *m* Esther Parks; George[7]);
4–George (1757-1827), Haddam, Conn.; served in Am. Rev.; *m* 1782, Susan (Smith) Brooks (1760-1828; Jonathan Smith[6], *m* Martha Brooks);
3–Ezra (1789-1881), Higganum, Conn.; *m* 1812, Sarah Hubbard (1790-1865; Thomas[4], *m* Sarah Boardman);
2–Benjamin (1827-1915), of Indianapolis, Ind.; *m* 1852, Mary Adams Gray (1831-1919; Adams[8], *m* Mary Davis); issue: I–Alice Gray (*b* 1853; *m* John Stone, 1846-1919); II–Carrie Adams (*b* 1855; *m* Frank B. Ferris, 1856-1923); III–Joseph Adams (*b* 1858; *m* 1896, Mary Fuller, 1869-1922); IV–Benjamin Carver (*b* 1860; *m* 1883, Mary Ann Johnston, *d* 1894); V–Margaret Elizabeth (*b* 1863; *m* 1907, Dr. Thomas Jefferson Murray); VI–Horatio Nelson (1 above); VII–Preston Telford (*b* 1867; *m* Laura Esther Halliday, qv).
1–*m* June 21, 1892, Burnette L. Bloomer, *b* Indianapolis, Ind., Aug. 1, 1866; dau. of Isaac L. Bloomer, of Indianapolis, *m* Katherine Hoshour; issue: 1–Esther, *b* Evanston, Ill., Sept. 22, 1894; *m* Apr. 27, 1920, Charles Booth, son of Charles Henry Alling, *m* Josephine Hill (issue: Charles B., Jr.; Prudence Kelsey; Joan; Elizabeth Josephine); 2–Burnette Catherine, *b* Indianapolis, Jan. 13, 1898; 3–Mary Alice, *b* Evanston, Ill., May 14, 1902; *m* Apr. 10, 1926, Wallace Herndon, son of Jay Herndon Smith, *m* Lida Wallace (issue: Jay Herndon, 2d); 4–Virginia, *b* Evanston, Apr. 24, 1905; 5–Millicent Ford, *b* Evanston, Jan. 29, 1908.
1–Ed. Butler U. (Sigma Chi). Began as clerk in a local agency and then was apptd. spl. agent of the London Assurance Corpn., for Ia., Neb., Mo., Kan.; state agent of Norwich Union Fire Ins. Soc. for Ind. and Ill., 1890-1901; in the latter year appointed asst. manager of western dept. of Sun Ins. Office, mgr., 1904; apptd. U.S. mgr. of Hamburg Bremen Fire Ins. Co., 1913; U.S. mgr. of London and Scottish Assn. Corpn., 1919-27; dep. mgr. of Northern Assn. of London, 1924-27; pres. Underwriters Trust Co., 1929-30, chmn. since 1930. Dir. Ins. Clerks' Mutual Benefit Assn. Mem. N.G. of Ind., 1881-90, of N.Y., 1918. Mem. S.A.R., I.A.G. Mason (K.T.). Conglist. Clubs: Down Town Assn., Transportation, Drug and Chemical, Highland Golf. Summer place: Higganum, Conn. Residence: 20 Clinton Av., Montclair, N.J.

1–**KELSEY, Laura Esther Halliday (Mrs. Preston Telford),** *b* Cairo, Ill., Oct. 17, 1869.
9–Jacob **Parker** (*d* ante 1669), from Eng., 1635, settled at Chelmsford, Mass.; town clk.; sgt. Train Band; *m* Sarah–;
8–Jacob (1652-94), of Malden, Mass.; *m* Joanna Call (1659-1734);
7–Thomas (1680-1760), of Malden; *m* 1702, Rebecca Danforth (1683-1758; Ens. Jonathan[8]; Jonathan[9], brother of Gov. Thomas Danforth, of Mass.);
6–David (1710-60), *m* 1740, Mary Upham (1715-95; g.g.dau. of Phineas Upham, in King Philip's War);
5–William (1745-1825), *m* 1772, Mary Warner (1753-1811), of Gloucester, Mass.;
4–William (1775-1855), of Newburyport, Mass.; *m* 1802, Betsey Wyatt;
3–Eliza (1805-61), of Rutland, O.; *m* 1822, Samuel **Halliday** (1799-1880), from Scotland, 1818; auditor Meigs Co., O., 20 yrs.;
2–Henry Laing (2 below).
8–George **Wyatt,** settled at Salem, Mass.; *m* Elizabeth–;
7–George (bap. 1702), in King Philip's War; *m* Hannah Lovett;
6–George (bap. 1727-1800), of Danvers, Mass.; Am. Rev.; *m* 1750, Sarah Stone (1726-74);
5–Joshua (1756-1822), Am. Rev.; *m* 1784, Elizabeth Shaw (1759-1828);
4–Betsey (1784-1869), of Beverly, Mass.; *m* William **Parker** (4 above).
4–William **Parker**;
3–Louisa, of Ripley, O.; *m* 1st, 1842, Joseph Matthew **Evans** (1819-51);
2–Laura Esther (1846-98), *m* 1867, Henry Laing **Halliday** (1842-96), banker and grain mcht.; issue: I–Eliza Parker (*b* 1868; *m* George H. Capen); II–Laura E. (1 above); III–Henry Evans (*b* 1872; *m* Nellie G. Galigher); IV–Douglas (1876-1915; *m* Emma Beebe, *d* 1925).
1–*m* Dec. 12, 1894, Preston Telford Kelsey, *b* St. Mary's, O., Oct. 4, 1867; U.S. mgr. Sun Ins. Office, New York City, since 1919; pres. Patriotic Ins. Co. of America, N.Y., since 1922; dir. Sun Indemnity Co.; v.p. Bank of Montclair; retired from active business, 1928 (see Who's Who in America); brother of Horatio N. Kelsey (qv for genealogy); issue: 1–Martha, *b* Cairo, Ill., Oct. 13, 1896; Northwestern U., 1919; *m* Dec. 3, 1919, Richard A., son of Richard H. Aishton, of Evanston, Ill. (issue: Richard H., II; Preston K.); 2–Laura, *b* Indianapolis, Ind., July 25, 1899; Northwestern; and 3–Lila (twins), *b* Indianapolis, July 25, 1899; *m* June 15, 1921, Wallace C., son of James M. Speers, of Montclair, N.J. (issue: Wallace C., Jr.; Laura); 4–Preston Halliday, *b* Indianapolis, Sept. 5, 1903; Dartmouth, '25; *m* Oct. 11, 1929, Suzanne, dau. of Thomas I. Van Antwerp, of Albany, N.Y.
1–Ed. Packer Collegiate Inst., Brooklyn. Mem. D.C.W., D.A.R., I.A.G., Episcopalian. Clubs: Montclair Woman's, Montclair Music, etc. Residence: 57 Union St., Montclair, N.J.

1–**KEMP, William Webb,** *b* Placerville, Calif., Feb. 6, 1873.
4–Joseph Alexander **Kemp** (1777-1832), of Delhi and Albany; *m* 1804, Elizabeth Jillson (*d* 1822);
3–William (ca. 1808-ca. 1866), of New York and later Ohio; *m* Caroline Hale (1808-90), of Watertown, N.Y.;
2–William (2 below).
5–Augustinus **Clapsaddle** (*d* 1777), lt. in French and Indian War; maj. Am. Rev.; *m* 1763, Barbara Wentz;
4–John (*b* 1777), *m* Barbara Helmer (George F.[5] [1740-1823], lt. in Am. Rev., pensioned, *m* Margaret Myers, 1757-1818);
3–Nancy (1808-86), *m* 1826, Aaron **Frazee** (1799-1863);
2–Caroline Elizabeth (1839-1911), *m* 1865, William **Kemp** (1829-83), cooper and Calif. pioneer; issue: I–Emma (*b* 1867; *m* George W. Askew); II–Frances (*b* 1869-*d* infancy); III–William Webb (1 above).
1–*m* Jan. 1, 1907, Grace Hayes (Aug. 14, 1869-Apr. 8, 1929); dau. of William Hayes, atty. at law, San Francisco, *m* Mary Bosqui; issue: 1–Marylyn Hayes, *b* San Diego, Calif., Mar. 23, 1908.
1–B.A., Stanford, 1898 (Phi Pi Phi, Phi Delta Kappa), grad. student same, 1904-05, U.Calif., 1905-06; research in archives of London, Eng., summer 1911; Ph.D., Columbia, 1912. Prof. edn. and dean Sch. of Edn., U.Calif., since 1923. Author (see Who's Who in America). Mem. S.A.R., Episcopalian. Republican. Club: Commonwealth. Residence: 1950 San Antonio Av., Berkeley, Calif.

1–**JACOBSON, Arthur Clarence,** *b* Brooklyn, N.Y., Sept. 28, 1872.
7–Hendrick (Jacobszen, Jacobsen) **Jacobson** (*d* 1694), from North Holland, settled in New Amsterdam, 1649; *m* 2d, Annetje, dau. of Simon Fell, from France, who *m* 1656 Anneken, dau. of Adrian Vincent, who came in the "Draetvat," and settled in New Amsterdam, 1657;
6–Jacob Hendricksen (*b* 1686), of New York; *m* Jannetje–;
5–Jacob (1720-1809), began to write name Jacobson; of New York and Albany; on Sir Will-

iam Johnson's muster rolls, 1767, of troops organized to protect the frontier against Indians; owned large estate at Bethlehem, Albany Co.; patentee of Jerseyfield, Herkimer Co., 1770; *m* 1756, Maria Evertsen Jansen;
4-Johannes (1767-1843), of Albany; *m* Maria Jansen;
3-Evert (1797-1847), of Albany; *m* 1822, Maria Dunham (1800-67);
2-John (2 below).
9-Jan Everts, in the "Gilded Beaver," to New Amsterdam, 1658; settled at Beverwyck (Albany), 1661; *m* Annetie Hendricks;
8-Evert **Jansen** (*d* 1726), *m* Maria Evertse;
7-Jan Evertse, *m* 1697, Maria Veders (*d* 1728, aet. 52; Simon Volkertse Veeder[8], qv);
6-Evert Evertsen, *m* Marytje Veeder;
5-Maria Evertsen (bap. 1733), *m* Jacob **Jacobson** (5 above).
10-Philip **du Trieux** (*b* 1585), in New Amsterdam, 1624; apptd. marshal of New Amsterdam, 1638; received patent for land in New Amsterdam, 1640; *m* Susanna de Chiney (living as late as 1654);
9-Susanna, 4th native-born child to be *m* in New Amsterdam; *m* Evert Jansen **Wendel** (qv);
8-Diewer (Debora), *m* Myndert **Wemp** (1649-90), justice Schenectady, 1689; killed in Schenectady massacre (Jan Barentse[9], from Netherlands to Beverwyck, 1643, owned land at Albany, Troy and Schenectady, *m* Maritie Mynders);
7-Susanna, *m* 1697, J. Symonse **Veeder** (will dated 1746), of Rensselaerwyck, 1720 (Simon Volkertse[8], qv);
6-Marytje (bap. 1705), *m* Evert Evertsen **Jansen** (6 above).
6-Jelles **de la Grange** (desc. of Johannes de la Grange, a Huguenot from LaRochelle, arrived at New Amsterdam, ca. 1656); on Sir William Johnson's muster rolls, 1767; assigned land bounty rights as a member of Col. Philip Schuyler's regt. during Am. Rev.; *m* Annatie—;
5-Antje, *m* 1770, Evert **Jansen** (bap. 1746), on Sir William Johnson's muster rolls, 1767; assigned land bounty rights as a mem. Col. Philip Schuyler's regt. during Am. Rev. (Evert Evertsen[6], same as 6 above);
4-Maria (bap. 1774-1861), *m* Johannes **Jacobson** (4 above);
3-Evert, *m* Maria Dunham (3 above);
2-John (1827-92), mem. New York Produce Exchange; *m* 1852, Mary Duggan (1831-96; Daniel[3] [1800-49], *m* Margaret Coughlan); issue: I-E. Wilbur (1854-1914; *m* Cornelia Ellsworth Rogers); II-Frank B. (1857-1929); III-John (1861-84); IV-M. Louise (1870-1929; *m* Adolph Huhn); V-Arthur Clarence (1 above).
1-*m* Nov. 26, 1896, Catherine Heinrichs, *b* Ottawa, Can., Feb. 7, 1874; dau. of Peter Frederick Heinrichs, of Ottawa, *m* Catherine Smith; issue: 1-Mary Catherine, *b* Brooklyn, N.Y., Sept. 28, 1897; ed. Conn. Coll. for Women and Columbia U.; *m* June 13, 1919, Louis Beverley Nicol Gnaedinger (issue: Arthur Beverley); 2-Margaret Helena, *b* Brooklyn, May 30, 1900; A.B., Conn. Coll. for Women, '21.
1-M.D., Long Island Coll. Hosp., 1894; Brooklyn Hosp. and New York Post-Grad. Med. Sch., 1895. Physician, dept. of hosps., since 1929; editor Medical Times, since 1926; Author (see Who's Who in America). Episcopalian. Democrat. Club: Authors' (London). Residence: 24 Clinton St., Brooklyn, N.Y.

1-**KENDALL, Effie Estelle Larrabee (Mrs. Perry G.),** *b* Hallsport, N.Y., Nov. 24, 1869.
9-Thomas **Selden** (qv);
8-Thomas (bap. 1645-1734), of Hartford, Conn.; *d* at Hadley, Mass.; *m* Felix Lewis (bap. 1658-1738; Capt. William[9], of Farmington, Conn., *m* Mary Hopkins; William[10], qv);
7-John (1675-1744), Hadley, Mass.; *m* 1698, Sarah Harrison (1675-post 1711; Isaac[8], wounded in Falls Fight, King Philip's War, *m* Martha, dau. Richard Montague);
6-Jonathan (1711-76), Granby, Mass.; *m* 1732, Mercy Ingram;
5-Jonathan (1740-1808), Whitestown, N.Y.; pvt. in Am. Rev., 1777, his powder horn now owned by Miss France Remmington, of Allen, Mich.; *m* Mehitable Cady (ca. 1735-ca. 1825), of Canandaigua, N.Y.;
4-John (1764-1843), Belleville, Can.; *m* his 1st cousin, Rhoda Green (1769-1833; Eliphalet[5], *m* Mercy, dau. of Jonathan Selden, *m* Mercy Ingram);
3-Rev. Joseph Willard (1803-63), Hallsport, N.Y.; died during service in Civil War; *m* 3d, 1843, Almeda Wheeler (1822-74; John[4], of Whitesville, N.Y., *m* Zilpha Hall);
2-Eliza Lugena (2 below).
9-Lt. Samuel **Smith** (qv);
8-Ens. Chileab (ca. 1635-1731), Hadley, Mass.; *m* 1661, Hannah Hitchcock (ca. 1645-1733; Luke[9], qv);
7-Hester (*b* 1674), *m* 1696, Nathaniel **Ingram** (*b* 1674; John[8], *m* Elizabeth Gardner);
6-Mercy (1702-80), *m* Jonathan **Selden** (6 above).
2-Eliza Lugena Selden (*b* 1849), of Hallsport, N.Y.; *m* 1866, Cyrenus Austin **Larrabee** (1844-1904), served 4 yrs. in Civil War; postmaster, at Port Allegany, Pa., 14 yrs.; jeweler, eye specialist; issue: I-Pauline Rosanna (*b* 1867; *m* Eugene Austin Robertson); II-Effie Estelle (1 above); III-Almeda Roselle (*b* 1872; *m* Charles Lamberson Cassingham); IV-Manville Angelo (1881-83); V-Lawrence Lyle (*b* 1883); VI-Florence Fern (*b* 1888; *m* Frank Burnham McLeary).
1-*m* Sept. 2, 1891, Perry Guy Kendall, *b* nr. Waterford, Pa. (Apr. 18, 1865-Jan. 9, 1917); son of Darwin Rufus Kendall, of Waterford, Pa.; issue: 1-Clyde Larrabee, *b* Port Allegany, Pa., Aug. 31, 1892; grad. Bliss Elec. Sch., '14; sgt., U.S. Signal Corps during World War; *m* June 21, 1922, Ethel Loree, dau. Theodore Allen Trimble, of Kings Mills, O. (issue: Larrabee Trimble, *b* 1923; Robert Keith, *b* 1924); 2-Guy Carleton, *b* Coudersport, Pa., Nov. 16, 1894; ed. Genesse Wesleyan Sem., '14; corpl., Ordnance Dept., U.S.A., World War; *m* Nov. 22, 1919, Ottilla Bertha, dau. of Christopher Kalweit, of Cleveland, O. (issue: Pauline Martha, *b* 1920; Evelyn Roselle, *b* 1927); 3-Kenneth Courtland, *b* Waterford, Pa., Sept. 30, 1896; *m* Sept. 11, 1920, Edna Elizabeth, dau. of John Louis Seligmann, of Buffalo, N.Y. (issue: Marian Louise, *b* 1924).
1-Ed. Chautauqua Lit. and Scientific Circle, '03. Taught school. Mem. D.F.P.A., D.A.R., M.E. Ladies' Aid Soc. (pres. 7 yrs.). Republican. Club: Shakespeare (pres. 4 yrs.). Residence: 2719 East Boul., Shaker Heights, Cleveland, O.

1-**KENNA, Edward Dudley,** *b* Jacksonville, Ill., Nov. 17, 1861.
3-John **Kenna** (1810-41), from Ireland, 1830; settled at Catskill, N.Y.; *m* 1829, Honor Flannery (1807-67), of Ireland;
2-Michael Edward (2 below).
7-Robert **Pilcher** (*b* 1708), from Eng.; settled in Va.; *m* Phoebe Chapman;
6-James (*b* 1729), of Fredericksburg, Va.; *m* Phoebe Fielding;
5-Joshua (1749-1810), of Culpeper Co., Va.; *m* Nancy Ballard;
4-Shadrach (*b* 1772), *m* Sarah Proctor (1771-1866);
3-Jeptha Dudley (1808-87), *m* 1836, Hannah Smith (1815-54);
2-Ellen (1838-1912), *m* 1857, Michael Edward **Kenna** (1834-1904), mcht., Jacksonville, Ill.; issue: I-Edward Dudley (1 above); II-Ernest Menard (*b* 1871); III-Eugene (1875-82).
1-*m* June 2, 1894, Madeline Kerens, *b* Ft. Smith, Ark., Aug. 24, 1871; dau. of Richard C. Kerens, capitalist of St. Louis, and former ambassador to Austria-Hungary; issue: 1-Richard Kerens, *b* St. Louis, Apr. 25, 1895; ed. Harvard; 2-Mary Dudley, *b* Chicago, Feb. 9, 1897; ed. in Eng.; 3-Edward Dudley, Jr. (Feb. 5, 1903-Sept. 15, 1905); 4-Catherine Irene, *b* Mentone, France (Apr. 5, 1908-Feb. 16, 1923); 5-John Kenna, *b* Eridge Sussex, Eng., Dec. 25, 1912; ed. Eng.
1-Ed. Drury Coll.; (hon. A.M., Knox Coll., 1900). Admitted to Mo. bar, 1880; gen. atty., St.L.-&S.F.Ry., 1889-95; gen. solicitor for the receiver, A.T. & S.F.Ry., 1895-98, and 1st v.p. same, 1898-1905 (see Who's Who in America). Clubs: Chicago (Chicago), Metropolitan (New York and Washington), Travellers (Paris), Wellington, Sportsman's (both of London). Winter residence: Riviera, France. Address: Metropolitan Club, New York, N.Y.

1-**KENNEDY, Clara Hart (Mrs. Thomas),** *b* Woodford Co., Ill.
7-Edward **Hart** (qv);

6–Jonathan (*b* ca. 1650), *m* Hannah Budd (*b* 1657);
5–Monmouth (ca. 1690-1761), *m* Sarah Ogden;
4–Joseph (1726?-1807), *m* Elizabeth Gedney;
3–Joseph (1756-1836), *m* Tamar Budd;
2–Allen (2 below).
8–Lt. John **Budd** (qv);
7–John (ca. 1620-1684), *m* Mary Horton (Barnabas[8]);
6–Hannah (*b* 1657), *m* Jonathan **Hart** (6 above).
8–John **Gedney** (1603-88), from Eng. in the "Mary and Ann," 1637; *m* Mary–;
7–Eleazer (1642-83), *m* 1665, Elizabeth Turner (Robert[8], of Boston, *m* Elizabeth Freestone);
6–Eleazer (1665-1722), *m* Anna Mott (?);
5–Eleazer (ca. 1698-1783), *m* Rebecca Turner (Daniel[6]; Lawrence[7]);
4–Elizabeth, *m* Joseph **Hart** (4 above).
8–Henry **Fowler** (*d* ca. 1687), Providence, R.I., and Mamaroneck, N.Y.; *m* Rebecca–;
7–Henry (1658-will dated 1730), Providence, R.I., Eastchester, N.Y.; *m* Abigail Hoyt (Moses[8], *m* Elizabeth–);
6–Henry (1679-1734), Eastchester and Mamaroneck, N.Y.;
5–Henry (1717-62), Mamaroneck, N.Y.; *m* Tamar– (*b* 1716);
4–Sarah (*b* 1744), *m* Joseph **Budd** (1732-1822), White Plains, N.Y.;
3–Tamar (1763-1826), *m* Joseph **Hart** (3 above);
2–Allen (1803-79), *m* 2d, 1853, Martha (Baldridge) Patterson (1833-1925).
1–*m* July 12, 1894, Thomas Kennedy, attorney; issue: 1–Kaywin, A.B., U.Ill., LL.B., Northwestern U.; capt., assigned as wireless telephone officer of 130th Field Signal Bn., 4th A.C., in France and served with Army of Occupation; *m* Dec. 18, 1920, Bernice Philips; 2–Thomas Hart, Culver Mil. Acad., Stanford U., Columbia U., Northwestern Law Sch.; commd. lt. from training sta., Ft. Sheridan and Camp Grant, Ill.
1–Mem. Col. Daughters, D.A.R. Residence: 1201 Broadway, Normal, Ill.

1–**KEPNER, Harry Valandigham,** *b* Arcanum, O., Apr. 2, 1867.
4–Jacob **Kepner** (1780-1848), of Port Royal, Juniata Co., Pa.; *m* Miss Grass;
3–Jacob (1806-88), of Juniata Co.; *m* Catherine Knawel (1808-80);
2–Harrison Agustus (2 below).
6–Johannes Henrich (Brumbach) **Brumbaugh,** from Rotterdam, arrived Phila., Pa., Sept. 30, 1754; settled nr. Washington, Md.;
5–Jacob (1734-1816), farmer, Huntingdon Co., Pa.;
4–Henry (1778-1856), farmer, Baker, Darke Co., O.;
3–George (1816-86), farmer, Greenville, O.
2–Harrison Agustus **Kepner** (1836-1905), merchant, Arcanum, O.; *m* 1859, Sarah Brumbaugh (1839-93); *m* 2d, 1895, Josephine Ivester (1858-96), issue (1st marriage): I–Willamina Alverda (*b* and *d* 1861); II–Clara Catherine (*b* 1862; *m* Nathen C. Bloom); III–Harry V. (1 above); IV–Bertha May (1877-91); issue (2d marriage): I–Helen Beatrice (*b* 1896; *m* Harold Wright).
1–*m* June 3, 1891, Clara May Fritchle, *b* Mt. Hope, O., Sept. 21, 1869; dau. of Agustus C. Fritchle, of Mt. Hope; issue: 1–Ralph Merril (Mar. 13, 1893-Apr. 25, 1895); 2–Harold Raymond, *b* Mt. Hope, O., Sept. 18, 1895; B.A., Ohio Wesleyan, '17; B.S., M.I.T., 1920, M.S., 1925; *m* July 6, 1926, Barbara, dau. of Dr. Charles M. Kent, of Forestville, Conn. (issue: Janet); 3–Dana Ewart, *b* Denver, Colo., Mar. 25, 1898; B.S., M.I.T., '21; *m* July 28, 1923, Beryl, dau. of Charles H. Fradd (issue: Barbara); 4–Dorothy May, *b* Denver, Oct. 24, 1909; student Ohio Wesleyan U.
1–A.B., Ohio Wesleyan U., '90 (Alpha Tau Omega), A.M., 1897; studied Harvard, 1894, U.Mich., 1895, U.Colo., 1896; (D.Sc., U.Denver, 1916). Educator since 1890, principal West High Sch., Denver, since 1919. Pres. Union Securities Co.; pres. bd. trustees State Teachers Coll., Western State Coll., Adams State Normal Sch. (see Who's Who in America). Mason (33°, K.T.). Methodist. Clubs: Colo. Schoolmasters' (ex-pres.), Lions (ex-pres.), Rocky Mountain Country. Residence: 607 E. 10th Av., Denver, Colo.

1–**KERN, Margaret Ethel Kelley (Mrs. George Thomas W.),** *b* Richmond, Va., Feb. 13, 1874.
10–Dr. John **Woodson** (qv);
9–Col. Robert (1634-post 1707), Prince Edward Co., Va.; *m* 1656, Elizabeth Ferris (Richard[10] [1596-1637], of "Curles," Henrico Co., Va.);
8–Robert (1660-1729), *m* Sarah Lewis (sis. of John Lewis, of "Warner Hall"); *m* 2d, Rachel Watkins;
7–Joseph (*b* 1685), of Henrico and Goochland cos.; *m* 1709, Elizabeth Mattox;
6–Joseph (1715-83), *m* 1737, Elizabeth Parsons (Joseph[7]);
5–Joseph (1749-1838), of Genitoe; capt. in Am. Rev.; *m* 1770, Mildred Redford (*d* 1810);
4–Robert (1775-1822), *m* 1805, Elizabeth Pledge;
3–Joseph (*d* 1848), *m* 1828, Julia Ann Edwards;
2–Louisa Rebecca (2 below).
9–Col. Richard **Lee** (qv);
8–Hancock (1653-1709), of "Ditchley"; burgess, Northumberland Co., 1688; naval officer; justice; collector of Va.; *m* 1st, 1675, Mary Kendall; *m* 2d, Elizabeth or Sarah Allerton;
7–Richard (1691-1740), *m* 1720, Judith Steptoe;
6–Kendall (*d* 1780), *m* 1749, Betty Heale;
5–Elizabeth, *m* Thomas **Edwards** (1752-98);
4–Richard, *m* Sally Williams (Jesse[5], *m* Charlotte Franklin);
3–Julia Ann (1805-59), *m* Joseph **Woodson** (3 above);
2–Louisa Rebecca (1841-1908), *m* 1862, Elias Henry **Kelley** (1837-1912), mem. Young's Grays, Co. I, 19th Va. Regt., 1861-65; bldg. contractor (Richard[3], of Hanover Co., Va., *m* 1831, Ann Peace, dau. of Rev. William Wood, of Hanover Co.); issue: I–Annie Bell (1866-1901; *m* Marion B. Sutton); II–Charles Lee (1868-71); III–Henry Spiller (*b* 1872; *m* Effie Bowles, see Vol. I, p. 166); IV–Loulie Coleman (*b* 1872); IV–Margaret Ethel (1 above); V–Aylett Richmond (1881-1906).
1–*m* June 19, 1901, George Thomas Walker Kern, *b* Roanoke Co., Va., Dec. 25, 1873; pharmacist and ophthalmologist; served with Richmond Light Inf. Blues (state vols.), 1917–; S.C.V.; mem. bd. of instrn. Richmond, 1917-18; son of George Michael Kern (*d*), of Roanoke Co., Va.; issue: 1–Margaret Eugenie, *b* Richmond, Va., Apr. 1, 1904; artist, musician.
1–Writer. Hostess for R.C., Westhampton Debarkation Hosp., No. 52; awarded 800 hr. service pin, A.R.C. Mem. D.A.R., U.S.D. 1812 (past state historian), U.D.C. (past historian, Richmond Chapter), A.P.V.A., The Service Legion (for civilian war service, 1917-18; organizer, hon. pres.), Council of Defense (asso. dir.), Va. War History Commn. (only woman mem. of Richmond branch), League of Fine Arts, Woman's Munition Reserve (dir.). Residence: 3000 Monument Av., Richmond, Va.

1–**KERR, Albert Boardman,** *b* Clearfield, Pa., Mar. 17, 1875.
7–John **Kerr** (*d* Sadsbury Tp., Chester Co., Pa., 1743), of Unicorn Plantation, Talbot Manor, Md.;
6–Josiah (1715-84), of Bart Tp., Lancaster Co., Pa.; commr. of Middle Octorara Presbyn. Ch., 1741; removed to Mt. Pleasant Tp., nr. Gettysburg, Pa.; *m* Mary Dinwiddie (David[7]);
5–Alexander (1744-75), *m* 1769, Sarah Murray;
4–John (1774-1858), of Reedsville, Pa.; *m* Nancy Conner (sister of Commodore David Conner, midshipman, War 1812, cdr. U.S.N., Mex. War); see Vol. I, p. 129, for Conner lineage;
3–James (1816-1903), non-commd. officer in Mex. War; buried at Reedsville, Pa.;
2–James (2 below).
9–Emanuel **Buck** (1626-1712), from Eng. to Wethersfield, Conn., 1647; *m* 1647, Sarah Deming; *m* 2d, Mary Kirby;
8–Ezekiel (1650-1715), *m* Rachel Andrews;
7–Enoch (*b* 1683), *m* Mary Beebe;
6–Daniel (1737-1814), served in Am. Rev.; *m* Ann Denton (*d* 1777);
5–Ichabod (1758-1849), served in Am. Rev.; *m* 1781, Lucy Boardman;
4–Sarah Boardman (1788-1849), *m* Ephraim **Smith** (see Vol. I, p. 521, for Smith lineage);
3–Henry Boardman (1809-57), *m* Laura Matilda Gibbs;
2–Julia Boardman (*b* 1852), *m* 1874, James **Kerr** (1851-1908), coal operator, financier, Clearfield, Pa.; mem. 51st Congress, 1889-91; issue: I–Albert B. (1 above); II–Frederick B. (*b* 1876; U.S.M.A., '99; comd. 23d Regt. U.S. Engrs. in World War; *m* Emily Bigler); III–Walter

KERR

Arms: Vert, a chevron argent, three mullets sable.
Crest: A unicorn's head couped argent, horn and mane or.

Boardman (*b* 1882; *m* Mary Canby); IV–James (*b* 1893).
1–*m* Oct. 8, 1913, Rosamond Burr, *b* Boston, June 8, 1889; dau. of Winthrop Burr (see Vol. I, p. 520, for genealogy).
1–B.A., Yale, '97 (Alpha Delta Phi, Scull and Bones). Lawyer; practiced in New York and Washington; Am. counsel for Royal Bank of Can., 1905-18; chief counsel, Bur. Industrial Housing and Transportation, U.S. Dept. of Labor, 1918. Author (see Who's Who in America). Mem. Assn. Bar City of New York. Democrat. Presbyn. Clubs: Yale, Union (New York), Metropolitan (Washington), Travellers (Paris), Authors (London). Residence: Villa Unicorn, Golfe-Juan A.M., France.

1–**KERR, Willis Holmes,** *b* Jamestown, Pa., June 26, 1880.
7–David **Kerr,** from Ireland 1708, settled at Camden and Phila., Pa., with his two bros., Robert and John;
6–John (*d* 1759), of Gettysburg, Pa.; *m* Martha–;
5–James (1752-1825), Shortcreek, Harrison Co., O.; *m* Agnes Carrick;
4–Samuel (1792-1882), *m* 1815, Ann Smith;
3–James (1818-86), of Cadiz, O.; *m* 1847, Julia Ann Carrick;
2–David Ramsey (2 below).
5–John **Sherrard** (1750-1809), from Ireland, settled at Smithfield, O.; *m* 1784, Mary Cathcart (1751-1833);
4–Robert Andrew (1789-1874), of nr. Steubenville, O.; *m* 1816, Mary Kithcart (1798-1823);
3–Mary Anne (*b* 1817), *m* 1848, Joseph Welsh **Hill** (1811-77);
2–Martha Sharon (*b* 1850), *m* 1879, David Ramsey **Kerr** (1850-1929), A.B., Franklin Coll., New Athens, O., 1874, A.M., 1877; Ph.D., Bellevue Coll., Neb., 1889; (D.D., U.Omaha, and Franklin Coll., O., 1891; LL.D., Westminster, 1912); pastor, 1876-89; pres. U.Omaha, 1891-1904, Bellevue Coll., 1889-1904, Westminster Coll., Fulton, Mo., 1904-11; prof. history and political science, Coll. of Emporia, Kan., 1911-12; asso. pres. Beechwood Sch. for Women, Jenkintown, Pa., 1912-16; again pres. Bellevue Coll., 1916-18, pres. emeritus, 1918; issue: I–Willis Holmes (1 above); II–James Fred (1882-1915; *m* Ethel Robinson); III–Mary Sherrard (*b* 1885; *m* David G. Page); IV–David Rhea (*b* 1887; *m* Olivia McCarty); V–Julia Ann Carrick (*b* 1890; *m* Will C. McCarty); VI–Robert Hill (*b* 1893; *m* Mildred Newell).
1–*m* June 14, 1904, Mary Wylie Nicholl, *b* Manchester, Eng., Nov. 11, 1879; dau. of Rev. William Nicholl, of Bellevue, Neb.
1–A.B., Bellevue (Neb.) Coll., 1900; A.M., Columbia, 1902; studied U. of Edinburgh, 1907-08. Librarian, Pomona Coll., Claremont, Calif., since 1925; dir. of libraries, Claremont Colleges, since 1927 (see Who's Who in America). Camp librarian, Camp Funston, Kan., Oct. 1917-June 1918; field rep. A.L.A. Library War Service, Washington, June-Dec. 1918; A.L.A. overseas war service, Paris, Dec. 1918-Sept. 1919. Congregational. Republican. Clubs: Collectors (N.Y.), Rotary (sec.), College. Residence: 470 W. 7th St., Claremont, Calif.

1–**KERR, Laurie King (Mrs. Peter),** *b* Portland, Ore., Apr. 22, 1877.
8–George **Colton** (qv);
7–Capt. Thomas (1651-1728), of Springfield, Mass.; lt. and capt., Springfield Co., 1685-92; served in French and Indian War, 1693; commd. capt. of E. Side Co. of Springfield, 1702; *m* 2d, 1691, Hannah Bliss (1665-1737);
6–Ebenezer (1696-1765), *m* 1733, Deborah Chandler (1709-69);
5–Jabez (1747-1819), of Longmeadow; grad. Yale, 1774; prof. Yale; *m* 1784, Mary Baldwin (1753-1839);
4–Simeon (1785-1868), Ashboro, N.C.; *m* 1812, Lucretia Woolworth (1788-1821);
3–Lucretia (1818-98), Chicago, Ill.; *m* 1841, in Longmeadow, Mass., John **King** (1805-91);
2–William Brown (2 below).
4–George **Messer,** *m* Elizabeth Cary;
3–Elizabeth, *m* Charles **Robinson;**
2–Laura (*b* 1857), of Dixon, Ill., and Portland, Ore.; *m* 1874, William Brown **King** (1844-1911); issue: I–Laurie (1 above); II–Mary Baldwin.
1–*m* Nov. 29, 1905, Peter Kerr, *b* Newton, Stewart, Scotland, Oct. 29, 1861; son of Thomas Kerr, of Scotland; issue: 1–Anne, *b* Portland, Ore., Sept. 22, 1906; 2–Jane, *b* Portland, Feb. 14, 1908.
1–Attended St. Helen's Hall, Portland. Mem. C.D.A., I.A.G. Clubs: Waverley Country, Town, Garden Club of America. Residence: Elk Rock, Portland, Ore.

1–**KILGORE, James,** *b* DeWitt Co., Tex., Jan. 15, 1865.
5–Thomas **Kilgore,** *m* Rebeccah–;
4–William (1735-1816), from Md. to Ohio; *m* 1770, Mary Armstrong (1750-1815; Archibald[5], *m* Elizabeth–);
3–William (1779-1851), of Md. and Ohio; *m* 1821, Anna R. Humphreys;
2–James Thomas (1825-1908), merchant; co. judge; *m* 1850, Caroline Elizabeth Bookwalter (1824-96); issue: I–Dr. William Humphrey (1851-1888; *m* Medora Guilemenot); II–Addison (*b* 1854; *m* Marvil Benson); III–Mary (*b* 1856; *m* Joseph B. Suttles); IV–Samuel Grafton (1858-1924; *m* Cassie Chase); V–Dr. Newton A. (*b* 1860; *m* Elizabeth Maurer); VI–Lee (*b* 1863); VII–James (1 above); VIII–Robert (1867-70); IX–Caroline Elizabeth (*b* 1870; *m* John F. Alford).
1–*m* Jan. 27, 1892, Lucy B. Pritchett (May 25, 1865-Apr. 3, 1894); dau. of Dr. E. H. Pritchett; issue: 1–John Edward, *b* Hayneville, Ala., Dec. 3, 1892; M.A., Southwestern U., '12; *m* Apr. 16, 1918, Lillian, dau. of George Amery, of McFadden, Tex. (issue: Lillian; John Edward); 2–Robert Hill (Mar. 23, 1894-June 17, 1894).
1–*m* 2d, Jan. 29, 1896, Faerie Blanton, *b* Houston, Tex., July 11, 1874; dau. of Thomas L. Blanton, of Houston; issue: 1–Frank Thomas (Jan. 23, 1898-Dec. 5, 1899); 2–Dr. Donald Gibson, *b* Cameron, Tex., Feb. 22, 1901; M.A., Southern Meth. U.; M.D., State Med. Coll., Galveston, 1923; *m* Gladys, dau. of Judge John Watson, of Cameron (issue: Donald Gibson, Jr.); 3–James Alford, *b* Palestine, Tex., Nov. 17, 1907; B.A., Southern Meth. U., '27.
1–B.A., Southwestern U., Georgetown, Tex., '89 (Phi Delta Theta), M.A., 1890 (D.D., 1910); studied U.Chicago 5 summers. Ordained ministry M.E. Ch., S., 1892; prof. philosophy of

religion, Southern Meth. U. (Dallas), 1915– (see Who's Who in America). Mason, K.P. Democrat. Club: Town and Gown. Residence: Southern Methodist University, Dallas, Tex.

1–**KING, Roy Stevenson,** *b* Xenia, Greene Co., O., Sept. 10, 1876.
11–Capt. William **King** (son of William, of E. Clayton, *m* Johann Beauchamp, a relative of the dukes of Devonshire); cdr. of the "Diamond"; from Eng. to America in his own ship, 1609; not known whether he settled or returned to Eng.;
10–Francis, to America with Giles Brent, 1653; *m* Miss Ashton;
9–Robert, *m* Mary Anne Peyton;
8–William (*d* 1702), *m* Judith Brent (George[9]);
7–Alfred, *m* Sophia Burgess (Capt. Edward[8], commr. Port of Londontown, Anne Arundel Co., justice Provincial Ct., capt. of fort, *m* Sarah, dau. Col. Samuel Chew; Col. William[9], qv);
6–Walter;
5–Zephaniah (*b* 1734), Port Tobacco, Charles Co., Md.; Am. Rev.; removed to Culpeper, Va., ca. 1800, later to Prince William Co.; lost at sea; *m* 1755, Dradah Clark;
4–Basil (1756-1844), Prince William Co., Va.; *m* 2d, 1789, Sarah Brookbank (1770-181–);
3–Vincent (1804-74), learned milling trade in mills of President John Quincy Adams, on Rock Creek, Georgetown, D.C.; buried at Xenia, O.; *m* 2d, 1836, Jane Gay Stevenson;
2–William Harrison (2 below).
6–Maj. John **Stevenson** (1728-98), believed to have come from Ireland, 1740; settled in Augusta Co., Va.; served in Indian wars; maj. in Gen. George Rogers Clark's Ill. Regt., 1778-83; *m* Miss Warwick (killed by Indians, ante Am. Rev.);
5–Samuel (1744-1825), to Lexington, Ky., 1779; a founder of Pisgah, Ky. and gave land to Pisgah ch., said to have been 1st ch. in Ky. and has never closed doors since; pvt. in Am. Rev.; *m* Jane Gay (John[6], settled on the Cow Pasture River, Augusta Co., *m* Jean Warwick);
4–James (1772-1864), *m* 1805, Ann Galloway (William[5] [1743-95], Am. Rev., of Cumberland Co., Pa., removed to Paris, Ky., *m* 1777, Rebecca Mitchell; George[6], from Ireland to Phila., Pa., settled in Cumberland Co.);
3–Jane Gay (1808-87), *m* Vincent **King** (3 above);
2–William Harrison (1840-1923), served in Co. F, 34th Ohio Vol. Inf., 1861-64; millwright; *m* 1865, Bertha Louise Ritter (1842-1912); issue: I–Minna Genieve (1866-69); II–Harry Ritter (1869-74); III–Roy Stevenson (1 above); IV–Bertha Dot (1879; *m* Edwin G. Fitzgerald); V–Ruby (1885-94).
1–*m* Feb. 19, 1903, Stella Gertrude Peterson, *b* Cincinnati, O., Mar. 16, 1872; dau. of John W. Peterson, of Xenia, O.
1–M.E., Ohio State U., '02 (Phi Kappa Phi, Sigma Xi); M.Sc., U. of Minn., 1907; (Sc.D., U. of Ga., 1922). Head of mech. engring. dept., Ga. Sch. of Tech., since 1923. Residence: 1293 Oxford Rd. N.E., Atlanta, Ga.

1–**KINDRED, John Joseph,** *b* Southampton Co., Va., July 15, 1864.
4–Henry **Kindred,** of Southampton Co., Va.;
3–Henry;
2–John J. (2 below).
8–John **Drewry** (son of Sir Drew Drewry), immigrated ca. 1650;
7–Samuel, was settled in Southampton Co., Va.;
6–John;
5–Samuel (*d* 1784), *m* —Simmons (—[6], mem. Va. House of Burgesses);
4–Humphrey (1761-1844), *m* 1787, Frances Simmons (1769-1825; John[5], burgess);
3–Samuel (*d* ca. 1862), of Southampton Co., Va.; *m* 2d, Eliza Avent;
2–Caroline Antoinette (*b* 1830), *m* 1859, John J. **Kindred** (*b* 1824), lawyer and scholar; issue: I–Mary Eliza (*b* 1861); II–John Joseph (1 above); III–Caroline Antoinette (*b* 1867; *m* William James Sebrell).
1–*m* July 10, 1892, Ella Welbon Cramer, *b* Poughkeepsie, N.Y.; A.B., Vassar; dau. of George E. Cramer; issue: 1–John Cramer, *b* Astoria, L.I., N.Y., Apr. 18, 1903; B.S., M.D., Randolph-Macon Coll.; *m* Dec. 21, 1929, Katherine Rebecca, *b* Richmond, Va., dau. of William Raleigh Carrier.

JOHN J. KINDRED

1–Ed. Suffolk (Va.) Mil. Acad., Randolph-Macon Coll., and U. of Va.; M.D., Hosp. Coll. of Medicine, Louisville, 1889; hon. grad. dept. mental diseases, U. of Edinburgh, 1892; LL.B., Stetson U., 1919. Clinical asst. and extra asst. physician under Sir Thomas S. Clouston, Royal Edinburgh Asylum for Insane; asst. physician N.Y. City Asylum for Insane, and at Hudson River State Hosp.; first asst. physician, Pa. State Hosp. for Insane, and as resident physician Md. Gen. Hosp., Baltimore; clinical asst., Bloomingdale Hosp. for Insane, New York; established a sanitarium at Stamford, Conn., 1895; established, 1897, and since owner, River Crest Sanitarium, Astoria, L.I., for mental and nervous diseases; also largely interested in real estate, building of homes and agr.; at present practicing his specialty of mental diseases in N.Y. City and is prof. of law and medical jurisprudence, Law Dept., John B. Stetson U., DeLand, Fla. Mem. 62d and 67th to 70th Congresses, 1911-13, and 1921-29, 2d N.Y. Dist. Mason. Democrat. Clubs: Pomonok Country, Manhattan Democratic. Summer home: Twilight Park, Haines Falls, N.Y. Residence: River Crest Sanitarium, Astoria, L.I., N.Y.

1–**KINNEY, Troy,** *b* Kansas City, Mo., Dec. 1, 1871.
8–Joel **Kinney,** from Ireland, 1660, with his brother Timothy, both soldiers in Oliver Cromwell's army; settled nr. Hartford, Conn.;
7–Joel, of Conn.;
6–Joel;
5–Joel, *m* 1765, Delight Kinney;
4–Joel (1768-1841), of Conn., Vt., and Livingston Co., N.Y.; *m* Elizabeth Holmes;
3–Sylvanus (1809-97), of N.Y. State and Lenawee Co., Mich.; *m* 1835, Hannah Crane (*d* 1849);
2–William Crane (1838-1908), of Mich. and Ill.; 1st lt., Co. E, Ill. Vols., 1861-65; alderman, Chicago, 1889-91; real estate broker; *m* 1869, Mary Candace Troy (1845-91; Edward[3], Methodist Minister, *m* —Stratton).
1–*m* June 9, 1900, Margaret Winifred West, *b* Peoria, Ill., July 11, 1872; studied Art Students League, New York, 1890-91, Julian Acad., Paris, 1891-95; pupil of Fleury, Lefebvre, Collin and Mercon; etcher, decorator and painter (see Who's Who in America); dau. of John Ackroyd West (1834-1915), from Eng. to U.S., 1855, treas. Knoxville Co., Ill., clk. Circuit Ct., Peoria Co., Ill., dep. clk. of Co. Ct., Peoria Co., *m* 1865, Margaret Jane McMillan (1834-1912), grad. Ingham U., LeRoy, N.Y., 1856, taught Ingham U., 1856-64, St. Marie's, Knoxville, Ill., 1864-65 (Daniel[3] [1801-95], of York, N.Y., *m* 1828, Margaret McNaughton [1806-86]; John[4], from Scotland, 1794, settled at Johnstown, N.Y.); issue: 1–John West, *b* New York, N.Y., Mar. 1903; M.E., Stevens Inst., '25; *m* Jan. 23, 1926, Mabel Irene, dau.

of Thomas Dolson, of Pompton Lakes, N.J., *m* Marguerite Delia– (issue: John West, Jr.).
1–B.A., Yale, '96 (D.K.E., Elihu Club); studied Yale Sch. of Fine Arts, and Chicago Art Inst. Artist and author (see Who's Who in America; The Etchings of Troy Kinney; Troy Kinney, Vol. IX, American Etchers). Mem. Chicago Soc. of Etchers, Brooklyn Soc. of Etchers, Architectural League of N.Y.; hon. mem. Phila. Print Club. Residence: Falls Village, Conn.

1–**KINSLEY, Carl,** *b* Lansing, Mich., Nov. 25, 1870.
9–Stephen **Kinsley** (ca. 1598-1673), from Eng., 1637; settled at Braintree, Mass., ca. 1640; rep., 1650; first ruling elder, 1653; removed to Dorchester, later to Milton; rep., 1666; *m* ca. 1624, Elizabeth– (*d* 1668);
8–Samuel (ca. 1630-62), Billerica, Mass.; *m* ca. 1655, Hannah Brackett (1634/35-1706), *b* Boston; removed to Braintree when married, and was killed by Indians in disturbances of 1706;
7–Samuel (1662-1713), Easton, Mass.; *m* ca. 1687, Mary Washburn;
6–Samuel (ca. 1689-post 1759), *m* ca. 1712, Mary Packard (ca. 1692-post 1747);
5–John (*b* 1721), Bennington, Vt.; mem. Capt. Dewey's co., and took part in Battle of Bennington; *m* 1746, Thankful Washburn;
4–Abisha (1766-1859), *m* 1793, Huldah Millard (1773-1813);
3–William (1804-65), Buffalo, N.Y.; *m* 1831, Carolyn Goodrich (1811-40);
2–William Wirt (2 below).
10–Francis **Cooke,** Mayflower Pilgrim (qv);
9–Jane, *m* ca. 1627, Experience **Mitchell** (*d* ante 1689);
8–Elizabeth (*b* ca. 1628), *m* 1645, John **Washburn**;
7–Mary (1661-ca. 1740), *m* Samuel **Kinsley** (7 above).
9–John **Washburn** (qv);
8–John (bap. in Eng. 1626-*d* 1686), of Duxbury and Bridgewater, Mass.; *m* 1645, Elizabeth Mitchell (*b* ca. 1628), same as 8 above;
7–John (1646-1719), *m* 1679, Rebecca Lapham (bap. 1645/46-1717), *d* Bridgewater, Mass.;
6–William (1686-1756), *m* 1715, Experience Mann;
5–Thankful (*b* 1723), *m* John **Kinsley** (5 above).
9–Thomas **Jewell** (qv);
8–Nathaniel (1648-1712), Plainfield, Conn.; *m* 1676/77, Mary (Smedley) Shepard;
7–Nathaniel (1678-ca. 1730), *m* 1704, Sarah Whitney;
6–David, Salisbury, Conn.; *m* 1741, Christiana Loomis;
5–Jonathan (1749-1833), of N. Adams, Mass.; *m* 1770, Betsey Dobbin;
4–Jesse (1778-1863), of Bolton, Vt., and Petaluma, Calif.; *m* 1803, Sarah Smith;
3–Jonathan (1805-94), Falls Ch., Va.; *m* 1835, Pamelia Bronson (1810-86);
2–Mary Ann (2 below).
10–John **Crane,** from Eng.; settled at Muddy Brook, Mass., 1637; dep. Gen. Ct., 1649;
9–Benjamin (ca. 1630-91), freeman, Wethersfield, Conn., 1658; *m* 1655, Mary Backus (*d* 1717; William[10], qv);
8–Jonathan (1658-1735), of Norwich and Windham, Conn.; dep. Gen. Ct., 1701-22; lt. in Indian War, 1704; *m* 1678, Deborah Griswold (1661-1704; Francis[9], *m* Mary, dau. of Thomas Tracy; Edward[10], qv);
7–Joseph (1696-1781), South East, N.Y.; *m* ca. 1719, Mary Couch (1695-1766; Samuel[8] [*d* 1739], of Fairfield, *m* Edora–; Simon[9] [*d* 1688], from Eng. to Fairfield, ca. 1640, *m* Mary [*d* 1691], dau. of Francis Andrews, *m* Anna, dau. Giles Smith);
6–Thaddeus (1728-1803), of N. Salem, N.Y.; lt. col. 4th Westchester Co. Regt., 1779; wounded in Battle of Ridgefield, 1777; mem. N.Y. Assembly, 1777-79, 1788-89; *m* 1st, 1751, Sarah Paddock (*d* 1777);
5–Sarah (1757-1829), *d* Bolton, Vt.; *m* Capt. Abram **Smith** (1754-1808), capt. Westchester Regt.;
4–Sarah (1781-1872), *m* Jesse **Jewell** (4 above);
3–Jonathan, *m* Pamelia Bronson (3 above);
2–Mary Ann (1838-1927), of Oberlin, O., and Falls Ch., Va.; *m* 1864, William Wirt **Kinsley** (1837-1923), left Oberlin Coll. to serve in Civil War; mem. P.B.K.; author of essays and books; issue: I–Lulu (*d* infancy); II–Carl (1 above); III–William Wirt, Jr. (*b* 1878; *m* 1907, Mabel Magoffin).
1–*m* June 1, 1901, Harriet Buchly (*d* 1910).
1–*m* 2d, June 7, 1913, Prudence Helen Ellis (qv); issue: 1–Colony, *b* Chicago, Ill., Mar. 13, 1914; 2–Stephanie, *b* Chicago, Dec. 10, 1917; 3–Penelope, *b* New York, N.Y., Apr. 27, 1926, and 4–Roger, twins (*d* May 9, 1926).
1–A.B., Oberlin, '93, A.M., 1896; E.E., Cornell, 1894. Instr. physics and elec. engring., Washington U., 1894-99; instr. and prof. applied physics, U. of Chicago, 1901-17; elec. expert for Signal Corps, U.S.A., on development of radio including invention, installation and test of first radio installation for army; maj. S.C., chief of section 10, Gen. Staff, U.S.A., etc. Consulting engr., engaged by U. S. Steel Corpn. on elec. research in New York (see Who's Who in America). Clubs: Cosmos (Washington), Engineers (N.Y. City), Westchester Co. Tennis. Residence: 22 Lynwood Rd., Scarsdale, N.Y.

1–**KINSLEY, Prudence Helen Ellis (Mrs. Carl),** *b* Charles City, Ia., Aug. 21, 1889.
8–Lt. Richard (Ellice) **Ellis** (qv);
7–John (1656-1727), of Dedham, Mass.; sgt. in Colonial army; *m* 1685/86, Elizabeth Fisher (*d* ca. 1724);
6–Ebenezer (*b* 1701), Dedham; *m* 1725/26, Elizabeth Barnard;
5–Asa (1744-1840), Bartlett, N.Y.; in Am. Rev.; *m* 1768, Phebe Smith;
4–Daniel (1786-1860), *m* 1808, Eliza Knapp (1784-1858), of Paris, N.Y.;
3–Charles Pickett (1810-90), Charles City, Ia.; *m* Sarah Ann Johnson (1819-99);
2–Charles Daniel (2 below).
9–Henry **Smith** (*d* 1687), from Eng., 1637, settled at Dedham, moved to Medfield, 1651; *m* Elizabeth– (*d* 1670);
8–Samuel (1641-91), *m* 2d, 1677, Sarah (Clark) Bowers (1651-1704);
7–Henry (1680-1743), *m* 2d, 1708, Mary Adams;
6–Jonathan (1714-84), *m* 1735, Abigail Wilkinson (*d* 1773), of Walpole;
5–Phebe (*b* 1747), *m* Asa **Ellis** (5 above).
10–Henry **Adams** (qv);
9–Ens. Edward (bap. 1629-1716), dep. Mass. Bay Colony; dep. Gen. Ct., 1689,92, 1702; *m* 1652, Lydia Rockwood (*d* 1676; Richard[10], *m* Agnes Bicknell);
8–Capt. Jonathan (1655-1718), of Medfield; *m* 1678, Mary Ellis (1660-1717);
7–Mary (1681-1725), *m* Henry **Smith** (7 above).
4–Obadiah **Wilbur** (1787-1841), of N.Y. State; *m* Urana Todd (*d* 1846), Quakeress;
3–Hervey (1811-88), Floyd, Ia.; *m* 1840, Angeline Moore (1820-1900; Philip[4] [1792-1866], *m* Sophia Roberts, 1794-1857);
2–Flora Ann (*b* 1854), *m* 1874, Charles Daniel **Ellis** (*b* 1850), lawyer; pres. First Nat. Bank of Charles City, Ia.; issue: I–Ida Mary (*b* 1875; *m* Malcolm Dana); II–Katharine Ruth (*b* 1879; *m* Robert LeMoyne Barrett); III–Melvin Wilbur (*b* 1881; *m* Mina Walleser); IV–Constance D. (*b* 1886); V–Prudence Helen (1 above); VI–Carlisle (*b* 1898; *m* Ellen Jennings).
1–*m* June 7, 1913, Carl Kinsley (qv for issue).
1–Ed. Rockford (Ill.) Coll.; A.B., Vassar, '10; medical courses at Chicago U. and Johns Hopkins. Residence: 22 Lynwood Rd., Scarsdale, N.Y.

1–**KIRKHAM, Thomas Atwood,** *b* Newington, Conn., Mar. 7, 1862.
8–Thomas **Kirkham** (qv);
7–Thomas, town shepherd, 1689; constable, Wethersfield; *m* 1684, Jane Butler;
6–Henry, in French and Indian War; *m* 1719, Martha Burr (*d* 1759; Samuel[7]);
5–Henry (*b* 1728), *d* of camp fever at Saratoga, N.Y.; served in Gen. Gates' Northern Army in Am. Rev.; *m* 1757 or 58, Eunice Butler;
4–John (1760-1815), fifer in Am. Rev., aet. 16; wounded at battle of Monmouth, N.J.; returned to Newington, Conn.; owned and operated a cloth mill introducing power looms; *m* 1785, Jeanette Stoddard (1767-1818; Capt. Jonathan[5], Am. Rev.);
3–William (1788-1868), owned homestead built on edge of Newington Mill Pond until 1840; sch. teacher, Hartford; removed to Springfield, Mass., ca. 1835; Conglist; fifer in Gov.'s

Footguard many yrs.; bought farm on main street of Newington which is still in possession of his descendants; *m* 1815, Sophia Leffingwell;
2-John Stoddard (2 below).
8-Thomas **Leffingwell** (qv);
7-Sgt. Thomas (1649-1723/24), to Norwich, Conn., with father, 1660; prominent citizen; freeman, 1671; rep.; *m* 1672, Mary Bushnell;
6-Capt. John (1688-1773), freeman, 1770; accumulated considerable estate; *m* 1710, Sarah Abel;
5-John (1721-95), gunsmith Am. Rev.; dea. 1st Congl. Ch.; *m* 1744, Hannah Edgerton;
4-Joshua (1762-1811), *m* 1787, Elizabeth Cook (*d* 1803);
3-Sophia (1796-1880), *m* William **Kirkham** (3 above).
7-Thomas **Atwood** (*b* Bromfield, Co. Essex, Eng., 1610-*d* 1682; son of Thomas), physician; soldier under Cromwell, capt. regt. dragoons at Marsden Moor; 1st appeared in N.E. at Wethersfield, 1663; practised his profession over a wide circuit as shown by his bills; built staunch ships for W.I. trade, built 1st shipyard on the Connecticut; *m* ca. 1667, Abigail–;
6-Josiah (1678-1758), of Farmington Parish; owned vessels engaged in W.I. trade, the losses from which made him surrender to his creditors, the Manor House in Eng., which he inherited from his father; *m* 1710, Bathsheba Latimer;
5-Asher (1729-1808), tanner; *m* 1757, Mary Mitchelson;
4-Ezekiel (1764-1853), of Hartford; served in Am. Rev., aet. 16; *m* 1793, Hannah Francis;
3-Josiah (1794-1863), *m* Prudence Kellogg (1790-1863);
2-Harriet Prudence (1827-82), *m* 1859, John Stoddard **Kirkham** (1826-1918), with Maj. Horace Goodwin on trip around Cape Horn to Calif., 1849; lost his health while seeking gold; returned home by way of Central America; crossed Isthmus by oxcart; sch. teacher and chmn. sch. bd., Newington; mem. Gen. Assembly, 1877; state senator, 1887; mem. Conn. Bd. Agr.; Conglist.; issue: I-Frances H. (1860-1903; *m* Henry Laurens Kellogg); II-Thomas Atwood (1 above); III-John Henry, Judge (*b* 1865; *m* 1896, Lilian S. West); IV-Mary Atwood (1866-1905; *m* Roderick Whittlesey Hine).
1-*m* May 23, 1906, Fanny Leffingwell Brown, *b* New Britain, Conn., Sept. 11, 1858; dau. of Martin Brown, of New Britain.
1-Mgr. father's farm, 12 yrs.; became partner of John A. Barri, in the Berkshire Mills Co., 1895-1900; established Berkshire Chem. Co., 1900; propr. and pres. since incorpn., 1913. Conglist. Clubs: Seaside, Brooklawn Country. Residence: 213 Courtland St., Bridgeport, Conn.

1-**KLEPPINGER, Stanley Jeremiah,** *b* Pennsville, Pa., June 20, 1899.
6-John Georg **Kleppinger** (1707-86), from the Palatinate, Germany, in the "St. Andrew Galley," 1737; settled at Kreidersville, Northampton Co., Pa.; *m* Anna Margaretta–;
5-Ludwig (1741-1827), served in 7th Co., 3d Bn., Northampton Co. Militia, in Am. Rev.; *m* 1768, Anna Maria Best (1751-1827);
4-Lewis (1790-1842), of Cherryville, Pa.; *m* 1815, Barbara Herman (1790-1872);
3-David (1817-79), *m* 1843, Lovina Kuntz (1820-91);
2-Jeremiah Wilson (2 below).
4-Samuel **Hummel** (1795-1867), *m* Mary Beil;
3-William (1831-98), *m* Matilda Solt (1836-82);
2-Amanda Rebecca (*b* 1856), of Kreidersville, Pa.; *m* 1877, Jeremiah Wilson **Kleppinger** (*b* 1854), of Cherryville, Pa.; issue: I-William David (1878-79); II-Wallace Edgar (*b* 1879; *m* Sallie B. Clymer); III-Minnie May (*b* 1881; *m* Edward C. Oswald); IV-Laura Estella (1882-1912; *m* Newton J. Oplinger); V-Elsie Jane (*b* 1884; *m* Victor E. Schaffer); VI-Harry Lewis (*b* 1887; *m* Eva R. Manbeck); VII-Nora Alice (*b* 1888; *m* Warren W. Wehr); VIII-Frank Albert (*b* 1890; *m* S. Florence Schappell); IX-Elvin Ellsworth (*b* 1891; *m* Irma I. Oplinger); X-Marvin Eugene (*b* 1895; *m* Mabel E. Easterday); XI-Stanley J. (1 above).
1-*m* Oct. 8, 1924, Lucy Anna Wehr, *b* Allentown, Pa., Nov. 6, 1896; dau. of Benjamin F. Wehr, of Allentown; issue: 1-Gerald Stanley, *b* Allentown, Apr. 13, 1926; 2-Lucile Edna, *b* Allentown, May 15, 1927.
1-Pub. sch. teacher, 1917-18; office sec., 1920–. Mem. Lehigh Co. (Pa.) Hist. Soc. United Brethren (supt. S.S., Grace U.B. Ch., Allentown). Residence: 631 N. St. Elmo St., Allentown, Pa.

HARRISON GRAY DYAR (1805-75).

1-**KNOPF, Perle Nora Dyar (Mrs. S. Adolphus),** *b* New York, N.Y., Jan. 2, 1868.
7-Thomas **Dyar** (1612-76), from Eng., 1632; settled Weymouth, Mass.; dea. in ch. under Rev. Samuel Torrey; *m* 1640, Agnes Reed, or Alice Read (*d* 1667);
6-John (1643-96), of Weymouth, Mass.; removed to Boston, ca. 1670; *m* 2d, 1678, Elizabeth–;
5-Joseph (1687-ca. 1720), of Boston, *m* 1717, Lydia Hough (*d* 1774);
4-Joseph (1719-80), *m* 2d, 1766, Amey Bumstead;
3-Jeremiah (1771-1829), *m* 1794, Susanna Wild (1776-1824);
2-Harrison Gray (1805-75), apprenticed to Lemuel Curtis, a clock and watch maker, 1820; when 12 yrs. old, had performed many experiments in chemistry; conceived idea of transmitting messages by electricity, extended wire line along "Causeway" or Lowell Rd., at Concord, Mass., line being hung from trees with glass phials as insulators, messages lightly recorded, 1826; erected 1st real line and dispatched 1st real message over it ever sent by such means in America; devised a code consisting of dots, dashes and spaces, with which the later "Morse Code," was almost identical; denounced when he proposed to erect a telegraph line between New York and Phila.; annoyed by extortionate law suit, charged with conspiracy; "Bank Conspiracy" affected his financial supporters, 1831; left the country, entrusted his plans and models with Charles Walker, a bro. in-law of S. F. B. Morse; spent several yrs. in Paris, where he was amply rewarded for other inventions; returned to America after 25 yrs.; in later yrs., in fit of despondence, had all his papers destroyed; *d* nr. Rhinebeck on the Hudson (see portrait); *m* 1865, Eleanora Rosella Hannum (*b* Adams, Mass., 1842-*d* Boston, 1888); issue: I-Harrison Gray (1866-1929; *m* 1889, Zella Peabody; *m* 2d, 1921, Wellesca Pollak Allen); II-Perle Nora (1 above).
1-*m* Oct. 19, 1889, Sigard Adolphus Knopf, M.D., *b* Halle, Germany, Nov. 27, 1857 (see Who's Who in America).
1-Residence: 16 W. 95th St., New York, N.Y.

1-**KNIGHT, Frederic Butterfield,** *b* Springfield, Mass., July 2, 1891.
6-John **Knight** (*d* 1800), of Kittery, Me., moved to Alfred, Me., 1765;

5–Thomas (*d* ca. 1835);
4–Daniel (*b* 1804), of Alfred, Me.; *m* Catharine Sawyer, of Portland;
3–Edward T. (1832-1906), Saco, Me.; *m* 1858, Sarah C. Boothby (1837-1914);
2–Rev. Frederic Harrison (2 below).
10–Benjamin **Butterfield** (qv);
9–Nathaniel (*b* 1642 or 43), *m* 1669, Deborah Underwood (1650-91; William[10], was at Concord, 1638);
8–Benjamin (*b* Chelmsford, Mass.-*d* 1715);
7–John (1699-1766), capt. in Indian wars;
6–Ephraim (*d* 1777), col. in French and Indian War, at battle of Lake George; selectman, Wilton, N.H., 1764-66; moderator, 1768; *m* 1732, Elizabeth Davis;
5–Abraham (1750-1833), pvt. in Am. Rev.; *m* 1771, Ruth Averill;
4–Ebenezer (1791-1865), pvt. in War 1812; *m* Sally Johnson;
3–George W. (1823-86), of Saugus, Mass.; *m* 1858, Salva Swain (1829-1906);
2–L. I. Marion (2 below).
11–Isaac **Allerton,** Mayflower Pilgrim (qv);
10–Remember (1614-55), of Plymouth, Mass.; *m* Moses **Maverick** (1610-68), of Marblehead and Salem;
9–Rebecca (1639-1759), *m* 1658, John **Hawkes** (1633-94), King Philip's War (John[10], from Eng. to Lynn, Mass., 1630);
8–Moses (1659-1709), *m* 1688, Margaret Cogswell;
7–John (1705-48), *m* 1732, Hannah Priest (*b* 1707);
6–Sarah, *m* 1761, James **Johnson;**
5–William, *m* Martha Proctor;
4–Sally (1800-64), of Salem and Saugus; *m* 1817, Ebenezer **Butterfield** (4 above);
3–George W., *m* Salva Swain (3 above);
2–L. I. Marion (*b* 1861), *m* 1887, Rev. Frederic Harrison **Knight,** Ph.D. (*b* Saco, Me., 1859-1922), issue: I–Howard Roscoe (*b* 1889; *m* 1917, Pauline Helms); II–Frederic Butterfield (1 above).
1–*m* June 16, 1922, Florence Mabel Brockhausen, *b* Milwaukee, Wis., Apr. 24, 1897; dau. of Frederick Brockhausen, of Milwaukee.
1–B.A., Boston U., 1913 (Beta Theta Pi, Phi Beta Kappa, Sigma Xi, Phi Delta Theta); M.A., Harvard, 1915; Ph.D., Columbia, 1920. Prof. education and psychology, State U. of Ia., since 1920; gen. editor Education Series, Longmans, Green & Co. Author (see Who's Who in America). Sgt. Med. Corps, U.S.A., Gen. Hosp., Plattsburg, N.Y., 1918-19. Methodist. Republican. Residence: 224 Richards St., Iowa City, Ia.

1–**KNOWLES, Morris,** *b* Lawrence, Mass., Oct. 13, 1869.
9–John **Knowles** (qv);
8–John (*b* 1661);
7–Ezekiel (*b* 1687), *m* Mary Wedgewood;
6–David (bap. 1725);
5–David (*b* 1751), *m* 1776, Mary Hobbs;
4–Morris (1780-1824), *m* 1801, Polly Caverly;
3–Morris (*b* 1810), *m* 1836, Sarah Green (*d* 1899);
2–Charles Edwin (2 below).
6–Ebenezer **Virgin,** from Eng. to Salisbury, Mass., 1766; to Dunstable, Mass., thence to Concord, N.H.;
5–William (1737-1803), *m* Mehitable Stickney;
4–Jeremiah (*b* 1765), to Rumford, Me., on the Swift River;
3–Harriet, *m* 1830, Jeremiah **Richardson** (1804-88; Jeremiah[4] [*d* 1819], *m* Betsy–, *d* 1840);
2–Ellen Britania (Dec. 20, 1844-Oct. 16, 1894), *m* 1866, Charles Edwin **Knowles** (1841-1922), carpenter and builder.
1–*m* Apr. 25, 1893, Mina P. McDavitt, *b* Albion, Me., Jan. 28, 1869; dau. William H. McDavitt, of Lawrence, Mass., formerly of Augusta and China, Me.; issue: 1–Helen Inez, *b* Lawrence, Mass., May 4, 1894; A.B., Vassar, '16; *m* Mar. 28, 1918, Harold N. Schreuder; 2–Morris, Jr., *b* Pittsburgh, Pa., July 16, 1904; Culver Mil. Acad., '24.
1–S.B., M.I.T., '91; (Dr. Engr., U.Pittsburgh, 1929). Pres. Morris Knowles, Inc. Formerly dir. dept. of municipal and sanitary engring., U.Pittsburgh. Chief engr. housing dept. Emergency Fleet Corpn. and supervising engr. Camp Meade, Md., and Camp McClellan, Ala., World War. Chmn. Pittsburgh City Plan Commn.; dir. Pittsburgh Chamber Commerce; mem. Corpn. M.I.T. (see Who's Who in America). Mem. O.F.P.A., S.A.R., I.A.G., N.E.H.G.S., Pa. Soc. Clubs: Duquesne, University (Pittsburgh), University (Phila.), Cosmos (Washington), City (N.Y. and Boston), Engineers (N.Y.). Residence: 5814 Stanton Av., Pittsburgh, Pa.

1–**KRAISSL, Anna Margaret Van Saun (Mrs. Frederick),** *b* Woodbridge, N.J., Mar. 4, 1869.
9–Jacob **Van** (Zauen) **Saun,** from Ransdorph, Holland; settled at New York; applied for land on Hackensack River, 1695, and patent was granted, 1696;
8–Jacob (bap. 1657), of N.Y., and Hackensack, N.J.; *m* 1678, Jannetje Lucas;
7–Jacob (bap. 1684), *m* 1705, Rachel Bougaert;
6–Isaac (bap. 1717), *m* 1739, Marytje (Maria) De Marest;
5–Lucas (bap. 1746), soldier in Am. Rev.; *m* 1773, Magdalena Berdan;
4–John L. (1793-1822), *m* 1812, Lany (Ellen) Van Voorhis (1793-1868; Albert[5], Am. Rev., *m* 1778, Rachel Hopper);
3–Albert J. (1814-86), *m* 1834, Margaret Weaver (1816-94; Jacob[4], *m* Jane, dau. of Abraham Van Keuren, Jr.; Michael[5], Am. Rev., *m* 1780, Margaret Buggs);
2–John A. (2 below).
8–Capt. Adrian **Post** (*d* 1677), from Harlengen, Holland, in the "New Amsterdam," 1650; settled on Staten Island, and started a colony which was destroyed by the savages, 1655; underwent severe hardships while trying to build a fortress, according to instructions from authorities, but was relieved by his friend, Gov. Cartaret, of N.J.; the West India Co. bought the island, 1661, and Capt. Post was a grantee; appointed gov.; nominated ens. of the villages of Bergen, 1663; elected to represent the town in Provincial Govt., 1673; lt. of militia, 1675;
7–Adrian (living 1713), from Holland; was petitioner in Acquackanack, N.J., patent; dea., 1699;
6–Johannis (bap. 1690-will proved, 1783), elder, 1734; *m* 1713, Elizabet Helmigse Van Houten;
5–Cornelius (1736-1812), pvt. Bergen Co., militia; served in Am. Rev., 1775-83; *m* 2d, Anna Maria Kough;
4–Casparus (1767-1842), *m* 1794, Fytje (Sophia) Paulusse (Paulison) (1754-1859);
3–Cornelius (1806-56), *m* 1827, Annaetje Van Houten (1809-86);
2–Sophia A. (1836-1912), Hackensack, N.J.; *m* 1st, Nicholas Kipp, of Woodridge; *m* 2d, 1859, John A. **Van Saun** (1835-1904), painter; issue (1st marriage): I–Nicholas (surname Kipp; *m* Sarah Ten Eyck); issue (2d marriage): I–Nellie (*m* Cornelius Kiel); II–Cornelius J.; III–Albert J. (*m* Emma Grawe); IV–Anna M. (1 above).
1–*m* June 22, 1897, Frederick Kraissl, *b* Austria, July 4, 1869; son of Edward Kraissl, of Austria; issue: 1–Frederick, *b* New York, July 8, 1899; A.B., Brooklyn Poly. Inst., '21; M.S., Columbia, 1922; *m* June 10, 1925, Alice, dau. of Charles Plenty, of Hackensack; 2–Cornelius J., *b* Vienna, Austria, July 31, 1902; M.D., Coll. of Physicians and Surgeons (Columbia), 1927.
1–Trenton State Normal Sch., special coll. course. Mem. D.F.P.A., D.R. (organizer and regent Hackensack Chapter, state registrar, dir. gen. loyal league work), Bergen Co., Hist. Soc. Mem. Reformed Ch. Republican. Summer place: Green Pond, N.J. Residence: N. Hackensack, N.J.

1–**KRAUSS, Elmer Frederick,** *b* Kraussdale, Pa., Sept. 7, 1862.
7–Melchoir **Krauss** (*died* Haarlem, Holland, May 28, 1733, on journey to America), from Silesia, Germany; *m* Anna Heidrick (1675-1755), from Silesia; with 5 children continued journey to America, arriving in Phila., Sept. 1733; settled in Lehigh Co., Pa., 40 miles north of Phila.;
6–Balthasar (1706-74), of Kraussdale, Pa.; *m* 1736, Susannah Hoffman (1708-91);
5–Balthasar (1743-1805), Am. Rev.; *m* 1769, Susannah Yeakel (1744-1820);
4–John (1770-1819), *m* 1795, Rosina Yeakel (1771-1872);
3–Anthony (1803-52), *m* 1825, Sarah Yeakel (1805-72);
2–Isaac Yeakel (1836-1914), mfr. of agrl. machinery; *m* 1861, Theodora Rosalie Waage

(1839-1928); issue: I–Elmer Frederick (1 above); II–Florence S. (*b* 1864-1917; *m* W. F. Dixon, *d* 1917); III–Edgar Anthony (*b* 1867; *m* Marguerite L. Bernd); IV–Charles O. (*b* 1869; *m* Ella L. Wambold, *d* 1929); V–Walter Isaac (*b* 1878).

1–*m* Oct. 27, 1887, Irene E. Hartzell (Dec. 27, 1860-Jan. 7, 1903); dau. of George W. Hartzell, of Allentown, Pa.; issue: 1–Irene Theodora, *b* Homestead, Pa., June 9, 1889; *m* 1913, Rev. D. E. Bosserman, of Ohio (issue: Irene; Elmer; Helen); 2–Rev. Paul Hartzell, *b* Homestead, Nov. 16, 1890; A.B., Muhlenberg, '12; *m* 1915, Helen Hitchcock, of Oak Park, Ill. (adopted: Constance); 3–Harold Frederick, *b* Minneapolis, Minn., Sept. 9, 1894; Wittenberg Coll.; *m* 1923, Elizabeth MacDonald, of Lincolnton, N.C. (issue: Harold; Jane); 4–Winfred Elmer (Sept. 13, 1896-July 4, 1902); 5–Ruth Sarah, *b* Leechburg, Pa., Oct. 19, 1899; ed. Chicago Teachers' Coll.; *m* 1922, Rev. H. A. Bosch, B.D., of New York (issue: Herbert; Robert).

1–*m* 2d, Sept. 20, 1904, Emma Alice King.

1–A.B., Muhlenberg, '84 (Chi Phi), A.M., 1887 (D.D., 1903); grad. Phila. Luth. Theol. Sem., 1887. Prof. N.T. exegesis, Evangelical Luth. Theol. Sem., Chicago, since 1900; acting pres., 1913-15, pres., 1915-20 (see Who's Who in America). Clubs: University, Rotary. Residence: 1618 S. 11th Av., Maywood, Ill.

1–**KRECH, Shepard,** *b* St. Paul, Minn., Feb. 22, 1891.

10–Edward **Shepard** (qv);

9–Sgt. John (*b* Eng., 1627-*d* 1707), *m* 1st, 1649, Rebecca Greenhill (1634-89; Samuel[10]);

8–Edward (*b* Cambridge, Mass., 1662);

7–John (*b* Middletown, Conn., 1688);

6–Elisha (*b* Middletown, 1736);

5–Cornelius (*b* Chatham, Conn., 1769);

4–David Shepard (*b* Marlboro, Conn., 1791), *m* Dolly Olmstead Foote;

3–David Chauncey (*b* Geneseo, N.Y., 1828-*d* St. Paul, Minn., 1920), prominent civil engr.; *m* Frances Aurelia–;

2–Caroline (*d* 1892), *m* Alvin William **Krech** (*b* Hannibal, Mo.-*d* May 3, 1928), pres. Equitable Trust Co., 25 yrs., chmn. bd. 5 yrs.; prominent in railroad reorganizations (William[3], country sch. teacher, nr. town of Eisenach, Saxony, where Luther translated the Bible, joined revolutionary movement with Carl Schurz and Gottfried Kinkel, sailed for S.A. ca. 1852, ship-wrecked off coast of La., landed at New Orleans, worked his way up the Mississippi River to Hannibal, Mo., later to St. Paul, Minn.).

1–*m* July 1, 1916, Mary Stevens, dau. of Charles Merrill Chapin; issue: 1–Shepard, Jr., *b* New York, Apr. 24, 1918; 2–Merrill Chapin, *b* New York, Sept. 18, 1919; 3–Mary Esther, *b* Boston, Dec. 12, 1921; 4–Alvin W., 2d, *b* New York, Jan. 10, 1925.

1–B.A., Yale, '13 (Alpha Delta Phi); Harvard Med. Sch., 1923; Presbyn. Hosp., 1925. At present asst. adjunct visiting surgeon, Bellevue Hosp.; instr. in surgery, Coll. of Physicians and Surgeons (Columbia U.). Commd. 2d lt., cav., Aug. 15, 1917; 1st lt., July 15, 1918; capt., inf., July 31, 1918; attached to 1st Brig., 1st, 77th and 98th divs.; in France, Sept. 7, 1917-Sept. 19, 1918. Mem. V.F.W., Squadron A N.Y. Cav., A.L., etc. Clubs: Racquet and Tennis, Yale (N.Y.), Yale, Harvard, Aesculapaean (Boston) Nat. Golf Links of America, Turf and Field, Westminster Kennel, Garden City Golf. Residence: 1060 Fifth Av., New York, N.Y.

1–**KRIEBLE, Vernon K.,** *b* Worcester, Pa., Mar. 4, 1885.

7–Christopher (Kribel) **Krieble** (1688-1741), from Germany, 1726; settled Lower Salford, Montgomery Co., Pa.; *m* Maria Heydrick (1693-1738; Melchior[8]);

6–Rev. Christopher (1724-1800), of Lower Salford; *m* 1748, Maria Dresher (1723-72; George[7], *m* Maria Beyer);

5–Abraham (1750-1818), *m* 1778, Rosina Hartrauft (1758-1816; George[6], *m* Maria Schmiedt);

4–Isaac (1779-1806), of Worcester, Pa.; *m* 1804, Regina Schultz (1783-1869; Rev. Melchior[5], *m* Salome Wagner);

3–Isaac S. (1806-81), *m* 1831, Christina Schultz (1812-83; William[4], *m* Salome Kriebel);

2–Jesse Schultz (1842-1915), farmer, Worcester, Pa.; *m* 1871, Susanna Zilling Kriebel (1846-1929; William[3], *m* Mary Zilling); issue: I–Malinda (1878-84); II–Ida (1880-82); III–Harvey (*b* and *d* 1883); IV–Vernon (1 above).

1–*m* June 22, 1912, Laura Cassel, *b* Lansdale, Pa., May 9, 1889; dau. of Abraham K. Cassel, of Lansdale; issue: 1–Gladys Verna, *b* Worcester, Pa., July 3, 1913; 2–Robert Henry, *b* Worcester, Aug. 22, 1916.

1–Ph.B., Brown U., '07 (Kappa Sigma, P.B.K., Sigma Xi); M.Sc., McGill, 1909, Ph.D., 1913. Demonstrator, dept. of chemistry, McGill, 1907-12; lecturer, McGill, 1912-14, asst. prof., 1914-20; Scoville prof. chemistry, Trinity Coll., Hartford, Conn., since 1920. Author (see Who's Who in America). Mem. Krieble Fam. Assn. Club: Twentieth Century, Congregational. Residence: 71 Vernon St., Hartford, Conn.

1–**KRIEGE, Otto Edward,** *b* Belleville, Ill., Nov. 20, 1865.

6– —**Rauzahn** (*b* ca. 1690), from Germany, aet. 8; settled in Pa.;

5–Conrad (ca. 1740-1818), of Pa.;

4–Christian (1771-1852), of Pa.; *m* 1794, Maria Barbara Shaeffer (1774-1855);

3–Anna Maria (1815-79), of Md.; *m* 1835, Solomon **Lehr** (1812-40);

2–Mary Elizabeth (1836-1917), of Ill.; *m* 1854, Eberhard Henry **Kriege** (1827-89), minister; issue: I–Amelia Juliana (1856-57); II–Louis Samuel (1858-1926; *m* Margaret Bassler); III–William Benjamin (1860-61); IV–John Henry (*b* 1862; *m* Carrie F. Frick); V–Emil Theodore (*b* and *d* 1864); VI–Otto Edward (1 above); VII–Albert Julius (1868-70); VIII–Carl Ferdinand (*b* and *d* 1871); IX–Frederick William (*b* and *d* 1873); X–Clara Elizabeth (*b* and *d* 1874); XI–Ollie Lydia (*b* 1876; *m* Ernest William Schonian, 1864-1929).

1–*m* Sept. 16, 1890, Emma Rosina Frick, *b* Denver, Colo., Feb. 17, 1867; dau. of Conrad Frick, of Denver; issue: 1–Edith Helene, *b* Arlington, Neb., June 12, 1891; A.B., Central Wesleyan Coll., '11; *m* Sept. 2, 1914, Prof. Paul Emil Hemke, Ph.D., Johns Hopkins, of Quincy, Ill. (issue: Harold Paul; Marjorie Helene; Emily Doris); 2–Herbert Frick, *b* Omaha, Neb., Mar. 14, 1895; B.A., Central Wesleyan, '16; M.S., U. of Mo., 1920; Ph.D., Ohio State, 1926; *m* Aug. 2, 1922, Mabel Ruth, dau. of Walter Hobbs, of Marcus, Ia. (issue: Owen Hobbs); 3–Winifred (*b* and *d* Sept. 18, 1901).

1–A.B., Central Wesleyan Coll., '88 (Sigma Tau Delta), A.M., 1890; student univs. Bonn and Berlin, Germany, Chicago and Denver (D.D., Baker U., 1906). Ordained M.E., ministry, 1890; pastorates, 1890-99; prof. psychology and ethics, 1899-1910, pres., 1910-25, Central Wesleyan Coll.; pres. New Orleans U., 1925– (see Who's Who in America). Mem. I.A.G., New Orleans Geneal. and Hist. Soc., La. Hist. Soc. Mason. Residence: 5300 St. Charles Av., New Orleans, La.

1–**KRIEGER, Agnes Checkley Keighler (Mrs. Louis C. C.),** *b* Baltimore, Md., Aug. 27, 1875.

11–Sir George **Yeardley** (qv);

10–Col. Argall (1621-55), mem. Council of Va., 1643; *m* 1649, Ann Custis;

9–Capt. Argall (*d* 1682), mem. Council of Va.; *m* 1670, Sarah Michael (*d* 1694; John[10], *m* Elizabeth, dau. of Capt. Adam Thorogood, qv);

8–Frances, *m* Maj. John **West,** Jr. (*d* 1718);

7–Sarah (*d* 1760), *m* Isaac **Smith**;

6–Isaac (1734-1813), *m* Elizabeth Custis Teackle;

5–Mary Ann, *m* William **Gilmor,** of Baltimore, Md.;

4–Ann, *m* Edward Greene **Williams** (1789-1829; Otho Holland[5] [1749-94], col. 6th Regt., Md. Line, bvt. brig. gen., Cont. Line, founder Williamsport, Md., 1st sec. Md. branch of Soc. Cin.);

3–Mary Smith (1822-1907), *m* Rev. Dr. John Campbell **White** (1820-65), bro. of William Pinkney Whyte, gov. Md., U.S. senator (for White lineage see Vol. III, p. 296);

2–Mary Williams (1845-1917), *m* Samuel Ames **Keighler** (1840-1901), mcht. (for issue see Vol. III, p. 296).

1–*m* Apr. 4, 1904, Louis Charles Christopher Krieger, *b* Baltimore, Feb. 11, 1873; ed. Royal Bavarian Acad. Fine Arts; artist, writer on botanical subjects; son of Henry Krieger,

from Hesse-Darmstadt, Germany, to Baltimore, 1867; issue: 1–Agnes Checkley, *b* Cambridge, Mass., May 28, 1909.
Residence: 1300 Mass. Av. N.W., Washington, D.C.

1–**KROWS, Arthur Edwin,** *b* New York, N.Y., June 22, 1892.
6–John **Krows,** from Germany, settled in Kingston, N.Y.; *m* Mareitje (Beem) Terpenning;
5–Leonard (1759-1838), served in Am. Rev.; *m* 1784, Deborah Ostrander (1763-1823);
4–John (1791-1867), of Esopus, N.Y.; *m* 1811, Elizabeth Clearwater (1793-1882);
3–William Timlow (1825-1904), of Kingston; *m* 1849, Eliza Jane Ferguson (1827-1910);
2–Edwin (2 below).
5–Francis **Cook** (described in family records as "an English gentleman"); *m* Rachel Van Zaun or Zanddt, of Paterson, N.J.;
4–Mary Ann, of Paterson; *m* William Henry **Myers** (1812-96), of Springfield, Ill.;
3–Francis Henry (*b* 1836), of New York; *m* 1863, Mary Louise Anthony;
2–Lavinia (2 below).
7–William **Baker,** of Camden, N.J.; *m* Elizabeth–;
6–Emily, of Elizabeth, N.J.; *m* Samuel **Robins,** of Phila. (family of French descent);
5–Hannah, *m* Abram **Dutcher,** of New York;
4–Lavinia (1838-1912), of Elizabeth, N.J.; *m* 1847, Peter **Anthony** (1828-1900), served on northern side in Civil War (Peter[5], *b* Alpine, N.J., his parents came from Portugal, *m* Laetitia [1785-1864], dau. of John Van Valen, soldier Am. Rev.);
3–Mary Louise (*b* 1848), of Alpine, N.J.; *m* Francis Henry **Myers** (3 above);
2–Lavinia (*b* 1864), of Alpine, N.J.; *m* 1884, Edwin **Krows** (1860-1919), of Staatsburg, N.Y.; sales mgr. Horton Ice Cream Co., New York; issue: I–Earl, D.D.S. (*b* 1885; *m* Grace Alton); II–Arthur Edwin (1 above).
1–*m* Oct. 9, 1914, his 2d cousin, Marion Soetemon, *b* Yonkers, N.Y., Mar. 28, 1887; dau. of Peter Soetemon (1842-1907), of Dutch desc., *m* Josephine Myers (1848-90; sister of Francis Henry Myers, above).
1–Studied playwriting with late William T. Price. Motion picture dir., specializing in social service films, since 1924. Author (see Who's Who in America). Republican. Residence: 64 Farragut Rd., Hastings-on-Hudson, N.Y.

1–**KULLING, Catherine Elizabeth Stewart Wood (Mrs. Otto W.),** *b* Phila., Pa.
5–William **Stewart** (1739-1810; desc. Earl of Bute), came from Ireland with his brothers, Archibald and James, and was one of the founders of the first Presbyn. Ch., of Hackettstown, N.J.; *m* 1st, Frances–;
4–James (1772-1834), *m* Elizabeth Culver;
3–Dr. Thomas Page (1798-1846), *m* 1824, Susan Sherred Beavers or Bevier (1802-77; Robert[4]);
2–Reuel (2 below).
9–Edward **Culver** (qv);
8–John (1640-1725), *m* Mary Winthrop (John[9]);
7–John (1670-1760), *m* his cousin, Sarah Winthrop;
6–Robert (1713-83), *m* Anne Clark (1717-post 1783; Stephen[7]);
5–Robert (1740-1814-15), *m* ca. 1763, Martha–;
4–Elizabeth (1776-1826), *m* 1796, James **Stewart** (4 above);
3–Dr. Thomas P., *m* Susan S. Beavers (3 above);
2–Reuel, M.D. (1829-1916), physician, Phila.; *m* 1853, Anna Rebecca Agey (*b* 1829; Jacob[3]); for issue see Vol. I, p. 663.
1–*m* Apr. 6, 1880, William Brewster Wood (July 25, 1851-Apr. 24, 1905); son of Thomas Wood, *m* Maria Jackson Flagg (desc. Elder William Brewster); issue: 1–Constance Brewster, *b* Phila., Pa., Jan. 7, 1881; *m* Apr. 18, 1910, Allen Rhoads Evans (issue: Beatrice, 1911-19).
1–*m* 2d, Nov. 8, 1913, Otto Walther Kulling.
1–Mem. Sons and Daughters of the Pilgrims (gov.-gen. nat. soc.), Nat. Soc. Women Descendants of the A. and H.A.Co. (rec. sec. nat.), D.A.R., U.S.D. 1812, League of Am. Pen Women. Editor "Pilgrim News Letter." Clubs: New Century, Woman's City, Phila. Music. Residence: "Wuntree," Meadowbrook, Pa.

1–**KUNKEL, Robert Sharp,** *b* Newville, Pa., June 8, 1864.
4–Michael **Long** (*d* 1802), soldier Am. Rev.; *m* Christina Stober;
3–Rebecca (1796-1869), *m* Aaron **Kunkel** (see Vol. II, p. 306, for Kunkel lineage);
2–John Atley (2 below).
5–Capt. James **Sharp** (*d* ca. 1795), French and Indian War; *m* Margaret McConnell (*d* 1769; Lt. Robert[6] [1707-76], French and Indian War, McConnellsburg, Bedford Co., Pa., was named and founded after the McConnell family, *m* Rosanna–, 1711-70); Sharpsburg, nr. Allegheny City, Pa., was founded and named after their son Matthew;
4–William (*d* 1806), pvt. Am. Rev.; *m* Jane McClintock (*d* 1812; Alexander[5], soldier Am. Rev., *m* Agnes, dau. of William Gamble, *m* Jane–);
3–Robert (1789-1858), *m* 1825, Rebecca Weaver;
2–Susan Emma (2 below).
6–Michael George **Eichelberger** (*d* 1789), prominent in Lancaster Co., Pa., affairs during Am. Rev.; *m* Christina–;
5–Margaret Magdalena, *m* 1761, Johan Wendel (Weber) **Weaver** (*d* 1772);
4–John Philip (1771-1827), *m* Elizabeth Brown (1775-1825);
3–Rebecca (1801-84), *m* Robert **Sharp** (3 above);
2–Susan Emma (1835-83), *m* 1863, John Atley **Kunkel** (*b* Cumberland Co., Pa., 1835-*d* 1921), col. Cumberland Co. militia, 1859-60; one of Abraham Lincoln's bodyguards from Harrisburg to Baltimore (for issue see **Vol. II, p. 306**).
1–*m* Nov. 5, 1890, Anna Hetherington, *b* Jersey City, N.J., Feb. 27, 1865; dau. of Samuel Read Hetherington (*b* N.Y., 1832-*d* Jersey City, 1882; *m* 2d, Ann Cecelia Laverty [Sept. 21, 1832-Dec. 26, 1921]; Edward[3]; Edward[4]; James[5], *b* ca. 1710]; John[3], *m* Sarah Read); issue: 1–Son (Aug. 13-Aug. 14, 1892); 2–John Atley (July 23, 1894-Feb. 12, 1895); 3–Lorraine, *b* Brooklyn, June 10, 1898; *m* Nov. 18, 1925, Willard Chase Peare, *b* Sept. 7, 1896 (issue: Patricia, *b* Aug. 17, 1926); 4–Margaret, *b* Brooklyn, Nov. 23, 1908.
1–Merchant, retired. Active in Am. Protective League and otherwise during World War. Mem. S.C.W., S.R., Pa. Soc. Club: Gipsy Trail (Carmel, N.Y.). Residence: 2107 Albemarle Terrace, Brooklyn, N.Y.

1–**LADD, Mary Lyman Andrews (Mrs. William M.),** *b* Cape Girardeau, Mo., Nov. 14, 1859.
8–William **Thornton,** of record in York Co., Va., 1646;
7–Francis (*b* 1651), settled in Stafford Co., Va., probably before 1700; *m* 1st, Alice Savage (Capt. Anthony[8], of Gloucester Co., Va.);
6–Anthony (1695-1757), St. Paul's Parish, Stafford Co., Va.; *m* Winifred Presley;
5–Anthony, sheriff Caroline Co., 1767; *m* 1st, Sarah Taliaferro;
4–Col. Anthony (1748-1828), of "Ormsby," Caroline Co., Va.; lt. col. militia; co. lt.; mem. Com. Safety in Am. Rev.; removed to Ky.; *m* 1772, Mary Rootes (Philip[5], of "Rosewall," King and Queen Co., Va.);
3–Lewis Beverley, *m* 3d, Eliza Curry;
2–Maria Rootes (2 below).
10–Hon. Henry **Corbin** (qv);
9–Winifred, *m* Col. LeRoy **Griffin**;
8–Thomas, *m* Elizabeth Lee;
7–Winifred, *m* Col. Peter **Presley,** of Northumberland Co., Va.:
6–Winifred, *m* Anthony **Thornton** (6 above).
5–James **Curry,** with wife, 2 sons and 3 daus., several brothers and their families, from Ireland, in the "Good Return," 1762; 15 weeks on voyage; all James' children *d* on voyage except son James; landed at Phila.; settled nr. Staunton, Augusta Co., Va.; *m* nr. Belfast, Ireland, 1750, —Warmick;
4–John, lived and *d* in Ky.; *m* Ann McConnell;
3–Eliza, *m* Lewis B. **Thornton** (3 above);
2–Maria Rootes Thornton (1829-1915), *m* 1856, Lyman Beecher **Andrews** (1829-59), educator.
1–*m* Feb. 24, 1885, William Mead Ladd, *b* Portland, Ore., Sept. 16, 1855 (see Who's Who in America); issue (all *b* Portland, Ore.): 1–William Sargent (see Vol. I, p. 184, for paternal lineage); 2–Charles Thornton, *b* Oct. 6, 1890; Amherst, '13; served with Spruce Div., Ore., World War; *m* Sept. 4, 1913, Lillian Ruth, dau. of Phillip Buehner, of Portland (issue: Martha Lillian; Meta Louise; Thornton); 3–Henry Andrews, *b* June 4, 1895; Amherst, '18;

served at Base Hosp. 46, Lorraine Front, France, World War; *m* June 6, 1922, Bernice, dau. of Daniel Langton (issue: Michael Daniel).
1–Winter place: Ojai, Calif. Residence: Dunthorpe, Portland, Ore.

1–**LAFFERTY, Virginia Turner (Mrs. Charles Albert),** *b* Heyworth, Ill., Dec. 16, 1882.
7–Nathaniel **Porter** (*d* 1749), from Scotland or Ireland, ca. 1718; settled finally in York Co., Pa., 1748; *m* Violet (*d* 1753), dau. James Ogelbay;
6–James (*d* 1775), of West Nantmeal Tp., Chester Co., Pa.; blacksmith; *m* Elizabeth–;
5–Nathaniel (1737-1818), Washington Co., Pa.; lt. col. in Am. Rev.; *m* 1766, Eleanor Gardner (*b* 1749; Francis[6], from Ireland, in Am. Rev., *m* Miss Wallace);
4–Margaret (1767-1849), *m* ca. 1801, Joseph **Turner** (1771-1847; Adam[6], of Westmoreland Co., Pa., *m* Mary–);
3–James (1802-78), Goshen, O.; *m* 1825, Margaret McKinnie;
2–William (2 below).
6–Archibald **Bard** (*d* 1765), from Ireland, settled at Newcastle, Del., ca. 1740; with others purchased 5,000 acres in Prince George Co., Md., called "Carroll's Delight," the ancestral home of the Bards;
5–Richard (1736-99), his wife, one child, a cousin Lt. Potter, and family servants were captured by the Delaware Indians, Apr. 3, 1758, from their home at the foot of South Mountain where they lived and where he owned a mill—the child was soon killed, Richard escaped and after 3 yrs. his wife was ransomed; settled in Cumberland Co., Pa.; mem. Pa. Conv. 1787; assisted his bros., David and William in laying out Bardstown, Ky.; was large slaveholder and owned large tracts of land in Ky., Md. and Pa.; *m* 1756, Catherine Poe (1737-1811; Thomas[6], from Ireland, *m* Mary Potter);
4–Elizabeth (1773-1824), *m* James **McKinnie** (1765-1811; Josiah[5], from Ireland to America before French and Indian War, settled in Franklin Co., Pa., *m* Isabel–);
3–Margaret (1804-84), *m* James **Turner** (3 above);
2–William (1838-1902), Heyworth, Ill.; *m* 1864, Mary Emma Hill (1841-1911; Samuel V.[3], *m* Mary Elizabeth, dau. of John Basford of Prince George Co., Md.; Godard[4], *m* Rachel Williams, of Alexandria, Va.); issue: I–Harry Hill (*b* 1864; *m* Dora Hanes); II–Mary Alice (*b* 1866; *m* Ingram C. Ryburn); III–Dr. Frank (1868-1928; *m* Hattie Cogswell); IV–Virginia (1 above).
1–*m* Sept. 15, 1904, Charles Albert Lafferty, *b* Le Roy, Ill., Nov. 7, 1873; son William S. Lafferty, of Le Roy (now Clinton), Ill.; issue: 1–Edith Elizabeth (Oct. 14, 1905-Jan. 14, 1924); Huron Coll., ex-'24.
1–Mem. D.A.R. (v.regent of S.D.). Mem. Huron Bd. of Education, 1923-27. Universalist. Republican. Residence: 536 Nebraska Av., Huron, S.D.

1–**LAKIN, (Marion) Hill,** *b* Yale, Ia., Mar. 13, 1904.
7–Abraham **Lakin** (*d* 1743), of Prince George's Co., Md.; received patent for land, 1717, called "Abraham's Fancie"; *m* 1717, Martha Lee (*b* 1699; William[8], *m* Ann–);
6–Joseph, of nr. Frederick Co., Md.; *m* Elizabeth Fee;
5–Samuel, *m* 1780, Sarah Musgrove;
4–Greenbury (1787-1869), *m* 1816, Margaret Dubukler (1793-1853);
3–William D. (1816-1907), of Brown Co., O.; *m* 1835, Susanna Harcout; *m* 2d, 1856, Delilia Joslen (*d* 1880);
2–Alvin Marion (2 below).
4–Thomas **Hill,** of Ky.; *m* Sarah Hough, of N.C.;
3–Charles Wesley (1843-1925), attended Ia. Wesleyan; grad. U.Mich. Law Sch.; served with Co. C, 4th Ia. Inf., Civil War; elected judge Dist. Ct. of Guthrie Co., Ia., 5 times and co. atty. twice; *m* Mary Jane Farnsworth (*b* 1853);
2–Lovina Charles (1872-1923), grad. Grinnell College, 1897; *m* Alvin Marion **Lakin** (1857-1920), physician and surgeon, of Yale, Ia.; issue: I–Marion Hill (1 above); II–Charles William (*b* Yale, Ia., June 19, 1907; grad. Epworth Mil. Acad.; student Drake U. and Olivet Coll.).
1–*m* Feb. 28, 1927, Helen Mae Scott (qv).
1–A.B., Drake U., '26 (P.B.K., Sigma Delta Chi). Reporter, Mason City Globe, Gazette, 1927; Blue Island (Ill.) Sun-Standard, 1927; editor Sun-Standard since 1928. Presbyterian. Republican. Residence: 2206 Grove St., Blue Island, Ill.

1–**LAKIN, Helen Mae Scott (Mrs. Marion Hill),** *b* State Center, Ia., Jan. 29, 1905.
6–Col. Lewis **Scott,** soldier in Am. Rev.;
5–Abram (1750-1830-40), of Greene Co., Pa.;
4–Laughlin (1810-90), of Grundy Co., Mo.; *m* Sally Nichols;
3–William Henry (1846-73), *m* 1865, Margaret Sheledy (1847-1929);
2–William Gilbert (2 below).
10–Henry **Kingman** (1592-*d* Bridgewater, Mass., 1690), from Wales to Weymouth, Mass., 1632; freeman, 1636; *m* Joanna– (*d* 1639);
9–John, *m* Elizabeth–;
8–Henry, *m* 1693, Bertha Howard (John[9]);
7–Jonathan (*b* 1708), *m* 1732, Mary Kieth;
6–Isaac (*b* 1747), Goshen, Mass.; Am. Rev.; *m* 1768, Content Packard (*b* 1747);
5–Isaac (1776-1867), *m* at Covington, Mass., ca. 1800, Mercy Bigelow (*d* 1867);
4–Charles Noble (*b* nr. Painesville, O., 1812-*d* Des Moines, Ia., 1885), *m* Eliza Ann Hendrix (*b* N.Y., 1819-*d* Spring Prairie, Wis., 1864);
3–Anson Hendrix (*b* Ashtabula Co., O., 1838-*d* 1916), served with Ia. cav. in Civil War; *m* 1872, Flora Silverthorne (1851-*d* Des Moines, Ia., 1925);
2–Mae Eliza (*b* 1880), *m* 1903, William Gilbert **Scott** (*b* 1873), of Parsons, Kan.
1–*m* Feb. 28, 1927, Marion Hill Lakin (qv).
1–Grad. Des Moines U., '27 (Tau Phi Xi). Residence: 2206 Grove St., Blue Island, Ill.

1–**LAMB, Frank Bird,** *b* Jackson, Pa., Oct. 24, 1863.
9–Thomas **Lamb** (*d* 1646), from Eng., settled at Roxbury, Mass., 1630; *m* 2d, 1640, Dorothy Harbittle (*d* 1698);
8–Abiel (1646-1709), of Framingham, Mass.; soldier in King Philip's War; *m* 1674, Elizabeth (Clark) Buckminster (*b* 1647; Hugh[9]);
7–Jonathan (1682-1749), of Spencer, Mass.; lt. in Capt. Isaac Clark's Co., Framingham; *m* 1708, Lydia Death (*b* 1682; John[8], *m* Mary Peabody);
6–Jonathan (1716-60), *m* 1737, Elizabeth Richardson (1718-80; Thomas[7], *m* Elizabeth Green);
5–David (1739-1814), in Am. Rev.; *m* 1760, Mary Howe (*d* 1773; Mathias[6], *m* Elizabeth Howe);
4–Joel (1767-1832), of Jackson, Susquehanna Co., Pa.; maj. of militia; *m* 1786, Lucy Corse (1766-1826; Gad[5], *m* Mary Wright);
3–Jairus (1791-1872), of Jackson, Pa.; *m* 1816, Elizabeth Hall;
2–Joel Hall (2 below).
9–Thomas **Lamb** (same as 9 above), *m* 1st, Elizabeth–;
8–John (ca. 1628-1690), of Springfield, Mass.; *m* Joanna– (*d* 1683);
7–Sarah (*b* 1660), *m* 1679, Jonathan **Bush** (1649-1738);
6–Jonathan (1681-1746), *m* 1709, Rachel Kibbe (1688-1786; Elisha[7], *m* Rachel Cook);
5–Aaron (1718-1805), *m* 1743, Alice French (1720-78; Richard[6]);
4–Elizabeth (1752-1830), *m* 1772, Joel **Hall** (1747-1843), of Enfield, Conn.;
3–Elizabeth (1789-1884), *m* 1816, Jairus **Lamb** (3 above).
6–John **Wood** (1648-1738), from Eng., settled at Groton, Conn.; *m* Mary Chapell (1669-1744; William[7]);
5–William (1702-94), of Groton; *m* Anner, or Honor, Adams (1706-96; James[6], *m* Honor Hall);
4–William (1750-1800), of Groton; served in Am. Rev.; *m* 1783, Sarah (Avery) Perkins (1754-1824; Simeon Avery[5],, *m* Sarah Niles);
3–Robertson (1789-1843), of New Milford, Pa.; *m* 1815, Lucretia Emeline Kingsley (1795-1879; Rufus[4], drummer in Am. Rev., *m* Lucinda Cutler);
2–Nancy Morgan (1826-1913), of Jackson, Pa.; *m* 1853, Joel Hall **Lamb** (1824-92), farmer of Jackson; issue: I–Frederick Willis (1856-63);

II–Sarah Jane (1858-63); III–Frank Bird (1 above); IV–George Elmer (1865-90; *m* Eleanor Forsyth); V–Myrtie Rose (1868-1908; *m* Herbert F. Smith).
1–*m* Apr. 3, 1890, Sarah Alice Neill, *b* Westfield, N.Y., Feb. 7, 1869; dau. of Hugh Neill, *m* Christina Ard; issue: 1–Grace Lucile, *b* Westfield, Apr. 25, 1892; attended Fairmont Sem.; *m* May 29, 1917, Steele Roberts, son of Henry Downes Sellers, *m* Belinda Roberts (issue: Steele Lamb, *b* 1920).
1–Grad. Afton (N.Y.) Acad., '81. Drug clerk, 1881-1900; mem. firm of Lamb & Cowan, druggists, Westfield, N.Y., 1901-23; retired. Mem. Bd. of Education, Westfield. Lamb family genealogist. Mem. S.A.R., N.E.H.G.S., I.A.G. Mason (32°). Methodist. Republican. Residence: 48 Elm St., Westfield, N.Y.

1–**LAMPREY, John Locke,** *b* St. Paul, Minn., Nov. 13, 1882.
8–Henry **Lamprey** (1616-1700), from Eng., ca. 1640, settled at Boston; removed to Hampton, N.H., ca. 1660; *m* 1640, Gillyen Morris (*d* 1670);
7–Benjamin (1661-1752), of Hampton, N.H.; served in Indian wars, 1724-25; *m* 1687, Jane Batchelder (*b* 1669; Nathaniel, Jr.[8], *m* 1656, Deborah Smith); *m* 2d, Mary– (*d* 1735);
6–Morris (1711-1809), of Hampton; *m* 2d, 1736, Rebecca Moulton (*b* 1716; John[7], *m* 1713, Rebecca Smith);
5–Lt. John (1748-1835), soldier in Am. Rev.; preacher; farmer; *m* 1773, Molly Marston (1748-1825; David[6], soldier Am. Rev., *m* 1741, Abigail Garland);
4–Morris (1778-1841), of N. Hampton, N.H.; *m* 1801, Nancy Locke (1785-1853; David[5], soldier Am. Rev., *m* 1758, Hannah Lovering);
3–David Marston (*d* 1868), *m* 1825, Sally Stearns (1805-51);
2–Uri Locke (1842-1906), *m* 1865, Jeannette Maud Robert (1845-1929); for issue and other lineages see Mrs. Francis H. Murray.
1–*m* Oct. 22, 1910, Carrie Kelly, *b* Minneapolis, Minn., Mar. 20, 1890; dau. of John Kelly, *m* in Minneapolis, 1884, Cornelia Jacobson (*b* Norway-*d* Minneapolis, Feb. 19, 1930); issue: 1–Nancy Locke, *b* Aug. 10, 1911; 2–John Locke, Jr., *b* May 10, 1915.
1–Attended Notre Dame U. and Exeter. Formerly newspaper man; now mfr. germicides, disinfectants, etc. Residence: 1784 Laurel Av., St. Paul, Minn.

1–**MURRAY, Lilian May Lamprey (Mrs. Francis H.),** *b* St. Paul, Minn., May 25, 1874.
7–Jean Baptiste **Robert,** from Parish of St. Sulpice, Quebec, Can.; *m* 1715, Genevieve Bois Proveau;
6–Luis (1716-88), *m* 1745, Marie Madeliene Mercier (Jean Baptiste[7], *m* 1718, Marie Barrette);
5–Louis (1746-1802), *m* Marie Madeliene Kiercereaux de Keriguac (*d* 1779);
4–Charles (1777-1835), *m* 1794, Marie Jeanne de Courtois (1780-1815; Col. Julien Louis[5], *m* 1770, Genevieve Hunaub);
3–Louis (1811-74), *m* 1841, Marie Rose Turpin (1828-82; g.g.g.dau. of Joseph du Motier, *m* 1769, Felicité Rollet);
2–Jeannette Maud (1845-1929), *m* 1865, Uri Locke **Lamprey** (1842-1906), of Manchester, N.H., later St. Paul, Minn.; attorney; issue: I–Miriam Stella (1867-68); II–Louis Robert (1872-73); III–Lilian May (1 above); IV–Jeannette Sarah (1876-1930; *m* 1894, Eugene A. Towle); V–Alma Irene (1877-83); VI–Rose Marie (1879-82); VII–John Locke (qv for Lamprey lineage); VIII–Elsa Cecelia (Mrs. Charles T. Redfield, qv).
1–*m* Oct. 4, 1898, Francis Henry Murray, *b* De Pere, Wis., Nov. 29, 1873; son of Michael Murray, *m* Helen Alice Dollard; issue (all *b* St. Paul, Minn.): 1–Jeannette Lamprey, *b* Aug. 26, 1900; 2–Locke Lamprey, *b* Feb. 18, 1902; 3–Norbert Dollard, *b* Feb. 13, 1906; 4–David Marston, *b* July 2, 1917.
1–Ed. Convent of the Visitation, St. Paul. Mem. D.A.R. Catholic. Residence: 990 Fairmount Av., St. Paul, Minn.

1–**REDFIELD, Elsa Cecelia Lamprey (Mrs. Charles T.),** *b* St. Paul, Minn., Oct. 6, 1884.
9–Isaac **Stearns** (qv);
8–John (1630-68), *m* 1653, Sarah Mixer (1634-56; Isaac[9], mariner, his ship was the "Dilligent," *m* Sarah–);
7–Lt. John (1654-1728), of Billerica; *m* 1st, 1676, Elizabeth Bigelow (1657-94; John[8], *m* Mary Warren);
6–John (1686-1776), *m* 1715, Esther Johnson (1691-1786; Capt. Edward[7], of Woburn);
5–Rev. Josiah (*b* 1732), grad. Harvard, 1757; ordained at Epping, 1758; active in Am. Rev.; *m* 1755, Sarah Abbott (1726-66; Uriah[6], *m* Sarah Mitchell);
4–John (1762-1843), of Deerfield, N.H.; Am. Rev., 1778; *m* 1783, Sarah Lane (1759-1845);
3–Sarah (1805-51), *m* 1825, David Marston **Lamprey** (1801-68);
2–Uri Locke (2 below).
9–William **Lane,** from Stepney, Eng., to Boston, Mass.; *m* Mary Kelways (William[10]);
8–William, *m* 1656, Mary Brewer (Thomas[9]);
7–William (1659-1749), *m* 1680, his 1st cousin, Sarah Brewer Webster (1661-1745), sister of Ebenezer, father of Daniel Webster (Thomas[8], qv, *m* 1st, 1657, Sarah Brewer, sister of Mary, 8 above);
6–Joshua (1696-killed by lightning, 1766), *m* 1711, Bathsheba Robie (1696-1783; Samuel[7]);
5–Joshua (1724-94), vol. at Saratoga, Am. Rev.; *m* Ruth Batchelder (Samuel[6]; g.g.dau. Rev. Stephen, qv);
4–Sarah (1759-1845), *m* John **Stearns** (4 above).
3–Sarah, *m* David Marston **Lamprey** (3 above);
2–Uri Locke (1842-1906), *m* 1865, Jeannette Maud Robert (1845-1929); for issue and other lineages see Mrs. Francis H. Murray.
1–*m* Nov. 28, 1906, Charles Toney Redfield, *b* Minneapolis, Minn., Mar. 17, 1867; son of George Davis Redfield, of Syracuse, N.Y.; issue: 1–Antoinette Lamprey, *b* Minneapolis, Jan. 19, 1908; B.S., U.Minn., '28; 2–Jacqueline Stearns, *b* Minneapolis, Sept. 17, 1910; 3–Francis Pettit, *b* St. Paul, Minn., May 16, 1912; 4–Mary Eugenia, *b* St. Paul, Dec. 1, 1914; 5–Louis Robert (Dec. 11, 1916-Nov. 19, 1923); 6–Joan Lamprey, *b* St. Paul, Aug. 13, 1918.
1–Mem. D.A.R. Residence: 670 Lincoln Av., St. Paul, Minn.

1–**LANE, Alfred Church,** *b* Boston, Mass., Jan. 29, 1863.
9–Thomas **Ruggles** (*b* Eng.-*d* Roxbury, Mass., 1644), *m* 1620, Mary Curtis;
8–Capt. Samuel (1629-92), selectman, rep. and capt. of Roxbury Co.; *m* Hannah Fowle (George[9], *m* Mary–);
7–Capt. Samuel (1658/59-1715/16), *m* 1680, Martha Woodbridge (ca. 1660-1738; John[8], qv, *m* Mercy, dau. of Gov. Thomas Dudley, qv);
6–Martha (1691/92-1740), *m* 1713, Job **Lane** (see Vol. I, p. 192);
5–John (1720-89), in Concord fight; *m* Sarah (Abbott) Hildreth (1726-1814);
4–Jonathan (1763-1808), *m* his cousin, Hannah Lane (1765-1848; Samuel[5], soldier in Am. Rev.);
3–Jonathan (1788-1860), *m* Ruhamah Page;
2–Jonathan Abbott (2 below).
8–Nathaniel **Page,** sheriff of Middlesex; *m* Susanna Lane (Job[9]);
7–Nathaniel (*d* Apr. 12, 1692), sheriff of Middlesex;
6–Nathaniel (1676-1755), *m* 1701, Susannah– (1682-1746);
5–John (1704-84), *m* 1730, Rebecca Wheeler (1712-55), of Concord;
4–Nathaniel, of Bedford, Mass.; carried the famous flag at the Concord fight;
3–Ruhamah (1788-1822), *m* Jonathan **Lane** (3 above).
5–Ichabod **Clarke** (*d* Sept. 20, 1805, aet. 90), of Stoughton, Mass.; *m* Sarah Whittemore, of Malden, Mass.;
4–Capt. Samuel (*b* Sharon 1750-1804), Am. Rev.; *m* Ursula Fillip Church;
3–Rev. Benjamin Franklin (1792-1872), *m* Sarah Chapin (*b* 1794; Israel[4], *m* Chloe Lombard);
2–Sarah Delia (1826-1918), *m* Jonathan Abbott **Lane** (1822-98), mcht., Boston; issue: I–John Chapin (1852-98; *m* Harriet Brewer Winslow); II–Augusta Benjamin (1854-56); III–Frederic Henry (1858-1919; *m* Louise Abbot Lane Moseley); IV–Alfred Church (1 above); V–Benjamin Clarke (*m* Florence Goodwin); VI–Lucius Page (1872-1903).
1–*m* May 15, 1896, Susanne Foster Lauriat, *b* Boston; dau. late Charles Emelius Lauriat, bookseller, Boston; issue: 1–Lauriat, *b* Brookline, Mass., Nov. 14, 1898; A.B., Harvard, '20; ambulance driver, Am. Field Service, May 5-Oct.

28, 1917, with French Army on Toul front; 2–Frederic Chapin, *b* Lansing, Mich., Nov. 23, 1900; Cornell, '21; A.M., Tufts, 1922; 3–Harriet Page, *b* Lansing, July 2, 1904; Smith Coll.

1–A.B., Harvard, '83, A.M., Ph.D., 1888; U. of Heidelberg, 1885-87; (Sc.D., Tufts, 1913). Geologist; was asst. state geologist of Mich., 1892-99, and state geologist, 1899-1909; Pearson prof. geology and mineralogy, Tufts Coll., since 1909. Head of dept. of mining, A.E.F. Univ., Beaune, France, 1919. Author (see Who's Who in America). Clubs: University, Boston City, Appalachian, Field and Forest. Residence: 22 Arlington St., Cambridge, Mass.

1–**LANE, Henry Higgins,** *b* Bainbridge, Ind., Feb. 17, 1878.
5–Thomas **Lane** (*b* 1740), of Loudoun Co., Va.;
4–James Hardridge, or Harden, removed from Va. to Ky.; Indian fighter; col. of militia;
3–Higgins (1812-77), removed from Ky. to Ind., 1844 (brother to Henry Smith Lane, gov. of Ind., U.S. senator from Ind., 1861-67, Indian commr., 1869), *m* Angeline Laurentine Thompson;
2–Rev. Edwin Thornton (2 below).
9–Col. William **Ball** (qv);
8–Capt. William (1641-94), justice, 1680; burgess, 1685; apptd. to lay boundaries bet. Northumberland and Lancaster cos., 1687; *m* 3d, ca. 1675, Margaret Downman (Rawleigh[9]);
7–Samuel (1686-1751), vestryman, St. Mark's Parish, Culpeper Co., Va.; *m* 1717, Ann Katherine Tayloe (*d* 1751);
6–Judith (*d* 1771), *m* John **Hackley,** also vestryman St. Mark's Parish;
5–Judith Ball (1759-1815 or 25), *m* 1775, Thomas **Jameson** (1743-1827), ens. Culpeper Co. troops in Am. Rev.; removed to Mt. Sterling, Montgomery Co., Ky., 1782 (Capt. Thomas[6], of Rockbridge Co., Va., justice; James[7] [*d* 1736], of Essex Co., Va., *m* Margaret–);
4–Elizabeth, *m* Lloyd **Thompson;**
3–Angeline Laurentine (1818-81), removed to Putnam Co., Ind., 1844; *m* Higgins **Lane** (3 above).
8–John **Darnall** (ca. 1647-1684; son of Sir Philip, of Birds Place, Eng., *m* dau. of Lord Talbot); from Eng. to Md.; settled at "Portland Manor," Anne Arundel Co.; sec. to Lord Baltimore; *m* Susanna Bennett (g.dau. of Richard[10], qv);
7–John;
6–Isaac (*b* ca. 1742), *m* Stacia McDonald;
5–Levi;
4–William G., *m* his cousin, Emelia Darnall (Daniel[5]; Isaac, 6 above);
3–Dr. Milton (1826-62), *m* Mary Elizabeth Dunington (1831-1920; Alexander[4], of Port Tobacco, Md., *m* Lavisa Sellers);
2–Jessie Fremont (*b* 1856), *m* 1876, Rev. Edwin Thornton **Lane** (*b* 1851), retired clergyman of Oklahoma City, Okla.; issue: I–Henry Higgins (1 above); II–Mary Elizabeth (1879-1909); III–Son (*b* and *d* 1891).
1–*m* Dec. 25, 1905, Mary Juno Harper, *b* Elmwood, Ill., Dec. 3, 1881; dau. of Samuel Alexander Harper (1840-1915), of Peoria, Ill.; issue: 1–Edwin Harper, *b* Norman, Okla., Nov. 18, 1906; B.S. in E.E., U. of Kan., '28; *m* July 12, 1930, Lorene Elizabeth, dau. of Frederick Adams Virkus, of Chicago; 2–Henry Wallace, *b* Chicago, Ill., Aug. 31, 1911; U. of Kan.; 3–Eleanor Hope, *b* Norman, Okla., May 6, 1916.
1–Ph.B., DePauw U., '99 (Sigma Chi, P.B.K.); A.M., Ind. U., 1903; studied at Cornell, 1903-04 (Gamma Alpha), U. of Chicago, 1904-05 (Sigma Xi); Ph.D., Princeton, 1915. Prof. biology, Hiram (O.) Coll., 1905-06; instr. zoology and embryology, U.Okla., 1906-08, prof. zoology, 1908-20; prof. zoology and embryology, Phillips U., Okla., 1920-22; prof. and head of dept. of zoology, U. of Kan., 1922–. Author (see Who's Who in America). Disciples of Christ. Republican. Clubs: University, Old and New, Cosmopolitan. Residence: 1737 Mississippi St., Lawrence, Kan.

1–**LANE, John Edward,** *b* Whately, Mass., Feb. 12, 1872.
8–William **Lane,** from Eng., settled at Boston, 1650;
7–William (1659-1749), of Boston, Mass., and Hampton, N.H.; *m* 1680, Sarah Webster (1660-1745);
6–Joshua (1696-1766), of Hampton; *m* 1717, Bathsheba Robie (1696-1765);
5–Samuel (1718-1806), of Stratham, N.H.; *m* 1741, Mary James (1722-69);
4–Jabez (1760-1810), of Stratham; *m* 1783, Eunice Colcord (1763-1836);
3–Charles (1796-1884), of Newfields, N.Y.; *m* 1821, Hannah French (1802-41);
2–John William (1827-1911), clergyman; *m* 1868, Mary Haynes (1841-1922); issue: I–Charles William (1869-70); II–Samuel (*b* and *d* 1871); III–John Edward (1 above); IV–Aleck Forbes (1873-75); V–Amy Sanders (*b* 1874; *m* William P. Powell); VI–Wallace Rutherford (qv for maternal lineages); VII–Wilfred Clary (1878-1925; *m* Lila Woodbury); VIII–Susan Klein (*b* 1881).
1–*m* May 19, 1909, Alice Treat Rogers, *b* Derby, Conn., Feb. 9, 1874; dau. Clark N. Rogers, of Derby.
1–B.A., Yale, '94, M.A., 1897, M.D., 1903. Studied univs. of Göttingen, Berlin, Geneva and Paris abt. 2 yrs. Began practice, New Haven, 1903; specializes in dermatology and syphilology; clin. prof. dermatology, Yale U. School of Medicine, 1920-22 (see Who's Who in America). Residence: 300 Lawrence St., New Haven, Conn.

1–**LANE, Wallace Rutherford,** *b* Whately, Mass., Aug. 12, 1876.
10–Walter **Haynes** (qv);
9–John (1621-97), of Sudbury, Mass.; dea.; freeman, 1646; selectman, 1666; surveyor, 1672; *m* 1642, Dorothy Noyes (*d* 1715; Peter[10]);
8–James (1660-1732), one of the defenders of the garrison house, Sudbury, 1676; *m* 1689, Sarah Noyes (1669-1756; Joseph[9], *m* Mary Darnell);
7–James (1692-1755), *m* 2d, 1720, Mary Rugg (*d* 1777; John[8]);
6–James (*b* 1721), served in Am. Rev.; *m* 1st, 1741, Eleanor Lee (*d* 1759);
5–Joseph (1742-1822), Princeton, Mass.; in Am. Rev.; *m* 1763, Hannah Stratton, of Leicester, Mass.;
4–Samuel (1764-1844), Guilford, N.Y.; *m* 1788, Louisa Brooks (*b* 1768; Charles[5], *m* Mary Hapgood);
3–Samuel (1789-1859), Townsend, Mass.; *m* 2d, Eliza Spaulding;
2–Mary (2 below).
9–Edward (Spalding) **Spaulding** (qv);
8–Dea. Andrew (1652-1713), *m* 1674, Hannah Jefts (1654/55-1730; Henry[9], of Woburn);
7–Andrew (1678-1753), selectman; teacher; *m* 1701, Abigail Warren (*d* 1768; Jacob[8]; Arthur[9], of Weymouth, Mass.);
6–Jacob (1703-76), *m* 1726, Susana Pierce;
5–Eleazer (1728-1812), *m* 1753, Elizabeth Proctor;
4–Thaddeus (1758-1836), *m* 1790, Olive Blood;
3–Eliza (1804-63), *m* 1826, Samuel **Haynes** (3 above);
2–Mary (1841-1922), *m* 1868, Rev. John William **Lane** (1827-1911), clergyman, of North Hadley, Mass.; for issue and Lane lineage see John Edward Lane.
1–*m* July 2, 1901, Gertrude Gardner, of Swansea, Mass.; dau. of William F. Gardner, of Swansea, *m* Esther Marion Cook; issue (all *b* Des Moines): 1–Esther Haynes, *b* May 27, 1902; *m* George T. Moore; 2–Josephine Gardner, *b* Apr. 3, 1904; *m* George D. Busher; 3–John Wallace, *b* Oct. 9, 1908; student Brown U.
1–Brown U., 1895-97 (Beta Theta Pi; hon. A.M., 1928); LL.B., Yale, 1900 (Book and Gavel Soc., Phi Alpha Delta). Admitted to Conn. bar, 1900; practiced at Des Moines, Ia., 1901-10, also prof. law, Highland Park Coll., and lecturer on patent law, Drake U. and U. of Neb.; settled in Chicago, 1910, and since mem. Parkinson & Lane (see Who's Who in America). Congregational. Republican. Clubs: University (Chicago and Washington), Mid-Day, Glen View, Brown (pres. 1923), Yale, Evanston Country, R.I. Country, Fall River Yacht. Residence: 1042 Michigan Av., Evanston, Ill.

1–**NORTON, Mary Latham (Mrs.),** *b* Hapeville, Ga., Mar. 12, 1891.
14–Dougal **Campbell** (*b* Inverary, Argyll, Scotland, ca. 1474; g.son of 1st Earl of Argyll, Bradalbane line);
13–Duncan (*b* ca. 1504), officer in English Army; went to Ireland;

CAMPBELL

Arms: *Or and sable, gyronny of eight, one and four for Campbell; two and three argent, lymphead her sails furled and oars in action, all sable, flag and pennants flying gules, for Lorne.*
Crest:—A boar's head fesswise couped or.
Motto: *Vix ea nostra voco.*

12–Patrick (*b* ca. 1544), eldest son;
11–Hugh (*b* ca. 1579);
10–Andrew (*b* ca. 1609);
9–Duncan (*b* ca. 1645), of "Drumboden," Londonderry, Ireland; *m* 1672, Mary McCoy; their sons settled in Pa. and Va.;
8–James (1682-1753), of Augusta Co., Va.; constable, 1746-47; capt. of foot soldiers, 1752, Augusta Co.; *m* 1720, Margaret– (ca. 1700-ca. 1750);
7–Margaret (1735-post 1777), *m* ca. 1755, her cousin Archibald **Rhea,** II (1720-74; William[8] [ca. 1687-1777], *m* Elizabeth, dau. of James Clark [*d* 1774], *m* Elizabeth–; Matthew or Charles Campbell[9], imprisoned with Argyll and was sentenced to be executed, fled from prison to Ireland and changed his name to Rhea, 1685 [both he and Duncan Campbell were in the Siege of Londonderry], *m* 1687, Janet Baxter; he was son of Sir Niel Campbell or Sir Duncan Campbell, Sir Niel was son of the 8th Earl of Argyll, Sir Duncan Campbell was of Auchinbreck);
6–John (1760-1840), soldier in Cont. Army from Va.; *m* ca. 1785, Mary De Loach (ca. 1765-1840);
5–Paphry, or Popia (*b* 1790), of E. Tenn.; *m* 1813, Elias **Breazeale** (1785-1855);

LATHAM

Arms: *Erminois, on chief indented azure, three besants, over all a bend gules.*
Crest: *On a wreath on a rock proper an eagle with wings elevated erminois, preying on a child proper swaddled azure.*
Motto: *Sans changer.*

4–Mary Katherine (1815-99), of Blount Co., Ala.; *m* 1831, William **Latham** (1810-60; Charles[5] [1766-1855], served in War 1812, *m* Susan Graves [ca. 1780-ca. 1854]; Franklin[6] [*d* 1783], Stafford Co., Va., *m* Nancy–; Stephen[7] [*d* 1746], Stafford Co., *m* Frances–);
3–John Calhoun (1832-75), pioneer merchant and planter, Gadsden, Ala.; capt. 49th Ala. Arty., C.S.A.; Methodist; *m* 1854, Mary Katherine Witt (1832-80; Dr. Abner[4], *m* Ann Airhart);
2–Augustus Franklin (1858-1921), *m* 1885, Maude Witt (qv).
1–*m* July 31, 1911, William Augustus Norton, *b* Corning, Ia., Aug. 14, 1888; son of Charles Crane Norton, banker, of Corning; issue: 1–Charles Crane, II, *b* Des Moines, Ia., Oct. 31, 1914.
1–Ed. Miss Hanna's Sch. for Young Ladies, Atlanta, Ga.; Young Ladies' Sch. of Jacob Tome Inst., Port Deposit, Md. Heraldic artist, genealogist. Mem. Nat. Campbell Assn. (chmn. for America for Campbell Memorial Belfry Tower), C.D.A., D.A.C., Huguenot Soc. Founders of Manakin in Colony of Va. (life mem., organizing pres., nat. pres., 1922-29), Huguenot Soc. of S.C., D.A.R. (organizing regent Mme. DeLafayette Chapter, 1920-22, state librarian, 1922-24, chapter v.regent and chapter corr. sec.), U.S.D. 1812, U.D.C., Calif. Geneal. Soc., East Tenn. Hist. Soc., Societe de l'Histoire du Protestantisme Français, Paris. Presbyterian. Democrat. Residence: 2545 Polk St., San Francisco, Calif.

Arms: *Gules, on pale three mullets or.*

1–**LATHAM, Maude Witt (Mrs. Augustus F.),** *b* Atlanta, Ga., June 17, 1869.
7–William **Witt** (ca. 1675-1754), Huguenot refugee, came from Southern France, 1699, settled at Manakintown, Powhatan Co., Va.; *m* —(*d* ca. 1741); issue: John, Benjamin, William, Abner, Sarah, Agnes, Charles, Lewis, David (all reared families in Va.);
6–John (ca. 1710-1782), of Amherst Co., Va.; *m* 1740, Lucy– (ca. 1720-post 1782);
5–John (1750-1825), of Knox Co., Tenn.; *m* 1770, Elizabeth Luttrell;
4–Jesse (1776-1846), of Rhea Co., Tenn.; *m* 1795, his cousin, Margaret Witt (1772-1847; David[5] [ca. 1752-ca. 1832], *m* Ann Luttrell, sister to Elizabeth, above; John[6], above);
3–Abner (1799-1865), physician, McMinn Co., Tenn., and Blount Co., Ala.; *m* 1822, Ann Airhart (1805-91; Henry[4] [ca. 1762-67-1842], soldier Am. Rev., *m* Jane, dau. of Samuel Carr [1748-1809], of Pa., soldier Am. Rev., *m* Ann– [*d* 1812]; Peter[5] [ca. 1740-1810], Pa. soldier in Am. Rev., *m* Polly–, *d* ca. 1815);
2–Horace H. (2 below).
12–Thomas **Sturman** (*d* 1645), Puritan gentleman; lived in Md.; mem. Md. Assembly, 1642; owned land in Va.; burgess from St. Michael's Hundred, 1642; *m* Ann–;
11–John, *m* 2d, Elizabeth–;
10–John (1650-1723), *m* 2d, Anna Elizabeth Spens (1650-1723; Patrick[11] [1633-*d* Va., 1689], lt. of horse, Va., 1665-67, *m* Dorcas–, 1633-1708);
9–Dorcus (1675-*d* Westmoreland Co., Va.), *m* 1694, Thomas **Sanford** (ca. 1670-1749);
8–Thomas (ca. 1695-*d* Westmoreland Co., Va., 1770), *m* Margaret–;
7–Patience (ca. 1715-post 1800), *m* John **Luttrell,**

Sr. (ca. 1700-1760; Simon[8] [ca. 1680-1723], *m* Elizabeth–, *d* post 1723);
6–Hugh (ca. 1732-ca. 1803), from Westmoreland Co., Va., to Ga.; *m* Elizabeth–;
5–Elizabeth (ca. 1752-ante 1823), *m* John **Witt** (5 above).

HOUSTON

Arms: Or, a chevron chequie argent and azure, between three martlets sable.
Crest: A sandglass winged proper.
Supporters: Greyhounds proper, collared and chained reflex, or.
Motto: Tempore.

5–John **Houston** (ca. 1730-1802), from Ireland to S.C., ca. 1772; served in Am. Rev.; *m* Jean Houston (ca. 1735-post 1802);
4–John (1760-1835), served in Am. Rev.; *m* Mary Wilson (1768-1843);
3–John (1788-1850), *m* Eunice Fowler (ca. 1805-65; Thomas[4] [*b* ca. 1770], of S.C.);
2–Arkansas Adelaide (1839-82), *m* 1858, Horace Hitchcock **Witt** (1830-1901), maj., 7th Ga. Regt., C.S.A.; mcht.; Mason (K.T.); issue: I–Claude Young (*b* and *d* 1860); II–Horace Houston (1862-63); III–Robert Abner (1863-64); IV–Maude Witt (1 above); V–Charlie Allen (1871-96; *m* 2d, Mrs. Mattie Williams Casey); VI–Horace Hill (*b* 1888; *m* 1908, Violette Le Claire Dorn, *b* 1891); VII–Grover Cleveland (1891-1908).
1–*m* Aug. 25, 1885, Augustus Franklin Latham (Apr. 19, 1858-Aug. 17, 1921), son of John Calhoun Latham; issue: 1–Mary (Mrs. Mary Latham Norton, qv).
1–Mem. Huguenot Soc. of the Founders of Manakin (pres. Calif. soc., nat. registrar, 1922-29), D.A.R. (chapter registrar, 1920-25). Residence: 2506 Polk St., San Francisco, Calif.

LUTTRELL

Arms: Or, six martlets sable, over all a bend of the second.
Crest: A plume of five feathers argent, issuing from a ducal coronet or.

1–**LATHAM, Rex Knight,** *b* North Loup, Neb., June 19, 1883.
10–John **Alden,** Mayflower Pilgrim (qv);
9–Joseph (1624-97), *m* Mary Simmons;
8–Joseph (1667-1747), *m* 1690, Hannah Dunham (1671-1747);
7–Eleazer (1694-1773), *m* 1720, Martha Shaw (1700-69);
6–Eleazer (1723-1803), *m* 1748, Sarah Whitman (1726-1818);
5–Hannah (1762-1838), *m* 1782, Levi **Latham** (1757-1816);
4–Nathaniel (1783-1849), *m* 1808, Jane Robbins (1791-1863);
3–Orange Lorenzo (1816-72), *m* 1838, Sarah Cheever Whitman (1822-1907);
2–Norman Wadsworth (1848-1912), *m* 1871, Louise Imogene Knight (1851-1910); issue: I–Grace (*b* 1873; *m* Harry A. Wright); II–Ernest Eugene (*b* 1876; *m* Elizabeth Norfolk); III–Rex Knight (1 above); IV–James Knight (1886-1913), and V–Genevieve, twins (*b* 1886).
1–*m* Sept. 4, 1914, Florence Alberta Jackson, *b* May 28, 1886; dau. of Col. A. M. Jackson, of Alton, Ill.; issue: 1–Rex Knight, Jr., *b* Alton, Sept. 16, 1917; 2–Albert Jackson, *b* Lexington, Mo., June 30, 1919; 3–James Knight, *b* Lexington, Nov. 25, 1921.
1–Ed. Mich. State Normal Coll., Albion Coll., U.Mich. (Sigma Nu). Engaged in agrl. development of south Mississippi since 1925. Mil. instr., 1909-25 (see Who's Who in America). Mason (Shriner), Elk, Rotarian. Residence: East Beach, Gulfport, Miss.

1–**BODINE, Frank Chamberlain,** *b* Plymouth, O., June 24, 1855.
8–Jean **Bodine** (*d* 1695), from France; settled at S.I., N.Y.;
7–Jean (*b* 1645), came with father; *m* 1st, —Croherm;
6–Isaac (*d* 1752), removed to Somerset Co., N.J., 1700; *m* Catelym–; *m* 2d, Lemelyke–;
5–Abraham (*b* 1717), *m* Mary Low (Cornelus[6]);
4–John (1743-ca. 1788), served in Am. Rev.; *m* Lementje Cozine (1744-1808);
3–Peter (1784-1849), removed to Pa., thence to Ohio; *m* 1814, Susan Ervin (*b* 1796; Peter[4], served in Am. Rev., *m* Elizabeth Armstrong);
2–Abram **Bodine** (1821-81), *m* 1848, Mercy Cordelia Chamberlain (1824-1905), removed to Plymouth, O.; issue: I–Ada O. (*b* 1852; *m* Rev. John Teney); II–Frank Chamberlain (1 above); III–Laurie Agusta (Mrs. Clark W. Latimer, qv for other lineages).
1–*m* May 16, 1888, Jennie Peck, *b* Providence, R.I., Jan. 12, 1862; dau. of A. A. Peck; issue (all *b* Mansfield, O.): 1–Harold Chamberlain, *b* Feb. 6, 1889; *m* Mar. 4, 1915, Florence Myers; 2–Roger Campbell, *b* May 15, 1894; *m* Apr. 23, 1926, Mabel Hill; 3–Chester Carpenter, *b* Oct. 17, 1895; *m* Sept. 4, 1925, Marion Phillips.
1–Attended U.Cincinnati. Instr. Pasadena Junior Coll. Presbyterian. Residence: 725 E. Walnut St., Pasadena, Calif.

1–**LATIMER, Laurie Agusta Bodine (Mrs. Clark W.),** *b* Plymouth, O., Mar. 9, 1858.
10–Gov. Thomas **Dudley** (qv);
9–Ann (*d* 1672), the "First American Poetess"; *m* 1628, Gov. Simon **Bradstreet** (qv);
8–Dorothy (1630-72), *m* 1654, Rev. Seaborn **Cotton** (1633-86; John[9], qv);
7–Rev. John (1658-1710), *m* 1686, Anne Lake (1663-1737; Capt. Thomas[8], killed by Indians, *m* Mary, dau. Dep. Gov. Stephen Goodyear, qv);
6–Thomas (1695-1770), *m* 1700, Martha Williams (*d* 1743; Robert[7], mem. A. and H.A. Co. of Boston);
5–Thomas (1730-1808), Pomfret, Conn.; minute man, 1775; *m* 1st, 1753, Sarah Holbrook;
4–Willard (1757-1829), Hartland, Vt.; minute man; *m* 1781, Mercy Gallup;
3–Mercy (1792-1880), *m* 1814, Samuel **Chamberlain** (1788-1863);
2–Mercy (2 below).
9–William **Sabin** (ca. 1600-1663), from La Rochelle, France; called "The Patriarch," of Rehoboth, Mass.; *m*—; *m* 2d, 1663, Martha Allen;
8–Benjamin (1646-1725), *m* 1st, Sarah Polley;
7–Mehitable (1677-1707), *m* 1695, Samuel **Warner,** of Woodstock, Conn.;
6–Mehitable (1698-1789), *m* 1719, Ebenezer **Holbrook,** of Pomfret, Conn.;
5–Sarah (1719-77), *m* Thomas **Cotton** (5 above).
9–Capt. John **Gallup** (qv);
8–John (ca. 1615-1676), killed at the Swamp Fight in King Philip's War; *m* 1634, Hannah Lake (John[9], *m* Margaret Reade);
7–Benadam (1655-1727), served in Colonial wars; *m* Hester Prentiss (*d* 1751; John[8], *m* Hester–);
6–Capt. Joseph (1695-1760), *m* 1720, Eunice Williams;
5–Elisha (1727-1800), minute man in Am. Rev.; *m* 1747, Mercy Denison;

4–Mercy (1753-1838), *m* 1781, Willard **Cotton** (4 above).
9–William **Denison** (qv);
8–Capt. George (1620-94), capt. of New London Co. forces in King Philip's War; *m* ca. 1640, Bridget Thompson; *m* 2d, Ann Borodel;
7–William (1655-1715), served in King Philip's War; *m* Sarah (Stanton) Prentiss (1655-1713; Thomas Stanton[8], qv);
6–George (*b* 1692), *m* 1717, Lucy Gallup;
5–Mercy (*b* 1729), *m* Elisha **Gallup** (5 above).
2–Abram **Bodine** (1821-81), *m* 1848, Mercy Cordelia Chamberlain (1824-1905), for issue and Bodine lineage see Frank C. Bodine.
1–*m* Apr. 9, 1890, Clark W. Latimer, *b* Mansfield, O., Feb. 16, 1859; son of George Latimer, of Mansfield; issue: 1–Rachel Mercy, *b* Portage, Wis., May 21, 1893; ed. Lawrence Coll., Appleton, Wis.; *m* Aug. 10, 1918, David, son of John Jones (issue: Barbara Rachel; Laurie Margery); 2–Margery Bodine, *b* Portage, Wis., Feb. 6, 1899; ed. U.Wis., Columbia U.
1–Mem. D.C.G., D.A.R. Residence: Portage, Wis.

1–**LAURENS, Henry,** *b* Charleston, S.C., Oct. 15, 1885.
7–Andre **Laurens** (qv);
6–Jean Samuel (1696-1747), *m* 1715 or 16, Esther (Hester) Grasset;
5–Henry (1724-92), pres. Cont. Congress, 1777-78; minister to Holland, and to negotiate peace with Eng., 1782-83; *m* 1750, Eleanor Ball (Elias[6]);
4–Henry (1763-1821), *m* 1792, Eliza Rutledge;
3–Keating Simons (1817-53), *m* Elizabeth Peyre Ashby;
2–Henry Rutledge (1847-1918), capitalist, Charleston, *m* Charlotte Hume Simons (1857-1918); issue: I–Henry (1 above); II–Martha Rutledge (*b* 1886; *m* William Morrison Patterson); III–John (*b* 1888; *m* Mary Holmes, dau. Alexander Rose); IV–Eleanor Ramsay (*b* 1890; *m* Louis de Berniere McCrady); V–Frederick (*b* 1892; *m* Natalie Breckenridge Robertson); VI– Rutledge (see Vol. III, p. 300, for Rutledge lineage); VII–Andrew (see Vol. III, p. 300, for Simons lineage); VIII–Samuel Lord (*b* 1898).
1–*m* June 17, 1915, Dorothea Mary Dexter (qv); issue (all *b* New Haven, Conn.): 1–Henry, Jr., and 2–John, 2d (twins), *b* Sept. 14, 1918; 3–Franklin Davenport, *b* Mar. 18, 1922.
1–A.B., Coll. Charleston, '07 (Kappa Alpha, Southern), A.M., 1908; Ph.D., Harvard, 1911. Prof. physiology, Tulane U. Was in C.W.S., in World War. Mem. Soc. Cincinnati of the State of S.C. Clubs: Round Table, New Orleans Country. Home: Charleston, S.C. Residence: 3102 Prytania St., New Orleans, La.

1–**LAURENS, Dorothea Mary Dexter (Mrs. Henry),** *b* New Haven, Conn., July 20, 1888.
9–Thomas **Dexter** (qv);
8–William (1630-94), Barnstable, Mass.; *m* 1653, Sarah Vincent;
7–Benjamin (1670-1732), *m* 1696, Sarah Arnold (Rev. Samuel[8] [1644-1709]; Rev. Samuel[9], *m* Elizabeth–);
6–Noah (1697-1745);
5–Benjamin (1734-1804);
4–Noah (1762-1814);
3–Rodolphus William (1806-62);
2–Franklin Bowditch (2 below).
9–John **Davenport** (qv);
8–John (ca. 1635-1676), *m* Abigail Pierson;
7–Rev. John (1668-1731), B.A., Harvard, 1687; *m* 2d, Mrs. Elizabeth Morris Maltby;
6–Col. Abraham (1715-89), B.A., Yale, 1732; soldier Am. Rev.; *m* Elizabeth Huntington;
5–John (1752-1830), B.A., Yale, 1770; soldier Am. Rev.; *m* Mary Wells;
4–John Alfred (1783-1864), B.A., Yale, 1803;
3–Theodosia (1810-83), *m* Russell Canfield **Wheeler** (1795-1847);
2–Theodosia Mary (*b* 1847), *m* 1880, Franklin Bowditch **Dexter** (1842-1920).
1–*m* June 17, 1915, Henry Laurens (qv for issue).
1–Residence: 3102 Prytania St., New Orleans, La.

1–**LAWRENCE, Graham,** *b* Shelbyville, Ky., Jan. 9, 1870.
6–Henry **Acton** (*b* 1732), of Prince George Co., Md.; *m* Esther– (*b* 1731);
5–Smallwood (1758-1844), Clark Co., Ky.; mem. Md. Flying Camp, in Am. Rev.; *m* Mary Wilson (1760-1819);
4–Thomas (1796-1881), of Clark and Henry cos., Ky.; *m* 1817, Sarah Kelly (1798-1865; Joseph[5], capt. in War 1812, *m* Elizabeth Mallory);
3–Mildred (1827-70), *m* 1844, Willis Albert **Lawrence** (1816-1907);
2–Joseph (2 below).
6– ———**Graham** (*d* ante 1760), of Prince Edward Co., Va.; *m* Mary–, living in Prince Edward Co., 1760;
5–Samuel (*d* Shelby Co., Ky., post 1797), *m* 1767, Elizabeth Morrison;
4–William (*b* Prince Edward Co., Va., ca. 1780-*d* Shelby Co., Ky., 1826), *m* in Ky., 1798, Martha (Patsy) Shillideay;
3–Baker Shillideay (1805-84), of Shelby Co., Ky.; *m* 1832, Margaret (Peggy) Smith (Nicholas[4], *m* Elizabeth Potts);
2–Sarah Elizabeth (2 below).
6–Edward (Shillidia, Shillady) **Shillideay** (*d* ante 1771), purchased land in Prince Edward Co., Va., 1754;
5–George, soldier Am. Rev.; *m* Esther Baker (*d* Shelby Co., Ky.), listed in 1793 tax list as widow;
4–Martha, *m* William **Graham** (4 above);
3–Baker S., *m* Margaret Smith (3 above);
2–Sarah Elizabeth (1843-85), *m* 1867, Joseph **Lawrence** (1844-1924), of Clark and Shelby cos., Ky.
1–*m* Oct. 19, 1898, Mary Adam Carrithers (qv); issue: 1–Eleanor Graham (qv).
1–Ed. Central U., Richmond, Ky.; grad. Center Coll., Danville, Ky., and Louisville U. Local surgeon for C.&O.R.R., and L.&N.R.R. Capt., M.C., U.S.A.; service at Evacuation Hosp., Unit No. 55, Camp Oglethorpe, Ga., World War. Trustee Presbyn. Ch., Shelbyville. Mem. Ky. and Southern Med. Assns., A.L. Residence: Shelbyville, Ky.

1–**LAWRENCE, Mary Adam Carrithers (Mrs. Graham),** *b* Shelbyville, Ky.
6–William **Hutchinson** (*d* Middlesex, now Mercer, Co., N.J.); one of the justices of the Quorum for Middlesex under the Crown, 1749;
5–John (*b* Middlesex Co., N.J.-*d* Prince William Co., Va., Feb. 1780), soldier Am. Rev.; *m* in N.J., Sarah Johnson (*b* N.J.-*d* Loudoun Co., Va.);
4–Mary (1759-1827), *m* Benjamin **Stout** (1756-1827), soldier Am. Rev. (see Vol. III, p. 300, for Stout lineage);
3–Joseph Hutchinson (1787-1860), *m* 1833, Martha Veech (1807-48; George[4] [his family had found refuge in Ireland from the troubles of Scotland], from Ulster, Ireland, to America, Apr. 1780, with brothers, John and James, to Shelby Co., Ky., where he *d*; surveyor, *m* 2d, 1793, Eleanor, dau. of John Bowman);
2–Mary Eleanor (1836-1911), *m* 1855, Adam Porter **Carrithers** (1827-1905).
1–*m* Oct. 19, 1898, Graham Lawrence (qv for genealogy and issue).
1–Mem. C.D.A., D.F.P.A., D.A.R., U.S.D. 1812., I.A.G. Residence: Shelbyville, Ky.

1–**LAWRENCE, Eleanor Graham,** *b* Shelbyville, Ky.
10–Rev. James **Ashton** (bap. 1603-1683/84), from Eng., 1639; settled at Providence, R.I.; commr., 1650,52-54,58,59,63; judge Ct. of Trials, 1652; dep. Gen. Assembly, Newport, 1665;
9–Rev. James (*d* 1705), Middletown, N.J.; dep. Gen. Assembly, Portland Pt., N.J., 1669; overseer for Middletown, 1677; 1st minister of Bapt. Ch., Middletown; associate with patentees, 1672; *m* Deliverance Throckmorton (*b* ca. 1640; John[10], qv);
8–Rebecca (*b* 1672/73), *m* 1688, David **Stout** (*b* 1667), of Amwell Tp., N.J. (Richard[9], qv);
7–James (1694-1731), of Amwell Tp.; *m* 1712, Catherine Simpson (1692-1749);
6–Jonathan (1723-87), Prince William Co., Va.; *m* ca. 1744, Elizabeth Hixson (*d* ante 1787), of Hunterdon Co., N.J.;
5–Benjamin (1756-1827), *m* Mary Hutchinson (1759-1827);
4–Joseph Hutchinson (1787-1860), Shelby Co., Ky.; vol. Ky. mounted inf., War 1812; *m* 1833, Martha Veech (1807-48);
3–Mary Eleanor (1836-1911), *m* 1855, Adam Porter **Carrithers** (1827-1905; Adam[4], *m* Elizabeth [Miller] Montgomery);

2-Mary Adam (qv), *m* 1898, Graham **Lawrence** (qv).
1-Grad. Louisville Conservatory of Music; ed. Science Hill, Shelbyville, Ky., Mary Baldwin Sem., Staunton, Va., Miss Moxley's Sch., Rome, Italy (Beta Pi Omega, Mu Phi Epsilon). Mem. D.A.R., U.S.D. 1812. Presbyn. Residence: Shelbyville, Ky.

1-**LEA, Luke,** *b* Nashville, Tenn., Apr. 12, 1879.
7-James **Lea,** from Eng., settled in King and Queen Co., Va.; bought land in Spotsylvania Co., bet. 1750-60, moved to Orange Co., N.C., settled finally nr. Leasburg, N.C.; served in French and Indian War, 1758;
6-James (1718-88), soldier N.C. militia, later pvt. in Am. Rev.; *m* Anne Tolbert (*b* 1718);
5-Rev. Luke (1739-1813), *m* Elizabeth Wilson (1739-92);
4-Luke (1783-1851), mem. 23d and 24th Congresses, from Tenn.; *m* Susan Wells McCormack;
3-John McCormack (1818-1903), mayor of Nashville, judge of Circuit Ct.; *m* Elizabeth Overton;
2-Overton (1846-1912), lawyer; *m* Ella Cocke (*b* 1846), C.D.A.; issue: I-Luke (1873-74); II-Laura (*b* 1876; *m* Rev. W. C. Robertson); III-Overton (1877-1903); IV-Luke (1 above); V-Elizabeth (*b* 1884; *m* J. O. Murdock).
1-*m* Nov. 1, 1906, Mary Louise Warner (Nov. 29, 1886-Mar. 8, 1919), dau. of Percy Warner, of Nashville, Tenn.; issue: 1-Luke, Jr., *b* Nashville, Tenn., Mar. 24, 1908; 2-Percy Warner, *b* Denver, Colo., October 31, 1909.
1-*m* 2nd, May 1st, 1920, Percie Warner, *b* May 21, 1896 (sister of first wife).
1-A.B., U. of the South, '99, A.M., 1900; LL.B., Columbia U., 1902. Editor and pub. Nashville Tennessean, Memphis Commercial Appeal, and Knoxville Journal. U.S. senator, 1911-17. Lt. col. and col., 114th F.A., with A.E.F. 10 months. Mem. I.A.G. (see Who's Who in America). Address: Tennessean Bldg., Nashville, Tenn.

1-**LEARNED, H(enry) Barrett,** *b* Exeter, N.H., Mar. 21, 1868.
9-William **Learned** (qv);
8-Isaac, probably came with father; *m* 1646, Mary Stearns, of Watertown;
7-Benoni (1657-1738), selectman, treas., deacon, rep. Gen. Ct., Sherborn, Mass.; *m* 2d, ca. 1690, Sarah Wright;
6-Capt. Edward (1705-75), *m* 2d, in 1737, Abigail Morse, of Sudbury;
5-Benjamin (1741-1818), Dublin, N.H.; served in French and Indian War aet. 13; *m* 1st, 1765, Elizabeth Wilson, of Sturbridge, Mass.;
4-John Wilson (1766-ca. 1855), *m* in 1797, Hannah Wight, of Sherborn (g.dau. of Joseph Twitchell);
3-Calvin (1804-80), *m* 1st, 1832, Hannah Dunster Barrett (Joel[4], of Ashburnham, Mass.);
2-John Calvin (2 below).
9-John **Wakefield** (qv);
8-John (ca. 1640-1703), *m* ca. 1663, Deliverance-;
7-John (1668-1735), *m* in 1693, Elizabeth Collins Walker;
6-Joseph (1701-32), *m* 1726, Copia (Bridge) Love, widow of Richie Love (Reverend Thomas Bridge[7]);
5-Thomas (1727-91), soldier Am. Rev.; *m* 1750, Dorcas Pratt (Timothy[6]);
4-Timothy (1756-1849), soldier Am. Rev.; town clk., selectman, rep.; del. Mass. Constl. Conv., 1820; *m* 1st, 1778, Susanna Bancroft (Joseph[6]);
3-William (1787-1875), *m* 1812, Sally Parker (William[4]);
2-Lucelia (1834-1917), *m* 1864, John Calvin **Learned** (1834-93), Unitarian minister, St. Louis; pres. St. Louis Pub. Library (for issue see Vol. I, p. 681).
1-*m* June 14, 1899, Emily Cheney, *b* at Hartford, Conn., Oct. 15, 1864; dau. Col. Frank Woodbridge Cheney, of S. Manchester, Conn.; issue: 1-John, *b* S. Manchester, Conn., Aug. 20, 1900; Williams, '22; 2-Frank Cheney, *b* New Haven, Conn., Apr. 1, 1903; *m* June 17, 1930, Frances Richmond Fletcher, of Wellesley Hills, Mass.; A.B., Conn. Coll. for Women, '27; A.M., Wellesley, 1930; 3-Horace Bushnell, *b* New Haven, July 5, 1904; 4-Mary Bushnell (Mar. 13-Sept. 13, 1906); 5-Emily Barrett, *b* New Haven, July 3, 1908; 6-Barrett (Dec. 7, 1909-Oct. 24, 1924).
1-A.B., Harvard, '90, A.M., 1897; A.M., U.Chicago, 1894; Ph.D., Yale, 1909. Educator and writer. Chmn. publication com. Am. Hist. Assn. V.p. Bd. of Edn., Washington, 1919-1921. Spl. agt. of Bur. of Investigation of Dept. of Justice, at Washington, 1917-19 (see Who's Who in America). Clubs: Cosmos (Washington), Keene Valley Country, Century (N.Y.). Mem. Inst. Am. Genealogy. Summer place: Keene Valley, Essex Co., N.Y. Residence: 2123 Bancroft Pl. N.W., Washington, D.C.

1-**LeBRUN, Maria Olivia Steele (Mrs. Michel M.),** *b* Brooklyn, N.Y.
10-John **Steele** (qv);
9-Lt. Samuel (1626/27-1685), dep. Conn. Ct.; *m* Mary Boosey (Hon. James[10]);
8-Capt. James (1664-1713), *m* Ann Welles (g.dau. Thomas Welles, qv);
7-Dr. Joseph (1690-1750), *m* Elizabeth Hollister (John[8]; John[9], qv);
6-Ebenezer (1727-1821), soldier Am. Rev.; *m* Sarah Sage;
5-Josiah (1758-1825), soldier Am. Rev.; *m* Susan Lewis;
4-Allyn (1779-1828), *m* Lucy (Jerome) Hart;
3-Ebenezer Hart (1802-186-, during Civil War), *m* Marilla Richards;
2-Oliver Richards (2 below).
8-Thomas **Selden** (qv);
7-Joseph (bap. 1651-1724), served in King Philip's War; *m* 1677, Rebekah Church (Dea. Edward[8], of Hadley, Mass.; Richard[9], an original propr. Hartford, Conn., and Hadley, Mass.);
6-Capt. Samuel (1695-1745), ens., lt., and capt., 3d Co. of Foot, Lyme, Conn.; dep., 1744; dea.; *m* Deborah Dudley (1701-99; Lt. Joseph[7]; Dea. William[8] [1639-1701], dep. from Saybrook, Conn., 1682-87, 1692-95, *m* Mary Roe; William[9], *d* 1683);
5-Col. Samuel (1723-76), raised and equipped his own regt. in Am. Rev.; captured in the retreat from New York and *d* from fever; his powder horn is in possession of the Boston Hist. Soc.; *m* 1745, Elizabeth Ely (g.-g.dau. of Richard Ely, qv; g.g.g.dau. of Reynold Marvin, qv);
4-Lt. Samuel (1748-1819), soldier Am. Rev.; *m* Deborah Colt;
3-Joseph (1796-1858), War 1812; *m* Mary Ann Kirtland;
2-Elizabeth (1830-91), *m* 1859, Oliver Richard **Steele** (1828-75); issue: I-Joseph Selden (*m* Eva Bewley); II-Elizabeth Selden (*m* George W. Smith); III-Maria O. (1 above).
1-*m* Sept. 21, 1892, Michel Moracin LeBrun, *b* Germantown, Pa., Aug. 6, 1856; son of Napoleon LeBrun, *m* Adele Lajus; issue: 1-Olivia, *m* George J. Strong; 2-Pierre Napoleon, *m* Margaret Eleanor Boyle; 3-Elizabeth Selden, *m* Roland N. Dakin.
1-Ed. pvt. schs. and Barnard Coll. Mem. Magna Charta Dames, N.J. Soc. C.D.A., D.F.P.A., D.C.G., D.A.R., I.A.G. Residence: Haddon Hall, 57 Union St., Montclair, N.J.

1-**LEE, George Hewit,** *b* Fair Haven (now part of New Haven), Conn., June 5, 1859.
8-John **Hill** (*d* 1689), from Eng. to Guilford, Conn., ante 1645; *m* Frances- (*d* 1673);
7-James (1646-1707), *m* 1682, Sarah Griswold (1662-1729);
6-Daniel (1692-1745), *m* 1714, Mindwell Wilcox (ca. 1694-1770; Obadiah[7]; William[8], qv);
5-Dea. Timothy (1722-81), *m* 1748, Elizabeth Stevens (1727-1801; Nathaniel[6]; Nathaniel[7]; William[8]; John[9]);
4-Mindwell (1769-1856), *m* Jonathan **Lee** (1762-1844), of Madison, Conn.; pvt. Am. Rev., 1778-80; served with coast guard at Guilford, received pension, 1832;
3-Jonathan Trumbull (1803-87), of Madison; *m* 1827, Betsey Barnes Judd (1803-47; Eber[4], *m* 1803, Betsey Barnes; Jonathan[5]);
2-Rev. William Brown (2 below).
9-William **Blake** (qv);
8-James (1623-1700), of Dorchester; selectman, constable, dea. in ch. and ruling elder, 14 yrs.; sgt. in mil. co.; *m* Elizabeth Clapp (1634-93; Dea. Edward[9]);
7-James (1652-1732), selectman, 1700-05; *m* 1684, Ruth Batchelder (1662-1752);

6–James (1688-1750), surveyor, selectman, assessor and town treas., 25 yrs.; town clk., 24 yrs.; *m* Wait Simpson (1684-1753);
5–Samuel (1715-54), surveyor; *m* 1740, Patience White (1714-86);
4–Patience (1747-1810), *m* 1769, Abraham **Howe** (1746-1811);
3–Edward (1783-1877), Portland, Me.; mfr. and merchant; *m* 1815, Suviah Marston (1789-1864; David[4], *m* Sarah, dau. of Othniel Tarr);
2–Elizabeth Payson (1833-1925), of Portland, Me.; *m* 1854, Rev. William Brown **Lee,** D.D. (1828-1901), of New Haven, and Madison, Conn.; Presbyterian minister; issue: I–Edward Trumbull (1855-1913; *m* Mary Martin; *m* 2d, Josephine Skinner); II–William Alexander (*b* 1856; *m* Harriet Warner); III–George Hewit (1 above); IV–Wallace Howe (*b* 1861; *m* 1887, Elizabeth Fortmiller, *b* 1862); V–Bessie Frances (*b* 1868; *m* William M. Fleming); VI–Lewis Earle (*b* 1870; *m* Caroline Maxwell); VII–Herbert Marston (*b* 1873; *m* 1903, Ethel Judson Bates, *b* 1873).
1–*m* June 10, 1885, Nettie Annie Cooke (qv); issue: 1–Louisa, *b* Corvallis, Ore., Apr. 18, 1886; B.S., U.Wash.; went to India under Foreign Mission Bd., of Presbyterian Ch., U.S.A., 1913; 2–Charles Marston, *b* Corvallis, Feb. 7, 1888; B.A., Miami U., Ohio, '10, M.A., U.Cincinnati, ca. 1915; *m* June 11, 1913, Alice Stewart (issue: Jonathan Stewart, Sarah Rebecca, Walter Marston; Margaret Isabella; Ellen Norville; Stewart Munro); 3–Ruth, *b* Pendleton, Ore., Feb. 17, 1890; B.S., Whitworth Coll., '15; teacher; attended Moody Inst., Chicago, 1925-26; 4–Walter Cooke, *b* Seattle, Wash. (Mar. 24, 1892-Nov. 16, 1918); B.A., Whitman, '14; commd. 2d lt., June 1917; to France with 146th F.A., Dec. 1917, 66th F.A. Brig.; participated in Champagne Marne, Aisne Marne, St. Mihiel, Meuse Argonne; commd. 1st lt., May 1918; gassed at Romagne, Oct. 31, 1918; *d* of pneumonia at Souilly, buried in American Cemetery, Romagne, France; 5–Arthur Trumbull, *b* Seattle, Wash., Nov. 24, 1894; B.S., Whitman, '17; enlisted, April 1917; commd. 2d lt., June 1917; to France with 364th Inf., 91st Div., June 1918; commd. 1st lt., 1918; served at St. Mihiel, Argonne, and Belgium; wounded Oct. 31, 1918, at Spitaals Bosschen Wood; awarded D.S.C., French Croix de Guerre and Belgian Cross; *m* Sept. 14, 1921, Katherine, dau. of Corwin S. Shank, of Seattle, *m* Jennie Baker (issue: Virginia, *b* 1922; Edward Trumbull, *b* 1926); 6–Harold Newton, *b* Seattle, Wash., Aug. 6, 1899; B.A., U.Ore., 1921 or 22; M.A., 1924; Ph.D., Harvard, 1930; prof. philosophy, Newcombe Coll., New Orleans, 1925; *m* June 6, 1924, Norma, dau. of Frank Soule, of St. Anthony, Ida.; 7–Florence, *b* Cincinnati, O., June 3, 1902; A.B., Pacific Coll., '25; *m* May 31, 1927, Cecil Floyd Lienard (issue: George Hewit, *b* 1929).
1–A.B., Williams, '79 (D.K.E.); grad. Hartford Theol. Sem., 1884. Pastor Plymouth Congl. Ch., 1885, Corvallis, Ore., 1886-88, Pendleton, 1888-90, Taylor Congl. Ch., Seattle, 1890-99, College Hill Presbyn. Ch., Cincinnati, 1899-1904, of Batavia, O., 1905-08, Ballard Presbyn. Ch., Seattle, 1908-15, and Newberg, Ore., 1915-30; retired. Republican. Residence: 509 N. Edwards St., Newberg, Ore.

1–**LEE, Nettie Annie Cooke (Mrs. George H.),** *b* nr. Salem, Ore., Sept. 22, 1857.
8–Henry **Cooke** (1615-61), from Eng., at Salem, Mass., 1638; butcher; propr. Dorchester, 1638; removed to Plymouth, 1640; *m* 1639, Judith Birdsall (*d* 1689; Henry[9], from Eng., 1632);
7–Samuel (1641-1702), Wallingford; *m* 1st, 1667, Hope Parker (1650-ante 1690; Edward[8], *m* Elizabeth Potter);
6–Samuel (1668-1725), farmer; *m* 2d, Elizabeth Bedell (*b* 1669; Robert[7]);
5–Asaph (1720-92), of N. Adams, Mass.; *m* 1744, Sarah Parker (*b* 1725; Joseph[6], *m* Sarah Curtis; John[7]; Edward[8], from Eng., 1639);
4–Joseph (1757-1845), Granville, N.Y., 1785; removed to Adams, 1806; one of Stark's 400 men in Battle of Bennington; had 3 bros. in Battle of Lexington; *m* ca. 1784, Rachel Langdon (1757-1833; Lewis[5], *m* —Cooley; Lt. Paul[6]; Capt. Philip[7]);
3–Charles Langdon (1788-1861), Monroeville, O., 1838; served in militia, War 1812, in Battle of Sackett's Harbor; regtl. adj. 1813; *m* 1814, Lois Benton;
2–Joseph (2 below).
8–Andrew **Benton** (1599-1666), from Eng. to Watertown, Mass., ca. 1630, settled at Milford, Conn., 1639; *m* 1649, Hannah (*d* 1670), dau. George Stocking;
7–Samuel (1658-1746), *m* ca. 1679, Sarah Chaterton (*b* 1661; William[8]);
6–Jacob (1698-1761), *m* 2d, 1728, Elizabeth (de Hinnesdell) Hinsdale (*b* 1703; Barnabas[7]; Barnabas[8]; Dea. Robert[9], qv);
5–Barnabas (*b* 1735), *m* Elizabeth Hinnesdell (Joseph[6]; Barnabas[7], same as 7 above);
4–William (1770-1830), of Adams, N.Y.; *m* Lois Kellogg (1774-1857; Azariah[5], *m* Hannah Catlin; Lt. Jacob[6]; Dea. Samuel[7]; Lt. Joseph[8], qv);
3–Lois (1796-1861), *m* Charles Langdon **Cooke** (3 above).
8–Samuel **Moore,** to Litchfield, N.H., ca. 1730; maj. French and Indian War, 1759; *m* Deborah Butterfield (Lt. Joseph[9], *m* Sarah Fletcher);
7–Dea. James (*d* 1770); a miller, Merrimac;
6–John, *m* Margaret Goff;
5–David (1744-1831), *m* Janet Moore (1747-1831; James[6], *m* Elizabeth Gregg);
4–Isabella (1773-1845), of Charleston, Va.; *m* Robert **Walker** (1764-1837; David[5], *m* Sarah Alexander);
3–Daniel Alexander (1807-35), Chester, Vt.; *m* 1832, Anna Duncan Heald;
2–Susan Isabella (2 below).
9–John **Heald** (*d* 1662); from Eng.; settled at Concord, Mass., 1635; freeman, 1641; *m* Dorothy–;
8–John (*b* 1639), of Concord;
7–Timothy (*b* 1660), of Concord;
6–Dea. Amos (1709-75), of Townsend, Mass.; *m* 1731, Elizabeth Billings (1709-77; Daniel[7]; Nathaniel[8]; John[9]);
5–Dea. Daniel (1739-1833), of Chester, Vt.; Am. Rev.; *m* 1760, Abigail Wheeler (1740-1828), of Lincoln, Mass. (Lt. Thomas[6], *m* Mary, dau. of Joseph Munro);
4–Amos (1767-1849), Chester, Vt.; *m* 1802, Lydia Edwards (Capt. Ebenezer[5], Am. Rev.);
3–Anna Duncan (1807-84), of Chester, Vt.; *m* Daniel Alexander **Walker** (3 above).
8–Robert **Edwards,** from Eng., 1640;
7–John (1686-1760), *m* Mary Melvin;
6–Nathaniel (1721-1800), *m* 1750, Hannah Prescott (1730-1807; Ebenezer[7], *m* Hannah Farnsworth; James[8], qv);
5–Capt. Ebenezer (1757-1826), of Acton, Mass.; minuteman, Lexington Alarm; *m* 1778, Lucy Wheeler (1759-87; Dea. James[6], *m* Mary Clark; Capt. James[7]; Samuel[8]; Moses[9], qv);
4–Lydia (1783-1864), *m* Amos **Heald** (4 above);
3–Anna D., *m* Daniel A. **Walker** (3 above);
2–Susan Isabella (1834-*d* Newberg, Ore., 1919), crossed the plains by ox team, 1851; taught in the Ore. Inst. (now Willamette U.), 1851-52; author 1st volume of poems printed and bound in Ore., "Tears and Victory," she declined to have her poems published with Joaquin Miller; *m* 1852, Joseph **Cooke** (1825-1917), of Ohio, 1838; removed to Salem, Ore., 1851; to San Francisco, 1895; issue: I–Charles Langdon (1855-58); II–Nettie Annie (1 above); III–Clyde Benton (*b* 1860); IV–Daniel Clinton Tyng (*b* 1866; *m* 1893, Edith Harris); V–Allyn Heald (1869-98; *m* 1895, U. Grace Bushnell); VI–Gaylord Walker (*b* 1872; *m* 1891, Belle Keel, *d* 1895; *m* 2d, Hattie Watkins; *m* 3d, 1919, Esther Hopple).
1–*m* June 10, 1885, Rev. George Hewit Lee (qv for issue).
1–B.S., Willamette U., 1877. Mem. Oregon Pioneer Soc. Presbyterian. Residence: 509 N. Edwards St., Newberg, Ore.

1–**LEEDS, William Bateman,** *b* 905 Fifth Av., New York, Sept. 19, 1902.
9–Thomas **Leeds** (*d* 1687), from Eng. to Shrewsbury, Monmouth Co., N.J., 1676;
8–Daniel (ca. 1652-1720), came in the "Shield," 1678; settled at Burlington, N.J.; purchased 1,000 acres in Gloucester (now Atlantic) Co., N.J.; this became Leeds Pt.; councillor; surveyor gen.; mem. N.J. Assembly, 1682; justice Supreme Ct.; compiler and author of 1st almanac, 1687; *m* 2d, 1682, Dorothy **Young** (Robert[9], of Burlington);
7–Japheth (1683-1736), of Burlington Co., N.J.;

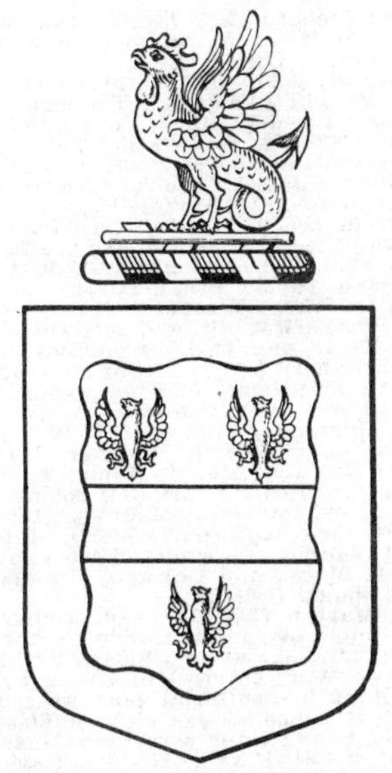

LEEDS

Arms: Argent, a fess gules, between three eagles displayed sable, within a bordure wavy of the second.
Crest: A staff raguly fess-ways vert, thereon a cockatrice gules, wings expanded.
Motto: Vigilate.

inherited Leeds Pt., ca. 1710; *m* Deborah Smith;
6–John (*b* 1708), landowner, Galloway Tp., Gloucester Co.; *m* 2d, 1751, Sarah (Mathis) Coate (John Mathis[7], *m* Alice [Andrews] Higbee);
5–Vincent (1756-1841), landowner, Richmond, Ind.; *m* Catherine Smith (1754-1825; Noah[6], *m* Judith Steelman, widow of Job Carr);
4–Warner Mifflin (1791-1850), of Richmond; *m* 1819, Elizabeth Bateman (1789-1857), of Springboro, O.;
3–Noah Smith (1825-80), of Richmond; *m* 1857, Hannah Ann Starr (1829-1905; Charles[4]);

WILLIAM B. LEEDS (1861-1908).

2–William Bateman (1861-1908), of Richmond; became owner of large tin plate industry (see portrait); *m* 1883, Jeannette Irene Gaar (*b* 1862); *m* 2d, 1900, Nonnie May Stewart (*b* 1873); issue (1st marriage): I–Rudolph Gaar (*b* 1886; *m* 1906, Florence Katherine Smith, *b* 1887); issue (2d marriage): I–William Bateman (1 above).
1–*m* Oct. 9, 1921, Princess Xenia, *b* St. Petersburg, Russia, Aug. 22, 1903; dau. of Grand Duke George, of Russia, *m* Princess Marie, sister to King Constantine, of Greece; issue: 1–Nancy Helen Marie, *b* 16 E. 64th St., New York, Feb. 24, 1925.
1–Ed. Wixenford, Wokingham, Berks, Eng., pvt. sch., and Eton Coll., Windsor, Eng. Pres. Mayfair Products, Inc., New York, and Air Services, Inc., Roosevelt Field, L.I., N.Y. Mem. Ohio Soc. of N.Y., Royal Thames Yacht, N.Y. Yacht, Seawanhaka, Corinthian Yacht. Residences: "Kenwood," Oyster Bay, L.I., N.Y.; 30 Beekman Pl., New York, N.Y.

1–**LEGG, Frances Jane Goodson (Mrs. James W.),** *b* Louisville, Ky., Sept. 20, 1876.
5–William **Goodson** (*d* 1746), of Kent Co., Md.;
4–Thomas (1730-1815), of Frederick Co., Md., and Augusta Co., Va.; *m* 2d, Sarah Riddell (*d* 1816; their dau. Sarah, *m* Col. James King, founder of Bristol, Tenn.);
3–Joseph (*b* 1776), *m* 1800, Ann Peck;
2–Jacob Peck (2 below).
8–Richard **Borden** (qv);
7–John (1640-1716), *m* 1670, Mary Earle (William[8] [*d* 1715], *m* Mary, dau. of John Walker; Ralph[9], qv);
6–Benjamin (1692-1743), settled in Monmouth Co., N.J.; to Va., 1734, or earlier; one of the original justices of the peace, Orange Co., Va., 1734; propr. of "Borden's Great Tract," Rockbridge and Botetourt cos., Va.; *m* Zeruiah Winter (William[7] [*d* 1733], *m* 1688, Hannah [Grover] Gardiner, dau. of James Grover, mem. 1st Assembly of N.J., 1668, *m* Rebecca–):
5–Lydia (ca. 1720-post 1797), *m* 1745, Jacob **Peck** (1700-1800 or 1801), originally called Johann Jakob Beck; from Wurttemburg, Ger., to Pa., 1740; settled near Sharpsburg, Md., thence to Fincastle, Va.;
4–Adam (1753-1817), soldier in Am. Rev.; settled at Mossy Creek (now Jefferson City), Tenn., 1788; mem. 1st Legislature of Tenn.; large planter and slave owner; *m* 1777, Elizabeth Sharkey;
3–Ann (*b* 1778), *m* Joseph **Goodson** (3 above);
2–Jacob Peck (1822-95), *m* 1853, Rebecca Morrison (1829-1905; Joseph[3], of Adair Co., Ky., *m* Rebecca Allen); issue: I–Charles P. (1854-93; *m* Adelaide Boutz); II–Ella S. (*d* 1907; *m* Griffen S. Martin); III–Ida K. (1863-1921; *m* Warren L. Reynolds); IV–Edward F. (*b* 1864; *m* Mary Allen); V–Frances J. (1 above); VI–Joseph A. (1878-1925; *m* Lalla R. Rascoe).
1–*m* July 29, 1903, James Walter Legg, *b* Rutledge, Tenn., Apr. 9, 1864; son of James Pryor Legg, *m* Nancy Peck.
1–Club: Marietta Golf. Presbyterian. Democrat. Residence: 514 Church St., Marietta, Ga.

1–**LEIGH, William Robinson,** *b* Maidstone, Berkeley Co., W.Va., Sept. 23, 1866.
5–Ferdinando **Leigh** (*d* ca. 1779), Gent., from Eng., bet. 1732-38; settled at West Point, on York River; *m* Widow West (dau. of William Cole[6], *m* Mary–);
4–Rev. William (1740-87), of Dale Glebe, Petersburg, Va.; ordained in Eng., 1772, by Bishop of London; *m* Elizabeth Watkins;
3–Benjamin Watkins (1781-1849), lawyer; author of Leigh's Reports; U.S. senator from Va.; *m* 2d, Susan Colston;
2–William (1814-89), lt., U.S.N.; maj., C.S.A.; farmer; *m* Ella Wickham; *m* 2d, Mary White Colston (1832-1918; Edward[3], *m* Sarah Jane Brockenbrough; Rawleigh[4], *m* Elizabeth Marshall, sis. of John Marshall, Chief Justice of U.S.A.); issue (2d marriage): I–Benjamin Watkins (*b* 1855; *m* 1918, Olive Buckingham); II–Edward Colston (*b* 1858); III–Raleigh T. C. (*b* 1863); IV–William Robinson (1 above); V–Thomas Watkins (*b* 1869); VI–Elizabeth K. M. (1873-1922).
1–*m* Anna Seng; issue: 1–William Colston, *b* New York, June 1902.
1–*m* 2d, June 4, 1921, Ethelinda Horton Traphagen (qv).
1–Ed. under pvt. tutor; studied art, Md. Inst., 1880-83, Royal Acad., Munich, 1884-89. Artist, Author (see Who's Who in America). Clubs: Salamagundi, Adventurers. Residence: 1680 Broadway, New York, N.Y.

HENRY TRAPHAGEN (1768-1857).

1–**LEIGH, Ethelinda Horton Traphagen (Mrs. William Robinson),** *b* New York, N.Y., Oct. 10, 1883.
8–William Jansen **Traphagen** (1616-89), from City of Lemgo, Co. of Lippe, Westphalia, 1647; erected first house nr. the pond at Bushwick, 1660; among those who bought the Newtown lands from the Indians, 1656; *m* 2d, 1661, Joosie Noortryck;
7–Hendrick (1668-ca. 1723), *m* Sarah–;
6–Rulif (1702-61), *m* Cornelia Potman (*b* 1711);
5–Henry (1731-1803), trustee of Queens (now Rutgers) Coll., 1782; *m* 1753, Hannah Van Deren (1733-90);
4–Henry (1768-1857), see portrait; *m* 1803, (Neetje) Eleanor Van Vorst (1768-1824; Cornelius[5] [1728-1818], lt. col. in Am. Rev., from Bergen Co., N.J.);
3–Henry Mackaness (1809-84), wealthy and influential citizen of Jersey City, N.J.; *m* 1834, Sarah Conselyea;
2–William Conselyea (2 below).
5–William **Conselyea,** *m* Maria Skillman;
4–Judge William (1784-1851), *m* Phebe Duryea (1786-1870; Peter[5], *m* Sarah Meserole);
3–Sarah (1810-66), *m* Henry Mackaness **Traphagen** (3 above);
2–William Conselyea (1837-96), grad. Rutgers Coll.; lawyer and senator of N.Y.; *m* 1874, Caroline Ross Maxwell; issue: I–Eleanor Van Vorst (*m* William Bisland Williams); II–John Maxwell; III–Caroline; IV–Ethelinda H. (1 above); V–William Conselyea; VI–Conselyea (*m* Janet Voorhis); VII–Maxwell (*m* Sarah Neilson Stearns).
1–*m* June 4, 1921, William Robinson Leigh (qv).
1–Studied at Nat. Acad. Design, Cooper Union, Chase School, Art Students League, N.Y. School of Art and in Paris. Instr. and lecturer on costume design and costume illustration, Cooper Union; formerly instr. at Brooklyn Teachers' Assn., and N.Y. University; founder and dir. Traphagen School of Fashion. Author (see Who's Who in America). Residence: 1680 Broadway, New York, N.Y.

1–**LEIPER, Henry Smith,** *b* Belmar, N.J., Sept. 17, 1891.
5–William (Leeper) **Leiper,** of Va.;
4–George Reynolds (1799-1861), of Shippensburg, Pa.; *m* 1820, Julietta Buchanan Galbraith;
3–Lt. Col. Bartram Galbraith (1824?-1870), began to write name Leiper; of Pittsburgh, Pa.; pvt., Co. K, 1st Pa. Vols., Mexican War; lt. col., 1st Ky. Vols., Civil War; *m* 1860?, Harriet Elizabeth McCarrell (*d* 1867?; Dr. Joseph[4] [*b* 1795], grad. Washington Coll., 1815);
2–Rev. Joseph McCarrell (2 below).
10–Richard **Smith** (*b* 1600?), from Eng. with his father, Richard, Sr., 1632, settled at Mass. Bay Colony, at Watertown, and later at Wethersfield, Conn., 1634;
9–Joseph (*d* 1673), of Wethersfield; *m* 1657, Lydia Wright (Thomas[10]; Thomas[11], an original propr., dep. for Wethersfield, 1643);
8–Joseph (1657-1733), of Wethersfield; freeman, Hadley; sgt. and selectman; *m* 1681, Rebecca Dickinson (*d* 1731; John[9], *m* Frances, dau. Nathaniel Foote; Nathaniel[10]);
7–Dea. John (1687-1777), of Belchertown, Mass.; dea. and selectman of Hadley; in 1736 the Gen. Ct., Boston, issued to him authority for the town and parish organization of Belchertown; *m* 1709, Elizabeth Hovey (1688-1758; Thomas[8] [1648-1739], lt. and selectman of Hadley, *m* Sarah, dau. Maj. Aaron Cook, qv);
6–Capt. Elijah (1723-70), capt. of a co. under Col. Ephriam Williams, 1755, in expdn. against Crown Point; in Battle of Lake George, 1755; *m* 1750, Sibyl Worthington (1727-1827; Daniel[7]);
5–Rev. Ethan (1762-1849), Hanover, N.H.; grad. Dartmouth, 1790; Congl. minister; drummer boy in Am. Rev.; *m* 1793, Bathsheba Sanford (*b* 1771; Rev. David[6], of Medway, Mass.);
4–Rev. Stephen Sanford (1797-1871), editor; pastor at Quincy, Newton, Westminster, and Warren, Mass., and Chicago, Illinois; *m* Lucretia Bishop (1804-71);
3–Henry Martyn (1830-95), grad. Amherst Coll., 1851; studied law in Detroit but entered journalism; mnging. editor Chicago Tribune during Civil War; enlisted in Ill. regt., but remained at his editorial post at request of President Lincoln; was close adviser of the President, and later served in Mass. Legislature; *m* 1854, Harriet Hudson (1836-75; Hon. Charles[4], selectman and historian of Lexington);
2–Fanny Heywood (1860-95), *m* 1890, Rev. Joseph McCarrell **Leiper** (1864-95); issue: I–Henry Smith (1 above); II–Bartram Galbraith (*b* 1893; *m* Mary Gudger); III–McCarrell Hudson (*b* 1894; *m* Christine Habeggar).
1–*m* May 15, 1915, Eleanor Lansing Cory, *b* Englewood, N.J., Nov. 28, 1890; dau. of David Uzal Cory, *m* Mary Wickes; issue: 1–Juliet McCarrell, *b* New York, June 23, 1916; 2–Henry Martyn Welling, *b* Peitaiho, China, July 27, 1918.
1–B.A., Amherst, '13 (Beta Theta Pi, Delta Sigma Rho); grad. Union Theol. Sem., N.Y. City, 1917; M.A., Columbia, 1917; studied Chinese at N. China Union Lang. Sch., Peking, 1919. Ordained Presbyn. ministry, 1915; traveling sec., Student Vol. Movement, 1913-14; actg. pastor Rutgers Presbyn. Ch., N.Y. City, 1914-16; served with Army Y.M.C.A. in Siberia, 1918; missionary, A.B.C.F.M., Tientsin, China, 1918-23; asst. sec. A.B.C.F.M., N.Y. City, 1922-23; editor Congl. Nat. Council's Commn. on Missions since 1923; asso. editor Am. Missionary magazine, 1924–; author (see Who's Who in America). Residence: 1 Paulin Boul., Leonia, N.J.

1–**Le NOIR, Mollie Bishop Gibson (Mrs. Charles O.),** *b* Flint, Mich., Oct. 15, 1886.
7–Eleazer **Bishop** (1669-1755), who was kidnapped by an English ship from Isle of Jersey at age of 7, and brought to New London, Conn., 1676, where Richard Dart paid a yoke of oxen for his passage and with whom he lived until 1704, when he *m* Dart's dau. Sarah (*b* 1680);
6–Nicholas (1722/23-1780), capt. in British Army during French and Indian war, raised a co. for defense of Boston in Am. Rev.; *m* 1749, Hannah Douglas (1732-1834; Robert[7]);
5–Jonathan (1754-1839), *m* Anna Allen;
4–Giles (1785-1837), *m* Phoebe Waite;
3–Giles, *m* 1843, Betsey Tupper;
2–Betsey (2 below).
9–Richard **Waite** (qv);
8–Thomas (1641/42-1722/23), *m* Sarah Cutler;
7–Thomas (1678-1725), *m* Mary Bronson;
6–Richard (1711-90), *m* Elizabeth Marvin;
5–Capt. Richard (1739-1810), *m* Lucy Griswold;
4–Phoebe, *m* 1809, Giles **Bishop** (4 above).
9–Judge Simon **Lynde** (qv);
8–Judge Nathaniel (1659-1729), *m* Susannah Willoughby;
7–Nathaniel (1692-1749/50), *m* Sarah (Pratt) Buckingham;
6–Susannah, *m* Ens. Thomas **Griswold** (see Vol. II, p. 89, for Griswold lineage);
5–Lucy, *m* Richard **Waite** (5 above).

10–Thomas **Tupper** (qv);
9–Thomas (1638-1706), mem. Council of War; town clk.; selectman 14 yrs.; rep. Gen. Ct.; *m* 1661, Martha Mayhew (1642-1717; Gov. Thomas[10], qv);
8–Thomas (1668-1744?), *m* Mary–;
7–Thomas (1698-1739), *m* Remember Perry (Parry);
6–Mayhew (*d* 1804), *m* 1st, Elizabeth Tiffany;
5–John (1780-1865), *m* Betsy Goff (Charles[6] [1758-1832], *m* Deborah Hill; Comfort[7] [1734-1819], *m* Susannah Guernsey; Robert[8], *m* at Rehoboth, 1733, Anna Horton);
4–Reuben (1801-69), *m* Carolina Olmstead;
3–Betsey, *m* Giles **Bishop** (3 above);
2–Betsey (1844-1908), *m* 1869, William Law **Gibson** (1841-1904), banker; issue: I–Mollie Bishop (1 above); II–Arthur (1888-1911); III–Guy Waters (1890-1910).
1–*m* July 5, 1917, Charles Owen Le Noir, *b* Orrville, Ala., Jan. 12, 1887; son of Judge Charles Le Noir, of Magnolia Springs, Ala., *m* Julia Owen Johnson.
1–Mem. I.A.G. Residence: 536 Riverside Av., Jacksonville, Fla.

1–**LENT, Eugene,** *b* San Francisco, Calif., Sept. 12, 1863.
9–Abraham (de Rycke, Riker) **Rycken** (1615-1689), from Holland to New Amsterdam, ca. 1638; patented land, 1640, and again, 1654; *m* Gertie Hermansen (Henrick[10]);
8–Ryck, eldest and only son to assume surname **Lent**; *m* Catryna Syboutsen (Harch[9]); and thru:
4–Abram;
3–Peter Waldron, *m* Catherine Forbes;
2–William Mandeville (1818-1903), *m* Frances Emeline Harrison LaForge (1830-1902), for issue see Vol. I, p. 937.
1–*m* Apr. 17, 1900, Berthe Marion (Welch) Russell, dau. of Andrew Welch; issue: 1–Frances Welch, *b* San Francisco, Calif., Jan. 24, 1901; *m* 1922, Hugh Beverley Porter (issue: William M. L.); 2–Ruth d'Alte, *b* San Francisco, July 18, 1903; *m* Jan. 10, 1923, Hermon Leonard Underhill, of Owego, N.Y., A.B., Yale, '17; v.p. Peoples Trust Co., Binghamton, N.Y.; lt. Air Service, U.S.A., 1918-19; mem. Yale Club, Bankers Club of America (both N.Y. City); (issue: Ruth; Gene; Hermon).
1–A.B., Harvard, '85 (Zeta Psi, D.K.E., Hasty Pudding, Inst. of 1770); LL.B., U.Calif., 1895. Lawyer. With A.R.C. in France, Mar.-Nov. 1918. Clubs: Pacific Union, University, Town and Country, San Francisco Golf, Burlingame Country. Residence: 2100 Jackson St., San Francisco, Calif.

1–**LEWIS, Arthur Henry,** *b* New Albany, Ind., Mar. 13, 1869.
8–Benjamin **Lewis,** from Wales, 1669; settled at New Haven, Conn.; removed to Stratford, Conn., 1675; *m* Hannah Curtis (1654-1728; Sgt. John[9]);
7–Edmund (1683-1758), judge Co. Ct. of Stratford; *m* 1702, Hannah Beach (1681-1756);
6–Nathaniel (1719-1807), *d* Ripton, Conn.; *m* 1740, Ruth Beardslee;
5–Isaac, D.D. (1746-1840), of Greenwich, Conn.; chaplain, Col. Philip B. Bradley's Conn. State regt., Brig. Gen. James Wadsworth's Brigade; *m* Hannah Beale (1743-1829);
4–Isaac, D.D. (1773-1854), grad. Yale Coll., 1794; *m* Catherine Everton (1775-1826; Jacob[5], of Cherry Valley, Conn.);
3–Isaac (1810-97), of New York, and Boston; *m* 1833, Cornelia Malvina Donaldson (1816-64);
2–William Henry (2 below).
10–Thomas **Welles** (qv);
9–John (1621-59), *b* Eng., *d* Stratford, Conn.; *m* 1647, Elizabeth Bourne;
8–Sarah (1659-1713), *m* 1677, Benjamin **Beach**;
7–Hannah (1681-1756), *m* Edmund **Lewis** (7 above).
6–Joseph **Culbertson** (1700-80), from Ireland; settled at Culbertson Row, Pa., bet. 1728-42; *m* 1735, Mary Breckenridge (*b* Ireland 1710-*d* 1791);
5–Col. Robert (1755-1801), of Cumberland Co., Pa.; capt. 5th Bn., Cumberland Co. Militia, Col. Joseph Armstrong's regt.; lt. col. 1st Bn., Cumberland Co. Militia, May-Aug., 1780; loaned money to govt. during Am. Rev.; *m* 1778, Annie Duncan (1755-1827; William[6], of Middle Spring, Cumberland Valley, Pa.);
4–William (1787-1824), of New Market, York Co., Pa.; *m* 1810, Julia Stuart (1787-1857; William[5], of Palmyra, Dauphin Co., Pa., q.m. to Gen. Sullivan);
3–Mary Ann (1811-80), *m* 1833, Daniel **Snively** (1802-72), of Greencastle, Pa.;
2–Julia Frances (1840-87), of New Albany, Ind.; *m* 1862, William Henry **Lewis** (1836-1906), sec.-treas., Chicago, Indianapolis, and Louisville, R.R. Co.; issue: I–Edward Mann (*b* 1863; maj. gen. U.S.A.; *m* 1888, Harriet Russell Balding, *b* 1867); II–William Andrew (1867-94); III–Arthur Henry (1 above); IV–Julia Culbertson (1874-75); V–Francis Snively (*b* 1876; *m* Adelaide Sara Terry); VI–Adelaide Louisa (*b* 1879; *m* Harry Heffrin).
1–*m* Jan. 2, 1917, Lilian Irene Howard, *b* Minneapolis, Minn., Dec. 13, 1881; dau. of Joseph Charles Howard, *m* Lillie M. Pulford.
1–Mgr. Minneapolis Club. Mem. S.R. Presbyterian. Summer place: Aloha Lodge, Excelsior, Lake Minnetonka, Minn. Residence: Leamington Hotel, Minneapolis, Minn.

REV. SCHUYLER COLFAX FULMER (1859-1912).

1–**LEONARD, Lenna Fay Fulmer (Mrs. Charles H.),** *b* South Bend, Ind., Dec. 2, 1883.
7–Thomas **Fulmer** (prob. son of Coenradt Felmore, from Palatinate, ca. 1710, *m* Christiana–; both given grants of land in Burnetsfield Patent);
6–Christian, served in Am. Rev.;
5–Christian (1767-*d* Jerseyfield, Herkimer Co., N.Y., 1813), farmer; *m* 1784, Anna Eva Marseilles (1767-1841);
4–Jacob (1789-1851), buried in N. Liberty, Ind.; *m* 1823, Polly Stockwell (1802-70), she *m* 2d, 1857, Christian Fulmer, Jacob's brother;
3–Jacob Christian (*b* prob. Herkimer Co., N.Y., 1827-*d* Elkhart, Ind., 1895), farmer; *m* 1857, Rosina Hayes;
2–Schuyler Colfax (2 below).
6–Henry **Hayes** (*d* Oppenheim, Fulton Co., N.Y.; buried at Ukersbusch), possibly from Bavaria; minister Reformed Ch.; *m* Catherine (Beliangar) Bellinger (*d* aet. 85);
5–Jacob H. (1784-1828), *m* Charity Rarick (1781-1850);
4–Reuben (1812-1891-92), laborer; *m* 1834, Elizabeth Fulmer (1808-63; Christian[5], 5 above);
3–Rosina (1835-*d* Walkerton, Ind., 1890), *m* Jacob C. **Fulmer** (3 above).
8–Henry **Woodward** (*d* ante 1734), from Eng., settled at Patuxent River, Anne Arundel Co., Md.; *m* 1690, Mary Garrett (James[9]);
7–William (1700-74), *m* Jane–;
6–William Garrett (*b* 1725), *m* Dinah Davidge Warfield;
5–Maria Graham (1763-1834), *m* 2d, 1795, Augustine **Gambrill,** III (1773-1830), vestryman (Augustine[6] [*b* 1733], *m* Sarah Sappington [*b* 1745]; Augustine[7] [*b* 1705], *m* Comfort–);

4–George Garrett (1796-1830), *m* 1817, Julia Ann Brown (*d* 1832);
3–Arthur James (1824-87), Baltimore; *m* 1850, Sarah Leedy (1830-76; "Big" John[4] [1779-1851], first white man in Richland Co., O., distiller and farmer, *m* 1806, Elizabeth [1790-1870], dau. of Lewis Keith; Abraham[5], served in Am. Rev., *m* Catherine Long; Abraham[6]);
2–Caroline (2 below).
10–Capt. John **Browne,** from Eng., 1659, settled nr. Crownsville, Anne Arundel Co., Md.; granted 500 acres of land for bringing in settlers;
9–Elinor, *m* 1670, Richard **Warfield** (1640-1703 or 04);
8–Richard (1676-1755), one of first organizers of public schools in Anne Arundel Co., 1723; presiding justice, 1735-37; vestryman; burgess, 1716-37; *m* 1698, Ruth Cruchley (Thomas[9]);
7–Alexander (1701-73), of "Warfield's Contrivance," Md.; *m* 1723, Dinah Davidge (*b* 1705; Maj. John[8], *m* Elizabeth Hudson);
6–Dinah D. (1742-ante 1771), *m* William Garrett **Woodward** (6 above).
2–Rev. Schuyler Colfax **Fulmer** (1859-1912), see portrait; *m* 1882, Caroline Gambrill (1859-92); *m* 2d, Eleanor Mead (b 1868); issue (1st marriage): I–Lenna Fay (1 above); II–Caroline Fern (*b* 1886; *m* Henry Howard Steward); III–Gladys Gambrill (*b* 1891; *m* Paul H. McConnell).
1–*m* July 5, 1916, Charles Hendricks Leonard, *b* nr. Cloverdale, Ind., Oct. 13, 1884; son of John A. Leonard, *m* Adeline McClure.
1–Ph.B., Franklin Coll., Ind., '09. Prin. high schools, Atlanta, Ind., 1910, Arcadia, Ind., 1911-12; asst. prin. high school, Zionsville, Ind., 1913-15; prin. high school, Conover, O., 1918-19; teacher in Detroit Intermediate School, since 1920. Mem. D.A.R., I.A.G. Linconia Literary Soc. (charter mem.). Baptist. Republican. Residence: 2662 Pasadena Av., Detroit, Mich.

1–**LEWIS, Frederick Humphreville,** *b* Philadelphia, Pa., May 14, 1858.
9–William **Lewis** (qv);
8–William (*b* 1620), Farmington, Conn.; *m* Mary Hopkins (William[9]);
7–William (bap. 1656-1737), *m* Sarah Moore (Isaac[8]);
6–Capt. Jonathan (1697-probably 1769), Kensington and New Britain, Conn.; *m* Elizabeth Newell (Thomas[7]);
5–Adonijah (1722-99), soldier French and Indian War; *m* Mary Bronson (James[6]);
4–Seth (1772-1849), New Britain, Conn., and Phila., Pa.; *m* Lydia Wright (Thomas[5]);
3–William Goodwin (1806-66), Phila.; *m* Eliza Lucy Southworth (Samuel[4]);
2–Henry Martyn (2 below).
8–Constant **Southworth** (qv);
7–William (1659-1719), Saybrook, Conn.; *m* 1705, Martha (Kirtland) Blaque (*b* 1667; Nathaniel Kirtland[8]);
6–Lt. Andrew (1709-72), *m* 1732, Temperance Kirtland (John[7]);
5–Capt. Andrew (1733-1810), *m* Anna (Buck?);
4–Samuel (1771-1841), *m* 1794, Hannah Shipman (1771-1827);
3–Eliza Lucy (1806-83), *m* 1830, William G. **Lewis** (3 above).
8–John **Humphreville** (*b* in Eng.), at New Haven, 1664; propr. there, 1685;
7–Samuel (1666-1748), of New Haven; *m* Experience Miller (1673-1754; Thomas[8]);
6–John (1702-51), of New Haven; *m* 1723, Rebekah Clark (1698-1749; Samuel[7]);
5–Lemuel (1737-98), of West Haven; ens., 8th Co., 2d Regt., 1777; *m* 1761, Mary Beecher (*b* 1741; Samuel[6]);
4–Lemuel (1770-1828), Northfield, Conn.; *m* 1799, Ursula Preston (1780-1882; John[5]);
3–Harriet (1812-97), Phila., Pa.; *m* 1836, George Washington **Smith**;
2–Frances Amelia (1836-1900), Phila.; *m* 1856, Henry Martyn **Lewis** (1831-1906), pres. S. S. White Co., Phila., Pa.; issue: I–Frederick Humphreville (1 above); II–Harriet Southworth (Mrs. Albert M. Barnes, qv for other lineages); III–Nellie (Mrs. Edward C. Cutler, see Vol. II, p. 253), IV–Henry Bertram (see Vol. I, p. 687).
1–*m* Nov. 2, 1882, Alice Marilla Law, *b* Carlisle, Pa., Feb. 8, 1860; dau. of Benedict Law, of Carlisle and Phila., *m* Anne Celestia Southworth; issue: 1–Eleanor Stiles, *b* St. Paul, Minn., July 26, 1883; *m* Apr. 19, 1902, Carlton M. Goodman (issue: Louise H.; Katherine E.; Bertha Barron); 2–Henry Martyn, Jr., *b* St. Paul, Dec. 5, 1884; pvt., sgt. and 1st lt., Signal Corps, construction and engring. duties in U.S., World War; *m* 1924, Marian Orr; 3–Charles Frederick, *b* Phila., July 28, 1886; 2d lt., Co. A, 2d Bn., 307th Engrs., June 14, 1917; capt., Aug. 14, 1917; maj., Apr. 30, 1918; with A.E.F. in France, May 29, 1918-July 11, 1919; *m* Sept. 18, 1919, Frances Louise Morris); 4–Alice Margaret, *b* Phila., Mar. 19, 1890; *m* Dec. 26, 1913, James MacFarlane Andrew; 5–Marion Whitney, *b* Phila., Feb. 10, 1898; *m* Sept. 13, 1921, H. Milner Weatherly.
1–U.Pa., '78. Civil engr. Commd. maj. of engrs., 1917; trained at Camp Lee, Va., Dec. 1917-Apr. 1918; on staff of Chief of Engrs., Washington, later with troops at Camp Humphrey. Mem. S.A.M.E.; life mem. Am. Soc. C.E. Club: Engineers (New York). Residence: Charlottesville, Va.

1–**LEWIS, Carll Andrews,** *b* New Haven, Conn., Jan. 2, 1862.
8–John **Lewis** (*d* 1691), settled at Westerly, R.I., 1661;
7–John (*d* 1735), *m* Ann– (*d* 1747);
6–John (*b* 1698), *m* 1718, Mary Burdick (*b* 1699; Benjamin[7], *m* Mary Reynolds; Robert[8], qv);
5–John (*b* 1719), *m* 1738, his cousin, Thankful Lewis (*b* 1720; Joseph[6], *m* Mary Wilcox; John[7]; John[8]);
4–Simeon (1753-1822 or 23), *m* 2d, 1803, Fanny (Gardner) Lewis, widow of his brother Jeptha;
3–Enoch Burrows (1805-74), of Hampton, Conn.; *m* 1st, 1831, Sarah Knowles;
2–John Gardner (2 below).
8–George **Gardner** (*d* 1677), from Eng.; *m* Herodias (Long) Hicks; *m* 2d, Lydia, dau. of Robert Ballou, *m* Susanna–;
7–George (1634-1724), of Kingston, R.I.; *m* 1670, Tabitha Tefft (1653-1722; John[8] [*d* 1676], of Portsmouth, 1655, *m* Mary–, *d* 1679);
6–John (*d* 1752), of Exeter, R.I.; *m* 1717, Mary Rathbone (*b* 1697; Joseph[7]; John[8]; John[9]; Richard[10]);
5–Samuel (1727-1815), of Hopkinton, R.I.; *m* 2d, 1764, Lucretia Burdick; (his sister Mary [1723-1807], *m* 1739, Jireh Mumford, same as 6 above);
4–Fanny (1766-1869), *m* 2d, 1803, Simeon **Lewis** (4 above).
8–Henry **Knowles** (1609-70), at Portsmouth, 1644; Warwick, R.I., 1655; *m* a dau. of Robert Potter;
7–William (1645-1727), of Warwick; *m* Alice Fish (*d* 1734; Thomas[8], *m* Mary–);
6–John (*d* 1772), of Richmond, R.I.; *m* 1718, Elizabeth Warner (1697-1771; John[7]; John[8]; John[9]);
5–Samuel (*d* 1799), *m* 1772, Sarah Mumford (1753-1835; Jireh[6]; Peleg[7]; Peleg[8]; Thomas[9], qv);
4–Joseph Mumford (1774-1848), of Dorrville, R.I.; *m* 1802, Dorcas Tillinghast (1778-1861; John[5]; Pardon[6]; John[7]; Pardon[8]; Pardon[9], qv);
3–Sarah (1805-54), of Hampton, Conn.; *m* 1831, Enoch Burrows **Lewis** (3 above).
9–Stephen **Hart** (qv);
8–Capt. Thomas (1644-1726), of Farmington, Conn.; dep. Gen. Ct., 1690-1711, speaker, 1700-06; *m* Ruth Hawkins (1649-1724; Anthony[9], one of patentees of Conn. under charter from Charles II, 1662, dep., gov.'s asst., *m* 2d, Ann, dau. of Gov. Thomas Welles, qv);
7–Thomas (1680-1773), of Kensington, Conn.; *m* 1702, Mary Thompson (1680-1763; John[8]; Thomas[9]);
6–Elijah (1711-72), *m* 1734, Abigail Goodrich (1714-1809; Allyn[7]; John[8]; William[9], qv);
5–Elijah (1735-1800), of New Britain, Conn.; *m* Sarah Gilbert (1737-1809; Ebenezer[6]; Johathan[7]);
4–Aaron (1761-1829), *m* 1790, Sarah Francis (1769-1847; Josiah[5]; Thomas[6]; John[7]; Robert[8]);
3–Aaron (1805-45), *m* 1827, Abigail Bronson Andrews (1806-77; Dr. John[4]; Moses[5]; John[6]; Daniel[7]; John[8]);
2–Jane Abigail (1837-1907), grad. New Britain State Normal Sch.; teacher; *m* 1860, John Gardner **Lewis** (1834-1915), grad. New Britain State Normal School; principal Webster School, New Haven, Conn., 50 yrs.; issue: I–

Carll Andrews (1 above); II–Robert Hart (*b* 1864; *m* 1903, Caroline Elizabeth Merrow); III–Mary Mumford (*d* 1887); IV–John Newton (1869-70); V–Harry Blakeman (*b* 1872; *m* 1920, Helen Hoge, divorced; *m* 2d, 1927, Helen D. Cummings); VI–Sarah Knowles (*d* young); VII–Dwight Milton, M.D. (*m* 1909, Helen Fuller); VIII–Newton Francis (*m* 1900, Sidney Elizabeth Roberts, divorced; *m* 2d, 1904, Nannie Leona [Reed] Saunders).

1–*m* June 23, 1886, Carrie Louise Lincoln (Feb. 7, 1861-Feb. 26, 1918); dau. of William Henry Lincoln, of Hampton, Conn., *m* Emma Woodworth; issue (all *b* Hampton, Conn.): 1–Edith Palmer, *b* Apr. 16, 1887; A.B., Oberlin, '15; *m* Oct. 18, 1916, Earle Vincent, son of Albert E. Harrison, of N. Branford, Conn., *m* Isabel Rose (issue: Margaret Lewis; Lincoln Rose); 2–Ethel Knowles, *b* Mar. 25, 1889; hosp. dietician; 3–John Gardner, *b* Sept. 26, 1891; Middlebury (Vt.) Coll., ex-'17; *m* Sept. 25, 1917, Lucy Belle, dau. of Irving E. Hopkins, of Hampton, Conn., *m* Jennie F. Mills (issue: Gardner; Barbara Jane); 4–Bessie Lincoln, *b* May 30, 1894; *m* Oct. 27, 1921, Nathan Albert, son of Albert E. Harrison (issue: Albert Carll; Shirley Lewis).

1–B.A., Yale, '83 (P.B.K., PsiU.); post-grad. in Greek as Clark scholar, 1883-84. Principal Guilford (Conn.) Inst. and High School, 1885-88, 1898-1913; classical instr., Hillhouse High School, New Haven, 1888-91; mgr. Lincoln Farm, Hampton, Conn., 1891-98, 1913-18; prin. Ft. Covington (N.Y.) Acad. and High School, 1918-24; supt. of schools, Guilford, Conn. Editor and publisher Lewisiana, a monthly inter-family paper of the Lewises, 1893-1907; has done much genealogical work, and is an authority on the history of the Lewis family in America. Mem. Am. Hist. Assn., Loyal Lewis Legion, I.A.G., etc. Residence: North Branford, Conn.

1–**LINCOLN, Francis Church,** *b* Boston, Mass., Sept. 8, 1877.

9–Thomas **Lincoln** (*d* 1692), from Eng. to Hingham, Mass., with his brother Stephen, 1638/-39;

8–Caleb (1645-1715);

7–Luke (1695-1770), to Lancaster, Mass.;

6–Mark (1732-98), of Leominster, Mass.; *m* Mary Carter, of Lancaster;

5–Abel, *m* Mary Marshall;

4–Abel (1793-1836), *m* 1819, Phebe Griffin (*d* 1870; Ebenezer[5]; James[6]);

3–Varnum (1819-1907), Universalist minister, Andover, Mass.; *m* 1844, Emeline Sprague;

2–Charles Thayer (2 below).

8–Nicholas (Sprake) **Sprague** (*d* ca. 1740), prob. from Eng.; of Billerica, Mass.;

7–Nicholas ("Nicholas Sprake, Jr."), of Billerica; *m* 1st, 1721, Elizabeth Burge;

6–Samuel (1725 or 26-ante 1789), *m* 1st 1749, Judith Pollard (1728-80; Edward[7], *m* Judith Hezeltine);

5–Ens. Samuel (1750-1836), Am. Rev. pensioner; fought in Battle of Bunker Hill; *m* 1777, Anna (Sprake) Sprague (1756-95; Nicholas[6], *m* Margaret–, *d* post 1794);

4–Jonathan (1785-1880), *m* Lydia Tarbox;

3–Emeline (1820-1907), *m* 1844, Varnum **Lincoln** (3 above).

11–Richard **Warren,** Mayflower Pilgrim (qv);

10–Elizabeth, *m* 1636/37, Richard **Church** (qv);

9–Joseph (1638-1711), of Little Compton, R.I.; *m* 1660, Mary Tucker (1640-1710; John[10], of Hingham);

8–Joseph (1663-1715), *m* 1688, Grace Shaw (1666-1737; Anthony[9], of Boston);

7–Caleb (1701-69), *m* 1721, Deborah Woodworth (1703-33);

6–Ebenezer (1725 or 26-1825), *m* 1754, Hannah Wood (1734-1815);

5–Joseph (1764-1840), *m* 1793, Elizabeth Taylor;

4–Nathaniel (*b* 1801), *m* 1825, Sarah C. Wood (1803-55);

3–Francis Taylor (1832-96), of Boston; *m* 1855, Helena Antoinette Simmons;

2–Lena Simmons (2 below).

11–John **Alden,** Mayflower Pilgrim (qv);

10–Elizabeth (1624-1717), *m* 1644, William **Pabodie** (1620-1707);

9–Mercy (*b* 1649), *m* 1669, John **Simmons** (*d* 1715; Moses[10], qv);

8–William (1672-1765), Little Compton, R.I.; *m* 1696, Abigail Church (1680-1720; Joseph[9]; Richard[10], qv);

7–Joseph (1702-78), *m* 1726, Rebecca Wood (1704-95);

6–John (*b* 1726/27), *m* 1746, Lydia Grinnell (*b* 1726);

5–Sgt. Benoni (1755-1835), pvt. and sgt. in Am. Rev.; master gunner on the "Trumbull," and lost an arm in an engagement on Lake Champlain, 1776, also served on the "Alliance"; *m* 1784, Nancy Bailey (1767-1855; Cornelius[6]);

4–Valentine (1802-85), Boston; *m* 1826, Mary Ann Lombard (1809-43; Peter[5]; Isaac[6]; Thomas[7]; Thomas[8]; Jedediah[9]; Thomas Lumbert[10]);

3–Helena Antoinette (1833-1904), *m* Francis Taylor **Church** (3 above);

2–Lena Simmons (*b* 1856), *m* 1876, Charles Thayer **Lincoln** (1849-79), glove mfr., Boston, Mass.; issue: I–Francis Church (1 above); II–Charles Thayer (*b* 1879; *m* 5th, 1928, Barbara Gauthier).

1–*m* June 19, 1901, Gertrude Whipple Appleton, *b* Roxbury, Mass., 1876 (divorced, 1923); dau. of George Herman Appleton, of Roxbury; issue: 1–Leslie Appleton, *b* Dover, N.H., Apr. 10, 1905; 2–Francis Appleton, *b* Boston, Mass., Apr. 6, 1914.

1–*m* 2d, Dec. 22, 1923, Florence May (Curtis) Hill, *b* Phila., Dec. 24, 1887; dau. of William Curtis, of Phila.; issue: 1–William Theodore, *b* Rapid City, S.D., Nov. 12, 1924; 2–Robert Charles, *b* Rapid City, Aug. 18, 1926.

1–S.B., mining engring., M.I.T., '00 (Sigma Xi); E.M., N.M. Sch. of Mines, 1904; A.M., Columbia, 1907, Ph.D., 1911. Prof. mining, S.D. State Sch. of Mines, since 1923. Author (see Who's Who in America). Residence: Rapid City, S.D.

Tilson
A.D. 1580.

Arms: Azure, a bend coticed or, between two garbs of the second.
Crest: A bear's head argent, issuing from a mural crown, gules.

1–**LINK, Jessie May Tillson (Mrs. John Alexander),** *b* Adamsville, Que., Can., June 22, 1866.

9–Edmond (Tilson) **Tillson** (*d* 1660), from Eng. to Plymouth, Mass., 1638; *m* Joanna–;

8–Ephraim (1636-1716), freeman, 1670; surveyor of highways, 1674,76,80; *m* 1666, Elizabeth Hoskins (*b* 1646; William[9], *m* Ann Hinde);

7–Edmund (1667-1762), of Plympton, Mass.; constable; *m* 1st, 1691, Elizabeth Waterman (1669-1705; Dea. John[8], *m* Anna, dau. Samuel Sturtevant; Robert[9], qv);

6–John (1692-1729), *m* 1712, Joanna Dunbar (1692-1756; Joseph[7], *m* Christian Garnet; Robert[8], *m* Rose–);

5–Ephraim (1728-1808), of Halifax, Mass.; in

Am. Rev.; *m* 1752, Mercy Sears (1736-1807; Edward[6], *m* Desire–; Josiah[7]; Silas[8]; Richard[9], qv);
4–Ephraim (1760-1833), in Am. Rev.; *m* 1782, Fear Waterman;
3–Welcome (1800-77), began to write name Tillson; bought Bryant homestead at Cummington, Mass., 1834; *m* 1820, Leah Tower;
2–Charles Waterman (2 below).
9–Isaac **Allerton,** Mayflower Pilgrim (qv);
8–Mary (1616-99), *m* 1635, Elder Thomas **Cushman** (1608-91), from Holland in the "Fortune," 1621; ruling elder of Mass. Colony, 1649 (Robert[9], qv);
7–Eleazer (*b* 1656), *m* 1687, Elizabeth Combs;
6–Lydia (1687-1771), *m* 1709, John **Waterman** (1685-1768; Dea. John[7], same as 8 above);
5–Capt. John (1718-90), Am. Rev.; *m* 1740, Fear Sturtevant (1719-90);
4–Fear (1758-1823), *m* Ephraim **Tillson** (4 above).
10–Richard **Warren,** Mayflower Pilgrim (qv);
9–Mary (*d* 1678), *m* 1628, Robert **Bartlett** (qv);
8–Joseph (1639-1711), of Plymouth; *m* 1662, Hannah Pope (1637 or 39-1709/10);
7–Benjamin (*b* 1669), *m* 1702, Sarah Barnes (*b* 1680);
6–Benjamin (1707-86), Stoughton; in Am. Rev.; *m* 1737, Hannah Stevens (1712-99);
5–Edward (1745-1815), Cummington, Mass.; Am. Rev.; *m* 1772, Zilpha Cole (1754-1813; Ephraim[6], Am. Rev.; Capt. Joseph[7], Am. Rev.; John[8]; James[9]; James[10], qv);
4–Rachel (1780-1814), of Cummington; *m* 1802, Ambrose **Tower** (1777-1813; Nathaniel[5], *m* Leah, dau. Peter Tower; Nathaniel[6]; Thomas[7]; Benjamin[8]; John[9], qv);
3–Leah (1802-76), *m* Welcome **Tillson** (3 above).
9–Abraham **Shaw** (qv);
8–John (1630-1704), of Weymouth, Mass.; *m* Alice Phillips (Dea. Nicholas[9], at Weymouth, 1640);
7–Joseph (1664-1718), *m* 1686, Judith Whitmarsh (1669-1760; John[8], *m* Sarah, dau. of John Harding; John[9], *m* Alice–);
6–Joseph (*d* 1744), *m* 1716, Mary Blanchard (John[7], *m* Abigail Phillips; Nathaniel[8]; Thomas[9]);
5–Capt. Ebenezer (1718-96), Abingdon; capt. in Lexington Alarm, 1775; *m* 1740, Anne Colson (1725-99; John[6], *m* Susannah, dau. Thomas Lincoln);

SYLVANUS SHAW (1766-1852), and his wife PERSIS WILDER STODDARD (1773-1852). Drummer at 13 years of age in Am. Rev.; pvt., 1781-82; under General Washington 3 mos.; also in Capt. Thomas Cushing's co. for defense of Castle and Governors Island in Boston Harbor. For many years precentor, Presbyterian Church, Cummington, Mass.

4–Sylvanus (1766-1852), of Cummington; in Am. Rev. (see portrait); *m* 1792, Persis Wilder Stoddard (1773-1852; Laban[5], Am. Rev., *m* Persis, dau. Theophilus Wilder; Hezekiah[6]; Hezekiah[7]; John[8]; John[9], *m* Ann–);
3–Brackley (1797-1848), tanner; *m* 1822, Sillinda Mason (1795-1858; Joseph[4], *m* Hannah Woods; Ichabod[5], *m* Ruth–);
2–Sarah Stoddard (1840-1903), to Toronto, Can.; *m* 1859, Charles Waterman **Tillson** (1836-90), *b* Bryant homestead Cummington, Mass.; tanner; issue: I–Byron William (1860-1927; *m* Evangeline Sanderson Flesher; *m* 2d, Charlotte Georgina Hincks); II–Ernest Charles (1864-65); III–Jessie M. (1 above).
1–*m* Dec. 23, 1885, John Alexander Link (Nov. 29, 1857-Apr. 9, 1908); son of Alexander Link, of Gravenhurst, Can.; issue: 1–Charles Alexander, *b* Toronto, Ont. (Feb. 8, 1887-July 2, 1894); 2–Ernest Tillson, *b* Gravenhurst, Ont., Mar. 2, 1890; *m* Aug. 22, 1916, Katharine Newton, grad. Superior Normal, dau. of Louis D. Newton, of Superior, Wis. (issue: Katharine; Margaret; Dorothy); 3–Sarah Margaret, *b* Superior, Wis., Feb. 13, 1894; A.B., Carroll Coll., '16 (B.X.O.); *m* Apr. 2, 1919, Ira Irl Tubbs, A.B., William Jewell, 1912, son of Rev. E.H.H. Tubbs, of Council Grove, Kan. (issue: Margaret; Helen; William Irl); 4–Jessie Miriam, *b* Superior, Aug. 25, 1896; A.B., Carroll Coll., '17, Mus. B., 1917 (B.X.O.); *m* Jan. 26, 1918, William L. Baird, B.S., U.Wis., '13, son of W. G. Baird, of Waukesha, Wis. (issue: Jessie Anne; Jane C.).
1–Ed. Convent of the Presentation of Mary (Granby, Que.), 1880-81; Richard Inst. (Toronto), 1882-84, and pvt. tutors. Mem. S.M.D., D.A.C., D.A.R. (chapter v.regent and chaplain), Descs. Robert Bartlet of Plymouth Soc., W.C.T.U. Presbyn. Republican. Residence: 1511 N. 19th St., Superior, Wis.

1–**LINDLY, Bayard Blachly,** *b* Washington Co., Pa., Aug. 20, 1841-*d* Jan. 5, 1929.
9–Richard **Treat** (qv);
8–Col. Robert (1622-1710), founder of Newark, N.J.; pres. United Colonies, 1684; gov. of Conn., 1683-98; *m* 1st, 1645, Jane Tapp (*d* 1703; Edmund[9], magistrate and asst. gov. New Haven Colony);
7–Mary (1649-1704), *m* Dea. Azariah **Crane** (1647-1730), dep. N.J. Provincial Assembly, a founder of Cranetown (now Montclair), N.J.;
6–Hannah (*d* post 1710), *m* 1677, John **Plum** (1658-1710), from Conn. to Newark, N.J. (Samuel[7]; John[8], qv);
5–Sarah (1698-1750), *m* John (Lindsly) **Lindly** (1693/94-1750), one of 1st judges of Morris Co., N.J. (John[6]; Francis[7], qv);
4–Levi (1731-1801), with commissary dept. of N.J., Am. Rev.; from Morris Co., N.J., to Washington Co., Pa.; *m* 2d, Anna Davison (1744-1818);
3–William (1786-1855), commr. for the poor at time of death; *m* Sarah (Squier) Squires (1791-1853);
2–John Milton (2 below).
9–Thomas **Blachly,** of Hartford, Conn., 1640, New Haven, 1643, Branford, 1645; signed agreement with those who migrated from Branford to settle Newark, but he did not go;
8–Aaron (*b* 1644), *m* Mary Dodd, of Guilford, Conn.;
7–Ebenezer (*b* 1677), lived at Dix Hills, Huntington Tp., L.I.;
6–Ebenezer (*b* 1709), *d* The Ponds, nr. Pompton, Milford Tp., N.J.; *m* Hannah Miller;
5–Ebenezer (1735-1805), a "practitioner of medicine," a founder of the N.J. Med. Soc., 1766; *m* 1758, Mary Wick (1739-96; Henry[6], *m* Mary Cooper);
4–Dr. Ebenezer (1760-1812), Paterson, N.J.; entered the Am. service under age; was at battles of White Plains, Valley Forge; surgeon's mate 10th Regt., N.C. Line, etc.; asst. surgeon to a regt. Pa. Line; practiced medicine; *m* Elizabeth Spencer;
3–Henry Wickham (1786-1849), studied medicine in New York, located in Washington Co., Pa.; *m* 1806, Hannah Loveridge (*d* 1886 aet. 97), had 4 sons who became physicians;
2–Eliza (1818-99), *m* 1839, John Milton **Lindly** (1814-58), surveyor, Washington Co., Pa.; issue: I–Bayard B. (1 above); II–Colin Melville (*b* 1846; *m* 1870, Flora Horn); III–Sarah Hannah (*b* 1849; *m* 1869, Richard R. Thomas).
1–*m* May 21, 1863, Clarriet Hanna, *b* Washington Co., Pa., Aug. 19, 1841; dau. of Thomas Hanna, of Washington Co.; issue: 1–John Milton (qv); 2–Jennie Franc (Oct. 27, 1867-

1922), *m* Jan. 25, 1899, William Bailey Ridgeway (issue: Philip Lindly, 1899-1900; Clarriet Adaline, *b* Mar. 9, 1904; Wilma J., *b* Oct. 16, 1907).
1–Settled in Henry Co., Ia., 1866. Atty.-at-law. Pres. Bank of Winfield, Ia., which he founded 1885. Was mayor of Winfield. Residence: Winfield, Ia.

1–**LINDLY, John Milton,** *b* nr. Lindly's Mills, Washington Co., Pa., Nov. 17, 1864.
10–Jared **Spencer** (qv);
9–Samuel (ca. 1646-1705), *m* Hannah Blackford Willey;
8–Isaac (1678-1751), *m* 1707, Mary Selden;
7–Samuel (1708-58), capt. French and Indian War, *d* in service; *m* 1732, Jerusha Brainerd;
6–Col. Oliver (*b* Conn., 1736-1811), wealthy tanner, Elizabethtown, N.J.; 1st maj., 1st Regt., Essex Co. Militia, 1776; lt. col., 1776; commd. col. of additional cont. regt. (known as Spencer's), 1777; wounded at Battle of Brandywine, 1777; took part with his regt. in Sullivan's expdn., 1779; moved to Cincinnati, O., 1791; comd. 1st regt. of southwestern Ohio; one of first judges in Ohio; *m* ca. 1758, Anna Ogden;
5–Elizabeth (1761-1839), *m* Dr. Ebenezer **Blachly** (1760-1812);
4–Henry Wickham (1786-1849), *m* Hannah Loveridge;
3–Eliza (1818-99), *m* John M. **Lindly** (1814-58);
2–Bayard Blachly (2 below).
10–Samuel **Whiting** (qv);
9–Elizabeth (1645-1733), *m* Rev. Jeremiah **Hobart** (1630-1715);
8–Dorothy (1670-1732), as widow of Daniel Mason, *m* 2d, 1707, Hezekiah **Brainerd** (1681-1727), mem. Council of Conn.;
7–Jerusha, *m* Samuel **Spencer** (7 above).
10–John **Ogden** (qv);
9–Jonathan (1646-1732), of Elizabeth, N.J.; *m* Rebekah– (1648-1723);
8–Robert (1687-1733), *m* 1st, Hannah Crane (1691-1726; Jasper[9], *m* Joana, dau. of Samuel Swain, to America, 1635);
7–Hon. Robert (1716-87), patriot Am. Rev.; speaker N.J. Assembly; del. Cont. Congress; chmn. Com. of Safety, Elizabethtown, N.J., Am. Rev.; *m* Phoebe Hatfield;
6–Anna (1740-1823), *m* Oliver **Spencer** (6 above).
11–Cornelius **Melyn** (qv);
10–Maria, *m* Matthias **Hatfield** (1640-87);
9–Abraham (1670-1708), *m* Phebe–;
8–Dea. Matthias (1698-1779), *m* Hannah Miller (1699-1783; Samuel[9] [1674-1759]; William[10], will proved Oct. 4, 1711);
7–Phoebe (1720-96), *m* Robert **Ogden** (7 above).
2–Bayard Blachly **Lindly** (qv), *m* 1863, Clarriet Hanna.
1–*m* Jan. 21, 1924, Claudia Yewell (qv); issue: 1–Buford Yewell, *b* Burlington, Ia., Jan. 28, 1926.
1–Grad. State U.Ia., '89. Publisher; cashier Bank of Winfield, Ia. State Senator, 1915-19; mem. Dem. State Central Com., 1916-22; sec. Iowa Pharm. Assn., 1905-11, and treas., 1911–; mem. Henry Co. Bd. of Edn., 1919–; sec. Winfield Sch. Bd., 1898–. In World War was mem. of Henry County Council of Defense, chmn. for Henry Co. for U.S. Pub. Service Reserve, and co. chmn. for finding employment for the returning soldiers, local chmn. for the liberty bond campaigns, and minuteman. Apptd. by the gov., 1920, mng. bd. of Ia. State Hist. Soc.; mem. D.C.G., S.C.W., S.A.R., I.A.G., Iowa and Am. Pharm. assns., Ia. and Am. Bankers assns.; life mem. Ia. State Hist. Soc., Ia. Acad. Science. Club: Grant (Des Moines). Residence: Winfield, Ia.

1–**LINDLY, Claudia Yewell (Mrs. John Milton),** *b* Owensboro, Ky., Dec. 1, 1884.
8–Charles (Ewell) **Yewell** (ca. 1660-1722), from Eng., ca. 1690; settled in St. Mary's Parish, Lancaster Co., Va.; bought land nr. Corotoman Creek and 1,000 acres of "Tolliver's Mount"; *m* ca. 1705, as her 1st husband, Mary Ann Bertrand (1690-1749 or 50; Rev. John[9], from France during the persecution of Louis XIV, to Eng., thence to America, clergyman Ch. of Eng.);
7–Soloman (1716 or 18-1760), capt. of Lancaster Co., Va.; *m* 1746, as widow of Thomas Taylor, Eve Ball (1713-78; Maj. James[8], *m* Mary Conway-Daingerfield);
6–Col. James, began to write name Yewell; of Va.; *m* Mary Yewell;
5–James;
4–Martin, *m* Nancy Foreman;
3–Maj. Harrison (1812-84), of Owensboro, Ky.; maj. militia; *m* 1836, Sarah Eliza Lewis;
2–Vardaman Harrison (2 below).
10–Robert **Lewis** (qv);
9–John (*b* 1635), of "Warner Hall"; *m* Isabella Warner;
8–Col. John (1669-1725), mem. Royal Council; co. lt.; judge Supreme Ct.; *m* his cousin, Elizabeth Warner;
7–John, of Va.; maj.; *m* Frances Fielding;
6–Capt. Henry, soldier in Am. Rev.; *m* Ann Buford;
5–Thomas, *m* Ann Rice;
4–Henry (*b* 1789), *m* Volinda Clagget Linthicum;
3–Sarah Eliza (1820-90), *m* Maj. Harrison **Yewell** (3 above).
11–Richard **Buford** (*b* 1617), from Eng. in the "Elizabeth," 1635; settled in Christ Ch. Parish, Lancaster (now Middlesex) Co., Va.; *m* 1635, Miss Vause (John[12]);
10–John (1642-1722), *m* 1662, Elizabeth Parrott (*b* 1645; Richard[11] [*d* 1686], from Barbados, an early settler in Lancaster Co., Va., 1649, sr. justice, 1673-86, commr., 1656, high sheriff, 1657, *m* Margaret–, *d* 1687);
9–Thomas (1663-1716), *m* Mary– (*d* 1720);
8–Thomas (1682-1761), *m* Elizabeth– (*b* 1675);
7–John (*d* 1787?), *m* Judith Caloway;
6–Ann, *m* Henry **Lewis** (6 above).
2–Vardaman Harrison **Yewell** (*b* 1851), farmer, Owensboro, Ky.; *m* 1877, Ella Robinson Yeager (*b* 1859); issue: I–Ned (*b* 1878); II–Vardaman Harrison (*b* 1880; *m* Nettie Cave); III–Annabell (*b* 1882; *m* Jerome S. Russell); IV–Claudia (1 above); V–John Vardaman (1887-1928; *m* Jewell Huston).
1–*m* Jan. 21, 1924, John Milton Lindly (qv for issue).
1–Mem. D.A.R. (organizing regent Winfield Chapter). Baptist. Democrat. Residence: Winfield, Ia.

EDWIN CLARK LITCHFIELD (1815-85), photograph of bust taken at Florence, Italy, 1864.

1–**LITCHFIELD, Grace Denio,** *b* New York, N.Y., Nov. 19, 1849.
8–Laurence **Litchfield** (qv);
7–Josiah (1647-1708), *m* Sarah Baker;
6–Nicholas (1680-1750), *m* Bathsheba Clarke;
5–Israel (*b* 1714), *m* 1st, Penelope Burdin;
4–David (*b* 1760), *m* Keziah Morse;
3–Elisha (1785-1859), 5 times a mem. and once speaker N.Y. Assembly; mem. Congress, 1821-25; *m* 1st, Percy Tiffany;
2–Edwin Clark (2 below).
5–Daniel **Hubbard,** *m* Diantha Ward;

4–Rev. Bela (1739-1812), B.A., Yale, 1758; *m* Grace Dunbar Hill;
3–Thomas Hill (1781-1857), B.A., Yale, 1798; mem. 15th and 17th Congresses; *m* his cousin, Phebe Hubbard;
2–Grace Hill (1819-81), *m* 1841, Edwin Clark **Litchfield** (1815-85), grad. Hamilton Coll., N.Y., 1832; admitted to bar aet. 21; removed to New York, 1848, to Brooklyn, 1857 (see portrait); issue: I–Francese Hubbard (1844-1927; *m* Lawrence Turnbull); II–Edward Hubbard (see Vol. I, p. 691); III–Henry Percy (*d* 1919); IV–Grace Denio (1 above).
1–Ed. privately and abroad. Author (see Who's Who in America). Residence: 2010 Mass. Av., Washington, D.C.

1–**LITTLEHALE, Paul Bradner,** *b* New York, N.Y., Oct. 6, 1886.
9–Richard **Littlehale** (*d* 1663), from Eng. in the "Mary and John," to Ipswich, Mass., 1633; one of original 91 proprs. of Newbury, 1635; a first settler of Pentucket (now Haverhill), 1640; town clk. 20 yrs.; magistrate; *m* 1647, Mary Lancton;
8–Isaac (1660-1718), *m* 1686, Elizabeth Davis;
7–John (1691-1750), *m* 1715, Hannah Colburn;
6–Abraham (1725-1810), soldier in Am. Rev.; *m* 1744, Mary Stearns;
5–Roger Langdon (1769-1845), *m* 1791, Mary (Polly) Griffin;
4–Daniel (1792-1859), *m* 1818, Joanna B. Davis;
3–Daniel Stearns (1823-55), *m* 1848, Elmira Brown;
2–Wilbur Stearns (1850-99), *m* 1881, Etta E. House.
1–*m* June 2, 1915, Aimee McPherson, *b* Phila., Pa., Sept. 1, 1888; mem. S.M.D., D.F.P.A., C.D.-A., D.A.R., H.S.; dau. of William Charles McPherson, *m* Mary Emma Ryder; issue: 1–Bradner McPherson, *b* Elizabeth, N.J., Oct. 30, 1916; 2–Langdon Ryder, *b* Elizabeth, Feb. 11, 1920.
1–Ed. Powder Point Prep. Sch., Duxbury, Mass. Pres. and dir. Littlehale Advertising Agency, Littlehale Pub. Co., and Littlehale Ltd. Mem. O.F.P.A., S.R., N.E.H.G.S.; fellow Am. Geog. Soc.; mem. Ship Model Soc. (R.I.). Clubs: Aldine, Echo Lake Country. Residence: 114 Orchard St., Cranford, N.J.

1–**LIVINGOOD, Lily Broadwell Foster (Mrs. Charles J.),** *b* Cincinnati, O., Feb. 17, 1872.
6–John **Lytle** (1703-77), from Ireland, 1723, settled nr. Carlisle, Pa.;
5–Capt. William (1728-97), capt. of co. at Ft. Hamilton, nr. Carlisle; *m* 1761, Mary Steele (1736-1809);
4–Gen. William (1770-1831), maj. gen. Ohio militia; surveyor-gen. of Northwest Ty.; *m* 1798, Eliza Noel Stahl (1779-1821), of Phila.;
3–Gen. Robert Todd (1804-39), of Williamsburg, O.; mem. 33d Congress; surveyor-gen. of Northwest Ty.; *m* 1825, Elizabeth Smith Haines (1804-41), of N.J.;
2–Josephine Roberta, *m* 1853, Dr. Nathaniel **Foster** (1819-82), from Ireland to Cincinnati, O., 1830; issue: I–Anna Haines (1856-1916); II–William Lytle (1867-1917); III–Lily Broadwell (1 above).
1–*m* Dec. 30, 1896, Charles J. Livingood, *b* Reading, Pa., Feb. 6, 1866; son of Jacob S. Livingood, of Reading; issue (all *b* Cincinnati): 1–Josephine Lytle, *b* Oct. 3, 1900; Westover Sch., Middlebury, Conn.; *m* Apr. 14, 1926, Virginius Cornick Hall; 2–John Jacob, *b* Mar. 7, 1903; Princeton U., '25; 3–Elizabeth Treon, *b* Oct. 26, 1907; Westover Sch.
1–Residence: 2766 Baker Pl., Walnut Hills, Cincinnati, O.

1–**LIVINGSTON, Philip,** *b* New York, N.Y., Nov. 9, 1861.
7–Col. Robert **Livingston** (qv);
6–Philip (1686-1749), 2d lord of the manor; sec. for Indian affairs; co. clk.; mem. Provincial Council; *m* Catherine Van Brugh (Peter[7], mayor of Albany);
5–Robert (1708-90), 3d lord of the manor; *m* 1st, Mary Tong;
4–Walter (1740-97), del. Provincial and Cont. congresses; commr. U.S. Treas.; *m* Cornelia Schuyler (Peter[5]);
3–Maria, *m* Philip Henry **Livingston** (1769-1831; Philip[4]; Philip[5]; Philip[6], same as 6 above);
2–Livingston (2 below).
7–Timothy **Williamson** (killed in King Philip's War, 1676), *m* Mary Howland (Arthur[8]);
6–George (1675-1742), *m* 1700, Mary Crisp (George[7], *m* Hepsibah Cole);
5–Caleb (1715-95), *m* 1737/38, Sarah Ransom (Robert[6], *m* Sarah Thomas);
4–George (1754-1822), Middlebury, Conn.; *m* 1778, Mary Foster (Capt. William[5], *m* Hannah Durkee);
3–William Durkee (1779-1846), pres. Me. Senate; 2d gov. of Me.; *m* 1st, 1806, Jemima Montague Rice (*d* 1822);
2–Mary Celia (1819-96), *m* 1859, Livingston **Livingston** (1809-72), lawyer.
1–*m* Apr. 16, 1890, Juliet Birckhead Morris (*d* 1908); dau. of William H. Morris, of Morrisania, N.Y.
1–*m* 2d, Jan. 5, 1910, Juliette Turner Benedict, *b* New York; C.D.A.; dau. of James Augustus Benedict, New York; issue: 1–Philip, Jr., *b* New York, Oct. 5, 1911; 2–Benedict, *b* New York, Jan. 19, 1914.
1–A.B., Harvard, '84; LL.B., Columbia, 1887 (Delta Phi). Lawyer, retired (see Who's Who in America). Mem. Co. K, 7th Regt., N.G.N.Y., 1885-92; lt. and capt. 12th Regt., 1909-11; office of adj.-gen., 1917; capt. and insp. small arms practice, 22d Engrs., N.Y. Guard; maj., Insp. Gen.'s Dept., N.Y. Guard, 1918-19. Mem. S.C.-W., D.C.G., S.N.S. (mem. bd. govs.), C.L.M., S.C. (v.p. R.I. Soc.), S.R. (registrar N.Y. Soc.), M.O.W.W. Pres. Bar Harbor Horse Show. Clubs: Union, New York Yacht, Riding, Tuxedo, Army and Navy (N.Y.), Bar Harbor Swimming (pres.), Bar Harbor Yacht, Kebo Valley Golf. Summer place: "Far View," Bar Harbor, Me. Residence: 20 E. 80th St., New York, N.Y.

1–**LOCKWOOD, Benoni,** *b* Wilmington, Del., Sept. 3, 1866.
9–Roger **Williams** (qv);
8–Mercy (1640-1711), *m* ca. 1659, Resolved **Waterman** (1638-70; Richard[9]);
7–John (1666-1728), *m* Anne Olney;
6–Resolved (1703-52); *m* 1732, Sarah Carr (*b* 1708; Edward[7], *m* Hannah, dau. of John Stanton; Caleb[8], qv);
5–Phoebe (1748-1845), *m* Benoni **Lockwood** (*b* 1733); see Vol. I, p. 694, for Lockwood lineage;
4–Benoni (1777-1829), *m* 1798, Phoebe Greene;
3–Benoni (1805-51), *m* Amelia Cooley;
2–Benoni (2 below).
10–John **Greene** (qv);
9–James (1626-98), *m* 1658, Deliverance Potter; *m* 2d, 1665, Elizabeth Anthony;
8–Peter;
7–Thomas;
6–Stephen (1734-1819), *m* 1754, Mary Rhodes;
5–Rhodes (1755-1821), *m* 1780, Phebe Vaughn (*b* 1761; Christopher[6], *m* Wait, dau. of John Wightman; Christopher[7]; Christopher[8]; George[9]; John[10]);
4–Phoebe (1781-1837), *m* Benoni **Lockwood** (4 above).
10–Zachariah **Rhodes** (1603-63), a 1st settler of Pawtuxet, R.I., joined Roger Williams in Bapt. belief; *m* 1646, Joanna Arnold (1617-92; William[11], qv);
9–Malachi (*d* 1682), *m* 1675, Mary Carder (*d* 1693; Richard[10]);
8–Malachi (*d* 1714), *m* 1701, Dorothy Whipple (*d* 1728; John[9]);
7–Malachi (*b* 1701), *m* 1731, Deborah Wightman (George[8]);
6–Mary (1732-1827), *m* Stephen **Greene** (6 above).
10–George **Cotton** (*d* 1699);
9–Gardner (1644-89);
8–John (1659-1727), *m* 1690, Joanna Wolcott (*d* 1755);
7–John (1697-1766), *m* 1726, Mercy Stebbins (*d* 1780);
6–Solomon (1735-1821), *m* 1755, Lucy Cooley (1730-1802);
5–Roxana, *m* 1790, Chauncy **Cooley** (1766-1838; Josiah[6]);
4–Franklin (1790-1857), *m* Abigail Harwood (1791-1848; John[5], 1739-1835);
3–Amelia (1812-72), *m* Benoni **Lockwood** (3 above).
8–Joseph **Willing,** *m* 1676, Ava Lorde;
7–Thomas (1679-1760), *m* 1704, Anne Harrison (*d* 1747; Thomas[8], *m* Dorothy, dau. of Simon Wayne, regicide; Thomas[9], regicide);
6–Charles (1710-54), *m* Anne Shippen (1710-90; Joseph[7], *m* Abigail, dau. of Thomas Gross; Edward[8], qv);
5–Thomas (1731-1821), *m* Ann McCall (1745-81; Samuel[6], *m* Anne Searle; George[7]);

4–Dorothy (1772-1847), *m* Thomas William **Francis** (1767-1815), of Phila. (Tench[5], *m* Ann Willing; Tench[6]; John[7]; Very Rev. John, D.D.[8]);
3–Anne (1802-64), *m* James Asheton **Bayard** (1799-1880); see Vol. I, p. 694, for Bayard lineage;
2–Florence (1842-98), *m* Benoni **Lockwood** (1838-1909), mgr. London Assurance Co.; maj. 9th Pa. Cav., 1861-64; 1st pres. Tariff Assn., N.Y.; issue: I–Florence Bayard (*m* C. Grant LaFarge); II–Benoni (1 above); III–Frances Willing (*m* Henry Wharton).
1–*m* May 8, 1898, Mary Isabel, dau. George T. Bonner; issue: 1–Benoni, Jr., *b* at New York, Apr. 12, 1899; Harvard, '22; 2–Mary Isabel, *b* Murray Bay, Can., July 5, 1901; *m* May 7, 1921, LeRoy King Rhinelander; 3–Florence Bayard, *b* Saunderstown, R.I., Sept. 23, 1903.
1–*m* 2d, Mar. 2, 1921, Julia (Chapin) DuVillard-Bourne, *b* Bridgeport, Conn.; dau. Chester W. Chapin, pres. B.&A.R.R.
1–A.B., Columbia, '87; LL.B., New York U., 1896. Lawyer. Clubs: Travellers (Paris), Racquet and Tennis, St. Anthony, Assn. of the Bar (N.Y.). Residence: Chateau Grandvault, Loches, France.

LOCKWOOD

Arms: Argent, a fesse between three martlets sable.
Motto: Avito viret honore.

1–**LOCKWOOD, Francis Cummins,** *b* Mt. Erie, Ill., May 22, 1864.
11–Robert **Lockwood** (qv);
10–Joseph (1638-1717), of Fairfield, Conn.; *m* only child of Robert Beacham;
9–Richard (*b* 1678), Worcester Co., Md., ca. 1700; *m* Mary Aydlock or Aydlott;
8–Armwell (1709-51), Kent Co., Del.; *m* Mary Holland (1712-89);
7–Richard (1736-86), justice of peace, 1771,77, and was among the last to be apptd. by the Duke of York; mem. Conv. which assembled at New Castle, Del., 1776, to organize the state of Del.; one of the small number of men present at the Council held 1777; in Am. Rev.; *m* Margaret Jackson (1737-1814);
6–John (1759-1811);
5–Caleb (1777-1855), removed to St. Louis, Mo., 1850;
4–John, *m* 1st, Anne Kirsley;
3–Daniel Cummins (1796-1868), of Smyrna, Del.; *m* 1826, Elizabeth Wakeman Battelle (Cornelius[4], of Phila., *m* Elizabeth–);
2–John Hughes, D.D. (1837-1916), of Salina, Kan., and Pasadena, Calif.; minister; *m* 1859, Ruth Locke (1844-1923); issue: I–Mary Elizabeth (*b* 1860); II–William Battelle (1862-1928; *m* May Taylor); III–Francis Cummins (1 above); IV–Annie Maria (*b* 1866, *m* Rev. Dan McGurk, D.D.); V–Charles Daniel (see Vol. I, p. 694); VI–George Moore (1872-1925); VII–Eva Belle (*b* 1874; *m* I. F. Bull); VIII–Minnie Blanche (*b* 1876; *m* Will Carhart); IX–Frederick (1878-79); X–Richard Crooks (*b* 1884; *m* Mae Shaw).
1–*m* Dec. 24, 1901, Mary Bly Pritner, *b* Keats, Kan., Aug. 8, 1879; A.M., Kan. State Agrl. Coll.; dau. of Calvin B. Pritner; issue: 1–Elizabeth Pritner, *b* Meadville, Pa., Oct. 27, 1905; A.B.,

REV. JOHN HUGHES LOCKWOOD, D.D. (1837-1916), orator, temperance advocate and humanitarian. Chaplain, 49th Ill. Vet. Vol. Inf., 1862-65. Presiding elder in the Methodist Episcopal Church 20 yrs.; member of General Conference of M.E. Church, 1884 and 1888; with A. P. Collins founder of Kansas Wesleyan University. Chaplain G.A.R., Department of Kansas.

Wellesley, '26; 2–Mary Margaret, *b* Meadville, Nov. 26, 1907; A.B., U.Ariz., '29.
1–A.B., Baker U., '92 (Delta Tau Delta, P.B.K.), A.M., Wesleyan, 1902, Ph.D., Northwestern U., 1896. Prof. English, Mt. Union Coll., 1898-99; prof., Kan. State Agrl. Coll., 1899-1901, Allegheny Coll., 1902-16; dean and prof. English lit., U.Ariz., since 1916. Author (see Who's Who in America). Mem. I.A.G. Clubs: Literary, Old Pueblo. Residence: Tucson, Ariz.

1–**LOGAN, Marvel Mills,** *b* Brownsville, Ky., Jan. 7, 1874.
7–William **Logan,** from Scotland or Ireland, 1680; settled Phila., Pa.;
6–David (1690-1750), of Rockbridge and Augusta cos., Va.;
5–Gen. Benjamin (1743-1802) pioneer of Shelby Co., Ky.; gen. Indian wars; with Col. Beauquette in expdn. against Indians of north; also in expdn. to N.W. Ohio and Ind., and with Daniel Boone in Ky.; mem. Ky. Constl. Conv., 1792,99; *m* 1770, Anne Montgomery (1748-90; William[6], in Am. Rev.);
4–Judge William (1776-1821), judge Ky. Ct. of Appeals; U.S. senator from Ky.; *m* 1797, Alicia Wallace;
3–M. M. (1808-86), of Brownsville, Ky.; *m* 1827, Almira Merrill (1810-34);
2–Gillis F. (1832-1915), lt. Union Army; farmer; *m* 1865, Georgiana Houchin; issue: I–David A. (*m* Elizabeth Cook); II–Spencer G. (1872-1922; *m* Louella Simmons, *d* 1907); III–Marvel Mills (1 above); IV–Jesse W. (*m* Maude Garner); V–Ion (*m* James Smith); VI–John A. (*m* Mary James); VII–Wilda (*m* Sydney B. Johnson); VIII–Grover (*d* 1929); IX–Rowan (*m* Martha Self).
1–*m* Sept. 25, 1896, Della Haydon, *b* Glasgow Junction, Ky., Oct. 29, 1874; dau. of Wiley J. Haydon, of Va.; issue (all *b* Brownsville, Ky.): 1–Victor Hubert, *b* May 12, 1899; A.B., U. of Ky., '21; 2–Agnes, *b* Feb. 26, 1902; A.B., Western State Teachers Coll., '24; 3–Leland Hallowell, *b* July 12, 1905; ed. Washington and Lee U., and U. of Ky.; 4–Ralph Hunter, *b* Nov. 15, 1910; ed. Center Coll.
1–Judge Ct. of Appeals, of Ky., since 1927 (see

Who's Who in America). Pres. Bowling Green Rock Asphalt Co.; v.p. Inter-Co. Land Co.; dir. Mammoth Cave Nat. Park Assn.; dir. edn. foundation of Western State Normal Sch. Clubs: Pendennis, XV. Mason. I.O.O.F. (Grand Sire), Elk. Residence: 650 14th St., Bowling Green, Ky.

1–**LOMBARD, Alice Maud Allen (Mrs. Louis),** *b* Pittsfield, Mass., Jan. 2, 1864.
8–Samuel **Allen** (qv);
7–Samuel (1634-1719), an original settler at Northampton, Mass., 1657; *m* Hannah Woodford;
6–Samuel (1675-1739), dea. in Jonathan Edward's ch., Northampton; *m* Sarah Rust;
5–Joseph (1712-79), *m* Betty Parsons (desc. Joseph Parsons, qv);
4–Thomas (1743-1810), A.B., Harvard, 1762; the "Fighting Parson of Bennington," *m* Elizabeth Lee, of Salisbury (desc. Gov. William Bradford, qv);
3–Jonathan (*b* 1773), capt. War 1812; *m* Elizabeth Marsh, of Dalton, Mass.; *m* 2d, Eunice Williams Larned;
2–Thomas, LL.D. (1813-82), A.B., Union, '32; pioneer ry. builder in the southwest; pres. St.L.,I.M.&S.Ry.; philanthropist; mem. 47th Congress; *m* Ann Clementina Russell (1823-97; William[8], to St. Louis, 1804); issue: I–Elizabeth Larned (1843-1909; *m* William Rhind Donaldson, *d* 1917); II–William Russell (1847-1916; *m* Louise Woodward); III–Frances Mary (*d* infancy); IV–Thomas (1849-1924; *m* Eleanor Whitney; *m* 2d, Alice Ranney); V–George Washington (1852-1917; see his son George W. H., Vol. III, p. 504); VI–Bradford (1854-84; *m* Helene Greer); VII–Annie Lee (Mrs. Louis Chauvenet, see Vol. I, p. 204); VIII–Grace (1860-64); IX–Alice M. (1 above).
1–*m* Sept. 28, 1899, Louis Lombard, *b* Lyons, France, Dec. 15, 1861; naturalized Am. Citizen; composer and author (see Who's Who in America); issue: 1–Thomas Allen, *b* Chateau de Trevano, Switzerland, Apr. 4, 1901; *m* Feb. 1927, Petranella Conti; 2–Aïda (*b* Cairo, Egypt, Jan. 13, 1903-*d* Barcelona, Spain, Feb. 14, 1921); 3–Lois, *b* Chateau de Trevano, Oct. 31, 1904; 4–Zuleika, *b* Chateau de Trevano, Aug. 27, 1906.
1–Mem. D.A.R. Residence: Chateau de Trevano, Lugano, Switzerland.

1–**LONG, Hallock Porter,** *b* Canton, Me., Sept. 14, 1891.
11–Robert (Longe) **Long** (qv);
10–Robert (1619-48), from Eng. with parents; mariner; 1635; *m* Elisabeth Hawkins;
9–Samuel (1647-71), blacksmith, Malden, Mass.; *m* 1669, Elizabeth Pinkham;
8–Robert (1669-1736), Nantucket, Mass.; mariner, whaler, and landowner; *m* ca. 1695, Sarah Skiff (*d* 1757; James, Jr.[9], *m* Sarah Barnard);
7–John (*d* 1784), *m* ca. 1735, Jane Luce (*d* 1785);
6–Robert (1748-80), mariner; *m* 1768, Sarah Gardner (*d* 1789; Peleg[7], *m* Eunice Gorham);
5–Peleg (*b* 1768), *m* 1789, Sarah Coffin (*d* 1836; Joseph[6], *m* Elizabeth Jillings); probably had son;
4–Caleb (ca. 1790-1825), Roxbury; *m* ca. 1806, Phebe Caswell (*b* ca. 1788-*d* ca. 1870), Berkeley, Mass.;
3–Jonathan Deane (1819-89), Brookline, Mass.; grad. Worcester Acad.; merchant and contractor; took trip over the Panama Isthmus, 1854, to fill govt. contract on the Presidio, San Francisco; *m* 1846, Mary Hoyt Morgan (1826-92; John[4], *m* Hannah Colby Hoyt);
2–Rev. Joseph Mansfield (2 below).
10–John **Alden** (qv);
9–Capt. Jonathan (1627-97), administrator of his father's estate, and the house he built in Duxbury still stands and is preserved and owned by the Alden Kindred of America; *m* 1672, Abigail Hallett (Andrew[10], *m* Anna Besse);
8–Anna (*d* 1705), Bridgewater, Mass.; *m* 1699, Josiah **Snell** (Thomas[9]);
7–Dea. Zachariah (1704-68), *m* 1730, Abigail Hayward (Joseph[8], *m* Hannah Mitchell);
6–Ebenezer (1738-1813), Cummington, Mass.; in Am. Rev.; mem. Mass. Gen. Ct.; judge Ct. of Sessions; *m* 1764, Sarah Packard (Capt. Abiel[7], *m* Sarah Ames);
5–Thomas, D.D. (1774-1862), N. Brookfield, Mass.; grad. Dartmouth, 1795; author; *m* 1800, Tirzah Strong (Judah[6], *m* Martha Alvord);
4–Dea. Thomas (1809-93); *m* 1st, 1836, Lucretia Porter (Col. Moses[5], *m* Amy Colt);
3–Capt. Moses Porter (1839-1909), grad. Amherst, 1861; served in Civil War, 1861-65; Presbyn. clergyman; Hartford Theol. Sem., 1868; *m* 1862, Mary C. Hallock (Gerard[4], *m* Elisa Allen);
2–Eliza C. (*b* 1868), of Hartford; *m* 1888, Rev. Joseph M. **Long** (*b* 1862), of Brookline, Mass.; B.A., Harvard U., '85; grad. Newton Theol. Sem., 1888; issue: I–Dorothy M. (*b* 1889); II–Capt. Hallock Porter (1 above); III–Gertrude E. (*b* 1895; *m* 1918, Prof. Walter R. Ballard, U. of Md.); IV–Carleton M. (*b* 1897; *m* 1921, Dorothy F. Fisher); V–Katherine E. (*b* 1900; *m* 1925, Bernard A. Bartoo); VI–George A. (1902-23); VII–Bryant A. (*b* 1911).
1–Not married. Grad. Georgetown U., 1913. Lawyer. Served in World War, 1917-19. Residence: 400 5th St. N.W., Washington, D.C.

1–**LONG, Theodore Kepner,** *b* Greenwood Township, Millerstown, Pa., Apr. 26, 1856.
6–John Nicholas **Long** (*d* 1767), from the Rhine country in the "Samuel of London," 1736; settled in Lancaster Co., Pa., where he purchased 4 tracts of land; *m* Anna–;
5–Abraham (1743-94), *m* Maria–;
4–David (1771-1859), settled in Cumberland Co., Pa.; *m* Catharine Hershey (1771-1849);
3–Abraham (1796-1854), stock raiser and farmer; *m* 1817, Mary Cauffman (1794-1848);
2–Abraham (1826-1902), stock raiser and farmer; *m* 1851, Catharine Kepner (1823-1916; David[3] [1787-1851], *m* Susanna Bunn, 1804-51); for issue see Vol. I, p. 938.
1–*m* Nov. 25, 1885, Kate Carson, *b* Eau Galle, Wis., Nov. 1859; dau. William Carson, of Eau Claire, Wis.; issue: 1–William Carson (Oct. 1, 1886-1912); U.Mich., '06.
1–LL.B., Yale, '78 (Theta Sigma). Lawyer, retired. Was alderman, Chicago, 1909-15. Chairman of Lake Shore Reclamation Commn., which instituted and successfully prosecuted sundry suits for the settlement of the title to Chicago's lake front from Grant Park to Jackson Park, thus making it possible to carry on successfully the work of beautifying the lake shore; mem. committee on bathing beaches, which developed a plan for the construction of bathing beaches and recreation piers on the lake front; mem. Ill. Legislature, 1920-21. Founded Carson Long Institute (military school), at New Bloomfield, Pa., in memory of his son William Carson Long, of which he is pres. (see Who's Who in America). Clubs: Union League, Midlothian, South Shore, Kenwood. Summer place: "The Maples," New Bloomfield, Pa. Residence: E. 535 20th Av. North, St. Petersburg, Fla. Address: "The Maples," New Bloomfield, Pa.

1–**LONGYEAR, Edmund Joseph,** *b* Grass Lake, Mich., Nov. 6, 1864.
9–Pieter (Winnen) **Winne,** *m* Aechie Jans;
8–Pieter, *m* Jannetje Albertz;
7–Pieter, *m* Jannetje Pier;
6–Pieter, *m* Antje Merken;
5–Pieter, *m* Arrientje Van Etten;
4–Annatje (1752-1843), *m* Johannes **Longyear** (see Vol. II, p. 174, for Longyear lineage);
3–Peter (1784-1845), *m* 1808, Jerusha Stevens (see Vol. III, p. 308, for Spencer-Stevens lineage);
2–Isaac (2 below).
9–Elder Henry **Cobb** (qv);
8–James (1634-95), *m* Sarah Lewis (1643-1735; George[9]);
7–Hannah (*b* 1671), *m* 1695, Joseph **Davis** (*b* 1662; Robert[8] [1609-93], from Eng., ca. 1650, *m* 1646, Anna–);
6–Dea. Gersham (1702-90), *m* 1731, Mary Hinckley;
5–Samuel (*b* 1734), *m* 1757, Mary Gorham;
4–Ebenezer (1765-1818), *m* 1790, Mary Paine (see Vol. III, p. 308, for Mayflower lineage);
3–Robert (1808-69), *m* 1835, Orpha Pomeroy;
2–Roanna (2 below).
9–Samuel **Hinckley** (qv);
8–Samuel (1642-1727), *m* Mary Fitz Randolph (Edward[9]);
7–Joseph (1672-1753), *m* Mary Gorham (Col. John[8]; Capt. John[9], qv);
6–Mary (*b* 1704), *m* Dea. Gersham **Davis** (6 above).
8–Capt. John **Gorham** (qv);
7–James (1650-1707), *m* Hannah Huckins (1653-1727; Thomas[8]);

6–Ebenezer (1696-1776), *m* Temperance Hawes (1705-67; Joseph[7], *m* Mary, dau. of Jeremiah Howes; John[8]; Edmond[9]);
5–Mary, *m* Samuel **Davis** (5 above).
10–Stephen **Hopkins** (qv);
9–Giles (1605-90), *m* 1639, Catherine Welden;
8–Stephen (1642-1718), *m* 1667, Mary Merrick;
7–Judah (1677-1748), *m* 1702, Hannah Mayo;
6–Stephen, *m* Rebecca Mayo (John[7]; John[8]; John[9]; John[10]);
5–Desire (*d* 1821, aet. 76), *m* Joseph **Foster** (1735-1801); see Vol. III, p. 308, for Foster lineage;
4–Deborah (*d* 1851, aet. 85), *m* John **Pomeroy** (see Vol. II, p. 174, for Pomeroy lineage);
3–Orpha (1807-85), *m* Robert **Davis** (3 above);
2–Roanna (1837-1925), *m* 1857, Isaac **Longyear** (1829-69), building contractor (for issue see Vol. II, p. 174).
1–*m* Apr. 16, 1890, Nevada Estelle Patten, *b* Boonville, Ind., Jan. 30, 1868; dau. of George Washington Patten (1844-1922; John Warren[3] [1793-1865], *m* Eliza Davis; Richard[4] [*d* 1801], *m* Ruth Owen), *m* Matilda Metz; issue: 1–Clyde Stanley, *b* Duluth, Minn., May 27, 1891; Coast Arty. Training Sch., Sept. 10-Nov. 22, 1918; *m* Sept. 15, 1917, Marion Ruth, dau. of John Eugene Hodge, of Los Angeles, Calif. (issue: John Edmund); 2–Robert Davis, *b* Petoskey, Mich., July 11, 1892; Williams, '14; pvt., 11th Co., C.A.C., Aug. 4-Sept. 23, 1918; Coast Arty. Training Sch., Sept. 23-Nov. 28, 1918; commd. 2d lt.; *m* Dec. 3, 1918, Barbara Elizabeth, dau. of Charles Brayton Lyon, of Minn. (issue: Roanne Elizabeth; Martha Patten); 3–Philip Owen, *b* Hibbing, Minn., Jan. 23, 1896; A.B., Williams, '19; E.M., U. Calif., 1923; U.S.A. Ambulance Service, 9 months at Allentown, Pa., and 14 months in France; Croix de Guerre; *m* June 21, 1927, Hildred Isabel, dau. of Maurice Joseph Taylor, of Colorado Springs, Colo.; 4–Margaret, *b* Hibbing, Oct. 20, 1899; Mills, '23; *m* Sept. 12, 1927, Ralph Haswell, son of Harry Elmer Lutz, of Seattle, Wash.; 5–Richard Patten, *b* Minneapolis, Minn., Apr. 12, 1905; 6–Edmund Joseph, Jr., *b* Excelsior, Minn., Sept. 6, 1906.
1–E.M., Mich. Coll. of Mines, '88. Mining engr., specializing in the exploration and development of mineral lands. Mem. S.R., I.A.G. (life). Clubs: Minneapolis (Minn.), Pasadena (Calif.) Golf. Residence: Altadena, Calif.

HENRY LOOMIS, D.D. (1839-1920), agent for American Bible Society at Yokohama, Japan.

1–**LOOMIS, Henry Meech,** *b* Yokohama, Japan, July 19, 1875.
10–Joseph **Loomis** (qv);
9–Dea. John (1622-88), Windsor, Conn.; dep. Gen. Ct.; *m* 1648, Elizabeth Scott (1625-96; Thomas[10], of Hartford);
8–Thomas (1653-88), of Hatfield, Mass.; *m* 1680, Sarah White (*b* 1662; Lt. Daniel[9], *m* Sarah Crow; John[10]);
7–John (1681-1755), of Lebanon, Conn.; *m* 1706, Martha Osborne (*b* 1687);
6–Israel (1715-1801), *m* 1737, Esther Hunt (1718-42; Ebenezer[7], *m* Hannah Clark);
5–Israel (1742-1821), *m* 1765, Rebecca Bingham (1743-1814; Dr. Eleazar[6], *m* Miriam Phelps);
4–Eleazer (1766-1847), of Otsego, N.Y.; *m* Julia Coleman (1768-1836);
3–Noah Coleman (1792-1857), of Burlington, N.Y.; *m* 1821, Maria Meech (1799-1843);
2–Henry, D.D. (1839-1920), see portrait and biography; *m* 1872, Jane Herring Greene (1845-1920); issue: I–Louise Ropes (*b* 1874); II–Henry Meech (1 above); III–Clara Denison (*b* 1877); IV–Evarts Greene (qv for Mayflower lineage); V–Jean Herring (*b* 1882; *m* Prof. James Everett Frame, D.D., see Who's Who in America); VI–Roger Sherman (qv);
1–*m* Nov. 10, 1908, Eleanor Wighton Wallace *b* Harrisburg, Pa., Oct. 2, 1879; dau. of Thomas Laird Wallace, *m* Annie M. Wallace, of Harrisburg.
1–B.S., M.I.T., '97. Asst. sec., Nat. Canners Assn. Chemist with various organizations since 1897 (see Who's Who in America). Club: Cosmos. Mem. A.A.A.S., Am. Chem. Soc., M.O.L.L. Congregationalist. Residence: 2115 P St. N.W., Washington, D.C.

1–**LOOMIS, Evarts Greene,** *b* San Rafael, Calif., Dec. 13, 1879.
10–William **Brewster,** Mayflower Pilgrim (qv);
9–Jonathan, *m* Lucretia Oldham;
8–Benjamin (1633-1710), *m* 1659/60, Ann Darte (*d* 1708);
7–Daniel (1667-1735), *m* 1st, 1686, Hanna Gager (1666-1727);
6–John (1695-1776), *m* 1725, Dorothy Treat (1702-95);
5–Sybil (1735-ca. 1758), *m* as his 1st wife, ante 1758, Hezekiah **Meech** (bap. 1734-ca. 1760);
4–Daniel (bap. 1758-post 1812), *m* 1780, Zerviah Witter (bap. 1760-1812);
3–Maria (1799-1843), *m* Noah C. **Loomis** (1792-1857);
2–Henry, D.D. (1839-1920), see portrait and biography; *m* 1872, Jane Herring Greene (1845-1920); for issue and other lineages see Henry Meech Loomis.
1–*m* Oct. 14, 1908, Amelia Curtis Brown, *b* Worcester, Mass., July 1, 1881; dau. of William T. Brown, *m* Kate A. Curtis; issue (all *b* Newark, N.J.): 1–Evarts Greene, Jr., *b* July 26, 1910; 2–David Greene, b Oct. 15, 1912; 3–Margaret (*b* and *d* 1916).
1–B.S., Worcester Poly. Inst., '01. Draftsman and designer with Françis H. Richards, New York, 1901-02; engr. in charge of design and installation of golf ball mfg. plant, 1902-03, in London and Glasgow; draftsman; designer and asst. mgr., Wildman Mfg. Co., Norristown, Pa., knitting machine mfrs., 1904-08; chief engr. The Arlington Co., Arlington, N.J. (now the DuPont Co. mfrs. of celluloid and lacquers), 1908-17; consulting engr. specializing in designing new processes and new machinery in various lines, since 1917. Pres. Evarts G. Loomis Co. Presbyterian. Republican. Residence: 275 Montclair Av., Newark, N.J.

1–**LOOMIS, Roger Sherman,** *b* Yokohama, Japan, Oct. 31, 1887.
9–John **Prescott** (qv);
8–Jonathan (ca. 1646-1724), *m* Elizabeth Hoar (John[9]);
7–Benjamin (1687-1777), grad Harvard, 1709; ordained, 1713, over ch. in 2d precinct of Salem, Mass., now Peabody, which he served 45 yrs.; *m* 1715, Elizabeth Higginson (John[8], of Salem, espoused cause of patriots with zeal in Am. Rev.);
6–Benjamin (1717-78), grad. Harvard, 1736; justice; mcht., Salem; *m* 1741, Rebecca Minot (James[7], *m* Martha Lane);
5–Rebecca (1742-93), *m* 1763, Roger **Sherman;**
4–Mehitable (1773 or 74-1851), as Widow Barnes, *m* 2d, 1804, Jeremiah **Evarts;**
3–Mary (1806-50), *m* 1829, Rev. David **Greene;**
2–Jane Herring (1845-1920), *m* 1872, Rev. Henry **Loomis** (1839-1920), see portrait and biography

(for issue and other lineages see Henry Meech Loomis).
1–*m* Aug. 27, 1919, Gertrude Schoepperle (July 15, 1881-Dec. 11, 1921); dau. of Vinzens Schoepperle, of Oil City, Pa., *m* Elizabeth Klein.
1–*m* 2d, June 6, 1925, Laura Alandis Hibbard, *b* Chicago, Ill., June 18, 1883; dau. of Frederick Alan Hibbard, of Chicago.
1–B.A., Williams '09; M.A., Harvard, 1910; B.-Litt., Oxford U., 1913. Instr. English, U. of Ill., 1913-18; instr. and lecturer in English, Columbia, 1920-26, asst. prof. English, since 1926. Pvt., corpl., sgt. (1st class), Psychological and Re-education Divs., Med. Dept., U.S.-A., May 4, 1918-Aug. 18, 1919. Residence: 454 Riverside Dr., New York, N.Y.

1–**LOPEZ, Edith Lockett (Mrs. Joseph E.),** *b* Marion, Ala., Jan. 15, 1865.
8–Thomas **Lockett** (1645-86), of Henrico Co., Va.; *m* Margaret Osborne;
7–Thomas (1673-1745), of Henrico and Goochland cos.; *m* Martha Osborne;
6–Thomas (1700-1774-75), of Goochland and Cumberland cos.; *m* Elizabeth Judith Townes (*d* 1781-82);
5–Stephen (1733-92), of Prince Edward Co., Va.; *m* Mary Clay;
4–Henry Wilson (1775-1846), *m* Susan Watkins;
3–Napoleon (1813-67), *m* 1834, Mary Clay Lockett;
2–Samuel Henry (2 below).
9–John **Clay** (qv);
8–Charles (1638-86), *m* Hannah Wilson (John[9], of Henrico Co.);
7–Henry (1672-1750), *m* Mary Mitchell (William[8], *m* Elizabeth–);
6–Charles (1716-89), *m* 1741, Martha Green;
5–Mary (1742-1823), *m* Stephen **Lockett** (5 above).
7–Henry **Watkins** (1638-1714/15), of Henrico Co.;
6–Thomas (*d* 1760), of Swift Creek, Cumberland Co.;
5–Benjamin (1725-81), of Chesterfield Co., Va.; clk of ct.; burgess; mem. Com. of Safety; *m* 1755, Elizabeth Cary;
4–Susan (1774-1832), *m* 1803, Dr. Henry Wilson **Lockett** (4 above).
9–Miles **Cary** (qv);
8–Thomas (ca. 1647-1708), of "Windmill Point"; constructed fort at Old Point Comfort, 1666; capt.; maj.; justice, Warwick Co.; *m* ca. 1669, Anne Milner (Capt. Francis[9], of Nansemond Co., sheriff, justice);
7–Miles (1671-1724), of Potash Creek; clk. of ct., Warwick Co.; capt. in co. militia; *m* 1695, Elizabeth Cocke (Richard[8], of Bremo, Henrico Co.);
6–Miles (1701-66), of Peartree Hall; clk. of ct., Warwick Co.; *m* ca. 1726, Hannah Armistead
5–Elizabeth (*d* 1801), *m* Benjamin **Watkins** (5 above).
9–William **Armistead** (qv);
8–Anthony (1645-post 1700), mem. Gov. William Berkeley's cts.-martial in 1676, to try the Bacon insurgents; justice; capt. of horse, 1680; burgess; mem. of com. to report revision of the laws which were approved by the Gen. Assembly; *m* Hannah Elyson (*d* 1728; Dr. Robert[9], qv);
7–William (*d* 1715/16), high sheriff, Elizabeth City Co., 1695; burgess; maj. of militia; *m* ante Nov. 20, 1696, Hannah Hind (Hines) (*b* 1673; Thomas[8], *m* Hannah–);
6–Hannah, *m* Maj. Miles **Cary** (6 above).
8–Henry **Watkins** (same as above), *m* Rachel–;
7–Thomas (*d* 1760), of "Swift Creek," Cumberland Co.;
6–Thomas (1714-83), of "Chickahominy," Henrico Co.; *m* 1733/34, Frances Anderson (*d* 1783; Col. Henry[7], of Henrico Co., *m* Prudence, dau. Edward Stratton, *m* Martha Shippey);
5–Francis (1745-1826), of Prince Edward Co.; mem. Com. Safety, 1775; clk. of ct.; *m* 1765, Agnes Woodson;
4–Selina A. (1788-1864), *m* 1811, Samuel L. **Lockett** (1782-1852);
3–Mary Clay (1814-85), *m* Napoleon **Lockett** (3 above).
9–Dr. John **Woodson** (qv);
8–Robert (1634-post 1707), *m* Elizabeth Ferris;
7–Richard, *m* Ann (Smith?);
6–Richard (ca. 1706-1773-74), of "Poplar Hill," Prince Edward Co., Va.; *m* Anne Madelin Michaux (Abraham[7] [1672-1717], *m* 1692, Susanne Rochet, Huguenot refugees to Va., 1700);
5–Agnes (1748-1820), *m* Francis **Watkins** (5 above).
9–Samuel **Clark** (ca. 1619-ca. 1690), from Eng.; came to Wethersfield, Conn., 1636; one of the 20 men who bound themselves, 1640, to establish for themselves a home at Rippowams (now Stamford), Conn.; he is supposed to have lived at Milford, 1669, then moved to Hempstead, L.I., and to have lived at New Haven, Conn., 1685; *m* Hannah Fordham (Rev. Robert[10]);
8–William (1645-1712), he with 15 others purchased land in (now) Bedford Tp., Westchester Co., N.Y., 1680, of Mohegan Indian chiefs; Bedford was called the "Hop Lands," also "Katonahs Land"; organized a Congl. ch., 1680;
7–Nathan (ca. 1666-will dated 1726), one of 29 land holders of Bedford, to whom Queen Anne confirmed 23,000 acres, 1704; freeholder, 1713-14; *m* ca. 1700, Clemence–;
6–Nathan (1704-ca. 1755), freeholder, Bedford, 1741; purchased 265 acres nr. Cornwall landing, 1748; *m* 1st, 1728 or 29, Miss Miller;
5–Jeremiah (1730-1808), purchased 218 acres of land lying west of his father's, 1762; mem. Provincial Congresses, 1775,76,77; mem. State Assembly, 1778-79, 1780-85, 1788-89; ruling elder Presbyn. ch., New Windsor, 1783; mem. Com. of Safety, 1777-78; judge Ct. Common Pleas, 1788; supervisor, 1791, 1793-94; town clk., 1799-1803, 1804-06; *m* 1752, Martha Newman;
4–Hon. William Augustus (1768-1843), supervisor, 1801,03,04,11; justice; sheriff, Orange Co., N.Y.; judge Ct. Common Pleas, 1814; mem. Assembly, 1803; *m* 1794, Sally Selleck (*b* 1774; Abraham[6]);
3–William H. (1804-ca. 1880), *m* 2d, Jean Emslie (*b* in Scotland-*d* 1890);
2–Cornelia C. (1841-42-1912), *m* 1859, Samuel Henry **Lockett** (1837-91); issue: I–Jean Emslie (*b* 1862; *m* 1882, Eugene F. Fuller; issue: a–Marguerite F., *m* Sept. 1, 1906, Clarke Gibson Dailey, issue: Gibson Fuller, *b* May 8, 1910; b–Frederick Lockett, *m* Agnes Jennings); II–Edith (1 above); III–Henry Watkins (*b* 1869; *m* May Keeler); IV–Samuel Hobart (1871-1917; *m* Addie McMichael [issue: a–Samuel Hobart, *m* Gretel Volkman, issue: Samuel Hobart, Jr., Donald; b–Donald McMichael, *m* Florence Holman, issue: Sally Joan]); V–Ettie Boyd (1873-1920; *m* George Morgan).
1–*m* June 5, 1889, Joseph E. Lopez, *b* Union Hill, Ala., Sept. 27, 1862; grad. U.Tenn.; civil engr.; pres. Cont. Ins. Co.; son of Joseph E. Lopez, *m* Aloysia Roland Bassan.
Residences: 28 E. 63d St., New York, N.Y., and Oceana, Va.

1–**LORING, Katharine Peabody,** *b* Boston, Mass., May 21, 1849.
9–Andrew **Greely** (qv);
8–Philip (1644-1717/18), Salisbury, Mass.; *m* 1670, Sarah Isley (1644-1710);
7–Jonathan (1672-1750), *m* 1697, Jane Walker (*d* 1721);
6–Philip (1711-46), *m* 1740, Hannah Stubbs (*b* 1722);
5–Jonathan (1741-81), capt. mcht. vessel, served as privateer in Am. Rev.; killed during engagement with English privateer off Marblehead; *m* 1768, Mary Hichborn (1742-1819);
4–Ann (1769-1819), *m* Caleb **Loring** (see Vol. II, p. 175, for Loring lineage);
3–Charles Greely, LL.D. (1794-1867), A.B., Harvard, 1812, LL.D., 1850, fellow, 1838-57; fellow and acad. mem. Mass. Hist. Soc.; lawyer, orator, state senator, author; *m* 1st, Anna Pierce Brace (1798-1836);
2–Caleb William (1819-97), A.B., Harvard, '39; lawyer; *m* 1846, Elizabeth Smith Peabody (1822-69), for issue see Vol. II, p. 175.
1–Ed. Pvt. schs. Trustee Beverly (Mass.) Public Library; pres. Beverly Hist. Soc.; life mem. A.L.A., etc. Residence: Prides Crossing, Mass.

1–**LOVE, Hazelle Marie Roberts (Mrs. Raymond V.),** *b* Rockford, Minn., Sept. 27, 1891.
8–John **Bull** (1674-1736), lived Providence Tp., Phila. Co., Pa.; *m* Elizabeth– (1676-1736);
7–Richard (1714-99), Raccoon Valley, Cumberland Co., Pa.; *m* Elizabeth Pawling (*b* 1719; Henry[8], of Padsbury, Eng., mem. Duke of York's expdn.);
6–Henry (1749-1816), of Chester Co., Pa.; built

stone grist and saw mill of stone, and a dwelling which is still standing; mem. 3d Co., 5th Bn., Cumberland Co. Militia; *m* 1769, Grace Brown (*d* 1838);
5–Jemima (1787-1830), *m* 1810, Francis **Jordon** (1787-1845);
4–Samuel (1815-75), minister; *m* Rebecca Ann Jones (1811-80);
3–Sarah (1841-1914), settled St. Anthony's Falls (now Minneapolis), Minn.; *m* 1861, Daniel H. **Buckwalter** (1840-1915), owned flour mill, Minneapolis;
2–Bessie A. (1862-1927), of N. Hollywood, Calif., and Havre, Mont.; *m* 1882, Orlando Chester **Roberts** (*b* 1861); for issue: see Mrs. Russell H. Barney, p. 44.
1–*m* Apr. 9, 1916, Raymond Vasco Love, *b* Columbia, Ia., Mar. 5, 1891; son of Alpheus E. Love; issue: 1–Dorothy Eileen, *b* May 14, 1918.
1–Grad high school, Mem. D.A.R. (organizing regent), O.E.S., Woman's Club. Episcopalian. Residence: 621 First Av., Havre, Mont.

1–**LOW, William Gilman,** *b* Brooklyn, N.Y., Apr. 9, 1844.
8–John **Porter** (1596-1676), from Eng., was at Hingham, Salem and Danvers, Mass.; *m* Mary–;
7–Joseph (1638-1714), *m* 1664, Ann Hathorne (Maj. William[8]);
6–Nathaniel (1671-1756), *m* 1701, Eleanor Dorman;
5–Elijah, *m* 1721/22, Dorothy Clark;
4–Thomas, *m* Ruth Allen (*b* 1759-60; Capt. Edward[5], *m* Ruth, dau. of Gamaliel Hodges);
3–Mary (1786-1872), *m* 1807, Seth **Low** (see Vol. I p. 939, for Low lineage);
2–William Henry (1816-45), *m* 1842, Anne Davison Bedell (1819-90), who *m* 2d, 1851, Abiel Abbot Low (bro. of William Henry), founder of A. A. Low & Bros., mchts. in the China trade, pres. New York Chamber of Commerce, etc.
1–*m* Jan. 15, 1873, Lois Robbins Curtis, *b* Lynn, Mass., Sept. 6, 1850; dau. of Benjamin Robbins Curtis (1809-74), asso. justice Supreme Court of U.S.; issue: 1–William Gilman, Jr., *b* Far Rockaway, L.I., June 24, 1875; B.A., Yale, '97; M.A., Columbia, 1899, LL.B., 1900; *m* Apr. 19, 1901, Rhoda, dau. of Herbert Marshall Howe, of Phila.; 2–Anna Curtis, *b* Brooklyn, Nov. 25, 1876; *m* 1905, Herbert Grant Watson, now British minister to Guatemala; 3–Lois Curtis, *b* Newport, R.I., Aug. 1, 1878; 4–Benjamin Robbins Curtis, *b* Fairhaven, Mass., June 22, 1880; B.A., Yale, '02; LL.B., Harvard, 1905; lawyer; capt. and maj. U.S.A., World War (see Who's Who in America); *m* Feb. 15, 1922, Virginia, dau. of Theodore B. Wagner (issue: Caroline, *b* 1923; Malcolm Scollay, *b* 1926); 5–Rosamond Curtis, *b* Fairhaven, Aug. 8, 1882; *m* June 1, 1905, Rev. John Henry Chapman; 6–Harriette, *b* Fairhaven, Aug. 8, 1884; 7–Esther Hope, *b* Bristol, R.I., June 16, 1888; *m* Apr. 21, 1910, Rev. Francis K. Little.
1–A.B., Columbia, '65, LL.B., 1867, A.M., 1868. Lawyer. Pres. Hospital Saturday and Sunday Assn. of Brooklyn, etc. (see Who's Who in America). Summer places: "The Bungalow," Bristol, R.I., and "Happyland," Bedford Hills, Westchester Co., N.Y. Residence: 58 Remsen St., Brooklyn, N.Y.

1–**LOWE, Boutelle Ellsworth,** *b* Marion, N.Y., Mar. 24, 1890.
9–Thomas (Low) **Lowe** (*d* 1677; son of Capt. John Low, master of ship "Ambrose" and vice adm. of the fleet which brought Gov. Winthrop's Colony, 1630, lost at sea and never settled in N.E.); settled Chebacco Parish, Essex Co., Mass., 1641; *m* Susannah– (ca. 1598-1684);
8–Dea. Thomas (1632-1712), of Ipswich; commoner, 1668; dea., 1678; built "Old Low House" still standing in Essex, Mass.; in King Philip's War, and received grant of land in Narragansett Tp. (now Buxton, Me.), for his services; *m* 1660, Martha Borman (Thomas[9], *m* Margaret–);
7–Jonathan (1665-1750), *m* 1692, Mary Thomson;
6–Jonathan (*b* 1708), Fitchburg, Mass.; *m* Sarah Perkins (*b* 1711; Abraham[7], *m* Abigail Dodger);
5–Jonathan (1748-1842), began to write name Lowe; minute man in Am. Rev.; *m* 1776, Sarah Perkins (1754-1842);
4–John (1789-1847), Ashford, Cattaraugus Co., N.Y.; farmer; *m* 1818, Fanny Boutelle (1796-1890);
3–Boutelle Asaph (1826-1912), Springville, N.Y.; farmer; insurance; *m* 1850, Harriet Atwood Pierce (1830-1928; Dea. Thomas[4], *m* Catherine Weber);
2–Rev. Ralph Weber (1859-1927), grad. Rochester U., '83, Rochester Theol. Sem., 1888; Bapt. ministry nearly 40 yrs.; *m* 1888, Clara Elizabeth Ellsworth (1864-1917; Charles H.[3], 18th Conn. Vols., *m* Eliza R. Rowley); issue: I–Boutelle Ellsworth (1 above); II–Ernest Howard (1894-1913); III–Vassar Weber (1900-24).
1–*m* June 28, 1926, Louise Alberta Caroline Klein, *b* New York, Sept. 17, 1905; dau. of Albert William Klein, of Yonkers, N.Y., *m* Caroline Wilhelmina Rau.
1–A.B., Denison, '11 (Pi Gamma Mu, Alpha Delta Tau, Lambda Chi Alpha, P.B.K.); A.M., U. of Rochester, 1912; Ph.D., Columbia U., 1918. Head dept. social sciences, Hackensack H.S., since 1920. Author, educator (see Who's Who in America). Mem. Sons Vets. Civil War. Baptist. Republican. Residence: 125 Lawrence Av., Hasbrouck Hts., N.J.

1–**LOWE, Gertrude Merrell (Mrs. William Baird),** *b* Bay City, Mich., Nov. 22, 1870.
9–Robert **Paddock** (qv);
8–Zachariah (1636-1727), *m* 1659, Deborah Sears (1639-1732; Richard[9], qv);
7–Zachariah (1664-1718), *m* 1st, Bethia Hall (1667-1707 or 08; Dea. John[8], *m* Priscilla Bearse);
6–David (*b* 1705), Yarmouth; *m* 1727, Mary Foster;
5–David (1734 or 37-1794), of Harwich, Mass.; *m* 1762, Miriam Belden (1744-1823; Daniel[6], *m* Esther Smith);
4–Horace (1775-1860), *m* Abigail E. Benjamin (1777-1849);
3–Maria, *m* John Jackson **Merrell**;
2–James Chandler (2 below).
10–Rev. Thomas **Foster,** *m* Abigail Wimes (Matthew[11], of Eng.);
9–Sgt. Thomas (1600-82), came in 1634;
8–Dea. John (1642-1732), *m* ca. 1663, Mary Chillingsworth (*d* 1702; Thomas[9]);
7–Dea. Chillingsworth (1680-1764), *m* 1705, Mercy Freeman (1687-1720);
6–Mary (*b* 1709), *m* David **Paddock** (6 above).
2–Lt. James Chandler **Merrell** (1838-1929); see Vol. I, p. 698, Vol. II, p. 47, and Vol. III, p. 311, for other lineages), *m* Julia Rose Wild (1852-1920); issue: I–Gertrude (1 above); II–Elizabeth Wilhelmina (*b* 1872; *m* 1900, John Watrous Case); III–John Hastings (see Vol. II, p. 47); IV–Edna Augusta (*b* 1882; *m* Brace Morgan Parker); V–Charles Albert (*b* 1885).
1–*m* June 28, 1899, William Baird Lowe, *b* Detroit, Mich., Jan. 27, 1871; mng. dir. of Detroit Free Press.; issue: 1–Helen Rosemary (Mrs. William J. Chesbrough, qv); 2–William Baird, Jr. (Jan. 7, 1913-Jan. 8, 1913).
1–U.Mich., ex-'93. Mem. D.A.R., I.A.G., College Club. Residence: 1818 Iroquois Av., Detroit, Mich.

1–**CHESBROUGH, Helen Rosemary Lowe (Mrs. William J.),** *b* Detroit, Mich., Oct. 16, 1900.
20–Sir Nicholas **Lambert,** Lord and Knight of Skipton, Durham and Owlton;
19–Sir Alan, Knight of Owlton;
18–Sir William, *m* Lady Joanne de Umfraville, dau. Lord of Riddesdale;
17–Robert, of Owlton;
16–Henry, of Ongar, Essex, Eng.;
15–Elizabeth (*d* 1509), *m* Thomas **Lyman** (*d* 1509; son of Henry);
14–Henry, *m* Alicia, dau. of Simon Hyde;
13–John, *m* Margaret, dau. of William Girard;
12–Henry, High Ongar (*d* 1587), *m* Phyllis (Phillis) Scott, dau. of John Scott;
11–Richard (qv), *m* Sarah, dau. of Roger Osborne;
10–Richard (1617-62), *m* as her 1st husband, Hepzibah Ford (*d* 1683; Thomas[11], came in the "Mary and John," 1630);
9–Sarah, *m* 1666, John **Marsh,** Jr. (*b* 1643; John[10], from Eng., 1636, *m* Ann, dau. of Gov. John Webster, qv);
8–Sarah (*b* 1673), *m* 1694, Lt. John **Merrell** (1669-1748; John[9]; Nathaniel[10]);
7–Caleb (1707-35), *m* Mercy Sedgwick (Capt. Samuel[8]; William[9]; Gen. Robert[10], qv);

6–Capt. Abijah (1734-1823), minute man in Am. Rev.; *m* 1st, Sarah Barton (William[7]);
5–Caleb Barton (1764-1842), soldier Am. Rev.; *m* Sarah Jackson (Col. Giles[6], Am. Rev.);
4–John Jackson (1797-1866), *m* Maria Paddock;
3–James Chandler (1838-1929), *m* 1870, Julia Rose Wild (1852-1920); see Vol. II, p. 47;
2–Gertrude Merrell (qv), *m* 1899, William Baird **Lowe** (*b* 1871; Thomas[3], *m* Mary Ann, dau. of Charles Lee Poole).
1–*m* June 7, 1924, William James Chesbrough (see Vol. II, p. 48); issue: 1–William Lowe, *b* Detroit, Mich., June 1, 1926; 2–Richard McCormick, *b* Detroit, Dec. 16, 1929.
1–Ed. Liggett Sch.; Wells Coll., ex-'23. Mem. Junior League. Residence: 1015 Yorkshire Rd., Grosse Pointe, Mich.

PHINEAS KIMBALL (b May 1, 1822-d Oct. 1900), photograph taken in 1850.

1–**LUBBE, Augusta Bernardine Kimball (Mrs. George A.),** *b* W. Fairlee, Vt., Aug. 23, 1867.
9–Henry **Wolcott** (qv);
8–Capt. Simon (1624-87), freeman, 1673; dep. 1673; cdr. Simsbury Train Band, 1673; capt. of Ft. at Simsbury, Conn.; selectman, 1674; trooper from Windsor under Maj. Mason, 1657; *m* 1657, Joanna Cook (1638-57); *m* 2d, 1661, Martha Pitkin (1638-1719), sister of William Pitkin, atty. gen. and treas. (Rev. William[9], *m* Elizabeth Stanley);
7–Henry (1670-1747), lt. Windsor Train Band; an original propr. Tolland and Wellington, Conn.; capt. French and Indian War; *m* 1696, Jane Allyn;
6–Lt. Henry (1697-1757-58), dep. Gen. Assembly, 1717,21,22; mem. Council, 1725; *m* Dec. 27, 1716, Abagail Cooley;
5–Penelope (1724-1816), *m* 1749, John **Colton** (1729-1813), Am. Rev.; see Vol. I, p. 700, for Colton lineage;
4–John (1754-1833), Am. Rev.; *m* 1786, Hannah Pomeroy (1763-1849); see Vol. II, p. 185, for Pomeroy lineage;
3–Abigail (1788-1858), *m* 1805, Phineas **Kimball** (1780-1869); see Vol. I, p. 700, and Vol. III, p. 311, for Kimball lineage;
2–Phineas (2 below).
9–Hon. Matthew **Allyn** (qv);
8–Capt. Thomas (*d* 1695/96), *m* 1658, Abigail Warham (*b* 1638; Rev. John[9], M.A., Oxford, 1619, minister first ch. of Windsor);
7–Jane (1670-1702), *m* Henry **Wolcott** (7 above).
8–Ens. Benjamin **Cooley** (qv);
7–Benjamin (1656-1731), *m* Abigail (du Bagg) Bagg (1673-1739; John Bagg[8], came to Springfield, Mass., 1657, *m* 1659, Hannah, dau. of Henry Burt, qv);
6–Abigail (*b* 1695-Nov. 16, 1740), *m* Henry **Wolcott** (6 above).
2–Phineas **Kimball** (1822-1900), see portrait; *m* 1866, Bernardine Ic-King (*b* 1842; Bernard[3]); for issue see Vol. II, p. 185.
1–*m* June 1, 1899, George Anthony Lubbe, *b* Quincy, Ill., Mar. 5, 1865; son Bernard Lubbe; issue: 1–Charles Kimball, *b* Peoria, Ill., Feb. 9, 1901.
1–Mem. D.A.R., I.A.G., Nat. Soc. Women Desc. A. & H. A. Co. Summer Place: West Fairlee, Vt. Residence: 217 Columbia Terrace, Peoria, Ill.

1–**LOWRIE, Charles Nassau,** *b* Warriors Mark, Pa., Apr. 8, 1869.
4–John (Lawrie) **Lowrie** (1749-1840), from Loch Rutten, Scotland, to New York, 1793; settled finally in Butler Co., Pa., 1798; *m* Catherine Cameron;
3–Walter (1784-1868), U.S. senator from Pa., 1819-25; sec. U.S. Senate, 1825-36; sec. Presbyn. Bd. of Fgn. Missions, 1836-68; *m* 1st, 1808, Amelia McPherrin (*d* 1832; Rev. John[4]);
2–Jonathan Roberts (2 below).
6–Charles John (Von) **Nassau** (son of Charles Henry, who was chief jager-meister to Frederick August, I, King of Saxony); went to Holland, thence to America, 1745, settling in Pa.;
5–Charles William, merchant, Phila.; *m* Hester Clymer;
4–William, importing merchant, Phila.; treas. Presbyn. Bd. of Domestic Missions, etc.; *m* Ann Parkinson;
3–Charles William, D.D. (1804-78), A.B., U. of Pa., 1821; 4th pres. Lafayette Coll., 1848-50; *m* 1826, Hannah Hamill;
2–Matilda Hamill (2 below).
6–Robert **Todd,** of Trappe, Pa.; *m* Isabella–;
5–Col. Andrew, pvt. Pa. Line in Am. Rev.; *m* Hannah Boyer;
4–Isabella, *m* Robert **Hamill,** of Norristown, Pa.;
3–Hannah, *m* Rev. Charles William **Nassau** (3 above).
2–Jonathan Roberts **Lowrie** (1823-85), lawyer; *m* 1848, Mary A. Lyon (1824-63); *m* 2d, 1866, Matilda Hamill Nassau (1840-1919); issue (1st marriage): I–Sara Roberts; II–Dr. William (*m* 1887, Bertha Finney); III–Roberts (*m* 1889, Sue Brisbin); issue (2d marriage): I–Charles Nassau (1 above).
1–*m* Nov. 5, 1905, Isabelle, dau. of Alexander Forrest, of Halifax, N.S., Can.; issue: 1–Charles Nassau, Jr., *b* New York, N.Y.; 2–Barbara Forrest, *b* New York.
1–Ph. B., Yale-S., '91. Landscape architect, New York, since 1896. Mem. N.Y. State Fine Arts Commn., N.Y. City Commn. on Plan and Survey. Mem. Am. Soc. Landscape Architects (past pres.), S.R., etc. Clubs: Century (N.Y.), Carteret (N.J.). Residence: 1001 Park Av., New York, N.Y.

1–**LOWTHER, Granville,** *b* Doddridge Co., Va. (now W.Va.), Jan. 19, 1848.
7–William **Lowther** (qv);
6–Robert (*d* 1780), *m* 1736, Aquilla Reese, of Plumstead Tp., Bucks Co., Pa.;
5–William (1742-1814), col. Am. Rev.; *m* Sudna Hughes (Thomas[6], killed by Indians, 1778, while defending Ft. Lowther);
4–William (1768-1859), *m* 1789, Margaret Morrison (*b* 1768; Alexander[5], *m* Mary Lowther);
3–Alexander (1791-1864), *m* Sarah Ireland (Alexander[4], *m* Elizabeth Ragan, White Oak, W. Va.);
2–Jesse (1823-1909), farmer; justice of the peace; *m* Hannah Leeson (1827-1911; William[3]); for issue see Vol. I, p. 699.
1–*m* Dec. 22, 1869, Elizabeth Ann Boyce (1850-89), dau. Thomas Boyce, Whitlesy, Eng.; issue: 1–Ada May, *b* at Palermo, Ill., Sept. 19, 1871; *m* May 15, 1889, Horace S. Wilkinson (see Vol. III, p. 584); 2–John Franklin, *b* Cherry Point, Ill., Apr. 5, 1874; Syracuse U., '02; *m* Mar. 24, 1914, Kathryn (*b* Nov. 20, 1885), dau. Jared Bush; 3–Charles C. (see Vol. I, p. 700); 4–Lola Edith, *b* Cherry Point, Ill., Dec. 22, 1878; Syra-

cuse U.; served with Y.M.C.A., in France, 18 months; 5–Mabel Elizabeth (Mrs. William Tefft Schwarz, see Vol. III, p. 585).
1–Ed. pub. schs. and under pvt. tutors; (D.D., Baker, 1899). Congl. minister, horticulturist (see Who's Who in America). Mem. S.A.R. Residence: Seattle, Washington.

JAMES T. LUKENS (1807-84), was the first to manufacture mineral water, or soda water, in fountains for the trade; The business began at Philadelphia in 1832, and in 1843 Mr. Lukens sold out to the Lippincotts, who have continued the business ever since.

1–**LUKENS, Herman Tyson,** *b* Phila., Pa., Jan. 29, 1865.
6–Jan **Lukens** (qv);
5–Abraham (1703-76), of Towamencin, Pa.; *m* 1st, 1727, Mary Marle (1702-70; Thomas[6], *m* Margaret–);
4–William (1734-84), to Haverford, Pa., 1782; *m* 1762, Catherine Evans (1740-1818; Edward[5], *m* Elizabeth Griffith);
3–Amos (1775-1845), *m* 1803, Sarah Tyson (1779-1842; James[4], *m* Sarah Harper);
2–James Tyson (2 below).
7–Jan **Lukens,** as above;
6–William (1687-1740), of Horsham, Pa.; *m* 1710, Elizabeth Tyson (1690-1765; Rynear[7], qv);
5–William (1713-1803), *m* 2d, 1752, Elizabeth Pennington (1735-1815; Daniel[6], *m* Elizabeth Michener);
4–Joseph (1772-1842), Phila.; *m* 1794, Ann Webster (1773-1835; Naylor[5], *m* Martha Fisher);
3–Martha (1797-1883), of Conshohocken, Pa.; *m* 1819, John **Jones** (1795-1886; Isaac[4], *m* Elizabeth Yerkes).
2–James Tyson **Lukens** (1807-84), carriage maker and merchant, Phila.; *m* 1835, Phebe Lewis (1805-54); *m* 2d, 1858, Elizabeth Jones (1830-1906), of Phila.; issue (1st marriage): I–John Lewis (1836-ca. 1870; *m* Purnelia Catharine Jones; *m* 2d, Mary Jane Crigler); II–Edward Hicks (1840-70; *m* Mary Jane Yeo); issue (2d marriage): I–Anna Jane (1859-60); II–Howard Jones (1861-95; *m* Florence M. Jenkins, 1863-1928); III–Herman Tyson (1 above).
1–*m* June 29, 1897, Eleanor Lee Spencer, *b* Baltimore, Md.; dau. of John M. Spencer, of Baltimore, *m* Elizabeth Jenkins.
1–A.B., U. of Pa., '85 (P.B.K.), A.M., 1888; Ph.D., Jena U., Germany, 1891; P.D., Clark U., 1896. Teacher biology, Northwest Division H.S., Chicago, 1891-94; lecturer on edn., Bryn Mawr Coll., 1896-97; head training teacher, State Normal Sch., California, Pa., 1898-1907; teacher, Francis W. Parker Sch., since 1907. Author (see Who's Who in America). Clubs: City, Collegiate. Mem. Soc. of Friends. Residence: 506 Arlington Pl., Chicago, Ill.

1–**LUCKEY, Leonard Wilson Arnold,** *b* Adams Co., Ind., Oct. 6, 1857.
5–Andrew **Luckey,** from Londonderry, Ireland, ca. 1735; settled in Chester Co., Pa.; removed to Cumberland Co., Pa.;
4–Robert (ca. 1753-1797), miller; of Cumberland, Westmoreland, and Washington cos., Pa.; pvt. in Cumberland Co. militia, 1779-82; suffered heavy financial loss thru sympathy with the colonies; *m* 1779, Catherine MacIlvaine (1755-1835; John[5], of Shippensburg, Pa.);
3–Andrew (1781-1856), Decatur, Ind., where he died; *m* 1st ca. 1805, Mary Mahaffee (ca. 1789-1834), of Wayne Co., O.;
2–George W(ashington) (1822-86), farmer, Decatur, Ind.; commr. Adams Co., Ind., 1869-75; pvt. Co. E, 107th Vol. Inf., *m* 1841, Drusilla Arnold (1820-85; Samuel[3], of Sharon, Medina Co., O., *m* Elizabeth Plum); issue: I–Mary Elizabeth (1842-1923; *m* P. B. Kern); II–Louisa Isabel (1845-1920; *m* John Brock); III–Lavina Ellen (1849-89; *m* George B. Cline); IV–Martha Drusilla (1851-1928; *m* John P. Spuller); V–George Washington Andrew (*b* 1855; see Who's Who in America and Am. Men of Science; *m* Bertha M. Musson); VI–Leonard Wilson Arnold (1 above); VII–J(ames) Thomas W(ilkerson) (1862-1929; *m* Mary E. Wolfe; *m* 2d, Nettie Louisa Kimbrough).
1–*m* Sept. 14, 1882, Lucy Ellen Stone (*b* Decatur, Ind., Feb. 21, 1861-*d* Indianapolis, Ind., Nov. 26, 1919); issue: 1–Herbert Arnold, *b* Decatur, Ind., Jan. 20, 1884; A.B., U. of N.Y., '01; B.L., Indiana Coll. of Law, 1904; pres. Indianapolis Life Underwriters' Assn.
1–*m* 2d, June 1, 1921, Ethel Irene Zwick, *b* Indianapolis, Ind., Sept. 4, 1890; issue: 1–Leonard, Jr., *b* New York, Apr. 27, 1925.
1–Grad. teachers course, Northern Ind. Normal Coll., 1880, A.B., Northern Ind. U., '85, M.A., 1887, Ph.D., 1892; B.D., McCormick Theol. Sem., Chicago, 1890; (D.D., Divine Metaphysics, Harvard, 1924. Pastor, First Ch., Crown Point, 1889-94, First Ch., Castile, N.Y., 1894-1901, Sixth Ch., Indianapolis, 1901-05, Grace Ch., 1919-20. Author. Presbyterian. Residence: 43 W. 84th St., New York, N.Y.

1–**LUDEY, Patty Spence (Mrs. Charles Addison),** *b* Bradford, Pa., Oct. 18, 1893.
10–Richard **Warren,** Mayflower Pilgrim (qv);
9–Anne, *m* 1633, Thomas **Little** (qv);
8–Hannah (*d* 1710), *m* 1662, Stephen **Tilden** (bap. 1629-1711; Nathaniel[9], qv);
7–Mary (1668-1718), *m* 1692/93, James **Thomas;**
6–John (1700-85), *m* Hannah Spofford (1708-95);
5–Malachi (1747-94), *m* 1770, Mary McCall (1747-1813);
4–William (1782-1855), Chatham, N.Y.; *m* 1808, Emma Halsey (1792-1877);
3–Patty Smith (1823-92), *m* 1857, Uriah Lewis **Davis** (1812-97);
2–Dora Sophia (2 below).
9–James **Pitney** (qv);
8–Sarah (1628/29-1682), *m* John **Thomas** (*b* 1629), from Eng. in the "Hopewell" to Marshfield, Mass.;
7–James (1663-ca. 1718), *m* Mary Tilden (7 above).
2–Dora Sophia Davis (see Vol. III, p. 428), *m* 1886, Horatio Moses **Spence** (1852-1924); issue: I–Davis (1889-1924); II–Patty (1 above).
1–*m* Mar. 11, 1914, Charles Addison Ludey, *b* Bellaire, O., July 7, 1874; son of Chris Ludey, of Woodsfield, O., *m* Emma A. Headley; issue: 1–Emma Suzanne, *b* Parkersburg, W.Va., Apr. 14, 1920; 2–Patsy Joan, *b* Parkersburg, Aug. 30, 1924.
1–Ed. Marietta Acad., '10 (Beta Theta). Mem. C.D.A., D.A.R. Residence: "Seven Gables," Parkersburg, W.Va.

1–**LUTZ, Ralph Haswell,** *b* Circleville, O., May 18, 1886.
7–John Michael **Lutz** (1689-ca. 1760), from Wurttemberg, Germany, to Pa.; settled in Lower Saucon Tp., Bucks (now Northampton) Co., Pa., ca. 1710; pvt. in Pa. militia, 1758; in transport service in French and Indian War; an organizer of Williams Lutheran Ch., Lower Saucon Tp.;

HON. SAMUEL LUTZ, centenarian, farmer, surveyor, legislator, life-long student (b March 13, 1789, in Upper Saucon Tp., Lehigh Co., Pa.-died Sept. 1, 1890, in Saltcreek Tp., Pickaway Co., Ohio).

6-Ulrich (1738-90), of Springfield Tp., Bucks Co., Pa.; also owned plantation of 426 acres, Northumberland Co., Pa.; pvt. Bucks Co. militia and associator in Am. Rev., 1775; *m* ca. 1760, Elizabeth (Deiss) Dice (1743-1818), family from Zweibrüken, Germany, 1741; two uncles in giant regt. of Frederick William, I;
5-John Jacob (1762-1824), landowner and farmer, Northumberland Co., Pa., and Pickaway Co., O.; boy soldier in Am. Rev.; pioneer in Ohio, 1802; *m* 1788, Elizabeth Demuth (1756-1842; Rev. Demuth[6], Dunkard minister, Quakertown, Pa., bro.-in-law of Christopher Sauer, noted German printer of Phila.);
4-Hon. Samuel (1789-1890), of Saltcreek Tp., Pickaway Co., O. (see portrait and biography); *m* 1811, Elizabeth Fetherolf;
3-John A. (1824-1900), A.B., Wittenberg Coll., 1853, M.A., 1855; admitted to Ohio bar, 1855; settled at Circleville, Pickaway Co.; genealogist and local historian; *m* 1855, Mary Humphreys;
2-Harry Elmer (2 below).
7-Peter **Fetherolf,** from Germany ca. 1720; settled in Berks Co., Pa.;
6-Jacob, farmer, landowner, Albany Tp., Berks Co.; pvt. Berks Co. militia in Am. Rev.;
5-Philip (1765-1844), *m* Catherine Lesher (1768-1844);
4-Elizabeth (Dec. 15, 1793-Apr. 15, 1868), *m* Samuel **Lutz** (4 above).
6-Robert **Humphreys** (*d* 1809), from Co. Tyrone, Ireland, to Pa., with his bros. Samuel and John, 1755; removed to Greenbrier Co., Va., 1780; *m* in Ireland, Elizabeth-;
5-John (1764-1857), came with his father; to Mason Co., Ky., 1793; went with Gen. Simon Kenton to Clark Co., O., 1799, settled nr. Springfield; *m* 1790, Jane Ward;
4-James (1791-1858), *m* 1824, Catherine Keifer (*d* 1883; George[5], of Clark Co., O., *m* Margaret, dau. Michael Hivner, of Washington Co., Md., *m* Catherine-; George[6], *m* Margaret Shisler);
3-Mary (1832-94), *m* John A. **Lutz** (3 above).
8-James **Ward** (*b* 1672), from Ulster, Ireland, with his sons, William, James and John, ca. 1735, to Pa.;
7-James (*b* ca. 1700), from Pa. to Augusta Co., Va.;
6-Capt. James (1727-74), killed by Indians in battle of Pt. Pleasant; *m* 1748, Phebe Lockhart (*d* 1779; Jacob[7], Indian scout, killed by Indians in Va., 1783);
5-Jane (1771-1849), *m* John **Humphreys** (5 above).

8-Peter (Horswell) **Haswell** (son of an early immigrant to Plymouth Colony), settled at Little Compton, R.I.; *m* 1692, Elizabeth-;
7-Peter (*b* 1708);
6-John (*b* 1729), *m* 1750, Mary Wilcox (William[7], of Tiverton, *m* Priscilla Pabodie);
5-Philip (1754-1838), Providence, R.I.; in Am. Rev.; *m* 1776, Mercy West (1756-1830); their g.son, Charles Creighton Hazewell, of Boston, was noted editor and encyclopedist;
4-James Coleman (1792-1846), began to write name Haswell; settled at Circleville, O., 1819; *m* 1814, Hannah Knowles;
3-Andrew Jackson (1826-1905), *m* 1860, Mary Ann May (1831-1909; Michael[4], *m* Lydia, dau. of Rev. Conrad Rieman, German Luth. minister, grad. Heidelberg U., active in Pa. and Ohio; Francis[5], of Frederick Co., Md., *m* Catharine Groce);
2-Florence May (2 below).
9-Henry **Knowles** (1609-70), from Eng. to Warwick, R.I.; *m* ca. 1640, Miss Potter (Robert[10], from Eng. to Lynn, 1630, at Warwick, 1641);
8-William (1645-1727), *m* Alice Fish (*d* 1734; Thomas[9], from Eng., settled at Portsmouth, R.I., 1643);
7-Daniel (1690-1759), *m* 1721, Hannah-;
6-Edward (1739-1824), *m* 1764, Mary (Molly) Bowen (Thomas[7], of Rehoboth, Mass., *m* Elizabeth Pidge);
5-Benjamin (*b* 1770), of Providence; *m* 1793, Hannah States (1773-1820; Peter[6], ens. in French and Indian War);
4-Hannah (1796-1855), *m* James Coleman **Haswell** (4 above);
3-Andrew Jackson, *m* Mary Ann May (3 above);

HARRY ELMER LUTZ, of Seattle, lawyer, editor, author, banker, born Sept. 18, 1860, in Circleville, Ohio, and resident of Pacific Coast from 1890.

2-Florence May (1863-1908), of Circleville; *m* 1885, Harry Elmer **Lutz** (*b* 1860), A.B., Wittenberg Coll., 1879, M.A., 1881; studied in Europe 2 yrs.; admitted to Ohio bar, 1883; owner and editor Circleville Union Herald, 6 yrs.; postmaster under Presidents Arthur and Harrison; removed to Seattle, Wash., 1890; pres. Bank of Clallam Co., 29 yrs. (see portrait); issue: I-Ralph Haswell (1 above); II-Donald Haswell (*b* 1887; *m* Clara Dean); III-Harold Haswell (*b* 1896; *m* Martha Knapp); IV-Hugh Ward (*b* 1898; *m* Helen Walsh).
1-*m* Sept. 12, 1927, Margaret Longyear, *b* Hibbing, Minn., Oct. 20, 1899; dau. of Edmund Joseph Longyear, of Minneapolis, Minn., and Altadena, Calif.
1-A.B., Stanford U., '06 (Kappa Sigma, Delta Chi, P.B.K.); studied law same univ.; LL.B., U. of Wash., 1907; Ph.D., Heidelberg, 1910. Asso. prof. history and dir. Hoover War

Library, Stanford U., since 1920. Author (see Who's Who in America). Student 1st O.T.C., Presido, Calif., 1917; commd. 1st lt., U.S. Inf.; assigned to hdqrs. 40th Div.; with A.E.F. in France, assigned hdqrs. 1st Army in Argonne; later with Am. Mil. Mission, Berlin, with Supreme Econ. Council, in Paris, and spl. mission to Poland; hon. disch., Sept. 6, 1919. Mem. S.A.R., etc. Republican. Presbyn. Clubs: Bohemian, Commonwealth, University (San Francisco), College (Seattle). Residence: Stanford U., Calif.

1-**LUDLOW, Myra Margarette Hunt (Mrs. Jacob L.)**, *b* Little York, N.J., Oct. 15, 1864.
8-Ralph **Hunt** (*d* 1677), at Newtown, L.I., N.Y., 1656; freeman; freeholder; schepen; commd. lt. provincial troops of N.Y. by Gov. Nicholas, 1665; *m* Ann-;
7-Samuel (will dated 1717), removed to Maidenhead, now Lawrenceville, N.J.; *m* Abigail-;
6-Thomas, *m* Abigail-;
5-Edward, *m* Mary-;
4-John, *m* Anna Taylor;
3-George, *m* Mary Insley;
2-Edward Insley (1832-1911), *m* 1857, Sarah Lesh (1834-92).
1-*m* Jan. 5, 1887, Jacob Lott Ludlow (Dec. 20, 1862-Aug. 18, 1930); son of Capt. Samuel Ludlow, of Spring Lake, N.J.; issue: 1-Annie Hunt, *b* Winston-Salem, N.C., Dec. 9, 1887; ed. Bryn Mawr and Agnes Scott colls.; *m* Nov. 17, 1909, Joseph F. Cannon; 2-Margarette Hunt, *b* Easton, Pa., Sept. 1, 1890; Agnes Scott Coll.; *m* Mar. 18, 1915, Henry Belo Shelton; 3-Louise Hunt, *b* Winston-Salem, Aug. 11, 1892; Agnes Scott Coll.; *m* Nov. 7, 1919, R. McBrayer.
1-Mem. C.D.A., D.A.R. Residence: 434 Summit St., Winston-Salem, N.C.

1-**LUKENS, Charles**, *b* W. Mansfield, O., Feb. 10, 1869.
7-Jan (Lücken) **Lukens** (qv);
6-Joseph (*b* 1705), *m* 1728, Susanna Marle (1704-71);
5-Peter (*d* 1811), Berks Co., Pa.; *m* 1753, Martha Jones (1726-1803);
4-Jonathan (1758-1843), to Frederick Co., Va., ca. 1780; *m* 1791, Lydia Fawcett (1761-1834);
3-Joseph Fawcett (1795-1871), to Warren Co., O., 1822, to Logan Co., O., 1833; farmer; *m* 1819, Elizabeth Fawcett (1791-1865);
2-John Fawcett (1824-1903), of W. Mansfield, Logan Co., O.; educator, surveyor and civil engr.; farmer; *m* 1863, Louisa Keturah Swartz (1828-1910), of Marlboro, O.
1-*m* Sept. 27, 1893, Lotta Grace Painter, *b* E. Liberty, O., Aug. 17, 1869; dau. of Alfred Painter, of E. Liberty; issue: 1-John Alfred, *b* W. Mansfield, O., Oct. 8, 1897; M.D., U.Mich., 1922; *m* 1927, Margaret, dau. of Dr. H. H. Sugg, of Mt. Vernon, Ind.; 2-Ruth Lotta, *b* Toledo, O., Aug. 17, 1904; A.B. in edn., U.Mich., '28.
1-B.L., Central (Ohio) Coll., '87; M.D., Ohio State U., 1892; post-grad. work in Phila. and interne in Wills Eye Hosp., Phila., 1898-1900. School teacher 1887-90; practiced medicine, 1892-98; limited practice eye, ear, nose and throat, Toledo, O., 1900-30; chief of staff Flower Hosp., Toledo, 1928-30. Pres. Acad. of Medicine, Toledo and Lucas Co., O., 1917-18; pres. Ohio State Med. Assn., 1920-21. Methodist. Republican. Clubs: Sylvania Golf, Torch. Residence: 2410 Warren St., Toledo, O.

1-**LUMMIS, Wilbur Sayre**, *b* E. Orange, N.J., Oct. 10, 1881.
7-Edward (Lumas, Lamos) **Lummis** (*b* 1606), from Eng. to Ipswich, Mass., 1648;
6-Samuel (*b* June 7, 1639), wrote name Lamos; *m* Sarah Smith; *m* 2d, Hannah Divoll;
5-Edward (1667-1754), Cohanzy, N.J.;
4-Edward (1733-1803), of Lower Penns Neck, N.J.; *m* 2d, Elizabeth Waters;
3-Samuel (1793-1826), began to write name Lummis; of N.Y. City; *m* Eliza Valentine;
2-James Valentine (2 below).
5-Stephen **Young**;
4-Aaron (1782-1858), *m* Mary Dyle (Diel or Doyle);
3-James Robert (1822-1914), *m* Janet Thompson.
2-James Valentine **Lummis** (1825-1906), painter, Newark, N.J.; *m* 1848, Mary Elizabeth Mott (1828-70); *m* 2d, Harriet Garland (Young) Hedden (1847-1929); issue (1st marriage): I-Elnathan Carpenter (*b* 1849; *m* Annie Paulina Cooper); II-Hannah F. (1851-53); III-James Valentine, Jr. (1853-84); IV-Edward Price (1856-1926; *m* Jennie Cochrane; *m* 2d, Martha J. Clark); V-David G. Wendell (1858-77); VI-Maria Louisa (1862-1928; *m* George W. Fredricks); VII-William Grant (*b* 1863; *m* Nellie Grover Wilson); VII-Samuel Mott (*b* 1865); IX-Mary Elizabeth (*b* 1867; *m* Fredrick Deer); issue (2d marriage): I-Harry (1873-90); II-Wilbur Sayre (1 above); III-Nellie Winey (*b* 1883; *m* David L. James; *m* 2d, William Burtt; *m* 3d, Harry Christine).
1-*m* May 6, 1913, Ethel Faith Hoffman, *b* Newark, N.J., Feb. 21, 1889; dau. of Isaac P. Hoffman, of Newark; issue: 1-Wilbur Sayre, Jr., *b* Newark, July 18, 1915.
1-Insurance underwriter. Methodist. Residence: 200 Montclair Av., Newark, N.J.

1-**LUTTRELL, John Augustine Adams**, *b* Amissville, Va., Sept. 11, 1878.
7-Robert **Luttrell** (son of Simon, Gent. of the Bed Chamber to Charles, II); came from Ireland; settled in Prince William Co., Va., bet. 1690-1706; *m* his cousin, Anne, dau. of Viscount Gormanston;
6-Richard, of Fauquier Co., Va.;
5-Richard, commd. ens. in Am. Rev.; *m* probably Miss Willis, of Culpeper Co.;
4-Burrell (*d* Nov. 26, 1831), *m* Hannah Button (*d* 1844; Harmon[5]);
3-Richard (*d* Feb. 11, 1874), famous fox hunter; *m* Elizabeth Bywaters (*d* July 6, 1870), of Culpeper Co.;
2-Burrell Edmond (2 below).
5-Thomas **Nelson** (*b* ca. 1775; desc. of "Scotch Tom," traditional); prosperous farmer Fauquier Co., nr. Warrenton;
4-William (*b* ca. 1795);
3-James Richard (ca. 1817-1861), of Culpeper Co.; *m* Mary Conway Griffin (Edward[4], *m* Grace Ball, cousin to Martha Washington, mother of George);
2-Mary Ritchie (1840-1909), *m* 1861, Burrell Edmond **Luttrell** (1838-1915), served as courier for Gens. J. E. B. Stuart and Beauregard during Civil War; taken prisoner during battle of Strasburg, Point Lookout Prison, 14 months to end of war; issue: I-Capitola L. (*married* John S. Hughes); II-Richard Edmond, *m* Ada Browning); III-Hugh Montgomery (*b* 1868; *m* Atlanta Singleton); IV-William Franklin (*b* 1870-*d* 1923); V-Charles Nelson (1872-1896); VI-James Warren (1874-1907); VII-David Russell (*b* 1876; *m* Edna Clarke); VIII-John Augustine A. (1 above).
1-*m* Oct. 10, 1906, Virginia Quarrier Snodgrass, *b* Parkersburg, W.Va., Dec. 15, 1876; dau. of Judge Kinnaird Snodgrass, of Parkersburg; issue: 1-Mary Ritchie Nelson (Oct. 22-31, 1907); 2-John A. A., Jr., *b* Parkersburg, W.Va., Feb. 12, 1913; 3-Burrell Kinnaird, *b* Waynesboro, Pa., Dec. 9, 1917.
1-Ed. Rappahannock Acad. Now retired. Mem. S.A.R. (state sec. Okla., 1917, now mem. Va. soc.), Sulgrave Instn. Resdience: Williamsburg, Va.

1-**LYON, Scott Cary**, *b* Washington, Pa., Oct. 20, 1884.
4-Ezekiel **Lyon**, of eastern Tennessee:
3-James Adair (1814-82), D.D., Princeton, 1836; Presbyterian minister and educator (see Encyclopaedia of the Presbyterian Church in the U.S.A., 1884); *m* Adelaide Eliza Deaderick;
2-James Adair (2 below).
5-John Paul **Barringer** (1721-1807), from Wurttemburg, to Pa., 1743, settled at Mt. Pleasant, N.C., 1749; *m* Catharine Blackwelder;
4-Gen. Paul (1778-1844), of Cabarrus Co., N.C.; served in War 1812; many yrs. mem. N.C. Legislature; *m* Elizabeth Brandon (Capt. Matthew L.[5], Rowan, N.C., soldier Am. Rev.);
3-Paul, merchant and planter of Oxford, Miss.; *m* Mary Carson;
2-Elizabeth (1853-1928), of Oxford; *m* James Adair **Lyon** (1852-1915), B.A., Princeton U., '72, A.M., 1875, Ph.D., 1880; LL.B., U. of Miss., 1873; prof. mathematics, York (Pa.) Collegiate Inst., 1874-76; prof. mathematics and natural sciences, Highland U., Kan., 1876-78; prof. chemistry, Washington and Jefferson, 1878-85; prof. natural sciences, Southwestern Presbyn. U., 1885-; issue: I-James Adair

(Tulane U.; *m* Elizabeth Antrim); II–Paul Barringer (*d* 1883); III–Theodoric Cecil (*d* 1927); IV–Scott Cary (1 above); V–Elizabeth Barringer (*m* William E. Cox).
1–*m* Dec. 22, 1909, Malline Bradford, *b* Center, Ala., June 27, 1886; dau. of William Bradford, M.D., of Cedartown, Ga.; issue: 1–William Adair, *b* Clarksville, Tenn., Mar. 17, 1911; 2–Malline Bradford, *b* Clarksville, Apr. 22, 1913.
1–B.A., Southwestern Presbyn. U., '04, M.A., 1905 (D.Sc., 1926); M.A., Tulane, 1909. Prof. mathematics, Ala. Presbyn. Coll., 1909-10; prof. chemistry, 1910-17, prof. biology and dean, 1917-25, Southwestern Presbyn. U.; prof. biology, Davidson Coll., since 1926. Mason. K.P. Club: Kiwanis. Residence: Davidson, N.C.

MOSES LYMAN, eighth in descent, first born son.

1–**LYMAN, Moses,** *b* Windsor Locks, Conn., July 17, 1865.
10–Richard **Lyman** (qv);
9–John (1623-90), *m* Dorcas Plumb;
8–Moses (1662-1701), *m* Ann–;
7–Capt. Moses (1689-1762), *m* Mindwell Sheldon (1692-1780);

FLORENCE (VAN FLEET) LYMAN, wife of Moses Lyman, eighth in descent, and mother of Moses Van Rensselaer Lyman, ninth in descent. Ancestors came from Utrecht, Holland in 1662 to New Amsterdam.

6–Dea. Moses (1713-68), *m* Sarah Hayden, or Heighton (1716-1808);
5–Col. Moses (1743-1829), served corp. to col. Am. Rev.; *m* 1st, Ruth Collins (*d* 1775);
4–Moses (1768-1844), *m* Elizabeth Buell;
3–Moses (1810-83), *m* Mary Ann Holley;
2–Moses (1836-1917), *m* 1863, Ellen Augusta Douglas (1840-71); for issue see Vol. II, p. 376.
1–*m* Aug. 17, 1892, Florence Van Fleet, *b* Williamsport, Pa., Feb. 18, 1862; dau. of S. Van Rensselaer Van Fleet, *m* Elvira DuBois, of Williamsport, Pa.; issue: 1–Moses Van Rensselaer (Dec. 20, 1896-May 11, 1897).
1–Ed. Waverly (N.Y.) High Sch., Poughkeepsie Mil. Acad., and M.I.T. Mechanical engineer, C.,M.&St.P. Ry., Springfield Foundry, Baush Machine Tool Co. Jr. warden, St. Andrew's-in-Longmeadow Episcopal Ch. Mem. S.A.R., Longmeadow Hist. Soc., Institute of Am. Genealogy, Mass. Hort. Soc., etc. Clubs: Springfield Garden, Springfield Country, Suffield (Conn.) Country. Mason (K.T., Shriner). Residence: 16 Westmoreland Av., Longmeadow, Mass.

1–**LYON, George Armstrong,** *b* Erie, Pa., Oct. 7, 1879.
6–John **Lyon** (1705-80), of Scottish ancestry; from Ireland to Pa., 1763; settled in Cumberland Co., now Milford Tp., Juniata Co.; warrant for his tract, 270 acres, dated 1766; received a grant of 20 acres for the use of the Presbyn. ch. of Tuscarora, where he is buried; *m* 1728, Margaret Armstrong (*d* ca. 1793), sister of John Armstrong (James[7], of Ireland; Edward[8], of Scotland);
5–William (1729-1809), to Carlisle, Pa. ca. 1750; he and his uncle, John Armstrong, laid out the town of Carlisle, 1751; 1st lt., Pa. regt., 1757-59; with expdn. against Ft. DuQuesne, 1758; magistrate, 1764; mem. Com. of Safety, 1776; prothonotary for Cumberland Co., 1779,91, 1802-05; clk. of Orphans Ct. of Cumberland Co., 1779,91, 1802,05; *m* 2d, 1768, Ann Fleming (*b* 1748);
4–Samuel (*b* 1775), mcht., Baltimore, Md.; *m* 1800, Betty Brown, of Wilmington, Del.;
3–Rev. George Armstrong, D.D. (1806-71), *m* 1829, Mary Sterrett (*d* 1871);
2–George Armstrong (2 below).
8–John **Vincent,** Huguenot, from France to New York, naturalized, 1687; *m* Susanne Nuquerque;
7–Levi (1676-1763), settled nr. Newark, N.J.; *m* Esther Tourneau;
6–John (1709-1801), *m* Elizabeth Doremus;
5–Cornelius (1737-1812), of Milton, Pa.; *m* Phebe Ward;
4–John (1772-1860), asso. judge Ct. Common Pleas, Erie Co.; moved to Waterford, Pa.; *m* 2d, Nancy Anderson;
3–Bethuel Boyd (1803-76), civil engr., iron founder, banker, Erie, Pa.; *m* 1834, Sarah Ann Strong;
2–Rose (2 below).
8–Elder John **Strong** (qv);
7–John (1626-98), *m* 2d, 1664, Elizabeth Warriner;
6–Jacob (1673-1750), *m* 1698, Abigail Bissell;
5–Timothy (1719-1803), vol. with Am. soldiers at relief of New London; *m* 2d, 1770, Abi Collins;
4–Capt. Martin (1770-1858), *m* 2d, 1798, Sarah Drake;
3–Sarah Ann (*d* 1901), *m* Bethuel Boyd **Vincent** (3 above);
2–Rose (1842-94), grad. Farmington Sch.; *m* Rear Admiral George Armstrong **Lyon** (1837-1914), Dartmouth, '58; issue: I–George Armstrong (1 above); II–B. B. Vincent.
1–*m* June 1, 1914, Marjorie Randolph Van Wickle, *b* Cleveland, O., Sept. 12, 1883; dau. of Augustine Stout Van Wickle, of Hazleton, Pa.
1–B.A., Yale, '00; LL.B., Harvard, 1904. Mem. firm of N. W. Halsey & Co., bankers, New York, N.Y. Clubs: Tennis and Racquet (New York), Exchange, Yale (Boston), The Country Longwood Cricket. Residence: 209 Newton St., Brookline, Mass.

1–**LYON, T(homas) Lyttleton,** *b* Pittsburgh, Pa., Feb. 17, 1869.
5–James **Lyon,** never came to America, brother of John, below;
4–Benjamin (1752-1826), came to America, 1763, with his uncle John, below; finally settled in Milford Tp., Cumberland Co., now Juniata Co.; served in Capt. Hendrick's co. of rifle-

men from Cumberland Co. in expdn. against Quebec; participated in battles of Long Island, Brandywine, Paoli, and Germantown; promoted lt., 1776, 1st lt., 1777, capt., 1778, resigned 1779; settled at Shirleysburg, Huntingdon Co., Pa., 1811; *m* 1780, Mary Lyon (*b* 1748; John[5], below);
3-John (1782-1868), head of Lyon, Shorb & Co., iron mfrs., Huntingdon, Centre, Blair, Clarion and Allegheny cos., Pa.; *m* 3d, 1820, Margaret E. Stewart (1796-1835; Samuel[4], of Ireland; Samuel[5], of Scotland);
2-James Benjamin (2 below).
5-John **Lyon** (1705-80), of Scottish ancestry; from Ireland to Pa., 1763; settled in (now) Juniata Co.; *m* 1728, Margaret Armstrong (*d* ca. 1793; James[6], of Ireland; Edward[7], of Scotland);
4-William (1729-1809), to Carlisle, Pa., ca. 1750; he and his uncle, John Armstrong, laid out the town of Carlisle, 1751; 1st lt., Pa. regt., 1757-59; with expdn. against Ft. DuQuesne, 1758; magistrate, 1764; mem. Com. of Safety, 1776; prothonotary for Cumberland Co., 1771, 91, 1802,05; clk. of Orphans Ct. of Cumberland Co., 1779,91, 1802,05; *m* 2d, 1768, Ann Fleming (*b* 1748);
3-George Armstrong (1784-1855), atty. at law; pres. Carlisle Bank; *m* 1815, Anna Glovina Savage;
2-Anna Margaret (2 below).
9-Thomas **Savage** (qv);
8-Capt. John (1624-78), burgess, Northampton Co.; received royal grant of 6,000 acres; *m* 2d, 1668, Mary Robins (Col. Obedience[9], burgess and cdr. of Accomac Co., Va., 1632);
7-Thomas (1669-1728), justice; *m* 1695, Alicia Harminson (Thomas[8], was in Va., 1622, burgess);
6-Thomas (*d* 1737), *m* 1722, Esther Lyttleton;
5-Nathaniel Lyttleton (*d* 1795), officer in Am. Rev.; *m* Anne Reynolds;
4-Thomas Lyttleton (1740-1813), clk. of ct., Northampton Co.; *m* 1796, Margaret Teackle (*b* 1778);
3-Anna Glovina (1797-1876), *m* George Armstrong **Lyon** (3 above).
9-Col. Nathaniel (Littleton) **Lyttleton** (qv);
8-Col. Southey (1645-79), officer colonial army; burgess; served against Indians and under Gov. Berkeley in Bacon's Rebellion; justice; sheriff, 1663; *m* Elizabeth Bowman (Sir Edmund[9], from Eng. to Accomac, Va., burgess, 1663);
7-Col. Nathaniel (*d* 1703), sheriff; justice; *m* Susanna Waters (Col. William[8], *m* Isabel Harmanson);
6-Esther (*d* 1764), *m* Thomas **Savage** (6 above).
2-James Benjamin **Lyon** (1821-1909), glass mfr., Pittsburgh; *m* 1850, Anna Margaret Lyon (1827-97); issue: I-Ellen Douglas (*b* 1852; D.A.R.); II-John Glamis (*b* 1855; *m* 1882, Adelina C. Langworthy); III-Margaret Stewart (*b* 1858; D.A.R.; *m* 1895, J. Ernest Yalden); IV-James Benjamin (*b* 1860); V-George Alexander (1863-1917); VI-Mary Lowrie (*b* 1866; D.A.R.; *m* 1890, Augustus P. Murdoch); VII-Thomas Lyttleton (1 above).
1-*m* Mar. 22, 1899, Bertha Laura Clark, *b* Lincoln, Neb., Oct. 20, 1874; dau. of John Revere Clark, *m* Amelia B. Gaston; issue: 1-John Lyttleton, *b* Lincoln, Neb., Feb. 4, 1901; Cornell, '22; *m* July 23, 1923, Mary Frances, dau. of Jesse William Fox, of Scott, Miss.; 2-George Clark, *b* Lincoln, June 6, 1906; Cornell, 1929.
1-B.S.A., Cornell, '91 (Phi Gamma Delta, Sigma Xi), Ph.D., 1904; studied agrl. chemistry, U. of Goettingen, 1893-94. Prof. agronomy, Cornell, since 1906. Author (see Who's Who in America). Address: Cornell University, Ithaca, N.Y.

1-**LYNCH, Harriet Louise Husted (Mrs. Jerome M.)**, *b* New York, N.Y., Aug. 16, 1864.
9-Robert **Husted** (1596-1652), from Eng., 1636, settled at Stamford, Conn.; witness to Indian deed, 1640; received land grant, 1642; *m* Elizabeth– (*d* 1654);
8-Angell (ca. 1620-1706), witness to Indian deed, 1640; an original patentee, named in the patent granted to Greenwich, 1665;
7-Samuel (1670-1741), *m* Elizabeth–;
6-Joseph, *m* Deborah Ferris;

RICHARD WATSON HUSTED (1835-1927), one of the three founders of the New England Conservatory of Music, and treasurer of Boston University for 35 years.

5-Nathaniel (*b* 1748), corpl. Am. Rev.; *m* Hannah Webb;
4-Nathaniel (1774-1849), moved to Alford, Mass., 1797; *m* 1796, Anna Stoddard;
3-John B. (1804-96), Watertown, Mass.; *m* 1831, Harriet E. McLellan;
2-Richard Watson (2 below).
9-Anthony **Stoddard** (qv);
8-Solomon (1643-1729), A.B., Harvard, 1662; settled at Northampton; first librarian of Harvard Coll.; *m* 1670, Esther (Warham) Mather (1644-1736; Rev. John[9], from Eng. to Dorchester, 1630);
7-Rev. Anthony (1678-1760), Congl. pastor, Woodbury, Conn.; *m* 1st, 1700, Prudence Wells (*d* 1714);
6-Elisha;
5-Elisha;
4-Anna, *m* 1796, Nathaniel **Husted** (4 above).
6-Hugh **McLellan** (*b* 1710), from Londonderry, 1733, settled at "Narragansett No. 7," Me.; *m* his cousin, Elizabeth McLellan;
5-Alexander (*d* 1779), of Gorham, Me.; capt. in Am. Rev.; *m* Margaret–;
4-James (*b* 1777), *m* 1799, Lydia Osgood;
3-Harriet E. (1800-91), *m* 1831, Rev. John B. **Husted** (3 above).
9-John **Osgood** (1595-1651), from Eng. to America, 1637; rep. Mass. Gen. Ct.; settled at Andover, Mass., 1651; *m* ca. 1627, Sarah Booth (*d* 1667);
8-Stephen (ca. 1638-1690/91), *m* 1663, Mary Hooker;
7-Stephen (1670-1749);
6-Stephen (1709-72), *m* 1730, Dorcas Ballard;
5-Stephen (*d* 1812), of Hallowell, Me.; *m* Mary Foster;
4-Lydia (*b* 1779), *m* James **McLellan** (4 above).
6-Dr. Neil **McLean** (*b* 1702), came to America 1736, settled at Hartford; *m* Hannah (Stillman) Caldwell;
5-Lachlan (1739-1813), of Windsor, Conn.; *m* Lucy Humphrey;
4-William (1774-1884), *m* Mrs. Lois Gillette Andrews;
3-Amasa Andrews (1806-87), *m* Louisa Elliston Quinn;
2-Annie (2 below).
6-James **Quinn** (*b* 1745), from Ireland 1769, settled in Washington Co., Pa.; *m* Sarah Henthorn, of Md.;
5-John;
4-Matthew Henthorn (1782-1866), *m* Harriet Louise Elliston (*d* 1822; Joseph Thorp[5], of Nashville, Tenn., *m* Louisa Mullen);
3-Louisa Elliston, *m* Amasa A. **McLean** (3 above);
2-Annie (1842-99), *m* 1860, Richard Watson **Husted** (1835-1927), see portrait; issue: I-Harriet Louise (1 above); II-Elizabeth Waterhouse (*m* Andrew Parker); III-Richard McLellan

(1881-1921; *m* Nora Hodgson); IV–Susan Chadwick (*b* 1882; *m* Albert R. Ross).

1–*m* Jan. 1, 1901, Jerome Morley Lynch, M.D., *b* in Ireland, Jan. 10, 1870; ed. Queen's Coll., Dublin, and Queen's Coll., Edinburgh; came to America 1893; M.D., Rush Med. Coll., Chicago, 1895; surgeon; author (see Who's Who in America).

1–Ed. Young Ladies' Collegiate Inst., Hyde Park, Mass. Author: A Little Game with Destiny; Two Bad Brown Eyes; Patricia; Told by Two; and various short stories. Episcopalian. Dir. Vet. Journalists of Boston; Mem. I.A.G., Pen Women's League, Authors League of America. Clubs: Women's Nat. Golf and Tennis (Glen Head, L.I.), Women's Nat. Country (Washington). Summer residence: Camp Carcassonne, Wolfeboro, N.H. Winter residence: 205 E. 61st St., New York, N.Y.

1–**McADAMS, Fannie Bristol Armstrong (Mrs. Charles L.)**, *b* Independence, Kan., Sept. 17, 1878.

6–Robert **Dyer** (1716-58), from Eng.; settled at Ft. Seybert, Va.; *m* Hannah Britton (Lord Britton[7], of Eng.);

5–Col. James (*b* 1750), of Ft. Seybert; *m* 2d, 1780, Jane Raleston;

4–Esther (1791-1865), of Va.; *m* 1810, Abraham **Trumbo** (1786-1865; George[5], *m* Margaret [Rockafellow] Oates);

3–Margaret (1814-96), of Ottawa, Ill.; *m* 1834, John Strawn **Armstrong** (1810-99);

2–Benjamin (2 below).

10–Robert **Hawkins**, from Eng. in the "Elizabeth and Ann," 1635; settled at Derby, Conn.;

9–Joseph (1642-82), *m* 1668, Abigail Holbrook;

8–Joseph (1669-1733), *m* 1693, Elizabeth Gunn (*b* 1672), of Milford, Conn. (Tebomah[9], *m* Sarah Lane);

7–Capt. Zachariah (1716-1806), Oxford, Conn.; soldier Am. Rev.; *m* 1st, 1737, Sarah Davis (Samuel[8], *m* Mercy Bennett);

6–Sarah (1739-1818), *m* 1761, Sgt. Justus **Bristol** (1736-1820; Eliphalet[7], to Southbury, Conn.; Eliphalet[8], *m* Esther Peck; Henry[9], of Eng., *m* Lydia, dau. of Francis Brown, *m* Mary Edwards);

5–Enoch (1765-1823), *m* 1794, Sally White (1774-1853), of New Haven;

4–Bennett (1795-1827), of Volney, Vt.; *m* 1817, Freelove Morgan (1797-1870; Joseph[5], Am. Rev., *m* Eunice Doolittle);

3–Norris Bennett (1819-1903), Fulton, N.Y.; *m* 1845, Mary Eddy (1824-90);

2–Melitta Melinda Freelove (1846-1905), *m* 1863, Edward Engle; *m* 2d, 1870, Benjamin Marple **Armstrong** (1842-89); issue (1st marriage): I–Carrie L. (*b* 1864; *m* Dr. A. W. Evans); issue (2d marriage): I–Fannie B. (1 above).

1–*m* 1st, Jan. 19, 1898, Charles Lee McAdams, *b* Newborn, Ill. (Mar. 25, 1872-Sept. 8, 1911); son of Dr. Charles E. McAdams, of Wichita, Kan., *m* Margaret Voorhees; issue: 1–Carl Armstrong, *b* Independence, Kan., Oct. 29, 1901; ed. U.Okla. and U.Kan.; *m* Sept. 1, 1923, Georgia, dau. of Jake Tyler Haynes, of Parsons, Kan., *m* Minnie Rannenberg (issue: Charles Armstrong).

1–Ed. Liberty (Mo.) Female Coll., 1897, and Central Coll. (Lexington). Mem. D.A.C., D.F.P.A., D.A.R. (chapter regent, 4 yrs.), Red Cross (mem. exec. bd. and chmn. of auxiliary organizations), O.E.S. Clubs: Country, Social. Summer place: Bovey, Minn. Residence: Independence, Kan.

1–**Mac ARTHUR, Ruth Alberta Brown (Mrs. William A.)**, *b* Searsmont, Me., Nov. 14, 1881.

4–Mathew **Hastings**, of St. George, now Tennant's Harbor, Me.; *m* Hannah Barter;

3–Jane, *m* 1st, Charles **Brown**;

2–William Mathew (2 below).

6–Benjamin **Cooper** (1757-1843), from Cambridge, Mass., to South Thomaston, Me.; *m* Lydia Bartlett (*d* 1821);

5–Benjamin, *m* 2d, Hannah Pillsbury (Joseph[6], from Kittery, Me., to nr. Ash Point or S. Thomaston, Me., blacksmith, *m* Sarah Emery);

4–Mary, *m* 1st, Joseph **Frost**;

3–Nathan, served with 19th Me. Vols., and 26th Me. Cav.; killed in the Battle of the Wilderness, 1864; *m* as her 1st husband, Ruth Ann Lovitt Googins (1834-78; Abram[4], *m* Salome Robbins);

2–Vesta Ella (*b* 1858), *m* William Mathew **Brown** (1852-1927), pres. Long Beach Sash & Door Co., 24 yrs.; issue: I–Walter Melville (*b* 1877; *m* Bessie M. Vickers); II–Grace Edith (*b* 1879); III–Ruth Alberta (1 above); IV–Jennie May (*b* 1884); V–Edna Leona (1889-95); VI–Vesta Estella (*b* 1892); VII–William Howard (*b* and *d* 1895).

1–*m* May 3, 1911, William Austin MacArthur, *b* Portage la Prairie, Can., Sept. 1, 1882; son of Charles MacArthur, of Can.; issue: 1–Ruth Marion, *b* Long Beach, Calif., Mar. 9, 1912; 2–Myron (*b* and *d* 1913); 3–William Charles and 4–Walter Austin (twins), *b* Billings, Mont., May 12, 1916; 5–Meredith Jean, *b* Long Beach, Apr. 7, 1921; 6–Merle Elladice, *b* Long Beach, Jan. 30, 1924.

1–Student U.Minn., 1900-02. Author (see Who's Who in America). Methodist. Republican. Residence: 1525 Redondo Av., Long Beach, Calif.

SILAS McBEE, D.C.L. (1853-1924), educated University of the South; editor, The Churchman, 1896-1912; founder and editor, The Constructive Quarterly, New York.

1–**McBEE, Mary Vardrine**, *b* Lincolnton, N.C., Sept. 24, 1879.

6–Vardry **McBee**, of Scottish descent, settled in Va.;

5–Vardry, Tryon Co., N.C.; soldier Am. Rev.; *m* Hannah Echols;

4–Vardry (1775-1864), Greenville, S.C.; *m* 1804, Jane Alexander;

3–Vardry Alexander (*b* 1818), Lincolnton, N.C.; *m* 1847, Mary Elizabeth Sumner;

2–Silas (2 below).

7–William **Sumner**, from Eng., 1690; settled at Manor Plantation nr. Suffolk, Va.;

6–Dempsey (*d* 1779), vestryman, 1740; rep. Chowan Co. in House of Commons, 1744,45,57,59; justice, 1750; *m* Martha Baker;

5–Jethro (*b* 1758), of N.C.; soldier Am. Rev.; state senator, 1780-82; *m* Elizabeth Turner, of Va.;

4–Benjamin (*b* 1801), Gates Co., N.C.; *m* Sarah Duke Hunt;

3–Mary Elizabeth (1829-1907), *m* Vardry Alexander **McBee** (3 above).

9–Laurence **Baker**, settled in Surry Co., Va., 1644;

8–Henry (*d* 1712);

7–William, *m* Martha Norsworthy;

6–Martha, *m* Dempsey **Sumner** (6 above).

7–William **Duke**, from Eng., 1709; *m* 1735, a dau. of Thomas Edward Green;

6–Green, *m* ——Parkham, of Va.;

5–Elizabeth, *m* Thomas **Hunt**;

4–Sarah Duke, *m* Benjamin **Sumner** (4 above).

2–Silas **McBee** (1853-1924), see portrait and biography; *m* Mary Estelle Sutton (1854-91; Joseph[3], *m* Emma Cassidy Estelle); *m* 2d.

Louise Post, of Great Neck, L.I.; issue (1st marriage): I–Emma Estelle (*b* 1878); II–Mary Vardrine (1 above); III–Malinda Sumner (*b* and *d* 1881); IV–Lucy Lee (1884-87); V–Silas (*b* 1887; *m* Corina Spenitti).
1–A.B., Smith Coll., '06 (Phi Kappa Psi, Alpha Kappa Psi); A.M., Columbia, 1908; studied at U. of Jena, Germany. Teacher at Fairmount Sch., Monteagle, Tenn., 1907; founder, 1909, and prin. Ashley Hall (pvt. sch. for girls), Charleston, S.C. (see Who's Who in America). Episcopalian. Address: Ashley Hall, 172 Rutledge Av., Charleston, S.C.

1–**McCALL, Howard Henry,** *b* Longstreet, Ga., Oct. 19, 1867.
6–Francis **McCall** (*b* ca. 1710), from Ireland, of Scotch descent; was in Pa., 1731, where he married; removed to Mecklenburg Co., N.C.; mem. colonial militia, 1766; patriot in Am. Rev.; constable, 1779;
5–Charles (1732-1814), of Pa., Va., Mecklenburg Co., N.C., settled in the Cheraw Dist., S.C.; granted 200 acres in Effingham Co., Ga., for his services in Am. Rev.; magistrate, Bullock Co.; commr., 1800; justice, 1792; judge of ct. many yrs.; state senator, 1799, 1801,02; mem. House of Rep. from Bullock Co., 1798, 1803,05,-06,08; mem. Constl. Conv. of 1798; *m* 1755, Celete Ann (Nancy) Williams (*d* ante 1814; Robert[6], pastor of Welch Neck Bapt. Ch.);
4–Rev. William (1765-1830), of Lynche's Creek, Cheraw Dist., S.C.; received land grant in Effingham Co., Ga., for his services in Am. Rev.; a first settler of Screven Co.; planter and large landowner; minister of Missionary Bapt. Ch.; *m* 1st, 1789, Ann (Nancy) Fletcher (1767-96; William[5] [*d* aet. 132], of Telfair Co., Ga., Am. Rev.);
3–Rev. Moses Nathaniel (1792-1885), of Screven Co., Ga.; teacher aet. 21; lt. War 1812; officer in Seminole War, 1818, in which he was severely wounded; chaplain in C.S.A.; magistrate and judge of Inferior Ct.; rep. state Legislature, 1825; minister of Middle Ground Ch., Little Ogeechee Bapt. Ch., and preached till he was 90 yrs. of age; *m* 1st, 1820, Carolina M. Griner (*d* 1835), of Bulloch Co.;
2–Rev. Moses Nathaniel (2 below).
7–Robert **Daniell** (*b* 1646), from the Barbados, 1679; settled in the Carolinas; landgrave, 1698; dep. gov.; colonial gov. of S.C., col. of militia; *m* 2d, ca. 1702, Martha Wainwright;
6–John (1707-1812), of New Hanover Co., N.C.; mem. colonial militia; *m* 1736, Sarah Raven (*b* 1717), of Charleston, S.C. (John[7], *m* Elizabeth, dau. of George Beadon);
5–Stephen Beadon (1745-1820), of Brunswick Co., N.C.; soldier Am. Rev.; *m* 1769, Rebecca Howe (Gen. Robert[6], of N.C., Am. Rev., *m* Sarah Grange);
4–George W. (1782-1845), of N.C., and Dublin, Ga.; soldier in War 1812; *m* 2d, 1807, Mary Gornto, or Gonto (1783-1835), of N.C.;
3–David Gonto (1808-84), of Laurens Co., Ga.; officer C.S.A.; *m* 1829, Mary J. (Garnett) Bettison (1808-81; John Garnett[4]; Thomas[5], Am. Rev.);
2–Janie Warren (1838-81), of Savannah, Ga.; *m* 1864, Moses Nathaniel **McCall** (1831-85), ed. Mercer Coll.; pastor of Sylvania (Ga.) Bapt. Ch., 1860; head of Sylvania Acad.; capt. of cav., 5th Regt., Ga. State troops, C.S.A., throughout the war, known as the "Fighting Chaplain"; from Longstreet, Ga., to Cochran, Ga., 1880; pres. Monroe Female (Bapt.) Coll., Forsyth, Ga., and was pastor of the ch.; issue: I–Howard Henry (1 above); II–George Daniell (1870-1914); III–Philip Boardman Warren (*b* 1872; *m* Bertha [Spates] Boughner).
1–*m* Nov. 14, 1894, Ettie Augusta Tidwell (qv for issue).
1–Ed. Joe Brown Coll. for Boys, Dalton, Ga.; A.B., Mercer, '87 (Kappa Alpha). Pres. and owner, Paragon Box Co., Atlanta, Ga. Mason. Baptist. Democrat. Residence: Georgian Terrace Hotel, Atlanta, Ga.

1–**McCALL, Ettie Augusta Tidwell (Mrs. Howard H.),** *b* Atlanta, Ga., June 30, 1870.
7–John **Tidwell,** from Eng., ca. 1700; settled on the Potomac River, Westmoreland Co., Va.; in 1705, the town Yeocomico was established on land grant of Richard, who came from Eng. with his brothers John and Robert;
6–John of Va., and S.C.;
5–William Carr (ca. 1745-1782), of Westmoreland Co.; in Am. Rev.; *m* 1779, Mary de Graffenreid (*d* 1782, dropped dead upon hearing the news of her husband's death; Baker[6], of Va., and Chester Co., S.C., *m* Sarah Vass);
4–William (1780-1835), vol. in War 1812; pioneer settler in Coweta Co., Ga.; large landowner in Pike and Meriwether cos.; *m* 1803, Mary Amelia Jones (*d* ante 1834; William[5], *m* Mary–);
3–William de Graffenreid (1818-72), of Coweta Co.; vol. aet. 18, in Creek Indian War, 1836; vol. C.S.A., aet. 42; lt. of Home Guards; lt. "Joe Brown's Militia," 1863; fought in Battle of Atlanta; home burned, 1864, and plantation raided on Sherman's "March to the Sea"; settled in DeKalb Co., Ga., after the war; *m* 1838, Angelina Westmoreland (1819-85; Reuben[4], *m* Keziah Simmons);
2–Reuben William (2 below).
10–William **Judson** (qv);
9–Joseph (1619-90), from Eng. with his parents aet. 15; of Woodbury and Stratford, Conn.; freeman, 1658; dep., 1659; rep. Gen. Assembly, 13 yrs.; ens.; lt. Train Band; soldier King Philip's and Narragansett wars, 1676; commr. of Woodbury; *m* 1644, Sarah Porter (*d* 1696, aet. 70; John[10]);
8–James (1650-1721 or 21), ens. and capt.; rep. Conn. Gen. Assembly, 30 sessions; ens. Train Band; capt. militia; lt. of Dragoons, 1690, of foot, 1697; *m* 1st, 1680, Rebecca Welles (1655-1717; Thomas[9]; Gov. Thomas[10], qv);
7–David (1693-1761), of Stratford; auditor of the treas., 1735; rep. Conn. Gen. Assembly, 1731,35,41; capt. Train Band; *m* 1713, Phebe Stiles (1696?-1765; Ephraim[8], *m* Bathsheba Curtiss, of Stratford);
6–Daniel (1728-1813), ens. in colonial army, 1762; capt. Train Band, 1768; rep. Gen. Assembly, 1774-75; justice; served in Am. Rev., apptd. inspector of all fire arms and fire locks for Fairfield Co., Conn., after Battle of Lexington; *m* 1st, 1752, Sarah Curtiss (1731-1808; Capt. Stiles[7], *m* Rebecca Judson);
5–Silas (1754-1808), soldier Am. Rev.; served with sea-coast patrol at burning of Fairfield; *m* 1777, Mary Whiting;
4–Isaac (1781-1844), of Huntington, Conn.; *m* Avis Shelton;
3–David Newton (1818-81), to Eatonton, Ga., 1835, aet. 17; thence to Warrenton, Athens, and Atlanta, 1855; soldier C.S.A.; *m* 1840, Sarah Folsom Hale;
2–Elizabeth Augusta (2 below).
10–Gov. William **Bradford,** Mayflower Pilgrim (qv);
9–William (1624-1704), *m* 1st, 1651, Alice Richards (1627-71; Thomas[10]);
8–Alice (*b* 1661), of Plymouth; *m* 1st, 1680, Rev. William **Adams** (1650-85; William[9], from Eng. on the "Elizabeth and Ann");
7–Elizabeth (*b* 1681), *m* 1st, 1696, Rev. Samuel **Whiting** (*d* 1725), first minister at Windham, Conn. (Rev. John[8], *m* Sybil Collins);
6–Samuel (1720-1803), to Stratford, Conn.; col. 4th Conn. Regt. during Am. Rev.; *m* 1743, Elizabeth Judson (1723-93), head of Stratford Daughters of Liberty during Am. Rev.;
5–Mary (1760-1811), *m* Silas **Judson** (5 above).
7–Daniel **Shelton** (1668-1728), from Yorkshire, Eng., with his brother, 1686; settled in Conn.; lt. of Train Band, 1717; large landowner and part owner of the "Endeavor"; *m* Elizabeth Welles (*b* 1670; Samuel[8]; Gov. Thomas[9], qv);
6–Samuel (1705-72), large landowner; *m* 1735, Abigail Nichols (*d* 1794; Capt. Joseph[7], *m* Mary Curtiss);
5–Agur (1758-1845), of Ripton, Conn.; *m* 1779, Abigail Newton (*d* post 1845; Rev. Christopher[6]);
4–Avis (1786-1859), of Huntington, Conn.; *m* Isaac **Judson** (4 above).
10–Thomas **Hale** (qv);
9–Thomas (1633-88), from Eng. with his parents; settled finally at Newbury, Mass.; *m* as her 1st husband, 1657, Mary Hutchinson (bap. 1630; Richard[10], *m* Alice Bosworth);
8–Thomas (1659-1730), capt. militia; justice; grand juror, 1692; selectman of Newbury, 1695-98; rep. Gen. Ct., 1713-14; *m* 1682, Sarah Northend (1661-1732; Ezekiel[9], *m* Edna [Halsted] Bailey);
7–Thomas (1683-will dated 1744), capt. militia; justice; selectman of Newbury, 1721; *m* 1704,

Anna Short (1682-1770; Henry[8], *m* Sarah Whipple);
6–Oliver (1721-1808), sgt., ens., lt.; soldier Am. Rev.; *m* 1758, his cousin, Judith Hale (1738-90; Daniel[7]; Thomas[8], same as 8 above);
5–Oliver (*b* 1762), served in Am. Rev.; *m* 1st, 1784, Lydia Coffin (1764-1801; Eliphalet[6], *m* Lydia Emery);
4–Eliphalet (1793-1860), merchant at Warrenton, Ga., many yrs.; paymaster U.S.V. in Indian wars in Fla.; Mason; *m* 1819, Ann (or Nancy) Stewart (1796-1851; William[5], of Beach Island, S.C., *m* Mary Parker);
3–Sarah Folsom (1823-96), of Warrenton, Ga.; *m* David Newton **Judson** (3 above);
2–Elizabeth Augusta (Nov. 10, 1847-Nov. 4, 1898), *m* Sept. 20, 1868, Reuben William **Tidwell** (Dec. 30, 1840-Mar. 16, 1915), of Atlanta, and "Poplar Grove," DeKalb Co., Ga.; merchant; capt. cav., maj., C.S.A.; Mason (Shriner, K.T.); issue: I–Lilien Reube (*b* 1869); II–Ettie Augusta (1 above); III–William de Graffenreid (*b* 1872; *m* Clio Mary Smith); IV–Charles Reuben (*b* 1874; *m* Janie Gillespie McMahan); V–Albert L. (*b* 1877; *m* Edna Floride McCall); VI–Minnie Avis (*b* 1879; *m* George S. Obear, Jr.); VII–Reuben Frank (*b* 1884; *m* Louise Duncan).
1–*m* Nov. 14, 1894, Howard Henry McCall (qv); issue: 1–Howard Henry, *b* Atlanta, Ga., Nov. 21, 1895; grad. Marist Coll.; B.A., U.Ga. (Kappa Alpha, P.B.K.); served in World War, cited for bravery in France; *m* Apr. 14, 1920, Harriet White, dau. of John A. Benedict, of Athens, Ga., *m* Mary Louise Coates (issue: Elsa Roberts; Howard Henry, III).
1–Ed. Mrs. Byer's Select Pvt. Sch., Atlanta. Mem. B.O.R., D.A.C. (parliamentarian), D.F.P.A., D.C.W., D.A.R. (state "War" regent, Ga., 1916-18; hon. state regent, v.p. gen.), U.D.C. (state registrar), Ga. Hist. Soc., N.E.H.G.S.; life dir. Ga. Fed. of Women's Clubs. Trustee Tallulah Falls (Ga.) Industrial Sch., State Teacher's Coll. (Athens, Ga.), 1924-34, Rabun Gap-Nacoochee (Ga.) Sch. Democrat. Baptist. Summer place: "Poplar Grove," De Kalb Co., Ga. Residence: Georgian Terrace Hotel, Atlanta, Ga.

Arms: Argent, on a cross gules, five mullets or.
Crest: Out of a ducal coronet or, a demi-lion affrontee gules.

1–**McBRIDE, Mabel Louise Adams (Mrs. William W.),** *b* Warren, O., Mar. 6, 1865.
9–John **Adams** (*d* 1633), from Eng., 1621; settled at Plymouth, Mass.; mem. council which incorporated Plymouth; *m* 1623, Ellen Newton (*d* 1681);
8–James (*b* 1626-*d* at sea), of Plymouth; *m* 1646, Frances Vassall, of Scituate, Mass. (William[9]);
7–Richard (1651-1728), wounded in "Great Swamp Fight," with Narragansett Indians; *m* 1679, Rebecca Davis, of Scituate (Robert[8]);
6–William (1690-1727), of Sudbury, Mass.; *m* 1723, Susannah Woodword (David[7]);
5–Phineas (1726-79), pvt. Am. Rev., later in "The Guards"; *m* 1751, Lydia Fitch;
4–Asael (1754-1821), of Canterbury, Conn.; pvt. Am. Rev.; *m* 1779, Olive Avery (*d* 1813);
3–Asael (1786-1852), with parents from Canterbury, to Liberty, O., 1802; *m* 1814, Lucy Mygatt;
2–George (2 below).
10–Joseph **Mygatt** (qv);
9–Jacob (*b* 1633), of Hartford, Conn.; *m* 1655, Sarah Whitney (*d* 1704);
8–Joseph, *m* Sarah Webster;
7–Joseph (1678-1724), Hartford; *m* Elizabeth Stephens;
6–Joseph (1720-49), of Danbury, Conn.; *m* Elizabeth Starr;
5–Eli (1742-1807), Danbury; col. in Am. Rev.; *m* 1759, Abigail Stevens (*d* 1767);
4–Comfort Starr (1763-1823), of Danbury, Conn., and Canfield, O.; *m* 1783, Lucy Knapp (*d* 1804);
3–Lucy (1794-1885), *m* Asael **Adams** (3 above);

GEORGE ADAMS (Dec. 19, 1822-Mar. 9, 1905), educated at Western Reserve Academy (now College), Hudson, O.; admitted to the bar but never practiced; merchant at Warren, Ohio.

2–George (1822-1905), see portrait and biography; *m* 1852, Elizabeth B. Dana (1829-71); *m* 2d, 1873, Elizabeth Fleming; issue (1st marriage): I–Anna Carey (1853-1908; *m* Dr. Henry Parsons); II–Lucy Dana (*b* 1855; *m* 1880, Dr. Charles A. Wilson); III–Elizabeth Dana (1857-1907; *m* 1883, Charles M. Van Gorder; IV Grace Harding (1860-1912; *m* 1888, DeForest Edwards); V–George Dana (*b* 1863; *m* Grace Field; *m* 2d, Pearl Biddle); VI–Mabel Louise (1 above); VII–Francis Howard (1866-83); VIII–Helen Ranney (*b* 1868; *m* 1892, George Southmayd, *d* 1924); IX–Henry Stiles (*b* 1871; *m* Florence Vandenburg, *d* July 16, 1927; *m* 2d 1928, Mary Tompkins).
1–*m* July 14, 1887, William Woodin McBride, *b* New Columbus, Pa., Apr. 30, 1862; son of George McBride; issue (all *b* Omaha, Neb): 1–Mabel Louise (1888-1913), grad. Chicago Art Inst.; 2–Ruth Elizabeth, *b* Dec. 4, 1889; *m* Oct. 12, 1912, Harvey James, son of James Wing, of Appleton, Wis. (issue: Priscilla Ruth; Robert Harvey; Elizabeth Dana); 3–Grace Emory, *b* Feb. 14, 1891; grad. Am. Conservatory of Music, Chicago; *m* Sept. 1, 1917, Harvey P., son of Ole P. Thorsen, of Chicago (issue: William McBride; Richard Adams); 4–Dana Adams (1902-03); 5–George Adams, *b* July 23, 1905; B.S., U.Mich., 1928, M.S., 1929; 2d lt., R.C., U.S.A.; *m* June 16, 1928, Helen Carrol Buchan, of Detroit, Mich.
1–Mem. S.M.D., C.D.A., D.A.R. Club: Omaha Athletic. Conglist. Residence: 409 Huntoon St., Topeka, Kan.

1–**McCALL, John Oppie (surname taken on adoption by Charles W. McCall),** *b* Geneva, N.Y., Oct. 4, 1879.
6–John **Mead,** of Conn.; brig. gen., 4th Conn. brig., Am. Rev.; *m* Ann–;
5–Ann, *m* John **Eells,** of Walton, N.Y.; corpl. Am. Rev., 1779;
4–Ann, *m* Lewis **Raymond** (William[5] [*b* 1734], Am. Rev., *m* 1760, Priscilla Hayden);
3–Elizabeth, *m* Samuel **McCall,** of Marshall, Mich.;
2–Carrie Isabel (*d* 1888), *m* John **Oppie** (1854-80), of Griggstown, N.J.; minister Dutch Reformed Ch., Geneva, N.Y.
1–*m* Dec. 6, 1911, Irene Tingler, *b* Buffalo, N.Y., Nov. 30, 1890; dau. of Christopher J. Tingler, of Buffalo, *m* Florence Amelia Legge; issue (all *b* Buffalo, N.Y.): 1–Elizabeth Raymond, *b* Oct. 17, 1912; 2–Patricia Willis (July 8, 1914-Dec. 2, 1915); 3–Helen Irene, and 4–John Oppie, Jr., twins, *b* July 17, 1916; 5–Nancy, *b* Jan. 2, 1920.
1–B.A., Yale, '01 (Delta U., Xi Psi Phi); D.D.S., U.Buffalo, 1904. Prof. of periodontia, New York U. Coll. of Dentistry (see Who's Who in America). Founder, fellow and ex-pres. Am. Acad. Periodontology; fellow Am. Coll. of Dentistry; mem. Nat. Dental Assn. Presbyterian. Republican. Club: Larchmont Shore. Residence: 4 Cambridge Ct., Larchmont, N.Y.

1–**McCARTY, James Dixon,** *b* Talladega Co., Ala., Oct. 25, 1860.
4–Peter **McCarty** (*b* 1742), of Bucks Co., Pa.; prob. son of Silas McCarty, from Ireland to Plumstead Tp., Bucks Co., Pa., 1718;
3–James (1784-1856), from Ala. to Smith Co., Tex., 1854; *m* Elizabeth Funderburgh (Isaac[4], capt. Am. Rev., from S.C. to Ga.);
2–William Anderson (2 below).
7–Thomas **Adair** (*b* Antrim Co., Ireland, 1680), to Pa., 1730;
6–Joseph (*b* Antrim Co., Ireland, 1711), to Pa., 1730;
5–Joseph (*b* Pa., 1733), to S.C., 1750;
4–John (*b* S.C., 1758), to Ga., 1800;
3–James (1806-45), *m* Sarah Dean (1810-1904);
2–Amanda Jane (1839-1928), *m* 1856, William Anderson **McCarty** (1825-63), farmer of Ala.; joined Co. K, 18th Ala. Regt.; mortally wounded in Battle of Chickamauga, Sept. 21, 1863; *m* 2d, 1875, Frederick A. Moore; issue (1st marriage): I–John Green (1856-63); II–George Weyman (1858-1922; *m* Sarah Rucker); III–James Dixon (1 above); IV–Willie Octavia (*b* 1863; *m* Walker Dunson).
1–*m* Oct. 16, 1888, Mary May, *b* Knoxville, Tenn., Apr. 23, 1868; dau. of Edwin Forrest May; issue (all *b* Atlanta, Ga.): 1–James Dixon, Jr., *b* Mar. 19, 1890; M.E., Ga. School of Tech., '12; *m* Apr. 19, 1928, Susan Barnard, dau. of James Burch Carson, of Vonore, Tenn. (issue: James Dixon, III); 2–Edwin Forrest, *b* Nov. 24, 1891; B.S., U. of Ga., '13; 3–Helen, *b* Oct. 5, 1896; *m* Nov. 3, 1923, Dr. Daniel Collier, son of Robert L. Elkin, of Lancaster, Ky. (issue: Daniel Collier, Jr.); 4–William Anderson, *b* Dec. 8, 1901; attended Washington and Lee U.; *m* Dec. 31, 1928, Elizabeth Newman; 5–Mary, *b* Sept. 15, 1906; *m* May 18, 1927, Edgar, son of Edgar Dunlap, of Atlanta, Ga. (issue: Edgar, Jr.).
1–Pres. A. D. Adair and McCarty Bros, Inc., 1921-30. Mem. I.A.G. Presbyterian. Democrat. Residence: 815 Piedmont Av. N.E., Atlanta, Ga.

1–**McCASLIN, Robert Horace,** *b* Sweetwater, Tenn., June 2, 1883.
5–William (McCausland) **McCaslin** (descended from Baron MacCausland, of Ulster, went to Ireland during reign of James VI); from Ireland with his bro., 1740; settled in Va.; served in Am. Rev.;
4–John, removed to N.C.;
3–William, from Buncombe Co., N.C., to Monroe Co., Tenn.; *m* 2d, 1841, Lydia Misemer;
2–Joseph Henry (2 below).
6–William **Magill** (1715-49; son of William [*b* 1670], from Scotland to Ireland, 1714), from Ireland bet. 1725-40; settled in Augusta Co., Va.;
5–James, served in 12th Va. Regt., Am. Rev.; *m* 2d, Mary McMeans;
4–Nathaniel (*b* 1797), planter; *m* 1824, Jane Rankin;
3–James Franklin (1825-1901), of Monroe Co., Tenn.; planter; ruling elder in Presbyn. Ch. over 50 yrs.; *m* 1850, Margaret Johnston;
2–Margaret Ella (*b* 1858), *m* 1881, Joseph Henry **McCaslin** (*b* 1852), merchant, Sweetwater, Tenn.; issue: I–Robert Horace (1 above); II–Ross (*d* infancy); III–Reese (*d* infancy); IV–Esther Alice (*d* infancy); V–Lynn Bachman (*d* infancy); VI–Henry Herbert (*b* 1890; *m* Alice Whitner).
1–*m* June 6, 1906, Grace N. Pollard, *b* Richmond, Va., Oct. 27, 1883; dau. of Dr. John Pollard, of Richmond; issue: 1–Susie Virginia, *b* Bowling Green, Ky., June 3, 1913; 2–Robert Horace, Jr. (Apr. 14, 1915-June 7, 1919).
1–B.S., Sweetwater Mil. Coll., '00; A.B., Maryville (Tenn.) Coll., 1903; grad. Union Theol. Sem.; (D.D., Richmond Coll., 1910). Pastor Cleveland, Tenn., Bowling Green, Ky., and Montgomery, Ala., 1906-22, Riverside Presbyn. Ch., Jacksonville, Fla., 1922– (see Who's Who in America). Trustee Ala. Presbyn. Coll., Southwestern Presbyn. U., Columbia Theol. Sem., Davidson Coll., Stillman Inst., Palmer Coll. Mason (Shriner, K.T.). Clubs: Civitan, Fla. Country, Timuquana. Residence: 2149 Herschel St., Jacksonville, Fla.

1–**McCAULEY, Edward, Jr.,** *b* Washington, D.C., Aug. 13, 1875.
5–John **McCauley,** *m* Isabella Brown;
4–John, of Phila.; *m* Sarah Stewart (Col. Charles[5], of Eng., *m* Sarah Harding; Robert[6]);
3–Commodore Charles Stewart (1796-1861), *m* 1831, Lilia Elizabeth Dickins;
2–Edwards (2 below).
5–John **Dickins** (1747-98; son of John, *m* Elizabeth Aston); studied at Eton; came from Eng. to N.C., 1773?; clergyman; founder of the M.E. Ch. in America; preached in Va. and N.C., 1776-82; as early as 1780 he suggested to Bishop Asbury, the plan of Cokesbury Coll. at N. Abingdon, Md., the first Meth. academic instn. in America; took charge of the John Street Ch., New York, 1783, and was the first Am. preacher to receive Thomas Coke and approve his scheme for organizing the denomination; established the Meth. Book Concern, Phila., 1789; *m* Elizabeth Yancey (*b* 1759; Jacomas[6], *m* Anna Kimbrough; Richard[7]);
4–Asbury (1780-1861), of Phila.; asso. with Joseph Dennie in founding the "Portfolio," Phila.; chief clk. U.S. Treas. Dept., 1816-36, and in the State Dept., 1833-36; sec. of the U.S. Senate, 1836-61; *m* 1804, Lilias Arnot;
3–Lilia Elizabeth (1807-93), *m* Commodore Charles S. **McCauley** (3 above).
8–John **Arnot,** *m* Katherine Melville;
7–Dr. Hugo (*d* 1768), *m* Christian Cook;
6–Christian (*d* 1773), *m* Duncan Pollack (*d* 1765);
5–Sir Hugo (1749-86), *m* 1770, Margaret Bennett (*d* 1826; William[6], *m* Margaret, dau. of James MacDuff);
4–Lilias (1779-1859), *m* Asbury **Dickins** (4 above);
3–Lilia E., *m* Charles S. **McCauley** (3 above);
2–Edward (1848-1929), *m* 1872, Frances Steele (1852-1922); issue: I–Frances S. (1873-80); II–Edward, Jr. (1 above); III–Lilia (Mrs. Wolcott Tuckerman, qv for maternal lineages); IV–Annie (*b* 1884; *m* Charles O'Donnell Lee, *d* 1917); V–Caroline Addison (1888-89); VI–Mary Morris (*b* 1892; *m* Cdr. H. S. Howard, U.S.N.).
1–*m* Feb. 8, 1913, Jean Oliver, *b* Pittsburgh, Pa., Feb. 16, 1888; dau. of George T. Oliver, of Pittsburgh; issue: 1–Barbara, *b* Constantinople, Turkey, Nov. 27, 1913; 2–Edward, 3d, *b* Brookline, Mass., June 15, 1915; 3–George Oliver (Sept. 5, 1916-June 1918); 4–John Arnot, *b* Washington, D.C., Apr. 16, 1918; 5–Michael, *b* Honolulu, T.H., Apr. 21, 1921.
1–Grad. U.S.N.A., 1896. Promoted ens., 1898; lt. (j.g.), 1901; lt., 1903; lt. cdr., 1909; cdr., 1915; capt., 1918. Served in Spanish-Am. War, in P.R. and P.I., Spanish-Am. War; duty in Office of Naval Intelligence, Washington, Sept. 1915; asst. dir. of same, Mar. 1916-July 1918; spl. duty abroad, several months; comdg. U.S.S. George Washington, Oct. 1918-Nov. 1919, taking President Wilson to and from France both times for Peace Conf. also bringing the King and Queen of Belgium for visit to U.S. and return; comdg. U.S.S. Huntington, 1919-20; comdg. Mine Force, Pacific Fleet, 1920-

21; asst. comdr. 12th Naval Dist., 1921-22; retired Nov. 1922. Now mem. firm of Hibbs & McCauley, naval architects and marine engrs., San Francisco. Awarded Spanish-Am. War, West Indies and Philippine campaign medals, Victory Medal, Navy Cross; Officer Legion of Honor (France); Officer Order of Leopold (Belgium). Mem. Loyal Legion, D.S. Episcopalian. Republican. Clubs: Metropolitan, Alibi (Washington), New York Yacht (New York), Pacific-Union, St. Francis Yacht, Olympic (San Francisco), Burlingame Country, San Mateo Polo. Residence: Burlingame, Calif.

1-**TUCKERMAN, Lilia McCauley (Mrs. Wolcott),** *b* Minneapolis, Minn., July 15, 1882.
5-William **Steele** (1707-80), of Lancaster Co., Pa.; *m* Rachel Carr, or Kerr (1726-98);
4-Gen. James (1764-1845), *m* Mary Humes (1782-1864; James[5], *m* Elizabeth, dau. of James Hamilton, *m* Mary Miller);
3-Franklin (1814-80), *m* 1842, Anne Eliza Barney;
2-Frances (2 below).
8-Jean Paul **Jaquette,** from Dutch West India Co., Brazil, 1654, settled in Del.; v.dir. Dutch Colony in Del., 1655; *m* Susanne Carpentier;
7-Peter (1690-1740), of Del.; *m* —Ingelborg;
6-Suzanne (*d* 1766), of Del.; *m* Gunning **Bedford** (1720-1802; Gunning[7], *m* Mary–; William[8]);
5-Anne (1755-1808), of Phila.; *m* 1780, Commodore Joshua **Barney** (1759-1818), master's mate, sloop "Hornet," 1775; lt., Cont. Navy, 1776 (William[6] [*d* 1772], *m* Frances Holland Warts [*d* 1791]; William[7]);
4-William Bedford (1781-1833), *m* 1808, Mary Chase (1786-1872; Samuel[5], *m* Hannah K., dau. of Dr. Samuel Giles, *m* Mary Hart; Rev. Thomas[6], *m* Matilda Walker; Rev. Samuel[7], *m* Elizabeth Tookey);
3-Anna Eliza (1824-81), of Washington; *m* Franklin **Steele** (3 above);
2-Frances (1852-1922), *m* 1872, Edward **McCauley** (1848-1929); for issue and paternal lineages see brother, Edward McCauley, Jr.
1-*m* Nov. 25, 1903, Wolcott Tuckerman, *b* New York, N.Y., Apr. 7, 1880; son of Walter Cary Tuckerman, of New York; issue: 1–Florence Fenno, *b* Washington, D.C., Dec. 20, 1904; *m* Jan. 10, 1925, Loring, son of Clarence Andrews, of New York (issue: Oliver Wolcott; Joel Loring; Gavin); 2–Lilia McCauley, *b* Washington, Oct. 2, 1906; *m* July 1927, Walter R. Gherardi, Jr., son of Admiral Walter R. Gherardi, U.S.N., of Washington (issue: Lilia Rockwell; Florence Neville); 3–Frances Steele, *b* Washington, Dec. 1, 1908; 4–Viola Wolcott, *b* Washington, June 1, 1912; 5–Clara Louise, *b* Los Angeles, Calif., 1916.
1-Artist, landscape painter. Dir. and chmn. Braille work for the blind, Santa Barbara Chapter, A.R.C. Mem. C.D.A., Washington Soc. of Artists, Nat. Assn. of Women Painters and Sculptors, Art Guild of the Fine Arts Soc. of San Diego, San Francisco Art Assn., Santa Barbara Art League, Am. Federation of Art. Clubs: National Arts (New York), Little Town (Santa Barbara), Montecito Country, Valley (Montecito). Episcopalian. Republican. Residence: Carpinteria, Calif.

1-**McCLELLAN, Catherine Ficklin Cave (Mrs. Malcolm),** *b* Moberly, Mo., Oct. 9, 1886.
9-George **Bledsoe** (will proved 1704), settled in Northumberland Co., Va.;
8-William (*d* 1770), sheriff, Spotsylvania Co., Va., 1723; capt. Colonial militia, 1729; *m* 1st, Elizabeth– (living 1727), widow of Charles Stevens;
7-Hannah, *m* 1720, Benjamin **Cave** (*d* 1762), Orange Co., Va., 1725; lt. colonial militia, Spotsylvania Co., 1730; received patent for 1,000 acres on Rapidan River, 1728; one of 1st justices of Orange Co., 1734; 1st sheriff, 1734; burgess, 1753-61;
6-John (*d* 1810), from Culpeper Co., Va., to Woodford (now Scott) Co., Ky.;
5-Richard (ca. 1772-1836), to Boone Co., Mo., ca. 1814; early settler at Columbia, Mo., 1816; 1st justice, 1821; built and preached in Old Bear Creek Christian Ch., 1821; *m* 1st, 1792, Sarah Wood (Thomas[6], of Woodford Co., Ky.);
4-William (*d* 1860), settled in Caddo Parish, La., 1859; *m* his 1st cousin, Mary Cave (1802-76; William[5], of Culpeper Co., *m* Frances, dau. Julius Christy; John[6], same as 6 above);
3-Franklin (1830-82), grad. U. of Mo., 1849; removed to Natchitoches, La., 1859; served in Co. A, 6th La. Cav., C.S.A.; head of pvt. sch., Moberly, Mo., 1875; *m* 1858, Catherine E. Galbreath;
2-Willard Percy (2 below).
7-Malcolm (name originally McGhorm, meaning "of blue") **Blue** (*d* 1770), from Scotland with the McNiell colony after the battle of Culloden, 1746; settled in Fayette Co., N.C.; *m* Sarah Smith (*d* 1812, aet. 102);
6-Duncan (*b* 1741), came with his father; served in Am. Rev.; *m* his cousin, Effie Blue; *m* 2d?, Margaret Graham;
5-Niel (*d* 1852), served in War 1812; from Ky. to Audrain Co., Mo.; *m* Elizabeth Galbreath (*b* 1783; Niel[6], from Scotland during Am. Rev., held prisoner by Brit. for remainder of war, settled in Cumberland Co., N.C.);
4-Flora (1814-69), *m* 1836, her 1st cousin, Daniel **Galbreath** (1809-92; Torquil[5]; Niel[6], same as 6 above);
3-Catherine E. (1837-63), *m* Franklin **Cave** (3 above).
8-William **Ficklin** (*d* 1756), from Eng., ca. 1720; settled in Brunswick Parish (now King George Co.), Va.; *m* Sarah–;
7-William (*b* ca. 1728), of St. George's Parish, Spotsylvania Co.; served in Am. Rev.; *m* Mary Marye;
6-John (1755-1819), pvt. Va. troops in Am. Rev.; to Jessamine Co., Ky., ca. 1780; *m* Mary–;
5-Jared (1782-1835), Mercer Co., Ky.; *m* Elizabeth Bowman Dunklin;
4-Joseph (1809 or 11-1871), to Mo., post 1849; served as mem. bodyguard to Gen. Sterling Price, C.S.A.; settled finally at Columbia, Mo.; *m* 1831, Eleanor Wilson Brown (1815-49; William[5], *m* Nancy, dau. of James Cecil; William[6]);
3-Prof. Joseph (1833-87), v.p. and head of math. dept., U.Mo., 1865-87; *m* 1856, Penelope Terrill;
2-Octavia (2 below).
9-Cornelius **Bowman,** from Germany to Pa.; later removed to Va.; settled in Augusta Co.; *m* Ann–;
8-George, of Pa.; removed to Va.; *m* 1731, Mary Hite (Joist[9], qv);
7-(John) Jacob, (1733-80), removed to Tumbling Shoals, Reedy River, S.C., ante 1768; shot in door of his mill by Tories; *m* Sarah–;
6-Mary (1768-1836), *m* 1788, Capt. John **Dunklin** (1765-1834), of Laurens Co., S.C.; served at New Orleans in 1812; from Ky. to New Madrid Co., Mo. (Joseph[7], from Wales to Laurens Co., ca. 1750, *m* Jane Caroline Worthen);
5-Elizabeth Bowman (1789-1839), *m* Jared **Ficklin** (5 above).
10-William (Tyrrell) **Terrill** (*b* 1635), from Eng., 1657 or 58; settled in New Kent Co., Va.; *m* Martha–;
9-William (1653-1727), St. Paul's Parish, Hanover Co., Va.; *m* Susannah Waters;
8-Timothy (*b* ca. 1658 or 68), began to write name Terrill; St. Peter's Parish, New Kent Co.; *m* Elizabeth Foster (John[9]);
7-Robert (1697-1787), Orange Co., Va.; *m* 1st, Mary Foster (John[8], *m* Anne, dau. Capt. Augustine Moore, of "Chelsea"); *m* 2d, Judith Towels;
6-Edmund (1740-84), sgt. in Am. Rev., 3 yrs.; capt. Culpeper militia; *m* 1760, Margaret Willis (1741-*d* 1812, Ky.);
5-John (1768-1850), Howard Co., Mo.; *m* 1789, Rebecca Cornelius (1773-1845);
4-James (1797-1885), *m* 1819, Susanna Mosby Cave (1802-80; William[6], of Boone Co., Ky., *m* Margaret, dau. John Threlkeld, Am. Rev.; William[6]; Benjamin, 7 above);
3-Penelope (1837-93), of Howard Co., Mo.; *m* Prof. Joseph **Ficklin** (3 above);
2-Octavia (1862-92), *m* 1885, Judge Willard Percy **Cave** (*b* 1859), cum laude grad. U. of Mo., '83; mayor of Moberly, Mo., 4 terms; acting circuit judge (he *m* 2d, Fannie E. Lango); issue: I–Catherine Ficklin (1 above); II–Helen Mar (*b* 1890; *m* Homer Cresap Teachenor).
1-*m* Mar. 18, 1907, Malcolm McClellan, *b* Atlanta, Ga., Sept. 18, 1884; son of Walter Gross McClellan, of Talladega, Ala.; issue (all *b* Jacksonville, Fla.): 1–Roby Blount, *b* July 31,

1908; U.Fla., '31; 2–Margaret Cave, *b* June 17, 1911; 3–Willard Cave, *b* Sept. 18, 1914.
1–Mem. D.A.R., U.D.C., Mo. Hist. Soc., etc. Clubs: Woman's, Garden. Residence: 1648 Osceola St., Jacksonville, Fla.

1–**MacCRACKEN, Edith Constable (Mrs. John Henry),** *b* Mamaroneck, N.Y., Aug. 31, 1884.
8–Cornelius **Bolmer** (*d* 1748), from Laon, Picardy, to Flushing, L.I., 1710; naturalized 1711;
7–Cornelius (*d* 1768), naturalized 1711; *m* 1732, Jane Van Alstyne (*d* 1742), of Brooklyn;
6–Peter (*d* 1793), *m* Catherine Worden;
5–Matthew (1758-1828), of N.Y. City; Am. Rev.; *m* Margaret (Leonhard) Leonard (1764-1817; William[6] [*b* Eden Kofen, Palatinate, 1734-*d* 1805], capt. Am. Rev., *m* Mary Christina–);
4–William (1784-1866), *m* 1807, Anne Brevoort;
3–Manuel Texido (1821-96), *m* 2d, Georgiana Eleanor Buckmaster;
2–Louise (2 below).
9–Jan Hendricksen van **Brevoort** (ca. 1630-1714), asst. alderman from Out Ward, 1702-03, 1707-14; constable, overseer, "authorized man"; surveyor of highways; *m* 1668, Annetje Bastiaens;
8–Hendrick (1670-1718), of N.Y.; *m* 1699, Maryken Van Couwenhoven;
7–Johannes (*b* 1700) *m* 1726, Annetje Idesse;
6–Henry (*b* 1735), *m* 1758, Maria Anthony (1739-94; Nicholas[7] [*b* 1693], *m* 2d, 1733, Hester Roome [1701-92]; Nicholas[8] [1657-ca. 1693], *m* Engeltje Schoonmaker, of Kingston; Allard[9] [1620-85], one of 1st five schepens of New Amsterdam, sheriff, 1664-73, orphan master, 1658, officer of city, 1664, *m* 1656, Henrica Wessels);
5–Abraham (1762-94), *m* 1788, Ann Devoor (David[6] [1717-80], *m* 1740, Mary Van Vleckeven; David[7] [1693-1760], *m* 1715, Jannetie, dau. of Abram de la Montagne, *m* 1689, Rebecca Ideus, or Ides);
4–Anne (1789-1821), *m* William **Bolmer** (4 above).
6–James **Buckmaster** (*d* 1785), from Eng., 1740; capt. pvteer. in Am. Rev.; *m* 1768, Sarah Hills (1743-1815);
5–George (1770-1829), chmn. com. of defence, New York, 1812; *m* 1795, Eleanor Whitfield (1777-1824);
4–Thomas Henry (1801-73), *m* 1826, Margaret Williams (1809-83);
3–Georgiana Eleanor (1827-93), *m* Manuel Texido **Bolmer** (3 above);
2–Louise (1861-1928), *m* 1881, Frederick Augustus **Constable** (1849-1905; James Mansell[3] [1812-1900], from Storrington, Sussex, Eng., to New York, 1835, *m* 1844, Henrietta, dau. of Aaron Arnold); issue: I–Marie Louise (*b* 1882); II–Edith (1 above).
1–*m* Apr. 20, 1910, John Henry MacCracken (see Vol. I, p. 651, for genealogy); issue: 1–Louise, *b* New York, Feb. 25, 1911; 2–Constable, *b* New York, May 4, 1913.
1–Ed. Miss Spence's Sch., '04. Mem. H.S., D.A.R. Clubs: Apawamis, Internat. Garden. Residence: 9 E. 83d St., New York, N.Y.

1–**McCONNELL, Lucy Evelyn Michaux (Mrs. Thomas M.),** *b* Halifax Co., N.C., Oct. 17, 1864.
6–Abraham **Michaux** (1672-1717), fled from France to Va., 1701; settled at Manakin Town, Henrico Co., Va.; *m* 1692, Susanna Rochet (*d* 1744); tablet to their memory is in First Presbyn. Ch., Greensboro, N.C.;
5–Jacob, of Goochland Co., Va.; *m* Judith Woodson;
4–Capt. Joseph (1739-1807), of Cumberland Co., Va.; capt. in Cont. Line 3 yrs.; *m* 1761, Judith Woodson (1747-1803; John[5]; Benjamin[6]; Col. Robert[7]; John[8], qv);
3–Joseph (1771-1837), of Cumberland Co.; *m* 1808, Judith (Crump) Mosby (*d* 1817); *m* 2d, 1822, Anne Meade Randolph;
2–John LaFayette (2 below).
10–John **Rolfe** (qv);
9–Thomas (*b* 1615), *m* Jane Poythress;
8–Jane (*d* 1676), *m* 1675, Col. Robert **Bolling** (qv);
7–Col. John (1676-1729), of "Cobbs," on the Appomattox, Va.; burgess; *m* Mary Kennon;
6–Jane (1703-66), of "Cobbs," below Petersburg, Va.; *m* Col. Richard **Randolph** (1690-1748), of "Curles" (William[7], qv);
5–Richard, of "Curles"; *m* Nancy Meade (David[6], *m* Susanna, dau. of Sir Richard Everard, gov. of the Colony of N.C., 1725-31; Andrew[7], qv);
4–Ann, *m* Brett **Randolph** (*b* 1760);

REV. JOHN LA FAYETTE MICHAUX (1824-98), editor and publisher of the Watchman and Harbinger, during the Civil War, the Central Protestant, 1874-92, and The Daily Workman (Photograph taken at age 34).

3–Anne Meade (1787-1836), of "Capua," Powhatan Co., Va.; *m* 1822, Joseph **Michaux** (3 above).
7–Gideon **Macon,** *m* Martha Matthews?;
6–Gideon (1682-1761), *m* Priscilla Jones, of King and Queen Co., Va.;
6–Capt. Harrison (ca. 1745-1790), *m* ca. 1772, Hannah Glenn;
5–Nathaniel (1778-1843) *m* Nancy Glenn (*d* 1827);
3–George Washington (1805-80), *m* 1827, Ellen Green (1811-44; Simon[4], *m* Priscilla, dau. of Atkins McLemore, mem. House of Commons from Bute Co., N.C., 1778);
2–Sarah McLemore (1831-94), *m* 1855, John LaFayette **Michaux** (1824-98), editor and publisher (see portrait); issue: I–Leonidas Macon (1856-1926; *m* 1892, Loulie Borden Miller); II–Edward Randolph, M.D. (*b* 1859; *m* 1902, Cornelia Roberson); III–John Summerfield (*b* 1861; *m* 1903, Lola Carraway); IV–Lucy Evelyn (1 above); V–Annie Glenn (Mrs. Thomas Henly Crocker, qv).
1–*m* Dec. 19, 1883, William Franklin Moss (June 27, 1848-Oct. 3, 1901); son of R. H. Moss, Sr., of Clarksville, Va., *m* Laura A. Clack.
1–*m* 2d, Oct. 28, 1909, Rev. Thomas Maxwell McConnell, D.D. (July 13, 1851-Jan. 9, 1927); son of William King McConnell, of Washington Co., Va., *m* Esther Carson Maxwell.
1–Grad. Greensboro Coll. for Women, 1883. Mem. D.B.R., D.A.R. (organizing regent Samuel Doak Chapter, Morristown, Tenn., regent Guilford Battle Chapter, Greensboro, N.C.), U.D.C., Guilford Co. Hist. Assn., I.A.G. Presbyterian. Democrat. Residence: 836 W. Market St., Greensboro, N.C.

1–**McCREARY, George Boone,** *b* New Concord, O., Dec. 9, 1875.
9–Jan Jooste(n) **Van Metre** (*d* 1706), from Holland, 1662, settled at Wyltwick (Kingston), N.Y.; *m* 1646?, Macyken Hendricksen;
8–Jooste Jans (1656-95), of Marbletown, N.Y.; *m* 1682, Sara DuBois;
7–Jan (1683-1745), of Somerset Co., N.J.; migrated to Va., 1744; *m* 1710, Margerat–;
6–Elizabeth (1715-92), *m* 1733, Thomas **Shepherd** (1705-76), founded Shepherdstown, Va. (now in W. Va.), 1732;
5–Col. David (1734-95), of Frederick Co., Va.; built fort at Wheeling, 1774; mem. Augusta Co. Com. of Safety, 1775; lt., Ohio Co., Va., by appmt. of Patrick Henry, and empowered to raise a co. of militia, 1776, as commissary for stations along the Ohio from Grave Creek to Ft. Pitt, 1776; col. in command of Ft. Henry (Wheeling) during attacks by Indians, June 28-Sept. 15, 1777; col. in the Brodhead expdn., Cochocton campaign, 1781; *m* 1756, Rachel Teague;
4–Ruth (1766-1846), *m* John **Mills** (1752-1833), of

Shepherdstown and Elm Grove, W.Va.; ens., lt., Cont. Army, in western Va. and Pa., 1780-81;
3-Sarah (1792-1847), *m* 1816?, George **McCreary** (1791-1872), of Guernsey Co., O.;
2-Henry (1837-1923), of New Concord, O.; served in 78th Regt., Ohio Vet. Vol. Inf., Civil War, 1861-65; physician; college teacher; *m* 1875, Samantha A. Stevenson (1845-77); *m* 2d, 1883, Mary Martha Paden; issue (1st marriage): I-George Boone (1 above); issue (2d marriage): I-Ralph Marion (*b* 1884; *m* 1912, Ada Wray); II-Mary (*b* 1885; *m* Neal Alexander Ranson); III-Grace Gordon (*b* 1889), and IV-Helen Holmes, twins (*b* 1889; *m* 1918, Roscoe Conklin Garrison); V-Eva Elizabeth (*b* 1892; *m* 1915, Lawrence A. Darrah).
1-*m* Sept. 24, 1901, Lova Ruth Fowler, *b* Kansas City, Mo., Jan. 20, 1883; dau. of Frank S. Fowler, of Salt Lake City, Utah; issue: 1-Lova Dorothy, *b* Salina, Kan., July 15, 1906; *m* July 27, 1927, Francis Prior Moore, son of Samuel Wagoner Moore, of St. Louis, Mo. (issue: Francis Prior, Jr.); 2-Jane Elizabeth, *b* Sterling, Kan., Dec. 6, 1911; attending Muskingum Coll.; 3-Robert Henry, *b* Holland, Mich., Aug. 28, 1915.
1-A.B., Muskingum Coll., '95, M.A., 1902 (D.D., 1924); grad. Pittsburgh Theol. Sem., 1898; student U.Chicago, 1901; Ph.D., Grove City (Pa.) Coll., 1914. Pastor of home mission churches, 1900-05; educator since 1905; prof. philosophy of religion, Xenia Theol. Sem., 1924-30; prof.-elect in the new Pittsburgh Xenia Theol. Sem., beginning 1930 (see Who's Who in America). Mem. S.A.R., etc. United Presbyterian. Clubs: Alpha Tau Epsilon, Apollo. Address: 616 W. North Av., N.S., Pittsburgh, Pa.

1-**McCREARY, Florence Marian Gail (Mrs. James Black),** *b* East Aurora, N.Y., Aug. 11, 1869.
10-Edmond (Gale) **Gail** (qv);
9-Abel, to Jamaica, L.I.; *m* Dinah-;
8-John (*d* ca. 1750), Goshen, N.Y.; propr.; served with Capt. Peter Schuyler's Co., 1692; *m* Mary-;
7-Joseph, Stamford, Conn.; *m* Rebeckah-;
6-William (*b* 1735), surveyor, 1760; *m* 1758, Rebeckah Jagger;
5-Isaac (*b* 1760), began to write name Gail; *m* 1779, Anna Lockwood;
4-Rev. Samuel (1790-1872), *m* Hannah Brown (1788-1872);
3-Rufus (1807-63), *m* Maria Storm (1810-71);
2-William Henry (2 below).
10-Jeremy **Jagger** (*d* 1658), one of 1st settlers of Wethersfield, Conn.; to Stamford, 1641; master of trading vessel; served in Pequot War; *m* Elizabeth-;
9-John (will probated 1684), Southampton, L.I.; *m* Hannah-;
8-Jonathan (*b* 1655), *m* 1700, Rebecca Holmes;
7-John (1702-43), *m* 1732, Rebecca Ingersoll;
6-Rebeckah (*b* 1734), *m* Joseph **Gale** (6 above).
10-Robert **Lockwood** (qv);
9-Jonathan (1634-88), rep. Conn. Legislature, 4 yrs.; *m* Mary Ferris (Jeffrey[10], qv);
8-Gershom (*d* ante 1762), dep. Conn. Colonial Ct., 1726; *m* Hannah-;
7-Nathan (1704-61), *m* Sarah-;
6-Thaddeus (will dated 1808), Greenwich, Conn.; *m* ca. 1740, Sarah-;
5-Annie, *m* Isaac **Gale** (5 above).
2-William Henry **Gail,** M.D. (1840-1914), *m* Julia Wallace (1844-90); issue: I-James Wallace (*b* and *d* 1867); II-Florence Marian (1 above); III-Clarence Wallace (*b* 1874; *m* Emily Trowbridge); IV-William Wallace (qv).
1-*m* Sept. 18, 1890, James Black McCreary, *b* Oil City, Pa., July 28, 1869; capt. A.R.C., in France during World War; son Robert DuBois McCreary, of Great Bend, Pa.; issue: 1-James B. (Sept. 9, 1893-July 5, 1919), to France with Richard Norton Ambulance Service as driver, 1916; joined 1st French Foreign Legion, returned home on sick leave, hon. disch.; attempted to join Am., then French forces, rejected; joined Y.M.C.A. and served as trouble man in France, sent to Prague where he died; 2-Gail, *b* East Aurora, N.Y., Sept. 18, 1895; *m* Apr. 26, 1913, Laurence Jerome, son Ira B. Lesh, of Orlando, Fla. (issue: Laurence Jerome, Jr.).
1-Ed. Normal Sch., Buffalo, N.Y. Residence: The Stuyvesant, Buffalo, N.Y.

1-**McDOWELL, Mary Eliza,** *b* Cincinnati, O., Nov. 30, 1854.
7-Ephraim **McDowell** (qv);
6-Capt. John (*b* Ireland, 1714-1742), killed by Indians while defending the settlers; capt. of arty., Va. militia; *m* Magdelen Wood (Michael[7], of Albemarle Co., Va., *m* Mary Campbell, of House of Argyle);
5-Samuel (*b* Pa., 1735-1817), with family to Ky.; pres. 9 convs., one of which drafted the 1st Constn., 1792; apptd. 1st U.S. judge of Ky. by President Washington; a founder of Danville, Ky.; burgess; del. "Colony Conv. in Richmond," Va., 1775; one of 1st trustees of Augusta Co. Acad. (now Washington and Lee U.); col. militia, Am. Rev.; *m* Mary McClung (William[6], of Augusta Co., Va.);
4-Samuel (1764-1830), called "Judge Samuel of Mercer"; ran away aet. 13 to join Am. Rev., later with Gen. LaFayette at surrender of Cornwallis; mem. campaign against Indians in Can.; *m* Anne Irvin (1763-1816; Abram[5], of Va. and Ky., *m* Mary Dean);
3-Abram Irvin (*b* 1793), clk. of Ohio Supreme Ct., of common pleas and ct. of bank many yrs.; mayor of Columbus, O.; in father's regt. under Gen. Isaac Shelby, of Ky., in Canadian campaign, War 1812; *m* 1817, Eliza Selden Lord;
2-Malcolm (2 below).
9-Thomas **Lord** (qv);
8-William (*b* 1623), large landowner in Saybrook, 1648, and Lyme, buying from Indians;
7-Thomas (1645-1730), *m* 1693, Marah Lay;
6-Thomas (1694-1762), *m* Esther Marvin (1707-92);
5-Abner (1733-90), Lyme, Conn.; col. in Am. Rev.; *m* Temperance Colt;
4-Abner (*b* 1760), pvt. Am. Rev.; with family to Clarksburg, W.Va., 1791; removed to Vienna on Ohio River, ca. 1794; removed to farm nr. Marietta, O., 1802; *m* 1st, 1782, Mary Selden (1761-1800);
3-Eliza Selden (1795-1817), Marietta, O.; *m* Abram Irvin **McDowell** (3 above).
7-Charles **Gordon** (*d* 1738), from Scotland with his kinswoman, Katherine Gordon Barclay, wife of John Barclay, propr. of E. Jersey; settled at Freehold, Monmouth Co., N.J., 1683; one of 1st three elders of "Old Tennent Ch.," the first Presbyn. ch. of N.J.; *m* Lydia Hampton (John[8], of Monmouth Co., *m* Jean-);
6-David (1717-83), Freehold, N.J.; *m* 2d, 1747, Rebecca Andrews;
5-William (1748-98), minute man in Am. Rev.; *m* Lydia Parent;
4-Lewis (1781-1844), to Cincinnati, O., 1810; in War 1812; *m* Eleanor Wyckoff (1783-1862; William[5], of Monmouth Co., *m* Lydia Brown);
3-Archibald (1809-45), ship builder; mem. Ohio Legislature; *m* 1830, Mary Hanson (*b* 1812; Anthony[4], *m* Barbara Shaffer, of Md.);
2-Jane Welsh (1832-1916), *m* 1852, Malcolm **McDowell** (1827-1903), inventor, metallurgist and mech. engr.; served under bro., Gen. Irvin McDowell, Civil War; served thruout war; after war removed with family to Chicago; issue: I-Archibald Gordon (*d* in infancy); II-Mary Eliza (1 above); III-Jennie (*d* aet. 8); IV-Malcolm (*b* 1860; *m* Jessie Randolph; *m* 2d, Fannie Randolph); V-Gordon (*b* 1863; *m* Belle Winne); VI-Anne (*b* 1865; *m* Herman Rogers Powers; *m* 2d, Maj. Eugene Owen Hopkins); VII-Hanson (*d* 1868; *m* Violet Greenwald); VIII-Irvin (*b* 1871; *m* Ethel Remwick).
1-Head resident, U. of Chicago Settlement since 1893 (see Who's Who in America). Clubs: Woman's City, Chicago Woman's, The Cordon. Residence: 4630 Gross Av., Chicago, Ill.

1-**McGUIRE, Ulysses Melville,** *b* Jennings Co., Ind., Apr. 7, 1856.
4 or 5-Francis **McGuire** (1763-1806), from Ireland, settled at Charleston, Ind.; and thru:
3-George Washington (*d* 1845), of Paris, Ind.; *m* 1833, Elizabeth Matthews (*d* 1858);
2-William Edward (1834-74), of Paris, Ind.; farmer; teacher in common schools; *m* 1855, Nancy Violetta Deputy (1837-1912); issue: I-Ulysses Melville (1 above); II-William Felix (1858-1922; *m* Luella Craig; *m* 2d, Darthulia James; *m* 3d, Mrs. Christine Downs); III-James Horace (1860-1915; *m* Ernestine Abrams); IV-Flora May (*b* 1865; *m* Howard

Newby; *m* 2d, Rev. Lewis King); V–John Elmore (*b* 1867; *m* Rose Byfield).

1–*m* Mar. 7, 1880, Elba Graham (Feb. 11, 1856-June 12, 1914); dau. of William J. Graham, of Paris Crossing, Ind.; issue: 1–Ella May, *b* Paris Crossing, Ind., May 28, 1881; *m* 1904, Joseph Randolph (issue: Carl; Wayne); 2–Mary Agnes, *b* Paris Crossing, Jan. 8, 1883; *m* 1905, Walter Freeland Wood, of Pleasantville, Ind. (issue: Elizabeth; Madge; Gertrude; Ada; Mary; Agnes; Walter, Jr.); 3–Arthur Graham, *b* Crothersville, Ind., Oct. 30, 1884; Danville Normal Coll.; *m* Dona, dau. of John Gravemyer, of Sullivan, Ind. (issue: John Ulysses; Helen; Ruth; Dona; Rebecca; Virginia); 4–Elbert Clive, *b* Crothersville, Oct. 11, 1886; U.Chicago; *m* Ruby, dau. of Jack Hays, of Sullivan, Ind. (issue: Harvey; Joseph Clive); 5–Clarance Vane, *b* Rensselaer, Ind., June 2, 1889; *m* Frances Smith, of Lansing, Mich. (issue: Robert; Frances; Phebe); 6–Paul Raymond, *b* Anderson, Ind., June 18, 1893; *m* 1917, Myrtle, dau. of Alonzo Harrington, of Bicknell, Ind. (issue: Bruce Graham; John Ulysses; Don Alonzo); 7–Edith Fern, *b* Anderson, Feb. 18, 1898; A.B., Franklin; *m* 1922, John Barnett, of Indianapolis (issue: Lois Jean).

1–Student, Hanover (Ind.) College, Southern Bapt. Theol. Sem.; (D.D., Franklin Coll., 1921). Ordained Bapt. ministry, 1881; pastor various village chs. until 1892; then successively pastor Anderson, Sullivan, Washington Lawrenceburg, Princeton and Greencastle, all of Indiana; editor The Baptist Observer 4 yrs.; asst. editor The Baptist, 1921, also 1925-29, editor, 1929-30 (see Who's Who in America). Mason. Residence: 6121 Greenwood Av., Chicago, Ill.

1–**McHATTON, Thomas Hubbard,** *b* Brooklyn, N.Y., Nov. 12, 1883.

6–William **McHatton** (1693-1801, aet. 108), from North of Ireland; *m* Margaret– (*b* 1705);

5–John (1739-1831), soldier in French and Indian War; capt. in Am. Rev.; *m* 1767, Martha– (1744-1821);

4–Robert Lytel (1778-1835), in Ky. Legislature, 1814-16, in U.S. Congress, 1826-29; lived at Dry Run, 4 miles from Georgetown, Ky.; *m* Kitty Emerson;

3–James Alexander (1814-72), rep. from La. to Charleston Conv., 1860; the first Confederate Flag to be raised in La. was at his plantation, Arlington, on the Miss. River, 3 miles below Baton Rouge; connected with Confederate intelligence, 1863-64; emigrated to Cuba 1864; *d* without taking oath of allegiance to U.S. (unreconstructed); *m* 1852, Eliza Chinn;

2–Henry Chinn (2 below).

8–John (Chynn) **Chinn,** from Eng. in the "James," to Lancaster Co., Va.; *m* Elizabeth Travers;

7–~~Raleigh~~ (1700-41), *m* ~~Esther~~ Margaret Ball (1685-1751; ~~Col. Joseph^{8};~~ Col. William^{9}, from Eng. to Lancaster Co.), she was half sister of Martha Washington, mother of Gen. George;

6–Charles (1723-87), *m* Syntha Davis;

5–John (1766-1839), *m* Mildred Higgins;

4–Richard Henry (*d* 1847), judge, New Orleans, 1840; *m* 1814, his ~~first cousin~~, Betsy Holmes (1798-1846; Robert^{5}, *m* Susan, dau. of John Chinn, 5 above);

3–Eliza (1832-1912), author "From Flag to Flag," and "Social Life in Old New Orleans"; *m* 1st, James Alexander **McHatton** (3 above).

11–William **Hubbard** (qv);

10–William (1621-1704), M.A., Harvard, 1642; minister and writer, wrote a history of Mass., 1640-80; *m* 1646, Mary Rogers (g.dau. of John Rogers, pres. Harvard Coll., 1684);

9–John (1648-1709), to Boston, 1680; merchant; treas. Suffolk Co.; *m* 1671, Ann Leverett (Gov. John^{10});

8–John (1677-1705), grad. Harvard, 1695; Congl. clergyman; *m* Mabel (Haynes) Russel (g.dau. John Haynes, qv);

7–Daniel (1706-41), posthumous son; A.B., Yale, 1727; lawyer; sheriff, 1735; *m* Martha Coit (John^{8}, of New London);

6–Capt. Russell (*b* 1732), A.B., Yale, 1751; Am. Rev.; *m* 1755, Mary Grey (*b* 1728);

5–Thomas (1758-95), *m* Mary Hallum;

4–Amos (*b* 1791), *m* Eliza Lanman;

3–Thomas (1828-67), *m* 1849, his cousin, Sarah Lanman;

2–Eliza (2 below).

7–James **Lanman,** from Eng., settled at Boston, 1692; *m* 1714, Joanna Boylston (Dr. Thomas^{8}, *m* Mary Gardiner);

6–Peter (*b* 1725), moved to Norwich, Conn., 1750, and engaged in commerce; *m* Marriana Sarah Coit (Col. Samuel^{7});

5–James (1769-1841), grad. Yale, 1788; U.S. senator from Conn., 1819-25; judge Supreme Ct. and Ct. of Errors; mem. both houses of the Conn. Legislature; mayor of Norwich; *m* 1794, Mary-Ann Griswold Chandler (g.dau. Matthew Griswold, qv);

4–Col. Charles James (1795-1870), *m* 1819, Marie Guy (Antoine^{5}, *m* Angelique Bordeau);

3–Sarah, *m* her cousin, Thomas **Hubbard** (3 above);

2–Eliza (*b* 1861), *m* 1880, Henry Chinn **McHatton,** M.D. (1856-1917), practiced medicine in Macon, Ga., 34 yrs.; pres. Ga. Med. Assn.; specialist on malaria, tuberculosis and children, on which subjects he wrote many papers and pamphlets; issue: I–James Alexander (*d* infancy); II–Thomas Hubbard (1 above).

1–*m* June 14, 1911, Marie Lustrat, *b* Vichy, France, Sept. 11, 1885; dau. of Joseph Lustrat, of Vichy, France, came to U.S., 1892, naturalized citizen, 1903, prof. Romance languages, U. of Ga., and State Normal Sch., Athens, since 1897; *m* 1880, Élinore Maria Moure, of Vichy, France; issue: 1–Marie Lustrat, *b* Athens, Ga., Dec. 13, 1912; A.B., U.Ga.; 2–Eleanor Elizabeth (July 17, 1917-Jan. 15, 1924).

1–B.S., Springhill Coll., Mobile, Ala., 1903, Sc.D., 1907; B.S., Mich. Coll. Agr., 1907, M.S. Hort., 1921; studied Cornell U., Ia. State Coll. Agr. Prof. and head div. of horticulture since 1911, also in charge extension work in horticulture, U.Ga. (see Who's Who in America). Capt. Air Service Production, U.S.A., Jan.-Dec. 1918; maj. C.W.S., O.R.C., 1923; lt. col. C.W.S. Reserve, 1926. Mem. S.C.W., A.L., Reserve Officers Assn. Democrat. K.C. Clubs: Cloverhurst, Athens Country. Summer place: Freedom Lodge, Margret, Fannin Co., Ga. Residence: 847 Milledge Av., Athens, Ga.

1–**McILHENNY, Edward Avery,** *b* Avery Island, La., Mar. 29, 1872.

4–Robert **McIlhenny** (*d* 1790; of the clan of Argylls, of Scotland, went to Ireland ca. 1685); came from North of Ireland to Phila., Pa., thence to Md.; *m* 1778, Barbara Barr;

3–John (*b* 1780), *m* 1811, Ann Newcomer;

2–Edmund (2 below).

9–Christopher **Avery** (qv);

8–James (1620-1700), *m* 1643, Joanna Greenslade;

7–James (*b* 1646), *m* 1669, Deborah Stallyon;

6–Benjamin (*b* 1696), *m* 1734, his cousin, Thankful Avery;

5–Daniel (*b* 1740), *m* his cousin, Deborah Avery;

4–Dudley (*b* 1770), *m* 1807, Mary Ann Brown;

3–Daniel Dudley (*b* 1812), *m* in 1837, Sarah Craig Marsh;

2–Mary (1838-1915), *m* Edmund **McIlhenny** (1815-1890), banker and mfr., Avery Island, La. (for issue see Vol. I, p. 708).

1–*m* June 6, 1900, Mary Matthews, *b* New Orleans, La., Dec. 18, 1874; dau. William H. Matthews, *d*, of New Orleans; issue (all *b* Avery Island, La.): 1–Rosemary, *b* Feb. 9, 1901; *m* June 11, 1919, Lt. Harold G. Osborn (issue: Harold Gray, Jr., *b* Jan. 27, 1925; Rosemary McIlhenny, *b* Sept. 1, 1926); 2–Pauline, *b* July 22, 1902; *m* Nov. 18, 1923, Fisher Simmons (issue: Fisher Edward, Jr., *b* Dec. 14, 1924; Edward Avery McIlhenny, *b* Sept. 15, 1928); 3–Lela, *b* Sept. 22, 1903; *m* June 3, 1925, Alfred Whitney Brown (issue: Anne Newcomer, *b* Oct. 3, 1926; Lela McIlhenny, *b* May 13, 1929).

1–Lehigh, '94 (Phi Delta Theta). Pres. McIlhenny Co., mfrs. tabasco sauce. Mem. New Orleans Zool. Soc., La. State Parks Assn., Am. Game Protective Assn., Am. Museum of Natural History, Am. Ornithologists Union, Game Conservation Soc., N.Y. Zool. Soc., N.Y. Bot. Gardens, Am. Geog. Soc., Canadian Camp, Am. Genetic Soc., Biol. Soc. of Washington, Am. Soc. Mammologists, Nat. Parks Assn., Archaeol. Soc. of America, U.S. Chamber of Commerce, Intercoastal Canal Assn., Inland Bird Banding Assn., Agassiz Assn., etc. Clubs: Boston (New Orleans), Arctic, Explorers (New York), Camp Fire (Chicago). Residence: "Mayward Hill," Avery Island, La.

1–**McINTOSH, Elizabeth Weaver Ellis (Mrs. George Thorburn),** *b* Cleveland, O., Nov. 7, 1853.
7–Lt. John **Ellis** (*d* 1677), from Eng.; settled at Sandwich, Mass., ca. 1643; *m* 1645, Elizabeth Freeman (*b* in Eng., 1625; Edmund[8], qv);
6–John (*b* 1661), *m* 1700, Sarah Holmes (*b* 1680; Nathaniel[7], *m* Mercy Frunce);
5–John (1704-92), Gelead, Conn.; *m* 1731, Rose Jennings (1710-82; Isaac[6], *m* Rose Goodspeed);
4–Sgt. John (1735-1803), Pittsfield, Mass.; soldier Am. Rev., 1778; *m* 1760, Elizabeth Sawyer (1741-1813);
3–Jonathan (1770-1836), to Ypsilanti, Mich., 1827; *m* 1796, Wealthy Lawrence;
2–Elijah (2 below).
8–John **Lawrence** (qv);
7–Peleg (1647-92), Groton, Mass.; *m* 1668, Elizabeth Morse (*b* 1647; Joseph[8], of Dedham, *m* 1638, Hannah Phillips; Samuel[9]);
6–Joseph (1688-1756), Plainfield, Conn.; *m* 1713, Mary– (*d* 1769);
5–Thomas (1714-54), *m* Sarah Warren (1715-99);
4–Thomas (1748-1825), of Dalton, Mass.; soldier Am. Rev.; *m* 1768, Abigail Britton (1745-1823), of Westmoreland, N.H. (Ebenezer[5], *m* Tabitha–);
3–Wealthy (1775-1825), *m* Jonathan **Ellis** (3 above).
6–Jacob **Weaver,** *m* Catherine Harter;
5–George J. (*d* 1811), soldier Am. Rev.; *m* 1754, Anna Elizabeth DuBois, of Livingston Manor, N.Y.;
4–Nicholas George (1762-1838), soldier Am. Rev.; *m* 1785, Gertrude Dygert;
3–Capt. Nicholas N. (1791-1853), soldier War 1812; *m* 1814, Elizabeth Shoemaker;
2–Mary Elizabeth (2 below).
7–Werner **Dygert,** at Livingston Manor, 1710; in Montreal expdn., 1711; granted land at Stone Arabia, 1723;
6–Peter, from Germany 1710; *m* Elizabeth Fox;
5–William (1723-1802), served in French and Indian War and Am. Rev.; *m* Maria Elizabeth Ecker;
4–Gertrude (1767-1851), *m* Nicholas G. **Weaver** (4 above).
6–Lt. Thomas (Schumacher) **Shoemaker** (qv);
5–Capt. Rudolph (*d* 1788), patentee under Burnetsfield Grant, 1725; capt. 1st Grenadiers Co., 1768; justice; capt. militia, Am. Rev.; *m* Gertruyd Herkimer (*d* 1806), sister Gen. Nicholas Herkimer (Johan Jost[6], *m* Catharina–; Jurgh[7]);
4–Maj. Johan Jost (1747-ca. 1797), maj. Am. Rev.; *m* 1775, Mary Smith (Robert[5], *m* Mary Ile);
3–Elizabeth (1790-1874), *m* Nicholas Nicholas **Weaver** (3 above).
2–Elijah **Ellis** (1810-89), of Ypsilanti, Mich., and Cleveland, O.; *m* 1837, Almira Warner (*d* 1839; Lawrence[3]); *m* 2d, 1852 or 53, Mary Elizabeth Weaver (1815-97), of Utica, N.Y.; issue (1st marriage): I–Emma A. (1838-1915; *m* 1864, John S. Jenness); issue (2d marriage): I–Elizabeth Weaver (1 above); II–John Courtland (*b* 1855; *m* 1881).
1–*m* Nov. 4, 1874, George Thorburn McIntosh (1849-1924), son of Alexander McIntosh, from Scotland, 1833; issue: 1–Mary Mabel, *b* Feb. 5, 1876; D.F.P.A., D.A.R.; *m* 1902, Albert Rees Davis (*d* 1919); *m* 2d, Nov. 12, 1925, Capt. Warren J. Clear, U.S.A., *b* Belmont, Mass., son of James Clear, of Newton, Mass., *m* Elizabeth Kelly; 2–Edith Agnes, *b* Cleveland, May 28, 1883; *m* Sept. 28, 1907, James Hiram Foster (issue: George McIntosh, *b* 1909; Mary Stanley, *b* 1911; James Hiram, Jr., *b* 1913; Elizabeth McIntosh, *b* 1915).
1–Mem. D.F.P.A., D.A.C., C.D.A. (hon. mem.), D.A.R. (treas. Western Reserve Chapter, 1898-1900; v.regent, 1902-06; regent 1906-08; state treas. Ohio, 1902-06; hon. mem. Ohio State Officer's Club), U.S.D. 1812 (regent Com. Perry Chapter, 1914-16; state pres., 1917-20; mem. Assn. of State Presidents), I.A.G., Soc. of N.E. Women. Residence: 2200 Devonshire Dr., Cleveland Heights, O.

1–**WEVER, Sara Flagg Childress (Mrs. William Feimster),** *b* Richmond, Tex., Oct. 6, 1857.
9–Alexander **Shapleigh** (qv);
8–Catherine, *m* James (Treeworthy) **Treworgye,** agent in Me. for Gov. Gorges;
7–Elizabeth (1639-1719), *m* 1657, Hon. John **Gilman** (1624-1708; Edward[8], qv);
6–Catherine (*b* 1684), *m* Peter **Folsom** (1682-1718);
5–Peter (1714-92), *m* Mary Folsom (1722-91);
4–Samuel (1761-1849), *m* Anna Shephard;
3–Isaac (1792-1865), physician; *m* 1825, Lucia Davis Morton;
2–Harriet Ann Elizabeth (2 below).
7–Samuel **Shephard** (*d* 1707), of Haverhill and Salisbury, Mass.; *m* 1673, Mary Page Dow (bap. 1646-1718);
6–John (1682-prob. 1732), *m* 1711/12, Rachel Morrill (*b* 1692);
5–Isaac, of Deerfield, N.H.; *m* 1747, Martha Brown (bap. 1730);
4–Anna (*d* 1804), *m* Samuel **Folsom** (4 above).
9–George **Morton** (qv);
8–Ephraim (1623-93), *b* on passage to America; *m* 1644, Anna Cooper (*d* 1691);
7–George (*d* 1727), *m* 1664, Joanna Kempton;
6–Timothy (1682-1748), *m* 1701, Mary Rickard (bap. 1688-1734/35);
5–Silas (*b* 1727), *m* 1748, Martha Morton;
4–Silas (1752-1840), capt. Am. Rev., at Valley Forge; *m* 1792, Elizabeth Foster;
3–Lucia Davis (1806-72 or 74), *m* Isaac **Folsom** (3 above);
2–Harriet Ann Elizabeth (1833-1910), *m* 1852, Capt. Patrick Henry **Childress** (1814-79), wholesale grocer and commission mcht., of Galveston, Tex.; for issue and other lineages see sister, Mrs. Robert H. McIntosh.
1–*m* Oct. 21, 1880, William Feimster Wever, *b* Olin, N.C., Oct. 1, 1856; son of George Wever, of Olin; issue (all *b* Wills Point, Tex.): 1–Clara Madge, *b* Dec. 22, 1881; ed. E. Tex. State Teachers' Coll.; *m* July 20, 1901, William R., son of John R. Taylor, of Selma, Ala. (issue: Estelle; Sara Louise; Herma); 2–Ralph William, *b* Apr. 18, 1884; 3–Harriet Wave (Aug. 9, 1892-Dec. 31, 1925) Belhaven Coll., Jackson, Miss.; *m* Apr. 24, 1919, John A., son of John A. McNabb, of Houston, Tex.; 4–Doris Elizabeth, *b* Feb. 25, 1895; *m* Apr. 18, 1918, Rhom, son of Dillard S. Carr, of Whitewright, Tex. (issue: Wave Wever; William Herbert, 1923-25).
1–Ed. Arcadia (Mo.) Coll. Methodist. Democrat. Residence: Mineola, Wood Co., Tex.

1–**McINTOSH, Mary Sanderson Childress (Mrs. Robert Hardy),** *b* Galveston, Tex., Dec. 16, 1867.
8–John **Folsom** (qv);
7–Dea. John (1640-1715), of Exeter, N.H.; rep. Gen. Assembly; *m* 1675, Abigail Perkins (Abraham[8]);
6–Jonathan (1685-1740), of Exeter; *m* Anna Ladd (Nathaniel[7]);
5–Mary (1722-91), of Exeter; *m* Peter **Folsom** (1714-92; Peter[6]);
4–Samuel (1761-1849), of Deerfield Parade; *m* Anna Shephard;
3–Isaac (1792-1865), of Batesville, Ark; physician; *m* 1825, Lucia Davis Morton;
2–Harriet Ann Elizabeth (2 below).
9–George **Morton** (qv);
8–Ephraim (1623-93), *b* while on passage to America; *m* 1644, Anna Cooper (*d* 1691);
7–Thomas (*b* 1667), of Plymouth; *m* Martha Doty (Edward[8], *m* Sarah Faunce);
6–Thomas (1700-31), *m* Hannah Nelson;
5–Martha (*b* 1729), *m* 1748, Silas **Morton;**
4–Silas (1752-1840), of Plymouth, capt. Am. Rev., at Valley Forge; *m* 1792, Elizabeth Foster;
3–Lucia Davis (1806-72 or 74), *m* Isaac **Folsom** (3 above).
10–Richard **Warren,** Mayflower Pilgrim (qv);
9–Mary (*b* in Eng.-*d* 1677), *m* Robert **Bartlett** (qv);
8–Lidia (1648-91), as Widow Barnabe, *m* John **Nelson,** of Plymouth;
7–Samuel (1683-ca. 1735), *m* Bathsheba Nichols (*d* 1717);
6–Hannah (*b* 1707), *m* Thomas **Morton** (6 above).
9–Sgt. Thomas **Foster** (ca. 1600-82), from Eng.; settled in Dorchester, Mass.; *m* 1638, Elizabeth– (*d* 1694/95);
8–Dea. John (1642-1732), *m* Mary Chillingworth (Thomas[9]);
7–Hon. John (*b* 1666), of Marshfield, Mass.; *m* Hannah Stetson (Thomas[8], of Scituate, *m* Sarah Dodson; Robert[9], qv);
6–Samuel (1698-1778), of Kingston, Mass.; *m* 1722, Margaret Tilden (*b* ca. 1696; Nathaniel[7],

of Scituate, *m* 2d, 1693, Margaret Dodson; Joseph[8], Elder Nathaniel[9], qv);
5–Robert (*b* 1737), *m* Elizabeth–;
4–Elizabeth (*b* 1767), *m* Silas **Morton** (4 above);
3–Lucia Davis, of Pembroke, Mass.; *m* Isaac **Folsom** (3 above);
2–Harriet Ann Elizabeth (1833-1910), of Batesville, Ark.; *m* 1852, Patrick Henry **Childress** (1814-79); issue: I–Clara Howard (*b* 1854; *m* Cromwell Dawson); II–Sarah Flagg (Mrs. William F. Wever, qv for other lineages); III–Emma Maude (1860-99; *m* James M. McKain); IV–Patrick Henry (1862-1928; *m* Lucy Cole); V–George Ferguson (*b* 1865; *m* Mae Torbett); VI–Mary S. (1 above); VII–Lucia Folsom (*b* 1870; *m* 1893, Rev. J. J. Clark).
1–*m* Sept. 16, 1896, Robert Hardy McIntosh, *b* Newton, Miss., May 17, 1866 (William D.[2]; William L.[3]; Alexander[4]); adopted dau., Katherine, *b* Dec. 25, 1914.
1–Mem. D.A.R. (regent Sarah McCalla Chapter), Folsom Family Assn., Stetson Family Assn. Methodist. Democrat. Residence: Cameron, Tex.

1–**MACKAY, Anna Augusta Morrell (Mrs. Daniel Ellis),** *b* Smithtown, L.I., N.Y., Dec. 1, 1847.
8–Richard **Smith** (1615-92), called "The Patentee"; founded Smithtown, L.I., 1683; *m* Sarah Folger (*d* 1708);
7–Daniel, *m* Ruth Tooker;
6–Daniel, *m* Hannah Brewster;
5–Caleb (1724-1800), grad. Yale, 1744; judge of Ct. Common Pleas; of "Willow Pond"; patriot during Am. Rev.; *m* Martha Smith (Maj. William[6]; Col. William[7], gov. of Tangier, received grant of St. George's Manor, L.I., from King William, III);
4–Paul Theodore (1759-1813), *m* Elizabeth Van Wyck (*d* 1847; Abraham[5], of Huntington, L.I.);
3–Theodorus, *m* 1819, his cousin, Eliza Conklin;
2–Martha E. (1821-72), *m* 1838, Joseph Smith **Morrell,** M.D., of New York.
1–*m* Jan. 6, 1866, Daniel Ellis Mackay (Apr. 1, 1845-Aug. 13, 1910), son of Daniel Mackay, *m* Sarah Acey; issue: 1–Donald Stuart, *b* Brooklyn, N.Y., Oct. 25, 1868; *m* Elizabeth Conklin, killed instantly in automobile accident, July 12, 1929 (issue: Donald Harold, *m* Mildred Cort; Dorothy, *m* Apr. 1916, John Kenneth Taylor [issue: Elizabeth; Donald Kenneth]); 2–Joseph Walter (May 10, 1870-Mar. 21, 1917), *m* Aug. 1916, Mary Stieges; 3–Charles Ellis, *b* Brooklyn, Feb. 1, 1879; *m* Mar. 1, 1905, Edith Aline, dau. Robert Block (issue: Charles Ellis; Aline Edith).
1–Mem. D.F.P.A., C.D. 17th C., D.A.R., Hist. Soc. of Huntington, L.I. Episcopalian. Republican. Residence: 39 Gibson Av., Huntington, L.I., N.Y.

1–**McKAY, Oscar Reed,** *b* Mason, Ill., Nov. 1, 1861.
4–Richard **McKay** (*b* probably ca. 1745), from Scotland; settled in Md.; removed later to Plum Run, Nelson Co., Ky., where he had land grant; ship pilot, Chesapeake Bay; served in Troop 2, Light Dragoons, Cont. Army, Am. Rev.; *m* 1st, Nancy Anna Hebb; *m* 2d, Mrs. Shumate (no issue); *m* 3d, Mary Murphy; issue (1st marriage): 1–William (*m* Mary McCarty); 2–Elizabeth (*m* —Moxley); 3–Katherine (*m* —Froman); 4–Elenor or Nellie (*m* George O'Neal; *m* 2d, —Losson); 5–Samuel (*m* Nancy Murray); 6–John (*m* Sallie Edwards); 7–Uriah (below); 8–Richard (*m* Sallie Murphy); issue (3d marriage): 1–Sarah (*m* —Cooms); 2–Nancy (*m* —Wilson);
3–Uriah (1782-1830), known as Hugh; removed with family from Md. to Ky. aet. 14; lived in Madison, Ind., and returned to Ky.; settled at Taylorsville; *m* Elizabeth O'Neal (1786-1891), of Plum Run, Ky.;
2–Rev. Uriah (1821-1909), Bapt. minister; *m* 1857, Mary Adelaide Billingsley; issue: I–Theodore W. (*b* 1858; *m* Elizabeth Blanshan); II–Allen (*b* 1860); III–Oscar Reed (1 above); IV–Edwin B. (*b* 1864); V–Arthur Neal (*b* 1868; *m* La Verne Morris); VI–Adelaide (*b* 1870; *m* William A. McGriff).
1–*m* Sept. 3, 1890, Mary Gertrude Lankton, *b* Elbridge, N.Y., Dec. 8, 1868; dau. of James Lankton, of Elbridge; issue: 1–Ralph Lankton, *b* India, Sept. 29, 1893; attended Colgate and Purdue; served with 23d Engrs., A.E.F., World War; *m* June 9, 1920, Mary Jane, dau. of George Collins, *m* Sallie– (issue: Robert C.).
1–A.B., Colgate, '87 (D.D., 1913); grad. Colgate Div. Sch. Ordained Bapt. ministry, 1890; missionary in India, 1891-94; pastor at Warsaw, N.Y., Lafayette and Bluffton, Ind., 1894-1921; dir. religious edn., Ind. Bapt. Conv., 1921-25; asso. pastor First Bapt. Ch., Indianapolis, 1925– (see Who's Who in America). Mason. Odd Fellow. Republican. Residence: 55 N. Arlington St., Indianapolis, Ind.

1–**MacKAYE, Arthur Loring,** *b* Perth Amboy, N.J., Dec. 19, 1863.
4–William (Kay, McKay) **MacKaye** (of the Clan MacKay), from Scotland, 1800, settled in the Scotch colony, Argyl, N.Y.; *m* Sarah (Wilkinson) McCracken, sister of Gen. Joseph Wilkinson, mil. aide to Gen. Gates at Battle of Saratoga;
3–Col. James Morrison (1804-88), prominent abolitionist; *m* Emily Benton Steele;
2–James Steele (2 below).
9–John **Steele** (qv);
8–John (*d* 1653, before his father), *m* 1645, Mercy Warner (Andrew[9]);
7–Samuel (1652-1710), *m* 1680, Mercy Bradford (*d* 1720; Maj. William[8]; Gov. William[9], qv);
6–Daniel (1697-1770), *m* 1725, Mary Hopkins;
5–Timothy (1736-1806), *m* Sarah Seymour (1740-1808);
4–Oliver (1781-1826), newspaper publisher at Savannah, Ga., and New Haven, Conn.; *m* 1803, Sarah Loring (David[5]);
3–Emily Benton (1806-49), *m* 1833, Col. James Morrison **MacKaye** (3 above).
9–Robert **Buffum** (qv);
8–Caleb (1650-1731), *m* 1672, Hannah Hope;
7–Benjamin (1686-1735), *m* Elizabeth Buxton;
6–Joseph (1717-96), Smithfield, R.I.; *m* 1736, Margaret Osborne (1719-1805; William[7]; William[8]);
5–William (1741-1829), *m* 1767, Lydia Arnold (1749-1828; Thomas[6], *m* Patience Cook; Richard[7]; Richard[8]; Thomas[9]);
4–Arnold (1782-1859), Eagleswood, N.J.; 1st pres. N.E. Anti-Slavery Soc., 1832; *m* 1804, Rebecca Gould;
3–Rebecca (1811-1911), *m* Marcus **Spring** (1810-74), of Uxbridge, Mass. (g.son of Rev. Amos Spring, chaplain with force of Gen. Benedict Arnold in march across Me.);
2–Jeanie (2 below).
8–Daniel **Gould** (Jeremiah[9]; Richard[10]; Richard[11]; Thomas[12]; Richard[13]; Thomas[14]), from Eng., 1637; asso. with Roger Williams in R.I.; *m* 1651, a dau. of John Coggeshall (qv);
7–Thomas;
6–Thomas (1698-1786), Middletown, R.I.; *m* 1723, Sarah Anthony (1697-1798; John[7]; John[8]);
5–John (1736-1811), *m* 1761, Sarah Coggeshall (1737-1816; James[6], *m* Hannah, dau. of Thomas Brooks; Benjamin[7]; John[8]; John[9]);
4–Rebecca (1781-1872), *m* Arnold **Buffum** (4 above).
2–James Steele **MacKaye** (1842-94), disciple of Delsarte; author, actor, theatrical mgr.; 1st lt., a.-d.-c., Civil War; *m* Jeanie Spring (1843-1921); *m* 2d, Mary Keith Medbury (1844-1924); issue (1st marriage): I–Arthur Loring (1 above); II–Beatrice Emily (1865-72); issue (2d marriage): I–Harold Steele (1866-1928; *m* Helen Lane); II–William Payson (1869-89); III–James Medbery (see Vol. I, p. 709); IV–Percy Wallace (*b* 1875; *m* Marion Morse); V–Benton (*b* 1879); VI–Hazel (*b* 1880).
1–*m* Feb. 4, 1885, Maud Miller (1864-1906), dau. of Joaquim Miller, of Calif.
1–*m* 2d, Apr. 19, 1889, Flora Cutler (*b* 1865), dau. of Charles D. Cutler; issue: 1–David Loring, *b* Brooklyn, N.Y., Feb. 15, 1890; capt. Hdqrs. Co., Fort Shafter, T.H.; adj. 1st Hawaiian Regt., 1917-18; A.B., Calif. State Coll., '30; *m* July 1919, Anna Virginia Trook (issue [all *b* Honolulu, T.H.]: David Steele, Mary Loring, Martin V.).
1–*m* 3d, Dec. 14, 1899, Laura Elida Hansen Florud, *b* Oslo, Norway, Oct. 8, 1868; dau. of Lars Hansen Florud.
1–Writer; formerly mem. Rep. Territorial Com., Hawaii; discoverer of Coral Gardens of Kaneohe, Hawaii. Author (see Who's Who in America). Congregationalist. Republican. Residence: 740 Solano Av., Los Angeles, Calif.

1–**McKAY, Herbert Couchman,** *b* Vigo Co., Ind., Apr. 8, 1895.
3–John Wallace **McKay** (*b* Westmoreland Co., Va., 1830-*d* 1905), of Neoga, Ill.; *m* Sarah Jane Moreland (*b* Trimble Co., Ky., 1838-*d* 1873);
2–Isaac Newton (2 below).
7–George **Brown** (desc. Edward Brown, who came from Eng., 1634, and settled in the Lord Baltimore colony), of nr. Baltimore; *m* 1730, Nancy Stevenson;
6–Edward (1734-1823), Frederick Co., Md.; ship capt. and owner; *m* Margaret Durbin;
5–Nicholas (1765-1858), ens. in Capt. Heister's Co. of Berks Co. (Pa.) Bn.; *m* 1792, Sarah Whitaker (1769-1859; Thomas[6], served in Capt. James Gibson's Co., 4th Bn., Cumberland Co. Militia, 1777, under Col. James Wilson);
4–Basil (1793-1854), of Cumberland Co., Ill.; lumberman; Bapt. preacher and sch. teacher; *m* 1817, Abigail Turner (1800-78);
3–James Sutton (1822-1902), of Vigo Co., Ind.; *m* 1st, 1848, Almira Grover (*b* Kirkesville, O., 1828-*d* 1864);
2–Keziah Jemima (*b* 1858), of Vigo Co.; *m* 1885, Isaac Newton **McKay** (1852-1918), contractor; issue: I–Charles Wesley (*m* Emily Elizabeth Longley); II–Herbert Couchman (1 above).
1–*m* Dec. 23, 1918, Hazel Irene Doane, *b* Cincinnati, O., Aug. 25, 1898; dau. of James Alexander Doane (1879-1929), of Indianapolis, Ind.; issue: 1–Patricia Dolores, *b* Santiago de las Vegas, Cuba, Dec. 6, 1919; 2–Betty Louise, and 3–Florence Margaret (twins), *b* Eustis, Fla., Dec. 17, 1921.
1–Spl. student Ind. State Normal Sch., 3 yrs. (Theta Nu Epsilon). Amateur photographer at 10, professional at 18; editor motion picture dept. Photo Era since 1923; recognized as a pioneer in amateur cinematography in U.S.; mem. advisory bd. N.Y. Inst. Photography, 1924, bd. dirs., since 1925, also dean. Bacteriologist Base Hosp., Camp Taylor, Ky., World War. Author (see Who's Who in America). Mason. Episcopalian. Republican. Residence: Eustis, Fla.

1–**McKEE, Angie Buchanan (Mrs. J. Langdon),** *b* Grand Rapids, Mich., Nov. 4, 1872.
7–Thomas **Bingham** (qv);
6–Dea. Abel (1669-1745), of Windham, Conn.; *m* Elizabeth (or Mary) Odell;
5–Jonathan (1712-1800), *m* 2d, 1735, Sarah (Upton) Vinton (1710-1803);
4–Elisha (1740-1821), Enfield, N.H.; corpl. in Am. Rev.; *m* 1770, Hannah Slapp (1748-1793 or 94);
3–Rev. Abel (1786-1865), Sault St. Marie, Mich.; lt. in War 1812; *m* 1809, Hannah Olmstead Brown;
2–Sophia Hascal (2 below).
10–Stephen **Hopkins** (qv);
9–Constance (ca. 1608-1677), *m* 1627, Hon. Nicholas **Snow** (qv);
8–Mary (*d* 1704), *m* 1650, Thomas **Paine** (1610-1706), of Eastham; rep. Gen. Ct., 1671; dep., 1672-90; selectman; treas., 1674-94 (Thomas[9], qv);
7–Elisha (1658-1735), a founder of Canterbury, Conn.; town clk.; selectman; rep. Gen. Assembly, 1711-34; *m* 1685, Rebecca Doan (1669-1738; John[8], *m* Hannah Bangs);
6–Rebecca (*b* ca. 1710), *m* 1737, at Canterbury, Conn., Edward **Cleveland**;
5–Rebecca Doan, *m* Daniel **Brown**;
4–Rev. Solomon (1757-1815), Wheatland, N.Y.; served in Am. Rev.; *m* Sarah or Sally Nash (1770-1848);
3–Hannah Olmstead (1794-1868), *m* Rev. Abel **Bingham** (3 above);
2–Sophia Hascal, *m* 1854, John Claudius **Buchanan,** D.D.S. (*b* Ithaca, N.Y., May 15, 1823-*d* 1902), gunsmith, Grand Rapids, Mich.; lt., Co. D, 8th Mich. Vol. Inf., Civil War; (Samuel[3], gunsmith, War 1812; John[4], Am. Rev.); issue: I–Mary Angie (1855-57); II–Claude Robinson (*m* Matilda Sharp, *d* 1916; *m* 2d, Bertha Falbe); III–Bingham Stuart (1860-1925); IV–Robbert Russell (1866-1901; *m* Maria Parsons Foster); V–Clara Bettine (1868-69); VI–Angie Sophia (1 above).
1–*m* Mar. 18, 1912, James Langdon McKee, *b* Grand Rapids, Mich., Oct. 31, 1859; son of James Henry McKee, of Grand Rapids; issue: 1–Dau. (*b* and *d* Apr. 11, 1913); 2–Gilbert Langdon, *b* Grand Rapids, Mich., Dec. 17, 1914; 3–Duncan Buchanan, *b* Grand Rapids, Nov. 7, 1915.
1–Mem. D.F.P.A., S.M.D. (Mass.), D.A.R., U.S.D. 1812. Baptist. Republican. Clubs: Women's City, St. Cecilia, etc. Summer place: Lamont, Mich. Residence: 505 Gladstone Av. S.E., Grand Rapids, Mich.

1–**McKEEHAN, Joseph Parker,** *b* Carlisle, Pa., Nov. 20, 1876.
6–John **McKeehan** (*d* 1783), from North of Ireland, settled at Newville, Cumberland Co., Pa.;
5–John (1736-1813), of Newville; elder Big Spring Presbyn. Ch.; roll capt. in Col. William Irvine's regt., 7th Pa. Cont. Line; *m* Elizabeth McKeehan (1745-1822);
4–George (1766-1827), of Abbotstown, Pa., and Emmittsburg, Md.; called capt.; *m* 1801, **Jane Johnstone**;
3–Joseph Gladney (1810-85), of Central, Pa.; *m* 1839, Elizabeth Catherine Hesser (1818-1902);
2–Joseph Hamlin (2 below).
6–Richard **Parker** (*d* ante 1750), from Ireland with wife to Pa., 1725; *m* Janet–;
5–James (1731-1803), of Pa.; pvt. Capt. John Carothers' co. of militia; *m* Mary Eleanor Boyd;
4–Andrew (1752-1805), of Cumberland Co., Pa.; *m* Margaret Williams (1766-1846), of William's Grove, Pa.;
3–Richard (1797-1867), of Carlisle, Cumberland Co., Pa.; *m* 1849, Hadasseh Graham;
2–Mary Graham (2 below).
6–Epraim **Lytle** (1714-76), from Ireland to Lancaster, Pa., 1726;
5–Ruth, *m* James **Graham** (1745-1804), 2d lt., Am. Rev.;
4–John (1789-1829), *m* Ann Elinor Taylor (1791-1830);
3–Hadasseh (1826-1908), *m* Richard **Parker** (3 above);
2–Mary Graham (*b* 1853), *m* 1872, Joseph Hamlin **McKeehan** (1848-76), law partner of Col. A. K. McClure, Phila.; issue: I–Matilda McClure (*m* Paul A. A. Core); II–Joseph Parker (1 above).
1–*m* June 6, 1917, Helen Wile, *b* Gettysburg, Pa., July 1, 1882; dau. of Henry B. Wile, D.D., of Carlisle, Pa.; issue: 1–Joseph Parker, Jr., *b* Baltimore, Md., Mar. 1, 1923.
1–A.B., Dickinson, Coll., '97 (P.B.K., Beta Theta Pi), A.M., 1899, LL.B., 1902. Prof. law, Dickinson Sch. of Law, since 1902. Spl. dep. atty. gen. Commonwealth of Pa., 1926-27; v.p. Carlisle Deposit Bank & Trust Co.; trustee Carlisle Hosp. (see Who's Who in America). Mem. Cumberland Co. Hist. Soc. Presbyterian. Republican. Club: Carlisle Country. Residence: 300 S. College St., Carlisle, Pa.

1–**McKENZIE, Daisette Dudley Stocking (Mrs. William P.),** *b* Mansfield, O., Aug. 31, 1863.
3–Sidney **Stocking**, *m* Lovisa Tennant;
2–Zalmon Stuart (2 below).
8–Francis **Dudley** (1640-living 1702), settled in Concord, Mass., 1663; *m* Sarah Wheeler;
7–Samuel (*b* 1682), *m* Abigail King;
6–Samuel (1705-ca. 1750), *m* Abigail Waters;
5–Stephen (1735-ca. 1785), Am. Rev.; *m* Lydia Harwood;
4–Stephen (1760-1826);
3–Lyman (1793-1876), *m* Susannah Burnham;
2–Eliza (1826-1906), *m* Benjamin Johns; *m* 2d, 1852, Zalmon Stuart **Stocking** (1819-99); issue (1st marriage, surname Johns): I–Sarah (*d* in infancy); II–Roberta Eugenia (*b* 1848-1920; *m* Charles H. Bulkley, *d*); issue (2d marriage, surname Stocking): I–Lida (*m* Arthur Lee Stone), and II–Leila, twins (1854-92; *m* Henry S. Blossom, *d*); III–Dudley, and IV–DeWitt, twins (*b* 1858-*d* infancy); V–Daisette Dudley (1 above).
1–*m* Aug. 1, 1901, William Padraic McKenzie, *b* Almonte, Ontario, Feb. 17, 1861; son of Rev. William McKenzie, of Scotland, *m* Catherine Shiells; issue: 1–Guilford Stuart, *b* Cambridge, Mass., May 23, 1902; *m* Feb. 4, 1930, Gertrude Louise Wheeler.
1–Mem. Woman's City Club (Boston), Concord (Mass.) Country. Residence: 10 Concord Av., Arsenal Sq., Cambridge, Mass.

1–**McKINNEY, Herbert Rowe,** *b* Sault Ste. Marie, Mich., June 7, 1896.
9–John **Bellows** (1623-83), from Eng. in the "Hopewell," 1635; settled at Concord, Mass., 1645; later an original propr. of Marlborough; *m* 1655, Mary Wood (*d* 1707);

8–Benjamin (1676-1750), Lunenberg, Mass.; *m* 1703, Dorcas (Cutler) Willard (*d* 1747);
7–Benjamin (1712-77), a founder of Walpole, N.H.; served in Indian wars, 1754-55; grant given him, 1752; surveyor; Bellows Falls, Vt., named for him; *m* 1st, 1735, Abigail Stearns (1708-57);
6–Peter (1738-1825), in Am. Rev., at Ticonderoga; *m* 1764, Mary Chase (1751-1830);
5–Solomon (1776-1832), Charlestown, N.H.; *m* 1799, Mary Norvil Hoyt (1776-1843);
4–William Edwy (1806-87), Climax, Mich.; pub. sch. official; *m* 1832, Lavinia A. Harris (1809-64);
3–Charles FitzRoy (1832-1907), of Ypsilanti, Mich.; newspaper editor and pub.; founder Mich. State Normal Coll.; Mason (Grand Master for Mich., 1883); *m* 1855, Julia E. Walter (1833-1925);
2–Jessie Lavinia (1866-1906), of Ypsilanti; pres. Bd. of Edn., Sault Ste. Marie, 1904-06; *m* 1886, Peter T. **McKinney** (1860-1929); for issue see Vol. II, p. 60.
1–*m* Aug. 1, 1925, Jessica Thomas, *b* Ft. Wayne, Ind., Oct. 13, 1900; dau. of Charles E. Thomas, of Ft. Wayne.
1–Newspaper writer, with The Detroit News, since 1920. Served in Mexico, 1916-17, and with A.E.F. in France, 1917-18; with 32d Div., 125th Inf.; mil. instr., Camp Funston, Kan., and Camp Beauregard, La., 1918-19; 2d lt. inf., U.S.R. Mem. S.A.R., A.L., 32d Div. Assn. Episcopalian. Clubs: Detroit Union League, Players, Red Arrow, Mich. Union League. Residence: 2627 John R St., Detroit, Mich.

1–**McKINLAY, Arthur Patch,** *b* Osborn, Mo., Apr. 8, 1871.
9–Thomas **Benedict** (qv);
8–Dea. Samuel (will dated 1720), of Southhold, L.I., Norwalk and Danbury, Conn.; *m* Rebecca Andrews (Thomas[9], of Fairfield, Conn.);
7–Abraham (1681-will proved 1779), of Norwalk; *m* Sarah (Hickok);
6–Jabez (*d* 1804), Cornwall, Conn.; *m* Charity Booth;
5–Sarah (1763-1843), *m* John **McKinlay** (1757-1811), Highlander; of Johnstown, N.Y.; soldier in Am. Rev.;
4–John (1782-1864), *m* Sallie Cameron (*d* 1846);
3–Angus (1812-96), *m* 1847, Frances Forbes;
2–George Angus (2 below).
9–John (Fobes) **Forbes** (*d* 1661; son of Rev. John, moderator of Gen. Assembly of Scottish Ch., 1620); came from Scotland, 1623, settled at Duxbury, Mass.; moved to Bridgewater, 1645; original propr.; *m* Constance Mitchell, passenger on "Little Ann" (sister of Experience Mitchell);
8–Hon. Edward (1650-1732), dea. Bridgewater, Mass.; rep. Mass. Gen. Ct., 1703,08,09,11,12,15,22; *m* 1676, Elizabeth Howard (John[9], *m* Martha, dau. of Thomas Hayward);
7–William (1698-1764), *m* 1725, Thankful Dwelly (*b* 1706; John[8], *m* Rachel Buck; Richard[9]);
6–Abner (*b* 1727), Uxbridge; *m* 1750, Phoebe Leach;
5–Absalom (1751-78), in Am. Rev.; Sutton, Mass.; *m* 1771, Martha Hall (1751-1821; Hon. Willis[6]; Dea. Percival[7]; John[8]);
4–Dr. Jotham (1776-1828), surgeon 34th U.S. Inf., War 1812; to Sandusky Co., O., 1820; *m* 1805, Nancy Olmstead;
3–Frances (1825-1910), *m* Angus **McKinlay** (3 above).
11–Hon. Francis **Cooke,** Mayflower Pilgrim (qv);
10–Jane, *m* Experience **Mitchell;**
9–Elizabeth, *m* John **Washburn,** Jr. (*b* 1621; John[10], qv);
8–Joseph (*b* 1646), *m* Hannah Latham (Robert[9], *m* Susanna, dau. of John Winslow, *m* Mary, dau. James Chilton, Mayflower Pilgrim, qv);
7–Hepzibah (*d* 1750), *m* 1702, Benjamin **Leach** (*d* 1764), of W. Bridgewater (Giles[8]; Lawrence[9]);
6–Phoebe (*b* 1727), *m* Abner **Forbes** (6 above).
10–James (Olmsted) **Olmstead** (qv);
9–Nicholas (1612-84), *m* 1640, Sarah Loomis (1617-67; Joseph[10], qv);
8–Dea. Joseph (1654-1726), *m* Elizabeth Butler (1643-1729; Dea. Richard[9], *m* Elizabeth Bigelow);
7–James (1677-1744), *m* Mary Bull (*b* 1685; Capt. Joseph[8], *m* Ann, dau. of Michael Humphreys; Capt. Thomas[9]);
6–James, *m* 1750, Mary White (*b* 1728; Hugh[7], *m* Mary Stone; Ens. Daniel[8]; Nathaniel[9]; Elder John[10]);
5–James (1751-1811), began to write name Olmstead; officer Am. Rev.; *m* 1774, Mary Beaumont (1749-1835);
4–Nancy (1779-1825), *m* Jotham **Forbes** (4 above).
9–Nicholas **Patch** (bap. 1597; son of Nicholas, of S. Petherton, Somersetshire, Eng., *m* Jane–), arrived Salem, Mass., 1636; *m* 1623, Elizabeth Owley;
8–Thomas (*b* 1638), Wenham, Mass.; rep., 1689; *m* 1670, Mary Scott (Thomas[9]);
7–Isaac (1682-1762), *m* Edith Edwards;
6–Ebenezer (1719-77), *m* 1746, Sarah Wright (*d* 1793);
5–Jacob (1747-1818), in Am. Rev.; *m* 1772, Mary Hazen (1743-1828; Benjamin[6], *m* Betty, dau. Daniel Nutting);
4–Zara (1784-1827), of Groton; *m* 1806, Susanna Nutting;
3–Rufus (1819-91), grad. Western Reserve Coll., 1841; taught at Western Reserve; at Marshall, Mich., and Ontario, Ind.; *m* 2d, 1846, Julia Ann Upson;
2–Julia Brace (2 below).
9–John **Nutting,** of Woburn, 1650; original propr. Groton; killed by Indians; *m* 1650, Sarah Eggleston (Stephen[10]);
8–John (*d* 1717), *m* 1674, Mary–;
7–Jonathan (*b* 1689), made first pair of shoes at Groton, 1706;
6–William (1712-76), went with son to Lexington, at the "Alarm"; *m* Joan Boynton (Benoni[7]);
5–William (1752-1832), corpl. of minute men; introduced Irish potato into Groton; taught school; musician; made his house a clinic to test and popularize the use of vaccine for small pox; *m* Susanna (French) Danforth (Col. Joseph French[6], of Dunstable);
4–Susanna (1781-1821), *m* Zara **Patch** (4 above).
8–Thomas **Upson** (*d* 1655), of Hartford, Conn., 1638; propr. Farmington, Conn.; *m* 2d, 1646, Elizabeth Fuller;
7–Stephen (1650?-1735), of Farmington, Conn.; *m* 1682, Mary Lee (*d* 1715 or 16; John[8], of Gen. Ct., 1710,12,29);
6–Stephen (*b* 1686), *m* Sarah Bronson (Isaac[7]);
5–Benjamin (*b* 1720), in Am. Rev.; *m* 1743, Marah (Mary) Blakesley (*b* 1726 or 27; Dea. Moses[6]);
4–Jesse (1756-1838), in Am. Rev.; settled at Mendham, N.J.; practiced medicine; justice, probate judge 25 yrs.; served in Legislature 50 yrs.; moved to Greenfield, Ind., 1838; *m* 2d, Polly (Mary) Dayton (*d* 1848; Robert[5]; Jonathan[6]; Samuel[7]; Robert[8]; Ralph[9]);
3–Julia Ann (1823-69), *m* Rufus **Patch** (3 above);
2–Julia Brace (1849-97), *m* 1868, George Angus **McKinlay** (1847-1928), Presbyterian minister; issue: I–Evelyn (1869-70); II–Arthur Patch (1 above); III–Roslyn (1873-95); IV–Joseph France (*b* 1877; *m* Ethel Patten; *m* 2d, Evelyn Fortner); V–Alice Cornelia (*b* 1879; *m* William Miller); VI–Edwin Lawrence (*b* 1884; *m* Edna Millikan; *m* 2d, Beatrice Curley); VII–Muriel (*b* 1896).
1–*m* Feb. 21, 1914, Jessie Goddard, *b* Monroe, Wis.; dau. of Anson Wesley Goddard, of Monroe, *m* Sarah Frances McMannes.
1–A.B., U.Ore., '93 (P.B.K.); A.M., Harvard, 1904, Ph.D., 1906. Chmn. dept. classical languages, U.Calif., prof. Latin, 1929–. Author (see Who's Who in America). Presbyterian. Republican. Summer place: McKinlay Orchards, Route 1, Salem, Ore. Residence: 1326 Lucile Av., Los Angeles, Calif.

1–**MacKINNON, Charlotte Hodgkins (Mrs. Arthur Custer),** *b* Bay City, Mich., July 23, 1874.
9–Thomas **Catlin** (qv);
8–John, of Hartford, Conn.; *m* 1665, Mary Marshall (Capt. Samuel[9]);
7–Samuel (*b* 1673), *m* 1702, Elizabeth Norton, of Farmington, Conn. (John[8]);
6–John (1703-68), *m* 1731, Margaret Seymour;
5–Theodore (*b* 1735), *m* 1750, Mary Goodwin;
4–Able, *m* Betsy Hollister;
3–William (1817-63), chaplain in Civil War, wounded; buried in Nat. Cemetery, Annapolis; *m* 2d, 1845, Ruth Ann Beardsley;
2–Cerelia Elizabeth (2 below).
10–William **Beardsley** (qv);
9–Joseph (1634-1712), from Eng. with his parents; settled Cupheag (now Stratford), Conn., 1639;

freeman, 1668; *m* 1665, Abigail Dayton, of L.I.;
8–John (1668-1735), blacksmith, of Mass.; *m* Abigail Wakelyn (*d* 1735);
7–Abraham (1696-1775), of Stratford; *m* 1723, Esther Jeans (*d* 1772; William[8], warden Christ's Ch., Stratford, 1732);
6–Michael (*b* 1740), of Catherine, N.Y.; *m* 1763, Eunice Mallet;
5–James (1771-1851), cooper; removed to Beardsley Hollow, 1801; *m* 1795, Hannah Beach;
4–Stephen (*b* 1801), Odessa, N.Y.; *m* Sally Bennett;
3–Ruth (1827-1913), *m* William **Catlin** (3 above);
2–Cerelia Elizabeth (1847-82), of Watkins, N.Y., *m* 1871, Ward W. **Hodgkins** (*b* 1844); issue: I–Jessie Lyle (1872-92); II–Charlotte (1 above); III–Nina Fray (1881-82).
1–*m* Oct. 19, 1899, Arthur Custer MacKinnon, *b* Cleveland, O., Aug. 3, 1870; son of John Donald MacKinnon, of Bay City, Mich., *m* Agnes Kirk; issue (all *b* Bay City): 1–Jessie Hodgkins, *b* May 28, 1902; *m* June 30, 1925, Hugo T., son of Nicholas Swanson, of Ishpeming, Mich. (issue: Charlotte Marie; Arthur Nicholas); 2–Mary Kirk, *b* June 9, 1904; B.A., Mich. State Coll., '26; 3–Charlotte Agnes, *b* May 14, 1911.
1–Mem. D.F.P.A., D.A.R. Congregationalist. Republican. Residence: 1214 Center Av., Bay City, Mich.

1–**MacLEAN, William Bradley,** *b* Great Barrington, Mass., Oct. 25, 1862.
6–Allan (McLean) **MacLean** (qv);
5–Alexander (1747-1806), boatswain's mate on Am. ship; capt. 10th Co., 19th Regt. of Conn.; *m* Johannah Smith;
4–Alexander (1772-1843), built and operated cotton mills at Talcottville, Conn.; established home at "McLean Hill"; *m* Betsy Thrall;
3–Alexander (1794-1828), Vernon, Conn.; *m* Mary Meekins;
2–Edwin W. (1821-75), mcht.; postmaster at Rockville, Conn.; mcht. at Great Barrington, Mass.; *m* 1847, Nancy Griswold (*d* 1849); *m* 2d, 1849, Julia Hannah Ladd (1832-1910); issue (2d marriage): I–George Edwin (*b* 1850; *m* 1874, Clara Stanley Taylor, 1849-1922); II–Minnie Rose (*b* 1856; *m* Nelson Peter Lewis, see Who's Who in America); III–William Bradley (1 above).
1–*m* Sept. 14, 1889, Addie May Lockwood, *b* Minneapolis, Minn., Sept. 30, 1866; dau. of Addison Lockwood; issue: 1–Edwin Lockwood (qv).
1–Ed. public schools of Great Barrington, Mass.; Williston Sem., East Hampton, Mass., 1879-80. Corpl., Troy Citizens Corps, 6th Separate Co., 5th Brig., 3d Div., N.G.N.Y., 1882-85. Was in shirt and collar business, Troy, N.Y., 1880-85; grain business, Duluth, Minn., 1886-87, 1890-91, Minneapolis, Minn., 1888-89, 1892-1921; mem. and sec. of Minn. State Bd. of Grain Appeals, Minneapolis, 1922-31. Mem. Co. A, Home Guards, Minneapolis, 1917-18. Clubs: Duluth Boat, Lurline Boat, Minikahda, Linwood Gun, Lake of Isles Driving (pres., 1900-07), Calhoun Beach (founder, life mem., mem. bd. govs., 1928-29, chmn. rowing and ice racing coms.). Residence: 3035 Humboldt Av. S., Minneapolis, Minn.

1–**MacLEAN, Edwin Lockwood,** *b* Duluth, Minn., Aug. 9, 1890.
11–Joseph **Loomis** (qv);
10–Thomas (1624-89), of E. Windsor; freeman, 1654; served in King Philip's War; *m* 1st, 1653, Hannah Fox (*d* 1662; Henry[11] [*d* 1640], from Eng., settled at Windsor, Conn.);
9–Thomas (1655/56-1746), *m* 1682, Hannah Porter (1662/63-1739/40; John[10], *m* Mary Standley);
8–Ens. Jabez (1696/97-1771), *m* 1720, Mary Ferry (*d* 1788, aet. 86; John[9], *m* 3d, Mary Cooley);
7–Mary (*b* 1723), *m* 1744, Allan (McLean) **MacLean** (qv);
6–Alexander (1747-1806), *m* Johannah Smith;
5–Alexander (1772-1843), *m* Betsy Thrall;
4–Alexander (1794-1828), *m* Mary Meekins;
3–Edwin Washington (1821-75), *m* 2d, 1849, Julia Hannah Ladd (1832-1910);
2–William Bradley (qv), *m* 1889, Addie May Lockwood (see Vol. I, p. 197, for Lockwood lineage).
1–*m* Apr. 3, 1920, Gladys Lenore Mabie, *b* Chicago, Ill., Apr. 4, 1892; dau. of Gordon Montague Mabie, of Delavan, Wis., and New York; issue (all *b* Minneapolis): 1–Alan Lockwood, Jan. 16, 1922; 2–Donald Edwin, Dec. 5, 1923; 3–Jean Fiske, *b* Apr. 29, 1926.
1–A.B., U.Minn., '11; Yale Law School, 1912-13 (Book and Gavel, Phi Alpha Delta); LL.B., U.Wash., 1916; post-grad., LL.B., Cambridge U. (Eng.), 1919. Second lt., then 1st lt., inf., U.S.A., June 1917; capt. U.S.A., Aug. 1917; served with 39th, 49th, 55th, 34th regts., U.S. Inf.; overseas service, July 1918-Dec. 1919, France, England, Germany, Belgium, Holland, Italy; battles of St. Mihiel, and Meuse-Argonne; poisoned at Le Mans, France, Aug. 1918, and at Gievres, France, Aug. 1919; hon. discharged, Nov. 1921. Practiced law at Minneapolis since Nov. 1921; mem. Minn. Ho. of Rep., 2 terms, 1923-26; mem. Minn. Senate, 1927-30. Dir. Boy Scouts of America. Mem. S.A.R., A.L., V.F.W., Disabled Am. Vets. of World War, Forty et Eight Soc., Mil. Order of the Cootie. Clubs: Army and Navy (Washington), Calhoun Beach (founder, life mem.), King's Coll. Assn. (Cambridge, Eng.). Residence: 3033 Knox Av. S., Minneapolis, Minn.

1–**McLESTER, James Somerville,** *b* Tuscaloosa, Ala., Jan. 25, 1877.
6–Joseph **McLester** (*b* ca. 1700), from Scotland, settled in N.C., 1730;
5–Joseph (*b* ca. 1730);
4–James (*b* 1751), served in Am. Rev. in 10th Regt. from N.C.; *m* Nancy Tompkins;
3–James A. (*b* 1811);
2–Joseph (*b* 1848), mcht.; *m* 1875, Nannie Somerville (1849-95); issue: I–James S. (1 above); II–Janie (*b* 1880; *m* R. E. Meade); III–Dora (*b* 1882; *m* Paul E. Chalifoux); IV–Susie (*b* 1884; *m* R. N. Hawkins).
1–*m* Oct. 29, 1903, Ada Bowron, *b* S. Pittsburg, Tenn., May 8, 1882; dau. of James Bowron, of Birmingham, Ala.; issue (all *b* Birmingham): 1–Anna, *b* July 31, 1904; A.B., Wellesley, '26; *m* Oct. 29, 1927, William W., Jr., son of W. W. French, of Birmingham (issue: Ada); 2–James Bowron, *b* July 17, 1906; A.B., U.Ala., '26, M.D., Harvard, 1930; 3–Jane, *b* May 2, 1922.
1–A.B., U.Ala., '96 (Phi Delta Theta, Phi Beta Kappa, Alpha Omega Alpha), M.D., U.Va., 1899; post-grad. work Göttingen, Freiberg, 1901-02; Berlin and Munich, 1907-08. Prof. pathology, later prof. medicine, Birmingham Med. Coll., 1902-12; prof. medicine, U.Ala., since 1919. Maj., chief of med., Base Hosp., Camp Sheridan, 1917; lt. col. A.E.F., c.o. Evacuation Hosp. 20, 1918; consultant A.E.F., 1918; col. M.R.C., U.S.A. Author (see Who's Who in America). Presbyterian. Democrat. Clubs: Country, Roebuck Country. Residence: 3917 Cliff Rd., Birmingham, Ala.

1–**McLOUTH, Clarence Deleon,** *b* Dover Tp., nr. Adrian, Mich., Nov. 21, 1860.
5–Laurence **McLouth** (1724?-1803), served in Am. Rev.; *m* Mary (Molly) Pratt (1737-1803; Peter[6], *m* Mary Lincoln);
4–Peter (1763-1834), served on brig "Shark," 1781, taken prisoner; served on the "Marquis de La Fayette," 1781-82; served in Mass. militia, Am. Rev.; *m* Lavina Wells (*d* 1792); *m* 2d, Lydia Osgood (*d* 1834);
3–William Wells (1792-1860), pioneer settler, Lenawee Co., Mich.; *m* Betsy Ketchum (1797-1873; Eleazer[4], of Williamston, Mass.);
2–Orville (1831-88), farmer and teacher; *m* Mary Ann Smith Ludlum (1838-88; Samuel[3] [1796-1868], of Clayton, Mich.); issue: I–Clarence Deleon (1 above); II–Herbert Grason (1864-1926; *m* Jennie Reed); III–Lenora (*b* 1868-*d* infancy).
1–*m* Sept. 1, 1886, Mary Ann Potts, *b* Palmyra, Mich., July 2, 1861; dau. of John Potts, of Palmyra, *m* Mary Elliott; issue: 1–Clarence Louis, *b* Ypsilanti, Mich., Sept. 20, 1887; *m* Mar. 1917, Alice Shelly Muir; 2–Mary Louise (July 3, 1890-Mar. 5, 1893); 3–Ada Alice, *b* Ypsilanti, Mich., Apr. 21, 1892; 4–Margaret Potts, *b* Muskegon, Mich., Mar. 6, 1894; *m* Jan. 1920, Thomas Emerson Freelon Hotchkiss (issue: Thomas Freelon, *b* Oct. 23, 1920); 5–Helen Ludlum, *b* Muskegon, June 12, 1895; *m* Mar. 1923, Charles Walter Spaulding (issue: Charles Walter, *b* Apr. 25, 1924); 6–Laurence Deleon (*b* Muskegon, May 31, 1902-*d* Sept. 7, 1928, Los Angeles, Calif.), *m* Aug. 18, 1928, Mary, dau. of Samuel Hefflin, of Long Beach, Calif.
1–Ed. Mich. State Normal, 1887. High school

teacher. Mem. I.A.G. Residence: 1450 Clinton St., Muskegon, Mich.

1–**MacMILLAN, Cornelia Spencer,** *b* nr. Rowland, N.C., May 4, 1875.
5–William **MacMillan** (1720-1800), from Scotland after defeat in battle of Culloden, 1746; settled nr. Elizabethtown, Bladen Co., N.C.; pvt. in Am. Rev.; *m* 1743 or 44, Catherine Hamilton (1724-1822), of Scotland:
4–Thomas (1771-1862), farmer, Cumberland Co., N.C.; *m* Isabella Graham (1770-1841; Alexander[5], from Scotland, 1780, *m* Mary McConnac);
3–William (1802-93), sch. teacher; *m* 1836, Ann Peterson MacNeill (1816-98; Daniel[4], *m* Margaret Black);
2–Hamilton (2 below).
7–Andrew **Robeson** (qv);
6–Col. Thomas (1698-1773), built homestead "Walnut Grove" on land granted him by George, II, 1735, on Cape Fear River, Bladen Co., N.C.; *m* 1736, Sarah Singletary (*d* 1775);
5–Col. Thomas (1740-85), del. Hillsboro Congress, 1775; mem. Provincial Congress, Halifax, 1776; comd. famous 69th Bladen Co. Militia, in battle of Elizabethtown in Am. Rev., 1781; *m* 1763, Mary Bartram;
4–William (1771-1825), *m* 1796, Ann Coddington (a Coddington, of N.J., and N.C., *m* Ann McKonky);
3–John Alexander (1799-1866), *m* 1824, Eliza Street Gillespie (1810-98);
2–Elizabeth Gillespie (2 below).
8–John **Bartram,** Huguenot, from Eng. to Darby, Delaware Co., Pa., 1682;
7–John William, *m* Elizabeth Smith; their son, John, called the "Botanist Royal of America";
6–Col. William (1711-70), "Ashewood," Colony of Westbrook, Bladen Co.; scientist; justice, 1739-51; mem. Gen. Assembly, 1739,46; mem. Colonial Assembly, 1740; *m* 2d, Elizabeth Locke;
5–Mary *m* Col. Thomas **Robeson** (5 above).
2–Elizabeth Gillespie Robeson (1834-1906), *m* 1863, Hamilton **MacMillan** (1837-1916), grad. U. of N.C.; lawyer and author, "Sir Walter Raleigh's Lost Colony"; served in Co. F, 1st N.C. Vols., C.S.A. issue: I–Francis Purdie, dau. (1864-65); II–William Graham (1866-90); III–Mary Eliza (*b* 1868); IV–Janie Robeson (*b* 1870; *m* B. W. Townsend); V–John Robeson (*b* 1872; *m* Nettie M. Pridgen); VI–Cornelia Spencer (1 above); VII–David Gillespie (*b* 1879).
1–Ed. Flora MacDonald Coll., Red Springs, N.C. Historian, Robeson Co. Mem. D.R., U.D.C. Residence: Red Springs, N.C.

1–**McMURRY, Lida Antoinette Brown (Mrs.),** *b* Kiantone, N.Y., Feb. 6, 1853.
9–John **Alden,** Mayflower Pilgrim (qv);
8–Joseph (1634/35-1697), of Bridgewater; *m* 1659, Mary Simmons (Moses[9], qv);
7–John (1674-1730), *m* ante 1702, Hannah White (1681-1732; Capt. Ebenezer[8]);
6–Lydia, *m* Samuel **Eddy** (1710-46; Samuel[7]; Obadiah[8]; Samuel[9], qv);
5–Nathan (*b* 1733), *m* Eunice Sampson;
4–Isaac (1774-1833), *m* Betsy McCary;
3–Eunice, *m* Alva **Brown;**
2–Russell McCary (2 below).
9–Capt. Miles **Standish,** Mayflower Pilgrim (qv);
8–Alexander (1627-1702), *m* Sarah Alden (1629-87; John[9], 9 above);
7–Lydia, *m* Isaac **Sampson;**
6–Ephraim, *m* Abigal–;
5–Eunice, *m* Nathan **Eddy** (5 above).
2–Russell McCary **Brown** (1823-88), fruit grower, Normal, Ill.; *m* Electa Louisa Sherman (1827-1900; see Vol. I, p. 74, for Sherman lineage); issue: I–Isaac Eddy (1849-1917; *m* Emma Stewart; *m* 2d, Mary Johnson); II–Lida Antoinette (1 above); III–Lillie May (1857-1917; *m* Eugene P. Fairchild); IV–Elmer Ellsworth (see Vol. I, p. 74).
1–*m* Aug. 7, 1878, William Paterson McMurry, *b* Ind., Oct. 26, 1852; son of Franklin McMurry, of Ind.; issue: 1–Fred Russell, *b* Normal, Ill., July 3, 1879; U.Ill.; A.B., Columbia U., M.A., same; *m* Oct. 14, 1905, Nettie Lawrence (issue: Lawrence William, *b* Apr. 3, 1909; Howard Vernon, *b* Mar. 28, 1912; Henry Lewis, *b* Mar. 28, 1912); 2–Karl Franklin, *b* Normal, Oct. 31, 1880; A.B., U.Ill.; M.A., U.Calif.; *m* Oct. 5, 1904, Minnie, dau. of John Hiett, of Monmouth, Ill. (issue: Helen, *m* 1927, Donald Newton; Elmer Brown; Vernon Bruce).
1–Grad. Ill. State Normal U., 1874 (Mu chapter, Kappa Delta Pi). Primary teacher, Normal, Ill., 1884-91; primary training teacher, State Normal U., 1891-1900, State Normal Sch., DeKalb, Ill., 1900-17. Author (see Who's Who in America). Presbyterian. Republican. Clubs: Polo Woman's, Halcyon. Summer place: Bass Lake, Pentwater, Mich. Residence: 309 N. Congress St., Polo, Ill.

1–**McQUEEN, Sue Moore,** *b* Wilmington, N.C., 1876.
23–King Robert Bruce;
22–Margery, *m* Walter–, High Steward;
21–King Robert, II.;
20–Lady Margaret Stewart, *m* John–, Lord of the Isles;
19–Donald, Lord of the Isles;
18–Alexander, Lord of the Isles;
17–Austin Moore;
16–Donald Gallich;
15–Donald Gruamach;
14–Donald Gorm Moore;
13–Donald Gorm Sassarrach;
12–Archibald;
11–Donald Gorm Oig;
10–Sir James;
9–Donald Oig;
8–Sir James Moore;
7–Sumerled or Soirle;
6–Austin Moore;
5–Flora, *m* Archibald **McQueen;**
4–Col. James (*b* Isle of Skye, Scotland, ca. 1760-*d* 1824), to America ca. 1772; founder of Queensdale; mem. N.C. Legislature from Robeson Co., 1794, 1802,03;
3–Dr. Edmund;
2–Henry Clay (*b* 1846), banker; *m* 1871, Mary Agnes Hall; issue: I–Sue Moore (1 above); II–Agnes (*b* 1888; *m* 1911, William P. Emerson).
1–Residence: 318 S. Front St., Wilmington, N.C.

1–**MADDOX, William Rolland,** *b* Tecumseh, Mich., Sept. 3, 1901.
6–Nathan **Maddox;**
5–Michael (1773-1845), *m* 1795, Mary Frailey;
4–Daniel Frailey (1806-98), *m* 1829, Mary Williams Hewitt;
3–Addison Hewitt (1830-1918), *m* 1868, Elizabeth Hedrick;
2–William Hedrick (2 below).
10–Thomas **Hewitt** (*d* ca. 1662), mariner from Eng. to Mass., ca. 1651; *m* 1659, Hannah Palmer (*b* 1634; Walter[11], qv);
9–Benjamin (*b* 1662), *m* 1683, Marie Manning (Edmund[10] [*d* 1683], *m* Ellen–);
8–Benjamin (bap. 1692), *m* 1707, Ann Palmer (bap. 1683; Gershom[9], *m* Ann, dau. of George Denison, g.dau. of William Denison, qv; Walter[10], qv);
7–Walter (*b* 1710), (not authenticated); *m* 1746, Elizabeth Dethick;
6–Daniel (*d* 1824), Am. Rev.; *m* Desire Williams (*d* 1789);
5–Darthick D. (1778-1857), *m* Bridget Roland (*d* 1856);
4–Mary Williams (1805-79), *m* Daniel Frailey **Maddox** (4 above).
11–Nicholas **Newlin** (qv);
10–Nathaniel (1665-1729), *m* 1685, Mary Mendenhall (Thomas[11] [*d* 1682], *m* Jeane–);
9–Nathaniel (1690-1751), *m* 1710, Jane Woodward (Richard[10] [1630-1700], *m* Jane–);
8–Nathaniel (*d* 1766), *m* 1735, Hester Metcalf (Thomas[9], *m* Elizabeth Taylor?);
7–Mary (1740-1818), *m* 1757, Gaius **Dickinson** (1737-1800; Joseph[8], from Eng. to Pa. ca. 1725, *m* Elizabeth, dau. of Gayen Miller, from Eng. to Chester Co., Pa., ca. 1688; Daniel[9]);
6–Joseph (1761-1832), *m* 1782, Elizabeth Nusum (1763-1860 or 66; Richard[7], *m* Hannah–);
5–Gaius (1783-1858), *m* Mary Hall;
4–Ruth (1808-74), *m* 1826, Lewis **Hedrick** (1800-71; Philip[5], *m* Letitia Foley);
3–Elizabeth (1833-1917), *m* Addison Hewitt **Maddox** (3 above).
10–John **Spring** (qv);
9–Lt. John (*b* 1630), selectman, Cambridge, 1686–, for 8 yrs.; dep. 3 yrs.; *m* 1656, Hannah Barsham (*d* 1710; William[10], of Watertown, *m* Anable–);

8–Ens. John (1678-1754), selectman 12 yrs.; *m* 1703, Joanna Richards (*d* 1743), of Dedham;
7–Ephraim (*b* 1708), grad. Harvard, 1728; *m* 1729, Mrs. Sarah Bowen;
6–Thomas (*b* 1737), Granby, Conn.; *m* Mary Gossard;
5–Sylvester (1767-1861), *m* 1789, Sarah Dibble (1771-1850; Moses[6]; Abraham[7]);
4–Milton (1806-88), from Pittsfield, Mass., to Portage Co., then to Fulton Co., O.; *m* 1834, Eunice Atwater Hall;
3–Cornelius Milton (1842-1916), farmer and cheese mfr., Wauseon, O.; *m* 1869, Sarah Ann Eldridge (see Vol. III, p. 606, for Eldridge lineages);
2–Ada Florence (2 below).
9–Nicholas (Gozard, Gozzard) **Gossard**;
8–John (*b* 1682);
7–Aaron (*b* 1708), of Simsbury, Mass.; *m* 1738, Mary Huxley, of Suffield (*b* 1712; Jared[8], *m* Mary Norton; Thomas[9]);
6–Mary, *m* Thomas **Spring** (6 above).
10–John **Hall** (qv);
9–Sgt. Thomas (1649-1711), given 50 acres of land in consideration of father's services in Pequot War, 1698; *m* 1673, Grace Watson (1653-1731; Edward[10], *m* Grace–);
8–Thomas (1676-1752), *m* 1711, Abigail Atwater (*b* 1685; John[9], *m* Abigail, dau. of Moses Mansfield);
7–Joshua (1722-1810), *m* Hannah Hall (*b* 1725; Samuel[8], *m* Hannah Brown);
6–Giles (1747-1826), *m* 1770, Lois Ives (*b* 1754; see Vol. III, p. 606, for Cooke-Ives lineage);
5–Abel Ives (1778-1853), Atwater, O.; *m* 1801, Eunice Bunnell (1776-1852; see Vol. III, p. 606, for Atwater-Bunnell lineage);
4–Eunice Atwater (1810-1904), *m* Milton **Spring** (4 above);
3–Cornelius M., *m* Sarah Ann Eldridge (3 above);
2–Ada Florence (see Vol. III, p. 605), *m* 1899, William Hedrick **Maddox** (*b* 1872), A.B., Ohio Wesleyan, '95; M.D., Ohio State U., 1898; 1st lt., M.C., U.S.A., July 10, 1917; capt., Nov. 6, 1917; assigned to 341st Inf., 86th Div., Camp Grant, Ill.; with A.E.F. in France, Sept. 30, 1918-June 12, 1919.
1–*m* Sept. 2, 1926, Virginia Isabella Sherman, *b* Ironton, O., July 25, 1903; A.B., Ohio Wesleyan, '26; dau. of John T. Sherman, *m* Carrie Marie Smith.
1–A.B., Ohio Wesleyan, '23 (Kappa Sigma, Phi Mu Alpha); M.A., U.Cincinnati, 1924. Teacher in Ironton High School, 1924-25; instr. political science, Ohio Wesleyan U., 1925-27, U.Mich., 1927–. Book review editor, Mich. Municipal Review. Residence: 1104 Forest Av., Ann Arbor, Mich.

1–**MAGEE, James Dysart,** *b* Morrisdale Mines, Pa., Aug. 22, 1881.
4–William **Magee** (*d* 1817), *m* 1799, Martha Stewart (*b* 1775);
3–James (1801-55), *m* 1826, Nancy Anna Lessig (1807-91);
2–William Archibald (2 below).
6–Arthur **Patterson** (1697-1763), from North Ireland, 1724, settled in Rapho Tp., Lancaster Co., Pa.; elder in Donegal Presbyn. Ch., 1733-39; mem. Colonial Assembly, 1743-54; collector, 1744-56; *m* Ann Scott (1699-1792);
5–William, of Lancaster Co.; 2d lt. of foot, 1st Lancaster Co. Bn., 7th Co., Flying Camp, 1776; made a prisoner of war at Battle of L.I. and died during captivity; *m* Elizabeth Dysart;
4–Eleanor (1769-1827), *m* Alexander **Dysart** (*b* in Ireland), settled in Sinking Valley, Pa.;
3–Joseph (1811-93), of Hollidaysburg and Altoona, Pa.; *m* 1843, Mary Ann Wigton (1821-1907);
2–Lizzie (1849-1925), of Hollidaysburg and Altoona; *m* 1878, William Archibald **Magee** (1849-1909), was state sec. Ia. Y.M.C.A.; issue: I–Anna Mary (*b* 1879); II–James Dysart (1 above); III–Elizabeth Stewart (*b* 1889).
1–Not married. A.B., Des Moines Coll., '02 (Delta Mu Delta); A.M., U. of Chicago, 1906, Ph.D., 1913. Office sec., Des Moines Y.M.C.A., 1902-04; asst. in mathematics, Kan. State Agrl. Coll., 1906-09; instr. economics, Western Reserve U., 1910-13; asst. and asso. prof. economics, U. of Cincinnati, 1913-19; asso. prof. economics, New York U., 1919-22, prof. since 1922, head of dept. since 1923. Author (see Who's Who in America). Presbyterian. Republican. Residence: 2715 Webb Av., New York, N.Y.

1–**MAGRUDER, Bruce,** *b* Washington, D.C., Dec. 3, 1882.
9–Alexander **Magruder** (qv);
8–Col. Samuel (*d* 1711), of "Good Luck," Prince George's Co., Md.; high justice and capt. militia; burgess, 1704-07; *m* Sarah Beall (*d* 1734; Col. Ninian[9], qv);
7–John (1694-1750), of "Dumblane," Prince George's Co.; burgess, 1728-45; *m* 1715, Susannah Smith (Nathan[8], *m* Elizabeth Coale);
6–Col. Jadok (1730-1811), col. Md. Line in Am. Rev.; *m* 2d, Rachel (Pottenger) Cooke (1732-1807);
5–Dr. Jadok (1765-1809), physician, Montgomery Co., Md.; *m* 1790, Martha Wilson (1772-1837);
4–Jadok (1795-1832), lawyer; *m* 1822, Rachel Cooke (*d* 1855);
3–Julian (1824-88), M.D., U.Pa., 1846; physician and farmer; *m* Margaret Ann Johnson;
2–George Corbin Washington (2 below).
10–Col. John **Washington** (qv);
9–Laurence (ca. 1661-1697), *m* 1690, Mildred Warner (Col. Augustine[10], of "Warner Hall");
8–Augustine (1694-1743), *m* 1st, 1715, Jane Butler (1699-1728; Caleb[9]); *m* 2d, Mary Ball (mother of General Washington);
7–Augustine (*b* 1720), *m* 1743, Anne Aylett (Col. William[8]);
6–Col. William Augustine (1757-1810), *m* 1st, 1777, his half first cousin, Jane Washington (1758-91; Col. John Augustine[7], *m* Hannah Bushrod; Augustine[8], 8 above);
5–Bushrod (1785-1831), *m* his cousin, Henrietta Bryan Spottswood (see Vol. III, p. 302, for Spottswood lineage);
4–Ann Eliza (1807-51), *m* 1831, Rev. William P. C. **Johnson** (1806-52), P.E. priest;
3–Margaret Ann (1835-96), *m* Dr. Julian **Magruder** (3 above);
2–George Corbin Washington (*b* 1855; bro. of Mrs. William Leonard, see Vol. III, p. 302), *m* 1882, Nannie Marshall (*d* 1906); issue: I–Bruce (1 above); II–Marshall (*b* 1885; *m* Anne Louise Peyton); III–Eleanor (*b* 1887; *m* 1908, Lt. Herndon Sharp); IV–Lyles (*b* 1892; *m* Betty, dau. of Arthur, son of Julian Magruder, 3 above).
1–*m* Feb. 15, 1912, Ferol Clara Lott, *b* San Antonio, Tex., Mar. 15, 1891; dau. William Cleveland Lott, of San Antonio; issue: 1–Bruce, Jr., *b* Washington, D.C., Feb. 12, 1922; 2–William Marshall, *b* Evanston, Ill., May 26, 1923.
1–Ed. Emerson Inst., George Washington U. Maj. U.S.A.; served in Philippines, on Mexican border and as lt. col., Gen. Staff, 35th Div. and at G.H.Q. in France. Address: c/o Adj. Gen., U.S.A., Washington, D.C.

1–**MALTBY, Arthur Norman,** *b* Verona, N.Y., Mar. 7, 1854-*d* Nov. 23, 1928.
7–William **Maltby** (1645-1710), from Eng., ante 1663; to Branford, Conn., 1672; cornet of New Haven Co. troops, 1673; rep. Gen. Ct.; commr.; owned 3 ships; *m* 2d, Hannah (Hosmer) Willard (Thomas Hosmer[8], *m* 1st, Frances–);
6–Daniel (1679-1731), *m* 1702, Esther Moss (*b* 1678; John[7], *m* Martha Lathrop; John[8], from Eng., an early settler of New Haven, Conn., mem. 1st Gen. Ct., 1639,40,49,64);
5–Joseph (1712-lost at sea, 1762), attended Yale Coll.; sea master; *m* 1735, Elizabeth Pratt (1714/15-1798; Jonathan[6], Hartford, Conn., *m* Elizabeth–; John[7]; John[8]);
4–William (1742-1812), *m* 2d, 1774, Catherine Lee (1755-98; Stephen[5]);
3–John (1778-1856), *m* 1805-06, Lucy Cox;
2–Norman (2 below).
9–Edward **Winship** (qv);
8–Edward (1654-1718), *m* Rebecca Barsham;
7–Elizabeth, *m* Walter **Russell**;
6–William, *m* Martha–;
5–Elizabeth (bap. 1715-1768), *m* Capt. Matthew **Cox** (*d* 1756);
4–William (bap. 1750-1779), was one of the "Indians" of the "Boston Tea Party"; *m* Mary (Molly) Sawin;
3–Lucy (1787-1844), of Andover, N.Y.; *m* John **Maltby** (3 above);
2–Norman (1814-76), *m* 1841, Lovina Maria Wright (1816-86); issue: I–Lucy Jane (1844-1910; *m* 1875, Edward Payson Powell, 1833-1915); II–Helen Lovina (*b* 1846; *m* 1868, William Taylor Thornton, *d*); III–Mary Persis

(*b* 1848; *m* 1890, John P. Victory, 1837-1909); IV–William John (1850-1928; *m* 1880, Emma Aurelia Leake, *b* 1858); V–Arthur N. (1 above).
1–*m* Oct. 6, 1886, Martha Stanley Humphreys (qv); issue: 1–Louise, *b* Sedalia, Mo., Nov. 15, 1889; *m* Oct. 12, 1920, Maurice J. McNellis, of Kansas City, Mo. (issue: Maurice Maltby; Louise Maltby).

1–**MALTBY, Martha Stanley Humphreys (Mrs. Arthur N.),** *b* Cole Co., Mo., July 3, 1858.
7–John **Humphreys** (ca. 1685-1723), missionary for the Soc. for the Propagation of the Gospel; *m* 1702, Catherine (Davis?), of Pa.;
6–David (1704-73), *m* 1730, Catherine Lewis (1709-1755 or 56; Evan[7], *m* Magdalen–);
5–John (1745-96), ens. Light Horse Harry Lee's dragoons, Am. Rev.; *m* 1772, Ann North (1750-1825; Roger[6], *m* Ann Rambo);
4–David (1775-1850), ens., Capt. George Washington Humphrey's (his brother) co., War 1812, lost right arm at Battle of Bladensburg; *m* 1797, Catherine Keyes (1778-1844; Capt. Humphrey[5], *m* Sarah Hall; Gersham[6]; Solomon[7]; Robert[8]);
3–George (1800-76), *m* 1826, Janet Lingen Henderson;
2–David English (2 below).
9–Edward **Dorsey** (qv);
8–Sarah, *m* Matthew **Howard** (will dated 1691), asso. justice of Anne Arundel Co.; commr. port of entry;
7–Sarah, *m* 2d, 1701, Capt. John **Brice** (1670-1713), from Eng. to Annapolis, Md., ca. 1698;
6–John (1705-66), justice, Anne Arundel Co., 1731-54; judge Provincial Ct., 1754-56; judge Ct. of Oyer and Terminer, 1760-62,66; *m* 1730, Sarah Frisby;
5–Sarah (*b* 1735), *m* 1761, Richard **Henderson** (1736-1802; Rev. Richard[6], *m* Janet Cleland, of Scotland);
4–John (1768-1809), *m* 1800, Lydia Ridgley Perry (*d* 1859; Charles[5], *m* Priscilla Johns);
3–Janet Lingen (1809-36), *m* George **Humphreys** (3 above).
10–Richard **Frisby** (*b* 1590/91), of French Huguenot origin; in the "Jonathan," to Va., 1619;
9–James (will proved 1673), *m* Mary–;
8–James (will proved 1704), of Cecil Co., Md.; *m* Sarah–;
7–James (1678-1719), *m* 1713, Ariana Vanderheyden (*b* 1690; Matthias[8], *m* Anna Margaretta, dau. of Augustine Herman, the 1st foreigner ever naturalized in America, the Lord of Bohemia Manor, on the Eastern Shore of Md., made an Am. citizen by act of the Provincial Assembly, 1673);
6–Sarah (1714-82), *m* John **Brice** (6 above).
2–David English **Humphreys** (1827-86), corp., Col. Doniphan's Mo. mounted vols., Mexican War, aet. 19; mcht., St. Louis, Mo.; *m* 1854, Frances Melvina Goode (1833-72; Thomas[3], *m* Eliza Royal Jones); issue: I–Janet Lingen (*b* 1855; *m* Charles A. Batterton); II–Martha S. (1 above); III–Louise Minor (*b* 1865; *m* William Hancock Powell).
1–*m* Oct. 6, 1886, Arthur Norman Maltby (qv for issue).
1–Mem. C.D.A., D.A.R., F.F.V., U.S.D. 1812, U.D.C., I.A.G., Mo. Valley Hist. Soc. (librarian and genealogist). Residence: 4130 Walnut St., Kansas City, Mo.

1–**MANGANO, Mabel Austin Farnham (Mrs.),** *b* Suffield, Conn., Sept. 7, 1878.
9–John **Farnham,** from Eng., settled at Dorchester, Mass., 1640; *m* Elizabeth–;
8–Henry (ante 1636-1700), mem. A. and H. A. Co.; dep. Gen. Court; removed to Killingworth, Conn.; *m* Joanna Kalsoe Rutke (*d* 1689; John[9]);
7–Peter (1652-1703), *m* 1688, Hannah Willcoxen (1665-1708);
6–John (1702-81), Litchfield, Conn.; *m* 1725, Hannah Crittenden (1703-77; Ens. Joseph[7], *m* Mary Hoyt; Abraham[8]; Abraham[9]);
5–Seth (*b* 1733), owner of supposed copper mine at Litchfield South farms; in Battle of Saratoga, 1777; *m* 1766, Dinah Woodruff Gibbs (*b* 1740; Benjamin[6], *m* Dinah, dau. Capt. Nathaniel Woodruff; Benjamin[7]; Samuel[8]; Giles[9]);
4–Seth (1777-1831), *m* 1802, Asenath Bradley (1778-1861; Richard[5], minuteman, Battle of Lexington, *m* Olive Miner);
3–William Henry (1811-1902), *m* 1837, Huldah Miranda Pickett (1812-1901; Rufus[4], Danbury, Conn., *m* Harriet Turrill);
2–Seth Taylor (2 below).
10–Richard **Austin** (qv);
9–Capt. Anthony (1635/36-1708), an orig. settler and propr. Suffield, Conn.; lt. 1681; town clerk, 1681 to death; commr. several terms; sch. master 11 yrs.; capt. militia, 1697; *m* 1664, Esther Higgins (1642-1697/98), of Rowley, Mass.
8–Nathaniel (1678-1760), *m* Abigail Hovey (1682-1764);
7–Thomas, *m* Dec. 13, 1737, Hannah Hale;
6–Thomas (1742-1816), sgt. 4th Conn. Regt., 1777; *m* 1768, Lucy Rising;
5–Thomas (*b* 1771), *m* 1796, Pamelia Loomis (*b* 1775; Israel[6], Am. Rev., *m* Abigail Saxton; Benjamin[7]; William[8]; Lt. Samuel[9]; Joseph[10], qv);
4–Alfred (1797-1834), *m* Maria De Lacey Smith;
3–Edward (1825-1901), *m* 1846, Eveline Chloe Gillette;
2–Julia Maria (2 below).
9–John **Harmon** (qv);
8–Joseph (*b* 1646), of Springfield, Mass.; surveyed Southfield (now Suffield), Conn., 1670; with bro. Nathaniel was one of 1st proprs.; mem. 1st bd. selectmen; town treas.; capt. militia, 1708; *m* Hannah Filley or Philly (*b* July 3, 1653), Windsor, Conn.;
7–Nathaniel (*b* 1695), Suffield; *m* 1st, Sarah Smith (*d* 1720);
6–Phineas (June 4, 1720-May 31, 1802), Suffield; *m* 1744, Hannah Barbour (*b* Dec. 8, 1720);
5–Paul (1768-1852), *m* 1793, Eunice Remington (Stephen[6], *m* Sarah, dau. James Barlow; John[7]; Thomas[8]; John[9], qv);
4–Julia (1800-35), *m* 1819, Frederick **Gillette** (*b* 1798), of Granville, Mass. (Frederick[5], *m* Sibyl, sis. Eunice Remington, 5 above; Thomas[6], Am. Rev.; Thomas[7]; Samuel[8]; John[9]; Jonathan[10], qv);
3–Eveline Chloe (1824-1907), *m* Edward **Austin** (3 above);
2–Julia Maria (1848-1924), *m* 1877, Seth Taylor **Farnham** (1847-84), A.B., Brown U., '74; grad. Rochester Theol. Sem., 1877; ordained Bapt. minister, 1877; issue: I–Mabel Austin (1 above); II–Mary Cantwell (*b* 1880); III–Julia Eveline (1882-84).
1–*m* Jan. 31, 1907, Antonio Mangano, *b* Acii, Italy, Dec. 7, 1869; A.B., Brown U., '99; A.M., Columbia, 1903; B.D., Union Theol. Sem., 1903; D.D., Colgate Sem., 1918; prof. in charge Italian dept., Colgate Theol. Sem., 21 yrs.; issue: 1–Richard Farnham, *b* Jamaica, L.I., May 17, 1908; 2–Philip Austin, *b* Richmond Hill, L.I., Mar. 23, 1910; 3–Arthur Dietz, *b* Hampton Falls, N.H., July 31, 1911.
1–A.B., Vassar, '02; post-grad., Harvard U., 1904. Mem. D.A.R., Nat. Soc. N.E. Women (Rochester Colony), N.E.H.G.S., A.A.U.W. Baptist. Clubs: Vassar, Travelers. Residence: 21 Thayer St., Rochester, N.Y.

1–**MANGUM, Mary Ball (Mrs. William Wynan),** *b* Clark Co., Ky.
5–William **Ball** (1718-83; desc. William Ball, from Eng., settled in Pa., 1691 or 1700); capt., Fauquier Co., Va., Am. Rev.; established iron works at Falmouth, Va.; supplied pig iron to govt. for ammunition; *m* 1741, Martha Bloomfield (1720-90);
4–Thomas (1754-1820), *m* 1781, Mary Reed (1762-1822);
3–John S. (Apr. 29, 1802-Feb. 7, 1832), *m* Susan Mitchum (Feb. 15, 1803-Sept. 22, 1868);
2–William Thomas S. (2 below).
9–Giles **Webb,** of Gloucester Co., Va.; burgess, 1658-60;
8–John, *m* Mary Sanford;
7–James (1673-1716), *m* Sarah–;
6–James (1705-71), vestryman South Farnam Parish, Essex Co., Va., bet. 1731-50; *m* 1731, Mary Edmonson (James[7], vestryman South Farnam Parish, Essex Co., bet. 1731-50);
5–James (*b* 1734), Essex Co.; signer Assn. in the Northern Neck of Va. against the Stamp Act, 1766; vestryman of Old South Farnham Ch., 1750-79; *m* Mary Smith;
4–William Smith (1768-1845), grad. Med. Coll., Phila., under Dr. Benjamin Rush, 1790; removed to Clark Co., Ky.; and thru:
2–Rebecca Morton (2 below).
9–Nicholas **Meriweather** (qv);
8–Col. David (1690-1744), planter, Louisa Co.,

Va.; *m* Anne Holmes (*d* 1735/36; George[9], of King and Queen Co., Va.);
7–Francis (*b* 1717), clk. of Essex Co.; *m* ante 1704, as her 2d husband, Mary Bathurst;
6–Lucy (*d* post 1740), *m* Capt. Francis **Smith** (*d* 1762), del. Cont. Congress, 1778,82 (Capt. Nicholas[7], Essex Co., *m* Elizabeth Crawford; Col. Nicholas[8], came to Va., 1650); among their children was Hon. George, gov. of Va.;
5–Mary, *m* James **Webb** (5 above).
13–Laurence **Bathurst,** lived at Cranebrook in Kent, Eng.;
12–Robert, *m* a dau. of William Saunders, of Horsmanden in Kent;
11–John, *m* Mary, dau. of Edward Dodge, of Wortham, Kent;
10–Robert, *m* 2d, Elizabeth, dau. and heiress of Robert Waller, of Clarkenwell in Middlesex;
9–Edward (*b* 1615), knighted 1643; created baronet, 1643; *m* 2d, Susan, dau. of Thomas Rich, of Gloucester;
8–Lancelot, from Eng. to Va., ca. 1683; granted 1,200 acres in New Kent Co., Va., 1683; clk. of com. of private causes in the House of Burgesses, 1688; examiner of records, 1689; high sheriff, New Kent Co., 1698; prom. lawyer, Charles City, 1680;
7–Mary, *m* 2d, Francis **Meriweather** (7 above).
2–William Thomas S. **Ball** (*b* 1828), col. C.S.A.; *m* 1850, Rebecca Morton Webb (1830-52); *m* 2d, Mary E. King; issue (1st marriage): I–Mary (1 above); issue (2d marriage): I–Livingston King (*b* 1860-*d* infancy); II–William Marion (1861-1925; *m* 1890, Louise Topp; *m* 2d, 1903, Isabelle Topp; *m* 3d, 1916, Lena Blocker); III–Minnie (*b* 1863; *m* King Pickett Parks).
1–*m* Mar. 25, 1874, William Wynan Mangum, Jr. *b* Benton, Miss., Mar. 25, 1847-*d* New Orleans, La., 1921); issue: 1–Mary Campbell (*b* Avon Plantation, Lake Lee, Washington Co., Miss., Mar. 22, 1876-*d* Shreveport, La., Apr. 1928), ed. Sophie Newcomb Coll. of Tulane U., New Orleans; *m* 1904, William F., son of William T. Hardie, of New Orleans (issue: Ella Mangum, *b* Oct. 1905, ed. Woman's College of Ky.); 2–William Ball, *b* Greenville, Miss., Dec. 10, 1881; ed. Tulane U.; *m* 1910, Eliza W. Whitney; 3–Lillian (*b* Jan. 22, 1883-*d* infancy).
1–Mem. C.D.A., Huguenot Soc. of S.C., D.A.R., I.A.G. Residence: 3118 Centenary Boul., Shreveport, La.

MAROT

Arms: Or, a saltire gules, between four fleurs de lis azure.

1–**MAROT, Mary Louise,** *b* Dayton, O., Oct. 16, 1870.
6–Pierre **Marot** (*b* ca. 1680), prob. from Eng. or Ireland to Rotterdam; sailed from Rotterdam, 1733, with wife and 7 children, to Phila., Pa.; took oath of allegiance, Sept. 18, 1733; *m* ca. 1706/07, Ann Tedit or Iedet;
5–Philip (1716-91), on Phila. tax list, 1762; *m* Mary (Saul?);
4–Joseph (1761-98), *m* 1784, Elizabeth Woodcock (*b* Wilmington, Del., 1761-*d* 1823; William[5], *m* Elizabeth Lea);
3–Joseph (1792-1868), Quaker; publisher, firm Marot & Walters, Phila.; from Wilmington, Del., to Bloomington, Ill.; *m* at Phila., Mary Richards (1800-65; Jonathan[4], *m* Ann Baldwin);

BENJAMIN MAROT (1836-1915).

2–Benjamin (1836-1915), of Dayton and Cincinnati, O.; served Civil War, 1861-65 (see portrait); *m* 1868, Harriet Burnham Sowers (*b* 1843; Thomas H.[3], *m* Mary Ann Richardson); issue: I–M. Louise (1 above); II–E. Blanche; III–Helen (*m* Wilfred Taylor).
1–Student, Wellesley, 1889-91; B.S., U.Chicago, '94 (P.B.K.). Founder, with Malvina Howe, of Miss Howe and Miss Marot's School, Dayton, O., 1905; moved school to Thompson, Conn., 1913 (now owner). Founder and pres. Marot Junior Coll. (see Who's Who in America). Clubs: York (New York), Quinnatisset Golf. Residence: Thompson, Conn.

1–**MANN, Gertrude Edith,** *b* Somerset, N.Y., June 6, 1880.
10–Richard (Man) **Mann** (qv);
9–Richard (1652-1728), received a grant at Hebron, Conn., for services in King Philip's War; settled there ca. 1703; *m* Elizabeth Sutton (*b* 1662; John[10]; George[11]);
8–Nathaniel (1693-1758), *m* 1st, 1713, Mary Root (1689-1728; Jacob[9]; Thomas[10]);
7–John (1720-1806), *m* 1st, 1740, Margaret Peters (1724-89; John[8]; William[9]; Andrew[10]);
6–Elijah (1751-1836), Onondaga Co., N.Y.; *m* 1771, Mary Perkins (*d* 1781);
5–Elijah (1777-1858), Oswego Co., N.Y.; *m* 1800, Mary Phelps (1782-1847; Frederick[6]; Joseph[7]; Joseph[8]; Joseph[9]; Timothy[10]; William[11]);
4–Thompson (1805-92), of Somerset, Niagara Co., N.Y.; *m* 1827, Euphemia Stewart (1808-71);
3–Oscar Elijah (1833-1901), *m* 1856, Hannah Elizabeth Merritt;
2–Willis Thompson (2 below).
10–Resolved **Waldron** (1610-90; desc. Baron Rudolph Van Waldron, who was granted a coat of arms and large manor, 1128, by Dutch Govt. for valor displayed in the Second Crusade in the taking of Jerusalem, 1099); came from Holland with Gov. Peter Stuyvesant; obtained a patent from the Dutch Govt., of which he was magistrate for 18 yrs., for a tract of land in the northern part of Manhattan Island where he founded and laid out the town of New Harlem; built "Waldron's Hall," a large stone structure; *m* 2d, 1653, Lady Teneca Van Nagle, of Gröningen, Holland;
9–Samuel (1670-1737), *b* New Amsterdam; *m*

1692, Neeltje Bloodgood (*b* 1670; Capt. Frans J.[10], *m* Lysbeth Jans);
8–Francis (1697-1765), of "Clover Hall," North Branch, Somerset Co., N.J.; *m* 2d, 1721, Catharine Brunneal;
7–Francis (*b* 1739), *m* 1760, Nellie Hagerman;
6–Samuel (1762-1838), of Amwell, Hunterdon Co., N.J.; *m* 1783, Nellie Van Fleet;
5–Margaret (1790-1850), *m* 1805, William **Wisner** (1782-1860), of Niagara Co. Ens. David[6], Am. Rev., *m* Sarah Blain; Lt. Thomas[7], Am. Rev; Adam[8]; Johannes[9], qv);
4–Delilah (1813-99), *m* 1830, Isaac **Merritt** (1802-53), N.Y.;
3–Hannah Elizabeth (1837-1909), *m* Oscar Elijah **Mann** (3 above).
10–Adrian Gerritsen (Van Vliet, Vliedt) **Van Fleet,** came from Utrecht, Holland in the "Trouw," 1662; *m* Agatha Jane Spruyt, of Utrecht;
9–Jan (*b* ca. 1650), wrote name Van Vliet; of Marbletown, Ulster Co., N.Y.; *m* 1684, Judith Hoosey (Hussei or Horsjes; Frederick[10], *m* Margaret–);
8–Frederick (*d* ca. 1795), began to write name Van Fleet; of Readington, N.J.; *m* 1718, Maria Biggs;
7–Thomas (1729-1812), *m* Margaret Wyckoff (1730-92);
6–Nellie (*b* 1766), *m* Samuel **Waldron** (6 above).
2–Willis Thompson **Mann** (*b* 1857), fruit grower, Geneva, O.; *m* 1879, Carrie Rosamond Townsend (1859-1914).
1–Ed. Alma Ladies Coll., St. Thomas, Ont. Librarian, Pub. Library, Barstow, Fla., 1918-20, Pub. Library, DeLand, since 1920. Mem. D.A.R. Methodist. Residence: DeLand, Fla. Address: DeLand Public Library, DeLand, Fla.

1–**MANSFIELD, Virginia Lee Maker (Mrs. Edward Augustus, III),** *b* Richmond, Va., Feb. 8, 1898.
10–Nicholas **Norton** (1610-90), from Eng., to Weymouth, Mass., 1635; later settled at Edgartown; served in Pequot War; *m* Elizabeth– (*d* 1690);
9–Joseph (1651-1741), 1st rep. from Edgartown to the 1st Gen. Ct. of Mass., 1692; sheriff, 1699; justice, Ct. of Common Pleas, 1702; *m* 1673, Mary Bayes (Thomas[10]);
8–Joseph (1676-1734), *m* 2d, Mary Green Pease;
7–Enoch (1700-68), *m* 1725, Hepsebah Daggett (1706-42);
6–Amy (*b* 1736), to Addison, Me., 1770; *m* 1760, Seth **Norton** (1736-1830); sgt. in Am. Rev.; mem. of crew of the "Unity," took the Brit. sloop "Margaretta," 1775;
5–Elihu (1761-1835), removed to Addison, Me.; pvt. Am. Rev.; also mem. of crew of "Unity," 1775; *m* Sarah Beal (Manwarren[6], of Beals, Me.);
4–Joseph (1784-1859), Jonesport, Me.; *m* Elizabeth Cummings (1792-1877);
3–William (1816-91), *m* 1841, Mary Jane Kelley (1817-1903);
2–Bessie (*b* 1858), *m* 1880, Capt. John Wilbur **Maker** (1859-1922), served during World War as master mariner under U.S. Shipping Bd.; issue: I–Capt. Le Roy (*b* 1886; *m* Jessie Jenkins); II–Virginia Lee (1 above).
1–*m* April 7, 1924, Edward Augustus Mansfield, III, *b* Jonesport, Me., June 17, 1897; son of Hon. George F. Mansfield, of Jonesport.
1–Ed. Ewell Conservatory, Norfolk, Va., State Normal Sch., Machias, Me. Former teacher in pub. schs. Mem. D.F.P.A. (charter mem. and state historian of Me. chapter), D.A.R., O.E.S. Conglist. Democrat. Residence: Jonesport, Me.

1–**MANSUR, Marion Emma Upham (Mrs. Clarence W.),** *b* Dorchester, Mass., Dec. 10, 1892.
9–John **Upham** (qv);
8–Lt. Phineas (ca. 1635-ca. 1676), Malden, Mass.; soldier in Indian wars; took command of the forces which made an assault upon the Indian fort Canonicus, 1675, when the capt. was killed; *m* 1658, Ruth Wood (1636-96);
7–Thomas (1668-1735), Reading, Mass.; *m* 1693, Elizabeth Hovey (*d* 1703);
6–Dea. Abijah (1698-1775), Weston, Mass.; dea., 30 yrs.; rep. Gen. Ct.; selectman; *m* 1725, Elizabeth Spring (1704-94);
5–Lt. Phineas (1747-89), lt. in Am. Rev.; *m* 1769, Lydia Myrick (1748-1828);
4–Amos (1789-1872), Dorchester, Mass.; grocer for 60 yrs.; "Upham's Corner" named for him; *m* 1819, Abigail Humphreys (1789-1878);
3–Charles Amos (1822-94), wheelwright; *m* 1849, Eliza Ann Kelton (1828-99);
2–Charles James (*b* 1856), *m* 1890, Emma Eugenia Sellon (*b* 1866); issue: I–Marion Emma (1 above); II–Charles Kelton (*b* 1899).
1–*m* Nov. 1, 1916, Clarence Whiston Mansur, *b* Wilton, N.H., Jan. 11, 1888; son of Gilman Russell Mansur, of Malden, Mass.; issue: 1–Kelton Upham, *b* Dorchester, Mass., July 1, 1918; 2–Paul Gilman, *b* Roxbury, Mass., Nov. 26, 1919; 3–Anne Eugenia, *b* Roxbury, Feb. 11, 1922.
1–Ed. Boston U., and Simmons Coll. Mem. D.C.-W., D.R. (3 yrs. councillor, dist. v.p., present state vice regent), W.C.T.U., O.E.S., etc. Residence: 32 Spruce St., Malden, Mass.

1–**MANVILLE, Edward Britton,** *b* New Haven, Conn., Dec. 25, 1879.
8–John (Mandeville) **Manville,** from France, probably settled at Woodbury, Conn.;
7–Nicholas (*d* 1751), of New York, and Woodbury, Conn.; *m* Marah– (1710-1811);
6–John (*b* 1736), Woodbury; mem. 11th Co., Col. D. Wooster's Regt., French and Indian War, 1758; *m* 1759, Elizabeth Weed (1736-1818);
5–Simeon (1760-1825), of Woodbury; mem. Capt. David Leavenworth's co., Col. Mosely's regt. of militia at Horseneck, 1779; *m* 1783, Electa Benham (1766-1863);
4–Uri (1787-1861), Middlebury, Conn.; *m* 1807, Betsey Strong (1784-1875);
3–Burritt (1814-84), New Haven, Conn.; *m* 1836, Augusta Hinman (1815-94);
2–Henry Lampson (1841-1905), in Co. B, 5th Calif. Inf., Civil War; pres. B. Manville & Co., carriage mfrs., New Haven; *m* 1879, Estelle Blackman Wilson (*b* 1849); issue: I–Edward Britton (1 above); II–Henry Burritt (*b* 1886; *m* Elsbeth Gehrke).
1–*m* Aug. 26, 1912, Eunice Katherine Hallett, *b* Oil City, Pa., Sept. 8, 1880; dau. of Inman Arnold Hallett, of Oil City, *m* Catherine Sadler; issue: 1–Margaret Jane, *b* Highland Park, Mich., Nov. 3, 1922.
1–Student Yale, 1897-1900; Guilmant Organ Sch., New York, 1902-03; fellow Am. Guild of Organists, 1915; Mus. Doc., 1920. Organist and dir. music, Woodward Av., Presbyn. Ch., Detroit, since 1919; mem. faculty Detroit Inst. Musical Art, since 1914, pres. since 1922 (see Who's Who in America). Commd. 1st lt. inf., U.S.A., Ft. Sheridan, Ill., Nov. 26, 1917; served in France, Jan. 1918-Apr. 1919; instr. Officers' Specialist Centre, Langres; mem. 119th Inf. M.G. Co.; hon. discharged Apr. 12, 1919. Mem. S.A.R., A.L., La Societe Des 40 Hommes et 8 Chevaux (cdr.). Mason (32°, K.T.), etc. Clubs: Army and Navy, Torch, Bohemian. Residence: 52 Putnam Av., Detroit, Mich.

1–**MANWARING, Wilfred Hamilton,** *b* Ashland, Va., Sept. 14, 1871.
5–George **Manwaring** (1767-1848), of New London, Conn.; removed to Oxford, N.Y., ca. 1808; *m* Lucy–;
4–Giles (1797-1863), *m* 1817, Ruth Goff;
3–Leonard S. (1821-91), Guilford, N.Y.; preacher, farmer; *m* 1846, Lydia Hamilton (1828-92);
2–Theodore Perry (2 below).
9–Michael **Griswold** (*d* 1684), from Eng. to Wethersfield, Conn., ca. 1644; *m* Ann–;
8–Thomas (*b* 1646), *m* 1672, Mary–;
7–Michael (*b* 1680), *m* Mary Gilbert;
6–Phineas (*b* 1714), *m* 1739, Martha Hurlban;
5–Miles (1740-1804), Mt. Upton, N.Y.; *m* 1764, Abigal Blinn;
4–William (1774-1854), *m* Abigal Ford (?);
3–Abel Ford (1807-46), *m* 1830, Elizabeth Beckwith (1806-97);
2–Mary Frances (*b* 1846), *m* 1870, Theodore Perry **Manwaring** (1848-1916), agriculturist, Ann Arbor, Mich.; issue: I–Wilfred H. (1 above); II–Mabel (*b* 1873; *m* Eugene Kennedy); III–Alice (*b* 1875; *m* Claude Morris).
1–*m* June 14, 1917, Ava Mautner, *b* Saginaw, Mich., Aug. 25, 1881; dau. Louis P. Mautner, mcht. and banker of Saginaw; issue: 1–John Hamilton, *b* Brookline, Mass., Sept. 10, 1919; 2–Frederick Wolcott, *b* San Francisco, Calif., July 11, 1921.
1–B.S., U.Mich. '95; M.D. Johns Hopkins, 1904;

studied Berlin, Leipzig, Frankfort-on-the-Main, Vienna and London, 1907-10. Fellow and asst. in pathology, U. of Chicago, 1904-05; asso. prof. pathology and bacteriology, Ind. U., 1905-07; traveling fellow in pathology and bacteriology, Rockefeller Inst. for Med. Research, 1907-08; asst. in same, 1910-13; prof. bacteriology and exptl. pathology, Stanford U., since 1913. Author (see Who's Who in America). Residence: Stanford University, Calif.

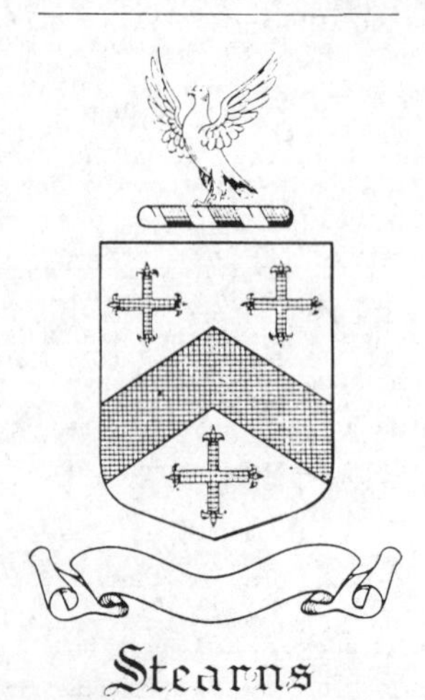

Stearns

Arms: Or, a chevron between three crosses flory sable.
Crest: A cock starling proper.

1–**MARINER, Ada M.,** *b* Canton, Ill., Feb. 8, 1856.
8–Richard **Everett** (qv);
7–John (1646-1715), *m* Elizabeth (Johnson) Pepper (1645-1714), of Roxbury;
6–Isreal (1681-1751), *m* 1710, Sarah Culver;
5–Ebenezer (1722-1810), *m* Lucy Moulton;
4–Olive (*b* 1760), *m* 1779, John **Lord**;
3–Esther (*b* 1784), *m* 1806, Buell **Mariner**;
2–Henry (2 below).
8–Isaac **Stearns** (qv);
7–Isaac (1633-76), *m* 1660, Sarah Beers (Capt. Richard[8], qv);
6–Isaac (1665-1741), *m* 1696, Elizabeth Stone (*b* 1670; Simon[7], qv);
5–Rev. Ebenezer (*b* 1711), *m* 1733, Thankful Clapp (1712-61);
4–Capt. Eliphlet (1736-1803), *m* 1760, Miss Clark (*b* 1737);
3–Phineas (1779-1866), *m* 1801, Mary Cooper (1784-1865);
2–Lucretia (1824-84), *m* 1849, Henry **Mariner** (1818-1908), farmer; issue: I–Mary E. (1850-86; *m* 1874, William Stewart; issue: Lucretia Mariner [*b* 1874], *m* 1912, W. W. Weir; Isabelle C. [*b* 1878], *m* 1912, Louis Legg); II–Ada M. (1 above).
1–B.S., Lombard Coll., '78, B.M., 1881; B.O., Boston Sch. Oratory, 1888. Teacher oratory, Buchtel Coll., Akron, O., 1885-90, Pasadena, Calif., 1891-93. Now engaged in real estate. Mem. C.D. 17th C., D.A.R. Residence: Bushnell, Ill. Address: c/o Charles E. Flack, Macomb, Ill.

1–**MARTIN, Rosalind Ewing (Mrs. C. Griffin),** *b* Lookout Mountain, nr. Chattanooga, Tenn., July 28, 1894.
7–William (Ewin) **Ewing,** from Scotland, settled in Rockingham Co., Va.; *m* Anne Shannon;
6–Andrew (1740-1813), ed. at Log Coll., Neshaminy, Pa.; one of the commrs. for laying out town of Nashville; clk of ct., Davidson Co., 1783-1813; *m* 1760, Susannah Shannon (1738-1818; Thomas[7]);
5–Nathan (1776-1830), of Nashville; *m* Sarah Hill (Dan[6], served in Battle of Guilford C.H.);
4–John Overton (1800-26), *m* 1823, Lemira Douglas (William[5] [1779-1831], *m* 1800, Jemima Lattimore);
3–John Overton (*b* 1826), *m* 1852, Sarah Edwards Bass (1833-82; John M.[4] [1804-78], *m* 1829, Mary Malvina Chenault, dau. of Felix Grundy, Atty. Gen. of U.S. under President Van Buren);
2–Henry Overton (2 below).
11–Richard **Warren,** Mayflower Pilgrim (qv);
10–Nathaniel (1624-67), *m* 1645, Sarah Walker (*d* 1700);
9–Alice (1656-92), of Plymouth; *m* 1674, Thomas **Gibbs** (1636-1732);
8–Abigail (*d* ante 1741), *m* 1697, Jireh **Swift** (ca. 1665-1749; William[9]; William[10], qv);
7–Jabez (1700-67), of Sandwich, Mass.; *m* 1729, Abigail Pope (*d* ca. 1776);
6–Abigail (*b* 1740), *m* 1759, Peleg **Chamberlain** (1736-1808), sgt. in Am. Rev. (Peleg[7]; William[8]; Joseph[9]; William[10]; Henry[11], from Eng. in the "Diligent," settled at Hingham, Mass., 1638);
5–Leander (1766-1822), of Litchfield, Conn.; *m* 1788, Mercy Berry (*d* 1822);
4–Leander (1804-84), of Ferrisburg, Vt.; *m* 1827, Susanna Willey (*d* 1887);
3–Hiram Sanborn (1835-1916), of Franklin, Ohio; *m* 1867, Amelia Isabella Morrow (1841-1916);
2–Minnie Morrow (*b* 1869), *m* 1892, Henry Overton **Ewing** (1860-1905), lawyer; issue: I–Margaret Louise (*b* 1893); II–Rosalind (1 above); III–Winifred (*b* 1899; *m* William Lusk McAllester).
1–*m* June 3, 1925, Cyrus Griffin Martin, *b* Chattanooga, Tenn., Sept. 3, 1894; son of Francis Martin, of Chattanooga.
1–Mem. S.M.D., C.D.A., D.A.R. (ex-chapter regent), U.S.D. 1812 (chapter regent), A. L. Auxiliary (v.p. Davis King Summers Post), E. Tenn. Hist. Soc. Presbyterian. Clubs: Junior League of Chattanooga, Komos, Chattanooga Woman's. Residence: 412 E. 2d St., Chattanooga, Tenn.

1–**MARTIN, Gertrude Bishop (Mrs. Edgar Stanley),** *b* Newark Valley, N.Y., Oct. 12, 1876.
10–John **Livermore** (qv);
9–Lt. John (1638-1719), Weston, Mass.; freeman, 1690; selectman, 1692; collector, 1692-93; assessor, 1695; in King Philip's War; *m* 1st, Hannah–;
8–Joseph (1675-1770), rep. Gen. Ct., 1738-40,42,43,-48,49; *m* Elizabeth Stone (1678-1764), of Framingham;
7–Josiah (1699-1761), *m* 1723, Thankful Harrington (1701-59);
6–Moses (1729-97), to Spencer, Mass., 1751; grand juror, Supreme Judicial Ct., 1774; soldier Am. Rev.; *m* 1750, Hannah Allen (1731-1817);
5–Isaac (1752-1838), pvt. Am. Rev.; *m* Hannah– (*d* 1827);
4–Larned (1783-1854), *m* 1807, Hannah Brown (1787-1878);
3–Samantha Jane (1819-85), *m* Lewis Daniel **Bishop** (*b* 1815);
2–Curtis Le Monte (2 below).
9–Nicholas **Wade** (1616-83), from Eng., 1635; settled at Scituate, Mass.; *m* Elizabeth Ensign (*d* 1708);
8–Thomas (*b* 1648), *m* 1672, Elizabeth Curtis (*b* 1649);
7–Ichabod (*b* 1685), Rehoboth, Mass.; *m* Elizabeth Cole;
6–Ichabod (1742-1810), pvt. Am. Rev.; capt. Light Inf. at Tiverton, 1777; *m* 1762, Mary Peck (*b* 1744);
5–Lewis (*b* 1766), *m* 1786, Rebeckah Peck (*b* 1765);
4–Lewis (1791-1862), musician in Capt. Silas Shepherd's Co., 3d Regt., Dean's Mass. Militia, War 1812; *m* 1814, Haraeta Bowen (1795-1879);
3–Lewis (1815-71), *m* 1840, Nancy Ann Brink (1820-78);
2–Ruth Emma (1852-76), *m* 1870, Curtis Le Monte **Bishop** (1849-1927), merchant of Newark Valley, N.Y.; issue: I–Helena Ardelle (*b* 1873); II–Gertrude (1 above).
1–*m* Dec. 24, 1898, Edgar Stanley Martin, *b* Gorham, N.Y., Mar. 8, 1873; grad. N.Y. State Coll. for Teachers, '98 (Phi Delta, Pi Gamma Mu), attended Central U., 1901. Dir. editorial dept., Nat. Council, Boy Scouts of America, and sec. editorial bd., Nat. Council, since 1915; son of William Martin (1838-1922), of Gorham,

N.Y., *m* 1872, Elizabeth McIntyre (*b* 1845); g.son of Bernard Martin (1779-1873), from Ireland, settled at Ferguson's Corners, Ont. Co., N.Y., 1844, *m* 1812, Alice Smith (1788-1877); issue: 1–Clinton Stanley, *b* Newark Valley, N.Y., June 16, 1902; ed. Dartmouth, 1925; 2–Margaret Elizabeth, *b* Racine, Wis., Mar. 3, 1909; ed. N.Y. School of Fine and Applied Art, 1930; 3–Ruth Alice, *b* Stanley, N.Y., July 26, 1910; ed. Stuart Hall, Staunton, Va., '28, and Katherine Gibbs Secretarial Sch., N.Y. City, 1929.

1–N.Y. State College for teachers, 1897. Teacher, Albany, N.Y., 1898-99. Mem. D.A.R., U.S.D. 1812, Daus. of the Union. Episcopalian. Republican. Clubs: Woman's of Orange, Contemporary of Newark. Residence: 222 N. Walnut St., E. Orange, N.J.

1–**MARTIN, Edwin Scott,** *b* Farmville, Va., March 4th, 1881.
5–John Todd **Martin,** *m* Elizabeth Anderson;
4–David Robertson (1785-1856), *m* 1817, Elizabeth S. Thompson (1799-1888);
3–John Todd Anderson (*d* 1859), *m* 1854, Elizabeth Bruce Robertson (1836-1915);
2–John Robertson (2 below).
8–Abner **Nash,** of Tenby, Wales;
7–John (*d* 1776), known as "Gentleman John Nash", of Templeton; justice of peace, Henrico and Prince Edward cos., Va., 1738-54; burgess, 1755-65; col. of militia, regt. raised for defense of frontier, 1757;
6–Anne, *m* Thomas **Haskins;**
5–Jane (1781-1856), *m* 1801, Col. Thomas **Scott** (1775-1837; James[6] [1735-1805], *m* 1753, Elizabeth Osborne, 1735-82);
4–Betsey Anne (1802-28), *m* 1820, Dr. John Turner **Ligon** (1797-1854);
3–Louise Jane (1821-80), *m* Edwin Wilson **Scott** (1827-55);
2–Jane Haskins (1855-1917), *m* 1879, John Robertson **Martin** (1855-1916); issue: I–Edwin Scott (1 above); II–Bessie Robertson (*b* 1882; *m* Dr. Charles Bledsoe Crute, *b* 1880); III–Lula Ligon (*d* aet. 4); IV–John Robertson, Jr. (died in infancy).
1–*m* Nov. 30, 1904, Mary Booth Walker, *b* Farmville, Va., Nov. 1, 1882; dau. of Col. Charles M. Walker, of Farmville, *m* Ella E. Warren; issue: 1–Mary Scott, *b* Farmville, Feb. 11, 1912; ed. Teachers Coll., Farmville; Stuart Hall, Staunton, Va.; 2–Virginia Walker, *b* Farmville, Apr. 16, 1917.
1–B.S., V.M.I., '01 (Kappa Alpha). Entered gen. ins. business, 1902; apptd. gen. agt. for Am. Nat. Life Ins. Co., 1907; apptd. state mgr. for Va. and eastern N.C., for Pacific Mutual Life Ins. Co., Los Angeles, 1912; pres. Farmville Hotel Corpn.; pres. Southside Community Hosp. Mem. City Council, Farmville, 10 yrs. Capt. Co. I, Va. State Militia, 1902-03. Mem. M.E. Ch., S. Democrat. Residence: Farmville, Va.

1–**MARTIN, William McChesney,** *b* Lexington, Ky., July 2, 1874.
5–John **Martin,** *m* Jane Greggs;
4–James (1758-1848), soldier in Am. Rev.; settled in Jessamine Co., Ky., after war; *m* 1788, Judith Young (1772-1841);
3–Lewis Y. (1806-58), of Jessamine Co.; *m* 1826, Ann B. Shreve (1810-87);
2–Thomas Lewis (1852-1925), of Lexington, Ky., and St. Louis, Mo.; grain dealer; *m* 1873, Hettie McChesney (1853-1908); issue: I–William McChesney (1 above); II–Martha Curry (*b* 1877; *m* Felix E. Anderson); III–Louis Wynne (*b* 1879; *m* Dorcas Carleton); IV–Thomas Lewis (*b* 1885).
1–*m* Nov. 21, 1905, Mary Rebecca Woods, *b* Chicago, Ill., June 15, 1876; dau. of Archibald Woods, of St. Louis, Mo., *m* Mary Matthews; issue: 1–William McChesney, Jr., *b* St. Louis, Mo., Dec. 17, 1906; A.B., Yale, 1928; 2–Malcolm Woods, *b* St. Louis, Feb. 21, 1912; Yale, class of 1933.
1–A.B., Washington and Lee U., '95 (P.B.K., Sigma Nu, Phi Delta Phi); LL.B., St. Louis Law Sch. (Washington U.), 1900. Chmn. and federal reserve agent, Federal Reserve Bank of St. Louis, 1914-1928, governor since 1929. Author (see Who's Who in America). Trustee Washington and Lee U., Memorial Presbyn. Ch. of St. Louis. Mem. Mo. Hist. Soc., Ky. Soc. Clubs: Noonday, University, Racquet, Glen Echo Country. Residence: 5055 Waterman Av., St. Louis, Mo.

1–**MARVEL, Josiah,** *b* Georgetown, Del., Jan. 18, 1866.
7–John **Marvel** (1632-1707), from Eng. to Va. before 1663, later moved to Worcester Co., Md. (now in Del.); *m* Ann–;
6–Thomas, *m* Elizabeth Huggins;
5–Robert (1737-75), *m* Rachel Chase;
4–Philip, *m* Elizabeth Short;
3–Josiah, *m* Lovey Tindale;
2–Josiah Phillips (1825-97), county treas.; sheriff; prothonotary of Sussex Co., Del.; *m* Harriet Ann Pepper (David[8]); for issue see Vol. III, p. 325.
1–*m* Apr. 20, 1898, Mary Belle Jackson, *b* Salisbury, Md., Oct. 16, 1875; sister of William Purnell Jackson (see Vol. I, p. 153, for genealogy); issue (all *b* Wilmington, Del): 1–Jackson, *b* Mar. 20, 1899; 2–Jane, *b* Aug. 8, 1900; 3–Mary, *b* May 23, 1902; 4–Josiah, Jr., *b* Nov. 26, 1904; 5–Ann, *b* Aug. 30, 1907; 6–William *b* Sept. 29, 1909; 7–Robert, *b* Dec. 22, 1911; 8–Hugh, *b* Mar. 2, 1913.
1–Mem. law firm Marvel, Marvel, Layton & Morford, Wilmington, Del. Past pres. Del. State Bar Assn., Wilmington Chamber Commerce, Wilmington Associated Charities, Wilmington Boy Scout Council; elected pres. Am. Bar Assn., 1930. Clubs: Metropolitan, Racquet (Washington), Wilmington Country, Concord Country, Vicmead Hunt (Wilmington). Mem. Inst. Am. Genealogy. Residence: "Nanticoke," Greenville, Del.

DANIEL SMITH MAPES (1833-1906).

1–**MAPES, Lester Dunbar,** *b* New York, N.Y., Jan. 14, 1866.
6–Thomas **Mapes** (qv);
5–Sgt. Jonathan (1670-1747), of Southold, L.I.; sgt. militia; *m* 3d, 1733, Mary Terry (1701-55);
4–Daniel (ca. 1734-post 1790), under-sheriff at Goshen, Orange Co., N.Y., 1776; signer of Assn. Test; had charge of suspects and British prisoners;
3–Selah (1782-1860), of Orange Co.; *m* 4th, 1829, Sophia (Slason) Hoyt;
2–Daniel Smith (2 below).
8–George (Slosson, Slawson) **Slason** (*d* 1695), in Lynn, Mass., as early as 1637; owned land at Duxbury, 1638; witnessed signing of deed of eastern part of Stamford, Conn., by Indians, 1645; selectman, Stamford, 1671;
7–Eleazer (will proved 1699), wrote name Slosson; selectman, Stamford, 1690; *m* Mary Lawrence;
6–James, *m* 1702, Mehitable Ambler (*d* 1736/37);

5–Deliverance (*b* 1710), began to write name Slason; lost 3 sons in French and Indian War; served in Am. Rev.; *m* 1733 or 34, Hannah Hait (*b* 1710/11);
4–Nathaniel (1745-1835), capt. Am. Rev.; *m* 1787, Hannah Whitney;
3–Sophia (1791-1867), *m* Augustus Hoyt; *m* 2d, Selah **Mapes** (3 above).
8–Henry **Whitney** (1620-73), from Eng.; bought land at Southold, L.I., 1649; *d* Danbury, Conn.; *m* 2d, Sarah Ketcham, a widow;
7–John (*d* 1720), of Norwalk, Conn.; *m* 1674/75, Elizabeth Smith (*d* post 1741);
6–Nathan (*d* post 1739), *m* ca. 1715, Sarah–;
5–Eliasaph (1716/17-1817), Stamford, Conn.; dea. Middlesex Ch.; taken prisoner, 1781, by British and sent to L.I.; *m* 1744, Mary Bishop (1722-1814);
4–Hannah (1760-1814), *m* Nathaniel **Slason** (4 above).
10–Richard **Warren,** Mayflower Pilgrim (qv);
9–Elizabeth (*d* 1670), *m* 1635/36, Richard **Church** (qv);
8–Abigail (1647-77), *m* 1666, Samuel **Thaxter** (1641-1725), of Hingham, Mass.; constable, 1671 (Thomas[9], granted house and lot, Hingham, 1638, freeman, 1642, *m* Elizabeth–);
7–Sarah (*b* 1668), *m* 1691, Peter **Dunbar** (1668-1720; Robert[8], thought to have been sent as prisoner by Cromwell to Mass. Colony, ca. 1652, *m* Rose–, *d* 1700);
6–Elisha (1699-1773), *m* 1727, Mercy Hayward;
5–Elisha (1735-ca. 1790), Am. Rev.; *m* 1757, Rebecca Wade;
4–Simeon (1758-93), Am. Rev.; *m* 1781, Phebe Howard;
3–Moses (1792-1855), of N.Y.; *m* 1820, Jane King;
2–Mary Almira (2 below).
9–Thomas (Hayward) **Howard** (*d* 1681), from Sandwich, Eng., in the "Hercules," with wife and 5 children, ca. 1634; in Duxbury, Mass., ante 1638; held land 1640; admitted freeman, 1646; original propr. Bridgewater, 1645; *m* Martha–;
8–Nathaniel, *m* Hannah Willis;
7–Samuel, *m* 1st, Elizabeth–;
6–Samuel (1706-82), to Taunton, Mass.; *m* 1736, Susanna Edson (*d* 1767);
5–Samuel (ca. 1736-1797), began to write name Howard; Am. Rev.; *m* ca. 1757, Charity Stacy;
4–Phebe (1759-1838), *m* Simeon **Dunbar** (4 above).
8–Adria or Aurie (Konninck, Koning) **King** (son of Jan Konninck, of Amsterdam); from Holland with his wife and four sons in the "Spotted Cow," 1663; settled N.Y. City; leather tanner; *m* Elizabeth Damen;
7–Hyman or Harman (*b* 1655), *m* 1683, Marritya Andrussa;
6–Abraham (*b* 1694), *m* 1716, Susana DeForrest;
5–Johannes (1729-ca. 1806), *m* Mary–;
4–Stephen, began to write name King; *m* Mary Sandford;
3–Jane (1799-1890), *m* Moses **Dunbar** (3 above);
2–Mary Almira (1833-1915), *m* 1864, Daniel Smith **Mapes** (1833-1906), Co. E, 7th Regt., N.G., N.Y.; mustered in Apr. 30, 1861; served at Washington, Ft. Federal Hill, Maryland and in N.Y. during the draft riots; forwarding agent (see portrait); issue: I–Lester Dunbar (1 above); II–Florence Adeline (*b* 1869; *m* Frederick Horace Beers, qv); III–Emma Louise (*b* 1871).
1–*m* Mar. 24, 1897, Edith Louise Tuthill, *b* New York, N.Y., Oct. 11, 1873; dau. of Samuel Burnet Tuthill (1837-85), asst. surgeon on U.S.S. Lancaster and U.S.S. Narragansett, during Civil War, *m* Elizabeth Smith (1847-1929); issue: 1–Gerard Sinclair, *b* Brooklyn, Feb. 6, 1899; B.S. in chemistry, Brooklyn Poly. Tech., '21; 2–Bruce Allan, *b* Brooklyn, Aug. 16, 1901; ed. Pratt Inst., 1925; *m* May 20, 1924, Evelyn Florence, dau. of William Edgar Chandler, *m* Annie Moulter, of Brooklyn, and Red Bank, N.J. (issue: Bruce Allan, *b* May 9, 1925; Chandler, *b* Nov. 9, 1926); 3–Donald Lester, *b* Berlin, Germany, July 5, 1914.
1–Ed. German schools, Brooklyn Poly. Inst., 1879-82. Certified public accountant. With Commn. for Relief in Belgium, in Brussels during World War, 1 yr.; special accountant to Herbert C. Hoover, in Belgium and London, 2 yrs. Mem. Am. Inst. of Accountants. Conglist. Republican. Residence: 317 Jefferson Av., Brooklyn, N.Y.

1–**BEERS, Frederick Horace,** *b* Brookfield, Conn., Feb. 25, 1869.
8–Anthony **Beers** (lost at sea, 1676; son of James Bere, of Gravesend), mariner; name first appears on record at Watertown, Mass., where he took the freeman's oath, 1657; removed to Roxbury, 1655, to Fairfield, Conn., 1658; *m* Elizabeth–;
7–John (1652-83), known as "John of Stratford"; soldier, severely wounded in battle of Narragansett, 1675, for which he received a grant of relief; *m* Mary–;
6–Samuel (1679-1725), Newtown, Conn.; *m* 1706, Sarah Sherman (*b* 1681);
5–Nathan (1718-1805), *m* Lydia Hawley (1725-96);
4–Ebenezer (1747-1826), *m* Ann (Hard) Nettleton (1755-1811);
3–Ebenezer (1787-1856), *m* Phebe Botsford (1787-1850);
2–Horace (1821-92), farmer, Brookfield, Conn.; *m* 1845, Emily Terrill (1824-99); issue: I–Sophia E. (1847-1929; *m* 1871, William J. Kellogg, see their dau. Mrs. Arthur S. Mansfield); II–Herbert Booth (1849-1878); III–Edward Terrill (1856-78); IV–Frederick Horace (1 above).
1–*m* Oct. 15, 1890, Florence Adeline Mapes, *b* New York, N.Y., Dec. 18, 1869 (sister of Lester Dunbar Mapes, qv for genealogy); issue: 1–Muriel Whitcomb, *b* Brookfield, Conn., Sept. 30, 1891; Conn. Agrl. Coll., 1910; 2–Hazyl, *b* Brookfield, Mar. 6, 1894; N.H. Normal Sch. of Gymnastics; *m* June 16, 1920, Earl, son of William Young, of Hartford, Conn. (issue: Beverly).
1–B.S., Trinity Coll., '89; given hon. recognition at Conn. Agrl. Coll., 1929, for services to agrl. and rural life. Instr. in Trinity Coll., 1889-90; farmer, Brookfield Centre, Conn., since 1890. First selectman, Brookfield, 2 yrs.; pres. Fairfield Co. Farm Bureau, 3 yrs.; sr. warden and treas. St. Paul's Ch., 25 yrs.; chmn. sch. com., 10 yrs. Episcopalian. Republican. Residence: "Beersford," Brookfield Centre, Conn.

1–**MANSFIELD, Florence Emily Kellogg (Mrs. Arthur S.),** *b* New Fairfield, Conn., June 13, 1875.
9–Daniel **Kellogg** (1630-88; son of Martin, g.son of Phillipe); came from Eng. ca. 1651, settled at Norwalk, Conn., ante 1656; townsman several times; dep. Gen. Ct., 1670-83; *m* 1655, Bridget Bouton (*d* 1689; John[10], of Norwalk);
8–Samuel (1673-1757), *m* 1704, Sarah Platt (1678-1750);
7–Martin (1711-56), *m* Mercy Wood (*d* 1783);
6–Martin (1740-1824), New Fairfield, Conn.; p.m. in Am. Rev.; *m* 1762, Mercy Benedict (1742-1811);
5–Martin (1763-1813), *m* Rachel Stevens (1766-1831);
4–Hanford Martin (1788-1870), *m* 1816, Sarah Bulkley (1792-1851);
3–Barzillai Bulkley (1818-82), *m* 1845, Emeline Johnson (1821-80; Daniel[4], *m* Lamira Wheeler; John[5]; Ichabod[6]; Lt. Col. Ebenezer[7]; Jeremiah[8]; Thomas[9]; Robert[10], from Eng.);
2–William Johnson (1848-1907), farmer; *m* 1871, Sophia Esther Beers (1847-1929; sister of Frederick Horace Beers, qv for Beers lineage); issue: I–Florence Emily (1 above); II–Herbert Beers (*b* 1882; *m* Mary A. Bateman).
1–*m* Sept. 2, 1896, Arthur Sherman Mansfield (qv); issue: 1–Lina Beers, *b* Brookfield Centre, Conn., Aug. 15, 1897; New Haven Normal Sch. of Gymnastics; A.B., Brenau Coll., 1922; M.A., Columbia, 1926.
1–Ed. Woodside Sem., Hartford, Conn. Mem. D.F.P.A., D.A.R., I.A.G. Episcopalian. Republican. Residence: Brookfield Centre, Conn.

1–**MANSFIELD, Arthur Sherman,** *b* Brookfield Centre, Conn., May 28, 1861.
10–Edmond **Sherman** (*b* 1572), from Eng. in the "Elizabeth," to Boston, Mass., before 1630, with sons Edmond, John and Samuel; *m* Joan Mackin;
9–Samuel (1618-1700), Stamford, Conn., 1640, finally settled at Stratford, ca. 1650; dep.; magistrate; prominent in church and military affairs; *m* 1640, Sarah Mitchell (Matthew[10], of Cambridge);
8–Samuel (1641-1719), soldier in Indian war of 1675; *m* 1665, Mary Titherton (*d* 1749; Daniel[9], of Stratford);
7–Daniel (1668-1740), farmer, Newtown; *m* 1694, Rebecca Wheeler (1672-1751; John[8]);

6–Samuel (1709-47), *m* 1st, 1729, Elizabeth– (*d* 1736);
5–Justin (*b* 1729), *m* Hepsabeth Botsford;
4–Eli (1764-1850), *m* Polly Phelps;
3–Justin (1791-1841), *m* 1814, Phoebe Main, of New Milford, Conn.;
2–Julia Maria (1831-97), *m* Timothy **Mansfield** (1806-91).
1–*m* Sept. 2, 1896, Florence Emily Kellogg (qv for issue).
1–Formerly farmer, coal dealer and miller, now retired. Mason. Residence: Brookfield Centre, Conn.

1–**MARQUIS, Rollin Ruthwin,** *b* Murray, Ind., Dec. 28, 1853.
6–William **Marquis,** from Ireland, 1720, settled in Frederick Co., Va.;
5–John;
4–Robert, *m* Hannah Crawford;
3–James Crawford (1795-1846), Cross Creek Village, Washington Co., Pa.;
2–Robert Crawford (2 below).
3–Dr. John (Riddle) **Riddile,** *b* Steubenville, O.; ed. Jefferson Coll., Canonsburg, Pa.; physician, Fredericksburg, O.; removed to Bluffton, Wells Co., Ind., 1839; *m* Rhoda Winters;
2–Martha (1824-1907), *m* 1845, Robert Crawford **Marquis** (1821-85), Darlington, Beaver Co., Pa.; farmer, mcht.; issue: I–John Riddle (1846-48); II–James Kirk (1847-48); III–Sarah Florinda (1849-76); IV–Infant (*b* and *d* 1850); V–Emily Orelia Jane (1851-59); VI–Rollin R. (1 above); VII–Martha Elmira (1856-1922; *m* Jacob L. Wade); VIII–Mary Etta Bell (1860-66); IX–Robert Crawford (*b* 1862; *m* Olive Reed, 1860-1916); X–Cora Margaretta (1865-1924).
1–*m* May 8, 1883, Clara Jane McCormick (*b* Fredericksburg, O., 1860-*d* 1892).
1–*m* 2d, Feb. 18, 1896, Ida Irene Shumaker, *b* Pierceton, Ind., Aug. 29, 1870; dau. of George M. Shumaker (Martin[3]); issue: 1–Rollin Howard, *b* Sedalia, Mo., Nov. 25, 1896; A.B., Maryville, '21; *m* Oct. 18, 1924, Carmen, dau. of Hardie Park, of Culleoka, Tenn. (issue: Rollin Park, *b* 1925); 2–Leone Irene, *b* Quincy, Ill., Jan. 26, 1898; A.B., Wooster, '20; *m* Aug. 10, 1923, Howard Tillman Kuist; 3–Dean Wilson, *b* Cedar Falls, Ia., Dec. 15, 1900; A.B., Wooster, '22; M.D., Cornell U. Med. Coll., 1926; *m* Apr. 6, 1929, Helen Van Derveer, dau. of Pliny A. Boyd, of Bloomfield, N.J.; 4–Donald George, *b* Winterset, Ia., Jan. 10, 1905; U. of Wooster, 1927; *m* June 30, 1928, Eleanor Bagley, of Cambridge, Wis.; 5–Robert Irwin, *b* Irwin, Pa., Apr. 6, 1908; Rose Poly., U. of Ariz.
1–A.B., Wooster U., '80, A.M., 1883 (D.D., 1905); B.D., Western Theol. Sem., 1883. Pastor Southside Presbyn. Ch., Vincennes, Ind., since 1929. Author (see Who's Who in America). Republican. Residence: Winona Lake, Ind.

1–**MARSH, L(indus) Cody,** *b* Cleveland, O., Sept. 30, 1883.
10–George **Marsh** (*d* 1647), from Eng. with 4 children; settled at Hingham, Mass., 1635; freeman, 1636; *m* Elizabeth– (she *m* 2d, Nov. 1648, Richard Brown, of Weymouth);
9–Thomas (1618-58), freeman, 1654; *m* 1649, Sarah Beal (*b* Eng., 1624-1710; John[10], *m* Nazareth Hobart);
8–Thomas (1651-1724/25), *m* 1675, Sarah Lincoln (1650-1738; Thomas[9], *m* Margaret Langer);
7–Thomas (1678-1726), *m* 1708, Mary Burr (1686-1747; John[8], *m* Mary Warren);
6–John (1724-1803), *m* 1747, Hannah Lincoln (1725/26-1803; Ebenezer[7], *m* Hannah Allyne);
5–Shubal (1766-1857), *m* 1794, Elizabeth Foxcroft (*b* 1771; Rev. Samuel[6], grad. Harvard, 1754, pastor Congl. ch., Gloucester, Me.);
4–Thomas (*b* 1795), Dayton, O.; *m* 3 times, 1st, Miriam Saxton (*d* 1832), Dover, Me. (adopted dau. of Capt. Smith, Salem);
3–Shubal (*b* 1827), Collinwood, Butler Co., O.; *m* 1st, Dec. 25, 1849, Auzelia Parker (*d* 1876), of Lexington, Ky.;
2–Andrew (*b* Nov. 2, 1857), Goshen, O.; *m* Sept. 15, 1880, Harriet Eliza Cody (1862-1904; sister of Lydia Sarah Cody, qv for Cody lineage); issue: I–Lindus Cody (1 above); II–Roy Parker (*b* 1885; *m* 1910, Katherine Robinson); III–Edith (*m* C. E. Murray).
1–*m* July 25, 1909, Eleanor Blake, *b* Nov. 19, 1884 (divorced), dau. of Charles R. Blake, of St. Louis, Mo.
1–*m* 2d, Dec. 21, 1923, Anne Barraud Cocke, *b* Bremo Bluff, Va., Oct. 19, 1900; dau. of Charles Pollard Cocke; issue: 1–Andrew, *b* Washington, D.C., Nov. 25, 1924; 2–Anne Barraud, *b* Albany, N.Y., Oct. 13, 1928.
1–A.B., Kenyon, '07 (Delta Tau Delta, Phi Beta Pi); post-grad., Columbia, George Washington and Johns Hopkins. M.D., Albany Med. Coll. Formerly Episcopal clergyman, now engaged in medico-psychological research. Capt. U.S.A. with A.R.C. in Siberia; dir. and asst. dir. of Red Cross work among troops in Siberia. Address: Kings Park State Hospital, Kings Park, L.I., N.Y.

1–**CODY, Lydia Sarah,** *b* East Cleveland (now Cleveland), O., Dec. 17, 1863.
7–Philip (le Gody) **Cody** (will probated 1743), from France, 1694; settled at Beverly, Mass., later at Hopkinton; held town offices; mem. First Congl. Ch.; *m* Martha–;
6–Joseph (1700-will probated 1756), Beverly and Hopkinton; *m* 1722, Mary Martin;
5–Philip (*b* 1729), Worcester Co., Mass.; *m* 1754, Abigail Emerson;
4–Philip (1770-1850), Cleveland, O.; *m* Lydia Martin (1764-1846);
3–Philip (1816-46), physician, Sheboygan, Wis.; *m* Harriet M. Sherwin (1820-54);
2–Lindus (2 below).
5–Josiah **Farnsworth** (*b* ca. 1714), of Greenville, N.Y.;
4–Solomon, served in Am. Rev. from Salem, Washington Co., N.Y.;
3–Whitcomb (g.son of Scotaway Whitcomb, Am. Rev.);
2–(Sarah) Amelia (1843-1928), D.A.R.; *m* 1861, Lindus **Cody** (1840-1926), Cleveland, O., and Babson Park, Fla.; religious worker; helped establish community churches in Cleveland; real estate, grove owner; issue: I–Harriet Eliza (*m* Andrew J. Marsh; see their son, Lindus Cody Marsh); II–Lydia Sarah (1 above); III–Henry Bissell (*b* 1866; *m* Elma Canfield); IV–Frank Lindus (*b* 1867; *m* Ida Rowene Baker); V–Mary Amelia (*b* 1871); VI–Leonard Farnsworth (*d* infancy); VII–Arthur Philip (*b* 1875; *m* Marie Davis); VIII–Jane Ethelind (*m* 1904, Sam Higginbottom); IX–Grace Isabel (*b* 1882); X–Gertrude Louise (*b* 1885; *m* William H. Wheaton).
1–A.B., Boston U., '88; grad. student at Cornell, 1891-92, at Columbia U.; fellow, Barnard Coll., 1897-98, 1898-99. Teacher in acad. dept., Tillotson Inst., Am. Missionary School for the Colored, 1888-89; teacher acad. dept., Dearborn-Morgan School, Orange, N.J., 1889-90; sociological writer, and speaker on "child study," general extension of Florida State U. Republican. Residence: Lake Shore Boul., Willoughby, O.

1–**MARTINDALE, Earl Henry,** *b* Greenwich, O., Jan. 22, 1885.
7–Edward **Martindale** (*b* 1690), from Eng.; settled in Hatfield, Mass., to Westfield, Mass.; *m* Ruth Smead;
6–Lemuel, of Hatfield or Westfield, Mass.;
5–Uriah (1758-1842), Westfield; Am. Rev.; *m* 1st, 1781, Chloe or Cloe Hitchcock (1755-1816);
4–Darius (1791-1860), Greenfield, Mass.; *m* 1817, Mary E. Northrop (*b* 1797);
3–Cyrus Sylvester (1817-78), Hartford, Conn.; Presbyn. minister; chaplain, Civil War; *m* 1838, Sarah Jane Neale (1815-96), of Cork, Ireland;
2–Henry Cyrus (1845-1928), M.E. minister, Kirtland, O.; pvt., Baty. C, 1st Ohio Light Arty.; dept. cdr. Ohio G.A.R., 1920; *m* 1873, Christine McBride (*d* 1874); *m* 2d, 1875, Mary Elizabeth Broadwell (1847-1914; Luther[3], *m* Mary E. –); issue (2d marriage): I–Edith Gertrude (*b* 1878; *m* 1902, John Orceneth Hathaway, *b* 1871); II–Earl Henry (1 above).
1–*m* June 28, 1911, Elsie Lydia Marty, *b* Cleveland, O., June 28, 1888; dau. of John M. Marty, of Cleveland; issue: 1–George Earl, *b* Cleveland, O., May 1, 1915; 2–Robert Henry, *b* Cleveland, Dec. 9, 1919.
1–B.S., Case Sch. Applied Sci., '08 (Tau Beta Pi), E.E., 1912. With Ill. Steel Co., Gary, Ind., 1908-09, Nat. Carbon Co., Cleveland, 1909-19; pres. and gen. mgr. The Martindale Electric Co., since 1919 (see Who's Who in America). Capt. engrs., U.S.A., 1917-19, overseas, Feb. 1918-Jan.

1919. Mem. Am. Inst. E.E., A.L. Clubs: Lakewood Country, Cleveland Chamber of Commerce. Residence: 1260 West 4th St., Cleveland, O.

1-**MASON, Thomas William,** *b* Wilkes-Barre, Pa., *b* Jan. 30, 1884.
8-Hugo (Freer, Frere) **Frear** (*d* 1698), Huguenot, from France, settled at New Paltz, N.Y., 1677; an original patentee of New Paltz; *m* Mary Haye (*d* 1695);
7-Abraham, of New Paltz; *m* 1694, Aagian Titesort;
6-William (*b* 1700), Kingston, N.Y.; *m* 1729, Maryanette Van Kuykendall;
5-Abraham (1740-1823), began to write name Frear; Wyoming Valley, Pa.; *m* 1788, Sarah Patterson Mitchell (1760-1845);
4-William (1792-1874), Eaton, Pa.; marched to defense of Baltimore in War 1812; Baptist minister; *m* 1818, Hannah Wheelock;
3-George (1831-94), Wilkes-Barre; Baptist minister; chaplain and capt. in Civil War; *m* 1858, Malvina Rowland (1835-1914; Newton[4], *m* Elizabeth Mathias);
2-Elizabeth Rowland (2 below).
8-Samuel **Steere** (1673-1745), *m* Hannah Field;
7-Jonah (1720-98), Gloucester, R.I.; in Am. Rev.; *m* 1741, Lydia Harding Whipple (1723-79);
6-Simeon (1746-1817), of R.I.; *m* Mary Walker (*b* 1753);
5-Sophia (*b* 1773), Eaton, Pa.; *m* Esock **Wheelock**;
4-Hannah (1800-89), *m* William **Frear** (4 above);
3-George, *m* Malvina Rowland (3 above);
2-Elizabeth Rowland (*b* 1861), of Wilkes-Barre, Pa.; *m* 1882, George Evans **Mason** (1859-1919); issue: I-Thomas William (1 above); II-Mary Frear (1886-1926; *m* Ray C. Weale); III-George Frear (*b* 1890; *m* Virginia Davis); IV-Elizabeth Glencora (*b* 1893; *m* Charles R. Hammonds); V-David Rowland (*b* 1905; *m* Florence Clouse).
1-*m* Sept. 9, 1909, Ruth E. Carrel, *b* Union City, Mich., Dec. 21, 1884; dau. of Rev. Morton D. Carrel; issue: 1-George Morton, *b* Battle Creek, Mich., Sept. 4, 1912; 2-Thomas William, Jr., *b* State College, Pa., Aug. 15, 1921.
1-B.S., Pa. State Coll., '08 (Delta U., Alpha Chi Sigma, Phi Lambda Upsilon), M.S., 1912. Instr. chemistry, Mich. State Coll., 1908-09; prof. chemistry, St. Olaf Coll., 1909-10; instr., Pa. State Coll., 1911-15, asst. prof., 1915-21, asso. prof. since 1921. Mason (K.T.). Mem. I.A.G. Baptist. Republican. Residence: 135 W. Prospect Av., State College, Pa.

1-**MASSECK, Clinton Joseph,** *b* Grand Rapids, Mich., Feb. 24, 1886.
9-Maj. Robert **Pike** (1616-1706), from Eng. in the "James," 1635; cdr. Essex Regt.; mem. Com. of Safety, 1689; and thru:
7-John, *m* Mary Hook (*b* 1707; Joseph[8]; desc. Humphrey Hook, from Eng., settled in Dover, N.H.);
6-Maj. Humphrey (1741-1817), Salisbury, Mass.; in Am. Rev.;
5-Abigail, *m* —**Hendrick**;
4-Susanne (ca. 1807-1884), *m* 2d, 1832, Joseph **Masseck** (1807-48), from France, 1830, settled at Saco, Me.;
3-Joseph Sewall (1838-1914), *m* ca. 1859, Sarah Frances Hurd (1841-1915; Dr. Stephen[4], *b* 1807);
2-Clinton Sewall (1861-1923), mcht., Lowell, Mass.; *m* 1884, Mary Lee Elmore (*b* 1861; John Howell[3], *m* Elizabeth, dau. of Capt. Jacob Frieze, to Fredericksburg, Va., ca. 1825); issue: I-Clinton Joseph (1 above); II-Holman Fletcher (*d* infancy).
1-*m* July 26, 1911, Annie Laurie Danforth, *b* Oxford, Me., May 12, 1888; dau. of James Danforth, *m* Mary Haskell; issue: 1-Ruth, *b* St. Louis, Mo., Jan. 28, 1914.
1-A.B., cum laude, Tufts Coll., '08 (Delta U.); A.M., Harvard, 1911; Docteur de l'universite de Paris, 1913. Instr. English, Tufts Coll., 1908-11, Washington U., 1913-17; editor The Dial, summer 1916; spl. investigator, adv. dept. Capper Farm Press, Topeka, Kan., 1919-20, dir. of sales, 1920-22. Lecturer in advertising N.Y. Univ. since 1924; adv. account executive the Borden Co., H. K. McCann Co. Commd. capt., 353d Inf., 89th Div., U.S.A., Aug. 15, 1917; arrived in France, June 1918; maj., Apr. 30, 1919; served as adj., later operations officer of regt. during trench development period; Euvezin Sector, St. Mihiel, and Meuse-Argonne offensive; comdt. at Neuenberg and elsewhere in Army of Occupation, Germany, 5 mos.; grad Army Sch. of the Line, Langres, France; hon. discharged, June 19, 1919; maj. O.R.C. Awarded Croix de Guerre with gold star; citation from comdg. gen. 32d French A.C. Author (see Who's Who in America). Republican. Club: Harvard. Address: c/o H. K. McCann Co., 285 Madison Av., New York, N.Y.

1-**MASTIN, Margaret Louise Crawford (Mrs. William M.),** *b* Mobile, Ala., Mar. 30, 1856.
8-William **Ball** (qv);
7-Joseph (1649-1718), burgess; of "Epping Forest," Lancaster Co., Va.; *m* 1676, Elizabeth Romney (*d* 1706; William[8], of London);
6-Annie (*b* 1686), *m* 1708, Col. Edwin **Conway** (1681-1763), burgess, of Va. (Col. Edwin[7]; Edwin[8], qv);
5-Elizabeth, *m* Christopher **Garlington** (whose father came from Eng. ante 1651);
4-Mary, *m* 1763, Rev. James **Creswell,** came to Md. bet. 1740-50; ordained Presbyn. ministry, settled on "Rose Hill Plantation," Laurens, S.C.; mem. Provincial Congress, 1775;
3-Robert (1769-1850), *m* 1812, Mary Davis (1791-1861);
2-Zemula Walker (1822-1904), *m* 1842, Col. James **Crawford** (1807-81), col., 21st Ala. Regt., Civil War; capt. Mexican and Indian wars; commn. mcht., Mobile, Ala.; issue: I-Mary J. (*b* 1843; *m* 1870, D. W. Marmaduke); II-Robert Creswell (1845-1902; *m* 1869, Louise Blevens); III-Zemula (*b* 1852; *m* 1873, Leslie Marmaduke); IV-Margaret L. (1 above); V-James W. (1859-1907; *m* Corinne Phillipe).
1-*m* 1882, Dr. William MacDowell Mastin, *b* Mobile, Ala., July 3, 1853; son of Dr. Claudius H. Mastin, of Mobile, *m* Mary MacDowell; issue: 1-Zemula C., *b* Mobile, Dec. 8, 1885.
1-Mem. C.D.A. Residence: 706 Government St. Mobile, Ala.

1-**MATHER, Kirtley Fletcher,** *b* Chicago, Ill., Feb. 13, 1888.
10-Richard **Mather** (qv);
9-Timothy (1628-84), of Dorchester; *m* 1650, Catherine Atherton (Maj. Gen. Humphrey[10], qv);
8-Atherton (1663-1734), *m* 2d, 1705, Mary Lamb (bap. 1681);
7-Richard (*b* 1708), Windsor, Conn.; *m* 1734, Lois Burbank (*b* 1714/15);
6-Elihu (1741-78), served in Am. Rev.;
5-Thomas (1768-1863), *m* Hannah Woodruff (1769-1846);
4-Alonzo Thomas (1802-46), mcht. and farmer, Monkton, Vt.; *m* Betsey Jordan (1803-63);
3-Asher Elihu (1823-99), of Battle Creek, Mich.; D.D., Kalamazoo Coll.; chaplain in Union Army during Civil War; Baptist minister; *m* Laura Lucretia Lord (1827-1909; Jared S.[4], *m* Polly Everest; Asa[5], Am. Rev.);
2-William Green (2 below).
9-Joseph **Northrop** (qv);
8-Joseph (1649-1700), *m* Marian Blakeman (*b* 1670; Rev. Aaron[9]);
7-Moses (1695-1746), of Milford, Conn.; *m* 1721, Abigail Cornell;
6-Amos (1730-1810), of Ridgefield, Conn.; ens. in Am. Rev.; *m* 1758, Hannah Calkins;
5-Barzillai (1768-1821), of Madison Co., N.Y.; *m* Marjory Rockwood (1769-1833);
4-Sabrina (1803-49), *m* 1828, Elijah W. **King** (1798-1864; Daniel[5], *m* Ruth Wells);
3-Nehemiah Huntington (1833-1922), mcht.; Jackson, Mich.; *m* Juliette Hewitt (1839-93; Alden[4], *m* Julia Crary);
2-Julia Sabrina (*b* 1860), *m* 1884, William Green **Mather** (*b* 1855), passenger agent, M.C. R.R.; issue: I-Asher King (1886-1928; *m* Ruth Elizabeth Delzell); II-Kirtley Fletcher (1 above); III-Ruth (*b* 1890); IV-Juliette Edla (*b* 1896); V-Harriet Livingston (*b* 1898); VI-William Green, Jr. (*b* 1901; *m* Florence Mildred Minchin).
1-*m* June 12, 1912, Marie Porter, *b* Weston, Mich., May 12, 1889; dau. of Herbert Walker Porter; issue: 1-Florence Margaret, *b* Kingston, Ont., June 13, 1916; 2-Julia Carolyn, *b* Columbus, O., Mar. 16, 1920; 3-Jean Marie, *b* Cambridge, Mass., Sept. 15, 1929.

1–B.S., Denison U., '09 (P.B.K.); Ph.D., U.Chicago, 1915 (Sigma Xi); (Sc.D., Denison U., 1929). Instr., U.Ark., 1911-12, asst. prof., 1912-14; fellow U.Chicago, 1914-15; asso. prof. geology, Queen's U., Kingston, Ont., 1915-17, prof. paleontology, 1917-18; prof. geology, Denison U., 1918-24; asso. prof. physiography, Harvard, 1924-27, prof. geology since 1927, chmn. dept. of geology and geography since 1925. Geologist U.S. Geol. Survey, since 1919. Author (see Who's Who in America). Baptist. Clubs: Twentieth Century (pres. since 1929), Harvard, Authors, University (Boston), Colonial (Cambridge). Residence: 15 Channing Rd., Newton Centre, Mass.

1–**MATLACK, Cora Tebbs (Mrs.),** *b* Covington, Ky., Sept. 3, 18–.
5–Daniel **Tebbs** (*b* Va.), *m* at least twice;
4–Daniel Heath (*b* 1755), of Va.; *m* Sarah Heath;
3–William Travis (*b* at sea during Am. Rev., on his father's ship, 1778-*d* 1848), of Va., and Fleming Co., Ky.; *m* Nancy Miller; *m* 2d, 1807, Margaret Robertson (1777-1845; George[4] [1749-ca. 1806], Am. Rev., *m* Susan Simpson, 1749-1811);
2–Willoughby Heath (2 below).
6–Isaac **Clemons,** aet. 9, landed at Salem, Mass., early in 1700, with bro. Jacob, aet. 7, "they became separated never to meet again, Jacob settled in Canada";
5–John (*b* Danvers, Mass.-*d* 1790), colonial soldier, 1755; founder of Hiram, Me.; settled there 1780; *m* 1757, Abigail Southwick (1730-1834; desc. Lawrence and Cassandra Southwick, landed at Salem, 1630, Quaker exiles who *d* at Shelter Island, 1660);
4–John (1763-1845), soldier Am. Rev., aet. 16; settled at Hiram, Me., 1790; *m* 1789, Mary McLellan (both buried on farm, at Hiram);
3–Cary (1790-1844), pioneer resident of Covington, Ky.; *m* 1813, Mary Merrill (*b* Cazenovia, N.Y., 1792-*d* 1882);
2–Martha (1831-88), *m* 1847, Samuel Cloon (1824-61); *m* 2d, in Covington, Ky., 1864, as his 2d wife, Willoughby Heath **Tebbs** (1815-83), capt. in Seminole War, 1838, a.-d.-c. to Brig. Gen. Rodgers; mayor of Covington, Ky., 1870; issue (mother's 1st marriage, surname Cloon): I–George B.; II–Will Wilshire; III–Sallie Clifford (*m* Richard Bacon Jones, see their son Clifford Cloon Jones); issue (2d marriage): I–Grace (1865-1914; *m* William Klappert, see their dau. Mrs. Earl William Wagner); II–Cora (1 above).
1–*m* Jan. 4, 1893, Dr. Harry Crout Matlack; issue: 1–Elizabeth Tebbs, *b* Covington, Ky., June 1, 189–; *m* 1916, Enos William Abare (issue: William Tebbs); 2–Harry Clemons, *b* Home City, Hamilton Co., O., May 6, 1900; U.S.N.R., served in World War, submarine-chaser fleet at Corfu, Greece; on S-C. 215 at Battle of Durazzo, Oct. 2, 1918, wounded at Durazzo, spent 3 weeks in hosp. in Montenegro; on surrendered Austrian battleship "Zrinyi"; served on Am. Food Comm. in Austria, 1919; *m* 1925, Catherine Gaughn (issue: Harry Clemens, II).
1–Mem. C.D. 17th C., Colonial Daughters (registrar gen.), D.A.R. Mem. Christian Ch. Residence: 123 W. Parkwood Dr., Dayton, O.

1–**WAGNER, Ruth Tebbs Klappert (Mrs. Earl William),** *b* Cincinnati, O., Nov. 27, 1892.
4–Henry **Klappert** (*b* Zurich, Switzerland-*d* 1881), enlisted at Cincinnati, O., in Co. C, 47th Ohio Inf., discharged 1862; re-enlisted 1864, Co. I, 108th Ohio Inf., pvt., Capt. Heintz' co., hon. disch., 1865;
3–John Jacob (1826-1904), in Civil War, 1861-65; *m* Mary Elizabeth Dohrman (1823-1907);
2–William (2 below).
7–Hugh **McLellan** (1710-87), from Antrim, Ulster, Ireland, 1735, settled at Gorham, Me.; patriot in Colonial and Rev. wars; selectman, 1768; frontier protection, 1746-47; scout, 1748; provided for soldiers' families during Am. Rev.; mem. com. on new constn., 1778; ruling elder; *m* Elizabeth McLellan (1708-1804), saved Ft. Narragansett, Gorham, Me., 1750; both lineal desc. of Sir Hugh McLellan, Clan Argyl-Campbell, Scotland, knighted 1515;
6–Lt. Cary (1745-1805), of Gorham; colonial constable, 1774; lt. of minute-men, 1775; marched to Lexington Alarm; ens., Hart Williams' Co.; recommended by council to be commd. by Gen. Washington, 1775; made daring escape from prison ship "Jersey"; *m* 1st, 1767, Eunice Elder (1745-84; Samuel[7], will probated York Co., 1753, came to America, 1720, *m* Mary Huston);
5–Mary (1767-1832), *m* 1789, John **Clemons** (1763-1845), soldier Am. Rev., aet. 16; settled at Hiram, Me., 1790; both buried on farm, at Hiram;
4–Cary (1790-1844), pioneer resident of Covington, Ky.; *m* 1813, Mary Merrill (*b* Cazenovia, N.Y., 1792-*d* 1882);
3–Martha (1831-88), *m* 2d, Willoughby Heath **Tebbs** (see their dau. Mrs. Cora Tebbs Matlack for Tebbs lineage);
2–Grace Tebbs (1865-1914), of Covington, Ky.; *m* 1885, William **Klappert** (1856-1929), founder William Klappert Ins. Agency, Cincinnati; issue: I–Cora Tebbs (1886-96); II–Grace (*d* infancy); III–Martha E. (*m* William J. Whitacre); IV–Henrietta V. (*m* Alfred E. Meyer); V–Ruth Tebbs (1 above); VI–William L.; VII–Hugh McLellan; VIII–Tebbs R.; IX–John S.; X–Charles E.
1–*m* Mar. 14, 1914, Earl William Wagner, *b* San Diego, Calif., Oct. 18, 1889; son of Rev. Edwin R. Wagner, of Dayton, O., *m* Dora Hawker; issue: 1–Grace Tebbs, *b* Buffalo, N.Y., Dec. 1, 1914; 2–Ruth Clemons, *b* Cincinnati, O., June 6, 1920; 3–Janet McLellan, *b* Cincinnati, Sept. 16, 1923.
1–Attended U.Cincinnati, 2 yrs. Mem. C.D. 17th C. (asst. nat. sec.), Colonial Daughters (sec. Cincinnati Chapter), D.A.R. (chapter registrar), Cincinnati Colony N.E. Women, Dames of Court of Honor. Presbyterian. Clubs: Hyde Park Garden, Riverside Culture (sec.). Residence: 3588 Mooney Av., Hyde Park, Cincinnati, O.

1–**MATSON, Clarence Henry,** *b* Kirtland, O., Apr. 6, 1872.
8–Sgt. Thomas **Matson** (1607-77), from Eng. with Winthrop, 1630, settled at Boston, later at Braintree, Mass.; *m* post 1631, Amy Chambers (*d* 1678);
7–Joshua (1640-86), shipmaster, Boston; *m* Elizabeth Thomas (Capt. Nathaniel[8], from Eng. to Marshfield, Mass., 1640; William[9], gov.'s asst. of Plymouth Colony);
6–Nathaniel (1682-1776), Lyme, Conn.; ship carpenter; *m* 2d, Joanna Ely (1700-76; Judge William[7]; Richard[8]);
5–William (1732-1804), *m* 1763, Eunice Skinner (*d* 1814; Dea. Aaron[6], of Colchester, Conn.);
4–David (*b* 1766), to Ohio, 1824; *m* 1797, Lois Sill;
3–George (1799-1841), magistrate, Black River, O.; postmaster during Van Buren's administration; *m* 1826, Emaline Augusta Bottum (1805-35; William[4], of Norwich, Conn., *m* Amy–);
2–William Augustus (2 below).
9–John **Sill** (*d* 1647), from Eng. to Saybrook, Conn., with wife, 1637; *m* Joanna–;
8–Capt. Joseph (*d* 1696), *m* 1677, Mrs. Sarah Marvin (George Clark, Jr.[9]);
7–Joseph (1678-1765), *m* 1705, Phoebe Lord (Richard[8], *m* Elizabeth Hyde);
6–John (1710-96), *m* 1731, Phoebe Fither, of L.I.;
5–David Fither (1733-1795?), *m* 1768, Sarah Griswold;
4–Lois (*b* 1771), *m* David **Matson** (4 above);
3–George, *m* Emaline A. Bottum (3 above);
2–William Augustus (1827-1908), to Kan., 1878; Methodist minister over 50 yrs., first in Ohio, later in Kan.; *m* 1855, Mary Ann Whelpley (1835-1902; Daniel[3] [*b* White Plains, N.Y., 1794-1883], civil engr. on Erie Canal, from Dayton, N.Y., to Kirtland, Lake Co., O., ca. 1840, *m* Mabel Anderson, 1800-78); issue: I–Henry Wallace (*b* 1857-*d* infancy); II–Emma Louise (1858-62); III–Elmer Elton (*b* 1861; *m* Ina C. Mead); IV–Wayland Albert (*b* 1864-*d* infancy); V–William Austin (*b* 1864; *m* Martha D. Crumrine); VI–Caroline Ruby (*b* 1867; dean of women Kan. Wesleyan U., see Who's Who in America); VII–Clarence Henry (1 above).
1–*m* June 29, 1898, Loretta May Collins (qv), issue: 1–Rev. William Archie, *b* Topeka, Kan., June 30, 1899; A.B., U.Southern Calif., '22; B.D., Garrett Biblical Inst., 1925; *m* Sept. 1925, Martha, dau. of Rev. A. D. Wagner, of Alhambra, Calif. (issue: Wesley Alfred); 2–Marguerite, *b* Salina, Kan., Oct. 17, 1900; A.B.,

U.Southern Calif., '25; *m* Oct. 26, 1926, Joseph Rogers Walker (issue: Hugh Kelso, III); 3–Elizabeth, *b* Topeka, May 4, 1902; A.B., U.-Southern Calif., '24; 4–Clarence (Ted), *b* Topeka, Mar. 2, 1906.

1–Studied at Kan. Wesleyan U. 2 yrs. Newspaper and magazine writer at Salina and Topeka, Kan., and Los Angeles, Calif., 1891-1912; sec. and traffic mgr., harbor dept., Los Angeles, 1912-20; trade promotion, 1920–; mgr. dept. foreign commerce and shipping, Los Angeles Chamber of Commerce (see Who's Who in America). Mem. Pacific Geog. Soc. Methodist. Republican. Clubs: Los Angeles Athletic, Surf and Sand, Hollywood Athletic, Pacific Coast, Los Angeles City, Calif. Yacht. Residence: 1035 W. 35th Pl., Los Angeles, Calif.

1–**MATSON, (Loretta) May Collins (Mrs. Clarence H.),** *b* Solomon, Kan., Oct. 10, 1876.

9–Henry **Collins** (qv);
8–John (*b* London, Eng., 1632-lost by shipwreck at sea, 1679); *m* Abigail Johnson (Richard[9], from Eng., 1630);
7–John (1679-1755), name originally William, renamed by mother; Quaker; farmer Lynn, Mass.; *m* 1703 or 04, Susannah Daggett (1685-1753; William[8], *m* Rebecca–);
6–John (*b* Charleston, R.I., 1716-*d* Hopkinton, R.I., 1778), Quaker preacher; *m* 1744, Mehitable Bowen (*b* 1725; Daniel[7], *m* Mehitable Chaffee; Richard[8]; Richard[9]; Richard[10]);
5–John (1745-1843), in Conn. militia, Am. Rev.; *m* Mary Elizabeth Smith;
4–John (1771-1844), Brookfield, N.Y.; *m* 1796, Lucy Burdick (1779-1833; Thompson[5], Am. Rev., *m* Tabitha Wilcox);
3–Oliver (1805-65), West Lodi, O.; *m* Sarah Noel (1806-76; parents were French and German from Alsace);
2–Andrew Perry (2 below).
6–Alexander **Blair** (*d* 1798; of Scotch Irish descent), from Armagh Province, Ulster; in Am. Rev., from Pa.; *m* Elizabeth Cochran;
5–William (*b* 1760), Am. Rev.; *m* Catherine Evans (Thomas[6], *m* Mary Rutledge);
4–Thomas (*b* Ky., 1789-*d* 1875), to Ohio, 1799; to Ind., 1819, where he was commr. for organizing Schuyler Co.; mem. 1st Wis. Territorial Legislature, and 1st Ia. Legislature; ruling elder Presbyn. Ch. 50 yrs.; *m* 1816, Margaret Job;
3–Newton (1817-83), to Solomon, Kan., 1866, with wife and 10 children; *m* 1841, Emily Houston (*d* 1906; Caleb[4], *m* 1815, Elizabeth Purdy; Samuel[5], Am. Rev.);
2–Sarah Elizabeth (2 below).
9–Andrew **Job,** from Kent, Eng., with wife, ca. 1650; *m* Elizabeth–;
8–Andrew (1650-1722), high sheriff under William Penn; *m* 1692, Elizabeth Vernon (Thomas[9], from Cheshire, Eng., to Pa., 1682);
7–Thomas Vernon (*d* 1780), *m* 1725, Elizabeth Maxwell (*d* 1782), the famous English runaway, niece of Daniel DeFoe;
6–Archibald, expelled by Quakers with sons, Morris and Thomas, for mil. activities, 1777; high sheriff, Cecil Co., Md., several terms; *m* 1752, Margaret Rees (Morris[7], *m* Sarah–);
5–Morris (1753-1803), repaired arms in Am. Rev., "scout"; moved to Baltimore to do iron and copper work on Cont. frigate "Constellation," 1782; *m* 1779, Lydia Bond;
4–Margaret (1788-1877), *m* Thomas **Blair** (4 above).
9–John **Sharpless** (qv);
8–John (1666-1747), *m* 1692, Hannah Pennell (1673-1721; Robert[9], Eng. Quaker, to Pa. with wife, 1686, *m* Hannah–);
7–Anne (1708-86), *m* 1726, Samuel **Bond** (1692-1783; Richard[8], *m* Sarah, dau. of Allen Robinet, purchased land from William Penn, 1681, *m* Margaret–);
6–Richard (1728-1819), mem. Md. House of Delegates, 1776-94; to Va., 1799; *m* Mary Jarmen (*b* 1733);
5–Lydia (1760-1821), *m* Morris **Job** (5 above).
2–Sarah Elizabeth Blair (*b* 1850), taught 1st sch. in Solomon, Kan., 1867; *m* 1868, Andrew Perry **Collins** (1835-1908), A.B., Ohio Wesleyan, '60, A.M., 1863; 1st lt., Civil War; farmer nr. Solomon, Kan.; co. supt. schs.; mem. Kan. Legislature, 4 yrs.; mem. Kan. State Bd. of Agr., 10 yrs.; Gen. Conference M.E. Ch., 1888; founder Kan. Wesleyan U. (1st pres. bd. trustees); issue: I–Oliver Edwin (*b* 1869; *m* Maud Schultz); II–Sarah Edith (*b* 1870; *m* Prof. George James Hagerty; *m* 2d, John Lewis Bishop); III–Albert Noel (*b* 1872; *m* Harriet May Thompson); IV–Frank Newton (*b* 1874; *m* Ruby–); V–(Loretta) May (1 above); VI–Ruth Emily (*b* 1883; *m* Melvin C. Schaible).
1–*m* June 29, 1898, Clarence Henry Matson (qv for issue).
1–Residence: 1035 W. 35th Pl., Los Angeles, Calif.

1–**MATTHEWS, Eleanor N. Adams (Mrs. Randolph),** *b* Lebanon, O., Sept. 13, 1879.

5–William **Adams** (1748-1852), from Ireland, settled nr. Yorktown, Pa., prior to Am. Rev.; pvt. 2d Pa. Regt. in Am. Rev.; removed to Henry Co., Ky., 1792; *m* his cousin, Mary Adams (William[6]);
4–John (1769-1824), an original settler at Lebanon, O.; *m* 1806, Christian Fox (1787-1834; Charles[5], *m* Mary–; Absolam[6], of Washington Co., Pa.);
3–William (1817-66), of Lebanon, O.; *m* 1838, Celia Ann Treleyn Mortimer (1816-1914; John Bushel[4], Member of Parliament, from Eng. to Phila., 1820, book dealer and newspaper editor at Phila., *m* Ann Davis);
2–John Mortimer, M.D. (2 below).
5–Thomas **Maxwell,** from Dumfriesshire, Scotland, 1760, settled in Trenton, N.J.; *m* —Hamilton;
4–Thomas (1767-1820), *m* Rachel Chambers;
3–Nathaniel V. (1809-86), *m* Eleanor Denise (1811-98; Sidney[4], *m* Anna Conover);
2–Eleanor (1844-1928), *m* 1876, John Mortimer **Adams** (1843-1925), M.D., Jefferson Med. Coll., 1866; practiced medicine at Cincinnati nearly half a century; 2d lt., Co. G, 35th Ohio Vol. Inf., Civil War, cited for distinguished bravery; Mason (32°), G.A.R.
1–*m* Apr. 17, 1929, Randolph Matthews, *b* Cincinnati, O., Sept. 16, 1874; son of C. Bentley Matthews, *m* Mary Ann Randolph Thomson.
1–A.B., U.Cincinnati, '02 (Kappa Alpha Theta), A.M., 1904; research student, Oxford U., Eng., 1904,07,10; Ph.D., Yale, 1914. Teacher of English in private schools of Cincinnati, prior to 1914; instr. English, U.Cincinnati, 1911-12; prof. English, Oxford Coll. for Women, 1915-18, pres., 1918-28. Author (see Who's Who in America). Mem. D.A.C., D.A.R., League of Am. Pen Women, A.A.U.W. Presbyterian. Republican. Residence: Oxford, O.

1–**MAUCK, Joseph William,** *b* Cheshire, O., Aug. 17, 1852.

4–Daniel **Mauck** (ca. 1735-1803), of Hamburg, Va.; *m* ca. 1777, Rebecca Baker (ca. 1745-1805), her father was a London merchant, who came to Va. in 1700;
3–Joseph (1780-1856), of Hamburg; *m* 1802, Elizabeth Whaley (1784-1855; Thomas[4] [*d* 1791], of Page Co., Va., *m* Margaret Pugh, *d* 1791);
2–Joseph (2 below).
5– —**Sigler,** from Germany to America;
4–Adam (1759-ca. 1830), Methodist minister in Va. and Cumberland, Md.; *m* Elizabeth Michael (1763-*d* Meigs Co., O., 1843);
3–Ely (Eli), M.D. (1794-1848), to Meigs Co., O., ca. 1818; surgeon's mate, 1st Regt., 1st Brig., Ohio Militia, 1819, surgeon, 1822; apptd. by ct., dir. to lay out town of Pomeroy, at the Meigs Co., "seat of justice," 1820; elected, 1831, asso. judge, Common Pleas Ct., for 7 yrs.; *m* 1820, Melinda Phelps (1801-34; Judge James Enos[4] [*b* Granby, Conn., 1772-*d* 1822], to Phelps Corners, Meigs Co., O., 1803; student of law, farmer, inn-keeper, mem. Legislature, ca. 1819; asso. judge, Common Pleas Ct., Meigs Co., ca. 1819-1822, *m* Philinda, dau. of Jacob Rice, to Meigs Co., O., ante 1818);
2–Adaline Rosetta (1823-1905), *m* 1841, Joseph **Mauck** (1820-82), of Cheshire, O.; farmer, dealer in produce and lumber; issue: I–Amos Orlando (1842-1916); II–Viola Ruama (1846-89); III–Sigler Whaley (*b* 1849); IV–Melinda Caroline (1850-87); V–Joseph William (1 above); VI–Judson Curtis (1854-62); VII–Adaline Rosetta (1864-71).
1–*m* Dec. 25, 1877, Emily Maude Ames (1853-79), dau. of Bishop Henry Ames, of Hudson, Mich., *m* Delia P. Murray.
1–*m* 2d, Dec. 25, 1884, Mary Frances **Ball** (Aug.

7, 1860-Feb. 21, 1926); dau. of Lucius Stiles Ball, of Green, O.; *m* Maria P. Bingham; issue: 1–Ruth Viola, *b* Minneapolis, Minn., Dec. 16, 1886; A.B., Hillsdale Coll., '07; *m* Sept. 5, 1911, Albert Leland, son of Joseph H. Walrath, of Canajoharie, N.Y. (issue: Frances Lydia; Marcia Joy); 2–Katherine Joy, *b* Minneapolis, Feb. 21, 1889; A.B., Hillsdale, '11; *m* Sept. 10, 1914, Cary Walker, son of Francis Little Hayes, of Oak Park, Ill. (issue: Alden Cary; Richard Mauck; Philip Thayer; David Francis); 3–Doris Lucina, *b* Clay Co., S.D., Sept. 16, 1893; A.B., Hillsdale, '15; *m* Aug. 27, 1921, Hugo A., Jr., son of Hugo A. Friedrichs, of St. Louis, Mo. (issue: William Mauck; Ruth Marian; Elisabeth Helen); 4–Willfred Otto, *b* Highland Park, Ill., Oct. 21, 1899; A.B., Hillsdale, '21; M.A. Columbia U., 1926; attended Johns Hopkins U., and London School of Econ. and Polit. Science; *m* Sept. 4, 1924, Wilhelmena Octavia, dau. of William O. Robinson, of E. Orange, N.J.

1–A.B., Hillsdale, '75 (Delta Tau Delta), A.M., 1877 (LL.D., Hillsdale, 1895, and U. of S.D., 1927); partial post-grad. course, Johns Hopkins. Prof. Greek, 1876-79, Latin 1881-83, Hillsdale Coll.; in pub. and banking business, Chicago and Minneapolis, 1883-91; pres. U. of S.D., 1891-97; in mfg. and railroading, Chicago, 1897-1902; pres. Hillsdale Coll., 1902-22, now emeritus. Pres. Gen. Conf. Free Baptists since 1904; mem. exec. com. Federal Council of Chs. since 1908; pres. Mich. Sch. Masters' Club, 1915-16; del. to Universal Christian Conf., Stockholm, 1925, and to World Conf. on Faith and Order, Lausanne, 1927. Republican. Mason. Residence: Hillsdale, Mich.

1–**MAURER, Angeline Peake Rockwell (Mrs. William A.)**, *b* Onawa, Ia., Nov. 26, 1870.
8–John **Rockwell** (*d* 1673; son of John), *m* Elizabeth Weed (Jonas[9], of Wethersfield, Conn.);
7–Joseph (*d* 1714), *m* Mary–;
6–Jonah (1710-1741-43), settled at Wilton; *m* Dorothy–;
5–Joseph (1739-1823), served in Colonial and Rev. wars; *m* 1762, Sarah Mead (*b* 1742; Jeremiah[6], *m* Hannah St. John);
4–Stephen (1775-1840), *m* 1793-94, Phebe Clinton;
3–Samuel (1796-1881), *m* 1822, Anna Rhodes (1805-82; Jabez[4], *m* Anna Blakeman);
2–David James (2 below).
8–Lawrence **Clinton** (*b* 1643), of Ipswich, Mass., Providence and Newport, R.I.; *m* 3d, Margaret (Painter) Morris (*b* 1667);
7–Thomas (bap. ante 1709-1761), Wallingford, Conn.; *m* 1st, 1718, Hope Downs (1697/98-1729; Ebenezer[8], *m* Mary Humphreville; John[9]);
6–John (*b* 1721), Ballston, N.Y.; *m* 1746, Elizabeth Beecher;
5–Sgt. John (1752-1832), Fly Neck, N.Y.; *m* 1st, Mary Scribner (1748/49-1805; Zaccheus[6], of Norwalk, Conn.);
4–Phebe (*b* 1774), *m* Stephen **Rockwell** (4 above).
10–Thomas **Trowbridge** (qv);
9–William (bap. 1633-1688), *m* 1656, Elizabeth (Lamberton) Sellivant (Capt. George Lamberton[10], lost at sea 1646, at New Haven, 1641, *m* Margaret–);
8–Dea. Thomas (1659-1750), *m* 1684, Abigail Beardsley (*b* 1664; Samuel[9]; William[10], qv);
7–Elizabeth (1705-32), *m* 1726, Isaac **Beecher** (1698-1784; Eleazer[8]; Isaac[9]; John[10]);
6–Elizabeth (*b* 1729), *m* John **Clinton** (6 above).
5–Moses **Peake,** Montgomery Co., Fla.; *m* Mercy–;
4–Eleazer, *m* Mary Voorhis (Garret[5], *m* Lovina–);
3–Elijah, Onawa, Ia., 1866; *m* Angeline Warner;
2–Alice (2 below).
10–Joseph **Loomis** (qv);
9–John (1622-88), Windsor, Conn.; *m* 1648/49, Elizabeth Scott (1625-96);
8–Dea. Samuel (1666-1754), Colchester, Conn.; *m* 1688, Elizabeth White (1667-1737; Lt. Daniel[9], *m* Sarah Crow);
7–Daniel (1709/10-1784), *m* 1731, Hannah Witherell (1703-79);
6–John (1741-1811), *m* 1760, Rachel Harris;
5–Rachel (1765-1851), *m* 1786, Oliver **Warner,** removed to Warren, Herkimer Co., N.Y., post 1790 (Nathan[6], of Conn.);
4–Nathan (1788-1841), *m* 1811, Hannah De Long (Francis[5]);
3–Angeline (1814-1901), *m* 1842, Elijah **Peake** (3 above).
11–Hon. William **Thomas** (qv);
10–Capt. Nathaniel (1606-75), of Marshfield, Mass.; *m* 1637, Elizabeth– (*d* post 1651);
9–Hon., Judge and Col. Nathaniel (1643-1718), *m* 1663, Deborah Jacob (1643-96);
8–Dorothy (1670-1755), *m* 1688, Judge Joseph **Otis** (1666-1754; John[9], of Scituate, *m* Mary Jacob);
7–Rachel (1713-61), *m* 1735, Jonathan **Harris** (1705-61), of Colchester (Capt. James[8], *m* Sarah, dau. of Samuel Rogers; James[9]);
6–Rachel (1737-1827), *m* John **Loomis** (6 above).
2–David James **Rockwell** (1845-1925), *m* 1866, Alice Peake (1845-1905).
1–*m* Oct. 24, 1893, J. Frank Brinsmaid.
1–*m* 2d, June 14, 1923, William A. Maurer, *b* Sandusky, O., June 1, 1855; son of Francis Xavier Maurer.
1–Mem. C.D.A., D.A.R. (chapter regent, 1918-19), I.A.G. Episcopalian. Republican. Summer place: Swastika Cottage, Okoboji, Ia. Residence: 831 2d Av., Council Bluffs, Ia.

–**MAXEY, Chester Collins,** *b* Ellensburg, Wash., May 31, 1890.
8–Edward **Maxey** (son of Walter, *b* in Wales, to France bet. 1660-75, *m* a French woman), from France to America bet. 1686-88; settled nr. Baltimore, Md.;
7–Justiman (*b* ca. 1686), of Lynchburg, Va.;
6–Jesse (*b* Va., 1750-*d* Gallatin Co., Tenn., 1808), served in Va. militia, Am. Rev.; *m* 2d, Elizabeth Lovoins;
5–William (*b* Va., 1770-*d* Jefferson Co., Ill., 1838), *m* 1793, Mary Emily Allen;
4–William M.A. (1812-86), country doctor; *m* 1830, Edda Owens;
3–Simeon W. (1832-1909), to Ellensburg, Wash.; sgt. in Civil War; commr. of horticulture in Wash.; was in charge of state horticultural exhibits at World's Fair, Chicago, 1893, and in many national exhibitions; one of 1st men to see possibilities of fruit industry in Pacific Northwest and had one of first commercially successful orchards in that region; *m* ca. 1857, Minerva Whittenberg;
2–Morton Monous (2 below).
5–William **Maxey** (same as 5 above);
4–Charles Hardy (*b* Jefferson Co., Ill., ca. 1801 or 02), *m* 1824, Sally Bruce;
3–Susan, *m* 1861, George A. **Collins,** of Va.;
2–Leota (*b* 1867), *m* 1889, Morton Monous **Maxey** (1860-97), of Ellensburg; railroad man and stockraiser; issue: I–Chester C. (1 above); II–Aurel LaVerne (1891-1907).
1–*m* June 17, 1915, Elnora Henrietta Campbell, *b* Great Falls, Mont., Aug. 10, 1890; dau. of William Martin Campbell, of Spokane, Wash., *m* Martha Cameron; issue: 1–Marilyn, *b* Spokane, Wash., June 24, 1920; 2–Aurel, *b* Cleveland, O., Apr. 24, 1923.
1–B.A., Whitman Coll., '12 (Beta Theta Pi); A.M., U.Wis., 1914; Ph.D., Columbia, 1919. M. C. Moore prof. polit. science, Whitman Coll., since 1925. Author (see Who's Who in America). Republican. Clubs: International (Geneva), Kiwanis, Inquiry. Residence: Walla Walla, Wash.

1–**MAXWELL, Charles Joseph,** *b* St. George, W.Va., Feb. 23, 1871.
7–John **Smith** (*b* Co. Monaghan, Ulster, Ireland, 1655);
6–John (*b* Co. Monaghan, Ireland, 1686-*d* 1765), from Ireland, 1720; settled in Chester Co., Pa.; *m* in Ireland, 1713, Susanna–;
5–Mary (*b* Chester Co., ca. 1735-*d* Weston, [W.] Va., 1799), *m* 1760, Alexander **Lewis** (*b* 1730-*d* Harrison Co. [W.] Va., 1814);
4–Jane (1767-1835), *m* 1785, Thomas **Maxwell** (*d* 1796; Robert[5] [*d* 1792], Am. Rev.);
3–Levi (1788-1884), *m* 1823, Sarah Haymond, see Vol. II, p. 95, for Haymond lineage;
2–Rufus (2 below).
6–Luke (Bonifant) **Bonnifield** (*b* ca. 1700), lived in Md.;
5–Gregory, *m* Sarah Henley;
4–Samuel (1752-1848), Am. Rev.; *m* Dorcas James;
3–Arnold (1799-1886), *m* 1825, Elizabeth Minear; see Vol. II, p. 95, for Minear lineage;
2–Sarah Jane (1834-97), *m* 1852, Rufus **Maxwell** (1829-1907), see Vol. II, p. 95, for issue.
1–Not married. A.B., U.Nashville, '91. Traveling

rep., Ginn & Co., sch. book pubs., 1904–. Mem. S.A.R., I.A.G. Club: Dallas Athletic. Residence: 1913 Bryan St., Dallas, Tex.

1–**MAYHEW, Edward Elliot,** *b* Chilmark, Mass., Nov. 20, 1851.
4–Theophilus **Mayhew** (1752-1829), *m* Elizabeth Tilton (1758-1844);
3–George (*b* 1782); *m* Clarissa Mayhew; *m* 2d, Mehitable Mayhew;
2–Edward (*b* 1818), of Chilmark, Mass.; *m* Jane Ann Swett.
1–*m* July 6, 1882, Florence Brown Blackwell (qv); adopted son: Walter Lloyd, *b* Nov. 21, 1888.
1–Residence: Chilmark, Mass.

1–**MAYHEW, Florence Brown Blackwell (Mrs. Edward E.),** *b* New York, N.Y., Nov. 7, 1856.
7–John **Brown** (*b* Eng., 1628-*d* 1714), to Reading, Mass.; *m* 2d, 1681, Sarah–;
6–Capt. Nathaniel (*b* Killingly, Conn., 1688), *m* 1713, Deborah Briant (*d* 1745; one of 7 daus. of Simon Briant);
5–Briant, or Bryant (bap. Killingly, Conn., 1717), *m* 1739, Hepzibah Chandler, of Woodstock, Conn.;
4–Joseph (1749-1812), Thompson, Conn.; ens.; *m* 1774, Elizabeth Gary (1750-1845; Joseph[6], of Pomfret, Conn.);
3–Joseph (1784-1877), to Henrietta, Conn.; *m* Abby Morse;
2–Antoinette L. (2 below).
9–Samuel **Morse** (qv);
8–Joseph (1615-54), *m* 1st, Hannah Phillips;
7–Hon. Capt. Joseph (1649-1717), *m* 3d, Mrs. Hannah Dyer;
6–Joseph (1679-1754), *m* Prudence Adams;
5–Jacob (1717-1800), *m* Mary Merrifield;
4–Abel (1766-1808), *m* Rebecca Brown;
3–Abby (1793-1873), *m* Joseph **Brown** (3 above);
2–Antoinette Louisa (1825-1921), *m* 1856, Samuel Charles **Blackwell** (*b* Bristol, Eng., 1823-1901); for Blackwell lineage and issue see Vol. III, p. 319.
1–*m* July 6, 1882, Edward Elliot Mayhew (qv).
1–Library trustee, 1890–. Local preacher in N.E. Southern M.E. Conference. Residence: Chilmark, Martha's Vineyard, Mass.

1–**MAYNARD, James Pickands,** *b* Marquette, Mich., Nov. 20, 1887.
10–Jonathan **Gillett** (qv);
9–Joseph (1641-75), *m* Elizabeth Hawks (John[10]);
8–John (1671-1755), *m* Experience Dewey (Josiah[9], *m* Hepsibah Lyman);
7–Ebenezer (1705-76), *m* Mary Ordway (Jacob[8], *m* Rebecca Wright);
6–Mary, *m* William **Torrey** (1747-83); see Vol. III, p. 326, for Torrey lineage;
5–Olive (1780-1856), *m* Abel **Goodwin**; see Vol. I, p. 720;
4–William (1808-54), *m* Mary Lyon;
3–William Wallace (1838-77), *m* Anna Roney Pickands;
2–Helen Pickands (2 below).
11–Thomas **Stoughton** (qv);
10–Thomas (*d* 1684), *m* 1655, Mary Wadsworth (William[11]);
9–John (*b* 1657), *m* Elizabeth Bissell (1666-88; Thomas[10], *m* Abigail, dau. of Dea. John Moore; John[11], qv);
8–John (1683-1746), *m* 1706, Eunice Bissell (Thomas[9], *m* Esther, dau. of Elder John Strong; Thomas[10], same as 10 above);
7–Martha (1711-98), *m* Samuel **Strong** (1705-89); see Vol. III, p. 326;
6–David (*b* 1736), *m* 2d, Jane Groves;
5–Mary (*d* 1829), *m* Eliakim **Lyon** (1779-1856); see Vol. III, p. 326;
4–Mary (1815-93), *m* William **Goodwin** (4 above).
9–Owen **Evans** (*d* 1723), *m* Elizabeth–;
8–Robert (*d* 1746), *m* 1717, Ellen Griefith;
7–Catherine (*b* 1718), *m* Peter **Jones** (Peter[8], *d* 1747);
6–Samuel, *m* Anna Lobdell;
5–Rebecca (1779-1862), *m* Thomas **Pickands** (*b* Belfast, Ireland-*d* 1811);
4–Rev. James D. (1802-76), *m* Louisa Sparks (1805-92; Henry[5], *m* Rachel Landenberger);
3–Anna Roney (1837-1901), *m* William W. **Goodwin** (3 above).
10–Pierre **Cresson**, *m* Rachel Cloos;
9–Jacques (*d* 1684), *m* Marie Reijnart or Reynard;
8–Solomon (1674-1746), *m* Anna Watson;
7–Rebecca (1713-94), *m* Isaac **Lobdell**;
6–Anna, *m* Samuel **Jones** (6 above).
2–Helen Pickands Goodwin, *m* 1882, Alfred Foot **Maynard** (see Vol. I, p. 720, for genealogy).
1–Not married. U.Mich., '17. Residence: Marquette, Mich.

1–**MAYO, Chester Garst,** *b* Burlington, Vt., Dec. 11, 1881.
10–Rev. John **Wing**, from Eng. to Lynn, Mass., 1632; removed to Sandwich, Mass.; *m* Deborah Batchelder (Stephen[11], qv);
9–Daniel (*d* 1697), *m* 1641, Hannah Swift;
8–John (1656-1717), *m* 1683, Martha Spooner;
7–Samuel (1704-73), *m* 1728, Anne Barlow;
6–Jonathan (1731-1819), *m* Phebe Handy;
5–Charles (*b* 1754), *m* Phebe Johnson;
4–Horace, *m* 1819, Eunice Rogers (Heman[5]);
3–Lt. Heman Rogers (1826-1905), Burlington, Vt.; *m* 1850, Juliet Green;
2–Mary Caroline, *m* 1881, Henry Thomas **Mayo** (qv for Mayo lineage).
1–*m* Apr. 30, 1908, Aida Manderson McLean, *b* Phila., Pa., Dec. 7, 1877; dau. of Charles Clothier McLean, of Phila.; issue: 1–Amanda Belknap Manderson, *b* Phila.; *m* Lt. Hayne Davis Boyden, U.S. Marine Corps.
1–U.Calif., '03 (Gamma Eta Kappa, Pi Gamma Mu). Capt. U.S.N.; served in Philippines, 1901, Mexico, 1914, and World War; chmn. Federal Traffic Bd., 1921-24 (see Who's Who in America). Clubs: St. Botolph (Boston), New York Athletic, Army and Navy (Washington). Residence: "Mayo Farm," Huntington, Vt.

1–**MAYO, Henry Thomas,** *b* Burlington, Vt., Dec. 6, 1856.
7–John **Mayo** (qv);
6–Thomas (1676-1750), *m* Elizabeth Davis;
5–Maj. Joseph (1720-76), officer Am. Rev.; sheriff; *m* Esther Kenrick;
4–Col. Joseph (1747-1817), Warwick, Mass.; officer Am. Rev.; *m* Lucy Richards;
3–Col. Nathaniel (1774-1867), *m* Hannah Simonds;
2–Capt. Henry (1802-89), lived to be the oldest steamboat captain in active service in U.S.; *m* Elizabeth Eldredge (1816-88); for issue see Vol. I, p. 721.
1–*m* Mar. 9, 1881, Mary Caroline Wing, Burlington, Vt.; issue: 1–Chester Garst (qv for Wing lineage); 2–George, *b* Olympia, Wash., Apr. 5, 1887; B.S., U.Calif., '11; maj., Engr. Corps, U.S.A.; *m* May 22, 1917, Dorothy (*b* Aug. 19, 1890), dau. of Charles H. Thompson (issue: George, Jr., *b* Nov. 29, 1918; Henry Thomas, *b* Sept. 27, 1923).
1–Grad. U.S.N.A., '76. Promoted through the grades to rank of rear admiral, June, 1913. Served on the original Kearsarge, the Monocacy, the old Tennessee, the schooner Earnest, and on the Yantic, a small wooden bark rigged cruiser of 900 tons; the service on latter vessel included cruise to the Arctic, 1883, for the relief of the Greely Expdn.; served on the Jamestown, Bennington, Thetis, Wisconsin, etc. Hoisted his flag as a rear admiral in command of the 4th Battleship Div., Atlantic Fleet, Dec. 1913, and in Apr. 1914, occurred the "Tampico incident" which caused Admiral Mayo to demand that the Mexican Govt. hoist the U.S. flag and fire a national salute of 21 guns, in addition to making public apology and punishing the Mexican officer who was responsible for the arrest of an American officer and boat crew summarily removed from a boat from the U.S.S. Dolphin while this boat was flying the American flag. In June 1915, was apptd. 2d in command Atlantic Fleet with the rank of vice admiral and was placed in command of the battleship squadrons, still retaining command of the 1st Div.; apptd. c.-in-c. Atlantic Fleet with rank of Admiral, June 1916; commanded Atlantic Fleet during the entire period of the U.S. participation in World War, this command included all naval forces in the Atlantic and European waters. Rep. U.S. Navy Dept. at an Allied Naval Conference, London, Sept. 1917, and, while abroad inspected U.S. naval forces and bases in Great Britain and France; in 1918 made another trip abroad and inspected all our naval activities in Great Britain, France and Italy; in Jan. 1919, the designation of his command was changed to "U.S. Fleet." Retired Dec. 8,

1920, having reached the age of 64 but was recalled to active duty Aug. 1924, and apptd. gov. of the U.S. Naval Home at Phila., serving as such for 4 yrs. Residence: Burlington, Vt.

1-**MAZYCK, William Gaillard,** *b* Cordesville, S.C., Oct. 12, 1846.
6-Isaac **Mazyck** (1661-1735), from Belgium, 1686, settled at Charleston, S.C.; *m* 1693, Marrianne Le Serrurier (1675-1732);
5-Paul (1702-49), of Charleston; *m* 1729, Catherine Elizabeth Chastaigner (1711-49);
4-Alexander (*b* 1736), *m* 1770, Elizabeth Charlotte Broughton;
3-Nathaniel Broughton (*b* 1777), *m* Christiana Boston Harris (1776-1858);
2-Alexander Harris (2 below).
7-Pierre **Gaillard,** *m* Jacquette Jolain;
6-Pierre, *m* Elizabeth Le Clair, widow of John Melet;
5-Theodore, *m* Margaret Serre;
4-Theodore, *m* Elinor Cordes;
3-Bartholomew, *m* Sarah Donom;
2-Emma Anna (1814-75), *m* 1831, Alexander Harris **Mazyck** (1808-69), rice planter; librarian Charleston Library Soc.; issue: I-Alexander Harris (1835-1913; *m* Anne Hume); II-Paul de l'Isle (*d* infancy, 1838); III-Bartholomew Gaillard (1839-1916); IV-James Simons (1841-1906; *m* Sarah A. Delgar); V-Henry Chastaigner (1844-1919; *m* Alice E. Tilton); VI-William Gaillard (1 above); VII-Mary Catharine (1848-1923; *m* William Izard Bull); VIII-Sarah Christianna (*d* infancy, 1855); IX-Emma Anna (1855-1922; *m* J. Waring Witsell).
1-*m* Oct. 12, 1869, Henrietta Vallée Ronan, *b* Charleston, S.C., May 7, 1847; dau. of William Ronan, *m* Harriet Frances Vallée McCay; issue (all *b* Charleston, S.C.): 1-Marion, dau. (Oct. 2, 1870-Dec. 3, 1928); 2-Ethel, *b* Nov. 27, 1876; 3-Vallée, *b* Nov. 25, 1878; 4-William Gaillard, *b* Jan. 25, 1886; *m* June 22, 1919, Alberta, dau. of William Buck Wright (issue: William Gaillard; Mae Wright, *b* July 24, 1923; Alberta Congdon, *b* July 4, 1928).
1-In ry. service 28 yrs. from apprentice in machine shop to treas.; with Charleston Daily News, 1871-72; sec. and treas. Equitable Fire Ins. Co., since orgn. Q.m. and adj. 2d Bn. S.C. Vols. Mem. Huguenot Soc. of S.C. (v.p.), Elliott Soc. Science and Art (sec. and treas), St. George's Soc. (sec. and treas.), S.C. Soc. (life), S.C. Agrl. Soc. (life), Fellowship Soc. (hon. mem.), St. Andrew's Soc. Former librarian Charleston Library Soc.; hon. curator, conchology, The Charleston Museum. Mason (32°, K.T., grand historian Grand Lodge of S.C.). Episcopalian. Democrat. Residence: 56 Montague St., Charleston, S.C.

1-**MEADE, Rosemary Brooks Kinkead (Mrs. Herbert A.),** *b* Libertyville, Mo., May 29, 1901.
8-Thomas (Kincaid) **Kinkead** (1705-50; desc. David I, King of Scotland); came from Ireland to Cumberland Co., Pa., to Augusta Co., Va.; *m* Margaret Lockhart;
7-William (1736-1823), adj. in Am. Rev.; *m* 1756, Eleanor Guy (1740-1825), captured by Indians, rescued by Capt. Bouquet's expdn., after 3 mos. captivity;
6-Andrew (1764-post 1810), began to write name Kinkead; *m* ca. 1787, Ann Poage (John[7], *m* Mary-);
5-Samuel (1791-1863), *m* 1810, Lettice Blanks;
4-Andrew B. (1811-52), St. Francois Co., Mo.; *m* 1837, Rebecca Elgin (1814-1904; George[5], *m* Sophia Cartwright);
3-Nicholas A. (1845-1926), *m* 1875, Harriet E. Marks;
2-Zeno D. (2 below).
11-Robert **Booth** (ca. 1610-1657), from Eng. to York Co., Va., 1640; clk., 1640-47; burgess, 1653-54; *m* Frances-;
10-Anna (1647-1716), as Widow Dennett; *m* 2d, ca. 1680, William **Clopton** (1655-ante 1733), from Eng., settled in York Co., Va., 1655, later in New Kent Co.; constable of Hampton Parish;
9-Walter;
8-William, *m* Cassandra-;
7-Cassandra (1743-1822), *m* 1764, Josephus **Perrin** (ca. 1743-1803), pvt. Am. Rev.;
6-Lydia (1764-1840), *m* 1st, Shadrach **Blanks** (1760-1809);
5-Lettice (1791-ante 1863), *m* Samuel **Kinkead** (5 above).
7-George **Marks** (ca. 1737-1809), corpl. Am. Rev.; *m* Catrin-;
6-George (ca. 1764-1808), from Ireland to Bethel, Pa.; *m* Sarah Cruise (*d* post 1814);
5-George (1793-1865), *m* 1821, Polly McFarland (1801-71; Reuben[6], *m* 1st, Martha Campbell);
4-Davis Fulton (1824-75), pvt. in Civil War; *m* 1850, Elizabeth Ann Dobbins (1830-1905; William Shaw[5], *m* Sarah Dedman; William Shaw[6]);
3-Harriet E. (*b* 1851), *m* Nicholas A. **Kinkead** (3 above).
8-Llewellyn **Davis** (ca. 1685-1720), from Wales, to Chester Co., Pa., 1701; *m* 1709, Bridget Jones;
7-Llewellyn (1720-94), *m* Magdalene- (1732-1809);
6-Llewellyn (*d* 1809), tobacco planter; lt. in Am. Rev., 1779-83; *m* 1776, Martha Jones;
5-Llewellyn (1779-post 1844), *m* 1802, Margaret Martin;
4-Margaret (1805-77), *m* 1825, James **Brooks** (1803-85; Thomas[6], *m* Amanda Boone);
3-Maj. James Francis (1843-1926), aide to Gov. Fletcher, during Civil War; *m* 1875, Florence Adele Turnbaugh;
2-Edna Rose (2 below).
8-Rev. Thomas **Jones** (1702-88), ordained Bapt. minister, 1740; *m* 1729, Martha Morris (1706-99), both from Wales;
7-Thomas (1733-1800), maj. in Am. Rev.; del. to Provincial Conv., 1776; founder of "The Associators"; *m* Mary Broomfield;
6-Martha (1762-1829), *m* Llewellyn **Davis** (6 above).
7-John **Buchanan** (*b* in Ireland), *m* Jane Russell (Samuel[8]);
6-Sarah, *m* William **Morrison,** from Ireland before Am. Rev., settled in Huntingdon Co., Pa.; linen mcht.;
5-James Dickinson (1793-1870), mounted ranger in War 1812; 1st cousin of President James Buchanan; *m* 1814, Lydia Lee (1798-1877; Samuel[6] in War 1812, capt. in Indian wars, Black Hawk War, *m* Phoebe, dau. of Aaron Atherton);
4-Nancy Ann (1822-1911), *m* 1836, John Jay **Turnbaugh** (1810-73; John[5], *m* Barbara-; John[6], from Alsace to Pa.);
3-Florence Adele (*b* 1860), *m* James Francis **Brooks** (3 above);
2-Edna Rose, *m* 1897, Zeno Davis **Kinkead** (see Vol. III, p. 293).
1-*m* Feb. 15, 1928, Herbert Aylett Meade (qv).
1-Ed. Loretta Acad., 1921; Bapt. Sanatarium Sch. of Nursing, 1926. Residence: 828 Marshall Av., Webster Groves, Mo.

MRS. CORA ANNA (BUCKNER) MEADE (1874-1928).

1-**MEADE, Herbert Aylett,** *b* Granite City, Ill., May 30, 1907.
4-William **Meade** (*b* Scotland), *m* Miss Brennan (*b* Ireland);

3–John (1829-92), in Civil War; *m* Sarah Dykes (*d* 1907; James[4], *m* Jane Molynieux);
2–John C. (2 below).
10–John **Buckner** (qv);
9–Richard (ca. 1678-1731), of "The Neck"; clk. of House of Burgesses, 1714; *m* Elizabeth Cooke;
8–William (1699-1760), justice; tobacco agt.; surveyor; *m* Judith (Aylett) Hawes;
7–Thomas, *m* Elizabeth Taliaferro;
6–Robert (1758-post 1800), *m* 1782, Mary Hawes (1764-post 1800; Samuel[7], *m* 1751, Ann Walker; Samuel[8], *m* Ann, dau. of Hon. Nicholas Spencer, *m* Frances–);
5–Henry (*b* 1783), *m* 1807, Kate Taliaferro Buckner;
4–William (*b* ca. 1816), *m* Elizabeth Barlow;
3–Aylett Hawes (*b* 1847), *m* Medora Richardson (*b* 1850; Allen[4], *m* Bessie Bolin);
2–Cora Anna (2 below).
11–Capt. John **Aylett,** from Eng., 1656, to the Northern Neck of Va.; *m* Annie–;
10–Maj. William (*d* 1723), justice, York Co.; vestryman, Bruton Parish; *m* Sybella Hubard;
9–Capt. William (ca. 1673-1735), clk. of Essex Co., 1702-04; in Indian wars; *m* Annie Ashton (*d* ante 1750; Col. Henry[10], burgess, Westmoreland Co.; John[11], *m* Elizabeth Hardidge);
8–Judith, as Widow Hawes, *m* 2d, William **Buckner** (8 above).
17–Nicholas **Martian** (qv);
16–Elizabeth, *m* Col. George **Reade** (qv);
15–Mildred (1640-94), *m* 1665, Augustine **Warner** (1642-81), mem. Royal Council, 1675-77; speaker (Augustine[16], qv);
14–Sarah, *m* Lawrence **Townley** (*b* 1660);
13–Alice, *m* Maj. John **Grymes** (*d* 1708), vestryman, Christ Ch., 1694-1708; justice, Middlesex Co., 1706 (Lt. Gen. Thomas[14]);
12–Rev. Charles (*d* 1706), rector York Parish, 1644; *m* Frances Jennings (Edmond[13], qv, *m* Frances, dau. of Henry Corbin, qv);
11–Sarah, *m* Robert **Taliaferro,** from Eng. to Va., 1656;
10–Lt. Col. John (ca. 1672-1720), lt. of rangers; justice, sheriff and burgess, Essex Co., Va.; *m* Sarah Smith (Maj. Laurence[11], came to Va., ante 1650);
9–Laurence, sheriff, Essex Co., 1720; *m* Sarah Thornton (Francis[10], settled Va., ante 1700, *m* Alice, dau. of Capt. Anthony Savage, *m* Winifred; dau. of Col. Peter Presley);
8–Francis (*d* 1757), col., Spotsylvania Militia; *m* 1730, Elizabeth Hay (Robert[9], of York Co.);
7–Elizabeth, *m* Thomas **Buckner** (7 above).
2–Cora Anna Buckner (1874-1928), see portrait; *m* 1893, John C. **Meade** (*b* 1866).
1–*m* Feb. 15, 1928, Rosemary Brooks Kinkead (qv).
1–Ed. Washington U., Sch. of Fine Arts. Residence: 828 Marshall Av., Webster Groves, Mo.

1–**MEARS, Mary,** *b* Oshkosh, Wis., Jan. 2, 1870.
5–Thomas **Mears,** came from Gurnsey, Eng.;
4–Thomas, sgt. on Lexington Alarm roll of Capt. Daniel Robbins' co. of militia; marched on Alarm of Apr. 19, from Lancaster to Cambridge; *m* 1764, Mary Stuart (1744-1831; desc. of Mary Stuart, Queen of Scotts, thru James VI, of Scotland);
3–Thomas (1775-1832), owned large gang saw mills on tributary streams of the Ottawa river; built the first steamboat at Hawksbury, 1823; *m* 1805, Polly Harrison (1786-1857; Noah[4] [1759-89], Am. Rev., *m* Hulda Bacon);
2–John Hall (1827-87), inventor many mechanical devices; mcht.; *m* 1864, Mary Elizabeth Farnsworth (1830-1907), author under pen name of "Nelly Wildwood"; issue: I–Louise (1866-1925; illustrator; *m* Frank B. Fargo); II–Mary (1 above); III–Helen Farnsworth (1872-1916; sculptor).
1–Ed. State Normal School, Oshkosh, Wis., and abroad. Author (see Who's Who in America). Clubs: Colony (Peterborough, N.H.), MacDowell, Pen and Brush (New York). Forwarding address: Pen and Brush Club, 16 E. 10th St., New York.

1–**MEDBURY, Lorena Hortense Robinson (Mrs. Harold L.),** *b* Bloomington, Ill., Feb. 4, 1902.
11–John **Whitmarsh** (*b* 1596), from Eng. with Rev. Joseph Hull's Co., 1635; selectman and town treas.; *m* Alice or Elsie–;
10–John, King Philip's War; *m* 1654, Sarah Harding (John[11]);
9–Ebenezer (1658-1718), *m* 1682, Christian Bayley (Thomas[10], *m* Ruth Porter);
8–Mercy (1683-1737), *m* 1706, Andrew **Ford** (see Vol. III, p. 400);
7–Jacob (1711-94), pvt. Am. Rev.; *m* 1733, Sarah Poole;
6–Luke (1742-1810), pvt. Am. Rev.; *m* 1766, Hannah Reed;
5–Adam (1784-post 1823), *m* ca. 1807, Susanna Hersey (1784-post 1847; John[6], *m* Experience Thomas; John[7]; William[8]; William[9]; William[10]);
4–John Chandler (1823-1904), *m* 1847, Sarah Ann Coomes (1822-1910; Alexander[5]; John[6], Am. Rev.; John[7], Am. Rev.; Richard[8], qv);
3–Hiram (1850-88), *m* 1876, Rosalie Hund (*b* 1853);
2–Georgiana (2 below).
11–Hon. William (Read) **Reed**;
10–Alice (*d* 1667), *m* as his 1st wife, Hon. Thomas **Dyer** (1612-76), at Weymouth, 1632; freeman, 1644; rep., 1646; dea.; clothworker, innkeeper;
9–Abigail (*b* 1647), *m* ca. 1666, Lt. Jacob **Nash** (ca. 1640-1717/18), freeman, Weymouth, 1666; lt.; rep., 1689-90 (Capt. James[10], at Weymouth, 1628, freeman, 1645, rep. Gen. Ct., *m* ante 1626, Alice, dau. Robert Burges, of Eng.);
8–Sarah (*b* 1688), *m* ca. 1710, Hon. Samuel **Poole** (*b* 1690; Capt. Joseph[9]; Edward[10], qv);
7–Sarah (1717/18-1788), *m* Jacob **Ford** (7 above).
10–William **Reed** (1605-63), from Eng. to Weymouth, 1635; dep. Gen. Ct.; *m* Avis Deacon;
9–William (1639-1706), constable, 1675; selectman; *m* 1675, Esther Thompson (1652-1706; Lt. John[10], *m* Mary, dau. Francis Cooke, Mayflower Pilgrim, qv);
8–John;
7–Ezekiel;
6–Hannah (1746-1824), *m* Luke **Ford** (6 above).
2–Georgiana Ford (see Vol. III, p. 400, for other lineages); *m* 1897, James Edwin **Robinson** (1844-1920), of Bloomington.
1–*m* Mar. 6, 1922, Harold Laverry Medbury (see Vol. II, p. 198).
1–Ed. Ill. State Normal U. Mem. S.M.D., D.F.P.A., D.A.C. (state treas.), D.A.R., U.S.D. 1812. Residence: 617 Normal Av., Normal, Ill.

1–**ROBINSON, James Edwin,** *b* Bloomington, Ill., Oct. 19, 1904.
6–James **Robinson,** who had to flee Scotland, as result of writing a burlesque article about the King; *m* Mary McKinnie, dau. of Widow McKinnie, who came to the colonies on account of trouble growing out of the settlement of her husband's estate (sister of Lord Leich, of Scotland);
5–Maj. William (1743-1815), *m* Margaret S. Roach (1745-1815);
4–Lt. Col. James (1787-1856), War 1812; *m* 1811, Amelia Wood (1788-1815; John[5] [1744-1829], *m* Margaret, dau. of James Robinson, same as 6 above);
3–Henry Mortimer (1814-86), *m* 1842, Nancy Allison;
2–James Edwin (2 below).
7–Sampson **Archer,** from North of Ireland, 1737; took up claim of 1,000 acres nr. Natural Bridge, Va.; lt. militia, Augusta Co., Va., 1758;
6–Elizabeth, held captive by Indians abt. 7 yrs.; *m* Robert **Renick** (killed by Indians, July 25, 1757, in Va.);
5–Margaret (*b* 1751), was held captive by the Indians; *m* **—Kincaid**;
4–Margaret (1785-1857), *m* 1804, Daniel **Allison** (1778-1864);
3–Nancy (1818-48), *m* Henry M. **Robinson** (3 above);
2–James Edwin (1844-1920), *m* Oct. 5, 1897, Georgiana Ford (see Vol. III, p. 400).
1–*m* May 12, 1928, Catherine Margaret Shipley. Address: Bloomington, Ill.

1–**MEIGS, Basil,** *b* Washington, D.C., Dec. 7, 1899.
11–Vincent **Meigs** (qv);
10–John (1612-71), was at Weymouth and Rehoboth; took oath of fidelity at New Haven, 1644, and admitted freeman; admitted planter at Guilford, 1654; assisted in the escape of the regicides Whalley and Goffe, 1661; constable at Guilford; *m* 1632, Thomasine (or Tamazin) Fry, of Weymouth, Eng.;
9–Dea. John (1641-1713), one of the 12 patentees of Guilford; *m* 1st, 1665, Sarah Wilcox (*d*

RETURN JONATHAN MEIGS, 3d (1801-91).

1691; William[10], of Stratford); *m* 2d, Lydia Crittenden (*d* 1729), widow of Isaac;
8–Capt. Janna (1672-1739), first magistrate of East Guilford, Conn.; rep. Gen. Assembly; capt. Train Band; *m* 1698, Hannah Willard, of Wethersfield, Conn. (1674-1749; Josiah[9], *m* Hannah Hosmer; Maj. Simon[10], qv);
7–Return (1708-82), lt. of Train Band or 2d Co. of 6th Conn. Regt.; rep. Conn. Gen. Assembly from Middletown, 1747; *m* 1st, 1732, Elizabeth Hamlin (1711-62; Jabez[8]); *m* 2d, 1763, Jane Doane;
6–Col. Return Jonathan (1740-1823), see portrait and biography, Vol. III, p. 328; *m* 1st, 1764, Joanna Winborn (*d* 1773), of Middletown, Conn. (their son Return Jonathan, was gov. of Ohio, federal judge, and Postmaster Gen. of the U.S.); *m* 2d, 1774, Grace Starr (*d* 1807);
5–John (1771-1807), of Ky., *m* 1797, Parthenia Clendenin (1779-1839), of Charlestown, W. Va.;
4–Return Jonathan, 3d (1801-91), lawyer; rode the circuit in Tenn.; atty. gen. of Tenn., 1838; author Meigs' Reports of Supreme Court Decisions in Tenn., Meigs' Digest of Laws; mem. state senate; after moving to Washington, D.C., organized Supreme Court of the district, and its clk. 30 yrs.; *m* 1825, Sally Keys Love (1804-58; John[5], of Washington, Tenn.);
3–Return Jonathan (1830-1913), first asst. clk. of U.S. Ct. for D.C., 50 yrs. (see portrait); *m* 1854, Elizabeth Martin (1833-1915), of Buchanan, Botetourt Co., Va. (their dau. Elizabeth M., *b* Mar. 2, 1863, succeeded her father as asst. clk. U.S. Ct. for D.C.);
2–George Clendenin (1873-1907), grad. Columbia School of Law; q.m. sgt. Co. F, 1st D.C. Vol. Inf. in Spanish-Am. War, 1898; *m* 1897, Mamie Higgins (*b* 1880; Edward[3], sec. of Ter. of Utah, 1866, *m* 1869, Alice, dau. of John Tyssowski, dictator of Cracow during Polish Rev., 1846).
1–Not married. Ed. Cornell and George Washington U. Engineer. Mem. Soc. Cincinnati (Conn.). Residence: 3025 15th St. N.W., Washington, D.C.

1–**MELLOR, Elizabeth Wharton Mendelson (Mrs. Walter),** *b* 1886.
7–Thomas **Wharton** (qv);
6–Joseph (1707-76), *m* Hannah Carpenter (John[7]; Samuel[8], treas. Province of Pa.);
5–Charles (1748-1838), *m* Hannah Redwood (William[6]; Abraham[7]);
4–William (1790-1856), *m* Deborah Fisher (Samuel R.[5]; Joshua[6]; Thomas[7]; John[8], qv);
3–William (1830-1907), *m* Anna Walter;
2–Mary (1859-1930), *m* Walter **Mendelson** (*b* 1858; Simon[3] [1822-1910], from Eng., 1853, *m* Rebecca MacGarr).
1–*m* Oct. 11, 1919, Walter Mellor (see Vol. III, p. 328); issue: 1–Louise, *b* Dec. 30, 1920.
1–Residence: Scotforth Rd., Mt. Airy P.O., Phila., Pa.

1–**MELVIN, Marion Edmund,** *b* Camden, Miss., Sept. 23, 1876.
5–William **Melvin,** from Ireland, 1772, settled in Cecil Co., Md., later in Washington Co., Pa.; *m* Margaret–;
4–William (*b* North of Ireland), *m* Margaret McCraig (*b* North of Ireland);
3–Robert (1811-90), *m* Nancy Waller;
2–Edmund Waller (2 below).
8–Sir William **Waller** (*b* 1597), mem. Parliament, 1640–; knighted by Charles I;
7–Edmund, from Eng. latter part of 17th Century, settled in Spotsylvania Co., Va.;
6–Col. John, of Va.;
5–Rev. William Edmund (1746-1830), *m* Mary Smith;
4–Stephen (*b* 1773), of Ky.;
3–Nancy, *m* Robert **Melvin** (3 above).
5–Henry **Parish** (1757-1847), soldier Am. Rev. from S.C.;
4–Elender (1786-1872), *m* 1804, Henry **Cobb** (1781-1850);
3–Telitha (1815-1909), *m* James A. **McMurtray** (1810-75);
2–Elizabeth Ann (1848-1911), *m* Edmund Waller **Melvin** (1850-1911), merchant and planter; issue: I–Marion Edmund (1 above); II–Walter Gibson (1878-1908); III–James Henry (*b* 1880; *m* Mary Staples); IV–Robert Alexander (*b* 1882); V–George McMurtray (*b* 1884; *m* Mildred Gwinn); VI–John Whitworth (*b* 1887; *m* Mamie Shelby).
1–*m* Nov. 7, 1900, Susie Priestley Reid, *b* Canton, Miss., Nov. 8, 1875; dau. of James A. Reid, of Canton, Miss.
1–A.B. Southwestern Presbyn. U. (Clarksville, Tenn.), '98; A.M. and B.D., 1900 (D.D., 1912). Presbyn. minister, 1900-08; pres. Chamberlain Hunt Acad., Port Gibson, 1908-14; supt. schools and colleges for Synod of Miss., Presbyn. Ch. in U.S., 1914-17; field sec. dept. of edn., same, 1917-21, raising abt. $5,000,000 for colleges; gen. sec. dept. of stewardship and ch. finance, 1921-27; pres. Westminster Coll., Fulton, Mo., since June 1, 1927. Author (see Who's Who in America). Mason. Democrat. Clubs: Noon Day, Athletic (St. Louis), Rotary. Residence: Fulton, Mo.

1–**MERCER, Edith Huling Crawford (Mrs. Hugh Victor),** *b* Marietta, O., Jan. 10, 1875.
4–John **Crawford** (1756-1805), from Ireland, 1793, and settled at Salem, O.; *m* ante 1790, Eleanor Coulter (1760-1839);
3–John (1797-1852), named as one of original incorporators in charter for Marietta Coll., 1835; *m* 1822, Martha Babcock (1803-54);
2–William Herr (2 below).
10–Dea. Samuel **Chapin** (qv);
9–Josiah (1634-1726), Mendon, Mass.; *m* 1st, Mary King (1639-76), Weymouth, Mass.;
8–Capt. Seth (1668-1746), Medford, Mass.; *m* 2d, 1691, Bethiah Thurston (1671-1744; Dea. John[9], *m* Mary Wood);
7–Dea. John (1698-1770), of Mendon; *m* 1718, Dorcas– (1694-1767);
6–Joshua (*b* 1728), New Marlboro, Mass.; *m* 1750, Mary Hayward (*b* 1729);
5–Peter (1756-1839), Am. Rev.; *m* 1780, Elizabeth Austin (1758-1838);
4–Seymour (1782-1861), Medina, O.; *m* 1803, Achsah Hulet (1784-1835);
3–William Harlow (1804-91), Marietta, O.; *m* 1833, Hannah Earl (1807-83);
2–Cornelia Maria (1834-1900), *m* 1856, William Herr **Crawford** (1830-98), oil producer, and ry. executive; issue: I–Martha (*b* 1859; *m* Simcoe Chapman); II–Harry Chapin (*b* 1861; *m* Clara Lee Welles); III–John Harlowe (1866-1927; *m* Katherine Pratt); IV–Frank Earl (*b* 1869-1910); V–Edith Huling (1 above); VI–Cornelia Earl (*b* 1875).
1–*m* Aug. 18, 1904, Hugh Victor Mercer, *b* Salem Ill., Jan. 26, 1869; son of Silas Mercer, *m* Caroline Gaston; issue (both *b* Minneapolis, Minn.): 1–Caroline Gaston, *b* Apr. 13, 1908; B.A., Vassar, '29 (P.B.K.); 2–Victoria Louise, *b* May 28, 1913.
1–Mem. D.F.P.A. (v.p., 1928), D.A.R. (chapter regent, 1924-26), Needlework Guild of Am. (sec. Minneapolis branch). Clubs: Woman's, Minikhada, Encampment Forest Assn. Republican. Residence: 3800 Zenith Av. S., Minneapolis, Minn.

1–**MERONEY, William Penn,** *b* Plano, Tex., Jan. 7, 1881.
4–Nathan **Meroney** (1763-1834), of Chatoogaville, Ga.; *m* Sarah– (1762-1840);

3-William (1791-1872), of Chatoogaville; *m* 1816, Elizabeth Griffith (1795-1876; James[4] [*d* aet. ca. 71], *m* Ann-, *d* 1798, aet. 25);
2-William Lowndes (1834-1903), of Comanche, Tex.; grad. Ga. Med. Coll., 1875; attended Coll. Physicians and Surgeons, Columbia U., 1874-75, Bellevue Hosp. Med. Coll., 1874-75; Univ. City of N.Y., med. dept., 1874-75; licensed to practice medicine at Centre, Ga., 1857; left Ala. for Tex., 1867, reaching Bonham; practiced medicine at Dallas, Plano, Weatherford and Comanche, Tex.; 1st lt. Co. E, 12th Ala. Regt., C.S.A., promoted to capt., resigned to serve as army surgeon the rest of Civil War; *m* Mary Elizabeth Cunningham; *m* 2d, 1880, Lucetta (Howard) Forman (*d* 1884); issue (1st marriage): I-Albert Lee (1866-1920; *m* 1893, Susan Elizabeth Todd); issue (2d marriage): I-William Penn (1 above); II-Emma Viola (*d* infancy 1884).
1-*m* Feb. 10, 1904, Ada Kathreen Reid, *b* Proctor, Tex., July 29, 1882; dau. of Rayford H. Reid, of Proctor; issue: 1-Howard Maxwell, *b* Waco, Tex., Jan. 31, 1906; A.B., Baylor, '26; A.M., U.Tex., 1928; 2-Charles Arthur, *b* Groesbeck, Tex., Mar. 22, 1909; A.B., Baylor '30; 3-William Albert, *b* Waco, Tex., July 28, 1922.
1-Student A. and M. Coll. of Tex., 1896-97, 1897-98; grad. Howard Payne Coll., Brownwood, Tex., 1903, A.B., Baylor, 1907 (Alpha Kappa Delta); Th.B., Southwestern Bapt. Theol. Sem., 1912; Th.M., Southern Bapt. Theol. Sem., 1917, Th.D., 1919; A.M., U.Chicago, 1922. Pastor, 1904-19; prof. sociology, Baylor U., since 1922, also head dept. of sociology. Author (see Who's Who in America). Mason. Baptist. Democrat. Residence: 1417 S. 7th St., Waco, Tex.

1-**MERRELL, Irving Seward,** *b* Syracuse, N.Y., Oct. 12, 1875.
10-Nathaniel (Merrill) **Merrell** (qv);
9-John, *m* Sarah Watson;
8-John, *m* Sarah Marsh;
7-Nathaniel, *m* Ester Warner;
6-Caleb, *m* Susannah Tompkins;
5-Nathaniel (1756-1823), of Waterbury, Conn.; capt., Am. Rev.; *m* Honor Doud (*d* 1796);
4-Caleb (1783-1864), *m* Sally Packard (1790-1871);
3-Oliver Dunbar (1811-99), Greene, N.Y.; *m* Polly Lewis;
2-Gaius Lewis (2 below).
9-John **Lewis,** from Eng., 1636, settled at Scituate, Mass.; *m* Sarah-;
8-Joseph (*d* 1680), from Eng. with his father; was at New London, Conn., 1666, Windsor, 1675, Simsbury, 1677; *m* 1674, Elizabeth Spencer (John[9]);
7-Joseph (1676-1749), Waterbury; *m* 1703, Sarah Andrews (Abraham[8], *m* Rebecca Carnington);
6-Joseph (1705-49), *m* 1727, Mary Slaughter (*d* 1738; John[7]);
5-Abraham (1737-1819), corpl. Am. Rev., dismissed after Burgoyne's surrender; *m* 1767, Ruth Judd (Joseph[6], *m* Elizabeth Royce);
4-Ansel, *m* Lydia Merrell (Caleb[6], *m* Susannah Tompkins);
3-Polly (1811-1900), Greene, N.Y.; *m* Oliver Dunbar **Merrell** (3 above);
2-Gaius Lewis (1843-1909), Syracuse, N.Y.; mfg. food products; *m* 1874, Mary Antoinette Seward (1846-1911); issue: I-Irving Seward (1 above); II-Lewis Charles (*m* Nettie M. Hoes, divorced; *m* 2d, Della Michaels); III-Oliver Edward (*m* Rosalind Wilson Brownell); IV-Arthur Howard (*d* 1887).
1-*m* Jan. 4, 1899, Carolyn Louise Snow, *b* Syracuse, N.Y., Oct. 15, 1874; dau. of Charles Nesley Snow, *m* Harriet Lavinia Powers; issue (all *b* Syracuse): 1-Seward Snow, *b* Nov. 7, 1899; attended M.I.T.; 2-Mary Antoinette, *b* Sept. 16, 1901; attended Smith Coll.; *m* Sept. 8, 1928, William Raynor, son of Lewis Raynor Stevens, of Maple View, N.Y. (issue: Antoinette Merrell); 3-Harriet Powers, *b* Feb. 1, 1906; attended Smith Coll.
1-B.S. in Mech. Engring., M.I.T., '96. Entered employ of Merrell-Soule Co., Syracuse, upon leaving coll. Developed and patented numerous processes for preservation of foods and machinery for producing the same (see Who's Who in America). Chmn. Draft Bd. No. 3, Syracuse, World War. Unitarian. Republican. Clubs: Onondaga Country (Syracuse), Skaneateles Country, Jungle Country (St. Petersburg). Residence: Skaneateles N.Y.

1-**MERRILL, George Arthur,** *b* Portland, Me., Sept. 9, 1866.
10-Nathaniel (Merrell) **Merrill** (qv);
9-Nathaniel (*d* 1683), of Newbury, Mass.; *m* 1661, Joanna Ninian (*d* 1718);
8-John (1663-1705), Haverhill; *m* Lucy Webster (*b* 1664);
7-John (1696-1773), founded Concord, N.H.; chosen dea., 1730; operated 1st ferry across Merrimac River at Concord; *m* 1723, Lydia Haynes (*b* 1678);
6-Lt. Thomas (1724-89), fought in French and Indian War and in Am. Rev.; founder of Conway, N.H.; *m* Phebe Abbott (1727-55);
5-Thomas (1748-1821), Am. Rev.; *m* Hannah Ambrose (*b* 1744);
4-Samuel (1777-1852), Winterport, Me.; *m* Sally Mason (*d* 1804);
3-Henry (1804-45), Newport, Me.; *m* Mary Whitney (1811-47);
2-Henry Franklin (2 below).
9-John **Whitney** (qv);
8-Benjamin (1643-1723), York, Me.; *m* Sarah- (*d* 1690);
7-Nathaniel (*b* 1680), *m* Sarah Ford;
6-Elder Nathan (1707-1804), *m* 1748, Elizabeth Melcher;
5-Asa (1754-1806), Gorham, Me.; *m* 1775, Patience Weston (1751-84; Thomas[6], *m* Patience, dau. of Capt. John Phinney);
4-Rev. Samuel (1777-1859), abolitionist preacher, one of authors of constn. under which Me. was admitted to the Union; *m* Mary Rich (1778-1822; James[5]; Lemuel[6]; Samuel[7]; Richard[8]);
3-Mary Whitney (1811-47), *m* Henry **Merrill** (3 above).
8-Francis **Grant** (1643-1717), settled at Marblehead, Mass.; *m* 1668, Susanna Coombs (1642-1729);
7-Francis (1673-1712), *m* 1702, Priscilla Hawkins (*b* 1685);
6-John (*b* 1705), *m* Elizabeth Carder (?);
5-Thomas (1752-1827), was in Marblehead regt. which manned the boats when Washington escaped with his army from L.I.; served as rear guard to hold back the British as Washington retreated to White Plains, across the Hudson, and thru N.J.; manned the boats again when Washington's army crossed the Delaware, and again when they recrossed the Delaware Christmas Eve, and captured the Hessians; *m* 1777, Elizabeth Babcock (*b* 1755; William[6]; William[7]);
4-Francis (1788-1873), Sedgwick, Me.; *m* 1812, Mercy Gray (1789-1844);
3-Thomas Baldwin (1813-91), San Francisco, Calif.; *m* 1836, Paulina Tolpy Ober;
2-Aurelia Maria (2 below).
8-Richard **Ober** (1641-1716), from Asbury, Eng., to Beverly, Mass., 1668; *m* 1671, Abigail Woodberry (1655-1742);
7-Hezekiah (1681-1739), *m* 1702, Anna Morgan (1685-1774);
6-Samuel (*b* 1705), *m* 1727, Elizabeth Bootman (*b* 1707);
5-William (*b* 1735), town clk., Beverly, Mass.; to Sedgwick, Me.; *m* 1760, Hannah Munroe (*b* 1740);
4-Samuel (1778-1869), *m* 1800, Martha Freeman (1781-1833; Reuben[5]; Capt. Joshua[6]; Col. Edmund[7]; Dea. Thomas[8]; Maj. John[9], *m* Mercy, dau. of Gov. Thomas Prince, qv, *m* Patience, dau. of William Brewster, qv);
3-Pauline Tolpy (1818-1900), *m* Thomas Baldwin **Grant** (3 above);
2-Aurelia Maria (1837-99), *m* 1855, Henry Franklin **Merrill** (1833-1907), of Portland, Me., Boston, Mass., and San Francisco, Calif.; in Civil War, 1861; issue: I-Albert Henry (*b* 1856; *m* Mollie Slater); II-Frederick Thomas (*b* 1858; *m* Lillian A. Stevens; *m* 2d, May Cassidy); III-Mary (*b* 1861; *m* Dr. John N. Blood; *m* 2d, George B. Miller); IV-Frank Whitney (*b* 1864; *m* Katherine Shepston; *m* 2d, Minnie [Lutgen] Schutte); V-George Arthur (1 above).
1-*m* June 11, 1895, Sarah Elizabeth McKie, *b* Hecker, Ill., April 13, 1866; dau. of Nathaniel McKie, of San Diego, Calif.; issue: (all *b* San Francisco): 1-Grant, *b* Oct. 23, 1899; B.S., U.Calif., '23; 2-Aurelia Marie, *b* Aug. 13, 1901; A.B., Stanford U., '23; *m* Aug. 19, 1924, Claude E. Peavy, of

Ventura, Calif. (issue: Merrill; Claudia Jane); 3–Ernest Nathaniel, *b* Feb. 12, 1903; B.S., Stanford U., '25; *m* Nov. 8, 1928, Eleanor, dau. of George Otis Hall, of San Mateo, Calif. (issue: Peter Stephen).

1–B.S., U.Calif., '88; post-grad., 1893-94. Teacher Cogswell Polytechnic Coll., San Francisco, 1888; head of dept. of science, 1889; v.prin., 1891; prin., 1892-93; dir. of endowments since 1894 (see Who's Who in America). Mem. S.M.D., S.R., Calif. Geneal. Soc., Civil Legion of World War. Unitarian. Progressive Republican. Residence: Redwood City, Calif.

1–**MERRILL, Leon Stephen,** *b* Solon, Me., Dec. 22, 1864.

8–Nathaniel (Merrell) **Merrill** (qv);

7–Daniel (1642-1717), of Newbury, Mass.; *m* 1667, Sarah Clough (1646-1706);

6–Stephen (1688-1755), *m* 1710, Mary Carr (1678-1744);

5–Stephen (1713-93), Salisbury, Mass.; capt. Am. Rev.; *m* 1740, Joanna French (*d* 1807);

4–Ezra (*b* 1746), *m* 1775, Molly Stevens;

3–Benjamin (1783-1858), Solon, Me.; *m* ca. 1809, Rachel Durrell (1790-1868);

2–Stephen **Merrill** (1828-1916), farmer, Solon, Me.; mem. Me. House of Rep., 1889-90; *m* 1855, Jerusha Dean (1830-1901; Benjamin[3], *m* Jane Green); issue: I–Albert Carroll (*m* Annie Coleman); II–Leon Stephen (1 above).

1–*m* Aug. 12, 1884, Alice Estelle Wilson (May 7, 1865-*d* 1928), dau. of Allen Baker Wilson, *m* Helen Moore; issue: 1–Gladys Helen, *b* Solon, Me., Aug. 1, 1893; B.A., U. of Me., '15; 2–Earl Stephen, *b* Solon, Oct. 12, 1895; B.A., U. of Me., '16; M.D., Harvard Med. School, 1920; *m* Aug. 1, 1922, Mary Homan.

1–M.D., Med. School of Me. (Bowdoin), '89 (Alpha Zeta, Phi Kappa Phi); (Sc.D., U. of Me., 1922). Druggist, 1889-1900; mgr. Solon Creamery Co., 1900-08; state dairy insr., 1907-10; prof. agrl. extension, U. of Me., since 1910, and dean Coll. of Agr., since 1911. Federal Food Administrator for Me., 1917-19. Mem. S.A.R., Me. Hist. Soc., etc. Congregational. Republican. Odd Fellow (Grand Sire, 1927-28). Clubs: Century, Rotary (Bangor, Me.). Residence: Orono, Me.

1–**MERRILL, Robert Dodge,** *b* Newburyport, Mass., Nov. 6, 1871.

9–Nathaniel (Merrell) **Merrill** (qv);

8–Abel (1643-89), of Newbury, Mass.; *m* Priscilla Chase (*b* 1649; Aquila[9], qv);

7–Thomas (*d* 1756), Southampton, Mass.; *m* Judith Kent (*d* 1751; John[8]);

6–Thomas (1710-1801), of Southampton, Mass.; *m* Hannah Bagley (*b* 1712);

5–Nathan (1736-1801), pvt. Am. Rev.; *m* 1760, Edna Griffin (1739-1809);

4–Orlando Bagley (1763-1855), Newburyport, Mass.; shipbuilder; built sloops of war "Wasp" in 1813, and "Pickering" for the U.S. Govt.; *m* 1791, Hannah Poor (*d* 1802);

3–John (1793-1861), grad Bowdoin Coll.; rep. Mass. Legislature several times; mem. Gov.'s Council; *m* 1814, Elizabeth Dodge;

2–George (2 below).

9–William **Dodge** (qv);

8–Capt. William (1640-1720), King Philip's War; rep., 1690; *m* Joan Larkin Hall (1647-94);

7–Robert (1686-1764), Beverly, Mass.; *m* Lydia Woodbury (1691-1759);

6–Isaac (1710-69), *m* Lois Herrick (1714-52);

5–Col. Robert (1743-1823), Hamilton, Mass.; Am. Rev., and in 23 battles, present at surrender of Burgoyne; rep., 1801-13; *m* 1765, Mary Boardman (1745-1824);

4–Robert (1775-1819), Newburyport; *m* Elizabeth Wade (*d* 1863);

3–Elizabeth (1796-1870), *m* 1814, John **Merrill** (3 above).

8–George (Abbott) **Abbot** (qv);

7–Benjamin (1661-1703), of Andover, Mass.; *m* 1685, Sarah Farnum;

6–Benjamin (1686-1748), *m* 3d, 1729, Abigail– (*d* 1783);

5–Abiel (1735-64), *m* 1761, Phebe Ballard (1738-1815);

4–Benjamin (1763-1821), *m* 1785, Johanna Holmes (1765-1828);

3–Francis Holmes (1797-1874), Orange, N.J.; *m* Mary Wade;

2–Emily Dodge (2 below).

9–Jonathan **Wade** (*d* 1683), from Eng. in the "Lion," to Boston, 1632, settling at Charlestown, Mass.; removed to Ipswich, 1636; rep. Gen. Ct., 1669,81,82; *m* Susanna–;

8–Thomas (1651-96), col. Middle Essex Regt.; justice; *m* 1670, Elizabeth Cogswell;

7–Thomas (1673-1737), capt. Ipswich co., 1695; *m* 1700, Elizabeth Thornton;

6–Timothy (1712-63), *m* Ruth Woodbury (1715-1802);

5–William (1742-93), *m* 1769, Mary Crocker;

4–Col. Thomas (1770-1827), *m* Elizabeth Merrifield (1767-1837);

3–Mary (1804-47), *m* 1826, Francis Holmes **Abbot** (3 above);

2–Emily Dodge (1830-89), *m* 1850, George **Merrill** (1827-1910), insurance auditor; issue: I–Mary Elizabeth (*b* 1852); II–George Francis (1857-58); III–Francis Gordon (*b* 1859; *m* Almira Stelle); IV–Emily Dodge (1861-1920); V–Helen Abbot (*b* 1864); VI–William Pierson (*b* 1867; *m* Clara Seymour Helmer); VII–Robert Dodge (1 above).

1–*m* Sept. 28, 1909, Ruth Elizabeth Dowling, *b* Canton, N.Y., Mar. 14, 1876; dau. of George Dowling, of Yonkers, N.Y.; issue: 1–Barbara (*b* Dec. 23, 1917-*d* infancy); adopted dau.; Jean Brooks, *b* New York, Feb. 22, 1922.

1–A.B., Rutgers, '93 (Delta U., P.B.K.); Union Theol. Sem., 1896; Presbyterian pastor, Brentwood, N.Y., 1896-1905, Babylon, N.Y., 1905-18, Seneca Falls, N.Y., since 1919. Republican. Residence: 66 State St., Seneca Falls, N.Y.

1–**MERRILLS, Frederick E.,** *b* Belleville, Ill., Jan. 14, 1889.

10–Nathaniel (Merrell, Merrill) **Merrills** (qv);

9–John (1635-1712), Hartford, Conn.; *m* 1663, Sarah Watson;

8–John (1669-1748), W. Hartford; *m* 1694, Sarah Marsh;

7–Nathaniel (1702-72), Waterbury, Conn.; *m* 1729, Esther Warner;

6–Ephraim (*b* 1733), *m* 1753, Jerusha Tompkins;

5–Jeptha (1756-1838), E. Bloomfield, N.Y.; Am. Rev.; *m* Mary Royce (*d* ca. 1826);

4–Sylvester (1793-1852), Belleville, Ill.; 1st co. supt. of schs., St. Clair Co., Ill.; *m* 1817, Susanna Varner (1798-1889);

3–Frederick (1818-85), began to write name Merrills; *m* 1859, Catherine Boyakin (1824-89);

2–Frederick Boyakin (2 below).

8–Anthony **Badgley**, settled at Flushing, L.I., ante 1700; sgt., Capt. Wright's co., 1715; *m* Elizabeth–;

7–John (1700-ca. 1759), lt. in Capt. N. Davis' militia, 1747; *m* Euphemia–;

6–Anthony (*d* 1768), Hardy Co., Va.; *m* 1747, Elizabeth–;

5–Rev. David (1749-1824), from Elizabeth, N.J., to Hardy Co., Va., 1768, to Ill., 1796-97; organized 1st Bapt. ch. west of Ohio River, at New Design, nr. Waterloo, Ill.; *m* 1769, Rhoda Valentine (1752-1835);

4–Job (1788-1854), *m* 1810, Micha Wilderman (1793-1856), of Pa.;

3–Simon Peter (1828-1908), *m* 1856, Mary Loretta Wilderman (1836-1918);

2–Virginia (*b* 1864), *m* 1887, Frederick Boyakin **Merrills** (1864-1920), master in chancery, St. Clair Co., Ill., 1902; Mason (Grand Master of Ill., 1907); issue: I–Frederick E. (1 above); II–Marshall C. (*b* 1892; *m* May DuBois); III–Virginia; IV–Wayne (*b* 1903).

1–*m* Aug. 15, 1915, Mary Turner, *b* Belleville, Ill., Jan. 9, 1890; daughter of L. D. Turner; issue: 1–Mary Josephine, *b* April 6, 1917; 2–Virginia Turner, *b* Feb. 10, 1919.

1–A.B., Harvard, '11; A.M., U. of Ill., 1912; Admitted to bar, 1913; dir. First Nat. Bank, St. Clair Co. Title Guaranty Co. Clubs: Harvard-Yale-Princeton (Chicago), University (St. Louis), St. Clair Country. Residence: 621 E. C St., Belleville, Ill.

1–**METCALF, Mary Richards (Mrs. George R.),** *b* Erie, Pa., July 27, 1861.

9–James **Penniman** (qv);

8–Lt. Samuel (1655-1704/05), lt. of Braintree Militia Co.; *m* 1673/74, Elizabeth Parmenter (*b* 1657; Robert[9], *m* Leah Saunders, widow of John Wheatley);

7–Joseph (bap. 1692), selectman, Mendon, Mass., 1742-43; *m* Anne Farnum (prob. John[8], *m* Mary–, of Mendon);

6–David (1727-1814), *m* 1747, Elisabeth Phipini (Phippeny);
5–Paul (1763-1837), *m* Philadelphia Earle;
4–Mehitable Snow (1790-1880), *m* Luther **Gilson** (see Vol. III, p. 330);
3–Caroline Earle (1813-92), Watertown; *m* David **McAllaster** (see Vol. III, p. 329);
2–Adelaide Philadelphia (2 below).
11–James **Blood** (*d* 1683), from Eng. to Concord, Mass., ca. 1638; *m* Ellen– (*d* 1674);
10–Richard (ca. 1617-1683), from Eng., one of original petitioners for Groton, Mass., and its largest propr.; *m* Isabel–;
9–James (*d* 1692), killed by Indians; *m* Elizabeth Longley (*d* 1677);
8–Elizabeth (1675-1759), *m* Samuel **Shattuck** (see Vol. III, p. 330);
7–Elizabeth (1705-84), *m* 1732, John **Shedd** (1706-64; Samuel[8], *m* Elizabeth, dau. of Capt. Jerathmeel Bowers, *m* Elizabeth Worthington; Daniel[9], *m* Mary–);
6–Elizabeth (*b* 1733), *m* 1st, 1752, Samuel **Gilson** (see Vol. III, p. 330);
5–Samuel (1752-1826), Chesterfield, N.H.; pvt. Lexington Alarm, 1775; *m* 1778, Sarah Lane;
4–Luther (1785-1839), Watertown, N.Y.; *m* 1810, Mehitable Snow Penniman (4 above).
10–John **Whipple** (qv);
9–Capt. John (1625-83), *m* Martha Reyner (*d* 1679; Humphrey[10], *m* Mary–);
8–Susanna (1662-1713), *m* 1680, John **Lane** (1661-1714; Job[9], qv);
7–Job (1689-1762), dea. 1738-62; lt. of troop; *m* 1713, Martha Ruggles;
6–Job (1718-96), wounded at Concord, 1775; *m* 1746/47, Susanna Fassett (1725-75; Capt. Josiah[7]; Patrick[8]);
5–Sarah (1751-1817), *m* Samuel **Gilson** (5 above).
10–Thomas **Ruggles** (*b* in Eng.-*d* at Roxbury, Mass., 1644), *m* 1620, Mary Curtis;
9–Capt. Samuel (1629-92), selectman, rep. and capt. of Roxbury Co.; *m* Hannah Fowle (George[10], *m* Mary–);
8–Capt. Samuel (1658/59-1715/16), *m* 1680, Martha Woodbridge;
7–Martha (1691/92-1740), *m* Job **Lane** (7 above).
10–Gov. Thomas **Dudley** (qv);
9–Mercy (1621-91), *m* 1639, John **Woodbridge** (1613-1694/95);
8–Martha (1659-1738), *m* 1680, Capt. Samuel **Ruggles** (8 above).
10–John **Trumbull** (*d* 1657), *m* in Eng., 1635, Elinor Chandler (*d* 1648/49);
9–Ruth (*b* 1645), *m* 1664, Samuel **Perley** (*b* 1640);
8–Sarah (1665-1693/94), *m* 1681, Capt. Joseph **Andrews** (1657-ca. 1732; Robert[9], *m* Grace–);
7–Sarah (1683/84-1732), *m* 1706, Paul **Averill** (*b* 1677; William[8], *m* 1661, Hannah, dau. John Jackson, of Ipswich; William[9], qv);
6–Paul (1711-1805-06), *m* 1737, Zerviah Howe;
5–John (1740-1815), pvt. and served 3½ mos. with the army in Can., 1776; *m* 1760, Mary Bradford;
4–Anna (1777-1862), *m* 1798, Francis **McAllaster** (see Vol. III, p. 329);
3–David (1800-80), *m* 1832, Caroline Earle Gilson (3 above).
9–James **Howe** (qv);
8–Capt. John (*d* 1728, aet. 92), *m* Mary Cooper (1642-1676/77; Peter[9], *m* Emma–);
7–John (*b* 1669/70), *m* 1697, Sarah Cave (1673/74-1730; Thomas[8], *m* Mary–);
6–Zerviah (bap. 1715), *m* 1737, Paul **Averill** (6 above).
9–Samuel **Shattuck** (1620-98; son of Damaris, widow, immigrant);
8–Mercy (1655-1710), *m* 1680, Lt. Andrew **Elliott** (bap. 1651-1688; Andrew[9], qv);
7–Grace (*b* ca. 1683), *m* 1707, William **Bradford** (bap. 1686-1760; William[8], *m* Rachel, dau. of John Rayment);
6–William (bap. 1715-1791), *m* 1737, Mary Lambert (1718-70; Samuel[7], *m* Mary Squire);
5–Mary (bap. 1742-1814), *m* 1760, John **Averill** (5 above).
4–Anna, *m* Francis **McAllaster**;
3–David, *m* Caroline Earle Gilson;
2–Adelaide Philadelphia (1833-1913), *m* 1853, John Stevens **Richards** (1821-97); for issue see Mrs. William W. Michener.
1–*m* Sept. 3, 1885, George Ralph Metcalf, *b* Erie, Pa., Sept. 26, 1858; son of Prescott Metcalf, *m* Abagail Wilder; issue: 1–John Richards, *b* Erie, Pa., Oct. 24, 1889; O.T.C., Aug. 23, 1917; commd. capt. C.A.C., Nov. 26, 1917; service in coast defenses of the Delaware, the Potomac, and Port of Embarkation, Newport News, Va.; *m* Nov. 28, 1914, Marion Elizabeth Rilling, *b* Erie, Oct. 4, 1891 (issue: Mary Rilling, *b* May 20, 1917; John Richards, Jr., *b* Dec. 13, 1918); 2–George Ralph, Jr., *b* Erie, Nov. 24, 1894; *m* June 1, 1929, Eleanore Clark Hulburd, *b* Nov. 25, 1903.
1–Ed. Mrs. Piatt's School for Girls, Utica, N.Y. Mem. Presque Isle Chapter (Pa.) D.A.R., Pa. Soc. C.D.A., Gov. Thomas Dudley Family Assn., Nat. Soc. Magna Charta Dames, Inst. Am. Genealogy; enrolled founder and life mem. Soc. Descendants of Knights of the Most Noble Order of the Knights of the Garter; pres. Visiting Nurse Assn. Clubs: Art, Woman's. Residence: 214 W. 9th St., Erie, Pa.

1–**MICHENER, Adelaide Richards (Mrs. William W.)**, *b* Erie, Pa., Mar. 31, 1864.
10–Capt. Ralph **Earle** (qv);
9–Dep. William (*d* 1715/16), *m* Mary Walker (John[10], *m* Katherine–);
8–Ens. Ralph (*b* 1660), *m* Mary (Carr) Hicks (Robert Carr[9], of Newport, R.I.);
7–Robert (1706-96), *m* 1726, Mary Newhall (*b* 1704; see Vol. III, p. 330);
6–Eseck (1741-1823), *m* 1762, Mehitable Snow;
5–Philadelphia (1767-68-1821), *m* ca. 1785, Paul **Penniman**;
4–Mehitable Snow (1790-1880), *m* Luther **Gilson**;
3–Caroline E., *m* David **McAllaster**;
2–Adelaide Philadelphia (2 below).
10–Richard **Snow** (*d* 1677), Woburn, Mass.; *m* Avis–; *m* 2d, Anne–;
9–John (ca. 1640-1706), *m* Mary Green (*b* 1644);
8–Zerubbabel (1672-1733), *m* 1697, Jemima Cutler;
7–John (1706-77), *m* 1729, Abigail Brigham (1708-90; Gershom[8], *m* Mehitable Warren);
6–Mehitable (*d* 1810), *m* Eseck **Earle** (6 above).
8–Patrick **Fassett** (*d* 1713, aet. 85), of Malden, Mass.; *m* Sarah–;
7–Capt. Josiah (1687-1740), *m* Sarah–; *m* 2d, Esther–;
6–Susanna (1725-75), *m* 1746, Job **Lane**, Jr., of Bedford;
5–Sarah (1751-1817), *m* 1778, Samuel **Gilson** (1752-1826);
4–Luther, *m* Mehitable Snow Penniman (4 above);
3–Caroline E., *m* David **McAllaster**;
2–Adelaide Philadelphia (1833-1913), Erie, Pa.; *m* 1853, John Stevens **Richards** (1821-97; John[3], from Wales, 1800, *m* Ann Henton, also from Wales, 1801); issue: I–Harry (*b* 1858; *m* 1880, Sarah M. Eliot); II–Mary (Mrs. George Ralph Metcalf, qv for other lineages); III–Adelaide (1 above).
1–*m* Oct. 12, 1892, William Weaver Michener (Nov. 3, 1857-Sept. 30, 1908); son of John Hanson Michener; issue: 1–John Hanson (see Vol. III, p. 330).
1–Mem. Nat. Soc. Magna Charta Dames, Gov. Thomas Dudley Family Assn., D.A.R., I.A.G., N.E.H.G.S. Residence: Hotel La Salle, 30 E. 60th St., New York, N.Y.

1–**MICHELS, Ruth Rough (Mrs. Leo L.)**, *b* New Albany, Ind., July 13, 1889.
7–Cornelius **McCarty**, *m* Nancy Bozeley;
6–Thomas (1756-1828), *d* in Hardin Co., Ky.; *m* 1777, Elizabeth McCarty (1759-1836);
5–James (1781-1842), *m* 1803, Mary Nancy Lusk (1785-1865; John[6] [1754-1820], Am. Rev., *m* 1780, Miss McMurtrie);
4–Elizabeth (1805-64), *m* 2d, 1832, William Hamilton **Smith**;
3–William H. (1834-1921), *m* 1852, Fanny Ophelia Garnette (1833-1918);
2–Cora Elizabeth (*b* 1858), *m* 1878, John Wesley **Rough** (1854-1918), issue: I–Eva Grace (*b* 1884; *m* 1906, Vinton Spencer Nunemacher); II–Ruth (1 above).
1–*m* Nov. 27, 1913, Leo Lawrence Michels, *b* Kaukauna, Wis., Jan. 24, 1891; 2d lt., Baty. C, 62d C.A.C. 1918; served 3 mos. in Saumur Arty. Sch., 6 mos. in France; son of John H. Michels; issue: 1–Ruth Louise, *b* Gilbert, Minn., Apr. 27, 1922.
1–Grad. American Coll. of Physical Edn. Mem. D.A.R. (chapter regent), O.E.S., White Shrine. Residence: Virginia, Minn.

1–**MICHENER, Carroll Kinsey**, *b* Fillmore Co., Minn., Aug. 11, 1885.

8–John **Michener,** Quaker; from Eng. to Phila., 1682; *m* Sarah–;
7–William (*b* 1696), of Pa.; *m* 1720, Mary Kester;
6–Mordecai (1723-95), *m* 1748, Sarah Fisher (1722-1812; John[7], *m* Elizabeth–; John[8], from Eng. with William Penn, 1682);
5–John (1750-1837), to Ohio, 1788; *m* 1779, Martha Longstreth (1755-1815; Daniel[6], *m* Grace Michener);
4–Daniel (1780-1853), Mt. Pleasant and Smyrna, O.; *m* 1804, Anna Kinsey (1784-1844; George[5], *m* Mary–);
3–John Longstreth (1819-96), to Fillmore Co., Minn., 1856 or 57; farmer; *m* 1840, Mary Blackledge (1813-66; Joseph[4], *m* Rachel Grisell);
2–Daniel Kinsey (2 below).
5–David **Blakeslee** (desc. Thomas Blakeslee [1615-74], from Eng. in the "Hopewell," to Boston, 1635, settled at Hartford, Conn., later at New Haven, dep. Conn. Gen. Ct., 1667-69, *m* Sussanna Ball, of Boston), capt. Am. Rev.;
4–Hiram, *m* Lenora Woodworth (grand niece of Samuel Woodworth, author "The Old Oaken Bucket");
3–Samuel Larue (1836-1906), *m* Elenora Heuston (Thomas[4], from North of Ireland, *m* Elnora McEwen);
2–Ida Lena (1864-1916), *m* 1884, Daniel Kinsey **Michener** (1846-1929); of Ind., and Fillmore Co., Minn.; shared the pioneer farming experiences of his father in Minn., specialized in horticulture; served in Minn. Legislature, 1884-85; chmn. co. commrs., Fillmore Co.; justice, supervisor, town treas., assessor, mem. of sch. bd.; probate judge, 1909-28; issue: I–Carroll Kinsey (1 above); II–Clarice Evelyn (*b* 1887; *m* Merrill G. Benjamin); III–Laura Elnora (*b* 1892; *m* Dr. Floyd V. Newell); IV–Lucile Alice (*b* 1894; *m* Edmund T. Streissguth); V–Allene (*b* 1899; *m* M. R. Anderson).
1–*m* Feb. 15, 1921, Sarah Amelia Spensley, *b* Madison, Wis., May 30, 1897; dau. of Calvert Fredric Spensley (*d*), of Madison; issue: 1–Mary Florence, *b* Minneapolis, Minn., Nov. 25, 1923; 2–Fredric Spensley, *b* Minneapolis, Dec. 3, 1925.
1–A.B., U.Minn., '07 (Sigma Nu), post-grad. courses in history and sociology, 1914. Reporter and city editor, Duluth (Minn.) News Tribune, 1907-10; editorial staff, Denver (Colo.) Republican and San Francisco Chronicle, 1910-11; sporting editor, Commercial Advertiser, Honolulu, T.H., 1911-12; cable editor, China Press, Shanghai, 1912-13; reporter, Minneapolis Morning Tribune, 1914-15, city editor, 1916-17; asso. editor, the Bellman, 1917-19; managing editor since 1924, of Northwestern Miller and other trade journals. Author (see Who's Who in America). Served as pvt., F.A., U.S.A., World War; commd. 1st lt., F.A., O.R.C., 1918; 1st lt., 4th Inf., Minn. N.G., 1919, resigned 1921. Mem. I.A.G., Minn. Hist. Soc., A.L. Mason. Episcopalian. Republican. Clubs: University, Country, 5:55. Residence: 1203 Mt. Curve Av., Minneapolis, Minn.

1–**MILAM, Nena Mitchell (Mrs. Herbert M.),** *b* Cartersville, Ga., June 5, 1862.
8–John **Skinner** (qv);
7–John (1641-90), of Hartford, Conn.; *m* 1662, Mary Easton (*d* 1695; Joseph[8], from Eng. to Cambridge, an original propr. of Hartford);
6–Thomas (1680-1761), *m* 1705, Sarah Grant (*b* 1684; Samuel[7], *m* Anna, dau. Samuel Filley; Samuel[8], *m* Mary, dau. John Porter, qv; Matthew[9], qv);
5–Ashbel (1716-92), Harwinton, Conn.; selectman, 1778-80; patriot Am. Rev.; *m* 1746, Maria Holcomb;
4–Arad (1756-1828), *m* 1st, 1789, Mary Baker;
3–Julius (1795-1872), buried at Cartersville, Ga.; *m* 1822, Lucinda Houston (1803-64; James[4], *m* Mary Hughey);
2–Margaret (2 below).
8–Thomas **Holcomb** (1601-57), from Eng., 1630; settled at Dorchester, Mass., 1634; removed to Windsor, Conn., 1636; *m* Elizabeth– (*d* 1679);
7–Sgt. Benajah (1644-1736), *m* 1667, Sarah Eno (1649-1732; James[8], *m* 1st, 1648, Anna Bidwell, 1634-57);
6–Corpl. Samuel (1683-1722), *m* 1709, Martha Phelps (*b* 1688; Timothy[7], *m* Mary, dau. Edward Griswold, qv; William[8], qv);
5–Maria (1722-78), *m* Ashbel **Skinner** (5 above).
10–William **Rockwell** (qv);
9–Joan (*b* 1625), *m* 1642, Jeffrey **Baker** (*d* 1655), of Windsor, Conn.;
8–Joseph (1655-91), *m* 1676/77, Hannah (Cook) Buckland (*b* 1655; Nathaniel Cook[9], *m* Lydia, dau. Richard Voare);
7–Joseph (1678-1754), *m* 1st, 1702, Hannah Pomeroy (1682-1705; Caleb[8], *m* Hepzibah, dau. Jeffrey Baker, above; Eltweed[9], qv);
6–Joseph (1703-82), *m* 1730/31, Margaret Gibbs, of E. Windsor;
5–Seth (1733-1816), Am. Rev.; *m* 1762, Mercy or Mary Skinner (1743-1819), of Coventry;
4–Mary (1763-1809), *m* Arad **Skinner** (4 above);
3–Julius, *m* Lucinda Houston (3 above);
2–Margaret (1831-1915), *m* 1856, William Arnold **Mitchell** (1822-95), of Cartersville, Ga.; issue: I–Willie Julius (1859-61); II–Nena (1 above); III–Eugene Weldon (1865-1922; *m* Bessie Harris); IV–Augustin Young (1871-1911; *m* Marie Jarion).
1–*m* Dec. 22, 1909, Herbert Marshall Milam, *b* nr. Cartersville, Ga., Jan. 24, 1862; son of James C. Milam, of Cartersville.
1–Mem. D.F.P.A., D.A.C., D.A.R., U.D.C. Residence: 31 3d St. N.E., Atlanta, Ga.

1–**MILLER, Florence Hazen (Mrs. Benjamin G.),** *b* Sylvia, Kan., Aug. 13, 1880.
9–Edward **Hazen** (*d* 1683), from Eng. to Rowley, Mass., ante 1649; selectman, 1650,51,54,60-61,65,68; judge of delinquents, 1666; *m* Hannah Grant (*d* 1715);
8–Thomas (1657-1735), removed to Boxford, Mass.; freeman, 1689; at Norwich, Conn., 1711; *m* 1682/83, Mary Howlet (*d* 1727; Thomas[9]; Sgt. Thomas[10], an early settler at Ipswich, 1632/33);
7–Thomas (1690-1776), *m* Sarah Ayer (*d* 1753);
6–Thomas (1719-82), mem. Com. of Safety, Cumberland Co., Vt., Am. Rev.; owned 1,500 acres; *m* 1742, Ann Tenney (1726-1802);
5–Daniel (1761-1814), scout during last 2 yrs. of Am. Rev.; *m* 1789, Olive Bartholomew (1759-1845);
4–Rev. Jasper (1790-1882), founder and pastor, 35 yrs., Christian Ch., Woodstock, Vt.; *m* 1813, Abigail C. Thomas (1792-1878; Elias[5], sgt., Am. Rev.);
3–Daniel Thomas (1816-94), *m* 1842, Hannah Elizabeth Webster (1822-94; Ozias[4]; Stephen[5], corpl. Am. Rev.; desc. John Webster, qv);
2–Daniel Webster (2 below).
5–John **Kinnamon** (*b* ca. 1757-1831), first known in America, 1774; *m* Eleanor– (will made 1843);
4–George (*b* 1788), of Stokes Co., N.C.; War 1812; *m* Patience Daniels;
3–Samuel (1818-91), of Randolph Co., N.C.; removed to Plevna Tp., Reno Co., Kan.; *m* Grizillia Ledford (1813-85; John[4]);
2–Eliza Frances (1856-1921), *m* 1877, Daniel Webster **Hazen** (*b* 1849); issue: I–Rufo Arling (1878-1928; sgt., Co. H., 20th Kan., Spanish-Am. War; *m* Nina Nicholas); II–Florence (1 above); III–Daniel Francis (*b* 1893; *m* Bess Miller).
1–*m* Nov. 16, 1911, Benjamin George Miller, *b* Lancaster Co., Neb., Oct. 3, 1877; son of John Gotlieb Miller, of Lancaster Co.
1–Active in civic work. Originator of the "Living Christmas Tree," the "Internat. Peace and Good Will Code," the Neb. State Flag. Responsible for the internat. music entitled "The Living Christmas Spirit" being written. Mem. D.F.P.A., D.A.R., C.A.R. (organized Crete Soc.). Residence: Crete, Neb.

1–**MILLER, Clarence Altha,** *b* Fairchance, Pa., Feb. 11, 1890.
8–Abraham **Miller** (1707-54; g.son of Martin Miller of Ashford, Kent, Eng., *m* Priscilla–), settled in Frederick Co., Md.; *m* Frances–;
7–David (*d* 1783), *m* Cathrine–;
6–Henry (1743-93), *m* Catharine–;
5–David (*d* 1842), of Fayette Co., Pa.; *m* Catharine Getzendanner;
4–William (1806-91), *m* Mary (Polly) Davis (*d* 1871; James[5], Am. Rev., *m* Kezia Phillips; Owen[6], French and Indian War);
3–Albert Samuel (1842-1904), Fairchance, Pa.; *m* 1864, Frances Elizabeth Britt;
2–F(rank) Pierce (2 below).
8–Joseph **Brunner,** from Germany to Phila., Pa., Sept. 15, 1729; *m* Barbara–;
7–Ann Barbara, *m* Christian **Getzendanner**

(1700-67), from Switerland, landed at Phila., Sept. 15, 1729;
6–Baltis (1736-95), Am. Rev.; *m* 1758, Anne Steiner;
5–Catharine, *m* David **Miller** (5 above).
7–Robert **Britt,** from Ireland to Phila., 1705; and thru his g.son:
5–Robert (1772-1846), *m* Mary Lloyd (1772-1862; John[6], from Ire., 1775);
4–Robert (1805-90), *m* 1831, Asenath Greenlee (1808-82; William[5], *m* Mary Ramsey; Samuel[6]; Michael[7], from Ire. to Del., 1714);
3–Frances Elizabeth (1844-1903), *m* Albert Samuel **Miller** (3 above).
9–Ezra **Darby,** from Devonshire, Eng., 1620; settled at Elizabeth Town, N.J.;
8–William, of Scotch Plains, N.J.; *m* Elizabeth–;
7–Dea. William (1693-1775), *m* Mary– (1699-1761);
6–Samuel (1730-ante 1774);
5–Samuel (1752-1850), of Trembly's Pt., N.J.; in Am. Rev.; *m* Hannah Darby (1760-1850; William[6]; William[7], 7 above);
4–Samuel (1784-1848), Preston Co., W.Va.; *m* 1808, Elizabeth Benson (1790-1853; William[5]; William O.[6], Am. Rev.);
3–Harrison Hagan (1832-1916), Fayette Co., Pa.; *m* Nancy Elizabeth Huntley;
2–Anna Belle (2 below).
9–William **Goodrich** (qv);
8–William (1697-1787), *m* Rachel Savage (1703-87; Capt. John[9], *m* Mary Ranney);
7–Capt. Stephen (1732-1823), Am. Rev.; *m* Dorothy– (*d* 1794);
6–Lucretia, *m* 1791, David **Huntley** (*b* 1760);
5–Stoddard (*b* 1792);
4–Robert (*d* 1883), *m* Mary McKean (*d* 1884-85; James[5]);
3–Nancy Elizabeth (1830-1908), *m* Harrison Hagan **Darby** (3 above);
2–Anna Belle (*b* 1864), *m* 1887, F(rank) Pierce **Miller** (*b* 1866), ry. employee; issue: I–Clarence Altha (1 above); II–Ray Arleigh (*b* 1892; *m* Florence Edna Graham); III–Kenneth Roy (*b* 1902, *m* Mary Hunnicutt).
1–*m* Sept. 7, 1910, Daisy May Curstead, *b* Oliphant Furnace, Pa., Apr. 22, 1889; dau. Arthur Curstead, of Oliphant Furnace (William[3], *m* Eliza Ann Price; John[4], *m* Elizabeth Littell; Daniel[5], from London soon after Am. Rev., *m* Mary Ward); issue: 1–Dorothy Agnes, *b* Uniontown, Pa., May 24, 1911; ed. Holy Trinity H.S., '29; Georgetown U. Hosp. Training Sch. for Nurses, 1930; 2–Reland Rita, *b* Washington, D.C., Nov. 1, 1912; ed. Holy Trinity H.S.
1–LL.B., George Washington U., '19 (Phi Delta Phi), LL.M., 1921. Lawyer, mem. firm of Hitt, Miller & Munson; legal author and teacher. Served N.G., D.C., 3 yrs.; O.T.C., Plattsburgh, N.Y. Mem. Foxhall Village Citizens' Assn. (pres., 1928) Washington Bd. of Trade, Am. Soc. Legal Authors, Am. Bar Assn., D.C. Bar Assn. Club: University. Republican. Residence: 4416 Greenwich Pkway., Foxhall Village, Washington, D.C.

1–**MILLER, Francis Garner,** *b* Lanark, Ill., June 2, 1866.
6–John **Moffett,** *m* Mary Christian;
5–Capt. William, *m* Mary Gardiner;
4–Capt. John, *m* Isabella Davis;
3–Abram Gobble, *m* Sarah Ann Davis;
2–Isabella Jane (1841-84), *m* 1860, Isaiah **Miller** (1838-1922), farmer; issue: I–William Washington (*b* 1861; *m* Sadie Rush); II–Sarah Ann (*b* 1864; *m* Dr. Andrus Carson); III–Francis G. (1 above); IV–Carrie (*b* 1868); V–Nellie Frances (*b* 1870; *m* Frank W. Beedle); VI–Emma Mae (*b* 1872; *m* John W. VanKirk); VII–Hattie Belle (1874-77); VIII–Charles Warren (*b* 1877; *m* Gertrude Wolf); IX–Nannie Grace (*b* 1879; *m* Frederick Potter); X–Minnie Inez (*b* 1881; *m* Dr. C. M. Kennedy).
1–*m* Sept. 15, 1906, Evelyn Depew Miller, *b* Adel, Ia., Sept. 25, 1873; dau. George W. Miller, *m* Katharine Scruggs; issue: 1–Frances Depew (Feb. 25-26, 1921).
1–B.Ph., State U. of Ia., '00 (Delta Chi, Sigma Xi, Alpha Zeta), B.S. Agr., Ia. State Coll., 1901; post-grad. work, degree Master Forestry, Yale, 1903. Supt. pub. schools in Ia., 1893-99; prof. forestry, U. of Neb., 1903-07; prof. forestry and dean, Coll. of Forestry, U. of Wash., 1907-12; prof. and head of dept. forestry, Wash. State Coll., 1915-17; prof. forestry and dean School of Forestry, U. of Ida., since 1917 (see Who's Who in America). Republican. Club: Kiwanis. Residence: Moscow, Ida.

1–**MILLER, Allie Spencer Everhart (Mrs. Edmund B.),** *b* Jefferson Co., Ky., June 28, 1865.
5–George **Everhart,** from Germany to Pa.; served in Am. Rev.; removed to W. Va.; settled in Berkeley Co., Va.; *m* in Germany, Barbara Brindle;
4–George (1781-1834), removed to Ohio, 1810; ran flatboats from Cincinnati, to New Orleans; *m* 2d, 1814, Elizabeth Wells (*d* 1833);
3–George Washington (1814-91), steamboat capt. and famed river pilot, Cincinnati to New Orleans; *m* 1834, Hanna Peterson;
2–George Fountain (2 below).
8–Israel **Peterson,** from Sweden, 1635; settled in N.J.;
7–Olaf, of N.J.; and thru his g.son:
5–Charles (1758-1834), removed to Ohio, 1834;
4–George (1786-1848), *m* 1st, Rebecca Jenkins (1789-1828; Zephaniah or John[5], from Eng., 1774, *m* Rebecca–);
3–Hanna (1816-49), *m* George Washington **Everhart** (3 above).
10–Francois (Laroux) **La Rue** (1606-88), Huguenot; from Rochelle, France, to N.Y., 1627;
9–Abraham (*d* 1712), to America ca. 1680; record of him at Kingston, N.Y.; later on S.I.; constable, 1694, 1706; *m* 1st, ante 1688, Magdelaine Gille;
8–Peter (1688-1783), lived nr. Phila., removed to Bucks Co., Pa., thence to Frederick Co., Va.; *m* Miss Cresson (Joshua[9], of L.I.; Pierre[10], from Holland);
7–Isaac (1712-95), removed from Hunterdon Co., N.J., to Shenandoah Valley, Va.; large landowner in Augusta Co., Va., and Ky.; *m* 1st, Phebe Carman (1725-1804; James[8], Bapt. minister, *m* Margaret Duwys);
6–Jacob (1744-1821), large landowner; removed to Nolin, Ky., 1798; *m* 1st, 1765, Mary Frost (1747-1804; William[7], fought in Dunsmore expdn., 1774);
5–Jacob (1769-1851), of Ky. and Ill.; *m* 1st, 1796, Phebe Hodgen (1777-1825; Robert[6], Am. Rev.);
4–Mary (1796-1834), *m* 1816, Judge John McNeilla **Morris** (1789-1865), War 1812; resided at Elizabethtown, Ky. (William[5], Am. Rev.);
3–Margaret McNeilla (1817-67), *m* 1839, Thomas **Lewis** (1809-92; Henry[4], of Ky., *m* Lavinia, dau. of John Myrtle; Thomas[5], from Va. to Jefferson Co., Ky., *m* Jane Baxter);
2–Laura Adelaide (*b* 1845), *m* 1863, George Fountain **Everhart** (1835-1915), merchant.
1–*m* Sept. 5, 1883, Edmund Boston Miller, D.D. (Feb. 2, 1853-1925), of Greenville, S.C., and DeSoto, Miss.; issue: 1–Edith Burton, *b* Louisville, Ky., May 20, 1884; A.B., Blue Mountain Coll., 1901; *m* Sept. 19, 1909, Edmond Ebenezer Stevens (issue: Allie Laura, *b* Nov. 1, 1916; Edmond Miller, *b* Jan. 28, 1919); 2–Laura Townes, *b* Grenada, Miss., May 7, 1891; ed. Blue Mtn., Miss., 1906-08; teacher, vocalist; *m* Apr. 8, 1916, James A. Martin, Jr.; 3–Edmund Fountain, *b* West Point, Miss., June 28, 1899; Ph.G., U.Miss., '21; *m* Oct. 23, 1924, Elizabeth, dau. of Walter Garland Anderson (issue: Edmund Anderson, *b* Aug. 9, 1927); 4–Lewis Lee, *b* West Point, June 30, 1901; B.S., A. and M. Coll., 1924 (Kappa Kappa Psi); *m* Aug. 11, 1924, Eula Mae, dau. John Lemuel Bennett, of Columbus, Miss.
1–Ed. in voice, Ouachita Coll., 1896; studied under Madam Fox, Chicago. Mem. D.A.R. Club: New Century. Residence: 55 E. Broad St., and Miller Av., West Point, Miss.

1–**MILLER, Florence Erminie Valentine (Mrs. John A.),** *b* Mercer Co., Ill., Nov. 8, 1869.
9–Richard **Valentine** (*d* 1687), from Eng., 1644, settled at Hempstead, L.I.;
8–Richard (will dated 1725), *m* Sarah Halstead (Timothy[9]);
7–Richard (will dated 1768), of Hempstead Harbor;
6–Richard (1700-66), Scotch Plains, N.J.; *m* 1725, Phebe Haines (1705-83; James[7]; Benjamin[8], *m* Johanna Jennings);
5–Obadiah (1730-88), Am. Rev.; *m* 1761, Mary Mulford;
4–William (1765-1839), Urbana, O.; *m* 1787, Joanna Crane (1769-1859; Joseph[5], *m* Ruth Miller);

3–Daniel (1803-65), Mercer Co., Ill.; *m* 1830, Jane McPherrin Taylor (1809-99; Robert[4], *m* Elizabeth McPherren, 1786-1838);
2–Levi Crane (2 below).
10–Lion **Gardiner** (qv);
9–Mary (1638-1727), of L.I.; *m* 1658 (?), Jeremiah **Conklin** (1634-1712; Ananias[10]);
8–Mary (*d* 1743), *m* Thomas **Mulford** (will probated 1732; William[9]);
7–Ezekiel, *m* 1714, Abiah Osborn (Jonathan[8]; William[9]);
6–Jonathan (1718-89), *m* 1740, Esther Conklin (bap. 1715-1776; Cornelius[7]);
5–Mary (1741-77), *m* Obadiah **Valentine** (5 above).
5–Ebenezer **Evans**, *m* Sarah– (*b* 1758);
4–John (1782-1850), *m* Sarah Conklin (1784-1874); both buried at Bunker Hill, Ill.;
3–John (*b* 1814), *m* 1847, Mary Love (1827-1916; Charles[4], *m* Mary, dau. of Alexander Mitchell; George[5]);
2–Flora (1848-1928), *m* 1868, Levi Crane **Valentine** (1843-1901), farmer; issue: I–Florence E. (1 above); II–Harriet Amanda (*b* 1873; *m* Joseph William Martin, M.D.); III–Frances Jeannette (*b* 1879; *m* Ralph O. Davis); IV–Leslie Crane (*b* 1890; *m* Johanna Rump).
1–*m* Dec. 12, 1888, John Alexander Miller, *b* Scott Co., Ia., June 26, 1867; atty. at law; son of James Evander Miller, of Kearney, Neb., *m* Ann Jane Duncan; issue: 1–Alice Ruth, *b* Poole, Neb., Oct. 24, 1889; A.B., U.Neb., '15; *m* Apr. 6, 1923, George Elwyn, son of George Walbridge DeWolf, of Gibbon, Neb., *m* Evelyn Gilman (issue: George Elwyn, II); 2–Effie Irene, *b* Poole, May 2, 1891; A.B., U.Neb., '13; *m* Sept. 26, 1917, Harry Edwin, son of John O. Cotton, of Kearney, *m* Caroline Burton (issue: Dorothy Anne; Marian Elizabeth); 3–Norma Katharine (Feb. 19, 1898-Feb. 6, 1900); 4–Gertrude Valentine, *b* Kearney, Neb., Jan. 7, 1901; U.Neb.; *m* Sept. 2, 1922, George Alfred Haslam, M.D., son of George James Haslam, M.D., of Fremont, Neb., *m* Mary Dern (issue: George James; John Alfred).
1–Mem. D.F.P.A., D.A.R., D.A.C., N.E.H.G.S. Author: "Valentine—1644-1908." Presbyterian. Republican. Residence: 421 W. 22d St., Kearney, Neb.

1–**MILLER, Lewis Bennett,** *b* Cooke Co., Tex., May 27, 1861.
3–John **Miller** (1795-1859), whose father *d* in Eng.; came from Eng. to Va., later to Ky. and Tenn.; *m* ante 1819, Dorcas Holloway (*b* ca. 1800), *d* in Alabama during Civil War;
2–Henry (2 below).
4–Robert **Osborn** (ca. 1765-ca. 1851), of Vermilion Co., Ill., ca. 1819; removed to Bates Co., Mo., 1838; *m* ca. 1790, Mary Price (*d* ca. 1851);
3–Joseph (1800-42), *m* ca. 1820, Lydia Copeland (1801-80; Charles[4], of Scotland);
2–Lurilla (*b* 1834), of Vermilion Co.; *m* 1855, Henry **Miller** (1830-1926), of Lawrence Co., Tenn., and Bates Co., Mo.; removed to Tex., 1849; lived in Erath and Cook cos.; farmer, merchant; issue: I–Columbus Cass (1857-58); II–Lewis Bennett (1 above); III–Charles Herbert (*b* 1866; *m* Ella Stockton);
1–Not married. A.B., Tex. Christian U., '81. Teacher Greek and Latin, Tex. Christian U., 1881-84; teacher pub. schs. of Tex., 1885-87; ry. office work, Keokuk, Ia., and St. Louis, 1888-91; with Crowell Pub. Co., Springfield, O., 1892-93. Author (see Who's Who in America). Christian Church. Summer Address: Hico, Tex., Route 5, Box 80. Residence: 815 Florence St., Ft. Worth, Tex.

1–**MILLER, Warren Hastings,** *b* Honesdale, Pa., Aug. 21, 1876.
7–Phillippus Jakob (Müller) **Miller,** Burgomaster of Codramstein, Bavarian Palatinate;
6–Philippus William (1710-61), began to write name Miller; settled at Phila., 1739; *m* 1745, Eva Christina–;
5–William (1761-91), of Phila.; capt., Pa. Line, Am. Rev.; *m* 1782, Susannah Hertzog;
4–Joseph (1783-1871), of Phila.; *m* Mary Smith (1811-54);
3–Daniel Sutter, D.D. (1813-88), rector St. Mark's P.E. Ch.; mem. Phila. Sanitary Commn.; *m* Jane Patterson Horner (1820-88; James T.[4], *m* Lettice, dau. of Gen. Brown, on Washington's staff, Am. Rev.);
2–Everard Patterson (2 below).
9–Thomas **Hastings** (qv);
8–John (1654-1718), of Watertown, Mass., *m* Abigail Hammond (1656-1717);
7–Joseph (1698-1785), *m* Lidia Brown;
6–Jonas (1729-71), *m* Mary Benjamin;
5–Jonas (1762-1844), of Frances Lethe (1764-1842);
4–Richard L. (1791-1854), of Boston; *m* Lois Warren; *m* 2d, Jerusha Lawrence Green;
3–Warren (1821-73), of New York; *m* Sophia Rodgers Purviance (1823-1905; William Young[4], of Baltimore);
2–Sophia Degen (*b* 1856), D.A.R.; *m* 1874, Everard Patterson **Miller** (*b* 1852), of Phila., Pa.; rector P.E. Ch.; issue: I–Warren H. (1 above); II–Margaret (*b* 1877; *m* Hobart Brown Upjohn); III–Dorothy Purviance (*b* 1884); IV–Everard P., Jr. (*b* 1886; *m* Lucy Baker); V–Marian (*b* 1889; *m* Rev. Francis Bliss).
1–*m* Nov. 15, 1899, Susan Barse, *b* Adrian, Mich., Aug. 21, 1875; dau. of J. Frederick Barse (1849-1916), *m* Adelaide Elizabeth King (1854-1920); issue: I–Barse, *b* New York, Jan. 24, 1904; grad. Pa. Acad. of Fine Arts (Cresson scholarship); *m* Feb. 23, 1924, Mary, dau. of William Smith, of Wilmington, Del. (issue: Barse; Mills; Helen); 2–Adelaide Warren, *b* Three Rivers, Mich., Mar. 23, 1905; *m* May 7, 1923, Douglas Neville, son of Robert Parker, of New Orleans, La. (issue: Douglas; Beatrice); 3–Purviance, *b* Bayonne, N.J., Dec. 11, 1910; 4–Beatrice Pixley (May 7, 1915-Oct. 17, 1926).
1–M.E., Stevens Inst. Tech., '98 (Theta Xi). Constrn. engr., Am. Sparklet Co., Fairbanks-Morse Co., C.C.C.&St.L.Ry., and Standard Oil Co., 1900-08; writer, in Paris, France, 1909-10; editor Field and Stream, New York, and v.p. Field & Stream Pub. Co., 1910-18. Author (see Who's Who in America). Able seaman, N.J. Naval Reserve, U.S.S. Portsmouth, 1896-98; ens. U.S.N., 1898-99; chief engr. U.S.S. Glacier, 1898-99; lt. (j.g.), Apr. 1918; lt., July, 1918-Apr. 1919; now in Fleet Reserve U.S.N. Mem. U.S.W.V., A.L. Republican. Episcopalian. Residence: Grapevine Rd., E. Gloucester, Mass.

SPENCER MILLER

1–**MILLER, Spencer,** *b* Waukegan, Ill., Apr. 25, 1859.
7–Joseph **Miller** (1617-97; 13th child, 9th son of "Maister" Thomas Miller, M.A., of Bishop's Stortford, Co. Herts, Eng., *d* 1627, *m* Agnes–; and grandson of John Myllar [died 1584], *m* Joan Thorowgood, also of Stortford); came in the "Hopewell," 1635, to N.E., settled at Cambridge; *m* Mary Pope (Walter[8], of Charlestown);
6–Samuel (1678-1759), *m* Elizabeth Child (Richard[7]; William[8]);
5–Dea. Samuel (1718-83), *m* Elizabeth Hammond

(Lt. Thomas[6]; Nathaniel[7]; Thomas[8], *b* in Eng., 1603);
4–Moses (1745-1834), *m* Sarah Gray (Robert[5]; John[6]);
3–Rev. Moses (1776-1855), *m* Bethiah (Avery) Ware (1780-1848);
2–Samuel Fisher (2 below).
9–John **Howe** (qv);
8–Josiah, *m* Mary Haynes (John[9]; Walter[10], *b* 1583);
7–Josiah (1678-1766), *m* Sarah Bigelow (Samuel[8]; John[9]; Randall[10]; Robert[11]);
6–Lt. Abraham (1709-90), *m* Martha Potter (Ephriam[7]; Robert[8]; Robert[9]; Nicholas[10]);
5–Ephraim (*b* 1733), *m* Sarah Gilbert (Nathaniel[6] Nathaniel[7]; Dea. Henry[8]; Thomas[9]);
4–William (*b* 1759), *m* Abigail Crosby;
3–William (1792-1865), *m* Almira Lyon (Benjamin[4]; Capt. Benjamin[5]; Caleb[6]; John[7]; John[8]; William[9], of Roxbury);
2–Charlotte (1826-63), *m* Samuel Fisher **Miller** (1822-70); issue: I–Annie (1852-1919); II–Mary (*b* and *d* 1855); III–Walter (*b* 1857; *m* Rowena Fobes); IV–Spencer (1 above); V–Samuel Fisher (*b* 1861; *m* Marion E. Sleeper); VI–Sidney Walker (1863-1910).
1–*m* Jan. 1, 1884, Hattie Maria Ruggles (*b* Moline, Ill., June 6, 1858-*d* Jan. 8, 1930); dau. of Willard G. Ruggles, of Worcester, Mass. (Benjamin[3]; Joseph[4]; Rev. Benjamin[5]; Capt. Samuel[6]; Capt. Samuel[7]; Thomas[8], of Roxbury); issue: 1–Marguerite Ruggles, *b* Worcester, Dec. 10, 1888; *m* Pierrepont Edwards Grannis (issue: Peter Edwards; Harriet Ann); 2–Spencer, Jr., *b* Worcester, July 2, 1891; B.A., Amherst, '12; M.A., Columbia; *m* Oct. 27, 1928, Margaret Montague, dau. of Alpheus Geer, of Nutley, N.J.; 3–Helen Emerson, *b* S. Orange, N.J., Jan. 25, 1897; *m* Jan. 1, 1921, Aurelio Giorni (issue: Helena Linda; Yolanda; Aurelia Maria).
1–B.S., in M.E., Worcester Poly. Inst., '79 (Dr. Engring., same). Engr. and inventor. Mem. Naval Consulting Board since 1915 (see Who's Who in America). Clubs: Cosmos, University (Washington), Engineers (New York), Orange Tennis. Residence: S. Orange, N.J.

1–**MILLIKAN, Robert Andrews,** *b* Morrison, Ill., Mar. 22, 1868.
5–William **Millikan** (ca. 1720-ca. 1800), from Ireland; settled at Washington, Mass., ca. 1760; *m* Mary McKnight (ca. 1725-ca. 1825);
4–Alexander (ca. 1760-ca. 1799), *m* Hannah Franklin (ca. 1775-1870);
3–Daniel Franklin (1796-1879), from Mass. to the Western Reserve, 1832, thence to Lyndon, Whiteside Co., Ill., 1838; *m* Aurelia Pease (ca. 1798-1873);
2–Rev. Silas F. (2 below).
8–John **Andrews** (*d* 1679), from Wales to Boston, 1656; settled at Taunton; *m* Hannah Jackson (*b* 1636);
7–Capt. John (1661-1742), *m* 1st, Alice Shaw (1666-1735);
6–Samuel (*d* 1756), *m* 2d, Mary Pitts;
5–Capt. John (1729/30-ca. 1767), *m* Elizabeth Talbot;
4–Capt. John (1765-1807), *m* Patience Hathaway (1772-1804);
3–Randall (1794-1877), Rochester, N.Y.; *m* 1818, Avis Mason (1798-1843);
2–Mary (1834-1917), *m* 1865, Rev. Silas Franklin **Millikan** (1834-1915), Congl. minister in Ill., Ia., and Kan.; issue: I–Allan Fairchild (*b* 1866; *m* Mary Plumb); II–Robert Andrews (1 above); III–Max Franklin (*b* 1870; *m* Arline James); IV–Grace (*b* 1872; *m* John Behr, *d*); V–Marjorie (*b* 1874; *m* George Johnson, M.D.); VI–Mabel (*b* 1878; *m* Rev. Robert E. Brown).
1–*m* Apr. 10, 1902, Greta Blanchard, *b* Rochester, Pa., July 16, 1876; dau. Clinton R. Blanchard, of Oak Park, Ill.; issue (all *b* Chicago, Ill.): 1–Clark Blanchard, *b* Aug. 23, 1903; Yale, '25; 2–Glenn Allan, *b* May 23, 1906; Harvard, '27; 3–Max Franklin, *b* Dec. 2, 1914.
1–A.B., Oberlin, '91; Ph.D., Columbia U., 1893; (Sc.D., Oberlin, 1911, Northwestern, 1913, U. Pa., 1915, Columbia, and Amherst, 1917, U. Dublin, 1924, Yale, 1925, King John Casimir U., 1926, Leeds U., 1927, U. of Ghent, 1927; LL.D., U.Calif., 1924, U.Colo., 1927). Prof. physics, U. of Chicago, 1896-1921; dir. Norman Bridge Lab. of Physics, and chmn. exec. council Calif. Inst. of Tech., since 1921. First exchange prof. to Belgium of C.R.B. Foundation, 1922; vice chmn. Nat. Research Council, Washington, since 1917; Am. mem. Com. on Intellectual Cooperation of League of Nations, 1923. Awarded Comstock prize for research in electricity, Nat. Acad. Sciences, 1913; Edison medalist Am. Inst. E.E., 1922; Hughes medalist Royal Soc. of Great Britain, 1923; Nobel prize in physics, 1923. Author (see Who's Who in America). Lt. col. Signal Corps, U.S.A., 1918, and chief of science and research div. of Signal Corps, during World War. Residence: 300 Palmetto Drive, Pasadena, Calif.

1–**MILLS, Thomas Caldicott,** *b* Toronto, Can., Jan. 2, 1863.
8–George **Mills** (*b* 1585-*d* aet. 89), signed petition to Gov. Stuyvesant for charter for Jamaica, L.I., 1656, also petition for ratification of said charter, later; *m* probably Rebecca–;
7–Samuel (1631-1726), *m* 1659;
6–Timothy (1667-1751), *m* Elizabeth–; *m* 2d, Sarah Longbottom;
5–Jacob (1710-79), Am. Rev.; *m* 1753, Mary Hawkins (*d* 1794, aet. 69; Capt. Eleazar[6]);
4–Isreal (1754-1818), *m* 1778, Martha Smith (*d* 1793);
3–David Smith (*d* 1851), *m* 1810, Lydia Tone (1790-1859; Hon. William[4], of South River, N.J.);
2–Montraville Walsingham (1833-1904), *m* 1854, Mary Josephine Goadby (1836-1914; James[3]).
1–*m* Oct. 17, 1893, Emilie Zella Ward (qv for issue).
Residence: Hollis, L.I., N.Y.

1–**MILLS, Emilie Zella Ward (Mrs. Thomas Caldicott),** *b* N.Y. City, Mar. 20, 1866.
9–William **Ward** (qv);
8–Sgt. John (1626-1708), ens. Newton co. during King Philip's War; dep. Mass. Gen. Court; *m* 1650, Hannah Jackson (1631-1704; Edward[9]);
7–Edward (1671-1749), of Newton, Mass.; *m* Grace Lovering (*d* 1754, aet. 67);
6–Samuel (1720-54), Natick, Mass.; *m* 1747, Miriam Morse (1725-93; Samuel[7]; Daniel[8]; Samuel[9]; Samuel[10]);
5–John (*b* 1748), Am. Rev.; *m* 1771, Martha Shed;
4–Samuel (1772-1830), *m* 1799, Joanna Bird;
3–James Otis (1803-55), established the Ward Line of packets, New York, Cuba, South America; *m* 3d, 1839, Hannah D. Fairbanks (1805-62);
2–George Edgar (2 below).
9–Daniel (Shed) **Shedd** (*b* ca. 1620), from Eng., 1640; settled at Braintree and Billerica, Mass.; *m* Mary Tarbell (?);
8–Zachariah (1656-1736), served in King Philip's War; *m* 1st, Mrs. Anne Bray;
7–James (1680-1749), of Billerica; *m* 1712, Mary Adams (*d* 1715; Roger[8], *m* Mary Baker);
6–James, *m* 1740, Mary Weld (Joseph[7], *m* Elizabeth Chamberlain);
5–Martha (1753-1806), *m* John **Ward** (5 above).
10–Thomas **Bird** (ca. 1613-1667), from Eng., ca. 1642; settled at Dorchester, Mass.; bailiff, 1654; selectman, 1657; *m* Anne– (*d* 1673);
9–Thomas (*b* 1640), *m* 1665, Thankful Atherton (1644-1714; Humphrey[10], qv);
8–Joseph (1666-1711), *m* Miriam–;
7–Aaron (1690-1745), *m* 1712, Mary Hooper (*d* 1745);
6–Aaron (1732-1807), Dorchester; *m* Ann– (*d* 1811);
5–Aaron (*b* 1756), *m* 1775, Johannah Glover (1758-1826; Enoch[6], *m* Susannah Bird);
4–Joanna (1781-1848), *m* Samuel **Ward** (4 above).
4–Samuel **Joyce** (*d* 1823), of N.Y. City; *m* Isabella– (*d* 1862, aet. 90);
3–Samuel (1811-61), *m* 1841, Ellen Zelinda Murphy (1808-92; Gabriel[4], of Ireland, *m* Mary Gammond);
2–Emily Josephine (1846-77), *m* 1865, George Edgar **Ward** (1843-92), ship chandler, N.Y. City; issue: I–Emilie Zella (1 above); II–Henry Murdoch (*b* 1868; *m* Josefa Schaller); III–Edward Mortimer (*b* 1872; *m* Mary [Post] Clapp).
1–*m* Oct. 17, 1893, Thomas Caldicott Mills (qv); issue: 1–Mary Josephine (Dec. 16, 1894-Oct. 5, 1920); 2–George Ward, *b* Denver, Colo., Aug. 4, 1896; enlisted as ambulance driver, June 1, 1917; 2d lt., Q.M.C., Sept. 22, 1918; *m* June 30, 1920, Elizabeth Gertrude, dau. John T. Ryan, of N.Y. City; 3–Henry Mortimer, *b* Denver, Aug. 3, 1898; sgt., inf., Harvard R.O.T.C., 1918.
1–Mem. C.D. XVII C., D.R., N.E. Women, Fair-

banks Family Assn. Residence: Hollis, L.I., N.Y.

1–**MILTON, Inez Lopez Seymour (Mrs. Samuel B.)**, *b* Brooklyn, N.Y., June 15, 1877.
5–Col. Sir Felix **Seymour** (1725-98; g.son of Earl of Hertford, Eng.); brought from North of Ireland to Va., by his father, 1735, who returned to Eng. and was prob. lost at sea; left with a Mr. Renick; settled nr. Moorefield (now W.Va.), Va.; built homestead at Seymourville, Grant Co., W.Va., 1st magistrate, Hardy Co., Va.; col., French and Indian War; officer Am. Rev.; *m* 1st, 1753, Margaret Renick (1734-78; William[6], of Va., *m* Ann Hamilton);
4–James (1766-1843), Seymourville, Grant Co., W.Va.; *m* Elizabeth Hutton (1774-1846; Col. Moses[5], officer Am. Rev.);
3–Col. John (1800-78), of nr. Reisterstown, Md.; served in Mexican War; *m* 1830, Lydia Ann Hutz (1813-98; Daniel[4], *m* Lydia Ann Perry, sister of Commodore Perry);
2–John Marshall (2 below).
7–John Jacob **Pouder** (desc. Catherine Pouder, weathy heiress of William Pouder, III, *m* her cousin, King of France, *m* 2d, Henry II, of Eng.; family held various titles and fought in the Thirty Years' War), Huguenot; fled thru Belgium to America, 1730; *m* Miss Leonard;
6–Jacob Leonard, *m* Margaret Boone, 1st cousin of Daniel Boone, the pioneer;
5–Jacob (*b* 1762), *m* Christina Diehl (1772-1837; Capt. John[6], of Berks Co., Pa., *m* Christina Bosseman; Frederick[7]);
4–Judge Jacob (1794-1870), judge Orphans' Ct., Carroll Co., Md.; mem. State Senate; *m* 1818, Elizabeth Boyer (Gabriel[5], *m* Elizabeth Arter; Lt. Casper[6]; Jacob[7]);
3–John Diehl (1823-95), *m* 1846, Elizabeth Hindes Hindman;
2–Mary Hindes (2 below).
7–Rev. James **Hindman** (*d* 1713), from Eng., 1710; settled in Talbot Co., Md.; *m* Mary Lockerman (Jacob[8]; Govert[9]);
6–Jacob (1711-76), *m* Mary Trippe (Henry[7], of Dorchester Co., Md.);
5–Dr. John (1754-1827), trustee 1st free sch. in America, on Eastern Shore of Md., 1787; treas. of Md.; *m* 1783, Mary Ann Latcha (Maj. Abram[6]);
4–Gabriel (1790-1854), *m* 1813, Maria Elizabeth Null;
3–Elizabeth Hindes (1832-83), *m* John Diehl **Pouder** (3 above).
10–Christopher **Gist** (1655-91), settled in Baltimore Co., Md., ante 1682; mem. Grand Jury; justice, 1689; *m* 1682, Edith Cromwell (1663-94), sister of Sir Oliver Cromwell;
9–Capt. Richard (1684-1748), surveyor, Western Shore of Md.; commr. for laying out Baltimore, 1729; justice; presiding magistrate; mem. Provincial Assembly; *m* 1704, Zipporah Murray (James[10], of Baltimore, *m* Jemima, dau. of Capt. Thomas Morgan); had 4 sons in French and Indian War;
8–Edith (*b* 1709), *m* Abram **Vaughn** (*b* 1707);
7–Maj. Gist (1724-post 1800), *m* 1744, his cousin, Rachel Gist (*b* 1725);
6–Maria Ann (*b* 1745), *m* 1765, Lord Richard **Richards** (*b* Eng., 1718);
5–Rachel (1770-1830), *m* 1789, Capt. George **Null** (*b* Eng., 1750-1802; Lord Conway[6]);
4–Maria Elizabeth (*b* 1795), *m* Gabriel **Hindman** (4 above);
3–Elizabeth H., *m* John D. **Pouder** (3 above);
2–Mary Hindes (1847-1922), *m* 1869, John Marshall **Seymour** (1839-91), broker and real estate, Glyndon, Md.; served in Co. F, 7th Va. Regt., C.S. Cav., in War between the States; issue: I–Daisy Belle (*m* George W. Percy; *m* 2d, Wilfrid Geist Fronheiser); II, III, and IV–(*d* infancy); V–Wivie (*d* aet. 2); VI–Frank (*d* aet. 3); VII–Inez Lopez (1 above); VIII–William Perry (*b* 1881; *m* Mrs. Anna Livingston; *m* 2d, Mrs. Rowell).
1–*m* 1897, Thomas Chalmers McConnell, *b* Angola, Ind., ca. 1860; son of Dr. George William McConnell, of Ind., *m* Eliza Bonar, of Pa.; issue: 1–Chalmers Seymour, *b* Phila., Pa., Aug. 9, 1899; holds S.A.R. medal for service, World War; sec. Washington Soc., S.A.R.; entered U.S. diplomatic service; asst. sec. Gen. Claims Commn., U.S. and Mexico.
1–*m* 2d, June 15, 1909, Col. Samuel Burleigh Milton, *b* Washington, D.C., June, 1860; son of George LaFayette Milton, of N.Y., *m* 1859, Ophelia S. Baggett, of Va.
1–Ed. Franklin Acad. Composer and soloist. Awarded bronze medal of France for service, World War; two Congressional medals for saving life from drowning (only woman in U.S.A. to be thus honored); six A.R.C. medals; certificate from Sec. of War for World War service. Mem. C.D.A. (Md.), Colonial Cavaliers, H.S. (S.C. and D.C.), D.A.R., Boone, Arter, and Boyer family assns., Southern Soc. of D.C., U.D.C. (historian), League of Am. Pen Women (won Mrs. Larz Anderson's prize for best musical composition in the League), Milton Life Saving and Swimming Club (founder). Summer place: "Seyton," on Chesapeake Bay, Calvert Co., Md. Residence: 3545 16th St. N.W., Washington, D.C.

1–**MINARD, John Putney**, *b* Spofford, N.H., Aug. 2, 1902.
11–Gov. William **Bradford**, Mayflower Pilgrim (qv);
10–Maj. William (1624-1701), treas. and dep. gov. of Mass.; *m* 1st, 1651, Alice Richards (*d* 1671; Thomas[11]);
9–Hannah, *m* 1683, Joshua **Ripley** (1658-1739; John[10], *m* Elizabeth, dau. of Rev. Peter Hobart);
8–Hannah, *m* 1711, Samuel **Webb** (*b* 1690; Samuel[9], *m* Mary, dau. of Capt. Samuel Adams);
7–Joshua (1722-1808), Rockingham, Vt., which he rep. in conv. leading to Vt. independence; *m* 1744, Hannah Abbe (1724-1815; John[8], *m* Mary Palmer; John[9]; John[10]);
6–Jehiel (1745-1813), of Rockingham; *m* 1770, Mary Eastman (1751-1811; Samuel[7], *m* Thankful Reed; Philip[8]; Philip[9]; Roger[10], qv);
5–Jehiel (bap. 1777-1836), *m* Sybil Olcott (Elias[6], *m* Sybil Dutton; Timothy[7]; Timothy[8]; Thomas[9]);
4–Caroline (1801-89), *m* John **Minard** (1798-1882);
3–Henry O. (1841-1915), *m* Elizabeth Wilcox (1843-1917);
2–Charles Edward (2 below).
11–Barnard **Capen** (qv);
10–Honor (*d* 1680), *m* William **Hannum** (*d* 1677), from Eng. in the "Mary and John," 1630; settled at Dorchester, Mass., ante 1639; at Windsor, Conn., 1639; at Northampton, Mass., ca. 1654;
9–John (1636-1712), original settler of Northampton; *m* 2d, 1675, Esther Langton (1649-1712; George[10], *m* 2d, Hannah, widow of Edmund Haynes);
8–William (1690-1756), Belchertown; *m* 1717, Mary Hutchinson (*d* 1785);
7–Moses (1718-1802), *m* 1748, Lydia (Warner) Cowdry (*d* 1796);
6–David (1763-1848), Pelham, Mass.; *m* 1788, Elizabeth Barker;
5–Henry (1794-1869), Weston, Vt.; in War 1812; *m* 1820, Submit, or Mitty, Abels (1796-1852);
4–Putney S. (1827-1906), Putney, Vt.; *m* 1st, 1852, Lucy E. Shattuck (*d* 1860; Ashley[5]; Parker[6]; Nathaniel[7]; Nathaniel[8]; Jeremiah[9]; Samuel[10]; John[11]; William[12]);
3–Oella E. (*b* 1853), *m* 1874, Duane S. **Taylor** (1851-1919; James M.[4]; James[5]; Reuben[6], officer Am. Rev.; Samuel[7]; Abraham[8]; Abraham[9]; William[10], qv);
2–Lucy Oella (*b* 1875), *m* 1901, Charles Edward **Minard** (*b* 1874), supt. Wild & Stevens, Boston; issue: I–John Putney (1 above); II–Oella (*b* 1907).
1–*m* Mar. 19, 1927, Ruth Genevieve Bernard, *b* Chicago, Ill., July 9, 1905; dau. of N.J. Bernard, *m* Edna Chiniquy.
1–B.S. in E.E., Norwich U., '22. Purchasing agt., Nachman Springfilled Corpn., Chicago. First lt., 318th Cav., 65th Div., U.S.A. Reserve. Mason (K.T.). Residence: 3131 S. Harlem Av., Berwyn, Ill.

1–**MINER, Roy Waldo**, *b* North Adams, Mass., Feb. 24, 1875.
9–Thomas **Miner** (qv);
8–Ephraim (1642-1724), of Taugwonk, N. Stonington, Conn.; rep. Gen. Ct.; selectman; in King Philip's War; *m* 1666, Hannah Avery (1644-1721; Capt. James[9], *m* Joanna Greenslade);
7–James (1682-1726), rep. Gen. Ct.; selectman; *m* 1705, Abigail Eldredge (1688-1720; Daniel[8], *m* Mary–);

6–Charles (1709-86), *m* 1740, Mary Wheeler (*b* 1720; Thomas[7], *m* Mary Miner);
5–Christopher (1745-1803), *m* 1765, Mary Randall (*b* 1746; Lt. John[6], *m* Mary Holmes):
4–Cyrus (1777-1845), Leyden, Mass.; *m* 1802, Fanny Clark (1781-1877; Thomas[6], *m* Fanny Brown);
3–Cyrus Clark (1804-87), *m* 1827, Freelove Packard;
2–Anson Dwight (2 below).
10–John **Alden** (qv);
9–Joseph (1624-97), Bridgewater, Mass.; *m* Mary Simmons (Moses[10], qv);
8–Isaac, *m* 1685, Mehitable Allen (*b* 1664; Samuel[9]);
7–Mehitable (*b* 1687), *m* 1711, Benjamin **Richards** (*b* 1686; Joseph[8], *m* Sarah–);
6–Mehitable (*b* 1712), *m* 1736, David **Packard** (*b* 1713; David[7], *m* Hannah Ames);
5–Abraham (1749-1835), Enfield, Mass.; *m* 1774, Freelove Dyer (1755-1841);
4–Cyrus (1775-1835), *m* Hannah Griswold (1777-1834);
3–Freelove (1807-94), Leyden, Mass.; *m* Cyrus Clark **Miner** (3 above).
5–William **Ingraham** (1746-1821), Am. Rev.; *m* Esther Carpenter (Elisha[6], Am. Rev.);
4–Ezra, *m* Ruth K. Bliss (Obadiah[5], Am. Rev.);
3–Mary Bliss, *m* Jeremiah **Wilbur**;
2–Ella (*b* 1844), *m* 1866, Anson Dwight **Miner** (1840-94), well known educator in western Mass.; issue: I–Guy Wilbur (*b* 1867; *m* Helen May Smiley); II–Edith May (1870-1923; *m* Rev. Edward Moore Parrott); III–Roy W. (1 above); IV–Howard Dwight (*b* 1879; *m* Katherine Dampman White; *m* 2d, Louise Belle Kollock); V–Agnes Eugenia (*b* 1880; *m* Harold Bugbee Payne); VI–Robert Bodley (*b* 1886; *m* Martha Fehlhaber).
1–*m* Sept. 15, 1903, Anna Elizabeth Carroll (Aug. 30, 1873-Oct. 20, 1924); issue (all *b* New York, N.Y.): 1–Dwight Carroll, *b* Nov. 4, 1904; B.A., Columbia U., '26, M.A., 1927; instr. in history at Columbia; and 2–Dorothy Eugenia (twins), *b* Nov. 4, 1904; B.A., Barnard Coll., '26; Carnegie Fellow, U.London, 1927; engaged in research in France and Italy; 3–Roy Waldo, Jr., *b* June 14, 1907; Columbia U., '32; and 4–son (twin; June 14-June 16, 1907).
1–*m* 2d, June 23, 1926, Eunice Thomasina Thomas, *b* Adamston, W.Va., Aug. 9, 1900; dau. of Frank Kent Thomas, of Fredericksburg, Va.
1–A.B., Williams, '97 (P.B.K., Delta Tau Delta); Ph.D., Columbia, 1923; (hon. Sc.D., Williams, 1927). Master of Latin and biology, Berkeley School, 1900-04; asso. headmaster, Kelvin School, New York, 1904-05; asst. curator invertebrate zoology, Am. Mus. Natural History, 1905-16, asso. curator, 1917-21, curator marine life since 1922. Author and marine explorer (see Who's Who in America). Episcopalian. Republican. Clubs: Williams Coll., Explorers. Residence: 120 W. 70th St., New York, N.Y.

1–**MINOR, George Henry,** *b* Deposit, N.Y., Sept. 27, 1866.
9–Thomas **Minor** (qv);
8–Capt. John (*b* Charlestown, Mass., 1635-1719), a 1st settler at Woodbury, Conn.; capt., French and Indian War; town clk. and leading man of town many yrs.; mem. Gen. Ct., 20 yrs.; dea.; *m* 1658, Elizabeth Booth (1641-1732; Richard[9], of Stratford, *m* Elizabeth Hawley);
7–Ephriam (1675-1762), rep. Gen. Ct., 1724,34,35; sgt. in militia; *m* 1701, Rebecca Curtiss (*d* 1763);
6–Jehu (1705-90), dea.; *m* 1731, Mary Judson (*d* 1762);
5–James (1733-94), *m* 1753, Mary Crissey (*d* 1779); *m* 2d, 1780, Aner Eastman (*d* 1831);
4–Philo (1781-1864), to Conventryville, N.Y., 1802; farmer; *m* 1803, Polly Stilson (*d* 1848);
3–George (1803-80), merchant and lumberman, Coventryville; *m* 1828, Sally M. Wattles (*d* 1838); *m* 2d, 1839, Ann Eliza Smith (*d* 1882);
2–James Smith (2 below).
4–Hubbard **Burrows,** of Conn., a pioneer in Delaware Co., N.Y.;
3–Henry, *m* Cynthia Smith;
2–Mary Elizabeth (1842-1905), *m* 1865, James Smith **Minor** (1840-1914), merchant and mfr., Deposit N.Y.; dea. and clk. of Presbyn. ch. many yrs.; issue: I–George Henry (1 above); II–William Burrows (1868-1900); III–Ella Maria (1869-70); IV–Henrietta Julia (*b* 1871); V–James Albert (*b* 1872; *m* 1922, Julia McCullough); VI–Harriet May (1874-1928); VII–Ralph Smith (*b* 1876; *m* 1904, Josephine Chittenden); VIII–Clark Haynes (*b* 1878; *m* 1909, Edith A. Schott, *d* 1929); IX–Edith Stowe (*b* 1880).
1–*m* Aug. 12, 1913, Sara Porter Strong, *b* Fort Atkinson, Wis., June 1, 1884; dau. of Ernest R. Strong, of Ft. Atkinson; issue: 1–George Henry, *b* New York, N.Y., Apr. 16, 1915; 2–Mary Porter, *b* Montclair, N.J., Apr. 25, 1918; 3–William Strong, *b* Montclair, July 20, 1920.
1–A.B., Hamilton Coll., '90 (D.K.E., Theta Nu Epsilon, P.B.K.), A.M., 1893; law dept., Lake Forest U., Chicago, Ill., 1895. Prof. mathematics, Park Coll., Mo., 1890-92; instr. mathematics, Northwestern U., 1892-95; admitted to Ill. bar, 1895, N.Y. bar, 1896; practiced at Buffalo, 1896-1903; with law dept., Erie R.R., N.Y. City, 1903; land and tax agt. at Cleveland, O., 1904-05; asst. gen. solicitor at N.Y. City, 1905-19; v.p., dir., sec., same rd. and its allied and subsidiary cos. (about 60) since 1919. Author (see Who's Who in America). Presbyterian. Republican. Clubs: Nat. Republican, New York Railroad, Machinery. Summer place: Deposit, N.Y. Residence: Upper Montclair, N.J.

1–**MITCHELL, Emma Downs Judson (Mrs. Frank H.),** *b* Southbury, Conn., June 16, 1862.
9–Thomas (Miner) **Minor** (qv);
8–Capt. John (1634-1719), capt. in Colonial and Indian wars; town clk. for many yrs.; a first settler of Woodbury, Conn.; *m* 1658, Elizabeth Booth (1641-1732; Richard[9], *m* Elizabeth Hawley);
7–Ephraim (1675-1762), *m* 1701, Rebecca Curtiss (*d* 1763);
6–Capt. Mathew (1708-78), *m* 1734, Sarah Preston; *m* 2d, Widow Mary Sanford; *m* 3d, Widow Mary Minor;
5–Capt. and Dea. Mathew (1753-1835), capt. N.Y., militia, 1776, Am. Rev.; *m* 1st, Phebe Root (1754-86);
4–Sarah (1778-1820), *m* 1798, Asa **Judson** (1774-1847);
3–Samuel (1811-47), *m* 1835, Almira Turrill (1815-54);
2–Jay Roy (2 below).
8–John **Downs,** from Eng., 1646; settled at New Haven, Conn.;
7–Ebenezer (1667-1711), of New Haven; *m* Mary Umphreville;
6–Ebenezer (1707-90), of Southbury, Conn.; capt. French and Indian War; mem. Com. of Safety, Am. Rev.; *m* 1727, Dinah Bristol (1705-93);
5–Ens. Moses (1735-1823), *m* Ann Hinman (1737-1810);
4–Nathan (1761-1819), *m* Susanna Tuttle (1763-1850);
3–Henry (1792-1856), *m* 1815, Sarah Ann Botsford (1797-1877);
2–Mary (1838-81), *m* 1861, Jay Roy **Judson** (1836-1905), farmer.
1–*m* Feb. 26, 1879, Frank Holbrook Mitchell (Feb. 5, 1856-Sept. 9, 1921); son of Charles L. Mitchell, of Newtown, Conn.; issue (all *b* Newtown, Conn.): 1–Laura Merwin, *b* Aug. 2, 1880; *m* Oct. 27, 1904, George Edward Camp (1876-1924), son of Oliver G. Camp, *m* Laura Warner, of Waterbury, Conn. (issue: Merwin Gaylord; Nelson Mitchell; Margaret Holbrook); 2–Wallace Nathan (see Vol. III, p. 335, for Mitchell lineages); 3–Clara Olive, *b* Aug. 10, 1899.
1–Mem. S.D.P., D.F.P.A., D.A.C., D.A.R., I.A.G., Washington Sulgrave Instn., etc. Residence: Newtown, Conn.

1–**MINOR, Lynn Overton,** *b* Plattsmouth, Neb., May 4, 1890.
9–Doodes (Maindort) **Minor** (qv);
8–Doodes (1640-1694 or 95), began to write name Minor; *m* Elizabeth Cocke (Maurice[9]);
7–Garret (1679-1720), justice, Middlesex Co., Va.; *m* 1706, Diane Vivian (*d* 1718; John[8]);
6–John (1707-55), planter, Spotsylvania Co., Va.; justice; received Crown patent for "Gale Hill," 1735; *m* 1732, Sarah Carr (1719-74; Thomas[7], *m* Mary Dabney);
5–Garret (1744-99), Louisa Co., Va.; *m* 1767, Mary Overton Terrell (1750-1830; Richmond[6], *m* Nancy, dau. of William Overton, from Eng. to Va.);
4–Samuel Overton (1793-1838), *m* Lydia Laurie Lewis;

3-Samuel Overton (1820-80), *m* 1841, Elizabeth White Carter (1825-1906 or 07; John[4]);
2-Peter Carr (2 below).
10-Robert **Lewis** (qv);
9-John (*b* 1635), burgess; justice; *m* 1666, Isabella Warner;
8-Col. John (1669-1725), mem. Royal Council; *m* 1692, Elizabeth Warner (1672-1719; Col. Augustine II[9], *m* Mildred, dau. of Col. George Reade, qv);
7-Col. Robert (1704-66), of "Belvoir," Albemarle Co., Va.; burgess, 1744; *m* ante 1725, Jane Meriwether;
6-Nicholas (1734-1808), capt. minute men; col. Va. militia, Am. Rev.; *m* 1760, Mary Walker;
5-Thomas Walker (1763-1807), *m* Elizabeth Meriwether;
4-Lydia Laurie (1795-1833), *m* Samuel Overton **Minor** (4 above).
10-John **Walker,** burgess, 1645,46,56;
9-Lt. Col. Thomas, burgess, 1663-66;
8-Thomas, burgess, 1732;
7-Dr. Thomas (1715-94), of "Castle Hill," Va.; 1st explorer in Tenn., 1748; maj. Va. troops, with Braddock at his defeat and death; burgess; *m* 1741, Mildred (Thornton) Meriwether (Col. Francis Thornton[8], *m* Mary Talliaferro; Francis[9]; William[10], qv);
6-Mary (*b* 1742), *m* Nicholas **Lewis** (6 above).
9-Nicholas **Meriwether** (qv);
8-David (*d* 1744), *m* Anne Holmes (*d* 1735 or 36; George[9]);
7-Thomas (1714-56), *m* Elizabeth Thornton (*d* 1756);
6-Nicholas (1736-72), *m* 1759 or 60, Margaret Douglas (*b* 1737; Rev. William[7]);
5-Elizabeth (1771-1851), *m* Thomas Walker **Lewis** (5 above).
2-Peter Carr **Minor** (1860-1901), of Louisiana, Mo., and Plattsmouth, Neb.; *m* 1889, Katherine Vallery (*b* 1866); issue: I-Lynn Overton (1 above); II-Madeline (*b* 1892; *m* Percival H. Field).
1-*m* Oct. 17, 1914, Ellen Campbell Pollock (qv); issue (all *b* Plattsmouth, Neb.): 1-Herbert Pollock, *b* Mar. 26, 1917; 2-Eleanor Patricia, *b* Dec. 21, 1919; 3-Charles Carter, *b* Apr. 20, 1923.
1-Mason. Rotarian. Residence: 714 Main St., Plattsmouth, Neb.

1-**MINOR, Ellen Campbell Pollock (Mrs. Lynn O.),** *b* Plattsmouth, Neb., Oct. 17, 1891.
5-James **Pollock** (ca. 1728-1812; son of Dr. Thomas Pollock, of Ireland, *m* Mary Cochran), from Ireland, settled at Westmoreland Co., Pa.; *m* ca. 1770, Mary Heron (*d* 1820);
4-Judge Thomas (1772-1847), *m* 2d, Susan Henderson (Rev. Joseph Washington[5]);
3-Thomas (1826-1913), *m* 1859, Mary Renick Kerr;
2-Thomas Herbert (2 below).
7-Robert **Lyle** (1698-1765; son of John, from Scotland to North of Ireland, 1681), from Ireland to N.Y., 1742; removed to N.J.; *m* 1747, Mary Gilleland;
6-Eleanor (*b* 1758), *m* William **Kerr** (*d* Cross Creek, Washington Co., Pa., 1807, aet. 69);
5-James (1782-1847), of Northampton Co., Pa.; *m* 1803, Hannah Mason (1784-1842; William[6]);
4-James Mason (1809-46), *m* 1831, Rebecca Dinsmore;
3-Mary Renick (1833-1914), *m* Thomas **Pollock** (3 above).
9-Thomas **Renick,** from Ireland, 1733; in Pa., 1738;
8-William (*b* Ireland, 1704-*d* Paxtang, Pa., ante 1763);
7-Alexander (*b* 1736), pvt., Pa. Troops, Am. Rev., *d* of camp fever before reaching home; *m* Esther Makemie (John[8], *d* 1766);
6-Mary (1765-1859), *m* Robert **Hamilton**;
5-Esther (1784-1859), *m* James **Dinsmore** (1782-1831; James[6], Am. Rev., *m* 2d, Rebecca, dau. of Squire Walker; Adam[7]; John[8]);
4-Rebecca (1808-95), *m* James M. **Kerr** (4 above).
7-James **Patterson** (1708-92), from Ireland, settled in Lancaster Co., Pa., 1728; *m* Mary Montgomery;
6-William (1733-1818), Am. Rev.; *m* 1758, Rosanna Scott;
5-Thomas (1764-1841), *m* 1795, Elizabeth Findley (William[6], Am. Rev., *m* Ewing Caruthers, *d* 1825);
4-James (1798-1861), Washington Co., Pa.; *m* 1820, Eliza Walker (1802-86; Alexander[5]; David[6]);
3-James Madison (1836-1903), *m* 1857, Ellen Hodgens Campbell;
2-Lida Walker (2 below).
8-Alexander **Rea,** from Ireland to N.J., 1734;
7-Samuel (*b* N.J., 1734-*d* Northampton Co., Pa., 1813), col. Am. Rev., *m* 1761, Ann McCracken (1736-81);
6-William (1762-1835), *m* 1788, Jane Mason;
5-Anna (1788-1858), *m* 1808, David **Campbell** (1784-1858; John[6] *m* [Mary ?] Hammond);
4-Samuel (1811-90), *m* 1835, Jane McGugin (1813-1900; David[5]; Daniel[6]);
3-Ellen Hodgens (1838-97), *m* James Madison **Patterson** (3 above);
2-Lida Walker (*b* 1870), *m* 1890, Thomas Herbert **Pollock** (*b* 1867), of Plattsmouth, Neb.; pres. Farmers State Bank; issue: I-Ellen C. (1 above); II-Alice Mary (*b* 1902; *m* Virgil Walker Perry); III-Edith Lillian (*b* and *d* 1909).
1-*m* Oct. 17, 1914, Lynn Overton Minor (qv for issue).
1-Attended Northwestern U., 1910-11 (Gamma Phi Beta). Mem. D.A.R. (past regent), P.E.O. past pres.). Residence: 714 Main St., Plattsmouth, Neb.

1-**MITCHELL, Nellie Harrington (Mrs. Clement C.),** *b* North Branch, Mich., Dec. 13, 1880.
11-William **Arnold** (qv);
10-Gov. Benedict (1615-78), Providence, R.I.; *m* 1640, Damarius Wescott;
9-Dr. Caleb (1644-1719), Portsmouth, R.I.; *m* 1666, Abigail (Wilbour) Porter (Capt. Samuel Wilbour[10]);
8-Samuel (*b* 1677), *m* 1706, Mary George (Samuel[9]);
7-Joseph (1710-76), Exeter, R.I.; *m* 2d, 1737, Hannah Gifford (Yelverton[8], *m* Anna Northrup);
6-Capt. Stephen (*b* 1739), *m* 1760, Martha (Gardner) Hovens (*d* 1819; Nicholas Gardner[7]);
5-Honor (1760-1848), Stephentown, N.Y.; *m* 1783, Samuel **Carpenter** (1760-1810; Joseph[6], *m* Sarah Greenman);
4-Nicholas (*b* 1786), *m* 1809, Rachel Mead (1793-1872);
3-Rachel Miranda (1820-80), North Branch, Mich.; *m* 1847, John **Harger** (1803-87);
2-Ella Miranda (1853-1920), *m* 1875, Walter Wallace **Harrington** (1853-1927), merchant; issue: I-Bertha (*b* 1877; *m* 1905, James Hersey Vandecar); II-Nellie (1 above); III-(Lulu) Grace (*b* 1885; *m* 1907, Harry Haines Ford); IV-Edith (*b* 1886; *m* Russell V. Hunter); V-Paul Walter (*b* 1892).
1-*m* Sept. 7, 1904, Clement Clinton Mitchell, *b* Hillsdale, Ont., Nov. 11, 1877; son of Thomas Mitchell; issue: 1-Harrington Caulkins, *b* Wilmette, Ill., Mar. 30, 1906; 2-Clement Clinton, Jr., *b* Wilmette, July 1, 1907.
1-Mem. D.A.R., Wilmette Country Club, Westmoreland Golf, Commonwealth (Boston). Residences: Alden Park Manor, Boston, Mass., and 814 Linden Av., Wilmette, Ill.

1-**MITCHELL, Emily Dean Judson (Mrs. Roy E.),** *b* Vernon, N.Y., May 17, 1882.
10-William **Judson** (qv);
9-Lt. Joseph (1619-90), *m* 1644, Sarah Porter (*d* 1696);
8-Capt. James (1650-1720/21), *m* 1680, Rebecca Wells (1655-1717);
7-David (1693-1761), *m* 1713, Phebe Stiles (1696?-1765);
6-Daniel (1728-1813), *m* 1751, Sarah Curtiss (1731-1808);
5-Silas (1754-1808), Kirkland, N.Y.; will dated Mar. 21, 1808, probated Mar. 22, 1809, Oneida Co., N.Y.; *m* 1777, Mary Whiting (Capt. Samuel[6]);
4-Ephriam (1777-1817), *m* 1799, Polly Curtis (1781-1857);
3-Ard (1815-86), *m* 1843, Emily Sheldon Norton (1816-80);
2-John Dean (2 below).
10-Gov. William **Pynchon** (qv);
9-Mary (*d* 1657), *m* 1640, Capt. Elizur **Holyoke** (*d* 1676);
8-Hannah (1644-79), *m* 1661, Capt. Samuel **Talcott** (1634-91), dep. and asst.; capt. Hartford Co. troop, 1681 (John[9], qv);
7-Sgt. Nathaniel (1678-1758), *m* 1703, Elizabeth Robbins (*d* 1768; Joshua[8]; Gentleman John[9]);

6–Joseph (1722-88), *m* 1748, Sarah (Kilburn) Kilbourn (1725-1814);
5–Jonathan (1754-1847), minute man in Am. Rev.; *m* 1785, Sarah Hubbard (*d* 1830);
4–Siah (1788-1822), transported govt. stores, War 1812; *m* 1812, Charlotte House (1792-1886);
3–Jonathan (1814-96), *m* 1st, 1836, Lucy Ann Shepard (1813-45);
2–Lucy Ann (1844-1925), *m* 1879, John Dean **Judson** (1853-1882); issue: I–Jonathan Talcott (*b* and *d* 1880); II–Emily Dean (1 above).
1–*m* Sept. 1, 1908, Roy Ernest Mitchell, M.D., *b* Porter's Mills, Wis., Mar. 17, 1876; son of Squire Freeman Mitchell, *m* Laura Ann Shaw McIntosh; issue: 1–Marjorie Dean, *b* Middletown, N.Y., July 11, 1909; U.Minn., '31; 2–Mancel Talcott, *b* Eau Claire, Wis., Jan. 28, 1912; U.Minn., '32; 3–Doris, *b* Eau Claire, Oct. 4, 1916.
1–Grad. Pratt Inst., '04. Mem. D.A.R. (chapter regent). Residence: 504 4th Av., Eau Claire, Wis.

JOHN WESLEY CAMPBELL (1841-76).

1–**MOHLER, Lavinia Ellen Campbell (Mrs. Thomas H.),** *b* St. Albans, W.Va., Feb. 29, 1864.
4–William **Whitton,** *m* Milly Witt (William[5]);
3–Angeline, *m* Henry Thruxton **Campbell** (1816-71), served in 11th W.Va. Regt., Civil War;
2–John Wesley (2 below).
9–Leonard **Calvert** (qv);
8–William (1642-82), St. Mary's, Md.; mem. Council of Md.; justice; *m* 1662, Elizabeth Stone (Gov. William[9], of Md., *m* Verlinda Cotton);
7–George (1666-post 1734), Charles Co., Md.; *m* 1688, Elizabeth Doyne;
6–John, Prince William Co., Va.; *m* 1710, Elizabeth Harrison (Thomas[7]; Burr[8]; Cuthburt[9]);
5–Jacob (1720-72), *m* 1750, Sarah Crupper (Richard[6]);
4–Francis (1751-1823), Bedford Co., Va.; pvt. Am. Rev.; *m* 1791, Elizabeth Witt (Lewis[6], *m* Anne Mills; William, or Guillaume[6], Huguenot, see 4 above);
3–John Lewis (1803-63), Kanawha Co., Va.; *m* 1825, Elizabeth Ann Slack;
2–Adaline (2 below).
7–Henry **Huddleston** (1665-1706), from Eng., 1688, settled in Bucks Co., Pa.; *m* 1701, Elizabeth Cooper (*b* 1673; William[8], qv);
6–Henry (1706-70), *m* 1727, Mary Wilkinson (William[7]);
5–Abraham (1741-85), Bedford Co., Va.; *m* 1761, Mary Patterson (1743-1825; Joseph[6]);
4–Nancy (1780-1862), Kanawha Co., Va.; *m* 1798, John **Slack** (1778-1826; Abraham[5], of Bucks Co., Am. Rev.);
3–Elizabeth Ann (1807-82), Kanawha Co.; *m* John Lewis **Calvert** (3 above);
2–Adaline (*b* 1843), *m* 1862, John Wesley **Campbell** (1841-76), served in 11th W.Va. Regt., Civil War; issue: I–Lavinia Ellen (1 above); II–James Albert (1866-84); III–John Mills (*b* 1868; *m* 1892, Sadie Brown, 1868-1908); IV–Frank Allen (1870-87); V–Emma Florence (*b* 1871; *m* 1891, George Crittendon Moore); VI–Myron Grant (*b* 1874; *m* 1898, Virginia Tasker); VII–Lucy May (*b* 1876; *m* 1906, Chastine Bickers).
1–*m* July 16, 1884, Thomas Howard Mohler, *b* Long Meadow, Augusta Co., Va., May 2, 1863; son of Daniel Freeman Mohler (1829-96), of Augusta Co., Va., *m* 1851, Ellen Elizabeth Sillings (1827-92); issue: 1–Edith May, *b* Williamsburg, Ky., Sept. 11, 1886; Marshall Coll.; *m* Feb. 15, 1911, Robert Cornell Sweet (issue: Robert Mohler, *b* Feb. 5, 1916).
1–Mem. C.D.A., Founders of Manakin Town, Va., Huguenot Soc., Soc. of Ark and Dove, D.A.R. Congregationalist. Clubs: Thursday Literary, Delphian. Residence: St. Albans, W.Va.

1–**MITCHELL, William Samuel,** *b* Bloomfield, Ia., Sept. 27, 1877.
5–Houston **Mitchell** (*b* 1756), from Ireland, 1781, settled in Washington Co., Pa.; *m* 1781, Isabel Worton, or Whorton (1758-98);
4–John Houston (1798-1884), Hillsboro, O.; capt. and later maj. in Ohio Militia; *m* 1821, Ellen Fenner (1804-95);
3–James William (1823-91), *m* 1847, Mary Ann Boyd Glenn (1826-1913);
2–William Samuel (2 below).
5–Dr. Robert **King** (1744-1802), Blandford, Mass.; *m* 1768, Bridget Knox;
4–Capt. Dr. Robert (1777-1851), Portage Co., O.; *m* Bridget Morgan; *m* 2d, Tasa Hall;
3–Joel Elisha (1813-90), Fairfield, Ia.; surgeon, 20th Ill. Vol. Inf.; in charge mil. smallpox hosp., Louisville, Ky., 1862; *m* 1835, Emmiline Barnes;
2–Emma (*b* 1856), *m* 1875, William Samuel **Mitchell** (1849-1912), Bloomfield, Ia.; issue: I–William Samuel (1 above); II–Glenn Adney (1881-1912).
1–*m* Sept. 27, 1905, Axie Lute, *b* Wayland, Ia., Dec. 15, 1882; dau. of John Henry Lute, of Mt. Pleasant, Ia.; issue: 1–Alan Lute, *b* Oil City, Pa., Jan. 12, 1912; 2–William Samuel, Jr., *b* Buffalo, N.Y., May 25, 1915.
1–A.B., Ia. Wesleyan U., '00 (Beta Theta Pi), A.M., 1903; S.T.B., Boston U. Sch. of Theology, 1904; (D.D., Grove City Coll., 1915, Allegheny Coll., 1915). Ordained M.E. ministry, 1906; asst. pastor Epworth Memorial Ch., Cleveland, O., 1905-08; pastor Stone Ch., Meadville, Pa., 1908-11, Grace Ch., Oil City, Pa., 1911-15, Plymouth Ch., Buffalo, N.Y., 1915-19; prof. evangelism and head of dept., Boston U. Sch. of Theology, 1919-20; pastor Calvary Ch., Phila., 1920-23, Wesley M.E. Ch., Worcester, Mass., since 1923. Author (see Who's Who in America). Republican. Mason (32°). Clubs: Union League, City (Phila.), Economic, Union (Worcester), Itinerants (Boston). Residence: 690 Pleasant St., Worcester, Mass.

1–**MOLL, Justus Reiniger,** *b* Mason City, Ia., Apr. 16, 1893.
4–Alexander Joseph **Moll** (1797-1841), builder of macadamized roads in Germany; to N.Y.; *m* Marie Bernardina Beckhaus (1798-1877), of Sparkhill, N.Y.;
3–Justus Bernard (1838-1917), C.M.&S.P. ry. official, Chicago; *m* 1865, Melvina Amanda Gurley;
2–Alexander Henry (2 below).
8–William **Gurley,** of Scotch descent; to Southampton Co., Va., ca. 1700;
7–John (*d* 1771);
6–John (*d* 1794), planter, Johnston Co., N.C.; *m* Elizabeth–;
5–Capt. Lewis, capt. Co. Light Horse, N.C., 1781; *m* Gracie Wiggs;
4–Daniel E. (1815-73), planter, Goldsboro, N.C.; *m* 1838, Edith Phillips (Dickson[5], planter, Johnston Co., N.C., *m* 1814, Edith Oliver);
3–Melvina Amanda (1847-86), *m* Justus B. **Moll** (3 above).
10–Jeremiah **Meacham** (1613-95), from Eng., settled at Salem, Mass.; *m* in Eng., Margaret–;
9–Jeremiah (1644-1743), *m* 1673, Mary Trask (*b* 1652; Henry[10], *m* Mary Southwick);
8–John, *m* 1697, Mary Cash (*b* 1675; William[9], *m* Elizabeth Lambert);
7–Jeremiah (*d* 1766), *m* 1732, Rebecca Hawkins

(1712-86; James[8], of Marblehead, Mass., *m* Elizabeth–);
6–John (1750-1808), New Salem, Mass.; minute man Am. Rev., at Battle of Bunker Hill with his bro. Capt. William Meacham, who fell in the retreat across Charleston Neck; *m* 1772, Sarah Hall (*b* 1748; Samuel[7], 1709-92);
5–Jacob (1782-1839) Fair Haven, Vt., Lake George, N.Y., and Montezuma, Ill.; served in War 1812 at Sackett's Harbor, N.Y.; *m* 1802, Lucy Simonds (1783-1844; Joel[6], Am. Rev., Vt., *m* Patience [1746-1832], dau. of Samuel Hall);
4–Rev. Ahira Griswold (1803-76), of Benson, Vt., and Mont Meacham, Ill.; editor, Battle Creek, Mich.; physician, atty. at law, Meth. minister; *m* 1825, Polly Knight Gault (1808-89; William[5], *m* Mahala Knight; James[6], *m* Lydia–);
3–Eliza Ainsworth (1827-1917), Lowville, N.Y.; *m* 1857, Gustavus George **Reiniger** (1827-69), lawyer, Charles City, Ia., and Union, Mo. (Gustav[4], *m* Rosalia Durr; George Michael[5], *m* Charlotte Wider, of Vaihengen, Germany);
2–Viola Belle (*b* 1866), of Union, Mo., living 1930, Washington, D.C.; *m* 1892, Alexander Henry **Moll** (1866-1921), ry. official, Mason City, Ia., Pueblo, Colo., Seattle, Wash., and Springfield, Mo.
1–*m* Jan. 10, 1917, Cleadie Edith Atkinson, *b* Phillipsburgh, Mo., May 6, 1894; dau. of William Hoeting Atkinson, farmer of Phillipsburg (George[3]); issue: 1–William Alexander, *b* Springfield, Mo., Jan. 13, 1918.
1–U.Wash. (Beta Tau Phi). Atty.-at-law. U.S. Bd. of Arbitration, 1928. Pres. Assn. Community Clubs of Springfield, Mo. Mem. S.R., U.D.C., I.A.G., Mo. Hist. Soc., Mo. Bar Assn., etc. Baptist. Mason, K.P. Democrat. Address: 305 E. Olive St., Springfield, Mo.

1–**MONTGOMERY, George Redington,** *b* Marash, Turkey, June 17, 1870.
7–Hugh **Montgomery** (1690-1767), from Ireland, settled at Casco Bay, Portsmouth, N.H., 1718; soldier in French and Indian War; *m* Jane McGregor (Rev. James[8]);
6–Hugh (*b* 1726), of Londonderry, N.H.;
5–Hugh (1750-1839), of Acworth, N.H.; pvt. in Am. Rev.; *m* Mary Campbell;
4–William, of Walden, Vt.; *m* Mary Dodge;
3–Sereno (1809-88), mem. Vt. Legislature; *m* 1st, Hannah Foster (1811-39);
2–Giles Foster (1835-88), of Walden; *m* 1863, Emily Redington (*d* 1899), issue: I–William Owen (1864-84); II–Marshall Foster (*b* 1868; *m* Margaret Louise Abell); III–George R. (1 above); IV–Charles (*d* infancy); V–Mary Williams (*b* 1874; *m* Gutzon Borglum).
1–*m* June 23, 1902, Emily Emerson (Nov. 3, 1875-May 1, 1903); dau. of Rev. Frederick Emerson; issue: 1–Roger, *b* Bridgeport, Conn., Apr. 25, 1903; Ph.B., Yale, '25; *m* Dec. 31, 1929, Jean Baur.
1–*m* 2d, Aug. 7, 1907, Helen Perkins, *b* New Haven, Conn., Mar. 19, 1880; issue: 1–Marshall Hugh, *b* New York, N.Y., May 16, 1909; Middlebury, '31; 2–Giles Newton, *b* New York, Dec. 15, 1911; Middlebury, '33.
1–A.B., Yale, '92 (Phi Gamma Delta), LL.B., 1894, B.D., 1900, Ph.D., 1901; U. of Berlin, 1897-98. Ordained Congl. ministry, 1901; pastor Olivet Ch., Bridgeport, Conn., 1901-04; prof. philosophy, Carleton Coll., 1904-05; asst. minister Madison Sq. Presbyn. Ch., New York, 1906-16; spl. asst. to Am. ambassador at Constantinople, 1916; in air service, Paris, 1917; sec. of Paris div., Y.M.C.A., 1918; attached to Peace Conf., Dec. 1918; tech. advisor to Commn. on Mandates in Turkey, 1919; asst. prof. French, Yale U., 1919-20; dir. The Armenia American Soc., 1920-23; asst. sec. Federal Council of Chs., since 1922; author (see Who's Who in America). Republican. Clubs: Wee Burn, Noroton Yacht, Yale Graduate. Residence: Boston Post Road, Noroton, Conn.

1–**MOORE, Donald Kimball,** *b* Chicago, Ill., July 16, 1882.
4–Daniel **Moore** (1783-1867), *m* 1st, ca. 1814, Jane–(1797-1834);
3–John (1821-82), *m* 1846, Rebecca Johnson (1823-1917; Uriah[4] [1779-1847], *m* 1802, Zeruiah Van Gelder, 1783-1880);
2–William John (2 below).
11–Edward (Browne) **Brown,** of Inkburrow, Eng.; *m* Jane, dau. of Thomas Lide;
10–Nicholas (*b* Eng.-*d* 1673), Reading, Mass., 1644; *m* Elizabeth–;
9–Cornelius (*d* post 1675), began to write name Brown; *m* 1665, Sarah Lamson (*d* 1683);
8–Samuel (1675-post 1720), *m* Mary–;
7–Jeremiah (*b* 1708), *m* 1737, Anna Burnap (1713-51; Thomas[8], *m* Sarah Walton; "Master" Thomas[9]);
6–Samuel (1740-post 1780), pvt. Am. Rev.; *m* 1762, Bridget Bryant;
5–Catherine (1767-1868), *m* 1793, Demas **Kimball** (1770-1865);
4–John (ca. 1796-1864), *m* Eliza Pease (1810-89; Oliver[5], *m* Ruth Hubbard; Henry C.[6]; Dea. Ezekiel[7]; Isaac[8]; Capt. John[9]; Robert[10], qv);
3–Dr. Henry Chandler (1836-1915), *m* 1857, Finwell (called Fanny) Bortle;
2–Henrietta (2 below).
10–Dea. Thomas **Kendall** (1615-81), *m* ca. 1641, Rebecca– (1618-1703);
9–Mary (1647-88), *m* 1664, as his 1st wife, Abraham **Bryant** (*b* 1647);
8–Kendall (*b* 1680), *m* 1704, Elizabeth Swayne (1684-1754; Maj. and Dr. Jeremiah Swain[9], *m* Mary, dau. of Francis Smith; Jeremiah[10]);
7–Jeremiah (1714-1804), *m* 1734, Ruth Thompson;
6–Bridget (1746-post 1800), *m* Samuel **Brown** (6 above).
10–Abraham **Van Deursen** (*b* 1607; son of Pieter, *m* Maria Jans–), early settler in New York; *m* 1629, Tryntje Melchiors (*d* post 1678);
9–Teunisse (*b* ca. 1631), *m* 1653, Helena Robberts;
8–Robbert (*b* 1665), *m* 1689, Cornelia Van Buren (ca. 1665-post 1718; Marten[9], *m* 1st, Maritje, dau. of Pieter Quackenbosch, from Holland; Cornelis Maesen[10], *m* Catelijntje Martens);
7–Robbert (1700-77), *m* 1724, Christiana Roorpagh;
6–Marten (1737-1815), pvt. Am. Rev.; *m* 1764, Elizabeth Oostrander;
5–Marytje (1767-1858), *m* 1783, Capt. Peter **Bortle** (1763-post 1809; Peter[6] [*b* ca. 1740], *m* 1762, Eleanor Vredenburg);
4–Nelson (1807-76), *m* 1829, Paulina Baker Caldwell (1810-91; Dr. Increase M.[5], *m* Betsy Baker; William[6]; Lt. Col. Joseph[7]; Joseph[8]);
3–Finwell (Fanny) (1836-1913), *m* Dr. Henry C. **Kimball** (3 above);
2–Henrietta (*b* 1858), *m* William John **Moore** (*b* 1858).
1–*m* May 9, 1916, Vivian Elsie Lyon (qv for issue).
1–Residence: 458 Briar Pl., Chicago, Ill.

1–**MOORE, Vivian Elsie Lyon (Mrs. Donald K.),** *b* Quincy, Mich., Nov. 23, 1887.
11–Edward **Bosworth** (qv);
10–Jonathan (1613-1687/88), *m* Elizabeth– (1614-1705);
9–Joseph (*d* 1693/94), *m* 1680, Esther Smith (*b* 1661; "Mr." Daniel[10], *m* Esther Chickering; Henry[11]);
8–Judith (1689/90-1733), *m* 1712, Lt. Noah **Butterworth** (1689-1736; Capt. John[9], *m* Hannah, dau. of Robert Wheaton; Dea. John[10]);
7–Hannah (1716-49), *m* 1734, as his 1st wife, Jonah **Titus** (1710-83), see Vol. III, p. 337;
6–Joel (1740-ca. 1820), pvt. French and Indian War and Am. Rev.; *m* 1762, Mary Treat (1744-ca. 1802), see Vol. III, p. 337;
5–Sarah (1771-1852), *m* 1793, William **Lyon** (1771-1823);
4–Rev. Daniel (1795-1842), pvt. War 1812; pastor of "Old Stone Ch.," Walworth, N.Y., 18 yrs.; *m* 1815, Polly Strickland;
3–Newton Thomas (1822-79), *m* 1843, Caroline Matilda Smith (1826-95; Anson[4]; Jerold, or Jared[5]);
2–Frank Almon (2 below).
6–Jacob **Fink** (ante 1765-post 1790), from Germany; pvt. Am. Rev.;
5–Johnston (1785-ca. 1850), pvt. War 1812; *m* Susan Myers (*b* 1786; George[6]);
4–Henry (1813-99), pvt. Civil War; *m* ca. 1836, Elizabeth Goldsborough;
3–James Madison (1837-1918), pvt. Civil War; *m* 1859, Isabella Sommers;
2–Mary Emma (2 below).
6–Robert **Goldsborough,** *m* Elizabeth–;
5–Robert (1795-1840), War 1812; *m* Catherine Cor-

bin (1791-1875; John[6], pvt. Am. Rev., *m* Sarah Morris);
4-Elizabeth (1818-95), *m* Henry **Fink** (4 above).
7-Johannes (Sommer) **Sommers,** from Germany, settled at Germantown, Pa.; *m* Margaretha-;
6-Capt. Jacob (1749-1817), in Am. Rev.; *m* 1772, Anna May Dauber (1752-1827);
5-Jacob (1775-1842), served War 1812; *m* 1799, Elizabeth Bright (1779-1842);
4-Gideon Bright (1806-77), began to write name Sommers; *m* 1837, Mary Loper (1812-1905; John[5], War 1812, *m* Elizabeth Trepania);
3-Isabella Bright (*b* 1840), *m* James Madison **Fink** (3 above);
2-Mary Emma (*b* 1864), *m* 1885, Frank Almon **Lyon** (1855-1921), distinguished lawyer; state senator, Hillsdale, Mich.
1-*m* May 9, 1916, Donald Kimball Moore (qv); issue: 1-Patricia Lyon, *b* Hillsdale, Dec. 7, 1917.
1-Piano diploma, Hillsdale Coll., 1905; St. Mary's Coll., Notre Dame, Ind., ex-'08; U.Mich., ex-1908 (Pi Beta Phi); artist's diploma, Univ. Sch. of Music, Ann Arbor, 1908 (Mu Phi Epsilon). Teacher of piano and German, Hillsdale Coll., 1909-14. Mem. C.D.A., D.C.G., D.A.R. (Mich. state consulting registrar, and state genealogist, 1921-24; state rec. sec., 1924-1927), U.S.D. 1812, O.E.S. (Mich. grand organist, 1908-09), Mich. Authors' Assn., I.A.G., N.E.H.G.S., Mich. Hist. and Pioneer Soc., Bunker Hill Country Club. Summer place: 25 S. Broad St., Hillsdale, Mich. Residence: 458 Briar Pl., Chicago, Ill.

1-**MOORE, Hugh Benton,** *b* Huntland, Tenn., Jan. 11, 1874.
6-Patrick **Moore,** from Ireland, ca. 1700, settled in what is now Moore Co., S.C.; killed in Battle of Cowpens;
5-Robert, also killed in Battle of Cowpens; *m* Betty Scissom;
4-John, of Moore Co., S.C.; *m* Mary Richardson;
3-Stephen L. (ca. 1799-1863), *d* in U.S. military prison at Alton, Ill.; *m* 1828, Lucy McDougal; they had five sons in the C.S.A.;
2-Horatio R. (2 below).
4-David **Hunt,** of Huntland, Tenn.; maj. in Andrew Jackson's Army; participated in the Battle of New Orleans, 1812; *m* Elizabeth Larkin;
3-Clinton A. (1810-81), Huntland, Tenn.; *m* Tappie Lipscomb (1818-1906);
2-Annie (*b* 1840), Huntland, Tenn.; *m* 1860, Horatio R. **Moore** (1833-1926), lawyer and farmer; issue: I-Elma (*m* George C. Rutledge); II-William Lipscomb (*m* Ollie Haney); III-Annie (*m* William W. Vanzandt); IV-Maymie (*m* Charles G. Renegar); V-Hugh Benton (1 above); VI-Hunt C. (*m* Belle E. Smith).
1-*m* Sept. 5, 1905, Helen Edmunds (qv).
1-Began as messenger T.&P. Ry. Co., Dallas, 1890; pres. and gen. mgr. Tex. City Terminal Ry. Co. since 1917. Commd. capt. O.R.C., 1916; apptd. transportation officer on staff of Gen. Pershing, May 1917; arrived in France, June 10, 1917; supt. army transport service at St. Nazaire, later gen. supt. at principal ports of France; promoted to newly created position of dir. of Army Transport Service of all ports and steamship operations of A.E.F. in Europe, Jan. 1918; promoted col.; hon. discharged Feb. 1919. Awarded D.S.M. (U.S.); Legion of Honor (French). Mem. Baltic Soc., S.A.M.E. Mason (K.T., 32°). Democrat. Club: Houston Yacht. Residence: Texas City, Tex.

1-**MOORE, Helen Edmunds (Mrs. Hugh B.),** *b* Black River Falls, Wis., Jan. 8, 1882.
7-James **Edmunds** (*d* 1734), from Eng. with brothers, William and Andrew, early in 17th Century; to Providence, R.I.;
6-James (*b* 1731);
5-Obadiah (*b* 1759), *m* Abigail Jenks;
4-Obadiah (*b* 1788), Danby, Vt.; *m* 1806, Lydia Mores;
3-John (*b* 1821), Butler Co., Pa.; *m* Hortensia Hadley;
2-Jesse Herschell (*b* 1853), Henderson Co., Ill.; *m* 1875, Frances Rowena Beach; issue: I-Jessie (*b* 1876; *m* 1899, Ferdinand H. Rohde); II-John (*b* 1878; *m* 1918, Leona Hall); III-Helen (1 above).
1-*m* Sept. 5, 1905, Hugh Benton Moore (qv).
1-Residence: Texas City, Tex.

1-**MOORE, Olin Harris,** *b* Mount Airy, N.C., Jan. 27, 1885.
8-John **Moore,** from Eng., 1646, settled in Upper Norfolk Co., Va.; *m* Elizabeth-;
7-Thomas (will dated 1743), Isle of Wight Co., Va.; inherited land from his father in Nottoway Parish;
6-Thomas (will dated 1765), Isle of Wight Co.;
5-Barham, Sussex Co., Va.;
4-Rev. Thomas (will probated 1834), Greensville Co., Va.; joined Va. Conf. of M.E. Ch., 1809; served various charges in Va. and N.C., Richmond, Portsmouth, Petersburg and Lynchburg among them; del. to Gen. Conf., 1816; retired from active ministry, 1819, and settled in Greensville Co., Va.; *m* 1819, Judith Stewart;
3-John Robert, M.D. (1825-82), Halifax Co., N.C.; M.D., Jefferson Med. Coll., 1847; *m* 1851, Lucy Elizabeth Burges (1827-1902);
2-Rev. Matthew Henry (*b* 1857), of N.C., Colo., and Mo.; pastor; presiding elder, editor and author; now a retired mem. of the Mo. Conf. M.E. Ch., South; *m* 1884, Mary Eugenia Thomas (*b* 1861); issue: I-Olin Harris (1 above); II-Henry Thomas (*b* 1886; *m* Marie Blaine); III-Mary Eugenia (*b* 1888; *m* Dr. F. P. Gaunt); IV-John Robert (*b* 1890; *m* Alice Beer); V-Randolph Lee (*b* 1892); VI-Lucy Burges (*b* 1894; *m* Maj. E. E. MacMorland); VII-Ethel (*b* 1896; *m* Dr. E. M. Fisher).
1-Not married. A.B., U. of Mo., '02; A.M., Harvard, 1904, Ph.D., 1913; studied Ecole Pratique des Hautes Etudes, Paris, France. Prof. Romance languages, Ohio State U., since 1920. Author (see Who's Who in America). Methodist. Clubs: Country, University. Residence: Columbus, O.

1-**MOORE, Gertrude Baker (Mrs. William C.),** *b* Logan, O., July 10, 1869.
8-Edward **Baker** (ca. 1610-ante 1687), from Eng., with Gov. Winthrop, ca. 1630; settled at Lynn, Mass.; removed to Northampton, 1658; *m* ante 1640, Joan- (*d* 1693);
7-Timothy (1647-1729), of Northampton; *m* 2d, post 1676, Widow Sarah (Hollister) Atherton (*d* 1691);
6-John (1680-1762), *m* 1709, Rebecca Clark (1687-1774);
5-Aaron (1726-1802), soldier Am. Rev.; *m* 1747, Jemima Clark (1728-1815);
4-Timothy (1749-1816), soldier Am. Rev.; Addison Co., Vt.; *m* ca. 1770, Prudence Brooks (*b* 1750);
3-Luman (1802-72), removed from Addison Co., Vt., to Logan, O.; *m* 1827, Sarah Hart (1806-88);
2-Thomas Edwin (1828-1904), of Lancaster, and Logan, O.; capt., Co. G, 90th O.V.I., wounded at Stone River; *m* Oct. 10, 1850, Mary Tower (1830-1922).
1-*m* Nov. 7, 1894, William Collins Moore, *b* Logan O., June 21, 1868; son of Meredith Darlington Moore, of Logan.
1-Mem. D.F.P.A., I.A.G. Residence: 70 Auburn Av., Columbus, O.

1-**MOORMAN, Lewis Jefferson,** *b* Leitchfield, Ky., Feb. 9, 1875.
8-Thomas **Moorman,** came in the "Bona Nova," to Va., 1619; granted land by London Co., 1619;
7-Charles (*d* 1757); of nr. Green Spring, Louisa Co., Va.; Quaker; entered 400 acres of land in Albemarle Co., Va., on a stream since known as Moorman River, 1735; *m* 1703, Elizabeth Reynolds;
6-Achilles, *m* Elizabeth Adams;
5-William, *m* 1st, Jane Haden;
4-James Haden (*b* 1776), *m* 1st, his cousin, Elizabeth Moorman (*b* 1777; Andrew[5], *m* Judith Clark);
3-Andrew Clark (1800-53), *m* 1823, Nancy Booker Owen;
2-Lemuel (1832-1917), *m* 1853, Martha Elizabeth Wortham (1837-1920; James H.[3], *m* Martha Rogers); issue: I-Ida (1854-55); II-James Clark (*b* 1857; *m* Nannie Strickler); III-Charles Wortham (*b* 1860; *m* Mary Elizabeth Talbott); IV-Harriett Ann (1862-1924; *m* Robert J. Bassett); V-Robert Lee (*b* 1864; *m* Mamie Thomas); VI-John Webb (*b* 1867; *m* Jessie McBeath); VII-William Gordon (1871-1927; *m* Eva Myer Herndon); VIII-Lewis Jefferson (1 above).

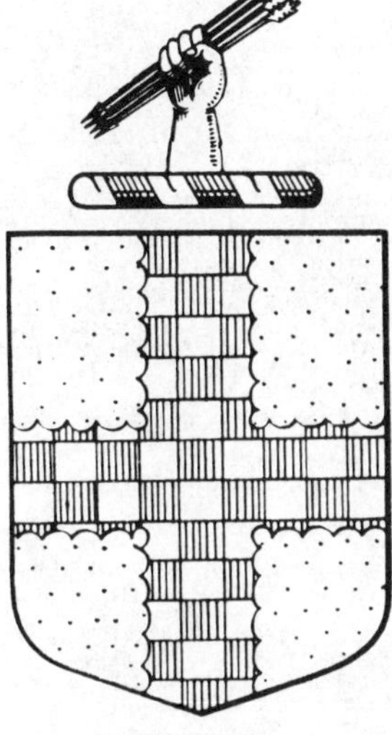

MOORMAN

Arms: Or, a cross engrailed chequy argent and gules.
Crest: A cubit arm erect holding arrows.
Motto: Esse quam videri.

1–*m* Apr. 27, 1909, Mary Davis Christian, *b* Lynchburg, Va., Aug. 12, 1888; issue (all *b* Oklahoma City, Okla.): 1–Elizabeth Dabney, *b* Feb. 20, 1910; ed. Pine Manor, Wellesley, Mass., 1929; 2–Mary Christian, *b* Feb. 14, 1913; 3–Lewis Jefferson, Jr., *b* Aug. 28, 1917.
1–B.S., Georgetown (Ky.) Coll., '98; M.D., U.-Louisville, 1901; post-grad. work, New York Polyclinic Med. School, 1903; U.Vienna, 1909. Began practice at Jet, Okla., 1901; moved to Oklahoma City, Okla., 1907; med. dir. Okla. Cottage Sanatorium since 1914; founder, 1923, since med. dir., Moorman Farm Sanatorium; prof. clinical medicine, U.Okla., since 1926 (see Who's Who in America). Presbyterian. Democrat. Clubs: Men's Dinner, Oklahoma City Golf and Country. Residence: 1301 Classen Boul., Oklahoma City, Okla.

1–**MORGAN, Charles Stillman,** *b* Niles, Mich., Dec. 29, 1891.
10–Rev. James **Noyes** (qv);
9–Rev. James (*b* 1640), settled at Stonington, Conn.; grad. Harvard; a founder and first trustee Yale Coll.; pastor of the first ch. at New Haven; *m* Dorothy Stanton;
8–Capt. Thomas (*b* 1679), Stonington, Conn.; *m* Elizabeth Sanford;
7–James (1714-93), served in colonial militia; *m* Grace Billings;
6–Peleg (*b* 1741), capt. 8th Conn. Inf.; *m* Prudence Williams;
5–Desire (1770-1843), *m* Joseph **Eldridge**;
4–Julia F. (1804-69), Truxton, N.Y.; *m* 1835, Dr. Stillman **Richardson** (1805-75);
3–James T. (1836-1914), Niles, Mich.; *m* 1855, Mary E. Clark (1836-1923);
2–Edith Amelia (*b* 1862), *m* 1882, Leander James **Morgan** (1854-1916), local official, later bookkeeper; issue: I–Edna Richardson (1884-1913; *m* Floyd G. Wicks); II–Floyd Henry (1885-1907); III–Ruth Caroline (*b* 1886; *m* Charles H. Miller); IV–Charles Stillman (1 above); V–Eleanor Frances (*b* 1897; *m* Freeman H. Shelton); VI–Dorothy Elizabeth (*b* 1902; *m* Allen J. Nieber).
1–*m* Jan. 6, 1917, Florence M. Gross, *b* Marietta, O., May 15, 1890; dau. of Henry A. Gross, of Marietta; issue: 1–Jeanne Noyes, *b* Marietta, O., Mar. 5, 1918; 2–Suzanne Elizabeth, *b* Washington, D.C., Jan. 29, 1920.
1–A.B., U.Mich., '14 (Pi Gamma Mu); post-grad. work, summers 1915,16; Ph.D., Yale, 1920. Principal economist, Interstate Commerce Commission, since 1927. Lecturer on transportation, U. of Md., 1924-25, Grad. Sch. of Am. U., Washington, 1927–. Author (see Who's Who in America). Clubs: Michigan Union (Ann Arbor), University, Cosmos (Washington). Residence: 5721 Chevy Chase Parkway, Washington, D.C.

1–**MORPHY, Katherine Ledwich Hazlehatch Meroney (Mrs. William James),** *b* Kershaw Co., S.C., Mar. 23, 1876.
9–Capt. John **Jefferson,** from Wales; among the first settlers in Va.; lived at Osborne's on the James; burgess, 1619;
8–Thomas, *m* Mary Branch (William[9], *m* Jane–; Christopher[10], *m* Mary Addie);
7–Capt. Thomas (1677-1735), *m* 1698, Mary Field (Maj. Peter[8] [*b* 1648], of St. Peter's Parish, New Kent Co., Va., *m* Judith, dau. of Hon. Henry Soane, speaker of Va. House of Burgesses; James[9] [*b* 1604], came to Va. in the "Swan");
6–Field (1702-65), vestryman, St. James Parish; justice of the peace, 1749; high sheriff; his estate was called "Occonechee"; *m* 1st, Mary Frances Robertson (*d* 1750, aet. 44);
5–Phoebe, *m* Capt. Alexander **Clark,** served in Am. Rev.; mem. N.C. Assembly from Chatham Co. (William[6]);

REV. WILLIAM BRITTON MERONEY (1769-1816).

Photograph from the alabaster bust of the Lord Bishop of Hereford, Theophilus Field (b or bap., Jan. 22, 1547-d June 2, 1630), the father of James Field (b 1604), who came to Virginia in the "Swan," and was the father of Maj. Peter Field, of New Kent Co., Va.

MERONEY

Arms: Argent, three crosses crosslet or, between as many boars' heads couped above the shoulders argent, langued gules.
Crest: A lion rampant argent, holding between the paws a sceptre or halbert or.
Motto: Amicis semper fidelis.

4–Winifred Webb (*d* 1817, aet. 48), as Widow Mott, *m* 2d, Rev. William Britton **Meroney** (1769-1816), Presbyn. clergyman, see portrait (Capt. Philip de Lancey[5] [*d* 1830], served with 1st Md. Bn. of the Flying Camp in Am. Rev.; was at the battles of Brandywine, White Plains, and surrender of Cornwallis, also went in southern campaign under Gen. Greene, *m* 1st, Sarah Nelson);
3–Col. John Alexander (1802-37), of Rowan Co., N.C.; *m* 1825, Mary Hendricks (a relative of V.P. Thomas A. Hendricks);
2–John Swift (1829-1909), of "Holly Hill," Kershaw Co., S.C.; *m* 1857, Margaret Sloan, of Camden, S.C. (Col. Hiram[3]); *m* 2d, 1865, Katherine Elizabeth O'Neill (Reid) Palmer, of Charleston, S.C.; issue (2d marriage): I–Marie Louise (*b* 1866-*d* infancy); II–Oscar John Daly Reid (*b* 1868; *m* Miss Muller); III–John Patrick Reid (*b* 1870; *m* Anna Jay); IV–Charles (*d* infancy); V–Alma Amelia Hilary (*b* 1872; *m* John Calhoun Williams); VI–Katherine Ledwich Hazlehatch (1 above).
1–*m* Nov. 4, 1921, William James Morphy, *b* "Drumheriff House," Ireland, 1852; son of John Morphy, master of "Drumheriff," his estate nr. Dungannon, Ireland.
1–Democrat. Residence: Wood-Norton, Wayne Av. and Johnson St., Germantown, Phila., Pa.

1–**MORGAN, Jacob Levi,** *b* Rowan Co., N.C., Feb. 7, 1872.
4–Nathan **Morgan** (1756-1842), of Rowan Co., N.C.; weaver and tailor; served in Am. Rev.; *m* 1778, Naomi Poole (1760-1851);
3–David (1789-1878), owner of farm in Rowan Co.; *m* 1812, Elizabeth Hoffner (1791-1887);
2–Jacob (2 below).
4–Joel **Hodge** (prob. son of John, of Eng.), of Rowan Co., N.C.;
3–Jesse (1792-1864), of Rowan Co.; *m* 1st, Ruhama Palmer (1792-1840).
2–Jacob **Morgan** (1818-98), farmer, Rowan Co., N.C.; soldier in Civil War; *m* 1851, Sarah Amanda Hodge (1829-72); *m* 2d, 1873, Mary Lucinda Casper (1843-1929); issue (1st marriage): I–David Calvin (*b* 1853; *m* Elizabeth Catharine Morgan); II–Lucinda Catherine (1855-*d*); III–Julian Elizabeth (*b* 1858; *m* Moses L. Morgan); IV–John Franklin (*b* 1860; *m* Amanda V. Trexler); V–Abram Alexander (*b* 1863-*d*); VI–Ally Amanda (*b* 1866; *m* John H. Bame); VII–Nancy Jane (*b* 1869; *m* W. Liberius Ludwig); VIII–Jacob Levi (1 above); issue (2d marriage): I–Mary Adeline (*b* 1874; *m* Henry E. Hodge); II–Martha Ellen (*b* 1875); III–Travis Eli (1877-*d*); IV–Colonel Ellis (*b* 1880; *m* Edie R. Morgan); V–Delinda Belle (*b* 1881; *m* Walter Eagle); VI–Richard Luther (*b* 1884; *m* Daisy L. Bame); VII–Margaret Lillie (*b* 1886); VIII–Minnie Virginia (*b* 1889).
1–*m* May 25, 1903, Elizabeth Virginia Clay Shoup, *b* Gurleyville, Ala., Sept. 30, 1875; ed. Mont Amoena Female Sem.; dau. of Rev. John B. Shoup; issue: 1–Gladys, *b* Enochville, N.C., Mar. 30, 1904; A.B., Lenoir-Rhyne Coll., '25; M.A., U. of N.C., 1928; 2–Ruth (May 18, 1905-May 26, 1907); 3–Karl Ziegler, *b* Enochville, Sept. 27, 1907; A.B., U. of N.C., '29, M.A., 1930; 4–Katharine, *b* Mooresville, Sept. 10, 1910; N.C. Coll. for Women, 1931; 5–Lois, *b* Raleigh, N.C., Feb. 14, 1917.
1–A.B., North Carolina Coll., '99; (D.D., Lenoir-Rhyne Coll., Hickory, N.C., 1922); grad. Southern Luth. Theol. Sem., 1902. Ordained Luth. ministry, 1902; pastor Haven and Christ Luth. churches, Salisbury, N.C., 1902-03, and Enochville pastorate, Rowan Co., N.C., 1903-07; sec. synodical home missions of N.C. Luth. Synod, 1907-17; pastor Holy Trinity Ch., Raleigh, 1911-19; pres. United Evangelical Luth. Synod of N.C. since 1919 (see Who's Who in America). Historian of Morgan Family Assn. of Rowan Co., N.C. Democrat. Residence: Salisbury, N.C.

1–**MORRIS, Fred Barton,** *b* nr. Carlinville, Ill., Dec. 23, 1875.
7–William **Witt** (1675-1754), from France, 1699; settled at Manakintown, Va.; later at Richmond;
6–Charles (1712-81), Halifax Co., Va.; *m* Lavinia Harbour;
5–Elijah (1756-1801), Jefferson Co., Tenn.; capt. Am. Rev.; *m* 1776, Miss Hutchinson (*d* ca. 1795);
4–Eli (1785-1851), Greene Co., Ill.; *m* 1806, Nancy McNealy (1790-1860);
3–Mary (1812-42), Carrollton, Ill.; *m* 1831, Lorenzo Dow **Morris** (1805-87; g.son Robert Morris [1733-1806], a "Signer");
2–George Washington (2 below).
9–John **Haynes** (qv);
8–John (1636-70), grad. Harvard, 1656; vicar of Stanway; clk. nr. Copford Hall, Co. Essex, Eng.;
7–John, from Eng. to Carolina, 1700; *m* Mary Deane;
6–John, *m* Mary Edings;
5–John (*b* Eng., ca. 1758), from Eng. aet. 16; served in Am. Rev. from N.C., 3 yrs.; lived in Person Co., N.C.; to Barren Co., Ky., 1797; *m* in N.C., Mary Stice;
4–Rev. William (1784-1830), *m* 1810, Annie Henley (1790-1868);
3–Lewis (1812-73), *m* 1848, Catherine Norton (1823-63).
2–George Washington **Morris** (1836-1914), of Orange, Calif.; farmer; *m* 1867, Nancy White (*d* 1873); *m* 2d, 1874, Mary Catherine Haynes (1857-95); *m* 3d, 1896, Mary F. Spotts (*d* 1929); issue (1st marriage): I–Eli William (*b* 1868; *m* Sadie E. Stealey); II–Orsa Dow (1870-1900; *m* Nora A. Backus); III–Reid (1873-94); issue (2d marriage): I–Fred B. (1 above); II–Orado Bird (1878-94); III–Annie Galena (*b* 1882; *m* William Perry Banes).
1–*m* June 7, 1910, Clara Dessa Logan, *b* Beaver Co., Pa., Aug. 24, 1880; dau. Matthew Logan, *m* Eliza Jane Banks, of Beaver Falls, Pa.; issue: 1–Louise Logan, *b* Beaver, Pa., Aug. 5, 1912.
1–Teacher's training course, Western Normal Coll., Bushnell, Ill., 1892. Teaching school, 1895-99; cattle raising, 1898-1907; railroad work, 1911-30. Mem. Huguenot Soc. of Founders of Manakin in Colony of Va., 1699. Odd Fellow. Residence: 180 W. Indianola Av., Youngstown, O.

1–**MORRIS, Lawrence Johnson,** *b* Chester Co., Pa., Sept. 26, 1870.
8–Anthony **Morris** (qv);
7–Anthony (1681/82-1763), of Phila.; mem. Pa. Assembly; alderman and asso. justice City Ct.; *m* Phoebe Guest;
6–Anthony (1705-80), *m* 1730, Sarah Powell (Samuel[7], *m* Abigail Wilcox);
5–Capt. Samuel (1734-1812), *m* Rebecca Wistar (Caspar[6], *m* Catherine, dau. of Dirck Jansen; Johannes Caspar[7]);
4–Israel Wistar (1778-1870), *m* Mary Hollingsworth (Levi[5], *m* 1768, Hannah, dau. of Stephen Paschall; Zebulon[6], *m* 1st, 1727, Ann, dau. of Col. Francis Maulden; Henry[7], same as 7 below);
3–Dr. Caspar (1805-84), *m* 1829, Ann Cheston;
2–James Cheston (2 below).
9–Richard **Cheston** (*d* ca. 1660);
8–Richard (*d* ca. 1665), *m* Joan–;

7–Richard (ca. 1664-1747), *m* 1698/99, Margery Blount (Thomas Blunt[8], *m* Margery–);
6–Daniel (bap. 1712-1758), *m* 1742, Francina Augustina Frisby;
5–James (*b* 1747), *m* Anne Galloway;
4–James (1779-1843), shipping and importing merchant, Baltimore; *m* Mary Ann Hollingsworth;
3–Ann (1810-80), *m* Dr. Caspar **Morris** (3 above).
9–Richard **Galloway** (*d* 1663), of Md.; *m* Hannah–;
8–Samuel (1659-*d* in London, Eng., 1720), *m* 2d, in London, 1689, Anne Webb (*d* 1722; Borrington[9]);
7–John (*b* 1693/94), *m* 1st, 1718, Mary Thomas (*d* 1755; Samuel[8], *m* Mary Hutchins; Lt. Philip[9], qv);
6–Samuel (*d* 1785), *m* 1745, Anne Chew;
5–Anne, *m* James **Cheston** (5 above).
9–Samuel **Chew** (qv);
8–Benjamin, *m* Elizabeth Benson (*d* 1700);
7–Dr. Samuel, chief justice, Del.; *m* 1st, 1715, Mary Galloway (Samuel[8], same as 8 above);
6–Anne, *m* Samuel **Galloway** (6 above).
8–Valentine **Hollingsworth** (qv);
7–Henry, *m* 1688, Lydia Atkinson;
6–Zebulon (1696-1763), *m* 2d, Mary Jacobs;
5–"Col." Samuel (1757-1830), *m* 1782, Sarah Adams (George[6], *m* Elizabeth, dau. of George Hilles);
4–Mary Ann, *m* James **Cheston** (4 above).
10–Christian Barentsen **Van Horn** (qv);
9–Barent Christiansen (*b* 1657), *m* Geertje Claessen (*b* 1662; Dirck[10], *m* Myrtie Roelofs);
8–Christian, rep. Pa. Gen. Assembly, 1723-32, 1734-37; *m* Williamtje Van Dyck (1681-1760; Hendrick[9]);
7–John (1713-60), *m* 1739, Lena Van Pelt (Joseph[8], *m* Catherine–; Anthony Teunisse[9]; Teunis Jansen Lanen[10]);
6–Catherine (bap. 1741), *m* 1764, John **Suber** (bap. 1720-estate administered 1783; John Peter[7], *m* Magdalen–);
5–Catharine, *m* Isaiah **Van Horn** (*d* 1802), see Vol. III, p. 340;
4–Sarah (1796-1838), *m* 1812, Aaron **Winder** (1759-1824);
3–Mary (1814-77), *m* 1837, Lawrence **Johnson** (*b* Hull, Eng., 1801-1860), head of L. Johnson & Co., typefounders, Phila.;
2–Mary Ella (1841-1912), *m* 2d, 1870, James Cheston **Morris** (1831-Nov. 29, 1923); see Vol. I, p. 267.
1–Not married. Penn Charter School, '85; A.B., Haverford, '89. Mem. firm of Lawrence Johnson Co., Phila.; formerly v.p. and dir. Abrasive Co., and Phila. Warehouse Co., etc. Mgr. Pa. Hosp. Phila. Dispensary, Pa. Epileptic Hosp.; dir. Phila. Dispensary, Pa. Epileptic Hosp.; dir. Phila. Bourse. Mem. S.C.W., Colonial Soc., Welcome Soc., S.R., I.A.G. (life mem.), Md. Hist. Soc., Hist. Soc. Pa., Acad. Natural Sciences. Clubs: Phila., Rittenhouse, University, University Barge, Merion, etc. Summer place: "Fernbank," near West Chester, Pa. Residence: St. James Pl., below 22d St., Philadelphia, Pa.

1–**MORRIS, S(idney) Kent,** *b* Jersey City, N.J., Dec. 8, 1894.
8–Daniel **Morris**;
7–Stephen;
6–Maj. Joseph (1732-78), served in Am. Rev.; *m* 1759, Hannah Ford (1740-83);
5–Lt. Jonathan Ford (1760-1810), doctor; *m* 1784, Margaret Smith Euen (1758-1844);
4–William Cullen (1789-1870), *m* 1819, Mary Magdalen Stryker (1796-1857);
3–Dr. Theodore Frelinghuysen (1831-1907), *m* 1855, Gertrude Vreeland Johnston (1835-89);
2–Dr. Austin Flint (1869-1906), Rutgers Coll., '92; M.D., Bellevue Hosp. Med. Sch., N.Y. Univ., 1893; *m* 1893, Helen Lincoln Kent (*b* 1868), of Chicago, Ill.; issue: I–S. Kent (1 above); II–Alberta (*b* 1896; *m* Arthur Gilbert Bissell).
1–Not married. Yale-S., ex-'19. Pvt. and sgt. heavy arty., Hdqrs. Co., at Ft. Totten, N.Y., June 10, 1917-Sept. 1918; O.T.C. at Ft. Monroe, Va., discharged, Nov. 21, 1918. Mem. S. C., I.A.G. (life). Clubs: Yale (N.Y.), Chevy Chase (Washington). Residence: Pequest Farms, Belvidere, N.J.

1–**MOSELEY, Franklin Shackelford,** *b* Montgomery, Ala., Jan. 15, 1899.
6–Robert **Moseley** (*d* 1796), of Edgefield Dist., S.C.; *m* 1st, Mary–;
5–Edward (1771-1834), to Ala., 1818; a first settler, Montgomery Co.; farmer, home on Pinchona Creek, ca. 18 miles south of Montgomery; co. commr., 1823-26; mem. com. to select site for first Montgomery Co. Court House; overseer poor; mem. No. 1, Old Bethel Primitive Bapt. Ch. (third Bapt. ch. in co.); *m* Martha Butler (1775-1831; James[6], of Edgefield Dist., *m* Winifred, dau. of Robert Brooks);
4–Anderson Wade (1801-70), farmer; staunch Primitive Bapt.; gave ground for Tabernacle Meth. Ch. (stands today on old Moseley place); *m* Rebecca McLemore (1805-80; William[5], from Jones Co., Ga., to Ala., 1818, justice, mem. State Legislature, 1823,25,34, donated land for Elim Primitive Bapt. Ch., 2d Bapt. ch. in co., *m* Julia, dau. of John Perry; James[6]);
3–Adkin McLemore (1828-95), Mason; steward Meth. ch.; *m* Martha Jane Canaday (1837-88; John[4], of Society Hill, Ala., *m* Elizabeth Kirkpatrick);
2–Franklin McLemore (2 below).
7–Francis **Shackelford,** of N.C.; *m* Sarah–;
6–John (1712-81), of Georgetown Dist., S.C.; *m* Ann– (*b* 1714);
5–Francis (1739-1823), of Marion Dist., S.C.; soldier Am. Rev.; *m* Rebeccah– (1738-1818);
4–George (1779-1852), to Montgomery Co., Ala., 1818; mem. Bethel Primitive Bapt. Ch.; *m* Annette Jeter (1806-70; Eleazer[5], to Ala., 1818, justice, *m* Ann–; William[6]);
3–Madison (1838-1905), served in C.S.A., an escort of Pres. Jefferson Davis; lt., 2d Ala. Cav.; *m* Sophronia Jane Ledbetter;
2–Lela (2 below).
6–James **Ledbetter,** *m* Mary–;
5–Osborne, *m* Mary Delbridge (Thomas[6], Am. Rev., *m* Nancy Gwaltney);
4–David Egbert, from Brunswick Co., Va., to Ala., 1834; *m* Polly Harrison Smith (Cuthbert[5], *m* Joanna Neale, a 1st cousin to Julia Neale, mother of "Stonewall" Jackson);
3–Sophronia Jane (1843-95), *m* Madison **Shackelford** (3 above);
2–Lela (*b* 1872), *m* 1896, Franklin McLemore **Moseley** (*b* 1872), of Montgomery, Ala.; received 1st elec. and mech. engr.'s degree, Ala. Poly. Inst., 1892 (highest honors), won fellowship; steward and trustee, Meth. Ch.; mem. Lion's Club (pres.), Business Men's Evangelistic Club, Crescent Lake Country Club; issue: I–Annie Lula (*b* 1897; *m* John Burkhart Mayson); II–Franklin S. (1 above); III–Adkin Madison (*b* 1901; *m* Lucia Murphree); IV–Edward McLemore (1902-20, accidently killed while doing Ala. N.G. duty in mining dist. nr. Birmingham); V–Robert Samuel (*b* 1906); VI–Henry David (*b* 1908).
1–Attended Ala. Poly Inst., 1919-21 (Sigma Nu). With Moseley Electric Co., 1921-26; with engring. dept., Fla. Power & Light Co., Miami, 1926-28. Admitted to Ala. Conference of the Southern Meth. Ch., 1928, as preacher on trial. Mem. S.A.R., A.L. Address: Evergreen, Ala.

1–**MOSELEY, Thomas Bedford,** *b* "Oakland," Halifax Co., Va., Dec. 6, 1855.
9–William **Moseley,** from Eng., 1649, settled in Norfolk Co., Va., establishing the homestead "Rolleston Hall," named for Rolleston Hall in Eng., the original family seat; had land grants in Lynhaven Parish on Broad Creek, Lower Norfolk Co., Va.; *m* Susanna Cockroft;
8–William (*d* 1671), commr. Lower Norfolk Co., 1660; *m* Mary Gookin;
7–Edward (will recorded 1736), col. and justice Princess Anne Co.; high sheriff, 1707-08; Knight of the Golden Horseshoe, 1710-22; burgess; *m* Mrs. Bartho Taylor;
6–Hillary (*d* 1760), *m* Nancy Bedford;
5–Col. Edward Hack (*d* 1782), burgess from Princess Anne Co., 1766-74; sheriff; vestryman; rep. of the Colony Counties; loyalist in Am. Rev., and friend of Benedict Arnold; *m* 1st, Mary Bassett (*d* 1755, aet. 38);
4–Hillary, of Charlotte Co., Va.; *m* 1785, Nancy Bedford;
3–Hillary (1792-1856), Charlotte, Va.; *m* 1822, Margaret Boulding (1799-1849);
2–Charles Hillary (1824-1906), Halifax Co., Va.; planter; *m* 1848, Sarah Ann Marable (1827-1905); issue: I–Clifton Hillary (1848-1922; *m* Bettie

Lipscomb); II–Ella O. (1850-1926; *m* Col. William T. Lipscomb); III–Henry E. (1853-1923; *m* Mit Edmonson, *d* 1928); IV–Thomas Bedford (1 above); V–Charles A. (1857-1921; *m* Sue Summers); VI–George G. (1862-1920; *m* Thomasa Niterville); VII–Sallie (*b* 1864; *m* Rev. W. B. Oliver); VIII–Richard E. (*b* 1866; *m* Bettie Guthrie).
1–*m* Minnie Wilkinson (1866-June 29, 1894).
1–*m* 2d, June 29, 1898, Evelyn Simms (qv for issue).
1–Mem. T.B. Moseley & Son, Real Estate and Fire Ins. Mem. I.A.G. Address: Raleigh, N.C.

1–**MOSELEY, Evelyn Simms (Mrs. Thomas Bedford),** *b* Charleston, W.Va., June 9, 1873.
5–James (Sims) **Simms,** *m* Elizabeth (prob.) Nalle, of Va.;
4–Edward (1762-1825), of Still Valley, Rappahanock Co., Va.; pvt. Va. Militia; *m* 1786, Amy Sims (1766-1845; William[5]);
3–Albert Gallatin (1800-72), Culpeper, Va.; educator; *m* 1830, Salome Baptiste Meredith (1814-77; Joseph[4], *m* Mary Baptiste);
2–Albert Meredith (1847-1918), Culpeper, Va.; Bapt. minister for 50 yrs.; *m* 1872, Mary Stewart (1851-1926); issue: I–Evelyn (1 above); II–Robert Nirwana (*b* 1876; *m* 1908, Virginia Egerton, *b* 1885); III–Matt Meredith (*b* 1878; *m* Dr. Robert Benjamin Adair).
1–*m* June 29, 1898, Thomas Bedford Moseley (qv); issue: 1–Albert Meredith, *b* Raleigh, N.C., Sept. 17, 1902; A.B., Wake Forest Coll., '23 (Zeta Psi, Phi Delta Phi); U. of N.C.; atty.; 2–Thomas Bedford, Jr., *b* Raleigh, Apr. 14, 1905; partner with father, T. B. Moseley & Son.
1–Attended Baylor Coll., 2 yrs.; grad. normal class, teachers for deaf, Sch. for Deaf, N.C. Mem. D.A.R., U.D.C. Clubs: Woman's, Cosmos. Residence: Raleigh, N.C.

1–**MULFORD, Gertrude Hodgman (Mrs. Linden C.),** *b* Grand Ridge, Ill., June 29, 1872.
8–Josiah **Webber,** was at Reading, Mass., in 1668, when his son Josiah was born;
7–Josiah (1668-1749), was adopted by Thomas **Hodgman** (*d* 1729), and took his name; *m* 1st, 1691, Elizabeth– (1668-1712);
6–Thomas (1692-1739), Stoneham, Mass.; *m* 1713 or 1714, Abigail Geary (1697-1767);
5–Samuel (1734-81), Lexington; *m* 1755, Abigail Cutler (1728-97);
4–Amos (1755-1822), Stillwater, N.Y., 1787; responded to the Alarm, 1775; *m* 1784, Jemima Stone (1758-1822);
3–Leonard (1791-1883); *m* 1815, Jeannette Morey (1792-1871);
2–Leonard (1828-1915), *m* 1855, Lizzie Irwin (1835-1902), from Ireland, 1851 (William[3], *m* Eliza Corscadden, both *d* in Ireland); issue: I–Lansing Henry (*m* Eliza McCormick); II–Mabel Isabel (*m* George Crawford); III–Mary (*d* young); IV–Fanny (*d* young); V–Gertrude (1 above).
1–*m* 1892, Linden C. Mulford, *b* Pana, Ill., Aug. 7, 1870; pres. Mulford Motors Co., and Streator Chamber of Commerce; Mason (past cdr. K.T.); son of H. Mulford, of Streator, Ill.; issue: 1–Linden, *b* Jan. 19, 1910; student U.Chicago Law School.
1–Grad. Ottawa Normal Coll. Mem. D.F.P.A., D.A.C., D.A.R. Presbyterian. Republican. Summer place: Pilgrim, Mich. Residence: 227 La Salle St., Streator, Ill.

1–**MUNSON, Thomas Burton Hill,** *b* Seymour, Conn., July 13, 1863.
8–Thomas **Munson** (qv);
7–Samuel (1643-93), ens. King Philip's War; rector and head master, Hopkins Grammar School, New Haven; constable; founder of Wallingford; selectman, townsman, auditor, recorder; treas. Church Soc.; advocate at Gen. Assembly; chosen to compile "The Court Laws"; *m* 1665, Martha Pritchard Bradley (William[8], *m* Alice Pritchard);
6–Caleb (1682-1765), first selectman, grandjuror, tithingman; *m* 1706, Elisabeth Herman (*d* 1739);
5–Caleb (1709-47), farmer; *m* 1735, Abigail Brockett (1711-1800; John[6]);
4–Caleb (1747-1826), first collector, Middlebury, Conn.; *m* 1781, Lucy Roberts (Gideon[5], of Waterbury);
3–Joseph (1786-1869), selectman, justice; first trustee of M.E. Soc.; *m* Lucinda Wooster;
2–Thomas Hamilton (2 below).
8–Edward **Wooster** (*d* 1689), from Eng., settled at Derby, Conn.; *m* Tabitha Tomlinson (*d* 1691);
7–Thomas (1656-1713), Milford, Conn.; *m* Phebe Tomlinson (1656-1739), of Stratford, Conn.;
6–Thomas (1692-1777), *m* Sarah Hawkins (1693-1785);
5–Thomas (1716-1800), Oxford, Conn.; *m* Lois Hawkins (*b* 1728; Eleazer[6], *m* Damaris Wooster);
4–Thomas (1757-1800), Lancaster, N.H. (or Vt.); *m* Elizabeth Bishop;
3–Lucinda (1791-1877), *m* Joseph **Munson** (3 above).
5–John **Hill,** *m* Margaret–;
4–Thomas (1747-1814), Basking Ridge, N.J.; capt. Am. Rev.; *m* Charity Joralemon, of Brooklyn;
3–Thomas (1794-1875), Weymouth, O.; *m* Mary Wilson (1798-1862; Joseph[4], *m* Charity MacAllister);
2–Mary Etta (1836-98), *m* 1859, Thomas Hamilton **Munson** (1831-1905), Bridgeport, Conn.; contractor, Wheeler & Wilson Co.; issue: I–Thomas Burton Hill (1 above); II–Mary Wooster (*b* 1866; *m* William J. Sutton, *d* 1920); III–Kate May (1868-69); IV–George Harris (1869-1922); V–Arley (*b* 1871; *m* James A. Hare); VI–Gertrude Edna (*b* 1873; *m* Fred Adee Hulst); VII–Alexander Joseph (1876-1918).
1–*m* Sept. 30, 1886, Frances Amelia Mills, *b* Green Farms, Conn., Oct. 1, 1864; dau. of Charles Henry Mills, of Stratford, Conn.; issue: 1–Raymond Burton, *b* Stratford, Conn., Nov. 12, 1888; A.B., Yale '09, A.M., 1910; *m* June 30, 1915, Bertha Wilkes, of Stratford (issue: Ruth Wilkes); 2–Vincent Hill, *b* Stratford, Mar. 31, 1901; *m* Mar. 1920, Mildred Harrington Atwood, of Oakville, Conn. (issue: Ferne Virginia; Gertrude Elsie).
1–Ed. Denmark (Ia.) Acad. Contractor, Wheeler & Wilson Co. Served 7 yrs. in Nat. Guard. I.O.O.F. (Noble Grand). Methodist. Democrat. Residence: "Fairview," Groton, Conn.

1–**MURRAY, Georgiana Groot (Mrs. Henry H.),** *b* Westbury, Wayne Co., N.Y., Jan. 10, 1876.
8–Symon Symonse **Groot** (*d* post 1699), from Holland to Beverwyck, 1631; settled at Schenectady; in service of Dutch West India Co.; boatswain of "Prince Maurice," New Amsterdam, 1645; owned Island in Mohawk River, 1667; carried prisoner to Canada, 1690, with his 5 sons; signed oath of allegiance, 1699; *m* Rebecca du Trieux (Philip[9], qv);
7–Symon Symonse (*d* ante 1734), of Schenectady, N.Y.; taken prisoner to Can. by French and Indians, 1690, returned 1691; pvt. in first mil. co. in Schenectady, 1715; *m* Geertruy Rinckhout (*d* 1734; Jan[8], of Albany);
6–Cornelius (1708-81), gave civil service during Am. Rev. together with his bro. Philip; *m* 1739, Elisabeth Pootman (Putnam; bap. 1717; Cornelius[7], *m* Jacomyntje Viele; Jan[8]);
5–Abraham Cornelius (1741-1818), served in 2d Schenectady mil. co., pvt. in Am. Rev.; *m* 2d, 1780, Elsje McKinney (bap. 1760-1833; Daniel[6], *m* Margaret Stanhouse);
4–Cornelius Abraham (1782-1849), Auburn, N.Y.,

settled on Cold Spring Farm; *m* 1806, Angelica Truax;
3–Abraham Cornelius (1813-90), *m* 1835, Sarah Knower;
2–Cornelius Abraham (2 below).
10–Phillippe (du Trieux) **Truax** (qv);
9–Philip (bap. 1619-murdered probably by Indians, Sept. 8, 1653), probably came with father;
8–Isaac (1642-ca. 1706), went to Schenectady, 1670; taken prisoner to Can. during Buckendal massacre, 1690; *m* Maria Williamse Brouwer (William[9], in Beverwyck, 1657);
7–Abraham (1683-1770), began to write name Truax; lt. in colonial war, 1733; *m* ante 1712, Christina DeLaGrange (1695-1773; Gillis[8], *m* Jane Molenaer);
6–Philip (bap. 1720), Schenectady; *m* 1747, Angelica Fairly (*b* 1726; Johannes[7], *m* Metje, dau. of Jan Pieterse Mebie);
5–John P. (bap. 1755-1817), *m* 1780, Cornelia Barheydt (bap. 1761-1827; Cornelius[6], *m* Rachel Yates);
4–Angelica (bap. 1785-1837), *m* Cornelius A. **Groot** (4 above).
10–Rev. Thomas **Weld** (qv);
9–Thomas (1626-82), *m* 1650, Dorothy Whiting (1628-94; Rev. Samuel[10], qv);
8–Joseph (*b* 1666), *m* Sarah–;
7–Daniel (1697-1761), *m* 1720, Elizabeth Tucker (1701-84);
6–Noah (*b* 1725);
5–Elizabeth (1752-1802), *m* 1773, Benjamin **Knower** (1754-1806), Am. Rev. (Daniel[6], French and Indian War and Am. Rev., *m* Abigail Whittemore);
4–Samuel (1793-1839), *m* 1814, Maria Donnelly (1793-1829; Thomas[5], Am. Rev., *m* Ruth Pettenger; Peter[6], colonial wars and Am. Rev.);
3–Sarah (1819-83), *m* Abraham C. **Groot** (3 above);
2–Cornelius Abraham (1837-97), grad. Union Coll., 1862; M.D., Albany Med. Coll., 1864; asst. surgeon, Civil War; physician and surgeon; Mason; Baptist; *m* 1865, Anna Maria Stevens (1845-1905); issue: I–Stella Alice (*b* and *d* 1866); II–Edith Stevens (1868-1922); III–Sarah Louise (1873-1906; *m* Harry Prescott Hoskins); IV–Mary E. Knower (*m* Francis Edward O'Brien, M.D.); V–Georgiana (1 above); VI–Abraham Cornelius (*m* Helen Barney; *m* 2d, Belle Kiley); VII–William Marcy (1878-96).
1–*m* Sept. 14, 1898, Henry Hotchkiss Murray, *b* Viola, Del., Mar. 16, 1871; son of George Henry Murray, of Viola, Del., *m* Olive I. Purinton, issue: 1–Cornelia Groot, *b* Riverton, N.J., Aug. 5, 1912.
1–Mem. D.F.P.A., Huguenot Soc. of N.J., D.A.C., D.A.R., U.S.D. 1812, N.E.H.G. Soc., N.J. Hist. Soc., Burlington Co. Hist. Soc. Residence: Riverton, N.J.

1–**NASH, Elizabeth Todd,** *b* Madison, Conn., Oct. 25, 1864.
8–Thomas **Nash** (qv);
7–Lt. Timothy (1626-99), Hadley, Mass.; lt. of militia; rep. Gen. Ct.; *m* 1657, Rebeckah Stone (ante 1641-1709; Rev. Samuel[8], came in the "Griffin," 1633, a founder of Hartford, 1636, chaplain in Pequot War);
6–Lt. John (1667-1743), rep. Gen. Ct., 1701-31; *m* 2d, 1691, Elizabeth Kellogg (1673-1750; Lt. Joseph[7], qv);
5–Samuel (*b* 1709), *m* 1734, Margaret Merrill (1709-59);
4–William (1743-1821), New Haven, Vt.; *m* 1766, Susannah Phelps (1748-1819; Lt. David[5]);
3–Col. David (1774-1852), *m* 1804, Elizabeth (Todd) Wilcox (1782-1849; Timothy Todd[4]);
2–John Wilcox (2 below).
9–John (called "John of Hartford") **Wilcox** (qv);
8–John (*d* 1676), soldier in Pequot War; *m* 2d, 1650, Catherine Stoughton (Thomas[9]);
7–Israel (1656-89), *m* 1677/78, Sarah Savage (1657-1723/24; John[8], *m* Elizabeth Dubbin);
6–Thomas (1687-1726), *m* Anna North (John[7]);
5–Thomas (1720-78), *m* 1744, Freelove Bradley (Stephen[6]);
4–Jonathan (1752-1818), Am. Rev.; *m* Elizabeth Todd (Timothy[5], Am. Rev.);
3–Col. Jonathan Samuel (1791-1875), was host to LaFayette at Madison, Conn.; *m* 1815, Chloe Hand;
2–Catherine Artemesia (2 below).
9–John **Hand** (qv);
8–Joseph (1638-1724), leading mem. of Guilford Colony, 1670-1724; *m* Jane Wright (Benjamin[9], 1610-77);
7–Joseph (1671-1699), sea capt.; lost at sea; *m* Esther Wilcox (1673-98);
6–Jannah (1693-1767), *m* Dorothy Griswold (1693-1775; John[7]);
5–Daniel (1732-1816), capt. Am. Rev.; *m* Siba Smith (*d* 1772; Elnathan[6]);
4–Daniel (1762-1821), *m* Artemesia Meigs (1777-1812; Daniel[5]);
3–Chloe (1791-1875), *m* Jonathan S. **Wilcox** (3 above);
2–Catherine Artemesia (1824-1903), *m* 1856, John Wilcox **Nash** (1823-82), mfr.; issue: I–Frances J. (*b* 1858; *m* George W. King, *d* 1929); II–Daniel Hand (1860-67); III–Catherine Gertrude (1862-1904); IV–Elizabeth Todd (1 above); V–Alice M. (1868-1904).
1–Ed. Lee's Acad., Madison, Conn., and N.E. Conservatory of Music, Boston. Hist. writer and genealogist. Author: Fifty Puritan Ancestors, 1902. Mem. D.F.P.A., D.A.R., etc. Residence: "Meadowbrook," Madison, Conn.

1–**NELSON, Ida Frances Wyman (Mrs. Henry L.),** *b* Brooklyn, N.Y., Nov. 2, 1851.
7–Francis **Wyman** (qv);
6–Benjamin (1674-1735), *m* Elizabeth Hancock (*b* 1686?), of Cambridge;
5–Benjamin (1706-74), *m* 1st, Esther Richardson;
4–Benjamin (1739 or 1740-1774), *m* Elizabeth Swain;
3–Benjamin (1767-1836), *m* Hannah Boynton (Lt. Joseph[4], minute man at Battle of Lexington, and served later in Cont. Army, *m* Sarah Tarbell, of Groton);
2–Luther Boynton (2 below).
8–Samuel **Hale** (1603-93), from Eng. ante 1637; settled at Hartford, Conn.; *m* Mary–;
7–Thomas (1653-1723), *m* Naomi Kilborn;
6–Thomas (1684-1750), *m* Mercy–; *m* 2d, Susannah Smith;
5–Moses (*b* 1728), of Rutland, Vt.; *m* Mary Edwards (David[6], of Middletown, Conn.);
4–William (1767-1809), *m* Sarah Perry, of Rutland;
3–William Hiram (1799-1839), *m* Mary Bowen Cooke (Thomas[4], of Providence, R.I., *m* Sarah Hall).
2–Luther Boynton **Wyman** (1804-79), shipping merchant; *m* 1831(?), Cecilia Warren (*d* 1847); *m* 2d, 1849, Frances Ann Hale (1826-1901); issue (1st marriage): I–Benjamin Franklin (*d* 1907; *m* Mary Anderson; *m* 2d, Mary Greene); II–Helen Cobb (1838-1911; *m* William H. Mallory); III–Luther Boynton, Jr. (1843-71); IV–Cecil Augustus (1847-95; *m* Esther Williams); issue (2d marriage): I–Ida Frances (1 above); II–Leon Hale (1856-1920; *m* Emma Marshall).
1–*m* Oct. 14, 1873, Henry Loomis Nelson (1846-1908); son of Theophilus Nelson, of Brooklyn, *m* Catherine Lyons; issue: 1–Madelon Wyman, *b* 1874; *m* Oct. 24, 1895, Lt. James Marks Williams, U.S.A. (*d* 1922; issue: Elinor Forniss, *b* West Point, N.Y., 1897; *m* 1927, Frederick Newborn Fisk); 2–Melville Egleston (1875-84); 3–George Lyons (1877-80); 4–Eileen White (1882-87); 5–Rose Hawthorne (*b* and *d* 1887).
1–Residence: Canterbury Hotel, 750 Sutter St., San Francisco, Calif.

1–**NELSON, William Bonneau,** *b* Stateburg, S.C., July 16, 1871.
7–Col. Moses **Thomson,** of Irish descent; removed from Pa. to Amelia Tp., Orangeburg Dist. S.C., 1730; col. or lt. col.; justice; *m* Jane–;
6–Gen. William (1727-96), capt. of rangers, 1750-59; and for services in the Cherokee War was promoted to maj.; col. 1765; mem. S.C. Assembly, 1765-69; mem. 1st Provincial Congress of S.C., 1775; brig. gen., Mar. 1, 1776; *m* 1755, Eugenia Russell (1737-1809; Capt. Charles[7], *m* Mary Heatly);
5–Col. William Russell (1761-1807), lt., 3d S.C. Regt., Cont. line, resigned Oct. 1778; col. militia; *m* 1783, Elizabeth Sabb (1761-1838);
4–Charlotte, *m* Derrill Hart, M.D.; *m* 2d, Col. Robert Howell **Goodwyn**;
3–Caroline (Goodwyn), *m* William Bonneau **Murray** (see Vol. I, p. 419, for Murray-Bonneau lineage);

2-Charlotte Thompson (*b* 1848), *m* 1869, Samuel Edgar **Nelson** (1844-1900); issue: I-William B. (1 above); II-Sarah Robinson (*b* 1873; *m* 1908, Nelson Burgess Murray); III-Caroline Goodwyn (*b* 1875; *m* 1904, Frank Hilton McLeod, M.D.); IV-Van der Horst Guignard (*b* 1878; *m* 1909, Mary Thompson Richardson); V-Emma Jane (*b* 1882; *m* 1927, Joseph James Murray); VI-Charlotte Thompson (*b* 1888; *m* 1911, Jenkins Mikell Pope, M.D.).
1-*m* Nov. 11, 1903, Mary Virginia Anderson (qv); issue: 1-Samuel Edgar, *b* at Stateburg, S.C., Aug. 3, 1904; 2-Mary Virginia, *b* Charleston, S.C., Mar. 1, 1906; 3-William Bonneau, *b* Stateburg, Sept. 1, 1908; 4-Catherine Elizabeth, *b* Montgomery, Ala., Sept. 9, 1911; 5-William Wallace, *b* Montgomery, Nov. 5, 1913.
1-Residence: 534 Cloverdale Rd., Montgomery, Ala.

1-**NELSON, Mary Virginia Anderson (Mrs. William B.),** *b* Stateburg, S.C., Oct. 26, 1872.
8-John **Briscoe** (qv);
7-Col. Philip (1648-1724), of St. Mary's, Charles Co., Md.; burgess, 1699-1700; justice Charles Co. Ct., 1694-1701; *m* 1st, Susanna Swann (*d* 1740; Col. Samuel[8]);
6-Edward (*d* 1725), *m* Susanna Gerard;
5-Priscilla, *m* 1750, Richard **Anderson** (*d* 1778), of Charles Co., Md.;
4-Col. Richard (1752-1835), col., 7th Md. Line, Am. Rev.; *m* 1787, Ann Wallace (1768-1814; William[5]);
3-Dr. William Wallace (1789-1864), Sumter Co., S.C.; *m* Mary Jane Mackenzie (1788-1832), see Vol. I, p. 419, for Mackenzie lineage;
2-Dr. William Wallace (2 below).
9-Samuel (Child) **Childs** (*d* 1676), from Eng. to Plymouth Colony, ca. 1620; killed by Indians;
8-Richard (*b* 1624), *m* 1649, Mary (Linnett) Linnell (Robert[9], from Eng., 1638);
7-Dea. Richard (*b* 1653), *m* 1679, Elizabeth Crocker (*b* 1660; John[8], *m* 1st, 1659, Mary Bodfish; William[9], qv);
6-Timothy (*b* 1686), began to write name Childs; *m* 1714, Hannah (Chapin) Sheldon (Japhet Chapin[7], Springfield, Mass., *m* Abilenah, dau. of Samuel Cooley, of Milford; Dea. Samuel[8], qv);
5-Capt. Timothy (*b* 1720), *m* 1744, Mary Wells (Jonathan[6], ens., Father Rastle's war, selectman Deerfield; Jonathan[7], boy hero, Turners' Falls Fight, selectman, Deerfield);
4-Lt. Timothy, M.D. (1748-1824), lt. and surgeon, Am. Rev. and War 1812; mem. Mass. Legislature; *m* Rachel **Easton;**
3-Thomas (1796-1853), U.S.M.A., 1813; served War 1812, and Mexican War; col. U.S.A. and bvt. brig. gen.; *m* 1819, Ann Eliza Coryton (Josiah[4]);
2-Mary Virginia (2 below).
9-Eltweed **Pomeroy** (qv);
8-Medad (1638-1716), town clk., Northampton, Mass.; mem. Gen. Assembly; asso. justice, Hampshire Co.; commr. to United Colonies; *m* 1st, 1661, Experience Woodward (*d* 1686; Henry[9], from Eng., 1639);
7-Ebenezer (1669-1754), sheriff, Hampshire Co.; mem. Royal Council; capt.; maj.; *m* 2d, Sarah King (1671-1747; Capt. John[8]);
6-John (1695-1736), capt. Indian wars; *m* 1718, Rachel Sheldon (1701-74);
5-Eunice (bap. 1733-*d* 1778), *m* 1753, James **Easton** (bap. 1728-*d* 1796), col. Am. Rev. (Joseph[6]; Joseph[7], from Eng.);
4-Rachel (*b* 1760), *m* 1778, Dr. Timothy **Childs** (4 above);
3-Thomas, *m* Ann E. Coryton (3 above);
2-Mary Virginia (1833-1912), *m* 1855, Dr. William Wallace **Anderson** (1824-1911), maj. and ranking surgeon from S.C. in C.S.A.; issue: I-Elizabeth Waties (*m* Mark Reynolds); II-Ann Catherine (Mrs. William L. Saunders [Oct. 8, 1864-June 25, 1928], see Vol. I, p. 419); III-William Wallace (see Vol. I, p. 419); IV-Mary V. (1 above); V-Benjamin Mackenzie (*d* Apr. 12, 1929; see Vol. I, p. 419).
1-*m* Nov. 11, 1903, William Bonneau Nelson (qv for issue).
1-Mem. C.D.A., D.A.R., U.D.C. Residence: 534 Cloverdale Rd., Montgomery, Ala.

1-**NEWBERRY, Truman Handy,** *b* Detroit, Mich., Nov. 5, 1864.
9-Thomas **Newberry** (qv);
8-Maj. Benjamin (1624-89), *m* 1646, Mary Allyn (1628-89; Matthew[9], qv);
7-Thomas (1657-88), *m* 1676, Ann Ford;
6-Sgt. Joseph (1684-1751), *m* 1708, Sarah Loomis (*b* 1689; Jonathan[7] [1664-1707], of Windsor, *m* 1688, Sarah, dau. of George Graves; Nathaniel[8] [1626-88], mem. Windsor Troop of Horse, King Philip's War, *m* 1653, Elizabeth, dau. Dea. John Moore; Joseph[9], qv);
5-Benjamin (1721-1804), *m* 1745, Jerusha Stoughton;
4-Capt. Amasa (1752-1835), soldier Am. Rev.; *m* 1784, Ruth Warner;
3-Elihu (1788-1860), *m* 1815, Rhoda Phelps;
2-John Stoughton (2 below).
8-Richard (Hendee) **Handy** (1611-70), came in the "Hopewell," 1634, was at Norwich and Killingsworth, Conn.; *m* 1661, Hannah Elderkin;
7-Richard (*d* 1759), *m* 1734, Anna Parmelee (1717-1803);
6-Jairus (*b* 1734), *m* 1755, Naomi Ward (1737-1821);
5-William (1760-1823), Am. Rev.; *m* 2d, 1786, Martha Parker (1764-1843);
4-William (1787-1869), *m* 1806, Eunice Parmelee;
3-Truman Parmelee (1807-98), banker, Cleveland, O.; *m* 1832, Harriet Newcomb Hall;
2-Helen Parmelee (1835-1912), *m* 1859 as his 2d wife, John Stoughton **Newberry** (1826-87), A.B., U.Mich., '45; lawyer and mfr.; mem. 46th Congress (for issue see Vols. I and III).
1-*m* Feb. 7, 1888, Harriet Josephine Barnes (qv for genealogy); issue: 1-Carol Barnes, *b* Detroit, Nov. 7, 1888; *m* June 19, 1912, Frank Wilkes Brooks, Jr. (issue: Frank Wilkes, III, *b* Mar. 29, 1913; Oliver Newberry, *b* Oct. 30, 1916); 2-Barnes (twin), *b* Detroit, Dec. 8, 1891; *m* June 28, 1915, Elizabeth Goddard Binney (issue: Elizabeth Goddard, *b* July 3, 1918; Helen Barnes, *b* Sept. 15, 1920; Barnes, Jr., *b* June 29, 1921; Carol Hope, *b* June 1925-*d* Nov. 1925; William Binney, *b* Feb. 6, 1928); 3-Phelps (twin), *m* Jan. 18, 1916, Christina Muir Van-Husen (issue: Phelps, Jr., *b* May 29, 1918; Truman Handy, II, *b* Dec. 21, 1922; Christina Muir, IV, *b* Apr. 1, 1925).
1-Ph.B., Yale-S., '85 (M.A., 1910). Mfr. and capitalist, Detroit. Lt. (j.g.), U.S.N., on bd. U.S.S. Yosemite, Spanish-Am. War, col. and a.-d.-c. on staff of gov. of Mich., 1899; lt. cdr., U.S.N. R.F., June 6, 1917, and asst. to comdt. 3d Naval Dist., New York. Asst. sec. of the navy, 1905-08; Sec. of the Navy, Dec. 1, 1908-Mar. 6, 1909, in Cabinet of President Roosevelt; U.S. senator from Mich., 1919-23 (see Who's Who in America). Mem. S.C.W. Clubs: Union, University, N.Y. Yacht, St. Anthony (New York), Chicago (Chicago), Yondotega, Detroit (Detroit). Residence: Grosse Pointe Farms, Mich.

1-**NEWBERRY, Harriet Josephine Barnes (Mrs. Truman H.).**
8-William **Barnes** (*d* 1699), from Eng. to Easthampton, L.I., 1644; several tracts of land were allotted to him, 1653; *m* Elizabeth-;
7-Stephen, of Branford, Conn., 1700; *m* Mary Barnes;
6-Stephen, *m* Martha Whedon;
5-Asa (1745-1819), of Southington, Conn.; served in Am. Rev.; mem. of numerous coms.; *m* Phebe Adkins;
4-Eli (*d* 1827), Barnesville, Conn.; *m* 1812, Susan (Morris) Bradley;
3-Alfred Smith (1817-88), founder A. S. Barnes & Co., pub. of New York; *m* 1st, 1841, Harriet Elizabeth Burr (Gen. Timothy[4], War 1812; Timothy[5], soldier Am. Rev.; desc. Benjamin Burr [*d* 1681], soldier in Pequot War);
2-Alfred Cutler (2 below).
9-Thomas **Morris** (qv);
8-Eleazer (1648-1710), *m* Anna Osborn (*b* 1663);
7-James (*b* 1686), *m* 1715, Abigail Rowe (*b* 1689);
6-Amos (1726-1801), officer Am. Rev.; *m* Lydia Camp;
5-Amos (1750-1801), soldier Am. Rev.; *m* Betsey Woodward;
4-Susan (1784-1854), *m* Eli **Barnes** (4 above);
3-Alfred Smith, *m* Harriet Elizabeth Burr (3 above);
2-Alfred Cutler, *m* Josephine E. Richardson.
1-*m* Feb. 7, 1888, Truman Handy Newberry (qv for issue).
Residence: Grosse Pointe Farms, Mich.

1–**NEWCOMB, Harry Turner,** *b* Owosso, Mich., Jan. 4, 1867.
8–Edward **Turner** (1633-1717), *m* 1656, Mary Sanford (Richard^{9}, *m* Margery–, of Boston);
7–John (*b* 1669), *m* Susanna Merrills (John^{8}, *m* Sarah Watson);
6–John (*b* 1703), *m* 1726, Abigail Richards (Dea. Thomas^{7}, *m* Mary Parsons);
5–Samuel (*b* 1730), *m* Sarah–;
4–Josiah (*b* 1776), *m* Mary Doherty or Daugherty;
3–Josiah (1811-1907), *m* 1835, Eveline Ellsworth;
2–Lucia (2 below).
8–Josiah **Ellsworth** (qv);
7–Thomas (1665-1750);
6–William (1702-59), *m* 1737, Mary Oliver, of Boston;
5–Oliver (1747-1821), *m* Mehitable Warner;
4–Dr. William Chauncey (*b* 1778), *m* 1st, Bethana Johnson;
3–Eveline (1817-85), *m* Josiah **Turner** (3 above);
2–Lucia, *m* Henry Martyn **Newcomb** (1831-1918), see Vol. I, p. 741, for Newcomb lineage, and issue.
1–*m* Oct. 11, 1893, Lucy Theodora Comstock, *b* Owosso, Mich., May 11, 1869; dau. John E. Comstock, of Owosso (his g.g.father, lt. John Comstock, 1734-1776, was killed at battle of White Plains); issue: 1–Comstock (Jan. 31, 1895-Aug. 16, 1901); 2–Ellsworth, *b* Washington, D.C., Dec. 16, 1899; *m* Mar. 4, 1922, Lt. James Clark McGuire; 3–Winifred Wheeler, *b* Wayne, Pa., Sept. 5, 1901; *m* Oct. 8, 1921, Lt. Armon D. A. Crawford, U.S.N.; 4–Josiah Turner, *b* Kensington, Md., Sept. 24, 1903; *m* July 12, 1926, Ann E. Bookhout; 5–Lucy Lamson, *b* Kensington, Dec. 17, 1904; *m* Oct. 21, 1927, Donald Stillwell Warman; 6–Maryland, *b* Bethesda, Md., June 26, 1907; *m* June 27, 1925, Malcom Murray Brigham; 7–Holly, *b* Bethesda, Aug. 20, 1908; 8–Simone, and 9–Janet (twins), *b* Bethesda, Feb. 6, 1910; 10–Harry Turner, 2d, *b* Bethesda, Oct. 12, 1911.
1–LL.B., Columbian, 1891, LL.M., 1892. V.p. and gen. counsel, D. & H. R.R. (see Who's Who in America). Mem. S.C.W. Clubs: Metropolitan, City, Bankers (New York), Cosmos, University (Washington). Residences: "Holly Farms," New Preston, Conn., and Rye, N.Y.

1–**NEWCOMER, Caroline Annie Stoddard (Mrs. Jesse D.),** *b* Litchfield, Conn., June 13, 1857.
9–John **Stoddard** (1620-64), from Eng.; settled at Wethersfield, Conn., ante 1645; sergeant; juror, 1642-43; *m* Mary Foote (ca. 1623-post 1685);
8–John (1646-1703), *m* Elizabeth Curtis (*d* 1679);
7–John (1674 or 75-1727), Litchfield, Conn.; *m* Sarah Camp (1677-1742);
6–Moses (1700 or 01-1777), *m* Ruth Goodwin (1707-77);
5–Obed (1743-77), in Battle of L.I., and White Plains, Am. Rev.; *m* Mary Harrison (*b* 1747; Ens. Gideon^{6});
4–Gideon (1768-1846), *m* Anna Kilbourne (1767-1843);
3–William (1804-84), Tama, Ia.; *m* Betsey Henderson (1810-74), Exeter, N.H.;
2–Albert (1829-70), Toledo, Ia.; *m* Delia E. McCall (1833-97); issue: I–Caroline A. (1 above); II–Charles Allen (1858-1924); III–Albert Levi (1860-1909; *m* Viola M. Dow).
1–*m* at Marion, Ia., Jesse D. Newcomer, *b* Connellsville, Pa., Jan. 18, 1845; son of John Newcomer, of Connellsville, and Toledo, Ia.; issue: 1–Carl Stoddard, *b* Eldora, Ia., Apr. 7, 1878; *m* Mabel Brewer; *m* 2d, Eleanor Alexander McClain; 2–Jay Stoddard, *b* Eldora, Dec. 27, 1879; *m* June Gertrude Porter.
1–Taught sch., 3 yrs. Mem. Congl. Ch. choir 54 yrs. Mem. D.F.P.A., D.A.R. (chaplain Ia. soc.). Republican. Clubs: Woman's, Treble Clef, Garden. Residence: Eldora, Ia.

1–**NEWHALL, John Breed,** *b* Lynn, Mass., Oct. 1, 1862.
9–Allen **Breed** (qv);
8–Allen (*b* 1626), *m* ante 1660, Mary– (*d* 1671);
7–Samuel (1669-1755), *m* 1691/92, Anna Hood (*b* 1672; Richard^{8}, *m* Mary, dau. of Anthony Newhall);
6–Jabez (1695/96-1778), *m* 1723, Desiah Bassett (John^{7}, *m* Abigail, dau. of Thaddeus Berry; William^{8}; William^{9});
5–Nathan (1726-1803), *m* 1754, Kezia Buxton (James^{6}, *m* Elizabeth–; John^{7}; Anthony^{8}, from Eng., at Salem, 1637);
4–Kezia (1765-1849), *m* 1787, Rufus **Newhall** (Ephraim^{5}, *m* Abigail Denmark; Joseph^{6}; Corpl. Thomas^{7}; Thomas^{8});
3–John (1788-1865), *m* 1817, Delia Breed;
2–Charles (2 below).
9–George (Puddington) **Purinton** (*d* post 1649), from Eng.; was at York, Me., 1640; alderman, 1641; *m* Mary–, she was licensed to sell wine, 1649; she *m* 2d, ante 1661, Capt. John Davis, of York;
8–John (*d* ca. 1692), removed to Cape Porpoise; recd. grant, 1681; town clk.; selectman, 1690; *m* Mary (Hussey?);
7–James (ca. 1663-1718), lost at sea; *m* Lydia– (ca. 1671-1737);
6–John, husbandman of Salisbury; *m* 1720, Theodate Swett (1695/96-1738; Moses^{7}; Capt. Benjamin^{8}; John^{9});
5–James (1723-1811), cordwainer; *m* 1746, Anna Breed (*b* 1726; Samuel^{6}, of Lynn, Mass.; Samuel^{7}; Allen^{8}; Allen^{9}, qv);
4–Theodate (1749-1836), *m* Samuel **Breed** (1747-1836);
3–Delia (1789-1863), *m* John **Newhall** (3 above).
8–Michael **Emerson** (qv);
7–Jonathan (1669-1736), of Haverhill, comd. a garrison against the Indians, 1690, 1701; with John Swan, set up a grist mill, 1705; chmn. bd. selectmen, 1708; a grantee of Chester, N.H.; *m* 1699, Hannah Day (John^{8}, *m* Sarah, dau. of Moses Pingry; Robert^{9}, qv);
6–Nathaniel (1703-ante 1741), *m* 1728, Mehitabel Eastman (*b* 1701; Jonathan^{7}, *m* Hannah, dau. of Peter Green; Thomas^{8}; Roger^{9}, qv);
5–Samuel (1736-1819), to Plymouth, N.H., 1770; selectman, 27 yrs.; mem. Com. Safety and muster-master, Am. Rev., town clk.; del. Provincial Congress; rep.; del. 2d Constl. Conv., 1781; co. treas.; justice Ct. of Common Pleas; chief justice, Grafton Co.; *m* 1763, Mary Little (1742-1815; Nathan^{6}, *m* Hannah, dau. Nathaniel Mighill; Moses^{7}; Capt. Joseph^{8} George^{9}, qv);
4–Samuel (1768-1842), Rumney, N.H.; *m* 1797, Virtue Spencer (*b* 1775; Hobart^{5}, *m* Eunice, dau. William Barnes; Maj. Gen. Joseph^{6}, Am. Rev.; Dea. Isaac^{7}; Samuel^{8}; Jared^{9}; Jared^{10});
3–Euphemia Celia (1802-88), *m* 1829, Benjamin **Moulton**;
2–Hester Celia (1834-91), *m* 1856, Charles **Newhall** (1826-67); issue: I–John Breed (1857-1861); II–Hattie Celia (1859-1861); III–Avis Ella (1861-1865); IV–John Breed (1 above); V–Hattie Celia (1864-1927).
1–*m* Dec. 6, 1893, Gertrude J. Cutler, *b* San Francisco, Calif., July 21, 1872; dau. of Elijah Boardman Cutler, of San Francisco; issue (all *b* Lynn, Mass.): 1–Hester Moulton, *b* Oct. 19, 1894; Radcliffe Coll., '16; *m* 1917, Benjamin Beuhring, son of James Frederick Brown, of Charleston, W.Va. (issue: Gertrude Woodbridge; James Frederick; Benjamin Beuhring; Elizabeth Newhall); 2–Avis Edna, *b* Sept. 1, 1896; Ed. Garland Sch. for Home-making; 3–Frances Ella, *b* Nov. 12, 1898; Simmons Coll., '20; *m* Donald Kent, son of Rev. Benjamin Mead Wright, of Greenwich, Conn. (issue: Benjamin Mead; Emily Jane; Priscilla); 4–Charles Boardman, *b* June 8, 1902; Harvard, '23; Harvard Law Sch., 1926.
1–Harvard, '85; Harvard Law Sch., 1888. Has been pres. Lynn Common Council, mem. Lynn Sch. Bd., mem. Mass. Legislature; trustee and v.p. of Lynn Inst. for Savings; sec. Bd. of Trade, 1891; trustee Lynn Pub. Library 1891; treas. Lynn Home for Aged Women. Universalist. Republican. Club: Oxford. Residence: 23 Atlantic St., Lynn, Mass.

1–**NICKLIN, Benjamin Patten,** *b* Chattanooga, Tenn., Jan. 24, 1873.
11–George **Calvert** (1579-1632), 1st Lord Baltimore, *m* 1st, 1604, Anne (1579-1622), dau. of George Mynne;
10–Leonard (1606-47), came with the "Ark" and the "Dove," expdn., 1633; gov. of Md., 1633-47; *m* Anne, dau. of Richard Brent;
9–William (1642-82), dep. gov. and prin. sec. of Md., 1669-82; *m* Elizabeth Stone (Gov. William^{10}, of Md.);
8–George (*b* 1666), *m* 1688, Elizabeth Doyne;
7–John (1690-1739), *m* Elizabeth Harrison, of Va.;

6–George (1712-82), burgess; capt. Am. Rev.; *m* 1st, 1740, Anne Crupper (Richard[7]);
5–John (1742-90), *m* 2d, 1772, Helen Bailey (John[6], of "Hunting Ridge," Baltimore Co., Md.; George[7]);
4–Elizabeth (1777-1833), *m* 1802, Capt. Joseph **Nicklin** (1776-1853);
3–John Bailey (1803-91), *m* 1830, Catherine T. Pendleton;
2–John Bailey, II (2 below).
12–William **Strother,** of Newton, Northumberland, Eng.; *m* Agnes, dau. of Sir Thomas Grey;
11–William, of Newton; *m* Jane, dau. of John Selby, of Twysell;
10–Lancelot (*d* 1611), of Towberry Towers; *m* Elinor (*b* 1570), dau. of John Conyers, of Sockhurne;
9–William (1598-1667), had Tythe of Akeld for life and was known as of Kirknewton;
8–William (1630-1702), came to Sittingbourne Parish, Rappahannock Co., Va., 1664; *m* Dorothy Savage (*d* post 1716);
7–William (1673-1726), sheriff; capt. and vestryman of King George Co., Va.; *m* Margaret Thornton (*b* 1678; Lt. Col. Francis[8], *m* Alice, dau. of Capt. Anthony Savage, of Gloucester Co., Va.,);
6–Anthony (1710-65), *m* Behethland Storke (see Vol. II, p. 187);
5–Benjamin (1750-1807), midshipman in Cont. Navy; *m* 1778, Catherine Price (see Vol. III, p. 351);
4–Elizabeth (1784-1822), *m* Benjamin **Pendleton** (see Vol. I, p. 743);
3–Catherine T. (1806-74), *m* John B. **Nicklin** (3 above);
2–John Bailey **Nicklin,** II (1843-1919), pvt. and drum maj. Pa. troops, 1861-65; mayor of Chattanooga, Tenn., 1887-89; Mason (33°); *m* 1871, Elizabeth Kaylor (1850-1925); issue: I–Benjamin Patten (1 above); II–Dwight Pendleton (see Vol. I, p. 743); III–Samuel Strang; IV–John Bailey, III (see Vol. I, p. 743, and Vol. II, p. 187).
1–*m* Oct. 31, 1910, Margaret Anne Peele Hayes, *b* O'Fallon, Ill., Sept. 17, 1885; dau. of James Hayes, *m* Ida Helen Soothoff.
1–Ed. public schools; grad. Inf. and Cav. School, 1903. Pvt., corpl., sgt., Troop I, 1st Cav., U.S.A., Jan. 22, 1895-July 6, 1898; 2d lt., June 22, 1898; 1st lt., Mar. 2, 1899; capt., July 29, 1903; maj., May 15, 1917; lt. col. (temp.), Aug. 5, 1917-June 12, 1918; col. N.A., May 11, 1918-Mar. 31, 1920; col. U.S.A., July 1, 1920. Silver star citation. Participated in Indian campaigns, Spanish-Am. War, Philippine Insurrection, Mexican Expdn., Boxer Rebellion, World War. Mem. Soc. Ark and the Dove, D.C.G., S.C.W., S.C., S.A.R., Am. Clan Gregor Soc., M.O.F.W., U.S.W.V., Soc. Dragon, Mil. Order Carabao, Order Spanish-Am. War, A.L., etc. Clubs: Army and Navy (Washington and Manila). Residence: 516 Poplar St., Chattanooga, Tenn.

1–**NIMS, Norman Granville,** *b* Keene, N.H., Aug. 24, 1868.
8–Godfrey **Nims** (ca. 1650-1705), from France, 1667, settled at Northampton, later at Deerfield, Mass.; *m* 1677, Mary (Miller) Williams (*d* 1688; William Miller[9]);
7–Ebenezer (1687-ca. 1760), of Deerfield; *m* Sarah Hoyt (1686-1761);
6–David (1716-1803), first settler at Keene, N.H.; *m* 1742, Abigail Hawks (1719-99);
5–David (1742-1826), Roxbury, N.H.; *m* 1768, Jemima Carter (1747-1832), of Lancaster, Mass.;
4–Matthew (1773-1849), *m* 1802, Lucy Brown (1778-1871), of Swansey, N.H.;
3–John Gilman (1813-83), *m* 1843, Charlotte K. Stone (1817-1900; Oliver[4]; John[5]; Oliver[6]; Simon[7]; Simon[8]; Simon[9]; Simon[10], qv);
2–Albert Gilman (2 below).
6–James **Thompson** (ca. 1671-1755), from Ireland, ca. 1718, settled at Holden, Mass.; *m* ca. 1700, Jeannette– (ca. 1667-1744);
5–Samuel (ca. 1700-1756), *m* 2d, 1727, Margaret Clark (1706-88);
4–Thomas (1742-1813), Keene, N.H.; *m* 2d, 1782, Sarah Scott;
3–Daniel (1794-1876), *m* 1822, Sally Putnam;
2–Harriet Augusta (2 below).
7–John **Scott** (*d* ante 1722), first mentioned at Roxbury, Mass., in 1672; in King Philip's War at the storming of the Narragansett stronghold, 1675, one of the few survivors; *m* 1672, Mary Duncan (1651-ca. 1722);
6–Joseph (*b* 1682), *m* 2d, 1708, Hannah Prior;
5–Benjamin (1725-ca. 1806), *m* 2d, 1757, Azubah Cheney;
4–Sarah (1758-1840), *m* Thomas **Thompson** (4 above).
9–John **Putnam** (qv);
8–Thomas (1615-86), *m* 1st, 1643, Ann Holyoke (*d* 1665);
7–Edward (1654-1747), *m* 1681, Mary Hale;
6–Joseph (1687-1773), *m* 1721, Lydia Flint;
5–Oliver (1722-bet. 1789-94), pvt. Am. Rev.; *m* 1743, Hannah Brown;
4–William (1744-1800), *m* 1766, Bethiah Putnam (1748-1813; desc. Nathaniel Putnam, brother of John, 9 above);
3–Sally (1799-1882), *m* Daniel **Thompson** (3 above);
2–Harriet Augusta (1843-1928), *m* 1866, Albert Gilman **Nims** (1844-92), farmer; issue: I–Norman Granville (1 above); II–Walter Thompson (*b* 1870; *m* Sarah Emma Barrett); III–Stella Harriet (1873-83); IV–Lester Albert (1880-1905).
1–*m* **Sept. 9, 1896, Elizabeth Maria Cass (June 21,** 1868-Feb. 16, 1925); dau. of Francis B. Cass, of Keene, N.H.; issue: 1–Elinor (qv for Cass lineage).
1–*m* 2d, Sept. 17, 1927, Mildred Anna Willey, *b* Boston, Dec. 20, 1891; dau. of Wheelock Willey, of Saugus, Mass.
1–S.B. in Architecture, M.I.T., '90. With firms of Andrews, Jaques & Rantoul, Boston and Chicago, McKim, Mead & White, New York, Carrere & Hastings, New York; associate mem. York & Sawyer, New York, architects. Councilman, Malden, Mass., 1902. Mem. Chamber of Commerce, Hist. Soc. of Cheshire Co., Keene, N.H. Republican. Clubs: Technology, Transportation (New York). Residence: 9 Livingston Av., Yonkers, N.Y.

1–**NIMS, Elinor,** *b* Malden, Mass., May 20, 1898.
10–John **Cass** (ca. 1620-1675), from Eng. ca. 1644, settled at Hampton, N.H.; *m* 1647 or 48, Martha Philbrick;
9–Samuel (*b* 1659), *m* 1681, Mercy Sanborn (*b* 1660);
8–John (*b* 1687), Mendon, Mass.; *m* 1712, Hannah Gove;
7–Daniel (1722-98), one of first settlers, Richmond, N.H., 1762; served Am. Rev.; *m* 1744, Mary Cook;
6–Jonathan (1756-1838), *m* 1779, Zilpah Martin (*d* 1798);
5–Martin (*b* 1781), *m* Margaret Allen;
4–Josiah Brigham (1810-66), Swansey, N.H.; *m* 1831, Eliza Willis;
3–Francis Brigham (1832-1902), *m* 1855, Cynthia Southwick Bolles;
2–Elizabeth Maria (1868-1925), *m* 1896, Norman Granville **Nims** (qv).
1–A.B., Vassar, '19 (Pi Gamma Mu); N.Y. Sch. of Social Work, 1924-25; Ph.D., U.Chicago, 1926. Agent, dept. of child welfare, Westchester Co., N.Y., 1919-23; instr. sociology, U.Ky., 1926-27; instr. social economy, Grad. Sch. of Social Service Administration of U.Chicago, 1927-28; asst. prof. and actg. head of sociology dept., U.Ky., 1928-29; instr. dept. child welfare, Sch. of Applied Social Sciences of Western Reserve U., 1929-30. Mem. A.A.U.W. Presbyterian. Republican. Residence: 2117 Adelbert Rd., Cleveland, O.

1–**NOBLE, Lucy Seward (Mrs. Bostwick Roberts),** *b* Fayetteville, N.Y., July 17, 1853.
8–Lt. William **Seward** (qv);
7–Caleb (1662-1728), Durham, Conn.; *m* 1686, Lydia Bushnell;
6–Thomas (*b* 1694), *m* 1720, Sarah Camp;
5–Amos (*b* 1726), *m* 1751, Ruth Rogers;
4–Col. Nathan (1758-1815), New Hartford, N.Y.; capt. and later col. in Utica militia; *m* Martha Gridley;
3–Timothy Gridley (1789-1862), Fayetteville, N.Y.; *m* 1809, Elizabeth Dudley (1790-1877);
2–Nathan (2 below).
11–William **Brewster,** Mayflower Pilgrim (qv);
10–Patience (*d* 1634), *m* 1624, Gov. Thomas **Prence** (qv);
9–Mercy, *m* 1649, John **Freeman** (1627-1719);
8–Edmond (1657-1717), Eastham, Mass.; dep. and selectman; *m* Sarah Mayo (*b* 1660);

7–Sarah, *m* 1701, Benjamin **Higgins** (*b* 1681);
6–Sarah (1706-66), *m* 1724, Jesse **Smith** (1703-82);
5–Jesse, soldier Am. Rev.; *m* 1760, Lydia Gregory (1739-91);
4–Ephraim (1761-1815), capt. Am. Rev.; *m* 1783, Miriam Thurston (Joel[5], Am. Rev.);
3–Anna (1794-1873), *m* 1817, David **Collin** (1794-1884);
2–Harriette (1824-55), *m* as his 1st wife, 1848, Nathan **Seward** (1814-69), merchant and banker, Fayetteville; he *m* 2d, Ada L. Hoag (*d* 1918); issue (1st marriage): I–Harriette Collin (1849-1927; *m* David N. Hurd, *d* 1916); II–Anna (1850-1876); III–Lucy (1 above); IV–Elizabeth Dudley (*b* and *d* 1855); (2d marriage): V–Ada Elizabeth (1862-83); VI–Mary Lavinia (1865-66).
1–*m* May 21, 1873, Bostwick Roberts Noble, *b* Franklin, N.Y., Aug. 31, 1848; son of Charles Noble, of Franklin, *m* Marcia Roberts; issue: 1–Anna Seward, *b* Lowell, Mich., June 15, 1874; grad. Liggett Sch., Detroit; *m* Sept. 18, 1895, Charles Farwell Lawson, son of Dr. B. Howard, of Detroit (issue: Seward Noble, *b* Detroit, Dec. 21, 1898, grad. U. of Mich., *m* 1924, Dorothy Ballantyne [issue, Joan, *b* Feb. 22, 1927]; Margaret Anna, *b* Detroit, Sept. 7, 1906; ed. "House in the Pines," Norton, Mass.); 2–Charles, *b* Vassar, Mich., Aug. 10, 1876; *m* Sept. 27, 1897, Mary Louise, dau. of Lewis Fenton, of Lexington, Mich., *m* Elizabeth Shortridge; 3–Anna-Lucile, *b* Brown City, Mich., July 4, 1898; U. of Mich.; *m* Jan. 11, 1924, Orison Steddom, son of Charles White, of Detroit.
1–Ed., Utica (N.Y.) Sem. Mem. S.M.D., D.A.C., C.D.A., D.F.P.A., D.C.G., D.A.R., U.S.D. 1812 (past state pres.), Huguenot Soc., N.E. Women's Colony (past pres. Fla.), League Am. Pen Women. Clubs: Woman's City (Detroit), Woman's (St. Petersburg, Fla.). Summer residence: 112 Center St., Fayetteville, N.Y.

1–**NORRIS, Charles,** *b* Hoboken, N.J., Dec. 4, 1867.
10–Richard **Warren,** Mayflower Pilgrim (qv);
9–Elizabeth, *m* 1636/37, Richard **Church** (qv);
8–Col. Benjamin (1639-1717/18), comdr. of troops, "Mass. Bay and Plymouth Colonies," King Philip's War; *m* Alice Southworth (*b* 1646; Constant[9], *m* Elizabeth Collier);
7–Edward (1680-1706), commd. capt. and served with his father in expdn. against French and Indians; *m* Martha Burton (1677-1750);
6–Dea. Benjamin (1704-81), grad. Harvard, 1727; *m* 2d, 1731, Hannah Dyer (Col. Gyles[7], mem. A. & H. A. Co. of Boston, 1680);
5–Hannah Dyer, *m* Edward **Weld** (see Vol. III, p. 619);
4–Benjamin (1758-1839), Am. Rev.; *m* 1792, Abigail Perkins;
3–Abby (1799-1886), *m* John A. **Stevens** (see Vol. I, p. 746);
2–Frances Ann (2 below).
8–Edmund **Perkins** (qv);
7–Edmund (1683-1762), *m* 1709, Mary Tarvis or Ferris;
6–William (1716-60), of Boston; *m* Elizabeth Palfrey;
5–Col. William (1742-1802), capt. of Kruse's regt. of arty., 1775; capt. 3d Regt. Cont. Arty., 1777; maj., 1778-83; apptd. col. at close of War; comd. "Castle William," in Boston Harbor; *m* 1763, Abigail Cox;
4–Abigail (1773-1840), *m* 1792, Benjamin **Weld** (4 above);
3–Abby, *m* John A. **Stevens** (3 above);
2–Frances Ann (1835-1906), *m* 1857, Joseph Parker **Norris** (1824-94), see Vol. I, p. 746 for Norris lineage and issue.
1–*m* Sept. 3, 1908, Eugenie Johanna Gebhart, *b* Feb. 18, 1892; dau. of Johann Gebhart.
1–Ph.B., Yale-S., '88 (Theta Xi); M.D., Columbia, 1892. Physician; apptd. chief med. examiner for City of N.Y., Jan. 31, 1918. Fellow N.Y. Acad. Medicine; mem. A.M.A., Soc. Am. Bacteriologists and Pathologists, Soc. Exptl. Biology and Medicine, etc. Mem. S.R. Club: University. Residence: 344 W. 72d St., New York.

1–**NORTON, Thomas Herbert,** *b* Rushford, Allegheny Co., N.Y., June 30, 1851.
8–Thomas **Norton** (ca. 1580-ca. 1648), from Eng.; one of the founders of Guilford, Conn., 1639; town miller; *m* 1631, Grace Wells, of Shelton, Surrey, Eng.;
7–Thomas (*d* 1712), at Saybrook, Conn.; *m* 1671, Elizabeth Mason (1654-99; Nicholas[8], of Saybrook);
6–Samuel (1681-1767), Durham, Conn.; *m* 1713, Dinah (Birdsey) Beach (1688-1765; John Birdsey[7], from Eng. to Milford, Conn., 1639, and later at Stratford);
5–Col. Ebenezer (1715-85), judge; dep. 22 terms; agent of Conn. during Am. Rev.; a founder of Goshen, Conn.; *m* 1740, Elizabeth Baldwin (1722-1811);
4–Ebenezer (1748-95), of Goshen; dep.; soldier Am. Rev.; *m* 2d, 1782, Charity Mills (1759-1843);
3–Dea. Lewis Mills (1783-1860), inventor, mfr.; historian; genealogist; *m* 1805, Laura Foote (1786-1855);
2–Rev. Robert (2 below).
9–William **Horsford** (*d* 1656), from Eng. to Dorchester, Mass., 1633; removed to Windsor, Conn., 1635; dep. Gen. Ct.; returned to Eng., 1655; *m* 2d, Widow Jane Fowkes (*d* 1692);
8–John (*d* 1683), of Windsor, *m* 1657, Philippa Thrall;
7–Timothy (*b* 1662), *m* 1st, 1689, Hannah Palmer (1666-1702; Timothy[8]; Sgt. Nicholas[9], from Eng., and an early settler of Windsor);
6–Daniel (1695-1777), S. Canaan, Conn.; *m* 1721, Elizabeth Stewart (*d* 1783);
5–Capt. Daniel (1723-88), *m* 1748, Martha Dibble (*b* 1719);
4–Roger (1755-1818), Charlotte, Vt.; *m* 1778, Mary Brown (1754-1812; Jerediah[5]; John[6]);
3–Col. Jerediah (1791-1875), Moscow (now Leicester), N.Y.; mem. N.Y. Assembly; 32d Congress; soldier War 1812; *m* 1816, Charity Maria Norton (1790-1859);
2–Julia Ann Granger (1822-1918), *m* 1847, Rev. Robert **Norton** (1822-1907), of Rushford, N.Y., St. Catherine, Ont., Lockport, N.Y.; grad. Auburn Theol. Sem., 1857; Presbyterian minister; issue: I–Thomas Herbert (1 above); II–Grace (1860-90).
1–*m* Dec. 27, 1883, Edith Eliza Ames (*b* Lockport, N.Y., Dec. 6, 1864-*d* New York, Oct. 30, 1929); dau. of Col. James D. Ames (see Who's Who in America); issue: 1–Robert Ames, *b* Cincinnati, O., Feb. 13, 1896; B.A., Yale, '18, LL.B., 1921; 2d lt., U.S.A. inf., 1917-18; admitted to bar, 1921; practices at New York and Pittsburgh; *m* Sept. 11, 1923, Barbara, dau. of Marcus Baker, of Washington.
1–A.B., Hamilton, '73 (D.K.E., P.B.K.), hon. Sc.D., 1896; Ph.D., Heidelberg, 1875. Chemist, coll. prof., U. of Cincinnati, 1883-1900; consul to Turkey, 1905-06, to Germany, 1906-14. Author. Editor (see Who's Who in America). Mem. S.C.W., S.R., S.A.R., Soc. War. 1812. Clubs: Chemists (N.Y.), Cosmos (Washington), Literary, Chess (Cincinnati), Brandywine Chess (Wilmington, Del., champion, 1920). Address: Box 115, R.F.D. No. 9, Pittsburgh, Pa.

1–**NOURSE, Robert Lee,** *b* Cloverport, Ky., Sept. 27, 1864.
9–Francis **Nourse** (1619-95), from Eng., 1639; settled at Salem, Mass.; *m* Rebecca Blessing Towne (1621-92);
8–John (*b* 1650), *m* 1st, 1672, Elizabeth Smith;
7–John (*b* 1673), *m* 1700, Elizabeth (Spring) Gale (*b* 1678);
6–John (*b* 1701), *m* Bathsheba Newton Rugg (*b* 1703);
5–Abraham (1732-93), *m* 1753, Zerviah Clayes Morse (1735-1805);
4–Asa (1754-1803), *m* 1781, Lois Glover (1762-1800);
3–Newell (*b* 1792), *m* 1819, Harriet Morton Bullard (*b* 1797);
2–Charles Augustus (1820-80), planter, Holliston, Mass., *m* 1841, Frances Bridges (1827-68); for issue see William H. Nourse.
1–*m* Nov. 27, 1889, Marie I. Crawford (1869-1921); dau. of Maj. (Dr.) Samuel K. Crawford; issue: 1–Robert Lee, Jr., *b* Ashland, Wis., Sept. 20, 1895; B. Litt., Princeton, '17; twice cited and awarded Croix du Guerre, World War; *m* June 30, 1920, Mildred, dau. of Robert W. Faris, of Boise, Ida. (issue: Ann Marie, *b* May 23, 1927; Faris, *b* July 24, 1928); 2–Norman Crawford, *b* Ashland, Mar. 30, 1897; B. Litt., Princeton, '18; cited and awarded Croix du Guerre, World War; *m* Jan. 28, 1926, Gwenn Hinerman, of Boise, Ida. (issue: Norman Crawford, *b* Oct. 3, 1927);
1–*m* 2d, Sept. 26, 1923, Anna Elnora Brakel, *b*

Alton, Ill., Nov. 10, 1884; M.A., U.Wash. (P.B.K.); dau. of Samuel Houston Brakel, of Portland, Ore., *m* Anna Lawson Davis; issue: 1–Marianna, *b* Boise, Nov. 23, 1924.
1–M.D., Rush Medical Coll. (Med. Dept., U. of Chicago). Physician and surgeon (specialist eye, ear, nose and throat); practiced at Washburn, Wis., 1889-91, Chicago, 1891-93, Ashland, Wis., 1893-97, Hailey, Ida., 1897-1905. After 2 yrs. study New York and Europe, specialized in practice, Boise, Idaho, since 1907. Sec. Ida. State Bd. Medical Examiners, 1899-1905; pres. state Med. Assn., 1905; fellow Am. Coll. Surgeons; mem. S.A.R. Mason (32°), Elk. Rotarian. Presbyterian. Democrat. Residence: Boise, Ida.

1–**NOURSE, William H.,** *b* in Ky., Mar. 29, 1861.
9–Francis **Nourse** (1619-95), from Eng., 1639; settled at Salem, Mass.; *m* Rebecca Blessing Towne (1621-92);
8–John (*b* 1650), *m* 1st, 1672, Elizabeth Smith;
7–John (*b* 1673), *m* 1700, Elizabeth (Spring) Gale (*b* 1678);
6–John (*b* 1701), of Framingham, Mass.; *m* Bathsheba Newton Rugg (*b* 1703);
5–Abraham (1732-93), of Framingham; pvt. in Capt. Jesse Eames Co., under Col. Samuel Bullard's 5th Middlesex Co. Regt., Framingham, Mass.; *m* 1753, Zerviah Clayes Morse (1735-1805);
4–Asa (1754-1803), of Framingham; pvt. in same co. with his father; *m* 1781, Lois Glover (1762-1800), of Sudbury, Mass.;
3–Newell (*b* 1792), of Framingham; *m* 1819, Harriet Morton Bullard (*b* 1797), of Holliston, Mass.;
2–Charles Augustus (1820-80), planter, of Holliston, Mass.; *m* 1841, Frances Bridges (1827-68); issue: I–Charles B. (1844-72); II–Ellinor (*b* 1847; *m* Isaac K. Moran, *d*); III–Frances E. (1849-72); IV–Julia L. (1854-1921; *m* John L. Hester); V–James E. (1858-1922; *m* Belle Russell, *d* 1920); VI–George (1860-66); VII–William H. (1 above); VIII–Robert Lee (qv).
1–*m* July 24, 1883, Sally Clarke (*d* Feb. 6, 1885); issue: 1–Charles Clarke (*d* aet. 6 mos).
1–*m* 2d, Oct. 20, 1886, Georgia L. Underhill (*d* May 3, 1923); issue: 1–Horace Lee, *b* 1888; *m* 1910, Marvel Felts; 2–Frances Pearl (1890-1926), *m* 1925, Claude Johnson; 3–Will Cecil (1892-94); 4–Mary Lou (1894-1909); 5–Mabel Ruth, *b* 1897; *m* 1918, Louie Hiett; 6–Arthur Augustus, *b* 1898; U.S. Navy, Aug. 1917-Aug. 1919; 7–Georgia Allien, *b* 1901.
1–Residence: 879 N. Belvedere St., Memphis, Tenn.

1–**NUTTING, Eliza Ann Steele Adams (Mrs. John D.),** *b* Danville, Vt., Jan. 22, 1881.
8–Sgt. Daniel **Adams** (1652-1713), resided at Simsbury, Conn.; in King Philip's War; rep. Conn. Assembly, 1699-1703; dep. Gen. Ct.; *m* 1677, Mary Phelps (1658-1715; Samuel[9], *m* Sarah Griswold);
7–Daniel (ca. 1678-1712/13), of Simsbury; *m* 1700, Thanks Shepard (1683-1724; Abraham[8], *m* Judith Philbrook Sill; Ralph[9], qv);
6–James (1712-87), in Am. Rev. from Vt.; town officer, Tinmouth; *m* 1736, Sarah Callender (1716-85; Philip[7], of Sheffield, Mass., *m* Mary Eaton);
5–James (1737-1813), in Am. Rev. from Mass.; *m* 2d, 1762, Submit Purchase (1735-1797; Jonathan[6], *m* Margaret Worthington; Thomas[7]; Thomas[8]; Thomas[9]);
4–Charles (1773-1845), Waterford, Vt.; fifer War 1812; *m* 1796, Rebecca Morgan;
3–Cornelius (1807-61), Danville, Vt.; drafted for Mexican War; *m* 2d, 1832, Harriet Brown (1805-81; Asa[4], *m* Esther Nichols; Ephraim[5]);
2–Charles (2 below).
10–Robert **Morgan** (1600-1690-94), a cooper; from Wales, 1636; *m* Margaret Norman (Richard[11], of Mass.);
9–Samuel (1637-98), cooper, Beverly, Mass., 1681; *m* 1658, Elizabeth Dixey (*d* 1690; Capt. William[10], *m* Ann–);
8–Samuel (1666-1700), cooper; *m* 1692, Sarah Herrick;
7–John (1693-1752), *m* ca. 1718, Sarah Whittredge (*d* 1762; Lt. Thomas[8], *m* Charity Livermore);
6–John (1721-92), in Am. Rev.; *m* 1st, 1745, Margaret Larcom (1726-48; David[7], *m* Lucy Downing);
5–Cornelius (1747-post 1820), of Vt.; in Am. Rev.; *m* 1769, Mehitable Preston (bap. 1754; Nehemiah[6], *m* Annis Bradford);
4–Rebecca (1778-1858), Waterford, Vt.; *m* 1796, Charles **Adams** (4 above).
7–Richard **English** (1690-1748), from Eng. in the "Swallow" to Newport, R.I.; settled at Lebanon, Conn., 1717; *m* 1712, Mary Hinksman (1688-1748; John[8], of R.I.);
6–John (1718-61), *d* Nova Scotia, where he had taken his family, 1760; *m* 1738, Abigail Newcomb (*b* 1715; Dea. John[7]; Simon[8]; Lt. Andrew[9]; Capt. Andrew[10], qv);
5–Richard (1741-78), Andover, Conn.; *m* 1762, Freedom Strong (1747-1839; Capt. John[6]; Lt. Jedediah[7]; Jedediah[8]; Jedediah[9]; Elder John[10], qv);
4–Joel (1766-1852), *m* 1788, Tryphena Strong (1770-1846);
3–Henry Walbridge (1805-85), *m* 1834, Eliza Ann Steele (1804-80; Stephen[4], fifer Am. Rev.; Capt. Stephen[5]; Rev. Stephen[6]; Lt. James[7]; James[8]; George[9], qv);
2–Chloe Tryphena (2 below).
9–John **Strong** (qv);
8–Jedediah (1637-1733), *m* 1662, Freedom Woodward (1642-81; Henry[9], from Eng., 1639);
7–Jedediah (1667-1709), Lebanon, Conn., 1696; killed by Indians; *m* 1688, Abiah Ingersoll (John[8]);
6–Lt. Jedediah (*b* 1700), Lebanon, Conn.; *m* 1722, Elizabeth Webster (*b* 1700; Capt. John[7]);
5–Benajah (1734/35-1815), of Bethel, Vt.; a first settler at Hartford, Vt., 1764; in Am. Rev.; *m* 1758, Mary Bacon;
4–Tryphena (1770-1846), *m* Joel **English** (4 above).
10–John **Howland,** Mayflower Pilgrim (qv);
9–Desire (*d* 1683), *m* 1643, Capt. John **Gorham** (qv);
8–James (1650-1707), of Barnstable, Mass.; *m* 1673/74, Hannah Huckins (1653-1727/28; Thomas[9], to America ante 1638, *m* Rose Hyllier);
7–Experience (1678-1733), *m* 1697, Thomas **Lothrop** (1673-1757), to Barnstable, Mass. (Hon Joseph[8], *m* Mary Ansel; Rev. John[9], qv);
6–Lydia (ca. 1715-91), *m* 1734, Ebenezer **Bacon** (*b* 1708; Dea. Samuel[7]; Nathaniel[8], qv);
5–Mary (1738-90), *m* Benajah **Strong** (5 above).
10–George **Hubbard,** from Eng., 1633; *m* Mary Bishop;
9–John (ca. 1630-1702), *m* 1648/49, Mary Merriam;
8–John (1655-1748), *m* ca. 1676, Mary Wright (Thomas[9], from Eng.);
7–Isaac (*b* 1679), *m* ca. 1700, Hannah Dickinson (Nehemiah[8]; Nathaniel[9]; William[10]);
6–Isaac (*b* 1701), *m* Hannah Goodrich (1707-73; Col. David[7]; Ens. William[8]);
5–Lt. George (1739-1818), in Am. Rev.; commd. lt., 1777; 1st settler in Claremont, N.H., 1778; *m* 1760, Thankful Hatch (1742-1802; Jonathan[6]; Joseph[7]; Joseph[8]; Jonathan[9]; Thomas[10], from Eng to Barnstable, ca. 1634);
4–Chloe (1763-1843), *m* Stephen **Steele** (1752-1831);
3–Eliza Ann, *m* Henry Walbridge **English** (3 above).
2–Charles **Adams** (Dec. 21, 1840-Apr. 26, 1909), farmer, of Danville and Peacham, Vt.; served with Co. G, 4th Vt. Vols., Civil War, 3 yrs.; in Andersonville Prison, 5 mos.; wounded in head by rebel gun while on way to prison at Florence, S.C.; paroled Feb. 1865, and sent to St. John's Hosp., at Annapolis; disch. Apr. 21, 1865; *m* 1867, Mary Gibbs (1843-71), of Barnard, Vt.; *m* 2d, 1875, Chloe Tryphena English (Feb. 8, 1847-Apr. 2, 1921); issue (1st marriage): I–Alice (Mar. 21-Mar. 31, 1869); II–Daniel Lemuel (*b* Apr. 27, 1870); III–Mary (1871-72); issue (2d marriage): I–Fred English (1879-82); II–Eliza Ann Steele (1 above).
1–*m* Oct. 11, 1916, John David Nutting, *b* Northfield, Minn., Nov. 6, 1881; son of John C. Nutting; issue: 1–Helen Adams, *b* Northfield, Minn., Apr. 13, 1918; 2–Ruth Elizabeth, *b* Northfield, July 3, 1920.
1–A.B., Mt. Holyoke, '02. Teacher Latin and German, Malone, N.Y., Camden, N.Y., Washington (Pa.) Sem., Hood Coll. (Frederick, Md.), Tucson, Ariz., Carleton Coll. (Northfield, Minn.). Mem. Northfield Sch. Bd. since 1921, etc. Mem. D.A.R., I.A.G., Colony N.E. Women, A.A.U.W. (pres. Northfield branch, 1916-18), P.E.O. (chapter pres., 1924-26). Congregationalist. Republican. Residence: Northfield, Minn.

1–**OLIPHANT, Henrietta Margaret Drum (Mrs. Hughes),** *b* San Francisco, Calif., Aug. 17, 1862.
7–David **Morgan,** from Wales to America ca. 1700; *m* Mary–;
6–Evan (*d* 1763), *m* Joanna Biles (George[7], *m* Martha Kirkbridge, or Kirkbride, dau. of Joseph, *m* Phoebe, dau. of Randall Blackshaw, who came in the "Welcome" with William Penn, 1682; William[8], large landowner in Bucks Co., Pa., before arrival of William Penn);
5–George (1743-1810), of "Prospect," nr. Princeton, N.J.; col. Cont. Army; explorer; *m* Mary Baynton;
4–Col. John (1770-1817), Morganza, Pa.; *m* Margaret Bunyan;
3–Judge Thomas Gibbes (1799-1860), *m* 2d, Sarah Hunt Fowler (desc. Earl of Airlie);
2–Lavinia Maria (2 below).
9–Thomas **Budd,** came to America, 1668;
8–John, *m* Rebecca Baynton;
7–Mary, *m* Peter **Baynton;**
6–John (1726-73), *m* 1747, Elizabeth Chevalier;
5–Mary (*b* 1749), *m* 1764, George **Morgan** (5 above).
10–Willem **deKay** (qv);
9–Jacobus Tunis (*d* 1691), *m* 1658, Hillegonda Theunisse (*d* 1707);
8–Jacobus (*b* 1672), *m* 1694, Sarah Willet (Col. Thomas[9]);
7–Col. Thomas (1697-1758), Orange Co., N.Y.; soldier French and Indian War; *m* 1723, Christina (1707-84), dau. Thomas Duncan, of Scotland;
6–Maj. George (1728-59), *m* 1754, Julianna Gale (*b* 1735);
5–Juliana, *m* 1772, James **Bunyan;**
4–Margaret, *m* 1795, John **Morgan** (4 above);
3–Judge Thomas G., *m* 2d, Sarah Hunt Fowler (3 above);
2–Lavinia Maria (1839-1912), *m* Brig. Gen. Richard Coulter **Drum** (1825-1909), served pvt. to brig. gen. and adj. gen. U.S.A., served through Mexican and Civil wars.
1–*m* June 23, 1883, Henry Jackson Hunt, Jr. (1855-86); lt. U.S.N.; son of Brig. Gen. H. J. Hunt, *m* Emily Caroline de Russey; issue: 1–Richard Coulter Drum, *b* Washington, D.C., Apr. 14, 1884; *m* June 6, 1906, Evelyn Cronin (issue: Richard C. D.; Frederick Talley); 2–Henry Jackson (see Vol. I, p. 400, for Drum and Hunt lineages).
1–*m* 2d, Oct. 23, 1888, Hughes Oliphant (Jan. 19, 1850-Mar. 7, 1920); Princeton, '70; son of Samuel Duncan Oliphant, of Uniontown, Pa.; issue: 1–Thomas Gibbes Morgan, *b* Bathesda, Md., Dec. 19, 1889; *m* Apr. 4, 1912, Ruth Horney (issue: Thomas G. M., Jr.; Richard Horney); 2–Margaret Coulter, *b* Washington, June 23, 1892; Chevy Chase Sem.; *m* Will Curtiss McGraw (issue: Lavinia Morgan); 3–Maryon Campbell, *b* Bethesda, Apr. 8, 1894; *m* Mary C. Wallace (issue: Maryon C., Jr.).
1–Mem. C.D.A., D.A.R., Guadalupe (Mexican War), I.A.G., Club of Colonial Dames, Washington Club, Chevy Chase Club. Residence: The Ontario, Washington, D.C.

1–**ORVIS, Francis Wayland,** *b* New London, Pa., Oct. 12, 1855.
8–George **Orvis** (qv);
7–Roger (1657-1737), presented with a sword cane, 1676, by order of King James II, of Eng., in recognition of his services in the Indian wars; the cane is still in the family; *m* 1692, Miriam Handerson (1671-1747);
6–David (1697-1760), *m* 1719, Hannah Gaylord (*b* 1700);
5–Eleazer (1719-1805), *m* 1743, Hannah North (1727-1816);
4–Jesse (1772-1858), *m* 1792, Susannah Holden;
3–Jesse (*b* 1803), *m* 1st, Betsy Rowley (*d* 1842);
2–Edward Everett (2 below).
9–Elder John **Strong** (qv);
8–Thomas, "the Trooper," *m* 2d, Rachel Holton;
7–Adino, *m* Eunice–;
6–Adino, *m* Deborah Prime;
5–Capt. Benajah, Am. Rev.; *m* Jane Cochrane;
4–Salmon, *m* Elizabeth Jagger;
3–Jane E., *m* Origen **Atwood,** of Ithaca, N.Y.
2–Edward Everett **Orvis** (1826-84), *m* 1849, Jane Eliza Atwood (*d* 1870); *m* 2d, Anna Eliza Bailey (for issue see Vol. III, p. 355).
1–*m* Jan. 1, 1884, Emma Gertrude Heacock (Sept. 30, 1855-Jan. 10, 1930); dau. of Samuel Heacock, of Benton, Pa., *m* Susan Winner; issue: 1–Ora Lucile, *b* Brooklyn, N.Y., Aug. 6, 1887; *m* Nov. 14, 1910, Wesley W. Fulkersin (issue: Francis A.; Elton J.; Walter B.; Pearl Marcia); 2–Eugene Luvois, *b* Bloomsburg, Pa., Sept. 26, 1888; *m* Aug. 19, 1922, Marie Isabel, dau. of Charles Carlstrand, *m* Mary Brophy; 3–Harold Heacock, *b* Brooklyn, N.Y., Mar. 22, 1891; *m* June 25, 1921, Leora Alice, dau. of Thomas Chapelle, *m* Alice Parker, of Baltimore, Md. (issue: Harold Heacock; Leora Marie; Barbara); 4–Edward Ernest, *b* Brooklyn, Nov. 26, 1892; *m* May 3, 1924, Elise Kennedy, dau. of William Hall Cocks, of Port Washington, N.Y., *m* Agnes Bennett (issue: Jean Elizabeth).
1–Printer, publisher and stationer. Author: History of the Orvis Family in America. Mason. Residence: 189 Stanley Pl., Hackensack, N.J.

1–**OTIS, Philo Adams,** *b* Berlin Hts., O., Nov. 24, 1846.
9–John **Otis** (qv);
8–John (1621-84), Barnstable, Mass.; *m* 2d, 1653, Mary Jacob (Nicholas[9], from Eng., 1633, *m* Mary–);
7–Joseph (1666-1754), judge Ct. Common Pleas; *m* his cousin, Dorothy Thomas (1670-1755; Judge Nathaniel[8], *m* Deborah, dau. of Nicholas Jacob; Nathaniel[9]; William[10], qv);
6–Dea. Joseph (1712-ca. 1793), *m* 1738, Elizabeth Little;
5–Nathaniel (1742-1815), *m* Amy Gardiner, or Gardner;
4–Asahel (1768-1837), *m* Mary Chester;
3–Joseph (1792-1844), *m* Nancy Billings;
2–James (2 below).
9–Thomas **Little** (qv);
8–Rev. Ephraim (1650-1717), rep. Gen. Ct.; *m* 1672, Mary Sturtevant (Samuel[9]);
7–Capt. David (1681-1779), of Scituate, Mass.; *m* Elizabeth Southworth (1686-1743; Capt. William[8], *m* Rebecca, dau. William Pabodie, *m* Elizabeth, dau. John Alden, the Mayflower Pilgrim, qv);
6–Elizabeth (*b* 1719), *m* Joseph **Otis** (6 above).
10–Thomas **Makepeace** (qv);
9–Esther, *m* 1655, John **Browne** (qv);
8–Elizabeth (*b* 1657), *m* 1678, Augustine Jean (1647-1720), from Isle of Jersey, to Reading, Mass., 1675; anglicized name to John **Gustine;** served in King Philip's War (Edward Jean[9], *m* Esther Le Rossignol);
7–John (1691-1777), *d* Frankfort, Sussex Co., N.J.; *m* Mary– (1692-1762);
6–Jemima (*b* 1720), *m* Corpl. David **Gardner** (1720-98), Am. Rev. (Stephen[7]; Benoni[8]; George[9]; Thomas[10], qv);
5–Amy (1745-1815), *m* Nathaniel **Otis** (5 above).
8–George **Adams** (qv);
7–Sgt. Daniel (1652-1713), in King Philip's War; a founder of Simsbury, Conn.; rep. Conn. Assembly; *m* 1677, Mary Phelps (1658-1715; Samuel[8]);
6–Daniel (ca. 1678-1712), *m* 1700 Thanks Shepard (1683-1724; Abraham[7], *m* Judith Sill; Ralph[8], qv);
5–James (1712-87), of Vt.; *m* 1736, Sarah Callender; and prob. thru:
4–Daniel (1745-1816), Dorset, Vt.; *m* Elenor (Jackson) Allen (*d* 1837; Abraham Jackson[5], of Wallingford, Vt.);
3–Dea. Philo (1787-1864), Huron, O.; *m* 2d, Laurena Baldwin (1785-1862; Benjamin[4], of Dorset);
2–Margaretta Graves Jackson (1824-66), *m* 1845, James **Otis** (1818-95), realtor, Chicago; issue: I–Philo Adams (1 above); II–Laurena Baldwin (1848-87; *m* Charles H. Starkweather); III–Walter Joseph (see Vol. I, p. 629); IV–Arthur James (1855-70).
1–*m* June 26, 1890, Alice Jeannette, dau. of Homer B. Sanford, of Bridgeport, Conn.; issue: 1–James Sanford, *b* Chicago, Ill., Aug. 30, 1896; B.A., Yale, '19; commd. ens., lt. (j.g.), and lt., U.S. Naval Aviation; with A.E.F. in France, June 27-Nov. 30, 1918; flight cdr., Northern Bombing Group; awarded Navy Cross.
1–B.A., Western Reserve, '68 (D.K.E.). Active in real estate business in Chicago, since 1895. Actively identified with musical enterprises

and author of many hymns and anthems; a founder of Apollo Musical Club (pres. 1890-93); sec. bd. trustees, Chicago Symphony Orchestra since 1894 (see Who's Who in America). Republican. Clubs: Chicago, University, Midlothian. Residence: 1709 Prairie Av., Chicago, Ill.

1-**OTKEN, Charles Henry,** *b* Summitt, Miss., Jan. 3, 1878.
8-Luke **Lea,** from Eng., settled in Va.;
7-James, from Eng., settled in King and Queen Co., Va.; bought land in Spotsylvania Co., bet. 1750-60, moved to Orange Co., N.C., settled finally nr. Leasburg, N.C.; served in French and Indian War, 1758;
6-James (1718-88), pvt. Am. Rev.; *m* Anne Tolbert (*b* 1718);
5-Rev. Luke (1739-1813), Am. Rev.; recorder of land patents, Frankland, Tenn.; *m* 1759, Elizabeth Wilson (1739-92);
4-Zachariah (1776-1845), capt. War 1812; mem. Legislature from Amite Co., Miss.; senator, 1820; *m* 1800, Sabrina Clay (1783-1842);
3-James Everett (1819-78), of Amite Co., Miss.; soldier C.S.A.; *m* 1846, Frances Powell (1827-86; Josiah[4] [1773-1846], 1st lt., War 1812, *m* Jane Brix);
2-Emily Jane (2 below).
8-John **Clay** (qv);
7-Charles (1638-86), soldier "Gt. Rebellion of 1676"; *m* Hannah Wilson (John[8], Sr., of Henrico Co., Va.);
6-Charles, *m* Sarah–;
5-James (*d* 1790), *m* Margaret Muse (1737-1832);
4-Sabrina (1783-1842), *m* Zachariah **Lea** (4 above);
3-James E., *m* Frances Powell (3 above);
2-Emily Jane Lea (1847-1918), *m* 1866, Charles Henry **Otken** (1839-1911), served in 45th Miss., Lowrey's Brig., Claiborne's Div., Hardee's Corps, C.S.A.; educator, minister and writer; founder and pres. Lea Female Coll., Summit, Miss., 1877-94; pres. McComb (Miss.) Female Inst., 1894-99; co. supt. edn., Pike Co., Miss., 1911; issue: I-Mary Frances (*b* 1867; *m* Benjamin F. Lewis, qv); II-Charles Henry, M.D. (1 above); III-Perla Clay; IV-John J. G.; V-Lois Bridgeforth; VI-Frances Powell (D.A.R.); VII-Luther Boyce, M.D. (*m* Frances Hodges).
1-*m* 1925, Ella Marosko, *b* Paige, Tex., Feb. 21, 1896; dau. of Friedrich Marosko, of Berlin, Germany; issue: 1-Henry Lea, *b* Aug. 9, 1926; 2-Charles Clay, *b* Nov. 6, 1927; 3-Francis Powell, *b* Jan. 27, 1930.
1-M.D., Chicago Coll. of Medicine and Surgery, 1909. Physician and surgeon. Mem. A.M.A., Southern Med. Soc., Tex. State Med. Soc., etc. Mason. Residence: Falfurrias, Tex.

SAMUEL WADDY SHELTON (b in Hanover Co., Va., 1758, d in Boyle Co., Ky., 1833), served in the Revolutionary War.

1-**OTT, Suzanne Elizabeth Shelton (Mrs. Henry J.),** *b* Danville, Ky., Aug. 27, 1860.
8-John **Shelton** (*d* 1706), built "Rural Plains," Hanover Co., Va., 1670; will filed in Westmoreland Co., Va.; *m* Jane–;
7-William, *m* 1698, Hannah Armistead;
6-Samuel (1703-93), Albemarle Co., Va.; *m* Judith Clough;
5-Samuel (1736-1826), will recorded in Albemarle Co.; *m* Sarah Waddy;
4-Samuel Waddy (1758-1833), see portrait; *m* 1781, in Hanover Co., Jane Henderson;
3-Thomas (1798-1872), Boyle Co., Ky.; *m* 1818, Pauline Noel;

JAMES THOMAS SHELTON (b in Boyle Co., Ky., April 10, 1834, d at Independence, Mo., April 15, 1917), son of Thomas Shelton, who served in the War of 1812; grandson of Samuel Waddy Shelton, who served in the Revolutionary War.

2-James Thomas (1834-1917), landowner, Danville, Ky. (see portrait); *m* 1856, Lucinda Frances Yeager (see Vol. III, p. 360, for other lineages and issue).
1-*m* Nov. 14, 1882, Henry Joseph Ott, *b* Independence, Mo., Sept. 26, 1856.
1-Ed. Caldwell Coll., Danville, Ky. State treas. Daughters Am. Colonists; regent Independence Pioneers Chapter D.A.R.; state chmn. Americanism D.A.R., also serving with Nat. chmn. of Americanism D.A.R.; mem. U.S.D. 1812; ex-pres. U.D.C.; mem. Browning Soc., Mary Paxton Literary Club, Mo. State Hist. Soc. Summer place: Minocqua, Wis., Residence: 710 W. Maple Av., Independence, Mo.

1-**OWEN, William Henry, Jr.,** *b* New York, N.Y., Oct. 11, 1874.
8-John **Owen** (1624-1698/99), from Wales to Boston, 1640; *m* 1640, Rebecca Wade;
7-Nathaniel, *m* Sarah Palmer;
6-Nathaniel, *m* Mary Griswold;
5-Nathaniel (1735-1821), in the Am. Army at the time of its retreat from L.I.; *m* Mary Pinney;
4-Hezekiah, *m* Elizabeth Thrall;
3-Edward Hezekiah, *m* Jane Augusta Livingston;
2-William Henry (*b* 1841), retired mcht., New York; *m* 1865, Mary Lavinia Brooks (*b* 1844); issue: I-Mary Lavinia (*b* 1870; *m* Bertram Harold Borden); II-William Henry, Jr. (1 above).
1-Not married. B.A., Yale, '97, M.A., 1899; B.D., General Theol. Sem., 1903. P.E., clergyman; rector Holy Trinity Church, New York City. Examining chaplain to the bishop of N.Y.; trustee Cathedral of St. John the Divine. Mem. S.C.W., O.F.P.A., S.R., S.V., M.O.L.L. Clubs: Graduate (New Haven), Yale, Union League (New York). Residence: Butler Hall, 88 Morningside Drive, New York.

1–**PADELFORD, Frank William,** *b* Haverhill, Mass., Apr. 6, 1872.
9–Jonathan **Padelford** (1628-60), from Eng.; of Cambridge, Braintree and Taunton, Mass.; *m* 1652, Mary Blanford (1632-1676; John[10], of Sutton and Sudbury, Mass.);
8–Jonathan (1656-1710), *m* Hannah Flint (1658-85);
7–Jonathan (1679-1747), *m* ante 1706, Hannah King (1691-1735; Philip[8], *m* Judith Whitman);
6–Zachariah (1710-65), *m* Martha Allen (1715-70);
5–Zachariah (1733-1803), *m* Rachael Reynolds (1732-1804);
4–Zachariah (1755-1846), *m* Abigail Williams; *m* 2d, Lydia Padelford;
3–Sedate (1784-ca. 1863), *m* Margaret Barney; *m* 2d, Martha Crane;
2–Adoniram Judson (2 below).
11–Elder William **Brewster,** Mayflower Pilgrim (qv);
10–Jonathan (1593-1661), *m* 1624, Lucretia Oldham;
9–Ruth (1631-77), *m* John **Pickett** (*d* 1667);
8–Mary (*d* 1735), *m* 1672, Benjamin **Shapley** (1645-1706; Nicholas[9]);
7–Ruth, *m* Capt. John **Morgan** (*b* 1667);
6–Mary (1698-1776), *m* James **Morgan** (1693-1770; James[7]; James[8]; James[9]);
5–John (1735-99), *m* 1759, Dorothy Avery;
4–Amos (1774-1845), *m* 1804, Jemima Stoddard (1785-1847);
3–William Pitt (1805-82), *m* 1831, Eunice W. Chester (1810-79);
2–Julia Smith (1837-93), *m* 1862, Adoniram Judson **Padelford** (1831-1914), A.B., U. of Rochester, 1858; grad. Rochester Theol. Sem., 1860; D.D., Colby, 1893; Bapt. minister, 1860-1911, at Fall River and Haverhill, Mass., Providence, R.I., Calais, Me.; for issue and other lineages see Frederick Morgan Padelford.
1–*m* Aug. 3, 1897, Grace Clementine Ilsley (Apr. 13, 1871-Mar. 24, 1919); dau. of Rev. George Boardman Ilsley, D.D., of Bangor, Me.; issue: 1–Norman Judson, *b* Haverhill, Mass., Nov. 18, 1903; *m* June 11, 1929, Helen Proctor, of Shanghai, China.
1–*m* 2d, Feb. 15, 1922, Gertrude Lois Ilsley, *b* June 13, 1873; also dau. Rev. George Boardman Ilsley, D.D.
1–A.B., Colby Coll., Me., 1894 (D.K.E., P.B.K.), A.M., 1897; grad. Rochester Theol. Sem., 1897 (D.D., Colby, 1911; LL.D., Denison, 1927). Ordained Bapt. ministry, 1897; pastorates, 1897-1908; gen. sec. Mass. Bapt. Missionary Soc., 1908-13; exec. sec. Bd. of Education of the Northern Bapt. Conv., 1913–. Author (see Who's Who in America). Clubs: University, Boston City, Boston Theol. (Boston), Clergy (New York), Union League (Chicago). Residence: Newton Centre, Mass.

1–**PADELFORD, Frederick Morgan,** *b* Haverhill, Mass., Feb. 27, 1875.
11–Elder William **Brewster,** Mayflower Pilgrim (qv);
10–Jonathan (1593-1661), *m* 1624, Lucretia Oldham;
9–Ruth, *m* John **Pickett** (*d* 1667);
8–Mary, *m* Capt. Samuel **Fosdick;**
7–Anna, *m* Thomas **Latham;**
6–Mary (*b* 1716), *m* 1735, Capt. Parke **Avery** (1710-97; Ebenezer[7], *m* Dorothy Parke; Lt. James[8]; Capt. James[9]; Christopher[10], qv);
5–Dorothy, *m* 1759, John **Morgan** (1735-99);
4–Amos (1774-1845), *m* 1804, Jemima Stoddard (1785-1847);
3–William Pitt (1805-82), *m* 1831, Eunice W. Chester;
2–Julia Smith (2 below).
8–Capt. Samuel **Chester** (*d* 1710), from Eng.; settled at Boston; removed to New London, 1663; *m* Mary–;
7–Capt. John (1692-1776), *m* 1716, Mary Starr (1696-1774, desc. Elder William Brewster);
6–Benajah (1724-83), *m* Jerusha Starr (1737-60);
5–Starr (1760-1812), *m* Mary Morgan;
4–Nicholas, *m* 1802, Mary Smith;
3–Eunice W. (1810-79), *m* William Pitt **Morgan** (3 above);
2–Julia Smith (1837-93), *m* 1862, Adoniram Judson **Padelford,** D.D. (1831-1914); issue: I–Lillian B. (1870-71); II–Frank William (qv for other lineages); III–Frederick Morgan (1 above).
1–*m* July 6, 1899, Jessie Elizabeth Pepper, *b* Upland, Pa., Mar. 20, 1874; sister of Charles Hovey Pepper (see Vol. I, p. 733 for genealogy); issue (all *b* Seattle, Wash.): 1–Morgan Grassie, *b* Oct. 10, 1902; 2–Eunice Brewster, *b* June 12, 1907; *m* Oct. 17, 1927, James W. Clise, Jr. (issue: Anne Gordon, *b* Aug. 4, 1928); 3–Philip Sidney, *b* June 8, 1912; 4–Charles Gordon, *b* June 23, 1915.
1–A.B., Colby, '96, A.M., 1899, Ph.D., Yale, 1899. Prof. English, 1901–, dean Grad. Sch., 1920–, and asst. dean of faculties, 1927–, U. of Wash. Author (see Who's Who in America). Summer place: "Woldmere," Kingston, Wash. Residence: 4710 20th Av. N.E., Seattle, Wash.

1–**PAINE, N(athaniel) Emmons,** *b* New Hartford, Oneida Co., N.Y., July 14, 1853.
9–Thomas **Paine** (qv);
8–Peter (*b* 1616/17), *m* Mary Folger (John[9], of Nantucket, whose brother, Peter, was g.-father of Benjamin Franklin);
7–Capt. John (*d* 1706/07), *m* Jemima Alsop (Joseph[8]);
6–Alsop (1698/99-1795), *m* Phoebe Mary Moore;
5–John (1740-1815), *m* Mary Booth (John [?][6]; John[7]; Richard[8]);
4–Ezra (1767-1828), *m* Elizabeth Weeks (see Vol. III, p. 362, for Weeks lineage);
3–John Alsop (1795-1871), physician; *m* Amanda Kellogg (see Vol. I, p. 755, and Vol. III, p 362);
2–Horace Marshfield, A.M., M.D. (1827-1903), physician (see portrait Vol. III, p. 362); *m* 1852, Charlotte Mann (1828-1904); see Vol. I, p. 754 for Mann lineage.
1–*m* June 5, 1879, Harriet Banks Gould (Dec. 10, 1853-July 8, 1905); dau. William Gould, publisher, banker, Albany, N.Y.; issue: 1–William Gould (*b* and *d* Nov. 10, 1886); 2–Alice, *b* Westborough, Mass., Nov. 17, 1888; Wellesley, '12; *m* June 5, 1915, Charles Henry Paul; 3–Nathaniel Emmons, Jr., *b* Westborough Oct. 1, 1890; Harvard, '13; 2d lt., F.A., Aug. 15, 1917; 1st lt., U.S.A., Oct. 30, 1918-Jan. 31, 1919; 4–Mary, *b* W. Newton, Mass., July 28, 1892; Wellesley, '15; *m* June 15, 1916, Sydney Dakin Chamberlain.
1–*m* 2d, Feb. 14, 1907, Martha Lee Gilmor, *b* Kennett Square, Pa., Oct. 9, 1867; dau. Rev. John Scott Gilmor, W. Alexander, Pa., later Stony Point, N.Y.
1–A.B., Hamilton, '74, A.M., 1877; M.D., Albany Med. Coll., 1875. Physician (see Who's Who in America). Mem. S.M.D., Inst. Am. Genealogy, etc. Residence: 1640 Washington St., W. Newton, Mass.

1–**PAINTER, Cora Herndon (Mrs. William Rock),** *b* Carroll Co., Mo., Sept. 3, 1865.
9–Dr. John **Woodson** (qv);
8–Robert (1632-post 1707), of Fleurdin Hundred, Va.; *m* ca. 1656, Elizabeth Ferris (Richard[9], of "Curlees");
7–Mary, of "Curlees"; *m* 1704, George **Payne** (*d* 1744), justice, Goochland Co., Va., 1728-29; sheriff, 1734-37;
6–Josias (1705-85), Goochland Co.; burgess from Goochland Co., 1761-65; *m* 1730, Ann Fleming (they were the g.parents of Dolly Madison);
5–Agnes (*b* 1739), Goochland Co.; *m* 1759, William **Mitchell** (1730-96), high sheriff, Goochland Co., 1773; justice, 1776;
4–Patsy Ann (*b* 1762), *m* 1784, Archelaus **Perkins** (1760-1849), ens., lt., and at close of Am. Rev. was made maj.; high sheriff, 1818; sheriff and collector, 1819; moved to Mo., 1830;
3–Ann Reed (1793-1872), *m* 1812, James **Herndon** (1791-1857), sgt. in War 1812; moved to Mo. 1830;
2–Isaac Otey (1824-1901), *m* 1st, 1851, Mary Brent Sterne (1834-60); *m* 2d, 1863, Sarah Amanda Day (1836-1915); issue (1st marriage): I–Leolelia Henry (*b* 1857; *m* 1891, John Gibson Hale); issue (2d marriage): I–Cora (1 above).
1–*m* Jan. 12, 1888, William Rock Painter, *b* Carrollton, Mo., Aug. 27, 1863; formerly lt. gov. of Mo., now state senator; son of Samuel Lee Painter, of Carrollton, *m* Sallie Ann Rock; issue (all *b* Carroll Co., Mo.): 1–Amanda Herndon, *b* Oct. 24, 1888; U.Mo.; *m* April 7, 1915, Eugene F., son of Henry Huston Salisbury, of Webster Groves, Mo., now of Chicago, Ill. (issue: William Painter; Henry Huston); 2–Sarah Ann, *b* June 7, 1891; U.Mo.; *m* Dec. 19, 1917, Charles Hudson, son of Dr. St. Cloud Cooper, of Ft. Smith, Ark. (issue: Sarah Painter); 3–Herndon William (July 27, 1902-Dec. 30, 1919).

1–Chmn. bd. mgrs., Arrow Rock Tavern. Baptist. Democrat. Mem. C.D.XVIIC., D.C.W., D.A.R. (chaplain gen. nat. soc.), U.S.D. 1812 (nat. rec. sec., pres. Mo. state soc.), D.A.C., U.D.C., Mo. Valley Hist. Soc., Am. War Mothers, League Am. Pen Women, P.E.O. Club: Magazine. Residence: 603 N. Main St., Carrollton, Mo.

1–**PALMER, William Lincoln,** *b* Portland, Me., Sept. 19, 1868.
11–Lord James **Prescott** (*d* 1582/83), purchased manor of Driby, Lincolnshire, Eng., 1579/80; *m* 1st, Alice, dau. of Sir Richard Molyneux (*d* 1581), Kt. of Sefton, Co. Lancaster, Eng.;
10–John, *m* Elizabeth Manby (Francis[11], of Elsham);
9–James (bap. 1607-1639), of Heighington; *m* Mary Copeland (John[10], of Ross, Co. Hereford);
8–James, came to N.H., 1665 (qv);
7–Jonathan (Aug. 6, 1675-Jan. 6, 1755), settled at Hampton (now Kensington), N.H.; admitted to ch., 1749; one of petitioners of Kensington, 1736; worked at Ft. William and Mary, 1696; mem. of scouting party under Capt. John Gilman, 1710; *m* 1695, Elizabeth–;
6–Jonathan (July 16, 1696-Jan. 19, 1746), selectman, Hampton Falls; capt. in expdn. against Louisburg, 1744-45; *m* Apr. 3, 1721, Judith Gove (*b* Dec. 18, 1700; Ebenezer[7], *m* Judith Sanborn; Lt. Edward[8], *m* Hannah, dau. Capt. William Titcomb; John[9]);
5–Jonathan (Oct. 8, 1723-Dec. 10, 1809), settled at Kensington; signed Assn. Test, 1776; served in N.Y. campaign thruout Am. Rev.; removed to Gilmanton, 1793; *m* Oct. 24, 1745, Rachel Clifford (*b* Dec. 18, 1723; Samuel[6], *m* Sarah, dau. Samuel Dow; Israel[7]; John[8]; George[9]);
4–Jonathan (Feb. 21, 1759-June 4, 1813), to Gilmanton, N.H., with his father; *m* Sept. 17, 1780, Lydia Tuck;
3–Martha (July 4, 1789-Mar. 23, 1879), *m* as his 2d wife, Jonathan **Palmer** (see Vol. II, p. 55);
2–James Monroe (2 below).
9–Robert **Tuck** (qv);
8–Edward (*d* 1652), *m* Mary Philbrick (Thomas[9]);
7–Dea. John (1652-1742), Hampton, N.H.; *m* 1678, Bethia Hobbs (1659-1738; Morris[8], *m* Sarah, dau. William Eastow);
6–Jonathan (1697-1781), *m* 1721, Tabitha Towle (1697-1766; Benjamin[7], *m* Sarah, dau. Michael Bowden; Philip[8], *m* Isabella, dau. Francis Austin);
5–Samuel (1731-89), Kensington, N.H.; *m* 1754 Martha Blake (1733-1821; Philemon[6], *m* Lydia, dau. John Boulter; Philemon[7], *m* Sarah, dau. Henry Dearborn; Jasper[8]);
4–Lydia (*b* Sept. 8, 1762), *m* Jonathan **Prescott** (4 above);
3–Martha, *m* Jonathan **Palmer** (3 above);

REV. JAMES MONROE PALMER (1822-97), A.B., Colby College, '47; Congregational minister.

2–James Monroe (Oct. 5, 1822-May 23, 1897), see portrait; *m* 1853, Caroline Frances Bacon (see Vol. II, p. 55, for genealogy and Vol. III, p. 363, for portrait).
1–*m* Apr. 14, 1892, Jennie Christine Giesler (July 22, 1873-Apr. 1, 1919), for whom the new $750,000 Palmer Memorial Cancer Hosp., Boston, was named; dau. of Charles A. Giesler, of Princeton, Me.; issue: 1–Jennie Carolyn, *b* Dorchester, Mass., Nov. 22, 1894; *m* June 28, 1920, Sheldon Smith Mayo (issue: Priscilla, *b* Aug. 1, 1922; Alden Sheldon, *b* Feb. 9, 1927); 2–Marion Prescott, *b* Boston, Mass., Sept. 29, 1897; *m* June 17, 1918, Walter Lafayette Abbott, Jr. (issue: Walter P., *b* Nov. 19, 1919); 3–William Lincoln, Jr., *b* Cambridge, Mass., July 7, 1909.
1–*m* 2d, June 19, 1922, Frances Hunt Johnson, *d* Feb. 17, 1925 (see Vol. II, p. 56, for genealogy).
1–*m* 3d, Feb. 2, 1927, Marian W., *b* Apr. 4, 1875; dau. of Horace Wiley Brackett, *m* Aug. 12, 1862, Maranda I. Stone, both of Belfast, Me.
1–Grad. Gordon Coll., Boston, '91. Realtor, genealogist, Boston. Mem. S.M.D., S.C.W., S.A.R., etc. Residence: Boston and Cambridge, Mass.

1–**PARKER, Francis LeJau,** *b* Abbeville, S.C., June 24, 1873.
7–John **Parker** (*d* ca. 1695), from Eng. to Jamaica, B.W.I.; came to S.C.; settled at "Hayes," St. James Parish, Goose Creek; *m* Sarah–;
6–John (*d* 1735), of "Hayes" and Parker's Ferry, for which he held the charter; mem. House of Commons, 1723-24,1728-29; *m* Jane–;
5–John (1735-1802), mem. Commons for St. James, Goose Creek, 1761-62, et seq.; mem. Conv. and Provincial Congress, 1774-75; senator from St. James, 1779-88; mem. Privy Council, 1779; *m* Mary Daniel;
4–Thomas (1760-1820), of "Woodlands," adjoining "Hayes"; served with Charles Town regt., S.C. militia, 1779; U.S. dist. atty. for S.C., 1792-1820; *m* Mary Drayton (William Henry[5], chief justice of the colony, pres. Provincial Congress, mem. Colonial Congress, Phila., 1779);
3–Thomas (1793-1844), atty., Charleston; removed to Rocky Grove Plantation, Abbeville Dist., S.C., ca. 1823; served in Seminole War in Florida; *m* Eleanor Legaré Frost (Rev. Thomas[4], of Charleston; g.g.dau. Francis LeJau, formerly of Angers, France, 1st rector at Goose Creek Ch.);
2–William Henry (2 below).

7–Robert **Wardlaw** (*b* ca. 1670), from Scotland to America; prob. Pa.;
6–William (ca. 1700-1762), from Scotland to Pa., ca. 1720; removed to Augusta (now Rockbridge) Co., Va., 1740-45; *m* ca. 1730, Jane Harper;
5–Hugh (1740-1802), removed from Va. to Ninety-Six Dist. (later Abbeville Co.), S.C., 1767; served as capt. of militia in Revolutionary forces; justice, Abbeville Co. Ct., 1797-1800; *m* 1st, 1763, Elizabeth Coalter (1744-90), by whom had 12 children; *m* 2d, Mrs. Mary (Logan) Miller; no issue;
4–James (1767-1842), clk. Abbeville Co. Ct. nearly 40 yrs.; *m* 1796, Hannah Clarke (1778-1825; Francis[5], of Phila., *m* Alice Rice); their son Francis Hugh, was 1st chancellor and justice Ct. of Appeals, 1859, also mem. com. of three which drafted Ordinance of Secession;
3–David Lewis (1799-1873), grad. with 1st honor, S.C. Coll., 1816; elected to Legislature 6 terms, 1826-36; speaker S.C. Ho. of Rep., 1836; judge, 1841; asso. justice Ct. of Appeals, 1865-68; del. to State Conv., which adopted Ordinance of Secession, 1860; *m* 1825, Sarah Rosalie Allen (1807-45);
2–Lucia Garvey (1833-97), *m* 1856, William Henry **Parker** (1828-1905), grad. S.C. Coll., 1846; admitted to bar, 1850; commr. in equity, 1856-69; capt. and adj., 19th S.C. Vols., C.S.A., 1862; mem. Legislature, many yrs.; pres. S.C. Bar Assn., 1887; issue: I–Sarah Allen (1856-58); II–Ellen Elizabeth (1858-59); III–Edward Frost (1860-72); IV–William Henry (1861-1924; mem. Charleston bar; *m* Elizabeth Robertson; 2 sons, Ens. William Henry, Jr., and Lt. Louis T. Parker, U.S.A., had service in World War); V–Rosalie Simkins (1863-70); VI–Lewis Wardlaw (1865-1916; mem. Greenville, S.C., bar and pres. Parker Mills; *m* Margaret Smith, *d* 1928; son Lt. Austin S. Parker, served in World War); VII–Allen Wardlaw (1867-91); VIII–Margaret Wardlaw (1869-70); IX–Thomas Drayton (*b* 1871; cdr. U.S.N., retired; *m* Rose Florence Bland); X–Francis LeJau (1 above); XI–Lucia Wardlaw (*b* 1875; served with A.R.C. in France, 1917-19).
1–Not married. U.S.M.A., '94; honor grad., Army Sch. of the Line, 1908; grad. Army Staff Coll., 1909; Army War Coll., 1920. Commd. 2d lt., 5th Cav., 1894, and promoted thru the grades to rank of brig. gen., N.A., 1918; chief of Bureau of Insular Affairs, with rank of brig. gen., 1929–. Served on Tex. Border, in Cuba, Porto Rico, Philippine Islands during Philippine Insurrection and later with civil govt.; in China, Roumania, Russia; with A.E.F. in France as cdr., 171st Inf. Brigade; in Mexico; with Plebiscitary Commn., Tacna-Arica, 1925-26; with Electoral Mission, Nicaragua, 1928; and at various camps in U.S. (see Who's Who in America). Address: Bureau of Insular Affairs, War Dept., Washington, D.C.

1–**PARKER, George Pleasant,** *b* Bedford Co., Va., Nov. 17, 1863.
5–probably William **Parker** (*d* 1805), said to have come from Md. via Fauquier Co., Va., and settled in Pittsylvania Co., Va., before Am. Rev.;
4–George (1769-1859), *m* 1797, Frances Oaks (1773-1858);
3–Ammon Hancock (1807-80), Bedford Co., Va.; *m* 1835, Frances H. Goggin;
2–Robert William (2 below).
8–Thomas **Moorman,** from Eng., 1670, settled in Nansemond Co., Va.; *m* Elizabeth–;
7–Charles (1690-1757), *m* 1710, Elizabeth Reynolds (*d* 1765; Christopher[8]);
6–Thomas (ca. 1710-1766), *m* 1730, Rachel Clark (*d* 1792; Christopher[7], Hanover Co., capt. Colonial army, justice Louisa Co., *m* ca. 1709, Penelope–);
5–Rachel (ca. 1754-post 1802), *m* 1773, Stephen **Goggin** (1752-1802), 1st lt. Bedford Co. militia during Am. Rev. (Stephen[6], from Ireland, settled in Bedford Co., Va., ca. 1759, *m* 2d, Susannah Terry);
4–Stephen (1789-1872), *m* 1808, Janet Robertson (1792-1875; Jeffry[5], *m* Nancy Dickerson; Nicholas[6]; Nicholas[7]);
3–Frances H. (1812-77), *m* Ammon H. **Parker** (3 above).
7–Alexander **Walker** (desc. George Walker, Gent., from Eng., 1607, with Capt. Newport and Capt. John Smith), of Surry, Charles City and Prince George cos., Va.; ordained and licensed to preach in Va., 1699;
6–David, mem. vestry of Bristol Parish, Va., 1735-43, later vestryman and ch. warden of Bath Parish; *m* Mary–;
5–David (1731-post 1791), of Dinwiddie Co., Va.; lt. in Am. Rev.; *m* 1756, Peletiah Jones (*d* ante 1791; William[6], *m* Mary–);
4–Robert Munford (1772-1827), Bedford Co.; *m* 1796, Mary Smith (1777-1811; Isham[5], *m* Patience–);
3–Dr. James Alexander (1802-69), physician, Bedford Co.; *m* 1837, Nancy Moorman Jopling;
2–Rebecca Louise Fitzhugh (2 below).
6–Thomas **Jopling** (1708-89), living in Albemarle Co., Va., 1749; capt. of minutemen of Amherst Co.; *m* 1743, Hannah–;
5–Josiah (1747-97), pvt. Am. Rev.; *m* 1767, Elizabeth Ware;
4–James (1769-1852), Bedford Co.; *m* 1793, Nancy Martin (1776-1827; Pleasant[5], *m* Rebecca Jopling; Thomas[6]; John[7]; Abram[8]);
3–Nancy Moorman (1814-73), *m* 1837, Dr. James A. **Walker** (3 above);
2–Rebecca L. F. (1840-67), *m* 1860, Robert William **Parker** (1838-65), farmer; last man in C.S.A. killed in Civil War, shot at Appomattox, Va., April 9, 1865; issue: I–Robert Moorman (1861-1902; *m* Sallie Viola Wappett); II–George Pleasant (1 above); III–Frances Rebecca (*b* 1865; *m* Robert W. Dooley).
1–*m* Nov. 11, 1903, Lula Eastman Jeter (qv for issue).
1–Sr. mem. Parker-Ayres Hardware Co., Bedford, Va.; dir. Piedmont Label Co., Overstreet-Smith Lumber Co. Mem. Town Council of Bedford, 1926,28. Mem. S.V., etc. Mason, Elk. Methodist. Democrat. Summer place: Hemlock Hut, Peaks of Otter, Thaxton, Va. Residence: 516 Blue Ridge Av., Bedford, Va.

1–**PARKER, Lula Eastman Jeter (Mrs. George P.),** *b* Bedford Co., Va., Aug. 3, 1873.
7–John **Jeter,** from Eng., settled nr. Port Royal, Caroline Co., Va.; *m* 2d, Elizabeth–;
6–Thomas (*d* 1765), *m* Winifred–;
5–Henry (ca. 1744-1821), 1st lt. Bedford Co. militia during Am. Rev.; *m* Elizabeth Bell (1747-1833);
4–Sovereign, *m* 1st, 1806, Matilda Vaughan (*d* 1833; James[5], pvt. Amelia Co. militia, *m* Mary, dau. of Thomas Jeter);
3–Fielden Harris (1810-94), *m* 1st, Virginia Ann White;
2–Thomas Alexander (2 below).
6–Henry **White** (*d* 1802; probably son of Daniel [*d* 1790], of Culpeper Co., Va.); *m* perhaps Catherine–;
5–Jacob (1765-1832), Am. Rev.; *m* 1781, Hannah Spiers (*d* 1816);
4–Jacob Washington (1792-1829), *m* 1812, Matilda Buford;
3–Virginia Ann (1820-77), *m* Fielden H. **Jeter** (3 above).
11–Richard (Beaufort) **Buford** (qv);
10–John (1642-1722), *m* 1662, Elizabeth Parrat (*b* 1645; Richard[11], from Barbados, an early settler in Lancaster Co., Va., 1649);
9–Thomas (1663-1716), *m* ca. 1681, Mary– (*d* 1720);
8–Thomas (1682-1761), *m* ca. 1703/04, Elizabeth– (*b* 1675);
7–John (1707-87), began to write name Buford; *m* ante 1735, Judith Philippe (*d* post 1785; dau. of Claude Philippe de Richebourg, from France to Va., 1700);
6–James (1740-post 1798), capt. Am. Rev.; *m* 1761, Elizabeth Bramblett (William[7]);
5–William (*d* 1794), *m* 1783, Martha Hill Logwood;
4–Matilda (1793-1876), *m* Jacob Washington **White** (4 above).
7–Edmund **Logwood** (*d* in Chesterfield Co., Va., 1775), from Eng.; *m* in Eng., Jane Eke;
6–Thomas (1740-1821), capt. Am. Rev.; *m* Ann Aiken, of Chesterfield Co., Va.; *m* 2d, Mrs. Martha Minnis, of Bedford Co., Va.;
5–Martha Hill, *m* 1st, William **Buford** (5 above).
5–James (Mayse) **Mays** (*d* 1792; desc. from William Mays, minister at "Kecoughtan," in Va., 1617); settled in Bedford Co., 1777; *m* Mary–;
4–James (*d* 1847), *m* 1802, Patsy Wright (*d* 1850; Joseph[5]; Thomas[6]);
3–Joseph Wright (1811-1900), began to write name Mays; *m* 1841, Malinda Wright (1812-79; Anthony[4], *m* Betsy Mayse; John[5], Am. Rev.; Thomas[6]);

2–Laurie Cornelia (1851-76), *m* 1872, Thomas Alexander **Jeter** (1841-85), teacher, county official, tobacconist; issue: I–Lula Eastman (1 above); II–Laura M. (*b* 1875; *m* Jesse Thornhill Davidson, II).
1–*m* Nov. 11, 1903, George Pleasant Parker (qv); issue (all *b* Bedford, Va.): 1–Georgette, *b* Aug. 2, 1907; B.S., Coll. of William and Mary, '30; 2–Laura Jeter, *b* June 1, 1911; Coll. of William and Mary, '32; 3–Virginia Hamilton (July 6, 1913-Sept. 29, 1919); 4–Josephine Mays, *b* June 27, 1914.
1–Ed. Hollins Coll. Mem. Huguenot Soc. Founders of Manakin, D.A.R.; pres. Bedford Co. Federation of Women's Clubs, 1917-19. Methodist. Democrat. Co-author: "Our Kin," history and genealogies of some of the old families of Bedford Co., Va. Residence: 516 Blue Ridge Av., Bedford, Va.

1–**MURPHY, Robert Neal,** *b* Sampson Co., N.C., July 22, 1889.
6–Patrick (McMurdock) **Murphy** (1720-85), from Scotland to Wilmington, N.C., 1774; settled in New Hanover Co., N.C.; Presbyn.; *m* in Scotland, Elizabeth Kelso (1724-98);
5–Hugh (*b* Scotland, 1754), pvt. Bladen Co., N.C., militia, Am. Rev.; *m* Catherine McMillian;
4–Archibald, Bladen Co.; *m* Elizabeth Mulford;
3–Hugh Neal (*d* 1865), settled in Sampson Co., N.C.; served in War Between the States, 1861-65; *m* Olive Page;
2–John Robert, grist mill owner and planter, Sampson Co., Presbyn.; *m* Ella Lula Balkcum; issue: I–Effie (*d* aet. 21); II–Robert N. (1 above); III–Margaret Lula (*m* Robert Sidney Mebane); IV–Hugh Tate (*b* 1892; served in World War; *m* —Bahr).
1–*m* Dec. 25, 1912, Anne Jacobs Boykin (qv).
1–C.P.A. course, Va. Mechanic's Inst. Flour broker. Mason. Episcopalian. Residences: 2501 Stuart Av., Richmond, Va., and 514 Princess St., Wilmington, N.C.

1–**MURPHY, Anne Jacobs Boykin (Mrs. Robert N.),** *b* Wilmington, N.C., Jan. 4, 1893.
8–Edward **Boykin** (*d* 1728), received grant of 525 acres in Isle of Wight Co., Va., 1685, for bringing 11 persons into the colony of Va.; received other grants, 1704,13,14,15,24; had 1,100 acres in 1704; *m* Ann– (*d* 1725);
7–Edward (ca. 1676-will dated 1743), Northampton Co., N.C.; received grants in Isle of Wight Co., Va., 1725,31,47; *m* Judith–;
6–Solomon (*d* 1771), had land grant in Brunswick Co., Va., 1753; removed to St. George's Parish, Ga., ante 1765; *m* Esther–;
5–Byus, or Bias (*d* 1812), soldier Am. Rev.; received bounty grants in Ga. for services; settled in Sampson Co., nr. Clinton, N.C.; *m* Sarah Peebles, of Va.;
4–Gen. Thomas (1785 or 86-1829), capt. Co. 5, detached from Sampson Co. militia, during War 1812, later commd. gen. Sampson Co. militia; mem. House of Commons, 1815,21,22,27,28; senator, 1824-31; *m* 1808, Elizabeth Fennell (1788-1844; Nicholas[5], received land grant from George, III, for services, received another grant from state of N.C., 1794, pvt. in Am. Rev., *m* Margaret, dau. of James Robinson);
3–Robinson Fennell (1819-98), planter, Sampson Co.; *m* 1842, Cynthia Ann Hobbs;
2–Byus Franklin (2 below).
11–Robert **Middleton** (will 1696), from Eng. to York Co., Va., later moving to Westmoreland Co.; received grant of 700 acres, 1665, 1,120 acres in Westmoreland Co., Va., 1666; *m* Mary–;
10–John, *m* Elizabeth– (will 1733);
9–John (will 1741), granted 640 acres by King George, II, in Onslow Co., N.C., 1736; *m* Sarah–;
8–James (will 1801, proved 1805), 1st lt., Independent Co., 1771, capt. militia, 1776; senator, 1780; mem. House of Commons; received land grant 1774, and on head Waters of Maxwell Swamp, 1779; *m* Mary Nixon; and thru:
6–James (will dated 1793), Duplin Co., N.C.; *m* Sarah–;
5–Isaac (will dated 1820), *m* Jane–;
4–Sarah (*b* 1797), *m* as his 1st wife, Abraham **Hobbs** (*b* 1791);
3–Cynthia Ann (1820-85), *m* Robinson F. **Boykin** (3 above).
7–Nicholas (Bourden) **Bowden,** of King and Queen Co., Va.; received land grant in Isle of Wight Co.; *m* Prudence–;
6–Nicholas (1741-will 1813), received 170 acres in Duplin Co., N.C.;
5–Baker, began to write name Bowden;
4–Lemuel, owned "Bottle Branch" and "Stag Park," two large plantations in New Hanover Co., N.C.; *m* Susan Cowan Kinneair;
3–Lt. Lemuel Henry (1825 or 26-1891), lt., Co. I, 10th Regt. Light Arty.; alderman, Wilmington, N.C., 8 yrs.; *m* Mary Jane Flournoy (Jacobs) King, widow of James Alexis King;
2–Julia Augusta (2 below).
8–Nicholas (Jacob) **Jacobs** (qv);
7–Joseph (1646-1708), a founder of Bristol, R.I., 1681; *m* ca. 1670, Hannah Bosworth (*b* 1650; Nathaniel[8], built the first house at Bristol, 1680, still occupied by descendants);
6–Benjamin (*b* Hingham, Mass., 1680), with father to R.I.;
5–Benjamin (1743-95), sgt. in Am. Rev.; Mason; *m* 1765, Susanna Beal (1747-85);
4–Joseph (*b* 1775), to Wilmington, N.C., 1803; *m* 2d, 1810, Jane Larkins (Col. William S.[5]);
3–Mary Jane Flournoy (1822-87), as Widow King, *m* 2d, Lemuel Henry **Bowden** (3 above).
10–Richard **Warren,** Mayflower Pilgrim (qv);
9–Ann, *m* 1633, Thomas **Little** (qv);
8–Patience (*d* 1723), *m* Joseph **Jones** (1659-1714);
7–Thomas (1679-1723), *m* Catharine Caswell (*d* 1761);
6–Sarah (1717-50), *m* Elijah **Beal** (1714-89);
5–Susanna (1747-85), *m* Benjamin **Jacobs** (5 above).
2–Byus Franklin **Boykin** (1847-1900), student, Wake Forrest Coll.; pvt. in War Between the States; *m* 1889, Julia Augusta Bowden (*b* 1859), grad. Davenport Female Coll.; mem. D.A.R.; issue: I–Mary Lemuel (*b* 1891; mem. D.A.C., D.A.R., U.D.C., U.S.D. 1812); II–Anne Jacobs (1 above); III–Augusta Bowden (*b* 1894; *m* Curtis Wayne Spencer); IV–Byus Frank (1896-1918); V–Owen Moore (*d* aet. 3 mos.); VI–John Robinson (*b* 1899; *m* 1924, Mary Elizabeth Newell); VII–Ida Love (*d* infancy).
1–*m* Dec. 25, 1912, Robert Neal Murphy (qv).
1–Mem. U.D.C., U.S.D. 1812. Episcopalian. Residences: 2501 Stuart Av., Richmond, Va., and 514 Princess St., Wilmington, N.C.

1–**NIMMO, Annie Boyd Ball (Mrs. Walden C.),** *b* Baltimore, Md., Jan. 3, 1870.
9–Edward **Dorsey** (qv);
8–Col. Edward (1645-1705), of "Major's Choice," Anne Arundel Co., Md.; justice, 1679-89; asso. judge High Ct. of Chancery, 1695-96; burgess, 1694-97, 1701-05; capt., 1686; maj., 1687; maj. of troop of horse, 1689; col., 1702; *m* 1st, 1675, Sarah Wyatt (Nicholas[9]);
7–Capt. Joshua (1686-1747), justice, Baltimore Co., 1712-14; capt. militia, 1742; *m* 1711, Ann Ridgely (*d* 1771; Henry[8], *m* Catherine, dau. of Col. Nicholas Greenberry; Col. Henry[9]);
6–Nicholas (1725 or 28-1792), of "Huntington Quarter," Annapolis Junction; *m* Elizabeth Worthington (*d* 1804; Capt. John[7], *m* Helen, dau. Capt. Thomas Hammond; Capt. John[8], from Eng.);
5–Sarah (1771-1828), *m* 1788, William **Ball** (1768-1841), War 1812; justice, Baltimore Co., 1827; sheriff, 1824-27;
4–William (1790-1863), *m* 1814, Elizabeth Dorsey;
3–Owen Dorsey (1817-98), *m* Elizabeth Frances Boyd (1817-1904);
2–David Charles (2 below).
9–Matthew **Howard,** patented land in Lower Norfolk, Va., 1650; removed to Severn; *m* Ann–;
8–Capt. Cornelius (1635-80), ens., Anne Arundel Co. militia, 1661; burgess, 1671-75; justice, 1678; *m* Elizabeth (Sission?);
7–Joseph (*d* 1736), *m* Margery Keith;
6–Henry (1712-73), justice; *m* Sarah Dorsey (John[7], *m* Honor, dau. Thomas Elder; Col. Edward, 8 above);
5–Honor (*d* 1817), removed to "Elioak"; *m* 4th, Michael **Dorsey** (*d* 1812; Michael[6], *m* Ruth, dau. Capt. Lancelott Todd, 1674-1735);
4–Elizabeth (1785-1857), *m* William **Ball** (4 above);
3–Owen Dorsey, *m* Elizabeth Frances Boyd (3 above);
2–David Charles (*b* Frederick, Md., Apr. 4, 1844-*d* DeVere Place, Baltimore Co., Md., Apr. 29, 1926), *m* 1867, Anne DeVere (for issue see Vol. I, p. 61).

1–*m* Aug. 24, 1895, Walden Carey Nimmo (*b* Baltimore, 1866-*d* 1923), son of James Nimmo, of Baltimore; issue: 1–Ruth Natali, *b* Baltimore, Sept. 14, 1897; grad. Goucher Coll., '20; *m* James C., son of Thomas Heath Harlan, of Mo.
1–Mem. Md. Hist. Soc. Residence: 3207 N. Calvert St., Baltimore, Md.

1–**ORR, Harriet Norton (Mrs. L. R.),** *b* Earlville, Ill., Aug. 31, 1859.
9–Nicholas **Norton** (1610-90), from Eng. to Weymouth, Mass., 1635, later at Martha's Vineyard; in Pequot War; *m* Elizabeth– (*d* 1690);
8–Joseph (1651-1741), 1st rep. from Edgartown to the 1st Gen. Ct. of Mass., 1692; sheriff, 1699; justice Ct. of Common Pleas, 1702; *m* 1673, Mary Bayes (Thomas[9]);
7–Ebenezer, *m* Deborah Mayhew;
6–Peter (1718-92), Am. Rev.; *m* Sarah Bassett;
5–Samuel (1743-1801), lt. Am. Rev.; *m* 1766, Mrs. Mollie (Davis) Norton (1744-1820; Meletiah Davis[6], lt. col. sea coast regt. during Am. Rev., *m* Jemmiah Dunham);
4–Henry (1770-1844), *m* 1792, Hannah Gower (1775-1864);
3–William Gower (1808-94), *m* 1830, Elmira Parker (1812-78; Josiah, Jr.[4], Am. Rev., *m* 2d, 1802, Ruth Paine);
2–William Henry (2 below).
11–John **Howland,** Mayflower Pilgrim (qv);
10–Hope (*b* ca. 1630), *m* John **Chipman** (1621-1708);
9–Hope (1652-1728), *m* 1670, John **Huckins** (1649-78);
8–Mary (1673-1743), *m* ca. 1691, Nathan **Bassett** (ca. 1666-1743);
7–Samuel (1693-1770), *m* Martha– (*d* 1762);
6–Sarah (1720-1804), *m* ca. 1740, Peter **Norton** (6 above).
10–Henry **Smith,** from Eng. in the "Diligent," 1638, to Hingham, Mass., to Rehoboth, 1645;
9–Ens. Henry (ante 1638-1676), *m* 1657, Elizabeth Cooper;
8–Ens. Joshua (1658-1719), *m* Mary Peck (Nicholas[9]);
7–Dea. Joshua (1695-1745), *m* 1721, Mary Whittaker (*b* 1700);
6–Joshua (*b* 1724), soldier Am. Rev.; *m* 2d, 1756, Elizabeth (Perren) Walker:
5–Daniel (1761-1826), pvt. Am. Rev.; *m* 1785, Mary Bliss (1763-1842; Ephriam[6], Am. Rev., *m* Sarah Reed);
4–David (1788-1863), *m* 1810, Susannah Brown;
3–Daniel B. (1813-96), *m* 1835, Harriet Burt;
2–Harriet Adelaide (2 below).
9–Chad **Brown** (qv);
8–Jeremiah (post 1638-1690), *m* Mary–; *m* 2d, ante 1680, Mary– (widow of Thomas Cook);
7–Joseph (post 1680-1764), *m* ca. 1703, Sarah Pray (John[8], *m* Sarah Brown);
6–Joseph (*b* 1726/27-*d* Cheshire, Mass., 1807), *m* 2d, 1752, Hopestill (Dexter) Peck (1726-1815; James Dexter[7], *m* Hannah Wilkinson);
5–Simon (1756-1810?), *m* 1782, Elizabeth Topliff;
4–Susannah (1786-1864), *m* David **Smith** (4 above).
9–Richard **Burt** (*d* 1647), from Eng., 1638; settled at Taunton, Mass.;
8–Richard (*b* Eng., 1629), arrived with father, 1638; *m* Charity–;
7–Abel (*b* 1657), *m* Grace Andrews;
6–Joseph, *m* Abigail–;
5–Elijah (1740-1817), *m* 1786, Sarah Williams (1771-1855);
4–Williams (*b* Berkley, Mass., 1790-*d* Earlville, Ill., 1853), *m* Lucy (Bowen?);
3–Harriet (1817-76), *m* Daniel B. **Smith** (3 above);
2–Harriet Adelaide (1837-74), *m* 1854, William Henry **Norton** (1831-1904), supt. water works; postmaster, Earlville; enlisted in Co. A, 104th Ill. Inf., 1862, discharged Oct. 7, 1864, for disability; he *m* 2d, Elizabeth Cook Hall; issue (1st marriage): I–Lawrence John (*b* 1855; *m* Alice Kellum, 1861-1927); II–Finette (*b* 1857; *m* Acker MacEachron); III–Harriet (1 above); IV–Maude (*b* 1861; *m* Samuel Wright Felton); issue (2d marriage): I–Vere (*b* 1879; *m* Henry W. Vroman).
1–*m* Aug. 23, 1883, Levi Ray Orr, *b* Freeland Corners, De Kalb Co., Ill., Dec. 3, 1860; son of David Orr (1818-93), of Wayne Co., O. (Samuel[8], from Ireland, settled in Wayne Co., O., *m* Mary Burnett, of N.J.), *m* Martha Jane McAfee (1825-97), from Ireland with parents to Wayne Co., O., 1837, to Ill., 1860; issue: 1–Ray Norton (May 28, 1885-Oct. 1, 1886); 2–Florence Ione, *b* Earlville, Ill., Nov. 22, 1887; Grinnell Coll., 1910; *m* Sept. 10, 1913, Alexander William Murray (issue: Marjorie Goodwin; Jean Orr); 3–Marjorie Adelaide, *b* Earlville, Oct. 6, 1890; *m* Sept. 6, 1916, Reuben N. Aspergren (issue: Brooke D.; Harriet Ann); 4–Marian Goodwin, *b* Des Moines, Ia., Aug. 14, 1894; grad. Wheelock Kindergarten Coll., 1917; Grinnell Coll., 1913-14; *m* Nov. 17, 1917, Lt. Norman Riley Hays; Grinnell Coll., '14; Harvard Law, 1917; entered 1st O.T.C., Ft. Snelling, Minn., commd. 2d lt. Aug. 15, 1917, 1st lt., Nov. 17, 1917, in service 25 months; commd. capt., Apr. 1919 in France, cited for gallantry in action (issue: Mary Harriet; Lorin Nelson, III; Lee Orr); 5–Lee Norton (June 9, 1898-Mar. 11, 1900).
1–Teacher and principal public schools. Mem. S.M.D., Desc. of Pilgrim John Howland, D.F.P.A., D.A.R., Daus. of Union Vets. of Civil War. Residence: 1418 3d Av., Cedar Rapids, Ia.

1–**PADDOCK, Abby Sanborn,** *b* Minneapolis, Minn., June 27, 1888.
10–Robert **Paddock** (*d* 1650), from Eng. to Duxbury, Mass., 1634; mem. mil. co., Plymouth, 1643; *m* Mary– (*d* 1650);
9–Zachariah (1640-1727), of Yarmouth; *m* 1659, Deborah Sears (Richard[10], qv);
8–Zachariah (1664-1718), *m* Bethia Hall (1667-1708; John[9], *m* Priscilla Bearse; John[10]);
7–Ichabod (1687-1750), *m* Joanna Faunce (1690-1758; Thomas[8], *m* Jean Nelson; John[9]);
6–Thomas (*b* 1723), *m* Hannah Thomas (William[7]);
5–Stephen (1766-1849), *m* Millicent Farnsworth (1779-1845);
4–Ora F. (1796-1867), *m* 1st, Sarah Williamson (1798-1829);
3–Henry Augustus (1823-84), Ft. Covington, N.Y.; *m* 1851, Mary Elizabeth Gove;
2–George Bridges Rodney Gove (2 below).
9–John **Gove** (*b* Eng., 1604), of East Smithfield, Sweden Court, London, Eng.; dealer in brass; to Charlestown, Mass., with wife and 3 children soon after 1647; *m* 1625, prob. Sarah Mott; *m* 2d, prob. Mary, dau. of Edward Gifford, of Eng.;
8–Dea. John (*b* Eng., 1627-1704), *m* 2d, 1677, Mary Woodward (Woodhead?) (1644-1700); *m* 3 times;
7–Jonathan (1682-1747), *m* 1st, 1706, Lydia Cooper (*d* 1740; Samuel[8]);
6–Dea. John (1707-60), *m* 1737/38, Tabitha Livermore (1711-69; Dea. Thomas[7], *m* Mary Bright);
5–Dr. Jonathan (1746-1818), A.M., Harvard, 1768; *m* 1st, 1770, Mary Hubbard (*b* 1748; Nathan[6], *m* Mary Patterson);
4–George B.R. (1778-1865), *m* 1804, Hannah Woodbury (1786-1861; Jesse[5], *m* Abigail Boutwell; Peter[6]; Josiah[7]; Josiah[8]; Peter[9]; John[10]);
3–Mary Elizabeth (1827-96), *m* Henry A. **Paddock** (3 above).
11–Stephen (Bachiler) **Batchelder** (qv);
10–Ann, *m* —(Samborne) **Sanborn** (prob. William, of Brimpton Berks.);
9–Lt. John (qv); *m* 1st, Mary Tuck;
8–John (ca. 1649-1727), *m* 1674, Judith Coffin (1653-1724; Tristram[9], qv);
7–Abner (1694-1780), *m* 1715, Rachel Shaw (Caleb[8]);
6–John (1723-1802), of Hampton Falls, Falmouth and Standish, Me.; began to write name Sanborn; *m* 1st, 1748, Lucy Sanborn (*d* 1775);
5–Peter (1751-1827), soldier Am. Rev.; *m* 1780, Lydia Richardson;
4–Rufus (1784-1859), *m* 1806, Sarah Cram (1787-1848);
3–George W. (1827-1908), *m* Abigail Brown (1831-1912; Cyrus[4], *m* Mary Burnham; Ephriam[5]; David[6]; Ephriam[7]; Thomas[8]; Thomas[9]);
2–Mary Abby (*b* 1858), *m* 1887, George Bridges Rodney Gove **Paddock** (1860-1928), merchant, farmer of Minneapolis, Minn.; issue: I–Abby S. (1 above); II–Henry Augustus (*b* 1890; *m* 1913, Pearl Berg); III–Elizabeth Gove (*b* 1894); IV–Rodney Bridges (*b* 1896; *m* 1921, Ruth Johnson); V–Daniel Mosher (*b* 1901; *m* 1922, Mabel Holmberg); VI–Mary Louise (*b* 1903).
1–Grad. Teachers State Coll., St. Cloud, Minn. Teacher, Junior High Sch., 20 yrs., now retired. Mem. D.A.R. Presbyterian. Residence: Willmar, Minn.

1-**PALMER, Howard,** *b* Norwich, Conn., Nov. 28, 1883.
9-Walter **Palmer** (qv);
8-Gershom (1644-46-1718), *m* 1667, Ann Denison (1649-94; Capt. George[9]);
7-George (1680-1728), *m* 1711, Hannah Palmer (*b* 1694);
6-Rev. Gershom (1725-1810), *m* 1747, Dorothy Brown (*d* 1808);
5-Rev. Reuben (1759-1822), *m* 1780, Lucretia Tyler (1764-1855);
4-Gideon (1793-1854), *m* 1813, Mercy M. Turner;
3-Hon. Elisha Hurlbut (1814-95), *m* 1837, Ellis Loomis;
2-George Smith (2 below).
7-Thomas **Turner** (*b* Scituate, Mass., ca. 1700-*d* 1792), settled at New London, Conn., ca. 1720; *m* 1727, Patience Bolles (both buried in 1st burying ground, New London);
6-Matthew (*b* 1733), *m* Mary Fargo;
5-Isaac (1754-1829), *m* 1776, Anna Comstock (*d* 1831);
4-Mercy Maria (1795-1870), *m* Gideon **Palmer** (4 above).
9-Dea. Joseph **Loomis** (qv);
8-Dea. John (1622-88), dep. Gen. Ct.; *m* Elizabeth Scott (*d* 1688; Thomas[9], of Hartford);
7-Dea. Samuel (*b* 1666), *m* Elizabeth White (*d* 1754);
6-Daniel (*b* 1709), *m* Hannah Withrell (*d* 1784);
5-John (1741-1811), *m* Rachel Harris (1737-1827);
4-Joel (1773-1867), *m* Ellis Chappell (1779-1853);
3-Ellis (1816-93), *m* Elisha H. **Palmer** (3 above).
10-Christopher **Avery** (qv);
9-Capt. James (*b* Eng., ca. 1620), in New London, Conn., Mar. 1651; *m* 1643, in Boston, Joanna Greenslade;
8-James (1646-1728), *m* 1669, Deborah Stallyon (*d* 1729);
7-Capt. Christopher (1679/80-1753), *m* 1704, at Preston, Conn., Abigail Parke;
6-Dea. John (1705-89), *m* Anne Stanton (1708-50);
5-Isaac (1743-1812), sgt., Lexington Alarm; *m* 1766, Mercy Williams (1745-1814);
4-Isaac (1771-1856), pvt. War 1812; *m* 1809, Abigail Amelia Guillaud (1784-1824), see Vol. III, p. 361;
3-Abigail Amelia (1819-90), *m* 1840, Dwight Wight **Cook** (1813-77);
2-Ida Amelia (1855-96), *m* 1879, as his 1st wife, George Smith **Palmer** (*b* 1855), B.A., Yale, '78; pres. Palmer Bros. Co., mfrs. cotton goods.
1-Not married. B.A., Yale, '05; LL.B., Harvard, 1908; admitted to bar and practiced at Boston. Sec. Palmer Bros. Co., 1919-29. Explored and surveyed Selkirk Mts., B.C., 1907-15; Canadian Govt. named "Mt. Palmer" in recognition of the work accomplished. Made many expeditions in remote portions of Canadian Rockies, 1916-27. Mem. Am. Inst. Mining Engrs.; fellow Royal Geog. Soc.; corr. mem. Geog. Soc. Phila.; mem. New London Co. Hist. Soc. (v.p.). Clubs: Century (N.Y.), British Alpine, Am. Alpine (pres. 1926-29). Author (see Who's Who in America). Residence: Hotel Mohican, 281 State St., New London, Conn.

1-**PALMER, John Simmons, 2d,** *b* Providence, R.I., Feb. 14, 1881.
11-Richard **Warren,** Mayflower Pilgrim (qv);
10-Elizabeth, *m* Richard **Church** (qv);
9-Joseph (1638-1711), *m* 1660, Mary Tucker (1640-1710; John[10]);
8-Abigail (1680-1720), *m* 1696, William **Simmons** (1672-1765), see Vol. III, p. 362;
7-Joseph (1702-78), *m* 1726, Rebecca Wood (1704-95);
6-Edward (1730-1803), *m* 1753, Mary Robinson (1738-77);
5-Lt. Jonathan (1755-1803), Am. Rev.; *m* 1778, Elizabeth Smith (1757-1819);
4-Elizabeth (1785-1853), *m* 1806, Gideon **Palmer** (1781-1854), see Vol. I, p. 613;
3-John Simmons (1824-1908), *m* 1848, Frances Prentice (1828-1906);
2-Julius (1854-1920), banker, jewelry mfr.; *m* 1878, Jessie Fearing Richmond (*b* 1857), see Vol. III, p. 362, and Vol. I, p. 613.
1-*m* June 14, 1911, Abbie Easton Greene, *b* Newport, R.I., Mar. 5, 1886; dau. Frederick Greene, Newport, R.I. (desc. John Greene), *m* Lizzie Chaffee Easton (desc. Gov. Nicholas Easton); issue (all *b* at Providence, R.I.): 1-Julius, *b* March 13, 1912; 2-Elizabeth, *b* Feb. 1, 1914; 3-Frances, *b* Dec. 19, 1915; 4-Jane Easton, *b* Mar. 30, 1917; 5-Ruth Richmond, *b* Aug. 13, 1921; 6-Richard Simmons, *b* Apr. 18, 1927.
1-Brown U., ex-'05 (Zeta Psi). Mem. S.M.D., S.A.R., N.E.H.G.S., I.A.G. (life). Clubs: Squantum, Bristol Yacht (ex-commodore), Barrington Yacht, Turks Head. Summer place: Warwick, R.I. Residence: 83 Arlington Av., Providence, R.I.

1-**PARKER, Amelia Day Campbell (Mrs. Alton B.),** *b* Cambridge, N.Y., Oct. 6, 1871.
9-Robert **Day** (qv);
8-John (*d* 1730), of Hartford, Conn.; *m* Sarah Butler;
7-John (1677-1752), of Colchester, Conn.; *m* 1696, Grace Spencer (1677-1714);
6-Benjamin (1704-77), *m* 1729, Margaret Foote (*d* 1801);
5-Benjamin (1731-1811), one of the original grantees of Royalton, Vt.: fence viewer; soldier in Am. Rev.; *m* 2d, 1764, Eunice (Rood) Young;
4-Sylvester (1770-1813), *m* 1794, Rachel Parkhurst (1775-1859);
3-Oel (1807-89), carpenter, of Royalton; *m* 1836, Mary Ann Wood (*d* 1878);
2-Amelia Parsons (2 below).
9-Myles **Standish** (qv);
8-Capt. Josiah (1634-90), *m* Sarah Allen, of Braintree;
7-Dea. Josiah (*d* 1753), Norwich, Conn.; *m* Sarah- (*d* 1741);
6-Mehitable, *m* Jabez **Rood**;
5-Eunice (1735-1806), of Colchester; *m* 2d, 1764, Benjamin **Day** (5 above).
2-Amelia Parsons Day (1853-1923), of Cambridge, N.Y.; *m* 1871, Andrew Arthur **Campbell** (*b* 1850), of Ireland; *m* 2d, William Henry Goddard; issue (1st marriage): I-Amelia D. (1 above); II-Effie May (*b* 1873; *m* 1896, Nelson Clark Bennett, *d* 1918); issue (2d marriage; surname Goddard): I-Bertah Belle (*b* 1880; *m* 1903, LeRoy Burbee); II-Oel D. (*b* 1882, adopted name Parker); III-Emma Louise (*b* 1884; *m* 1920, Edward Carrigan).
1-*m* Jan. 16, 1923, Alton Brooks Parker, *b* Cortland, N.Y. (May 14, 1852-*d* May 10, 1926), chief judge, N.Y. State Ct. of Appeals; Dem. nominee for Presidency, 1904 (see Who's Who in America); son of John Brooks Parker, of Cortland, N.Y., *m* Harriet Stratton.
1-Mem. S.M.D., Nat. Soc. C.D., D.A.C., D.F.P.A., D.A.R. (state historian N.Y.; nat. v.chmn. hist. research and preservation of records com.), I.A.G., N.Y. Colony N.E. Women (dir.). Trustee Schuyler Mansion (Albany); gov. Thomas Jefferson Memorial Foundation. Clubs: Women's Press (N.Y.), Ulster Country Garden, N.Y. State Officiers D.A.R. (dir.). Residence: Esopus, N.Y., and Hotel Savoy-Plaza, New York, N.Y.

1-**PARKER, Frances Augusta Reed (Mrs. D. Lindsay),** *b* Darien, Conn., Jan. 31, 1855.
7-John **Bouton** (qv);
6-Elizabeth (1679-1760), of Norwalk, Conn.; *m* 1698, Edmund **Warren,** or Waring (1673-1749);
5-Joseph (1723-1809), *m* 1754, Elizabeth Bixbee;
4-James (1757-1803), served in Am. Rev.; *m* 2d 1795, Hannah Selleck (1778-1806);
3-Phebe (1796-1872), *m* 1817, Hiram **Sanford** (1794-1855), War 1812; postmaster, Redding, Conn. (Elias[4], patriot Am. Rev., *m* Hannah Youngs; Seth[5], Conn. Assembly; Capt. Samuel[6]; Ezekiel[7]; Ezekiel[8]; Thomas[9], qv);
2-Phebe Maria (2 below).
9-Stephen **Hopkins,** Mayflower Pilgrim (qv);
8-Giles (1607-92), *m* 1639, Katherine Whelden (*d* 1689; Gabriel[9], of Eastham, Mass.);
7-Joshua (*b* 1657), Eastham; *m* 1681, Mary Cole (1658/59-1733/34; Daniel[8], *m* Mary-);
6-Phoebe (*b* 1702), *m* 1724/25, Moses **Bixbee** (1704-76);
5-Elizabeth (1731/32-1808), *m* 1754, Joseph **Warren** (5 above);
4-James, *m* 2d, Hannah Selleck (4 above);
3-Phebe, *m* Hiram **Sanford** (3 above);
2-Phebe Maria (1831-1915), Liberty, N.Y.; *m* 1854, Lewis Seymour **Reed** (1820-87; John[3], of Norwalk, Conn., *m* 3d, Martha Hoyt).
1-*m* Dec. 10, 1874, David Lindsay Parker (Dec. 25, 1848-July 17, 1915); son of James Parker,

of Dublin, Ireland; issue: 1–Ethel, *b* Darien, Conn., Sept. 15, 1876; Packer Inst., Brooklyn; *m* May 27, 1903, John Morris, son of John Morris Robinson, of St. John, N.B. (issue: Ruth Beverly; John Morris; Frances Parker; Catherine Mary); 2–Lindsay Reed, *b* Brooklyn, Feb. 5, 1878; E.E., Columbia, 1901.
1–Mem. S.M.D., D.A.R., I.A.G. Episcopalian. Residence: 108 2d St., Jackson, Mich.

1–**PARSONS, Charles Francis,** *b* Mankato, Minn., Jan. 18, 1872.
9–Capt. Thomas **White** (qv);
8–Lt. Ebenezer (1648-1703), Weymouth; *m* Hannah Phillips (Lt. Nicholas[9]);
7–Ebenezer (1672-1756), grad. Harvard, 1692; settled as pastor, Bridgehampton, L.I., 1695-1748, over 53 yrs.;
6–Sylvanus (1700-82), grad. Harvard, 1722; Presbyn. pastor, Southampton, L.I., 1727-82, 55 yrs.; *m* Phebe Howell (Lt. Hezekiah[7], of Southampton);
5–Sylvanus, Jr. (*b* 1730), removed to Orange Co., N.Y., post 1754; settled on 300 acres of land, Blagg's Cove, which has become the "White Homestead"; *m* 1754, Eunice Herrick;
4–Nathan Herrick, *m* Frances Howell (desc. Edward Howell, qv);
3–Albert Smith (1803-64), grad. highest honors, Union Coll., 1822; from Orange Co., N.Y., to Lafayette, Ind., 1829; U.S. senator from Ind., 1839-45; U.S. dist. judge, 1864; *m* 1843, Harriot Wilson Randolph (1822-93), see Vol. I, p. 758;
2–Frances Howell (1849-95), *m* 1869, S. DeWitt **Parsons** (1834-1916); issue (living): I–Charles Francis (1 above); II–John Randolph (see Vol. I, p. 758).
1–Not married. LL.B., U.Mich., '93 (Delta Chi). Judge, 4th Circuit Ct. of H.T., 1904-16; U.S. atty., Dist. of Hawaii, 1925; judge 2d Div., 1st Circuit Ct., H.T., Feb.-Oct., 1926; asso. justice Supreme Ct. of Hawaii, Oct. 25, 1926– (see Who's Who in America). Mem. S.A.R., I.A.G. Clubs: University, Oahu Country (Honolulu), Yacht (Hilo). Residence: Honolulu, H.T.

GEORGE HENRY PARTRIDGE (1830-65).

1–**PARTRIDGE, George Henry,** *b* Medford, Minn., Aug. 21, 1856.
8–George **Partridge** (*d* 1694 or 95), from Eng., 1636, settled at Duxbury, Mass.; constable, 1646; surveyor of highways; mem. grand-jury; in Capt. Miles Standish's co.; an original purchaser of Middleborough; *m* 1638, Sarah Tracy (*d* 1695; Stephen[9], qv);
7–John (1657-1731), selectman, 1716; moderator, 1721; mem. grand jury, 1728; trustee, 1723-31; *m* 1st, 1684, Hannah Seabury (1668-ante 1700; Samuel[8], *m* Patience Kemp; John[9]);
6–George (1690-1768), *m* 1st, 1712/13, Lydia Keen (Josiah[7]; Josiah[8], *m* 1st, Abigail, dau. of Thomas Little, *m* Anna, dau. of Richard Warren, Mayflower Pilgrim, qv); *m* 2d, Hannah Bradford, dau. of Dea. John Foster;
5–James (*d* 1770), *m* 1744, Thankful Stevens (*b* 1725; Henry, Jr.[6]);
4–Stephen (1747-1826), Canaan, Conn.; *m* 1772, Sarah Brookins (1750-1838);
3–Harvey (1786-1875), Albert Lea, Minn.; *m* 2d, 1826, Laura Maxson;
2–George Henry (2 below).
9–Richard (Maxon) **Maxson,** from Eng. to Boston, 1634; a founder of Portsmouth, R.I., 1638;
8–Rev. John (1638-1720), first white child *b* on island, R.I.; pastor Bapt. ch., Westerly, R.I.; *m* ca. 1664, Mary Mosher (Rev. Hugh[9], an original purchaser of Misquamicut [Westerly], from the Indians, 1676);
7–Rev. John (1666-1747), ordained pastor Bapt. Ch., Westerly, 1719; *m* Judith Clarke (Joseph[8]);
6–John (*b* 1701), *m* 1724, Thankful Randall (Matthew[7], *b* 1671);
5–Matthew (*b* 1727), of R.I.; *m* 1748, Martha Potter;
4–Thomas, *m* Hannah–;
3–Laura (1793-1868), *m* Harvey **Partridge** (3 above).
8–Robert **Francis** (1629-1712), from Eng., settled at Wethersfield, Conn., 1645; *m* Joane– (1629-1705);
7–Sgt. John (1658-1711), served in colonial wars; *m* 1683, Mercy Chittenden (*d* 1745);
6–Thomas (1690-1774), *m* 1718, Abigail Griswold (Jacob[7]);
5–Josiah (1722-98), *m* 1746/47, Millicent Stoddard (Nathaniel[6]);
4–Justus (1750-1827), *m* 3d, 1786, Lois Andrus (Hezekiah[5]; Daniel[6]; Daniel[7]; John[8]);
3–Anson (1790-1868), *m* Betsey Hatfield;
2–Mary Elizabeth (*b* 1832), *m* 1855, George Henry **Partridge** (1830-65), sgt., Co. E, 10th Minn. Inf., Civil War; farmer (see portrait); issue: I–George Henry (1 above); II–Sarah Lillian (1858-96; *m* 1881, George Odlum); III–Harvey Earl (*b* 1859; *m* 1883, Mattie Louise Curtis).
1–*m* Jan. 25, 1882, Sarah Adelaide Wyman (qv for issue).
1–B.S., U.Minn., '79 (Chi Psi). Railroad and land surveyor, 1877-81; cashier and credit man, Wyman, Mullin & Co., 1881-1905; partner in Wyman, Partridge & Co., wholesale dry goods, 1890–, pres. since 1923; dir. Northwestern Nat. Bank, Minn. Loan & Trust Co., Minneapolis. Regent U. of Minn., 1913–. Mem. S.M.D. Unitarian. Democrat. Clubs: Minneapolis, Lafayette, Minnikahda, also University (New York and Chicago). Residence: 1 Groveland Terrace, Minneapolis, Minn.

1–**PARTRIDGE, Sarah Adelaide Wyman (Mrs. George H.),** *b* Marion, Ia., Oct. 8, 1859.
8–Francis **Wyman** (qv);
7–Samuel (1667-1725), of Woburn, Mass.; *m* 1692, Rebecca Johnson (1665-1734; Matthew[8]; Edward[9]);
6–Samuel (1700-67), *m* 1730, Mary Pierce;
5–Samuel (1731-82), soldier Am. Rev.; *m* 1759, Mary Merriam (*b* 1731);
4–Jonathan (1774-1823), *m* 1797, Abigail Adams (John[5], *m* Mary–);
3–Dr. Henry (1803-91), *m* 1st, ca. 1833, Prudence Berry (ca. 1819-37; Capt. John[4], *m* Sarah McDonald);
2–Oliver Crowell (1837-1923), *m* 1858, Charlotte Eleanor Mullen (1840-80; Lannen[3], *m* Sarah Julian); *m* 2d, 1889, Bella Maria Ristine; issue (1st marriage): I–Prudence (*b* 1858; *m* 1907, Charles Carroll Ladd); II–Sarah A. (1 above); III–Henry (*b* 1861); issue (2d marriage): I–Katherine (*b* 1889; *m* 1916, James A. Vaughan).
1–*m* Jan. 25, 1882, George H. Partridge (qv); issue (all *b* Minneapolis, Minn.): 1–Helen Adelaide, *b* Jan. 14, 1883; *m* Apr. 21, 1909, Francis Talmage, son of Francis Dodge, *m* Magdalene Talmage (issue: Virginia Mary, *b* Jan. 18, 1912); 2–Marion Elizabeth, *b* Sept. 12, 1885; *m* Dec. 13, 1907, Edward S., son of Charles J. Mills, *m* Mary Quimby (issue: George Partridge, *b* Oct. 17, 1908; Edward Ensign, *b* Nov. 25, 1911; Charles James, *b* Apr. 26, 1913); 3–Charlotte Wyman, *b* Oct. 3, 1887; *m* Dec. 21, 1909, John Gilman, son of Lu-

cius Pond Ordway, *m* Jessie Gilman (issue: Sarah Prudence, *b* Dec. 23, 1910; Katherine Pond, *b* Apr. 3, 1916; Charlotte Partridge, *b* May 26, 1917; Helen Partridge, *b* May 16, 1920; John Gilman, Jr., *b* Nov. 29, 1922); 4–Georgiana Henriette, *b* May 29, 1901; *m* Mar. 7, 1923, Curtiss Griffith, son of Henry Seymour Noble, *m* Gertrude Griffith.

1–Attended U.Minn. (Kappa Kappa Gamma). Mem. S.D.P., D.A.C. Clubs: Minnikahda, Lafayette, Woodkil Country, Woman's. Democrat. Residence: 1 Groveland Terrace, Minneapolis, Minn.

1–**PATTEN, Jeanie Maury Coyle (Mrs. John D.)**, *b* Washington, D.C., Sept. 11, 1855.
9–William **Ball** (qv);
8–Capt. William, Jr. (1641-94), from Eng. to Lancaster Co., Va., with parents; justice, burgess; *m* 2d, Miss Hanes, of "Bay View," Northumberland Co., Va.;
7–Maj. James (1678-1754), of "Bewdley"; burgess; *m* 2d, as her 2d husband, 1707, Mary Conway (1686-1730; Edwin[8]; Edwin[9], qv);
6–Sarah (*b* 1711/12), *m* 1736, Charles **Ewell** (*b* ca. 1713; Charles[7] [ca. 1660-1722], from Eng. to Va., 1690, settled in St. Mary's Parish, Lancaster Co., *m* 1705, Mary Ann [1690-1749/50], dau. of Rev. John Bertrand, *m* Charlotte de Jolie);
5–Mariamne (1740-1814), *m* 1760, Dr. James **Craik** (1730-1814), from Scotland to Va., 1750; surgeon 1st Va. Regt. in French and Indian War; was at Braddock's defeat; asst. dir. gen. hosp. dept. in Am. Rev.; mem. S.C.; in 1832, his heirs received from Va. 6,000 acres of land for services; attending physician at death of George Washington;
4–Mariamne, *m* Roger **West** (*d* 1801);
3–Ann Margaret (1794-1819), *m* Alexander **Moore** (ca. 1786-1843);
2–Jane Jackson (Apr. 11, 1817-Aug. 15, 1884), *m* Randolph **Coyle** (Oct. 8, 1812-Aug. 22, 1869), civil engr., performed much pioneer govt. work and whose diary was valuable aid in establishing boundaries of N.H., 1840-41 (see Vol. I, p. 760, for Coyle lineage and issue).
1–*m* Dec. 8, 1875, John Dewhurst Patten (see Vol. I, p. 760, for genealogy and issue).
1–Mem. C.D., D.A.R., D.C., Residence: The Ontario, Washington, D.C.

1–**PATTERSON, Mary Eliza Van Wie (Mrs. Eleazar A.)**, *b* Van Wie's Point, Albany Co., N.Y., Mar. 27, 1847-*d* July 5, 1930.
7–Hendrick **Van Wie** (*d* 1690), from Holland, 1664, settled at Ft. Orange; bought tract of land at Van Wie's Point, Albany Co., N.Y., 1679; *m* Eytje Ariaansz;
6–Gerrit (*d* 1746), *m* Agnietze Caspars Conyn;
5–Hendrick (*b* 1703), *m* 1732, Catherine Cornelia Waldron, of Albany, N.Y.;
4–Gerrit P. (*b* 1739), in 3d Rensselaerwyck Bn., Albany Co. Militia in Am. Rev.; *m* 1762, Catharina Lansing, of Albany (Johannes[5], *m* Janetta Van Vechten);
3–Peter G. (1780-1846), *m* 1810, Mary Marten (1780-1864),
2–Peter P. (1817-94), *m* 1846, Mary Margaret Patterson (1822-84), of Glenmont, N.Y. (Archibald[3] [*d* 1877], of Scotland; *m* Pamela Frazier, of Glenmont); issue: I–Mary Eliza (1 above); II–Pamela Frazier (1850-Feb. 27, 1930); III–Peter, Jr. (1853-1920; *m* 1883, Elizabeth Williams).
1–*m* Dec. 13, 1876, Eleazar A. Patterson (Feb. 19, 1846-Jan. 31, 1916); civil engr.; mem. 26th Regt., N.Y. Cav.; G.A.R.; son of Andrew Patterson (1815-1903), of Rouse's Point, N.Y., *m* Almira Marney (1825-1900); issue: 1–Mildred Van Wie, *b* Van Wie's Point, Albany Co., N.Y.; B.S., Teachers Coll., '22, M.A., 1925; grad. work at Cornell and Columbia univs.; contributor to ednl. magazines; mem. N.Y. State Fort Crailo Commn., 1930–; mem. Dutch settlers Soc. of Albany (founder), Fort Crailo Assn. (founder and pres.), Nat. Assn. for the Study of Edn., N.Y. State Hist. Assn., A.A.U.W., Gansevoort Chapter D.A.R.; 2–May M. (June 6, 1880-Apr. 28, 1908); Milne High Sch.; Albany Normal Coll.
1–Mem. Dutch Settlers Soc. of Albany. Dutch Reformed. Republican. Residence: 1710 6th St., Rensselaer, N.Y.

1–**PATTON, James Blaine**, *b* Washington C.H., O., June 12, 1881.
6–James **Patton** (*b* 1723), from Scotland, 1746; settled in Stafford Co., Va.; *m* 1746, in Scotland, Eleanor Gordon; both buried in Gordon Burying Ground, Falmouth, Stafford Co., Va.;
5–George (1759-1813), of Stafford Co.; sgt. Am. Rev.; *m* 1784, Sarah Stringfellow (1766-1848; James[6], *m* Susanna–);
4–Thornton (1793-1869), of Stafford Co.; *m* 1818, Sarah Anne McInteer or McEnteer (1799-1844; Alexander?[5]);
3–James Moreau (1819-92), of Fayette Co., O.; *m* 1848, Eleanor Waln (1833-71; Joseph[4] [1797-1857], *m* Eleanor Dick, 1795-1859);
2–Joseph Henry (2 below).
8–Samuel **Littler** (*d* 1727), from Eng., tradition says with William Penn; settled at Nottingham, Pa.; *m* 1707, Rachel Minshall Taylor, dau. of John Minshall, of Eng.;
7–John (*d* 1748), of Chester Co., Pa., and Va.; *m* 1728, Mary Ross (*b* 1706);
6–John (1740-1819), of Frederick Co., Va.; Am. Rev.; *m* Rosanna–;
5–Samuel (1773-1827), of Va. and Ohio; *m* 1799, Sarah Standfield (1779-1840);
4–Elizabeth (1807-63), of Highland Co., O.; *m* 1824, James **Dunnell** (1802-80);
3–William (1825-1903), *m* Sarah Zimmerman (1832-76);
2–Sarah Elizabeth (*b* 1853), of Fayette Co., O.; *m* 1870, Joseph Henry **Patton** (1849-94), lawyer, Washington C.H., O.; issue: I–Glenn R. (*m* Anna Fox; *m* 2d, Fernande Bedel); II–Daisy V. (*m* George Haynes); III–Eleanor (*m* Jesse Grant); IV–James B. (1 above).
1–*m* July 4, 1911, Marguerite B. Courtright (qv for issue).
1–In hardwood lumber business. Mem. S.A.R. (N.J.), S.R. (Ohio). Mason (K.T., Shriner). Club: Columbus Lumberman's. Republican. Presbyn. Residence: 2215 Bryden Rd., Bexley, Columbus, O.

1–**PATTON, Marguerite Boggs Courtright (Mrs. James B.)**, *b* Circleville, O., Feb. 5, 1889.
9–Jan Bastiaensen (Van Kortryk, Van Kortright, Cortright) **Courtright** (*b* 1618), Huguenot; from Leerdam, Holland, 1663; settled at New Amsterdam, N.Y.; *m* at Beest, Holland;
8–Hendrick Jansen (1648-1741), trustee and freeholder of Rochester, Ulster Co., N.Y.; pvt. militia; *m* 1672, Catherine Hansen Weber (*d* 1740; Hans[9], "master at arms," Harlem);
7–Cornelius Hendricksen (*b* 1680), freeholder at Marbletown and Rochester, Ulster Co.; pvt. militia; *m* 1701, Christina Roosekrans (*b* 1671; Harmon H.[8], *m* Widow Magdalena [Dircks] Caper);
6–Johannes or John (1714-83), Sussex Co., N.J.; capt. and maj. in Am. Rev.; *m* 1735, Margaret Dennemerken;
5–Abram (1748-1825), from Pa. to Ohio, 1803; pvt. Am. Rev.; *m* Effie Drake, or Dreek;
4–John (1779-1863), began to write name Courtright; Fairfield Co., O.; capt. War 1812; *m* 1st, Elizabeth Grubb (1780-1852);
3–Jesse Drake (1811-73), large landowner; Pickaway Co., O.; mem. Legislature; *m* 1831, Sarah Stout (1808-81);
2–Judge Samuel Wilson (2 below).
10–Thomas **Swartwout** (1607-70), from Groningen, ante 1653; settled at New Amsterdam; *m* 1630, Adrientje Symons;
9–Roeloff (1634-1714), Ulster Co., N.Y.; *m* 1657, Eva Albertse Bratt;
8–Cornelia (1667-1714), *m* 1688, Hendrick Claessen **Schoonhoven** (*b* 1667);
7–Eva (*b* 1689), *m* 1719, Dirk **Kermer** (*b* 1697);
6–Christina (*b* 1726), *m* 1749, John (Dreek) **Drake**;
5–Effie (1752-1824), from Sussex Co., N.J., to Fairfield Co., O., post 1803; *m* Abram **Courtright** (5 above).
2–Samuel Wilson **Courtright** (1842-1913), of Circleville, O.; lawyer and judge; *m* 1865, Jennie Rosealtha Martin (1843-1914); for issue see sister Mrs. Clark K. Hunsicker.
1–*m* July 4, 1911, James Blaine Patton (qv); issue: 1–James Courtright, *b* E. Orange, N.J., Jan. 5, 1913; 2–Robert Miller, *b* Orange, N.J., Apr. 2, 1915.
1–Mem. D.A.C., D.F.P.A., D.A.R., U.S.D. 1812, I.A.G., Ohio State Officers Club (D.A.R.). Presbyterian. Republican. Residence: 2215 Bryden Rd., Bexley, Columbus, O.

1–**HUNSICKER, Burdick Courtright (Mrs. Clark K.),** *b* Circleville, O., Oct. 17, 1878.
7–John Michael (Staudt, Stoudt) **Stout** (*b* Palatinate), to America, 1760, in the "Samuel," with three brothers; settled in Phila., Pa.; Huguenot;
6–George Michael (1712-76), *m* Barbara–;
5–George Wilhelm (1748-1820), of Pa.; ens., 7th Co., 6th Bn., Berks Co. Militia, in Am. Rev.; *m* Christiana Weidenhammer (1752-1817; Johannes[6] [*b* Kurpfalz, 1727], *m* Margareth Ehteigie);
4–George (1771-1846), began to write name Stout: from Berks Co., Pa., to Ohio, 1808; *m* Mary Dunkle (1771-1840);
3–Sarah (1808-81), Fairfield Co., O.; *m* 1831, Jesse Drake **Courtright** (1811-73);
2–Samuel W. (2 below).
4–Nimrod **Martin,** *m* Priscilla Bright;
3–Zachariah Reese (*b* Cumberland Co., Pa.), *m* Rebecca Bright, of Fairfield Co., O.;
2–Jennie Rosealtha (1843-1914), *m* 1865, Samuel Wilson **Courtright** (1842-1913); issue: I–Florence B. (*b* 1870; *m* Eagleton F. Dunn); II–Burdick (1 above); III–Marguerite B. (Mrs. James B. Patton, qv for Courtright lineages).
1–*m* June 2, 1903, Clark Kinder Hunsicker, *b* Williamsport, O., Nov. 17, 1877; son of John Webb Hunsicker, of Woodlyn, Williamsport, O. (Samuel[3] [1805-51], *m* Elenor Webb; Jacob[4] [1775-1857], *m* Eva, dau. of Samuel Parrett, pvt. Am. Rev.); issue: 1–Margaret Martin, *b* Pickaway Co., O., Sept. 12, 1912; 2–Clark K., Jr., *b* Pickaway Co., Oct. 30, 1919.
1–Miss Armstrong's Finishing Sch., Avondale, Cincinnati. Mem. D.A.R. (organizing regent Pickaway Plains Chapter), I.A.G., O.E.S., Ohio State Archaeol. and Hist. Soc. Club: Monday Study. Presbyterian. Democrat. Residence: Circleville, O.

1–**PAUL, Helen McGraw Longyear (Mrs. Carroll),** *b* Marquette, Mich., Jan. 20, 1885.
6–Jacob (Langjahr) **Longyear** (*b* 1720), from Bavaria to Ulster Co., N.Y., ca. 1750; *m* Maria Kok (or Cox);
5–Johannes (1754-1824), soldier in Am. Rev.; *m* Annaatje Winne;
4–Peter (1784-1845), *m* 1808, Jerusha Stevens;
3–John Wesley (1820-75), mem. 38th and 39th Congresses, 1863-67; U.S. district judge for eastern Mich., 1869-75; *m* Harriet Munro (1826-1917);
2–John Munro (2 below).
10–Pieter (Winnen) **Winne** (*b* in Ghent, Flanders-*d* ca. 1692), rented a farm in Bethlehem nr. Albany from a Rensselaer patroon ca. 1652; *m* Aechie Jans;
9–Pieter, *m* ca. 1660, Jannetje Alberz;
8–Pieter (*b* Curacao, West Indies, bap. Kingston, 1661), *m* 1682, Jannetje Pier;
7–Pieter (bap. 1691), *m* 1720, Antjen Merken;
6–Peter, *m* 1749, Arriantje Van Etten;
5–Annaatje (1752-1843), *m* Johannes **Longyear** (5 above).
10–Ens. Gerrard **Spencer** (qv);
9–Thomas (*d* 1670), *m* Elizabeth Bates;
8–Gerrard (*d* 1753 or 54), *m* 1702, Sarah Douglas;
7–Jonathan (*b* 1705), *m* 1733, Content Platts (Frederick[8], *m* Elizabeth Fox);
6–Capt. Reuben (1739-1806), Am. Rev.; *m* Elizabeth Snyder (1746-1807);
5–Hannah (*d* 1856), *m* 1783, Peter **Stevens** (1759-1810);
4–Jerusha (1789-1865), *m* Peter **Longyear** (4 above).
10–John **Beecher** (*d* 1637), *m* Hannah Potter;
9–Isaac (1623-90), *m* Mary–;
8–John (1646-1712), *m* Elizabeth Roberts;
7–Ebenezer (1686-1763), *m* Hannah Mix;
6–Caleb (1724-84), *m* Abigail Wheeler;
5–Burr (1756-1823), Am. Rev.; *m* Anna Eunice Smith;
4–Marcus Lyman (1782-1866), War 1812; *m* Fanny Johnson;
3–Samuel Peck (1817-81), of Battle Creek, Mich.; *m* Caroline Matilda Walker (1828-96);
2–Mary Hawley (*b* 1851), *m* 1879, John Munro **Longyear** (1850-1922), see Vol. I, p. 696.
1–*m* Mar. 25, 1911, Carroll Paul, *b* Tokyo, Japan, May 5, 1882; B.S., Dartmouth, '03, C.E., 1904; B.S. in architecture, M.I.T., 1909; lt. U.S.N.; son of Prof. Henry Martyn Paul (see Vol. III, p. 257); adopted children: Beatrice, *b* 1923; Howard, *b* 1924; Philip Martyn, *b* 1928; Judith, *b* 1928.
1–Residence: 505 E. Ridge St., Marquette, Mich.

1–**PEASE, Mae Townsend (Mrs. Henry H.),** *b* Phila., Pa., May 28, 1881.
6–Capt. John **Brisbane** (1730-1822), came to America, 1749; *m* Isabella Simmons (*d* ca. 1770);
5–John (1760-1845), entered Cont. Army aet. 16; *m* 1783, Mary Clark (1765-1834);
4–William (1784-1822), *m* Sarah Sterrett (1786-1854);
3–Dr. William (1823-80), lt. col., 49th Pa. Vols. in Civil War; *m* 1854, Mary Ann Rozet Bicking 1829-94;
2–Ellen Bicking (*b* 1858), *m* 1878, Dr. Eugene **Townsend** (1856-1928), U.Pa., '77.
1–*m* Feb. 27, 1906, Henry Hildreth Pease, *b* Wilkes-Barre, Pa., Jan. 2, 1878; issue: 1–Henry H., Jr., *b* Wilkes-Barre, Pa., Jan. 28, 1907; Princeton, '28; 2–Pauline Townsend, *b* Wilkes-Barre, Jan. 29, 1909.
1–Residence: 2307 Delancy Place, Phila., Pa.

Arms: Quarterly, first and fourth argent, on a chevron engrailed gules, three crosses formée of the field.
Crest: A cubit arm erect habited azure, holding on one stalk enfiled with a scroll three roses gules, leaves vert.

1–**PECK, Robert Halford,** *b* San Francisco, Calif., Mar. 15, 1875.
9–Joseph **Peck** (qv);
8–Ens., lt. and capt. Nicholas (bap. 1630-1710), Seekonk, Mass.; mem. Council of War; capt. French War; *m* 2d, Rebecca– (*d* 1704);
7–Jonathan (1666-1717), of bet. Bristol and Warren, R.I.; *m* Elizabeth Throop (1687-1729; William[8]);
6–Dea. Thomas (1711-70), of Swansea, Mass.; *m* Mary Kingsley (1713-1804; Jonathan[7], of Rehoboth; Eldad[8]);
5–Capt. Peleg (1736-1807), of Swansea; served in Am. Rev.; *m* Phebe Mason (1736-78; Hezekiah[6]; Isaac[7]; Sampson[8], qv);
4–Nicholas (1762-1837), of Swansea, Ashfield, Mass., Dutchess Co., and Grand Isle, N.Y.; *m* Eunice (Clark) Barney (*d* 1842; Dea. John Clark[5]; John[6]; Lt. William[7]);
3–Charles (*born* 1794), of Grand Isle, N.Y., and Ohio; *m* Polly Martin (Jonah[4]);
2–Charles Manley (2 below).
9–Ralph **Earle** (qv);
8–William (*d* 1715/16), *m* Mary Walker (John[9]);
7–Ens. Ralph (1660-1757), *m* Mary (Carr) Hicks (Robert Carr[8]);
6–Robert (1706-96), *m* ca. 1726, Mary Newhall (*b* 1704; Lt. Thomas[7], *m* Mercy Stebbins [Samuel[8]; John[9]; Rowland[10], qv]; Thomas[8], *m* Rebecca, dau. of Thomas Greene, *m* Rebecca, dau. of Joseph Hills, *m* Rose–);
5–Capt. George (1735-1806), served in Am. Rev.; *m* Mary Baker (1738-1824; Thomas[6], *m* Azubah Rice);
4–Frederick (1759-1847), served Am. Rev.; *m*

Elizabeth Young (1771-1825; Dr. John[5], Am. Rev.; William[6], Am. Rev.);
3-Halford (1811-1902), *m* Elizabeth Barker (Joshua[4], *m* Aurelia Sherman [Abishai[5], Am. Rev.; Jabez[6]; Philip[7]; Samuel[8]; Henry[9]]; Joshua[5]; Barnabas[6]; John[7]; John[8]; Sir Robert[9]);
2-Anne Barker (2 below).
10-Richard **Warren,** Mayflower Pilgrim (qv);
9-Nathaniel (1624-67), *m* 1645, Sarah Walker (*d* 1700);
8-Elizabeth (1654-90), *m* William **Greene,** Sr. (*d* 1685);
7-William (1684-1756), *m* Desire Bacon (1688/89-1730; John[8]; Nathaniel[9], qv);
6-Mary (*b* 1710), *m* Barnabas **Barker** (John[7]; John[8], immigrant);
5-Joshua (1740-1804), *m* Mary Copeland (1740-1829);
4-Joshua (*b* 1774), *m* Aurelia Sherman (4 below);
3-Elizabeth (*d* 1895), *m* Halford **Earle** (3 above).
9-John **Alden,** Mayflower Pilgrim (qv);
8-Ruth (1634-74), *m* 1657, John **Bass** (1633-1716; Samuel[9], qv);
7-Mary (*b* 1669), as widow of Christopher Webb, *m* 2d, 1694, William **Copeland** (1656-1716; Lawrence[8], of Braintree, *m* Lydia Townsend);
6-Joseph, *m* Elizabeth Tolman;
5-Mary (1740-1829), *m* Joshua **Barker** (5 above).
10-John **Howland,** Mayflower Pilgrim (qv);
9-Desire, *m* Capt. John **Gorham** (qv);
8-Desire, *m* 1661, John **Hawes** (*b* 1640; Edmond[9], from Eng., 1635, settled at Yarmouth, Mass.);
7-Benjamin (1682/83-1722), *m* Dorcas Smith;
6-Jedidah (*b* 1709), *m* Jabez **Sherman** (1704-74), lt. British Navy (Philip[7]; John[8]; Hon. Philip[9], qv);
5-Abishai, served in Am. Rev.; *m* 1777, Mercy Goodspeed;
4-Aurelia, *m* Joshua **Barker** (4 above);
3-Elizabeth, *m* Halford **Earle** (3 above).
2-Charles Manley **Peck** (1831-1901), expert accountant; *m* 1854, Isabella Linton (*b* 1830); *m* 2d, 1872, Anne Barker Earle (*b* 1848); issue (1st marriage): I-Alice May (*b* 1855; *m* Charles Ward Takway; *m* 2d, John Butterworth); issue (2d marriage): I-Allan Earle (1873-1925; surgeon U.S.N.; *m* Anna Dixon); II-Robert Halford (1 above); III-Isabel (*b* 1877; *m* Prof. Elliot Jones).
1-*m* 1900, Elizabeth B. Anderson (*d* 1904).
1-*m* 2d, Apr. 15, 1907, Mabel Rodney Steele, *b* Brooklyn, N.Y., Mar. 12, 1881; dau. of John Wesley Steele (*d* 1903), of Brooklyn (Robert[3]); issue: 1-Rodney Halford, *b* Ft. Ontario, N.Y., July 10, 1908; cadet U.S. Coast Guard Acad., '31; 2-Ruth, *b* Ft. Ontario, Mar. 30, 1910; Agnes Scott Coll., '31; 3-Robert Earle, *b* Ft. Sam Houston, Tex., June 9, 1913; 4-Rosemary, *b* Ft. Shafter, H.T., Dec. 23, 1916; 5-John Steele, *b* Washington, Aug. 10, 1921.
1-U.S.M.A., '99; honor grad. Inf. and Cav. Sch.; Staff Coll.; field officers' course, Ft. Benning; Arty. Sch. Trier (Treves), Germany. Second lt., 1st lt., capt., maj., lt. col., col. U.S. Army, 1918, retired. Awarded: D.S.C., D.S.M., Officer Legion of Honor, France, two army citations, Croix de Guerre, Victory Medal. Editor genealogical and patriotic-historic soc. page of Atlanta American. Mem. S.M.D. (sec. Ga. Soc.), D.C.G., S.A.R., I.A.G.; sec. and genealogist, Atlanta Geneal. Soc. Congregationalist. Residence: 1078 Arlington Ave. S.W., Atlanta, Ga. Office: 82 Marietta St., Atlanta, Ga.

1-**PEARSON, Nella Jane,** *b* Boston, Mass., Dec. 31, 1864.
9-William **Eaton** (ca. 1605-1673), from Eng. in the "Hercules and Sandwich," 1637; settled at Watertown, Mass., at Reading, Mass., 1642; *m* Martha Jenkins (*d* 1680);
8-John (1633-91), *m* 1658/59, Elizabeth Kendall (*b* 1642/43; Dea. Thomas[9], *m* Rebecca-);
7-Rebecca (1664/65-1732), *m* 1680, Capt. Thomas **Nichols** (ca. 1655-1736/37), of Reading, Mass. (Richard[8], *m* Anna-);
6-Daniel (*b* 1707), of Reading, Mass.; *m* 1729, Elizabeth Batchelder;
5-Elizabeth (1732-93), *m* Sgt. Amos **Pearson** (1734-85), minute man at Lexington (see Vol. I, p. 948, for Pearson lineage);
4-Hiram (1770-1856), *m* Alice Barron;
3-William (1807-87), Boston; *m* 1830, Lucinda Maria Greenleaf (1811-87; David[4]; Bickford[5]; David[6]);
2-William Henry (2 below).
9-John (Batchelor) **Batchelder** (*d* 1676);
8-John (1636-1705), *m* 1662, Sarah- (*d* 1685);
7-John (1665/66-1732), *m* 1696, Sarah Poore (*b* 1671; John[8], *m* Mary, dau. of William Titcomb);
6-Elizabeth (1710-1746/47), *m* Daniel **Nichols** (6 above).
9-Ellis **Barron** (1608-76), *m* Grace-;
8-John (ca. 1638-1693), *m* 1664, Elizabeth Hunt (*d* 1704; William[9], qv);
7-Moses (1669-1742), *m* 1702, Sarah Power (1683-1743; Walter[8], qv);
6-Timothy (bap. 1706/07-ante 1766), *m* 1725/26, Hannah Fletcher (*b* 1706; Dea. Joshua[7]; Joshua[8]; William[9]; Robert[10], qv);
5-Ens. Joshua (1749-1828), *m* Lavina Derby (1760-88), see Vol. I, p. 948;
4-Alice (1779-1816), *m* Hiram **Pearson** (4 above);
3-William, *m* Lucinda M. Greenleaf (3 above);
2-William Henry (1832-1926), *m* 1861, Nancy Delia Benjamin (1833-1917), for issue and maternal lineages see Vol. I, p. 948.
1-Ed. public and private schools. Mem. D.A.R., D.R., N.E.H.G.S. Clubs: Women's City (Boston), Women's Republican of Mass. Residence: 367 Otis St., West Newton, Mass.

HERVEY BATES (1795-1876), founder of Indianapolis, Ind.; was appointed first sheriff of Marion Co., Ind., and invested with authority to organize the county government and place its legal machinery in motion. He built one of first three log cabins in the "New Purchase" at Indianapolis. Organized and was pres. for 10 years of the first bank in Indianapolis, the Indianapolis Branch of the State Bank; organized and was pres. of first insurance co. and the first gas, light and coke co. in the city; was pres. of first railroad finished to Indianapolis; stockholder in first hotel and in 1852 built the "Bates House," long one of the finest hotels in the West, from the balcony of which Lincoln delivered his famous address.

1-**PERRIN, Hervey Bates,** *b* Indianapolis, Ind., Nov. 8, 1884.
7-Thomas **Perrin** (1675-1753), from Eng. to Hartford, Conn., 1719; settled at Hebron; *m* 1714, Sarah Phelps (*d* 1742), from Westfield, Sussex, Eng.;
6-Thomas (1716-89), from Eng. with parents; *m* 1739, Jerusha Porter (1712-54);
5-Solomon (1744-1834), buried at Vernon, Conn.; *m* 1773, Anna Kellogg (1746-1826);
4-Solomon (1781-1833), Staunton, Va.; *m* 1810, Sarah Neal Bott (1795-1851), of Staunton;
3-James Joel (1829-1903), Lafayette, Ind.; *m* 1851, Margaret Cason (1829-1902; Judge Cason[4], of Thorntown, Ind.);
2-John (2 below).
11-Rev. John **Wheelwright,** from Lincolnshire, Eng., to Mass., 1636; driven from Boston by

the Puritans, 1637; founder of Exeter, N.H.; settled at Wells, Me.;
10–Abigail, *m* Rev. Abraham **Pierson** (qv);
9–Grace (*b* 1650), *m* 1666, Samuel **Kitchell** (1635-90; Robert[10], qv);

JOHN BRUEN (1646-97), m a dau. of Dea. Richard Lawrence, of Branford, Conn.; his father Hon. Obadiah Bruen, came to Plymouth and Gloucester, 1640; was a founder of New London (then Pequot), and of Newark, N.J.; one of commissioners to purchase land from Indians for New Jersey settlement; named as grantee of Royal Charter of King Charles, 1662.

8–Dea. Abraham (1679-1741), judge; *m* 1703, Sarah Bruen (1679-1745; John[9] [1646-97], see portrait, *m* Esther [*b* 1651], dau. of Dea. Richard Lawrence, of Branford, Conn.; Hon. Obadiah[10] [1606-80; desc. Charlemagne, thru King John and six of his barons who signed the Magna Charta, and 15th from Robert LeBrun], came to Plymouth and Gloucester, 1640, grantee of Royal Charter, 1662);
7–Judge Joseph (1710-79), of N.J.; *m* 1732, Rachel Bates (1712-89);
6–Moses (1740-1820), a founder of Cincinnati, O.; lt. Am. Rev.; *m* 1st, Phebe Hedges (*b* 1740);
5–Mary (*d* Cincinnati, 1799), *m* 1787, Daniel **Bates** (1763-1845), from Morris Co., N.J., to Sandusky, O.; drummer boy Am. Rev.; master of transportation under Gen. Anthony Wayne in Indian wars (Capt. David[6], of Whippany,

JOHN PERRIN, for 10 years chairman of the board and federal reserve agent, Federal Reserve Bank of San Francisco.

Morris Co., N.J., capt. Am. Rev., maj. Morris Co. militia, justice, *m* Annabella Dodd);
4–Hervey (1795-1876), founder of Indianapolis, Ind.; see portrait; *m* 1819, Sidney Sedgwick (1798-1872; John[5], *m* Janette Kent; Benjamin[6]; Benjamin[7]; Joshua[8], *m* Elizabeth, dau. of Henry Fisher [their g.g.dau. *m* President John Quincy Adams]; Thomas[9]);

MAJOR HERVEY BATES (1834-1929), commissioned major, 132d Ind. Vol. Inf., raised by Gov. Oliver P. Morton in answer to Lincoln's call for volunteers.

3–Maj. Hervey (1834-1929), of Indianapolis; maj. 132d Ind. Inf., Civil War; see portrait; *m* 1857, Charlotte T. Cathcart (1838-1907), from Phila. to Indianapolis (Andrew[4] [1808-71], from Girvan, Scotland, to Indianapolis);
2–Ellenor Cathcart (*b* Oct. 14, 1859), C.D.A., D.A.R.; *m* Oct. 3, 1883, Hon. John **Perrin** (*b* Jan. 17, 1857), see portrait, see Who's Who in America for biography; issue: I–Hervey B. (1 above); II–John Bates (Jan. 16, 1887-Oct. 29, 1913).
1–*m* Feb. 16, 1916, Alice Louise Schaf, *b* Indianapolis, Ind., July 31, 1889; dau. of Joseph Charles Schaf; issue: 1–John, *b* Pasadena, Calif., Jan. 27, 1927.
1–B.A., Yale, '07 (D.K.E., Elihu), M.A., 1910. Investment securities. Commd. capt. of cav., May 14, and capt., F.A., Aug. 8, 1917; assigned to 304th F.A., 77th Div., and in France and Army of Occupation, Germany; c.o. 1st Bn., 304th F.A., during Argonne campaign. Mem. B.O.R., S.C.W., S.R., M.O.L.L., M.O.W.W., M.O.F.W., A.L. Fellow Royal Geog. Soc. Clubs: Yale, Fencers, (New York), Midwick Country (Pasadena). Ranches: Sinaloa, Mexico. Residence: 415 State St., Pasadena, Calif.

1–**PERRINE, Irving**, *b* Wallkill, N.Y., Aug. 5, 1884.
8–Daniel (Perrin, Perine) **Perrine** (*b* 164– *d* 1719), from France, 1665, settled at Elizabethtown, N.J.; *m* 1666, Maria Thorel (*b* 164– *d* ante 1687); *m* 2d, Elizabeth– (*d* 1719);
7–Peter (1667-1743), New Dorp, S.I.; *m* 1704, Ann Holmes (*b* 1670);
6–James (*d* 1798), Perth Amboy, N.J.; *m* 1745, Neeltje (Elenor) Stotholf (*d* 1803);
5–John (*d* 1801), Middlesex Co., N.J.; *m* 1772, Sophie Burgess;
4–James W. (1780-1849), Perrine's Bridge, N.Y.; *m* 1st, 1801, Catherine Freer (*d* 1834);
3–John (1801-60), *m* 1831, Rachel Deyo (1806-75);
2–Alfred (2 below).
8–Balthus Barentzen **Van Kleeck** (1644-1717), from Holland ante 1663, first mentioned in affidavit as witness to a shooting in Flatbush, N.Y., 1663; founded Poughkeepsie, 1702; capt. in Dutchess Co. militia, 1700; lived at Albany, 1676-82, Bergen, N.J., 1683-97, Poughkeepsie, 1697-1717; mem. 16th and 17th Colonial Assemblies; largest landowner in Dutchess Co.; *m* 1676, Tryntje Janse Buys (post 1654-post 1725);

7–Barent (ca. 1677-post 1748), Poughkeepsie; col. in French and Indian War, capt. 1715, maj., 1728, lt. col., 1737, col., 1740; *m* 1701, Antoinette Parmentier (*b* 1684);
6–Peter (bap. 1725), *m* 1746, Antoinette Frear (Freer);
5–Levi (*b* bet. 1754-57), in Am. Rev., massacred by Indians on return;
4–Levi (1777-1862), *m* 1st, 1801, Elizabeth Way (1783-1827);
3–Levi L. (1817-88), Montgomery, N.Y.; *m* 1843, Mahala Green (1819-97), of Greenville, N.Y.;
2–Agnes Estella (1852-1920), *m* 1870, Alfred **Perrine** (1842-1908), merchant, druggist, Wallkill, N.Y.; issue: I–Charles (*b* 1871; *m* Elizabeth Van Wagenen); II–Eva (*b* 1873; *m* Webster H. Hare); III–Leroy L. (*b* 1877; *m* Cora E. Fay); IV–Mabel (*b* 1881; *m* Ernest O. Greiner); V–Irving (1 above); VI–Henry Ivey (*b* 1886; *m* Ethel Ray); VII–Ina Mildred (*b* 1891; *m* Alfred Inge); VIII–Frances E. Willard (*b* 1895).
1–*m* Aug. 25, 1910, Hilda Aurelia Sweet, *b* Elmira, N.Y.; dau. of Frank Benjamin Sweet, of Ithaca, N.Y. (James S.[3], of Binghamton, N.Y.); issue: 1–Phyllis Sweet, *b* Oklahoma City, Okla., Nov. 12, 1915.
1–A.B., Cornell, '07 (Phi Gamma Delta, Sigma Gamma Epsilon, Sigma Xi), A.M., 1911, Ph.D., 1912. Consulting geologist and oil operator since 1917 (see Who's Who in America). Pres. Belle Isle Royalty Co., Unidos Royalty Co., City Oil Co.; v.p. Randado Oil Corpn.; dir. Flag Oil Corpn., Diversified Royalties, Inc., Mid-Continent Royalty Owners Assn., Kilpatrick Bros. Lumber Co., Nat. Aid Life Ins. Co., Am. Fidelity Ins. Co. Sec. and dir. Okla. City Community Fund; dir. Okla. City Chamber of Commerce, Okla. Co. Chapter A.R.C. Mem. I.A.G., Conn. Hist. Soc. Mason (32°, K.T.), Elk. Residence: 506 W. 14th St., Oklahoma City, Okla.

1–**PERROW, Elizabeth Egglestone Stone (Mrs. F. Kirkpatrick),** *b* Pittsylvania Co., Va., Aug. 5, 1881.
8–Thomas **Carter** (qv);
7–Thomas (1672-1733), of "Barford," Lancaster Co., Va.; justice, Lancaster Ct., 1705-29; capt. militia; *m* 1695, Arabella Williamson;
6–Thomas (1696-1735), nr. Corotoman River; *m* 1720-25, Joanna Miller;
5–Thomas (1734-1817), of "Greenrock," Pittsylvania Co.; in Am. Rev.; *m* 1764, Winifred Hobson (1745-1831);
4–Rawley Williamson (1788-1847), sgt., War 1812; *m* 1809, Annie Jennings Robertson (1792-1863);
3–Dr. George Adcock (1834-92), to Danville, Va.; maj.; C.S.A.; *m* 1858, Bettie Anne Womack;
2–Kate Williamson (2 below).
8–William **Womack** (1690-1762), of St. James, Northam Parish, Goochland Co., Va.;
7–William (1710-91), Cumberland Co.; *m* 1735, Mary–;
6–William (*b* 1736), Halifax Co.; *m* 1765, Mary (Mollie) Allen (*b* 1746);
5–Allen (1766-1849), Pittsylvania Co.; *m* 1789, Sallie Watson Womack (1766-1828);
4–Allen Watson (1801-80), Chatham, Va.; *m* 1833, Kathryne W. Stone (1816-49);
3–Bettie Anne (1841-1912), Danville, Va.; *m* Dr. George A. **Carter** (3 above);
2–Kate Williamson (1859-1900), *m* 1879, James Banister **Stone** (1852-1915), planter, Pittsylvania Co.; issue: I–Samuel Marion (*b* 1880; *m* Effie Mucklow); II–Elizabeth Egglestone (1 above); III–Mary Emma (*b* and *d* 1884); IV–George Carter (qv); V–Mary Hightower (*b* 1889; *m* Samuel Stone Gregory); VI–Katie Womack (*b* 1890); VII–Dr. James Banister, Jr. (qv).
1–*m* June 21, 1905, Fletcher Kirkpatrick Perrow, *b* "Oak Grove," Campbell Co., Va., Mar. 1, 1874; son of Fletcher C. Perrow, of Lynch's Station, Campbell Co., Va.; issue: 1–Fletcher Kirkpatrick, Jr., *b* Anniston, Ala., Mar. 28, 1906; A.B., Birmingham-Southern Coll., '28; M.S., Columbia (Sch. of Business), 1929; 2–James Banister Stone, *b* Lynchburg, Va., Sept. 8, 1909; Birmingham-Southern Coll.; 3–Elizabeth Stone, *b* Anniston, Ala., Mar. 3, 1915.
1–Ed. Woman's Coll., Richmond, Va. Mem. D.F.P.A., D.A.R., U.D.C. Methodist. Summer place: Hurt, Va. Residence: 314 E. 7th St., Anniston, Ala.

1–**STONE, James Banister, Jr.,** *b* Hurt, Pittsylvania Co., Va., Jan. 18, 1893.
9–Richard **Anderson** (*b* 1639), of New Kent and King and Queen cos., Va.; *m* 1680, Margaret– (*d* 1767);
8–Richard (1681-1767), of King and Queen Co., Va.;
7–Paulin (*b* 1701), *m* 1723, Judith Jones (*b* 1702; Capt. Roger[8]);
6–Richard (1723-96), capt. King and Queen Co. militia, Am. Rev.; to Pittsylvania Co., 1784; *m* 2d, 1761, Jane Foster;
5–Thomas (1765-1815), of Pittsylvania Co.; *m* 1792, Polly Haley (1774-1862);
4–Churchill (1803-61), *m* 1826, Rebecca W. Thompson (*b* 1809);
3–Elizabeth Egglestone (1831-55), *m* Samuel Marion **Stone** (1825-81);
2–James Banister (1852-1915), *m* 1879, Kate Williamson Carter (1859-1900); for issue and other lineages see Mrs. F. Kirkpatrick Perrow.
1–Not married. B.A., U.Va., '15 (Pi Mu, P.B.K., Alpha Omega Alpha), M.D., 1919. Interne, N.Y. Nursery and Child's Hosp., Apr.-June 1919; Interne, Bellevue Hosp., New York, 1919-21, resident physician, children's med. div., same, 1922. Baptist. Democrat. Clubs: Country of Virginia, University, Virginia Boat. Residence: 2042 Park Av., Richmond, Va.

1–**STONE, George Carter,** *b* Pittsylvania Co., Va., June 8, 1887.
9–William **Stone,** mariner, from Eng. to Va., 1619; *m* Mary Vernon;
8–William (*d* 1707), Gloucester Co., Va.; removed to Richmond Co., Va.; *m* Sara– (*d* 1718);
7–Joshua (*d* 1774), *m* Virginia Howard;
6–Joshua (1725-1822), capt. of militia during Am. Rev., being sworn into service 1780, Pittsylvania Co.; co. surveyor; *m* 1748, Mary Coleman (1730-post 1822);
5–John (1754-1824), Pittsylvania Co.; Am. Rev.; *m* 1st, 1777, Dolly Hoskins (1761-1802);
4–Rev. James Hoskins (1778-1854), *m* 1803, Elizabeth Fitzgerald (1785-1865);
3–Samuel Marion (1825-81), justice, Pittsylvania Co.; *m* 1850, Elizabeth Egglestone Anderson (1830-ca. 1855);
2–James Banister (1852-1915), *m* 1879, Kate Williamson Carter (1859-1900); for issue and other lineages see Mrs. F. Kirkpatrick Perrow.
1–*m* July 12, 1916, Mary Carter Younger (qv); issue: 1–Mary Carter, *b* Altavista, Va., Nov. 5, 1922.
1–B.S., Va. Poly. Inst., '08, C.E., 1909; C.E., Cornell, 1911. Engr. with Lockwood, Greene & Co., Boston, Mass., 1911-16; mgr. estate, Hurt, Va., 1916-18; consulting engr., Altavista, Va., 1918; Dir. Altavista Development Corpn., Altavista Ice Co., Altavista Laundry Co. Mem. Town Council, 2 terms. Mason, Odd Fellow. Mem. Corda Fratres Assn. of Cosmopolitan Clubs, University Club (Buffalo), Lions Club, Am. Soc. C.E., Boston Soc. C.E. Baptist. Democrat. Residence: Altavista, Va.

1–**STONE, Mary Carter Younger (Mrs. George Carter),** *b* "Longwood," Granville Co., N.C., Mar. 19, 1889.
7–Rev. Daniel **Taylor,** from Eng., 1703, settled at Blissland Parish, New Kent Co., Va., as missionary and rector;
6–Rev. Daniel (1704-42), B.A., Trinity Coll., Oxford, Eng.; rector St. John's Parish, King William Co., Va.; *m* Alice Littlepage (Richard[7], *m* Frances–; Richard[8], vestryman and sheriff, St. Peter's Parish, 1685);
5–William (1732-1820), Lunenburg Co., Va.; burgess, 1765; supported resolutions brought forward by Patrick Henry against unjust taxation of the colonies by Parliament; clk., Mecklenburg Co. Ct., 1763-1814; *m* 1767, Martha Waller (1747-88; Judge Benjamin[6]; Edmund[7]; Col. John[8]);
4–Thomas (*d* 1824), Lunenburg Co.; *m* 1800, Martha (or "Patsy") Gregory (*d* 1853; Roger[5], see 5 below);
3–William Louis (1813-97), "Longwood," Granville Co., N.C.; col. militia, 1861-65; *m* 1845, Sallie Mary Gregory;
2–Anna Gregory (2 below).
9–Capt. John **West** (qv);
8–Col. John (1632-post 1689), West Point, Va.; first child born of English parents on the York River, Va.; taken prisoner during

Bacon's Rebellion, and later sat on the court martial which tried Bacon's men; col. of militia, and burgess for New Kent Co., Va., 1685-86; *m* Unity Croshaw (Maj. Joseph[9]);
7–Capt. Thomas, King William Co., Va.; burgess, 1702-06;
6–Agnes, *m* Richard **Gregory,** of "Mount Pleasant," King William Co.;
5–Roger (1729-1803), Mecklenburg Co.; *m* 2d, 1776, Fanny Garland Loury (*d* 1816);
4–Herbert (1777-1821), of "Effingham," Dinwiddie Co., Va.; *m* 1803, Lucy Osborne Thweatt (James[5], *m* Lucy Peterson);
3–Sallie Mary (1821-1902), *m* Col. William Louis **Taylor** (3 above).
2–Rev. Robert Hobson **Younger** (1852-1904), M.E. minister; *m* Mary Robertson, of Pittsylvania Co.; *m* 2d, 1888, Anna Gregory Taylor (*b* 1861), of "Longwood," and Stovall, Granville Co., N.C.; issue (1st marriage): I–Robert Nicholas (1880-1921; *m* Blanche Haynes); issue (2d marriage): I–Mary Carter (1 above); II–Sallie Gregory (*b* 1891; *m* Hastings Wyman Baker); III–Anna Linville (*b* 1894; *m* Henry Haynes King); IV–Cora Taylor (*b* 1901).
1–*m* July 12, 1916, George Carter Stone (qv for issue).
1–Ed. Blackstone (Va.) Female Inst., 1905, Randolph Macon Woman's Coll., 1913. Mem. D.A.R., U.D.C., Va. Federation of Music Clubs. Methodist. Democrat. Residence: Altavista, Va.

1–**PETERS, Frederick,** *b* Poughkeepsie, N.Y., July 21, 1869-*d* Fishkill, N.Y., July 20, 1930.
6–Dr. Charles **Peters** (will probated in N.Y., Apr. 3, 1733), from Wales or Cornwall; early settler of Hempstead, L.I.; name entered in N.Y. census for 1703; *m* Mary Hewlett (George[7], *m* Mary Bayles; graves at Hempstead marked G.H. 1722: M.H. 1733: aged 78);
5–John (1721-1806), warden, St. George's Ch., Hempstead, L.I., 1752-59; *m* 2d, 1752, Elizabeth Smith (Joseph[6]; Joseph[7]; John[8]);
4–Samuel (1761-1819), removed to Beekman, Dutchess Co., N.Y., 1800; *m* Hannah Van Wyck (1767-1847);
3–Hewlett (1792-1875), *m* Elizabeth Swartwout;
2–John (2 below).
9–Tomys **Swartwout** (*b* 1607), from Holland to New Amsterdam, 1652; patentee Midwout, now Flatbush, L.I.; schepen; *m* 1631, Hendrickjen Barentse Otsen;
8–Roeloff (bap. June 1, 1634-*d* Hurley, N.Y., May 1715), to Beverwyck, now Albany, 1656; returned to Holland to secure agrl. implements and the services of some young farmers for a projected settlement on Esopus Creek; sheriff of Esopus; *m* 1st, Eva (Bratt) De Hooges (*d* ca. 1689; Albert Andriessen Bratt[10], *m* Barentse Van Rotmers, of Amsterdam);
7–Thomas (ca. 1660-ca. 1723), *m* Elizabeth Gordinier (1662-1749);
6–Jacobus (1692-1749), Wiccopee, Dutchess Co., N.Y.; justice; asst. to judge, Ct. of Common Pleas, 1743; *m* 1714, Gieletjen Nieuwkerk (bap. 1691);
5–Thomas (bap. 1715), *m* Mary Garseling;
4–Jacobus (bap. 1754), ens. Am. Rev.; *m* Martha Van Wyck;
3–Elizabeth (1793-1843), *m* Hewlett **Peters** (3 above).
8–Cornelius Barentse **Van Wyck** (desc. Chevalier Hendrick Van Wyck, of Wyck nr. Teck, Holland, living in 1400), to New Amsterdam, 1660; *m* Anna Polhemus (Theodorus[9], 1st Dutch Ref. minister on L.I.);
7–Theodorus (1668-1753), *m* Margaretta Brinckerhoff (1675-1741; Abraham Joris[8], *m* Altie, dau. of Jan Stryker; Joris[9]);
6–Judge Theodorus (1697-1776), Fishkill, N.Y.; purchased 900 acres, 1736; judge Ct. of Common Pleas, 1750; mem. 2d Provincial Congress; *m* Elizabeth Creed (1698-1764; William[7]);
5–William (1727-93), his notable civil service during Am. Rev. gave him the name "the Enemy of the King"; *m* Martha Carman (1732-72);
4–Martha (*b* 1760), *m* Jacobus **Swartwout** (4 above).
9–Cornelius Barentse **Van Wyck** (8 above);
8–Theodorus (7 above);
7–Cornelius (1694-1761), of Fishkill; *m* Hannah Thorne (1700-71);
6–Theodorus C. (1720-54), *m* 1st, Cathelyna Adriance (*d* 1746);
5–Capt. Cornelius (*d* 1776), capt. Am. Rev., killed in Battle of White Plains; *m* Sarah Carman;
4–Sarah (1774-1865), *m* 2d, William **Doughty** (1770-1854), of Green Haven (Joseph[5], *m* Syche Wiltsie);
3–Siche (1809-94), *m* 1830, Gilbert **Flagler** (1805-74), of Green Haven (Zacharias[4], *m* Catherine Collins);
2–Martha (1835-1918), *m* 1863, John **Peters** (1812-71), of Beekman; issue: I–John (1864-1921); II–James Delamater (1867-88); III–Frederick (1 above).
1–*m* Nov. 17, 1898, Iva Lowther (see Vol. III, p. 370).
1–Field agt. with Albany Ins. Co. Mem. S.R. Mason. Methodist. Residence: Fishkill, N.Y.

1–**PETERS, William Richmond,** *b* New York, N.Y., Apr. 13, 1850.
7–Andrew **Peters** (ca. 1634-1713), from Eng. to Mass., 1658; King Philip's War; *m* Mercy Beamsley;
6–Samuel (1674/75-1736), *m* Phoebe Frye;
5–John (1705-97), *m* 1st, Phoebe Carlton;
4–John (1741-1821), *m* Mary (Dyer) Cushing;
3–Edward Dyer (1785-1856), *m* Lucretia McClure;
2–Thomas McClure, S.T.D. (1821-93), B.A., Yale, '41; rector St. Michael's P.E. Ch., New York; *m* 1847, Alice Clarissa Richmond (1828-1904); for issue see Vol. I, p. 309.
1–*m* June 11, 1879, Helen Russell Heiser (*b* New York, June 25, 1852-*d* Oct. 11, 1929); dau. Henry Anthon Heiser, of New York; issue (all *b* N.Y. City): 1–Isabel, *b* Oct. 13, 1881; 2–Alice Richmond, *b* June 16, 1883; 3–William Richmond (Dec. 13, 1887-August 17, 1912); B.A., Yale, '08; 4–Thomas McClure, *b* June 28, 1888; B.A., Yale, '12; 5–Helen (May 18-Nov. 11, 1890).
1–Ed. pvt. schools in N.Y., and Yale 1 year, 1870. Formerly importer and mfr. of chemicals; now retired. Mem. S.C.W., S.R. Clubs: Century, Down Town, Metropolitan, etc. Residences: 6 E. 69th St., New York, N.Y., and Oyster Bay, L.I.

WILLIAM CUDWORTH DARBY (b Chesterfield, N.H., May 5, 1786-d Elmwood, Ill., Mar. 18, 1870), settled in the west, 1852.

1–**PETTERSEN, Nellie M. Darby (Mrs. Benjamin),** *b* Elmwood, Ill., Jan. 7, 1870.
7–Thomas (Daby, Derby, Dabie) **Darby** (1657-1749), of Concord, Mass.; to Stow, Mass., 1684; in King Philip's War, 1676; dea. first ch. at Stow; *m* Mary–;
6–John (1687-1767), petitioner for creation of town of Harvard, 1731; ch. pew third in rank; *m* Hannah– (*d* 1747);

5–Simon (*b* 1714), began to write name Darby; *m* Mercy Wilson (1717-51; John[6]);
4–Thomas (*b* 1739), signed Assn. Test, 1776; served in Am. Rev.; *m* 2d, 1784, Orpah Jillson;
3–William Cudworth (1786-1870), of Chesterfield, N.H., and Elmwood, Ill. (see portrait); *m* 2d, 1823, Mary Hale Mann;
2–Henry Harrison (2 below).
9–William (Gilson) **Jillson,** from Eng. to Scituate, 1630, with Winthrop fleet; *m* Frances Damon;
8–James, *m* Mary–;
7–Nathaniel (*d* 1751), *m* Elizabeth–;
6–Nathaniel, *m* 1723, Ruth Boyce;
5–Jonathan (1729-1803), signer Assn. Test at Richmond, N.H.; in Am. Rev.; made first spinning wheel in N.H.; *m* Chloe Cargill;
4–Orpah (*b* 1758), *m* Thomas **Darby** (4 above).
9–Richard **Mann** (drowned 1665), to Plymouth aet. 14 with Elder Brewster's fam. in Mayflower, 1620; one of Conihasset partners; in King Philip's War; *m* Rebecca–;
8–Richard (1652-1728), of Scituate; in Indian wars; *m* Elizabeth Sutton (*b* 1662; John[9], *m* Sarah–);
7–Nathaniel (1693-1728), founded Mansfield, Conn., 1720; *m* 1713, Mary Root;
6–John (*b* 1720), large property owner; *m* 1740, Margaret Peters (1724-89; Rev. Samuel, D.D., LL.D.[7], 1st rector P.E. ch., Hebron, Conn., 40 yrs., noted Tory, sent to Eng. by Conn. Royalists, and wrote History of Conn., pub. London, 1783, also wrote "Blue Laws of Conn."; John[8], removed from Boston to Hebron, 1717; William[9]; William[10], with two bros., Thomas, Hugh, from Eng., 1634, bought entire peninsula on which Boston stands, built ch. and manse at Andover, Mass., for son-in-law, Rev. Fry);
5–John (1743-1825), founded Orford, N.H., 1765; *m* 1765, Lydia Porter;
4–Jared (1770-1837), public official; *m* 1794, Mindwell Hale;
3–Mary Hale (1799-1880), *m* William Cudworth **Darby** (3 above).
10–John **Porter** (qv);
9–Samuel (1626-87), *m* 1659, Hannah Stanley;
8–John (1666-1702), Lebanon, Conn.; *m* Mary Butler;
7–John (1694-1753), *m* Esther Deane;
6–John (1723-83), Hebron; in Am. Rev.; *m* 1741, Lydia Tarbox (*d* 1751);
5–Lydia (1742-1815), *m* John **Mann** (5 above).
9–Thomas **Hale** (qv);
8–Thomas (1633-88), *m* 1657, Mary Hutchinson;
7–Samuel (1674-1745), Bradford, Mass.; *m* Martha Palmer (Walter[8]);
6–Jonathan (*b* 1701/02), Bradford; *m* 1729, Susannah Tuttle;
5–Dr. Samuel (1745-1820), surgeon Am. Rev.; *m* 1771, Mindwell Tillotson (1745-1815; Daniel[6], g.son of John, Archbishop of Canterbury);
4–Mindwell (*b* 1775), *m* Jared **Mann** (4 above).
10–Dea. Samuel **Edson** (qv);
9–Joseph (1649-1711), *m* 2d, Mary Turner;
8–Benjamin (1689-1758), *m* 1715, Joanna Orcutt;
7–Benjamin (*b* 1716), *m* Joanna Thayer (*b* 1718);
6–Jacob, Pelham, Mass.; selectman, 1780; soldier Am. Rev.; *m* 1759, Elizabeth Packard;
5–Elizabeth (1765-1850), *m* 1785, James **Harkness,** soldier Am. Rev. (William[6], from Scotland; William[7]);
4–Anna (1790-1837), *m* 1809, Ichabod **Smith** (1782-1856);
3–Edson Fayette (1816-93), banker; *m* 1841, Sarah Angeline Hungerford;
2–Ellen (2 below).
10–Thomas **Hungerford** (qv);
9–Thomas (1648-1714), of Hartford, Lyme and E. Haddam, Conn.; selectman; *m* Mary Green;
8–Thomas (1673-1750), New London, Conn.; *m* Elizabeth Smith (Matthew[9], *m* Mary Cutler; Matthew[10]; Matthew[11]);
7–Benjamin (1705-90), New Cambridge, 1748; *m* 1730, his cousin, Jemima Hungerford (*d* 1769);
6–Matthew (1733-1809), *m* 1756, Rachel Spencer;
5–Joseph (1761-1832), in Am. Rev.; *m* 1791, Sarah Tuttle (Noah[6], *m* Thankful Royce);
4–Joseph Lyman (*d* 1855), of Camden, N.Y., and Leehigh, Ill.; *m* 1822, Laura Huntley;
3–Sarah Angeline (1822-98), of Elmwood, Ill.; *m* 1841, Edson Fayette **Smith** (3 above);
2–Ellen (1848-1923), *m* 1866, Henry Harrison **Darby** (1840-1901); ed. Knox College, Civil War Service; issue: I–William Edson (1867-1912; Spanish-Am. War service; *m* Minnie Louisa Case; *m* 2d, Mary Lucette Dickinson); II–Nellie M. (1 above); III–Henry Harrison, Jr. (1880-97).
1–*m* Aug. 23, 1910, Benjamin Pettersen, *b* Bergen, Norway, Dec. 14, 1864; son of Wilhelm Christian Rosendahl Pettersen, of Bergen; issue: 1–Harry Darby *b* Ortonville, Minn., Sept. 9, 1912.
1–B.L., U. of Ill., '91; U. of Chicago. Prin. normal dept., Plate Coll. Inst., Kearney, Neb.; prin. high schools, Dillon, Mont., Moscow, Ida., Ortonville, Minn.; asst. supt. schools, Hedrick, Ia.; v.-p. Inland Empire Teachers' Assn.; mem. N.E. Colony, D.A.R. (organizing regent, 1922-26, and regent, 1926-30), O.E.S., etc. Residence: Sisseton, S.D.

1–**PEYTON, Albert Hovey,** *b* Huntington, W. Va., Mar. 17, 1893.
10–John **Peyton** (1596-post 1622), from Eng., 1622, settled at Acquia on the Potomac River, Va.; *m* ante 1620, Ellen Packington;
9–Henry (ante 1622-1659), of Acquia, Va.; *m* Ellen–;
8–Henry (*b* 1656), *m* Anne–;
7–Col. Valentine (1688-1754), justice Prince William Co., 1743; sheriff, 1749; burgess, 1736; vestryan Overwharton Parish, 1749; *m* Frances Harrison (Capt. Thomas[8], of Chappawamsic);
6–Craven (*d* 1781), vestryman Shelbourne Parish, 1771-76; justice Loudoun Co., 1764,66,67,68,70,71; personal friend of Washington, who mentions him in his diary; *m* ante 1760, Anne West;
5–Col. Francis (*d* 1836), vestryman Christ Church, Alexandria; *m* ante 1784, Sarah West (*d* post 1836);
4–Capt. Thomas West (ante 1784-1819), on first vestry of St. Paul's Ch., Alexandria, 1810; justice, 1814; capt. of militia War 1812; *m* 1811, Sophia Matilda Dundas;
3–Capt. Thomas West (1819-63), New Orleans, La.; capt. in C.S.A.; wounded and taken prisoner at Stone River; *m* 1850, Sarah O'-Dowd (*b* 1833);
2–Capt. Thomas West (2 below).
11–Anthony **West** (*d* 1652), from Eng., 1622, settled in Accomac Co., Va.; *m* ante 1622, Anne– (*d* post 1652);
10–Lt. Col. John (ante 1622-post 1692), Northumberland Co.; *m* Matilda Scarborough;
9–Maj. John (*d* post 1749), lt., Westmoreland Co. militia, 1690; maj., 1703; surveyor; *m* ca. 1690, Sally (or Susannah) Pearson;
8–John (*d* ante 1748), of West's Grove; vestryman; *m*— (*d* post 1739), a dau. of Burr Harrison of Chappawamsic;
7–William (ante 1719-69), of West's Ordinary and Leesburg, Va.; surveyor; justice Loudoun Co., Va., 1757; trustee Leesburg, 1758; *m* Mary–;
6–Anne (*d* 1805), *m* Craven **Peyton** (6 above).
6–James **Dundas** (1734-post 1787), from Scotland, 1757, settled at Phila., Pa.; officer Phila. militia, and as "Mr. Dundas of Reading" lent money to the government in Am. Rev.; *m* 1758, Elizabeth Moore (*d* 1787; James[7]; John[8], of Manor);
5–Lt. John (1760-ante 1819), ens. Phila. Militia, 1780; *m* 1785, Agnes Hepburn (1771-1820; Thomas[6]);
4–Sophia M. (1791-post 1864), of Alexandria and Cabell Court House, Va.; *m* Thomas W. **Peyton** (4 above).
8–Ullrich (Meuller) **Miller,** from Zweibruken, Germany, with son Jacob and family; burgher; settled in York Co., Pa.;
7–Jacob (1698-1776), from Germany, Sept. 2, 1749; to Shenandoah Valley, 1752; original trustee Woodstock or Muellerstadt; *m* Barbara–;
6–Christian (*b* Germany, 1744-*d* Woodstock, Va., 1838), sgt. Va. militia, Am. Rev., pensioner; *m* 1771, Catherine Wiseman (1746-1837);
5–John (1781-1846), lived nr. Point Pleasant, Va., and Gallipolis, O.; Mason 40 yrs.; *m* 1806, Sophia Clendennin;
4–Margaret Catherine (1818-59), *married* Thomas **Thornburg,** mem. Va. Assembly from 1857 to Civil War; mem. W.Va. Constl. Conv., 1872;
3–Ellen Eliza (1842-1915), *m* 1866, Capt. William Marshall **Hovey** (1842-1923), U.S.A., Civil War;
2–Mary Thornburg (2 below).
8–Archibald **Clendennin** (*d* 1749), from Scotland ante 1733, settled in Shenandoah Valley, Va.:

lived in "The Calf Pasture," Rockbridge Co., Va.; moved to "Lower Cow Pasture";
7-Capt. Charles (*d* post 1786), capt. in Battle of Point Pleasant; gave his name to Charleston, W.Va.;
6-Maj. William (1753-1828), Kanawha Co., Va. (now W.Va.); capt. Augusta Co. militia in Am. Rev., maj. Kanawha Co. militia, 1789; gent. justice, 1789; original trustee Charleston, W.Va., 1794; sheriff Kanawha Co., 1792-93; justice Mason Co., 1804; mem. Gen. Assembly of Va., 1804; *m* 1783, Margaret Handley (1762-1835; John[7]);
5-Sophia (1783-1823), *m* John **Miller** (5 above).
2-Mary Thornburg Hovey (1867-1902), *m* 1890, Capt. Thomas West **Peyton** (1860-1912), of Huntington, W.Va.; capt. W.Va. N.G.; issue: I-Capt. Thomas West, IV (*b* 1891; *m* Gay Zenith Vaughan); II-Albert H. (1 above); III-John Thornburg (*b* 1897; *m* Mrs. Bertha Mae Ullman), IV-Lt. Robert Edwin (*b* 1901).
1-*m* July 30, 1919, Betty Tyler (qv for issue).
1-Ed. Morris Harvey Coll. Entered W.Va. N.G. and promoted to 2d lt.; Mexican border service, 1916; apptd. to regular army, 1917; trained at Ft. Leavenworth; 1st lt., 1917, capt., Co. H, 51st Inf., with which organization to France, 1918-19. Address: c/o Mrs. Bert Albert Tyler, Edgewood, Dalton, Ga.

1-**PEYTON, Betty Tyler (Mrs. Albert Hovey),** *b* Evanston, Ill., Dec. 18, 1896.
10-Job **Tyler** (qv);
9-Moses (1641-1727), *m* Prudence Blake (1647-89);
8-Ebenezer (1673-1743), *m* Elizabeth Walker (1668-1745);
7-David (1710-1805), *m* 1735, Martha Howard (*d* post 1768), of Lynn;
6-Ebenezer (1747-1823), in Battle of Saratoga, Am. Rev.; signed Assn. Test in N.H.; *m* Jerusha Chapman (*d* 1834);
5-Joseph (1772-1853), *m* 1792, Mehitable Ladd (*d* post 1819);
4-Asa Ladd (1794-1882), served War 1812, pensioned; *m* 1817, Fanny Tupper (1796-1871);
3-Horace Chamberlain (1838-79), *m* 1859, Abigail Matilda Piper (1841-1922);
2-Bert Albert (2 below).
9-Richard **Hubbell** (qv);
8-Samuel, Jr. (*b* 1670), *m* Elizabeth-;
7-Nathan (1699-1761), *m* Martha Finch (1701-55);
6-Capt. Gershom (1729-1802), capt. of Train Band, ens. in French and Indian War; lt. Am. Rev.; *m* 2d, Sarah Wakeman (*d* 1769);
5-Sarah (1765-1815), *m* 2d, 1802, Gideon **Kellogg** (1767-1807);
4-Ozias (1805-86), *m* Daphne Eliza Cook;
3-Gideon (1846-1911), *m* 1868, Emily Euphemia Donaldson (1850-92);
2-Bertha (2 below).
10-Capt. Thomas (Cook) **Cooke** (*b* 1603-will proved June 20, 1677), from Eng. to Boston, 1635/36; settled at Portsmouth, R.I.; dep., 1664; *m* 2d, Mary-;
9-John (1631-91), dep. Gen. Ct.; *m* 1670, Mary Borden (*d* ante 1691);
8-Thomas (*d* 1726), *m* Mary Cory;
7-Stephen (1703-1803), *m* Mary- (1714-90);
6-Benjamin (1740-post 1790), Am. Rev.; *m* 2d, 1771, Naomi Shrieve;
5-Stephen (1774-1820), served War 1812; *m* ante 1806, Thankful Creel;
4-Daphne Eliza (1810-78), *m* Ozias **Kellogg** (4 above);
3-Gideon, *m* Emily E. Donaldson (3 above);
2-Bertha (see Vol. II, p. 236), *m* 1895, Bert Albert **Tyler** (*b* 1868).
1-*m* July 30, 1919, Albert Hovey Peyton (qv); issue: 1-Virginia, *b* Camp Grant, Ill., May 19, 1920; 2-Sarah West, *b* Ft. Sam Houston, Tex., Aug. 25, 1923.
1-Ed. Shorter Coll., Rome, Ga. Mem. D.F.P.A., D.A.R. Address: c/o Mrs. Bert Albert Tyler, Edgewood, Dalton, Ga.

1-**PHELPS, Edmund Joseph, Jr.,** *b* Minneapolis, Minn., Dec. 11, 1891.
9-Thomas **Richardson** (qv);
8-Nathaniel (1651-1714), *m* Mary- (*d* 1719);
7-Joshua (1681-1748), *m* Hannah- (*d* 1768);
6-Joshua (1716-74), *m* 1739, Eunice Jennison (1719-48);
5-Nathaniel (1742-96), *m* 1771, Eunice Putnam (1751-1846; David[6], *m* Rebecca Perley);
4-Capt. William Putnam (1785-1826), sea captain; *m* 1807, Deborah Lang (1785-1845; Edward[5], *m* Rachel Ward);
3-Charles Frederic (1818-1852 or 53), *m* 1842, Ruth Cheever Shepard (1820-1907; Jeremiah[4], *m* Ruth Cheever);
2-Louisa Anne (*b* 1849), C.D.A.; *m* 1874, Edmund Joseph **Phelps** (1845-1923); for issue and Phelps lineage see brother, Richardson Phelps.
1-*m* Oct. 16, 1920, Katharine Marfield, *b* Winona, Minn., July 30, 1896; dau. of James Russell Marfield, of Minneapolis, *m* Helen Horton; issue (all *b* Minneapolis, Minn.): 1-Marcella Marfield, *b* Mar. 5, 1922; 2-Ruth Shepard, *b* Oct. 6, 1923; 3-Edmund Joseph, 3d, *b* Mar. 9, 1928.
1-B.A., Yale, '14. Landscape architect. Served in Am. Ambulance Service with French Army at Verdun, Apr.-Nov. 1917; enlisted in French Army and grad. as aspirant, Fontain bleau Arty. Sch., June 1918; attached to 17th Regt. Light Arty. and comd. baty. at Montdidier; awarded Croix de Guerre. Residence: Wayzata, Minn.

1-**PHELPS, Richardson,** *b* Minneapolis, Minn., Jan. 6, 1887.
9-William **Phelps** (qv);
8-Nathaniel (*b* Tewkesbury, Eng., 1627-*d* 1702), *m* 1650, Elizabeth Copley (*d* 1712);
7-William (1657-1745), *m* 1678, Abigail Stebbins (1660-1748; John[8]);
6-Ebenezer (1697-1769), *m* 1740, Sarah Taylor (1706-92);
5-Ebenezer (1740-1821), *m* 1764, Phebe Wright (1743-1826);
4-Asahel (1775-1826), *m* 1802, Polly Sears;
3-Joseph Edmund (1805-95), farmer; *m* 1826, Ursula Wright (1806-76; Daniel[4], *m* Achsah Clark);
2-Edmund Joseph (Jan. 17, 1845-Oct. 12, 1923), see Vol. I, p. 949; *m* Sept. 16, 1874, Louisa Anne Richardson (*b* June 30, 1849), C.D.A.; issue: I-Ruth Shepard (*b* 1876; *m* 1929, Paul Morand); II-Richardson (1 above); III-Edmund Joseph, Jr. (qv for Richardson lineage).
1-*m* Feb. 7, 1916, Anne Foley, *b* St. Cloud, Minn., July 1, 1893; dau. of Thomas Foley, of St. Paul, Minn., *m* Jessie Craig; issue (all *b* St. Paul): 1-Anne Foley, *b* Nov. 13, 1917; 2-Richardson, Jr., *b* Apr. 1, 1919; 3-Craig, *b* Feb. 21, 1921.
1-B.A., Yale, '10. Pres. Phelps & Co. (ins.), Minneapolis. Enlisted U.S.A., Jan. 1918; apptd. 2d lt., A.S., Mar. 1918; joined A.E.F., July 1918; served thru St. Mihiel and Argonne offensives as asst. adj. to Gen. William Mitchell, chief of the A.S., 1st Army; disch. New York, Feb. 1919. Trustee Minneapolis Soc. of Fine Arts; dir. Minneapolis Orchestral Assn., Minneapolis Bd. of Underwriters. Club: Minneapolis. Address: Foshay Tower, Minneapolis, Minn.

1-**PHELPS, Edith Foster (Mrs. Oscar Acken),** *b* South Windsor, Conn., Jan. 21, 1867.
8-Christopher **Foster** (qv);
7-John (*b* 1634), from Eng.; trustee of Southampton, 1676; town overseer;
6-John (*b* 1662), justice, L.I., 1724; signed Andros patent in L.I.; *m* 1689, Hannah Abbott;
5-Abraham (1702-84), Windsor, Conn.; sgt. French and Indian War; *m* 1727, Elizabeth Moore;
4-Thomas (1737-1826), S. Windsor; soldier French and Indian War; ens. in Am. Rev., enlisted 1778; *m* 1761, Martha Elmer (1742-1812);
3-William (1781-1870), *m* 1806, Eunice Dart (1786-1860);
2-Ralph (2 below).
8-John **Warham** (1595-1670), from Eng.; a founder of Windsor; *m* 1637, Jane- (*d* 1655);
7-Sarah (1642-78), *m* 1664, Return **Strong**;
6-Abigail (1666-1733), *m* 1693, John **Moore** (*b* 1665);
5-Elizabeth (1702-1800), *m* 1727, Abraham **Foster** (5 above).
8-William **Buckland** (qv);
7-William (*d* 1691), of E. Hartford; *m* Elizabeth-;
6-William (1674-1724), surveyor, 1708,15; *m* as her 1st husband, Elizabeth Hills (John[7], one of the 1st settlers of Hartford);
5-Sgt. William (*d* 1758), soldier French and Indian War, *m* 2d, Meribah- (*d* 1794, aet. 72);
4-George W. (1757-1845), Springfield, Mass.; pvt. Am. Rev.; *m* 1781, Elizabeth-;

3–Norman (1796-1844), guardian of real estate in Manchester; selectman, 1827-28, 1839-43; *m* Joanna Marilla Wright (*d* 1863);
2–Chloe (1829-1910), *m* 1851, Ralph **Foster** (1824-1900), selectman, Hartford, 9 yrs.; issue: I–George (*b* 1852); II–Alice (1853-1903; *m* Edgar F. Burnham); III–Hattie M. (*b* 1865); IV–Edith (1 above).
1–*m* Oscar Acken Phelps, of Hartford, Conn.; son of John Phelps, of Guilford, Conn.; issue (both *b* Hartford): 1–Dorothy Foster, *b* Feb. 2, 1897; Mt. Holyoke, '18; 2–Alice Buckland (1898-1928); Mt. Holyoke, '20.
1–Ed. New Britain Normal Sch. Teacher S. Windsor, 2 yrs., Arsenal Sch., Hartford, 3 yrs., Willimantic Normal, 2 yrs. Mem. S.D.P. (dir.), D.F.P.A., D.A.C., D.A.R., Soc. N.E. Women (registrar), Y.M.C.A. Clubs: Woman's (Hartford), Woman's Saturday Afternoon of Wethersfield (pres. 1927-29). Conglist. Republican. Residence: 280 Wolcott Hill Rd., Wethersfield, Conn.

1–**PHELPS, Ryland Thornton,** *b* "Rosedale", Greensville Co., Va., Mar. 17, 1888.
5–Edward **Phelps**;
4–Edward, *m* Fanna Spruill;
3–Jeremiah, *m* Debora Fortune;
2–Rev. William Girard (2 below).
5–James **Phelps**;
4–Penelope, *m* Capt. James **Fortune,** Irish sea capt., of Currituck Co., N.C.; lost at sea on trip to Bermuda;
3–Debora, *m* Jeremiah **Phelps** (3 above);
2–Rev. William Girard (July 14, 1832-Dec. 5, 1918), Episcopal minister; *m* 1865, Mary Randolph (Aug. 20, 1844-May 23, 1930), see Vol. III, p. 371, for lineages; issue: I–Edward Randolph (1866-1918; *m* Sallie B. Field); II–Charlotte Mead (*b* 1868; *m* William Linton Stables); III–William Girard (*d* infancy); IV–Everard Stockdell (*b* 1871; *m* Sarah Ann Queen); V–Mary Margaret (*b* 1872; *m* Frederick Ferrin Bingham); VI–Virginia Stockdell (*d* infancy); VII–Fannie Randolph; VIII–Mary Harrison; IX–David Randolph (*m* Florence Schirmacher); X–Richard Roscoe (*b* 1882; *m* Margaret Anderson Petar); XI–Anna Harrison (*b* 1884); XII–Robert Randolph (*d* infancy); XIII–Ryland Thornton (1 above).
1–*m* Oct. 19, 1910, Mary Irene Morrison (qv); issue (all *b* Graham, Va.): 1–Mary Randolph, and 2–William Girard (twins), *b* Nov. 21, 1911; 3–James Davidson Morrison, *b* Jan. 25, 1915.
1–B.S., Washington and Lee Univ., '10. Civil engineer. R.A. Mason. Residence: 300 Frederick St., Bluefield, W.Va.

1–**PHELPS, Mary Irene Morrison (Mrs. Ryland T.),** *b* nr. Lexington, Va., Feb. 11, 1881.
9–Samuel **Chapin** (qv);
8–Henry (*d* 1718), *m* 1664, Bethia Cooley (1643-1711; Benjamin[9], qv);
7–Benjamin (1682-1756), ens.; dea. of Chicopee ch., 1752; *m* 1st, 1704, Hannah Colton;
6–Benjamin (1708-62), *m* 1735, Anna Howard, of Springfield, Mass.;
5–Benjamin (1736-78), from Mass. to Va., ante 1775; one of 22 surgeons of the Va. State Navy; died in service and was entitled to 6,000 acres of land; heirs delayed 14 yrs. to file claim and it was rejected; *m* 1760, Margaret Colton (*b* 1738; Benjamin[6]; Ephraim[7]; George[8], qv);
4–Gurden (1765-1811), *m* 1793, Margaret (the "Beautiful Peggy") Reeder (1774-1843; Thomas[5], of Md., *m* Nancy–);
3–Charles (1795-1863), prominent Mason, Alexandria, Va.; *m* 1827, Mary Ann Martha Newton Wise (1809-72);
2–Laura (2 below).
9–Thomas **Cooper** (1617-75), from Eng. in the "Christian," 1635, settled at Boston; removed to Windsor, Conn., 1641, thence to Springfield, 1645; mem. 1st Bd. of Selectmen, 17 yrs.; dep. Gen. Ct., 1668; *m* 2d, Mary Slye;
8–Mary (*b* 1651), *m* Isaac **Colton** (1646-1712; George[9], qv);
7–Hannah (1688-1739), *m* Benjamin **Chapin** (7 above).
2–Laura Chapin (1853-1903), *m* 1875, James Davidson **Morrison** (1830-1902), capt. C.S.A.; lawyer; editor Rockbridge Citizen; mem. Va. Assembly, 1872-75; for issue and other lineages see Vol. III, p. 371.
1–*m* Oct. 19, 1910, Ryland Thornton Phelps (qv for issue).
1–Mem. D.A.R., O.E.S. Residence: 300 Frederick St., Bluefield, W.Va.

1–**PICKENS, Carrie Rankin Read (Mrs. William Letcher),** *b* McMinnville, Tenn., Oct. 12, 1863.
9–Nicholas **Martian** (qv);
8–Elizabeth, *b* in France; *m* Col. George **Reade** (qv);
7–Thomas, of Va.; *m* 1688, Lucy Gwynne;
6–Clement (1707-63), Charlotte Co., Va.; *m* 1730, Mary Hill;
5–Clement (1736-1770), *m* 1757, Mary Nash (1733-1812; Col. John[6]);
4–John Nash (1763-1826), *m* Elizabeth Julia Spencer;
3–Sion Spencer (1791-1845), *m* 1819, Hardinia Jefferson Spencer;
2–John Thomas (2 below).
9–Henry **Corbin** (qv);
8–Frances (*b* 1653), *m* Edmund **Jennings** (1659-1727);
7–Priscilla, York Co., Va.; *m* William **Hill**;
6–Mary (*d* 1786), Lunenburg Co., Va.; *m* Clement **Read** (6 above).
2–John T. **Read** (1825-1900), physician and surgeon, Chattanooga, Tenn.; *m* 1848, Laurena Caroline Rankin (1827-1903); issue: I–Eliza Roberson (*d* infancy); II–Laura Barksdale (1851-78; *m* Samuel McCall); III–Mary Hardinia (*b* 1854; *m* William Watson Frater); IV–Harriet Stone (*b* 1857; *m* Rev. Harrison H. Sneed, *d* 1927); V–Samuel Roberson (*b* 1860; *m* Elizabeth H. Sims, *d* 1909; *m* 2d, Katherine Lenoir Key); VI–Carrie Rankin (1 above).
1–*m* Apr. 23, 1889, William Letcher Pickens (July 15, 1851-Nov. 2, 1898); son of William Kennedy Pickens, of Cleveland, Tenn.; issue: 1–Henry Berlin (qv for Pickens lineage); 2–John Read, *b* Chattanooga, Apr. 23, 1896; ed. Davidson Coll., N.C.; served on Mexican border, 9 months, and in World War, 2 yrs.
1–Grad. Ward Sem., '81. Mem. Magna Charta Dames, C.D.A., U.D.C., D.A.R. (chapter treas., 3 yrs.), I.A.G. Dir. Tuberculosis Sanitarium Assn. Club: Chattanooga Woman's. Episcopalian. Democrat. Residence: 710 Walnut St., Chattanooga, Tenn.

1–**PICKENS, Henry Berlin,** *b* Chattanooga, Tenn., Aug. 3, 1893.
8–Andrew **Pickens,** *b* in Scotland; with his family, was expelled, 1661, because of religious faith; to France, where they were forced to flee when the Edict of Nantes was revoked, 1685; returned to Scotland;
7–Robert (or Israel), *m* in France, Widow Esther Jane Bonneau;
6–Robert (*b* 1697), in Ireland; came to America, 1755, and settled in S.C.;
5–Robert (*b* 1747), capt., a.-d.-c. to his cousin, Gen. Andrew Pickens during Am. Rev.; *m* 1774, Dorcas Holburn (*b* 1760);
4–John (1775-1827), Pendleton Dist., S.C.; *m* 1799, Nancy Bowen (1779-1859);
3–William Kennedy (1812-55), *m* Mary Ann Egleston White;
2–William Letcher (1851-98), *m* 1889, Carrie Rankin Read (qv).
1–*m* July 8, 1920, Christine Valentine Stoehr, *b* Hartford, Conn., April 11, 1900; dau. of Henry Valentine Stoehr, of New Haven; issue: 1–Andrew Read, *b* Birmingham, Ala., Dec. 12, 1921.
1–B.S., Yale, '15; grad. Chattanooga Law Sch., 1917. Insurance broker. Commd. 2d lt., O.T.C., Fort Oglethorpe, Ga., Aug. 15, 1917; assigned to Intelligence Dept., 81st Div.; arrived in France, Aug. 15, 1918; participated in engagements in Vosges sector and Battle of the Argonne; returned to U.S.A., Sept. 1919; commd. 1st lt., May 19, 1919; slightly gassed; in hospital in France 3 mos.; disch., Sept. 29, 1919. Residence: 137 E. 66th St., New York, N.Y.

1–**PILLSBURY, Helen (Nelle) Pendleton Winston (Mrs. Charles Stinson),** *b* St. Paul, Minn., Oct. 16, 1878.
8–Cyprian **Stevens** (*b* ca. 1648; son of Col. Thomas, of London); came from Eng., 1660; one of the earliest settlers of Lancaster, Mass.; served in King Philip's War, and his house was used as a garrison; *m* 1st, 1671,

Mary Willard (1653-ca. 1685; Maj. Daniel[9], qv);
7–Simon (1677-1758), Boston; *m* 1701, Mary Wilder (*b* 1679; Lt. Nathaniel[8], served in Indian wars, *m* Mary, dau. of Thomas Sawyer, qv; Thomas[9], a founder of Lancaster, *m* Mary, dau. of John Prescott, qv; John[10]);
6–Joseph (ca. 1720-ante 1810), *m* 1745, Dorothy Sawyer (*b* 1726);
5–Lemuel (1753-post 1781), Newfane, Vt.; Am. Rev.; *m* ca. 1772, Hannah Green (ca. 1750-1795);
4–Gardner (1782-1845), *m* 1806, Deborah Harrington (1786-ca. 1872);
3–John Harrington (1820-1900), *m* 1850, Helen F. Miller;
2–Katherine Duane (2 below).
6–Giles **Miller** (1725-1804), officer Conn. militia, Am. Rev.; *m* Elizabeth Parsons;
5–Giles (1758-1825), *m* Janet McCallum;
4–Abner (*b* 1787), *m* Sally Lyman;
3–Helen F. (1822-1902), *m* John H. **Stevens** (3 above);
2–Katherine Duane (1852-1911), *m* 1876, Philip Bickerton **Winston** (1845-1901), of Minneapolis.
1–*m* Dec. 7, 1901, Charles Stinson Pillsbury (see Vol. III, p. 373); issue (all *b* Minneapolis): 1–Philip Winston, *b* Apr. 16, 1903; Yale, '24; 2–Mary Stinson, *b* Nov. 14, 1904; *m* Dec. 7, 1929, Oswald Bates Lord, of New York; 3–Katharine Stevens, *b* Oct. 11, 1905; *m* May 24, 1930, Elliott Bates McKee, of Paris, France, and Washington, D.C.; 4–Helen Winston, *b* Nov. 18, 1907.
1–Mem. C.D.A., D.F.P.A. Summer place: "Dunbarton," Wayzata, Minn. Residence: 100 E. 22d St., Minneapolis, Minn.

1–**PLEASANTS, Missouri Alston (Mrs. William H., Jr.),** *b* "Saxham Hall," Warren Co., N.C., June 11, 1867.
8–John **Alston** (qv);
7–John (*d* 1704), *m* Anne Wallis (*b* ca. 1645; John[8]);
6–Col. John (1673-1758), from Eng.; first Am. record, 1711, Chowan Co., N.C.; asso. justice Supreme Ct. of N.C., 1725; col. N.C. militia; *m* Mary Clark;
5–Maj. Philip (1706-83), Warren Co.; *m* 1746, Winifred Whitmel;
4–Thomas Whitmel (*b* 1755), apptd. lt. col., Nov. 23, 1777, on resignation of his bro. Col. William Alston, Am. Rev.; *m* 1786, Lucy Faulcon (*b* 1763; Nicholas[6], of Surry Co., Va., *m* Lucy Wyatt);
3–Nicholas Faulcon (1787-1818), *m* 1812, Elizabeth Crawford Davis;
2–Archibald Davis (2 below).
7–Thomas **Whitmel,** from Surry Co., Va., to N.C., where he was commr. of Indian affairs and justice; sr. warden first Anglican (old Glebe) ch. built in N.C. at Windsor, Bertie Co.; *m* Mary–;
6–Thomas (1688-1735), col. Bertie Co. militia; *m* 1712, Elizabeth Hunter Bryan (*b* 1690; Lewis[7], believed to have come from Eng. to Bertie Co., 1713, *m* 1688, Elizabeth Hunter, of Surry Co.);
5–Winifred (1721 or 1729-1795), *m* Philip **Alston** (5 above).
5–Thomas **Davis,** public printer, Am. Rev.; *m* Hartwell Hodge;
4–Archibald, pvt. and musician, Am. Rev.; *m* Elizabeth Hilliard (Isaac[5], Am. Rev., *m* Leah Crawford);
3–Elizabeth Crawford (1787-1869), *m* Nicholas F. **Alston** (3 above);
2–Archibald Davis (June 11, 1817-May 4, 1899), *m* 1843, Missouri Florida **Alston** (1824-68; Hon. Willis[3], mem. U.S. Congress, *m* Sarah Madeline, dau. of Joshua Potts, Am. Rev.); see Vol. I, p. 123 for maternal lineage.
1–*m* Sept. 14, 1892, William Henry Pleasants, Jr. (Sept. 14, 1869-Apr. 11, 1918); son of William H. Pleasants, of Louisburg, N.C., *m* Sarah Carlisle.
1–Summer place: "Saxham Hall," Warren Co., N.C. Residence: Cor. Church St. and Sunset Ave., Louisburg, N.C.

1–**ALSTON, William Wiggins,** *b* Oxford, N.C., Feb. 12, 1923.
10–John **Alston** (qv);
9–John (*d* 1704), *m* Anne Wallis (*b* ca. 1645; John[10]);
8–Col. John (1673-1758), from Eng.; first Am. record 1711, Chowan Co., *m* Mary Clark (John[9] [*d* 1689]; g.dau. of John Palin, chief justice of N.C.);
7–Joseph John (1700-81), of Halifax, N.C.; mem. Gen. Assembly, 1744-46; *m* Elizabeth Chancy;
6–Capt. John (1740-84), capt. 3d N.C. Regt. in Am. Rev.; *m* Ann Hunt Macon (Gideon[7], *m* Priscilla, dau. of Edward Jones, *m* Abigail Shugan);
5–Congress Willis (1770-1837), mem. Provincial House of Commons, N.C.; state senator; mem. 8th to 13th (1803-15) and 19th to 21st (1825-31) Congresses, chmn. Ways and Means Com., during War 1812; *m* 1817, Sallie M. Potts (Joshua[6], asst. Q.M. Gen. in Am. Rev.);
4–Charles Julian Poydroas (1818-ca. 1875), *m* ca. 1857, Mary Janet Clark;
3–Leonidas (1861-1927), *m* 1882, Aline Wiggins;
2–William Wiggins (2 below).
9–Thomas **Whitmel,** went from Surry Co., Va., to N.C., where he was commr. of Indian affairs and justice; sr. warden of the first Anglican (old Glebe) ch. built in N.C. at Windsor, Bertie Co.; *m* Mary–;
8–Thomas (1688-1735), col. Bertie Co. militia; *m* 1712, Elizabeth Hunter Bryan (*b* 1690; Lewis[9], believed to have come from Eng. to Bertie Co., N.C., 1713, *m* 1688, Elizabeth Hunter, of Surry Co., Va.);
7–Elizabeth, *m* Col. William **Williams,** adj., Am. Rev., mem. Provincial Congress, Halifax, Apr. 4, 1776, and Constl. Conv., Oct. 1776;
6–Gen. William, *m* Elizabeth–;
5–Martha Boddie, *m* William McKinzie **Clark;**
4–Mary J., *m* Charles J. P. **Alston** (4 above).
7–Robin **Jones,** from Wales to Va.; removed to N.C.; agent for Lord Granville; lawyer, ed. Eng.; atty. gen. of N.C., 1761; *m* 1737, Sarah Cobb;
6–Willie (1741-1822), ed. Eton Coll., Eng.; to Halifax, 1763; mem. Provincial Congress, 1774,76; Am. Rev.; actg. gov. until Richard Caswell was elected, 1776; *m* 1776, Mary Montford (Col. Joseph[7] [1724-76], from Eng. to N.C., 1750, clk. of ct., Halifax, 1758, mem. Colonial Assembly, 1762-73, col. Halifax militia, apptd. Provincial Grand Master of Masons of and for North America, received commn. 1772, from the Duke of Beaufort, Grand Master of Masons of Great Britain, *m* 1753, Priscilla, dau. of Col. Benjamin Hill, of Bertie Co.);
5–Sarah, *m* 1812, Gov. Hutchings G. **Burton** (1782-1836), ed. Chapel Hill; read law under Judge Henderson; rep., Mecklenburg Co., House Commons, 1810,17; atty. N.C., 1810-16; elected Congress, 1819, served 2 terms; gov. N.C., 1825-27 (John[6] [*d* ca. 1785], of Va., officer Am. Rev.);
4–Bettie (Berta), *m* Mason L. **Wiggins,** senator, 1854,56, 1864-66;
3–Aline, *m* Leonidas **Alston** (3 above);
2–William Wiggins (1888-1926), *m* Lucy Patton; issue: I–Florence Patton (*b* Oxford, N.C., 1919); II–William Wiggins, Jr. (1 above); III–Lucy P. (*b* Oxford, N.C., 1925).

1–**POGUE, Mary Isabella Crawford (Mrs. Henry),** *b* Cincinnati, O.
10–Sir William **Lovelace** (bap. 1583-1627; son of Sir William, of Bethersden [*b* 1561], *m* Elizabeth, dau. of Sir Anthony Aucher); mem. Va. Co., incorporator of the 2d Va. Charter, 1609; *m* 1610, Dame Anne, dau. of Sir William Barne, *m* Anne, dau. of Sir Edwin Sandys, Archbishop of York;
9–Anne (ca. 1610-1652), *m* 1628, Rev. John **Gorsuch** (*d* ca. 1647);
8–Charles (1644-1716), from Va. to Md., 1659; *m* Sarah Cole (*d* ante 1690; Thomas[9], *m* Priscilla–);
7–John (*b* ca. 1678, living 1723), *m* ante 1717, Elizabeth–;
6–Charles (1720-1806), *m* ante 1742, Susannah–;
5–Anne (*b* ca. 1749-*d* probably 1789), *m* 1769, William **Jones** (1747-1830);
4–Anne (*b* 1780-*d* Cincinnati, O., 1844), *m* James **Butler** (*d* 1860);
3–Emily (1804-62), *m* 1833, Peter **Smith** (1805-64);
2–Susan Etherington (*b* Cincinnati, O., 1834-*d* Rome, Italy, 1907), *m* 1851, John **Crawford** (*b* Ireland, 1826-*d* Covington, Ky., 1897); merchant; issue: I–Emily Armstrong (*d* infancy); II–Mary I. (1 above); III–Elizabeth King; IV–Blanche (*d*).
1–*m* Nov. 4, 18–, Henry Pogue (*b* Ireland, May 5,

1830-*d* Cincinnati, Jan. 15, 1903); issue: 1-Blanche Crawford, *b* Cincinnati; *m* Oct. 18, 1910, William Walker Smith (see Vol. III, p. 576); 2-Mary Elsie, *b* Cincinnati; 3-Charlotte (*d* infancy); 4-Susan Natalie, *b* Ft. Hamilton, N.Y.; *m* John Langdon Gates (issue: Muriel Isabella; Natalie Pogue); 5-Henry, *b* Cincinnati, O.; *m* Constance Lewis (issue: Constance; Henry, Jr.; William Armstrong); 6-John Crawford, *b* Cincinnati; *m* Faye Elliott (issue: Patricia; John Crawford, Jr.; Elliott; Robert Ross); 7-Elizabeth (*d* infancy); 8-Margaret, *b* Cincinnati; *m* Victor Louis Tyree (issue: Mary Isabella Pogue; Millard Hite).

1-Dir. H. & S. Pogue Co., Cincinnati. Mem. C.D.A., C.D.XVIIC. (v.p. gen. Ohio chapter), Colonial Daus. of America (2d v.regent nat. soc., Cincinnati Chapter), Dames of the Court of Honor (pres. gen. nat. soc.), D.A.R., I.A.G. (life), Cincinnati Geneal. Soc., F.F.V., Mary Washington Soc., Cincinnati Museum (life), Audubon Soc. (life). Episcopalian. Clubs: Cincinnati Country, Cincinnati Woman's, Three Arts. Residence: Hotel Alms, Cincinnati, O.

1-**POGUE, Thomas Lightfoot,** *b* Maysville, Ky., Nov. 28, 1868.
6-Col. Robert (Poage) **Pogue** (*b* in Va.);
5-William (1735-78), sgt. in command of Ft. Russell on the Clinch River, southwestern Va., 1774; *m* 1762, Ann Kennedy;
4-Robert (1765-post 1833), *m* Martha Jane Hopkins (*b* 1767);
3-William Lindsey (1794-1880), *m* Ann McCormick (*b* 1797);
2-Henry Edgar (1825-90), Washington (Pa.) Coll., ex-'45; of Maysville, Ky.; *m* 1853, Frances Ann Wood (1833-1908); issue: I-John Fleming (1854-1917; *m* 1893, Nellie Patterson); II-Henry Edgar (1859-1919; *m* 1891, Anna Belle Maltby); III-James Wood (1861-1915; *m* 1887, Madge Ellis); IV-Province McCormick (see Vol. III, p. 569); V-Thomas Lightfoot (1 above).
1-*m* June 21, 1911, Margaret Edwards, *b* Cincinnati, O., Sept. 27, 1886; dau. of William Edwards; issue: 1-Virginia, *b* Sept. 21, 1912; 2-Margaret (Peggy), *b* June 16, 1914; 3-Thomas L., Jr., *b* Oct. 26, 1915; 4-Barbara, *b* Jan. 14, 1922.
1-A.B., Washington and Jefferson, '91; law student, U.Va., 1891-92; B.L., Cincinnati Law School, 1893. Began practice of law, 1893; mem. firm of Pogue & Pogue and Pogue, Hoffheimer & Pogue, 1896-. Pros. atty., Hamilton Co., Ohio, 1912,13,14. Clubs: University, Cincinnati Country. Residence: 1733 E. McMillan St., Walnut Hills, Cincinnati, Ohio.

1-**POMEROY, Franklin Thomas,** *b* Paris, Ida., Sept. 15, 1870.
8-Eltweed **Pomeroy** (qv);
7-Joseph (1652-1734), of Northampton; *m* 1677, Hannah Lyman (1660-1736);
6-Noah (1700-79), of Windsor, Conn.; *m* 1724, Elizabeth Sterling (1700-79), of Lynn;
5-John (1733-1810), of Somers, Conn.; *m* 1762, Esther Kibbie (1731-1808);
4-Jude (1769-1852); *m* 1793, Mary Root (1771-1862);
3-Martin (1798-1879); *m* 1817, Sybil Hunt (1798-1846);
2-Francis Martin (1822-82), pioneer to Utah with Brigham Young, 1847; removed to Idaho, 1863, to Mesa, Ariz., 1877; *m* 1844, Irene Haskell; *m* 2d, Sarah Matilda Colborn (1834-1926); issue (2d marriage): I-Mary Ursula (*b* 1860; *m* 1881, Solomon F. Kimball); II-Talma Emerson (*b* 1863; *m* 1886, Sarah Melissa Johnson); III-William Edley (*b* 1865; *m* Isabelle Robson); IV-Franklin Thomas (1 above); V-Sarah Rosina (*m* Adam Rufus Brewer); VI-Edward Leslie (*b* 18-; *m* Serena Mcguire).
1-*m* Mar. 28, 1893, Sophia Isadora Morris, *b* Rockville, Utah, Apr. 10, 1873; dau. of Hyrum Bowles Morris, *m* Eleanor Crawford, of Ky. and Ill.; issue (all *b* Mesa, Ariz.): 1-Franklin Ivan, *b* Jan. 26, 1894; capt. Baty. B, Manhattan Coll., Kan.; *m* Aug. 12, 1923, Ann Tanner (issue: Ivan Dwayne; Francyne; Carrwin Jeffrey); 2-Karl Francis, *b* Feb. 13, 1899; *m* Aug. 12, 1922, Elizabeth Herold, *b* Dec. 18, 1897; 3-Adah Eleanor, *b* Mar. 11, 1902; ed. State Teachers Coll.; *m* May 29, 1925, Owen Woodruff Allen (issue: Owen W., Jr., Eleanor Shirleen); 4-Gladys, *b* Dec. 11, 1904; ed. Ariz. State Teachers Coll.; 5-George Hyrum (Nov. 16, 1907-May 7, 1913); 6-Ralph (Sept. 25, 1910-Oct. 2, 1910), and 7-Roland Eltweed (twins), *b* Sept. 25, 1910; attending Ariz. State Teachers Coll.; 8-Margery Rohesia, *b* Jan. 4, 1914; 9-Dorothy Nastilla, *b* Aug. 21, 1916.
1-Grad. Latter Day Saints Coll., Salt Lake City, '91. Asst. mgr. 2,000 acres ranch, 1891-94; preaching mission, southern states, 1895-98; bookkeeper, 1899-1900; mcht., 1901-07; real estate business, 1907-22; sec. and treas. Magma Chief Copper Co., 1916-24; pub. Genealogical and Hist. Mag., since 1924. Justice, city clk., mem. Ariz. Legislature, 7th session, etc. Dir. Ariz. State Mutual Bldg. & Loan Assn. Mem. I.A.G., Geneal. Soc. of Utah; sec. and historian Pomeroy Family Orgn. of America and Europe. Latter Day Saints Ch. (mem. High Council, Stake Presidency). Democrat. Summer Place: Groom Creek, Ariz. Residence: 246 W. 1st Av., Mesa, Maricopa Co., Ariz.

1-**POMEROY, Robert Watson,** *b* Auburn, N.Y., Feb. 24, 1868.
8-Eltweed **Pomeroy** (qv);
7-Caleb (1642-91), original settler at Northampton; freeman, 1663; subscribed to Harvard Coll. fund; took part in Falls Fight, 1676; *m* 1665, Hepzibah Baker (*b* 1646; Jeffrey[8], *m* Joan Rockwell);
6-Eldad (1679-1760), among first settlers Easthampton, 1730; *m* 1705, Sarah Wait (*b* 1687; William[7], *m* Sarah Kingsley);
5-Ebenezer (1715-66), of Southampton; *m* 1740, Rachel Searle (Nathaniel[6], *m* Priscilla-);
4-Gen. Timothy (1750-93), minute man in Bennington engagement; corpl. in Am. Rev.; known as gen. of militia after the declaration of peace and the organization of state troops for home protection against the Indians; *m* 1777, Phoebe Pomeroy (1754-85); *m* 2d, Anna Burt;
3-Rev. Medad (1792-1867), of Cayuga Bridge, later Albany, N.Y.; *m* 1819, Lilly Maxwell (1797-1857);
2-Hon. Theodore Medad (1824-1905), minister of the Gospel, Auburn, N.Y.; *m* 1855, Elizabeth Leitch Watson (*d* 1892); issue: I-Janet Watson (1858-92); II-Lillias (*b* 1860; *m* Charles Irving Avery); III-Josephene (*m* Frank Rufus Herrick); IV-Robert Watson (1 above); V-Theodore Medad (*b* 1874; *m* Mabel Wadsworth).
1-*m* June 24, 1895, Lucy Bemis, *b* July 15, 1869; dau. of Jonathan W. Bemis, of New York, *m* Lucy Wyeth; issue: 1-Lucy, *b* Buffalo, N.Y., July 1, 1900; 2-Robert Watson, *b* Buffalo, July 1, 1902.
1-B.A., Yale, '91; LL.B., Harvard, 1895. Asso. in law firm of Rogers, Locke & Milburn, 2 yrs.; then opened office for himself and has practiced law continuously since. Dir. Niagara Falls Power Co., Buffalo Gen. Electric Co., Shredded Wheat Co., Buffalo Abstract & Title Co., Internat. Ry. Co., Peoples Bank of Buffalo, Casualty Co. of America, Western N.Y. Water Co., Eastern Oil Co.; trustee Fidelity Trust Co. of Buffalo, Buffalo Gen. Hosp., Charity Organization Soc. of Buffalo, Buffalo Fine Arts Acad., Mt. Hermon Boys Sch., First Presbyn. Ch. of Buffalo; pres. Pomeroy Family Organization. Winter place: Miami, Fla. Residence: 230 Park Av., New York, N.Y.

1-**POND, Irving Kane,** *b* Ann Arbor, Mich., May 1, 1857.
9-Samuel **Pond** (qv);
8-Lt. Samuel (1648-1718), of Branford, Conn.; dep. Gen. Ct.; *m* 1669, Miriam Blatchly (1652-1694);
7-Samuel (*b* 1679), *m* 1704, Abigail Goodrich;
6-Philip (1706-49), *m* Thankful Frisbie;
5-Dan (1726-83), *m* Mehitable (Mabel) Munson (1730-93);
4-Benjamin (1768-1814), War 1812; judge Ct. Common Pleas, Essex Co., N.Y.; mem. N.Y. Legislature; 12th Congress, 1811-13; *m* Abigail Ashley (*d* 1835);
3-Jared (1790-1856), *m* Sept. 25, 1825, Statira Bartlit;
2-Elihu Bartlit (2 below).
11-William **Brewster,** 4th signer of the Mayflower Compact (qv);

10–Patience (ca. 1600-1634), *m* Aug. 5, 1624, Gov. Thomas **Prence** (qv);
9–Mercy (1631-1711), *m* Feb. 13, 1649/50, Maj. John **Freeman** (1627-1719; Edmund[10], qv);
8–John (1651-1721); *m* 1st, Dec. 18, 1672, Sarah Merrick (1654-96; William[9]);
7–John (1678-1767), *m* 1st, ca. 1700/01, Mercy Watson (1683-1768);
6–Phoebe (*b* 1711), *m* 1st, Jan. 16, 1728/29, Thomas **Ashley**;
5–Thomas, *m* 1st, Zeruah Richards;
4–Abigail (*d* 1835), *m* Benjamin **Pond** (4 above).
2–Elihu Bartlit **Pond** (1826-98), newspaper publisher, Ann Arbor, Mich.; *m* Nov. 20, 1849, Mary Barlow Allen (Oct. 7, 1825-July 11, 1915); for issue see Vol. III, p. 375.
1–*m* June 9, 1929, Katharine Lattimer de Nancrède, of Ann Arbor, Mich.
1–C.E., U.Mich., '79 (hon. M.A., 1911). Mem. firm of Pond & Pond, architects, Chicago. Fellow and pres., 1910-1911, A.I.A.; mem. Nat. Inst. Arts and Letters, etc. (see Who's Who in America). Author: The Meaning of Architecture (listed by the Am. Library Assn. and regarded as standard). Clubs: Chicago Literary, Cliff Dwellers, Little Room, University. Residence: 14 W. Elm St., Chicago, Ill.

1–**PORTER, William Arthur,** *b* Montgomery Co., Ind., Feb. 28, 1880.
9–Peter **Porter** (1602-58), from Eng. in the "Tiger," 1622 the boat left Eng., Sept. 1621, in company with the Warwick, but the two were separated and the Tiger was captured by the Turks, escaping after all the rigging had been removed; Peter settled in Va., where Norfolk now is; mem. Capt. Epes' co. of Indian fighters, 1623-24, along eastern shore of Va.; removed to Md., 1649; *m* 1636(?), Frances–;
8–Peter (1640-76), of Anne Arundel Co., Md.; killed by Indians, 1676, after he had "killed 7 Indians with one shot"; *m* 1674, Sarah Howard (1645-81; Samuel[9]; Matthew[10]);
7–Peter (1675-1755), *m* 1702, Lois Shipley (Adam[8]);
6–Peter (1704-75), *m* 1736, —Shipley;
5–Adam (1738-1823), Bath Co., Va., 1784; *m* 1760, Delilah Tivis (Robert[6]);
4–John (1787-1853), Montgomery Co., Ind.; *m* 1811, Nancy Agnes Bratton (1789-1824; Capt. James[5]; Capt. Robt.[6]);
3–John Reason (1821-76); *m* 1845 Mary Hanna Caldwell;
2–James Albert (2 below).
7–Alexander **Caldwell** (*b* 1723), of Scotch-Irish descent; from Wales to Phila., Pa. 1740; *m* in Wales a distant cousin, Mary Colwell;
6–Alexander (1752-1821), Nicholas Co., Ky.; Am. Rev.; *m* 1774, Elizabeth Stephenson (*b* 1752, *d* 1814);
5–David B. (1775-1852), Carlisle, Ky.; *m* 1801, Elinor McClenehan;
4–James M. (1803-68), Montgomery Co., Ind.; *m* 1823 Nancy Sample (Robert[6], *m* 1790, Mary Hanna);
3–Mary Hanna (1827-88), *m* 1845, John Reason **Porter** (3 above).
5–Christopher **Peck,** of Henderson, Ky.;
4–Jacob Oliver (1801-73), *m* Mariah Nox Lane (1809-1906);
3–Strawder Wall (1844-1926), Montgomery Co., Ind.; *m* Elizabeth Frances Wall (1844-80; Ephriam[4]);
2–Mary Louisa (*b* 1862), *m* 1878, James Albert **Porter** (*b* 1855), farmer, Crawfordsville, Ind.; issue: I–William Arthur (1 above); II–Effie Ellen (*b* 1883; *m* William Hiram Wise); III–Nellie Viola (*b* 1885; *m* Thomas Stark Brown); IV–Nina Gertrude (*b* 1890; *m* Ison Owens); V–Fern (1898-1902); VI–Maude May (*b* 1900; *m* Reuben Joseph Ely).
1–*m* Aug. 12, 1906, Vella Hybarger (qv); issue: 1–William Arthur, Jr., *b* Des Moines, Ia., Nov. 5, 1909; ed. U. of Minn., '31.
1–B.A., Wabash Coll., '04 (Alpha Tau Omega); M.A., U.of Minn., 1924. Taught sch., 1904-05, 1908; managed Porter Lyceum Bureau, 1908-14; built houses, Miami, Fla., 1914-16; attended Harvard Law School, 1916-18; wheat farmer, Montana, 1918-21; now prin., Henry Jr. High School, Minneapolis. Mem. S.A.R. Mason (32°), Elk. Republican. Residence: 5100 Lyndale Av. S., Minneapolis, Minn.

GEN. HORACE PORTER (Photo. by Gessford, New York).

1–**PORTER, Horace** (*b* Huntingdon, Pa., Apr. 15, 1837-*d* New York, May 29, 1921).
4–Robert **Porter,** from Ireland, 1720; settled at Londonderry, N.H.;
3–Andrew (1743-1813), col. in Am. Rev.; brig. gen. Pa. militia, 1801; maj. gen. and surveyor gen. of Pa., 1809-13; declined the Secretaryship of War 1812, tendered by his friend President Madison;
2–David Rittenhouse (1788-1867), gov. of Pa., 1839-45; *m* 1820, Josephine McDermott (1803-74; William[3]).
1–*m* Dec. 23, 1863, Sophie K. McHarg (1841-1903), dau. of John McHarg, of Albany, N.Y.; issue: 1–Horace (Oct. 22, 1864-Sept. 17, 1890); 2–Clarence (1872-March 1917); 3–Elsie (Mrs. Edwin Mende, see Vol. I, p. 724).
1–Ed. Lawrence Scientific Sch. (Harvard); grad. with honors, U.S.M.A., 1860; (LL.D., Union U., 1894, Princeton, 1906, Williams, 1907, Harvard, 1910). Diplomat, soldier; five times brevetted for distinguished service on the field of battle; a.-d.-c. to Gen. Grant, 1864-65; sec. to Pres. Grant, 1872; received Congressional Medal of Honor for Chickamauga, 1863; asst. sec. of war, 1866; retired from army service and became v.p. Pullman Palace Car Co. Am. ambassador to France, 1897-1905, apptd. by Pres. McKinley; first American to receive Grand Cross of Legion of Honor from France; American del. with Joseph Choate to Peace Conference at the Hague, 1907; recovered body of Paul Jones at personal expense in Paris, 1905; received by unanimous vote, the thanks of Congress and privilege of the floor of both houses for life. His biography, "An American Soldier and Diplomat," published by Elsie Porter Mende. Former residence: 277 Madison Av., New York, N.Y.

1–**PORTER, Vella Hybarger (Mrs. William Arthur),** *b* Montgomery Co., Ind., Nov. 12, 1889.
7–William **White,** from Eng.; settled on the Potomac, Va.; removed to Washington Co., Va.; farmer.
6–William, Greenville Co., Tenn.; *m* Mary Johnson;
5–William (1776-1873), capt. War 1812; removed to Ind., 1815; *m* 1796, Ann W. Balch;
4–William Bloomer (1797-1847), *m* 1824, Elizabeth Isabel White (no relation, 1802-92);
3–Amanda Lorena (*b* 1829), *m* 1847, James McGill **Hybarger,** of Fountain Co., Ind.;
2–Charles Ellis (2 below).
7–James **Balch,** *b* London, Eng.; ed. in Md.; *m* Ann Bloomer, from Wales;
6–Hezekiah James, D.D., (1750-1821), Presbyn. minister; grad. Coll. of N.J., 1766; author of the Mecklenburg Declaration of Independence and of the sub-com. of three who

revised it; *m* 1774, Susannah Lavinia Garrison (1758-1834);
5–Ann Wilks (1776-1832), *m* William **White** (5 above).
2–Charles Ellis **Hybarger** (*b* 1863), Montgomery Co., Ind.; mill owner; *m* 1885, Libby Titus (*b* 1863); issue: I–Voyle (*b* 1885; *m* Ida Newkirk); II–Vella (1 above); III–Mary (1892-1917; *m* Ray Miller); IV–Harry (*b* 1897; *m* Naomi Nelson).
1–*m* Aug. 12, 1906, William Arthur Porter (qv for issue).
1–Residence: 5100 Lyndale Av. S., Minneapolis, Minn.

1–**POUND, Roscoe,** *b* Lincoln, Neb., Oct. 27, 1870.
8–James **Mathewson** (1624-82), from Eng. to Providence, R.I.; dep. R.I., 1680; *m* Hannah Field (John[9], qv);
7–Thomas (1673-1735), *m* Martha Field (Thomas[8], *m* Martha, dau. of Thomas Harris, qv);
6–Thomas, *m* Sarah Smith;
5–Philip (1737-96), *m* Lydia Angell;
4–Philip (1765-1828), *m* Deidama Phillips;
3–Olivia (1808-85), *m* Joab Stafford **Biddlecombe** (see Vol. III, p. 378);
2–Laura J. (2 below).
9–Rev. Chad **Brown** (qv);
8–Daniel (1645-1710), Smithfield and Providence, R.I.; *m* 1669, Alice Hearnton;
7–Sarah (*b* 1677), *m* Thomas **Angell** (1672-1744; John[8] [1646-1720], soldier King Philip's War, one of those who "staid and went not away" when the greater part of Providence was destroyed by the Indians in 1676, *m* Ruth Field; Thomas[9], qv);
6–Jeremiah (1707-85), *m* 1730, Mary Mathewson;
5–Lydia, *m* Philip **Mathewson** (5 above);
4–Philip, *m* Deidama Phillips (4 above);
3–Olivia, *m* Joab S. **Biddlecombe** (3 above);
2–Laura J. (1841-1928), *m* 1869, Stephen Bosworth **Pound** (1833-1911; see Vol. I, pp. 195, 196, for other lineages); issue: I–Roscoe (1 above); II–Louise (see Vol. I, p. 196); III–Olivia (*b* 1874).
1–*m* June 17, 1899, Grace Gerrard, of Columbus, Neb.
1–A.B., U.Neb., '88, A.M., 1889, Ph.D., 1897; (hon. LL.M., Northwestern, 1908; LL.D., Mich., 1913, Neb., 1913, Mo., 1916, Chicago, 1916, Brown, 1919, Harvard, 1920, Cambridge [Eng.], 1922 Union, 1923, Pittsburgh, 1926, Colorado, 1927, George Washington, 1928). Asst. prof. law, 1899-1903, dean law dept., 1903-07, U.Neb.; prof. law, Northwestern U., 1907-09, U.Chicago, 1909-1910; Story prof. law, 1910-13, Carter prof. jurisprudence, 1913–, dean Law Sch., 1916–, Harvard U. (see Who's Who in America). Residence: 304 School St., Watertown, Mass.

1–**POWERS, Shirley Richard,** *b* Kankakee, Ill., Mar. 16, 1865.
5–Laurence **Powers,** on Ch. of Eng. tax list at Hebron, Conn.; *m* 1729/30, Widow Elizabeth (Downing) Stagers (John Downing[6], *m* Elizabeth–, of New London, Conn.);
4–John (1730-62), *b* Groton, Conn.; served French and Indian War; died Dec. 15, 1762, of smallpox or camp fever on L.I.; *m* 1755, Elizabeth Phelps (*b* 1739; Lt. Nathaniel[5], of Hebron, Conn.; *m* Mary Curtice; Capt. Nathaniel[6]; Lt. Timothy[7]; William[8], qv);
3–John (1762-1837), Warren Co., N.Y.; in Am. Rev., ca. 5 yrs.; *m* 2d, 1815, Anna (Napier) Myers (1785-1860);
2–Sidney (1816-89), of Petersburg, N.Y.; removed to Kankakee, Ill.; *m* 1861, Adelena Doyle (1836-79; Ephraim[3], *m* Martha Kyle); issue: I–Jessie (*b* 1862; *m* George H. Holmes); II–Shirley (1 above).
1–*m* Aug. 8, 1898, Mrs. Sarah Ann (Loughran) Robinson, *b* Co. Tyrone, Ireland, Feb. 14, 1865; dau. of Michael Loughran, *m* Catherine Slane, of Co. Tyrone; issue: 1–Hattie, *b* Salida, Colo., Dec. 24, 1899; *m* Nov. 10, 1927, William C. Singer (issue: Caroline, *b* Santa Monica, Calif., Oct. 20, 1929); 2–Helen, *b* Salida, Apr. 10, 1902; *m* May 19, 1923, Elmer F. Belt (issue: Robert Powers, *b* Santa Monica, Calif., Oct. 20, 1926).
1–Life-long railroad man. Address: 1112 Tenth St., Santa Monica, Calif.

1–**PRALL, Clara Dayle Borden (Mrs. Charles E.),** *b* Essex, Ia., Apr. 20, 1892.
10–Brian **Pendleton** (qv);
9–Capt. James (1628-1709), King Philip's War; selectman of Stonington; *m* 1656, Hannah Goodenow (1639-ca. 1725; Capt. Edmund[10]);
8–Joseph (1661-1706), town clk. of Westerly; *m* 2d, 1700, Patience Potts (1683-1731; William[9]);
7–Col. William (1704-86), served in Am. Rev.; mem. first ch. of Stonington, Conn.; apptd. to form ch. of Westerly; *m* 1725, Lydia Burrows (1703-50; John[8]);
6–Lt. Peleg (1733-1810), lt. R.I. arty. train in Am. Rev.; *m* 1758, Ann Park;
5–Green (1774-1863), Searsport, Me.; master mariner; *m* 1795, his cousin, Nancy Park (1776-1839);
4–Green (1804-74), mariner; *m* 1828, Mary Brooks (1806-65; Solomon[5]);
3–Brooks Solomon (1833-1912), Essex, Ia.; sea capt.; in 76th Ohio Vols., Civil War; justice and notary public; *m* 1858, Lucretia Scribner;
2–Ada Marie (2 below).
10–Richard **Park** (qv);
9–Thomas (1628/29-1690), *m* 1653, Abigail Dix (1637-91; Edward[9], *m* Jane Wilkinson);
8–John (1656-1718), wounded in colonial wars; *m* 2d, 1694, Elizabeth Miller;
7–Joseph (1705-77), A.B., Harvard, 1724; Indian missionary in R.I.; *m* 1732, Abigail Greene (*d* 1772, aet. 68);
6–Ann (1739-1817), *m* Peleg **Pendleton** (6 above).
7–Uriah **Scribner** (*b* 1722), Norwalk, Conn.; *m* 1746, Marthia Scrivener (*b* 1724);
6–Asa (1757-90), Ridgefield, Conn.; pvt. and sgt., Am. Rev.; *m* 1779, Rachel Olmstead (*b* 1760);
5–Harvey (1783-1861), Homer, O.; *m* 1800, Lydia Jelliff (1784-1872);
4–Asa (1805-45), *m* 1825, Esther Jelliff (1809-72);
3–Lucretia (1836-1926), Essex, Ia.; *m* Brooks S. **Pendleton** (3 above);
2–Ada Marie (1860-1922), *m* 1878, Aaron Avery **Borden** (1836-1906).
1–*m* June 16, 1915, Charles Edward Prall, *b* W. Concord, Minn., Mar. 1, 1891; son of Oscar E. Prall; issue: 1–Charles Edward, Jr., *b* Clarion, Ia., Aug. 15, 1918.
1–A.B., U.Neb., '14 (Delta Gamma). Teacher, Jr. High Sch., and High Sch., Essex and Rock Rapids, Ia. Joint author: Tiny Tale and other Stories. Mem. D.A.R., D.A.C. Congregational. Clubs: Colonial Daughters Bridge, University Women's, Current Events, Outlook. Residence: Fayetteville, Ark.

1–**PRATT, Helen Price Throop (Mrs. Ransom),** *b* Palmyra, N.Y., May 2, 1856.
7–William (Throope) **Throop** (*d* 1704), from Eng.; settled nr. Hartford, Conn., later at Barnstable and Bristol; *m* 1666, Mary Chapman (1643-1732);
6–Dan (1670-1727), *m* 1712/13, Deborah Church;
5–Capt. Dan (1715-71), began to write name Throop; Lebanon, Conn.; *m* 1737, Susanna Carey (1717-54);
4–Benjamin (1745-1842), Palmyra, N.Y.; capt. in Am. Rev.; *m* 1775, Rachel Brown (1753-1851);
3–Benjamin (1784-1834), *m* 1814, Nancy Gardner (1796-1887);
2–Benjamin Franklin (2 below).
9–Richard **Warren** (qv);
8–Elizabeth (ante 1620-1669/70), *m* 1635, Richard **Church** (qv);
7–Joseph (1638-1711), *m* 1660, Mary Tucker (1640-1709/10);
6–Deborah (1672-1752), *m* Dan **Throop** (6 above).
2–Benjamin Franklin **Throop,** M.D. (1822-63), Palmyra, N.Y.; physician and surgeon astronomer; *m* 1853, Harriet Ellen Walker (1827-60).
1–*m* Dec. 31, 1879, William Edgar Purdy (June 22, 1854-Apr. 6, 1927), son of William S. Purdy, M.D., of Corning, N.Y.; issue (all *b* Corning, N.Y.): 1–Isabel Townsend, *b* Feb. 6, 1881; *m* Dec. 28, 1901, William Wilson Pratt, M.D., son of William Sylvester Holt, D.D., of Portland, Ore. (issue: Helen Frances; Barbara Richmond); 2–Lawrence Dorman, *b* Apr. 8, 1883; *m* Aug. 10, 1921, Clara Maud, dau. of Abram Eves, of Los Angeles, Calif. (issue: William Throop); 3–Harriet Walker, *b* Sept. 8, 1885; *m* Sept. 18, 1913, Allen Tremain, son of Zephaniah Jefferson Hatch, of Oakland, Calif. (issue: Nancy Tremain; Priscilla Throop).
1–*m* 2d, May 7, 1928, Ransom Pratt, *b* Corning, N.Y., Aug. 22, 1857; son of George Wollage Pratt, M.D., of Corning, N.Y.

1–B.A., Elmira Coll., '76 (trustee Alumnae Assn.). Mem. D.F.P.A. (v.p. Calif. chapter), S.M.D. (dir. Calif. Soc.), C.D.A. (dir. Calif. Soc.), D.A.R. (dir.), Calif. Hist. Soc. (dir.), A.A.U.W., Calif. Writers' Club, Stevenson Soc. of America, Dickens Fellowship. Presbyn. Republican. Residence: 2737 Alcatraz Av., Berkeley, Calif.

1–**PRATT, Waldo Selden,** *b* Philadelphia, Pa., Nov. 10, 1857.
8–William **Pratt** (qv);
7–William (1653-1718), *m* 1680(?), Hannah Kirtland (Nathanael[8]);
6–Benjamin (*b* 1681), *m* 1702, Anna Bates (*b* 1678; Samuel[7], *m* Mary, dau. Robert Chapman, qv);
5–Jared (1711?-1764), *m* 1740, Abigail Clark;
4–Ezra (1757-1806), *m* 1783, Temperance Southworth;
3–Selden Mather (1805-81), *m* 1828, Rebecca Clark Nott;
2–Lewellyn (2 below).
9–William **Pratt** (qv);
8–Lydia (*b* 1659), *m* 1679, John **Kirtland** (Nathanael[9]);
7–John (*b* 1681), *m* 1702(?), Temperance Buckingham (1684-1714; Rev. Thomas[8]);
6–Temperance (*b* 1710), *m* 1732, Andrew **Southworth** (*b* 1709; William[7], *m* Martha [Kirtland] Blague; Constant[8], qv);
5–Nathan (*b* 1735), *m* Hannah Wheeler;
4–Temperance (*d* 1842), *m* Ezra **Pratt** (4 above).
8–John **Nott** (*d* 1681), from Eng., 1640, settled at Wethersfield, Conn.; rep. Gen. Ct.;
7–John (1648-1710), *m* 1683, Patience Miller;
6–Abraham (1696-1756), *m* Phebe Tapping (*b* 1699);
5–Josiah (1732-1814), *m* Zeruiah Clark (1725-1816);
4–Clark (1770-1838), *m* 1796, Wealthy Pratt (1775-1850; Abraham[5]; David[6]; Samuel[7]; William[8], qv);
3–Rebecca C. (1807-69), *m* Selden M. **Pratt** (3 above).
8–Anthony **Gulliver** (1619-1706), from Eng., 1642; settled at Milton, Mass.; *m* Lydia Kingsley;
7–Nathaniel (*d* 1743), *m* Hannah Billings;
6–John (*b* 1690), *m* Margaret Hunt;
5–John (1727-1804), lt. Am. Rev.; *m* Sarah Trescott;
4–Gershom (1756-1840), capt. Am. Rev.; *m* Phoebe Harvey;
3–John (1792-1879), War 1812; *m* Sarah Putnam;
2–Sarah Putnam (2 below).
9–John **Putnam** (qv);
8–Nathaniel (1619-1700), *m* Elizabeth Hutchinson (1629-88);
7–Capt. Benjamin (1664-1715), *m* 1st, 1686, Hannah Tarrant;
6–Rev. Daniel (1696-1759), A.B., Harvard, 1717; *m* 1718, Rebecca Putnam (*b* 1691 or 95; John[7]);
5–Daniel (1721-1773 or 74), rep. Gen. Ct.; *m* Hannah Ingalls (1723-61);
4–Henry (1755-1806), officer in Am. Rev.; *m* 1st, 1775, Mary Hawkes (1756-94);
3–Sarah (1790-1865), *m* John **Gulliver** (3 above).
10–Isaac **Allerton,** Mayflower Pilgrim (qv);
9–Mary (1612-99), *m* Thomas **Cushman** (1608-91; Robert[10], qv);
8–Sarah, *m* as his 2d wife, 1661, John **Hawkes** (1632-94);
7–Adam (*b* 1664), *m* Elizabeth–;
6–John (*b* 1690), *m* Mary–;
5–Adam (*b* 1714), *m* 2d, 1747, Lydia Wiley;
4–Mary (1756-94), *m* Henry **Putnam** (4 above).
2–Lewellyn **Pratt** (1832-1913), A.B., Williams, 1852, A.M., 1855 (D.D., 1877); educator, 1866-88; pastor, 1871-1913 (see Who's Who in America, Vol. VII); *m* 1855, Sarah Putnam Gulliver (1823-1913); issue: I–Waldo S. (1 above); II–Theodore Putnam (1863-67).
1–*m* July 5, 1887, Mary Elizabeth Smyly, *b* San Francisco, Calif., July 31, 1852; dau. of James W. Smyly (*b* Newport, R.I.), of Stonington, Conn., *m* Mary Richmond (*b* Hull, Eng.); issue: 1–son (*b* Hartford, 1888-*d* infancy).
1–A.B., Williams, 1878, A.M., 1881 (L.H.D., 1929); Johns Hopkins U., 1878-80; Mus. D., Syracuse, 1898. Educator since 1882; musician; author (see Who's Who in America). Residence: 86 Gillett St., Hartford, Conn.

1–**PRESTON, Theodosia Trigg (Mrs. David A.),** *b* Abingdon, Va., Mar. 3, 1880.
12–Richard **Branch** (*b* ante 1500-*d* 1544), of Abingdon, Eng.; of Norman origin; woolen draper; head of a civic fraternity and master of the Holy Cross until 1544; *m* Elizabeth Beauforest (*d* 1556; Thomas[13], of Cornwall, Eng.; Thomas[14], of Deane, Co. Gloucester);
11–William (post 1524-1604), gov. of the Hosp. of the Holy Cross, 44 yrs.; mayor of Abingdon, 1566-72; *m* 2d, Katherine Jennings (*d* 1597; Thomas[12], *m* Alice, dau. of Richard Bright, of Colleen);
10–Lionel (bap. 1566-1605), *m* 1596, Valentia Sparke;
9–Christopher (1600 or 02-1681 or 82), from Eng. to Va., 1619/20; his will dated 1678 in Henrico Co., Va.; land patent, 1630, of 100 acres, "Arrowhattocks," Henrico Co., Va.; permanent home was on "Kingsland," Chesterfield Co., Va.; patented 350 acres, 1636; burgess, 1629; justice, Henrico Co., 1650; tobacco inspector, 1639; *m* 1619, Mary Addie (Francis[10], of Darton in Yorkshire);
8–Thomas (1623-93), *m* Elizabeth Gaugh;
7–Matthew (*d* 1726);
6–Matthew, *m* 1749, Ridley Jones (*b* 1730);
5–Peter (*b* ca. 1760-65), *m* 1785, Judith Jones;
4–Peter Jones (1796-1873), *m* 1822, Rachel Findlay (1790-1835);
3–Rachel (1828-88), *m* 1850, Joseph E. C. **Trigg** (1822-1901); see Vol. III, p. 381;
2–Lilburn (2 below).
9–Peter **Jones,** *m* Margaret Wood;
8–Peter, *m* 1668, Mary Batte (*d* 1741);
7–Peter (*b* 1691), *m* 1727, Dorothy Chamberlayne (1710-82; Maj. Thomas[8], *m* Elizabeth Stratton);
6–John (1746-1819), Am. Rev.; *m* 1761, Martha Redford (ca. 1746-1823);
5–Judith (*b* ca. 1765), *m* Peter **Branch** (5 above);
4–Peter Jones, *m* Rachel Findlay (4 above);
3–Rachel, *m* Joseph E. C. **Trigg** (3 above);
2–Lilburn (1851-88), *m* 1878, Sarah Vance Thompson (*b* 1859); for issue and other lineages see Vol. III, p. 381.
1–*m* as his 2d wife, Nov. 8, 1911, David Alexander Preston, *b* Dec. 29, 1869; son of Samuel A. Preston, of Londonderry, Ireland, to America, 1848; issue: 1–David Alexander, Jr., *b* Abingdon, Va., Dec. 12, 1914; 2–Byrd C., *b* Abingdon, Jan. 6, 1918.
1–B.S., Martha Washington Coll., '97. Mem. D.A.C., D.A.R., U.S.D. 1812, U.D.C., Booklovers' Club. Residence: Abingdon, Va.

1–**POOL, Minnie Alice Lewis (Mrs. Sherman I.),** *b* Apple River, Ill., Oct. 27, 1866.
9–Rev. Francis **Doughty,** from Eng.; preacher at Taunton; planter, Dorchester, 1639; received grant at "Maspeth," now Newtown, L.I.; 1st Puritan minister in New York City, 1st to preach in English language there; *m* 1st, Bridget–;
8–Elias (*b* Eng., ca. 1632-*d* bet. 1692-1701), of Flushing, L.I.; *m* 1658, Sarah– (*d* 1726);
7–William (*b* 1676), *m* Phebe Taylor (*d* 1714);
6–William (1710-will dated 1771), Dutchess Co., N.Y., ante 1757; *m* Margaret–;
5–Phebe (living 1790), *m* 1753, Morris **Lewis** (ca. 1730-post 1790), Nine Partners, Pine Plains, N.Y.;
4–Joseph, in Dutchess Co. militia; *m* Sarah Odell (Joseph[5], Am. Rev.; *m* Martha Manning; Joshua[6]; Isaac[7]; William[8]; William[9]);
3–Joshua Odell (1800-42), Chautauqua Co., N.Y.; *m* 1825, Melinda Haven Sawyer;
2–James Sawyer (2 below).
9–Edward **Hall** (*d* 1670), from Eng. to Duxbury, Mass., ca. 1634, settled at Rehoboth, Mass., 1645; *m* Hester–;
8–Benjamin (1668-1726), *m* Sarah Fisher (Cornelius[9], *m* Sarah Everett; Anthony[10], qv);
7–Edward (1698-1765), propr. of Wrentham, 1734; sgt., ens. and lt. Colonial service; removed to Uxbridge, 1740; *m* Hannah Fisher (Eleazar[8], *m* Hannah Leonard; Cornelius[9]; Anthony[10], qv);
6–Edward (1727-1807), lt. Colonial service, moved to Coryden, N.H.; selectman, 1784-86; constable; moderator; *m* 1748, Lydia Brown (1730-1819; John[7]; William[8]); four sons in Cont. Army;
5–James (1757-1835), Am. Rev.; *m* 1775, Huldah Cooper (1759-1847; Dea. John[6], *m* Mary Sherman; Samuel[7]; Samuel[8]; Dea. John[9]);
4–Chloe (1787-1869), *m* ca. 1805, Manassah **Sawyer** (1783-1837), War 1812; from Canada to Georgia Plains, Vt.;

3–Melinda Haven (1806-83), *m* 1st, Joshua Odell **Lewis** (3 above).
9–Rowland **Stebbins** (qv);
8–John (1626-78), Northampton, Mass.; *m* 1st, 1646, Anne (Munson) Munden (*d* 1656; Thomas Munson[9], of Hartford);
7–John (1647-1724), of Springfield and Deerfield; in King Philip's War; carried captive to Canada, 1704, he, his wife and son John were redeemed, 1706, and returned to Deerfield; *m* 1683/84, Dorothy Alexander (1660-living 1733; John[8], *m* Beatrice–; John[9]);
6–John (1686/87-1760), Deerfield; *m* 2d, 1735, Hannah Allen (1698-living 1772; Edward[7], *m* Mercy Painter; Edward[8]);
5–Lt. David (1741-1816), Conway, Mass.; 2d lt. Am. Rev.; *m* 1765, Rhoda Sheldon (1748-1826; Abner[6], *m* Lucy Bardwell; Capt. Ebenezer[7]; John[8]; Isaac[9], qv);
4–David (1775-1835), Chautauqua Co., N.Y.; *m* 1798, Irena Collins (1777-1859);
3–Lyman (1799-1871), Galena, Ill.; *m* 1824, Almira Eggleston;
2–Harriet Almira (2 below).
9–Richard **Ingraham** (*d* 1683; son of Arthur), to America bet. 1638-42, settled at Rehoboth;
8–Jarrette (1635-1717/18), *m* 1st, 1662, Rebecca Searles;
7–Joseph (*b* 1677), *m* 1700, Mary Shepardson (Daniel[8], of Attleboro);
6–Jarret (1709-81), Colchester, Conn.; *m* 1729, Marcey Taylor;
5–Daniel (1737-1823 or 24), in French and Indian War and Am. Rev.; *m* Margaret Hill, or Hills (Ebenezer[6], *m* 1737, Margaret Ingraham);
4–Lucy (1777-1853), *m* 1798, Eliab **Eggleston** (1762-1838), drummer boy in Am. Rev. aet. 14; wounded in the head, pensioned (Isaac[5], *m* Mary Hill?);
3–Almira (1806-95), *m* Lyman **Stebbins** (3 above);
2–Harriet Almira (*b* 1840), *m* 1859, James Sawyer **Lewis** (1833-1905), corpl. and sgt., Co. E, 96th Ill. Vol. Inf., 1862-63; issue: I–Arthur James (1860-79); II–Helen Almaretta (1862-63); III–Charles Henry (*b* and *d* 1865); IV–Minnie Alice (1 above); V–Frank Lyman (*b* and *d* 1868); VI–Harry Haven (1870-1917); VII–Ernest Edward (*b* 1871; *m* Amy Frances Haflich); VIII–Inez Viola (*b* 1874; *m* Charles D. Arnold).
1–*m* Nov. 24, 1898, Sherman Ira Pool, *b* Upper Sandusky, O., May 20, 1864; son of Ira Pool, of Upper Sandusky, *m* 2d, Lucy Ann (Eggleston) Dille.
1–Taught in the public schools of Jo Daviess Co., Ill., 1884-98; writer. Mem. D.F.P.A. (state registrar, Ia., 1918-31), D.A.R. (regent Rev. Dames Chapter, 1908-13, organizing regent and regent Clock-Reel Chapter, 1913-17; state historian, 1913-17); dir. western div. nat. com. preservation of historic spots, D.A.R., 1917-18; mem. Pocumtuck Valley Mem. Assn., Ill. State Hist. Soc. Club: Southside Community. Residence: Waverly, Bremer Co., Ia.

1–**POLAND, Dan Grigsby,** *b* Ardmore, Okla., June 30, 1901.
9–Thomas **Poland,** of Henrico Co., Va.; *m* Eleanor–;
8–Thomas (*d* 1754), of Henrico Co.;
7–John or Joe, of Chesterfield Co., Va.;
6–Thomas, served in Am. Rev.;
5–Nelson, from Chesterfield Co., Va., to Montgomery, Ala.; *m* a dau. of William Moseley[6], Am. Rev.; Col. William[7]; William[8]; Capt. William[9]; William[10]);
4–William H. (1827-90), *m* 1854, Kezzia Pytchlynn (1824-58; John[5], of St. Thomas and Prince Island, friend and interpreter for Gen. George Washington, and it was his influence that caused the Choctaws and Chickasaws to espouse the cause of the Americans in the Am. Rev., and kept them from joining the British; friend and mouthpiece of the Great Chief Apushmataha of the Choctaws; *m* 1804, Sophia, dau. of Ebenezer Folsom, *m* Nitka, a Choctaw);
3–William Pytchlynn (*b* 1855), Marshall, Tex.; *m* 1878, Emma Lucy Garrett (*b* 1860; Capt. Robert Calvin[4], in Mexican War, and C.S.A., *m* Lucy Jane Long; Jesse[5]; Jesse[6]);
2–Robert Pytchlynn (2 below).
9–John **Grigsby** (*b* 1640), from Eng. to Stafford Co., Va., 1660; *m* Jane Rosser;
8–Thomas (*b* 1710), *m* 1735;
7–William (*b* 1740), capt. in Am. Rev., 1778;
6–Horatio (*b* 1760), in War 1812; *m* 1782, Susan Owen;
5–Milding (*b* 1785), *m* 1810, Elizabeth Fulks;
4–David (1814-61), *m* 1848, Mahalah Roberts;
3–Daniel Jefferson (1849-1926), *m* Lily Gex;
2–Emer Mildred (2 below).
9–John **Craig** (*d* 1704), from Scotland, settled in Va.; *m* 1704, Jane Taliaferro, came to Va. with bros. James and John;
8–Taliaferro (1704-95), capt. militia; oldest defender of Bryant's Station when attacked by British under Caldwell and Indians led by Simon Girty, 1782; *m* 1730, Mary (Polly) Hawkins (1715-1804), oldest of 20 women of Bryant's Station, 1782, who, knowing that the Indians were in ambush nr. the spring made the defense possible;
7–Benjamin (1755-1824), *m* Nancy Sturman, assisted in the defense of Bryant's Station;
6–Sally (1771-1856), *m* 1789, John M. **Price**;
5–Cyrena Anne (1792-1868), *m* 1816, John Anthony **Gex** (1791-1863), from Switzerland to Vevay, Ind.; banished by Napoleon as the Gex family belonged to the nobility;
4–Silas (1826-1906), *m* 1850, Emer Jane Keene;
3–Lily, *m* Daniel J. **Grigsby** (3 above).
10–Mr. Henry **Keene** (*d* post 1672), from Eng.; *m* 1623, Anne Halle;
9–Richard (bap. 1628-1653), from Eng. to Md., 1653; *m* bet. 1652-56, Mary Hodkins;
8–Capt. John (1659-1723), justice, Dorchester Co., Md., 12 yrs.; *m* Mary Hopewell;
7–Richard (*d* 1787), *m* 1714, Susannah Pollard;
6–William (*b* in Md.-*d* in Ky.);
5–William (*d* 1859), *m* 1817, Anne West;
4–Emer Jane, *m* Silas **Gex** (4 above);
3–Lily, *m* Daniel J. **Grigsby** (3 above);
2–Emer Mildred, *m* 1900, Robert Pytchlynn **Poland** (*b* 1880), oil broker, Ardmore, Okla.
1–*m* Nov. 3, 1926, Adolyne Jeannette Young, *b* Bonham, Tex., Nov. 11, 1903; dau. of Judge R. Bruce Young, 48th Dist. Ct., Ft. Worth, Tex.
1–Spl. student U.Okla., 1922-23 (Alpha Tau Omega pledge). Automobile distributor. Mem. Scions Colonial Cavaliers, S.A.R., Sons Tex. Republic, S.C.V. Clubs: Dornick Hills Country (Ardmore, Okla.), Ft. Worth Club. Mason (K.T., Shriner). Episcopalian. Democrat. Residence: Ardmore, Okla.

1–**PRESTON, Annie Lewis White (Mrs. John),** *b* Seguin, Tex., Apr. 12, 1861.
8–Maj. Lawrence **Smith** (will dated 1700), came from Eng. ante 1675; settled in Gloucester Co., Va.; *m* Mary–;
7–William (*d* ca. 1734), Spotsylvania Co., Va.; *m* Elizabeth Ballard (Thomas[8], York Co., *m* Katherine Hubard);
6–Francis (*d* post 1771), Hanover Co., Va.; *m* ca. 1738, Elizabeth Waddy (Anthony[7], Hanover Co., *m* Sara Parke);
5–Susanna (*b* 1739), *m* 1761, Col. William **Preston** (1729-83), surveyor under Washington; sheriff and burgess, Augusta Co.; burgess and justice, Botetourt Co.; col. of militia; co. lt. of Fincastle; officer in Am. Rev. (John[6], qv);
4–Margaret Brown (1782-1835), *m* 1802, her cousin, John **Preston** (1781-1864), of "Walnut Grove," Washington Co., Va.;
3–Margaret Rhea (1806-60), *m* 1825, James Lowery **White,** Jr. (see Vol. III, p. 382);
2–John Preston (1832-1905), grad. Emory and Henry Coll., '50, U.Va., 1853; admitted to bar, 1853; raised, and was capt. Co. E, 6th Tex. Inf., C.S.A., 1861; entire co. captured and prisoners, 1862; later provost marshal under Gen. Bragg in Tex.; ordnance officer, 1863-64 in La., etc.; resumed law practice at Seguin, Tex., 1864; judge 22d jud. dist. of Tex., 1874-76; judge of the first Ct. of Appeals of Tex., 1876-79, and chief justice, 1879-94; court reporter, 1894-1905; author of legal text books; *m* 1853, Annie Stuart Lewis (see Vol. III, p. 382, for other lineages).
1–*m* Apr. 16, 1879, Dr. John Preston (see Vol. III, p. 381); issue: 1–Walter White, *b* Seguin, Tex., Apr. 18, 1880; *m* June 23, 1903, Annie Marie Frederick Bonham (issue: Walter Bonham; Lewis Frederick; Frances Marie); 2–John Lewis, *b* Seguin, Mar. 24, 1883; *m* Oct. 15, 1913, Lenora McKellar (d.s.p.); 3–James Rhea, *b* Seguin, Feb. 2, 1885; 4–Fannie Rhea, *b* Austin,

Tex., Feb. 24, 1890; *m* June 2, 1923, Dr. Thad. W. Riker (issue: Malcolm Preston); 5–Robert White, *b* Terrell, Tex., Feb. 24, 1892; pvt., corpl. and q.m. sgt. of Inf., 1918-19; 6–Anne-Lewis, *b* Lockhart, Tex., July 24, 1898; *m* June 29, 1926, Laurance V. Phillips; 7–Margaret Lynn, *b* Abilene, Tex., July 24, 1904; *m* Apr. 10, 1926, George M. Ritchie (issue: John Preston, *b* Apr. 27, 1928).
1–Ed. Farmville Female Coll., Va. Mem. C.D.A., D.A.R., U.D.C., A.L. Auxiliary, I.A.G. Residence: 709 W. 22d St., Austin, Tex.

1–**PRICE, Caroline C. Beall (Mrs. Francis L.),** *b* Coffeeville, Tex., June 4, 1851.
9–Col. Ninian **Beall** (qv);
8–John (*b* Scotland 1651-1711);
7–Alexander (1691-1743), *m* Elizabeth Dick (step dau. of Dr. Patrick Hepburn);
6–Ninian, *m* Ruth–;
5–Capt. Andrew (1721-81), Am. Rev.; *m* his cousin, Margaret Beall;
4–Richard (*d* 1832), *m* Eleanor Magruder;
3–William Magruder (*d* 1870), *m* Letitia Bland Phillips;
2–William Phillips (2 below).
9–Alexander **Magruder** (qv);
8–Capt. Samuel (1654-1711), of "Good Luck," Prince George's Co., Md.; civil and mil. officer, 1676; gentleman justice, 1695; capt. Md. militia, 1696; burgess, 1704-07; *m* Sarah Beall (*d* 1734; Ninian[9], qv);
7–Ninian, I (1686-1751), *m* Elizabeth Brewer (*b* 1690; John, II[8], *m* Sarah, dau. of Henry Ridgely, qv; John, I[9], mem. Md. Assembly, commr., 1657-61, *m* Elizabeth Heathcote);
6–Samuel (1708-86), *m* Margaret Jackson (John[7], *m* Ruth Beall);
5–Ninian Beall (1738-1801), *m* Rebecca Young (*d* 1801);
4–Eleanor (*b* 1772), *m* Richard **Beall** (4 above);
3–William M., *m* Letitia B. Phillips (3 above);
2–William Phillips (1822-86), surgeon C.S.A.; *m* 1850, Myrtilla Isabella McKisick (1826-1906); issue: I–Caroline C. (1 above); II–Pope Linton (*b* 1860; *m* Seigar Tisdale); III–Myrtilla (*b* 1863); IV–Madeleine Isabella (Mrs. Edmund M. Longcope, see Vol. I, p. 695).
1–*m* May 17, 1870, Capt. Francis Lewis Price (*b* in Ceylon, 1837-1884); son of a British Army officer; issue (all *b* Georgetown, Tex.): 1–William Francis, *b* Oct. 3, 1873; *m* Dec. 27, 1897, Jennie Bedell (issue: Dorothy); 2–Winfred Llewellyn, *b* Oct. 9, 1877; *m* Oct. 16, 1895, George Lee Hume (1872-1908), banker (issue: Winfred, *b* in 1896; George [girl], *b* 1899; Millicent, *b* 1905); 3–Annie Millicent, *b* June 26, 1880; *m* Dec. 18, 1912, Herman Pfaefflin (issue: Francis [girl], *b* 1914).
1–Mem. D.F.P.A., C.D.A. (pres. Tex. soc.), O.C., D.B.R. Residence: 2612 Guadeloupe St., Austin, Tex.

1–**PRICE, William Raleigh,** *b* Belington, W.Va., Aug. 7, 1875.
4–William **Price,** of Morgantown, W.Va.;
3–William (ca. 1800-ca. 1890), of Belington, W.Va.; *m* Anne Wright, or Right (ca. 1800-ca. 1875);
2–Albert (2 below).
4–William **Bonner** (1759-1847), of York Co., Pa., and Bath Co., Va.; *m* Hannah– (1790-1868);
3–William (1810-59), of Belington, W.Va.; *m* Caroline Corley (1819-97; William[4] [*d* 1859], *m* Catherine, dau. of Henry Whitman, *m* Elizabeth Wilson; Minoah[5], *m* Hannah–);
2–Sofia (1845-97), *m* Albert **Price** (1847-1915), of Belington, W.Va., and Buffalo, N.Y.; issue: I–Harrison Jackson (*b* 1868; *m* Lucille Longuemare); II–Columbus C. (*b* 1870; *m* Henrietta Macauley); III–Ambrose Booten (*b* 1871; *m* Nellie Cleveland); IV–Helen S. (*b* 1873; *m* Col. A. J. Harris); V–William Raleigh (1 above); VI–Marion (*b* 1878).
1–*m* Jan. 14, 1899, Catharine M.F. Hirlimann, *b* Strassburg, Germany, 1869 (adopted dau. of Alexander Bartels, of Wolfenbuttel, Germany); issue: 1–Irma Ingeborg, *b* Louisville, Ky., Nov. 1, 1899; 2–Frederick William, *b* Rochester, N.Y., July 19, 1902.
1–*m* 2d, Aug. 7, 1922, Frances Paget, *b* Owego, N.Y., July 23, 1879; dau. of Silas Edgar Paget, of Owego.
1–A.B., Cornell U., '98; Ph.D., Columbia, 1911; post-grad. work, Cornell, Berlin and Paris. Instr., Male High School, Louisville, Ky., 1900-02, high schools and U. of Rochester, N.Y., 1902-06, High Sch. of Commerce, N.Y. City, 1906-11; state supervisor modern foreign langs., U. of State of N.Y., since 1911; author (see Who's Who in America). Mem. I.A.G. Baptist. Republican. Clubs: Cornell, Nat. Arts, Town Hall (New York), University, Internat. Torch (Albany). Summer residence: R.D. 2, Owego, N.Y. Residence: 2059 Davidson Av., New York, N.Y.

1–**PRICHARD, Jacob A.,** *b* Harlan, Ia., Dec. 13, 1859.
7–Roger **Prichard** (*d* 1670/71), from Eng., 1640, settled at Wethersfield, Conn.; at Springfield, 1643; Milford, 1653; *m* 1653, Elizabeth (Pruden) Slough (James Pruden[8]);
6–Benjamin (*b* 1657), of Milford; *m* 1683, Rebecca Jones;
5–James (bap. 1698-1749), *m* 1721, Elizabeth Johnson (*b* 1701; George[6], *m* Hannah Dorman);
4–Isaac (1734-98), Waterbury, Conn.; *m* 1758, Lois Bronson;
3–Jared (1760-1836), enlisted aet. 16, served with Conn. troops in Am. Rev., 1776-80; moved to Ohio, 1807; *m* 2d, 1820, Elizabeth Smith (1784-1871);
2–Edwin (2 below).
8–John **Bronson** (qv);
7–Sgt. Isaac (1645-1719), 1st sgt. of Train Band; mem. Legislature 3 sessions; *m* 1669, Mary Root (*d* 1696; John[8], qv);
6–Isaac (1670-1751), of Middlebury; *m* 1701, Mary Morgan (*d* 1749; Richard Rhys[7], to Boston, 1660, a first settler of Waterford, *m* 1664, Hopestill Merrick);
5–Isaac (1707-99), patriot, at whose house LaFayette stopped, and where Count Rochambeau made his hdqrs. at Breakneck Hill in Waterbury, 1781; *m* 1st, 1734, Eunice Richards;
4–Lois (1735-1824), *m* Isaac **Prichard** (4 above).
8–Thomas **Richards** (ca. 1600-1638/39), one of the 62 original settlers to whom "were granted lotts to have onely by the town's courtesie with liberty to fetch wood and keep swine or cows on the common";
7–Obadiah (*d* 1702), propr. Farmington, 1672; *m* Hannah–; *m* 2d, Rachel– (*d* 1725);
6–Thomas (1685-1726), *m* as her 1st husband, 1714, Hannah Upson (*b* 1695; Stephen[7], *m* Mary, dau. of John Lee; Thomas[8], from Eng. to Hartford, *m* 2d, Elizabeth Fuller);
5–Eunice (1716-49), *m* Isaac **Bronson** (5 above).
2–Edwin **Prichard** (1822-1904), farmer, in Ohio, and Ticonic, Ia.; *m* 1848, Abbie Rounds (1829-1911; John[3], *m* Catherine Hover, or Hoover); issue: I–Catherine (*b* 1849; *m* Bradford H. Harrington, *d*); II–Minerva Jane (1851-1928; *m* Alonzo Tyler, *d*); III–Jared (*b* 1852; *m* Sarah Hewitt, *d*); IV–John (*b* 1855; *m* Ida Nichols); V–Jacob A. (1 above); VI–Abbie (*b* 1869; *m* Lester Harding, *d*).
1–*m* Feb. 22, 1891, Emma Grace Jones (qv); issue: 1–Vernon Edwin, *b* Smithland, Ia., Jan. 25, 1892; Morningside Coll., 2 yrs.; U.S.M.A., 1915; actg. adj. of 17th regt. with General Pershing in Mexico, 1916; served overseas in World War 1½ yrs.; *m* Sept. 6, 1916, Charlotte, dau. of Frederick Blessé, of Eagle Pass, Tex., *m* Nita Gibbs; 2–George Webster, *b* Smithland, Mar. 13, 1894; B.A., Morningside Coll., '13; LL.B., Ia. U., 1916; commd. 2d lt. at first O.T.C.; served overseas 1 yr., was captured by Germans and escaped, received a divisional citation for bravery and presence of mind; county atty., 2 terms. State commander, A.L., 1929; now practicing law; *m* Dec. 25, 1917, Jane Irene, dau. of McClellan Bigelow, of Whiting, Ia., *m* Irene Crawford (issue: George Webster, Jr.; Barbara); 3–Elbert Morris, *b* Smithland, Feb. 19, 1898; B.A., Morningside, '19; LL.B., Ia. U., 1922; commd. 2d lt., 1918, served six mos.; practicing law; *m* July 12, 1923, Louise Bowe (issue: Robert Daniel); 4–Helen (1900-05); 5–Leslie Arthur, *b* Onawa, Ia., Oct. 29, 1901; Morningside Coll., 3 yrs.; U.S.M.A., 2 yrs.; LL.B., Cumberland U., 1929; capt. Tex. N.G.; practicing law.
1–B.A., Cornell, '85, M.A., 1887; LL.B., U.Ia., 1889. Practiced law since 1889, and farm owner and manager since 1900. Served in 3d U.S. Cav. in Spanish-Am. War, one of the "cowboy" regts. Mem. U.S.W.V. Republican. Mason. Odd Fellow. Residence: Onawa, Ia.

1–**PRICHARD, Emma Grace Jones (Mrs. Jacob A.),** *b* Tamaroa, Ill., Dec. 25, 1869.
11–Francis **Cooke,** Mayflower Pilgrim (qv);
10–Jane (ca. 1612-ante 1666), *m* 1627, Experience **Mitchell** (1601-89);
9–Elizabeth (1627-ante 1684), *m* 1645, John **Washburn** (1621-86; Hon. John[10], qv);
8–Joseph (*b* 1650), *m* Hannah Latham (Robert[9], *m* Susannah, dau. of John Winslow (qv), *m* Mary, dau. of James Chilton, Mayflower Pilgrim, qv);
7–Hepzibah (*d* 1750), Bridgewater, Mass.; *m* 1702, Benjamin **Leach** (post 1672-1764; Giles[8]; Lawrence[9]);
6–Sarah (*b* 1711), *m* 1732, her 1st cousin, Timothy **Leach** (*b* 1707; John[7]; Giles[8]; Lawrence[9]);
5–Jonathan (1741-1829), Marathon, N.Y.; in Am. Rev.; *m* 1763, Abigail Leach (1746-ante 1784);
4–Sarah (1777-1868), *m* 1793, James **Jones** (1767-1828);
3–Thomas (1807-80), *m* 1828, Hannah Adams (1807-82; Preserved[4], *m* Martha Sheldon; Edward[5]);
2–Morris L. (2 below).
10–Roger **Conant** (qv);
9–Sarah, *m* ante 1648, John **Leach** (*d* 1659), from Eng., 1629, with his father Lawrence;
8–John (bap. 1648), Wenham, Mass.; *m* Mary–;
7–Richard (*d* 1719), *m* 1703 or 04, Hannah Balch (1676-living 1739; John[8], *m* Hannah Denning);
6–Richard (1711-1805), of Torrington, Conn.; *m* Rebecca Bugbee;
5–Abigail (bap. 1746), *m* 1763, Jonathan **Leach** (5 above).
9–Lawrence **Leach,** from Eng., 1629; founded ch. at Salem; built and operated first iron foundry in the colonies; *m* Elizabeth–;
8–Giles (1632-post 1705), *m* 1656/57, Anne Nokes;
7–John (1665-1743), *m* Alice–;
6–Timothy (*b* 1707), *m* 1732, his 1st cousin, Sarah Leach;
5–Jonathan (1741-1829), Marathon, N.Y.; in Am. Rev.; *m* 1763, Abigail Leach (1746-ante 1784);
4–Thomas (1766-1828), *m* Anna Bradley (1772-1855);
3–Ann (1795-1841), *m* Harvey **Webster** (1801-70).
2–Morris L. **Jones** (1832-1901), merchant, Smithland, Ia.; *m* 1855, Lois Smith; *m* 2d, 1867, as her 3d husband, Jerusha (Webster) Spencer (1834-79); *m* 3d, 1880, Eva Harris; issue (1st marriage): I–Frank (1858-1926); issue (2d marriage): I–Emma Grace (1 above); issue (3d marriage): I–Myra (*b* 1881; *m* W. D. McConnell).
1–*m* Feb. 22, 1891, Jacob A. Prichard (qv for issue).
1–Mem. bd. trustees Public Library 25 yrs. Mem. S.M.D., D.A.R., Spanish War Vets. Auxiliary, Old Plymouth Colony Descs., Woman's Relief Corps, A.L. Auxiliary, O.E.S. Club: Woman's. Residence: Onawa, Ia.

1–**PRINDLE, Edith Isabella,** *b* Chicago, Ill., Dec. 2, 1879.
8–Thomas **Tobey** (*d* 1710), settled at Sandwich, Mass.; *m* 1650, Martha Knott;
7–Jonathan (*d* 1741), *m* Rembrance, or Remember– (*d* 1732);
6–Samuel (1707-91), *m* 1735, Experience Ellis;
5–Stephen (1747-1847), Lee, Mass.; *m* 1772, Lydia Ellis (1755-99; Nathaniel[6], *m* Remember Bourne);
4–Lydia (1785-1855), *m* 1811, James **Pearl** (1786-1861);
3–Caroline Miriam (1813-55), *m* 1832, Abijah Le Gore **Prindle** (1808-83), enlisted in Co. D, 52d Ill. Vol. Inf. as musician;
2–Jason Richards (2 below).
6–John Charles **Hedenberg** (*b* ca. 1731-*d* at sea 1768), from Sweden, settled in New York; *m* 1762, Jane Van Aalst;
5–John Charles (1763-1818), *m* 1784, Sarah Cadmus (1766-1830; Peter[6], *m* Blandina Kip);
4–James Van Aalst (1796-1867), *m* 1817, Sarah Arents (1799-1843; Stephen[6], *m* Anna–);
3–John Wesley (1820-1902), *m* 1849, Isabella Challacombe (1827-92; John[4], *m* Elizabeth Parminter);
2–Isabella Arents (*b* 1850), *m* 1872, Jason Richards **Prindle** (1844-1900), served in 52d Ill. Vol. Inf., Civil War; issue: I–Miriam Elisabeth (*b* 1873; *m* Dr. Granville Blackburn Waller); II–Arents Le Gore (*b* 1875; *m* Irma Cilka Chapek); III–Richard Hedenberg (*b* 1877; *m* Amy Elizabeth Butler); IV–Edith Isabella (1 above); V–Catherine Sarah (*b* 1882; *m* Hamilton Roddis); VI–Lucy Adelaide (*b* 1885; *m* Rev. John Holcombe Holloway).
1–Northwestern U., ex-'03 (Pi Beta Phi); 2 yrs. at Armour Inst. Teacher domestic arts, 1904-05, at Tome Inst., Port Deposit, Md., and at Industrial Sch., Wilmington, Del., 1907-08. Mem. D.A.R., Woman's Relief Corps, I.A.G. Methodist. Republican. Residence: 804 W. Pierce St., Kirksville, Mo.

1–**PURDON, John,** *b* Hong Kong, China, Aug. 16, 1862.
4–John **Purdon,** merchant; elder Old Scots Ch., Phila., Pa.; *m* 1765, Mary Ross (Judge James[5], of Pittsburgh); her brother, or cousin, was U.S. Senator Ross, friend of General Washington, and had charge of General Washington's estates in Pa.;
3–John (1782-1835), lawyer, Phila.; author of Purdon's Digest of the Laws of Pa.; *m* 1821, Mary Brian Boyle;
2–James (2 below).
5–David **Williams,** a Welsh Friend; came to Pa. ca. 1700, settled at Charlestown, Chester Co.; *m* Nannie Williams;
4–Martha, *m* James **Boyle** (son of Earl of Olery), capt. in Wayne's brig., and served thru Am. Rev.;
3–Mary Brian (*d* 1860), *m* John **Purdon** (3 above).
9–Francis **Cooke,** Mayflower Pilgrim (qv);
8–John (*d* 1695), chief magistrate and gen. agent; *m* 1634, Sarah Warren (*d* 1696; Richard[9], Mayflower Pilgrim, qv);
7–Sarah (1635-1713), *m* 1652, Arthur **Hathaway** (1635-1711);
6–Thomas (1665-1748), *m* 1697, Hepzibah Starbuck;
5–Jethro (1720-1803), *m* aet. 21, Hannah West (1719-70);
4–Stephen (1744-1825), *m* 1764, Abigail Smith (1743-1831);
3–Sylvia (1790-1883), *m* 1811, Gideon **Nye** (1786-1875);
2–Lydia Swain Hathaway (2 below).
8–Edward **Starbuck** (ca. 1604-1690), from Eng. to Dover, N.H., settled at Nantucket, Mass., 1659; *m* 1636, Katharine Reynolds;
7–Nathaniel (1638-1719), *m* 1662, Mary Coffin (1645-1717; Tristram[8], qv);
6–Hepzibah (1680-1740), *m* Thomas **Hathaway** (6 above).
2–James **Purdon** (Feb. 19, 1822-Nov. 3, 1886), China merchant; banker, Phila.; *m* Nov. 29, 1853, Lydia Swain Hathaway Nye (1826-99); issue: I–Sylvia Hathaway (*b* 1855; *m* 1888, Edward Martin); II–Mary Grame (1858-1925); III–Clara Nye (1860-1914); IV–James (1861-1915); V–John (1 above).
1–*m* Nov. 3, 1897, Frances Nelson (Bogert) O'Brien (*d* May 23, 1904); C.D.A.; dau. of Theodore Peacock Bogert, Providence, R.I.; adopted Frances Hope (dau. of deceased wife and her first husband, Richard O'Brien), Barnard, '05; *m* May 6, 1908, Sheldon Leavitt, Jr.
1–*m* 2d, Nov. 28, 1906, Marcia Latham Richardson, *b* Lexington, Ky., July 4, 1879; dau. of late Charles E. Richardson, of Lexington; issue: 1–John, *b* New York, N.Y., Jan. 6, 1908.
1–LL.B., Columbia, '83 (Zeta Psi). Lawyer. Clubs: Assn. of the Bar, Columbia University. Residence: Abbott Boul., Palisade, N.J.

1–**PYLE, Flora May Marquis (Mrs. Joshua J.),** *b* Washington Co., Pa., July 7, 1862.
7–William **Marquis,** from Ireland, ca. 1720, settled nr. Winchester, Frederick Co., Va.; *m* Margaret–;
6–Thomas (*d* 1762), of Winchester, Va.; *m* Mary Colville;
5–William (1745-1815), *m* Elizabeth Vance (William[6], 1718-88);
4–Anne (1780-1819), *m* as his 1st wife, her cousin, James **Marquis** (*b* 1779; Rev. Thomas[5], lt. in Am. Rev., *m* Jane Park);
3–William (1804-55), of Cross Creek, Washington Co., Pa.; *m* 1826, Letitia Griffith (1804-82);
2–Eli (2 below).
5–Joseph **Reed** (*b* Ireland, 1733-*d* 1804, buried in Chanceford Graveyard, York Co., Pa.), from Ireland, ante 1763; to York Co., Pa., 1763; miller, farmer; mem. Pa. Legislature, 1780, presented

act leading to liberation of slaves; del. to Congress, 1787-88; col. Am. Rev.; *m* 1763, Jeannette Brotherton (*b* Ireland, 1745-*d* 1838, buried in Cross Creek Graveyard, Washington Co., Pa.);
4-Nickolas (*b* Reeds Mills, York Co., Pa.-*d* 1854), to Cross Creek Tp., Washington Co., Pa., ca. 1797; *m* Elizabeth Fulton (James[5], of York Co.);
3-William (1801-77), *m* 1828, Isabella Curry;
2-Isabella Matilda (Jan. 16, 1836-1865), *m* Feb. 29, 1860, Eli **Marquis** (1836-1907), farmer and stockraiser, Cross Creek Village, Washington Co., Pa. (he *m* 2d, Nancy A. Mc Nary, 1836-79); issue (1st marriage): I-(*d* infancy); II-Flora May (1 above); III-(*d* infancy); issue (2d marriage): I-Joseph McNary (1867-1904; *m* Francie Allen); II-William Edmund (*b* 1868; *m* Sadie Beabout); III-Rosabella Jane (*b* 1870; *m* George B. Lowry).
1-*m* Oct. 7, 1884, Joshua James Pyle, *b* nr. Cross Creek Village, Washington Co., Pa.; son of William H. Pyle, *m* Mary R. Lyons.
1-Mem. D.A.R. (historian 10 yrs., geneal. research chmn. 6 yrs.), I.A.G. Asso. editor local newspaper, 10 yrs. Rebekah, Ladies Auxiliary Patriarch Militant I.O.O.F., etc. Presbyterian. Democrat. Residence: Santa Ana, Orange Co., Calif.

1-**RAILEY, James Alderson,** *b* Bolivar, Mo., Dec. 29, 1886.
8-William **Randolph** (qv);
7-Isham, of Goochland Co., Va.; *m* 1717, in London, Jane Rogers;
6-Elizabeth (1727-82), *m* 1750, Capt. John **Railey** (1721-83), of Stonehenge, Chesterfield Co., Va.; capt. Am. Rev.;
5-Martin (1764-1810), of Albemarle Co., Va.; *m* 1794, Elizabeth Mayo;
4-Daniel Mayo (1796-1858), of Weston, Mo.; *m* 1816, Lucy Jane Elizabeth Watson (1801-63; John[5], *m* Jane Hord, dau. of Richard Price);
3-Egbert Watson (1830-1920), *m* 1854, Mary Elizabeth McAdow (1836-1927; Samuel[4], *m* Julian Bean);
2-Daniel McAdow (2 below).
8-William **Mayo** (qv);
7-Daniel (1733-81), *m* Mary-;
6-Col. William (1754-1802), of Powhatan Co., Va.; col. of Va. Line, Am. Rev.; *m* Catharine Swann (*d* 1806);
5-Elizabeth (1777-1856), *m* Martin **Railey** (5 above).
2-Daniel McAdow **Railey** (*b* 1863), wholesale paper business; *m* 1886, Anna Alderson (*b* 1867); issue: I-James Alderson (1 above); II-Bert W. (*b* 1889; *m* Helen Clagett); III-Mabel (1892-97).
1-*m* May 19, 1917, Winifrede Repp, *b* Arkansas City, Kan., Sept. 17, 1890; dau. of William A. Repp, of Kansas City, Mo.
1-Engaged in insurance business. Ens. U.S.-N., World War. Christian Scientist. Republican. Club: Mission Hills Country. Residence: 817 W. 61st Terrace, Kansas City, Mo.

1-**RAILEY, William Edward,** *b* Woodford Co., Ky., Dec. 25, 1852.
7-William **Randolph** (qv);
6-Isham (1687-1742), of Goochland Co., Va.; adj. gen. of the Colony; col. of militia; burgess; *m* 1717, Jane Rogers (*d* 1760);
5-Elizabeth (1727-82), *m* 1750, Capt. John **Railey** (1721-83), from Eng. to Chesterfield Co., Va.;
4-Thomas (1754-1822), farmer, Woodford Co., Ky.; Am. Rev.; *m* 1786, Martha Woodson (1764-1834; Col. John[5]);
3-Peter Ives (1793-1832), farmer; *m* 1817, his cousin, Judith Woodson Railey;
2-Richard Henry (2 below).
9-Dr. John **Woodson** (qv);
8-Col. Robert (1634-ca. 1707); *m* 1656, Elizabeth Ferris (Richard[9]);
7-John (1658-1716), merchant, Henrico Co., Va.; *m* Judith Tarleton (Stephen[8]);
6-Josiah (1702-ca. 1736), *m* Mary Royall (Joseph[7]);
5-Col. John (1730-89), vestryman, 1756; mem. of conv., 1774-76; high sheriff of Goochland Co.; col. of militia; burgess; *m* 1751, Dorothy Randolph (*d* 1794; Col. Isham, 6 above);
4-Judith (1767-1831), *m* 1793, William **Railey** (Capt. John[5]);
3-Judith Woodson (1799-1842), *m* Peter Ives **Railey** (3 above).
7-William **Randolph** (qv);
6-Thomas (ca. 1683-1729), of Goochland Co., Va.; *m* 2d, 1712, Judith Fleming;
5-Mary Isham (*b* 1718), *m* 1733, Rev. James **Keith**;
4-Lt. Isham (1737-87), Am. Rev.; mem. Va. Legislature; *m* 1778, Charlotte Ashmore (*d* 1801);
3-Katherine (1784-1854), *m* 1802, William Strother **Hawkins** (1772-1858; William[4]; Capt. Moses[5]);
2-Katherine Keith (1825-1902), *m* 1852, Richard Henry **Railey** (1823-88), farmer, Woodford Co., Ky.; issue: I-William Edward (1 above); II-Bertha Hontas; III-P. Woodson.
1-*m* May 26, 1886, Annie H. Owsley, *b* Lincoln Co., Ky., Oct. 7, 1856; dau. of Capt. Henry Ebsworth Owsley; issue: 1-Jennie Farris, *b* Louisville, Ky., June 28, 1887; *m* 1917, Douglass Wheeler King, *b* Oct. 20, 1885.
1-Officer, Ky. Legislature, 1874-83; col. on staff of Gov. Luke P. Blackburn, 1883; officer, Internal Revenue Service, 1886-90. Author: The Pioneer Families of Woodford County, Ky.; Raileys and Kindred Families; Interesting Faces and Relics to be seen in the rooms of The Ky. State Hist. Soc. Mem. S.A.R., Ky. State Hist. Soc. (curator). Mason (K.T.). Residence: Frankfort, Ky.

1-**RAMBO, Ormond, Jr.,** *b* Phila., Pa., Dec. 7, 1888.
13-Henry (Grubbe) **Grubb** (*d* 1581), elected to Parliament for Wiltshire, 1571;
12-Thomas (*d* 1617), of Potterne, Devizes, Wiltshire;
11-Thomas (*b* 1581), began to write name Grubb; M.A., Oxford U.; rector, Cranfield, Bedfordshire;
10-John (1610-67), royalist; after execution of Charles I, settled in Cornwall; *m* Helen Vivian;
9-John (*b* 1652), from Eng. in the "Kent," 1677; received grant at Upland (now Chester), Pa., 1679, and at Grubb's Landing, New Castle Co. (now Del.), Pa., 1682; *m* Frances Vane;
8-John (1684-1758), *m* Rachael Buckley (1690-1752; John[9], *m* Hannah Sanderson);
7-Richard (1720-70), *m* 1745, Mary Dutton (*b* 1721);
6-George (*d* 1791), Am. Rev.; *m* Sasanna Collett;
5-Margaret (1778-1864), Mill Creek Hundred, Del.; *m* 1800, Peter **Rambo** (1778-1825); see Vol. III, p. 389, for Rambo lineage;
4-John (1804-39), *m* 1824, Margaret Cramp (1803-84);
3-Peter Grubb (1825-90), grad. U.Pa.; attended Princeton Theol. Sem.; ordained minister; pres. of Race & Vine St. Pass. Ry.; sec.-treas. Neafie & Levy Ship-building & Engring. Co., Chester, Pa.; *m* 1849, Sarah Luffberry (1822-1913);
2-Ormond (2 below).
7-Robert **Kennedy** (1693-1776), from North of Ireland; settled in Bucks Co., Pa., 1730;
6-William (1743-83), Curly Hill, Bucks Co.; pvt. Plumstead Co., 1775; 1st lt., 7th Co., 2d Bn., 1776; maj. 3d Bn., 1780; *m* Agnes Greer;
5-Col. Robert (1770-1849), Plumstead, Pa.; *m* 1792, Jean McCalla (1770-1823; William[6], capt. Am. Rev.);
4-Robert (1811-30), *m* Elinor (Day) Dey (1803-57);
3-Amos Dey (1833-1923), Phila.; *m* 1st, 1858, Mary Elizabeth Miller (1838-62);
2-Ida Louise (1860-1909), Phila.; *m* 1887, Ormond **Rambo** (*b* 1859), lawyer; v.p. Presbyn. Bd. of Pensions, U.S.A.; pres. Phila. Sch. of the Bible; for issue see Vol. III, p. 389.
1-*m* Oct. 25, 1919, Edna M. Stead, *b* Phila., Pa.; dau. of Wesley Stead, *m* Fannie R. Webb, of Phila.
1-Grad. DeLancy Sch., Phila. Broker. Mem. B.O.R., Swedish Colonial Soc., O.F.P.A. (treas. gen., 1930-, treas. Pa. Soc., 1926-29), S.R., Hist. Soc. of Pa., Geneal. Soc. of Pa., I.A.G.; fellow Royal Philatelic Soc. of London. Clubs: Manufacturers, Overbrook Golf. Residence: Merion Station, Pa.

1-**RAMSEY, Avis Beatrice Wise (Mrs. John E.),** *b* Poseyville, Ind., Apr. 18, 1888.

5–Abraham **Wise** (1767-1849), v.p. Washington Temperance Soc., the first temperance soc. of Daviess Co., Ind., 1832; *m* 1790, Dolly Day (1776-1862);
4–Lewis (1802-42), of Washington, Ind.; *m* 1823, Debora Jones (1806-1900; Ebenezer[6], Am. Rev., *m* Mary Roten);
3–William (1826-97), Poseyville, Ind.; *m* 1852, Susannah Moore (1830-84; Thomas[4], *m* Sarah Allison);
2–Oran Adolph (2 below).
6–Simon **Williams** (*b* 1753), of S.C.; *m* Polly Ann– (*b* 1759);
5–Bennet (1783-1837), of Ky.; *m* 1807, Polly Martin (1788-1847; James[6]);
4–John (1808-46), of Ind. and Ky.; *m* 1829, Elizabeth Allen (1810-1902; Lee, Levi or LeRoy[5], *m* Betsy Graham);
3–Zreldia (*b* 1845), Mt. Vernon, Ind.; *m* 1860, George **Wade** (1833-1915; William[4], *m* Cathrine Boyle);
2–Dora Elizabeth (*b* 1870), *m* 1887, Oran Adolph **Wise** (*b* 1863), farmer.
1–*m* Dec. 31, 1912, John Edmund Ramsey, *b* Hopkinsville, Ky., Apr. 25, 1887; son of Dr. John E. Ramsey, of Gallatin, Tenn., and Hopkinsville, Ky., *m* Hallie Wright.
1–Mem. I.A.G. Clubs: Woman's, Community, Cherry Valley Golf. Residence: 52 Kensington Rd., Garden City, L.I., N.Y.

1–**RAND, John Langdon,** *b* Portsmouth, N.H., Oct. 28, 1861.
9–Francis **Rand,** from Eng. to Portsmouth, N.H., 1631; received large land grants; killed by Indians, Sept. 29, 1691;
8–Thomas (*b* 1645), of Rye (Portsmouth), N.H.;
7–probably William;
6–probably Thomas, *m* May 22, 1722, Hannah Pray;
5–Ephraim (1737-76), Rye, N.H.; with Arnold at Quebec; *d* of smallpox on the retreat nr. Saratoga, N.Y.; *m* Sept. 25, 1757, Mary Smith;
4–David (1772-1851), of N.H.; served War 1812; *m* 1798, Polly Salter;
3–Reuben (*b* Oct. 9, 1798), of Portsmouth; *m* Mary Rand;
2–John Sullivan (Feb. 11, 1827-Mar. 30, 1916), of Portsmouth; *m* May 3, 1859, Elvira W. Odiorne (Apr. 15, 1830-Feb. 12, 1913).
1–*m* July 23, 1895, Edith G. Packwood, *b* Baker, Ore., Apr. 21, 1871; dau. of William H. Packwood; issue: 1–Irving, *b* Baker, Ore., Oct. 27, 1896; *m* May 24, 1926, Helen Biggs; 2–Langdon, *b* Mar. 22, 1901; *m* Leona Reinhardt (issue: John Langdon, *b* Oct. 8, 1927; Catharine, *b* Mar. 13, 1929).
1–A.B., Dartmouth, 1883. Admitted to the bar, Wash. Ty., 1885, Ore., 1886. Asso. justice Supreme Ct. of Ore., 1921-29, chief justice, 1929–. Mem. Ore. Senate, 1903,05 (see Who's Who in America). Mem. S.A.R. Mason (32°, K.T., Shriner), Elk, K.P., Kiwanis. Residence: Salem, Ore.

1–**RANKIN, Florence West (Mrs. Homer D.),** *b* Cleveland, O., Jan. 28, 1882.
10–Francis **West** (1606-92), from Eng.; settled at Duxbury, Mass.; *m* 1639, Margery Reeves;
9–Samuel (1643-89), Duxbury; *m* 1668, Tryphosa Partridge (*d* 1701);
8–Francis (1669-1731), a founder of Tolland, Conn.; *m* 1696, Mercy Minor;
7–Amasa (bap. 1704), Am. Rev., 1780; *m* 1st, Amy Hatch; *m* 2d, 1757, Bathsheba Gibbs;
6–Oliver (1733-1816), Lee, Mass.; pvt. Am. Rev.; *m* 1757, Thankful Nye (1737-1806);
5–Ebenezer, Am. Rev.; *m* 1779, Mehitable Nye;
4–Ephraim (1783-1867), of Lee; *m* 1807, Polly Ingersoll (1783-1859; Jared[5], Am. Rev., *m* Elizabeth [Noble] Kniblow);
3–William Kniblow (1812-62), of Hinckley, O.; *m* 1826, Irena A. VanDeusen (1817-1902; Andrew[4], *m* Orpha Joyner [Octavius[5], *m* Esther Hollenbeck; Robert[6], Am. Rev., Mass., *m* Lucy Loomis]);
2–Elmer Adams (2 below).
9–John **Ingersoll** (qv);
8–Thomas (*b* 1668), Westfield, Mass.; *m* 1692, Sarah Ashley;
7–Capt. David (1699-1773), *m* 1720, Lydia Child, of Springfield;
6–William (1724-1815), Lee, Mass.; mem. Com. Corr. and Safety, 1777; *m* 1746, Lydia Ingersoll (1727-1804);
5–Elijah (*b* 1766), *m* 1786, Mary (Polly) Barlow (1764-1807);
4–Nathan (1791-1858), *m* 1812, Polly Perry (1790-1880);
3–Lucy (1819-62), *m* 1839, John **Kelly** (1808-87);
2–Mary Adeline (1852-1926), *m* 1876, Elmer Adams **West** (1844-1919), Cleveland, O.; issue: I–Lucy Irene (1879-1912; *m* Charles Rees Morgan); II–Florence (1 above).
1–*m* Oct. 18, 1904, Homer Day Rankin, *b* Cambridge, O., June 18, 1875; son of W. H. H. Rankin, of Cambridge, *m* Sarah Dawson; issue (both *b* Cleveland, O.): 1–Elmer West, *b* Dec. 4, 1905; Miami U.; 2–Mary Jean, *b* Sept. 24, 1916.
1–Mem. D.F.P.A., D.A.R. Presbyn. Republican. Residence: 1427 E. 110th St., Cleveland, O.

1–**RAWSON, Edward Stephen,** *b* in Ohio, Aug. 14, 1868.
9–Edward **Rawson** (qv);
8–William (1651-1726), of Boston; English mcht., ship owner; colonial dep.; *m* 1673, Ann Glover (*d* 1730);
7–Nathaniel Glover (*b* 1682), *m* 1714, H. Thompson;
6–Hon. Edward (*b* 1724), lawyer; mem. Com. of Safety and Constl. Conv.; *m* 1747, Deborah Warren;
5–Hon. Levi (1748-1843), lawyer; insp. of troops; town commr.; *m* 1776, Thankful Rawson;
4–Col. Warren (*b* 1777), lawyer; rep. 14 terms; *m* 1802, Mary Adams (cousin of Presidents John Adams and John Quincy Adams);
3–Joseph (1808-91), capitalist, of Mendon and Boston, Mass., and Ohio; *m* 1833, Mary Whiting Richards, of West Roxbury, Mass.;
2–Warren (1839-98), B.S., Harvard, '61; of Mass. and Ohio; prominent in civic affairs of Cincinnati, where Warren Av. and Rawson St. were named for him; *m* 1865, Frances Delphine Williams (*b* 1847), mem. S.M.D. (James Madison[3]).
1–*m* Apr. 7, 1896, Elizabeth Pendleton Rogers, *b* Hyde Park, N.Y.; mem. S.M.D., C.D.A.; dau. of Nathaniel Pendleton Rogers (desc. Col. Nathaniel Pendleton and Archibald Rogers); issue: 1–Delphine de Normandy Bard, *b* New York, N.Y., Feb. 15, 1900.
1–A.B., Harvard, '90; A.M., LL.B., Columbia, 1894. Lawyer and financier of Mass. and R.I.; member of New York, Ohio and R.I. bars. Del. Rep. Nat. Conv., Chicago, 1908. Mem. S.M.D., S.C.W., S.R., S.C., etc. Clubs: Metropolitan (Washington); Metropolitan, Racquet and Tennis, Automobile, Harvard (New York), University (Boston), Newport (R.I.) Country. Residences: Rhode Island Av., Newport, R.I., and Lenox, Mass.

1–**RAY, Louise Crenshaw (Mrs. Benjamin F.),** *b* nr. Greenville, Ala., May 17, 1890.
6–William **Crenshaw,** *m* Susannah Brooke Carr (Capt. William[7]; Col. Thomas[8]);
5–Charles (1749-1814), *m* 1775, Eunice White (Thomas[6], *m* Betty Lee);
4–Judge Anderson (1782-1847), served on Supreme Ct., 1821-47; judge of Chancery Ct.; Crenshaw Co. named in his honor, 1865; *m* 1816, Mary Chiles;
3–Frederick William (1824-1902), Greenville, Ala.; *m* 1850, Caroline Womack;
2–Thaddeus Henry (2 below).
10–Lt. Col. Walter **Chiles** (qv);
9–Col. Walter (*d* 1672), Jamestown, Va.; burgess; *m* Mary Page (Col. John[10], qv);
8–John (*d* 1723), of Va.; mem. Assembly, 1723; *m* Eleanor Webber (Henry[9]);
7–Henry (*d* 1763), of Spotsylvania Co.; *m* Mary Carr (Col. Thomas[8], had land grants in King William Co., 1701; justice, high sheriff);
6–William, of Va.; *m* Agnes White (Thomas[7], *m* Betty Lee);
5–Thomas (1763-1842), of Spotsylvania Co.; *m* Judith Leake; *m* 2d, Elizabeth Tillman;
4–Mary (1790-1873), Abbeville, S.C.; *m* Anderson **Crenshaw** (4 above).
8–William **Leake,** from Eng., ca. 1685, settled in Henrico Co., Va.; *m* ca. 1687, Mary Bostick;
7–Walter (*d* 1756), *m* Judith Mask;
6–William, *m* Judith Moseley, Buckingham Co., Va.;
5–Judith, *m* Thomas **Chiles** (5 above).
7–Richard **Womack** (*b* Va. 1710-*d* 1791), to Burke Co., Ga., 1765; *m* Ann–;

6–Abraham (1742-1804), Hancock Co., Ga.; *m* Martha Mitchell (1744-82; Edward[7]);
5–Mansel (1770-1826), to Butler Co., Ala., ca. 1817; *m* Mary Lewis (*d* 1855);
4–Jacob Lewis (1806-77), Greenville, Ala.; *m* Agnes Chiles (1809-90; Thomas, 5 above, *m* 2d, Elizabeth Tillman);
3–Caroline (1832-67), *m* Frederick William **Crenshaw** (3 above);
2–Thaddeus Henry (1862-1911), Greenville, Ala.; mem. Ho. of Rep., 1900; *m* 1886, Anne Haddon Calvin (*b* 1865; Joseph[3], D.D. [1830-67], from Ireland to La., ca. 1847, pres. coll. at Oakland, Miss., *m* 1858, Caroline Crenshaw, 1832-99); issue: I–Thaddeus Henry, Jr. (*b* 1887; *m* Martha Dominick); II–Louise (1 above); III–Mary Eunice (*b* 1893; *m* Calvin Poole); IV–John Calvin (*b* 1899); V–Joseph Frederick (*b* 1903); VI–Ann Earle (*b* 1906).
1–*m* Jan. 23, 1918, Benjamin Franklin Ray, *b* Alexander City, Ala., Dec. 11, 1885; son of Edward Washington Ray; issue: 1–Anne Innes, *b* Birmingham, Ala., June 28, 1919; 2–Mary Crenshaw, *b* Birmingham, Feb. 23, 1922.
1–A.B., Woman's Coll., Ala. '08. Writer. Mem. C.D.A., Poetry Soc. America, League Am. Pen Women. Residence: 920 S. 31st St., Birmingham, Ala.

1–**REA, Edith Oliver (Mrs. Henry R.)**, *b* Pittsburgh, Pa., Nov. 17, 1865.
3–Henry William **Oliver** (1809-82), from Ireland to Pittsburgh, 1842; *m* Margaret Brown;
2–Henry William (2 below).
3–James **Cassidy**, from Ireland, 1826, *m* Edith Anne Porter;
2–Edith Anne (*d* 1919), *m* 1862, Henry William **Oliver** (1840-1904), capitalist, Pittsburgh.
1–*m* Apr. 3, 1889, Henry R. Rea (1863-1919), M.E., Stevens Inst. Tech., '84; son of William Rea; issue: 1–Edith Anne, *b* Pittsburgh, Aug. 9, 1890; 2–Henry Oliver (see Vol. III, p. 390, for Rea lineage).
1–Chmn. bd. Oliver Iron & Steel Co., and Oliver & Snyder. Awarded medal by Nat. Inst. Social Sciences (see Who's Who in America). Clubs: Colony (New York), Allegheny Country. Residence: "Farmhill," Sewickley, Pa.

1–**REDFIELD, Jennie Louise**, *b* Waupaca, Wis., June 7, 1858.
8–William (Redfyn) **Redfield** (*d* 1662), from Eng., settled at Boston, ca. 1639; *m* Rebecca– (*d* post 1662);
7–James (ca. 1646-1723), at Saybrook, Conn., 1683; had charge of a fort nr. the mouth of the Conn. River during King Philip's War; twice received a grant of land on Pipe Stove's Point; moved to Fairfield, 1693; *m* Elizabeth How (*b* 1645; Jeremy[8]; Edward[9], qv);
6–Theophilus (1682-1759), of Killingworth, Conn.; *m* 1706, Priscilla Grinnell;
5–George (1725-1812), *m* 1750, Trial Ward (*d* 1762; Ira[6], *m* Lydia–);
4–Seth (*b* 1757), Am. Rev.; *m* 1st, 1779, Sarah Pierson (*d* 1802; Samuel[5], *m* Rachel–);
3–Cleaveland (1787-1860), Cavendish, Vt.; *m* 1815, Sarah Beckley (1794-1856; Josiah[4], *m* Mary–);
2–Josiah Beckley (2 below).
9–John **Alden**, Mayflower Pilgrim (qv);
8–Elizabeth (1623/24-1717), *m* 1644, William **Paybodie** (1619/20-1707);
7–Lydia (1667-1748), *m* Daniel **Grinnell** (1668-1740);
6–Priscilla (1689-1770), *m* Theophilus **Redfield** (6 above).
2–Josiah Beckley **Redfield** (1829-1901), printer, Cavendish, Vt.; capt. 8th Wis. Vols.; postmaster; city councilman; Mason; *m* 1853, Susan Helen Cook (1838-67); *m* 2d, 1867, Margaret Ellen (Reed) Lloyd (1835-1916); issue (1st marriage): I–Willis Cleaveland (1856-83; *m* Katharine Archer); II–Jennie Louise (1 above); III–Melvin Harvey (*b* 1860; *m* Frank Roselle Smith); issue (2d marriage): I–Josiah Beckley, Jr. (*b* 1874; *m* Margaret Hoey).
1–Taught school, Omaha, Neb., 1879-1920; principal, Lincoln Sch., 1885-1911, Castelar Sch., 1911-20, retired. Mem. D.F.P.A., D.A.R., Tex. Hist. Soc., Donna Civic League (pres.), Donna Delta Delphian Soc. (pres.), Woman's Club, Rio Grande Valley Federation of Women's Clubs. Residence: Donna, Texas.

1–**REED, Ellen Augusta**, *b* Windsor, Conn., June 24, 1865.
7–Dr. Philip (Reade, Read) **Reed** (1624-96), from Eng., ca. 1660; freeman, 1660; soldier King Philip's War; *m* Abigail Rice (*d* 1709; Richard[8], *m* Elizabeth–);
6–Dr. Jacob (1673-1709), Simsbury, Conn.; began to write name Read; *m* 1699, Elizabeth Law (*d* 1738; John[7] [*d* 1707/08], *m* 1659/60, Lydia [1641-1732/33], dau. of Roger Draper, freeman 1639, Concord);
5–John (*b* 1708), *m* 1736 or 37, Hannah Holcomb (*d* 1756?);
4–Abner (1755-1822), began to write name Reed; West Granby, Conn.; corpl. Am. Rev.; *m* 1783, Mary Spring (1762-1832), of Salmon Brook, Conn. (Thomas[5] [1737-1825], *m* Mary, dau. of Aaron Gosard or Goddard, *m* Mary Huckley);
3–Shalor (1797-1872), *m* 1816, Laura Farnham;
2–Charles Wilson (2 below).
8–Ralph **Farnham** (qv);
7–Ralph (*b* Eng., 1633), *m* 1650, Elizabeth Holt (Nicholas[8], of Andover, Mass., *m* Elizabeth Hed);
6–Ralph, *m* Sarah Sterling (William[7], of Andover, *m* Elizabeth–);
5–Joseph, pvt., Am. Rev.; *m* Lydia Howard, of Hampton;
4–Benjamin (*b* 1736), *m* 1777, Abigail Robey; *m* 2d, Sarah Barber (Lt. Thomas[5]);
3–Laura (1792-1876), *m* Shalor **Reed** (3 above).
4–Rev. William **Hodge** (1789-1843), from Scotland, 1824, settled at Riverhead, L.I., N.Y.; *m* Elizabeth Lamont (1789-1872);
3–George Lamont (1814-67), papermaker, Windsor, Conn.; *m* 1838, Hannah Maria Pelton (1810-93);
2–Jane Elizabeth (1839-1918), *m* 1859, Charles Wilson **Reed** (1834-80), grocer, New Haven, Conn.
1–Ed. Misses Nott's Ladies' Sem., New Haven and Suffield Sch., Suffield, Conn. Taught in Windsor, New Haven, Seymour and North Haven, Conn., grade and high schools. Mem. I.A.G., Reade Soc. for Historic-Genealogical Research (life). Conglist. Republican. Residence: 1178 Whalley Av., New Haven, Conn.

1–**REED, William Blose**, *b* Delmont, Pa., June 5, 1874.
6–James **Reed** (1710-99), from Northern Ireland, ca. 1728, settled at Hamiltonbann Tp., successively a part of Chester, Lancaster, York, and Adams cos., Pa.; said to have been a col. in a Highland regt. of associators and militia before Am. Rev.; *m* Margaret Floyd;
5–Gen. William (1752-1813), Adams Co., Pa.; officer Am. Rev.; state senator from Pa., 1801; mem. Constl. Conv., 1790; maj. gen. militia; adj. gen. of Pa. during War 1812; *m* 1774 or 75, (Nancy) Agnes Miller (1753-1818; John[6], of Millerstown, now Fairfield, Pa., an early settler on Marsh Creek, in the section for a long time in dispute between the proprs. of Md. and Pa., settled in the "Carroll Tracts," laid out the town which for many yrs. bore his name);
4–Capt. Samuel (1784-1819), left Adams Co., ca. 1808 or 09, settled at New Alexandria, Westmoreland Co.; was the first to successfully mfr. salt on the Conemaugh River; his home still stands on the south side of the William Penn Highway in New Alexandria, where it is an inn; *m* 1805, Mary Agnew (1783-1817; David[5], Am. Rev., of York, now Adams Co., Pa.; James[6], capt. of the associators, 1755; James[7], of Lancaster Co., from Northern Ireland);
3–William Jefferson (1808-93), connected with what is said to have been the earliest paper mill west of the Allegheny mtns., that of General Markle at Millgrove, Westmoreland Co., Pa.; partner in paper mill located at New Alexandria; co. commr. Westmoreland Co.; *m* 1834, Elizabeth Campbell (1812-84);
2–Robert Agnew (1846-1912), millwright and carpenter; *m* 1871, Mary Ann Blose (1842-1916; Daniel[3]; Daniel[4]; Daniel[5]); issue: I–Rev. Harry B., D.D. (*b* 1872; *m* Myra Gertrude Jones); II–William Blose (1 above); III–Dr. John Milligan (*b* 1880); IV–Bess (Lizzie Estella) (*b* 1883; *m* Oscar W. A. Oetting).
1–*m* Sept. 10, 1903, (Carrie) Adelma Eakman, *b*

Pittsburgh, Pa., Jan. 16, 1878; dau. of John Morrison Eakman, of Johnstown, Pa., later Pittsburgh, *m* Harriet E. Davis; issue: 1–John Robert, *b* Pittsburgh (Ingram), Pa., Sept. 25, 1906; A.B., George Washington U., '28, LL.B., 1930; 2–Harriet Adelma, *b* Mount Hope, W.Va., Nov. 14, 1915.

1–With Pa. R.R., 1890-99; Pittsburgh Coal Co., 1899-1911; auditor New River Co., Macdonald, W.Va., and its affiliated cos., 1911-18; sec. Nat. Coal Assn., Washington, resigned 1922; engaged in the prosecution of tax claims against the govt., 1922–; tax adviser Nat. Coal Assn. Author: Bituminous Coal Mine Accounting, 1922. Sec. Fayette Co. Red Cross during World War. Mem. S.A.R., I.A.G., Nat. Assn. of Cost Accountants. Presbyterian (elder 25 yrs.). Republican. Mason. Residence: 6700 Connecticut Av., Chevy Chase, Md.

1–**REES, Lucy Arzelia Jenks (Mrs. John L.),** *b* St. Clair, Mich., Sept. 4, 1861.
7–Robert **Lane** (1639-1718), from Eng.; settled at Newport, N.H.; *m* 1665, Sarah Pickett;
6–John (1674-1759), dep. Gen. Assembly, 20 yrs.; justice, New London Co.; dea.; *m* 2d, 1711, Hannah Parks;
5–Robert (1713-94), *m* 1744, Mary Thatcher (*b* 1717);
4–Jesse (1746-1809), *m* 1770, Hester Wright (1752-1832);
3–Hester (1784-1850), Newport, N.H.; *m* 1803, Jeremiah Whipple **Jenks** (1786-1852);
2–Robert Henry (1827-98), St. Clair, Mich.; postmaster, 20 yrs.; mayor, 4 terms; *m* 1854, Mary Sherburne Clarke (1829-1910); for issue and other lineages see Mrs. P. Roger Cleary, p. 111.
1–*m* Sept. 25, 1889, John Livermore Rees, *b* Eagle River, Mich., Feb. 10, 1860; son of Seth Rees, of Houghton, Mich., *m* Eugenia Livermore; issue: 1–Aileen, *b* Houghton, Mich., Nov. 3, 1892; ed. Kindergarten Coll., Cleveland, O.; *m* Oct. 12, 1912, Charles Francis, son of Francis Newpher, of Cleveland, *m* Carrie Briggs (issue: Charles Richard, *b* June 30, 1915; Janet Elizabeth, *b* June 10, 1920).
1–Mgr. Gratiot Inn Hotel, Port Huron, Mich. Mem. D.A.R. Republican. Summer residence: Gratiot Inn, Port Huron, Mich. Residence: 3220 Warrington Rd., Cleveland, O.

1–**REICHELT, Marie Louise Ward (Mrs. John A., Jr.),** *b* Grenada, Miss., July 8, 1873.
9–William **Ward** (qv);
8–Obadiah (ca. 1632-1718), rep. Gen. Ct. from North Marlboro, Mass., 1689; *m* 1st, 1669, Mary– (*d* 1706);
7–Obadiah (1672-1752), *m* 1st, Elizabeth– (*d* 1709);
6–Jabez (1708-67), magistrate, New Marlboro, Mass.; *m* 1730, Phoebe Eager (1703-75);
5–Maj. Jedediah (1741-1805), Am. Rev.; *m* Esther Post (1744-1809; Gideon[6], *m* Mary Chase);
4–Jedediah (1776-1825), removed to N.Y. State; *m* 1803, Catherine Gaylord (*d* 1835);
3–Volney James (1816-91), tanner and inspector of leather during Civil War; *m* 2d, 1842, Eliza Ann McCombs;
2–John Clark (2 below).
5–John **McCombs** (1747-1832), Am. Rev.; *m* Elizabeth Marshall (1748-1839);
4–Robert (1775-1843), *m* 1809, Elly Stewart (1789-1856; William[5], Am. Rev., *m* Mary Kerr);
3–Eliza Ann (1815-54), *m* Volney J. **Ward** (3 above).
6–William **Wallace** (1720-93), *m* Mary Burns (1730-1815; John[7], Am. Rev.);
5–John (1750-1835), *m* 1780, Mary Bradford (1760-1840; Capt. Andrew[6], Am. Rev., *m* Hannah, dau. of Col. John Goffe, Am. Rev., *m* Hannah Griggs);
4–Asa (1789-1815), *m* 1814, Nancy Averill (1792-1837; John[5], *m* Anna, dau. of James Woodbury, Am. Rev., *m* Hannah Trask; John[6], *m* Mary Bradford);
3–Asa (1815-77), *m* 1848, Mary Felicite Denie (1832-1916; John Augustus[4], of France, *m* Cecelia Felicite Ordan);
2–Rose Louise (1854-1924), *m* 1872, John Clark **Ward** (1845-1923), pvt. Co. H, 155th Ohio Inf., 1864; printer; cdr. Columbia Post, G.A.R., Chicago; issue: I–Marie Louise (1 above); II–William Wallace (*b* 1875; *m* 1902, Wilhelmina Caroline Bottenhagen); III–Edna Cecelia (*b* 1878; *m* John William Elliott); IV–Ella Felicite (*b* 1880; *m* 1906, Burt John Dickens).
1–*m* Oct. 18, 1893, John Augustus Reichelt, Jr. (Dec. 14, 1871-Oct. 19, 1928); son of John A. Reichelt, *m* Louise Cowlin, of Chicago; issue: 1–Ruth, *b* Chicago, Aug. 31, 1895; Northern Ill. State Teachers Coll.; *m* Aug. 25, 1915, Robert Edmund, son of Charles William Pettis, of Deerfield, Ill. (issue: Jean Roberta); 2–Elizabeth, *b* Crystal Lake, Ill., July 22, 1900; Northern Ill. State Teachers, '23; *m* June 30, 1920, Carl Theodore, son of Frank Anderson, of Deerfield, Ill. (issue: Dorothy Jean); 3–Dorothy, *b* Chicago, Feb. 20, 1902; Northern Ill. State Teachers, '21; U.Ill., 1924; *m* Dec. 12, 1925, Dr. Charles Coleman, son of Frank L. Gates, of Globe, Ariz.; 4–Ward (Nov. 30, 1904-Dec. 23, 1916); 5–Helen, *b* Chicago, Apr. 28, 1908; Northern Ill. State Teachers Coll., '27; 6–Wallace Ward, *b* Deerfield, Ill., June 12, 1910; Lake Forest Coll., 1932.
1–Newspaper correspondent and historian; visiting teacher Deerfield-Shields H.S. Mem. D.A.R., Highland Park Woman's Club. Summer place: Crystal Lake, Ill. Residence: Deerfield, Ill.

1–**REIMERS, Nellie May Cady (Mrs. John J.),** *b* Cambridge, Ill., Oct. 17, 1879.
9–Sgt. Nicholas **Cady** (1615-1700), from Eng., 1630, with William Knapp, who later became his father-in-law; settled at Watertown, Mass.; oath of fidelity, 1652; mem. Train Band, 1653; constable of Groton, 1685; *d* at Groton, Mass.; *m* 1648, Judith Knapp (William 10, above);
8–Capt. Joseph (1666-1742), of Watertown; capt. of Train Band; rep. Gen. Ct.; *m* 1689, Sarah Davis (*b* 1667; Samuel[9], *m* Mary Waters; Barnabas[10], from Tewksbury, Eng., 1635);
7–Stephen (1701-85), *m* 1723, Abigail Lee (1703 or 1704-1782; Samuel[8], *m* Mary–);
6–Samuel (1724-99), Am. Rev.; *m* 1746, Elizabeth Winter (1728-1831; Samuel[7], *m* Elizabeth Philbrick; John[8], *m* Hannah, dau. of James Cutler, qv; John[9], from Eng., 1634);
5–Jeremiah (1752-1848), Killingly, Conn.; mem. "Boston Tea Party"; present at Battle of Bunker Hill; soldier throughout Am. Rev.; *m* 1772, Hannah Warner;
4–Stephen (1786-1863), *m* 1810, Cynthia Robinson;
3–Lyman Spalding (1826-1908), *m* 1848, Anna Mascall (1833-1920; Richard[4], *m* Abigail, dau. of Moses Elston, *m* Thankful Howard; John[5], from London, Eng., 1830, *m* Elizabeth Neeves);
2–Lyman Edgar (2 below).
11–William **Lewis**, from Wales, 1632; *m* Sarah Cathcart;
10–William (qv);
9–Capt. William (1620-90), Farmington, Conn.; *m* 1644, Mary Hopkins (William[10], qv);
8–Felix (bap. 1658-1738), *m* Thomas **Selden** (bap. 1645-1734; Thomas[9], qv);
7–Ebenezer (1679-1740), *m* ca. 1710, Elizabeth Clark (1685-post 1746; John[8]);
6–Ruth (*b* 1717), *m* 1741, Aaron **Warner** (1717-87), pvt. in Capt. David J. Burt's Co., and in Col. John Whitcomb's Regt., which marched on the alarm of Apr. 19, 1775;
5–Hannah (1754-1829), *m* Jeremiah **Cady** (5 above).
9–John **Studley,** from Kent, Eng.; *m* Elizabeth–;
8–Benjamin (*b* 1661), *m* 1683, Mary Merritt (John[9], *m* Elizabeth Wyborne; Henry[10], from Eng., settled at Plymouth, 1626);
7–Eliab (1706-85), *m* 1729, Mary Briggs (1707-97; Joseph[8], *m* Deborah Holbrook; Capt. Cornelius[9], *m* widow of Samuel Russell, Mary, dau. of Humphrey Turner, in Plymouth, 1628; Walter[10], from Eng., to Plymouth, and settled at Scituate, Mass., 1643);
6–Elizabeth, *m* 1754, John **Robinson** (*b* 1732; Gain[7], from Scotland, 1717, *m* Margaret Watson);
5–Isaac (*b* 1760), *m* 1790 or 91, Hannah–;
4–Cynthia (1794-1869), *m* Stephen **Cady** (4 above).
5–John (MacElnay) **MacNay** (1753-1841), *b* York Co., Pa.; pvt. Am. Rev.; *m* 1779, Hannah Brown;
4–Joseph (*b* 1785), began to write name MacNay; *m* 1814, Margaret Hunter (*b* 1786);

3-Samuel Hunter (1822-1904), *m* ca. 1857, Sarah Elizabeth Lewis (1832-65; Samuel[4], *m* 1822, Sarah Elizabeth, dau. of Otha Holland; John[5]);
2-Sarah Elizabeth (1859-96), *m* 1877, Lyman Edgar **Cady** (1855-1927), architect; issue: I-Nellie May (1 above); II-Roy Edgar (1885-1918; *m* 1908, Mabel Hartman).
1-*m* Sept. 12, 1900, John Jacob Reimers, *b* Denmark, Oct. 30, 1878; son of John Reimers, from Denmark to Fremont, Neb., 1881; issue: 1-Gerald Fletcher, *b* Omaha, Neb., Dec. 7, 1903; *m* Dec. 14, 1926, Lois Hall (issue Dana, *b* prematurely, Aug. 21, 1927).
1-Mem. D.A.C., D.F.P.A., D.A.R., Neb. Hist. Soc., Neb. Geneal. Soc., W.C.T.U., Neb. Children's Home Soc. (life mem.), Woman's Club. Residence: Genoa, Neb.

1-**REMINGTON, Harvey Foote,** *b* Henrietta, N.Y., June 28, 1863.
9-John **Remington** (1617-67), from Eng. to Rowley, Mass., 1637; *m* Elizabeth-;
8-Thomas, *m* Mehitable Walker;
7-John (*b* 1661), *m* 2d, Hannah Hale (widow);
6-Daniel (*b* 1706), *m* Sarah Winchell;
5-Thomas (*b* 1733), *m* cousin, Mary Remington;
4-Thomas (*b* 1763), Suffield, Conn.; *m* Olive Nelson;
3-Alvah (*b* 1797), *m* 1st, Mercy Gorton (Thomas[4]);
2-William Thomas (2 below).
8-Nathaniel **Foote** (qv);
7-Robert (*b* 1627), *m* Sarah Potter (William[8]);
6-Joseph (*b* 1666), *m* 1690, Abigail Johnson;
5-Dr. Ichabod (*b* 1711), *m* 2d, Demaris Finch (Daniel[6]);
4-Heli (1755-1827), *m* 2d, Ruth Polly (*d* 1832; Hiram[5]);
3-Harvey (1795-1842), *m* Amy Northrup (William[4], drum maj. Am. Rev.);
2-Sarah Ann (1829-1904), *m* William Thomas **Remington** (1820-76), farmer, Caledonia, N.Y.; for issue see Vol. I, p. 307.
1-*m* May 28, 1889, Mary Agnes Brodie, *b* Apr. 7, 1864; dau. of late Thomas Brodie, Caledonia, N.Y.; issue: 1-William Brodie, *b* June 14, 1890; lt., Aviation Service, World War; *m* Feb. 18, 1915, Dorothy Childs (*b* Apr. 29, 1889), dau. Frederick Cross, Rochester, N.Y. (issue: William B., Jr., *b* 1918; Frederick Cross, *b* 1919); 2-Thomas Howard, *b* Sept. 4, 1891; grad. U. Rochester and Harvard Law Sch.; maj. in World War; twice cited for meritorious service; lt. col., R.C., 391st Inf.; *m* Aug. 15, 1917, Edith Ryder (issue: Ann Ryder, *b* 1918; Jane Ryder, *b* 1920; Thomas Ryder, *b* 1927); 3-Agnes, *b* Sept. 11, 1893; grad. Smith Coll.; *m* Apr. 3, 1922, John Eugene Harmon (issue: John Remington, *b* 1923; Eugene Elisha, *b* 1925; Marion MacPherson, *b* 1927); 4-Harvey Foote, *b* June 25, 1895; grad. U. of Rochester; ens. in U.S.N., World War; *m* Apr. 18, 1923, Kathryn Ellen Madison (issue: Agnes Brodie, *b* 1924); 5-John Warner, *b* Jan. 10, 1897; grad. U. Rochester and Harvard Law Sch.; lt. (j.g.), U.S.N., World War; *m* June 17, 1922, Margaret Leighton Alcock (issue: Edith Allen, *b* 1923; John Leighton, *b* 1926; Martha Brodie, *b* 1928); 6-Harriet, *b* July 31, 1898; grad. Nat. Cathedral Sch.; Ordnance Dept. World War; *m* Sept. 22, 1923, Alden H. Sulger (issue: Sarah Ann, *b* 1924; Alden Harwood, *b* 1928); 7-Francis Kirk, *b* Nov. 3, 1902; grad. U.Rochester; Harvard Law Sch.; *m* Jan. 28, 1928, Carolyn Sibyl Lyon (issue: Carol Sibyl, *b* Dec. 25, 1928).
1-Ed. Geneseo State Normal Sch.; LL.B., Union Coll., 1887. Lawyer. Trustee and mem. exec. com. Bapt. Missionary Conv. of N.Y., and N.Y. Bapt. Edn. Soc. (Colgate Rochester Div. Sch.); pres. bd. Keuka Coll.; trustee Rochester Pub. Library; sec. Monroe Co. Bapt. Home for the Aged. Pres. Empire State Soc. S.A.R., 1919-1921; pres. gen. Nat. Soc. S.A.R., 1925-26; pres. Rochester Hist. Soc., 1918-21; trustee Am. Scenic and Historic Preservation Soc.; pres. Rochester Bar Assn., 1923; mem. I.A.G. (see Who's Who in America). Clubs: Rochester, Monroe Golf. Summer place: "Strathmore Lodge," Fourth Lake, Adirondack Mts. Residence: 300 Winton Rd. S., Rochester, N.Y.

1-**RENNER, Frank Linfield,** *b* Natchez, Miss., Sept. 12, 1870.
7-Augustin Jean (John) **Gustine** (1647-1719; son of Edmond Jean de le Tacq [1597-1674], *m* 1638, Esther, dau. of Jean le Rossignol); from Isle of Jersey 1675, settled at Falmouth (now Portland), Me.; sgt. in King Philip's War, and received a grant of land from Thomas Danforth, gov. of Me., belonging to Mass. Bay Colony; *m* 1677, Elizabeth Browne (*b* 1657; John[8], *m* Esther Makepeace);
6-Samuel (*b* 1681), Stonington, Conn.; *m* 1712, Abigail Shaw (*b* 1695);
5-Lemuel (*b* 1724), apptd. by an act of the Colonial Assembly of Conn., 1776 "to be surveyor of lands for the County of Litchfield"; *m* 1748, at Saybrook, Conn.;
4-Dr. Joel Trumbull (1759-1839), of Conn., Va., and Georgetown, D.C.; marched with men of Conn. to relief of Boston in Lexington Alarm; pvt. and corpl., 1775, sgt., 1776; was in battles of Bunker Hill and Long Island; charter mem. and founder of first Med. Soc. of Washington, D.C.; *m* Anne (Nancy) Taylor Green;
3-Mary Ball (1781-1874), *m* 1810, Daniel **Renner** (ca. 1772-ca. 1832), of Georgetown, Md.;
2-Daniel Gustine (2 below).
8-Col. William **Ball** (qv);
7-Capt. William (1641-94), burgess; *m* Margaret Williamson, of Rappahannock Co., Va.; *m* 2d, Miss Hanes (or Harris), inherited "Bay View," Northumberland Co., Va.; *m* 3d, Margaret Downman;
6-Samuel (1686-1751), vestryman St. Mark's, Culpeper Co.; *m* 1717, Ann Catherine Taylor, of Lancaster, Va.;
5-Patty or Mary, *m* Robert **Green**; one of the 16 justices of the peace for Culpeper Co., Va., who drew up and signed a protest to Gov. Fauquier against the imposition of the Stamp Act and resigned their commissions, Oct. 21, 1765 (William[6], an Englishman from Ireland with his uncle, William Duff, a Quaker, to Va., settled in King George Co., ca. 1710, settled in what is now Culpeper Co., took up large tracts of land in what was Essex, 1712, Spotsylvania, 1721, Orange, 1735, and Culpeper, 1749, burgess, vestryman St. Mark's Parish, *m* Eleanor Dunn, of Scotland);
4-Anne (Nancy) Taylor (*d* 1843), 1st cousin to George Washington; *m* Dr. Joel Trumbull **Gustine** (4 above);
3-Mary Ball, *m* Daniel **Renner** (3 above);
2-Daniel Gustine (ca. 1822-1876), of Georgetown, D.C., and Natchez, Miss.; soldier in Mexican War; cotton planter; *m* Elizabeth Matt (*d* 1858); *m* 2d, 1863, Minerva Ann Hooter (1844-1926); issue (1st marriage): I-Cornelia (1851-91; *m* William A. Guning); II-Charles Huffman (1853-88; *m* Emma Clark); III-Daniel Eustis (1855-87; *m* Carrie Welch); issue (2d marriage): I-Mary Theodosia (*b* 1864; *m* William Percy Fraser, *d* 1915); II-Eloise America (1866-91; *m* Benjamin Drake Watkins, M.D., *d* ca. 1905); III-Tom Rea (1868-1911); IV-Frank Linfield (1 above).
1-Not married. Sec., Ins. Exchange of Memphis, Tenn., 1896-1903; state agent, Liverpool & London & Globe Ins. Co., since 1903. Mason. Democrat. Clubs: Chess, Checkers, etc. Address: 422 Canal Bank Bldg., New Orleans, La.

1-**REYNOLDS, Charles Waugh,** *b* Cincinnati, O., Nov. 10, 1871.
10-Robert **Reynolds** (qv);
9-Nathaniel (1627-1708), a founder of Bristol, R.I.; *m* 1st, 1657, Sarah Dwight (1638-63; John[10]);
8-Nathaniel (1662-1717), *m* 1685, Ruth Lowell (?; 1665-1716);
7-Nathaniel (1693-1719), *m* 1716, Mary Snell (1689-1737);
6-Thomas (1719-95), *m* 1748, Elizabeth Turner (1729-1816);
5-Joseph (1751-1831), *m* 1772, Jemima Perkins (1753-1816);
4-Luke (1782-1810), *m* 1806, Alice Austin (1789-1848);
3-Luther Cullender (1807-67), *m* 1828, Charlotte Rhoda Jackson (1804-89);
2-Orrin A. (1838-1912), postmaster, Covington, Ky., 13 yrs.; *m* 1869, Mary Barry Lyle (1847-1912); for issue see Vol. III, p. 395.
1-*m* Apr. 5, 1904, Sarah Graham Graves, *b* Hop-

kinsville, Ky., Mar. 27, 1878; dau. of Otho Graves; issue: 1–Maryanna, *b* Covington, Ky., Dec. 18, 1904; *m* Oct. 3, 1924, Archie Howard, son of Otto Carpenter (issue: Elizabeth Ann, *b* May 31, 1925); 2–Robert Graham, *b* Dayton, Ky., Sept. 19, 1907; ed. U.Ky., and U.-Cincinnati; 3–Sarah Elizabeth, *b* Covington, Ky., Mar. 18, 1911; ed. U.Ky.

1–Med. Coll. of Ohio U., Cincinnati. Physician. Mem. Covington Bd. of Edn., 1922–, pres., 1929–. Mem. S.M.D., O.F.P.A., S.R., I.A.G. Residence: 48 W. 4th St., Covington, Ky.

1–**RICE, Edgar Whitman,** *b* Sudbury, Mass., May 30, 1879.

9–Edmund **Rice** (qv);

8–Joseph (bap. 1637-post 1684), a petitioner for Marlboro; *m* 1677, Widow Sarah (Prescott) Wheeler (*b* 1637; John Prescott[9], *m* Mary Platts);

7–Dea. Jonathan (1679-1772), of Sudbury; *m* 1702, Ann Derby or Darby (1681-1773; Thomas[8]);

6–William (1708-80), trial justice; *m* 1737, Mary Estabrook;

5–Capt. William (1737-1819), trial justice, and held ct. in his house; rep. to Gen. Ct.; Am. Rev.; *m* 1772, Sarah Noyes (1746-1821; Joseph[6], *m* Elizabeth Gilbert; Joseph[7]; Joseph[8]; Rev. James[9], qv);

4–Capt. William (1782-1860), capt. Sudbury militia; *m* 1810, Charlotte Whitman;

3–John Whitman (1822-1905), farmer and veterinary, Sudbury; *m* 1847, Martha Almarine Gerry;

2–Edgar Whitman (2 below).

9–John **Whitman** (qv);

8–John (*d* 1713), Weymouth; *m* 2d, Abigail Hollis (Samuel[9], *m* 2d, Abigail–; John[10], qv);

7–John (*d* 1772), magistrate and dea.; very wealthy and influential; inherited large tract of land at Stow, where he settled; *m* 3d, Widow Margaret (*d* 1758), dau. of Rev. Thomas Clark;

6–Zachariah (1722-93), Am. Rev.; *m* Elizabeth Gates (1727-91; Daniel[7], *m* Anna–; Stephen[8]; Stephen[9]);

5–Zachariah (1747-1806), Westminster; prominent in town affairs; constructed many houses; *m* Abigail Wood (1750-1816; Jonathan[6], Am. Rev., *m* Abigail, dau. Cornet Joseph Daby);

4–Charlotte (1786-1857), *m* William **Rice** (4 above).

10–Walter **Haynes** (qv);

9–Dea. John (1621-97), *m* 1642, Dorothy Noyes (1626-1715; Peter[10]);

8–James (1660-1732), *m* 1689, Sarah Noyes (1669-1756; Joseph[9]; Rev. James[10]);

7–Ahijah (1701-87), *m* 1726, Elizabeth Smith (*d* 1778; Thomas[8]; Thomas[9]; John[10]);

6–Israel (1728-1808), Am. Rev.; *m* 1755, Sarah Da(r)by;

5–Israel (*b* 1777), *m* 1803, Mary Gleason (1784-1867; Samuel[6], Am. Rev., *m* Hannah Brigham);

4–Orisa (1805-83), *m* Charles **Gerry** (1802-77; David J.[5]; Thomas[6]; Thomas[7]; Thomas[8]; Thomas[9]; William[10]);

3–Martha A. (1825-98), *m* John W. **Rice** (3 above).

10–John **Whitcomb** (*d* 1671), planter Dorchester, 1633, Lancaster, 1652; *m* Frances–;

9–Josiah (1638-1718), Lancaster; *m* Rebecca Waters (Laurence[10], propr. Watertown, 1636, Lancaster, 1653, *m* Ann, dau. Richard Linton);

8–Mary, *m* Simon **Willard** (*b* 1678; Henry[9], *m* Mary, dau. of Sgt. John Lakin; Simon[10], qv);

7–Unice (*b* 1703), *m* 1724, Lt. Joseph **Daby** (1703-67; Joseph[8]; Thomas[9]);

6–Sarah (1736-1821), of Stow; *m* Israel **Haynes** (6 above).

2–Edgar Whitman **Rice** (1853-95), farmer; chmn. Rep. Town Com. many yrs.; justice; Mason; *m* 1877, Alice Emily Puffer (*b* 1855); issue: I–Edgar Whitman (1 above); II–Lydia Miles (*b* 1880; *m* 1908, Frank W. Morse, 1880-1916); III–Alice Almarine (Mrs. Harry A. Feltus, qv); IV–Laura Augusta (*b* 1886).

1–*m* Oct. 3, 1906, Grace Helen Feltus, *b* New Auburn, Minn., June 19, 1879; dau. of Henry A. Feltus, of Minneapolis.

1–B.S. in Chemistry, U.Minn., '02. Chemist in iron, sugar, and alkaloid plants, 1902-07; supt. sugar refineries, 1907-09, in Tex., La., and N.J.; chief chemist Nat. Sugar Refinery, Yonkers, N.Y., since 1909. Mem. Am. Chemical Soc. Mason. Residence: 117 Radford St., Yonkers, N.Y.

1–**FELTUS, Alice Almarine Rice (Mrs. Harry A.),** *b* Sudbury, Mass., June 12, 1883.

9–George **Puffer** (ca. 1600-39), from Eng.; settled at Boston; was granted 20 acres of land at Mt. Wollaston (afterwards, Braintree); farmer and "boatman"; constable;

8–James (ca. 1624-1692), from Eng.; settled at Braintree; *m* 1656, Mary Ludden (1636-1700; James[9]);

7–Capt. Jabez (1672-1746), capt. Sudbury Co.; *m* 1702, Mary Glazier (*d* 1749);

6–Capt. Samuel (1707-76), capt. Sudbury Co.; *m* 1732, Dorothy Haynes (*b* 1710; James[7]; Dea. John[8]; Walter[9]);

5–Phineas (1741-1817), Am. Rev.; *m* Molly Stratton (*d* 1817);

4–Capt. Dea. Samuel (1756-1842), dea. Congl. Ch. 35 yrs.; capt. militia; *m* 1785, Joanna Eames;

3–Samuel (1808-64), sch. teacher and farmer; *m* 2d, 1851, Sophronia Miles Brown;

2–Alice Emily (2 below).

9–Thomas **Buckminster** (*d* 1656), from Wales; received grant of land at Boston, 1640; freeman, 1646; lived at Muddy River (now Brookline); *m* Joan–;

8–Joseph (*d* 1668), *m* Elizabeth Clark (*b* 1647; Hugh[9], qv);

7–Col. Joseph (1666-1747), cdr. of a co. of grenadiers in expdn. to Port Royal; comd. a regt. in colonial militia; owned lands at Framingham, 1693; *m* 1686, Martha Sharp (John[8]);

6–Joanna (*b* 1690), *m* 1712, John **Eames** (1687-ante 1740), selectman, Framingham, 17 yrs.; rep. Gen. Ct., 12 yrs.; commr. of peace (John[7], *m* 2d, Elizabeth–; Thomas[9], qv);

5–Aaron (*b* 1721), Framingham; *m* 1748, Ann McCollester (*b* 1727; John[6], *m* Ann–);

4–Joanna (1766-1820), *m* Samuel **Puffer** (4 above).

9–William **Brown** (will probated 1676), gent., from Eng., 1639; freeman, 1641; dea.; capt.; rep. Sudbury under new charter; *m* 1641, Mary Bisby or Bixby (Thomas[10], from Eng. in the "Hercules," 1635);

8–Hopestill (*b* 1656), Sudbury; *m* 1685, Abigail Haynes (1657-1737; Josiah[9], from Eng. in the "Confidence," *m* Elizabeth, dau. of Peter Noyes; Walter[10]);

7–Hopestill (*b* 1691), *m* 1718, Dorothy Parris (*d* 1724/25; Rev. Samuel[8]; Thomas[9], London mcht.);

6–Hopestill (*b* 1721), *m* 1746, Sarah Loring (*b* 1717; Rev. Israel[7]; Dea. John[8]; Thomas[9], qv);

5–John (1755-1837), Am. Rev.; *m* 1783, Alice How (*b* 1763; David[6], Am. Rev.; David[7]; Samuel[8]; John[9]);

4–I(srael) How (1791-1879), *m* 1816, Lucy Adams (1790-1876; Reuben[5], Am. Rev.; Nathan[6], Am. Rev.; Obadiah[7]; John[8]; Edward[9]; Henry[10], qv);

3–Sophronia Miles (1819-97), *m* Samuel **Puffer** (3 above);

2–Alice Emily (*b* 1855), *m* 1877, Edgar Whitman **Rice** (1853-95); for issue and other lineages see Edgar Whitman Rice.

1–*m* Sept. 30, 1903, Harry Arthur Feltus, *b* New Auburn, Minn., Dec. 11, 1881; son of Henry Arthur Feltus, of Minneapolis; issue (all *b* Minneapolis): 1–Mildred, *b* June 13, 1911; 2–Barbara, *b* June 8, 1913; 3–Keith, *b* Feb. 13, 1915.

1–Mem. D.F.P.A., D.A.R., U.S.D. 1812, P.E.O. Episcopalian. Republican. Residence: 132 W. Rustic Lodge Av., Minneapolis, Minn.

1–**RICE, Paran Flint,** *b* Syracuse, N.Y., Sept. 7, 1859.

8–Thomas **Flint** (qv);

7–Lt. John (*d* 1687), of Concord, Mass.; lt., 1677; dep. Mass. Gen. Ct., 1677,79,80,82; *m* 1667, Mary Oakes (*d* 1690);

6–John (1677-1746), *m* 1713, Abigail Butterick (1687-1746);

5–John (1722-92), *m* 1744, Hepzibah Brown (1725-85);

4–Edward (1749-1812), *m* 1770, Hepzibah Fletcher (1750-1820);

3–Charlotte (1793-1879), to Syracuse, N.Y.; *m* 1814, Thomas **Rice** (*b* Ashby, Mass., 1794-*d* Oran, N.Y., 1843);

2–Thomas (2 below).
9–Edward **Dorsey** (qv);
8–Hon. John (1663-1714), *m* Pleasance Ely;
7–Edward (*d* 1714), *m* Ruth Todd;
6–John (Patuxent John), *m* Elizabeth Hill;
5–Ely (*d* 1794), lt., 1776; capt. 2d Md. Regt., 1776, Am. Rev.; *m* Deborah Dorsey (*d* 1807);
4–Eleanor (1761-1834), *m* 1779, Daniel **Dorsey** (1757-1823);
3–Upton (1788-1856), *m* 1815, Ann Starett;
2–Mary Ann (1827-1910), *m* 1846, Thomas **Rice** (1817-91), for issue and other lineages see Vol. III, p. 395.
1–*m* Aug. 3, 1915, Ruth Gleason Perkins (qv); issue: 1–Mary Dorsey, *b* San Francisco, Calif., Sept. 15, 1918.
1–Student Phillips Exeter Acad., 1878; Syracuse U., '83 (Psi U.); LL.B., U.Southern Calif. Admitted to Calif. bar, 1898, and practiced at Los Angeles. Mem. O.F.P.A., S.C.W., S.R., I.A.G. Club: University. Residence: 368 Arroyo Terrace, Pasadena, Calif.

1–**RICE, Ruth Gleason Perkins (Mrs. Paran F.),** *b* Newburyport, Mass., Nov. 1, 1880.
9–John **Perkins** (qv);
8–Dea. Thomas (1616-86), of Topsfield, Mass.; served against Indians, 1643; *m* ca. 1640, Phoebe Gould (1620-63; Zaccheus[9]);
7–Thomas (1659-1719), *m* 1683, Sarah Wallis (*b* 1658; Nicholas[8], *m* Sarah, dau. of Humphrey Bradstreet; Robert[9]);
6–Samuel (1699-1764), *m* 1723, Margaret Towne (1700-57);
5–Thomas (1724/25-1801), in Lexington Alarm, served 1777, Am. Rev.; *m* 1760, Martha Day Wilder (1735-76; Palatiah[6], *m* Abigail Giddings);
4–Thomas (1773-1853), Newburyport, Mass.; *m* 1804, Elizabeth Storey (1778-1864; Daniel[5], *m* Ruth Burnham);
3–Henry Coit (1804-73), *m* Harriett Davenport;
2–Henry Russell (Apr. 2, 1838-Aug. 20, 1913), *m* July 6, 1868, Georgiana Prescott Reed (*b* Aug. 14, 1845).
1–*m* Aug. 3, 1915, Paran Flint Rice (qv for issue).
1–Residence: 368 Arroyo Terrace, Pasadena, Calif.

1–**RICE, Willie Emily,** *b* Marshallville, Ga., May 18, 1891.
5–Aaron **Rice** (1758-1822), of Va.; later at Ridge Spring, S.C.; soldier in Am. Rev.; *m* 1778, Eleanor Rodden (1758-1819);
4–Jesse (1793-1865), of Barnwell Dist., S.C.; *m* 1815, Sarah Wroton (1797-1842; Isaiah[6] [1772-1807], *m* Rebecca, dau. of John Hickman, *m* Elizabeth Bright);
3–William Henry (1817-85), *m* 1844, Emily Anne Buckner;
2–William Henry (2 below).
7–John **Morrison** (1700-83), from Ireland, settled in Montgomery, Orange Co., N.Y., ca. 1760; *m* 1722, Prudence Gwyn;
6–John (1730-90), pvt. 2d Regt. Ulster Co. Militia; also 16th Regt. Albany Co. Militia; *m* 1750, Elizabeth Scott (1731-91);
5–Joseph (1756-1817), in Am. Rev. from S.C.; *m* 1778, Elizabeth Barton (1758-90);
4–Margaret (1786-1865), of Colleton Dist., S.C.; *m* 1814, Benjamin **Buckner** (1783-1826; Bernard[6], *m* Sarah Heape);
3–Emily Ann (1821-75), of Beaufort Dist.; *m* 1844, William Henry **Rice** (3 above).
5–John **Beverley** (1753-1842), of Va.; removed to Anson Co., N.C.; *m* 1783, Frances Morris (1766-1839; William[6], *m* Martha Airly?);
4–William (1801-93), Anson Co.; *m* 1824, Elizabeth Patrick;
3–Nancy (1833-92), Macon Co., Ga.; *m* 1851, William Madison **Dykes** (1824-91; John Elijah[4], *m* Rebecca Truluck);
2–Claudia (2 below).
6–John **Patrick** (1751-82), of Md.; removed to Lincoln Co., N.C.; commr. of labor during Am. Rev.; *m* 1772, Mary Patrick (*b* 1753);
5–Pernal (1776-1856), *m* 1804, Catherine Parsons (1788-1855);
4–Elizabeth (1810-88), *m* 1824, William **Beverley** (4 above);
3–Nancy, *m* William Madison **Dykes** (3 above);
2–Claudia (*b* 1868), of Marshallville, Ga.; *m* 1888, William Henry **Rice** (*b* 1851), fire insurance agent, Marshallville; issue: I–Willie Emily (1 above); II–Ethel Beverley (*b* 1894; *m* William Harbour Lee);
1–Attended Agnes-Scott Coll., Decatur, Ga.; Von Ende School of Music, N.Y., 1916. Piano and violin teacher, Marshallville, Ga., 1919-20; violin teacher, Fort Valley, 1924-27, at Montezuma, 1927-30. Mem. D.A.R. (treas. Stephen Hopkins Chapter), I.A.G. Democrat. Residence: Marshallville, Ga.

1–**RICHARDSON, Mabel Kingsley,** *b* Lodi, S.D., Sept. 21, 1874.
5–Abiel **Richardson** (*d* 1765), *m* Cambridge, Mass., July 9, 1751, Abigail Converse;
4–Godfrey (*b* 1757), soldier Am. Rev., at Bunker Hill; *m* Annie Burlingame;
3–Timothy (1800-76), *m* 1829, Nancy Brooks;
2–George William (2 below).
8–William **Brooks** (*b* Eng., 1610-*d* Deerfield, Mass., 1688), to Va. in the "Speedwell," 1635; in Mass. Bay Colony, 1653; to Deerfield, 1658; *m* 1654, Mary Burt (Henry[9], *m* Eulalie March);
7–Benjamin (1671-1755), Springfield, Mass.; in Colonial wars; *m* Mary–;
6–Benjamin (*b* 1693), *m* Hannah Walker (Edward[7]);
5–Edward (1727-76), Am. Rev.; *m* Anna Hayward (1733-1822; Ephriam[6], *m* Johanna–);
4–Reuben (1763-1843), *m* Annie Terry;
3–Nancy (1806-62), *m* Timothy **Richardson** (3 above);
2–George William (1842-1917), *m* 1871, Anna Kingsley (1849-1916); for issue see Vol. III, p. 217.
1–A.B., U. of S.D., '02 (P.B.K.); B.L.S., U.Ill., 1917. Mem. D.A.R. (state regent, 1925-27), A.A.U.W., I.A.G. Residence: 204 N. Yale St., Vermillion, S.D.

1–**RICHARDSON, Anne (Pritchett) Spady (Mrs. William W.),** *b* Culpeper, Va., Nov. 25, 1879.
5–James **Pritchett,** deed to sons, recorded 1794; *m* 1745, Anne Hankins, of Spotsylvania Co., Va.;
4–Benjamin, of Orange Co., Va.; *m* 1798, Mary (Polly) Herndon;
3–Robert, clk., Green Co., Va., Ct.; *m* 1822, Elizabeth (Eliza) Hunton;
2–Edgar Herndon (2 below).
6–Sir Edwin (or Edward) **Walker,** Baronet, from Wales, ca. 1730-40; *m* Mary Daniels, of Caroline Co., Va.;
5–Capt. William (*d* 1807), Am. Rev.; *m* in Madison Co., Va., 1792, Anne Merry (Prittyman[6], burgess, officer Am. Rev.);
4–Frances, *m* 1796, Alexander **Hunton**;
3–Elizabeth (Eliza), *m* Robert **Pritchett** (3 above).
10–Benjamin **Harrison** (qv);
9–Benjamin (1645-1712), of "Wakefield," Surry Co., Va.; one of 1st trustees of Coll. of William and Mary; *m* Hannah Churchill;
8–Benjamin (1673-1710), of "Berkley," Charles City Co., clk. Coll. of William and Mary; clk. of Gen. Council of Va.; atty. gen. of the colony; burgess; *m* 1695, Elizabeth Burwell (1677-1734; Lewis[9], *m* Abigail Smith; Lewis[10], qv);
7–Col. Benjamin (1695-1745), of "Berkley"; sheriff; maj. Charles City Co. militia; burgess 10 yrs.; *m* 1722, Anne Carter (*b* 1704; "King" Robert[8]);
6–Robert (1732-97), received land known as "Bicres," from Benjamin and Elizabeth, his wife, 1760; *m* 1753, Elizabeth T– (*b* 1733);
5–Robert (1755-97), of "Bicres"; in Am. Rev.; *m* 1777, Henrietta Maria Hardyman (1751-1836; William[6], *m* Angelica, dau. Sir Francis Epes, qv);
4–Robert (1780-1812), of "Bicres," and "Racefield"; comd. Ft. Powhatan during War 1812; *m* 1803, Charlotte Thomas Pretlow (1785-1860), of Southampton Co., Va.;
3–William Henry (1804-65), of "Bicres," Prince George Co.; *m* 1826, Agnes Peebles Heath;
2–Jane Hardyman (2 below).
9–Sir Robert **Heath** (*b* 1576), shareholder Va. Co., 1616; atty. gen. under Charles, I; patentee of the Carolinas; lord propr.; *m* Margaret Miller;
8–Edward John (*b* 1603), *m* 1640, Margaret Mennes;
7–Howell (*b* 1655), *m* Mary Tarleton;
6–Col. Charles Tarleton (*b* 1700), *m* Bettie Harrison;

5-William (1731-71), *m* 1750, Margaret Bonner (1731-1804 or 08);
4-Jesse (*b* 1766), *m* Agnes Peebles;
3-Agnes Peebles (*b* 1808), of "Curoton"; *m* William H. **Harrison** (3 above);
2-Jane Hardyman (1841-1925), *m* 1862, Rev. Edgar Herndon **Pritchett** (*b* Stanardsville, Orange Co. [now Green Co.], Va., 1828-*d* 1881); issue: I-Hartwell Heath (*d* 1885); II-Agnes Heath (*m* Frank Major Bogge); III-Edgar Herndon (*m* Evelyn Stinton); IV-Anne (1 above); V-Jane Stringfellow.
1-*m* Apr. 3, 1902, George Jarvis Spady (1858-1927); issue: 1-Teackle Robins Jarvis, *b* Cape Charles, Va., June 28, 1904; A.B., V.M.I., '25 (Kappa Alpha); mem. S.A.R.
1-*m* 2d, June 11, 1912, William W. Richardson, *b* Hampton, Va., Aug. 18, 1878; son of John W. Richardson, of Hampton, Va., *m* Emma Wood.
1-Ed. Southern Female Coll., Petersburg, Va. Mem. D.C.W., D.A.R. (state librarian; vice regent, historian, Hampton Chapter, etc.), Sulgrave Instn., Kenmore Assn., U.S.D. 1812. Clubs: Hampton Rds. Golf, Tidewater, Woman's (Newport News, Va.). Residence: "Little Berkley," Old Point Rd., Hampton, Va.

1-**RICHMAN, Carl Louis,** *b* New Palestine, Ind., June 17, 1893.
7-Frederick Reinhart **Waltz,** from Switzerland, settled at New York, 1731;
6-John Reinhart, of Switzerland, settled nr. Baltimore, 1744;
5-Frederick (1749-99), of Berks Co., Pa.; *m* 1779, Mary Seltzer;
4-Daniel (1793-1868), of Pershing, Ind.; *m* Hannah Kimmel (1791-1846);
3-Joseph (1813-84), of Arcadia, Ind.; *m* 2d, 1852, Margaret Anna Bardonner (1828-98);
2-Margaret Katherine (*b* 1867), of Tipton, Ind.; *m* 1890, Charles Joseph **Richman** (*b* 1869), state agt., Am. Fire Ins. Co., of N.J.; issue: I-Ralph Edward (*b* 1891; *m* Grace Elinor Schulenborg); II-Carl Louis (1 above); III-Luther Anton (*b* 1896; *m* Katherine Olga Long); IV-Mary Margaret (*b* 1899; *m* Claude Leslie Sumner); V-Paul George (*b* 1903); VI-Florence Janet (*b* 1907); VII-Irene Martha (*b* 1909).
1-Not married. A.B., St. John's Coll., '17. Teacher, Tipton Co., Ind., 1911-14; with insurance publishers, Cincinnati and Chicago, 1919-22; teacher English, Elwood (Ind.) High School, 1922-24. Genealogist for the Waltz, Richman, Merlau-Meier, and Bardonner associations. Mem. I.A.G. Lutheran. Democrat. Residence: 303 S. Independence St., Tipton, Ind.

1-**RICHMOND, Carl Adams,** *b* Rochester, Vt., Apr. 30, 1874.
9-John **Richmond** (qv);
8-John (1627-1715), town officer; *m* Abigail Rogers (1641-1727; John[9]; Thomas[10], Mayflower Pilgrim, qv);
7-Edward, *m* Mercy-;
6-Josiah (1697-1763), *m* Mehitable Deane (1697-1746);
5-Ephraim (1735-1816), in colonial wars and Am. Rev.; *m* 1766, Ann Deane (1744-1836; John[6], *m* Abigail White);
4-Capt. Elias (1777-1847), *m* 1798, Lucy Chaffee (1776-1827; Amos[5], Am. Rev., *m* Anna Brown; John[6]; John[7]; Joseph[8]; Thomas[9]);
3-Horace Locke (1801-71), *m* Phebe Eaton;
2-Alfred (2 below).
9-John **Hoar** (*d* 1704; son of Charles Hoare, sheriff of Gloucester, Eng., *m* Joanna Hinkesman or Hinchsman); from Eng. with his widowed mother to Braintree, Mass., ca. 1640, settled at Concord, 1660; *m* Alice Lyle;
8-Daniel (*b* 1650), *m* 1st, 1677, Mary Stratton (Samuel[9]);
7-Capt. Leonard (1682-1771), *m* Esther Bowman;
6-Nathan (1720-1801), Brimfield, Mass.; Am. Rev.; *m* 1751, Miriam Colton;
5-Esther (*b* 1753), *m* 1777, Eldad **Hitchcock** (1757-1829), Westminster, Vt.; minute man Am. Rev. (Moses[6]; Nathaniel[7]; Dea. John[8]; Luke[9], qv);
4-Melinda (1784?-1845), Westminster; *m* Asa **Eaton** (1778 or 80-1858), Rochester, Vt. (Rev. Asa[5], *m* Abigail Goodale; James[6], Am. Rev.; Thomas[7]; John[8]; John[9], qv);
3-Phebe (1805-47), *m* Horace Locke **Richmond** (3 above).
9-Robert **Adams** (qv);
8-Sgt. Abraham (1639-1714), *m* Mary Pettengill (1652-1705; Richard[9], qv);
7-Isaac (*b* 1678/79), *m* Hannah Spoffard (*d* 1775);
6-Capt. Isaac (1713-97), *m* 1743, Mercy Wood (1720-94);
5-Capt. Samuel (1750-1813), Am. Rev.; *m* 1773, Lucy Spoffard (1753-1813);
4-Isaac (1776-1848), Gilead, Me.; *m* 1803, Olive Wight (1777-1856; Joel[5], Am. Rev., *m* Elizabeth Twitchell; Seth[6]; Ephraim[7]; Ephraim[8]; Thomas[9]);
3-Dr. Samuel (1806-77), grad. Bowdoin Coll., 1831; of Jacksonville, Ill.; prof. physics and chemistry, Illinois Coll., 40 yrs.; *m* 1836, Mary Joanna Moulton;
2-Emily (2 below).
9-Thomas **Moulton** (*b* ca. 1614), from Norfolk Co., Eng., to Newbury, Mass., 1637; *m* Martha-;
8-Hon. Jeremiah (*d* 1727), York, Me.; mem. Mass. Gen. Ct. and Council; *m* Alice Chadbourne Donnell (*d* 1744);
7-Col. Jeremiah (1688-1765), *m* Hannah- (*d* 1760);
6-Col. Jeremiah (1713-77), in Indian wars; comd. regt. at Louisburg, 1745; *m* 1737, Hannah Sayward (*d* 1757);
5-Brig. Gen. Jotham (1743-77), York, Me.; Am. Rev.; *m* 1765, Joanna Tilden;
4-Dr. Jotham (1771-1857), Bucksport, Me.; *m* 1802, Mary Joanna Farrar (1772-1865; Humphrey[5], Am. Rev., *m* his cousin, Lucy, dau. Dea. Samuel Farrar; Dea. George[6]; George[7]; Jacob[8]; Jacob[9], from Eng. to Lancaster, Mass., 1658);
3-Mary Joanna (1810-87), *m* Dr. Samuel **Adams** (3 above);
2-Emily (1846-1921), *m* 1873, Alfred **Richmond,** M.D. (1844-1912), of Rochester, Vt., Jacksonville, Ill., and Claremont, Calif.; issue: I-Carl Adams (1 above); II-Frank Adams (*b* 1876; *m* 1924, Hilda Wright); III-Ruth (*b* 1884; *m* 1915, Charles Grant Burgess).
1-*m* June 26, 1901, Katharine Augusta Fall, *b* Farmington, N.H., Mar. 10, 1866; ed. Wellesley Coll.; mem. I.A.G., N.E.G.H.S., Soc. for Preservation of N.E. Antiquities, N.H. Hist. Soc.; sister of Henry Clinton Fall (see Vol. III, p. 184, for genealogy).
1-B.S., Pomona Coll., 1900; M.P.L., George Washington U., 1907; grad. student, U.Chicago. Lawyer. Spl. counsel, Signal Corps, World War. Mem. P.B.K., Am. Geog. Soc., A.A.A.S., Appalachian and Green Mtn. clubs. Summer Place: Tyngsboro, Mass. Residence: 195 Broadway, and Butler Hall, 88 Morningside Dr., New York, N.Y.

RICHMOND

Arms: Argent, a cross patonce fleury azure, between four mullets gules.
Crest: A tilting spear argent, headed or, broken in three parts, one piece erect the other two in saltier enfiled with a ducal coronet of the last.

1-**RICHMOND, Mildred,** *b* Geneseo, Ill., Oct. 21, 1888.
10-John **Richmond** (qv),
9-John (1627-1715 or 18), *m* 1663, Abigail Rogers

(1641-1727; John[10]; Thomas[11], Mayflower Pilgrim, qv);
8–Lt. Joseph (*b* 1663), Taunton, Mass.; in Canadian Expdn., 1711; owned the "Rogers 100 acre lot" until 1724; *m* 1685, Mary Andrews (Henry[9], of Taunton);
7–Joseph (1686-1750), *m* 1st, Hannah Deane (*b* 1682);
6–Dea. Joseph (1723-92), *m* 1st, 1743, Elizabeth Hackett (1720-70);
5–Joseph (1756-1821), Middleboro, Mass.; Am. Rev.; *m* 1st, 1779, Prudence Waldron (1760-89);
4–Benjamin (1783-1830), *m* 1807, Abigail Deane (1790-1850; Philip[5]; Philip[6]; Ephraim[7]; Ezra[8]; Walter[9], qv);
3–Isaiah (1809-99), pioneer of Tazewell Co., Ill.; pioneer nurseryman of Geneseo, Henry Co., Ill., 1855; *m* 1833, Eliza Angell Fenner;
2–Joseph Warren (2 below).
9–Capt. Arthur **Fenner** (qv);
8–Maj. Thomas (1652-1718), gov.'s asst., 1707-17; "Maj. of the Main," 1712; *m* 2d, 1682, Dinah Borden (1664-1761; Thomas[9]; Richard[10], qv);
7–Hon. Richard (1695-1773), mem. Gov.'s Council, 1740; justice, 1732,37; *m* 1716, Abigail, dau. of Nicholas Sheldon, *m* Abigail Tillinghast; *m* 2d, Abigail (Clemence) Thornton, dau. of Richard Clemence;
6–Jeremiah (1730-90), mem. Gen. Assembly, 1776; Am. Rev.; *m* 1751, Anne Warner (*b* 1727?; Ezekiel[7]; John[8], 1645-70);
5–Samuel (1755-1830), one of the "Scituate Hunters," 1792; *m* 1776, Lydia Ralph (1758-1820; David[6], of Hope, nr. Scituate);
4–Jeremiah (1785-1848), *m* 1810, Mary Angell (1793-1853; Ezekiel[5]; Ezekiel[6]; Daniel[7]; John[8]; Thomas[9], qv);
3–Eliza Angell (1812-78), *m* Isaiah **Richmond** (3 above).
9–George **Varnum** (*d* 1649), from Eng., 1635, settled at Ipswich, Mass.; soldier in Indian wars; *m* 1617?, Hannah–;
8–Samuel (1619-98), officer in King Philip's War; moved to Dracut, Mass.; *m* 1645, Sarah Langton (Roger[9]);
7–John (1669-1715), first white child *b* in Merrimac Valley; first town clk. of Dracut, 1702-13; *m* 1700, Dorothy Prescott (1681-1722; Jones[8]);
6–Abraham (1710-60), *m* 2d, Rachel– (*d* 1748);
5–Capt. William (1746-1814), Am. Rev.; to Thornton, N.H., 1779; land surveyor, laid out highways; *m* 1768, Sarah Coburn (1749-1806; John[6], *m* Sarah Richardson; John[7]; John[8]; Ezra[9]; Edward[10], qv);
4–Dorothy (1772-1850), *m* John **McLellan** (*d* 1817);
3–Benjamin (1813-93), pioneer of Saginaw, Mich.; *m* 1845, Emeline Palmer;
2–Clara (2 below).
9–Lt. William **Palmer** (*d* 1661/62), at Yarmouth, Mass., as early as 1639; rep. Gen. Ct., Plymouth; lt., 1642, under Capt. Myles Standish; went to Newtown, L.I., 1652-53, where he was magistrate, 1658-60; *m* Judith, dau. of James Feake, goldsmith, of London, Eng.;
8–James (1656-1717), Greenwich, Conn.; *m* Sarah Denham (Thomas[9], first preacher at Rye, N.Y.);
7–Samuel (*d* 1733), *m* 1715, Hannah (Knapp) Cross (*b* 1676);
6–Samuel (1719-96), Am. Rev., from Claverack, Albany Co., N.Y.; *m* his cousin, Hester or Esther Palmer (1730-99; William[7], *m* Rachel Fowler);
5–James (1753-1808), Am. Rev.; probably removed to Danby, Vt., ante 1790; *m* Elizabeth– (1752-1818);
4–Zachariah (1785-1864), War 1812; received bounty land; *m* 1809, Elizabeth Whitney (1792-1850; John[5], *m* Lydia–);
3–Emeline (1827-90), *m* Benjamin **McLellan** (3 above);
2–Clara (*b* 1854), *m* 1881, Joseph Warren **Richmond** (1840-1921), a local authority on horticulture; issue: I–Mildred (1 above); II–Warren McLellan (*b* 1895).
1–A.B., U.Mich., '11. High school teacher, Villa Grove and Geneseo, Ill., Lewistown, Mont., and LaCrosse, Wis., 1912-28. Mem. D.A.R. (regent). Congregational. Republican. Residence: Geneseo, Henry Co., Ill.

1–**RITCHIE, Elisha Bishop,** *b* Tenn., Dec. 19, 1874.
6–Alexander **Ritchie,** *m* Jane–;
5–Alexander (1739-1818), *m* 1761, Mary Wilson (*d* 1807);
4–Alexander (1764-1848), emigrated from N.C. to southwest Va., thence to Hawkins Co., Tenn., probably about 1796 or 97; *m* 1792, Elizabeth Doherty (*d* 1839);
3–Robert (1811-99), *m* 1846, Margaret King (*d* 1894);
2–Taylor Overton (1847-1922), farmer and stockman; *m* 1868, Martha Anne Bishop (1849-91); issue: I–Jennie C. (*b* 1870); II–Robert L. (*b* 1872; *m* Susan Griggs); III–Elisha Bishop (1 above); IV–Arch B. (*b* 1877; *m* Dee Graybill); V–Margaret (*b* 1879; *m* H. Theodore Tate).
1–*m* Apr. 26, 1898, Anne Menefee, *b* Stanford, Ky., Mar. 13, 1874; dau. of John Newell Menefee, of Stanford, *m* Eleanor Cowan; issue: 1–George Menefee, *b* Mineral Wells, Tex., Jan. 22, 1902; LL.B., U.Tex., '24; *m* Apr. 10, 1926, Margaret, dau. of Dr. John Preston, of Austin, Tex., *m* Annie W. Preston (issue: John Preston, *b* Apr. 27, 1928).
1–A.B., Carson-Newman Coll., 1895. Practicing atty., since 1897; pres. Strawn Merchandise Co., and v.p. and gen. mgr. Strawn (Tex.) Coal Co.; pres. Burton-McKee Oil Corpn., v.p. and dir., State Nat. Bank, Mineral Wells, Tex.; dir. Strawn Nat. Bank; in ranching business since 1922. City atty., Mineral Wells, 1900-04; co. judge Palo Pinto Co., Tex., 1904-08; mem. Tex. Legislature, 1913-14. Mem. I.A.G. Baptist. Democrat. Residence: Mineral Wells, Tex.

1–**ROBERTS, Eunice Byram (Mrs. Arthur John),** *b* Cedarpoint, Kan., Feb. 20, 1884.
9–Nicholas **Byram** (1610-88), "Kidnaped by sailors and taken to W. Indies; ransomed, but never returned to Eng.;" settled at Bridgewater, Mass., 1634, and bought land of Moses Simmons, Philip Delano and George Soule; *m* 1635, Susanna Shaw (*d* 1698; Abraham[10], *m* Bridget Best, of Eng.);
8–Nicholas (1640-1729), sea capt.; served in French and Indian War; *m* 1676, Mary Edson (1647-1727; Dea. Samuel[9], *m* Susanna Orcutt; Thomas[10]);
7–Capt. Ebenezer (1692-1753), rep. Gen. Ct. at Plymouth, 1738-41; *m* 1714, Hannah Hayward (1694-1761; Joseph[8], *m* Hannah, dau. of Experience Mitchell);
6–Ebenezer (1716-62), Mendham, N.J.; one of principal founders of Third Ch. of Christ at Bridgewater; *m* 1738, Abigail Alden (1721-62; Ebenezer[7] [1693-1776], *m* 1717, Anna, dau. of Lt. Joseph Keith; Isaac[8], *m* 1685, Mehitable, dau. of Samuel Allen; Joseph[9] [1624-97], *m* 1659, Mary, dau. of Moses Simmons, came from Eng. in the "Fortune," 1621; John[10], Mayflower Pilgrim, qv);
5–Joseph (1753-1829), Morris Co., N.J.; *m* 1776, Esther Douglass (1756-1840; Capt. John[6], *m* Esther Leach; Thomas[7]; Robert[8]; William[9]);
4–Joseph (1791-1864), to Ill.; *m* 1814, Abigail Thompson Harris (1793-1881);
3–Joseph William (1825-94), Knoxville, Ill.; to Lawrence, Kan., 1864, later to Cedarpoint, Kan.; *m* 1851, Maria Jane Ross (1828-1905; James[4], *m* Mary Plummer);
2–Lemuel Wade (2 below).
5–Phillipe (de la Colombe) **Columbia** (1750-1825), from France, 1776; lt. in Cont. Army, 1776, capt., 1777, a.-d.-c. to LaFayette and DeKalb, Oct. 1779; settled in Ohio; *m* 1790, Margaret– (1756-1838);
4–John (1795-1840), began to write name Columbia; *m* 1819, Lucy B. Clark (1797-1882);
3–Amy (1828-72), *m* 1847, Joseph L. **Crawford** (1825-93);
2–Margaret Amanda (*b* 1861), of Clements, Kan.; *m* 1880, Lemuel Wade **Byram** (*b* 1857), farmer, stockman; issue: I–Byron Rees (*b* 1881; *m* Della Laughridge); II–Eunice (1 above); III–Floy (*b* 1886; *m* William S. Laughridge); IV–Joseph Lee (*b* 1888; *m* Margaret Zickafoose); V–Jennie (*b* 1891; *m* Evert L. Truex); VI–Frank Elias (*b* 1894); VII–Amy Maria (*b* 1896; *m* John Ross Overstreet); VIII–Mayme (*b* 1899; *m* William Perry Brown); IX–Ethel (*b* 1902; *m* Ernest Frank Matti); X–Beth (*b* 1905; *m* Leslie E. Mann).
1–*m* June 14, 1909, Dr. Arthur John Roberts, *b* Emporia, Kan., Feb. 19, 1885; son of William H. Roberts, from Wales to Emporia, Kan.,

m Grace Thomas; issue: 1–Dorothy, *b* Caney, Kan., Feb. 21, 1911; ed. Okla. Coll. for Women.
1–Grad. Kan. State Teachers Coll., '08. Mem. D.A.R. Residence: 1521 S. 17th St., Chickasha, Okla.

1–**ROBERTS, George McKenzie,** *b* Vergennes, Vt., Dec. 28, 1886.
11–Isaac **Cummings** (q.v);
10–Isaac (1633-1721), sgt., Narragansett War, 1675; selectman, treas., constable, Topsfield, Mass.; *m* 1659, Mary Andrews (1638-1718; Robert[11], *d* 1668);
9–John (1666-ca. 1722), *m* Susannah Towne (1670/71-1766; Joseph[10] [1639-1713], *m* Phebe Gould [1620-ca. 1691]; William[11] [1600-72], *m* 1620, Joanna Blessing);
8–Joseph (1689/90-1729), *m* 1712, Abigail Estey (1692/93-1729/30; Isaac[9], *m* 1689, Abigail Kimball [*b* 1667]; Isaac[10], *m* Mary [*b* 1634, executed as a witch, 1692], dau. of William Towne, 11 above; Jeffrey[11]);
7–Jacob (1717-1814), *m* 1740/41, Mary Marble (Freegrace[8], *m* Mary Sibley; Samuel[9], *m* Rebeckah [*b* 1654], dau. of Robert Andrews, 11 above);
6–Daniel (1743-92), Am. Rev.; *m* 1765, Rachel Hayden;
5–Rachel (1775 or 76-1817), *m* 1797, Daniel **Hewitt**;
4–Dr. Simon (1803-88), *m* Elizabeth Cogswell Converse (1803-97);
3–Elizabeth Cogswell (1832-97), *m* 1850, George Clapp **Roberts** (1821-93);
2–George Simon (*b* 1860), *m* 1885, Florence Loise McKenzie (1863-1905); for issue and other lineages see Vol. II, p. 195.
1–Asst. treas. Internat. Gen. Electric Co., N.Y. Mem. S.C.W., N.E.S., S.R., S.A.R. (treas. gen., 1922-26), N.E.H.G.S., N.Y.G.B.S., Windsor (Conn.) Hist. Soc., Schenectady Co. Hist. Soc., N.Y. State Hist. Assn., Gov. and Co. of Mass. Bay in N.E., Dudley Family Assn. (v.p.), Denslow Family Assn., Vt. Soc. of N.Y. (sec.), I.A.G. Address: 120 Broadway, New York, N.Y.

FLORANCE LOVELESS KEENEY ROBERTSON

1–**ROBERTSON, Florance Loveless Keeney (Mrs. John Edwin),** *b* "Loveless Farm," Meridian, Cayuga Co., N.Y., Nov. 28, 1884.
10–Alexander **Keeney** (*d* 1680), from Eng. ante 1662, settled at Weathersfield, Conn.; *m* Alice Colfax (*d* 1683);
9–Ebenezer, of Derby, Conn.; *m* a dau. of Abraham Colt, of Glastonbury, Conn.;
8–John, of Stratford and Glastonbury, Conn.;
7–John (*b* 1712), served in Am. Rev.;
6–Mark (1740-1804), in French and Indian War and Am. Rev.; *m* 1759, Abigail B. Lee (1739-1804);
5–Jeremiah (*b* 1768), of Ithaca, N.Y.; doctor;
4–John J. (1792-1863), of Hannibal, N.Y., *m* 1816, Rebecca Bessey (1800-63);
3–Isaac (1820-93), of Hannibal; *m* 1843, Mary Collins;
2–Isaac Thair (2 below).
8–Francis (Lovelace) **Loveless** (1620-75), from Eng. ante 1650, settled in Va., 1650-53; gov. of N.Y., 1667-73; *m* Mary Iver; *m* 2d, Blanche Talbot;
7–Edward (*d* 1714);
6–John, of Dutchess Co., N.Y.; 63 acres of the Jumel estate, a portion of which now belongs to Trinity Ch., was deeded by him in 1715 to the Trinity Ch. Corpn.;
5–John (*d* 1803), began to write name Loveless;
4–George (ca. 1772-1816), of Meridian, Cayuga Co., N.Y.;
3–Solomon (1801-76), *m* Mary Moses Goss (1809-93);
2–Cora Eulalia Goss (1851-1920), *m* 1881, Isaac Thair **Keeney** (1856-1928), farmer, builder and engr.
1–*m* July 15, 1913, John Edwin Robertson, *b* Eureka, Kan., Feb. 25, 1878; son of William Robertson, *m* Sophronia Bell.
1–B.A., U.Southern Calif., '11 (Beta Phi), M.A., 1929. High school teacher, farm mgr. in N.Y.; research investigator, Washington, D.C.; teacher of adults, day and evening school, Los Angeles, Calif.; traveled extensively thruout U.S., Canada, Mexico, and Europe; writer of poems and articles for ednl. mags., also travel articles. Methodist. Residence: 2447 S. Orange Dr., Los Angeles, Calif.

1–**ROBERTSON, Lucy Maria Beekman (Mrs. Thomas M.),** *b* Tallula, Ill., Dec. 20, 1867.
9–Maarten **Beekman,** to America, 1638; *m* Susannah Jans;
8–Hendrick, *m* Annetje Quackenbosh;
7–Marten (1685-1757), *m* 1724, Elizabeth Waldron (1700-60);
6–Samuel (1729-1808), *m* 1765, Elizabeth Waldron;
5–Samuel (1766-1850), *m* 1787, Helena Ten Broeck (1768-1855);
4–Cornelius Ten Broeck (1789-1860), *m* 1813, Elizabeth Todd (*d* 1860);
3–William Todd (*b* 1815), *m* 1841, Mary Conover Spears (*b* 1825);
2–John Todd (2 below).
9–Anthony **Colby** (1590-1661), from Eng. to Boston, 1630; founder of Amesbury, Mass., 1632; *m* Susannah Haddon (*d* post 1684);
8–Isaac (1640-ante 1691), of Amesbury and Haverhill, Mass.; *m* Martha Jewett;
7–Anthony (*b* 1687), of E. Haverhill, Mass.; snow shoe man in war; *m* Mary–;
6–Isaac (*b* 1709), *m* Sarah Davis;
5–William Davis (1753-1812), of Hopkinton, N.H.; soldier in last French and Indian War; *m* Elizabeth Straw (1753-1840);
4–Timothy (1782-1866), Hopkinton; *m* Lydia Herrick (1778-1866);
3–Jonathan (1808-85), Petersburg, Ill.; *m* Lydia Ingalls;
2–Sarah Sharpe (2 below).
9–Edmund **Ingalls** (qv);
8–Henry (1627-1718/19), Andover, Mass.; *m* 1st, Mary Osgood (*d* 1686);
7–James (1669-1735), *m* Hannah Abbott (*d* 1753);
6–James (1695-1767), Pomfret, Conn.; *m* Mary Stevens (1693-1773);
5–Ephriam (1724-1805), *m* Mary Sharpe;
4–Ephriam (1764-1831), *m* Lucy Goodell (*d* 1829);
3–Lydia (1809-58), *m* Jonathan **Colby** (3 above).
10–William **White,** Mayflower Pilgrim (qv);
9–Resolved (1614-1690 or 94), *m* 1st, 1640, Judith Vassall (1619-80; William[10]);
8–John;
7–Abigail (1676-1753), *m* William **Sharpe** (1673-1751; Lt. John[8] [1643-76], *m* Martha Vose; Robert[9] [1615-53], from Eng., 1635);
6–John (1703-79), *m* Dorcas David (*d* 1754);
5–Mary (1733-1809), *m* Ephriam **Ingalls** (5 above).
2–John Todd **Beekman** (1843-88), farmer; served 3 yrs. in Civil War; *m* 1867, Sarah Sharpe Colby (1842-1917); issue: I–Lucy M. (1 above); II–Flora Belle (*d* infancy); III–Francis Ingalls (*d* infancy); IV–Jonathan Colby (*b* 1875; *m* 1898, Kate Emily Golden).
1–*m* Aug. 25, 1892, Thomas Morton Robertson

(Sept. 11, 1863-June 28, 1915); son of Dr. Colin Morton Robertson, of Ky.; issue: 1–Harris Morton, *b* Tallula, Ill., May 14, 1893; Ill. Coll., '25; *m* June 17, 1918, Lucille, dau. of J. Z. Fox, of Chapin, Ill., *m* Elizabeth Burnham (issue: Helen Lucille); 2–Arthur, *b* Tallula, Aug. 18, 1896; U.Ill., '18; *m* Feb. 21, 1920, Hazel Gertrude, dau. of U. G. Mills, of Urbana, Ill. (issue: Barbara; Thomas; Colin).
1–Ed. Geneseo Collegiate Inst., '87. Mem. D.A.R., S.U.V. Auxiliary, A.L. Auxiliary. Residence: 415 S. 10th St., Petersburg, Ill.

1–**ROUNDS, Viola Estelle Huntley (Mrs. William A.),** *b* Medina Co., O., Jan. 9, 1865.
4–Ezekiel **Huntley** (1780-1853; desc. John [*d* 1676], at Boston, 1652, Roxbury, 1659, later at Lyme, Conn., *m* 1st, Jane–, *m* 2d, Mary Barnes of Lyme); *m* 1803, Ruth Miner (1787-1851; Elisha[5]);
3–William A. (1804-75), *m* ca. 1829, Eunice Newton;
2–Carter (2 below).
10–Joseph **Loomis** (qv);
9–Nathaniel (ca. 1626-1688), freeman, 1654, admitted to the ch., 1663; mem. Windsor Troop of Horse in King Philip's War; *m* 1653, Elizabeth Moore (*b* 1638; Dea. John[10], *m* Abigail Moore);
8–Josiah (1660/61-1735), to E. Windsor, Conn., 1700; *m* 1683, Mary Rockwell (1662/63-1738; Samuel[9], *m* Mary Norton);
7–Lt. Caleb (1693-1784), *m* 1728, Joannah Skinner (Dea. John[8], *m* Sarah–);
6–Caleb (1728-74), Colchester, Conn.; *m* 1755, Ann Strong;
5–Jacob (1756-1840), one of the 27 settlers of Russell, Mass.; selectman, 1807-08; *m* 1775, Thankful Hubbard (*d* 1844, aet. 92);
4–Anna (*b* 1783), *m* 1804, John **Newton** (*d* 1835);
3–Eunice (1808-80), *m* William A. **Huntley** (3 above).
8–Robert **Follett** (1625-1708), settled at Salem, Mass.; *m* 1655, Persus Black;
7–Benjamin (1676-1752), of Salem, and Windham; lt. in French War; *m* 1707, Patience Doulee;
6–Benjamin (1715-ante 1788), Wyoming, Pa.; *m* 1736, Hannah Woodward (*d* 1757);
5–Eliphalet (1741-78), killed in Wyoming massacre; *m* 1764, Elizabeth Dewey (1743-1832; Martin[6], *m* Elizabeth Dewey Follett; Ens. Jededias[7]; Jededias[8]; Thomas[9], qv);
4–Benjamin (1774-1831), *m* 1803, Mercy Noble (1776-1830; Josiah[6], Am. Rev., *m* Olive Hill; John[6]; Mark[7]; Thomas[8]);
3–Eliza (1809-81), of Cleveland, O.; *m* ca. 1835, Charles M. **Cook** (1801-77), of Medina Co., O.;
2–Mary Elizabeth (1838-1906), of Weymouth, O.; *m* 1861, Carter **Huntley** (1830-1904), farmer, Granger, O.; issue; I–Elnora Olive (*b* 1862; *m* Scott S. Bennett); II–Viola Estella (1 above); III–Royal Noble (*b* 1867).
1–*m* Jan. 29, 1896, William Albert Rounds, *b* Medina Co., O., Apr. 8, 1865; son of Hirom Luther Rounds, *m* Mary Nancy Watters.
1–Ed. Normal School, Ada, O. Mem. D.A.R., I.A.G., Cleveland Geneal. Soc. Methodist. Residence: 5711 Franklin Boul., Cleveland, Ohio.

1–**ROCKEY, Phila Jane Watson (Mrs. Alpha E.),** *b* Fulton, Mo., Sept. 28, 1857.
8–John **Watson,** *m* Margaret Smith;
7–John (1646-1730), *m* Anna, or Sarah–;
6–Cyprian (1689/90-1753), *m* 1715, Elizabeth Steele (James[7]; James[8]; George[9]);
5–Zachariah (*d* 1757), *m* Hannah–;
4–Amariah (1751-1837), *m* 1783, Eleanor Burr;
3–Samuel (1783-1845), *m* Mary Richardson;
2–Isaac Richardson (2 below).
7–Samuel **Richardson** (ante 1652-1719), from Eng.; bought 5880 acres in Pa., 1686; mem. Provincial Council, 1688-89, 1695-96; judge Co. Ct., and justice, 1688-1704; mem. Assembly, 1691-94, 1696-98, 1700-03, 1706,07,09; alderman, 1703-19; *m* 1st, Eleanor– (ante 1657-1703);
6–Joseph (ca. 1675-1751), *m* 1696, Elizabeth Bevan (1678-1739; John[7], from Eng. in the "Morning Star," to Phila., 1683, returned to Wales and *d* there 1704, *m* Barbara, dau. of William Aubray);
5–Edward (1711-51), *m* Ann Jones (William[6]);
4–John (1748-1823), in Am. Rev. and War 1812; *m* 2d, Rachel Farquhar (1764-1838; Allen[5], *m* Sarah–);
3–Mary (1786-1856), *m* Samuel **Watson** (3 above).
9–William **Dyer** (qv);
8–Samuel (1635-ca. 1678), *m* Anne Hutchinson (bap. 1643-1717; Capt. Edward[9]; William[10], qv);
7–Edward (1670-post 1717), *m* 1695, Mary Greene (*b* 1677; William[8], *m* Mary, dau. John Sayles, qv; John[9], *m* Ann, dau. William Almy, qv; John[10], qv);
6–Samuel (1704-60), *m* 1725/26, Tabitha Niles (*d* 1795; Nathaniel[7], *m* Mary, dau. of Robert Hannah; Nathaniel[8]; John[9]);
5–George (1735-1817), *m* 1760, Anne Nichols (1738-1812; Joseph[6], *m* Mary, dau. of Capt. Ishmael Spink; Capt. Benjamin[7]; Thomas[8]);
4–Daniel (1764-1842), *m* 1787, Susannah Olin (*d* 1845; Maj. Gideon[5], Am. Rev., *m* 1st Patience Dwinnel; John[6]; John[7]);
3–Daniel Harris (1797-1870), *m* 1820, Phila Beverstock;
2–Phila Maria (2 below).
10–Jacob **Barney** (qv);
9–Jacob (1634-1692/93), of Salem, Swansea and Rehoboth; *m* 2d, 1660, Ann Witt (*d* 1701; Jonathan[10]);
8–Lt. Joseph (1673-1730/31), *m* 1692, Constance Davis (*b* 1674; James[9], *m* Elizabeth–; James[10]);
7–Daniel (1697-1784), rep. Mass. Gen. Ct.; *m* 1726, Alice or Elsa Wheaton (ca. 1700-1766; Ephraim[8], *m* Mary Mason; Robert[9], qv);
6–Constant (1731-1819), mem. Com. of Safety; served in N.H. militia; *m* 1753, Hannah Carpenter (1734-1814; Abiah[7], *m* Experience, dau. of Preserved Abell; Abiah[8]; Samuel[9]; William[10]);
5–Jeffery Amherst (1760-1847), in N.H. militia; *m* 1781, Phila Aldrich (1761-1847; Capt. Abner[6], sgt. French and Indian War, *m* Elizabeth Cooke; David[7]; Jacob[8]; George[9]);
4–Urania (1782-1852), *m* 1801, Silas **Beverstock** (1780-1866);
3–Phila (1803-82), *m* Daniel Harris **Dyer** (3 above);
2–Phila Maria (1823-1904), *m* 1843, Isaac Richardson **Watson** (1819-75); issue: I–Samuel Dyer (*d*; *m* Susan Dickerson, *d*); II–Helen Adeline (*d*; *m* George M. Eves); III–Henry Albert (*d* infancy); IV–Phila J. (1 above); V–Mary Richardson (*d*; *m* Nicholas Altmyer); VI–Susan Estella (*d*; *m* Fred. Marsh Goodwin).
1–*m* Oct. 7, 1880, Alpha Eugene Rockey (July 5, 1857-Mar. 28, 1927); capt., M.R.C., 1917; chief of surgical service, Camp Lewis, Washington, 1918-19; maj., M.R.C., 1918-19; lt. col., Med. Section, O.R.C., July 16, 1919–; son of Paul Warren Rockey; issue: 1–Paul Rockey, *b* Iowa City, Ia., Oct. 11, 1883; capt., M.R.C., U.S.A., 1917–; maj., 1919; served in France; *m* Selma Schempf; 2–Eugene Watson, *b* Iowa City, Aug. 14, 1886; capt., Med. Section, O.R.C., U.S.A., 1918, served in France, 1918-19; *m* Alice Mary Carey.
1–Ed. Iowa Acad., Iowa City, Ia. Mem. Magna Charta Dames (regent), C.D.A. (state historian Ore.), D.A.R., I.A.G. Residence: 225 Riverside St., Portland, Ore.

1–**ROWELL, Ruth Frances Hobbs (Mrs. Edward P.),** *b* Kortright, N.Y., Oct. 2, 1848.
7–Josiah **Hobbs** (1649-1741), from Eng. in the "Arbella"; settled at Boston, 1671; farmer and cordwainer; served in Capt. Josiah Sill's Co., King Philip's War; Narragansett grantee; *d* Lexington, Mass.; *m* 1st, Tabitha–;
6–Josiah (1685-1779), of Weston, Lexington, Boston, Mass.; farmer; *m* 1708, Esther Davenport (1690-1778);
5–Ebenezer (1709-62), selectman, Princeton, Mass.; *m* 1734, Eunice Garfield (*b* 1710);
4–Dea. Elisha (1743-1807), *m* 1764, Lois Hastings (1742-1807);
3–Jonas (1772-1862), Delhi, N.Y.; *m* 1st, 1793, Anna Hastings (1772-ante 1803);
2–Joseph Hastings (2 below).
8–Miles **Merwin** (1623-97), from Wales, 1630, aet. 7, in the "Mary and John," with his aunt Mrs. John Branker; farmer, tanner; *m* 1st, Elizabeth (Baldwin) Canfield (*d* 1664);
7–Miles (1658-1721), Milford, Conn.; *m* 1681, Hannah (Wilmot) Miles (*b* 1645);
6–Hon. Daniel (1688-1766), Durham, Conn.; large landowner; *m* 1710, Sarah Botchford, or Botsford (1683-1764);
5–Lt. Miles (1719-86), Milford; cornet of horse,

10th Regt., 1757; Am. Rev.; *m* 1743, Mary Talcott (*d* 1793);
4–Rev. Daniel (1746-1820), Am. Rev.; Methodist minister, as were his 3 sons; *m* 1769, Rebecca Seward (1743-1815), of Stonington, Conn.;
3–Rev. Lewis (1781-1866), Valatie, N.Y.; *m* 1805, Ruth Reynolds (1786-1833);
2–Rachel (1806-85), *m* 1822, Joseph Hastings **Hobbs** (1794-1852); issue: I–Rev. Lewis Merwin (1824-1906; *m* Barbara Miller); II–Rev. Henry Asher (1826-1908; *m* Susan Hartman); III–Nancy Maria (1828-1912; *m* Cornelius Merwin; *m* 2d, Peter Hotaling); IV–Flora Jane (*b* 1832-*d*; *m* John Fenstermacher); V–Orpha Maria (1835-54; *m* Harvey Soper); VI–Frances Adelia (1839-184–); VII–Susan Elizabeth (1841-1926; *m* Dr. Nathaniel Williams); VIII–Charles (1843-184–); IX–Abram Dewitt (1845-1924; *m* Josephine Simmons); X–Ruth Frances (1 above).
1–*m* Oct. 23, 1872, Edward Payson Rowell (Nov. 4, 1845-Feb. 6, 1914); son of Alvah Rowell, of Walton and Franklin, N.Y.; issue: 1–Clara Merwin, *b* State Center, Ia.; ed. Los Angeles State Normal; 2–Henry Dewitt, *d*; 3–Julia Wakeman, *d*.
1–Ed. Kinderhook and Mechanicsville, N.Y., acads. Taught sch., Delaware Co., N.Y., 1867, in Mattewan, N.Y., 1869-71, Los Angeles Co., 1890-98. Conglist. Republican. Residence: 1648 3d Av., Los Angeles, Calif.

LUCIEN MERRIAM ROYCE (b Bristol, Conn., Dec. 21, 1838-d Meriden, Conn., May 23, 1907), entered drug business, Hartford, Conn., 1855; enlisted as pvt. Co. A, 25th Conn. Vols., 1862; med. officer in charge of officers' hospital, Baton Rouge, La., to 1863; surgeon's steward, U.S.N., 1863-65, service on U.S.S. "Acacia." Grad. Coll. of Pharmacy (Columbia U.), 1866; engaged in wholesale drug business, New York, and retail at Brooklyn. Mem. All Saints' P. E. Church, Brooklyn.

1–**ROYCE, Helen Elizabeth,** *b* Windsor, Conn., Oct. 11, 1873.
8–David **Atwater** (qv);
7–Jonathan, *m* Ruth Peck (Rev. Jeremiah[8], *m* Joanna Ketchel; William[9]);
6–David (*d* 1727), *m* Ruth Bradley (Nathaniel[7], *m* Ruth Dickerman; William[8], qv);
5–Stephen, *m* Elizabeth Yale (John[6], *m* Sarah Payne; Capt. Thomas[7], Thomas[8], qv);
4–Isaac (1758-1839), Am. Rev.; *m* Lucy (Meriam) Merriam (Joseph[5], Am. Rev., *m* Sarah Austin; Joseph[6]; John[7]; William[8]; Joseph[9], from Eng. in the "Castle," 1638);
3–Sarah Elizabeth (1807-87), *m* Enos **Royce** (1803-74), see Vol. II, p. 199, for Royce lineage;
2–Lucien Merriam (2 below).
10–John **Hollister** (qv);
9–John (1644-1711), *m* Sara Goodrich (William[10], qv);
8–Thomas (1672-1741), *m* 1695, Dorothy Hills (Joseph[9], *m* Elizabeh–; William[10]);
7–Lt. Gideon (1699-1785), *m* 1723, Rachel Talcott (1706-90; Nathaniel[8], *m* Elizabeth, dau. of Joshua Robbins; Samuel[9]; John[10]);
6–Nathaniel (1731-1810), Am. Rev.; *m* 1754, Mabel (Mehitabel Mathison) Matson (1739-1824; Thomas[7], *m* Rachel Fox; Thomas[8]; Thomas[9]; Thomas[10]);
5–Gideon (1776-1864), *m* Mary Olmstead (*d* 1827; Samuel[6], *m* Jerusha Pitkin; Nehemiah[7]; Joseph[8], Nicholas[9]; James[10], qv);
4–Edwin Madison (1800-70), dry goods mcht. and paper mfr.; *m* Gratia Taylor Buell (1801-88; Maj. John Hutchinson[5], a.-d.-c. to Gen. Washington, *m* Sarah [Taylor] Metcalf; Benjamin[6]; Benjamin[7]; Samuel[8], William[9]);
3–Edward Hubbell (1826-75), Civil War; *m* Emily Harriet Phelps;
2–Emma Gratia (2 below).
10–William **Phelps** (qv), *m* 1st–;
9–Samuel (1625-69), *m* Sarah Griswold (Edward[10], qv);
8–Josiah (*b* 1667), *m* Sarah Winchel (Nathaniel[9], *m* Sarah Porter; Robert[10], from Eng. to Dorchester, Mass., 1634);
7–Josiah (1708-91), capt. Am. Rev.; *m* Ann Griswold (Benjamin[8], *m* Elizabeth Cook; George[9]; Edward[10], qv);
6–Josiah (1735-1820), capt. Am. Rev.; *m* Ann Denslow (Joseph[7], *m* Ann Holcomb; Henry[8]; Nicholas[9]);
5–Josiah (*died* 1828), *m* Polly Phelps (Aaron[6], Am. Rev., *m* Susannah Wells; Lt. Daniel[7], Am. Rev.; William[8]; Samuel[9]; William[10], qv);
4–Josiah (1789-1861), War 1812; *m* Emily Allyn, see Vol. II, p. 199 for Allyn lineage;
3–Emily H., *m* Edward H. **Hollister** (3 above);
2–Emma Gratia (*b* 1852), *m* Oct. 15, 1872, Lucien Merriam **Royce** (1838-1907), see portrait and biography; issue: I–Helen Elizabeth (1 above); II–Lucy Atwater (1876-Sept. 19, 1928); III–Robert Hollister (*b* 1880).
1–Adelphi Coll., '95. Teacher. Mem. S.M.D., D.F.P.A., D.A.C., D.A.R., U.S.D. 1812, Daughters of Vets. of Civil War. Club: College (Hartford). Summer place: "Nehemiah Royce" House, Wallingford, Conn. Residence: 5 Pliny Ct., Hartford, Conn.

1–**ROYSTER, Lawrence Thomas,** *b* Norfolk, Va., Aug. 18, 1874.
5–Nathaniel **Royster,** of Halifax Co., Va.; *m* Elizabeth Maynard, of Mecklenburg Co., Va.;
4–Littleberry (*d* in Ky., 1822), said to have *m* a Miss Savage;
3–John Woodson, M.D. (1794-1842), *m* 1829, Susan Bacon Wilkinson;
2–Lawrence (2 below).
9–Thomas **Savage** (qv);
8–Capt. John (1624-78), justice and burgess; *m* 1st, Ann Elkington; *m* 2d, Mary Robins (Col. Obedience[9], burgess and cdr. of Accomac Co., Va., 1632);
7–Capt. Thomas (1663-1728), *m* 1702, Alicia Harmonson (Thomas[8], was in Va. 1622, lawyer, burgess);
6–Thomas, *married* Esther Littleton (see Vol. III, p. 404, for Littleton lineage);
5–Nathaniel Littleton (1755-93), officer Am. Rev.; *m* 1783, Ann Reynolds (1757-1800);
4–Susan (1784-1828), *m* 1802, George **Wilkinson** (1780-1830);
3–Susan Bacon (1803-70), *m* Dr. John Woodson **Royster** (3 above);
2–Lawrence (1841-1907), *m* 1867, Alice Josephine Ridley (1840-1914).
1–*m* Dec. 9, 1903, Ola Park (qv).
1–M.D., U. of Va., 1897 (Sigma Chi, Alpha Omega Alpha, Phi Beta Kappa, Sigma Xi, Phi Beta Pi). Prof. and head dept. pediatrics, U. of Va. (see Who's Who in America). Mem. Soc. Cincinnati. Residence: University, Va.

1–**ROYSTER, Ola Park (Mrs. Lawrence T.),** *b* Jefferson, Tex., Nov. 30, 1877.
7–Ezekiel **Park,** of Highfield Hall, Eng.;
6–Thomas, *m* Esther Coke;
5–Joseph, *m* Esther Sankey (Rev. Richard[6], trustee Hampden-Sidney Coll., *m* Esther, dau. of James Thompson, ruling elder in Presbyn. Ch., g.dau. John Thompson, of Ireland);
4–Joseph Littlejohn, *m* Sarah Owen Musgrove (Maj. H.[5], *m* Jane, dau. of W. H. Owen; Admiral Musgrove[6], *m* an Indian princess);
3–John Thompson Sankey, *m* Tabitha Ann

Skinner (Judge William[4], of Augusta, Ga.);
2–Oscar Brantly (2 below).
4–David Calhoun **Caldwell,** *m* Lucy Anne Cabiness;
3–John Madison, *m* Emily G. Bell (Capt. Henry[4], *m* Elizabeth Gee);
2–Willie Ola, *m* Oscar Brantly **Park.**
1–*m* Dec. 9, 1903, Lawrence Thomas Royster (qv).
1–Ed. Hollins Coll., Va. Mem. D.A.R. Residence: University, Va.

1–**RUDOLPHY, Jay Besson,** *b* Hoboken, N.J., Nov. 30, 1887.
3–John Leonhard **Rudolphy** (1819-90; Rudolphé family originated in France); came from Germany to New York, 1850; was wholesale druggist and author of Pharmaceutical Directory and Handbook; *m* Anna Louise, dau. of Ernst August Robbelen, distinguished physician of Hameln, Germany;
2–Charles Bruno (2 below).
7–Samuel **Green** (*d* 1760), prominent in N.J.; freeholder; assessor, justice, gen. surveyor; supposed to be pioneer settler of Hope Tp.; *m* Hannah–;
6–Margaret, *m* John **Opdyck** (1710-77), resided in Old Amwell (now Delaware) Tp., Hunterdon Co., N.J.; farmer, miller, merchant; justice (see Vol. III, p. 405 for Opdyck lineage);
5–Margaret (1751-1820), *m* John **Besson** (1750-1842), ens. in Am. Rev. (see Vol. I, p. 808 for Besson lineage);
4–John (1773-1838), *m* Rachel Trout;
3–Jacob (1811-90), *m* 1838, Sarah Carhart Runkle (desc. Edward Fuller, qv);
2–Almira Josephine (2 below).
6–Adam **Runkle,** came to America bet. 1735-45; *m* ca. 1749, Mary Youngblood (John[7]);
5–Jacob (1763-64-1824), *m* 1791, Euphemia Eick (1772-1834; Phillip[6], farmer nr. New Germantown, N.J.);
4–Phillip (1792-1833), *m* 1815, Sarah Carhart;
3–Sarah C. (1816-96), *m* Jacob **Besson** (3 above).
8–Thomas **Carhart** (qv);
7–Robert (1693-1745), *m* Mary Catherine Bowne;
6–Cornelius (1729-1810), capt. 3d Regt., Hunterdon Co., 1778, 3d maj., 1781, Cont. Army; *m* 1754, Willimpia Coleman;
5–Cornelius (1765-1818), *m* 1785, Sarah Dunham (see Vol. II, p. 199 for Dunham lineage);
4–Sarah (1794-1873), *m* Phillip **Runkle** (4 above);
3–Sarah C., *m* Jacob **Besson** (3 above);
2–Almira Josephine (1842-1914), *m* 1877, Charles Bruno **Rudolphy** (1851-92).
1–*m* Feb. 20, 1930, Edith Rondinella (qv).
1–M.D., Coll. of Physicians and Surgeons (Columbia), 1915; Grad. Sch. of Medicine of U. of Pa. Physician; asso. in opthalmology; Grad. Sch. of Med., U.Pa.; on staff of Phila. Gen. Hosp. and Pa. Hosp. First lt. and capt. M.C., U.S.A. active duty, Aug. 27, 1917-Oct. 4, 1919. Mem. S.M.D., S.R., Hist. Soc. of Pa. Residence: 4043 Walnut St., Philadelphia, Pa.

1–**RUDOLPHY, Edith Rondinella (Mrs. Jay Besson),** *b* Philadelphia, Pa., Mar. 28, 1896.
9–Anthony **Yerkes,** probably *b* in Holland; settled at Germantown, Phila.; juror, 1702; burgess, 1702-04; purchased a large plantation on Pennypack Creek in Manor of Moreland, 1709; *m* 1st, Margaret–;
8–Herman (*b* Holland [?] 1689-*d* in Manor of Moreland, 1751), *m* 1711, Elizabeth Watts (1689-1756; Rev. John[9]);
7–John (1714-90), *m* Alice McVaugh (*b* 1717);
6–Silas (1752-79), *m* Hannah Craft (ca. 1758-1830);
5–Silas (1779-1868), *m* 1806, Mary Leech;
4–Charles Tyson (1808-83), pres. Kensington Nat. Bank; *m* 1st, Elizabeth Link Broom (1810-42);
3–Charles Tyson (1837-1905), financier and railroad magnate, Chicago; *m* 1859, Susanna Guttridge Gamble;
2–Elizabeth Laura (2 below).
9–Tobias **Leech** (1652-1726), from Eng. to Phila., 1682; mem. Pa. Assembly, 1713-19; founder Trinity P.E. Ch., Oxford, Pa., 1698; *m* 1679, Hester, or Esther, Ashmead;
8–Isaac (1692-1744), was elected coroner of Phila. Co., 1727; commissioned one of the justices of the courts of Phila. Co., 1741; *m* Rebecca Hall (ca. 1709-1785; g.dau. of Thomas Rutter, *b* Eng., came to Pa., 1682; mem. of Assembly);
7–Isaac (ca. 1730-1763), *m* 1753, Martha Thomas (*b* 1730);
6–Isaac (1754-1834), *m* 1781, Sarah Holcombe (*d* 1825);
5–Mary (1786-1858), *m* Silas **Yerkes** (5 above).
2–Elizabeth Laura Yerkes, *m* 1895, Lino Francesco **Rondinella,** B.S., M.E., U. of Pa. (Pasquale[3], *m* Elizabeth Gifford Esler, g.g.dau. of Adam Esler, lt. in Am. Rev.).
1–*m* Feb. 20, 1930, Jay Besson Rudolphy, M.D. (qv).
1–A.B., Bryn Mawr Coll., 1919. Residence: 4043 Walnut St., Philadelphia, Pa.

Original RUBINCAM homestead in America, built in pre-Revolutionary days; during the Battle of Germantown it was used as a hospital for wounded American soldiers.

1–**RUBICAM, Arthur Benfer,** *b* Plymouth Meeting, Pa., Apr. 5, 1900.
6–Charles William (Rubakam, Revacomb, Rubincam) **Rubicam** (*d* July 1748; son of Rev. John Philip Rubakam, *m* Margaret Catherine–); came from Wanfried, Germany, settled at Germantown, Pa., 1725; *m* Barbara Rittenhouse;
5–Peter (Revacomb) (*d* July 2, 1799), served First Co., 7th Bn., Pa. Militia, Am. Rev.; *m* July 17, 1772, Hannah Potts;
4–Ezekiel (1773-1853), (Rubincam), *m* 1805, Mary Strode (*d* 1806);
3–Richard (Oct. 20, 1806-Nov. 8, 1882), *m* Mar. 12, 1843, Mary Ann Eckel (1824-76);
2–Albert Rittenhouse (July 26, 1852-Aug. 20, 1926), *m* 1883, Ida May Pyke (*b* 1864); issue: I–Ethel May (1884-90); II–Howard Albert (*b* and *d* 1885); III–Grace Warder (1887-88); IV–Harold Albert (*b* and *d* 1889); V–Marion Alberta (*b* 1891; *m* John Lloyd Balderston); VI–William Gladstone (1894-96); VII–Arthur Benfer (1 above).
1–Not married. Advertising. Mem. S.A.R. Summer place: Raccoon Island, Lake Hopatcong, N.J. Residence: 121 E. 17th St., New York, N.Y.

1–**RUBICAM, Raymond,** *b* New York, N.Y., June 16, 1892.
7–Rev. John Philip (Rubakam) **Rubicam,** of Wanfried, Germany; *m* Margaret Catherine– (*d* 1727), who, as his widow, came to America, ca. 1725; settled at Germantown, Pa.;
6–Charles William (*d* 1748), of Germantown, *m* 1671, Barbara Rittenhouse;
5–Peter (*d* 1799), of Chester Co., Pa.; served 1st Co., 7th Bn., Pa. Militia, Am. Rev.; *m* Hannah Potts;
4–Ezekiel (1773-1853), *m* 1805, Mary Strode;
3–Richard (1806-82), of Phila.; *m* 1843, Mary Ann Eckel (1824-76);
2–Joseph (1846-97), fruit importer, Phila.; *m* 1865, Sarah Bodine (1849-1921); issue: I–Josephine (*d* infancy); II–Harry Cogswell (*b* 1871; *m* Kitty Wallen); III–Charles Bodine (*b* 1873; *m* Sue Holter); IV–Anna Merritt *married* George Beck); V–Richard Strode (*b* 1882; *m* Elizabeth Brittingham); VI–Florence Eckel (1884-1929; *m* J. Howard Scribner); VII–Edward (*d* infancy); VIII–Raymond (1 above).
1–*m* Nov. 30, 1916, Regina McCloskey, *b* Phila.,

Pa., June 14, 1893; dau. of George Charles McCloskey, of Phila.; issue (all *b* Phila.): 1–Kathleen Bodine, *b* Sept. 21, 1917; 2–Jane Collins, *b* Oct. 5, 1919; 3–Anne Wilson, *b* Dec. 27, 1922.

1–Pres. Young & Rubicam, Inc., advertising; dir. Young & Rubicam, Inc. Clubs: Scarsdale Golf, Ardsley, Golfers, Advertising, Automobile, Mid-York (dir.), New York, (New York) and Huntingdon Valley Country, Art Club of Phila. Residence: Richbell Rd., Scarsdale, N.Y.

SACKETT

Arms: Argent, a chevron between three mullets of six points sable.
Crest: An eagle's head and neck erased or.
Motto: Aut nunquam tentes, aut perfice.

1–**VERNOR, Maude Estelle Sackett (Mrs. Russel L.),** *b* Nashville, Ill., Jan. 29, 1895.
10–Simon **Sackett** (1602-35), from Eng. to Newton (now Cambridge), Mass., 1630; *m* Isabel–;
9–John (1632-1719), Newton, *m* 1659, Abigail Hannum (1640-90; William[10], of Newton, *m* Honor Capen, of Dorchester, Windsor, Northampton);
8–William (1662-1700), *m* 2d, 1689, Hannah Graves (1666-post 1696; Isaac[9], *m* 1645, Hannah Church);
7–Jonathan (1696-1773), Westfield; *m* 2d, 1725, Ann Filer (*d* post 1743; Zebulon[8], *m* Experience Strong);
6–Reuben (1732-1803), Hebron and E. Greenwich, Conn.; *m* 1752, Mercy Finney (*d* post 1771; John[7], *m* Ann Toogood);
5–Dr. Samuel (1754-1833), *m* Greenwich, Conn.; physician and surgeon's mate, Conn. militia, 1779; surgeon, Westmoreland Co., Pa., militia, 1782; *m* 1777, Sarah Manning (ca. 1753-1813; Samuel[6] [1725-90], *m* 1749, Abigail Clark, *d* 1758);
4–Dr. David Filer (1780-1864), Litchfield Co., Conn.; *m* 1807, Martha Millikin (1787-1874; William[5], *m* Margaret Lackey);
3–Samuel B. (1810-99), *m* 1832, Lucinda Preston;
2–John Preston (1837-1913), settled at Nashville, Ill. (see portrait); *m* 1879, Mary Lurinda Corgan (*b* 1852; John W.[3] (1829-86), *m* 1848, Sarah Ellen Reeves, 1833-76); issue: I–Lucinda Ellen (Mrs. Pringle Williams, qv for Preston lineage); II–Alice Garnet (*b* 1882; *m* 1909, Otto H. Buhrman); III–Mary Edith (*b* 1887; *m* 1916, William F. Jurgens); IV–Eben John (*b* 1889; *m* 1908, Margaret M. Crandell; *m* 2d, 1925, Jeannette DeWolfe); V–Maude Estelle (1 above); VI–Madge Adelle (*b* 1895; *m* 1924, Leonard Halstead).
1–*m* Feb. 22, 1918, Russel La Rue Vernor, *b* Nashville, Ill., Oct. 30, 1894; son of Dan H. Vernor, of Nashville, *m* Elzona Hook; issue: 1–Russel La Rue, Jr., *b* Cushing, Okla., Jan. 5, 1919; 2–John Sackett, *b* Nederland, Tex., Sept. 20, 1926.
1–Residence: Nederland, Tex.

JOHN PRESTON SACKETT (b Millford, Kosciusko Co., Ind., Dec. 18, 1837-d 1913), settled at Nashville, Ill., 1866, where he was a farmer and builder.

1–**WILLIAMS, Lucinda Sackett (Mrs. Pringle),** *b* Nashville, Ill., July 4, 1881.
6–John **Preston,** Friend, from Eng., ante 1750; *m* Miss Tucker;
5–John (1750-1820), *m* 1774, Rebecca Vicker (1753-1834);
4–John (1776-1838), *m* 1804, Lucinda Tansil (*b* 1788);
3–Lucinda (1816-82), *m* 1832, Samuel B. **Sackett** (1810-99);
2–John Preston (1837-1913), see portrait; *m* 1879, Mary Lurinda Corgan (*b* 1852); for issue and Sackett lineage, see Mrs. Russel L. Vernor.
1–*m* Aug. 11, 1915, Pringle Williams, *b* Foristell, Mo., Aug. 13, 1872; son of N. E. Williams, of Foristell.
1–Ed. normal colleges at Carbondale, and Normal, Ill. Mem. D.F.P.A., D.A.R., U.S.D. 1812, W.R.C., Wednesday Club, Bay View Reading Club. Residence: 3220 Linden Pl., E. St. Louis, Ill.

1–**SAFFORD, Kate Putnam,** *b* Gallipolis, O., June 10, 1851.
9–Thomas **Safford** (*d* 1667), from Eng.; first mentioned in Ipswich, Mass., 1641; *m* Elizabeth– (*d* 1670);
8–John (*b* 1633), prob. from Eng.; *m* Sarah Low, or Lowe, of Ipswich;
7–Thomas (1672-1754), *m* 1698, Eleanor (Cheney) Shatswell (Daniel Cheney[8]);
6–Joseph (1704-ca. 1757), Hardwick, Mass.; *m* 1728, Mary Chase;
5–Challis (1733-71), *m* 2d, Lydia Warner;
4–Jonas (1763-1834), Gallipolis, O.; *m* Joanna Merrill;
3–Robert (1794-1854), *m* Jane Davis Putnam;
2–Jonas Putnam (2 below).
9–John **Putnam** (qv);
8–Lt. Thomas (bap. 1614-86), Salem, Mass.; *m* 1st, 1643, Ann Holyoke (*d* 1665);
7–Dea. Edward (bap. 1654-1747), *m* 1681, Mary Hale;
6–Elisha (1685-1745; 1st cousin of Gen. Israel Putnam), *m* Susanna Trask Fuller (Jonathan[7], *m* Susan Trask);
5–Rufus (1738-1824), settled at Marietta, 1788; soldier in French and Indian War; chief engr. with rank of col., Am. Rev.; built the fortification of Dorchester Heights, 1775; brig. gen., U.S.A., 1783; dir. of the Ohio Co., and surveyor gen. of the U.S., 1793-1803; *m* 2d,

1765, Persis Rice (Zebulon[6], of Westboro, Mass.);
4–Judge Edwin (1776-1843), *m* 1800, Eliza Davis (1781-1845);
3–Jane Davis (1804-28), *m* Robert **Safford** (3 above);
2–Jonas Putnam (1823-88), *m* Lucy Caroline Knapp (1827-1928); issue: I–Kate Putnam (1 above); II–Romaine Vinton (1853-60); III–Frank Knapp (*b* 1855; *m* Rachel Boles).
1–Kindergartner, 1889-1921; librarian, of Windsor (Conn.) Public Library, since 1909. Mem. D.A.R. Residence: 323 Broad St., Windsor, Conn.

1–**SAGE, John Parker,** *b* Tidioute, Pa., Feb. 25, 1879.
8–David **Sage** (qv);
7–Jonathan (1674-1712), of Cromwell, Conn.; *m* ca. 1705, as her first husband, Anna Bidwell (ca. 1678-1748; Joseph[8]; John[9]);
6–Jonathan (*b* 1711), of Cromwell; *m* ca. 1738, Hannah Gibson or Gipson (*b* 1713/14; Samuel[7], *m* 1st, Hannah Whitmore; Roger[8]);
5–Jonathan (*b* 1739), French and Indian War; at siege of Louisburg; *m* 1765, Mary Bole (1745/46-1810);
4–Jonathan (1768-1823), Shaftsbury, Vt.; pioneer settler in n.w. Pa.; *m* Mercy Read;
3–Jonathan Read (1801-39), Franklin, Pa.; *m* 1824, Sarah Parker (1797-1870; John[4]);
2–John Parker (2 below).
9–Dolor **Davis** (qv);
8–Samuel, Concord, Mass.; *m* 1st, 1665, Mary Mead, or Meddowes (*d* 1710);
7–Lt. Simon (1683-1763), Rutland, Mass.; *m* 1713, Dorothy Hale (1692-1776);
6–Simon (1714-54), *m* Hannah Gates (1713-60);
5–Elizabeth (*b* 1742), *m* 1760, John **Read** (1737-1813; Daniel[6]; Thomas[7]; Thomas[8]; Thomas[9], from Eng.);
4–Mercy (1767-1814), *m* Jonathan **Sage** (4 above).
9–James **Cole,** from Eng., 1632; settled at Saco, Me.; at Plymouth, Mass., 1633; surveyor of highways; constable; soldier in Pequot War; first settler of Cole's Hill, just back of Plymouth Rock; *m* 1624, Mary Lobel (*d* 1660; Mathieu[10] [1538-1616], physician to James I, of Eng.);
8–John (1637-77), of Swansea, Mass.; original propr.; *m* 1667, Elizabeth Ryder (Samuel[9]);
7–John (*b* 1672), *m* 1st, 1693, Mary Lewis (*d* 1711; Hezekiah[8]);
6–Seth (1708-72), *m* 1730, Experience Luther;
5–Esau (*b* 1732), Oneida Co., N.Y.; in Am. Rev.; *m* 1768, Mary Chase;
4–Joseph (*b* 1770), Herkimer Co., N.Y.; *m* Hannah– (1775-1822);
3–Peleg Slade (1808-88), Warren, Pa.; pub. "People's Monitor," one of the first newspapers in Warren Co.; *m* 1st, Louisa Brown (1811-39);
2–Sariette (2 below).
9–Capt. John **Luther,** from Eng., 1635; settled at Swansea; first settler of Gloucester; killed by Indians while on trading voyage to Delaware Bay, 1644;
8–Hezekiah (1640-1723), *m* 1st, Elizabeth–;
7–Dea. Nathaniel (1664-1719), *m* 1693, Ruth Cole (1666-1718; daughter of Hugh[8], sgt. in King Philip's War, rep. and dep. Gen. Ct., *m* Mary Foxwell; James[9], qv);
6–Experience (*b* 1710), *m* Seth **Cole** (6 above).
2–Sariette Cole (1836-1913), *m* 1857, John P. **Sage** (1832-1905); issue: I–Frank Henry (1858-1905; *m* Lola Gertrude Trescott); II–Miles Whitney (1860-62); III–Ralph Clapp (*b* 1862; *m* 3d, Alice Loretta Rowan); IV–Gertrude Elizabeth (*b* 1865; *m* 1st, John Thomas Wood; *m* 2d, James William Foley); V–Cora (*b* 1867; *m* 1st, Hugh Henry Griffin; *m* 2d, Harold Jackson); VI–Sarah Matilda (1872-1907; *m* as his 3d wife, Franklin K. Barnhart); VII–Miles W. (*b* 1875; *m* Lona May Barb); VIII–Maude (*b* and *d* 1878); IX–John Parker, Jr. (1 above).
1–*m* 1st, Jan. 8, 1898, Mabel Emma Morrison (Jan. 13, 1882-Jan. 9, 1902); dau. of Eugene Hiram Morrison, *m* Harriet Louisa Sillaway; issue: 1–Russell Morrison (qv); 2–Eugene John, *b* Newcastle, Pa., Nov. 29, 1901.
1–*m* 2d, Mar. 15, 1905, Hilma Wilhelmina Levine, *b* Hugnerud, Warmland, Sweden, June 20, 1880; dau. of Nels Emanuel Levine, from Sweden to Pa., 1887; *m* Mina Casja Bjornson; issue: 1–Sarah Eleanor Levine, *b* Tidioute, Pa., Dec. 8, 1907; 2–Charles Philip, *b* Tidioute, May 20, 1916.
1–Undertaker. I.O.O.F. Presbyn. Republican. Residence: Tidioute, Pa.

1–**SAGE, Russell Morrison,** *b* Worthington, Ind., Aug. 28, 1899.
13–John **Whitney** (qv);
12–John (*d* 1692), *m* 1642, Ruth Reynolds (Robert[13], the Immigrant);
11–Ruth (*b* 1645), *m* 1st, 1664, John **Shattuck** (1647-75; William[12], qv);
10–John (1666-1709), *m* Mary Blood (1672-1756; James[11], Richard[12]; James[13]);
9–Mary (*b* 1699), *m* 1722, John **Gilson** (1697-1756; John[10], of Groton, *m* Sarah–; Joseph[11]);
8–John (1726-87), pvt. Am. Rev.; at Battle of Bunker Hill; *m* 1747, Hannah Green;
7–John (1750-1811), pvt. Am. Rev.; early settler at Warren, Pa., 1803; *m* 1769, Patience Graves;
6–Lydia (1769-1851), *m* as his 3d wife, 1787, John **Owen** (1741-1843), of Carroll, N.Y.; pvt. Am. Rev. (John[7]);
5–Phoebe (*b* 1796), *m* 1815, Ephraim **Morrison** (1784-1845; James[6]; Samuel[7], from Ireland);
4–Hiram (1816-97), of Warren Co., Pa.; *m* his 1st cousin, Joanna Hadley (1819-1910; Stephen[5], of N.J., m 1808, Elizabeth Owen; Robert Headley[6], of N.J.; Robert[7], of Conn.; Robert[8]);
3–Eugene Hiram (1847-1906), of Warren Co., Pa.; *m* 1870, Harriet Louisa Sillaway (1851-1909; Harvey[4] of Erie Co., N.Y.; *m* Eunice, dau. Moses Cheney);
2–Mabel Emma (2 below).
12–Thomas **Graves** (*d* 1662), Hartford, 1645; removed to Hatfield, Mass.; *m* Sarah– (*d* 1666);
11–John (*d* 1677), *m* 1st, Mary Smith (*d* 1668; Lt. Samuel[12], qv);
10–Samuel (*d* 1731), Sunderland, Mass.; *m* Sarah– (*d* 1734);
9–Noah (*b* 1695), *m* Rebecca Wright (1700-44; Benoni[10], *m* Rebecca Barrett);
8–Reuben (1724-78), *m* 1748, Hannah Fuller;
7–Patience (1749-1823), *m* John **Gilson** (7 above).
2–Mabel Emma Morrison (1882-1902), *m* 1898, as his first wife, John Parker **Sage,** Jr. (qv).
1–*m* Aug. 21, 1922, Florence Louise Schmidt (divorced, 1924).
1–*m* 2d, Aug. 21, 1926, Evelyn Elizabeth, dau. of Benjamin Tracy, of Cleveland, O., *m* Laura Price; issue: 1–Russell Eugene, *b* Cleveland, O., July 19, 1927.
1–Grad. Cincinnati Coll. of Embalming. Embalmer. Mason. U.S. Navy, 1917-19, U.S.S. South Carolina, active war duty. Presbyterian. Republican. Residence: 7000 Carnegie Av., Cleveland, O.

1–**SAMPSON, William Shattuck, III,** *b* Cincinnati, O., Oct. 23, 1867.
6–Alexander **Sampson** (son of Alexander), from Eng. to Boston, early part of 18th Century; *m* in 1724, Rebecca Shattuck;
5–Alexander (1729-85), *m* Hepsibah Hastings (*b* 1737);
4–Stephen (1767-1823), *m* 1787, Mehitabel Morse (1770-1803);
3–William Shattuck (1800-78), settled at Cincinnati, O., ca. 1830; *m* Anna Maria Coolidge;
2–William S., Jr. (2 below).
11–Edmund **Sherman** (1572-1641), came to Mass., 1634;
10–Grace (1615-91), *m* John **Livermore** (1606-1684);
9–Hannah, *m* John **Coolidge** (1630-1691), Watertown (John[10], qv);
8–John (1662-1713), *m* Mary–;
7–Isaac (1685-1761), *m* Hannah Morse (1689-1710);
6–Capt. John (*b* 1714), *m* Anne Russell;
5–Isaac (1747-1822), *m* Abigail Bacon;
4–Isaac (1772-1812), *m* Rebecca Hastings (*b* 1774);
3–Anna Maria (1805-1844), *m* William Shattuck **Sampson,** I (3 above).
10–Edmund **Rice** (qv);
9–Matthew, of Sudbury, Mass., *m* 1654, Martha Lamson;
8–Deborah (*b* 1659), *m* Lt. Thomas **Sawin** (1657-1738);
7–John (1689-1760), *m* Johanna Lyon (*b* 1690);
6–Abigail (*b* 1724), *m* John **Bacon** (1721-75), lt. Am. Rev.;
5–Abigail (*b* 1747), *m* Isaac **Coolidge** (5 above).
8–Thomas **Evans** (*d* 1738, aet. 87 yrs.), Gwynedd, Pa.; from Wales;

7–Robert (*d* ca. 1753 aet. 80);
6–Cadwallader (1709-70), *m* Ann Pennell;
5–Cadwallader, *m* 1770, Eleanor Thomas;
4–Eleanor, *m* Joseph **Wright** (*d* 1844), Quaker, from Ireland to Baltimore, Md., ca. 1801;
3–Smithson Evans (1807-91), auditor Franklin Co., O., 1843-47; mayor of Columbus, O., 1843-1844; treas. Little Miami R.R. Co.; *m* 1832, Matilda Martin (William T.[4] [1788-1866], mayor of Columbus, 1824-26, *m* Amelia, dau. of Nathaniel Ashcom, of Md., *m* Sarah Reeder; James[5], capt. Am. Rev.);
2–Virginia A. (1835-1909), *m* 1865, William S. **Sampson,** Jr. (1834-1900), mfr., Cincinnati, O. (for issue see Vol. I, p. 813).
1–*m* Apr. 20, 1903, Abigail Singleton Donham (qv for genealogy and issue).
1–LL.B., U.Cincinnati, 1889. Practiced law at Cincinnati; represented iron firm in Mexico, 1903-04; retired, 1915. First lt., San. Corps, U.S.A., 1918-19; with U.S. Interdepartmental Social Hygiene Bd., 1919-22; lecturer, N.J. State Dept. of Health; now chief of State Social Hygiene Bur. Mem. S.D.P., S.C.W., S.R. Address: 110 Prospect Av., Princeton, N.J.

1–**SAMPSON, Abigail Singleton Donham (Mrs William S., III),** *b* Clermont Co., O., Feb. 1, 1870.
9–Edward **Higbee,** from Eng. to Mass., ca. 1630; landholder at New London, Conn., 1647; bought a farm at Hartford from an Indian sachem, 1664; freeman, 1667; landholder at Huntington and Jamacia, L. I.; *m* Jedidah Skidmore (Thomas[10]);
8–Edward (*d* 1716), landholder at Middletown, Conn., 1673, and Huntington, N.Y.; went to Middletown, Monmouth Co., N.J.; *m* ca. 1684, Abigail Adams (*b* 1660; John[9], *m* Abigail, dau. of Richard Smith, of Wethersfield; Jeremy[10] qv);
7–John (*d* 1715), landholder at Huntington, N. Y., and Burlington Co., N.J.; *m* Alice Andrews (see Vol. III, p. 408);
6–Edward (*b* 1714), landholder, Gloucester (now Atlantic) Co., N.J.; *m* 1738, his cousin, Jemima Risley;
5–John (*b* 1739), landholder, Gloucester Co.; *m* Mary Smith (*b* 1738; John[6], of L.I.; *m* Mary–);
4–Absalom (1761-1833), landholder, Gloucester Co.; pvt. at battle of Chestnut Neck, N.J., Am. Rev.; *m* 2d, 1823, Julia Ann Steelman (see Vol. III, p. 408);
3–Abigail Steelman (1826-85), *m* 1845, Stephen Benton **South** (1819-85; see Vol. III, p. 407);
2–Helena Elizabeth (2 below).
10–Gerrit Wolfertsen **Van Cowenhoven,** from Amersfort, Holland, 1630, to New Netherland; burgher, New Amsterdam; one of the "Eight Men," 1643; magistrate of Flatlands, 1644; *m* Neeltje–;
9–Pieter (ca.1614-75), schepen of New Amsterdam; surveyor-gen. of colony, 1655; *m* 1665, Aeltje (Sybrants) Roelfs;
8–Petrus (bap. 1669-will probated 1704), of Gloucester (Atlantic) Co., Galloway Tp.; name changed to **Conover**; *m* Mary–;
7–Esther, *m* Richard **Risley,** III;
6–Jemima, *m* her cousin, Edward **Higbee** (6 above).
2–Robert Warren **Donham** (*b* 1840), landowner; bank director; Clermont Co., O; *m* 1868, Helena Elizabeth South (1846-1915), see Vols. I and III.
1–*m* Apr. 20, 1903, William Shattuck Sampson, III (qv); issue: 1–Gail Elizabeth, *b* Mar. 16, 1907; Bryn Mawr, '28; mem. Soc. Magna Charta Dames (life), S.D.P.; clubs: Bryn Mawr (N.Y.City), College, Present Day (Princeton), University League (Princeton), sec. English-Speaking Union (Princeton Chapter).
1–Author of travel sketches and poems; contributor to "The Gypsy," poetry magazine; listed in Braithwaite's Anthology of Am. Verse since 1926; awarded first prize for "Midsummer Moon," a lyrical drama in competition of Cincinnati MacDowell Soc., 1922. Mem. S.D.P., C.D.A., D.A.R. Summer place: "Clermont Lodge," at Forest Beach, near Harbor Point, Mich. Residence: 110 Prospect Av., Princeton, N. J.

1–**SANDERS, Lucy Taylor (Mrs. Robert Stuart),** *b* Paris, Ky., Feb. 22, 1881.
8–Edward **Taylor** (*b* ca. 1650; son of John, of Briggs House, York Co., Eng., *m* Mary–); from Eng., 1692; settled nr. Garret's Hill (now Pigeon Hill), N.J.; succeeded to property of his bro. Matthew, who *d* 1688; became large landowner; *m* Catherine–;
7–Edward (*b* 1678), settled at Colts Neck, Freehold, N.J.; grand juror, 1695; *m* Catherine Morford (Thomas[8], settled at Colts Neck, ante 1670);
6–Joseph (1720-66), Upper Freehold, N.J.; *m* 1743, Elizabeth Ashton;
5–William (1744-1830), Ross Co., O.; pvt. Am. Rev.; *m* 1768, Lucy Imlay (1752-1817);
4–Joseph (1770-1830), *m* 1797, Jane Irwin (1779-1847; Jared[5]);
3–Joseph (1806-73), *m* 1837, Priscilla Bell;
2–Irwin (2 below).
6–William **Bell,** weaver; from Scotland to Phila., Pa., 1754;
5–William (1763-1801), from Del. to Greenfield, O.; *m* 1784, Mary Brady (1765-1857; Michael[6], from Ireland to America, 1761);
4–Josiah, *m* Margaret Young (*b* 1794; Jacob[5], *m* Tamar–);
3–Priscilla (1817-92), *m* Joseph **Taylor** (3 above).
5–William **Caldwell** (1754-1829), from Ireland; sgt., 2d Pa. Regt., Am. Rev.; *m* 1782, Ann Sutherland, of Pa.;
4–Eliza N. (*b* 1795), *m* 1814, Samuel **Hall** (1787-1835), removed from Va. to Ky.;
3–James (1820-94), Harrison and Bourbon cos., Ky.; *m* 1850, Nancy Ann Huston;
2–Elizabeth Huston (2 below).
10–Capt. Thomas (Halliday, Holloday) **Holladay,** settled in Va., 1656; living at Jamestown, Va., 1660;
9–Anthony (will probated 1718), wrote name Holladay; settled in Isle of Wight Co.; lawyer; burgess; sheriff, 1698; justice; *m* widow of Col. John Brewer, of Isle of Wight Co.;
8–Joseph (1669-1712/13), *m* Charity–;
7–Capt. John (*d* 1742), wrote name Holloday; capt. of rangers; justice; magistrate of Spotsylvania Co.; *m* Elizabeth Brocas;
6–Joseph (*d* 1795), *m* Betty Lewis;
5–Stephen (*b* 1760), with Va. militia in Am. Rev.; removed to Clark Co., Ky.; *m* 1783, Anna Hickman (1754-1836; James[6], *m* Hannah Lewis; Edwin[7]; Thomas[8]);
4–Elizabeth (1795-1833), wrote name Holladay; *m* 1819, John **Huston** (1772-1845), of Clark Co., Ky. (James[5], spy in French and Indian War, mem. Va. militia in Am. Rev., *m* 1746, Nancy, dau. John McCreery, from Ireland to Md., ca. 1730, capt. of foot, Augusta Co., Va.; James[6]);
3–Nancy Ann (1820-93), Paris, Ky.; *m* James **Hall** (3 above);
2–Elizabeth Huston (1850-1905), *m* 1873, Irwin **Taylor** (1845-1918), died at Oak Park, Ill.; *b* and reared in Ky.; served in Union Army under Gen. Lew Wallace, 1861-65; student law; an editor Cooperative Law Book Pub. Co.; librarian 4th Appellate Ct., Rochester, N.Y., ca. 25 yrs.; issue: I–Huston; II–Joseph Irwin (*m* Virginia Cooper); III–Mary Bell; IV–James Hall (*m* Nina Atkinson); V–Elizabeth Caldwell (*m* George G. Mulliner); VI–Lucy (1 above).
1–*m* Oct. 23, 1907, Robert Stuart Sanders (see Vol. III, p. 408); issue: 1–Irwin Taylor, *b* Millersburg, Ky., Jan. 17, 1909; Washington and Lee U., '29; 2–Stuart, II, *b* Millersburg, Nov. 8, 1910; Washington and Lee, '31.
1–A.B., Wellesley Coll., '03. Mem. D.A.R. Residence: 3650 Spottswood Av., Memphis, Tenn.

1–**SANDERS, Elizabeth Ann Grigsby (Mrs. William L.),** *b* Klamath Co., Ore., Dec. 10, 1903.
9–Wolfort **Webber** (*d* 1670), from Holland, 1640; *m* Anneke–;
8–Arnout, *m* 1675, Annetje Cornelius;
7–Rachel (1688-1782), *m* 1713, John **Horn**;
6–Sarah (1721-1806), *m* 1742, James **Pearce,** of Bergen Co., N.J.;
5–Stephen (*b* 1764), *m* 1787, Mary B. Kinney;
4–Aaron (*b* 1804), *m* 1825, Elizabeth Crandall;
3–Anna Mariah (1840-1924), *m* 1855, Henry Anderson **Grigsby** (1836-1908);
2–Basil Sinclair (2 below).
12–Everardus **Bogardus** (qv);
11–William (*b* 1638/39), lt. colonial militia, 1684; apptd. comptroller of Windmill, 1656; postmaster of the province, 1687; apptd. Dutch

public notary by Gov. Nicoll; *m* 1st, 1659, Wyntje Suybrandt;
10–Anetjee (bap. 1663), *m* 1683, Jacobus **Brower** (*b* 1656);
9–Suybrandt (*b* 1683), *m* 1706, Sarah Webber (*b* 1685);
8–Jacob (*b* 1707), *m* 1727, Claesjie Bogart (1709-29);
7–Mary (*b* 1728), *m* 1745, John **Williams**;
6–Mary B. (*b* 1745), *m* 1762, Louis **Kinney** (1735-1822);
5–Mary B. (*b* 1766), *m* Stephen **Pearce** (5 above).
2–Basil Sinclair **Grigsby** (*b* 1863), of Klamath Falls, Ore.; stockman and capitalist; *m* 1884, Emma Retta Faith (1866-1921); issue: I–Ida (*b* 1885; *m* James D. Grimes); II–Adah (*b* 1886; *m* Ozro L. Brown); III–June (*b* 1890; *m* Henry A. Grimes); IV–Virgil Vernon (*b* and *d* 1893); V–Elizabeth Ann (1 above).
1–*m* Dec. 25, 1921, William Lewis Sanders, *b* St. Louis, Mo., Dec. 12, 1897; son of Walter Sanders, of Upland, Calif.; issue: 1–Betty Jane, *b* Klamath Falls, Ore., Feb. 24, 1923.
Residence: 708 N. 9th St., Klamath Falls, Ore.

1–**SANFORD, John L.,** *b* Baltimore, Md., June 9, 1872.
5–Robert **Sanford** (1745-92), of Fairfax Co., Va.; *m* 1768, Jean Sanders (1748-92);
4–George (1770-1837), of Alexandria, Va.; *m* 1800, Elizabeth Lowry (1776-1841);
3–John L. (1810-93), of Baltimore, Md.; *m* 1835, Mary Hoyle Knight (1814-94);
2–N. Knight (2 below).
6–John **Iglehart,** settled in Prince George Co., Md.;
5–John (1745-1813), *m* 1766, Mary de Noon;
4–Richard (*b* 1772), *m* 1800, Anne Hammond;
3–John Hammond (*d* 1867), *m* 1838, Anne Eliza Warner (1806-1869);
2–Annie Maria (1846-1907), *m* 1871, N. Knight **Sanford** (1846-1925), merchant, Baltimore, Md.
1–*m* Dec. 7, 1909, Mary Jennings Carroll (Mar. 18, 1880-Nov. 1, 1927); dau. of St. John Carroll, *m* Susan Placide; issue (all *b* Baltimore, Md.): 1–John L., Jr., *b* Nov. 13, 1910; attended Georgetown U.; *m* Aug. 31, 1929, Elizabeth Davis, of Berlin, Md.; 2–Anne Iglehart, *b* Dec. 19, 1911; 3–David Hoyle, *b* July 27, 1917; 4–William L., *b* Apr. 12, 1919.
1–LL.B., U.Md. Attorney at law; pres. commrs. of opening sts. and annex improvement commn., 1913-16; mem. Legislature, 1900-01. Author: An Introduction to English History; Addresses; French Chateaux; and articles on various literary and hist. subjects. Pres. St. George's Soc. of Baltimore; bd. of mgrs. Masonic Temple; trustee Masonic Home Fund. Hon. life mem. Halifax Law Soc.; life mem. Yorkshire Archael. Soc., Brontë Soc., Halifax Antiquarian Soc.; mem. S.W. 1812, Md. Hist. Soc. Episcopalian. Clubs: Authors (London), Baltimore Country, Annapolitan. Residence: 2729 N. Charles St., Baltimore, Md.

1–**SANTEE, Ellis Monroe,** *b* Hughesville, Pa., Aug. 13, 1862.
6–Capt. John **Santee** (*b* Easton, Pa., 1730-*d* 1807), ancestors presumably from Eng.; capt. militia in Am. Rev.;
5–Valentine (1748-1828);
4–John (1772-1852);
3–Elijah (1809-84);
2–John Clark (2 below).
5–John **Gray** (*b* Germany);
4–Jacob (1788-1841);
3–John (ca. 1812-1890);
2–Elizabeth (1840-1905), *m* 1859, John Clark **Santee** (1834-95), mfr. shingle machines (for issue see Vol. I, p. 816).
1–*m* Dec. 22, 1883, Beulah Hortense Barber (Oct. 17, 1858-1921); dau. John S. Barber, of Cortland, N.Y.
1–*m* 2d, June 1, 1922, Martha Jane Wood, *b* Cramer Hook, Pa., Mar. 31, 1860; dau. James Wood (1833-99), from Eng. to Phila., ca. 1841; removed to Muhlenburg, Pa.; served in Civil War, 1864-65; *m* 1854, Frances Catherine Roberts (*b* 1833; Elisha[3], Luzerne Co., Pa., *m* Dorcas Moore).
1–M.D., Homeo. Med. Coll. of Mo., 1890. Physician, retired (see Who's Who in America). Compiled Santee Genealogy, 1899 and 1927. Mem. I.A.G. Home: "Brookside Maples," Muhlenburg, Pa. P.O. address: Hunlock Creek, Pa., R.F.D. No. 2.

1–**SAVAGE, Charles Albert,** *b* Stockbridge, Mass., Sept. 4, 1866.
3–Joseph **Savage,** from Eng. with his father; settled at Montreal, Can.; *m* Abby Jones Lyman;
2–Albert Buckley (2 below).
9–Henry **Adams** (qv);
8–Ens. Edward (1630-1716), *b* Eng.; settled with 3 other bros. at Medfield; ens.; selectman; rep. Gen. Ct., 1689,92,1702; *m* 1st, Lydia Rockwood (*d* 1676; Richard[9], *m* Agnes Bucknell);
7–Henry (1663-1747-49), to Providence, R.I., and thence to Canterbury; *m* 1691, Patience Ellis (1668-95; Thomas[8]);
6–Joseph (1706-69), one of the 5 who formed 1st ch. at New Marlboro, Mass., 1744; *m* 1738, Miriam Cleveland (1718/19-1766; Moses[7], *m* Mary Johnson);
5–Simeon (1746-1825), sgt. and capt. from Sandisfield and New Marlboro; Am. Rev.; served in Arnold's expdn. against Quebec; *m* Dinah Spalding (Samuel[6]);
4–Aaron (1771-1847), adopted on death of his mother by his g.father Spalding; *m* 1792, Betsey Smith (*d* 1847; Capt. Ebenezer[5], officer Am. Rev., guarded Maj. André);
3–Dr. Lucius Smith (1804-80), Stockbridge, Mass.; *m* Eliza A. Prentice;
2–Sarah Williams (*b* 1839), *m* 1865, Albert Buckley **Savage** (1840-89), iron merchant, Montreal, Can.; later, life ins. business, St. Paul, Minn.; issue: I–Charles Albert (1 above); II–Frederick Adams (*b* 1870; *m* Anne Hoge); III–Arthur Harold (*b* 1872; *m* Louise Cochran); IV–Francis Joseph (*b* 1875; *m* Rachel Hoge).
1–*m* July 31, 1911, Clara Blanche Hull, *b* Dec. 30, 1882; dau. of Clark Hull, of Minneapolis, Minn.; issue: 1–Albert Buckley, *b* Minneapolis, Dec. 22, 1912; 2–Robert Hull, *b* Minneapolis, May 18, 1914.
1–U. of Minn., '89 (D.K.E.); A.B., Johns Hopkins, 1895, Ph.D., 1903. Prof. Greek, chmn. dept., U. of Minn. Author (see Who's Who in America). Republican. Episcopalian. Residence: 2216 Doswell Av., St. Anthony Pk., St. Paul, Minn.

1–**SAYLES, Robert Wilcox,** *b* Pawtucket, R.I., Jan. 29, 1878.
8–John **Sayles** (qv);
7–John (1654-1727), *m* Elizabeth Olney;
6–Richard (1695-post 1775), *m* 1720, Mercy Phillips;
5–Israel (1726-1801), *m* post 1748, Mercy Whipple;
4–Ahab (1760-1849), *m* 1786, Lillis Steere;
3–Clark (1797-1885), *m* 1822, Mary Ann Olney;
2–Frederic Clark (2 below).
10–Chad **Brown** (qv);
9–John (1630-1706), *m* Mary Holmes (Obadiah[10], qv);
8–Martha, *m* Joseph **Jenckes** (1656-1740);
7–Obadiah, *m* 1713, Alice Eddy (*b* 1694);
6–Martha, *m* Daniel **Hopkins** (*d* 1786);
5–Amey, *m* 1760, Emor **Olney** (1741-1830);
4–Paris (1770-1850), *m* Mercy Winsor;
3–Mary Ann (1803-78), *m* Clark **Sayles** (3 above).
10–Francis **Cooke,** Mayflower Pilgrim (qv);
9–John (*d* 1695), Dartmouth; *m* 1634, Sarah Warren (Richard[10], qv);
8–Elizabeth (*d* 1715), *m* 1661, Daniel **Wilcox** (Edward[9]);
7–Edward (*d* 1718), *m* Sarah Manchester;
6–Josiah (*b* 1701), *m* Patience Chase (*b* 1699; Benjamin[7], *m* Amie Borden; William[8]; William[9], qv);
5–William (1731-1813), *m* Betsey Horswell;
4–Thomas (*d* 1843), *m* 1782, Keziah Bennett;
3–Robert (1802-64), *m* 1826, Deborah Cook (1803-60; William[4], *m* Deborah Cory; Isaac[5]; Thomas[6]; Joseph[7]);
2–Deborah Cook (1841-95), *m* 1861, Frederic Clark **Sayles** (1835-1903), see Vol. III, p. 641, for issue.
1–*m* June 1, 1904, Adelaide Kimball Burton, dau. James C. Burton, of Providence, R.I.; issue: 1–Deborah Wilcox, *b* Norwich, Conn., Feb. 23, 1906; 2–Robert Wilcox, Jr. (qv).
1–A.B., Harvard, '01 (Delta U.). Geologist; research asso., div. of geology, Harvard U. Also manufacturer of cotton goods (see

Who's Who in America). Summer place: York Village, Me. Residence: 263 Hammond St., Chestnut Hill, Mass.

1–**SAYLES, Robert Wilcox, Jr.,** *b* Chesnut Hill, Mass., Apr. 28, 1915.
9–William **Burton** (*d* 1714), *m* Hannah Wickes (John[10], qv);
8–John (1667-1749), *m* Mary–;
7–John (*d* 1799), *m* Mary–;
6–George (1751-76), *m* 1770, Rosanna Potter;
5–George (1776-1847), *m* Rhoda Andrews;
4–John (1800-60), *m* 1830, Phoebe Congdon;
3–James Congdon (1831-85), *m* 1863, Josephine Adelaide Kimball;
2–Adelaide Kimball (2 below).
10–Stukeley **Westcott** (qv);
9–Jeremiah, *m* 1665, Eleanor England;
8–Benjamin (1684-1765), *m* Bethiah Gardiner;
7–Dorcas (*d* ca. 1734), *m* James **Congdon** (1686-1757);
6–Ephraim (1731-94), *m* Phoebe Sheldon (Nicholas[7], *m* Penelope Congdon; Nicholas[8], *m* Abigail, dau. Pardon Tillinghast, qv);
5–Nicholas (1769-1848), *m* 1793, Phoebe Battey (1772-1841);
4–Phoebe (1806-72), *m* John **Burton** (4 above).
10–Richard **Kimball** (qv);
9–John (1631-98), *m* ca. 1655, Mary Bradstreet;
8–Joseph (1675-1761), *m* Sarah Warner;
7–Philemon (*b* 1704), *m* 1734, Catherine Lewin;
6–Asa (1737-97), *m* 1762, Hannah Sweet;
5–John (1764-1842), *m* Dorothy Hoyt;
4–Jefferson Liberty (1805-77), *m* 1837, Mary Amanda Gardiner;
3–Josephine Adelaide (1840-83), *m* James C. **Burton** (3 above).
10–"Surgeon" John **Greene** (qv);
9–James (bap. 1626), *m* 1665, Elizabeth Anthony (*d* 1698; John[10], qv);
8–Jabez (1673-1741), *m* 1697/98, Mary Barton (*d* 1712/13; Benjamin[9], *m* Susannah, dau. Samuel Gorton, qv);
7–Rufus (1712-84), *m* 1734/35, Martha Russell (*b* 1716; Joseph[8], *m* Mary Tucker; Joseph[9]; John[10], qv);
6–Joseph (1745-1825), *m* 1770, Patience Sheffield (1748-1839; Caleb[7], *m* Lydia, dau. Ebenezer Cook);
5–Catherine (*b* 1783), *m* 1810, Augustus Mumford **Gardiner**;
4–Mary Amanda (1818-48), *m* Jefferson L. **Kimball** (4 above);
3–Josephine A., *m* James C. **Burton** (3 above);
2–Adelaide Kimball (*b* 1881), *m* 1904, Robert Wilcox **Sayles** (qv).
1–Residence: 263 Hammond St., Chestnut Hill, Mass.

1–**SCHOONMAKER, Harriet Emeline Warner (Mrs. James),** *b* Cameron Mills, N.Y., Apr. 8, 1861.
8–John **Peckham** (qv);
7–Thomas (ca. 1646-1709), weaver, Newport, R.I.; original propr., E. Greenwich, R.I., 1677; dep. Gen. Assembly, 1708; *m* 2d, Hannah (Weeden) Clark (*d* post 1722; William Weeden[8]);
6–Daniel (*b* 1692), freeman, Newport, 1713; at Westerly, R.I., 1733; *m* 1720, Mary Ross (1700-68; William[7], *m* Hannah–);
5–Abel (1733-will recorded 1825), Westerly, R.I.; pvt. Am. Rev.; served with his three sons in War 1812; *m* 1754, Rebecca Burdick (*d* 1779);
4–Peleg (1759 or 62-1858), Am. Rev.; *m* 1787, Elizabeth Stetson (1769-1845);
3–Isaih (1796-1863), *m* 1818, Nancy Bishop Darrow (1799-1873);
2–Elizabeth Bishop (1827-98), *m* William Henry **Warner** (1825-96), contractor; issue: I–Ellen Sophia (*d* aet. 5); II–Lucy Antoinette (*d* 1856); III–William Henry (*b* 1862; *m* J. O. Waginius); IV–Mary Elizabeth (*d* 1891); V–Edward (*d* 1890; *m* Mayette Knickerbocker); VI–Harriet E. (1 above).
1–*m* July 1, 1886, James Schoonmaker (June 7, 1857-Feb. 10, 1927), of St. Paul, Minn.
1–Ph.B., Alfred U., 1884. Taught school in N.Y. State, 2 yrs., in Pa., 4 yrs. Mem. D.F.P.A. (1st pres. Minnesota Chapter), D.A.R., U.S.D. 1812. Unitarian. Republican. Residence: c/o Mrs. R. J. Knight, Newport, Minn.

1–**SCHOONMAKER, Elizabeth Mabel Fowler (Mrs. William E.),** *b* Margaretta Tp., O., Mar. 27, 1879.
8–Ambrose **Fowler** (*d* 1704), from Eng.; settled at Windsor, Conn., ca. 1639; *m* 1646, Jane Alvord (*d* 1684);
7–John (1648-post 1706), Westfield, Mass.; *m* Mary or Mercy Miller;
6–Isaac (1697-1790), *m* 1728, Abigail Pixley (*d* 1759);
5–Ebenezer (1729-post 1764), *m* 1755, Catherine Root (1725-87);
4–Medad (1760-1849), mem. Saratoga expdn. in Am. Rev.; *m* 1st, Louisa Falley (1763-1807);
3–Harvey (1797-1876), Margaretta, O.; *m* 2d, Ellen Hubbard;
2–Richard Falley (1846-1926), contractor and builder; *m* 1871, Mary Eliza Lyman (1849-1901); issue: I–Harvey Lyman (1876-1909; *m* Nellie Ophelia Storrs); II–Elizabeth or Besse (1 above).
1–*m* June 15, 1898, Benjamin Knapp Richardson, *b* Brooklyn, N.Y., Oct. 10, 1870; son of Andrew H. Richardson, of Brooklyn; issue (both *b* Fernandina, Fla.): 1–Helen Fowler (1903-04); 2–Frederick Fowler, *b* Sept. 16, 1904; *m* Oct. 16, 1925, Carol Thelma Parker.
1–*m* 2d, Sept. 30, 1925, William Everett Schoonmaker, *b* Yonkers, N.Y.; son of Everett Bogardus Schoonmaker, of Yonkers, *m* Louise Lockwood.
1–Mem. D.F.P.A. Episcopalian. Residence: 46 W. Cayuga St., Oswego, N.Y.

1–**SCOTT, Jack (John William),** *b* Buena Vista, Ky., July 15, 1892.
6–Samuel **Scott,** to Mercer Co., Ky.;
5–Joseph; or William;
4–David (1807-77), of Garrard Co., Ky.; *m* 1830, Polly Vance (1807-61; Jacob[5], of Garrard Co., *m* Luvina Scott);
3–John W. (*d* 1915), of Garrard Co.; *m* 1859, Jalila Crow;
2–Augustus (2 below).
5–Sam **Crow** (1773-1838), *m* Polly Douglas;
4–Rev. James E. (1814-93), Garrard Co.; *m* 1835, Eleanor Robison (1814-63; Tom[5], *m* Delitha Riley);
3–Jalila (1840-1914), *m* John W. **Scott** (3 above).
7–William **Ford**;
6–Rev. Reuben (1742-1823), Baptist minister; of Va.; *m* 1770, Mary Bowles;
5–Timothy (1773-1839), Goochland Co., Va.; *m* 1793, Betsy Webber (1776-1844; Rev. William[6]);
4–Rev. William (*d* 1858), Garrard Co.; *m* 1818, Sallie S. Poore (*b* 1793; John[5] [1760-1817], Am. Rev., *m* 1788, Jane Stratton; Robin[6], of Powhatan Co., Va.);
3–James Madison (1825-90), of Garrard Co.; War 1812; *m* 1847, Martha Kersey;
2–Elizabeth (2 below).
5–Meredith **Kersey** (*b* 1769), from Va. to Garrard Co., Ky.; *m* 1794, Luiza Pulliam (*b* 1777);
4–William (1807-64), of Garrard Co.; *m* 1830, Ann Brown (1808-87; Leroy[5], *m* Sallie Graham; John[6], *m* Ruth Mitchel);
3–Martha (1831-57), *m* James Madison **Ford** (3 above);
2–Elizabeth (1854-1925), Methodist; *m* 1883, Augustus **Scott** (1860-1930), of Buena Vista, Garrard Co., Ky.; issue: I–Nellie (*b* 1884; *m* 1902, Leslie Ruble); II–Mattie Belle (*b* 1887; *m* 1925, Stanley Nooe); III–John W. (1 above).
1–*m* Jan. 28, 1915, Lula Ephriam Nooe (qv for issue).
1–Farmer. Mason. Democrat. Methodist. Residence: Buena Vista, Ky.

1–**SCOTT, Lula Ephriam Nooe (Mrs. Jack),** *b* Burgin, Ky., Apr. 2, 1890.
5–John **Hopper,** of Va.; lived in Bourbon Co., Ky., 1791; mem. Battle Run Bapt. Ch.; *m* Barbara–, from Germany;
4–Elijah (*d* 1831), Bourbon Co., Ky.; *m* 2d, 1805, Susanna Latham (John[5], Stafford Co., Va., *m* Mary–);
3–Polly, *m* 1827, Ethelbert Mandaville Joseph Robert **Nooe** (1807-76; Zepha[4] [*d* ante 1821], *m* 1803, Sarah Susanna Kirtley);
2–John Augustus (2 below).
7–Jean (John) **Lillard,** from France ca. 1668, settled on James River, near Richmond, Va.; *m* 1700, Mildred Jones; *m* 2d, Mrs. Martha Littlejohn, of Prince William Co.;
6–Benjamin (*b* ca. 1701), Culpeper Co., Va.; in French and Indian War at Du Quesne with Va. troops under Washington, and in Lord

JOHN AUGUSTUS NOOE (1843-1917).

Dunmore's War under Col. William Fleming, and later at Ft. Pitt under Cresap; *m* 1724, Elizabeth Lightfoot (William[7], uncle of "Light Horse Harry" Lee, the father of Gen. Robert E. Lee);
5–Capt. John (1737-1801), of Culpeper Co.; Am. Rev.; *m* 1st, 1758, Susanna Ball (1738-82; Samuel[6], *m* Anne Taylor; Capt. William[7]; Col. William[8], qv);
4–Ephriam (1772-1838), Anderson Co., Ky.; *m* 1795, Margaret Prather;
3–Ephriam (1820-1901), of Anderson Co.; *m* 1842, Martha McQuiddy (1819-1907; James[4], *m* Jane, dau. of Lewis Perry; John[5], pvt. in Va. Line);
2–Florence (2 below).
9–Jonathan **Prather,** of Calumet Co., Md.; *m* Jane–;
8–Col. Thomas (*d* 1712), *m* Martha Sprigg (Col. Thomas[9], qv);
7–Col. Thomas (*b* 1704), *m* 1725, Elizabeth Claggett (Capt. Thomas[8], *m* Mary [Nutter] Hooper; Capt. Thomas[9], from Eng. to Md., ca. 1670);
6–Lt. Thomas Claggett (1726-58), killed at Battle of Loyalhanna; colonial soldier; *m* Margaret–;
5–Thomas (1751-86), Am. Rev.; from Va. to Ky., settled at Ft. Harrod; *m* Mary–;
4–Margaret (1777-1858), *m* Ephriam **Lillard** (4 above);
3–Ephriam, *m* Martha McQuiddy (3 above);
2–Florence (1849-96), of Lawrenceburg, Ky.; *m* 1872, John Augustus **Nooe** (1843-1917), A.M., Ky. U. (now Transylvania U.); elder Christian Ch.; a founder of Burgin (Ky.) High School; issue: I–Mary Irvine (1873-74); II–James Franklin (*b* 1874; *m* 1901, Lillie Smith); III–Mattie Lillard (1876-1918; *m* 1904, John S. Buster); IV–Walter Ray (1878-1925; *m* 1903, Susan Mary Crews); V–Stanley O. (*b* 1879; *m* 1925, Mattie B. Scott); VI–Joseph R. (*b* 1882; *m* Burke Henderson, divorced); VII–Maggie May (1884-86); VIII–Lula Ephriam (1 above); IX–Florence Augusta (*b* 1893; *m* 1913, Walter Coleman).
1–*m* Jan. 28, 1915, Jack (John William) Scott (qv); issue: 1–John William (Jack, Jr.), *b* Burgin, Ky., Nov. 5, 1919.
1–A.B., Radnor Coll., '08. Mem. D.A.R., O.E.S. Democrat. Residence: Buena Vista, Ky.

1–**SCOTT, Baker Perkins Lee,** *b* Bridgetown, Va., Oct. 29, 1896.
5–Benjamin **Scott,** Northampton Co., Va.; in War 1812; *m* Sept. 23, 1796, Sally Nottingham;
4–Benjamin N. (1800-30), *m* 1824, Mary Ann Goffigan (*b* 1803; James[5], War 1812, *m* 1802, Polly, dau. Nathaniel Goffigan, *m* 1772, Frances, dau. Levine Dunton);
3–James Benjamin (1827-91), *m* 1847, Emily Sarah Williams (1829-1903; Thomas[4], *m* 2d, 1814, Margaret, dau. George Luker);
2–Benjamin Thomas (2 below).
6–John **Dixon**;
5–Clear, *m* 1775, William **Hallett**;
4–Thomas, *m* 1815, Sallie Trower;
3–Decina C. (1819-88), *m* 1844, Nathaniel G. **Downes** (1824-1905; Thomas[4], *m* 1820, Elizabeth [Bell] Nottingham);
2–Sallie Elizabeth (1853-1923), *m* 1875, Benjamin Thomas **Scott** (1848-1904), Bridgetown, Va.
1–*m* Jan. 16, 1923, Grace Rebecca Manville (see Vol. III, p. 171); issue: I–Baker, P. L., Jr., *b* Eastville, Va., Feb. 1, 1924; 2–Grace Manville, *b* Eastville, Aug. 8, 1927; 3–Emily Thomas, *b* Nov. 22, 1929.
1–Ed. V.P.I., 3 yrs. Left coll. to enter U.S.N.; commd. lt. Air Service, U.S.N. Residence: Eastville, Va.

1–**SCOTT, Rose Moss (Mrs. William T.),** *b* Edgar Co., Ill., Dec. 13, 1869.
10–Andrew **Cockrell,** from Eng. to Md., 1635; removed to Va.;
9–John;
8–John, *m* Lucretia Neale (Daniel[9]; Lt. Daniel[10], from Ireland to Va.);
7–Thomas;
6–John; his son, Rev. Simon, was noted Bapt. minister;
5–Nancy (1732-1807), *m* Reverend Nathaniel **Moss** (see Vol. II, p. 71, for Moss lineage);
4–Moses (1758-1838), of Va.; pvt. Am. Rev.; captured by Indians, taken to Can.; *m* 2d, Lucretia Williams;
3–William Henry Harrison (1814-52), *m* 1833, Mary Chrisman;
2–John Chrisman (2 below).
9–Samuel **Fuller,** Mayflower Pilgrim (qv);
8–Mary (1644-1720), *m* Joseph **Williams** (1647-1720);
7–Capt. John (1680-1741), *m* Mary Knowlton (1681-1749);
6–Capt. Joseph (1723-76), *m* Eunice Wheeler (1727-1804);
5–John (1747-1813), Marlboro, Vt.; *m* 1776, Abigail Phelps (1748-1815);
4–Lucretia, *m* as his 2d wife, Moses **Moss** (4 above).
6–Henry **Chrisman** (1744-1838), in Capt. Gregory's Co., Northampton (Pa.) militia, Am. Rev.; *m* Mary– (1746-99);
5–John (1768-69-1844), Fleming Co., Ky.; *m* 1789, Martha Gross (1768-1856);
4–John (1790-1878), *m* Jane Sommerville (*b* Ireland, 1781-*d* Ill., 1866);
3–Mary (1812-94), *m* William H. Harrison **Moss** (3 above);
2–Judge John Chrisman (1840-1915), *m* 1867, Nancy Susan Sousley (see Vol. II, p. 71, for Sousley lineage and issue).
1–*m* July 16, 1894, William Thomas Scott, *b* Edgar Co., Ill., Dec. 20, 1866; mgr. of Epps Farms of 4,000 acres, Edgar Co.; son of James Thomas Scott, of Edgar Co.; issue: 1–John Robert, (see portrait Vol. II, p. 71), *b* Chrisman, Ill., Jan. 26, 1896; De Pauw U.; pvt. 59th Inf., 4th Div., U.S.A., 1917; with A.E.F. in France, May 14-Dec. 28, 1918; transferred to Mobile Hosp. 39, Oct. 20, 1918-19.
1–Mem. D.F.P.A., D.A.C., S.D.P. (gov. Ill. Soc.), D.A.R. (state historian, 1927-29), U.S.D. 1812, Edgar Co. Hist. Soc., Ill. Tuberculosis Assn. (sec.), League of Am. Pen Women. Residence: "Willrose Farm," Chrisman, Ill.

1–**SCRANTON, Anna Belle Jenks (Mrs. Gilmore G.),** *b* San Beach (now Harbor Beach), Mich., Aug. 4, 1877.
10–Joseph (Jenckes) **Jenks** (qv);
9–Joseph (1632-1716), founder of Pawtucket, R.I.; gov.'s asst.; *m* Esther Ballard (1633-1717);
8–Maj. Nathaniel (1662-1723), *m* 1686, Hannah Bosworth (1663-1723; Benjamin[9], *m* Hannah, dau. Nathaniel Morton, sec. Plymouth Colony, 40 yrs., and g.dau. John Howland, Mayflower Pilgrim, qv);
7–Jonathan (1688-1745), *m* 1707, Mary Slack;
6–Jonathan (1718-87), *m* 1736, Hannah Pullen;
5–Jeremiah (1739-1811), lt. Am. Rev.; *m* 1776, Lucy Whipple (1746-1819);
4–Jeremiah Whipple (1780-1852), *m* 1803, Hester Lane (1784-1850; Jesse[5], pvt. Am. Rev.);

3–Jeremiah (1810-93), lumberman; *m* Relief Huestis;
2–George Walton (1838-98), pvt., 2d and 1st lt., Co. D, 10th Mich. Vol. Inf., 1861-63; lumberman, mfr., capitalist; *m* 1867, Arabella Willard Knapp (1848-1915, Henry[3], of Jeddo, Mich.); surviving issue: I–George J. (*b* 1869; *m* Bertha Wells); II–Anna Belle (1 above).
1–*m* Feb. 25, 1908, Gilmore Gridley Scranton. (July 21, 1863-Dec. 30, 1924); son of Myron W. Scranton, Sault Ste. Marie, Mich.; for issue see Vol. II, p. 78.
1–Mem. I.A.G. Residence: Harbor Beach, Mich.

1–**SCRUGGS, Marian Stuart Price (Mrs. Gross R.),** *b* Jessamine Co., Ky., July 10, 1869.
8–John **Walker,** of Wigton, Scotland; *m* Jane McKnight;
7–Capt. John, from Scotland to Chester Co., Pa., 1726; settled in Augusta Co., Va., 1737; *m* 1702, Katherine Rutherford (John[8], *m* Isabel, dau. of Rev. Joseph Alleine, of Eng.);
6–Capt. James (*b* 1707), granted 3,000 acres for services in French and Indian War; *m* 1737, Mary Guffey (or McGuffey);
5–Elizabeth, Augusta Co.; *m* 1760, John **Stuart** (1740-1831), officer Am. Rev. (John[6], *m* Elizabeth Archer; Stuart ancestors emigrated from Scotland to Pa., 1740; went to the "Borden Tract" of Va., later settled on Walker's Creek, Rockbridge Co., Va.);
4–Rev. Robert (1772-1856), Lexington, Ky.; *m* 1802, Hannah **Todd;**
3–Mary Jane (1804-89), Jessamine Co., Ky.; *m* as his 2d wife, Maj. Daniel Branch **Price** (1789-1860; see Vol. I, p. 539);
2–Capt. Robert Stuart (2 below).
7–Robert **Todd** (1697-1775), from Ireland, settled in Montgomery Co., Pa.;
6–David (1723-85), Lancaster Co., Pa.; French and Indian War and Am. Rev.; *m* Hannah Owen (1729-1805);
5–Gen. Levi (1756-1807), maj. Am. Rev.; maj. gen. Ky. militia; *m* 1779, Jane Briggs (1761-1800; Samuel[6], sgt. Am. Rev., *m* Mary, dau. of David Logan, *m* Jane, dau. of David McKinley, *m* Esther–, progenitors of Pres. Wm. McKinley);
4–Hannah (1781-1834), *m* Robert **Stuart** (4 above).
9–John **Settle** (son of Josias of Bedfordshire, Eng., will 1667), *m* Elizabeth (Slaughter);
8–Francis (will 1707), *m* Mary Jackson (Daniel[9]);
7–John (*d* 1738), *m* Amey Arnold (Isaac[8]);
6–Isaac (1700-52), *m* 1726, Charity Browne (Maxfield[7]; William[8]);
5–George (1732-1820), *m* Mary (Martin);
4–Thomas (1755-1816), *m* 1814, Priscilla, widow Jefferson;
3–Mary Anne (1816-65), *m* John **Butler** (1813-70; see Vol. I, p. 539);
2–Margaret Harrison (*b* 1843), *m* 1866, Capt. Robert Stuart **Price** (1842-1917), co. clk., Jessamine Co.; underwriter; issue: I–Marian Stuart (1 above); II–Robert Butler (*b* 1874; *m* Susan, dau. of Thomas Coffey).
1–*m* Nov. 18, 1890, Gross Robert Scruggs (see Vol. I, p. 539, for genealogy); issue: 1–Margaret, *b* Dallas, Tex., Feb. 18, 1892; Bryn Mawr, '13; *m* June 6, 1912, Raymond Percy Carruth (see Vol. I, p. 540); 2–Stuart Briscoe (see Vol. I, p. 539).
1–Ed. Mary Nash Coll. First v.p. C.D.A. in Tex.; charter mem. Internat. Soc. Desc. of Barons of Runnemede; mem. O.C., D.F.P.A., Huguenot Soc. of S.C., D.A.R., U.S.D. 1812, I.A.G., Club of Colonial Dames (Washington), Matheon Club, Dallas Art Assn., Woman's Club (bd. govs.). Residence: 3715 Turtle Creek Pkway., Dallas, Tex.

1–**SCUDDER, Henry Townsend,** *b* New York, N.Y., Sept. 7, 1854.
8–Thomas **Scudder** (qv);
7–Thomas (*d* 1690), from Salem to Southold, L.I., 1651; moved to Huntington, N.Y., where he became a propr. by grant and purchase of 1,000 acres; *m* Mary Leedlam;
6–Timothy (1655-1740), inherited valuable landed estate from his father; *m* Sarah Wood (*d* 1738);
5–Timothy (1696-1778), capt. militia, 1759; signer of Assn. Test, 1775; *m* 1728, Mary Whitehead;
4–Henry (1743-1822), 2d lt. Am. Rev.; mem. N.Y. Conv. to adopt Constn. of U.S., 1788; mem. N.Y. Assembly, 1790; *m* Phoebe Carll;
3–Henry (1778-1863), *m* 2d, Elizabeth Newlett;
2–Henry Joel, A.M., LL.D. (1825-86), B.A., Trinity, '46; lawyer of New York; mem. 43d Congress, 1873-75; *m* 1853, Louisa Henrietta Davies (1834-64; see Vol. I, p. 821, for Davies lineage); *m* 2d, 1866, Emma Willard (1835-93); issue (1st marriage): I–Henry Townsend (1 above); II–Charles Davies (1856-92; *m* Louisa W. Evarts); III–Edward Mansfield (*b* 1858); IV–Mary English (1859-82); V–Elizabeth (1861-65).
1–*m* June 5, 1889, Margaret Mott Weeks, dau. of Jacob Mott Weeks, of Glen Cove, N.Y. (desc. Francis Weeks, who settled at Oyster Bay, L.I.); issue (all *b* at Brooklyn, N.Y.): 1–Edna Hewlett, *b* Apr. 28, 1890-*d* Oct. 10, 1916; *m* Archibald K. Coles; 2–Henry Holloway, *b* Sept. 24, 1895; Yale, '17; 1st lt. and capt. Bty. C, 308th F.A., 78th Div., A.E.F.; *m* June 17, 1922; 3–Dorothy Weeks, *b* Mar. 31, 1899; *m* Aug. 17, 1917, John Alden Thayer.
1–A.B., Columbia, '74 (Phi Kappa Psi), A.M., 1877; grad. Berkeley Div. Sch., 1877. P.E. clergyman; rector emeritus Christ Church, Tarrytown, N.Y. Mem. S.C.W., S.R., M.O.F.W. Clubs: University, St. Nicholas, Columbia University. Summer place: Northport, L.I. Residence: 303 W. 80th St., New York.

1–**SCULL, Florence Townsend Somers (Mrs. Martin V. B.),** *b* Linwood, N.J., July 12, 1864.
7–John **Somers** (1640-1723), from Eng., 1681; settled at Upper Somers' Point, Dublin (now Somerton), Pa., ante 1693; located in what is now Somers' Point, N.J.; constable, Great Egg Harbor, 1693; bought 3,000 acres, "Somerset Plantation," 1695; rep. to 4th Assembly, 1708; mem. Legislature, 1709; *m* 1685, Hannah Hudgkins (1667-1738);
6–Richard (1693-1760), surveyor; built "Somers Mansion," still owned by descendants of family; *m* 1726, Judith Letart (1712-63);
5–John (1727-97), capt. Am. Rev., wounded in action at Red Bank, N.J., 1777; *m* 2d, 1784, Hannah (Spicer) Ludlam (1735-1800), widow of Reuben Ludlam;
4–Jesse (1763-1859), dep. collector of port of Great Egg Harbor, 1799; collector and insp. of the revenue, 1804,09-10; postmaster, 1811; *m* 1790, Deborah Ludlam (1775-1835; dau. of Widow Ludlam, above);
3–Richard L. (1809-71), *m* 1837, Anna Braddock (1813-97), of Medford, N.J.;
2–Job Braddock (2 below).
9–John **Stites** (qv);
8–Richard (1640-1702), from Eng.; of Hempstead, L.I., 1656; *m* Mary–;
7–Henry (1662-1748/49), removed to Cape May, ante 1689; whaleman; *m* 1693, Hannah Garlick (Joshua[8], *m* Elizabeth–);
6–Isaiah (ca. 1705-1767), whaleman, of Cape May Co.; *m* 1738, Rhoda Crowell (*d* 1751 or 60; Josiah[7], *m* Mary Whilldin);
5–John (*d* ante 1797, aet. 47), *m* 1773, Sarah Townsend (1750-1824);
4–John (1782-1867), capt. of militia at Cape May during War 1812; *m* 1811, Melicent Young (1793-1884);
3–Rhoda (1813-1909), *m* 1835, Abijah **Corson** (1809-63), sea capt.;
2–Louisa Stites (1837-88), *m* 1863, Job Braddock **Somers,** M.D. (1840-95), Linwood, N.J.; issue: I–Florence Townsend (1 above); II–Lucien B. C. (*b* 1872).
1–*m* Apr. 10, 1892, Martin V. B. Scull, *b* Mar. 2, 1862; son of Joseph Scull, of Scullville, N.J.
1–Ed. Alfred U., 1881-83. Mem. D.F.P.A., Pilgrim Soc., D.A.C. (treas. N.J. Soc.), D.A.R. (ex-chapter regent), N.J. State Hist. Soc., Atlantic Co. Hist. Soc. (ex-pres.), A.A.U.W. Club: Woman's (Atlantic City, N.J.). Residence: Somers' Point, N.J.

1–**SEAY, Adelia Davis Smith (Mrs. Charles Howard),** *b* Nashville, Tenn., Feb. 19, 1883.
6–John **Quicksall,** of Crosswicks, Burlington Co., N.J.; *m* Miss Robbins;
5–John (*d* 1783), of Burlington, N.J.; Quaker; recruited a company of 100 men, equipped them at his own expense and was elected their capt. during Am. Rev.; the co. was incorporated in the 1st Regt. of Burlington

Co. Vols.; served gallantly under Washington; *m* Elizabeth Hunt (*d* 1783);
4–Sarah (1777-1832), *m* John **Anderson** (1770-1822), Lexington, Ky.;
3–William (1796-1857), Nashville, Tenn.; *m* 1826, Paulina Payne (1804-47), Franklin Co., Ky.;
2–Anna Maria (1839-Aug. 5, 1920), *m* May 1, 1855, John L. **Smith** (*b* Versailles, Ky., Sept. 29, 1832-*d* Mar. 22, 1907), architect, Nashville, Tenn. (Charles[3] [1797-1868], of Hanover Co., Va., *m* Mahala Christopher [1803-92], of Woodford Co., Ky.); issue: I–William Anderson (*b* 1859); II–Clarence M. (*b* 1863); III–Minnie Louise (1877-99); IV–Adelia D. (1 above); V–Nannie Mai (*b* 1885); VI–Lucille B. (*b* 1888; *m* Joseph Plunket Brennan).
1–*m* Jan. 14, 1908, Charles Howard Seay, *b* Nashville, Tenn., Feb. 19, 1883; son of Rev. Rufus Wiley Seay (*b* nr. Grant, Smith Co., Tenn., Oct. 28, 1849-*d* Franklin, Tenn., June 1, 1927), mem. Tenn. Meth. Conference, 54 yrs. (Daniel[3], *m* Elizabeth Ledbetter); issue: 1–Dorothy Elizabeth, *b* St. Louis, Mo., Nov. 19, 1909; Washington U. (Delta Delta Delta).
1–Mem. I.A.G. Residence: 7162 Cambridge Av., University City, Mo.

1–**SELDEN, Edwin Van Deusen,** *b* Pittsburgh, Pa., Dec. 23, 1858.
8–Thomas **Selden** (qv);
7–Joseph (ca. 1651-1724), *d* Hadlyme, Conn.; *m* Rebecca Church (g.dau. Richard Church, qv);
6–Capt. Samuel (*b* May 17, 1695), *m* Deborah Dudley (g.g.dau. William Dudley, Guilford, Conn.);
5–Col. Samuel (Jan. 11, 1723-Nov. 11, 1776), cdr. 1st Regt., from New London Co., Conn.; *d* a prisoner of war; *m* Elizabeth Ely (desc. Richard Ely (qv);
4–Dr. George (1763-1817), physician; removed to Millersburg, Ky.; *m* Olive West (Eleazer[5], *m* Olive Redington; desc. Francis West, of Duxbury, Mass.);
3–George (*b* Aug. 17, 1796), Vienna, Va.; lawyer; *m* Louise Sophie Shattuck (Jared[4], *m* 1799, Marie Madelaine Sophie de Vincent de Mazade);
2–George Shattuck (1822-94), lawyer, Phila., Pa.; *m* 1842, Elizabeth Wright Clark (1824-94; Connor[3], from Ireland, 1801, mcht., Meadville, Pa.; g.g.dau. of Aaron Wright, served in Col. Thompson's regt., Pa., marched to the relief of Boston, 1775).
1–*m* Jan. 2, 1901, Cornelia Fuller, dau. Rev. Samuel Earp, Ph.D. (*b* in Eng.), P.E. clergyman, of Oil City, Pa., *m* Mary Elizabeth, dau. Col. Robert Johnston, Saltzburg, Pa. (desc. Maj. John Johnston, officer Am. Rev.); issue (all *b* at Oil City, Pa.): I–John Earp, *b* Jan. 27, 1902; Princeton U.; II–Edwin V. D., Jr., *b* July 5, 1903; Princeton U; III–Elizabeth, *b* Mar. 28, 1905; IV–George Samuel, *b* Feb. 1, 1907; 5–William Kirkpatrick, *b* Nov. 11, 1911.
1–Ed. private sch., Meadville, Pa., public sch., Episcopal Acad., Phila., Pa. Oil refiner. Col., 21st Inf., N.G.Pa., 1898-1900. Mem. O.F.P.A., S.R., etc. Residence: Oil City, Pa.

1–**SELLECK, (Alice) Isabella,** *b* Northumberland, N.Y., Sept. 27, 1861.
9–David **Selleck** (ca. 1614-1654), from Eng., settled at Dorchester, Mass., 1633; removed to Boston, 1641; soap maker, ship owner, and coast trader; *m* ca. 1637, Susannah Kibby (Henry[10], mem. A. and H.A. Co., *m* Rachel–);
8–Capt. John (*b* 1643), Stamford, Conn.; *m* 1669, Sarah Law (1639-1732; Richard[9], *m* Margaret, dau. of Thomas Kilbourne);
7–Lt. Nathaniel (1678-1712), *m* 1700, Sarah Lockwood (1678-1765; Lt. Jonathan[8], *m* Mary Ferriss; Robert[9], qv);
6–David (1700-50), *m* 1722/23, Mercy Waterbury (1705/06-60; Lt. David[7], in King Philip's War, *m* 2d, Sarah Weed; John[8]);
5–Thaddeus (*b* 1735), in French and Indian War, 1755,57, and Am. Rev.; *m* Anna–;
4–Miles (1766-1837), Luzerne, N.Y.; *m* ca. 1792, Jemima Olmsted;
3–Jonas (1810-86), Holland, N.Y.; *m* 1st, 1834, Achsah Stone;
2–Jerome Bradley (2 below).
9–Richard **Olmsted** (qv);
8–John (1649-1705), Norwalk, Conn.; *m* 1670, Mary Benedict;
7–Daniel (*b* 1682), Ridgefield, Conn.; *m* 1711, Hannah Ketchum;
6–Samuel (1715-88), mem. Conn. Gen. Ct., 1775,76, 78; *m* 1737, Abiah Smith (1716-96);
5–Daniel (1738-1814), *m* 1766, Jemima Smith;
4–Jemima (*b* 1770), Balston, N.Y.; *m* Miles **Selleck** (4 above).
8–Nicholas **Stone** (1615-89), from Eng., settled at Boston, 1651; *m* Hannah–;
7–Josiah (1654-1717), *m* 1685, Mary Greenough (*b* 1662);
6–Daniel (*b* 1694), Hopkinton, Mass.; *m* 1726, Mary Wood;
5–Josiah (*b* 1730), Coleraine, Mass.; Am. Rev.; *m* 1760, Mary Sanford (*b* 1732);
4–Joseph (1772-1841), Luzerne, N.Y.; *m* ca. 1794, Abigail Call (1776-1838);
3–Achsah (1816-45),*m* Jonas **Selleck** (3 above);
2–Jerome Bradley (1837-1909), to South Glens Falls, N.Y., 1899; farmer; *m* 1859, Mary Jane Bentley (1837-71; Cornelius[3], *m* Mary Brayton); issue: I–Isabella (1 above); II–Mary Elizabeth (*b* 1863; *m* John Menge); III–Phoebe (1865-1917); IV–George Henry (*b* 1867; *m* Amy Gray Noyes); V–Sarah Helen (1868-88).
1–Grad. Glens Falls Acad., '80. Taught rural and village schools; asst. principal, South Glens Falls H.S., 1894-1921, with exception of 1 yr. during which acted as principal; retired. Mem. I.A.G., N.Y. Hist. Assn. Republican. Club: Woman's Civic. Residence: 6 Harrison Ave., South Glens Falls, N.Y.

1–**SHAFFER, Frank Holmes,** *b* Cincinnati, O., Mar. 31, 1857.
9–Edward **Doty,** Mayflower Pilgrim (qv);
8–Capt. Samuel (ca. 1643-1715), New Piscataway, N.J.; commd. lt. mil. co., 1675; *m* 1678, Jane Harman;
7–Samuel (1679-1750), *m* 1700, Elizabeth Hull (*b* 1679);
6–John (1707-57), *m* Oey T. Killman;
5–Anna (1739-1828), Basking Ridge, N.J.; *m* 1760, Zephaniah **Lewis** (1734-77);
4–Thomas (1765-1831), *m* 1789, Susanna McCoy (1773-1821; Gavin[5], famous hero of Am. Rev.);
3–David Lewis (1797-1840), Hamilton, O.; *m* 1821, Sarah Voorheis (1802-87);
2–Susan Ann (1824-94), *m* 1845, William **Shaffer** (1817-93), removed from Westmoreland Co., Pa., to Cincinnati; issue: I–Sarah Catherine (1846-63); II–Ella Keck (1848-1925, *m* Charles L. F. Huntington, 1845-1926); III–Nettie Jane (*b* 1851); IV–Lewis William (1854-98; *m* 1883, Sallie Smith); V–Frank Holmes (1 above); VI–Frederick David (*b* 1859; *m* Lena Arnold); VII–Stanley (1861-1928; *m* Esther Williams); VIII–Grace Gray (*b* 1868; *m* 1897, James R. Reeder, *d* 1929).
1–*m* Sept. 25, 1883, Alicia Adelaide Bakewell (qv for issue).
1–B.A., Yale, '77; LL.B., U.Mich., 1881. Attorney. Mem. S.M.D. Residence: 2260 Park Av., Walnut Hills, Cincinnati, O.

1–**SHAFFER, Alicia Adelaide Bakewell (Mrs. Frank H.),** *b* Louisville, Ky., June 14, 1862.
3–William Gifford **Bakewell** (1762-1821; of noble descent; owner of Manor of Crich, Bakewell, Derbyshire, Eng.); came from Eng. on tour of inspection, and decided to remain, and relinquished his titles and property in Eng.; settled at New Haven, Conn.; removed to "Fatland Ford," nr. Phila., Pa.; entertained many celebrities, among them Darwin, Audubon and Washington; *m* 1786, Lucy Green (1765-1804);
2–William Gifford (2 below).
9–John **Howland,** Mayflower Pilgrim (qv);
8–Hope (1629-83), *m* 1646, John **Chipman** (qv);
7–Desire (1673-1705), Barnstable, Mass.; *m* 1693, Melatiah **Bourne** (1673-1742), Sandwich, Mass.;
6–Bathsheba (1703-ca. 1787), *m* 1st, William **Newcomb** (*b* 1702);
5–Sarah (*b* 1737), *m* 1760, Benjamin **Fessenden** (1739-83), of Sandwich;
4–Rebecca (1762-1830), *m* 1782, Maj. Nathan **Dillingham** (1759-1836), drummer and fifer in Am. Rev. aet. 17; commd. maj. in War 1812 (John[5], Am. Rev.; Simeon[6]);
3–Charles (1799-1834), propr. boys' prep. sch., Pittsfield, Mass.; *m* 1827, Martha Heaton;
2–Maria Allen (2 below).
6–Samuel **Heaton,** from Ireland in early 18th Century; *m* Sarah Hancock (nr. relative of John Hancock);
5–Isaac (*b* 1730), soldier colonial wars; *m* 1760, Hannah Bowen (Henry[6], *m* Anna–);

4–Henry, Am. Rev.; mem. Pa. Legislature; *m* 1789, Martha Morgan (dau. of Gen. Morgan, Am. Rev.);
3–Martha (1806-79), *m* 1st, Charles **Dillingham** (3 above).
2–William Gifford **Bakewell** (*b* Eng. 1799-1871), removed with his sister and bro.-in-law, John James Audubon, to Ky., ca. 1810, settled at Louisville; shipping and commn. mcht.; removed to New Orleans, 1848; administrator of Gordon estate; owned mansion on Jefferson and 8th Sts.; *m* Alicia Adelaide Matthews (*d* 1847); *m* 2d, 1854, Maria Allen Dillingham (1830-1918); issue (2nd marriage): I–Lucy Audubon (1859-86; *m* Ira S. Millikin); II–Alice Adelaide (1 above); III–Ann Gordon (*b* 1865; *m* Robert Tyler, *d*); IV–Willie (*b* 1871; *m* Harry T. Crittenden).
1–*m* Sept. 25, 1883, Frank Holmes Shaffer (qv); issue: (all *b* Cincinnati, O.): 1–Lucy Kennedy, *b* Oct. 5, 1885; Smith, '08; 2–Annie Bakewell (Apr. 18, 1888-Jan. 27, 1911); Smith, '09; 3–Susan Lewis, *b* Dec. 11, 1892; Smith Coll., and U.Cincinnati, '16; 4–Frank Holmes, Jr., *b* Aug. 18, 1896; Yale, '18; *m* Apr. 10, 1926, Elizabeth, dau. of Charles Blake, of Cincinnati; 5–William Bakewell, *b* July 21, 1899; Yale, '21; *m* May 14, 1927, Mary Beekman, Smith Coll., '22; dau. of Albert Beekman Mills (issue: William Bakewell, *b* Jan. 1, 1929); 6–Frederic Stanley, *b* Dec. 19, 1902; Yale, '23; *m* Oct. 29, 1927, Margaret Sherlock, dau. of William Ernst Minor (issue: Frederic Stanley, *b* Sept. 7, 1928).
1–Ed. U.Cincinnati. Mem. S.M.D. Residence: 2260 Park Av., Walnut Hills, Cincinnati, O.

1–**SHAW, George Guilford,** *b* Dayton, O., May 20, 1865.
7–John **Shaw,** a Quaker, from Eng. on William Penn's 2d voyage, 1699; settled at Northampton, Mass.; *m* Susanna–;
6–James (1694-1761), *m* 1718, Mary Brown;
5–Alexander (1734-90), *m* Sarah Brown, widow (*d* ca. 1812);
4–George (1760-1801), *m* Mary Wilson (*b* 1763);
3–David (1796-1860), *m* 1819, Nancy Speer Andrews, of Dayton, O.;
2–George Wilson (2 below).
8–Daniel (Perrin) **Perrine** (qv);
7–Peter (1667-1743), *m* Ann Holmes;
6–James (*b* 1720), *m* 1745, Neltje Stoothof;
5–James (1746-1826), *m* 1773, Hannah Bennett (*b* 1753);
4–John (*b* 1774), *m* 1800, Sarah Voorhies (*b* 1771);
3–James (1801-64), *m* 1830, Julia Ann Darst;
2–Mary P. (*b* 1833), *m* 1852, George Wilson **Shaw** (1822-1907), of Dayton, O.; issue: I–Ella Nora (1854-77); II–Nancy Andrews (*b* 1856; *m* 1879, John Bradley Greene, *d* 1893); III–James Perrine (1859-81); IV–Julia Perrine (*b* 1863; *m* 1890, Frank Jefferson Patterson, *d* 1901); V–George Guilford (1 above).
1–*m* Jan. 24, 1901, Sophia Craighead (qv for issue).
1–Ed. Williston Sem., Easthampton, Mass. Banker, mfr.; pres. Dayton Paper Novelty Co. Clubs: Buz Fuz, Bicycle, Vingt-et-un, Dayton Country, Miami Valley Hunt and Polo. Residence: "Fairforest," Hills and Dales, Dayton, O.

1–**SHAW, Sophia Craighead (Mrs. George G.),** *b* Dayton, O., Feb. 16, 1868.
8–Rev. Robert **Craighead** (*d* 1711), a native of Scotland, pastor Presbyn. ch. of Donoughmore, Ireland, 34 yrs.; subsequently minister at Londonderry, when the gates of the city were closed against the Papal forces of James, II, whose purpose was to massacre the Protestants; escaped during the second day of the siege, and made his way to Glasgow, Scotland; later returned to Ireland and *d* in Londonderry;
7–Rev. Thomas (ca. 1660-1739), ed. in Scotland as physician; later studied divinity; pastor in Ireland for several years; from Ireland to N.E., 1715; to the "Jerseys," 1723; to Lancaster Co., Pa., 1733; *m* in Scotland, Margaret– (1664-1738);
6–John, mcht., Phila.; purchased a large tract of land nr. Carlisle; *m* Rachel R–;
5–Thomas (1737-1807), *m* Margaret Gilson (1738-1813);
4–Thomas (1768-1852), miller and farmer; *m* 1796, Rebecca Weakley (1773-1858);
3–Dr. John Boyd (1800-68), ed. Dickinson Coll.; M.D., U.Pa., 1826; removed from Pa. to Mansfield, O., 1827, thence to Dayton, 1830; *m* 1st, 1829, Mary Wallace Purdy (1811-39);
2–William (2 below).
4–Reed **Wright** (1774-1845), from Va. to Ohio; *m* Sarah Turner Mastin (1784-1876);
3–Francis Mastin (1810-69), state and co. auditor; *m* 1837, Sophia Adams Corwin (1813-59; Moses Bledsoe[4] [*b* 1790], *m* Margaret Fox, *b* 1791);
2–Sophia Margaret (1838-1920), *m* 1865, William **Craighead** (1838-1905), grad. Miami U., '55; lawyer, Dayton, 1859-1905; issue: I–Sophia (1 above); II–Jeannette (1872-73).
1–*m* Jan. 24, 1901, George Guilford Shaw (qv); issue: 1–George Wilson, *b* Dayton, O., June 5, 1902; Yale, '19; 2–William Craighead (*b* and *d* Jan. 1904); 3–Margaret Craighead, *b* Dayton, Aug. 28, 1906.
1–Ed. Cooper Sem., Dayton, O. Residence: "Fairforest;" Hills and Dales, Dayton, O.

1–**SHAW, George Wright,** *b* Bradford, Vt., June 13, 1864.
10–Abraham **Shaw** (qv);
9–John (1630-1704), Weymouth, Mass.; *m* 1652, Alice Phillips (Nicholas[10]);
8–Nicholas (1662-1717), *m* 1686, Deborah Whitmarsh (1659-1717; Nicholas[9]);
7–Benjamin (1706-32), Abington, Mass.; *m* 1727, Hannah Tirrel;
6–William (1730-1810), Bridgewater, Mass.; *m* 1st, 1753, Hannah West (*d* 1772);
5–Dan (1758-1814), Lyme, N.H., Bradford, Vt.; selectman; soldier in Am. Rev.; later col. of militia; *m* 1780, Joanna Perkins (1761-1803), of Middleboro, Mass. (Dea. Isaac[6]);
4–Abraham (1791-1876), Bradford, Vt.; *m* 1813, Mary Jenkins (1793-1855; Joseph[5]);
3–Joseph Wright (1814-70), E. Somerville, Mass.; furniture mfr.; *m* 1835, Almyra A. Tisdale (1818-1902; Asa[4], *m* Sarah Barnard, dau. of Ebenezer Wright, of Hanover, N. H.);
2–John Everett (2 below).
8–Gideon **George,** from Eng., settled at Salem, Mass., 1662; removed to Rowley;
7–John (1662-1715), Haverhill; *m* 1697, Ann Swaddock (*d* 1763); she *m* 2d, Nathan Simons 1718;
6–Gideon (1712-87), Kingston, N.H.; Am. Rev.; *m* 1733, Elizabeth Jewett (1718-86; Dea. Daniel[7], of Rowley, Mass.);
5–Gideon (1740-1823), in Am. Rev.; present at Burgoyne's Surrender; *m* 1758, Deborah Stevens;
4–Stephen (1771-1853), of Bradford, and Newbury, Vt.; *m* 1797, Sarah Towle (*d* 1865);
3–Sargent Towle (1813-1904), merchant, Bradford; *m* 1833, Melissa Greenleaf (1818-1901; Lowell[4]);
2–Orinda Ann (1839-91), *m* 1862, John Everett **Shaw** (1837-82), of Boston, merchant; *m* 2d, George A. Hawkins; issue (1st marriage): I–George Wright (1 above); II–Delia Evelyn (*b* 1867).
1–*m* Aug. 17, 1887, Emily May Merritt, *b* Tecumseh, Mich., May 12, 1864; dau. of Selah Oliphant Merritt, of Tecumseh, Mich. (William Henry[3], of Hillsdale, Mich.); issue: 1–Emily Wright, *b* Walla Walla, Wash., June 9, 1888; *m* Daniel E., son of John Lawrence Harris, of Berkeley, Calif.; 2–Genevieve (July 10, 1890-*d* infancy); 3–Harry Romeyn, *b* Corvallis, Ore., Aug. 17, 1891; served in World War, overseas; *m* Feb. 17, 1920, Vena Marie Doty, of Oakland, Calif.; (issue: Romeyn Gordon, *b* 1921); 4–Frances Lucile, *b* Corvallis, Oct. 4, 1893; *m* Apr. 1, 1916, Joseph W. Loughlin, of Oakland, Calif.; (issue: Joseph Barry, *b* 1918); 5–Margaret Gwendolyn (Aug. 15, 1896-July 1, 1921); *m* May 31, 1920, Joseph Marvin, of Berkeley, Calif.
1–A.B., Dartmouth, '87 (Phi Delta Theta), A.M., 1889; Ph.D., Willamette U., 1895. Prof. natural science, Whitman Coll., Walla Walla, Wash., 1887-89, Pacific U., Forest Grove, Ore., 1889-91; prof. chemistry, Ore. Agrl. Coll., Corvallis, 1891-99; later prof. agrl. chemistry and agronomy, U.Calif.; chief appraiser, Federal Land Bank, Berkeley, Calif., 1915-18; supervisor of farm loans, Security-First Nat. Bank, of Los Angeles, 1920–. Mem. O.F.P.A., S.R. Conglist. Republican. Residence: 2220 West Boul., Los Angeles, Calif.

1–**SHAW, Fern Eva West (Mrs. Hartley),** *b* Fort Dodge, Ia., 1877.

9–Francis **West** (1606-92), from Eng., 1639; settled at Duxbury, Mass.; freeman, 1656; surveyor of highways, 1658; constable, 1661; mem. Grand Inquest; *m* 1639, Margery Reeves;
8–Samuel (1643-89), Duxbury, Mass.; constable, 1664; *m* 1668, Tryphosa Partridge (*d* 1701; George[9], *m* Sarah Tracy);
7–Dea. Francis (1669-1731), Preston, Stonington and Tolland, Conn.; 1st dea. of Tolland ch.; *m* 1696, Mercy Miner (1673-1751; Dr. Joseph[8], in King Philip's War; Thomas[9], qv);
6–Amasa (*b* 1704), Tolland, Conn.; in Am. Rev.; *m* 1st, 1730, Amy Hatch (1713-1756; Joseph[7], *m* Amy Allen);
5–Oliver (1733-1816), in Am. Rev.; mem. Com. Corr. at Lee, Mass., 1777; mem. 1st Bd. of Selectmen; *m* 1757, Thankful Nye (1736-1806; Capt. Ebenezer[6], *m* Sarah Newcomb);
4–Joshua (1775-1854), Lee, Mass., thence to Ohio; *m* 1798, Mary Newell (1778-1862; Josiah[5], *m* Ruth Root);
3–Josiah Newell (1805-77), Tabor, Ia.; *m* 1827, Louisa Hinckley (1808-49; Silas[4], *m* Anne Bradley);
2–Henry Silas (1840-1923), from Windham, O., to Ia., to Neb., to Los Angeles, Calif.; served in Civil War, spent ten months in Confed. prison at Tyler, Tex.; *m* 1870, Nina Jones (*b* 1849; Wiley[3], *m* Isabelle Van Dyke Frost, of N.C. and Tenn.); issue: I–Iva C.; II–Fern E. (1 above).
1–*m* Sept. 17, 1901, Hartley Shaw, *b* Bloomfield, Ind., June 2, 1874; son of Lucien Shaw, of Glendale, Calif.; issue (all *b* Los Angeles, Calif.): 1–Dorothy, *b* Dec. 26, 1902; *m* July 12, 1928, John Bernard, son of John Faust; 2–Evelyn, *b* July 17, 1904; *m* Oct. 12, 1928, Arthur Edwin, son of John Lawrie; 3–Lucien West, *b* Jan. 30, 1910.
1–U.Calif., '00. Mem. S.M.D., D.F.P.A., D.A.C., D.A.R., I.A.G. Clubs: Women's University (Los Angeles), Glendale Coll. Women's. Conglist. Residence: 212 W. Chevy Chase Drive, Glendale, Calif.

1–**SHAWVER, John Laney,** *b* Bellefontaine, O., Apr. 6, 1859.
5–Daniel **Shawver** (*b* 1734), served in battle of Dresden, Saxony, 1756, with brother George; both arrived in America, 1758; Daniel settled at Germantown, Pa.; aided in constrn. of forts about Phila.; George settled in Va.;
4–Daniel, III (*b* 1760), of Hanover, Pa.;
3–Daniel, IV (1781-1864), of Greensburg, Pa.; *m* Mary E. Shultz (1783-1867; George[4], from Germany, Am. Rev., *m* Elizabeth Shumaker);
2–Elias (2 below).
6–Andrew **Kirkpatrick** (1710-79), left Watties Neach, Co. Dumfries, Scotland, 1725; came in company with bro. Alexander, from Belfast, Ireland, to N.J., 1736; settled nr. Basking Ridge; aided Cont. Army during Jersey campaign by giving food;
5–Capt. John (1738-1822), 1st lt., later capt., 2d Regt., Sussex Co. Militia, Am. Rev., 1776-81; elder Yellow Frame Ch.; *m* 1759, Lydia Lewis (1742-1831), made clothing for Cont. Army; sent cattle to feed army; sent venison to Valley Forge (Edward[6]; Samuel[7], to America, 1732);
4–Andrew (1761-1814), War 1812; *m* 1789, Phoebe Read (1762-1814; Joseph[5], *m* Sarah–);
3–Martha (1791-1882), *m* 1807, Amos **Williams** (1783-1855), served in War 1812 (John[4], pvt. 1st Regt., Sussex Co. Militia, Am. Rev., *m* Rebecca–);
2–Sarah (1821-92), *m* Elias **Shawver** (1817-84), contractor and builder; issue: I–Samuel W. (1840-71; *m* Caroline Williams); II–Mary A. (1841-42); III–Eliza J. (1842-68; *m* Simon Anstine); IV–Matilda E. (1844-55); V–Sarah E. (1846-95; *m* Simon K. Miller); VI–David B. (1850-1918; *m* Louisa A. Earl); VII–William F. (1853-1917; *m* Udora Dowell); VIII–John L. (1 above); IX–Arie L. (1863-1921; *m* Cory L. Lane).
1–*m* Apr. 8, 1885, Mary E. Miller, *b* Gretna, O., Nov. 1, 1864; dau. of John N. Miller of Gretna; issue (all *b* Bellefontaine, O.): 1–Charles Ernest, *b* Feb. 21, 1886; Chicago Sch. Architecture, '06; *m* Apr. 7, 1909, Leigh A. Wolfinger (issue: Christine, *b* 1914; Myron E., *b* 1924); 2–Grace Viola, *b* Mar. 21, 1890; Ohio Northern U., '08; *m* Aug. 24, 1911, Clyde L. Lynn (issue: Ralph J., *b* 1913; Dorothy L., *b* 1915; Kenneth C., *b* 1924); 3–Frances Kate, *b* Sept. 7, 1892; Chautauqua Inst., '08; *m* Mar. 18, 1914, Ray T. Miksch (issue: Mary E., *b* 1915; Byron J., *b* 1917; Robert T., and Russell S., *b* 1919); 4–Lawrence, *b* Feb. 9, 1898; *m* Mar. 8, 1922, Agnes A. Shick (issue: Charles L., *b* 1922; Janet L., *b* 1926); 5–Lucile (July 28-Dec. 2, 1904).
1–Ed. Wittemberg Coll., 1883; Chicago Sch. Architecture, 1894. Educator for 15 yrs.; lecturer; editor, 15 yrs. Author: Artistic Architecture; Plank Frame Construction; The Empress Eugenie; The Kirkpatricks; The Shawvers; That Registered Calf. Mem. S.R., etc. Winter place: DeLand, Fla. Residence: Shady Nook Pl., Bellefontaine, O.

1–**SHELDON, Mary Thomas Rogers (Mrs. William O.),** *b* E. Bridgewater, Mass., Feb. 21, 1867.
6–John **Rogers** (*d* 1661), of Duxbury and Scituate, Mass.; *d* in Weymouth, Mass.;
5–Thomas, of Marshfield, Mass.;
4–Samuel (1766-1838), of E. Bridgewater, Mass.; *m* 1790, Betty Allen;
3–Charles (1799-1880), *m* 1821, Sarah Thompson;
2–Wales (2 below).
9–Samuel **Allen** (qv);
8–Samuel (*b* 1632), settled in E. Bridgewater, Mass., 1660; was 2d town clk.; deacon; *m* Sarah Partridge (*b* 1639; George[9], of Duxbury, Mass.);
7–Ebenezer (1674-1730), *m* 1698, Rebeckah Scate;
6–Jacob (*b* 1702), *m* 1730, Abigail Kingman (1705-70; Henry[7], *m* 2d, Bethiah Newcomb);
5–Capt. Jacob (1739-77), Am. Rev.; *m* 1762, Abigail Bailey (*b* 1738; Israel[6]; John[7]; John[8]);
4–Betty (1768-1831), *m* 1790, Samuel **Rogers** (4 above).
8–John **Thompson** (qv);
7–John (1648-1725), Middleboro, Mass.; *m* Mary Tinkham (1664-1731);
6–Jacob (1710-59), *m* 1735, Mary Howard;
5–Ebenezer (1737-1832), Halifax, Mass.; *m* Elizabeth Besse (1741-1820);
4–Maj. Nathaniel (1761-1839), maj. militia; *m* 1785, Sarah Thayer (1764-1810);
3–Sarah (1801-72), *m* Charles **Rogers** (3 above).
9–William **Gerrish** (qv);
8–John (1646-1714), *m* 1666, Elizabeth Waldron (Maj. Richard[9], qv);
7–Timothy (1684-1755), *m* 1706, Sarah Eliot (*b* 1684; Robert[8], a Welshman, *b* in Eng., 1643, first settler of Portsmouth, N.H., councilor of N.H., 1692-1715, *m* Sarah–);
6–John (1710-50), *m* 1734, Margery Jackson (*b* 1711; Dr. George[7], *m* Joanna, dau. of William Pepperell, qv);
5–John (*b* 1735), Dover, N.H.; *m* 1760, Abigail Grace Phillips (1734-1812; Andrew[6], *m* Sarah–);
4–Andrew (*b* 1774), Kittery, Me.; *m* Ruth Ellis (1779-1815);
3–Ira (1810-96), Fairhaven, Mass.; *m* 1830, Eveline Eldredge (1811-75; Killey[4]);
2–Sarah Louisa (1843-1918), *m* 1866, Wales **Rogers** (1825-89), of E. Bridgewater; issue: I–Mary Thomas (1 above); II–Charles Wales (*b* 1869; *m* Maud Savage); III–Harrie Gerrish (1872-73).
1–*m* Aug. 15, 1887, William Oren Sheldon, *b* N. Billerica, Mass., Feb. 2, 1860; son of Oren Sheldon; issue: 1–William Mallory, *b* Summertown, Tenn., July 22, 1891; B.S., Carnegie Inst. Tech., '11; *m* Oct. 30, 1915, Mercedes I. dau. of Jacob Roeser (issue: William Oren); 2–Evart Rogers, *b* Summertown, Sept. 14, 1893; ed. Middlebury, 1911; *m* June 4, 1916, Dorothy Helen, dau. of Henry Vincent Hucker (issue: Rogers Hucker); 3–Miriam, *b* New Bedford, Mass., July 21, 1896; ed. Art Students League of New York; *m* Dec. 28, 1929, Arthur F. son of Henry L. Wolff; 4–Lawrence Kimball, *b* Fairhaven, Mass., Mar. 11, 1898; sgt., U.S.A., World War; LL.B., Cleveland Law School, 1926; *m* Nov. 16, 1929, Twila Marie, dau. of Thomas J. Greene; 5–Allyn Wight, *b* Newark, N.J., June 5, 1903; Wharton Sch., U.Pa., ex-'25; *m* Oct. 21, 1929, Mary T., dau. of Edward Clinton Letchman.
1–Librarian, E. Bridgewater Public Library, 1883-87. Mem. D.A.R., N.E.S., Lakewood Woman's Club. Republican. Residence: 1475 Clarence Av., Lakewood, O.

1–**SHEPARD, Lola Adeline,** *b* Gurnee, Ill., Mar. 7, 1878.
10–Samuel **Morse** (qv);

9-John (1611-ca. 1657), from Eng.; 34th signer of town covenant of Dedham, owned land there, 1636; to Boston, 1654; tailor; returned to Eng., 1655; *m* Annas, or Annis Chickering (*d* 1691);
8-Joseph (1640-89), *m* Priscilla Colburn (1646-1731);
7-Rev. Joseph (1671-1732), *m* Amity Harris (*d* 1732);
6-Amity, *m* 1735, Thomas **Shepard** (*d* 1782);
5-Jacob (1737/38-1798), pvt. Am. Rev.; *m* 1765, Bathsheba Puffer (1745-1809; John[6]; John[7]; Matthias[8]; George[9]);
4-Thomas (1766-1835), *m* 1792, Elizabeth Richards (1766-1843; Benjamin[5] [1738-1816], pvt. Am. Rev., *m* 1763, Mary Belcher [1742-1820]; William[6]; Jeremiah[7]; Nathaniel[8]; Edward[9]);
3-Joel Richards (1807-81), *m* 1835, Adeline Capen (1815-59; Asa[4] [1785-1873], *m* 1812, Mary [Dickerman Clapp], a widow [1788-1873]; James[5], Am. Rev., *m* Elizabeth Cummings; Edward[6], Am. Rev.; Jonathan[7]; Samuel[8]; John[9]; Bernard[10]);
2-Henry (2 below).
10-George **Parkhurst** (1618-1698/99), from Eng. ca. 1635; at Watertown, Mass., 1642; *m* 1st, 1643, Sarah Browne;
9-John (1644-1725), *m* ca. 1670, Abigail Garfield (1646-1726);
8-John (*b* 1671/72), *m* Abigail Morse (*b* 1677; desc. Joseph, 1587-1646);
7-Josiah (*b* 1706), Weston, Mass.; *m* 1735, Sarah Carter;
6-Josiah (1736/37-1832), mem. Train Band at Weston, 1757; *m* 1758, Elizabeth Bigelow (*b* 1738), of Newton (Nathaniel[7]; Joshua[8]; Joshua[9]; John[10]);
5-John (1760-1836), pvt. Am. Rev.; *m* 1st, 1783, Sarah Bullard (*d* 1818);
4-Josiah (1789-1882), *m* 1813, Rachel Harkness (1794-1868);
3-Cordelia (1827-85), *m* 1845, Horace Leonard **Chandler** (1819-78; George[4] [1797-1855], Lake Co., Ill., War 1812; *m* 1818, Julia Ann Dickinson, *b* 1803);
2-Ella Louise (1850-1913), *m* 1867, Henry **Shepard** (1845-1911), farmer.
1-B.A., Lake Forest Coll., 1902. Librarian. Mem. D.A.R., I.A.G., A.A.U.W. Residence: 409 Franklin St., Waukegan, Ill.

1-**SHEPARD, Perry Melville,** *b* Chicago, Ill., Feb. 13, 1883.
9-Robert **Lay** (1617-89), *m* 1647, Sarah– (1616-76);
8-Phebe (1651-99), *m* 1667, Capt. John **Denison** (1646-98; Capt. George[9]; William[10], qv);
7-Phebe (bap. 1690-1775), *m* 1706, Lt. Ebenezer **Billings** (1684-1760; Ebenezer[8]; William[9], qv);
6-Abigail (1707-89), *m* Dea. Samuel **Prentice** (1702-73), Stonington (Samuel[7]; Thomas[8]; Capt. Thomas[9], qv);
5-Dorothy (1727-72), *m* 1743, Capt. Isaac **Shepard** (see Vol. II, p. 202);
4-John (1765-1837), *m* 1790, Anna Gore;
3-Job (1801-55), *m* 1833, Abigail Sage Ellsworth (see Vol. III, p. 639);
2-Henry Martyn (2 below).
11-John **Thompson,** gentleman, of Preston, Northamptonshire, Eng.; *m* Alice–;
10-Bridget (*d* 1643), *m* 1640, Capt. George **Denison** (1618 or 21-1694; William[11], qv);
9-Hannah (*b* 1643), *m* 1659, Nathaniel **Chesebrough** (bap. 1630-1678; William[10], qv);
8-Anna (1660-1751), *m* 1685, Samuel **Richardson** (1659/60-1712/13; Amos[9]);
7-Anna (1688-1727 or 29), *m* 1715/16, William **Avery** (*b* ca. 1687; John[8]; Capt. James[9], qv; Christopher[10], qv);
6-Richardson (*b* 1717/18), *m* 1740, Sarah Plumb (*b* 1711; Joseph[7]; John[8]; Robert[9]; John[10], qv);
5-Anna (1744-1829), *m* 1764, Judge Obadiah **Gore** (see Vol. III, p. 639);
4-Anna (1772-1805), *m* John **Shepard** (4 above).
10-Robert **Blott** (*d* 1665), *m* Susannah– (*d* 1660);
9-Mary (*d* ante 1654), *m* Thomas **Woodford** (qv);
8-Mary (*d* 1684), *m* 1653, Isaac **Sheldon** (ca. 1629-1708; Isaac[9], qv);
7-Mindwell (1666-1735), *m* 1687, Lt. John **Lyman** (1660-1740; Lt. John[8]; Richard[9], qv);
6-Elizabeth (*b* 1702), *m* 1722, Abner **Moseley** (*b* 1669; Joseph[7]; Lt. John[8]; John[9], qv);
5-Mary (1737 or 1738-1823), *m* 1758, Lt. Solomon **Ellsworth** (1737-1822);
4-John (1773-1823), *m* Ruth Stoughton;
3-Abigail Sage, *m* Job **Shepard** (3 above).
10-Emanuel **Downing** (*d* 1653 or 1656; son of Rev. Emanuel); *m* Lucy Winthrop (bap. 1601-post 1656; Adam[11], among his sons was the first gov. of Mass.);
9-Mary (*d* 1647), *m* Anthony **Stoddard** (qv);
8-Rev. Samuel or Solomon (1644-1729), *m* 1670, Hester or Esther Warham (bap. 1644-1736; Rev. John[9]);
7-Esther (1672-1771), *m* 1694, Rev. Timothy **Edwards** (1669-1758; Richard[8]; William[9], qv);
6-Ann (1699-1790), *m* 1734, Capt. John **Ellsworth** (1697-1784);
5-Ann (1741-1819), *m* Col. Lemuel **Stoughton** (1731-93; Nathaniel[6]; John[7]; Anc. Thomas[8]; Mr. Thomas[9], qv);
4-Ruth (1776-1859), *m* John **Ellsworth** (4 above).
8-Rev. John **Bradner,** *m* ca. 1720, Miss Colville (Lord Robert[9]);
7-Rev. Benoni (1733-1804), *m* Rebecca Bridges (1732-77);
6-Elizabeth, *m* John **Stuart** (*d* 1770);
5-Judge Nathan (1758-1844), *m* 1784, Anna Morton (*b* 1759; Rev. James[6]);
4-Henry Young (1784-1870), *m* 1811, Deborah Beebe (*d* 1814);
3-Col. Charles Beebe (1814-81), *m* 1841, Frances Maria Welles;
2-Frances W. (2 below).
9-John **Talcott** (qv);
8-Capt. Samuel (1634/35-1691), *m* 1661/62, Hannah Holyoke (1644-78; Hon. Elizur[9], *m* Mary, dau. of Col. William Pynchon, qv);
7-Dea. Benjamin (1674-1729), *m* 1698/99, Sarah Hollister;
6-Col. Elizur (1709-97), *m* 1730, Ruth Wright (1711-91; Daniel[7], *m* Elinor, dau. Edward Benton; James[8]; Thomas[9]);
5-Prudence (1757-1839), *m* 1780, George **Welles** (1756-1813); see Vol. II, p. 202;
4-Gen. Henry (1780-1833), *m* 1812, Sarah Spalding (see Vol. II);
3-Frances Maria, *m* Charles B. **Stuart** (3 above).
10-Mathew **Marvin** (qv);
9-Sarah (1632-1702), *m* 1648, Ens. William **Goodrich** (qv);
8-Sarah (1649-1700), *m* 1667, John **Hollister** (ca. 1644-1711; Lt. John[9], qv);
7-Sarah (1676-1715), *m* Dea. Benjamin **Talcott** (7 above).
2-Frances Welles Stuart (*b* 1848, *m* 1869, Judge Henry Martyn **Shepard** (1837-1904); for issue and other lineages, see Vol. II, p. 202, Vol. III, p. 639.
1-*m* Sept. 18, 1920, Eleanor Ogden West (qv); issue: 1-Frederick West, *b* Chicago, Ill., May 15, 1922; 2-Deborah Stuart, *b* Indianapolis, Ind., Mar. 14, 1925.
1-Hobart, ex-'03 (Sigma Phi). Pres. The Wire Hardware Co., 1910-14, and treas. of its successor, the Cassady-Fairbank Mfg. Co., 1914, and v.p. of its successor, The Washburn Co., 1922-24, all of Chicago; v.p. The Haley M-O Co., at Indianapolis, 1924-26, and at Geneva, N.Y., 1926, pres. 1928. Maj., Q.M.C., and participated in 4 campaigns of A.E.F. in France; on eligible list of Gen. Staff, U.S.A.; maj., staff specialist, O.R.C. Trustee Hobart Coll., 1922–. Mem. S.A.R., A.L., I.A.G. Clubs: Saddle and Cycle, Racquet, University (Chicago), Country (Rochester, N.Y.), Country (Geneva, N.Y.). Residence: 803 S. Main St., Geneva, N.Y.

1-**SHEPARD, Eleanor Ogden West (Mrs. Perry M.),** *b* Pittsfield, Mass., Sept. 18, 1892.
10-Rev. John **Ward** (1606-93; son of Rev. Nathaniel), *m* Alice Edmunds;
9-Elizabeth (1647-1714), *m* 1663, Nathaniel **Saltonstall** (Richard[10]; Sir Richard[11], qv);
8-Elizabeth (*b* 1668), *m* ca. 1684, Rev. John **Denison** (1665-89; John[9]; David[10], William[11], qv);
7 Hannah (1689-1772), *m* 1710, Nathaniel **Kingsbury** (Joseph[8]; Henry[9]; Henry[10]);
6-Hannah (1719-95), *m* 1738, John **Chapman** (1714-74; John[7]);
5-Hannah (1753-1814), *m* 1774, Abel **West**;
4-Abel (1780-1871), *m* Matilda Thompson (1782-1866; Thomas[5]);
3-John Chapman (1811-93), *m* 1844, Lydia Maria Goodrich (1816-95; Maj. Butler[4]; Caleb[5]; Gideon[6]; Ephraim[7]; William[8], qv);
2-Frederick Thomas (*b* 1855), *m* 1886, Anna Sheldon Ogden (for issue and other lineages, see Vol III, p. 639).

1–*m* Sept. 18, 1920, Perry Melville Shepard (qv for issue).
1–Residence: 803 S. Main St. Geneva, N.Y.

1–**SHIELDS, Amelia Eliza Kittrell (Mrs. Van Winder),** *b* Lexington, N.C., Sept. 13, 1857.
5–Jonathan **Kittrell** (*d* 1812), capt. militia, Granville Co., N. C., 1771; justice;
4–Joshua (*d* 1802), *m* his cousin, Ruth Kittrell;
3–Benjamin (1798-1836), *m* 1819, Martha Long; *m* 2d, 1822, Eliza T. Howze;
2–Benjamin Anderson (2 below).
8–Col. William **Burgess** (qv);
7–Capt. Edward (*d* 1722), commr. Port of Londontown, Anne Arundel Co.: justice Provincial Ct.; capt. of foot; *m* Sarah Chew (Col. Samuel[8], *m* Ann, dau. of William Ayres, of Va.; John[9], qv);
6–Sarah, *m* 1709, Benjamin **Gaither** (*d* 1741), of "Gaither's Fancy," Howard Co., Md. (John[7], *m* Ruth Mosely);
5–Edward, *m* Eleanor Whittle;
4–Burgess, *m* 1791, Amelia Martin;
3–Sarah (*b* 1796), *m* 1824, Robert **Foster**;
2–Amelia Emma (1830-64), *m* 1854, Benjamin Anderson **Kittrell** (1831-65); lawyer; issue: I–Louisa Melissa (*b* 1855, *m* James Madison Wesson); II–Amelia Eliza (1 above); III–Sarah Letitia (1860-1909; *m* Robert Walter Lassiter).
1–*m* Feb. 27, 1878, Rev. Van Winder Shields, D.D. (July 3, 1849-*d* May 13, 1927); son of William Bayard Shields; issue: 1–Bayard Benoist, *b* Aberdeen, Miss., Feb. 19, 1879; U.South, '98; Washington and Lee U. 1904-06; 2–Robert Benoist, *b* New Berne, N.C., July 31, 1881; U. South, '00; *m* Nov. 15, 1912, Cora Julie, dau. of Benjamin F. Bowen (issue: Robert Benoist; Benjamin Bayard); 3–Van Winder (Apr. 17, 1885-Aug. 1886); 4–Van Winder (*b* New Berne, Sept. 10, 1889-*d* Pasadena, Calif., June 27, 1929); U.South, '08; Washington and Lee, '11; *m* Feb. 27, 1918, Janet Phelan (issue: Robert Bayard, *b* Mar. 6, 1929); 5–Amelia Dunbar, *b* Jacksonville, Fla., Nov. 22, 1895; C.D.A.; Junior League, Washington, D.C.; *m* May 10, 1916, Carl Robertson, son of William Kurtz, *m* Eleanor Robertson (issue: Amelia Shields; Carl Robertson, Jr.);
1–Mem. C.D.A. (hon. pres. Fla. Soc.), Ladies' Friday Musical Club, Old Settlers' Garden Club (hon. mem.). Residence: 3319 Pine St., Apt. 8, Jacksonville, Fla.

1–**SHIPMAN, Mary Francis Whiton (Mrs. Leander Kenny),** *b* West Stafford, Conn., July 21, 1867.
9–Thomas **Whiton** (1588-1664), from Eng. to Plymouth, Mass., 1635; *m* Audrey–; *m* 2d, Winnyfreed Harding;
8–James (1624-1710), came with father; settled at Hingham, Mass.; *m* 1647, Mary Beal (1622-96; John[9], qv);
7–James (1651-1725), *m* Abigail Rickard (1655-1740; Giles[8], *m* Hannah Dunham);
6–Joseph (1687-1777), Ashford, Conn.; *m* 1713, Martha Tower (1693-1719; Samuel[7], *m* Silence Damon);
5–Elijah (1714-84), Westford, Conn.; apptd. justice for Windham Co., by Gen. Assembly, 1777-79; *m* 1st, 1741, Priscilla Russ (*d* 1756; Joseph[6], *m* Priscilla Moore);
4–Joseph (1745/46-1817), *m* Joanna Chaffee (1748-1820; David[5], *m* Martha Walker);
3–Heber (1782-1828), W. Stafford, Conn.; *m* 1808, Marcia Gay (1784-1848; Ebenezer[4], *m* Elizabeth Leavens; Lusher[5]; Lusher[6]; Nathaniel[7]; John[8], qv);
2–David Erskine (2 below).
9–John **Alden,** Mayflower Pilgrim (qv);
8–Joseph (*d* 1697, aet. 73); *m* Mary Simmons (Moses[9], qv);
7–Joseph (1667-1747), *m* 1690, Hannah Dunham (*d* 1748, aet 78; Daniel[8]);
6–Mary (1699-1782), *m* 1719, Timothy **Edson** (*b* 1694; Joseph[7]; Samuel[8], qv);
5–Hannah (*b* 1720), *m* 1758, Israel **Howe**;
4–Israel (1759-1845), *m* 1784, Hannah Washburn;
3–Achsah (1798-1871), *m* 1820, James **Francis** (1794-1870; John[4], *m* 1792, Anna Gladding);
2–Asenath (2 below).
10–John **Washburn** (qv);
9–John, *m* 1645, Elizabeth Mitchell (Experience[10], *m* Jane, dau. Francis Cooke, Mayflower Pilgrim, qv);
8–Samuel (1651-1720), called "Sergeant"; *m* 1st, Deborah Packard (Samuel[9]);
7–Samuel (1678-1752), *m* Abigail–;
6–Solomon (*b* 1708), *m* 1732, Martha Orcutt (1703-89; William[7]);
5–Solomon (1734-1816), ens. Am. Rev.; *m* 1757, Mary Warner (1737-1812; John[6], *m* 2d, Catherine–; Nathaniel[7]; John[8]; William[9]);
4–Hannah (1764-1850), *m* Israel **Howe** (4 above);
3–Achsah, *m* James **Francis** (3 above);
2–Asenath (1833-1902), *m* 1856, David Erskine **Whiton** (1825-1904), mfr.; issue: I–Rosella Lenette (1860-65); II–Lucius Erskine (*b* 1862; *m* Viola Emma King); III–Mary F. (1 above).
1–*m* Apr. 23, 1890, Leander Kenny Shipman, M.D., *b* New London, Conn., June 25, 1853; son of Joseph A. Shipman, of Waterford, Conn.
1–Ed. Wesleyan Acad. Mem. D.F.P.A., S.M.D., D.A.R., I.A.G., United Workers of New London (dir.). Conglist. Republican. Residence: 160 Hempstead St., New London, Conn.

1–**SHIPP, John Edgar Dawson,** *b* Chattahoochee Co., Ga., Oct. 4, 1858.
7–William **Shipp** (*d* 1657), from Eng., settled in Va. ante 1637; vestryman colonial church, Lower Norfolk; appt. by Gen. Assembly as a tobacco viewer, Va. crop, 1639; court of Lower Norfolk held at his home considering affairs of ch., 1640-42; *m* twice;
6–Francis (*d* 1695), *m* Sarah–;
5–William (*d* 1735), *m* Mary–;
4–Willis (*d* 1782), of Craven Co., N.C.; *m* Mary–;
3–William (*d* 1832), *m* Nancy Roach–;
2–William Wesley (1814-84), mem. Ga. Gen. Assembly from Chattahoochee Co.; *m* 1856, Mary Frances McLester (1838-1927; Dr. James[3] [1804-69], *m* Caroline Wooldridge, 1820-95).
1–*m* Freddie Brooks (1858-1918), dau. of Dr. Terrell Brooks (1821-89), surgeon C.S.A., *m* Nancy Matthews (1837-1915); issue: 1–Ethel *m* Roy Sheffield Bell; 2–Dr. Terrell Brooks; 3–Edgar Jr., *m* Sara Cannon; 4–Freddie, *m* Lucius Lamar McCleskey; 5–H. B., *m* Florence Walters.
1–A.B., Auburn, '79 (Sigma Alpha Epsilon). Atty. and writer; pres. Americus Book Co., and collector of rare editions. Author: Giant Days or Life and Times of William H. Crawford; various educational and historical articles. Mem. Ga. Legislature, 1883-84. Founder of town of Cordele, Ga., 1889; chmn. Bd. of Edn., Sumter Co., Ga. Baptist. Residence: Americus, Ga.

1–**SHIRER, Lillian Whiting (Mrs. Hampton L.),** *b* Milford, Kan., Feb. 14, 1868.
8–Nathaniel **Whiting** (qv);
7–Samuel (1649-1727), of Dedham, Mass.; *m* 2d, 1702, Mary Fairbanks (1667-post 1727; Jonathan[8], *m* Dorothy Shepard);
6–Zachariah (1704-63), of Dedham; *m* 1729, Elizabeth Phillips (1708-post 1768);
5–Zachariah (1747-1814), ens. Am. Rev.; *m* 1769, Desire Guild (1749-1807; Joseph[6], *m* 3d, Beulah Peck);
4–Capt. Gerry (1775-1827), Francestown, N.H.; *m* 1798, Abigail (Nabby) Starrett (1778-1831; William[5], Am. Rev., *m* Abigail Fisher);
3–Dea. Harris (1805-47), New Boston, N.H.; *m* 1832, Mary Dodge (1807-70; Simeon[4], *m* Martha Fairfield);
2–Albe Burge (2 below).
10–John **Whitney** (qv);
9–Thomas (1629-1719), Stow, Mass.; *m* 1654, Mary Kedell or Kettle (1637-1708/09);
8–Thomas (1656-1742), Bolton, Mass.; soldier King Philip's War; *m* 1679, Elizabeth Lawrence (1659-1741; George[9], of Watertown, Mass., *m* Elizabeth Crispe);
7–Nathan (1689-1761), Stow, *m* 1719, Mary Holman (Jeremiah[8], *m* Abigail–);
6–Nathan (1723-1801), Conway, Mass.; *m* 1752, Tabatha Barnett (*b* 1724);
5–Aaron (1752-91), Conway, Mass.;
4–Chester (1783-1852), Waterbury, Vt.; *m* Polly Waite Green (1784-1854);
3–Baxter (1812-89), *m* 1836, Mary Ann Kneeland (1814-87; Richard[4]);
2–Katherine Amelia (1838-1907), *m* Nov. 15, 1858, Albe Burge **Whiting** (Nov. 10, 1835-May 14, 1928), of Lamoille Co., Vt.; issue: I–Harris Lyon (1861-1924; *m* 1885, Georgia Frances Murdock); II–Mary Helen (*b* 1863; *m* 1883, Harry L. King); III–Wallace Albe (*b* and *d* 1864); IV–

Katharine Louise (*b* 1866; *m* 1892, Tallmadge S. Hand); V–Lillian (1 above); VI–Annie Julia (1872-76).
1–*m* Jan. 3, 1889, Hampton Lafayette Shirer, *b* Muskingum Co., O., Jan. 7, 1861; son of Daniel G. Shirer, *m* Cordelia King; issue: 1–Mary Helen, *b* Topeka, Kan., Oct. 30, 1892; B.A., Washburn, '15; *m* June 1, 1916, Thomas Amory, son of Robert Ives Lee (issue: Barbara, *b* Nov. 4, 1922; Mary, *b* June 26, 1924); 2–Hampton Francis, *b* Topeka, Oct. 10, 1894; A.B., Washburn, '16; A.B., M.I.T., 1918; *m* May 20, 1917, Pauline Haynes (issue: Sarah Elizabeth, *b* Oct. 5, 1920; Hampton Whiting, *b* Aug. 8, 1924).
1–Mem. D.F.P.A., D.A.C., D.A.R., Kan. State Hist. Soc. Conglist. Republican. Residence: 1157 Fillmore St., Topeka, Kan.

1–**SHNABLE, Mary Alice Davis (Mrs. Emile R.),** *b* nr. Vernon, N.Y., Dec. 9, 1856.
8–William **Stone** (1618-83), from Eng., 1639, settled at Guilford, Conn., 20 miles east of New Haven; propr. of the first inn; farmer; *m* 2d, 1659, Mary, widow of Richard Hughes;
7–William (1642-1730), *m* 1st, 1673, Hannah Wolfe (*d* 1712);
6–William (1676-1753), *m* 1701, Sarah Hatch (1681-1751);
5–Jehial (1704-80), *m* 1730, Ruth White (1703-74);
4–William (1740-1814), of Harwington, Conn.; *m* 1763, Sarah (Johnson) Sage (1748-1830);
3–Joseph (1777-1852), moved to Oneida Co., N. Y., 1795; capt. militia in War 1812; organizer and dir. Nat. Bank of Vernon, N.Y.; *m* 1803, Polly Langdon (1782-1854);
2–Mary Ann (2 below).
8–Thomas **Morehouse** (*d* 1658), from Eng., 1653, settled at Fairfield, Conn.; bought 24 acres on Lasco Hill; dep. Gen. Ct. at Hartford; *m* Isabella Keller;
7–Samuel (1637-87), of Fairfield; lt. of military co. and marshal of Fairfield; *m* Rebecca Odell (William[8], from Eng., 1639, *m* Rebecca–);
6–Thomas (*b* 1665), of Fairfield;
5–Andrew (*b* 1725), mem. Assembly, 1777-79; *m* 1746, Phoebe Hurd (1730-83);
4–Lucy (1749-1847), Saybrook, Conn.; *m* 1st, 1770, John **Langdon** (1740-87), Fishkill, N.Y.;
3–Polly (1782-1854), *m* Joseph **Stone** (3 above);
2–Mary Ann (1816-1903), *m* 1845, Isaac Barnes **Davis** (1820-99), dep. sheriff, poor master, Madison Co. (Isaac[3], *m* Roxalana, dau. of Roger Wilson); issue: I–Frederick Barnes (1846-95); II–Jane (1848-84; *m* John J. Rivenburgh); III–Anna (*b* 1850); IV–Frank (1852-60); V–Maria K. (*b* 1854; *m* J. Wesley Walrath); VI–Mary Alice (1 above); VII–John Carey (*b* 1860).
1–*m* June 20, 1883, Emile Ralph Shnable, *b* Chicago, Ill., Jan. 14, 1856; C.E., Cornell, '81; sr. partner firm of Shnable & Quinn, engrs. and contractors; son of Jacob Schnable (1826-1922), from Alsace, to Chicago, *m* Barbara Sigwalt (1828-76), also from Alsace; issue: 1–Olga Edith (Feb. 25-Aug. 19, 1888); 2–Barnes Davis, *b* Ravenswood, Ill., Jan. 24, 1891; Armour Inst.; *m* Oct. 7, 1914, Anita Mae, dau. of Charles Brooks, of Park Ridge, Ill. (issue: Jean Brooks, *b* Feb. 14, 1916; Jack Davis, *b* Apr. 23, 1918); 3–Earl Potter, *b* Ravenswood, July 31, 1895; M.E., U.Wis.; *m* July 12, 1924, Beatrice Mellor, dau. of William E. Hudson, of Wilmette, Ill.
Residence: 1005 Michigan Av., Wilmette, Ill.

1–**SHOVER, Eliza Crosby Gibbes (Mrs. Hayden C.),** *b* Augusta, Ga., June 4, 1870.
7–Robert **Gibbes** (1645-1715; son of Robert); came from Eng. to S.C. ca. 1681; chief justice, 1708; gov., 1709-12; *m* 2d, Mary–;
6–William (1689-1733), *m* 1716, Alice (1700-39), dau. of Ralph Culcheth, of Ireland;
5–William (1723-80), mem. secret com. of five, Council of Safety at Charleston, Am. Rev.; del., Provincial Congress; *m* 2d, 1748, Elizabeth Hasell (1725-62; Rev. Thomas[6], M.A., Cambridge U., came from Eng., 1705, *m* Elizabeth, dau. of John Ashby, of S.C.);
4–William Hasell (1754-1834), lawyer; capt.-lt. Ancient Bty. of Arty. at Charleston, Am. Rev.; master in chancery of S.C.; *m* 2d, 1808, Mary Philp Wilson (1772-1844; Dr. Robert[5], from Scotland to S.C., a founder of Charleston Med. Coll., 1789, *m* 1759, Ann, dau. Alexander Chisolm, *m* Judith Radcliff);
3–Dr. Robert Wilson (1809-66), surgeon gen. S.C., 1861-65; twice mayor of Columbia; author Gibbes Documentary History of S.C.; *m* 1827, Caroline Elizabeth Guignard;
2–Capt. Washington Allston (2 below).
11–Rev. John **Foster,** of Barbados;
10–Margaret, *m* 1st, Col. Benjamin **Berringer**;
9–Margaret (*b* 1669), *m* Gov. James **Moore** (*b* Eng., 1644-*d* S.C., 1706), gov., 1700-02;
8–Gen. James (*d* 1724), *m* Elizabeth– (Noyville or Beresford?);
7–Margaret (ca. 1707-1775), *m* 1738, Col. William **Sanders** (ca. 1705-1742), mem. Assembly, 1725-26; atty. gen., 1728 (William[8]; Lawrence[9]);
6–James, *m* 1785, Sarah Slann (Andrew[7], *m* Anne, dau. of Thomas Waring; Peter[8]);
5–Elizabeth, *m* John Gabriel **Guignard**;
4–James S., *m* 1801, Caroline Richardson (Capt. William[5], *m* 1768, Ann Magdalene Guignard, 1750-1810);
3–Caroline Elizabeth, *m* Dr. Robert Wilson **Gibbes** (3 above);
2–Capt. Washington Allston (1841-1927), capt. Co. D, 16th S.C. Vols., C.S.A.; capt. Co. C, 16th and 24th S.C. Regts., consolidated, 1861-65; Mason; *m* 1869, Elizabeth Forster Hunt (1851-90; Dr. Samuel[3], *m* 1850, Eliza Panthea Crosby; William[4]; Samuel[5]; John[6]; Samuel[7]; Capt. Thomas[8]; Ephraim[9]); issue I–Eliza Crosby (1 above); II–Elizabeth Guignard (*b* 1872); III–Mary Thomas (*b* 1875; *m* Francis Waring Plumb); IV–Caroline (*b* 1879; *m* John Tilkey Bailie).
1–*m* Oct. 12, 1897, Hayden Crosby Shover, *b* Fond du Lac, Wis., Jan. 25, 1870; son of Sidner J. Shover; issue (all *b* Chicago, Ill.): 1–Elise Caroline, *b* Feb. 20, 1901; Oglethorpe U., '22; mem. C.D.A., D.F.P.A., D.A.C.; 2–Martha, *b* Nov. 4, 1902; Oglethorpe, '22; mem. C.D.A., D.F.P.A., D.A.C., D.A.R.; 3–Robert Gibbes (June 28-July 26, 1910).
1–Sec. of Woman's Auxiliary of All Saints' P.E. Ch., Atlanta. Mem. C.D.A. (sec. Atlanta circle, 1918-19), D.A.C., D.F.P.A., Huguenot Soc. S.C., D.A.R., U.D.C. Residence: 14 Ridgeland Way, Atlanta, Ga.

1–**SHUFORD, Ada Church (Mrs. Charles S.),** *b* Louisville, Ky., Jan. 3, 1881.
8–George **Boone,** III (qv);
7–Samuel (1711-45), *m* 1734, Elizabeth Cassel (Arnold[8], of Pa.);
6–Samuel (1736-1805), *m* 1766, Jane Foulke Hughes;
5–Rachel (1767-1836), *m* Alexander Hamilton **Merrifield** (1765-1847; John[6], from Eng. to Va.);
4–Matilda (1803-41), *m* 1824, George L. **Rogers** (1793-1892), Meth. minister; known as hero of three wars, served in War 1812 and Mexican War, suffered losses of money and property in Civil War; his son Capt. and Dr. John was killed in battle (Edwin[5], Am. Rev);
3–Cynthia (1831-1906), *m* 1850, William L. **Ball** (1823-1908);
2–Mary Martha (2 below).
9–Edward **Foulke** (qv);
8–Jane (1685-1766), *m* Ellis **Hughes** (*b* 1686);
7–Judge John (1714-66), mem. Pa. Assembly; judge Ct. Common Pleas; *m* 1742, Hannah Boone (1718-46; George, IV[8] [1690-1753], arrived at Phila., 1712, surveyor for William Penn, magistrate, *m* 1713, Deborah [1691-1759], dau. of William Howell, from Wales to Pa., 1682; George, III[9], qv, 8 above);
6–Jane Foulke (1745-1830), *m* Samuel **Boone** (6 above).
2–Mary Martha Ball (*b* 1853), Louisville, Ky.; *m* 1877, Joseph Foster **Church** (1845-1906), engr. and contractor; sgt. Civil War; issue: I–Ada (1 above); II–Joseph Foster (*b* 1884; sgt. U.S.A., World War); III–Milton Lawrence (*b* 1890; *m* Rose Garing); IV–Mattye (*b* 1892).
1–*m* June 26, 1901, Charles Sylvanus Shuford, *b* Pisgah Forest, N.C.; ed. A. and M. Coll., Raleigh, N.C.; Mason (K.T., 32°); son of Perry Sylvanus Shuford, *m* Mary Orr; issue: 1–Mary Italyne, *b* Albany, Ala., Feb. 12, 1903; *m* Nov. 21, 1922, Edwin Vincent, son of Robert F. Caulfield, *m* Lula Amory (issue: Patricia Shuford).
1–Ed. pub. and pvt. schs.; specialized in music. Mem. D.A.R., U.D.C. Chmn. speakers com. all Liberty Loan campaigns and food con-

servation, Mobile Co., Ala., World War; pres. Mobile Co. Sch. Improvement League, Woman's War League; mem. bd. of control of Mobile Infirmary. Summer place: Virginia Beach, Va. Residence: Norfolk, Va.

1–**SHULER, Luella May French (Mrs. William B.),** *b* Butler Co., O., May 26, 1862.
10–Richard **Treat** (qv);
9–Honor, *m* 1637, John **Deming** (qv);
8–Mary (*b* 1655), Middletown, Conn.; *m* 1670, John **Hurlburt** (1642-90);
7–Mehetable (1690-1744), *m* 1714, Nathaniel **White** (1685-1743);
6–Nathaniel (1715-1767), Portland, Conn.; *m* 1737, Mary Sage (*b* 1720);
5–Margaret (*b* 1741), Middletown; *m* 1759, William **Bartlett** (*b* 1737);
4–Josiah (1767-1856), Chatham, Conn.; *m* Anna Latham (*d* 1832);
3–Dr. William Henry (1807-84), St. Lawrence Co., N.Y.; *m* 1836, Eliza Andrews;
2–Amanda (2 below).
11–John **Howland** (qv);
10–Desire (1623-83), of Plymouth; *m* 1643, Capt. John **Gorham** (qv);
9–Desire (1644-1700), of Plymouth; *m* 1661, Capt. John **Hawes** (1637-1701), capt. of Yarmouth Co., 1700; rep. Legislature at Boston, 1697-98; grand juryman;
8–Elizabeth (1662-1732), Yarmouth; *m* 1683, Thomas **Daggett** (1658-1726), lt. in militia; capt., 1691; justice county ct.;
7–Jemima (*b* 1694), Edgartown, Mass.; *m* Malachi **Butler** (*b* 1689);
6–Benjamin (1729-1804), Windham; *m* 1753, Dorcas Abbot (1729-89);
5–Dorcas (1766-1857), Nottingham, N.H.; *m* 1786, Jonathan **Cilley** (1762-1807); asst. treas. Order of the Cincinnati, 1794-99, v.p. 1799-1802;
4–Sarah (1789-1862), *m* 1812, Hugh **Andrews** (1774-1822);
3–Eliza (1814-41), Eaton, O.; *m* Dr. William Henry **Bartlett** (3 above);
2–Amanda (1840-78), Hamilton Co., O.; *m* 1859, Nathaniel G. **French** (1834-1900); issue: I–William H.B. (1860-61); II–Luella May (1 above); III–Matilda Bartlett (*b* 1864; *m* Arthur Letherby); IV–Ransford M. (*b* 1866; *m* Vashti Morrow); V–Harry G. (1869-1910); VI–Charlotte E. (1872-1911).
1–*m* Oct. 24, 1883, William Baron Shuler, *b* Hamilton, O., Aug. 5, 1860; son of Asa Shuler, of Hamilton; issue: 1–Frank Berger, *b* Hamilton, May 20, 1885; Ohio State U., '08; *m* Oct. 21, 1915, Mattie, dau. of Calvin Hemp (issue: Mary; Frances; Asa William); 2–Marie, *b* Hamilton, Aug. 26, 1886.
1–Mem. S.M.D., C.D.XVIIC., D.C.W., D.A.R., I.A.G., Soc. of N.E. Women. Methodist. Republican. Club: Woman's. Residence: 712 Dayton St., Hamilton, O.

1–**SIGMON, Vivian Marie Lewis (Mrs. Martin L.),** *b* Texarkana, Tex., Sept. 11, 1884.
10–Nicholas **Martian** (Nicolas Martiau), qv;
9–Elizabeth, *m* Col. George **Reade** (qv);
8–Mildred, *m* Col. Augustine **Warner** (1642-81), speaker Va. House of Burgesses;
7–Elizabeth, *m* her cousin, Col. John **Lewis** (1669-1725), mem. Royal Council; judge Supreme Ct. (John[8], *m* Isabella Warner; Gen. Robert[9]);
6–Col. Robert (1704-66), of Belvoir; *m* Jane Meriwether;
5–John (1726-89), *m* Catherine Fauntleroy (Col. William[6], of Naylor's Hole, Richmond Co., *m* Apphia, dau. of John Bushrod, Gent., of Westmoreland Co.; William[7], Rappahannock Co., *m* Katherine, dau. of Col. Samuel Griffin, of Northumberland Co.; Maj. Moore[8], qv);
4–John (1753-1817), *m* 1776, Elizabeth Kennon (1754-1825; William[5], of Chesterfield Co., *m* Elizabeth, dau. of Col. Charles Lewis, *m* Mary, dau. of John Howell, Gent.);
3–Augustine (1784-1854), *m* 1809, Louise Brooking;
2–Dr. Francis Brooking (2 below).
10–Col. John **Walker** (*d* 1688), *m* 1622, Sarah– (*d* 1656);
9–Ann (*b* 1624), *m* 1666, John **Paine,** Jr. (*d* 1669);
8–Elizabeth (1668-1714), *m* Henry **Thacker** (1663-post 1690);
7–Frances (1696-1724), *m* 1717, Lord Thomas **Vivian** (1694-1787);
6–Frances (1719-66), *m* Robert **Brooking** (1700-69);
5–Col. Francis Vivian (1736-1808), col. accounts, 1779-80, Amelia Co., Va., Am. Rev.; *m* 1763, Elizabeth Brodnax (1742-1806);
4–William (1764-1840), *m* 1790, Elizabeth Barret;
3–Louise (1791-1856), *m* 1809, Augustine **Lewis** (3 above).
7–William **Brodnax** (1675-1727; son of Robert, of Eng., and desc. Robert Brodnax, *m* 1416, Alicia Scappe); came from Eng. to Va., 1700, settled at Jamestown; rep. James City Co. in House of Burgesses, 1718,20,22,23,26; *m* Rebecca (Champion) Travis;
6–Edward, justice, 1745; burgess, Gen. Assembly, 1745-46; *m* Elizabeth Hall (Thomas[7]);
5–Lt. Col. Stephen Edward (1748-1840), served in Am. Rev.; *m* Elizabeth Rebecca Danzee (John J. C.[6]);
4–Edward Brooking, in War 1812; *m* his 1st cousin, Frances Vivian Brooking;
3–Mariah (1823-90), *m* 1843, Joseph **Mann** (*d* 1879; Col. John[4], of Amelia Co., *m* Elizabeth Brooking, 1791-1856);
2–Elizabeth B. (2 below).
11–Sir Richard Vyvyan, Knight, burgess for Tregory;
10–Charles Vyvyan, of Cornwall;
9–John **Vivian,** of Eng.;
8–John, *m* Margaret Smith;
7–Thomas, *m* 1717, Frances Thacker (Henry[8]);
6–Frances, *m* Robert **Brooking**;
5–Col. Francis Vivian, *m* Elizabeth Brodnax;
4–Frances Vivian, *m* her 1st cousin, Edward Brooking **Brodnax** (4 above);
3–Mariah, *m* Joseph **Mann** (3 above);
2–Elizabeth Brodnax (*b* 1847), *m* Dr. Francis Brooking **Lewis** (1835-90).
1–*m* Feb. 5, 1903, Martin L. Sigmon, *b* Vanndale, Ark., Oct. 19, 1875; son of Eli Sigmon, *m* Mary Jane Gardner; issue: 1–Frances Vivian Lewis, *b* Little Rock, Ark., May 31, 1904; Vassar, '27; *m* June 6, 1928, Ens. E. Glenn Cooper, son of James O. Cooper, *m* Anna Bell Manee.
1–Ed. Ursuline Acad., Arcadia, Mo. Mem. bd. Boys' Industrial Sch.; mem. Ark. Post Park Commission, apptd. by Gov. Harvey Parnell. Mem. D.B.R., D.F.P.A., Huguenots of Va., D.A.R. (state regent), U.S.D. 1812 (hon. state pres. nat. corr. sec., 1926), D.A.C. (past state pres.), I.A.G., F.F.Va., Va. Cavaliers, Yellow Rose, Knights of the Golden Horse Shoe. Residence: Vivian Manor, Monticello, Ark.

1–**SIMPSON, J(efferson) Beard,** *b* Shullsburg, Wis., June 11, 1859.
5–Alexander **Simpson** (1721-88), Scotch-Irish descent; bought land at Windham, N.H., 1747; *m* Janet Templeton (had three sons in Battle of Bunker Hill);
4–Alexander (1756-1838), soldier Am. Rev.; removed to Watertown, N.Y.; *m* Mary Rogers (Samuel[5], soldier Am. Rev.);
3–Sylvanus (1791-1848), served in War 1812; removed to Ohio; *m* Susannah Herrington (g.-dau. of Benjamin Carpenter, officer Am. Rev., lt. gov. of Vt., 1778);
2–Philemon Baldwin (2 below).
7–John (Baird) **Beard** (1675-1748), came from Scotland, settled in Bucks Co., Pa.;
6–Thomas, *m* Hannah Stuart;
5–James (1730-1802), in Am. Rev.; *m* Isabelle–;
4–James (1765-1831), *m* Sarah Lowry (Matthew[5]);
3–John (1794-1832), removed to Ohio, 1824; *m* Hannah Doane;
2–Mary (2 below).
10–John **Doane** (qv);
9–Daniel (1636-1712), *m* Hepsibah Cole (Daniel[10]);
8–Daniel (*d* 1743), *m* Mehitable Twining (William[9]);
7–Eleazer (1691-1757), removed to Bucks Co., Pa.; *m* Susannah–;
6–John, *m* Hannah Wilson;
5–Eleazer, *m* Mary Kinsie (Jonathan[6]; Edmund[7]; Edmund[8]);
4–Jonas (1773-1829), *m* Pamelia Price (John[5]; Nathan[6]; David[7]; James[8]);
3–Hannah, *m* John **Beard** (3 above);
2–Mary (1822-1915), *m* 1843, Philemon Baldwin **Simpson** (1818-95), LL.B., U.Cincinnati, 1843; removed to Wis., 1847; mem. Wis. Senate, 1858-61.
1–*m* Nov. 8, 1888, Luella Allan (qv for issue).
1–A.B., U.Wis., '79. Admitted to the bar, 1881;

county judge of LaFayette Co., Wis., since 1910. Residence: Shullsburg, Wis.

1-**SIMPSON, Luella Allan (Mrs. J. Beard),** *b* Scales Mound, Ill., May 16, 1860.
8-Robert **Proctor** (*d* 1697), Freeman, Concord, Mass., 1643; a petitioner for Chelmsford, 1653; *m* 1645, Jane Hildreth (Sgt. Richard[9], *m* 1st, Sarah-);
7-Samuel (1655-1740), *m* Sarah-;
6-Thomas (1698-1774), *m* 1722, Hannah Barron (*b* 1703; Isaac[7]; Moses[8]; Ellis[9]);
5-Leonard (1734-1827), minute man at Lexington Alarm; capt. Am. Rev.; removed to Proctorsville, Vt.; *m* 1st, Lydia Nutting (Josiah[6]; Ebenezer[7]; John[8]);
4-Leonard (1764-1812), seaman and soldier Am. Rev.; *m* 1792, Experience Hildreth (Hosea[5], marched on Lexington Alarm; Joseph[6]; Joseph[7]; Richard[8]);
3-Abel (1800-88), fifer War 1812; removed to Scales Mound, Ill.; *m* 1831, Mary Moffatt;
2-Emily (2 below).
7-William **Moffatt**, at Newbury, Mass., 1681; a propr. of Killingly, Conn., 1709; *m* Mehetable-;
6-Joseph (*b* 1703), *m* Mary Waters (Daniel[7]);
5-Aquilla (1740-post 1796), sgt. Am. Rev.; *m* Elizabeth-;
4-Joseph (1771-1850), *m* Mary Piper (1778-1822; Elisha[5], of N.H., *m* Sarah, dau. Ebenezer Barker, civil officer during Am. Rev.; Samuel[6]; Samuel[7]; Nathaniel[8]);
3-Mary (1806-65), *m* Abel **Proctor** (3 above);
2-Emily (1834-1900), *m* 1858, George **Allan** (1842-64), settled at Scales Mound, Ill. (James[3], from Scotland to Can., 1842); issue: I-Luella (1 above); II-David (*b* 1862-*d* infancy).
1-*m* Nov. 8, 1888, Jefferson Beard Simpson (qv); issue (all *b* Shullsburg, Wis): 1-Jefferson Allan, *b* Nov. 25, 1889; A.B., U.Wis., '10, LL.B., 1913; enlisted as pvt. when U.S. entered the war; capt., Co. M, 337th Inf., 86th Div., A.E.F.; *m* Sept. 1, 1923, Jessie Allen (issue: Jefferson Allan, *b* Nov. 9, 1924); 2-Mary Olive, *b* Sept. 25, 1891; A.B., U.Wis., '12; *m* Nov. 29, 1919, Heiskell Bryan Whaling, Ph.D., prof. economics, U. Cincinnati (issue: Allan Heiskell, *b* 1922; Alice Mary, *b* 1926); 3-Alexander Lewis, *b* Sept. 23, 1898; LL.B., U.Wis., 1927.
1-Mem. D.F.P.A., D.A.R. Residence: Shullsburg, Wis.

1-**SIMS, Almon James,** *b* Waynesboro, Tenn., Aug. 12, 1892.
6-Henry (Simms) **Sims,** from Ireland, ca. 1768, with his brothers, Robert and Parish; settled in N.C.; he and his two brothers were soldiers in Am. Rev.;
5-Robert (1783-1842), of N.C.; removed to Giles Co., Tenn., 1820, thence to Wayne Co., 1834; *m* 1813, Frances H. Merritt (1797-1871), came from Eng., an orphan in the care of friends;
4-Matthew Joseph (1816-90), farmer and sch. teacher; owned merchandise store and tannery at Waynesboro, Tenn.; Chancery Court clerk 10 yrs., *m* 1837, Dorothy Greeson (1819-86; Henry[5], *m* Betsy Cook, both from Germany to Bedford Co., Tenn.);
3-John Shields (1838-1927), Waynesboro, Tenn.; 1st sgt., Co. H, Tenn. Mounted Inf., Union Army, in Civil War; farmer and tanner; *m* 1859, Edith Melinda Caroline Youngblood (1841-1915; Josiah[4] [*b* 1818], of Rutherford Co., Tenn., *m* Mary Horton; William[5], *m* Edith Reed);
2-Matthew Josiah (2 below).
4-David Harrison **Davis,** of Va.; missionary Bapt. preacher, of Wayne Co., Tenn.; *m* Matilda Wakefield, of Ind.;
3-Joseph Noah (1844-1920), large landowner and farmer; private in Union army; *m* Nancy Jane Copeland (1849-1906);
2-Cammilla Ellen (*b* 1873), Wayne Co., Tenn.; *m* 1891, Matthew Josiah **Sims** (*b* 1868), farmer and stockman; issue: I-Almon James (1 above); II-Mergie Elenor (*b* 1893; *m* Sam Carson); III-Raymon (*b* 1896; *m* Lena Foster); IV-Wilbur Shields (1901-18); V-Vernon Wakefield (*b* 1908).
1-*m* Apr. 11, 1917, Sammy Clark, *b* Eagleville, Tenn., Nov. 20, 1898; dau. of Erasamus Lee Clark, of White and Rutherford cos., Tenn.; issue: 1-Almon James, *b* Nashville, Tenn., Mar. 11, 1918; 2-Annie Fain, *b* Nashville, Feb. 1, 1920; 3-Wilbur Joseph, *b* Knoxville, Tenn., May 6, 1922; 4-Frank Clark, *b* Knoxville, Jan. 21, 1927.
1-Ed. U. of Mo. Editor, Agrl. Bulletin and Agrl. Extension News Service, U. of Tenn. since 1920. Half-owner and editor of Lawrence Democrat, Lawrenceburg, Tenn., 1916; reporter, State News and Agrl. editor, Nashville Tennessean, 1917-20. Author. Pres. Am. Assn. of Agrl. Coll. Editors, 1925; sec. Tenn. Press Assn., 1928; mem. E. Tenn. Hist. Soc. Missionary Baptist. Republican. Summer place: Fountain City, Route 2. Address: Knoxville, Tenn.

1-**SLACK, Katherine Woolsey (Mrs. Charles W.),** *b* Gilroy, Santa Clara Co., Calif., May 25, 1861.
8-George **Woolsey** (qv);
7-Thomas (*b* 1655), *m* Ruth-;
6-Richard (1697-will proved, 1782), *m* Sarah Fowler (William[7], *m* Mary, dau. of John Thorn; Joseph[8]; John[9]);
5-John, *m* Chloe Peck;
4-John (1759-1848), *m* Deborah Ann Wright;
3-John (*b* Newburgh, N.Y., May 6, 1781-*d* Apr. 1, 1854), *m* Elizabeth Bradshaw (Dec. 5, 1781-Jan. 16, 1875), from Boylestown, N.Y., to DeLong, Ill.;
2-James Bradshaw (2 below).
9-William **Teller** (1616 or 1620-1701; son of Rev. Romanus, desc. nobles of Kempton, nr. Switzerland, author of religious works, refugee in Holland during Thirty Years War); came from Holland to Albany (Ft. Orange), N.Y., 1639; apptd. watchmaster ("wachmeister") by Dutch India Co.; tax collector, justice, alderman; co. lt., 1669; a patentee of Schenectady; removed to N.Y., 1692; *m* 1st, ca. 1641, Margaret (Mary Douchen, Dusen or Donekson) Donckesen;
8-William (1657-1711), large landowner in Westchester Co.; owned Teller's Point; *m* Oct. 16, 1686, Rachel Kierstede (*b* 1665; Dr. Hans[9], *m* Sarah, dau. of Jans Roelofson, from Holland, 1633, settled at New Amsterdam, *m* Anneke Jans Webber, 1602-63);
7-William (*b* Dec. 25, 1690) *m* Mary Caniff (Canoff);
6-Margaret (*d* 1811, aet. 78), *m* 1761, Benjamin **Woolsey** (*d* 1795; Richard[7], same as 6 above);
5-Rev. Henry (*d* June 23, 1848), *m* Feb. 18, 1784, Sarah Woolsey (June 16, 1762-Dec. 14, 1839);
4-Abigail (May 14, 1792-Feb. 20, 1845), *m* Rumsey **Reeve;**
3-Henry (Mar. 27, 1815-June 11, 1891), of Rensselaerville, N.Y.; *m* at Willoughby, O., Charlotte Shaw (John[4], *m* Johanna, dau. of John Woolsey, 4 above; Isaiah[5], teamster in Am. Rev., *m* Charlotte Haver);
2-Hannah Melissa (Oct. 13, 1836-Jan. 31, 1926), *m* Jan. 3, 1856, James Bradshaw **Woolsey** (Mar. 4, 1822-Aug. 6, 1919), of Ashtabula, O.; issue: I-Mary; II-Katherine (1 above); III-Walter P. (*m* cousin, Effie Reeve); IV-Philip S. (*d* Nov. 30, 1917); V-Chester H. (*m* Sarah Chambers); VI-Frank R. (*m* Helene Johnson); VII-Audubon J. (*m* Myrtle Priestly); VIII-Roydon I. (*m* Zoe Larkins); IX-Mark H. (*m* Florence Parker).
1-*m* Aug. 5, 1886, Charles William Slack, *b* Mifflin Co., Pa., Dec. 12, 1859; son of Uriah Slack; issue: 1-Edith, *b* San Francisco, Feb. 29, 1888; 2-Ruth, *b* San Francisco, Dec. 22, 18-; *m* Apr. 23, 1912, Edgar T. Zook.
1-Ed. U. of Calif Mem. D.A.R., I.A.G. Clubs: Century, Francisca, Women's City. Residence: 2224 Sacramento St., San Francisco, Calif.

1-**SMALLEY, Frank Mather,** *b* Syracuse, N.Y., May 25, 1877.
9-Rev. Richard **Mather** (qv);
8-Timothy (1628-84), *m* Catherine Atherton; *m* 2d, Elizabeth Weeks;
7-Atherton (1663-1734), of Dorchester, Mass.; *m* 2d, 1705, Mary Lamb;
6-Richard (*b* 1708), of Suffield, Conn.; *m* 1733, Lois Burbank;
5-Zachariah (1743-1816), of Fayette, Seneca Co., N.Y.; *m* 1769, Lucy Gaylord (1741-1837);
4-Lucius (1788-1879), of Middlesex, N.Y.; *m* 1817, Jane Ackerman;
3-Abram (1822-1906), of Rushville, N.Y.; *m* 1852, Elizabeth A. Low (1825-1923);
2-Mary Jane (1855-1926), *m* 1876, Frank **Smalley**

(*b* 1846), vice chancellor emeritus Syracuse U.; issue: I–Frank Mather (1 above); II–Carrie Elizabeth (1879-1903).
1–*m* Dec. 31, 1901, Helen Pettit Spencer, *b* Ft. Wayne, Ind.; dau. of M. V. B. Spencer, of Ft. Wayne; issue (all *b* Syracuse, N.Y.): 1–Jane Mather, *b* Mar. 20, 1912; 2–Robert Warren, *b* Feb. 17, 1915; 3–Margaret Spencer, *b* Feb. 25, 1916.
1–A.B., Syracuse U., '98 (D.K.E., Phi Delta Phi); studied law, Syracuse U., 1898-1900. With Middle States Inspection Bureau, New York, 1902; sec. Glens Falls Ins. Co., since 1920, v.p. since 1926, pres. since 1929; also pres. Commerce Ins. Co.; v.p. Glens Falls Indemnity Co., Commerce Casualty Co. (see Who's Who in America). Fellow Ins. Inst. of America; mem. N.Y. State Hist. Soc., I.A.G. Club: Glens Falls Country. Summer place: Assembly Point, Lake George, N.Y. Residence: 33 Horicon Av., Glens Falls, N.Y.

1–**SMILEY, John Jay,** *b* Marion, O., Apr. 1, 1875.
6–Francis **Smiley** (*b* 1689), from Ireland 1727, settled at Haverhill, Mass.; *m* 1718, Agnes Wilson;
5–Dea. William (*b* 1725), grad. Dartmouth Coll.; *m* 1753, Sarah Robinson;
4–John, *m* Betsy Stanley;
3–Jay (*b* 1794), *m* 1822, Dollie Johnson (1800-73);
2–Henry Johnson (1826-99), *m* 1869, Maria Zook (1842-1916).
1–*m* Apr. 17, 1906, Dale Aye (qv for issue).
1–Residence: College Hill, Manhattan, Kan.

1–**SMILEY, Dale Aye (Mrs. John Jay),** *b* in Ohio, Nov. 17, 1876.
10–William **Hyde** (qv);
9–Samuel (1637-77), removed to Saybrook with his father, thence to Norwich, 1660; *m* 1659, Jane Lee (Thomas[10], of Eng.);
8–Samuel (1665-1742), of Norwich and Lebanon, Conn.; *m* 1690, Elizabeth Calkins (*b* 1673; John[9], an original propr. of Norwich, *m* Sarah–; Hugh[10], qv);
7–Elijah (1705-83), *m* 1st, 1730, Ruth Tracy (1711-73; John[8], *m* Elizabeth Leffingwell; John[9]; Thomas[10], a founder of Norwich, Conn., served 27 sessions in Conn. Legislature, lt. in New London Dragoons);
6–Andrew (*b* 1732), pvt.; kept general store at Lebanon, Conn.; *m* Hannah Thomas;
5–Andrew (1757-1845), guard along Hudson; sent out on various forays from Lenox, Mass.; *m* Rebecca Galpin (*d* 1820);
4–Rebecca (1792-1871), *m* 1820, Jacob **Aye** (1793-1871);
3–William S. (1821-1908), guard during Civil War, at Camp Chase, Columbus, O.; *m* 1844, Sarah Jane Mitchell (1829-1906);
2–Melville C. (1851-1928), stockman; *m* 1874, Minnie Devore (1852-1922; J. W.[3], *m* Ann Eliza Martin); issue: I–Dale (1 above); II–Gertrude (*b* 1883; *m* Harry D. Barker).
1–*m* Apr. 17, 1906, John Jay Smiley (qv); issue: 1–Henry Devore, *b* Marion, O., Aug. 3, 1908; 2–Esther Gertrude, *b* Marion, Apr. 24, 1911.
1–Mem. I.A.G. Residence: College Hill, Manhattan, Kan.

1–**SMITH, Abigail M.,** *b* Detroit, Mich., Mar. 3, 1888.
8–John **Smith,** prob. from Dartmouth, Eng., settled at Burrells Mills, ca. 1650; *m* Deborah Howland;
7–Deliverance, *m* Mary Tripp;
6–Humphrey, *m* 1737, Mary Wilcox;
5–Humphrey, *m* 1770, Sylvia Howland;
4–Benjamin H., *m* 1794, Sylvia Slocum;
3–Ahijah, *m* 1828, Eliza Goodrich;
2–Horace G. (2 below).
9–Sylvester **Eveleth** (*d* 1689), from Eng.; baker, Boston, 1642; selectman at Gloucester, 1647,49,-51; *m* Susanna– (1594-1659);
8–Isaac (1642-85), *m* 1677, Abigail Coit;
7–Job (*b* 1682), *m* 1708, Abigail Sargent;
6–Isaac (*b* 1711), *m* 1737, Rachel Sargent (*d* 1738);
5–Isaac (1738-post 1790), of Rehoboth, Mass.; pvt. Am. Rev.; *m* 1762, Emma Bucklin (1742-85);
4–John (*d* 1820), of Bingham Place, Shrewsbury, N.J.; *m* 1809, Mary Williams (*d* 1882);
3–John C. (1814-45), *m* 1842, Julia Patten (1813-78);
2–Mary G. (*b* 1843), of New York, N.Y.; *m* 1866, Horace G. **Smith** (1840-1927).
1–Mem. D.F.P.A., D.A.R. Episcopalian. Residence: 8162 E. Jefferson Av., Detroit, Mich.

1–**SMITH, Elizabeth Ryder Williams (Mrs. Edward I., Jr.),** *b* Phila., Pa., Dec. 14, 1885.
10–Thomas **Ryder** (ante 1614-1697), from Eng.; settled at Dorchester, Mass., 1634; bought land at Hashamomack, L.I., 1659; *m* Elizabeth Lane (*d* 1650);
9–John (bet. 1635-40-1681), practiced law at New York, 1665;
8–John (bet. 1665-67-1734), *m* 1690, Andriante Hercke Krankheyt (Hercks[9]);
7–John (*d* 1763), *m* 1732, Bridget Farrington (*d* 1761);
6–John (1732-1812), pvt., Putnam Co., N.Y., Militia, 1777-78; served in N.Y. Line, 3 yrs., Am. Rev.; *m* Sarah Sprague (or Hannah Keeler?);
5-Absalom (1767-1839), *m* 1st, 1792, Tamson Townsend (1767-1819);
4–Chauncey (1806-50), *m* 1829, Dianthan Maria Boughton (1808-97);
3–John (1833-75), *m* 1856, Emma Leach (1836-1908);
2–Elizabeth (1864-85), *m* 1884, George **Williams** (1864-1901), settled at Phila., Pa.
1–*m* Aug. 22, 1914, Edward Iungerich Smith, Jr., *b* Phila., Pa., Dec. 12, 1887.
1–Studied in Paris, France. Mem. S.M.D., D.F.P.A., H.S. Residence: 2410 Golf Rd., Phila., Pa.

1–**SMITH, Frank Marshall,** *b* Phila., Pa., Aug. 16, 1866.
9–Francis **Smith** (*b* ca. 1600);
8–Samuel (*b* ca. 1633);
7–Samuel (*b* ca. 1667);
6–Jasiel (*b* ca. 1700);
5–Lt. Jasiel (1734-1810), *m* 1757, Anna Crossman (1734/35-1823), for Crossman lineage see Vol. III, p. 575;
4–Seba (*b* 1767), of Boothbay, Me.; *m* 1788, Apphia Stevens (*d* aet. 84);
3–Marshal (*b* 1798), *m* 1823, Nancy Anna Murray Montgomery (1800-75);
2–William Marshall (1838-1922), *m* 1865, Mary Alice Beath (1840-1927), for Beath lineage see Vol. III, p. 575; for issue see Vol. I, p. 964.
1–*m* June 21, 1893, Clara Thatcher Everhart, *b* Martinsburg, Pa., Nov. 19, 1869; dau. of Marshall Henderson Everhart; issue (all *b* Great Falls, Mont.): 1–Aldridge Everhart, *b* June 7, 1894; *m* Oct. 22, 1920, Julia Jacobs, dau. of Samuel J. Heron; 2–Dorothy Alice, *b* Jan. 1, 1896; *m* July 9, 1921, Irving Taft Atwater (issue: Robert Taft, *b* Oct. 1, 1923; Richard Marshall, *b* May 14, 1926); 3–Marjorie Helen, *b* Nov. 16, 1897; *m* Sept. 4, 1929, Lt. Augustus D. Sanders, U.S.A.
1–E.M., Columbia Sch. of Mines, '89. Mining engr.; smelter dir. Bunker Hill Smelter of Bunker Hill & Sullivan Mining & Concentrating Co., Kellogg, Ida.; pres. Northwest Lead Co., Seattle, Wash. (see Who's Who in America). Mem. S.A.R., Mining and Metall. Soc. of America, Am. Inst. Mining and Metall. Engrs. (past v.p. and dir.), Northwest Mining Assn. (past pres.). Mason (32°, K.T., Shriner). Clubs: Columbia U. (N.Y.), City, Rotary, Country, University. Residence: W. 54 8th Av., Spokane, Wash.

1–**SMITH, George Albert,** *b* West Cambridge (now Arlington), Mass., Oct. 15, 1861.
7–John **Morison** (1628-1736), from Scotland, settled for a time in Ireland at or near Londonderry and ca. 1720, settled at Londonderry, N.H.;
6–John (1678-1776), *m* Margaret Wallace;
5–Elizabeth (1723-1808), *m* William **Smith** (1723-1808), justice; del. 4th Provincial Congress of N.H. (Robert[6] [1681-1766; family originally from Scotland], came from Ireland to Lexington, Mass., 1736, settled at Peterborough, N.H., ca. 1757, *m* Elizabeth Smith, 1683-1757);
4–Samuel (1765-1842), founder Village of Peterborough, N.H.; mem. 13th Congress, 1813-15; *m* Nov. 10, 1793, Sally Garfield (1771-1856; Elijah[6], *m* Jane Nichols);
3–Samuel Garfield (1799-1842), mfr., agt. of cotton mills; *m* Sarah Dorcas Abbot (see Vol. II, p. 211, for Abbot lineage);
2–Samuel Abbot (1829-65), A.B., Harvard, '49; grad. Harvard Div. School, 1853; minister 1st Congl. Parish (Unitarian), W. Cambridge,

now Arlington, Mass., 1854-65; *m* 1854, Maria Eliza Edes (see Vol. II, p. 211, for Edes lineage); issue: I–Abbot Edes (*b* 1855; *m* Alice M. Prouty); II–Maria Ellen (1857-1925); III–George Albert (1 above); IV–Samuel Herbert (1864-1902; *m* 1892, Mary Helen Horton, issue: Agatha, *b* Jan. 5, 1893, *m* Aug. 10, 1914, Frank C. Elwell).

1–*m* Feb. 26, 1895, Anna Putnam (July 30, 1872-Dec. 18, 1912); dau. of Charles Putnam, of Lexington, Mass. (George, D.D.[3], minister First Ch., Roxbury, Mass.); issue (all *b* Arlington, Mass.): 1–Samuel Abbot, *b* Dec. 9, 1895; Harvard, '18, A.B., 1919; served in U.S.N. as seaman, naval aviator, ensign, lt. (j.g.); *m* June 17, 1920, Priscilla, dau. of Lyman Whitman Gale (see Vol. I, p. 113; issue: Anna Putnam, *b* Aug. 24, 1921; Lyman Whitman, *b* Oct. 11, 1924; Gale, *b* Feb. 23, 1928); 2–Elizabeth Abbot (Dec. 12, 1897-Feb. 26, 1898); 3–Charles Putnam, *b* Mar. 22, 1899; A.B., Harvard, '21; corpl., U.S.A., Aug. 10, 1918; 2d lt., Sept. 16, 1918; discharged, Dec. 26, 1918; *m* June 6, 1923, Elizabeth Hunnewell, dau. of Harry J. Carlson, of Newton Centre, Mass., *m* Carrie Elizabeth Cornforth (issue: Elizabeth Hunnewell, *b* Oct. 2, 1925); 4–Elizabeth Abbot, *b* Aug. 21, 1900; 5–Anna Putnam (Nov. 29, 1905-Aug. 10, 1906).

1–S.B., M.I.T., '83. Wall paper mfr. since 1886, and treas. Thomas Strahan Co., Chelsea, Mass., both before and since its incorporation, 1900. Summer place: Coffins Beach, West Gloucester, Mass. Residence: 41 Academy St., Arlington, Mass.

1–**SMITH, Helen Norman,** *b* New York, N.Y., Sept. 1, 1899.

10–Jean (Miserol) **Meserole** (*d* 1695), from France, 1663, settled in Bushwick (now Williamsburgh), N.Y.; *m* 1662, Jennie Carton (*d* 1712), from Holland;

9–Jan (1662-1712), *m* 1682, Marytje Covert;

8–Jan (*d* 1756), *m* Elizabeth Praa;

7–Jacob (*d* 1782), began to write name Meserole; *m* 1745, Jannetje Stryker (1724-1811);

6–John I. (1754-1834), Brooklyn, *m* 1781, Elizabeth Titus (1758-1841);

5–Francis (1784-1819), of Williamsburgh; *m* 1804, Letty Brower;

4–Maria A. (1810-82), *m* 1832, Charles **Smith** (1804-41);

3–Henry (1833-97), of Plainfield, N.J.; *m* 1854, Mary Ann Hagar (1832-1906; William[4], *m* Mary King Smith; William H.[5]; William[6]; Joseph H.[7]; William H.[8]; William H.[9]; William[10]);

2–Clarence Meserole (2 below).

6–Col. Crean **Brush** (1725-78), from Dublin, Ireland, settled at New York; practised law there; mem. last 2 Provincial Assemblies, N.Y.; removed to Westminster, Vt., where he was given grant of land; *m* —Cushing (Ethan Allen *m* his step-daughter);

5–Elizabeth Martha (*b* 1758), *m* Thomas **Norman** (*d* 1814), from Drogheda, Ireland;

4–John Echlin (1791-1842), of Caldwell, Lake George, N.Y.; *m* 1822, Jane Ann Thurman;

3–Thomas James (1834-1907), of Montclair Heights, N.J.; *m* 1873, Sophia Speer;

2–Jane (2 below).

8–John **Thurman** (*b* 1695), from Eng., settled in N.Y., 1732;

7–Francis (1727-1756-57), *m* Susannah Matthews, of Eng.;

6–Richardson (1755-1806), of Thurman, Lake George, N.Y.; *m* Catharine Low (1761-1840);

5–James Low (1783-1826), of Warrensburgh, N.Y.; *m* Catherine Cameron (*b* Scotland 1777-*d* 1864);

4–Jane Ann (1805-83), of Thurman; *m* John Echlin **Norman** (4 above).

10–John Hendrick **Speer** (*d* Passaic, N.J.), from Holland, settled in New York; removed to Bergen; later in N.J.; *m* Maria Franse;

9–Frans (bap. 1683-will proved 1771), of Horseneck, N.J.; *m* Dircktie Cornelisse;

8–Cornelius, *m* 1735, Susanna Vincent, widow of Johannes Van Giesen;

7–John, or Johannes, *m* Metje Van Giesen;

6–Reynier (1767-1825), of Speertown, N.J. (now Montclair Hghts. and Upper Montclair); *m* Maria Jacobusse (1768-1842);

5–John R. (*d* 1853), *m* 1811, Leah Sigler (*d* 1853);

4–Rynier (1817-75), *m* Charity Mandeville (1813-95; Henry[5], *m* Sophia Brown; Yellas, or Yellis[6]);

3–Sophia (1844-1926), *m* Thomas James **Norman** (3 above);

2–Jane (*b* 1874), of Montclair, N.J.; *m* 1897, Clarence Meserole **Smith** (*b* 1872), mfr.; issue: I–Helen Norman (1 above); II–Muriel Lefferts (*b* 1903; *m* Webb Wilson).

1–B.S., Columbia, '22. Instr. physical edn., Teachers Coll., Columbia U., 1924-25; prof. and dir. physical edn. for women, U. of Cincinnati, since 1923. Mem. I.A.G. Clubs: Jr. League (New York), Clovernook Country (Cincinnati). Residence: 103 E. 75th St., New York, N.Y.

1–**SMITH, Henry Villiers Brown,** *b* Brooklyn, N.Y., Mar. 20, 1868.

9–John **Smith** (1595-1648), miller; from Eng.; left Dorchester with Roger Williams, 1635; a founder of Providence Plantations, R.I.; established 1st grist mill; town clk., 1641; del. to Portsmouth, to organize govt. under new charter; *m* Alice– (*d* 1650);

8–John (*d* 1682), ens. and dep., 1666-72; town clk., 1672-76; *m* Sarah Whipple (1642-87);

7–Elisha (1680-1766), *m* Experience Maury;

6–Noah (1705-46), *m* 2d, Anna–;

5–Noah (1734-post 1790), ens. Smithfield, R.I., militia, 1750-60; lt., 1765-66; messenger to Gen. Assembly, Providence, during Am. Rev.; *m* 1763, Keziah Man (*b* 1741);

4–Esquire (1765-post 1821), *m* Amy Brown (1770-1814);

3–Hon. Squire (1799-1855), of Norwich, N.Y.; mem. N.Y. Legislature; *m* 1826, Prudence Randall (1800-37);

2–Maj. George Henry (1833-1905), organizer and cdr., U.S. Mil. Telegraph Corps during Civil War, hdqrs. St. Louis, Mo.; *m* 1855, Mary Frances Brown (*b* 1835); issue: I–Herbert Wood (*b* 1859; *m* Frances Laura Letcher); II–George Henry, Jr. (*b* 1862; *m* Hallie Edna Getchell, *d*); III–Mary Frances (*b* 1864); IV–Henry Villiers Brown (1 above); V–Julia Breed (*b* 1873; *m* Walter King Adams); VI–Olive Randall (Mrs. Frank C. Buckley, qv); VII–Paul Litchfield (1878-79).

1–*m* Sept. 3, 1890, Bessie Florence Wilcox, *b* Wadalupe, Ia., July 22, 1871; dau. of Orion Norman Wilcox (1842-1921), *m* Hester Pauline Archer (1843-1921), of Malone, N.Y.; issue (all *b* Crossville, Tenn.): 1–Leonard Villiers (*b* and *d* 1892); 2–Nellie Chadbourne, *b* May 21, 1895; *m* 1925, Cyrus Frank Rea; 3–Hester Mary, *b* May 23, 1902; 4–Florence Elizabeth, *b* July 20, 1905.

1–Ed. public and private schools, St. Paul, Minn. Newspaper business in Crossville, Tenn., 1889; studied law, admitted to bar, Tenn., 1897, N.M., 1911; held varied positions, corporate and public, in Tenn. and N.M.; special practice for 20 years in real estate and probate law and examination of land titles. Mem. S.A.R. Mason (R.A.). Club: Twin Lakes. Residence: Santa Rosa, N.M.

1–**BUCKLEY, Olive Randall Smith (Mrs. Frank C.),** *b* St. Paul, Minn., Oct. 28, 1875.

12–John **Tilley,** Mayflower Pilgrim (qv);

11–Elizabeth (1607-87), *m* ante 1624, John **Howland** (qv);

10–Desire (1623/24-1683), of Marshfield; *m* 1643, Capt. John **Gorham** (qv);

9–Temperance (1646-1715), *m* 1st, ca. 1663, Edward **Sturgis** (1642-78), of Yarmouth (Edward[10], qv);

8–Fear (*d* 1753), of Stonington, Conn.; *m* 1698, Joshua **Holmes** (1678-1729), of Stonington (Joshua[9], *m* Abigail [Ingraham] Chesebro; Robert[10], of Stonington, soldier in King Philip's War);

7–Abigail (1703-32), Stonington; *m* 1728, Jedediah **Brown** (1709-32; John[8], of Stonington, *m* 1692, Elizabeth Miner; Thomas[9], of Lynn, Mass., *m* Mary, dau. Thomas Newhall, of Lynn);

6–Lucy (1730-65), of Stonington; *m* 1750, Capt. John **Randall** (1730-1802), served in Am. Rev. (John[7] [1701-61]; John[8] [*b* 1666]; John[9], 1629-84);

5–Lucy (1751-1831), Stonington; *m* 1768, Amos **Breed** (1744-85);

4–Elias (1782-1849), *m* 2d, 1807, Betsey Randall (1784-1868; Thomas[6] [1741-1831]; John[6] [1701-

61]; John[7] [*b* 1666]; John[8], 1629-84, see 8 above);
3–Mary Elizabeth (1811-87), of Norwich, N.Y.; *m* 1830, Henry Villiers **Brown** (1808-62; Hezekiah[4]; Jesse[5]; Richard, Jr.[6]; Richard[7]; Henry[8], of Providence);
2–Mary Frances (*b* 1835), *m* 1855, Maj. George Henry **Smith** (1833-1905), for issue and Smith lineage see Henry V. B. Smith.
1–*m* Dec. 7, 1895, Frank Cornelius Buckley, *b* Mt. Pleasant, Mich., Dec. 7, 1874; son of Thomas Buckley, of Mt. Pleasant; issue: 1–Randall, *b* Duluth, Minn., Aug. 5, 1913.
1–Mem. S.M.D., D.A.R. (past state cons. registrar), U.S.W.V. Auxiliary, etc. Residence: 1706 21st St., Superior, Wis.

1–**SMITH, Herbert Shelmire** (June 25, 1865-Apr. 1, 1911).
9–Samuel **Smith** (qv);
8–Lt. Philip (1634-85), lt., dea., and rep.; *m* ca. 1657, Rebecca Foote (*d* 1701; Nathaniel[9], qv);
7–Jonathan (1663-1737), of Hatfield, Mass.; *m* 1688, Abigail Kellogg (Joseph[8], qv);
6–Stephen (1697-1760), Amherst, Mass.; *m* Mary Ingraham (John[7], *m* Mehitable Dickinson);
5–Stephen (1749-1813), in Am. Rev.; *m* Dorothy Mattoon (Ebenezer[6], *m* Dorothy Smith; Dr. Nathaniel[7]; Ichabod[8]; Lt. Philip[9]; Lt. Samuel[10]);
4–Arad, *m* Salome Elmer (1781-1827; Elijah[5]);
3–Adolphus (1800-79), *m* 1824, Nancy Dodge (*b* 1804; Maj. Thomas[4], War 1812, *m* Hannah Kezar);
2–Silas Chester (2 below).
8–Rev. Thomas **Dungan,** from Eng., settled at E. Greenwich, R.I.; removed to Cold Springs, Pa., 1682, founded Baptist ch. there; *m* Elizabeth Weaver;
7–Jeremiah (1673-1761), *m* 1702, Deborah Drake (1686 or 87-1721; Capt. George[8], *m* Mary Oliver);
6–Clement (1717-60), *m* 1739, Eleanor Craven (James[7]);
5–Elias (1742-1804), Am. Rev.; *m* ca. 1767, Diana Carrell (James[6], *m* Dianna Van Kirk);
4–Rebecca (1780-1851), *m* George **Shelmire** (1777-1850; Capt. John[5], Am. Rev., *m* Catherine Lashar);
3–Elias Dungan (1803-59), *m* 1826, Maria Vanderpool (1799-1865; Jabez[4], *m* Polly Conrad);
2–Martha Adelia (1839-1914), *m* 1864, Silas Chester **Smith** (1841-78).
1–*m* June 24, 1889, (Lulu) May Alida Purdy (qv for issue).

1–**SMITH, (Lulu) May Alida Purdy (Mrs. Herbert S.),** *b* Greece, Monroe Co., N.Y., May 1, 1868.
8–Francis **Purdy** (ca. 1595-1658), from Eng., settled at Fairfield, Conn., ca. 1635; *m* Mary Brundage (*b* 1628; John[9], *m* Rachel Hubbard);
7–Francis (*d* 1722), *m* Mary Lane (?);
6–Francis (*b* ca. 1672), *m* Sarah Brown (*b* ca. 1692; Peter[7], *m* Martha Disbrow);
5–Ebenezer (1707-1806), Westchester Co., N.Y.; *m* Mary June (1716-1819; Thomas[6]);
4–James (1750-1828), Am. Rev.; *m* his cousin, Phebe Purdy (1744-1840);
3–Nathaniel (1786-1861), N. Norwich, Chenango Co., N.Y.; *m* 3d, Julia Ann Northrop;
2–Dwight Ephriam (2 below).
8–Joseph (Northrup) **Northrop** (qv);
7–William (1666-ca. 1736), *m* Mary Peck (Joseph[8]);
6–Joseph (1698-1775), *m* 1725, Ruth Allen (*d* 1780; Henry[7]);
5–Heth (1754-1825), Am. Rev.; *m* 1777, Anna Newton (*d* 1856);
4–Ephriam (1786-1853), dea.; *m* 1812, Ruth O'Kelley Bunker (1795-1887; Benjamin[5], *m* Ruth Tracy O'Kelley; Benjamin C.[6]; Benjamin[7]; Benjamin[8]; Jonathan[9]; George[10]);
3–Julia Ann (1816-84), *m* 1839, as his 3d wife, Nathaniel **Purdy** (3 above).
9–William **Hartwell** (ca. 1613-1690), from Eng., settled at Concord, Mass., 1636; *m* Jazan– (*d* 1695);
8–John (1640-1702 or 03), *m* 1st, 1664, Priscilla Wright (*d* 1680);
7–Ebenezer (1665 or 66-1723 or 24), *m* 1690, Sarah Smedley (1670-1715);
6–Ebenezer (1698 or 99-1739), Groton, Mass.; *m* 1727, Rachel Farnsworth (*b* 1704; John[7], *m* Hannah Aldis);
5–Oliver (1739-1836), Am. Rev.; *m* 2d, Hannah Benedict;
4–Ebenezer (1767-1856), of Plymouth, Chenango Co., N.Y.; *m* 1795, Rachel Mead;
3–Hiram (1810-61), to Greece, Monroe Co., N.Y., 1855; *m* 1837, Celia Eccleston, (1819-78; David[4], *m* 1st [Polly] Bridget, dau. of Rev. Hazard Burdick, Am. Rev.; David[5], Am. Rev., *m* Katherine Fanning);
2–Aurilla Lewis (2 below).
9–William **Mead** (qv);
8–John (ca. 1634-1699), *m* 1657, Hannah Potter (William[9]);
7–Jonathan (ca. 1665-1726 or 27), *m* ca. 1688, Martha Finch (Joseph[8]);
6–Jonathan (1689-1726), *m* ca. 1718, Sarah Husted (*b* 1687; Joseph[7]);
5–Jonathan (ca. 1727-1804), 1st lt. in Am. Rev.; *m* 1750, Sarah Thompson (1736-1800; Amos[6], *m* Rebecca–);
4–Rachel (1776-1857), *m* 1795, Ebenezer **Hartwell** (4 above);
3–Hiram, *m* Celia Eccleston (3 above);
2–Aurilla Lewis (1841-1917), *m* 1867, Dwight Ephriam **Purdy** (1843-1919), farmer; issue: I–(Lulu) May Alida (1 above); II–Katherine Grace (*b* 1874; *m* William Monroe Grover); III–Hartwell Mead (1879-1915; *m* Anna Maude Ball).
1–*m* June 24, 1889, Herbert Shelmire Smith (qv); issue (all *b* Spencerport, N.Y.): 1–Helen Louise, *b* June 21, 1891; Normal Training School; *m* Apr. 10, 1917, Ivon Northrop, son of Nehemiah H. Brown, *m* Belle Northrop (issue: Richard Nehemiah); 2–Grace Marguerite, *b* Aug. 21, 1892; B.A., U. of Rochester; *m* Mar. 10, 1917, Robert Lewis, son of Lincoln Thomas, *m* Susan Francis (issue: Francis Herbert, Ruth Gertrude); 3–Gertrude Lillian, *b* Apr. 5, 1896; Buffalo Gen. Hosp. Training; *m* Aug. 23, 1923, Herbert Kimball, son of George Herbert Cummings (issue: Dorothy Adell; Donald Herbert); 4–Robert Winfield, *b* Aug. 26, 1897; *m* Aug. 1, 1925, Pearl Doty, dau. of Elmer Ellsworth Sharp, *m* Maude Cromwell; 5–William Seward (Nov. 30, 1898-Sept. 26, 1926), served in World War; *m* July 22, 1921, Lillian Lawler, dau. of John Lawler, *m* Mary Duncan (issue: Donald Duncan); 6–Ralph Hartwell, *b* Feb. 1, 1911; grad. Brockport Normal Sch., '30.
1–Mem. I.A.G., N.E.H.G.S. Congregational. Republican. Residence: Cayuga, N.Y.

1–**SMITH, Annie Morrill (Mrs. Hugh M.),** *b* Brooklyn, N. Y., Feb. 13, 1856.
9–Thomas **Ruggles** (1584-1644), to America, 1637;
8–Capt. Samuel (1629-92), *m* 1654, Hannah Fowle;
7–Samuel (1658-1715), *m* Martha Woodbridge;
6–Samuel (1681-1749), *m* Elizabeth Whiting;
5–Dorothy (1721/22-1804), *m* as his 2d wife, Rev. Isaac **Morrill** (see Vol. II, p. 213);
4–Nathaniel (1757-1828), *m* 1781, Hannah Jaquith;
3–Micajah (1782-1814), *m* 1807, Susannah Floyd;
2–Henry Edwin, M.D. (2 below).
8–Abraham **Jaquith,** from Eng. to Charlestown, Mass.; admitted to ch., 1643; freeman, 1655-56; *m* Anna Jordan;
7–Abraham (*b* 1644), Woburn, Mass.; *m* 1671, Mary Adford;
6–Abraham (1672/73-1753), *m* 1700, Sarah Jones;
5–Capt. Benjamin (1716-1801), *m* Hannah–;
4–Hannah (1757-1826), Wilmington, Mass.; *m* Nathaniel **Morrill** (4 above).
7–Capt. John **Floyd** (ca. 1636-1701/02), from Eng. to Mass.; large landowner nr. Lynn, Mass., 1662; removed to Malden, settled nr. Rumney Marsh, ca. 1670; lt. in King Philip's War; *m* ca. 1661, Sarah Doolittle (*d* 1717, aet. 75; John[8], of Rumney Marsh);
6–Ens. Hugh (1663-1730), *m* Elinor–;
5–Hugh (1704-89), Chelsea, Mass.; *m* 1st, 1729, Mary Baker (1706-51);
4–Hugh (1732/33-1800), served in Lexington Alarm, 1775; *m* 1759, his cousin, Rachel Floyd (*b* 1739; Samuel[5]; Ens. Hugh[6]);
3–Susannah (1780-1860), of Chelsea; *m* 1st, 1807, Micajah **Morrill** (3 above).
9–Rowland **Stebbins** (qv);
8–Lt. Thomas (1620-83), *m* 1645, Hannah Wright;
7–Samuel (1646-1708), *m* 1679, Joanna Lamb;
6–Samuel (1683-1767), *m* 1707, Hannah Hitchcock (1684-1756);
5–Moses (1718-post 1779), *m* 1749, Dorcas Hale;

4–Esther (1755-1827), *m* 1788, James **Langdon** (see Vol. II, p. 213);
3–James Davenport (1792-1887), *m* Sarah Phelps;
2–Cynthia (2 below).
8–Henry **Phelps**, from Eng. in the "Hercules," 1634; settled at Salem; *m* 2d, Eleanor Tresler (Thomas[9]);
7–John (ca. 1644-1685), Reading, Mass.; *m* Widow Abigail Upton (prob. sister of Obadiah Antrum);
6–John (1670/71-1721), Salem; *m* 1700/01, Elizabeth Putnam;
5–Joseph (1704-53), *m* Mrs. Elizabeth (Burnap) Smith;
4–Ebenezer (1745-1831), settled finally at Coesse, Whitley Co., Ind.; *m* 1788, Sarah Brown (1768-1847);
3–Sarah (1797-1862), *m* Rev. James Davenport **Langdon** (3 above);
2–Cynthia (1823-61), *m* 1841, Henry Edwin **Morrill,** M.D. (1813-74).
1–*m* June 9, 1880, Hugh Montgomery Smith (Sept. 21, 1848-Aug. 30, 1897).
1–Ed. Packer Collegiate Inst., ex-'74. Crytogamic botanist; editor and pub. "The Bryologist," 1898-1914. Genealogist since 1913. Author (see Who's Who in America). Mem. D.A.R., I.A.G., Brooklyn Inst. of Arts and Sciences, Bronxville Colony N.E. Women. Residence: 64 Sagamore Road, Apt. L 4, Bronxville, N.Y.

1–**SMITH, L(ewis) Worthington,** *b* Malta, Ill., Nov. 22, 1866.
5–Nathan **Goodspeed** (1760-1837), contractor; leader of mil. bands; *m* Mary Andrus;
4–Asahel, *m* Esther Parker (*d* 1835);
3–Elizabeth Oshea (*b* 1806), *m* George **Smith**;
2–Dwight A. (2 below).
8–Benjamin **Lewis** (1676-1759), of New Haven, and Stratford, Conn.; *m* Hannah Curtis (1654/55-1728; Sgt. John[9], early settler of Stratford);
7–Joseph, *m* Phebe Judson (James[8]);
6–Thomas, *m* Eunice Wells (Robert[7]);
5–Wells (*d* 1836), *m* Anna–;
4–Isaac, *m* 1st, Polly Craft (*d* 1811);
3–Joseph Clark (1798-1877), *d* Bridgeport, Conn.; *m* 1824, Sarah Marianne Phelps;
2–Sarah Elizabeth (2 below).
9–William **Phelps** (qv);
8–Nathaniel (1627-1702), from Eng. with his father; removed to Northampton, Mass.; *m* 1650, Elizabeth Copley;
7–Dea. Nathaniel (1653-1719), of Windsor, Conn.; removed to Northampton, 1656; *m* 1676, Grace Martin;
6–Capt. Timothy (*b* 1697), *m* Abigail Merrick (1702-91), of Springfield, Mass.;
5–Samuel (*b* 1742), Suffield, Conn.; *m* 1768, Lucy Kent;
4–Samuel Merrick (1770-1841), grad. Yale, 1795; minister Presbyn. ch. at N. Salem, N.Y.; later at Ridgefield, Conn.; *m* Eliza Wallace (1781-1857; Uriah[5]);
3–Sarah Marianne (1804-43), *b* Weston, Conn., *d* Bridgeport, Conn.; *m* Joseph Clark **Lewis** (3 above);
2–Sarah Elizabeth (1837-1919), *m* 1864, Dwight A. **Smith** (*d* 1913), merchant, farmer, Malta, Ill.; 1st sgt. in Civil War; for issue, see Vol. I, p. 831.
1–*m* Aug. 24, 1897, Jessie Belle Welborn (qv for issue).
1–Studied Beloit, Wis.; Ph.B., Fairfield Coll., Neb., '89; studied U. of Neb.; A.M., Cotner U., 1901. Prof. English, Drake U., since 1902. Author (see Who's Who in America). Mem. S.A.R. Clubs: Iowa Press and Authors' (pres. 1915-16, 1922-24), Prairie (pres. 1916-17, 1928-29), Authors (London), Poetry Soc. of America. Republican. Congregationalist. Residence: 4023 Cottage Grove Av., Des Moines, Ia.

1–**SMITH, Jessie Belle Welborn (Mrs. L. Worthington),** *b* Indianola, Neb., Mar. 19, 1880.
8–James **Welborn,** from Wales, in the "Sea Venture," 1609, which was wrecked, and he arrived in Jamestown, Va., 1610; settled in Accomac Co., Va.;
7–John;
6–Capt. Thomas (1640-1702), mem. Bd. of Justices and high sheriff, Accomac Co.; *m* Arcadia Toft (Henry[7], *m* Anne–);
5–Samuel, settled in N.C., ca. 1700; surveyor; *m* Mary (or Mason?);
4–William (1762-1839), soldier in Am. Rev.; *m* Heptzabah Starnes;
3–William (1808-89), *m* 1835, Tylitha Cumi Floyd, of Va. (1811-90?);
2–Jesse Davis (1850-1915), landowner, stock breeder; *m* 1871, Belle Hodges Shaw (*b* 1855; Crandall[3], *m* Experience Hodges); issue: I–Son (*d* at birth); II–William Crandall (*d* infancy); III–Daisy Minard (*d* infancy); IV–Jessie Belle (1 above); V–Dorothy D. (*m* Alvin L. Williamson); VI–Georgia Gladys (*m* Elbert Jerome Briggs).
1–*m* Aug. 24, 1897, Lewis Worthington Smith (qv); issue: 1–Marjorie Elizabeth Welborn, *b* Tabor, Ia., Oct. 19, 1900; A.M., Drake, '26.
1–Author, playwright, etc. Pres. Ia. Press and Authors Club, 1919-20. Residence: 4023 Cottage Grove Av., Des Moines, Ia.

1–**SMITH, Martin Sidney,** *b* N. Scituate, R.I., Dec. 21, 1844.
8–Christopher **Smith** (*d* 1676), from Eng., settled at Providence, R.I., ante 1670; sgt. and dep. Gen. Ct. of Mass., 1655; "Antient Friends of Providence"; *m* Alce–;
7–Edward (1635-93), sgt.; mem. Colonial Assembly, 1665-83; *m* 1663, Amphyilis Angell (Thomas[8], founder with Roger Williams of Providence Plantations, *m* Alice, dau. of James Ashton);
6–Joseph (1680-1734), *m* 1706, Patience Mowry (Nathaniel[7], *m* Joanna, dau. of Edward Inman; Roger[8], *m* Mary, dau. of John Johnson);
5–Jacob (*b* 1706), *m* 1727, Dinah Harris (Richard[6]; Thomas[7]; Thomas[8], of Providence Plantations);
4–Jeremiah (*b* 1733), *m* 1759, Lavina Olney (Obediah[5], *m* Lydia Hawkins);
3–Israel (1765-1838), *m* Amey Phillips (Jeremy[4], *m* Elsie, dau. Lt. Gov. William West);
2–Martin (2 below).
8–Christopher **Smith** (above);
7–Edward (above);
6–Joseph (above);
5–Joseph, *m* Lydia Dexter;
4–Simon (1737-1831), *m* Elizabeth Sayles;
3–Ziba (1772-1844), *m* Lydia Waterman (Resolved[4]);
2–Mary (1803-59), *m* Martin **Smith** (1800-70), farmer.
1–*m* 1880, Marcelia Dexter (July 16, 1861-Oct. 11, 1914); dau. of Joseph W. Dexter, of N. Scituate, R.I.; issue (all *b* N. Scituate, R.I.): 1–Howard Dexter, *b* July 27, 1881; *m* July 1, 1909, Grace Weed, dau. of Dr. Fred T. Nye, of Beloit, Wis. (issue: Dorothy G.; Margret; Dexter N.); 2–Mary E. (Feb. 28, 1883-Apr. 16, 1902); 3–Lydia W. (Oct. 11, 1884-May 26, 1919); *m* 1907, Luther W. Patterson; 4–Benjamin H., *b* June 12, 1888; 5–Helen M. (Mrs. Howard W. Steere, qv).
1–A.B., A.M., Brown, '67 (P.B.K.). Farmer. Mem. R.I. Gen. Assembly, 1874-76, 1879-84; R.I. Senate, 1891-92, 1894-95. Second lt., Co. K, 14th R.I. Heavy Arty., in Civil War. Cdr. Rodman Post No. 12 G.A.R., 1887, 1918-29. Mem. M.O.L.L. Residence: North Scituate, R.I.

1–**STEERE, Helen M. Smith (Mrs. Howard Whipple),** *b* Scituate, R.I., Aug. 13, 1890.
9–John **Peckham** (qv);
8–Thomas, *m* 1st–; *m* 2d, Hannah W. Clarke;
7–Thomas (1693-1764), *m* Sarah Browne;
6–Jeremiah (*d* 1765);
5–Jeremiah (*b* 1754), of Newport, R.I.; *m* 2d, 1802, Elizabeth Whitman;
4–Isaac Chapman (1803-72), *m* Johanna Weatherhead (*d* 1901);
3–Elizabeth Whitman (1844-1920), *m* Joseph W. **Dexter** (1834-69), of N. Scituate, R.I.;
2–Marcelia (1861-1914), *m* Martin Sidney **Smith** (qv).
1–*m* Sept. 2, 1914, Howard Whipple Steere, *b* Apr. 22, 1888; son of Thomas Whipple Steere; issue: 1–Lloyd Bertram, *b* Mar. 15, 1916; John Howland Sch., '29.
1–Ed. R.I. Coll. of Edn. and Brown U. Teacher mathematics, John Howland Sch., since 1926. Mem. Town Council, 1921-22. Mem. O.E.S., Grange (master, 1921-22; master of ladies' degree team, 1921-29). Conglist. Republican. Residence: Chepachet, R.I.

1–**SMITH, Richard Alexander,** *b* Chatham Co., N.C., 1868.
8–Alexander **Smith,** from Eng. to Lancaster Co., Va., 1653; owned land in Middlesex Co.;

listed as one to furnish armor and supplies to militia, 1687; vestryman, Christ Ch., Middlesex Co., 1683-90; *m* Mary Anne Coke, of London;
7–Lt. John, mem. of Quorum; *m* Jane Cocke (Nicholas[8]);
6–Samuel (will proved 1737), Caroline Co., Va.; *m* 1726, Anne Amiss;
5–Col. Samuel (1729-1800), removed to "Abrams' Plains," Granville Co., N.C., ca. 1776; justice of ct., 1774; maj. Granville Co. militia, 1776; col. in Am. Rev.; mem. N.C. Senate several terms; *m* 1761, Mary Webb (James[6], of Essex Co., *m* Mary Edmonson);
4–Samuel (1765-1818), had estate in Caswell Co., N.C.; *m* 1792, Elizabeth Harrison (1772-1838; Thomas[5], of Caswell Co., *m* Mary Kennon);
3–Robert Kennon, M.D. (1806-87), Chatham Co., N.C.; *m* 1827, Mildred Hayes Howze (1811-60; Isaac[4], *m* Sarah Willis Ward);
2–Richard Alexander (1828-1904), M.D., U. of N.C. and U. of Pa.; removed to Raleigh, Wake Co., N.C.; *m* Bridgetta Kerrigan (1834-1905), from Donegal Co., Ireland to Phila., Pa.
1–Married; issue: 1–Katharine Pannill; 2–Richard A., Jr.
1–Supt. elec. affairs, Norfolk and Portsmouth, Va., many yrs. Residence: Norfolk, Va.

1–**SMITH, William Basil**, *b* Barren Co., Ky., Oct. 20, 1859.
10–Cuthbert **Fenwick** (1613-55), of Fenwick Towers, Northumberland, Eng.; sailed in "The Ark," Nov. 22, 1633; landed, 1634, and settled at Baltimore; held various offices under Gov. Leonard Calvert; *m* 2d, Widow Jane (Eltonhead) Moryson, of Va. (1600-60; Richard Eltonhead[11], of Lancashire, Eng.);
9–Richard (*d* 1722), of Md.; *m* Dorathy Plowden;
8–John (*d* 1734), of Md.; *m* Winifred Plowden;
7–Robert (*d* 1778 or 79), St. Mary's Co., Md.; *m* Susanna Ford (*d* 1784);
6–John (*d* 1781), civil officer, collector of taxes, St. Mary's Co.; *m* 1st, Elizabeth Guyther;
5–Robert (*d* 1808), of Md. and Ky.; *m* 1762, Ann Elizabeth Manning (*d* 1765);
4–Catherine (1765-1835), Frankfort, Ky.; *m* 1785, Robert **Holton** (*d* 1804), soldier in Am. Rev.;
3–Maria (1791-1870), Franklin Co., Ky.; *m* Benjamin **Luckett** (1787-1866), ens. 2d Regt. Ky. Vols., 1813;
2–Mary Elizabeth (1819-94), Frankfort, Ky.; *m* 1851, Basil Gaither **Smith** (1806-89), planter; issue: I–Maria (*b* 1852; *m* Samuel Pedan); II–Benjamin Luckett (1855-1928; *m* Sallie Ritter); III–Llewelyn Holton (*b* 1857; *m* Sabina Wichard); IV–W. Basil (1 above); V–Humphrey Marshall (*b* 1862; *m* Louise Neideffer); VI–Catherine Quarles (*d* infancy).
1–*m* Nov. 23, 1880, Annie Laurie Huggins (qv for issue).
1–Ed. Western Ky. Normal Sch., '78. Chicken fancier, farmer. Taught sch. aet. 16; passed law examination, 1879; published paper at Lockhart, Texas; published Glasgow (Ky.) Times with J. M. Richardson, 9 yrs.; established, with two other men, the First Nat. Bank of Glasgow, of which he is pres. Baptist. Republican. Residence: Wayside, Glasgow, Ky.

1–**SMITH, Annie Laurie Huggins (Mrs. W. Basil)**, *b* Barren Co., Ky., Sept. 24, 1858.
5–Simon, Simeon or Simmonds **Everett** (*d* 1822; desc. Charles, from Eng., settled at Williamsburg, Va., 1632), of Bedford Co., Va.; *m* 2d, Elizabeth Nelms (*d* 1823; Susannah Vaughan Nelms[6]);
4–Samuel (1782-1864), removed to Ky., ante 1810; *m* 1810, his cousin, Nancy McCoy (*b* 1773; Daniel[6], soldier in Am. Rev.);
3–Elizabeth Ann (1814-80), *m* 1830, Zion Recorder **Huggins** (1808-78), pioneer nurseryman and horticulturist (Reuben[4], *m* Mary McQuillen);
2–William Edmund (1834-84), farmer and merchant; originator of Huggins apple brandy; *m* 1857, Sallie Ermine Reynolds (1837-1915; Meredith S.[3], *m* Sallie Ritter); issue: I–Annie Laurie (1 above); II–Eugenia (1861-1908; *m* 1884, Dr. J. S. Leech); III–Emma (*d*); IV–Eddie (*d*); V–Virginia (*d*); VI–Willie Ermine (*m* James D. Ebert); VII–Nellie (*d*); VIII–Maud Howard; IX–Zion Meredith (*m* Minnie Parrish, *d* 1908).
1–*m* Nov. 23, 1880, William Basil Smith (qv); **issue**: 1–Edmund Huggins, *b* Lockhart, Tex., Nov. 27, 1881; ed. Ky. Mil. Inst., '01; LL.B., Yale, 1905; *m* Nov. 15, 1905, Cora, dau. of Tom McVay, *m* Elizabeth Parker (issue: Basil H.; Tom P.; Edmund McVay; Robert); 2–Jennie Jean, *b* Glasgow, Ky., Nov. 15, 1883; ed. Fairmont, Washington, D.C., '04; *m* Apr. 25, 1912, Vincent Reynolds, son of John W. Jones and Bell Reynolds (issue: Vincent R., *d* infancy; Howard Malcolm); 3–Harry Gorin, *b* Glasgow, Mar. 28, 1885; ed. K.M.I., and U. of Ky.; *m* Oct. 7, 1909, Lyda, dau. of W. B. Gwynne, of Del Ray, Fla., *m* Elizabeth Gardner (issue: Edna Gwynne); 4–Sarah Luckett, *b* Glasgow, Apr. 10, 1889; ed. Liberty Coll., Curry Sch., and Bush Temple, Chicago; *m* Mar. 29, 1916, Ernest B., son of Frank Warder, *m* Alice Yates (issue: Ernest Smith); 5–Howard Basil, *b* Glasgow, Aug. 4, 1891; ed. U. of S.C., and Center Coll., Ky.; 2d lt. in World War; *m* Nov. 23, 1922, Frances, dau. of Herman Leibing, of Terre Haute, Ind., *m* Ella Bohannon (issue: Howard B.; Robert Sydney); 6–Malcolm Rhodes, *b* Glasgow, Oct. 23, 1893; ed. Dixon Acad., Tenn., and K.M.I.; 7–Robert Hendricks (Aug., 1887-July, 1888).
1–Ed. Glasgow Normal, '77. Mem. D.A.R. (Edmund Rogers Chapter historian, regent, 1924-27). Residence: Wayside, Glasgow, Ky.

1–**SMYSER, Lewis Tyler**, *b* Louisville, Ky., Oct. 28, 1897.
5–Jacob **Smyser** (1767-1829), *m* Nancy Frey;
4–John Wesley (1801-53), *m* Mary Elizabeth Smith;
3–Jacob Lewis (*b* 1834), *m* 1861, Frances Lithgow;
2–Harry Lee (2 below).
6–David **Lithgow**;
5–Walter (1787-1813), *m* Frances Stevenson;
4–James Smith (1812-92), *m* Hannah Cragg;
3–Frances (1842-1925), *m* Jacob L. **Smyser** (3 above).
10–Robert **Tyler** (*d* ca. 1674), from Eng., 1663, settled on the Patuxent River, "Bough," Md.; justice, Calvert Co., 1670; *m* 1663, Joanne Ravens;
9–Robert (1671-1738), of Prince George Co., Md., 1671-1738; peace commr.; served in lower house of Gen. Assembly 15 yrs.; elected speaker, 1712, but declined to serve; *m* 1694, Susannah Du Val;
8–Edward (1696-ante 1733), *m* 1716, Elizabeth Duvall (Samuel[9]);
7–Edward (1719-1802), settled at Cross Creek, Va. (now Williamsburg, W.Va.); del. Va. Conv., 1781; came to Ky. with George Rogers Clark, settled at Louisville; moved to Jeffersontown, Jefferson Co., 1783; *m* 1749, Nancy Langley (1732-1820);
6–Edward (1769-1840), *m* 1788, Ann Hughes (1766-1817; Isaac[7], *m* Sarah Leak);
5–Levi (1789-1861), *m* 1810, Eliza Oldham (1792-1840; Samuel[6], *m* Ann Lipscomb);
4–Henry Samuel (1815-83), *m* 1837, Rebecca Ann Gwathmey (1815-92); see Vol. III, p. 425, for Gwathmey lineage;
3–Isaac Hughes (1838-83), *m* Jane Louise Owen (1846-1929);
2–Rebecca Gwathmey (see Vol. III, p. 425); *m* 1894, Harry Lee **Smyser** (*b* 1864).
1–*m* Mar. 4, 1919, Sarah Marshall Ide, *b* Troy, N.Y., Sept. 2, 1897; dau. of Alba Marshall Ide, *m* Gertrude Knight; issue (all *b* Louisville, Ky.): 1–Frances, *b* July 31, 1920; 2–Cynthia Ide (Nov. 8-10, 1924); 3–Marshall Ide, *b* Aug. 21, 1926; 4–Sarah Tyler, *b* Dec. 27, 1928.
1–Ed. Rensselaer Poly. Inst., 1919. Treas. Alemite Lubricator Co. of Ky. Ens., U.S.N., World War. Mem. S.C.W., S.A.R. Clubs: Wynn Stay, Louisville Country. Residence: Blankenbaker Lane, Upper River Rd., Louisville, Ky.

1–**SNEDEKER, Charles Dippolt**, *b* New Brunswick, N.J., July 17, 1861.
8–Jan **Snedeker** (*b* ca. 1620), from Holland, 1642; settled at Flatbush, L.I., *m* Annetje Buys;
7–Gerret Janse (*b* ca. 1645), *m* Willemtje Vooks;
6–Christiaen (*b* ca. 1669), *m* 1689, Pietertie Ariaense;

5–Isaac (bap. 1708), *m* Catherine Hegeman;
4–Isaac (bap. 1761), *m* Sarah–;
3–Jacob (*b* 1802), *m* 1822, Catharine Stults (*b* 1801);
2–Cornelius (1830-81), *m* 1853, Mary Catherine Stonaker (1833-1912).
1–*m* Jan. 23, 1894, Mary Davison, *b* New Brunswick, N.J., Mar. 11, 1863; dau. of John J. Davison, of New Brunswick; issue: 1–Charles D., Jr. (*b* and *d* 1897).
1–Retail clothing business, at New Brunswick, N.J., 1883-94; sec. and treas. Perth Amboy Dry Dock Co. 1894-1928, since pres.; also pres. First National Co. of Perth Amboy; v.p. First Nat. Bank of Perth Amboy; dir. First Nat. Bank of Carteret, N.J. Pres. Bd. of Water Commrs. of Perth Amboy 10 yrs. Mem. Holland Soc. of New York, I.A.G.; fellow Am. Geog. Soc., N.J. Hist. Soc., Maritime Assn. of the Port of New York, etc. Clubs: Automobile of America, Colonia Country (pres.). Residence: Perth Amboy, N.J.

JOHN TALMAN MACK (b Rochester, N.Y., July 26, 1846-d Sandusky, O., July 8, 1914), A.B., Oberlin Coll., '70, A.M., 1872; for many years editor and publisher of the Sandusky Daily Register; a founder of the Associated Press, and pres. Associated Ohio Dailies 25 years; trustee Ohio State University 21 years; vestryman, and supt. Sunday School of Grace Episcopal Church 25 years.

1–**SNYDER, Alice Ritchart Mack (Mrs. Reginald Clare),** *b* Sandusky, O., Aug. 27, 1876.
8–John **Mack** (1653-1721), from Scotland, 1669, settled at Salisbury; later at Concord, Mass.; landed propr. at Lyme, Conn.; *m* 1681, Sara Bagley (*b* 1663; Orlando[9], *m* Sara, dau. of Anthony Colby);
7–Jonathan (1695/96-1768), *m* 1727, Sara Bennett (Caleb[8]; Henry[9], *m* Sara, dau. of Henry Champion, founder of Saybrook);
6–Joseph (1728-92), Am. Rev.; Alstead, N.H.; *m* 1st, Lois Tiffany (*d* ante 1782; Lt. Nathan[7]; Consider[8], *m* Abigail Niles; Humphrey[9]);
5–Nathan, Wilbraham, Mass.; Am. Rev. from N.H.; *m* 1st, 1774, Molly Diggens (Dickens) (1754-1810);
4–Sewell Tiffany (ca. 1775-76-1812), of Wilbraham; said to have been an Episcopal minister; *m* 1801, Hannah Cady (1778-1852);
3–Isaac Foster, Sr. (1806-86), ed. Monson (Mass.) Acad.; prin. first free common school at Cincinnati; organized, and was many yrs. supt. of the first free school system at Rochester, N.Y.; moved to Wis. and laid out town of Broadhead; editor Broadhead Independent, lawyer, farmer; sch. supt. and village pres.; later pres. Englewood (Ill.) Bd. Edn.; *m* 1st, 1831, Clarissa Beebe;
2–John Talman (2 below).
9–John **Beebe,** III (*d* 1650), *d* at sea, on his journey from Eng. to America; *m* Rebecca Ladd, from Eng., 1650, settled at New London, Conn.;
8–Samuel (1633-1712), *m* 1st, 1660, Agnes Keeney; *m* 2d, Mary Keeney, sister of 1st wife;
7–Jonathan (1674-1761), Millington, Conn.; large landowner; *m* Bridget Brockway (1671-1756);
6–William (1700-88), ens. of Train Band at Parish of Millington, 1743; *m* 1st, Phoebe–; *m* 2d, Eleanor–;
5–Asa (1730-1813), Winhall, Vt.; sold cattle for army during Am. Rev.; minuteman in Am. Rev.; in "Danbury Raid," 1777; *m* 1763, Lydia Day (1743-1813);
4–Asa (1764-1851), rep. for Winhall, Bennington Co., Vt., 1796-1816; first town clk. of Winhall; *m* 1790, Sara Day (1769-1849);
3–Clarissa (1809-48), Greece, Monroe Co., N.Y.; *m* 1831, Isaac Foster **Mack** (3 above);
2–John Talman (1846-1914), see portrait and biography; *m* 1873, Flora Alice Davenport (1849-1925); issue: I–John Davenport (*b* 1875; *m* Mrs. Blanche [Ford] Emmick); II–Alice Ritchart (1 above); III–Ethel Beebe (*b* 1879; *m* Albert Charles Blinn); IV–Egbert Hiram (*b* 1881; *m* Dorothy Schumaker); V–Cornelia Penelope (*b* 1886; *m* Charles Jacob Stark).
1–*m* Oct. 20, 1897, Reginald Clare Snyder, *b* Findlay, O., Sept. 25, 1873; son of William Edward Snyder, of Findlay, *m* Sara Helen Duduit; issue: 1–Alice Davenport, *b* Findlay, O., Mar. 19, 1899; Smith, '22; *m* June 28, 1924, Dudley Allen, son of Albert Union White, of New London, O. (issue: Alice Mack, *b* Sept. 22, 1925; Dudley Allen, Jr., *b* Apr. 15, 1930).
1–Mem. D.A.C. (nat. historian, 1928-31), D.A.R., U.S.D. 1812. Episcopalian. Residence: Norwalk, O.

1–**SOMERVILLE, Anne Keith Frazier (Mrs. Robert N.),** *b* Chattanooga, Tenn., May 14, 1888.
8–William **Randolph** (qv);
7–Col. Thomas (1685-ca. 1731), of "Tuckahoe"; *m* Judith Fleming (Col. Charles[8], *m* Mary Bolling; Sir Thomas[9]);
6–Mary Isham, *m* 1733, Rev. James **Keith** (qv);
5–Alexander (1748-1824), *m* 1778, Mary (Thornton) Gallihue (*b* 1753; Charles Gallihue[6], Am. Rev.);
4–Charles Fleming (1782-1864), *m* Elizabeth Douglas Heale;
3–Alexander (1814-76), *m* 1840, Sarah Ann Penelope Foree (1823-1914; Augustine Pryor[4], *m* Nancy Pugh; desc. Peter Foree, from France, officer Am. Rev., *m* Sarah Pryor, of Charleston, S.C.);
2–Louise Douglas (2 below).
9–Nicholas (Haile) **Heale,** planter, York Co., Va., 1654;
8–George (*d* 1698), began to write name Heale; burgess, Lancaster Co., 1693-96; *m* Ellen–;
7–William (*d* 1732), *m* Priscilla Downman (William[8], from Eng. to Va., 1608, *m* Million, dau. of Raleigh Travers, from Eng. to Va., burgess, *m* Hannah, dau. of Col. Joseph Ball);
6–George (1728-1808), Fauquier Co., Va.; burgess; *m* Sarah Smith;
5–Philip (*b* 1753), *m* 1779, Katherine Douglas (William[6], from Scotland to Va., Am. Rev., *m* Elizabeth Offut);
4–Elizabeth D., *m* Charles Fleming **Keith** (4 above).
10–George **Reade** (qv);
9–Mildred, *m* Speaker Augustine **Warner** (1642-81), of "Warner Hall" (Augustine[10], qv);
8–Mary (*d* 1700), *m* Col. John **Smith** (*d* 1698), of "Purton" (Speaker John[9]);
7–Philip (1695-1743), of Northumberland Co.; *m* Mary Matthews (g.dau. of Gov. Samuel Matthews, of Va.);
6–Sarah (*b* 1732), *m* George **Heale** (6 above).
2–Louise Douglas Keith, *m* 1883, James B. **Frazier** (*b* 1856), gov. of Tenn., 1903-07; U.S. senator, 1905-11; issue: I–Anne Keith (1 above); II–James B., Jr. (*b* 1890); III–Thomas Alexander (*b* 1895); IV–Louise Douglas (*m* John Porter Fort).
1–*m* Nov. 20, 1912, Robert Nugent Somerville, *b* Greenville, Miss., 1886; son of Robert Somerville, *m* Nellie Nugent; issue: 1–Keith, *b*

Chattanooga, Tenn., May 30, 1914; 2–Ashton, *b* Cleveland, Miss., Feb. 12, 1917.
1–Ed. Ward-Belmont Sch., Nashville, and The Castle, Tarrytown, N.Y. Mem. C.D.A., D.A.R. (state regent), Soc. Sponsors of U.S.N., National Officers Club. Residence: "Somervilla," Cleveland, Miss.

1–**SMITH, Edward Luther,** *b* Towanda, Pa., Apr. 27, 1862.
5–Jonas **Smith** (1737-1800), *m* Mercy Buxton (1744-1822; Charles[6], *m* Mercy Lounsbury; Clement[7], *m* Elizabeth Ferris; Clement[8], *m* Judith–);
4–Jesse (1766-1843), *m* Jane Miller (1766-1844);
3–Jesse (1807-71), *m* 1828, Anna Lent;
2–Myron (2 below).
9–Hercules **Lent,** trustee Dutch Ch., at Peekskill, N.Y.; *m* Catrena Seboutin (Hendrickson[10]);
8–John, *m* Catrena Van Tassell (Jacob[9], of Sleepy Hollow);
7–Abram, *m* Mary de Ronda;
6–Hendrickson, *m* Mary de Pew;
5–Henry, patriot Am. Rev.; *m* Catherine Croft (John[6], *d* ante Am. Rev.);
4–Joseph (1786-1869), pioneer of Bradford Co., Pa.; War 1812; *m* Mary Ann Johnson;
3–Anna (1811-50), *m* Jesse **Smith** (3 above).
7–Moses **Johnson,** of Woodbury, Conn.; *m* Prudence Jenner (Samuel[8]);
6–John (*b* 1719), *m* Mary Judd (Daniel[7], *m* Mercy Mitchell; William[8]; Dea. Thomas[9], qv);
5–John, *m* Anne Hinman (Samuel[6], *m* Amy Twitchel; Capt. Wait[7], Am. Rev.; Benjamin[8]; Sgt. Edward[9], qv);
4–Mary Ann, *m* Joseph **Lent** (4 above).
6–Benjamin **Scott** (of the family of Scotts, of Harden, House of Buccleuch, Scotland), defeated in battle of Culloden, 1746; came from Scotland; settled at Suffield (now Conn.), Mass.; in French and Indian War, 1755-57, and on expdn. to Quebec;
5–William (1744-1803), came with his father; Am. Rev.; *m* 1766, Anne Boise (William[6], *m* Mary Hamilton; David[7]);
4–George (1784-1834), settled in Pa., 1805; *m* Lydia Strope (Henry[5], *m* Catherine, dau. Rudolph Fox, 1st white settler at Towanda, 1770);
3–Luther Henry (1820-1904), *m* Marietta Learned Brown;
2–Frances Marion (2 below).
10–William **Learned** (qv);
9–Isaac (1623-57), of Watertown, Mass.; *m* 1646, Mary Stearnes (bap. 1626; Isaac[10], qv);
8–Isaac (1655-1737), *m* Sarah Bigelow (John[9]);
7–William (1688-1747), *m* Hannah Briant (Simon[8], *m* Hannah Spear);
6–Samuel (1718-70), in French and Indian War; *m* Rachel Green (Henry[7], *m* Judith, dau. Ephraim Guile; Henry[8]; Henry[9]; Thomas[10], qv);
5–William (1752-1828), Am. Rev. and War 1812; *m* Mrs. Angell;
4–Betsey (ca. 1778-ca. 1824), *m* ca. 1803, Ephraim **Brown** (Joseph[5]; Briant[6]; Capt. Nathaniel[7]; John[8]);
3–Marietta Learned (1820-1902), *m* Luther Henry **Scott** (3 above);
2–Frances Marion (1840-1922), *m* 1861, Myron **Smith** (1830-1908), contractor and builder; issue: I–Edward Luther (1 above); II–Clara (*d* infancy).
1–*m* June 15, 1886, Mildred Louise Rahm (qv for issue).
1–Ed. Susquehanna Collegiate Inst. Formerly owned and operated public utilities. Mem. H.S. (Pa.), S.R. Mason (K.T., Shriner). Clubs: Scranton City, Shepherd Hills Country, Towanda Country, Irem Temple Country. Summer place: "Pleasant View," Lake Wesauking, Pa. Residence: 363 York Av., Towanda, Pa.

1–**SMITH, Mildred Louise Rahm (Mrs. Edward L.),** *b* Towanda, Pa., June 5, 1867.
8–John Conrad **Weiser** (1660/61-1746), from Germany, 1709; settled at Livingston Manor, N.Y., 1710; capt., Queensbury Co. of Palatines, Brit. Army, 1711; settled in Berks Co., Pa., 1723; *m* Anna Magdalen Ubele (*d* Germany, 1709);
7–Christopher Frederick (1699-1768), *m* Elizabeth– (*b* 1702); *m* 2d, Marie Catherine Roeder;
6–Maria Catherine (1733-62), *m* 1754, Conrad **Rahm** (1728-82), from Metz, Alsace-Lorraine, in the "Europa," settled nr. Phila., 1745; corpl., German Cont. Regt. at Valley Forge; crossed Del. River with Gen. Washington;
5–John Michael (1755-95), pvt. Am. Rev.; 2d lt., 1777; *m* 1780, Sophia (Toot) Ross (*b* 1754-55; David Toot[6]; Jonas[7], of Dauphin Co., Pa.);
4–Melchoir (*b* 1781), as q.m. Dauphin Co. militia, War 1812; *m* Sarah Kapp (1781-1849; Michael[5], Am. Rev.; Michael[6], from Germany in the "Pennsylvania," 1732);
3–David (1811-82), of Schuylkill, Columbia and Bradford cos.; *m* 1838, Hannah Pugh Davis (1816-82; John Pugh Davis[4], *m* Sarah, dau. John Cleaver, Am. Rev.; Benjamin[5], of Am. Rev.; James[6]; Morris[7]; James ap David[8], from Wales to Chester Co., Pa., 1701);
2–John Melchoir (2 below).
7–William **Ennes,** Ulster Co., N.Y.; *m* ante 1694, Cornelia Vier Vant;
6–William (*b* 1711/12), Am. Rev.; *m* 1739, Elizabeth Quick (Thomas[7], of Milford, Pa., *m* Margrieta Decker);
5–Cornelius (1761-1836), Am. Rev.; *m* Eleanor Decker (1756-91);
4–Levi (1782-1858), *m* Mary Adams (1788-1869; James[5], *m* Mary Ann Dunn);
3–Alexander (1816-79), *m* 1837, Eleanor Stevens;
2–Anna Amelia (2 below).
9–Cyprian **Stevens** (son of Col. Thomas, of London, Eng.); from Eng., 1660; settled at Lancaster, Mass.; *m* 1st, 1671, Mary Willard (1653-ca. 1685; Maj. Simon[10], qv);
8–Simon (1677-1758), Boston; *m* 1701, Mary Wilder (1679-ca. 1728; Lt. Nathaniel[9], *m* Mary, dau. Thomas Sawyer, qv; Thomas[10]; John[11]);
7–Jonathan (bap. 1710), *m* 1732, Mary Tracy (Solomen[8]; Dr. Solomen[9]; Lt. Thomas[10], qv);
6–Asa (1734-78), Am. Rev.; killed in Wyoming Massacre (name on monument); *m* Sarah Adams (*d* 1787; Ahaziah[7], of Canterbury, Conn.; Henry[8]; Samuel[9]; Lt. Thomas[10]; Henry[11], qv);
5–Jonathan (*b* Wilkes-Barre, Pa.-*d* 1850), Am. Rev.; to Standing Stone, Pa., after Am. Rev.; surveyor and asso. judge, Bradford Co., Pa.; *m* Eleanor Adams (Abner[6], Am. Rev.; Isaac[7]; Richard[8]); *m* 2d, Elizabeth (Waite) Shipley;
4–Asa (1790-1879), *m* Phoebe Vought (*b* 1795; Achitius[5], War 1812; Joseph Christian[6], from Holland, Am. Rev.);
3–Eleanor (*b* 1818), *m* Alexander **Ennes** (3 above);
2–Anna Amelia (1844-1926), Standing Stone, Pa.; *m* 1866, John Melchoir **Rahm** (1839-1915), supt. maintenance of way, L.V.R.R., 1867-97.
1–*m* June 15, 1886, Edward Luther Smith (qv); issue (all *b* Towanda, Pa.): 1–David Rahm, *b* Apr. 30, 1888; Lehigh U., '12; capt. and maj. inf., U.S.A., at Ft. Niagara, N.Y., and Camp Meade, World War; lt. col. O.R.C., 1922; *m* Anna Louise Eilenberger (see Vol. III, p. 421); 2–Eleanor Scott, *b* Jan. 14, 1894; grad. Birmingham Sch. for Girls (Pa.), '13, Drexel Inst., '16; *m* Apr. 12, 1918, Steacy Ernest, son of J. Harold Webster, of Chestnut Hill, Pa.; 3–Elizabeth Learned (May 18-28, 1906).
1–Ed. Susquehanna Collegiate Inst., 1883; Bliss Sch. for Young Ladies (Rochester, N.Y.), 1883-85. Dir. Towanda Pub. Library. Mem. S.D.P., C.D.A., H.S. of Pa., D.A.R. (regent 7 yrs.), U.S.D. 1812 (v. regent 8 yrs.), Bradford Co., Pa., Hist. Soc. (pres. 2 yrs., librarian 4 yrs.), Nat. Soc. N.E. Women. Residence: 363 York Av., Towanda, Pa.

1–**SMITHEY, Dorothy Muffly Strickland (Mrs. Louis Philippe),** *b* Roanoke, Va., Oct. 28, 1894.
8–Capt. Christopher **Clark,** gent. (*b* Eng., ca. 1700-*d* 1754), received land grant, Albemarle Co., Va.; *m* Penelope Massie Bolling (g.dau. of Earl of Shaftsbury);
7–Micajah (1718-1801), Am. Rev.; *m* 1736, Judith Adams (*b* 1716; Robert[8], *m* Mourning Adams);
6–Dr. Micajah (1741-1849?), *m* 1761, Mildred Martin (*b* 1742; Thomas[7], settled in Albemarle Co., ante 1764, *m* Anne, dau. of Charles Moorman; John[8], burgess);
5–Dr. Robert (1764-1820), *m* 1791, Nancy Venable Moorman;
4–Dr. Thomas Martin (1799-1871), of Patrick Co., Va.; *m* 1821, Susan Elizabeth Cobb (1806-89);
3–Martha Hunt (1824-1910), *m* 1856, Matthew Will-

iam **Strickland** (1819-1900; James Cabaniss[4], of Halifax Co., Va.);
2–Dr. James Thomas (2 below).
8–Abraham **Venable** (qv);
7–Abraham (1700-68), capt. militia, Louisa Co., Va.; owned immense tracts of land in Hanover, Louisa, Goochland and Albemarle cos., Va.; justice, Hanover Co., ante 1742, Louisa Co., 1742; capt. colonial militia; burgess, 1742-62; vestryman, St. Paul's Parish, Hanover Co., ante 1742, Fredericksville Parish, 1742-61, Trinity Parish, 1762-68, *m* ca. 1723, Martha Davis (1702-65; Robert[8], *m* Abadiah Lewis);
6–Mary (*b* 1739), *d* Breckinridge Co., Ky.; *m* Charles **Moorman** (1737-98), Am. Rev.;
5–Nancy Venable, *m* Robert **Clark** (5 above).
6–Nicholas **Muffly,** from Rotterdam, Holland, 1737, as cabin passenger on the "William," landed in Phila.; took oath of allegiance; naturalized; bought farm in Bucks (now Carbon) Co., Pa.;
5–Peter (*d* 1816), *m* Catherine Regina Wanamaker;
4–Lucas Henry (*b* Carbon Co., Pa., 1812-*d* 1858), *m* Nancy Davis Eckert;
3–Sidney Theodore (1840-1908), *m* 1865, Mary Eliza Brewer;
2–Nettie (2 below).
7–Henry **Eckert,** English Quaker; to America with Quaker colony, 1732 or 35; settled in Phila.;
6–William, from Bucks Co. to Lancaster (now York) Co., Pa.;
5–Jacob (*b* York, Pa., 1780), *m* Ann Hewings (*b* 1783; John[6], *m* Sarah–);
4–Nancy Davis (1810-80), *m* Lucas H. **Muffly** (4 above).
10–John **Brewer** (1622-64), one of the 100 invited Puritans to go to Va. from Mass.; burgess; mem. Council; from Va. to Anne Arundel Co., Md.; built "Brewerton," on South River; *m* 1640, Elizabeth Heathcoat (*d* 1667);
9–John (1644-90), commr., 1667; justice; del., 1660-62; burgess; *m* 1685, Sarah Ridgley (Col. Henry[10], qv);
8–John (1686-1730), Anne Arundel Co.; *m* 1704, Dinah Battee (*d* 1732; **Ferdinand**[9], **grad. Oxford**, Eng., justice Anne Arundel Co., 1683-94);
7–Joseph (*b* 1713), *m* 1736, Mary Stockett (*b* 1704; Thomas[8]; Thomas[9]);
6–Joseph (*b* 1744), *m* 1768, his cousin, Jane Brewer (*b* 1746; John[7], *m* 1727, Eleanor MacCubbin);
5–John (*b* 1776 or 78), *m* 1st, 1800, Elizabeth Jeannette Gaston (Capt. George[6], French naval officer with LaFayette, *m* Anne–);
4–Dr. William (1804-78), *m* 1837, Mary Elizabeth Rawlings (1821-88; William[5], *m* Mary Eliza Miles);
3–Mary Eliza (1848-81), *m* Sidney T. **Muffly** (3 above);
2–Nettie (*b* 1866), *m* 1885, Dr. James Thomas **Strickland** (*b* 1857), physician, Roanoke, Va.; issue: I–Jeannette (*b* 1890; *m* 1910, Philip Barnhart Weaver, *b* 1883); II–Dorothy M. (1 above).
1–*m* Jan. 1, 1925, Louis Philippe Smithey, *b* Marengo, Va., June 7, 1890; son of Rev. William Rosser Smithey, of Amelia Co., Va., *m* Namie Greene (desc. Gen. Nathanael Greene, Am. Rev.).
1–Ed. Va. Coll., Roanoke, Hollins (Va.) Coll., Washington (D.C.) Coll., Corcoran Art Sch. Atty. at law, interior decorator. Mem. D.A.R., U.D.C., A.L. Auxiliary (past pres.), Am. Fed. of Arts. Clubs: Roanoke Country, Roanoke Woman's, Delphian. Residences: 2 Thompson St., Annapolis, Md.; 802 Wycliffe Av., Roanoke, Va.

1–**SONNER, Wenonah Ermine Peckinpaugh (Mrs. Thomas B.),** *b* Alton, Ind., Jan. 1, 1878.
5–George Peter **Peckinpaugh** (*d* 1785), from Germany, 1760, *d* at Brownsville, Pa.;
4–John (1783-1867), of Cape Sandy, Ind.; *m* 1st, 1804, Christine Rice (*d* 1812; Nicholas[5], served in 3d Co., 6th Bn., 1780-81, 5th Co., 6th Bn., 1782, 1st Co., 4th Bn., 1783, Am. Rev., *m* Mary Ann Marilda Elizabeth Hickman);
3–Nicholas Rice (1810-59), of nr. Alton, Ind.; *m* 1832, Eleanor Sheckell (1815-89);
2–Abraham Nicholas **Peckinpaugh** (1839-1912), lumberman, Alton, Ind.; *m* 2d, 1874, Ruth Elizabeth Wilson (1840-1927); for issue and maternal lineages see Mrs. Sidney J. Hatfield, p. 252.
1–*m* July 9, 1896, Thomas Bayard Sonner, *b* Harrison Co., Ind., Feb. 24, 1866; son of Amos Sonner, of Harrison Co., Ind., *m* Eliza Dean; issue: 1–Ruth Peckinpaugh, *b* Alton, Ind., June 22, 1899; *m* Jan. 26, 1918, Ford Patrick Tracey (issue: Ford; Thomas Sonner; Ruth Elizabeth).
1–Attended Ward-Belmont Coll. Mem. S.M.D., D.A.R., Soc. of Ind. Pioneers. Methodist. Democrat. Residence: 3925 Broadway, Indianapolis, Ind.

1–**SPAULDING, Forrest Brisbine,** *b* Nashua, N.H., May 4, 1892.
10–Edward (Spalding) **Spaulding** (qv);
9–Andrew (1652-1713), of Chelmsford, Mass.; *m* 1674, Hannah Jefes (*d* 1730);
8–Henry (1680-1720), *m* 1703, Elizabeth Lund (*b* 1684; Thomas[9]);
7–Henry (1704-92), pvt. colonial wars, 1757; *m* 1725, Lucy Proctor (*d* 1742),
6–Samuel (1727-97), Merrimack, N.H.; lt. in Am. Rev.; in Battle of White Plains; *m* 1753, Sarah Woods (1730-1815; Samuel[7], *m* Mary Parker);
5–Henry (1760-1857), Francestown, N.H.; *m* 1787, Joanna Russell (1766-1853), of Dunbarton, N.H.;
4–Leonard (1802-90), *m* 1831, Ede Farrington (1800-56), of Greenfield, N.H.;
3–Ebenezer Farrington (1835-1919), of Francestown, N.H., Janesville, Wis., and Boston, Mass.; asst. surgeon, 7th Wis. Regt., Civil War; *m* 1864, Ada H. Pearson (*d* 1925), of Janesville, Wis.;
2–Maj. Hollon Curtis (2 below).
4–David **Brisbine,** of Ohio; *m* Margaret Stevens;
3–Napoleon B., of Lancaster, Pa.; *m* Harriet Chamberlin;
2–Lucile (*b* 1868), *m* 1890, Maj. Hollon Curtis **Spaulding** (1865-1925), of Janesville, Wis., Boston, Mass., and Nashua, N.H.; capt. Ordnance Dept., World War; served as port q.m., Halifax, N.S., promoted to rank of maj.; electrical engr.
1–*m* Aug. 28, 1916, Genevieve Anderson Pierson, *b* Omaha, Neb., Sept. 10, 1892; dau. of John L. Pierson, of Burlington, Ia. (Johnson[3], of Burlington); issue: 1–John Pierson, *b* Brooklyn, N.Y., June 25, 1917; 2–Jean, *b* New York, N.Y., Jan. 17, 1920.
1–Phillips Exeter Acad., 1908; Williston Sem., 1908-09; diploma Library Sch., N.Y. Public Library, 1913. Librarian, Des Moines, (Ia.) Public Library, 1917-19, and since 1927 (see Who's Who in America). Mason (32°). Episcopalian. Republican. Clubs: Hermit, Rotary, Prairie, Pow-wow, Wakonda Country. Summer place: Colebrook, Conn. Residence: 520 42d St., Des Moines, Ia.

1–**SPEARS, Maude Lucile Dawson (Mrs. George Thomas),** *b* Wills Point, Tex., Dec. 29, 1877.
10–Alexander **Shapleigh** (qv);
9–Catherine (1608-living 1674), *m* 1st, James **Treworgye** (1595-ante 1650), agent in Me. for Gov. Gorges;
8–Elizabeth (1639-1719), *m* 1657, Hon. John **Gilman** (1624-1708), of Exeter, N.H.; councillor, selectman, asso. judge; dep. Gen. Ct.; rep. and speaker; lt. and capt. Exeter militia; judge Common Pleas Ct. (Edward[9], qv);
7–Catherine (*b* 1684), *m* Peter **Folsom** (1682-1718);
6–Peter (1714-92), *m* Mary Folsom;
5–Samuel (1761-1849), Deerfield, Me.; *m* Anna Shepherd;
4–Isaac (1792-1865), Batesville, Ark.; *m* Lucia Davis Morton;
3–Harriet (1833-1910), *m* 1852, Patrick Henry **Childress** (1814-79);
2–Clara Howard (2 below).
9–John **Folsom** (qv);
8–Dea. John (1640-1715), of Exeter, N.H.; mem. Gen. Assembly; *m* 1675, Abigail Perkins;
7–Jonathan (1685-1740), *m* Anna Ladd;
6–Mary (1722-91), *m* Peter **Folsom** (6 above).
10–George **Morton** (qv);
9–Ephraim (1623-93), *m* on passage to America; *m* 1st, 1644, Anna Cooper (*d* 1691);
8–George, *m* 1664, Joanna Kempton;
7–Timothy (1682-1748), *m* 1711 or 12, Mary Rickard (*d* 1734);

6–Silas (*b* 1727), *m* 1748, Martha Morton;
5–Silas (1752-1840), lt. Am. Rev.; bvtd. capt.; mem. S.C. (Mass.); *m* 1792, Elizabeth Foster (*b* 1769).
4–Lucia Davis (1806-72), *m* Isaac **Folsom** (4 above);
3–Harriet, *m* Patrick Henry **Childress** (3 above);
2–Clara Howard (*b* 1854), *m* 1876, Abraham Cromwell **Dawson** (1854-1921), of Athlone, Ireland; cotton dealer; issue: I–Maude Lucile (1 above); II–Mamie Mae (1886-87).
1–*m* Feb. 22, 1899, George Thomas Spears, *b* Butler, Ga., Sept. 12, 1871; son of Mark Lucius Spears, Ga.; issue: 1–Maude Lucile (May 7, 1900-1903); 2–George Thomas, *b* Grand Saline, Tex., Oct. 1, 1904; Tex. Mil. Coll.; *m* Sept. 16, 1926, Ruby, dau. Charles J. Clark, of Breckenridge, Tex. (issue: George Thomas, III); 3–Clara Mary, *b* Terrell, Tex., Apr. 14, 1908; B.S., Coll. of Industrial Arts of Tex. U., '29.
1–Grad. Hawthorne Coll., '95. Teacher in Tex. public schs., 1896-98, and during World War. Mem. D.A.R. (organizing regent, Silas Morton Chapter, named for Capt. Silas Morton, 5 above). Mem. M.E. Ch., South. Clubs: Delphian, Fine Arts, Wednesday Study. Residence: 107 N. McAmis Av., Breckenridge, Tex.

1–**SPENCER, Bunyan,** *b* nr. Coshocton, O., July 16, 1854.
4–Joseph **Spencer** (*b* 1757), supposed to have been capt. of militia in Am. Rev.; *m* 1781, Margaret Foreman (1758-94);
3–William (1786-1839), *m* 1st, 1810, Katherine Prior (1794-1831; Timothy[4], soldier Am. Rev.);
2–Joseph Cephas (2 below).
5–James **Dunn,** of N.J.;
4–Caleb, from Sussex Co., N.J., to Muskingum Co., O., 1804;
3–Elizabeth (June 16, 1784-Nov. 12, 1865), *m* Nov. 24, 1807, John (Fittz, Fits, Fitts) **Fitz** (Feb. 2, 1787-Mar. 29, 1844), to Muskingum Co., O.;
2–Jane (Oct. 8, 1816-Dec. 31, 1899), *m* Oct. 15, 1835, Joseph Cephas **Spencer** (1813-89); for issue see Vol. II, p. 367.
1–*m* Aug. 28, 1884, Emily Jerusha Gear, *b* Downieville, Calif., Apr. 5, 1864; dau. of Hiram L. Gear, *m* Cornelia Van Clief; issue: 1–Gladys, *b* San Francisco, Calif., July 24, 1885; Denison U., '22; grad. Conservatory of Music, '20; asst. librarian Ohio Wesleyan U.; 2–William Gear (see Vol. II, p. 367, for Gear lineage); 3–Cornelia, *b* San Francisco, Jan. 6, 1888; Denison, '10; *m* June 8, 1917, William Lee Smith (issue: Harold Eugene; Elizabeth Jane; Emily Gear; Rosa Lee); 4–Eudora, *b* San Francisco, Mar. 15, 1890; ed. Denison U.; *m* Feb. 21, 1918, John A. Blackburn; 5–Emily, *b* Oakland, Calif., May 13, 1893; Denison U.; *m* Sept. 14, 1915, Rev. Roy B. Deer (issue: Gordon Spencer; Margaret Emilie; Donald Spencer); 6–Herman Gear, *b* Alexandria, O., Feb. 19, 1897; commd. 2d lt. in field arty. during World War; supt. of schs., Utica, O.; *m* May 31, 1923, Dorothy Martin (issue: James Martin; Robert Gear);
1–A.B., Denison, '79 (Alpha Delta Tau, Phi Beta Kappa, Tau Kappa Alpha), A.M., 1882; B.D., Bapt. Union Theol. Sem., 1885; (D.D., Colgate, 1922). Ordained Bapt. ministry, 1885; pastor Hamilton Square Ch., San Francisco, 1885-88, Emmanuel Ch., San Jose, Calif., 1889-90; prof. Greek and v.p., Calif. Coll., 1890-94; pastor Alexandria, O., 1894-1902; prof. philosophy and dean, Denison U., since 1902, acting pres., 1925-27. Author (see Who's Who in America). Residence: 204 S. Pearl St., Granville, O.

1–**SPENCER, Luella Grace Reynolds (Mrs. Charles F.),** *b* Prophetstown, Ill., May 27, 1871.
5–James **Reynolds,** probably in Am. Rev. from North Kingston, R.I.; moved to St. Armands Can., 1804, thence back to Hancock, Berkshire Co., Mass.; *m* Suzannah–;
4–Griffin (1772-1841), *m* 1792, Martha Gardner (1775-1854; Nathaniel[5], at Battle of Bennington, *m* 1762, Martha [Polly] Brown);
3–Nathaniel Gardner (1794-1865), in War 1812; clk. for Gen. Dearborn, "being a tolerable penman"; *m* 1819, Phoebe Bates Brace;
2–Phineas Bates (2 below).
8–Stephen **Brace** (1644-92), from Eng. to Hartford, Conn., 1660; *m* 1666, Elizabeth– (1644-1724);
7–Henry (1680-ante 1751), ens. of Train Band; *m* 1706, Ann Collier (1687-1758; Joseph[8], *m* Elizabeth Sanford);
6–Capt. Henry (1713-87), lt. 4th Co., Hartford, 1743; *m* 1740, Elizabeth Cadwell (1713-66; Thomas[7]);
5–Capt. Abel (1740-1832), capt. Am. Rev.; mem. Conn. Gen. Assembly; *m* 1760, Keziah Woodruff;
4–Orange (1765-1812), killed in War 1812; *m* 1787, Sarah Bates;
3–Phoebe B. (1801-76), *m* Nathaniel G. **Reynolds** (3 above).
9–Matthew **Woodruff** (qv);
8–Matthew (1646-91), *m* Mary Plum (1644-1708; Robert[9], of Milford, *m* Mary, dau. of Sylvester Baldwin, came in the "Martin," 1638, he *d* on passage, his widow, Sarah Bryan, settled at New Haven, Conn.);
7–Ens. Samuel (*d* 1732), *m* Mary Judd;
6–James (1708-87), in Am. Rev.; *m* Lydia Goodrich Curtis (*b* 1721; Capt. Thomas[7], *m* Mary Goodrich; Joseph[8]; Thomas[9]);
5–Keziah (*b* 1742), *m* Capt. Abel **Brace** (5 above).
10–James **Bates** (qv);
9–James (1624-92), *m* Ann Withington (Henry[10], of Dorchester);
8–Samuel (1648-99), Saybrook, Conn.; *m* 1676, Mary Chapman (Robert[9], *m* Ann Bliss);
7–Stephen (*b* 1689), *m* 1715, Patience Seward (*b* 1694; Joseph[8], of Guilford and Durham, Conn., *m* Judith, dau. of William Bushnell, of Saybrook; Lt. William[9], qv);
6–Stephen (*b* 1722/23), *m* Lois– (1729-91);
5–Phineas (1749-1829), served in Lexington Alarm; *m* 1771, Esther Curtiss;
4–Sarah (1772-1835), *m* 1787, Orange **Brace** (4 above).
9–William **Curtiss,** settled at Stratford, Conn., 1639; *m* Widow Elizabeth–;
8–William (*d* 1676), *m* Sarah Marvin Goodrich (*b* 1630);
7–James, *m* Hannah–;
6–David (1725-82), Am. Rev.; *m* Thankful Thompson (1721-88);
5–Esther (*b* 1751), *m* 1771, Phineas **Bates** (5 above).
2–Phineas Bates **Reynolds** (1820-1901), a pioneer of northern Ill., 1835; served in Co. K, 34th Ill. Vols., Civil War; to Neb., 1880, to Holyoke, Colo., 1888, and to Lexington, Neb., where he *d*; *m* 1857, Elizabeth Gardiner May (1836-1912); issue: I–Fannie May (1858-60); II–Anna Barbara (1860-1926; *m* Whitney L. Irwin); III–Edward Bates (1863-1917; *m* Emma Libolt; *m* 2d, Edna Reese); IV–Jennie May (Mrs. Harry V. Temple, qv for maternal lineages); V–Samuel Stillman (*b* 1867; *m* Velma S. Nye); VI–Luella Grace (1 above); VII–Robert Logan (*b* and *d* 1873); VIII–Herbert Brace (*b* 1875; *m* Myrtle A. Roberts); IX–Bessie Logan (1877-1910; *m* Westray J. Johnson).
1–*m* Oct. 26, 1892, Charles Fielding Spencer, *b* Spencer's Grove, Ia., May 31, 1864; son of Charles Henry Spencer; issue (all *b* Lexington, Neb.): 1–Charles Harold, *b* Sept. 16, 1901; *m* Sept. 26, 1929, Mary, dau. of Milton Williman Strong, of Ohio; 2–Herbert Logan, *b* Sept. 1, 1908; 3–Eloise Elizabeth, *b* Mar. 7, 1910.
1–Editor geneal. dept. The Nebraska Farmer; founder Lue R. Spencer Genealogical Circulating Library (D.A.R. Neb.). Mem. S.M.D., D.F.P.A., D.A.R. (past state regent), P.E.O. (past state pres.). Residence: 2511 R St., Lincoln, Neb.

1–**TEMPLE, Jennie May Reynolds (Mrs. Harry Vane),** *b* Prophetstown, Ill., Dec. 30, 1864.
9–John **May** (qv);
8–John (1631-71), Roxbury, Mass.; *m* 1656, Sarah Brewer (*b* 1638; Daniel[9], from Eng. to Boston, 1632, freeman, Roxbury, 1634, *m* Joanna–; Daniel[10], of Roxbury);
7–John (1663-1730), *m* 1684, Prudence Bridge (1664-1723; John[8], of Roxbury, *m* Prudence Robinson);
6–Hezekiah (1696-1783), Wethersfield, Conn.; dea.; gave aid in Am. Rev.; *m* 1721, Anne Stillman (1698-1767; George[7], from Eng., 1684, from Hadley, Mass., to Wethersfield, Conn., 1704, merchant, selectman of Hadley, 1686, dep. Mass. Gen. Ct., 1698, juror, 1705, *m* 2d,

Rebecca F., dau. Lt. Phil Smith, of Hadley, *m* Rebecca, dau. Nathaniel Foote, qv);
5–Samuel S. (1724-93), gave grain and money for relief of Boston during siege in Am. Rev.; *m* 1746, Mary Peirce (1727-90);
4–James (1764-post 1840), *m* 1790, Hannah Stillman;
3–Samuel Stillman (1796-1877), Bath, N.Y.; architect and builder; dea. 1st Presbyn. Ch., 50 yrs.; brig. gen. N.Y. militia; *m* 1830, Barbara Logan (1812-96; Robert[4], from Limerick, Ireland, *m* Polly Rowe);
2–Elizabeth Gardiner (2 below).
9–Edward **Doty,** Mayflower Pilgrim (qv);
8–Edward (1637-1689/90), *b* Plymouth, Mass.; drowned Plymouth Harbor; *m* 1662/63, as her 1st husband, Sarah Faunce (*d* 1695; John[9], *m* Patience, dau. of George Morton, qv; Thomas[10]; Thomas[11]; Bonham[12]);
7–Samuel (1681-1750), mariner, trading with Barbados; his vessel "Six Friends" pressed into gov. service, 1710, in expdn. against Nova Scotia; capt. Train Band, 1727; rep. from Saybrook to Gen. Assembly, 1732-37; *m* 1706, Anne Buckingham (Rev. Thomas[8], a founder of Yale Coll., *m* Esther, dau. of Thomas Hosmer, of Hartford);
6–Sarah (1708-32), *m* as his 1st wife, 1727, Benjamin **Stillman** (*b* 1705; George[7], above);
5–Capt. Samuel Doty (1731-72), *m* 1757, Susannah Lord (1734-59; Capt. Samuel[6], lt. Train Band, 1757, *m* Hannah, dau. Ens. Samuel Watrous; Thomas[7], qv);
4–Hannah (1771-1840), *m* James **May** (4 above);
3–Samuel S. *m* Barbara Logan (3 above);
2–Elizabeth Gardiner (1836-1912), *m* 1857, Phineas Bates **Reynolds** (1820-1901); for issue and paternal lineages see sister Mrs. Charles F. Spencer.
1–*m* Sept. 6, 1881, Harry Vane Temple (1853-1912); son of Nathaniel Temple, of Wadestown, W.Va.; organized 1st Nat. Bank of Lexington, Neb., 1882, of which he was pres.; issue (all *b* Lexington, Neb.): 1–Guy, *b* 1884; U.-Neb., 1902-05; *m* 1908, Julia Olsson (issue: Dorothy May, *b* 1911; Harry Vane, *b* 1914); 2–Leroy Bates, *b* 1889; U.Neb.; *m* 1911, Hilda Sandberg (issue: Elizabeth, *b* 1913; Jane, *b* 1914; Louise, *b* 1921); 3–Paul Nathaniel, *b* 1894; A.B., U.Neb., '16; lt. F.A., 1917-18; *m* 1921, Marie White (issue: Paul Nathaniel, Jr.); 4–Ruth, *b* 1897; Northwestern U., 1921; *m* 1921, Preston H. Owen (issue: Temple H., *b* 1922); 5–Marjorie May, *b* 1900; U.Neb.; *m* 1922, Muir Penick.
1–Mem. S.M.D., D.F.P.A., D.A.R., U.S.D. 1812, P.E.O. Residence: 1011 N. Mariposa Av., Los Angeles, Calif.

1–**SPENCER, Emily Mason Adams (Mrs. Henry Francis),** *b* Medway, Mass., Aug. 23, 1870.
9–Henry **Adams** (qv);
8–Ens. Edward (1630-1716), of Medfield, Mass.; *m* 1652, Lydia Rockwood (*d* 1676; Richard[9], *m* Agnes Bicknell);
7–John (1657-1751), *m* 1682, Deborah Partridge (1662-ante 1695; John[8], *m* Magdalen Bullard);
6–Obadiah (1687-1765), West Medway, Mass.; *m* 1716, Christian Sanford (1697-1777; Dea. Thomas[7]);
5–Stephen (1729-95), assessor, 1776; *m* 1773, Mary (Molly) Littlefield (1753 or 54-1813; Ephraim[6], *m* Sarah Bullard);
4–Capt. Eli (1779-1832), Readfield, Me.; *m* 1801, Esther Harding (1769-1814; Lt. Abraham[5], *m* Abigail Adams);
3–Elizabeth (1802-75), Holliston, Mass.; *m* 1827, Thomas Bacon **Adams** (1799-1860; James[4], *m* Sarah Bacon);
2–James Thomas (2 below).
9–Richard **Rockwood** (*d* 1660), from Eng., 1636; settled at Dorchester; *m* Agnes– (1598-1643), widow of Zachery Bicknell;
8–Nicholas (1628-1680), Braintree, Mass:; *m* 1st, Jane Adams;
7–Nathaniel (*d* 1721), of Wrentham, Mass.; *m* 1698, Joanna Ellis (*b* 1677; Thomas E.[8], of Medfield, Mass.);
6–Benjamin (1702-72), *m* 1745, Ruth Mann (1720-1811; Thomas[7], *m* Hannah–);
5–Elisha (1750-1831), Am. Rev.; *m* 1778, Eunice Clark (1753-1838; Elijah[6], Am. Rev., *m* Bathsheba Harding);
4–Benjamin (1783-1868), *m* 1810, Lucy Ware (1787-1870; Josiah[5], Am. Rev., *m* Lois Ware);
3–Benjamin (1812-55), *m* 1835, Sarah Rebecca Pond (1815-1901; Jacob[4], *m* Rebecca Perry);
2–Eunice Angenette (*b* 1848), *m* 1869, James Thomas **Adams** (1844-1928); issue: I–Emily Mason (1 above); II–George Thomas (*b* 1872; *m* Carrie Louise Seigler); III–Walter Rockwood (*b* 1876; *m* Mary Blake); IV–Harry James (*b* 1879; *m* Mertice E. Shaw).
1–*m* Dec. 17, 1895, Henry Francis Spencer, *b* Norton, Mass., Aug. 6, 1868; son of Henry Green Spencer of Millis, Mass.; issue: 1–Eunice Hope (Nov. 6, 1896-Nov. 13, 1926); B.S., Simmons Coll., '19; *m* June 14, 1924, Everett Oyler, son of Dr. William E. Waters (*d* 1924), of New York (issue: Hope Spencer); 2–Orville Holland, *b* Framingham, Mass., Jan. 30, 1900; Mass. Agrl. Coll.; *m* Sept. 3, 1924, Sylvia May, dau. Charles Henry Clement, of Derry, N.H.
1–Mem. D.A.R. Conglist. Republican. Residence: 483 Washington Av., West Haven, Conn.

1–**SMITH, Abbie Nellie Adams (Mrs. George H.),** *b* Newfane, Vt., Oct. 25, 1887.
10–Henry **Adams** (qv);
9–Edward (1630-1716), Medfield, Mass.; *m* 1st, 1652, Lydia–;
8–John (1657-1751), *m* 1682, Deborah Partridge (1662-95; John[9]; William[10]);
7–Obadiah (1687-1765), *m* 1716, Christian Sanford (1697-1777; Thomas[8]; Robert[9]; Richard[10]);
6–Obadiah (1721-1803), Am. Rev.; *m* 1744, Sarah Partridge (1725-1817; John[7], of N. Bellingham, Mass.; John[8]; John[9]; William[10]);
5–Samuel (1755-1840), Am. Rev.; *m* 1777, Mrs. Chloe Legge (1760-1854);
4–William (1792-1870), Dover, Vt.; *m* Betsey Haskins (1795-1865; William[5], of Dover; Samuel[6]; Samuel[7]; John[8]);
3–Marcus W. (1826-1900), *m* 1853, Sarah F. Bellows;
2–Herbert Marcus (2 below).
8–John **Bellows** (1623-83), from Eng. in the "Hopewell," 1635; settled at Concord, 1645; an original propr. at Marlborough; *m* 1655, Mary Wood (*d* 1707; John[9]);
7–John (1666-post 1749), *m* 1st, Hannah– (*d* 1719);
6–Joseph (*b* 1711), *m* 1749, as her 2d husband, Abigail (Pike) Ward;
5–Charles (1754-1839), *m* Eleanor Bellows (1760-1840; Jotham[6]; John[7]; John[8]; John[9]);
4–Ward (1801-89), of Dover, Vt.; *m* 1823, Sally Wheelock (1798-1872; Seth[5]; Joseph[6]; Ephraim[7]; Eleazer[8]; Ralph[9]);
3–Sarah F. (1836-1928), *m* Marcus W. **Adams** (3 above).
10–Samuel **Morse** (qv);
9–Joseph (1615-54), Medfield, Mass.; *m* as her 1st husband, 1638, Hannah Phillips (*d* 1676);
8–Lt. Samuel (1639-1717/18), *m* 1st, 1664/65, Elizabeth Wood (*d* 1682; Nicholas[9]);
7–Hon. Joshua (1679-1749), *m* 2d, ante 1708, Mary Paine (1680-1746/47; Samuel[8]; Stephen[9]; Moses[10]);
6–Rev. Ebenezer (1717/18-1802), *m* 1745, Persis Bush (1727-88);
5–Dr. John (1746-1822), Newfane, Vt.; *m* 1769, Elizabeth Andrews (1746-1833; Thomas[6]; John[7]; Joseph[8]; Robert[9]);
4–Thomas (1786-1840), *m* Lucinda Wood (1790-1871; Solomon[5]; Solomon[6]; Isaac[7]; John[8]);
3–Franklin B. (1817-90), *m* Mary Warner;
2–Abbie (2 below).
10–William **Warner** (*d* 1648; son of Samuel, of Boxsted, Eng.), from Ipswich, Eng., in the "Globe," 1637; settled at Ipswich;
9–John (1616-92), of Brookfield, Mass.; *m* 1st–;
8–Samuel (1640-ca. 1703), early settler Dunstable, propr., 1682; *m* 2d, 1685, Mary (Martin) Swallow;
7–Capt. Eleazer (1686-1776), New Braintree, Mass.; *m* 1722, Prudence Barnes (1704-70; Thomas[8]; Thomas[9]);
6–Phineas (1726-95), *m* 1752, Martha Nash (*d* 1811; John[7]; Thomas[8]; Timothy[9]; Thomas[10]);
5–Alpheus (1753-1800), *m* 1774, as her 1st husband, Meribah Hilyard;
4–Roswell (1777-1849), Dover, Vt.; *m* Betsey Bicknell (1779-1848; William[5]; Zachariah[6]; Zachariah[7]; John[8]; Zachary[9]);
3–Mary (1819-1900), *m* Franklin B. **Morse** (3 above);
2–Abbie (*b* 1862), *m* 1883, Herbert Marcus **Adams**

(1854-1905), farmer; issue: I–Florence May (*b* 1885; *m* 1908, Charles Homer Palmer, *b* 1884); II–Abbie N. (1 above).
1–*m* Sept. 3, 1912, Dr. George Hathorn Smith, *b* Harrison, Me., Sept. 25, 1885; prof. immunology and bacteriology, Yale Med. Sch.; son of Rev. John L. Smith, of Hampton, N.H.; issue: 1–Allan Hathorn, *b* Norwood, Pa., Sept. 8, 1913; 2–Bryce Adams, *b* Glenolden, Pa., Apr. 29, 1915; 3–Miriam, *b* New Haven, Conn., Oct. 15, 1920; 4–Charlotte, *b* New Haven, Mar. 26, 1922.
1–Mem. D.F.P.A., D.A.R. Residence: 474 Washington Av., West Haven, Conn.

1–**SPENCER-MOUNSEY, Creighton,** *b* Tarrytown, N.Y., Apr. 20, 1863.
8–Ens. Gerard **Spencer** (qv);
7–Samuel (*d* 1705), of Millington Soc., E. Haddam; *m* 1st, 1673, Hannah Willey (1643-ca. 1681; Isaac[8], *m* Joanna–);
6–Isaac (1678/79-1750/51), dep. for Haddam and E. Haddam, 1734-41; dea. of E. Haddam Ch., 1734; *m* 1707, Mary Selden (*b* 1689; Joseph[7], *m* Rebecca, dau. of Edward Church; Thomas[8]);
5–Maj. Israel (1732-1813), capt. in Burrall's Cont. regt., 1776; maj. in McKinstry's N.Y. levies, 1781; dep. E. Haddam, 1778-80; *m* 1753, Elizabeth Marsh;
4–Jared Wilson (1760-1809), of Hadlyme; orderly sgt. in Canfield's Conn. regt., 1782-83; *m* 1783, Margaret Wiggins (1763-1842; John[5], *m* Mary, dau. of Ens. John King; John[6]; John[7]; John[8]);
3–Jared Wilson (1784-1866), of Brooklyn; *m* 1811, Charlotte Billings;
2–James Selden, D.D. (2 below).
10–Rev. John **Wilson** (1588-1667; son of Rev. Dr. William Wilson, canon of Windsor, St. Paul's and Rochester, *m* Isabel, dau. of John Woodhall, of Walden, Essex, *m* Elizabeth Grindall); from Eng. in the "Arbella," 1630, with Winthrop; founder and first pastor 1st Ch. of Boston at Charlestown, 1630; chaplain in Pequot expdn., 1637; *m* ca. 1617, Elizabeth Mansfield (*d* 1658; Sir John[11], *m* Elizabeth–);
9–Rev. John (1621-91), pastor, Medfield, 1651; *m* ca. 1648, Sarah Hooker (Rev. Thomas[10], qv);
8–Dr. John (1660-1728), capt. Braintree military co., 1696; justice, 1700; *m* 1683, Sarah Newton (1662-1725; Rev. Roger[9] [qv], *m* Mary, dau. of Thomas Hooker, qv);
7–Sarah (*b* 1684), *m* 1701, John **Marsh** (1679-1745; Lt. Alexander[8], *m* Mary, dau. of Gregory Belcher, of Braintree, *m* Catherine–);
6–John (1702-55), *m* 1727, Submit Woodward (*b* 1704; Smith[7], of Dorchester, *m* Thankful, dau. of John Pope; Robert[8]; Robert[9]; Nathaniel[10]);
5–Elizabeth (1729-1801), *m* Maj. Israel **Spencer** (5 above).
8–William (Billing) **Billings** (qv);
7–Ens. Ebenezer (ca. 1661-1727), in King Philip's War, 1675; *m* 1681, Anne Comstock (Daniel[8], *m* Paltiah, dau. of John Elderkin; William[9]);
6–Lt. Ebenezer (1684-1760), lt. of 2d mil. co. of Stonington, 1731; dep. for Stonington, 1721-22; *m* 1706, Phebe Denison (1690-1775; Ens. John[7], *m* Phebe, dau. of Robert Lay; Capt. George[8], *m* 2d, Ann, dau. of John Borodell, gent.; William[9], qv);
5–John (1708-61), *m* 1743, Elizabeth Page;
4–Ens. Daniel (1749-1801), ens., 10th Regt., Conn. Cont. Inf., 1776; *m* 1779, Catharine (Eldredge) Geer;
3–Charlotte (1789-1884), *m* 1811, Jared Wilson **Spencer** (3 above).
9–William **Denison** (qv);
8–Capt. George (1620-94), dep. for Stonington, 1671-94; capt. and 2d in command of Conn. forces, 1676; *m* 1st, ca. 1640, Bridget Thompson (1622-43; John[9], *m* Alice–);
7–Hannah (*b* 1643), as widow of Nathaniel Cheesebrough, *m* 2d, 1680, Capt. Joseph **Saxton** (1656-ca. 1715), in King Philip's War, 1675 (Thomas[8], *m* Ann, dau. of William Cope);
6–Mary (1681-1750), as widow of Benjamin Minor, *m* 2d, 1713, Joseph **Page** (*b* 1680; John[7], *m* Faith, dau. of Robert Dunster, *m* Alice Fletcher; John[8]);
5–Elizabeth (*b* 1717), *m* 1743, John **Billings** (5 above).
8–Sgt. Samuel (Eldred) **Eldredge** (ca. 1620-1697), at Cambridge by 1641; joined A. and H.A.Co., 1641; sgt., 1659; *m* ca. 1641, Elizabeth–;
7–Capt. Daniel (*d* 1726), capt. Kingstown mil. co., 1702; dep. for Stonington, 1709, Kingstown, 1715; justice, Kingstown, 1713-17; *m* probably ca. 1687, Mary– (*d* ca. 1750);
6–Capt. Daniel (1690-1737), dep. for Groton, 1727, 29,30,34; capt. of 3d mil. co. of Groton, 1733; *m* 1711, Abigail Fish (ca. 1690-1784; Capt. Samuel[7], *m* Sarah, dau. of Aaron Stark; John[8]);
5–Charles (1720-95), *m* 1741, Mary Starr;
4–Catharine (1754-1817), as widow of Samuel Geer, *m* 1779, Ens. Daniel **Billings** (4 above).
9–William **Brewster,** Mayflower Pilgrim (qv);
8–Jonathan (1593-1659), came in the "Fortune," 1621, to Plymouth; freeman on 1st list, 1633; freeman-dep., 1637; mil. cdr., 1637; dep. for Duxbury, 1639-44; mem. Duxbury mil. co., 1643; dep. for New London, 1650-59; *m* 1624, Lucretia Oldham (*d* 1679);
7–Hannah (*b* 1641), *m* 1664, Samuel **Starr** (ca. 1640-ca. 1688), co. marshal, 1674-ca. 1688 (Dr. Thomas[8]; Comfort[9], qv);
6–Capt. Jonathan (1674-1747), dep., Groton, 1712-28; mem. Gov.'s Council, 1712-21; capt. of Groton Co. mil. co., 1721-27; *m* 1699, Elizabeth Morgan (1678-1763; Capt. James[7]; James[8], qv);
5–Mary (1722-79), *m* Charles **Eldredge** (5 above);
4–Catharine, *m* Ens. Daniel **Billings** (4 above);
3–Charlotte, *m* Jared Wilson **Spencer** (3 above);
2–James Selden, D.D. (1821-1914), of Tarrytown, N.Y.; *m* 1844, Annie Maria Mildeberger (1821-54; John[3]); *m* 2d, 1862, Mary Frances Mounsey (1840-1915; John Mark[3], *m* Frances, dau. of William George; Thomas[4]); issue (1st marriage): I–Seymour Hobart (Very Rev. Francis Aloysius Spencer, O.P.; 1845-1913); II–Selden Mildeberger (1854-81; *m* 1881, Ida May Bayles); issue (2d marriage): I–Creighton (1 above), surname changed by court order, 1916, from Spencer to Spencer-Mounsey; II–Irving (*b* 1865; *m* 1902, Margaret Brathwaite); III–Frederick Mounsey (1867-1915; *m* 1893, Helen Pamela Lawrence); IV–Harold Eldredge (*b* 1871); V–Ernest Knowlton (*b* 1874); VI–Katharine Kingsland (*b* and *d* 1881); VII–Kingsland Noel (*b* 1882; *m* 1906, Elsie Leigh Marshall).
1–*m* Apr. 26, 1898, Joanna Livingston Mesier, *b* Wappingers Falls, N.Y., Jan. 10, 1865; dau. of Henry Mesier (Matthew[3]; Pieter[4]; Pieter[5]; Abraham[6]; Pieter Janzen[7]), *m* Elizabeth Carmer Wetmore (Apollos Russel[3]; Noah[4]; Noah[5]; Samuel[6]; Samuel[7]; Thomas[8]); issue: 1–Henry Mesier, *b* Hempstead, N.Y., Apr. 19, 1899; 2–John de Monceux (Oct. 22, 1900-July 10, 1903).
1–A.B., Columbia, '84; Gen. Theol. Sem., New York, 1887. Rector of St. John's, Delhi, N.Y., 1892-93, St. George's, Hempstead, N.Y., 1893-1901, Christ Ch., Tarrytown, N.Y., 1901-07, St. Thomas', New Windsor, N.Y., 1907-11, St. John's, Bisbee, Ariz., 1911-13, Christ Ch., W. Collingswood, N.J., 1913-14; archdeacon of Kan., 1914-17, of E. Okla., 1917-22; now rector Trinity Ch., Northport, N.Y. Mem. S.M.D., S.C.W., S.R., I.A.G., N.Y.G. and B. Soc. Mason (K.T., 32°). Democrat. Clubs: Authors (London), University (New York). Residence: Trinity Rectory, Northport, N.Y.

1–**SPINING, Arthur Milton, Sr.,** *b* Springfield, O., Oct. 25, 1867.
7–Humphrey (Spinnage) **Spining** (*b* 1630-will executed 1689), from Eng. with his uncle, Humphrey Spinage, 1637, to New Haven, Conn.; founder of Elizabeth, N.J., 1666; took oath of allegiance and fidelity, 1665; had a grant of 218 acres from Lord Carteret, 1657; *m* 1657, Abigal Hubbard;
6–Edward (1666-1726), *m* Anna Lee;
5–Ebenezer (1712-71), *m* 1749, Phoebe Williams;
4–Isaac (1759-1825), pvt. in Am. Rev.; judge Circuit Ct., Dayton, O.; *m* 1785, Catherine Pierson (1767-1818; John[5], Am. Rev.);
3–Pierson (1786-1857), contractor, Springfield, O.; *m* 1812, Mary Schooly (1790-1876; John[4] [1761-1834], Am. Rev., *m* Mary Earl, 1763-1833);
2–Isaac Milton (2 below).
4–John **Taylor** (*d* in Am. Rev.), soldier Am. Rev.; revenue officer, and was poisoned by smugglers, whom he was trying to apprehend in a hotel in Can.;
3–Pascal (1802-65), *m* Mary Jane Sweet (1803-66);
2–Harriet Louisa (1827-1900), *m* 1851, Isaac Milton **Spining** (1813-78); issue: I–John Franklin (*b* 1852; *m* 1887, Emma Snedaker); II–Pierson Taylor (1854-1928); III–William Vernon (*b* 1856; *m* Clara E. Stutesman, *d* 1921); IV–Carrie

Louisa (*b* 1857; *m* William DeVaney, 2d; *m* 2d, Omar Sylvester); V–Milton (1860-1865); VI–Arthur Milton (1 above).
1–*m* July 3, 1888, Mary Estella Wade (qv); issue (all *b* Springfield, O.): 1–Mary Louise, *b* Oct. 12, 1890; 2–Edith Cecelia, *b* Jan. 12, 1892; 3–Susie Wade, *b* Mar. 29, 1895; *m* Sept. 27, 1917, Carl Wilbur Tuttle (issue: Wilbur Spining; Mary Jane); 4–Katherine Pierson, *b* Apr. 2, 1899; *m* July 21, 1923, Edgar Roy Wyant (issue: Edgar Roy, Jr.; Estella Katherine); 5–Arthur Milton, *b* Oct. 13, 1904.
1–Ed. Nelson's Business Coll. Mgr. and treas., Springfield Coffin & Casket Co. Mem. S.A.R. (pres. George Rogers Clark Chapter). Presbyn. Mason. Clubs: Springfield Shrine (sec. and treas.), Springfield Masonic (treas.). Residence: 263 S. Belmont Av., Springfield, O.

1–**SPINING, Mary Estella Wade (Mrs. Arthur M.),** *b* Avondale, Cincinnati, O., Feb. 22, 1867.
8–Benjamin **Wade** (ca. 1646-ca. 1700), *m* ca. 1670, Ann Looker (1649-1727; William[9]);
7–Robert (*d* 1766), *m* Elizabeth–; *m* 2d, Sarah–;
6–Robert (*d* 1756), in French and Indian War; taken prisoner and *d* in France; *m* Elizabeth–;
5–David (1733-79), *m* 2d, Sarah Everett (1721-64);
4–David Everett (1763-1842), pvt. in Am. Rev. aet. 14; one of 1st trustees of Cincinnati; *m* 1786, Mary Jones (1765-1811; Rev. John[5], Am. Rev.);
3–Melancthon Smith (1802-68), brig. gen. Civil War; *m* 1823, Eliza Armstrong (1804-61; Col. John[4], Am. Rev.);
2–John Armstrong (2 below).
7–John **Ashcraft** (will dated 1732), of S. Groton, New London Co., Conn.; *m* Mary–;
6–John (*b* 1725), *m* Mary–;
5–Gibson (1749-1823), Am. Rev.; *m* 1772, Deborah Smith (1748-1832);
4–Samuel (1782-ca. 1850), of N.J.; *m* 1806, Ann Clutch (1787-1847);
3–Jesse (1816-73), of Cincinnati, O.; *m* 1841, Mary Ann Miller (1815-79);
2–Cecelia Adelaide (1844-1924), *m* 1864, John Armstrong **Wade** (1843-1915), lt. in Civil War; issue: I–Melancthon Smith (1865-1925; *m* Emma Timmerman); II–Mary Estella (1 above); III–Susie May (1869-94; *m* J. Frank Hayes); IV–Cecelia Adelaide (*b* 1870; *m* David Cooper); V–Frances Louise (*b* 1872; *m* Charles A. Fay); VI–Bessie Pearl (*b* 1878; *m* Judge Frank Martin Krapp); VII–John Armstrong (*b* and *d* 1880); VIII–Jesse Ashcraft (*b* 1881; *m* Mabel D. Troutman); IX–Charles Edwin (*b* 1884; *m* Lena Pfeiffer).
1–*m* July 3, 1888, Arthur M. Spining, Sr. (qv for issue).
1–Mem. D.A.R. Residence: 263 S. Belmont Av., Springfield, O.

1–**STANDISH, Sherwood Hubbard,** *b* at Detroit, Mich., June 26, 1883.
9–George **Hubbard** (1601-84), from Eng., 1635; *m* Elizabeth Watts;
8–Nathaniel (1652-1738), *m* 1682, Mary Earl;
7–Nathaniel (1690-1765), *m* 1716, Sarah Johnson;
6–Noahdiah (1735-1816), *m* Phoebe (Fairchild) Crowell;
5–Noahdiah (1765-1859), officer War 1812; first white settler in Jefferson Co., N.Y.; *m* 1794, Eunice Ward;
4–Hiram (1794-1888), *m* Charille Sherwood;
3–John Sherwood (1829-1910), *m* Sara (Lovett) Bartlett;
2–Carrie (*b* 1858), *m* 1878, Fred Dana **Standish** (see Vol. I, p. 486, for Standish lineage).
1–*m* Apr. 14, 1910, Mary Boyd, dau. Clifton Wood Bransford (see Vol III, p. 517); issue: 1–Virginia Caroline, *b* Racine, Wis., Aug. 19, 1911; 2–Margaret Richards, *b* Milwaukee, Mar. 31, 1917; 3–Sherwood Hubbard, Jr., *b* St. Louis, Apr. 12, 1921.
1–B.S. in M.E., U.Mich., '05 (Psi U., Sigma Xi). Gen. mgr. G.H.R. Foundry Co., Dayton, O. Address: P.O. Box 1021, Dayton, O.

1–**VAN WORMER, Sara Truax,** *b* Glenville, N. Y., Mar. 5, 1861.
4–Peter **Van Wormer** (1749-1808), Albany Co., N. Y.; Am. Rev.; *m* Rachel Van Hosen (*b* 1752);
3–Caspar (1770-1859), *m* 1794, Eve Van (Dyke) Dycke (1775-1851; Hendricus[4] [1731-post 1787], Am. Rev., of Corry's Bush, Schenectady, N. Y., *m* 1753, Engeltje Mebie);

2–John Cornelius (2 below).
5–Claas Frederick **Van Patten,** came from Holland; *m* Aeffie Bradt (Aaron[6], *m* Cateline de Vos);
4–Capt. Johannes (1739-1809), of Schenectady; capt. Am. Rev.; *m* 1762, Neltje Vedder (1741-1805; Simon[5]);
3–Simon I. (1775-1851), *m* 1797, Eve Conde;
2–Nancy (1820-1906), *m* 1844, John Cornelius **Van Wormer** (1813-89); for issue see Vol. III, p. 609.
1–Mem. D.A.R., Phi Mu. Residence: 648 N. Garfield Av., Pocatello, Ida.

1–**STANDROD, Drew William, Jr.,** *b* Malad, Ida., May 6, 1891.
10–Philip (du Trieux) **Truax** (qv);
9–Philip (bap. 1619-murdered probably by Indians, Sept. 8, 1653), probably came with father;
8–Isaac (1642-ca. 1706), first white child *b* New Amsterdam; settled in Rotterdam, 1670; *m* Maria Williamse Brouwer (William[9] [*d* 1668], of Albany, N.Y., in Beverwyck, 1657);
7–Isaac (bap. 1690), *m* Schenectady, 1719, Catalina van Benthuysen (bap. 1700; Martin[8], *m* Feitje Boorsboom);
6–Peter (1723-97), began to write name Truax; *m* 1748, Jacoba Bogardus (Cornelius[7], 1st minister at Schenectady, N.Y.; *m* a dau. of Dominie Cornelius Van Santwood, of Leydon, Holland, *m* Anna Staats);
5–Catelyntje (bap. 1752-1843), *m* 1770, Adam **Conde** (1748-1824), Am. Rev. (Adam[6], high sheriff, Albany, 1724, was killed in Beechdale massacre, 1748, *m* 1736, Catherine, dau. of Jesse De Graff);
4–Eve (*b* 1780), *m* 1797, Simon I. **Van Patten** (1775-1851);
3–Nancy (1820-1906), *m* 1844, John C. **Van Wormer** (1813-89); see their dau. Sara T. for other lineages;
2–Eve Emma (*b* 1849), *m* 1888, Drew William **Standrod.**
1–*m* Aug. 1, 1916, Helen Carey Crockett, *b* New York, N.Y., Jan. 28, 1895 (divorced July 23, 1922).
1–*m* 2d, July 28, 1928, Lucy Carolyn, dau. of William J. Hostetler.
1–Ed. Whitman Coll., '10; U.Pa., 1914. Lawyer; pres. Pioneer Motor Co., 1919-20; asst. city atty. of Los Angeles, 1921; sec. Lamb Oil & Drilling Co., Amarillo, Tex., 1926; law practice, Pocatello, Ida., 1926-27. First lt., U.S.A., Nov. 14, 1917, capt., 361st Inf., 91st Div., May 9, 1918; served at Presidio Training Camp, San Francisco, and Camp Lewis, Wash.; comdt. cadets, V.P.I., Blacksburg, Va., May-Dec. 1918; maj. comdg. 414th Inf., O.R.C.; civilian aide to Sec. of War, 1923-27. Residence: 648 N. Garfield Av., Pocatello, Ida.

1–**STARK, Mildred Althea Foote (Mrs. Clifford),** *b* Morrisville, N.Y., June 20, 1878.
10–Nathaniel **Foote** (qv);
9–Nathaniel (1620-55), of Wethersfield, Conn.; *m* 1646, Elizabeth Smith (*d* 1655; Lt. Samuel[10], of Wethersfield, rep. 13 yrs., asso. judge Co. Ct., 8 yrs.);
8–Nathaniel (1647-1703), leader of settlement at Colchester, Conn., but died before completing home there; in King Philip's War; *m* Margaret Bliss (Nathaniel[9]; Thomas[10], qv);
7–Nathaniel (1682-1774), *m* 1st, Ann Clark;
6–Nathaniel (1712-1811), *m* Patience Gates (Daniel[7]);
5–Nathaniel (1742-1829), *m* 2d, Patience Skinner (Israel[6]);

4–Asa (1785-1859), *m* Betsey Gates;
3–Nathaniel (1813-1901), lawyer, master in chancery, Morrisville, N.Y.; *m* Olivia M. Knox (1814-93);
2–Arthur Asa (2 below).
10–William **Bradford** (qv);
9–William (1624-1706), *m* 1st, 1650, Alice Richards (1627-71);
8–Alice (1662-1745), *m* 1680, Rev. Williams **Adams** (1650-85);
7–Elizabeth (1681-1766), *m* 1696, Rev. Samuel **Whiting** (1670-1725);
6–Samuel (1720-1803), col. Am. Rev.; *m* Elizabeth Hudson (*d* 1793);
5–Elizabeth, *m* Judson **Lewis**;
4–William, *m* Atlanta Curtis;
3–Alfred C., *m* Eusebia Curtis;
2–Kate Cora (*b* 1858), *m* 1877, Arthur Asa **Foote** (*b* 1851), U.S.M.A., ex-'76; lawyer, W. Eaton, N.Y.; issue: I–Mildred Althea (1 above); II–Lewis Arthur (*b* 1879; *m* Isabel Donnelly); III–Ethel Knox (*b* 1881; *m* Dana Fox Stark); IV–Robert Nathaniel (1883-95); V–Leon Laertes (1888-98).
1–*m* Sept. 3, 1901, Clifford Stark, *b* Niven, Pa., Feb. 3, 1870; son of Somers J. Stark, of Elmira, N.Y.; issue: 1–Dana Foote (June 2, 1902-Apr. 10, 1925), Colgate, '23; died as result of an accident, in Shanghai, China, while in service of the Internat. Banking Corpn. of N.Y.; 2–Lewis Clifford, *b* Syracuse, N.Y., June 30, 1903; Colgate, '25; *m* Sept. 28, 1929, Mary Viola Willis, of Rochester, N.Y.; 3–Anna Kate, *b* Rochester, N.Y., Mar. 2, 1913; 4–Ethel Althea, *b* Rochester, Sept. 6, 1920.
1–Summer place: Hatch's Lake, W. Eaton, N.Y. Residence: 104 Croydon Rd., Rochester, N.Y.

1–**STARK, Frances Kate Bouldin (Mrs. Horatio O.),** *b* Nesbitt, Miss., Jan. 3, 1879.
11–Thomas **Bouldin** (*b* 1523), of Shelbourne, Eng.;
10–Thomas, of Warwick Co., Eng.;
9–Thomas (*b* 1580), to Va. in the "Swann," 1610; *m* Mary–;
8–William (ca. 1620-1691), of Pa.; *m* Ann–;
7–William (ca. 1650-1717), took 887 acres in Gloucester Co., Va., 1688; *m* Elizabeth– (*d* 1710);
6–John (ca. 1680-1711), of Md.; *m* Mary–;
5–Col. Thomas (1706-83), of "Golden Hills," nr. Drakes Branch; capt. French and Indian War, 1758; high sheriff, Lunenburg Co., 1759; lt. col. of militia, Charlotte Co., 1773, and was staunch patriot during Am. Rev.; vestryman Rough Creek Episcopal Ch., which he built; *m* 1731, Nancy Clark, of Md. (niece of Maj. Wood of English Navy); among their sons, Maj. Wood, was lt. 14th Va. Regt., Am. Rev., later maj., *m* Joanna, sister of Gov. John Tyler, of Va. and aunt of Pres. John Tyler;
4–Thomas (1736-1827), Henry Co., Va.; *m* 1759, Matilda Moseley (will probated 1827);
3–Green (1760-1835), from Va. to Ala.; *m* 2d, Margaret (Jiggetts) Driver;
2–Ephraim (1828-93), mcht. and planter, Nesbitt, Miss.; *m* 1853, Maria Hobbs Bridgforth; *m* 2d, 1861, Kate Jones, of Batesville, Miss.; *m* 3d, Elizabeth Baugh, of Elkton, Tenn.; *m* 4th, 1874, Susie Jane Boyd (1839-1916); issue (1st marriage): I–Alice (*m* W. S. McWilliams, *d* 1928); II–Robert (*d* aet. 9); III–Lilian (*m* Dana Daniel Boyd); issue (2d marriage); I–Marshall Jones (*m* Elizabeth Huddlestone; *m* 2d, Mary Helen Alcorn); II–Van Lewis (*d* infancy); issue (3d marriage): I–Sir Dhu (*d* aet. 18); II–Joe Hilery (*m* Minnie McGrew, *d* 1904); III–Anne (1872-1903; *m* William B. Coggin); issue (4th marriage): I–Grace Boyd (*b* 1875); II–E. Russell (1877-1905); III–Frances Kate (1 above); IV–Henry Malcolm (1881-1923).
1–*m* Dec. 15, 1903, Horatio Osborn Stark, *b* Evergreen, La., Oct. 12, 1875; son of Theodore Osborn Stark, of New Orleans, La., *m* Dora Lambeth; issue (all *b* Bunkie, La.): 1–Dorothy Lambeth, *b* Dec. 16, 1907; Gulf Park Coll., '27; B.A., Miss. State Coll., '29; 2–Frances Bouldin, *b* Aug. 2, 1909; Gulf Park Coll., '28; attending U.Tex.; 3–Meredith Osborn, *b* May 12, 1911; Gulfport H.S., 1928; entering U.Miss.; 4–Robert Boyd, *b* May 28, 1915.
1–Ed. Dick White Coll., '96. Mem. D.A.R. Episcopalian. Democrat. Club: Gulfport Woman's. Residence: 1100 32d Av., Gulfport, Miss.

1–**STEARNS, Daisy Loula Cushman (Mrs. Roy Sumner),** *b* Middlebury, Vt., Aug. 2, 1880.
10–Robert **Cushman** (qv);
9–Elder Thomas (1608-91), to America, aet. 14; when his father went back to Eng., 1621, Thomas was left with Gov. Bradford, with whom he remained until manhood; freeman, Plymouth, 1633; apptd. ruling elder in ch. at Kingston, 1649; *m* Mary Allerton (1609-99);
8–Rev. Isaac (1647/48-1732), *m* ca. 1675, Mary Rickard (1654-1727);
7–Ichabod (1686-1736), *m* 1712, Patience Holmes (*d* post 1736);
6–Sgt. Ichabod (*b* 1725), mem. 2d Bristol Co. Regt.; *m* 1751, Patience Macfern;
5–Ichabod (1757-1805), Hartland, Vt.; pvt. Am. Rev.; *m* 1782, Molly Morton;
4–Ichabod Morton (1787-1847), Middlebury, Vt.; *m* 1822, Mary (Chase) Montgomery;
3–Horace Dawes (1824-1908), *m* 1844, Susan Almedia Pinney (1826-1920);
2–Edward Pinney (2 below).
10–George **Morton** (qv);
9–Ephraim (1623-93), *m* 1st, 1644, Ann Cooper (*d* 1691);
8–Eleazer (*b* 1659), *m* Rebecca Dawes; *m* 2d, Martha Wheaton;
7–Nathaniel (1695-lost at sea), *m* Rebecca Clarke Ellis;
6–Ichabod (1726-1809), of Middleboro; Am. Rev.; *m* 1749, Deborah Morton (*d* 1789; Ebenezer[7]);
5–Molly (1758-1841), *m* Ichabod **Cushman** (5 above).
2–Edward Pinney **Cushman** (*b* 1854), mcht., Middlebury, Vt.; *m* 1879, Julie Pierce White (*b* 1855); issue: I–Daisy Loula (1 above); II–Harry Leon (*b* 1883; *m* Grace Vittum).
1–*m* June 10, 1908, Dr. Roy Sumner Stearns, *b* Bristol, Vt., Apr. 19, 1877; son of Ansel Stearns, of Bristol, *m* Julia Farr.
1–Ed. Hellmuth Ladies Coll., London, Ont., Canada. Mem. D.F.P.A., D.A.R. Conglist. Republican. Summer place: Lake Lytle Beach, Portland, Ore. Residence: 964 Tolman Av., Portland, Ore.

1–**STEDMAN, Livingston Boyd,** *b* Boston, Mass., Feb. 2, 1864.
9–Isaac **Stedman,** from Eng. in his own ship "Elizabeth," to Scituate, Mass., 1635, moved to Boston, at Muddy River, 1650;
8–Thomas, *m* Mary Watson;
7–Thomas, *m* Mary–;
6–Joseph, *m* Mary–;
5–Josiah, *m* Hannah Curtis;
4–Josiah, *m* Miriam White Baxter;
3–Daniel Baxter (1817-99), *m* Miriam White Stedman;
2–Daniel Baxter (1840-1905), merchant, Boston; *m* Susan Livingston Boyd (1838-1920); for issue see Vol. III, p. 625.
1–*m* Apr. 29, 1891, Ann Bonneville Leiper, Colonial Dame; dau. Thomas Irvine Leiper, of Chester, Pa.; issue (all *b* Seattle, Wash.): 1–Daniel Baxter, *b* Sept. 15, 1892; U.Wash., spl., '19; pvt., 164th Ambulance Corps, A.E.F.; 2–Lewis Leiper, *b* Feb. 24, 1895; U.S.N.A., '15; lt. U.S.N., resigned; LL.B., U.Wash., 1924 (Order of Coif, Phi Delta Phi); lawyer; mem. Seattle, Wash. State and Am. bar assns.; *m* July 14, 1626, Evelyn A. Wallin; 3–Livingston Boyd, Jr., *b* Oct. 29, 1898; served pvt. to 2d lt., aviation pilot, instr. flying, resigned; capt., U.S. Marine Corps Reserves, aviation section on active duty; *m* Feb. 7, 1928, Kathryn Geisel.
1–A.B., Harvard, '87 (P.B.K., Phi Delta Phi), A.M., 1891; Harvard Law Sch. Atty.-at-law, Seattle, Wash. Pres. Seattle Bar. Assn., 1913-14; mem. Wash. State and Am. bar assns., S.R. Mason (K.C.C.H., Shriner). Clubs: University (past pres.), Harvard (past pres.), Nile Shrine Luncheon (pres.), Seattle Golf. Residence: The Highlands, R.F.D., No. 2, Seattle, Wash.

1–**STEELE, Charles Edwin,** *b* Philadelphia, Pa., Sept. 4, 1869.
10–George **Steele** (qv);
9–James (ca. 1623-1681), served in Pequot and King Philip's wars; *m* 1st, Anna Bishop (*d* 1676; John[10], of Guilford, Conn., *m* Anne–);

STEELE

Arms: Argent, a bend chequy sable and ermine, between two lions' heads erased gules, a chief azure.

Crest: Out of a ducal coronet or, a demi-ostrich with wings endorsed or.

8–Lt. James (1658-1712), of Hartford; *m* Sarah Bernard (*d* 1730; Bartholomew[9]);
7–Jonathan (1693-1753), *m* 1715, Dorothy Mygatt (1696-1775; Joseph[8]);
6–James (1720-97), of Hartford;
5–James (*b* 1757), of Hartford;
4–Gurdon (1788-1843), Boston; *m* 1809, Nancy (Green) Risborough (1779-1834);
3–James (1813-82), *m* 1834, Ellen Maria Keith (1816-97);
2–George Passarow (1839-1909), treas. of a stationery co., Boston; *m* 1862, Emma Victoria MacLauchlin (1840-1910); issue: I–Julia (*b* 1865-89); II–Charles Edwin (1 above).
1–*m* Oct. 12, 1892, Iola Swords, *b* S. Norwalk, Conn., Sept. 25, 1871; dau. of William Henry Swords; issue: 1–Dorothy, *b* S. Norwalk, May 19, 1895; *m* Apr. 10, 1920, Edward Bradley, son of Louis Flower Anschutz, *m* Emma Bradley (issue: Bradley Steele, *b* June 10, 1921).
1–Mem. S.A.R., I.A.G., N.E.H.G.S., Soc. Preservation of N.E. Antiquities, Am. Mus. Natural History. Episcopalian. Republican. Residence: Eton Hall, Scarsdale, N.Y.

1–**STETSON, C(aleb) Rochford,** *b* Boston, Mass., Apr. 16, 1871.
9–Robert **Stetson** (qv);
8–Joseph (1639-1732), of Scituate, Mass.; *m* 2d, Prudence–;
7–Robert (1670-1760), *m* 1692, Mary Collamore (Capt. Anthony[8]);
6–Amos (1703-77), *m* Margaret Thayer;
5–Amos (1730-79), *m* Experience French;
4–Amos (*b* 1777), *m* Hannah Hunt;
3–Caleb (1801-85), *m* Susannah Hunt;
2–George R. (2 below).
9–Christopher **Avery** (qv);
8–Captain James (qv);
7–Samuel (1664-1723), Groton, Conn.; *m* 1686, Susannah Palmer (1665-1747);
6–Humphrey (1699-1788), Wyoming Valley, Pa.; *m* 1st, 1724, Jerusha Morgan (1704-63);
5–Samuel (1731-1806), *m* Sybil Noyes;
4–Elisha (1761-1835), *m* Sybil Avery;
3–Samuel (1791-1867), *m* Mary Ann Wood Candler (Capt. John[4], fought on the "Constellation" and in Am. Rev.);
2–Helen Sybil (1840-1907), *m* George Rochford **Stetson** (1833-1923); for issue see Vol. I, p. 841.
1–*m* June 30, 1914, Helen Stetson Richards, *b* at Boston, Mass., June 20, 1875; dau. of Henry C. Richards, *m* Helen L. Stetson, of Boston.
1–A.B., Harvard, '94; studied medicine, Johns Hopkins U., 1894-95; grad. Gen. Theol. Sem., 1898 (S.T.D., Columbia, Gen. Theol. Sem., Hobart; D.D., St. Stephen's, U. of the South). Rector of Trinity Parish (P.E.), New York, since 1921 (see Who's Who in America). Mem. S.M.D., S.C.W. Clubs: Cosmos, Chevy Chase, University (Washington), Century, University, Ardsley, Harvard, Grolier (New York). Residence: 56 Park Av., New York.

EDWARD LOT GAYLORD (b Bristol, Conn., 1827-d Bridgeport, Conn., 1915), a pioneer of locks and was pres. Eagle Lock Co., Bridgeport.

1–**STEVENS, Anna May Gaylord (Mrs. Frederick S.),** *b* Terryville, Conn., May 22, 1855.
10–William (Gaillard) **Gaylord** (qv);
9–Walter (1622-89), of Exeter, Eng., and Windsor, Conn.; *m* 1st, 1648, Mary Stebbins (*d* 1657);
8–Joseph (1649-1711), Durham, Conn.; *m* 1670, Sarah Stanley (1651-1711);
7–John (1677-1753), Wallingford, Conn.; *m* Elizabeth– (1678-1751);
6–Edward, *m* 1733, Mehitable Brooks;
5–Capt. Jesse (1735-1807), Waterbury, Conn.; chosen "to seat the meeting house," 1753; took oath of fidelity, 1775; surveyor of highways, 1785; *m* 1756, Rachael Hungerford (1735-1828);
4–Lot (1774-1816), Bristol, Conn.; *m* 1796, Sarah Allen (1772-1843);
3–Ransom (1800-92), Oshkosh, Wis.; *m* Pamila Alcott (1805-33; Joseph C.[4], *m* Anna Bronson, their son, Amos Bronson Alcott, educator and philosopher, was the father of Louisa May Alcott);
2–Edward Lot (2 below).
9–Lt. Thomas **Miner** (qv);
8–Clement (1640-1700), *m* 1st, 1662, Widow Frances Willey (*d* 1673);
7–Lt. Clement (*b* 1668), *m* 1698, Martha Mould;
6–Hugh (1710-45), *m* 1731, Demaris Champlin (1713-53);
5–Sgt. Christopher (1733-1820), farmer; sgt. Am. Rev.; Bapt. minister, Granville, Mass.; *m* 2d, 1758, Abigail Way;
4–David (1769-1839), *m* Mary Bishop (*d* 1817);
3–David (1791-1843), Southwick, Mass.; *m* 1817, Emma Kennedy (1795-1874);
2–Mary Rebecca (1831-1909), Terryville, Conn.; *m* 1850, Edward Lot **Gaylord** (1827-1915), see portrait and biography; issue: I–Anna May (1 above); II–Edward (1863-64); III–Jesse Ransome (1867-1902).

1–*m* June 22, 1876, Frederick Sylvester Stevens (1848-1906), of Danbury, Conn.; son of Sylvester Stevens of Danbury; issue: 1–Louise May, *b* Bridgeport, Conn., Oct. 10, 1880; *m* July 8, 1918, Louis F., son of George Nutting, *m* Rosetta Jackson (issue: Doris Stevens, *b* Bridgeport, 1920); 2–Nellie Starr, *b* Stratford, Conn., Mar. 28, 1884; Mt. Holyoke, '07 (P.B.K.); 3–Ferris Alcott, *b* Bridgeport, Mar. 27, 1888; *m* June 30, 1921, Margaret A. O'Day; 4–Edith Mary, *b* Bridgeport, Mar. 7, 1892; *m* Nov. 4, 1911, Lewis A., son of Lewis T. Young, of Phila., Pa. (issue: Frederick Alexander, *b* 1913; Torrence, *b* 1916).

1–Ed. pvt. schools. Mem. D.F.P.A., D.A.R. (rec. sec. Conn., 5 yrs.). Episcopalian. Residence: 1482 Iranistan Av., Bridgeport, Conn.

STEVENS and allied paternal lineages of MARY ELIZABETH STEVENS, CARRIE LOUISE STEVENS (*m* Charles E. Ellis), and ELIZA STEVENS (*m* Nathan Cook Osgood).

8–William **Stevens** (qv);

7–John (1650-1724), *b* Newbury; went to Hampstead, Mass., where he became a large landowner; *m* 1669, Mary Chase (see Chase below);

6–Otho (1702-71), ensign, Gloucester, Mass.; *m* 1723, Abagail Kent (see Kent below);

5–Otho (1732-59), ensign, mentioned among those especially distinguished in French and Indian War; was with Wolf's Brigade at storming of Quebec and died from injuries received while climbing the Heights of Abraham; *m* 1752, Abigail Emerson (see Emerson below);

4–Simon (1756-1825), Canterbury; *m* Elizabeth Boynton (see Boynton below);

3–Edmund (1778-1854), *b* and lived at Canterbury save last 3 years which he spent with his son at Dover, N.H.; *m* 1807, Betsey Shepard (see Shepard below);

WILLIAM SHEPARD STEVENS (1816-97).

2–William Shepard (1816-97), financier, manufacturer of "New England Flint and Emery Paper," firm name Wiggin & Stevens; after the plant in Dover, N.H., was destroyed by fire it was rebuilt in Malden, Mass.; Wiggin & Stevens, and Baeder & Adamson in Phila. were the largest, and for many years, practically the only manufacturers of this commodity in this country. After the death of William Shepard Stevens and the permanent illness of his son, Everett Jewett Stevens, the plant was sold and passed out of the family; was connected with the Strafford Nat. Bank, Dover, N.H., from its reorganization to a national bank, and was its pres., 1868-97; was also v.p. Strafford Savings Bank, dir. Boston & Maine R.R., 1870-97, and interested in other important enterprises. Served as mayor of Dover, 3 terms, 1870-73, also member board of education many years, etc.; rep. in N.H. Legislature 8 years; Mason (see portrait); *m* 1st, 1839, Mary R. Jewett (*d* 1849); issue:

I–Cordelia (*d* aet. 2);

II–Everett Jewett (*b* Ossipee, N.H., May 11, 1847-*d* Malden, Mass., Nov. 1, 1924); lived in Malden from 1874 until his death; mayor of Malden, 1894-98; pres. First National Bank many years; mem. board of education many years; trustee Malden Hospital to which he left money at his death; rep. Mass. Legislature, 1899-1903; junior partner firm of Wiggin & Stevens, mfrs. of "New England Flint and Emery Paper," Malden, Mass., until death of senior partners when he became head of the business; *m* Oct. 28, 1874, Abbie Emery, Somersworth, N.H. (*b* Mar. 28, 1851-*d* Jan. 13, 1917); dau. of William Emery, *m* Ann Maria Locke; issue: 1–Gertrude Emery, *b* Malden, Mar. 18, 1877; *m* Jan. 14, 1897, George C. Dutton (*b* Oct. 13, 1868), son of Benjamin Franklin Dutton, *m* Harriet M. Conant (issue: i–Gertrude Stevens, *b* May 30, 1902; ii–Benjamin Franklin, 2d, *b* June 4, 1904; iii–Harriet Conant, *b* Mar. 30, 1911; iv–George Conant, Jr., *b* Oct. 11, 1914); 2–Alice Madelaine, *b* Malden, Jan. 18, 1880; *m* Dec. 6, 1905, Paul T. Wise (*b* Mar. 26, 1879), son of Daniel P. Wise, *m* Grace Bates; business of Paul T. Wise, of firm of Chelsea Fibre Co., estab. by Pratts who were donors of The Pratt Institute of Brooklyn (issue: i–Parker Stevens, *b* Dec. 16, 1906; ii–Everett Stevens, *b* Oct. 19, 1910; iii–Pauline, *b* June 27, 1915); 3–Helen Morette, *b* Malden, May 19, 1883-*d* at home, Riverton, N.J., Apr. 20, 1930; *m* A. Russell Gausler (*b* Aug. 29, 1881), son of Augustus C. Gausler, *m* Clara Becker; business Philadelphia (issue: i–Russell Stevens, *b* Mar. 8, 1911-*d* Feb. 22, 1927; ii–Helen M., *b* Apr. 27, 1919),

William Shepard Stevens, *m* 2d, Sarah Varney Bangs (1823-65); for issue see under Bangs lineages following.

14–Thomas **Chase,** of Chesham, Eng.;

13–John, of Chesham;

12–Matthew, of Chesham; *m* Elizabeth, dau. of Richard Bould;

11–Thomas (bap. 1506), of Hundrick Parish, Chesham;

10–Richard (bap. 1542), *m* 1564, Joan Bishop;

9–Aquilla (bap. 1580), *m* 1606, Martha Jelliman;

8–Aquilla (1618-70), from Chesham, Eng., to N.E. with his brother Thomas; at Hampton, ante 1640, at Newbury, 1646; *m* Anne Wheeler (1620-87; John[9] [*d* 1670], from Salisbury, Eng., founder of N.H., a sea capt., *m* Anne– [*d* 1662]; Dominic, or Doming[10], will dated 1615, of Eng., *m* Mercy–);

7–Mary (*b* 1650), *m* 1669, Hon. John **Stevens** (7 above).

9–Thomas **Kent** (*d* 1658), from Eng. to Gloucester, Mass., ante 1643; had house and land in what is now Essex, Mass.; an original propr.;

8–Thomas (*d* 1696), among those drafted in King Philip's War; an original propr. of Gloucester; *m* 1658, Joan Penny (Thomas[9] [*d* ca. 1692], *m* Ann– [*d* 1667], *m* 2d, 1668, Agnes Clark [*d* 1682], *m* 3d, 1683, Joan Braybrook);

7–Josiah (1660-1725), *m* 1689, Mary Lufkin;

6–Abagail (*d* 1771), *m* Otho **Stevens,** Sr. (6 above).

13–George **Emerson,** atty. of Rysome Manor, Hollington, Gt. and Little Fenton, Co. York, and of Stratford Loughsome and Stanstead Montfichet, Ugley, Berden and Bolyngton, Co. Essex; *m* Alice Wyatt, dau. or sister of Henry Wyatt, of Co. York, and later Sir Henry Wyatt, of Allington Castle, Co. Kent;

12–Ralf, armiger, of Sigston and Foxton, Co. York, Fines York;

11–Thomas (ante 1540-1595), of Great Dunmow, Co. Essex; *m* Joan–;

10–Robert (1561-1620), of Gt. Dunmow and Bishop's Stortford; *m* 1578, Susan Crabbe;

9–Thomas (1584-1666), bap. Bishop's Stortford, 1584; collector for the poor, 1636; probably came to America, 1636; at Ipswich, Mass., as early as 1638, when his name appears as a propr. of that town; selectman, 1646; *m* in Eng., 1611, Elizabeth Brewster (Elder Will-

Arms: *Vert and or, on a bend engrailed azure, three lions passant argent.*
Crest: *A lion rampant vert, bezantée, holding a battle-axe gules, headed argent.*

iam[10], Mayflower Pilgrim, qv); their son Joseph was the ancester of Ralph Waldo Emerson;

EMERSON HOUSE

Built about 1640 on land overlooking the Ipswich River, by Thomas Emerson, the first Emerson in America, ancestor of Ralph Waldo Emerson. Thomas Emerson's grave is in the old burial yard with the Emerson arms on the stone; also the grave of his son Nathaniel, with the arms of Ralph of Foxton carved on the stone.

8–Robert (ca. 1612-1694), *b* at Bishop's Stortford; lived at different times at Haverhill, Ipswich and Hempstead; said to have been killed by the Indians; *m* 1635, Elizabeth Grave; *m* 2d, Frances–; *m* 3d, 1660, Ann, or Anna, Grant (Thomas[9], *m* Jane–);
7–Benjamin (1679-1734), *m* 1707, Sarah Philbrick;
6–Lt. Benjamin (*b* 1716), *m* 1736, Hannah Watts (see Ayer-Watts below);
5–Abigail (1737-1833), *m* 1st, Otho **Stevens,** Jr. (5 above).
11–Thomas **Ayer,** of Wiltshire, Eng.; *m* Elizabeth Rogers;
10–John (1590-92-will proved 1657), from Eng. in the "James," 1635, settled at Newbury, Mass.; removed to Salisbury, where he received land, 1640,43; removed to Ipswich, 1645/46, to Haverhill, 1647; *m* Hannah– (1598-1686 or 88);
9–Thomas (1630/31-1686), freeman, Haverhill, 1650; landowner; *m* 1656, Elizabeth Hutchins (*d* 1710; John[10], of Newbury);
8–Elizabeth (1659-95), *m* Samuel **Watts** (see Emerson-Watts below);
7–Capt. Samuel, *m* Abagail Duston;
6–Hannah (*b* 1718), *m* Benjamin **Emerson** (6 above).
13–John **Emerson** (*d* 1561), of Sereby, Co. Lincoln; *m* Isabelle–;
12–George (will dated 1573, proved 1574), the elder; of Sereby;
11–Alexander (*d* 1605), of Sereby; yeoman; *m* Jennett (*d* 1612), dau. of John Hornsey;
10–Thomas (*d* 1657), of Howsham in Cadney; *m* ca. 1612, Margaret Froe;
9–Michael (qv); *m* Hannah Webster (John[10] [*d* 1646], of Ipswich, *m* Mary Shatswell);

DUSTIN MONUMENT

Erected in memory of Hannah Dustin, famous for killing, scalping and escaping from the Indians, who had taken her captive, in Haverhill, Mass., Mar. 15, 1697, to an island opposite Penacook, now Concord, N.H., from which island she escaped.

8–Hannah (1657-post 1709), one of the most famous women of early N.E. (see illustration); *m* 1677, Thomas **Duston** (ca. 1650-1698; Thomas[9] [1627-1703], *m* 1649, Joan–; Thomas Durston[10] [*b* 1598], *m* 1626, Elizabeth Burgess);
7–Abagail (1690-1727), *m* ante 1706, Capt. Samuel **Watts** (7 above).
8–John **Boynton** (1614-70; son of William, of East Riding of Yorkshire, Eng., at Kingston, Wintringham, descended from Bartholomew de Boynton, who was seized of the manor of Boynton, 1067, and was succeeded in his estate by his son Walter); he and his brother William came to N.E. with the Rev. Ezekiel Rogers, 1638, they settled at Rowley, Mass.; *m* Ellenor (or Ellen) Pell (*d* 1694), of Boston;

BOYNTON

Arms: *Or, a fess between three crescents gules.*
Crest: *On a wreath, a goat passant sable, guttee d'argent, beard, horns, and hoofs or.*
Motto: *Il tempo passa.*

7–Sgt. Caleb (1649-1708), officer King Philip's War; *m* 1674, Hannah Harriman (1655-1708; Leonard[8] [*d* 1691], at Rowley, 1649, freeman, 1657, selectman, 1665-72; *m* Margaret–);
6–Ebenezer (1688-1761), of Byfield Parish, Rowley; removed to Weston, Middlesex Co., Mass., 1726; *m* 1st, Sarah Grout (*d* 1727/28; Caleb[7]);
5–Caleb (1724-97), *m* Rachel–; *m* 2d, Lydia Bullard (*b* 1728; Benjamin[6], *m* Judith Hill; Benjamin[7], *m* Martha, dau. of Thomas Pigge; Benjamin[8], settled at Watertown, ante 1637,

received land grant, freeman, *m* Mary, dau. of Henry Thorpe, of Watertown); *m* 3d, 1753, widow Abagail Richardson, of Medway;
4–Elizabeth (1754-1825), *m* Simon **Stevens** (4 above).

SHEPARD

Arms: Ermine, on a chief sable, three pole-axes argent.
Crest: On a mount vert, a stag courant, reguardant proper, attired or.

8–John **Shepard** (qv);
7–Samuel (1641-1707), took oath of allegiance at Haverhill, 1677; removed to Salisbury; *m* 1673, Mary (Page) Dow, widow of John Dow (bap. 1646-1717; John Page[8] [*d* 1687], of Hingham and Haverhill, *m* Mary, daughter of George Marsh, from Eng. to Hingham, 1635, an original propr., *m* Elizabeth–; John[9] [1586-1676], from Eng. with Gov. Winthrop to Boston, 1630, Dedham, 1636, freeman, 1640, *m* 1st, Phoebe–, *m* 2d, Mary Paine);
6–Israel (1684-1769), at Epping, N.H., 1741, where he signed a petition; moved to Gilmanton, N.H., where he *d*; *m* 1718, Mary True (among their sons was Rev. Samuel, famed in N.H. annals); (see Bradbury-True below);
5–Joseph (1725-93), Epping, N.H.; *m* Anna Sanborn (see Sanborn below);
4–John (1754-1844), moderator and selectman, Gilmanton; a founder of Gilmanton Acad.; dep. Gen. Ct., 1807,08,12; *m* Elizabeth Gilman (see Gilman below);
3–Betsey (1783-1842), *m* Edmund **Stevens** (3 above).

BRADBURY

Arms: Sable, a chevron ermine, between three round buckles, the tongues hanging downward.
Crest: A demi-dove volant argent, fretty gules, holding in beak a slip of barberry vert.

16–Robert **Bradbury,** of Ollerset, Co. Derby;
15–William, of Broughing, Co. Hertfordshire;
14–Robert, of Littlebury, Co. Essex;
13–William, of Littlebury, Co. Essex;
12–Matthew, of Wicken Bonant, Co. Essex;
11–William, of Wicken Bonant, Co. Essex;
10–Wymond, of the Brick House, Wicken Bonant; *m* Elizabeth Whitgift (William[11]; Henry[12]; John[13]);
9–Capt. and Judge Thomas (1610/11-1694/95), freeman, Salisbury, 1640; town clk.; school teacher; justice; dep. from Salisbury to Mass. Gen. Ct., 1651,52,56,57,60,61,66; capt. militia; recorder, Norfolk Co., 6 yrs.; asso. judge; *m* 1636, Mary Perkins (Sgt. John[10], *m* Judith–);
8–Jane (1645-1700), *m* 1668, Henry **True** (1645-1735), ens. Salisbury Foot Co., 1682; lt., 1691; capt., 1703-04; commr. of N.H. boundary, 1705; rep. Mass. Gen. Ct., 1689,95,1707 (Henry[9] [*d* ca. 1659], from Eng. to Halifax, thence with Richard Saltonstall to Salem, where he owned a home in 1644, *m* ca. 1644, a dau. of John Pike [*d* 1654], from Eng. in the "James," 1635, to Newbury, Mass., to Ipswich, to Salisbury where he died, atty., 1636-37, *m* Sarah–);
7–Lt. William (ca. 1674-1768), of "Rocky Hill," Salisbury; lt., capt., 1705; rep. Gen. Ct., 1717; selectman and assessor; *m* 1691, Elinor Stevens (1674-1768; Lt. Benjamin[8] [1650-1689/90], *m* 1673, Hannah [1649-1711], dau. of Thomas Barnard, from Eng. to Salisbury, ca. 1634, chief magistrate of Nantucket, one of the 9 original purchasers of Nantucket, killed by the Indians; Sgt. John[9] [ca. 1611-1688/89], of Salisbury, *m* Katherine or Catherine–, *d* 1682);
6–Mary (1695/96-1767), *m* 1718, Israel **Shepard** (6 above).
18–Nicholas (Samburne, Sambourne, Sanborne) **Sanborn,** held Biddle Stone Manor, 1392;
17–Sir William (*b* 1390), wrote name Sambourne; *m* Ann, dau. of Sir William Lushill;
16–Nicholas, of Fernham, nr. Faringdon, Berks Co., and Lushill in Wilts; *m* Katherine, dau. of Sir John Lushill;
15–Walter, of Lushill in Wilts, and of Southcot in Co. Berks, *m* Margaret Drew (Thomas[16], of Leagry in Wilts, and of Southcot in Berks; Lawrence[17], *m* Lucy Restwold, of Vache in Bucks);
14–Drew (ca. 1449-will proved 1506), *m* Joan, dau. of Thomas Cricklade, the lord of various manors, Studleigh, Cricklade, Ford, in Wilts and Lanaride in Somerset;
13–Henry, *m* Elizabeth, dau. of Richard Richards, of Burfield;
12–Thomas, *m* 3d, Joan, dau. of Henry Polstede, of Albury and Surrey;
11–Richard (*b* 1550), *m* Elizabeth, dau. of Richard Stampe, of Cholsey, Co. Berks;
10–John (*b* 1590), began to write name San-

Arms: Argent, three bars gules between eight escallop-shells sable, three, two, two, one.
Crest: On a pellet a falcon rising argent.

borne; *m* 1619, Ann Bacheler (Rev. Stephen[11], qv);
9–Lt. John (qv); began to write name Sanborn;
8–Richard (*b* 1655), *m* 1676, Ruth Moulton (William[9] [1617-80], from Eng. with Robert Page, founder Hampton, N.H., one of the petitioners for the town's incorporation, large landowner, some of the land he owned is said to be still occupied by descendants, selectman many yrs. and moderator, *m* Margaret Page [Robert[10] (1604-79) *m* Lucy– (*d* 1665); Robert[11] (1577-1617), *m* Margrette Goodwynge or Goodwin; Robert[12] (ante 1550-1587), *m* Martha–]; Robert Moulton[10], in descent from Sir Thomas de Moulton, 4th baron by that name in Eng., Lord of Moulton and of Egremont, who was the most trusted friend of Richard Coeur de Lion, and went with him on his crusade to the Holy Land; during an illness Coeur de Lion made Sir Thomas ruler in his place);
7–Ens. John (1681-1727), ens. French and Indian War; *m* as her 1st husband, 1701, Sarah Philbrick (see Roberts-Philbrick below);
6–Dea. Daniel (1702-98), an original propr. of Sanbornton; dea. of the ch.; justice for Stratford Co.; *m* 1725, Catherine Rollins (see Rollins below);
5–Anna (1728-1807), *m* Joseph **Shepard** (5 above).
10–Edward **Gilman** (will dated 1573), of Caston, Eng.; *m* 1550, Rose Rysse;
9–Robert (1559-1631), *m* Mary– (*d* 1618);
8–Edward (qv);
7–Hon. John (1624-1708), came to N.E. with father in the "Diligent"; settled at Exeter, N.H., ca. 1648; councillor, 1680-83; selectman; asso. judge Old Norfolk Co., 1677,79; dep. Gen. Ct., 1692,97; rep. and speaker, 1693-97; lt. Exeter militia, 1669; capt.; judge Common Pleas Ct.; *m* 1657, Elizabeth Treworgie (1639-1719; James[8] [*d* ante 1650], in Me. as early as 1635, *m* Catherine [*d* bet. 1676-82], dau. of Alexander Shapleigh [1585-ante 1650], from Eng. in his own ship the "Benediction," to Kittery, Me., mcht. and shipowner, agent for Sir Fernando Gorges, in N.E.);

Arms: Vert, a chevron argent, between three escallops or.
Crest: An arm vested gules, turned up argent, holding in the hand proper a chaplet vert, garnished with roses of the first.
Motto: Fideli certa merces.

6–Hon. Nicholas (1672-1749), judge Ct. Common Pleas, 1729, Superior Ct., 1732-40; *m* 1697, Sarah Clarke (see Somerby-Clarke below);
5–Dr. Josiah (1710-93), "a leading physician of Exeter for more than half a century"; clk. of proprs. of Gilmanton more than 30 yrs.; draftsman of a plan of that town; one of the proprs.; *m* 1731, Abagail Coffin (see Coffin below);
4–Elizabeth (1760-1840), *m* 2d, 1779, John **Shepard** (4 above).
10–Henry **Somerby** (*d* 1607; desc. Osbert de Somerby, living in 1156); immigrant; *m* Margaret–;
9–Richard, *m* as her 1st husband, Margaret–;
8–Henry (1612-52), from Eng. in the "Jonathan," 1639, with his brother Anthony; capt., later col., of militia at Newbury; dep. Mass. Gen. Ct. 11 terms; *m* Judith Greenleaf;
7–Elizabeth, *m* 1663, Nathaniel **Clarke** (qv);
6–Sarah (1678-1748), *m* Judge Nicholas **Gilman** (6 above).
11–Nicholas **Coffin** (*d* 1613), Devonshire, Eng.; *m* Joan–;
10–Peter (*d* 1628), *m* Joanna Thember, or Kember (*d* 1661);
9–Tristram (1605-81), from Devonshire, Eng., 1642; at Salisbury and Haverhill, Mass., 1642; removed to Newbury ca. 1648; returned to Salisbury, 1654-55; one of the 9 original founders of Nantucket, 1660, and became one of the most important men on the island; chief magistrate about 8 yrs.; lt., 1654; commr., 1665; *m* in Eng., ca. 1630, Dionis Stevens (*d* post 1682; Robert[10], of Brixton);
8–Hon. Peter (1631-1715), from Brixton, Co. Devonshire, Eng., to Dover, N.H., where he lived some yrs.; to Exeter where he died; one of the 9 original proprs. of Nantucket, where he was magistrate; capt.; dep. from Dover, N.H., to Mass. Gen. Ct., 1672,73,97; councillor of N.H., 1692-1712; lt. King Philip's War, 1675; acting gov. of N.H., 1692-97, 1703-15; chief justice of the province, 1697; asso. justice, 1699-1714; *m* Abagail Starbuck (Elder Edward[9] [1605-90], from Eng. to Dover, N.H., ca. 1635, leading elder in the ch., among "associates chosen by the first proprs."; one of commrs. chosen by Dover and Kittery to lay out the dividing bounds between said towns, first rep. from Dover, 1643-46; chief magistrate at Nantucket, to which place he removed, *m* Katherine Reynolds);
7–Tristram (*b* 1665), *m* 1684, Deborah Colcord (*b* 1664; Edward[8] [1616/17-1682], from Eng. to Portsmouth, N.H., ca. 1631, at Exeter, 1638, Hampton, N.H., ca. 1631, at Hampton, 1644, at Saco, Me., a founder of N.H., served in King Philip's War, gov. of the plantation at Dover, dep. Gen. Ct. at Boston, *m* Ann or Anne Page);
6–Capt. Eliphalet (1689-1736), of Gilmanton, N.H.; selectman; moderator; capt.; *m* 1710, his cousin, Judith (Coffin) Noyes (see Coffin below);
5–Abagail (*b* 1711), *m* Dr. Josiah **Gilman** (5 above).
11–Nicholas **Coffin,** above;
10–Peter, above;
9–Tristram, Sr., above;
8–Tristram, Jr. (1632-1704), lt. Newbury Co., 1683; dep., 1696-1702; *m* 1652, Judith Greenleaf (see Greenleaf below);
7–James (1659-1720), judge Ct. Common Pleas, 1696-1718, chief justice 1708-18; commr. of Oyer and Terminer, 1704; judge of probate, 1700-20; *m* 1685, Florence Hooke (William[8] [ca. 1638-1721], *m* Elizabeth Dyer [*d* 1717]; Gov. William[9] [*d* 1667], A.B., and A.M., Trinity Coll., 1620, minister in Eng., came to N.E., ca. 1630; first charter councillor under Gorges, 1640, at Agamenticus [now York], Me., gov. Province of Me.; dep. Salisbury [Mass.] Gen. Ct., returned to Eng., 1656, *m* Elenor Whalley [sister of Whalley, the friend of Cromwell]; Humphrey[10], alderman, Bristol, Eng.);
6–Judith (1686-1736), as Widow Noyes, *m* 2d, 1710, Capt. Eliphalet **Coffin** (6 above).
10–John **Greenleaf** (*b* 1574), *m* Margaret–;
9–Capt. Edmund (ca. 1590-1671), from Eng. to N.E., ca. 1635, settled at Newbury, Mass.; among the first proprs. of Newbury; freeman and ens., 1639; comd. a co. which marched against the Indians, 1637; lt. Mass. provincial forces, 1642; "ancient and experienced lt. under Capt. William Gerrish," 1644; capt., 1645; removed to Boston, 1650; *m* Sarah Dole (William[10], *m* 1622, Joane Hale; Richard[11] [will proved 1609], of Rangeworth, Gloucestershire, Eng., *m* Dorothy–);
8–Judith (1625-1705), *m* 2d, Tristram **Coffin** (8 above).
10–Gov. Thomas **Roberts** (*d* 1674), historic founder of N.H.; gov. of Dover Colony; pres. of the ct.;

GREENLEAF

Arms: *Argent, three saltires humette vert.*
Crest: *An arm embowed couped at the shoulder, holding in the hand a fireball, all proper.*

9–Ann, of Dover Neck; *m* as his 2d wife, James **Philbrick** (1632-76), sea capt.; drowned in the Hampton River nr. Cole's Creek (Thomas[10], qv);
8–Lt. James (1657-1723), sea capt. of Hampton; did much trading with N.E. coast towns and the W.I.; selectman; surveyor; lt. militia in French and Indian War; *m* Hannah Perkins (1656-1739; Isaac[9] [*d* 1685], founder of Hampton, N.H., *m* Susanna– [*d* 1685]; Isaac[10] [*d* ante 1639], of Ipswich and Sandwich, *m* Alice–, widow of Edmund Perkins);
7–Sarah (1682-1761), *m* 1701, Ens. John **Sanborn** (7 above).
9–James (Rawlings) **Rollins** (1605-91), emigrated to America, 1632, with the settlers of Ipswich, Mass.; at Newbury, 1634; at Bloody Point, Dover, N.H., where he built a large house on the beautiful shores of Piscataqua, the house still stands (1930), and until within a few years was occupied by some member of the family; *m* Hannah–;
8–Thomas (1641-1706), justice of sessions; one of the company of Edward Gove; mem. of the dissolved assembly of N.H.; lived at Bloody Point until ca. 1668, when he removed to Exeter; *m* ca. 1670, Rachel Cox (Moses[9] [1594-1687], from Eng. to Hampton as early as 1640, one of the Edward Gove co. that inaugurated the famous rebellion, selectman of the town, later moved to Exeter, *m* Alice–);
7–Lt. Thomas (1671-1756), resided at Stratham, N.H.; lt. Stratham Military Co.; in French and Indian War; *m* 2d (?), Sarah Philbrick, widow of John Sanborn, above;
6–Catherine, *m* 1725, Dea. Daniel **Sanborn** (6 above).

BANGS and allied maternal lineages of MARY ELIZABETH STEVENS, CARRIE LOUISE STEVENS (*m* Charles E. Ellis), and ELIZA STEVENS (*m* Nathan Cook Osgood).

9–Edward **Bangs** (1592-1678), from Eng. in the "Ann," to Plymouth, Mass., 1623; mem. Plymouth mil. co., 1643; removed to Eastham, Mass., 1644; capt. of the guard against Indians; he and Gov. Prence (qv) "raised each a man and a horse" at his own expense for two years when the military were required to arm and equip three troop horse as the proportion of Eastham; dep. Gen. Ct., 1652; *m* Lydia Hicks; *m* 2d, Rebecca Tracy;
8–Capt. Jonathan (1640-1728), of Eastham; ens. company of foot and capt. militia; selectman and town treas. of Eastham; dep. Old Colony Ct., and rep. Gen. Ct.; *m* 1664, Mary Mayo (see Mayo below);
7–Capt. Edward (1665-1746), Eastham, Mass.; *m* Ruth Allen (see Allen below);
6–Ebenezer (*b* 1702), Brewster, Mass.; *m* 1727, Anna Sears (see Brewster-Freeman-Sears below);
5–Barnabas (1728-1808), *b* at Harwich (now Brewster), Mass.; went early to Gorham, Me.; pvt. at Lexington Alarm and later matross in Am. Rev.; *m* 1751, Loruhama (Leurania or Luraney) Elwell (John[6], *m* Abigail Sawtelle; William[7]; Thomas[8]; Robert[9]);
4–James (*b* 1752), *m* 1789, Elizabeth Estes (see Estes below);
3–Cyrus (1792-1867), Dover, N.H.; mem. Society of Friends; *m* 1817, Matilda Varney (see Varney below);
2–Sarah Varney (2 below).

Bangs

Arms: *Sable, a cross engrailed ermine, between four fleurs-de-lis or.*
Crest: *A Moor's head full faced couped at the shoulders proper, on the head a cap of maintainance gules, turned up ermine, adorned with a crescent issuant therefrom a fleur-de-lis.*

10–Rev. John **Mayo** (*d* 1676), grad. from an English univ.; from Eng., 1638, at Barnstable, 1639; freeman, 1640; removed to Eastham, 1646, and took charge of the church in that town until 1655, when he went to the historic "Second" or "North" Church, Boston, as first pastor, 1655-73; removed to Cape Cod, 1673; *m* Thomasine– (*d* 1682);
9–Capt. Samuel (1625-1663/64), mariner; shipmaster at Boston, 1663; one of the purchasers of Oyster Bay, L.I., 1653; *m* Thomasine Lumpkin (*d* 1709; William[10] [*d* 1671], of Yarmouth, 1639, constable, surveyor of highways, 1652, rep., 1652, foreman of coroner's jury, *m* Thomasine–);
8–Mary (1649/50-1711), *m* Capt. Jonathan **Bangs** (8 above).
10–George **Allen** (1568-1648), from Eng., settled first at Martha's Vineyard, later at Lynn, 1636, at Sandwich, 1637; dep. from Sandwich to Plymouth Gen. Ct., 1640-42,44; *m* Catherine–;
9–Samuel (1596-1669), at Dorchester, 1628; freeman, Braintree, 1635; *m* Ann–; *m* 2d, Margaret–, widow of Edward Lamb;
8–James (1636-1714), settled at Chilmark, 1660; *m* Elizabeth Perkins;
7–Ruth (1669-1738), *m* Capt. Edward **Bangs** (7 above).
9–Richard **Sears** (qv); desc. Emperor Charlemagne;
8–Paul (1637-1708), capt., comdg. a co. of militia in Narragansett War; *m* 1658, Deborah Willard (George[9] [*b* 1614], *m* Dorothy, probably Dunster; Richard[10] [*d* 1617], *m* 3d, Joan Morehead; Simon[11], *m* Elizabeth–);
7–Paul (1669-1739/40), *m* 1693, Mercy Freeman;
6–Anna (*b* 1706), *m* Ebenezer **Bangs** (6 above).
11–Elder William **Brewster** (*b* 1566/67), 4th signer of the Mayflower Compact; a ruling elder of the church at Plymouth, 1620-44; dep., 1636; chaplain of a mil. co.; *m* before 1593, Mary– (*d* 1637);
10–Patience (1600-34), *m* 1624, Gov. Thomas **Prence** (1600-73), from Eng. to Plymouth, 1621; asst., Plymouth Colony, 1635, and gov., 1634,38,57,72; removed to Duxbury, 1635, to Eastham, 1645; mem. Council of War, and served in Pequot

BREWSTER

Arms: Sable, a chevron ermine, between three estoiles argent.
Crest: A wolf's head erased argent.

War; he and Edward Bangs (qv) "raised each a man and a horse" at his won expense for two years when the military were required to arm and equip three troop horse as the proportion of Eastham; commr. United Colonies, 1645; was the first to establish public schools in this country;

9–Mercy, *m* Maj. John **Freeman** (1627-1719), of Eastham, Mass.; dep. Mass. Gen. Ct.; judge Ct. Common Pleas; one of Council of War; selectman; lt., 1659; capt. King Philip's War; maj. and gen. cdr. of the Barnstable co. militia (Edmund[10], qv);

8–Dea. Thomas (1653-1715), settled at Brewster and was petitioner for the incorporation of the town of Harwich; helped to found the first ch., 1700; first town clk.; selectman; dea. of the ch.; *m* 1673, Rebecca Sparrow (1655-1740; Capt. Jonathan[9] [ca. 1633-1706], *m* Rebecca Bangs; Richard[10] [1580-1660], dep. Plymouth Gen. Ct., *m* Pandora–);

7–Mercy (*b* 1674), *m* Paul **Sears** (7 above).

8–Robert (Este) **Estes** (*b* 1645; desc. Albert Azo, of Italy, Marquis of Liguria, *b* 1087); *m* Dorothy, of Dover, Eng.;

7–Richard is said to have come from Eng., 1684, arrived at Boston; mem. Society of Friends; *m* 1697, Elizabeth Beck (*b* 1663; Henry[8], *m* Jane, dau. of Dea. John Cate, son of James Cate, Jr.; Thomas[9], *m* Mary Frost; Henry[10], from Eng. to America, 1635, *m* Ann Frost);

6–Benjamin (1698-1775), was called "joiner," "housewright," "millwright"; large landholder; of Salem and Reading, Mass., Portsmouth, N.H., Kittery, Berwick and Wells, Me.; *m* Elizabeth–;

5–Henry (*d* 1792), yeoman; extensive landholder; *m* Mary Varney (see Varney below);

4–Elizabeth, *m* 1789, James **Bangs** (4 above).

9–William **Varney** or Verney (*d* 1654), came probably via Barbados from Eng. to America, about the middle of 17th Century; at Ipswich, Mass., 1649; *m* Bridget– (*d* 1672);

8–Humphrey, of Gloucester, Ipswich, Salem and Salisbury, settled permanently at Dover, 1659; *m* Esther Starbuck (Elder Edward[9] [1604/05-1690], chief magistrate Nantucket); *m* 2d, Sarah Starbuck, sister of 1st wife;

7–Ebenezer (*b* 1670), husbandman, Dover, N.H.; mem. Soc. of Friends; *m* ca. 1689/90, Mary Otis (see Otis below);

6–John (*b* 1701), brother of Paul below; *m* Sarah Robinson (see Roberts-Robinson below);

5–Mary (*d* 1763), *m* Henry **Estes** (5 above).

11–Richard **Otis** (ca. 1550-1611), of Glastonbury, Somerset Co., Eng.;

10–John (1581-1657), probably came to America ca. 1630, to Plymouth Colony, thence to Hingham; *m* 1st, Margaret–;

9–Richard (prob. *b* 1626-*d* 1689), in great Indian Massacre; came with father; probably admitted inhabitant of Boston, 1655; selectman, Dover, N.H.; *m* 1651, Rose Stoughton (Sir Anthony[10], *m* Agnes, dau. of Robert Pierce; Laurence[11], *m* Rose, dau. of Richard Ive, of London; Thomas[12], *m* Elizabeth, dau. of Edward Lewkenor; Lawrence[13], *m* Ann Comb; Gilbert[14], *m* Mary, dau. of Edward Bankesey; Thomas[15], of Stoughton in Surrey);

OTIS

Arms: Argent, a saltire engrailed between four crosses crosslets fitchée azure.
Crest: An arm in armor embowed, the hand grasping a dirk.

8–Stephen (1652-89), *m* Mary Pitman (William[9] [1632-82], *m* Barbara Evans);

7–Mary (*b* ca. 1670), *m* Ebenezer **Varney** (7 above).

9–Gov. Thomas **Roberts** (*d* 1673), historic founder of N.H.; gov. of Dover Colony; pres. of the ct.; Gov. Roberts and William Hilton among the earliest and most influential of first settlers in N.H., built houses on what are now opposite sides of street at Dover Point; afterwards Gov. Roberts moved further up the Neck toward what is now Dover and became owner there of very extensive holdings of land running down to the Piscataqua river on one side and the Cochecho on the other; the "Bound Oak," over 500 years old, which marked the boundary line between the extensive tracts of land which he gave to his two sons, is still standing and of great interest to visitors; there are still standing Roberts' houses at Dover Neck; a new stone was placed at his grave a few years ago, in place of the crumbling one there, by the Society of Colonial Wars (see illustration);

Stone at the grave of GOV. THOMAS ROBERTS, in the Roberts' burying plot, erected by the Society of Colonial Wars.

8–John, *m* Abagail Nutter (Hatevil[9] [1604-75], founder of N.H.);

7–Mary (1695-1771), *m* Timothy **Robinson**;

6–Sarah, *m* John **Varney** (6 above).

8–William **Varney** (9 above);

7–Humphrey (8 above);

6–Ebenezer (7 above);

5–Paul (1715-82), brother of John above; *m* 1742, Elizabeth Mussey (see Mussey below);

4–James (1759-1815), *m* 1793, Sarah Allen (see Curtis-Jenkins-Allen below);

3–Matilda (1797-1874), *m* 1817, Cyrus **Bangs** (3 above).

8–John **Mussey,** from Eng. to Ipswich, ca. 1640; *m* Lydia–;
7–Thomas (ca. 1635-ca. 1710), resided at Cape Porpoise (now Kennebunkport); constable; served in Indian wars; spent last years at Salisbury;
6–James (*b* ca. 1680), removed from Cape Porpoise to Mendon, ca. 1735; Friend; town clk., Arundel, 1725; *m* 1705, Judith Whitehouse (Thomas[7] [*b* ca. 1640], from Eng. with his father, aet. ca. 18, freeman, Dover, 1665, *m* ca. 1670, Elizabeth [*b* 1649], dau. of Dea. John Dam [ca. 1610-1690], *m* Elizabeth Pomfret; Thomas[8] [*d* 1707], *m* a dau. of Lt. William Pomfret [ca. 1600-1680], from Eng. to Wales with Capt. Thomas Wiggin's company, settled at Dover Neck, 1633, town clk., lt. of a militia co. for defense of Dover, *m* Elizabeth–);
5–Elizabeth (1720-63), *m* 1742, Paul **Varney** (5 above).
14–John **Curtis,** of Malestock;
13–William, of Malestock;
12–Eustis, of Malestock;
11–William, of Walton, Warwick Co., Eng.;
10–John (will proved 1690), of Boston, Co. Middlesex, N.E.; mariner; belonging to His Majesty's Ship the English "Togger"; *m* 1610, Elizabeth Hutchings;
9–Thomas (1619/20-1706), from Eng. to Portsmouth, N.H., ca. 1640; bought land of Sir Fernando Gorges at York, Me., 1645; later at Scituate, Mass., 1680; *m* Elizabeth–;
8–Hannah, *m* ante 1680, Jabez **Jenkins** (ca. 1655-1697; Reginald[9] [1608-83], came to America ca. 1634, served with John Winter at Richmond Island, 1634-39, settled at Kittery, Me., Friend, *m* ca. 1647, Ann–; Reginald[10], of Dorchester, Mass., is undoubtedly the man who removed, says Winthrop, to Cape Porpoise, Me., and was there killed by the Indians 1632);
7–Hannah, *m* Francis **Allen** (will proved bet. 1744-49), of Kittery or Eliot, Me.; was in service with John Winter at Richmond's Island, 1634-39 (Robert[8] [1637-1701], of English origin, landholder, Kittery, Me., *m* Hannah, dau. of John White, *m* Lucy–; Robert[9]);
6–Francis (1697-ante 1759), *m* 1724, Mary Pettigrew (see Ball-Pettigrew below);
5–Elijah (*d* ca. 1772), tanner and farmer; *m* 2d, 1760, Elizabeth (Dennet) Jenkins (see Dennet below);
4–Sarah (1764-1851), *m* James **Varney** (4 above).
10–William **Ball,** of Wiltshire, Eng., had six sons who came to America in the "Planter," 1635 (of whom one, William, went south and was ancester of George Washington's mother, Mary Ball);
9–John, went first to Watertown, then to Agamenticus and Dover; *m* Elizabeth Fox, or Mary Clark (perhaps both);
8–John (*b* 1636), bought land at Spruce Creek, Kittery, Me.; served in Indian war; *m* Joanna (Wheelwright?);
7–Elizabeth, *m* 1706, Francis **Pettigrew** (*b* ca. 1680), settled at Kittery, Me., ca. 1700;
6–Mary (*b* 1707), *m* Francis **Allen** (6 above).
8–Alexander **Dennet** (ca. 1639-1698);
7–Alexander (ca. 1670-1733), settled at Eliot, Me., 1681, owned land there but returned to Portsmouth, where he died; *m* 1st, Mehitable Tetherly (Gabriel[8] [ca. 1628-1696], from Eng. to Portsmouth, N.H., ca. 1650; bought land at "Boiling Rock," and resided there until his death; sea capt., lumberman, farmer, *m* Susanna–);
6–Ebenezer (ca. 1692-ca. 1758), *m* 1714, Abagail Hill (see Strong-Hill below);
5–Elizabeth, *m* 2d, Elijah **Allen** (5 above).
10–Richard **Strong,** of Somersetshire, Eng.;
9–Elder John (1605-99), from Eng. in the "Mary and John," to Nantasket, Mass., 1630; settled at Dorchester, 1630, at Hingham, 1635; freeman, 1637; rep. Gen. Ct., 1641-44, later at Windsor, Conn., and Northampton, Mass.; *m* 2d, 1630, Abagail Ford (Thomas[10], from Eng. in the "Mary and John," 1630, rep., 1640,41,43);
8–Elizabeth, *m* John **Hill,** inherited land from his father at Dover, N.H. (John[9] [*d* 1647], moved from Plymouth to Boston, 1630, freeman, 1642; taxed at Dover, N.H., 1639, grantee of "Nashaway," 1640, *m* Elizabeth–);
7–Samuel (1659-1713), *m* 1680, Elizabeth Williams (William[8] [*b* ca. 1635], of Oyster River, inherited "Williams Farm," owned and occupied by the Williams family until after the Am. Rev., constable, *m* Margaret [*b* ca. 1640], dau. of Thomas Stevenson, from Eng. to Dover, N.H., ca. 1640, tax payer, 1649, *m* Margaret–; William[9] [ca. 1610-1685], from Eng. with Capt. Thomas Wiggin's co., 1633, one of the founders of the settlement at Dover Neck, first settler at Oyster River and large landholder there, *m* Alice–);
6–Abagail (*b* 1689), *m* Ebenezer **Dennet** (6 above);
5–Elizabeth, *m* Elijah **Allen** (5 above);
4–Sarah, *m* James **Varney** (4 above);
3–Matilda, *m* Cyrus **Bangs** (3 above);
2–Sarah Varney (1823-65), *m* 1851, as his 2d wife, William Shepard **Stevens** (see above); issue:
I–Mary Elizabeth, *b* June 25, 1852; has always lived in the old homestead, "Garrison Hill," Dover, N.H., and was born there. Mem. Colonial Dames of America; one of the two founders, 1893, of Tuesday Club (still flourishing), mem. of other clubs and organizations at various times; a trustee of Wentworth Home for the Aged, from the time of its organization to the present time, also mem. of admission com. and mem. of bd. of managers until resignation in 1924. Hobbies: Book collecting, curio collecting, genealogy, etc. Residence: "Garrison Hill," Dover, N.H.;
II–Carrie Louise, *b* Sept. 1, 1857-*d* Aug. 9, 1899; *m* Charles E. Ellis, *b* Nov. 21, 1854-*d* July 19, 1917; son of Ephraim C. Ellis, of New Bedford, Mass.; issue: i–Marguerite Stevens, *b* May 6, 1883; *m* May 6, 1907, Clarence R. Kilbourne, *b* Aug. 30, 1879; son of Lincoln P. Kilbourne [their son, Radcliffe Ellis Kilbourne, *b* July 23, 1908, Dartmouth Coll., '30]; ii–Mildred C., *b* Oct. 21, 1886-*d* Sept. 29, 1926; *m* Oct. 1908, Arthur K. Pope, Jr., son of Arthur K. Pope, Sr.; home: Hingham, Mass.; business, insurance, Boston; iii–Caroline Stevens, *b* Aug. 9, 1899; *m* Oct. 1921, Donald Thayer, concert singer, son of William C. Thayer, Sr. [their children: Carla Thayer, Jean Thayer, Donelda Thayer, Sylvia Patricia Thayer];
III–Eliza, *b* Dec. 28, 1860; *m* Sept. 22, 1886, Nathan Cook Osgood (see Osgood, Vol. III, p. 356), *b* Aug. 24, 1857-*d* Apr. 3, 1926. Home: 15 Chestnut St., Salem, Mass.; issue: i–Katharine, *b* June 5, 1887; *m* May 23, 1914, Henry Wagner Wright, son of Samuel Henry Wright, lawyer, Chicago; grad. Yale, an architect of firm Frohman, Robb & Little, Boston, architects of the cathedral now under construction in Washington, D.C., which Mr. Wright and another member of the firm are superintending; Mr. Wright is himself architect of the Gothic Chapel now being erected at Trinity College, Hartford, Conn., the corner-stone of which was laid June, 1930 [issue: Peter Brewster Wright, *b* July 27, 1915, student at Middlesex, Concord, Mass.]; residence: Topsfield, Mass);
IV–Annie Howell (*d* aged 2 yrs.).

1–**STEVENS, W(illiam) Bertrand,** *b* Lewiston, Me., Nov. 19, 1884.
6–Benjamin **Stevens** (*d* 1791), member Louisburg Expdn. and scout; *m* Sarah Pride;
5–Nathaniel (*b* 1741), soldier Am. Rev.; *m* Elizabeth Sinclair;
4–Frederick (1774-1834), *m* Betty Gilkey;
3–Isaac Gilkey (1820-1902), *m* Mariam Fernald;
2–Albion Morse (*b* 1860), *m* Ada Mary (*b* 1864), dau. Hugh McKenzie, of Can.
1–*m* Oct. 10, 1911, Violet Heathcote Bond, *b* N.Y. City, Feb. 5, 1883; dau. late William E. Bond, of New York; issue: 1–Ellen Hewson, *b* New Canaan, Conn., Aug. 14, 1912; 2–Ann Heathcote, *b* New York, Dec. 12, 1913; 3–Edith McKenzie, *b* New Canaan, July 22, 1916; 4–Emily McIlvaine, *b* San Antonio, Tex., Jan. 10, 1919.
1–A.B., Bates Coll. as of '06; B.D., Episcopal Theol. Sch., 1910; A.M., Columbia, 1911; Ph.D., New York U., 1916; (LL.D., U.Southern Calif., 1921; D.D., Bates, 1922). Consecrated bishop coadjutor of Los Angeles, 1920; bishop of Los Angeles, 1928 (see Who's Who in America). Mem. S.C.W., S.R., P.B.K., Phi Gamma Delta. Summer place: Del Mar, Calif. Residence: 2277 S. Hobart Boul., Los Angeles, Calif.

HOLLINGSWORTH HALL

1–**STEWART, J(oseph) Adger,** *b* Rockdale Co., Ga., Jan. 23, 1877.
10–Valentine **Hollingsworth** (qv);
9–Thomas (1661-1733), New Castle Co., Pa.; *m* 1st, Margaret–;
8–Abraham (1686-1748), Frederick Co., Va.; *m* 1710, Ann Robinson (*d* 1749);
7–George (*b* 1712), *m* 1st, 1734, Hannah McCoy (Robert[8]);
6–Abraham (1739-91), Laurens Co., S.C.; *m* 1762, Margaret Wright;
5–Joseph (1765-1844), Newton Co., Ga.; *m* 1789, Rosannah Nichols (1767-1839);
4–Joseph (1797-1859), *m* 1815, Ann Jane Carr Rogers (1795-1881; Andrew[5], *m* Lettie Franks);
3–Julia Ann (1819-1911), *m* 1837, John Lewis **Stewart** (1810-86; Alexander[4], *m* Sarah Stripling);
2–Joseph Alexander (2 below).
10–Giles **Webb** (*b* ca. 1620), from Eng., settled in Va.; burgess of Nansemond Co., 1658-60;
9–John (*b* ca. 1645), of Essex Co., Va.; *m* Mary Sanford;
8–James (1673-1716), *m* Sarah–;
7–James (1705-71), *m* 1731, Mary Edmonson (Benjamin[8], of Essex Co.);
6–James (1734-73), justice, Essex Co.; signer of Northern Neck Assn. against the Stamp Act, 1766; *m* Mary Smith (Col. Francis[7], of Essex Co., *m* Lucy Meriwether);
5–Francis (1759-1811), midshipman Va. state navy during Am. Rev.; *m* 1786, Frances Walker (Freeman[6], *m* Frances Belfield);
4–John (1794-1870), in War 1812; *m* 1815, Ann Thomason (John Conner[5], of Hancock Co., Ga., *m* Narcissa Lewis);
3–Martha A. E., *m* James Hardwick **Robinson** (Cornelius[4], *m* Kessiah Hardwick);
2–Carrie Julia (1852-1927), *m* 1873, Joseph Alexander **Stewart** (1845-90), of Newton Co., Ga.; merchant and planter; issue: I–James H. Robinson (*b* 1874); II–J. Adger (1 above); III–Estelle (*b* 1880; *m* George Kearsley Selden); IV–Daisy (*b* 1882; *m* Walter F. Roberts); V–Eloise (*b* 1884; *m* James Perry Champion); VI–Frances (*b* 1886; *m* Hugh Battey); VII–Anita (*b* 1889; *m* R. B. Armstrong).
1–*m* Apr. 26, 1899, Ann Carter, *b* Louisville, Ky., July 15, 1876; dau. of John Allen Carter; issue (all *b* Louisville, Ky.): 1–John Carter, *b* Feb. 26, 1900; U.Wis., '22; *m* Apr. 26, 1926, Patty A., dau. of T. Kennedy Helm (issue: Elizabeth Nelson); 2–Joseph Adger (Apr. 17, 1901-Jan. 30, 1902); 3–Joseph Alexander, *b* Feb. 17, 1904; A.B., Yale, '26; *m* Apr. 10, 1929, Virginia B., dau. of S. Clay Lyons (issue: Anne Carter); 4–Jean Hollingsworth, *b* Apr. 29, 1911; Vassar, '31.
1–Ga. Sch. of Tech. '96 (Sigma Alpha Epsilon). Purchasing agent, Ohio Falls Car Co., 1896-99; pres., Louisville Forge Co., 1899-1905; pres. Am. Tool Co., 1905-08, Louisville Axe & Tool Co., since 1908; pres. Cheatham Electric Switch Co. since 1901. Capt. U.S.A. during World War. Mem. S.C.W., S.A.R., S.C., I.A.G., Va. Hist. Soc., S.C. Hist. Soc. Mason (32°). Methodist. Democrat. Clubs: Pendennis, Louisville Country, Audubon Country, Les Cheneaux. Summer place: Les Cheneaux, Mich. Residence: 2525 Ransdell Av., Louisville, Ky.

1–**STEWART, Mary Ridgely,** *b* Montclair, N.J., Nov. 9, 1906.
10–Henry **Ridgely** (qv);
9–Henry (1669-1700), *m* Katherine Greenbury (Nicholas[10], qv);
8–Col. Henry (1690-1749), *m* Elizabeth Warfield (*d* 1719; Benjamin[9]);
7–Greenberry, *m* Lucy Stringer;
6–Richard (*d* 1824), judge, Howard Co.; *m* Elizabeth Dorsey (Ely[7], *m* Deborah–);
5–Matilda Chase, *m* —**Baer** (?);
4–Lydia, *m* William Henry **Stewart**;
3–Shellman Baer (*b* Baltimore, Md., 1848-*d* 1897), *m* 1869, Lorraine Tiffany (1849-1924; Samuel Slater[4], *m* Isabella, dau. William Cooper Mead, g.dau. William Mead, qv);
2–William Henry (*b* 1870), *m* 1898, Anna Doyle (*b* 1871); issue: I–John Shellman (1899-1900); II–Mary R. (1 above).
1–Ed. Kimberley Sch. (Montclair, N.J.), Miss Porter's Sch. (Farmington, Conn.). Mem. Junior League. Summer place: 163 Ocean Av., Sea Bright, N.J. Residence: 67 Prospect Av., Montclair, N.J.

1–**STICE, James Allen,** *b* Waverly, Ill., Oct. 8, 1866.
5–Andrew **Stice,** from Germany, settled in Rowan Co., N.C., ante 1766; *m* Katron Collins;
4–Andrew (1766-1818), Madison Co., Ill.; *m* Nancy Green Wilson (1771-1852; William[5], pvt. Am. Rev.);
3–Andrew (1803-55), Waverly, Ill.; *m* Nancy Armstrong;
2–James P. (2 below).
6–James **Armstrong,** from Ireland, settled in Lancaster Co., Pa., ante 1725;
5–John (1725-95), led expdn. against Indians, 1756; brig. gen. Cont. Army, 1776, same in Pa. militia 1777; cdr. at Brandywine and Germantown; maj. gen., 1778-80; del. Cont. Congress, 1778-80;
4–Joshua (1756-1844), pvt. Pa. militia in Am. Rev.; *m* Sarah Morris (Morris[5], of Rockingham Co., Va.);
3–Nancy (1803-60), *m* Andrew **Stice** (3 above);
2–James P. (1826-99), farmer, Waverly, Ill.; *m* 1848, Margaret Conlee (1833-1919); issue: I–Andrew Jackson (1851-1926; *m* Elizabeth Wood; *m* 2d, Janette Seymore); II–Sarah E. (1854-1924; *m* Harvey Spires); III–Isaac Douglas (1859-1908; *m* Caroline Hazelrigg); IV–James Allen (1 above).
1–*m* Sept. 2, 1891, Hattie Keplinger, *b* Waverly, Ill., June 26, 1870; dau. of B. F. Keplinger; issue: 1–Earl Franklin, *b* Waverly, Ill., June 24, 1892; grad. McKendree Coll., '15; served in World War 7 months; *m* Mar. 12, 1918, Edna Mae, dau. of Charles Klitzing (issue: Glen Franklin; Betty Mae; James Arnold); 2–J. Maurice (see Vol. III, p. 433).
1–Grad. Ill. Coll., '91 (Sigma Phi). Mercantile business and public utility business 35 yrs.; pres. Nat. Trail Telephone Co., Altamont, Ill. Mem. Ill. Hist. Soc., I.A.G. Methodist. Democrat. Residence: Shelbyville, Ill.

1–**STIEFEL, Eleanor Brooke Perry (Mrs. Charles Valentine),** *b* Queenstown, Md., Apr. 9, 1897.
9–Henry **Wallis** (*d* 1699);
8–Samuel (*d* 1724), planter, Kent Co.; mem. Colonial Assembly of Md., 1722-24; *m* 1700; Ann–;
7–John (1709-61), *m* 1747, Hannah Rasin;
6–John (1749-89), *m* 1st, Sophia Brookes;
5–John (1775-1828), *m* 1803, Sarah Everett Comegys (1783-1830);
4–Francis Ludolph (1804-55), *m* 1826, Emily Thomas (1803-96);
3–Francis Adolphus (1828-1904), *m* Mary Georgiana Willson;
2–Henrietta Eleanor (2 below).
10–Capt. Richard **Smith,** from Eng., 1649; settled in Calvert Co., Md.; atty. gen. of Md., 1651-60; mem. Assembly, 1651-67; *m* in Eng., Eleanor Hatton Somerset;
9–Capt. Richard (*b* Eng., 1651-*d* 1714), 1st surveyor gen. of Md., apptd. 1693; capt. of militia, Calvert Co.; *m* 2d, Widow Barbara (Morgan) Rousby (Col. Henry Morgan[10], *m* Frances Sayer);
8–Capt. Richard, *m* Elizabeth (Hutchens) Brooke, widow of Roger Brooke;
7–Margaret, *m* Dr. Thomas **Willson,** of Kent Co., Md.;
6–Dr. Thomas Bennett, *m* 1776, Mary Theresa Hall (Francis[7] [1729-1819], *m* Martha Neal);
5–Dr. Thomas B. (1778-1859), *m* 1806, Ann Maria

Smythe (1784-1823; Thomas[6], *m* Margaret Hands);
4–George Hayward (1810-73), *m* 1837, Eleanor Brooke;
3–Mary Georgiana (1842-1906), *m* Francis **Wallis** (3 above).
11–Gov. Leonard **Calvert** (qv);
10–Ann (1644-1714), of Md.; *m* 1664, Baker **Brooke** (1628-79);
9–Baker (1666-98), of De La Brooke Manor, St. Mary's Co., Md.; *m* 1690, Katherine Marsham (1672-1712);
8–Leonard (1692-1736), *m* 1722, Ann Darnall (1705-79);
7–Capt. Leonard (1728-85), of "Black Walnut Thicket," Prince George Co., Md.; was capt. in command of the "Horatio," which traded between Eng. and Md.; *m* 1753, Elizabeth Maxwell (1735-98), of Eng.;
6–Hester (1755-1835), of Prince George Co.; *m* 1781, Capt. Henry **Hill** (1750-1830), Am. Rev.; in battles of L.I., and Valley Forge; fitted out a company at his own expense;
5–Mary Ann Hoskins (1795-1847), *m* 1814, James **Brooke** (1758-1822), of Charles Co., Md.; mem. of Md. Legislature (Richard[6]);
4–Eleanor (1820-77), *m* George Hayward **Willson** (4 above);
3–Mary Georgiana, *m* Francis **Wallis** (3 above);
2–Henrietta Eleanor (*b* 1868), of Kent Co., Md.; *m* 1895, Elton Howard **Perry** (1862-1923), merchant, of Queen Anne Co., Md.; issue: I–Eleanor Brooke (1 above); II–Henry Elton (*b* 1898; *m* Mary Armstrong).
1–*m* June 4, 1923, Charles Valentine Stiefel, D.D.S., *b* Washington, D.C., Sept. 13, 1895; son of Charles Leo Stiefel, *m* Mary Noonan; issue: 1–Eleanor Brooke, *b* N. Woodside, Md., Apr. 8, 1929.
1–Ed. Mt. Saint Agnes Coll. (Baltimore). Mem. D.F.P.A., D.A.R., U.D.C. Catholic. Democrat. Address: N. Woodside, Montgomery Co., Md.

1–**STILLMAN, Stanley,** *b* Sacramento, Calif., Aug. 23, 1861.
7–George **Stillman** (qv);
6–George (1679-1760), from Eng., 1699; settled at Westerly, R.I.; *m* Deborah Crandall (1675-1737);
5–Joseph (1716-92), *m* Mary Maxson (1718-91);
4–Joseph (1743-1825), *m* Eunice Stillman (1751-1837);
3–Joseph (1779-1861), *m* Elizabeth Ward Maxson (1783-1869);
2–Jacob Davis Babcock (2 below).
9–Nathaniel (Welles) **Wells** (*b* 1600), from Eng., 1629, settled at Wellstown, R.I.;
8–Thomas (1626-1700 or 16), of Wellstown; *m* 1655, Naomi Marshall (1637-68);
7–Thomas (1663-1716), *m* 1691, Sarah Rogers;
6–Edward (*b* 1694), of Hopkinton, R.I.; *m* 1725, Elizabeth Randall (*b* 1704);
5–Joseph (*b* 1729), *m* Mercy Lillibridge;
4–Samuel (1758-1802), *m* Susan Potter (1763-1825);
3–William Davis (1797-1889), *m* Abbie Gavitt (1803-77).
2–Jacob Davis Babcock **Stillman** (1819-88), A.B., Union, '43, M.D., Columbia, 1847; physician and surgeon, Calif. pioneer of '49; *m* Caroline Bliss Maxson (1822-52); *m* 2d, Mary Gavitt Wells (1834-1923); for issue, see Vol. I, p. 317.
1–*m* Feb. 26, 1895, Josephine Welsh, *b* San Francisco, Calif., June, 1875; dau. of Captain Charles Welsh, of Baltimore, Md.; issue: 1–Elizabeth Lane, *b* San Francisco, May 6, 1900; Vassar, '22; *m* Nov. 26, 1925, Russell Anderson Mackey (issue: Mary Stillman, *b* Oct. 24, 1927; Elizabeth Courtney, *b* Aug. 15, 1929); 2–Stanley, Jr., *b* San Francisco, July 10, 1903; *m* June 26, 1928, Lucy Wilkinson Anderson (issue: Stanley, III, *b* Oct. 29, 1929).
1–A.B., U.Calif., '82 (Zeta Psi); M.D., Cooper Med. Coll., 1889. Prof. surgery, Stanford Med. Sch., 1909-26, now emeritus. Surgeon, U.S.N.-R.F., 1917, dir. Navy Base Hosp. No. 2; cdr. M.C., U.S.N.R.F., 1919 (see Who's Who in America). Fellow Am. Surg. Assn., Am. Coll. Surgeons; mem. Societe Internationale de Chirurgie. Clubs: Pacific Union, Bohemian. Summer place: Belvedere, Marin Co., Calif. Address: Stanford U. Hospital, San Francisco, Calif.

1–**STOCKING, Helene Schuyler Stanton (Mrs. George Eldredge)** *b* Low Moor, Ia., May 27, 1867.

Arms: Argent, two chevrons sable, a border engrailed of the last.
Crest: A fox passant proper.

9–Thomas **Stanton** (qv);
8–Capt. John (1641-1713), of Hartford; soldier King Philip's War; *m* 1664, Hannah Thompson (*d* 1713);
7–John (*b* 1665-will probated 1775), Preston, Conn.; *m* 2d, Mary Starkweather (*b* 1689);
6–Daniel (1708-75), *m* 1737, Mrs. Dinah (Galusha) Starkweather (*d* post 1754);
5–John (1746-1818), sgt. Am. Rev.; *m* Huldah Freeman (1757-1807);
4–John Warren (1775-1850), *m* 1st, Hannah Corbin;
3–Henry (1803-41), Charlestown, N.Y.; *m* 1829, Christiana Van Valkenburg;
2–Henry (2 below).
8–Clement **Corbin** (qv);
7–James (*b* 1665), removed to Brookline; *m* 1697, Hannah Eastman (*d* 1728);
6–James, Dudley, Mass.; *m* Susanna Bacon (*d* 1794);
5–Elkanah (*b* 1752), *m* Hannah Harlow (*b* 1750);
4–Hannah (1782-1850), *m* John Warren **Stanton** (4 above).
6–Lambert **Van Valkenburg**, from Holland; *m* Catherina Van Vechten;
5–Jacobus (1753-1812?), Albany Co., N.Y.; *m* 1775, Catharina Sixby;
4–Garret (*b* 1780), *m* 1806, Jane Clough or Clow;
3–Christiana (1810-98), *m* Henry **Stanton** (3 above);
2–Henry (1834-82), Canajoharie, N.Y.; *m* 1859, Mary Elizabeth Carey (*b* 1838); issue: I–Savilla Maria (*d*; *m* Marvin Carr); II–Alfa Louise (*m* Dr. J. E. Fraser, *d*); III–Helene Schuyler (1 above).
1–*m* May 16, 1888, George Eldredge Stocking, *b* Lynville, Ill., Jan. 2, 1864; son William Stocking, of Rochelle, Ill.; issue (all *b* Rochelle, Ill.): 1–Elizabeth A., *b* Sept. 15, 1889; grad. St. Mary's Episcopal Sch.; *m* Walter Pickle (1884-1919), (issue: Elizabeth Jean); *m* 2d, John A. Borden, of Phila.; 2–Lydia Lillian (*b* Dec. 3, 1891-*d*), grad. St. Mary's Episcopal Sch.; *m* Oct. 22, 1918, Millard Webb, of Los Angeles, Calif. (issue: Barbara Jane); 3–Helene Stanton, *b* Oct. 18, 1897; grad. St. Mary's Episcopal Sch.; *m* James Leonard Winslow, of San Antonio, Tex. (issue: Helene Stocking).
1–Mem. D.F.P.A., D.A.R., I.A.G., Soc. N.E. Women. Residence: Rochelle, Ill.

1–**STOLL, Richard Charles,** *b* at Lexington, Ky., Mar. 21, 1876.
6–Robert **Frier,** from Eng. to Va., but removed to Ky. and settled in Fayette Co., ca. 1788; mem. 1st Constl. Conv. of Ky. and one of the first trustees of Fayette Co.;
5–Peggy, *m* George **Vallandingham** (*b* 1761), soldier Am. Rev.;
4–Jane (*b* 1788), Fayette Co., Ky.; *m* Joseph **Scrugham** (*b* Va., 1777), soldier War 1812;
3–Mary Jane (*b* 1824), Lexington, Ky.; *m* George **Stoll** (*b* Phila., 1819; Gallus[4] [*b* Wurttemberg, Germany, 1792], to America, 1817);
2–Richard Pindell (*b* Lexington, Ky., 1851-*d* 1903),

pres. Lexington City Nat. Bank; *m* Elvina Stoll.
1–*m* Sept. 24, 1919, Angelene, dau. George W. Chesnut, of Danville, Ky.; issue: 1–Richard Pindell, *b* Lexington, Ky., Oct. 2, 1920.
1–B.A., Ky. State Coll., '95 (P.B.K.); LL.B., Yale, 1897; (LL.D., U.Ky., 1913). Gen. Counsel, Ky. Traction & Terminal Co., 1911-21; circuit judge, 22d jud. dist. of Ky., 1921–. Dir. First Nat. Bank & Trust Co., Lexington; v.p. Lexington Water Co. Del. Rep. Nat. Conv., 1912,16,20; mem. Ky. State Bd. of Election Commrs., 1914-15; trustee and v.chmn. of bd. U.Ky. Mem. Am. Bar Assn., Am. Law Inst., Ky. State Bar Assn. (treas. 1906-08, pres. 1922-1923), Lexington Bar Assn. (pres. 1920), Judicial Council of Ky., Ky. Trotting Horse Breeders Assn. (dir.); pres. Circuit Judges of Ky., 1928–. Chmn. com. pub. safety, Ky. Council of Defense and chief for Ky. of Am. Protective League, during World War. Mem. S.R. Clubs: Yale, Republican (of New York), Queen City, University (Cincinnati), Pendennis (Louisville), Lexington, Lexington Country. Residence: 444 W. 3d St., Lexington, Ky.

WILLIAM ADDISON STONE (1863-1924).

1–**STONE, William Addison** (Dec. 15, 1863-Feb. 24, 1924).
9–Simon **Stone** (qv);
8–Dea. Simon (1630-1708), Watertown, Mass.; *m* 1655, Mary Whipple (1634-1720);
7–Dea. Simon (1656-1741), Groton, Mass.; soldier King Philip's War; *m* 1685, Sarah Farnsworth (1663-1731; Matthias[8]);
6–Dea. Simon (1686-1785), capt. and deacon; *m* 1712, Sarah– (*d* 1767, aet. 78);
5–Simon (*b* 1714), dea.; *m* 1739, Eunice– (1716-91);
4–Aaron (1745-1814), *m* 1773, Elizabeth Rea, or Ray (*b* 1755);
3–Aaron (1790-1872), *m* 1815, Margaret Hayden (1793-1842);
2–William Augustus (1824-99), farmed an original Federal Govt. deed farm; *m* 1st, 1857, Caroline Lamb (1830-69); for issue see Vol. III, p. 313.
1–*m* June 22, 1898, Harriette Osborn McCalmont (qv for issue).
1–M.D., U.Mich., '85. Psychiatrist; alienist, Travers City Hosp. for Insane, 1886; asst. supt. Kalamazoo State Hosp., 1891-1910; consultant dept. med. jurisprudence, U.Mich., 1905-06. Author: Dementia Americana-Brainstorm; Endemic Infantile Paralysis; Hereditary Afflictions, etc. Mem. S.A.R.; hon. mem. Mich. N.G. Fellow A.M.A., Am. Psychiatry Assn.; mem. Am. Anthropol. Assn., etc.

1–**STONE, Harriette Osborn McCalmont (Mrs. William A.),** *b* Franklin, Pa., Jan. 13, 1867.
9–Nicholas **Noyes** (qv);
8–John (1645-91), freeman, 1674; *m* 1668, Mary Poore (1651-1716, Daniel[9]);
7–John (1677-1719), *m* 1703/04, Mary Thurlon (*b* 1682);
6–Elizabeth (1708-87), *m* 1728, William **Adams** (1706-1765-66), of Newbury, Mass.;
5–Capt. Benjamin (1735-1817), present at Burgoyne's surrender; *m* 1760, Mary Harriman (1739-1818);
4–Pattie (1780-1847), *m* 1796, Samuel **Plumer** (1772-1820);
3–Mary Harriman (1799-1848), *m* 1818, John **McCalmont** (1788-1877);
2–Samuel Plumer (1823-1904), lawyer; *m* 1859, Harriet Osborn (1836-1913); for issue see Vol. III, p. 313.
1–*m* June 22, 1898, William Addison Stone, M.D. (qv); issue: 1–Helen McCalmont, *b* Kalamazoo, Mich., Mar. 22, 1900; A.B., Bryn Mawr, '21; U.London (Eng.), six mos., 1922; acting prof. collegiate biology, Western Mich. State Normal Coll., 1922-23; D.A.R.; *m* Sept. 20, 1924, Archibald Irvine, son of John A. McColl, M.D., of Grand Rapids, Mich.; 2–William Addison, Jr., *b* Kalamazoo, June 27, 1902; The Hill Sch., '20; B.S., Yale-S., 1924; B.F.A., Yale, 1928; mem. S.A.R.; Engrs. R.O.T.C.; Yale Club (N.Y.).
1–Woman's Med. Coll. of Pa., 1893. Physician, Warren (Pa.) State Hosp. for Insane and Kalamazoo (Mich.) State Hosp. for Insane. Mem. C.D.A., D.A.R. (hon. regent for life), I.A.G., A.M.A. Mem. Bd. of Edn., 2 terms. Residence: 1102 W. Main St., Kalamazoo, Mich.

1–**STONER, Winifred Sackville, II (Countess de Bruché),** *b* Norfolk, Va., Aug. 19, 1902.
10–Alexander **Stoner** (1587-1667; son of Alexander Stoner [1532-1600], desc. Sir John Stoner, Knight of the Garter under Edward III, of Eng.); from Eng. with Capt. Newport, to Jamestown, 1607; *m* 1609, Anne Neville (1588-1638);
9–John (1610-80), in Winchester, Va.; established schools; inventor; *m* 1640, Mary Worthington (1612-98);
8–James (1642-1732), of Winchester; inventor; *m* 1704, Elizabeth Grey (1684-1782);
7–Charles (1705-70), of Baltimore, Md.; established schools in Md.; *m* 1747, Winifred Winthrop (1727-81);
6–Edward (1749-1820), served in Am. Rev.; *m* 1770, Mary Maybury (1750-1822);
5–John (1772-1868), removed to Calif.; founded a boys' school; *m* 1802, Mary Neville (1780-1865);
4–Edward (1804-80), established schools in Mich.; *m* 1824, Elizabeth Merrill (1804-82);
3–John (1825-99), established library in Pa.; *m* 1845, Katherine Woods (1821-1904);
2–Col. James Buchanan (1861-1925), of E. Berlin, Pa., surgeon, U.S. Public Health Service; served in campaigns against cholera, yellow fever, bubonic plague, etc.; *d* after service in World War; *m* 1900, Lady Winifred d'Estcourte Sackville (*b* 1883), M.D.; Ph.D., etc.; founder of natural edn. system (see Who's Who in America).
1–*m* Aug. 7, 1921, Count Charles P. de Bruché, *b* Paris, France (1883-Aug. 7, 1922); son of Count Charles de Bruché, of Paris, France.
1–Ed. at home and by travel. Internationally known as lecturer and author (see Who's Who in America). Mem. Authors' League of America, Authors' Guild, League Am. Pen Women, U.S.A. Natural Edn. Forum, Internat. Natural Edn. Assn., League for Fostering Genius (pres. and dir.), Authors and Composers (London, Eng.). Summer place: Chateau de Radingham, France. Residence: 418 Central Park West, New York, N.Y.

1–**STONE, Henry S.,** *b* Livermore, Ia., Sept. 13, 1869.
11–Rev. Joseph **Hull** (qv);
10–Tristram (1624-67), *m* 1643, Blanche–;
9–Joseph (1652-post 1709), *m* 1676, Experience Harper (Robert[10], *m* 1654, Deborah, dau. of Edmond Perry, *m* Sarah–);
8–Joseph (1676-1748), *m* 1700, Ann Gardner (*d* 1710; William[9], *m* Elizabeth–; George[10]);
7–Ann (1702-58), *m* 1721, Robert **Knowles** (1680-1758; William[8]; Henry[9]);
6–Joseph (1730-1809), *m* 1753, Bathsheba Segar;
5–Robert (1758-1812), *m* 1782, Lucy Ann Rodman;
4–Henry (1786-1877), *m* 1809, Susanna Anthony;
3–Henry A. (1811-95), *m* Mary K. Collins;
2–Lucy L. (2 below).

10–John **Anthony** (1607-73), emigrant 1634; *m* Susanna Potter;
9–Abraham (1650-1727), *m* 1671, Alice Wodell (William[10], *m* Mary–);
8–William (1675-1744), *m* 1695, Mary Coggeshall (*b* 1675; John[9], *m* Elizabeth Timberlake; Maj. John[10]; Gov. John[11], qv);
7–Abraham (*b* 1696), *m* 1716, Elizabeth Gray (*b* 1695; Edward[8], *m* Mary Smith; Edward[9]);
6–Philip (1723-77), *m* 1750, Mary Goddard (*b* 1726; Beriah[7], *m* Anna Smith; Henry[8], *m* Mary, dau. of Zoeth Howland and g.dau. of Henry Howland, qv);
5–Abraham (*b* 1751), *m* 1782, Lettishe Smith (*b* 1757; Benjamin[6], *m* Susanna Wood; Benjamin[7]; Hezekiah[8]; John[9]);
4–Susanna (*b* 1786), *m* Henry **Knowles** (4 above).
10–Henry **Collins** (1609-87), emigrated 1635; *m* Ann– (*b* 1605);
9–John (1632-79), *m* Abigal Johnson (Richard[10], *m* Alice–);
8–John (1679-1755), *m* 1705, Susanna Daggett (1685-1753; William[9], *m* Rebecca, dau. of Arthur Wormstall, *m* Rebecca Sadlock);
7–Hezekiah (1707-75), *m* 1735, Cathrine Gifford;
6–Joseph (1738-1827), *m* 1764, Bathsheba Hoxie (1740-1823; Solomon[7], *m* Mary Davis; John[8]; Lodwick[9]);
5–Joseph (1767-1824), *m* 1789, Hannah Sheffield (Samuel[6], *m* Eliza–);
4–Sheffield (1793-1824), *m* 1814, Eliza Knowles (John[5], *m* Mary Hoxie; John[6]; John[7]; William[8]; Henry[9]);
3–Mary K. (1815-1905), *m* 1830, Henry A. **Knowles** (3 above);
2–Lucy Lettia (1847-1911), *m* 1868, Eber **Stone** (1824-75); for issue see Vol. III, p. 434.
1–*m* Dec. 31, 1891, Lois Frances Rowe (qv).
1–Farmer, hardware mcht., real estate broker. Mason. Residence: Humboldt, Ia.

1–**STONE, Lois Frances Rowe (Mrs. Henry S.),** *b* Dec. 13, 1872.
9–Jonas **Eaton** (*d* 1674), emigrated 1637; *m* Grace–;
8–Jonathan (1655-1743), *m* 1689, Mary–;
7–Samuel (1702-68), *m* 1722, Ruth Russell (*b* 1699; John[8], *m* Elizabeth Palmer; John[9]; John[10]);
6–Samuel (*b* 1722), *m* 1748, Millicent Wheeler (*b* 1731; Uriah[7], *m* Abigal Rice; Obadiah[8]; Obadiah[9]);
5–Elizabeth (*b* 1751), *m* Moses **Noyes** (see Vol. III, p. 434);
4–Abel (1775-1818), *m* 1808, Sophia S. Hatch (see Vol. III, p. 434);
3–Charles (1812-81), *m* 1837, Nancy P. Warren;
2–Mary Elizabeth (1839-1905), pioneer of Ia.; *m* 1860, Franklin **Rowe** (*d* 1906; Lucian[3], *m* Lucy–); for issue see Vol. III, p. 434.
1–*m* Dec. 31, 1891, Henry Samuel Stone (qv); for issue see Vol. III, p. 434.
1–Mem. D.A.R. (chapter regent), O.E.S. (White Shrine), W.C.T.U., Woman's Club (pres.), Service Star Mothers. Residence: Humboldt, Ia.

1–**STORK, William Boteler,** *b* Baltimore, Md., Apr. 8, 1871.
4–Karl Augustus Gottlieb (Storch) **Stork** (1764-1831), from Germany 1788, settled at Salisbury, N.C.; Lutheran clergyman; 1st pres. of N.C. Synod; *m* 1790, Christina Beard (*d* 1832; Louis[5], of Salisbury, N.C.);
3–Theophilus, D.D. (1814-74), of Phila., Pa.; Lutheran; *m* 1837, Mary Jane Lynch (*d* 1846; William[4], *m* Eliza Boteler);
2–Charles Augustus (2 below).
9–John **Ellis** (*d* 1697), from Eng. 1640, settled at Dedham, Mass.; founder of Medfield, selectman many yrs.; *m* 1655, Joan (*d* 1704), widow of John Clapp;
8–Joseph (1662-1726), selectman 7 yrs.; *m* 1688, Lydia Lovell (1665-94; Alexander[9], *m* Lydia Leland);
7–Joseph (1691-1757), large landowner, Medway, Mass., and vicinity; *m* 1716, Elizabeth Partridge (1696-1718; Eleazer[8], *m* Elizabeth Smith);
6–Joseph (1718-1808), *m* Melatiah Metcalf (Michael[7]);
5–Amos (1744-1817), capt. 4th Bellingham Co., 4th Mass. Militia, Am. Rev.; *m* Hannah Hill (1748-1829; Joseph[6]);
4–Nathan (*b* 1777), merchant, Blue Hill, Me.; *m* Sally Osgood (*d* 1814);
3–Nathan (1812-98), shoe mfr., Andover, Mass.; *m* Susan Lovett Gardner (1812-89; Capt. John[4], master mariner, *m* Joanna Lovett);
2–Maria Holbrook (1841-1913), *m* 1863, Rev. Charles Augustus **Stork,** D.D. (1838-83), Lutheran clergyman (see portrait); issue: I–Mary Ellis (*d* infancy 1866); II–Charles Gardner (1867-71); III–William Boteler (1 above); IV–Francis Osgood (1872-73); V–Amy Lynch (*b* 1879; *m* John Angus Kydd).
1–*m* May 22, 1901, Lisetta Helen Martyn (Mar. 21, 1872-Sept. 6, 1919).
1–*m* 2d, his 1st cousin, Oct. 15, 1923, Belle Warner Stork, *b* Baltimore, Md., Aug. 21, 1889; dau. of William Lynch Stork, of Baltimore; issue: 1–Dorothea von Asseburg, *b* Brooklyn, N.Y., July 19, 1925.
1–M.I.T., ex-'95. Draftsman, R.I. Locomotive Works, and motive power dept. B. & M. R.R., 1895-96; enlisted in U.S.N., Apr. 20, 1897, commd. chief machinist, Mar. 3, 1909; lt., Dec. 31, 1921; retired Nov. 30, 1927. Mem. of joint merchant vessel bd. in 1st Naval Dist. during World War. Mem. I.A.G., N.E.H.G.S., Md. Hist. Soc. Lutheran. Republican. Summer place: "Sea Crest," East Chop, Mass. Residence: 700 Park Av., Baltimore, Md.

REV. CHARLES AUGUSTUS STORK, D.D. (b Jefferson, Md., Sept. 4, 1838-d Phila., Pa., Dec. 17, 1883), ed. Gettysburg (Pa.) Prep. School; Hartwick Sem., N.Y.; grad. Williams Coll., '57; Andover (Mass.) Theol. Sem.; prof. Greek, Newberry (S.C.) Coll., 1859-60; in charge of St. James' Lutheran Mission, Phila., 1861; assistant pastor of St. Mark's English Lutheran Church, Baltimore, 1861-64, pastor, 1865-81; pres. of Gettysburg Theol. Sem., 1881-83.

1–**STOUT, Claude D.,** *b* Albion, Dane Co., Wis., May 13, 1881.
10–Edward **Fuller,** Mayflower Pilgrim (qv);
9–Samuel (*b* 1615-*d* Barnstable, Mass., 1683), *m* 1635, Jane Lathrop (*d* ante 1683; John[10], qv);
8–Hannah (*b* Scituate, Mass., 1636-*d* Piscataway, N.J., 1685), *m* 1658/59, Nicholas **Bonham** (will proved Dec. 18, 1684), a first settler Piscataway, N.J., ca. 1660 (George[9]);
7–Hezekiah, *m* 1690, Mary Dunn (*b* 1671; Hugh[8], *m* 1670/71, Elizabeth, dau. of Francis Drake, *m* Mary–);
6–Hannah (*b* 1695), *m* Benjamin **Stout** (see Vol. III, p. 437, for Stout lineage);
5–Ezekiel (will dated 1795) settled nr. Lost Creek, Harrison Co., W.Va.; *m* Sarah Drake;
4–Hezekiah (*b* 1777), *m* his cousin, Mary Stout;
3–Milton (*b* 1799), *m* 2d, 1822, Elizabeth Hoffman (1805-94);
2–Hezekiah Milton (1827-1904), *m* 1875, Harriet Bond (*b* 1851), for issue and Bond lineage see Vol. III, p. 437.
1–*m* Dec. 26, 1911, Viola May Sisson (see Vol. III,

p. 437); issue: 1–David Bond, *b* Stoughton, Wis., Mar. 7, 1913.
1–Atty. at law; mem. Legal Advisory Bd. Mem. Knickerbocker Soc., Milwaukee Philatelic Soc. Residence: 531 13th Av., Wauwatosa, Wis.

1–**STRACHAUER, Gertrude Louise Hale (Mrs. Arthur C.),** *b* Minneapolis, Minn., Oct. 31, 1874.
9–John (Heald) **Hale** (*d* May 24, 1662), from Berwick on Tweed, Eng., 1635; settled at Concord, Mass.; *m* Dorothy–;
8–John, *m* 1661, Sarah Dean (*d* 1689);
7–John (1666-1721), *m* 1690, Mary Chandler (1672-1759), buried at Concord;
6–Timothy (1696-1736), *m* as her 1st husband, Hannah– (later Howe);
5–Timothy (1722-85), removed to Me., 1770; *m* Elizabeth Stevens;
4–Josiah (1759-1826), began to write name Hale; settled at Norridgewock, Me.; *m* Phebe Emerson (1762-1829; Ezekiel[5], *m* Catherine, dau. of Rev. Joseph Door);
3–Eusebius (1806-80), minister; his parish on Long Island objected to his abolitionist tendencies and he removed to N.Y.; was later recalled to same parish on L.I.; *m* 1st, 1831, Philena Dinsmore;
2–William Dinsmore (2 below).
6–David **Dinsmore,** from Scotland, 1714; settled at Londonderry, N.H.; owned "Chester Farm" (Robert[7]; Robert[8]; John[9]; Laird[10] of Achenmead, Scotland, 1620);
5–Arthur, *m* ca. 1774, Margaret Fulton, of Chester, N.H.;
4–William Wilson, *m* 1808, Lucy Gould, of Norridgewock, Me.;
3–Philena (1809-46), *m* Eusebius **Hale** (3 above).
9–Benjamin **Hammond** (son of William Hammond, of London, *m* Elizabeth Penn, aunt of William Penn); came from Eng. with his mother and three sisters, in the "Griffith"; landed at Boston, 1634; *m* 1650, Mary Vincent (John[10]);
8–Samuel (*b* 1655), to Rochester, Mass., with his brother John, 1680; a founder 1st Congl. ch., Marion, Mass.; *m* ca. 1680, Mary Hathaway (Arthur[9], *m* Sarah, dau. of John Cook, *m* Sarah Warren, and g.dau. of Francis Cook, qv);
7–Thomas, of New Bedford; *m* 1721, Sarah Spooner (William[8], *m* Alice, dau. of Nathaniel Warren, son of Richard Warren, qv);
6–Samuel (*b* at Dartmouth), as a youth, was a whaler; *m* 1755, Hannah Shepherd;
5–Luthan H., farmer, Fleming, Cayuga Co., N.Y.; *m* 1781, Mary Rood or Rude;
4–John, of Rushford, Allegheny Co., N.Y.; War 1812; Mason; *m* 1810, Huldah Tibbels;
3–Horatio Nelson (1812-64), of Rushford, surveyor and sch. teacher; *m* 1840, Sophia Louisa Bennett (1815-1904; Oliver Cromwell[4], entered the Am. Rev. aet. 15, as an officer's orderly, *m* 1783, Huldah Bushnell).
2–William Dinsmore **Hale** (1836-1915), postmaster, Minneapolis, 16 yrs.; *m* 1864, Sarah Baker (*d* 1868), of Cannon Falls, Minn.; *m* 2d, 1870, Flora Annette Hammond (*b* 1844); issue (2d marriage): I–Nelle Philena (1871-1924; *m* 1900, George Wilbur Bestor, *d* 1919); II–Gertrude Louise (1 above); and III–Florence Aurora, twins (*d* 1875); IV–Arthur Dinsmore (*b* 1878; *m* 1903, Maybelle Darling); V–William Hammond (*b* 1880; *m* 1920, Mary Everett Rhodes *b* 1889).
1–*m* June 9, 1909, Dr. Arthur Clarence Strachauer, *b* Minneapolis, Minn., May 1, 1883; son of Clarence Strachauer, of Minneapolis; issue: 1–Hermann Hale, *b* Minneapolis, July 29, 1910.
1–Ed. U.Minn. (Kappa Kappa Gamma), N.E. Conservatory of Music, and musical study at Florence, Italy. Mem. D.A.R., etc. Clubs: Minneapolis Woman's, Minikahda. Universalist. Republican. Residence: 1720 James Av. South, Minneapolis, Minn.

1–**STRINGFELLOW, Nan Cannon (Mrs. William W.),** *b* Concord, N.C.
8–James **Cannon,** in Dorchester Co., Md., 1683; *m* Rose (or Rosanna) Pope (Robert[9], of Dorchester Co., will proved 1701, *m* Eliza–, will probated 1716);
7–James (will proved 1711/12), planter, Dorchester Co., Md.; *m* Mary–;
6–James (*b* ca. 1700), *m* 1724, in Harford Co., Md., Mary Bowen (or Boren);
5–James (1731-84), settled in Mecklenburg Co., N.C., 1768; tailor; purchased 124 acres in Rowan Co., 1769; *m* Margaret Alexander;
4–James (1762-1837), farmer and cabinet maker; from the Catawba River settlement to Poplar Tent, then in Mecklenburg Co. (now Cabarrus Co.); purchased 2 tracts of 150 and 105 acres in Mecklenburg Co.; claimed to have served in Am. Rev.; *m* 1790, Ann Black (1771-1857; "Heroic Pioneer" William[5]);
3–Joseph Allison (1808-87), farmer; *m* 1843, Eliza Caldwell Long (1821-1905; David[4], *m* Margaret, dau. of William Andrews, *m* Barbara Caldwell);
2–David Franklin (2 below).
8–Joseph **Alexander,** will probated in Cecil Co., Md., 1730;
7–James (*d* 1779), named among first purchasers of the Munster lands in Cecil Co., Md., 1714; acquired considerable land in Md. and N. C.; ruling elder of the New Castle Presbytery, 1725, and frequently after that in those of the Synod of Phila.; *m* 1st, Margaret McKnitt;
6–Theophilus (will probated 1768), of Cecil Co.; *m* Catherine– (probably a dau. of Michael Wallace);
5–Margaret (*d* 1802), *m* James **Cannon** (5 above).
6–Martin **Phifer,** Sr. (1720-91), from Berne, Switzerland, to Pa., 1738; settled first in Lunenburg Co., Va., where he received large grants of land; established "Cold Water," on Cold Water Creek in Mecklenburg Co., N.C.; large landowner, planter; justice; maj. Mecklenburg Bn., 1768; statesman; *m* 1745, Margaret Blackwelder (1722-1803; Caleb[6], *m* Mary–, Rev. patriots);
5–Caleb, col. Am. Rev.; councilor of state; mem. N.C. House and Senate; *m* Barbara Fullenwider;
4–Esther, *m* Nathaniel **Alexander;**
3–Nancy, *m* John B. **Moss;**
2–Mary, *m* David Franklin **Cannon** (*b* 1844-*d*), pres. Cannon Mills, Concord, N.C.; issue: I–David Franklin (*m* Mattie Lee); II–Joseph Archibald (*m* Neppie Borden); III–Nan E. (1 above); IV–John Moss (*d*).
1–*m* William Whittingham Stringfellow, *b* Hyde Park, N.Y.; son of Rev. Horace Stringfellow.
1–Ed. Peace Inst., Raleigh, N.C. Residence: "Amicenza," Anniston, Ala.

1–**STRONG, Sydney Dix,** *b* Seville, O., Jan. 25, 1860.
8–John **Strong** (qv);
7–Lt. Return (1640/41-1726), large landowner at Windsor, Conn.; dep. Gen. Ct., 1689-90; *m* 1664, Sarah Warham (1642-78; Rev. John[8], of Windsor, *m* Jane–);
6–Samuel (1675-1741), Windsor; q.m. Hartford Co. troop; *m* 1699, Martha Buckland (1678-1770; Nicholas[7], *m* Martha Wakefield; Thomas[8]);
5–Samuel (1705-89), Union, Conn.; commr. land tax; *m* 1733, Martha Stoughton (1711-98; John[6], *m* Sarah Fitch);
4–David (1736-1811), Stafford, Conn.; capt. Am. Rev.; *m* 1st, 1760, Sarah Warner;
3–John Stoughton (1771-1863), to Marlboro, Vt.; to northern Ohio, founded Strongsville, 1816; *m* 1795, Tamar Whitney (1779-1856; Dea. Jonas[4], *m* Tamar Houghton);
2–Lyman Whitney (2 below).
9–Gov. William **Bradford,** Mayflower Pilgrim (qv);
8–Maj. William (1624-1704), dep. gov. Mass.; *m* 1651, Alice Richards (1629-71; Thomas[9]);
7–Alice (1662-1735 or 45?), *m* 1st, as his 2d wife, 1680, Rev. William **Adams** (1650-85), A.B., Harvard, 1671 (William[8]; William[9]);
6–Abiel (*b* 1685), *m* 1707, Rev. Joseph **Metcalf** (1682-1723), A.B., Harvard, 1703 (Dea. Jonathan[7], *m* Hannah Kenrick; Michael[8], *m* Mary, dau. Jonathan Fairbanks, qv; Michael[9], qv);
5–Delight (1719-50), Falmouth, Mass.; *m* 1737, Thomas **Warner** (1705-56), Mansfield, Conn.;
4–Sarah (1740-77), buried in "Old Stafford St. Cemetery," Stafford, Conn.; *m* David **Strong** (4 above);
3–John Stoughton, *m* Tamar Whitney (3 above);
2–Lyman Whitney (1817-81), merchant, farmer, Seville, O.; *m* 1843, Ruth Maria Dix (1827-65; John Childs[3], *m* Huldah Porter); issue: I–Arthur Tappan (1845-62); II–Lyman Whitney,

Jr. (1849-1914; *m* Harriet Martin); III–Timothy Dowd (*b* 1851; *m* 1872, Lodieska Sophia Dailey); IV–Sarah Elizabeth (1854-1914; *m* Adelbert Lorenzo Spitzer); V–Charles Sumner (1856-1909; *m* Harriet Hulda Neifer); VI–Sydney Dix (1 above).

1–*m* Nov. 20, 1884, Ruth Maria Tracy, *b* Mansfield, O. (Dec. 25, 1863-Oct. 11, 1903); dau. of Frederick E. Tracy, of Mansfield; issue: 1–Anna Louise, *b* Friend, Neb., Nov. 24, 1885; 2–Tracy, *b* Mt. Vernon, O., Aug. 6, 1887; *m* 1910, Edith Robbins, of McCool, Ind. (issue: Robbins, *b* Nov. 24, 1912; Tracy, Jr., *b* Sept. 12, 1915; Ruth Adelaide, *b* Aug. 24, 1918); 3–Ruth Maria, *b* Mt. Vernon, July 24, 1890; *m* 1912, Charles Howard Niederhauser (issue: Ruth Louise, *b* July 27, 1913; John Strong, *b* Sept. 26, 1916; Sydney, *b* May 25, 1919).

1–A.B., Oberlin, '81 (Phi Kappa Psi), B.D., 1884 (D.D., 1898). Pastor Congl. chs. at Friend, Neb., Mt. Vernon, O., Cincinnati, O., Oak Park, Ill., and Seattle, Wash. Author and lecturer. Residence: 508 Garfield St., Seattle, Wash. Address: 12 Park Av., New York, N.Y.

1–**STRONG, Albert,** *b* Windham, O., Oct. 27, 1861.

11–George (Stronge) **Strong** (*d* ca. 1635), mentioned as a mfr. of serge at Chard, Co. Somerset, Eng.; will of 1627, proved 1636 in Prerogative Ct., Canterbury; lived to great age;

10–John (*d* 1613), of Chard; deathbed will mentions son John, an unborn child, and his father George; wife's name missing, perhaps Eleanor;

9–Elder John (qv);

8–Lt. Return (1641-1726), Windsor, Conn.; dep. Gen. Ct., 1689-90; *m* 1664, Sarah Warham (1642-78; Rev. John[9]);

7–Samuel (1675-1741), q.m. Hartford Co. troop; *m* 1699, Martha Buckland (1678-1770);

6–Samuel (1705-89), Union, Conn.; commr. land tax; *m* 1733, Martha Stoughton (1711-98); three sons in Am. Rev.;

5–David (1736-1811), Stafford, Conn.; capt. Am. Rev.; *m* 1760, Sarah Warner (see Vol. III for Warner-Bradford lineage);

4–John Stoughton (1771-1863), a founder of Strongsville, O.; *m* 1795, Tamar Whitney (1779-1856; Jonas[5]; Samuel[6]; Nathaniel[7]; Nathaniel[8]; John[9]; John[10], qv);

3–Warner (1804-56), *m* 2d, 1829, Salome Burrell (1804-56; Jabez[4]; Abraham[5], Am. Rev.);

2–Frederick (2 below).

9–Thomas **Arnold** (qv);

8–Eleazer (1651-1722), Providence; town council; justice; dep., 1686, et seq.; *m* Eleanor Smith (*d* 1722);

7–Joseph (*d* 1746), Smithfield; *m* 1716, Mercy Stafford (1694-1753; Amos[8]; Samuel[9]; Thomas[10], qv);

6–Benjamin (1719-ca. 1789), *m* 1741, Anne Dexter (*b* 1718; James[7]; John[8]; Gov. Gregory[9], qv);

5–Simeon (*b* 1749), Scituate; *m* 1772, Freelove Olney (Obadiah[6]; Thomas[7]; Thomas[8]; Thomas[9], qv);

4–Elisha (1777-1845), Hopewell, N.Y.; *m* 1802, Patience Comstock (1775-1854; desc. William Comstock, qv);

3–Cornelia (1805-79), *m* 1830, Joseph **Angell** (see Vol. III, p. 438, for Angell lineage);

2–Elizabeth (1838-1907), *m* 1861, Frederick **Strong** (1835-1919), Pacific Grove, Calif. (for issue see Vol. III, p. 438).

1–*m* Nov. 20, 1895, Effa May Lyons (qv).

1–A.B., Grinnell, 1884. Retired newspaper publisher. Mem. S.M.D., S.A.R. Mason (32°, K.T.). Residence: 617 S. 12th St., Ft. Dodge, Ia.

1–**STRONG, Effa May Lyons (Mrs. Albert),** *b* Hardin, Ia., Aug. 1, 1865.

4–William **Lyons** (1755-1848 or 49), of Scotch descent; from North of Ireland to Pa., ante 1776; soldier in Am. Rev., wounded in battle of Fort Washington, re-enlisted twice after recovery; removed to Harrison Co., O.; *d* in Morgan Co.; *m* Margaret Gibson;

3–John (1794-1875), Harrison Co., O.; soldier War 1812; elder Presbyn. ch., 40 yrs.; *m* Mary Riggs (1794-1875);

2–David W. (2 below).

4–John **Wallace** (1760-1832), Chester Co., Pa.; Am. Rev.; to Moorfield, O.; *m* Margaret Anderson (1767-1848);

3–Rev. William (1787-1841), ed. Jefferson Coll.; Presbyn. pastor and founder of churches in southeast Ohio; *m* Mary W. McWilliams (1797-1869; David[4], one of the first pioneers west of the Ohio);

2–Sarah Ann (1822-75), *m* 1842, David Wallace **Lyons** (1822-95), ed. Franklin Coll., and Western Theol. Sem.; pioneer minister and organizer of churches in Iowa; large land owner; issue: I–William Wallace (1843-1924; *m* Wilma L. Cromett); II–Mary Amanda (1845-1915; *m* George C. Lawton); III–Sophia Jane (1848-86; *m* David Secor); IV–Sarah Ellen (1851-1916; *m* David Secor); V–David McWilliams (1854-57); VI–Susan Marie (1859-1902; *m* Hollis Joy); VII–Caroline Belle (*m* Dr. Andrew Engberg); VIII–Effa May (1 above).

1–*m* Nov. 20, 1895, Albert Strong (qv).

1–Ed. Cornell and Grinnell Colls. Mem. D.A.R., P.E.O., O.E.S. Residence: 617 S. 12th St., Ft. Dodge, Ia.

1–**STRONG, Ethel Gwendolen Johnson (Mrs. Jacob Corrington),** *b* Kenton, O., Jan. 19, 1872.

8–Henry **Crane** (qv);

7–Benjamin (1657-1721), rep. Gen. Ct. from Taunton, 1703, from Dighton, 1721; *m* 1688, Mary–;

6–Benjamin (1716-1743), *m* Mary Myrick;

5–Bernice (1742/43-1828), Berkley, Mass.; in Am. Rev.; *m* 1763, Joan Axtelle (*d* aet. 101 yrs.);

4–Capt. Barnabas (1775-1860), *m* 1805, Hannah Crane;

3–George Washington (1809-83), *m* 1834, Louisa Maria Briggs (1815-95);

2–Louise Maria (2 below).

10–Gov. William **Bradford** (qv);

9–William (1624-1704), *m* Alice Richards (*d* 1671);

8–Samuel (1668-1714), *m* 1688/89, Hannah Rogers;

7–Hannah (*b* 1689), *m* 1709, Nathaniel **Gilbert** (1683-1765), served on expdn. to Crown Pt., 1755 (Ens. Thomas[8]; Thomas[9]; Thomas[10], bro. Jonathan, qv);

6–Wealtha, *m* 1744, Ebenezer **Hathaway** (*d* 1791);

5–Tryphena (1745-1812), *m* 1763, Capt. Benjamin **Crane** (*b* 1740; Seth[6]; Benjamin[7]; Henry[8]);

4–Hannah (1783-1825), *m* Barnabus **Crane** (4 above).

11–Thomas **Rogers**, Mayflower Pilgrim (qv);

10–John, rep. Gen. Ct.; *m* 1639, Ann Churchman;

9–John (*d* 1738), Barrington, R.I.; *m* 1666, Elizabeth Pabodie (*b* 1644; William[10], *m* Elizabeth, dau. John Alden, qv);

8–Hannah (*b* 1668), *m* Samuel **Bradford** (8 above).

2–Artemus Bell **Johnson** (1843-1917), A.B., Oberlin Coll., '64; judge Ct. of Common Pleas, 1889-99; to Kenton, O.; *m* 1866, Louise Maria Crane (1845-87); *m* 2d, 1893, Annie E. Welch; issue (1st marriage): I–Cedric Edgar (*b* 1868; *m* Helen Hoskins); II–Ethel G. (1 above); III–Dr. Burke Lamartine (*b* 1874; *m* Edna Sullivan); IV–Kent Percival (*b* 1876; *m* Harriet Duncan); V–Cecil Amy (1879-1921; *m* Fred Murcott Harpham); VI–Louise Artemas (1886-1921; *m* Earl Everett Whaley).

1–*m* Mar. 17, 1901, Dr. Jacob Corrington Strong, *b* Carmi, Ill., July 11, 1867; son of Samuel Strong, of Carmi; issue: 1–Artemus Jacob, *b* Santa Paula, Calif., Mar. 18, 1902; A.B., Stanford, '24; M.D., Stanford Med. Sch., 1928; resident physician and surgeon San Francisco hosp.; 2–Gwendolen Mary, *b* Santa Paula, Oct. 6, 1906; A.B., Pomona Coll., '28.

1–Ed. Oberlin (O.) Coll., 1888-94. Taught physical edn., Kenton, O., 1894-98. Trustee Santa Paula (Calif.) grammar sch., 1915-30 (pres. bd., 1924-30). Mem. D.F.P.A., S.M.D., D.A.R. Universalist. Democrat. Club: Ebell. Residence: Santa Paula, Calif.

1–**STUBBS, Elizabeth Saunders Blair (Mrs. William C.),** *b* Mobile, Ala., Jan. 23, 1853.

9–Edward **Saunders** (1624-72), from Eng., settled in Northumberland Co., Va., 1635; *m* 1660, Mary Webb (*d* 1683);

8–Ebenezer (1661-93), *m* 1684, Elizabeth Presley (Col. Peter[9], burgess 1657, *m* Elizabeth, dau. of Richard Thompson; William[10], from Eng. to Va., 1642, *m* Jane–);

7–Edward (*b* 1686), *m* 1717, Winifred–;

6–William (1718-79), Lancaster Co.; *m* 1738, Elizabeth (Betty) Hubbard (1721-89; Thomas[7] [*d*

1745], of Lancaster Co., *m* Mary–; Thomas[8], *m* Sarah–);
5–Thomas (1739-1808), of Brunswick Co.; in Am. Rev.; *m* 1764, Ann Turner;
4–Turner (1782-1853), of Va., Ala., and Miss.; *m* 1st, 1799, Frances Dunn (1779-1824; Ishmael[5] [1748-1828] of Brunswick Co., Va., and Lawrence Co., Ala., *m* Mildred Dudley);
3–James Edmonds (1806-96), of Va. and Ala.; *m* 1824, Mary Frances Watkins (1809-89);
2–Mary Lou (1832-59), Courtland, Ala.; *m* 1852, Henry D. **Blair** (1825-55), mcht., Mobile, Ala. (John James[3] [1793-1844]; James[4], Lancaster Co., S.C.).
1–*m* July 28, 1875, William Carter Stubbs, Ph.D. (1843-1924); son of Jeff. W. Stubbs, *m* Ann Walker (Carter) Baytop.
1–Genealogist since 1875. Author. Published numerous books in collaboration with her husband. Mem. D.A.R., U.D.C., I.A.G., New Orleans Geneal. and Hist. Soc., hist. societies of Ala., La., and Va. Democrat. Residence: 701 Howard Av., New Orleans, La.

BRIG. GEN. THOMAS W. SWEENY, U.S.A. (1820-1892). Lt., N.Y. vols., 1846; in War with Mexico participated in Siege of Vera Cruz, battle of Cerro Gordo, capture of Puebla, battles of Contreras (wounded), and Churubusco (twice wounded, losing right arm); bvtd. capt.; 2d lt., 2d U.S. Inf., 1848; 1st lt., 1851; Yuma Indian War (Calif.), 1851-52 (wounded); Sioux Expedition, 1855-56, as aide to Gen. W. S. Harney; in Civil War, capt., 2d U.S. Inf. and brig. gen. Mo. vols., 1861; defense of St. Louis Arsenal; capture of Camp Jackson; expedition to and capture of Forsyth, Mo.; battle of Wilson's Creek (wounded); col., 52d Ill. Vols., 1862; battle of Shiloh, where, according to Gen. Sherman he "saved the day" (thrice wounded); battle of Iuka; siege of Corinth; brig. gen. vols., 1862; Atlanta campaign; bvtd. lt. col. and col. U.S.A.; retired with the full rank of brig. gen. U.S.A., 1870. Received a silver medal from the City of New York for his services in the War with Mexico; received a gold-mounted sword from the City of Brooklyn, Aug. 1862, for his services in the Civil War. Gen. Sweeny was one of the officers included in the Thanks of Congress to the officers and men of Gen. Lyon's army for their services at the battle of Wilson's Creek.

1–**SWEENY, William Montgomery,** *b* New York, N.Y., Aug. 29, 1871.
6–Francis **Cook** (1729-1813), from York Co., Va., to Guilford Co., N.C., ante Am. Rev.; thence to Wilkes (later Elbert) Co., Ga., ca. 1783 (had three sons in Am. Rev.);
5–Nancy, *m* James **Reagan** (*d* 1827), soldier colonial militia of N.C.; removed from Guilford Co., N.C., to Knox Co., Tenn.;
4–James (1780-1855), *m* 1805, Mary Dandridge Morrison (1784-1839);
3–Francis Washington, M.D. (1821-65), pvt. C.S.A.; *m* 1845, Sarah Cecilia Refo (1826-1910; Caesar[4], *b* in France);
2–Eugenia Octavia (1846-1923), *m* 1867, Brig. Gen. Thomas William **Sweeny,** U.S.A. (1820-92), from Ireland, 1832; served in Mexican and Civil wars, and Indian campaigns (see portrait); issue: I–Thomas Francis (*b* 1868); II–William Montgomery (1 above).
1–*m* Oct. 28, 1928, Mrs. Lenora E. (Higginbotham) McFarlane (qv).
1–Coll. City of N.Y., ex-'90. Author, editor (see Who's Who in America, Vol. 12). Mem. S.C.W., S.C., Aztec Club of 1847 (former pres.), M.O.F.W. Club: Army and Navy (Washington). Residence: 126 Franklin St., Astoria, N.Y.

Hickinbotham.

Arms: *Argent, a rose gules, barbed vert, seeded or.*
Crest: *A dexter and a sinister arm discharging an arrow from a bow, all proper.*
Motto: *By aim and by effort.*

1–**SWEENY, Lenore Elizabeth Higginbotham (Mrs. William M.),** *b* Bedford Co., Va.
7–John **Higginbotham,** from Ireland, with wife ca. 1735; settled in Goochland Co.; later in Albemarle Co.; *m* Frances Riley;
6–Aaron (*d* 1785), *d* Amherst Co., Va.; vestryman and ch. warden, Amherst Co.; capt. militia, 1769; *m* Clara (Green?);
5–Aaron (*d* 1794), ens., Amherst Co. militia, 1769; *m* Dec. 4, 1775, Nancy Croxton (Samuel[6]);
4–Aaron (1789-1852), *m* May 22, 1817, Elizabeth Steward Sandidge;
3–Alexander Brown (June 23, 1818-Dec. 1, 1888), served C.S.A.; *m* Eliza Frances Plunkett;
2–Cyrus Aaron (2 below).
7–William **Sandidge** (*d* 1747), Spotsylvania Co., Va.; *m* Anne Taylor (John[8], *m* Catherine, dau. of Philip Pendleton, settled in Caroline Co., Va., 1674; Col. James[9], settled in King and Queen Co., Va., ante 1650);
6–John (*d* 1803), *d* Amherst Co.;
5–Benjamin (*d* 1829), *m* Elizabeth Childress (Joseph[6]);
4–Elizabeth Steward (Jan. 26, 1796-Jan. 7, 1850), *m* Aaron **Higginbotham** (4 above).
6–John **Plunkett** (*d* 1758), *m* Mildred Hawkins;
5–Benjamin (*d* 1829), *m* 1792, Frances Ham (Stephen[6], Am. Rev., *m* Mildred, dau. of Capt. John Rucker);
4–Willis Rucker (Mar. 2, 1796-Aug. 6, 1883), *m* July 23, 1818, Margaret Finley Shields;
3–Eliza Frances (June 14, 1819-Aug. 7, 1908), *m* Alexander Brown **Higginbotham** (3 above).
7–James **Shields** (*d* 1749), from Ireland with 3 brothers and parents, landed at New Castle,

Del., Feb. 26, 1737; father and one brother *d* on voyage settled in Cecil Co., Md.; removed to Rockingham Co., Va.; *m* Jane Montgomery, of Shippensburg, Pa.;
6–John (ca. 1740-1802), Amherst Co., *m* June 26, 1768, Margaret Finley;
5–James (Mar. 9, 1772-Sept. 7, 1837), *m* Mar. 2, 1797, Elizabeth Higginbotham (July 11, 1778; Aaron[6], *m* Nancy, dau. of Samuel Croxton; Aaron[7], *m* John[8], 7 above);
4–Margaret Finley (Mar. 27, 1801-Apr. 2, 1831), *m* Willis Rucker **Plunkett** (4 above).
16–John **Finley,** of Forfarshire, Scotland; mem. of Clan of Finley, a Highland family in the vicinity of Elgin and Inverness, a sept of the great Highland confederation Clan Chattan, one of the most ancient and noble families in Scotland;
15–John, *m* Janet Rogers;
14–Andrew, *m* Janet Hayes;
13–James, *m* Elizabeth, dau. of William Warrender;
12–John, *m* Sarah Craigie;
11–James, *m* Margaret Mackie;
10–Alexander, *m* Catherine Jennings;
9–James (Dec. 4, 1687-1752), from Dublin, Ireland, 1720; *d* Greens Tp., Pa.; *m* Jan. 10, 1706, Elizabeth Patterson (Robert[10]);
8–John (1706-73), from Ireland with parents; to Augusta Co., Va., 1737; thru French and Indian War; *m* 1723, Thankful Doak (James[9], with wife Elizabeth and 5 children, from Ireland to New Castle, Del., 1708);
7–John (1724-91), Augusta Co., Va.; French and Indian War; surveyor of Augusta Co., 1758,69; commissary Washington Co. militia, 1776; *m* Apr. 22, 1741, Mary Caldwell (1726-69; David[8]);
6–Margaret (Nov. 2, 1746-1802), *m* John **Shields** (6 above).
6–John **Higginbotham,** *m* Frances Riley, as above;
5–James (Dec. 25, 1729-Mar. 14, 1813), maj., 1769; col. Amherst Co. militia, Am. Rev.; surveyor of Amherst Co.; vestryman and ch. warden; *m* May 30, 1779, Rachel Campbell (1755-Mar. 28, 1809; Henry[6], *m* Charity–);
4–Joseph Cabell (Aug. 9, 1782-Nov. 18, 1842), served War 1812; col. Amherst Co. militia; *m* 1803, Lucy Wills (1784-1854; James[5], *m* Mildred–);
3–Joseph Cabell (1821-Mar. 29, 1894), *m* Feb. 7, 1849, Angelina Elizabeth Plunkett, sis. Eliza Frances Plunkett, 3 above;
2–Althea Jane (Oct. 7, 1852-Oct. 13, 1921), *m* Oct. 21, 1874, Cyrus Aaron **Higginbotham** (Aug. 25, 1852-Apr. 15, 1896), of Nelson Co., Va.; issue: I–Lillian Brown (*b* 1876; *m* 1900, Leo William Kasehagen, Sr.); II–Minnie Rosamund (*b* 1880; *m* 1912, Royston St. Noble); III–Lenore E. (1 above); IV–Annie Cabell (*b* 1887; *m* 1908, Howard W. Johnson); V–Raymond Clyde (*b* 1889; *m* 1918, Katie Lee Wright, *d* 1928; *m* 2d, Mrs. —Lewis); VI–Ida Rice (*b* and *d* 1894); VII–Janie Corinne (*b* 1895; *m* 1920, Clarence Edward Berger).
1–*m* Apr. 27, 1905, James M. McFarlane (1864-1917).
1–*m* 2d, Oct. 28, 1928, William Montgomery Sweeny (qv).
1–Mem. D.A.R., U.D.C., A.P.V.A., Va. Soc. Residence: 126 Franklin St., Astoria, N.Y.

1–**SWEET, James Sylvester Perry,** *b* Waupun, Wis., Apr. 30, 1853.
9–John **Sweet** (1595-1637), from Eng., settled at Salem, Mass., 1630; later at Providence, R.I.; *m* 1618, Mary– (ante 1600-1681);
8–James (1622-95), Warwick, R.I.; *m* 1655, Mary Greene (*b* 1633; John[9]);
7–Benoni (1663-1752), N. Kingstown, R.I.; *m* 1680, Elizabeth Sweet (Samuel[8]);
6–James (*b* 1687), *m* Mary Sweet; *m* 2d, Ann Weeden;
5–Job (*b* 1724), of S. Kingston, R.I.; *m* Jemima Sherman; *m* 2d, Sarah Kingsley;
4–Rufus (*b* 1753), *m* Elizabeth Clark;
3–Samuel Clark (1790-1863), of Boston, Erie Co., N.Y.; *m* 1816, Hannah Perry;
2–Sylvester Damon (2 below).
9–Jonathan (Fairbanks) **Fairbank** (qv);
8–George (*d* 1683), from Eng. to Dedham, Mass.; *m* Mary Adams;
7–Dr. Jonathan (*b* 1662), of Medway; *m* 1st, Sarah–;
6–Dr. Jonathan (*b* 1689), *m* ca. 1726, Hannah Cooledge;
5–Lt. Joshua (1727-81), Am. Rev.; *m* Lydia Ellis;
4–John (1776-1838), *m* 1789, Experience Bailey (*b* 1771);
3–Ellis (1796-1875), *m* 1817, Anna Canada (1797-1886);
2–Julina (1826-1910), *m* 1846, Sylvester Damon **Sweet** (1820-76), of Ripon, Wis.; farmer; inventor; mech. engr.; issue: I–Royal (1850-1924; *m* Meribah Hillebert; *m* 2d, Etta Davis); II–James Sylvester Perry (1 above); III–Lucien Abel Arthur (*b* 1859; *m* Lucy Churchyard); IV–Luella Belle Eliza (*b* 1866; *m* Wellington Stewart, *d*).
1–*m* Aug. 14, 1876, Amelia Grout (*d* 1884); issue: 1–Lucien Samuel Sylvester, *b* Winnemucca, Nev.; A.M., U.Wis., '02; *m* June 19, 1929, Blanche Lovett.
1–*m* 2d, July 1, 1891, Julia Melvina Goodyear, *b* Mankato, Minn., Feb. 21, 1866; dau. of Robert Goodyear (Lyman[3]; Stephen[4]; John[5]; Stephen[6], qv).
1–Attended Ripon Coll., Oshkosh Normal Sch., Nat. U.Ill. Teacher, 1870-75; high school prin., 1876-84; normal school pres., 1884-90; pres. Rosa Business Coll., since 1891; also pres. J. S. Sweet Pub. Co. since 1893. Mayor of Santa Rosa, 1898-1902; del. Dem. Nat. Conv., St. Louis, 1900. Mem. S.A.R. Mason. Residence: 607 Cherry St., Santa Rosa, Calif.

1–**TAINTOR, Starr,** *b* Stratford, Conn., Aug. 27, 1871.
10–William **Sargent** (qv);
9–John (1639-1716), *m* 1662, Deborah Hillier (1643-69);
8–Joseph (1663-1717), *m* 1685, Mary Green (1668-1759);
7–Sarah (1695-1740), *m* 1713, Samuel **Newhall** (1689-1733; Thomas[8]; Thomas[9]; Thomas[10], qv);
6–Mary (1721-45), *m* 1740, Rev. Thomas **Skinner** (1712-62; Nathaniel[7]; John[8]; John[9], qv);
5–Mary (1742-1823), *m* 1766, Charles **Taintor** (see Vol. III, p. 441, for Taintor lineage);
4–Charles (1772-1827), *m* 1800, Sarah Fox;
3–Charles (1805-64), *m* 1830, Catherine Elkins Musier (1803-55; John[4], *m* Sarah, dau. of John Guest, *m* Sarah Jordon);
2–Henry Fox (2 below).
11–William **Brewster** (qv);
10–Jonathan (1593-1659), *m* 1624, Lucretia Oldham (1600-1678/79);
9–Mary (1627-97), *m* 1645, John **Turner** (Humphrey[10], qv);
8–Ezekiel (1650-1704/05), *m* 1678, Susannah Kenny (*b* 1662; John[9], of New London, Conn., *m* Sarah Douglas);
7–Ezekiel (*b* 1699), *m* 1729, Borodel Denison (*b* 1712; Joseph[8], of Stonington, *m* Prudence Miner);
6–Prudence (1732-1823), *m* 1751, Samuel **Fox** (1724-1810);
5–Jesse (1754-1834), *m* 1777, Ruth Hall, of Plainfield, Conn.;
4–Sarah, *m* Charles **Taintor** (4 above).
10–Rev. Peter **Bulkeley** (qv);
9–Dorothy (1589-1676), *m* 1610, Thomas **Lord** (qv);
8–Anne (1621-88), *m* 1637, Thomas **Stanton** (qv);
7–Dorothy (1652-1743), *m* Rev. James **Noyes** (1640-1719), grad. Harvard, 1659; settled at Stonington, Conn., 1664; trustee Yale Coll., 1701-19; chief sachem of Narragansett Indians (Rev. James[8], qv);
6–John (1685-1751), *m* Mary Gallup (Lt. William[7]);
5–Joseph (1731-1820), *m* 1763, Prudence Denison;
4–Joseph (1768-1852), *m* 1811, Eunice Chesebrough;
3–William Chesebrough (1813-94), *m* Jane R. Keown (James[4]);
2–Frances Leeds (2 below).
10–Christopher **Avery** (qv);
9–Capt. James (qv);
8–Capt. John (1654-1715), *m* 1675, Abigail Chesebrough (*b* 1656; Samuel[9]; William[10], qv);
7–Mary (1680-1762), *m* 1698, Lt. William **Denison** (1677-1730; John B.[8]; Capt. George[9]; William[10], qv);
6–Avery (1712-75), *m* 1734, Thankful Williams (1717-67; John[7]; John[8]; Isaac[9]; Robert[10], qv);
5–Prudence (1743-1818), *m* Joseph **Noyes** (5 above).
10–Walter **Palmer** (qv);

9–Grace (*b* in Eng.), *m* 1634, Thomas **Miner** (qv);
8–Manasseh (1647-1728), *m* 1670, Lydia Moore (*d* 1720);
7–Hannah (*b* 1676), *m* 1698, Elihu **Chesebrough** (*b* 1668; Elisha[8]; William[9], qv);
6–Elihu (1704-69), *m* 1740, Esther Dennis (1710-68);
5–William (1745-1840), *m* 1774, Esther Williams (1743-1814);
4–Eunice (1781-1844), *m* Joseph **Noyes** (4 above);
2–Frances Leeds Noyes (1838-1923), *m* 1869, Henry Fox **Taintor** (1833-1908), pres. H. F. Taintor Mfg. Co., New York (for issue see Vol. III, p. 441).
1–*m* Nov. 1, 1905, Mabel Koons, *b* Phila., Pa., May 12, 1878; issue (all *b* New York): 1–Mabel Musier, *b* Mar. 6, 1909; 2–Frances Noyes, *b* Sept. 19, 1910; 3–Catharine Koons, *b* May 8, 1912.
1–A.B., Columbia, '93 (Alpha Delta Phi). See Vol. I, p. 748 and Vol. III, p. 441, for biography. Residence: Ralsey Rd., Stamford, Conn.

JOSEPH CRUICKSHANK TALBOT, D.D., LL.D., son of Elisha and Sarah Saunders Talbot (b Alexandria, Va., Sept. 15, 1819-d Indianapolis, Ind., Jan. 15, 1883); m 1850, Matilda Ware, in Louisville, Ky., no issue; ed. Pierpont Acad., and Church Theol. Sem., Alexandria, Va., and General Theol. Sem., New York. Founded, and rector St. John's Parish, Louisville, 1848-53; rector Christ's Church, Indianapolis, 1853-59, and built the present "Rubble Stone" church at Meridian St. and Monument Pl., the earliest example of Gothic architecture in the West; elected missionary bishop of the Northwest, 1859, comprising 11 states and territories; was the first bishop of "The English Church" in America, sent west of the Missouri River; in 1862 he made a missionary trip of more than 7,000 miles by wagon, coach, horseback, often afoot, through Neb., Colo., N.M., Utah, Ariz., Nev. and Calif. to San Francisco; returned to Ind., 1866, as assistant to Bishop George Upfold, whom he succeeded in 1872; del. to the Lambeth Conference, London, 1867, receiving degree of LL.D., from U. of Cambridge, Eng. Of Bishop Talbot, his contemporaries, Bishop Smith (Ky.), Bishop Seymour (Ill.), Bishop Daniel S. Tuttle (Mo.), said and wrote: "He blazed the way for Randall in Colorado, Clarkson in Nebraska, Tuttle in Wyoming, Utah, Idaho, Montana, and Whitaker in Nevada. He was a man of vigorous mental and physical force, strong convictions, possessed of a genial, lovable personality, he was a strong preacher, the ideal bishop." Bishop Daniel S. Tuttle, of Missouri, who had followed Talbot to the West in 1867, wrote: "The man, his unselfish devotion of his life to his work, his enthusiasm and success inspired me to enter the ministry."

1–**TALBOT, John Saunders,** *b* Louisville, Ky., Apr. 21, 1858.
7–Richard **Talbot** (qv);
6–John (1660-1707), *m* Sarah Mears (*b* 1673; John[7], of "The Cliffs," Calvert Co., Md., *m* Sarah Thomas);
5–Joseph (*b* 1706), *m* 1745, Mary Birckhead (Abraham[6], from Eng. to Md., ca. 1663-64);
4–Joseph, *m* Anna Plummer;
3–Elisha (*b* Alexandria, Va., 1782-1832), *m* 1806, Sarah Saunders (*b* 1784; John[4], *m* Mary Pancoast); among their sons was Joseph Cruickshank, D.D., LL.D. (see his portrait and biography above);
2–William Washington (*b* Alexandria, Va., 1823-64), *m* 1855, Cordelia Anne Hewes (*b* Baltimore, Md., 1839; Capt. Aaron[3], formerly resident of Baltimore and Philadelphia, *m* Adeline Watts); issue: I–James William (May 13, 1856-Jan. 15, 1860); II–John S. (1 above); III–Charles Hewes (*b* Nov. 21, 1860); IV–Richard Arthur (Mar. 13, 1863-June 4, 1864).
1–*m* June 3, 1890, Harriet Eleanor Smith, *b* Terre Haute, Ind., July 24, 1862; dau. of Charles Carter Smith, *m* Phebe Sandford; issue: 1–Helen Laura, *b* Denver, Colo., Sept. 9, 1891.
1–Privately tutored 2 yrs. in Latin, English and mathematics, preparing for study of law; 2 yrs., Indianapolis, Ind., high school, coached and tutored by Bishop Talbot of Indiana. Entered service Pa. Ry. System as junior clerk, Indianapolis, 1877, thereafter continuously engaged in railway freight traffic service until "Armistice Day," Nov. 11, 1918, in official positions of responsibility with eastern and western trunk line railway systems. Thereafter engaged in the investment securities field, Chicago and Terre Haute; retired 1930. Mem. St. Mark's Parish, Evanston, Ill., and St. Stephen's Parish, Terre Haute, Ind. Mem. S.A.R. (Chicago and Terre Haute chapters), English-Speaking Union. Clubs: Chicago Athletic (Chicago), Exmoor Country (Highland Park, Ill.), Terre Haute Country. Address R. 220, National Bldg., Cor. 6th and Wabash Av., Terre Haute, Ind.

1–**TALBOTT, Bertha Clarinda Hall (Mrs. William H.),** *b* Poolesville, Md., Sept. 30, 1864.
4–Joseph **Hall** (*d* 1824), of Sugarland Hundred, Md.; served in Am. Rev.; *m* Elizabeth, prob. Soper (*d* ante 1824);
3–Thomas (1800-54), *m* 1826, Rebecca Poole Pile (1806-1846-47);
2–Thomas Randolph (2 below).
10–Thomas **Fitch** (qv);
9–Thomas (1640-84), *m* Ruth Clark (bap. 1642);
8–Mary (*b* 1668), *m* Daniel **Terrill** (1660-1727);
7–Ephraim (*b* 1702), *m* Elizabeth Lines (*b* 1703);
6–Elizabeth, *m* 1745, Thomas **Beecher**;
5–Thomas (*b* 1746), of Woodbury, Conn.; *m* 1775, Phoebe Sanford (1755-post 1802);
4–Hopestill (1777-1823), *m* 1800, Abigail Rathbone (1779-1879);
3–Sarah R. (1818-59), of Tioga Co., Pa.; *m* 1834, Samuel Kent **Phillips** (1810-81);
2–Clarinda Beecher (1842-1914), *m* 1860, Thomas Randolph **Hall** (1828-84), merchant; extensive landowner; issue: I–Lulu J. (*m* Arthur Poole Fletchall); II–Bertha Clarinda (1 above); III–Sara Randolph (*m* S. N. C. Williams; *m* 2d, Edmund LaFayette Hardcastle); IV–Thomas Randolph (1871-1927; *m* Beulah B. White); V–Mortimer Beecher (*b* 1874; *m* 1915, Virginia Pyrl Van Winkle); VI–Anne Estelle (*b* 1878; *m* R. S. Owens).
1–*m* Sept. 2, 1885, William Hyde Talbott, *b* Poolesville, Md., July 5, 1861; atty.; son of Benson Talbott, of Poolesville; issue: 1–Marie Hyde, *b* Poolesville; *m* May 17, 1921, Walter Grove Ellison (issue: William Talbott; John Randolph; Leslie Warren); 2–William Randolph, *b* Poolesville; sgt. 313th M.G. Co., 79th Div., with A.E.F. in France, Sept. 26, 1917-June 1919; participated in Meuse-Argonne, Montfaucon, Tryon, Grand Montagne; *m* July 1, 1918, Laura M., dau. John J. Higgins, of Rockville, Md. (issue: William Randolph).
1–Mem. woman's section of Md. Council of Defence, World War. Mem. C.D.A., D.C.W., D.B.R. (rec. sec. and an organizer), D.A.C. (an organizer and nat. treas.), O.C., D.A.R. (ex-v.p. gen.), U.S.D. 1812, U.D.C., Nat. Mary Washington Memorial Assn., Md. Hist. Soc.,

I.A.G. (life), N.E.H.G.S., Nat. Geneal. Soc. Huguenot Soc., F.F.V. Residence: Rockville, Md.

1–**TALIAFERRO, Samuel Walker,** *b* Roseville, Ill., May 11, 1865.
5–Samuel **Taliaferro** (ca. 1729-1798), built one of the first houses in Charlottesville; was a vol. mail carrier during Am. Rev.; a "signer" for Albemarle Co.; *m* Anne– (*d* 1802);
4–Francis (1750-1826), Guthrie, Ky.; sgt. 3 yrs. in Am. Rev.; dep. sheriff of Albemarle Co., Va.; commr. of revenue, St. Anne's Parish, Albemarle Co.; a "signer" for Albemarle Co.; *m* 1795, Letitia Hughes (1761-1843);
3–Samuel Walker (1798-1879), planter, Todd Co., Ky.; *m* 1829, Sally McClung Moore;
2–David Moore (2 below).
6–Andrew **Moore** (1675-1748), came from Ireland; mem. army of Va.; *m* Isabel Baxter (1680-1760);
5–David (1722-83), Augusta Co., Va.; served in colonial wars and in Am. Rev.; *m* 1743, Mary Evans (1720-96);
4–David (1764-1826), Trenton, Ky.; *m* 1782, Janet McClung (*d* 1804; John[5], *m* Rebecca Stewart);
3–Sallie McClung (1804-91), of Guthrie, Ky.; *m* Samuel Walker **Taliaferro** (3 above).
5–John **Kelley** (*b* ca. 1756), of N.J.; *m* Olive Pierson (ca. 1770-1841), buried in ch. cemetery at Somerville, N.J.;
4–Nathaniel Pierson (ca. 1786-1844), Neshanic, N.J.; *m* 1807, Margaret Van Doren (1787-1862);
3–Isaac Vernard (1815-97), Somerville; *m* 1836, Catherine Maria Vorhees (1818-89);
2–Sarah Jane (1837-1921), of Roseville; *m* 1861, David Moore **Taliaferro** (1830-1918), of Roseville, Ill.; physician; breeder of short horn cattle; supervisor and town clk. of Roseville Tp.; issue: I–Myrtie (*b* 1862; *m* Eli Dixson); II–Samuel Walker (1 above); III–Sallie McClung (*b* 1866); IV–Catherine (*b* 1869; *m* 1893, William N. Brown, *d* 1928); V–Francis Isaac (1872-83); VI–Jennie (1876-94).
1–*m* Sept. 13, 1887, Chirena Blanche Johnston (Feb. 18, 1866-Sept. 24, 1914); dau. of Eli C. Johnston, of Roseville, Ill.; issue: 1–DeMoss Moore, *b* Roseville, June 21, 1888; *m* Sept. 29, 1909, Finette, dau. of Charles O. Pinney, of Roseville (adopted Marcia Ellen).
1–*m* 2d, Oct. 17, 1916, Leah Munger Sutton (qv); issue: 1–Mary Ellen, *b* Peoria, Ill., July 9, 1921; 2–Sally Jane, *b* Peoria, Sept. 10, 1923.
1–Ed. Monmouth Coll., and U. of Ill. (Phi Kappa Psi). Farmer till 1889; pharmacist, Tampa, Fla., till 1892; postmaster, Roseville, Ill., 1892-97, pharmacist, 1897-1907, cashier First Nat. Bank, 1907-14; farmer, 1914-16; pharmacist, Peoria, Ill., since 1916. Supervisor, mem. city council, one term; pres. city council, 1 term; tp. treas.; mem. bd. edn., 18 yrs., Roseville. Trustee Western Ill. Teachers' Coll., 4 yrs. Mem. S.A.R. Rotarian, Mason, Elk. Presbyterian. Democrat. Residence: 103 Hanssler Place, Peoria, Ill.

1–**TALIAFERRO, Leah Munger Sutton (Mrs. Samuel Walker),** *b* Rose Center, Mich., Mar. 31, 1891.
8–William **Sutton,** Quaker, from Eng.; settled at Eastham, Mass.; yeoman; town clk. and constable, Woodbridge, N.J.; *m* 1st, 1666, Damaris Bishop (*d* 1682; Richard[9], *m* Alice–);
7–Richard (1676-1732), farmer, Piscataway, N.J.; *m* 1702, Sarah Rognon (or Runyon; Vincent[8], Huguenot, founder of the Runyon family in America, *m* Anne Boutcher, an Englishwoman);
6–Jonas (1721-97), farmer, Sand Brook, N.J.; *m* 1764, Elizabeth Runyon;
5–Nathan (*b* 1767), Herkimer Co., N.Y.; *m* ca. 1787, Elizabeth Robbins (*b* 1769; John[6], *m* Elizabeth–);
4–John (1793-1856), farmer, Lapeer Co., Mich.; *m* 1816, Widow Joanna (Bird) Williamson (1789-1832; Elisha Bird[5], of Beattystown, N.J., *m* Rachel Osmun; James[6], early settler of Mansfield Tp., Warren Co., N.J.);
3–Peter (1817-98), pioneer of Oakland Co., Mich.; *m* 1837, his 2d cousin, Frances Bird (1821-84; Thomas[4], from N.J., to Mich., ca. 1840, *m* Sarah Swayze; John[5], *m* Frances, dau. of William Stewart; Elisha[6], above);
2–Charles Milan (2 below).
3–George **Munger** (1823-90), from Eng., ca. 1850; finally settled in Rose Tp., Oakland Co., Mich.; farmer; *m* 1st, ca. 1850, Elizabeth Eads (1821-65), from Eng. with her husband on wedding trip;
2–Mary Ellen (*b* 1858), Holly, Mich.; *m* 1882, Charles Milan **Sutton** (1858-91), farmer and merchant (she *m* 2d, 1921, Eli Bird, 1849-1927); issue (mother's 1st marriage): I–Otto Clare (*b* 1886; *m* Caroline Tock, 1888-1928); II–Leah Munger (1 above).
1–*m* Oct. 17, 1916, Samuel Walker Taliaferro (qv for issue).
1–Ed. Mich. State Normal Coll. Taught commercial course, Roseville (Ill.) Tp. H.S., 1912-16. Mem. D.A.R. Presbyterian. Republican. Residence: 103 Hanssler Pl., Peoria, Ill.

1–**TARDY, Clarence Minge,** *b* Mobile, Ala., Mar. 27, 1864.
9–Col. John **West** (qv);
8–Col. John (1633-91), of "West Point," Va.; the first English child *b* on York River; sr. justice Colonial Gen. Ct.; burgess; *m* Unity Croshaw (Maj. Joseph[9], of "Poplar Neck," York Co.);
7–Capt. Nathaniel (1655-1724), of "West Point;" burgess, 1702; *m* ca. 1699, Martha Bigger, widow of Gideon Macon;
6–Unity (ca. 1700-1753-54), *m* ca. 1719, Capt. William **Dandridge,** R.N. (*d* 1743), of "Elsing Green," King William Co.; mem. Council, 1728; burgess (brother of John Dandridge, of New Kent Co., Va., father of Martha Washington);
5–Mary, *m* 1745, Col. John **Spotswood** (1728-56), of "Germannos;" lt., cdr.-in-chief, Spotsylvania Co.; burgess (Gov. Alexander[6], qv);
4–Capt. John (1747-1811), owned part of old "Horse Shoe" grant; "Orange Grove," "Sidley Lodge"; capt. Am. Rev., wounded at Brandywine; col. militia; *m* 1771, Sallie (Sarah) Rowzie (Col. Edwin[5], of "Farmer's Hall," Essex Co., burgess);
3–Elliott (ca. 1785-1837), *m* Sarah Dandridge Littlepage;
2–Mary (2 below).
7–Richard **Littlepage** (*d* 1688), from Eng. to New Kent Co., Va., 1660, where he received 1143 acres of land, 1664, and 400 additional acres in partnership with James Turner; received 800 acres, 1684; sheriff; burgess, 1684; vestryman, St. Paul's Parish, 1685; *m* Judith Turner;
6–Richard (*d* 1717), received 2367 acres, 1701, and 4486 acres, 1702; vestryman, 1703-09; justice, 1715; *m* Frances Arnott;
5–James (1714-69), clk., Louise Co., 1742; mem. Grand Jury, 1745; burgess, Hanover Co., 1764; *m* Sarah Carter;
4–John Carter (1752-post 1830), pvt. Va. Cont. Line, Am. Rev.; *m* Sarah Dandridge;
3–Sarah Dandridge (1790-1854), *m* Elliott **Spotswood** (3 above).
8–John **Carter** (qv);
7–Col. Robert, "King" (1662-1732), of "Corotoman," Lancaster Co.; speaker House of Burgesses; treas. of Va.; pres. Council; actg.gov.; *m* 1st, 1688, Judith Armistead (1665-99; Col. John[8], qv);
6–John (1690-1743), barrister of the Middle Temple; *m* 1723, Elizabeth Hill (*d* 1777; Edward[7], of "Shirley," Va.; Edward[8]);
5–Sarah (1729-60), *m* James **Littlepage** (5 above).
2–Mary Spotswood (1828-90), *m* 1860, Balthazar **Tardy** (*b* France, 1802-*d* Huntsville, Ala., 1879), cotton buyer; issue: I–Lucy Matthews (1861-63); II–Clarence Minge (1 above); III–Sarah Lilian (Feb. 22, 1867-July 17, 1927, Mrs. William A. Rose, see Vol. I, p. 766); IV–Rosalind (1871-90; *m* 1889, Thomas H. Benners).
1–*m* Dec. 29, 1885, Annie Laurie Southerne (qv).
1–Ed. Presbyterian Coll., Clarksville, Tenn. Wholesale grocer. Mem. D.C.G. Club: Roebuck Country. Residence: 1119 Hickory St., Birmingham, Ala.

1–**TARDY, Annie Laurie Southerne (Mrs. Clarence M.),** *b* Petersburg, Va., Nov. 4, 1866.
8–Joseph **Morton,** came to America, 1680; created landgrave of S.C., 1681; commd. gov. of S.C., 1682,85; apptd. admiralty officer, 1697; commr. free schools, S.C., 1709; *m* Eleanor Blake (Benjamin[9]);
7–Elizabeth, *m* Capt. Christopher **Wilkinson, of**

Eng.; mem. Assembly, 1720,21,23; commr. trade; justice, tax collector;
6–Francis, *m* Miss Braileford;
5–Ann, *m* Edmund **Peters** (*b* 1733), of Va.; served in Col. William Byrd's Regt., 1758; removed from Cumberland Co., Va. to S.C., where he received patent of land;
4–Mary, *m* Gibson **Southerne** (1753-1833), soldier in Am. Rev. (see Vol. I, p. 766);
3–John Whirley (1802-54), *m* Elizabeth Callahan (William[4]; Joel[5], officer in Am. Rev.);
2–John Peters (2 below).
9–Lemuel (Reddick) **Riddick,** from Ireland; settled in Nansemond Co., Va.; vestryman 40 yrs.; *m* Miss Willis, of Va.;
8–Joseph (1689-1759), *m* Priscilla Parker (*b* 1700; Abraham[9]);
7–Isaac (1716-88), Am. Rev.; *m* 1733, Hannah Perry (*b* 1716);
6–Mirriam (*b* 1735), *m* Joel **Hollowell** (1732-74); see Vol. I, p. 766;
5–Silas (1754-90), *m* 1774, Mirriam Riddick (1755-93; Hon. Joseph[6], *m* Ann Stallings);
4–Arthur (1775-1818), Bertie Co., N.C.; *m* 1797, Elizabeth Sharrock (1776-1814; Thomas[5]);
3–William D. (1800-90), Huntsville, Ala.; *m* 1830, Mary Elizabeth Echols;
2–Mary Winifred (2 below).
12–Richard **Cobbs,** *m* Sibyl Sheetz, of Holland;
11–Joseph (*b* 1588), from Amsterdam to Va., 1613, in the "Treasurer";
10–Joseph;
9–Ambrose, *m* Anne–;
8–Robert, *m* Elizabeth Allen (Rev. Daniel[9]);
7–Martha, *m* Dudley **Richardson,** maj. in Am. Rev.;
6–Sarah, *m* George **Booker,** Jr.; mem. Com. Safety, Elizabeth City, Va., 1775;
5–Grace, *m* Absolem **Farmer**;
4–Mary Elizabeth, *m* William **Echols**;
3–Mary Elizabeth, *m* William D. **Hollowell** (3 above);
2–Mary Winifred (1839-1916), of Birmingham, Ala.; *m* 1865, John Peters **Southerne** (1825-83), pres. Union Bank of Columbia, S.C.; col. on staff of Gov. Wade Hampton; auditor and treas. Greenville & Columbia R.R.; for issue and other lineages, see Vol. I, p. 766.
1–*m* Dec. 29, 1885, Clarence Minge Tardy (qv); issue (all *b* Huntsville, Ala.): 1–Clarence Southerne (Jan. 16, 1887-July 16, 1887); 2–Matthews Hollowell, *b* Oct. 29, 1888; pvt. to 2d lt., engrs., Nov. 29, 1917-Aug. 19, 1919; in France, Jan. 1918-July 1919; 2d lt. U.S.R.; *m* Nov. 1917, Mary Seal Grubb (*d* 1923); *m* 2d, Apr. 30, 1927, Margaret Frances McDuffie, *b* Oct. 23, 1896 (issue: Virginia Anne, *b* Sept. 11, 1929); 3–Mary Rosalind (July 20, 1890-Oct. 11, 1918); *m* Apr. 22, 1914, Warren Henderson Buchanan; 4–Annie Southerne, *b* Dec. 8, 1895.
1–Ed. Columbia Female Coll. Mem. C.D.A., D.C.G., F.F.V., D.F.P.A., D.A.R., U.S.D. 1812, U.D.C., Scions Col. Cavaliers. Member Poetry Soc. of Ala., League of Am. Pen Women. Residence: 1119 Hickory St., Birmingham, Ala.

1–**TATUM, Edith Brittain Crenshaw (Mrs. George H.),** *b* Greenville, Ala., Sept. 2, 1877.
6–William **Crenshaw,** *m* Susannah Brooke Carr (Capt. William[7]; Col. Thomas[8]);
5–Charles (1749-1814), *m* 1775, Eunice White (Thomas[6], *m* Betty Lee);
4–Judge Anderson (1782-1847), served on Supreme Ct., 1821-47; was judge of Chancery Ct.; Crenshaw Co., named in his honor, 1865; *m* 1816, Mary Chiles;
3–Walter Henry (1817-78), A.B., U. of Ala., with its 1st class, 1834; speaker Ala. House and pres. Ala. Senate; judge Butler Co., etc.; *m* Sarah Anderson Crenshaw (Abner[4], *m* Charlotte Perry Elmore);
2–Edward (2 below).
10–Lt. Col. Walter **Chiles** (qv);
9–Col. Walter (*d* 1672), Jamestown, Va.; burgess; *m* Mary Page (Col. John[10], qv);
8–John (*d* 1723), mem. Va. Assembly, 1723; *m* Eleanor Webber (Henry[9]);
7–Henry (*d* 1763), of Spotsylvania Co., Va.; *m* Mary Carr (Col. Thomas[8], had land grants in King William Co., 1701; justice of ct., high sheriff);
6–William, of Va.; *m* Agnes White (Thomas[7], *m* Betty Lee);
5–Thomas (1763-1842), of Spotsylvania Co., Va.; *m* Judith Leake; *m* 2d, Elizabeth Tillman;
4–Mary (1790-1873), Abbeville, S.C.; *m* Judge Anderson **Crenshaw** (4 above).
8–William **Leake,** from Eng., ca. 1685, settled in Henrico Co., Va.; *m* ca. 1687, Mary Bostick;
7–Walter (*d* 1756), *m* Judith Mask;
6–William, *m* Judith Moseley, of Buckingham Co., Va.;
5–Judith, *m* Thomas **Chiles** (5 above).
2–Edward **Crenshaw** (1842-1911), capt. C.S.A.; lawyer; *m* Sarah Edith Brittain (1856-87; Rev. William[8], of Ireland); issue: I–Arthur (*b* 1875; capt. U.S.N.; *m* Theodora M. Jacobs); II–Edith Brittain (1 above); III–Saxon (*d* infancy).
1–*m* Feb. 21, 1900, George Hamlet Tatum, *b* La Grange, Ga., Dec. 10, 1876; son of Seth Tatum (1822-1904), *m* Sarah Elizabeth Stinson; issue: 1–Sarah Edward, *b* Greenville, Ala., Feb. 3, 1901; *m* May 31, 1918, Walter Prentice Smith (issue: Sarah Tatum, *b* 1919).
1–Author. Mem. C.D.A., U.D.C., League Am. Pen Women, Poetry Soc. of Ala., etc. Residence: The Pines, Greenville, Ala.

1–**TAULMAN, Joseph Edwin,** *b* nr. Bryan, Tex., Feb. 18, 1867.
8–Dow Harmanse (Talma, Taelman, Taleman, Tallman) **Taulman** (ca. 1624-1687), from Holland with his wife and 3 children, in the W.I. Co.'s ship "Brownfish"; settled at New Amsterdam, 1658, later at what is now Bergen Co., N.J.; *m* Dirckie Teunise (*b* ca. 1624);
7–Harman Douwenszen (1655 or 57-1690), began to write name Taelman; *m* 1686, Griete Minnens (Minne Johannes [Minnelay][8], *m* Rensje Feddans);
6–Douwe Harmanse (1689-1779), wrote name Taleman and Talema; though in his 90th yr. rendered aid to the Am. cause during Am. Rev. in the way of supplies and information; killed by Tories; *m* 1715, Maria Haring;
5–Harmanus (1731-96), wrote name Taleman and Taulman; to N.W. Territory, O., 1792; 2d Regt., Orange Co., N.Y., Militia during Am. Rev.; *m* 2d, 1774, Katrina Blauvelt (1743-86);
4–John (1779-1833), began to write name Taulman; War 1812 and Black Hawk War; *m* 1810, Elizabeth Burns (1792-1876; John[5], of Va.);
3–Evan L. (1813-1900), postmaster, Milton, Ky.; mem. Home Guard in Civil War; *m* Laura Maria Comstock (1820-1901; Botsford[4]);
2–Francis Asbury (1841-1910), from Ky. to Tex. before Civil War; pvt. Co. G, 32d Tex. Cav., C.S.A.; captured at Blakely, Ala., 1865, and kept a prisoner on Ship Island nearly 30 days; merchant; *m* 1866, Emma Jane Hill (1846-1914); issue: I–Joseph Edwin (1 above); II–Oscar Evan (*b* Aug. 4, 1868; *m* Minnie Lloyd); III–Julia Laura Pearl (*b* June 20, 1875; *m* Harry Sweetman; *m* 2d, William Henry Christopher).
1–*m* Apr. 27, 1901, Araminta Inez McClellan (qv); issue (all *b* Hubbard, Tex.): 1–Wilhelmina Dorothy, *b* Feb. 15, 1902; *m* Nov. 30, 1921, Robert Elbert Smith (qv); 2–Katrina Mildred, *b* July 27, 1903; *m* Jan. 16, 1926, J. E. Storey (qv); 3–Parker Harmanus, *b* Dec. 22, 1907; 4–Daniel Comstock, *b* Oct. 26, 1912.
1–Photographic artist and compositor. Sgt., 1st lt., capt., Tex. N.G.; assisted in recruiting co. for World War. Mem. S.A.R. Residence: 2711 Av. E, Ft. Worth, Tex.

1–**TAULMAN, Araminta Inez McClellan (Mrs. Joseph E.),** *b* Limestone Co., Tex., Jan. 11, 1881.
4–William **McClellan** (*b* Scotland, ca. 1752-ca. 1809), from Ireland; lived in S.C., N.J., and Pa.; *m* Miss Epperson;
3–Samuel (ca. 1790-92-1855), in War 1812, and was at Battle of New Orleans; *m* Mildred (Womack) Foster-Henderson;
2–James Wyatte (2 below).
6–George **Crist,** from Germany; enlisted Apr. 21, 1761, 1st N.Y. Regt., "Old French War" (7 yrs.' War);
5–George (1768-1845), *m* 1793, Elizabeth Gerard (*d* 1807), a widow;
4–Stephen (1799-1867), *m* 1822, Annie Parker;
3–Sarah Livonia (1838-1912), *m* 1854, John Ellis **Chaffin** (1831-70), soldier C.S.A., 1861-65 (John Eli[4], from Eng. when a small boy);
2–Mary Amanda (2 below).
6–John **Parker** (Sept. 5, 1758-1836), of Md. and Va.; killed by Comanche Indians at Parker's

Fort massacre in Tex., May 19, 1836; *m* Sarah White (*d* 1824; Benjamin[7], of Md. or Va.);
5–Daniel (1781-1844), pioneer preacher; emigrated to Tex., 1833; organized a church in Ill. and brought it to Tex. in a body, travelling in wagons and holding services on the way; it was the first regularly constituted Protestant ch. in Tex.; mem. of the "first consultation" which met to organize the Republic of Texas; assisted in Indian warfare and in gaining the Independence of Tex. from Mexico; uncle of Cynthia Ann Parker who was captured by Comanche Indians at Parker's Fort massacre, Tex., 1836; *m* 1802, Martha Dixon (*d* 1846);
4–Annie (1803-55), *m* Stephen **Crist** (4 above);
3–Sarah L., *m* John Ellis **Chaffin** (3 above);
2–Mary Amanda (1859-1905), *m* 1875, James Wyatte **McClellan** (1844-1903), newspaper man, writer and farmer; soldier C.S.A., 1861-65; issue: I–Della, and II–Ella (twins, both *d* infancy); III–Mildred Livonia (*b* Mar. 17, 1878; *m* Edward Roach); IV–Mary Elizabeth (*b* Mar. 28, 1879; *d* young); V–Araminta Inez (1 above); VI–Willie (dau. *b* Jan. 16, 1884-*d* infancy); VII–Ada Wyatte (*b* July 1, 1885; *m* Herbert R. Twaddell); VIII–Samuel James (Oct. 11, 1887-May 25, 1930; *m* Vera Massey); IX–Sarah Womack (*b* Sept. 14, 1889; *m* Wermer J. Lange); X–John Archelaus (*b* Mar. 17, 1891; *m* Maud Gibson); XI–Daniel Crist (Sept. 22, 1895-Dec. 24, 1911).
1–*m* Apr. 27, 1901, Joseph Edwin Taulman (qv for issue).
1–Local. sec. A.R.C., and co. chmn. Com. of Defense during World War. Mem. D.A.R.; U.S.D. 1812 (v.regent), Daus. of the Republic of Tex. (v.p.), U.D.C.; sec. Oakwood Cemetery Assn. Residence: 2711 Av. E, Ft. Worth, Tex.

1–**SMITH, Robert Elbert,** *b* in Tex., July 24, 1899.
4–Archibald **Smith,** *b* in Md., whose father came from Ireland and landed in Md.; *m* Sarah Reynolds;
3–Manaen (*d* June 22, 1886), emigrated to Tex. before the Republic; was in battle of San Jacinto, Apr. 21, 1836; received grant of land from Mexico; *m* Matilda Haley (*b* Mo.), *m* 2d, May 4, 1856, Mrs. Ellen Chandler White;
2–Thomas Haley (Jan. 1, 1850-May 22, 1924), *m* July 21, 1870, Nancy Montgomery Boyd (Nov. 20, 1855-Sept. 11, 1905).
1–*m* Nov. 30, 1921, Wilhelmina Dorothy, dau. of Joseph Edwin Taulman (qv); issue: 1–Nancy Inez, *b* Dallas, Tex., Sept. 6, 1922; 2–Robert Elbert, Jr., *b* Henrietta, Tex., Sept. 6, 1923.
1–In govt. service in post office. Second lt., U.S.R. Residence: Rockdale, Tex.

1–**STOREY, J. E.,** *b* Freestone Co., Tex., Oct. 2, 1905.
4–Anthony **Storey** (Apr. 30, 1792-Mar. 18, 1869), *m* Jan. 7, 1819, Margaret Means;
3–Julius William (Jan. 22, 1830-Dec. 31, 1902), capt. C.S.A., Civil War; *m* 1854, Angeline Wills;
2–John Edwin (2 below).
4–William Jackson **Drake** (Aug. 27, 1815-Aug. 21, 1866), *m* Nancy Tinsley Busby;
3–Matthew Montgomery (Oct. 6, 1841-May 7, 1910), served 4 yrs. in Hood's Tex. Brig., C.S.A.; wounded, spent 6 mos. in Federal prison; *m* 1st, 1868, Susan Ferrell;
2–Helen Martha (*b* Nov. 14, 1869), *m* Oct. 28, 1891, John Edwin **Storey** (Oct. 20, 1870-Apr. 30, 1921).
1–*m* Jan. 16, 1926, Katrina Mildred, dau. of Joseph Edwin Taulman (qv); issue: 1–Patricia Anne, *b* Ft. Worth, Tex., Feb. 1, 1929.
1–Lab. technician. Residence: 3304 Av. L, Ft. Worth, Tex.

1–**TAYLOR, Frederic William,** *b* Weeping Water, Neb., Apr. 13, 1860.
9–William **Taylor** (1618-96), from Eng. ca. 1635; settled at Concord, ca. 1638/39; *m* Mary Merriam (*d* 1699; Joseph[10]);
8–Abraham (1656-1729), in King Philip's War; *m* 1681, Mary Whitaker (1661-1756; John[9], *m* Elizabeth–);
7–Abraham (1682-1743), *m* 1st, 1706, Sarah Pellet (1685-1710; Thomas[8], *m* Mary Dean);
6–Dea. Samuel (1708-92), *m* 1733, Susannah Perham (1713-98; Joseph[7], *m* Dorothy, dau. James Kidder; John[8]);
5–Reuben (1736-1813), New Ipswich, N.H.; capt. Am. Rev.; *m* 1761, Lucy Kendall (1737-1814; John[6], *m* Deborah, dau. John Richardson; Jacob[7]; Francis[8] [qv]; Henry[9], from Eng.);
4–Zebedee (1765-1845), *m* 1796, Ruth Spaulding;
3–George (1797-1842), *m* 1825, Relief Nichols;
2–William (2 below).
9–Edward **Spaulding** (qv);
8–Andrew (1652-1713), landowner, New Ipswich, N.H.; *m* 1674, Hannah Jeffts (1654-1730; Henry[9], *m* Hannah Bieths);
7–Henry (1680-1720), of Chelmsford; *m* 1701/02, Elizabeth Lund (*b* 1684; Thomas[8]; Thomas[9], at Boston, 1650);
6–Thomas (1707-95), *m* 1730/31, Mary Adams (1707-88; Joseph[7], *m* Mary–; Capt. Samuel[8], from Eng.; Henry[9]);
5–Thomas (*b* 1737), Am. Rev.; *m* 1757, Rachel Chandler (*b* 1732; William[6], *m* Susannah Burge; William[7]; Thomas[8]; William[9], qv);
4–Ruth (1769-1853), *m* Zebedee **Taylor** (4 above).
9–Richard **Nichols** (*d* 1674), of Ipswich, later at Reading; freeman, 1638; *m* Annis– (*d* 1692);
8–Thomas, mem. Amesbury mil. co., 1665; *m* Mary Moulton;
7–John, "snowshoe man," 1708; *m* 1701/02, Abagail Sargent (*b* 1665; William[8], of Gloucester, 1649);
6–William (*b* 1706);
5–William, Am. Rev.; *m* 1749, Miriam Ward;
4–Levi (1763-1817), Am. Rev.; *m* 1788, Eleanor Boutelle (1765-1855; James[5], *m* Elizabeth Smith; James Boutwell[6]; James[7]; James[8]; James[9], qv);
3–Relief (1804-42), *m* George **Taylor** (3 above).
8–Robert **Isbell** (ca. 1620-ca. 1655), of New London, Conn., 1650; *m* Ann– (*d* 1689);
7–Eleazer (ca. 1645-1677), *m* 1668, Elizabeth French (Thomas[8], planter, *m* Mary, dau. John Button);
6–Robert (1675-1718), *m* 1698, Miriam Carter (*d* 1728);
5–Noah (1717-1801), *m* 2d, 1748, Jerusha Ward (Pelatiah[6]; Peter[7]; Andrew[8]; Andrew[9]);
4–Nathan (1765-1839), *m* 1780, Abigail Smith (1764-1830);
3–Nathan (1801-56), *m* 1823, Sophia Jarvis;
2–Sophronia Elvira (2 below).
7–Thomas **Jarvis** (ca. 1640-ca. 1700), at Huntington, L.I., 1670; owned various pieces of real estate;
6–Thomas (1669-1732), *m* 2d, 1726, Abigail Smith;
5–William (1727-72), French and Indian War; weaver; settled at Fly Creek, N.Y.; trustee, town of Huntington; *m* Mary Wright (1730-1804);
4–Dr. Joseph (1752-1806), surgeon Am. Rev.; to New Baltimore, N.Y., 1805; *m* 1783, Abigail Church (*b* 1763);
3–Sophia (1801-72), *m* 1823, Nathan **Isbell** (3 above);
2–Sophronia Elvira (1834-98), *m* 1855, William **Taylor** (1830-85), corpl. in mil. co. against Neb. Indians during Civil War; trustee of tp., Adams Co., Ia., nurseryman; issue: I–Thomas Herbert (*b* 1856; *m* Jettie Hurlbut); II–Frederic William (1 above); III–Alice May (*b* 1861); IV–Hattie Minerva (*b* 1863); V–George Nathan (*b* 1866); VI–Emma Sophronia (*b* 1872); VII–Charles Isbell (*b* 1880).
1–*m* Nov. 5, 1885, Stella Arnold (*b* Dec. 6, 1859-July 9, 1891); dau. of Solomon Brooks Arnold, of Vt.; issue: 1–Jettie Arnold, *b* Creston, Ia., Sept. 24, 1886; *m* Oct. 1, 1915, John Harvey Gray; 2–Herbert Solomon, *b* Omaha, Neb., Feb. 19, 1888; 2d lt., U.S. inf.; 1st lt., 346th M.G. Bn., 91st Div.; with A.E.F. in France over a yr.; cited for bravery; given 3 mo.'s course at U. of London; *m* Dec. 23, 19–, Bonnie Snoke (issue: Richard Warren); 3–Mary Stella, *b* Omaha, June 23, 1891; *m* Aug. 11, 1914, Ruskin M. Lhamon.
1–*m* 2d, Apr. 12, 1898, Marion Treat, *b* Sharon, Wis., Apr. 10, 1869; dau. of Fayette Treat; issue: 1–William Treat, *b* Buffalo, N.Y., Sept. 26, 1900; *m* May 16, 1925, Gladys Buck; 2–George Frederic, *b* Denver, Colo., Mar. 6, 1908.
1–Ed. in horticulture by father. Expert agriculturist. V.p. Am. Rubber Producers, Inc., since 1927. Author (see Who's Who in America). Fellow Royal Geographical Soc., etc. Mem. A.A.A.S.; Officer Legion of Honor (France); Knight of the Order of Jesus Christ (Portugal); Order of the Rising Sun

(Japan); Order of the Crown (Italy). Republican. Conglist. Clubs: Circumnavigators (New York), University (Los Angeles), Authors (London), University (Manila). Residence: 3939 W. 7th St., Los Angeles, Calif.

1-**THAYER, Ernest Wentworth,** *b* Weymouth, Mass., Oct. 10, 1871.
9-Richard **Thayer** (qv);
8-Richard (1625-1705), Braintree, Mass.; soldier in Indian wars; *m* 1651, Dorothy Pray (1634-1705; Quinton[9]);
7-Richard (1655-1729), *m* 1679, Rebecca Micall (*b* 1659; James[8], *m* Mary Farr);
6-John (1688-1768), *m* 1715, Rebecca French (1694-1762; Dependence[7], *m* Rebecca, dau. of John Fenno; John[8];
5-Richard (1727-1800), *m* 1752, Susannah Wild;
4-Barnabas (1759-1833), Weymouth; Am. Rev.; *m* 1781, Lucy Nash (1761-1836; Job[5], *m* Abigail Haynes; Lt. Joseph[6]; Capt. Jacob[7]; James[8]);
3-Josiah (1791-1863), *m* 1817, Mary Colson (1794-1875; Bolter[4], Am. Rev., *m* Sarah, dau. of Josiah Holbrook, Am. Rev.; Thomas[5]; John[6]);
2-Prince Lyman (2 below).
9-John **Hayden,** *m* Susannah-;
8-Samuel, *m* 1664, Hannah Thayer (Richard, 9 above);
7-Sarah (1667-1725), *m* 1689, John **Wild** (*d* 1732);
6-Jonathan (1698-1756), *m* Sarah Randall (John[7], *m* Susanna Benson; John[8]; Robert[9]);
5-Susannah, *m* Richard **Thayer** (5 above).
9-William **Eaton** (1604-73), of Co. Kent, Eng.; settled at Reading, Mass.; *m* Martha Jenkins (*d* 1680);
8-John (*d* 1695), *m* 1668, Elizabeth Kendall (*b* 1642; Thomas[9]; Henry[10]);
7-William (1670-1734), *m* 1695, Mary Swaine (*b* 1674; Dr. Jeremiah[8], *m* Mary, dau. of Lt. John Smith; Jeremiah[9]);
6-Jeremiah (1698-1754), Lynnfield, Mass.; *m* 2d, 1730, Hannah Osgood, of Andover;
5-Jeremiah (1740-91), Haverhill; Am. Rev.; *m* 1761, Lydia Flint (1739-80; Capt. Thomas[6], *m* Priscilla, dau. of Joseph Porter; Thomas[7]; Capt. Thomas[8]; Thomas[9]);
4-Osgood (1770-1830), Westford; *m* 1797, Joanna Leighton (1776-1803; Francis[5], Am. Rev., *m* Lydia Fitch; John[6]; John[7]; John[8]);
3-Osgood (1799-1877), Reading; *m* 1825, Hannah Wentworth;
2-Caroline (2 below).
8-Elder William **Wentworth** (qv);
7-John (*b* ante 1649), of Dover, N.H.; *m* Martha-;
6-Shubael (*d* 1759), Stoughton, Mass.; farmer and blacksmith; *m* 1st, 1717, Damaris Hawes (1696-1739);
5-Sion (1725-76), Canton; blacksmith and large landowner; *m* 1753, Hannah Pettingill (1733-80);
4-David (1763-1855), of Strong, Me.; *m* 1791, Elizabeth Brown (1772-1843);
3-Hannah (1801-71), *m* Osgood **Eaton** (3 above);
2-Caroline (1831-1902), Wilton, Me.; *m* 1856, Prince Lyman **Thayer** (1825-1916), mfr.; issue: I-Abbie Caroline (*b* 1856; *m* 1880, Charles W. Elliot); II-Louis Prince (*b* 1859; *m* Isadora Lee Derby); III-Helen Jeannette (1861-1902; *m* Thomas Purvis); IV-Mary Hannah (1865-68); V-Lizzie Emaline (1868-1920; *m* Dr. William Holyoke); VI-Ernest Wentworth (1 above).
1-*m* Aug. 24, 1898, (Grace) Margaret Harwood (qv for issue).
1-Retired. Mgr. Upland (Calif.) Citrus Assn.; treas. Boyle-Dayton Co., Los Angeles. Mason. Conglist. Republican. Summer place: 1222 East Bay Front, Balboa, Calif. Residence: 953 Elden Av., Los Angeles, Calif.

1-**THAYER, Grace Margaret Harwood (Mrs. Ernest W.),** *b* Springfield, Mo., July 16, 1872.
9-Boniface **Burton** (qv);
8-John (1608-84), Quaker, Salem, Mass.;
7-Isaac (1647-1706), in King Philip's War; *m* Hannah-;
6-Jacob (1688-1770), Preston, Conn.; *m* 2d, 1729, Mary Herrick (*d* 1745);
5-Josiah (1741-1803), capt. Am. Rev.; *m* 1763, Susannah Winans (*b* 1744; James[6], Am. Rev., *m* Sarah Reynolds);
4-John (1764-1822), Albany, N.Y.; *m* 1795, Catherine Eights (1776-1845; Abraham[5], 2d lt., Am. Rev., *m* Catherine Brooks);
3-Stephen (1813-89), Blandford, Mass.; *m* 1835, Charlotte Jackson;
2-Margaret Jane (2 below).
9-Edward **Jackson** (qv);
8-Sebas (1642-90), Cambridge, Mass.; in King Philip's War; *m* 1671, Sarah Baker (1650-1726; Thomas[9]);
7-Edward (1672-1748), in Indian war, 1722; *m* ca. 1695, Mary Newton;
6-Edward (1698-1738), *m* 1720, Abigail Gale (Abraham[7], *m* Sarah Fiske);
5-Abraham (1721-1807), Am. Rev.; *m* 1745, Mary Hyde (1728-68; Timothy[6]);
4-Ezra (1764-1834), *m* 1787, Mary Woodward (1767-1852; Caleb[5], *m* Hannah Cheever; Abraham[6]; George[7]; George[8]; Richard[9], qv);
3-Charlotte (1812-68), *m* Stephen **Burton** (3 above);
2-Margaret Jane (1842-1915), of Crystal Lake, Ill.; *m* 1864, Alfred Perez **Harwood** (1838-1929); for issue and Harwood lineage see Mrs. Butler Ames Woodford.
1-*m* Aug. 24, 1898, Ernest Wentworth Thayer (qv); issue: 1-Alfred Harwood, *b* Kansas City, Mo., June 10, 1899; A.B., Stanford U., '21, E.E., 1922; *m* Oct. 1, 1926, Marian Elizabeth, dau. of Watson Vernon, of Aberdeen, Wash. (issue: Margaret Harwood, *b* 1927); 2-William Lyman, *b* Upland, Calif., July 26, 1901; A.B., Stanford, '25, E.E., 1926; *m* Mar. 25, 1925, Arlene Vivian, dau. of Simeon Joseph White, of Pomona, Calif. (issue: William Wentworth, *b* 1926; Jean Beatrice, *b* 1928).
1-Pomona Coll., ex-'97. Mem. C.D.A., D.F.P.A. (pres. Calif. Soc., 1925-26), D.A.C., D.C.W., D.A.R. (chapter regent, 1920-21), I.A.G., N.E.-H.G.S. (life). Clubs: Women's Athletic, Friday Morning (Los Angeles), Friday Afternoon (Ontario). Residence: 953 Elden Av., Los Angeles, Calif.

1-**WOODFORD, Emma Burton Harwood (Mrs. Butler A.),** *b* Crystal Lake, Ill., Sept. 23, 1865.
9-George **Harwood,** 1st treas. Mass. Co.;
8-Nathaniel (1626-1716), from Eng.; settled at Boston; in Concord, Mass., 1665; *m* Elizabeth-(*d* 1715);
7-Peter (1671-1740), *m* 1700, Mary Fox (1673-1742; Eliphalet[8], *m* Mary Wheeler);
6-Benjamin (1713-58), *m* 1733, Bridget Brown (1715-62; Eleazer[7], *m* Abigail, dau. Roger Chandler);
5-Zachariah (1742-1821), of Bennington, Vt.; served in Battle of Bennington; *m* 1767, Lovina Rice (1751-1808; Oliver[6], Am. Rev., *m* Hannah Barret, or Bartlett; Charles[7]; Thomas[8]; Thomas[9]; Edmund[10], qv);
4-Perez (1772-1859), *m* 1791, Lucinda Finch (1773-1844; Joshua[5], Am. Rev., *m* Reuhamah Brewer);
3-Hiram (1799-1891), *m* 1830, Eliza Haswell (1800-99; Anthony[4], Am. Rev.);
2-Alfred Perez **Harwood** (1838-1929), *m* 1864, Margaret Jane Burton (1842-1915); issue: I-Emma Burton (1 above); II-Maria Louise (1867-68); III-Mary Lillian (1869-76); IV-Grace Margaret (Mrs. Ernest W. Thayer, qv for maternal lineages); V-Alfred James (1874-90); VI-Frank Haswell (*b* 1875; *m* Mildred Allen Spencer).
1-*m* May 8, 1889, Butler Ames Woodford (qv); issue (all *b* Upland, Calif.): 1-Alfred Oswald, *b* Feb. 27, 1890; B.A., Pomona Coll., '13; Ph.D., U. of Calif., 1923; *m* Feb. 21, 1929, Gwendolyn, dau. of Ralph Waldo Green, of Seattle, Wash.; 2-Mary Lillian, *b* Aug. 7, 1892; B.A., Pomona, '15; Wellesley, 1917; 3-Marjorie Burton, *b* Sept. 23, 1894; B.A., Pomona, '16; M.A., Columbia U., 1918; 4-James Beach, *b* Dec. 29, 1899; ed. U. of Calif.; *m* Oct. 27, 1923, Margaret Jane, dau. of Harry D. Roe, of Claremont, Calif. (issue: James Beach, Jr.); 5-Katharine Louise, *b* July 30, 1902; B.A., Pomona, '25; *m* Aug. 31, 1928, Warner, son of L. J. Bentley, of Claremont, Calif.
1-Mem. D.A.C., D.F.P.A., C.D.A., D.C.W., D.A.R. Residence: 639 Yale Av., Claremont, Calif.

1-**WOODFORD, Butler Ames,** *b* West Avon, Conn., Apr. 22, 1860.
8-Thomas **Woodford** (qv);
7-Joseph (*d* 1701), Farmington, Conn.; *m* Rebecca Newell (1643-1700; Thomas[8], *m* Rebecca Olmstead);
6-Joseph (1676-1760), *m* 1st, 1699, Lydia Smith (*b* 1684; Joseph[7], *m* Lydia-; William[8]);

5–Joseph (*b* 1705), *m* 1728, Sarah North (1711-77; Thomas[6], *m* Martha, dau. of Isaac Roys, Thomas[7]; John[8]);
4–Isaac (1753-1831), Avon, Conn.; *m* 1774, Sarah Fuller (1754-1822);
3–Zerah (1794-1881), War 1812; *m* 1820, Minerva Potter;
2–Oswald Langdon (2 below).
9–Gov. John **Webster** (qv);
8–Lt. Robert (1627-76), Hartford, *m* 1652, Susanna Treat (1629-1705);
7–John (1653-94), Middletown, Conn.; *m* Sarah Mygatt (Jacob[8]; Joseph[9]);
6–Capt. John (1680-1753), Southington, Conn.; *m* 1712, Abiel Steele;
5–Susannah (*b* 1728), Hartford; *m* 1746, Ebenezer **Scott** (1723-78);
4–Jerusha (*b* 1753), *m* Philemon **Potter** (*b* 1754);
3–Minerva (1796-1871), *m* Zerah **Woodford** (3 above).
9–Gov. William **Bradford,** Mayflower Pilgrim (qv);
8–Maj. William (1624-1704), *m* 1651, Alice Richards;
7–Mercy (1660-1720), *m* 1680, Samuel **Steele** (1652-1709/10; John[8]);
6–Abiel (*b* 1693), *m* 1st, 1712, Capt. John **Webster** (6 above).
9–Richard **Butler** (qv);
8–Thomas (1637-88), Hartford; *m* 1658, Sarah Stone (Rev. Samuel[9], *m* Elizabeth Allen);
7–Thomas (1661-1725), *m* 1691, Abigail Shepherd (1665-1750; John[8], *m* Rebecca, dau. of Samuel Greenhill; Edward[9]);
6–Isaac (1693-1777), Waterbury; grad. Yale, 1722; *m* 1722, Sarah Marshfield (*d* 1753);
5–Samuel (1726-98), Norfolk; Am. Rev.; *m* 1751, Mary Goodwin (*b* 1729; Stephen[6], *m* Sarah, dau. of Joseph Gillet; Nathaniel[7]; William[8]; Ozias[9]);
4–Hezekiah (1761-1846), *m* Hepzibah Burr (1768-1842; Oliver[5], *m* Sarah Canfield; Ebenezer[6]; John[7]; Samuel[8]; Benjamin[9]);
3–Dr. Elizur (1794-1854), *m* 2d, 1830, Lucy Ames (1793-1870; Eli[4], *m* Eunice, dau. of Samuel Parker; Amos[5]; Samuel[6]; Robert[7]; Robert[8]);
2–Esther Post (1831-1905), *m* 1859, as his 2d wife, Oswald Langdon **Woodford** (1827-70), minister and missionary, West Avon, Conn.; issue: I–Butler Ames (1 above); II–Abbie Marean (*b* 1861); III–Kittie (1866-69); IV–Esther Minerva (*b* 1867).
1–*m* May 8, 1889, Emma Burton Harwood (qv for issue).
1–Retired. Manager Upland Lemon Growers' Exchange, Ontario-Cucamonga Fruit Exchange, and gen. mgr. Calif. Fruit Growers' Exchange. Trustee First Nat. Bank, Claremont, Calif., Pomona Coll., La Verne Fruit Exchange, La Verne Orange Assn. Club: Red Hill Country. Conglist. Republican. Residence: 639 Yale Av., Claremont, Calif.

1–**THAYER, John Eliot,** *b* Boston, Mass., Apr. 3, 1862.
9–William **Colburn,** came with Sir Richard Saltonstall, 1630; *m* Margery–;
8–May, as widow of John Barrell, *m* 2d, 1659, as his 2d wife, Daniel (Turrell) **Turell** (*d* Jan. 23, 1699), from Eng., to Mass., settled at Boston, removed to Medford; capt. Boston militia, 1653;
7–Samuel (1659-1738), *m* Lydia Stoddard (Anthony[8]);
6–Lydia, *m* as his 2d wife, Cornelius **Thayer** (*b* 1684), see Vol. I, p. 855, for Thayer lineage;
5–Nathaniel (*b* 1710), *m* 1733, Ruth Eliot;
4–Rev. Ebenezer (1734-92), grad. Harvard, 1753; minister at Hampton, N.H., 26 yrs.; *m* Martha Cotton;
3–Rev. Nathaniel (1769-1840), mem. 1st graduating class of Phillips Exeter Acad.; grad. Harvard, 1789; educator, clergyman; *m* 1795, Sarah Parker Toppan (*b* 1775);
2–Nathaniel (2 below).
8–Andrew (Aliot) **Eliot** (qv);
7–Andrew (1650-88), of Beverly; drowned off Cape Sable, Sept. 12, 1688; *m* 1680, Mercy (Shattuck) Trask (1655-1710);
6–Andrew (1683-1749), mcht., Boston; lost much of his property in the great Cornhill fire, 1711; *m* 2d, 1707, Mary Herrick (1675-1760);
5–Ruth (1711-46), *m* Nathaniel **Thayer** (5 above).
8–John **Cotton** (qv);
7–John (1639/40-1669), A.B., Harvard, 1657; minister at Wethersfield, Haddam, and Killingworth, Conn., and Edgarton, Mass.; removed to Charleston, S.C., 1697; *m* 1660, Joanna Rosseter (1642-1712; Dr. Briah [Brian, Bray, Bryor][8], freeman, Dorchester, 1631, physician, *m* Elizabeth Alsop; Edward[9], qv);
6–Rev. Roland (1667-1721/22), grad. Harvard, 1685; minister Sandwich, Mass., 1694-1721, *m* 1692, Elizabeth (Saltonstall) Denison;
5–John (1693-1757), minister, Newton, 1714-57; *m* 1719, Mary Gibbs (1699-1761; Robert[6]);
4–Martha (1727-1809), *m* Ebenezer **Thayer** (4 above).
9–Sir Richard **Saltonstall** (qv);
8–Richard (1610-94), dep. Mass. Bay Colony, 1633-37; asst.; sgt.-maj., Essex Regt., 1641; *m* Muriel Gurdon;
7–Col. Nathaniel (*d* 1707), asst., 1679-86; col., 1680; councillor, 1689; judge, 1692; commr., 1683; *m* Elizabeth Ward;
6–Elizabeth (*d* 1726), *m* Roland **Cotton** (6 above).
2–Nathaniel **Thayer** (1808-83), founder of firm of John E. Thayer & Bros., bankers; benefactor of Harvard Coll.; *m* June 10, 1846, Cornelia Patterson Van Rensselaer (1808-83), see Vol. I, p. 855, for Van Rensselaer lineage and issue.
1–*m* June 22, 1886, Evelyn Duncan Forbes, *b* Clinton, Mass.; dau. of Franklin Forbes; issue (all *b* Lancaster, Mass.): 1–John Eliot, Jr., *b* Aug. 19, 1887; Harvard, '10; *m* April 6, 1911, Katherine Bayard, dau. of Samuel Warren, of Boston; 2–Evelyn, *b* Aug. 1, 1888; *m* Oct. 4, 1913, Isaac Tucker Burr, Jr.; 3–Nora Forbes, *b* Sept. 6, 1889; *m* Jan. 2, 1913, Francis Abbot Goodhue (see Vol. I, p. 293); 4–Natalie, *b* Mar. 24, 1895; *m* Dec. 12, 1917, Lawrence Hemenway (see Vol. I, p. 23); 5–Duncan Forbes, *b* Feb. 14, 1900; Harvard, '23.
1–A.B., Harvard '85 (A.M., 1910). Formerly pres. 1st Nat. Bank of Clinton; chmn. selectmen Town of Lancaster. Hobby: Ornithology; has built a mus. in Lancaster, open to the public, containing one of the most complete collections of specimens of N. Am. birds extant (see Who's Who in America). Clubs: Harvard (of New York), Somerset, Algonquin, Myopia Hunt, Harvard, The Country. Residence: Lancaster, Mass.

DAVID R. THOMAS (1839-1912).

1–**THOMAS, Lowell (Jackson),** *b* Woodington, O., Apr. 6, 1892.
5–David **Thomas** (1765-1847), of Bucks Co., Pa.; *m* Elizabeth Weaver;
4–Charles (1797-1872), Hollansburg, O.; soldier War 1812; *m* 1824, Mercy Sackett;
3–David R. (1839-1912), 44th Ohio Vol. Cav., Civil War (see portrait); *m* 1861, Pheriba Jackson (1841-1921);

2–Harry George (2 below).
10–Simon **Sackett** (*d* 1635), from Eng. in the "Lyon"; landed off Boston, Feb. 5, 1631; settled at Newtown, Mass.; *m* Isabel–;
9–John (1632-1719), *m* 1659, Abigail Hannum (1640-90);
8–William (1662-1700), Westfield, Mass.; *m* 1689, Hannah Graves;
7–Jonathan (1696-1773), *m* 1725, Ann Files;
6–Reuben (1732-1803), Greenwich, Conn.; *m* 1752, Mercy Finney;
5–Cyrus (*b* 1764), Am. Rev.; in St. Clair's campaign against the Indians of the northwest, 1791; *m* 1792, Nancy Stapleton (*d* 1859);
4–Mercy (*b* 1797), *m* Charles **Thomas** (4 above);
3–David R., *m* Pheriba Jackson (3 above);
2–Harry George (*b* 1869), physician Asbury Park, N.J.; lt. col. M.C., A.E.F., 1916-20; with Army of Occupation after the Armistice; *m* 1890, Harriet May Wagner (*b* 1869); issue: I–Lowell Jackson (1 above); II–Helen; III–Pheriba.
1–*m* Aug. 4, 1917, Frances Ryan, *b* Dec. 7, 1894; dau. of Harry Philip Ryan, of Denver, Colo.; issue: 1–Lowell Jackson, *b* London, Eng., Oct. 5, 1923.
1–B.S., U. of Northern Ind., '11; B.A., M.A., U. of Denver, 1912; M.A., Princeton, 1916. Author, lecturer, explorer and editor. Chief of civilian mission sent to Europe by Pres. Wilson to prepare historical record of World War; attached in turn to Belgian, French, Italian, Serbian, American, British, and Arabian armies; made historical and pictorial record of German revolution and reported to Peace Conference. Asso. editor Asia Magazine, 1919-23 (see Who's Who in America). Fellow Am. Geog. Soc., Royal Geog. Soc.; hon. life mem. English-Speaking Union. Clubs: Princeton, Explorers, Advertising (New York). Residence: "Clover Brook," Pawling, N.Y.

1–**THOMAS, Marie Louise Wade (Mrs. Sewell),** *b* St. Louis, Mo., Sept. 17, 1886.
9–Sir Philip **Bigoe** (*d* 1631), Huguenot; glass mfr. with glasshouses at Newton, Tuamagh Parish, Gloster, glasshouse nr. Shinrone, Port Arlington, and Newton nr. Neagh, Co. Tipperary, Ireland;
8–Catherine, *m* Ananias **Henzell** (*d* 1676?), Huguenot, from France to Ireland;
7–Bigoe, of Barnagrathy in Kings County; capt. in army of King William, III, served 5 yrs.; *m* Rebecca, dau. of Capt. John Andrews;
6–Philip, *m* Miss Armstrong, dau. of Robert Armstrong;
5–Catherine Armstrong (*d* 1815), *m* 1770, Dan **Cualahan** (*d* 1796), of Kings County;
4–Mary (1775-1841), *m* 1815, Festus **McDonough**;
3–Catherine (1818-93), *m* Thomas **Wade** (1816-91; James[4], of Ireland, *m* 2d, Jane Gilsenan);
2–Festus John (1859-1927), was brought to America, 1860; banker; pres. Anderson-Wade Realty Co., 1888-99 (see Who's Who in America, Vol. 14); *m* 1883, Katherine V. Kennedy (*d* 1929); issue: I–Stella (*b* 1884; *m* Lee Petit Warren); II–Marie Louise (1 above); III–Florence Josephine (*b* 1889); IV–Festus John, Jr. (*b* 1899; *m* Catherine L. Crunden).
1–*m* Apr. 10, 1912, (Charles) Sewell Thomas (see Vol. III, p. 577); issue: 1–Lenore Marie, *b* Denver, Colo., Dec. 26, 1922.
1–Ed. Georgetown Visitation Convent. Mem. Junior League. Residence: 380 Gilpin St., Denver, Colo.

1–**THOMAS, Augusta Annie Dillman (Mrs. Thomas Lewis),** *b* Pottsville, Pa., Nov. 28, 1872.
7–Christopher **Kalbach,** from Germany, 1750, settled in Tulpehocken Tp., Berks Co., Pa.;
6–Adam (*d* 1801), *m* Anna Maria–;
5–Susanna, *m* Anthony **Dillman,** of Brunswick Tp., Berks Co., Pa.;
4–Capt. Peter (1781-1858), Fountain Springs, Pa.; capt. 149th Regt., 2d Brig., 6th Div., Pa. Militia, War 1812; lumberman and farmer; *m* 1806, Susanna Kraus (1786-1879; George[5]);
3–Daniel Kraus (1809-92), Llewellyn, Pa.; capt. of a canal boat; school teacher; mine foreman; farmer; Republican; *m* 1835, Catherine Dunkelberger (1814-88; Jacob[4], *m* Magdelina Schneider);
2–Daniel Dunkelberger (2 below).
6–Hans Dieter (Bauman) **Bowman** (*d* 1761), from Germany, 1727, settled at Hosensack, Marlborough Tp., Phila. Co., Pa.; contributed to the cause of the colonies in the Colonial wars; *m* Eve Elizabeth–;
5–Capt. Heinrich (1751-1824), capt. Northampton Co., Pa., militia, and ranger of the frontier in Am. Rev.; *m* 1770, Catherine Dreisbach (1754-1825; Col. Jost[6], mem. Pa. Com. of Observation during Am. Rev., and Northampton Co. militia);
4–Maj. John Dieter (1773-1853), War 1812; co. commr. of Carbon Co., Pa.; owned vast lands and was a contractor, builder and lumberman; *m* 1796, Margarethe Newhard (*d* 1854; Peter[5], *m* Catherine, dau. of Jacob Miller, Am. Rev.);
3–Peter (1814-1901), Mahanoy City, Pa.; began to write name Bowman; first treas. of Carbon Co.; mem. Pa. Legislature 2 yrs.; contractor and coal operator many yrs.; Mason; *m* 1840, Polly Romich (1820-65; Conrad[4], *m* Catherine Minnich);
2–Isabel Catherine (*b* 1841), attended Arcadian Inst., Orwigsburg, Pa., and Miss Allen's School for Girls, Pottsville; mem. D.R., U.S.D. 1812; *m* 1869, Daniel Dunkelberger **Dillman** (1836-72), grad. Poughkeepsie Law Sch.; school teacher; lawyer; traveled to Calif. by way of Cape Horn, 1864, but finally returned, settling at Pottsville; chmn. Rep. Co. Com., 1872; served in Co. H, 6th Pa. Vols., and 2d Regt., Pa. Militia, 1862; corpl. 27th Regt. Vol. Militia, 1863; mem. G.A.R., Odd Fellow, Mason, etc.; issue: I–Daniel Walter (*b* 1869); II–Robert John (1871-76); III–Augusta Annie (1 above).
1–*m* Feb. 21, 1901, Thomas Lewis Thomas, *b* Duncott, Minersville, Schuylkill Co., Pa., May 11, 1861; Mason, Odd Fellow, son of Henry Thomas, (1819-85), of Mahanoy City, Schuylkill Co., Pa., from Wales, *m* Mary Lewis (1832-1913); issue (all *b* Mahanoy City, Pa.): 1–Augusta Dillman (*b* and *d* Nov. 24, 1901); 2–Muriel Isabel, *b* Mar. 3, 1904; B.A., Swarthmore, '25; M.A., Radcliffe, 1926; teacher of English, in Mahanoy City High School; mem. D.A.R., D.R., U.S.D. 1812, College Club of Phila., A.A.U.W.; 3–Harold Lewis (Dec. 18-Dec. 28, 1905); 4–Vivian Mary, *b* June 20, 1908; Bancroft School; Wilson Coll., 2 yrs.; A.B., Smith, '30; mem. D.R., U.S.D. 1812.
1–B.E. and M.E., West Chester Teachers Coll., '93. Taught primary grades of Mahanoy City Public Schools 7 yrs., and 1 yr. in grammar grade. Chmn. Mahanoy City Chapter A.R.C., 1917-1920. Mem. D.R., D.A.R., U.S.D. 1812, I.A.G., Patriotic Order of True Americans, Rebekah. Episcopalian. Republican. Summer place: Asbury Park, N.J. Residence: 420 E. Mahanoy Av., Mahanoy City, Pa.

1–**THOMPSON, Norman Frederick,** *b* Perry, Ga., June 27, 1856.
9–Anthony **Thompson** (qv);
8–John (1632-1707), New Haven, Conn.; *m* 1656, Ann Vickers (George[9], *m* Rebecca, dau. of David Phiffeny, at Boston, 1650, *m* Sarah–);
7–Capt. Samuel (1669-1749), *m* 1695, Rebecca Bishop (1673-1734; Hon. James[8], *m* 2d, Elizabeth, dau. of Micah Tompkins);
6–Dea. Gideon (1704-59), Goshen, Conn.; *m* 1729, Lydia Punderson;
5–David (1731-1807), Poultney, Vt.; *m* 1760, Hannah Griswold;
4–Judge Amos (1771-1849), *m* 1796-98, Dotha Brace;
3–Norman Brace (1801-74), Rockford, Ill.; *m* 1827, Seraph Howe Ruggles;
2–Norman Cornelius (2 below).
9–John **Punderson** (*d* 1681), from Eng., settled at New Haven; *m* Margaret–;
8–Dea. John (1643-1729), *m* 1667, Damaris Atwater (1648-1711; David[9], qv);
7–Thomas (1678-1742), *m* 1704, Lydia Bradley (1685-1757; Dea. Abraham[8]; William[9], qv);
6–Lydia (1708-1802), *m* Dea. Gideon **Thompson** (6 above).
9–Edward **Griswold** (qv);
8–George (*d* 1704), Windsor, Conn.; *m* 1665, Mary Holcomb (*d* 1708; Thomas[9], *m* Elizabeth–);
7–Benjamin (*b* 1671), *m* 1693, Elizabeth Cook (*b* 1673; Moses[8], *m* Elizabeth, dau. of Daniel Clark, qv; Maj. Aaron[9], qv);

6–Zacheus (*b* 1705), *m* 1728, Mary Griswold (1707-1806; Francis[7]; Joseph[8]; Edward[9], qv);
5–Hannah (1739-1826), *m* David **Thompson** (5 above).
10–Gov. John **Webster** (qv);
9–Lt. Robert (1627-76), Hadley, Mass.; *m* ca. 1652, Susanna Treat (bap. 1629-1705; Richard[10], qv);
8–Dea. Jonathan (1657-1735), *m* 1681, Dorcas Hopkins (*d* 1694; Stephen[9]; John[10]);
7–Mary (bap. 1688), Harwinton, Conn.; *m* 1705/06, John **Brace** (*b* 1677; Stephen[8], from Eng., settled at Hartford, ca. 1660);
6–Elisha (ca. 1710-ca. 1751-52), *m* Jerusha–;
5–Elisha (1745-1807), Harwinton; *m* Irene Catlin (1744-94; Isaac[6]; Samuel[7]; John[8]; Thomas[9], qv);
4–Dotha (1780-1817), *m* Judge Amos **Thompson** (4 above).
9–Thomas **Ruggles** (1584-1644; son of Thomas); from Eng., settled at Roxbury; *m* 1620, Mary Curtis (ca. 1586-1674/75; William[10]);
8–Capt. Samuel (1629-92), *m* 1655, Hannah Fowle (1640-69; George[9]);
7–Capt. Samuel (1658-1715/16), *m* 1680, Martha Woodbridge (ca. 1660-1738; Rev. John[8], qv);
6–Rev. Timothy (1685-1768), Rochester, Mass.; *m* 1710, Mary White (1688-1749; Benjamin[7]; John[8]);
5–Capt. Benjamin (1713-90), Hardwick, Mass.; *m* 1736, Alice Merrick (Nathaniel[6]; Ens. William[7]; Lt. William[8]);
4–Thomas (bap. 1750-1808), Oakham, Mass.; *m* 1778, Hannah Winslow (1761-1832; Thomas[5]; Col. Thomas[6]; Kenelm[7]; Kenelm[8]; Kenelm[9], qv);
3–Seraph Howe (1806-74), *m* Norman Brace **Thompson** (3 above).
8–William **Blackmer** (*d* 1676), from Eng., settled at Scituate; killed by Indians; *m* Elizabeth Banks;
7–Peter (1667-1717), Rochester, Mass.; *m* Elizabeth– (ca. 1673-1711);
6–William (*b* 1699), Ware, Mass.; *m* Sarah–;
5–William (1736-1822), Barnard, Vt.; *m* Lydia Record (1738-1820);
4–Solomon (1767-1813), *m* 1796, Miriam Benedict;
3–Hiram (1801-85), Rockford, Ill.; *m* 1822, Phoebe R. Townsend;
2–Laurentia J. (2 below).
10–Thomas **Benedict** (*b* 1617), of Eng.; *m* Mary Bridgman;
9–Samuel, Norwalk, Conn.; *m* 2d, 1678, Rebecca Andrews (Thomas[10], of Fairfield, Conn.);
8–Nathaniel, *m* Sarah–;
7–John;
6–John, of Kent, Conn.; *m* Lucy– (*d* 1794);
5–Samuel (1744-1820), *m* 1771, Mary Dibble (1746-1825; Lt. John[6]; Wakefield[7]; Ebenezer[8]; Thomas[9]);
4–Miriam (1775-1834), *m* Solomon **Blackmer** (4 above).
9–Thomas **Townsend** (qv);
8–John (1640-1726), Lynn, Mass.; *m* 1668, Sarah Pearson (*d* 1689; John[9]);
7–George, Taunton; *m* 1705, Elizabeth Crane (*b* 1663; John[8]; Henry[9], qv);
6–George (*d* 1749), *m* Margaret–;
5–Job (1739-1820), Barnard, Vt.; *m* 1768, Phoebe Richmond (1741-1817; Josiah[6]; Josiah[7]; Edward[8]; John[9]; John[10], qv);
4–George (1769-1843), Taunton; *m* Polly Richmond (1766-1857; Lemuel[5]; Josiah[6]; Edward[7]; John[8]; John[9], qv);
3–Phoebe R. (1801-82), *m* Hiram **Blackmer** (3 above);
2–Laurentia J. (1832-1917), *m* 1853, Norman Cornelius **Thompson** (1828-98), Yale, ex-'49; banker and mfr., Rockford, Ill.; issue: I–Norman Frederick (1 above); II–Arthur Edward (*d*); III–Norma Cornelia; IV–Amos Lawrence.
1–*m* Jan. 10, 1883, Adaline Eliza Emerson, *b* Aug. 13, 1859; dau. of late Ralph Emerson, and sister of Mrs. William E. Hinchliff (see Vol. I, p. 358); issue (all *b* Rockford, Ill.): 1–Norman Frederick, Jr. (see Vol. I, p. 952); 2–Ralph Emerson, *b* Feb. 1, 1888; Yale-S., '09; *m* 1911, Emma Missouri Moffett (issue: Gretchen Adaline; Ralph Emerson, Jr.; Harris Barnum); 3–Adalyn (Dec. 4, 1889-Feb. 5, 1915); *m* Alan C. Dixon.
1–B.A., Yale, '81 (Delta Kappa, He Boule, D.K.E., Skull and Bones). Chmn. bd. Manufacturers Nat. Bank & Trust Co., Rockford, Ill. Mem. S.M.D., S.C.W., B.O.R., I.A.G. Clubs: University (Chicago), University, Rockford Country, Elks, Harlem Hills, Mid-Day. Residence: 427 N. Church St., Rockford, Ill.

1–**LATHROP, Mary Emerson (Mrs. Edward Potter),** *b* Rockford, Ill., Apr. 6, 1863.
9–John **Talcott** (qv);
8–Capt. Samuel (1635-91), *m* 1661, Hannah Holyoke (Elizur[9]);
7–Dea. Benjamin (1674-1727), *m* 1st, Sarah Hollister (John Jr.[8]);
6–Capt. Samuel (1708-68), *m* 1732, Hannah Moseley;
5–William (1742-1807), officer Am. Rev.; *m* Mary Carter;
4–Capt. William (1784-1864), War 1812; *m* Dorothy Blish (desc. Edward Fuller, Mayflower Pilgrim);
3–Wait (1807-90), *m* Elizabeth Anna Norton;
2–Adaline Elizabeth (1837-1915), *m* 1858, Ralph **Emerson** (1831-1914), prominent mfr., financier and philanthropist, Rockford, Ill. (for issue and other lineages, see Mrs. William E. Hinchliff, Vol. I, p. 358).
1–*m* Edward Potter Lathrop.
Residence: 105 Douglas St., Rockford, Ill.

1–**THOMISON, Maude,** *b* Dayton, Tenn., Apr. 18, 1891.
5–John **Thomison**;
4–John (*d* 1812), of Fincastle, Va.; *m* 1809, Nancy Preston (John[5], of Fincastle, Botetourt Co., Va.);
3–William Preston (*b* 1812), *m* 1836, Nancy Smith;
2–Walter Farfield (2 below).
5–Absolom **Smith** (1753-1827), of Madison Co. and Salem, Va.; *m* Mary Phillips;
4–John (*b* 1779), *m* Rhoda Pates, of Va.;
3–Nancy (*b* 1816), of Salem, Va.; *m* William Preston **Thomison** (3 above);
5–William **Darwin** (*b* 1762), of S.C.; *m* 1792, Jane Adams, of S.C.;
4–Thomas A., of Madison Co., Ala.; *m* 1816, Susanah White Clements;
3–Capt. William Perry (1830-94), of Evensville, Tenn.; *m* Adelia Gillespie;
2–Ella (2 below).
8–Rev. George **Gillespie** (*b* 1618), from Scotland to Westminister Assembly, 1643;
7–George, *m* Elizabeth Duval, came to America from Scotland, 1740;
6–Col. George, *m* Elizabeth Allen, of Va.;
5–Col. George, *m* Anne Neilson (William[6], *m* Jane Lewis; Thomas[7], *m* Elizabeth Douglas in Scotland, came to America, 1740);
4–Robert, *m* Hannah Luty;
3–Adelia, *m* William Perry **Darwin** (3 above);
2–Ella (*b* 1874), mem. U.D.C.; *m* 1890, Walter Farfield **Thomison** (*b* 1859), physician Dayton; issue: I–Maude (1 above); II–Clara (*b* 1894; *m* P.J. Broun); III–Dr. Walter A. (*b* 1898; *m* Shirley Gaskins).
1–Ed. Campbell-Hagerman Coll., Lexington, Ky., Ward Seminary, Nashville, Tenn. Mem. I.A.G. Presbyterian. Residence: Dayton, Tenn.

1–**THRELKELD, Hansford Lee,** *b* Union Co., Ky., Feb. 17, 1868.
6–William **Threlkeld** (*d* 1766), from Eng., settled in King George Co., Va.; *m* Ruth–;
5–Benjamin (*d* 1794), Culpeper Co., Va., and Mason Co., Ky.; *m* ca. 1767, Ann Booth (1749-1828; James[6], of King George Co., *m* Ellen–);
4–Daniel (1773-1828), Union Co., Ky.; *m* 1796, Delilah Nichols (John[5], Mason Co., Ky.);
3–James (1805-89), *m* 1830, Mary Simms Peters;
2–Uriel Hansford (2 below).
7–Henry **Floyd** (*b* ca. 1695), from Wales, settled in Prince William Co., Va.;
6–Henry (ca. 1720-1816), sgt. Am. Rev.; *m* Ann Helm (*d* 1805);
5–Lt. Henry Helm (1761-ca. 1850), pvt. Am. Rev.; lt. under George Rogers Clark, in the conquest of Illinois; *m* 1783, Frances Crosby, of Fauquier Co., Va. (George[6], of Fauquier Co.);
4–Elizabeth Crosby (*b* 1790), *m* John **Peters,** of Union Co.;
3–Mary Simms (1813-84), *m* James **Threlkeld** (3 above);
6–William Tarlton **Taylor** (ca. 1738-ca. 1804);
5–William Tarlton (1759-1811), Am. Rev.; *m* 1778, Elizabeth Hampton;

4–John Hampton (*b* 1782), Loudoun Co., Va.; *m* Joanna Weeks;
3–William Tarlton (1808-69), *m* 1831, Jane Day (1814-97);
2–Mary Catherine (1840-1926), *m* 1859, Uriel Hansford **Threlkeld** (1833-1916), farmer, Union Co., Ky.; pvt. 10th Ky. Partisan Rangers under Gen. Adam Johnson, dea. Bapt. Ch.; Mason; issue: I–Sue Emma (*b* 1863; *m* Len M. Daniel); II–Ella Mathers (*b* 1866; *m* William N. Menifee); III–Hansford Lee (1 above); IV–Mary Elizabeth (*b* 1870); V–James Preston (*b* 1872; *m* Mary Allison Waller); VI–Bertha Taylor (*b* 1874; *m* Daniel F. Shacklett); VII–William Thomas (*b* 1877; *m* Georgia Powell); VIII–Louis Posey (*b* 1880; *m* Jennie Roberts); IX–Polk Laffoon (*b* 1886; *m* Willie Belle "Pollye" Mauney).
1–*m* Feb. 26, 1902, Bettie Berry Waller, *b* Morganfield, Ky., Aug. 3, 1870; dau. of Thomas Small Waller, of Morganfield; issue: 1–Thomas Waller, *b* Ft. Crook, Neb., Jan. 22, 1905; A.B., Vanderbilt, '27; LL.B., Vanderbilt Law School, 1929.
1–Grad. U.S.M.A., '92; distinguished grad., Army School of the Line, 1910; grad. Army Staff Coll., 1911, Army War Coll., 1917. Served in Spanish-Am. War in Cuba, at Battle of San Juan Hill, and at siege and surrender of Santiago (citation with silver star) served in Philippine Campaign, and in the World War in France; retired from active service as col., July 14, 1920, at own request after more than 33 years' service. V.p. and dir. Union Co. Building & Loan Assn. Dea. Baptist Ch. Democrat. Mem. S.A.R., I.A.G., Ky. Hist. Soc., U.S. Inf. Assn., Assn. of Grads. U.S.M.A., Filson Club. Residence: Morganfield, Ky.

1–**THROCKMORTON, Alice Grandin,** *b* Jersey City, N.J., Oct. 30, 1875.
9–John **Throckmorton** (qv);
8–Job (1650-1709), *m* 1684/85, Sarah Leonard (1663-1743/44; Henry[9], *m* Mary–);
7–Judge John (1688-1741), *m* 1712, Mary Stillwell (1690-1739; Capt. Jeremiah[8]);
6–Joseph (1720-1800), *m* 1747, Mary Forman;
5–James (1754-1838), Am. Rev.; *m* 1783, Frances Barberie (1756-1813; John[6], *m* Gertrude Johnson; Peter[7]; John[8]);
4–Thomas Coffin (1784-1868), War 1812; *m* 1808, Elizabeth Craig;
3–Barberie (1813-70), *m* 1840, Sarah Maria Grandin;
2–Barberie Woodburn (2 below).
10–Robert (Foreman) **Forman** (ca. 1605-1671; son of Rev. William), to Holland from Eng., one of 45 patentees of Flushing, L.I.; magistrate, Hempstead; *m* Johanna– (*b* in Holland);
9–Aaron (*b* 1637), *m* Dorothy–;
8–Samuel (1662-1740), commd. high sheriff of Monmouth Co., 1695; *m* 1683/84, Mary Wilbur;
7–Capt. John (1701-48), *m* Jane Wyckoff;
6–Mary (1725-66), *m* Joseph **Throckmorton** (6 above).
10–Samuel (Wilbore) **Wilbur** (qv);
9–Samuel (*d* 1679), from Eng., 1633; capt., 1669; gov.'s asst., 1665,66,77,78; dep. Gen. Assembly, 1664-65, 1669-70; commr.; *m* Hannah Porter (John[10], from Eng., 1633, a founder of R.I., *m* Margaret Odding, widow);
8–Mary (1667-1728), *m* Samuel **Forman** (8 above).
8–John **Craig**, *m* Ursula–;
7–Archibald (1678-1751), *m* Mary–;
6–William (1727-1806), *m* Eleanor Rhea (1733-1807);
5–Maj. James, ens. Am. Rev.; *m* Esther Rhea (1758-1838);
4–Elizabeth (1791-1863), *m* Thomas C. **Throckmorton** (4 above).
7–Daniel **Grandin** (1694-1739), *m* Mary Throckmorton (1695-1739);
6–Daniel (1723-90), *m* Sarah Throckmorton (1721-61);
5–William (1751-1813), *m* Ame Lewis (1764-1853);
4–Philip, *m* Amanda Robinson;
3–Sarah M. (1820-43), *m* Barberie **Throckmorton** (3 above).
9–Claas Arians **Sip,** *m* Geertje Aurianse (*d* 1691);
8–Jan Arianse (1662-1729), *m* 1684, Johanna Van Vorst;
7–Ide (1695-1762), *m* 1725, Antje Van Wagenen (*d* 1749);
6–Garret (1739-75), *m* Jannetje Merseles (1740-1825);
5–Peter (1767-1852), *m* 1789, Elizabeth Vreeland (*d* 1827);
4–Garret (1791-1868), *m* 1811, Margaret Newkirk (1790-1886);
3–Peter (1815-55), *m* 1839, Ann Winne Van Winkle (1820-88);
2–Margaret Ann (1842-1925), *m* 1868, Barberie Woodburn **Throckmorton** (1843-82), lawyer; Civil War; issue: I–Margaret Sip (*b* 1869; *m* Elias H. Sisson, Jr.); II–Alice Grandin (1 above).
1–Mem. D.F.P.A., D.A.R., Alden Kindred of America. Residence: 2540 Boulevard, Jersey City, N.J.

EBEN JENKS LOOMIS (b Nov. 11, 1828-d Dec. 2, 1912), student Lawrence Scientific School of Harvard U.; mathematician, astronomer and author; senior assistant Nautical Almanac Office, 1859-1900; member and historian of the eclipse expedition to West Africa, 1889-90.

1–**TODD, Mabel Loomis (Mrs. David),** *b* Cambridge, Mass., Nov. 10, 1856.
9–Joseph **Loomis** (qv);
8–Nathaniel (1626-88), freeman, 1654; admitted to the ch., 1663; mem. Windsor Troop of Horse, King Philip's War; *m* 1653, Elizabeth Moore (1638-1728; Dea. John[9], *m* Abigail–);
7–Jonathan (1664-1707), of Hartford, Conn.; *m* 1688, Sarah Graves (*d* 1699; Marshall George[8], *m* Elizabeth, who was probably a Mitchell);
6–Dea. Nathaniel (1690/91-1769-70), *m* Mary Dyer;
5–Dyer (1727-66), *m* 1755, Sarah (Fuller) Merrell (Samuel Fuller[6], *m* Mary Blodgett);
4–Rev. Josiah (1767-1852), Bapt. clergyman; removed to N.Y. State, 1820, thence to Springvale, Fairfax Co., Va.; *m* 1790, Susannah Howes (1773-1865; Josiah[5], *m* Mary Sears);
3–Prof. Nathan (1794-1876), A.M., Amherst; conducted a pvt. sch. for boys, both in N.Y. State and Va.; computer Nat. Observatory, Springvale, Fairfax Co., Va.; one of the first writers for Am. Ephemeris and Nautical Almanac, Cambridge, Mass.; mem. Mass. Legislature, 1860,63; teacher, mathematician, civil engr.; *m* 1820, Waitie Jenks Barber (1797-1860; Joseph[4], of Eng., *m* Experience Palmer);
2–Eben Jenks **Loomis** (*b* 1828), see portrait and biography; *m* 1853, Mary Alden Wilder (*b* 1831; Rev. John[8], *m* Mary W. F., dau. of Nehemiah Jones, *m* Polly Alden, desc. John Alden).
1–*m* Mar. 5, 1879, David Todd, *b* Lake Ridge, N.Y., Mar. 19, 1855; astronomer (see Who's Who in America); son of Sereno Edwards

Todd, of Brooklyn; issue: 1–Millicent (Mrs. Walter Van Dyke Bingham, qv).
1–Ed. Georgetown Sem.; N.E. Conservatory, Boston. Author, writer and lecturer (see Who's Who in America). Mem. D.A.R. (founder Mattoon Chapter, and hon. regent), Amherst Hist. Soc. (pres.), Conn. Valley Hist. Soc. (v.p.), Fla. Hist. Soc., Mass. State Federation of Women's Clubs (dir.), etc. Clubs: Boston Authors; Boston Ex Club, Springfield Cosmopolitan (hon.). Residence: "Matsuba," Coconut Grove, Fla.

1–**BINGHAM, Millicent Todd (Mrs. Walter V.),** *b* Washington, D.C., Feb. 5, 1880.
9–Cornet Joseph **Parsons** (qv);
8–Hon. Joseph (1647-1729), 1st justice; capt. Train Band, Northampton; rep., 1693-1724; *m* Elizabeth Strong (1648-1736; John[9], *m* Abigail Ford);
7–Ebenezer (1677-1744), ens. and capt.; selectman, Northampton, 1721-23; *m* 1703, Mercy Stebbins (1683-1753; Samuel[8], *m* Mary French);
6–Elihu (1719-85), of Stockbridge; *m* 1750, Sarah Edwards;
5–Sarah (1760-1837), *m* 1781, Dea. David **Ingersoll** (1759-1839), of Lee, Mass. (William[6], Am. Rev., *m* his cousin, Lydia, dau. Moses Ingersoll; Capt. David[7]; Thomas[8]; John[9], qv);
4–Lucretia (*b* 1788), *m* Josiah **Todd** (*b* 1781);
3–Sereno Edwards (*b* 1820), *m* Rhoda Peck;
2–David (2 below).
10–William **Edwards** (qv);
9–Richard (1647-1718), wealthy mcht., New Haven; *m* 1667, Elizabeth Tuttle (*b* 1645; William[10], *m* Elizabeth–);
8–Rev. Timothy (1669-1758), grad. Harvard, 1691; pastor at East Windsor, Conn., 1694; chaplain colonial forces of Conn., 1711; *m* 1694, Esther Stoddard (1672-1770; Rev. Solomon[9], A.B., Harvard, 1662, distinguished theologian, *m* Esther Warham Mather; Anthony[10], qv);
7–Rev. Jonathan (1703-58), grad. Yale, 1720; distinguished Calvinistic theologian; 3d pres. Princeton; *m* 1727, Sarah Pierrepont;
6–Sarah (1728-1805), *m* Elihu **Parsons** (6 above).
10–James (Pierpont) **Pierrepont** (qv);
9–John (1617-82), Ipswich, 1640; Roxbury, 1656; *m* Thankful Stow (*d* 1668; John[10]);
8–Rev. James (1659/60-1714), A.B., Harvard, 1681; pastor First Congl. Ch., New Haven; a founder of Yale Coll.; *m* 3d, 1698, Mary Hooker (1673-1740; Rev. Samuel[9], *m* Mary, dau. Thomas Willet, qv; Rev. Thomas[10], qv);
7–Sarah (1710-58), *m* Jonathan **Edwards** (7 above).
2–Prof. David **Todd** (*b* 1855), see Who's Who in America, *m* 1879, Mabel Loomis (qv).
1–*m* Dec. 4, 1920, Lt. Col. Walter Van Dyke Bingham (qv).
1–A.B., Vassar, 1902 (P.B.K.); studied univs. of Paris, Grenoble, Berlin and at Harvard; M.A., Radcliffe Coll., 1917, Ph.D., 1923. Geographer. Author (see Who's Who in America). Residence: 110 Washington Pl., New York, N.Y.

1–**BINGHAM, Walter Van Dyke,** *b* Swan Lake, Ia., Oct. 20, 1880.
8–Dea. Thomas **Bingham** (qv);
7–Thomas (1667-1710), Norwich, Conn.; *m* 1692, Hannah Backus (1676-1762; Lt. William[8], *m* Elizabeth Pratt);
6–Nathaniel (1704-56), sgt. French and Indian War; *m* ca. 1724, Margaret Elderkin;
5–John (1727-1804), Am. Rev.; *m* 1750, Susannah Burnham (1731-95);
4–Asa (1769-1847), Ellsworth, O.; *m* 1793, Hannah Lord;
3–Oliver Abel (1801-83), *m* Martha Rothwell;
2–Lemuel Rothwell (2 below).
8–Stephen **Tracy** (qv);
7–John (1633-1718), Duxbury; *m* Mary Jane Prince, or Prence (Gov. Thomas[8], *m* Mary Collier);
6–Stephen (1673-1769), *m* 1707, Deborah Bingham (1683-1733; Dea. Thomas[7], qv);
5–Thomas (1725-1822), Windham, Conn.; pvt. Am. Rev.; mem. Com. Safety; *m* 1751, Elizabeth Warner (*b* 1727; Lt. Joseph[6], *m* Elizabeth Allen);
4–Joseph (1763-1829), Hartford, Vt.; *m* 1792, Ruth Carter (*b* 1772; Ezra[5], *m* Mary Fifield);
3–Samuel (1808-89), *m* Emeline Newton (1814-1900);
2–Martha Evarts (1836-1919), *m* 1857, Lemuel Rothwell **Bingham** (1831-1908), mcht.; issue: I–Martha Emma (*b* 1858; *m* George N. Luccock); II–Mary Tracy (*b* 1863; *m* Willis G. Banker); III–Hon. Lewis Lemuel (*b* 1867; twin; *m* Ella Craig); IV–Lizzie Alice (*b* 1867; *m* Charles R. Frazier); V–Samuel (*b* and *d* 1870; twin); VI–Susan Adelaide (1870-93); VII–Walter Van Dyke (1 above).
1–*m* Dec. 4, 1920, Millicent Todd (qv).
1–U.Kan., 1897-98; B.A., Beloit (Wis.) Coll., 1901 (Sigma Xi, P.B.K.); U.Chicago, 1905-06; U.Berlin, 1907; M.A., Harvard, 1907; Ph.D., U.Chicago, 1908; (Sc.D., Beloit, 1929). Psychologist. Dir. Personnel Research Federation, Inc., since 1924 (see Who's Who in America). Exec. sec. com. on classification of personnel in the army, 1917-18; lt. col., personnel branch, Gen Staff, U.S.A., 1918-19. Clubs: City (N.Y.), Cosmos (Washington). Residence: 110 Washington Pl., New York, N.Y.

1–**TOPPING, Charles Tallman,** *b* Cedar Point, Kan., Mar. 26, 1888.
10–William **Ward** (qv);
9–William (1649-97), *m* 1679, Hannah (Brigham) Eames (1650-1719; Thomas Brigham[10], qv);
8–Col. William (1680-1767), rep. Gen. Ct.; col. of militia; *m* 1702, Jane Cleveland (1681-1745; Samuel[9], *m* Jane Keyes; Moses[10], qv);
7–Charles (1722-45), *d* at capture of Louisbourg; *m* 1st, 1742, Abigail Pike (1724-84; William[8], *m* Mary Flagg);
6–William (1743-1819), mem. Com. of Safety in Am. Rev., Poultney, Vt.; ens. 8th Co., 2d Regt., Vt. Militia; present at Burgoyne's surrender at Saratoga; judge Co. Ct., Rutland Co., 6 yrs.; 1st probate judge, Fair Haven, 22 yrs.; justice, 40 yrs.; 1st rep. Vt. Legislature; dea. over 40 yrs.; *m* 1763, Lucy Church (1748-1846; Noah[7], *m* Lydia Barnard);
5–Lorenzo (1785-1846), *m* 1806, Abigail Cleveland (1789-1880; see Vol. II, p. 81, for Cleveland lineage);
4–Lucy (1811-96), *m* 1829, Alexander **Topping** (1809-88; Hezekiah[5]);
3–Henry (1835-1927), lt. in Civil War; civil engr., lawyer; *m* 1857, Mary Rine Tallman;
2–George (2 below).
6–James **Tallman** (*d* ante 1818), from Eng., settled at Winchester, Vt.; served in Am. Rev., 1777-83; *m* 2d, Mary Holland;
5–Peter (*d* 1833), St. Clairsville, O.; clk. of ct. Belmont Co., O.; *m* Sarah (Jenkins) Berry (*d* 1833);
4–John C. (1812-76), also clk. of ct. Belmont Co.; cashier, Belmont Co.; *m* 1835, Ellen Rine (1814-1902; John[5], silversmith, *m* Charlotte, dau. of James Wood, *m* Chlotilda Haggerty);
3–Mary Rine (1836-1909), *m* Henry **Topping** (3 above);
2–George (*b* 1858), *m* 1887, Louise Elvira Grinnell (see Vol. II, p. 80).
1–*m* July 27, 1914, Maud Kirk Smith, *b* Janesville, O., July 27, 1881; dau. of William Henry Smith, of Chicago; issue: 1–Louise Josselyn, *b* Pittsburgh, Pa., Sept. 22, 1915; 2–Mary Cornelia, *b* Pittsburgh, Nov. 5, 1917.
1–Kan. State Agrl. Coll., 1908. Inventor; mechanical engineer, manufacturing "The Topping Pony-Ditcher"; pres. Chas. T. Topping Machinery Co., Cleveland; also associated with Industrial Brownhoist Corpn. Residence: 3287 Beechwood Av., Cleveland Heights, Ohio.

1–**TOWER, Earle Jasper,** *b* Ferryville, Wis., May 20, 1898.
10–John **Tower** (qv);
9–Jeremiah (1645/46-1676), of Hingham, Mass.; *m* 1670, Elizabeth (Goodale) Rowlands (*d* 1723; Richard Goodale[10], *m* Mary–);
8–Jeremiah (1671-1743), *m* 1698/99, Hannah Hobart (1675-1749; John[9], *m* Hannah, dau. of Simeon Burr; Edmund[10]; Edmund[11], qv);
7–Peter (1701-68), *m* 1727, Patience Garnet, or Gardner (1703-ca. 1767; Stephen[8], *m* Sarah, dau. of John Warren);
6–Malachi (1737/38-1806), responded to Lexington Alarm; *m* 1760, Ruth (Hayward) Wilder (1733-69; Nehemiah[7], *m* Bethiah Shaw);
5–Malachi (1761-1833), mem. Sullivan's expdn. to R.I., 1778; mem. Capt. Ward's co. of guards at Boston, 1778; *m* 1783, Bathsheba Weatherbee, of Dedham;
4–John Hancock (1794-1856), Towerville, Wis.;

schoolmaster, merchant and starch mfr.; *m* 1817, Phebe Poland (1791-1860; Joseph[5], answered Bennington Alarm, *m* Rachel Hathaway; Joseph[6]);
3–John Hancock (1819-1901), pioneer Wis. miller; *m* 1843, Jane Adelia Woodruff (*b* 1822), of Essex, Vt. (Nathan[4], *m* 1816, Annie Campbell);
2–William Hancock (2 below).
10–Richard **Newton** (qv);
9–Moses (1645 or 46-1736), propr. of iron works; wounded during attack on Marlborough, King Philip's War; *m* 1st, 1668, Joannah Larkin (ca. 1645-1713; Edward[10], *m* Joanna–);
8–Moses (1669-1736), King Philip's War; *m* 1695, Sarah Howe (1675-1733; Isaac[9], *m* Frances Woods; John[10]);
7–Elisha (1701-ca. 1791), Shrewsbury; *m* 1728, Sarah Tomlin (1708-ca. 1798; Isaac[8], *m* Mary Wait);
6–Solomon (1741-1822), *m* 2d, 1782, Widow Lydia (Rice) Hemenway (1746-1826; Zebediah Rice[7]; James[8]; Thomas[9]; Edmund[10], qv);
5–Solomon (*b* 1783), Trimble, O.; *m* 1804, Patience Hastings (*b* 1782; Eliakim[6]; John[7]; Daniel[8]; Dea. Thomas[9]);
4–Dennis (1817-1893 or 95), physician; *m* Eliza Adams (1822-1909; James[5], of Bishoptown, O.);
3–Solomon (1842-70), Ferryville, Wis.; Co. E, 174th Ohio Vols., 1864-65; *m* Eliza Jane Tanner (Jacob[4], *m* Mary Warner);
2–Hannah Phebe (1866-1915), *m* 1881, William Hancock **Tower** (1859-1902), horticulturist; issue: I–Floyd L. (*b* 1882); II–Alma Jane (*b* 1884; *m* George Merritt Marks); III–Myra Bernice (*b* 1886; *m* Rudolph J. Cheska); IV–Zella (1888-1919; *m* William B. Davis); V–John Harvey (*b* 1895); VI–Earle Jasper (1 above).
1–*m* May 1, 1926, Yvonne Smith (qv).
1–A.B., U. of Wis., '21. Adv. staff of Aluminum Goods Mfg. Co. Mem. Tower Geneal. Soc., Manitowoc Co. Hist. Soc., A.L. Republican. Residence: 925 S. 12th St., Manitowoc, Wis.

1–**TOWER, Yvonne Smith (Mrs. Earle Jasper),** *b* Green Bay, Wis., June 18, 1902.
7–Jonathan **Smith**;
6–John (1763-1855), wagoner of N.J. militia, 1777-81; *m* 1789, Sarah Gould (1770-1872);
5–Jonathan Huger (1790-1864), *m* Phebe Condict Beach;
4–John Mills (1820-94), Green Bay, Wis.; *m* 1844, Emily Blandin Torrey;
3–Henry Condict (*b* 1845), of Green Bay; *m* 1870, Louisa Berger (*b* 1848);
2–Edwin George (2 below).
11–Thomas **Axtell** (1619-46), to Sudbury, Mass., ante 1642; *m* ante 1639, Mary– (she *m* 2d, John Maynard);
10–Henry (1641-76), killed in Wadsworth Massacre, King Philip's War; *m* 1665, Hannah Merriam (George[11], *m* Sarah Diker);
9–Daniel (*b* 1673), of Berkley; *m* 1702, Thankful Pratt (*b* 1683; William[10] *m* Elizabeth Baker; Sgt. Thomas[11]);
8–Henry (1715-53), Mendham, N.J.; *m* 1737, Jemima Leonard (1717-ca. 1797; Benjamin[9], *m* Hannah Phillips; Isaac[10]; Solomon[11]);
7–Maj. Henry (1738-1818), *m* 1st, 1760, Mary Beach (*d* 1766); *m* 2d, 1767, Phebe (Condict) Day (1740-1829; Peter Condit[8], *m* Phebe Dodd; Peter[9]; John[10], from Wales, 1678);
6–Lurana (1767-1820), Morris Co., N.J.; *m* 1788, Samuel **Beach** (1762-1824);
5–Phebe Condict (1792-1864), *m* 1819, Jonathan H. **Smith** (5 above).
10–Capt. William **Torrey** (qv);
9–William (1638-1718), of Weymouth; *m* Deborah Green (1649-1729; John[10]);
8–Lt. John (1673-1730), *m* 1700, Mary Symmes (1677-1758; William[9], *m* Mary, dau. of Nathaniel Sparhawk; Rev. Zachariah[10]);
7–Lt. Samuel (1706-45), lt. Conn. regt. Louisbourg expdn.; *d* while on duty there; *m* 2d, 1738, Martha Strickland (Jonah[8], *m* Martha–);
6–William (1744-1820), Williamstown, Mass.; *m* 1771, Hannah Wheeler (*d* 1824; Dea. Nathan[7]);
5–Ephraim (1782-1829), Bethany, Pa.; *m* 1806, Eunice Lewis (1790-1870);
4–Emily Blandin (1821-98), Green Bay, Wis.; *m* John Mills **Smith** (4 above).
3–Henry Condict, *m* Louisa Berger (3 above);
2–Edwin George (*b* 1873), of Green Bay; v.p. Smith Bros. Co., gardeners and wholesale produce; *m* 1901, Fannie Ansorge (*b* 1872; Killian[3]); -issue: I–Yvonne (1 above); II–Harold Ansorge (*b* 1903).
1–*m* May 1, 1926, Earle Jasper Tower (qv).
1–Oshkosh Normal, '21. Teacher, Manitowoc Jr. High Sch., 1921-26. Mem. D.A.R. Mem. A.L. Auxiliary, Girl Scout Council. Residence: 925 S. 12th St., Manitowoc, Wis.

1–**TOWNER, Frances Marsh (Mrs. Frank H.),** *b* Rockford, Ill., Aug. 20, 1879.
7–William **Marsh** (*d* 1724), surveyed and laid out Plainfield, Conn., and finally settled there; commissary during Indian wars; wounded in Narragansett fight, 1675; *m* Elizabeth Yeamans (*b* 1659);
6–James (1690-1749), *m* Hannah Shepard (1695-1770 or 76);
5–Jonas (1712-88), *m* Mercy Merrill (1712-1802);
4–Nathaniel (1746-95), pvt. in Conn. troops, 1776, and in 13th Mass. Regt. in Am. Rev., 1779; *m* Delight Wilson;
3–William Lowry, M.D. (1790-1834), physician, Goshen, Conn.; *m* 1821, Emeline Bradford;
2–William L. (2 below).
9–Gov. William **Bradford,** Mayflower Pilgrim (qv);
8–Maj. William (1624-1704), *m* ca. 1673, Widow Mary Wiswell;
7–Lt. Joseph (1674-1747), Montville, Conn.;
6–Capt. John (1717-87), lt. in Train Band; capt., 1755; *m* 1736, Esther Sherwood (1717-52);
5–John (1739-1818), *m* 1764, Mary Fitch (1744-80);
4–James Fitch (1765-1837), *m* 1790, Mary Merwin (1770-1828);
3–Emeline (1798-1852), Cornwall, Conn.; *m* 1821, Dr. William Lowry **Marsh** (3 above);
2–William L. (1832-1920), New London, Conn.; *m* 1865, Charlotte Morgan Beebe (1843-1909); issue: I–Carlie Emeline (*b* 1867); II–Frances (1 above).
1–*m* June 2, 1903, Dr. Frank Hough Towner, *b* Washington, D.C., June 19, 1879; asst. surgeon, U.S.N.; issue: 1–Helen Marsh, *b* Washington, Mar. 21, 1905.
1–Ed. Mt. Vernon Sem., Washington. Mem. S.M.D., D.F.P.A., D.C.W., D.A.R. Conglist. Republican. Clubs: City, Republican. Residence: 217 Butler Av., Providence, R.I.

1–**TRACY, Sherman Weld,** *b* Brevard, N.C., Nov. 29, 1866.
8–Stephen **Tracy** (qv);
7–John (1633-1718), Windham, Conn.; *m* 1660, Mary Prence (Gov. Thomas[8], qv);
6–Stephen (1673-1769), farmer, Windham, Conn.; *m* 1707, Deborah Bingham (1683-1733; Dea. Thomas[7], qv);
5–Thomas (1725-1821), Hartford, Vt., 1774; propr. same; served Vt. frontier militia, under Capt. Joshua Hazen; mem. Com. Safety, Am. Rev.; *m* 1751, Elizabeth Warner (*b* 1727; Lt. Joseph[6], *m* Elizabeth, dau. of William Allen; Isaac[7]; Isaac[8]; Andrew[9]);
4–Joseph (1763-1829), farmer, Hartford, Vt.; *m* 1792, Ruth Carter (1772-1845; Ezra[5], *m* Mary, dau. of Benjamin Fifield, of Fryesburg, Me.; Dr. Ezra[6]; Ephraim[7]; John[8]; Thomas[9]);
3–Myron (1798-1855), Hudson, O.; Congl. minister; *m* 1829, Sarah Weld (1807-73; Samuel[4], of Braintree, Vt., *m* Sarah Hayden; Rev. Ezra[5]; John[6]; Edmund[7]; Thomas[8]);
2–Samuel Joseph (1835-81), of Indianapolis, Ind., Hudson and Fostoria, O.; capt. Co. H, 177th Ohio Inf., Civil War; merchant; *m* 1865, Arminda Catherine Hogshead (1847-92; William P.[3], of Brevard, N.C., *m* Mary Edna Manley; Walter[4]; Walter[5]); issue: I–Sherman Weld (1 above); II–Laura Edna (*b* 1868; *m* William G. Klinepeter); III–Carman Francis (*b* 1869).
1–*m* Feb. 14, 1889, Mary Alice Carr, *b* nr. Warsaw, Ind., Jan. 21, 1867; dau. of George Crawford Carr, of Warsaw and Knox, Ind.; issue: 1–Agnes Veronica (Feb. 18, 1890-Jan. 16, 1910); 2–Oswald Crawford, *b* Kankakee, Ill., Feb. 10, 1895; ed. Kemper Mil. Acad.; *m* July 3, 1928, Mary Alice, dau. of Charles C. Reniff, of Amboy, Ill.
1–Telegraph operator, station agent, r.r. accountant, and operating officer, N.Y. Central R.R., 1887-1912; v.p. Chicago Tunnel Co., 1912-16, since pres. same and affiliated corpns. Mem. N.E.G.H.S. Clubs: Union League, Traffic, Olympia Fields Country. Republican. Residence: 7739 Yates Av., Chicago, Ill.

1–**TRAXLER, Dean Lake,** *b* Leavenworth, Kan., Nov. 6, 1893.
5–Christopher **Traxler,** emigrated from Holland; *m* Mary–;
4–Henry (1769-1849), *m* Elizabeth Coon;
3–Philip (1803-76), *m* 1830, Prudence Bodine;
2–Benjamin Franklin (2 below).
10–John **Emery** (qv);
9–Jonathan (1652-1723), *m* Mary Woodman (*b* 1654; Edward[10] [1628-94], *m* Mary, dau. William Goodridge; Edward[11], Newbury, Mass., 1635);
8–John (*b* 1678), *m* Hannah Morse (1681-1732; Joshua[9] [1653-91], *m* Joanna [1661-91], dau. of Thomas Kimball; Anthony[10], qv);
7–Joshua (*b* 1709), *m* Sarah Smith (Samuel[8], *m* Abigail, dau. of Michael Emerson, *m* Hannah Webster; Nathaniel[9], *m* Elizabeth Ladd);
6–John, *m* Abigall Webster (*b* 1730; Samuel[7]; Stephen[8]; Stephen[9]; John[10]);
5–John (1753-1823), *m* Abiah Page (1757-1837; Amos[6]; Thomas[7]; Cornelius[8]; John[9]);
4–Samuel (1788-1860), Haverhill, Mass.; *m* 1814, Betsy Young;
3–Ruby Maria (1829-1902), *m* 1847, Dr. Matthew Bullock **Van Petten** (see Vol. III, p. 579);
2–Mary Josephine (2 below).
9–Samuel **Getchell;**
8–Samuel;
7–Nathaniel;
6–Susanna (*b* 1727/28), *m* 1746, John **Young** (*d* 1785):
5–Jesse (1751-1804), lt. Am. Rev.; in expdn. against Can.; *m* 1778, Ruby Richardson;
4–Betsy (1791-1863), *m* Samuel **Emery** (4 above).
9–Samuel **Richardson** (qv);
8–Samuel (1646-1712), served in King Philip's War; *m* 4th, 1680, Sarah Hayward (1655-1717);
7–Ebenezer (1686-1756), *m* 1718, Elizabeth Kendrick;
6–Ebenezer (*b* 1720), *m* 1747, Katherine Brewster (see Vol. III, p. 579);
5–Ruby (1756-1821), *m* Jesse **Young** (5 above).
2–Mary Josephine Van Petten (*b* 1856; sister of Mrs. Henry C. Burnham, see Vol. III, p. 104), *m* 1877, Benjamin Franklin **Traxler** (*b* 1852); for issue see Vol. III, p. 579.
1–Not married. A.B., Northwestern U., '15 (Wranglers, Delta Theta Phi), LL.B., 1917. Mem. law firm of Church, Traxler & Kennedy, Chicago. Served as 2d lt., F.A., U.S.A., Sept. 6, 1917-Sept. 12, 1919; instr. Saumur Arty. Sch., France. Mem. S.M.D., S.A.R., M.O.W.W., A.L. Clubs: University (Chicago and Evanston), Midland (Chicago), Shawnee Country. Residence: 711 Emerson St., Evanston, Ill.

1–**TROUTMAN, Ella Augusta Hammer (Mrs. John Hamilton),** *b* Orwigsburg, Pa., Feb. 11, 1851.
5–George Frederick **Hammer,** from the Rhine provinces of Germany, 1763, settled at Hamburg, Pa.;
4–John, *m* Elizabeth Helwig;
3–Joseph, *m* Phoebe Huntzinger;
2–William Alexander (1827-95), mcht.; tax commr., Newark, N.J.; pres. N.J. State Tax Commn.; prominent in affairs of Reformed Episcopal Ch.; *m* Martha Augusta Beck (1827-61; John[3], of Lititz, Pa.); *m* 2d, 1862, Anna Maria Nichols Lawton (1840-1910); issue (1st marriage): I–Ella Augusta (1 above); II–Martha Virginia (1852-1926); III–John Beck (1856-80); IV–William Joseph (*b* 1858; *m* 1894, Alice Maude White, 1863-1906); issue (2d marriage): I–Alfred L. (1865-68); II–Edwin Wesley (qv for Howland-Lawton lineage); III–Mary Lawton (*b* 1874; *m* 1906, William Clarence Allen, 1877-1907; *m* 2d, 1910, Harold Francis, 1875-1926).
1–*m* Sept. 28, 1882, John Hamilton Troutman (1856-1918); see portrait and biography; issue: 1–Percival Hammer (qv for Troutman lineage).
1–Residence: Shirley-Savoy Hotel, Denver, Colo.

1–**TROUTMAN, Percival Hammer,** *b* Philadelphia, Pa., June 5, 1883.
5–John Peter Christian **Troutman** (1742-89; son of John Balthasar Trautman, Sr. [*b* 1707], of Zweibrucken, Germany, senator, censor and inn keeper, *m* Maria Magdalena Schnellin); came from Germany ca. 1770, settled at Frankford, Pa.; said to have been the first silk importer in America; served in a Pa. regt. during Am. Rev.; *m* 1775, Elizabeth Falkrod, of Frankford;
4–George Christian (1781-ca. 1829), said to have been one of the first bridge builders in Pa., having constructed many important bridges; *m* 1803, Sarah Hamilton;
3–Lewis Wernwag (1818-ca. 1871), Pottsville, Pa.; *m* ca. 1840, Annie Esler (1818-1907), of Phila.;
2–John Hamilton (1856-1918), see portrait and biography; *m* 1882, Ella Augusta Hammer (qv for Hammer lineage).
1–*m* Jan. 1, 1908, Amy Wellington Broad, *b* Boston, Mass., Dec. 14, 1883; dau. of Wilmot Edgar Broad (1847-1907), built first toll road into the San Joan Basin, *m* Arabella Augusta (1845-1924; desc. John Alden thru her mother), dau. of Thomas Faunce (desc. of Thomas Faunce, first ruling elder Plymouth Ch.); issue: 1–Dorothy Louise, *b* Denver, Colo., Apr. 16, 1912; student Colo. Woman's Coll.
1–Farming, wholesale produce and manufacturing food stuffs, 1906-23; pres. Union Trust Co., Denver, Union Deposit & Savings Co., Del., Union Deposit Co., offices from coast to coast. Candidate for lt. gov. of Colo., 1914. Trustee First Presbyn. Ch., Canon City, Colo., 1919-23, Central Presbyn Ch., Denver, 1924-28 (mem. of Session, 1930). Mem. S.A.R. Residence: 2200 Birch St., Denver, Colo.

JOHN HAMILTON TROUTMAN (b Phila., Pa., Mar. 3, 1856-d Denver, Colo., Oct. 3, 1918); left school at age of 15 on death of father; became associated with John Price Wetherill and August Heckscher in management of coal properties, 1879, and joined with them in the organization of the Lehigh Zinc Co., 1881, which was merged with N. J. Zinc Co., 1897; gen. mgr. of a subsidiary, Mineral Point Zinc Co., at Chicago, 1897-1900; gen. mgr. Empire Zinc Co., Denver, 1900-18. Elder Central Presbyn. Ch., and was active in civic and social affairs of Denver.

1–**TROWBRIDGE, Wallace,** *b* Franklin, La., Aug. 1873.
8–Thomas **Trowbridge** (qv);
7–Thomas (1631-1702), from Eng. with parents; *m* 1657, Sarah Rutherford (1641-87);
6–Thomas (1663/64-1711), New Haven, Conn.; *m* 1685, Mary Winston (1667-1742);
5–Daniel (1703-52), B.A., Yale, '25; shipping mcht.; *m* 1731, Mehetable Brown (1711-97);
4–Newman (1738-1816), *m* 1778, Rebecca (Dodd) Cable (1751-1808);
3–Isaac (1789-1877), *m* 1835, Mehitable (Wire) Hall (1806-45);
2–Newman (1838-86), *m* 1872, Elizabeth Graham Wallace (1848-1912; George[3] [*d* Sheridan, Kan., 1869; buried in Springfield, O.], from Ayr, Scotland, with wife, 1847, supt. construction Kan. Pacific R.R., *m* Isabella Smith); issue: I–Wallace (1 above); II–George Graham (*b* 1875; *m* Elizabeth Short); III–Harry Lorraine (*b* 1878; *m* Marion Short); IV–Paul Wire (*b* 1881; *m* Mary Foster).

1-*m* Feb. 11, 1904, Mary Jane Kemper (qv for issue).
1-Sugar and ice mfr. Mem. S.A.R. Residence: Pass Christian, Miss.

WILLIAM PETER KEMPER (b St. Mary's Parish, La., 1826-d there, 1890).

1-**TROWBRIDGE, Mary Jane Kemper (Mrs. Wallace),** *b* Glencoe, St. Mary's Parish, La., Feb. 25, 1866.
5-Bernard **Reynolds** (*b* Russell Co., Va., 1768-*d* 1833), *m* Lucy Johnston;
4-Bernard (1793-1870), *m* Monica McKeon;
3-Elizabeth (*d* 1871), *m* John Michal **Rogers**;
2-Monica Reynolds (1838-1909), see portrait; *m* 1858, William Peter **Kemper** (*b* 1826, posthumous son, *d* 1890), sugar planter (see portrait); issue: I-Stephen Young (1858-59); II-Eliza Blanche (1860-93; *m* Carroll Barton); III-William Byrne (*b* 1861; *m* Alice Potter); IV-Kate Gilman (*b* 1863; *m* Dr. William P. Simmons); V-Mary Jane (1 above); VI-James Parkerson (qv); VII-Walter Young (*b* 1871; *m* Leonora Barton); VIII-Charles Delaware (*b* 1873; *m* Emma Frere; *m* 2d, Frances Bush).
1-*m* Feb. 11, 1904, Wallace Trowbridge (qv); issue: 1-Wallace, Jr., *b* New Orleans, La., Nov. 5, 1906.
1-Attended Winchester (Va.) Junior Coll., 1881-83. Mem. D.A.R. Episcopalian. Democrat. Residence: Pass Christian, Miss.

1-**KEMPER, James Parkerson,** *b* St. Mary's Parish, La., Aug. 5, 1868.
7-John **Kemper** (*b* 1692; son of John George [1663-1731], *m* 1691, Agnes Kleb; g.son of Johann [1635-70], of Germany, *m* 1655, Anna Low); came from Germany, settled in Spotsylvania Co., Va., 1714; *m* 1716, Ailsey (or Alice) Utterbach;
6-John Peter (1717-88), of Va.; *m* 1738, Elizabeth Fishback, of Cedar Grove, Va.;
5-Peter (1743-1829), Cedar Grove, Va.; *m* Isabella Nicholls;
4-Nathan (1775-1832), Fauquier Co., Va., and St. Mary's Parish, La.; *m* 1801, Nancy Whitaker;
3-William Peter (1802-25), *m* 1825, Eliza Hulick (1801-62);
2-William Peter (*b* 1826, posthumous son, *d* 1890), sugar planter (see portrait); *m* 1858, Monica Reynolds Rogers (1838-1909), see portrait; for issue see Mrs. Wallace Trowbridge.
1-*m* Mar. 19, 1896, Cordelle Alexander, *b* St. Mary's Parish, La., Feb. 9, 1872; dau. Theodore Sessions Alexander; issue: 1-Cordelle, *b* New Orleans, La., Aug. 5, 1897; U.Mich.; *m* June 1928, Lyman J. Ballard; 2-James Lawson, *b* New Orleans, Jan. 5, 1900; B.E., Tulane U., '23; 3-Richard Rogers, *b* St. Mary's Parish, La., Sept. 28, 1906.

MONICA REYNOLDS (ROGERS) KEMPER (b Boston, Mass., 1838-d St. Mary's Parish, La., 1909).

1-Md. Agrl. Coll., 1882-84; B.E., U.Ala., '87, C.E., 1894. With L. & N. and Ga. Pacific rys., 1887-89; with Thompson-Houston Electric Co., Lynn, Mass., 1890; electrical business, St. Paul and Chicago, 1890-93; in practice of civil engring. since 1894, also mgr. sugar plantation. Author (see Who's Who in America). Mem. S.A.R. Episcopalian. Republican. Residence: 4610 Corondelet St., New Orleans, La.

1-**TUCKER, Mary Lightfoot Coleman (Mrs. Clifton D.),** *b* Winston-Salem, N.C., Jan. 10, 1902.
11-John **Rolfe** (qv);
10-Thomas (*b* 1615), *m* Jane Poythress;
9-Jane (*d* 1676), *m* 1675, Robert **Bolling** (qv);
8-Col. John (1676-1729), of "Cobbs"; burgess; *m* 1697, Mary Kennon (Dr. Richard[9], qv);
7-Anne (*d* 1800), of Va.; *m* James **Murray**;
6-Margaret (*b* 1748), *m* Thomas **Gordon**;
5-Anne (1776-1821), *m* 1795, Henry Embry **Coleman** (1768-1837), lt. col. in War 1812; comd. 6th Regt., Va. Militia, 1814 (John[6], lt., Am. Rev.);
4-Thomas Gordon (1802-62), Halifax Co., Va.; *m* 1828, Anne Sims Clark (1807-73);
3-Dr. John Clark (1829-98), Halifax Co.; capt., Co. C, 3d Va. Cav., C.S.A.; *m* 1861, Anne Lightfoot Edmunds (1840-99);
2-John (1869-1929), *m* 1899, Mary A. Conrad (*b* 1877); issue: I-Mary L. (1 above); II-Elizabeth Edmunds (*m* Edward Monroe); III-Frances Murray (*b* Sept. 11, 1907; *m* Zach Toms), and IV-John Carrington, twins (*b* Sept. 11, 1907); V-Mildred Gordon (*b* July 26, 1912); VI-Henry Edmunds (*b* Jan. 16, 1916).
1-*m* Mar. 22, 1924, Clifton Dwight Tucker, *b* Fitchville, O., Mar. 19, 1878; son of Edgar L. Tucker; issue: 1-Pocahontas Rolfe, *b* San Fernando, Calif., Dec. 9, 1925.
1-Mem. D.A.R., U.S.D. 1812, U.D.C. Residence: 708 4th Av., San Fernando, Calif.

1-**TUCKER, Elmer Austin,** *b* Winston-Salem (Waughtown), N.C., Sept. 28, 1871.
5-Thomas **Tucker** (1750-living 1833), from Calvert Co., Md., 1790, to Stokes (now Forsyth) Co., N.C.; removed to Morgan Co., Ga., thence to Warren Co., Tenn.; gave the trustees of Loves Meth. Ch. an acre of ground to establish a church, provided in the deed Meth. ministers only should be allowed to preach in the ch.; this ch. still owns the land; served in Am. Rev., granted pension, 1833; *m* Nancy Ann–;
4-Francis (1777-1862), moved to nr. Moravia P.O., Appanoose Co., Ia.; *m* 1805 or 06, Millie Crews (1778-1843; James[6], of Granville Co., N.C.);

3–Edmund (1810-71), Winston-Salem, N.C.; *m* 1841, Hannah Elnora Light;
2–Francis Augustus (2 below).
5–Henry **Ripple** (1758-1835), from Germany; with Gotlieb Schrober founded the first Sunday School in N.C. at Hopewell Ch., Stokes (now Forsyth) Co., N.C.; *m* Catharine– (1765-1825);
4–Sarah (1788-1832), *m* 1812, John Simon (Leicht) **Light** (1780-1861), from Germany; made spinning wheels and wooden wheel clocks; bought land in Bagge Town, and moved to it, 1812; joined the Moravian Congregation at Friedland; bought of Michael Riminger a dwelling house and 45½ acres, 1821; this house was built by Mr. Rominger, 1806, was occupied by John Simon Light until 1861, then by his son, Peter Edwin Light, until his death, 1910, it is still standing and is in good condition, it is located in a part of Winston-Salem called Waughtown;
3–Hannah Elnora (1817-1906), *m* Edmund **Tucker** (3 above).
6–Joh. Bernhardt Eytel, or Barnett **Idol** (ca. 1734-bet. 1785-86), from Germany in the "St. Andrew," 1752, as an indentured servant; settled in Bucks Co., Pa.; removed to Stokes Co., N.C., 1776; *m* ca. 1760, Elizabeth Meier (*d* ca. 1798; Conrad[7], of Switzerland);
5–Jacob (1761-1851), Stokes Co., in Am. Rev., pensioned; *m* 1782, Chloe Johnson (1759-1859 or 60; Henry[6] [*d* ca. 1809], agent for Gen. Greene in procuring supplies for his army);
4–Phoebe (1789-1845), *m* Risden **Charles** (1783-1863), of Davidson Co., N.C. (Elisha[5], *m* Elizabeth–, will dated 1831);
3–Risden Jefferson (1821-68), of Forsyth Co.; missionary Bapt. preacher; *m* 1842, Mary Louisa Morris (1824-99; Aaron[4] [1783-1876], *m* Jane Thomas [1792-1872]; John[5]);
2–Nancy Elizabeth (*b* 1849), *m* 1870, Francis Augustus **Tucker** (1846-1911); issue: I–Elmer Austin (1 above); II–Curtis Houston (*b* 1872; *m* 1917, Ida May Harrelson); III–Arthur Gilbert (1875-1903); IV–Irvin Burchard (*b* 1878; *m* 1910, Bessie Richardson); V–Luther Jefferson (*b* 1880; *m* Lillie Hogan); VI–Roscoe Conklin (*b* 1882; *m* 1906, Rosalie Anderson); VII–Thomas Settle (*b* 1887; *m* 1923, Ulah Jordan); VIII–Minnie (1889-90).
1–*m* Apr. 2, 1893, Mary Florence Thomas, *b* Davidson Co., N.C., Nov. 7, 1875; dau. of William Newton Thomas (1839-97; William[8] [1804-84], *m* Catharine Leonard [1808-81]; Alexander[4] [1758-1842], from Pa. to N.C., post 1790, according to family tradition, *m* 1st, Hannah–, *b* 1758, *m* 2d, 1803, Hannah [Gray] McDorman [1775-1854], dau. James Gray, 1753-1844); issue: 1–Lillian, *b* Davidson Co., N.C., June 19, 1894; *m* Oct. 4, 1916, John D. (*b* May 15, 1889), son of John Stockton (issue: Jean Vivian, *b* Aug. 7, 1925); 2–Sadie (Mar. 3, 1896-Mar. 7, 1897); 3–Frances Cameron, *b* Winston-Salem, Feb. 4, 1914.
1–Clerk Winston-Salem Post Office, 1898; with railway mail service, 18 yrs.; with Post Office Dept. at Washington 4 yrs.; supt. of mails, Winston-Salem, N.C., since 1923. Mem. I.A.G. Residence: 947 W. End Boul., Winston-Salem, N.C.

1–**TULLY, Emily Learned (Mrs. John J.),** *b* San Francisco, Calif., May 2, 1860.
9–William **Learned** (qv);
8–Isaac (1623-57), *m* 1646, Mary Sternes (1626-63);
7–Benoni (1657-1738), selectman; treas.; rep. Gen. Ct., Sherborn, Mass.; *m* 1st, 1680, Mary Fanning (1662-88);
6–Thomas (1682-1729), *m* Mary Mason (1685-1770);
5–Jonathan (1708-81), *m* 1730, Hannah White (1709-post 1747);
4–Jonas (bap. 1748-1821), minuteman at Cambridge, 1776; settled at Dedham; *m* 1787, Hannah Titterton (1759-1831);
3–George (1804-80), *m* 1827, Emily Holbrook (1805-87);
2–Andrew Meneely (Nov 29, 1830-Apr. 9, 1863), settled at San Francisco, Calif., 1857; *m* 1859, Kate Derrick (Jan. 21, 1838-Feb. 24, 1927; Peter[3]); issue: I–Emily Learned (1 above); II–Alfred Mosher (1862-1914).
1–*m* John James Tully, *b* Worcester, Mass., July 7, 1862; son of John Tully (1836-1918), of Ireland; issue: 1–Emily Eugenie, *b* Sierra City, Calif.; *m* June 1, 1910, Emile Huguenin, *b* Switzerland, June 2, 1885 (issue: Katherine, *b* Sept. 13, 1912; Jeanne, *b* Dec. 18, 1913; William, *b* July 19, 1915; Barbara, *b* May 22, 1921); 2–Amoretta (Jan. 26, 1890-Nov. 18, 1890); 3–Jasper William, *b* San Francisco, Nov. 3, 1891; 1st lt., World War, stationed at Camp Lewis; *m* Sept. 25, 1919, Leslie Brown (June 25, 1895-May 10, 1929; issue: Robert, *b* Sept. 27, 1920; Thomas, *b* May 19, 1924); 4–Genevieve, *b* Stockton, Calif., Aug. 21, 1895.
1–Mem. C.D.A., D.F.P.A., D.A.R. Residence: 609 Sutter St., San Francisco, Calif.

1–**TURNER, Albert Milford,** *b* Litchfield, Conn., Feb. 26, 1868.
8–Nathaniel **Turner** (*d* 1646), from Eng. with Winthrop's Fleet, 1630; freeman, 1630; dep. Gen. Ct. of Mass., 1634-36; mem. A. and H. A. Co.; mem. Gen. Ct. of N.H., 1639; dep. Congress of United Colonies;
7–Isaac (1640-99), New Haven; *m* 1668, Mary Todd (*d* 1676; Christopher[8], *m* Grace Middlebrook);
6–Joseph (1672-1759), *m* 1708, Sarah Hotchkiss (Lt. Samuel[7] [1645-1705], *m* Sarah Talmadge);
5–Thomas (*b* 1716), *m* 1740, Sarah Humiston (1723-87; John[6] [1686-1767], *m* Hannah Ray);
4–Titus (1741-1828), Litchfield; *m* 1765, Sarah Blakeslee (1740-1809; Jacob[5] [1706-67], *m* Elizabeth Barnes);
3–Eber (1782-1857), Northfield, Conn.; *m* 1809, Malitta Wilmot (*d* 1863; Asa[4] [1752-1804], Am. Rev., *m* Esther Curtiss);
2–Abraham Manning (2 below).
9–William **Filley,** from Eng., settled at Windsor, Conn., 1640; *m* 1642, Margaret–;
8–Samuel (1643-1712), *m* 1663, Ann Gillett (1639-1711/12; Jonathan[9], qv);
7–Jonathan (*b* 1672), *m* 1700, Deborah Loomis (*b* 1679 or 80; Dea. John[8]; Dea. John[9]; Joseph[10], qv);
6–Lt. Jonathan (*b* 1703), *m* 1728, Mary Wilson (*b* 1710);
5–Jonathan (1732-1805), *m* 1755, Sarah Butler;
4–Gurdon (*b* 1769), *m* Eunice Phelps (William[5], Am. Rev., *m* Ana Bishop);
3–Gurdon (1796-1866), Litchfield, *m* 1818, Polly Crampton (1796-1876; Elon[4], Am. Rev., *m* Avis Webster);
2–Elizabeth (1828-94), *m* 1849, Abraham Manning **Turner** (1824-88), farmer, Northfield, Conn.; issue: I–Caroline Louisa (1851-1921; *m* Henry Munger); II–Phebe Maria (*b* 1853; *m* Edward Bumstead); III–Dwight Filley (1856-75); IV–Albert Milford (1 above).
1–*m* 1894, Mary Seaton (divorced, 1921).
1–*m* 2d, July 14, 1923, Helen Catlin, *b* Litchfield, Conn., Oct. 30, 1875; dau. of John Howard Catlin, Northfield, Conn.
1–Ph.B., Yale-S., '90. Civil engr. with A.B. Hill, New Haven, 1892-1905; engr. of construction, Conn. Lime Co., 1905-09; pres. and mgr., Mass. Lime Co., Sheffield, Mass., 1910-14; field sec., Conn. State Park and Forest Commn. since 1914. Mem. S.A.R., I.A.G., New Haven Colony and Conn. Hist. socs. Conglist. Clubs: Appalachian Mtn., Adirondack Mtn., Green Mtn. Residence: Northfield, Conn.

1–**TURNER, Maurice Worcester,** *b* Brooklyn, N.Y., Mar. 24, 1857.
5–John **Turner,** of Eng.;
4–John;
3–Gov. John (*b* Eng.), high sheriff, Armagh, Ireland; *m* 1st, Mary Morrison (*b* Scotland-1824);
2–John (2 below).
9–Rev. William **Worcester** (qv);
8–Samuel (*d* 1680/81), *m* 1659, Elizabeth Parrott (*b* 1640);
7–Francis (*d* 1717), *m* 1690/91, Mary Cheney (1671-1759);
6–Rev. Francis (1698-1783), *m* 1720, Abigail Carlton (1696-1774);
5–Capt. Noah (1735-1817), marched from Hollis, N.H., 1775, at the head of a co. to reinforce Washington at Cambridge; *m* 1757, Lydia Taylor (1733-72);
4–Noah, A.M., D.D. (1758-1837), the "Apostle of Peace"; of Hollis, N.H., and Brighton, Mass.; hon. A.M., Dartmouth, 1791; S.T.D., Harvard, 1818; fifer in Am. Rev. aet. 16, at Bunker Hill and Bennington; "Worcester House," built

1688, and used as post office, 1817, of which he was first Brighton postmaster; ordained minister, 1787; author; Christian philanthropist; *m* 1779, Hannah Brown (1760-97);
3-Rev. Samuel (1793-1844), *m* 1817, Sarah Sargent;
2-Emma (2 below).
8-William **Sargent,** to Bridgeton, Barbados, returned to Eng. and thence to America, 1633, settled at Ipswich, Mass.;
7-William (*d* ante 1707), called "the Second"; *m* 1677/78, Mary Duncan (Peter[8], *m* Mary Epes);
6-Maj. Epes (1690-1762), *m* 1st, 1720, Esther Maccarty (1701-43; Florence[7], *m* Sarah Nework; helped establish the first Episcopal ch. in N.E.);
5-Capt. Winthrop (1727-93), took part in the siege of Louisburg, 1745; mem. Com. of Safety, 1775; govt. agt. at Gloucester during the war; wealthy shipowner, with David Pearce he owned "General Stark" a privateer out of Gloucester, mounting 18 guns; *m* 1750, Judith Sanders (1731-93; Capt. Thomas[6], *m* Judith, dau. of Capt. Andrew Robinson, said to have been the g.son of Rev. John Robinson, of Leyden);
4-Fitz William (1768-1822), *m* 1789, Anna Parsons (bap. 1769-1860; Capt. Thomas[5], *m* Sarah Sawyer);
3-Sarah (1793-1883), *m* 1817, Rev. Samuel **Worcester** (3 above);
2-Emma (1836-1920), *m* 1853, John **Turner** (*b* Ireland, 1823-*d* New York City, 1893), M.D., Pa. Homeopathic Med. Coll., 1853; Mason (32°); naturalized, 1854; issue: I-John, Jr. (1854-58); II-Maurice Worcester (1 above); III-Anna Sargent (1860-1920).
1-*m* June 30, 1878, Abby Rebecca Lamb Corliss (qv for issue).
1-M.D., Boston U. Sch. of Med., 1889. Asst., 1891-1903, and prof. theory and practice of medicine, Boston U., 1903-12; asst. physician, Mass. Homœopathic Hosp., 1903-12; med. dir., N.E. Bapt. Hosp., 1892-99. Pres. Internat. Hahnemannian Assn., 1911; mem. Am. Inst. of Homoeopathy, Mass. Homoe. Med. Soc., etc. Mem. O.F.P.A. (sec. Mass. Soc.), S.R., Soc. of The Gov. and Co. of Mass. Bay in N.E. Club: Boston New-Church (Swedenborgian). Mason. Summer place: "Poplar Lawn," Jackson, N.H. Residence: 786-788 Washington St., Brookline, Mass.

1-**TURNER, Abby Rebecca Lamb Corliss (Mrs. Maurice W.),** *b* Brighton, Mass., Nov. 3, 1858.
7-George **Corliss** (qv);
6-John (1648-98), *m* 1684, Mary Wilford (*b* 1667), of "Merrimack," Mass. (Gilbert[7]);
5-John (1686-1766-69), died in the same chair in the homestead in which his father and g.-father died; *m* 1711, Ruth Haynes (1691-1787; Jonathan[6], *m* Sarah-);
4-Joshua (1733-1819), Hampstead, N.H.; minuteman in Am. Rev.; *m* 1759, Abigail Marsh; *m* 2d, Molly Wells Colby (*d* 1825), a widow;
3-John (1768-1815), N. Yarmouth, Me.; *m* 1793, Mehitable Jewett;
2-Charles (2 below).
8-Maximillian **Jewett** (qv);
7-Joseph (*b* bet. 1655-57), *m* Rebecca Law (William[8], *m* Mary-);
6-Jonathan (1678/79-1745), *m* 1699, Mary Wicom (*d* 1741/42; John[7], *m* 1673, Abigail Kimball);
5-Mark (*b* 1713), Newbury, *m* 1737, Mary Chute;
4-Moses (*d* aet. "over 90"), Ware, N.H.; *m* Mary Meade (*d* 1774);
3-Mehitable (1774-1831), *m* John **Corliss** (3 above).
7-Joseph (Collings) **Collins,** supposed to have come from Ireland; was at Eastham, Mass., soon after 1644; *m* 1st, 1671, Ruth Knowles; *m* 2d, Sarah-;
6-John (*b* 1674), *m* 1702, Hannah Doane;
5-David (*b* 1715), *m* Dexiah Hawes;
4-David (1747-1832), *m* Deborah Sears;
3-Reuben (1783-1868), *m* 1808, Elizabeth R. Matthews;
2-Rebekah Wing (2 below).
8-James **Matthews** (*d* 1668), *m* Sarah-;
7-Thomas (*b* 1655);
6-John (ca. 1683-1776), *m* 1707/08, Hannah Sturgis (*b* 1687; Thomas[7], *m* 1680, Abigail Lothrop);
5-David (*b* 1727), *m* 1st, Sarah Hedge;
4-Thomas (*b* 1755), *m* 1774, Phoebe Matthews;
3-Elizabeth R. (1787-1864), *m* Reuben **Collins** (3 above).
10-John **Howland,** Mayflower Pilgrim (qv);
9-Desire (*d* 1683), *m* 1643, Capt. John **Gorham** (qv);
8-Desire (1644-1700), *m* 1661, John **Hawes** (*b* 1640; Edmond[9]);
7-Ebenezer (1678-1727), *m* Sarah Norton (*d* 1741-42, aet. 65);
6-Desire (1704-64), *m* 1724, John **Hedge** (1702-61);
5-Sarah (1729-84), *m* 1748/49, David **Matthews** (5 above).
10-Elder William **Brewster,** Mayflower Pilgrim (qv);
9-Patience (ca. 1600-1634), *m* 1624, Gov. Thomas **Prence** (qv);
8-Sarah (*d* 1706), *m* Jeremiah **Howes;**
7-Prence (1659-1753), *m* Dorcas Joyce (Hosea[8], *m* Elizabeth, dau. of John Chipman, qv, *m* Hope, dau. of John Howland, qv);
6-Dorcas (1702-76), *m* 1723, James **Matthews** (1700-bet. 1750-51; Banjamin[7]; James[8]; James[9]);
5-Benjamin (1725/26-1771), *m* 1751, Hannah Webber (*d* 1818);
4-Phoebe (*b* 1752), *m* 1774, Thomas **Matthews** (4 above);
3-Elizabeth R., *m* Reuben **Collins** (3 above);
2-Rebekah Wing (1816-61), *m* 1840, Charles **Corliss** (1812-90), farmer and stock broker; issue: I-Joseph Sylvanus (1841-1919; served in Civil War, 90 days); II-Elizabeth Collins (1844-1915); III-Henry Madison (1847-1920); IV-Abby Rebecca (1850-52); V-Abby Rebecca Lamb (1 above).
1-*m* June 30, 1878, Maurice Worcester Turner (qv); issue: 1-Theodore (*b* and *d* Somerville, Mass., Oct. 15, 1879); 2-Beatrice Constance, *b* 10 Savin Hill Av., Savin Hill, Dorchester, Boston, Nov. 24, 1883.
1-Mem. S.M.D., D.F.P.A. (treas., Mass. Chapter). Residence: 786-788 Washington St., Brookline, Mass.

CHURCHILL

Arms: *Sable, a lion rampant argent, debruised with a bendlet gules.*
Crest: *Out of a ducal coronet or, a demi-lion rampant argent.*
Motto: *Dieu defend le droit.*

1-**TURNER, (Marie) Christine Robertson (Mrs. Percy P.),** *b* Temple, Bell Co., Tex., May 17, 1898.
8-William **Churchill** (qv);
7-Armistead (1704-63), justice of the peace; col. of militia; collector for Rappahannock River; warden and vestryman; *m* Hannah

Harrison (Col. Nathaniel[8], of Wakefield, Surry Co., *m* Mary [Cary] Young; Benjamin[9], atty. gen., 1697-1702, commr. to Eng. from Va. Colony; Benjamin[10], qv);
6–William (1726-99), clk. of Middlesex Co.; mem. Council; warden and vestryman, Christ Ch.; *m* Elizabeth Carter (Robert "King"[7], of "Corotoman");
5–Thomas, *m* 1801, Elizabeth Burwell Berkeley;
4–Elizabeth Edmonia, *m* 2d, Rev. John **Cooke,** rector of Hanover Parish;
3–Charles, *m* 1856, Susan Gatlin Reavis;
2–Mary Gatlin (2 below).
11–Capt. Nicholas **Martian** (qv);
10–Elizabeth, *m* Col. George **Reade** (qv);
9–John, *m* Mary Lilly;
8–Margaret, *m* Thomas ("Scotch Tom") **Nelson** (qv);
7–Mary, *m* Edmund **Berkeley,** burgess, 1736-40 (Edmund[8], of "Barn Elms," *m* Lucy, dau. of Lewis Burwell, of Carter's Creek);
6–Edmund (1730-1802), of "Barn Elms," burgess, 1772-74; mem. final sessions of House of Burgesses, 1775; mem. of the convs., 1775,76; *m* 2d, 1768, Mary Burwell;
5–Elizabeth Burwell, *m* Thomas **Churchill** (5 above).
8–Martin **Franck,** from Germany to N.C., ca. 1710, settled on Trent River where he had large tracts of land; mem. N.C. Assembly, 1712; justice, Craven Co., N.C.;
7–Suzannah, *m* William **Herritage,** Gent., crown lawyer, presented by Queen Anne with a pair of diamond knee buckles; came to N.C. ante 1737, had a large practice as lawyer in and around New Bern; clk. House of Burgesses about 30 yrs.;
6–Sarah, *m* 1758, Richard **Caswell** (*b* 1729), removed to N.C., aet. 17; surveyor of the colony; clk. of ct., Orange Co.; mem. Colonial Assembly, 1754-71, speaker, 1770-71; col. of militia, Dobbs Co., 1771; comd. the right wing in Battle of Alamance, 1771; mem. Provincial Congress, organized at New Bern, 1774; del. Cont. Congress, 1774-76; treas. of N.C., 1775; elected gov. of N.C., 6 times, the 1st gov. under the Constn.; would receive no pay for services; received the thanks of Congress for gallant service at Battle of Moore's Creek;
5–Suzannah, *m* John **Gatlin,** of N.C.;
4–Sarah Catherine, *m* Judge Turner **Reavis,** 6th Jud. Dist. Ala.;
3–Susan Gatlin, *m* 1856, Charles **Cooke** (3 above);
2–Mary Gatlin (*b* 1860), mem. C.D.A., I.A.G.; *m* 1885, Huling Parker **Robertson** (*b* 1856), of Bell Co., Tex.; issue: I–Huling Parker, Jr. (*m* Wilhelmina Pegram); II–Marie Christine (1 above).
1–*m* Jan. 6, 1921, Dr. H. C. **Bailiff** (May 10, 1888-May 27, 1923); son of John Henry Bailiff.
1–*m* 2d Dec. 18, 1928, Percy Pamorrow Turner, *b* in Va., Dec. 28, 1892; son of Leonidas Grant Turner.
1–Grad. Temple (Tex.) H.S., 1916; grad. Dana Hall, Wellesley, Mass., 1917; Scoville Sch., New York, 1917-18; George Washington U., 1918-19; special studies in music and art. Mem. C.D.A., D.C.G., D.A.R. (state officer), C.A.R., U.D.C., Daus. Rep. of Tex., Pi Beta Phi. Episcopalian. Residence: San Antonio, Tex.

1–**TYNDELL, Charles Noyes,** *b* Fall River, Mass., May 2, 1876.
8–Thomas (Tyndale, Tindell) **Tyndell,** from Eng. ca. 1678, settled at Trenton, N.J.; *m* Isabel–;
7–John (*b* 1721), *m* Elizabeth–;
6–William (*b* 1745), *m* Mary Cubberly;
5–John (*b* ca. 1767), *m* Elizabeth Hammell;
4–Aaron (*b* ca. 1790), began to write name Tindell; *m* Abby–;
3–Charles (1815-58), *m* Rebecca Skillman;
2–Rev. Charles Henry (2 below).
8–Nicholas **Noyes** (qv);
7–Cutting (1649-ante 1734), *m* Elizabeth Knight;
6–Cutting (1676-1757), *m* Elizabeth Toppan;
5–Jacob (1704-86), *m* Jane Titcomb;
4–Joseph (*b* 1736), *m* Hannah Knapp;
3–George Rapall, D.D. (1798-1868), A.B., Harvard, 1818; Hancock prof. Hebrew, Harvard Div. Sch.; eminent theologian and author; *m* 1828, Eliza Wheeler Buttrick;
2–Martha Willson (2 below).
9–Maj. Simon **Willard** (qv);
8–Elizabeth (*d* 1690), *m* 1653, Robert **Blood** (*d* 1701);
7–Elizabeth (1656-1733), *m* 1677, Samuel **Buttrick** (1654-1726; William[8], to N.E., 1635, aet. 18);
6–Jonathan (1690-1767), *m* 1718, Elizabeth Wooly (1700-72);
5–Maj. John (1731-91), cdr. of the minutemen of Concord and the action at Concord North Bridge, Apr. 19, 1775; gave the famous order to fire, and himself fired the first shot on the American side in the Revolution; *m* Abigail Jones;
4–Stephen;
3–Eliza W. (1804-68), *m* George Rapall **Noyes** (3 above);
2–Martha Willson (1841-1916), *m* Rev. Charles Henry **Tyndell** (1841-1919), P.E. priest.
1–*m* Oct. 3, 1900, Rebecca Holmes Lewis (qv); issue: 1–Cary Noyes, *b* Front Royal, Va., July 23, 1901; *m* Dec. 18, 1924, Peyton Jacquelin Marshall (see Vol. II, p. 335; issue: Peyton Jacquelin, II, *b* Nov. 7, 1927); 2–Rebecca Holmes, *b* Winchester, Va., July 29, 1903; *m* Aug. 30, 1930, Francis Ryland Washington (qv).
1–Colgate, ex-'94; grad. Theol. Sem., Alexandria, Va., 1900; (S.T.D., Dickinson, 1921). Deacon, 1900, priest, 1901, P.E. Ch.; rector Christ Ch., Williamsport, Pa., 1914-23, St. Luke's, Memphis, Tenn., 1923-30, now rector St. Stephens, Terre Haute, Ind. (see Who's Who in America). Dep. to Gen. Conv. P.E. Ch., 1916,19,-22,25. Mem. Pi Gamma Mu, 1928. Study: 215 N. 7th St., Terre Haute, Ind.

1–**TYNDELL, Rebecca Holmes Lewis (Mrs. Charles N.),** *b* Jefferson Co., W.Va., Jan. 5, 1881.
7–William **Lewis,** from Wales, settled in Northumberland Co., Va.:
6–Vincent (*b* 1707), Loudoun Co., Va.; *m* Ann Longwith;
5–James (1754-1823), *m* 1775, Elizabeth Berkley (*d* 1811);
4–John Hancock, M.D. (1779-1833), *m* 1807, Mary Muse (*b* 1788; Battaile[5], Jefferson Co., Va., *m* Margaret Tate);
3–Lt. James Battaile, U.S.N. (1810-73), *m* 1841, Ann Catherine Hume (1814-83);
2–Robert Hume (2 below).
8–Thomas **Jones,** from Eng. to Va. ca. 1620; *m* Anne Spottswood;
7–Thomas, Williamsburg, Va.; *m* Elizabeth Pratt;
6–Gabriel (*b* Williamsburg, Va., 1724-1806), burgess; del. Cont. Congress; mem. Va. Conv. of 1788; *m* 1748, Margaret Strother;
5–Capt. Strother (*b* 1758), on Washington's staff in Am. Rev.; *m* 1780, Frances Thornton;
4–William Strother (*b* 1783), *m* 1825, Ann Cary Randolph (desc. William Randolph, of Turkey Island);
3–Beverley Randolph (1832-1912), *m* Rebecca J. Tidball;
2–Ann Cary Randolph (1859-1908), *m* 1872, Robert Hume **Lewis** (1843-1922), served in C.S.A., 1861-65.
1–*m* Oct. 3, 1900, Charles Noyes Tyndell (qv for issue).
Residence: 1613 S. 6th St., Terre Haute, Ind.

1–**WASHINGTON, Francis Ryland,** *b* Alexandria, Va., Aug. 18, 1897.
9–John **Washington** (qv);
8–Lawrence (1661-97), *m* 1690, Mildred Warner (Col. Augustine[9], *m* Mildred, dau. Col. George Reade, qv);
7–Augustine (1694-1743), *m* 2d, 1730/31, Mary Ball (1706-89; Col. Joseph[8]; William[9]; William[10], qv); they were parents of Gen. George Washington, and Elizabeth ("Betty") Washington, who *m* Fielding Lewis;
6–John Augustine (1736-87), *m* 1756, Hannah Bushrod (1736-post 1765; Col. John[7]; John[8]; Richard[9], qv);
5–Corbin (1765-ca. 1800), *m* 1787, Hannah Lee (1766-1801; Col. Richard Henry, "Light Horse Harry"[6]);
4–John Augustine (1787 or 90-1832), *m* 1814, **Jane** Charlotte Blackburn;
3–John Augustine (1821-61), killed at Cheat Mtn., W.Va.; lt. col. on Gen. Lee's staff; was the last private owner of Mount Vernon; *m*

1843, Eleanor Love Selden (1824-60; see their dau. Mrs. Julian Howard);
2–Lawrence (1854-1920), at the time of his death was the last male member of the Washington family *b* at Mount Vernon; reference librarian, Library of Congress; *m* 1876, Frances Lackland, of Jefferson Co., W.Va.
1–*m* Aug. 30, 1930, Rebecca Holmes, dau. of Charles Noyes Tyndell (qv).
1–Ed. Shenandoah Valley Mil. Acad., Va. Poly. Inst. Comdt. and instr. English, Shenandoah Valley Mil. Acad., 1921-30; asst. business mgr., 1923-30; with Standard Oil Co. of N.J., 1930–. Residence: 106 College Av., Salisbury, Md.

1–**HOWARD, Eleanor Love Selden Washington (Mrs. Julian),** *b* "Mt. Vernon," on the Potomac, Va., Mar. 14, 1856.
8–Richard **Lee** (qv);
7–Col. Richard (1647-1714), of "Mt. Pleasant," Westmoreland Co., Va.; house burned bet. 1716-30, still known as "Burnt House Fields"; burgess, 1677; mem. Council, 1676 and 80-98; naval officer and receiver of Va. duties for Potomac; *m* 1674, Laetitia Corbin (1657-1706; Henry[8], qv);
6–Thomas (1690-1750), mem. Council; pres. and cdr.-in-chief of Va.; apptd. gov., 1750; *m* 1722, Hannah Ludwell (1701-49; Col. Philip[7], pres. Council, rector of William and Mary Coll., *m* 1697, Hannah, dau. Benjamin Harrison, of Southorpe Parish, Surry Co.; Philip[8], came to Va., ca. 1660, dep., sec., gov. Carolinas, 1693, *m* 1st, as her 3d husband, 1667, Lucy, dau. Capt. Robert Higginson, Indian fighter, *m* Joanna Tokesy);
5–Richard Henry (1732-94), of "Chantilly"; burgess, 1757-92; pres. Cont. Congress; col. Cont. forces; a "signer"; *m* 1st, 1757-58, Anne Aylett (*d* 1768; William[6], of King William Co., *m* Anne–; Philip[7]; Capt. John[8], from Eng., 1656, settled in King William Co.);
4–Hannah (1766-1801), *m* 1787, Corbin **Washington** (1765-ca. 1800); for Washington lineage see Francis Ryland Washington;
3–John Augustine (1787 or 90-1832), kept 2 substitutes in War 1812, because he was not physically fit to serve; *m* 1814, Jane Charlotte Blackburn;
2–John Augustine (2 below).
6–Richard **Blackburn,** of Eng.; *m* Mary Watts;
5–Thomas (1740-1807), justice, Prince William Co., Va., 1769; mem. Com. of Safety, 1775; wounded in Battle of Germantown, Am. Rev.; a.-d.-c. to Gen. Washington; said to have been architect of "Mt. Vernon"; *m* Christian Scott (James[6], from Scotland to Va., 1739, removed to Prince William Co., rector Dittingham Parish, *m* Sarah, dau. Gustavus Brown);
4–Maj. Richard Scott, U.S.A. (*d* 1804 or 05), *m* ante 1787, Judith Ball;
3–Jane Charlotte (1787-1855), *m* John Augustine **Washington** (3 above).
10–Col. William **Ball** (qv);
9–Capt. William (1641-94), justice, 1680; burgess, 1685; *m* Miss Harris, of "Bay View," Lancaster Co., Va.;
8–William (1676-1744/45), surveyor, Northumberland Co., 1724; *m* Hannah Heale;
7–Capt. William (*d* 1744), justice; sheriff; capt. Lancaster Co., 1727-37; *m* Margaret Ball (Capt. Richard[8], *m* Sarah Young);
6–William, burgess, Lancaster Co., 1757-58; del. 1781; *m* 1741, Letitia Lee (*b* ca. 1730; Henry[7], *m* Mary, dau. Richard Bland, g.dau. Theodoric Bland, qv);
5–Mary (*b* 1748), *m* 1765, John **Ball** (George[6], *m* Judith, dau. Meryman Payne);
4–Judith, *m* Maj. Richard Scott **Blackburn** (4 above).
7–Samuel **Selden** (will probated 1720), from Eng., 1690; justice, Elizabeth City Co.; *m* Rebecca Yeo (Sir James[8]);
6–Joseph (*d* 1727), justice, Elizabeth City Co., 1723; sheriff, 1725; *m* Mary Cary (Col. Miles[7], royal naval officer for York River, etc., *m* Mary, dau. Col. William Wilson; Col. Miles[8], qv);
5–Col. Cary (1723-ca. 1792), capt., 1751; lt. col., 1763, col., Elizabeth City Co., 1767; magistrate Co. Ct.; mem. Com. of Safety; dep collector of customs; clk. Elizabeth City Ct., 1782; *m* ca. 1755, Elizabeth Jennings;
4–Dr. Wilson Cary (1761-1835), ed. by his brother-in-law, famous Dr. James McClurg; surgeon Va. Arty., Am. Rev.; *m* 2d, 1794 or 95, Eleanor Love (1772-1816; Samuel[5], of Charles City Co., Md., mem. Com. Safety and Com. Observation during Am. Rev., mem. Md. Conv., 1774-76, *m* Elizabeth, dau. of Col. John Courts; Samuel[6], sgt. Va. Line, *m* Elizabeth Courts, dau. of Charles Jones, Gent.);
3–Wilson Cary (1796-1845), *m* 1822, Louisa E. F. Alexander;
2–Eleanor Love (2 below).
10–John **Alexander** (*d* 1677), from Scotland; settled in Stafford Co., Va., 1652-59; called the founder of Alexandria, Va.; gave land which is site of Christ's Ch.; *m* Miss Graham, dau. John Graham, of Scotland;
9–Capt. John, *m* ? a dau. of Philip Fitzhugh;
8–Robert (*d* 1704), *m* Grace Ashton;
7–Robert (1688-1725), *m* 1st, Anne Fowke (Col. Gerard[8], of Charles City Co., Md., *m* 2d, Sarah Burdette; Col. Gerard[9], *m* Ann, dau. Adam Thoroughgood, qv);
6–John (1711-63), *m* 1731, Susan Pierson (1717-88);
5–Charles (1737-1806), gave right of way thru "Preston," for "King's Highway," to the Potomac River; mem. com. for establishment Va. militia, 1775; furnished supplies for minutemen of Alexandria in Am. Rev.; *m* 1771, Frances Brown (*d* 1823; Rev. Richard[6], M.D., Charles City Co., *m* Helen Bailey; Dr. Gustavus[7], from Scotland, owned "Rich Hill," Charles Co., Md., *m* 1710, Frances, dau. Gerard Fowke);
4–Charles (1772-1812), *m* 1800, Mary Bowles Armistead;
3–Louisa Elizabeth Fontaine (1805-26), *m* Wilson Cary **Selden** (3 above).
7–Rev. Peter **Fontaine** (1691-1757; g.g.g.son John de la Fontaine, martyred Huguenot); came from Eng. to Va., 1716; rector Westover Parish, Va., over 40 yrs.; *m* 1st, 1714, Elizabeth Fourreau;
6–Col. Peter (*b* 1720), surveyor, Halifax Co.; co. lt.; *m* Elizabeth Winston (Lt. William[7], *m* Sarah, dau. George Dabney; Isaac[8], from Eng., settled nr. Richmond, 1704, *m* Mary Dabney);
5–Mary, *m* Bowles **Armistead** (William[6], *m* Mary, dau. James Bowles; Henry[7]; John[8]; William[9], qv);
4–Mary Bowles, *m* 1st, Charles **Alexander** (4 above);
3–Louisa Elizabeth Fontaine, *m* Wilson Cary **Selden** (3 above);
2–Eleanor Love (1824-60), *m* 1843, Lt. Col. John Augustine **Washington** (1821-61), last pvt. owner of "Mt. Vernon"; mem. Gen. Lee's staff, C.S.A.; killed in W.Va. during War Between the States; issue: I–Louisa Fontaine (1844-1927; *m* 1871, Col. Roger Preston Chew, C.S.A., *d* 1921); II–Jane Charlotte (1846-1924; *m* 1869, Nathaniel Hite Willis, C.S.A., *d* 1914); III–Eliza Selden (1847-1909; *m* as his 3d wife, Col. Robert W. Hunter, C.S.A., *d* 1916); IV–Anna Maria (1851-1927; *m* 1872, Rt. Rev. Beverley Dandridge Tucker, D.D., C.S.A., see Vol. I, p. 864); V–Lawrence (1854-1920; *m* 1876, Frances Lackland; see their son Francis R.); VI–Eleanor L.S. (1 above); VII–George (1858-1905; *m* 1885, Emily Serena Porterfield).
1–*m* May 5, 1880, Julian Howard (July 10, 1853-May 17, 1884); son of Charles Howard, of Richmond, Va.; issue: 1–Sarah Smith, *b* "Ingleside," Richmond Co., Va., Mar. 28, 1881; *m* Oct. 22, 1903, Hugh Milton, *b* June 7, 1881, son of Thomas M. Caldwell (issue: Eleanor Washington, *b* Dec. 27, 1906; Jane Kearsley, *b* Aug. 10, 1908; Anne Howard, *b* Apr. 10, 1910; Hugh Milton, Jr., *b* May 24, 1918).
1–Ed. pvt. schs. Mem. D.B.R., C.D.A., D.A.R. (hon. v.p. gen.), C.A.R (nat v.p.), U.D.C., Nat. Mary Washington Memorial Assn. (pres.), etc. Clubs: Washington (hon. life mem.), Cameron (Alexandria, Va.). Residence: 1332 I St. N.W., Washington, D.C.

1–**TYNES, Narcissa Pendleton (Mrs. Conrad F.),** *b* Marion, Va., Nov. 3, 1876.
9–Col. John **Catlett** (1630-70), from Eng. to Va.; killed by Indians at Port Royal; *m* 1654, Elizabeth (Underwood) Slaughter, widow of Francis Slaughter (Capt. William Underwood[10]);

8–John (1658-1724), burgess; *m* Elizabeth Gaines (Col. Daniel[9], of Essex Co., *m* Margaret Bernard; Thomas[10]; Sir John[11]);
7–John (*d* 1789), *m* 1726, Mary Grayson (John[8], *m* Susannah–);
6–Judith (*d* 1798), godmother to President James Madison; *m* 1740, John **Bowie** (qv);
5–Catherine (1747-95), *m* 1765, James **Pendleton** (1740-93), burgess, justice, high sheriff; col. Am. Rev. (see Vol. II, p. 230 for Pendleton lineage);
4–William (1777-1820), *m* 1800, Nancy Strother;
3–James F. (1805-78), lawyer; *m* 1829, Narcissa Cecil;
2–Col. William Cecil (2 below).
9–William **Strother** (1630-1702), from Eng. to Va., ca. 1650; *m* ca. 1651, Dorothy Savage (*d* 1716);
8–William (1653-1726), high sheriff, King George Co., Va.; *m* ca. 1694, Margaret Thornton (*b* 1678; Francis[9], *m* 1st, Alice, dau. Capt. Anthony Savage; William[10], qv);
7–Francis (1700-52), *m* Susan Dabney (John[8]; Cornelius[9]);
6–John (1721-95), capt. French and Indian War, 1756-57; *m* Mary Willis Wade (Joseph[7], *m* Sarah–);
5–John (1756-1819), capt. Am. Rev.; *m* 1783, Helen Piper (*b* 1756);
4–Nancy (1784-1819), *m* William **Pendleton** (4 above).
8–Thomas **Witten,** *m* —Bulkeley;
7–Thomas (*b* 1672);
6–Thomas (1719-94), 1st white settler of Tazewell Co., Va.; sgt., Am. Rev.; *m* Elizabeth Cecil (*b* 1719);
5–Nancy (1755-1843), *m* William **Cecil** (Samuel[6], from Md. to Pulaski Co., Va., *m* Rebecca White; John[7]; John[8], from Eng. to St. Mary's, Md., ca. 1658);
4–Samuel, *m* Sally Poston;
3–Narcissa (1815-87), *m* James F. **Pendleton** (3 above).
5–George Michael **Bittle** (*b* 1759), from Prussia, 1780; Am. Rev.; *m* Anna Maria Beale (*b* 1761);
4–Thomas (*b* 1783), War 1812; *m* Mary Baer (*b* 1786; Philip[5], officer Am. Rev., *m* Elizabeth Loerne);
3–David Frederick (1811-76), founder Roanoke Coll.; *m* Louisa Catherine Krauth (1816-88; Charles[4], *m* Catherine Doll);
2–Julia Francke (1849-1916), *m* 1875, Col. William Cecil **Pendleton,** C.S.A. (*b* 1847), lawyer; issue: I–Narcissa (1 above); II–Fred W. (*m* Mary Kelly); III–Louise (*m* Walter L. Hodges); IV–Julia (*m* Glenn M. St. Clair); V– Sarah (*m* Edwin A. Turpin); VI–Ruth Holland.
1–*m* Apr. 11, 1900, Conrad F. Tynes, *b* Tazewell, Va., Feb. 3, 1877; son of Capt. Achilles James Tynes (1833-1914), of Tazewell, Va.; issue: 1–A(chilles) James, *b* Tazewell, Va., Mar. 12, 1903; *m* Dec. 1925, Mary Virginia, dau. B.C. Snidow, of Princeton, W.Va.; 2–Conrad F., Jr., *b* Tazewell, Nov. 13, 1912; 3–Nancy Pendleton, *b* Bluefield, W.Va., Nov. 10, 1918.
1–B.A., Martha Washington Coll., '95. Mem. C.D.A., Huguenot Soc. Founder of Manakin Town, Va., D.A.R. Residence: Bluefield, W.Va.

1–**TYNES, William Vernon,** *b* Nansemond Co., Va., July 26, 1883.
6–Timothy **Tynes** (*d* 1752), vestryman, Benns (St. Luke's), Isle of Wight Co., 1743; *m* Elizabeth–;
5–Robert (*d* 1773), vestryman, 1759;
4–Robert (*d* 1819), capt. 29th Va. Vols., Isle of Wight Co., War 1812; *m* Martha Jordan;
3–Henry Lexington (1801-74), *m* 2d, Anne Caroline Powell (1812-65; Matthew[4], *m* Elizabeth Pruden; Benjamin[5]);
2–Henry Lexington (2 below).
4–James Hunter **Godwin,** *m* Harriett Corbell;
3–James Ed., *m* Margaret A. Darden;
2–Rose (*b* 1857), *m* Henry Lexington **Tynes,** of Nansemond Co.; issue: I–Henry Lexington; II–Ruth Godwin; III–James Hunter Godwin; IV–William Vernon (1 above); V–Dr. Matthew Powell (*m* Elizabeth W. Smith); VI–Helen Jordan (*m* Harry B. Hearn); VII–Adlyn Darden.
1–*m* Feb. 24, 1915, Ethel Virginia Matthews (qv); issue: 1–William Henry, *b* Norfolk, Va., Sept. 21, 1916; 2–Clarence Matthews, *b* Norfolk, Dec. 29, 1921.
1–Residence: 829 Brandon Av., Norfolk, Va.

1–**TYNES, Ethel Virginia Matthews (Mrs. William V.),** *b* Roanoke, Va., Nov. 18, 1895.
6–William **Matthews** (*b* 1725), of Albemarle Co., Va.;
5–William (1758-1825), soldier Am. Rev.; present with Gen. Washington at battles of Brandywine, and Germantown; *m* 1799, Jane Dunbar Hall (1778-1836; Nathan[6], Am. Rev.);
4–John Barley (1800-56), Albemarle Co., Va.; *m* 1822, Catherine Burford (1800-50; William[5], Am. Rev.);
3–John W. (1839-1909), Nelson Co., Va.; served under Stonewall Jackson, 3 yrs., in C.S.A.; *m* 1862, Mary Harris;
2–Melville N. (2 below).
5–Thomas **Ware** (1762-1851), of Albemarle Co., Va., later in Henry Co.; in Am. Rev., with LaFayette at Charlottesville, Williamsburg and surrender at Yorktown; *m* 1787, Mildred Bryant (*b* 1770), of Buckingham Co.;
4–Mary (1815-80), *m* 1837, Nelson B. **Harris** (1817-88), of Nelson Co.;
3–Mary (1841-89), *m* John W. **Matthews** (3 above).
6–Morris **Floyd** (1775-1860), of Amherst Co.; constable; 2d Bn., 121st Regt., Va. Militia, 1821; *m* 1797, his cousin, Sallie Floyd (1776-1845; Lt. Charles[7] [1752-97], Am. Rev., *m* Martha Davis [1754-1806]; Josiah[8]);
5–Elizabeth (1800-86), *m* 1818, as his 2d wife, Isaac **Hanes** (1780-1863);
4–Sarah (1819-1907), *m* 1836, Col. John **Kelly,** of Botetourt Co., Va.;
3–Sarah Virginia (1842-1913), *m* 1868, David Walker **Gillespie** (1826-91), sgt. Co. B, 5th Va. Cav., C.S.A. (David L.[4] [1783-1856], *m* 1805, Nancy [1789-1843], dau. of Joseph King [1759-1821], pvt. 14th Va. Regt., Cont. Line, Am. Rev., of Fluvanna Co., *m* 1779, Mourning–; John[5] [*d* 1811], served in 9th Va. Regt., Am. Rev., of Fluvanna Co.);
2–Oscela (*b* 1873), *m* 1891, Melville N. **Matthews** (*b* 1869); issue: I–Clarence William (*b* 1892; *m* Sarah Barnes); II–Ethel Virginia (1 above); III–Mayme Crystal (*b* 1899; *m* Arthur Lloyd Cruser); IV–Hattye Elizabeth (*b* 1904; *m* Claude William Kyle).
1–*m* Feb. 24, 1915, William Vernon Tynes (qv for issue).
1–Mem. D.A.R. Residence: 829 Brandon Av., Norfolk, Va.

1–**VadeBONCOEUR, Mary Edith Bovell (Mrs. Prudent A.),** *b* Arcola, Ill., June 12, 1880.
9–Richard **Hubbell** (qv);
8–Richard (1654-1738), *m* 2d, 1692, Hanna Sillway (or Silliman);
7–Richard (1696-1787), Am. Rev.; *m* 1725, Penelope Fayerweather (1704-91);
6–Hezekiah (1728-84), *m* 1752, Anne Patterson;
5–Aaron (1761-1848), Am. Rev.; *m* Sarah Silliman (1767-1851);
4–Ellen (1783-1880), *m* 1811, Daniel S. **Odell** (*d* 1821);
3–Mary Elizabeth (1821-91), *m* 1838, George P. **Warden;**
2–Adaline M. (1857-86), *m* 1878, James Wilson **Bovell** (1851-81; Stephen[3]); *m* 2d, 1884, William S. Crawford.
1–*m* Jan. 7, 1903, Prudent A. VadeBoncoeur, *b* Ashkum, Ill., Dec. 7, 1877; son of Thomas VadeBoncoeur, of Kankakee, Ill.; issue: 1–Bovell Joseph, *b* Kankakee, May 21, 1906; St. Viator Coll., '31.
1–Grad. nurse, Ill. State Hosp., Kankakee, 1903. Mem. C.D.A., D.A.R., Women of Mooseheart Legion. Catholic. Residence: 1204 S. East Av., Kankakee, Ill.

1–**VALENTINE, John A.,** *b* Soso, Miss., June 24, 1868.
4–William **Valentine** (*b* 1783), lived in S.C. since 1808; *m* Elizabeth Moore;
3–Allen (1808-1901), *m* 1830, Cyntha Welch;
2–Richard H. (1843-1925), farmer; *m* Sarah J. Coats (1848-1903).
1–*m* Apr. 1, 1891, Mary I. Copeland, *b* Soso, Miss., Oct. 22, 1873; dau. of S.J. Copeland, of Soso; issue (all *b* Soso, Miss.): 1–Edward Leroy, *b* Oct. 14, 1893; *m* July 21, 1924, Rubye, dau. of Milledge W. Carr (issue: Mary E.); 2–Bessie I., *b* Feb. 1, 1896; *m* Oct. 4, 1913, James

B. Harper (issue: Louise; Kimbrill; Willford); 3–Hettie E., *b* Dec. 18, 1897; *m* June 21, 1919, John F. Harper (issue: Sybil); 4–Richard L., *b* Dec. 23, 1899; 5–Linnie, *b* Jan. 31, 1903; *m* Dec. 8, 1928, Thomas D. Broome; 6–Stephen E., *b* Oct. 17, 1908.

1–Studied Miss. A. and M. Coll., 2 yrs. Farmer and teacher, 1891-1900; worked in store, 1901-04; farmer 1904-06; postmaster, since 1906. Mayor of Soso, Miss., 2 terms. Methodist. Democrat. Residence: Soso, Miss.

1–**VAN HEUSEN, Maude,** *b* Seneca, Ill., Aug. 26, 1881.

9–Jan Franse (Van Hoesen) **Van Heusen** (*d* 1703), from Holland ante 1645, settled at Fort Orange, later at Beverwyck, N.Y.; *m* Volke Jurrianse;

8–Johannes (*d* post 1720), of Claverack; *m* 1658, Jannetje Jan De Ryck (*d* ante 1709; Jan Cornelise[9]);

7–Jan Hanneson, of Claverack and Loonenburgh; *m* 1711, Tannekie Witbeck (*b* 1693; Hendrick Janse[8], *m* Lyntje, dau. of Peter Winne; Jan Thomas[9]);

6–Jacob (1722-1807), *m* 1745, Annatje Van Loon (1725-1807; Albertus[7], *m* Maria, dau. of Casper Jacobse Halenbeck; Jan[8]);

5–Albert (*b* 1750), Am. Rev., 1776-83; *m* ante 1771, Sophia Delyne (Cornelius[6], *m* Alida–; Benjamin[7]);

4–John A. (1785-1869), *m* 1811, Judith Van Wormer (1792-1842; Cornelius[5], *m* Catharine, dau. of Hendrick Hendricksen; Lawrence[6]);

3–Cornelius (1814-60), *m* 1844, Caroline Rulison (1823-80; Cornelius[4], *m* Catherine Elwood);

2–William Anderson (2 below).

9–Abel **Wright** (1631-1725), from Eng., settled at Lebanon, Conn.; *m* 1659, Martha Kitcherall (Samuel[10]);

8–Abel (1664-1745), *m* 1691, Rebecca Terry (*b* 1673; Samuel[9], *m* Anna Lobdell);

7–Ephraim (1704-1758-59), *m* 1724, Hannah Wood (*d* 1737; Thompson[8], *m* Martha Foster);

6–Ephraim (1735-1808), Hartland, Conn.; Am. Rev.; *m* Lucretia Holdridge;

5–Bildad (1768-1853), Mayfield, N.Y.; War 1812; *m* 1790, Chloe Shipman (1768-1845; Jonathan[6], *m* Abigail Fox);

4–Joel Shipman (1803-84), *m* Jennet Templeton (1800-66; Thomas[5], *m* Margaret Stewart, both from Scotland);

3–Orrin Wentworth (1828-1907), Johnstown, N.Y.; *m* 1853, Eleanor Dunning (1825-81; Josiah[4], *m* Sarah Joslin);

2–Helen Emeline (1856-1909), *m* 1878, William Anderson **Van Heusen** (1846-1901), engr.; issue: I–Allie M. (*b* 1879); II–Maude (1 above); III–Edith (*b* 1882; *m* Frank N. Becker).

1–Mem. Dutch Settlers Soc. of Albany, D.A.R. Baptist. Republican. Club: Century. Residence: 33 Stewart St., Amsterdam, N.Y.

1–**VAUGHAN, Margaret Anne Stites (Mrs. Horatio Nelson),** *b* Fayetteville, W.Va., Nov. 26, 1857.

8–Dr. John **Stites**, (qv);

7–Richard (*b* Hempstead, L.I., 1640-*d* 1702);

6–William (1676-1727), Elizabethtown, N.J.; *m* Mary–;

5–John (1706-82), Springfield, N.J.; *m* 2d, Margaret Hampstead (1716-84);

4–Maj. Benjamin (*d* 1804), *m* Hannah Warren;

3–Nathaniel (1799-1873), *m* Margaret McKibben (1800-63);

2–Dr. John (1827-1916), physician, Cincinnati, O.; *m* 1850, L. Virginia Manser (1827-98); issue: I–Catherine Morris (1852-1917; *m* William H. Orr); II–Eunice (1855-1863); III–Margaret Anne (1 above); IV–H. Virginia (*b* 1863; *m* James C. Ernst); V–Angie E. (*b* 1868; *m* William O. Powell; *m* 2d, William L. Strow).

1–*m* May 8, 1880, Horatio Nelson Vaughan (May 18, 1833-Aug. 8, 1916); son of John Vaughan, of Springfield, N.H.

1–Ed. high school, College of Music, Cincinnati. Mem. D.F.P.A., D.A.R., Women's Club. Residence: 108 N. Chicago St., Pontiac, Ill.

1–**VENABLE, Albert Sidney,** *b* Victoria Co., Tex., Sept. 3, 1862.

6–Abraham **Venable** (qv);

5–Abraham (1700-65), of New Kent Co., Va.; capt. militia, Louisa Co.; co. lt.; burgess 20 yrs.; said to have been the most influential Venable who ever lived in Va.; vestryman St. Paul's, Trinity and Fredericksburg parishes; *m* ca. 1723, Martha Davis (1703-65; Robert[6], *m* Abadiah Lewis);

4–Nathaniel (1733-1804), of "Slate Hill," Prince Edward Co.; planter; justice; burgess, 1766-69; mem. Va. Assembly; mem. Va. Senate, 1780-82; vestryman St. Patrick's Parish; a founder of Hampden-Sidney Coll.; *m* 1755, Elizabeth Woodson;

3–William Lewis (1780-1824), A.B., Hampden-Sidney; lt. in Capt. Samuel V. Allen's co. of cav., 1st Regt., Va. Militia, War 1812; trustee Hampden-Sidney 16 yrs.; *m* 1808, Frances Watkins Nantz (1793-1859);

2–William Goodridge (2 below).

8–Dr. John **Woodson** (qv);

7–Robert (1634-1707), Prince Edward Co.; *m* ca. 1656, Elizabeth Ferris (Richard[8], of Curls Neck; Nicholas[9], to Va., 1619);

6–Col. Richard (ca. 1662-1730), *m* Anne Smith (Obadiah[7], of Henrico Co., *m* Mary dau. of William, son of Lt. Col. Richard Cocke, qv, *m* Mary, dau. of Lt. Col. Walter Aston, qv);

5–Richard (1690-1773), of "Poplar Hill," Prince Edward Co.; *m* 1715, Anne Madeline Michaux (*b* 1693; Abraham[6], Huguenot refugee to Va., settled at Manakin Town, *m* 1692, Susanne Rochette);

4–Elizabeth (1740-91), *m* Nathaniel **Venable** (4 above).

6–Col. George **Carrington** (qv);

5–Judge Paul (1733-1818), burgess and judge Ct. of Appeals of Va.; *m* Margaret Read (1739-76; Col. Clement, Jr.[6]; Thomas[7]; Col. George[8], qv);

4–Gen. George (1756-1809), lt. col. in Am. Rev.; *m* 1784, Sallie Coles Tucker (*b* 1765);

3–Emily Eaton (1805-71), *m* 1824, Dr. Paul Carrington **Venable** (1793-1876; Samuel Woodson[4]; Nathaniel[5], 4 above);

2–Sallie Tucker (1825-97), *m* 1845, William Goodridge **Venable** (1819-1908), farmer and merchant, Prince Edward Co.; during the Civil War, he offered his services several times to his beloved Southland; Gen. J. B. Magruder said: "Go home, Mr. Venable, and do what you can to furnish the sinews of war, I know where your heart is, you are too valuable a man to be shot down in the ranks"; he gave all that he made on his large plantation, outside of a living, during the entire war; issue: I–David (1846-*d* young); II–Frederick Nantz (1848-1861); III–Mildred Lightfoot (*b* 1850; *m* William Francis Lyte); IV–Paul Carrington (1852-1908; *m* Georgiana Carpenter); V–Sallie Emily (1855-97); VI–Frances Proctor (1857-58); VII–William Goodridge (1859-1929; *m* Sadie Heiskell Anderson, *d* 1907); VIII–Albert Sidney (1 above); IX–George Curtis Moore (1867-75).

1–*m* Oct. 25, 1893, Sallie Elizabeth Garden, *b* Prince Edward Co., Va., Feb. 27, 1868; dau. of Thomas James Garden, supt. of public schools, Prince Edward Co.; issue: 1–Sidney Johnson, *b* Van Buren, Ark., Nov. 13, 1894; A.B., Southwestern Presbyn. U., '16; B.D., Union Theol. Sem. Va., 1918; *m* Dec. 17, 1918, Leucia Reynolds, dau. of James A. Butler, of Millersburg, Ky. (issue: Alice Garden; Sidney Johnson; Leucia Butler).

1–A.B., Austin Coll., '89 (D.D., 1924); B.D., Union Theol. Sem., 1892. Ordained Presbyn. ministry, 1892; pastor Van Buren, Ark., 1892-95, Bayview, Va., 1895-1907, Glasgow, Va., 1907-08, Sherman, Tex., 1908-10, Lewisburg, Tenn., 1910-12, Millersburg, Ky., 1913-18; McAfee, Ky., 1919-21, Farmville, N.C., 1927. Principal Bayview High Sch., 1896-1900; pres. Sayre Coll., 1917-19; supt. home missions, Roanoke (Va.) Presbytery, 1921-27. Democrat. Residence: Farmville, N.C.

1–**VENN, Maria Garnett (Mrs. Henry Straith),** *b* Washington, D.C., Sept. 2, 1875.

7–John **Garnett** (will proved 1713), from Eng., settled in Gloucester Co., later removed to Essex Co., Va.; *m* Ann–;

6–James (1692-1765), burgess, 1742-47; justice, Essex Co., 1720-40; *m* 2d, Elizabeth Muscoe (*d* 1736; Salvator[7], burgess and vestryman);

5–Muscoe (1736-1803), of "Elmwood," Essex Co., Va.; mem. Com. of Safety, Am. Rev.; builder of the "Elmwood" estate before Am. Rev.; *m* 1767, Grace Fenton Mercer (1751-1814; John[6],

GARNETT

Arms: *Gules, a lion rampant argent, ducally crowned or, within a bordure engrailed of the last.*
Crest: *A dexter arm holding a swan's head erased proper.*
Motto: *Diligentia et honore.*

from Ireland, settled at "Marlborough," Stafford Co., Va., *m* 2d, 1750, Ann, daughter of Dr. Mungo Roy, first of family in Va., from Scotland);
4–Muscoe (1786-1869), of "Prospect Hill," Essex Co.; *m* 1807, Maria Willis Battaile;

DR. ALEXANDER YELVERTON PEYTON GARNETT (1819-88).

3–Dr. Alexander Yelverton Peyton (1819-88), grad. U.Pa., 1841; asst. surgeon U.S.N., promoted to surgeon, 1848, resigned 1850, to accept the chair of clinical medicine in the Nat. Med. Coll., Washington; mem. examining bd. of surgeons C.S.A., 1861, and subsequently was surgeon in charge of the two military hosps. in Richmond, Va.; was family physician of Jefferson Davis, of all the mems. of the Conf. cabinet, and of General Lee and family; prof. clinical medicine, Nat. Med. Coll., 1867-70, upon resignation was made emeritus prof.; dir. Children's Hosp., St. Ann's Asylum for Foundlings, and mem. bd. of advisory and consulting surgeons and physicians to the Columbia Hosp. for Women; v.p. A.M.A., 1885, pres., 1887; pres. Med. Soc. and Med. Assn., Washington, Southern Memorial Assn., Pathological Soc.; *m* 1848, Mary Elizabeth Wise;
2–Henry Wise (2 below).
9–John **Washington** (qv);
8–Lawrence (1661-97), of Westmoreland Co.; burgess, 1684, 1691-92; *m* 1690, Mildred Warner (*d* 1700; Col. Augustine, 2d[9], *m* Mildred Reade);
7–Mildred Warner (1696-1747), aunt and godmother of General Washington; part owner of the property later known as Mount Vernon; *m* 2d, 1733, as his 3d wife, Col. Henry **Willis** (1691-1740), founder of Fredericksburg, Va.; burgess;
6–Col. Lewis (1734-1813), first cousin and schoolmate of General Washington; lt. col. 10th Va. Regt., 1776-78; *m* 1st, Mary Champe (Col. John[7], of Lambs Creek, King George Co., *m* Jane–);
5–Mary Champe (*d* 1792), *m* as his 1st wife, Hay **Battaile,** of "Hayfield," Caroline Co., Va.; moved to Ky., ca. 1819;
4–Maria Willis, *m* 1807, Muscoe **Garnett,** 2d (4 above).
9–John **Wise** (1617-95), from Eng., settled on Eastern Shore of Va.; *m* Hannah Scarburgh (Capt. Edmund[10], of Eng. and Va.);
8–John (*d* 1717), of Accomac, Va.; *m* Matilda West (*d* 1722);
7–Col. John (*d* 1767), *m* Scarburgh Robinson;
6–Col. John (1723-69), *m* Margaret Douglas (1736-1808);
5–Maj. John (1765-1812), *m* 2d, 1799, Sarah Corbin Cropper (1777-1813);
4–Hon. Henry Alexander (1806-76), *m* 1st, 1828, Anne Jennings (1808-37);
3–Mary Elizabeth (1829-98), *m* 1848, Alexander Y. P. **Garnett** (3 above);
2–Henry Wise (1849-97), prominent lawyer, Washington; *m* 1874, Marion Morson (1849-88; James Marion[8], lawyer, of Fredericksburg, Va., later resided at Dover-on-James-River, Va., which estate was looted by Dahlgren's raiders in the Civil War, *m* Ellen Carter Bruce); issue: I–Maria (1 above); II–Ellen (*b* 1877); III–Dr. Alexander Yelverton Peyton; (*b* 1881; *m* Mildred Harper Poor); IV–Henry Wise (*m* Maud Vincent).
1–*m* Sept. 26, 1906, Henry Straith Venn (Nov. 29, 1869-Jan. 3, 1908); son of The Rev. Henry Venn, canon of Canterbury (Eng.) Cathedral; issue: 1–Henry Garnett (July 3-6, 1908).
1–Ed. Norwood Inst., Washington. Mem. C.D.A. Ams. of Royal Descent, D.A.R., S.P.V.A., I.A.G., etc. Summer place: "Iron Hill," Alleghany P.O., Alleghany Co., Va. Residence: 2013 Q St. N.W., Washington, D.C.

1–**VILES, Annie Ethel Johnson (Mrs. Blaine S.),** *b* Lynn, Mass., Oct. 9, 1878.
8–Thomas **Breck** (1633-1703), from Eng., settled at Sherborn, Mass.; with others built a fort on the northern Bank of Boggaston Pond for the protection of their families, defending it repeatedly against Indians; *m* Mary Hill (*b* 1636);
7–Esther (1679-1774), *m* 1699, John **Richardson** (1679-1759);
6–John (1701-67), of Medfield, *m* 1730, Jemima Gay (1705-82);
5–Elisha (1743-98), of Wrentham, went on call at Lexington; *m* 1771, Abigail Lawrence (1749-1827);
4–Abigail (*b* 1778), Franklin, Mass.; *m* 1810, Nathan **Metcalf** (1765-1843);
3–Julianna (1819-1902), *m* 1839, Stephen Carlton **Johnson** (1813-87);
2–William Carlton (1851-1912), shoe mfr., Hallowell, Me.; *m* 1876, Annie Copp (*b* 1851).
1–*m* June 30, 1904, Blaine Spooner Viles, *b* North New Portland, Me., July 22, 1879; son of Edward Payson Viles, of Showhegan, Me.; issue: 1–Dorothy Johnson, *b* Newport, N.H., May 30, 1905; 2–William Payson, *b* Newport, July 16, 1906.
1–Ed. Lasell Sem., 1899. Mem. D.C.W. (organizing regent), D.A.R. (v.regent Koussinoc Chapter, regent, v.state regent, state regent),

etc. Republican. Residence: 154 State St., Augusta, Me.

1–**VAN HORN, Arthur Wesley,** *b* Hackensack, N.J., Mar. 15, 1860.
9–Garrit Hendericksen **Blauvelt** (1620-83), from Holland to Rensselaerwyck, N.Y., 1637; settled at New Amsterdam, 1646; *m* 1646, Marretje Moll (ante 1625-ante 1679; Lambert Huybertsen[10], of Bushwyck);
8–Huybert, *m* Willemtje Ariaens;
7–Gerrit, *m* Jan. 12, 1704, at Tappen, N.Y., Katrina Meyer;
6–Huybert (*b* Oct. 14, 1716), *m* Alida Verveelen;
5–Sarah (June 22, 1756-1806), *m* Cornelius **Van Horn** (1747-1824); see Vol. III, p. 457, for Van Horn lineage;
4–Cornelius, Jr. (1790-1845), *m* Lavina Vanderbeck (1789-1876), of Paramus, Bergen Co., N.J.;
3–John (1813-90), *m* Martha Terhune;
2–Cornelius (2 below).
9–Albert Albertse (Terheun) **Terhune** (qv);
8–Albert Albertse, Jr. (1651-1709), *m* Hendrikje S. Van Voorhees (*d* 1705);
7–Derk (Richard), (bap. 1702), *m* 1727, Katherine Kip;
6–Albert (bap. 1728), *m* Mary, or Maria, Demarest;
5–Albert (*b* 1771), *m* his cousin, ca. 1793, Rachel Terhune;
4–Martin (1795-1839), *m* Catherine Ackerman (1799-1853);
3–Martha (1820-81), *m* John **Van Horn** (3 above);
2–Cornelius (1838-1906), *m* 1859, Almira Van Saun (1838-75); for issue and other lineages see Vol. III, p. 457.
1–*m* Dec. 14, 1889, Jessie McKinney (divorced 1893); issue: 1–Josephine Elizabeth, *b* Apr. 30, 1892.
1–*m* 2d, Jan. 7, 1905, Harriet Rohrer, *b* Canton, O., July 25, 1863; dau. of Henry Rohrer, *m* Harriet Rowland.
1–Architect, 1883-1930. Sec.-treas., N.D. State Bd. of Architecture, 1917-30. Mem. H.S., S.A.R., I.A.G., A.O.U.W. K.P. Residence: 209 Seventh St., Bismarck, N.D.

1–**VAN RENSSELAER Florence.** *b* Melville Park, Baltimore, Md., Nov. 7, 1875.
9–Kiliaen **Van Rensselaer** (qv);
8–Col. Jeremias (1632-74), 3d patroon; from Holland to Albany, 1642; *m* 1662, Maria van Cortlandt (1645-89; Oloff Stevensen[9], qv);
7–Kiliaen (1663-1719), 4th patroon; *m* 1701, his cousin, Maria Van Cortlandt (*b* 1674);
6–Stephen (1707-47), *m* 1729, Elizabeth Groesbeck (bap. 1707-1756; Stephanus[7], *m* 1699, Elizabeth, dau. of Johannes Lansing, *m* Gertie Van Schaick);
5–Stephen (1742-69), *m* 1764, Catharine Livingston;
4–Elizabeth (1768-1841), as widow of John Bradstreet Schuyler (1762-95); *m* 2d, 1800, John **Bleecker** (1760-1833);
3–Catharine Westerlo (1809-86), *m* 1826, Cornelius Glen **Van Rensselaer** (1801-71), see Vol. I, p. 869, for paternal Van Rensselaer lineage;
2–Dr. John Jeremiah (2 below).
8–Robert **Livingston** (qv);
7–Philip (1686-1749), 2d lord of the manor; sec. for Indian affairs; co. clk.; mem. Provincial Council; *m* 1707, Katherine Van Burgh (*d* 1756; Peter[8], mayor of Albany);
6–Philip (1716-78), B.A., Yale, 1737, M.A., 1740; speaker, Provincial Assembly; a "signer"; *m* 1740, Christina Ten Broeck (1718-1801; Col. Richard [Dirck Wessels][7], recorder, Albany);
5–Catharine (1745-1810), *m* 1st, Stephen **Van Rensselaer** (5 above).
4–Thomas **Taylor** (*b* 1788-*d* Baltimore, Md., Sept. 6, 1838), from England or Ireland; captured on own ship, 1812; taken to Tower of London for 7 months; on return to America destroyed all proof of origin; in partnership with Alexander Brown, of Baltimore; *m* 1811, Ruth Gorham, of Md.;
3–Col. Charles Rutherford Taylor Bang (1814-Mar. 15, 1900), of Baltimore; *m* Sept. 10, 1835, Georgianna Millemon (George[4], of Havre de Grace, Md., *m* Roseanna Coleman);
2–Florence Rutherford (Nov. 1, 1844-Apr. 1, 1913), *m* Oct. 20, 1864, Dr. John Jeremiah **Van Rensselaer** (Sept. 13, 1836-June 18, 1911), A.B., Rutgers, '57; M.D., Albany Med. Coll., 1859; maj. and surgeon U.S.V., 1861-65; issue: I–Lyndsay (*b* July 22, 1870); II–Florence (1 above).
1–Mem. C.D.A., C.L.M.A., H.S.A., D.A.R., Nat. Geneal. Soc., Md. Hist. Soc., N.Y.G.B.S., I.A.G. Club: Women's Nat. Republican. Summer place: "Sagtikos Manor," Bay Shore, L.I. Residence: 3 E. 82d St., New York, N.Y.

1–**VAUGHAN, George Tully,** *b* Arrington, Nelson Co., Va., June 27, 1859.
15–John **Finley** (living 1457; desc. Kenneth McAlpin, A.D. 864), of Clan of Finley;
14–John (living 1463), *m* Janet Rogers;
13–Andrew F. (living 1508), *m* Janet Hayes;
12–James (*b* ca. 1530), *m* Elizabeth Warrender;
11–John (*b* ca. 1570), *m* Sara Craigie;
10–James (*b* ca. 1610), *m* Mary Mockie;
9–Alexander (*b* ca. 1640), *m* Catherine Jennings;
8–James (*b* ca. 1670), *m* Elizabeth Patterson;
7–John (*b* ca. 1700), *m* 1723, Thankful Doak;
6–John (*b* 1724), *m* Mary Caldwell;
5–Margaret (*b* 1746), *m* John **Shields** (*b* 1740; James[6] [*b* ca. 1718], *m* Jane Montgomery);
4–James (1772-1839), *m* 1792, Elizabeth Higginbotham (1778-1837), see Vol. III, p. 459;
3–Egbert Oswald (1818-83), *m* Sarah Ellen Brent; see Vol. III, p. 459;
2–Francis Ellen (1842-1905), *m* Dr. Washington Lafayette **Vaughan** (1833-82), physician (for issue see Vol. II, p. 241).
1–*m* June 27, 1883, Maria Townsend Venable, *b* Amherst Co., Va., Dec. 21, 1862; C. D. A.; dau. William Goodwin Venable, of Farmville, Va.; issue: 1–Vera, *b* Lowesville, Va., May 13, 1884; Randolph-Macon Coll., '08; *m* Apr. 19, 1911, William R. Crute (issue: Elizabeth Nevil; May Venable); 2–William Washington (see Vol. II, p. 241, for Venable lineage).
1–M.D., U.Va., 1879 (Kappa Sigma, Phi Chi, Alpha Omega Alpha); M.D., N.Y.U., 1880; post-grad. courses, New York Polyclinic, U.Berlin, Jefferson Med. Coll., Phila.; (LL.D., Georgetown, 1919). Prof. surgery, Georgetown U. Med. Sch., since 1897; chief surgeon Georgetown U. Hosp.; surgeon Tuberculosis Hosp. and consulting surgeon St. Elizabeth Hosp., Washington Asylum Hosp. and Veteran's Bureau; author (see Who's Who in America). Asst. surgeon, Jan. 1888, surgeon, Apr. 1900, asst. surgeon gen., 1902-06, U.S. Pub. Health and Marine Hosp. Service; maj. and brig. surgeon 7th A.C. during Spanish-Am. War; operating surgeon, U.S.N., in Mexican embroglio at Vera Cruz, 1914; surgeon U.S.S. Leviathan during World War; cdr. Med. Reserve Corps, U.S.N. Mem. S.C.W., S.C., S.A.R., N.M.O.S.A.W., Assn. Mil. Surgeons of U.S., M.O.W.W., A.L., Inst. Am. Genealogy. Clubs: Cosmos, University, Army and Navy. Residence: 1718 I St. N.W., Washington, D.C.

1–**VOLK, Douglas (Stephen Arnold Douglas Volk),** *b* Pittsfield, Mass., Feb. 23, 1856.
4–Henry **Volk**, Harrington, Bergen Co.; *m* Maria Outwater;
3–Garrett (*b* 1788), of Wells, Montgomery Co., N.Y., and Stockbridge, Mass.; *m* 1809, Elizabeth Gesner (1790-1851);
2–Leonard Wells (2 below).
5–Aaron **Barlow** (*b* 1735);
4–Nathaniel (*b* 1767), *m* Betsey King;
3–Jonathan K. (*b* 1789), of Bethany, Genesee Co., N.Y., and Brandon, Vt., *m* 1814, Honor Douglas, of Brandon (she was aunt of Stephen A. Douglas);
2–Emily Clarissa (1832-95), *m* Leonard Wells **Volk** (1828-95), sculptor (for issue see Vol. I, p. 872).
1–*m* June 25, 1881, Marion B. Larrabee (*b* Chicago, Ill., Mar. 6, 1859-*d* Jan. 11, 1925); dau. William M. Larrabee, of Chicago; her ancestors landed in Maine from England, soon after the Mayflower; issue: 1–Leonard Douglas (July 19, 1882-Apr. 30, 1901); 2–Wendell, *b* N.Y. City, Apr. 16, 1884; capt. engrs., overseas, World War; 3–Marion Douglas, *b* Minneapolis, Jan. 1, 1888; *m* Sept. 16, 1913, Dr. E. R. Bridge, of Brunswick, Me.; 4–Gerome, *b* Minneapolis, July 18, 1900; corp., overseas, World War.
1–Studied art at Rome, Italy, and at Paris with Gerome, 1873-78. Artist; organized Minneapolis Sch. Fine Arts, 1886-93; exhibitor at Paris Salon, 1875-78; represented in many art gal-

leries and museums thruout U.S. Commissioned to paint from life, 1919, portraits of King Albert, General Pershing, and Lloyd George, for collection of war portraits, for Nat. Gallery, Washington; painted several portraits of Lincoln from his father's life mask and bust of Lincoln. Decorated: Officer Order of Leopold II, 1920, by King Albert; recipient of many medals and prizes (see Who's Who in America). Clubs: Century, Nat. Arts. Summer place: Center Lovell, Oxford Co., Me. Address: National Arts Club, New York, N.Y.

1–**VOORHEES, Edward Kinsey,** *b* Monroe, Butler Co., O., Dec. 6, 1862.
9–Steven Coerte (Van) **Voorhees** (qv);
8–Coerte Stevense (1637-1702 or 09), capt. King William's War; in French and Indian invasion of New York and in march on Albany; magistrate, 1664 and 73; rep. Gen. Assembly, 1664; del. Conv. at New Orange (Albany); *m* Marretje Van Couwenhoven (Gerrit Wolfertse[9], *m* Aeltje, dau. Cornelis L. Cool; Wolferte G.[10], from Holland to Albany, 1630, removed to New Amsterdam, was granted earliest patent of land on L.I.);
7–Gerrit Coerte (*d* 1704), *m* Mensie Janse;
6–Coerte Gerritse (*d* 1750), began to write name Voorhees; *m* Neeltje Hegeman (Joseph A.[7], *m* Femmetje Remsen);
5–Gerrit (1739-1816), mem. Somerset Co. (N.J.) militia, Am. Rev.; *m* Ann Beekman (Gerardus Christopher[6], *m* Catharine Van Dyke);
4–Coert (1761-1816), served with father in Am. Rev.; *m* Jane Hoagland;
3–John K(oert), (1798-1873), *m* Mary Rynearson;
2–Ellison Hoagland (2 below).
9–Elbert Elbertse **Stoothoof** (1620-88), from Holland to Flatlands, L.I.; *m* Aeltje Lambertse (Cool) Couwenhoven (Cornelis L. Cool[10], and widow of Gerrit W. Van Couwenhoven, 9 above);
8–Maj. Gerret Elbertse (*d* 1729), *m* Joanna Nevius (Johannis[9], *m* Ariaentje Blyck);
7–Adrianna, *m* Harmanus (Hooglandt) **Hoagland** (*b* 1681; Christoffel[8], alderman, New York, 1667, *m* Catharine, dau. Marten Cregier);
6–Christopher (1708-66), *m* Neeltje Van Voorhees (Albert C.[7]; Coerte S.[8]; Steven C.[9], as above);
5–Christopher (1746-1822), began to write name Hoagland; *m* Maria Bergen (George[6], *m* Maria, dau. Jacob Probasco);
4–Jane, *m* Coert **Voorhees** (4 above).
9–Arent Theunissen (Van Hengel) **Rynearson,** killed during Indian uprising on S.I., Sept. 1655; *m* Tryntie Reyniers;
8–Reynier Arentsen, *m* Jannetje Aukes Van Nuyse;
7–Auke Reyniersen (*d* 1740?), *m* Ida Vonk (Cornelius[8], of Southampton, L.I., *m* 1667, Madeline Hendricks);
6–Reynier (*d* 1773 or 74), mem. Kings Co. militia, 1715; of Somerset Co., N.J.; *m* Geertje Vohleman;
5–Barent (*d* 1773), began to write name Rynearson; *m* Elizabeth DuBois (Abraham[6], *m* Marie Larzalere; Abraham[7], *m* Margaret, dau. Christian Deyo; Louis[8], lead expdn. against Indians, 1663 and 70, 1st elder New Paltz Ch., *m* Catharine Blanchan);
4–Nicholas (1769-1822), *m* Jane Ellison (Ezekiel[5], *m* Ariaantje, dau. Johannes Bennet);
3–Mary (1800-63), *m* John K. **Voorhees** (3 above);
2–Ellison Hoagland (1836-1920), of Warren Co., O., Pella, Ia., and Garnett, Kan.; *m* 1860, Eugenia Boyd (1841-1920; Andrew[3]; Thomas[4], aet. 15, was wagoner in Braddock's campaign); issue: I–Viola May (1861-86; *m* 1880, Horace Kay Herbert, *d* 1920); II–Edward K. (1 above); III–Harry Lincoln (1865-1907; *m* Flora Judy); IV–Mary Elsie (*b* 1867; *m* 1892, Mathew Steidly Gilfry, 1851-1901); V–Albert Boyd (1869-84); VI–Jessie Wheeler (*b* 1873-*d* infancy); VII–Charles Gill (1874-81); VIII–Andrew Ellison (*b* 1877; *m* Margaret–).
1–*m* Oct. 17, 1893, Imogen Southerland (qv for issue).
1–In railroad service since 1880; gen. freight agt., St.L.&S.F.R.R., 1904-11; mem. com. on uniform (freight) classification, Chicago, 1912-17; mem. southern classification com., Atlanta, 1917–. Mem. H.S., S.A.R., I.A.G., Atlanta Geneal Soc. (2d v.p. and treas.). Clubs: Traffic (Atlanta, Chicago). Residence: 554 Boulevard Terrace N.E., Atlanta, Ga.

1–**VOORHEES, Imogen Southerland (Mrs. Edward K.),** *b* Memphis, Tenn., Oct. 21, 1868.
5–John **Southerland** (*d* 1796?), of Edgecombe Co., N.C.;
4–John (*d* ante 1813), *m* Clara Llewellyn (John[5], *d* 1793?);
3–John Llewellyn (1792-1873), ens. N.C. troops, 1814; *m* Martha Eliza Reeves;
2–James (2 below).
8–John **Clayton** (1665-1737), from Eng. to Va., 1705; burgess, recorder; *m* Anne Page;
7–Samuel (1685-1735), Caroline Co., Va.; *m* 1702, Elizabeth Pendleton (1685-1761; Philip[8], qv);
6–George (1720-65), *m* Barbara–;
5–John (1754-1783?), lt. and capt. Brunswick Co., Va., 1777 and 79; *m* Temperance Hill (Green[6], *m* Grace, dau. William Bennett; their son Rev. Green Hill, was del. to 3 Provincial Congresses, N.C., 1774,75,76, maj. N.C. troops and treas. Halifax Dist., mem. Council of State, 1783);
4–Mary, *m* 2d, Willis **Reeves** (1778-1848), of Orange Co., N.C., and Fayette Co., Tenn.;
3–Martha Eliza (1810-55), *m* John L. **Southerland** (3 above).
9–John **Ogden** (qv);
8–David (1639-1692), an original associate, Elizabeth, N.J., 1665; *m* 1676, Elizabeth (Swaine) Ward (1654-1706; Capt. Samuel Swaine[9], *m* Johanna Ward; William[10], dep. gov. Conn., 1644);
7–Thomas (1684-1760), *m* Dinah– (1686-1731);
6–David (1712-65 or 77?), *m* Anne Burwell;
5–Mary (1743-1814), *m* Alexander **Carmichael** (1734-1817), lt. Light Dragoons, Morris Co., N.J., 1776; judge, Morristown, N.J., 1786;
4–Ann, *m* Stanton **Latham** (*d* 1817), headmaster, Collegiate Sch., Ref. Dutch Ch., New York City, 1791-1810;
3–Francis Stanton (1808-80), editor "Recorder," Randolph, Tenn., 1834, "Enquirer," Memphis, Tenn., 1836, "Eagle," Memphis, 1843; postmaster, Memphis; *m* Jane Catherine Smith;
2–Imogen (2 below).
7–James **Turner,** *m* Kerenhappuch Norman;
6–Sarah, *m* James **Smith**;
5–James Turner, soldier Am. Rev., Va. line; of Halifax Co., Va., Richmond Co., N.C., and Maury Co., Tenn.; *m* in Charles Co., Md., 1784, Constantia Ford;
4–James Norman (1789-1875), *m* Sarah Jenkins (Philip[5], *m* Elizabeth, dau. of Barton Hungerford);
3–Jane Catherine, *m* Francis S. **Latham** (3 above).
9–Thomas **Allison,** witness law suit, Feb. 29, 1659; contract is recorded between Richard Smyth of "Potomocke" planter, and "Thomas Allison, son of Thomas Allison of Gaston in the county of Lancaster, husbandman, for seven years service," Aug. 8, 1659; "overseer of the Right honorable the Governor's servants," July 29, 1661;
8–Elizabeth, *m* Edward **Ford** (will dated Charles Co., Md., Jan. 16, 1693);
7–Edward, with Barton Warren, was assigned Pew 6 in William and Mary Parish Ch., Charles Co., Md., June 8, 1752;
6–Charles Allison (will dated Jan. 23, 1783);
5–Constantia, *m* James T. **Smith** (5 above).
2–Imogen Latham (1846-1920), *m* 1867, James **Southerland** (1834-75), lt. Bluff City Grays, Memphis; Co. A, Forrest's old regt., C.S.A.; paroled at Gainesville, Ala., 1865; issue: I–Imogen (1 above); II–Katherine (*b* 1869); III–James (1872-94); IV–Mary (*b* 1875).
1–*m* Oct. 17, 1893, Edward Kinsey Voorhees (qv); issue (all *b* Memphis, Tenn.): 1–Mary Katherine, *b* Mar. 2, 1896; B.A., Northwestern U., '17 (Kappa Alpha Theta); 2–Imogen Southerland, *b* Nov. 26, 1897; B.A., Northwestern U., '18 (Kappa Alpha Theta); *m* Jan. 30, 1926, Edward Delmar Anderson, B.S. in M.E., Purdue U. (issue: Mary Katherine, *b* Apr. 26, 1928); 3–Edward K., Jr., *b* Oct. 27, 1899; attended Northwestern U. (Beta Theta Pi); ens., U.S.N.R. Flying Corps.
1–Mem. D.A.R., Va. Hist. Soc., Atlanta Woman's Club. Residence: 554 Boulevard Terrace N.E., Atlanta, Ga.

1–**WADSWORTH, Charlotte Abigail Harrison (Mrs. Harry A.),** *b* Cornwall, Conn., Sept. 3, 1866.
9–Richard **Harrison,** from Eng., settled at Branford, Conn., ca. 1644;
8–Ens. Thomas (1630-1704), of New Haven and Branford; *m* 1st, 1652, Dorothy– (*d* ante 1666), widow of John Thompson;
7–Nathaniel (1658-1727), Branford; *m* ca. 1690, Hannah Frisbie (1669-1723);
6–Daniel (1694-1752), *m* 1722, Hannah Hoadley (1694-1748; Samuel[7]);
5–Noah (1737-1823), Cornwall, Conn.; *m* 1st, 1767, Hannah Rogers (1737-85);
4–Edmund (1768-1867), *m* 1795, Ruth Hopkins (1769-1852; Elijah[5], Am. Rev., *m* Lois Fuller; Sylvanus[6]; Judah[7]);
3–John Rogers (1807-80), *m* 1833, Eleanor Bradford (1809-90; Ens. James F.[4], *m* Mary Merwin; Corpl. John[5], Am. Rev.; Capt. John[6]; Lt. Joseph[7]; William[8]; William[9], qv);
2–George Chandler (2 below).
8–Christopher **Todd** (qv);
7–Samuel (1645-1714), of New Haven, Conn.; *m* 1668, Mary Bradley (1653-1724);
6–Daniel (1687-1724), *m* 1721, Desire Tuttle (*b* 1697);
5–Daniel (*b* 1725), Derby, Conn.; *m* 1748, Sybil Carrington (*b* 1731);
4–Daniel (*b* 1751), *m* 1775, Eunice Hitchcock;
3–Carrington (*b* 1798) Cornwall; *m* 2d, 1832, Harriet Shepherd (1794-1853);
2–Rebecca Ann Louisa (1837-1902), as Widow White, *m* 2d, 1862, George Chandler **Harrison** (1840-1907), town treas. and clk.; farmer; judge Probate Ct., 30 yrs.; issue: I–Cynthia Rebecca (*b* 1863; *m* 1891, Francis Henry Monroe); II–Eleanor Harriet (1864-1904; *m* 1890, Mark R. Holliday, *d* 1904); III–George Edward (1865-96; *m* 1888, Mrs. Flora A. [Moore] Bosley); IV–Charlotte Abigail (1 above); V–Kate Jane (*b* 1868; *m* 1890, Henry D. Whitney); VI–John Rogers Carrington (*b* and *d* 1869); VII–Ruth Hopkins (1871-87); VIII–Gertrude Chandler (1873-1918; *m* 1901, Arthur Kenyon Harrison); IX–Annie Shepherd (1875-95); X–Mary Merwin (1876-78); XI–Mabel Todd (*b* 1878; *m* 1905, Harold Ira Arms); XII–John Rogers (*b* 1882; *m* 1904, Nellie Marion Swanson).
1–*m* Mar. 2, 1909, Harry A. Wadsworth, *b* Hudson, O., June 15, 1855; son of Harvey A. Wadsworth, of Windham, O.
1–Ed. Rocky Dell Inst., Lime Rock, Conn., and Housatonic Valley Inst., Cornwall, Conn. Mem. S.M.D., D.F.P.A., O.E.S. Democrat. Residence: Garretsville, O.

1–**WAGGONER, Alice Fidelia Tower (Mrs. John Henry),** *b* Smyrna, N.Y., Nov. 18, 1861.
9–Clement **Bates** (qv);
8–Joseph (ca. 1630-1706), *m* 1659, Esther Hilliard (*d* 1709; William[9], of Boston, *m* Esther–);
7–Joshua (*b* 1671), *m* 1695/96, Rachel Tower (*b* 1674/75; Ibrooke[8], *m* Margaret, dau. of John Hardin, of Braintree; Comdt. John[9], qv);
6–Solomon (*b* 1706), *m* 1732, Deborah Studley (*b* 1703; Benjamin[7], *m* Mary Merritt; John[8]);
5–Corpl. James (*b* 1743), Am. Rev.; *m* 1765, Abigail Litchfield;
4–Abigail (1774-1856), *m* 1794, Shubael **Tower** (see Vol. III, p. 462, for Tower lineage);
3–Dea. Obadiah (1807-80), Oxford, N.Y.; *m* 1830, Fidelia Munroe;
2–Edwin Murray (2 below).
10–Widow Martha **Vinal** (*d* 1664), came from Eng. with 3 small children to Scituate, Mass., 1636; owned considerable property; an original Conihasset partner;
9–John (*b* ca. 1632/33), *m* Elizabeth Baker (Rev. Nicholas[10]);
8–John, *m* Mary Woodworth (Thomas[9], *m* Deborah, dau. Sgt. John Damon; Walter[10]);
7–Jacob (*b* 1691), *m* 1716, Elizabeth Simmons (*b* 1686; Aaron[8], *m* Mary, dau. Walter Woodworth; Moses[9], qv);
6–Priscilla (*b* 1723), *m* 1742, Ens. Samuel **Litchfield** (*b* 1715), of Scituate; constable, 1756-58 (Samuel[7], *m* Abigail, dau. Isaac Buck; Josiah[8]; Lawrence[9]);
5–Abigail (*b* ca. 1747), *m* James **Bates** (5 above).
8–William **Munroe** (qv), *m* 2d, Mary Ball;
7–David (1680-1755), Canterbury, Conn.; *m* Deborah–;
6–Samuel (1720-77), Windsor, Conn.; served in French and Indian War and Am. Rev.; *m* Abigail– (1722-1817 or 18);
5–Isaac (1746/47-1825), *d* at Plymouth, N.Y.; served Am. Rev., pensioned;
4–Dan (*d* 1854), *m* Deborah Sexton (1778-1822; James[5], of Colchester, Conn., *m* Deborah Fox);
3–Fidelia (1806-67), *m* Obadiah **Tower** (3 above);
2–Edwin Murray (1835-1910), *m* 1859, Emily Jeanette Morley (1831-1924); see Vol. III, p. 462, for issue and other lineages.
1–*m* May 15, 1902, John Henry Waggoner, *b* Oramel, Alleghany Co., N.Y., Sept. 18, 1871; son of Charles Wesley Waggoner, (John Henry[3], *m* 3d, Eleanore, dau. of Nehemiah Sears), *m* Lucinda Dake.
1–Ed. in music, piano and organ. Mem. S.M.D., D.F.P.A., D.A.R., Nat. Soc. N.E. Women, and Bunker, Bates, and Tower family assns. Club: Cosmopolitan. Baptist. Residence: 225 Lovering Av., Buffalo, N.Y.

1–**WAID, Earnest David,** *b* Liberty Center, O., Apr. 21, 1880.
9–Thomas **Canfield** (qv);
8–Thomas, *m* 1674, Rebecca Adkinson;
7–Thomas, *m* 1705, Mary Camp;
6–Gideon (*b* 1717), *m* 1740, at Durham, Conn., Anna Robinson;
5–Dan (*b* 1754), served Lexington Alarm, and in 1777-78, 1779 Am. Rev.; *m* 1775, Comfort Newton;
4–Titus (*b* 1784), *m* 2d, 1813, at W. Bloomfield, N.Y., Orpha Gilman;
3–Orpha Gilman (1824-64), *m* 1845, Williams **Waid**;
2–Charles Heman (1851-1925), *m* 1876, Elizabeth T. Hack; issue: I–Luman (1878-80); II–Earnest D. (1 above); III–Anna (*b* 1882; *m* Wallace Knowles; *m* 2d, Dent Lugabill); IV–Will Carleton (*b* 1883; *m* Alta Mae Lutton); V–Paul H. (*b* 1885; *m* May Adams; *m* 2d, Mildred Bliss); VI–Dottie Dimple (*b* and *d* 1890); VII–Gladys Margaret, twin (*b* 1890; *m* George E. Walker); VIII–Benson Foraker (*b* 1892; *m* 1919, Hazel W. Foreman).
1–*m* Dec. 25, 1906, Nelle Williams (qv); issue: 1–David Williams, *b* Cambridge, Mass., Aug. 12, 1918; 2–Frances Helen, *b* Columbus, O., June 10, 1921.
1–B.Sc. Agr., Ohio State U., '06. Coll. teacher and extension work 10 yrs.; farm management 4 yrs.; agrl. co-operative work 10 yrs. Methodist. Republican. Residence: Wauseon, O.

1–**WAID, Nelle Williams (Mrs. Earnest David),** *b* Wauseon, O., Aug. 24, 1882.
6–John **Williams,** from Eng., settled in Anne Arundel Co., Md.; *m* Elizabeth Cheney Pierce (1717-1813);
5–Jeremiah (1759-1842), pvt. Am. Rev.; *m* 1784, Mary Gaither (1761-1845);
4–Elisha (1795-1863), Huntingdon Co., Pa.; *m* 1816, Hannah A. Harrison (1798-1859);
3–Jeremiah (1822-94), Wauseon, O.; *m* 1847, Matilda Biddle;
2–Tilden (2 below).
6–Andrew **Biddle** (1740-1812), from Germany, settled in Md., 1760; 1st lt., Frederick Co., Md.; later train master of supplies; *m* 1766 or 67, Christina Cover (*d* 1777);
5–Jacob (*b* 1770), *m* 1792, Rachel Todd;
4–Samuel (1798-1867), Beaver Co., Pa.; *m* 1817, Elizabeth Knight (1800-77);
3–Matilda (1825-94), *m* Jeremiah **Williams** (3 above);
2–Tilden (1851-1915), Wauseon, O.; farmer and insurance agent; *m* 1879, Emma Frances Pocock (1857-1910); issue: I–Herma Helen (*b* 1880; *m* Carl William Waldeck); II–Nelle (1 above).
1–*m* Dec. 25, 1906, Earnest David Waid (qv for issue).
1–Mem. D.A.R., O.E.S. Methodist. Republican. Residence, Wauseon, O.

1–**WAKEFIELD, Sherman Day,** *b* Bloomington, Ill., July 12, 1894.
10–Capt. William **White,** Mayflower Pilgrim (qv);
9–Resolved (1614-1690?), *m* 1st, Judith Vassall;
8–Elizabeth (*b* 1652), *m* Obadiah **Wheeler**;
7–Joseph (1690-1780), *m* Abigail Butterfield;
6–Phebe (*b* 1728), *m* Jotham **Wilder,** Am. Rev.;
5–Susannah (1751-1847), *m* Thomas **Sawyer,** soldier Am. Rev. and War 1812;
4–Susan (1787-1836), *m* Joseph **Wakefield** (1779-1842), War 1812 (see Vol. II, p. 320);

3–Dr. Cyrenius (1815-85), *m* 1843, Harriet Richardson (1820-92; Josiah[4]; Tilley[5]; Tilley[6]; Josiah[7]; Capt. James[8]; Nathaniel[9]; Thomas[10], qv);
2–Dr. Homer (2 below).
10–Hon. Thomas **Willet** (qv);
9–Mary (1637-1712), *m* Rev. Samuel **Hooker**;
8–Hon. John (1664-1746), judge Superior Ct., Conn. Colony; *m* Abigail Standley;
7–Joseph (1705-64), *m* Sarah Lewis;
6–Joseph (1751-99), *m* Mary Ingersoll;
5–Dr. Joseph (1786-1820), *m* Eliza Sampson;
4–Jane Eliza (1817-76), *m* Benjamin Franklin **Sherman** (see Vol. II, p. 320);
3–Benjamin Franklin (1845-77), *m* Lydia Woodward Pearson;
2–Julia Pearson (2 below).
11–Hon. John **Webster** (qv);
10–Mary, *m* John **Hunt**;
9–Mary (*d* 1690), *m* John **Ingersoll**;
8–Jonathan (1681-1760), *m* Sarah (Newton) Miles;
7–Rev. Jonathan (1713-78), grad. Yale, 1736; chaplain in Seven Years' War; *m* Dorcas Moss;
6–Mary (1748-1805), *m* Joseph **Hooker** (6 above).
11–Rev. Thomas **Hooker** (qv);
10–Mary (*d* 1675), *m* Rev. Roger **Newton**;
9–Samuel (1646-1708), *m* Martha Fenn;
8–Sarah (1687-1748), as Widow Miles, *m* 2d, Jonathan **Ingersoll** (8 above).
10–Thomas **Lincoln** (*d* 1692), the husbandman, of Hingham, Mass.; *m* Margaret Langer;
9–Susanna (1646-1730), *m* Joseph **Barstow**;
8–Samuel (1683-1730), *m* Lydia Randall;
7–Joseph (1725-1800), *m* Mary (Bliss) Webster;
6–Michael (1754-1837), soldier Am. Rev., 6 yrs.; *m* Ruth Abbott;
5–Dea. Henry (1787-1849), *m* Harriet Webster;
4–Lydia Woodward (1815-1908), *m* Merrill **Pearson**;
3–Lydia Woodward (1849-1914), *m* Benjamin Franklin **Sherman** (3 above);
2–Julia Pearson (*b* 1875), *m* 1893, Dr. Homer **Wakefield** (*b* 1865), retired physician, New York; issue: I–Sherman Day (1 above); II–Elizabeth Ann (*b* 1896; *m* 1916, Stephen Higginson Tyng, IV, 1897-1918); III–Harriet Jane (*b* 1896; *m* Philip Penhale Whritner).
1–Not married. Grad. Meadville Theol. School, 1923; Ph.B., U.Chicago, 1924; B.S., Sch. of Library Service, Columbia, 1928. Librarian and bibliographer; genealogist of the Wakefield family. Pvt., corpl., sgt. and sgt. 1st cl., engrs., U.S.A., Sept. 10, 1918-May 31, 1919. Mem. A.A.A.S., A.L.A., Rationalist Press Assn. (London), First Humanist Soc. of N.Y. Summer residence: "The Owl's Nest," Spencer Hill, Winsted, Conn. Permanent address: Bloomington, Ill.

1–**WALDRON, George Washington,** *b* Sherburne, N.Y., Mar. 1, 1857.
8–Resolved **Waldron** (qv);
7–William (1647-post 1710), *m* 1671, Engeltie Stoutenburg (Peter[8]);
6–Peter (1675-1725), *m* 1698, Tryntie Vandenbergh (Cornelius[7]);
5–Cornelius (1705-56), *m* 1732, Jannettie Van Ness;
4–Garrett (1738-1829), pvt. in Am. Rev.; *m* 1761, Catherine Van Denburgh;
3–Evert G. (1773-1860), of Northumberland, N.Y.; War 1812; *m* 1797, Elizabeth Van Derwerken;
2–Ebenezer B. (1810-95), farmer; *m* 1839, Lavinia R. Benton (1818-1906; John[8], *m* Sarah Gillett); issue: I–John B. (*d* infancy); II–James Albert (*b* 1851; *m* Mary Jane Deuel); III–George Washington (1 above).
1–*m* Oct. 13, 1886, Florence Adelia Burns, *b* Gloversville, N.Y., Apr. 6, 1856; dau. of William Burns, *m* Helen A. Orton.
1–With Brooklyn Daily Eagle 41 yrs. Mem. I.A.G. Baptist. Residence: 570 Rugby Rd., Brooklyn, N. Y.

1–**WALKER, Annie Laurie,** *b* Snow Hill, Tex., Oct. 4, 1877.
7–William **Butler,** from Scotland, 1700; settled Culpeper Co., Va.; *m* Mildred Lewis;
6–John (*b* 1700), of Culpeper Co., Va.;
5–James (*b* 1754), pvt. Am. Rev.;
4–Austin (1799-1870), Granville Co., N.C.; *m* 1825, Frances Davis (*b* 1805; Joseph[5], Am. Rev.);
3–Louisa (1827-1915), of Maury Co., Tenn.; *m* 1845, George Washington **Walker** (1822-80), of Lauderdale Co., Ala.; served C.S.A.;
2–John Wesley (2 below).
7–Edward **Bliven** (g.father [*b* 1643], from Eng., 1664; settled at Salem, Mass.), of Westerly, R.I.; *m* Freelove–;
6–John (*b* 1721), soldier Am. Rev. from Westerly; *m* 1758, Elizabeth–;
5–John (*b* 1760), of Westerly; *m* Elizabeth–;
4–John (*b* 1795), of Ky.; *m* 1820, Catherine Harris Ryan (*b* 1800);
3–Abram (1823-1900), of Morgan Co., Ala.; soldier C.S.A., present at Siege of Vicksburg; *m* 1845, Sarah Ann Forman (1824-1900; Elijah[4] [*b* 1797], of N.C., *m* 1815, Catherine Strickland [1798-post 1850]; John[5]);
2–Sarah Jane (1852-1915), of Morris Co., Tex.; *m* 1875, John Wesley **Walker** (*b* 1847), retired farmer, of Omaha, Tex.; co. commr., and justice of peace, Morris Co., Tex., 1892-94; issue: I–Annie Laurie (1 above); II–Jesse Abram (1880-1898); III–Lulu Ola (*b* 1882; *m* William Henry Wright); IV–Katherine (*b* 1887; *m* William Bliss Robison, *d*); V–James William (*b* 1889).
1–Ed. North Tex. State Normal Sch. (now Teachers Coll.); A.B., Baylor U.; grad. work, U.Chicago. Teacher in high schools in Texas at Henderson, 1909-10, Hearne, 1913-17, Marshall, 1917-19, Ft. Worth, 1919–. Teacher of Latin U.Tex., summer, 1928. V.p. Classical Assn. Tex., 1922, sec.-treas., 1929; chmn. Latin Sect. City Inst. of Ft. Worth, 1929-30. Mem. A.A.-U.W. Baptist. Democrat. Residence: C/o John Wesley Walker, Omaha, Tex.

1–**WALKER, Amy Gertrude Littlehale (Mrs. James G., Jr.),** *b* Wakefield, Mass., Nov. 18, 1886.
9–Richard **Littlehale** (*d* 1663), from Eng. in the "Mary and John," to Ipswich, Mass., 1633; one of original 91 proprs. of Newbury, 1635; a first settler of Pentucket, or Haverhill, 1640; town clk. 20 yrs.; magistrate; *m* 1647, Mary Lancton;
8–Isaac (1660-1718), *m* 1686, Elizabeth Davis;
7–John (1691-1750), *m* 1715, Hannah Colburn;
6–Abraham (1725-1810), soldier Am. Rev.; *m* 1744, Mary Stearns;
5–Roger Langdon (1769-1845), *m* 1791, Mary Griffin;
4–Isaac (1798-1856), *m* 1819, Harriet Butterfield;
3–Albert (1822-85), *m* Achsa Maria Briggs (David[4], *m* Joanna Safford);
2–Ernest Jerome (2 below).
9–Benjamin **Butterfield** (qv);
8–Joseph (1649-1720), *m* 1674, Lydia Ballard, of Andover;
7–Lt. Joseph (1680-1757), to Tyngsboro, 1711; *m* Sarah Fletcher;
6–Capt. Reuben (1727-1816), capt. Am. Rev.; *m* Mary Richardson (*b* 1728; Capt. William[7], *m* Elizabeth Colburn; Lt. Josiah[8]; Capt. Josiah[9]; Ezekiel[10], qv);
5–Abner Richardson (1764-1851), *m* 1791, Hepzibah Buttrick (1788-1859; Joseph[6], Am. Rev., *m* Sarah Brown; Jonathan[7]; Samuel[8]; William[9]);
4–Harriet (1800-1904, aet. 104), *m* Isaac **Littlehale** (4 above).
11–John **Alden,** Mayflower Pilgrim (qv);
10–Ruth (*d* 1674), *m* 1657, John **Bass** (1633-1716; Samuel[11], qv);
9–Samuel (1660-1751), *m* 1696, Mary Adams (*d* 1706);
8–Samuel (1700-68), *m* Hannah White;
7–Hannah (*b* 1725), *m* Dea. Jonathan **Wild**;
6–John (1751-1831), soldier Am. Rev.; *m* Jemima Spear;
5–Sally (*b* 1773), *m* Daniel **Curtis** (William[6], of Stoughton, *m* 1751, Deborah Wales, of Braintree);
4–Daniel (1794-1861), *m* Zilpha (Drake) Clark;
3–Sarah Curtis (1836-1901), *m* 1855, Charles **McCarty**;
2–Lucy Brown (2 below).
8–Thomas **Drake** (qv);
7–Benjamin (*b* 1677), *m* Sarah Pool (1678-1775);
6–Richard (1717-73), *m* 1742, Famer Manley (1724-72; Thomas[7], *m* Lydia Field);
5–Edward (1763-1830), soldier Am. Rev.; *m* 1788, Hannah White (1767-1850);
4–Zilpha (1802-89), *m* 2d, Daniel **Curtis** (4 above);
3–Sarah C., *m* Charles **McCarty**;

2–Lucy Brown (*b* 1862), *m* 1884, Ernest Jerome **Littlehale** (1854-1906).
1–*m* Jan. 19, 1916, James Greig Walker, Jr., *b* San Francisco, Calif., June 18, 1882; attended M.I.T.; LL.B., Boston U. Law Sch., 1908; son of James Greig Walker (*b* Scotland, 1836-*d* San Francisco, Calif, 1914), *m* Josephine E. Kinney (Robert Crouch^3, pioneer in Ore., 1847, mem. 1st Territorial Legislature, mem. Constl. Conv., *m* Eliza Lee Bigelow; Samuel^4, *m* Polly, dau. of John Gibbons, Am. Rev.); issue: 1–Curtis Kinney, *b* Astoria, Ore., Feb. 20, 1917; 2–Edna Littlehale, *b* Seaview, Pacific Co., Wash., July 10, 1918; 3–Robert Bigelow, and 4–Olive Drake (twins), *b* Portland, Ore., June 30, 1921.
1–Mem. S.M.D. (founder Ore. Soc., sec.), D.F.-P.A. (pres. Ore. Chapter), D.A.R. (organizing regent), C.A.R. (past state dir. and hon. state dir.). Club: Portland Hunt. Summer place: "Bleak House," Seaview, Wash. Residence: 676 Halsey St., Portland, Ore.

WOOD

Arms: Per pale gules and argent; first, a leg in armour embowed between two spears; second, a chevron of the first, between three lions rampant.
Crest: An arm in armour embowed holding a spear.

1–**WALKER, Nina Chinn (Mrs.),** *b* Washington, D.C., Jan. 28, 1873.
7–John (Chynn) **Chinn,** from Eng. in the "James," to Lancaster Co., Va., *m* Elizabeth Travers (their son Raleigh *m* Esther Ball, half-sister of Mary Washington, mother of George);
6–John (1691-1737), *m* Margaret Ball (Capt. William^7; Col. William^8, qv);
5–Charles (1723-87), *m* ~~Seth~~ Davis; Cynthia
4–John (1766-1839), *m* Mildred Higgins;
3–Richard Henry, law partner of Henry Clay; mem. Ky. Ho. of Rep., 1831, and Senate, 1833-36; *m* Betsy Holmes;
2–Richard Henry (2 below).
6–Thomas **Thomas** (1722-86), from Wales; *m* Ann–;
5–Seth (1748/49-1827), Chester Valley; *m* Prudence Edwards (William^6, *m* Sarah–);
4–Elizabeth (1786-1865), *m* Amos **Davis**;
3–Elizabeth (1814-1906), *m* Robert Serrell **Wood** (1808-53), of Osmington House, Dorsetshire, Eng.; retained his landed English estate and settled, 1840, at "Mt. Hermon," his estate, which is now a portion of the Soldier's Home, D.C.;
2–Virginia S. (2 below).
7–Lewis **Davis,** *m* Florence Laird;
6–William, *m* Elizabeth Fauset;
5–William (1739-1822), *m* Prudence Powell (Samuel^6, *m* Susan–);
4–Amos (1783-1868), *m* Elizabeth Thomas (4 above);
3–Elizabeth, *m* Robert S. **Wood** (3 above);
2–Virginia Serrellina (1843-1923), *m* 1870, Richard Henry **Chinn** (1826-1900), planter in Cuba; issue: I–Elizabeth Bertha; II–Nina (1 above).
1–*m* Feb. 24, 1897, James Wilson Grimes Walker (see Vol. I, p. 483); issue: 1–Elizabeth Grimes, *b* Washington, D.C., Nov. 30, 1897; *m* Oct. 22, 1921, John Williams Davis (see Vol. IV, p. 140); 2–John Grahame, *b* Brookline, Mass., Oct. 2, 1899; 3–Robert Serrell Wood, *b* Brookline, Nov. 16, 1900; 4–Herbert Wood, *b* Brookline, Dec. 18, 1901.
1–Mem. The Washington Club. Residence: 2222 Q St., Washington, D.C.

1–**WALKER, Robert Turner,** *b* Lyme, N.H., Oct. 16, 1867.
9–Richard **Walker** (1611-87), from Eng. in the "Elizabeth," 1635, settled at Lynn, Mass.; capt.; *m* 1636/37, Jane Talmadge (*d* 1641; Thomas^{10}, qv);
8–Richard (*b* 1638), *m* 1661, Sarah Story (*b* 1641; William^9);
7–John (*b* 1664), of Chelmsford, Mass.; *m* 1685, Lydia Colburn (*b* 1666; Edward^8);
6–Edward (*b* 1688), of Newington, N.H.; *m* 1710, Deliverance Gaskin (John^7; Daniel^8);
5–Seth (1725-69), of Newington; *m* 1752, Ann Tripe (1728-1818; Sylvanus^6; Sylvanus^7);
4–William (1759-1832), of Barnstead, N.H.; in Am. Rev.; *m* 1784, Elizabeth Shackford (1761-1843; Capt. Samuel^5, Am. Rev.; Capt. William^6; Samuel^7; William^8);
3–Joseph Alcott (1802-64), *m* 1823, Abigail Wiggin Murray;
2–Augustus Chapman (2 below).
9–Capt. Thomas **Wiggin** (*d* 1667), of Stratham, N.H.; dep.gov. of N.H.; *m* in Eng., 1632/33, Catherine ~~Mason~~ Whiting;
8–Andrew (1635-1710), of Exeter, N.H.; *m* 1659, Hannah Bradstreet (*d* ca. 1707; Simon^9, qv);
7–Judge Andrew (1671-1756), Stratham, N.H.; *m* 1st, 1697, Abigail Follett (*d* 1742; Nicholas^8; Nicholas^9);
6–Bradstreet (1713/14-1752), *m* as her 1st husband, Phebe Sherburne (bap. 1715; Capt. Joseph^7, *m* Phebe, dau. Edward Ayers; Henry^8, *m* Sarah, dau. Thomas Wiggins, son of Gov. Thomas Wiggin, 9 above; John^9);
5–Abigail (1741-1816), *m* Timothy **Murray** (bap. 1740-1774; Timothy^6);
4–Dea. Timothy (1773-1815), *m* 1796, Elizabeth Chapman (1774-1846; David^5, *m* Elizabeth, dau. of Caleb Clark, Am. Rev.; Samuel^6; Samuel^7; Samuel^8; Edward^9);
3–Abigail W. (1797-1856), *m* Joseph A. **Walker** (3 above).
9–Matthew **Grant** (qv);
8–Samuel (1631-1718), *m* 1658, Mary Porter (*b* 1638; John^9);
7–Nathaniel (*b* 1672), *m* 1699, Bethia Warner (*b* 1680; Robert^8; Andrew^9);
6–Benjamin (1708-95), *m* 1736/37, Anna (Wood) Hunt (1710-83; Josiah Wood^7; Thomas^8);
5–Benjamin (1745-76), lt., 3d Co., 12th N.H. Regt.; *m* 1770, Sarah Sloan (1750-1845; John^6; William^7);
4–Alanson (1775-1849), *m* 1799, Polly Fairfield (1780-1842; Walter^5; Walter^6; Walter^7; John^8);
3–Sidney S. (1816-93), *m* 1837, Louisa Turner (1817-95; David^4, *m* Lavina Jenks; David^5; Israel^6; Philip^7; John^8; Humphrey^9);
2–Maria Churchill (1838-1917), *m* 1862, Augustus Chapman **Walker,** M.D. (1833-1918), Dartmouth, ex-'62, granted A.B., 1871, A.M., 1873; M.D., Harvard, 1866; asst. surgeon, 133d N.Y. Vol. Inf., Sept. 24, 1862-Sept. 1864; surgeon on staff of Col. James J. Byrne, 18th N.Y. Cav., Sept. 10, 1864-June 14, 1865; physician and surgeon, Greenfield, Mass.; an original companion M.O.L.L.; issue: I–Robert T. (1 above); II–Sidney Grant (*b* 1869); III–William Augustus (1872-1905).
1–Not married. S.B., M.I.T., '90. Architect. Mem. Mil. Order Loyal Legion. Residence: 75 Charles St., Boston, Mass.

1–**WALLACE, Henry Agard,** *b* nr. Orient, Ia., Oct. 7, 1888.
8–Michael **Finley** (qv);
7–John (1713-58), of Shippensburg, Pa.; killed by Indians; *m* Martha Berkeley;
6–Clements (1735-75), of Westmoreland Co., Pa.; *m* 1761, Elizabeth Carnahan;

5–Martha (1775-1847), *m* 1793, Randall **Ross** (1755-1847);
4–Martha (1811-76), *m* 1835, John **Wallace** (1805-72), first man to introduce tile drainage in western Pa.;
3–Henry (1836-1916), of Des Moines, Ia.; minister U.P. Ch.; 1st editor "Wallaces' Farmer"; mem. Roosevelt's Country Life Commn.; pres. Conservation Congress; *m* 1863, Nancy Ann Cantwell (1839-1909);
2–Henry Cantwell (2 below).
9–Daniel **Brodhead** (qv);
8–Capt. Richard (1666-1758), of Marbletown, N.Y.; *m* 1692, Magdalena Jansen (1668-1707);
7–Capt. Daniel (1693-1755), removed from Albany to Pa., 1737; owner and founder of Dansbury (later called Stroudsburg), Pa.; served in Indian wars, 1714; justice, Bucks Co., 1747; *m* 1719, Hester Gerritse Wyngart (1697-1759); their son, Gen. Daniel, was cdr. western forces, Ft. Pitt, 1778, Am. Rev.;
6–Garret (1733-1804), Smithfield, Pa.; justice; ens. Am. Rev.; *m* 1759, Jane Davis;
5–Samuel (1776-1815), Tioga, N.Y.; *m* Hannah Shoemaker (1776-1850);
4–Elijah Shoemaker, *m* 1830, Mary Agard;
3–John Avery (1836-70), N.Y. City; capt. in Union Army during Civil War; *m* 1865, Mary Ann Matilda White;
2–May (2 below).
11–Theophilus **Eaton** (qv);
10–Hannah (1632-1707), *m* 1659, Dep. Gov. William **Jones** (1624-1706), from Eng., 1660; settled at New Haven;
9–Isaac (1671-1741), *m* 1692, Deborah Clarke (1672-1733 or 35; James[10], *m* Deborah, dau. John Peacock; James[11]);
8–Samuel (*b* 1693), Wallingford, Conn.; *m* 1719, Sarah– (*d* 1760);
7–Eaton (*b* 1730), Litchfield, Conn.; *m* 1756, Elizabeth Catlin (*b* ca. 1733);
6–Lucina (*b* 1758), *m* Noah **Agard** (1756-1840), served in Am. Rev. aet. 19;
5–Horace (1785-1850), presiding elder, Meth. Ch., Susquehanna and Berkshire dists.; *m* 1808, Polly Stone (1783-1867);
4–Mary (1810-48), Tioga Co., N.Y.; *m* Elijah Shoemaker **Brodhead** (4 above).
9–John (Levins) **Leavens** (1581-1647), from Eng. to Boston, Mass., 1632; freeman, Roxbury, 1634; *m* 2d, 1639, Rachel Wright;
8–John (1640-96), Woodstock, Conn.; selectman; *m* 2d, 1674, Elizabeth Preston (*b* 1655);
7–Justice Joseph (1683-1773), a founder of Killingly; *m* 1707/08, Judith Sabin (1690-1751);
6–Capt. John (1734-99), served at Lexington Alarm; removed to Belpre, O.; *m* 1762, Esther Williams (1744-1828);
5–Matilda (*b* 1783), Marietta, O.; *m* 1803, John **White,** of Fearing Tp., O.;
4–James Howell (1814-73), pvt. in "Gray Beard" Regt., Civil War; Meth. minister, *m* 1838, Emmeline Guitteau (1817-80);
3–Mary Ann Matilda (1841-67), Mt. Pleasant, Ia.; *m* John Avery **Brodhead** (3 above):
2–May (*b* 1867), Des Moines, Ia.; *m* 1887, Henry Cantwell **Wallace** (1866-1924), mgr., asso. editor and editor, Wallaces' Farmer; pres. and treas. Wallace Pub. Co., Capital City Printing Plate Co.; dir. Central State Bank; Sec. of Agr., in Cabinet of President Harding, 1921; issue: I–Henry Agard (1 above): II–Annabelle (*b* 1891; *m* Angus D. McLay); III–John Brodhead (*b* 1894; *m* Mary Margaret Powell); IV–James Wilson (*b* 1896; *m* Virginia Stubbs); V–Mary Olive (*b* 1898; *m* Charles Bruggmann); VI–Ruth Elizabeth (*b* 1901).
1–*m* May 20, 1914, Ilo Browne, *b* St. Charles, Ia., Mar. 10, 1888; dau. of the late James L. Browne, of Indianola, Ia., issue (all *b* Des Moines, Ia.): 1–Henry Browne, *b* Sept. 18, 1915; 2–Robert Browne, *b* July 13, 1918; 3–Jean Browne, *b* June 30, 1920.
1–B.S., Ia. State Coll. '10 (Delta Tau Delta, Alpha Zeta, Sigma Delta Chi), hon. M.S. in Agr., 1920. Asso. editor, 1910-24, and editor since 1924, Wallaces' Farmer. Author (see Who's Who in America). Pres. Hi-Bred Corn Co.; v.p. Wallace Pub. Co. Mem. Corn Belt Meat Producers' Assn. (sec. since 1921). Residence: 3821 John Lynde Rd., Des Moines, Ia.

1–**WARD, Flora Lusk (Mrs. Charles C.),** *b* Parsons, Kan., Mar. 14, 1881.
9–Anthony Jacobus (Henckel) **Hinkle** (bap. 1668-1728), preacher, ordained Giessen U., 1692; from Germany, settled at Phila., Pa., 1717; *m* Maria Elisabetha– (1671-1744);
8–John Gerhard Anthonius (1698-1736), *m* 1720, Anna Catherine– (*d* 1789);
7–George (1727-78), of Hinkletown, Pa.; innkeeper; *m* ca. 1753, Barbara Rowland (*d* 1791; Jacob[8], *m* Barbara–);
6–John (1760-1828), Louisville, Ky.; large landowner; *m* 1780, Catherine– (1764-1828);
5–Jacob (1785-1862), established and owned Edinburgh (Ind.) "Review," 1854; printed July 12, 1808, "Missouri Gazette," the first newspaper west of Mississippi River; *m* 1805, Nancy Kennedy (1789-1869; Rev. John[6], *d* 1801);
4–Mary Ann (1813-96), *m* 1827, David S. **Laughlin** (1801-61), steamboat pilot and capt. on Ohio and Miss. rivers;
3–Nancy (*b* 1839), *m* 1854, David Winston **Lusk** (1834-89); historian, newspaper publisher and editor; collector of internal revenue (Dr. Winston C. N.[4]);
2–Harry H. (2 below).
9–William (Haward, Howard) **Hayward** (qv);
8–Samuel (1646-1713), original propr. of Mendon, Mass.; *m* Mehitable Thompson (dau. of John, from north of Wales, 1622/23, *m* 2d, 1645, Mary, dau. of Francis Cooke, Mayflower Pilgrim, qv); *m* 2d, Elizabeth–, widow of Robert Millard;
7–Benjamin (*b* 1689), *m* Anna or Hannah–;
6–Thomas (1719-93), *m* 1st, 1746, Elizabeth (bap. 1729), dau. of Eleazer Giles; *m* 2d, —; *m* 3d, 1773, Elizabeth Young (1728-74);
5–Eliezer or Eleazer (1753-89), Groton, Vt.; pvt. Am. Rev.; *m* 1784, Keziah Shed;
4–Benjamin (1788-1860), Rutland, Vt.; *m* 1816, Elizabeth Marshall;
3–Horace (1824-78), trustee, Olney, Ill.; supervisor, Richland Co., Ill.; circuit judge, 1873; pres. Graysville & Mattoon R.R.; dir. First Nat. Bank; Mason (32°); *m* 1852, Ellen Jane McCollough (1831-98);
2–Tinnie Elisabeth (2 below).
9–Daniel **Shed** (qv);
8–John (1654-1736/37), took oath of fidelity, 1677; landowner, 1679; selectman, 1700,01,05; served in King Philip's War; sgt. and ens. Billerica militia co.; *m* 1676/77, Sarah Chamberlaine (1655-1735/36; William[9], qv);
7–Benjamin (1696-1770), *m* 1st, 1719, Abial Manning (1698-1736/37; Samuel[8], *m* Abihaielo, dau. of John Wight; William[9]; William[10], from Eng. to Mass. Bay Colony, 1634, *m* 2d, Susanna–, *d* 1650);
6–Benjamin (1727-60), *m* 1755, Keziah Butterfield (1733-1805; David[7], *m* Keziah, dau. of Benjamin Shettleworth; Jonathan[8]; Samuel[9]; Benjamin[10], qv);
5–Keziah (*b* 1760), *m* Eliezer, or Eleazer **Hayward** (5 above).
10–Thomas (Pers) **Pierce** (qv);
9–Thomas (1617/18-1683), Woburn, Mass.; selectman, 1660; sgt. in King Philip's War; *m* 1635, Elizabeth (*d* 1688), dau. of Ryse (Rice) Cole[10];
8–Benjamin (*d* 1739), Woburn; *m* 1688, Mary Read (Reed) (1670-1746; Ralph[9], *m* Mary, dau. of Anthony Pierce; William[10], from Eng. in the "Defense" 1635);
7–Thomas (1702-68), *m* 1st, 1722, Hannah Locke (1701-43; James[8], *m* Sarah Cutter; William[9], from Eng. in the "Planter");
6–Thomas (1726/27-1768), *m* 1750, Mary Haven (*b* 1728; Joseph[7], *m* Martha, dau. of Thomas Walker; Moses[8]; Richard[9], qv);
5–Mary (*b* 1768), *m* 1788, Elijah **Marshall** (1766-1838; John[6], of Derry, N.H., *m* Martha Horton);
4–Elizabeth (1792-1871), *m* Benjamin **Hayward** (4 above).
9–Isaac **Leet,** from Eng. to Burlington, N.J., 1685; *m* Elizabeth–;
8–Daniel (1685-1727), *m* Susannah Horseman (Marmaduke[9], of N.J.);
7–Isaac (1726-1802), built at own expense a blockhouse fort, on Chartier's Creek (Shurtee's), Washington Co., Pa., 1776; commr. of Oyer and Terminer, 1778; *m* Rebecca Vahan (Vaughn; William[8], of N.J.);
6–Rebecca (1755-1840), Washington Co., Pa.; *m* 1781, Enoch (Dey) **Dye** (1753-1830), pvt. Will-

iam Leet's Co., 3d Bn., Washington Co., Pa. militia in Am. Rev.;
5–Mary (1781-1843), *m* 1802, Samuel **Carrothers** (1780-1865), landowner, Mansfield, O.;
4–Rebecca Dye (1813-79), *m* John **McCollough** (1807-56);
3–Ellen Jane (1831-98), *m* Horace **Hayward** (3 above);
2–Tinnie Elisabeth (1857-94), *m* 1875, Harry H. **Lusk** (1855-1902), propr. and pub. of Olney (Ill.) "Journal," 1872, Parsons (Kan.) daily and weekly "Sun," 1878-1902; postmaster, 1889-94, 1896-1901.
1–*m* July 12, 1909, Charles Cresap Ward, *b* Randolph Co., W.Va., June 2, 1877; son of Jacob Loman Ward (1848-1918).
1–Ed. Mary Inst., St. Louis, Mo.; George Washington U., Washington, D.C.; Newspaper Inst. of America. Law clk., U.S. Land Office, Waterville, Wash.; law clk., Interior Dept., Washington; dir. Westlake Finance Co., Los Angeles. Mem. D.A.R., U.D.C. (registrar), U.S.D. 1812 (state historian), Haigler Family Assn. (historian), Shed Family Assn., Henckel Family Assn., Nat. Geneal. Soc. Residence: 241 S. Catalina St., Los Angeles, Calif.

1–**WARD, James Alfred,** *b* Yankton, S.D., Sept. 8, 1879.
10–William **Ward** (qv);
9–Samuel (1641-1729), of Marlborough, Mass.; *m* 1667, Sarah How (1644-1707);
8–Samuel (1678-1737), *m* Mary–;
7–Ephraim (*b* 1705), Southboro, Mass.; *m* 1733, Susannah Weeks (1712-40);
6–Ephraim (1733-1820), Bradford, N.H.; Am. Rev.; *m* 1755, Elizabeth Priest (*d* 1816);
5–Abner (*d* 1841), Sutton, N.H.; *m* Polly Davis;
4–Isaac (1788-1856), Cornish, N.H.; in War 1812; *m* 1816, Catherine Davis;
3–Stephen Davis (1819-64), Warrenville, Ill.; *m* 1844, Miriam Susannah Douglas (1819-1900);
2–James Alfred (*b* 1847), furniture mfr., Fort Smith, Ark.; fought in Civil War; *m* 1870, Emma Krebs (1852-1926); issue: I–Carl (1871-81); II–James Alfred (1 above); III–Miriam Douglas (*b* 1883; *m* Henry Frank Goodnow).
1–*m* Nov. 2, 1903, Cornelia Rand, *b* Huntsville, Ala., May 22, 1882; dau. of Jackson Rand; issue (all *b* Fort Smith, Ark.): 1–James Alfred, III, *b* June 27, 1905; Ph.B., Yale, '27 (a founder of Chi Psi Chapter at Yale, mem. Elihu Club, letter in crew); *m* Aug. 3, 1923, Virginia Elizabeth, dau. of Harry Clendening; 2–Evelyn Carlock, *b* Feb. 23, 1907; attended Miss Wright's School, Bryn Mawr, Pa.; *m* Dec. 27, 1928, Robert Scott, son of Robert Scott Robertson (issue: Robert Scott, III); 3–Miriam Chambless, *b* Mar. 26, 1916.
1–B.S., Ala. Poly. Inst., '99 (Phi Delta Theta). Pres. Ward Furniture Mfg. Co. Capt., 345th Inf., 87th Div., during World War; 6 mos. service in France. Mem. bd. govs. Am. Furn. Mart, Chicago; dir. Nat. Assn. Furn. Mfrs., First Nat. Bank, Ark. Valley Trust Co., Fort Smith, Midland Valley R.R. Co. Mem. I.A.G. Presbyterian. Democrat. Clubs: Southern Yacht (New Orleans), Hardscrabble Country, Furniture Club of America. Residence: Fort Smith, Ark.

1–**WARNOCK, Miss Charley,** *b* Union Springs, Ala., Apr. 8, 1870.
7–George **Walton** (*d* 1765), one of the first justices in Brunswick Co., Va.; *m* Elizabeth Ledbetter (*d* 1775);
6–Isaac Rowe (*d* 1770), burgess, Brunswick Co., 1761-65; *m* Elizabeth–;
5–Isaac Rowe (1765-1833), of Brunswick Co.; *m* 1st, 1787, Elizabeth Allen (1770-1805; William^{6}, lt. in Am. Rev.);
4–Cidney Jane (1788-1826), *m* 1803, Warren **Webb,** of Greensville Co., Va.;
3–Minerva (1806-43), *m* 1826, James K. B. **Delbridge** (1796-1866);
2–Mary Jane (1839-1907), of Bulloch Co., Ala.; *m* 1859, James Theophilus **Warnock** (1835-1903), grad. Jefferson Med. Coll.; served in C.S.A. (Rev. John^{3}, from Ireland to Ohio, 1823, *m* Jane Boyd); issue: I–James Edward (1865-1903; *m* Louise Burruss); II–Charley (1 above); III–Samuel Delbridge (*m* Nina Maner); IV–Simon P. (*m* Nancy Bethune); V–Mary Lillian (*m* Henry St. George Tucker).
1–Mem. D.A.R., I.A.G. Episcopalian. Residence: 6501 Three Chopt Rd., Richmond, Va.

1–**WARREN, Laura Alden Cranston (Mrs. Frank Manley,** *b* Denver, Colo., Mar. 3, 1881.
8–John **Cranston** (qv);
7–Samuel (1659-1727), Newport, R.I.; *m* 1st, 1680, Mary Hart (1663-1710; Thomas^{8}, of Newport, *m* Freeborn, dau. of Roger Williams, qv);
6–Thomas (1692-1721), *d* at sea; *m* ante 1717/18, Patience Gardiner (*b* 1687);
5–Peleg (1717/18-1805), Foster, R.I.; *m* 1747, Sarah Carr (1722-91);
4–James (1764-1832), Waterloo Tp., O.; *m* 1787, Ruth Austen (1767-1858);
3–Earl (*b* 1812), *d* Alexandria, La.; *m* 1839, Jane Montgomery (1823-99);
2–Earl (2 below).
10–John **Alden,** Mayflower Pilgrim (qv);
9–John (post 1627-1697), *m* Mary Simmons (*d* post 1697);
8–John (1674/75-1730), *d* Middleboro, Mass.; *m* ante 1702, Hannah White (1681-1732);
7–John (1718-1821), Middleboro, Mass.; *m* 1739, Lydia Lazell (1723-1749);
6–John (1739 or 1740-will probated 1817), *m* 1766, Lois Southworth (1741-post 1817);
5–Gideon Southworth (1780-1809), New Bedford, Mass.; *m* 1803, Priscilla Le Baron;
4–Francis LeBaron (1804-42), *m* 1828, Eudora Rowland Sampson;
3–Eudora Rowland (1831-64), of Easton, Md.; *m* 1849, Nicholas **Martin** (1829-58);
2–Laura Alden (2 below).
10–William **Bradford,** Mayflower Pilgrim (qv);
9–William (1624-1703/04), *m* 3d, post 1674, Mary (Atwood) Haynes (*d* 1714/15);
8–David (ca. 1690-1730), *m* 1713/14, Elizabeth Finney (1695-living 1746);
7–Lydia (1719-56), *m* 1743, Lazarus **Le Baron** (1698-1773);
6–William (1751-1816), *m* 1774, Sarah Churchill (1750-96);
5–Priscilla (1781-1846), *m* Gideon Southworth **Alden** (5 above).
11–Miles **Standish,** Mayflower Pilgrim (qv);
10–Alexander (ca. 1620-ca. 1702), *m* ante 1660, Sarah Alden (ca. 1629-ante 1686);
9–Sarah (ca. 1667-1740), *m* ante 1694, Benjamin **Soule** (1665-1729);
8–Hannah (1696/97-1776), *m* 1718, George **Sampson** (1690/91-1774);
7–Zabdiah (1727-76), in Am. Rev. from Plympton; *m* 1752, Abiah Whitmarsh (1724-1800);
6–George (1755-1826), *m* 1780, Hannah Cooper (1761-1836);
5–Zabeliel (1781-1828), *m* 1804, Ruth Lobdell (1784-1837);
4–Eudora R. (1807-52), *m* 1828, Francis Le Baron **Alden** (4 above);
3–Eudora Rowland; *m* Nicholas **Martin** (3 above);
2–Laura Alden (1857-1903), of Jacksonville, Ill.; *m* 2d, 1874, Earl **Cranston** (*b* 1840); issue: I–Eudora (*b* and *d* 1877); II–Ethel (*b* 1879); III–Laura Alden (1 above); IV–Ruth (*b* 1887).
1–*m* Oct. 8, 1902, Frank Manley Warren, *b* Portland, Ore., Aug. 25, 1876; son of Frank M. Warren, of Portland; issue (all *b* Portland, Ore.): 1–Anna Elizabeth, *b* Aug. 3, 1905; *m* Feb. 20, 1930, Gordon Berkeley, son of Rev. Hugh Donald Leitch, of Drumheller, Alberta, Can.; 2–Laura Alden, *b* July 30, 1913; 3–Frank Manley, *b* Sept. 10, 1915; 4–Nancy Jane Cranston, *b* Oct. 14, 1916.
1–Ed. Portland Acad. Mem. C.D.A., I.A.G., Town Club. Residence: 881 Westover Rd., Portland, Ore.

1–**WARRING, Susan Browning Whited (Mrs. Francis W.),** *b* Morrison, Ill., Mar. 16, 1870.
11–Edward **Bosworth** (qv);
10–Jonathan (*b* ca. 1611), lived at Cambridge, Hingham, Rehoboth, Swansea, Mass.; *m* Susanna–;
9–Jonathan (*d* 1687), Swansea and Rehoboth; *m* 1661, Hannah Howland (John^{10}, qv);
8–Joseph, *m* Esther Smith;
7–Esther, *m* Solomon **Drown;**
6–Benjamin (*b* 1719), *m* Hannah Kent;
5–Sgt. Benjamin (1747-1826), Am. Rev.; *m* Rachel Scott;
4–Ann, *m* John **Maxfield** (*b* 1792);
3–Nathaniel Drown (1813-88), *m* Susan Browning Sherman (1815-68);

2–Mary Alice (1844-1925), *m* 1862, William Moses **Whited** (1841-1903; Freeman F.[8] [1813-44], *m* Sally Bennett [1818-1902], of Steuben Co., N.Y.); for issue see Vol. III, p. 469.
1–*m* Dec. 23, 1891, Francis Wilber Warring (Sept. 9, 1859-June 13, 1923); son of Amos Warring, of Albany, N.Y.; issue: 1–Arthur Hutton, *b* Columbia, S.D., Nov. 26, 1892; *m* July 7, 1914, Gladys Idelle, dau. of Lyman G. Dingman, of Sioux Falls, S.D.
1–Grad. Morrison (Ill.) H.S., 1887; grad. C.L.S.C., Chautauqua, N.Y., 1894; English course, U.Chicago, 1896; art course, Yankton Coll., 1911; religious edn. and church pageantry course, Yankton Coll., 1922. Past pres. Yankton Women's Club; past grand matron O.E.S. of S.D.; ex-state regent D.A.R.; state dir., C.A.R., 1930-33; life mem. and state chmn. Internat. Council of Women; trustee Carnegie Library; state v.p. Nat. L.A.P.W., 1930-32. Residence: 1100 Walnut St., Yankton, S.D.

1–**WASSELL, Charlie Louise Jones Hartley (Mrs. Sam M.),** *b* Conway, Ark., Sept. 11, 1886.
5–Moses **Taylor,** served in Am. Rev.; *m* ca. 1754, Elizabeth Prevatt;
4–Rev. John Prevatt (1783-1843), *m* Hueann Carr (1781-1861);
3–Mary Ann (1818-1905), *m* 1840, John Mason **Jones** (1811-86), 1st lt. Forrest's cav., C.S.A. (John Seaborn[4], *m* Mary–);
2–Charles William (1864-86), *m* 1885, as her 1st husband, Leona Hall Winton (1865-1900), see Vol. II, p. 247 for maternal lineage; she *m* 2d, 1889, James Thomas Markham.
1–*m* June 23, 1908, Maynard Leslie Hartley (Dec. 11, 1882-Oct. 6, 1918); son of John Hartley, issue: 1–Maynard Leslie, *b* Little Rock, Ark., July 7, 1909.
1–*m* 2d, June 10, 1923, Sam McConaughey Wassell, *b* Little Rock, Ark., Apr. 13, 1883; son of Samuel S. Wassell, of Little Rock, *m* Elizabeth McConaughey.
1–Mem. S.M.D., D.A.R., U.S.D. 1812 (1st v.p. for Ark., 1928-29), U.D.C., A.A.U.W., L.A.P.W., Taylor Family Assn. Clubs: Central College (pres.), Country. Residence: 1305 Broadway, Little Rock, Ark.

1–**WATKINS, Corinne Louise Wheeler (Mrs. Thomas D.),** *b* Austin, Minn., May 9, 1873.
9–Sgt. Ephraim **Wheeler** (*d* 1669/70), from Eng., 1635; was one of first settlers of Fairfield, Conn.; *m* Ann Turney (Robert[10]);
8–Dea. Isaac (1642-1712), one of first nine men in church at Stratfield (Bridgeport), Conn.; *m* Ann–;
7–Sgt. Samuel (*d* 1707/08), *m* Hannah Wheeler (Sgt. John[8]; Thomas[9]);
6–Samuel (1700-73), *m* Abigail Lacey (*d* post 1773; Edward[7]; Edward[8]; Edward[9]; John[10]);
5–Jedediah (1726-1811), cooper and farmer; *m* Elizabeth Rundell;
4–Eli (*b* 1773), capt. militia, 1808-10; *m* 1795, Grissel Osborn (1776-1868; Ens. Eleazer[5], Am. Rev.; Eleazer[6], lt. in French and Indian War; Sgt. David[7]; Capt. John[8]; Capt. Richard[9]);
3–Orange Hall (1804-89), St. Paul, Minn.; *m* 1832, Eve Tucker (1813-85; Dr. Benjamin[4]);
2–Eber Osborn (1839-89), lawyer; *m* 1869, Katherine Jane Fleck (1843-76; Jacob[3]; Jacob[4]); *m* 2d, Mina Moore (1838-1912); issue (1st marriage): I–Corinne Louise (1 above); II–Paul Clifford (1876-1918); issue (2d marriage): I–Alice Moore (*b* 1882).
1–*m* Sept. 14, 1898, Thomas David Watkins (Sept. 4, 1870-Dec. 25, 1912); son of John Watkins, of West Exeter, Otsego Co., N.Y.; issue (all *b* Utica, N.Y.): 1–John Wheeler, *b* Apr. 5, 1901; Cornell U.; *m* May 23, 1925, Emily Beatrice, dau. of Samuel A. Batty, of Utica (issue: Joanne Beatrice, *b* Aug. 25, 1929); 2–Winifred Corinne (Feb. 11, 1903-Jan. 17, 1904); 3–Thomas David, Jr., *b* Jan. 31, 1904; Cornell, '28; *m* June 8, 1928, Margaret Eileen Mitchell (issue: Corinne Mitchell, *b* June 15, 1929; Sally Elizabeth, *b* Aug. 3, 1930); 4–Wheeler Wynne, *b* July 26, 1909; Utica Free Acad., '26.
1–Mem. C.D.XVIIC., D.A.R., Soc. N.E. Women, U.S.D. 1812 (regent), Americans Armorial Ancestry, Herkimer Home Assn. Residence: 1521 Kemble St., Utica, N.Y.

1–**WAY, Glenn Charles,** *b* Ransomville, N.Y., Sept. 3, 1881.
9–James **Way** (*d* 1685), from Eng., 1652, settled at Newtown, N.Y.; elected "overseer" in Newtown, 1676, although a Quaker; *m* Ede–;
8–Francis (*d* 1712), of Newtown; *m* Elizabeth–;
7–James (1694-1767), of Newtown; apptd. one of six trustees to defend Newtown in a suit with Bushwick, 1764; *m* 1716, Hannah Leverich (*d* 1729; John[8]; Caleb[9]; Rev. William[10], settled at Salem, 1633);
6–John (*b* 1725), of Halfmoon, N.Y.; *m* 1st, Sarah–; *m* 2d, Catherine Tenbach;
5–probably Benjamin or Josiah (both Am. Rev.);
4–David B. (1795-1865), left an orphan aet. 7, brought up by Matthew Calkins till 12; served in 13th U.S. Inf., 1814-15; Baptist clergyman; settled nr. Niagara Falls, 1823; *m* 1818, Phoebe Sherman (1799-1861);
3–Henry D. (1822-1911), of Niagara Co.; *m* 1852, Amanda Markley (1832-1910; Jonah[4], *m* Hannah Dirstine);
2–William Henry (2 below).
9–Sgt. Nicholas **Cady** (1615-1700), from Eng., 1630, with William Knapp, who later became his father-in-law, in the group headed by Sir Richard Saltonstall; settled at Watertown; took oath of fidelity, 1652; mem. Train Band, 1653; constable of Groton, 1685; *m* 1648, Judith Knapp (William[10]).
8–Capt. Joseph (1666-1742), of Watertown; capt. of Train Band; rep. Gen. Ct.; *m* 1689, Sarah Davis (*b* 1667; Samuel[9], *m* Mary Waters; Barnabas[10], from Eng.);
7–Stephen (1701-85), *m* 1723, Abigail Lee (1703 or 04-1782; Samuel[8], immigrant, *m* Mary–);
6–Samuel (1724-99), Am. Rev.; *m* 1746, Elizabeth Winter (1728-1831; Samuel[7], *m* Elizabeth Philbrick; John[8], *m* Hannah, dau. of James Cutler, qv; John[9], from Eng., 1634);
5–Samuel (1759-1813), *m* Keziah Richardson;
4–Joseph (*b* 1788), settled at Yates, Orleans Co., N.Y., 1805; *m* Lavinia Tyler (John[5], *m* Ruby Bennett);
3–Permelia Bahama (1832-61), *m* 1851, James Madison **Foster** (*b* 1832; James[4], *m* Willina Thomas);
2–Jennie E. (1855-1927), Niagara Co., N.Y.; *m* 1880, William Henry **Way** (1856-1928); issue: I–Glenn Charles (1 above); II–Clark Henry (*b* 1883; *m* Teresa Donahue); III–James Elton (*b* 1885; *m* Mary Jane Beggs); IV–Alta May (*b* 1892; *m* Roger H. Schweigert).
1–*m* Nov. 27, 1901, Effie Blanche Shippy, *b* Lewiston, N.Y., Apr. 9, 1883; dau. of Oren Oscar Shippy, of Lewiston; issue (all *b* Niagara Falls, N.Y.): 1–Howard William, *b* Mar. 29, 1905; *m* May 15, 1926, Dorothy M., dau. of Fred Pries, of Dunkirk, N.Y. (issue: Lois Marilyn; Jean Marie); 2–Harold Glenn, *b* Mar. 19, 1908; 3–Donald Verne, *b* May 9, 1919.
1–School teacher, 1899-1904; salesman, 1904-07; customs inspector, 1907-14; immigrant inspector, since 1914. Trustee and treas. St. James M.E. Ch., since 1914. Mem. I.A.G. Mason. Republican. Residence: 1631 Niagara Av., Niagara Falls, N.Y.

1–**WATKINS, John Elfreth,** *b* Vincentown, N.J., Feb. 12, 1875.
11–John **Stockton,** Lord of Stockton Manor, Walpos Parish, Cheshire, Eng.;
10–Richard (ca. 1630-1707), from Eng. ante 1656; settled at Flushing, L.I.; lt. of Flushing Troop of Horse, 1665; converted to Quaker faith; moved to Burlington, N.J., 1660; *m* 1652, Abigail–;
9–Richard, acquired from William Penn 6,400 acres in center of which, 1682, he founded Princeton, N.J.; built "Marven," ancestral home of later Stocktons (including his descendant, Richard, who was a "signer"); *m* Susannah (Witham) Robinson (Robert Witham[10]), widow of Thomas Robinson;
8–Elizabeth (*b* 1684), *m* 1703, William **Budd** (William[9]; Rev. Thomas[10], the Quaker martyr, confined until his death in Ilchester jail, Eng., for refusing an oath; Rev. John[11], prelate of the Episcopacy, and direct desc. of John Budd, Earl of Sussex);
7–Rebecca, *m* Joseph **Lamb** (Joseph[8]);
6–Rebecca, *m* Joshua **Shreve** (*d* 1819); see Vol. III, p. 582;

5-Leah (1771-1855), *m* Joseph **Burr** (*b* 1768); see Vol. III, p. 582;
4-Joshua (1794-1865), of Vincentown; *m* Mary Euphemia Newbold (g.g.g.dau. of Michael Newbold, from Eng. to N.J., 1680);
3-Rebecca Shreve, *m* Guy **Bryan** (1815-88); see Vol. I, p. 358;
2-Helen (1855-84), *m* 1873, John Elfreth **Watkins** (1852-1903); see Vol. I, p. 358, for issue.
1-*m* June 1, 1899, Corinne Clements (see Vol. II, p. 248, for genealogy).
1-Journalist since 1894; gen. mgr. Public Ledger Syndicate, Phila., since 1917 (see Who's Who in America). Residences: Cedarbrook Rd., Merion Golf Manor, Ardmore, Pa., and Avalon, N.J.

1-**WAY, Thomas Lewis,** *b* Johnstown, N.Y., Nov. 10, 1885.
11-Jan **Gardinier** (alias Flodder);
10-Jacob Jense (*d* ante 1688), *m* Josyna- (*d* 1669);
9-Hendrick (ca. 1660-1694), *m* Neeltie Classe;
8-Nicholas (1684-1758), *m* 1713, Rachel Winne (1690-1758; Adam[9], *m* Anna Lockerman; Pieter[10], original settler, 1652);
7-Capt. Jacob (1730-91), *m* Dirkje Van De Worken;
6-Nicholas, *m* Rachel Barhydt;
5-Jacob N. (1784-1838), *m* 1801, Maria Veeder;
4-Volkert (1806-41), *m* 1828, Mary G. Schuyler (1810-44);
3-Maria (1831-72), *m* 1847, Simeon **Forgue** (1818-72);
2-Olive (2 below).
9-Simon Volkert **Veeder** (qv);
8-Volkert Simon (1698-1732/33), *m* Jannetje Schemerhorn (Reyer[9], *m* Arianntje Bratt; Jacob Janse[10], qv);
7-Johannes (*d* 1798), *m* 1738, Catharine Mebie (*b* 1720; Abraham[8], *m* Annatje Vedder);
6-Lt. Col. Volkert (1740-1813), *m* 1762, Elizabeth Smith;
5-Maria (1785-1826), *m* Jacob N. **Gardinier** (5 above).
10-Abraham Isaacse **Ver Planck** (qv);
9-Catalyn (*d* 1708), *m* David (Pieterse) **Schuyler** (*d* 1690), bro. of Philip Pieterse, and they were the first of the name in America;
8-Abraham (1663-1726), *m* 1691, Gertrude Ten Broeck (Dirk Wesselse[9], qv);
7-David (*b* 1692), *m* 1725, Maria Hansen;
6-Abraham (*b* 1735), *m* 1763, Eva Beekman;
5-David (*b* 1769), *m* 2d, Margaret Marselies;
4-Mary G. (1810-44), *m* Volkert **Gardinier** (4 above);
3-Maria, *m* Simeon **Forgue** (3 above);
2-Olive (*b* 1863), *m* 1884, John Lewis **Way** (1843-1912), from Eng., settled at Johnstown, N.Y. (Thomas Palmer[3] [1821-89], *m* 1842, Eliza Susannah Lewis); issue: I-Thomas Lewis (1 above); II-William Forgue (1888-1916); III-Olive Way (*b* 1892; *m* Thomas J. King).
1-*m* Jan. 17, 1912, Edith F. Merrill (Mar. 28, 1888-May 25, 1919); dau. of Cyrus H. Merrill, of Johnstown, N.Y.; issue: 1-Thomas Howland, *b* White Plains, N.Y., Aug. 23, 1915.
1-*m* 2d, Sept. 8, 1921, Fannie Margaret Payne, *b* Shelter Island, N.Y.; dau. of William Otis Payne, of Shelter Island; issue: 1-William Otis, *b* Albany, N.Y., May 28, 1923.
1-Grad. Rensselaer Poly. Inst. Engr. in charge of work on N.Y. State highways, Barge Canal and N.Y. City subways; partner in Snyder & Way Lumber Co., Johnstown, N.Y.; pres. Johnstown Savings & Loan Assn.; dir. Johnstown Business Men's Assn., Johnstown Y.M.C.A., Northeastern Retail Lumbermen's Assn. Mem. Johnstown Hist. Soc. Deacon Presbyterian church. Republican. Clubs: Colonial, Fulton County Auto (v.p.). Summer Residence: Camp on East Carogo Lake, Fulton Co., N.Y. Residence: 2 First Av., Johnstown, N.Y.

1-**WAYNE, May Clark (Mrs. Norris W.),** *b* Decatur, Ill., July 29, 1898.
10-Thomas **Thayer** (*d* 1665), from Eng., 1630, settled at Braintree, Mass.; shoemaker; *m* 1618, Margery Wheeler (1599-1672);
9-Fernando (1625-1713), Mendon, Mass.; *m* 1652, Huldah Hayward (*d* 1690; William[10], came in the "Ann and Elizabeth," 1635, *m* Margery-);
8-Ebenezer, *m* 1695, Martha White (*b* 1675; James[9], *m* Sarah Baker; Edward[10], came in the "Abigail," 1635, *m* Margery-);
7-Ebenezer (*b* 1699), Bellingham, Mass.; *m* 1724, Sarah Wheelock;
6-Jeremiah (1725-1805), signed the Assn. Test in Richmond, N.H., 1776; *m* 1747, Alice Holbrook;
5-Nathan (1769-1845), Warren, Vt.; *m* 1793, Sally Abbott (1765-1838);
4-Aaron (1797-1863), *m* 1824, Esther Field (1802-79; Anthony[5], *m* Sarah Franklin; Anthony[6]; Anthony[7]; Benjamin[8]; Anthony[9]; Robert[10]);
3-Erastus (1834-1924), Pontiac, Ill.; *m* 1861, Mary Elizabeth Blair;
2-Martha Ann (2 below).
12-John **Alden,** Mayflower Pilgrim (qv);
11-Elizabeth (1623 or 24-1717), Little Compton, R.I.; *m* 1644, William **Peabody** (1620-1707; John[12], came ca. 1635, *m* Isabel-);
10-Mercy (*b* 1649), *m* 1669, John **Simmons** (Moses[11], qv);
9-William (1672-1765), *m* 1696, Abigail Church (Joseph[10], *m* Mary Tucker; Richard[11], *m* Elizabeth, dau. Richard Warren, qv);
8-Mercy (1697-1768), *m* 1725, James **Bennett** (James[9], *m* Ruth Rogers [John[10], *m* Elizabeth, dau. of William Peabody, *m* Elizabeth, dau. of John Alden, qv; John[11], *m* Ann Churchman; Thomas[12], qv]);
7-James (*b* 1726), *m* 1753, Susanna Davenport (*b* 1730);
6-James (1758-1841), Bolton, Vt.; served 7 enlistments as pvt. and seaman in Am. Rev., pensioned, 1832; *m* 1779, Patience Shrieve (1760-1841; John[7], *m* Almy Head; Daniel[8]; Daniel[9]; Thomas[10]; William[11]);
5-Betsey (1789-1824), *m* 1810, Nathaniel **Stockwell** (1791-1875), corpl., Vt. militia, War 1812, received bounty land, and widow received pension;
4-Nancy (1813-94), Warren, Vt.; *m* 1836, James **Blair** (James[6], *m* Betsey Cox; James[6]);
3-Mary E. (1842-1917), *m* 1861, Erastus **Thayer** (3 above).
2-Orrin Ferris **Clark** (*b* 1859), supt. transportation, Grand Trunk R.R. (Lt. Addison[3], *m* Sarah Helen Bowen; Orrin[4], *m* Ellen Kilpatrick); *m* 1st, 1883, Minnie Case (1866-92); *m* 2d, 1897, Martha Ann Thayer (*b* 1868); issue (1st marriage): I-Ora (1885-95); II-Helen (1888-1926; *m* Leland Griffing; *m* 2d, Nicholas Chatham); issue (2d marriage): I-May (1 above); II-Orrin F., Jr. (1903-21; *m* Delight Rigby).
1-*m* May 5, 1921, Norris Wagner Wayne, *b* Porter Tp., Cass Co., Mich., Mar. 5, 1900; son of John Wayne, of Bristol, Ind.; issue: 1-William John, *b* Porter Tp., Cass Co., Mich., Apr. 23, 1922; 2-James Clark, *b* Porter Tp., Dec. 15, 1923.
1-Attended U. of Chicago, Spring term, 1918; attended Ypsilanti Normal, summer terms 1918,19, fall term, 1920, winter, 1920-21; studied music at Battle Creek (Mich.) Conservatory and Am. Conservatory, Chicago. Taught school, Randall Beach, Mich., 1918-19, Kessington, Mich., 1919-20; amateur genealogist. Mem. D.A.R., I.A.G., Alden Kindred of America. Presbyterian. Republican. Residence: 2214 Mather Av., Elkhart, Ind.

1-**WEARY, Ruth Jordan (Mrs. Franklin G.),** *b* St. Joseph, Mo., Oct. 6, 1886.
6-John **Jordan** (1694-1758), from Ireland; of Scotch-Irish descent; Presbyn.; settled nr. Phila., Pa.; *m* Elizabeth- (1694-1779);
5-Francis (1733-1804), Cumberland Co., Pa.; served in 6th Bn., 4th Co., 8th Class, Pa. troops in Am. Rev.; *m* 1759, Catherine Kendall (*d* 1804);
4-Amos (1762-1843), *m* 1784, Sarah Davis;
3-Jeremiah (1805-84), La Porte, Ind.; *m* 1827, Margaret Foresman;
2-William Amos (2 below).
7-Col. Caleb **North,** from Ireland to Phila., 1729; *m* Jane Eckerly;
6-Roger (1704-85), *m* 1733, Ann Rambo (*d* 1798; Gunner[7]; Peter G.[8]);
5-Sarah, *m* Elisha **Davis**;
4-Sarah (1762-1844), *m* Amos **Jordan** (4 above).
5-Robert **Foresman** (1725-1803), of Mt. Bethel, Pa.; *m* Jane All (1748-1803);
4-Robert (*d* 1829), Lycoming Co., Pa.; *m* 1785, Catherine Jacoby (1769-1831; Henry[5]; Peter[6], from Germany, 1741, settled in Bucks Co., Pa.);

3–Margaret (1809-68), *m* Jeremiah **Jordan** (3 above).
11–William **Pynchon** (qv);
10–Mary (*d* 1657), Springfield, Mass.; *m* 1640, Elizur **Holyoke** (*d* 1676; Capt. Edward[11], settled at Lynn, 1630);
9–Hannah (1644-77), *m* 1661, Samuel **Talcott** (1634-91), grad. Harvard, 1658; capt. Troop of Hartford Co.; original propr., Glastonbury (John[10], qv);
8–Nathaniel (1678-1758), sgt. of Train Band; *m* 1703, Elizabeth Pitkin (*d* 1768);
7–Rachel (1706-90), *m* 1723, Gideon **Hollister** (1699-1785), lt. of militia (Thomas[8]; John[9]; John[10], qv);
6–Nathaniel (1731-1810), *m* 1754, Mehitable Mattison (1739-1824);
5–David (1758-1836), Oswego, N.Y.; soldier 8th Regt. Conn. Line, Am. Rev.; *m* 1782, Hope Clark (1760-1855);
4–Mabel (1783-1847), Exeter, N.Y.; *m* 1815, Roswell **Harding** (1781-1867);
3–Benjamin D. (1816-1904), mem. first Territorial Senate (council) of Kan.; capt. Co. K, 9th Kan. Regt., Civil War; first settler of Wathena, Kan.; twice register of deeds, Doniphan Co.; *m* 1847, Emily Williams;
2–Clara (2 below).
9–Thomas **Williams** (1632-92), from Wales, settled at Wethersfield, Conn., bet. 1645-56; *m* Rebecca–;
8–Jacob (1664-1712), *m* Sarah Gilbert;
7–Stephen (*b* 1693);
6–Jehiel (1733-1810), *m* Ann Edwards (1735-1810);
5–Wait (*b* 1764), *m* Abigail Treadway;
4–Russell Trumbull (1806-57), *m* Caroline Knickerbocker (1808-82);
3–Emily (1826-1906), *m* Capt. Benjamin D. **Harding** (3 above);
2–Clara (*b* 1851), Minneapolis, Minn.; *m* 1872, William Amos **Jordan** (1844-92), bank cashier, St. Joseph, Mo.; issue: I–Riverda Harding (*b* 1873; *m* Mary Vinette Hoover); II–Helen (*b* 1876); III–Ruth (1 above); IV–Loring Kenneth (*b* 1888; *m* Grace Wilma Hoover); V–William Amos, 2d (*b* 1893; *m* Marion Porter).
1–*m* Sept. 9, 1909, Franklin Grimm Weary, *b* Humeston, Ia., Oct. 2, 1886; son of Dr. Franklin Grimm Weary, of St. Joseph, Mo.; issue: 1–Clara Frances, *b* St. Joseph, Mo., Oct. 9, 1915; 2–Franklin Grimm, Jr., *b* Richmond, Mo., Aug. 17, 1924.
1–Grad. Mo. State Normal School; 1 yr. at Randolph-Macon Woman's Coll. Mem. D.A.R., etc. Methodist. Residence: Richmond, Mo.

1–**WEEKS, Jennie Esther Guile (Mrs. Charles Warren),** *b* Louisiana, Mo., Feb. 26, 1877.
7–George **Stillman** (qv);
6–Nathaniel (1691-1770), Wethersfield, Conn.; *m* 1731, Sarah Allyn (1708-94);
5–Allyn (1732-1803), Enfield, Conn.; capt. comdg. the brig "Jason" in Am. Rev.; contributed to the aid of Boston, 1777; *m* 1767, Prudence Kingsbury (1746-88);
4–Samuel Allyn (1778-1849), Wethersfield; *m* 1813, Mabel Terry (*d* 1833);
3–Samuel Allyn (1821-1903), Enfield; *m* 1845, Jane Eliza Burt (1827-1907);
2–Emma Jane (1850-95), *m* 1874, Judson Monroe **Guile** (1852-1918), lawyer; issue: I–Minnie Burt (*m* Elmer E. Brackett); II–Jennie E. (1 above); III–Mabel Terry (*b* 1878); IV–Henry Franklin (*b* 1880; *m* Frieda Edsell); V–Emmett (1891-93).
1–*m* Dec. 11, 1902, Charles Warren Weeks, *b* Osage, Ia., Mar. 15, 1876; son David Parker Weeks, of Woodstock, Minn.; issue: 1–Margaret, *b* Manila, P.I., Oct. 30, 1903; *m* Jan. 30, 1925, Charles Alvin Pyle, son of John F. Pyle, of Rockport, Ind. (issue: Ruth); 2–Charles Stillman, *b* Ft. Crook, Neb., Jan. 12, 1905; U.S.N.A., '25; 3–Phoebe, *b* Iowa City, Ia., Jan. 25, 1907; *m* Sept. 10, 1929, Azro P. Fiedler, of Thomasboro, Ill.; 4–Esther, *b* Lincoln, Neb., Dec. 31, 1918.
1–B.A., U. of Neb., '97. Mem. D.F.P.A. Presbyn. Republican. Clubs: University, Social Science. Residence: 812 W. Green St., Champaign, Ill.

1–**WEINMANN, Jeanne Fox (Mrs. John Francis),** *b* Little Rock, Ark., Sept. 19, 18–.
8–Thomas **Fox** (qv);
7–Isaac (1657-1735), Concord, Mass.; *m* Abigail Osborn (1661-1718; Thomas[8], of Charlestown, *m* Sarah–);
6–Ebenezer (1689-1752), Medford; *m* Jane Stedman (1699-1719);
5–David (1720-1804), New London, Conn.; Am. Rev.; *m* Mary (Mercy) Chapman (1726-1814; Benjamin[6], *m* Lydia–);
4–Stephen (1760-1842), East Haddam, Conn.; Am. Rev.; *m* Mary Bates (1776-1844);
3–John (1795-1885), Wayne Co., Ind.; War 1812; *m* Katharine Miller (*d* 1845);
2–John Wesley (1843-74), atty.; judge U.S. Dist. Ct., eastern dist. of Ark.; *m* 1873, Anna Jeannette Compton (1852-90); she *m* 2d, Frank M. Parsons.
1–*m* Oct. 25, 1895, Richard Lambert Raleigh (1869-1912); son of Patrick Raleigh, of Little Rock, Ark.; issue: 1–Cecil Baring, *b* St. Louis, Mo., Oct. 18, 1896; ed. Culver Mil. Acad.; capt. U.S.M.C., World War; *m* Oct. 24, 1928, Lucile, dau. of Charles Stewart, of Greenwood, Ark.
1–*m* 2d, July 3, 1902, John Francis Weinmann, *b* Cleveland, O., May 15, 1877; son of John Weinmann, of Conway, Ark.
1–Ed. pvt. schools, and Galloway Woman's Coll., 1890. Mem. U.D.C. (state pres.), D.A.C. (state regent), D.F.P.A. (past state pres.), D.A.R. (former state treas. and parliamentarian), U.S.D. 1812 (former regent, state pres., and nat. historian), Ark. Pioneers, A.L. Auxiliary, Societe Academique d'histoire Internationale (Paris); Ark. regent for Kenmore Assn. Clubs: Sylvan Hills Golf, Lakeside Fishing, Woman's Nat. Dem. (Washington). Presbyterian. Democrat. Residence: 2214 Battery St., Little Rock, Ark.

1–**WEIS, Frederick Lewis,** *b* Cranston, R.I., Aug. 22, 1895.
9–Dea. Nicholas **Clap** (1612-79), from Eng., 1633, settled at Dorchester, Mass.; *m* his cousin, Sarah Clap (*d* 1650);
8–Nathaniel (1640-1707), *m* Elizabeth Smith (1647-1722; Lawrence[9]);
7–Ebenezer (1678-1750), *m* Hannah Clap (1681-1747; Maj. Samuel[8]; Capt. Roger[9]);
6–Sgt. Ebenezer (1705-52), *m* 1727, Hannah Pierce (1708-57; John[7]; Thomas[8]; Robert[9]);
5–Capt. Lemuel (1735-1819), 1st lt., Lexington Alarm, 1775; capt. Am. Rev.; *m* 1768, Rebecca Dexter (1739-1823; Rev. Samuel[6]; Capt. John[7]; John[8]; Richard[9]);
4–Richard, Gent. (1780-1861), *m* 1807, Mary Blake (1784-1875; Adj. Jonathan[5]; Samuel[6]; Dea. James[7]; Dea. James[8]; Dea. James[9]; William[10]);
3–Mary (1825-1908), *m* 1852, Charles Frederick **Weis** (1820-1905), from Germany to N.E., 1845 (Johann Daniel Adolf[4]; Johannes[5]; Johann Albert[6]; Johann Adam[7]; Johann Adam[8]; Daniel[9]);
2–John Peter Carl (2 below).
9–Edmond **Lewis** (1601-51), from Wales, 1634, settled at Watertown, 1634, at Lynn, 1642; *m* Mary– (1602-58);
8–Capt. Dea. John (1631-1710), innholder; lt., King Philip's War, 1675-76; *m* 1659, Hannah Marshall (1640-99; Capt. Thomas[9]);
7–Lt. John (1660-1711), *m* 1683, Elizabeth Brewer (*b* 1660; Crispus[8]);
6–Thomas (1708-74), *m* 1741, Elizabeth Hutchinson (Thomas[7]; Hananiah[8]; Edward[9]);
5–Dea. Thomas (1750-1813), dea. 2d Ch., Boston; soldier Am. Rev.; large ship owner and merchant at Boston; owned Lewis Wharf, still standing; *m* 1770, Sarah Merry (1750-1835; Ralph[6]; Ralph[7]; Walter[8]; Walter[9]);
4–Thomas (1771-1824), ship owner and merchant; owned Lewis Wharf, Boston; *m* 1813, Polly Clap;
3–Hon. Abiel Smith (1814-95), Framingham, Mass.; mem. Mass. Senate, 1856; ship owner and commn. mcht., A. S. & W. G. Lewis & Co.; *m* 1865, Harriet Phipps Richardson (1841-71; George[4]; William[5]; Capt. Benjamin[6]; Benjamin[7]; Benjamin[8]; Isaac[9]; Thomas[10]);
2–Georgina (2 below).
10–Richard **Warren,** Mayflower Pilgrim (qv);
9–Anna (*b* ca. 1612), *m* 1633, Thomas **Little** (*d* 1671);
8–Ephraim (1650-1717), *m* 1672, Mary Sturtevant (1651-1717/18; Samuel[9]);

7–Mercy (1678-1755), *m* Job **Otis** (1677-1758; John[8]; John[9]; Richard[10]);
6–Ephraim (1708-94), *m* 1733, Rachel Hersey (1714-93; James[7]; James[8]; William[9]);
5–Priscilla (1742-1836), *m* William **Clap** (1733-1807; Samuel[6]; Joseph[7]; Maj. Samuel[8]; Dea. Thomas[9]);
4–Polly (1780-1865), *m* Thomas **Lewis** (4 above);
3–Hon. Abiel Smith, *m* Harriet Phipps Richardson (3 above);
2–Georgina (*b* 1868), *m* 1891, John Peter Carl **Weis** (*b* 1866), pres., The Narotex Co., textile mfrs., Lincoln, R.I.; issue: I–John Lewis (1892-93); II–Robert Lewis (*b* 1893; *m* Mae Dawson Collett); III–Frederick Lewis (1 above); IV–Richard Clap (*b* 1897); V–Marian Lewis (*b* 1898; *m* 1921, Maj. Paul Adams Merriam); VI–Eva Lewis (*b* 1902; *m* Rev. Richard Allen Day); VII–Francis Wilson (1905-26); VIII–Mary Blake (*b* 1906).
1–*m* Nov. 6, 1926, Elizabeth Williams Stone (qv for issue).
1–Grad. U.S.N.A., '17; Ens., U.S.N., 1917, lt., 1917-18; retired; B.D., Meadville Theol. Sch., 1922, S.T.M., 1928; Cruft fellow, U. of Strassbourg (France), 1922-24; studied U.Chicago and Harvard. Minister, Third Religious Soc., Dorchester, Mass., 1924-29; minister First Church of Christ, Lancaster (founded 1653), since 1929. Author, editor, genealogist. Sec. and treas. Unitarian Ministerial Union, 1926-28. Mem. Mass. and R.I. socs. S.M.D., 1919-29, R.I. Soc. S.C.W., 1919-29, R.I. Soc. S.A.R., 1919-30, I.A.G. Republican. Residence: Lancaster, Mass.

1–**WEIS, Elizabeth Williams Stone (Mrs. Frederick L.),** *b* Braintree, Mass., Dec. 17, 1904.
12–Elder William **Brewster,** Mayflower Pilgrim (qv);
11–Patience (*d* 1634), *m* 1624, Gov. Thomas **Prence** (qv);
10–Mercy (1631-1711), *m* 1649/50, Maj. John **Freeman**;
9–John (1651-1721), *m* 1672, Sarah Merrick;
8–Mercy (1687-1720), *m* 1705, Dea. Chillingsworth **Foster**;
7–Dea. James (1705/06-1788), Rochester, Mass.; *m* 1729, Lydia Winslow;
6–Mary (1732-1825), Hardwick; *m* 1754, Col. Timothy **Paige**;
5–Capt. Timothy (1757-1821), *m* 1780, Mary Robinson;
4–Martin (1791-1872), Providence, R.I.; *m* 1817, Mary Ann Billings;
3–Martha Pomeroy (1832-92), Templeton; *m* 1854, William **Stone**;
2–William Sidney (2 below).
11–Gov. Thomas **Dudley** (qv);
10–Mercy, *m* Rev. John **Woodbridge** (qv);
9–Martha (1660-1723), *m* 1680, Capt. Samuel **Ruggles** (1658-1716);
8–Rev. Timothy (1685-1768), Rochester; *m* 1710, Mary White;
7–Capt. Benjamin (1713-90), Hardwick; *m* 1736, Alice Merrick;
6–Mary (1738-1835), *m* 1758, Lt. Daniel **Billings**;
5–Barnabas (1769-1824), M.A., Brown, 1791; *m* 1792, Martha Pomeroy;
4–Mary Ann (1795-1875), *m* 1817, Martin **Paige** (4 above);
3–Martha Pomeroy, *m* William **Stone** (3 above);
2–William Sidney (*b* 1862), *m* 1888, Mary Elizabeth Russell (*b* 1863); *m* 2d, 1902, Ellen Reed Dewson (*b* 1871); issue (1st marriage): I–Barbara Russell (*b* 1890; *m* Hon. Major Willis Kennedy Hodgman, Jr.); II–Roger Pomeroy (*b* 1895; *m* 1926, Carol Rix); issue (2d marriage): I–Elizabeth Williams (1 above); II–Virginia (*b* 1907); III–Mary Dewson (*b* 1909).
1–*m* Nov. 6, 1926, Frederick Lewis Weis (qv); issue: 1–Robert Pomeroy, *b* Taunton, Mass., June 12, 1928; 2–Virginia Stone, *b* Clinton, Mass., June 10, 1930.
1–Ed. Lincoln School, Providence, R.I., 1922; Bridgewater Normal School, 1925. Residence: Lancaster, Mass.

1–**WELBORN, John Scott,** *b* Randolph Co., N.C., Dec. 5, 1871.
10–John (Wellborn) **Welborn,** from Wales, in the "Sea Venture," 1609, which was wrecked, and he arrived at Jamestown, Va., 1610, settled in Accomac Co., Va.;
9–John;
8–Capt. Thomas (1640-1702), of Accomac Co., Va.; *m* Arcadia–;
7–Samuel, settled in N.C., ca. 1700; surveyor; *m* Mary Chapley;
6–Thomas (*d* 1778), will recorded in Guilford Co., N.C.;
5–John (1757-1825), Randolph Co., N.C.; capt. militia in Am. Rev.; *m* 1776, Jane McGee (1760-1835; Col. John[6] [1716-1774], officer, English army, later of Randolph Co., N.C.; *m* Martha McFarlane [1735-1820], of Orange Co., N.C., who *m* 2d, 1779, William Bell);
4–Rev. John (1779-1830), *m* 1st, 1799, Mary Parsons (*d* 1819);
3–William J. (1808-92), *m* 1830, Eleanor Smith (1811-68);
2–William Clark (1835-78), of Randolph Co., N.C.; *m* 1861, Roxie Brandon (1843-1920), of Yadkin Co., N.C.
1–*m* Dec. 20, 1899, Cadia Barbee (see Vol. III, p. 642, for genealogy).
1–Owner of Welborn Supply Co.; dir. High Point Savings Bank, North State Telephone Co. Mason. Clubs: Commercial, High Point Country, Sedgefield Country. Residence: High Point, N.C.

1–**WELCH, Maude Ivy Greene (Mrs. William J.),** *b* Odell, Ill., Mar. 7, 1874.
9–John **Greene** (1606-95), from Eng. ca. 1639; settled at Narragansett, R.I.; *m* 1642, Joan Beggarly;
8–Benjamin (ca. 1665-1717), Quidnesset, R.I.; *m* 1687, Humility Coggeshall (1671-1719);
7–John (ca. 1688-1752), *m* 1708, Mary Aylesworth (1688-ante 1741; Arthur[8], immigrant);
6–Benjamin (*b* 1719), of West Greenwich; *m* 1742, Mercy Rogers (*b* 1712);
5–Caleb (1744-90), West Greenwich; lt. Am. Rev.; *m* 1773, Welthian Ellis (*b* 1753; Gideon[6]; Jeremiah[7]);
4–Thomas (*b* 1774), *m* ca. 1792, Dorcas–;
3–Caleb (1793-1840), of N. Y. State; soldier in War 1812; *m* 1810, Mary Oaks (1793-1881; Abraham[4]; William[5]; Nathaniel[6]; Nathaniel[7], immigrant);
2–Hon. Leander (2 below).
5–Malachi **Fitz Randolph,** *m* Sarah Bonham (Zedekiah[6] of N.J.);
4–Zedakiah (1748-1835), Am. Rev.; *m* 1779, Sarah Coryell (1759-1840; Abraham[5], Am. Rev., *m* Esther Heath);
3–Abraham (1797-1879), *m* 1826, Abigail Day Willcox (1807-78);
2–Marilla J. (Apr. 2, 1832-Aug. 27, 1913), *m* 1847, Hon. Leander L. **Greene** (Jan. 24, 1825-Sept. 8, 1906), retired farmer and banker, Genoa, Neb.; issue: I–Gurley J. (1848-1909; *m* Belle Miller); II–Franklin H. (1850-1915; *m* Elida Brown); III–Okeley E. (1854-1922; *m* Maude Perrigo); IV–Maude Ivy (1 above).
1–*m* Jan. 18, 1916, William J. Welch, *b* Genoa, Neb., Dec. 24, 1863; son of Jonas Welch, of Columbus, Neb.
1–M.B., Gates Coll., in piano and organ. Mem. D.F.P.A., D.A.C., D.A.R. (chapter regent). Conglist. Clubs: Woman's (pres.), Lakeside Country. Residence: Genoa, Neb.

1–**WENDELL, Arthur Rindge,** *b* Quincy, Mass., Feb. 22, 1876.
8–Rev. Nathaniel **Rogers** (qv);
7–Rev. John (1631-84), grad. Harvard, 1649; 5th pres. Harvard Coll., 1683-84; *m* Elizabeth Denison (1641-1723);
6–Rev. Nathaniel (1669-1723), grad. Harvard, 1687; minister at Portsmouth, N.H.; *m* Sarah Purkis (or Purchase);
5–Hon. Daniel (1715-95), mem. His Majesty's Council many yrs.; resigned account of the acts of the British Parliament; *m* Mehitable Rindge (1725-1803; John[6], below);
4–Mark (1762?-1801), *m* Susanna (Shores) Gardiner (1765-1850);
3–Mehitable Rindge (1792-1859), *m* 1816, Jacob **Wendell** (see Vol. I, p. 348, for Wendell lineage);
2–George Blunt (2 below).
8–Daniel **Rindge** (*d* Feb. 1661), of Roxbury, Mass., 1639, Ipswich, 1648; *m* Mary Kinsman (Robert[9]);
7–Isaac, *m* Elizabeth Dutch, a widow (John

Dutch[8] [*b* 1646], *m* Elizabeth Roper; Robert[9], *m* Mary-);
6-John (1695-1740), apptd. by Gen. Assembly to be its agent to go to Eng. and establish the boundaries bet. provinces of N.H. and Mass., 1731-32; apptd. by the king as a mem. of Benning Wentworth's Council, 1738-40; *m* Ann Odiorne (1701-62; Jothan[7], 1675-1748);
5-Isaac (*b* 1735), *m* Sarah Parr;
4-John Parr, *m* Sarah Lewis;
3-Artemisia (1801-66), *m* 1829, Jacob Weeks **Thompson** (see Vol. I, p. 348, for Thompson lineage);
2-Mary Elizabeth (1838-97), *m* 1861, George Blunt **Wendell** (1831-81), capt. mcht. marine (for issue see Vol. I, p. 348).
1-*m* Nov. 8, 1902, Grace Frances Peck, *b* N.Y. City; dau. of William Ward Peck, of New York; issue: 1-Eleanor Sherburne, *b* N.Y. City, Dec. 16, 1906.
1-A.B., Harvard, '96 (Pi Eta). V.p. and treas. The Wheatena Corpn.; trustee Individual Underwriters, Fireproof Sprinklered Underwriters and Metropolitan Inter-Insurers, New York; v.p. and mgr., Rahway (N.J.) Savings Instn.; pres. Industrial Bldg. & Loan Assn., Rahway; dir. Central Stamping Co., New York. Commr., 2d v.p. and treas., Union County (N.J.) Park Commn.; dir. U.S. Trade Mark Assn. Mem. O.F.P.A., I.A.G., Holland Soc. of New York. Clubs: Harvard, University (New York), Harvard, Baltusrol Golf, Canoe Brook Country of N.J. Summer address: Berkeley Hotel, 78 Piccadilly, London, W. 1, Eng. Residence: Wendelsora, Beekman Terrace, Summit, N.J.

1-**WERNER, Grace Harrington (Mrs. Joseph G.)**, *b* Annawan, Ill., Aug. 12, 1874.
11-William **Carpenter** (qv);
10-William (1605-59), settled at Rehoboth; rep., 1641,43; dep., 1645; constable, 1641; propr. and town clk., 1643-49; capt. 1642; *m* Abigail-;
9-William (1631/32-1703), town clk., Rehoboth, 1656; dep., 1668; *m* 1st, 1651, Priscilla Bennet;
8-Ephraim (*b* 1683), *m* Hannah Read;
7-Ephraim (*b* 1709), *m* Ferviah Carpenter;
6-Jonathan (*b* 1732), *m* Abagail Walker;
5-Jonathan, corpl., capt. and col. in Am. Rev.; *m* Olive Sessions;
4-Marshall (*b* 1795), Randolph, Vt.; capt. and maj. in War 1812; *m* Lucy Martin;
3-Marshall Darwin, *m* Dorcas Connor;
2-Emma Viola, *m* 1869, Prof. George B. **Harrington** (1844-1909), educator, Bureau Co., Ill. (Daniel[3]); issue: I-Ward (*d* aet. 4); II-Grace (1 above); III-dau. (*d* infancy).
1-*m* Dec. 19, 1920, Joseph G. Werner, *b* Kenosha, Wis.; issue: 1-Marie Viola, *b* Chicago, Ill., Dec. 18, 1923; ed. Roycemore Priv. Sch., Evanston, Ill.
1-Ed. Northwestern U., Chicago Musical Coll., and Columbia Sch. of Music. Mem. D.F.P.A., D.A.R., U.S.D. 1812. Conglist. Clubs: Rogers Park Woman's, Friends of Drama. Residence: 6757 Sheridan Rd., Chicago, Ill.

1-**WESCOTT, Edgar Hilt**, *b* La Porte, Ind., July 25, 1878.
4-Joshuah **Mason** (1778-1852), *m* 1801, Amy Raymond (1780-1851);
4-Harriet (1806-88), *m* Stephen **Wescott** (1803-89);
2-Clarence Edgar (2 below).
9-Tristram **Coffin** (qv);
8-James (1640-1720), *m* 1663, Mary Severance (John[9], from Eng. to Ipswich, Mass., 1634, original propr. at Salisbury);
7-Nathaniel (1671-1721), *m* 1692, Damaris Gayer (1673-1764; William[8], *m* Dorcas-);
6-Benjamin (*b* 1705), Quaker; gave money to Am. Rev.; *m* 1726, Judidah Hussey (1708-59; Batchelder[7], *m* Abigail, dau. of John Hall; Capt. Christopher[8], *m* Theodate, dau. Rev. Stephen Bachellor);
5-William (1730-1816), *m* 1758, Heptizibah Barney (Benjamin[6], *m* Lydia-);
4-Albert (1766-1818 or 19), *m* Mary Fay (1770-1849);
3-Charles Griffin (1801-78), *m* 2d, 1833 or 36, Margaret Ann Hughes (1806-63);
2-Mary Louise (1848-1929), *m* 1868, Clarence Edgar **Wescott** (1841-1924).
1-*m* Sept. 28, 1904, Clara Edna Street (qv); issue: 1-Helen Rude, *b* Plattsmouth, Neb., Oct. 6, 1907; 2-Edgar Street, *b* Plattsmouth, Mar. 18, 1910.
1-Ed. Plattsmouth High School and U. of Neb. Merchant; organist. Mason. Methodist. Club: Rotary. Residence: Plattsmouth, Neb.

1-**WESCOTT, Clara Edna Street (Mrs. Edgar H.)**, *b* Red Oak, Ia., July 26, 1876.
8-Daniel **Street** (1658-1738), *m* Hannah (West) East (John West[9]);
7-James (1692-1753), *m* Mary Griffith (*b* 1702; Robert[8], *m* Alice-);
6-Daniel (1731-1801), *m* Mary Foster (1730-1816; Thomas[7], *m* Lucy-);
5-James (1756-1828), *m* Elizabeth Walton (1755-1836);
4-Griffith (1781-1830), *m* Mary Egbert (1777-1873; Abraham[5]);
3-Jonathan (1819-1916), licensed M.E. preacher; *m* 1843, Adaline Wharton (1820-95);
2-William Lewis (2 below).
10-William **Blake** (qv);
9-James (bap. 1624-1700), sgt. in mil. co.; selectman; *m* 1651, Elizabeth Clapp (1634-93; Dea. Edward[10], *m* Prudence-);
8-James (1652-1732), *m* 2d, 1684, Ruth Bachellor (Nathaniel[9], *m* Deborah Smith; Nathaniel[10]; Rev. Stephen[11]);
7-Increase (1699-1770?), *m* 1724, Anna Gray (1704-51; Edward[8], *m* Susannah Harrison);
6-Increase (1726-95), Am. Rev.; *m* 1st, 1754, Anna Crafts (1734-62; Thomas[7], *m* Anna White);
5-James (1762-1839), *m* 1784, Rebecca Cunningham (1760-1835; David[6], *m* Elinor-);
4-Sally (1793-1878), *m* Nathaniel **McCulloch** (1793-1867), Bapt. minister (Joseph[5], from Ireland, soldier Am. Rev., *m* 1771, Sarah Spring);
3-William (1823-1905), Adventist minister and farmer; *m* 1844, Hannah Rude;
2-Mary Amelia (2 below).
10-Myles **Standish** (qv);
9-Josiah, *m* 2d, Sarah Allen;
8-Josiah, *m* Sarah-;
7-Mehitable, *m* Jabez (Rood) **Rude** (will dated 1758);
6-Josiah Standish, *m* Mary Foster;
5-Thaddeus (1763-1826), *m* 1789, Mary Bennitt Twitchell (*b* 1762);
4-Thaddeus (1794-1833), began to write name Rude; *m* 1817, Betsey Vincent (David[5], Am. Rev., *m* Elizabeth Hall);
3-Hannah (1824-1905), *m* William **McCulloch** (3 above);
2-Mary Amelia (1849-1930), D.A.R.; *m* 1868, William Lewis **Street** (1844-1909), Civil War vet.; mem. G.A.R.; issue: I-Walter Winfield (*b* 1869; *m* Hattie Woodard); II-Mary Elma (*b* 1874; *m* Schuyler Colfax Morgan); III-Clara Edna (1 above).
1-*m* Sept. 28, 1904, Edgar Hilt Wescott (qv for issue).
1-Teacher of voice, concert singer, choir director. Mem. S.M.D., D.A.R. (state v.regent), O.E.S., P.E.O., Woman's Club. Methodist. Residence: Plattsmouth, Neb.

1-**WHALLON, Edward Payson**, *b* Putnamville, Ind., Mar. 30, 1849.
4-James **Whallon**, from Ireland to Somerset Co., N.J., 1760; lt. Am. Rev.; *m* Sarah Smith;
3-James (1770-1849), soldier War 1812; settled at Cincinnati, 1800; *m* Alley Hagaman;
2-Thomas (2 below).
7-Adrian **Hagaman**, from Holland to N.J., 1650; *m* Katryna Margits;
6-Hendrick, *m* 1685, Adrientje, or Adrianna Bloodgood (Capt. Franz Jansen Bloetgoet, or Bloodgood[7], from Holland to New Amsterdam, 1659, with his wife, Lysbeth Jans; he was chief officer of Dutch militia, privy councillor, 1675, to deliver the colony to the British, magistrate, etc.);
5-Adrian (*b* 1686), *m* Maria Van Vliet;
4-Simon (*b* 1727), *m* Aaltje-;
3-Alley (1773-1847), *m* James **Whallon** (3 above).
4-James (Bigel) **Bickle** (Huguenot ancestry), from Eng. to Staunton, Va.; *m* Mary Hughes;
3-James Hughes (1792-1844), soldier War 1812; from Staunton, Va., to Centerville, Ind., 1837; *m* Rebecca Bridgland (1794-1839; John[4], from Holland to Staunton, Va., 1790);
2-Harriet Susanna (1822-1908), *m* 1842, Rev. Thomas **Whallon** (*b* Springdale, O., 1812-*d* Chicago, Ill., 1891), Presbyn. minister; chaplain 101st Ind. Vol. Inf., Civil War.
1-*m* Nov. 17, 1873, Margaret Ellen Kitchell (see Vol. III, p. 475, for genealogy and issue).

1-A.B., A.M., Hanover, Ind., Coll., '68; McCormick Theol. Sem., Chicago, 1868-70; grad. Union Theol. Sem., 1872; Ph.D., U.Wooster, 1885 (D.D., 1892; LL.D., Hanover Coll., 1925). Presbyn. clergyman, editor, author (see Who's Who in America). Mem. Inst. Am. Genealogy. Residence: 103 Wentworth Av., Wyoming, Cincinnati, O.

1-**WHEELER, Lydia Genevieve Thatcher (Mrs. Robert C.),** *b* Pueblo, Colo., May 3, 1886.
10-Rev. Robert **Jordan** (qv);
9-Dominicus (killed by Indians, 1703), *m* 1681, Hannah Tristram;
8-Dominicus (1683-1749), *m* ca. 1715, Joanna Bray;
7-Nathaniel (*b* 1718), col. Am. Rev.; *m* 1740, Hannah Woodbury, of Beverly, Mass.;
6-Tristram (*b* 1743), *m* Hannah Lassell, of Saco, Me.;
5-Tristram (1770-1826), of Cape Elizabeth, Me.; *m* 1797, Rebecca Hayden (1774-1835);
4-Larkin Lassell (*b* 1798), *m* 1820, Sarah P. Frost (1800-59);
3-Jacob Osborne (1826-1911), of Denmark, Me.; *m* 1853, Lucia Ann Peabody;
2-Luna Ada (2 below).
10-Lt. Francis **Peabody** (qv);
9-Capt. John (1642-1720), dep. Boxford, Mass. to Gen. Ct.; *m* 1st, 1665, Hannah Andrews (1642-1720; Robert[10], *m* Grace-);
8-Ens. David (1678-1826), *m* Sarah Pope (1685-1756; Capt. Seth[9] [1648-1727], a propr. of Dartmouth, N.H.; Thomas[10] [1608-86], *m* 2d, Sarah, dau. of John Jenney);
7-John (1714-65), *m* 1736, Mary Chadwick;
6-Dea. Moses (1744-1826), Am. Rev.; *m* 1767, Hannah Foster (1744-1825; Lt. Jeremiah[7], *m* Abigail Wood);
5-John (1768-1835), *m* 1793, Edith Beaman (*d* ca. 1851);
4-Calvin (1798-1879), *m* 1st, 1822, Lucinda Pember (*d* 1836);
3-Lucia Ann (1830-1901), *m* 1853, Jacob Osborne **Jordan** (3 above);
2-Luna Ada (see Vol. III, pp. 444, and 626), *m* 1876, Mahlon Daniel **Thatcher** (1839-1916), founder and pres. First Nat. Bank of Pueblo, Colo., 1871; mayor of Pueblo, 1877.
1-*m* Oct. 27, 1908, Robert C. Wheeler; issue: 1-Winifred, *b* Chicago, Ill., June 23, 1911; 2-Robert Thatcher, *b* Chicago, Oct. 24, 1915.
Residence: 1447 Astor St., Chicago, Ill.

1-**WHITE, Lou Lee Tomlinson (Mrs. James Phelps),** *b* Taylor, Tex., Oct. 21, 1879.
3-Wylie **Tomlinson** (*b* 1809), of Ga., and of Iredell Co., N.C.; *m* ca. 1830, Amanda Hitchcock;
2-David Young (2 below).
5-Benjamin **Bailey** (1755-1813), of Chesterfield Co., Va.; served as 1st lt. in Va. militia in Am. Rev.;
4-Thomas T., M.D. (1808-70), of Charlottesville, Va.; removed to Houston, Tex., 1845; *m* in Va., 1830, Catherine Wigglesworth;
3-Lou (1831-1910), *m* Walter Pliney **Anderson** (1824-85), enl. in C.S.A. from Yorktown, Tex.; served in many southern battles in Civil War;
2-Zoa (*b* 1854), *m* 1877, David Young **Tomlinson** (*b* 1855), contractor and architect; issue: I-David Young, Jr. (*b* 1878; *m* 1905, Bertha Irons); II-Lou Lee (1 above).
1-*m* July 22, 1903, James Phelps White, *b* Gonzales, Tex., Dec. 21, 1856; son of Thomas J. White, of Gonzales; issue (all *b* Roswell, N.M.): 1-James P., Jr., *b* May 31, 1904; N.M. Mil. Inst., 1919-23; Washington and Lee U.; *m* June 28, 1927, Mary D., dau. John B. Beers, of Roswell; 2-Zoa Elizabeth, *b* Mar. 6, 1906; ed. U. of Tex., and U. of Mo., '28; three months in Europe 1928; *m* Apr. 16, 1929, Horace Hamilton McGee, of Mexico, Mo.; 3-Thomas David, *b* Dec. 14, 1908; grad. as capt., N.M. Mil. Inst., '29; 4-George Littlefield, *b* Dec. 14, 1908; grad. as capt., N.M. Mil. Inst., '29.
1-Mem. D.A.R., I.A.G., O.E.S. Presbyterian. Club: Woman's. Residence: 200 N. Lea Av., Roswell, N.M.

1-**WHITE, Ula Lee Terrill (Mrs. Sydney R.),** *b* Terrill, Ky., Mar. 9, 1882.
9-William (Tyrrell, Terrell) **Terrill** (*b* 1635), from Eng. ante 1667, settled in New Kent Co., Va.; *m* Martha-;
8-William (*d* 1727), Hanover Co., Va.; Susannah Waters;
7-Timothy (*b* 1668), New Kent Co.; *m* Elizabeth Foster (John[8], of New Kent Co.);
6-Robert (1697-1786), planter, Orange Co.; *m* Mary Foster;
5-Robert, planter, Culpeper Co.; *m* Judith Towles (*b* 1733; Stokeley[6]);
4-William (1764-1830), planter, Madison Co., Ky.; *m* 1793, Malinda Bernard (1774-1846; Charles[5], *m* Sarah Small);
3-William Towles (1805-76), planter, Madison Co.; *m* 1829, Parthenia W. Maupin;
2-Daniel Maupin (2 below).
7-Gabriel **Maupin** (qv);
6-Daniel (1699-1788), Albemarle Co., Va.; *m* Margaret Via (*b* 1701);
5-Daniel (1727-1803), pvt. Va. militia, Colonial wars; *m* Mary Elizabeth Dabney (Cornelius[6], *m* Sarah Jennings);
4-Daniel (1760-1832), Madison Co., Ky.; orderly sgt., Va. troops at Yorktown; *m* 2d, 1805, Margaret McWilliams;
3-Parthenia W. (*b* 1812), Madison Co.; *m* William Towles **Terrill** (3 above).
7-Alexander **Cleaveland** (1659-1770), from Eng., settled in Albemarle Co., Va.; *m* Mildred Presley (1667-1770);
6-Alexander (1700-76), planter; *m* Margaret Doolittle (1710-85);
5-Elizabeth (1753-1846), *m* 1779, John **McWilliams** (1751-1824), pvt. Va. troops in Am. Rev.;
4-Margaret (*b* 1781), *m* Daniel **Maupin** (4 above).
7-John **Bottom** (*d* 1737), Henrico Co., Va.; *m* Elizabeth-;
6-John, of Henrico Co.;
5-Susannah, *m* 1782, Thomas **Francis** (*d* 1801);
4-Lewis (1790-1855), pvt. Ky. troops, War 1812; *m* 1813, Ede Kennedy (1791-1876; Joseph[5], ens. and lt. Va. militia during Am. Rev., apptd. capt. 1783, 1st sheriff of Madison Co., Ky., *m* 1788, Martha Perrin; John[6], from N.C. to Boonesborough, Va., now Ky., 1775);
3-Susan (1822-46), *m* John Broaddus **Francis** (Thomas[4], *m* Mary Broaddus; Thomas[5], same as 5 above);
2-Martha Ann (1846-84), *m* 1868, Daniel Maupin **Terrill** (1836-1904), planter, Madison Co., Ky.; issue: I-Arthur Middleton (*m* Nancy Settle); II-Helen B. (*m* William Orme Mays, *d*); III-Ruth (1877-1903; *m* James Bailey Rosson, *d*); IV-Ula Lee (1 above); V-Johnnie Francis (*m* Robert Terrill Dunn).
1-*m* Sept. 22, 1906, Sydney Ray White, *b* Friendsville, Md., Aug. 26, 1883; son of Richard Benton White (1838-92), of Friendsville, Md. (Richard[3] [1794-1871]; William[4]); issue: 1-Richard Daniel, *b* Columbus, O., Mar. 10, 1912; midshipman, U.S.N.
1-Ed. Jessamine Female Inst., Nicholasville, Ky. Mem. D.A.R. Christian. Democrat. Residence: The Broadmoor, Washington, D.C.

1-**WHITE, William Allen,** *b* Emporia, Kan., Feb. 10, 1868.
8-Nicholas **White** (qv);
7-John (1649-1726), resided in that part of Taunton which became in 1731, Raynham; surveyor, clk. of military co., selectman; large landowner; *m* 1679/80, Hannah Smith (Samuel[8], *m* Susanna Reed);
6-John (1681-ca. 1758), carpenter, surveyor, millwright; selectman of Raynham, 1733; assessor, town treas.; built first meeting house in Raynham; *m* 1709, Elizabeth Crossman (Samuel[7], *m* Elizabeth Bell);
5-George (*d* 1767), *m* 1745, Hannah Bryant (Dr. Timothy[6], *m* Hannah Hodges);
4-John (1749-1834), sgt. Am. Rev.; order for bounty coat dated Camp before Boston, Dec. 21, 1775; *m* 1772, Martha Keith;
3-John (1775-ca. 1831), *m* 1798, Fear Perry;
2-Allen (2 below).
7-Rev. James **Keith** (*d* 1719, aet. 76), from Scotland, 1662; first minister of Bridgewater, Mass.; *m* Susanna Edson (Dea. Samuel[8]), *m* 2d, 1707, Mary, widow of Thomas Williams;
6-Josiah (*d* 1754), *m* 1703, Mary Lathrop (Samuel[7]);
5-Josiah (*b* 1706), *m* 1730, Ruth Manly;
4-Martha (1754-1816), *m* John **White** (4 above);
3-John, *m* Fear Perry (3 above);
2-Dr. Allen, M.D. (*b* 1819), *m* Mary A. Hatton.
1-*m* Apr. 27, 1893, Sallie Lindsay, *b* Nicholasville, Ky., Dec. 3, 1870; dau. of Joseph N. Lindsay, of Kansas City, Mo.; issue: 1-Will-

iam Lindsay, *b* Emporia, Kan., June 17, 1900; Harvard, '24; 2–Mary (*d* May 1921).
1–Propr., editor Emporia Daily and Weekly Gazette. Author (see Who's Who in America). Clubs: Nat. Arts, Century (New York), Colonial (Cambridge, Mass.), Cosmos (Washington), University (Chicago). Residence: 927 Exchange St., Emporia, Kan.

1–**TALLEY, Elisabeth Nisbet Furman (Mrs. James N.),** *b* Sumter Co., S.C., May 11, 1874.
8–Abram **Martin** (of noble English family), to Albemarle Co., Va., 1680; colonial officer;
7–John (1685-1750), mem. Va. Assembly; *m* Letitia–;
6–John (1710-87); *m* Ann Farish;
5–Letitia (*d* bet. 1818-23), *m* James **Carter** (*d* Sept. 14, 1780);
4–Farish (*b* Jan. 1781-1861), *m* 1811, Eliza McDonald (1789-1865);
3–Catherine (1824-51), *m* 1845, John Howard **Furman** (1824-1902), see Vol. III, p. 200, for Furman lineage;
2–Farish Carter (2 below).
11–Michael **Bacon** (qv);
10–Michael (*b* Eng., 1579-*d* 1648), *m* Alice–;
9–Michael (1640-1707), *m* 1660, Sarah Richardson (*d* 1694);
8–Michael (*d* 1733), to Dorchester, S.C., ante 1716; *m* 1694, Joanna Way (Aaron[9], *m* Joan Sumner; Henry[10], original settler, Dorchester, Mass., 1630);
7–Joseph (*d* 1764), *m* Mary Quarterman;
6–Rebecca, *m* 1757, Thomas **Quarterman**; see Vol. III, p. 584, for Quarterman lineage;
5–Joseph (1764-1801), *m* 1787, Elizabeth Quarterman (*d* 1817);
4–Anne (1793-1826), *m* 1812, Louis **LeConte** (1782-1838), see Vol. III, p. 201, for LeConte lineage;
3–Joseph (1823-1901), *m* 1847, Caroline Elizabeth Nisbet (1828-1915);
2–Emma Florence (*b* 1847), sister of Joseph Nisbet LeConte (see Vol. III, p. 201); *m* 1869, Farish Carter **Furman** (1846-83), served in C.S.A.; planter and lawyer; judge Co. Ct.; state senator; mem. Constl. Conv.; issue: I–Katherine Carter (Mrs. John R. L. Smith, see Vol. III, p. 200); II–Elisabeth N. (1 above).
1–*m* Oct. 10, 1895, James Nicholas Talley, *b* Nashville, Ga., Aug. 31, 1869, son of Hamilton McDuffie Talley, of Valdosta, Ga.; issue: 1–Farish Furman, *b* Macon, Ga., Dec. 6, 1897; U.Ga., '17; *m* Aug. 10, 1920, Sarah Ethel, dau. of Joseph Humphrey, of Hardwick, Ga. (issue: Farish Furman, Jr.); 2–Joseph LeConte, *b* Macon, Ga., Feb. 15, 1901; U.Ga., '23; *m* Aug. 28, 1926, Pauline Ada, dau. of N. R. Thomas, M.D.; 3–Emma LeConte, *b* Scottsboro, Ga., June 9, 1907; Randolph-Macon Woman's Coll., '28 (P.B.K.); C.D.A.; *m* Sept. 8, 1928, Ralph B. Shaw (issue: Carolyn Carter, *b* Oct. 30, 1929).
1–Mem. C.D.A., D.A.R., U.D.C. Residence: 1014 Vineville Av., Macon, Ga.

1–**WHITE, Elizabeth Nisbet Davis (Mrs. William C.),** *b* Columbia, S.C., July 11, 1884.
7–John **Means,** of Co. Down, Ireland;
6–John (1717-89), of Scotch descent; from Ireland to Boston, 1743; *m* 1747, Isabella Harper (1729-93);
5–Thomas (1767-1828), from Boston, to Fairfield Dist., S.C.; *m* 1789, Sarah Milling (1773-1816; David[6], from Ireland to S.C. ante Am. Rev., *m* Sarah Burney; Alexander[7], of Ireland);
4–Robert (1796-1836), grad. S.C. Coll., 1813; Presbyn. minister; *m* 1815, his cousin, Sarah Eloise Means (1798-1883; John[6] [1758-1811], bro. of Thomas, 5 above, *m* 1787, Mary Milling [1772-1820], sister of Sarah, 5 above);
3–Isabella Harper (1830-71), *m* Lt. Col. Henry C. **Davis** (1823-86), see Vol. III, p. 584, for Davis lineage;
2–Robert Means (2 below).
11–Philip (Kirkland) **Kirtland,** from Eng., 1635, granted 10 acres of land at Lynn, Mass., 1638;
10–Nathaniel (1616-86), came in the "Hopewell" to Lynn; selectman, 1678; *m* Parnell–;
9–Lt. John (1659-1716), adopted by his uncle and aunt (John Westall, *m* Susanna Kertland), of Saybrook, Conn.; lt., Indian wars, 1702,08; *m* 1679, Lydia Pratt (*b* 1659; Lt. William[10], qv, *m* Elizabeth, dau. of John Clark, of Hartford, one of 19 patentees named in Royal Charter from Charles II);
8–Lydia, *m* Robert **Griffing**;
7–Samuel;
6–Moses, *m* Sarah Stillwell (for Stillwell lineage see Vol. III, p. 584);
5–Elizabeth, *m* James **Edwards**;
4–Sarah Stillwell, *m* 1824, Alfred Moore **Nisbet** (James[5], *m* Penelope Cooper; John[6] [1738-1817], from Lancaster Co., Pa., to Statesville, N.C., 1748, mem. Com. of Safety, Am. Rev., mem. Congress, 1774-76, *m* Mary Osborne);
3–Caroline Elizabeth (1828-1915), *m* 1847, Joseph **LeConte** (for LeConte lineage see Vol. III, p. 584);
2–Sarah Elizabeth (1850-1915), *m* Jan. 3, 1877, Robert Means **Davis,** LL.D. (Apr. 9, 1849-Mar. 13, 1904), A.B., U. of S.C.; sec. Dem. party during reconstruction period; head of Mt. Zion Inst., Winnsboro, S.C., where he introduced 1st graded school system, outside of Charleston; journalist; prof. history and political science, U. of S.C., 20 yrs.; for issue see Vol. III, p. 584.
1–*m* June 17, 1913, William Cozby White, *b* Rock Hill, S.C. (Aug. 17, 1882-July 12, 1920); son of Rev. James Spratt White, *m* Caroline Crawford Dudley; issue: 1–Sarah LeConte, *b* Atlanta, Ga., Mar. 29, 1914; 2–William Harris Crawford, *b* Atlanta, Aug. 21, 1915.
1–B.A., Winthrop Coll., '04. Teacher Columbia city schs., 1904-13. Mem. C.D.A., H.S.S.C., D.A.R. Clubs: Woman's, Forest Lake. Summer place: "Treetops," Saluda, N.C. Residence: 1130 Maple St., Columbia, S.C.

1–**WHITEHEAD, Susan Thurston (Mrs. Robert H.),** *b* W. Medford, Mass., June 26, 1883.
8–Daniel **Thurston** (*d* 1693), from Eng., 1632; settled Newbury, Mass.; *m* 1655, Anna Pell (Joseph[9], of Lynn, Mass.);
7–Joseph (*b* 1667), *m* 1695, Mehitable Kimball;
6–Joseph (1698/99-1780), *m* 1725, Mary (Lane) Finson (1697-1792; John Lane[7], served in Indian wars, *m* Dorcas, dau. of John Wallis, of Falmouth, Mass.; James[8]);
5–Capt. John (1737-1814), Rockport, Mass.; Am. Rev.; *m* 1760, Eunice (Gott) Stockbridge;
4–William (1778-1852), *m* 1800, Nancy Foster;
3–George Washington (1810-76), Bristol, Me.; *m* 1842, Sarah McKay (Donald[4], of Can., *m* Margaret McPherson);
2–Henry William (2 below).
9–Charles **Gott,** from Eng., 1628; settled Gloucester, Mass.; first dea. Salem Ch.;
8–Charles (1648-1708), rep. Gen. Ct.; commr.; clk. of Train Band; dep. Mass. Bay Colony;
7–Lt. Samuel (*d* 1767), *m* 1697, Margaret Andrews (1676-1722);
6–Stephen (*b* 1705), Gloucester, Mass.; *m* 1729, Eunice Emmons;
5–Eunice (1738-1832), as widow of Benjamin Stockbridge, *m* Capt. John **Thurston** (5 above).
9–Lt. John **Andrews** (*b* abt. 1621-*d* ante 1708; son of Robert of Eng., and Elizabeth–); came from Eng.; settled Ipswich, Mass.; corpl. 3d co. at Chebacco, Pequot War, 1639; received land grant for services; *m* 1650, Jane Jordan (*d* post 1708; Stephen[10], from Eng. to Ipswich in the "Mary and John," 1634, *m* Susanna–);
8–Ens. William, of Ipswich; *m* 1672, Margaret Woodward (*b* 1655/56; Ezekiel[9], from Eng., *m* Ann Beamsley);
7–Margaret (1676-1722), *m* Lt. Samuel **Gott** (7 above).
10–Reginald **Foster** (qv);
9–Abraham (*b* 1618), of Ipswich; *m* 1655, Lydia Burbank (Caleb[10], of Rowley, *m* Martha Smith; John[11]);
8–Caleb (1677-1766), *m* 1702, Mary Sherwin (*b* 1679; John[9], from Eng. in the "Susan and Ellen," 1635, aet. 24 yrs., *m* Frances, dau. of Edward Lomas);
7–Caleb (*b* 1708), Am. Rev.; *m* 1729, Priscilla Buxton (John[8], *m* Mary, dau. of John Small);
6–Nathan, of Ipswich; *m* Marian–;
5–John (bap. 1760), Pemaquid, Mass.; said to have been in Battle of Bunker Hill; *m* Susanna Robinson;
4–Nancy (*b* 1783), *m* William **Thurston** (4 above);

3-George Washington, *m* Sarah McKay (3 above);
2-Henry William (1845-1910), mfr., Saddle River, N.J.; *m* 1867, Margaretta Gilmore (1843-81); *m* 2d, 1882, Sarah Jane Dove (*b* 1859); issue (1st marriage): I-Ida May (*b* 1874; *m* Fred Ashworth); II-Lottie Alice (*b* 1877; *m* Edgar Wilford, *d* 1917); issue (2d marriage): I-Susan (1 above); II-Henry Nathaniel (*b* 1889; *m* Meta Wise).
1-*m* Oct. 14, 1903, Robert Henley Whitehead, *b* Rockmart, Ga., Aug. 25, 1876; son of William Andrew Jackson Whitehead (*d* 1929), of Rockmart.
1-Pres. and organizer A.R.C., Burlington, N.C., 1917-18. Mem. D.A.C., D.F.P.A., D.A.R., (organizing regent and regent Battle of Alamance Chapter), I.A.G. Clubs: Music, Woman's Guild (ex-pres.). Residence: 500 W. Davis St., Burlington, N.C.

1-**WHITING, Segar,** *b* Hampton, Va., Jan. 18, 1859.
8-James **Whiting** (1608-ca. 1658), from Eng. in the "George," with Rev. George Keith, 1617; patented land in Gloucester Co., Va., 1642; *m* 1643, Ann-;
7-Henry (*b* 1650), burgess, Gloucester Co., 1680-84; mem. Council, 1691; treas. of Va., 1692; *m* 2d, Elizabeth Beverley (prob. dau. of Robert Beverley, historian);
6-Maj. Henry (1680-1728), sheriff, 1723; *m* Anne Beverley;
5-Col. Thomas (1712-81), of Abingdon Parish, Gloucester Co., Va.; burgess, 1755; King's atty.; pres. Naval Bd. during Am. Rev., at Williamsburg; mem. Conv. of 1776; *m* Elizabeth Beverley (*d* 1749); *m* 2d, Elizabeth Thruston; *m* 3d, Anne Seawell;
4-Thomas Beverley (*b* 1758), *m* Elizabeth (Kennon) Perrin;
3-Kennon (1796-1886), *m* Anne Wythe Mallory (1803-71; Johnson[4], of Norfolk);
2-Henry Clay (1832-99), mcht. and banker; capt. C.S.A.; *m* Mary Simkins Segar (1835-84; Joseph[8] [1804-80], *m* Mary E. Simkins, 1808-86); issue: I-Segar (1 above); II-Katherine B. C. (*b* 1861; *m* William G. Young); III-Livingston Faison (1864-1913; *m* Mary Buchanan); IV-Virginia Fairfax (*b* 1867; *m* Hon. Charles J. Faulkner, *d*); V-Mattie Kennon.
1-*m* Nov. 15, 1882, Robena Susan Spady, *b* Northampton Co., Va., Sept. 7, 1861; dau. of Dr. Thomas Fitchette Spady, of Northampton Co.; issue (all *b* Hampton, Va.): 1-Henry Clay, *b* Jan. 14, 1884; Blackstone Mil. Acad.; Hampden-Sidney Coll.; *m* Nell, dau. of Goodwin Lee, of Hampton, Va. (issue: Harry C., Jr.; Bessie Ballard; Nellie Lee); 2-Kate Spady (Jan. 15, 1886-Sept. 13, 1924); Hampton Female Coll.; *m* July 15, 1922, Clarke, son of H. S. Thompson, of Hampton, Va. (issue: Kate Whiting); 3-Mary Kenna, *b* Oct. 16, 1887; Hampton Female Coll.; *m* Apr. 24, 1912, Albert R. Masters (issue: Mollie Whiting; Ann Jarvis; Louise Warner); 4-Thomas Spady, *b* Aug. 15, 1894; V.M.I.; capt. U.S.M.C., severely wounded at Chateau Thierry; received Croix de Guerre with palm; *m* Dec. 29, 1917, Bessie, dau. of Charles Blassenham, of Newport News, Va. (issue: Shirley Lee; Thomas S., Jr.; Charles Segar); 5-Maria J., *b* July 23, 1897; Hampton Female Coll.; *m* Mar. 10, 1923, Paul W. Wyatt, of Hampton.
1-Ed. Columbia Coll. (Georgetown U.), Washington. Cashier of Bank of Hampton; accountant. Treas. Elizabeth City County, Va. Presbyterian. Democrat. Residence: Hampton, Va.

1-**WHITLOCK, Brand (Joseph Brand Whitlock),** *b* Urbana, O., Mar. 4, 1869.
7-Thomas **Whitlock** (1620-1703), from England to Mass., moved to Middletown, N.J., ca. 1640, *m* Susanna Stock;
6-John;
5-James, *m* 2d, Jane Cruiser;
4-John (1775-1830), *m* Lydia Howell (1776-1842);
3-Elias (1797-1880), *m* Mary Johnston (1805-86; Luke[4]);
2-Rev. Elias D., D.D. (2 below).
5-Thomas **Brand,** from Scotland to Va., 1746;
4-Thomas, *m* Frances Carter;
3-Joseph Carter (1810-1898), *m* Lavinia Hickman Talbot (desc. Thomas Hickman, from Eng. to Va., ca. 1683);
2-Mallie Lavinia, *m* Rev. Elias D. **Whitlock,** D.D. (1843-1913), M.E. minister; for issue, see Vol. I, p. 886.
1-*m* June 29, 1892, Susanne Lamb Brainerd (Feb. 13, 1874-Oct. 31, 1892), dau. Gideon R. Brainerd, of Springfield, Ill. (desc. Rev. David Brainerd, celebrated Indian missionary, revivalist, author).
1-*m* 2d, June 8, 1895, Ella Brainerd, *b* Sept. 25, 1876 (sister of 1st wife).
1-LL.D., Brown, 1916; Ohio Wesleyan, 1917, Kenyon, 1919; Litt.D., Western Reserve, 1919; Docteur en Droit, Université Libre de Bruxelles, 1919; Docteur en Droit, U. of Lourain, 1927. Lawyer, author, diplomat; mayor of Toledo, O., 1905-1913; E.E. and M.P. to Belgium, Dec. 2, 1913, A.E. and P., Sept. 1919-Feb. 1, 1922. Decorated: Grand Cordon de l'Ordre de Léopold, Belgium, 1917; Croix Civique de la Première Classe, 1919; Grand Croix de Saint Sava, Serbia, 1921; Grand Cross Order Rising Sun, Japan, 1922; Commemorative Cross, Comité National, Belgium, 1921; Grand Officer de la Légion d'Honneur, France, 1929; elected by common council Bourgeois de Bruxelles, 1918, Citoyen d'Honneur d'Anvers, 1918, Bourgeois de Liège, 1918, de Gant, 1921. Awarded gold medal, Nat. Inst. Social Sciences, 1914, for social service. Member Am. Acad. Arts and Letters, Royal Acad. of Belgium, Belgian Royal Academy of French Language and Literature; hon. mem. "Grand Serment Royal des Arbalètriers de St. Georges," etc. (see Who's Who in America). Clubs: Cercle du Parc, Royal Golf (Brussels), Century, Players (New York), Cliff Dwellers (Chicago), Authors (Boston), Inverness, Toledo, Toledo Country; Cannes Country, Mougins (A.M.), France. Residence: Toledo, O. Address: Hotel des Anglais, Cannes (A.M.), France.

1-**WILHELM, Martha Sophronia Torrey (Mrs. Louis),** *b* Charlton, Mass., Mar. 28, 1870.
8-William **Torrey** (qv);
7-William (1638-1718), *m* 1669, Deborah Greene (1649-1728; Dep.Gov. John[8]);
6-Phillip (1681-1754), *m* 1708, Mary Marsh (1683-1781; Thomas[7]);
5-William (1728-70), *m* 1753, Mehitable Crane (1733-1813; John[6]; John[7]; Henry[8]);
4-Caleb (1758-1808), *m* 1791, Mary Miller (1773-1855; Phillip[5]);
3-Caleb (1801-71), *m* 1831, Mary Tyler (1804-93; Solomon[4]);
2-Edwin Tyler (2 below).
8-John **Partridge** (1620-1706), from Eng., 1650; *m* 1655, Magdalene Bullard (John[9]);
7-Eleazer (1664-1736), *m* 1705, Elizabeth Allen (1669-1733, William[8]);
6-Benjamin (1713-1805), *m* 1737, Sarah Allen (1716-1801);
5-Job (1742-1823), *m* 1769, Deborah Fairbanks (1747-1827);
4-Benjamin (1777-1853), *m* 1798, Milcah Pond (1778-1858);
3-Leonard (1810-59), *m* 1838, Sophronia Morse (1819-1913);
2-Melvina (1846-93), *m* 1869, Edwin Tyler **Torrey** (1844-1925); issue: I-Martha S. (1 above); II-Lewis Edwin (*b* 1874; *m* Edith Newton, issue: Mary Torrey); III-Alice Melvina (*b* 1884; *m* William Nathan Middleton; issue: Keith Torrey).
1-*m* Nov. 24, 1892, Louis Wilhelm, *b* in Germany, Mar. 27, 1870; son of Bernhard Augusta Wilhelm, of Germany; issue: 1-Karl, *b* 1893; *m* 1920, Jennie Macauley; 2-Paul, *b* 1896; *m* 1918, Doris Askam; 3-Ruth, *b* 1898; *m* 1921, Chancey W. Hulse; 4-Bernhard, *b* 1901; *m* 1928, Juliette Visetely; 5-Hazel Elizabeth, *b* 1902; *m* 1922, Eldon S. Robinson.
1-Mem. D.F.P.A., D.A.R., D.A.C. Fairbanks Assn., New Haven Colony Hist. Soc. Residence: 432 Norton St., New Haven, Conn.

1-**WILLETT, Clara Goddard (Mrs. Norman),** *b* Decorah, Ia., May 4, 1867.
5-Robert **Goddard** (*d* 1807, aet. 79), of Grafton, Mass.; *m* 1759, Elizabeth- (*d* 1826, aet. 86);
4-Nahum (*b* Petersham, Mass., 1776), *m* 1800, Sallie Richardson;

3–Robert, *m* Maria Bailey;
2–Clark Nahum (2 below).
6–James **Richardson,** *m* Miss Paige;
5–Johnson (*b* 1760), pvt. Am. Rev.; *m* 1788, Sibel Stanley;
4–Rufus (1790-1847), *m* 1813, Lydia Fales (1793-1847);
3–Rufus (1818-90), *m* 1840, Eliza Durkee;
2–Jane (2 below).
6–Capt. Joseph **Durkee** (1733-1812), ens., lt. and capt. in Am. Rev.; *m* 1753, Elizabeth Fiske (1735-92; David[7]);
5–John (1762-1828), *m* 1785, Sarah Holt (1761-1813);
4–John (*b* 1785), *m* Eunice Ranney;
3–Eliza (1821-1902), *m* Rufus **Richardson** (3 above);
2–Jane (1842-1917), *m* 1861, Clark Nahum **Goddard** (1835-1909), mcht.; issue: I–Harry Clark (*b* 1865; *m* Frances Barrow); II–Clara (1 above); III–Herbert (*b* 1877; *m* Mary Ayres); IV–Frederic Richardson (*b* 1879; *m* Edna Daskam).
1–*m* June 28, 1899, Norman Willett, *b* Chambly, Can., Aug. 15, 1853; grad. Grinnell Coll., '74; son of Capt. George Rice Willett (1826-98), of Can., moved to Decorah, Ia., 1857; lawyer; judge; capt., 3d Ia. Regt., Civil War; *m* Olinda Clemintina Kellogg (1826-1900, sister of Brainerd Kellogg, see Vol. I, p. 168).
1–Mem. D.A.R., P.E.O. Vice-chmn. Rep. Com., sec. Library Bd. Congregationalist. Residence: 510 Jefferson St., Decorah, Ia.

1–**WILLIAMS, Donald Ward,** *b* Willows, Calif., Oct. 29, 1880.
5–Samuel **Williams** (1755-1835), of Barnstead, N.H.; served in 2d Regt. Cont. Line from Barnstead, left service, 1783; served Capt. Bradford's co., 21st U.S. Inf. in War 1812; *m* 1777, Sobriety Bunker (Jonathan[6]);
4–Joshua (1786-1867), New Portland, Me.; *m* 1805, Ruth Philbrick (Titus[5], Mt. Vernon, Me.);
3–Joseph Philbrick (1807-81), *m* 1831, Betsey Pease (1814-50; Abraham[4], *b* 1787); their son, Abram Pease (1832-1911), was U.S. senator from Calif.;
2–Ward Spooner (2 below).
8–John **North,** of Cloneen, Ireland, came to Pemaquid, Me.; *m* Lydia–;
7–Capt. John, Pemaquid; *m* Elizabeth Lewis; their son was Gen. William North;
6–Mary, *m* 1760, Dr. John **McKecknie,** of Waterville, Me.;
5–Elizabeth, *m* Samuel **McFarland,** of Winslow, Me.;
4–David, *m* Louisa Stevens (Isaac[5]);
3–Isaac Stevens (1822-1908), Fairfield, Me.; *m* 1850, Julia Cummings.
2–Ward Spooner **Williams** (1841-1904), mcht., New Richmond, Wis.; *m* 1870, Estelle McFarland (1850-88); *m* 2d, 1890, Carrie S. Houston; issue (1st marriage): I–Freda Jeanette (1875-1902); II–Harry McFarland (*b* 1877; *m* Mary Wells); III–Donald Ward (1 above); issue (2d marriage): I–Ward Sawyer (*b* 1890; *m* Elizabeth Brown); II–Abram Parker (*b* 1893; *m* Mazie Thompson).
1–*m* Oct. 6, 1909, Alice Kenrick, *b* Fairfield, Me., Nov. 7, 1883; dau. of Edward Payson Kenrick, of Fairfield; issue: 1–Edward Abram, *b* Redwood City, Calif., May 4, 1913.
1–Spl. student, Carleton Coll., 1897. Asst. cashier and dir., Bank of New Richmond, Wis., 1905-11; cashier and dir., Redwood City (Calif.) Commercial Bank, 1911-18; Dir. San Mateo Co. Bldg. & Loan Assn., and Industrial Finance Co., Palo Alto; pres. Calif. Finance & Loan Co. of Burlingame. Dir. Redwood City Chamber of Commerce; trustee Sequoia Union High School. County Food Administrator, San Mateo Co., 1918. Mem. S.A.R., I.A.G., Bunker Family Assn. Conglist. Republican. Club: Kiwanis. Residence: 610 Edgewood Rd., Redwood City, Calif.

1–**WILLIAMS, Henry Lane,** *b* Hartford, Conn., July 26, 1869.
9–Richard **Williams** (qv);
8–Nathaniel (*d* 1692), *m* 1668, Elizabeth Rogers (*d* 1724);
7–Nathaniel (1679-1726), *m* 1709, Lydia King (1688-1748);
6–Nathaniel (*b* 1711), *m* 1737, Mary Atherton (*d* 1778);
5–Seth (bap. 1746-1818), lt. in Capt. Hall's Co., Gen. Godfrey's Brig., R.I.; *m* Mary Snow (*d* 1818);
4–Zephaniah (1777-1853), *m* Olive Howe (1776-1855);
3–Giles (1807-69), *m* Fanny Maria Gallup (1814-1863);
2–Job, L.H.D. (1842-1909), B.A., Yale, '64, M.A., 1867; principal, Sch. for the Deaf, Hartford; *m* 1868, Catherine Stone (1845-1909); issue: I–Henry Lane (1 above); II–Alice Stone (*d*); III–Arthur Collins (*d*); IV–Charles Gallup (*b* 1885; *m* Lilian Sills).
1–*m* Nov. 24, 1897, Nina Meadows Boyd, *b* Richmond, Va., July 15, 1876; dau. of Samuel Charles Boyd, of Md. and Va.; issue: 1–Henry Lane, Jr., *b* Phila., Pa., Aug. 31, 1898; prepared for Coll. at St. Paul's Sch., Garden City, L.I., and William Penn Charter Sch., Phila., entered Yale as a Sophomore from U. of Minn., ex-'20; B.A., Yale, '21 (Alpha Delta Phi); M.D., U.Pa., 1924 (Alpha Kappa Kappa); mem. staff Mayo Clinic, Rochester, Minn.
1–B.A., Yale, '91 (Alpha Delta Phi); M.D., U. Pa., 1895 (Alpha Nu Pi Omega). Physician; asst. prof. of gynecology, Coll. of Medicine and Surgery, U.Minn. Dist. med. officer, Dist. 10, Federal Bd. for Vocational Edn. and U.S. Veterans' Bureau; surgeon (R.) U.S. Pub. Health Service; zone surgeon, U.S. Fidelity & Guaranty Co. Mem. O.F.P.A., S.A.R. Summer place: "Bonny Riggs," Prescott, Wis. Residence: Hampshire Arms, Minneapolis, Minn.

1–**WILLS, James Stapleton,** *b* Gala, Va., Nov. 21, 1883.
9–Col. John **West** (qv);
8–Col. John (1641-93), capt., maj., lt. col., and col.; sat on ct. martial of Nathaniel Bacon, Jr., 1676; *m* 1667, Unity, or Ursula, Croshaw (1647-75; Maj. Joseph[9], of York Co., Va.);
7–Capt. Thomas (1673-1706);
6–Col. Francis (1708-53), *m* Jane (Cole) Bingham (1708-41; William Cole[7], of Warwick Co.; William[8], sec. of Va.);
5–William (1735-88), Am. Rev.; *m* Letitia Martin (1750-88);
4–Col. Robert (1776-1816), of Gloucester Co.; *m* 1809, Mary Beverley Grymes;
3–Ann Maria Grymes (*b* 1814), *m* 1836, Joseph Van Meter **Carper** (1812-64);
2–Virginia Taylor (2 below).
8–William **Randolph** (qv);
7–Sir John (1683-1737), knighted for service to Walpole; first native born Virginian to receive knighthood; speaker Va. Ho. Burgesses; treas. of the Colony; *m* Susanna Beverley;
6–John (1727-84), of Williamsburg, Va.; king's atty. Gen. for Colony of Va.; known as "John Randolph, the Tory"; *m* Ariana Jennings (their son Edmund was gov. of Va., 1786-88, was first Atty. Gen. of U.S. in Washington's Cabinet; Sec. of State during Washington's 2d administration);
5–Susana, *m* her cousin, Maj. John Randolph **Grymes**;
4–Mary Beverley (1782-1858), *m* Col. Robert **West** (4 above);
3–Anna Maria Grymes, *m* Joseph V. M. **Carper** (3 above);
2–Virginia Taylor (1849-1927), of Botetourt Co., Va.; *m* 1880, James Reid Willis **Wills** (1851-1926), planter; issue: I–Margaret Josephine (*b* 1881; *m* Henry Woodhouse Davis); II–James Stapleton (1 above); III–John Beverley Grymes (1886-1909); IV–James Reid (*b* 1888; *m* Eva Wright); V–Wyndham Randolph (*b* 1891); VI–Joseph Lemuel (1893-1930; *m* Ellen Clare Chiles).
1–*m* June 11, 1913, Nancy Wyndham Walkup, *b* Glen Wilton, Va., May 7, 1891; dau. of Arthur Middleton Walkup, M.D., of Botetourt Co.; issue (all *b* Louisa, Va.): 1–Josephine Wauchope, *b* June 13, 1914; 2–Anne Middleton, *b* Feb. 21, 1916; 3–James Wyndham, *b* Sept. 2, 1918.
1–Ed. Va. Poly. Inst., '06; special work, Med. Coll. of Va., 1907-08,08-09. Educational work with extension div. Va. Poly. Inst. Pres. Va. Assn. Co. Agrl. Agents; mem. Va. Acad. of Science. Clubs: Commonwealth (Richmond), Roanoke (Va.) Country. Presbyterian. Democrat. Residence: Fincastle, Va.

1–**WILSON, Mary Scott Spencer (Mrs. David C.),** *b* St. Charles, Mo., Dec. 1, 1889.
9–Nicholas **Spencer** (ca. 1620-1689), from Eng., ca. 1659; settled in Westmoreland Co., Va.; *m* 1666, Frances Mottrom (will proved 1720);
8–John;
7–William Nicholas;
6–Thomas (1721-93), Charlotte Co., Va.; mem. Com. Safety, 1775; presiding justice, 1782; officer Am. Rev.; *m* 1741, Elizabeth Julia Flournoy;
5–John (1745-1828), lt. Am. Rev.; *m* 1765, Sarah Watkins (1748-86; Thomas[6], *m* Frances, dau. of Col. Henry Anderson; Thomas[7], of Swift Creek; Henry[8]);
4–Henry (1778-1844), *m* 1802, Sarah Bouldin;
3–Robert Bouldin (1818-1902), Botetourt Co.; *m* Mary Jane Scott;
2–James Morton (2 below).
9–John **Buckner** (qv);
8–Elizabeth, *m* James **Williams,** from Wales to King and Queen Co.;
7–Elizabeth (1695-1740), *m* 1720, Jean Jacques (John James) **Flournoy** (1686-1740), from France to Va., 1700; Huguenot refugee;
6–Elizabeth Julia (*b* 1721), *m* Thomas **Spencer** (6 above).
10–Thomas **Bouldin** (*b* 1580), to Va., 1610; *m* Mary–;
9–William (ca. 1620-1691), to Pa.; *m* Anne–;
8–William (1650-1717), *m* Elizabeth–;
7–John (1680-1711), from Pa. to Md.; *m* Mary–;
6–Col. Thomas T. (1706-83), to Charlotte Co., Va.; *m* 1731, Nancy Clark;
5–James (1732-1801), *m* 1762, Sallie Watkins (William[6], justice, mem. House of Dels., Dinwiddie Co., Va., *m* Mary Osborne; William[7]);
4–Sarah (1780-1841), *m* Henry **Spencer** (4 above).
8–William **Daniel** (*d* 1715), Middlesex Co.; vestryman, Christ Ch.; justice of ct.;
7–Robert (*d* 1720), *m* 1687, Margaret Price (*b* 1670; Robert[8], *m* Jane–);
6–James (1709-61), sheriff, Albemarle Co.; *m* Jane Hicks;
5–John, *m* ca. 1770, Elizabeth Morton;
4–Nancy, *m* Rev. William Nelson **Scott** (1789-1857; Archibald[5], from Scotland to Augusta Co., Va., minister, trustee Liberty Hall Acad. [now Washington and Lee U.], 1782, *m* Frances Ramsay);
3–Mary Jane (1822-88), *m* Robert B. **Spencer** (3 above).
9–John **Woodson** (qv);
8–Robert (1634-ca. 1707), *m* Elizabeth Ferris;
7–Richard (*b* 1662), *m* Anne (Smith?);
6–Agnes (1711-1802), *m* ca. 1735, Joseph **Morton** (1709-82), mem. Com. of Safety, Charlotte Co., 1775; justice of ct., Prince Edward and Charlotte cos.; founder Briery Presbyn. Ch.; trustee Hampden-Sydney Coll., 1775;
5–Elizabeth (1754-1828), *m* John **Daniel** (5 above).
10–William (Tyrell) **Terrill** (*b* Eng.; g.g.son George Tyrell, desc. Edward, I, *m* Eleanor Montague); came from Eng., 1657/58; settled in New Kent Co., Va.; *m* Martha–;
9–William (*d* 1727), settled in St. Paul's Parish, Hanover Co.; *m* Susannah Waters;
8–Timothy (*b* ca. 1658 or 68), began to write name Terrill; settled in New Kent Co.; *m* Elizabeth Foster (John[9]);
7–Robert (1697-1787), Orange Co., Va.; *m* Mary Foster (John[8], *m* Anne, dau. Capt. Augustine Moore, of "Chelsea"); *m* 2d, Judith Towles (1690-1786);
6–William;
5–William, of Orange Co.;
4–William Henry, of Warm Springs, Va.; *m* Elizabeth Pitzer;
3–George Parker, of Salem, Va.; *m* Sarah Brent Dold;
2–Maria Louise (1860-1900), *m* 1886, James Morton **Spencer** (1854-1921), ed. Union Theol. Sem., Va., 1882-84; minister and evangelist; pres. Synod Coll., Fulton, Mo., 1901-06, Sayre Coll., 1906-21; author (see Who's Who in America, Vol. 9); Mason; issue: I–Frank Terrill (1888-1908); II–Mary Scott (1 above); III–James Morton (*b* 1891); IV–Sarah Brent (*b* 1893; *m* Harrison B. Walton); V–Louise Greenwood (*b* 1895); VI–Frances Boyle (*b* 1896; *m* Robert S. Dennis); VII–Anne Gray (*b* 1897; *m* O. D. Chapman); VIII–John Grant (*b* 1899).
1–*m* Aug. 8, 1916, David Cooper Wilson, *b* Clarinda, Ia., Jan. 30, 1882; son of David C. Wilson, of Tarkio, Mo.; issue: 1–David Spencer, *b* Seattle, Wash., July 20, 1917.
1–A.B., U.Ky., '10 (Beta Sigma Omicron), A.M., 1912. Teacher, Nicholasville High School, 1910-11, Sterling Coll., 1913-15, Ardmore High School, 1915-16. Mem. Huguenot Soc., U.D.C. Presbyterian. Democrat. Residence: Hampden-Sydney, Va.

1–**WILSON, Frederica Minerva Faulkner (Mrs. Kyde),** *b* Vevay, Ind., July 15, 1883.
5–Nicholas **Blankenbaker** (1758-1849), Culpeper Co., Va., to Ky.; of Shelby Co. (now Clark's Station), Ky.; pvt. Am. Rev., pensioned; *m* Fannie Wilhite (1764-1815);
4–Samuel (1790-1871), *m* 1811, Martha Roney (1790-1870);
3–Minerva Emery (1813-90), *m* William **Faulkner** (1822-90);
2–Jasper William (1851-1921), *m* Josephine Thomas Boerner (1857-1904); issue: I–Adah Boerner (*b* 1879; *m* William Edgar Newkirk); II–Frederica Minerva (1 above).
1–*m* Apr. 10, 1907, Kyde Wilson, *b* Liberty, Ind., Oct. 31, 1875; son of Garrett D. Wilson, of Liberty; issue: 1–Faulkner, *b* Burney, Ind., Aug. 10, 1908; DePauw, '29.
1–Mem. D.A.R. (regent John Conner Chapter), Woman's Edn. Assn. (a founder). Residence: 1801 Virginia Av., Connersville, Ind.

1–**WILSON, William Garrick,** *b* N.Y. City, Feb. 23, 1871.
5–William **Wilson** (*d* 1824), pvt. Pa. troops in Am. Rev.;
4–David (1791-1881), soldier War 1812; *m* Abigail Porter (Elijah[5], drum maj. in Am. Rev.);
3–R. Porter (1823-92), *m* 1846, Caroline Easton;
2–Odell (2 below).
10–Joseph **Easton** (1602-88), from Eng., 1632, settled at Hartford, Conn.;
9–Joseph (1648-1711), *m* Hannah Ensign;
8–Joseph (1669-1735), *m* Sarah Spencer;
7–Samuel (1702-61), *m* Sarah–;
6–Lemuel (1730-84), *m* Elizabeth Buckland;
5–Ashbel (1757-1836), artificer in Am. Rev.; *m* 1784, Sarah Arnold;
4–Julius (*b* 1791), *m* 1817, Artimisia Manchester;
3–Caroline (1822-80), *m* R. Porter **Wilson** (3 above);
2–Odell (*b* 1854), mfr.; *m* 1870, Kate Garrick (1854-1892); for issue see Vol. II, p. 224.
1–*m* June 24, 1895, Margaret Elizabeth Gribben (*b* Cleveland, O., Jan. 9, 1870-*d* Aug. 31, 1929); dau. of Morgan Gribben, of Cleveland; issue (all *b* Cleveland, O.): 1–Margaret Mary, *b* July 15, 1899; *m* June 24, 1919, William H. Hoffman, lt., M.G. Bn., 83rd Div., A.E.F. (issue: William Wilson, *b* Aug. 4, 1925); 2–Robert William Garrick, *b* Sept. 21, 1904; *m* Feb. 1, 1928, Lucille Constance Gaffney (issue: William Garrick, II, *b* Oct. 26, 1928); 3–Ruth Katherine, *b* Sept, 18, 1908; *m* Oct. 29, 1929, Aldo Mario Ermini.
1–Mgr. in Ohio for Aetna Life Ins. Co. and affiliated companies. Was capt., A.R.C., World War. Mem. S.A.R., I.A.G., Cleveland Geneal. Soc. Clubs: American (Paris), Metropolitan, Embassy (New York), Everglades (Palm Beach), Hartford (Hartford, Conn.), Union, Shaker Heights Country, Midday, Athletic, Advertising (Cleveland). Residence: 1010 Wade Park Manor, Cleveland, O.

1–**WING, George Homer,** *b* Conway, Mass., Apr. 9, 1870.
10–Rev. Stephen **Batchelder** (qv);
9–Deborah (*b* ca. 1592), from Eng. with her father and her four sons in the "William and Francis," 1632, settled at Lynn, Mass.; *m* 1609/10, Rev. John **Wing,** grad. Queen's Coll., Oxford U., 1604; preached at Flushing and Middlebury, Holland (*d* ante 1632);
8–John (*d* 1699), from Eng. with mother; to Yarmouth, Mass.; *m* 1st, Elizabeth–;
7–Ananias (*d* 1718), Brewster, Mass.; King Philip's War, 1676; *m* Hannah– (*d* 1730);
6–John (1702-73), French and Indian War; *m* 1722, Mary Knowles (will probated 1773; Richard[7]);
5–John (1732-1822), to Conway, Mass., *m* Abigail Snow;
4–Isaiah (1761-1834), fifer Am. Rev., 1777; *m* 1786, Zeluida Allis (1761-97);
3–Lucius Bliss (1789-1870), *m* 1824, Abigail Wilson (1793-1867);

2–Edward Everett (1836-1922), farmer; Conway, Mass.; *m* 1859, Helen Jane Newman (1837-1926); issue: I–Frederick Lucius (1860-89; *m* Fannie Hopkins); II–Frank Edward (1865-1923; *m* Edith Smith); III–Laura Wilson (*b* 1868; *m* 1890, Charles Lyman Parsons); IV–George Homer (1 above).
1–*m* Feb. 28, 1900, Laura Josephine Snell (Dec. 3, 1870-July 26, 1921); dau. of Joseph A. Snell; issue: 1–Everett Homer, *b* Springfield, Mass., Feb. 27, 1902; *m* May 1923, Florence, dau. of William Priest (issue: Everett George and Edward William, twins, *b* 1924).
1–Mem. S.A.R. Summer place: "Gunyah," Holland, Mass. Residence: 42 Berkeley St., Springfield, Mass.

ELIZABETH ROLL THOMPSON WOOD (1801-95), of Ridgeville, Indiana; a pioneer woman who practiced medicine over several counties. She imported flowers, medicinal herbs and garden stock from the east and distributed specimens as a public service. She gave four sons to the Civil War, two of whom were killed, and five to the Indian wars of Minnesota, George and William being killed in the Spirit Lake Massacre.

1–**WOOD, Charles Jelleff,** *b* Ridgeville, Ind., Nov. 16, 1882.
4–James **Wood** (1761-1839), of N.C., Botetourt Co., Va., and New Madison, O.; pvt. Am. Rev.; *m* 1793, Jemima Phillips (*b* 1774; John[5]);
3–Samuel (1794-1847), pvt. War 1812; *m* 1819, Elizabeth Roll Thompson;
2–Alexander (2 below).
8–Hur **Thompson,** from Scotland, settled in Elizabethtown, N.J.; one of the "Elizabethtown Associates" who purchased an historic tract of 500,000 acres of Indian lands;
7–John, also an "Elizabethtown Associate";
6–Thomas (1712-1803), of Union Tp. nr. Rahway River; served Am. Rev.; *m* Hannah Rushmore;
5–Abner (*d* 1815), *m* Mary Ross;
4–Smith (1764-1827), soldier War 1812; *m* Sarah Roll;
3–Elizabeth Roll (1801-95), of Elizabethtown, N.J., and Ridgeville, Ind. (see portrait); *m* Samuel **Wood** (3 above).
8–Jan (Mangler, Mangelsen, Manglesee) Manglese (descendants are known as **Roll**), an Indian trader, at Beverwyck (Albany) as early as 1656; purchased tract from Indians nr. Schenectady, N.Y., 1681; settled New York City; a taxable inhabitant in the list of voters for the North Ward, 1701; *m* a dau. of Peter Andriaensen von Voggelum;
7–Johannes (Mangle Janse), (first of this line to adopt the name **Roll**);
6–John (*b* Staten Island, N.Y.), sgt., Am. Rev., N.J. Line;
5–Isaac, of Springfield, N.J.; pvt., Am. Rev., N.J. Line; *m* Sarah Cauldwell (James[6]);
4–Sarah or Sally (*d* 1803), *m* Smith **Thompson** (4 above);
3–Elizabeth R., *m* Samuel **Wood** (3 above);
2–Alexander (see portrait and biography), *m* 1882, Carrie Belle Jelleff (1862-87); issue: I–Charles J. (1 above); II–Ellen Adaline (qv for maternal lineages).
1–*m* Nov. 25, 1925, Minnie Jane Readling, *b* Sept. 26, 1881, dau. of David Monroe Readling (1857-1904), of Concord, N.C., *m* A. Catherine Wallace (*b* 1852).
1–A.B., Hillsdale (Mich.) Coll., '05; LL.B., Indiana U., 1910 (Alpha Tau Omega, Delta Sigma Rho). Lawyer. Capt., F.A., World War, disabled. Founded J. Earl Carpenter Post, A.L., Ridgeville, Ind. Address: Ridgeville, Ind.

ALEXANDER WOOD (1832-1912), of Ridgeville, Ind.; A.B., Ridgeville Coll., '79, A.M., 1880; lawyer; founded city of Jackson, then Springfield, Minn.; commanded opposite Little Crow in Battle of New Ulm, Minn., in Indian War (From a daguerreotype taken at 21, when he was admitted to the Indiana bar).

1–**WOOD, Ellen Adaline,** *b* Ridgeville, Ind., June 19, 1884.
10–Ralph (Hemenway, Hemmenway) **Hemingway** (qv);
9–Samuel (1636-1711), *m* 1661, Sarah Cooper (*b* 1645; John[10]);
8–Sarah (1663-1725), *m* 1684, Thomas **Goodsell** (1646-1713), from Eng.;
7–Samuel (1684/85-1745), sgt.; *m* Mary Frisbie (1685-1760; Jonathan[8]; Edward[9], immigrant, helped found Branford, Conn., signer of the Plantation and Church Covenant, 1668);
6–Isaac (*b* 1715), *m* 1737, Elizabeth Penfield (*b* 1717; Isaac[7]);
5–Jacob (1763-1821), *m* 1785, Phebe Warner;
4–Patience (1801-85), *m* 1822, Dr. Cyrus **Jelleff** (1799-1873), physician; to Jay Co., Ind., 1836, from Painted Post, N.Y.;
3–Dr. Fitz Allen (1829-80), *m* 1854, Katherine Fitzpatrick (1831-1873 or 74; William[4]);
2–Carrie Belle (2 below).
10–John **Warner** (qv);
9–John (*d* 1707), of Waterbury and Farmington, Conn.;
8–Capt. Ebenezer (1677-1755), of Woodbury, Conn.; dep. Gen. Assembly, 1722-23; *m* 1704, Martha Galpin (1685-1745; Benjamin[9]; Philip[10]);

7–Benjamin (1709-1806), physician; commd. capt., 1755; *m* 1st, 1736, Silence Hurd (1715-85), parents of Col. Seth Warner associated in command with Gen. Ethan Allen (Benjamin Hurd[8]; Benjamin[9]; John[10]);
6–Daniel (1741-77), soldier Am. Rev., killed in Battle of Bennington, Vt.; *m* 1765, Patience Norton (*b* 1748; George[7], mortally wounded at Battle of Trenton; George[8]);
5–Phebe (1768-1849), *m* Jacob **Goodsell** (5 above).
2–Carrie Belle Jelleff (1862-87), of Decatur, Ind.; *m* 1882, Alexander **Wood** (1832-1912), of Ridgeville, Ind. (see portrait and biography); issue: I–Charles Jelleff (qv for Wood lineages); II–Ellen Adaline (1 above).
1–Teacher. Founded Woman's Auxiliary of J. Earl Carpenter Post, A.L., Ridgeville. Mem. D.A.R. Congregational. Residence: Ridgeville, Ind.

1–**WOOD, Clara Louise,** *b* Chicago, Ill., Apr. 8, 1872.
10–Joseph **Peck** (qv);
9–Nathaniel (1641-76), *m* Deliverance– (*d* 1675);
8–Nathaniel (1670-1751), *m* 1695, Christian Allen (*d* 1702);
7–Nathaniel (1699-1756), lt. colonial forces; *m* Alice Fish;
6–Thomas (*b* 1726), R.I.;
5–Peleg (1760-1849), *m* 1779, Betsey Sweet (*d* 1838);
4–Pardon (1784-1829), *m* 1808, Sophia Burnham;
3–Eliza J. (1817-1901), *m* 1843, George W. **Hawes** (1815-80; Ebenezer[4] [1778-1862], of N.Y., *m* 1800, Betsey Hills, 1784-1822);
2–Helen J. (2 below).
9–Thomas **Burnham** (qv);
8–Richard (1654-1731), in Narragansett expdn., 1675; *m* 1680, Sarah Humphrey (1659-1726; Michael[9], *m* Priscilla Grant);
7–Richard (1692-1754), *m* 1715, Abigail Easton (*b* 1687; John[8] [1646-1716], *m* Elizabeth– [*d* 1711]; Joseph[9] [1602-88], from Eng., 1633);
6–Aaron (1719-60), *m* 1748, Hannah Pitkin;
5–Simeon (1757-88), *m* 1779, Jerusha Rockwell;
4–Sophia (1788-1825), *m* Pardon **Peck** (4 above).
9–William **Pitkin** (qv);
8–Roger (1662-1748), capt., 3d Co., Hartford Militia, 1698; ens., 1704; *m* 1683, Hannah Stanley (1662-1703; Capt. Caleb[9] [1642-1718], *m* Hannah, dau. of John Cowles, qv; Timothy[10] [1603-48], to America, 1634, *m* Elizabeth–);
7–Caleb (1687-1773), *m* Dorothy Hills (1697-1746; Lt. Jonathan[8] [*b* 1665], *m* Dorothy [1667-1733], dau. of Samuel Hale, qv; William[9] [*d* 1683], came in ship "Lyon," 1632, *m* 3d, Mary Warner Steele, dau. of Andrew Warner, qv);
6–Hannah (1722-1807), *m* Aaron **Burnham** (6 above).
2–Helen Jerene Hawes (1847-1911), *m* 1870, Marshall William **Wood** (see Vol. III, p. 492).
1–Mem. D.A.R., I.A.G. Residence: 1424 Franklin St., Boise, Ida.

1–**WOOD, Ira Wells,** *b* Wilkes-Barre, Pa., June 19, 1856.
8–John **Bissell** (qv);
7–John (*d* 1697), in King Philip's War; q.m. county troop of Hartford, 1677; *m* 1658, Isabel Mason (Maj. Gen. John[8], qv);
6–Jeremiah (*b* 1677), *m* 1705, Mehitable White (Lt. Daniel[7], of Hatfield, Mass.);
5–Mabel, *m* Lampson **Wells** (Wills, Wyllys);
4–Capt. Hezekiah (1736-1817), Am. Rev.; *m* Sarah Trumbull;
3–Dea. Ira (1783-1857), *m* Persis Pease;
2–Emily Hannah (2 below).
9–John **Drake** (qv);
8–Elizabeth (1621-1716), *m* as his 2d wife, 1653, William **Gaylord** (1616-56; Dea. William[9], qv);
7–Nathaniel (*b* 1656), *m* 1st, 1678, Abigail Bissell;
6–Josiah, *m* 1713, Naomi Burnham;
5–Sabra, *m* Capt. Ammi **Trumbull**;
4–Sarah, *m* Hezekiah **Wells** (4 above).
8–Dea. Samuel **Chapin** (qv);
7–Japhet (1642-1712), *m* 1st, 1664, Abilene Cooley (1642-1710);
6–Jonathan (1688-1761);
5–Rebecca, *m* Dea. Joseph **Sexton**;
4–Elizabeth, *m* Dea. Samuel **Pease** (desc. John Pease, capt. A. and H.A.Co.);
3–Persis, *m* Dea. Ira **Wells** (3 above);
2–Emily Hannah (*d* 1891), *m* Isaac **Wood** (1815-89; Moses[3], from Eng., 1819, settled at Wilkes-Barre, Pa.); issue: I–Horace (*d* aet. 7); II–Isaac Trumbull (*m* Stella Helena Buist); III–Emily (Mrs. James F. Rusling, 1847-1927; see Vol. I, p. 897); IV–Ellen Persis (see Vol. I, p. 897); V–Ira Wells (1 above); VI–Edward Scott; VII–William Phelps.
1–Not married. A.B., Princeton, '77, A.M., 1880. Counsellor-at-law; mem. 58th Congress, 1904-05, for unexpired term of William M. Lanning (resigned); reelected to 59th to 62d Congresses, 1905-13 (see Who's Who in America, Vol. 12). Club: Republican. Residence: 138 E. State St., Trenton, N.J.

1–**WOOD, Edna Hilliard White (Mrs. J. Robert),** *b* Oxford, N.C., Oct. 29, 1889.
7–George **White** (*d* 1736), from Eng., settled on the Roanoke River, Va.; granted 145 acres land in Brunswick Co., 1735;
6–George (ca. 1722-1792), Am. Rev.; *m* 1748, Susannah Read;
5–Coleman Read (1765-1835), *m* 1st, 1786, Selah Bradford (1767-1811; Thomas[6], Am. Rev., *m* Mary–);
4–John (1796-1865), *m* 1825, Hixey Cole (1800-85; John[5], *m* Susannah–);
3–Dr. William Coleman (1827-1903), Jefferson Med. Coll.; surgeon in Civil War; Mason; *m* 1855, his cousin, Sallie Agnes White (1835-91; Edmund[4], *m* 2d, 1833, Mary Williamson, dau. of Thomas Hilliard, *m* Sallie Bowdoin; John[5], capt. Am. Rev., *m* 1772, Agnes, dau. of Abraham Mayfield; George[6], same as 6 above);
2–Dr. Edmund Thomas (2 below).
8–James **Taylor** (qv);
7–John (1696-1780), *d* in Granville Co., N.C.; *m* 1716, Catherine Pendleton (1699-1774; Philip[8], to Va., 1676, *m* Isabella Hart, or Hurt);
6–Mary (1718-57), *m* 1735, Joseph **Penn** (ca. 1710-post 1763);
5–Frances (*b* 1756), *m* 1771, John **Hunt** (1752-1818), Am. Rev. from N.C. (John[6] [*d* ante 1768], *m* Mourning–, *d* 1823);
4–John Penn (1789-1850), *m* 1811, Sarah Longmire (*b* 1792; William[5]);
3–James Thomas (1833-79), *m* 1861, Helen George;
2–Ida Penn (2 below).
10–Gov. Edward **Digges** (1621-75; son of Sir Dudley; g.son of Gen. Thomas, *m* Anne St. Leger; direct desc. Alfred the Great); came from Eng., settled at "Belfield," Va., 1650; mem. council, 1654; auditor general, 1670-75; gov., 1655-57; *m* Elizabeth Page (*d* 1691);
9–Catherine, *m* 1677, William **Herndon,** of New Kent Co., Va.;
8–Edward (1678-1745), *m* 1698, Mary Waller;
7–John (*b* ca. 1708), *m* Sarah Pomfret;
6–George (1734-96), from Fredericksburg, Va., to Orange Co., N.C.; Am. Rev.; *m* Sarah– (*d* 1802);
5–Zachariah, *m* 2d, 1824, Lydia Clifton;
4–Sylvinia (*d* 1883), *m* David **George,** served in Civil War;
3–Helen (1840-76), *m* James Thomas **Hunt** (3 above);
2–Ida Penn (*b* 1862), *m* 1883, Dr. Edmund Thomas **White** (1858-1928), A.B., Trinity (Duke U.), '79; M.D., Vanderbilt, 1882; practiced in Oxford and Granville cos., N.C.; tobacconist; pres. Bank of Granville from 1895; trustee Duke U.; served on War Board during World War; issue: I–Helen Agnes (*b* 1885); II–Edna Hilliard (1 above); III–Ida Hixey (*b* 1894; *m* 1920, Ewing Linwood Smith).
1–*m* Jan. 25, 1928, J(ames) Robert Wood, *b* Oxford, N.C., Sept. 23, 1875; son of James Knight Wood (*b* 1844), *m* 1865, Fanny Leonard; g.son of James Madison Wood (1815-1902), *m* Mary M. Smith.
1–Ed. Westminister, Richmond, Va. Sec. home service dept., A.R.C. during World War. Mem. D.A.R. (sec.), Taylor Family Assn. Clubs: Oxford Woman's (past pres.), Tuesday Study. Residence: Oxford, N.C.

1–**WOODRUFF, Stephen Albert,** *b* St. Louis, Mo., Dec. 24, 1876.
9–John **Woodruff** (qv);
8–John (1650-1703), of Southampton, L.I.; *m* Sarah–;
7–Nathaniel (ca. 1680-1726), *m* 1705, Abigail Leek;
6–Stephen (*d* 1769), Westfield, N.J.; *m* Hannah Crane (*b* 1728; Jonathan[7]);

5–Stephen (1755-1826), Hamilton Co., O.; *m* 2d, Catherine– (*b* 1776);
4–Stephen Lyon (1799-1864), *m* 1819, Elizabeth Markley (1799-1882);
3–Joab (1821-64), Cincinnati, O.; *m* 1840, Sarah A. Robbins (1824-94);
2–Samuel Ridgway (2 below).
4–John **Lanphear** (*b* 1773), *m* 1803, at Poughkeepsie, N.Y., Elizabeth Gullen (Gullien?), sister of Mary Gullien Van Renssalaer;
3–Joseph (*b* June 4, 1812), *m* Jane Bigelow (*b* Nov. 28, 1818);
2–Emma Jane (*b* 1842), *m* 1866, Samuel Ridgway **Woodruff** (1842-1906), of Cincinnati, O., and Necedah, Wis.; farmer; soldier Civil War; issue: I–Joseph Arthur (*b* 1867; *m* Elsie Malotke); II–Stephen Albert (1 above).
1–*m* Dec. 18, 1897, Mary Ethel Pearson, *b* Guelph, Ont., Can., Mar. 29, 1879; dau. of John Pearson, of Chicago; issue (all *b* Chicago, Ill.): 1–Margaret Emma, *b* June 13, 1899; U.Ill., 1920-21; 2–Jane Alice, *b* Mar. 15, 1901; *m* June 22, 1922, Carl Francis, son of Charles Naffz, of Madison, Wis. (issue: Helen Marie, *b* Apr. 21, 1923; Charles Stephen, *b* Mar. 21, 1925; Joan Louise, *b* Dec. 15, 1926); 3–Samuel John, *b* Oct. 1, 1902; U.Ill., 1921-22; 1st lt., 108th Engrs. Corps; 4–Stephen Albert, *b* Dec. 23, 1903; B.S., Wheaton Coll., '29; Evangelical Theol. Sem., Dallas, Tex.; 5–David Pearson, *b* Feb. 15, 1910.
1–Printer, 1893-1906; asst. editor, Farm Implement News, Chicago, 1906-11; publishing agent, Moody Bible Inst., 1911-25; sales mgr., Kable Brothers Co. Inc., since 1925. Mem. Springer Family (pres.), Bible Rescue Mission (pres.). Methodist. Republican. Club: Kiwanis. Residence: 6066 N. Harlem Av., Chicago, Ill.

1–**WOODS, James Haughton,** *b* Boston, Mass., Nov. 27, 1864.
6–Samuel **Woods** (qv);
5–Samuel (1722-1808), *m* 1772, Abigail Whitney (1741-1826);
4–Leonard, D.D. (1774-1854), A.B., Harvard, 1796; theologian, author; *m* 1799, Abigail Wheeler;
3–Samuel (1800-84), *m* 1825, Mary Hale Lowe;
2–Joseph Wheeler (2 below).
9–William **White,** Mayflower Pilgrim (qv);
8–Resolved (1615-1690 or 94), came with his parents; *m* 1st, 1640, Judith Vassall (1619-80; William[9]);
7–Elizabeth (*b* 1652), *m* 1672, Obadiah **Wheeler** (*b* 1651; Obadiah[8], from Eng. to probably Concord, Mass., where he was an original propr.; freeman, 1641; *m* 1st, Susannah–, *d* 1649);
6–Joseph (1690-1780), Lancaster, Mass.; *m* 1st, 1726/27, Abigail Butterfield (1702-64; Jonathan[7], *m* Ruth Wright);
5–Rev. Joseph (1734/35-1793), B.A., Harvard, 1757, M.A., 1760; del. Provincial Congress, 1774-75; rep. Gen. Ct., 1775; register of probate, Worcester Co., 1775-93; *m* 1st, 1760, Mary Greenleaf;
4–Abigail (1776-1846), *m* 1799, Leonard **Woods** (4 above).
10–Edmund **Greenleaf** (qv);
9–Stephen (1628-90), capt., 1686; drowned while on expdn. against Port Royal, 1690; *m* 1651, Elizabeth Coffin (1630-78; Tristram[10], qv);
8–Capt. Stephen (1652-1743), in King Philip's and Indian wars; *m* 1676, Elizabeth Gerrish (1654-1712; William[9], qv);
7–Rev. Daniel (1680-1763), *m* 1701, Elizabeth Gookin (1681-1762; Samuel[8]; Daniel[9], qv);
6–Dr. Daniel (1702-95), surgeon at siege of Louisburg, 1745; in Am. Rev.; *m* Silence (Nichols) Marsh (1702-62; Israel Nichols[7], *m* 1688, Mary, dau. of Roger Sumner, g.dau. of William Sumner, qv; Thomas[8], qv);
5–Mary, *m* Rev. Joseph **Wheeler** (5 above).
2–Joseph Wheeler **Woods** (1829-1912), mcht.; *m* 1858, Caroline Frances Fitz (1837-1911); issue: I–Harriette Appleton (*b* 1859; *m* 1879, Philo Woodruff Sprague); II–Joseph Fitz (*b* 1863; *m* Harriette G. Cotton Smith); III–James H. (1 above); IV–Arthur (*b* 1870; see Who's Who in America; *m* 1916, Helen Morgan Hamilton); V–Herbert Richardson (*b* 1872; *m* Aline Griffin).
1–*m* July 17, 1907, Gertrude, dau. of Elbert Irving Baldwin (1829-94), *m* 1855, Mary Jeannette Sterling.
1–*m* 2d, 1927, Elizabeth Robinson.
1–A.B., Harvard, '87; Cambridge Theol. Sch., 1887-89; U.Berlin, 1889-91; Oxford, 1891; U.-Strassburg, 1894-97; Ph.D., Strassburg, 1896. Prof. philosophy Harvard, since 1913; author, editor (see Who's Who in America). Fellow Am. Acad. Arts and Sciences; mem. Am. Philol. Assn., Am. Oriental Soc., Royal Asiatic Soc., Am. Philos. Assn., Deutsche Morgenländische Gesellschaft. Clubs: Harvard, Century (New York), Union, Harvard (Boston), Corde Artistique et Littéraire (Paris). Residence: 29 Follen St., Cambridge, Mass.

1–**WOODS, Weightstill Arno,** *b* Versailles, Mo., June 10, 1885.
5–Robert **Woods** (*d* 1811), from Ireland with his two brothers aet. 10, 1730; settled at Franklin, Bedford Co., Va.; *m* Elizabeth Middleton;
4–John (*d* 1800), *m* 2d, Agnes Hairston (Robert[5], from Ireland, 1730);
3–Samuel Hairston (1798-1876), *m* 1822, Sicily Patterson (1807-68), removed to Morgan Co., Mo., 1855;
2–Peter George (2 below).
4–William (Parks) **Parkes** (1780-1828), of N.C.; *m* 1809, Elizabeth Henderson (1785-1850);
3–Weightstill Avery (1820-88), began to write name Parkes; of Versailles, Mo.; *m* Tilitha J. Embry (1829-58; Talton[4], *m* Sarah Duncan);
2–Susan Harriet (1851-1909), *m* 1868, Peter George **Woods** (1844-1919), physician, banker, farmer and stock raiser; issue: I–Edna (1869-93; *m* Joseph H. Banks, *d* 1894); II–Eva (*b* 1872; *m* Rev. David Cary Peters); III–George (*b* and *d* 1875); IV–Nancy Mosel (*b* 1879; *m* Dr. Edgar Peyton Yarnell); V–Herbert Spencer (1881-1920); VI–Weightstill Arno (1 above).
1–*m* Dec. 24, 1914, Mary Leona Holderness, *b* San Diego, Calif., Nov. 1, 1891; dau. of William H. Holderness, of Ohio; issue: 1–Peter Holderness, *b* Chicago, Ill., Sept. 3, 1916; 2–Leona Harriet, *b* La Grange, Ill., Aug. 9, 1919; 3–Mary June, *b* Hinsdale, Ill., Apr. 30, 1921; 4–Weightstill William, *b* Chicago, June 27, 1925.
1–A.B., U. of Mo., '11 (Phi Delta Phi, Acacia, P.B.K.); J.D., U. of Chicago, 1913. Lawyer since 1913. Mason. Clubs: Quadrangle, Interfraternity (Chicago), La Grange Country. Residence: La Grange, Ill.

1–**WOODWARD, Ruth Helen Wassell (Mrs. Clarence Stephens),** *b* Little Rock, Ark., Dec. 24, 1879.
6–William **Spotts,** from Scotland, 1742; in Am. Rev.;
5–Lt. John (*b* 1755), with Washington at Valley Forge;
4–George (1779-1843), to Louisville, Ky., 1829; *m* 1806, Sarah Croxton (1788-1851; Archibald[5], of Eng., *m* Margaret Heinmon);
3–Margaret (1815-95), *m* 1838, John **Wassell** (1813-81), from Eng.;
2–Albert (2 below).
11–John **Dunham** (qv);
10–John (1620-92), *m* 1643, Dorothy–;
9–John (1649-96), *m* 1680, Mary Smith (Rev. John[10], *m* Susanna, sister of Gov. Thomas Hinckley);
8–Ebenezer (1684-1767), *m* 1707, Anne Ford (*d* 1777);
7–Seth (1708-72), *m* 1735, Judith Paulk (*d* 1767);
6–Joseph (*b* 1745), *m* 1770, Abigail (Hovey) Jennings (James Hovey[7], *m* Joanna Bassett);
5–Josephus (1772-1838), *m* 1795, Elizabeth Huntington (1781-1872; Jonas[6]);
4–Samantha (1799-1864), *m* 1821, Daniel **McAlmont** (1794-1839; John[5], officer during Am. Rev.);
3–Corydon (1827-62), served in Rust's brigade in War Between the States; *m* 1855, Sarah Helen Cheever (1833-60);
2–Leona Helen (2 below).
9–Michael **Findley** (*b* 1680), from Ireland to Phila., 1734;
8–John (1708-57), *m* 1729, Martha Barclay (*b* 1712);
7–James (1730-1809), *m* 1749, Mary Patterson (1732-1810);
6–Robert W. (1750-1840), served in 2d Pa. Regt., 1777, Am. Rev.; transferred to c.-i.-c. guard at Yorktown, 1780, and served to close of war; *m* 1780, Rebecca Bradley (1752-1821; James[7], *m* Elizabeth Pelham, who established and supported a hosp. for sick and wounded nr. Charlotte, N.C., their three sons, John, James and Francis were killed in Am. Rev.);

5–John Patterson (1783-1825), *m* 1805, Sarah Strain (1787-1852);
4–Elvira Heney (1812-47), *m* 1832, James Stuart **Cheever** (1810-79; John Mann[5], *m* Maria Saulsbury; Joseph[6], *m* Eliza Stuart);
3–Sarah Helen (1833-60), *m* Corydon **McAlmont** (3 above);
2–Leona Helen (*b* 1856), *m* 1877, Albert **Wassell** (*b* 1851), of Little Rock, Ark.; issue: I–Ruth Helen (1 above); II–Corydon McAlmont (*b* 1884; *m* Irene Yarnell); III–John Randolph (1889-1919; *m* Lucile McRae).
1–*m* Aug. 14, 1913, Clarence Stephens Woodward, *b* Nashville, Tenn., Mar. 10, 1876; son of Benjamin C. Woodward.
1–Mem. D.A.R. (hon. state regent), U.S.D. 1812. Residence: 2005 Scott St., Little Rock, Ark.

1–**WOODWORTH, Paul,** *b* Caseville, Mich., Sept. 3, 1869.
8–Jasper **Crane** (qv);
7–Dea. Azariah (1649-1730), dep. N.J. Provincial Assembly; a founder of Cranetown (now Montclair), N.J.; *m* Mary Treat (Gov. Robert[8]; Richard[9], qv);
6–Azariah, *m* Rebecca–;
5–Moses, *m* Sussanna Brant;
4–Elizabeth (1787-1830), *m* Caleb **Woodworth** (1786-1850);
3–Stephen Elias (1815-87), *m* Rachel Bell;
2–Thomas Bell (2 below).
9–Christopher **Smith** (*d* 1676), sgt. and dep. Gen. Ct. of Mass., 1655; "Antient Friend of Providence"; *m* Alice–;
8–Edward (1635-93), sgt.; mem. Colonial Assembly, 1665-83; *m* Anphillis Angell (Thomas[9], founder with Roger Williams, of Providence Plantations);
7–Joseph (1680-1734), *m* Patience Mowry (Nathaniel[8]; Roger[9]);
6–Jacob (*b* 1706), *m* Dinah Harris (Richard[7]; Thomas[8]; Thomas[9], of Providence Plantations);
5–Rufus (*b* 1741), *m* Mary Sayles;
4–Jacob (1767-1855), *m* Elizabeth Mowry;
3–Philip Martin (1805-96), *m* Harriet Ann Nichols;
2–Mary Gertrude (2 below).
9–Roger **Mowry** (*d* 1666), from Eng.; settled Boston ca. 1631; *m* Mary Johnson;
8–Nathaniel (1644-1718), *m* Johannah Inmans (Edward[9]);

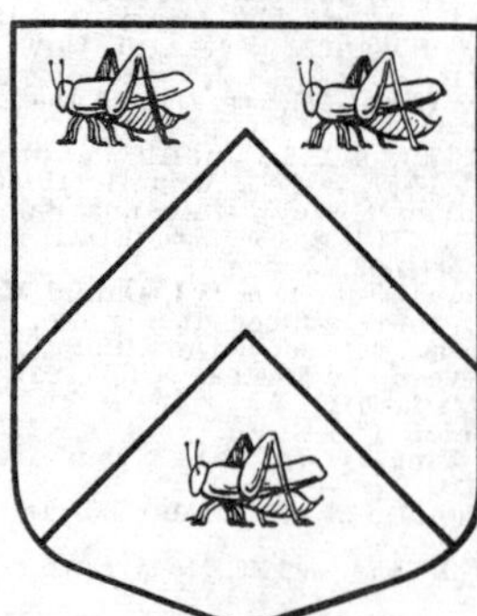

WOODWORTH

Arms: Argent, a chevron sable, between three grasshoppers vert.

Crest: A demi-woman couped at the knees, vested gules, hair dishevelled or, in the dexter hand a honeysuckle proper, stalked and leaved vert.

7–Henry;
6–Uriah;
5–Philip;
4–Elizabeth (1768-1861), *m* Jacob **Smith** (4 above);
3–Philip Martin, *m* Harriet Ann Nichols (3 above);
2–Mary Gertrude (1843-1913), *m* 1864, Thomas Bell **Woodworth** (1841-1904); for issue and other lineages see Philip Bell Woodworth.
1–*m* Nov. 22, 1916, Margaret C. Carolan, *b* Richmond, Ind., Nov. 9, 1889; dau. of Peter J. Carolan; issue: 1–Philip, *b* Bad Axe, Mich., Jan. 5, 1918; 2–James Fred, *b* Bad Axe, Mar. 3, 1921.
1–Ed. Mich. State Coll., '90; LL.B., U.Mich., 1893. Admitted to bar, 1893, and practised at Caseville, 1893-1901, Bad Axe, Mich., 1901–; gen. atty. for Mich. Electric Power Co. and Mich. Public Service Co. Elected pros. atty. of Huron Co., 1900, re-elected three successive terms; presdl. elector, 1928; del. several Rep. Nat. convs. Mason (K.T., Shriner), Elk. Mem. Mich. and Huron Co. bar assns. Clubs: Bad Axe Rotary, Bad Axe Community, Verona Hills Golf, Detroit Yacht, Detroit Republican, Michigan "M." Residence: Bad Axe, Mich.

1–**WOODWORTH, Philip Bell,** *b* Auburn, N.Y., Oct. 19, 1865.
9–Walter **Woodworth** (*d* 1685/86), from Eng. to Plymouth, 1633; one of the early settlers and officials of Scituate, Mass., 1635; surveyor; juror; mem. First Ch.;
8–Benjamin (1647-1728/29), Lebanon, Conn.; *m* 2d, Hannah Damon (John[9]);
7–Caleb (1704-75), first white settler at Salisbury, Conn.; *m* Jane Munger (*b* 1705; Samuel[8]; Nicholas[9]);
6–Gershom (1728-1810), Mayfield, N.Y.; capt. French and Indian War; present at massacre of Ft. William and Henry; *m* 1749, Rosanna Evarts (1733-95; Josiah[7]; John[8]; James[9]; John[10], of Guilford, Conn.);
5–Caleb (1763-1810), soldier in Am. Rev.; mem. N.Y. State Gen. Conv., 1801; *m* 1781, Rebecca Travers (1759-1844; Nicholas[6]; Sebastian[7]; John[8]);
4–Caleb (1786-1850), *m* 1808, Elizabeth Crane;
3–Stephen Elias (1815-87), *m* 1840, Rachel Bell (1822-45; Thomas[4]; William[5]);
2–Thomas Bell (2 below).
9–John **Sayles** (qv);
8–John (1654-1727), *m* Elizabeth Olney (1666-99; Thomas[9]; Thomas[10], qv);
7–Richard (1695-1775), *m* 1720, Mercy Phillips (Richard[8]; Michael[9]);
6–Richard (*b* 1723), *m* 1741, Abigail Hawkins (John[7]; William[8]; William[9]);
5–Mary (1742-70), *m* Rufus **Smith** (*b* 1741);
4–Jacob (1767-1847), *m* Elizabeth Mowry (1768-1861);
3–Philip Martin (1805-96), *m* Harriet Ann Nichols;
2–Mary Gertrude (2 below).
10–Francis **Nichols** (qv);
9–Isaac (*d* 1695), *m* 1646, Margaret Sherman;
8–Isaac (1654-90), *m* Mary Baldwin (*b* 1653; Richard[9]; Sylvester[10]);
7–Richard (1678-1755), *m* 1702, Comfort Sherman (*d* 1726; Theophilus[8]; Samuel[9], qv);
6–Theophilus (1703-74), *m* 1723, Sarah Curtis (1702-69; Ebenezer[7]; William[8], qv; John[9]);
5–William (1724-94), *m* Ann Burritt (1729-76; Stephen[6]; Josiah[7]; Stephen[8]; William[9]);
4–Stephen E. (1762-1822), *m* 1786, Roby Kennicott (1768-1844);
3–Harriet Ann (1807-48), *m* 1830, Philip M. **Smith** (3 above);
2–Mary Gertrude (1843-1913), *m* 1864, Thomas Bell **Woodworth** (1841-1904), Cazenovia, '62; atty. at law, Caseville, Mich.; mem. Mich. Legislature; presdl. elector; writer of lumber laws of Mich.; issue: I–Philip Bell (1 above); II–John Gilmore (1867-68); III–Paul (qv for other lineages); IV–Robert Shank (1873-96); V–Fred Langdon (*b* 1877; int. rev. collector, Detroit); VI–Gertrude Elizabeth (*b* 1878).
1–*m* Aug. 11, 1893, Lucy Merrylees Clute, *b* Newark, N.J., Aug. 29, 1873; dau. of Oscar Clute, pres. Fla. U.; issue: 1–Paul Merrylees (qv); 2–Robert Clute, *b* Chicago, Apr. 13, 1902; Purdue, '26; 3–Gertrude Elizabeth, and

4–Marion Merrylees (twins), *b* Chicago, Jan. 24, 1909.
1–B.S., Mich. State Coll., '86 (Phi Delta Theta), Sc.D., 1920. Engineer and atty.; mem. Rummler & Rummler & Woodworth, since 1923. Asst. prof. physics and engineering, Mich. State Coll., 1892-99, dean, Lewis Inst., Chicago, 1899-1917; pres. Rose Poly. Inst., Terre Haute, Ind., 1921-23. Civilian officer, War Plans Div., 1918-21 (see Who's Who in America). Mem. Bar Supreme Ct. of Ind. Mem. Am. Inst. E.E., Western Soc. Engrs., Am. Bar Assn., Chicago Bar Assn., Chicago Patent Law Assn., O.F.P.A. Clubs: University, Cornell, Mich. State Coll. Club. Residence: Glen Ellyn, Ill.

1–**WOODWORTH, Paul Merrylees,** *b* E. Lansing, Mich., July 12, 1894.
11–Roger **Tyler,** at Lynn, Mass., ante 1640; New Haven, 1650; *d* at Branford, 1673;
10–George (*b* 1650), *m* Hannah–;
9–Isaac (1680-1718), *m* 1704, Abigail Pond (*b* 1677; Samuel[10]; Samuel[11], qv);
8–Ann (*b* 1710), *m* 1731, Josiah **Evarts** (1705-55;)
7–Rosanna (1733-95), *m* 1749, Gershom **Woodworth** (1728-1810);
6–Caleb (1763-1810), *m* 1781, Rebecca Travers (1759-1844);
5–Caleb (1786-1850), *m* 1808, Elizabeth Crane;
4–Stephen Elias (1815-87), *m* 1840, Rachel Bell;
3–Thomas Bell (1841-1904), *m* 1864, Mary Gertrude Smith;
2–Philip Bell (2 below).
10–Richard **Treat** (qv);
9–Robert (1624-1710), *m* Jane Tapp (1627-1703; Edmund[10]);
8–Mary (1652-1704), *m* Azariah **Crane** (1647-1730; Jasper[9], qv);
7–Azariah (*b* 1682), *m* Rebecca– (*d* 1739);
6–Moses (1731-95), Am. Rev.; *m* Catherine Littell;
5–Elizabeth (1787-1830), *m* Caleb **Woodworth** (5 above).
10–William **Bunnell** (qv);
9–Nathaniel (ca. 1640-1696), *m* 1665, Susannah Whitehead (1650-1735; Isaac[10]; John[11]);
8–Lydia (*b* ca. 1680), *m* ca. 1700, Samuel **Littell** (John[9]; Benjamin[10], qv);
7–David (1718-90), *m* 1738, Susannah Craig (1716-53; Andrew[8]; Andrew[9]);
6–Catherine (1743-94), *m* Moses **Crane** (6 above).
10–Jacob Walingh **Van Winkle** (ca. 1599-1656), at New Amsterdam, ca. 1624; leading merchant; returned to Holland, 1633,35 and 41; *m* in Holland, ca. 1642, Tryntje Jacob;
9–Symon Jacobse (bap. 1653), *m* 1677, Annatje Sip (Arian Hendrickse[10]);
8–Marinus (1700-67), *m* 1721, Geesje Van Wagenin (Hendrick[9], *m* Margaretje Straatmaker);
7–Catrintje, *m* 1763, Abraham **Van Riper** (1731-70; Jurian[8]; Thomas[9]; Jurian[10]);
6–Altie, *m* 1787, Reynier **Van Giesen** (1760-1831; Abraham[7]; Reynier[8]; Abraham[9]; Reynier[10]);
5–Ann (1797-1875), *m* 1820, Thomas **Bell** (1796-1878; William[6], *m* Mary Gilmore);
4–Rachel (1822-45), *m* Stephen Elias **Woodworth** (4 above).
11–Richard **Osborn** (qv);
10–Sarah, *m* ca. 1620, John **Peet** (1597-1678);
9–Benjamin (1640-1704), *m* 1662, Phebe Butler (Richard[10], qv);
8–Mary (*b* 1683), *m* 1702, Josiah **Burritt** (*b* 1681; Stephen[9]; William[10]);
7–Stephen (*b* 1705/06), *m* 1723, Ann Sherman (*b* 1697; Daniel[8]; Samuel[9]; Samuel[10], qv);
6–Ann (1729-76), *m* ca. 1750, William **Nichols** (1724-94)
5–Stephen Ely (1762-1822), *m* 1786, Roby Kennicott;
4–Harriet Ann (1807-48), *m* 1830, Philip Martin **Smith** (1805-96);
3–Mary G. (1843-1913), *m* Thomas Bell **Woodworth** (3 above).
11–Roger **Williams** (qv);
10–Mary (1633-81), *m* 1650, John **Sayles** (qv);
9–Deborah, *m* 1680, Caleb **Carr** (qv);
8–Mercy (1683-1776), *m* 1705, Esek **Brown** (1679-1772; James[9]; Chad[10], qv);
7–Elizabeth (*b* 1708), *m* 1729, Robert **Sherman** (1705-85; Eber[8]; Peleg[9]; Philip[10], qv);
6–Roby (1729-1831), *m* 1751, John **Kennicott** (*b* 1728; John[7]; John[8]; Roger[9], *m* Joanna, dau. of Daniel Shepardson);
5–Roby (1768-1844), *m* Stephen E. **Nichols** (5 above).
8–Johannes **Clute** (ca. 1640-1725), famous Indian trader; *m* Baata Van Schlichtenhorst (Gerrit[9], *m* Aeltje Lansing; Brandt Arentse[10]);
7–Gerardus (1697-1746), *m* 1725, Machtelt Heemstraat (*b* 1704; Dirke[8], *m* 1700, Claasje Quackenbos, dau. of Peter Quackenbos; Takel Dirkse[9]);
6–Jacob (1736-96), Am. Rev.; *m* 1761, Maayke Lansing (bap. 1745; Hendrick[7]; Jacob[8]; Hendrick[9]; Gerrit[10], qv);
5–Richard (*b* 1768), *m* Anna Frazier;
4–Richard (1808-61), *m* 1831, Lucy Clements (1812-50; John[5]; Johannis[6]; Pieter[7]; Jan[8]);
3–Oscar (1837-1902), *m* 1868, Mary Merrylees (*b* 1840; William[4]; Peter[5]);
2–Lucy Merrylees (*b* 1873), *m* 1893, Philip Bell **Woodworth** (qv).
1–*m* Dec. 31, 1924, Ruth Hull Tobey (qv); issue: 1–Philip Tobey, *b* Chicago, Ill., July 15, 1926; 2–Robert Titus, *b* Wausau, Wis., June 25, 1930.
1–Grad. Lewis Institute, 1913; U.Ill., 1920. Technical engr., Portland Cement Assn. Wason Research Medalist, 1930. Served with A.E.F. in France and Germany. Mem. O.F.P.A., Western Soc. Engrs. Residence: 256 Van Damin St., Glen Ellyn, Ill.

1–**WOODWORTH, Ruth Hull Tobey (Mrs. Paul M.),** *b* Norway, Mich., May 22, 1894.
8–Thomas **Tobey** (*d* 1711), from L.I. to Sandwich, Mass., ca. 1640; *m* 1650, Martha Knott (*d* 1720; George[9]);
7–Samuel (*d* 1737), *m* 1696, Abiah Fish (*b* 1678; Ambrose[8]; John[9]);
6–Samuel (1715-81), *m* 1738, Bathsheba Crocker (*b* 1717; Timothy[7]; Joseph[8]; William[9], qv);
5–Timothy (1745-1812), *m* 1773, Mary Halloway (*d* 1835);
4–Silas (1789-1864), *m* Julia A. Hardin (1810-74);
3–Timothy (1826-1906), *m* Lucy Ann Gorham;
2–Silas Bertram (2 below).
12–Roger **Williams** (qv);
11–Mary (1633-81), *m* John **Sayles** (qv);
10–Mary (*b* 1652), *m* 1680, John **Holmes** (1649-1712; Obadiah[11], qv);
9–Susanna, *m* 1703, Valentine **Wightman** (1681-1749; George[10], *m* Elizabeth, dau. Gilbert Updike);
8–Mary (1704-77), *m* 1724, Joshua **Rathbone** (1696-1779; John[9]; John[10]; John[11]);
7–Job (*b* 1736), *m* Abigail Russell;
6–Martha (1760-1850), *m* 1779, Solomon **Cleveland** (1754-1843; Enoch[7]; Deliverance[8]; Edward[9]; Moses[10], qv);
5–Abigail (1789-1879), *m* 1806, Lorenzo **Ward** (1785-1841; William[6]; Charles[7]; William[8]; William[9]; William[10], qv);
4–Sarah (1814-95), *m* 1834, James Thomas **Gorham** (1811-53; Thomas[5]; James[6]; John[7]; Joseph[8]; Jabez[9]; John[10], qv);
3–Lucy Ann (1835-1909), *m* Timothy **Tobey** (3 above).
10–Robert **Titus** (qv);
9–John (1627-89), *m* Rachel–;
8–John (1650-97), *m* 1677, Sarah Miller (1655-1712; John[9]);
7–John (1678-1758), *m* 1712, Mary Palmer (1691-1746; Samuel[8]; Jonah[9]; Walter[10], qv);
6–Ebenezer (*b* 1714), *m* 1738, Mehitable Garnsey;
5–Comfort (*b* 1741), *m* Dorothy Gore (*b* 1646; Samuel[6]; Samuel[7]; Samuel[8]; John[9]);
4–Sylvanus (*b* 1772), *m* Catherine Rodman Carpenter (*b* 1781; James[5]; Daniel[6]; Solomon[7]; Samuel[8]; William[9]; William[10], qv);
3–George (1816-86), *m* Polly Hull (1826-96; William[4], *m* Polly Person, desc. John Pearson, qv);
2–Edith Rodman (*b* 1863), *m* 1889, Silas Bertram **Tobey** (*b* 1861), educator; issue: I–Ruth Hull (1 above); II–Paul Titus (*b* Aug. 10, 1895; *m* Katherine Van Arsdale Neilson); III–Alice Marjorie (*b* May 5, 1897); IV–Edith Louise (*b* Sept. 21, 1901); V–Silas Bertron (*b* Sept. 10, 1905; *m* Jeanette Piltz).
1–*m* Dec. 31, 1924, Paul Merrylees Woodworth (qv for issue).
1–Grad. U.Wis., 1917 (Kappa Kappa Gamma). Was librarian in Cleveland Pub. Lib. and Ind. State Normal Coll. Residence: 256 Van Damin St., Glen Ellyn, Ill.

1–**WORMLEY, John Marion,** *b* Macomb, Ill., Nov. 25, 1863.

5–Johannes (Wurmle) **Wormley** (1727-89), from Germany in the "Patience," to Phila., Pa., 1753; settled in Lancaster Co.; removed to Cumberland Co., ca. 1776, settled on west bank of Susquehanna River; owned 600 acres, on which Wormleysburg was founded, 1815; *m* 1st, 1753, Anna Maria– (had 3 sons in Am. Rev.);
4–Engelhart (1755-1827), of Lancaster Co., Pa.; began to write name Wormley; pvt. 3d Bn., Cumberland Co., militia in Am. Rev.; in Battle of L.I.; commd. officer 6th Regt. in War 1812; *m* 1784, Mary Elizabeth Rupley (1755-1815);
3–George Elder (1794-1887), of Newton, Ia.; *m* 1816, Barbara Kiner (1798-1859);
2–Samuel Stuart (1833-1905), teacher, farmer and mechanic, Newton; *m* 1859, Susan Shoopman (1842-1915); issue: I–George Washington (1860-1926; *m* Mary E. Spencer); II–Thomas Jefferson (*b* 1862; *m* Alta Lint); III–John Marion (1 above); IV–Samuel Arthur (1866-1919; *m* Maggie McGurne); V–Arminta Ann (*b* 1868; *m* George O. Kelly); VI–Cora Belle (*b* 1870; *m* Hiram Hand); VII–Lulu Elaine (1872-1928; *m* Harry Lockery Kelly); VIII–Mary Elizabeth (Mrs. Wilbert Eugene Harriman, qv); IX–Henry Wilson (1876-87); X–Patience (Mrs. Henry C. Korf, qv); XI–James Garfield (*b* 1881; *m* Effel Foreman); XII–David Frederick (*b* 1883; *m* Leona Benjamin).
1–*m* Sept. 21, 1893, Frances Rock, *b* Chambersburg, Pa., Mar. 14, 1868; dau. of John Rock, of Chambersburg; issue (all *b* Kingsley, Ia.): 1–Edna Belle, *b* July 7, 1894; Morningside Coll., '18; *m* June 2, 1928, Francis McQuire, of Sioux City, Ia.; 2–Susan Marion, *b* Apr. 16, 1896; Morningside Coll., '18; *m* Oct. 15, 1923, William L. Sandborn, of Moville, Ia. (issue: Suzanne); 3–Henry Wilson, *b* May 13, 1898; B.A., U.Ia., '21, Law Sch., 1923, served in 4th Co., 4th Bn., U.S. Inf., at Central Training Sch., during World War; 4–John McKinley, *b* Mar. 26, 1901; U.Ia., '26; *m* June 30, 1926, Beatrice Pfabe, of Davenport, Ia.; 5–Frances Barbara, *b* June 28, 1903; *m* Jan. 10, 1923, Virgil Wright (issue: Frances Anne); *m* 2d, Oct. 10, 1927, Bruce R. Clark; 6–George Thomas, *b* July 29, 1910; U.Ia., '32; 7–Woodrow Wilson, *b* July 9, 1912; 8–Charles Hughes, *b* Sept. 27, 1916; 9–Paul (*b* and *d* Nov. 15, 1917).
1–*m* 2d, Feb. 14, 1923, Vera Abby Low (qv).
1–LL.B., State U.Ia., '89; studied at Hazel Dell Acad. Atty. and banker. Mayor, Kingsley, Ia.; mem. 37th and 38th Assemblies of Ia. Chmn. Co. Council of Defense during World War. Mem. S.A.R. Elk, Odd Fellow. Winter place: Ft. Myers, Fla. Residence: Kingsley, Ia.

1–**WORMLEY, Vera Abby Low (Mrs. John M.),** *b* Green Mountain, Ia., June 13, 1887.
4–John **Low** (1792-1866), *m* 1816, Rhoda Sheppard;
3–William (1820-83), *m* 1844, Sarah Chapman;
2–Thomas Powers (2 below).
9–Kenelm **Winslow** (qv);
8–Lt. Job (1641-1720), rep. 1st Gen. Ct., Mass., 1692; *m* Ruth–;
7–James (1687-1773), 1st Quaker at Falmouth (now Portland), Me.; *m* Elizabeth Carpenter;
6–Benjamin (1717-96), Am. Rev.; *m* 1738, Hope Cobb;
5–William (1750-1834), *m* 1770, Phebe Pope (1751-1824);
4–Daniel (*b* 1789), *m* 1815, Irene Briggs (*b* 1793);
3–Robert (1831-1902), *m* 1854, Phebe Shepard (1831-73);
2–Mary Abby (2 below).
11–John **Tilley,** Mayflower Pilgrim (qv);
10–Elizabeth (*d* 1687), *m* 1623, John **Howland** (qv);
9–Hope (1629-83), *m* 1646, Elder John **Chipman** (qv);
8–Hope (1652-1728), *m* 2d, 1682, Dea. Jonathon **Cobb** (1660-1728), of Barnstable, Mass. (Henry[9], qv);
7–Dea. Samuel (1683-1767), *m* Abigail Stewart, or Stuart (1686-1766);
6–Hope (1716-97), *m* Benjamin **Winslow** (6 above).
2–Mary Abby Winslow (*b* 1864), *m* 1886, Thomas Powers **Low** (*b* 1856), farmer, Green Mountain, Ia.; issue: I–Vera Abby (1 above); II–Tura Isabel (*b* 1889; *m* Carl L. Cole); III–Sarah Mildred (*b* 1890; *m* William J. Young); IV–Avis Erma (*b* 1893; *m* George L. Owings); V–Carol Franciene (*b* 1900; *m* William Stuart Somers); VI–Margaret Irene (*b* 1904).
1–*m* Feb. 14, 1923, John Marion Wormley (qv).
1–Formerly pvt. sec. to the treas. State of Ia., and senatorial sec., Ia. State Senate. Mem. S.D.P. (state corr. sec.), S.M.D. (asst. dep.gov. gen., D.A.R., P.E.O., A.L. Auxiliary. Club: Sioux City Woman's. Residence: Kingsley, Plymouth Co., Ia.

1–**KORF, Patience Wormley (Mrs. Henry C.),** *b* Newton, Ia., Mar. 7, 1878.
Sister of John Marion Wormley, qv for genealogy.
1–*m* Aug. 9, 1905, Henry Christopher Korf, *b* Newton, Ia., Apr. 25, 1876; son of the late Henry Korf, of Newton; issue: 1–Wilhelmina June, *b* Newton, June 30, 1910; ed. Ferry Hall, 1927-28; B.S., U. of Ia., '31.
1–Ed. Newton Normal Coll., '98; Ia. State Coll., 1901. Sec. to pres. of Ia. State Coll., 1901-05. Mem. D.A.R., P.E.O. (pres., v.p., sec.), Camp Fire Girls (pres. bd. sponsors). Conglist. Republican. Clubs: Newton Woman's (1st v.p.), Newton Country. Residence: Newton, Ia.

1–**HARRIMAN, Mary Elizabeth Wormley (Mrs. Wilbert Eugene),** *b* Newton, Ia., Feb. 4, 1874.
4–Jacob **Shoopman,** of Va.; removed to Ky., 1829, where he died same yr.; *m* Polly Owens;
3–Thomas F. (1810-1900), from Tenn. to Bethel Tp., McDonough Co., Ill., 1833; *m* 1831, Patience Smedley;
2–Susan (1842-1915), *m* 1859, Samuel Stuart **Wormley** (1833-1905); for issue and Wormley lineage see John Marion Wormley.
1–*m* Oct. 4, 1894, Wilbert Eugene Harriman (Dec. 4, 1871-Mar. 17, 1909); son Walter Franklin Harriman, of Hampton, Ia.; issue (all *b* Ames, Ia.): 1–Loretta Marie, *b* Dec. 11, 1895; B.S., Ia. State Coll., '19; *m* Oct. 12, 1918, Raymond Curtis, son Curtis B. Jones, of Ames, Ia. (issue: Raymond Walter); 2–Walter Franklin, *b* Nov. 10, 1897; B.S., Ia. State Coll., '20; M.D., U.Pa., 1924; *m* Aug. 23, 1927, Mildred B., dau. Isaac Elmer Allan, of Phila., Pa. (issue: Walter Franklin); 3–Dorothy May, *b* Nov. 1, 1902; B.S., Ia. State Coll., '23; *m* Apr. 28, 1923, Walter M., son Thomas Sutton, of Burlington, Ia. (issue: Harriman).
1–Ed. Newton Normal Training Coll., 1890-92; Ia. State Coll., 1892-95. Teacher in country schs., 1890-91, in Hazel Dell Acad., 1892, in Newton Normal Coll., 1893; in Ames grade and junior high schs. since 1911. Mem. P.E.O. (pres. chapter, 1901-02), Pythian Sisters, Parent-Teachers Assn. Conglist. Republican. Clubs: Woman's, Golf and Country, Book and Basket. Residence: 119 12th St., Ames, Ia.

1–**WORTZ, Carl Henry,** *b* Independence, Kan., Mar. 29, 1890.
6–Oliver **Kelly** (1757-1829), matross, Capt. Clark's Co. Arty., Cont. Troops; *m* 1778, Jane Morris (*b* 1759), sister of Robert Morris, financier, Am. Rev. (Robert[7], from Eng. to Oxford, Md., 1747);
5–Dennis (1782-1849), *m* 1803, Mary Jones (1782-1863);
4–Susan (1815-1903), *m* Elisha **Martin** (*b* Cincinnati, O., 1812-*d* Winchester, Ind., 1898);
3–Lt. John K. (1837-97), lt., Co. C, 69th Ind. Inf., Civil War; *m* at Winchester, Ind., Ann Eliza Quinn (1837-1922);
2–Lizzie Bell (*b* 1866), *m* 1884, Christian Henry **Wortz** (*b* 1863).
1–*m* June 22, 1920, Ed Dell Haglin (qv for issue).
1–Biscuit mfr., Fort Smith. Second lt., inf., World War, bn. supply officer, Camp McArthur, Tex. Mem. A.L. Clubs: Hardscrabble Country, Rotary. Mason (Shriner). Presbyn. Residence: 127 May Av., Fort Smith, Ark.

1–**WORTZ, Ed Dell Haglin (Mrs. Carl Henry),** *b* Ft. Smith, Ark., May 30, 1898.
6–Robert **Creekmore** (*b* Scotland?), *m* Elizabeth Bachellor;
5–Balentine Bachellor (*b* 1784), *m* 1807, Mary Brown (*b* 1786; Abel[6]);
4–David Herbert (*b* 1817), served in Co. G, 2d

Tenn. Inf., U.S.A., Civil War; took census Scott Co., Tenn., 1860, Crawford Co., Ark., 1870, Alma and Richland tps., Crawford Co., 1880; justice, Huntsville, Tenn., 5 yrs.; served as one of 3 who constituted Co. Ct., 1873; elected co. judge, 1874; G.A.R.; Baptist; *m* 1843, Elizabeth Meadows (*b* 1820; John[5], Am. Rev.);
3–Randolph Brown (1846-93), served in 49th Ky. Vols., Civil War; U.S. marshal, Indian Ty.; mcht., Van Buren, Ark.; *m* 1867, Mary Emeline Chastain;
2–Martha Adella (2 below).
9–Pierre **Chastain** (1660-1728), from France, 1699, settled at Manakintown; ch. warden, 1719; *m* 1680, Marie Madeline de la Rochefoucauld;
8–John (Jean), (*d* 1762), of Va.; *m* Charlotte Judith Amonet;
7–Peter (Pierre), (*b* 1728), of Va.;
6–Rev. John, of Buckingham Co., Va.; Baptist minister; *m* 1762, Mary O'Bryan;
5–Edward (1769-1834), *m* 1787, Hannah Brown (*b* 1771; Daniel[6]);
4–Edward B. (1809-89), *m* Nancy M. Rogers;
3–Mary Emeline (1851-1905), *m* Randolph B. **Creekmore** (3 above).
7–James **Adams** (will probated, Hancock Co., Ga., 1796); *m* Mary–;
6–William (will probated Hancock Co., 1808); *m* Jane–;
5–Amy G. (*b* 1799), *m* 1814, John Calvin **Rogers** (1796-1875), served in Garrison's co., Ga. militia, War 1812; to Ark. while employed in transferring Cherokees to Indian Ty., 1843;
4–Nancy M. (1816-91), *m* Edward **Chastain** (4 above);
3–Mary E., *m* Randolph B. **Creekmore** (3 above);
2–Martha Adella (*b* 1874), *m* 1897, Edward **Haglin** (*b* 1860), realtor; issue: I–Ed Dell (1 above); II–Edward, Jr. (1901-21).
1–*m* June 22, 1920, Carl Henry Wortz (qv); issue: 1–Carl Haglin, *b* Ft. Smith, Ark., May 9, 1921; 2–Amrita Ed Dell, *b* Ft. Smith, Nov. 16, 1922.
1–Ed. Belcourt Sem., Washington, D.C. Auxiliary to lady bd. of mgrs. Sparks Memorial Hosp. Mem. D.A.C., Huguenot Soc. of the Founders of Manakin, Va., U.S.D. 1812. Club: Fortnightly Study. Presbyterian. Residence: 127 May Av., Fort Smith, Ark.

1–**WYKOFF, Leward Cornelius,** *b* Alliance, O., June 22, 1892.
10–Claes Corneliszen (Wijkhoff, Wyckoff, Wikoff, Wicoff) **Wykoff** (1597-1674), from Amsterdam, Holland, settled at New Amsterdam, 1636; *m* 1623, Margaret Van der Goos (*d* 1633);
9–Pieter Claesen (1625-97), of Flatlands, L.I.; wrote name Wijkhoff; *m* 1646, Grietje Van Ness (Cornelius[10], *m* 1st, Mayken Vandon Burghgraf);
8–Nicholas (1646-1730), wrote name Wyckoff; *m* 1673, Sarah Monfoort (Peter[9]);
7–Peter (1673-1757), wrote name Wikoff; *m* 1695, Willemptje Jansen Schenck;
6–Jacobus (*b* 1713), Somerset Co., N.J.; *m* Catalina Gulick (Joachim[7]);
5–Joachim (1749-1841), Brooke Co., W.Va.; wrote name Wicoff; in Am. Rev.; *m* 1772, Hannah Yerkes (1755-1844);
4–Cornelius (1787-1867), Jefferson Co., O.; began to write name Wykoff; *m* 1810, Leah Critser (1789-1869);
3–John M. (1830-1908), Richmond, O.; *m* 1852, Eliza Jane Frye (1827-91);
2–William Frye (1870-1923), minister, Cleveland, O.; *m* 1889, Margaret Blanche Bright (*b* 1870); issue: I–Leward Cornelius (1 above); II–Ruth Lois (*b* 1904; *m* Ralph P. Reed).
1–*m* Oct. 10, 1917, Dorothy Kathryn Young, *b* Cleveland, O., Aug. 2, 1894; dau. of Dr. Thomas C. Young; issue: 1–Mary Louise, *b* Cleveland, Dec. 16, 1920; 2–Nancy Ann, *b* Cleveland, May 13, 1925.
1–A.B., Western Reserve U., '13 (Alpha Tau Omega, Delta Theta Phi). Admitted to Ohio bar, 1915. In mil. service, 1917-18. Mem. S.A.R., I.A.G., Cleveland Geneal. Soc. Republican. Clubs: Hermit, Nisi Prius. Residence: 3223 E. 137th St., Cleveland, O.

1–**WYMAN, Fred,** *b* Schroon, N.Y., Oct. 10, 1857.
7–Lt. John **Wyman** (*d* 1684), from Eng. ca. 1640, settled at Woburn, Mass.; *m* 1644, Sarah, dau. of Miles Nutt;
6–Jacob (*d* 1742), *m* 1687, Elizabeth Richardson (*d* 1739);
5–Daniel (1715-59), of E. Sudbury; sgt. militia, French and Indian war, 1757-59; *m* 1738, Rebecca Cook (*d* 1744);
4–Daniel (1739-87), Brookfield, Mass.; entered army for invasion of Canada aet. 19 yrs.; *m* 1763, Betty Stone (*d* 1809);
3–Joseph (1774-1860) Schroon, N.Y.; capt. War 1812; *m* 1800, Phebe Potter (1780-1849), of Pawlet, Vt.;
2–Daniel (2 below).
8–George **Phelps** (qv);
7–Jacob (1649-89), Windsor, Conn.; *m* 1672, Dorothy Ingersoll (*b* 1654);
6–Israel (*b* 1681), *m* 2d, 1714, Rachel Jones, a widow;
5–David (1716-1803), *m* 1737, Margaret Colton (1714-1810);
4–John (1756-97), lt. Am. Rev.; *m* 1st, 1779, Anna, Baker (*d* 1797);
3–Elihu (1782-1856), *m* 1816, Margaret Cruikshank;
2–Anna (1825-82), *m* 1844, Daniel **Wyman** (1816-93), grain dealer; flour mfr., Schroon, N.Y.; issue: I–Joseph Wallace (1845-1904; *m* 1871, Mary R. Brevoort); II–Charlotte Elizabeth (1847-1917; *m* 1872, Fred I. Breed); III–David Franklin (1849-1930; *m* 1872, Jane M. Barnett); IV–Eugene (1851-1914; *m* 1882, Addie R. Parsons); V–Emma Louise (1855-1930; *m* 1886, Cassius D. Hayward); VI–Fred (1 above); VII–Mary B. (1861-1924; *m* Frank H. Pierce).
1–*m* Feb. 9, 1887, Millie Lindsay (Mar. 14, 1863-Dec. 27, 1905); dau. of James Edwin Lindsay, of Davenport, Ia.; issue: 1–Edith Helen, *b* Davenport, Ia., Jan. 5, 1888; grad. Vassar Coll., '10; *m* Sept. 28, 1910, Charles H., son of William H. Wilson (issue: Richard Wyman, *b* Jan. 13, 1913; John Oliver, *b* Oct. 20, 1916).
1–*m* 2d, Aug. 23, 1917, Margaret B. Lindsay, *b* Galena, Ill., Mar. 13, 1865; dau. of Andrew Lindsay.
1–Accountant, Lindsay & Phelps, 1878-1905; sec. (Minn.) Lumber Co., since 1910; pres. Southland Lbr. Co., 1915-1927; sec. and treas., The Sound Timber Co. since 1916; v.p. North Am. Timber Co., 1930–; pres. Warren & Ouachita Valley Ry. Co., 1915; pres. Southern Lumber Co., 1915–. Mem. Chamber of Commerce, I.A.-G., Francis Wyman Assn. (v.p.). Presbyterian. Clubs: Outing, Country. Residence: 49 Hillcrest Av., Davenport, Ia.

DR. JOHN SPENCER GAYLORD (1849-1928).

1–**WRIGHT, Jessie Cordelia Gaylord (Mrs. Frank Clark),** *b* Muscotah, Kan., Nov. 10, 1880.
10–William (Gaillard) **Gaylord** (qv);
9–Walter (1622-89), of Exeter, Eng., and Wind-

sor, Conn.; *m* 1st, 1648, Mary Stebbins (*d* 1657; Edward[10]);
8–Joseph (1649-1742), Durham, Conn.; *m* 1670, Sarah Stanley (1652-post 1680; John[9], from Eng., 1634, *m* Sarah Scott);
7–John (1677-1753), Bristol, Conn.; *m* 1701, Elizabeth Hickox (1681-1726; Joseph[8], *m* Mary Carpenter);
6–Joseph (1722-92), began to write name Gaylord; in Am. Rev.; *m* 1750, Ruth Mathews (1736-91; Capt. Caleb[7], *m* 2d, Ruth Merriam);
5–Chauncey (1759-1844), Otisco, N.Y.; Am. Rev.; *m* Ruth Bunnell (*d* 1835);
4–Jesse (1784-1864), Dundee, N.Y.; *m* 1817, Dema Cowles, or Coles (1794-1854; Isaac[5], *m* Lucy Driggs);
3–Leman Royce (1820-1902), Muscotah, Kan.; *m* 1847, Catherine Mary Spencer (1820-1909; John[4], from Eng., *m* Elizabeth Alexander);
2–John Spencer (2 below).
10–Sir Robert (Parke) **Parks** (qv);
9–Samuel (*d* post 1684), Stonington and Plainfield, Conn.; *m* 1671, Martha–;
8–William (1678-1750), *m* 1699, Jane Brodwyn;
7–Isaac (1703-27), *m* 1725, Elizabeth Clerk;
6–Isaac (*b* 1726), began to write name Parks; *m* Lydia–;
5–Capt. Abijah (1748-1813), Dalton, Mass.; in Am. Rev.; *m* 1772, Mary Dean (Lemuel[6], *m* Mary Lawrence; Jonathan[7], *m* Sarah Alcott Douglas);
4–Abijah (1787-1875), Sheffield, O.; *m* 1811, Lucinda Weston (1788-1875; Jonathan[5], *m* Anna Gillett; Jonathan[6]; Zachariah[7]; Edmond[8], *m* Rebecca, dau. John Soule, g.dau. George Soule, Mayflower Pilgrim, qv; Edmond[9], *m* Miss De La Noye);
3–Alonzo Augustus (1812-74), *m* 1855, Cordelia Siley Garfield (1826-1906);
2–May Garfield (*b* 1856), *m* 1880, John Spencer **Gaylord** (1849-1928), physician, Muscotah, Kan. (see portrait); issue: I–Jessie Cordelia (1 above); II–Kent Kellogg (*b* 1890; *m* Ethel Alice Loftin).
1–*m* Dec. 30, 1903, Frank Clark Wright, *b* Muscotah, Kan., Sept. 8, 1879; son of Albert Augustus Wright, of Muscotah; issue: 1–Albert Gaylord, *b* Muscotah, Nov. 24, 1904; U.Cincinnati, '24; 2–Francis (Frank) Heath, *b* Marysville, Kan., May 27, 1909; U.Cincinnati, '28.
1–Ed. Oberlin (O.) Conservatory, 1898-1900. Church soloist. Mem. S.M.D., C.D.A., D.F.-P.A., D.A.R., Delta Tau Delta Dames, O.E.S. Conglist. Republican. Residence: 362 Terrace Av., Cincinnati, O.

1–**YARBOROUGH, Edith Graham,** *b* Louisburg, N.C., Mar. 19, 1868.
5–Henry **Yarborough** (*d* post 1793), of Va.; *m* Martha Robinson;
4–Nathaniel (*d* post 1797), *m* Mary Mildred Fuller (1768-1853);
3–Richard Fenner (1797-1851), *m* 1825, Elizabeth Agnes Rebecca Brown (1809-61; John[4], *m* Rebecca Dupre);
2–Richard Fenner (2 below).
7–Maj. Richard **Foster** (1619/20-post 1670), from Eng. to Va., 1635; burgess, Lower Norfolk Co., 1655-56; mem. Council, Albemarle, N.C., 1670;
6–John (*b* ca. 1653), of Chowan Co., N.C.; *m* Ann Williams; *m* 2d, Elizabeth– (tradition says Hutchinson);
5–Richard (*b* ca. 1703), clk. Co. Ct., Chowan Co., 1733; *m* Susannah–;
4–Peter (1756-post 1798), of Mathews Co., Va.; soldier Am. Rev.; received grant of land, Wake Co., N.C.; *m* 1776, Ann Hall (*d* post 1798);
3–William Edward (1795-1843), *m* 1833, Mary Eleanor Wiatt;
2–Eleanor Scott (2 below).
10–Rev. Hawte (Wyatt) **Wiatt** (qv);
9–Edward (1619-90), patented land in Gloucester Co., 1662; owned "Boxley," "Oakley," "Old Upton," "New Upton," plantations; *m* Jane Conquest (1622-98);
8–Conquest (1645-1720), sheriff, Gloucester Co., 1705,07; vestryman, Petsworth Parish; *m* Sally–;
7–Conquest (1673-post 1735), vestryman, Petsworth Parish, 1727; *m* 2d, ca. 1730, Martha Gaines;
6–Capt. John (1732-1805), ch. warden, Petsworth Parish, 1755; *m* 1756, Mary Todd;
5–Dr. William Edward (1762-1802), sheriff, Gloucester Co., 1802; *m* 1781, Mary Graham (*d* 1815; John[6], *m* Elizabeth, dau. Catesby Cocke);
4–John Todd Cocke (1781-1855), col. War 1812; *m* 1810, Cecilia Dabney (1788-1837; George[5], *m* Ann Nelson);
3–Mary Eleanor (1812-94), *m* William E. **Foster** (3 above).
12–Sir William **Barne** (ca. 1568-*d* Va., 1619), knighted, 1603; of Woolwich, Eng.; mem. Va. Co. of London; incorporator 2d Charter, 1609; *m* Ann, dau. of Edwin Sandys, archbishop of York;
11–Ann (*d* 1633), *m* Sir William **Lovelace** (bap. 1583/84-*d* 1627), of Woolwich; knighted, 1609; mem. Va. Co. of London; incorporator 2d Charter, 1609;
10–Anne, *m* Rev. John **Gorsuch** (*d* 1647);
9–Anne (*b* 1638/39), *m* Capt. Thomas **Todd** (qv);
8–Thomas (1660-1724/25), justice, Gloucester Co., 1698-1702; *m* Elizabeth Bernard (William[9], qv);
7–Christopher (1690-1743), of "Toddsbury"; *m* bet. 1718-21, Elizabeth Mason (1701-64; Lemuel[8], lt. col., *m* Mary Thelabel; Col. Lemuel[9]; Lt. Francis[10], from Eng. to Lower Norfolk Co., 1613);
6–Mary (1725-94), *m* John **Wiatt** (6 above).
2–Eleanor Scott Foster (1840-1925), *m* 1859, Richard Fenner **Yarborough** (1834-1910), mcht.; issue: 10 children, those living 1929 are: I–Mary Wiatt; II–John Brown (*m* Susie M. Webb); III–Edith Graham (1 above); IV–William Henry (*b* 1870; *m* 1900, Eloise Hill, see Vol. III, p. 495; see their son (Charles) Hill Yarborough, Vol. III, p. 496, for paternal lineage); V–Eleanor Nelson (*m* James Redmond Collie).
1–Attended Louisburg Coll. Mem. C.D.A. Residence: Louisburg, N.C.

1–**YAWKEY, Cyrus Carpenter,** *b* Chicago, Ill., Aug. 29, 1862.
5–Johann Georg **Yawkey,** from the Palatinate in the "Harle," 1736, settled near Phila.; *m* Catherine–;
4–George (1771-1844), *b* nr. Phila. and lived there until 1807; lived in Waterloo on Senaca Lake, N.Y., 1807-16, in Stark Co., O., 1816-44; *m* 1803, Elizabeth Hoover (1771-1836);
3–John Hoover (1806-89), *b* near Phila.; lived in Waterloo, 1807-16, Stark Co., O., 1816-24, Massillon, O., 1824-51, Flint, Mich., 1851-58, Saginaw, 1858-63, Bay City, 1863-85, Detroit, 1885-89; *m* 1828, Lydia Clyman (1807-88);
2–Samuel W. (2 below).
8–William **Carpenter** (qv);
7–Samuel (1644-1682 or 83), Rehoboth, Mass.; *m* 1660, Sarah Readaway;
6–David (1675-1701 or 02), *m* 1697, Rebecca Hunt;
5–David (1701-87), *m* 1724, Joannah Walker (1704-86);
4–John (1733-1821), Am. Rev.; *m* 3d, 1801, Mary (Carpenter) Ide;
3–Cyrus (1802-63), Guilford, Vt.; *m* 1st, 1825, Elvira Louise Gale (1808-41);
2–Mary Uliaetta (1833-1919), *m* 1855, Samuel W. **Yawkey** (1830-82), lumberman; lived in Massillon, O., 1830-50, Saginaw, Mich., 1850-57, Chicago, Ill., 1857-63, Saginaw, 1863-82; issue: I–John Cyrus (1860-96); II–Cyrus Carpenter (1 above); III–Mary Elvira (1866-1928; *m* 1889, Frederick Moir White).
1–*m* Oct. 13, 1887, Alice Maud Richardson, *b* Saginaw, Mich., Oct. 25, 1863; dau. of Noah C. Richardson, of Saginaw; issue: 1–Leigh, *b* Saginaw, Mich., Aug. 23, 1888; *m* Aug. 15, 1911, Aytchmonde Perrin, son of Stephen Crittenden Woodson, of Kansas City, Mo. (issue: Cyrus Yawkey, *b* 1914; Nancy Leigh, *b* 1917; Alice Richardson, *b* 1918; Margaret Perrin, *b* 1920).
1–Grad. Mich. Mil. Acad., Orchard Lake, '81. Clerk in retail hardware store, Saginaw, 1881-83; mem. firm of Yawkey & Corbyn, retail hardware mchts., Saginaw, 1884-89, Yawkey & Lee Lumber Co., Hazelhurst, Wis., 1889-93; treas. and gen. mgr. Yawkey Lumber Co., Hazelhurst, 1893-1903; pres. Yawkey Lumber Co., Hazelhurst and Wausau, Wis., since 1903; also Alexander-Yawkey Timber Co., Wis. & Ark. Lumber Co., C. Francis Colman Co., Hazelhurst Land Co.; v.p. Yawkey-Bissell Lumber Co., Wausau Southern Lumber Co., Marathon Lumber Co.; sec-

treas. Cisco Lake Lumber Co.; dir. McCloud River Lumber Co., B C Spruce Mills, Ltd., Wis. Box Co., Masonite Corpn.; pres. Marathon Paper Mills Co.; v.p. Wausau Paper Mills Co., Ontonagon Fibre Co.; dir. Tomahawk Kraft Paper Co.; pres. Minn. Northern Power Co., Montana-Dakota Power Co., Northwest States Utilities Co.; dir. Marathon Electric Mfg. Co.; v.p. Am. Nat. Bank. Pres. Marathon Co. (Wis.) Park Commn., since 1920; chmn. Co. Bd., Oneida Co., Wis., 1891-93; mem. Wis. Assembly, 1895-96. Capt. Mich. N.G., 1888, maj., 1889; capt. Wis. State Guard, 1917, maj., 1918, col., 1919. Mem. I.A.G., A.L. (hon.), V.F.W. (hon.), Reserve Officers Assn. (hon.). Universalist. Republican. Mason (32°, K.T.). Clubs: Rotary, Wausau, Wausau Country. Residence: 403 McIndoe St., Wausau, Wis.

1–**YODER, Albert Henry,** *b* nr. Nora Springs, Ia., Feb. 15, 1866.
5–Conrad **Yoder** (*d* 1790), from Switzerland, first appeared in America, 1751; settled in Catawba Co., N.C.; *m* Christine Klein (*d* 1767);
4–Jacob (1767-1843), *m* Catherine Dellinger (1782-1862);
3–Henry (1804-72), *m* Ruth Ann Rader (1813-73);
2–William Henry (2 below).
8–Laurens Andriessen **Van Buskirk** (qv);
7–Thomas (1662-1748), officer King's rangers; capt., maj. and col., colonial troops of N.J.; *m* 2d, 1720, Volkertie Collier;
6–Michael (*b* 1721), of Hunterdon Co., N.J.; ens. Md.; soldier French and Indian War; *m* ca. 1745, Mary Van Deventer (*b* 1726);
5–Isaac (1760-1843), Monroe Co., Ind.; almost continuously engaged for several yrs. in Indian border warfare; pvt., Va. militia, Am. Rev.; *m* Jerusha Littell (1756-1827);
4–Michael (1782-1856), War 1812; 1st commr., Monroe Co., Ind.; asso. judge; *m* Elizabeth Bilderback (1787-1871);
3–Capt. Isaac Shelby (1815-64), in Mexican and Civil wars; *m* 1838, Elizabeth Gabbert (1815-97);
2–Catherine Adelaide (1846-1921), *m* 1864, William Henry **Yoder** (1846-1924); for issue see Vol. I, p. 445.
1–*m* June 11, 1894, Susan Norton Griggs, *b* Madison, Ind., Nov. 5, 1869; dau. of Joseph Emerson Griggs, of Indianapolis; issue: 1–Leverett Griggs, *b* Indianapolis, Aug. 3, 1895; pvt., Co. C, 1st Wis. Inf., June 30, 1916, federalized; grad. U.S.M.A., Oct. 30, 1918; 2d lt., Corps of Engrs., U.S.A. (regular), Nov. 1, 1918; 1st lt., May 13, 1919; A.E.F., June 21-Sept. 10, 1919; *m* Feb. 14, 1920, Dorothy, dau. of Omer Arnaide Cloutier; 2–Miriam, *b* Vincennes, Ind., Sept. 10, 1896; U. of N.D., '21; *m* Aug. 17, 1921, Miles K. Lander (issue: Edward King; Robert Griggs); 3–Charlotte, *b* Vincennes, Feb. 26, 1899; U. of N.D., '22; 4–Albert, *b* Seattle, Wash., Feb. 21, 1902; U. of N.D., '25; 5–Frederic, *b* Seattle, Mar. 19, 1904; U. of N.D., '30; 6–Paul, *b* Tacoma, Wash., Oct. 8, 1908, U. of N.D., '30.
1–A.B., Ind. U., '93. Education since 1893; dir. university extension, U. of N.D., since 1919 (see Who's Who in America). Mem. S.A.R., I.A.G. (council). Residence: 507 Reeves Drive, Grand Forks, N.D.

1–**YOUNG, Howard Brown,** *b* Crestline, O., July 5, 1873.
6–George **Brown** (*d* 1756), *m* Mary–;
5–William (1738-1833), *m* Mary–;
4–George (1773-1828), *m* Alice Hardesty (1770-1848);
3–Susannah (1794-1854), *m* Jacob **Young**;
2–Dr. Peter Brown (1832-1923), physician; surgeon in Civil War; *m* 1862, Sarah Margaret Gormly (1837-1906); issue: I–Willis Gormly (1863-64); II–Howard Brown (1 above).
1–*m* Sept. 5, 1903, Lucia Ella Pattison, *b* Buffalo, N.Y., July 31, 1874; dau. of Judge Albert E. Pattison, of Buffalo, N.Y., and Denver, Colo. (desc. Adam Patterson, from Ireland, 1730, settled at Coleraine, Mass.); issue: 1–Genevieve Pattison, *b* Denver, Sept. 5, 1907; U. Denver, 1928.
1–M.D., U.Denver, 1899. (Beta Theta Pi). Physician. Sumer place: Shawnee, Colo. Residence: 3856 Tejon St., Denver, Colo.

1–**YOUNG, Iva Anne Higbee (Mrs. John W.),** *b* Carversville, Bucks Co., Pa., Feb. 16, 1861.
9–Edward **Higbee,** from Eng. to Mass., ca. 1630; landholder at New London, Conn., 1647; bought a farm at Hartford from an Indian sachem, 1664; freeman, 1667; was at Huntington and Jamaica, N.H.; *m* Jedidah Skidmore (Thomas[10], *m* Ellen–);
8–Edward (*d* 1716), landholder at Middletown, Conn., 1673, and Huntington, N.Y.; went to Middletown, Monmouth Co., N.J.; *m* ca. 1684, Abigail Adams (*b* 1660; John[9] [ca. 1637/38-1670], *m* 1657, Abigail, dau. of Richard Smith, of Wethersfield, Conn., *m* Rebecca–; Jeremy[10], qv);
7–John (*d* 1715), landholder at Huntington, N.Y., and Burlington Co., N.J.; *m* 1712, Alice Andrews (Edward[8], *m* Sarah, dau. of Jacob Ong; Samuel[9]; Edward[10]);
6–Edward (*b* 1714), landholder, Gloucester (now Atlantic) Co., N.J.; *m* 1738, Jemima Risley (Richard[7], *m* Esther Conover; Peter[8], *m* Mary–; Richard[9], same as 7 below);
5–John (*b* 1739), *m* Mary Smith (*b* 1738; John[6], *m* Mary–);
4–Absalom (ca. 1761-1833), landholder, Gloucester Co.; pvt. Am. Rev.; *m* Rachel Scull (*d* post 1816; Joseph[5], Am. Rev., *m* Sarah–);
3–Joseph (1798-1867), landholder, Atlantic Co., N.J.; *m* 1823, Ann Risley;
2–Mahlon Risley (2 below).
8–Richard **Risley** (ante 1615-1648), from Eng. in the "Griffin," to Mass. with Rev. Thomas Hooker, 1633; at Hartford, Conn., 1636; participated in the adoption of the "Fundamental Order," Jan. 14, 1638;
7–Richard (*b* 1648), *m* Rebecca Adams (John[8], *m* Abigail Smith);
6–Jeremiah (1690-ante 1767), *m* Dinah Gaile (Samuel[7], *m* Mary–, widow of Peter Conover);
5–Samuel, Am. Rev.; *m* Judith Somers (Richard[6], *m* Judith Letart);
4–Richard, *m* 1801, Hannah Leeds (Daniel[5], Am. Rev.; *m* Mary Steelman; John[6]; Japheth[7]; Daniel[8]; Thomas[9]);
3–Ann (*b* 1802), *m* Joseph **Higbee** (3 above).
8–Thomas **Walmsley,** to Pa. with William Penn in the "Welcome," 1682; *m* Elizabeth Rudd;
7–Thomas, *m* Mary Paxson;
6–Mary (*d* 1754), *m* ca. 1720, John **Worthington** (*d* 1777), settled in Montgomery Co., Pa., 1705;
5–Thomas (1726-98), settled at Churchville, Pa.; *m* Hannah Duncan;
4–John (*b* 1753), farmer nr. Carversville; *m* Hannah Pugh;
3–Joseph Pugh (1796-1860), *m* ca. 1832, Ann Eliza Engles (1812-90);
2–Mary Ellen (2 below).
11–Henry **Howland** (qv);
10–Abigail (*d* 1692), *m* 1658, John **Young** (*d* 1690), had a grant of land at Salem, 1638;
9–Abigail (1660-1715), *m* 1683, Stephen **Twining,** of Eastham, Mass. (William[10], *m* Elizabeth, dau. of Stephen Deane, came to Plymouth in the "Fortune," 1621);
8–Stephen (1684-1772), large landowner, Newtown, Pa.; *m* 1709, Margaret Mitchell (1685-1784; Henry[9], *m* Elizabeth [Fowes] Foulds);
7–Elizabeth (1712-44), *m* 1730, Isaac **Kirk** (1703-ca. 1781; John[8], from Eng., settled in Delaware Co., Pa., 1687);
6–Margaret (1739-ca. 1781), *m* 1760, John **Scarborough** (1734-1813; Robert[7], *m* Elizabeth–; John[8]; John[9]);
5–Rachel (1765-1848), *m* Ajax **Osmond** (*b* 1768; John[6], *m* Miriam–);
4–Margaret (1793-1862), *m* Michael **Engles,** of Phila.;
3–Ann Eliza (1812-90), *m* 1832, Joseph P. **Worthington** (3 above);
2–Mary Ellen (1834-1915), *m* 1856, Mahlon Risley **Higbee** (1825-78), Mercer Co., Ill., 1856; went to Calif. twice during gold rush; landowner; issue: I–Ida M. (1859-1908); II–Iva A. (1 above); III–Richard Risley (*b* and *d* 1864).
1–*m* as his 2d wife, June 30, 1920, John Whalen Young, *b* Princeton, Ill., Oct. 13, 1858; son of James A. Young, *m* Delcinia Weller.
1–Grad. Northern Ill. Coll.; attended State U., Normal, Ill. Teacher in graded schools of Ill. more than 25 yrs., pensioned, 1915. Mem. D.A.R., P.E.O. Residence: 1305 30th St., Rock Island, Ill.

1-**ZEITLER, Josephine Ashford Cortner (Mrs. Henry B.),** *b* Courtland, Ala., Sept. 6, 1895.
6-William **Michie,** of Albemarle Co., Va.; "signer"; corpl. Am. Rev.; *m* Anne Mills;
5-Sarah, *m* Robert **Clifton**;
4-Gabriella (1817-1900), *m* William F. **George** (1812-95);
3-Sarah Elizabeth (*b* 1849), *m* 1870, Matthew **Cortner** (*b* 1831), 1st lt., C.S.A.;
2-Robert George (2 below).
7-Theophilus **Hunter** (will dated 1798, recorded Wake Co., N.C., Feb. 5, 1799);
6-Edith, *m* 1786, Britain **Sanders** (will recorded Wake Co., Feb. 2, 1799);
5-Britain, commr. army accounts, 1792, Wake Co.; eligible for participation in the lottery of 1805; on record Oglethorpe Co., Ga., 1804; *d* Madison Co., Ala.;
4-William, War 1812; *m* Sarah Fox;
3-Oliver P. (*d* 1879), *m* 2d, Josephine Fletcher;
2-Clara Ashford (2 below).
11-Col. John **West** (qv), *m* Ann, dau. of Sir Francis Knollys, K.G.;
10-Col. John (1633-91), of West Point, Va.; the first English child *b* on York River; sr. justice, Colonial Gen. Ct. and burgess; *m* Unity Croshaw (Maj. Joseph[11]);
9-Anne, *m* Henry **Fox,** burgess;
8-Henry;
7-William, *m* Sarah Avent (Col. Thomas[8], of Surry Co., Va.);
6-John, *m* Celia Bonner (John[7], *m* Sarah Hicks);
5-Isaac, *m* Phada Hailey;
4-Sarah (*b* 1807), *m* William **Sanders** (4 above).
10-Benjamin **Harrison** (qv);
9-Benjamin (1645-1712/13), burgess for Surry Co., 1680-82; mem. Council from 1698 until his death; *m* Hannah– (1651-1698/99);
8-Nathaniel (1677-1727), apptd. to the Council, 1713; co. lt. of Surry and Prince George, 1715; auditor gen., 1724; *m* Mary Cary;
7-Elizabeth, *m* Rev. John **Cargill,** of Surry Co., Va.; ordained, 1707, by Bishop of London; clergyman for Colony of Va. (Rev. John[8], K.B., from Scotland to Va., 1708);
6-Capt. John (*d* 1777), mem. Com. of Safety of Sussex Co., Va.; in French and Indian War; *m* 1st, 1762, Sarah Avery (*d* 1766);
5-Elizabeth, *m* Richard **Fletcher** (John[6], Brunswick Co., Va.);
4-Nathan (*d* 1858), Morgan Co., Ala.; *m* 2d, 1837, Sarah A. Smith;
3-Josephine (*d* 1879), Grenada, Miss.; *m* Oliver P. **Sanders** (3 above);
2-Clara Ashford (*b* 1873), *m* 1893, Robert George **Cortner** (*b* 1871), cotton merchant, broker; issue: I-Carolyn (*b* 1893; *m* Wilburn Blanks Smith); II-Josephine A. (1 above); III-Robert M. (1897-1902); IV-Sanders A. (*m* Inez Teasley).
1-*m* Nov. 24, 1910, Henry Bartlett Zeitler, *b* Mooresville, Ala., June 18, 1885; Mason (32°); S.A.R.; 1st v.p. Bella Mina (Ala.) Bank; son of Andrew J. Zeitler, of Mooresville; issue: 1-Anne Cortner, *b* Decatur, Ala., Nov. 15, 1913; grad. Salem Acad.; student Randolph-Macon Woman's Coll. Kappa Delta); 2-Carolyn Cortner, *b* Decatur, Ala., July 23, 1919.
1-Mem. O.C., C.D.A., D.A.R., Ala. Hist. Soc. Presbyterian. Democrat. Residence: Mooresville, Ala.

1-**ZUG, Nellie Louise Austin (Mrs. Robert M.),** *b* Suffield, Conn., May 4, 1853.
9-Thomas **Kent** (qv);
8-Samuel (*d* 1691), from Eng.; *m* 1654, Frances Woodall;
7-Samuel (1661-1740), *m* 3 times, 1st, 1683, Priscilla Hunter;
6-Samuel (1684-1772), *m* 1710, Hester Phelps;
5-Amos (*b* 1713), of Suffield; *m* 1st, 1743, Sarah Austin;
4-Amos (1744-post 1800), *m* 1st, 1773, Lydia Bush;
3-Lydia (1776-1868), *m* 1803, Gustavus **Austin** (1764-1855), see Vol. III, p. 67;
2-Thomas Jefferson (1804-91), schoolmaster and farmer, Suffield, Conn.; *m* 1847, Charlotte Louise Hayden (1824-1900); see Vol. III, p. 67, for issue.
1-*m* Oct. 4, 1893, Robert Morse Zug, *b* Detroit, Mich., Nov. 7, 1851; son of Samuel Zug, of Detroit.
1-Ed. Conn Literary Inst., Suffield. Mem. D.B.R., Noble Order of the Garter, S.M.D., S.D.P., D.F.P.A., C.D.A., H.S.S.C., D.A.C., D.C.W., D.A.R., Order LaFayette, U.S.D. 1812, Daus. of the Union, 1861-65, Colony of N.E. Women. Clubs: Women's Athletic (Los Angeles), Pacific Coast (Long Beach). Residence: Pacific Coast Club, Long Beach, Calif.

ABRAHAM ZUNDEL (1836-1917).

1-**ZUNDEL, George Lorenzo Ingram,** *b* Brigham City, Utah, Dec. 23, 1885.
4-Johann Eberhard **Zundel** (1761-1819; son of Johannes [1719-98], of Wurttemburg, Germany, who *m* 2d, Maria Catherine Glos); came from Germany, 1805; settled with family at Economy, Butler Co., Pa., under leadership of Georg Rapp, with whom they had fled from religious persecution; removed to New Harmony, Ind., where he *d*; widow and family returned to found Economy, Beaver Co., Pa., with Rapp's Harmony Soc.; *m* 1787, Julia Ann Pflueger (1764-1815);
3-Jacob (1796-1880), from Germany with parents; withdrew from Harmony Soc. at Economy, Pa., and helped to form the New Philadelphian Soc. which bought the village of Phillipsburg (now Monaca), Beaver Co., Pa.; this soc. soon disbanded and 1836, he and family joined the Latter Day Saints and went from Kirtland, O., to Nauvoo, Ill., and finally removed to Salt Lake Valley; *m* ca. 1833, Sara Forstner (1809-98; Johann Georg[4] [*b* 1771], to America, 1805, *m* Anna Maria [*b* 1770], dau. Johannes Zoll, *m* Anna Maria Stearla);
2-Abraham (2 below).
4-Samuel **Ingram** (1779-1843), of Eng.; *m* Kezia Coggins (1800-92), she came to America with 2 children;
3-James (1833-1913), from Eng., 1851 with his mother and sister, Mary Ann; landed New Orleans, La.; removed to Brigham City, Box Elder Co., Utah; *m* 1858, Charlotte Holland (1839-1916; John[4] [1808-94], early convert to Latter Day Saints in Eng., came to America, 1860, and settled in Salt Lake Valley, *m* Ann King [*b* 1805], dau. of John Renall);
2-Mary Ellenor (1866-*d* Oakland, Calif., Apr. 19, 1930), of Brigham City, Utah; *m* as his 2d wife, 1884, Abraham **Zundel** (1836-1917), *b* Phillipsburg (now Monaca), Pa., and went with parents to Salt Lake Valley; is said to have been first man to use water for irrigation in present state of Idaho; mem. of party sent to colonize Limhi, in Salmon River Valley, Idaho, and carried mail by pony express from Limhi to Salt Lake City; mem. Utah State Constl. Conv., and was elected state senator to first Utah Legislature; mayor of Willard, Utah, 1901-02; bishop of Willard Ward, Ch. of Jesus Christ of Latter Day Saints (see portrait); issue: I-George Lorenzo Ingram

(1 above); II–Fanny Louise (1890-1901); III–Ruth (1893-94); IV–Mary Ellenor (*b* 1894; *m* William J. Glover); V–Assenath (1897-1906); VI–Oliver (*d* infancy); VII–Theodore Roosevelt (*d* infancy).
1–*m* Sept. 14, 1910, Rose Mae Bell, *b* Logan, Cache Co., Utah, June 18, 1886; dau. of Eli Bell (1834-95), *m* Louisa Ann McClellan (1840-1916); 1–adopted son, Robert Clayburn, *b* Mar. 20, 1924.
1–B.S., Utah Agrl. Coll., '11; M.S., Cornell, 1915; Ph.D., Yale, 1929. Instr. botany and horticulture, Utah Agrl. Coll., 1911-12; instr., Box Elder H.S., Brigham City, 1912-13; asst. prof. biology, Brigham Young Coll., 1915-17; asst. pathologist, U.S. Dept. Agr., in charge cereal disease control for state of Wash., 1917-19; extension plant pathologist, Wash. State Coll., 1919-26; asst. botanist to Dr. G. P. Clinton, Conn. Agrl. Experiment Sta., New Haven, Conn., 1926-28; now asst. prof. plant pathology, Pa. State Coll. Residence: 304 S. 1st West St., Brigham City, Utah. Address: Pa. State Coll., State College, Pa.

1–**ALLEN, Elizabeth Orvis,** *b* Oshkosh, Wis., July 17, 1901.
9–Thomas **Sayre** (qv);
8–Francis, of Southampton, L.I.; *m* Sarah Wheeler; and thru his g.son;
6–Joshua (*d* 1806);
5–Paul (*b* 1760), Southampton, *m* 1784, Mary Halsey;
4–Hannah (1801-68), *m* 1826, Dr. Charles **Orvis** (1796-1858), War 1812;
3–Eliza S. (1840-1903), *m* Timothy Rush **Allen** (1843-1910);
2–Silas Marsh (2 below).
10–Thomas **Halsey** (qv);
9–Thomas (ca. 1627-1697), of Southampton, *m* Mary–;
8–David (1662-1731), *m* Hannah–;
7–Abram (1685-1759), *m* Amy Halsey (Daniel[8]);
6–David (1722-1805), *m* Mary Cooper;
5–Mary (*b* 1764), *m* Paul **Sayre** (5 above).
2–Silas Marsh **Allen** (*b* 1867), *m* 1895, F. Isabelle Strong (*b* 1867); see Vol. III, p. 27; issue: I–Marjorie Strong (Mrs. William J. Montgomery, qv); II–Elizabeth Orvis (1 above).
1–U.Wis., 1926. Mem. S.D.P., D.A.R., Daus. G.A.R., etc. Presbyterian. Residence: 73 Fulton St., Oshkosh, Wis.

1–**MONTGOMERY, Marjorie Strong Allen (Mrs. William J.),** *b* Oshkosh, Wis., Feb. 8, 1897.
9–James **Allen** (qv);
8–Joseph (1652-1703), of Medfield, Mass.; *m* 1673, Hannah Sabine (1654-1730; William[9]);
7–Nehemiah (1699-1785), *m* Mary Parker (*d* 1785);
6–Timothy (1744-1813), of Dedham; soldier in Am. Rev.; present at Battle of Lexington; *m* 1768, Hannah Moffit (1748-1813);
5–Col. Timothy (bet. 1788-90-post 1855), of Sturbridge, Mass., and Brookfield, N.Y.; *m* 1812, Clarissa Marsh (1789-1846);
4–Silas Marsh (1813-59), of Allenville, Wis.; *m* Phoebe Louise King (1817-1901; David[5], *m* Phebe, dau. of David Bunce);
3–Timothy Rush (1843-1910), of Allenville; *m* 1864, Eliza S. Orvis;
2–Silas Marsh (2 below).
9–George **Orvis** (qv);
8–Samuel (1653-post 1709), of Farmington, Conn.; *m* Deborah–;
7–Samuel (1685-1734), soldier in colonial wars; *m* 1707, Rachel Andrus (1686-post 1738; Abraham[8], of Waterbury, *m* Rebecca, dau. of John Carrington);
6–William (1710-74), *m* 2d, 1750, Martha (Severance) Burt (*d* 1754);
5–Gershom (1754-1824), Am. Rev.; *m* 1776, Asenath Parmenter (1757-1840; Jason[6], Am. Rev., *m* Abigail Frazzell);
4–Dr. Charles (1796-1858), *m* Hannah Sayre;
3–Eliza S. (1840-1903), *m* Timothy Rush **Allen** (3 above);
2–Silas Marsh (*b* 1867), *m* F. Isabelle Strong (*b* 1867); see Vol. III, p. 27; issue: I–Marjorie Strong (1 above); II–Elizabeth Orvis (qv for other lineages).
1–*m* Oct. 8, 1927, William J., son of Rev. Andrew J. Montgomery, D.D., of Mt. Vernon, N.Y.
1–U.Wis., 1921. Technician, Camp Pike, World War. Mem. A.A.U.W. Residence: 110 Elvin Av., Hamilton, O.

1–**ANDERSON, Clifford LeConte,** *b* Macon, Ga., July 7, 1862.
4–William Henry **Anderson,** from Scotland, settled in northern Va.;
3–Hezekiah, *m* Martha Robertson;
2–Clifford (2 below).
7–Guillaume **Le Conte** (qv);
6–Pierre (1704-68), physician in N.J.; *m* 2d, Valeria Eatton;
5–John Eatton (1739-1822), *m* Jane Sloan;
4–Louis (1782-1838), scientist and planter in Ga.; *m* Anne Quarterman (among their sons were John, 3d pres. U.Calif., and Joseph, distinguished scientist);
3–William (1812-41), *m* Sarah A. Nisbet;
2–Anna (1836-1922), *m* Jan. 13, 1857, Judge Clifford **Anderson** (1833-99), many yrs. atty. gen. of Ga.; prof. of law, Mercer U. (his sister Mary, was the mother of Sidney Lanier, distinguished poet and musician; see Vol. I, p. 193); for issue see Vol. I, p. 418.
1–*m* Sept. 10, 1884, Kittie, dau. Wilson J. Van Ryke, Minneapolis, Minn.; issue: 1–Adora, *b* Atlanta, Ga., Dec. 10, 1888; Agnes Scot Coll., '06; *m* Apr. 20, 1910, John Gelzer, Jr.; 2–Clifford Van Dyke, *b* Atlanta, May 11, 1891; U.Ga., '11; served on Mexican border with 5th Inf., Ga. N.G., 1916; 2d lt., 1916; 1st lt., 1917; with 1st M.G. Co., 122d Regt., 31st Div., in France, Sept. 1918-June 1919.
1–*m* 2d, Apr. 30, 1910, Mary Alice, dau. Andrew Jackson Van der Grift, Greenville, S.C.; issue: 1–Jackson Van der Grift, *b* New York, N. Y., July 20, 1911.
1–A.B., Mercer, '80, LL.B., 1883. Sr. mem. law firm Anderson & Rountree, Atlanta, Ga. Served in N.G. Ga., 1883-1912, retired, Oct. 1912, with rank of brig. gen. Mem. Ga. Council of Defense, 1917-18 (see Who's Who in America). Hobby: Collector of books; has a large library of best literature, largely in special editions, probably largest private library in South. Mem. I.A.G.; pres. Atlanta Geneal. Soc., 1930–. Clubs: Capital City, City, Lawyers (Atlanta), Army and Navy (New York). Residence: Atholl, 3703 Peachtree Road, Atlanta, Ga.

1–**ANDREWS, Hardage Lane, Jr.,** *b* Boonville, Mo., Oct. 25, 1889.
10–John **Wilson** (1630-90), from Scotland (?), 1656, settled in Anne Arundel Co., Md.; *m* 1663 (?);
9–John (1665-1702), planter and landowner; *m* 1688, Margaret–;
8–William (1690-1753), Harford Co., Md.; Quaker; *m* 1715, Rachel Child;
7–William (1716-80), *m* 1740, Cassendra Gover (1712-80);
6–Samuel (1743-1802), *m* 1765, Mary Lee (1730-1800);
5–William Lee (1770-1836), *m* 1798, Sarah Chew Lee;
4–Mary Lee (1799-1871), Baltimore, *m* 1815, William **Sharpe** (1788-1821), War 1812 (John[5], maj. Am. Rev., *m* Martha Young; John[6], killed in Indian wars, *m* Jemima, dau. James Alexander; James[7], from Scotland to Lancaster Co., Pa.);
3–Martha Caroline (1819-88), of Ala. and Tenn.; *m* 1837, as his 2d wife, Thomas Jefferson **Dobyns** (1801-65), lawyer; col. in C.S.A. (Thomas[4], War 1812; Edward[5], from Eng. to Culpeper Co., Va., Am. Rev., settled in Mason Co., Ky., *m* Frances Kaye);
2–Jennie (2 below).
11–John **Chew** (qv);
10–Col. Samuel (1625-77), of Va., and Anne Arundel Co., Md.; high sheriff, burgess, judge; *m* 1655 (?), Anne Ayers (1635-95);
9–Samuel (1660-1718), *m* 1682, Anne– (*d* 1702);
8–John (1687-1718), *m* 1708, Elizabeth Harrison (Richard[9], *m* Eliza Smith);
7–Sarah (1713-60), *m* 1732, Charles **Worthington** (1701-73), of Harford Co., Md.;
6–Sarah Chew (1746-post 1803), Quaker; *m* 1765, Josiah **Lee** (*b* 1741);
5–Sarah Chew (1778-1841), of Harford Co.; *m* 1798, William L. **Wilson** (5 above);
4–Mary L., *m* William **Sharpe** (4 above);
3–Martha C., *m* Thomas J. **Dobyns** (3 above);
2–Jennie (1853-1925); see Vol. I, p. 423; *m* 1880, Charles Edward **Andrews** (1849-1917; David J.[3] [1809-93], *m* 1833, Margaret Baird, 1818-1901).
1–*m* Jan. 12, 1917, Mittie Stephens Huff, *b* Marshall, Mo., Mar. 15, 1892; dau. of J. S. M.

Huff, of Kansas City; issue: 1–John Hampton, *b* Schenectady, N.Y., May 19, 1924; 2–Hardage Lane, III, *b* Schenectady, Apr. 26, 1921.
1–B.S. in E.E., U.Mo. With Gen. Electric Co., 1910–, and as chief engr. transportation dept., 1929–. Clubs: Railroad (New York), Mohawk (Schenectady), Erie, Kahkwa, Hunters Lodge (Erie). Residence: 439 Arlington Rd., Erie, Pa.

1–**ARCHER, Shreve Maclaren,** *b* Yankton, S.D., Sept. 29, 1888.
5–John **Archer** (*b* July 13, 1764), who went from Phila., Pa., to Montgomery Co., O., ca. 1798; *m* Sarah Rockhill (widow of James Craft);
4–John (*b* Oct. 6, 1789), *m* 1813, Sarah Bailey;
3–William Shreve (*b* Dec. 23, 1823), mfr. of linseed oil; served in 131st Ohio Regt.; *m* Oct. 12, 1847, Sarah Jane Mixer;
2–George Alfred (2 below).
10–Thomas (Sheriff) **Shreve** (*d* 1675), Plymouth, Mass., 1642; *d* Portsmouth, R.I.; *m* Martha–;
9–Caleb (1652-1740), changed name to Shreve; *m* 1680; Sarah Areson (Diedrick[10], from Amsterdam to Flushing, L.I.);
8–Benjamin (*b* 1706), *m* 1729, Rebecca French;
7–William (1737-1812), 1st maj., 1st Regt., Burlington Co., N.J., Militia, 1776, lt. col., 1777, col., 1778; *m* 1756, Anna Ivins;
6–Jeremiah Warden (*b* 1757), *m* 1775, Sarah Beck;
5–Rebekah (*b* 1776), *m* 1791, John **Bailey,** of nr. Natural Bridge, Va.;
4–Sarah (*b* 1796), *m* John **Archer** (4 above).
5–Col. James **Cunningham** (g.son of James Cunningham, Scotchman who came from Ireland, 1718); prominent in organizing the 6th Lancaster Co. Bn. and was its first maj., 1776, promoted to rank of col.; stationed at Lancaster as commr. for army supplies 1777; mem. Phila. Gen. Assembly, and later mem. Supreme Exec. Council of Pa., reelected 1782 and 1783; went to Ky., 1784, and with friends built their log cabins, 1785, about 20 miles back of the present town of Covington; moved to Beargrass Creek, Jefferson Co., Ky.; moved to Losantiville (now Cincinnati), O., 1789; *m* 1787, Jeanette Park;
4–Robert, *m* Abigail Williams (Miles[5]);
3–James F. (1810-70), of Glendale, O.; *m* 1846, Harriett Harkness;
2–Harriett Harkness (2 below).
8–Christoffel **Hooglandt** (*b* 1634), from Holland; *m* Catrina Cregier;
7–Christopher (bap. 1669), *m* 1695, Sarah Tallet;
6–Martin (*b* 1704), *m* 1732, Phoebe Van Winkle;
5–Christopher (*b* 1742), *m* 1773, Fannie Gordon;
4–Mary (*b* 1800), *m* 1817, Anthony **Harkness**;
3–Harriet (1817-70), *m* 1846, James Findlay **Cunningham** (3 above);
2–Harriet Harkness (*b* 1855), see Vol. II, p. 72; *m* 1884, George Alfred **Archer** (*b* 1850), see Vol. II, p. 72, and Vol. III, p. 588.
1–*m* Sept. 26, 1912, Doris Cowley, *b* White Bear Lake, Minn., June 26, 1892; dau. of Augustus M. P. Cowley; issue (all *b* St. Paul, Minn.): 1–Helen Harriet, *b* July 4, 1913; 2–Georganna, *b* Nov. 16, 1914; 3–Barbara, *b* May 15, 1917; 4–Doris Leslie, *b* July 5, 1921; 5–Shreve McLaren, *b* Dec. 27, 1922.
1–Yale-S., '10. Pres. Archer-Daniels-Midland Co., mfrs. of linseed and other vegetable oils, 1930; dir. St. Paul Fire & Marine Ins. Co., First Nat. Bank, First Bank Corpn. (St. Paul), Northwestern Nat. Bank, Northwest Bancorporation (Minneapolis). Capt., Co. B, 6th Minn. N.G., 1917. Clubs: Minnesota, Minneapolis, University, White Bear Yacht. Residence: 990 Summit Ave., St. Paul, Minn.

1–**ASH, Gordon Monges,** *b* Phila., Pa., Oct. 17, 1869.
7–Tobias **Leech** (1651-1726), from Eng. to Phila., 1682; mem. Pa. Assembly, 1713-19; founder of Trinity P.E.Ch., Oxford, Pa., 1698; *m* 1679, Hester Ashmead (1659-1727; John[8]);
6–John (1683-1745), *m* Mary Harrison;
5–Rebecca (1726-1803), *m* 1749, Capt. Henry **Ash** (*d* 1761), from Ireland to Phila., ante 1749, of "Ashbrook";
4–Col. James (1749-1830), see portrait; *m* 2d, 1804, Rachel (Morgan) Douglass;
3–Dr. Thomas Forrest (1806-38), M.D., U.Pa., 1827; *m* 1831, Mary Reeves (1810-76; Thomas[4], of Phila.; desc. Biddle Reeves [*d* 1789], and Walter Reeves [*d* 1698], from Eng. to N.J., 1681);
2–Thomas Reeves (2 below).
7–Thomas **Morgan** (1659-1746), of royal descent, from Wales to Pa., ante 1720, founder of Morgantown, Pa.; *m* Elizabeth–;
6–Col. Jacob, Sr. (1716-92), capt. French and Indian War; judge Berks Co., Pa., 1769-77; mem. Supreme Exec. Council of Pa., 1777-78; col. Am. Rev.;
5–Gen. Jacob, Jr. (1742-1802), see portrait; *m* 1763, Barbara (Lesher) Jenkins (Capt. John Lesher[6], 1711-94);
4–Rachel (1772-1817), *m* 2d, Col. James **Ash** (4 above).
8–William **Matlack** (1648-aet. ca. 90), from Eng. to N.J., 1677, in the "Kent," *m* 1682, Mary Hancock (1664-1728), from Eng., 1681, in the "Paradise";
7–Timothy (1695-1752), from Pensauken, to Haddonfield, N.J., 1726; a Quaker; *m* 1720, Mary Haines; *m* 2d, 1730, Martha Burr (Henry[8], *m* Elizabeth–), widow of Josiah Haines;
6–Col. and Hon. Timothy (1730-1829), see portrait; *m* 1758, Ellen Yarnall;
5–Martha (1770-1826), *m* 1785, Guy **Bryan** (1755-1829), of Phila.; pres. Am. Fire Ins. Co.; dir. 2d U.S. Bank (William[6], from Eng. to Bucks Co., Pa., *m* Rebecca–);
4–Ellen Matlack (1785-1826), *m* 2d, 1806, John **Harland,** Jr. (1782-1863; John[5] [1753-1828], from Eng. to Phila., *m* Jane Newland, 1751-1835);
3–Charles Deighton (1807-35), *m* 1828, Delphine B. Pease (1807-79);
2–Ellen Margaretta (2 below).
8–Hon. Francis **Yarnall** (1660-1721), from Eng., 1684, to Pa.; mem. Provincial Assembly; *m* 1686, Hannah Baker (Joseph[9], from Eng. to Pa., mem. Provincial Assembly, founder of Edgemont, Pa., *m* Mary–);
7–Rev. Mordecai (1705-72), minister Society of Friends; *m* 1st, 1733, Catharine Meredith (*d* 1741);
6–Ellen (1736-91), *m* Timothy **Matlack** (6 above).
2–Ellen Margaretta Harland (1835-1913), *m* 1857, Thomas Reeves **Ash** (1833-1906), banker, Phila. (for issue see Vol. I, p. 429).
1–*m* Nov. 15, 1913, Jeannie Morrison Drill, *b* Knoxville (Merryland Tract), Frederick Co., Md., Feb. 3, 1873; mem. Order LaFayette; hon. mem. Imperial Order Yellow Rose; dau. of Henry Clay Drill, Frederick, Md.
1–Princeton, ex-1890. Writer. Mem. S.C.W., Imperial Order Yellow Rose, Knights Golden Horseshoe, Scions Colonial Cavaliers, Order LaFayette (chevalier cdr. general for the U.S.), Order Washington, S.A.R., S.R., Nat. Geneal. Soc., George Washington-Sulgrave Instn.; founder-mem. Institute of American Genealogy (council); past chmn. for Frederick Co., Md., Nat. Patriotic Council; herald, Soc. Desc. of Knights of Most Noble Order of the Garter; 1st v.p. gen. Desc. Signers of the Secret Pact, etc. Mason (32°, K.T.). Mem. Bachelors Cotillion (Washington). A founder the First Naval Bn. of Pa. Residence: "White Oak Springs Farm," Frederick, Md.

1–**ASHBAUGH, Robert Frederick,** *b* Galion, O., Oct. 25, 1854.= d Jan 8, 1933.
5–John **Sells** (ante 1720-1781), Am. Rev., killed in battle at Yorktown, Va.; *m* 1742, Sally Haak;
4–Ludwick (1743-1833), Am. Rev.; mem. Pa. Assembly, 1780; coronor, 1788; *m* 1771, Catherine Deardorff (1749-1828; Abraham[5], Am. Rev.);
3–Sophia (1784-1847), *m* 1806, John **Ashbaugh** (1782-1853);
2–Frederick (2 below).
8–Daniel **Clark** (qv):
7–Daniel (1654-ante 1746), locksmith, Hartford, Conn., until 1710: removed to Colchester; served in one Indian war; enlisted in expdn. to Louisburg just prior to his death; *m* 1678, Hannah Pratt (Daniel[8], *m* Hannah–; John[9], qv);
6–Aaron (bap. 1687-1744), weaver, Mansfield, Conn.; prominent in colonial affairs; *m* 1711, Susanna Wade (Robert[7], *m* Abigail, dau. Jonathan Royce, *m* Deborah, dau. Hugh Caulkins, qv);
5–Israel (1734-1811), pvt. Indian wars, 1760,61,62; prominent in Mansfield; settled finally at Chaplin, 1810; *m* Esther Wilson (*b* 1738; Joseph[6], *m* Abigail Bugbee);
4–Israel (1757-1827), Am. Rev., 1775-83, pensioned

for services, 1818; settled in Delaware Co., O., 1802 or 03; large landowner, Delaware and Marion cos.; *m* 2d, ca. 1787, Mary Kendall (*d* ante 1810; Isaac[5], Am. Rev., *m* Mary Russell);
3–Harvey (1797-1873), Ashford, Conn.; prominent agriculturist and stock dealer at Marion, O.; capt. of militia; *m* 1820, Nancy Travis (1804-88; Robert[4], *m* Eleanore Grace);
2–Matilda (1821-70), *m* 1836, Frederick **Ashbaugh,** M.D. (1807-77), grad. Botanic Med. College, '41; issue: I–Orrilla Mirium (*d* infancy); II–Oliver Marion (*d* infancy); III–Orrin Milton (*m* Chloie Courtright); IV–Nancy Sophia (*d* infancy); V–John Harvey (*m* Ora Tabor; *m* 2d, Clara Wilson); VI–Enoch Clark (*m* Josephine Latham); VII–Ellen Almira (*m* H. H. Arnold; *m* 2d, Berry Stewart); VIII–Robert Frederick (1 above); IX–Adella Matilda (*m* William Christy); X–Olive Laura (*m* Leslie McKitrick).
1–*m* June 17, 1886, Osta Ina Poling (qv for issue).
1–Ed. Normal School, Valparaiso, Ind., and Ada, O. Mason contractor. Mem. S.A.R., S.A.W. Mason, I.O.O.F. Baptist. Residence: 220 N. Jefferson St., Sigourney, Ia.

1–**ASHBAUGH, Osta Ina Poling (Mrs. Robert F.),** *b* Union Co., O., Dec. 11, 1864.
4–Samuel **Poling** (1767-1854), Randolph Co., Va.; *m* 1786, Sarah– (1767-1863);
3–James (1806-93), farmer, Marysville, O.; *m* 1831, Mary Carpenter;
2–Cyrus (2 below).
5–John **Hill** (1759-1839), large landowner in Randolph Co., Va.; Am. Rev.; *m* 1782, Barbara–;
4–Catherine (1783-1855), *m* 1809, Solomon **Carpenter** (1784-1837);
3–Mary (1811-81), *m* 1831, James **Poling** (3 above).
5–Simon **Hornbeck** (1730-1800; desc. Warnaar [Hoornbeeck], from Holland, 1661, settled at Wiltwyck, later Kingston, N.Y., *m* 1670, Anna de Hooges, *m* 2d, 1692, Margarita Ten Eyck); was of Hampshire Co., Va., 1784; went with Daniel Boone to Bourbon Co., Ky.; *m* Margaret Alkire;
4–Michael (1774-1830), Pickaway Co., O.; instructer; *m* 1801 or 02, Sarah Phillips (*d* 1833; aet. 52 yrs.; dau. of Cdr. Phillips of British Army);
3–Dorothy (1813-85), *m* 1839, Elisha Mitchel **Wheeler** (1813-62), served in Civil War, aet. 48, Co. F, 31st Ohio Vol. Inf. (John[4], Am. Rev., *m* Tabitha Warrington);
2–Samantha Jane (1843-1929), *m* 1860, Cyrus **Poling** (1836-98), of Hayden, Ind.; farmer; issue: I–Reuben Frederick (1863-1922; *m* Bessie Gordon); II–Osta Ina (1 above); III–Frenchie Lawrence (*d* infancy).
1–*m* June 17, 1886, Robert Frederick Ashbaugh (qv); issue: 1–Lura Gertrude (Dec. 28, 1888-Oct. 24, 1895).
1–Trustee, Sigourney (Ia.) Public Library since 1914 (sec. of the bd. since 1921). Mem. D.A.R., Iowa State Hist. Soc. Baptist. Republican. Clubs: Sigourney Woman's, Delphian, Chautauqua Circle. Residence: 220 N. Jefferson St., Sigourney, Ia.

1–**AUGIR, Viola Juliet,** *b* McHenry, Ill., Nov. 6, 1855.
7–Robert (Augur) **Augir** (*b* in Eng.; son of John, *m* Ann); came from Eng., 1668, settled at New Haven, Conn.; *m* 1673, Mary Guilbert (1651-1731; Dep.Gov. Mathew[8], *m* Jane–);
6–John (1686-1726), shoemaker; *m* 1710, Elizabeth Bradley (Isaac[7], from Eng. to Conn., *m* Elizabeth–);
5–John (ca. 1716-1804), mem. North Branford Congl. Ch., 1780; *m* 1744, Rachel Barnes (*d* 1805);
4–John (1748-1827), served at Lexington Alarm; *m* 1st, 1776, Dinah Page (1752-95; Daniel[5], *m* Dinah, dau. of Israel Baldwin; Daniel[6]);
3–Dea. Robert (1785-1862), began to write name Augir; moved to Racine Co., Wis., 1839; bought 280 acres at East Troy, Wis.; chmn. School Board; dea. Free Baptist Ch.; *m* 1805, Abigail Hough (1786-1862; Zephaniah[4], *m* Sabra Smith);
2–Franklin Page (2 below).
8–Joseph **Bixby** (qv);
7–Benjamin (1650-1727), *m* Mary–;
6–Nathan;
5–Solomon;
4–Ichabod;
3–Ebenezer (1782-1868), *m* Hannah Flint (1784-1863; James[4], *m* Jerusha Lillie);
2–Lavinia Lillie (1821-1909), *m* Franklin Page **Augir** (1818-93), clergyman Free Baptist Ch.; issue: I–Arvilla Leila (1848-71); II–Newell Galusha (1849-1918); III–Emmer Estella (1851-71); IV–Wayland Bixby (1853-1926); V–Viola Juliet (1 above); VI–Lillie Felicia (1857-1910; *m* 1881, Arthur Stewart Van de Mark); VII–Edmund Fairfield (*b* 1858; *m* 1884, Ella Van Aken).
1–Ph.B., Hillsdale (Mich.) Coll., '81 (Kappa Kappa Gamma). Woman's dept., Mutual Life Inst. of N.Y., at Phila., 1898-1908; real estate operator, Brooklyn, N.Y., and Morrisville, Pa., 1908-24; retired. Mem. bd. of women's commrs., Hillsdale Coll. Baptist. Residence: 1818 Montrose St., Los Angeles, Calif.

1–**BAKER, Horace Henry,** *b* Buckley, Ill., Apr. 14, 1884.
11–Thomas **Blakeslee** (ca. 1615-1674), from Eng. in the "Hopewell," 1635; settled at Boston, *m* 1644, Susanna Ball;
10–Aaron (1644-99), at New Haven, Conn., 1677; *m* 1665, Mary Dodd (bap. 1651; Daniel[11], at Branford, Conn., 1644, *m* 1646, Mary–);
9–Ebenezer (*b* 1677), mem. Episcopal Ch.; New Haven;
8–Capt. Thomas (1700-78), first capt. in Northbury Soc.; *m* Mary– (*d* 1792);
7–David (1722-81), Woodbury, Conn., 1753; Am. Rev.; *m* 2d, 1752, Abigail Howe (1723-92; Jonathan[8], *m* Sarah Hapgood; Capt. Daniel[9]; Abraham[10]);
6–Eli (1753-1826), *m* 1773, Lettice Curtis;
5–Charles (1778-1856), *m* 1802, Elizabeth Smith;
4–Jacob Smith (1811-53), *m* 1831, Esther Parmelee;
3–Angeline A. (1836-1913), *m* 1856, Horace **Lincoln** (1820-85; Leonard[4]);
2–Julia Emogene (2 below).
11–Richard **Curtis** (1611-81), from Eng., settled at Dorchester, Mass., and later at Wallingford; *m* 1st, 1642, Elizabeth–; *m* 2d, 1657, Sarah– (widow of John Strange);
10–Isaac (1658-1712), *m* 1682, Sarah Foote (*b* 1662; Robert[11]; Nathaniel[12], qv);
9–Isaac (*b* 1683), *m* 1st, 1706, Abigail Tuttle (Simon[10]; William[11], qv);
8–Lt. Daniel (1707-50), *m* 1727, Lettice Ward;
7–Ebenezer (*b* 1728), *m* 1751 or 52, Annise Warner (*b* 1734 or 35; Ens. John[8]; Dr. Ephraim[9]; Dr. John[10]; John[11], qv);
6–Lettice (1756-1839), *m* 1773, Eli **Blakeslee** (6 above).
17–Thomas **Sherman** (1420-93), Suffolk Co., Eng.; *m* Agnes–;
16–John (*d* 1504), *m* Agnes, dau. Thomas Fuller;
15–Thomas (1490-1551), "Gentleman"; *m* Jane (*d* 1572), dau. of John Waller;
14–Henry (1520-90), *m* Agnes– (*d* 1580);
13–Edmund (1548-1600), *m* 1570, Anne Pilette (*d* 1584);
12–Edmund (1572-1641), from Eng. in the "Elizabeth," settled at Wethersfield, Conn., 1635; *m* ca. 1598, Joan Makin (Thobias[13]);
11–Hester (bap. 1606-1666), *m* Andrew **Ward** (1597-1635; Richard[12], Lord Mayor of Gorleston, Eng., *m* Anne Guiville);
10–Andrew (1645-91), *m* 1668, Tryall Meigs (1646-90; John[11]; Vincent[12], qv);
9–William (1678-1767), *m* 1701, Lettice Beach (1679-1767; John[10]; Thomas[11], qv);
8–Lettice (1711-49), *m* Lt. Daniel **Curtis** (8 above).
10–James **Smith** (*b* in Eng., will proved 1676), of Weymouth, Mass.; freeman, 1654; *m* Joanne–;
9–Nathaniel (*b* 1639), freeman, 1681; *m* Experience–;
8–Nathaniel (will probated 1725), *m* Ann Hoskins (*b* 1678; William[9], from Eng. ca. 1630, *m* Sarah Casewell);
7–Jacob, *m* Elizabeth–;
6–Lt. Jacob (1738-1807), Am. Rev.; of Northfield, Conn.; *m* Mary Lewis;
5–Elizabeth (1779-1856), *m* 1802, Charles **Blakeslee** (5 above).
11–Dea. James **Hurst** (*d* 1657), dep. Gen. Ct. in Mass.; *m* Gartend– (*d* 1670);
10–Patience (*d* 1648), *m* 1631, Henry **Cobb** (ca. 1596-1678);
9–Hannah (1639-1729 or 30), *m* 1661, Edward **Lewes** (ca. 1634-1703; George[10], removed to Barnstable, 1638, *m* Sarah Jenkin);
8–John (*b* 1666), of Barnstable, Mass.;
7–Gershom (*b* 1704);

6–Mary (1742-1823), *m* Lt. Jacob **Smith** (6 above).
10–John (Parmely, Parmele) **Parmelee** (*d* 1659), from Eng. with Rev. Henry Whitfield, 1639; *m* Hannah Bradley;
9–John (1618-1687 or 88), freeman, 1649; Guilford, Conn.; *m* 1659, Hannah Plane (*d* 1687; William[10], *m* Ann–);
8–Job (1673-1765), *m* 1699, Betsy Edwards (*d* 1761 (Thomas[9], *m* Abigail–; William[10]);
7–Thomas (1712-87), *m* 1739, Sarah Gould (1723-78; John[8], *m* Mehitable, dau. of Thomas Cooke; Benjamin[9]);
6–Reuben (1755-1813), *m* 1780, Betty Thorp;
5–Chester (1782-1852), War 1812; *m* 1805, Hadassah Mitchell (1787-1881);
4–Esther (1809-95), *m* 1831, Jacob Smith **Blakeslee** (4 above);
3–Angeline A., *m* Horace **Lincoln** (3 above);
2–Julia Emogene (1860-1919), *m* 1883, Joseph G. **Baker** (1849-1913; Henry[3] [*b* Eng., *d* 1863], of Fairport, N.Y., 1853, *d* at Ottawa, Ill., *m* in Eng., 1848, Elizabeth West, 1828-1901); issue: I–Horace Henry (1 above); II–Florence Louise (*b* 1890; *m* Ira Everett Burtis); III–Joseph Lincoln (1897-1921).
1–*m* Nov. 25, 1909, Glenna Mildred Bonar (qv); issue: 1–Frederick Bonar, *b* El Paso, Ill., Feb. 24, 1911; Morgan Park Mil. Acad., 1930.
1–Ed. Morgan Park (Ill.) Acad., '02; LL.B., U.-Mich., 1906. Lawyer. Residence: El Paso, Ill.

1–**BAKER, Glenna Mildred Bonar (Mrs. Horace H.),** *b* Panola, Ill., Apr. 28, 1884.
6–William **Bonar** (*b* in North Ireland, 1722), of Scotch parents; came to America, ca. 1739; *m* Miss Garrel, Roanoke, Va.;
5–John B. (1763 or 64-1829), Moundsville, Va., 1790; *m* Rebecca Calhoun (1765 or 66-1848);
4–James C. (1789-1858), War 1812; *m* Sarah Magers (1799 or 1800-1856; Elias[5], *m* Elizabeth Arnold);
3–John M. (1818-73), removed to Ill., 1853; *m* 1849, Celicia Jones (1829-1905; Samuel[4], *b* in Wales, came to America with his father, *m* Susanna Weigle);
2–Joseph L. (2 below).
14–Guille **Le Rossignol** (*b* ca. 1500), of Isle of Jersey; *m* Perinne Dyaume (Thomas[15]);
13–Helier (*d* ante 1600), *m* Marie Hacquoil (George[14], *m* Georgette–);
12–William (*d* ca. 1620), *m* Margaret De Carteret (George[13], *d* ca. 1620);
11–Jean (*d* 1661), *m* Rachael Le Gresley;
10–Esther (1612-72), *m* 1638, Edmund **Jean** (1597-1674);
9–Augustine Le Rossignol (1647-1719), anglicised name to John **Gustine**; served in King Philip's War; *m* 1678, Elizabeth Browne;
8–Samuel (*b* 1680), *m* 1712, Abigail Shaw (*b* 1695; Daniel[9], *m* Ruth–);
7–Amos (*b* 1726), *m* 1746, Patience Gardiner (*b* 1726);
6–William (1752-90), Am. Rev.; *m* 1773, Pricilla–(1754-1824);
5–William (1781-1868), *m* 1805, Hannah– (widow of Jacob Hipple);
4–John (1810-94), *m* 1830, Mary Childers (1809-90), to Fulton Co., Ill., 1839 (James[5], *m* Mary Anderson);
3–William (1831-65), wounded in Civil War at Dallas, Ga.; *m* 1856, Mary Elida Pritchard;
2–Harriet (2 below).
20–John **Browne**, "Esq.," of Stamford, Lincoln Co., Eng.; mayor of Stamford, 1376-77;
19–John, of Stamford;
18–John (*d* 1442), draper; alderman of Stamford, 1414; buried in All Saints Ch. which was erected at his own expense; *m* Margery– (*d* 1460);
17–John (*d* bet. 1462-70), draper; alderman; *m* Agnes– (*d* 1470);
16–Christopher (*d* 1516-18), granted coat of arms in 1480; of Stamford; *m* 1st, Agnes Bedingfield;
15–Christopher (*d* 1531-38), of Swan Hall, Hawkedon, Suffolk; estate was called "Deans" and "Swaynes"; *m* Anne–;
14–Christopher (*d* bet. 1568-74), of Swan Hall;
13–Thomas (will dated 1590), of Swan Hall; *m* Joan–;
12–John (*d* 1616), *m* Margaret–;
11–John (bap. 1601), from Eng. in the "Lion," 1632, to Boston, 1632; freeman, 1634; *m* Dorothy–;
10–John (*d* 1697), *m* 1655, Esther Makepeace (Thomas[11], qv);
9–Elizabeth (*b* 1657), *m* Augustine Le Rossignol Jean **Gustine** (9 above).
7–Elijah **Laws** (*d* ca. 1770), Culpeper Co., Va.;
6–John (1757-1840), Am. Rev.; *m* 2d, 1815, Margaret Randall;
5–William (1784-1863), *m* Sarah Robinson (1786-1825; Maximillian[6], Am. Rev., *m* Lucinda Grundy);
4–Harriet (1816-99), *m* 1833, Alexander **Pritchard** (*d* 1847), circuit rider; preacher (Benjamin[5], War 1812);
3–Mary Elida (1840-1921), *m* William **Gustine** (3 above);
2–Harriet (*b* 1862), *m* 1883, Joseph L. **Bonar** (*b* 1859); issue: I–Glenna Mildred (1 above); II–Faerie Virginia (*b* 1888; *m* Percy Henry Andrews); III–Joseph Leslie (*b* 1889; *m* Alice Clark); IV–Donald Gustine (*b* 1900).
1–*m* Nov. 25, 1909, Horace Henry Baker (qv for issue).
1–Ed. Ill. Wesleyan Coll. of Music, 1903, and U. Ill., 1906. Mem. D.A.R. Residence: El Paso, Ill.

1–**BEADLE, Christine Swalm Spofford (Mrs. Walter J.),** *b* Georgetown, Mass., Nov. 16, 1896.
9–John **Spofford** (1612-78), from Eng. to Rowley Mass., 1639; *m* Elizabeth Scott (*b* 1626);
8–John (1648-96), soldier King Philip's War; *m* 1675, Sarah Wheeler (1652-1737);
7–Capt. John (1678-1735), *m* Sarah Poor (*b* 1692);
6–Daniel (1721-1803), col. Essex Co. militia; *m* 1742, Judith Follansbee (*b* 1720); see Vol. III, p. 576, for Follansbee lineage;
5–Dr. Amos (1751-1805), *m* Irene Dole;
4–Sewell (1792-1865), *m* Elizabeth Nelson (1794-1828); see Vol. III, p. 577, for Nelson lineage;
3–George Milton (1824-1912), *m* 1852, Sarah Peabody Hood (1828-1923); see Vol. I, p. 834, for Hood lineage;
2–Charles Milton (2 below).
9–Richard **Dole** (qv);
8–Abner (1672-1740), *m* Mary Jewett (1674-95);
7–Henry (1695-1766), *m* Mary Hale (*b* 1704);
6–Moses (*b* 1740), *m* Ruth Peabody;
5–Irene (*d* May, 1826), *m* Dr. Amos **Spofford** (5 above).
2–Charles Milton **Spofford** (see Vol. I, p. 834, and Vol. III, p. 576, for other lineages), *m* 1896, Florence Corwin Swalm (*d* 1917; George A.[3], of Middletown, N.Y., *m* Eliza M., dau. of David S. Corwin).
1–*m* June 3, 1922, Walter Jay Beadle, *b* Lima, N.Y., Feb. 24, 1896; son of Clifford J. Beadle, of Rochester, N.Y.; issue (all *b* Phila., Pa.): 1–Sarah Spofford, *b* Nov. 22, 1924; 2–Spofford Jay, *b* May 12, 1928; 3–Elizabeth Ocumpaugh, *b* Oct. 10, 1929.
1–A.B., Vassar, '18. Residence: 7108 McCallum St., Mt. Airy, Philadelphia, Pa.

1–**BEAMAN, Alexander Gaylord** (*b* Alexander Gaylord Emmons, took surname of step-father, 1892), *b* West Hartford, Conn., June 23, 1885.
8–Richard **Goodman** (1632-75), killed in King William's War; *m* Mary Terry (1635-92; Stephen[8], of Windsor, Mass.);
7–Richard (1663-1730), *m* 1703, Abigail Pantry;
6–Timothy (1706-86), W. Hartford, Conn.; *m* 1735, Joanna Wadsworth (Joseph[7], *m* Joanna Hovey);
5–Richard (1748-1834), *m* Nancy Seymour (Capt. Timothy[6], *m* Lydia Kellogg);
4–Childs (1791-1866), *m* 1822, Sarah Porter;
3–Amelia Sarah (1824-1910), *m* 1843, Nodiah F. **Emmons**;
2–Alexander Franklin (1850-85), *m* 1884, Anna Gabel (she *m* 2d, George Crichton Beaman).
1–*m* Apr. 10, 1926, Adelaide Bereman Walton, *b* Los Angeles, Calif., Oct. 4, 1895; dau. of Charles Strong Walton; issue: 1–Gaylord Walton, *b* Feb. 11, 1927.
1–Grad. high school, Joliet, Ill., '01; Gregg School, Chicago. Officer and dir. various finance corpns. Editor Scottish Rite Bulletin 18 yrs.; editor Los Angeles Cdry. Bulletin 4 yrs.; mng. editor Masonic Digest, 1924-27. Mason (all bodies). Mem. S.C.W., S.R., I.A.G.; F.R.G.S.; F.A.G.S., etc. Clubs: Los Angeles Athletic, Pacific Coast, Surf and Sand, Hollywood Athletic, Santa Monica Athletic, Zamorans (gov.), Uplifters (sec.), Midnight Mission (dir., sec., treas.); hon. mem. Holly-

wood Shrine Club, Santa Fe Masonic Club, Doric Club, etc. Residence: 2284 Moreno Drive, Los Angeles, Calif.

1–**BEAN, Mary Cloud,** *b* Botetourt Co., Va., Mar. 5, 1868.
9–Rev. Charles **Grymes** (*b* 1612), had a parish in York Co., Va., 1644;
8–Maj. John (1660-1709), of "Grymesby," Middlesex Co., Va.; receiver gen., justice, vestryman; *m* Alice Townley;
7–Col. the Hon. John (1691-1748), of "Brandon," Middlesex Co.; burgess, councillor, auditor gen.; vestryman Christ Ch., 1711-48; *m* 1715, Lucy Ludwell;
6–Philip (1721-62), of "Brandon"; burgess, councillor, receiver gen. of the Colony; *m* 1742, Mary Randolph;
5–Maj. John Randolph (ca. 1746-1797), *m* in London, 1778, his 1st cousin, Susannah Beverley Randolph;
4–Mary Beverley (1782-1859), *m* 1st, Robert **West** (see Vol. III, p. 595);
3–Anna M. G. (1814-87), *m* Joseph Van Meter **Carper** (see Vol. III);
2–Ariana Williamson (2 below).
11–Augustine **Warner** (qv);
10–Augustine (1642-81), of "Warner Hall," Gloucester Co., Va.; *m* ca. 1665, Mildred Reade (George[11], qv, *m* Elizabeth, dau. of Nicholas Marteau, qv); their dau. Mildred, *m* Lawrence Washington and became the g.mother of George Washington;
9–Sarah, *m* Lawrence **Townley**;
8–Alice, *m* John **Grymes** (8 above).
10–Thomas **Ludwell,** of Eng.; *m* Jane Cottington (James[11], of Bruton Parish, Eng.; Philip[12], of Godminster, Somerset);
9–Philip (qv);
8–Philip, *m* Hannah Harrison (Benjamin[9], of Wakefield, the first home in Va. of the Harrisons);
7–Lucy, *b* at "Rich Neck"; *m* Col. John **Grymes** (7 above).
11–Robert **Randolph,** of Eng., *m* Rose, dau. of Thomas Roberts, of Eng.;
10–William, of Little Houghton, Northamptonshire; *m* 2d, Dorothy (Lane) West;
9–Richard (1621-71), half brother of Thomas Randolph the poet; of "Morton Hall," Warwickshire; *m* Elizabeth Ryland (Richard[10]);
8–William (qv);
7–Sir John (1693-1737), treas. of Colony of Va.; speaker House of Burgesses; atty. gen. of Va.; *m* Susannah Beverley;
6–Mary (*d* 1768), *m* Philip **Grymes** (6 above).
10–Maj. Robert **Peyton** (*d* 1686), of the family of Isleham, Eng.;
9–Maj. Robert (1640-94), to Va., 1679; *m* 1668, in England;
8–Elizabeth, *m* Col. Peter **Beverley** (*d* 1728), speaker House of Burgesses; treas. of Colony, 1710-23; surveyor gen.; brother of Robert, the historian of Va. (Maj. Robert[9], to Middlesex Co., Va., 1663, *m* Mary Keebe [*d* 1678], *m* 2d, 1679, Catherine Hone);
7–Susannah, *m* Sir John **Randolph** (7 above).
11–Peter **Jennings** (*d* ca. 1651), of Silsden, nr. Yorkshire; *m* Anne–;
10–Jonathan (*d* ca. 1649), of Ripon; *m* 1625, Elizabeth Parker (Giles[11], of Newby);
9–Sir Edmund (ca. 1626-1695), high sheriff of Yorks; M.P. Ripon; *m* Margaret Barkham (Sir Edward[10], of Totnam High Crosse);
8–Edmund (ca. 1659-1727), to Va., 1680; *m* Frances Corbin (*d* 1713; Henry[9], qv);
7–Edmund (*d* 1756), sec. of Colony of Md.; *m* 1728, as her 3d husband, Ariana (Vanderheyden) Frisby Bordley;
6–Ariana (1729-1808), *m* John **Randolph** (1727-84), mem. House of Burgesses for William and Mary Coll.; atty. gen. of Va. at outbreak of Am. Rev.; loyalist; went to Eng. and died there but body was returned to Va., 1785, and interred in Chapel of William and Mary Coll. Sir John[7]; William[8], qv);
5–Susannah Beverley (*d* 1790), *m* 1778, in London, her 1st cousin, Maj. John Randolph **Grymes** (5 above).
2–William Bennett **Bean** (1835-1915), 1st lt. Baltimore Light Arty., C.S.A.; teacher; merchant; *m* 1866, Ariana Williamson Carper (1845-1906); for issue see Vol. III, p. 595.
1–Summer place: "Cloud Aerie," Afton, Va. Residence: Locust Valley, Long Island, N.Y.

1–**BEVAN, (Claire) Evelyn Wahrer (Mrs. William A.),** *b* Salem, Ia., Aug. 18, 1881.
10–William **Clayton** (qv);
9–Honour, *m* James **Brown,** of Chichester;
8–Jeremiah, *m* Mary Royal, of Scotland;
7–Patience (1712-83), *m* 1735, as his 2d wife, Joshua **Hadley** (1703-64), of Pa. and Va. (Simon[8] [1676-1756], desc. landed proprs. in Somerset, Eng., came from Ireland, 1712, settled at Steyning Manor, Pa., justice many yrs. from 1726, also judge New Castle cts., *m* 1697, Ruth [Miller ?] Keran, 1677-1750);
6–Joshua (*b* 1743), Chatham Co., N.C.; *m* 1761, his first cousin, Ruth Lindley (1745-98; Thomas[7], mem. Provincial Assembly of Pa., *m* Ruth Hadley);
5–Thomas (1763-1832), of N.C. and Ind; *m* 1783, Mary Newlin;
4–John (1788-1869), Orange Co., N.C.; *m* Hannah Hadley (1792-1834; Joshua[5], *m* Elizabeth Barker);
3–Dinah (1820-95), Mooresville, Ind.; *m* 1842, Hiram **McCracken** (1822-90; Henry[4], *m* Mary Ann Yates);
2–Sarah (2 below).
9–Nicholas **Newlin** (qv);
8–Nathaniel (1665-1729), mem. Provincial Assembly; trustee provincial loan office; *m* 1685, Mary Mendenhall (Thomas[9], of Eng., *m* Joan–);
7–John, *m* Mary Woodward;
6–John, went from Pa. to N.C.; *m* Mary Pyle;
5–Mary (1763-1845), *m* Thomas **Hadley** (5 above);
4–John, *m* Hannah Hadley (4 above);
3–Dinah, *m* Hiram **McCracken** (3 above);
2–Sarah (*b* 1853), of Fort Madison, Ia.; *m* 1876, Karl Friedrich **Wahrer** (1850-1922), physician, Fort Madison (August[3], *m* Rosina Fiedler); issue: I–Carl William (*b* Jan. 11, 1879; *m* Julia Howe McConn); II–Claire Evelyn (1 above); III–Frederick Louis (*b* Feb. 8, 1888; *m* Josephine Gableman).
1–*m* Dec. 29, 1915, William Alfred Bevan, *b* Skewen, Wales, Dec. 11, 1876; son of Alfred Bevan, of Brecon, Wales, *m* Margaret Davies.
1–Ed. Knox College, Galesburg, Ill. (Delta Delta Delta). High school teacher, 1903-13. Mem. Society of Friends. Republican. Mem. A.A. U.W., Ames Women's Club, etc. Residence: 525 Welch Av., Ames, Ia.

1–**BLACKBURN, Ellen Ada,** *b* Fayette Co., Tex.
8–John **Alexander** (*d* 1677; son of Sir William, Earl of Stirling, Baron of Nova Scotia, and Viscount of Canada); came from Eng. to Va., ante 1659; patented land in Northampton Co., Va., 1659; received grant in Westmoreland Co., 1664; settled in Stafford Co.; purchased the Howison's Patent, 1669; *m* Tabitha Smart;
7–Philip (*d* ca. 1705), *m* Sarah Ashton (*d* 1749; desc. Sir Thomas de Assheton, lord of Assheton, g.son of Orin Fitz Edward, *m* Emma, dau. of Albert de Greesley);
6–Philip (1704-53), King George Co., Va.; *m* 1726, Sarah Hooe (1708-58; desc. Robert Hoo, of Hoo, Co. Kent, Eng., *d* ca. 1000 A.D.);
5–Frances (*b* 1728), *m* 1749, John **Stuart** (Rev. David[6], *b* in Scotland, *m* Jane Gibbons);
4–Philip (1760-1830), of Md. and Va. and Washington, D.C.; *m* 1792, Mary Fell Baynes (*b* ca. 1770);
3–John Philip (1810-81), Washington, D.C., and Charles and Prince George cos., Md.; *m* 1832, Mary Eleanor Dent;
2–Ellen Anna (2 below).
9–Adam **Thoroughgood** (qv);
8–Ann (*b* ca. 1632), Princess Ann Co., Va.; *m* 1661, Gerard **Fowke** (*d* 1669; Roger[9], of Eng., *m* Mary Bayley);
7–Elizabeth (*b* ca. 1664), of Md.; *m* 1684, Lt. Col. William **Dent** (1660-1705), burgess, speaker of the house, atty. gen.; (desc. King Edward, I, of Eng.);
6–Col. George (1690-1754), of Md.; *m* ca. 1712, Ann Herbert;
5–Capt. George (*d* 1785), *m* Eleanor Hawkins (desc. Sir Richard Hawkins, mem. Va. Council, 1607);
4–George (*d* 1833), of Charles Co., Md.; *m* Elizabeth Yates;
3–Mary Eleanor (*d* 1881), *m* 1832, John Philip **Stuart** (3 above);
2–Ellen Anna (1845-1917), *m* 1864, Mr. Prince; *m*

2d, Samuel Edward **Blackburn** (1835-99); issue (mother's 2d marriage): I–Ellen Ada (1 above); II–Ruth Almira (*m* Walter Oliver Stephens); III–Alice Almeda (*m* James Boone Rhodes); IV–Willie Alberta (*m* James Powell Murray, *d*); V–Edward Stuart (*m* Margherita De Cou).
1–Attended U. of Tex. (Delta Kappa Gamma). Teacher of mathematics, Allan High School, Austin, Tex. N.E.A., P.T.A. (life), etc. Residence: 704 W. 28th St., Austin, Tex.

DR. WILLIAM MORROW BEACH (b Amity, O., May 10, 1831-d nr. London, O., May 5, 1887); M.D., Starling Med. Coll., 1853; studied at Coll. Phys. and Surgeons and Bellevue Hosp. Med. Coll., New York; author of article "Milk Sickness," in Handbook of Medical Science, which is still the authority. Asst. surgeon, 20th and 78th Ohio Vol. Inf., 1862-64; surgeon, 118th Ohio Vol. Inf., 1864-65. Mem. Ohio Gen. Assembly, 1869-71, Senate, 1871-73.

1–**BIDWELL, Mary Beach (Mrs. Forrest A.),** *b* LaFayette, O., July 9, 1862.
8–Thomas **Beach** (qv);
7–John (1655-1709), a founder of ch. at Wallingford, Conn., 1675; *m* 1678, Mary Royce (ca. 1658-1709; Jonathan[8], *m* Mary Spinning or Spinage);
6–John (1690-1773), Goshen, Conn.; tithingman, 1726; moderator, Goshen, 1739; selectman, 1742; capt. of Train Band; rep. Gen. Assembly, 1757-61; *m* 2d, 1717, Mary Royce (1695-1767; Samuel[7], *m* Sarah Baldwin);
5–Amos (*b* 1724), *m* Sarah Royce (*d* 1820; Josiah[6], *m* Abigail Clark); had 8 sons in Am. Rev.;
4–Obil (1758-1846), Am. Rev. 3 yrs.; removed to Amity, Madison Co., O.; *m* 1782, Elizabeth Kilbourne (1765-1826; Roswell[5], *m* Irene Stone);
3–Uri (1789-1832), woolen mfr., Amity, O.; *m* 1816, Hannah (Noble) Gorham;
2–William Morrow, M.D. (1831-87), see portrait and biography; *m* 1860, Lucy Eleanor Wilson (*b* 1844; James[3], of Madison Co., O., *m* Eleanor Smith).
1–*m* June 29, 1887, Edward Everett Cole (Mar. 17, 1853-Feb. 7, 1909); son of Judge Philander Blakesly Cole, of Marysville, O., *m* Dorothy Witter.
1–*m* 2d, Forrest Alvin Bidwell, *b* Amity, O., Nov. 10, 1860; son of Lawson Bidwell, of Amity, *m* Jane Harrington.
1–A.B., Rutgers Female Coll., '82. Mem. D.F.P.A. (mem. Ohio exec. bd.), D.A.R (organizing regent), U.S.D. 1812 (regent Jonathan Alder Chapter, 1927-29), I.A.G., Beach Family Assn. (pres.). Presbyterian. Republican. Residence: London, Madison Co., O.

1–**GOSE, Eugenie Burruss Blocker (Mrs. John Thomas),** *b* Mimosa Hall Plantation, Tex., Mar. 7, 1872.
5–John **Webster** (1743-1839), Am. Rev.; removed from Caroline Co., Va., to Ala., 1817; settled at Tuscaloosa;
4–John Johnston (1796-1854), removed to Tex., ca. 1833; owned "Mimosa Hall Plantation"; *m* 1821, Miriam Richardson Brown (1799-1844);
3–John Brown (1822-64), of "Mimosa Hall Plantation"; *m* 1846, Julia Maria Mead Steele (see their son Louis B. Webster);
2–Eliza Jane (2 below).
10–Thomas **Sheppard,** from Eng. to Va., 1623; burgess, Elizabeth City Co., 1632-33;
9–Lt. Col. John, burgess, James City Co., 1644, from Elizabeth City Co., 1652,53, et seq.;
8–Anne (*d* ca. 1740), *m* 3d, 1695, Rev. James **Wallace** (1668-1712), from Scotland; settled in Elizabeth City Co., 1692;
7–James, prominent citizen of Elizabeth City Co.; justice, 1727; *m* Martha Westwood;
6–James (*d* ca. 1777), ed. William and Mary Coll.; burgess, 1769-71; mem. Com. of Safety, 1775; capt. Va. militia; *m* ca. 1758, Elizabeth Westwood (1741-1824; William[7]);
5–Martha, *m* Edward (?) **James;**
4–Mary Catherine (1789-1840), *m* 1805, Rev. William Moore **Steele** (1780-1857);
3–Julia Maria Mead (1829-72), *m* John Brown **Webster** (3 above);
2–Eliza Jane (1850-1926), *m* 1868, Albert Butler **Blocker** (1844-1923), planter at "Mimosa Hall," Tex.; served in Co. A, 3d Tex. Cav., C.S.A.; for issue and Blocker lineage see Douglass V. Blocker.
1–*m* Dec. 4, 1904, John Thomas Gose, *b* Shelbina, Mo., May 23, 1871; asst. atty. gen. of Mo.; son of John S. Gose, of Shelbina; issue: 1–George Blocker, *b* Shelbina, Mo., Apr. 4, 1910; ed. U. of Calif. at Los Angeles (Delta Tau Delta).
1–Mem. D.A.R., U.D.C. Residence: 644 Heliotrope Drive, Los Angeles, Calif.

ALBERT BUTLER BLOCKER (1844-1923), from a daguerreotype taken at the age of 16; Co. A, 3d Tex. Cav., C.S.A.

1–**BLOCKER, Douglass Vaughan,** *b* Blocker, Tex., Aug. 2, 1886.
6–Michael (Blucher) **Blocker,** from Prussia, obtained grant in Edgefield Dist., S.C.; *m* Anna– (1725-1814);
5–John (1749-1814), Am. Rev.; *m* 2d, 1775, Juliana Johnston (1755-1818);
4–Gen. Jesse (1780-1831), served in War 1812; built home on his estate "Cedar Grove," nr. Edgefield, S.C.; *m* Eliza Malone (1787-1855);
3–William Johnson (1811-59), *m* Mary Douglass Butler;
2–Albert Butler (2 below).

7–William **Butler** (*d* aet. 112), from Ireland, 1700; large landowner nr. Culpeper Ct. Ho., Va.;
6–John (1733-1817);
5–William (1752-1836), removed from Va. to Lawrence Co., Ala.; in Am. Rev.; *m* Mary Kabler;
4–Rev. Jesse (1780-1824), of Va., later in Ala.; *m* Mary Hill Burruss (1795-1869);
3–Mary Douglass (1813-95), *m* William Johnson **Blocker** (3 above);
2–Albert Butler (1844-1923), planter at "Mimosa Hall," Tex.; pvt. Co. A, 3d Tex. Cav., C.S.A.; *m* 1868, Eliza Jane Webster (1850-1926); issue: I–William Webster (1869-1908; capt. Spanish-Am. War); II–Eugenie Burruss (Mrs. John T. Gose, qv for maternal lineages); III–Albert Butler (1873-1910); IV–Louis Edwin (1875-90); V–Eliza Miriam (*b* and *d* 1878); VI–Mary Steele (*b* 1879; *m* H. P. Mabry); VII–Charles Preston (1882-1901); VIII–Francis Howard (1884-1911); IX–Douglass Vaughan (1 above); X–Westwood Wallace (*b* 1891; *m* Kathrene Hall).
1–*m* Dec. 30, 1914, Ethel Van Hook, *b* Marshall, Tex., Apr. 11, 1889; dau. of Albert Van Hook; issue: 1–Douglass Vaughan, Jr., *b* Beaumont, Tex., Sept. 3, 1918.
1–Asst. to 3d v.p., Gulf Refining Co. of La. Mason, Hoo Hoo; mem. Mid-Continent Oil & Gas Assn. Residence: 1556 Irving Pl., Shreveport, La.

1–**WEBSTER, Louis Beauregard,** *b* Mimosa Hall, Harrison Co., Tex., Dec. 8, 1858.
4–John **Webster** (1743-1839), of Tuscaloosa Co., Ala.; enlisted in Cont. Army, served under George Washington, and witnessed the surrender of Cornwallis at Yorktown;
3–John Johnston (1796-1854), of Tuscaloosa, Ala., and Tex.; building contractor and planter; built the first brick public buildings at Tuscaloosa, Ala.; *m* 1821, Miriam Richardson Brown (1799-1844);
2–John Brown (2 below).
5–Rev. John **Steele** (1715-79), from Ireland, settled at Carlisle, Pa.; pastor first Presbyn. Ch. at Carlisle; capt. of a company from Carlisle, under General Armstrong, 1758, Indian wars; capt. and chaplain in Am. Rev.; *m* Margaret– (1721-79);
4–Capt. John (1744-1812), lawyer, Carlisle; capt. Am. Rev.; *m* 1772, Agnes Moore (*b* 1757; Rev. John[6], from Ireland to Pa., built 1st Presbyn. Ch. at Carlisle, Pa., capt. and chaplain Am. Rev.);
3–Rev. William Moore (1780-1857), of Carlisle, Pa., Ala., and Tex.; P.E. clergyman in Ala. and Tex.; *m* 1805, Mary Catherine James (1789-1840);
2–Julia Maria Mead (1829-72), *m* 1846, John Brown **Webster** (1822-64), ed. U. of Ala.; lawyer and planter; issue: I–William Edwin (1847-1923; *m* Emma Perry, *d*); II–Miriam Richardson (*b* 1849; *m* Dr. Ben Baldwin, *d*); III–Eliza Jane (1850-1926; *m* Albert Butler Blocker; see their dau. Mrs. John T. Gose); IV–Louis Beauregard (1 above).
1–*m* Feb. 25, 1880, Tralucia Rives, *b* nr. Jefferson, Tex., July 20, 1860; dau. of William Green Rives, of Jefferson; issue: 1–Louis Beauregard, Jr., *b* "Mimosa Hall," Tex., June 8, 1881; *m* Dec. 2, 1918, Lena, dau. of Dr. John Young Murry, of Arkadelphia, Ark.; 2–Lida Mae (Mrs. Henry Haynes Dugan, qv for Rives, Wyche and Harrison lineages); 3–Abbie Haywood (Mrs. Milton Moore Smith, qv for Haywood lineage).
1–Ed. East Tenn. U.; A. and M. Coll. of Tex. Engaged in oil business in Tex. and La. to 1923, now retired. Methodist. Democrat. Residence: 543 Jordan St., Shreveport, La.

1–**DUGAN, Lida Mae Webster (Mrs. Henry Haynes),** *b* "Mimosa Hall," Harrison Co., Tex., July 7, 1884.
10–William **Rives** (*b* ca. 1636), from Eng. to Va., ca. 1653;
9–George (1660-post 1719), trader;
8–Col. William (ca. 1683-1746), Prince George Co., Va.; *m* Elizabeth (Foster?), (*d* 1759);
7–Timothy (ca. 1710-post 1772), Brunswick Co., Va.; gentleman justice of the county, 1751; *m* Hester (Birchett?);
6–William (ca. 1737-1783), settled in Camden Dist., S.C.; *m* ca. 1760, Lucy Wyche;
5–William (ca. 1767-1804), resident of Richland Co., Camden Dist., S.C., in first federal census, 1790; *m* Rebecca (Jackson?);
4–John Green (1800-45), *m* 1825, Elizabeth Perry Harrison;
3–William Green (1831-87), *m* 1858, Mary Ann Haywood (1840-86);
2–Tralucia (2 below).
9–Henry **Wyche** (1648-1712; son of Rev. Henry, *m* Ellen, dau. of Ralph Bennett); settled in Surry Co., Va., 1679;
8–George (will dated 1753); Surry Co.;
7–Peter (will dated 1756), Brunswick Co., Va.; *m* Alice, probably dau. of Thomas Scott, of Prince George Co.;
6–Lucy, *m* William **Rives** (6 above).
6–Reuben Henry **Harrison** (ante 1760-1794; desc. Richard or Benjamin Harrison, brothers who came from Eng. with 3 bros.), served in Am. Rev.; *m* 1782, Sarah Burgess (1765-1831);
5–William Henry (ca. 1786-1825), removed from S.C. to Ala., thence to Tex.; *m* 1807, Ann Perry (*d* 1815), of Longtown, Fairfield Dist., S.C.;
4–Elizabeth Perry (1808-70), *m* 1825, John Green **Rives** (4 above);
3–William Green, *m* Mary Ann Haywood (3 above);
2–Tralucia (*b* 1860), *m* 1880, Louis Beauregard **Webster** (qv for other lineages).
1–*m* June 26, 1907, Henry Haynes Dugan, *b* Bells, Tex., Mar. 29, 1881; son of William Preston Dugan, of Bells; issue: 1–Haynes Webster, *b* Sherman, Tex., Mar. 23, 1913.
1–Studied at Sam Houston Normal, Huntsville, Tex. Mem. D.A.R. Methodist. Democrat. Residence: 3002 Wheeles St., Shreveport, La.

1–**SMITH, Abbie Haywood Webster (Mrs. Milton M.),** *b* Jefferson, Tex., Nov. 18, 1896.
7–Col. John **Haywood** (1685-1758), first of the name in N.C.; emigrated from New York, 1741, and settled at the mouth of Conoconarie Creek, Halifax Co.; col. provincial troops of N.C.; mem. Assembly, 1746-52; commr. of coast fortifications, 1748; treas. of the northern cos. of the Province, 1752-54; surveyor for Earl of Granville; one of the lords proprs. of Carolina; *m* Mary Lovett;
6–Maj. Egbert (1730-1801), of Halifax Co.; maj. of N.C. militia, 1775-76; mem. Com. of Safety 1774-75; mem. com. to procure arms and ammunition for Cont. Army, 1776; mem. Provincial Congress of N.C. 1776; justice Ct. of Pleas and Quarter Sessions, 1776; mem. N.C. House of Commons, 1777-78; *m* Sarah Ware;
5–William, *m* Abigail Jones;
4–Eliza (1820-1908), *m* 1836, William Henry **Haywood** (1810-77);
3–Mary Ann (1840-86), *m* 1858, William Green **Rives** (1831-87);
2–Tralucia (*b* 1860), *m* 1880, Louis Beauregard **Webster** (qv for other lineages).
1–*m* Dec. 11, 1920, Milton Moore Smith, *b* Columbus, Tex., Sept. 29, 1895; son of Loundes George Smith, of Columbus; issue: 1–Louis Milton, *b* Shreveport, La., Nov. 26, 1923.
1–Ed. Kidd Key Coll. Methodist. Democrat. Residence: 341 Albany St., Shreveport, La.

1–**BOND, Benjamin Davis,** *b* Kohala, Hawaii, Jan. 21, 1853.
7–William **Bond** (qv);
6–Col. Jonas (1664-1727), *m* 1688/89, Grace Coolidge (1663/64-1699; John[7], *m* Hannah, dau. of John Livermore; John[8]);
5–Jonas (1691-1768), *m* 1718, Hannah Bright (1694-1786; Nathaniel[6], *m* Mary, dau. of Simon Coolidge; Sgt. Henry[7]; Henry[8]);
4–Col. William (1733-76), col. 25th Mass. Cont. Line in Am. Rev.; *m* Lucy Brown;
3–Elias (1774-1865), Hallowell, Me.; *m* 2d, 1804, Rebecca Davis;
2–Rev. Elias (1813-96), missionary in Hawaii; *m* Ellen Mariner Howell (1817-81; John[8], *m* Eleanor Douglass); for issue see Vol. II, p. 272.
1–*m* Sept. 5, 1889, Emma Mary Renton, *b* Honolulu, Hawaii, Nov. 16, 1866; dau. of James Renton; issue (all *b* Kohala, Hawaii): 1–Benjamin Howell, *b* Dec. 30, 1890; A.M., Valparaiso, '11; LL.B., Indiana Law School, 1913; *m* Dec. 14, 1921, Hazel Beatrice Hoffman, of Honolulu (issue: Benjamin Howell, Jr., *b* Oct. 30, 1923; Charles Hoffman, *b* Jan. 23, 1928; Renton, *b* Mar. 31, 1930); 2–Alice Renton, *b*

July 15, 1893; A.B., Oberlin, '14; *m* Feb. 27, 1919, William Patterson Alexander, of Honolulu (issue: William Patterson, III, *b* Apr. 26, 1920; Benjamin Bond, *b* Nov. 14, 1921; Henry Arthur, *b* Mar. 14, 1925); 3–Kenneth Davis, *b* June 3, 1895; A.B., U.Mich., '20; *m* Nov. 7, 1925, Kathryn Isobel Lyman, of Hilo, Hawaii (issue: Kenneth Lyman, *b* Sept. 4, 1926; Charlotte Marjorie, *b* Apr. 9, 1928); 4–James Douglass, *b* May 10, 1899; A.B., U. Mich., '19, A.M., 1922; B.S., Audubon Sugar Sch., 1922; *m* Sept. 6, 1924, Dorothy Ruth Allen (issue: James Douglass, Jr., *b* Aug. 28, 1928; Janet Emmaton, *b* July 9, 1930).
1–A.B., Amherst, '79, A.M., 1883; M.D., U.Mich., 1882; post-grad. med. work at New York. Physician; actg. asst. surgeon, U.S.P.H.S. Mem. S.A.R. Residence: Kohala, H.T.

1–**BOOKER, George Edward, 3d,** *b* Orange, Va., July 11, 1898.
9–Edward **Booker,** from Eng. to York Co., Va., 1648; mem. Council same yr.;
8–Capt. Richard (ante 1652-post 1704), of Gloucester Co., Va.; *m* 2d, 1694, Hannah (Hand) Marshall (Richard Hand[9], *m* Frances Purefoy, of the extinct baronetcy of that name who had a seat in Leicestershire, called "Drayton");
7–George, *m* 1st, Grace Richeson;
6–Richard (*b* 1764), *m* Martha Bronskill;
5–Edward (*d* 1800), lt. in Am. Rev.; was at siege of Yorktown; *m* Edith Cobbs Anderson;
4–William (1789-1855), capt. in War 1812; *m* Nancy Dudley Agee (1799-1869);
3–George Edward, D.D. (1823-99), B.A., Randolph-Macon, '56; M.A., 1858; founder Southside Acad., Farmville, Va.; chaplain, capt. and maj., C.S.A.; *m* 2d, 1869, Mary Frances Eubank (*b* 1848);
2–George Edward, Jr., D.D. (see Vol. II, p. 116), *m* 1896, Annie Parham Howle (*b* 1869; James David[8], of "Elm Shade," Sussex Co., Va., *m* Emma Parham).
1–Not married. Ed. in private schools; Randolph-Macon Coll. (Phi Delta Theta, Blacki Ribbon Society), Sutherlin medal, U. of Va.; LL.B., U. of Richmond. Lawyer; commissioner in chancery of several courts. Served in S.A.T.C. during World War. Mem. Soc. of Colonial Wars, Richmond Alumni of U. of Va., Soc. of Alumni of Randolph-Macon College. Club: The Country. Residence: 1710 Grove Avenue, Richmond, Va.

SALMON LOOMIS HAIGHT (1804-81), and his wife EMILY FOWLER (1809-95).

1–**BROWN, Mary Emily Haight (Mrs. Edward D.),** *b* Dundee, Mich., July 7, 1871.
10–William **Mann** (*b* Eng., ca. 1607-*d* 1662), settled at Cambridge, Mass.; *m* 1643, Mary Jarred, of Eng.; *m* 2d, 1657, Alice Tiel;
9–Rev. Samuel (1647-1719), of Wrentham, Mass.; A.B., Harvard, 1665; taught at Dedham, 5 yrs.; *m* 1673, Esther Ware (1655-1734; Robert[10], qv);
8–Theodore (1680-1761), dea. of ch. at Wrentham; selectman; rep., 1722; *m* 1702, Abigail Hawes;
7–Phoebe (1706-90), *m* 1732, John **Guild** (*b* 1690; John[8] [1649-1722 or 23], of Dedham and Wrentham, *m* 1677, Sarah [*b* 1658], dau. of Anthony Fisher, *m* Joane Faxon; John[9], qv);
6–Samuel (1734-1816), pvt. and corpl. Am. Rev.; *m* 1760, Ruth Nims (1744-1804);
5–Samuel (1762-1844), of Bridgewater, Mass., and Cohocton, N. Y.; *m* 1780, Lydia Essen (1761-1806);
4–Lydia Essen (1783-1855), of Leyden, Mass.; *m* 1802, Dijah **Fowler** (1782-1849), farmer at Bridgewater and Oneida, N.Y., until 1816, when he moved to North Cohocton, Steuben Co., where he built first grist mill (Mark[5], *m* Miriam Sterling Warner; Capt. Dijah[6] [1717-1804], *m* Abigail, dau. of Sgt. Isaac Bigelow; John[7]; Mark[8]; Capt. William[9]; William[10], qv);
3–Emily (1809-95), of N. Cohocton, N.Y., Saline and Tecumseh, Mich.; *m* 1826, Salmon Loomis **Haight** (1804-81), rep. Mich. State Legislature, 1848 (George Washington[4], of Leyden, N.Y., *m* Cynthia Loomis); see portrait;
2–Samuel Guild (2 below).
8–Joseph **Parsons** (qv);
7–Jonathan (*b* 1657), of Northampton, Mass.; *m* 1682, Mary Clarke (Nathaniel[8]);
6–Nathaniel (*b* 1685), of Northampton; *m* Abagail Bunce;
5–Elisha (1731-1805), of Northampton; signer Articles of Assn., Black Creek Dist., Charlotte Co., 1775; Am. Rev.; *m* 1770, Lucy Alvord;
4–Stephen (1780-1848), of Northampton; *m* 1803, Zeruiah Pierce (1783-1852);
3–Almira (1806-83), of Leroy and Forestville, N.Y., Northampton, Mass., Milan and Dundee, Mich.; *m* 1828, Cyrus G. **McBride** (Daniel[4], *m* Abagail Meade);
2–Louisa Priscilla (1843-1913), *m* 1862, Samuel Guild **Haight** (1841-1915), farmer; issue: I–Alonzo Walter (*b* 1864; *m* Isabelle Cowie Brillinger); II–Mary Emily (1 above).
1–*m* Nov. 2, 1898, Edward Dancey Brown, D.D.S., *b* Brownsville, Ont., Can., May 1866; son of Benajah M. Brown, of Brownsville, Ont.; issue: 1–Arthur Haight, *b* Dundee, Mich., Nov. 28, 1899; D.D.S., U.Mich.; *m* Oct. 5, 1927, Muriel E., dau. of Elmer H. Halladay, of Tecumseh, Mich. (issue: Annette Louise, *b* Dec. 14, 1929). Residence: 501 Evans St. S., Tecumseh, Mich.

1–**ELLIOTT, Marion Hamilton Hall (Mrs. James F.),** *b* Covington, Ky., May 27, 1891.
5–Benjamin **Hall,** of New London, Conn.; sea capt. between Conn. and W.I., during Am. Rev.;
4–Stephen (1797-1861), of Calhoun Co., Mich.; justice of the peace; capt. militia; dea. Bapt. Ch.; *m* 1822, Clarissa Dibble (*b* 1801; Andrew[5], of Genesee Co., N.Y.);
3–Alfred D. (1824-1896 or 97), of Tecumseh, Mich.; justice of the peace in Calhoun Co.; pres. and treas. of Farmers' Mutual Fire Ins. Co.; supervisor 6 yrs., chmn. 1 yr.; rep. Mich. Legislature, 1876, 78; *m* 2d, 1865, Engelina Heesen (1838-91; Rudolph[4], *m* Petronella Taute);
2–William Elmer (2 below).
5–George **Hamilton,** from Scotland 1750; settled in Cumberland Co., Pa.; is said to have fought in Am. Rev.;
4–Samuel (*d* 1853), St. Marys, O.; *m* Mary Weaver;
3–George Washington (1820-74), contracted and built buildings in the South until the Civil War, when he and his brother David, went North; had a store in Louisville, Ky., and dealt in ship furnishings; went to Tecumseh, Mich., 1869; built and conducted a flour mill; *m* Lydia Maria Haight;
2–Emilie May (2 below).
10–Joseph **Loomis** (qv);
9–Lt. Samuel (ca. 1628-1689), freeman, 1654; admitted to the ch., 1661; lt., removed to Westfield, Mass., bet. 1672-75; *m* 1653, Elizabeth Judd (Thomas[10]);
8–William (1672-1738), *m* 1703, Martha Morley (1682-1753; Thomas[9], *m* Martha Wright);
7–Benjamin (1708-87), removed to Southwick, Mass., 1773; *m* 1st, 1734, Elizabeth Mosley;
6–Benjamin (1750-1814), removed to Remsen, N.Y.; *m* 1771, Lucy Leonard;
5–Cynthia (1784-1813), of Pompey, N.Y.; *m* 1779, George W. **Haight**;
4–Salmon Loomis (1804-81), *m* 1826, Emily Fowler

(see Mrs. Edward D. Brown for Fowler-Guild-Mann lineage);
3–Lydia Maria (1835-1924), *m* 1870, George Washington **Hamilton** (3 above);
2–Emilie May (*b* 1873), of Tecumseh; *m* 1890, William Elmer **Hall** (*b* 1870), ed. Mich. Agrl. Coll.; grad. U.Ky.; issue: I–Marion Hamilton (1 above); II–Lydia Winnifred (*b* 1896; *m* 1917, Elmer Hunt Green); III–Jeannette Fowler (*b* 1903; *m* 1926, Andrew Northrup).
1–*m* May 19, 1909, James Floyd Elliott, *b* Tecumseh, Mich., July 25, 1881; son of James Elliott, of Tecumseh, *m* Addie E. Rainey; issue: 1–George Hamilton, *b* Tecumseh, Mich., May 8, 1916.
1–Mem. O.E.S. Methodist. Republican. Residence: 204 Evans St. S., Tecumseh, Mich.

1–**BROOKS, John Pascal,** *b* Kittery, Me., Sept. 24, 1861.
6–William **Brooks** (*b* 1685), of Kittery (now Eliot), Me.; *m* 1709, Mary Fogg (*b* 1689; Daniel[7], of Kittery, *m* Hannah Libby; Samuel[8]);
5–Joshua (*b* 1712), *m* 1733, Anne Staple (*b* 1716);
4–William (*b* 1755), *m* 1777, Mary Gowell (bap. 1757-1814);
3–Asa (1798-1872), *m* 1822, Abigal Tobey (1798-1884);
2–James W. (2 below).
8–Gowen **Wilson,** of Kittery, Me.;
7–Joseph (1650-1710), *m* 1683, Hannah Endel;
6–William (*b* 1686), *m* 1711, Hopewell (Furbish) Hutchins;
5–William (*b* 1711), *m* Edah Briar;
4–Edmund (1743-1825), *m* Susanna Gunnison;
3–Gowen (1788-1878), *m* Nancy Fernald;
2–Anna A. (1826-1917), *m* 1854, James William **Brooks** (1830-1908); issue: I–Anna Luella (*d* young); II–Lillian (*b* 1858; *m* 1887, William Linwood Fernald); III–John Pascal (1 above); IV–Gowen Wilson (1867-1920).
1–*m* June 25, 1888, Maude Pepperrell Perkins (1863-92); dau. of Rev. Aaron Perkins, of Red Bank, N.J.; issue: 1–Raymond Wentworth, *b* Red Bank, Aug. 30, 1889; *m* 1918, Annette Hester; 2–Elizabeth Maude, *b* Bethlehem, Pa., May 1, 1891.
1–*m* 2d, June 4, 1903, Belle Clark Pearson, *b* Atchison, Kan., Dec. 26, 1872; dau. of Alexander Pearson, of Lexington, Ky.
1–B.S., Dartmouth, '85, M.S., 1893, Sc.D., 1915. Prof. civil engring., State U. of Ky.; asso. prof. civil engring, U.Ill.; pres. Clarkson Coll. of Tech., Potsdam, N.Y., since 1911. Author (see Who's Who in America). Mem. Am. Soc. C.E., Soc. Promotion Engring. Edn., etc. Republican. Residence: Potsdam, N.Y.

1–**BROOKS, William Frederick** (Mar. 1, 1863-Mar. 19, 1928).
9–Capt. Thomas **Brooks** (qv);
8–Joshua (ca. 1630-1697), Concord, Mass.; *m* 1653, Hannah Mason (*b* 1636; Capt. Hugh[9]);
7–Ens. Daniel (1663-1733), *m* 1692, Anne Merriam (1669-1757; John[8]; Joseph[9]);
6–Job (*b* 1698), *m* 1721, Elizabeth Flagg (*b* 1701; Ebenezer[7]; Gershom[8]; Thomas[9]);
5–Daniel (1738-1820), Acton, Mass.; soldier Am. Rev.; *m* 1757, Caroline Prescott (1736-1806; Amor[6]; Samuel[7]; Capt. Jonathan[8]; John[9]);
4–Lt. Col. Job Frederick (1765-1822), lt. col. militia, Westmoreland, N.H.; *m* 1799, Polly Babcock (1770-1847);
3–William (1806-80), *m* 1832, Louisa Ayer Swan (1812-94); see Vol. II, p. 276, for Swan lineage;
2–Frederick William (2 below).
6–Amos **Babcock,** *m* Ann Watkins (desc. Dep.-Gov. William Jones and Gov. Theophilus Eaton);
5–Amos, *m* Peggy Peabody (desc. Lt. Francis Peabody);
4–Polly (1770-1847), *m* Job F. **Brooks** (4 above).
7–Miles **Oakley** (1615-98), mayor of Westchester, N.Y.; *m* Mary Wilmot;
6–John;
5–Thomas, *m* Patience Skidmore;
4–Samuel, *m* Abigail Wood;
3–Timothy (*d* 1842), *m* Sophronia Wheeler;
2–Annie (2 below).
5–Judge Martin **Ryerson** (1751-1831), of Pompton, N.J.; *m* 1778, Sophronia Van Winkle;
4–Ann (1788-1821), *m* Maj. James **Wheeler** (1783-1852);
3–Sophronia (1811-89), *m* Timothy **Oakley** (3 above);
2–Annie (1839-1905), *m* 1862, Frederick William **Brooks** (1833-83), of Battle Creek, Mich. (for issue see Vol. II, p. 276).
1–*m* Jan. 11, 1888, Caroline Bell Langdon, *b* Minneapolis, Minn., June 30, 1866; ed. Ogontz Sch.; mem. C.D.A., D.F.P.A., D.A.R., Pilgrim Soc., I.A.G., etc.; dau. of Robert Bruce Langdon, ry. builder and v.p. M., St.P.&S.S.M. Ry., of Minneapolis (see his son, Cavour Smith Langdon, below); issue: 1–Robert Langdon, *b* Minneapolis, Minn., Dec. 15, 1889; Yale, '14; *m* Oct. 27, 1915, Katherine Lawler, *b* Dec. 15, 1889, dau. of John Lawler, of St. Paul, Minn. (issue: Caroline Langdon, *b* Aug. 4, 1916; Robert Langdon, II, *b* Nov. 4, 1917; John Lawler, *b* Dec. 6, 1919; William Pennington, *b* Oct. 30, 1922; Glenn Sturgis, *b* Nov. 14, 1926).
1–B.S., Worcester Poly. Inst. Mem. firm Backus-Brooks Co., lumber; pres. Leader, Inc.; dir. Minn. Loan & Trust Co. Mem. Minn. Senate, 1919-27 (reelected for 3d term, 1927); chmn. Rep. Nat. Com. 1924-28. Clubs: Minneapolis, Minnekahda, Lafayette, Aero (pres.), etc. Residence: 1928 Stevens Av., Minneapolis, Minn.

1–**LANGDON, Cavour Smith,** *b* New Haven, Vt., Sept. 11, 1861.
9–George (Langton) **Langdon** (*d* 1676), settled at Wethersfield, Mass., 1636, removed to Springfield, 1646, to Northampton, 1653; surveyor of highways, Springfield; *m* Hannah– (widow of Edmund Haynes);
8–Dea. John, *m* Mary (Seymour) Gridley (widow of Capt. John Gridley);
7–Joseph (bap. 1659-1736), of Farmington, Conn.; *m* 1st, 1683, Susannah Root (John[8]);
6–Ebenezer (*b* 1701), *m* 1727, Jemima Cowles (*b* 1707; Capt. Isaac[7]; Samuel[8]; John[9]);
5–Capt. Noah (1728-1819), Tyringham, Mass.; capt. 1st Berkshire Co., Mass. militia; *m* Rebecca Porter (1731-1819; Ebenezer[6], *m* Anna Porter; Timothy[7]; Dea. Thomas[8]; Dea. Thomas[9]);
4–Seth (1759-1851), New Haven, Vt.; corpl. Mass. militia, 1777-81; *m* 1784, Anne Dowd (1763-1824; Capt. Giles[5]; David[6]; John[7]; Henry[8]);
3–Seth (1799-1881), *m* 1821, Laura Squire;
2–Robert Bruce (2 below).
8–George **Squire** (*d* 1691), Fairfield, Conn., 1644; sgt. colonial wars;
7–Lt. Thomas (Fairfield, Conn., Mar. 11, 1643-Apr. 9, 1712, Woodbury), *m* Elizabeth–;
6–Ebenezer (bap. Woodbury, Aug. 1697-*d* 1732), *m* Ellen–;
5–Lt. Andrew (Woodbury, 1731-Jan. 2, 1824), lt. in Indian wars; pvt. Am. Rev. in Berkshire Co. Regt.; to Lanesboro, Mass., 1759; *m* Mar. 22, 1755, Huldah Bronson (May 22, 1730-Dec. 16, 1783; Timothy[6], *m* Abigail Jenner), sister of Col. Eli Bronson, of Manchester, Vt.;
4–Wait (Lanesboro, July 5, 1767-Jan. 9, 1858), *m* Jan. 18, 1790, Hannah Powell (Feb. 23, 1769-Nov. 17, 1822; Lt. Col. Miles[5], cdr. of minute men at Lexington, *m* Jemima, dau. of Benjamin Adkins; Robert[6]; William[7]; Thomas[8]);
3–Laura (1801-77), *m* Seth **Langdon** (3 above).
8–Edmund **Rice** (qv);
7–Corpl. Thomas (1620-81), *m* Mary King (Thomas[8]);
6–Perez, *m* Lydia– (1701-93);
5–Mehitable (*d* 1782), *m* Lt. Joseph **Willoughby,** Am. Rev. (John[6]);
4–Susanna, *m* at Bennington, Vt., Hezekiah **Smith** (1765-1813);
3–Dr. Horatio Augustus (1790-1862), *m* 1829, Jerusha Reeve Bell (1799-1865; Harvey[4]; Sgt. Solomon[5], Am. Rev.; John[6]);
2–Sarah A. (1839-1911), *m* 1859, Robert Bruce **Langdon** (1826-95), capitalist, Minneapolis, Minn.; ry. builder and v.p. M.,St.P.&S.S.M. Ry.; state senator 13 yrs.; issue: I–Cavour Smith (1 above); II–Martha Aurelia (*b* 1863; *m* 1886, Hiram Calvin Truesdale, *b* 1860); III–Caroline Bell (*b* 1866; *m* 1888, William Frederick Brooks, qv); IV–Frances Gertrude (1869-70); V–Linton Shepard (*b* and *d* 1872).
1–*m* Dec. 27, 1893, Mabel Shaw, *b* Minneapolis, Minn., Apr. 17, 1868; dau. of Judge John M. Shaw; issue: 1–Elizabeth (Feb. 2, 1898-May. 15, 1907); 2–Mabel Ellen, *b* June 2, 1899; *m* Apr. 27, 1921, Howard Ives McMillan (*b* Aug. 5, 1897), son of John D. McMillan (issue: Cavour Langdon, *b* Jan. 22, 1922; Elizabeth Langdon, *b* Feb. 21, 1924; Howard I., Jr., *b* June 6, 1929).
1–V.p. Farmers & Mechanics Savings Bank;

pres. Pine Land Co., Minneapolis Syndicate; dir. M.,St.P.&S.S.M. Ry. Co., Northwestern Nat. Bank, Minneapolis Lloyds, Minneapolis Fire & Marine Ins. Co. Clubs: Minneapolis, Lafayette, Minikahda, Woodhill Country. Residence: 2200 Pillsbury Av., Minneapolis, Minn.

1–**BROWN, Martha Estella Tenney (Mrs. Arthur),** *b* Vancouver, Wash., Dec. 20, 1871.
10–Thomas **Tenney** (qv);
9–Daniel (1653-1748), *m* 1st, 1680, Elizabeth Stickney (1661-94; desc. Lt. Samuel Stickney);
8–Thomas (1681-1746), *m* 1705, Sarah Tenney (bap. 1685; Thomas[9]; Thomas[10], same as 10 above);
7–Moses (1707-70), was on muster roll for invasion of Canada and was at Crown Point; *m* 1733, Susanna Rockwood (1709-36);
6–Josiah (*b* 1734), *m* 1759, Mary Shirar (or Shearer);
5–Josiah (1760-1837), Am. Rev.; *m* ca. 1779, Levinah Keyes (*b* 1760; desc. Col. William Ward [1680-1767], who had grant of 1,000 acres nr. conway, Mass.; Andrew Stevenson [*b* 1612], from Eng., settled in Cambridge ante 1648 where he was a propr.; James Patterson, qv);
4–Obed (1793-1858), *m* 1816, Electa Ann (Curtis) Steele (1794-1857; desc. Capt. Nathaniel Merriam);
3–Chauncey Brewer (1817-87), *m* 1838, Martha Cleveland Brewer (1809-81; desc. John Butterworth [*b* 1630], a Baptist church was organized in his home, Swansea, Mass., 1663);
2–Horace Dewey (1838-1923), farmer; *m* 1862, Ellen Goddard (1846-1904); issue: I–Joseph Hill (*b* and *d* 1864); II–George Washington (1865-90; *m* Emma Bartlett); III–Chauncey Edward (1868-97); IV–William Otterbein (*b* 1870; *m* Cora Pender); V–Martha E. (1 above); VI–Charles Wesley (*b* 1873; *m* Alice Maude Huston); VII–Mary Jane (1875-90); VIII–Henry Orville (1878-83).
1–*m* Sept. 28, 1891, Arthur Brown, *b* Elma, Wash., June 18, 1873; sea capt., mcht. marine, World War; son of Holabert Herrick Brown; issue: 1–Mary Agnes, *b* Jan. 9, 1893; *m* Dec. 1912, J. Arthur Perkins; 2–Horace Daniel (Sept. 7, 1894-96); 3–Chauncey Edward, *b* Dec. 26, 1897; *m* Nov. 1923, Alodia Englert Sutton; 4–Philip Arthur, *b* Mar. 7, 1899; *m* Nov. 1925, Hazel Bateman; 5–Anna Estella, *b* Jan. 11, 1902; *m* June, 1925, William Weaver; 6–William Joseph, *b* May 12, 1905; 7–Carlos Theodore and 8–Carroll Elbert (twins), *b* Dec. 8, 1907; 9–Margaretta Maude, *b* Aug. 31, 1911; 10–Arthur Orville, *b* June 18, 1913; 11–Frances Josephine, *b* May 12, 1915.
1–Residence: R.F.D. 3, Box 190, Vancouver, Wash.

Gordon

1–**BROWN, Caroline Lewis Gordon (Mrs. Orton B.),** *b* "Sutherland," Kirkwood (nr. Atlanta), Ga., Sept. 8, 1872.
6–Adam **Gordon,** from Scotland, with his brother Basil, in latter part of 17th Century, settled nr. Fredericksburg, Va.; *m* Sally Chapman;
5–Charles, mem. N.C. Colonial Assembly which framed Constitution of N.C.; *m* Mrs. Sarah Herndon;
4–Chapman (1757-95), soldier Am. Rev.; *m* Charity King;
3–Zachry Herndon (1790-1883), *m* Melinda Coxe;
2–John B. (2 below).
9–Gen. Robert **Lewis** (qv);
8–John (*b* 1635), "Warner Hall," *m* Isabella, dau. Augustine Warner, I;
7–Col. John (1669-1725), mem. Royal Council; county lieut.; judge Supreme Ct.; *m* his cousin, Elizabeth, dau. Augustine Warner, II (1642-81), speaker Va. House of Burgesses (*m* Mildred, dau. of Capt. George Reade, came to Va., 1637, was sec. of the colony and mem. Royal Council);
6–Robert, of "Belvoir," Albemarle Co., Va.; *m* Jane Meriwether (they had 3 sons in Am. Rev.);
5–Robert, mem. N.C. Colonial Assembly, 1723; Constl. Conv., 1776; *m* Frances, dau. Charles Lewis, of "The Byrd";
4–Nicholas Meriwether, *m* Elizabeth Sutherland;
3–Caroline Matilda, *m* Hugh Anderson **Haralson** (1805-54), maj. gen. Ga. militia, mem. 28th to 31st Congresses, 1843-51;
2–Frances Rebecca (see Vol. I, p. 625 for other lineages), *m* 1854, John Brown **Gordon** (Feb. 6, 1832-Jan. 9, 1904), see portrait and biography Vol. III, p. 92.
1–*m* Sept. 18, 1901, Orton Bishop Brown, *b* Portland, Me., Apr. 17, 1870; son of William W. Brown, of Portland, Me.; issue: 1–Gordon, *b* Aug. 17, 1902; 2–Wentworth, *b* Apr. 10, 1905; 3–Caroline Lewis, *b* Mar. 13, 1907.
1–Mem. C.D.A., D.A.R. Club: Colony (New York). Residence: 209 Church St., Berlin, N.H.

1–**BRUMBACK, Orville Sanford,** *b* Delaware Co., O., Dec. 2, 1855.
6–Probably: John Melchoir (Brombach) **Brumback,** from Holland in the "Halifax," to Phila., 1752;
5–Henry (1739-99);
4–John (*b* 1764), began to write name Brumback;
3–David (1797-1833), *m* Frutilda Bearnes;
2–John Sanford (2 below).
6–John **Purmort**;
5–John;
4–Joshua (*b* 1776), *m* Eunice Walworth (*b* 1773; Capt. Charles[5], officer Am. Rev.);
3–Minor (1799-1854), *m* Perlena Nettleton (1808-50; Jeremiah[4] [died 1816]; Jeremiah[5] [*b* 1718], *m* Debora–);
2–Ellen Perlena (*b* 1832), *m* John Sanford **Brumback** (1829-97), pres. VanWert (O.) Nat. Bank; issue: I–Orville Sanford (1 above); II–David LaDoyt (1861-1928); III–Estella (*b* 1863; *m* John P. Reed); IV–Saida (*b* 1870; *m* Ernest I. Antrim, see Vol. III, p. 507).
1–*m* Oct. 26, 1881, Jennie Carey (Oct. 15, 1860-Mar. 16, 1920); dau. of Simeon B. Carey (1822-1902), of Indianapolis, Ind., *m* Lydia King (1837-1924; Eldad[3] [1804-48], *m* Olive T. Ball [1809-47]; Charles[4] [1781-1824]; Aaron[5] [1754-82], adj., Col. Mosely's regt., *m* Hannah [1755-1819], dau. Col. John Mosely [1725-1880], col. 3d N.H. Co. Regt., Mass. Militia, Am. Rev., was also in Colonial Wars, and capt. in the Crown Point Expdn., 1756); issue (all *b* Toledo, O.): 1–Blanche B., *b* Mar. 4, 1885; A.B., Vassar, '06; *m* Sept. 19, 1906, Lyman Strong Spitzer (issue: Lydia Carey, *b* Oct. 7, 1909; Luette Ruth, *b* July 25, 1912; Lyman Strong, Jr., *b* June 26, 1914; John Brumback, *b* Mar. 6, 1918); 2–Lydia B., *b* Dec. 2, 1888; *m* June 1, 1910, Horace Ethan Allen (issue: Horace Ethan, Jr., *b* Jan. 27, 1913; Carey Brumback, *b* Feb. 27, 1918; Orville Sanford, *b* Sept. 11, 1919).
1–*m* 2d, May 18, 1922, Mae (Fuller) Cone, *b* Birmingham, O.; dau. of Stephen M. Fuller, Norwalk, O.
1–A.B., Princeton, '77, A.M., 1880; LL.B., U.Mich., 1879. Lawyer; mem. Ohio House of Rep., 1886-87. Mem. S.A.R., Sigma Chi, Am. Bar Assn., Toledo Bar. Assn., Chamber of Commerce, etc. Mason. Elk. Clubs: Toledo, Toledo Country, Toledo Automobile. Residence: 2004 Parkwood Av., Toledo, O.

1–**BUDD, Britton Ihrie,** *b* San Francisco, Calif., Sept. 7, 1871.
7–William **Budd** (qv);
6–Thomas (1686-1742), of Burlington Co., N.J.; *m* Deborah Langstaff (bap. 1703);

5–Levi (1726-90), of Phila., Pa.; *m* 2d, 1762, Elizabeth Sheilds (1735-98);
4–George (1764-1817), of Phila. (see portrait); *m* 1792, Suzannah Britton;
3–George Knight (Feb. 12, 1802-Sept. 24, 1875), settled at St. Louis, Mo., 1836, and established the private banking house of Budd and Co., later Budd & Park; elected city comptroller, 1850; one of the founders of the Boatmens Savings Bank, drafted its charter, and was dir. many years; pres. Bd. of Water Commrs., Park Bd., etc.; organized Real Estate & Savings Instn., 1858, drafted its charter, and was its first pres., 1858-74; acted as financial agent for Jay Cooke & Co., of Phila., at outbreak of Civil War, 1861; *m* 1830, Rebecca Neff Patterson (1810-98);
2–Wayman Crow (2 below).
10–John **Throckmorton** (qv);
9–John (*d* 1690), of Monmouth Co., N.J., 1669; rep. Gen. Assembly, 1675; justice; *m* 1670, Alice Stout (Richard[10] [1620-1705], one of the 12 patentees of Monmouth Co., N.J., 1665, mem. 1st Gen. Assembly (composed of deps. and patentees), Portland Point, N.J., 1671);
8–Rebecca, *m* John **Stillwell** (1660-1724), high sheriff, Richmond Co., S.I., 1693; justice, 1702; del. to Gen. Assembly, 1710-24 (Richard[9] [1634-88], apptd. 1664, under the Duke of York, justice of the West Riding of Yorkshire, comprising S.I. and the western portion of L.I., N.Y.; Nicholas[10] [1607-71], from Eng., 1638, settled on Manhattan Island);
7–Rebecca (*b* 1693), *m* Ebenezer **Saltar** (1696-1760; Judge Richard[8], qv, *m* Sarah [*b* 1669], dau. of John Bowne, qv, *m* Lydia, dau. Rev. Obadiah Holmes, qv);
6–Hannah (*d* 1785), *m* 1733, Richard **Britton** (*d* 1771), of S.I., N.Y.; removed to Monmouth Co., N.J., ca. 1733 (Nathaniel[7] [*d* ante 1732], of S.I., N.Y.; Nathaniel[8] [1662-1703], of L.I., N.Y.; Nathaniel[9] [*d* 1683], of Richmond Co., S.I., N.Y.);
5–John (1737-1816), moved from Monmouth Co., N.J., to Phila., Pa.; was taxed in Phila. Co., 1780, on an estate of 194,000 pounds (Pa. archives, Vol. 15); sketch of John Britton's home in Phila., 1802 (standing in 1912), by Joseph Pennell in "Our Philadelphia," p. 321, designated as N.E. cor. Front and Callowhill streets, land originally owned by William Penn; *m* Apr. 1, 1767, by Bishop White, at Christ Ch., Phila., Eleanor Waters (1748-99; Thomas[6] [*d* 1795] resided at "Bellwood," a property near Valley Forge, Pa., in possession of the Waters, Britton, and Budd families prior to the Revolution until 1816);
4–Suzannah (1768-1848), *m* George **Budd** (4 above);
3–George Knight, *m* Rebecca Neff Patterson (3 above);
2–Wayman Crow (1839-1917), one of the first mems. of the San Francisco Stock Exchange; firm Budd & Co., San Francisco, 1864; settled at Chicago, Ill.; stock and bond business, 1883; mem. Chicago Bd. of Trade, 1883; mem. Chicago Club; *m* 1864, Annabelle Parks (1846-1916); issue: I–Georgia Knight (qv for maternal lineage); II–Wayman C., Jr. (*b* 1869); III–Britton Ihrie (1 above); IV–Blanche (*b* 1874; *m* 1907, William Henry McFetridge, 1869-1926).
1–*m* Jan. 1, 1900, Katharine Doddridge Kreigh (*d* Jan. 1925); dau. of Charles W. Kreigh, of Chicago.
1–*m* 2d, Feb. 20, 1928, Marie, dau. of Daniel P. Sheehan, ry. builder, Evanston, Ill.
1–Became pres. Met. West Side Elevated Ry. Co., Chicago, 1910, Northwestern Elevated R.R. Co. and South Side Elevated R.R. Co., 1911, Chicago, North Shore & Milwaukee R.R., 1916, Public Service Co. of Northern Ill., 1923, Chicago Rapid Transit Co., 1924, Chicago, South Shore & South Bend R.R., 1925, C.,A.-&E. R.R. Co., 1925; officer or director in various other corpns. (see Who's Who in America). Trustee and mem. exec. com. Chicago Century of Progress Expn. to be held in 1933. Capt., maj. and lt. col., 11th Regt., Ill. N.G., 1917-18. Clubs: Chicago, Union League (v.p.), Industrial, City, The Attic, Evanston Country, Commercial, Mellody Farm Country, Knollwood Country. Office: 1218 Edison Bldg., Chicago, Ill.

GEORGE BUDD (1764-1817), of Philadelphia (Copy of miniature by Rembrandt Peale). George Budd married Nov. 22, 1792, Suzannah, daughter of John Britton (1737-1816), of Philadelphia. Among his descendants: George Knight Budd (1802-1876) St. Louis, Mo., and Britton I. Budd of Chicago

1–**BUDD, Georgia Knight,** *b* San Francisco, Calif., Feb. 14, 1867.
7–William **Budd** (qv);
6–Thomas (1686-1742), of Burlington Co., N.J.; *m* Deborah Langstaff (bap. 1703);
5–Levi (1726-90), of Phila., Pa.; *m* 2d, 1762, Elizabeth Sheilds (1735-98);
4–George (1764-1817), of Phila. (see portrait); *m* 1792, Suzannah Britton;
3–George Knight (Feb. 12, 1802-Sept. 24, 1875), settled at St. Louis, Mo., 1836, and established the private banking house of Budd & Co., later Budd & Park; elected city comptroller, 1850; one of the founders of the Boatmens Savings Bank, drafted its charter, and was dir. many years; pres. Bd. of Water Commrs., Park Bd., etc.; organized Real Estate & Savings Instn., 1858, drafted its charter, and was its first pres., 1858-74; acted as financial agent for Jay Cooke & Co., of Phila., at outbreak of Civil War, 1861; *m* 1830, Rebecca Neff Patterson (1810-98);
2–Wayman Crow (2 below).
7–Randall **Vernon** (1639-1725), Quaker; from Stanthorne, Cheshire Co., Eng.; settled in Nether Providence, Chester Co., on land acquired from William Penn by grant 1681; one of a committee apptd. by Friends of Chester Monthly Meeting to build a meeting house; mem. Pa. Assembly from Chester Co., 1687; justice of the peace, 1692; declined same office 1693; *m* 1670, Sarah Bradshaw (*d* 1718), of Stanthorne, Cheshire Co., Eng.;
6–Jacob (*d* 1740), of Thornbury, Chester Co., Pa.; Quaker; *m* 1701, Ann Yearsley (*d* 1740);
5–Mary (*b* 1722), of Thornbury; *m* 1753, at Concord Meeting, Richard **Parks** (*d* 1803; Richard[6], *m* Suzanna Carleton);
4–Jacob (*d* 1841), of Thornbury; Quaker; *m* 2d, Hannah Chamberlain (*d* ante 1813; John[5], of Birmingham, Delaware Co., Pa.);
3–John (*b* Thornbury, Jan. 9, 1810-*d* San Francisco, Calif., Dec. 17, 1879), Quaker; *m* 1842, Rebecca Sheilds Kimball (1816-66);
2–Annabelle (1846-1916), *m* 1864, Wayman Crow **Budd** (1839-1917), one of the first members of the San Francisco Stock Exchange; firm Budd & Co., San Francisco, 1864; settled at Chicago, Ill.; stock and bond business, 1883; mem. Chicago Bd. of Trade, 1883; mem. Chicago Club (for issue and other lineages see Britton I. Budd).

1–Mem. C.D.A. Winter residence: 1625 Plumosa Way, San Diego, Calif. Chicago address: c/o Britton I. Budd.

1–**BURNAM, Florence Kennedy,** *b* "Burnamwood," Richmond, Ky., Nov. 2, 1902.
6–Henry **Burnam,** from Eng. to Md., ca. 1760;
5–John (1762-1831), soldier Am. Rev.; *m* 1787, Ann Fort (Capt. Frederick[6], of Wake Co., N.C., Am. Rev., *m* —Newsome);
4–Thompson (1789-1872), *m* Lucinda Field;
3–Curtis Field (1820-1909), mem. Gen. Assembly; state senator; asst. sec. treas., 1875; lawyer, statesman; *m* Sarah Harris Rollins (see Vol. III, p. 102, for Rollins and other lineages);
2–Edmund Tutt (2 below).
7–William **Kennedy** (1695-1777), from Ireland to Bucks Co., Pa., 1730; *m* in Ireland, Mary Henderson;
6–James (1730-99), *m* Jane Maxwell (1748-84; John[7], from Ireland to Sussex Co., N.J., 1747, *m* Ann–);
5–Maxwell (1782-1845), col. War 1812; *m* his cousin, Margaret Maxwell (*b* 1781; Robert[6], lt. Am. Rev., *m* Eleanor Sloan; John[7], *m* Ann–);
4–Winfield Scott (1815-97), *m* 1837, Mary Malvina Slaymaker;
3–John Matthias (1840-1911), capt. Pittsburgh Rifles in Civil War; *m* 1866, Florence Graddy (1841-1926); see Vol. III, p. 102, for Graddy and other lineages;
2–Jessie Graddy (2 below).
11–Matthys (Blanshan) **Blanchan,** from Artois, France, in "Gilded Otter," to Wiltwyck, N.Y., Apr. 27-Dec. 7, 1660, with wife and family; patentee of New Paltz; in several expdns. against Indians, 1663;
10–Catarinen (Catherine), *m* at Mannheim, Germany, 1655, Louis **DuBois** (qv);
9–Abraham (1657-1731), *m* Margaret Deyo, or Doyan (Christian Deyo[10], from France, patentee and founder of New Paltz);
8–Leah (1687-1758), *m* 1712, Philip **Ferree** (1687-1753; John[9] [*d* in Palatinate], his widow, Maria Warrimbere, came from Palatinate to Kingston, N.Y., thence to Paradise, Lancaster Co., Pa.);
7–Joel (1730-1801), patriot Am. Rev.; *m* Mary Copeland (*d* 1752);
6–Isaac (1752-1829), *m* his cousin, Mary Ferree (1747-1806; Isaac[7], *m* Susan Green; Daniel[8]; John[9], same as 9 above);
5–Rebecca (1791-1827), *m* Matthias **Slaymaker** (1784-1862), see Vol. III, p. 102, for Slaymaker lineage;
4–Mary M. (1817-43), *m* Winfield S. **Kennedy** (4 above);
3–John M., *m* Florence Graddy (3 above);
2–Jessie Graddy (*b* 1869), *m* 1901, Edmund Tutt **Burnam** (1864-1911), for issue see Vol. III, p. 102.
1–A.B., Vassar, '25. Residence: "Yorick," Richmond, Ky.

1–**BURNSIDE, Don Gillham,** *b* Pt. Pleasant, W. Va., Jan. 1, 1891.
7–Robert **Burnside** (1700-ca. 1742), from Co. Tyrone, Ireland, prob. with group of Scotch-Irish from Ulster who settled in Shenandoah Valley, Va.; he settled (now) Bath Co.; *m* ca. 1725, Esther– (*d* 1756);
6–James (ca. 1728-1812), *d* Union, Monroe Co., Va.: one of 1st settlers in Monroe and Greenbrier cos., (now) W.Va., where he acquired many land tracts; served in colonial militia, Va., and in Am. Rev.; *m* ca. 1760, Isabella–;
5–James (*b* ca. 1764), he and bro. John, with others, commrs. to organize Monroe Co., 1799; had land tract in Boone Co., W.Va.; ens. Monroe Co. Militia; *m* Anne–;
4–Joseph (1794-1869), *d* Middleport, O.; engaged in rafting salt and lumber down Coal and Kanawha rivers; removed to Middleport, O., and was noted river man; funeral procession was on Ohio River in the "Oriole" to West Columbia, W.Va., where he was buried on top of hill overlooking river; *m* 1838, Lucinda Fields (*d* 1882; John William[5], *m* Mildred Taylor);
3–Joseph (1839-95), of Kanawha Co., Va.; served Co. A, 140th Regt., Ohio N.G. during Civil War; *m* 1863, Elizabeth Jane Martin (1844-1913; John[4], *m* Catherine Bartlett);
2–Edwin A. (2 below).
8–David **Morris** (*d* 1720), of Chester Co., Pa.; *m* 1685, Mary Philpin;
7–Isaac (1689-1734/35), *m* Sarah–;
6–Jonathan (ca. 1722-ca. 1790), *m* 1747, Mary West (ca. 1722-1807; John[7], *m* Sarah, dau. of Thomas Pearson, *m* Margery Smith);
5–David (1766-1834), *m* 1790, Mary Fulton (1768-1806; Robert, Sr.[6], to Phila., ca. 1750, *m* Mary Smith);
4–David (1800-68), Washington Co., Pa.; *m* 1824, Frances Millard (1801-40; Benjamin[5], *m* Mary–);
3–Robert Fulton (1840-1922), *m* 1859, Elizabeth Ann Humphrey;
2–Minnie Belle (2 below).
9–Michael **Humphrey** (qv);
8–Samuel (1656-1736), *m* Mary Mills (*b* 1662);
7–Samuel (1689-1759), *m* 1731, Mary Orton;
6–Noah (1747-1819), *m* 1774, Sarah Marshall (*b* 1750);
5–Seth (1781-1827), *m* 1804, Olive Smith;
4–Joseph S. (1805-89), of Washington Co., O.; *m* 1837, Elmira Muchler (1817-97; Godfrey[5], *m* Jerusha–);
3–Elizabeth Ann (1838-1916), *m* Robert F. **Morris** (3 above);
2–Minnie Belle (*b* 1867), *m* 1886, Edwin A. **Burnside** (1864-1922), designer of river steamers; chmn. exec. com. Kanawha River Improvement Assn., mem. Rivers and Harbors Congress of U.S., Soc. Naval Architects and Marine Engrs., Am. Soc. of M.E., Naval History Soc., v.p. Nat. Bd. Steam Navigation, etc.; issue: I–Morris C. (*b* 1887; *m* Louise M. Buck); II–Don Gillham (1 above); III–Max E. (*b* 1893; *m* Elizabeth Ruffner); IV–Mary Elizabeth (*b* 1900; *m* Wendell Reynolds).
1–*m* Jan. 8, 1921, Margaret Elizabeth Anthony, *b* Detroit, Mich., Nov. 27, 1895; dau. of Howard B. Anthony; issue: 1–Mary Elizabeth, *b* Detroit, Mich., Oct. 21, 1921; 2–Donna, *b* Detroit, Feb. 25, 1926.
1–Ed. W.Va. U., 1917. Electrical engr. Served in 12th F.A. Brig., radio officer, May 1917-Feb. 1919. Mem. S.A.R., N.E.H.G.S., I.A.G., A.L., M.O.W.W Club: Manufacturers Country. Residence: 5135 Pulaski Av., Germantown, Pa.

1–**BURR, George Alfred,** *b* Stockport, O., Sept. 8, 1863.
7–Henry **Burr** (*d* 1743), Quaker; came to America, with William Penn, 1682; settled at Mt. Holly, N.J.; *m* Elizabeth Hudson (Robert[8], of L.I., *m* Mary, dau. Richard Thredder, of London);
6–Joseph (*b* 1694), Quaker; *m* 1726, Jane Abbott (1701-67; John[7], from Eng. in the "Bristol Merchant" to Phila., *m* Anne Mauleverer);
5–William (1740-1833), Quaker; *m* Ann Edwards (William[6], *m* Martha Foulke [Hugh[7], *m* Ann Williams; Edward[8], qv]; John[7], *m* Mary Howell; Thomas[8]);
4–David (*b* 1777), of Belmont Co., O.; Baptist;
3–William (*d* 1854), killed while homesteading land nr. White Post, Kan.; *m* 1827, Elizabeth Maffitt (1804-92; Henry[4], of Loudoun Co., Va., *m* 2d, Margaret Brent);
2–Alfred (2 below).
7–Garrett Hendricks **De Weese,** Huguenot, from Holland to New York 1688; removed to Germantown, Pa., 1690; *m* Zytian–;
6–Cornelius (*b* Holland), *m* Margaret Koster (or Kuster);
5–Cornelius, *m* Margaret Richards (William[6], of Phila.);
4–Owen, emigrated to Ohio; *m* Mary Lee;
3–Hannah (*b* 1791), *m* Benjamin **Grimes,** settled at Stockport, O.;
2–Esther (1833-70), *m* 1853, Alfred **Burr** (1829-64), pvt. Co. C, 122d Inf. Ohio Vols., died from wounds received in Battle of the Wilderness; buried in Arlington Cemetery; issue: I–Alcinda Jane (*b* 1854; *m* Albert Allard; *m* 2d, William Lynn); II–Emma Louise (*b* 1855; *m* John Warren Wallace; *m* 2d, Beniah Elliott); III–John Warren (1858-79); IV–Clarence Everett (*b* 1860); V–George Alfred (1 above).
1–*m* Jan. 1, 1890, Virginia Stainback Hamlin (Oct. 20, 1868-Jan. 20, 1915); issue: 1–Alfred Hamlin (qv for Hamlin lineage); 2–Laura Esther, *b* Lebanon, O., Oct. 14, 1892; *m* Nov. 4, 1911, Allen Duckworth Stewart (issue: Laura Margaret, *b* Nov. 20, 1914; Mary Virginia, *b* Oct. 23, 1917; George Edward, *b* Sept.

27, 1920; Ruth Burr, *b* July 12, 1925; Martha Elizabeth, *b* Mar. 21, 1927); 3–Edward Everett, *b* Lebanon, O., Jan. 18, 1895; 4–George (*d* infancy, 1900).
1–Grad. Northern Normal U., Lebanon, O. Lawyer, Cincinnati, O., and Paragould, Ark., 35 yrs.; pastor M.E. Ch., Imboden, Ark., 4 yrs. Mem S.V. Mason. Residence: Imboden, Ark.

1–**BURR, Alfred Hamlin,** *b* Lebanon, Warren Co., O., Nov. 22, 1890.
9–Capt. John **Hamlin** (*d* 1720), *m* Elizabeth– (*d* ca. 1720);
8–John (*d* 1725), *m* Ann Goodrich (Maj. Charles[9]);
7–Charles;
6–Charles (*d* 1786), *m* 1757, Agnes Cocke;
5–Thomas (1758-1857), *m* 1807, Mary Ligon Stainback (Peter[6], of Nottoway Co., Va.);
4–Peter Stainback (1808-91), *m* 1832, Virginia Ann Michaux (1812-89);
3–Richard Franklin (1834-94), sgt., Co. H, 3d Ky. Mounted Inf.; *m* 1866, Laura Juliet Boggs (1846-86; Dr. Robert Ewart[4], *m* as his 2d wife, Juliet, dau. of Benjamin Kelly, of Md. and Ky.);
2–Virginia Stainback (2 below).
10–Richard **Cocke** (qv);
9–Thomas (1636 or 38-1696), of "Pickthorn Farm"; *m* 1663, Widow Margaret (Wood) Jones (*d* ca. 1719; Abraham Wood[10], from Eng., 1620, one of the four maj. gens. commanding the mil. establishment of Va.);
8–Stephen (1664-1717), of Prince George Co.; *m* 1st, 1688, Widow Sarah Marston;
7–Abraham (*d* 1759), of Nottoway and Lunenburg cos., Va.; sheriff of Amelia Co., Va., 1751; justice, 1745, et seq.;
6–Agnes, *m* Charles **Hamlin** (6 above).
11–Richard **Cocke** (qv); *m* 2d, Mary Aston;
10–William (1655-93), *m* 2d, ca. 1689, Sarah Flower, of James City Co.;
9–Mary, *m* Obadiah **Smith** (John[10], of Charles City Co., *m* Hannah Dwast);
8–Ann, *m* Richard **Woodson** (Robert[9], 9 below).
7–Judith (*b* 1703), *m* ca. 1722, Jacob **Michaux** (Abraham[8], *m* Suzanne Roché);
6–Capt. Joseph (1739-1807), *m* 1761, Judith Woodson;
5–Richard Waters, or Woodson (1779-1838), *m* 1800, Mary Mayo Macon;
4–Virginia Ann (1812-89), *m* Peter S. **Hamlin** (4 above).
10–Dr. John **Woodson** (qv);
9–Robert (*b* 1634), *m* Elizabeth Ferris (Richard[10], of Curles, Va.);
8–Benjamin (1666-1723), *m* 1688, Sarah Porter;
7–John (*b* 1696), *m* 1731, Mary Miller (William[8], of Lancaster Co.);
6–Judith (1747-1803), *m* Capt. Joseph **Michaux** (6 above).
11–Dr. John **Woodson** (qv);
10–John (1632-84), *m* 1654;
9–John (1655-1700), *m* 1677, Mary Tucker (*d* 1710; Samuel[10], *m* Jane–);
8–Mary Jane (*b* 1686), *m* her 2d cousin, Joseph **Woodson** (1664-1735; Robert[9], 9 above);
7–Tucker (1720-76), *m* 1760, Mary Netherland (*d* 1775; Wade[8]);
6–Sarah or Sally (1764-1824), *m* ca. 1780, William **Macon** (*b* Jan. 7, 1754; Henry[7], of New Kent Co., Va., *m* 1st, Rebecca, dau. of William Mayo, qv; John[8], *m* Ann–; Gideon[9], of New Kent and Isle of Wight cos., *m* Martha Woodward);
5–Mary Mayo (*d* 1813), *m* Richard Waters or Woodson **Michaux** (5 above).
2–Virginia Stainback Hamlin (1868-1915), *m* 1890, Rev. George Alfred **Burr** (qv).
1–*m* Oct. 26, 1914, Hazel Edna Wilson, *b* Paragould, Ark., Aug. 31, 1891; dau. of William Woodburn Wilson of Paragould and Little Rock, Ark.; issue: 1–William Alfred, *b* Little Rock, Ark., Apr. 29, 1918; 2–Mary Ann, *b* Little Rock, July 28, 1921.
1–B.S., Vanderbilt U., '14 (Sigma Alpha Epsilon). Sec.-treas., W. W. Wilson Stave Co., since 1921. Commd. 2d lt., adj. gen. dept., Feb. 4, 1919; served at Leon Springs, Tex., Trade Test School, Newark, N.J., in Adj. Gen. Dept. and Camp Pike, Ark. Mem. H.S., S.A.R., S.C.V., I.A.G., N.E.H.G.S., A.L. Clubs: Little Rock Country, Lakeside Country, Athletic Assn. (Little Rock), Shrine Country. Mason (32°). Residence: 1621 Gaines St., Little Rock, Ark.

The PORTER HOMESTEAD, at what was then called Judd's Meadows, then a part of Waterbury (Mattatuck), and now a part of Naugatuck, Conn.; still standing (1930); the north (left) end was built and occupied by 1691; the south (right) end was added between 1730-35.

1–**CARTER, Mabel Woodruff Porter (Mrs. Merritt E.),** *b* Naugatuck, Conn., Aug. 29, 1858.
8–Dr. Daniel **Porter** (*d* 1690), settled at Farmington, Conn., ante 1644/45; *m* Mary–;
7–Dr. Daniel (1652-1726), original propr., Waterbury; *m* 2d, ante 1699, Deborah Holcomb (1674-1765; Joshua[8]; Thomas[9]);
6–Capt. Thomas (1702-97), selectman; served in War between Eng. and France, 1756-57; *m* 1727, Mary Welton (*b* 1704; Stephen[7], *m* 1st, 1701/02, Mary, dau. of Joseph Gaylord; John[8], from Eng. ca. 1667, *m* Mary Upson);
5–Thomas (1736-1817), Am. Rev.; *m* 1758, Mehitable Hine (1739-1837; Daniel[6]; Samuel[7]; Thomas[8]);
4–Truman (1763-1838), dep. Gen. Ct.; Am. Rev.; justice; *m* 1784, Sarah Thompson (1763-1837; Jonathan[5]);
3–Julius (1790-1831), *m* 1811, Mabel Woodruff (1794-1842; Jonah[4]; John[5]; John[6]; Matthew[7]; Matthew[8], qv);
2–Richard Thompson (2 below).
7–John **Brockett** (*b* Eng., 1610-*d* Wallingford, Conn., 1690), came with Davenport and Eaton to New Haven, Conn.; surgeon, war bet. Holland and Eng., 1654; laid out Elizabethtown, N.J., 1664; a founder of Wallingford, 1667-70; dep.; commr.; signed Covenant, 1639;
6–John (1642-1720), physician; ed. Oxford, Eng.; *m* Elizabeth Doolittle (1652-1731);
5–Moses (1680-1764), *m* Lydia Ann Grannis (1706-42);
4–Abel (1725-1815), soldier French and Indian War and Am. Rev.; *m* 1755, Hannah Pierpont (1736-1816; Joseph[5]; Reverend James[6]; John[7]; James[8], qv);
3–Lyman (1780-1857), *m* Hannah Goodsell (niece of Timothy Goodsell of Watertown, and Dr. Isaac Goodsell, of Woodbridge);
2–Mary Anne (1820-1902), *m* 1844, Richard Thompson **Porter** (1819-70), Mason; issue: I–Helen Alice (1845-1924; *m* James L. Edwards); II–Mary Grace (*b* 1852; *m* —Hitchcock; *m* 2d, —Dorman); III–Emily Nancy (1854-78; *m* Walter Irwin); IV–Mabel (1 above); V–Albert Richard (*b* 1862; *m* Mary L. Scott); VI–Frank Harvey (1865-92).
1–*m* Bryant Pitcher.
1–*m* 2d, Oct. 15, 1890, Merritt E. Carter, *b* Meriden, Conn. (Feb. 14, 1856-July 9, 1914); son of Miles Carter, of Clinton, Conn.
1–Ed. Peoria (Ill.) pub. schs. and business coll., New Haven, Conn. Asst. official reporter Conn. Superior Ct., New Haven Co., 1891-1907, official reporter, 1907–. Mem. D.A.R., I.A.G., New Haven Colony of N.E. Women, Travel Club of America. Residence: 47 W. Park Av., New Haven, Conn.

1–**CATLIN, Robert Mayo,** *b* Burlington, Vt., June 8, 1853.
8–Thomas **Catlin** (qv);
7–John, *m* 1665, Mary Marshall;
6–Samuel (*b* 1673), Hartford, Conn.; *m* 1702, Elizabeth Norton (John[7]);

ROBERT MAYO CATLIN

5–John (1703-68), *m* 1728, Margaret Seymour;
4–Alexander (*b* 1738), capt. Am. Rev.; *m* 1767, Abigail Goodman;
3–Guy (*b* 1782), *m* 1808, Melinda Wadhams;
2–Henry Wadhams (2 below).
8–Richard **Treat** (qv);
7–Susanna (1629-1705), *m* 1652, Lt. Robert **Webster** (1627-76), of Middletown, Conn. (Gov. John[8], qv);
6–Elizabeth (1674-1754), *m* John **Seymour** (1664-1748);
5–Margaret (1707-92), *m* John **Catlin** (5 above).
7–Richard **Goodman** (1609-76), from Eng. to Cambridge, Mass., 1632; removed to Hartford, Conn., later to Hadley, Mass.; killed in King Philip's War; *m* 1659, Mary Terry;
6–Richard (*b* 1663), *m* 1703, Aligol Poutry;
5–Timothy (1706-86), *m* Johanna Wadsworth;
4–Abigail (*b* 1741), *m* Alexander **Catlin** (4 above).
8–William **Wadsworth** (qv);
7–Capt. Joseph, "Charter Oak Joe" (*b* 1647), capt. Hartford Train Band; *m* Elizabeth Barnard (*d* 1710);
6–Joseph (1682-1778), *m* Johanna Hovey (1684-1762);
5–Johanna (1710-68), *m* Timothy **Goodman** (5 above).
2–Henry Wadhams **Catlin** (1811-78), *m* Aug. 10, 1840, Mary Cobb Mayo (1816-56); issue: I–Helen (*b* 1841); II–Henry Guy (1843-1925); III–Albert Ormsby (1846-49); IV–Charles Albert (1849-1916); V–Robert M. (1 above); VI–Walter Moses (*b* 1856; *m* Louise Merk);
1–*m* June 15, 1882, Ann Elizabeth Robertson, *b* San Francisco, Calif., 1859; dau. of Gilbert Robertson, of San Francisco, Calif.; issue: 1–Bessie Margery, *b* Mineral Hill, Nev., Jan. 18, 1883; 2–Mary Helen, *b* San Francisco, Calif., Mar. 30, 1887; 3–Robert Mayo, Jr., *b* Kennilworth, Cape Colony, S. Africa, Feb. 4, 1900.
1–B.S., U. Vt., 1872, C.E., 1873 (hon. E.M., 1902; Sc.D., Rutgers, 1918). Mining engr. (see Who's Who in America). Eastern mgr. of mines, N.J. Zinc Co., since 1906. Life mem. Am. Inst. Mining and Metall. Engrs.; pres. Mine Mgrs. Assn. of The Witwatersrand, 1903-04; pres. Mech. Engrs. Assn. of the Witwatersrand, 1903-04; life mem. advisory bd. South African Instn. of Engrs. (past pres.). Residence: Franklin, N.J.

1–**CHAMBERLAIN, Sarah Estella M. Reese (Mrs. Edwin G.),** *b* Holmes Co., nr. Wilmot, Stark Co., O., July 28, 1872.
4–Lewis **Reese** (*d* Apr. 15, 1868, aet. 78 yrs. 9 mos. 24 days) from Fayette Co., Pa., Dec. 1820, to nr. Wilmot, Stark Co., O.; *m* Catherine Fisher (*d* Feb. 16, 1863, aet. 76 yrs. 26 days), both buried Mt. Eaton, Wayne Co., O.;
3–George (Oct. 15, 1820-Oct. 24, 1897), buried Wilmot, O.; *m* Jan. 11, 1844, Sarah McClintock;
2–James M. (2 below).
5–Walter **McClintock** (*b* prob. in Ireland, 1756), lived nr. Dublin; to America, 1790; settled in Va.; later moved to Harrison Co. nr. Cadiz, O.; *m* Isabel Moore;
4–James (*d* Sept. 13, 1865), served 21 yrs. as squire in Holmes Co., O.; Federalist, ardent Whig, "in 1856, became one of the best Republicans Holmes Co. ever had"; Winebrennarian; deed to his farm (a quarter section, west of Wilmot, O., $2.50 an acre, 1817), signed by President Monroe; *m* Mar. 1818, aet. 15, Mary Clark (*d* Oct. 5, 1871; Andrew[5], buried at Forest, Hardin Co., O., *m* Catherine, dau. of a Hollander);
3–Sarah (Feb. 26, 1824-Dec. 16, 1910), *m* George **Reese** (3 above).
10–Dea. Stephen **Hart** (qv);
9–John (1630-66), from Eng. with father, 1632; *m* 1651, Sarah–;
8–Capt. John (1655-Nov. 11, 1714), he alone of his father's family escaped being burned to death, Dec. 15, 1666; capt. colonial troops, Queen Anne's War, 1702; dep. Gen. Ct., 4 yrs.; *m* Mary Moore (*d* Sept. 19, 1738);
7–John (1684-Oct. 7, 1753), of Farmington, Conn.; elected 23 times to Conn. Gen. Ct.; *m* Mar. 20, 1706, Esther Gridley (*d* July 10, 1743); *m* 2d, Jan. 11, 1744, Hannah Hull (*d* Nov. 27, 1760);
6–John (Oct. 11, 1714-Dec. 18, 1772), of Kensington, Conn.; *m* 1744, Anna Hall; *m* 2d, Jan. 30, 1749, Huldah Gould (*d* Jan. 19, 1771); *m* 3d, May 28, 1772, Martha Foot;
5–Silas (May 9, 1760-Aug. 6, 1828), *b* Canaan, Conn., emigrated 1795, to Palmyra, N.Y.; post 1813, emigrated to Columbiana Co., O., returned 1823 to Palmyra; *m* 1787, Philae Swift;
4–Julia Maria (Sept. 5, 1801-Mar. 21, 1841), *m* 1820, William **Milner** (Jan. 26, 1794-Jan. 1, 1860), both buried Monroeville Cemetery, nr. Salineville, Columbiana Co., O.;
3–Philena (Nov. 1, 1821-July 4, 1905), *m* Feb. 22, 1844, James (Crumbleigh, Crumly) **Crumley** (June 7, 1816-Dec. 25, 1859), both buried on same cemetery lot as 4 above (William[4], came to Phila., ca. 1777, *m* Mary Druggin);
2–Margaret Annis (2 below).
11–Richard **Warren,** Mayflower Pilgrim (qv);
10–Nathaniel (1624-67), *m* 1645, Sarah Walker;
9–Alice (1656-92), *m* 1674, Thomas **Gibbs** (1636-1732);
8–Abigail (*d* ante Nov. 1741), *m* 1697, Jireh **Swift** (ca. 1665-Apr. 1749; William[9] [*d* 1705/06], *m* Ruth–; William[10], qv);
7–Jabez (1700-67), *m* 1729, Abigail Pope (*d* ca. 1776);
6–Elisha (1731-77), *m* 1756, Mary Ranson (*b* 1737);
5–Philae (1767-1813), *m* Silas **Hart** (5 above).
2–Margaret Annis Crumley (July 19, 1847-July 1, 1906), *m* Oct. 24, 1871, James M. **Reese** (Mar. 22, 1847-June 15, 1908), Civil War; issue: I–Sarah Estella M. (1 above); II–(Nellie) Mary Eleanor (*b* 1873; *m* 1919, James Ray, *d* 1929); III–(Jettie) Elida Juliet (1874-82); IV–Daisy Rebecca (*b* 1876; *m* 1900, John Smith); V–Cora Opal (1878-1915; *m* 1906, Walter Stabb); VI–Philena Margaret Clessing (*b* 1883; *m* 1901, Albert Atack).
1–*m* at Akron, O., Oct. 10, 1894, Edwin Grant Chamberlain; issue (all *b* Akron, O.): 1–Georgia Edwina, *b* Mar. 24, 1897; grad. Buchtel Acad. (Akron, O.), 1914; 2–Gladys Estella (qv for paternal lineages); 3–Armin Curtis, *b* Apr. 4, 1905.
1–Grad. Akron Central H.S., 1891. Mem. S.M.D., D.A.R. (chapter regent), U.S.D. 1812, D.U.V. Residence: 1526 18th St., Cuyahoga Falls, Ohio.

1–**CHAMBERLAIN, Gladys Estella,** *b* Akron, O., Mar. 25, 1903.
4–James **Chamberlain** (Jan. 8, 1797-July 27, 1876), from Va., Apr. 1823, to Ashland Co., O.; buried with wife in Clearcreek Church Yard; *m* June 22, 1826, Sarah Peterson (Dec. 8, 1806-Aug. 1896);

3–Weden Smith (Sept. 14, 1843-Aug. 10, 1914), O.V.I., Civil War; *m* Jan. 19, 1865, Maryette Wiard;
2–Edwin Grant (2 below).
11–Nicholas **White** (qv);
10–John (1649-1726), resided in that part of Taunton which became Raynham, 1731; surveyor, clk. of mil. co.; selectman of Taunton; large owner of real estate; *m* 1679/80, Hannah Smith (Samuel[11], *m* Susanna Reed);
9–John (1681-ca. 1758), carpenter, surveyor, millwright; selectman Raynham, 1733; assessor; town treas.; built 1st meeting house in Raynham; *m* 1709, Elizabeth Crossman (Samuel[10], *m* Elizabeth Bell);
8–George (*d* 1767), *m* 1745, Hannah Bryant (Dr. Timothy[9], *m* Hannah Hodges);
7–John (Dec. 23, 1749-1834), Am. Rev., sgt., Capt. James Keith's Co., Col. Paul Dudley Sargent's (28th) Regt., corpl., Capt. Keith's Co., order for bounty coat dated camp before Boston, Dec. 21, 1775; *m* Feb. 13, 1772, Martha Keith;
6–John (July 31, 1775-ca. 1831), *m* 1798, Fear Perry;
5–Arabella (Aug. 15, 1799-Apr. 18, 1879), *m* 1820, Calvin **Leach** (*b* Conn., 1792-Aug. 1846), buried Fitchville, O.;
4–Charlotte (1821-1867), *m* 1843, Josiah Milliard **Wiard** (Jerrymy or Jeremiah[5], *m* Hannah Carley, *b* on Mohawk River, N.Y., prob. at Constantia);
3–Maryette (Nov. 12, 1844-Jan. 15, 1928), *m* Weden Smith **Chamberlain** (3 above).
10–Rev. James **Keith** (*d* 1719, aet. 76), from Scotland, 1662; first minister of Bridgewater, Mass.; *m* Susanna Edson (Dea. Samuel[11]); *m* 2d, 1707, Mary, widow of Thomas Williams;
9–Josiah (*d* 1754), *m* 1703, Mary Lathrop (Samuel[10]);
8–Josiah (*b* 1706), *m* 1730, Ruth Manly;
7–Martha (1754-1816), *m* John **White** (7 above).
2–Edwin Grant **Chamberlain** (*b* Avon, Fulton Co., Ill., Sept. 15, 1867), contractor and builder, Akron, O.; I.O.O.F. (mem. Akron Lodge, 35 yrs.); *m* at Akron, O., Oct. 10, 1894, Sarah Estella M. Reese (qv for genealogy and issue).
1–B.A., U.Akron, 1923, B.E., 1927. Mem. S.M.D., D.A.R., U.S.D. 1812. Residence: 1526 18th St., Cuyahoga Falls, O.

1–**CHAMBERLIN, Elmer Henry,** *b* East Elba, N.Y., July 21, 1866.
8–Henry **Chamberlin** (1595-1674), from Eng. in the "Diligent"; settled at Ipswich, Mass.; admitted freeman 1638/39; settled at Hingham, 1638; *m* Jane–;
7–William (1620-78), *m* 2d, 1661, Sarah Jones;
6–Joseph (1665-1752), *m* 1688, Mercy Dickinson (1668-1735);
5–John (*b* 1707), *m* ca. 1730, Eunice Johnson (*b* 1709);
4–Benjamin (1750-1824), ens., 1st lt., Berkshire Co. militia, Am. Rev.; *d* at Amsterdam, N.Y.; *m* Lucy Day (1756-1843; Adonijah[5]; Capt. Benjamin[6]; John, Jr.[7]; John[8]; Robert[9]);
3–Charles (1799-1862), *m* 1819, Catherine Ann Howell (1797-1865);
2–Alvin (2 below).
8–Edward **Hinman** (qv);
7–Benjamin (1662-1713), dep., Woodbury, Conn., 1711; *m* 1684, Elizabeth Lamb (Samuel[8]; Thomas[9], came with Winthrop's fleet, 1630);
6–Wait (1706-75), capt. in colonial wars; *m* 1729, Ann Hurd (1706-85);
5–Bethuel (*b* 1742), sgt., ens., lt. in Am. Rev.; capt., 1784; *m* 1770, Hannah Hickok (*b* 1743);
4–Justus (1778-1838), *m* 1808, Ruth Buell;
3–Henry Delos (1809-69), *m* 1838, Mary Ann Crocker (James, Jr.[4]; James[5]; Jabez[6]; Samuel[7]; Thomas[8], to New London, Conn., ca. 1650);
2–Marie Louise (2 below).
11–John **Alden,** Mayflower Pilgrim (qv);
10–Elizabeth, *m* William **Pabodie** (*b* 1619);
9–Lydia (1667-1748), *m* 1683, Daniel **Grinnell** (*b* 1665);
8–Priscilla (*b* 1689), *m* 1706, Theophilus **Redfield** (1682-1759);
7–Daniel (1707-58), *m* 1728, Elizabeth– (1701-75);
6–Daniel (1729-88), rep. Gen. Ct.; clk. Com. of Corr., selectman, during Am. Rev.; *m* 1749, Margaret Crane (*b* 1725);
5–Ruth (1756-1839), *m* 1779, Job **Buell,** Jr. (1758-1819), Am. Rev. (Job[6], Am. Rev.; Samuel[7]; Samuel[8]; Samuel[9]; William[10], qv);
4–Ruth (1791-1849), *m* Justus **Hinman** (4 above);
3–Henry Delos, *m* Mary Ann Crocker (3 above);
2–Marie Louise (1841-1903), *m* 1863, Alvin **Chamberlin** (1832-1913); issue: I–Frank Merritt (*b* 1864); II–Elmer Henry (1 above); III–Ada Louise (*b* 1868).
1–Not married. Business manager. Mem. S.M.D., B.O.R., O.F.P.A. (registrar Pa. Soc., 1929-30), H.S., S.A.R. Mason. Residence: 135 Hansberry St., Germantown, Philadelphia, Pa.

ELIZABETH (CHANDLER) PAINE, wife of NATHANIEL PAINE.

1–**CHAMBERLIN, Henry Harmon,** *b* Worcester, Mass., Aug. 6, 1873.
5–Moses (Chamberlayne) **Chamberlin** (1756-1813), of Natick and Hardwick, Mass.; *m* 1783, Hannah Church (1763-1826), of Bristol, R.I. (desc. Capt. Benjamin Church, King Philip's War);
4–Harmon (1784-1858), *m* 1806, Arathusa Hinckley (1786-1872; desc. Gov. Thomas Hinckley, son of Samuel Hinckley, qv);
3–Henry Harmon (1813-89), *m* 1839, Charlotte Ramsey Clarke (*b* 1820);
2–William Wigglesworth (2 below).
9–Stephen **Paine** (qv);
8–Nathaniel (*d* 1678), came to N.E. with his father; *m* Elizabeth–;
7–Nathaniel (1661-1723), of Rehoboth, Mass.; *m* Dorothy Rainsford (John[8]);
6–Nathaniel (1688-1730), *m* Sarah Clarke;
5–Timothy (1730-93), crown mayor, Worcester, Mass., during Am. Rev.; *m* Sarah Chandler;
4–Nathaniel (1759-1840), *m* Elizabeth Chandler (see portrait);
3–Charles (1804-66), *m* Elizabeth Ferguson (*d* ante 1849); *m* 2d, Margaret Webb;
2–Elizabeth Ferguson (*b* 1849), *m* 1872, William Wigglesworth **Chamberlin** (1850-1910).
1–*m* June 1, 1907, Armida Theresa Zoraide Moja, *b* Lugano, Switzerland, May 21, 1888; dau. of Francesco Moja, of Varese, Italy; issue: 1–Harmon Paine, *b* Worcester, Mass., June 7, 1908; ed. Harvard.
1–A.B., Harvard, '95, A.M., 1896. Cnmn. Worcester com. Italian War Relief Fund, World War. Mem. Nat. Security League, Constl. Liberty League. Mem. Chamberlin Family Assn. Decorated Cavaliere della Corona d'Italia. Author (see Who's Who in America). Clubs: Worcester, Quinsigamond Boat; Harvard (Boston, New York); Pacific (Nantucket); Royal Societies, American (London). Summer place: Nantucket, Mass. Residence: 22 May St., Worcester, Mass.

1-**CHATFIELD, Frank H.,** *b* Centervile, Conn., Sept. 2, 1856.
8-George **Chatfield** (1624-71), from Eng. to Guilford, Conn., 1639; *m*. 2d, 1659, Isabel Nettleton:
7-John (*b* 1661), settled at Derby, Conn.; *m* 1684, Anna Harger;
6-Ebenezer, *m* Abigail Prindle;
5-Elnathan, *m* Hannah Northrop;
4-Joel (1757-1836), Woodbridge, Conn.; Am. Rev.; *m* Ruth Stoddard;
3-Oliver Stoddard (1797-1883), *m* Abigail Tuttle;
2-George Wooster (1829-1905), mcht. and mfr.; *m* 1853, Cornelia Ford (1830-1920; Elias[3], of Hamden, Conn.); issue: I-Andrew O. (1854-1919; *m* Ella Yates); II-Frank H. (1 above); III-Minotte Estes (*b* 1859; *m* 1880, Stella Stowe Russell, 1858-1916).
1-*m* Oct. 3, 1876, Emma Cornelia Ford, *b* Westville, Conn., June 7, 1859; dau. of David Ford, of Westville; issue: 1-Lena Gertrude, *b* New Haven, Conn., July 27, 1877.
1-Grad. Hopkins Prep. Sch. Traveling salesman. Residence: 204 Mt. Prospect Av., Newark, N.J.

1-**CLAY, May Stoner (Mrs. Sidney Green),** *b* Montgomery Co., Ky., May 9, 1872.
7-George **Boone** (qv);
6-Squire (*b* 1696), *m* Sarah Morgan (parents of Daniel, the pioneer);
5-George (1737-39-1820), Am. Rev.; *m* ca. 1764, Ann Linville (William[6], *m* Eleanor Bryan);
4-Mary (1776-1831), *m* 1793, Peter Burris **Tribble** (1774-1849; Rev. Andrew[5], *m* Sarah Ann, dau. Thomas Burris);
3-Nancy (1794-1872), *m* ca. 1812, George Washington **Stoner** (1787-1871; George Michael[4], Ky. pioneer, in Am. Rev., *m* Frances Tribble);
2-Lt. Col. Robert Gatewood (2 below).
10-Rev. Nathaniel **Rogers** (qv);
9-Rev. John (1630-84), Ipswich, Mass.; 5th pres. Harvard Coll.; *m* Elizabeth Denison (1640-1723; Maj. Gen. Daniel[10], *m* Patience, dau. Gov. Thomas Dudley, qv);
8-Rev. John (1666-1745), Ipswich; *m* 2d, 1691, Martha Whittingham (1670-1759; William[9], *m* Mary, dau. of Hon. John Lawrence, N.Y. City, qv);
7-William (1699-1749), removed to Md.; colonial officer; *m* 1720, Mary Caldwell, of Annapolis, Md.;
6-Thomas (1725-86), Charlotte Co., Va.; *m* Elizabeth Ann Carr (*d* 1793; Thomas[7], *m* Ann Elizabeth, dau. John Addison);
5-Nathaniel (1755-1804), Bourbon Co., Ky.; Am. Rev.; among those who framed the 2d Constn. of Ky., 1799; *m* 1st, 1783, Frances Cobbs (Capt. Charles[6], Am. Rev., capt. militia, *m* Anne Walton);
4-William (1784-1862), *m* 1806, Anne Cornick (Richard[5], *m* Olioth, dau. John Phelps);
3-Warren Brown (1810-64), *m* Marie Louise Lindsay;
2-Alice (2 below).
8-Col. William **Randolph** (qv);
7-Sir John (1689-1737); *m* 1718, Susanna Beverly (Peter[8], of Gloucester Co.);
6-Mary, *m* 1743, Philip **Grimes,** of Va., removed to Fayette Co., Ky.;
5-Stephen, *m* Sarah Garrard (Daniel[6], *m* Elizabeth, dau. William Montjoy; Col. William[7], from Eng. to Va., Am. Rev.; *m* Mary, dau. Stephen Lewis);
4-Lavinia G. (1801-40), *m* Col. Nimrod **Lindsay** (1789-1840; Thomas[5], *m* Margaret);
3-Marie Louise (1822-1906), *m* Warren Brown **Rogers** (3 above).
2-Lt. Col. Robert Gatewood **Stoner** (1837-98), breeder of trotting horses, Montgomery Co., Ky.; *m* 1867, Alice Rogers (1847-96); *m* 2d, Ida Hamilton; issue (1st marriage): I-Warren W. (*b* 1869; *m* Jennie Fox); II-May (1 above).
1-*m* Dec. 30, 1895, Sidney Green Clay (*b* Nov., 1872-1916); issue: 1-Alice Rogers, b Paris, Ky., June 20, 1898; *m* Jan. 22, 1919, Hiram Roseberry, of Paris, Ky. (issue: Bettie Lindsay; Clay).
1-Mem. D.F.P.A., D.A.R. (chapter regent), Filson Club. Affiliated with Disciples of Christ Ch. Democrat. Residence: Paris, Ky.

1-**CHAMBERLAIN, Lewis Birge,** *b* Vellore, India, Oct. 3, 1864.
8-William (Chamberlin) **Chamberlain** (qv);

JACOB CHAMBERLAIN (1835-1908), B.A., Western Reserve U., '56 (Alpha Delta Phi); New Brunswick (N.J.) Theol. Sem., 1859; Coll. Phys. and Surgeons, N.Y., 1859; M.D., Western Reserve Med. Coll., 1868; (D.D., Rutgers, Western Reserve, and Union, 1878; LL.D., Hope Coll., 1900, and Western Reserve, 1901); evangelistic and medical missionary, Palmaner and Madanapalle, India, 1859-1901; literary work in Telugu language, Coonoor, India, 1901-08; made extensive evangelistic tours, one of 6 months covering 2,000 miles; success as both physician and surgeon led Madras govt. to place two hospitals under him; chairman, 1873-94, of Union Com. on Revision of Bible in Telugu; author Telugu Hymn Book and Telugu Bible Dictionary; powerful and fascinating advocate of missions, his addresses bore notable fruit in America, Great Britain and Australia. Author: "In The Tiger Jungle"; "The Cobra's Den"; "The Kingdom in India." Pres. General Synod Reformed Church in America, 1878; first moderator South Indian United Church, 1902.

7-Jacob (1657-1712), of Billerica and Newton, Mass.; *m* Experience-;
6-Jacob (1691-1771), of Medford and Newton, Mass.; *m* ca. 1718, Susanna Stone (1694-1774; Dea. Simon[7], *m* Sarah Farnsworth);
5-Isaac (1728-57), of New Marlboro; *m* Mary Keyes (*d* 1806);
4-William Isaac (1756-1833), of Sharon, Conn.; lt. in Am. Rev.; *m* 1780, Elizabeth Sprague;
3-Jacob (1791-1876), of Sharon, Conn., and Hudson, O.; *m* 2d, 1826, Anna Nutting;
2-Jacob (2 below).
8-Richard **Birge** (*d* 1651), *m* Elizabeth Gaylord;
7-Daniel (1644-1697/98), *m* Deborah Holcomb (1650-86; Thomas[8], of Dorchester);
6-Cornelius (1694-1763), *m* Sarah Loomis;
5-Capt. Jonathan (1734-76), *m* Priscilla Hammond (*b* 1741);
4-Isaac (1764-1830), *m* Parmela Warner (1768-1838);
3-Chester (1796-1861), *m* Hannah Close (1801-60);
2-Charlotte Close (2 below).
9-Joseph **Loomis** (qv);
8-Dea. John (1622-88), of Windsor, Conn.; dep. Gen. Ct.; *m* 1648, Elizabeth Scott (1625-96; Thomas[9], of Hartford);
7-Dea. Joseph (1651-99), *m* 1675/76, Hannah Marsh (*b* ca. 1655);
6-Sarah (1693-1776), *m* 1721/22, Cornelius **Birge** (6 above);
2-Charlotte Close Birge (1836-1915), *m* 1859, Jacob **Chamberlain** (1835-1908), see portrait and biography; issue: I-Jacob Chester (1860-1905; *m* Anna Mary Irwin); II-William Isaac (*b* 1862; *m* Mary E. Anable; see their dau. Mrs. David F. Anderson); III-Lewis Birge (1 above); IV-Rufus Nutting (*b* 1866; *m* Louise Bruyere); V-Arthur Egerton (1867-78); VI-Charles Storr (*b* 1870; *m* Lulu Gaylord).
1-*m* June 16, 1897, Julia Frances Anable (qv);

issue: 1–Julie Stafford (Mrs. Alexander Buel Trowbridge, Jr., qv); 2–Anne Anable (Mrs. James Terwilliger, 3d, qv); 3–Mary Eleanor (Mrs. Irving Wayland Bonbright, Jr., qv).
1–B.A., Rutgers U., '86 (Delta U., P.B.K.), M.A., 1891 (D.D., 1926); New Brunswick (N.J.) Theol. Sem., 1891. Missionary, Madanapalle, India, 1891-1915; active developing Christian Endeavor, as exec. sec. South India Union several yrs., and United Society of India, Burma and Ceylon 2 yrs.; Indian Church Board, pioneer in devolution of authority to native church; Union Tuberculosis Sanitarium. Editor Progressive Bible Lessons Series and author of first volume. Author: Seshayya—a story of India; also numerous articles and addresses on missionary policies and problems. Requested by govt. to appear before two royal commissions; commissioned by Hindus and Mohammedans to represent them before govt. several times, and used by govt. to help in emergencies with Indians. Asst. corr. sec. Am. Bible Soc., New York, 1915-18, rec. and editorial sec. same, 1918–. Residence: Englewood, N.J.

1–**CHAMBERLAIN, Julia Frances Anable (Mrs. Lewis Birge),** *b* Westerlo, N.Y.
8–Anthony **Anable** (*d* 1673), from Eng. in the "Ann" to Plymouth, 1621; rep. to Gen. Ct., Scituate, 1634-35; apptd. to assist in revision of laws of the colony, 1636; rep. Gen. Ct., Barnstable, 1646-58; commr. and constable for Scituate; *m* 2d, 1645, Anna Clark;
7–Samuel (1645-78), *m* 1667, Mehitable Allyn;
6–John (1673-1732), *m* 1692, Experience Taylor;
5–Cornelius (*b* 1704), *m* Experience–;
4–John (1744-1815), *m* 1768, Hannah Stewart;
3–Joseph (1773-1831), *m* 1814, Alma Sheldon;
2–Maj. Samuel Low (1821-1913), maj. 7th N.Y. Heavy Arty., Civil War; took part in all battles of the Potomac; apptd. by General Grant, U.S. pension agt. for Va.; moved to Chicago, 1883, and engaged in real estate; *m* 1844, Sarah Roxcina Babcock (1826-1916); for issue see Vol. III, p. 29.
1–*m* June 16, 1897, Lewis Birge Chamberlain (qv for issue).
1–Residence: Englewood, N.J.

1–**TROWBRIDGE, Julie Stafford Chamberlain (Mrs. Alexander B., Jr.),** *b* Madanapalle, India, Apr. 22, 1899.
9–Stukeley **Westcott** (qv);
8–Mercy, *m* Samuel **Stafford** (1635-1718), dep. Gen. Ct. and asst. or senator for Warwick, R.I.;
7–Thomas (1682-1765), dep. Gen. Ct.; dep. Colonial Assembly, Warwick; rep. Colonial Assembly, Coventry, 1747; *m* 1719, Audrey Greene;
6–Alma (1728-99), *m* 1760, Capt. Samuel **Low**;
5–Isabel (1766-1847), *m* 1784, Asa **Sheldon**;
4–Alma (1785-1875), *m* Joseph **Anable** (1773-1831);
3–Maj. Samuel Low (1821-1913), *m* 1844, Sarah Roxcina Babcock (1826-1916);
2–Julia Frances (2 below).
10–Roger **Williams** (qv);
9–Mary (1633-99), *m* 1650, John **Sayles** (1633-1727), treas. and gen. asst., Providence; mem. Town Council; deputy;
8–Eleanor (1671-1714), *m* 1693, Richard **Greene** (John[8]; John[9], qv);
7–Audrey (died 1773), *m* Thomas **Stafford** (7 above).
2–Julia Frances Anable, *m* Lewis Birge **Chamberlain** (both qv).
1–*m* Alexander Buel Trowbridge, Jr.; issue: 1–Julie Stafford, *b* Englewood, N.J., July 14, 1924; 2–Alexander Buel, 3d, *b* Englewood, Dec. 12, 1929.

1–**TERWILLIGER, Anne Anable Chamberlain (Mrs. James, 3d),** *b* New Brunswick, N.J., Dec. 6, 1902.
10–Francis **Sprague,** from Eng. in the "Anne," 1623, settled at Plymouth and Duxbury, 1637; *m* Lydia–;
9–John (*d* 1676), killed in King Philip's War; *m* 1655, Ruth Basset (William[10], qv);
8–John (ca. 1656-1727/28), of Duxbury and Lebanon, Mass.; ens. and lt.; *m* 1st, Lydia– (*d* 1725);
7–John (ca. 1690-1760), Canaan, Conn.; *m* 1st, 1710/11, Mary Babcock (*d* 1721/22; Jonathan[8]; James[9]; Rev. James[10], qv);
6–Jonathan (1716-1807), Sharon, Conn.; served in French and Indian War; *m* 1745/46, Lydia Barrows (1726-67; Robert[7]; Robert[8]; John[9], qv); *m* 2d, 1773, Mary Keyes, widow of Isaac Chamberlain;
5–Elizabeth (*b* 1756), *m* 1780, William Isaac **Chamberlain** (1756-1833);
4–Jacob (1791-1876), Hudson, O.; *m* 2d, 1826, Anna Nutting;
3–Jacob (1835-1908), see portrait and biography; *m* 1859, Charlotte Close Birge (1836-1915);
2–Lewis Birge (qv for other lineages), *m* 1897, Julia Frances Anable (qv).
1–*m* James Terwilliger, 3d; issue: 1–James Rockefeller, *b* Englewood, N.J., Apr. 9, 1928.

1–**BONBRIGHT, Mary Eleanor Chamberlain (Mrs. Irving W., Jr.),** *b* Coonoor, India, July 1, 1904.
9–John **Boynton** (1614-70; son of William; desc. Bartholomew de Boynton, 1067); from Eng.; *m* Ellen (Eleanor, Helen) Pell, of Boston;
8–Joseph (1644-1730), of Groton, Mass.; *m* 1st, Sarah Swan (1646-1717/18);
7–Benoni (1681-1758), of Lunenburg; French and Indian War; *m* 1706, Ann Mighill (1685/86-1764; Stephen[8], *m* Sarah, dau. of Rev. Samuel Phillips, *m* Sarah, dau. of Samuel Appleton; Thomas[9]);
6–Jane, or Jean (1719-1803), *m* William **Nutting** (1712-76; Jonathan[7]; John[8]; John[9]);
5–Rev. William (1752-1832), *m* Susanna (French) Danforth (1757-1800; Col. Joseph French[6]; Joseph[7], *m* Elizabeth, dau. of John Cummings, Jr.; Samuel[8], *m* Sarah, dau. of John Cummings; Lt. William[9], *m* Elizabeth Godfrey);
4–Anna (1796-1860), *m* 1826, as his 2d wife, Jacob **Chamberlain** (1791-1876);
3–Jacob (1835-1908), see portrait and biography; *m* 1859, Charlotte Close Birge (1836-1915);
2–Lewis Birge (qv for other lineages), *m* 1897, Julia Frances Anable (qv).
1–*m* Irving Wayland Bonbright, Jr.; issue: 1–Irving Wayland, 3d, *b* Englewood, N.J., July 14, 1927; 2–Mary Birge, *b* Englewood, July 16, 1929.

1–**ANDERSON, Alma Birge Chamberlain (Mrs. David Forgham),** *b* Madanapalle, India, Apr. 14, 1897.
10–John **Greene** (qv);
9–John, dep.gov., R.I. Province, 1690-1700; *m* Ann Almy (William[10], qv);
8–Richard (1660-1711), *m* 1692, Eleanor Sayles (1671-1714; John[9], qv);
7–Audrey (1692-1773), *m* 1719, Thomas **Stafford** (1682-1765), see Vol. III, p. 29, for Stafford lineage;
6–Alma (1728-99), *m* 1760, Capt. Samuel **Low** (1729-1807), marched on the "Alarm to the Northward," Am. Rev.;
5–Isabel (1766-1847), *m* 1784, Asa **Sheldon** (1761-1848);
4–Alma (1785-1875), *m* 1814, Joseph **Anable** (1773-1831), see Vol. III, p. 29, for Anable lineage;
3–Samuel Low (1821-1913), *m* Sarah Roxcina Babcock;
2–Mary Eleanor (2 below).
10–Samuel **Chapin** (qv);
9–Henry (*d* 1718), of Springfield, Mass., 1659-1718; rep. Gen. Ct., 1689; *m* 1664, Bethia Cooley (1643-1711; Benjamin[10], qv);
8–Benjamin (1682-1756), *m* 1704, Hannah Colton (Isaac[9], *m* Mary, dau. Lt. Thomas Cooper; Q.M. George[10]);
7–Benjamin (1708-62), *m* 1735, Ann Howard, of Springfield;
6–Charles (*b* 1742), *m* 1766, Silence Kellog, of S. Hadley, Mass.;
5–William (1767-1837), *d* Greenfield, Saratoga Co., N.Y.; *m* 1796, Sally Brayton (1767-1815), of Providence, R.I.;
4–Lorinda (1806-72), *m* 1824, Josiah Hubbell **Babcock** (1801-36), of Broadalbin, Fulton Co., N.Y.;
3–Sarah Roxcina (1826-1916), *m* Samuel Low **Anable** (3 above); see their dau. Mrs. Lewis Birge Chamberlain;
2–Mary Eleanor (*b* Westerlo, N.Y.-*d* July 25, 1929), grad. Miss Anable's Sch., Phila.; a principal, Misses Anable's Sch., New Brunswick, N.J.; missionary to India, 1891-1905; contributor to Atlantic Monthly, The Century Mag.; author: **Fifty Years in Foreign Fields** (see Vol. III, p. 29, for other lineages); *m* June 18, 1891, William Isaac **Chamberlain** (*b*

Madras, India, Oct. 10, 1862), A.B., Rutgers, '82, A.M., 1886 (D.D., 1912); B.D., New Brunswick Theol. Sem., 1886; Ph.D., Columbia, 1900; evangelistic and ednl. missionary in the Arcot Mission (Madanapalle, Chittoor, Vellore), India, 1887-1905; established 1898, and pres. until 1905, Voorhees Coll., Vellore, India; prof. logic and mental philosophy, Rutgers, 1906-09; corr. sec., Bd. of Foreign Missions, Reformed Ch. of America, 1909– (see Who's Who in America); issue: I–Eleanor (1893-1904); II–Alma B. (1 above).

1–*m* Feb. 21, 1925, David Forgham Anderson, Flight Lt., Royal Air Force, Great Britain, D.F.C., A.F.C.; issue: 1–David Robin (*b* London, Eng., June 18, 1926-*d* Murree, India, Aug. 23, 1929); 2–William Alexander, *b* Srinagar, Kashmir, India, July 14, 1928.

1–Vassar, '19. Address: Royal Air Force, Drigh Rd., Karachi, Sind, India.

1–**CLOPTON, Malvern Bryan,** *b* St. Louis, Mo., Oct. 8, 1875.

7–Jesse **McIlvaine,** to America with William Penn, 1681;

6–Orville;

5–William (*b* Bucks Co., Pa., 1732-*d* Md., 1798), only survivor of wreck in Gulf of Mexico, when accompanying father on sailing vessel to W.I.; while floating on a cask picked up by a party of Spaniards who took him to New Orleans, and up the Mississippi and Missouri rivers to a point nr. where Jefferson City now is; started in quest of precious metal; discovered lead ore mistaking it for silver ore; returned to New Orleans leaving William and two of the party to guard their huts at New Madrid (founded 1740); Indians captured William, ca. 1750, he escaped to Kascaskia, Ill.; engaged in lead mining and flat-boating; helped transport a cargo of powder from New Orleans to Fort Pitt, 1775, for use in Am. Rev., returned to Bucks Co., Pa.; *m* in Bucks Co., 1776, Mary McIlvaine;

4–John (*b* Baltimore Co., Md., 1777-*d* Washington Co., Mo., 1843), made trip to lead mines nr. Potosi, Mo., 1795-96; to Limestone (now Maysville), Ky., 1799; removed family to Potosi, 1804; *m* 1799, Jane Hord, of Stafford Co., Va.;

3–Eveline (1804-85), *m* Dr. John Gano **Bryan** (1798-1860), see Vol. III, p. 126, for Bryan lineage;

2–Belle (1848-93), *m* 1873, William Hickman **Clopton** (1847-1912), ed. La. Grange (Ala.) Mil. Acad., 1860-61; Southern U., Greensboro, Ala., 1861-62; U.Va., 1865-68, LL.B., 1868; entered C.S.A., 1864, and served under Gen. Dan Adams as mem. of his escort, later with scouts for Dept. of Ala., and with Gen. Buford's escort; admitted to Mo. bar and practiced at St. Louis; apptd. U.S. atty. by President Cleveland, for Eastern Dist. of Mo., 1894; mem. Dem. State Central Com.; for issue and Clopton lineage see Vol. III, p. 126.

1–*m* Oct. 22, 1909, Lily (Lambert) Walker (Jan. 9, 1884-Nov. 19, 1911); dau. of Jordan W. Lambert, of St. Louis, Mo., formerly of Va., *m* Lily Winn.

1–M.D., U.Va., '07 (Kappa Sigma). Surgeon (see Who's Who in America). Mem. bd. directors and clinical prof. surgery, Washington U. Served as lt. col. Med. Corps, U.S.A., 1917-19; with Base Hosp. 21 and c.o. Mobile Hosp. 4, A.E.F. Fellow Am. Coll. Surgeons. Mem. I.A.G. Clubs: University, Racquet, St. Louis Country, Bogey, Round Table. Residence: 5391 Waterman Av., St. Louis, Mo.

1–**COOK, Cornelia Elisabeth Seamans (Mrs. Charles G.),** *b* Sabinsville, Tioga Co., Pa., Apr. 3, 1870.

6–Jacob **Whitman** (1716-1802), general sealer of weights and measures, R.I., 1778; dep. Gen. Assembly, 1764-65; mem. town council, 1769-73; *m* ca. 1744, Hannah Hartshorn (1725-1811);

5–Hannah (1751-81), *m* Thomas (Simmons) **Seamans** (1748-1824), fifer during Am. Rev.;

4–Israel (1770-1800), *m* 1789, Esther Chloe Phillips (1773-1857);

3–Jonathan (1794-1867), *m* 1819, Rebecca Tuttle;

2–Milo Phillips (2 below).

8–William **Tuttle** (qv);

7–Nathaniel (bap. 1652), of New Haven, and Woodbury, Conn.; *m* Sarah–;

6–Isaac (1688-1772);

5–Andrew (1739-1824), pvt. in defense of West Point, 1787; *m* Lydia Sturgis (1741-1814);

4–Ayers (1762-1837), guard & minuteman in Am. Rev.; present at battle of Bunker Hill; *m* 2d, 1792, Hannah Barnes;

3–Rebecca (1803-73), *m* 1819, Jonathan **Seamans** (3 above).

8–Thomas **Barnes** (*d* 1688), settled at Hartford, and Farmington, Conn., 1639-46; in Pequot War; sgt., 1651; *m* Mary Andrews (Andrus);

7–Thomas, Jr., *m* Mary Jones;

6–Thomas;

5–Timothy (1739-1831), Southington, Conn.; Am. Rev.; *m* 1760, Mariam Miller (1737-1818; Henry[6]);

4–Hannah (1763-ca. 1840), *m* 1792, Ayers **Tuttle** (4 above).

6–Samuel (Eldred) **Eldridge** (1720-85), pvt. Cont. Army, 1777; *m* 1750, Susanna Casey (1727-74);

5–John (1763-1823), of Exeter, R.I., and Groton, N.Y.; pvt. Am. Rev.; began to write name Eldridge; *m* 1784, Huldah Austin (1766-1840; Ellis[6], pvt. Am. Rev., *m* Sarah Aylesworth);

4–Thomas (1794-1868), War 1812; *m* 1810, Elisabeth Graham (1793-1865);

3–Thomas (1823-84), pvt. Co. L, 1st Pa. Mounted Vols., 1864; *m* 2d, 1848, Emeline Thompson;

2–Rachel (2 below).

6–John **Thompson,** *m* Ruth–;

5–John (1753-1823), sgt. Am. Rev.; present at Valley Forge; *m* 1st, 1783, Juda Merritt (1764-1852; Henry[6]; Isaac[7]; Henry[8]; John[9]; Henry[10]);

4–Alvah (1797-1870), *m* 1822, Polly Waklee (1803-81; John[5], Am. Rev., *m* 1785, Elizabeth Cummings);

3–Emeline (1832-1907), *m* 1848, Thomas **Eldridge** (3 above);

2–Rachel (*b* 1849), *m* 1867, Milo Phillips **Seamans** (1845-1914).

1–*m* Mar. 21, 1885, Charles Gould Cook, *b* Addison, N.Y., Jan. 1, 1866, son of Fayette Cook.

1–Ed. public grammar and high schools in Pa. Mem. I.A.G., N.Y. State Hist. Soc., D.A.R. (regent Onwentsia Chapter, 1924-26; N.Y. State dir. Nat. Soc., 1929-32), O.E.S. Residence: 58 Steuben St., Addison, N.Y.

BRADLEY

Arms: *Gules, a chevron argent, between three boars' heads couped or.*
Crest: *A boar's head couped or.*
Motto: *Liber ac sapiens esto.*

1–**COOPER, Mary Guyton Bradley (Mrs. Willard),** *b* Stewart Co., Ga., Aug. 17, 1891.

8–Isaac **Bradley** (ante 1650-1712), *m* Elizabeth– (1656-1712);

7–Samuel (1686-1758), *m* 1715, Sarah Robinson (1695-1728);

6–Dan (1724-post 1798), *m* 1st, Sarah Judd (1730-64);
5–Edmond (1757-1828), *m* 1781, Lydia Chidsey (1761-1834; Isaac[6]; Caleb[7]; Caleb[8], *m* Hannah Dickerman; John[9]);
4–Dan (1784-1827), *m* 1804, Amy Forbes (1782-1824; Levi[5], Am. Rev.; *m* Sarah Tuttle);
3–Forbes (1809-90), Russell Co., Ala.; *m* 1845, Theresa Ann Clark (1827-71; William[4], *m* Rebecca Peddy; Richard[5], from Wales to N.C., settled at Tarboro, N.C., moved to Ga. and *d* in Hancock or Jasper Co., *m* Miss Jones, *b* in Scotland);
2–Dan (2 below).

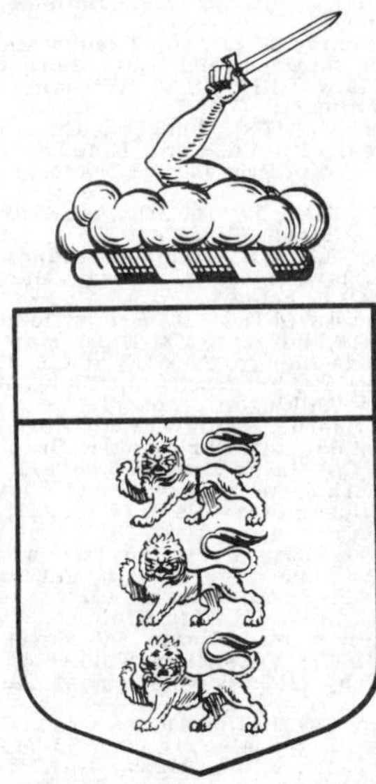

BRYAN

Arms: *Gules, three lions passant guardant in pale per pale or and argent; a chief of the second.*
Crest: *Issuing out of clouds a naked arm embowed the hand grasping a sword, all proper.*
Motto: *"Lank laidir au Nachtar" (The strongest hand is on high).*

9–William **Bryan,** Marquis of Thomond (qv);
8–Needham (1690-1770), justice, Bertie Co., N.C., 1732,39,45; sheriff and commr.; apptd. to council held at Bath, 1645; mem. Assembly, New Bern, 1750,59; settled at Snowfield, Bertie Co., N.C.; *m* 1st, 1711, Annie Rambeau (1695-1730);
7–Needham (1725-1800), mem. Colonial Assembly of N.C., 1771, of Wilmington, 1762; col. colonial militia of Johnston Co., N.C., at the battle of Alamance; mem. Provincial Congress, 1775; del. to that band of patriots which convened at New Bern, 1775; *m* 1st, 1749, Nancy Smith (Col. John[8], of Johnston Co., *m* Elizabeth Whitfield);
6–Needham (*b* 1750), capt. Johnston Co. Regt., 1774; mem. Provincial Congress, Halifax, 1776; del. Congress at Halifax which formed the state constn., 1776; *m* 1768, Sarah Hinton;
5–Clement, *m* Edith Smith (1772-1842; David[6] [1746-95], *m* 1771, Charity– [1756-1818], Samuel[7] [1709-83], *m* Edith–, 1717-85);
4–Loverd (1804-87), *m* Elizabeth Wyche (1809-77; Littleton[5]; George[6]; Peter[7]; George[8]; Henry[9]);
3–Whitfield Clement (1836-1913), *m* Margaret Guyton;
2–Emma (2 below).
7–Amos **Love,** *m* Mary–;
6–Amos (*d* 1798), 1st lt. in Am. Rev.; justice Onslow Co. Ct., N.C., 1759; *m* Mary–;
5–Amos (*d* 1835), on tax list of Pulaski Co., Ga., as early as 1805; 1st clk. Co. Ct., Laurens Co., Ga.; mem. Ga. Legislature; *m* Margaret James;
4–Mary Ann (1811-95), *m* 1829, Moses **Guyton** (1799-1870; Moses[5] [1750-1807], from France, settled in S.C., *m* 1782, Tabitha Saxon, 1764-1811);
3–Margaret (1839-92), *m* Whitfield Clement **Bryan** (3 above);
2–Emma (*b* 1862), *m* 1881, Dan **Bradley** (1856-1915): issue: I–Theresa (*b* 1882; *m* Park Dallis); II–Mary Guyton (1 above); III–Emma Bryan (*b* 1893; *m* H. W. Hemphill); IV–Margaret Love (*b* 1897; *m* Nathan A. Dykes).
1–*m* Oct. 11, 1911, Willard Cooper, *b* Columbus, Ga., Oct. 28, 1885; son of John Thomas Cooper; issue (all *b* Columbus, Ga.): 1–Lenora Newsom, *b* Sept. 28, 1912; 2–Mary Bradley, *b* June 20, 1914; 3–Margaret Susan, *b* Nov. 15, 1917; 4–Dan Bradley, *b* Nov. 27, 1922.
1–Ed. privately and at Agnes Scott, 1 yr. Mem. C.D.A., D.A.R., U.D.C., I.A.G. Residence: 813 Cooper Av., Wynnton, Columbus, Ga.

1–**COWING, Hattie Josephine Ammon (Mrs. John P.),** *b* Euclid, O., Sept. 30, 1868.
9–George (Sexton) **Saxton** (*d* 1688-90), from Eng. bet. 1635-45; settled at Westfield, Mass.; removed to Windsor, Conn.; *m* Catherine–;
8–James (1660-1741), Westfield; *m* Hannah Fowles; *m* 2d, Anna Bancroft; *m* 3d, Mary McCranny;
7–James (1702-83), *m* 1728, Abalena Gilbert;
6–James (*b* 1729), Sheffield, Mass.; lt. 1763; *m* Sarah Noble (1730-69);
5–Ebenezer (1753-1828), *m* Hannah Loomis (1757-1843);
4–Jehiel (1782-1865), capt. in War 1812; present at Battle of Plattsburg; *m* 1808, Polly Stewart (1789-1873);
3–Jehiel (1812-95), Cleveland, O.; *m* 1837, Emeline Axtell Morse (1821-98);
2–Josephine Mary (1844-92), *m* 1863, Col. John Henry **Ammon** (1840-1904), book publisher; col. in old 19th N.Y. Regt., Baty. I; issue: I–Hattie Josephine A. (1 above); II–Jay Ripley (*b* 1875; sgt. in Spanish-Am. War; *m* Miltone Horton; *m* 2d, Elizabeth Bates); III–Harry Ticknor (*b* 1876; *m* Margaret Odell); IV–Mark Anthony (*b* 1877; *m* Elizabeth Hone).
1–*m* Jan. 15, 1890, John Philo Cowing (Mar. 3, 1867-Sept. 5, 1926); son of George Cowing, *m* Helen Hutchinson; issue (all *b* Cleveland, O.): 1–John Ammon, *b* Nov. 17, 1890; attended Culver Mil. Acad.; *m* Nov. 13, 1917, Mary Rebecca, dau. of William DeWeese Ferree (issue: John DeWeese); 2–Jay Clinton, *b* July 13, 1892; World War Vet.; 3–Hattie Josephine (*b* and *d* Nov. 12, 1895).
1–Grad. Moses Brown Boarding School, '89. Mem. D.A.C., D.A.R., U.S.D. 1812 (state and local registrar, 4 yrs.), I.A.G., Cleveland Geneal. Soc. Episcopalian. Republican. Cleveland Emerson Club (past pres.). Residence: 1892 Knowles Av., East Cleveland, O.

1–**COX, Gordon Leland,** *b* Johnson City, Tenn., Mar. 8, 1888.
4–John **Cox**;
3–Thomas Jefferson (1814-59), *m* 1835, Caroline Hale (1817-54);
2–Pembrook Somerset (2 below).
5–John **Patton,** from Ireland ca. 1765, settled at Carlisle, Pa., later moved to N.C. (now Carter Co., Tenn.); owned a powder mill on Powder Branch of Buffalo Creek; his wife Mary (McKeehan) Patton made the powder used to fight in Battle of King's Mountain;
4–Samuel English (1799-1878), *m* 1830, Temperance Morgan (1811-60);
3–David Adams (1835-1924), *m* 1861, Mary Jane Swingle;
2–Margaret (2 below).
6–George **Haynes** (*b* 1736), *b* Frederick Co., Md., *d* Washington Co., Tenn.; soldier Am. Rev.; *m* Margaret McInturf;
5–Mary Magdalen (1787-1844), *m* 1807, George **Swingle** (1779-1836; George[6], *b* in Germany, *d* Frederick Co., Md., soldier Am. Rev.);
4–Benjamin Franklin (1816-1911), *m* 1838, Margaret Cockran (1822-98);
3–Mary Jane (1839-98), *m* 1861, David Adams **Patton** (3 above);
2–Margaret (*b* 1866), *m* 1886, Pembrook Somerset **Cox** (*b* 1849).
1–*m* Aug. 20, 1914, Evelyn Bearden (qv for issue).
1–Ed. U. of Tenn. (Pi Kappa Alpha). Mining engineer for Koppers Coal Co. Residence: Elkhorn, W.Va.

1–**COX, Evelyn Bearden (Mrs. Gordon L.),** *b* Knoxville, Tenn., Nov. 27, 1892.
7–Richard **Bennett** (ca. 1720-1786), maj. gen. in Colonial and French and Indian wars; moved to N.C. ante 1765; *m* ante 1750, Ann–;
6–Peter (1750-1822), capt. in Am. Rev.; sheriff, Granville Co., N.C., 1787-89; *m* 1773, Elizabeth Pomfret (1753-1845; John[7], of King William Co., Va., *m* Ann Hunt);
5–Nancy Ann (1774-1855), moved to Knox Co., Tenn., about 1800; *m* Richard **Bearden** (1770-1845);
4–Marquis ("Marcus") De La Fayette (1802-54), *m* 2d, ca. 1835, Sarah Morgan;
3–Rufus Morgan (1837-72), adj., 2d Tenn. Cav., C.S.A.; *m* 1864, Mary Moore Gaines;
2–Rufus Morgan (2 below).
9–Daniel **Trigg** (*d* 1716), *m* Susan–;
8–Abraham (1684-1718), Va.; *m* 2d, 1710, Judith Clarke;
7–William (1716-73), of Va.; *m* Mary Johns;
6–Daniel (1749-1819), capt. Am. Rev.; *m* 1777, Anne Smith (1755-95);
5–Elizabeth (1791-1859), *m* 1809, Rufus **Morgan** (1781-1826; Gideon[6], Am. Rev., *m* 1st, Patience Cogswell);
4–Sarah Frances (*b* 1817), *m* Marquis De La Fayette **Bearden** (4 above).
9–Dunken (Duncan) **Bohannon** (*d* 1754), from Eng. to Jamestown, Va., ante 1690; settled in King's Parish, now King and Queen Co., Va.; received land grants; *m* Sara–;
8–Robert (*b* 1707), removed to Broomfield Parish, Madison Co., 1730; *m* 1st, Balsheba–;
7–Elliott (*b* 1729), *m* Ann Walker;
6–Mildred, *m* Robert **Gaines** (*b* ca. 1740), of Orange Co.;
5–Ambrose (*died* 1840), Am. Rev.; *m* 1792, Mary Moore;
4–Matthew Moore (1809-93), *m* 1830, Margaret Luttrell;
3–Mary Moore (1842-92), *m* Rufus Morgan **Bearden** (3 above).
7–John **Moore** (*d* 1777), Louisa Co., Va.; *m* 1st, Frances Jouett (Matthew[8], Albemarle Co., Va.);
6–Matthew (*b* 1738), *m* 1757, Letitia Dalton (*b* 1742; Samuel[7], from Eng., *m* Nancy Redd, of Goochland Co., Va.);
5–Mary (1771-1867), *m* Ambrose **Gaines** (5 above).
9–William **Witt** (1675-1745), Huguenot, from France, 1699, settled at Manakintown, Va.; *d* in Albemarle Co., Va.;
8–John (1710-82), Amherst Co.; *m* 1st, Elizabeth–;
7–Abner;
6–Elizabeth (1757-1849), *m* 1776, James **Luttrell** (1755-1846), minuteman in Am. Rev.;
5–James Churchwell (1777-1824), Knox Co., Tenn.; *m* 1807, Martha Armstrong;
4–Margaret (1816-92), *m* Matthew Moore **Gaines** (4 above).
7–Robert **Armstrong** (1700-75), from Ireland 1735, settled at Phila., later moving to Abbeyville Dist., S.C.; *m* 1728, Alice Calhoun (*b* 1705), sister of James Calhoun, immigrant, and aunt of Patrick Calhoun;
6–Robert (1731-96), lt. Am. Rev.; *m* Margaret Cunningham (1740-1837; Samuel[7]);
5–Martha (1783-1863), Knox Co., Tenn.; *m* James Churchwell **Luttrell** (5 above).
6–Edmond **Williams** (*d* 1795), from Wales, settled in Mass.; auditor Washington and Sullivan dists., N.C., 1782; moved to N.C. bet. 1775-79; sheriff, 1788; *m* Lucretia Adams;
5–Sarah Adams (1783-1859), *m* John **Hoss** (Jacob[6], Am. Rev., *m* 1761, M. Boone);
4–Landon Carter (1817-91), *m* 1845, Lauretta P. Boren (1825-93);
3–Marietta (1848-74), *m* 1871, Alvin Jackson **Johnson** (1833-1901);
2–Anna May (2 below).
6–Benjamin **Drane** (1763-1842), *m* 1788, Rachel– (1769-1863);
5–Jane (1789-1847), *m* ca. 1804, Chana **Boren**;
4–Lauretta P. (1825-93), *m* 1845, Landon Carter **Hoss** (4 above);
3–Marietta, *m* Alvin J. **Johnson** (3 above);
2–Anna May (1873-1906), *m* 1891, Rufus Morgan **Bearden** (1868-1924), he *m* 2d, 1915, Ida Reeves Moore; issue (1st marriage): I–Evelyn (1 above); II–Rufus Morgan, III (*b* 1894); III–Glenn V. (*b* 1901; *m* Fay McLaughlin).
1–*m* Aug. 20, 1914, Gordon Leland Cox (qv); issue: 1–Gordon Leland, Jr., *b* Charleston, W.Va., Nov. 19, 1915; 2–Margaret Patton, *b* Kingston, W.Va., Jan. 26, 1917; 3–Donald Morgan, *b* Huntington, W.Va., Aug. 31, 1922.
1–Mem. D.A.R., U.D.C. Residence: Elkhorn, W.Va.

1–**CRAM, Elizabeth Carrington Read (Mrs. Ralph A.),** *b* Prince Edward Co., Va., June 5, 1873.
9–Nicholas **Martian** (qv);
8–Elizabeth (*d* 1687), *m* Col. George **Reade** (qv);
7–Thomas, *m* ca. 1688, Lucy Gwynn (desc. Hugh Gwynn, burgess; of Col. William Bernard, mem. Council; of Capt. Robert Higginson, in charge of troops against Indians, Middle Plantation);
6–Col. Clement (1707-63), col. French and Indian War, 1758; burgess; clk., Lunenburg Co., Va.; *m* 1730, Mary Hill (1711-86; William[7], *m* Priscilla Jennings);
5–Col. Isaac (*d* 1778), burgess, Charlotte Co., Va.; lt. col., 4th Va. Cont. Line; col., 1st Va. Cont. Army and 4th Va. Cont. Army; *m* Sarah Embra;
4–Isaac (1777-1824), 1st lt., 4th Va., War 1812; *m* 1802, Anne Mayo Venable;
3–Isaac (1806-79), A.B., Hampden-Sidney; LL.B., Harvard; lawyer; *m* 1831, Susan Mary Nash;
2–Clement C. (2 below).
7–Henry **Embra** (*d* 1763), lt., Brunswick Co., Va.; col. militia; burgess, 1736-40; *m* Martha Patteson (Jonathan[8], of New Kent Co., Va.);
6–Henry (*d* 1753), burgess, Lunenburg, 1748-49; *m* Priscilla Wilkinson (Joseph[7], *m* Priscilla Branch Skerne, widow, dau. of Thomas Branch, g.dau. of Christopher Branch, qv);
5–Sarah, *m* Col. Isaac **Read** (5 above);
4–Isaac, *m* Anne Mayo Venable (4 above);
3–Isaac, *m* Susan Mary Nash (3 above);
2–Clement Carrington (1837-93), capt. C.S.A.; chemist; *m* 1872, Mary Carrington Johnson (1847-1913); issue: I–Elizabeth Carrington (1 above); II–Susan Nash (Mrs. Shepperd Strudwick, qv); III–Mary Johnson (*b* 1878; *m* John Sinnickson Allen); IV–Maria Strudwick (*b* 1880); V–William Tucker (*b* 1882; *m* Sarah Kirby Hicks); VI–Clement Carrington (*b* 1884).
1–*m* Sept. 20, 1900, Ralph Adams Cram (see Vol. I, p. 569, for genealogy); issue: 1–Mary Carrington, *b* Brookline, Mass., Nov. 9, 1901; *m* Jerome Crosby Greene; *m* 2d, Richard H. Thurston, Jr.; 2–Ralph Wentworth, *b* Boston, Sept. 18, 1904; *m* Aug. 1929, Florence M. Heath; 3–Elizabeth Strudwick, *b* Sudbury, Mass., Aug. 29, 1913.
1–Mem. C.D.A. Club: Chilton (Boston). Summer place: "Whitehall," Sudbury, Mass. Residence: 71 Mt. Vernon St., Boston, Mass.

1–**STRUDWICK, Susan Nash Read (Mrs. Shepperd),** *b* Farmville, Va., June 24, 1875.
12–Lt. Col. Walter **Aston,** Gent. (1607-56), from Eng. to Va., 1628; judge and burgess; *m* 2d, Hannah Warham;
11–Mary, *m* ca. 1646, Lt. Col. Richard **Cocke** (qv);
10–William (1655-93), burgess; *m* 2d, Sarah Flower;
9–Mary (1690-1754), *m* Obadiah **Smith,** Sr. (*d* 1746), of Henrico Co.;
8–Ann, *m* Richard **Woodson** (*b* ca. 1662; Robert[9], *m* Elizabeth, dau. of Richard Ferris, of Curles, Henrico Co.; John[10], qv);
7–Richard, of "Poplar Hill," Prince Edward Co.; *m* Anne Micheaux (Abraham[8], Huguenot refugee from Holland to Va., *m* Susanne de la Roche);
6–Elizabeth (*d* 1791), *m* Nathaniel **Venable** (1733-1804), early patron of Hampden-Sidney Coll.; burgess (Abraham[7]; Abraham[8], qv);
5–Samuel Woodson (*b* 1756), A.B., Princeton, 1780; ens. in Am. Rev.; *m* 1781, Mary S. Carrington (1756-1837; Paul[6], lt. Charlotte Co., burgess, *m* 1st, 1755, Margaret, dau. of Clement Reade [1707-63]; Col. George[7], qv);
4–Anne Mayo (1784-1869), *m* Isaac **Read** (1777-1824);
3–Isaac (1806-79), A.B., Hampden-Sidney; LL.B., Harvard; lawyer; *m* 1831, Susan Mary Nash;
2–Clement Carrington (2 below).
9–Capt. Roger **Jones** (qv);
8–Frederick (will probated 1722), gent., of "Hayes," nr. Albemarle Sound, N.C., from Eng.; mem. Colonial Assembly, 1711; officer, French and Indian War, 1712; mem. Gov.'s

Council, 1716; chief justice, 1718; *m* ca. 1708, Jane Harding;
7–Frederick (*d* ante 1743), mem. Colonial Assembly, N.C., 1738; justice, Chowan Precinct, 1739; *m* as her 1st husband, Mary Vail (*b* 1706; Jeremiah[8], the Elder);
6–Harding (*d* 1759), grad. Yale, 1756; *m* 1756, Mary Whiting (1735-63; Rev. John[7]; Rev. Samuel[8]; Rev. John[9]; William[10], qv);
5–Mary (*b* 1758), *m* 1st, as his 2d wife, Gov. Abner **Nash** (1740 or 43-1787), of N.C.;
4–Frederick, LL.D. (1781-1858), A.B., Princeton, 1799; chief justice of N.C., 1852-58; *m* 1803, Mary Goddard Kollock (*b* 1781; Judge Shepard[5]; Shepard[6]; Simon[7]; Jacob[8]);
3–Susan Mary (1806-79), *m* Isaac **Read** (3 above).
7–John **Johnson**;
6–Jesse, *m* 1751, Elizabeth Watkins (Benjamin[7]);
5–Thomas (1760-1823), Cumberland Co., Va.; *m* 1793, Lucy Crowder (*d* 1846);
4–Ichabod (1801-42), *m* 1824, Jane Sterne Wood (*d* 1833);
3–William Thomas (1825-96), *m* 1846, Elizabeth Cabell Carrington (1825-93);
2–Mary Carrington (1847-1913), *m* 1872, Clement Carrington **Read** (1837-93); for issue and other lineages see Mrs. Ralph A. Cram.
1–*m* June 24, 1897, Shepperd Strudwick, *b* Hillsboro, N.C., Nov. 15, 1868; son of Dr. William Samuel Strudwick, of Hillsboro, Orange Co., N.C.; issue: 1–William Shepperd (June 11, 1898-Apr. 4, 1905); 2–Clement Read, *b* Columbia, Tenn., Apr. 16, 1900; U. of N.C., '22; 3–Shepperd, *b* Hillsboro, N.C., Sept. 22, 1907; U. of N.C., '29; 4–Edmund, *b* Hillsboro, Dec. 27, 1909.
1–Mem. U.D.C. Residence: Hillsboro, N.C.

DAVIS

Arms: Argent, a lion rampant sable, armed and langued gules.
Crest: On a ducal coronet argent, a lion's head erased sable, crowned of the first.

1–**CRENSHAW, Katherine McAden Davis (Mrs. Henry A.),** *b* Louisburg, N.C., Aug. 29, 1856.
6–Jonathan **Davis,** from Eng. to Hanover Co., Va., 1667; *m* Martha Drayton Vernon;
5–William, of Hanover Co.; *m* Catherine Staige;
4–William (ca. 1746-1825), *m* Martha Taylor Winston;
3–Jonathan (1769-1841), *m* 1809, Mary Pomfret Butler (1784-1851; Isaac[4], *m* Mary Hunt Pomfret; John[5]; William[6], from Scotland to Culpeper Co., Va., 1700);
2–Judge Joseph Jonathan (2 below).
8–James **Taylor** (qv);
7–Col. James (1674-1729), justice, King and Queen Co., Va., 1702-14; surveyor; located 10,000 acres in Caroline Co. and settled there; *m* 1699, Martha Thompson (1679-1762; dau. of Col. William, served in Royal Army; g.dau. Sir Roger Thompson);
6–James (1703-84), burgess, 1772-74; mem. Va. Conv., 1774-78; *m* Alice (Thornton) Catlett (Francis Thornton[7], burgess, Spotsylvania Co., 1726; William[8], qv);
5–Alice (*b* 1730), *m* Anthony **Winston** (*b* 1723), of Hanover Co.; mem. Va. Conv., 1775-76; del. Va. Ho. of Burgesses; capt. in Am. Rev. (Isaac[6], from Wales, ca. 1704, settled in Hanover Co., *m* 2d, Mary, dau. of Cornelius Dabney);
4–Martha Taylor, *m* William **Davis** (4 above).
6–Col. Nicholas **Long** (1728-98), of Halifax Co., N.C.; col. of minute men in Am. Rev., served at Cowpens, Camden, Yorktown; commissary gen., 1775; mem. Com. Safety, 1775; chmn. Provincial Congress, 1774; *m* 1752, Mary Reynolds (1736-58);
5–Gabriel (1754-1819), *m* Sarah Ann Richmond (1759-1843; William[6], came with his brother-in-law, Sir Peyton Skipwith, *m* 2d, Ann, dau. of Col. James Milliken, of Halifax Co., N.C.);
4–Martha Elizabeth (1789-1870), *m* Joel **King** (1778-1863; Dr. John[5], M.D., of Leicestershire, Eng., disciple of John Wesley, and the "father of Methodism" in America, "Green Hill," home in N.C.; Rev. John[6], clergyman Ch. of Eng.);
3–Sarah Helen (1811-87), *m* 1829, Robert John **Shaw** (1800-48), from Kilmarnoch, Scotland; grad. Edinburgh; studied law, Oxford, Eng.;
2–Katherine Elizabeth (1830-81), *m* 1852, Judge Joseph Jonathan **Davis** (1828-92), grad. Coll. of William and Mary, 1847; U. of N.C., 1849; mem. Congress, 1875-84; elected to Supreme Ct. of N.C., 1884-92; issue: I–Katherine M. (1 above); II–Robert Henry (*m* 1893, Annie Jones); III–Hugh L. (*d* 1914); IV–Mary Helen (*d* 1912; *m* 1892, James M. Allen).
1–*m* Nov. 15, 1882, Henry Austin Crenshaw, *b* Louisburg, N.C., Mar. 6, 1848; son of William Martin, of Louisburg; issue: 1–Katherine Elizabeth (Sept. 13, 1883-Jan. 27, 1890); 2–Helen Shaw, *b* Aug. 29, 1886; *m* June 7, 1911, Robert Lynn Bernhardt, of Salisbury.
1–Ed. St. Mary's Coll., Raleigh, N.C. Mem. C.D.A., Scions of Colonial Cavaliers, H.S.A., D.F.P.A., U.D.C. Residence: 202 W. Bank St., Salisbury, N.C.

1–**SAWYER, Florence Louise,** *b* Harrison Co., Tex., Mar. 9, 1868.
6–William **Sawyer,** from Eng. to Va., 1700; moved to Edgefield Dist., S.C.; in Am. Rev.; *m* Judith Sanford;
5–George (*b* 1732), *m* 1st, Elizabeth Byrd;
4–Henry (*b* 1767), *m* Elizabeth Warren;
3–George Vardell (1811-36), *m* 1832, Sophia Reilley (*b* 1814; James[4], from Ireland to Edgefield, S.C., *m* Gertrude Paisley, dau. of John Davis, *m* Mary Allison);
2–James Henry (2 below).
7–Jeremiah **Perry,** from Eng. to Tyrrell Co., N.C.; *m* 1694, Christian Blount (Thomas[8], *m* Jane–);
6–Jeremiah (*b* 1695), of Franklin Co., N.C.;
5–Joshua (1725-98), of Warren Co., N.C.; pvt. Am. Rev.; *m* 1750, Elizabeth Rush;
4–Jeremiah (1763-1846), of "Cross Roads," Franklin Co., N.C.; *m* 1802, Mary Hartsfield;
3–Levin K. (1810-65), of "Spring Hill," Harrison Co., Tex.; *m* 1831, Martha Pomfret Davis;
2–Martha Louisa (2 below).
7–John **Rush** (*d* 1699), comd. a troop of horse in Cromwell's Army; came to Pa., 1683; *m* 1648, Susanna Lucas;
6–Benjamin, Quaker; moved from Pa. to Spotsylvania Co., Va.; Am. Rev.; *m* Amy–;
5–Elizabeth (*b* 1734), *m* Joshua **Perry** (5 above).
6–Andrew **Hartsfield,** from Ireland to New York, thence to Phila., and later moved to Wake Co., N.C.;
5–Jacob (*b* Phila.), of Wake Co., N.C.; *m* Sarah (Lynn) McElroy (*b* 1739; Joseph Lynn[6], *m* Sarah Marshall);
4–Mary (*b* 1775), *m* Jeremiah **Perry** (4 above).
9–James **Taylor** (qv);
8–Col. James (1674-1729), justice, King and Queen Co., Va., 1702-14; surveyor of Va.; located 10,000 acres in Caroline Co.; *m* 1699, Martha (1679-1762), dau. of Col. William Thompson, of the Royal Army;
7–James (1703-84), burgess, 1772-74; mem. Va. Conv., 1774-78; *m* Alice (Thornton) Catlett (Francis Thornton[8], *m* Alice Savage);
6–Alice (*b* 1730), *m* Anthony **Winston** (*b* 1723), mem. Va. Conv., 1775; del. Va. House of Burgesses; capt. in Am. Rev. (Isaac[7], *m* Mary, dau. of Cornelius Dabney, *m* Sarah Jennings; Anthony[8], *m* Kezia Jones; William[9], from Eng. to Hanover Co., Va., 1687);
5–Martha Taylor, *m* William **Davis** (ca. 1746-1825; Rev. William[6], of Hanover Co., Va., *m* Catherine Staige; Jonathan[7], from Eng. to Han-

over Co., Va., 1667, *m* Martha Drayton Vernon);
4–Jonathan (1769-1841), *m* 1809, Mary Pomfret Butler (1784-1851; Isaac[5], *m* Mary Hunt Pomfret; John[6]; William[7], from Scotland to Culpeper Co., Va., 1700);
3–Martha Pomfret (1810-46), *m* 1831, Levin K. **Perry** (3 above);
2–Martha Louisa (1844-1918), *m* 1867, James Henry **Sawyer** (1834-75), planter, Harrison Co., Tex.; lt. C.S.A., Crumbar Bn., McGruder's Regt.; issue: I–Florence Louise (1 above); II–Levin Perry (1869-1926; *m* Ronda Marie Hood); III–James Henry (*b* 1875; *m* Felicia Demming).
1–Grad. Sam Houston Normal. Former teacher at Waco, Tex. Owner Ft. Worth Woman's Exchange. Residence: 715 Fifth Av., Ft. Worth, Tex.

JEREMIAH PERRY (1763-1846).

1–**DONALD, Senova Godwin Fulkerson (Mrs. James L.),** *b* Wellington, Mo., Jan. 3, 1871.
5–Capt. James **Fulkerson** (1737-99), Am. Rev.; *m* Mary Van Hook (1747-1830);
4–Peter, *m* Margaret Craig (Capt. Robert[5] [1744-1834], Am. Rev., mem. expdn. to S.C., and fought in Battle of King's Mountain, *m* 1st, Margaret Whitehill);
3–Jacob Van Hook, *m* Catherine Ewing (Nathaniel[4], *m* Jane Elinor [1778-1809]; Capt. Patrick[5] [1737-1819], of Cecil Co., Md., asst. dep., mem. Md. Conv., *m* Jane Porter, 1739-84);
2–Dr. Albert Preston (2 below).
7–Jeremiah **Perry,** from Eng. to Tyrrell Co., N.C.; *m* 1694, Christian Blount;
6–Jeremiah (*b* 1695), of Franklin Co., N.C.;
5–Joshua (1726-92 or 98), of Warren Co., N.C.; pvt., Am. Rev.; *m* 1749 or 50, Elizabeth Rush (*b* 1735);
4–Jeremiah (1763-1846), of "Cross Roads," Franklin Co., N.C. (see portrait); *m* Mary Hartsfield (*b* 1781);
3–Sarah Lynn (1812-67), *m* 1840, Richard W. **Godwin** (1812-67);
2–Carrie (1845-1910), *m* 1866, Dr. Albert Preston **Fulkerson** (1836-1904), surgeon; served in C.S.A. in Civil War; issue: I–Albert Putnam (*b* 1868; *m* Jessie L. Flook); II–Senova Godwin (1 above); III–Richard Wilkerson (*b* 1877).
1–*m* Dec. 28, 1897, Lewis A. Jaruagin (divorced); issue: 1–Richard Will, *b* Spokane, Wash., Jan. 14, 1899; ed. U. of Washington; *m* Jan. 21, 1922, Grace Kleinschmidt, of Seattle, Wash.
1–*m* 2d, Oct. 5, 1908, Lorengo D.S. Patton (1858-1910), who adopted Richard Will.
1–*m* 3d, Dec. 10, 1915, James LaPraik Donald, *b* Canada, Sept. 2, 1870; son of John Donald, of Kingston, Ont., and Scotland.
1–Ed. Elizabeth Aull Presbyn. Coll., Lexington, Mo. Mem. D.A.R., U.D.C. Baptist. Democrat. Residence: 204 N. Second St., Yakima, Wash.

1–**BOBBITT, Laura Scheherazade Blake (Mrs. William H.),** *b* nr. Raleigh, N.C., Apr. 25, 1864.
9–William **Blake** (qv);
8–James (bap. 1624-1700), *m* ca. 1651, Elizabeth Clap (1632-93);
7–James (1652-1732), *m* 1684, Ruth Batchelor (1662-1752);
6–Increase (1699-1770), *m* 1724, Ann Gray (1704-51);
5–Benjamin (1739-1809), Dorchester, Mass.; pvt. in Am. Rev., 1778; *m* 1763, Elizabeth Harris (1736-1813);
4–Ellis Gray (1768-1816), Southampton Co., Va.; *m* 1793, Mary Taylor;
3–Rev. Bennett Taylor (1800-82), Wake Co., N.C.; *m* 1837, Scheherazade Price (1805 or 10-1853);
2–Joseph (2 below).
7–Etheldred **Taylor** (*d* 1716), apptd. sheriff, Surry Co., Va., 1710; *m* Elizabeth Batts;
6–Col. Etheldred (ca. 1702-1755), served in Va. Militia; burgess, Southampton Co., Va., 1752-55; *m* Patience Kinchen;
5–Henry, of Southampton Co.; *m* Temperance Peterson;
4–Mary (1770-1811), *m* Ellis Gray **Blake** (4 above).
9–James **Taylor** (qv);
8–Col. James (1674-1729), justice, King and Queen Co., Va., 1702-14; surveyor of Va.; located 10,000 acres in Caroline Co. and settled there; *m* 1699, Martha (1679-1762), dau. of Col. William Thompson, of the Royal Army;
7–James (1703-84), burgess, 1772-74; mem. Va. Conv., 1774-78; *m* Mrs. Alice (Thornton) Catlett (Francis Thornton[8], burgess, Spotsylvania Co., 1726; William[9], qv);
6–Alice (*b* 1730), *m* 1747 or 49, Anthony **Winston** (*b* 1723), of Hanover Co., Va.; mem. Va. Conv., 1775-76; del. Va. Ho. of Burgesses; capt. in Am. Rev. (Isaac[7]);
5–Martha Taylor, *m* William **Davis** (ca. 1746-1825);
4–Jonathan (1769-1841), *m* 1809, Mary Pomfret Butler (1784-1851);
3–Lucy Caroline (1818-41), *m* Anthony Arrington **Person** (1817-76), settled at Sandy Creek plantation;
2–Lucy Caroline (1841-1918), *m* 1860, Joseph **Blake** (1839-1902), settled in Wake Co., N.C.; issue: I–John Bennett (*b* 1861-*d*); II–Henry Davis (*b* 1862); III–Laura S. (1 above).
1–*m* Oct. 29, 1884, William Haywood Bobbitt, *b* Tarboro, N.C., Oct. 24, 1861; son of Rev. James Burress Bobbitt, D.D., of Raleigh, N.C.; issue (both *b* Raleigh): 1–Bennett Blake, *b* Jan. 28, 1887; *m* 1918, Lucile Miller, of Kokomo, Ind. (issue: Cecilia, *b* Feb. 4, 1920; Jane, *b* Apr. 5, 1922); 2–Laura, *b* Aug. 15, 1888; *m* Edward Kennedy Reese.
1–Ed. Wesleyan Female Inst., Staunton, Va. Mem. Scions of Colonial Cavaliers, D.F.P.A., D.A.C., H.S.A., D.A.R., U.D.C. Residence: 1437 Fairfield Av., Indianapolis, Ind.

1–**GRAY, Mary Mabel Segraves (Mrs. Virgil Homer),** *b* Deer Creek Tp., Carr Co., Ind., Dec. 5, 1891.
6–John **Segraves** (*b* 1738; desc. Francis Segraves, from Eng., 1697, settled in Perquiman Co., N.C., *m* Lucretia–), served in 5th N.C. Regt. during Am. Rev.;
5–William (*b* 1768), *m* 1798, Leah Sealey (*b* 1778);
4–Ealem (1806-79), of Carroll Co., Ind.; *m* 1827, Martha Jane Moore (*b* 1810?);
3–William (*b* 1832), of Carroll Co.; *m* 1858, Anna Mary Magdalene Plank;
2–Alphonso (2 below).
8–Jacques (de la Planche) **Plank** (*b* 1759), from Picardy, 1720, settled in Oly Tp., Berks Co., Pa.;
7–Frederick (*d* post 1773), of Berks Co.;
6–Jacob (*b* 1755), of Berks Co.; pvt., 2d class, Capt. Mathias Henning's Co., 2d Bn., Lancaster Co., Pa., militia, during Am. Rev.;
5–Conrad (?), (*b* 1775), Lancaster Co.; *m* 1799;
4–Henry (1800-64), Lancaster Co.; *m* 1825, Madaline Guisie (*d* 1839; Adam[5]; Henry[6], Lancaster Co.);
3–Anna Mary Magdalene (1837-1922), *m* William **Segraves** (3 above).
8–Joseph Louis **Crockett** (*b* 1676; desc. of Antoine Desasuse Perronette de Crocketagne, a French Huguenot), from Ireland to New

York; settled in Wythe Co., Va.; *m* Sarah Stewart, of Ireland;
7–William (*b* 1709), of New Rochelle, N.Y.;
6–William, of Cumberland Co., Pa.; served in Am. Rev.;
5–William (1785-1858), of Cumberland Co.; *m* 1810, Nancy McNary Moss;
4–William Perry (1813-67), of Butler Co., O.; *m* 1835, Mary Anne Stanley (Moses[5], *d* in Carroll Co., Ind.);
3–John Stanley (1837-1923), *m* Mary Jane Circle;
2–Clara Catherine (2 below).
7–Peter (Zirkle) **Circle,** from Germany to Phila., Pa., 1725;
6–Samuel (*b* 1750), *m* 1770;
5–Immanuel (*b* 1778), of Fincastle, Va.; *m* 1800;
4–John (1806-81), *m* 1837, Clara Catherine Young (Francis[5], *m* Mary Rebecca–);
3–Mary Jane (1839-1911), *m* 1860, John Stanley **Crockett** (3 above);
2–Clara Catherine (1862-1928), *m* 1884, Alphonso **Segraves** (1859-1922); issue: I–William Everett (*b* 1885; *m* 1907, Lola Bowman); II–Otis Earl (*b* 1887; *m* 1908, Maebelle Noakes); III–Mary Mabel (1 above); IV–Minnie Ruth (*b* 1899; *m* 1918, Russell Seward); V–Lena Elizabeth (*b* 1901; *m* 1918, Donald G. Huston).
1–*m* Dec. 25, 1920, Virgil Homer Gray, *b* Harrison Tp., Cass Co., Ind., Feb. 9, 1896, son of George Gray, *m* Mary Jane Clark.
1–Ed. Cass Co. pub. schs., Ind. Business Coll., Logansport. Office mgr., Callahan & Crawford Construction Co., McAllen, Tex. Mem. D.A.R. Rebekah. Universalist. Republican. Residence: Royal Center, Ind. Winter address: C/o Miss Florence L. Sawyer, 715 Fifth Av., Ft. Worth, Tex.

1–**DARROW, Annie Eliza Pearson (Mrs. James P.),** *b* Solebury Tp., Bucks Co., Pa., May 28, 1862.
6–Aaron **Pearson** (*d* 1718), *m* Margaret Riggs;
5–Robert, *m* Margaret Longshore;
4–Crispin (ca. 1748-1806), reared by John Scarborough, the famous Quaker preacher; *m* 1769, Hannah Willson (1750-1817; John[5], of Warren Co., N.J., *m* Margaret Lundy);
3–John (1772-1858), *m* 1817, Elizabeth (Maskel) Wood (1774-1856);
2–Willson (2 below).
7–Joseph **Fell** (1668-1748), from Eng. to Buckingham, Bucks Co., Pa., 1704/05; *m* 1700, Bridget Willson (1673-1708);
6–Benjamin (1703-58), *m* 1728, Hannah Scarborough (1704-43);
5–John (1730-53), *m* Elizabeth Hartley (*b* 1733; Thomas[6]);
4–Seneca (*b* 1760), *m* 1783, Grace Holt (*d* 1845; Benjamin[5]);
3–Eli (1787-1859), *m* Rachel Bradshaw (*d* 1851);
2–Rachel Bradshaw (1824-1908), *m* 1849, Willson **Pearson** (1820-1900), of Bucks Co., Pa. (for issue see Vol. III, p. 36).
1–*m* Sept. 12, 1901, James P. Darrow, *b* Fayette N.Y., Oct. 2, 1846; son of James Darrow, *m* Sophia–, of Fayette.
1–Genealogist of Pearson Family. Mem. I.A.G. Residence: 1788 Casa Grande St., Pasadena, Calif.

1–**DAVIS, Mildred Watkins Dickinson (Mrs. Charles Hall, Jr.),** *b* Worsham, Va., Jan. 22, 1900.
12–Simon **Codrington** (qv);
11–Robert, of "Didmarton," Gloucestershire, Eng.; *m* Anne Stubbs (*d* 1618);
10–Christopher, from Eng. to West Indies; mem. Legislature, 1641; purchased land in St. John's Parish, Barbados, 1642 and 47;
9–Col. John (*d* 1685), mem. life guards, Barbados; treas., 1648; *m* Sarah Bate (Col. William[10], *d* 1680);
8–Henningham (1673-1744), *m* Dr. Paul **Carrington,** of Barbados;
7–Col. George (qv), *m* Ann Mayo;
6–Judge Paul (1733-1818), king's atty., Bedford Co., Va., 1756, Lunenburg, Mecklenburg, and Botetourt cos., 1767-70; burgess, Charlotte Co., 1765-75; mem. Convs. of Va., 1775 and 76; maj. Lunenburg militia, 1761; col.; co. lt.; presiding justice, Charlotte Co.; clk., Halifax Co., 1772; chmn. Com. of Safety, 1774-76; mem. convs., 1774-76; del., 1776-78; judge Gen. Ct., 1778; judge Ct. of Appeals, 1779-1807; *m* 1755, Margaret Reade;
5–Ann (1760-1838), *m* Col. William **Cabell** (1730-98), burgess, Albemarle Co., 1757-61, Amherst Co., 1761-75; co. lt., Albemarle Co. (Col. William[6], *m* Margaret, dau. of Col. Samuel Jordan, burgess, Buckingham Co., Va., 1767,69, *m* Ruth Meredith);
4–Clementina (*b* 1794), *m* 1815, Jesse **Irvine** (*d* 1876; William[5], *m* Martha, dau. of Jesse Burton; William[6], a Scotch settler, purchased land on the Otter river, where he built a house called "Otter," first justice of Bedford, *m* Mary Anthony);
3–Sarah Cabell, *m* Asa Dupuy **Dickinson** (1816-1884);
2–Thomas Harris (2 below).
10–Nicholas **Martian** (qv);
9–Elizabeth (*d* 1687), *m* Col. George **Reade** (qv);
8–Thomas, *m* ca. 1688, Lucy Gwynn (desc. Hugh Gwynn, burgess; of Col. William Bernard, mem. Council; of Capt. Robert Higginson, in charge of troops against Indians, Middle Plantation);
7–Clement (1707-63), col. French and Indian War, 1758; burgess; clk., Lunenburg Co., Va.; *m* 1730, Mary Hill (1711-86; Capt. William[8], *m* a dau. of Gov. Edmund Jennings, of Va.);
6–Margaret (1739-76), *m* 1755, Paul **Carrington** (6 above).
10–John **Woodson** (qv);
9–Robert (1634-post 1707), Prince Edward Co., Va.; *m* ca. 1656, Elizabeth Ferris (Richard[10], of Curles Neck);
8–Richard (ca. 1662-1730), *m* Ann Smith (Obediah[9], of Henrico Co., *m* Mary, dau. of William Cocke);
7–Richard (1690-1773-74), of "Poplar Hill," Prince Edward Co.; *m* 1715, Ann Madelin Michaux (*b* 1693; Abraham[8], *m* Susanne Rochet, Huguenot refugees to Va., 1700);
6–Elizabeth (1740-91), *m* 1755, Nathaniel **Venable** (1733-1804), burgess, 1766-69 (Abram[7], burgess 20 yrs., *m* Martha Davis; Abraham[8], qv);
5–Elizabeth Ann (1760-1826), *m* Col. Thomas **Watkins**;
4–Henry Anderson (1787-1850), *m* Mildred S. (Morton) Edmunds;
3–Richard Henry (1825-1905), *m* Mary Purnell Dupuy;
2–Mildred Stuart (1860-1902), *m* 1895, as his 1st wife, Thomas Harris **Dickinson** (1851-1916), sheriff of Prince Edward Co., Va., and farmer.
1–*m* Oct. 5, 1929, Charles Hall Davis, Jr., *b* Petersburg, Va., Nov. 29, 1902; son of Charles Hall Davis, of Petersburg.
1–B.S. in Education, State Teachers Coll., Farmville, Va., 1922; M.S. in English, U.Va., 1927. Taught English at Lee Junior High School, Roanoke, Va., 1922-23, in public high schools of Porto Rico, 1923-25, at State Teachers Coll., Farmville, Va., 1927-29. Mem. C.D.A. Episcopalian. Democrat. Residence: 705 Hendricks St., Anderson, Ind.

1–**DAVIS, Adeline Hamilton (Mrs. Frank V.),** *b* Momence, Ill., Sept. 1, 1860.
4–Thomas **Hamilton** (1750?-1825-30; son of Lord Hamilton); came from Eng., settled in Hardy Co., Va., later in Butler and Warren cos., O.; soldier Am. Rev.; *m* Sarah Seymour (or Beaver?; *d* bet. 1827-30);
3–Adam (1793-96-1875), Warren Co., O.; *m* 1818, Margaret Howard (Thomas[4], *m* Rebecca Malone);
2–Jacob Burnett (2 below).
10–Richard **Warren,** Mayflower Pilgrim (qv);
9–Sarah (*d* 1696), *m* 1634, John **Cook** (1612-95; Francis[10], Mayflower Pilgrim, qv);
8–Elizabeth (*d* 1715), *m* 1661, Daniel **Wilcox** (*d* 1702; Edward[9], of Portsmouth, R.I.);
7–John (*d* 1718), Tiverton, R.I.; *m* Rebecca– (*d* 1725);
6–Rebecca (*b* 1711), *m* 1728, Nicholas **Mosher** (*b* 1703; Nicholas[7], *m* Elizabeth–);
5–Deliverance (1730-1813), *m* 1758, Levi **Preston** (*b* 1738), Am. Rev. (Levi[6], *m* Elizabeth Harden);
4–Hannah (1771-1848), White Creek, N.Y.; *m* 1793, Elijah **Slocum** (1770-1850; Benjamin[5], *m* Rebecca Willcox);
3–Tryphena (1795-1857), *m* 1814, George **Wilber** (1789-1853; Nicanor[4], *m* Meribah Sherman);
2–Hannah Elizabeth (1831-61), *m* 1859, Jacob Burnett **Hamilton** (1821-1905), photographer,

Momence, Ill.; issue: I–Adeline (1 above); II–Eugene (1861-62).
1–*m* Jan. 19, 1881, Frank Virgil Davis, *b* Momence, Ill., May 15, 1852; son of Silas Davis, of Momence, *m* Rebecca Dashiell; issue: 1–Cassius Miles, *b* Chicago, Apr. 21, 1884; B.Sc. in E.E., U.Mich., '08; M.A., Union Coll.; *m* Sept. 6, 1911, Marguerite Stott (issue: Jane; Elizabeth; Evans Hamilton; Ann Bradford; Harriet Stott); 2–Frances Vivian, *b* Detroit, Mich., Nov. 30, 1901; B.Sc. in Edn., Ohio State U., '24; *m* June 5, 1926, Richard Harrison Evans, son of Judge Marcus Gaston Evans (issue: Elyse Marland).
1–Ed. The Alywick Sem., Washington, D.C. Mem. S.M.D., D.A.C., D.A.R., I.A.G., Wildbores in America. Residence: 2096 Iuka Av., Columbus, O.

1–**DAVIS, John Staige,** *b* Norfolk, Va., Jan. 15, 1872.
6–Andrew **Davis,** Jr., from Wales, settled in Middlesex Co., Va.; *m* 1757, Lucia Staige;
5–Staige (*d* 1812), Middlesex Co.; *m* 1792, Elisabeth Macon Gardiner (1776-1820);
4–John Andrew Gardiner (1802-40), prof. law, U.Va.; *m* Mary Jane Terrell;
3–Prof. John Staige (1824-85), prof. anatomy, U.Va.; *m* Lucy Landon Blackford;
2–Col. William Blackford (2 below).
7–Peter **Jefferson** (1708-57), of Shadwell, Albemarle Co.; whose father came from Wales and settled in Osbornes, Chesterfield Co., Va.: *m* 1738, Jane Randolph (1720-76; Isham[8], of Dungeness, Goochland Co., Va.); their son, Thomas, was third President of the U.S.;
6–Martha (*b* 1746), *m* 1765, Dabney **Carr** (1744-73);
5–Lucy (*d* 1804), *m* Richard **Terrell** (*b* 1802; Richmond[6], *m* Anne Overton);
4–Mary Jane (1803-79), *m* Prof. John Andrew Gardiner **Davis** (4 above).
9–John **Carter** (1608-69), from Eng., 1643, settled at Corotoman, Lancaster Co., Va.; *m* 3d, Sarah Ludlow;
8–Robert "King" (1663-1732), *m* 2d, Betty Landon (1684-1719), of Eng.;
7–Charles (1707-64), of Cleve, King George's Co.; *m* 2d, Ann Byrd (William[8]);
6–Landon (1751-1811), of Cleve; *m* 1st, Mildred Washington Willis (Col. Henry[7], *m* Mildred [Washington] Gregory, aunt and godmother of Gen. George Washington);
5–Lucy Landon (*b* 1776), of Cleve; *m* 1793, Gen. John **Minor** (1761-1816), of Fredericksburg, Va.;
4–Mary Berkeley (1802-96), *m* William Matthews **Blackford** (1801-64), of Lynchburg;
3–Lucy Landon (1828-59), *m* Dr. John Staige **Davis** (3 above).
10–Henry **Howland** (qv);
9–Zoeth (*d* 1676), of Dartmouth, Mass.; *m* 1656, Abigail;
8–Benjamin (1659-1727), *m* 1684, Judith Sampson;
7–Barnabas (1699-1773), *m* 1724, Rebecca Lapham (1707-36);
6–Benjamin (1727-98), *m* 1748, Anne Briggs (1725-68);
5–Barnabas (*b* 1749), *m* Olive Mosher;
4–Capt. Jethro (*d* 1824), Norfolk, Va.; *m* Mary Bingham, of Portsmouth, Va.;
3–William Jethro (1822-54), of Portsmouth; *m* Mary Jane Watts (1827-70);
2–Mary Jane (Kentie) (1851-1930), *m* 1871, William Blackford **Davis** (1848-1926), M.D., U.Va., 1870; asst. surgeon U.S.A., Jan. 9, 1877; col., M.C., U.S.A., Jan. 1, 1909; retired, Aug. 5, 1912.
1–*m* Oct. 26, 1907, Kathleen Gordon Bowdoin, *b* Baltimore, Md., Jan. 14, 1883; dau. of William Graham Bowdoin, of Baltimore; issue (all *b* Baltimore, Md.): 1–Kathleen Staige, *b* Nov. 17, 1909; 2–William Bowdoin, *b* Feb. 4, 1912; Princeton, 1934; 3–Howland, *b* Nov. 21, 1913.
1–Ph.B., Yale-S., '95; M.D., Johns Hopkins U., 1899; (hon. M.A., Yale, 1925). Resident house officer, Johns Hopkins Hosp., 1899-1900; resident physician, Union Memorial Hosp., 1900-03; asst. instr., asso., asso. prof. clinical surgery, Johns Hopkins Med. Sch.; visiting surgeon, Union Memorial Hosp., Hosp. for Women of Md., Children's Hosp. School; visiting surgeon (plastic surgery), dispensary surgeon, Johns Hopkins Hosp. Capt. M.C., U.S.A., 1917-19. Mem. S.A.R., Md. Hist. Soc. Episcopalian. Democrat. Clubs: Baltimore, Elkridge Fox Hunting, Fishers Island; Yale (New York). Residence: 215 Wendover Rd., Baltimore, Md.

1–**DEAN, Sidney Walter,** *b* Warren, R.I., June 1, 1871.
8–Walter (Deane) **Dean** (qv);
7–Dea. Ezra (*d* 1727), of Taunton, Mass.; *m* 1675, Bethiah Edson (1653-1732);
6–Dr. Ezra (1680-1737), *m* Abagail Brintnell, of Norton, Mass.;
5–Solomon (1731-84), *m* Mary William (1733-88);
4–Sylvester (1757-1817), Am. Rev.; *m* Abigail Halley (1758-1832), of Edgartown, Martha's Vineyard;
3–Amos (1794-1849), began to write name Dean; silk and woolen mfr., Glastonbury, Conn.; *m* 1814, Nancy Robinson Kempton (1790-1874), of Plymouth, Mass.;
2–Sidney (2 below).
9–Samuel **Eddy** (qv);
8–Zachariah (1639-1718), *m* Alice Padduck (1640-92);
7–Caleb (*b* 1678), *m* Bethiah Smith;
6–Edward (*b* 1703), *m* Elizabeth Comines, or Cummings;
5–Caleb (1738-70), *m* Sarah Cole (1746-1835);
4–Caleb (1768-1850), *m* Nabby Maxwell (1768-1861);
3–James M. (1811-1901), *m* Nancy Smith (1811-54);
2–Annie (*b* 1843), *m* Sidney **Dean** (1818-1901), of Glastonbury, Conn.; clergyman; mem. Congress (1855-1857, 1857-1859), from eastern dist. of Conn.; editor and publisher, Providence (R.I.) Evening Press, and Morning Star, (1864-80); author, lecturer; issue: I–Edward Sidney (1867-69); II–Sidney Walter (1 above); III–Arthur Kempton (1873-1919; *m* Florence Belle Anderson).
1–*m* Aug. 30, 1904, Marian Hamilton Perry (1884-Nov. 10, 1915); issue: 1–Sidney Walter, Jr., *b* Boston, May 20, 1905; B.A., Yale, '26; 2–Warren Kempton, *b* Boston, May 17, 1907; 3–Dorothy Marion, *b* Brookline, Mass., Nov. 29, 1909.
1–*m* 2d, June 3, 1916, Marguerite Mooers Marshall (qv).
1–Newspaper work at Brookline, Mass., 1892-1900; Boston Journal, 1900-04; managing editor Boston Herald, 1904-09, Boston Journal, 1909-11; editor of trade publications, New York City, since 1911; dir. Trades Reporting Bureau, Inc., New York, since 1920. Clubs: New York Press (trustee 7 yrs., pres., 1926-28), Adventurers, Rockaway Point Yacht. Summer place: Rockaway Point, L.I., N.Y. Residence: 37 Brunswick Rd., Montclair, N.J.

1–**DEAN, Marguerite Mooers Marshall (Mrs. Sidney W.),** *b* Kingston, N.H., Sept. 9, 1887.
9–Edmund **Marshall** (1608-73), from Eng., 1637; settled at Manchester, Mass.; removed to Ipswich; *m* Millicent–;
8–Benjamin (1646-1716), *m* 1677, Prudence Woodward (1660-1732);
7–Benjamin (1684-1747), *m* 1711, Bethia Goodhue (*d* 1752);
6–William (1726-1822), first rep. from Hampstead in N.H. Legislature; *m* 1756, Abigail Burnham (1726-90);
5–Samuel (1766-1840), Landaff, N.H.; *m* 1787, Lydia Eaton (*b* 1770);
4–James (1789-1858), Kingston, N.H.; *m* 1812, Mary Dudley (1792-1874);
3–James F. (1815-87), Kingston, N.H.; *m* 1850, Mary Miranda George (1833-82);
2–Herbert Walter (1852-1910), carriage mfr.; *m* 1882, Lela Mooers Brown (1857-1901); issue: I–Marguerite Mooers (1 above); II–Ethel Brown (*b* 1891; *m* Nathaniel Sherman).
1–*m* June 3, 1916, Sidney Walter Dean (qv).
1–A.B., Tufts Coll., '07 (P.B.K.). With Boston Herald, 1908-09, N.Y. Sunday and Morning World, 1909-10; columnist and special writer, Evening World (N.Y.), since 1910; writer of prose and verse for magazines. Author: The Drift, 1911 (see Who's Who in America). Clubs: Women's City (N.Y.), P.B.K. Alumnae. Residence: 37 Brunswick Rd., Montclair, N.J.

1–**DENBY, Edwin Hooper,** *b* Phila., Pa., Feb. 9, 1873.
17–Henry **Borden** (*b* bet. 1370-80), *m* Robergia–;
16–Thomas (*d* 1469), *m* Isabella–;
15–John, *m* Benett, dau. Thomas Tornor;
14–William (*d* 1531), *m* Joan–; *m* 2d, Thomasia–; *m* 3d, Rose–;

13–Edmund (*d* 1539), *m* Margaret–;
12–William (*d* 1557), *m* Joan–;
11–Thomas (*d* 1592);
10–Matthew (*d* 1620), of Headcorn, Kent; *m* Joan Reeder;
9–Richard (qv), *m* Jane Fowle;
8–John (1640-1716), *m* 1670, Mary Earle (William[9] [*d* 1715], *m* Mary, dau. of John Walker; Ralph[10], qv, *m* Joan Savage);
7–Benjamin (1692-1743), settled at an early age in Monmouth Co., N.J., in Va., 1734, or earlier; *m* Zeruiah Winter (William[8] [*d* 1733], *m* 1688, Hannah [Grover] Gardiner, dau. of James Grover, mem. 1st Assembly of N.J., 1668, *m* Rebecca–);
6–Benjamin (1715-58), *m* 1743, Mrs. Magdalen (Woods) McDowell (Michael Woods[7], *m* Mary Campbell);
5–Martha (1744-1822), *m* 1773, Benjamin **Hawkins** (1732-79);
4–Magdalen (*b* 1775), *m* 1801, Matthew **Harvey** (William[5], *m* Rebecca, dau. of Robert Caruthers);
3–Sarah Jane (*d* 1840), *m* 1829, Nathaniel **Denby** (1798-1845), see Vol. II, p. 101, for Denby lineage;
2–Edwin Robinson (2 below).
19–William **Whitfield,** of Whitfield Hall, Cumberland, Eng.; *m* dau. of Richard Holme, of the Manor of Alstonmore, Cumberland;
18–William, *m* Maude, dau. John Wheateley;
17–John;
16–William;
15–Richard;
14–Richard;
13–Myles;
12–Robert;
11–Robert, of Wadhurst; *m* Agnes, dau. William Atwood;
10–Jane, *m* Anthony **Fowle,** of Rotherfield;
9–Jane (1604-88), *m* Richard **Borden** (9 above).
2–Dr. Edwin Robinson (1834-75), fleet surgeon U.S.N.; *m* 1870, Laura Hooper (1838-1928; John[3] [1769-1855], *m* 1827, Mary [1797-1849], dau. of Robert M. Richardson [*b* 1753], *m* 1778, Comfort Ayres); for issue see Vol. III, p. 151.
1–*m* June 28, 1916, Sadie Campbell, *b* Brooklyn, N.Y., 1880; dau. of Felix Campbell, of Brooklyn, *m* Mary, dau. John Campbell, *m* Jane Carr.
1–Grad. Ecole des Beaux Arts, Paris, 1897. Architect, New York. Has devised an accumulating genealogical chart. Mem. N.Y. G.B.S., I.A.G. Clubs: Metropolitan, Manhattan, Riding, Tuxedo, Nat. Arts, MacDowell, Atlantic Yacht. Summer place: Bar Harbor, Me. Residence: 105 E. 53d St., New York, N.Y.

1–**DEANE, Mavrett Angelia,** *b* Whitingham, Vt., Nov. 15, 1856.
9–Richard **Sears** (qv);
8–Paul (1636-1707), Marblehead, Mass.; took oath of fidelity, 1657; capt. militia, served in Narragansett War; an original propr. of Harwich, Mass.; grand juror, 1667; *m* 1658, Deborah Willard (bap. 1645-1721; George[9], of Scituate, *m* Dorothy Dunster);
7–Capt. Samuel (1663/64-1741/42), one of first settlers, Harwich; constable, 1702; lt., 1706; capt., 1715; *m* 1684, Mercy Mayo (1664-1748/49; Dea. Samuel[8], *m* Tamzin Lumpkin; Rev. John[9], qv);
6–Judah (1699-1776), *m* 1731, Mary Paddock (*b* 1714);
5–Nathan (1741-1825), Rochester, Mass.; ens. Am. Rev.; *m* 1st, 1764, Rebecca Crowell (*b* 1742);
4–Paul (1765-1846), *m* 1790, Hannah Delano (*b* 1766);
3–Susan (1792-1861), Woodstock, Vt.; *m* John **Sanderson** (1783-1848);
2–Hannah (2 below).
9–John **Alden,** Mayflower Pilgrim (qv);
8–David (1646-1719), dep. Duxbury, Mass.; *m* 1670, Mary Southworth (Constant[9], qv);
7–Alice (1685-1774), *m* 1706, Judah **Paddock** (1681-1770; Zachariah[8]; Robert[9]);
6–Mary (*b* 1714), Yarmouth, Mass.; *m* Judah **Sears** (6 above).
8–Philip (De La Noye) **Delano** (qv);
7–Lt. Jonathan (1647-1720), an original propr. of Dartmouth; *m* 1678, Mercy Warren (*b* 1658);
6–Jabez (1682-1734), *m* 1710, Mary Delano (John[7], *m* Mary Weston);
5–Jabez (1723-68), Rochester, Mass.; *m* 2d, 1760, Ruth Goodspeed (1736-68);
4–Hannah (*b* 1766), *m* Paul **Sears** (4 above);
3–Susan, *m* John **Sanderson** (3 above);
2–Hannah (1829-1908), *m* 1854, Ebenezer Alexander **Deane,** M.D. (1825-1908), physician and surgeon; issue: I–Mavrett Angelia (1 above); II–Mary Luella (*b* 1859).
1–Ed. N.E. Conservatory of Music, Boston. Trustee Montague Public Library. Mem. S.M.D., D.A.R., I.A.G., Alden Kindred of America. Congregational. Republican. Club: Woman's. Address: Box 75, Montague, Mass.

1–**DICKINSON, Helen Winslow Dickinson (Mrs. Asa D.),** *b* Lakewood, N.J., July 8, 1885.
10–Francis **Cooke,** Mayflower Pilgrim (qv);
9–Jane, *m* Experience **Mitchell**;
8–Elizabeth, *m* 1645, John **Washburn** (*d* 1686);
7–Sarah (1675-1746), *m* 1697, John **Ames** (1672-1756);
6–Daniel (1712-78), *m* 1742, Hannah Keith (1718-1802);
5–Job (1752-1827), Am. Rev.; *m* 1782, Mary Dyke (1755-1813);
4–Azel (1783-1842), *m* 1811, Mercy Hatch;
3–Lois (1825-91), *m* 1851, Rev. Erastus **Dickinson** (1807-88);
2–Frederic Erastus (2 below).
11–Richard **Warren,** Mayflower Pilgrim (qv);
10–Anna (*b* ca. 1612), *m* Thomas **Little** (*d* 1672);
9–Mercy or Mary (*d* 1693), *m* 1666, John **Sawyer**;
8–Mercy (1668-1702), *m* 1686, Anthony **Eames** (*d* 1729);
7–Mercy (1687-1760), *m* 1711, Joseph **Phillips** (1685-1767);
6–Mercy (1725-85), *m* Benjamin **Hatch** (*b* 1721);
5–Charles (1755-1828), *m* 1787, Joanna Winslow;
4–Mercy (1789-1842), *m* Azel **Ames** (4 above).
10–Peter **Browne,** Mayflower Pilgrim (qv);
9–Mary, *m* Ephraim **Tinkham**;
8–Ebenezer (1651?-1718), *m* 1675, Elizabeth Burrowes (1654-1718);
7–Joanna (1685-1766), *m* 1709, Thomas **Macomber** (1684-1771);
6–Elizabeth, *m* 1740, Job **Winslow** (1715-87; Gilbert[7], *m* Mercy Snow; Capt. Nathaniel[8], *m* Faith Miller; Kenelm[9], qv);
5–Joanna (1755-1840), *m* Charles **Hatch** (5 above).
2–Frederic Erastus **Dickinson** (1860-1925), bus. mgr., The Independent, New York; *m* 1884, Julia Randall Smith (1860-1900).
1–*m* June 6, 1908, Asa Don Dickinson (see Vol. III, p. 154, for genealogy and issue).
1–Ed. New York Public Schools and Packer Collegiate Inst. Residence: 47 Amherst Av., Swarthmore, Pa.

1–**DORRANCE, Frances,** *b* Wilkes-Barre, Pa., June 30, 1877.
6–Rev. Samuel **Dorrance** (1685-1775), from Ireland, settled at Voluntown, Conn.; ordained at Voluntown, 1723; minister of the first permanent Presbyn. ch. in Conn.; *m* 1st, 1726, Elizabeth Smith (1705-50);
5–Lt. Col. George (1736-78), of Kingston, Luzerne Co., Pa.; *m* Elizabeth– (1747-96);
4–Col. Benjamin (1767-1837), mem. Pa. Legislature, 1808,10,12,14,19,20,30; col. militia; sheriff, Luzerne Co.; *m* 1795, Nancy Ann Buckingham (1767-1834; Jedediah[5], *m* Martha Clark, of Columbia, Conn.);
3–Col. Charles Dorrance (1805-92), *m* 1845, Susan E. Ford (1828-92; James[4], of Lawrenceville, Pa., *m* Maria Lindsley);
2–Benjamin (2 below).
9–Elder John **Strong** (qv);
8–Thomas (*d* 1689), *m* 1671, Rachel Holton;
7–Selah (1680-1732), *m* Abigail Terrey (1680-1761);
6–Selah (*b* 1713/14), *m* Hannah Woodhull;
5–Maj. Nathaniel (1737-78), *m* Amy Brewster (*b* ca. 1741);
4–Selah, *m* Ruth Woodhull (1770-1810);
3–Schuyler (1797-1845), Bath, N.Y.; *m* Frances Minerva Cruger (Gen. Daniel[4]);
2–Ruth Woodhull (1844-1925), *m* 1872, Benjamin **Dorrance** (1846-1922); issue: I–Anne (*b* June 26, 1873); II–Frances (1 above); III–Ruth (Aug. 9, 1879-Feb. 13, 1895).
1–Ed. Wyoming Sem., Kingston, Pa.; A.B., Vassar, '00; B.L.S., N.Y. State Library School, 1918; U. of Berlin, 3 semesters, 1911-14; Marine Biol. Lab., Woods Hole, summers 1900 and 1902; Columbia U., summer course 1912. Dir. Wyoming Hist. and Geological Soc., Wilkes-

Barre, Pa., mem. Pa. State Hist. Commn. Life mem. Hist. Soc. of Pa., Swedish Colonial Soc., N.Y. State Hist. Assn.; mem. I.A.G., Pa. Soc. Colonial Dames of America, U.S.D. 1812. Residence: Wilkes-Barre, Pa.

1–**DOTY, Minnie McNary (Mrs. Charles),** *b* Delafield, Wis., Aug. 27, 1860.
10–William **Hutchinson** (qv);
9–Edward (bap. 1613-1675), from Eng., 1633, settled at Portsmouth, R.I.; mem. A. and H. A. Co. of Boston, 1638; chief officer of cav. in Mass. forces during King Philip's War; mortally wounded by Indians in ambush nr. W. Brookfield, Mass.; *m* 1636, Catherine Hamby, of Eng.;
8–Ann (1643-1717), *m* Samuel **Dyer** (bap. 1635; William[9], qv);
7–Ann, *m* 1693, Carew **Clarke** (*d* 1759; Joseph[7]; Thomas[8]; John[9]; John[10]);
6–Ann (*b* 1698), *m* 1718, Samuel **Dunn**;
5–Batsheba, of N. Kingston, R.I.; *m* 1754, John **Dyer**;
4–Elizabeth (1754-1817), *m* Charles **Shepherd** (1744-1820), Am. Rev.;
3–Charles (1797-1838), of Hudson, N.Y.; *m* 1817, Mary Winters (*d* 1838);
2–Elizabeth (2 below).
10–Roger **Williams** (qv);
9–Mary (1633-81), *m* John **Sayles** (1633-81);
8–Mary (b 1652), *m* 1674, William **Greene** (1653-79);
7–Mary (1677-95), *m* Edward **Dyer** (1670-post 1717; Samuel[8], 8 above);
6–Edward (*b* 1701);
5–John, *m* Batsheba Dunn (5 above).
2–Elizabeth Shepherd (1822-1923), *m* 1849, Cornelius **McNary** (1820-1920), farmer; issue: I–John Cornelius (*b* 1851; *m* Emma–); II–Emily Agusta (*b* 1855; *m* Adolph Wittstruck); III–George (*b* 1857); IV–Minnie (1 above); V–Harvey (*b* 1862; *m* Rose–); VI–Susie (*b* 1864; *m* Otto Demour); VII–Ida Gray (*b* 1866); VIII–Addie (*b* 1869; *m* Justice Doty); IX–A. D. (*b* 1871; *m* Anna–).
1–*m* Jan. 1, 1879, Charles Doty, *b* Kendall Co., Ill., Nov. 30, 1846; served in 23d Ill. Regt. in Civil War; son of Robinson Doty, of Rutland, Vt.; issue (all *b* Ashkum, Ill.): 1–Charles Albert, *b* Oct. 22, 1879; attended Valparaiso U.; *m* Dec. 23, 1903, Maud, dau. of A. C. Smith, of Ft. Collins, Colo. (issue: Wendell); 2–Lucy Elizabeth, *b* Dec. 1, 1880; B.S., Valparaiso U.; *m* Feb. 9, 1905, Alfred Rosco Putnam, son of Michel Putnam (issue: Alfreda Putnam); 3–Ida Mae, *b* Mar. 23, 1886; B.S., Valparaiso U.; *m* Sept. 23, 1910, H.S. Cook, M.D., son of James Cook, of Gilman, Ill. (issue: Velma Mae; Marvin).
1–Attended Valparaiso (Ind.) U., and State U., Bloomington, Ind. Mem. D.A.C., D.A.R., I.-A.G., O.E.S., Woman's Club. Episcopalian. Republican. Residence: 413 N. Pennsylvania Av., Roswell, N.M.

1–**EASTER, Anita Tinges (Mrs. James W.),** *b* Wilmington, Del., Nov. 1, 1890.
5–John **Tinges** (1735-1801), settled at Boston, 1757; removed to Baltimore, 1775; *m* Ann Wheatherby;
4–Charles (1765-1816), of Baltimore; *m* 2d, 1806, Mary Harvey Hill (1781-1861);
3–George W. (1814-87), *m* 1840, Sarah White (1819-99);
2–Albert Howard (2 below).
9–John **Webster,** settled in Northampton Co., Va., 1632; mentioned in court record, Aug. 18, 1650;
8–John, of Delaware;
7–John (1667-1753), Harford Co., Md.; *m* Hannah Butterworth;
6–Isaac, *m* 1722, Margaret Lee (James[7]);
5–Samuel (1746-1817), *m* Margaret Adams;
4–John Adams (1787-1877), capt.; assisted in defense of Fort McHenry, 1812; *m* 1816, Rachel Biays;
3–John Adams (1821-75), capt. U.S. revenue service; *m* 1852, Amelia R. Patterson;
2–Margaret Jones (1860-98), *m* 1887, Albert Howard **Tinges** (1852-1900), of Baltimore; ed. Washington and Lee U.; civil engr., supervisor P.,W.&B. div. Pa. R.R.; issue: I–Henry Belin (*b* 1889; *m* Ruth Sheridan Geer); II–Anita (1 above); III–Charles Howard (*b* 1894; *m* Mildred Lee Carter White); IV–Elizabeth Baldwin (*b* 1896).
1–*m* Apr. 21, 1917, James Washington Easter, *b* Baltimore, Aug. 15, 1892; son of James Miller Easter, of Owings Mills, Md.; issue (all *b* Baltimore, Md.): 1–James Miller, *b* Apr. 11, 1919; 2–Margaret Webster, *b* Nov. 1, 1921; 3–John Hamilton, *b* Feb. 13, 1925.
1–Bryn Mawr Coll., 1 yr. Mem. Md. Hist. Soc., etc. Episcopalian. Clubs: Woman's City (Baltimore). Residence: Owings Mills, Md.

1–**EGBERT, James Chidester,** *b* New York, N.Y., May 3, 1859.
9–Govert **Egbert,** from Holland to New Amsterdam, 1660; settled at Elizabethtown, N.J., 1673; *m* ante 1674, Femmetjie Jans;
8–Tunis (*d* 1721), supervisor, S.I., 1704-09; *m* 1690;
7–Abraham (ante 1695-ante 1725), *m* Francyutje Parrin, Perrin or Perrins;
6–John (bap. 1720), *m* Margaret–;
5–John (1750-1830 or 32), in charge of powder wagons in Am. Rev.; *m* Hannah Little (1750-1840);
4–Enos (1778-1835), *m* 1801, Sarah Lyon (1784-1865);
3–James (1801-81), *m* 1826, Johanna Chidester (1797-1886);
2–James Chidester (1826-1904), clergyman; *m* 1855, Louisa Drew (1831-1905; George Gardiner[8], lost at sea as capt., 1833); issue: I–Annie Lake (*b* 1857); II–James Chidester (1 above); III–Rev. George Drew (*b* 1865; *m* Estelle Powers); IV–Marion D. (*b* 1870).
1–*m* June 12, 1884, Emma Gross Pennington, *b* Hoboken, N.J., Jan. 15, 1861; dau. of John Pennington, of Eng., later New York City; issue: 1–James C. Pennington (June 5, 1885-June 12, 1886); 2–Harry Drew (Aug. 24, 1886-Mar. 1, 1919); *m* Dec. 28, 1912, Edith, dau. of James Frederick Cowperthwaite, of Westfield, N.J. (issue: Marjorie Louisa; Edith Pennington); 3–George Pennington, *b* Jersey City, N.J., Mar. 28, 1889; Columbia, '10; *m* May 19, 1918, Mary Eloise, dau. of Ferdinand Hunting Cook, of N.Y. City (issue: George Pennington, *b* Jan. 14, 1930); 4–Lester Darling, *b* Jersey City, Mar. 4, 1892; Columbia, '14; *m* May 14, 1921, Beatrice Valerie, dau. of Ferdinand Hunting Cook (issue: John Pennington: Richard Cook).
1–A.B., Columbia, '81 (P.B.K.), A.M., 1882, Ph.D., 1884; (LL.D., Rutgers, 1926; Litt.D., Columbia, 1929). Educator since 1885; prof. Latin, Columbia U., since 1906, dir. Sch. of Business, since 1916. Pres. L.I. Coll. Hosp., 1917-30; pres. L.I. Coll. of Medicine, 1930–. Author (see Who's Who in America). Club: Century. Summer place: Bay Head, N.J. Residence: 325 Riverside Dr., New York, N.Y.

1–**ELLIS, Mary Rebecca,** *b* Richmond, Mo., July 21, 1867.
9–Lt. Col. William **Collier** (*b* Hertfordshire, Eng., 1620-*d* New Kent Co., Va., 1682), of York Co., Va., 1670; removed to New Kent Co., 1675; lt. col., New Kent Co. militia; *m* 1655, Sallie–(1636-80);
8–Charles (*b* Eng., 1660-*d* King and Queen Co., Va., 1735), owned large landed estates in York, New Kent, King and Queen, and Gloucester cos.; vestryman; *m* 1684, Mary Eyers or Eyres (*b* Norfolk, Va., 1665-*d* King and Queen Co., 1701; Robert[9], burgess from Norfolk);
7–John (1685-1765), of "Porto Bello," King and Queen Co.; vestryman; *m* 2d, 1706, Miss (Sarah?) Gaines;
6–John (1707-will probated 1749), inherited "Porto Bello"; to Hanover Co., Va.; capt., Va. regt., Carthagean expdn., 1740-42; owned large estates in Isle of Wight and Surry cos.; *m* his cousin, Ann Collier;
5–John (1742-1820), Charlotte Co.; Am. Rev.; apptd. maj. Va. militia; to Nicholas Co., Ky.; *m* Hannah Cary;
4–Franklin (*d* ante 1835); served several terms Ky. Legislature; *m* 1814, Mary M. Bayse;
3–Elizabeth (*b* Ky., 1817-*d* Mo., 1843), *m* 1834, Dr. Robert Binns **Ellis** (*b* Sussex Co., Va., 1812-*d* Nev., 1872; Robert[4], of Va.);
2–Robert Henry (2 below).
9–Capt. John **Marshall** (qv);
8–Thomas (1655-1704), Westmoreland Co., Va.; *m* 1685, Martha Jane Pendleton;

7–Capt. John (1700-52), of "The Forest"; capt. French and Indian War; *m* ca. 1722, Elizabeth Markham (1704-75; John[8], of Eng., *m* Mary Sedgbrook);
6–Mary (*b* 1738), *m* ca. 1758, Rev. William **McClanahan,** Bapt. minister; the "Fighting Parson," capt. Am. Rev. (Thomas[7], of Va., *m* Elizabeth Newman; William[8], *m* Margaret–);
5–Nancy, *m* Dr. Elizmond **Bayse,** Am. Rev. (Edmund[6], of Fauquier Co., *m* Winifred–);
4–Mary M. (*d* 1835), *m* Franklin **Collier** (4 above).
8–George **Felt** (*b* Eng., 1601-*d* 1682), came with Gov. Endicott 1628, settled at Salem, 1629; with 100 men founded Charleston, 1634; selectman; pioneer settler at Yarmouth, 1640; *m* Elizabeth Wilkinson (1601-94; Widow Prudence[9], *d* 1655);
7–Moses (*b* 1651), *m* Hannah Maine;
6–Aaron (1715-69), *m* 1739, Mary Waite (1717-60);
5–Peter (1745-1817), *m* 1769, Lucy Andrews (1749-1805; Jeremiah[6], of Ipswich, *m* Lucy–);
4–Hannah (1778-1842), *m* 1798, Stephen **Mansur** (1773-1865), see Vol. III, p. 179, for Mansur lineage;
3–Charles (*b* Temple, N.H., 1805-1847), *m* 1834, Rebecca Wills (1809-74; Josiah[4] [*b* Mt. Hadley, N.J., 1763], *m* Sarah Gallilee [*b* Md., 1772], of Phila., Pa.);
2–Emeline (1842-94), *m* 1860, Robert Henry **Ellis** (1835-1910), lawyer; capt. C.S.A.; for issue see Vol. III, p. 179.
1–Mem. D.A.R., U.S.D. 1812 (regent), U.D.C. (chapter pres.; Mo. state historian), Kansas City Quill Club. Genealogist. Compiler: The House of Mansur, 1926. Writer of poems, songs, feature articles. Residence: 4111 Warwick Boul., Kansas City, Mo.

1–**SHUMATE, May Black (Mrs. David L.),** *b* Pettis Co., Mo., Mar. 24, 1881.
6–Michael **Goodknight** (1689-1780), of Va. and Ky.; *m* 2d, 1762, Mary Landers;
5–John (1765-1841), served in War 1812; *m* 1785, Ruth Davis (1763-1850);
4–Michael (1789-1861), *m* 1811, Comfort McCormick;
3–Nancy (1818-74), *m* 1836, Milton **Durrell** (1815-69);
2–Sallie Ann (2 below).
6–Dr. John **McCormick,** from Ireland, bet. 1730-40, settled in Jefferson Co., Va.; grad. in medicine at Dublin Inst.;
5–George (1742-1820), of Va. and Ky.; capt. in Am. Rev. and War 1812; *m* 1770, Mary Chaplin (1738-1819);
4–Comfort (1789-1865), *m* 1811, Michael **Goodknight** (4 above);
3–Nancy, *m* Milton **Durrell** (3 above);
2–Sallie Ann (1852-86), *m* 1870, James **Black** (1847-89); issue: I–Ida Nora (1874-1924); II–Columbus (1877-1905); III–May (1 above); IV–Ottie (*b* 1884); V–Hettie (*b* 1887); VI–Bernice (1887-90).
1–*m* Mar. 3, 1897, David Larkin Shumate, *b* Johnson Co., Mo., Sept. 30, 1873; son of Martin Shumate (1846-1920), of N.C. and Mo., *m* Salina Thomas (1847-1904), of Tenn. and Mo.
1–Ed. high school and young ladies' coll. Mem. D.A.C., D.A.R., U.S.D. 1812 (post regent), U.D.C. (past pres.), Mo. Valley Hist. Soc., etc. Clubs: Kansas City, Kansas City Athletic, Presidents and Past Presidents Assembly, Blue Hills Country. Residence: 3703 Pa. St., Kansas City, Mo.

1–**ENSEY, Grace Ella,** *b* Covington, Ky.
8–Thomas **Benedict** (qv);
7–John (1640-post 1723 ?), *m* 1670, Phoebe Gregory;
6–Joseph, *m* 2d, 1720, Mary–;
5–Jonathan (ca. 1722-1800), *m* Lucy Castle;
4–Sylvia (1768-1846), *m* 1788, Thomas **Bull** (1762-1823; Thomas[5], *m* Martha–);
3–Alonson (1797-1858), *m* 1822, Hannah Leonard;
2–Chloe F. (2 below).
8–John **Leonard** (*d* 1676), of Springfield, Mass.; brother of James of Taunton, Mass.; *m* 1640, Sarah Heath or Held (*d* 1711);
7–Benjamin (1654-1724), *m* 1679/80, Sarah Scott (1663-1751);
6–Ebenezer (1687-1762), *m* 1722, Martha Miller (1695-1760);
5–Luther (*b* 1727), *m* 1749, Anna Bancroft;
4–Oliver (1749/50-1804), *m* 1785, Abiah Warriner;
3–Hannah (1800-85), *m* Alonson **Bull** (3 above).

GRACE E. ENSEY

8–William **Warriner** (*d* 1676), *m* 1639, Joanna Searle (*d* 1660);
7–Dea. James (1640/41-1727), *m* 1664, Elizabeth Baldwin (*d* 1687);
6–Ens. Ebenezer (1681/82-1737), *m* 1700/01, Joanna Dickinson (1684-1764; Hezekiah[7] [1645-1707], of Springfield, Mass., *m* 1679, Abigail Blakeman [1663-1716]; Nathaniel[8], qv);
5–Hezekiah (1724-85), *m* 1747, Mary Hitchcock;
4–Abiah (1756-1837), *m* 1785, Oliver **Leonard** (4 above).
8–Luke **Hitchcock** (qv);
7–Capt. Luke (1655-1726/27), *m* 1676/77, Sarah (Burt) Dorchester (1656-1746), widow of Benjamin Dorchester;
6–Capt. Ebenezer (1694-1776), *m* 1716/17, Mary Sheldon (see Vol. III, p. 539, for Pynchon-Sheldon lineage);
5–Mary (1723-1802), *m* Hezekiah **Warriner** (5 above).
2–Chloe F. Bull (1833-95), *m* 1858, William P. **Ensey** (*b* 1828).
1–Mem. C.D.A., D.C.G., life mem. I.A.G. Residence: The Newhouse, 1470 Grant Av., Denver, Colo.

1–**FAUNTLEROY, Powell Conrad,** *b* Winchester, Va., Sept. 21, 1869.
8–Col. Moore **Fauntleroy** (qv);
7–William (1656-1686), of "Crondall," Naylor's Hole, Rappahannock Co., Va.; *m* 1678, Katherine Griffin (1664-1728; Col. Samuel[8], *m* Sarah–);
6–Col. William (1684-1757), of "Naylor's Hole," Richmond Co., Va.; *m* 1712, Apphia Bushrod (Col. John[7], of Westmoreland Co., *m* Hannah Keene);
5–Lt. Col. William (1713-93), Va. militia; of "Naylor's Hole"; *m* 2d, 1737, Margaret (Peggy) Murdock (Jeremiah[6], *m* Jane–);
4–Joseph (1754-1815), of "Greenville," Frederick (now Clarke), Co., Va.; ens. in Am. Rev.; *m* 1787, Elizabeth Fouchee Fauntleroy (1772-1824; Capt. Bushrod[5], *m* Elizabeth Fouchee, of Northumberland Co., Va.);
3–Brig. Gen. Thomas Turner (1796-1883), of Warrenton, Va. (see portrait and biography); *m* 1821, Ann Magdalen Magill (1798-1862; Col. Charles[4], of Winchester, Va., Cont. Army, Rev. Army, 1776-83);
2–Archibald Magill (2 below).
6–Stephen **Ley,** from Germany to Va., 1750; *m* Marie Unchild;
5–Marie Clara, *m* Frederick **Conrad**;
4–Dr. Daniel, *m* 1798, Rebecca Holmes (Col. Joseph[5], came from North of Ireland, col. Am. Rev., removed to Winchester, Va., *m* 1767, Rebecca, dau. of Col. David Hunter, of Berkeley Co., Va.; their son David Holmes

Fauntleroy

Fantleroy

ANTE 1480

Arms: Gules, three infants' heads couped argent, crined or.
Crest: Fleur de lis or, between two angel's wings displayed azure.

[1769-1832], was gov. of Miss., 1817-19 and 1825-27);
3–Hon. Robert Young (1805-75), mem. Va. Constl. Conv., 1860, etc.; *m* 1829, Elizabeth Whiting Powell;
2–Sarah Harrison (2 below).

ARCHIBALD MAGILL FAUNTLEROY (b Warrenton Va., July 18, 1836-d Staunton, Va., June 19, 1886); grad. V.M.I., 5th in his class, 1856; med. dept. U. of Va., 1858; U. of Pa., 1859; commd. asst. surgeon U.S.A., June 23, 1860; resigned, May 9, 1861; commd. a.-d.-c. and med. dir. on staff of Gen. Joseph E. Johnston, C.S.A.; med. dir. of Army of N.C., 1862, and organized gen. hospitals at Danville, Va., etc.; later med. dir. of Shenandoah Valley, and organized and directed the gen. hospital at Staunton, Va., until end of the war; practiced at Staunton; organized Med. Board of Examiners of Va.; med. supt. of Insane Asylum at Staunton, 1877-86. Mason (32°).

9–William **Powell,** Gent. (descendant from Powells of Brecknock, Wales), of Jamestown, Va.; from Yorkshire to Va., 1611;
8–Cuthbert, of Lancaster Co., 1650; vestryman, 1664;
7–William, of Powell's Creek, Prince William Co.;
6–William (1711-87), *m* 1735, Eleanor Peyton (Col. Valentine[7], *m* Frances, dau. of Thomas Harrison; William[8], of Iselham, Eng.);
5–Lt. Col. Leven (1737-1810), maj., Loudoun Co. militia, 1775; lt. col., 16th Va. Regt. in Am. Rev.; in Valley Forge Campaign; *m* 1763, Sarah Harrison (1746-1812; Burr[6], of Chappawamic, *m* Anne, dau. of Mathew Barnes);
4–Maj. Burr (1768-1838), Va. militia; of "The Hill," Middleburg, Va.; *m* 1792, Catherine Brooke (Col. Humphrey[5], of Fauquier Co., Va., militia, *m* Anne, dau. of Mathew Whiting; g.g.g.dau. of Robert Brooke [1654-1712], *m* Catherine Booth, who came to Essex Co., Va., ca. 1675, from London, and desc. Humphrey Brooke of London, who was from White Church, Hampshire, Eng.);
3–Elizabeth Whiting (1809-72), *m* 1829, Hon. Robert Young **Conrad** (3 above);

THOMAS TURNER FAUNTLEROY (b in Richmond Co., Va., Oct. 8, 1796-d Leesburg, Va., Sept. 12, 1883); Ensign, Va. militia, War 1812; studied law in Winchester, Va., and admitted to the bar; settled in Warrenton; mem. Va. Legislature from Fauquier Co., 1823; editor of newspaper. Commd. maj., 1st U.S. Dragoons, June 8, 1836, and served in Seminole and Creek wars in Florida; his regt. took the Indians west and settled them in the Indian Ty.; built Fort Fauntleroy, N.M. (renamed in 1862 Fort Wingate); commanded cav. at Monterey, Mex., under Gen. Zac. Taylor and subsequently under Gen. W. Scott in campaign against City of Mexico; received thanks of Va. Legislature and recommended for promotion for service against Indians in 1845; lt. col., 2d U.S. Dragoons, June 30, 1846; col. 1st U.S. Dragoons, July 26, 1850. He was one of the first, and the second ranking officer of the line to resign his commission (May 13, 1861), and tender his services to Va., and for which he received the thanks of the Va. Legislature and was commissioned a brig. gen. provisional army and assigned to command of troops around Richmond; resigned C.S.A., 1862, and bought a farm on the Staunton River, Va., and moved there.

2–Sarah Harrison (1842-1908), *m* 1866, Archibald Magill **Fauntleroy,** M.D. (1836-86), grad. V.M.I., '56; U. of Va.; U. of Pa.; asst. surgeon U.S.A., 1860-61; med. dir. C.S.A., 1861-65; med. supt., Insane Asylum, Staunton, Va.; issue: I–Ann Magill (*b* 1867); II–Robert Young Conrad (*b* 1868; *m* Mary Pugh); III–Powell Conrad (1 above); IV–Elizabeth Whiting (*b* 1871; *m* Kennon Clark); V–Thomas Turner (1873-1912).
1–*m* Apr. 18, 1914, Mary Dalrymple Small, *b* York, Pa., Dec. 25, 1872; dau. of William Latimer Small, of York, *m* Mary Wilson.
1–M.D., U. of Va., 1893 (Kappa Sigma, Pi Mu); Army Med. Sch., 1896, Asst. surgeon U.S. Med.

Corps, Nov. 15, 1895; capt., 1900; maj., 1908; lt. col., 1916; col., 1917. Chief surgeon, 4th Corps Area, 1919-22; retired, 1922. Participated in Indian campaign in Ariz. and N.M., 1896; in Spanish-Am. War (Silver Star Citation), and the Cuban Occupation and Cuban Pacification, 1906-08. In direct and immediate charge of the successful eradication of the yellow fever epidemic in eastern Cuba in 1908 (since when no case has originated there), and for this work received the official commendation in the report of Dr. Carlos Finley, chief of the Cuban sanitary dept. Philippine Insurrection, 1899-1902; maj. and surgeon, U.S. vols. 1900, for service in the field; on Mexican Border, 1910; instr. at Army Med. Sch., Washington, 1911-13. Fellow Coll. Surgeons N. America; mem. Soc. Santiago de Cuba, Soc. of Carabao, V.F.W. Residence: 2123 California St. N.W., Washington, D.C.

1–**FARRELL, Louis,** *b* Nashville, Tenn., Dec. 17, 1878.
3–John **Farrell** (*b* Doagh, Co. Antrim, Ireland, 1809-*d* 1854), grad. U. Edinburgh; to New Orleans, La.; *m* 1838, Jane Barbara Kirkman (1807-93; Thomas[4] [1779-1826], from Ireland, 1805, settled at Phila., Pa., *m* Eleanora Jackson, 1774-1850);
2–Norman (2 below).
8–Simon **Miller** (*d* 1684);
7–Simon (*d* 1721), col. of Richmond Co., Va.; and prob. thru:
6–Eleanor, *m* Robert **Elliston**;
5–Robert (*d* 1809), of Culpeper Co., Va.; removed to Ky., 1789; *m* Elizabeth Triplett?);
4–Joseph Thorp (1779-1856), *m* 1800, Louisa Mullen (*d* 1816);
3–William Robert (1815-70), *m* 1841, Elizabeth Blackman Boddie;
2–Josephine (2 below).
9–William **Boddie** (qv);
8–John (1685-1720), *m* Elizabeth Thomas; both *b* Isle of Wight Co., Va.;
7–William (1710-72), *m* Mary Bennett, of Va.;
6–Nathaniel (1732-97), rep. Edgecombe Co., to Provincial Congress of N.C., Apr. 4, 1776; *m* 1762, Chloe Crudup (1745-81);
5–Elijah (1765-88), *m* 1787, Elizabeth Taylor, of Va.;
4–Elijah (1788-1851), *m* Maria Platte Elliott (1800-46);
3–Elizabeth Blackman (1820-1904), of Sumner Co., Tenn.; *m* William Robert **Elliston** (3 above);
2–Josephine (1847-1921), *m* 1869, Norman **Farrell** (1843-1918), wholesale hardware mcht.; issue: I–William Elliston (*b* 1870; *m* Emily Cottrell); II–Norman (*b* 1874); III–Louis (1 above); IV–Herbert (*b* 1882; *m* Ritchie Cheek); V–Josephine Elliston (*b* 1886); VI–Lizinka (*b* 1889; *m* Donald W. Southgate).
1–*m* Mar. 29, 1910, Mallie Gaines Wilson, *b* Pulaski, Tenn., Dec. 23, 1885; dau. of William Edwin Wilson, of Pulaski; issue: 1–Louis, Jr., *b* Manila, P.I., Jan. 27, 1911; 2–Elizabeth Elliston, *b* Nashville, Tenn., Oct. 19, 1912; 3–Jean, *b* Ft. Logan, Roots, Ark., Jan. 21, 1914; 4–Wilson, *b* Monteagle, Tenn., Aug. 10, 1915; 5–Norman, *b* Atlanta, Ga., July 11, 1917.
1–Vanderbilt U., '99 (Phi Delta Theta). Enlisted as pvt. Co. G, 26th Inf., Mar. 23, 1901; corpl. Co. K, 27th Inf.; 2d lt., 15th Inf., Oct. 9, 1903 and promoted thru the grades to rank of lt. col., 1927. Comdr. 3d Bn., 59th Inf., A.E.F.; participated in counter-offensive at Aisne-Marne; seriously wounded in action. Instr., General Service Schs., Ft. Leavenworth, 1929. Address: C/o Adj. Gen., U.S.A., Washington, D.C.

1–**FELLOWS, Raymond,** *b* Bucksport, Me., Oct. 17, 1885.
9–William **Fellows** (qv);
8–Isaac (1635 or 36-1721), of Ipswich, Mass.; soldier King Philip's War; *m* 1672, Joanna Boardman, or Boreman;
7–Jonathan (1682-1753), Ipswich; *m* 1718, Deborah (Batchelder) Tilton;
6–Abner (1720-86), New Chester (now Bristol), N.H.; mem. Com. of Safety, 1776; *m* 1740, Elizabeth Rowe;
5–Josiah (1757-1852), Am. Rev., 1776-80; drove a 4-oxen freight wagon bet. Boston and Bristol regularly; *m* 1780, Jemima Quimby (1757-1814);
4–Benjamin (1799-1880), Bristol; *m* 1821, Miriam Hoyt (1797-1866; Samuel[5], *m* Judith Blaisdell);
3–Milo (1821-1906), stone cutter, Bristol; worked on Bunker Hill monument; *m* 1850, Susan D. Locke;
2–Oscar F. (2 below).
8–Capt. John **Locke** (1627-96), from Eng.; settled at Portsmouth, N.H., 1640; killed by Indians, Rye, N.H.;
7–Edward (1662?-1739), Portsmouth, N.H.;
6–Thomas (*b* 1713), Rye, N.H.;
5–Levi (1745-1810);
4–Benjamin (1770-1858);
3–Susan D. (1828-99), *m* Milo **Fellows** (3 above).
9–Thomas **Sleeper** (1607-96), from Eng., 1640; granted land at Hampton,
8–Aaron (1661-1732), of Hampton, N.H.; *m* 1682, Elizabeth Shaw;
7–Moses (1685-1754), of Kingston, N.H.; *m* 1714, Margaret Sanborn;
6–David (1721-80), Am. Rev.; of Sandown, N.H.; *m* 1755, Ruth Jenness;
5–John (1760-1818), Am. Rev.; Sandown, N.H.; *m* 1785, Elizabeth Tilton (1765-1814; Sherburn[6], Am. Rev., *m* Huldah Prescott);
4–Rev. Walter (1790-1875), pioneer Meth. preacher; rode circuit among White Mountains of N.H.; *m* 1814, Nancy Plaisted (1790-1862);
3–Margarette (1828-1908), *m* 1855, Lewis W. **Fling** (1824-1917; Abel[4] [1795-1880], *m* Hopestill Harlow; Abel[5], Am. Rev., *m* 1793, Susan Alvord, *b* 1760);
2–Eva M. (*b* 1863), *m* 1883, Oscar F. **Fellows** (1857-1921), of Bucksport, Me.; practised law at Bangor; atty. Hancock Co., 4 yrs.; customs collector, 3 yrs.; speaker Me. Ho. of Rep., 1903; apptd. atty. U.S. Internat. St. John River Commn., 1909-16, by Pres. Roosevelt; issue: I–Raymond (1 above); II–Frank (*b* 1889; *m* Eleanor Maling).
1–*m* Feb. 11, 1909, Madge Gilmore (qv); issue (all *b* Bangor, Me.); 1–Margaret, *b* Nov. 22, 1909; U. of Me., '31; 2–Rosalie, *b* May 10, 1913; 3–Frank, *b* Nov. 26, 1914.
1–B.A., U.Me. (Phi Gamma Delta; Phi Delta Phi), hon. M.A., 1926; attended Law Sch., 1909. Admitted to bar, 1909, and began practice at Bangor; associated with bro. Frank; atty. gen. of Me., 1925-29. Mem. Legal Advisory Bd., Penobscot Co., Me.; trustee Me. State Hosps., 1910-12. Mem. Me. Hist. Soc., Bangor Hist. Soc. Republican. Summer place: Verona Island, Penobscot Bay, Me. Residence: 395 Union St., Bangor, Me.

1–**FELLOWS, Madge Gilmore (Mrs. Raymond),** *b* Dedham, Me., Dec. 15, 1884.
8–John **Gilmore** (1660-1741), from Scotland to Raynham, Mass., 1700; *m* Agnes– (*d* 1752);
7–James (1693-1773), *m* Thankful Tyrrel (1705-89; William, Jr.[8], Abington, Mass., *m* Abigal–);
6–Tyrrel (1744-75), minuteman in Am. Rev.; *d* as result of exposure on march to Lexington; *m* Hannah Cook (1745-1815), of Foxboro, Mass.;
5–Samuel (1765-1845), Am. Rev.; a first settler of Holden, Me.; *m* Reumah Hathorn (1767-1864), of Taunton;
4–David (1788-1868), *m* Sally Coombs (1794-1876), of Poland, Me.;
3–Tyrrel (1815-90), *m* 1844, Mary Wood Pearl (1815-88), of West Boxford, Me. (Peter[4], *m* Rebecca Spofford);
2–Pascal Pearl (2 below).
10–John **Alden,** Mayflower Pilgrim (qv);
9–Ruth (*b* 1634), *m* 1657, John **Bass** (*b* 1632; Samuel[10], qv);
8–Mary (*b* 1669), *m* 2d, 1694, William **Copeland** (Lawrence[9], of Braintree, *m* Lydia Townsend);
7–Benjamin (1708-90), *m* 1734, Sarah Allen (Benjamin[8], of Braintree, *m* Sarah–);
6–William (1748-1840), Norton, Mass.; minuteman, lt., Cont. Army 3 yrs.; *m* 1774, Martha White (1756-1800; Isaac[7], *m* Hannah Hews);
5–William (1778-1849), settled in Brewer, Me.; *m* 1802, Silence Lane (1781-1853; Joseph[6], of Norton, *m* Silence Wetherell);
4–Silence Lane (1804-92), *m* 1825, George **Wiswell** (1800-71; George[5], of Holden, Me., *m* Mary Morey);
3–Lauretta Sophia (1833-1901), *m* 1857, Henry Thomas **Hart** (1833-84; Samuel[4], *m* Sarah Allen);
2–Alma Maria (*b* 1859), *m* Oct. 25, 1881, Hon. Pas-

cal Pearl **Gilmore** (*b* 1845), of Dedham and Bucksport, Me.
1–*m* Feb. 11, 1909, Raymond Fellows (qv for issue).
1–Ed. East Me. Sem., Bucksport; Natl. Park Sem., Washington. Residence: 395 Union St., Bangor, Me.

MAJ. HUGH BRADY FLEMING, U.S.A. (1827-95), one of the heroes in the opening of the West.

1–**FLEMING, Hugh Neely, Jr.,** *b* Erie, Pa., Dec. 14, 1901.
6–Morrow **Lowry,** on whose large estates in Crawford Co., Pa., the slave houses still stand;
5–Robert, of Crawford Co., Pa.; *m* Janet L. Barr (James[6] [1738-1823], Presbyn. deacon);
4–Rebecca C. (1802-74), *m* 1822, Gen. James E. **Fleming** (1797-1880), Clinton Co., Pa.; wounded in War 1812 (Lt. George[5], Am. Rev., *m* Elizabeth White; desc. Sir Thomas Fleming, 2d son of Lord John, Earl of Wigton);
3–Maj. Hugh Brady, U.S.A. (1827-95), U.S.M.A., '52; to whom Kit Carson presented his Bible and sword (see portrait) *m* 1866, Maria Louise Neely;
2–Hugh Neely (2 below).
7–Thomas **Moorhead** (1697-1765), from Ulster Co., Ireland;
6–James (1732-1818); Am. Rev.; *m* 1769, Catherine Byars (1748-1813; John[7]);
5–Col. Thomas (1769-1858), *m* 1791, Jane Miller Young (1771-1862; Capt. Joseph[6] [1725-1823], buried at Greenmont Cemetery, Baltimore, 1st lt., 1777, capt., 1793, *m* 1768, Isabel Miller);
4–Matilda Miller (1797-1880), *m* Joseph **Neely** (1790-1873; Albert[5], *m* Phoebe Pearsall);
3–Marie Louise (1836-94), *m* Maj. Hugh Brady **Fleming** (3 above).
11–Col. John **Chew** (qv);
10–Col. Samuel (1634-77), burgess, councillor, chancellor and sec. Province of Md.; col. provincial forces of Md.; *m* 1658, Ann Ayres (*d* 1695; William[11], of Nansemond Co., Va.);
9–Benjamin (1671-1700), *m* 1692, Elizabeth Benson (John[10] [*b* 1639], from Wales, 1690, settled at "The Cliffs," Md., *m* Elizabeth Kinsey);
8–Elizabeth (1695-1727; aunt of Benjamin Chew [1723-1810], atty. gen. and chief justice of Pa.), *m* 1711, Kensey **Johns** (1689-1727; Richard[9], of "The Cliffs," Calvert Co., Md.; desc. of Sir Thomas Johns);
7–Mary (*b* 1725), *m* 1750, Brian **Philpott,** of Baltimore (Brian[8], Gent. [*b* 1695], from Newburg Co., Berks, Eng., settled in St. Mary's Co., Md.);
6–Mary (*d* 1840), *m* 1783, Thomas **Usher** (1760-1839), during siege of Baltimore by British fleet, Sept. 1814, he opened his graneries to the needy (Thomas[7] [*d* 1786], *m* Catherine–; Thomas[8] [*d* 1714], of Kent Co., Md., Gent., from Eng., *m* Elizabeth–);
5–John-Philpott (1787-1839), adj., 46th Md. Regt., Baltimore Co.; *m* 1815, Elizabeth– (1778-1827);
4–Mary Clara (1821-1903), *m* George Russell **Glasgow;**
3–Agnes Ann (1856-1905), *m* John William **Brown** (1840-95; Rev. John Murray[4], Brown U.);
2–Agnes Augusta (qv), *m* 1896, Hugh Neely **Fleming,** Yale, '89; secret service work during World War; capitalist and philanthropist.
1–Not married. U. of Va., '24; Columbia, 1927. Editor and publisher The Erie Observer. Associated Press war correspondent in Mexico. Mem. Loyal Legion. Residence: 202 W. 8th St., Erie, Pa.

1–**FLEMING, Agnes Augusta Brown (Mrs. Hugh Neely),** *b* San Francisco, Calif., May 5, 1876.
10–Michael **Griswold** (1597-1684), from Eng. to Wethersfield, Conn.; *m* Ann–;
9–Hester (1648-93), *m* 1668, Nathan **Bradley,** of Guilford;
8–Ann (*b* 1669), *m* 1688, Jonathan **Murray** (1667-1747), was mem. Clan Murray family of first rank in Scotland since 12th century, title head of clan is Duke of Athol, Earl of Mansfield buried at Westminster, 1793, member of family;
7–John (1703-89), *m* Sarah Buell;
6–John (1731-1820), *m* Mindwell Crampton (1738-1816; Jonathan[7]);
5–Seymour (1754-1813), Am. Rev.; *m* 1781, Philena Willett (1754-1806; Jonathan[6]);
4–Elizabeth (1784-1863), *m* 1804, Israel **Brown** (1778-1809);
3–John Murray (1807-83), *m* 1830, Sophie Augustine de la Mere (1811-69);
2–John William (2 below).
10–William **Buell** (qv);
9–Samuel (1641-1720), *m* 1662, Deborah Griswold (1646-1719; Edward[10] [1607-91], dep. atty. to Gen. Ct., 1658);
8–Maj. David (1679-1749), *m* 1701, Phoebe Fenner (*b* 1677);
7–Sarah (1710-43), *m* John **Murray** (7 above).
2–John William **Brown** (1840-95), *m* 1873, Agnes Ann Glasgow (1856-1905); see Vol. I, p. 917, for Usher-Glasgow lineage.
1–*m* Jan. 17, 1896, Hugh Neely Fleming (Jan. 2, 1868-1928); see Vol. I, p. 917; issue: 1–Hugh Neely, Jr. (qv).
1–Mem. Pa. Industrial Bd., D.A.R. Residence: 202 W. 8th St., Erie, Pa.

1–**FOOTE, Harriet Mason Hosford (Mrs. Charles Whittlesey),** *b* Hudson, O., Sept. 12, 1857.
9–Joseph **Youngs,** from Eng. to Southold, L.I.; *m* in Eng., 1632, Margaret Warren (*d* ca. 1658);
8–Joseph (1633-post 1706), of Southold; *m* Elizabeth– (*d* 1705);
7–Josiah, of Southold, L.I.; *m* Mary– (*d* 1705/06); *m* 2d, 1732/33 Widow Experience Landor (*d* 1738);
6–Bethniah, of Aquebogue, L.I.; *m* 1721, Noah **Hallock** (1696-1773; Peter[7]; William[8]; Peter[9]);
5–William (1730-1815), of Brookhaven, L.I., and Goshen, Mass.; in Am. Rev. with his sons Jeremiah and Moses; was in battle of Ticonderoga; *m* Alice Homan (ca. 1734-1816);
4–Bethniah (1765-1839), *m* 1785, Stephen Calkins **Hosford** (1763-1855; Joseph[5]);
3–Stephen (1791-1861), mcht. Williamstown, Mass.; mem. Assembly; *m* ca. 1816, Amy Brown;
2–Henry Brown (2 below).
9–John **Brown** (1574-1662), Gent.; from Eng., ante 1634; settled at Plymouth and Rehoboth; *m* Dorothy Kent (*d* 1673), "The name and memory of this colonial dame is perpetuated in Swansea, Mass., by the 'Dorothy Brown Rebekah Degree Lodge 122, I.O.O.F.' ";
8–Ens. John (*b* Eng., ante 1623-*d* 1662), *m* twice;
7–Capt. John (1650-1709), *m* 1672, Anne Mason (*b* 1650; Capt. John[8], of Pequot War);
6–Joseph (1690-1762), *m* 1st, 1719, Elizabeth Darling (Capt. John[7]; Dennis[8]);
5–Caleb (1720-68), *m* 1744, Rebecca Daggitt (*b* 1722; John[6]; Nathaniel[7]; John[8]; John[9]);
4–Caleb (1753-1827), moved from Cumberland, R.I., to Cheshire, Mass.; *m* 1773, Amy Mason (1758-1822; Pelatiah[5]; Pelatiah[6]; Sampson[7], qv);
3–Amy (1793-1866), *m* Stephen **Hosford** (3 above).
8–Sampson **Mason** (qv);

7–Bethia (*b* 1665), *m* 1688, John **Wood** (*b* 1667; Thomas[8]; John[9]);
6–Hopestill (*b* 1698/99), *m* 1721, John **Daggitt** (1698/99-1738; Nathaniel[7]; John[8]; John[9]);
5–Rebecca (*b* 1722), *m* Caleb **Brown** (5 above).
9–John **Potter** (ca. 1607-1642), from Eng., *d* in N.H.; *m* Elizabeth–;
8–John (1641-1706), of New Haven; *m* 1661, Hannah Cooper (1638-75; John[9], propr., N.H.);
7–John (1667-1712), of East Haven; *m* 1691/92, Elizabeth Holt (1674-1718; John[8]; William[9]);
6–Gideon (1700-58), of East Haven; *m* Mary Moulthrop (*b* 1701; Mathew[7]; Mathew[8]; Mathew[9]);
5–Capt. Stephen (1737-1810), served thruout Am. Rev., as ens., 1st and 2d lt., and capt.; *m* 1766, Sarah Lindsley (*b* 1742; Ebenezer[6]; John[7]; John[8]; John[9]);
4–Lucinda (1767-1848), of Branford, Conn.; *m* 1787, Benjamin **Plant** (1763-1812; Benjamin[5]; John[6]; John[7]);
3–Benjamin (1794-1876), *m* 1823, Sarah Mason;
2–Mary Eliza (2 below).
10–Richard **Ingraham,** came to America ca. 1638; *m* 1st, Ruth–; *m* 2d, Joan (Rockwell) Baker;
9–Elizabeth (*d* 1660), *m* 1647, Richard **Bullock** (ca. 1622-1667), of Rehoboth;
8–Mary (1650-1730), *m* Richard **Hail** (*d* 1720, aet. 80), came from Eng.; admitted to Swansea, 1677;
7–John (1678-1718), *m* Hannah Tillinghast (*d* 1731; Rev. Pardon[8] [1622-1717], from Eng.);
6–Lillis (1714-97), *m* 1731, Nathan **Mason** (1705-58; Isaac[7]; Sampson[8], qv);
5–Levi (1752-1844), pvt. in Am. Rev.; *m* Amy Tilson or Gilson (1751-1844);
4–Arnold (1774-1861), civil engr., worked on Harlem River High Bridge and Erie Canal; *m* 1795, Mercy Coman or Cooman (1776-1850);
3–Sarah (1798-1879), *m* Benjamin **Plant** (3 above).
9–Roger **Williams** (qv);
8–Mercy (1640-ca. 1705), *m* 1677, Samuel **Winsor** (1640?-1705; Rev. Joshua[9], *d* 1679);
7–Rev. Samuel (1677-1758), *m* 1703, Mercy Harding (1683-1771; Abraham[8]; Stephen[9]);
6–Mercy (1718-58), *m* 1740, Nedadiah **Angell** (1712-86; Daniel[7]; John[8]; Thomas[9], qv);
5–Hannah (*b* 1750), *m* Daniel **Coman** (1752-1839), pvt. Am. Rev., Capt. Daniel Brown's co. Mass. Militia (Richard[6]; Richard[7]);
4–Mercy (1776-1850), of Cheshire; *m* Arnold **Mason** (4 above);
3–Sarah, *m* Benjamin **Plant** (3 above);
2–Mary Eliza (1824-1907), *m* 1850, Henry Brown **Hosford** (1817-89), served in Sanitary Commn., Civil War; Congrl. minister; prof. Western Reserve Coll., 1853-58; issue: I–Sarah Amy (*b* 1851; *m* Rev. John Peter Jones [1847-1916], missionary in India, A.B.C.F.M.); II–Frances Juliette (*b* 1853; prof. Oberlin Coll.); III–Mary Eliza (*b* 1855; teacher); IV–Harriet Mason (1 above); V–Henry Hallock (*b* 1859; *m* Jennie Chamberlain); VI–Helen Plant (*b* 1863; *m* Dr. William Howard Aldrich, 1857-1929); VII–Daniel Mason (*b* 1866; *m* Erlena Johnson Beekman, *b* 1869).
1–*m* July 30, 1879, Charles Whittlesey Foote (Jan. 21, 1853-Aug. 4, 1922); son of Horace Foote (*d* 1887), of Tallmadge, O.; issue: 1–Frances Rosana, *b* Akron, O., May 26, 1880; 2–Charles Raymond, *b* Akron, Aug. 8, 1883; Pomona Coll., 1907; *m* 1909, Mabel Wright Brandes; 3–Robert Hosford (July 29, 1886-Feb. 27, 1888); 4–Harriet Ruth, *b* Cleveland, O., Jan. 10, 1889; Occidental Coll., 1910; *m* Christopher Gaskell, of San Diego, San Francisco, and Los Angeles (issue: Robert Christopher, *b* 1918; Harold Hosford, *b* 1921); 5–Helen Marjorie, *b* Claremont, Calif., Apr. 2, 1894; *m* Dec. 25, 1919, Elihu E. Suits, of Santa Monica, Calif. (issue: Charles Elihu).
1–Mem. D.A.R., Highland Park Ebell Club. Conglist. Residence: 4842 Malta St., Los Angeles, Calif.

1–**Du BOIS, Carrie Miner (Mrs. Frank C.),** *b* Tabor, Ia., Jan. 18, 1869.
9–Capt. Luke **Hitchcock** (qv);
8–John (1642-1712), dea., Springfield, Mass.; lt. Colonial Army; wounded at Turners Falls, Mass., 1676; mem. com. for settlement of Brookfield, Mass., 1686; with five others sent to relief of Brookfield and to fortify it; freeman, 1682; *m* 1666, Hannah Chapin;
7–Nathaniel (1677-1777), weaver, Springfield; a first settler of Brimsfield; *m* 1713, Abigail Lombard;
6–John;
5–John (1746/47-1822), *m* Lucy Colton;
4–John Colton (*b* 1791), *m* Irena Clark (1793-1876);
3–Lucy Colton (1812-67), *m* 1831, Madison **Miner** (1809-74), of Chester, O.;
2–Daniel I. (2 below).
4–Noah **Cooley** (*d* 1816), native of Longmeadow, Mass.; *m* Lydia Weatherell;
3–Warren (1810-90), *m* 1835, Ammerillus Seger (1816-89);
2–Lydia Jane (1836-1906), *m* 1859, Daniel Irenaeus **Miner** (1833-1909); issue: I–Gertrude Viola (1860-65); II–Sarah Luella (*b* 1861; B.A., Oberlin, '84, M.A., 1897, hon. Litt.D., 1914; missionary of A.B.C.F.M. in China since 1887; see Who's Who in America); III–Clifford Irenaeus (1864-65); IV–Mary (1867-70); V–Carrie (1 above); VI–Stella May (Mrs. Horatio C. Flagg, qv for Miner lineage); VII–Edith Maud (1881-1904).
1–*m* Jan. 1, 1895, Frank Cornelius Du Bois, *b* Star Prairie, Wis., Mar. 21, 1869; son of John C. Du Bois; issue: 1–Max Miner, *b* Hayward, Wis., July 1, 1896; B.S., Wash. State Coll., '22; *m* Feb. 15, 1928, Margaret Fayle; 2–Maud (Apr. 20, 1899-Apr. 21, 1899); 3–Paul Francis, *b* Tacoma, Wash., Jan. 3, 1900; *m* Oct. 5, 1920, Helen, dau. of John Castlio (issue: John Harold; Max Raymond; Ruth); 4–Harold Neil, *b* Tacoma, Sept. 4, 1901; *m* Sept. 2, 1922, Esther Josephine, dau. of James Fordham, of Seattle, Wash. (issue: Virginia Caroline).
1–Presbyterian. Republican. Residence: 1006 S. Madison St., Tacoma, Wash.

MINER

Arms: *Gules, a fesse argent, between three plates.*
Crest: *A mailed hand holding a battle-axe.*
Motto: *Spers et fidelis.*

1–**FLAGG, Stella May Miner (Mrs. Horatio C.),** *b* Bavaria, Kan., Jan. 19, 1875.
10–Thomas (Minor) **Miner** (qv);
9–John (1634-1719), town clk., Stratford; a first settler at Woodbury; interpreter to Indians; capt. militia; justice of the quorum; *m* 1658, Elizabeth Booth (*d* 1732);
8–John (1659-1731), Stratford; *m* Sarah Rose;
7–John (1697 or 98-1761), *m* Elizabeth–;
6–John (*b* 1737), *m* 1758, Sarah Dutton;
5–Justice (1762-1850), Woodbury, Conn.; *m* 1st, 1779, Mabel Plumb;

4–Philo (1780-1832), to Chester, O., 1802; *m* 1802, Sally Jackson;
3–Madison (1809-74), *m* 1831, Lucy Colton Hitchcock;
2–Daniel Irenaeus (1833-1909), of Chester, O.; missionary and educator; capt. of vols. in Civil War; *m* 1859, Lydia Jane Cooley (1836-1906); for issue see Mrs. Frank C. Du Bois.
1–*m* June 24, 1895, Horatio Cozens Flagg, *b* Mt. Clemens, Mich., June 14, 1873; son of Benjamin Franklin Flagg; issue: 1–Donald Horatio, *b* Hayward, Wis., Feb. 25, 1897; U. of Wash.; *m* July 9, 1926, Aline, dau. of Frank Weaver, of Shelton, Wash.; 2–Lawrence Miner, *b* Hayward, Oct. 5, 1899; B.S., Ore. Agrl. Coll., '24; *m* Sept. 10, 1923, Mildred, dau. of Willard D. Simmons, of Woodburn, Ore.
1–Accountant, Olympia Bldg. & Loan Assn. Mem. A.L. Auxiliary. Democrat. Mem.: Business and Professional Women's Club, Delphian Soc., Eastern Star. Residence: 327 Sherman St., Olympia, Wash.

1–**GAERTNER, Nelle Hornbeck (Mrs. Herman J.),** *b* Potomac, Ill., Sept. 18, 1875.
8–Warnaar (Hoornbeeck) **Hornbeck** (*b* 1645), from Holland ante 1660; at New Amsterdam 1660; mentioned at Esopus and Wiltwyck (now Kingston, N.Y.); was in rendezvous at Marbleton with Hurley soldiers, 1670; *m* 1670, Anna de Hooges (*d* 1688; Anthony[9], from the Texel in the "Cornick David," 1641, to New Amsterdam);
7–Johannes (bap. 1685), of Kingston; in expdn. to Can., 1711; in foot militia, Ulster Co., 1715; sgt., 1738; lt. col., mustered out 1758; *m* 1716, Urseltjen Westbroek (bap. 1697; Dirk[8], *m* Catharina Oosterhout);
6–Jonathan (bap. 1730), *b* Rochester, N.Y.; resided in South Branch; *m* 1751, Sara Vernooy (bap. 1732);
5–Benjamin (1754-1827), began to write name Hornbeck; served in Hampshire Co., Va., rangers, 1775; sgt. militia, 1781; justice, Randolph Co., 1806; sheriff, 1815; *m* 2d, 1782, Lydia Currence (1763-1840; William[6], Scotch-Irish immigrant, built Currence Ft., Harrison Co., Va., 1774, killed by Indians 1791);
4–Joseph (1791-1865), farmer, Vermilion Co., Ill.; *m* 1819, Nancy (Light?), (1797-1865);
3–Solomon (1820-99), farmer, merchant, Paxton, Ill.; *m* 1st, 1841, Catherine Currence (*d* 1852);
2–Lorenzo Dow (2 below).
7–Israel **Friend** (*d* 1753), from Prince George's Co., Md., 1733, settled in Frederick Co., Va., nr. Harpers Ferry; *m* Sarah–;
6–Jonas, sgt. in French and Indian War; constable, Rockingham Co., Va., 1767; justice, Randolph Co., 1777-81; built Friends Fort on Leading Creek, 1774; *m* Sarah–;
5–Nancy (1759-1851), *m* John **Currence** (1757-1849);
4–William B. (*b* 1796), *m* 1816, Elinder Daniels;
3–Catherine (*d* 1852), *m* 1841, Solomon **Hornbeck** (3 above).
7–Capt. Samuel **Stalnaker** (*d* 1775), of Holston, Va., 1746; trader, explorer and discoverer of Cumberland Gap; capt. in French and Indian War; mediator between Indians and early Va. govt.; built a stockade fort at Draper's Meadow;
6–Jacob, *b* in the Holston settlement, and migrated to Randolph Co., Tygarts Valley, 1772;
5–Katherine (1776-1857), *m* 1795, William **Daniels** (1772-1858), Scotch-Irish immigrant; rep. Randolph Co., Va., in Gen. Assembly, 1824,27,28;
4–Elinder (*b* 1799), *m* William B. **Currence** (4 above);
3–Catherine, *m* Solomon **Hornbeck** (3 above);
2–Lorenzo Dow (1845-1911), in the saddlery and harness business at Potomac and Paxton, Ill.; *m* 1874, Quiteria Wood (1851-1929; Joel[3], *m* Mary Ann, dau. of Robert Courtney of Monongalia Co., Va.; John[4]); issue: I–Nelle (1 above); II–Mary Ann.
1–*m* Aug. 16, 1894, Herman Julius Gaertner, *b* Clawsthal, Germany, July 11, 1866; son of Christian Gaertner, of Goettingen, Germany; issue: 1–Harold Hornbeck, *b* Wilmington, O., Jan. 14, 1896; North Ga. Agrl. Coll.; *m* Dec. 1927, Edna, dau. of Rolfe Bloodworth, of Covington, Ga.; 2–Wendell Wood (June 2, 1897-Oct. 7, 1897); 3–Marion Adolph, *b* Newnan, Ga., Nov. 3, 1899; A.B., Oglethorpe U.; M.S., Emory U.; *m* June 28, 1924, Irene, dau. of Rolfe Bloodworth (issue: Jane Bloodworth); 4–Herman Julius, Jr., *b* Birmingham, Ala., Apr. 13, 1903; Oglethorpe U.; U.Ga.; 5–Paul Courtney, *b* Clarkston, Ga., Mar. 4, 1905; A.B., Oglethorpe, 1925; *m* Feb. 2, 1928, Elizabeth, dau. Charles Alden Rowland, of Athens, Ga. (issue: Paul Courtney, Jr.); 6–**Nellie Jane**, *b* Decatur, Ga., Apr. 26, 1915.
1–Wilmington Coll., 1894-95; Oglethorpe U., 1921-22, A.B., 1925; U.Ga., 1922-23, 1923-25. Mem. Woman's Bd., Oglethorpe U. Mem. D.A.C., D.A.R., Chi Omega. Presbyterian. Democrat. Residence: 162 Peachtree Circle, Atlanta, Ga.

MARY (VAN CLEVE) McCLEAN-SWAYNIE (1787-1883), first white child to arrive at Dayton, Ohio.

1–**GILKES, Luella Shoemaker (Mrs. William H.),** *b* Chicago, Ill., Nov. 1, 1881.
8–John **Van Cleve,** from Holland to New Amsterdam ca. 1650;
7–Isabrant, came from Duchy of Cleves on the river Rhine, in Germany, and settled on Staten Island; *m* Jane Vanderbilt;
6–Benjamin, settled in Monmouth (now Freehold), N.J., 1734; *m* Sept. 9, 1734, at Middletown, N.J., Rachel Covenhoven;
5–John (*b* Freehold, N.J., 1749– killed by Indians, June 1, 1791, within the present corporate limits of Cincinnati), blacksmith; settled at Maidenhead, N.J., Nov. 1785; served as pvt. and guide to Morgan's Riflemen, 1773; also served in militia as guide when N.J. was the battlefield; pvt. and capt. in N.J. state troops and militia; removed overland from Freehold to nr. Washington, Monmouth Co., where he remained, 1786-89; thence to Cincinnati, Dec. 1789; *m* 1773, Catherine Benham (*b* 1756-*d* Aug. 8, 1837, Dayton, O.); she was the first female resident of Dayton, O., where she went Apr. 1, 1796; she *m* 2d, Samuel Thompson who was drowned in Mad River, nr. Cincinnati (John Benham[6], *m* Catharine Van Dyke, a stepdau. of ——Van Cleve, of Pleasant Valley, Monmouth Co., N.J.);
4–Mary (*b* Feb. 10, 1787-*d* Mar. 3, 1883); removed to Dayton at age 9 with parents (see portrait); *m* Dayton, O., 1804, John **McClean** (or McClain); she *m* 2d, 1826, Robert Swaynie;
3–Sarah Jane (*b* Dayton, O.), *m* Oct. 7, 1832, John **Swaynie** (*b* Dayton);
2–Luella (*b* Dayton, O., Nov. 12, 1854), *m* 1877, Rev. Clarence **Shoemaker,** of Lake Geneva, Wis.
1–*m* June 2, 1908, William H. Gilkes, *b* Nov. 15, 1870; asst. cashier Continental Illinois Bank & Trust Co., Chicago; issue: 1–Clarence, *b* Chicago, Mar. 5, 1909; Purdue U., '32; 2–Howard and 3–Robert (twins), *b* Chicago, Apr. 21, 1916.
1–Mem. D.A.R. Residence: 88 7th Av., LaGrange, Ill.

1–**GLOS, Frances Henrietta Wilcox (Mrs. Charles H.)**, *b* Spencerport, N.Y., Sept. 16, 1868.
10–William (Wilcockson) **Wilcox** (qv);
9–Samuel (1640-1713), rep. from Simsbury to Gen. Assembly, 1694-1712; *m* Hannah–;
8–William (1669-1733), *m* 1699, Elizabeth Wilson (*d* 1746; Samuel[9]);
7–Amos (1706-75), *m* 1728, Joanah Hillyer;
6–Amos (*b* 1730), capt. of a co. from Simsbury at Lexington Alarm, 1775; maj., 3d Bn., Conn. State Regt.; promoted lt. col., 1779; *m* 1749, Hannah Hoskins;
5–Joel (*b* 1765), Sandisfield, Mass.; *m* 1781, Lydia–;
4–William John (1782-1842), grad. Williams Coll., 1806; Congl. minister at Otisco, N.Y., 1808-26; removed to Napoli, N.Y., 1826, where he *d*; *m* 1808, Luranah Green;
3–Austin Green (1812-91), Lockport, N.Y.; minister and preacher; *m* 1836, Eliza Spalding (1809-76);
2–Cassius Marcellus (2 below).
9–Nicholas **Byram** (1610-88), from Eng. to N.E., ca. 1633, settled at Weymouth, Mass., at Bridgewater, 1666; *m* ca. 1635, Susanna Shaw (*d* 1698; Abraham[10], of Dedham);
8–Capt. Nicholas (1640-1727), King Philip's War, 1675-76; *m* 1676, Mary Edson (*d* 1727; Samuel[9], *m* Susanna Orcutt);
7–Josiah (1698-1760 or 61), *m* 1720, Hannah Rickard (1693-1771; Samuel[8], *m* Rebekah Snow);
6–Mehetabel (*b* 1730), *m* 1750, Daniel **Beal** (1729-ca. 1761-64), to Mendon, Mass., bet. 1758-60 (Samuel[7], *m* Mary Bassett);
5–Mehetabel (1758-1823), *m* 1777, Joseph **Green** (1754-1835), soldier Am. Rev.; after the war removed to Windsor and E. Windsor, and later to Williamstown, Mass., to Sodus, N.Y., 1810;
4–Luranah (1783-1845), *m* William John **Wilcox** (4 above).
9–Jonas **Weed** (*d* 1676), from Eng., 1630, settled at Watertown, Mass.; freeman, 1631; moved to Wethersfield, Conn., 1635, to Stamford, 1642; *m* Mary– (*d* 1690);
8–Jonas (*d* 1706), *m* 1670, Bethia Holly (*d* 1713; John[9], first settler of Stamford);
7–Jonathan (*b* 1684), *m* ca. 1714/15, Mary–;
6–Josiah (*b* 1716), *m* 2d, 1742, Abigail Bouton;
5–James (*b* 1745), sgt., later lt., 9th Co., 9th Regt., Conn. Militia, 1776-79;
4–James (1771-1833), Pulaski, N.Y.; built first court house of Oswego Co.; *m* 1793, Eunice Stevens (1776-1858; Ezra[5], of Stamford and Danbury, soldier 5th Cont. Regt.);
3–Ebenezer (1816-81), of Pulaski, N.Y., Racine, Wis., and St. Charles, Ill.; *m* 1840, Frances Sophia Young (1820-84; Ebenezer[4], *m* 2d, Diana Southwick);
2–Elizabeth (*b* Racine, Wis., 1843-*d* Corvallis, Ore., 1913), resided at St. Charles, Ill., Rochester and Spencerport, N.Y., Portland and Corvallis, Ore.; *m* 1866, Cassius Marcellus **Wilcox** (*b* Napoli, N.Y., 1844-*d* Salamanca, N.Y., 1925), dentist; issue: I–George Henry (*b* 1867; *m* Sarah Dorr; *m* 2d, Mary–); II–Frances Henrietta (1 above); III–Harriet (1870-71).
1–*m* July 31, 1895, Charles Henry Glos, *b* Oak Park, Ill., Jan. 5, 1873; Northwestern, 1894; atty.; son of Henry A. Glos, of Oak Park and St. Charles, Ill.; issue: 1–Karl Frederick, *b* St. Charles, Ill., Sept. 27, 1896; U.Ore., law dept., 1922; 2d lt. in France during World War; now capt.; adj. of 162d Inf., Ore. N.G.; atty.; *m* Aug. 10, 1920, Charlotte, dau. of Marshall MacDonald, of Oakland, Calif. (issue: Marshall Charles, *b* Apr. 1, 1922; Karl Frederick, II, *b* Feb. 22, 1924).
1–Studied music, Chicago Musical Coll., 1887. Conglist. Republican. Residence: 303 E. 47th St., Portland, Ore.

1–**GLOVER, Lena Verharen (Mrs. Harry E.)**, *b* Vinton, Ia., May 22, 1874.
9–Dr. Samuel **Fuller** (qv);
8–Rev. Samuel (1624-95), *m* 1654, Elizabeth Brewster (*d* 1713; desc. Elder William Brewster, qv);
7–Dr. Isaac (1675-1727), *m* 1709, Mary Platt (or Pratt);
6–Isaac (*b* 1712), Bridgewater, Mass.; *m* 1737, Sarah Packard (*b* 1719);
5–Lt. Isaac (1738-1803), officer Am. Rev.; *m* 1764, Mary Alden;
4–Eunice (1778-1858), Bridgewater; *m* 1805, Simeon **Drake** (1780-1863);
3–Charles Hewitt (1814-50), *m* 1837, Roxanna Bruce (1818-55);
2–Charlotte (2 below).
9–John **Alden,** Mayflower Pilgrim (qv);
8–Joseph (1624-97), farmer, Bridgewater, *m* 1659, Mary Simmons (Moses, Jr.[9]);
7–Dea. Joseph (1667-1747), *m* 1690, Hannah Dunham (1669-1747/48; Daniel[8], of Plymouth);
6–Daniel (1691/92-1767), *m* 1717, Abigail Shaw (1694-1755; Joseph[7]);
5–Mary (1743-1818), *m* 1764, Isaac **Fuller** (5 above).
2–Charlotte Drake (1845-1929), *m* 1871, Franklin **Verharen** (1843-1904), mcht.; issue: I–Lena (1 above); II–Lulu (*b* 1877; *m* 1906, —Lavell); III–Arthur Ward (*b* 1879; *m* Marguerite Ahern).
1–*m* Nov. 5, 1903, Harry Erastus Glover, *b* Manchester, Ia., Dec. 27, 1872; son of Henry Glover, of Manchester; issue: 1–Charlotte, *b* Spencer, Ia., May 3, 1914.
1–Ed. Sherwood Conservatory. Mem. S.M.D., D.A.C., D.A.R., Clef Club. Residence: Spencer, Ia.

BENJAMIN YOE (d 1812), after a portrait by Peale.

1–**GILL, Jane Henderson (Mrs. Robert Lee).**
4–John **Henderson,** of Clamperlane, Co. Donegal, Ireland; *m* Isabella Stuart;
3–Robert or James, came to Elkton, Md., 1794; his estate was called "Henderson Point"; *m* Jane M'Kierlie;
2–Gustavus Robert (2 below).
5–Alexander **Ross** (*b* 1741), a Highlander; *m* 1767, Jane McGaw (*b* 1741; John[6]);
4–Isabella (*b* 1768), *m* Alexander **M'Kierlie**;
3–Jane, *m* Robert or James **Henderson** (3 above).
7–William **Brinckle** (*b* ca. 1685), was in Kent Co., now Del., 1698; justice of the peace 4 terms; *m* 1706, Elizabeth Curtis;
6–Sarah (*b* 1715), *m* 1735, Spencer **Cole,** M.D. (*d* 1756);
5–Penelope (*b* ca. 1736), *m* Reynear **Williams** (*d* 1793);
4–John (*b* 1765), *m* 1787, Sarah– (*b* 1767);
3–John (*b* 1807), *m* Ann Eliza T. Collins;
2–Sarah Rebecca (2 below).
6–Stephen **Yoe,** *m* Rachel–;
5–Benjamin (*d* 1812), *m* Araminta Collins (Edward[6], *m* Ann Williams);
4–Rebecca (1796-1845), *m* 1813, Henderson **Col-**

ARAMINTA (COLLINS) YOE (after a portrait by Peale).

lins (1788-1872), pvt. vol. co. of light inf. comd. by Capt. Dr. John Adams, 7th Regt., Del. Militia, War 1812 (Thomas[5], pvt. Capt. Rhodes' 7th Co., Col. David Hall's Regt. of Foot, Del.);
3–Ann Eliza T. (*b* 1814), *m* John **Williams** (3 above);
2–Sarah Rebecca, *m* Gustavus Robert **Henderson** (1811-82), see portrait.

GUSTAVUS ROBERT HENDERSON (Jan. 19, 1811-May 8, 1882).

1–*m* Apr. 14, 1898, Robert Lee Gill (Dec. 20, 1870-Jan. 23, 1918), lawyer; son of Nicholas Rufus Gill; issue: 1–Robert Lee, Jr. (qv for Gill lineage).
1–Mem. I.A.G., Md. Hist. Soc. Clubs: Gibson Island, Baltimore Country. Residence: 11 Club Rd., Roland Park, Baltimore, Md.

GILL

Arms: Sable, a pale between four fleur de lis or, a canton argent.
Crest: The head of an eastern king couped at the shoulders in profile proper, crowned and collared, a chain passing from the rim of the crown behind to the collar, all or.

1–**GILL, Robert Lee, Jr.,** *b* Roland Park, Baltimore, Md., Jan. 28, 1907.
8–Stephen **Gill,** from Eng., 1695-1700, settled in the "Forest," Baltimore Co., Md.; one of the organizers of St. Thomas' or "Garrison Forest" Episcopal Ch.; mem. 1st vestry, 1747; *m* 1708, Elizabeth Hubbard;
7–John (1709-97), elder; *m* 1730, Mary Rogers (1712-97; Nicholas[8]), sister of Col. Nicholas Rogers, aide to Baron de Kalb in Am. Rev.;
6–Nicholas (1750-93), *m* Elizabeth Gill (*b* 1762);
5–Stephen (1781-1846), capt. Md. vols. in War 1812; *m* 1800, Phoebe Osburn (1774-1864; Joseph[6], of Baltimore Co.);
4–George Washington (1808-76), *m* 1828, Rebecca Ensor (1809-42; John[5]);
3–Nicholas Rufus (1838-1905), lawyer; *m* 1861, Eleanor Agnes Dowson Gill (1842-1903; Edward[4] [1788-1867], *m* 1835, Julia Ann Johnson; Edward[5] [1744-1818], *m* Mary McClain; John[6], the Elder, 7 above);
2–Robert Lee (1870-1918), lawyer (see portrait); *m* 1898, Jane Henderson (qv).
1–Not married. Princeton, '31. Mem. S.R., Md. Hist. Soc. Episcopalian. Clubs: Gibson Island, Baltimore Country. Residence: 11 Club Rd., Roland Park, Baltimore, Md.

ROBERT LEE GILL (b Baltimore, Md., Dec. 20, 1870-d Jan. 23, 1918), LL.B., U. of Md., 1893; lawyer.

1-**GORDON, Alice Gordon Hart (Mrs. Donald C.),** *b* Porte Colborne, Ont., Can., Mar. 5, 1876.
9-Nicholas **Hart,** of Taunton, 1643; of Boston, 1654; *m* Joan Rossiter (1615-85; Edward[10], qv);
8-Richard (*d* 1696), *m* Hannah Keen (*d* 1696; Richard[9], *d* on bd. the "Elizabeth," coming from Barbados);
7-Richard (1667-1745), *m* 1708, Amy Gibbs;
6-Stephen (1712-98), *m* 1736, Sarah Tabor;
5-Noah (1754-1830), *m* Cynthia Gray (*died* 1840; Phillip[6], in Am. Rev.);
4-Noah (1802-82), *m* 1823, Betsy Lyon (1801-88);
3-Welcome Washington (1824-90), Detroit, Mich.; *m* 1846, Margaret Hierlihy Burnham;
2-Capt. Frederick Closson (2 below).
9-Francis **Cooke** (qv);
8-Mary (1626-1714), *m* 1645, John **Thompson** (qv);
7-Mary (1650-1723), *m* 1672, as his 2d wife, Thomas **Tabor** (1636-1720; Philip[8], qv);
6-Sarah (*d* 1792), *m* 1736, Stephen **Hart** (6 above).
9-Thomas **Burnham** (qv);
8-William, of Hartford; received land grants from his father, 1684; *m* Elizabeth- (*d* 1717);
7-Rev. William (1684-1750), grad. Harvard, 1702; *m* 1704, Hannah Wolcott (1684-1748);
6-Josiah (1710-1800), *m* 1740, Ruth Norton (1724-62; John[7]);
5-Capt. Amos (1756-1815), Burlington, Vt.; *m* 1780, Susannah Hierlihy (1758-1800; Col. Timothy[6], *m* Elizabeth Wetmore);
4-Charles (1796-1855), Detroit, Mich.; *m* 1815, Thirza Closson (*b* 1800);
3-Margaret Hierlihy (1829-1907), *m* Welcome Washington **Hart** (3 above);
2-Capt. Frederick Closson (1848-1916), of Detroit; supt. transportation co.; *m* 1874, Adaline Gordon (1852-1919; John[3], *m* Sara Davis); issue: I-Alice Gordon (1 above); II-John Howard (*b* 1877; *m* Elfie Barnett); III-Frederick Closson (*b* 1883; *m* Gertrude Buell).
1-*m* Dec. 24, 1900, Donald Cassius Gordon, *b* Redford, Mich., May 12, 1867; son of Capt. George C. Gordon; issue (all *b* Detroit, Mich.): 1-Donald Hart, *b* Oct. 28, 1901; LL.B., Detroit Coll.; 2-Alice Virginia, *b* Dec. 5, 1904; A.B., Detroit Coll.; *m* Apr. 5, 1926, Percy H., son of Robert C. Hamly (issue: Robert Bruce; Alice Virginia; Katharine Patricia); 3-Wallace Emerson, *b* Sept. 25, 1907; A.B., Detroit Coll.; M.A., U.Mich.; *m* Sept. 10, 1930, Marion Patricia Searle, A.B., U.Mich., dau. of Clinton E. Searle.
1-A.B., City Coll., Detroit. Member S.M.D., D.A.R., I.A.G. Residence: 211 Westminster Av., Detroit, Mich.

1-**GIPSON, Emily Doolittle Benedict (Mrs. Eugene H.),** *b* Warsaw, N.Y., Sept. 22, 1878.
9-Thomas **Benedict** (qv);
8-John (*d* 1727), of Norwalk, Conn.; deacon, freeman, selectman and rep. Gen. Assembly 1722-25; *m* 1670, Phoebe Gregory;
7-Thomas (1682-1763), selectman 7 times; moderator of annual town meetings 11 times; rep. Gen. Assembly, 1737,40,44; worker in Congl. Ch.; *m* 1705, Millison Hyatt;
6-Thomas (1720-60), grand juror; surveyor; *m* 1740, Abigail Scrivener (*d* 1762);
5-Stephen (1743-1828), Attica, N.Y.; lt. 7 yrs. in Am. Rev.; *m* 3d, Lydia Betts (1756-1835);
4-Thomas (1789-1832), Norwalk, Conn.; in War 1812; farmer; *m* 1815, Sarah Brewster;
3-George Betts (1823-61), Avon, N.Y.; studied at Oberlin 1 yr.; lawyer; *m* 1849, Helen Lucelia Doolittle;
2-Charles Henry (2 below).
11-William **Brewster** (qv);
10-Jonathan (1593-1659), settled at New London, Conn.; *m* 1624, Lucretia Oldham (*d* 1679);
9-Benjamin (1633-1710), *m* 1653, Ann (Addis) Dart (*d* 1709);
8-Jonathan (1664-1704), *m* Judith Stevens;
7-Joseph (1698-1770), *m* Dorothy Witter;
6-Joseph (1726-75), ensign 5th co. militia, 1764, Norwich, Conn.;
5-Joseph (1759-1850), pvt. Am. Rev.; *m* Sarah Geer;
4-Sarah (1793-1872), *m* 1815, Thomas **Benedict** (4 above).
9-Abraham **Doolittle** (qv);
8-Abraham (1649-1732), of Wallingford; *m* 1680, Mercy Holt (1649-88);
7-Abraham (1684-1730), *m* 1710, Mary Lewis (*d* 1730);
6-Ambrose (1719-93), Am. Rev.; *m* 1749, Martha Munson (*b* 1729);
5-Reuben (1766-1847), *m* 1788, Thankful Bunnell (1761-1827); their son Reuben was father of U.S. Senator James Rood Doolittle, LL.D. of Wis.;
4-Chauncey (1801-71), a founder of Wethersfield Springs, N.Y.; built church and academy; *m* 1824, Emily Wilbor (1804-91; William[5], *m* Sarah-);

CHARLES HENRY BENEDICT (1851-95).

3-Helen Lucelia (1828-1903), *m* George Betts **Benedict** (3 above).
9-Richard **Adams,** *m* 1679, Rebecca Davis;
8-John (1686-1734), *m* 1710, Esther Cady;
7-John (1713-82), physician;
6-John (1739-93), E. Bloomfield, N.Y.; 2d lt. in Am. Rev., 1776-81; rep. from Alford, 1781-82; deacon; *m* Chloe- (1739-1803);
5-Joseph (1775-1839), *m* Eunice Throop (1783-1852; Benjamin[6], *m* Rachel Brown);
4-Benjamin (1808-82), *m* Janet Gibson (1810-99);
3-Oliver Benjamin (1833-95), Warsaw, N.Y.; surgeon in Civil War; *m* 1854, Harriet Newell Dwelle;
2-Allie (2 below).
9-Richard (Dwelley) **Dwelle** (ca. 1630-1692), from Eng., at Lancaster, later at Hingham, Mass., ca. 1660; settled at Scituate, ca. 1665; in King Philip's War; *m* 2d, Elizabeth Simmons (*d* 1708);
8-John (ca. 1660-1718), *m* 1692, Rachel Buck (*d* 1739);
7-Jedediah (1698-1738), *m* 1725, Elizabeth House;
6-Abner (1733-1803), Am. Rev.; *m* 1st, 1755, Elizabeth Brown;
5-Capt. Abner (1758-1826), began to write name Dwelle; Am. Rev.; *m* 1786, Miriam Martin (1770-1825);
4-Horatio Nelson (1807-77), *m* 1st, 1827, Eliza Ann Hurd (1811-41);
3-Harriet Newell (1837-1924), *m* Oliver Benjamin **Adams** (3 above).
2-Charles Henry **Benedict** (1851-95), lawyer, St. Paul, Minn.; U.S. consul in South Africa, 1893-95 (see portrait); *m* 1876, Allie Adams (1856-81), of Warsaw, N.Y.; *m* 2d, 1887, Belle Crouch (*b* 1865); issue (1st marriage): I-Emily Doolittle (1 above); II-Charles Adams (1881-1900).
1-*m* June 4, 1902, Eugene Henry Gipson (Aug. 9, 1877-Dec. 11, 1929); son of Henry Spencer Gipson; issue (all *b* Faribault, Minn.): 1-Gertrude Alice (May 24, 1904-Aug. 24, 1904); 2-Helen Emily, *b* Nov. 10, 1906; B.A., Oberlin, '29; 3-Eugenia Harriet, *b* July 2, 1911.
1-Ed. U. of Minn., 1902. Mem. D.A.R., I.A.G., Rice Co. Hist. Soc. Episcopalian. Democrat. Clubs: Monday, Country, Nature. Residence: 503 S. 3d St., Faribault, Minn.

1-**GOSS, Georgene Christy Brooke (Mrs. Alpha L.),** *b* Webster Groves, Mo., Nov. 23, 1896.

10–Gov. Thomas **Welles** (qv);
9–Hon. Samuel (1630-75), Wethersfield, Conn.; freeman, 1657; dep. Gen. Ct.; ens. of Train Band, lt., 1665; capt., 1670; commr., 1665-75; *m* 1st, ca. 1660, Elizabeth Hollister (John[10], qv);
8–Capt. Thomas (1662-Dec. 1711), *m* 2d, 1705, Jerusha Treat (1678-1754; Lt. James[9], *m* Rebecca Latimer);
7–Ichabod (Apr. 1712-1758), *m* Mary Hall (*b* 1714; Eliphalet[8], *m* Abigail Bushnell); *m* 2d, Abigail Bigelow;
6–Benjamin (1733-1804), in Conn. militia during Am. Rev.; *m* 1757, Lucy Talcott;
5–Benjamin (1758-1811), Bolton, Conn.; fifer in Conn. militia during Am. Rev.; *m* 1781, Mary Warner (*b* 1762; Dr. Ichabod[6], *m* Mary Lazell);
4–Elijah Gardner (1782-1855), New Hartford, Conn.; hon. M.A., Yale, 1808; Presbyn. minister; *m* 1806, Lucy Griffin;
3–George Griffin (1807-88), of Phila., Pa.; *m* 2d, 1843, Marie Josephine Brazeau Conrad (1819-97; Joseph Brazeau[4], *m* Julie Fishback);
2–Lucy Griffin (2 below).
11–Gov. William (Pincheon) **Pynchon** (qv);
10–Mary (*d* 1657), Springfield, Mass.; *m* 1640, Capt. Elizur **Holyoke** (1619-76; Edward[11], *m* Prudence–);
9–Hannah (1644-77), *m* 1661, Capt. Samuel **Talcott** (1634-91), grad. Harvard, 1658; lt. of Train Band, capt. of troops of Hartford, 1681 (John[10], *m* Dorothy Mott);
8–Dea. Benjamin (1674-1727), Wethersfield, Conn.; lt. of Train Band; *m* 1699, Sarah Hollister (1676-1715; John[9], *m* Sarah Goodrich);
7–Benjamin (1702-85), Bolton, Conn.; *m* 2d, 1736, Deborah Gillette;
6–Lucy (1737-93), *m* 1757, Benjamin **Welles** (6 above).
8–Maj. Jasper **Griffin** (qv);
7–Jasper (*b* 1675), Southold, L.I.; *m* 1696, Ruth Peck (*b* 1676; Joseph[8], of Lyme, Conn.; William[9]);
6–Lemuel (*b* 1704), of Lyme, *m* Phoebe Comstock;
5–George (*b* 1734), Am. Rev.; *m* 1762, Eve Dorr;
4–Lucy (1773-1852), *m* 1806, Rev. Elijah Gardner **Welles** (4 above).
9–Henry **Wolcott** (qv);
8–Anna (*d* 1704), *m* 1646, Matthew **Griswold** (qv);
7–Matthew, *m* Phebe Hyde (*b* 1663; Samuel[8], *m* Jane Lee);
6–Mary (*b* 1694), *m* 1719, Edmund **Dorr** (*b* 1692; Edward[7], *m* Elizabeth Hawley);
5–Eve (*b* 1733), *m* 1762, George **Griffin** (5 above).
2–Lucy Griffin Welles (*b* 1858), of St. Louis, Mo.; *m* 1877, Abraham William **Brooke** (*b* 1855), auditor and sec. of Am. Refrigerator Transit Co., 1889-1913 (George[3], *m* Ann Homes); issue: I–Marie Grace (*b* 1878; *m* Frank V. Grubs); II–Rosa Josephine (*b* 1880; *m* Wilbur Gear Miles); III–Lucy Claire (*b* 1882; *m* F. R. Hesse); IV–Agnes Welles (*b* 1885; *m* Roy Cunningham); V–Constance Griffin (*b* 1887; *m* J. P. Finkenaur); VI–Emelie Claire (*b* 1894; *m* Dr. C. E. Grizzell); VII–Georgene Christy (1 above); VIII–Adrian Welles (1899-1925).
1–*m* Sept. 2, 1917, Alpha Lloyd Goss, *b* Fayetteville, Ark., Mar. 8, 1891; grad. U. of Ark., '15; son of John Franklin Goss, *m* Mary Zillah, of Fayetteville; issue: 1–Adrian Franklin, *b* St. Louis, Mo., Apr. 18, 1918; 2–Alpha Lloyd, Jr., *b* Fayetteville, Jan. 4, 1922.
1–Mem. D.A.C., D.A.R. Presbyterian. Residence: Mt. Sequoyah, Fayetteville, Ark.

1–**GRANBERY, Marguerite Lee Shaffer (Mrs. Robert L.),** *b* "Bull Run Plantation," Chacahoula, La., July 14, 1862.
4–John **Shaffer,** of Winnsboro, S.C.; *m* Hepzibah Elizabeth Strother;
3–William Alexander (1796-1886), *m* 1829, Emily Bourgeois;
2–Capt. John Jackson (2 below).
8–Teige **Cantey** (*d* 1679), from the Barbados, 1672; settled at Dorchester, S.C., on Ashley River; received a land grant, 1672, another of 550 acres later; *m* Elizabeth–;
7–Capt. William (*d* ca. 1716), freeholder of the province; received grants, 1679,82,1713; commanded in the military attack on Charleston; mem. Assembly; comd. a company of which Capt. Fenwicks signally defeated and routed the enemy at Hobcaw's, Christ Church Parish; *m* Jane Baker (Judge Richard[8], judge, 1692, mem. Assembly, 1696, *m* Elizabeth–);
6–Samuel (post 1704-1762), overseer of Prince Frederick Parish, S.C.; *m* Anne–;
5–Joseph (1735-81), Craven Co., S.C.; repeatedly justice of the peace, and in 1767, mem. grand jury, St. Mark's Parish; received land grants as early as 1759; will found in probate court of Camden, 1781; *m* Ann–;

Arms: Azure, semée of crosses botonnée, a lion rampant reguardant argent, langued gules, charged with a mullet of the last.
Crest: A demi-wyvern vert, wings addorsed or, over all semée of pellets.

4–Thomas (1772-1809), of St. George's Parish; *m* Susannah Singletary;
3–Thomas Singletary (1797-1862), of Camden Dist., S.C., later of "Myrtle Grove Plantation," La.; sugar planter; in battle of New Orleans, 1814; vestryman, old Methodist Ch. of Baton Rouge, La.; *m* 1820, Anne Kenner Harbour;
2–Minerva Anne (2 below).
9–Richard **Singletary** (1585-1687), from Eng., settled at Haverhill, Mass.; *m* Susannah Cook;
8–Benjamine (*b* 1656), settled at Red Bank, S.C., ca. 1695; *m* 1678, Mary Stockbridge (*b* 1656);
7–Richard, of S.C.; *m* Sarah Stewart (sister of Thomas Stewart);
6–Joseph (*b* 1721/22), of St. Thomas and St. Denis parishes; *m* 1745, Hannah Dunham (John[7], received a warrant for 400 acres in Berkeley Co., S.C., 1708, lived in St. Thomas and St. Denis parishes, S.C., *m* Hannah–);
5–Benjamine (*d* 1811), of Goose Creek, St. James' Parish; *m* Hannah Darby (*b* 1718; Michael[6], *m* 1717, Mary Warnock);
4–Susannah (1770-1862), of S.C.; *m* 1795, Thomas **Cantey** (4 above).
7–William **Dalton** (*d* ante 1733; desc. Count de Alton, who went from Normandy with William the Conqueror); came from Yorkshire, Eng., 1685 or 90, settled in Gloucester Co., Va.; *m* 1st, Mary Dalton (widow of William Brockenborough);
6–Samuel (1699-1803, aet. 104), of Beaver Island, Mayo River, Va. (later Rockingham Co., N.C.); said to have been the wealthiest man in the Piedmont District of Va.; *m* 1740, Anne Dandridge Redd (George[7], *m* Anne Dandridge; Sir William Rufus Lyonel de Redd[8], *m* Catherine Moore);
5–Samuel (1745-91), of Beaver Island; *m* 1769, Charlotte Gallaline, of Pittsylvania Co. (she *m* 2d, 1793, Adonijah Harbour, whose first wife was Anne, dau. of Samuel Dalton);
4–Jane (1777-1833), of East Baton Rouge Parish, La.; *m* ca. 1792, Thomas Adonijah **Harbour** (*b* ca. 1772);
3–Anne Kenner (1803-74), of "Myrtle Grove Plantation," La.; *m* 1820, Thomas Singletary **Cantey** (3 above);
2–Minerva Anne (1835-1921), *m* 1855, Capt. John Jackson **Shaffer** (1831-1918), grad. Western Mil. Inst., 1851; capt., Co. F, 26th La. Inf., C.S.A.; comd. Braxton Bragg Camp, Thibodaux, La.; fought in the Battle of Chickasaw

CAPT. JOHN JACKSON SHAFFER (1831-1918).

Bayou, under Gen. S. D. Lee, in the defeat of Sherman; also in seige of Vicksburg, under the command of Gen. M. L. Smith, 1862; sr. warden, St. John's Episcopal Ch.; owned "Magnolia Plantation," "Isle of Cuba Plantation," and inherited part of "Crescent Farm Plantation," all plantations in Terrebonne Parish, La. (see portrait); issue: I–John Dalton (1858-1927; *m* 1882, Julia Culliffa, *d* 1920); II–Effie Maud (*b* 1860; *m* Samuel Isett Raymond); III–Marguerite Lee (1 above); IV–Thomas Alexander (*b* 1864; *m* Elise Wagoman Conway; *m* 2d, Mary [Altemus] Walker); V–Annie Laurie (1867-1922; *m* O. Z. Bartlett; *m* 2d, Rev. Dunham Van Syckel); VI–Bessie Emily (*b* 1870; *m* Charles Tew Madison; *m* 2d, Frederick Ransom Letcher).

1–*m* Jan. 20, 1885, Miles Coleman Mayes (*d* Sept. 27, 1887).

1–*m* 2d, Feb. 20, 1893, Robert Lee Granbery (*d* 1922).

1–Ed. Stuart Coll., Shelbyville, Ky.; Silvester Larned School, New Orleans. Has written a small book of poems not yet published. Was v.p. Crescent Magnolia Planting & Mfg. Co., Terrebonne Parish, La. Mem. Council of Defense, Girl Scouts of America. Mem. C.D.A. (N.J. Chapter), U.D.C. (New Orleans Chapter No. 72; charter mem. and treas. Maury Co. Chapter of Columbia, Tenn.), Confed. Memorial Assn. of New Orleans (life), Juda P. Benjamine Memorial Assn., New Orleans, St. John's Cemetery Assn., Thibodaux (first pres.), Am. Tree Assn., George Washington Bi-Centennial Treeplanting. Residence: Magnolia Plantation, Minerva Post Office, Terrebonne Parish, La.

1–**GRAY, Clarence Truman,** *b* Russell, Kan., Nov. 22, 1877.

10–John **Alden,** 7th signer of the Mayflower Compact (qv);

9–Sarah (*d* 1688), *m* Alexander **Standish** (1627-1702; Capt. Myles[10], qv);

8–Elizabeth, *m* 1682/83, Samuel **Delano** (1659-1728);

7–Elizabeth (1694-ante 1728), *m* 1720, Joseph **Chandler** (*b* 1694; Joseph[8]; Joseph[9]);

6–Benjamin (1721-77), Tinmouth, Vt.; owner and worker in irons; enlisted, 1775; pvt. in defense of Piscataquera Harbor, at Portsmouth; later sgt.; killed at Battle of Bennington, Aug. 16, 1777; *m* Elizabeth Jeffries (*d* aet. 88);

5–John (1757-1829), *m* Mary (Royce) Rice (1758-1826);

4–Zachariah Royce (1778-1862), *m* Fannie Bingham (1786-1857);

3–Eliza Reynolds (1821-98), *m* Rezin **Gray** (1822-87);

2–Zachariah Bingham (*b* 1851), farmer, *m* 1876, Lucinda Evangeline Anderson (*b* 1853); issue: I–Clarence Truman (1 above); II–Harry Anderson (*b* 1881; *m* Eura Coffman); III–Edith Lilly (*b* 1885; *m* Walter Ratcliff); IV–Olive (1890-1910).

1–*m* July 30, 1905, Bessie Lee Stretcher, *b* Elwood, Ind., July 30, 1879; dau. of William Wesley Stretcher, of Elwood; issue: 1–Truman Stretcher, *b* Spencer, Ind., May 3, 1906; B.S., U. of Tex., '26; B.A., U. of Tex., '27; M.S., M.I.T., 1929, D.Sc., 1930. 2–Margaret Elnora, *b* Chicago, Ill., July 30, 1916.

1–A.B., U. of Ind., '04; Ind. State Normal; Ph.D., U. of Chicago, 1916 (P.B.K., Sigma Xi, hon.). Prof. educational psychology, U. of Tex. (see Who's Who in America). Club: University. Residence: 3201 West Av., Austin, Tex.

GREGORY

Arms: *Per pale argent and azure, two lions rampant endorsed counterchanged.*
Crest: *Two lions' heads endorsed erased azure and argent, collared or.*

1–**GREGORY, Myron Stephen,** *b* Homer, Mich., Feb. 4, 1870.

10–Henry **Gregory** (qv);

9–John (*d* 1690), of New Haven; settled at Norwalk, Conn.; dep. Provincial Council, 1652-63;

8–John (*b* ca. 1639), of Cranberry Plain, Conn.;

7–John, *m* Mary Smith (Ebenezer[8], of L.I.);

6–John, *m* 1726, Mary–;

5–John (*b* 1727), *m* Naomi Thompson, dau. of a Scotch shipmaster;

4–Moses (1752-ante 1820), ship owner and master of privateer, Am. Rev.; settled in western N.Y., 1790; *m* Naomi Stevens (ca. 1774-ca. 1873);

3–Stephen Stevens (1810-86), settled in Albion Tp., Mich., 1837; *m* 1835, Lydia A. Knowles;

2–Omar (2 below).

10–Probably Rev. John **Knowles,** from Eng., 1639; settled at Watertown, Mass.; removed to Va., 1642; returned to Bristol, 1650;

9–Richard (*d* 1670-75), shipmaster; propr. of Plymouth, 1639; removed to Eastham, Mass., surveyor, 1670; *m* ca. 1639, Ruth Bower (*d* 1687; George[10], *m* Barbara–);

8–John (ca. 1640-1675), killed by Indians nr. Taunton, during King Philip's War; *m* 1670, Apphia Bangs (1651-post 1722; Edward[9], from Eng., *m* Rebecca–);

7–Col. John (1673-1757), cdr. of 2d Barnstable Regt.; *m* 1st, Mary Sears (1672-1745; Capt. Paul[8], *m* Deborah Willard; Richard[9]);

6–Seth (1700-52), Easthampton, Conn.; *m* 1723, Martha Remick (*d* 1760; Abraham[7], *m* Eliza-

beth, dau. of Dea. Samuel Freeman, *m* Mercy, dau. of Gen. Constant Southworth; Christian[8], from Eng.);
5–Daniel (ca. 1732-ca. 1770), Chatham, Conn.; *m* 1757, Sibbel Bacon (1735-ante 1796; Lt. John[6], *m* Sarah, dau. Joseph White; John[7]; Nathaniel[8], qv);
4–Seth (1760-1829), pvt. 3d Conn. Regt. in Am. Rev.; *m* 3d, 1804, Mehitable Bills (*b* 1778; Joel[5], corpl. Am. Rev.);
3–Lydia A. (1814-96), *m* Stephen S. **Gregory** (3 above).
7–Richard **Easton** (1680-1772), settled in N.J. ante 1732; *m* Elenor– (1698-1776);
6–Stephen (ca. 1725-1781), sgt. Eastern Bn., Morris Co., N.J., Am. Rev.; *m* twice;
5–Enos (1774-1838), *m* 1800, Sarah Drake;
4–Charles (1800-82), *m* 1822, Rachel B. Phillips (1802-70);
3–Myron Wilbur (1827-84), *m* 1850, Sally Aldrich;
2–Alice (2 below).
11–Robert **Drake** (ca. 1580-1668), from Eng.; at Exeter, N.H., 1643; settled at Hampton, N.H.;
10–Francis (*d* 1687), Portsmouth, N.H., 1661; a founder of Piscataway, N.J., 1667-68; justice; judge, Middlesex Co. Ct., 1682; 1st selectman, Piscataway; *m* Mary (Walker?);
9–Rev. John (1655-1739/40), pastor of Piscataway Bapt. Ch., 50 yrs.; *m* 1677, Rebecca Trotter;
8–Abraham (1685-will proved 1763), *m* Deliverance Wooden (*b* 1683);
7–Jacob (*b* ca. 1710), *m* Mary–; *m* 2d, Joan (Jane Chambers) Ayres;
6–Paul (1761-1828), Am. Rev.; *m* 1st, 1781, Mary Luce;
5–Sarah (1782 or 83-1827), *m* Enos **Easton** (5 above).
10–George **Aldrich** (qv);
9–Jacob (*b* 1652), *m* 1675, Hulda Thayer;
8–Jacob (*b* ca. 1676), *m* Margery Hayward (Samuel[9], *m* Mahitable Thompson);
7–Jacob (*b* 1711), *m* 1732, Mary Fletcher;
6–Stephen (*b* 1745), sgt. Am. Rev.; *m* 1766, Mary Thayer;
5–Stephen (*b* 1782), *m* Lucy A.–;
4–Russel E. (1802-83), Homer, Calhoun Co., Mich., 1867; *m* 1st, 1824, Eliza Marshall (1806-60);
3–Sally (1830-98), *m* Myron W. **Easton** (3 above);
2–Alice (1853-1926), *m* 1868, Omar **Gregory** (1849-1905), millwright; town treas. Litchfield, Mich., many yrs.; Mason.
1–*m* Feb. 29, 1892, Lydia Bolton, *b* London, Eng., Jan. 11, 1873; dau. of Joseph Bolton, from London, to Tekonsha, Mich.; issue: 1–Vera Zea, *b* Platte, Mich., Oct. 11, 1894; *m* 1917, Verne, son of Robert Teare (issue: Robert Myron; Philip Verne; Arthur Reynolds; Thomas Gregory; Beverly Jane); 2–Henry Reynolds, *b* Platte, Sept. 9, 1896; Mich. Agrl. Coll.; *m* Oct. 31, 1922, Gertrude, dau. of William Brandon, of Knobnoster, Mo. (issue: William Allen; Walter Myron; Omar Reynolds, and Ellis Stephen, twins); 3–Mynie Neleta, *b* Platte, Oct. 29, 1899; *m* 1920, Earl Hustin, of Elsie, Mich.; 4–Ellis Van Rensselaer, *b* Benzonia, Mich., Apr. 5, 1903; LL.B., Detroit Coll. Law, 1929; *m* Jan. 25, 1930, Edith Hickham; 5–Clark Stephen, *b* Ann Arbor, Mich., May 22, 1906; LL.B., Detroit Coll. Law, 1928; *m* June 8, 1928, Gertrude, dau. of Fenton J. Brink, of St. Johns, Mich. (issue: Helen Claire).
1–*m* 2d, Mar. 18, 1922, Lillian May (Long) Whelan (qv).
1–Ed. Mich. Agrl. Coll., 1888-91; M.D., U.Mich., 1906. Physician, specialist in neuro-psychiatry; lecturer, Okla. Gen. Hosp., Wesley Hosp.; prof. science, Benzonia Coll., Mich., 1899-1901. Justice of peace, 1893-94; supt. Benzie Co. schs., 1897-1903. Capt., M.C., neuro-psychiatric unit, 1917-19. Mem. S.A.R., I.A.G., A.L. Mason (32°, Shriner), Elk, Odd Fellow. Club: Civitan. Summer place: Nicoma Park, Okla. Residence: 2209 W. 22d St., Oklahoma City, Okla.

1–**GREGORY, Lillian May Long (Mrs. Myron S.)**, *b* Montezuma, O., Oct. 30, 1880.
8–Richard **Miles** (*d* 1713), from Wales, 1682 or 83, settled in Pa.; *m* in Wales, Sarah Evans;
7–James (1713-84), of Pa.; organizer of patriotic meetings; *m* 1734, Hannah Pugh (1715-79);
6–James (ca. 1736-1798), of Northumberland Co., Pa.; soldier Am. Rev.; *m* Susanna Rock;
5–Abiezēr (1768-1832), ens., Chester Co., Pa., militia, 1792; served in War 1812; *m* ca. 1796, Judith Jessup;
4–Susanna Rock (*b* Pa., 1799), *m* William P. **Long** (*b* Pa. 1794), from Northumberland Co., Pa., to Cincinnati, O.;
3–James Miles (1824-92), of Appleton City, Mo.; *m* 1848, Amanda Case Burdge;
2–Benjamin Franklin (2 below).
10–John **Jessup**, from Eng. to Stamford, Conn., 1637; settled at Southampton, L.I., 1649;
9–John (will dated 1710), of Old Town; *m* 1669, Elizabeth–;
8–Isaac (1673-1753), *m* Abigail–;
7–Stephen (*b* ca. 1710-will proved 1764), *d* Deerfield, Cumberland Co., N.J.; *m* Mary–;
6–John (*b* ca. 1731), to Hamilton Co., O., 1801; *m* Judith–;
5–Judith (1775-1839), *m* Abiezer **Miles** (5 above).
9–Jonathan **Burdge** (*d* 1681), settled at Hempstead, L.I.;
8–David, to Middletown, N.J., 1715;
7–Jonathan, of N.J.; *m* Dorothy–;
6–Richard (*b* 1728), *m* 2d, 1757, Hannah Huff (*b* 1725);
5–Jonathan (1760-1827), *m* 1782, Hannah Van Dusen (1759-1842);
4–Robert (1797-1872), Hillsdale, N.Y.; *m* Alley (Olivia) Whallon (1800-79);
3–Amanda C. (1827-1908); *m* James M. **Long** (3 above).
9–Adrian **Hagaman**, from Holland, 1650, settled at Flatbush, L.I., later in N.J.; *m* Katryna Margits;
8–Hendrick, of N.J.; *m* 1685, Adrientje Bloodgood;
7–Adrian (*b* 1686), *m* Maria Van Vliet;
6–Simon (*b* 1727), *m* Aaltje–;
5–Alley (1773-1847), *m* James **Whallon** (1770-1849), settled at Cincinnati, 1804; soldier War 1812 (James[6], from Ireland to Somerset Co., N.J., 1760, lt. Am. Rev., *m* ante 1759, Sarah, dau. of Ralph Smith);
4–Alley (1800-79), Hamilton Co., O.; *m* 1820, Robert **Burdge** (4 above);
3–Amanda C., *m* James M. **Long** (3 above).
2–Benjamin Franklin (*b* 1856), retired farmer; *m* 1877, Elizabeth Catherine Coburn (*b* 1858; Henry H.[3], vet. Civil War); issue: I–Ora A. (*b* 1878; *m* Bessie McVickers); II–Lillian May (1 above); III–Hallie Bertha (*b* 1883; *m* Stokley Linwood Shinn); IV–David Guy (1886-97); V–Amanda C. (1889-1925); VI–George F. (*b* 1891; *m* Kate McCorkle); VII–Anna Lee (*b* 1895; *m* Charles Ralph Kirkland).
1–*m* June 27, 1900, Ernest Alvan Whelan (*b* Feb. 22, 1876); son of Ely Hugh Whelan, of Appleton City, Mo.; issue: 1–Arthur Ernest, *b* Appleton City, Mo., May 1, 1901; 2–Ellen Edna, *b* Hill City, Kan., Sept. 27, 1909.
1–*m* 2d, Mar. 18, 1922, Dr. Myron Stephen Gregory (qv).
1–Mem. D.A.R., A. L. Auxiliary, Auxiliary Co. Med. Soc., Delphian Soc., O.E.S. Unitarian. Republican. Residence: 2209 W. 22d St., Oklahoma City, Okla.

1–**GRIGGS, Elvira Caroline Ingersoll (Mrs. Herbert S.)**, *b* Milwaukee, Wis., Mar. 31, 1883.
8–Thomas **Leavenworth** (*d* 1683), from Eng.; *d* at Woodbury, Conn.;
7–Dr. Thomas (1673-1754), *m* 1698, Mary Jenkins;
6–Rev. Mark (1711-97), B.A., Yale, 1737, M.A.; *m* 1739, Ruth Peck;
5–Col. Jesse (1740-1824), B.A., Yale, 1759; lt. in Gov.'s Foot Guards; was in Battle of Lexington; officer in Am. Rev.; *m* Catherine (Conkling) Frisbie;
4–Gen. Henry (1783-1834), see portrait and military record; *m* 1806, Elizabeth Morrison;
3–Col. Jesse Henry (1807-85), U.S.M.A., 1830; lt., 4th Inf., U.S.A., 1830-36; resigned to become civil engr.; built piers in Chicago harbor; commd. col., 2d Colo. Inf., 1862-63; raised and comd. Rocky Mtn. Rangers, for service against Indians; *m* 1832, Elvira Caroline Clark;
2–Harriet May (2 below).
8–Thomas **Clark**, first mate on the Mayflower; buried at Plymouth, Mass.;
7–Benjamin;
6–Thomas;
5–Stephen;
4–Festus, of Sackett's Harbor; *m* Elvira Caroline Calkins;

GEN. HENRY LEAVENWORTH (1783-1834), capt., 25th U.S. Inf., 1812; maj., 9th Inf., 1813, in War 1812; wounded in Battle of Lundy's Lane, 1814; lt. col., 5th Inf., 1818; col., 3d Inf., 1825; bvtd. lt. col., July 5, 1814, for distinguished services at the Battle of Chippewa, and col., July 25, 1814, for same at Niagara Falls; bvtd. brig. gen., July 25, 1824.

3–Elvira Caroline (*b* 1813), *m* Col. Jesse Henry **Leavenworth** (3 above);
2–Harriet May (1851-1927), *m* 1874, Avery Melvin **Ingersoll** (*b* 1849), was pres. Tacoma Warehouse & Elevator Co.; v.p. western div., C., M.&St.P. R.R.; now pres. Pacific Stevedoring Co. (son of Allan J.³, Wis. lumberman); issue: I–Jesse (*b* 1875; *m* Florence Ingall); II–Airs Elsie (*b* 1879; *m* Harry Markoe, Jr.); III–Elvira Caroline (1 above); IV–Marjorie (*b* and *d* 1885); V–Mary Janet (*b* 1889).
1–*m* June 15, 1903, Herbert Stanton Griggs, *b* St. Paul, Minn., Feb. 27, 1861; B.A., Yale, '82, LL.B., 1884; lawyer; v.p. Coll. of Tacoma; sec.-treas. St. Paul-Tacoma Lumber Co.; mem. Wash. State Hist. Soc., S.A.R., etc.; son of Col. Chauncey Wright Griggs (see Vol. I, p. 307, for genealogy); issue (all *b* Tacoma, Wash.): 1–Herbert S., Jr., *b* Jan. 27, 1906; Ph.B., Yale, '28; 2–Chauncey, *b* July 6, 1909; 3–Elvira Caroline, *b* Aug. 26, 1913; 4–Harriet, *b* Feb. 10, 1911; student Wellesley, '32.
1–Grad. Georgetown Convent, Washington, D.C. Residence: 923 Yakima Av. N., Tacoma, Wash.

1–**HARDIE, Martha Dickson Roe (Mrs. James F.),** *b* Ft. Worth, Tex., July 29, 1881.
9–Rev. George **Phillips** (qv);
8–Rev. Samuel (1625-96), Harvard, 1650; of Rowley, Mass., *m* 1652/53, Sarah Appleton (Samuel⁹, qv);
7–Rev. George (1664-1739), of Brookhaven, L.I.; *m* Sarah Hallett (*b* 1673);
6–Elizabeth (1702-88), *m* ca. 1741, Nathaniel **Roe** (1700-89), see Vol. II, p. 87, for Roe lineage;
5–James (1744-1815), officer Am. Rev.; *m* 1770, Elizabeth LeSoeur (1745-93; Jan⁶; William⁷);
4–John Eltinge (1774-1831), *m* 1796, Charlotte Merritt;
3–John Morey (1804-72), *m* 2d, 1842, Jeannette Kirtland Shipman;
2–Theodore Hart (2 below).
10–Robert **Seabrook** (1566-163–), of Stratford;
9–Alice (1587-ca. 1639), *m* ca. 1612, Thomas **Sherwood** (qv);
8–Jane (1636-85), *m* Thomas **Merritt** (qv);
7–Samuel (1672-1722), *m* ca. 1698, Elizabeth Underhill (Humphrey⁸; Michael⁹);
6–George (1711-59), *m* ca. 1731, Glorianna Purdy (1715-65; Samuel⁷; Judge Joseph⁸; Francis⁹);
5–George (1741-1822), *m* Mary Fowler (1744-99; Samuel⁶; John⁷);
4–Charlotte (*d* 1835), *m* John Eltinge **Roe** (4 above).
9–Edward (Shipton) **Shipman** (qv);
8–John (1664-1705?), *m* 1686, Martha Humphrey (*b* 1663; Michael⁹, qv);
7–John (1687-1742), of Saybrook, Conn.; *m* 1715, Elizabeth Kirtland (1688-1778; Lt. John⁸; Nathaniel⁹; Philip¹⁰);
6–John (1717-86), *m* 1742, Margaret Bushnell (Dea. Joshua⁷; Joshua⁸; Lt. William⁹; Francis¹⁰, qv);
5–Elias (*b* 1757), from Saybrook, Conn., to Binghamton, N.Y.; *m* 1781, Elizabeth Titus (*d* 1790), of L.I.;
4–Henry Titus (1782-ca. 1836), *m* 1800, Jeannette Kirtland (1784-1871; Capt. William⁵, *m* Azubah–);
3–Jeannette Kirtland (1818-1906), *m* John Morey **Roe** (3 above);
2–Theodore Hart (1849-1917), lumber dealer; *m* 1880, Elizabeth Walker Dickson (1846-1910); for issue and other lineages see Mrs. Charles A. Keith, see Vol. II, p. 87, and Vol. III, p. 604.
1–*m* Aug. 14, 1913, James Finley Hardie, D.D., *b* Selma, Ala., Jan. 29, 1880 (see Who's Who in America); issue: 1–Maybelle, *b* Austin, Tex., Dec. 22, 1916; 2–James Finley, Jr., *b* Houston, Tex., Sept. 27, 1924.
1–Ed. Mary Nash Coll., Sherman, Tex., 2 yrs.; N.E. Conservatory of Music, Boston, 2 yrs. Teacher of piano, 1902-09, at Littleton (N.C.) Coll., 1907-08, Presbyterian Inst., Blackshear, Ga., 1908-09; missionary, Southern Presbyn. Mission, Kashing, China, 1909-11. Democrat. Clubs: Virginia Dare Book, Charlotte Country. Residence: 425 Queen's Rd., Charlotte, N.C.

1–**HAWLEY, John Blackstock,** *b* Red Wing, Minn., May 27, 1866.
7–Joseph **Hawley** (qv);
6–Samuel (1647-1734), of Stratford, Conn.; *m* 2d, Widow Patience Hubbell;
5–Stephen (1695-1790), of New Milford, Conn.; *m* 1720, Mary de Forest (*b* 1696), of Stratford;
4–Rev. Stephen (1738-1804), of Bethany and New Haven, Conn.; *m* 2d, 1793, Mehetable Hotchkiss (1763-1827), of Bethany;
3–Isaac A. (1797-1867), removed to Geneva, N.Y., 1848; *m* 1831, Ann Eliza Boyer (1812-1902), of Caroline, Tompkins Co., N.Y. (Augustine⁴; Augustine⁵, a marquis, from France to America, 1700);
2–Augustine Boyer, M.D. (1833-78), *m* 1865, Harriet Bowman Blackstock (1844-85); issue: I–John B. (1 above); II–Edward Welles (*b* 1867; *m* Leulah Judson); III–Mary Everett (*b* 1869; *m* E. Zeh Hawkes, M.D.); IV–George Maxwell Blackstock (*b* 1870; *m* Ruth Wilson); V–Elizabeth McKennan (Mrs. Frederick B. Chute, qv for McKennan lineage); VI–William Sinclair (1873-75); VII–Augustine Boyer, Jr. (1875-83); VIII–Anne MacDonald (*b* 1876); IX–Henry Wilder (*b* 1877; *m* Jean Judson).
1–*m* Apr. 11, 1895, Sue Anna Terrell, *b* Ft. Worth, Tex., May 13, 1872; dau. of Joseph C. Terrell, of Ft. Worth; issue (all *b* Ft. Worth): 1–Judith Terrell, *b* Mar. 5, 1896; ed. Wellesley, 1916-17; *m* June 19, 1919, Dr. Henry M., son of Henry S. Winans, of Denver, Colo. (issue: Henry M., Jr.; Judith Hawley; Sue Terrell); 2–John Blackstock, Jr., *b* July 11, 1899; C.E., Cornell U., '21; *m* Nov. 3, 1925, Helen Winston, dau. of James S. Thurston, of Minneapolis, Minn. (issue: Terrell); 3–Harriet Elizabeth, *b* July 15, 1904; B.A., U.Tex., '28; *m* Sept. 17, 1929, Jacques Albert Fermaud, of Paris, France; 4–George Maxwell Blackstock, *b* Feb. 16, 1915.
1–B.S., U.Minn., '87 (Chi Psi), M.S., Tex. Christian U., 1926. Consulting hydraulic engr. Maj. engrs., U.S.A., 1917-19; engr. Water Bd., St. Paul, 1887-89; pvt. practice, Ft. Worth, 1890-97; mem. Hawley & Sands, 1893, alone on death of partner, 1923-27; mem. Hawley & Freese, since 1927 (see Who's Who in America). Mem. Am. Soc. C.E. (dir. 1915-17), S.A.-M.E. Unitarian. Clubs: Ft. Worth, Ft. Worth U., River Crest Country. Address: C/o Hawley & Freese, 411 Capps Bldg., Ft. Worth, Tex.

1–**CHUTE, Elizabeth McKennan Hawley (Mrs. Frederick B.),** *b* Red Wing, Minn., Sept. 10, 1872.

6–Rev. William **McKennan** (1719-1810), from the North of Ireland to the Barbados, ca. 1750; settled finally at Wilmington, Del., where he was a clergyman for over 50 yrs.; *m* Miss Wilson, of Winchester, Va.;
5–Col. William (1758-1810), capt. in Am. Rev.; was made col. at the close of the war; fought in the battles of Brandywine, Germantown (where he received wounds from which he eventually died), Monmouth, Yorktown, etc.; charter mem. of the Order of Cincinnati; *m* 1781 or 82, Elizabeth Thompson (1761-1839; niece of Thomas McKean, a "signer"; pres. of the Cont. Congress, 1781, at the time of Cornwallis' surrender at Yorktown, was chief justice of Pa. 22 yrs., and gov. of Pa., 3 terms); of their sons, William was U.S. circuit judge, 1869-91, and Thomas McKean Thompson was congressman, 1832-42, and Sec. of the Interior in Cabinet of Pres. Fillmore;
4–John Thompson (1791-1830), of Brownsville, Pa.; *m* 1816, Harriet Bowman (1789-1832);
3–Harriet Elizabeth (1821-1903), of Washington Co., Pa., and Minneapolis Minn.; *m* 1842, John MacDonald **Blackstock** (1821-52);
2–Harriet Bowman (1844-85), *m* 1865, Augustine Boyer **Hawley** (1833-78), M.D.; for issue and Hawley lineage see brother, John Blackstock Hawley.
1–*m* May 26, 1909, Frederick Butterfield Chute, *b* Minneapolis, Minn., Dec. 21, 1872, son of Dr. Samuel H. Chute, of Minneapolis; issue (both *b* Minneapolis): 1–Margaret McDonald (Aug. 20, 1910-*d* Sept. 20, 1923); 2–Frederick Hawley, *b* June 3, 1912.
1–U.Minn., 2 yrs. (Kappa Kappa Gamma). Asst. reference librarian, U.Minn., 13 yrs. Mem. D.A.C. Episcopalian. Republican. Club: Women's. Residence: 2205 Pleasant Av., Minneapolis, Minn.

Arms: Gules, a chevron or.

1–**HARTZELL, J(oseph) Culver,** *b* New Orleans, La., Sept. 10, 1870.
7–John George, Pfalzgraf, von **Herzel** (1680-1760; desc. Clan von Herzeele, Barons of the Reich); from Upper Consistory of the Palatinate, Germany, 1727; took oath of allegiance, Sept. 11, 1732; settled at Hartzells (now Drylands), Pa.; buried at Drylands Reformed Church; born, Mannheim, Grand-Duchy of Baden; *m* Anna Barbara–.
6–John George, Jr., of Bucks Co.; "took the sacrament 1740, and became a citizen"; *m* Catherine–;
5–John Adam (1742-1832), Westmoreland Co., Pa.; Am. Rev.; *m* Anna Maria Clara–;
4–Adam (1780-1840), *m* 1800, Catherine Bash (1783-1851);
3–Michael Bash (1810-99), Moline, Ill.; *m* 1836, Nancy Worman Stauffer;
2–Joseph Crane (2 below).
7–John **Stauffer** (*b* 1655; son of Daniel, of Alzheim, Zurick, Switzerland, desc. of the royal House of Hohenstaufen); from Switzerland, 1710; settled at Valley Forge, Chester Co., Pa.; *m* Widow Kinget (Heistand) Risser;
6–Henry, of Colebrookdale Tp., Pa.; *m* Magdalena Hess;
5–John (1760-1837), Lancaster Co., Pa.; Am. Rev.; *m* 1790, Ann (Nancy) Shelenburger (1765-1825; Jacob[6] [1724-1812], Am. Rev., *m* 2d Ann–, Ulrich[7], from Switzerland to Pa.);
4–John (*b* 1792), of Blairsville, Pa.; *m* 1814, Margaret Worman (*b* 1794);
3–Nancy Worman (1817-1909), of Blairsville; *m* Michael Bash **Hartzell** (3 above).
8–Edward **Culver** (qv);
7–John (1640-1725), of New Haven, Conn.; *m* Sarah Winthrop (Gov. John[8], qv);
6–John (1674-1760), of Schooley's Mtn., N.J.; *m* Sarah Franklin;
5–John (1700-75), *m* Abigail Crassman;
4–Phineas (1764-1840), of "Peach Orchard Plantation," Horseheads, N.Y.; Am. Rev.; *m* 1794, Phoebe Breese (1773-1854; John[5], Am. Rev., *m* 1769, Hannah Gildersleeve; John[6], from Eng., 1735, settled in N.J., *m* Dorothy Riggs; Rev. Sidney[7], of Eng.);
3–John Breese (1811-94), Chicago, Ill.; atty. state and U.S. courts; a founder Northwestern U.; promoted Ill. canal; *m* 1840, Margaret Ann Boyd (1819-70; John[4], of Leith, Scotland, *m* Jeanette Fuzzard);
2–Jennie (1844-1916), *m* 1869, Rt. Rev. Joseph Crane **Hartzell** (1842-1928), D.D., LL.D.; bishop M.E. Ch.; missionary bishop of Africa, 1896-1916 (see Who's Who in America); issue: I–Joseph Culver (1 above); II–John Wesley (*b* and *d* 1873); III–Jennie Culver (Sept. 23, 1874-Jan. 15, 1875); IV–Morton Culver (Feb. 17, 1876-Feb. 17, 1916); V–Robert Culver (*b* 1879).
1–*m* Aug. 31, 1893, Helen Hitchcock Thresher, *b* Monson, Mass., Sept. 1, 1869 (desc. John Alden, qv); dau. Eben Thresher, of Monson, Mass, and Riverside Calif., *m* Henrietta Hitchcock; issue: 1–Helen Henrietta (June 10-Oct. 10, 1894).
1–B.S., Chattanooga U., '92 (Phi Gamma Delta), M.S., Chattanooga, 1895, and Yale, 1899; M.D., Coll. Phys. and Surg., 1901; Ph.D., Munich, 1904; grad. student, Harvard, 1896, Johns Hopkins, 1897-98, Pisa, 1903, Ohio-Miami Med. Coll., 1915. Retired consulting engr. Prof. biology and chemistry, Ill. Wesleyan U. and U. of the Pacific, 1899-1910; consulting engr. in chemistry and metallurgy, 1910-13. Pres. and gen. mgr., Ohio Lesgas Corpn., 1921-25 (see Who's Who in America). Has pvt. library of nearly 5,000 books, bulletins, technical papers, reprints, among which are many rare publications; has collections of many curios, among which is a piece of the cloth from which the original Am. flag was made. Mem. Gov. and Co. of Mass. Bay in N.E. (freeman), Soc. of Desc. of First Citizens of the U.S., S.A.R., Pa. German Soc., I.A.G., etc. Club: Engineers (Cincinnati). Methodist. Republican. Residence: "Cedar Cottage," Madisonville Rd., Blue Ash, Ohio.

1–**HEIBLER, Madeleine du Pont (Mrs. Max),** *b* Wilmington, Del., Oct. 16, 1887.
11–Jehan **duPont** (1538-1604), *m* 1st, Guillemine Brière (ca. 1536-1581);
10–Abraham (1572-1640), *m* 2d, Marie Cossart;
9–Jean (1631-1710), *m* 1st, Marie du Busc (1632-76);
8–Jean (1662-1731), *m* Marie de la Porte (*b* 1674);
7–Samuel (1708-75), *m* Anne Alexandrine de Montchanin (1720-56);
6–Pierre Samuel (qv);
5–Eleuthère Irénée (1771-1834), *m* Sophie Madeleine Dalmas (1775-1828);
4–Alfred Victor (1798-1856), *m* Margaretta Elizabeth Lammot (1807-98);
3–Eleuthère Irénée (1829-77), *m* Charlotte S. Henderson (1835-77);
2–Alfred Irénée (*b* 1864), *m* 1st, 1887, Bessie Gardner (see Vol. III, p. 172).
1–*m* Max Heibler, of Germany.
1–Address: C/o Mrs. Bessie G. DuPont, Greenville, Del.

1–**HEITMAN, Henry Nading,** *b* Forsyth Co., N.C., Jan. 15, 1905.
7–Marcus **Hoehns** (1719-97), came from the Palatinate to America, 1738; *m* 1749, Anne Elizabeth Kerber (1727-1804);
6–John (1750-1822), *m* 1776, Maria Schor (1756-1825);
5–Anna Catherine (1786-1870), *m* 1812, Christian

Ripple (1784-1869; Henry[6] [1758-1835], *m* 1782, Catharina [1765-1825], dau. of Christian Frey, *m* Sarah–);
4–Philip (1813-93), *m* Melinda Frey (1813-52);
3–Elizabeth Catherine (1839-1914), *m* 1863, Orin Burgess **Heitman** (1845-1917; John A.[4] [1816-93], *m* Anna Kensy [1823-1910]; John Christian[5]);
2–Emory Philip (2 below).
5–Daniel **Wagner** (1792-1850), *m* Christina Eller (1794-1851);
4–Mathias (*b* 1820?), *m* Mary (Mollie) Hedrick;
3–John Peter (1845-1911), *m* 1865, Martha Jane Michael;
2–Claudia Irene (2 below).
5–Jacob **Michael** (1783-1832), *m* Susanna Koontz (1783-1855);
4–Henry (1820-95), *m* Louisa H. Myers (1831-1918; Col. John[5] [1804-83], *m* Jane [Jennie] Clopton, 1811-79);
3–Martha Jane (1850-1909), *m* John Peter **Wagner** (3 above);
2–Claudia Irene (1866-1918), *m* 1886, Emory Philip **Heitman** (*b* 1866), mercantile business; issue: I–Flossie M. (1888-91); II–Addie May (*b* 1890; *m* 1910, Charles Albert Hege, *b* 1886); III–Beecher Graham (*b* 1893; *m* 1916, Pansy Mae Phillipps, *b* 1897); IV–Eva Ruth (*b* 1896; *m* 1912, Carlie Columbus Shaver, *b* 1891); V–Frank Clifton (*b* 1901); VI–Henry Nading (1 above).
1–Not married. Grad. Shenandoah Jr. Coll., 1926. Residence: 8 E. Sprague St., Winston-Salem, N.C.

1–**HIGGINS, Eugene,** *b* Springport, Mich., Dec. 27, 1863.
9–Richard **Higgins** (qv);
8–Jonathan (1637-post May 21, 1711, prob. 1721), *m* 1st, 1660/61, Elizabeth Rogers (1639-1678?; Lt. Joseph[9]);
7–Elisha (1677 or 79-1750), *m* 1st, 1701, Jane Collins (1684-1738?; Joseph[8], *m* Ruth Knowles);
6–Elisha (1701 or 02-1777), *m* 1721, Sarah Lewis (1702-1732?);
5–Elisha (1727-1801), *m*– (*d* 1778);
4–Isaac (1750-1819), *m* 1784, Asenath Clark (1761-1824);
3–Samuel (1797-1863), *m* 1818, Julia Ann Skellenger (1798-1863; Nathan[4] [*d* 1823], *m* Nancy–);
2–Samuel Ross (1834-70), *m* 1861, Adaline Knowles (1839-1915); issue: I–Eugene (1 above); II–Annie or Anna (1865-*d* Oct. 24, 1929).
1–*m* Feb. 2, 1896, Edith Elvira Herrick, *b* Battle Creek, Mich., June 13, 1874; dau. of Joseph Morehouse Herrick, of Battle Creek, *m* Cornelia Anna Rogers; issue: 1–Marcia Cornelia, *b* Battle Creek, July 5, 1899; *m* Sept. 8, 1928, John Francis, son of William Henry Haughey, *m* Elizabeth Eunice Converse; 2–Adaline Edith (*b* and *d* 1901); 3–Florence Ann, *b* Lansing, Mich., Apr. 3, 1906.
1–Designer of special machinery. Dir. Jackson Engrs. Club. Residence: 1701 First St., Jackson, Mich.

1–**HIGHFILL, May Haralson (Mrs. LeRoy),** *b* St. Francisville, La., July 7, 1894.
7–Peter **Haralson,** capt. Danish army; went from Denmark to Holland, thence to Hanover Co., Va., 1715; *m* Miss Chambers;
6–Paul, *m* 1757, Nancy Lea (James[7], from Eng., soldier in N.C. militia, pvt. under his bro., Gabriel, of Orange Co., enlisted in 10th N.C. Cont. Regt., 1782, and served thruout the Siege of Yorktown, *m* Ann Talbert; James[8]; John[9], of Eng.);
5–Herndon, maj., Caswell Co., N.C.; capt. under Gen. Green; *m* 1791, Mary Murphey (Archibald[6], Am. Rev., *m* Jane DeBow);
4–Archibald (*b* 1792), lawyer; dist. atty. for La., 1822; *m* 1813, Theresa Lodoiska Augustine Pont-Brieullet (*b* 1795), only child of Capt. Pont-Brieullet, *m* Marie Louise Pillet, dau. of Francois Count de Portier, surnamed Pillet, *m* Mebainie de Messene, Countess D'Effeat, from the House of Orleans;
3–Bertrand (1820-74), Baton Rouge, La.; recorder 16 yrs., senator, register of land office, judge, lawyer; *m* 1856, Frances Temple Peirce;
2–Bertrand (2 below).
12–William **Dawes,** came to N.E. with first body of Puritans, 1628-29, who founded Boston and Salem; returned to Eng.; suffered in estate under Cromwell as he helped support the royal family during exile; after the return of Charles, II, 1663, he was made a baronet and the title descended through Thomas—John—Robert—William (Bishop of Chester—Archbishop of York—and finally Archbishop of Canterbury), and D'Arcy to William the last of the line on whose death, without progeny, the baronetcy became extinct, May 28, 1741;
11–William (1620-1703), from Eng. in the "Planter," 1635; mason; settled at Braintree, later at Boston; *m* Susannah Mills (John[12], from Eng. with Gov. Winthrop's fleet, *m* Susannah–);
10–Ambrose (1642-1705), mason and builder, Boston; freeman, 1671; lt., A. and H.A. Co., 1674; in King Philip's War, 1675; wounded at Ft. Pemaquid, 1692; *m* Mary Bumstead (bap. 1642-1706; Thomas[11], emigrated 1640, *m* Susannah–);
9–Thomas (1680-1750), mason and builder; *m* 1702, Sarah Story (*d* 1759), from Eng. ca. 1700;
8–Thomas (1706-ca. 1747-50), *m* Elizabeth Muderwood (Anthony[9], the chair-maker, *m* Jane, dau. of John Plaice, of Boston);
7–Thomas (1731-1809), architect of the State House, and of the Old Brattle Street Ch., Boston; dea. Old South Ch., 1786-1809; adj. Boston regt., and comd. the Coulrat Militia Co.; maj. Boston regt., 1771, col., 1773, until the provincial gov. was abolished; senator, rep., councillor; *m* 1752, Hannah Blake (*d* 1815; Increase[8], *m* Anne, dau. of Edward Gray; Dea. James[9]; Elder James[10]; William[11]);
6–Ann (1753-1812), *m* 1771, Capt. Joseph **Peirce** (1745-1828), founder and 2d capt. of the Grenadiers (Isaac[7], *m* Mary, dau. of Joseph Hardy, Isaac[8]; Samuel[9]; Thomas[10]; Thomas[11]);
5–Maj. Joseph Hardy (*b* 1773), *m* Frances Temple Cordis;
4–Col. Constantius (1801-39), of Boston; on duty at Baton Rouge, La., 1822; entered army as capt. of vols. under Gen. Houston in the War for the indepedence of Texas; *m* 1823, Mary Lintot Steer (1800-34);
3–Frances Temple (*b* 1826), *m* Bertrand **Haralson** (3 above).
10–Richard **Russel** (qv);
9–James (1640-1709), Charleston; freeman, 1668; rep., 1679; asst., 1680-86; councillor, 1692; judge; treas.; mem. A. and H.A. Co.; *m* 3d or 4th, 1684, Abigail (Curwen) Hawthorne;
8–Daniel (1685-1763), councillor 20 yrs.; treas. of Middlesex 50 yrs.; *m* 1710/11, Rebecca Chambers (*d* 1729);
7–Richard, *m* 1744, Mary Cary;
6–Rebecca Chambers (1746/47-1800), *m* 1770, Capt. Joseph Temple **Cordis** (*b* 1743);
5–Francis Temple (1776-1815), *m* 1791, Maj. Joseph Hardy **Peirce** (5 above).
10–Richard **Martyn** (*d* 1694), a founder of 1st ch. at Portsmouth, N.H., 1672; rep., 1672-79; speaker of house; councillor of province, 1680;
9–Michael (*b* 1667), of N.H.;
8–Mary, *m* 1722, as his 2d wife, Samuel **Cary** (*d* 1740, aet. 58);
7–Mary (1725-86), *m* 1744, Richard **Russel** (7 above).
9–James **Dashiell** (*b* 1634), from Eng. to Northumberland Co., Va.; surveyor of highways; judge of one of the commns. of the Quorum, 1694; burgess; *m* 1659, Ann Cannon;
8–Thomas (1666-1755), *m* 1686, Elizabeth Mitchell;
7–Col. George (1690-1748), colonial wars; *m* Elizabeth Fairfax;
6–George (*b* 1743), *m* 1760, Rose Fisher;
5–Rev. George (1770-1832), *m* 1791, Ester Handy;
4–Dr. Addison (1797-1847), *m* 1832, Anna C. O. Percy;
3–Rosa E. (1833-67), *m* Dr. Patterson Venable **Whicher** (*d* 1893);
2–Jennie Percy Dashiell (2 below).
6–Charles **Percy** (*b* in Eng. or Ireland-*d* 1794), *m* 1st, 1761, Margret– (*b* in Eng. or Ireland, 1745-*d* in London, 1785);
5–Robert (*b* in Ireland 1762), entered the British Navy and was promoted to lt., 1783, for gallant conduct nr. Quebec during Am. Rev., promoted to capt. after active service; came to U.S., 1802; *m* in Eng., Jane Middlemist (1772-1831);
4–Anna Christina O'Connor (1812-77), *m* Dr. Addison **Dashiell** (4 above);

3–Rosa Ester, *m* Dr. Patterson Venable **Whicher** (3 above);
2–Jennie Percy Dashiell (*b* 1864), *m* 1887, Bertrand **Haralson** (*b* 1860).
1–*m* June 30, 1914, LeRoy Highfill, *b* Fairgrove, Mo., Aug. 7, 1889; son of William Richard Highfill; issue: 1–Mary Haralson Rumble, *b* Natchez, Miss., July 19, 1915; 2–Jean Percy, *b* Gainesville, Fla., Dec. 28, 1918.
1–Mem. D.A.R. Residence: Cocoa, Fla.

1–**HILL, John Arthur,** *b* nr. Carrollton, O., June 10, 1880.
5–James **Hill** (1773-1839), moved from New York or Md. to Lee Tp., Carroll Co., O.; *m* Nancy– (1781-1837);
4–John (1802-77), farmer, Lee Tp.; *m* 1825, Rebecca Drake (1808-71);
3–Cheeseman (1830-1858-60), farmer, Lee Tp., *m* 1853, Eliza Jane Bothwell (1833-1915; George[4] [1781-1874], *b* in North Ireland, *m* 2d, Jane Armstrong, 1788?-1865);
2–James Ross (2 below).
5–Aaron **Marshall,** said to have lived at Pughtown (now in W.Va.);
4–Joshua (*d* 1876), farmer, Washington Tp., Carroll Co., O.; *m* 1820, Mary Roudebush (1803-1900; Tobias[5], *m* Sarah–);
3–Clark (1821-90), *m* Elizabeth Bartholemew (1823-90; George[4] [1798-1891], farmer, Carroll and Jefferson cos., O.);
2–Mary Eliza (1856-95), *m* 1879, James Ross **Hill** (1857-1926), farmer; issue: I–John Arthur (1 above); II–Alvah Leroy (*b* 1881; *m* 1909, Clara Mertis McCausland); III–Mabel Lunette (1884-99); IV–Robert Clark (*b* 1885; *m* 1920, Nettie Magee); V–Harry Harrison (*b* 1888; *m* 1916, Natalie West Berry); VI–Elizabeth Jane (*b* 1890); VII–Inez Mary (*b* 1891; *m* 1921, Jesse Johnson); VIII–Scott Marshall (*b* 1894; *m* 1921, Olive Magee).
1–*m* June 30, 1911, Evelyn Corthell, *b* Laramie, Wyo., May 4, 1886; dau. of Nellis Eugene Corthell, of Laramie; issue (all *b* Laramie, Wyo.): 1–Robert Morris, *b* May 15, 1912; 2–John Marshall, *b* May 17, 1913; 3–Ross Corthell, *b* Mar. 30, 1915; 4–Nellis Eugene, *b* Nov. 3, 1919; 5–Evelyn, *b* Aug. 10, 1921.
1–B.S., U.Wyo., '07 (Phi Kappa Phi, Lambda Gamma Delta). Spl. work in wool, Phila. Textile Sch., 1907; wool specialist, U.Wyo. Expt. Sta., since 1907; prof. textile industry, Wyo. Agrl. Coll., since 1912; dean Agrl. Coll. and dir. Expt. Sta., U.Wyo., since 1923 (see Who's Who in America). Capt. 166th Depot Brig., World War; capt. inf., O.R.C., U.S.A., 1919-22; maj. inf. sect. O.R.C., U.S.A., 1922-30; promoted lt. col. Inf. Reserves, U.S.A., Jan. 24, 1930. Republican. Clubs: Lions, American College, Quill. Residence: 264 N. 9th St., Laramie, Wyo.

1–**HOLSTEIN, Otto,** *b* Lexington, Ky., Jan. 14, 1883.
9–Edward **Gilman** (qv);
8–Lt. John (1626-1708), selectman; mem. 1st Provincial Council of N.H.; mem. Assembly, 1693-1697 (speaker 1693); judge Provincial Court; *m* 1657, Elizabeth Treworgye (1639-1719; James[9]);
7–John, II (1677-1748), original settler of Gilmanton, N.H.; chmn. 1st bd. of selectmen; capt., maj., and col. in Indian wars; moderator Ref. Gen. Assembly; *m* 1st, Elizabeth Coffin;
6–John (*b* 1712), lt., capt., and maj., N.H. forces; *m* Jane Deane (Dr. Thomas[7]);
5–Thomas (1747-1823), *m* Elizabeth Roberts (Rev. Daniel[6], grad. Harvard, 1725, pastor at Exeter);
4–Nathaniel Clark (*b* 1779), *m* Sarah Goodwin;
3–Oscar Fitzgerald (*b* 1815), *m* Belinda H. Fox;
2–Emilie Octavia, *m* Captain Otto **Holstein,** U.S.A., breeder of fine horses.
1–*m* Aug. 20, 1911, Esther San Martin, *b* at Lima, Peru, S.A., Sept. 16, 1896; dau. José J. San Martin (Spanish ancestry), of Lima, *m* Maria, dau. Luis Frayssenet, French soldier Franco-German War of 1870, German captive who escaped and fled from France to Peru; issue: 1–Otto, III, *b* Lima, Peru, Aug. 31, 1912; 2–Esther (*b* in Ecuador, Sept. 10, 1913, *d* San Antonio, Texas, May 10, 1914); 3–Marion, *b* El Paso, Tex., Dec. 15, 1916.
1–Railway and transportation expert. Lt., Philippine Constabulary, Philippine Insurrection; served 2 yrs. as officer and instr., Chinese Imperial Army at Hankow; organized and trained Field Co. A, Signal Corps (afterwards part of 10th Provisional Div.), for service on Mexican border; provost marshal at Lexington, Ky., during World War mobilization; made cdr. H.Q. Detachment, 63d F.A. Brig., later brig. communications and intelligence officer, then brig. adj. and instr. sch. for communications and liaison; served in France; after Armistice asst. chief transportation officer dist. of Paris; on spl. duty in Balkans with rank of capt.; mustered out as maj., Mil. Int. Sect., O.R.C.; now asst. G-2, Gen. Staff, 12th A.C., 2d Corps Area, with permission of indefinite absence from U.S. Col. and a.-d.-c. on staff of gov. of Ky., 1930. Prof. extraordinary of geography, Faculty of Philosophy and Letters, Nat. U. of Mexico. Decorated: Cdr. Order of Prince Danilo (Montenegro); Cdr. with star Order St. Stanislaus (Russia); Cdr. Order Polonia Restituta (Poland); Officer Order of St. Sava (Serbia); Croix de Guerre (Czecho-Slovakia, 2 awards), gold medal (Montenegro), Medalla de la Solidaridad (Panama), Fatiche de Guerra and Medaglia de Italia Unita (Italy). Mem. S.C., S.W. 1812, Aztec Club of 1847; fellow Royal Geog. Soc. (London), and of the principal geog. socs. of Europe and America; corr. academician of the Real Academia Hispano Americana de Ciencias y Artes de Cadiz, 1930. Clubs: Royal Societies (London), Circle National des Armees de Terre et de Mer (of Paris), Ends of the Earth, Explorers, Army and Navy. Address: Apartado Postal 1833, City of Mexico, Mex.

1–**HOOK, James William,** *b* Wapello Co., nr. Hedrick, Ia., Jan. 9, 1884.
8–Thomas (Hooke) **Hook** (ca. 1655-1697 or 98), from Eng., settled at Annapolis, Md., 1668; *m* ca. 1679, Annaple– (ca. 1658-ca. 1720);
7–James (ca. 1680-1738), of Prince George Co., Md.; began to write name Hook; a founder of Rock Creek Parish of the Episcopal Ch. in Md., 1719; *m* 1706, Margaret Thrasher (ca. 1686-ca. 1750; Benjamin[8]);
6–John (ca. 1718-1762), a founder of All Saints' Parish, Frederick Co., Md., 1742; *m* 1748, Sarah Simpson (ca. 1724-ca. 1798);
5–James (1749-1824), Greene Co., Pa.; capt. in colonial militia of Va.; transferred to Cont. Line as capt. in 13 Va. regts., 1776; served throughout Am. Rev.; *m* 1769, Mary Leith (1743-1815);
4–Stephen (1780-1856), Perry Co., O.; *m* 1803, Anne Subah Grant (1780-1816?; Capt. Noah[5], *m* 1st, Anne Richardson);
3–James Grant (1805-84), moved with family to Wapello Co., Ia., from Vinton Co., O., in covered wagon, 1865; *m* 1826, Sarah Lyle (1807-82; William[4]; John[5]; John[6]; James[7]; John[8]);
2–James (2 below).
7–Christian **Eller** (ca. 1724-1804), from Germany, settled in Lancaster Co., Pa., 1747; removed to Rowan Co., N.C., nr. Salisbury; *m* Mary Beefle (Paul[8]);
6–George (ca. 1745-1805), of Grayson Co., Va.; *m* ca. 1765, Christina (?) Bullen;
5–John (1769-1823), of Wilkes Co., N.C.; *m* 1792, Susanna Kerns (1766-1853), of Rowan Co.;
4–Simeon (1794-1850), capt. Wilkes Co. militia; *m* 1817, Fanny McNiel (1799-1856; James[5], *m* Mary Shepherd; Rev. George[6], from Scotland, 1750, founder of Baptist ch. in western N.C., chaplain in army of Col. Benjamin Cleveland, present at battle of Kings Mtn.; *m* 1754, Mary Coats);
3–Harvey (1819-1906), moved with family to Wapello Co., Ia., from Wilkes Co., N.C., in covered wagon, 1852; *m* 1841, Mary Caroline Vannoy (1823-1904; Jesse[4], *m* Mary–; Nathaniel[5]; John[6]);
2–Virginia (1845-97), of Wapello Co., Ia.; *m* 1867, James **Hook** (1839-1905), of Wapello Co.; enlisted 1861, 18th Ohio Vol. Inf., discharged Aug. 28, 1861; re-enlisted Sept. 9, 1862, 7th Ohio Vol. Cav., served thruout the war as mem. of Hospital Corps and as a dispatch carrier; issue: I–John (*b* 1870; *m* Jennie Lentner); II–Orin (*b* 1872; *m* Pearl Richards; *m* 2d, Idylmarch [Rockwell] Naugle); III–Wallace (*b* 1874; *m* Isis L. Edwards); IV–Sarah (*b*

1876; *m* Henry Edgar Passig); V–James William (1 above); VI–M. Glen (*b* 1889; *m* Elizabeth Clark).
1–*m* Sept. 17, 1907, Hattie Rosemond Bechtel, *b* Fort Dodge, Ia., Dec. 16, 1886; dau. of Carl Phillip Bechtel; issue (all *b* Marshalltown, Ia.): 1–James Phillip (Jan. 23, 1911-Mar. 15, 1911); 2–James William, Jr., *b* May 30, 1912; 3–Rose Virginia, *b* May 23, 1914.
1–B.M.E., Ia. State Coll., '05 (Kappa Sigma, Tau Beta Pi), M.E., 1912. Editor and mgr., Cody (Wyo.) Enterprise, 1905-06; engr. Globe Mchy. & Supply Co., Des Moines, Ia., 1906-09; sales mgr. and gen. mgr., C. A. Dunham Co., Marshalltown, Ia., 1909-16; pres. and dir. Allied Mchy. Co. of America, 1916-23; pres. The Geometric Tool Co., New Haven, Conn., since 1923; dir. and chmn. exec. com., Acme Wire Co.; dir. and mem. exec. com., First Nat. Bank & Trust Co., New Haven. Mem. Bd. of Edn., Tarrytown, N.Y., 1922-23; mayor's advisory air bd., New Haven, 1926-29; mem. from Conn., N.E. Council. Mem. S.C.W., Md. Hist. Soc., New Haven Hist. Soc. Republican. Clubs: Engrs., Machinery (N.Y.), Graduates, Lawn, Quinnipiack, Dissenters, New Haven Country. Residence: 98 Cold Spring St., New Haven, Conn.

1–**HOOTON, Mary Beidler Camp (Mrs. Ernest A.),** *b* Chicago, Ill., Aug. 11, 1889.
10–Edward **Frisbie** (*d* 1690), of Branford, Conn.; *m* Hannah (Culpepper ?);
9–John (1650-94), *m* Ruth Bowers (1657-1736; Rev. John[10], *m* Rebecca, dau. of Thomas Gregson);
8–John (1676-1736), of Branford; *m* Susanna Henbury (*d* 1767); Arthur[9]);
7–Israel (1709-87), *m* Elizabeth Grannis (1708-60; John[8], *m* Elizabeth Brockett; Edward[9]);
6–Lt. Jonah, or Jonas (*b* 1734), Am. Rev.; *m* 1758, Elizabeth Hickox;
5–Elizabeth (*b* 1761), *m* as his 2d wife, Heth **Camp** (bap. 1735-*d* 1800); see Vol. III, p. 253, for Camp lineage;
4–Heth Frisbie (1792-1849), *m* 1818, Phoebe Bates;
3–Ebenezer (1825-1909), *m* 1852, Frances E. Waller; see Vol. II, p. 304, for Waller lineage;
2–Arthur Bates (2 below).
12–Edward (Hyccocks, Hickocks, Hickox, Hickok) **Hickox** (*b* ca. 1562), of the "Landed Gentry," being addressed as Esquire; granted the right to "bear arms";
11–Thomas (ca. 1585-1611), *m* 1600, Elizabeth Sturley;
10–William (*b* 1609), wrote name Hickocks; from Eng. in the "Plaine Joan," 1635; "after remaining in N.E. for some years, returned to his family estates in Warwickshire and spent the remainder of his days as a justice of the peace"; *m* Elizabeth– (*d* 1655);
9–Sgt. Samuel (ante Feb. 28, 1638-1694), wrote name Hickox; at Farmington, 1673; an original settler of Waterbury; townsman, 1682; *m* Hannah Upson (Thomas[10], *m* Elizabeth Fuller);
8–Stephen (1684-1727/28), Durham; *m* Ruth Gaylord;
7–Samuel (*b* Durham, Conn., 1712), *m* Hannah–;
6–Elizabeth (bap. Sept. 17, 1738), *m* Jonah, or Jonas **Frisbie** (6 above).
11–William **Gaylord** (qv);
10–Walter (1622-89), of Windsor, Conn.; *m* Mary Stebbins (*d* 1657); *m* 2d, 1658, Sarah Rockwell (1638-83);
9–Joseph (1649-1742), Durham; *m* Sarah Stanley (*b* 1652; John[10], *m* Sarah Scott);
8–Ruth, *m* Stephen **Hickox** (8 above).
11–James **Bates** (qv);
10–James (1624-92), Haddam, Conn.; dep. Gen. Ct.; *m* Ann Withington (Henry[11], of Dorchester);
9–Samuel (1648-99), of Saybrook, Conn.; *m* 1676, Mary Chapman (Robert[10], *m* Ann Bliss);
8–James (1683-1718), began to write name Bates; *m* Hannah, or Anna Bull (*b* 1687), moved to Durham, Ct.;
7–James (*b* 1715), *m* Mary Curtis (*b* 1717; James[8], *m* Hannah Coe; Benjamin[9]; John[10]);
6–James (*b* 1740), *m* Ann Guernsey (*b* 1748; Ebenezer[7], *m* Rhoda–; Joseph[8]; Joseph[9]; John[10], of Milford);
5–Daniel (*b* 1769), *m* Anne Smithson (*b* 1771; Robert[6], *m* Phebe–; William[7]);
4–Phoebe (1792-1845), *m* Heth Frisbie **Camp** (4 above);
3–Ebenezer, *m* Frances E. Waller (3 above);
2–Arthur Bates (1860-1906), A.B., Lafayette, '84; lawyer; *m* 1887, Emma Beidler; see Vol. II, p. 304, for other lineages and issue.
1–*m* June 3, 1915, Ernest Albert Hooton, *b* Clemensville, Wis., Nov. 20, 1887 (see Who's Who in America); son of William Hooton, from Eng. to Randolph, Wis., 1883, M.E. minister; issue: 1–Jay Camp, *b* Boston, Mass., Jan. 26, 1918; 2–William Newton, *b* Chicago, Ill., June 15, 1920; 3–Emma Beidler, *b* Boston, June 24, 1924.
1–B.A., Smith Coll., 11. Life mem. I.A.G., N.E.H.G.S. Residence: 13 Buckingham St., Cambridge, Mass.

FAY

Arms: *Argent, six roses gules, three, two and one.*
Crest: *A cubit arm in armour embowed holding a dagger.*

1–**HURLBURT, Harriet Isabella Dodd (Mrs. Frederick B.),** *b* Boston, Mass., Sept. 30, 1869.
8–Dolor **Davis** (qv);
7–Samuel (1639/40-ante 1720), Concord, Mass.; *m* 1660 or 66?, Mary (Meads, Meddowes, Medow) Mead (*d* 1710);
6–Lt. Simon (1683-1763), early settler at Rutland, Mass.; later a founder of Holden, Mass.; moderator of 1st ten assemblies, Holden; *m* Dorothy Hale (1692-1776);
5–Rev. Joseph (1720-99), A.B., Harvard, 1740, A.M.; 1st pastor at Holden; *m* 1742, Catherine Jones (1721-1815; Capt. James[6], *m* Sarah Moore; Josiah[7], *m* Lydia, dau. Nathaniel Treadway; Simon[8], *m* Anna, dau. Dea. Simon Stone, qv);
4–Lemuel (July 14, 1756 or 1765?-1828), *m* 1788, Eunice Sherwin (1766-1818; Elnathan[5], *m* Eunice Brown);
3–Eliza (*b* 1797), *m* 1823, Benjamin **Dodd**;
2–William Goodell (2 below).
7–John **Fay** (qv);
6–Capt. John (1669-1747), dea. Congl. Ch., Westboro, 1727; 1st town clk.; selectman many terms; town treas., 1722; assessor; magistrate; *m* 1690, Elizabeth Wellington (1673-1729; Benjamin[7], *m* Elizabeth Sweetman);
5–Capt. Benjamin (1712-77), of Westboro; town treas., 1742-43,66-68; selectman 5 terms; comd. co. during French and Indian War; *m* 2d, 1765, Elizabeth (Hapgood) Stow (1725-84; Capt. Thomas Hapgood[6], of Shrewsbury, Mass.);
4–Col. Joel (1769-1830), *m* 1788, Hannah Rice Wood (*d* 1860; Dr. Joseph[5], *m* Martha Willard);
3–Charles Madison (*b* 1808), *m* Mary C. L. Montague;
2–Eliza Dodd (2 below).
10–Peter **Montague,** of Boveney Parish, Burnham, Buckinghamshire, Eng.; *m* Eleanor Allen (William[11], of Boveney Parish);
9–Richard (qv);
8–John (ca. 1655-ca. 1732), of Wethersfield, Conn.; settled at Hadley, Mass.; selectman, 1697; *m*

MONTAGUE

Arms: Quarterly, first argent, three fusils conjoined in fess gules, between three pellets sable; second, a griffin rampant; third, three legs in armour, conjoined at the thighs flexed in triangle; fourth, three fusils conjoined in fess of the second.
Crest: A griffin's head erased.

1681, Hannah Smith (*b* 1662; Chileab[9], of Hadley, *m* Hannah, dau. Luke Hitchcock);
7–Dea. Samuel (1695-1779), early settler at Sunderland; mem. of Mass. Provincial Congress; selectman; capt. militia; *m* Elizabeth White (John[8]);
6–Daniel (1725-1804), Am. Rev.; his home in Sunderland now occupied by his g.g.g.son Richard Montague; *m* 1750, Lydia Smith (Nathaniel[7]);
5–Medad (1755-1837), Am. Rev.; selectman; rep. Mass. Legislature; *m* Ruth Dinsmore;
4–Zebina (1789-1819), Grafton, Mass.; *m* Catharine Davis (Lemuel, 4 above);
3–Mary Catherine Lowden (*b* 1815), *m* Charles Madison **Fay** (3 above);
2–Eliza Dodd (1837-1913), *m* 1857, William Goodell **Dodd** (*d* 1869), paying teller of bank in Boston; issue: I–Helen Bigelow (1858-1902); II–Mary (1863-67); III–Harriet Isabella (1 above).
1–*m* Apr. 22, 1890, Frederick Butler Hurlburt (Dec. 10, 1867-July 24, 1925); son of Henry O. Hurlburt, of Honesdale, Pa.
1–Served with Nat. League for Women's Service, Navy Yard Canteen, Phila., during World War. Clubs: Phila. Art Alliance, Print, Women's Republican, Pa. Soc. N.E. Women, Le Coin d'Or. Summer place: Cove Cottage, Orr's Island, Me. Residence: 621 W. Hortter St., Germantown, Phila., Pa.

1–**HOLMES, Samuel Judd**, *b* New York, N.Y., Oct. 18, 1859.
9–John **Bronson** (qv);
8–Isaac (1645-1719), a first settler at Woodbridge, N.J., 1667; *m* 1669, Mary Root (*d* 1719; John[9], qv);
7–Samuel (*b* 1676/77);
6–Mercy (*d* 1737), *m* 1731, John **Judd** (see Vol. III, p. 236);
5–Samuel (1734-1825), capt. Am. Rev.; *m* 1763, Obedience Hopkins;
4–Sarah (1771-1821), *m* 1793, Israel **Holmes** (1768-1802), see Vol. II, p. 163 for Holmes lineage;
3–Samuel Judd (1794-1867), *m* 1822, Lucina Todd;
2–Samuel (2 below).
9–John **Hopkins** (1613-54), Cambridge, Mass., 1634; *m* Jane Strong (John[10], qv);
8–Stephen (1634-89), of Hartford; *m* Dorcas Bronson (John[9], qv);
7–Ebenezer (1669-1711), *m* 1691, Mary Butler (1670-1744; Samuel[8] [1639-92]; Richard[9], qv);
6–Isaac (1708-65), of Waterbury; *m* 1732, Mercy Hickox (*d* 1790; Dea. Thomas[7]; Sgt. Samuel[8]; William[9]; Thomas[10]);
5–Obedience (1737-1810), *m* Samuel **Judd** (5 above).
9–William **Ives** (qv);
8–Joseph (1648-94), *m* Mary Yale (*b* 1650; Thomas[9], qv);
7–Samuel (1677-1726), *m* Ruth Atwater (1688-1758; Jonathan[8], *m* Ruth Peck; David[9], qv);
6–Mary, *m* Caleb **Todd** (1700-37; Samuel[7]; Samuel[8]; Christopher[9], qv);
5–Hezekiah (*b* 1728), *m* Lydia Frost (Ebenezer[6]);
4–Hezekiah (1755-1836), of Cheshire, Conn.; *m* Mercy Holt (Joseph[5]; Samuel[6]; Joseph[7]; John[8]; William[9], qv);
3–Lucina (1796-1876), *m* Samuel Judd **Holmes** (3 above).
9–Humphrey **Bush** (1592-1662), from Eng. to Concord, Mass., ca. 1640;
8–John (*d* 1711), *m* 1662, Mary Pond;
7–Abiel, *m* 1688, Grace Barrett (1669-1739);
6–Grace (1696-1770), *m* 1718, Peter **Howe** (1695-1778; John[7]; John[8]; John[9], qv);
5–Rebecca (*b* 1728), *m* 1747, Eliakim **Howe** (1723-ca. 1800; Jonathan[6]; Thomas[7]; John[8], qv);
4–Mary (1757-1818), *m* 1779, Abner **Goodale** (1755-1823), Am. Rev. (Nathan[5]; John[6]);
3–David (1791-1858), *m* 1819, Millicent Warren;
2–Mary Howe (1829-1900), *m* 1856, Samuel **Holmes** (1824-97); for portrait, issue and other lineages, see Vol. III, p. 236.
1–*m* Mar. 18, 1886, Sarah Josephine Brautigam, *b* Jersey City, N.J., Oct. 14, 1860; dau. of Jacob Castor Brautigam, of Montclair, N.J., *m* Mary J. Nichols (*b* Eng.); issue (all *b* Montclair, N.J.): 1–Charles Samuel, *b* Dec. 23, 1886; Cornell, '10; *m* Feb. 19, 1913, Else Marie, dau. of Frederick Kraemer, of Brooklyn, N.Y. (issue: Mary Elsie, *b* 1913; Millicent Warren, *b* 1916; Winifred Kraemer, *b* 1919; Josephine Anne, *b* 1927); 2–Arthur Brautigam, *b* Oct. 1, 1888; Cornell, '11; *m* Sept. 23, 1916, Alice Blanche (1891-1918), dau. of Joseph W. Connelly (issue: Blanche Josephine, *b* 1918); *m* 2d, Nov. 27, 1923, Zillah De Lamater, dau. of Charles Vezin, of Yonkers, N.Y. (issue: Adah De Lamater, *b* 1924); 3–Warren Goodale, *b* Oct. 15, 1890; served pvt. to 1st sgt., 104th M.P. Co., 29th Div., 3d A.C., and with A.E.F. in France, 1918-19; *m* July 10, 1923, Harriet Fay, dau. of Louis R. Cobb, of Montclair, N.J. (issue: Kathryn Cobb, *b* 1924; Nancy Goodale, *b* 1926); 4–Ethel Josephine, *b* Jan. 6, 1897; *m* June 16, 1922, Adrien Tschudy von Schmid (issue: Patricia Hale, *b* 1924; John Goodale Tschudy, *b* 1928).
1–Mass. Agrl. Coll., '82. Realtor. Mem. S.A.R. Residence: 188 Park St., Montclair, N.J.

1–**HOPKINS, Walter Lee**, *b* Rocky Mount, Va., Dec. 26, 1889.
6–William **Hopkins** (*d* 1755), of New Kent Co., Va.; *m* Frances– (*d* 1755);
5–Francis (1737-1804), *m* 1760, Jane Cox (*d* 1815; Frederick[6], *m* Elizabeth–; Bartholomew[7], *m* Rebecca–; John[8], from Eng. to Va., 1642);
4–John (1775-1821), *m* 1800, Mary Turner;
3–Dr. William Leftwich Turner (1814-73), M.D., U. of Pa., 1838; *m* 1850, Julia Ann Muse;
2–William Leftwich Turner (2 below).
9–Ralph **Leftwich,** from Eng. to Va., patented lands in New Kent Co., Va., 1658;
8–Thomas (ca. 1660-ca. 1730), *m* 2d, ca. 1706, Mary North (Augustine[9], *m* Dorothy–);
7–Augustine (ca. 1712-1795), of Bedford Co., Va.;
6–Col. William (1737-1820), capt. in colonial and Indian wars; col. in Am. Rev.; *m* ca. 1757, Elizabeth Haynes (William[7], *m* Elizabeth–);
5–Sally (1762-1834), *m* Rev. James **Turner,** Presbyn. minister; soldier in Am. Rev. (Richard[6], *m* Nancy Johns; James[7]);
4–Mary (1779-1848), *m* 1800, John **Hopkins** (4 above).
8–John **Muse** (1633-1723), of Westmoreland Co., Va.;
7–John (1680-1722), of Westmoreland Co.; *m* Ann–;
6–John (ca. 1720-ante 1779), Westmoreland, Lancaster and Powhatan cos., Va.; *m* 1754, Frances Chattin;
5–Thomas (1757-1832), Pittsylvania Co.; *m* 1st, ca. 1781, Elizabeth Tidwell (1756-93);
4–Henry Lawson (1788-1845), Franklin Co.; mem. Gen. Assembly many yrs.; War 1812; *m* 1816, Elizabeth Swanson (1790-1866; William[5], *m* Ann–; William[6], *m* Mary McQuire);
3–Julia Ann (1824-1916), *m* 1850, Dr. William Leftwich Turner **Hopkins** (3 above).
6–John **Hancock** (ca. 1730-1802), of Goochland, Fluvanna and Patrick cos., Va.; *m* 1755, Elizabeth Madox (John[7], *m* Elizabeth–);
5–Lewis (1757-1828), of Fluvanna and Franklin cos.; *m* 1778, Celia (Duncan) Oglesby (George[6], capt. in Am. Rev.);
4–Benjamin (1782-1860), Franklin Co.; *m* 2d, 1817, Elizabeth Booth (1801-60; Col. Peter[5], *m* 1st, his 1st cousin, Elizabeth, dau. of George Booth; John[6]; Thomas[7]);

3–Col. Abram Booth (1825-1903), lt., Co. E, 57th Va. Regt. and col. 195th Va. Regt., C.S.A.; *m* 1847, Martha E. Walker;
2–Mary Ella (2 below).
6–Dudley **Glass** (*d* 1827), 2d lt., Capt. Milner's Co., Am. Rev.; *m* Frances Priddy (Prideaux); *m* 2d, Sally–;
5–Capt. John, of Halifax Co., Va., ca. 1800; moved to Franklin Co., 1815; *m* Maitland Simmons;
4–Frances Elizabeth (1807-97), *m* 1st, 1830, Moses **Walker** (1793-1833; Elisha[5], War 1812, *m* Judith, dau. of John Kirby, son of John Kirby, Am. Rev.);
3–Martha Elizabeth (1832-81), *m* Abram B. **Hancock** (3 above).
2–William Leftwich Turner **Hopkins** (*b* 1860), planter; *m* 1882, Mary Ella Hancock (1858-90); *m* 2d, 1895, Mary Ann Rebecca Smith (1864-1902); *m* 3d, Sallie Kathleen Stone (*b* 1875); issue (1st marriage): I–Dr. William Benjamin (*b* 1883; *m* Mary Conrad Nicholson); II–Oscar Leonidas (*b* 1886; *m* Ada Kirkland James); III–Abram Hancock (*b* 1888; *m* Catherine Walker Dabney Lee, grand-niece of Gen. Robert E. Lee); IV–Walter Lee (1 above); issue (2d marriage; I–Dr. Clack Dickinson (*b* 1896; *m* Mildred Carter Lee, grand-niece of Gen. Robert E. Lee); II–Mary Alma (*b* 1899; *m* David Bidwell Sabine); III–Annie Elizabeth (*b* 1900); IV–Lawson Muse (*b* 1901).
1–*m* Dec. 23, 1917, Alice Edington Peake, *b* Rocky Mount, Va., Dec. 31, 1898; dau. of Halifax Word Peake; issue: 1–Mary Edington, *b* Rocky Mount, Va., Mar. 8, 1919.
1–A.B., Washington and Lee U., '12, LL.B., 1914 (Kappa Chi, Theta Nu Epsilon, Phi Alpha Delta). Atty.-at-law. Sgt. Co. K, 318th Regt., 8th Div., Apr. 19, 1918, transferred to 155th Depot Brig. commd. 2d lt. of inf., June 1, 1918, transferred to inf. replacement and training camp at Camp Lee; transferred to Adj. Gen.'s office, Washington, where he was head of a dept. in the cable section; discharged Mar. 10, 1919, with rank of 1st lt. of inf., O.R.C. Asso. mem. Bd. of Contract Adjustment, War. Dept., 1919-20. Mem. of Staff of Gov. John Garland Pollard. Mem. Richmond City, Virginia and Am. bar assns., S.C.W., S.R., S.A.R., S.C.V. (adj.-in-chief), Va. Hist. Soc., A.L. Mason (Shriner), Odd Fellow, Elk. Democrat. Episcopalian. Club: Westmoreland. Residence: 1122 West Av., Richmond, Va.

1–**HYDE, Theophilus Rodgers,** *b* Waterbury, Conn., Sept. 22, 1890.
9–William **Hyde** (qv);
8–Samuel (*b* 1637), Hartford, Conn.; *m* 1659, Jane Lee, of E. Saybrook (Thomas[9], from Eng., 1641, *m* —Brown);
7–Jabez (1677-1762), of Norwich, Conn.; rep. Gen. Ct.; *m* 1709, Elizabeth Bushnell (1686-1768; Richard[8], rep. Gen. Ct. 8 sessions, *m* Elizabeth Adgate);
6–Phinehas (*b* 1720), *m* 1744, Anne Rogers (1726-76; Dr. Theophilus[7], *m* Elizabeth Hyde);
5–Dr. Phinehas (1749-1820), surgeon in Am. Rev.; *m* 1782, Ester Holdridge (1766-1810; William[6], *m* Prudence Gavitt);
4–John (1783-1861), *m* 1808, Lucy Ann Burrows (1789-1844; Enoch[5], *m* Esther Denison);
3–Theophilus Rogers (1824-1906), of Mystic, Conn.; *m* 1850, Fanny Hazard Brown (1829-1909; Elnathan[4], *m* Frances Gardener Hazard);
2–Theophilus Rogers (1855-1907), asst. sec. Scoville Mfg. Co., Westerly, R.I.; *m* 1880, Jane Pelton Burdon (1857-1925); issue: I–Hazel (*m* Lewis Rumford); II–Burdon Pelton (*m* Lois Allerton); III–Elsie (*m* Dr. Dudley Guilford); IV–Theophilus Rodgers (1 above); V–Charles Carroll (*d* aet. 12).
1–*m* June 25, 1915, Marion Meigs, *b* Pottstown, Pa., Oct. 23, 1891; dau. of John Meigs, late headmaster of The Hill School, Pottstown, Pa.; issue: 1–Marion, *b* Pottstown, Pa., Jan. 30, 1917; 2–Elsie, *b* Pottstown, Dec. 18, 1921.
1–Ph.B. in Engring., Yale-S., 1912, M.A. in Education and Psychology, 1916. Educator since 1912; headmaster Chestnut Hill Acad., 1923-30, The Lakeside Country Day School, Seattle, 1930–. Holds aviation pilot's license (see Who's Who in America). Congregational. Republican. Clubs: Yale (New York), Yale, Nat. Aero. Assn., Philadelphia Cricket, Philadelphia Aero. Address: The Lakeside Country Day School, Seattle, Wash.

HYNSON

Arms: *Azure, within a bordure ermine, a chevron or, between three suns, in splendor of the last.*
Crest: *A fleur-de-lis per pale, ermine and azure.*

1–**HYNSON, W(illiam) George,** *b* Baltimore, Md., Mar. 8, 1872.
10–Lt. Thomas **Hynson** (qv);
9–Col. John (*d* 1705), of Kent Co., Md.; high sheriff; del. to Assembly; justice; vestryman, St. Paul's Parish; *m* Anne–;
8–Capt. John (*d* 1708), high sheriff, Cecil Co.; vestryman, St. Stephen's Parish; *m* 1693, Mary Storp (John[9]);
7–Col. Nathaniel (1697-1755), high sheriff, Cecil Co.; vestryman, St. Stephen's Parish; *m* Mary–;
6–John (1717-61), of Kent Co.; *m* Frances–;
5–Benjamin (*d* 1791), *m* Anne Ricketts (Nathaniel[6]);
4–Benjamin (1786-1832), *m* Mary Ann Crow; *m* 2d, Anne (Mansfield) Hollis;
3–Benjamin Thomas (1815-77), of Baltimore; *m* 1836, Elizabeth Simpson (1816-53);
2–William George (1840-82), mcht., Baltimore; *m* 1865, Anna Maria Dushane (1843-1904; Col. Nathan Thomas[8]).
1–*m* Oct. 4, 1902, Lucy Erskine Bains, *b* Phila., Pa., Mar. 29, 1879; dau. George B. Bains, Jr., of Phila.; issue: 1–William George, Jr., *b* Baltimore, Mar. 19, 1905; Yale, '28; *m* June 14, 1930, Grace, dau. of Ellis W. Gladwin, of Bronxville, N.Y.; 2–Richard, *b* Baltimore, Dec. 14, 1919.
1–V.p., treas., and dir., U.S. Fidelity & Guaranty Co.; dir. Lawyers Surety Co., N.Y.; Fidelity Ins. Co., Canada; The Del Mar Co. Mem. Md. League for Nat. Defense and Am. Protective League during World War. Mem. I.A.G., H.S.A., N.E.H.G.S., Md. Hist. Soc. Episcopalian. Clubs: Maryland, Elkridge, L'Hirondelle (Ruxton), Chesapeake, Churchmen's. Residence: Ruxton, Md.

1–**JACKS, Lile T. (Elias Thomas Jacks),** *b* Meadow Valley, Plumas Co., Calif., Mar. 26, 1877.
First Jackses named in Md. wills were Richard and Thomas Jacks, Jr., devisees in will of their step-brother, John Powell, Jr. (*d* 1715/16), of Anne Arundel Co., Md., whose mother Elizabeth, *m* Thomas Jacks, Sr.;
4–Richard **Jacks** (1772-1841), pioneer; of Silver

Creek, Madison Co., Ky., and Howard, Clay and Platte cos., Mo.; joined father of Gen. Christopher ("Kit") Carson and the Madison Co. colony in Howard Co., Mo., extreme w. settlement, 1817; moved to (now) Clay Co., Mo., then extreme w. settlement, 1821; before Indians' removal from Platte Purchase of Mo., with family, selected, 1835, and entered choice lands in E. Platte Co., and took possession 1837, before organization of Platte; *m* 1797, Sophia Barnes (Elias[6], Md. desc., of Madison Co., Ky., *m* Rebecca Turner); their g.son, Benjamin Jacks, was first white child *b* in Platte Co.;

3–Elias Barnes (1802-70), mcht.; large slaveholder and owner of 1,039 acres, including 678 acres of suburbs of Kansas City, Kan.; mem. Willock's Mo. Mounted Inf. in Mexican War; *m* Polly Warden (St. Clair[4], cousin of Maj. Gen. Arthur St. Clair, cdr.-in-chief, U.S.A., and gov. N.W. Ty.);

2–Richard (2 below).

7–Capt. Alexander **Dunlap** (qv);

6–Ens. Robert (1740-81), of "Aspen Grove," Rockbridge Co., Va.; furnished money for founding McConnell's Sta., in (now) Lexington, Ky., which estate was lost to g.children by decision of Ky. Ct. of Appeals, 1805; ens., killed or lost at battle of Guilford C.H., because he refused to obey orders of his half bro., Capt. (later Maj.) James Bratton, to retreat; *m* Mary Gay;

5–Maj. William (1767-1834), of "Aspen Grove"; *m* Elizabeth Coursey;

4–William (1797-1870), owner of Indian trading sta. in Kan.; one of first men to explore that state; received high respect and honors from Plains Indians; returned to Mo.; *m* Mary Hite;

3–Narcissus Coursey (1833-62), *m* James **Bell**;

2–Florence Fremont (2 below).

7–William **Gay** (ca. 1729-1755), of Gay's Run, Augusta (now Rockbridge) Co., Va.; from Ireland to Pa., thence to Augusta Co., with bros. Capt. John, James, Robert, Henry and Samuel and sister Elinor, who *m* Capt. William (Kincaid) Kinkead; William, *m* Margaret Walkup (*b* nr. Belfast, Ireland), sister of Capt. James Walkup, a cdr. at battle of Walkup's Plantation, N.C., in Am. Rev., *m* Margaret Pickens, aunt of Gov. Israel Pickens, of Ala., and also sister of Lt. John Walkup, cdr. of Warm Springs Ft., Va. frontier in Am. Rev., whose g.son was Joseph Walkup, lt.-gov. Calif., 1858-59;

6–Mary, *m* 1st, Robert **Dunlap** (6 above).

7–William **Riddell**, King and Queen and Orange cos., Va.; *m* Joice Powell (same family as Lt. Gen. Ambrose Powell Hill, C.S.A., and Brig. Gen. Abraham Buford, C.S.A., of "Bosque Bonita," cav. officer and distinguished southern racing man);

6–Winifred, *m* 1st, Capt. James **Coursey**, officer in Am. Rev., and owner 2,000 acres, Orange Co., Va.;

5–Elizabeth (1768-1851), *m* Maj. William **Dunlap** (5 above).

7–Blasius (Bär) **Bear**, from Germany to Pa., 1740, removed to Va., 1763; convert from Catholicism, becoming Mennonite minister; landholder, Conewago Creek, York Co., Pa., and Frederick (now Page) Co., Va.;

6–Jacob, owner of lands on Bratton's Run, Rockbridge Co.; *m* Elizabeth Blosser;

5–Esther (*b* 1781), *m* Rev. Daniel **Hite** (Daniel[6], of Shenandoah [now Page] Co., Va., *m* Apolonia Keller);

4–Mary (1802-89), *m* William **Dunlap** (4 above).

7–Peter (Blaser) **Blosser** (*b* ca. 1715), from Switzerland to France, thence to America, 1739; Mennonite leader and minister, York (now Springettsburg) Tp., York Co., Pa., and Blosserville, Shenandoah (now Page) Co., Va.;

6–Elizabeth, *m* Jacob **Bear** (6 above).

5–John **Bell**, of Germany; his issue were heirs to large German estate; *m* Miss McDaniel, of Ky.;

4–William (*d* 1846), pioneer, large landholder and slaveholder, of Camden Point, Platte Co., Mo.; *m* Sultana Clemently Duncan (Scotch desc. of S.C., and Mo. pioneer of 1817);

3–James (1831-1915), of Platte Co., Mo., and Fannin Co., Tex.; *m* 1st, Narcissus Coursey Dunlap (3 above);

2–Florence Fremont (*b* 1854; her niece, Lena Brinkers, *m* [John] Morgan Haun, g.nephew of Henry P. Haun, U.S. senator from Calif., 1859-60); *m* 1871, Richard **Jacks** (1831-99), owner of "Jacks Hill," "Missouri Flat" and "Golden Enterprise" goldmines; goldmining ditchowner, lumberman, inventor and landowner (including Jacks Meadows), of Plumas Co., Calif.; business associate of U.S. Senator George C. Perkins, of Calif.; Calif. pioneer of 1850, with Platte Co. Overland Company; issue: I–Doniphan Richard (*b* 1871; *m* 1st, 1898, Elizabeth Ellen Boyle; *m* 2d, 1909, Mary Ottilia Ramelli); II–Mary Elizabeth (*b* 1873; *m* 1893, Charles Russell Thompson); III–Solon Pattee (*b* 1875; *m* 1904, Rose Edna Self); IV–Lile T. (1 above); V–Florence Josephine (*b* 1879; *m* 1908, William Clarence Reynolds); VI–Andrew Robinson (*b* 1881; *m* 1910, Mary Emeline Arms); VII–Ruth Perkins (*b* 1884; *m* 1913, John Lewis Mathews); VIII–Agnes Georgia (*b* 1887; *m* 1st, 1906, [John] Thomas Loveless; *m* 2d, 1912, William Frederick Werner).

1–*m* Sept. 21, 1913, Ethel Augusta Kluver, *b* San Francisco, Calif., Nov. 28, 1890; dau. Henry Kluver, pres. Schleswig-Holstein Verein of San Francisco, *m* Emma Helena Rebecca, dau. of Henry Dobbel, Calif. pioneer from Germany, and owner of parts of "Rancho Canada de Verde y Arroyo de la Purisima" and "Rancho Miramontes," San Mateo Co., Calif., the third largest landowner in San Mateo Co., about 1880.

1–Ed. St. Ignatius Coll., San Francisco, and LL.B., Golden Gate Law Coll., 1908. Superior judge, lawyer and judicial reformer. Admitted to bar, 1908, and practiced in San Francisco. "Drafted" with Judge Sylvain Lazarus, as candidates for police judges of City and Co. of San Francisco, by Bar Assn. of San Francisco, at only recall election ever held in history of that city, to reform administration and intolerable condition of police cts., and after campaign conducted solely by Bar Assn., was elected, Mar. 1, 1921, police judge of City and Co. of San Francisco, and served unexpired term, 1921-23; reelected, 1923, and served for term, 1924-28; reelected 1927, receiving highest vote ever received by a candidate in a contested election in history of San Francisco, and served, 1928; resigned, 1928; elected 1928, superior judge for City and Co. of San Francisco, for term, 1929-35. Has delivered addresses before many bodies and organizations on reform and administration of criminal justice. Four-minute speaker in World War. Mason (32°, Shriner, Sciot). Mem. Sierra-Plumas Soc. (past pres.), Am. Calif. and San Francisco bar assns.; mem. L.O.M. (past dictator for San Francisco), Woodmen of World (past consul-cdr.), etc. Summer place: Yosemite, Calif. Residence: 650 Ulloa St., San Francisco, Calif.

1–**KIRTLEY, James Samuel,** *b* Saline Co., Mo., Nov. 9, 1855.

6–Francis **Kirtley** (*d* 1763), from Wales to Va., 1710; known among his neighbors as "Sir Francis"; merchant, Falmouth, Va.; owner of large tracts; res. nr. Great Forks of Rappahannock river (now Culpeper Co.), Va.; capt. militia, Spotsylvania Co., Va., 1729; capt. of foot, Spotsylvania Co. in French and Indian War, 1756, discharged at Winchester, Va.; vestryman, St. Mark's Ch., Culpeper Co.; *m* 1st, Miss James;

5–William (*d* 1795), justice of Culpeper Co., 1762, et seq.; *m* Sarah Early (g.g.aunt of Lt. Gen. Jubal A. Early, C.S.A.);

4–Jeremiah (1754-1806), pioneer of 1796, of Boone Co., Ky.; *m* Mary Robinson (John[6]), Jeremiah's sister, Margaret Kirtley, *m* Simeon Buford, and their son, Hon. John Buford, was father of Maj. Gen. Napoleon Bonaparte Buford, U.S.V., and Maj. Gen. John Buford, Jr., U.S.V.; Simeon and Margaret (Kirtley) Buford's son Col. William Buford, *m* Frances Walker Kirtley (g.dau. of Capt. Francis Kirtley, II [bro. of William, 5 above] and Elizabeth Powell), and their son was Brig.

Gen. Abraham Buford, C.S.A., of "Bosque Bonita";
3–Rev. Robert (1786-1872), minister; lt. in War 1812; *m* Mary Thompson (cousin of Col. Manlius V. Thompson, lt. gov. of Ky. [uncle of Maj. Gen. Gustavus W. Smith, C.S.A., Sec. of War of C.S.A.]);
2–Maj. George Robinson (2 below).
7–Robert **Huey** (ca. 1700-1770), French Huguenot descent, Lancaster Co., Pa.;
6–Samuel, Lancaster Co.; *m* Mrs. Russell;
5–Robert, of Pa., Va., Ky., and Dayton, O.; served in Am. Rev.; *m* Agnes Elliott;
4–Samuel (1771-1831), *m* Jane Mason (*b* Va.);
3–William (1798-1870), of Boone Co., Ky.; *m* 2d, Mary Bradford (g.dau. of Fielding Bradford, who with his bro. John, established and edited the Kentucky Gazette, first Ky. newspaper);
2–Hariett Elizabeth (1827-99), *m* 1846, Maj. George Robinson **Kirtley** (1824-63), maj. 5th Mo. Cav., C.S.A., killed while col. comdg. at battle of Hartville; farmer, surveyor; issue: I–Mary Pauline (1847-1924); II–Septimus (1849-51); III–William Robert (1851-1909; *m* 1886, Elizabeth Roland Gray); IV–(Harriett) Ella (1853-1914; *m* 1873, Henry Clay Duncan); V–James Samuel (1 above); VI–Anne Elizabeth (*b* 1858); VII–Georgia Robinson (*b* 1860).
1–*m* Mar. 2, 1897, Mary Louise Kniffin, *b* Sedalia, Mo., Apr. 21, 1876; dau. Sylvester Westerfield Kniffin, lt., Union Army; issue: 1–George Sylvester, *b* Little Rock, Ark., Jan. 24, 1898; ed. William Jewell Coll., and Washington U., St. Louis, Mo.; *m* June 22, 1929, Margaret, dau. of Capt. Peter William Wey, U.S.A., retired; 2–Mary Adelaide, *b* Kansas City, Mo., Mar. 15, 1900; ed. U. of Chicago, and U. of Washington; 3–Bess Harriet, *b* Kansas City, June 23, 1901; Ph.B., U. of Chicago.
1–A.B., Georgetown (Ky.) Coll., '83 (D.D., 1894); studied Southern Bapt. Theol. Sem. and U. of Chicago. Minister for stronger churches of Baptist denomination since 1879; ad interim minister since 1917. Author. Trustee Shurtleff Coll., Alton, Ill., and Ouachita Coll., Ark. Club: Torch (see Who's Who in America). Residence: 1166 E. 54th Pl., Chicago, Ill.

1–**JACKSON, Jesse Benjamin,** *b* Paulding, O., Nov. 19, 1871.
5–Edward **Jackson,** of N.J.; *m* Martha Miller;
4–William (1777-1857), of Harrison Co., W. Va.; *m* 1789, Hannah Bennett;
3–Benjamin Basil (1821-1902), Antwerp, O.; sgt., Co. G, 14th Ohio Vol. Inf., 1861-65; *m* 1840, Elizabeth J. Champion (1823-1913);
2–Andrew Carl (1842-1923), of Paulding, O.; musician Co. G, 14th Ohio Vol. Infantry, 1861-5; school teacher; dep. co. clk; printer; *m* 5 times; *m* 1st, 1869, Lucy Anne Brown (1844-93; Elijah Jesse[3] [1818-ca. 1896], of nr. Paulding, O.; *m* ca. 1840, Mary Diantha Griffin [ca. 1820-ca. 1890], from Conn. and Mass.); issue: I–Jesse Benjamin (1 above); II–Coe Griffin (*b* 1874; *m* Rachel Onda Dines); (4 others *d* infancy).
1–*m* June 22, 1898, Rosebelle Berryman (Oct. 25, 1873-Jan. 11, 1928); dau. of Abram Berryman; issue: 1–Virgil Allen, *b* Paulding, O., June 18, 1900; attended British Mission School, Alexandretta, Syria, 1905-08; Franciscan Coll., Aleppo, Syria, 1908-15; Culver (Ind.) Mil. Acad., 1916-18; Miami Coll., Oxford, O., 1918-19; Kenyon Coll., Gambier, O., 1920-21; Ohio State U., 1921-24 (Delta U.); *m* Sept. 1924, Marguerite, dau. of Rev. L. S. Wees, of Urichsville, O. (issue: Jack Jesse; James Allen).
1–Engaged in real estate, mortgage loan and insurance, 1893-1905; enrolling clk., Ohio House of Rep., 1900-01; consul at Alexandretta, Syria, Turkey, 1905-08, Aleppo, Syria, 1908-23, Leghorn, Italy, 1923-28, Ft. William-Port Arthur, Ont., Can., since 1928 (see Who's Who in America). Q.M. sgt., 2d Ohio Vol. Inf., 1898-99, service in Cuba, in Spanish-Am. War. Decorated Officer of Order of Crown of Italy, 1922. Received with wife by Pope Pius XI in throne room of Vatican, June 1923. Mason. Methodist. Republican. Club: Fort William Tennis. Address: American Consulate, Fort William, Ont., Can.

1–**JENNINGS, W(illiam) Beatty,** *b* Bennettsville, S.C., Sept. 26, 1859.
7–Charles **Jennings** (*d* 1705), from Eng.; clk. of Elizabeth City Co., Va.; *m* 1680, Mary– (1651-1710);
6–Charles (1680-1747), *m* 2d, Jane Latimer (Edward[7]);
5–Col. John (1702-85), acting clk. of Elizabeth City Co., 1744; lived in Lunenburg Co., 1764; moved to Anson, N.C., 1774; high sheriff; *m* Lydia Batts (Thomas[6]);
4–Maj. John (*d* 1806), high sheriff of Anson Co., 1798; *m* Elizabeth Lanier;
3–Dr. Edmund (1792-1863), of Wadesboro, N.C.; *m* 1st, Isabella Beatty (1797-1824; Jonathan[4], of Yorkville, N.C.);
2–Dr. Jonathan Beatty (2 below).
10–John **Flood** (*d* 1661), to Va., in the "Swann," 1610; rep. Gen. Assembly, 1630,32,42,45; Charles City, 1638; capt.; Indian interpreter; lt. col., Surry Co.; in legislature, 1652-55; *m* ante 1625, Widow Margaret Finch;
9–Mary, *m* 1658, John **Washington** (1633-1719), from Eng., 1650 or 60, to Surry Co., Va.;
8–Richard (ca. 1660-1725), *m* Elizabeth Jordan (*d* ca. 1735; Arthur[9], *m* Elizabeth Baron);
7–Elizabeth, *m* Sampson **Lanier** (1682-1743; John[8], qv);
6–Sampson (1712-57), vestryman, St. Andrew's Parish; justice; high sheriff, Brunswick Co.; *m* 1740 or 42, Elizabeth Chamberlain (*d* 1749; Samuel[7]);
5–Burwell (*d* 1812), *m* 1st, Elizabeth Hill;
4–Elizabeth (*d* 1824), *m* Maj. John **Jennings** (4 above);
3–Dr. Edmund, *m* Isabella Beatty (3 above);
2–Dr. Jonathan Beatty (1817-89), of Bennettsville, S.C.; physician; *m* Sally McCully (John[8], of Columbia, S.C., *m* Eliza A., dau. of Nathaniel Haraden, sailing master on "Old Ironsides"); issue: I–William Beatty (1 above); II–Edmund Haraden (1861-1921; *m* Mary Hinsdale Mathews); III–Douglas (1863-1925; *m* Annie Crosland); IV–Isabelle Beatty; V–Sallie (1870-71).
1–*m* Sept. 12, 1893, Martha Judith Candis Huff (qv for issue).
1–A.B., Davidson Coll., N.C., '80; A.M., Princeton, 1882; grad. Princeton Theol. Sem., 1883; (D.D., Centre Coll., Ky., 1896). Minister, First Presbyn. Ch., Germantown, Pa., since 1906. Trustee Princeton Theol. Sem.; mem. Presbyn. Gen. Assembly, 1902,09,12,21. Author (see Who's Who in America). Clubs: Union League, Phi Beta Kappa Assn., Phi Alpha, Adelphoi. Residence: 6012 Greene St., Germantown, Philadelphia, Pa.

1–**JENNINGS, Martha Judith Candis Huff (Mrs. W. Beatty),** *b* Macon, Ga., Oct. 18, 1874.
6–William **Huff** (prob. son of Francis, who came in "Swan," 1620), of Va. and N.C.
5–William (*d* 1807), of Va.;
4–James (*d* post 1821);
3–Travis (*b* nr. Macon, Ga., 1807), *m* Candace Maund;
2–William Arnold (2 below).
9–Edward **Carleton** (1605-78; desc. Baldwin de Carleton, of Carleton Hall, Cumberland); came from Eng., settled at Rowley, Mass.; dep. Gen. Ct., 1643-48; *m* 1636, Ellen Newton (*b* ca. 1615);
8–Lt. John (ca. 1638-1668), *m* ante 1660, as her 1st husband, Hannah Jewett (*b* 1641);
7–Thomas (1667-1734), *m* 1694, Elizabeth Haseltine (1679-1708);
6–Elizabeth (1706-73), *m* 1724, Lt. Jeremiah **Stickney** (1702-63);
5–Mehitable (1743-1816), *m* William **Virgin** (1737-1803), of Concord, N.H.;
4–Abial (1771-1830), *m* 1795, Mehitable Stanley (*d* 1813);
3–Jonathan Ambrose (1808-81), *m* 1833, Judith Story Goodwin (1811-91);
2–Martha Ellis (1838-91), *m* 1860, Col. William Arnold **Huff** (*b* nr. Macon, Ga., Mar. 1, 1832-*d* Apr. 2, 1916), mayor Macon, Ga., 9 yrs.; mem. Ga. Legislature many yrs.; served in commissary dept. C.S.A.; issue: I–William Arnold, Jr. (*b* 1861-*d*); II–Albert (*b* 1862-*d*); III–Walter (*b* 1865); IV–Daisy (*b* 1866; *m* Ovid Sparks); V–Prentice (*b* 1868); VI–Travis (*b* 1870); VII–Martha J. C. (1 above); VIII–Edison Fitzgerald (*b* 1878).
1–*m* Sept. 12, 1893, William Beatty Jennings (qv); issue: 1–William Beatty, Jr. (June 21, 1894-Mar. 4, 1901); 2–Arnold Huff, *b* Louisville,

Ky., May 2, 1896; Princeton U., 1919; M.D., U.Pa. Med. Sch., 1924; 3–Judith, *b* Louisville, Sept. 29, 1897; 4–Martha Haraden, *b* Detroit, Mich., Nov. 26, 1902; A.B., Smith, '25; *m* Oct. 8, 1927, Cooper, son of J. Somers Smith, of Germantown, Pa., *m* Mary Nixon.

1–Ed. Southern Home Sch., Baltimore, and Wesleyan Coll., Macon. Mem. C.D.A. Residence: 6012 Greene St., Germantown, Philadelphia, Pa.

1–**JOHNSTON, Summerfield Key,** *b* Chattanooga, Tenn., May 16, 1900.

5–Joseph **Johnston** (1745-1825), from Ireland, 1770, settled at Graham's Forge, Va., moved to Tenn.; sgt. in Cont. Army, under Capt. Joseph Spencer; *m* 1781, Margaret Graham (1747-1825), from Ireland, 1770;

4–Josiah (1785-1861), of York Dist., S.C.; *m* Margaret Walker (John[5], from Scotland 1747, settled in Pa.);

3–James Miller (1813-81), of Cleveland; *m* Sarah Tucker (1828-1922; John[4], of Burke Co., N.C., *m* Mary Hagler; William[5], of Albemarle Co., Va.);

2–James Francis (2 below).

11–Jacob **Williams,** in French and Indian War; landowner in Isle of Wight Co., Va.;

10–John, of Isle of Wight Co.; landowner, 1661;

9–George (*b* 1685), *m* Sara Mann (Thomas[10], *m* Bridget, dau. William Hooker; John[11], of Va.);

8–George (1710-58), of Edgecombe Co., N.C.; *m* Priscilla Thomas;

7–Samuel (1733-88), of Northampton Co., N.C.; capt. in Am. Rev.; served in Franklin Legislature; mem. Jonesboro Conv., 1788; *m* 2d, Hannah Isbel;

6–George (1787-1832), of Greene Co., Tenn.; *m* Tempie Kyle;

5–Samuel (1807-98), founder of Chattanooga, Tenn.; *m* Rebecca Davis (William[6]; William[7], Am. Rev.);

4–Elizabeth (1828-54), *m* John **Divine** (1818-92);

3–Mary (1846-1927), *m* Summerfield **Key** (1832-91; John Ross[4], chancellor and judge);

2–Margaret Elizabeth (*b* 1873), *m* 1895, James Francis **Johnston** (1865-1930).

1–Not married. B.A., U.Va., class of '22 (Phi Kappa Sigma); LL.B., Harvard, 1925. Attorney; dir. Am. Trust & Banking Co., Cleveland Bank & Trust Co.; trustee Baylor's School. Mem. S.A.R., I.A.G., A.L. Presbyterian. Democrat. Clubs: Mountain City, Golf and Country, Meadowbrook. Summer place: McDonald, Bradley Co., Tenn. Residence: 505 Walnut, Chattanooga, Tenn.

1–**JONES, Hilton Ira,** *b* Mankato, Minn., May 9, 1882.

9–Lewis **Jones** (qv);

8–Josiah (1643-1714), in King Philip's War; capt., Watertown militia; *m* 1667, Lydia Treadway (1648-1743);

7–Nathaniel (1674-1745), selectman; capt. militia; rep. in legislature; *m* 1st, Mary– (*d* 1724);

6–Nathaniel (1707-95), of Sutton, Leicester and Charlton; *m* 1st, 1731, Hannah King (Ebenezer[7], *m* 1699, Hannah Manning);

5–Enos (1734-1803), soldier Am. Rev.; *m* 1st, 1758, Amplias Wadsworth (*d* 1785; Asael[6]);

4–Joel (1764-1845), soldier Am. Rev.; corpl., Capt. Charles Rood's Co. of Arty., N.Y. state militia, 1814; *m* 2d, 1795, Rhoda Sprague;

3–Volney (1800-86), *m* 1829, Esther Thruston;

2–Addison Sprague (2 below).

10–Richard **Warren,** Mayflower Pilgrim (qv);

9–Mary, *m* Robert **Bartlett** (qv);

8–Elizabeth (*d* 1713), *m* 1661, Anthony **Sprague** (1636-1719; William[9], qv);

7–Jeremiah (1682-1795, aet. 113), *m* 1706, Priscilla Knight (1685-1775);

6–Knight (1711-1804), *m* 1735, Mary Lewis (1717-46; Joseph[7]; Lt. James[8]; George[9]);

5–Knight (1740-1835), *m* 1767, Rhoda Marsh (1738-1817; Caleb[6]; Caleb[7]; Thomas[8]; Thomas[9]);

4–Rhoda (1768-1854), *m* Joel **Jones** (4 above);

3–Volney, *m* Esther Thruston (3 above);

2–Addison Sprague (1836-1915), teacher, farmer; sheriff; in charge at siege of New Ulm, Minn., in the Indian outbreak; *m* 1860, Alice Nancy Hilton (1841-1916); issue: I–Lucinda Phillette (1861-85; *m* 1884, Harmon Haggard); II–Volney Hayden (1864-86); III–Ernest Enos (*b* 1867; *m* 1892, Anna Tarter, *d*); IV–Mary Ora (1869-1912; *m* 1887, Charles James Howard, *d*); V–Friend Harry (*b* 1875; *m* 1894, Elizabeth Mary Mann); VI–Pearl Alice (*b* 1878; *m* 1917, Rev. Edward Benjamin Johnson); VII–Hilton Ira (1 above).

ADDISON SPRAGUE JONES (b Jan. 28, 1836-d July 9, 1915), became govt. clerk for the pack-train between Kansas City and Fort Salt Lake, 1856; surveyor at Ottawa, Kan. and layed out the sites of Lawrence, Ottawa and Ossawatamie; sheriff at Ossawatamie; drove from Kansas to Mankato, Minn.; in charge at the Indian siege of New Ulm, etc.

1–*m* June 16, 1908, Blanche Wilson Pinkerton, *b* DeSoto, Ia., Dec. 4, 1882; dau. of Colin McKenzie Pinkerton, of Des Moines, Ia.; issue: 1–Eugenia, *b* Chicago, Ill., Mar. 22, 1909; *m* Nov. 24, 1928, Clyde Peaster; 2–Hayden, *b* Muskogee, Okla., Feb. 15, 1911; 3–Llewellyn, *b* Mitchell, S.D., Mar. 17, 1913; 4–Virginia, *b* Mitchell, Sept. 20, 1916; 5–Joan (Jan. 2, 1919-Feb. 26, 1921); 6–Ernestine Harriette, *b* Evanston, Ill., Sept. 4, 1922; 7–Florice, *b* Evanston, June 26, 1925.

1–A.B., Parker Coll., Winnebago, Minn., 1903 (Sigma Phi Epsilon, Phi Kappa Phi, Pi Kappa Delta, Kappa Kappa Psi, Kappa Delta Pi); A.M., Drake U., 1904; Harvard U., 1906-08; fellow in chemistry, U.Chicago, 1908-09; Ph.D., U. of S.D., 1916. Educator, 1904-06, 1909-18; prof. chemistry and chem. engring., Okla. Agrl. and Mech. Coll., 1918-22; dir. of scientific research, The Redpath Bureau, since 1922 (see Who's Who in America). Mem. S.M.D., S.A.R. Mason (K.T.), Elk, K.P. Club: Engineers'. Residence: 1538 Forest Av., Wilmette, Ill.

1–**JUSTICE, Lula Cutlar (Mrs. Edwin J.),** *b* Wilmington, N.C., Mar. 4, 1873.

9–William **Swann** (1585-1637), from Eng., settled at Swann's Point, opposite Jamestown, Va.; allowed 1,200 acres of land for bringing 24 persons into Va. Colony; *m* Judith Swann (1589-1636);

8–Col. Thomas (1616-80), burgess, James City, 1645-49, Surry, 1657-58; mem. Council, 1660; justice of Surry Co. and lt. col. of militia, 1652; sheriff, 1652-53; surveyor of Surry and Isle of Wight cos.; *m* 2d, 1649, Sarah Codd (*d* 1654);

7–Samuel (*b* 1653), justice of Surry Co., 1674; maj. of militia, 1687; sheriff, 1676,78; burgess, 1677,80,82,84,86,92,93; removed to N.C. and was speaker of Assembly there ante 1715; *m* 2d, Elizabeth Lillington (1679-1725; Alexander[8], pres. of Council and actg. gov. of N.C., *m* Elizabeth Cooper);

6–Samuel (*b* 1704), of The Oaks, N.C., rep. N.C. in surveying state line between Va. and N.C.; speaker of Colonial Assembly 30 yrs.; revised the laws of N.C. called "Swann's Revisal," 1st book published in N.C.; *m* Jane Jones, of Va. (Chief Justice Frederick[7], of N.C., *m* Jane–; Capt. Roger[8], qv);

5–Jean (*d* 1781), of The Oaks; *m* 1758, her cousin, Fred **Jones** (*b* 1732), of Va.;

4–Ann, *m* Dr. Roger **Cutlar,** of Scotland;
3–Dr. Fred, of Wilmington, N.C.; *m* 1825, Louisa Bourdasoule Du Brutz (1808-99);
2–Du Brutz **Cutlar** (1831-96), atty.-at-law, Wilmington, N.C.; *m* 1864, Marianna Poisson (1839-91); issue: I–Du Brutz (1865-1905); II–Lila (1870-94); III–Lula (1 above); IV–Louis Julien Poisson (*b* 1876; *m* Kathryn Lassiter).
1–*m* Oct. 8, 1896, Edwin Judson Justice (June 30, 1867-1917); son of Judge N. H. Justice, of Rutherford, N.C.; issue: 1–Pauline Du Brutz, *b* Marion, N.C., July 15, 1897; U. of Calif., '17; *m* 1917, Cedric Sheerer, *d*; (issue: Cedric); *m* 2d, 1926, Oswald Granicher (issue: Bruce); 2–Martha, *b* Marion, Oct. 14, 1899; U. of Calif.; *m* 1920, Charles Nordyke, of Berkeley, Calif. (issue: Cutlar); 3–Louisa Cutlar, *b* Greensboro, N.C., Aug. 11, 1906; 4–Edwin Judson, Jr., *b* Greensboro, Oct. 5, 1910; U. of Calif., '33.
1–Ed. St. Timothy's Catonsville, Md. Mem. C.D.A., I.A.G. Episcopalian. Democrat. Residence: Menlo Park, Calif.

1–**KENDALL, Henry Hubbard,** *b* New Braintree, Mass., Mar. 4, 1855.
9–Francis **Kendall** (qv);
8–Thomas (1649-1730), *m* 1st, 1673, Ruth Blodgett (1656-96; Samuel[9], *m* Ruth Eggleden);
7–Thomas (*b* 1677), *m* 1701, Sarah Cheever (1686-1761);
6–Benjamin (*b* 1708), *m* 1733, Eunice Leland (*b* 1717);
5–Benjamin (1745-1841), soldier in Am. Rev.; *m* 1767, Keziah Twitchell (*b* 1749);
4–Jonathan, *m* Mary Nichols;
3–Hubbard (*b* 1796), of Gardner, Mass.; *m* Rhoda Sawin (*b* 1797);
2–Albert Asaph (2 below).
8–John **Bigelow** (qv);
7–Joshua (1655-1745), in King Philip's War; *m* Elizabeth Flagg (Thomas[8], qv);
6–Joshua (1677-1728), of Weston, Mass.; *m* 1701, Hannah Fiske (*b* 1680; Nathaniel[7]; Nathan[8]);
5–Joshua (1702-92), rep. Gen. Ct., 6 terms; *m* Lydia Hastings;
4–Asa (1738-1807), *m* Rebecca Richardson;
3–Dea. Amasa (1778-1872), *m* Hannah Lee;
2–Helen Maria (1835-1923), *m* 1854, Albert Asaph **Kendall** (1827-62), physician and surgeon, Newton, Mass.; surgeon, 12th Regt., M.V.M., Civil War, killed in battle; issue: I–Henry Hubbard (1 above); II–Frederick Albert (*b* 1860).
1–*m* Nov. 29, 1881, Annie Beecher Stearns, *b* Newton Centre, Mass., July 5, 1859; dau. of Rev. Oakman Sprague Stearns, D.D., of Newton Centre; issue: 1–Albert Stearns, *b* Washington, D.C., Jan. 7, 1883; A.B., Harvard, '05; M.I.T., 1907; *m* July 27, 1910, Harriet Reed, dau. of Charles Henry Means, of Geneva, N.Y. (issue: Anne Means, *b* 1914; Henry Stearns, *b* 1919); 2–Horace Bigelow, *b* Washington, Feb. 18, 1889; *m* Jan. 11, 1908, Doris Belle, dau. of Charles W. Whitney, of Troy, N.H. (issue: Charles Whitney, *b* 1910; Norma, *b* 1912); 3–Dorothy, *b* Newton Centre, Dec. 27, 1890; B.A., Radcliffe, '12; *m* Jan. 4, 1917, Horace Whitney, son of James M. W. Hall, of Cambridge and Newton, *m* Oriana Breed (issue: Kendall Whitney, *b* 1924; Richard, *b* 1926).
1–Under-grad. Worcester Poly. Acad., '74, M.I.T. '76; studied architecture with W. G. Preston, 1874-79. Asst. and prin. asst. to supervising architect, U.S. Treasury, 1879-87; private practice at Washington, 1887-89, at Boston, since 1889. Pres. Newton Centre Savings Bank, Boston Bapt. Social Union; pres. bd. Newton Theol. Instn.; trustee Gordon Coll. of Theology, Charlesbank Homes. Fellow A.I.A. (pres. 1920-22); ex-pres. Boston Soc. Architects, etc.; mem. S.A.R. Republican. Clubs: Boston City, Boston Art, Tiffin, Exchange, Engineers, Neighbors, Villagers (see Who's Who in America). Summer place: Restwood, Centre Harbor, N.H. Residence: 876 Beacon St., Newton Centre, Mass.

1–**KEYES, Frances Parkinson Wheeler (Mrs. Henry W.),** *b* Charlottesville, Va., July 21, 1885.
8–John **Holbrook** (*b* 1619), from Eng., 1630, settled in Mass.; capt. in King Philip's War; Mass. State Rep., 1651-74; *m* Lydia–;
7–Samuel (1654-95), *m* Mary Needham;
6–Obiah (*b* 1695), *m* 1717;
5–Samuel (1729-84), 2d headmaster for many yrs. of a famous boys' school in Boston, which in spite of all adverse circumstances, including the loss of his entire fortune because of his patriotic zeal, he kept open thruout the duration of the war, training many young patriots; one of the Sons of Liberty who dined at Lee, 1769; one of the men who took part in concealing the cannon in Boston when Gage attempted to secure the military stores; *m* 1755, Elisabeth Williams (*d* 1809);
4–Mary (1768-1833), *m* Jaddock **Wheeler** (1768-1841);
3–Melancthan Gilbert (1802-70), *m* 1848, Frances Parkinson;
2–John Henry (2 below).
6–William **Parkinson** (*d* 1791), from Ireland 1744, settled at Londonderry, N.H.; signer Assn. Test; *m* 1739, Esther Woods (*b* 1723); 5 sons in Am. Rev.;
5–Henry (1741-1820), grad. Princeton, 1764; enlisted May 4, 1775, pvt. in Capt. Reid's regt., fought at Battle of Bunker Hill; lt., July 4, 1775, and q.m. of 5th Cont. Line, comd. by Capt. John Stark; resigned 1777, on account of ill health; served at Ticonderoga, Crown Point, and probably at Trenton; pensioned 1819; town clk. of Francestown, N.H., 1777-80; justice, 1780; chmn. Com. Safety, 1779; established a boy's school at Concord, N.H., which later moved to Canterbury, and became famous as the "Canterbury School Master"; *m* 1778, Janet McCurdy (1756-1836);
4–Robert (1781-1849), of Columbia, N.H.; *m* 1810, Elisabeth Kelso;
3–Frances (1819-1904), *m* M. Gilbert **Wheeler** (3 above).
9–William **Johnson** (*d* 1677), from Eng., 1630; founder and principal municipal officer of Charlestown; *m* 1633, Elisabeth Story (*d* 1684);
8–Joseph (1637-1714), one of the founders, proprs., and principal municipal officers of Haverhill; "distinguished for enterprise and moral worth"; *m* 1666, Hannah Tenney (*b* 1642);
7–Thomas (1670-1742), *m* 1700, Elisabeth Page (1679-1752);
6–John (1711-62), founder and early settler of Hampstead, N.H.; procured the charter for that town, and was chosen its first selectman; magistrate; one of the justices of His Majesty's Court of Gen. Sessions for the Peace, in and for the Province of N.H. which sat at Portsmouth; *m* 1731, Sarah Haynes (*d* 1750);
5–Thomas (1742-1819), of Newbury, Vt.; capt. of the militia and of a company of minute men organized 1775; capt. at Ticonderoga, 1777, aide to General Lincoln; in charge of prisoners after surrender; mem. Bd. of War, 1777; captured at Peacham, Vt., by the British, 1781, and taken to Can., released the same year; apptd. lt. col.; rep. Newbury at Cornish Conv., 1778; town rep. to Legislature, 1786-1801; author of an interesting and remarkable diary and had an illuminating correspondence with George Washington on the subject of exchange of prisoners; *m* 1775, Abigail Carleton;
4–David (1778-1865), *m* 1812, Lucy Towne;
3–Edward Carleton (1816-78), of New York City; *m* 1847, Delia Maria Smith;
2–Louise Fuller (2 below).
10–Edward **Carleton** (qv);
9–Lt. John (1630-68), lt. col. of Haverhill div. of militia for Essex Co.; *m* Hannah Jewett (*b* 1641; Joseph[10], qv);
8–Edward (1664-1711), *m* Elisabeth Kimball (*b* 1669; Benjamin[9], *m* Mercy Hazeltine);
7–Benjamin (1693-1772), *m* Elisabeth Dalton;
6–Dudley (1722-1801), *m* Abigail Wilson (1725-99);
5–Abigail (1750-1833), *m* Thomas **Johnson** (5 above).
6–Elisha **Towne** (*b* 1706), *m* 1738, Sarah Rhodes;
5–John (1740-1830), of Boxford, Mass.; sgt. in battle of Bunker Hill; was one of the vets. who rode at the laying of the corner stone of Bunker Hill Monument, June 17, 1785; *m* 1763, Ann Cummings;
4–Lucy (1785-1820), *m* David **Johnson** (4 above).
7–Abijah **Smith** (1715-85), *m* 1738, Lydia Rogers (1721-1806);
6–Abijah (1740-86), of Leominster, Mass.; capt.

of a co. from New Ipswich in recognition of his services during the French and Indian War; at the Battle of White Plains, 1777; *m* 1764, Abigail Wheeler (1744-1815);
5–Samuel (*b* 1778), *m* Hope Hunt;
4–Adon (1804-74), *m* 1823, Louise Fuller (1804-59);
3–Delia Maria (1827-81), *m* Edward Carleton **Johnson** (3 above);
2–Louise Fuller (*b* 1848), *m* 1868, James Underhill; *m* 2d, 1880, John Henry **Wheeler** (1851-87), B.A., Harvard, '71, M.A., 1875; Ph.D., Bonn, 1879; prof. Latin, Bowdoin Coll.; head of Greek dept., U. of Va.
1–*m* June 8, 1904, Henry Wilder Keyes, *b* Newbury, Vt., May 23, 1863; U.S. senator (see Who's Who in America); son of Henry Keyes, of Newbury; issue: 1–Henry Wilder, Jr., *b* N. Haverhill, N.H., Mar. 22, 1905; B.A., Harvard, '26, LL.B., 1930; 2–John Parkinson, *b* N. Haverhill, Mar. 26, 1907; B.A., Harvard, '29; 3–Francis, *b* Boston, Dec. 4, 1912.
1–Ed. private schools, Boston, and Geneva, Switzerland; private tutors at home and in Berlin, Germany; (Litt.D., George Washington U., 1921). Author (see Who's Who in America). Regular contributor to Good Housekeeping Magazine, since 1920 (asso. editor, since 1923), Delineator since 1921; etc.; public speaker since 1917. Mem. C.D.A., D.A.R., C.A.R. (nat. v.p., 1921), N.H. Hist. Soc., Va. Hist. Soc., Women's Roosevelt Memorial Assn. (state chmn.), Civic Federation of N.H., L.A.P.W. Episcopal. Republican. Clubs: Graduate of Windsor School, National Woman's Press, Congressional, Congressional Country. Winter residence: 1509 16th St., Washington, D.C. Residence: "Pine Grove Farm," North Haverhill, N.H.

GEORGE DARIUS KILBORN (1853-1930), from an oil portrait by Konier.

1–**KILBORN, George Darius,** *b* on homestead, Champion Tp., Jefferson Co., N.Y., Apr. 6, 1853-*d* March 19, 1930.
8–Thomas (Kilbourne) **Kilborn** (1578-1636), from Eng., 1635, settled at Wethersfield, Conn.; *m* 1604, Frances Moody (1584-1650);
7–John (1624-1703), mem. Conn. Legislature; *m* Sarah Bronson (*d* 1711);
6–George (1668-1741), known as "Mr. George;" *m* 1689, Abigail Atwood (1668-1739 or 40; Capt. Thomas[7], capt. in Cromwell's army, physician Wethersfield, owner W.I. ships);
5–Hezekiah (*b* 1700), M.A. Yale, 1720; *m* 1722, Elizabeth Allyn (*b* 1700; Capt. Joseph[6]);
4–Elisha (1727-ca. 1815), of Sandisfield, Mass.; *m* 1748, Sarah Robbins;
3–Allen (1775-1841), *m* Rhoda Canfield;
2–Hiram Wellington (2 below).
7–John **Robbins** (*d* 1660), to America ante 1638; *m* ante 1641, Mary Welles (under 18, 1627-*d* 1659; niece of Gov. Thomas Welles);
6–Capt. Joshua (1651-post 1726), *m* 1680, Elizabeth Butler (1665-ca. 1736; Samuel[7], *m* Elizabeth–);
5–Capt. Jonathan (1694-1777), *m* Sarah Welles (1708-76; Capt. Robert[6], *m* Sarah Wolcott; Capt. Robert[7], *m* Elizabeth Goodrich; John[8], *m* Elizabeth Bourne; Thomas[9], qv);
4–Sarah (1729-1810), *m* Elisha **Kilborn** (4 above);
3–Allen, *m* Rhoda Canfield (3 above);
2–Hiram Wellington (1814-1902), of Champion, N.Y.; owner of stock farms; *m* 1840, Olive White (1825-1908); issue: I–Frances Ellen (1844-1914; *m* Henry Sherman); II–Frederick Norman (1850-1912); III–George Darius (1 above).
1–*m* Nov. 2, 1895, Katherine Wright Anderson, *b* July 23, 1867; dau. of Maj. J. N. Anderson.
1–Brown's Coll., Watertown, N.Y.; studied metallurgy and chem. analysis under tutor in own lab. at Rhinebeck, N.Y. Metallurgist with Colo. mines, samplers and smelters; mng. dir. Taylor Park Properties, 1890; mng. dir. Isabella Mines, 1898; operating and giving incidental attention to personally owned properties, Nev., 1908–; retired, 1919. Episcopalian.

1–**KLAYDER, Mary Twyman (Mrs. Paul A.),** *b* nr. Armstrong, Mo., Feb. 24, 1880.
8–Edward **Walker** (*d* 1776), immigrant to Culpeper Co., Va.; *m* Mary Daniel (William, Jr.[9]);
7–William (*d* 1808), capt. in Am. Rev. from Culpeper Co., Va.; *m* Ann Merry (Thomas[8]);
6–Elizabeth, *m* Capt. Francis **Kirtley** (*b* 1756), capt. in Am. Rev. (see Vol. III, p. 556);
5–Frances Walker (1787-1866), *m* Col. William **Buford** (1781-1848); see Vol. III, p. 556;
4–Margaret Kirtley (1806-81), *m* Joel **Twyman** (1797-1880);
3–Francis K. B. (1836-80), *m* Mary Jane (Tooley) Harvey;
2–Joel Kirtley (2 below).
5–John **Tooley** (1774-1843), *m* 1796, Emily Witt (*d* 1816; William[6], *m* Milly–);
4–Charles Porter (1800-63), *m* 1824, Eleanor Munro (1808-78; William[5], from Ky. to Howard Co., Mo., 1808, he and his wife were the first permanent white settlers of Howard Co., he, his wife and father and 2 bros. were stationed at Ft. Kincade during War 1812 for protection against the Indians, *m* 1806, Jerusha Williams; Daniel[6], Am. Rev.);
3–Mary Jane (1831-79), *m* 2d, 1853, Francis K. B. **Twyman** (3 above).
6–Thomas **Thorp** (*d* 1768), Essex Co., Va.; *m* Sarah Thorp;
5–Thomas (ca. 1752-1818), Am. Rev.; *m* 2d, 1791, Eleanor Jackson, with several of her children and their families emigrated from Madison Co., Ky., to Howard Co., Mo., 1821 (Jervis[6], of Bedford Co., Va., Am. Rev., *m* Mary–);
4–Jackson (1799-1849), *m* 1823, Harriett Bastin (Richard[5], *m* Polly Roper, with her small children, her bro., Jesse Mims Roper and his family, emigrated from Woodford Co., Ky., to Howard Co., Mo.; John[6], of Essex Co., Va., *m* Sarah–);
3–Mary Ann (1834-1916), *m* 1853, Reuben Parks **Briggs** (1827-1901; David Anderson[4], *m* Polly W., dau. of Reuben Parks, *m* Lois Ellen Merritt, emigrated 1826 to Pike Co., Mo.); see Vol. I, p. 672, for Briggs lineage;
2–Frances Belle (*b* 1856), D.A.R., O.E.S.; *m* 1877, Joel Kirtley **Twyman** (*b* 1855), Armstrong, Mo.; for issue and other lineages see Vol. III, p. 556.
1–*m* Apr. 27, 1904, Paul August Klayder, *b* Paterson, N.J., Jan. 2, 1877; son of Frederick Julius Klayder (1827-1920, Howard Co., Mo.), from Germany, 1866, settled at Paterson, *m* 1873, Pauline Fiedler (ca. 1843-1884), from Germany 1872; issue (all *b* Armstrong, Mo.): 1–Paul August, Jr., *b* Nov. 19, 1906; 2–Maryfrances Harriett (*b* Dec. 1908, *d* infancy); 3–Julius Kirtley Twyman, *b* Dec. 12, 1914; 4–Reuben William, *b* May 14, 1917.
1–Ed. Central Coll., Fayette, Mo. Compiler: The Twyman Family and Its Branches. Mem. D.A.R. (state librarian also state chmn. Memorial Cont. Hall Library, past regent and registrar Neodesha Chapter; organized Armstrong, Mo., chapter and regent 4 yrs.), I.A.G., Nat. Geneal. Soc., Ky., Mo. and Kan. state hist. socs. Collecting books and magazines for the Kan. Traveling Geneal. Library, which, thru her efforts, passed the D.A.R. State Bd.

at their conference, 1930. Residence: Neodesha, Kan.

1–**KRAMER, LeRoy,** *b* Wichita, Kan., Aug. 19, 1875.
4–George **Kramer** (1780-1870), of Frederick Co., Md.; *m* 1805, Barbara Ann Kramer (1782-1873);
3–Thomas (1817-1900), of Green Co., Pa.; *m* 1839, Judith Jacoby (1814-59; Henry[4]; George[5]; Peter[6]);
2–Henry Theodore (2 below).
5–James (Pritchartt) **Pritchart** (*d* 1832), served in Morgan's Light Horse Regt., was in battle of Cowpens and at surrender of Cornwallis at Yorktown; *m* Phoebe Abbott:
4–Mahala, *m* James **Baynum**;
3–John W., *m* Empress Sellman;
2–America (*b* 1855), *m* 1873, Henry Theodore **Kramer** (1839-1908), mcht. and banker, Darrtown, O.; in Civil War.
1–*m* June 6, 1900, Ethel Davis Gray (*d* Apr. 9, 1910); dau. of Oliver C. Gray, in C.S.A.
1–*m* 2d, Feb. 17, 1912, Margery Hull Hannegan, *b* Cedar Rapids, Ia., May 27, 1888; dau. of James E. Hannegan; issue: (all *b* Chicago, Ill.): 1–Julia Hull, *b* June 5, 1913; 2–LeRoy, Jr., *b* Jan. 13, 1915; 3–Henry Theodore, *b* Apr. 8, 1917.
1–Admitted to Kan. bar, 1895. Started railroading on St.L.&S.F. R.R..; became supt., later asst. to v.p.; asst. v.p., Rock Island R.R., Chicago, 1912-18; v.p. The Pullman Co.; v.p., dir. Gen. Am. Tank Car Corpn. since 1924; treas. Harbor Point Assn.; dir. Cont. Cushion Spring Co. Federal mgr. of "Frisco" and "Katy" rys. under govt. control. Mem. I.A.G. Episcopalian. Republican. Clubs: Chicago, Union League, Commonwealth, Glen View Golf, Harbor Point (Mich.) Country. Summer place: Harbor Point, Mich. Residence: 1320 N. State St., Chicago, Ill.

1–**LACY, Mate Almyra Medberry (Mrs. Robert J.),** *b* East Troy, Wis., Oct. 5, 1867.
10–John **Howland,** Mayflower Pilgrim (qv);
9–Lydia, *m* James **Brown** (1623-1710; John[10], qv);
8–Sgt. James (1655-1718), *m* 1678, Margaret Dennison (1657-1742; Capt. George[9]; William[10], qv);
7–Dorothy (*b* 1694), *m* 1718, Nathaniel **Medberry** (*b* 1691; John[8], *m* Sarah–);
6–Benjamin (1718-95), *m* Sarah–;
5–Nathan (1751-1816), *m* 1772, Rhoda Harris;
4–Abner (1774-1845), *m* 1796, Rhoda Blackmer;
3–Hiram (1799-1863), organizer and first Master Mason of the Masonic Lodge, E. Troy; *m* 1824, Nancy S. Chambers (1800-60);
2–George Washington (2 below).
10–Thomas **Harris** (qv);
9–Thomas (*d* 1710/11), Providence, R.I.; *m* Elnathan Tew (1643-1718/19);
8–Richard (1668-1750);
7–Jonathan (*d* 1785), *m* Mary Brown;
6–Abner (1730-68), *m* Amy Colwell;
5–Rhoda, *m* 1772, Nathan **Medberry** (5 above).
10–Joshua **Winsor** (*d* 1679), from Eng., settled at Providence, R.I.;
9–Samuel (1644-1705), *m* 1677, Mercy (Williams) Waterman (1640-1705; Roger Williams[10], qv);
8–Samuel (1677-1758), *m* 1703, Mercy Harding (1683-1771; Abraham[9], *m* Deborah–; Stephen[10]);
7–Martha (1703-97), *m* 1728, Robert **Colwell** (1702-97; Robert[8], *m* Amey Downing; Robert[9]);
6–Amy (1731-1821), *m* Abner **Harris** (6 above).
8–James **Blackmer** (1639-1709), *m* Mary Hawkins (*d* 1724);
7–John (*d* 1768), Gloucester, R.I.; *m* Jemima Kenney;
6–Henry, *m* 1739, Jane Arnold;
5–Stephen (*b* 1749), *m* 1773, Lydia A. White;
4–Rhoda (1776-1849), *m* Abner **Medberry** (4 above);
3–Hiram, *m* Nancy S. Chambers (3 above);
2–George Washington (1828-91), served in Co. E, 1st Heavy Arty., Civil War; *m* 1854, Mary Elizabeth Fryor (1832-1901); issue: I–George Hiram (1855-1927; *m* Naomi Bishop); II–Jerome (*b* 1857; *m* Bertha Skiff); III–John Seeley (*b* 1860; *m* Alice Healy); IV–William (1862-89); V–Carrie A. (*b* 1864; *m* George Brewster); VI–Mate Almyra (1 above); VII–Hattie Emily (*b* 1870; *m* George Tappen); VIII–Irving (*b* 1873).
1–*m* Aug. 26, 1886, Robert Joseph Lacy, *b* Mukwonago, Wis., Nov. 9, 1865; son of Patrick Lacy, of Mukwonago; issue: 1–John Raymond, *b* East Troy, Wis., Sept 18, 1888; joined 149th Aero Squadron, and sent to Wright Field, Dayton, O., thence to Eng.; hon. discharge, Mar. 29, 1919; *m* Mar. 12, 1921, Ludie Rebecca, dau. of James Briggs, of Wilburton, Okla. (issue: Doris Rae, *b* Sedalia, Mo., May 23, 1922).
1–Taught school, 1885; organizer and pres., East Troy Public Library, since 1917. Mem. S.M.D. (mem. bd., 1927-29), D.F.P.A. (sec., 1928-29), C.D.A. (mem. hist. com.), D.A.R. (chapter sec., 1924-25, regent, 1925-26, state consulting registrar, 1928-30), O.E.S., Women's Relief Corps (charter mem. East Troy), A.L. Auxiliary (pres., 1924-25). Conglist. Republican. Residence: East Troy, Wis.

AMASA JACKSON (1765-1824).

1–**KOOP, G(odfrey) Phelps,** *b* New York, N.Y., Aug. 9, 1867.
9–Edward **Jackson** (qv);
8–Sebas (*b* at sea 1642-1696), soldier King Philip's War; *m* Feb. 19, 1671, Sarah Baker;
7–Edward (Sept. 12, 1672-Mar. 27, 1748), *m* Mary Newton;
6–Michael (Feb. 28, 1709-Aug. 27, 1765), *m* 1733, Phebe Patten;
5–Gen. Michael (Dec. 18, 1734-Apr. 10, 1801), lt. during French and Indian War; chosen capt. on day of Battle of Lexington; maj., Gardner's regt. at Bunker Hill; lt. col., 1776; col. 8th Regt. Cont. Line, 1777; bvtd. brig. gen., 1783 (his 5 brothers and 5 sons were also soldiers Am. Rev.); *m* Ruth Parker (Ebenezer[6]);
4–Amasa (1765-1824), ens. in Am. Rev.: mem. Soc. Cincinnati; a founder and many yrs. pres. Union Bank, New York (see portrait); *m* Mary Phelps (Oliver[5], *m* Mary, dau. of Zachariah Seymour, of New Haven, Conn.);
3–Oliver Phelps, justice Supreme Ct. of La.; *m* Antonine Hugon des DeMaines;
2–Mary Elizabeth Phelps (1846-93), *m* Johannes **Koop** (1837-1894), banker and shipping merchant, New York (for issue see Vol. III, p. 636).
1–Not married. Awarded Médaille de Liege for valuable services rendered the town of Spa, Belgium. Relief work, Holland, 1915-18. Mem. S.C.W., S.A.R., Inst. Am. Genealogy. Club: St. Nicholas. Address: St. Nicholas Club, New York, N.Y.

1–**LAIRD, Mary Alletta Belin duPont (Mrs. Wm. Winder),** *b* "Nemours," near Wilmington, Del., Nov. 30, 1878.
5–Pierre Samuel **du pont** de Nemours (1739-1817), ex-pres. Constituent Assembly and of

the Counceil des Anciens, of France; sec. Provisional French Govt., 1814, statesman and author, arrived at Newport R.I., with his sons, Jan. 1, 1800; *m* Nicole-Charlotte-Marie-Louise Le Dee de Rencourt (or Roccourt) (1743-84);
4–Eleuthère Irénée (1771-1834), settled on Brandywine Creek, near Wilmington; founded the E. I. du Pont de Nemours Powder Co.; *m* 1791, Sophie Madeleine Dalmas (1775-1828);
3–Alfred Victor (1798-1856), of Eleutherian Mills, near Wilmington, head of the firm, 1837-50; *m* 1824, Margaretta Elizabeth LaMotte (1807-98);
2–Lammot (2 below).
4–Charles Augustus **Belin,** *m* Mary Alletta Haedrick;
3–Henry, *m* Isabella d'Andelot;
2–Mary (1839-1913), *m* 1865, Lammot **duPont** (1831-84), of Nemours, Christiana Hundred, Del.; A.B., U.Pa., '49; mem. E.I. duPont de Nemours & Co.; mfr. of gun powder and dynamite; issue: I–Isabella d'Andelot (1866-71); II–Louisa d'Andelot (1868-1926; *m* Charles Copeland); III–Pierre Samuel (see Vol. I, p. 224); IV–Sophia Madeleine (1871-94); V–Henry Belin (1873-1902; *m* Eleuthera du Pont Bradford); VI–William Kemble (1874-1907; *m* Ethel F. Hallock, see Vol. I, p. 224); VII–Irenee (*b* 1876; *m* Irene Sophie du Pont); VIII–Mary Alletta Belin (1 above); IX–Lammot (*b* 1880; *m* Natalie Driver Wilson; *m* 2d, Bertha Taylor; *m* 3d, Calolene Hinson Stollenwerck); X–Isabella Mathieu (*b* 1882; *m* Hugh Rodney Sharp); XI–Margarette Lammot (*b* 1884; *m* Robert Ruliph Morgan Carpenter).
1–*m* Oct. 14, 1904, William Winder Laird (Jan. 4, 1878-Nov. 19, 1927); son of Rev. William Henry Laird, rector at Brookville; issue (all *b* Windmar, Wilmington, Del.): 1–Mary Belin, *b* Dec. 10, 1907; 2–William Winder, Jr., *b* Feb. 18, 1910; M.I.T., 1933; 3–Alletta d'Andelot, *b* June 5, 1913; 4–Wilhelmina Wemyss, and 5–Rosa Packard, twins, *b* Aug. 24, 1916.
1–Life mem. I.A.G., etc. Residence: 3200 W. 17th St., Wilmington, Del.

1–**LAWSON, Roberta Emma Campbell (Mrs. Eugene B.),** *b* Al-lu-we, Indian Ty. (now Okla.), Oct. 31, 1878.
5–James **Campbell** (*d* 1839, aet. 82), from North of Ireland, settled first in Pa., later nr. Round Hill, Frederick Co., Va.; *m* Mary Reed;
4–William, *m* 2d, Mary Johnson;
3–Robert Madison (1809-92), moved to the Greenwood farm, nr. the head of the Opequon, 1843; later purchased "Stony Mead"; ruling elder Loudoun St. Presbyn. Ch., Winchester, Va.; ruling elder Round Hill Ch., 1880-92; *m* 1833, Rebecca Ann Lockhart;
2–John Edwards (2 below).
5–Robert **Lockhart,** of Ireland or Scotland; *m* Margery (Denney) Wilson, of Pa.;
4–Gen. Josiah, of Back Creek, Frederick Co., Va.; served in War 1812, and was in Hull's surrender; *m* Nancy O'Dell (Rev. Thomas[5], methodist minister, *m* Grace Austin, of Welsh descent);
3–Rebecca Ann (1815-97), *m* Robert Madison **Campbell** (3 above);
2–John Edwards (1847-1926), taught school in Mo.; *m* 1878, Emeline Journeycake (1852-1917; Rev. Charles[3], the last chief of the Delawares); issue: I–Roberta Emma (1 above); II–Robert Charles (1880-81); III–Herbert Lockhart (*b* 1885).
1–*m* Oct. 31, 1901, Eugene B. Lawson, *b* Shelbyville, Ky., May 27, 1871; son of William Henry Lawson; issue: 1–Edward Campbell, *b* Nowata, Ind. Ty., Oct. 7, 1905.
1–Ed. Hardin Coll., Mexico, Mo. Pres. Okla. Federation Women's Clubs, 1917-19 (dir. Gen. Federation, 1918-22, and chmn. music dir., 1926-28; 2d v.p. 1928-32); Okla. chmn. women's com. Council Nat. Defense, World War. Regent Okla. Coll. for Women; trustee U. of Tulsa. Presbyterian. Democrat. Mem. D.A.R., U.S.D. 1812, U.D.C. Clubs: Hyechka Music, 20th Century, Tulsa Woman's. Residence: Tulsa, Okla.

LEACH

Arms: Ermine, on a chief dancette gules, three ducal coronets or.
Crest: Out of a ducal coronet or, an arm proper entwined by and holding a snake vert.
Motto: Alla corona fidisimo.

1–**LEACH, F(ayette) Phelps,** *b* Bakersfield, Vt., Nov. 17, 1864.
9–Lawrence **Leach** (1580-1662), from Eng., settled at Salem, Mass., 1629; freeman, 1631; *m* Elizabeth– (*d* 1674);
8–Giles (*b* 1632), *m* 1656, Anne Nokes;
7–John (1665-1743), *m* Alice–;
6–Sgt. Solomon (*b* 1721), in French and Indian War; *m* 1743, Hannah Leach;
5–Ephraim (1761-1840), Enosburg, Vt.; pvt. Am. Rev.; *m* 1785, Chloe Shattuck (1766-1845; Samuel[6], *m* Chloe Field);
4–Tertius (1786-1864), of Waterville, Vt.; *m* 1812, Sophia Hawley (1795-1879);
3–Tertius Hawley (1813-81), of Clinton, Ia.; *m* 1st, 1835, Orisa Fanton (1812-90; James[4], *m* Rachel Colyer);
2–Horace Brayton (2 below).
10–Hon. John **Washburn** (qv);
9–John (*b* 1621), *m* 1645, Elizabeth Mitchell (Experience[10], *m* Jane, dau. of Francis Cooke, Mayflower Pilgrim, qv);
8–Joseph, *m* Hannah Latham (Robert[9], *m* Susannah, dau. of John Winslow, *m* Mary, dau. of James Chilton, Mayflower Pilgrim, qv);
7–Hepzibah (*d* 1750), *m* 1702, Benjamin **Leach** (*d* 1764; Giles[8]; Lawrence[9]);
6–Hannah (*b* 1725), *m* 1743, Sgt. Solomon **Leach** (6 above);
2–Horace Brayton Leach (1836-1919), farmer, E. Highgate, Vt.; *m* 1863, Caroline Alexandria Phelps (1840-1921); issue: I–Fayette Phelps (1 above); II–Elizabeth May (Mrs. Oscar Herbert Rixford, qv for other lineages); III–Albertine Louisa (*b* 1868; *m* Charles J. Read); IV–Frankie Orisa (*b* 1870; *m* Homer J. Cutler); V–Adelbert Horace (*b* 1877; *m* Bertha P. Mullen).
1–*m* Sept. 3, 1887, Josie L. Brown (Feb. 3, 1870-Nov. 22, 1894); dau. of Alfred Brown; issue: 1–Beatrice Josie, *b* Milton, Vt., Aug. 16, 1889; State Normal School, Johnson, Vt.; *m* Apr. 27, 1914, Frank A. Young, of Alburg, Vt. (issue: Kathleen Mary); 2–Hazel May, *b* E. Fairfield, Vt., Oct. 14, 1891; State Normal School; *m* Oct. 26, 1914, James Elsworth Allard, of Lyndon, Vt. (issue: Viola Beatrice; James Leach; Conrad Milton, *b* 1928).
1–*m* 2d, Sept. 6, 1896, Emma L. McManimon, *b* Waterville, Vt., June 20, 1868; dau. of William

McManimon; issue: 1–Edith Emma, *b* E. Fairfield, Vt., Sept. 16, 1897; *m* Aug. 22, 1917, Claude Clesson, son of Leslie Macy, of Swanton, Vt. (issue: Fern Alice; Keith Sherwood; Beverly Edith).
1–*m* 3d, Oct. 30, 1900, Lottie E. Martin, *b* Bedford, Que., Sept. 4, 1865; dau. of Arvide Martin.
1–B.A., Bakersfield (Vt.) Coll. Author and publisher of Leach Genealogy, vols. 1, 2, and 3, and of Hungerford Genealogy, 1st and 2d editions. Mem. S.M.D., I.A.G., N.E.H.G.S. (life mem. No. 58), United Commercial Travelers of America, Ia. State Traveling Men's Assn. Residence: East Highgate, Vt.

1–**RIXFORD, Elizabeth May Leach (Mrs. Oscar Herbert),** *b* Bakersfield, Vt., Jan. 7, 1866.
9–William **Phelps** (qv);
8–Capt. Timothy (1639-1719), apptd. capt. at Windsor, 1696, and went up to Great Falls on public service; lt. under Col. William Whiting; *m* 1661, Mary Griswold (bap. 1644-ante 1719; Edward[9], of Killingworth, Conn.);
7–Lt. Samuel (*b* 1675), *m* Abigail Eno (James[8]);
6–Lt. Samuel (1708-54), of Windsor and Harwington, Conn.; *m* Ruth Phelps (*b* 1706; William[7], *m* Ruth Barber);
5–Joel (*b* 1732), *m* 1757, Jerusha Nash (1736-96; Samuel[6], *m* Mary Merrick);
4–Phineas (1767-1813), *m* Lydia Lawrence (1762-1813; Jonathan[5], *m* Zervia–);
3–David Nash (1796-1884), Stanbridge, Que.; *m* 1821, Elizabeth Hungerford (1798-1878);
2–Caroline Alexandria (2 below).
9–William **Mead** (qv);
8–Joseph (1630-90), *m* 1654, Mary Brown;
7–Joseph (ca. 1657-1714), *m* Sarah Reynolds;
6–Jeremiah (1702-42), *m* 1725, Hannah St. John (*d* 1746);
5–Stephen (1728-1806), *m* 1751, Rachel Sanford;
4–Esther (1760-1836), *m* Isaiah **Hungerford** (1757-1833);
3–Elizabeth, *m* David Nash **Phelps** (3 above).
9–Thomas **Sanford** (qv);
8–Ezekiel (1637-83), *m* 1665, Rebecca Whelpley (*d* ca. 1697; Henry[9]);
7–Ezekiel (1668-1728/29), *m* 1696, Rebecckah Gregory (*d* post 1764; Samuel[8], of Chester Hill, Conn.);
6–Ephraim (1708-1761 or 62), *m* 1730, Elizabeth Mix (1715-77);
5–Rachel, *m* Stephen **Mead** (5 above).
2–Caroline Alexandria Phelps (1840-1921), *m* 1863, Horace Brayton **Leach** (1836-1919); for issue and Leach lineage see Fayette Phelps Leach.
1–*m* Sept. 8, 1889, Oscar Herbert Rixford (Dec. 27, 1860-Sept. 21, 1926); v.p. and clerk Rixford mfg. Co.; postmaster Highgate, Vt., 34 yrs.; issue: 1–Oscar Adelbert (qv for Rixford lineage).
1–Ed. Brigham Acad. Mem. Magna Charta Dames (state regent), H.S.A., S.M.D. (charter mem. Nat. Soc., sec. Vt. Soc.), D.A.C. (v.p.), D.F.P.A. (state historian), D.C.W., C.D.A., D.A.R., U.S.D. 1812, N.E. Women in Vt. (organizing pres.), Daus. of Vt., etc. Chmn. woman's finance com., Franklin Co., Vt., 1912-16; mem. advisory com. on education, Franklin Co.; town supt. schs., 1903-04; trustee Highgate Library, 15 yrs.; mem. Fed. of Women's Clubs; pres. Woman's Auxiliary St. John's Episcopal Ch. Republican. Residence: East Highgate, Vt.

1–**RIXFORD, Oscar Adelbert,** *b* East Highgate, Vt., Aug. 4, 1890.
6–William **Rixford,** the first of the name in America; *m* at Medway, Mass., 1751, Hannah Thayer, moved to Grafton, Mass.;
5–William (1754-1839), Winchester, N.H.; *m* Lucy Wilson;
4–Luther (1779-1859), mfr. of scythes, Winchester, 1812; to Highgate, Vt., 1837, and there laid the foundation of what has since become a large and the oldest plant for the manufacture of scythes and axes in America; *m* Sarah Hawkins (Stephen[5], *m* Fanny Parker);
3–Oscar S. (*b* Winchester, N.H., 1828-*d* 1911), with parents and seven brothers and sisters by ox team to E. Highgate, Vt., 1837; became pres. and mgr., Rixford Mfg. Co.; *m* May Flint Cutting (1838-1909);

MR. AND MRS. O. H. RIXFORD

2–Oscar Herbert (1860-1926), *m* 1889, Elizabeth May Leach (qv).
1–*m* Jan. 18, 1919, Mary Carolyn Hefflon, *b* Montreal, Quebec, June 6, 1899; dau. of Willard Hefflon; issue: 1–Mary-Elizabeth Lenora, *b* E. Highgate, Oct. 6, 1922; 2–Oscar Theodore, *b* E. Highgate, Vt., July 21, 1925.
1–Ed. St. John's Sch., Quebec, Can.; Goddard Sem., Barre. Mgr., Rixford Mfg. Co. Mem. State Legislature, 1915; selectman; town auditor. Mem. Vt. State Chamber of Commerce. Jr. Warden Episcopal Ch. Mem. S.M.D., Vt. Hist. Soc., Taquahunga Club. Residence: East Highgate, Vt.

1–**LIVEZEY, Walter Baker,** *b* Yardley, Pa., July 1, 1869.
9–Thomas **Livezey** (*d* 1691/92), from Eng. to Phila., 1681; purchased land from William Penn, 1681; mem. Grand Jury;
8–Jonathan (*d* 1698), *m* Rachel Taylor;
7–Jonathan (1692-1764), *m* 1717/18, Ester Eastburn (*d* 1788, aet. 94; Robert[8], of Phila.);
6–Jonathan (1719/20-1789), *m* 1st, 1747, Catherine Thomas (*b* 1721; Daniel[7], *m* Catherine Morris);
5–Daniel (1752-96), Southampton Tp., Bucks Co., Pa.; *m* 1778, Marjory Croasdale (*b* 1758; Robert[6], *m* Margery Hayhurst; Jeremiah[7], *m* Grace, dau. Robert Heaton; Ezra[8], Quaker, from Eng. to New York, 1683, settled in Bucks Co., Pa., *m* Ann Peacock);
4–Robert (1780-1864), of Solebury, Bucks Co.; *m* 1804, Sarah Paxon (1779-1865; Abraham[5], *m* Elizabeth Brown; Thomas[6], *m* Sarah Harvey; Henry[7], *m* Ann Plumley; James[8], from Eng. to Bucks Co., *m* Jane–);
3–Allen (1814-99), of Solebury; later at Yardley, Pa., 1895; *m* 1839, Mary Ann Gordon (1814-76);
2–Theodore (1840-1912), Newport News, Va., 1881; *m* 1865, Elizabeth Baker (1845-1917; John George[3], *m* Elizabeth Gamphur); issue: I–Henry Clay; II–Walter B. (1 above); III–Herbert Stanley.
1–*m* Nov. 8, 1893, Katherine Walker Poe (Dec. 14, 1870-July 7, 1895); dau. of George W. Poe, Newport News, Va.; issue: 1–Elizabeth Baker (June 27, 1895-Dec. 25, 1918); *m* Aug. 25, 1917, Anderson Dana Hodgdon, of St. Mary's Co., Md.
1–*m* 2d, Feb. 7, 1899, Ellen Allard Johnson (qv).
1–Ed. pub. schs. and Friends schs. (Phila.). Corpn. employee from jr. clerk to pres. Has been connected with interests of Huntington family since July 1886; dir. Old Dominion Law Co., Newport News Land Corpn., First Nat. Bank of Newport News. Mem. S.A.R. (chapter pres.), Newport News Pioneer Assn. (v.p.). Clubs: Engineers (New York), Westmoreland (Richmond), Tidewater, Golf and Country. Mason (32°). Quaker. Residence: Hampton, Va.

1–**LIVEZEY, Ellen Allard Johnson (Mrs. Walter B.),** *b* Newton, Mass., 1873.
9–Solomon **Johnson** (*d* 1685), from Eng. to Watertown, Mass.; an original propr. of Sudbury, 1639; *m* Eleanor–;
8–Solomon (*d* 1690), selectman, Sudbury, 1651-66; *m* 1st, Hannah–;
7–Caleb (1658-1715), *m* 1684, Agnes Bent (1661-1729; Peter[8], *m* Elizabeth–; John[9], qv);
6–Charles (1693-1777), *m* Grace Rice (1712-89; Ebenezer[7], *m* Bethiah Williams; Benjamin[8], *m* Mary, dau. of Capt. William Brown, of Sudbury; Edmund[9], qv);
5–Ebenezer (1741-1823), served from Sudbury at Lexington Alarm, 1775; *m* 1766, Elizabeth Rice (1748-1820);
4–Rev. Phineas (1778-1850), Brown U., 1799; M.A., 1802; *m* 1806, Mary A. Nash;
3–Phineas A. (1806-85), *m* 1828, Abigail Pratt (1802-76);
2–Samuel Watson (2 below).
9–Edmund **Rice** (qv);
8–Thomas, *m* Mary King;
7–Elisha (*b* 1679), *m* 1707, Elizabeth Wheeler;
6–Eliakim (*b* 1708), *m* 1730, Mehitable Livermore (*b* 1712; Daniel[7], *m* Mehitable Norcross; Lt. John[8]; John[9], qv);
5–Elizabeth, *m* Ebenezer **Johnson** (5 above).
10–Thomas **Nash** (qv);
9–Lt. Timothy (1626-99), lt. militia; rep. Gen. Ct.; *m* ca. 1657, Rebecca Stone (ante 1641-1709; Rev. Samuel[10], came in the "Griffin," 1633, a founder of Hartford, 1636, chaplain in Pequot War);
8–Lt. John (1661-1743), rep. Gen. Ct., 1707-31; *m* 2d, 1691, Elizabeth Kellogg (1673-1750; Lt. Joseph[9], qv);
7–Timothy (1699-1756), *m* 1722, Prudence Smith;
6–Rev. Judah (1728-1805), B.A., Yale, 1748; minister Montague, Mass., 52 yrs.; *m* 1753, Mary Terry (1728-1824; Dr. Terry[7], *m* Mary Helms; Capt. Samuel[8], *m* Hannah, dau. of Miles Morgan);
5–Judah (1759-1848), *m* 1786, Sarah Clapp (*b* 1770);
4–Mary Almira (1787-1859), *m* Phineas **Johnson** (4 above).
8–Edmund (Montfort) **Mountfort** (*b* Eng., 1629-1670; son of Simon), from Eng. to Boston, ca. 1640; *m* Elizabeth, dau. of Dea. John Farnham;
7–Jonathan (*b* 1673), *m* 1702, Hannah Nichols (bap. 1677);
6–Sarah (*b* 1712), of Boston; *m* 1744, John **Gardner** (*b* 1722);
5–Jonathan (1745-80), of Malden; *m* 1770, Abigail Knower (1750-80);
4–Abigail (1771-1817), as widow of John Sylvester, *m* 2d, 1801, Thomas **Pratt** (*b* 1780);
3–Abigail, *m* Phineas A. **Johnson** (3 above);
2–Samuel Watson (1838-1903), inventor and mfr. of ice making machinery; *m* 1861, Rebecca Teel (1839-1903; Thomas[3], *m* Susan Frost); issue: I–George Comb (*b* 1862; *m* Laura Brooks); II–Susan Teel (*b* 1864); III–Clara Louise (Mrs. Frederick Manville, qv for other lineages); IV–Ellen A. (1 above); V–Alice Rebecca (*b* 1875); VI–Edward Samuel (*b* 1876); VII–Isabelle Edna (Mrs. Reuben B. Eberly, see Vol. III, p. 170).
1–*m* Feb. 7, 1899, Walter Baker Livezey (qv).
1–Mem. C.D.A. (Va.), D.F.P.A., D.A.R. (regent). Club: Woman's (Newport News). Presbyn. Residence: Hampton, Va.

1–**MANVILLE, Clara Louise Johnson (Mrs. Frederick),** *b* Brighton, Mass., Nov. 26, 1868.
10–Rev. Zachariah **Symmes** (*b* Canterbury, Eng., 1593-*d* 1658; son of Rev. William), grad. Emanuel Coll., 1620; chosen lecturer St. Anthony's, London; rector Dunstable 8 yrs., but being harassed and persecuted in Bishops Ct. for non-conformity, came to America, 1634; pastor at Charlestown, Mass.; *m* Sarah–;
9–Rev. Zachariah (1637-1707), grad. Harvard, 1657; first minister at Bradford, Mass., where he preached 40 yrs.; *m* 1st, Susanna Graves (Rear Admiral Thomas[10], *m* Catherine Gray);
8–Zachariah (*b* 1674), *m* 1700, Dorcus Brackenbury (*b* 1682);
7–John B. (*b* 1705), *m* Elizabeth Winslow (1705-64; Nathaniel[8], *m* Elizabeth Holbrook; Kenelm[9], *m* Mercy Worden; Kenelm[10], bro. of Gov. Winslow of Plymouth);
6–Sarah (*b* 1729), *m* 1751, Thomas **Pratt** (*b* 1729; Thomas[7], *m* Lydia, dau. of Joseph Lynde; Thomas[8]);
5–Jacob (1754-1844), served at Lexington Alarm; *m* 1776, Phebe Jenkins (Nathaniel[6], *m* Abigail Baldwin);
4–Thomas (*b* 1780), *m* 1801, Abigail (Gardner) Sylvester;
3–Abigail (1802-76), *m* 1828, Phineas A. **Johnson** (1806-85);
2–Samuel Watson (2 below).
11–John **Green** (*b* London, Eng., 1593-1658), to N.E., 1632; town clk.; ruling elder, Charlestown, Mass.; *m* Perseverence Johnson (Rev. Francis[12], grad. Christ's Coll., Cambridge, 1581, M.A., 1585, pastor of 1st Independent Ch. in Eng., but being persecuted and imprisoned for non-conformity, established, with many of his exiled congregation, ch. in Amsterdam, of which he was pastor);
10–Jacob (*b* 1625), *m* 2d, 1662, Mary Bartholomew Whipple (William Bartholomew[11], *m* Anna Lord);
9–Dorcus (1665-82), *m* 1681, John **Brackenbury** (*b* 1657; John[10], mariner, *m* Amy Anderson; Richard[10]);
8–Dorcus, *m* Zachariah **Symmes** (8 above).
2–Samuel Watson **Johnson** (*b* Newton, Mass., 1838-1903), served with 43d, "Tiger" Regt., Mass. Vol. Light Inf., 1862-63; inventor and mfr. of ice making machinery; *m* Rebecca Teel (1839-1903); for issue and other lineages see sister Mrs. Walter B. Livezey.
1–*m* Nov. 11, 1896, Frederick Manville, *b* Whitehall, N.Y., Dec. 25, 1866; son of Taylor Manville; issue: 1–Ruth Viola, *b* Apr. 26, 1898; *m* May 28, 1918, Eugene, son of Oscar M. Dugger, of Andalusia, Ala. (issue: Frances Elizabeth; Clara Louise; Ruth Manville; Ellen Livezey); 2–Grace Rebecca, *b* June 6, 1900; *m* Jan. 16, 1923, Baker Perkins Lee, son of Benjamin T. Scott, of Bridgetown, Va. (issue: Baker P. Lee, Jr.; Grace Manville, Jr.; Emily Thomas).
1–Mem. C.D.A., D.F.P.A., D.C.W., D.A.R. Presbyterian. Residence: 311 61st St., Newport News, Va.

1–**LEAVITT, Scott,** *b* Elk Rapids, Mich., June 16, 1879.
8–Dea. John **Leavitt** (qv);
7–Israel (*b* 1648), of Hingham, Mass.; *m* 1678, Lydia Jackson;
6–Lt. Soloman (*b* 1682);
5–Jacob (1732-1814), Turner, Me.; minute man in Am. Rev.; *m* 1753, Sylvia Bonney (1734-1810);
4–Isaiah (1769-1845), *m* Lydia Ludden (1779-1866);
3–Alvin (1798-1868), *m* 1826, Susanna Dean (1799-1892);
2–Roswell (*b* 1843), Bellaire, Mich.; pvt. 17th Me. Vol. Inf., Civil War; mem. Me. House of Rep., 1868; mem. Mich. Senate, 1889; *m* 1877, Annie Carrie Lawrence (1858-79); issue: I–Scott (1 above); II–Clyde (*m* Ruby Gowan).
1–*m* Sept. 27, 1903, Elsie Edna Frink, *b* nr. Lewisville, Ore., Oct. 18, 1884; dau. of John Charles Frink, of Falls City, Ore.; issue: 1–Anna Josephine (July 10, 1904-Jan. 10, 1909); 2–Roswell, *b* Falls City, Ore., Sept. 14, 1906; B.F., U. of Mont., '30.
1–Student U. of Mich., 1899-1900. Homesteading and teaching, in Ore., 1901-07; apptd. ranger, U.S. Forest Service, 1907; apptd. supervisor, Lewis and Clark Nat. Forest in Mont., 1910, Jefferson Nat. Forest, 1913-18 (resigned); mem. 68th to 72d Congresses (1923-29), 2d Mont. Dist. Corpl. Co. L, 33d Mich. Vol. Inf., Spanish-Am. War; served in Santiago Campaign; dir. of employment and of Pub. Service Reserve, Mont., during World War. Mem. S.R., U.S.W.V., V.F.W. Mason, Workman, Woodman. Republican. Conglist. Residence: Great Falls, Mont.

1–**LONG, Chester I.,** *b* Perry Co., Pa., Oct. 12, 1860.
6–John Nicholas **Long** (*d* 1767), from the Rhine country in the "Samuel of London," 1736; settled in Lancaster Co., Pa., where he purchased 4 tracts of land; *m* Anna–;
5–Abraham (1743-94), *m* Maria–;
4–David (1771-1859), Cumberland Co., Pa.; *m* Catharine Hershey (1771-1849);
3–Christian (1793-1856), *m* 1812, Nancy Gabel (1793-1861);

2–Abraham G. (1812-91), *m* Mary Cauffman (1813-98).
1–*m* Feb. 12, 1895, Anna Bache (Aug. 18, 1860-Dec. 10, 1919); dau. John Bache; issue: 1–Agnes, *b* Washington, D.C., Oct. 20, 1895; *m* Feb. 12, 1925, Harry F. Gee, Jr.; 2–Margaret, *b* Kansas City, Mo., Nov. 2, 1897; *m* Jan. 18, 1922, W. E. Stanley. Also foster-dau., Vera Clemes, *b* Plymouth, Eng., Jan. 6, 1892; *m* Dec. 22, 1914, Roger S. Hurd.
1–Admitted to bar, 1885. Mem. Kan. Senate, 1889-93; mem. 54th, 56th and 57th Congresses, 1895-97, 1899-1903, 7th Kan. Dist.; reelected to 58th Congress, but before taking seat was elected U.S. senator for term, 1903-09; now mem. law firm Long, Houston, Depew & Stanley, Wichita, Kan.; associated with law firm Long, Chamberlain & Nyce, Washington, Chmn. Commn. to Revise Gen. Statutes of Kan. Mem. Am. Bar Assn. (mem bd. of editors of its jour.; pres. 1925-26), Kan. State Bar Assn. (pres. 1922), Wichita Bar Assn., Am. Soc. Internat. Law, etc. Residence: 3401 E. 2d St., Wichita, Kan.

1–**LORANGER, Louise Baker (Mrs. Hubert R.)**, *b* Flint, Mich., Aug. 5, 1896.
10–Isaac **Robinson** (qv);
9–John (*b* 1640), of Barnstable; rep. for Plymouth, 1689; *m* 1667, Elizabeth Weeks;
8–Fear (*b* 1676), *m* 1695, Thomas **Blossom** (1667-1726; Peter[9], *m* Sarah Bodfish; Thomas[10], qv);
7–Elizabeth (1705-34), *m* 1725, Israel **Butler**;
6–Benjamin (1727-1800), Am. Rev.; *m* 1757, Susanna Whiting (*b* 1734; Ephraim[7], *m* Abigail Mason);
5–Ormond (1775-1850), constable and collector, Loraine, N.Y.; assessor, 1805; in War 1812; *m* 1796, Abigail Rudd (1771-1857; Increase[6], sgt. Am. Rev., *m* Bathsheba Johnson);
4–Susan (1806-80), of Loraine, N.Y., and Farmington, Mich.; *m* 1831, John Halsey **Button** (1805-76), supervisor, Oakland Co., 1845-54; state rep., 1840 (John[5], *m* Cynthia Clark);
3–James Addison (1838-1909), mcht., Flint, Mich.; register of deeds, Genesee Co., Mich., 2 terms; postmaster, Flint, 1897-1909; *m* 1867, Maria Louise Barse (1847-1927; William[4], *m* Maria Louise Nichols);
2–Alta Louise (*b* 1870), of Flint and Midland, Mich. (see Vol. III, p. 48 for Barse and other lineages); *m* 1895, Fred Partridge **Baker** (*b* 1866; Charles[3], *m* Eliza Dymond, who came from Devonshire, Eng., 1856, settled at Flint, Mich.); issue: I–Louise (1 above); II–Frederic James (*b* 1899); III–Dymond (*b* 1902); IV–Mabel Button (*b* 1904).
1–*m* Nov. 16, 1918, Hubert Rivard Loranger, *b* Bay City, Mich., Sept. 7, 1896; son of Ubald R. Loranger; issue: 1–Hubert Rivard, Jr., *b* Detroit, Mich., Oct. 26, 1921; 2–Richard Baker, *b* Detroit, Apr. 5, 1925.
1–Mem. D.A.R., Woman's Nat. Aeronautical Assn. Presbyterian. Residence: 2242 Emerson Av., Dayton, O.

1–**LUCE, Helen May Prindle (Mrs. Franklin A.)**, *b* Durand, Wis., Feb. 7, 1858.
9–William **French** (qv);
8–Francis (1624-91), *m* 1661, Lydia Bunnell (*d* 1708; William[9], *m* Annie Wilmot);
7–Francis (1677-1751), of Derby, Conn.; *m* 1703, Anna Bowers (1669-1744; John[8]);
6–Samuel (1704-83), Am. Rev.; *m* 1733, Martha Chapman (1714-80; Daniel[7], *m* Katharine Wentworth;
5–Sarah (1738-1805), *m* 1756, Lt. Abraham **Smith** (1734-96), of Norfolk, Conn.; Am. Rev.;
4–Josiah (1769-1850), *m* 1795, Betsey Holbrook (1772-1836; Col. Daniel[5], Am. Rev.);
3–Betsey (1799-1867), *m* 1821, William Nelson **Prindle** (1799-1843);
2–William Frederick (1828-85), of Derby; *m* 1856, Eliza Amerette Packard (1836-1904); issue: I–Charles Smith (1856-57); II–Helen May (1 above); III–Katie Parthenia (1859-77).
1–*m* June 2, 1881, Franklin Augustus Luce (Oct. 31, 1854-Feb. 1, 1922); issue: 1–Katherine Prindle, *b* Chicago, Ill., May 12, 1885; *m* Oct. 17, 1910, Mahlon Daniel Thatcher (see Vol. III, p. 444; issue: Mahlon Daniel, III [July 2, 1912-July 5, 1929]; Helen Elizabeth, *b* Mar. 21, 1915; Katherine Eleanore, *b* June 18, 1917).
1–Mem. C.D.A., D.A.R., I.A.G., Art Inst., Chicago Antiquarian Soc. Episcopalian. Club: Chicago Women's. Residence: 1607 Elizabeth St., Pueblo, Colo.

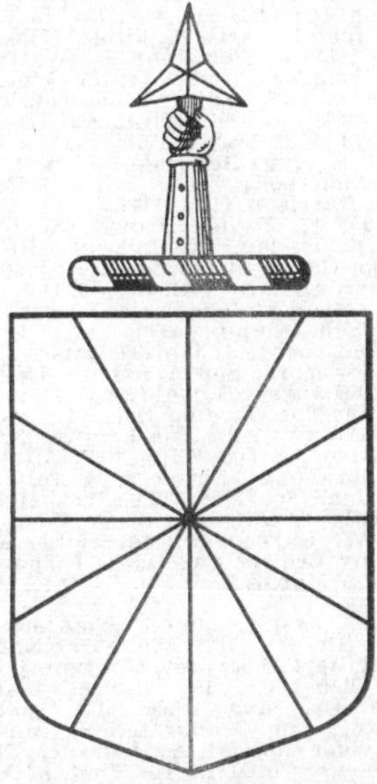

LOVEJOY

Arms: *Gyronny of twelve gules and or.*
Crest: *An arm from the elbow in armour, holding a galtrap.*

1–**LOVEJOY, Thomas Eugene,** *b* Spaulding, Macon Co., Ga., Sept. 16, 1875.
7–Joseph **Lovejoy** (1680-1748), from Eng., 1698, settled in Prince George Co., Md.; received grant of land from the crown; planter and slave holder; *m* 1705, Anne Lyon;
6–John (1708-60), of Prince George Co.; *m* 1729, Margaret Miles;
5–Edward (*b* 1738), moved to Fairfield Co., S.C., 1765; served in Am. Rev.; *m* 1769, Jemimi Morey;
4–Eleazer (1775-1834), moved to Jasper Co., Ga.; had extensive plantations, and was slave holder; *m* 1799, Mary Pennington;
3–Welcome Collingsworth (1822-76), of Montezuma, Ga.; *m* 1844, Catherine Parker (1827-1902);

PLEASANT HARRISON LOVEJOY (1848-1917).

2-Pleasant Harrison (1848-1917), served in Civil War and received the Confederate Cross; mayor of Hawkinsville, Ga., 6 terms (see portrait); *m* 1869, Henrietta McKenzie (1853-98; Joseph H.[3] [1821-86], *m* 1843, Martha Riggins); issue: I-Mattie Capitola (1870-79); II-Kate (*b* 1873; *m* 1889, John B. Watts); III-Thomas Eugene (1 above); IV-Welcome C. (1877-1914; *m* 1899, Edith Irene Gordon); V-Lena (*b* 1880; *m* 1904, Mirabeau H. Boyer); VI-Annie Lee (*b* 1882; *m* 1904, Russell J. Twitty); VII-Evelyn Gertrude (*b* 1886; *m* 1907, John L. Anderson); VIII-Hallie (*b* 1888); IX-Pleasant Harrison (1890-1914).

1-*m* Nov. 9, 1897, Fannie Brown (Sept. 5, 1878-Sept. 3, 1910); dau. of Harry C. Brown, of Talbotton, Ga., *m* Susan Dowdell; issue (all *b* Hawkinsville, Ga.): 1-Susan, *b* Oct. 26, 1898; ed. The Gardner Sch., New York, '18; pres. Gardner Sch. Alumni Assn.; *m* Oct. 22, 1921, George DeLancey, son of DeLancey P. Harris, of New York, and Annapolis Royal, N.S. (issue: DeLancey; Lovejoy); 2-Henrietta, *b* Feb. 9, 1900; The Gardner Sch., '19; sec. Gardner Sch. Alumni Assn.; *m* May 20, 1926, Hugh Addison, son of Dr. Wilmot P. Mitchell, of Brunswick, Me.; 3-Frances, *b* July 6, 1902; The Gardner Sch., '20; The Froebel League, '24; *m* July 9, 1924, Marion Wilson, son of Charles W. Harris, of Centreville, Md. (issue: Fanny Brown; Caroline); 4-Thomas Eugene, Jr., *b* Mar. 3, 1906; Ph.B., Yale, '28 (Zeta Psi).

1-Began as asst. cashier, Planters Bank, Hawkinsville, Ga., 1896; v.p. First Nat. Bank, Hawkinsville, 1905-09; pres. Montgomery (Ala.) Bank & Trust Co., 1909-13; pres. Manhattan Life Ins. Co., since May 1913; trustee and chmn. exec. com. Manhattan Savings Bank; mem. advisory bd. 5th Ave. Branch Chemical Bank & Trust Co. Mem. Ins. Inst. of America, Am. Civil Legion. Baptist. Clubs: Metropolitan, Bankers, Cragston Country, Chelsea Yacht. Summer place: Mount Beacon, N.Y. Residence: 655 Park Av., New York, N.Y.

1-**McARTHUR, Mary Delia Smith (Mrs. William T.),** *b* York, Pa., Nov. 18, 1878.

8-Edmund **Beauchamp** (*d* 1716), from Eng., settled in Somerset Co., Md.; commd. clk. and keeper of records of Somerset Co., 1666, when co. was first laid off; owned plantation situated on Armamessex River, Coventry Parish, Somerset Co.; *m* 1668, Sarah Dixon (*d* 1734; Ambrose[9]; *m* Mary Dixon);

7-Edmund (*b* 1676), of Armamessex River, Md.; clk. and keeper of records; *m* —Traherne;

6-Robert (*d* 1771), of "Contention," plantation on Armamessex River; removed to Kent Co., Del., 1762; *m* Esther-;

5-John, to Rowan Co., N.C., 1776; killed in Battle of Cowpens; *m* Sarah (Purdon?);

4-Stephen (1774-1847), *m* 1805, Nancy Call (1784-1852);

3-Sarah Purdon (1821-65), *m* John Wesley **Smith** (1815-87);

2-Rev. Stephen Morgan (1837-1903), of Davie Co., N.C., and York, Pa.; minister Monavian Ch.; manufacturer; *m* 1860, Emma Rebecca Fahs (1838-1914); issue: I-Charles Elmer (*b* 1863; *m* Virginia Noss, *b* 1865); II-S(tephen) Fahs (*b* 1864; *m* Lucy Neville Mitchell, see Vol. III, p. 576); III-Beauchamp Harvey (1869-1903); IV-Sarah Elizabeth Purdon (*b* 1872; *m* William Hubbard Hall, *b* 1865); V-Susan Ellen (*b* 1876; *m* Carey Elwood Etnier); VI-Mary Delia (1 above).

1-*m* June 16, 1904, William Taylor McArthur, M.D. (Dec. 31, 1867-Mar. 11, 1930); F.R.C.S., F.A.C.S. (see Who's Who in America, 1928); issue (all *b* Los Angeles, Calif.): 1-Elizabeth, *b* Mar. 4, 1907; ed. Vassar Coll.; *m* July 21, 1929, Henry Duque; 2-Mary Beauchamp, *b* Mar. 31, 1910; ed. Sarah Lawrence Coll.; 3-William Taylor, *b* Dec. 13, 1911; 4-Duncan Donald, *b* May 18, 1915.

1-A.B., Vassar, '00. Mem. board of Children's Hosp., Los Angeles. Moravian. Republican. Clubs: Women's Athletic, Beach, Westport Beach, Los Angeles Country. Summer place: Hilltop, Pasadena (Altadena). Residence: 2025 S. Western Av., Los Angeles, Calif.

1-**McAUSLAN, William Alexander,** *b* Providence, R.I., Nov. 17, 1872.

9-Abraham **Robinson** (*d* 1645), settled at Gloucester, Mass.; *m* Mary-;

8-Abraham (1644-1740), *m* 1668, Mary Harrenden (*d* 1725);

7-Abraham (1677-1724), *m* 1703, Sarah York;

6-Abraham (*b* 1704), *m* 1728, Lydia Day;

5-Ezekiel (*d* 1777), served in Am. Rev.; *d* in English prison ship; *m* 1765, Abigail Tarbox (*b* 1734);

4-Ezekiel (1770-1856), of Gardiner, Me.; *m* 1794, Eunice Bodge;

3-William S. (1796-1885), *m* 2d, 1831, Pamelia E. Gow (1801-45);

2-Amelia Bovey (2 below).

10-John **Howland,** Mayflower Pilgrim (qv);

9-Hope (1629-83), of Barnstable, Mass.; *m* 1646, John **Chipman** (qv);

8-Hope (1652-1728), *m* 2d, 1682, Jonathan **Cobb** (1660-1728; Henry[9], *d* 1679);

7-Dea. Samuel (1683-1767), Falmouth, Me.; *m* 1708, Abigail Stewart or Stuart (1686-1766);

6-Hannah (1712-91), Windham, Me.; *m* 1753, Zerubbabel **Hunnewell** (1716-1803), mem. Com. of Safety for Windham during Am. Rev.;

5-Susannah (1755-87), *m* 1778, Benjamin **Bodge** (1755-1831);

4-Eunice (1778-1848), *m* Ezekiel **Robinson** (4 above).

2-Amelia Bovey Robinson (1839-1911), *m* 1863, John **McAuslan** (1835-96), dry goods mcht.; issue: I-George Robert (*b* 1865); II-John Wallace (1866-94; *m* Fannie Olney Ashley); III-William Alexander (1 above); IV-Arthur Warden (1874-85); V-Harold Lee (*b* 1877; *m* Cleora Foster); VI-Frederic Troup (*b* 1879; *m* Mary Reoch); VII-Albert Hamilton (*b* 1881; *m* Frances Cornish).

1-*m* Feb. 18, 1897, Grace Ellen Barnaby, *b* Providence, R.I., Apr. 21, 1873; dau. of Abner Jones Barnaby, of Providence; issue: 1-Alexander (Dec. 23, 1898-Jan. 10, 1899); 2-Barnaby, *b* Providence, Nov. 4, 1900; Ph.B., Brown, '22; *m* June 29, 1928, Elsie Kreider, of Lancaster, Pa.; 3-Grace Amelia, *b* Providence, Apr. 3, 1905; A.B., Brown, '28; 4-Gloria Natalie, *b* Providence, July 25, 1913.

1-A.B., Brown, '96 (Delta Phi). In library business since 1904; trustee Ministry at Large, Providence. Mem. S.M.D., O.F.P.A., S.C.W., S.A.R., N.E.H.G.S., R.I. Hist. Soc., Hathaway Family Assn. (pres.), First Congl. Soc. (pres.). Unitarian. Republican. Clubs: Shelter Harbor Country, Westerly Shrine, Economic, Brown (Providence), City (Boston), Delta Phi (N.Y.). Summer place: Warwick, R.I. Residence: 47 Grotto Av., Providence, R.I.

1-**McCAMANT, Davis,** *b* Portland, Ore., July 24, 1896.

7-Alexander **McCamant** (*d* 1748), from Ireland to Lancaster Co., Pa., ca. 1725; *m* Mary Black;

6-William, *m* Mary Simpson;

5-James (*d* 1825), capt. Am. Rev.; *m* Abigail Graham (James[6], Am. Rev.);

4-Graham (1787-1851), *m* Mary Meadville;

3-Thomas (1840-1907), A.B., Lafayette, '61; lt. in Civil War; auditor gen. of Pa., 1888-92; *m* 1866, Delia Rollins;

2-Wallace (2 below).

9-James (Rawlins) **Rollins** (qv);

8-Thomas (*b* 1641), *m* 1670, Rachel Cox;

7-John (*d* 1776), *m* 1722, Mary Savary;

6-Nathaniel, *m* Lydia Clark;

5-Eliphalet (1758-1835), *m* Mary Jones;

4-Joseph (*b* 1797), *m* Mary Howard;

3-Delia (1843-1920), *m* Thomas **McCamant** (3 above).

9-Stephen **Davis,** of N.J.; one of those who asso. to "endeavor the carrying on of spiritual concernments as also civil and town affairs according to God and godly government," on the banks of the Passaic;

8-Thomas (*b* ante settlement of Newark-*d* 1738/39, aet. 78);

7-Jonathan;

6-Caleb (1717-83), Am. Rev.; *m* Ruth Bruen;

5-Joseph (1753-1827), minuteman in Am. Rev.; *m* Anna Crane;

4-Charles (*b* 1800), *m* Caroline Matilda Gildersleeve;

3-William M. (1840-1905), lawyer, Phillipsburg, N.J.; *m* Elizabeth Wakeman Weller (1845-1923);

2-Katherine Stimson (*b* 1867), *m* 1893, Wallace **McCamant** (*b* 1867), master in chancery U.S. Court for Dist. of Ore., 1894-1917; asso. justice Supreme Ct. of Ore., 1917-18; pres.-gen. Nat. Soc., S.A.R., 1921-22 (see Who's Who in America); issue: I-Davis (1 above); II-Thomas (*b* 1901; *m* Feb. 17, 1929, Katherine, dau. of Rev. Clayton Judy; issue: Wallace, III, *b* Feb. 13, 1930).
1-Not married. Oregon Agrl. Coll., '22. Served as pvt. Co. E, 162d Inf., in base censor's office, Paris, with A.E.F. during World War. Mem. Loyal Legion (Ore. Cdry.), Multnomah Athletic Club. Address: C/o Wallace McCamant, 236 King St., Portland, Ore.

1-**McCANN, Minnie Abigail Thompson (Mrs. Thomas E.),** *b* Lawrence, Kan., Oct. 30, 1868.
8-Richard **Bullock** (qv);
7-Samuel (1648-1718), of Rehoboth; *m* 2d, 1675, Thankful Rouse;
6-Seth (*b* 1693), *m* 1718, Experience Salisbury (*b* 1700);
5-Shubael (1746-1807), to Guilford, Vt., 1763-64; corpl., Cumberland Co. militia in Am. Rev.; *m* 1764 or 65, Mary E. Richardson (1747-1807);
4-Shubael (1776-1848), to Fairhaven, Vt., 1798; War 1812; *m* Elizabeth Dibble (*d* 1862; Thomas[5], Am. Rev.);
3-Shubel (1814-1903), of St. Clair, Mich.; *m* 1839, Abigail Weeks (1819-1901);
2-Eliza Jane (1843-1916), *m* 1863, George Coleman **Thompson** (1838-1921); issue: I-Cora Jane (*b* 1865; *m* Samuel Petri); II-Charles Shubell (*b* 1866; *m* Eva Purchase); III-Minnie Abigail (1 above); IV-Flora M. (*b* 1870; *m* Jack Stahl); V-George Edwin (1872-1913); VI-Walter (*b* 1874); VII-Anna Fay (*b* 1883; *m* Robert Ward).
1-*m* Aug. 29, 1888, Thomas Edward McCann, *b* Bayfield, Ont., Can., Apr. 5, 1867; son of Henry W. McCann; issue: 1-Russell Loyd, *b* Midland, Mich., June 10, 1889; *m* Nov. 23, 1909, Florence, dau. of John Broderick, of Saginaw, Mich. (issue: Thomas Edward, *b* Aug. 11, 1915; Margery Ruth, May 1, 1919); 2-W. D. Gordon, *b* Midland, Feb. 21, 1892; *m* Nov. 30, 1913, Helen, dau. of Burton H. Carter, of Midland (issue: Dorothy Jane, *b* Dec. 25, 1914; Burton Edward, Feb. 3, 1921; Margot Helen, *b* Jan. 4, 1922).
1-Mem. D.A.R., Monday Club. Residence: 608 W. Main, Midland, Mich.

1-**McCLURE, Roy Fleming,** *b* Braddock, Pa., Dec. 4, 1876.
7-John **McClure** (1696-1757), from Ireland, settled at Carlisle, Cumberland Co., Pa., 1725; *m* 1720, Janet McKnight (1702-80);
6-John (1723-1811), coroner, 1754-58; removed to Mifflin Tp. Allegheny Co., 1786; *m* Martha Denny (William[7]);
5-John (1766-1833), *m* Agnes Topping (1771-1858; Robert[6]);
4-Robert (1792-1859), *m* Elizabeth McClure;
3-Alexander (1818-80), McKeesport, Pa.; *m* 1842, Margaret McClure;
2-William Barnett (2 below).
8-Richard **McClure,** from Ireland, settled in Paxtang Tp. Lancaster Co., Pa.;
7-Richard (*d* 1774), of Paxtang Tp.; *m* Jean-;
6-Alexander (*d* 1803), of Mifflin Tp., Allegheny Co.; soldier in Am. Rev.; *m* Martha-;
5-Margaret (1762-1835), *m* 1782, Francis **McClure** (1740-1843; Samuel[6]);
4-Elizabeth (1794-1848), of Mifflin Tp.; *m* Robert **McClure** (4 above).
7-Richard **McClure** (same as 8 above);
6-Richard (7 above);
5-Andrew (1756-99), of Pa.; served in Am. Rev.; *m* 1775, Margaret Barnett;
4-William Barnett (1779-1862), of Pa.; clk. of courts at Pittsburgh, 1830-34; justice; co. commr., Allegheny Co.; elder Presbyn. ch.; *m* 2d, 1811, Margaret Ferguson (1791-1884; Samuel[5], from Ireland to Pa., 1773, *m* Mary Hearst);
3-Margaret (1816-91), *m* Alexander **McClure** (3 above).
8-John **Barnett** (1678-1734), from Ireland, settled in Lancaster Co., Pa., ante 1730; *m* in Ireland, Jennett-;
7-John (1705-85), of Paxtang Tp.; *m* Margaret Roan (1710-90);
6-Joseph (1726-1808), of Mifflin Tp.; *m* 1749, Elizabeth Graham;
5-Margaret (1752-1831), *m* Andrew **McClure** (5 above).
4-James **Fleming** (1762-1825), from Ireland, settled in Pa.; *m* Jane Magoffin (1770-1848; Alexander[5], of Ireland);
3-James (1801-85), of Pittsburgh; *m* 1827, Mary Patterson Criswell (1800-76; James[4], of Ireland, *m* Catherine McClure);
2-Rebecca Moreland (1845-1917), *m* 1875, Dr. William Barnett **McClure** (1849-1927), physician, Cattanooga, Tenn.; issue: I-Roy Fleming (1 above); II-George Cavan (*m* Flora Treuthart); III-William Alexander (*m* Mary Wheelock).
1-Not married. LL.B., U. of Chattanooga, 1907 (Delta Theta Phi), LL.M., 1919. Engaged in law practice since 1907; instr. law, Chattanooga Coll. since 1910 (trustee); sec. North Ga. Abstract Co. Mem. I.A.G. Presbyterian. Democrat. Residence: Chattanooga, Tenn.

1-**McDANIEL, Walton Brooks,** *b* Cambridge, Mass., Mar. 4, 1871.
7-Benjamin **Ashton,** *m* Eliza-;
6-Robert (1714-70), *m* Hannah Farnsworth;
5-Joseph (1754-98), *m* Elizabeth Parker;
4-Hannah, *m* 1808, John Bowman **McDaniel** (1784-1829), of Egypt, N.J. (William[5], desc. of Scotch invaders of the North of Ireland in the time of King James);
3-Joseph Ashton (1809-66), Jacobstown, N.J.; *m* 1830, Hannah Boyer (*b* 1810; Jacob[4], living at Phila., 1821);
2-Samuel Walton (2 below).
9-Capt. Thomas **Brooks** (qv);
8-Joshua, *m* 1653, Hannah Mason;
7-Benjamin (*b* ca. 1698), of Concord (now Lincoln), Mass.; *m* Sarah-;
6-Benjamin, of Townsend; *m* Elizabeth Green;
5-Abner, *m* Anna Hobart;
4-Samuel (1780-1863), of Townsend; *m* 1806, Jane Hill (1781-1857), of Newton, Mass.;
3-George Hobart (1808-92), of Brighton, Mass.; *m* 1831, Lucy Dana White (1810-95);
2-Georgianna Frances (1839-1920), *m* 1870, Samuel Walton **McDaniel** (1833-1905), capt., Co. I, 4th Pa. Vols., 1861, later chaplain same regt.; LL.B., Harvard, 1878; councilman and alderman of Cambridge, Mass.; mem. Mass. House of Rep.; asso. judge, 3d Middlesex Dist. Ct. many yrs.; issue: I-Walton Brooks (1 above); II-Ralph Boyer (1872-1923; *m* Helen Nolan).
1-*m* Aug. 2, 1899, Alice Corinne Garlichs, *b* St. Joseph, Mo., Apr. 27, 1872; dau. of Herman M. Garlichs, of St. Joseph.
1-A.B. (magna cum laude), Harvard, '93 (Delta U., P.B.K.), A.M., 1894, Ph.D., 1899. Prof. Latin, U. of Pa., since 1909. Author (see Who's Who in America). Unitarian. Democrat. Mem. Am. Philos. Soc. (councillor), Am. Philol. Assn. (ex-pres.), Archaeol. Inst. America, Classical Assn. of Atlantic States, Phila. Classical Soc., Ends of the Earth Club, Am. Classical League, Mediaeval Academy of America, A.A.A.S., Classical Assn. of England and Wales, Société des Études Latines of France, Am. Assn. Univ. Profs. (charter). Summer place: Oak Bluffs, Marthas Vineyard, Mass. Residence: 264 S. 44th St. W., Philadelphia, Pa.

1-**MacDONALD, Grace Joy (Mrs. James Davis),** *b* Springport, Mich., Dec. 22, 1872.
10-Thomas **Joy** (qv);
9-Ens. Joseph (1645-97), Boston and Hingham, Mass.; constable, carpenter and farmer; ens. in Hingham mil. co.; *m* 1667, Mary Prince (bap. 1649-1726; John[10], settled at Hingham ca. 1646; *m* Margaret-);
8-Joseph (1668-1716), *m* 1690, Elizabeth Andrews;
7-David (1693-1739), of Rehoboth, *m* 1718, Ruth Ford, of Pembrook, Mass.;
6-David (1724-1809), at Russia, Herkimer Co., N.Y., ante 1809; in French and Indian War; present at capture of Fort Ticonderoga, 1775; said to have been a platoon officer under Gen. Ruggles; justice; *m* 1747, Elizabeth Allen (*d* 1820, aet. 96);
5-David (1754-1813), in Am. Rev., July 17-Dec. 9, 1775; *m* 1776, Hannah Partridge (1757-1830);
4-Comfort (1787-1869), *m* 1810, Mary Breiner (1792-1844);
3-Alonzo (1825-69), *m* 1846, Phebe Z. Burgess (1831-91);
2-Ben A. (2 below).

11–Thomas **Andrews,** from Devonshire, Eng., ante 1635; a first settler of Hingham, 1643;
10–Joseph (1597-1679), constable, rep. and first town clerk of Hingham; *m* Elizabeth–' (*d* 1688);
9–Capt. Thomas (1632-90), constable, selectman, rep.; mem. of Council of Safety; died while on expdn. to Canada under Sir William Phipps; *m* Ruth– (1635-1732);
8–Elizabeth (1665-1743), *m* Joseph **Joy** (8 above).
2–Ben A. **Joy** (1847-1918), *m* 1871, Clarissa J. Ferris (1849-1919); issue: I–Grace (1 above); II–Mabel (*b* 1878; *m* Dr. G. M. Livingston); III–Alice C. (1879-1927; *m* H. L. Pinney).
1–*m* Aug. 26, 1896, James David MacDonald (July 27, 1866-July 2, 1925); son of William MacDonald, of Sault St. Marie, Mich.; issue: 1–Elizabeth Forbes, *b* Petoskey, Mich., Nov. 20, 1897; Randolph-Macon Woman's Coll.; *m* June 30, 1920, H. R. Hausen (issue: Robert; James); 2–Alice Joy, *b* Lapeer, Mich., June 28, 1901; A.B., U. of Mich., '27; *m* May 5, 1927, K. F. Campbell.
1–Ed. Albion Coll. Mem. D.A.R., I.A.G. Presbyterian. Republican. Residence: 49 Highland Av., Detroit, Mich.

1–**McHUGH, Lerah Gillett Stratton (Mrs. P. J.),** *b* Ft. Collins, Colo., May 4, 1868.
9–Samuel **Wright** (*d* 1665; son of Nathaniel, of London, Eng.); deacon; Springfield, Mass., 1639; *m* Margaret– (*d* 1681);
8–Samuel (bap. 1629-1675), *m* 1653, Elizabeth Burt (1630-91);
7–Benjamin (1660-1743), *m* 1st, 1680, Thankful Taylor (1664-1701; Capt. John[8] [1641-1704], *m* Thankful Woodward);
6–Remembrance (1683-1765), *m* Elizabeth– (1689-1769);
5–Reuben (1733-1807), soldier Am. Rev.; *m* Hannah Graves;
4–Hannah (*d* 1846), *m* 1789, Hezekiah **Stratton** (1766-1825); see Vol. II, p. 44, for Stratton lineage, and Vol. III, p. 559, for Smith-Stratton lineage);
3–Harris (1791-1872), *m* 1819, Sophie Ruggles (see Vol. II, p. 44, for Ruggles lineage);
2–Harris (2 below).
9–Thomas **Graves** (ante 1585-1662), from Eng. to Salem, Mass., ca. 1628; *m* Sarah– (*d* 1666);
8–John (*d* 1677), freeman, Wethersfield, Conn., 1654; *m* 1st, Mary Smith (Lt. Samuel[9], of Wethersfield);
7–Samuel (1657-1731), from Hatfield to Sunderland ca. 1725; *m* Sarah– (*d* 1734);
6–David (1693-1781), of "Bashan," Hatfield; removed to Whately, Mass., ca. 1730-33; *m* 1720, Abigail Bardwell (1699-1786; Robert[7], of Hatfield);
5–Hannah (1742-1807), *m* 1757, Reuben **Wright** (5 above).
9–Richard **Treat** (qv);
8–Richard;
7–Thomas (1668-1713), *m* Dorothy Bulkeley (1662-1757; Gershom[8], A.B., Harvard, 1655, 2d minister at New London, historian, *m* 1659, Sarah, dau. of Charles Chauncy, qv; Rev. Peter[9], qv);
6–Dorothy (1704-90), *m* Theophilus **Baldwin** (Barnabas[7], *m* Sarah–; Richard[8], qv);
5–Richard (1745-1823), served on com. of inspection for Branford, Conn.; *m* Alice Botsford;
4–Adah (*b* 1773), *m* 1794, David **Hickox** (1772-1830; John[5], *m* 1757, Eunice Warner; John[6]; Samuel[7]; Sgt. Samuel[8]; William[9]; Thomas[10]; Edward[11]);
3–Abiah (1800-87), *m* 1819, Elisha **Parke** (1793-1852); see Vol. III, p. 559, for Parke lineage;
2–Elizabeth (1830-1922), as Widow of William Keays, *m* 2d, as his 1st wife, 1866, Harris **Stratton** (1828-1908), mem. Colo. Legislature, 1876; sec. Colo. Agrl. College (see Vol. II, p. 44, for issue).
1–*m* Jan. 21, 1892, Dr. Peter Joseph McHugh, *b* Essex, Ont., Can., Sept. 17, 1863; of Irish descent; issue (all *b* Ft. Collins, Colo.): 1–Keith Stratton, *b* Feb. 22, 1895; U.Wis., '17; 1st lt., ordnance, Aug. 15, 1917; capt., July 1918; c.o., ordnance machine gun instruction, Camp Hancock, Ga., Apr. 22-Sept. 9, 1918; exec. officer engring. dept., A.E.F., Tours, France, Sept. 1918-Feb. 8, 1919; *m* Aug. 16, 1917, Frances, dau. of Benjamin Perry Brown, of Ottumwa, Ia.; 2–Jerome Antony (Mar. 15, 1897-July 16, 1920); Colo. Agrl., '20; 3–Joseph Weir, *b* Dec. 12, 1902; U.Ill., '24.
1–B.S., Colo. Agrl. Coll., '87. Pres. Colo. State Federation of Women's Clubs, 1912-14; state registrar Colo. D.A.R., 1920-26; mem. I.A.G. Residence: 137 Remington St., Ft. Collins, Colo.

1–**McLEAN, Grace Chalmers Patton (Mrs. Allan),** *b* St. Marys, Pa., Oct. 24, 1867.
11–Robert **Fletcher** (qv);
10–William (1622-77), settled at Chelmsford, 1653; selectman, 1654; commr. for Chelmsford, 1673; *m* 1647, Lydia Bates (*d* 1704);
9–William (*d*-1713), commd. lt., Boston, 1704, by Gov. Dudley; *m* 1677, Sarah Richardson (1659-1748);
8–William (1684-1744), *m* Tabitha–;
7–Stephen (1713-67), *m* 1741, Susanna Colburn (1721-1817);
6–Oliver (*b* 1743), *m* 1766, Tabitha Richardson;
5–Thankful (1766-1800), Hollis, N.H.; *m* 1790, William **Combs** (1758-1840), Am. Rev. (John[6], Am. Rev.);
4–William (1791-1849), *m* 1808, Jane A. Nutt (1792-1849), of Manchester (James[5], served thru Rebellion of 1786);
3–William H. (1820-95), of Manchester; *m* 1841, Grace Chalmers (1816-98);
2–Kate (2 below).
10–Ezekiel **Richardson** (qv);
9–Josiah (1635-95), of Woburn, Mass.; freeman, 1653; constable, 1667; selectman, 1668-88; capt. of a mil. co.; *m* 1659, Remembrance Underwood;
8–John (1669-1746), of Chelmsford, Mass.; *m* 1693, Elizabeth Farwell (1672-1729);
7–John (1711-64), *m* 1733, Esther Pierce (1710-1803);
6–Tabitha (*b* 1746), of Charlestown; *m* 1766, Oliver **Fletcher** (6 above).
9–Pieter **Winne** (*d* 1693), from Holland; magistrate, 1650-74; maj., 1689; commr. to treat with Indians, 1690; *m* Tanneke Adams;
8–Daniel, *m* 1698, Dirkie Van Ness;
7–William (*b* 1716), *m* Maria De Wandelaer (*b* 1715);
6–Dirkie (*b* 1748), *m* 1769, Guy **Young** (*b* 1749), lt. and capt. Am. Rev.;
5–Cathalynte (*b* 1771), *m* 1787, Jacob D. **Felthousen** (*b* 1765);
4–Nancy (*b* 1787-1825), *m* 1810, Stewart **Chalmers** (1782-1825);
3–Grace, *m* William H. **Combs** (3 above);
2–Kate (1843-1923), of Corry, Pa.; *m* 1867, John Vevers **Patton** (1844-1920), in Civil War; ry. supt.; issue: I–Grace Chalmers (1 above); II–Joseph Robinson (1868-1930; *m* 1893, Mary S. C. Uhl); III–Robert Baily (*b* 1871; *m* Jane Shea); IV–John Vevers, Jr. (*b* 1873); V–Stewart Spencer (*b* 1876); VI–Frank Hamilton (*b* 1881; *m* 1909, Eda D. Black).
1–*m* Oct. 12, 1914, Allan McLean, *b* Jersey City, N.J., Apr. 6, 1873; son of Alexander McLean, of Jersey City.
1–Mem. C.D.XVIIC., Dutch Settlers of Albany, D.A.R., Daus. of the Union, 1861-65, I.A.G., etc. Episcopalian. Republican. Residence: 1465 E. 19th St., Brooklyn, N.Y.

1–**MacNEAL, Arthur,** *b* Detroit, Mich., Jan. 6, 1868.
5–Edward Fitzgerald **MacNeal** (*b* 1732), officer in Am. Rev., served in New York;
4– ————, *m* Hannah Butterfield;
3–Abraham (1789-1869), of Sterling, N.Y.; *m* Elizabeth Durham (1791-1858; sister of James, Methodist preacher, Elmira, N.Y.);
2–Edward (1833-1922), merchant, railroad conductor, Fenton, Mich.; *m* 1855, Mary Paine (*d* 1864); *m* 2d, 1865, Jane Elizabeth Pratt (1841-1918); issue (1st marriage): I–Mary Adelaide (*b* 1858; *m* Dobson–; *m* 2d, William Howard); II–Edward (*b* 1861; *m* Lucy Reid); III–Cordelia (*b* 1864; *m* 1890, Edward Mann, *b* 1860); issue (2d marriage): I–Frank (*b* 1866; *m* Ella Bruce); II–Arthur (1 above); III–George Frederick (*b* 1879; *m* Ada Angell); IV–Ward J. (qv for maternal lineage);
1–*m* Mar. 7, 1893, Mina Kolb, *b* Battle Creek, Mich., Oct. 4th, 1867; dau. of William A. Kolb, *d*, *m* Sarah E.–; issue (all *b* Berwyn, Ill.): 1–Doris, *b* Feb. 28, 1894; A.B., U.Chicago, '15; *m* July 1917, Harold T. Moore, of Chicago, Ill.

(issue: Doris Elizabeth; Malcolm, adopted); 2–Kenneth F., *b* Dec. 20, 1895; grad. U.Chicago, 1919, Walton Sch. of Commerce; *m* Mar. 1921, Marguerite Gireaud, of Grenoble, France (issue: Richard Henri; Edward Arthur; Marguerite Louise); 3–Louise, *b* Sept. 18, 1898; A.-B., U.Chicago, '21; *m* Nov. 1926, Carleton H. Burlingame, of Los Angeles, Calif. (issue: Carleton, Jr.); 4–Florence, *b* Aug. 8, 1899; A.B., U. of Chicago, '20; *m* June 1927, Guy, son of John Noonan, of Darlington, Eng. (issue: John MacNeal); 5–Robert Arthur, *b* Nov. 9, 1909; student Northwestern U.

1–A.B., U. of Mich., '90 (Delta U.); M.D., Rush Med. Coll., 1892. Practicing physician, Berwyn, Ill., since 1892. Pres. Berwyn Med. Unit; High Sch. Bd. Med. Mem. local exemption bd. during World War. Mem. Life Founder of The Civil Legion. Mason. Republican. Residence: 3144 Wisconsin Av., Berwyn, Ill.

1–**MacNEAL, Ward J.**, *b* Fenton, Mich., Feb. 17, 1881.
5–Abraham **Osborn** (1753-1835), of Point Pleasant, N.J.; *m* Elizabeth Allen (1756-1839);
4–Jane (1787-1874), of Birdsall, N.Y.; *m* 1800, Thomas **Havens** (1778-1833);
3–Mercy (1811-91), of Chicago, Ill.; *m* 1829, George K. **Pratt** (1807-81; Stephen[4], of Livingston Co., N.Y., *m* Keturah Greene, *d* ca. 1845);
2–Jane Elizabeth (1841-1918), *m* 1865, as his 2d wife, Edward **MacNeal** (1833-1922); for issue see brother Arthur MacNeal.
1–*m* Dec. 28, 1905, Mabel Perry, *b* Ann Arbor, Mich., Oct. 21, 1881; dau. of W. S. Perry, supt. schs. of Ann Arbor, 1872-97, *m* Emma Blackman; issue: 1–Edward Perry (Oct. 4, 1906-Mar. 3, 1919); 2–Herbert P., *b* Urbana, Ill., Mar. 10, 1909; 3–Perry Scott, *b* Brooklyn, N.Y., Sept. 11, 1913; 4–Mabel Ruth, *b* Forest Hills, L.I., June 25, 1924.
1–A.B., U.Mich., 1901, Ph.D., 1904, M.D., 1905. Prof. and dir. of laboratories of pathology and bacteriology, New York Post-Grad. Med. Sch. and Hosp., since 1915, also mem. bd. trustees, 1921-24, v.chmn. med. bd. 1924-29. Author (see Who's Who in America). Capt. Med. R.C., 1917; lt. col., M.R.C., U.S.A., 1919; col., 1925; with A.E.F. in France to Feb. 1919. Republican. Club: Kew Gardens Tennis. Residence: 82 Rockrose Pl., Forest Hills, L.I., N.Y.

1–**McSWEENY, John**, *b* Westgate, Ia., Feb. 26, 1890.
5–David Wheeler **Morehouse** (desc. Thomas Morehouse, from Eng., 1628, settled at Stamford, Conn.), was of Meekerstown, Conn.; *m* Anna–;
4–Eli (1777-1855), of Greene Co., O.; *m* 1801, Hannah Knapp;
3–Eli (1804-55), of Colebrook, O.; *m* 1829, Angelina Webb;
2–Mary (2 below).
9–Richard **Webb** (qv);
8–Richard (1623-76), of Norwalk and Stamford; *m* Margery–;
7–Samuel, of Stamford;
6–Charles (*b* 1696), *m* 1723, Mary Smith;
5–Charles (1724-1800), col. in Am. Rev.; selectman, 1757, re-elected 19 times; rep. State Legislature, 1758, re-elected 23 times; *m* 1747, Mercy Holly (1729-1803);
4–Isaac (1766-1840), pvt. Am. Rev.; *m* 1791, Mary Weed (1771-1849);
3–Angelina (1812-1901), of Colebrook, O.; *m* 1829, Eli **Morehouse** (3 above);
2–Mary (1851-1926), of Westgate, Ia.; *m* 1874, John H. **McSweeny** (*b* 1853), farmer; issue: I–Lula A. (*b* 1875; *m* James B. Murphy); II–Henry (*b* 1881; *m* Margaret Mae Kinyon); III–Albert (*b* 1883; *m* Olive Lee Baker); IV–John (1 above).
1–*m* June 22, 1915, Shirley Louise Day, *b* Oelwein, Ia., Nov. 4, 1891; dau. of Edward Everett Day; issue: 1–Shirley Marguerite, *b* Oelwein, Ia., Feb. 7, 1920; 2–Albert Blair, *b* Cotter, Ia., May 28, 1924.
1–B.A., Upper Ia. U., '15 (Delta Upsilon Iota). Teacher, 1914-17; on cattle ranch, 1919-22; teaching since 1922. Served in 91st Div., Camp Lewis, Wash., Oct. 1917-June 4, 1918; F.A.O.-T.C., Zachary Taylor, Ky., June 4-Aug. 31, 1918; assigned to F.A. R.D. Camp, Jackson, S.C.; 56th F.A., Ft. Sill, Okla., F.A.R.C. since 1919. Mem. I.A.G., A.L. Mason, Odd Fellow. Methodist. Residence: Victor, Ia.

1–**MAERCKLEIN, Alice Rebecca Crane (Mrs. Herman Julius)**, *b* Hartford, Conn., Mar. 12, 1859.
8–Benjamin **Crane** (ca. 1630-1691), at Wethersfield, Conn., 1655 or earlier; *m* 1655, Mary Backus (*d* 1717; William[9]);
7–Lt. Jonathan (1658-1735), dep. from Windham to Gen. Ct.; *m* 1678, Deborah Griswold (1661-1704);
6–John (*b* 1687), of Windham; *m* 2d, 1716, Prudence Belding (*b* 1694);
5–Hezekiah (1721-1805), E. Windsor, Conn.; Am. Rev.; *m* 1746, Rachel Rockwell (1726-1809);
4–David (1748-1840), corpl. Am. Rev.; *m* 2d, 1779, Jerusha Smith (1759-1848);
3–Warren Smith (1802-60), of West Hartford; *m* 1828, Mary Kirtland Crampton (1808-35);
2–Warren Burdette (2 below).
8–Daniel **Cone** (1626-1706), of Haddam, Conn.; *m* ante 1662 Mahitabel Spencer (1642-91; Gerard or Jared[9]);
7–Nathaniel (1674-1732), of E. Haddam; *m* 1695 or 96, Sarah Hungerford (1679-1753; Thomas[8], *m* Mary Grey; Sir Thomas[9], qv);
6–James (1698-1774), lt. colonial troops, 1738; mem. Conn. Legislature, 1747-49; 1st clk. of Ecclesiastical Soc. of Millington (E. Haddam); *m* 1726, Grace Spencer (1702-67; John[7], *m* Elizabeth–);
5–Sylvanus (1734/35-1812), mem. Ft. Edwards expdn., 1755; Crown Pt. expdn., 1756; in French and Indian War; minute man in Am. Rev.; was at Battle of Bunker Hill; *m* Hannah Ackley (1742-1790; Gideon[6]);
4–Joseph Warren (1775-1848), of E. Haddam and Hartford; *m* 1796, Mahitabel Swan (1778-1849);
3–Sylvanus Franklin (1814-79), of Hartford; *m* 1835, Sarah Ann Terry Miller (1812-49);
2–Sarah Adelaide (1837-75), *m* 1857, Warren Burdette **Crane** (1832-60), mfr., W. Hartford, and Newington, Conn.
1–*m* Nov. 3, 1883, Herman Julius Maercklein, *b* Hartford, Conn., Dec. 30, 1856; son of Herman August Wilhelm Maercklein; issue (all *b* Hartford, Conn.): 1–Burdette Crane, *b* Oct. 12, 1884; A.M., Trinity, '06; 2–Marion Crane, *b* June 1, 1888; *m* Mar. 15, 1924, Dr. Philip Dudley Woodbridge (issue: Dudley Hooker); 3–Richard Cone, *b* Mar. 28, 1890; *m* Oct. 10, 1916, Marjorie Argyle, dau. of Harvey Burdette Goodwin (issue: Richard Goodwin; Margaret Marion).
1–Mem. S.M.D., I.A.G. Residence: 213 Laurel St., Hartford, Conn.

1–**MANDEVILLE, Ernest Wyckoff**, *b* Elmira, N.Y., Mar. 20, 1896.
11–Yellis Johnson **Mandeville**, from France via Holland ca. 1640, settled at New Amsterdam; *m* Elsie Hendricks (*d* 1701);
10–William;
9–Yellis (*d* 1778);
8–Jeremiah;
7–John, of Claverick;
6–Francis (*d* 1836), of Garland, Warren Co., Pa.;
5–Jeremiah (*b* 1787), War 1812; *m* 1812, Anna Atwater;
4–Nelson (*b* 1816), *m* Elizabeth Ann Hanford;
3–Edgar W., *m* Carrie E. Cassidy;
2–Hubert C. (*b* 1867), A.B., Union Coll., '88, L.H.D., 1923; lawyer; author (see Who's Who in America); *m* 1892, Mary F. Stoops; issue: I–William H. (*b* 1893; *m* Ruth Buck); II–Ernest Wyckoff (1 above); III–Mary (*b* 1902); IV–Hubert C., Jr., (*b* 1903).
1–*m* Sept. 17, 1919, Ruth Elizabeth Turner, *b* Benziner, Pa., July 26, 1896; dau. of William T. Turner, of Utica, N.Y.; issue: 1–Ernest Wyckoff, Jr., *b* Utica, N.Y., June 29, 1920; 2–Hubert Turner, *b* Utica, Sept. 11, 1922; 3–Michael Lloyd, *b* Long Branch, N.J., Sept. 24, 1923.
1–B.A., Union Coll., '17 (Psi U.); grad. Gen. Theol. Sem., 1924. Deacon, 1924, priest, 1925, P.E. Ch.; minister Christ Ch., Middletown, N.J., since 1923. With U.S. Secret Service, 1917-18; investigator for Westchester Co., N.Y., 1918-19. Editor The Chesterfieldian, 1919-20; news editor Churchman, nat. weekly of P.E. Ch., since 1923; editorial writer with Outlook; mem. staff Christian Century. Made study of Great Britain's liquor problem for

the Outlook, 1925. Author (see Who's Who in America). Club: Town Hall (New York). Residence: Middletown, N.J.

1–**MANGAM, Jennie Marie Webster (Mrs. Samuel A.),** *b* New York, N.Y., July 10, 1868.
9–Judge Simon **Lynde** (qv);
8–Judge Samuel (1653-1721), of Boston; prominent in town affairs, 1692-1708; one of majesty's justices, 1702-18; overseer of poor, 1691; merchant, and owned a brick house and brick warehouse on Cornhill St., and a pasture and orchard on Cambridge St.; owned land inherited from his father, in Freetown; donated the lot on which the first meetinghouse was built; owned an island in the Kennebec River; admitted to A. and H.A.Co., 1691; *m* 1674, Mary Ballord (*d* 1697/98; Jervis[9]);
7–Mary (1680-1724), of Boston; *m* 1702, John **Valentine** (*d* 1724), adv. gen. for N.E.; freeman 1675;
6–Samuel (1702-81), of Freetown, Mass.; constable, 1725; rep. Gen. Ct., 1728; selectman and assessor, 1751; *m* 1st, Abigail Durfee (*d* 1765), of Tiverton, R.I.;
5–Joseph (*b* 1734), *m* 1754, as her 1st husband, Hannah Hathaway (*b* 1738);
4–Abigail (1756-1800), *m* 1779, Samuel **Webster** (1741-1808), of Conn.; soldier Am. Rev.;
3–Samuel (1798-1843), of Freehold or Cairo, N.Y.; *m* 1822, Eliza Brown (1801-43; Jonathan[4] [*d* 1850, aet. 75], maj. War 1812, shipbuilder, New York, *m* Rhenanna–);
2–William Valentine (1827-83), of N.Y. City; *m* 1853, Amanda Melvina Jennings (1831-63); *m* 2d, 1865, Jennie Amanda Marie Solan (1842-90); issue (1st marriage): I–Samuel (1855-1929; *m* 1886, Anna Cecilia McBarron, 1861-1901); issue (2d marriage): I–Jennie Marie (1 above); II–William Valentine, Jr. (*b* 1870; *m* 1892, Elizabeth Cashow); III–Charles Carpenter (*m* 1899, Isabel Larkin).
1–*m* Jan. 8, 1896, Samuel Alfred Mangam, *b* Brooklyn, N.Y., Aug. 8, 1868; son of John William Mangam (1844-1900), of Brooklyn, *m* 1866, Almira M. Betts (1850-1922); issue: 1–Elliott Webster, *b* Brooklyn, Mar. 16, 1897; *m* Mar. 5, 1927, Winifred Irma, dau. of Otto Pfordte, of Cairo, Greene Co., N.Y., *m* Frieda Titel.
1–Ed. Normal (now Hunter) Coll., N.Y. City. Local historian of Cairo, N.Y. Mem. D.A.R., I.A.G., Greene Co. Hist. Soc. (life), L.I. Hist. Soc., Brooklyn Inst. of Arts and Sciences. Episcopalian. Republican. Summer place: Cairo, Greene Co., N.Y. Residence: 1307 Pacific St., Brooklyn, N.Y.

1–**MARSHALL, Harriet Putnam Ely (Mrs. George M.),** *b* Elyria, O., Oct. 9, 1864.
8–Nathaniel **Ely** (qv);
7–Samuel (*d* 1695), of Springfield; *m* 1659, Mary Day (1641-1725; Robert[8], *m* Editha Stebbins);
6–Dea. John (1678-1758), *m* 1703, Mercy Bliss (1680-1763; Samuel[7], *m* Mary Leonard);
5–Ens. John (1707-54), *m* 1733, Eunice Colton (1705-78; John[6], *m* Joanna–);
4–Justin (1739-1817), grad. Harvard, 1759; merchant, W. Springfield; rep. Gen. Ct. of Mass., 1777; interested in real estate in Mass., Vt., N.Y., and dist. of Me.; one of the original proprs. of the Conn. Reserve in Ohio under the Conn. Land Co.; *m* 1762, Ruth White (1744-1809; Capt. Joel[5], *m* Ruth Dart);
3–Heman (1775-1852), Elyria, O.; *m* 1818, Celia Belden;
2–Heman (2 below).
9–Richard **Belden** (qv);
8–John (1631-77), freeman, Wethersfield, 1657; trooper under Capt. John Mason, 1657-58; *m* Lydia Standish (Thomas[9], *m* Susanna–);
7–Joseph (*b* 1663), *m* 1693, Mary Willard (Josiah[8], *m* Hannah Hosmer);
6–Thomas (*b* 1700), *m* 1731, Mary Mix (*b* 1700; Rev. Stephen[7], *m* Mary Stoddard);
5–Thomas (*b* 1732), *m* 1753, Abigail Porter (*b* 1732; Hezekiah[6], *m* Sarah Wright);
4–Col. Ezekiel (1756-1824), *m* 1790, Mary Parsons (Rev. David[5], *m* Eunice Welles);
3–Celia (1796-1827), *m* 1818, Heman **Ely** (3 above).
8–Robert **Day** (qv);
7–Thomas (*d* 1711), *m* Sarah Cooper;
6–Thomas (1662-1729), *m* Elizabeth Merrick;
5–Thomas (1689-1772), *m* Mary Wells;
4–Rev. Jeremiah (1737-1806), B.A., Yale, 1756; *m* Abigail Noble (among their sons was Jeremiah, 9th pres. Yale Coll.);
3–Judge Thomas, LL.D. (1777-1855), B.A., Yale, 1797; sec. of state of Conn. 25 yrs.; *m* Sarah Coit;
2–Mary Frances (2 below).
8–John **Coit** (qv);
7–Joseph (*d* 1704), *m* 1667, Martha Harris (*d* 1713; William[8]);
6–Joseph (1673-1750), *m* 1705, Experience Wheeler (*d* 1759);
5–Col. Samuel (ca. 1708-1792), *m* 1730, Sarah Spaulding (*d* 1776);
4–Wheeler (1739-96), *m* 1774, Sibyl Tracy (*d* 1793; Samuel[5]);
3–Sarah, *m* 1813, Thomas **Day** (3 above).
2–Heman **Ely** (1820-94), banker, Elyria; mem. Ohio Legislature; *m* Mary Harris Monteith (1824-49); *m* 2d, 1850, Mary Frances Day (1827-95); issue (1st marriage): I–Celia Belden (1842-61); II–George Henry (see Vol. I, p. 98); III–Mary Monteith (*b* and *d* 1849); issue (2d marriage): I–Edith Day (Mrs. James De Long Williamson, see Vol. I, p. 98); II–Charles Theodore (*b* 1856; *m* 1881, Carrie Williams); III–Albert Heman (see Vol. I, p. 97); IV–Harriet Putnam (1 above).
1–*m* June 7, 1893, George Morley Marshall (see Vol. II, p. 188 for portrait and genealogy); issue: 1–Esther Philena, *b* Phila., Pa., June 8, 1895; B.A., Vassar, 1917; *m* June 11, 1921, Stephen G., son of Stephen W. Kent, of Summit, N.J. (issue: Stephen G., Jr.; George Marshall; Thomas Day); 2–Harriet Ely, *b* New Hope, Pa., Sept. 7, 1896; *m* Feb. 8, 1930, Robert Seabury Wentworth (Foote), of Germantown, Phila., Pa.; son of Charles Foote, *m* Mary Cecelia Wentworth; 3–Margaret Ely, *b* Phila., Apr. 24, 1898; *m* Jan. 4, 1922, Welsh, son of Dr. George Strawbridge, of Germantown, Phila., *m* Alice Welsh; 4–Celia Belden, *b* New Hope, Jan. 29, 1902; B.A., Sweet Briar, '24; *m* Dec. 27, 1929, Robert Darrah, son of Henry Miller, of Phila. (issue: Darrah Marshall); 5–Thomas, *b* New Hope, Oct. 8, 1905; Ph.B., Yale, '28.
1–Mem. C.D.A., I.A.G., Geneal. Soc. of Pa., Bucks Co. Hist. Soc. Presbyterian. Republican. Clubs: Civic, New Century, Art Alliance. Summer place: "Highland Cove," New Hope, Bucks Co., Pa. Residence: 1819 Spruce St., Phila., Pa.

1–**MERRILL, Henry Ferdinand,** *b* Hartford, Vt., June 15, 1853.
9–Nathaniel **Merrill** (qv);
8–Nathaniel (*d* 1683), of Newbury; *m* 1661, Joanna Ninian (*d* 1718);
7–John (1663-1705), Haverhill, Mass.; *m* Lucy Webster (*b* 1664);
6–John (1696-1773), founded Concord, N.H.; chosen dea., 1730; operated 1st ferry across Merrimac River at Concord; *m* 1723, Lydia Haynes (*b* 1678);
5–Lt. Thomas (1724-89), in French and Indian War and Am. Rev.; founder of Conway, N.H.; *m* Phebe Abbott (1727-55);
4–Enoch (*b* 1751), *m* Mary Ambrose;
3–Josiah Goodhue (1787-1872), Congl. minister, of Me. and N.H.; *m* Harriet Jones (1790-1865), of Standish, Me.;
2–Rev. Josiah (2 below).
9–Dea. Edward (Convers) **Converse** (qv);
8–Sgt. Samuel (*b* Charlestown, 1637), *m* Judith Carter;
7–Samuel (1662-1732), Killingly, Conn.; *m* Dorcas (Hepburn?);
6–Edward (1696-1784), Thompson, Conn.; *m* 1717, Elizabeth Cooper;
5–Jonathan (1723-61), *m* 1743, Keziah Hughes;
4–Dea. Jonathan (1760-1845), began to write name Converse; *m* 1783, Esther Whipple;
3–Adolphus Bolles (1794-1871), *m* Pamela Day;
2–Philomedia Henrietta (1827-69), *m* 1847, Rev. Josiah **Merrill** (1819-94), grad. Dartmouth, '41; Congl. minister, of Me., N.H., Vt. and Mass.; issue: I–Henrietta Augusta (1849-55); II–Caroline Adelaide (*b* 1851; *m* Rev. F. L. Allen, *d*); III–Henry Ferdinand (1 above); IV–James Converse (1856-1921); V–Frederick Josiah (*b* 1860; *m* May Sayre); VI–Helen Isadore (*b* 1861; *m* Lawrence Mayo); VII–Ida Augusta (1865-1924).
1–*m* Oct. 17, 1890, Emma Cornelia (Burnett) Hill (Feb. 20, 1852-June 20, 1916); dau. of

David C. Burnett; issue: 1–Helen Burnett, *b* Ningpo, China, Feb. 1, 1892; *m* Dec. 1922, Everitt Groff Smith (issue: Rosamond, *b* 1923; Geoffrey Groff, *b* 1927).

1–A.B., Harvard, '74 (P.B.K., Pi Eta). In service of Chinese Govt. as commr. of customs, dir. of Conservancy Bd. at Shanghai, and in other posts connected with customs and postal service extension, 1874-1916; retired and returned to America (see Who's Who in America). Decorated Imperial Order Double Dragon, and Civil Rank, 2d Class, China; patent of nobility, 2d Class, Corea, 1891; Chinese Order of Chia Ho, 1915. Fellow Royal Geog. Soc., London. Clubs: Shanghai, Country (Shanghai), Harvard (Boston), etc. Residence: 15 Raymond St., Cambridge, Mass.

1–**MERRITT, Flora Pinney (Mrs. Edward H.),** *b* Windham, Portage Co., Ohio, June 26, 1863.
6–Hendricks **Hover,** from Holland, ante 1738, settled in Sussex Co., N.J.; mem. Com. of Safety, 1775;
5–Emanuel (1748-1824), of Newton Tp., Trumbull Co., O.; capt. Sussex Co., N.J. Regt. during Am. Rev.; mem. Com. of Safety; *m* Mary Schoonover (*d* 1827);
4–Caty (1783-1865), *m* Reuben S. **Clark** (1773-1825);
3–Latallia (1817-68), *m* 1840, William P. **Ladd** (1817-93);
2–Gertrude Eliza (1842-84), *m* 1862, Bidwell **Pinney** (1841-65), owner of saw mill, Windham, Portage Co., O.; *m* 2d, 1872, George J. Williams (*d* 1898).
1–*m* Nov. 15, 1898, Edward H. Merritt, *b* Schulesburg, Wis., Feb. 14, 1864; pres. Trade Mark Title Co., Ft. Wayne, Ind.; son of Simeon Merritt; issue: 1–Florence, *b* Ft. Wayne, Ind., Mar. 20, 1900; commercial artist.
1–Ed. Miami U., Oxford, O., and Chicago Acad. Fine Arts. Mem. D.A.R., I.A.G. Residence: 225 W. Woodland Av., Ft. Wayne,. Ind.

1–**MERWIN, Mabel Anna Metcalf (Mrs. James),** *b* at Westmoreland, N.Y., Apr. 19, 1875.
10–Michael **Metcalf** (qv);
9–Michael (1620-54), Dedham, Mass.; *m* Mary Fairbanks;
8–Jonathan (1650-1727), *m* Hannah Kenrick;
7–Ebenezer, to Lebanon, Conn., 1711; *m* Margaret Ware;
6–Benjamin, *m* Sarah Abel;
5–Zebulon (1729-ca. 1800), *m* 1st, Lydia Bourne;
4–Charles, of Metcalf Hill, nr. Coopertown, N.Y., and Vernon, N.Y.; *m* 1st, Mary Fitch;
3–Nehemiah Fitch (*d* 1883), Westmoreland, N.Y.; *m* Delia Buel Clark;
2–Francis Marion (2 below).
9–Thomas **Fitch** (qv); – wrong
8–Rev. James, *m* Priscilla Mason (Capt. John[9]);
7–Nathaniel, *m* Anne Abel;
6–Nehemiah, *m* Elizabeth Veach;
5–Nehemiah, *m* Freelove Hackley;
4–Mary, *m* Charles **Metcalf** (4 above).
8–Daniel **Clark** (qv);
7–John (1656-1715), *m* 1685, Mary Crow (*b* 1665; Christopher[8], *m* Mary Burr);
6–Daniel (*b* 1704), *m* Elizabeth Abel;
5–Charles, *m* Anna Williams;
4–Erastus, *m* Lucretia Hyde Buel (James[6]; Capt. Josiah[6], *m* Lucretia Hyde; Abel[7]);
3–Delia Buel, *m* Nehemiah Fitch **Metcalf** (3 above);
2–Francis Marion (1844-1905), Westmoreland, N.Y.; *m* 1868, Mary Elizabeth Boag (John[3], of Scotland and England, and later Newark, N.J., *m* Sarah Bradley); issue: I–Mabel Anna (1 above); II–Winifred Christian Lucia (*b* 1887; *m* John Sawyer Fitch, qv).
1–*m* Jan. 14, 1905, James Merwin, *b* Utica, N.Y., Dec. 17, 1877; son of Justice Milton H. Merwin, of the Supreme Ct. of N.Y.
1–Ed. Houghton Sem., Clinton, N.Y. Mem. C.D.A., D.C.G., I.A.G. Residence: Clinton, N.Y.

1–**FITCH, John Sawyer,** *b* Albion, N.Y., Feb. 21, 1887.
9–Thomas **Fitch** (qv);
8–Capt. Thomas (1630-84), *m* 1662, Ruth Clark (George[9], of Milford, Conn.);
7–Thomas (1671-1731), *m* 1st, Sarah– (their son Thomas, was gov. of Conn., 1654-66);
6–James (1702-90), *m* Mary (Haynes) Buckingham (*d* 1789, aet. 90; William Haynes[7], *m* Mercy Marion);
5–Elijah, *m* Phebe Smith;
4–Zadock (*d* 1883), *m* Lucina Whipple;
3–Willard Rufus (1826-1921), *m* Maria Ransom;
2–Gurdon Willard (*b* July 3, 1858), *m* Oct. 15, 1885, Julia A. Sawyer.
1–*m* Apr. 15, 1918, Winifred Christina Lucia Metcalf, *b* Westmoreland, N.Y., Mar. 26, 1887; dau. of Francis Marion Metcalf, and sister of Mrs. James Merwin (qv); issue (*b* Rochester, N.Y.): 1–Mary Elizabeth Metcalf, *b* Oct. 18, 1920; 2–Julian Francis Metcalf, *b* Nov. 19, 1925.
1–A.B. and A.M., Hamilton Coll.; LL.B., Harvard. Admitted to bar, 1911; mem. firm Castle & Fitch; pres. North East Service, Inc.; treas. Electromatic Typewriters, Inc. Mem. N.Y. State Bar Assn., etc. Clubs: Genesee Valley, University, Munroe Golf. Residence: 420 Oxford St., Rochester, N.Y.

1–**MILLER, J(ohn) Peery,** *b* Bethel Tp., Clark Co., O., May 7, 1847.
8–Richard **Stout** (qv);
7–Jonathan (1651-1723), settled in Hunterdon Co., N.J.; organized the Baptist Ch. at Hopewell, 1715; *m* 1685, Anne Bollen (James[8], clk. first Colonial Congress in N.J.);
6–Samuel (*b* 1709), *m* 1729, Catherine Simpson, widow of his cousin;
5–Samuel (1730-1803), justice; mem. Legislature; capt. of a co., 3d Regt., Hunterdon Co., N.J., Militia; *m* 1753, Anna Van Dyke;
4–Catherine (1758-1831), *m* 1776, Rev. Peter **Smith** (1753-1816), from Wales; ed. at Princeton, N.J.; pvt. N.J. militia, Am. Rev.; physician and Baptist minister (Dr. Hezekiah[5], of the Jerseys);
3–Samuel (1778-1856), *m* 1801, Elizabeth McCleave (1780-1849; George[4] [*d* 1824], moved from Md. to Colerain, O., ca. 1790, served in Am. Rev.);
2–Joanna (2 below).
10–Thomasse Janse **Van Dyke** (1580-1665), from Holland; *m* Sytie Dirke;
9–Jan Thomasse (1605-73), *m* Tryntje Haegan;
8–Capt. Jan Janse (1650-1736), *m* Tryntje Thyssen Van Pelt;
7–Jan (1680-1764), *m* Annetje Verkerk Van Buren;
6–Jan (1709-78), lt. in a N.J. Regt. in Am. Rev.; *m* Margaret Barcolo;
5–Anna, *m* Samuel **Stout** (5 above);
4–Catherine, *m* Rev. Peter **Smith** (4 above);
3–Samuel, *m* Elizabeth McCleave (3 above);
2–Joanna (1806-91), *m* 1824, John **Miller** (1798-1863; Frederick[3] [1760-1822], *m* Mary Elizabeth Peery [1769-1844], probably moved to Botetourt Co., Va., soon after their marriage); they had issue: Mary (1789-1850; *m* Anthony Leffel, 1791-1870); Henry (1791-1886; *m* Charity Vantassel [1797-1858], *m* 2d, Sarah Beaty, *b* 1822); Elizabeth (1796-1874; *m* James P. Leffel, 1799-1887); John (above); Daniel (1802-78; *m* Elizabeth Neff, 1802-70); David (1805-67; *m* Sarah Smith, 1808-74); Delilah (1811-63; *m* William Gordon, 1802-70). Issue of John Miller and Joanna Smith: I–Harrison (1825-1917; *m* 1850, Sarah Wise, 1832-1905); II–Elizabeth (1827-84; *m* 1844, Alfred Hance, 1823-89); III–Samuel Smith (1829-1916; *m* 1856, Margaret Palmer, 1833-1922); IV–Milton Jennings (1831-1919; *m* 1863, Hannah Dean Allen, 1829-1917); V–Catherine (1834-1902; *m* 1868, Bolivar Judy, 1826-99); VI–Charity (1836-1908; *m* 1864, Jacob Wise, 1834-91); VII–son (*b* and *d* 1839); VIII–Cyrus (1840-42); IX–Almarinda (1843-47); X–dau. (*b* and *d* 1846); XI–J(ohn) Peery (1 above); XII–dau. (*b* and *d* 1850); XIII–George Clinton (*b* 1853; *m* 1881, Martha Ann Wolfe, 1848-96).
1–*m* Mar. 15, 1870, Elizabeth Ellen Stone (Sept. 30, 1850-Apr. 3, 1896); dau. of Robert Sanford Stone, of Brownsville, Pa.; issue (all *b* Yellow Springs, O.): 1–Mary Elsie, *b* Mar. 20, 1871; *m* June 30, 1897, Rev. Stephen G. Palmer, A.B., Antioch Coll. (issue: Elizabeth Lucile, *b* May 12, 1899; Elsie Gertrude, *b* Nov. 18, 1906); 2–Della Stone, *b* Aug. 17, 1873; Ph.B., Antioch, '97; *m* Oct. 4, 1900, Dr. Harvey V. Cottrell (issue: Donald Peery, *b* Feb. 17, 1902; Robert Roger, *b* July 6, 1906; Lois Eleanor, *b* May 23, 1907); 3–Hazel Kate, *b* Oct. 6, 1877; *m* Sept. 4, 1901, Prof. Lewis S. Hopkins (issue: Ralph Miller, 1902-08; Dorothy Dean,

b Mar. 30, 1906); 4–Edna Dean, *b* June 21, 1885; A.B., Antioch, '07; *m* July 9, 1913, John Hugh Birch, son of John M. Birch, of Yellow Springs (issue: John Miller).
1–Student, Antioch Coll., 1865-70, M.A., 1903. Teacher in public schools, 1870-82; prof. history, Antioch Coll., 1882-1915; retired; part time engaged in compiling family genealogy. Mem. Yellow Springs school and health bds.; trustee Antioch Coll. Pvt. Co. F, 153d Ohio Vol. Inf., Civil War. Mem. S.A.R., I.A.G., G.A.R. Republican. Residence: 204 Dayton St., Yellow Springs, O.

1–**MILLER, Richard Bateman,** *b* Middletown, O., May 24, 1910.
5–Peter **Miller,** of Clermont Co., O.; *m* Mary (perhaps Matheny);
4–Adam (1818-94), *m* 1838, Phoebe Shetterley (1811-74; Philip[5], *m* Elizabeth, perhaps Fisher; probably Andrew[6], of Northumberland Co., Pa., and later of Clermont Co., O., *m* Elizabeth–);
3–Henry (1841-1918), served in Civil War; *m* 1871, Maria Louisa Ackley;
2–Horace Otto (2 below).
5–John **Ackley** (*d* 1828), native of N.J.; pvt. in Capt. David Plunkett's Troop, 4th Regt., Light Dragoons, Cont. Troops, discharged 1783; resided in Greenwood Tp., Mifflin Co., Pa., 1814;
4–James A. (1807-86), of Clermont Co., O.; *m* Mary Ann Conrad;
3–Maria Louisa (1846-1923), *m* Henry **Miller** (3 above).
6–George **Conrad** (1766-1825), of Va., and later Clermont or Brown Co., O.; *m* Rachel McFarland (1757-1823), of Ky.;
5–Jacob (1792-1849), of Milford, O.; *m* 1816, Mariah Dimmitt (1801-63; Ezekiel[6], of Baltimore Co., Md., later of Clermont, O., *m* Phebe–);
4–Mary Ann (1818-49), *m* James A. **Ackley** (4 above).
4–Alfred Gilmore **Bateman** (1809-82), of Chillicothe, O.; *m* 1835, Sarah B. McCollister (1813-89; James[5], *m* 1810, Martha Clark; probably Robert[6]);
3–Clement Cullen (1850-1910), of Washington C.H., O.; *m* 1873, Jennie Bell;
2–Ada Bell (2 below).
7–William **Bell** (*d* 1794), from Ireland, Eng. or Scotland 1754 or 57, settled in Phila., Del. or N.J.; weaver; served in Am. Rev. from N.J.; *m* Ann–;
6–William (1761-1801), moved from N.J. to Phila., 1790, to Culpeper C.H., Va., 1794, to Greenfield, O., 1798; *m* 1785, Mary Brady (1765-1857; Michael[7], shipping master, from Ireland, 1761);
5–Joseph (1786-1862), of Washington C.H., O.; served in War 1812; *m* 1811, Sarah Young (1792-1874; Jacob[6], Am. Rev., *m* Tamer Warford, 1755-1837);
4–John Mitchell (1822-61), *m* 1848, Eliza Jane Backenstoe (1826-1901; Fletcher B.[5], of Frankfort and Washington C.H., O., *m* Jane Perry Eads);
3–Jennie (1849-1913), *m* Clement C. **Bateman** (3 above);
2–Ada Bell (*b* 1878), *m* 1907, Horace Otto **Miller** (*b* 1879), of Middletown, O.
1–Not married. Princeton, '31. Residence: 1112 S. Main St., Middletown, O.

1–**MINER, Alice Reed Dunshee (Mrs. Carl Shelley),** *b* Monticello, Ia., Apr. 25, 1887.
11–Francis (Cooke) **Cook** (qv);
10–Mary (1626-1715), *m* 1645, Lt. John **Thompson** (1616-96), from Eng., settled at Middleborough, Mass.;
9–Esther (1662-1706), *m* 1675, William **Reed** (1639-1706);
8–William (1682-1753), Weymouth, Mass.; *m* 1703, Alice Nash (1685-1751);
7–James (1716-62), Abington, Mass.; *m* 1739, Abigail Nash (1715-1808);
6–Solomon (1743-75), *m* 1765, Mercy Reed Terrell (1742-1808), a widow;
5–Molly (1766-1838), of Cummington, Mass.; *m* 1782, Asa **Gurney** (1758-1837), of Bridgewater, Mass.;
4–Alonzo (1802-52), *m* 1825, Orpha Reed (*b* 1805);
3–Marcia Abigail (1834-93), *m* 1859, John Adams **Chandler** (1833-1903), of Fryburg, Me.;
2–Kate Caroline (*b* 1863), of Monticello, Ia.; *m* 1883, William Hulin **Dunshee** (*b* 1856), pres. Chandler Pump Co., Cedar Rapids, Ia.; issue: I–Alice Reed (1 above); II–Frank Chandler (1891-1925; *m* Mary Mansfield); III–Walter Eastman (*b* 1898; *m* Katherine Gibson).
1–*m* Jan. 11, 1912, Carl Shelley Miner, *b* State Center, Ia., Aug. 5, 1879; son of Marvin Edward Miner, of Glencoe, Ill.; issue: 1–Barbara Dunshee, *b* Chicago, Ill., Jan. 1, 1913; 2–Carl Shelley, Jr., *b* Evanston, Ill., May 7, 1915.
1–Attended Vassar Coll. 2 yrs., U. of Chicago, 1 yr. Mem. I.A.G., Nat. Hort. Soc., Wild Flower Preservation Soc., League Women Voters. Republican. Clubs: Woman's Athletic, Glencoe Garden. Residence: 344 Palos Rd., Glencoe, Ill.

1–**MONNETTE, Orra Eugene,** *b* Dallas Tp., Crawford Co., O., Apr. 12, 1873.
11–Robert **Brassieur,** Sr. (ante 1600-1665), name transmuted to Brashear, etc.; was a French Huguenot of a family removing from France to Eng. soon after the revocation of the Edict of Nantes, 1685; they settled on the Isle of Thanet, off the northeast coast of Kent Co., Eng.; Robert immigated to America before 1636, for in that year he owned land in Elizabeth City, Va., and was a settler in Isle of Wight Co., Va., where, in 1649, appeared Thomas Brassieur, his son (Calendar of Va. Land Grants); a settlement was made upon Nansemond River and the family became prominent in Nansemond Co., Va., 1653; he and his family were related to the noted Fowke family of Va.; about 1658, he removed with his son, Benoist, to Calvert Co., Md., where he *d* 1665, called "Robert Brasheur, Sr.," his wife being then dead; in his will he names, "Mary Brashieur," who was his dau.-in-law, widow of Benoist Brassieur. It is indicated that he or a son *m* Elizabeth, dau. of Chandler Fowke of Va., son of Col. Gerard Fowke. When Robert Brassieur transported members of his family to Va. in 1653 while living in Nansemond Co., the following names are listed as immigrants: (Cabell), Katherine, Bennett (Benoist), Persie and Mary, who together with Thomas, John, Robert, Jr., and Margaret, who *m* in Isle of Wight, Thomas Jordan, were his children. Of these the most prominent in Va. was that Colonial, John Brassieur, who was so long a member of the House of Burgesses and *m* Mary, dau. of Thomas Cocke, and *m* 2d, Mary, dau. of Col. Robert Pike;
10–Benoist (Benjamin), (ante 1629-ante 1663), first lived in Nansemond Co.; in 1658, he removed to Calvert Co., Md., where he settled on "The Cliffts," neighbor to the Monnet family, similarly French Huguenot. In the Archives of Md. (Vol. III, p. 465), is preserved a rare document, in original language, of the "Denization of Benoist Brasseuir" (sic), under date of 1662; commr. of Calvert Co., Md.; in a summons, 1660, his name was anglicized to "Benjamin Brasheers"; *m* Mary–, died, leaving a will, 25th May, 1663, called "widow, of The Cliffts," naming children: sons Robert, Benjamin and John (not yet 21), and daus. Mary, Anne, Susanna, Martha and Elizabeth (not yet 16); the son, Robert, was 21 in 1677, but the son, Benjamin, had died in 1675; concerning the other children, their intermarriages with the Dalrymple, Sterling, Freeman, Kent, Scott and Monnet families of "The Cliffts," Calvert Co., Md., furnish a complete genealogical puzzle: John Brassieur (not 21 in 1663, *b* ca. 1652-1696), *m* Anne, dau. of Thomas Sterling, Sr., and wife, Christian, dau. of William Dalrymple, Sr., of Calvert Co., Md., by which Thomas Sterling became step-father to John Brassieur's sister Martha before her majority. Thomas Sterling was in Somerset Co., Md., in 1689, where he made affidavit he was 46 years old (Md. Arch. Vol. XVII, p. 315); Martha Brassieur (sister of John) (not 21 in 1663, *b* ca. 1658), was aged 17 in 1676, when Thomas Sterling (supra), was made her guardian; she *m* 1674, Henry Kent, Jr. (Henry) of Calvert Co., and had a dau. Martha Kent, who figures in these records;

9–Anne, sister of John and Martha Brassieur (supra), (not 21 in 1663, *b* ca. 1654), *m* William **Dalrymple,** Jr. (William, Sr.[10]), of Calvert Co., who was a brother to Christian Dalrymple, wife of Thomas Sterling (supra); William Dalrymple, Sr., was an original immigrant to Md., received grants of extensive acreage of land, had a colonial mansion, was magistrate and appears frequently in records, Calvert Co., Md.; in 1689, he with other residents of Calvert Co. signed document of Royal Allegiance, addressed to the King (Md. Arch., Vol. VIII, p. III); his name was transmitted to Dalrymple Tucker of colonial fame; living at "The Cliffts" he was neighbor to all foregoing families whose children intermarried; he had a daughter, Christian above, and others;

8–Jeannett (*d* 1757), *m* John Tucker; *m* 2d, John **Kent** (Henry, Jr.[9], *m* Martha Brassieur [supra], bringing in the Brassieur blood from a second collateral);

7–Elizabeth (Tucker) Dalrymple Kent (1709-post 1757), *m* ca. 1725, William **Monnett** (1702-ca. 1776); see Vol. I, p. 397 and Vol. III, p. 619, for Monnett lineage;

6–Isaac (ca. 1726-ca. 1798), soldier Am. Rev.; *m* Elizabeth Osborne;

5–Abraham (1748-1810), soldier Am. Rev.; *m* Ann Hilliary;

4–Jeremiah Crabb (1784-1864), *m* Aley Slagle;

3–Abraham (1811-81), *m* 1st, 1836, Catherine Braucher;

2–Mervin Jeremiah, see Vol. III, p. 619, for other lineages; began to write name **Monnette;** *m* 1869, Olive Adelaide Hull, see Vol. III, p. 620.

1–*m* 1st, Oct. 5, 1891, Ella Elizabeth Crim.

1–*m* 2d, Nov. 6, 1895, Carrie Lucile Janeway.

1–*m* 3d, Dec. 15, 1917, Helen Marie Kull, *b* Pittsburgh, Pa., Mar. 6, 1889; dau. of Christian G. Kull, *m* Helen Margaret Winkler (for Kull lineage, see Vol. II, p. 18, and for Winkler lineage, see Vol. III, p. 621); issue: 1–Helen Hull (qv).

1–B.A., Ohio Wesleyan U., Delaware, O., 1895; studied law; (LL.D., Lincoln Memorial U., 1930). Banker, publicist; vice-chairman bd. of dirs., chmn. regional bd. and dir., Bank of Italy, Nat. Trust & Savings Assn., and of Bank of America Nat. Trust & Savings Assn., San Francisco and Los Angeles. Pres. bd. of library commrs., Los Angeles Public Library since 1914; trustee Lincoln Memorial U. (Tenn.), and officer, dir. or mem. of many public or institutional boards. Councillor, life mem. and fellow I.A.G.; officer, hon. mem. or mem. many geneal. organizations U.S. and abroad. Author: Monnet Family Genealogy, 1911; Hull Family in America, N.J. branch, 1910-12; Brassieur Family, Md. and Va., 1929 (see Who's Who in America). Residence: 350 S. Oxford Av., Los Angeles, Calif.

1–**MONNETTE, Helen Hull,** *b* Los Angeles, Calif., Aug. 26, 1920. This lineage leads back to twelve of the Barons, Sureties for the Magna Charter, 1215, and has been accepted for Orra Eugene Monnette by the Baronial Order of Runnemede of Philadelphia, 1930. It is the Noble House of Hilton of Hilton Castle, Durham, Eng.;

11–Roger **Hilton,** of London, merchant, citizen and fishmonger, 4th son of William, Lord Hilton, and Margaret Metcalfe, and g.son of William, Lord Hilton, and Sibilla Lumley, both of royal descent;

10–Edward, believed to have immigrated to N.E., with his brother, William Hilton, in the "Fortune," 1621; if not, he came separately in the "Diligent"; called the "father of New Hampshire"; these two with David Thompson, fishmongers from London, began a plantation at Piscataqua, N.H., 1623; in a London list of fishmongers, 1641, the name of Edward Hilton is marked "New England"; received patent for land called "The Squamscott Patent" covering what is now known as Dover; about two leagues from the mouth of Piscataqua River, N.H., is to be found the more definite "Hilton's Point" which lies within a tract which was conveyed to Edward Hilton by the Council thru Capt. Thomas Wiggin and others, 1631; when Ed-

HILTON

Arms: *Quarterly, first, argent, two bars azure (for Hilton); second, vert, three lions rampant, two and one, collared or, chains fixed to the collar of the last, pendent between the legs and over the lions (for Tyson); third, gules, two lions passant in pale or (for Felton); fourth, gules, three swords conjoined at the pommels in fess, the points extended to the dexter and sinister chief points and middle base of escutcheon or (for Stapleton).*

Crest: *On a close helmet, Moses's head in profile glorified, adorned with a rich diapered mantle, all proper.*

Supporters: *Two lions azure.*

Motto: *Tant que je puis (As much as I can).*

ward Hilton, his brother, William and their families came, they were neighbors of Thomas Roberts, afterwards the first colonial governor of N.H.; Edward Hilton had a first wife, mother of his children, lived at Exeter, N.H., in 1642, was a justice or magistrate and held other public positions; associate, 1640; assistant 1641; *m* 2d, Jane, dau. of Mr. Alexander Shapleigh and widow of James Treworgy; he *d* before Mar. 6, 1670/71, when administration was granted to his sons, Edward, William, Samuel and Charles, two daus., unnamed, being represented by Christopher Palmer;

9–Mary (*b* ca. 1635), *m* John (Screven) **Scribner** (*d* 1675), from Kent, Eng., to Hampton, Mass., ca. 1652; settled later at Dover, Mass.; large landowner;

8–Thomas (1664-1718), of Exeter, later of Kingston; *m* 1708/09, Hannah Welch (*b* 1680; Philip[9], of Ipswich, *m* Hannah, dau. of Henry Haggett, of Salem and Wenham);

7–Samuel, I (1716-94), in Kingston until 1753; on expdn. to Louisburg, Cape Breton, 1745; 5th settler at Salisbury, N.H., 1753; sold into slavery by a capturing band of Indians, at Chamblee, Can.; *m* 1740, Hannah Webster (1721-1807; Ebenezer[8] [1667-1756], *m* 1709, Hannah Judkins, they were g.g.parents of Hon. Daniel Webster);

6–Samuel, II (1743-post 1806), moved to Poultney, Vt., then to Essex Co., N.Y., 1797, thence to Liberty Tp., Richland (afterwards known as Delaware) Co., O., 1805; *m* Hannah Rayno (Elias[7], of Kingston and Salisbury, N.H., *m* Mary Severance);

5–Samuel, III (1784-1880), see portrait Vol. III, p. 621; came with his father to Delaware Co.; removed to Marion, 1823, thence to Cardington, Marion Co.; in War 1812; civil officer; *m* 1810, Almira Clark (Israel[6], *m* Mary Kendall, of Windham Co., Conn., and Ohio);

4–Artemissa (1826-93), *m* 1845, George Washington **Hull** (see their g.son, Orra E. Monnette, Vol. I, p. 397, and Vol. II, p. 180, for Hull lineage);

3–Olive Adelaide (1849-1912), see Vol. III, p. 620, for portrait and other lineages; *m* 1869, Mervin Jeremiah **Monnette** (*b* 1847); see Vol. III, p. 619 for portrait and other lineages;

2–Orra Eugene (qv), *m* Dec. 15, 1917, Helen Marie Kull (*b* Mar. 6, 1889); see Vol. III, p. 621 for Kull lineage.

1–Ed. Westlake School for Girls, Holmby Hills, Westwood, Calif. Life mem. Nat. Soc. of Magna Charta Dames of America, Soc. of Descendants of Knights of the Most Noble

HELEN HULL MONNETTE

Order of The Garter, Soc. of Mayflower Descendants in the State of Calif. (the latter in descent from Edward Fuller, his son Samuel, and George Soule, Mayflower passengers, see Vol. II, p. 180, for this lineage); also, Society of Children of the Am. Rev. Residence: 350 S. Oxford Av., Los Angeles, Calif.

1–**MOODY, Anne Coleman Perkins (Mrs. Arthur W.),** *b* Newbury, Mass., Dec. 17, 1867.
8–Robert **Adams** (1601-82), from Eng.; at Ipswich, Mass., 1635, Salem, 1638/39, Newbury, Mass., 1640; tailor and yeoman; *m* 1st, ante 1635, Eleanor (Wilmot?), (*d* 1677);
7–Sgt. Abraham (1639-1714), corpl. in militia, 1685-93, sgt., 1703; *m* 1670, Mary Pettingell (1652-1705; Richard[8], *m* Joanne Ingersoll);
6–Richard (1693-1778), *m* 1717, Susanna Pike (1697-1754; John[7], *m* Lydia [Coffin] Little);
5–Richard (1726-88), *m* 1755, Sarah Noyes (1731-1821; Moses[6], *m* Hannah Smith [James[7]; Lt. James[8]; Thomas[9]]; Maj. Thomas[7]; Rev. James[8]);
4–Paul (1758-1833), Quaker; farmer, blacksmith and miller; *m* 1803, Hannah G. Keniston (1774-1844; Moses[5], of Amesbury, *m* Dolly–);
3–Rebecca Bartlet (1812-95), *m* 1832, Benjamin Creasey **Perkins** (*b* 1811; Joseph[4], *m* Eunice Noyes);
2–Paul Adams (*b* 1841), *m* 1864, Hannah Cary Cilley (Edward Aaron[3], *m* 1835, Alice, dau. of James Cary, *m* Hannah Poor); issue: I–Lewis (*b* 1865-*d* aet. 4); II–Anne Coleman (1 above); III–Paul Adams, Jr. (*b* 1872-*d*; *m* Maude Bryant).
1–*m* June 26, 1898, Arthur W. Moody, *b* Apr. 12, 1871; son of Nathaniel Warren Moody.
1–Mem. I.A.G.; founder and corr. sec. Sons and Daus. of the First Settlers of Newbury, Mass. Residence: "The Elms," Newbury, Mass.

1–**MONTGOMERY, Joseph, 2d,** *b* Harrisburg, Pa., Aug. 27, 1886.
6–John **Montgomery,** "originally from Ireland," ca. 1720-22, settled in Lancaster (now Dauphin) Co., Pa.; elder; *m* ca. 1725, Martha–;
5–Robert (1740-1806), of Paxton Tp., Lancaster Co., Pa.; schoolmaster; served in Lancaster Co. militia in Am. Rev.; overseer of roads; tax assessor; mem. first jury of Dauphin Co., 1785; moved to Lycoming Co., Pa., 1791, where he *d*; *m* ca. 1765, Agnes (Nancy) Montgomery (ca. 1749-1822);
4–James (1774-1844), of Harrisburg, Pa.; served in War 1812 in co. of Capt. Thomas Walker; justice of peace; pres. Harrisburg Council, 1818; clerk of the borough, 1829-37; Mason; *m* 1st, 1801, Susan Fedder (1784-1804);
3–James (1804-43), printer; *m* 1832, Sarah Ann Peipher (1809-93);
2–James Buchanan (2 below).
6–Valentine **Buchecker** (*d* 1760), from Holland in the "Two Brothers," to Phila., 1747; settled in Upper Saucon Tp., Northampton Co., Pa.; one of the first church wardens of Lower Saucon Reformed Ch.; *m* ca. 1733, Anna Maria Sherey (*d* ca. 1775);
5–Baltzer (1745-1821), of Upper Saucon Tp., Northampton (now in Lehigh) Co., Pa.; Am. Rev.; *m* ca. 1775, Margaret Windt (ca. 1745-1838; Andrew[6], *m* Elizabeth–);
4–Philip (1776-1852), War 1812; *m* 1796, Sarah Owen (ca. 1777-1855);
3–Edward Emanuel (1806-68), of Luzerne Co., Pa.; contractor and brickmaker; Civil War; *m* 1829, Rebecca Lynn;
2–Emma Lynn (2 below).
6–Peter (Lin) **Lynn** (*d* 1761), from Germany, 1737, to Phila.; settled in Lower Milford Tp. (now in Lehigh Co.), Pa., where he warranted land, 1738; mem. Great Swamp Ch.; *m* ca. 1739, Anna Margaret Brunner;
5–Dr. Felix (1740-1809), of Iron Hill, near Bethlehem, Northampton Co., Pa.; practiced medicine in Lower Saucon Tp.; justice of the peace; Am. Rev.; *m* 1760, Jacobina (Freever) Siegle (1730-1801);
4–Jonathan (1776-1853), Luzerne Co.; *m* 1802, Elizabeth Thomas;
3–Rebecca (1806-71), *m* Edward Emanuel **Buchecker** (3 above).
7–Rev. William **Thomas** (1678-1757), from Wales via Eng., to Phila., 1712; moved to Radnor (now in Delaware) Co., Pa.; purchased 440 acres at Hilltown, Bucks Co., Pa., 1718; founded the Baptist ch. of Hilltown; *m* ca. 1708, Ann Griffith (1680-1752);
6–Thomas (ca. 1711-1780), of Hilltown; *m* 2d, ca. 1750, Mary Williams;
5–Jonah (ca. 1754-ca. 1815), Am. Rev.; *m* ca. 1778, Sarah Freeman (*d* 1835; Richard[6]);
4–Elizabeth (1783-1822), *m* Jonathan **Lynn** (4 above);
3–Rebecca, *m* Edward Emanuel **Buchecker** (3 above);
2–Emma Lynn (*b* 1843), *m* 1865, James Buchanan **Montgomery** (1842-97), grad. Crittenden Commercial Coll., Phila.; started Peipher's New York Line, 1867, an overnight fast freight line bet. N.Y. City and Harrisburg, Pa., which was later merged with Peipher's Daily Line, ran bet. Phila. and Harrisburg, and was one of the last freight lines in the country to remain privately owned; issue: I–Arthur Ree (1867-1872); II–George Peipher (*b* 1870; *m* Katherine Kafka); III–Walter Leslie (*b* 1872; *m* Enneta Lynch Gross; *m* 2d, Sarah Evelyn Beckley); IV–Oliver Buchecker (*b* 1874; *m* Louise Moore); V–Edith Ray (*b* 1876; *m* Charles Henry Briner); VI–Frank Stanley (*b* 1881; *m* Lillian Earl Ott); VII– Joseph, 2d (1 above).
1–Not married. C.E., Pa. Mil. Coll., '10. Engaged in historical research. With U.S. Shipping Board, Emergency Fleet Corpn., Phila., during World War. Mem. S.A.R., I.A.G., Hist. Soc. of Dauphin Co., Pa. (treas.), Pa. German Soc. Mason. Presbyterian. Club: University. Residence: 309 Chestnut St., Harrisburg, Pa.

1–**MYLIN, Barbara Kendig,** *b* West Lampeter Twp., Lancaster Co., Pa., Jan. 7, 1885.
8–Rev. Hans **Herr** (qv);
7–Abraham (*b* 1660), of Manor, Pa.; *m* Anna–;
6–David (1722-71), *m* Barbara Hershey;
5–Abraham (1751-1823), of Millersville, Pa.; *m* Barbara Eshleman (1757-1839; Benedict[6]);
4–Fannie (1790-1849), *m* John **Kendig** (1774-1822);
3–Barbara (1814-1904), *m* 1832, Martin **Mylin** (1807-69; Abraham[4], *m* Elizabeth Barr);
2–Amos Herr (2 below).
5–Samuel **Hepburn** (1698-1795), from Scotland, settled at Northumberland, Pa., ca. 1775; *m* 1746, Janet–;
4–William (1753-1821), of Williamsport, Pa.; first pres. judge of Lycoming Co.; lt. col., 1792; brig. gen., 1800; maj. gen., 1807; *m* 2d, Elizabeth Huston (1779-1827; Thomas[5], Am. Rev., *m* Janet, dau. of Charles Walker; Hugh[6], from Scotland to Bucks Co., Pa.);
3–John (1806-78), *m* 1831, Caroline Wheeler;
2–Caroline Emily (2 below).
9–Thomas **Wheeler,** from Eng. in the "Defiance"; freeman, Concord, Mass., 1636/37; removed to Fairfield, Conn., 1644; *m* in Eng., 1613, Anne Halsey;
8–John (bap. 1624-89), Fairfield, Conn.; *m* Judith Turney (Benjamin[9]); *m* 2d, Elizabeth Rowland;
7–Joseph (1673-1759), *m* 1705, Deborah Nichols (Ephraim[8]);
6–Ephraim (1716-1806), *m* Martha Bulkeley

(Thomas[7], of Redding, Conn.);
5–Calvin (bap. 1742-1831), *m* 2d, 1766, Mary Thorpe (1745-1828; David[6]);
4–Ephraim (1779-1853), of Elmira, N.Y.; *m* 1802, Elizabeth Wakeman;
3–Caroline (1807-78), *m* 1831, John **Hepburn** (3 above).
9–Capt. John **Wakeman** (qv);
8–Rev. Samuel (bap. 1635-*d* 1692), *m* 1656, Hannah Goodyear (*d* 1721; Gov. Stephen[9], of New Haven, Conn.);
7–Capt. Joseph (1670-1726), *m* 1697/98, Elizabeth Hawley (1679-1753; Ebenezer[8], *m* Esther, dau. of Ens. William Ward);
6–Joseph (1703-62), *m* 1727, Abigail Allen (1705-1804; Gideon[7], *m* Annah Burr);
5–Gideon (1737-92), *m* 1759, Ann Adams (*b* 1740; Nathaniel[6], *m* Ann Silliman);
4–Elizabeth (1778-1833), *m* 1802, Ephraim **Wheeler** (4 above);
3–Caroline (1807-78), *m* John **Hepburn** (3 above);
2–Caroline Emily (1847-1925), *m* 1868, Martin Powell (1845-79); *m* 2d, 1884, Amos Herr **Mylin** (1837-1926), of Lancaster, Pa.; issue (1st marriage, surname Powell): I–Mary Caroline (*b* 1872; *m* Daniel H. Witmer); II–Elizabeth Hepburn (*b* 1874; *m* Benjamin Parmer; *m* 2d, William E. Parmer); issue (mother's 2d marriage): I–Barbara Kendig (1 above); II–Helen (1887-1905); III–Mercy Hepburn (*b* 1889; *m* Christian G. Hess).
1–Grad. First Pa. State Normal School, Millersville, Pa. Mem. D.A.R., I.A.G. Episcopalian. Republican. Residence: 455 S. Shippen St., Lancaster, Pa.

1–**NORBURY, Frank Parsons,** *b* Beardstown, Ill., Aug. 5, 1863.
8–Elisha **Doubleday,** from Yorkshire, Eng., to Boston, Mass., 1676; *m* Ann– (*d* 1711);
7–Elisha (1670-1715), *m* Mary Woodhead, of Boston;
6–William (*b* 1699);
5–Lydia (1733-1806), *m* 1758, Joseph **Norbury** (1722-69; desc. Sir John Norbury, treas. of Eng.), from Eng. to Cumberland Province, N.J., 1753; schoolmaster;
4–Heath (1760-1824), steward Phila. Hosp. on Tinicum Island, Delaware River, 1799; mem. Bd. Health; *m* 1783, Susanna Britt (1760-1856; John[6], Quaker);
3–Joseph Britt (1788-1846), maj., 2d Bn., 84th Regt., 2d Brig., 1st Div., Phila. Militia, for term of 7 yrs.; 1st lt., Vol. Corps, "Penn Township Guards," attached to 128th Regt., Pa. Militia, 1st Brig., 1st Div., Phila. Militia, War 1812; judge Ct. Common Pleas (see portrait, Vol. III, p. 566); *m* 1809, Rebecca Minschall Frick (1789-1833), for Frick lineage see Vol. III, p. 566;
2–Charles Joseph (2 below).
6–David **Harriman** (*b* Wales), of N.J., ranger on the frontier, 1778,83, Capt. Ritchie's Regt., also in 7th Class, return of Capt. Scott's Co. Militia, 4th Bn., Washington Co., Pa.;
5–Sarah, *m* Thomas **Spence** (desc. Duke of Argyle), from Scotland, settled in N.J.;
4–David (*b* N.J., ca. 1758-*d* Robertson Co., Tenn., 1839), served in 1st Pa. Regt., Cont. Line, pvt. on muster roll of Capt. Wilkin's Co., 6th Pa. Regt., pvt. 6th Regt., Cont. Line; *m* ca. 1782, Mary McElyea (*d* 1867, aet. 104; Ludovic[5], *m* Mary, dau. of William Powers, *m* Phillis [Dennison] Wright, from Ireland to N.C.);
3–Rev. Thomas (*b* N.C., ca. 1784-*d* nr. Anna, Ill., 1835), *m* ca. 1805 or 07, Catherine Carter (for Carter lineage see Vol. III, p. 566);
2–Elizabeth Peters (1822-1905), *m* 1839, Charles Joseph **Norbury** (1812-95), mcht., Beardstown, Ill. (for issue see Vol. III, p. 566).
1–*m* Oct. 2, 1890, Mary Elizabeth Garm, *b* Beardstown, Ill., Aug. 30, 1864; dau. of Henry Garm, of Beardstown; issue: 1–Frank Garm, *b* Jacksonville, Ill., Jan. 27, 1892; A.B., Ill. Coll., '12; A.M., U.Ill., 1913; M.D., Harvard, 1917; *m* Apr. 11, 1918, Mary Elson, dau. of Charles A. Barnes (issue: Ruth Margaret; Phyllis and Frank Barnes); 2–Elizabeth, *b* Jacksonville, Aug. 13, 1896.
1–Ed. Ill. Coll. (hon. A.M., 1903); M.D., L.I. Coll. Hosp., 1888. Pres. and med. dir. Norbury Sanitorium (see Who's Who in America). Residence: Springfield, Ill.

DONALD MYERS (1844-73).

1–**MYERS, Howard Charles,** *b* Manchester, N.S., June 17, 1869.
10–Rev. John **Lothrop** (qv);
9–Samuel (1623-1700), to New London, Conn., 1648; at Norwich, Conn., 1668; *m* 1st, 1644, Elizabeth Scudder (*d* ante 1690);
8–Sarah (1655-1706), *m* 1681, Nathaniel **Royce** (1639-1726; Robert[9]);
7–Sarah (1683-1733), *m* 1701, Lt. Hawkins **Hart** (1677-1735; Capt. Thomas[8], *m* Ruth, dau. of Anthony Hawkins; Dea. Stephen[9]);
6–Nathaniel (1702-50), *m* 1727, Martha Lee;
5–Josiah (*b* 1742), removed to Manchester, Guysboro Co., N.S., 1786, where he and his sons improved a tract of 1200 acres, near Chedabucto Bay and Milford Haven River; *m* 1765, Lydia Moss (they were g.parents of the Hart brothers, Reuben, Jairus and Levi, of Halifax, N.S., prominent West Indies merchants and traders; also, their son Tyrus, *m* Martha Ingraham, was g.father of Caroline Whitman who *m* Hon. James Cranswick Tory, gov. of N.S., and of Edward Cecil Whitman, mayor of Canso, N.S., pres. Bd. of Trade and gov. of Acadia U.);
4–Panthia (*b* 1775), *m* 1795, Charles **Myers** (1765-1840), soldier in English army, in the 60th, or Royal Am. Regt.; received grant of land in N.S.;
3–Charles (1801-92), farmer; dea. Boylston Bapt. Ch.; *m* 1833, Bridget Ross (1807-85; Donald[4], from Scotland, *m* 1795, Anne, dau. of Richard Morris, surveyor, *m* 1st, 1775, Bridget Griffith);
2–Donald (2 below).
10–Rev. John **Lothrop,** above;
9–Samuel, above;
8–Elizabeth (1648-ca. 1690), *m* 1669, Isaac **Royce** (*d* 1681), of Wallingford, Conn. (Robert[9]);
7–Elizabeth (1669-1760), *m* 1690, Capt. Stephen **Lee** (1667-1753; John[8], *m* 1658, Mary, dau. of Dea. Stephen Hart);
6–Martha (1702-ca. 1773), *m* 1727, Nathaniel **Hart** (6 above).
10–Rev. John **Lothrop,** above;
9–Samuel, above;
8–Martha (1657-1719), *m* 1677, John **Moss** (1650-1717; John[9]);
7–John (1682-1755), *m* 1708, Elizabeth Hall (1690-1759; Capt. Samuel[8], *m* Hannah Walker; John[9], qv);
6–Joseph (1714-75), of Cheshire, Conn.; *m* 1735, Lydia Jones;
5–Lydia (1740-1809), *m* Josiah **Hart** (5 above).
10–Rev. Henry **Whitfield** (1597-1657), from Eng. to Guilford, Conn., 1639; *m* 1618, Dorothy Sheafe (Rev. Thomas, D.D.[11] dean of Windsor, *m* Mary Wilson, 1575-1613);
9–Abigail (ca. 1622-1659), *m* 1648, Rev. James **Fitch** (qv);
8–Hannah (*b* 1653), *m* 1677, Thomas **Mix** (1655-1706; Thomas[9], qv);
7–Hannah (*b* 1685), *m* 1711, Theophilus **Jones** (*b*

1690; Nathaniel[8], *m* Abigail, dau. David Atwater, qv; Dep. Gov. William[9]);
6–Lydia (1714-88), *m* 1735, Joseph **Moss** (6 above);
5–Lydia (1740-1809), *m* 1765, Josiah **Hart** (5 above);
4–Lydia (1777-1874), *m* 1796, William **Simpson** (1766-1849), a native of Scotland;
3–Capt. William (1799-1864), farmer; Episcopalian; Liberal; *m* 1830, Sarah Boles (1808-83; Capt. Robert[4], of Ireland, *m* 1802, Rebecca, dau. of John Ryan, *m* Sarah Whittenbury; John[5], *m* Grace Woods);
2–Victoria (*b* 1846), *m* 1868, Donald **Myers** (1844-73), farmer, trader; local Baptist preacher; issue: I–Howard Charles (1 above); II–Louise; III–Dr. Laura T.
1–Not married. Began business career as trader in investment securities in Boston and New York, 1890; acting as trustee of personal trusts in New York and Los Angeles, since 1912. Mem. I.A.G. Baptist. Republican. Summer place: Glen Ranch, Calif. Residence: 5564 Echo St., Los Angeles, Calif.

1–**PARDO DUFOO, José Joaquín F., Furlong y Cordera,** *b* Nov. 1891.
5–James **Furlong Downes** (*b* Belfast, Ireland, 1740; son of Mathew Furlong, V Baron of Forth; g.son of John, of Wexford); from Ireland to Veracruz, Mexico, thence to Puebla de los Angeles; settled in Puebla, 1763; founder of Huexotitla Mills (flour) in Puebla; *m* at Puebla, Jan. 1772, Ana María de Malpica, Salcedo y Dios-dado, dau. of Marquis of Malpica, a Spaniard, settled in the Colonia of Virreinato;
4–Patricio Furlong Malpica (1776-1833), general of div., and gov. of the State of Puebla de los Angeles, 1829-33; took part in the Trigarante Army, 1821, as a capt. of Iturbide, the first Emperor of Mexico; *m* Nicolasa Kerny;
3–María Soledad Furlong Kerny, *m* Col. Agustín Fernández **De Pardo Ortiz De Zárate** (*d* at Jalapa, Aug. 1890; desc. of the Barons of San Carlos); military commandant of the City of Puebla on several occasions (his son Joaquín was the V Baron of San Carlos, because his uncle Francisco had no son but had a dau. who became a nun);
2–Joaquín Bernardo Fernández de Pardo Furlong (1845-1920), an engineer; *m* 1890, María Dolores Dufoo (Dufort) Cordera (desc. Dukes of Duras, of Delorge and of Civrac, France, Hijodalgo Spanish family of Cordera); dau. of Ramon Dufoo Vivanco, *m* Asuncion Cordera Nogueyra Maldonado, and grand dau. of José de Cordera (the Spaniard), who arrived at Veracruz, 1815, settled at Jalapa.
1–*m* Oct. 6, 1928, Amada Elvira Chávez Cobos; dau. of José Maria Chávez and of Octavia Cobos Hernandez; José María, son of José María, and grandson of Jesús Joaquín, the Spaniard, the first to arrive at Chihuahua, in the Northern part of Mexico.
1–Ed. under spl. professors at home, later at Maristas Coll. of Mex., thence College des Petits Freres de Marie, Paris. Hon. and founder mem. Real Sociedad de Genealogia, Mexican Branch; Cdr. of Holy Sepulchre and San Lazarus orders; Knight of LaFayette; Homenaje medal, etc. Mem. (1st class) Unione Cavalleresco (Rome), Centro de Accion Nobiliana (Madrid); hon. mem. Acad. Internat. d'Histoire (Paris). Residence: De la Baronia De San Carlos, Mexico, D.F., and Jalapa, Ver.

1–**PARROTT, Dale Kennedy,** *b* Batavia, O., June 12, 1876.
5–Nicholas **Parrott** (1761-1834), *m* 1783, Elizabeth Moran (1764-1834);
4–John (1787-1867), *m* 1810, Rachel Stigers (1791-1874; John[5], *m* Eleanor Stilwell; Adam[6], Am. Rev., *m* Sophia–);
3–Edmund (1815-63), *m* 1839, Margaret Lafever (1818-97; William[4], *m* Mary Price; Minard[5], from France, settled in Fredericktown, Knox Co., O., served in Am. Rev., *m* Charity Elinor Teets);
2–Judge John Shannon (2 below).
5–Hugh **Kennedy,** of Lancaster Co., Pa.; *m* Sarah–;
4–Robert (1772-1849), *m* 1801, Margaret White (1783-1849; Capt. Thomas[5], Am. Rev., *m* Mary, dau. of Robert McCurdy, killed at Braddock's defeat);
3–John W. (1813-83), *m* 1834, Martha Reed Dowdney (1816-1902; William Reed[4], *m* 1813, Eliza, dau. of Joseph Francis; Samuel[5], *m* Martha Reed);
2–May (1851-1907), *m* 1871, Judge John Shannon **Parrott** (1840-1912), judge Ct. of Common Pleas, 5th jud. dist. of Ohio, 1897-1909; issue: I–Edmund Kennedy (1872-1926; *m* Nancy Dimmitt); II–Dale Kennedy (1 above); III–Louise Kennedy (*b* 1880; *m* Rolland A. Norton); IV–Robert Kennedy (1884-1901).
1–*m* Mar. 18, 1900, Irma Ann Holter (qv); issue: 1–Elizabeth Holter, *b* Batavia, O., Jan. 2, 1901; ed. George Washington U.; *m* May 16, 1925, William E. Foley (issue: Irma Ann); 2–John Shannon, *b* Batavia, Apr. 23, 1902; attended Briarley Hall Mil. Acad.; *m* Aug. 12, 1924, Elisabeth, dau. of Samuel Comer (issue: John Samuel); 3–Dale Holter (Dec. 23, 1905-Aug. 11, 1906).
1–Ed. Hanover (Ind.) Coll. (Phi Delta Theta). Admitted to Ohio bar, 1900. Acting asst. commissioner Gen. Land Office. Served in Spanish-Am. War. Mem. U.S.W.V. Presbyterian. Residence: 3522 Northampton St. N.W., Washington, D.C.

1–**PARROTT, Irma Ann Holter (Mrs. Dale K.),** *b* Batavia, O., Dec. 4, 1879.
5–George **Holter,** of Frederick Co., Md.; *m* 1776, Margaret Arnold;
4–John (*d* 1819), *m* 1803, Mary Ann Elright (1782-1866);
3–Col. Alfred (1804-87), *m* Rachel Ann Phillips (1808-83; Wesley[4], *m* Harriet A. Lemaster);
2–Alfred Hanson Penn (2 below).
9–Moses **Cleveland** (qv);
8–Aaron (1654 or 55-1716), *m* 1675, Dorcas Wilson (John[9], *m* Hannah James);
7–Aaron (1680-1755), *m* 1701 or 02, Abigail Waters (1683-1761; Samuel[8], *m* Mary, dau. of Daniel Hudson; Laurence[9], *m* Ann Linton);
6–Aaron (1715-57), died at the home of Benjamin Franklin; *m* 1735 or 36, Susannah Porter;
5–Rev. Aaron (1738 or 44-1815), served in Am. Rev.; mem. Conn. House of Rep., 1779, and introduced bill for abolition of slavery; *m* 2d, 1788, Elizabeth (Clement) Breed;
4–Jeremiah Clement (1794-1836), *m* Elizabeth Robinson (1798-1865; Charles[5], *m* Aseanath Martin);
3–Aseanath Martin (1820-71), of Clermont Co., O.; *m* 1840, Wesley **Apple** (1815-89; Daniel[4]; Andrew[5]);
2–Evaline Amanda (2 below).
10–John **Porter** (qv);
9–Samuel (*d* 1689), of Windsor and Hadley, Conn.; *m* Hannah Stanley (*d* 1708; Thomas[10], qv);
8–Judge Samuel (1660-1722), *m* 1683 or 84, Joanne Cook (1665-1713; Capt. Aaron[9], *m* Sarah, dau. of William Westwood; Maj. Aaron[10], qv);
7–Rev. Aaron (1689-1722), *m* Susannah Sewall (1691-1747; Maj. Stephen[8]; Henry[9]);
6–Susannah (1716-88), *m* Aaron **Cleveland** (6 above).
10–Robert **Clement** (qv);
9–Robert (ca. 1634-1714), of Haverhill, Mass.; *m* 1653, Elizabeth Fawne (John[10]);
8–John (*b* 1653), *m* Elizabeth Ayer (Robert[9], *m* Elizabeth Palmer);
7–Nathaniel (1689-post 1754), *m* 1694, Sarah Merrill (1694-1748; Nathaniel[8], *m* Sarah Woodman; Edward[9]; Edward[10]);
6–Jeremiah (1724-84), patriot in Am. Rev.; *m* 1745, Mary Moseley (1726-post 1793; Increase[7], *m* Mary Hazen);
5–Elizabeth (1755-1826), of Norwich, Conn.; *m* 2d, 1788, Rev. Aaron **Cleveland** (5 above).
2–Evaline Amanda Apple (*b* 1854), of Olive Branch, O.; *m* 1877, Alfred Hanson Penn **Holter** (1847-1906), dep. auditor and government clerk; issue: I–Alfred Hanson (*b* 1877; *m* Teresa Agnes Clauson); II–Irma Ann (1 above); III–Aseanath Eloise (*b* 1883; *m* Leonard E. Hauck).
1–*m* Mar. 18, 1900, Dale Kennedy Parrott (qv for issue).
1–Mem. D.A.R. Residence: 3522 Northampton St., N.W., Washington, D.C.

1–**PAGE, Hugh Nelson,** *b* Norfolk, Va., May 15, 1882.

8–John **Page** (qv);
7–Col. Matthew (1659-1703), of "Rosewell," Gloucester Co., Va.; mem. Royal Council; an original trustee of Coll. of William and Mary; *m* ca. 1689, Mary Mann (1672-1707; John[8], of Timberneck, Gloucester Co.);
6–Mann (1691-1730), mem. Royal Council; *m* 2d, 1718, Judith Carter (Robert, "King," Carter[7]);
5–John (ca. 1720-ca. 1780), mem. Colonial Council and the last Royal Council; *m* ca. 1740 or 41, Jane Byrd (Col. William[6], of "Westover," Charles City Co.);
4–John (ca. 1743-1789), *m* 1764, Elizabeth Burwell (*d* 1811; Lewis[5], of York Co.);
3–Hugh Nelson (1788-1871), capt. U.S.N., War 1812, in Battle of Lake Erie; *m* 2d, 1848, Elizabeth P. Wilson (Holt[4], of Portsmouth, Va.);
2–Hugh Nelson (1852-1914), banker, Norfolk, Va.; *m* 1878, Sallie Newton (1858-1930); issue: I–Hugh Nelson (1 above); II–Thomas Newton (*b* 1883).
1–*m* June 3, 1914, Virginia Anderson, *b* Laurens, S.C., Oct. 25, 1888; C.D.A., D.A.R.; dau. of Albert Williams Anderson, of Augusta, Ga.; issue (all *b* Augusta, Ga.): 1–Virginia, *b* Oct. 28, 1915; 2–Hugh Nelson (1917-19); 3–Nelson, *b* Sept. 12, 1921; 4–Albert Anderson, *b* Oct. 9, 1923.
1–M.D., U.Va., '05 (Phi Gamma Delta, Nu Sigma Nu.). Prof. anatomy, U.Ga., 1911-21, now surgeon, Augusta, Ga. Residence: 800 Georgia Av., North Augusta, S.C.

1–**PARKER, Edith Virginia Dunham (Mrs. Barton L.)**, *b* DePere, Wis., May 17, 1872.
9–Dea. John **Dunham** (qv);
8–Benajah (1640-80), *m* 1660, Elizabeth Tilson (Edmund[9]);
7–Edmund (1661-1734), *m* 1681, Mary Bonham;
6–Jonathan (1693-1777), *m* 1714, Jane Pyatt (1695-1779; Reynier[7], *m* Elizabeth Sheffield);
5–David (1723-1807), *m* 1750, Rebecca Dunn;
4–Azariah (1760-1839), *m* 1792, Elizabeth Dunham (1772-1827; David[5], *m* Mary Dunn);
3–Jeptha (1795-1882), *m* 1815, Ann Runyon;
2–Jeremiah Stelle (2 below).
10–Edward **Fuller,** Mayflower Pilgrim (qv);
9–Dr. Samuel (*d* 1683), *m* Jane Lothrop (Thomas[10]; Robert[11]; John[12], of Eng.);
8–Hannah, *m* 1658, Nicholas **Bonham,** of Barnstable;
7–Mary (*b* 1661), *m* 1681, Edmund **Dunham** (7 above).
11–John **Howland,** Mayflower Pilgrim (qv);
10–Hope, *m* Elder John **Chipman** (qv);
9–Lydia (1654-1730), *m* 1674, John **Sargeant** (1639-1716);
8–Jonathan (1677-1754), *m* 1699, Mary Lynde (1678-1716);
7–Jonathan (1700-77), *m* 1726, Debora Richardson (1708-70);
6–Lucretia (1734-93), *m* 1750, Pliny **Lawton,** M.D. (1732-61), of Hampshire Co., Mass.;
5–William, M.D. (1759-1800), surgeon's mate, 5th Regt., Mass. Inf., 1777, later ordered to 1st Inf. where he served to end of war; nominated by President Washington, 1794, surgeon at West Point; mem. Order of Cincinnati; *m* 1784, Abigail Farrington (*b* 1763);
4–Charles (1787-1858), *m* 1809, Sophia Dobson Willson (1791-1844);
3–Joseph Grellet (1822-96), *m* 1844, Ellen Virginia Baird;
2–Frances Augusta (2 below).
5–Mathew **Carey** (1760-1839; son of Christopher, *m* Mary Sheriden); from Ireland; publisher and prominent citizen of Phila.; *m* ca. 1792, Bridget Flahaven (1771-1829), their son, Henry C., was prominent political economist;
4–Eliza Catherine (1795-1881), *m* 1822, Lt. Thomas James **Baird,** U.S.A. (1795-1842; Henry[5] [1763-1847], from Ireland, settled at Green Bay, Wis., *m* Ann Burnside, 1766-1852);
3–Ellen V. (1823-98), *m* Joseph G. **Lawton** (3 above);
2–Frances Augusta (1846-1913), *m* 1867, Jeremiah Stelle **Dunham** (1831-1908), business man, flour mills; issue: I–Lewis Augustus (*b* 1869; *m* 1910, Marguerite Augusta Blemel); II–Edith Virginia (1 above).
1–*m* Oct. 9, 1895, Barton Lessey Parker (qv); issue: 1–Stevens Dunham (June 29, 1898-July 8, 1898); 2–Alexandrine, *b* Green Bay, Wis., Dec. 26, 1899; A.B., Smith Coll., '21; *m* June 21, 1923, Howard Berridge, son of Victor Maxwell Tuthill, of Grand Rapids (issue: Virginia, *b* Apr. 15, 1924; Victor Parker, *b* Nov. 28, 1927; Howard Berridge, Jr., *b* Apr. 28, 1930).
1–Wells Coll. 2 yrs. Sec. and v.chmn. Brown Chapter Red Cross during World War, 1917-19. Mem. S.M.D., D.A.R., I.A.G. Episcopalian. Republican. Residence: 839 S. Quincy St., Green Bay, Wis.

1–**PARKER, Barton Lessey,** *b* DePere, Wis., Jan. 24, 1871.
8–Abraham **Parker** (1612-85), from Eng. ca. 1640; settled at Woburn, Mass.; freeman, 1645; founder of Chelmsford, 1653; soldier King Philip's War; *m* 1644, Rose Whitlock;
7–Moses (ca. 1657-1732), *m* 1684, Abigail Hildreth (g.dau. Richard Hildreth, a founder of Chelmsford);
6–Aaron (1689-1775), Westford, Mass.; *m* ca. 1712, Abigail Adams;
5–Lt. Moses, *m* 1744, Bridget Comings;
4–Isaac (1760-1825), drummer in Am. Rev.; *m* 2d, 1806 or 07, Catherine Hyde Wilson, a widow;
3–Hiram (1807-89), *m* 1st, 1829, Sally Crocker;
2–Elijah Fletcher (1843-1904), *m* 1868, Susan Lessey (*d* 1894); *m* 2d, 1901, Clarissa Williams; issue (1st marriage): I–Barton Lessey (1 above); II–Josephine Lessey.
1–*m* Oct. 9, 1895, Edith Virginia Dunham (qv for issue).
1–Residence: 839 S. Quincy St., Green Bay, Wis.

1–**PARMENTER, Elmer Ellsworth,** *b* Albion, Me., June 29, 1861.
9–Dea. John **Parmenter** (1588-1671), from Eng., 1635-39, settled at Sudbury, Mass.; selectman, dea., and commr.; *m* 1609, Bridget– (*d* 1660);
8–John (1612-66), from Eng. with father; propr. at Sudbury, and permitted to keep an ordinary, later known as the "Old Parmenter Tavern"; mem. of Maj. Willard's troopers of Dedham, and was known as "Major's man"; *m* 1639, Amy– (*d* 1681);
7–John (1640-1719), of Sudbury; *m* 1667, Elizabeth Cutler (*b* 1646);
6–John (1678-1768), of Sudbury; *m* Martha–;
5–Caleb (1722-95), Attleboro, Mass.; Am. Rev.; *m* Sarah Richardson (*b* 1720);
4–Caleb (1758-1850), Am. Rev., at battles of Lexington and Bunker Hill, promoted to rank of capt.; *m* 1780, Elizabeth Rounds (1758-1854; Rev. Nathaniel[5], of Attleboro, who there entertained the famous English clergyman, Whitefield, at his home, where he held service "under those great elms");
3–Joseph (1782-1866), Harlem (now China), Me.; War 1812; *m* 1802, Roxey (Roxana) Richardson (1784-1866);
2–Thomas (2 below).
7–Samuel **Richardson** (qv);
6–Stephen (1649-1717/18), *m* 1674/75, Abigail Wyman (*d* 1717/18);
5–Seth (*b* 1689/90), *m* Mary Brown;
4–Seth (*b* 1723), *m* Sarah French;
3–Roxey (Roxana) (1784-1866), *m* Joseph **Parmenter** (3 above).
10–Christopher **Webb** (*b* 1590), from Eng. ante 1645, settled at Braintree, Mass.; town clk.; removed to Billerica ca. 1655; *m* Humility–;
9–Christopher (1630-94), King Philip's War; dep. Gen. Ct.; town clk., 1678; rep., 1689-90; *m* 1654/55, Hannah Scott (*d* 1718; Benjamin[10]);
8–Christopher (1663-90), *m* 1686, Mary Bass (John[9], *m* Ruth, dau. of John Alden, qv);
7–Christopher (*b* posthumously, Aug. 16, 1690); *m* 1713, Anne White;
6–Samuel (*b* 1716), *m* 1740, Sarah Lincoln;
5–Christopher (1747-1845), *m* 1767, Betty Smith;
4–Dea. Samuel (1773 or 74-1853), *m* Sarah Ireland;
3–Christopher (1799-1875), *m* Eliza Ann Greenough (1798-1880);
2–Jane Greenough (1818-1910), *m* 1841, Thomas **Parmenter** (*b* at "Parmenter Hill," Harlem, now China, Me., 1818-*d* 1899), farmer; issue: I–Alvecia Miller (1842-1916; *m* 1862, Isaiah Wiggin, 1835-1907); II–John Greenough (1844-1903; *m* 1869, Maria Bradstreet Stinson, *b* 1849); III–Mary Isabel (*b* 1846; *m* 1886, George Washington Murch, 1843-1920); IV–Charles Alfred (1849-1924; *m* 1870, Georgia Anna Bragg, 1847-1917); V–Joseph Millard (*b* 1850; *m* 1873, Ella Janet Hurlburt, 1857-1925); VI–Elmer Ellsworth (1 above).

1-*m* Sept. 7, 1892, Mae Della Fall, *b* Albion, Me., May 22, 1866; dau. of Tristram Fall (1826-1915), of Albion; issue: 1-Ralph Colby, *b* China, Me., July 8, 1893; B.A., Bowdoin, 1916; 2d lt., Q.M. Dept., World War; *m* Aug. 18, 1920, Arline Louise (*b* Mar. 10, 1894), dau. of Fred Morton, of Portland (issue: Elizabeth Mae, *b* Sept. 21, 1922; Donald Morton, *b* July 1, 1924); 2-LeClare Fall, *b* Deering (now Portland), Me., Mar. 27, 1895; B.A., Bowdoin, '16; 1st lt., Aviation Sect., World War; *m* Apr. 23, 1918, Esther, dau. of Leroy Haley, of Biddeford, Me. (issue: Thomas Elmer, *b* Feb. 19, 1922; Robert Haley, *b* Sept. 19, 1925); 3-Mae Della, 2d, *b* Portland, Me., May 8, 1899; N.E. Conservatory of Music, 1928.

1-B.A., Colby Coll., '87, M.A., 1890 (D.K.E.). Began teaching at Branch Mills Village, China, Me., 1879; taught country dist. and free high schools in China, Albion, Vassalboro, Liberty and Vinal Haven, Me., 1879-87; first asst. in Mitchell's Mil. Boys' School, Billerica, Mass., 1887-94; supervising principal North School, Portland, since 1894. Elected supt. of schools, China, Me., 1884,85; supervisor of schools of China, Me., 22 districts, 1884-86. Life mem. S.M.D., O.F.P.A., S.A.R., I.A.G., Huguenot Soc. of N.E., N.E.A., Me. Charitable Mechanics Assn.; mem. Alden Kindred of America, S.C.W., S.W. 1812, Old Plymouth Colony Descs., Me. Hist. Soc. Mason (K.T. [life mem.], 32°), Odd Fellow. Conglist. Republican. Residence: 23 Nevens St. (Woodfords P.O.), Portland, Me.

1-**KNOWLTON, John Franklin,** *b* Montville, Me., Mar. 19, 1856.
9-William **Knowlton** (1584-1639), from Eng., 1632, settled at Hingham, Mass., 1635; *m* Ann Smith;
8-William (1615-55), of Ipswich; *m* Elizabeth Smith;
7-Thomas (1640-1717), Norwich, Conn.; *m* 1668, Hannah Greene;
6-Ebenezer (*b* 1674), *m* 1699, Sarah Lowell;
5-Ebenezer (*b* 1710), *m* 1734, Jane Philbrook;
4-David (1740-1805), ens. 15th Regt., 1774; 1st lt. in Col. Stickney's regt., 1776; *m* 1767, Mary Green (*b* 1745);
3-Ebenezer (1782-1841), *m* 1802, Abigail True (*d* 1868);
2-John Colby (2 below).
10-John **Alden,** Mayflower Pilgrim (qv);
9-Ruth, *m* John **Bass;**
8-Mary (*b* 1669), *m* 1686, Christopher **Webb** (1663-90; Christopher[9]; Christopher[10]);
7-Christopher (*b* 1690, posthumous son), *m* 1713, Anne White;
6-Samuel (1716-73), *m* 1740, Sarah Lincoln (ca. 1716-1813, aet. 97);
5-Christopher (1747-1845), Skowhegan, Me.; *m* 1767, Betty Smith (*d* 1826);
4-Dea. Samuel (1773 or 74-1853), *m* Sarah Ireland (1774-1857);
3-Christopher (1799-1875), Albion, Me.; *m* 1817, Eliza Ann Greenough (1798-1880);
2-Sarah Ann (1822-1905), *m* 1842, John Colby **Knowlton** (1822-87), served in Co. D., 19th Me. Vols., 1861-64; mill owner, justice of the peace, Montville, Me.; issue: I-Charles Edgar (1843-78; *m* Helen A. Blood); II-Mary Emma (*b* 1845; *m* 1869, Daniel Tarr); III-Caro Ella (1848-1927; *m* 1873, Francis Orlando Keating); IV-John Franklin (1 above).
1-*m* Dec. 4, 1878, Jessie Fremont Meservey, *b* Appleton, Me., Feb. 25, 1856; dau. of Charles Albert Meservey, of Appleton; issue: 1-Ethel May, *b* Rockport, Me., Dec. 3, 1879; Lasell Sem.; *m* Sept. 16, 1903, William E. Whiting, of Ellsworth, Me. (issue: Ruth Nelson, *b* Dec. 31, 1904, *m* Mar. 11, 1926, John Whitcomb); 2-Morris Wilson (Oct. 23, 1882-Mar. 7, 1926); Burdette's Bus., Coll.; George Washington Law School; lawyer, Interstate Commerce Commn., Washington; *m* Nov. 14, 1901, Ione M. Stone, of Kingwood, W.Va. (issue: Frances Jessie, *b* Jan. 4, 1908); 3-Charles Colby, *b* Bucksport, Me., Mar. 3, 1885; Bowdoin Coll.; M.D., Harvard Med. Sch.; *m* Sept. 19, 1909, Ella Eugenia, dau. of Charles L. Morang, of Ellsworth, Me. (issue: John Franklin, 2d, *b* Feb. 26, 1918); 4-Hazle Meservey, *b* Bucksport, Apr. 9, 1887; *m* Nov. 27, 1907, Kenneth MacKenzie Cameron (issue: Mary Knowlton, *b* May 30, 1910; Norah MacKenzie, *b* Mar. 30, 1916).
1-Ed. Commercial Coll., Augusta, Me.; Bucksport Sem. Clk. Supreme Jud. Ct., Hancock Co., Me., 1890-1910; practiced law at Ellsworth, Me., 1910-17, as partner of Judge Peters; sec. to Congressman John A. Peters, 1917-22; clk. U.S. Dist. Ct. of Maine, since 1922. Supt. schools Bucksport and Ellsworth, Me.; prof., East Me. Conf. Sem., Bucksport. Mem. S.M.D., Me. Hist. Soc. Mason (32°). Conglist. Republican. Club: Portland. Residence: 15 Amherst St., Portland, Me.

1-**PATTEN, Frank Chauncy,** *b* Rochester, N.Y., June 15, 1855.
8-William **Patten** (qv);
7-Thomas (1636-90), of Billerica, Mass.; *m* 1st, 1662, Rebecca Paine (1642-80; Thomas[8], *m* Rebecca-);
6-William (1671-1730), selectman, Billerica, 1720, 1723-25, 1728-30; rep. Gen. Ct., 1729-30; *m* 1st, Mary Rogers (*d* 1716, aet. 48; probably John[7]);
5-Thomas (1695-1747), cooper; *m* ca. 1730, Miriam Stearns (1705-47; Isaac[6], *m* Mary Miriam-);
4-William (1732-1801), in Am. Rev. 3 yrs.; *m* 1761, Rebecca Brown (*d* 1815, aet. 78; Josiah[5]);
3-Josiah (1765-1837), pioneer of Westmoreland, N.Y., lived on what was called "Van Eps Patent"; ens. mil. co., 1800; town clk., 1802-11; supervisor, 1811-19; *m* 1791, Asenath Hutchinson (1771-1858), of Andover, Conn.;
2-Horace (1801-80), of Rochester, N.Y., Groton, Mass., and Wis.; wagon maker, merchant and farmer; *m* 1833, Eliza Ann Dutton (*d* 1841); *m* 2d, 1844, Olive Maria Rice (1819-74; John[3]); issue (1st marriage): I-Mary Jane (*b* 1834; *m* Thomas Mead); II-Eliza (1838-1915; *m* 1867, Alexander J. Stewart, *b* 1835); III-Ann (*b* 1841; *m* 1872, Henry Kistler); issue (2d marriage): I-Simon Rice (1847-1926; *m* 1868, Eliza Estelle Hallock, 1850-1922); II-Frank Chauncy (1 above).
1-Not married. Ripon (Wis.) Coll., 1884-86; Columbia Coll. Library School, 1887-88; Harvard U. Grad. Sch., 1899-1901. Library asst., Ripon Coll. Library, 1882-86, Columbia Coll. Library, 1887-89, N.Y. State Library, Albany, 1889-92; librarian, Public Library, Helena, Mont., 1892-99; asst. librarian, New York Public Library, Mar.-June 1903; librarian, Rosenberg Library, Galveston, Tex., since 1903. Treas. N.Y. State Library Sch. Assn., 1895-96, pres., 1901-02; trustee Rosenberg Library Assn., since 1918, chartered 1900. Mem. S.A.R., A.H.A., Miss. Valley Hist. Assn., Tex. State Hist. Assn., Tex. Folk-Lore Soc., A.L.A., Tex. Library Assn., Galveston Chamber of Commerce, etc. Mason (32°, K.T.), Odd Fellow. Episcopalian. Club: Rotary. Address: Rosenberg Library, Galveston, Tex.

1-**PATTERSON, Mary Ward (Mrs. James L.),** *b* Pennington Point, Ill., Sept. 7, 1888.
8-Col. Robert **Bolling** (qv);
7-Robert (1682-1749), *m* 1706, Anne Cocke;
6-Anne (*b* 1713), *m* John **Hall,** of Bristol Parish, Va.;
5-John (*b* 1762), of Louisa Co., Va.; pvt. in Va. state arty. 3 yrs. for which he received a grant of land in Ky.; *m* 1785, Nancy- (1768-1825);
4-Joel (1786-1882), Sciota, Ill.; soldier in War 1812, enlisted in Washington Co., Ky., served 1812-13, pensioned, 1871; *m* 1st, 1812, Mary (Polly) Clarke (John[5], Am. Rev., drafted at Amherst, Va., aet. 16, pension dated 1834, *m* Anne Whitten);
3-Randolph (1823-98), *m* 1846, Almeda Lianda Woods;
2-Marcella Genevra (2 below).
9-John **Woods** (1610-78), original grantee of Sudbury, Mass., 1638; founder Marlboro, 1656; selectman, 1664-65; *m* Mary Parmenter (*d* 1699, aet. 80);
8-James (*d* 1718), dea. 1st ch., 1716; *m* 1678, Hopestill Ward (William[9], grantee of Sudbury, 1638, founder Marlboro, Mass., *m* Elizabeth-);
7-James (1687-1772), dea. of 1st ch., 1741; town clk., Marlboro; rep. Gen. Ct., 1750; assessor; *m* 1719, Dorothy Barnes (1698-1734; John[8], *m* Hannah-; Thomas[9]);
6-David (1720-1807), *m* 1744, Martha Wheeler;
5-Samuel (1751-1813), soldier in Am. Rev.; min-

ute man at Lexington Alarm, 1775; *m* 2d, 1778, Mrs. Phoebe Holton (1755-1845);
4–Salem (1799-1879), *m* 1823, Cornelia Grow;
3–Almeda Lianda (1829-1921), *m* Randolph **Hall** (3 above).
10–George **Wheeler,** at Concord, Mass., 1638; *m* Katherine–;
9–Thomas (*d* 1686), tithing man, 1680; *m* 1657, Hannah Harwood (George[10], *m* Hannah–);
8–John (1661-1712), *m* 1686, Elizabeth Wells;
7–John (*b* 1695), assessor, 1731-35; constable, parish clk., 1743; ens., 1735-36; committeeman; moderator town meetings; *m* 1717, Mary Hapgood;
6–Martha (1726-1819), *m* David **Woods** (6 above).
11–Elder and Lt. Edward **Howe** (*d* 1644), at Watertown, Mass., 1634; ruling elder in Watertown ch.; selectman; rep. Gen. Ct., he and Matthew Craddock of London owned the first mill at Watertown; *m* Margaret–, who *m* 2d, George Bunker, the owner of Bunker Hill;
10–Sufference (*d* 1682), *m* Nathaniel **Treadway** (*d* 1687), original grantee of land at Sudbury, 1638;
9–Elizabeth (*b* 1646), *m* 1664, Shadrach **Hapgood** (1642-75), from Eng. in the "Speedwell," aet. 14 yrs., 1656; ambushed and killed by Indians at Quaboag;
8–Thomas (*b* 1669), *m* 1690, Judith Barker (1671-1759; John[9], *m* Judith Symonds);
7–Mary (1694-1759), *m* John **Wheeler** (7 above).
10–William **Meade** (qv);
9–John (1634-99), Hempstead, L.I.; *m* 1657, Hannah Potter;
8–Jonathan (1665-1717), Greenwich, Conn.; *m* 1688, Martha Finch;
7–Jonathan (*b* 1689), Nine Partners, Dutchess Co., N.Y.; *m* 1726, Sarah Husted;
6–Jonathan (1727-1800), lt. in Am. Rev.; signer of the Articles of Assn., Dutchess Co., N.Y., 1775; *m* 1758, Sarah Guernsey;
5–Sarah (1768-post 1816), *m* Jacob **Grow** (1765-1816; John[6], *m* Mary, dau. of Edward Farrington);
4–Cornelia (1804-93), *m* Salem **Woods** (4 above);
3–Almeda Lianda, *m* Randolph **Hall** (3 above);
2–Marcella Genevra (*b* 1853), *m* 1873, Francis Cooke **Ward** (*b* 1845), served in Co. C, 50th Ill. Vols., Civil War (Daniel Dimmitt, or Dimick[3], *b* Prince Edward Island, *d* at Industry, Ill., resided at Port Huron, Mich., *m* in N.S., ante 1841, Harriett Newel Cooke, 1822-ca. 1861); issue: I–Cornelia Cooke (*b* 1875; *m* John Miller Paton); II–Walter Hall (*b* 1878; *m* Anna McLean); III–Bertha Almeda (*b* 1879; *m* Scott Sager Walterhouse); IV–Mary (1 above).
1–*m* June 17, 1908, James Lindley Patterson, M.D., *b* Union Star, Mo., Mar. 20, 1884; lt. and capt. in World War, with the 1st and 17th cavs.; issue (all *b* Woodward Co., Okla.): 1–Mildred Florence, *b* Feb. 26, 1911; 2–Marjorie Ward, *b* June 8, 1914; 3–James Lindley, *b* Apr. 9, 1923.
1–Mem. D.A.C., D.C.W., D.A.R., I.A.G., U.S.D. 1812. Residence: 205 N. 12th St., Duncan, Okla.

1–**PEARCE, Furman Octavius Barnes,** *b* Thomson, Ga., Nov. 25, 1878.
5–Capt. Daniel **Sparks** (1740-1810), of Va. and S.C.; planter; capt. of S.C. troops during Am. Rev.; *m* 1763, Miss Stephens (1745-74);
4–Elizabeth (1765-1815), *m* 1782, Silas **Pearce** (1760-1820), of Md. and S.C.;
3–James Heustess (1797-1856), of S.C.; planter; magistrate; capt. in Seminole War, 1832-37; *m* 1824, Ann Margaret Saunders (1796-1874);
2–Robert Hayne (2 below).
6–John (Dorsey) **Darsey,** of Md.; *m* Elizabeth–;
5–Joseph (1762-1823), of Md. and Ga.; planter; Am. Rev.; *m* 1791, Mary Bowdre (1772-1830);
4–James Madison (1809-59), of Ga.; began to spell name Darsey; scientific agriculturist; *m* 1828, Mary Sutton (1811-80);
3–Ann E. (1829-1901), *m* 1850, Virgilius M. **Barnes** (1827-85), of Ga.; planter, noted editor, judge;
2–Mary Harriet (1851-1917), *m* 1872, Robert Hayne **Pearce** (1834-1927), of S.C.; educator, public official; soldier C.S.A.; issue: I–Lulu Murray (*b* 1873; *m* Ira E. Farmer); II–Col. Earle D'A. (*b* 1876; *m* Jennie Dick Gray); III–Furman Barnes (1 above); IV–Eleanor (Pansy), (*b* 1882; *m* Thomas Allen Scott); V–Robert Hayne, Jr., (1885-1915); VI–Harold Maro (1887-1914).
1–*m* Aug. 10, 1910, Ellen A. Saint, *b* St. Landry Parish, La., May 5, 1887; dau. of Chapin A. Saint; issue: 1–Elizabeth Bowdre, *b* New Orleans, La.; 2–Harriet Murray, *b* New Orleans.
1–LL.B., Mercer U., Macon, Ga., '00. Engaged in legal and government work, 1900-08; asst. postmaster, Savannah, Ga., 1904-08; with South Atlantic Steamship Line, 1908-18, retiring as v.p. and gen. mgr.; gen. mgr. Steele Steamship Line, 1918-19; southern mgr. Norton, Lilly & Co. since 1918; also v.p. (advisory) Standard Fruit & Steampship Corpn., New Orleans, since 1926. Dir. and mem. of exec. com., Johnson Iron Works & Shipbuilding Co.; dir. Otis Mfg. Co., Gulfport Service Corpn. Ga. Militia, 1901-04; dir. of shipping, Shipping Control Com. (Army Transport Service) for Gulf Dist. during World War. Dir. New Orleans Assn. of Commerce. Mason (32°). Mem. S.A.R., La. Hist. Soc., I.A.G., New Orleans Geneal. and Hist. Soc. Episcopalian. Clubs: Boston, Louisiana, New Orleans Country, Recess, Hammond (La.) Country. Residences: "Sucasa" Hammond, La., and 1415 Audubon St., New Orleans, La.

1–**PERRY, Mary Jane Newton (Mrs. Charles H.),** *b* Greenfield, Mass., June 27, 1866.
8–Edward **Allen** (qv);
7–Edward, *m* 1683, Mercy Painter;
6–Edward, *m* 1721, Mercy Childs;
5–Elizabeth (1728-75), *m* Capt. Ebenezer **Arms** (1721-88), Am. Rev. (see Vol. III, p. 369);
4–Elizabeth, *m* 1778, Corpl. John **Newton** (1750-1827), Am. Rev. (see Vol. I, p. 757);
3–Obed (1795-1847), *m* 1841, Abigail Briggs;
2–Seth Smead (2 below).
9–Thomas **Wilder** (qv);
8–John, *m* 1673, Hannah–;
7–Thomas, *m* Sarah Hunt;
6–Jotham, *m* 1746, Phoebe Wheeler (see Vol. III, p. 369);
5–Abigail, *m* 1783, Thomas **Akeley,** Am. Rev. (Francis[6], one of the "Boston Tea Party," Am. Rev., *m* 1750, Tabitha Bull);
4–Phoebe, *m* Samuel **Briggs,** Plymouth, Vt.;
3–Abigail, *m* Obed **Newton** (3 above).
10–Thomas **Nash** (qv);
9–Lt. Timothy, *m* 1657, Rebekah Stone (Rev. Samuel[10]);
8–Lt. John, *m* 1691, Elizabeth Kellogg (Lt. Joseph[9], *m* 1667, Abigail Terry);
7–Enos, *m* 1735, Joanna Barnard;
6–Lt. Enos, Am. Rev., *m* 1771, Martha Gaylord;
5–Enos, *m* 1793, Sarah Wells;
4–Abel Wells, *m* 1820, Mary Mosher;
3–Julia Ann (1823-82), *m* George W. **Frary** (see Vol. I, p. 757);
2–Henrietta (2 below).
11–Dea. William **Gaylord** (qv);
10–William (1616-56), *m* 1st, 1644, Ann Porter (*d* 1653; John[11], qv);
9–William (1651-80), *m* 1671, Ruth Crow (John[10], *m* Elizabeth Goodwin);
8–Samuel (1676-1734), *m* 1702, Mary Dickinson (Nehemiah[9]);
7–Samuel, *m* Margaret Cook;
6–Martha, *m* Enos **Nash** (6 above).
9–Ens. Hugh **Mosher,** affiliated with Roger Williams as a preacher;
8–James, *m* 1714, Mary Davol;
7–John, *m* Elizabeth Lawrence (Zechariah[8]);
6–James, Am. Rev.; *m* Eunice Blood;
5–Jacob, *m* Mary Pierce;
4–Mary, *m* Abel Wells **Nash** (4 above).
11–John (Pers, Peirce) **Pierce** (qv);
10–Anthony (1609-78), of Watertown and Woburn, Mass.; *m* 2d, ca. 1634, Ann– (*d* 1682/83);
9–Daniel (1639/40-1723), settled at Groton; *d* at Waltham, Mass.; *m* Elizabeth– (*b* 1642);
8–Ephrahiam (1673-1740/41), a first settler at Lunenburg, Mass.; surveyor, sealer, selectman, assessor, mem. sch. com.; *m* Mary Whitney (1675-1749);
7–Simon, *m* 1737, Susanna Parker;
6–Solomon, Am. Rev., *m* 1771, Lucy Parker;
5–Mary, *m* Jacob **Mosher** (5 above).
2–Henrietta Frary (1849-1926), *m* Seth Smead **Newton** (1844-1925), farmer; for issue and other lineages see Vol. III, p. 369.
1–*m* June 27, 1892, Dr. Charles Herbert Perry

(May 10, 1869-May 3, 1918), grad. Harvard; vet. surgeon; son Charles M. Perry, Worcester, Mass.; issue: 1-Roger Newton (see Vol. III, p. 569, for paternal lineage) also Roger Newton, Jr. (qv).
1-Teacher before marriage, now teaching Americanization in Worcester. Mem. C.D.A. (Vt.), D.A.R., I.A.G. Residence: 82 Park Av., Worcester, Mass.

1-**PERRY, Roger Newton, Jr.,** *b* Worcester, Mass., Oct. 18, 1922.
12-Thomas **Gates**;
11-Stephen (*d* 1662), of Hingham; *m* Ann Hill (*d* 1682);
10-Stephen (1640-1706), Acton, Mass.; *m* Sarah Woodward (George[11], *m* Elizabeth Hammond);
9-Simon (*b* 1666), *m* 1688, Hannah Benjamin;
8-Benjamin (*d* 1756), Barre, Mass.; *m* Bethulia Rice (*b* 1704; Jonathan[9], *m* Ann Derby); 5 sons in Am. Rev.;
7-Esther (*b* 1739), *m* Phineas **Perry** (*b* 1735);
6-Luther (1770-1845), lawyer; *m* 1801, Harriet Howes;
5-Charles Howes (1804-55), Phillipston, Mass.; *m* 2d, 1835, Mary B. Peckham (1815-97); see Vol. III, p. 569;
4-Charles Mordecai (1839-97), Worcester; served in Civil War; *m* 1867, Ellen M. Garfield;
3-Charles Herbert, M.D.V. (1869-1918), *m* 1892, Mary Jane Newton (qv);
2-Roger Newton (2 below).
11-Samuel **Hinckley** (qv);
10-Gov. Thomas (1618-1706), commr. of United Colonies, 1678-92; gov. Plymouth Colony, 1681-86; *m* 2d, Mary Smith;
9-Reliance (1675-1759), *m* 1698, Rev. Nathaniel **Stone** (*d* 1755; Dea. Simon[10], *m* Mary Whipple; Simon[11], *m* Joan, dau. William Clark; David[12], *m* Ursula-; Simon[13], *m* Agnes-);
8-Nathaniel (1713-77), *m* 1742, Mary Bourne;
7-Abigail (1748-1826), *m* Edmund **Howes** (*b* 1742), retired English sea capt.;
6-Harriet (1783-1810), *m* Luther **Perry** (6 above).
11-Edmund **Rice** (qv);
10-Edward (1619-1712), *m* Ann-, or Agnes Bent (1625-1713);
9-Benjamin (1666-1749), *m* 1st, 1691, Mary Graves (1670-1736);
8-Azariah (1693-1779), *m* Hannah- (*d* 1754);
7-Jonas (1731-76), in French and Indian War; in battle of Concord Bridge, 1775; *d* in service; *m* Deborah Force;
6-Simon (1762-1812), *m* 1786, Sarah Bigelow;
5-Sophia (1798-1867), *m* 1822, Paul **Garfield** (1798-1860; Moses[6], of Princeton, Mass., *m* 1790, Abigail Mason);
4-Ellen M. (1839-1906), *m* 1867, Charles Mordecai **Perry** (4 above).
10-Thomas **Hastings** (qv);
9-Samuel (1665-1724), of Watertown; *m* Sarah Coolidge (Simon[10], *m* Hannah, dau. of Ellis Barron; John[11], qv);
8-Daniel (1702-77), *m* Sarah Ball (*b* 1700; James[9], *m* Elizabeth Fisk; John[10], qv);
7-Sgt. John (1738-1802), Am. Rev.; *m* 1762, Elizabeth Howe (1740-1813);
6-Eliakim (1763-1811), *m* 1782, Patience Moore (*d* 1816; Dea. Levi[7], Lancaster, Mass.);
5-Hezekiah (1797-1864), *m* Mary Lovell (*b* 1799; Jonathan[6]);
4-Jonathan Lovell (1821-64), Civil War; *m* 1848, Susan M. Stone;
3-Charles William (1855-1921), *m* 1878, Jane Cue (1858-1921; William[4], of Eng., *m* Jane Eaton);
2-Marion Iola (*b* 1893), *m* 1920, Roger Newton **Perry** (see Vol. III, p. 569).

1-**PHILLIPS, (Isabel) Carolyn Whipple (Mrs. Paul Maxon),** *b* New York, N.Y., May 12, 1896.
10-Capt. John **Whipple** (qv);
9-David (1656-1710), of Dorchester, Mass.; *m* 1677, Hannah Tower (1652-1722; John[10], qv);
8-Israel (1678-1720), of Providence, R.I.; *m* 1697, Mary Wilmarth (*b* 1678);
7-Nathaniel (1713-92), of Cumberland, R.I.; *m* 1736, Bethiah Slack;
6-Ichabod (1738-91), *m* 1st, 1762, Catherine Brown (1736-ante 1774);
5-Ichabod (1770-1856), of Richmond, N.H.; *m* 1793, Chloe Kempton (1767-1862; Stephen[6], served at Ticonderoga, 1777, *m* Catherina-);
4-Mason (1796-1880), *m* 1818, Lydia Curtis (1798-1877; Calvin[5], *m* Lydia, dau. of Capt. Nicholas Cook);
3-Calvin (1829-82), of McDonough, N.Y.; *m* 1861, Satira Augusta Smith (1837-1926; George Washington[4], *m* Mary Tyler Hovey);
2-Frederick Eli (2 below).
9-Sgt. Richard **Hubbell** (qv);
8-Richard (1654-1738), *m* Rebecca Morehouse;
7-Peter (1686-1780), *m* Katherine Wheeler;
6-Ephraim (1712-95);
5-Capt. Amos (1747-1817), capt. Am. Rev.;
4-Catherine (*b* ca. 1795), *m* 1818, Nathaniel **Ruland** (1797-1885);
3-William Parker (1825-1872), *m* 1849, Margaret Reynolds (1831-1911);
2-Isabella Maud (*b* 1866), of Brooklyn, N.Y.; mem. D.A.R.; *m* 1886, Frederick Eli **Whipple** (*b* 1864), of Syracuse, N.Y.; sec.-treas. Bond Co.; mem. O.F.P.A.; issue: I-Mark Mayor (*b* 1889; *m* Beatrice Adele Swarts); II-Carolyn (1 above).
1-*m* Oct. 23, 1926, Paul Maxon Phillips, *b* Dallas, Tex., Dec. 7, 1894; son of Mason Phillips, *m* Margaret Maxon.
1-A.B., Barnard Coll. (Columbia U.), '19 (Rho Sigma Phi, pres.); grad. work, Cornell U. Teacher of English, Latin, French, civics. Mem. D.F.P.A. Mem. Barnard College Club (New York), Mozart Soc., A.A.U.W., College Woman's Club of Westfield. Residence: 260 W. Jersey St., Elizabeth, N.J.

1-**PHILPUTT, Anna Elizabeth Maxwell (Mrs. Allan B.),** *b* Bloomington, Ind., Nov. 30, 1854.
6-Bezaleel **Maxwell** (1708-1808), from Scotland, settled in Lancaster Co., Pa., 1725; later in Augusta Co., Va., then in St. Ann's Parish, Albemarle Co., ca. 1750; *m* Rebecca Boyd;
5-Capt. John (1728-98), came with his father; capt. in Augusta militia in colonial wars; soldier in Am. Rev.; justice, 1770; removed to Garrard Co., Ky.; *m* Fannie Garner;
4-Bezaleel (1755-1834), Am. Rev.; present at surrender of British; *m* 1775, Margaret Anderson (1751-1828; John[5]);
3-Dr. David Hervey (1786-1854), founder Indiana U.; surgeon, War 1812; mem. conv. that organized State of Ind.; speaker Ind. House of Rep.; mem. Ind. Senate; pres. State Bd. of Internal Improvement; physician, Bloomington, Ind.; *m* 1809, Mary Dunn (1788-1880; Samuel[4]);
2-James Darwin (2 below).
5-Edward **Howe** (1723-80), from Eng. to Md.; propr. of Ellicott's Mills, nr. Baltimore;
4-Samuel (1750-1820), *m* Elizabeth Shouel;
3-Joshua Owen (1784-1868), *m* 1816, Lucinda Higgins Allison (1798-1870);
2-Louisa Jane (1819-1907), *m* 1843, James Darwin **Maxwell** (1815-92), of Bloomington, Ind.; grad. Ind. Coll., '33; M.D., Jefferson Med Coll., Phila., 1844; sec. bd. of trustees, Ind. U., 17 yrs., and trustee 32 yrs.; issue: I-Emma Turpin (1844-1915; *m* Vinson Carter); II-Mary Effie (1845-1920); III-Howard (1847-1907); IV-Allison (1848-1915; *m* Cynthia A. Routh); V-James Darwin, Jr. (1850-91); VI-David Howe (1852-1904; *m* Sophie Sheets); VII-Anna Elizabeth (1 above); VIII-Louise Allen (1857-1927); IX-Fannie Belle (*b* 1859); X-Juliette Martha (*b* 1861).
1-*m* Sept. 23, 1880, Allan B. Philputt (May 6, 1856-Apr. 19, 1925); son of Bearden Philputt, of Bedford Co., Tenn.; issue: 1-Louise Elizabeth (May 29, 1881-Jan. 6, 1903); 2-Grace Maxwell, *b* Bloomington, Ind., Feb. 9, 1886; A.B., Ind. U., '08 (P.B.K.); scholarship, Bryn Mawr Coll., 1908-09; Sorbonne, Paris, France, 1909-10; Lycee Descarter Tours, 1913-14; teacher French, Shortridge High School, during World War; instr. Romance Languages present time; asso. editor Modern Lang. Journal; *m* July 12, 1923, Prof. Bert E., son of Cyrus H. Young, *m* Kate Dunlap.
1-Grad. in music, Glendale (O.) Sem., 1872. Dir. Indianapolis Y.W.C.A., 1898-1923. Mem. C.D.A. (librarian), U.S.D., 1812, Soc. of Indiana Pioneers, etc. Republican. Residence: 3273 Central Av., Indianapolis, Ind.

1-**PIPES, Mary Louise Minor (Mrs. David W., Jr.),** *b* "The Cottage," West Feliciana Parish, La., Aug. 24, 1886.
9-Thomas (Miner) **Minor** (qv);
8-Clement, of New London, Conn.; *m* 1st, 1661, Frances Willey;

7–William (*b* 1670), *m* 1st, Anne Beckwith, of Lyme, Conn.;
6–Stephen (*b* 1705), Winchester, Va.; *m* ca. 1732, Atheliah Updike, of N.J.;
5–William (*d* 1804), of Va.; comd. Statler's Fort nr. Morgantown, W.Va.; *m* ca. 1759, Frances Phillips (*d* 1797), of Md.;
4–Stephen (*b* 1760), of Natchez, Miss.; maj. in Spanish army; commr. for Spain in establishing La. boundaries; *m* 3d, 1792, Katharine Lintot (1770-1844; Bernard[5], from Eng., *m* Katharine Trotter, of N.Y.);
3–William John (1808-69), of "Southdown," Houma, La.; *m* 1829, Rebecca Ann Gustine (*b* 1813), of Carlisle, Pa. (Dr. James[4], *m* 1808, Mary Ann Duncan; Dr. Lemuel[5]; Lemuel[6]; Samuel[7]; Jean[8]);
2–Henry Chotard (2 below).
6–Thomas **Butler** (qv);
5–Thomas (1748-1805), of Pa.; Am. Rev.; col. in U.S.A.; *m* 1784, Sarah Jane Semple (Robert[6], from Scotland to Cumberland Co., Pa., *m* 1st, Lydia Steele, of Pa.);
4–Thomas (1785-1847), of Pa. and La.; U.S. dist. judge; mem. Congress from La.; *m* 1813, Anne Madeline Ellis;
3–Pierce (1817-88), of La.; *m* 1840, Mary Louise Stirling (1818-45; William Henry[4], *m* Mary, dau. of Jacob Bowman; Alexander[5], Scotland to La., *m* 1782, Anne, dau. of John Alston, of N.C.);
2–Anna Louise (2 below).
9–John **Ellis**, burgess; *m* Susanna–;
8–John, of Henrico Co., Va.; *m* Elizabeth Ware;
7–John, *m* Elizabeth Smith (Obadiah[8], *m* Mary Cocke);
6–Richard, of Amelia Co., Va., Natchez Ty., Miss.; *m* Mary Cocke (Abraham[7]);
5–Abram (*d* 1816), *m* Marguerite Gaillard (Tacitus[6], of S.C., *m* Anne Madeline Le Grand);
4–Anne Madeline (1794-1878), *m* 1813, Thomas **Butler** (4 above);
3–Pierce, *m* Mary Louise Stirling; (3 above);
2–Anna Louise (1843-1906), *m* April 28, 1875, Henry Chotard **Minor** (1841-98), planter of "Southdown," Houma, La.; issue: I–John Duncan (*b* 1876; *m* Lucille Gillis); II–Margarett Gustine (*b* 1883; *m* Charles C. Krumbhaar); III–Mary Louise (1 above).
1–*m* Nov. 2, 1910, David W. Pipes, Jr., *b* New Orleans, La., Aug. 6, 1886; son of David W. Pipes, of East Feliciana Parish, La.; issue (all *b* New Orleans, La.): 1–David W. (*b* Feb. 25, 1912-Jan. 12, 1914); 2–Anna Fort, *b* May 16, 1914; 3–Henry Minor, *b* Mar. 17, 1916; 4–John Butler, *b* Jan. 27, 1919; 5–Katharine Minor, *b* Feb. 1, 1922; 6–Mary Minor, *b* Apr. 3, 1925; 7–Margarett Gustine, *b* Jan. 25, 1927.
1–Grad. Newcomb Coll., '06 (Kappa Kappa Gamma). Mem. C.D.A. Episcopalian. Residence: "Southdown," Houma, La.

1–**PITTS, Mary Bacot,** *b* Baltimore, Md., June 4, 1879.
8–Rev. Henry **Hall** (1676-1722), rector St. James' Parish, 1698-1722; commd. Commissary of the Bishop of London for Md., 1707, but declined; *m* 1701, Mary Duvall (Mareen[9] [*d* 1694], of Anne Arundel Co., Md.);
7–Maj. Henry (1702-56), mem. Colonial Assembly for Anne Arundel Co., 1740-48,51; justice, 1742; *m* 1st, 1723, Martha Bateman, of Prince George's Co., Md.;
6–Henry (1727-70), of Anne Arundel Co.; *m* 1748, Elizabeth Watkins;
5–Nicholas (1758-1821), of New Market, Md.; *m* 1st, 1779, Anne Griffith;
4–Elizabeth (1780-1830), *m* 1804, Rev. John **Pitts** (1772-1821), of Frederick Co. (Thomas[5], of Town Neck Hundred, Anne Arundel Co.);
3–Charles Hall (1814-64), of Baltimore; *m* 1844, Elizabeth Reynolds;
2–Charles Hall (2 below).
10–Thomas **Besson** (1616-79), mem. Gen. Assembly, 1657; burgess, Anne Arundel Co., 1666; *m* Hester–;
9–Anne, *m* Col. Nicholas **Gassaway** (qv);
8–Anne (1670-1742), *m* 1st, John **Watkins** (*d* 1696/97; John[9], of Anne Arundel Co.; John[10], of Nansemond Co., Va., *m* Frances–);
7–Nicholas (1691-1770), *m* Margaret Lamb (bap. 1703-1774; John[8], *m* Elizabeth Williams, ?);
6–Elizabeth (1727-89), *m* Henry **Hall** (6 above).
9–Nicholas **Greenberry** (qv);
8–Katharine, as Widow Ridgely, *m* 2d, John **Howard** (*d* 1704), of Anne Arundel Co. (John[9]; Mathew[10], *m* Anne–);
7–Katharine (*d* 1783), *m* 1717, Orlando **Griffith** (1688-1757), of Annapolis, Md. (William[8], from Eng. to Md., 1675, *m* Sarah, dau. of John Maccubbin);
6–Henry (1720-94), justice, Anne Arundel Co., 1755-61; mem. Assembly for Frederick Co., 1773-75; mem. Md. Conv. for Frederick Co., 1775; mem. Com. of Corr. for Frederick and later for Montgomery Co., 1775-76; *m* 2d, 1751, Ruth Hammond;
5–Anne (1762-91), *m* Nicholas **Hall** (5 above).
9–Maj. Gen. John **Hammond** (qv);
8–Maj. Charles (1674-1713), burgess, Anne Arundel Co., 1710-13; mil. officer, 1696; *m* Hannah Howard (Philip[9], *m* Ruth, dau. of John Baldwin; Mathew[10]);
7–John (*d* 1753), *m* Anne (Dorsey?), (*d* 1786);
6–Ruth (*d* 1782), *m* Henry **Griffith** (6 above).
6–John **Reynolds** (*d* 1784), of Sharpsburg Hundred, Washington Co., Md.;
5–Joseph (1747-1808), *m* 1774, Sarah Smith (1757-1821);
4–Robert Smith (1792-1832), of Vincennes, Ind.; *m* Martha Lansdale (ca. 1805-1831);
3–Elizabeth (ca. 1825-1855), *m* Charles Hall **Pitts** (3 above).
7–William **Lord** (*d* 1749), of Brunswick, New Hanover Co., N.C.; *m* Margaret Espey;
6–William (1732-80), *m* 1758, Sarah Espey (*b* 1736?; James[7], *m* Margaret–);
5–John (1765-1831), *m* Elizabeth Bradley;
4–Sarah Elizabeth (1799-1865), *m* 1813, John Rutherford **London** (1786-1832), of Wilmington, N.C. (John[5], from Eng., settled at Wilmington, N.C., *m* 1st, 1785, Peggy, dau. of Rufus Marsden; John[6], of Eng.);
3–Mary Bacot (1825-51), *m* 1850, Samuel Jones **Person** (1823-69; Benjamin[4], of Carthage, N.C., *m* Annie, dau. of Murdock Bethune, of Fayetteville, N.C.; Samuel[5], of Moore Co., N.C., *m* Tabitha–);
2–Mary Bacot (2 below).
10–Jeffrey **Sharples** (*d* 1661), *m* Margaret Ashley (*d* 1643/44);
9–John (1624-85), *m* 1662, Jane Moor (1632-1722);
8–John (1666-1747), *m* 1692, Hannah Pennell (1673-1721; Robert[9], *m* Hannah–);
7–John (1699-1769), *m* 2d, 1729, Elizabeth Ashbridge (1708/09-1767; George[8], of Goshen Tp., Pa., *m* 1st, 1701, Mary Malin);
6–Elizabeth (1734-1802), *m* 1755, Richard **Bradley** (John[7], of Eng.);
5–Elizabeth (ca. 1763-1847), *m* 1792, John **Lord** (5 above;
4–Sarah Elizabeth, *m* John R. **London** (4 above);
3–Mary Bacot, *m* Samuel Jones **Person** (3 above);
2–Mary Bacot (1851-81), *m* 1870, as his 1st wife, Charles Hall **Pitts** (1845-87): issue: I–Alice Dickinson (*b* 1874; *m* James Piper); II–Sophia Norris (*b* 1877; *m* William LeGendre); III–Mary Bacot (1 above); IV–Jane London (*b* 1881).
1–Mem. C.D.A., I.A.G., Md. Hist. Soc., Mount Vernon Club. Episcopalian. Democrat. Residence: 822 W. 40th St., Baltimore, Md.

1–**PLEASANTS, Lucile Rogers Randolph Gibson (Mrs. J. S.),** *b* West Point, Miss., Feb. 11, 1882.
10–William **Clack,** of Marden, Wiltshire, Eng.; *m* Mary Spencer (sister of Col. Nicholas Spencer, and cousin of Lord Culpeper, gov. of Va.);
9–Rev. James (*d* 1723), came to Va., 1679; rector of Ware Parish, Gloucester Co. 45 yrs.; *m* Jane–;
8–Capt. James (ca. 1690-1757), Gloucester, York and Brunswick cos.; *m* ca. 1718, Mary Sterling;
7–Col. John (ca. 1720-post 1783), spent 10 yrs. in Northern Neck, as surveyor and in mil. service; settled in Brunswick, 1748, when he qualified as lt. of co. militia; warden of St. Andrew's Parish, 1766; sheriff, 1755; burgess; *m* 1743, Mary Kennon (*b* 1728; Capt. Richard[8], *m* Agnes, dau. of Col. Robert Bolling, qv; Richard[9], qv);
6–Hon. Spencer (1746-1832), *b* in Loudoun Co., Va.; lived in Brunswick, several cos. in northern and western Va., Henry and Frank-

COL. JOSEPH TUCKER RANDOLPH (1818-91), lived in Sussex Co., Va., Limestone Co., Ala., Lowndes, Oktibbeha and Clay cos., Miss., Lake Co., Fla.; Confederate soldier; lt., Co. F, Perrin's Bn., Miss. State Cav.; later colonel of ordnance.

lin cos., Va., and Sevier Co., Tenn.; his training in surveying and military tactics was under supervision of George Washington, who sponsored him when he joined the Masons; soldier in Am. Rev., 1st lt., Co. A, Henry Co. militia; mem. 1st Legislature in Tenn., 1796, and as senator from Sevier Co., 1796-1832; mem. com. that drafted Constitution of Tenn.; *m* in Va., 1766, Mary Beavers (*b* 1745; desc. Chevalier Robert de Beauvilliers, the name was shortened to Beavill, and later changed to Beavers, when French names became unpopular, during the French and Indian War);
5-Catherine (1778-1850), *m* Rev. Elijah **Rogers** (1774-1841; Henry[6], *m* Elizabeth Lankford);
4-Robert H. (1796-1869), *m* 1st, 1825, Malinda Henderson;
3-Mary Catherine (1828-1904), *m* 1843, William Wellington **Gibson** (1812-76), of Vt., Mass., Ala. and Miss.; prominent educator, served with Confederacy in hosps. and in gathering supplies for army;
2-Col. Orville Abraham (2 below).
9-James **Moore** (son of Sir John), from Barbados to Charleston, S.C., 1675; gov. of S.C., 1700-03; *m* 1676, Margaret, dau. of Dame Margaret Yeamans, by her 1st husband Col. Berringer of Barbados;
8-John (*b* ca. 1678), moved to Bristol Parish, Prince George Co., Va.;
7-John (*b* ca. 1699), lived in Prince George and Surry cos. Va.; *m* 1719, Catherine-;
6-Betty Rutherford (1731-68), *m* 1748, George (Randolf) **Randolph** (*d* 1772), clk. of St. Mark's Parish Ch., 1769-1772;
5-Peter (1750-86) Am. Rev.; began to write name Randolph; of Sussex and Brunswick cos., Va.; *m* Frances Parham (1747-91; James, Sr.[6], of Brunswick Co., *m* Elizabeth-);
4-St. George (1781-1818), *m* Lucretia Tucker Chappell;
3-Joseph Tucker (1818-91), see portrait and biography; *m* 1st, 1842, Susan Marion Reed, or Reade;
2-Josephine Marion (2 below).
9-Thomas **Chappell** (*b* 1612), sailed from Gravesend, Eng., in the "America," June 23, 1635, aet. 23; settled in Charles City Co., opposite Westover at mouth of creek, still called "Chappell's Creek"; *m* a dau. of Lt. John Banister;
8-Thomas (ca. 1650-ante 1700), *m* Elizabeth Jones (James[9], *m* Sarah-);
7-James (1694-1769), Charles City, Prince George, Surry and Sussex cos., Va.; vestryman; high sheriff; called "James Chappell, Gentleman" in numerous land patents; *m* 1718, Elizabeth Briggs (1696-1744; Henry[8], called "The Interpreter" for southern Indians, *m* Miss Howell; Henry[9], of Southwark Parish, Surry Co., *m* Mary-);
6-Thomas (1719-90), lived in Surry, Southampton and Lunenburg cos.; *m* ca. 1745, his cousin, Mary Briggs;
5-Thomas (1749-1823), Southampton, Charlotte, Lunenburg and Sussex cos.; Am. Rev.; *m* 1772, Elizabeth Malone (*d* 1807; William[6], *m* Mary-; William[7]);
4-Lucretia Tucker (1784-1861), Sussex Co., Va., Limestone Co., Ala., Lowndes and Oktibbeha cos., Miss.; *m* 1801, St. George **Randolph** (4 above).
9-Henry **Briggs** (1635-86), of Southwark Parish; *m* Mary Ford, a widow;
8-Samuel (1673-1737), of Surry Co.; *m* Mary Bayley (Edward[9]);
7-William (*d* 1748), of Albemarle Parish, Surry Co.; *m* Mary Cook (William[8], *m* Rebecca, dau. of James Jones, and sister of Elizabeth Jones, who *m* Thomas Chappell, 8 above);
6-Mary, *m* Thomas **Chappell** (6 above).
10-Nicholas **Martian** (qv);
9-Elizabeth, *m* Col. George **Reade** (qv), ancestor of George Washington and descended from Plantaganet kings through his ancestor Sir William Gascoigne;
8-Robert (1644-1712), justice of York Co., Va.; *m* Mary Lilly (*d* 1722), dau. of John Lilly and heiress of Edward Mallson;
7-John (*b* ca. 1670), King and Queen Co., Va.;
6-William (1715-64), name on first poll list of Brunswick Co., 1748; vestryman, St. Andrew's Parish; *m* Elizabeth-;
5-John (*b* Brunswick Co., Va., 1757-*d* in Tenn., 1817), Am. Rev. and War 1812; *m* ca. 1778, Margaret- (1762-1829);
4-James (*b* 1793-*d* in Ala. ante 1850), War 1812; *m* 1824, Jane Norvell;
3-Susan Marion (1827-57) *m* Joseph Tucker **Randolph** (3 above).
12-Thomas (Neuville, Neville), **Norvell,** of Isle of Wight, came to Va. ante 1630; *m* Mary-;
11-William, of Isle of Wight; *m* Lydia-;
10-George (*d* 1686), vestryman, Bruton Ch., James City Co.; *m* a dau. of Capt. Hugh Bullock;
9-Hugh (*d* 1719), vestryman, Bruton Ch., James City Co.;
8-George, of St. Paul's Parish, Hanover;
7-James, of Hanover and Goochland; soldier colonial wars; paid for services in Lunenburg, 1758;
6-Spencer (*d* 1829), soldier in the Am. Rev. from Albemarle Co.; signer of Albemarle Declaration of Independence, 1758; *m* 1770, Frances Hill;
5-John P. (1775-1830), War 1812; moved to Tenn., ca. 1800; *m* — (*d* ante 1829);
4-Jane (*d* ante 1840), *m* James **Reade** (4 above);
3-Susan Marion, *m* Joseph T. **Randolph** (3 above);
2-Josephine Marion (1853-89), *m* Col. Orville Abraham **Gibson** (*b* 1845), Fayette, Miss.; entered Co. E, Oktibbeha Rescues, 1st Miss. Cav., C.S.A. (Gen. Stephen D. Lee. commander), Apr. 1862, mustered out May 26, 1865; issue: I-Orville W. (1874-1900); II-Virginia Marion (called May Byrd; *b* 1880; *m* 1st, William Lucian Owsley, see their son Randolph G. Owsley, Vol. III, p. 361); III-Lucile Randolph (1 above); IV-Joseph Tucker (*b* 1884); V-Augustus W. (1887-1917; corpl. Washington Arty., of New Orleans on Mexican border, 9 mos., 1916-17; entered World War, Apr. 10, 1917, mem. of 141st Arty., killed in accident while in service, Sept. 21, 1917).
1-*m* Oct. 14, 1902, John Stephen Pleasants (1872-1923); issue: 1-John Gibson (qv for Pleasants lineages).
1-Grad. in piano, N.E. Conservatory of Music, Boston; studied voice, Chicago Musical Coll. Church and concert singer. Mem. C.D.A., D.F.P.A., D.A.R., U.D.C., I.A.G., etc. Clubs: Town and Gown, Casa del Mar, Deauville Beach. Residence: 1186 Crenshaw Boul., Los Angeles, Calif.

1-**PLEASANTS, John Gibson,** *b* Laurel, Miss., Dec. 27, 1908.
5-William **Pleasants** (1756-1836; desc. John Pleasants [1645-98], came to Va., ca. 1665, set-

JOHN LANDIS PLEASANTS (1826-79), mem. Co. G, 4th Ala. Regt., Marion Light Inf., C.S.A.; lived most of his life at Asheville, N.C., where he owned the first department store; deacon Bapt. church.

tled in Henrico Co.; *m* 1670, Jane [Larcome] Tucker, *d* 1708); pvt. Am. Rev., pensioned;
4–Stephen (1779-1852), *b* in Va.; prominent Bapt. minister; monument erected to his memory in Person Co., N.C., by Beulah Assn.; *m* Mary Brown (1785-1867; Rev. William[5]);
3–John Landis (1826-79), see portrait and biography; *m* 1862, Cornelia Lawrence;
2–John Stephen (2 below).
9–William **Lawrence,** of Lancaster Co.; *m* Johannah Sydnor; and thru his g.son;
7–William (1734-60), fought in Spanish Alarm War; received land grant in Granville Co., N.C., 1756; *m* 1756, Deborah– (1740-91);
6–Abraham (1759-1838), Am. Rev.; *m* 1781, Leannah Jones (1763-1840);
5–William Twitty (1784-1832), *m* 1805, Lydia Pruitt (John[6], *m* Susannah Twitty);
4–Turner (1818-81), of Granville Co., N.C.; C.S.A.; *m* 1835, Priscilla Upchurch (1818-93; Ambrose[5], *m* Elizabeth Hill);
3–Cornelia (1836-1900), *m* 1862, John Landis **Pleasants** (3 above).
10–John **Gibson** (qv);
9–John (1641-79), King Philip's War; captured by Mogg Megone, Indian chief, 1677; *m* 1668, Rebecca Errington (*d* 1713; Abraham[10], *m* Rebecca, dau. of Robert Cutler, of Charlestown);
8–Timothy (1679-1757), large landowner and selectman, 1734-39, at Stow; *m* 1700, Rebecca Gates (1682-1754; Stephen[9], *m* Sarah Woodward [George[10], *m* Mary–; Richard[11]]; Stephen[10], *m* Ann Gates);
7–Isaac (1721-97), scout against Indians, 1749; selectman, 1767-77; town moderator, 1777; minute man and soldier in Am. Rev.; chmn. com. of seven, 1773 "to respond to Boston letter"; *m* 1744, Keziah Johnson;
6–Nathaniel (1753-1824), minute man and soldier in Am. Rev.; *m* 1776, Hannah Brown (1753-89; Daniel[7], *m* Anna Bright);
5–Persis (1783-1824), *m* 1806, Abraham **Gibson** (see Vol. III, p. 361, for Gibson lineage);
4–William Wellington (1812-76), *m* Mary Catherine Rogers;
3–Orville Abraham (*b* 1845), see portrait and biography; *m* 1869, Josephine Marion Randolph;
2–Lucile Rogers Randolph (2 below).
14–William **Johnson** (1500-76), of Canterbury, Eng.; *m* 1528, Alice, dau. of John Foreflode;

COL. ORVILLE ABRAHAM GIBSON (b 1845), entered Oktibbeha Rescues, Co. E, 1st Miss. Cav., C.S.A. (Gen. Stephen D. Lee, commander), April 1862, mustered out May 26, 1865; lt. col. on staff of cdr. U.C.V. and q.m. gen. for Miss. (Photograph from a daguerreotype taken at age 17, in 1862).

13–John (1531-98), *m* 1551, Joane Humfrey (*d* 1584);
12–William (1559-1637), *m* ca. 1587, Susan, dau. of John Porredge, of Westgate Court, Canterbury;
11–Capt. Edward (qv);
10–John (1635-1720); *m* 1657, Bethia Reed (*d* 1717; Capt. William[11], *m* Mabel–);
9–John (*b* 1658), *m* Mary Carley (William[10], *m* Jane–; William[11], of Lancaster);
8–Dea. Samuel (*b* 1692), *m* Rebecca Wilson (1698-1731; Samuel[9], of Woburn, *m* Elizabeth–);
7–Keziah (1725-66), *m* 1744, Isaac **Gibson**, (7 above).
10–Giles **Rogers** (1645-1730; John[11]; Thomas M.[12]; Bernard[13]; John[14], the martyr, burned at the stake, 1554/55; nephew of Thomas Rogers, the Mayflower Pilgrim); came to Va., 1670, and again in 1680; *m* in Eng., Rachel Eastham;
9–John (*b* 1680), *m* Mary Byrd (William[10], qv);
8–George (*b* 1721), *m* 1st, ca. 1740, a dau. of Henry Lee (?); *m* 2d, 1754, Frances Pollard;
7–Henry (*b* 1741), Am. Rev.; lived in Fauquier Co., Va., Chatham Co., N.C., and Sevier Co., Tenn.; *m* Elizabeth Lankford (Langford);
6–Rev. Elijah (1774-1841), under Col. Doherty in expdn. against Cherokees and was with Col. Doherty in 1803, when 8 cos. of East Tenn. militia, marched to Natchez to force surrender of New Orleans by Spaniards; pioneer Bapt. preacher in Sevier Co.; *m* 1794, Catherine Clack (1778-1850; Spencer[7], *m* Mary Beavers);
5–Robert Henderson (1796-1869), in Creek War, surveyor under Gen. Sevier in Ala.; sheriff of Sevier Co., Tenn.; shot through lungs by a criminal; lived in Sevier Co., Tenn., Blount Co., Ala., Natchitoches Parish, La., and Winston Co., Miss.; *m* 1825, Malinda Henderson; *m* 2d, 1838, Lucinda Hale;
4–Mary Catherine (1828-1904), *m* William Wellington **Gibson** (4 above);
3–Col. Orville A., *m* Josephine M. Randolph (3 above);
2–Lucile Rogers Randolph (qv), *m* John Stephen **Pleasants** (*b* High Point, N.C., 1872-*d* Los Angeles, Calif., Oct. 3, 1923), asso. with Stuart W. Cramer, of Charlotte, N.C., superintended equipment of new cotton mills in the South, 1895-1902; gen. mgr. Kosciusko, Miss., Cotton Mills, 1902-04; gen. mgr and v.p. cotton mills at Laurel, Miss., 1904-20; dir. Interstate Wholesale Grocers Inc., of New Orleans; trustee Laurel Bd. of Edn., 1918-20; four-minute speaker during World War; Baptist; Democrat.
1–B.A. (magna cum laude), U. of Southern

Calif., 1929 (Eta Kappa Nu, Kappa Alpha Order, Phi Kappa Phi); M.A., Calif. Inst. of Tech., awarded an assistanceship, 1930. Mem. S.A.R., Am. Inst. of E.E., Sigma Xi, Casa del Mar Club. Residence: 1186 Crenshaw Boul., Los Angeles, Calif.

1-**POMEROY, Horace Burton,** *b* Troy, Pa., June 3, 1879.
8-Eltweed **Pomeroy** (qv);
7-Joseph (1652-1734-39), of Windsor, Conn., and Northampton, Mass.; *m* 1677, Hannah Lyman (1660-1736);
6-Noah (1700-79), Somerset, Conn.; *m* 1724, Elizabeth Sterling (1700-79);
5-Daniel (1727-85), of Colchester, Conn.; *m* 1749, Naomi Kibbie (1726-93), of Coventry, Conn.;
4-Hon. Eleazor (1752-1811), *m* 2d, 1785, Priscilla Kingsbury (1756-1841);
3-Martin Ebenezer (1794-1866), *m* 1818, Laura Brewster (1795-1890), of Coventry;
2-Charles Burton (*b* 1839), of Troy, Pa.; *m* 1867, Sophia Weber (*b* 1841); issue: I-Edwin Soreno; II-John Webber; III-Adele; IV-Laura Brewster; V-Horace Burton (1 above); VI-Fayette Brewster.
1-*m* Nov. 17, 1909, Ethel Josephene Braman, *b* New York, N.Y., June 17, 1882; dau. of Chester Alwyn Braman, of New York; issue: 1-Horace Burton, Jr., *b* N.Y. City, Sept. 10, 1910; 2-Lawrence, *b* Rochester, N.Y., Jan. 21, 1913; 3-Josephene Adele, *b* Buffalo, N.Y., July 2, 1917; 4-Braman, *b* Buffalo, Feb. 21, 1920).
1-B.A., Yale, '03, M.A., 1906 (Psi U.). With Bankers Trust Co., New York, 1903-08; with Harris, Forbes & Co., New York, 1908-11; v.p., treas. and dir. Schoellkopf, Hutton & Pomeroy, Inc., Rochester, N.Y., since 1921. Mem. S.A.R., Buffalo Hist. Soc., Pomeroy Family Organization (v.p.). Presbyterian. Republican. Clubs: Kawartha Fishing, Fenelon Falls (Ontario), Yale, University (New York), Buffalo Athletic, Wanakena, Buffalo Country, Lake Shore Hunt (Buffalo). Summer place: Wanakah, N.Y. Residence: 550 Lafayette Av., Buffalo, N.Y.

1-**POPE, Curran,** *b* Louisville, Ky., Nov. 12, 1866.
8-Col. Richard **Johnson** (*d* 1699), mem. Va. Council, 1696; *m* 2d, in Va.;
7-William, capt. Va. militia, 1729; *m* Nan Chew (Larkin[8], *d* 1728);
6-William (1714-65), col. Va. militia; *m* 1742, Elizabeth Cove (Benjamin[7]);
5-Col. Robert ("Robin"), (1745-1815), Am. Rev.; Ky. pioneer, rep. 5th Ky. Dist., 1785; mem. Constl., Conv., 1792,99; mem. Legislature; *m* 1770, Jemima Suggett (1753-1814);
4-Col. James (1774-1825 or 26), senator, 1808; lt. col. War. 1812; presidential elector, 1821; elected to congress, 1825; *m* 1st, 1796, Nancy (Ann) Payne (1780-1847);
3-Nancy (1815-49), *m* 1834, Edmond Pendleton **Pope** (1809-57), see Vol. III, p. 570, for Pope-Thruston lineage;
2-Alfred Thruston (2 below).
10-John (De La) **Fontaine** (ca. 1500-1563), of France; Huguenot, martyred for his religion;
9-James (1549-1633), *m* twice;
8-Rev. James (1603-66), *m* 2d, 1641, Marie Chaillon (*d* aet. 63);
7-Rev. James (*b* 1658), from France to Eng., 1685; *m* 1686, Anne Elizabeth (Barnstaple) Boursiquot (*d* 1721);
6-Rev. Peter (*b* Va., 1696-*d* Charles City Parish, Va., 1757); *m* Elizabeth Wade;
5-Aaron (1753-1823), *m* 1773, Barbara Terrill (*d* 1797);
4-Anne Overton (1796-1819), *m* 1811, John Jeremiah **Jacob** (1778-1852), leading citizen and wealthiest banker of Louisville, Ky.; 1st pres. Nat. Bank of Ky. (for Jacob lineage see Vol. III, p. 570);
3-Matilda Prather (1815-80), *m* 1838, Col. Curran **Pope** (1813-62), U.S.M.A., '34;
2-Mary Tyler (1846-1906), *m* 1865, Alfred Thruston **Pope** (1842-91), judge Circuit Ct. of Ky. (for issue see Vol. II, p. 317).
1-Not married. M.D., U.Louisville, '89 (Phi Chi). Physician; med. dir. The Pope Hospital. Served in Ky. N.G. 6 yrs.; Mem. O.F.P.-A., S.C.W., S.C., S.A.R., M.O.L.L. Residence: 225 E. Walnut St., Louisville, Ky.

1-**POTTER, Harriet Wilkins (Mrs. Frederick E.),** *b* Suncook, N.H., Apr. 25, 1848.
8-Bray **Wilkins** (1610-1702; son of Lord John), from Wales, settled at Middleton, Mass.; original propr. Dorchester; mem. 1st church of Salem; *m* Ann Gingle;
7-John (*b* 1642); *m* Mary-;
6-John (*b* 1667), of Salem; *m* 1687, Elizabeth Southwick (Daniel[7], Quaker, *m* Esther Boyce);
5-John (1689-1733), *m* 1713, Mary Goodall (*b* 1696);
4-Josiah (1718-83), *m* Lois Bush (1721-96);
3-Jonathan (1755-1820), *m* 1787, Sarah Hall (1770-1826);
2-Jeremiah Hall (2 below).
8-Nicholas **Noyes** (qv);
7-John (*b* 1646), of Newbury, Mass.; *m* 1668, Mary Poore (*b* bet. 1648-57-*d* 1716);
6-Samuel (1692-1729), *m* 1714, Hannah Poor (*b* 1692);
5-John (1720-70), *m* 1741, Abigail Poor (1721-1814);
4-Benjamin (1742-1811), *m* Hannah Thompson (1744-1828), of Kingston, N.H.;
3-Judith (*b* 1777), *m* 1799, Robert **Thompson** (1774-1803);
2-Mary (1799-1879), *m* Jeremiah Hall **Wilkins** (1791-1864), of Concord, N.H., and Suncook.
1-*m* Oct. 2, 1873, Dr. Frederick Eugene Potter (July 3, 1839-Nov. 18, 1902), son of Frederick F. Potter, *m* Calister Lucas.
1-Mem. C.D.A., D.C.G., D.A.R., I.A.G. (life). Residence: 93 Islington St., Portsmouth, N.H.

CLARKSON CROLIUS (1773-1843), from a painting by Ezra Ames, 1825, in the library of the New York Historical Society.

1-**POWERS, Walter Hayward, III,** *b* 146 E. 74th St., New York, N.Y., Nov. 10, 1908.
10-Matthew **Woodruff** (qv);
9-Samuel (1661-1742), of Hartford and Farmington, Conn.; first white settler at Southington; *m* 1686, Rebecca Clark (1662-1737);
8-Hezekiah (1701-91), *m* 1730, Sarah Mason (*d* 1785);
7-Hezekiah (*b* 1735), to Colebrook, Conn., 1786; *m* 1761, Ruth Boardman;
6-Isaiah (1764-1832), *m* 1797, Sarah Parsons;
5-Elijah Parsons (1798-1847), *m* 1831, Mary C. Crolius;
4-Mary Henrietta (1833-1904), *m* 1854, George W. **Powers** (1824-95);
3-Walter Hayward (1855-93), *m* 1878, Katharine Staats Weaver;
2-Walter Hayward (2 below).
11-Samuel **Boardman** (qv);
10-Isaac (1642-1701), *m* Abiah Kimberly (1641-1722; Thomas[11], *m* Alice-);

9–Isaac (1666-1719), of Wethersfield, Conn.; *m* 1699, Rebecca Benton;
8–Ephraim (1711-61), *m* 1734, Mehitable Cole (1708-69);
7–Ruth (*b* 1737), *m* Hezekiah **Woodruff** (7 above).
11–Robert **Pease** (qv);
10–Capt. John (1634-89), of Salem, Mass.; as surveyor helped lay out Enfield; A. and H. A. Co., 1661, sgt. 1665, capt., 1668; *m* 2d, Dec. 8, 1669, Ann Cummings (ca. 1629-1689; Isaac[11], qv);
9–James (1670-1748), *m* 1695, Hannah Harmon;
8–Abigail (*b* 1708), *m* 1735, Rev. Nathaniel **Collins,** Jr. (1700-87); see Vol. III, p. 379 for Collins lineage;
7–Jerusha (1747-1826), *m* Elijah **Parsons** (1745-97; Thomas[8]; Phillip[9]);
6–Sarah (1773-1855), *m* Isaiah **Woodruff** (6 above).
8–Johan William (Crollius) **Crolius** (*b* 1700), to New York, 1718, or before; established a pottery, probably the first in New York City, which flourished until 1850; freeman, 1739; *m* 1724, Veronica Cortselius;

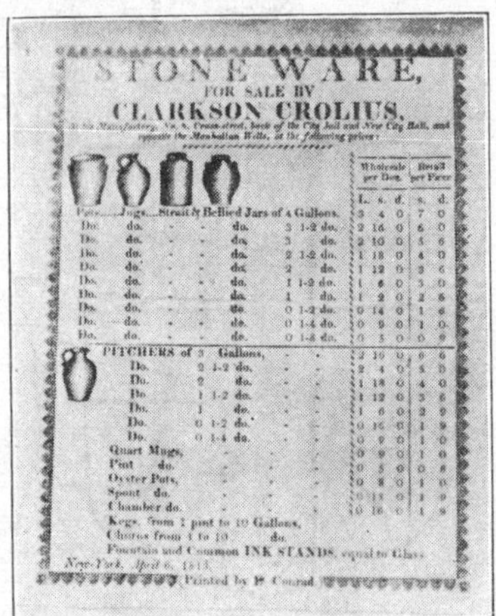

Stoneware advertisement, New York, 1813.

7–John (1733-1812), began to write name Crolius; potter; *m* 1753, Mary Clarkson (1733-99; William[8], London, Eng., to Albany, N.Y.);
6–Clarkson (1773-1843), asst. alderman, 6th ward, N.Y. City, 1802-05; mem. Assembly, 1806-07, 1815-25; speaker of the House, 1825; collector, 1838-44; as Grand Sachem or Sagamon of the Tammany Soc., May 13, 1911, laid the cornerstone of the new Tammany Hall; officiated at the laying of the cornerstone of the new City Hall, and, 1842, was the last surviving mem. of the Common Council, who was present at that event; active founder of the American Institute (v.p. many yrs.); maj. War 1812; *m* 1793, Elizabeth H. Meyer (*d* 1856; Frederick[7], *m* Lydia–);
5–Mary Clarkson (1803-83), *m* Elijah P. **Woodruff** (5 above).
10–Maj. Abram **Staats** (*d* 1694), from Holland to Albany, N.Y., 1642; settled on Staats' Island just below Albany in Hudson River; was surgeon, capt., 1669, and maj.; pres. Council; *m* Catrina Jochemse Wessels (Joachim[11]);
9–Capt. Joachim (1654-1712), of Albany; *m* 1678, Anna Barends (Rynderse) Reyndertse (1656-1707);
8–Capt. Barent (1680-1752), *m* 1701, Neeltje Gerritse (Neeltse Garretts) Vanden Berg (1684-1749);
7–Garret (*b* 1722), *m* 1747, Deborah Beekman (1726-63; Jacob[8], *m* Deborah Hansen; Johannes Martense[9], *m* J., dau. Jacob Jansen Schermerhorn [qv]; Marten[10], *m* Susanna–);
6–Jacob (1757-1819), *m* Elizabeth Lowe;
5–Catharine (1805-54), *m* William R. **Lansing** (1804-86);
4–Eliza (1830-63), *m* 1854, George Shearman **Weaver** (1826-1907), see Vol. III, p. 379 for Weaver lineage;
3–Katharine Staats (*b* 1856), *m* Walter H. **Powers** (3 above);
2–Walter Hayward **Powers** (qv); *m* 1907, Helen Gillette Ballard.
1–Ed. Rye Country Day School; Loomis Inst., Windsor, Conn. Mem. Drake Sparkman Yacht Brokers and Marine Ins. Co. Club: Larchmont Yacht. Residence: Windcrest Rd., Rye, N.Y.

FREDERICK EDWARD BALLARD (1853-1915).

1–**POWERS, Katharine Louise,** *b* Grace Church St., Rye, N.Y., June 14, 1913.
11–Joseph **Loomis** (qv);
10–Dea. John (1622-84), from Eng. to Windsor, Conn., 1638; freeman, 1640; dep. Gen. Ct., 1666-67, 1675-87; *m* 1648/49, Elizabeth Scott (1625-96; Thomas[11], from Eng. to Ipswich, Mass., 1634);
9–Sgt. Daniel (1657-1740), *m* 1st, 1680, Mary Ellsworth (*b* 1660; Sgt. Josiah[10], *m* Elizabeth Holcomb);
8–Daniel (1682-1754), *m* 1709, Elizabeth Barber;
7–Daniel (1710-58), *m* 1736, Sarah Enos;
6–Elijah (1747-95), to Georgia, Vt., 1788; *m* 1774, Althea (Burleigh) Burley (1751-99; John[7], from Eng. to Union, Conn., 1732, *m* Miriam, dau. of Nathaniel Fuller, *m* Ann Butterworth);
5–Mary (Polly) (1775-1858), *m* 1793, Joseph **Ballard** (1766-1836); see Vol. III, p. 379;
4–Loomis (*b* 1816), New York; *m* Mary Sophia White (1819-95);
3–Frederick Edward (1853-1915), *m* 1877, Elizabeth Boyd Keeler;
2–Helen Gillette (2 below).
11–John **Drake** (qv);
10–John (*d* 1688), Simsbury, Conn.; *m* 1648, Hannah Moore (*d* 1686; Thomas[11]);
9–Ruth (1657-1731), desc. Edward I, King of Eng. and Eleanor of Castile; *m* as his 2d wife, Samuel **Barber** (1648-1708/09; Thomas[10], qv);
8–Elizabeth (*b* 1684), *m* Daniel **Loomis** (8 above).
11–John **Bissell** (qv);
10–Samuel (1630-98), Windsor, Conn.; *m* 1658, Abigail Holcombe (bap. 1638-*d* 1688; Thomas[11]);
9–Abigail (1661-1728), *m* 1678, James (Eno) **Enos** (1651-1714);
8–James (1679-1762), *m* 1708, Hannah Phelps (1684-1728; Timothy[9], admitted freeman at Windsor, 1664, in Queen Anne's War, *m* Mary, dau. of Edward Griswold, qv, desc. Sir. Humphrey Griswold, of Malvern Hill, Eng.; William[10], qv);
7–Sarah (*b* 1717), Union, Conn.; *m* 1736, Daniel **Loomis** (7 above).
11–Matthew **Marvin** (qv);
10–Matthew (1627-1712), Norwalk, Conn.; *m* Mary–;
9–Sarah (*b* 1660), *m* Thomas **Betts**;
8–Sarah (*b* 1686), *m* 1712, Samuel **Keeler** (*d* 1763); see Vol. III, p. 379;

7–Matthew (*b* 1717);
6–Isaac (1759-1814), *m* 1781, Deborah Whitney;
5–William (1782-1822), *m* 1804, Deborah Lounsbury;
4–James Rufus (*b* 1818), New York; *m* Mary Louise Davidson (*b* 1826);
3–Elizabeth Boyd (*b* 1855), *m* Frederick E. **Ballard** (3 above).
10–Henry **Whitney** (*b* ca. 1620), 1st record, 1649, Southold, L.I.; *m* Widow Ketcham (*d* 1655);
9–John (*d* ca. 1720), Norwalk, Conn.; *m* 1674, Elizabeth Smith (*d* 1720; Richard[10]);
8–Joseph (1678-1741), *m* 1704, Hannah Hoyt (Zerubbabel[9]);
7–David (*b* 1721), *m* Elizabeth Hyatt;
6–Deborah (1758-1838), *m* Isaac **Keeler** (6 above).
10–Thomas **Hyatt,** from Eng. to Stamford, Conn.; *m* Elizabeth Russell;
9–Lt. Thomas, *m* 1677, Mary St. John (Matthias[10], qv);
8–Ebenezer, *m* Elizabeth–;
7–Elizabeth (1718-98), *m* David **Whitney** (7 above).
10–Robert **Lockwood** (qv);
9–Lt. Jonathan (1634-88), Fairfield, Conn.; *m* Mary Ferris (Jeffrey[10]);
8–Still John (1674-1758);
7–Jonathan (1719-98), *m* Mercy–;
6–Elizabeth, *m* 1781, Amos **Lounsbury**;
5–Deborah (1784-1849), *m* William **Keeler** (5 above).
2–Helen Gillette Ballard, *m* 1907, Walter Hayward **Powers** (qv).
1–Ed. Rye Country Day School; Les Fougeres, Lausanne, Switzerland. Residence: Windcrest Rd., Rye, N.Y.

1–**POWERS, Walter Hayward, II,** *b* New York, N.Y., June 11, 1880.
10–William **Phelps** (qv);
9–Lt. Timothy (1639-1719), *m* 1661, Mary Griswold (1644-90; Edward[10], qv);
8–Capt. Nathaniel (1677-1746), *m* 1700, Hannah Bissel (1682-1717; Samuel[9], from Eng., *m* Abigail Holcomb);
7–Lt. Nathaniel (1703-81), *m* 1726, Mary Curtis (1706-40; Samuel[8]; Thomas[9]);
6–Elizabeth (*b* 1739), *m* 1755, John **Powers** (1730-62), Petersburg, N.Y.; soldier French and Indian War (Lawrence[7], on Church of Eng. tax list, Hebron, Conn., *m* 1729, Elizabeth Stogers, dau. of John Downing, *m* Elizabeth–);
5–John (1762-1837), Chestertown, N.Y.; Am. Rev., 1777; *m* 1784, Susannah Palmer;
4–Col. Harvey, N.Y. militia in War 1812; at Plattsburg, N.Y., 1814; *m* Phebe Randall;
3–George W. (1824-95), dry goods mcht., N.Y. City; *m* 1854, Mary Henrietta Woodruff;
2–Walter Hayward (2 below).
9–John **Mack** (1653-1721), *m* Sarah Bagley;
8–Elizabeth (1687-1750), *m* 1707, Sgt. Edward **Sawyer** (1686-1766);
7–Isaac (*b* 1720), *m* 1740, Susanna Gillet;
6–Susannah (*b* 1742), *m* 1760, Stephen **Palmer** (*b* 1737);
5–Susannah (1763-1813), *m* John **Powers** (5 above).
8–John **Randall** (1629-84; son of Matthew, mayor of Bath, Eng., 1627); from Eng. to R.I., 1667;
7–Matthew (1671-1736), *m* 1693, Eleanor–;
6–Benjamin (1700-44), *m* 1735, Mary Babcock (*b* 1716; Capt. John[7], *m* Mary, dau. of Capt. William Champlin, *m* Mary, dau. of James Babcock);
5–Joshua (1756-1837), *m* (Selah) Celia Reynolds (Elisha[6]; Elisha[7]; Henry[8]; James[9], qv);
4–Phebe (1789-1834), *m* Col. Harvey **Powers** (4 above).
9–Gerrit Frederick **Lansing** (*d* ante Oct. 3, 1679), from Holland to New Amsterdam, 1640; *m* Elizabeth Hendrickse;
8–Gerrit, *m* Elsie Van Wythorst;
7–Everet (bap. 1704), *m* Annetje Cooper;
6–Obadiah (*b* 1740), *m* Cornelia Cooper (Obadiah[7], *m* Mary Fonda; Obadiah[8], *m* Cornelia Gardiner);
5–James (1780-1852), *m* Antoinette Witbeck (1783-1866; William[6]; William[7]; Jan Thomase[8]);
4–William R. (1804-86), *m* 1829, Catharine Staats (1805-54);
3–Eliza (1830-63), *m* 1854, George Shearman **Weaver** (1826-1907);
2–Katharine Staats (*b* 1856), Blind Brook Lodge, Rye, N.Y.; *m* 1878, Walter Hayward **Powers** (1855-93), stock broker, New York; for issue see Vol. III, p. 379.
1–*m* Apr. 10, 1907, Helen Gillette Ballard (see Vol. III, p. 379); issue 1–Walter Hayward (qv); 2–Whitney Ballard, *b* New York, Feb. 11, 1911; Choate Sch.; 3–Katharine Louise (qv); 4–Betty Bradford, *b* Port Chester, N.Y., Jan. 24, 1921.
1–E.E., Columbia, 1902 (Alpha Delta Phi, Nacoms). Treas., dir., Peet & Powers, Inc., electrical engrs. and contractors, New York. Lt., Squadron A Cav., N.G.N.Y., 1901-15. Trustee Village of Rye, N.Y., 5 yrs. Mem. S.M.D., I.A.G. Treas., vestryman, Christ's Ch., Rye, N.Y. Clubs: University, Columbia U. (New York), Apawamis, Manursing Island, Kenilworth Riding (Rye). Residence: Windcrest Rd., Rye, N.Y.

PRICE

Arms: Argent, a cross between four pheons azure.
Crest: Out of a ducal coronet or, a lion's head issuing proper.

1–**PRICE, Benjamin Luther,** *b* nr. Farmville, Cumberland Co., Va., Oct. 5, 1867-*d* May 7, 1928.
8–John **Price** (qv);
7–Mathewes (*b* 1615), ed. in Wales; came in the "George," to Jamestown, 1635; granted 150 acres, Henrico Co., 1638; *m* Miss Pugh or Miss Nelson (tradition differs as to these names);
6–John (1650-1711), Henrico Co.; *m* Jane Cannon;
5–Pugh (1690-1775), processioner, St. John's Ch., ca. 1743; to Prince Edward Co., Va., ca. 1747; settled nr. site of Hampden-Sidney Coll.; large landowner; *m* 2d, Jerusha Penick;
4–Charles (ca. 1757-1790), in Am. Rev.; *m* Betsey Haskins;
3–Benjamin Haskins (1780-1839), *m* 2d, 1816, Temperance (Watkins) Hundley (g.dau. of Col. William Morton, of Am. Rev.);
2–John Morton (1818-94), of "Weaver," Prince Edward Co.; purchased "Hopewell," which is still standing; rejected by C.S.A., so raised many provisions for the Confederate Army. Democrat; Presbyterian; *m* 1842, Martha Katherine Spencer (1823-1900); issue: I–Mary Plummer (1845-1909; *m* 1866, Sterling Daniel, 1841-81); II–Sion Stanley (*b* 1848; *m* 1872, Susan Ballantine Ligon, *b* 1848); III–John Morton (*b* 1851; *m* 1871, Maria Edmonia Gilliam, *b* 1849); IV–Nannie Elizabeth (*b* 1852; *m* 1873, Leonard Amos, *b* 1838); V–Walter Hoge (1855-82); VI–Ida Watkins (1857-83); VII–Benjamin Luther (1 above).
1–*m* Nov. 22, 1894, Isabella Carrie Grady (qv for issue).

1-Ed. Hampden-Sydney Coll.; B.D., Union Theol. Sem., 1894; (D.D., Southwestern Presbyn. U., 1916). Pastor at Glen Allan, Washington Co., Miss., 1890-92, Presbyn. Ch., Morrillton, Ark., 1892-94; organized and built 1st Presbyn. Ch., Alexandria, La., 1894, pastor, 1894-1927, pastor emeritus, 1927-28. Organized churches on the Atchafalaya River, 1895, at Marksville, 1896, at Bunkie, 1902, at Oakdale, 1915. Head clk. La. jurisdiction of the Woodmen of the World (clk. Alexandria Local Camp, over 30 yrs.), auditor Supreme Forest Woodmen Circle, over 12 yrs. Mason (32°, K.T.). Mem. S.A.R. Author: John Price the Emigrant, Jamestown Colony, 1620, with some of his descendants.

BENJAMIN LUTHER PRICE (1867-1928).

1-**PRICE, Isabella Carrie Grady (Mrs. B. L.),** *b* Mobile, Ala., Mar. 31, 1871.
7-Lt. Col. Walter **Chiles** (qv);
6-Walter, Jamestown, Va.; burgess, 1655,59,60-1663; *m* Mary Page (Col. John[7], qv);
5-John (*d* 1723), justice; mem. Assembly; messenger of Council; *m* 2d, Elizabeth Webber;
4-Henry, *m* Mary Carr;
3-Isabella, *m* John G. **Ulrick** (Capt. Peter[4], naval service in War 1812);
2-Agnes (1852-95), *m* Dominick Oliver **Grady** (1824-71), importer (desc. Count O'Gara, sought refuge in France during the invasion of Ireland by Oliver Cromwell, 1650).
1-*m* Nov. 22, 1894, Rev. Benjamin Luther Price, D.D. (qv); issue: 1-Martha Agnes, *b* Alexandria, La., Sept. 11, 1895; 2-John Kauffman, *b* Alexandria, Dec. 26, 1901; B.S., Davidson Coll., '22 (Kappa Sigma); M.I.T.; mgr. Fidelity Securities Co., Alexandria, La.; Mason (K.T., Shriner).
1-Newcomb Coll., '90. Mem. C.D.A. (sec., later chmn. Alexandria com.), D.A.R. (ex-chapter v.regent and regent, La. State chaplain and local registrar), U.D.C., I.A.G. Clubs: Up-to-date Fiction (sec. and treas. for 33 yrs.), Rainbow. Residence: 2111 White St., Alexandria, La.

1-**PUGSLEY, Cornelius Amory,** *b* Peekskill, N.Y., July 17, 1850.
9-John **Drake,** mem. Original Plymouth Company, London, 1606;
8-John (*d* 1659), came to Boston, 1630; settled at Windsor, Conn.; *m* Elizabeth- (*d* 1681, aet. 100);
7-Samuel (*d* 1689), removed to Fairfield, ca. 1650, thence to Eastchester, N.Y., 1663; *m* Anne (Barlow?);
6-John, settled at Peekskill Hollow; mem. N.Y. Assembly;
5-Jeremiah (1726-84), capt. Am. Rev.; *m* Martha Deason;
4-Elizabeth, *m* Samuel **Pugsley** (see Vol. II, p. 193, for Pugsley lineage);
3-Jeremiah, capt. War 1812; *m* Hannah Underhill Taylor;
2-Gilbert Taylor (1823-1912), farmer, Peekskill, N.Y.; *m* Julia Butler Meeker (see Vol. II, p. 193, for Meeker lineage and issue).
1-*m* Apr. 7, 1886, Emma Catherine Gregory (see Vol. III, p. 386); issue: 1-Chester Dewitt, *b* Peekskill, N.Y., Mar. 29, 1887; A.B., Harvard, '09; served at Camp Zachary Taylor, Ky., F.A., C.O.T.S.
1-Privately educated. Pres. Westchester Co. Nat. Bank, Peekskill, N.Y. Mem. 57th Congress, 1901-03. Pres. bd. trustees, Peekskill Mil. Acad.; pres. Field Library and Field Home, Peekskill; ex-pres., N.Y. State Bankers Assn.; ex-mem. exec. council Am. Bankers Assn.; mem. Westchester Co. Park Commn.; mem. Chamber of Commerce of N.Y. State (see Who's Who in America). Mem. S.A.R. (past pres. gen.), N.E. Soc. of N.Y., Am. Flag Assn. (pres.). Clubs: Lotos, Bankers. Summer place: Peekskill, N.Y. Residence. 12 W. 122d St., New York.

RAGLAND

Arms: Quarterly, France, azure, three fleur de lis or; and England gules, three lions passant-guardant in pale or, all within a bordure compony argent and azure.
Crest: A portcullis or, nailed azure, with chains pendent thereto of the first.
Supporters: Dexter, a panther argent, flames issuant from mouth and ears proper, gorged with a plain collar, and chained, or, and semée of torteaux, hurts, and pomies, alternately; sinister, a wyvern wings endorsed vert, holding in the mouth a sinister hand couped at the wrist gules.
Motto: Mutare vel timere sperno.

1-**RAGLAND, Harry Lee,** *b* Richmond, Va., Jan. 6, 1864.
5-John **Ragland** (*d* 1773), from Wales, 1720, settled in Va., near mouth of Chickahominy River; received about 16,000 acres in Louisa and Hanover cos. in different grants from the Crown; *m* his cousin, Ann, dau. of Duke of Beaufort;
4-Pettus, of Hanover Co.; corpl. "Hanover Petitioners" Co., Am. Rev.; *m* Elizabeth Davis;
3-Fendall (1780-1833), soldier War 1812; *m* 1806, Sarah Nelson;
2-Samuel Beaufort (1827-1903), of Richmond, Va.; lumber business, contractor and builder; Confed. soldier, corpl. "Castle Thunder," Richmond, at the time Dr. Mary Walker was held there as a prisoner of war; last year of war was clerical asst. in office of provost marshal Army of Northern Va.; clk. to Gen. Robert E. Lee in the siege of Petersburg, surrendered and was paroled at Appomattox; after war was extensively engaged in farming, residing at "Bleak Hill" in upper end of King William Co., later returning to Richmond, and again in building and contracting; *m* 1859, Sarah Elizabeth Pemberton (1838-69; William D.[3], 1813-73); issue: I-William Lauman (*b* 1860; *m* 1887, Mattie Ragland); II-Samuel B., Jr. (1862-1918; corpl. Spanish-Am. War; *m* Emma Jones); III-Harry Lee (1 above); IV-Elise Douglas (1866-91; *m* Frank Noel); V-Bettie Pemberton (1869-1900).
1-*m* Feb. 2, 1891, Frances Cecelia O'Hare (1863-

1904); dau. of Christopher S. O'Hare, of Washington, D.C., *m* Ann Elizabeth Shreve, of Va.; issue: 1–Joseph Pemberton, *b* Richmond, Va., May 16, 1897; B.S., A.M., M.F.S., Georgetown U.; 2d class seaman, World War; vice consul of career, stationed at Halifax, N.S.; *m* 1919, Ruth, dau. of John Shepard, of Scranton, Pa. (issue: Frances C.; Joseph P., Jr.; John Christopher).

1–*m* 2d, May 15, 1911, Ida Pitt Scudo Spittel, *b* Gotha, Thuringia, Germany, 1870; dau. Rechnungsrat Oscar Spittel, of Gotha; issue: 1–Harry Beaufort, *b* Washington, Dec. 27, 1912; C.A.R.

1–Copy editor, in U.S. Govt. Printing Office, 32 yrs.; retired. Club: Cleveland Park. Residence: 3230 Highland Pl. N.W., Cleveland Park, Washington, D.C.

1–**ROBERTS, Clarence Vernon,** *b* Phila., Pa., Aug. 25, 1862.

6–Thomas **Roberts** (bap. at Mallwyd in Mawddwy Co., Merioneth, N. Wales, Apr. 19, 1691; son of Robert, *m* Catherine Thomas, of Dynas; desc. John Griffith ap Howell of Nannau); came to America ca. 1715; was of Quakertown, Pa., 1720;

5–Thomas, *m* 1750, Letitia Rhea;

4–Israel, *m* 1782, Ann Foulke (John[5], *m* Mary–);

3–Lewis, *m* 1821, Harriet Brooke (Nathan[4], *m* Susannah–; desc. John Brooke, who came to Phila. from Yorkshire, Eng., 1699);

2–Lewis E. (2 below).

7–Edward **Foulke** (1651-1741; son of Foulke Thomas Lloyd; desc. Edward I, of Eng.), scholar and writer; from Merionethshire, Wales, in the "Robert and Elizabeth," to Phila., 1698, with 9 children; owned 700 acre estate; a founder of Gwynedd, Pa.; *m* Eleanor (Hughes) dau. of Hugh Cadwalader Rhys, *m* Gwenn–;

6–Hugh, *m* 1713, Ann Williams (John[7], *m* Mary–);

5–John, mem. Provincial Assembly, 1769-75; *m* 1755, Mary Roberts (Edward[6], *m* Mary–);

4–Edward, *m* 1797, Ann Roberts (Thomas[5], *m* Letitia–);

3–Joshua, *m* 1825, Caroline Green (William[4], *m* Mary–);

2–Jane, *m* 1860, Lewis E. **Roberts.**

1–*m* Apr. 2, 1895, Frances A. Walton, *b* Phila., Pa., Oct. 4, 1868; dau. of Barclay Walton (Silas[3]); issue: 1–Jane L., *b* Phila., Pa., Aug. 20, 1896; Columbia U., 1919-25; 2–Frances F., *b* Phila., May 17, 1909; Bradford (Mass.) Acad., '30.

1–Pres. Roberts & Mander Stove Co., Genealogist. Mem. I.A.G. Residence: 6439 Cherokee St., Philadelphia, Pa.

BARCROFT

Arms: Argent, a lion rampant sable.

1–**RUNK, Louis Barcroft,** *b* Phila., Pa., June 13, 1873.

7–Ambrose **Barcroft** (1681-1724; eldest son of Thomas Barcroft, gentleman, of Barcroft Hall and Noyna, Colne, Lancashire); from Eng. to Talbot Co., Md., post 1716; removed ante 1722, to Bucks Co., Pa.; drowned nr. Easton, Pa.; *m* 1702, Maria Walshman (*d* Eng., 1705);

6–Ambrose (1703/04-1784), from Eng., with father; *m* Hannah–;

5–Ambrose (1745-1817), *m* 3d, ca. 1786, Francena (Opdycke) Hogeland (1757-1809; Joshua Opdycke[6]);

4–Ambrose (1793-1881), *m* 1815, Anna Woolverton (1794-1883; John[5], Am. Rev.);

3–Fanny (1821-1911), *m* 1845, Peter Ten Broeck **Runk** (1818-60); see Vol. I, p. 343 for Runk lineage;

2–William Mentz (2 below).

9–Peter **Hill** (qv);

8–Roger (1631-98), *m* 1658, Sarah Cross (John[9], to America as an infant with father);

7–John (1666-1713), ens. and lt. King William's War; capt., 1693-1700; *m* 1694, Mary Frost (*b* 1676; Maj. Charles[8]);

6–Capt. Elisha (1710-64); *m* 1736, Mary Plaisted (1718-85; Elisha[7]);

5–Elisha (1743-98); *m* 2d, 1773, Elizabeth (Marshall) Clark (1744-1822; John Marshall[6]);

4–Elisha (1776-1850), *m* 1803, Lucy Ricker;

3–Marshall (1809-67); *m* 1835, Harriet Smallwood Field (1814-89; James[4], *m* Prudence, dau. Capt. Rufus Lincoln, Am. Rev., of Wareham, Mass.);

2–Elizabeth Cogswell (2 below).

7–Maturin **Ricker** (*d* 1706), from Eng. to Cocheco, N.H., ca. 1672;

6–Maturin, *m* Lucy Wallingford;

5–Ebenezer (1741-1815), *m* 1771, Elizabeth Wallingford (ca. 1753-1781; Thomas[6], Am. Rev.);

4–Lucy (ca. 1779-ca. 1850), *m* Elisha **Hill** (4 above).

2–William Mentz **Runk** (1846-92), mcht., Phila.; *m* 1872, Elizabeth Cogswell Hill (1850-85); *m* 2d, 1886, Evelyn Ten Broeck Runk (*b* 1854); for issue see Vol. I, p. 343.

1–*m* Oct. 23, 1907, Mary Amelia Rankin, *b* Lock Haven, Pa., July 16, 1875; D.A.R.; dau. of late William Washington Rankin, and sister of John Hall Rankin (see Vol. I, p. 343 for genealogy); issue (all *b* Germantown, Phila., Pa.): 1–Elisabeth Hill, *b* Dec. 10, 1908; 2–Mary Amélie, *b* Nov. 25, 1910; 3–John Ten Broeck, *b* Jan. 30, 1915.

1–A.B., Yale, 1893 (P.B.K., Zeta Psi), M.A., 1903; LL.B., U.Pa., 1896. Lawyer, and asst. trust officer, Provident Trust Co., of Phila. Maj. Ordnance Dept., U.S.A., Sept. 1, 1917-Sept. 10, 1919; maj., O.R.C., Apr. 7, 1920; lt. col., Jan. 11, 1929. Pres. Yale Alumni Assn. of Phila., 1914-15, P.B.K. Assn. of Phila., 1921-22, Episcopal Acad. Alumni Soc., 1922-24, Church Club of Phila., 1924-26. Church Advocate of the Diocese of Pa., 1914-28. Author: Fort Louisburg, Its Two Sieges and Site To-Day; The Birth of Our Flag and Flag Etiquette. Mem. S.C.W., O.F.P.A., S.R., M.O.F.W., Colonial Soc. of Pa., Inst. Am. Genealogy. Clubs: Cosmos (Washington), University (v.p.), Yale, Phila. Cricket. Summer place: "Mariner's Cottage," Avalon, N.J. Residence: 17 W. Upsal St., Germantown, Phila., Pa.

1–**ROEDEL, Mary Louise,** *b* Lebanon, Pa., Jan. 22, 1863.

4–John Henry (Readel) **Roedel** (*b* 1763), from Bavaria, settled in Shaefferstown, Lebanon Co., Pa.; *m* Eva Margaret (Yovonne) Heussler (1765-1829);

3–Philip Jacob (1804-88), dir. of Lebanon Nat. Bank; sec. and treas. Berks and Dauphin Turnpike cos.; chief burgess of the town of Lebanon; pres. of bd. Zion Lutheran Ch. 30 yrs.; *m* 1st, Justina Diller;

2–Henry Heussler (2 below).

7–Casper Elias **Diller** (1696-1796), from Heidelberg, settled in New Holland, Lancaster Co., Pa., 1733, farmer; *m* Barbara–;

6–Jean, or Hans, Martin (*b* 1725), *m* Christina–;

5–John (*b* 1748), *m* Magdalena–;

4–Adam (1784-1814), tanner, Lebanon; *m* Margaret Mark (1787-1861; Conrad[5], *m* Margaret Schaeffer);

3–Justina (1808-37), *m* Philip Jacob **Roedel** (3 above).

5–Johannes (Rudrauff) **Ruthrauff** (*b* 1727), from Germany, settled in Perkiomen region, Pa., 1753; *m* 1755, Anna Barbara Hoffman;

4–Rev. Johann (1764-1837), of Northampton Co., and Greencastle, Pa.; began to write name

Ruthrauff; *m* 1784, Ann Maria Hamma (*b* 1764; Valentine[5]);
3–Rev. Jonathan (1801-50), of Greencastle, and Lebanon, Pa.; *m* 1827, Ann Louisa Lochman (1808-78; Rev. John George[4], *m* Susan Hoffman; Nicholas[5], *m* Johanna Maria–);
2–Susan Lochman (1831-1911), *m* 1858, Dr. Henry Heussler **Roedel** (1832-1916), physician, Lebanon; issue: I–William Ruthrauff (1859-1922; *m* Lucy Hastings Wright); II–Mary Louise (1 above); III–Emma Margaret (*b* 1865); IV–Anna Louise (*b* 1870; *m* Rev. George Fulton).
1–V.p. and historian, E. Pennsylvania Missionary Soc. of the Lutheran Ch.; trustee. Lebanon Co. Health Council. Mem. D.A.R. (regent), I.A.G. Republican. Residence: 5 S. 6th St., Lebanon, Pa.

1–**ROWNTREE, Margaret Cunnyngham,** *b* Kansas City, Mo., May 6, 1894.
5–Claiborne (Johnston) **Johnson** (1759-1840), of Albemarle Co., Va.; pvt., Va. troops, Am. Rev., pensioned 1834; *m* 1794, Betsy Sims;
4–Thomas (1802-65), of Nelson Co., Va.; to Kansas, 1827; established the Shawnee Indian Mission in Kan.; Johnson Co., Kan., is named for him; *m* 1827, Sarah T. Davis (1810-74; Thomas[5]);
3–Andrew Monroe (1841-1902), Westport, Mo.; *m* 1864, Margaret Jane Bernard;
2–Mary Agusta (2 below).
7–John **Bernard,** from Eng., settled in Albemarle Co., Va., 1720; *m* ? Abney;
6–John (*b* 1736), served under Gen. Braddock during French and Indian War; *m* 1760, Elizabeth Barnett;
5–Allan (*b* 1763), in Am. Rev.; *m* 1787, Ann Mitchell;
4–Joab (1800-79), *m* 1838 or 39, Arabella Mather Bier;
3–Margaret Jane (1840-1920), *m* 1864, Andrew Monroe **Johnson** (3 above).
6–Jacob **Bier** (*b* 1741), from Germany to Frederick, Md.; *m* 1764, Eva Catherine Schley;
5–George Henry (1786-1822 or 23), of Baltimore; *m* 1812, Jane Augusta Cunnyngham (1797-1890; John[6] [1750-1847], from Scotland to Baltimore, 1765, *m* Margaret Mather, *d* 1856);
4–Arabella Mather (1816-99), *m* Joab **Bernard** (4 above);
3–Margaret Jane, *m* Andrew M. **Johnson** (3 above);
2–Mary Agusta (*b* 1865), *m* 1892, Harold **Rowntree** (*b* 1865), from Eng. to Kansas City, Mo.; chmn. bd. Nat. Pneumatic Co.; issue: I–Margaret Cunnyngham (1 above); II–Wornall (*b* 1897; *m* Duncan Arthur Talbot); III–Gertrude Aguirre (*b* 1899; *m* Joseph Dempf, divorced).
1–Mem. D.A.R., I.A.G. Residence: 2595 San Pasqual St., Pasadena, Calif.

1–**RUTTER, Mary Elizabeth McMurtrie (Mrs. David),** *b* Newark, N.J., June 19, 1852.
8–John **Ogden** (qv);
7–David (1643-1691/92), *m* 1676, Elizabeth Swaine (1649-91; Capt. Samuel[8]; William[9]);
6–Thomas (1684-1760), *m* Dinah Clauson (1686-1731);
5–Abigail, *m* — **Price**;
4–Rebecca, *m* —**Simpson**;
3–Elizabeth, *m* —**McMurtrie**;
2–William (2 below).
9–Joris Jansen **Rapalje** (qv);
8–Annetje (*b* 1646), *m* 1663, Martin **Ryerson** (qv);
7–Martin (1666-1748), *m* 1691, Anna Schout (1666-1743);
6–Joris;
5–Martin;
4–Martin;
3–Hon. David;
2–Catherine (1826-1906), *m* William **McMurtrie** (1820-1908), mcht., Newton, N.J.; for issue see Vol. I, p. 810.
1–*m* Nov. 22, 1871, David Rutter (1846-1900); son of late Dr. David Rutter (desc. Thomas Rutter, 2d mayor of Germantown, Pa.), *m* Esther Turner Ryerson, Phila.; issue: 1–Lynn Ryerson, *b* Chicago, Ill., Sept. 13, 1873; Princeton, '95; U.S.N.R.; *m* Dec. 7, 1898, Mabel, dau. of Judge Lysander Hill (issue: David Ryerson; John T.; Catherine Barton, *m* Cdr. Frank D. Wagner, U.S.N. [issue: Catherine Rutter; Esther Ryerson]); 2–William McMurtrie, *b* Evanston, Ill., Nov. 19, 1876; Williams, '98; investment banker; *m* Mar. 1912, Lucia, dau. of Charles Seymour Ford (issue: Elizabeth; Peter; Martha; Thomas); 3–Rhea Barton, *b* Evanston, Oct. 9, 1878; Williams, '00; investment banker; *m* Nov. 22, 1914, Elizabeth, dau. of Charles Hassell Bowen (issue: Elizabeth Bowen Brown; David McMurtrie); 4–Esther Ryerson (Sept. 13, 1883-May 1886).
1–Ed. Park Inst., Newark, N.J., Moravian Sem., and Wells Coll., '71. Clubs: Art Allianec, College (Phila.), York (New York). Residence: "Pine Top," Pine Forge, Berks Co., Pa.

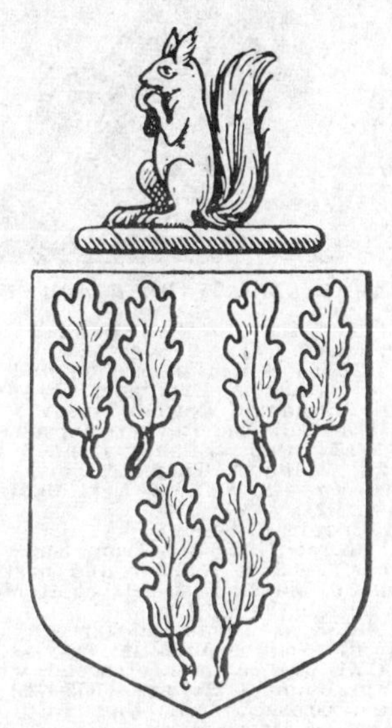

BALDWIN
Arms: *Argent, six oak leaves in pairs, two in chief and one in base vert, stalks sable, their points downward.*
Crest: *A squirrel sejant.*
Motto: *Vim vi repello.*

1–**RUPLEY, Orpha Ophelia Baldwin (Mrs. William C.),** *b* nr. Hillsdale, Mich., Apr. 17, 1878.
9–John **Baldwin** (qv);
8–Josiah (1642-83), *m* 1667, Mary Camp;
7–Samuel (*b* 1674), *m* Rebecca Wilkerson;
6–Caleb (1704-63), *m* Ann Tibballs;
5–Jared (1731-1817), removed from Conn. to Luzerne Co., Pa., 1795; q.m. in Am. Rev.; *m* 1753, Damares Booth (*d* 1816);
4–Jude (1775-1821), of Luzerne Co.; *m* 1797, Eleanor Watson (1782-1833);
3–Burr (1798-1855), of Williams Co., O.; *m* Lucy Ann Trux (1812-1865);
2–Joseph (1842-1909), grain dealer; pvt. in Civil War; *m* 1862, Mary Jane Andre (*b* 1843); issue: I–Laura Etta (*b* 1864; *m* Rufus H. Gephart *d*); II–Almon Burr (*b* 1867); III–Eva Lavilda (1871-98; *m* Dr. Harry C. Nickels *d*); IV–Orpha Ophelia (1 above).
1–*m* Mar. 4, 1901, William Cromwell Rupley, *b* N. Manchester, Ind., June 20, 1874; son of David Joseph Rupley, of Ind.; issue: 1–Joseph William, *b* Denver, Colo., Feb. 11, 1902; B.S., Whitman Coll., Wash., '23.
1–Ed. normal school. Mem. D.A.R. (registrar), Eastern Wash. State Hist. Soc., P.E.O. Presbyterian. Republican. Residence: 3425 N. Audubon St., Spokane, Wash.

1–**SADLER, Holmes Elias,** *b* Brockport, N.Y., May 19, 1851-*d* Oct. 10, 1929.
8–Dea. Samuel **Chapin** (qv);
7–Japhet (bap. 1642-1712), *m* 1st, 1664, Abilene Coley (1642-1710; Samuel[8], qv);

HOLMES ELIAS SADLER (1851-1929).

6–Samuel (1665-1729), *m* 1690, Hannah Sheldon (*b* 1670; Isaac[7], qv);
5–Caleb (1701-55), killed in French and Indian War; *m* Catharine Dickinson (*b* 1706; Nathaniel[6]; Nathaniel[7]; Nathaniel[8], qv);
4–Selah (1751-1830), Am. Rev.; *m* Jerusha Burnham (*b* 1752; Capt. Elisha[5]; Capt. William[6]; William[7]; William[8]; Thomas[8], qv);
3–Jerusha (ca. 1780-1815), *m* Levi **Sadler** (see Vol. I, p. 812);
2–Manley Chapin (2 below).
9–Samuel **Morse** (1587-1654), from Eng., in the "Increase," 1635, a founder and first treas. of Dedham, Mass.; first settled at Medfield, 1649; *m* Elizabeth–;
8–John (1611-57), *m* Annas Chickering;
7–Ruth (*b* 1637), *m* Joseph **Ellis**;
6–Mary (1671-1752), *m* as his second wife, ca. 1706, Capt. Samuel **Holmes** (1675-1725; John[7], *m* Sara–; George[8], from Eng. to Roxbury, Mass., 1636, *m* Deborah–);
5–Nathaniel (*b* 1715), a leader of "the Bennington Mob"; *m* 1740, Sarah Pettee;
4–Zephaniah (1743-1800), *m* Barbara McLucas (Lucas?), (1750-1821);
3–Joseph (1776-1825), *m* Sept. 29, 1803, Diantha Bellows (1787-1824);
2–Sara Farnsworth (2 below).
8–William (Pittee, Pittey, Petty) **Pettee** (ca. 1595-1679; probably son of John Pittey, of Roxbury); settled at Weymouth, Mass., ca. 1638; *m* Mary–;
7–Joseph (1639-92), *m* ca. 1671, Sarah–;
6–Joseph (ca. 1677-1759), *m* Mary–;
5–Sarah (*b* July 20, 1716), *m* Nathaniel **Holmes** (5 above).
8–William **Chandler** (qv);
7–Dea. John (ca. 1635-1703), *m* 1658, Elizabeth Douglas (William[8], qv);
6–Capt. Joseph (1683-1749), *m* 1708, Susannah Perrin (John[7]; John[8]);
5–Capt. Daniel (1729-90), Am. Rev.; *m* Violet Burnham (Jonathan[6]);
4–Tryphena (1758-1825), *m* James **Bellows**;
3–Diantha (1787-1824), *m* Joseph **Holmes** (3 above);
2–Sara Farnsworth (1814-93), *m* Manley Chapin **Sadler** (1803-69); issue: I–Julia Maria (1841-1902; *m* Charles Aiken Holmes, 1831-1901); II–Holmes Elias (1 above).
1–*m* Oct. 19, 1875, Mary Everit Coley, *b* New Haven, Conn.; dau. of John Hyde Coley (John Hyde[3]; Michael[4]; Capt. Ebenezer[5]; David[6]; Peter[7]; Peter[8]; Samuel[9]); issue: 1–Isabel Coley, *b* New Haven, Conn., June 27, 1876; *m* Jan. 10, 1906, Herman C. Ehrlicher; *m* 2d, May 14, 1929, Robert F. Clark; 2–Everit Jay, *b* Brockport, N.Y., May 1, 1879; *m* Oct. 8, 1902, Lorena Bilisoly; 3–Sara Farnsworth, *b* Emporia, Kan., Oct. 9, 1882.
1–B.A., Yale, '73; LL.B., Union, 1874. Lawyer. Residence: 1053 Faxon Av., Memphis, Tenn.

1–**SANDIDGE, Daisy,** *b* Harrison Co., Tex., Mar. 3, 1877.
9–John **Sandidge,** from Eng. to Loudoun Co., Va., for political reasons during the rule of Cromwell; and thru:
6–John (*b* Loudoun Co., Va.-*d* Franklin Co., Ga., post 1826), served in Am. Rev.;
5–Clayborne (1761-1843), pvt. under LaFayette, took part at Brandywine, Monmouth, Williamsburg, in defense of Richmond; present at the surrender of Cornwallis at Yorktown;
4–James (*b* Amherst Co., Va.-*d* in Ga.), *m* a dau. of Richard Shelton, soldier Am. Rev.;
3–Claiborn (*b* Amherst Co., Va.-*d* Elbert Co., Ga.), *m* 1802, Jane Higginbotham (John[4], from Ireland to Goochland Co., Va., 1736, *m* Frances Riley);
2–Andrew Jackson (2 below).
10–Richard **Cocke,** from Eng. to Henrico Co., Va.;
9–Thomas (1662-1707), *m* Mary Brazier;
8–James, *m* Elizabeth Pleasants;
7–Richard, of "Surry";
6–Nath (1746-1813), capt. 7th Va. militia, Am. Rev., 1776; *m* Rebecca Thompson;
5–James (*b* 1775?);
4–James Nath (*b* 1798?), *m* Julia Pleasants;
3–Julia (1824-ca. 1890), *m* 1843, Harris Ogilvie **Allen** (1807-76), moved to De Soto Co., Miss., 1850;
2–Mary Elizabeth (2 below).
10–John **Pleasants** (1644-98), from Eng. to Henrico Co., Va.; of "Curles"; Quaker; *m* Jane (Larcome) Luchen;
9–John (1671-1713), administrator of his father's estate; *m* Dorothy Cary (Maj. Thomas[10], *m* Anne, dau. of Capt. Francis Milner; Miles[11], qv);
8–Thomas (*b* 1695), *m* Mary Jordan (Robert[9], *m* Mary Belsen; Robert[9]; Thomas[10]; Thomas[11], from Eng. to Va.);
7–Thomas, *m* 1761, Elizabeth Brooke (*d* 1804), of Md.;
6–William Henry (*b* 1765?), *m* Mary Ladd;
5–Joseph (*d* 1814), *m* Martha Bates;
4–Julia, *m* James Nath **Cocke** (4 above).
3–Julia, *m* Harris O. **Allen** (3 above).
2–Andrew Jackson **Sandidge** (*b* 1821), *m* 1867, Mary Elizabeth Allen (1845-87); issue: I–Guy (1872-1900); II–Vera (1875-1912; *m* J. P. McCullough); III–Daisy (1 above); IV–Irl (*b* 1879; *m* Geraldine Palmore); also 3 children *d* infancy or childhood.
1–Grad. Baylor Coll., Belton, Tex.; studied U.-Chicago. Mem. Evanston Woman's Club. Episcopalian. Residence: 1510 Church St., Evanston, Ill.

1–**SCHERTZ, Helen Pitkin (Mrs. Christian d'-Augsbourg),** *b* New Orleans, La., Aug. 8, 1875.
7–William **Pitkin** (1635-94), from Eng., 1659, settled at Hartford, Conn.; freeman, 1662; prosecutor Colony of Conn., 1662; apptd. atty. gen. by the King, 1664; rep. Hartford in Colonial Assembly, 1675-90; treas., 1676; often apptd. commr. by the Colony to the United Colonies; apptd., with Maj. Talcott, to negotiate peace with the Narragansett and other Indian tribes; mem. Colonial Council, 1690-94; sent by the Colony to Gov. Fletcher of New York, to negotiate terms respecting the militia until Gov. Winthrop's return from Eng., 1693; with Samuel Chester and Capt. William Whiting was apptd. by the Gen. Ct. to run the division line bet. the Conn. and Mass. colonies; *m* 1661, Hannah Goodwin (1637-1724; Ozias[8]); their g.son, William, III, was elected gov. of Conn. by a majority so great that the votes were not counted;
6–Ozias (1678-1747), of Hartford; capt. of militia, 1714; mem. Colonial Assembly; asso. justice of Hartford Co., 1725-35; chief justice Supreme Ct., 1735; mem. Colonial Council, 1727-46; commr. of war in defense of frontier towns, 1743; *m* Esther (Burnham) Cadwell (*d* 1784; Richard Burnham[7]);
5–Daniel (1735-1815), of Hartford; selectman 13 yrs. from 1783; *m* 1763, Susannah Stanley (1742-1815);
4–Ozias (1778-1849), of Hartford; *m* 1805, Hannah Olmsted (1780-1864);
3–John Waldo (1808-73), of New Orleans, La.; Civil War; *m* Adaline Graham (*b* 1820; Commodore John[4], lost leg in War 1812);

2-John Robert Graham (1840-1900), grad. La. Law U. in civil law (a code that obtains only in La.); began practice of law, 1860; soon after Gen. Butler entered New Orleans, 1862, Mr. Pitkin declared himself for the Union in a public speech and became one of the foremost Republican figures and was attached to Farragut's fleet; master in chancery for Tex. & Pacific R.R.; E.E. and M.P. to the Argentine Republic, under President Harrison; declined the ministry to Mexico under the Arthur administration; *m* 1866, Helen Fearing Fuller (*d* 1874); *m* 2d, Annie Lovell; issue (1st marriage): I-Waldo Mills (*m* Marie Guitet); issue (2d marriage): I-Helen (1 above); II-Joseph Lovell (*b* 1879); III-Robert Graham (*b* 1881).

1-*m* Apr. 29, 1909, Christian d'Augsbourg Schertz (Mar. 31, 1872-Oct. 31, 1927); son of Joseph Schertz, of Imlingen, near Saarburg, Lorraine, then Germany, now France, *m* Marie d'Augsbourg.

1-Studied Newcomb Coll., New Orleans. Writer. Mem. U.S.D. 1812 (pres.), I.A.G., New Orleans Geneal. and Hist. Soc., La. Hist. Soc., Soc. for Preservation of Ancient Tombs, Nat. Inst. Social Sciences, La. Sunshine Soc. (pres.). Episcopalian. Republican. Clubs: Orleans, Le Petit Salon. Residence: 1300 Moss St., New Orleans, La.

1-**SCHOENFELD, Virginia Berkley Bowie (Mrs. Frederick),** *b* Baltimore Co., Md.

7-John **Bowie,** of Md. (qv);

6-Allen (1719-83), of Prince George's Co., Md.; justice, 1752-54; *m* 1744, Priscilla (*d* 1747), widow of Capt. William Finch, mariner;

5-Fielder (1745-94), capt. Prince George's Co. militia, 1776; *m* 1766, Elizabeth Eversfield (1745-94; Rev. John[6], *m* Eleanor Clagett);

4-Eversfield (1773-1815), *m* 1804, Elizabeth Ann Lane (*b* 1780; Capt. Lane[5], *m* Barbara Brooke);

3-Allen Perrie (1807-56), *m* 1831, Melvina Harper Berry;

2-Howard Strafford (2 below).

10-Robert **Brooke** (qv);

9-Maj. Thomas (1632-76), chief justice of Calvert Co., Md., 1667; *m* 1659, Eleanor Hatton (1642-1725; Richard[10], *m* Margaret-);

8-Col. Thomas (1660-1730), of Prince George's Co.; pres. Council; acting gov. of Md., 1720; *m* 1680, Anne- (*d* 1694);

7-Thomas (1683-1744), high sheriff, 1731; *m* 1705, Lucy Smith (*d* 1770; Col. Walter[8], *m* Rachel Hall);

6-Dr. Richard (1716-83), violent patriot during Am. Rev.; *m* 1767, Rachel Gantt (*d* 1793; Dr. Thomas[7], *m* Rachel Smith);

5-Sarah (1772-1834), *m* 1789, Samuel **Harper** (*b* 1765), of Alexandria, Va.;

4-Rachel Wells (*b* 1794), *m* 1811, Dr. John Eversfield **Berry** (1792-1855; Benjamin[5], *m* Deborah Eversfield);

3-Melvina Harper (1813-94), *m* 1831, Allen Perrie **Bowie** (3 above);

2-Dr. Howard Strafford (1846-1900), of Baltimore; *m* 1879, Laura Virginia Berkley (*b* 1848; Edris[3], of Fairfax Co., Va., and Baltimore, Md., *m* Virginia Enders); issue: I-Virginia Berkley (1 above); II-Edris Berkley; III-Allen Strafford; IV-Eleanor Howard (*m* Edward Raymond Turner).

1-*m* June 23, 1928, Maj. Frederick Schoenfeld, U.S.A., *b* New York, N.Y., Feb. 27, 1887; son of Maximilian Von Schoenfeld, of Brandenburg, Prussia, later of America, *m* Emilie Von Leuchter.

1-Mem. C.D.A., D.A.R., I.A.G., Md. Hist. Soc. Club: Baltimore Country. Residence: 811 Hamilton Terrace, Baltimore, Md. Address: Fort Eustis, Va.

1-**SCOTT, Everett B,** *b* Kearney, Neb., July 4, 1892.

5-Abraham **Scott**;

4-Capt. Abraham, of Waterloo, N.Y.; capt. of flatboat; *m* Sarah Campbell (1807-38; Samuel[6] [*b* 1773], *m* Mary Harper; Lord John[6] [1727-91], from Scotland to New York, *m* Lady Hannah-);

3-Francis Fernando Dicoello (1831-98), of Danville, Ill.; *m* Harriet Deloy (1832-1913);

2-Thomas Jefferson (1857-1929), register of deeds, Buffalo Co., Neb.; *m* 1887, Mary Estelle Grant (1859-1917); issue: I-Everett B (1 above); II-Susan S. (*b* 1894; *m* Gaylord Davis); III-Myron L. (qv).

EVERETT B. SCOTT

1-*m* June 28, 1924, Edna C. Froyd, *b* Paxton, Ill., Oct. 6, 1890; dau. of John A. Froyd; issue: 1-Joan Estelle, *b* Portland, Ore., Dec. 16, 1927.

1-Grad. U. of Neb., 1916. Investment securities. Enlisted in U.S.N., Omaha, Neb., June 1917; discharged June 1919, as ensign U.S.N.R.F., naval aviator No. 1657; instr. in flying, Pensacola and Miami, Fla. Mem. Phi Gamma Delta. Mason. Residence: 8610 Gregory Way, Los Angeles, Calif.

1-**SCOTT, Myron Lewis,** *b* Kearney, Neb., Apr. 9, 1898.

7-David **Grant** (*d* 1743), settled nr. Liberty Corners, Somerset Co., N.J.; *m* Martha-;

6-Capt. John (*d* 1792), of Somerset Co.; *m* Elenor-;

5-George (*d* 1820), of Washington Co., Pa.; pvt. Capt. Ross' Co., Am. Rev.; *m* Mary-;

4-John (1768-1854), of Sugar Creek Tp., Stark Co., O.; *m* Elizabeth Casner (1775-1852);

3-Michael (1815-83), of Ligonier, Ind.; *m* Susan Carr (1816-91; Benjamin[4] [1786-1861], Stark Co., O., *m* Maryan Jennings, *b* 1792);

2-Mary Estelle (1859-1817), *m* 1887, Thomas Jefferson **Scott** (1857-1929); for issue and Scott lineage see Everett B Scott.

1-Not married. U.S.M.A., 1918-19; A.B., Columbia, '21 (Beta Theta Pi); Columbia Law Sch., 1924. Admitted to N.Y. bar, 1926, to U.S. Supreme Ct., 1929. Counsel for farm mag., Am. Agriculturalist, 1926-29; with law firm of Taylor, Blanc, Capron & Marsh since 1928. Served in Squadron A, N.Y.N.G., 1922-23. Mem. West Point Grads. Assn., Assn. of Bar of City of N.Y., N.Y. Co. Lawyers Assn., Squadron A Ex-members Assn. Club: Columbia University. Residence: 228 W. 13th St., New York, N.Y.

1-**SEASTONE, Susan Sarah Bouton (Mrs. Charles V.),** *b* Anna, Ill., Mar. 9, 1880.

10-Isaac **Allerton** (qv);

9-Mary, *m* Elder Thomas **Cushman** (1608-91), came with his father in the "Fortune," 1621, to Plymouth Colony (Robert[10], qv);

8-Dea. and Ens. Elkanah (1651-1727), of Plymouth; *m* 1682, Martha Cook (1659/60-1722; Jacob[9], *m* Demaris, dau. of Stephen Hopkins, qv; Francis[10], qv);

7-Lt. Josiah (1687-1750), of Plympton, Mass.; *m* 1709, Susanna Shurtliff (1691-1763);

6-Isaiah (1730-1818), of Plympton; *m* 1753, Sarah Ring (1737-1809);

5-Jabez Newland (1766-1819), of Plympton; *m* 1791, Molly (Polly) Cooper;

4-Esther (1802-73), of Homer, N.Y.; *m* 1823, Rev. Enoch **Bouton** (1796-1843);

3-Thomas Fassett (1831-97), of Farmington, O.; *m* 1854, Sarah Jane Cady (1837-79);

2-Harvey Cady (2 below).

10-Capt. Myles **Standish** (qv);

9-Alexander, *m* Sarah Alden (John[10], qv);

8–Ebenezer (1672-1755), *m* ca. 1697, Hannah Sturtevant (1679-1759);
7–Zeruiah (1706/07-1778), *m* 1st, Andrew **Ring** (1696-1744);
6–Sarah (1737-1809), *m* Isaiah **Cushman** (6 above).
10–Francis **Cook** (qv);
9–Jane, *m* Experience **Mitchell** (1609-89), came in the "Anne," 1623;
8–Hannah, *m* Dea. Joseph **Hayward** (*b* 1673);
7–Thomas (*d* 1741), of Bridgewater, Mass.; *m* 1719, Bethia Waldo (1688-1775);
6–Edmund (1720-81), *m* 1751, Anna Snell (1732-76; Josiah[7], *m* Abigail Fobes; Josiah[8], *m* Anna, dau. of Jonathan and g.dau of John Alden, qv);
5–Waldo (1758-1834), *m* 1781, Lucy Bartlett (1762-1831);
4–Ira (1782-1850), *m* 3d, 1827, Olive McLaughlin (1791-1856);
3–Ira Alden (1828-93), went to Jonesboro, Ill., when young and changed his name to Oliver **Alden**; *m* 1853, Sarah Caroline Tripp (1838-1922);
2–Alice Dora (1858-1917), *m* 1877, Harvey Cady **Bouton** (1856-86), of Anna, Ill.; newspaper owner and publisher; issue: I–Susan Sarah (1 above); II–Winifred (*b* 1884; *m* Edward Leo Karraker); III–Ada Frances (*b* 1886; *m* Willis Hartline).
1–*m* June 25, 1900, Charles Victor Seastone, *b* New Boston, Ill., Apr. 18, 1872; son of John August Seastone, from Sweden to New Boston, Ill.; issue: 1–John Bouton, *b* Lafayette, Ind., Mar. 11, 1905; B.S., U. of Wis., '26; 2–Charles Victor, Jr., *b* Madison, Wis., Jan. 11, 1908; B.A., U. of Wis., '27.
1–Ed. Union Acad., Anna, Ill., 1898. Mem. S.M.D., D.F.P.A., D.A.R., U.S.D., 1812, I.A.G., Alden Kindred, Am. Fed. of Arts, Madison Art Assn., Madison Woman's Club, Madison Civic Music Assn. (dir.). Republican. Residence: 134 W. Gilman St., Madison, Wis.

KIMBERLEY.

AGINCOURT

Arms: Sable, a chevron or, guttée de sang, between three cinquefoils ermine.
Crest: A dexter arm couped and erect vested argent, and grasping a club in bend sinister or.

1–**SCOTT, Katherine Fairfax Kimberly (Mrs. William Dodds),** *b* Baltimore, Md., 1899.
10–Thomas **Kimberly** (Thomas Wodehouse, Earl of Kimberly, *b* ca. 1617- *d* 1671), from Eng. to Mass. on exploration trip, ca. 1633; returned in the "Hector," 1638; settled at Indian village which later became New Haven, Conn.; officer of mil. co.; dep. and marshal of the colony; *m* Alice– (1619-59);
9–Nathaniel (1645-1705), of New Haven; *m* Mary– (*d* 1705);
8–Nathaniel (*d* 1720), of Conn.; *m* Abigail–;
7–Zuriel, *m* Hannah Hill;
6–Nathaniel (1734-1802), pvt. Am. Rev.; *m* Mabel Thompson;
5–Nathaniel (*b* ca. 1758), enlisted as pvt. in Am. Rev. aet. 17;
4–William H. (*d* 1820), of New Haven; *m* 2d, 1812, Elizabeth Webb (1783-1866);
3–Edward (1819-89), of Baltimore, Md.; *m* 1845, Catherine Younglove Pierce (1828-99);
2–Harry (1846-96), *m* 1877, Elizabeth Jane Davis Wade; issue: I–Mary Elizabeth (*b* 1883; *m* Henry Rutledge Buist); II–Roberta (*b* 1885; *m* Philip Frederic); III–Harry Fairfax (*b* 1895; *m* Dorothy D. Bevan); IV–Katherine F. (1 above).
1–*m* Oct. 1, 1919, William Dodds Scott, M.D., *b* Fredericksburg, Va.; son of William Dodds Scott, of Fredericksburg.
1–Ed. pvt. schools (Baltimore, Md.). Mem. D.F.P.A. (former pres. Md. soc.), D.A.R. Residence: 3908 Hadley Square, W., Guilford, Baltimore, Md.

1–**SEYMOUR, Estella May,** *b* Port Leyden, N.Y., Aug. 11, 1872.
10–Richard **Seymour** (qv);
9–John (*d* 1713), freeman, Hartford, 1667; *m* Mary Watson (John[10], *m* Margaret–);
8–John (1666-1748), *m* 1693, Elizabeth Webster (bap. 1673-1745; Lt. Robert[9], *m* Susannah Treat; Gov. John[10], qv);
7–John (1694-1758), *m* Hannah Ensign;
6–John (1726-1809), in French and Indian War, 1756, and Am. Rev.; *m* 1749, Lydia Wadsworth (1731-1817);
5–John (*b* 1774), Houseville, nr. Lowville, N.Y.; *m* Lois Marsh (*b* 1773);
4–Jeremiah (1792-1876), *m* 1814, Sarah K. Cadwell (*d* 1865);
3–William (1815-87), of Port Leyden, N.Y.; *m* 1841, Harriet Demon;
2–George Kellogg (1848-1916), of Port Leyden; *m* 1871, Mary Jacobie (1852-1918); issue: I–Estella May (1 above); II–Grace (*b* 1876; *m* Charles Hand); III–Clara J. (*b* 1879; *m* Oscar C. Thayer).
1–A.B., N.Y. State Coll. for Teachers, '23, A.M., 1928. Teacher since 1906. Mem. D.A.R., I.A.G., Am. Hist. Assn., N.E.A. Residence: 101 Main St., Boonville, N.Y.

1–**SHRINER, Francis Earle,** *b* Union Bridge, Md., Sept. 11, 1890.
6–Abraham (Schreiner, Shryner) **Shriner** (*b* 1719), from southern Germany in the "Samuel," to Phila., 1739;
5–Capt. Peter (1748-1838), capt. 1st Bn., Pa. Militia, and was attached to Gen. Washington's army at Valley Forge; moved to Frederick Co., Md., after Am. Rev., and owned a large tract of land; *m* 1773, Margaret Ann Faust (1749-1825);
4–Jacob (1790-1866), of Carroll Co., Md.; *m* 1815, Elizabeth Stoner (1795-1881);
3–Peter Hanson (1821-94), *m* 1850, Rebecca Englar (1829-98);
2–Frank Jacob (2 below).
6–Leonard (Krumbein, Krumbine) **Grumbine,** from Bavaria, 1754; settled at Schaefferstown, Pa.; scout and ranger; soldier in Cont. Army; *m* 1754, Catharina–;
5–Peter (1761-1851), of Pa.; began to write name Krumbine; served in Cont. Army; *m* 1795, Catherine–;
4–William (1797-1862), of Carroll Co., Md.; began to write name Grumbine; *m* Comfort Howells (1804-53);
3–George Thomas (1838-1910), *m* 1866, Josephine LaMotte (1843-1914);
2–Rosa Belle (*b* 1867), *m* 1889, Frank Jacob **Shriner** (1866-1928), of Carroll Co., Md.
1–*m* Apr. 14, 1920, Thelma Walden Littlefield, *b* Middleburg, Md., Oct. 30, 1895; dau. of Fred Littlefield, of Middleburg.
1–Attended Md. Collegiate Inst.; Western Md. Prep. Sch.; U. of Md.; Johns Hopkins U. Mem. Council, Union Bridge, Md.; mem. Md. Legislature. Second lt., Air Service, U.S.A. Mem. S.A.R. (state registrar), Md. Hist. Soc., M.O.W.W. Episcopalian. Democrat. Mason (K.T., Shriner). Clubs: Gibson Island, Charcoal. Summer place: Gibson Island, Baltimore, Md. Residence: Union Bridge, Md.

1–**SLAUGHTER, Marcellus Leslie,** *b* Lynchburg, Va., Mar. 13, 1895.
11–John **Slaughter,** from Eng., settled in Va., ante 1620; received a land grant on Knight's Creek, Essex Co., Va., 1635;
10–Francis (1630-1656/57), capt. militia; justice, Rappahannock Co.; planter, mcht.; *m* 1652, Elizabeth Underwood (*d* 1673; Col. William[11], *m* Margaret–);
9–Francis (1653-1718), wealthy planter, Richmond Co.; *m* 1679, Margaret Hudson;
8–Robert (1680-1726), wealthy planter, Essex Co.; owned large tracts of land, Spotsylvania Co., 1719-23; *m* 1700, Frances Ann Jones (Lt. Col. Cadwallader[9], of Stafford Co., *m* Katherine–; Richard[10], wealthy mcht., London and Co. Devon, Eng.);
7–Francis (1701-66), large landowner, Culpeper

Arms: *Argent, a saltire azure.*
Crest: *Out of a ducal coronet or, an eagle's head between wings addorsed azure, beaked or.*
Motto: *Invictae fidelitatis praemium.*

and Orange cos.; col. militia; justice; vestryman and ch. warden; *m* 1729, Ann Lightfoot (1708-48; Maj. Goodrich[8], *m* Mary Chew; Col. John[9], mem. Va. Council, cdr.-in-chief, King and Queen Co., *m* Ann, dau. Lt. Thomas Goodrich);

6–John (*b* 1732), Culpeper Co.; mem. Com. Safety, Am. Rev.; *m* 2d, 1758, Elizabeth Suggett (*b* 1742; Edgecomb[7], of Richmond Co.);

5–Col. John Suggett (1759-1830), of "Clover Dale," Woodville, Va.; served under Washington in Am. Rev.; in battle of Saratoga and at surrender of Burgoyne; magistrate, high sheriff; *m* 1779, Susan Brown (1763-1833; Capt. William[6]);

4–Thomas Jefferson (1800-73), surveyor and teacher, Culpeper Co.; *m* 1826, Martha Moore (1811-61; Capt. Reuben[5]);

3–Reuben Moore (1826-94), served as flagbearer, C.S.A., 1861, and in Co. D, 4th Va. Cav. Co., Culpeper Co.; *m* 1862, Lucy Watson Turner (1847-80; George H.[4]);

2–Wilton Hamilton (*b* 1872), of "Longwood," Amherst Co.; *m* 1894, Ella Wright (*b* 1871); issue: I–Marcellus Leslie (1 above); II–Wilton Hamilton (*b* 1899); III–William Arthur (*b* 1901, *d* infancy).

1–*m* Jan. 23, 1917, Helen Temple Thomson, *b* Bedford, Va., Oct. 9, 1896; dau. Spottswood Edward Thomson (1864-1922; Dr. Alexander S.[3] [*b* 1827], *m* 1848, Margaret Rucker Hatcher; Jesse L.[4], *m* Rhoda Wharton; Anderson[5], from Scotland, *m* Miss Anderson); issue: 1–Margaret H., *b* Lynchburg, Va., June 25, 1922; 2–Shirley Penn, *b* Lynchburg, Nov. 4, 1925.

1–Ed. U.Va. Asst. sec. Craddock-Terry Shoe Co. Mason. Presbyterian. Residence: 308 Warwick Lane, Lynchburg, Va.

1–**FITZ-HUGH, Glassell Slaughter,** *b* Charlottesville, Va., May 1, 1907.

9–Col. William **Fitz-Hugh** (1651-1701), from Eng., 1670; settled at "Bedford," on the Rappahannock, Stafford Co. (now King George Co.), Va.; lt. col., Westmoreland Co., Va., 1683; burgess, 1678-87; col. Stafford Co., 1690; king's councillor; mem. Jamestown settlement; and distinguished lawyer (see portrait); *m* 1674, Sarah Tucker (1663-1701), she was only 11 yrs. of age when married, and her husband sent her back to Eng. to complete her education; at 27, she was a widow with 6 children; she *m* 2d, Col. James Taylor;

8–Capt. Henry (1686-1758), *b* "Bedford," Stafford Co., Va.; ed. Cambridge U., Eng.; burgess; high sheriff, of Stafford Co., Va.; *m* 1718, Susannah Cooke (1693-1749; Mordecai[9]);

7–Maj. Henry (1723-83), col. Stafford militia in Am. Rev. (see portrait); *m* 1746, Sarah Battaille (1731-83), of "Prospect Hill," Caroline Co., Va.;

6–Henry (1750-77), of "Bedford," Stafford Co.; *m* Elizabeth Stith (1754-86; Col. Drury[7], of Brunswick Co., Va.);

COL. WILLIAM FITZ-HUGH (1651-1701), the settler of "Bedford," on the Rappahannock.

MAJ. HENRY FITZ-HUGH (1723-83).

5–Henry (1773-1830), inheritor of "Bedford"; *m* 1791, Elizabeth Conway, of "Hawfield," Orange Co., Va.;

4–James Madison (1809-45), wealthy landowner; *m* 1830, Mary F. Stuart (*d* 1880);

3–Francis Conway (1839-1910), accountant; served in C.S.A.; *m* 1869, Margaret Conway (1840-83);

2–Glassell (Nov. 22, 1875-Mar. 29, 1917), druggist, Charlottesville, Va.; *m* June 19, 1906, Orie Charlotte Slaughter (for genealogy and issue, see Vol. III, p. 190).

1–Ed. Augusta Mil. Acad.; med. student, U.Va. (Zeta Psi). Presbyterian. Residence: 31 University Pl., University, Va.

1–**SHRYOCK, Joseph Grundy,** *b* Haddonfield, N.J., Sept. 2, 1880.

6–John (Hans Johannes) (Schreyack, Schryock) **Shryock** (1705-88; son of Friederick von Schrieck, originally from Bois Le Duc, Duchy of Brabant, and known as Van Schrieck who lived in the kingdom of Prussia); came from Germany in the "Hope," with two

brothers to Phila., 1733; took oath of allegiance; Lutheran; first settled in that part of Lancaster Co., which in 1749 was made York Co., later they migrated further west and south into the Cumberland and Shenandoah Valleys, finally settled at Elizabethtown (now Hagerstown), Md.; owned 162 acres in the "Manor of Springettsburg," York Co.; *m* 1st, 1736, Susanna Kirn or Kern (1713-50);
5–Leonard (1738-82), served with the King's army in French and Indian War, 1755-59, at the taking of Quebec; settled at "Toddy," near Elizabethtown (Hagerstown), Md.; sank the first tanyard in Hagerstown, 1762; commd. 2d lt., Capt. Michael Fackler's Militia from Washington Co., Md., 1777; farmer and landowner; *m* 1765, Maria Margaretha Streiter (*b* 1746; Rev. John Phillip[6], from Germany in the "St. Andrew Galley," 1737, to Phila., finally located near Harper's Ferry, Va., Lutheran minister, *m* Anna Julianna, dau. of Phillip Gottfried Wittmann, from Germany in the "Hope," 1733);
4–John (1771-1856), moved to Chambersburg, Franklin Co., Pa.; built "Hollywell" Mill, at Chambersburg, 1790, mfrs. of printing paper, and bank note paper purchased by U.S. Govt.; elected to town council 1803; *m* 1st, 1793, Rachel Aston (1776-1811; Owen[5], *m* Rachel Phipps; George[6]; George[7]; John[8]);
3–George Augustus (1799-1867), of Phila.; made experiments on straw pulp in father's mill, 1829; samples of the news print paper were used to print the Phila. Bulletin, and shipped to all parts of the U.S. and Europe; invented the grooved wood roll for the mfr. of binder boards and box boards; rebuilt the mill and dam at a cost of $35,000; built "mammoth" mill on Conococheague Creek near Chambersburg, 1832, which was burned in 1864 by raiding Confederate troops; *m* 1825, Sarah Evans Knight;
2–William **Knight** (2 below).
7–**Thomas Knight** (*d* 1725), *m* 1682, Martha Allin (*d* 1731; John[8]);
6–John (1684-1728), *m* 1718, Hannah Badcock (Henry[7], *m* Mary, dau. of Peter Browne, *m* Sarah Fisher);
5–Henry (1726-1807), *m* 1748, Elizabeth Harding (1720-88; Reuben[6], *m* Mary–; Thomas[7]);
4–Daniel (1759-1838), *m* 1796, Mary Ridgway (1774-1829; John[5]; Edward[6]; Thomas[7]; Richard[8]);
3–Sarah Evans (1805-80), *m* George Augustus **Shryock** (3 above).
6–John Henry (Schafer) **Schaeffer** (1690-1775), *m* 1715, Barbara Krieger (*d* 1772);
5–John Jacob (1720-74), *m* Susanna Maria Fickard (*d* 1772);
4–Frederick David (1760-1836), from Germany, settled at Frederick, Md.; *m* 1786, Rosina Rosenmiller (1764-1835; Lewis[5], *m* Barbara, dau. Capt. Nicholas Bittinger);
3–Charles Frederick (1807-79), began to write name Schaeffer; *m* 1832, Susanna Schmucker (1811-84; John George[4], from Germany, settled at Williamsburg, Pa., *m* Catharina, dau. of Samuel Gross; John C.[5]);
2–Virginia Susan (1845-1924), *m* 1871, William Knight **Shryock** (1844-1907), of Phila.; ed. Gregory Classical Inst.; studied law in the office of the Hon. Benjamin Harris Brewster; admitted to the bar, 1866; devoted his attention largely to Orphans' Ct. and real estate practice; pvt. 2d Keystone Light Arty., Independent Baty., Pa. Vol. Militia, 1863; issue: I–William Allen (*b* 1871; *m* 1901, Florence Burd English); II–Florence Virginia (1874-90); III–Edith Hill (1875-76); IV–Genevieve Augusta (*b* 1877); V–Bertha Estelle (1878-1916; *m* 1908, Eric Johnstone); VI–Joseph Grundy (1 above); VII–Harold Aston (*b* 1881).
1–*m* Apr. 6, 1904, Aimée Caroline Picolet d'Hermillon, *b* Phila., Pa., May 6, 1881; dau. of Jules Emmanuel Arthur Picolet, Baron d' Hermillon from France, naturalized citizen, Philadelphia; issue: 1–Joseph Richard, *b* Bala-Cynwyd, Montgomery Co., Pa., July 8, 1905; U. of Pa.; 2–Raymond deSouville, *b* Phila., Oct. 11, 1906; U. of Pa., '26, law, 1929.
1–Ed. College Jacques Amyot à Melun-Seine et Marne, France, 1896-97; grad. Eastburn Acad., 1897; C.E., Pa. Mil. Coll., 1900 (hon. M.C.E., 1921), studied 3 mos. in Dresden, Germany. Draughtsman, Am. Bridge Co., Pencoyd plant, 1900-03; designing engr., Va. Bridge & Iron Co., Roanoke, 1903-04; draughtsman and checker, Belmont Iron Works, Phila., 1904-06; designing engr. and salesman, Belmont Iron Works, Phila., 1906-22; chief engr., Eng. Est. Sales Adv., Belmont Iron Works, 1922-26; v.p., dir. and chief engr., Belmont Iron Works, since 1926. Mem. H.S. of Pa., Colonial Sons and Daus., Colonial Soc. Pa., Netherlands Soc. Pa., S.A.R., S.R., I.A.G., Geneal. Soc. Pa., Hist. Soc. Pa., Welsh Soc. Phila., Nat. Geneal. Soc., Pa. German Soc., N.E.H.G.S., Md. Hist. Soc., Pa. Soc., Geneal. Soc. N.J., Hist. Soc. York Co. (Pa.), Am. Hist. Assn., N.Y.G.B.S., Am. Soc. of C.E., Societe des Ingenieurs Civils de France, Zool. Soc. Phila. (life), Pa. Acad. Fine Arts. Clubs: Engineers, Art, Wynnefield, Philadelphia Country. Residence: Rolling Rd. and State Rd., Bryn Mawr, Pa.

1–**SMITH, Clara Estelle Clements (Mrs. Andrew R.)**, *b* Tuscaloosa, Ala., Dec. 22, 1871.
4–Reuben (Clement) **Clements,** Huguenot, from Bajonne, France, and wife Elizabeth Stuart (Scotch descent), of Edgefield C.H., Pendleton Co., S.C., went to Ala., 1819;
3–Hardy (1783-1867), preceded his parents in Ala.; wrote name Clements; civil engr.; planter; *m* 1st, 1822, Martha Hargrove (1801-30; Rev. Dudley[4], of Tuscaloosa Co., Ala.);
2–Rufus Hargrove (2 below).
8–Edward (Bugby) **Bugbee**, from Eng. with his wife Rebecca, and dau. Sarah, in the "Francis," to Roxbury, Mass., 1634;
7–Joseph (1640-1729), *m* Experience Pitcher;
6–Josiah (*b* 1684), Woodstock, Conn.; *m* Sarah Hubbard;
5–Josiah (*b* 1708), *m* Polycenia Arnold;
4–Amos (*b* 1749), soldier at Lexington Alarm; *m* 1782, Martha Woodward;
3–Francis (1784-1877), B.A., Yale, 1818; judge Superior Ct. of Ala.; *m* 1827, Lavinia Hudson Tarrant;
2–Martha Lavinia (2 below).
8–Lt. Thomas **Bancroft** (qv);
7–Sarah (1665-1723), *m* 1686, as his 2d wife, John **Woodward** (1649-1732; George[8]; Richard[9]);
6–Joseph (1688-1727), Canterbury, Conn.; *m* 1714, Elizabeth Silsby (1685-1727);
5–Joseph (1725-1814), Ashford, Conn.; officer Am. Rev.; *m* 1745, Elizabeth Perkins (1782-1823; Capt. John[6]);
4–Martha (1757-1847), *m* 1782, Amos **Bugbee** (4 above).
5–John **Nash,** of Culpeper Co., Va.; *m* Mary Long;
4–Malinda, of Asheville, S.C.; *m* Thomas **Tarrant**;
3–Lavinia Hudson (1803-82), *m* 1827, Francis **Bugbee** (3 above);
2–Martha Lavinia (1829-1906), *m* 1850, Rufus Hargrove **Clements** (1823-75), A.B., U.Ala., '45, A.M., 1848, LL.B., Harvard, 1847; lawyer, planter; rep. Ala. Gen. Assembly; issue: I–Francis Bugbee (see Vol. I, p. 555); II–Julius M. (*b* 1869; *m* Caroline Simonds); III–Clara Estelle (1 above).
1–*m* Nov. 16, 1893, Andrew Reid Smith, *b* Griffin, Ga., Sept. 8, 1869; banker; son of Charles Smith, of Rome, Ga., *m* Minnie Wingfield; issue: 1–Fenton Reid, *b* Tuscaloosa, Ala., Nov. 18, 1894; *m* June 16, 1923, Alice, dau. of Henry R. Bright, of Mt. Sterling, Ky.; 2–Francis Clements, *b* Tuscaloosa, June 28, 1898; B.A., U.Ala.; 3–Charles Singleton, *b* Demopolis, Ala., Oct. 18, 1902; B.A., U.Ala.; *m* Feb. 25, 1925, Eleanor, dau. of James Broun, of Biloxi, Miss. (issue: Andrew Reid, II).
1–M.A., Tuscaloosa Female Coll. Chmn. Co. Red Cross Chapter during World War; chmn. Fatherless Children of France for Demopolis; chmn. Y.W.C.A. during World War; manager of 4th dist. of Federation of Women's Clubs, 1919-20. Pres. women's organization of Trinity Ch., Demopolis. Mem. C.D.A., D.A.R., (regent), I.A.G., Colonial Book Club. Residence: Bluff Hall, Demopolis, Ala.

1–**SMELKER, Marie Frances Wrotnowski (Mrs. Van Archibald)**, *b* Clermont, Fla., Oct. 13, 1886.
9–Richard **Haines** (qv);
8–John (1666-1728), large landowner in Burling-

HAINES
Arms: Or, on a fess gules, three bezants, and in chief a hound courant sable.
Crests: An eagle displayed on a tortoise's back; (2) an eagle displayed azure, with a semee of 18 stars of 6 points argent.

ton Co., N.J., and Chester Co., Pa.; *m* 1684, Esther Borton (John[9], came in the "Griffin," 1675, mem. N.J. Assembly, 1682-85);
7-Jonathan, *m* 1711, Mary Matlock (William[8], *m* Mary Hancock);
6-Jonathan, *m* 1740, Hannah Sharp (William[7], *m* Mary Austin);
5-Nehemiah (*b* 1755), *m* 1783, Abigail Haines (*b* 1755; Noah[6], *m* Hannah Thorn, widow);
4-Sarah (*b* 1783), *m* 1809, John **Hoskins** (John[5], *m* Rachel Valentine);
3-Angelina (see portrait), *m* Edwin **Bladen**.

ANGELINA (HOSKINS) BLADEN

2-Arthur Francis **Wrotnowski** (1839-1911), see portrait and biography; *m* 1868, Josephine Rachel Thomas (*b* Medford, N.J., 1841-*d* New Orleans, 1883; Edward B.[3], of Lumberton, N.J., *m* Abigail Haines [*b* 1800] sister of Sarah, 4 above); *m* 2d, 1885, Angeline Haines Bladen (1859-1911); issue (1st marriage): 1-Florence (*b* 1872; *m* 1893, Charles F. de Ganahl, *b* 1869); issue (2d marriage): I-Marie F. (1 above); II-Janet (*b* 1889; *m* William W. Griffith); III-Arthur Corthell (*b* 1891; *m* Dulcine Brodersen).
1-*m* May 6, 1912, Dr. Van Archibald Smelker, *b* Dodgeville, Wis., Sept. 11, 1882; son of Jesse

COL. ARTHUR FRANCIS WROTNOWSKI (b Clermont, Ferran, France, Oct. 14, 1839-d Nogales, Ariz., Oct. 23, 1911), 1st lt. and adj., 1st La. Inf., Mar. 1863; lt. col., 1st Vol. Engr. Corps d'Afrique, Sept. 3, 1863, reorganized, Oct. 1864, as the 95th U.S. Colored Vol. Inf.; hon. mustered out on consolidation, Nov. 26, 1864.

P. Smelker, *m* Mary Greene; issue (all *b* Nogales, Ariz.): 1-Mary, *b* Mar. 8, 1913; 2-Betty, *b* Sept. 3, 1914; 3-Barbara, *b* May 1, 1917; 4-Van Archibald, *b* May 10, 1920.
1-Residence: Nogales, Ariz.

1-**SNYDER, Jennie Elmina Whetstone (Mrs. William H.),** *b* Tamaqua, Pa., Sept. 15, 1865.
5-Capt. Jacob (Wetzstein, Wetstein) **Whetstone** (1738-1833), capt. 1st Co., Dord Bn. militia, 3d Bn. from Langschwamp, a part of Maxatany Tp., Berks Co., Pa.; *m* 1770, Anna Maria Schoffer, or Shaeffer (Jacob[6], of Brunswick Tp., Berks Co., Pa.);
4-Isaac (1774-1850), of Pa.; *m* Persus Hunsicker (*d* ca. 1850);
3-John (1798-1848), Tamaqua, Pa.; *m* 1820, Barbara Moser;
2-Gideon (2 below).
5-Burkhardt **Moser** (1736-1807), pvt. 1st Co., 6th Bn., Northampton Co., during Am. Rev.; *m* 1762, Mary Agatha (Steininger) Lichtenwalner (John[6]);
4-Burkhardt (1763-1849), pvt. 1st Co., 1st Bn., Northampton Co., 1785; militia, Lynn Tp., 1794; lt. 1st Co., Troop of Light Horse, 1794; elected capt. 1st Co., 1st Regt. Northampton Co.; *m* 1783, Catherine Hornberger;
3-Barbara (1796-1879), *m* 1820, John **Whetstone** (3 above);
2-Gideon (1823-1907), coal operator, lumber mcht.; *m* 1845, Catherine Boughner (1821-1912; Abraham La Rue[3], *m* Catherine Vetter); issue: I-Anna Catherine (1845-1915; *m* Nathan Krause); II-Mary Ellen (1852-1927); III-Louisa (1856-1915); IV-Claudius Gideon (*b* 1859; *m* Mary Elba Caroline Fry); V-Martha (1862-1921; *m* Judiah Burd Irish); VI-Jennie Elmina (1 above).
1-*m* Oct. 16, 1888, William Heinrich Snyder (Dec. 6, 1862-Nov. 30, 1925); son of Carl Snyder; issue: 1-Paul La Rue, *b* Mahanoy City, Pa., Sept. 8, 1890; *m* Oct. 6, 1914, Florence Myrtle, dau. of Daniel D. Evans, *m* Hannah Fox (issue: Roger); 2-Roger William, *b* Hagerstown, Md., Nov. 26, 1915.
1-School teacher 3 yrs., music teacher 15 yrs.

Mem. D.A.R., U.S.D. 1812, I.A.G., Pa. German Soc., O.E.S. Lutheran. Republican. Residence: 27 E. Antietam St., Hagerstown, Md.

1–**SPENCER, Mary Kerr (Mrs. William Oliver),** *b* Yanceyville, N.C., Oct. 1, 1875.
11–Capt. Henry **Graves,** from Eng., 1608; settled in James City Co., Va.; burgess; *m* Katharine Graves;
10–Thomas, came with his father;
9–William (*b* 1689), of Gloucester Co., Va.;
8–John, of Gloucester Co.;
7–John (*b* 1728?), of Caswell Co., N.C.;
6–John Herndon (*b* Va. 1749-*d* 1829), of Caswell Co.; pvt. N.C. troops; capt. Am. Rev.; *m* 1770, Nancy Slade (*d* 1807);
5–Ann, *m* Bartlett **Yancey;**
4–James, *m* Zilphah Johnson;
3–Dr. Albert G., *m* Mary Graves Miles (g.dau. John Herndon Graves);
2–Eliza Catharine, *m* John H. **Kerr** (1844-1924); issue: I–Hon. John H. (*b* 1863; see Who's Who in America; *m* Lillian Ella Foote); II–Mary (1 above); III–A. Yancey (*m* Mary Oliver); IV–B. Graves (*m* Lucy Mason Jackson); V–Martha Frances (*m* Alexander H. Motz); VI–Nannie Emma (*m* Dr. Stephen A. Malloy).
1–*m* May 24, 1894, William Oliver Spencer, *b* Mocksville, N.C., Apr. 21, 1863; son of Oliver H. Spencer, of Mocksville; issue: 1–William Oliver, *b* Yanceyville, N.C., July 9, 1895; U. of N.C.; *m* Apr. 6, 1924, Fay Huntley, dau. of B. F. Huntley (issue: William Oliver, III; Mary Josephine); 2–John Kerr, *b* Yanceyville, Aug. 21, 1897; Duke U.; *m* Nov. 27, 1926, Kathleen Huntley, also dau. of B. F. Huntley (issue: John Kerr, Jr.; Huntley Spencer); 3–Frank Graves, *b* Winston-Salem, N.C., Dec. 29, 1906; Oak Ridge Mil. Inst.; *m* June 16, 1927, Helen Mickey, dau. R. H. Mickey.
1–Grad. Oxford Coll. Journalist. Mem. D.F.P.A. (state pres. of N.C.), D.A.R. (v.p. gen. Nat. Soc., state regent, N.C.), U.S.D. 1812 (state pres., N.C.), N.C. Hist. Soc.; trustee Traveller's Aid Soc. Clubs: Woman's (Winston-Salem). Nat. Officers D.A.R. Baptist. Democrat. Residence: 510 Brookstown Av., Winston-Salem, N.C.

Arms: (1) Gules, a pale fusillé argent; (2) argent, a lion rampant sable, crowned or.

1–**STATHAM, Mary Beaumont,** *b* Lynchburg, Va., June 13, 1856.
7–Hugh **Statham** (ca. 1640-1700), from Eng., 1667; first of the name found in Va., 1667, as tutor and guardian in family of John Percy (or Pearcy), and of John Grimstead; settled in Northumberland Co.; *m* Jane Love (*d* 1702/03), probably a dau. of Thomas Love, of Eng., *m* 1638, Penelope Turner;
6–Edmund, or Edward (*b* ca. 1666), of York, 1702; sec. with William Davis for John Howard, in Estate of late Rev. Cope D'Oyley; supposedly *m* a Miss Lawrence, but no proof;
5–Love (*d* 1781), patented land in Hanover Co., 1735; had large estates in Hanover and Louisa cos.; *m* Martha–;
4–Charles (ca. 1736-ca. 1817), of Amherst Co., Va., and Ga.; in 1785 census had 10 white and 17 blacks, Amherst Co.; pvt. in Va. cav., Am. Rev., 1784, refused to carry arms but drove supplies; *m* ca. 1762, Cecily (Brothers) Stewart;
3–Richmond (1767-1839), of Amherst and Appomattox cos.; served in War 1812; *m* 2d, 1814, Rhoda Hill (1788-1839), of Prince Edward and Amelia cos., Va. (William[4], *m* Rhoda [Gresham] Watkins Hill, of Amelia Co. Va., Widow of Col. Joel Watkins, of Rev. War);
2–Col. Charles Wesley (1819-89), of Appomattox Co.; as lt. in cav., C.S.A., 1861, helped to equip a company in Lynchburg, fought under Gen. Stonewall Jackson in northern Va.; col. in command of local forces at Lynchburg; on account of disability retired from active service, 1864; *m* 1845, Maria Virginia Ferguson (1825-1917; Thomas[3], of Lynchburg, *m* Elizabeth Catherine Beaumont, of Huddersfield, York., Eng., of royal descent of France and England); issue: I–Charles (*b* 1847-*d* infancy); II–Thomas Richmond (1848-1929; student U.-Va.; *m* Lelia Hobson, dau. of Calvin Ferguson, *m* Eleanora Johnson, of Nashville, Tenn. [issue: Virginia, *m* Rev. George W. Carter, Fairfax Co., Va., issue: Catherine, *m* Lt. James Bellinger Rasbach, U.S.A. in World War; issue: Virginia and Elizabeth]); III–Beaumont (*d* young); IV–Elizabeth (*b* 1852; *m* 1877, Page Morris, see Vol. I, p. 352, see their dau., Mrs. Wells Smith Gilbert, Vol. III, p. 32); V–William Woodville (1855-1903; cadet M.V.I.); VI–Mary Beaumont (1 above).
1–Ed. Va. Female Inst., Staunton, Va.; Miss Charlotte Hinsdale's School for Young Ladies, N.Y. City; tutored during several trips abroad. Pvt. sec. to Col. Charles W. Statham, Lynchburg, 1885-89; pvt. sec. to Rep. Page Morris, U.S. Congress, 1902-03; letters from Nat. Capitol to Minn. papers, 1896-1903; letters from abroad to Duluth Journal and other publications, 1907-11; engaged in genealogical work since 1896; compiler of Statham, Morris, Davis, Hill, Hollman, Lewis, Turner, Michell, Chiswell, Love, Gresham and Brothers genealogies. Mem. D.A.R., I.A.G. (life), Va. Hist. Soc., Nat. Geneal. Soc., Pasadena (Calif.) Hist. Soc., L.A.P.W. Clubs: Twentieth Century (founder and life hon. v.p.), etc. Residence: 1190 Oak Knoll Av., Pasadena, Calif.

1–**STRASSBURGER, Ralph Beaver,** *b* Norristown, Pa., Mar. 26, 1883.
6–Johann Andreas **Strassburger** (*b* 1716), from Germany, 1742; *m* 1751, Catharine Rosina Kolb (*d* 1771);
5–John Andrew (1754-1825), *m* 1781, Eva Yeager (1754-1835);
4–Rev. John Andrew (1796-1860), *m* 1818, Catharine Stout;
3–Reuben Y. (1823-72), *m* 1847, Elizabeth Ziegler Schwenk;
2–Jacob Andrew (2 below).
7–John Jacob **Stout** (*b* Switzerland, 1710-*d* Bucks Co., Pa., 1779), *m* 1739, Anna Miller, widow of John Leisse (or Lacy);
6–Abraham (1740-1812), *m* 1773, Mary Magdalena Hartzell (1751-1811; Jorg Heinrich[7], *b* Switzerland, 1692-*d* Bucks Co., Pa., 1784 or 88);
5–Henry Hartzell (1776-1854), *m* 1798, Elizabeth Kern (1778-1871; John Adams[6]; Christian[7]; Frederick[8]);
4–Catharine (1798-1838), *m* Rev. John A. **Strassburger** (4 above).
9–George **Markley** (*b* 1620-22), *m* Eva–;
8–Abraham (*b* 1664), *m* 1684, Anna Veronica–;
7–Jacob (1701-84), *m* 1722, Barbara Dodderer (1704-38; George Philip[8] [*d* 1741], *m* Veronica–, *d* 1752);
6–Veronica (1732-77), *m* 1751, George **Schwenk**

(1728-1803; Hans Michael[7] [1696-1773], *m* Mary Elizabeth–, *d* 1775);
5–Abraham (1759-1843), *m* Veronica Landis Bauer (1756-1840; Michael[6], *m* Veronica, dau. of Johannes Landis; Hans[7]);
4–Jacob (1787-1852), *m* ca. 1817, Magdalena Ziegler;
3–Elizabeth Z. (1821-1907), *m* Reuben Y. **Strassburger** (3 above).
8–Michael **Ziegler** (*b* Germany, 1680-*d* 1765), *m* Catherine–;
7–Andrew (1707-93), *m* 1730, Elizabeth Kolb (1715-84);
6–Michael (*b* 1735), *m* Miss Clemens (Jacob[7]; Gerhardt[8]);
5–Andrew (1770-1844), *m* 1792, Catherine Lederach (1769-1840; Henry[6]; Andreas[7]);
4–Magdalena (1795-1826), *m* Jacob **Schwenk** (4 above).
7–Johannes (Bieber) **Beaver,** to Pa., ca. 1741;
6–Jacob (1731-98), Lehigh Co., Pa.; *m* Christina Steinbrenner;
5–John (*d* 1827), *m* 1795, Catherine–;
4–Jacob (1796-1837), *m* 1821, Lydia Kerr (Henry[5] [1772-1853], *m* Maria Magdalena Cressman [1778-1832; Jacob[6], *m* Elizabeth, dau. of George Nase, *m* Catherine Bender; Anthony[7]; John[8]]);
3–Dr. Ephraim Kerr (1826-62), *m* Lucy Ann Solliday;
2–Mary (2 below).
6–Frederick (Sallade) **Solliday,** from France to Bucks Co., Pa.; *m* Barbara–;
5–John (1755-1842), Bucks Co.; *m* Elizabeth Hinckel (1761-1841; Leonard[6], [*d* 1816], *m* Magdalena–);
4–Dr. Joseph (1800-82), *m* 1820, Elizabeth Stein (*d* 1880; John[5], *m* Catherine Ohl [Michael[6], *m* Catherine, dau. of Johan Philip Mosser; Michael[7]]; Michael[6], *m* Catherine Brobst [Martin[7]; Jacob Philip[8]]; Jacob[7], *d* Lehigh Co., Pa.);
3–Lucy Ann (1831-59), *m* 1852, Dr. Ephraim Kerr **Beaver** (3 above);
2–Mary J. (1856-1913), *m* 1880, Jacob Andrew **Strassburger** (1849-1908), A.B., Ursinus, '73; lawyer, Norristown, Pa.; dist. atty., Montgomery Co.; for issue see Vol. I, p. 845.
1–*m* at West Wickham, Kent, Eng., May 11, 1911, May, dau. of Frederick G. Bourne; issue: 1–Johann Andreas Peter, *b* Phila., Pa., Jan. 3, 1916.
1–U.S.N.A., '05; (LL.D.). Ens., U.S.N., resigned, 1909. Consul gen. and sec. legation to Roumania, Bulgaria and Serbia, 1913-14; nominee for Congress, 1914. Lt. (j.g.) and lt., U.S.N., World War. Publisher; breeder of thoroughbred horses (see Who's Who in America), mem. of French Legion d'Honneur. Life mem. I.A.G., etc. Clubs: Travelers, Tennis, Sporting, Ile de Puteau (Paris), Metropolitan (Washington), University, Racquet and Tennis, N.Y. Yacht, Recess, Turf and Field, Army and Navy (New York), Racquet, Radnor Hunt, Rose Tree Hunt, Sunnybrook Golf (Pa.), Everglades, Palm Beach Country, etc. Residence: Normandy Farm, Gwynedd Valley, Pa.

1–**STICK, Gordon Malvern Fair,** *b* Nagoya, Japan, July 17, 1903.
5–Johann Kaspar (Stück) **Stick** (1752-1814), from Germany, 1775, settler at Sherman's, Mannheim Tp., York Co., Pa.; *m* 1776, Margaretta Sherman (*d* 1815);
4–Henry (1808-82), founder Stick's Tavern, York Co.; prospered as a merchant, farmer and community banker; *m* 1836, Mary Ann Thoman (1815-1903);
3–Henry Silas (1848-1917), of Sticks, York Co.; postmaster; built two schools; founded Glenville (Pa.) Acad., rep. Dun and Bradstreet; keeper of store and banker for the community; *m* 1869, Rebecca Koller (1850-1918);
2–Jacob Monroe (2 below).
7–John **Fair** (1742-1827), from Germany, settled at Hanover, Pa., later Manchester, Md.; fought in Am. Rev. in first Partisan Legion, comd. by Brig. Gen. Armand, Marquis de la Rouerie, 1782-83; *m* 1763, Barbara Fair (1745-1834);
6–George (1765-1831), "Wakefield Valley," Manchester, Md.; *m* 1784, Anna Margaretta Walker? (1767-1823);

VON STÜCK

Arms: Azure, a barry of six wavy argent and the first, a crayfish issuant from the party line, naissant and moving gules.
Crest: Out of a ducal coronet three ostrich plumes, one azure between two argent.

5–Peter (1790-1844), of "Peter's Luck," Alesia, Carroll Co., Md.; *m* 1808, Barbara Ziegler? (1784-1859);
4–Ephraim (1816-94), of "Meadowbrook," Glen Rock, York Co.; *m* 1841, Magdalena Warner (1820-72);
3–Hezekiah Warner (1849-1912), of "Fairview," Glen Rock; *m* 1868, Almira Jane Seitz (1849-1909);
2–Este Pearl (*b* 1876), *m* 1902, Jacob Monroe **Stick** (*b* 1877), ed. Ursinus Coll., and U.Pa.; entered ministry; went to Japan as missionary; brig. gen. on staff of Gen. Nishi and Nogi in Russo-Japanese War; received Order of the Rising Sun from Emperor of Japan; returned to U.S.A., 1909; nat. sec. Layman's Missionary Movement; asso. pastor Fifth Av. Presbyn. Ch., N.Y. City; exec. sec. of Men and Religion Forward Movement in U.S.; gen. sec. of Md. Tract Soc.; grad. from Chaplain's Training Sch., at Camp Zachary Taylor as 1st lt., 1918, and served in World War; grad. U.S. Army Service Schools, Ft. Leavenworth, Chaplain's course; now in charge of Reserve Officers Assn. of Md. and exec. sec. for III Corps Area Mil. Training Camps Assn. of U.S.A.; now maj. in Chaplain Corps of U.S. Army; etc.
1–*m* Jan. 1, 1927, Anne Howard Fitchett, *b* Baltimore, Md., Oct. 8, 1901; dau. of Thomas Howard Fitchett, of Baltimore and Glen Arm, Md., *m* Lillian Glenn Davis; issue: 1–Anne Howard Fitchett, *b* Baltimore, Mar. 25, 1928.
1–A.B., John Hopkins, '26 (Phi Gamma Delta; Omicron Delta Kappa; Pi Delta Epsilon; Pi Delta Pi). Rep. for Hynson, Westcott & Dunning, pharmaceuticals, Baltimore, 1926-27; investment banker, Gillet & Co., Baltimore, 1927-30; sales mgr., Funk Printing Press Co., N.Y. City, subsidiary of F.X. Hooper Co., Glen Arm, Md. First lt., 319th Inf. Reserve Corps, U.S.A. Mem. I.A.G., M.O.F.W., Md. Hist. Soc., Star-Spangled Banner Flag House Assn., Order of the Rising Sun (Japan), Scabbard and Blade, Reserve Officers Assn. Episcopalian. Republican. Clubs: Green Spring Valley Hunt, Tudor and Stuart, The Barnstormers. Residence: "Land of Promise," Glen Arm, Md.

1–**STURGES, Harold Merwin,** *b* E. Norwalk, Conn., July 26, 1893.
6–Thomas **Nash** (1743-1815), capt. of guards in

Col. Whiting's 4th Regt. of militia, comd. by Lt. Col. Jonathan Dimon; *m* Mary Burr (1750-84);
5–Joseph (*b* 1776), *m* Mary Squires;
4–Joseph (1806-85), *m* 1827, Angeline Baker (1806-84);
3–Emeline (1840-1912), *m* 1858, Sylvester **Sturges** (1837-1907);
2–Edward Frances (*b* 1869), mason builder; *m* 1891, Maude Alice Carr (*b* 1873); issue: I–Harold Merwin (1 above); II–LeGrand F. (*b* 1896; *m* M. Louise Bawden); III–Almeda G. (*b* 1899; *m* S. Edward Jennings); IV–Reba N. (*d* 1904).
1–*m* Nov. 2, 1918, Laura Starr Ford, *b* Detroit, Mich., Apr. 5, 1894; dau. of Allen P. Ford, *m* Eleanor Starr, of Bridgeport, Conn.; issue: 1–Jonathan Ford, *b* Bridgeport, Conn., June 17, 1919; 2–Nancy Allen, *b* Fairfield, Conn., Feb. 16, 1922; 3–Priscilla Merrill, *b* Fairfield, Mar. 29, 1925.
1–A.B., Clark U., '16 (Theta Kappa Nu, Pi Gamma Mu). Mgr. traffic inspection, Mich. State Telephone Co.; chemist, DuPont Co.; special agent Conn. Gen. Life Ins. Co., since 1922. Served in World War, discharged Jan. 3, 1919. Elder First Presbyn. Ch. Mem. S.A.R., I.A.G., Soc. Am. Mil. Engrs., Army Ordnance Assn., A.L., Disabled Am. Vets., Mason. Civitan Club. Residence: 332 Wakeman Rd., Fairfield, Conn.

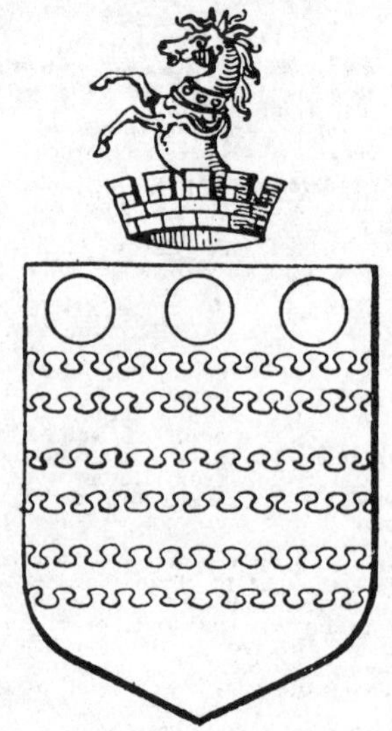

EMERY

Arms: *Argent, three bars nebulée gules, in chief as many torteaux.*
Crest: *Out of a mural crown a demi-horse argent, maned or, collared gules, studded of the first.*

1–**COX, Juliet Hazeltine Emery (Mrs. William Van Zandt),** *b* Washington, D.C., Jan. 21, 1858-*d* "Emery Place," Brightwood, D.C., Dec. 2, 1929.
8–John **Emery** (qv);
7–John (ca. 1628-ca. 1693), from Eng. with parents; resided in Newbury; freeman, 1654-55; selectman, 1671,74; way warden, 1679,86; surveyor of highways, 1690; styled sgt.; *m* 1648, Mary Webster (ca. 1630-1708/09; John[8], from Eng., at Ipswich, Mass., 1634, freeman, 1634-35, clerk of the bonds, 1642, pound warden, 1643, *m* Mary Shatswell);
6–Joseph (1662/63-1721), Andover, Mass.; *m* 1693, Elizabeth Merrill (1669-post 1712; Dea. Abraham[7], [1636 or 37-1722], selectman, 1684, a founder and warden 2d Episcopal church in Mass., 1714, *m* 1660, Abigail, dau. of John Webster, above; Nathaniel[8], from Eng., 1635, *m* Susanna–);
5–Joseph (1696-1776), to Pembroke, N.H., 1769; *m* 2d, 1738, Abigail Long (1699-1776; Shubael[6] [1661-1731], *m* 1695, Hannah [1670/71-post 1712], dau. of Dea. Abraham Merrill, above; Dea. Robert[7], *m* 1647, Alice Short);
4–Capt. Joseph, Gent. (1739-1821), 1st lt., 9th N.H. Militia, 1775; capt., 13th N.H. Militia, 1779; served 6 yrs. in Am. Rev.; on committee of Pembroke to consider N.H. Constn., 1792; deacon; *m* 1763, Hannah Stickney (4 below);
3–Dea. Jacob (1777-1870), "a man of honor and integrity respected by all"; *m* 1804, Jane Gault (1786-1862; Matthew[4] [1754-1824], 3 yrs. in Am. Rev., drummer in Gen. Stark's brig. at Bennington and Stillwater, *m* Elizabeth Buntin [1762-ante 1819; Capt. Andrew, Gent.[5], captured by Indians, 1747, with father, taken to Montreal, escaped 1748, capt. N.H. Cont. troops, 1775, mortally wounded at White Plains Oct. 28, 1776, *m* Jeannette–; Robert[6], *b* in Scotland, at siege of Londonderry, Ireland, 1689, from Londonderry to N.H., one of the first settlers of Allenstown, captured by Indians, 1747, but escaped, 1748, *m* Elizabeth–]; Andrew[5] [1714-97], signed N.H. Association Test, 1776, *m* Molly Ayer; Samuel[6], *m* Elsie Carlton);
2–Hon. Matthew Gault (2 below).
8–William **Stickney** (qv);
7–Amos (1635-78), from Eng. with parents ca. 1638; removed from Rowley to Newbury after marriage; *m* 1663, Sarah Morse (1641-1711; Anthony[8] [ca. 1607-1686], from Eng. in the "James," 1635, settled at Newbury, freeman, 1636, sealer of leather, 1677, fence viewer, 1675, *m* Mary–);
6–Benjamin (1673-1756), to Rowley, ante 1694; *m* 1700/01, Mary Palmer (1674-1747; Dea. Samuel[7] [1644-1719], *m* 1671, Mary Pearson [1651-1716; Dea. John[8] from Essex Co., Eng. among first settlers of Rowley, overseer 1649,54, selectman, 1667,70, rep. Gen. Ct., 1678, deacon, 1686, *m* Dorcas–]; Thomas[8], from Eng., a founder of Rowley, 1638, one of the weavers who in Rowley produced the first cloth manufactured in N.E., tything man, 1677, *m* 1643, Ann–);
5–Joseph (1705-56), dep. sheriff of Essex Co., 1737; *m* 1737, Hannah Goodridge (1712/13-1806; Samuel[6] [1681 or 82-1752], *m* 1710, Hannah, dau. of Colin Frazer; Benjamin[7], removed to Rowley, 1685, killed by Indians with wife and two children at evening prayers; William[8] [1605-1646/47], from Bury St. Edmunds, Suffolk, Eng., at Watertown, Mass., 1636, freeman, 1642, *m* 1632, Margaret–);
4–Hannah (1738-1834), *m* Capt. Joseph **Emery,** Gent. (4 above).
7–Robert **Hazeltine** (*d* 1674), from Eng., 1637, to Salem, Mass.; a founder of Rowley, 1637; freeman, 1642; one of the first three settlers of Bradford, 1649; established ferry between Bradford and Haverhill; overseer of highways and fences, 1662,64; *m* 1639 (the first marriage in Rowley), Ann– (*d* 1684);
6–Abraham (1648-1711), town clerk of Bradford, 1686-90; *m* 1671, Elizabeth Langhorne (*b* 1649; Richard[7] [1617-1668/69], selectman, 1660-61, *m* Mary Crosby);
5–Richard (*b* 1679), a founder of Chester (now Hooksett), N.H.; *m* 1702/03, Abigail Chadwick (John[6] [1651-1707], *m* Mary, dau. of Edmund, or Edward Barlow; John[7], 1601-81);
4–James (1719-1803), to Haverhill, 1768; *m* 2d, 1765, Hannah Kimball (4 below);
3–William (1776-1864), to Pembroke, N.H., 1800; *m* 1803, Abigail (Nabby) Emery (1780-1867; Capt. Joseph, Gent.[4], 4 above);
2–Mary Kittridge (2 below).
8–Richard **Kimball** (qv);
7–Cornet Benjamin (1637-95), Ipswich to Salisbury; at Rowley (which then included Bradford), 1663; of Bradford, 1670; cornet of troop of horse under Capt. Appleton, 1683-84; *m* 1661, Mercy (Marcy) Hazeltine (1642-1707/08; Robert[8], 7 above);
6–Richard (1665-1710/11), town clerk of Bradford for many years; *m* 1692, Mehitable Day (*b* 1669; John[7], *m* 1664, Sarah, dau. of Dea. Moses Pengry; Robert[8], from Eng. in the "Elizabeth," 1637, settled at Ipswich, freeman, 1641, selectman, 1643,63,69, tything man, 1677);
5–Stephen (1707/08-1756), Bradford; *m* 1736, Hannah Perley (*b* 1716; Lt. Jacob[6] [1670-1751], *m*

2d, 1709, Lydia, dau. of Joseph Peabody; Dea. Thomas[7]; Allan[8]);
4–Hannah (1743-1815), *m* James **Hazeltine** (4 above);
3–William, *m* Abigail Emery (3 above);

HON. MATTHEW GAULT EMERY (Sept. 28, 1818-1901), removed from Pembroke, N.H., to Baltimore, Md., 1837; settled at Washington, 1842; architect and builder; did much of the stone work of the Capitol; July 4, 1848, laid the corner-stone of the Washington Monument, the resolution of thanks which he received for this work is signed by John Quincy Adams, Henry Clay, and Robert C. Winthrop; organized a militia company, 1861, of which he was capt.; mem. bd. of aldermen of Washington, and the last mayor, 1870-71; regent Smithsonian Instn.; trustee Dickinson Coll., Carlisle, Pa.; regent, incorporator and treas., American U.; pres. bd. trustees, Metropolitan Methodist Ch.; pres. Second Nat. Bank, 1877-1901, etc.

2–Mary Kittridge (1824-1903), active in religious and charitable work in Washington; mem. board of lady mgrs. Washington City Orphan Asylum; *m* 1854, Hon. Matthew Gault **Emery** (1818-1901), see portrait and biography; issue: I–Matthew Gault, Jr. (1855-87); II–Juliet Hazeltine (1 above); III–William Reynolds (*d* infancy); IV–Mary A. (*m* William M. Hannay).
1–*m* Oct. 27, 1886, William Van Zandt Cox (June 12, 1852-July 24, 1923; son of Col. Thomas Jefferson Cox, see Vol. III, p. 441); B.A., Ohio Wesleyan, '74, M.A., 1884 (LL.D., 1919, Phi Beta Kappa); admitted to Ohio bar, 1877; removed to Washington, 1879; chief clerk U.S. Nat. Mus., 1886-1901; pres. Second Nat. Bank, 1901-14; held many offices in financial and civic orgns.; mem. Washington Bd. of Edn., 1906-11, pres. 1910-11; trustee Howard U.; chmn. Selective Service Bd., D.C., 1917-19; issue: 1–Emery, *b* Washington, May 23, 1888; U. of Mich., 1912; marine engineer; *m* June 5, 1914, Dagny L. Nelson, of N.D. (issue: Emery, Jr., *b* Mar. 6, 1916; Harold Nelson, *b* Oct. 20, 1918; William Van Zandt, II, *b* Nov. 7, 1923); resides Norfolk, Va.; 2–Hazel Van Zandt, *b* Washington, Feb. 14, 1890; *m* June 16, 1917, Charles O. Parks, of Washington (issue: Dorothy Whitcomb, *b* Aug. 10, 1918; Charles O., Jr., *b* Aug. 16, 1920; William Van Zandt, *b* Aug. 29, 1924); resides St. Petersburg, Fla.; 3–Theodore Sullivan, *b* "Emery Place," Brightwood, D.C., Aug. 17, 1894; historian; capt. U.S.F.A., A.E.F.; sometime instr. of law, U. of Va.; prof. and head of School of Jurisprudence, Coll. of William and Mary, Va.
1–Charter mem. D.A.R. and past chapter regent; former nat. pres. D.F.P.A.; succeeded mother on bd. of lady managers, Washington City Orphan Asylum, 1904, First Directress from 1916 (an office first held by Dolly Madison).

1–**SULLIVAN, Elizabeth Denison Cox (Mrs. Theodore G.),** *b* Zanesville, O., Feb. 3, 1854.
5–David **Sullivan** (*d* 1784), served in N.J. troops and Cont. Line in Am. Rev.; *m* Jane– (*d* 1776);
4–Judge Samuel (1773-1853), pioneer in Ohio, 1802; settled at Zanesville, 1809; judge Ct. Common Pleas; mem. Ohio Senate; treas. of Ohio; *m* Mary Freeman (1773-1863; Lt. Samuel[5], served in Del. horse troop in Am. Rev.);
3–Maria Matilda (1801-85), *m* 1822, Hon. Ezekiel Taylor **Cox** (1795-1873); see Vol. III, p. 440;
2–Col. Thomas Jefferson (2 below).
8–Gerret Dircksen **Kroesen** (*d* 1680), from Holland; patented land on S.I., 1677; *m* 1660, Neeltje Jans;
7–Dirck (bap. 1662-will probated 1731), *m* 1684, Elizabeth Kregier, of S. River, Del.;
6–Gerret (ca. 1685-1767), mem. Richmond Co. militia, 1729; *m* ca. 1710, Arientje Nevius (1690-1774; Cornelius[7], of S.I., *m* 1683, Agatha, dau. Joris J. Bowman, of "The Ferry," Brooklyn; Johannes[8], ed. Leyden U., from Holland as trader and mcht., 1650, *m* 1653, Arientje Bliejck, of Batavia, E. Indies);
5–Lt. Johannes (1729-1812), 2d lt., 4th Associators, Bucks Co. Militia, Am. Rev.; *m* Jannetje Nevins;
4–Elizabeth (1764-1849), *m* 1796, John **Van Zandt** (1769-1846); see Vol. III, p. 440;
3–James Monroe (1802-30), farmer; freighted products of his farms by flatboat to New Orleans; *m* 1822, Elizabeth Denison (1797-1884); see Vol. III, p. 440;
2–Lucy Ann (2 below).
10–Wolfert Gerretsen **Van Couwenhoven** (*d* 1662; son of Gerret); from Holland to New Netherlands, 1630 as manager for the vast estates of the Patroon Van Rensselaer, of Rensselaerwick, at Albany; later manager of "Bouwery No. 6" at New Amsterdam; bought lands from the Indians, 1636, and obtained patents for them from Gov. Van Twiller, these three "flats" were later known as Flatlands and New Amersfoort; *m* Neltje– (*d* 1661);
9–Gerret Wolfersen (*b* 1610), from Holland with his father to L.I., 1630; magistrate; *m* Altie Lambertse Cool (Cornelis Lambertse[10], a freeholder of Gowanus, 1639, patentee of Breuckelen, 1642, magistrate, 1644-45, etc.);
8–Marretje Garretse (*b* 1643), *m* ante 1664, Coerte Stevense **Van Voorhees** (1637-post 1702);
7–Alberte Coerte (will proved, 1748), of Flatlands and Utrecht; mil. service, 1691; *m* 4 times;
6–Margaret Albertse (ca. 1700-1784-85), widow of Peter Stoothoof, *m* 1728, David **Nevins** (bap. 1702), of Middlebush, N.J.;
5–Jannetje (1732-1816), *m* Lt. Johannes **Kroesen** (5 above);
4–Elizabeth, *m* John **Van Zandt** (4 above);
3–James Monroe, *m* Elizabeth Denison (3 above);
2–Lucy Ann (1828-1914), see Vol. III, p. 440, for portrait; *m* 1846, Col. Thomas Jefferson **Cox** (1823-66); see Vol. III, p. 441, for portrait and biography.
1–*m* Jan. 4, 1879, Theodore Greene Sullivan, *b* Zanesville, O. (Nov. 7, 1848-Nov. 20, 1925); son of Col. John H. Sullivan and g.son of Judge Samuel Sullivan (above); issue: 1–Algernon Sidney (July 17, 1880-*d* infancy); 2–Ethel Van Zandt (June 28, 1881-Sept. 28, 1927); Wellesley, '05; served in World War with A.R.C., the French Commn. and Hoover Commn. to Czecho-Slovakia; in exec. dept., Children's Bureau, 1917-19; decorated by City of Lyons, France, and twice by Czecho-Slovakian Commn.; *m* Dec. 17, 1919, Jean Paul Gaston Darrot, of Paris, served in World War; 3–Aileen (Dec. 25, 1887-*d* aet. 8); 4–Theodore Greene, Jr. (qv);
1–Grad. Putnam Female Sem., Zanesville, O., '75. Mem. C.D.A., D.F.P.A., D.A.R., Soc. N.E. Women, I.A.G. Organized and carried on unit for A.R.C. (awarded D.S.M. for work during World War). Summer place: Brookdale, Zanesville, O. Residence: Montclair, N.J.

1–**SULLIVAN, Theodore Greene, Jr.,** *b* Montclair, N.J., Apr. 19, 1895.
10–Mother **Phinney** (*d* 1650, aet. 80), from Eng. with two sons John and Robert, aet. ca. 68; spoken of as the oldest woman in the colony;

BENJAMINE PHINNEY (b Barnstable, Mass., June 10, 1744-d Lexington, Mass., Jan. 27, 1843).

9-John, came to Plymouth, 1638; freeman, 1639; removed to Barnstable; *m* 1st, Christiana-(*d* 1649);
8-John (1638-will dated 1718), served in Great Swamp Fight, King Philip's War, 1675; *m* 1664, Mary Rogers (1644-77; Joseph[9], *m* Hannah-; Thomas[10], Mayflower Pilgrim, qv);
7-Benjamine (*b* 1682), *m* 1709, Martha Crocker;
6-Zaccheas (*b* 1720), *m* Susanna Davis;
5-Benjamine (1744-1843), see portrait; *m* 1768, Susanna Morse (ca. 1747-1829; Capt. Theodore[6], master mariner of Falmouth, Mass., *m* Thankful [or Susanna?] Croocker);
4-Patience (1782-1844), as Widow Greene, *m* 2d, 1813, Samuel **Stowers** (1798-post 1866; John[5], sgt.-maj., 15th Mass. Regt., 1777, ens., 1778, lt., 1779, adj., transferred to 5th Mass. Regt., 1781; *m* Abigail [Stearns] Fullerton, dau. of Thomas Stearns);
3-Deidamia (1817-78), *m* 1845, Col. John H. **Sullivan** (1808-88; Judge Samuel[4], *m* Mary Freeman; David[5]);
2-Theodore Greene (2 below).
9-William **Crocker** (qv);
8-Joseph (*b* 1654-will dated 1720/21), of West Barnstable; freeman, 1678; sgt. of mil. co., "an officer of honor"; *m* 1677, Temperance Bursley (John[9], qv);
7-Martha (*b* 1689), *m* Benjamine **Phinney** (7 above).
2-Theodore Greene **Sullivan** (1848-1925), *m* 1879, Elizabeth Denison Cox (qv for other lineages).
1-*m* Apr. 27, 1918, Helen Louise McAdams, Dec. 18, 1898 (divorced Dec. 30, 1925); dau. of William Terry McAdams; issue: 1-Theodore Greene, 3d, *b* Newtonville, Mass., Dec. 10, 1922.
1-*m* 2d, June 19, 1926, Frances Louise Hoeg, *b* Brooklyn, N.Y., Feb. 21, 1904; dau. of Frederick Francis Hoeg; issue: 1-Barbara Aileen, *b* Brooklyn, Aug. 30, 1928; 2-Gertrude Van Zandt, *b* Brooklyn, Nov. 29, 1929.
1-B.S., Rutgers, '15; advanced degree work at M.I.T. Rubber technologist and chem. engr.; pres. Vansul, Inc., New York. During World War with E. I. du Pont de Nemours Co. in charge of mfg. high explosives, gases, etc. Mem. Chi Phi, Am. Chem. Soc., S.M.D. Mason. Residence: 179 Vreeland Av., Rutherford, N.J.

1-**TAYLOR, Margaretta Van Tuyl Metcalf (Mrs. George W.),** *b* Montgomery, Ala., Feb. 7, 1856.
9-Michael (Metcalfe) **Metcalf** (qv);
8-Michael (*b* Eng., 1620-1654), freeman, Dedham, Mass., 1642; *m* 1644, Mary Fairbanks (ca. 1620-1684; Jonathan[9], qv);
7-Dea. Jonathan (1650-1727), *m* 1674, Hannah Kenrick (*d* 1731; John[8]);
6-Jonathan, *m* 1701, Mary Avery (William[7]);
5-William, *m* 1739, Abigail Edwards (Rev. Timothy[6]);
4-Eliphalet, of Lebanon, Conn.; *m* 1775, Mary West (Joshua[5]);
3-William (*b* 1776), *m* 1808, Margaretta Van Tuyl;
2-Eliphalet Henry (1809-86), planter; *m* 1834, Mary Jones Bonner (*b* 1814; g.dau. William Green, capt. Am. Rev.); issue: I-William Van Tuyl (1835-92; served C.S.A.); II-Hamilton Bonner (1836-1922; *m* Anna Howard); III-John (*b* 1845; with Forrest's cav., C.S.A.; *m* Cora A. Farley); IV-Lucie Green (1848-1925; C.D.A., D.A.R., U.D.C.; *m* Henry Crommelin); V-Margaretta Van Tuyl (1 above).
1-*m* Jan. 13, 1881, George Washington Taylor, *b* Montgomery, Ala., Jan. 16, 1849; served in C.S.A.; mem. Congress, 1897-1915; son of Edward Fisher Taylor, *m* Anne Sewell Trezevant, of Columbia, S.C.; issue: 1-Mary, *b* Montgomery, Ala., Dec. 28, 1881; *m* June 26, 1907, Hughes Turnley Reynolds, of Rome, Ga. (issue: John H.; Margaretta Metcalf); 2-Edward, *b* Demopolis, Ala., Aug. 13, 1884; *m* June 28, 1924, Isabelle Stone (issue: Isabelle; Edward); 3-Lucie, *b* Montgomery, Ala., Feb. 15, 1887; *m* Oct. 14, 1909, W. Brown Morton (issue: Brown; Edward; Lucie); 4-Anne, *b* Demopolis, Ala., Dec. 23, 1888; *m* Jan. 30, 1918, William McRea Ford (issue: William McRea); 5-George Margaretta, *b* Montgomery, Sept. 27, 1892; *m* June 16, 1921, Howard M. Douglas (issue: Margaretta Van Tuyl).
1-Mem. C.D.A., U.D.C. Residence: 398 9th St., Brooklyn, N.Y.

1-**TODD, Sallie Oliphant (Gemmill) Mitchell (Mrs. William D.),** *b* Cresson, Pa., Nov. 16, 1858.
5-John **Gemmill,** from Scotland, settled in Mifflin Co., Pa.; bought a farm nr. Lewistown which he named "Kilmarnoch," after the place of his birth; *m* 1758, Elizabeth Porter;
4-Zachariah (1772-1812), *m* 1803, Mary Mytinger;
3-John (1806-76), *m* 1830, Rose Ann Jackson (1810-83);
2-Zachariah (2 below).
6-George Ludwig **Mytinger,** from Germany to Phila., 1754; *m* 1749, Margaretha Engleharat;
5-John Jacob (1750-93), served in Am. Rev.; signature on original rolls of Order of Cincinnati; *m* 1779, Elizabeth Matthieu;
4-Mary (1782-1860), *m* Zachariah **Gemmill** (4 above).
5-Andrew **Oliphant** (*d* 1790), in French and Indian War and Am. Rev.; *m* Ann Hughes;
4-John (1759-1836), *m* 1794, Sarah McGinnis (1778-1842);
3-Sarah Hughes (1811-90), *m* 1833, Alfred **Stewart** (1806-88);
2-Caroline (1836-1921), *m* 1858, Zachariah **Gemmill** (1831-99); issue: I-Sallie Oliphant (1 above); II-Rose (*b* Apr. 24, 1863; *m* 1883, Theodore Messner); III-Mary Stewart (*b* July 18, 1866; *m* 1891, John Roy; *m* 2d, 1929, George E. Southard); IV-Alfred Breston (June 4, 1870-Nov. 4, 1896); V-Bertha Talbot (*b* Sept. 16, 1873; *m* 1909, Marshall Parshall).
1-*m* Jan. 8, 1877, Willis Alvin Mitchell (Apr. 19, 1853-Feb. 15, 1897); son of John Hutchinson Mitchell; issue (all *b* Warren, Pa.): 1-Willis Gemmill, *b* Sept. 30, 1877; U.S.N.A., '99; served ens. to capt. U.S.N., resigned 1919; cadet U.S.N., Cuban blockade in Spanish-Am. War; with Atlantic Fleet during World War; *m* Sept. 3, 1906, Elizabeth Lapham Wakeman (issue: Willis Alvin, *b* July 15, 1911; Helen Annette, *b* Sept. 17, 1913; Elizabeth Lapham, *b* Apr. 28, 1916); 2-John (1880-87); 3-Harry Luzerne, *b* 1883; *m* 1908, Edith M. Davidson (issue: Charles Davidson, *b* Mar. 20, 1910; Caroline Stewart, *b* Mar. 5, 1912; Margaret Davidson, *b* Jan. 15, 1914).
1-*m* 2d, Apr. 3, 1913, William Dwight Todd, *b* Corning, N.Y., Apr. 21, 1854; son of Luzerne Todd.
1-Mem. D.A.R., U.S.D. 1812, Chautauqua Lit. and Scientific Circle, A.L. Auxiliary. Presbyn. Missionary Soc. Clubs: Woman's, Blue Stocking. Residence: 208 Conewango Av., Warren, Pa.

1-**TOMPKINS, Zula Smith (Mrs. Frederick Jay),** *b* Rockland Co., N.Y., May 31, 1869.
8-Samuel **Boardman** (qv);
7-Daniel (1658-1725), of Wethersfield, Conn.; *m* 1683, Mary Wright (1664-1746; Samuel[8]; Thomas[9]);
6-Timothy (1700-53), *m* 1721, Hannah Crane (1702-60; Israel[7]; Benjamin[8]);
5-John (1735-1817), of Rensselaerville, N.Y.; served in French and Indian War; *m* 1760, Lydia Dean (John[6]; John[7]; James[8]; Walter[9]);
4-Timothy (1764-1825), *m* 1789, Ruth Elliott (1771-1844);
3-Aurelia Caroline (1807-66), of Westerlo, Albany Co., N.Y.; *m* 1829, Caleb Haight **Smith** (1808-90; Jacob[4]; Daniel[5]);
2-Harvey Salem (2 below).
9-Rev. Johannes Theodorus **Polhemus** (*d* 1676), from Holland via Brazil, settled at New Amsterdam, N.Y., 1654; minister in Brooklyn; *m* Catharina Van Werven;
8-Theodorus (*d* 1722), of Jamaica, L.I.; magistrate; *m* 1677, Aertje Gysbertse (Teunis[9]);
7-Teunis (*d* 1743), *m* Sarah Emans (Andrew[8]);
6-Theodorus (*b* 1720), *m* 1741, Margrietje Remsen (*b* 1722; Aert[7]; Abraham[8]);
5-Abraham (1755-1831), of Rockland Co., N.Y.; soldier 2d Regt., Orange Co. Militia during Am. Rev.; *m* 1st, Margrietje Lydecker (1759-1801);
4-Theodorus (1795-1859), of Clarkstown, N.Y.; *m* 1817, Elizabeth DeClark (1798-1879; Daniel[5]; Jacobus[6]);
3-Jacob (1819-1900), of Rockland Co., N.Y.; *m* 1843, Catherine Sar Vant (1823-96; Peter[4]; Abraham[5]);
2-Leah Louise (*b* 1846), *m* 1868, Harvey Salem **Smith** (1840-1922), of Westerlo and Yonkers, N.Y.; issue: I-Zula (1 above); II-Aurelia (*b* 1870); III-George Boardman (*b* and *d* 1872); IV-Clara Louise (*b* 1875); V-Lloyd Lyman (*b* 1878); VI-Harry Lewis (*b* and *d* 1880).
1-*m* May 12, 1891, Frederick Jay Tompkins, *b* Harrison, N.Y., Apr. 26, 1868; son of William E. Tompkins; issue (all *b* Yonkers, N.Y.): 1-Fred Leslie, *b* Aug. 4, 1895; chief yeoman, 3d naval dist., U.S.N.R.F.; active duty July 12, 1917-May 12, 1919; mem. A.L.; *m* Apr. 26, 1919, Leah Tennie, dau. of Lewis Worster Munson (issue: Robert Frederick, *b* 1920; Richard Leslie, *b* 1922); 2-Edith Imogene and 3-Elsie Louise (twins), *b* Dec. 24, 1896; both D.A.R.; 4-Zula Viola, *b* Oct. 12, 1898; D.A.R.; 5-Percy Freeman, *b* Mar. 10, 1901; *m* Nov. 8, 1923, Dorothy Susan, dau. of John Cullen (issue: Percy Freeman, Jr., *b* 1924; Frederick Jay, II, *b* 1926).
1-Mem. D.A.R., I.A.G. (life), N.Y. State Hist. Assn. (life), Westchester Co. Hist. Soc., A.L. Residence: 560 N. Broadway, Yonkers, N.Y.

1-**TRUAX, Charles Frederick,** *b* Sauk Center, Minn., Oct. 19, 1869.
8-Philippe (du Trieux) **Truax** (qv);
7-Isaac (*b* 1642), one of original settlers of Schenectady, defender at time of massacre in 1690, and escaped to the fort at Albany with news of the battle; *m* Maria Williamse Brouwer;
6-Abraham (1683-1770), of Schenectady; began to write name Truax; *m* 1711, Christina de la Grange (*d* 1773);
5-Isaac (*b* 1715), served in early wars; veteran soldier in Schenectady, 1782, when dinner was given in Gen. Washington's honor; *m* 1741, Angeltje Beck (1715-58);
4-Johannes Isaacse (1749-1825), Ogdensburg, N.Y.; participated in battles of Bennington and Fort George during Am. Rev.; drowned in St. Lawrence River, 1825, while fishing; *m* Annatje van der Heyden;
3-Daniel van der Heyden (1798-1870), to Hastings, Minn., 1854; *m* ca. 1825, Sarah Wright (1807-86; Samuel[4], *m* Mary-);
2-James Wright (2 below).
9-Matthys **van der Heyden**;
8-Jacob Tyssen (Mathyssen), (*b* 1680 or 90), of Albany, N.Y.; mem. Burgher Militia Corps of New Amsterdam, 1653; *m* 1655, Anna Hals (*d* ca. 1691);
7-Dirk (ca. 1662-1738), fire master, assessor, constable, asst. alderman of 1st Ward, Albany; purchased present site of Troy, N.Y., 1707; *m* Rachel Jochemese Keteluyn (*d* 1754; Jochem[8], *m* Anna-);

CHARLES FREDERICK TRUAX

6-Jochem (bap. 1700-1746), *m* 1st, 1725, Anna Keteluyn (bap. 1690; Daniel[7], *m* Debora Viele);
5-Dirk Jochemse (bap. 1725), *m* 1754, Margarita Kittle;
4-Annatje (bap. 1754-1835), *m* Johannes Isaacse **Truax** (4 above);
3-Daniel van der Heyden, *m* Sarah Wright (3 above);
2-James Wright (1833-1902), served in Co. A, 2d Wis. Cav., 4 yrs., Civil War; wounded in battle; drove a Red River cart until 1875, when he began ry. work in which he continued actively until 1900; co. judge Williston, N.D.; *m* 1st, Chloe Anna Wheeler (*b* 1842); *m* 2d, 1875, Rose Belle (Colby) Stone (1846-95); issue (1st marriage): I-Ida (*m* William Temple); II-Minnie (*m* Arthur Fisher); III-Charles Frederick (1 above); issue (2d marriage): I-Frank Gordon (*d* infancy); II-Joseph Hentzelman (*b* 1888; *m* Abbie Johnson, *d*); III-Thura Helen (*b* 1886; *m* John E. Hires).
1-*m* June 28, 1901, Martha Dalziel Gibb, *b* London, Ont., Nov. 7, 1874; dau. of William Gibb, *m* Katie Carter, from Scotland to N.J., later to Lake Park, Minn., to Minot, N.D., 1886; issue (all *b* Minot, N.D.): 1-Charles Abraham, *b* June 30, 1903; 2-William Raymond, *b* May 18, 1905; 3-Theodore Gibb, *b* May 19, 1907.
1-Engaged in ry. work with his father, until 1889; mem. firm of Truax & Colcord, publishers of The Independent (weekly), Minot, N.D. Also engaged in cattle business. Pres. Minot Bd. Edn. Mason (K.T.). Presbyterian. Republican. Residence: Minot, N.D.

1-**TRUE, Gertrude Adelaide Reilly (Mrs. Dwight),** *b* at Somerville, Mass., May 12, 1875.
10-Henry **Adams** (qv);
9-Joseph (1626-94), *m* 1650, Abigail Baxter (1634-92);
8-Capt. John (1661-1702), *m* Hannah Webb (1665-ante 1694);
7-Samuel (1689-1747/48), *m* 1712, Mary Fifield (1694-post 1740);
6-Samuel (1722-1803), B.A., Harvard, 1740, M.A., 1743; mem. Legislature, justice, selectman; dea. Old South Ch.; "signer"; gov. of Mass.; statesman; "father of the Am. Rev."; *m* 1st, 1749, Elizabeth Checkley (1725-57; Rev. S.[7]);

5–Hannah (1756-1821), *m* 1781, Capt. Thomas **Wells**, officer in Am. Rev.;
4–Samuel Adams (1787-1840), *m* Margaret Gibbs, dau. of Maj. Gibbs, aide to Washington;
3–Catherine, *m* 1848, Gilbert H. **Reilly**, of Augusta;
2–John Adams (*b* 1849), lawyer, Boston; *m* 1874, Jeannie Adelaide Osborne (1855-95); *m* 2d, Myrta Green; issue (1st marriage): I–Gertrude (1 above); II–Mabel Wells (*b* 1877; *m* Frank Williams); III–Samuel Adams (1880-1911; *m* Hilda Grass); IV–Josephine May (*b* 1883; *m* Foster Sanborn Nims); V–Lucy Eugenia (*b* 1890; *m* Archibald Hector Robertson).
1–*m* June 15, 1898, Dwight True, *b* Chicago, Ill., June 22, 1873; son of Charles S. True, of Chicago; issue: 1–Dorothy, *b* Chicago, Mar. 29, 1899; U.Mich., 1921 (Eta Chapter Chi Omega); *m* June 16, 1923, Albert E., son of George Schoerger, of Pt. Clinton, O. (issue: Alan True, *b* 1926); 2–Marion, *b* Phila., Pa., June 14, 1901; U.Mich., 1922 (Eta Chapter Chi Omega); *m* Sept. 23, 1922, Eugene Harbeck (issue: Lawrence True, *b* 1924).
1–Mem. D.A.R., I.A.G., Detroit Hist. Soc. Universalist. Republican. Residence: 2676 Glendale Av., Detroit, Mich.

MELVILLE S. WADHAM

1–**WADHAM, Melville Samuel,** *b* Goshen, Conn., Dec. 20, 1846.
8–John (Wadhams) **Wadham,** from Eng., settled at Wethersfield, Conn., 1650; *m* Susannah–, a French girl;
7–John (1655-1718), *m* 1682, Hannah Bidwell (1658-96);
6–Noah (1695-1783), Goshen, Conn.; *m* 2d, 1718, Anne Hurlbut (1701-62);
5–Jonathan (1730-1812), *m* 1754, Judith Howe (1730-1813);
4–Moses (1759-1823), *m* 1783, Anne Collins (1762-1853; Cyprian[5], Am. Rev.);
3–Samuel (1786-1862), of Goshen; *m* 1812, Olive Towner (1782-1858);
2–Norman Towner (1813-82), wrote name Wadhams; woodworker, builder and wheelwright; *m* 1838, Mary Gillett (1815-50); *m* 2d, 1851, Mary R. Whittlesey (1820-77); issue (1st marriage): I–Delphene Elizabeth (1839-1922; *m* Herman C. Norris, *d* 1872); II–Melville Samuel (1 above); issue (2d marriage): I–Erwin Ray (1855-1928; *m* Amy Tuttle, *d* 1926); II–Frederic Eugene (1857-1911; *m* Harriet Beardsley, *d* 1930).
1–*m* Feb. 25, 1868, Sarah Jane Bassett, *b* Sandisfield, Mass., Dec. 11, 1848; desc. Gov. Bradford of Mass.; D.A.R.; dau. of Joseph Hamilton Bassett, of Norfolk, Conn.; issue: 1–Bertha Aurelia, *b* Torrington, Conn., Mar. 27, 1869; *m* May 18, 1891, Warner G. Brooke, son of George Brooke, of West Haven, Conn. (issue: George M.; Olive Ray; Walter C.); 2–Ernest Winfield, *b* Lee, Mass., Mar. 12, 1871; *m* Oct. 23, 1895, Virginia, dau. of E. L. Pettigrew, of Groton, Conn. (issue: Mildred Aurelia, *b* Oct. 19, 1896); 3–Arthur Wellesley, *b* Lee, Dec. 23, 1872; *m* Sept. 23, 1903, Olive M. W., dau. of Charles Bullivant, of New Haven (issue: Ruth Olive, *b* May 25, 1905); 4–Willis Melville (Mar. 10, 1875-Sept. 21, 1911); 5–Harold Earle, *b* West Haven, Conn., Oct. 18, 1881; *m* May 11, 1902, Mary Vaughan Keith.
1–Country store, 1864; gen. agent, sundries, life and fire ins., 1867-78; bookkeeper, etc., 1878-91; shipping clerk, since 1891. Served in Civil War, Jan.-May 1865. Mem. S.A.R., I.A.G., G.A.R., Patriotic Sons of America. Episcopalian. Democrat. Residence: 613 Washington Av., West Haven, Conn.

1–**WANNAMAKER, J(ohn) Skottowe,** *b* St. Matthews, S.C., Sept. 25, 1869.
12–Rev. Peter **Bulkeley** (qv);
11–Dorothy, *m* Thomas **Lord** (qv);
10–Richard (1610-62), *m* Sarah Graves;
9–Richard (1636-85), *m* 1665, Mary Smith (Henry[10], *m* Anne, dau. of William Pyncheon, qv);
8–Richard, *m* Abigail Warren;
7–Epaphras (*b* 1709), *m* Hope Phillips;
6–Hope (1736-99), *m* 1754, Amasa **Jones**;
5–Samuel Phillips (1759-1836), *m* Jane Bruce (Donald[6], *m* Margaret Lockhart);
4–Margaret Lockhart, *m* George Elmore **Salley** (1788-1828), capt. War 1812; state senator; for Salley lineage see Vol. III, p. 466;
3–Jane Bruce (*b* 1810), *m* Rev. Lucius **Bellinger** (*b* 1806);
2–Eleanor Margaret (1835-1900), *m* 1856, Capt. Francis Marion **Wannamaker** (1835-90), lawyer, St. Matthews, S.C.; capt. C.S.A.; for issue and other lineages see Vol. III, p. 466.
1–*m* June 24, 1896, Lillian Bruce Salley (qv for issue).
1–Banker and planter. Began as ry. agt. aet. 15; pres. St. Matthews Nat. Bank; pres. Banks & Wimberly Co., Calhoun Agrl. & Investment Co.; extensively engaged in farming. Writer, lecturer and economist (see Who's Who in America). Chmn. Bd. of Commrs. for formation of Calhoun Co., S.C. Mem. Am. Cotton Assn. (pres. since 1917), S.C. Bankers Assn. (pres. 1917-18), Farmers and Tax Payers League (pres.). Pres. S.C. State Dem. Conv. Mason, K.P. Mem. bd. dirs. Chicora Coll. (Columbia, S.C.), Roosevelt Mil. Acad., West Englewood, N.J. Residence: St. Matthews, S.C.

1–**WANNAMAKER, Lillian Bruce Salley (Mrs. John Skottowe),** *b* Orangeburg, S.C.
7–James **Bruce** (desc. family of Robert the Bruce), from Eng. to Va., ca. 1715; agent for Gov. Spotswood, 1710-22; *m* a relative of Anne Butler Brayne, wife of Gov. Spotswood; and thru:
5–Donald (*b* ca. 1742-living 1790), *m* 1767, Margaret Lockhart (1745-living 1790);
4–Jane (ca. 1768-1802), *m* 1787, Samuel Phillips **Jones** (1759-1836);
3–Margaret Lockhart (1788-1861), *m* George Elmore **Salley** (1788-1828);
2–Thomas Bennett (2 below).
8–Ephraim **Mikell** (1661-ca. 1728), from Eng. with Colony of Lord Cordrosa to Port Royal, S.C., 1682; settled at Edisto Island, S.C.; *m* Martha Sealey;
7–Ephraim, *m* Anne Scott;
6–John (1718-64), *m* Anne Fickling;
5–Ephraim, *m* Abigail Jenkins;
4–Elizabeth, *m* 2d, ca. 1802, Mungo **Mackay** (said to have been son of Eric Mackay, Lord Reay of Scotland);
3–George Chisolm, *m* Abigail Martha Jenkins (see Vol. III, p. 467);
2–Annie Chisolm (1837-1910), *m* Thomas Bennett **Salley** (1826-93), of Orangeburg, S.C. (for issue see Vol. III, p. 467).
1–*m* June 24, 1896, John Skottowe Wannamaker (qv); issue (all *b* St. Matthews, S.C.): 1–Lillian Mackay (May 9, 1897-May 2, 1898); 2–Francis Marion, *b* Sept. 24, 1898; Duke U., '19; 2d lt. in World War; *m* Nov. 10, 1923, Laurie Emily, dau. of Thomas Branson Moore, of Trenton, S.C.; 3–Jannie Bruce, *b* Jan. 4, 1900; Chicora Coll., '20; *m* June 30, 1921, John Blanton, son of Dr. George W. Belk (issue: Lillian; John B., Jr.; Jane Bruce; Bar-

bara Ella); 4–Thomas Salley (Sept. 9, 1902-July 23, 1903); 5–Ella Salley, *b* Feb. 26, 1904; Chicora Coll., '25; *m* May 23, 1925, William Lambert DePass, III, of Camden, S.C. (issue: William Lambert, IV; John Skottowe Wannamaker); 6–Frances Margaret, *b* Dec. 20, 1905; Chicora Coll., '27; *m* June 2, 1927, William Herbert, son of William Patterson Smith, of Clover, S.C.
1–Mem. D.A.R., U.D.C. Residence: St. Matthews, S.C.

1–**WARD, Henry Galbraith,** *b* New York, N.Y., Apr. 19, 1851.
7–William **Ward** (qv);
6–William (1649-97), of Sudbury and Marlborough; *m* 1679, Hannah (Brigham) Eames (1650-1719; Thomas[7], from Eng., to Cambridge, Mass., 1635, *m* Mercy Hurd);
5–Col. Nahum (1684-1754), sailor; Boston mcht.; militia officer; a founder of Shrewsbury; lawyer; 8 yrs. rep. Gen. Ct.; judge Ct. Common Pleas; *m* Martha How (1687-1755; Daniel[6], *m* Elizabeth Kerley);
4–Maj. Gen. Artemas (1727-1800), see portrait and biography; *m* 1750, Sarah Trowbridge;
3–Thomas Walter (1758-1835), of Shrewsbury; was on guard at Manchester, Vt., at time of Battle of Bennington; was mem. of cav. regt. which took part in the suppression of Shay's Rebellion; many yrs. sheriff of Worcester Co.; moderator and treas.; justice; spl. judge Ct. Common Pleas; *m* 1782, Elizabeth Denny (1760-1846);
2–Henry Dana (2 below).
7–Thomas **Trowbridge** (qv);
6–James (1636-1717), lt. in King Philip's War; rep. Gen. Ct.; *m* 2d 1674, Margaret Jackson (1649-1727; Dea. John[7]);
5–Rev. Caleb (1692-1760), *m* 2d, 1718, Hannah Walter (*b* 1699);
4–Sarah (1724-88), *m* Maj. Gen. Artemas **Ward** (4 above);
3–Thomas W., *m* Elizabeth Denny (3 above);
2–Henry Dana (1797-1884), of Phila., Pa., and N.Y.; A.B. Harvard, 1816, A.M., 1819; Episcopal clergyman; school principal; *m* 1st, Abigail Porter Jones (*d* 1837); *m* 2d, 1842, Charlotte Galbraith (1807-87; Richard[3], of Dublin, Ireland, *m* Rebecca Allen); issue (2d marriage): I–Henry Dana Artemas (1843-51); II–Charlotte Elizabeth (1845-1923); III–Artemas (qv in genealogy of Artemas Ward, Jr.); IV–Henry Galbraith (1 above).
1–*m* Aug. 13, 1891, Mabel Marquand (Oct. 29, 1860-Nov. 23, 1896); dau. of Henry Gurdon Marquand, *m* Elizabeth Love Allen; issue: 1–Galbraith (Aug. 9, 1892-Dec. 17, 1918); A.B., Princeton, '15; served with the American Ambulance Field Service to the French armies, Dec. 1916-June 1917; O.T.C., Plattsburg, N.Y., 1917; pvt. in Co. M, 306th Regt. Inf., 77th Div., 1918, overseas, became corpl. and later scout-sgt. in charge of 26 scouts; died of pneumonia in Camp Hospital No. 9 at Château Villain; posthumously cited for gallantry in Gen. Orders No. 24 of the 77th Div., 1919, and awarded posthumously D.S.C., May 3, 1923; 2–Marquand (Dec. 9, 1894-Oct. 18, 1918); entered Princeton, class of 1917; war degree A.B., July 1918; pvt. Co. C, 312th Inf., 78th Div., May 1918; killed in action at Talma Farm, Grand Pré; posthumously cited for gallantry in Gen. Orders No. 6 of 78th Div., Mar. 17, 1919. Both are buried in the American Cemetery, R. 17, Nos. 39 and 40, Romagne-sous-Montfaucon, Meuse-Argonne.
1–A.B., U. of Pa., 1870 (Phi Beta Kappa), A.M., 1873 (LL.D., 1917). Admitted to bar, in Phila., 1873; mem. law firm of Biddle (George and A. Sydney) & Ward, Phila.; later in New York as Robinson, Bright, Biddle and Ward; U.S. circuit judge, 2d Circuit, 1907, becoming senior judge of the Circuit Court of Appeals, now resigned on a pension. Mem. S.R. Clubs: University, Century, Church (New York), University (Phila.). Residence: 1018 Madison Av., New York, N.Y.

1–**WARD, Artemas, Jr.,** *b* Philadelphia, Pa., Nov. 9, 1875.
9–Richard **Mather** (qv);
8–Rev. Increase (1639-1723), A.B., Harvard, 1656; actg. pres., rector and pres. Harvard Coll., 1685-1701; *m* Maria Cotton (*d* 1714; Rev. John[9], qv);

MAJ. GEN. ARTEMAS WARD (1727-1800), A.B., Harvard, '48, A.M., 1851; lt. col. in Ticonderoga campaign, 1758; rep. and councillor in Gen. Ct.; mem. 1st and 2d Provincial Congresses of Mass.; 1st cdr.-in-chief of the Revolutionary forces; was 1st maj. gen. under George Washington; chief justice Ct. of Common Pleas for Worcester Co., Mass.; mem. Cont. Congresses; speaker Mass. House; rep. 2d and 3d U.S. Congresses.

7–Sarah (1671-1758), *m* Rev. Nehemiah **Walter** (1663-1750), A.B., Harvard, 1684;
6–Hannah (*b* 1699), *m* Rev. Caleb **Trowbridge** (1692-1760);
5–Sarah (1724-88), *m* 1750, Maj. Gen. Artemas **Ward** (see portrait and biography);
4–Thomas Walter (1758-1835), *m* 1782, Elizabeth Denny (1760-1846);
3–Henry Dana (1797-1884), *m* 2d, 1842, Charlotte Galbraith (see their son Henry Galbraith Ward for Ward lineage);
2–Artemas (2 below).
9–John **Alden,** Mayflower Pilgrim (qv);
8–Ruth (*d* 1674), *m* 1657, John **Bass** (1632-1716; Dea. Samuel[9]);
7–Joseph (1665-1733), *m* 1688, Mary Belcher (1668-1705);
6–Elizabeth (1704-74), *m* 1724, Daniel **Henshaw** (1701-81; Joshua[7] [1672-1747]; Joshua[8] [1638-1719], from Eng. to Dorchester, Mass., 1653; William[9]);
5–Elizabeth (1737-87), *m* 1757, Samuel **Denny** (1731-1817), lt. col. at Battle of Lexington;
4–Elizabeth (1760-1846), *m* Thomas Walter **Ward** (4 above);
3–Henry Dana, *m* Charlotte Galbraith (3 above);
2–Artemas (1848-1925), of New York; publisher, advertiser and manufacturer; collector of Americana, printed and manuscript, specializing in Central Mass. and early Revolutionary; tercen. mem. N.E.H.G.S.; life mem. Bostonian Soc., Soc. Preservation of N.E. Antiquities, N.Y.G.B.S., N.E. Soc. of N.Y.; Clubs: City, Aldine, Church and a founder of the Sphinx Club; *m* Dec. 3, 1872, Rebecca Dunwoody Robinson (1843-1921; Jonathan John[3] [1788-1869], *m* 1829, Mary J. Miles, 1803-87).
1–*m* Oct. 24, 1911, Grace Morley Robinson, *b* New York, Aug. 6, 1877; dau. of Dr. Frederick C. Robinson (*b* Eng., 1845-*d* New York, 1900), *m* Susannah Lyon.
1–A.B., Harvard, '99; LL.B., U. of Buffalo, 1903; mem. law firm Everett, Clarke, Benedict & Ward; pres. King Motor Car Co., Detroit, 1915-20. Mem. N.Y. Assembly 1908,09,10,11. Mem. S.A.R., S.M.D., S.A.E.; Clubs: Harvard, City, National Arts. Summer place: Shelter Island, N.Y. Residence: 40 E. 54th St., New York, N.Y.

1–**WATERBURY, Eugene Wells,** *b* Muskegon, Mich., May 23, 1873.

9–John **Waterbury** (1621-58), from Eng., settled at Watertown, Mass., 1630; removed to Stamford, Conn., 1646; *m* 1640, Rose Lockwood;
8–John (1650-88), of Stamford; *m* Mary–;
7–David (1684-1710), *m* 1707, Waitstill Green (1685-1730);
6–David (*b* 1708), *m* 1730, Mary Boughton;
5–Daniel (*b* 1742), lt. in Am. Rev.; 1st Co. minute men, Winchester Co., N.Y.; *m* 1761, Ann Bouton (*b* 1738);
4–Daniel (1764-1847), *m* 1786, Mary Stevens (1765-1838), of Salem, N.Y.;
3–Rev. Calvin (1809-74), of Andes, N.Y.; *m* 1836, Percilla Betts;
2–Stephen (1838-81), of Otsego Co., N.Y.; 1st Ill. Cav. and 23d Ia. Inf. during Civil War; physician and surgeon; *m* 1862, Lydia Ellen Overman (1843-1901); issue: I–Frank Calvin (*b* 1866; *m* Coral P. Chaffin); II–Fannie Jane (1868-1928; *m* Clark Hoagland); III–Milton Overman (1870-1914; *m* Charlotte M. Newton); IV–Eugene Wells (1 above); V–Addie (*b* 1876; *m* Merton H. Wick).
1–*m* Aug. 19, 1901, Arreta E. Gwin, *b* Coshocton, O., Oct. 16, 1873; dau. of Thomas Gwin (Jacob^{3}); issue: 1–Theodore Eugene, *b* Des Moines, Ia., Aug. 22, 1903; ed. Columbia; pharmaceutical chemist, 1925; *m* Dec. 8, 1929, Dorothy E., dau. of Eugene P. Hermann (issue: Lois Ann); 2–Helen Belle (twin), *m* May 23, 1926, James M., son of Frank Camp; *m* 2d, Nov. 25, 1928, Harry R., son of William L. Dotts.
1–Sec., treas., v.p., Waterbury Chemical Co., Des Moines, Ia., 31 yrs. Retired. Alderman, Des Moines, 1906-08; trustee Rutgers Presbyn. Ch., New York. Corpl. Troop B, 1st U.S. Vol. Cav. ("Rough Riders"), Spanish-Am. War. Mem. S.R., U.S.W.V., Army of Santiago, Rough Riders, I.A.G., Ia. Hist. Soc. Mason (Shriner). Republican. Club: Hollow Brook Country. Summer Place: Peekskill, N.Y. Residence: 170 W. 73d St., New York, N.Y.

1–**WATKINS, Rose Burwell Griffith (Mrs. Samuel Shelton),** *b* Owensboro, Ky., June 13, 1865.
7–William **Griffith** (1660-99), from Eng., settled on Severn River, Md., on present site of Annapolis, 1675; *m* Sarah MacCubbin (*d* 1716; John^{8}, *m* Elinor Carroll);
6–Orlando (*b* 1688), *m* 1717, Katherine Howard (1700-83; John, Jr.^{7}, *m* Katherine [Greenberry] Ridgely, dau. of Col. Nicholas Greenberry);
5–Hon. Henry (1720-94), mem. Assn. of Freeman of Md.; *m* 2d, 1751, Ruth Hammond (1733-82; John^{6}, *m* Ann, dau. of Maj. Edward Dorsey; Maj. Charles^{7}; Maj. Gen. John^{8}, qv);
4–Joshua (*d* 1845), *m* 1st, 1783, Elizabeth Ridgely (1765-97; William^{5}, officer Am. Rev., *m* Elizabeth Dorsey);
3–William Ridgely (1793-1848), *m* 1st, Arria Moseley (Thomas^{4}, Am. Rev., *m* Judith, dau. of John Finney, Am. Rev.);
2–Daniel Moseley (2 below).
6–Charles **Stewart** (*b* Edinburgh, 1710-1794; of royal descent), came from Scotland, 1735, settled in Ky.; *m* Sarah–;
5–Hannah (1741-73), *m* Judge John **Harris,** patriot during Am. Rev.;
4–Elizabeth (1765-1811), *m* Thomas **Todd** (1765-1826), Am. Rev.; chief justice of Ky., 1806-07; asso. justice Supreme Ct. of U.S., 1807-26;
3–Col. Charles Stewart (1791-1871), sec. of state of Ky.; minister to Colombia and to Russia; *m* 1816, Laetitia Shelby (1799-1868; Isaac^{4}, known as the "Hero of King's Mountain"; 1st gov. of Ky., 1792-96 and again 1812-16, officer War 1812, led Ky. forces at Battle of Thames; Evan^{5}, Am. Rev., *m* Letitia Cox; Evan^{6}, qv);
2–Virginia Shelby (1836-83), *m* 1857, Daniel Moseley **Griffith** (1826-93); issue: I–Letitia Shelby (1858-1904; *m* Henry Colston Watkins); II–Virginia Todd (1859-76); III–Joshua (*b* 1861; *m* Jettie Rothchild); IV–Florence (*b* 1863; *m* Harmon Miller); V–Rose Burwell (1 above); VI–Daniel Moseley (*b* 1867; *m* Sue Taylor Herr); VII–Ruth (1869-85); VIII–Charles **Todd** (1871-82); IX–Clinton (1873-1923; *m* 1918, Sara Young); X–Mary Ridgely (1876-1901; *m* 1900, Lee Davis Ray).
1–*m* Mar. 17, 1887, Dr. Samuel Shelton Watkins, II, *b* Owensboro, Ky., Aug. 8, 1863; son of Samuel Shelton Watkins, M.D., issue: 1–Sue Roberts, *b* Owensboro, Ky., Jan. 22, 1888; *m* June 30, 1910, William Keith, son of John Wellington McCulloch (issue: William Keith, Jr.; Rose Yandell; Mary Holmes); 2–Daniel Griffith, *b* Owensboro, Aug. 12, 1889; Center Coll., '09; *m* Feb. 5, 1927, Hazel Johnston.
1–Fairmount Coll. (Tenn.), '85. Mem. C.D.A., D.C.G., H.S., D.A.R. (past state vice regent; chapter regent, 3 times, now hon. life regent), U.S.D. 1812 (past Ky. state pres.). Clubs: Woman's; Married Ladies' Reading (oldest woman's club in Ky.). Residence: 116 W. Seventh St., Owensboro, Ky.

1–**WATRES, Effie Julia Hawley (Mrs. Louis Arthur),** *b* Hartford, Pa., Aug. 29, 1851.
8–Joseph **Hawley** (qv);
7–John (1661-1729), *m* 1686, Deborah Pierson (*d* 1739);
6–Nathan, *m* 1719, Silence Mallory (1698-1747; John^{7}, *m* Elizabeth, dau. of Nathaniel Kimberly; Peter^{8});
5–Nathan (*d* 1757), *m* 1st, 1746, Sarah–;
4–John (1750-1869), *m* 1st, Mary Newton (John^{5}, *m* 1st, Mary, dau. of Stephen Miles; John^{6}; John^{7}; Roger^{8}, qv);
3–John (ca. 1782-1866), of New Milford, Pa.; *m* 1st, Merab (Andrews) Hitchcock;
2–Nathan (2 below).
9–William **Andrews** (qv);
8–Nathan (bap. 1639-1712), *m* 1st, 1661, Deborah Abbott (*d* 1672; Robert^{9}, qv);
7–Nathan (1662-1713), *m* 1st, 1686, Elizabeth Miles (*b* 1666; John^{8}, *m* Elizabeth, dau. of John Harriman; Richard^{9});
6–Daniel (*b* ca. 1692-1760), *m* 1st, Mehitable Cook (1694-1742; Samuel^{7}, *m* 2d, Mary–; Henry^{8});
5–Nathan (1714-56), *m* 2d, Ruth Beach (1722-84; Gershom^{6}, *m* Deliverance, dau. of Daniel How; Thomas^{7}; John^{8}, qv);
4–Nathan (1750-88), of Cheshire, Conn.; *m* 1772, Phebe Thompson (*b* 1753; Samuel^{5}, *m* Rachel, dau. of Nathaniel Bunnell; Joseph^{6}; Joseph^{7}; John^{8});
3–Merab (1775-1830), *m* —Hitchcock; *m* 2d, John **Hawley** (3 above).
8–Rev. Thomas (Thacher) **Thatcher** (qv);
7–Peter (*b* 1651), Milton, Mass.; *m* 1st, 1677, Theodora Oxenbridge (Rev. John^{8}; Daniel^{9});
6–Peter (1688-1744), Middleboro, Conn.; *m* 1710/11, Mary Prince (ca. 1687-1771; Samuel^{7}, *m* Mercy, dau. of Thomas Hinckley; John^{8}; Rev. John^{9});
5–Peter (1715-85), Attleboro, Mass.; *m* 1749, Bethia Carpenter (1729/30-1793; Obadiah^{6}, *m* his cousin, Bethia Lyon, dau. of Daniel Carpenter; Obadiah^{7}; William^{8}; William^{9}, qv);
4–John (1759-1841), Am. Rev.; *m* 1780, Sally Richardson (1762-1840; Daniel^{5}, *m* Sarah, dau. of Noah Reed; Stephen^{6}; William^{7}; Stephen^{8}; Samuel^{9}, qv);
3–Daniel (1791-1861), Harford, Pa.; *m* 1813, Huldah Reed;
2–Julia Emily (2 below).
9–Samuel **Richardson** (qv);
8–Stephen (1649-1717/18), *m* 2d, 1674/75, Abigail Wyman (ca. 1660-1720; Francis^{9}, qv);
7–William (*b* 1678), removed to Stoneham; *m* 1703, Rebecca Vinton (*b* 1683; John^{8}, *m* Hannah, dau. of Thomas Green; John^{9});
6–Stephen (*b* 1714), *m* 1736, Hannah Coy (*b* 1718; Caleb^{7}, *m* Mary, dau. of Abraham Wellman; Caleb^{8}; Richard^{9});
5–Hannah (*b* 1744), *m* Amos **Sweet** (1734/35-will proved 1801), Wilkes-Barre, Pa.; Am. Rev. (John^{6}; Henry^{7}; John^{8}; John^{9});
4–Elizabeth (1771-1849), *m* Abel **Reed** (1768-1851), of Harford, Pa. (Noah^{5}; Daniel^{6}; Daniel^{7}; John^{8});
3–Huldah (1795-1859), *m* Daniel **Thatcher** (3 above);
2–Julia Emily (1814-84), *m* 1839, Nathan **Hawley** (1811-63); issue: I–Sarah Elizabeth; II–Anna Miller (*b* 1845; *m* Berthold Galland); III–Effie Julia (1 above).
1–*m* May 20, 1871, Louis Arthur Watres (LL.D., Lafayette Coll.), *b* Mt. Vernon (Winton), Pa., Apr. 21, 1851; lt. gov. of Pa., 1891-95; served Pa. N.G., 1877-1909, as capt., maj. and col.; pres. George Washington Masonic Nat. Memorial Assn., 1918; (see Who's Who in America); issue (all *b* Scranton, Pa.): 1–

Harold Arthur (Apr. 23, 1879-Sept. 15, 1905), A.B., Princeton, '01; studied U.Pa., 1901-02, Columbia, 1902-03; *m* Sept. 13, 1904, Dorothy Jackson, of Englewood, N.J.; 2–Laurence Hawley, *b* July 18, 1882; A.B., Princeton, '04; LL.B., Harvard, 1907; U.S. congressman from Pa., 1923– (see Who's Who in America); capt., 108th M.G. Bn., 28th Div., later commd. maj.; wounded in action during World War; awarded D.S.C. (U.S.); 3–Lovell (Jan. 16, 1885-Jan. 4, 1888); 4–Reyburn, *b* Mar. 7, 1887; *m* June 17, 1920, Isabel Elliott (issue: Harriett Hollister, *b* Apr. 17, 1921; Louis Arthur, *b* Dec. 31, 1922).

1–Mem. Magna Charta Dames, C.D.A., D.F.P.A., H.S.A. (Pa.), D.C.G., U.S.D. 1812. Scranton Colony N.E. Women. Club: Century. Summer place: Siasconset, Mass. Residence: Elmhurst Boul., Scranton, Pa.

1–**WEHMANN, Frances Winona Coggeshall (Mrs. Hermann),** *b* Hastings, Minn, June 26, 1867.

9–Thomas **Stevens** (*d* Sept. 19, 1658), landholder, Stamford, Conn., 1649; *m* Ann–;

8–Obadiah (ca. 1649-Dec. 24, 1702), *m* Dec. 18, 1678, Rebecca Rose;

7–Thomas (1679-1774), *m* Sarah–;

6–Daniel (1711-living June 22, 1801), *m* 1733/34, Judith Webb;

5–Jacob (*b* 1747), *m* 2d, 1771, Mary Prindle;

4–Enoch (*b* 1772), town officer, Stamford, Conn., 1800; owned land Poundridge, Westchester Co., N.Y.; *m* Anna–;

3–Harriet (1803-77), *m* as his 2d wife, Frederick **Coggeshall** (1795-1863), see Vol. III, p. 473;

2–Eri (1830-1901), *m* 1859, Julia Mary Bott (1834-1921), for issue see Vol. II, p. 69.

1–*m* June 10, 1891, Hermann Diedrich Daniel Wehmann, *b* Germany, May 29, 1861; flour exporter, Minneapolis; son of Gerhard Wehmann, of Germany; issue: 1–Charles Gerhard, *b* Minneapolis, July 2, 1894; U.Pa., '19; 2d lt., Aviation Corps, U.S.A., and with A.E.F. in France, World War; *m* Oct. 11, 1922, Helen Ludlam (issue: John Coggeshall, *b* July 15, 1923); *m* 2d, Cathleen French; 2–Hermann Coggeshall, *b* Minneapolis, Jan. 22, 1898; U.Pa., '21; *m* Oct. 18, 1923, Frieda Langley, dau. of Charles Edgar Halsted, of Westfield, N.J., *m* Ella Berry (issue: Halsted, *b* Dec. 28, 1926).

1–Mem. D.A.C., D.A.R., Woman's Club, Minneapolis Museum of Fine Arts. Residence: 2100 Pillsbury Av., Minneapolis, Minn.

1–**WELLER, Reginald Heber,** *b* Jefferson City, Mo., Nov. 6, 1857.

4–George **Weller** (Nov. 10, 1757-Boston, Mass., Feb. 10, 1825), *m* Boston, Mar. 10, 1789, Abigail Copeland (*b* Braintree, Mass., Apr. 8, 1759);

3–Rev. George (*b* Boston, Nov. 15, 1790-*d* Raymond, Miss., Nov. 9, 1841), *m* Harriet Caroline Birckhead;

2–Reginald Heber (2 below).

8–Thomas **Look** (*b* Scotland 1622), removed to Lynn, Mass.;

7–Thomas (Lynn, Mass., June 6, 1646-Dec. 1725), removed to Martha's Vineyard; *m* at Nantucket, Elizabeth Bunker;

6–Samuel (Mar. 1683-Jan. 14, 1772), *m* Oct. 19, 1704, Thankful Lewis (Apr. 1684-Jan. 24, 1769);

5–Noah (*b* Tisbury, Martha's Vineyard, Nov. 27, 1719-*d* Conway, Mass., Aug. 16, 1790), *m* Hannah Holley;

4–William (Nov. 3, 1774-June 14, 1860), *m* Sallie M. Childs (July 14, 1773-Nov. 8, 1837);

3–Horace (Apr. 27, 1798-Dec. 25, 1863), *m* Dec. 7, 1821, Emma Corbett Darrow (*b* Mar. 19, 1797);

2–Emma Amanda (1830-72), *m* 1850, Rev. Reginald Heber **Weller** (1828-1902), P.E. priest (for issue see Vol. I, p. 882).

1–*m* May 18, 1886, Bessie Brown, *b* Patch Grove, Grant Co., Wis., July 23, 1863; dau. Dan Thayer Brown (*b* Middletown, Conn., Mar. 25, 1824-*d* 1865), served 1st Wis. Cav., buried Jefferson Barracks, St. Louis, Mo.; *m* 1860, Sarah Elizabeth Glover; g.dau. Benjamin Brown (*b* Conn., 1790-*d* Patch Grove, Wis., Nov. 9, 1855), War 1812, *m* 1811, Elizabeth Sizer; issue: 1–Ruth, *b* Eau Claire, Wis., Aug. 19, 1887; Wellesley, '08; *m* Apr. 16, 1912, George B. Nelson (issue: James J.; Reginald Weller; George Bliss); 2–Reginald Heber, *b* Waukesha, Wis., Aug. 21, 1889; Harvard, '10; 2d lt., inf., Nov. 1917, 1st lt., Sept. 1918; platoon cdr., intelligence officer and a.-d.-c.; overseas, Jan. 1918-Apr. 1919; *m* Feb. 29, 1928, Charlotte Calthrop; 3–Dan Brown, *b* Stevens Point, Wis., Oct. 6, 1891; U.Wis., '13; 1st lt., inf., Aug. 1917, attached to supply co., 339th Inf., served at Archangel, Russia, July 1918-July 1919; *m* Feb. 13, 1926, Florence Poppenhagen; 4–Charles Grafton, *b* Stevens Point, Apr. 8, 1895; U.Wis., '17; Rush Med. Sch., 1921; 2d lt., inf., Nov. 1917; in France, Jan. 1918-Apr. 1919; *m* Aug. 6, 1921, Esther Montague Curtis; 5–Walter Trowbridge, *b* Stevens Point, Nov. 9, 1897; U.Wis., '19; *m* Feb. 1925, Mildred Harris; 6–Horace Look, *b* Stevens Point, Jan. 18, 1901; U.Wis. '22; *m* Jan. 4, 1927, Margaret Page Moore.

1–St. John's Acad., Jacksonville, Fla., 1867-75; U.South, 1875-77; B.D., Nashotah (Wis.) Theol. Sem., 1884 (D.D., 1901), P.E. bishop of Fond du Lac (see Who's Who in America). Residence: Fond du Lac, Wis.

1–**WELSH, Blanton Charles,** *b* Columbia, Pa., June 2, 1860.

5–William **Young,** from Scotland to Windham, Conn.;

4–Samuel (1740-1810), soldier Am. Rev., captured at Ft. Washington, N.Y.; *m* Lydia Drew (*d* ca. 1813);

3–Samuel (1785-1836), *m* 1818, Elizabeth Kline (1801-41; Col. Jacob[4], of Wrightsville, Pa., *m* Elizabeth, dau. George Withers, of Lancaster, Pa.);

2–Nancy Eunice (1831-94), *m* 1850, Brig. Gen. Thomas **Welsh** (1824-63), Columbia, Pa.; enlisted as pvt. in Co. E, 2d Ky. Inf., Mex. War, 1846; capt. first co. in Lancaster Co., 1861; lt. col., 2d Pa. Vols. in Shenandoah Valley; col., 45th Pa. Vols., 1862; comd. 2d Brig., 1st Div., 9th Corps, under Gen. Reno at South Mtn. and Antietem; brig. gen. Vols., 1863; under Burnside in Dept. of Ohio and under Gen. Grant at Vicksburg; issue: I–Alice (1851-1923); II–Mary Young (1853-1927); III–Effie (1855-1916); IV–Addie (1856-58); V–Lilian, M.D. (*b* 1858); VI–Blanton Charles (1 above); VII–Thomas Annie (dau., 1863-Aug. 2, 1929).

1–*m* Oct. 2, 1885, Emilie Benson (qv for issue).

1–Grad. U.S.M.A., '82. Commd. 2d lt., 15th Inf., 1882; served 1st lt., 1st Inf., 1891; retired reëntered U.S.A. as maj., Ordnance Dept., World War, Sept. 5, 1918-Nov. 5, 1919. Mem. Aztec Soc. Residence: 24 Upper Mountain Av., Montclair, N.J.

1–**WELSH, Emilie Benson (Mrs. Blanton C.),** *b* in the Brison Homestead, Millburn, N.J., Apr. 18, 1862.

7–Dirck **Benson** (qv);

6–Johannes (1655-1715), of Beverwyck, N.Y., later at Harlem; *m* 1680, Lysbet Van Deusen (*d* 1746; Matthew A.[7], of Beverwyck, *m* Helena–);

5–Matthew (1693-1758), of Harlem and Dey St., N.Y. City; *m* 2d, 1727, Hannah (Edsall) De-Groot (John Edsall[8]);

4–Benjamin (1732-79), of Bergen Co., N.J.; soldier Am. Rev., killed by British spies; *m* 1756, Catherine DeRonde (1738-1803; Hendrick[5], of Haverstraw, N.Y., *m* Catherine, dau. Hercules Lent);

3–Benjamin (1767-1823), *m* ca. 1790, Elizabeth Craig (ca. 1776-1854);

2–Col. Benjamin Whitney (2 below).

9–Obadiah **Bruen** (1606-1680/81; son of John, of Bruen Stapleford, Co. Cheshire, Eng., *m* 2d, Anne Fox); from Eng., settled at Plymouth, 1640-41; recorder and selectman, Gloucester, Mass., and New London, Conn., 1641-66; founder of Newark, N.J., 1666; *m* 1632, Sarah–;

8–John (1646-1695?), *m* Esther Lawrence (bap. 1651-living 1695);

7–Joseph (1677-1753);

6–Ruth, *m* Caleb **Davis** (*d* 1783);

5–Elizabeth (1745-1826), *m* Aaron **Carter** (1744-1804), Am. Rev.;

4–Elizabeth Hannah (1776-1844), *m* Benjamin **Marsh** (1774-1854);

3–Elizabeth Hannah (1810-81), of Madison, N.J.; *m* David Armstrong **Brison** (1811-99), Millburn, N.J. (John[4], built Brison Homestead, Short Hills Rd., Millburn, ante 1811).

2–Col. Benjamin Whitney **Benson** (1804-77), of Old Short Hills, Millburn, N.J., and N.Y. City; mem. N.Y. militia; buried in St. Ste-

phen's Cemetery, Millburn; *m* 1825, Esther Foster (1802-56); *m* 2d, 1857, Mary Kanouse Brison (1837-64); issue (2d marriage): I–Mary Elizabeth (1859-92; *m* 1880, James Frontiss Ives); II–Benjamin Lane (1860-76); III–Emilie (1 above).
1–*m* Oct. 2, 1885, Maj. Blanton Charles Welsh (qv); issue: 1–Dr. Thomas Whitney Benson (qv); 2–Emilie Benson, *b* Ft. Sheridan, Ill., June 29, 1892; *m* June 14, 1918, Paul Felton Wiggin, of Montclair, N.J. (issue: Blanton Culver, *b* 1922; Nancy Jane, *b* 1926; Paul Benson, *b* 1929).
1–Ed. at pvt. schs. Mem. executive bd. N.J. State Consumer's League; former mem. N.J. State Commn. for the Blind. Mem. Magna Charta Dames, C.D.A., Montclair Women's Club. Residence: 24 Upper Mountain Av., Montclair, N.J.

1–**WELSH, Thomas Whitney Benson,** *b* Ft. Buford, N.D., Sept. 11, 1886.
9–Nicholas **Carter** (1629-81), from Eng. to Stamford, Conn., 1652; settled at Elizabethport, N.J., ca. 1665;
8–Nicholas (*b* ca. 1658), of Newtown, L.I.;
7–Nathaniel (*d* 1794), *m* Hannah Price;
6–Aaron (1744-1804), Am. Rev.; *m* Elizabeth Davis;
5–Elizabeth Hannah (1776-1844), *m* Benjamin **Marsh** (1774-1854);
4–Elizabeth Hannah (1810-81), of Madison, N.J.; *m* 1836, David Armstrong **Brison** (1811-99);
3–Mary Kanouse (1837-64), *m* 1857, Col. Benjamin Whitney **Benson** (1804-77);
2–Emilie (qv), *m* 1885, Maj. Blanton Charles **Welsh** (qv).
1–*m* Aug. 27, 1912, Jennie Loraine Ellis, *b* Ithaca, N.Y., May 22, 1888; A.B., Cornell, '11; dau. of Warren J. Ellis, of Ithaca.
1–A.B., Cornell, '08 (Sigma Nu, Sphinx Head, Sigma Xi), Ph.D., 1913. Research chemist. Served as capt., C.W.S., Jan. 30, 1918-Sept. 15, 1919, at Edgewood Arsenal, Md., and Washington, D.C., later capt. O.R.C. Mem. S.A.R., Am. Chem. Soc. Residence: 3630 Gardiner St., Bayside, L.I.

1–**WHITAKER, Ralph Oral,** *b* Clark Co., O., Feb. 19, 1886.
7–Jonathan **Whitaker** (1690-1763), from Eng.; settled on L.I., later in N.J.; *m* Elizabeth Jervis (Eliphalet[8]);
6–Jonathan (1723 or 26-1786), Am. Rev.; *m* Mary Miller;
5–Jonathan, removed to Ohio, ca. 1800; in War 1812; *m* Mary Mitchell;
4–Stephen (*b* 1793), *m* Hulda Skinner;
3–Jonathan (1829-64), farmer, Clemont Co., O.; served in 90th Ohio Vol. Inf., Civil War; *m* Rebecca Phillips;
2–Granville Moody (2 below).
5–John **Clemans,** *m* Abigail Higbee;
4–William, *m* Catharine Ladd;
3–Enos, *m* Mary Ann Keys;
2–Ella (*b* 1861), *m* Granville Moody **Whitaker** (*b* 1857); issue: I–Homer (*m* Mary Knowles); II–Ralph Oral (1 above); III–Benjamin Harrison (*m* Lola Boyer); IV–Leroy (*m* Gladys McCrea); V–Darmel (*m* Kittie Whalen).
1–*m* June 15, 1909, F. Edythe Horney (qv).
1–Ed. Clark's Pvt. Art Sch. Former newspaper pub.; now automobile dealer. Mason. Clubs: London Country, London Gun. Residence: 199 N. Main St., London, O.

1–**WHITAKER, F. Edythe Horney (Mrs. Ralph Oral),** *b* Jeffersonville, O., Mar. 22, 1885.
8–Jeffery **Horney** (*d* 1738), settled in Md., 1685; assisted in bldg. Friends Meeting House, eastern Md.;
7–Jeffery (*d* 1779), of Caroline Co., Md.; *m* 1735, Deborah Bainor (*d* 1791);
6–William (1752-1829), 5th Md. Regt., Am. Rev.; *m* 1772, Hannah Chipman;
5–Daniel (1786-1865), served War 1812 and Civil War; *m* 1807, Margaret Calloway (1790-1855);
4–Jefferson E. (1810-84), *m* 1832, Margaret Griffith (1812-76; Elijah[6], War 1812, *m* Susannah, dau. Abraham Rinehardt, Am. Rev.; Samuel[6], of Md., Am. Rev., *m* Mary–);
3–Forris (1833-1912), Civil War; *m* 1858, Esther Williams;
2–Frank Albert (2 below).
12–John **Tilley,** Mayflower Pilgrim (qv);
11–Elizabeth, *m* 1623, John **Howland,** Mayflower Pilgrim (qv);
10–Hope (1629-83), *m* 1646, Elder John **Chipman** (qv);
9–John (1670-1756), of Barnstable, Mass.; *m* Mary Skiff (1671-1711; Stephen[10], *m* Lydia, dau. Anthony Snow, *m* Abigail, dau. Richard Warren, qv);
8–Perez (1702-81), Sandwich, Mass.; served in colonial wars;
7–Perez (*d* 1801), *m* 1751, Margaret Manlove (*d* 1803), of Del.;
6–Hannah (*b* 1753), *m* William **Horney** (6 above).
6–Charles **Botkin** (1738-1820), from Ireland as mem. Hessian forces to Va.; deserted and joined Cont. Army; pvt., 9th Va. Regt., Am. Rev.; *m* 1782, Jemima Karl (1763-1807);
5–Jeremiah (1784-1866), *m* 1806, Anna Ellsworth;
4–Margaret (1815-95), *m* 1835, Jesse **Williams** (1806-66; Thomas[5], of Va., *m* Esther, dau. William Innes, to America, 1796);
3–Esther (1838-1911), *m* Forris **Horney** (3 above).
10–Josiah **Ellsworth** (qv); and thru:
7–Moses, served in 2d Conn. Regt., Am. Rev.; *m* Mary Hinckle;
6–Moses (1767-1833), *m* 1783, Mary Magdaline Bumgartner (1762-1853);
5–Anna (1790-1864), *m* Jeremiah **Botkin** (5 above).
7–William **Brown** (1687-1757), of Va. and N.C.; *m* Margaret Fleming;
6–Joseph (1731-1815), Guilford Co., N.C.; *m* Mary Porter;
5–Joseph (1760-1800), pvt. Am. Rev.; *m* 1781, Jemima Broyles;
4–Absolem (1795-1865), Highland Co., O.; *m* 1816, Catharine Kessinger (1797-1875);
3–David (1822-1905), *m* 1846, Nancy McDaniel (Robert[4], *m* Rebecca Reese);
2–Catharine Maria (1861-1925), *m* 1883, Frank Albert **Horney** (*b* 1859); merchant; issue: I–F. Edythe (1 above); II–Esther Laura (*b* 1885; *m* 1909, Joseph Gallagher); III–Ralph Otho (*b* 1888; *m* 1910, Audrey Porter).
1–*m* June 15, 1909, Ralph Oral Whitaker (qv).
1–Mem. S.M.D., D.A.R. (state chmn. publicity), U.S.D. 1812, O.E.S. (worthy matron). Author: History of the Horney Family. Club: Woman's (pres.). Residence: 199 N. Main St., London, O.

1–**WHITE, Walter Charles,** *b* Cleveland, O., Sept. 9, 1876-*d* Sept. 29, 1929.
9–John **Livermore** (qv);
8–Samuel (1640-90), *m* Anna Bridge;
7–Jonathan (1678-1705), *m* Rebecca Barnes;
6–Jonathan (1700-1801), *m* Abigail Fiske Ball;
5–Susanna (1740-1816), *m* Joshua **Townsend** (1742-1812); see Vol. III, p. 583;
4–Abigail (1768-1839), *m* 1788, John **Greenleaf** (1767-1842); see Vol. III, p. 583, and Vol. II, p. 252;
3–Charles Ward (1805-96), *m* 1828, Louisa Harriet Greenwood;
2–Almira Louisa (2 below).
10–John **Holbrook**;
9–Thomas, *m* Margaret Bouker;
8–Nathaniel (1677-1716), *m* Mary Morse;
7–Nathaniel (1701-74), *m* 1728, Sarah Sanger;
6–James, *m* Sybil Clark (Solomon[7]; Solomon[8]; Joseph[9]; Joseph[10]);
5–Sybil (1760-1842), *m* 1780, Jonathan **Greenwood** (1755-1821); see Vol. III, p. 583;
4–Jonathan (1786-1846), *m* Phebe Temple;
3–Louisa Harriet (1808-40), *m* Charles W. **Greenleaf** (3 above).
9–John **Howe** (qv);
8–Thomas (1655-1733), of Marlborough, Mass.; col. militia; rep. Gen. Ct.; King Philip's War; *m* 1st, 1681, Sarah Hosmer (*d* 1724);
7–Thomas;
6–Ezekiel, *m* Elizabeth Rice (Edward[7]; Samuel[8]; Edmund[9]);
5–Rebecca (*b* 1754), *m* ca. 1777, Jonathan **Temple** (1752-96), Am. Rev.; see Vol. III, p. 583;
4–Phebe (1787-1856), *m* Jonathan **Greenwood** (4 above);
3–Louisa H., *m* Charles W. **Greenleaf** (3 above);
2–Almira Louisa (1837-1900), *m* 1858, Thomas Howard **White** (1836-1914), founder and pres. White Sewing Machine Co.; for issue see Vol. III, p. 583.
1–*m* Sept. 25, 1919, Mary Virginia Saunders (see Vol. II, p. 253); issue (all *b* Cleveland, O.): 1–Ann Heron, *b* July 7, 1920; 2–Mary Greenleaf, *b* Feb. 27, 1922; 3–Virginia Harrison, and

4–Walter Charles, Jr. (twins), *b* Sept. 28, 1923, both *d* infancy; 5–Walter Harrison, *b* June 4, 1926; 6–Martha Welles, *b* Oct. 30, 1927; 7–Catherine Coryton, *b* June 20, 1929.
1–B.S., Cornell, '98 (Alpha Delta Phi). Pres. White Motor Co.; dir. Union Trust Co., Garfield Savings Bank. Was chmn. citizens' advisory bd. for motor transport, and in France, Mar. 1-June 1, 1918. Chevalier de la Legion d'Honneur. Clubs: Metropolitan, University (New York), Union, Chagrin Valley Hunt, Kirkland Country (Cleveland). Residence: "Circle W Farms," Gates Mills, O.

1–**WHITE, Emma Augusta Eaton (Mrs. Edward F.),** *b* Black River Falls, Wis., Mar. 14, 1868.
9–John **Eaton** (1595-1668), from Eng., ante 1639, settled at Salisbury, Mass., at Haverhill, 1646; *m* ca. 1618, Anne– (*d* 1668);
8–Thomas (1618-1708), *m* 2d, 1659, Eunice Singletery (1641-1715);
7–Job (1671-1717), *m* 1695, Mary Simons (*d* post 1721);
6–Thomas (1701-post 1748), Salem, N.H.; *m* 1730, Mehitable Carter (*d* post 1749);
5–John (1733-1823), Bradford, N.H.; *m* Abigail Peaslee (1734-72);
4–John (1765-1844), Newbury, N.H.; pvt., 1st Regt. from Hopkinton, N.H., 1781-84; *m* 1788, Phebe Brockway;
3–Ebenezer (1809-72), *m* 1836, Hannah Cross (1808-74; Jesse[4], *m* Anna Dow);
2–Albridge (2 below).
8–Wolston **Brockway** (1638-1717), from Eng., settled at Lyme, Conn.; *m* Hannah Briggs (*d* 1687);
7–Wolston (*b* 1667), *m* 1688, Margaret–;
6–Ephraim (1703-72), *m* 1727, Susannah Currier;
5–Capt. Jonathan (1738-1829), *m* 1757, Phebe Smith (*d* 1791);
4–Phebe (1770-1851), *m* John **Eaton** (4 above).
9–Robert **Adams** (qv);
8–Sgt. Abraham (1639-1714), of Salem and Newbury, Mass.; corpl. in militia, 1685-93; sgt., 1703; *m* 1670, Mary Pettengill (1652-1705; Richard[9], qv);
7–Dr. Matthew (1686-1755), *m* 1707, Sarah Knight (1679-1778);
6–Matthew (1709-1765?), *m* 2d, 1744, Hannah Rawlins (1726-82);
5–Benjamin (1752-1819), New London, N.H.; pvt. on "Alarm Roll," Apr. 19, 1775; *m* 1772, Judith Adams;
4–Matthew (1778-1828), Newbury, N.H.; *m* 1805, Hannah Cheney (1783-1858);
3–John Langdon (1807-86), *m* 1832, Jane Felch (1810-55);
2–Almira Louisa (2 below).
10–Stephen **Dummer**, from Eng., 1638;
9–Jane (1628-1701), *m* 1646, Henry **Sewall**;
8–Anne, *m* William **Longfellow**;
7–Anne (1684-1758), *m* 1703, Abraham **Adams**;
6–William (1706-68), *m* 1728, Elizabeth Noyes;
5–Judith (*d* 1823), *m* Benjamin **Adams** (5 above).
2–Albridge **Eaton** (1836-1922), contractor and builder; *m* 1858, Almira Louisa Adams (1839-1918); issue: I–Charles Langdon (*b* 1859; *m* 1880, Minieski Washburn, 1860-1927); II–Nellie Jane (*b* 1861; *m* 1886, John Marion Braly, *b* 1862); III–Emma Augusta (1 above); IV–John Alvin (1874-1905).
1–*m* Sept. 17, 1900, Edward Franklin White, *b* Clarksburg, Ind., May 15, 1858; son of Joel Barlow White, of Indianapolis, Ind.; issue: 1–Mira, *b* St. Paul, Minn., May 13, 1903.
1–LL.B., U.Mich., 1894 (Pi Beta Phi, Phi Delta Delta); spl. studies in lit. and history, State U. of Ia. Attorney; began practice at Creston, Ia., 1894; legal editor West Pub. Co., St. Paul, Minn., 1897-1900, and Bobbs-Merrill Co., Indianapolis, 1915-20; dep. atty. gen. of Ind., 1921-25; reported Supreme and Appellate cts. of Ind., 1925-29. Mem. D.A.R. Republican. Mem. Gen. Federation of Women's Clubs (1st v.p. and legal adviser, 1924-28), Ind. Federation of Clubs (legal adviser), Woman's Press Club, Woman's Rotary Club. Residence: 5222 E. Michigan St., Indianapolis, Ind.

1–**WHITESIDE, Daisy Lenore,** *b* Belleville, Ill., Apr. 2, 1877.
7–Davis **Stockton** (*d* 1760), from N. of Ireland to Lancaster Co., Va., removed to Goochland (now Albemarle) Co.; entered land on Rockfish and Stockton's creeks, 1739; *m* Sarah– (she *m* 2d, Samuel Arnold);
6–Richard, *m* Agnes–;
5–Margaret, *m* ante 1775, John **Pulliam** (ante 1757-1813), of St. Clair Co., Ill.; Am. Rev.;
4–Nancy (1777-1859), *m* 1797, William Lot **Whiteside** (1770-1846), see Vol. III, p. 477;
3–Joseph Ogle (1811-75), Mexican War; *m* 1st, 1833, Margaret Angeline Badgley (1814-59);
2–Thomas Asbury (2 below).
5–George **Atchison,** justice, Ct. Common Pleas; from Pa. to Ill., *m* Elizabeth–;
4–Elizabeth (*b* Eng., 1781-*d* 184–), *m* as his 1st wife, Ichabod **Badgley** (1780-1856), of Belleville, Ill. (see Vol. III, p. 477);
3–Margaret A., *m* Joseph O. **Whiteside** (3 above).
9–Robert **Royce** (*d* 1676), from Eng. in the "Francis," settled at Stratford, Conn., 1648; at New London, 1660; dep., 1661; *m* Mary Sims, or Simms;
8–Nehemiah (ca. 1635-1706), Wallingford, Conn.; *m* 1660, Hannah Morgan (1642-1706; James[9], qv);
7–Lydia (1680-1751), *m* 1703/04, Capt. Daniel **Messenger** (*b* 1683), Harwinton, Conn.;
6–Samuel, *m* Mabel Buck;
5–Roderick (twin to Andrew), (1741-1823), Jericho, Vt.; Am. Rev.; *m* 1st, 1763, Tamesia Stephens;
4–John (1771-1846), from W. Stockbridge, Mass., to Vermont, 1783; moved to Ky., 1799; to Ill. Ty., 1802; mem. Legislature; assisted in forming 1st Constn. for State of Ill.; speaker of House, 1st Ill. Gen. Assembly; surveyor; prof. mathematics, Rock Spring Sem., 1st instn. of higher education west of Alleghanies (now Shurtleff Coll.); Black Hawk War; *m* 1796, Anne Lyon;
3–Matthew Lyon (1814-65), *m* 1839, Margaret Ann Gillham (1821-89; Thomas, Jr.[4] [*d* 1829], Am. Rev.; Thomas, Sr.[5], from Ireland to S.C., Am. Rev.);
2–Olive (1848-1928), *m* 1866, Thomas Asbury **Whiteside** (1843-1919), of Belleville, Ill.; sgt. Co. I, 117th Ill. Inf., Civil War; for issue see Vol. III, p. 477.
1–Ed. Ill. State Normal Sch., and Teachers Coll., St. Louis. Mem. D.A.R. (past chapter regent). Organizer and chmn. Jr. Red Cross, Madison, Ill. Residence: "Oakdale," R. 4, Belleville, Ill.

MISS ALIENNE WIGGINS

1–**WIGGINS, Alienne,** *b* Vance Co., N.C., Dec. 19, 1886.
6–Thomas **Wiggins** (*d* 1799), granted land in Granville (now Vance) Co., N.C., 1760; patriot Am. Rev.; *m* Tabitha– (*d* ante 1764);
5–Frederick (*d* 1836), register of deeds, Granville Co., several yrs.; *m* 1775, Sarah Smith;

m 2d, 1783, Mrs. Nancye Smith Jordan (*d* post 1836), sister of 1st wife;
4–John (*d* 1838), War 1812; *m* 2d, ca. 1820, Mary Jordan;
3–James Turner (1830-1909), soldier War between the States; *m* his 1st cousin, 1859, Ellen Fowler Burroughs;
2–Thomas Frederick (2 below).
7–John **Marshall** (*d* 1782), patriot Am. Rev.; *m* Tabitha Dixon (ca. 1734-1822);
6–Mary, *m* 1775, John **Wortham** (*d* 1830), Am. Rev., *d* Warren Co., N.C. (James[7] [*d* 1770], of English descent, of Brunswick Co., Va., owned land in Prince George's Co. on the James River, Va., and in N.C.);
5–Tabitha (*d* 1855), *m* Thomas **Jordan** (*d* post 1831, Warren Co., N.C.; Arthur[6] [*d* 1793], granted 600 acres of land in Granville Co., N.C., 1757, and 590 acres, 1762, *m* Elizabeth–, *d* post 1793);
4–Mary (*d* post 1838), *m* John **Wiggins** (4 above).
5–William **Burroughs**, to N.C. from Md.; *m* 1797, in Warren Co., N.C., Agnes Van Landingham (Dawson[6], *d* 1799);
4–James (*d* 1847), *m* 1837, Lucie Jordan (*d* 1886; sister of Mary Jordan, 4 above; dau. of Thomas[5], 5 above);
3–Ellen Fowler (1841-1904), *m* James T. **Wiggins** (3 above).
6–James (Baskette, Basquette) **Baskett** (*d* 1788; son of William [*d* 1764], who settled with James on Fishing Creek, N.C., and apptd. James executor of his will); granted land in Granville Co., 1761; Am. Rev.; *m* ante 1765, Youreth– (*d* post 1788);
5–Pleasant (*d* 1837), War 1812; *m* 2d, 1810, Hixie Brown (*d* ante 1837; Archibald[6]; William[7], *m* Peggy–);
4–Joseph Bonaparte (1810-88), *m* 1832, Mary Burroughs (1809-91; William[5], 5 above);
3–Agnes (1834-1907), *m* 1858, David Wilson **Wiggins** (1827-1913; Wilson[4], not known to be related to paternal line, *m* Judith Blanks);
2–Lucy Davis (*b* 1862), *m* 1885, Thomas Frederick **Wiggins** (*b* 1860), farmer and bank dir.; issue: I–Alienne (1 above); II–Clifton (*b* and *d* 1889); III–Frederick Carl (*b* 1890; *m* Emma Martesen); IV–Arthur (*b* 1892; *m* Eliza Mabry); V–Julius (*b* 1894; *m* Mary Royster Wortham); VI–Lucy Agnes (*b* 1896; *m* Joseph Perlyman Andrew); VII–James Burroughs (*b* 1897); VIII–Irene Cullom (*b* 1899; *m* William Robert Turner); IX–Harold Furman (*b* and *d* 1904).
1–Ed. N.C. Coll. for Women and Duke U. Teacher. Mem. D.A.R. (chapter historian), U.D.C., A.L. Auxiliary, I.A.G. Baptist. Club: Woman's. Residence: 303 Chestnut St., Henderson, N.C.

1–**BROWNELL, Baker,** *b* St. Charles, Ill., Dec. 12, 1887.
9–Thomas **Brownell** (qv);
8–Thomas (1649-1732), of Little Compton, R.I.; *m* Mary Pearce (1654-1736; Richard[9], *m* Susanna Wright);
7–Charles (1694-1774), ens.; *m* Mary Wilbert; *m* 2d, Mary Wood;
6–Charles (*b* 1745), *m* Content Shaw (Israel[7], *m* Sarah Wilbur, or Wilbert);
5–Israel, of Fulton Co., N.Y.;
4–Humphrey (*d* post 1850), of Lowville, N.Y.; *m* —Briggs; *m* 2d, Cynthia Packard;
3–Humphrey (*d* 1850), *m* 1837, Renew Willard;
2–Eugene A. (1841-1919), *m* 1867, Esther Burr Baker (*b* 1847); for issue and other lineages see Mrs. George W. Wilcox.
1–*m* July 31, 1915, Helena Van Arsdale Maxwell, *b* Grinnell, Ia., Nov. 14, 1897; dau. of Samuel Argyl Maxwell.
1–A.B., Northwestern, U. of Washington, Tuebingen, Germany, Cambridge, Eng.; A.B., Harvard, '10, A.M., 1911; traveling fellow in philosophy from Harvard, 1912-13; studied Northwestern, U.Wash., Tübingen (Germany), Cambridge (Eng.). Editorial writer, Chicago Daily News, 1920, Chicago Tribune, since 1920. Asso. prof. and prof. journalism, Northwestern U., 1920-25; prof. contemporary thought, same, since 1925, head of dept. since 1927. Author: "The New Universe," 1926. Served as sgt. on Mexican border, 1916; enlisted man, 2d lt., U.S.A., and ens., U.S.N., May 1917-Aug. 1919. Residence: 1200 Sherwin Av., Chicago, Ill.

1–**WILCOX, Lulu May Brownell (Mrs. George W.),** *b* St. Charles, Ill., June 29, 1868.
9–Maj. Simon **Willard** (qv);
8–Capt. Benjamin (1665-1730), *m* 1691, Sarah Lakin (1661-1740);
7–Maj. Joseph (1693-1774), *m* 1715, Martha Clarke (1694-1794);
6–Lt. Isaac (1724-1805), *m* 1746, Sarah Whipple (*b* 1729);
5–Solomon (1755-1808), *m* 1777, Lydia Johnson (1755-1830; Capt. Micah[6], *m* Phoebe Moore);
4–Johnson (1786-1858), *m* Renew Pierce (1792-1832; Reuben[5], *m* Abigail–);
3–Renew (1821-98), *m* 1837, Humphrey **Brownell**;
2–Eugene A. (2 below).
8–Thomas **Baker** (1618-1700), from Eng., settled at Milford, Conn., 1639; *m* Alice Dayton;
7–Thomas (1654-1735), of Topping;
6–Samuel (1702-67), *m* Mercy Schellinge (*b* 1699);
5–Jonathan (1736-1820), of White Creek and Saratoga, N.Y.; *m* Betsy–; *m* 2d, Sarah Morris;
4–Jonathan (1773-1850), of Pawling, N.Y.; *m* 1797, Esther Burr;
3–John Randolph (1812-99), of Mayfield, N.Y.; *m* 1836, Harriet Angeline Foote (1817-97; Elisha[4], *m* 1810, Pamelia Kennicutt; Elisha[5]; Joseph[6]; Daniel[7]; Samuel[8]; Nathaniel[9]; Nathaniel[10], qv);
2–Esther Burr (2 below).
9–Jehu **Burr** (qv);
8–Daniel (*b* ca. 1642), of Fairfield, Conn.; *m* 1678, Abigail Glover;
7–Daniel, *m* Abigail–;
6–Jabez, of Redding, Conn.;
5–Nathan (1745-1818), Am. Rev.; *m* Phoebe–;
4–Esther (1778-1840), *m* Jonathan **Baker** (4 above).
3–John R., *m* Harriet A. Foote (3 above);
2–Esther Burr (*b* 1847), *m* 1867, Eugene A. **Brownell** (1841-1919), of St. Charles, Ill., and Seattle, Wash.; pvt., Co. H, 13th Ill. Inf., Civil War; issue: I–Lulu May (1 above); II–Harriet Angeline (*b* 1870); III–Mary Frances (*b* 1875; *m* Dr. Lewis Lake Phelps); IV–Eugene Willard (*b* 1879; *m* Elizabeth Bronson); V–Baker (qv); VI–Willard Foote (1894-1917).
1–*m* Dec. 27, 1888, George Wheeler Wilcox (July 11, 1868-June 21, 1916); issue (all *b* Flandreau, S.D.): 1–Etta Lucinda (Sept. 12, 1889-Mar. 21, 1915); 2–Lyle Brownell (qv for Wilcox lineages); 3–Grace Ella (*b* and *d* 1892); 4–Harriet Angeline (Mar. 27, 1894-July 2, 1895).
1–Attended Northwestern U. and U.Wis. Mem. D.C.W., D.A.R., O.E.S., Woman's Club (pres.), Past Matrons' Club (pres.), Day Nursery Assn. (pres.), Rock River Country Club. Conglist. Republican. Residence: 311 Av. F, Sterling, Ill.

1–**WILCOX, Lyle Brownell,** *b* Flandreau, S.D., Aug. 30, 1890.
11–William (Wilcockson, Wilcocks, Wilcoxson) **Wilcox** (qv);
10–Sgt. Samuel (1640-1713), to Windsor, Conn., 1667; propr. of Simsbury, Patent, 1685; selectman; dep. Gen. Ct., 1694-1712; *m* Hannah–;
9–Sgt. William (1669-1732), *m* 1699, Elizabeth Wilson (*d* 1746; Samuel[10]);
8–Sgt. Amos (1706-55), *m* 1728, Joanna Hilyer;
7–Amos (*b* 1729), col.; mem. 18th Regt. from Simsbury; *m* 1749, Hannah Hoskins;
6–Joel (*b* 1765), Sandisfield, Mass.; Am. Rev.; *m* Lydia–;
5–Rev. William John (*b* 1782), pastor Otisco N.Y., Congl. Ch.; grad. Williams Coll., 1806; *m* 1808, Luranah Greene (*d* 1842; Capt. Joseph[6], *m* Mehitable Beals);
4–Lysander Byram (1810-1903), *m* Rachel Childs Ledyard;
3–Samuel Ledyard (1837-1901), St. Charles, Ill.; *m* 1859, Lucinda Wheeler (1837-97; Job[4], *m* Harriet Warner);
2–George Wheeler (2 below).
8–John **Ledyard** (1700-71), from Eng., settled at Southold, L.I., 1717; taught Latin and Greek, 1727, in school which later became Dartmouth Coll.; mem. of Assembly at Groton, Conn.; dep. and justice of peace, Hartford, 1753; *m* 1728, Deborah Youngs (Judge Benjamin[9]);
7–Youngs (1731-62), *m* Mary, or Aurelia, Avery (Ebenezer[8], lt. col. in Am. Rev.);
6–Maj. Benjamin (1753-1813), Aurora, N.Y.; Am.

Rev.; clerk Onondaga Co.; an original founder of N.Y. Soc. of Cincinnati; *m* 1775, Catherine Forman (1753-87; Samuel[7], col. in Am. Rev.);
5–Samuel, *m* 2d, Sophia Childs (Timothy[6], Am. Rev.);
4–Rachel Childs (1816-53), *m* 1836, Lysander Byram **Wilcox** (4 above);
3–Samuel Ledyard, *m* Lucinda Wheeler (3 above);
2–George Wheeler (1868-1916), Sterling, Ill.; *m* 1888, Lulu May Brownell (qv).
1–*m* June 29, 1921, Mae Elizabeth Grandon, *b* Adrian, Mich., Oct. 22, 1891; dau. of D. W. Grandon, *m* Elizabeth Dakin.
1–B.S., U.Wis., '17 (Beta Theta Pi). Served in 131st Depot Brig. from Ill. during World War. Past cdr. A.L. Mason (K.T., Shriner); past exalted ruler B.P.O.E. Clubs: Rotary, Sterling, Country. Residence: 311 Av. F, Sterling, Ill.

1–**WILLIAMS, Oscar Waldo,** *b* Mt. Vernon, Ky., Mar. 17, 1853.
7–David **Williams,** from Wales to Elk Harbor, Md., 1666;
6–Jesse, of Elk Harbor, and Newcastle Co., Del.;
5–David (ca. 1720-ca. 1760), of Newcastle Co.;
4–Jesse (1750-1835), sgt., ens., 9th Bn., Md. Militia; to Culpeper Co., Va., 1780; served in Va. Militia, Am. Rev.; of Stafford and Orange cos., Va., 1818-28; to Garrard Co., Ky.; of Rockcastle Co., Ky., 1828-35; *m* 1774, Rachel Gott, of Baltimore Co., Md.;
3–Richard Gott (1786-1876), of Richmond, Ky.; carried a trading expdn. from Westport, Mo., to Santa Fe, N.M., and Chihuahua, Mexico, 1826; *m* 1812, Catherine Holder;
2–Jesse Caleb (2 below).
9–Thomas **Gott,** settled in Nansemond Co., Va., 1642; to Anne Arundel Co., Md., 1650;
8–Richard (*d* 1661), from London, Apr. 1650, to Anne Arundel Co.,
7–Richard (1651-1715), *m* Eliza Holland (Anthony[8], *m* Isabel, dau. Thomas Parsons);
6–Richard (1690-ca. 1751), *m* Sarah Sparrow (Solomon[7]; Thomas[8]);
5–Richard (1728-post 1790), mem. Md. militia, Am. Rev.; *m* Susan–;
4–Rachel (1755-94), *m* Jesse **Williams** (4 above);
3–Richard G., *m* Catherine Holder (3 above);
2–Jesse Caleb (1819-1917), mcht., Cathage, Ill.; state senator 1871-72; *m* 1850, Mary A. Collier (1826-1910; John[3]; John[4], Am. Rev.); issue: I–Oscar Waldo (1 above); II–William David (1855-1916; *m* Jettie Pearson); III–Josiah Joplin (1858-1910); IV–Anna Susan (*b* 1862); V–Jessie (Mrs. Archie Elmer Hart, qv).
1–*m* Dec. 15, 1881, Sallie Wheat, *b* Louisville, Ky., Oct., 1860; dau. of Clayton Miller Wheat, of Dallas, Tex.; issue: 1–Oscar Waldo, Jr., *b* Dallas, Apr. 14, 1883; B.S., Carthage (Ill.) Coll.; *m* Nov. 18, 19–, Olive, dau. of Henry Strickler, of Keokuk, Ia. (issue: Olivia; Oscar Waldo, 3d; Mary Helen Irene); 2–Mary Ermine, *b* Dallas, Feb. 21, 1885; Carthage Coll.; *m* June 6, 1906, Charles H. Garnett (issue: Elizabeth; Williams K.; Sarah); 3–Susan Kathryn, *b* Santa Rosa, Tex., Mar. 4, 1892; A.B., Carthage Coll.; A.M., U.Ill.; *m* F. G. Walker (issue: J. C. and Junior, twins; David George; Harriet Anne; Susan Elizabeth); 4–Clayton Wheat, *b* Ft. Stockton, Tex., Apr. 15, 1895; A. and M. Coll. of Tex., '15; 2d lt., C.A.C., U.S.A., Aug. 15, 1917; in France and Eng., Sept. 12, 1917-Feb. 21, 1919; thrice recommended; 1st lt., C.A.C., June 10, 1919; *m* Chic Graham; 5–Jesse Caleb, *b* Ft. Stockton, Apr. 15, 1899; A. and M. Coll. of Tex., '19; 2d lt., inf., Sept. 17, 1918; instr., S.A.T.C., U. of W.Va. and Kenyon Coll., to Dec. 24, 1918.
1–LL.B., Harvard, '76; attended William Jewell Coll. (Mo.), Christian U. (Mo.), and Bethany Coll. (W.Va.). Lawyer; co. judge about 16 yrs. Fellow S.W. Hist. Soc. Residence: Fort Stockton, Tex.

1–**HART, Jessie Williams (Mrs. Archie Elmer),** *b* Carthage, Ill., Oct. 10, 1865.
7–Joseph **Callaway,** from Eng. to Va.;
6–Joseph (*d* Caroline Co., Va., ca. 1730);
5–Col. Richard (*b* Caroline Co., Va.-*d* 1780), officer in French and Indian War; signer of Watauga treaty; a founder of Boonesborough, Ky., 1775; burgess of Va. during Am. Rev.; killed by Indians; *m* 1st, Frances Walton (1727-66; Robert[6]);
4–Frances (1763-1806), *m* 1778, Capt. John **Holder** (*d* 1798), officer Am. Rev. (Luke[5]);
3–Catherine, *m* 1812, Richard Gott **Williams** (1786-1876);
2–Jesse Caleb (1819-1917), *m* 1850, Mary A. Collier (1826-1910); for issue and other lineages see Oscar Waldo Williams.
1–*m* Archie Elmer Hart.
1–A.B., Carthage Coll., '83, A.M., 1892. Mem. D.A.R. (chapter historian and chaplain), Calif. Carthaginians (sec.), King W.C.T.U. (pres.). Club: Friday Morning. Residence: 5227 Stratford Rd., Los Angeles, Calif.

1–**WILLIAMSON, Mary Ready Weaver (Mrs. William Henry),** *b* Nashville, Tenn., Aug. 8, 1877.
5–Dr. John **King** (1746-94), from Lancaster, Eng.; degree in medicine from Oxford; joined Methodist Soc. after hearing Wesley, and was disinherited by his father; in America, 1769; began preaching in Old Potter's Field, Phila., Aug. 1770; removed to Wilmington, N.C., where he was auditor of Dist. of Wilmington, 1770-81; *m* 1774, Sarah Seawell (Col. Benjamin[6], *m* Lucy Hicks);
4–Thomas Seawell (1786-1851), of Nashville, Tenn.; *m* Delia Cantrell Nolen (1795-1858);
3–Frances Louise (1823-89), *m* Dempsey **Weaver** (1815-80);
2–Thomas Shadrach (2 below).
9–John **Washington,** from Eng.; settled in Surry Co., Va.; *m* 1658, Mary Fford;
8–Richard (1660-1725), from Eng.; of Surry Co., Va.; *m* Elizabeth Jordan (*d* ca. 1735; Arthur[9], *m* Elizabeth Baron);
7–James (*d* 1776), of Northampton, N.C.; mem. Gen. Assembly, N.C., 1753,55,56; *m* Joyce Nicholson;
6–Joyce (*d* 1818), of Northampton, N.C.; *m* John **Long** (*d* 1782);
5–Susannah (1775-1808), *m* Archer **Cheatham** (1771-1822);
4–Gen. Richard (1799-1845), of Springfield, Tenn.; mem. state Constl. Conv., 1834; elected as a Whig to 25th Congress; gen. state militia; merchant; *m* 1817, Susan Saunders (1802-64);
3–William Archer, M.D. (1820-1900), of Nashville, Tenn.; grad. U.Pa.; *m* Mary Emma Ready (1827-64);
2–Martha Strong (2 below).
10–Elder John **Strong** (qv);
9–John (1626-97), *m* 2d, 1664, Elizabeth Warriner (*d* 1684);
8–John (1665-1749), of Windsor, Conn.; *m* 1686, Hannah Trumbull (Dea. John[9]);
7–Dea. David (1704-1801), of Windsor and Bolton, Conn.; *m* 1732, Thankful Loomis (1709-71; Moses[8], *m* 1694, Joanna Gibbs);
6–Judah (*b* 1738), farmer, Bolton, Conn.; *m* 176–, Martha Alvord (*b* 1747; Saul[7], *m* Martha Churchill);
5–Joseph Churchill, M.D. (1775-1844), of Bolton; *m* 1804, Catharine Neilson (1785-1810);
4–Martha Alvord (*b* 1807), of Knoxville, Tenn.; *m* 1825, Hon. Charles **Ready** (*b* Readyville, Tenn., 1802), grad. Greenville Coll.; lawyer; mem. Tenn. Legislature; mem. Congress, 1853-55, twice reelected;
3–Mary Emma, of Murfreesboro, Tenn.; *m* William A. **Cheatham** (3 above);
2–Martha Strong (1853-1919), of Nashville, Tenn.; *m* 1872, Thomas Shadrach **Weaver** (1850-1911), lawyer; issue: I–Thomas (1873-1918; *m* Mary T. Howell); II–Dempsey (*b* 1874; *m* Anna Russell Cole); III–Mary Ready (1 above); IV–William Cheatham (*b* 1884; *m* Irene Morgan); V–Richard Cheatham (1895-1913).
1–*m* June 8, 1909, William Henry Williamson, *b* Murfreesboro, Tenn., Nov. 8, 1873; son of William Henry Williamson, of Lebanon, Tenn.; issue: 1–Martha Cheatham, *b* Nashville, July 23, 1910; ed. Randolph-Macon; Sorbonne, Paris; 2–Mary Weaver, *b* Nashville, Sept. 8, 1911; ed. Ward-Belmont Jr. Coll.
1–Ed. Belmont Coll., and Xavier Scharwenka Conservatory of Music, N.Y. Mem. C.D.A. (mem. Nashville bd.), I.A.G. Centennial Club, Vanderbilt Aid Soc., Query Club, Art

Museum. Methodist. Democrat. Residence: 207 Louise Av., Nashville, Tenn.

1–**WILLSON, James Carruthers,** *b* Richmond, Ky., Oct. 22, 1884.
5–James **Willson** (1715-1809), from Ireland, settled at "Mount Pleasant," Rockbridge Co., Va.; *m* 1750, his first cousin, Rebecca Willson (1728-1820; Thomas[6], *m* Elizabeth Dinwiddie);
4–Matthew (1769-1830), of Rockbridge Co.; *m* 1810, Nancy Carruthers (1780-1857; Robert[5], *m* Ann, dau. of Archibald Alexander, capt. colonial militia);
3–James Carruthers (1811-63), *m* 1837, his cousin, Lavinia Willson;
2–William Matthew (2 below).
7–Col. John **Willson** (1702-73), from Ireland, settled in Augusta Co., Va.; mem. House of Burgesses, 1745-73; *m* 1723, Martha– (1696-1755);
6–Capt. Matthew (*d* 1804), of Augusta Co.; capt. of militia during Am. Rev.; *m* Eleanor Mitchell (John[7], *m* Elizabeth–);
5–Elizabeth (1761-1833), Rockbridge Co.; *m* her cousin, Moses **Willson** (1754-1826; James[6], Am. Rev., *m* Rebecca Willson);
4–James S. (1782-1864), *m* 1814, Tirzeh Humphreys (1787-1844; David Carlisle[5], Am. Rev., *m* Margaret, dau. of William Finley);
3–Lavinia (1820-52), *m* James Carruthers **Willson** (3 above).
5–James **Hanna** (*d* 1798), from Ireland, settled in Va.; removed to Mercer Co., Ky.; *m* Martha–;
4–Thomas (1766-1822), of Shelby Co., Ky.; *m* 1797, Margaret Smith (1777-1813; Col. John[5], *m* Margaret Dobbins);
3–William Chenoweth (1808-92), of Shelby Co.; *m* 1837, Agnes Morton;
2–Agnes Woodson (2 below).
7–Thomas **Morton** (1700-31), from Eng., settled in Henrico Co., Va.; *m* Elizabeth Woodson (Richard[8], *m* Ann Smith; Robert[9]; Dr. John[10], qv);
6–Richard (*d* 1815), *m* Judith Quin (John[7], Am. Rev., *m* Susanne, dau. of Abraham Michaux);
5–Quin (1749-1805), of Charlotte Co., Va.; served in Am. Rev.; *m* Mary Anderson (Charles[6], *m* Elizabeth Chambers);
4–William Quin (1794-1850), of Shelby Co., *m* 1816, Elizabeth Venable (1795-1869; Judge Joseph[5], *m* Elizabeth, dau. of Francis Watkins; James[6]; Abraham[7]; Abraham[8]);
3–Agnes (1819-74), *m* William Chenoweth **Hanna** (3 above);
2–Agnes Woodson (1851-1910), *m* 1877, William Matthew **Willson** (1839-1910), of Richmond and Shelbyville, Ky.; in Rockbridge Arty., C.S.A.; prof. of Creek and Latin, Central U.; issue: I–Margaret Lavinia (*b* and *d* 1879); II–William Hanna (*b* 1882; *m* Emma Elizabeth Ballard); III–James Carruthers (1 above); IV–Mary Agnes Morton (*b* 1889); V–Sallie Bird (*b* 1891; *m* Richard Patrick Roach).
1–*m* Jan. 2, 1913, Marion Stuart Burnam (Mar. 9, 1886-Mar. 30, 1923); dau. of Thompson Burnam; issue: 1–James Carruthers, III, *b* Louisville, Ky., May 3, 1914; 2–Betty Moran, *b* Louisville, Nov. 14, 1915.
1–*m* 2d, Mar. 25, 1927, Eda (Turner) Clarke.
1–With Harris Trust & Savings Bank, Chicago, 1908-12; established James C. Willson & Co., Louisville, 1912, James C. Willson & Co., New York, 1924; dir. Curtiss-Wright Corpn. and affiliated cos., Intercontinent Aviation, St. Louis Aviation, Aviation Securities of Chicago, of N.E., Transcontinental Air Transport, Petroleum Corpn. of America. Mem. S.A.R. Presbyterian. Republican. Clubs: Pendennis, Country (ex-pres.), Wynn Stay, Sleepy Hollow, Big Spring (Louisville), Whist, Hangar, Aviation Country, Sleepy Hollow Country, Turf and Field (New York), Weedigo Fish and Game (Can.). Summer place: "Kinmont," Shepherdsville, Ky., and "Moran Farm," Richmond, Ky. Winter place: Sea Island Beach, Ga., Kingsland, Ga. Residence: 1241 Cherokee Rd., Louisville, Ky.

1–**WILLIS, Park Weed,** *b* Umatilla Co., Ore., July 10, 1867.
5–Stephen **Willis** (*d* Mar. 27, 1820), from Wales to Va.;
4–Stephen, *m* 1782, Martha Wherry;

WILLIAM McCLELLAN WILLIS (1827-1904).

3–James Wherry (*b* S.C., Mar. 29, 1797-*d* Sept. 21, 1843), *m* Aug. 21, 1819, Ann Stewart (1800-84; Robert[4], *m* Margaret McCellan; William[5], from Clogh, Co. Antrim, Ireland, to Pa., linen Weaver, passport dated July 7, 1762, *m* Ann Park);
2–William McCellan (2 below).
9–Robert **Keyes** (*d* Newbury, Mass., July 16, 1647), from Co. Kent, Eng., settled at Watertown, Mass., ca. 1633; later of Newbury and Sudbury; *m* Sarah– (*d* July 7, 1680; she *m* 2d, Sgt. John Gage);
8–Elias (*b* May 20, 1643), from Watertown to Sudbury, Mass.; *m* Sept. 11, 1665, Sarah Blanford (*b* Nov. 27, 1642/43; John[9] [*d* 1687], of Sudbury, Mass., *m* Dorothy–, *d* 1703);
7–Thomas (1674-1742), *m* 1698/99, Elizabeth How (1675-1764), of Marlboro, Mass. (John[8] [1640-75], killed by Indians, in King Philip's War, *m* 1662, Elizabeth, dau. William Ward, qv; John[9], qv);
6–Dea. Cyprian (1706-1802), selectman, town clk., assessor, Shrewsbury, Mass.; dea. Congl. Ch.; *m* 1729, Hepsibah Howe (*d* 1792, aet. 86);
5–Cyprian (1735-ca. 1805), to Pittsfield, Mass.; *m* 1756, Martha Bush (John[6]);
4–Jotham (1772-*d* Marion, Linn Co., Ia., 1854),

MARY ARABELLA (KEYES) WILLIS (1833-1904).

from Rutland to Holden, Mass.; settled in Windsor, Morgan Co., O., 1817; *m* 1794, Mary Harriet Everett (*d* Marion, Ia., 1853);
3–Horace (*b* Waldo Co., Me., May 17, 1809–*d* Mar. 23, 1895), postmaster Pleasant Ridge, Kan.; *m* in Morgan Co., O., 1831, Sarah Reader;
2–Mary Arabella (1833-1904), *m* 1855, William McCellan **Willis** (1827-82), farmer (see portraits); issue: I–Sarah Ellen (*b* 1856); II–James Wherry (1861-1921; *m* Mary Jones; *m* 2d, Mary Stevenson); III–Albert Lincoln (*b* 1864; *m* Felicia Chamberlain); IV–Park W. (1 above); V–Frank Shinn (1869-1905); VI–child (*d* infancy); VII–Harry Moore (1874-1928).
1–*m* June 15, 1892, Georgeanna Clark, *b* Tallmadge, O., Apr. 1, 1864; D.A.R.; dau. Robert William Clark, of Milford, Conn.; issue: 1–Park Weed, Jr., *b* Seattle, Wash., Mar. 4, 1893; U.Pa., '16; *m* 1917, Beatrice (divorced), dau. F. H. Garrigues (issue: Suzanne); *m* 2d, July 3, 1924, Leota Geraldine Snider (issue: Park Weed, III, *b* Nov. 18, 1925); 2–Cecil Durand, *b* Seattle, Mar. 24, 1898; U.Pa., '22; *m* June 16, 1923, Elizabeth Palmer Bayley (issue: Mary Perham, *b* May 5, 1924; Elizabeth Margaret, *b* Aug. 17, 1925; Priscilla Alden, *b* Feb. 28, 1927).
1–U.Wash., 1883-84; Sc.B., Whitman Coll., '88, Sc.M., 1891 (P.B.K.); M.D., U.Pa., 1891. Physician and surgeon at Seattle, 1892– (see Who's Who in America). Served during World War in Med. Dept., Council of Nat. Defense, Washington. Clubs: Army and Navy (Washington), Rainier, College, Swinomish Gun. Summer place: Orchard Hill Farm, Redmond, Wash. Residence: 1316 Columbia St., Seattle, Wash.

1–**WILSON, John Graham,** *b* Factoryville, Pa., Feb. 9, 1869.
5–Joseph **Wilson** (*b* 1740), served on a privateer in Am. Rev.; moved to Basking Ridge, N.J., thence to Warwick, Orange Co., N.Y.; *m* Elizabeth Rickey;
4–Isaac (1768-1842), *m* 1793, Sarah Phillips (1775-1855; John[5] [1752-1846], pvt. in Am. Rev.; Francis[6], *b* at Bennington, Vt.);
3–Dr. John (1801-79), physician, Factoryville, Pa., 1827; m Elsie Capwell (1809-63; Jeremiah[4]; Stephen[5]; Stephen[6]; Stephen[7]);
2–Giles Slocum (2 below).
9–Walter (Dean) **Deane** (qv);
8–James (1648/49-1725), *m* 1673/74, Sarah Tisdale;
7–Jonathan, began to write name Dean; mem. Susquehanna Co.; *m* 1716, Sarah Douglas;
6–Ezra (1718-1807), settled in Wyoming Valley, 1769;
5–Jonathan (1741-1822), Am. Rev.; settled at Abington, Pa., 1800; *m* 1773, a dau. of Thomas Nichols;
4–Jeffre (1781-1871), *m* 1805, Sibyl Hall (1786-1878; Jonathan[5], of Plainfield, Conn.; Joshua[6], *m* Susana, dau. Jonathan Sprague);
3–Davis (1810-76), *m* 1832, Hannah Smith;
2–Helen Malvina (2 below).
10–Richard **Warren,** Mayflower Pilgrim (qv);
9–Nathaniel (1624-67), *m* 1645, Sarah Walker (*d* 1700);
8–Elizabeth (1654-89), *m* 1684, William **Green** (*d* 1685);
7–William (1684-1756), *m* 1709, Desire Bacon;
6–Warren (1712-85), *m* Mary Paine (*d* 1783; probably a dau. of John[7]; Dea. John[8]; Thomas[9], *m* Mary, dau. of Nicholas Snow, *m* Constance, dau. of Stephen Hopkins, Mayflower Pilgrim, qv);
5–Mary (1736-1810), *m* 1760, Thomas **Smith** (1738-1821), pvt. and corpl. in Am. Rev. (Thomas[6]; Matthew[7]; Matthew[8]; Matthew[9], *m* Sarah, dau. John Mack, qv);
4–Diodate (1772-1821), *m* 1797, Rachel Allsworth;
3–Hannah (1810-79), *m* Davis **Dean** (3 above).
11–John **Howland,** Mayflower Pilgrim (qv);
10–Desire (1623-83), *m* 1643, Capt. John **Gorham** (qv);
9–Desire (*d* 1700), *m* 1661, Capt. John **Haws** (1635-1701);
8–Mary (1664-1725), *m* 1686, John **Bacon** (*b* 1661);
7–Desire (1688-1730), *m* William **Green** (7 above).
8–John **Pettebone** (*d* 1713), Huguenot, from France to Eng., thence to America, bet. 1640-50; freeman, Windsor, Conn.; *m* 1664, Sarah Eggleston (1643-1713; Begat[9]);
7–Stephen (*b* 1669), *m* Deborah Bissell (Samuel[8]);
6–Noah (1714-91), to Wyoming Valley, Pa., 1771; mem. 1st alarm list, 24th Conn. Militia, battle of Wyoming, Pa., 1778; *m* Huldah Williams;
5–Esther (1747-1833), *m* William **Allsworth,** of Dutchess Co., N.Y., later of Providence, Pa.;
4–Rachel (1776-1848), *m* Diodate **Smith** (4 above);
3–Hannah, *m* Davis **Dean** (3 above);
2–Helen Malvina (1845-1913), *m* 1868, Giles Slocum **Wilson** (1840-1901), farmer; issue: I–John Graham (1 above); II–Paul Dean, D.D.S. (*b* 1871).
1–*m* Nov. 24, 1897, Louise C. Kent, *b* Montrose, Pa., Dec. 1, 1865; dau. of Henry J. Kent, of Montrose, *m* Emily W. Moore (see their g.-dau. Mrs. Ralph Lee Strock).
1–M.D., U.Mich., 1892. Physician. Mem. S.M.D. Residence: Factoryville, Pa.

1–**STROCK, Marion Kent MacCreary (Mrs. Ralph Lee),** *b* Montrose, Pa., July 29, 1900.
10–Louis **Du Bois** (qv);
9–Abraham (1656-1731), patentee of New Paltz; served in colonial wars; *m* 1681, Margaret Deyo (*b* 1659; Christian[10], eldest of 12 patentees of New Paltz);
8–Abraham, *m* Maria Larzalere;
7–Abraham;
6–Minna, settled in Great Bend, Pa.; Am. Rev.;
5–Abraham (1786-1867), *m* 1811, Juliet Bowes (1794-1855);
4–Catherine (1814-50), *m* 1832, Rev. James B. **Mac Creary** (1797-1887);
3–James B. (1835-1900), *m* 1863, Frances Bailey (*b* 1843);
2–William H. (2 below).
11–Gov. William **Bradford,** Mayflower Pilgrim (qv);
10–Maj. William (1624-1703), *m* Alice Richards;
9–Alice, *m* 1687, Maj. James **Fitch** (1647-1727), of Canterbury, Conn.;
8–Ebenezer (1689-1724), of Canterbury; *m* 1712, B. Brown;
7–Alice (1713-96), of Windsor and Groton, Conn.; *m* 1731, Capt. John **Fitch** (1705-60), of Windham, Conn.;
6–Lucy (1743-1804), *m* 1767, Robert **Geer** (1743-1834), grad. Yale, 1763; corpl. Am. Rev. (Ebenezer[7], *m* Prudence Wheeler; Robert[8]; George[9], qv);
5–Prudence (1768-1854), of Brooklyn, Pa.; *m* 1801, Capt. Amos **Bailey;**
4–Prudence (1804-63), of Montrose, Pa.; *m* 1825, Robert **Kent** (1801-78);
3–Henry J. (1832-94), of Montrose; *m* 1860, Emily W. Moore (1834-1903); their dau. Louise C. Kent, *m* John Graham Wilson (qv);
2–Martha Eliza (2 below).
11–William **Bailey** (*b* 1579), from Eng. in the brig "Prosperous," 1620, settled in Va.; landowner, 1626; *m* Mary–, who came 1 yr. later in the "George," bringing her son Thomas;
10–Thomas (1616-75), gen., King Philip's War; killed at Bloody Brook, Deerfield, Mass.; *m* 1655, Lydia Redfield (James[11]);
9–John (*b* 1661), *m* Elizabeth Smith;
8–Obadiah, *m* 1718, Elizabeth Williams (Richard[9], *m* Sarah–);
7–Obadiah (1728-80), of Groton, Conn.; *m* 1747, Azuba Rogers;
6–Obadiah (1750-1843), of Groton; *m* 1774, Esther Williams;
5–Capt. Amos (1777-1865), of Brooklyn, Pa.; *m* 1801, Prudence Geer (5 above);
10–James **Rogers** (1615-85), from Eng. in the "Increase," 1635, settled in New London, Conn.; rep. to Gen. Ct. 6 times; served in Pequot War; brought Bible of first Martyr, John Rogers, when he came to America; *m* Elizabeth Rowland (Samuel[11], of Stratford Conn.);
9–Samuel (1640-1713), *m* 1662, Mary Stanton (Thomas[10], *m* Ann Lord);
8–Jonathan (1680-1769), *m* 1708, Elizabeth Pemberton (Joseph[9]);
7–Azuba (*d* Whitestown, N.Y., aet. 100), *m* Obadiah **Bailey** (7 above).
9–John **Williams,** of Conn.;
8–Peter (1688-1739), of Preston, Conn.; *m* 1712, Micah Lambert (1689-1777; Michael[9], *m* Elizabeth Stark);
7–John (1715-96), *m* 1736, Susannah Latham (1717-99; Carey[8]);
6–Esther (1746-1833), of Groton, Conn.; *m* Obadiah **Bailey** (6 above).

2–Martha Eliza Kent (1869-1904), of Hallstead, Pa.; *m* 1899, William H. **Mac Creary** (*b* 1869).
1–*m* Mar. 2, 1920, Ralph Lee Strock, *b* Mechanicsburg, Pa., Dec. 3, 1898; son of George L. Strock; issue: 1–Jeanne Wilson, *b* Harrisburg, Pa., Dec. 11, 1920; 2–Bradford Kent, *b* Carlisle, Pa., Nov. 8, 1923.
1–Ed. Clark's Summit, Pa., '18, Pa. State Coll., 1918-20. Mem. S.M.D. Presbyterian. Republican. Residence: 311 Trinity Av., Ambler, Pa.

1–**WINSLOW, Lorenzo Simmons,** *b* Mansfield, Mass., Aug. 20, 1892.
11–Richard **Bowen** (qv);
10–Alice, *m* 1636, Robert **Wheaton** (qv);
9–Hannah, (*b* 1654), *m* 1674, John **Butterworth** (1651-1731), of Rehoboth, Mass.;
8–Elizabeth (1682-1708), *m* 1704, Daniel **Carpenter** (*b* 1669; William[9]; Capt. William[10]);
7–Bethiah (1706-88), *m* 1728, Obadiah **Carpenter** (1707-64), see Vol. III, p. 586;
6–Capt. Nehemiah (1731-99), *m* Elizabeth Sweet (1733-73);
5–Ezra (1753-1841), *m* 1779, Margaret Daniels;
4–James (1785-1865), *m* Nancy Day;
3–Nancy Maria (1824-1902), *m* Simmons **Winslow** (1809-1900), see Vol. III, p. 586;
2–George (2 below).
10–Jonathan **Fairbanks** (qv);
9–Mary (1622-76), *m* 1644, Michael **Metcalfe** (1620-54; Michael[10]);
8–Sarah (1648-1718), *m* 1677, Robert **Ware** (1653-1724; Robert[9]);
7–Ebenezer (1677-1750), *m* Bathyah Fisher (Josiah[8]; Anthony[9]);
6–Bethiah (*b* 1713), *m* 1737, Caleb **Day** (John[7]; John[8]; Ralph[9]);
5–Jesse, *m* Azubah Turner;
4–Nancy, *m* James **Carpenter** (4 above).
10–Lt. Griffin **Craft** (1600-89), from Eng. with Gov. Winthrop, 1630; settled at Boston; founder of Roxbury; dep. Gen. Ct.; selectman, 1650-73; mem. bd. commrs.; lt. Roxbury Mil. Co., 21 yrs.; *m* Alice– (*d* 1673);
9–John (1630-85), *m* 1654, Rebecca Wheelock (*d* 1667; Rev. Ralph[10], qv);
8–Rebecca (*b* 1664), *m* Isaac **Turner** (*b* 1654; John[9], *m* Deborah Williams);
7–Samuel, soldier colonial wars; *m* 1710, Mary Rockett (1681-1762; Josiah[8], *m* Mary Twitchell; Nicholas[9]; Richard[10]);
6–Samuel (1724-84), soldier King Philip's War; *m* Ruth Smith (*b* 1730; Henry[7]; Samuel[8]; Henry[9]);
5–Azubah, *m* Jesse **Day** (5 above).
11–Rev. John **Wing** (qv);
10–Daniel (qv), *m* 1641, Hannah Swift (William[11]);
9–John (1656-1717), *m* Martha Spooner (William[10]);
8–John (1689-1750), *m* Experience–;
7–Benjamin (1711-56), *m* Experience Barlow (Shubel[8]; Aaron[9]);
6–Shubel (*b* 1738), *m* 1758, Beulah Weston;
5–Eunice (*b* 1762), *m* 1783, Simon **Hathaway,** of Rochester, Mass.;
4–Simon (1793-1851), *m* Jerusha Barton (1792-1869);
3–Lorenzo Dow (1837-99), of Foxboro, Mass.; *m* Eliza I. Wolff (*b* Canterbury, Eng.);
2–Andree Bertha (*b* 1861), *m* 1882, George **Winslow** (*b* 1857); for issue see Vol. III, p. 586.
1–*m* Aug. 12, 1917, Albinia Daggett Fish, *b* Falmouth, Mass., July 11, 1889; dau. of Joseph Crowell Fish, of Falmouth; issue: 1–Peter Daggett Hathaway, *b* Greensboro, N.C., Aug. 12, 1920.
1–*m* 2d, Feb. 26, 1930, Garnette M. Vaughan Burks (qv).
1–C.E., Ohio Northern U., ex-'12; traveled and studied in Europe, 1912. Architect. Enlisted in 1st O.T.C., May 4, 1917, at Plattsburg, and Engr. O.T.C. at Am. U., Washington, D.C.; 2d lt. engrs., Aug. 15, 1917; 301st Engrs., Camp Devens, Aug. 15, 1917-Oct. 1, 1917; 1st lt. engrs., Mar. 1918; mem. Gen. Staff, G-I, G.H.Q. and 1st A.C., with A.E.F. in France; participated in Champagne-Marne, Aisne-Marne, Soissons, St. Mihiel, Meuse-Argonne, 1st Army Defensive Sector; overseas, Oct. 15, 1917-Nov. 1, 1919. Mem. S.M.D., S.C.W. (council Tenn. soc.), O.C.G., O.F.P.A., Order of LaFayette, S.A.-R., S.W. 1812, I.A.G., V.F.W., M.O.F.W., (reg. N.C. commandery), M.O.W.W., S.A.M.E., N.E.H.G.S., Fairbanks Family of America, A.L., Order of Pulaski (rec. gen.). Mason (K.-T.), I.O.O.F. Club: Sedgefield Country. Summer place: Quissett Harbor, Falmouth, Mass. Residence: Greensboro, N.C., P.O. Box 109.

1–**WINSLOW, Garnette Mabelle Vaughan Burks (Mrs. Lorenzo S.),** *b* "Foxhall," Sandidges, Amherst Co., Va.
14–Col. George **Reade** (qv);
13–Mildred, *m* ante 1671, Col. Augustine **Warner,** Jr. (1642-81; Augustine[14], qv);
12–Sarah, *m* Lawrence **Townley;**
11–Alice, *m* Maj. John **Grymes** (*d* 1708), of "Grymesby," on the Piankatank, Middlesex Co., Va. (Lt. Gen. Thomas[12], from Eng., 1642);
10–Charles, *m* Frances Jennings (Gov. Edmund[11], of Va.);
9–Sarah, *m* Robert **Taliaferro** (1626-87), from Eng., settled on the Rappahannock River, Va.;
8–Lt. Col. John (1656-1720), called "John the Ranger"; cdr. against the Indians, 1692; justice, Essex Co., Va.; sheriff, 1699; *m* 1682, Sarah Smith (Maj. Lawrence[9], *m* Mary–);
7–Capt. Richard, *m* 1726, Rose Berryman;
6–Charles (*b* 1735), Amherst Co.; *m* 1758, Isabella McCulloch (Roderick[7], qv);
5–Benjamin Berryman (*b* 1799), *m* 1822, Judith Anderson Crawford;
4–Elizabeth Elkin, *m* John Woodford **Broaddus;**
3–Ellen, *m* Alexander Hairston **Burks,** of Natural Bridge, Rockbridge Co., Va. (Samuel Cabell[4], *m* Elizabeth Hairston);
2–Franklin Taliaferro (2 below).
10–Thomas **Loving** (ca. 1610-1665), surveyor gen. Va.; burgess; *m* 1639, Elizabeth Kingston;
9–Charles (*b* ca. 1640);
8–James (*b* ca. 1675);
7–John (1705-69), *m* Susanne Lomax (*b* 1709; John[8], *m* Elizabeth, dau. Ralph Wormeley);
6–Capt. William (1740-92), Am. Rev.; *m* Elizabeth Hargrove;
5–Susan (1777-1816), *m* 1795, Capt. George **Vaughan** (1772-1846; William[6], *m* Ginetta, dau. Thomas Riddle; John[7], desc. Sir Walter Vaughan, from Wales to Va., ca. 1630);
4–George (1801-76), *m* Mary C. Edmunds (Rowland[5], *m* Elizabeth, dau. of Col. James Nevil, Am. Rev.);
3–Washington LaFayette (1833-82), *m* Frances Ellen Shields;
2–Hortense Washington (2 below).
8–John **Higginbottom** (ca. 1690-1760), *m* Frances Riley;
7–Aaron (ca. 1715-1785), capt., Amherst Co. militia, 1769; *m* Clara Green;
6–Aaron (1752-94), *m* 1775, Nancy Croxton;
5–Elizabeth (1778-1837), *m* James **Shields** (1772-1839; John[6], *m* Margaret, dau. of James Finley);
4–Egbert Oswald (1818-83), *m* Sarah Ellen Brent (James[5]; James[6]; William[7]; Hugh[8]; Hugh[9]; Hugh[10], to Va., 1639);
3–Frances Ellen (1842-1905), *m* Washington L. **Vaughan** (3 above);
2–Hortense Washington (*b* 1867), *m* 1889, as his 2d wife, Franklin Taliaferro **Burks** (1849-1921), inherited estate of "Fox Hall" which has been in the family since 1746, being land grant given Richard Taliaferro (7 above), by George, II (he *m* 1st, 1869, Nancy Ogden); issue (1st marriage): I–Woodford Elkin (*b* 1871; *m* Katherine Van Wagner); II–Ruby Nettie (*b* 1875; *m* Boyd W. Hamilton); III–Rose Berryman (1885-1925); issue (2d marriage): I–Reade Carrington (1891-92); II–Pearl Corinne (*b* 1894; *m* Ernest Rosser); III–Franklin Taliaferro (*b* 1896; *m* Roberta Drummond); IV–Garnette M. V. (1 above); V–Broaddus Vaughan (*b* 1904).
1–*m* Feb. 26, 1930, Lorenzo Simmons Winslow (qv).
1–Studied at Washington (D.C.) Sch. of Art, and Corcoran Sch. of Fine Arts. Portrait painter and illustrator. Mem. Knights of the Most Noble Order of the Garter, L.A.P.W., Arts Club (Washington). Residence: 904 Wharton St., Greensboro, N. C.

1–**BURTON, Margaret Sealy (Mrs. Frederick M.),** *b* Galveston, Tex., Mar. 24, 1876.
8–Ashby (or Abraham) **Womack** (1683-1756), from Eng., 1702, settled in Prince Edward Co., Va.;

7–Richard (1710-85), *d* in Hancock Co., Ga.;
6–Jesse (1739-1815), 1st lt. Am. Rev.; participated at Kings Mountain, and Guilford C.H.; received land grant for services in Am. Rev.; *m* 1st, Dorothy Prior (*b* 1740), believed to have been a Choctaw Indian princess, of Augusta, Ga.;
5–John (1776-1848), of "Womack's Hill," St. Stephan's, Washington Co., Va.; *m* 1797, Frances Coleman;
4–John (1799-1859), from Ala. to Montgomery, Tex., 1838; *m* Mrs. Tabitha Lord (1801-65);
3–Caroline (1828-63), of Montgomery, Ala.; *m* 1844, Peter James **Willis** (1815-74), of Potters Landing, Md.;
2–Magnolia (*b* 1855), *m* 1875, George **Sealy** (1835-1901); banker, philanthropist, pioneer R.R. builder, Galveston, Tex.; issue: I–Margaret (1 above); II–Ella (*m* E. R. Newell); III–George (*b* 1880; *m* Eugenia Taylor); IV–Caroline (Mrs. Norman B. Livermore, qv); V–Rebecca (Mrs. Clifford Day Mallory, qv); VI–Mary Constance (*b* 1887-*d* aet. 5); VII–Robert (*b* 1889); VIII–William (*b* 1891; *m* Catharine Richard).
1–*m* Apr. 29, 1902, Frederick Middleton Burton, *b* Liverpool, Eng., Aug. 8, 1876; son of Miles Kirk Burton, of Liverpool; issue (all *b* Galveston, Tex.): 1–Miles Kirk, *b* Aug. 24, 1903; Sewanee Mil. Acad.; Tex. A. and M. Coll.; U. of Tex.; 2–Margaret Sealy, *b* May 6, 1907; 3–Caroline, *b* Nov. 19, 1908; 4–Jane, *b* Mar. 28, 1911.
1–Leader in civic and charitable enterprises; organized the first Red Cross at Galveston during World War; organized the first troop of Boy Scouts, under another name, 1908, membership of 12 functioning 6 yrs.; organized an aid society for John Sealy City Hosp., 1899, and still pres.; organized a civic and charitable social club, "Merrie Wives," 1910, still pres.; v.p. State (Tex.) Fine Arts Assn.; dir. State Forestry Assn.; supervisor of town planting for city, county, of public parks, etc. for past 10 yrs. Author of several books of poetry and short stories; amateur singer. Mem. U.D.C., Dau. Tex. Republic, Art League, Y.W.C.A. Episcopalian. Democrat. Clubs: Women's (v.p.), Women's Civic League (pres.), etc. Summer place: Dickinson, Tex. Residence: 2323 Sealy Av., Galveston, Tex.

1–**LIVERMORE, Caroline Sealy (Mrs. Norman B.),** *b* Galveston, Tex., Aug. 7, 1883.
5–John (Willess) **Willis** (1742-1819), *b* in Great Gum Island Swamps, Sussex Co., Del.; sgt. under Thomas Montgomery, 14th regt., U.S. Inf., wounded in arm at Beaver Dam, Can., 1813, pensioned; served under Capt. Collins, whose company was called "The Blue Hen's Chickens," was wounded at battles of Brandywine and Germantown; served 7 yrs. in Cont. Army; *m* 1768, Nanna Short;
4–Short Adam (1782-1860), *b* in Sussex Co., Del.; was in bombardment of Lewistown, 1812; *m* 1812, Mary (Rich) Griffin (1788-1861; Peter Nixon[5] [1744-1805], *m* Prudence Lane; Peter[6], 1st lt. Caroline Co. Troops, Del., *m* 1739, Susanne Whitely);
3–Peter James (1815-74), *m* 1844, Caroline Womack;
2–Magnolia (*b* 1855), *m* 1875, George **Sealy** (1835-1901); for issue and other lineages see Mrs. Frederick M. Burton.
1–*m* Jan. 5, 1910, Norman Banks Livermore, *b* San Francisco, Calif., July 20, 1872; son of Horatio Putnam Livermore, of Boston; issue (all *b* San Francisco, Calif.): 1–Norman Banks, *b* Mar. 27, 1911; 2–George Sealy, *b* Mar. 18, 1914; 3–John Sealy, *b* Apr. 16, 1918; 4–Horatio Putnam, *b* May 29, 1922; 5–Robert, *b* June 12, 1926.
1–A.B., Vassar, '05. Mem. C.D.A., A.A.U.W. Clubs: Town and Country, Century, Meadow, Athletic, Woman's City, Garden, Vassar. Summer place: "Montesol," Calistoga, Calif. Residence: 1045 Vallejo St., San Francisco, Calif.

1–**MALLORY, Rebecca Sealy (Mrs. Clifford D.),** *b* Galveston, Tex., Dec. 17, 1885.
11–John **Chew** (qv);
10–Joseph (*d* 1715), Fredericksburg, Va.; *m* Miss Larkin;
9–Larkin (*d* 1729), Spotsylvania Co.; *m* Hannah Roy;
8–Anne, *m* 1732, William **Johnston,** of Scotland;
7–Hannah, *m* Francis **Coleman** (*b* 1700; James[8], *m* Mary Keys);
6–Francis (1744-1823), col. Am. Rev.; burgess; charter mem. Soc. Cincinnati; *m* Margaret Daniel (*b* 1750);
5–Frances (1781-1852), *m* John **Womack** (1776-1848);
4–John (1799-1859), *m* Tabitha Ford (1801-65);
3–Caroline (1828-63), *m* Peter J. **Willis** (1815-74);
2–Magnolia (*b* 1855), *m* 1875, George **Sealy** (1835-1901); for issue and other lineages see Mrs. Frederick M. Burton.
1–*m* Jan. 3, 1911, Clifford Day Mallory, *b* Brooklyn, N.Y., May 26, 1881; son of Henry R. Mallory, of Brooklyn; issue: 1–Margaret Pynchon; 2–Clifford Day, Jr.; 3–Barbara Sealy.
1–Ed. Spence School. Mem. Westchester Woman's Golf and Tennis Club. Episcopalian. Democrat. Residence: Old Church Road, Greenwich, Conn.

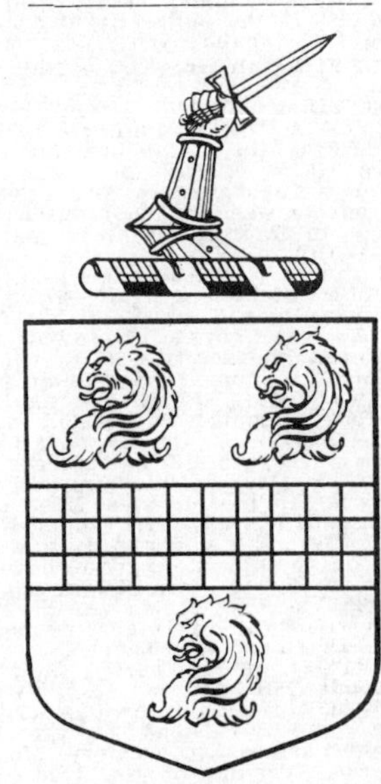

BELT

Arms: *Argent, a fess checky or and azure, between three lions' heads erased gules.*
Crest: *On a wreath, a hand and arm embowed in armour, grasping a sword proper pommel and hilt or.*
Motto: *Tempus edax rerum.*

1–**BELT, William Bradley Tyler,** *b* Richmond, Va., Aug. 1, 1871.
7–Humphrey **Belt,** from Eng. in the "America," to Jamestown, Va., 1635, aet. 20 yrs.; settled in Lower Norfolk Co., 1654; in Anne Arundel Co., Md., 1663; *m* Ann–;
6–John (1645-98), of Anne Arundel Co.; *m* Elizabeth Tydings (*d* 1738; Richard[7]);
5–Col. Joseph (1680-1761), patentee of Chevy Chase, Md., 1725; owned 1000 acres of land; keeper of the Greater Seal; gentleman justice, Prince George's Co., Md., 1726-28; burgess, 1725-37; commd. lt. col., 1725, col. of militia, 1728-61; mem. Col. George Beall's Troop of Horse, 1748; trustee for first free schools in Md.; owned Friend's Choice, Belt's Discovery, Belt's Hunting Quarter, Good Luck, Addition to Good Luck, Oronoko, Seneca Hills, Friendship, Arthur's Seat, Thompson's Lot, Belt's Pasture, and Chelsea; planter and surveyor; *m* 1st, Hester Beall (Col. Ninian[6], qv);

4–Tobias (1720-85), capt. Am. Rev.; *m* Mary Gordon (*d* 1795);
3–Thomas Hanson, *m* Eliza Key Heath;
2–Thomas H. (2 below).
7–Robert **Tyler** (qv);
6–Robert (*d* 1738), *m* Susanna DuVal (Mareen[7], qv);
5–Robert (*d* 1777), lt. col. Upper Bn., Prince George Co., Md.; *m* Eleanor– (1737-77);
4–Robert Bradley (1759-93), *m* 1783, Dryden Belt (*d* 1825; Col. Joseph[5]);
3–William Bradley (1788-1863), *m* Maria Davis (*d* 1866);
2–Maria (1830-1909), *m* as his 1st wife, 1850, Thomas H. **Belt** (*d* 1880).
1–*m* Oct. 11, 1893, Cecelia Mary Willis, *b* Sioux City, Ia., July 1, 1872; dau. of John G. Willis; issue: 1–Dorothy, *b* Omaha, Neb., May 10, 1901; grad. Miss Bennett's Sch., '22; *m* Oct. 20, 1923, Francis S., son of Frank H. Gaines (issue: Tyler Belt; Mary Theresa).
1–Ed. Racine (Wis.) Coll. With Northwestern Bell Telephone Co. since Jan. 9, 1889, pres. since 1919 (see Who's Who in America). Mem. S.A.R., I.A.G. Mason (32°). Episcopalian. Republican. Clubs: Omaha Country, University, Des Moines, Minneapolis. Residence: 320 S. Elmwood Rd., Omaha, Neb.

1–**BEACHLEY, Ralph Gregory,** *b* Hagerstown, Md., Aug. 12, 1895.
8–Gottfried **Miller** (1690-1778), from Mannheim, Prussia, 1695, settled at Phila.; employed by Benjamin Franklin in his printing shop at Phila., ca. 1740-50; *m* 1731; sons, Peter, George and Jacob were officers in Am. Rev.; Peter Miller went to General Washington at Valley Forge to intercede for the pardon of Michael Whitman;
7–Mary Margaret (1733-1810), of Phila.; *m* 1st, Capt. John **Stadleman** (1720-86), cdr. of Germantown Blues in Am. Rev.;
6–Mary (1756-1839), of Germantown; *m* 1777, Peter **Humrickhouse** (1756-1837), vol. Cont. Army, May 3, 1776, ens. Flying Camp; crossed the Delaware, July 4, 1776, and again, Dec. 24, 1776; took a number of Hessian prisoners who were in Trenton, Dec. 26, 1776; after the battle, he was apptd. officer of the day, and was sent by General Washington with a flag of truce to the enemies' lines to bury the dead; commd. capt., 1777; engaged in the battle of Germantown; apptd. by General Washington to take a cargo of powder for the Cont. Army to York Town and Fredericksburg, Va.;
5–Frederick (1791-1876), of Hagerstown, Md.; *m* 1814, Hannah Harry (1797-1880);
4–Louisa (1818-98), of Funkstown, Md.; *m* 1831, Simon **Knode** (1811-68);
3–Annie (*d* 1912), of Hagerstown; *m* 1863, J. H. **Beachley** (1838-1905), head of the largest mercantile business in western Md. many years; pres. Washington Co. (Md.) School Bd.; v.p. Hagerstown Spoke & Bending Co.; treas. M.E. Ch., Hagerstown, 35 yrs.;
2–Harry Knode (2 below).
6–William **Jacques** (1757-1836), from Ireland, 1776; ed. Oxford U., Eng., later in the school for training officers for British Army; commd. and came to America with the British Army during Am. Rev.; on staff of Gen. John Burgoyne; captured at Battle of Saratoga, 1777, and sent to prisoners' camp at Frederick, Md.; after the surrender of the British forces at York Town he resided at Williamsport, Md., later at Hancock, Md.; *m* 1780, Anna Fidlers (1755-1837);
5–Anna (1786-1859), of Hancock; *m* 1806, Joseph **Hixon** (1785-1863);
4–Mary (*b* 1809), of Hancock; *m* 1830, Moses **Gregory** (1798-1871);
3–Margaret (1834-1910), of Hancock; *m* 1862, James Harvey **Taylor** (1834-1910), served in Co. E, 45th Regt., Pa. Vol. Inf., Chambersburg; present at siege of Richmond; hon. discharged, July 17, 1865;
2–Alice (1865-1928), of Hagerstown; *m* 1893, Harry Knode **Beachley** (1865-1918), A.B., Dickinson Coll., '86, later A.M.; city treas., Hagerstown; pres. Washington Co. School Bd.; issue: I–Ralph Gregory (1 above); II–Catherine Louise (*b* 1901); III–Jack H. (*b* 1903; *m* Helen Mogart).
1–*m* Apr. 2, 1921, Carolyn Bates, *b* Waverly, Ia., Jan. 8, 1894; dau. of George L. Bates, of Waverly; issue: 1–Eleanor Louise Gregory, *b* Hagerstown, Md., Jan. 15, 1922.
1–Grad. Mercersburg Acad., 1914; Johns Hopkins U., 1914-16 (Phi Sigma Kappa); M.D., George Washington U., 1920 (Phi Chi); Dr. P. H., U.Ga., 1926. Asst. dir., Washington Co. Health Demonstration (field school for students of Johns Hopkins U. School of Hygiene and Public Health), 1922-23; deputy of county health units, S.C. State Bd. of Health, 1923-26; dep. state health officer of Md., 1926–; dir. Dept. of Student Health Service, Washington Coll., Chestertown, Md., 1930–. Pvt., M.C., 1918; capt., Med. O.R.C., 1924; capt., 1st Inf., Md. N.G. Methodist. Democrat. Residence: Chestertown, Md.

1–**DIMMICK, George Beck,** *b* Clarks Green, Pa., Aug. 10, 1862.
8–Elder Thomas (Dymocke) **Dimmick** (qv);
7–Dea. Shubael (bap. 1644-1732), of Barnstable; selectman, 1685-86; dep. to Colonial Ct., 1685-86,89; ens. militia co.; removed to Mansfield, Conn., where he died; *m* 1663, Joanna Bursley (*d* 1727, aet. 83 yrs.);
6–Shubael (1673-1728), *m* 1699, Tabitha Lothrop (*d* 1727, aet. 57 yrs.);
5–Shubael (1706-88), "ye 2nd, of Mansfield"; *m* 1739, Esther Pierce (*d* 1805, aet. 92 yrs.; Rev. Samuel[6]);
4–Edward (1748-1839), of Uniondale, Pa.; *m* 2d, 1789, Esther Tilden (*d* 1850; Joshua[5], *m* Eunice Carpenter);
3–Eber (1792-1841), *m* Roxana Mumford (Jireh[4]);
2–Eber (1834-98), 2d lt. Co. D, Pa. Vols., Civil War; sec. to Dr. B. H. Throop, capitalist; *m* 1861, Eleanor Mary Beck (1834-1921; George[3]); issue: I–George Beck (1 above); II–Eugene Eber (1864-70); III–James Orville (1866-1926; *m* Kate Johns); IV–Sarah Amelia (*b* 1869; *m* James A. Marvine, *d* 1908); V–Jesse (*b* 1871; *m* Jeanette Hallock); VI–Edgar Allen (1873-74); VII–Henry Laurens (*b* 1876; *m* Marguerete Koehler); VIII–Eleanor Lorencie (*b* 1880; *m* Dr. Daniel S. Gardner).
1–*m* Sept. 15, 1903, Elizabeth Fuller Hitchcock, *b* Scranton, Pa., May 19, 1873; dau. of Col. Frederick Lyman Hitchcock, 25th Regt. U.S.C.T. in Civil War (Daniel[3], of Wallingford, Conn.); issue (all *b* Scranton, Pa.): 1–Caroline Eleanor, *b* Aug. 28, 1904; B.S., N.Y. Univ., '27; 2–George Beck, *b* Mar. 1, 1906; 3–Elizabeth Kingsbury, *b* Aug. 6, 1913.
1–Clerk with First Nat. Bank of Scranton 43 yrs.; treas. and dir. of building and loan assn. Pa. N.G. 5 yrs. Mem. O.F.P.A., I.A.G. Mason. Presbyterian. Republican. Summer place: Lake Waynewood, Wayne Co., Pa. Residence: 1103 Richmont St., Scranton, Pa.

1–**CASSIDY, Perlina Barnum Sizer (Mrs. Gerald),** *b* Sizer's Ranch, nr. Las Animas, Colo., Mar. 4, 1869.
6–Antonio (de Sousier, de Sousa) **Sizer** (*b* 1707), from Terceria, Azore Islands, 1726, settled at Bridgeport, Conn.; *m* 1727, Sarah Tryon (1706-74; Abel[7]);
5–Lemuel (1736-1820), of Bridgeport; *m* 1753, Abigail Barnes;
4–Eli (1765-1845), *m* Jedida Prior (1755-1855);
3–Luther (1798-1877), Oneida Co., N.Y.; *m* Paulina Barnum;
2–Eber Rockwell (2 below).
8–Thomas **Barnum** (1625-95), from Eng., settled at Fairfield or Norwalk, Conn.; *m* 2d, Sarah Hurd (1648-1718);
7–Richard (*b* 1675), mem. Colonial Legislature; *m* Mary Hurd;
6–Joseph (*d* ante 1793), *m* 1731, Mary Breckinridge;
5–Col. Joseph (*d* 1790), *m* 1st, Keziah–; *m* 2d, Mabel–;
4–Seth (1754-1820), of Danbury, Conn.; *m* 1777, Abigail Bearss;
3–Paulina (1802-72), of Middletown, Conn.; *m* 1820, Luther **Sizer** (3 above).
8–Augustine (Bearse) **Bearss** (*b* 1618), from Eng. in the "Confidence," 1638, settled at Barnstable (Cape Cod), Mass., 1639;
7–Joseph (*b* 1652), in King Philip's War; *m* 1676, Martha Taylor (Richard[8], *d* 1728);
6–Josiah (*b* 1690), *m* 1716, Zerviah Newcomb (*b* 1698; Lt. Andrew[7], *m* 2d, Anna, dau. of Capt. Thomas Bayes, of Boston; Andrew[8]);
5–Thomas (1729-1814), began to write name

EBER ROCKWELL SIZER (b Steuben, Oneida Co., N.Y., Feb. 26, 1833-d 1900); father and grandfather associated in settlement with Baron Steuben, western frontiersman, 1855; Colorado pioneer, 1859; with Gen. Sherman to establish Ft. Abercrombe; with Col. Noble surveying boundary between Canada and United States; trader with Hudson Bay Co.; Indian trader, Denver, 1859, with Kit Carson; scout and interpreter with Kit Carson in Colo. and N.M. Indian wars, capturing and removing Navajos; in battles at Pigeon's Ranch and Apache Canon, N.M., against Gen. Sibley's Confederate army.

Bearss; *m* 2d, 1756, Esther (Lyon) Smith (*d* 1797);
4–Abigail (1760-1832), *m* Seth **Barnum** (4 above).
9–Hugh **Mosher** (1600-94), from Eng., 1630; ens.; ordained Bapt. Ch., 1674; *m* 1632, Lydia Maxon;
8–Hugh (1633-1713), an original owner of Westerly; large landowner; mem. ct. martial for trial of Indians, 1676; *m* Elizabeth Harndel (John[9]);
7–Capt. Nicholas (1664-1747), *m* 1687, Elizabeth–;
6–Nicholas (*b* 1703), *m* 1729, Rebecca Wilcox (*b* 1711; John[7]; Daniel[8], *m* Elizabeth Cooke [John[9], *m* Sarah, dau. of Richard Warren, qv; Francis[10], qv]; Edward[9], at Portsmouth, R.I., 1638);
5–Susannah, *m* John Simon **Covill,** British Officer at the time of Am. Rev., stationed in N.Y. City; at close of war removed to Can., where the rest of the family were born:
4–John Hurd, *m* Mary Dickson (David[5], *m* Sarah–);
3–Mary, *m* 1828, Daniel Stephens **Savage,** from Can. to Ia.; Methodist circuit rider;
2–Mary (*b* 1846), *m* John Madison Miles; *m* 2d, 1868, Eber Rockwell **Sizer** (1833-1900), see portrait; issue: (mother's 1st marriage, surname Miles): I–John Edgar (*b* 1867; *m* Eula Castleman); issue (mother's 2d marriage, surname Sizer): I–Perlina Barnum (1 above); II–Maggie Teresa (*b* 1873; *m* Herbert B. Swartz); III–Eber Rockwell, Jr. (*b* 1878); IV–James Harl (*b* 1880; *m* Mary Boswell).
1–*m* Nov. 29, 1890, John Boyd Davis (1867-Jan. 10, 1899); son of Robert H. Davis.
1–*m* 2d, Jan. 5, 1912, (Ira D.) Gerald Cassidy, *b* Cincinnati, O., Nov. 10, 1869; artist; son of Edwin B. Cassidy, *m* Olive Crouch.
1–Writer. Mem. D.A.R., I.A.G. Unitarian. Residence: 924 Canon Rd., Santa Fe, N.M.

1–**DODGE, Clarence Phelps,** *b* Honolulu. H.I., July 26, 1877.
10–William **Dodge,** from Eng. in the "Lion's Whelp," to Salem, Mass., 1629;
9–Richard (*d* 1671);
8–Richard (1643-1716), *m* Mary Eaton;
7–Daniel (1677-1740), *m* Joanna Benham;
6–David (*b* 1723), *m* Anna Low;
5–David (1742-1807), *m* Mary (Stuart) Earl;
4–David Low (1774-1852), distinguished mcht. and philanthropist, New York; *m* Sarah Cleveland (Rev. Aaron[5]);
3–William Earl (1805-83), a founder of Phelps, Dodge & Co.; railway builder, financier, philanthropist; pres. New York Chamber of Commerce, etc.; *m* Melissa Phelps;
2–David Stuart, D.D. (1836-1921), *m* 1860, Ellen Ada Phelps (*d* 1880), for issue and Phelps lineage see Walter Phelps Dodge, Vol. I, p. 913.
1–*m* Jan. 1, 1900, Regina Lunt (qv for issue).
1–B.A., Yale, '99 (Alpha Delta Phi). Former publisher and editor Colorado-Springs (Colo.) Gazette. Mem. 15th Gen. Assembly of Colo.; chmn. Progressive Party in Colo., 1914-16. Mem. Internat. Com. of Y.M.C.A. and of Nat. War Work Council; served in Y.M.C.A. war work six months in U.S. and 3 months overseas. Capt. O.R.C. (staff specialist). Trustee Am. U., Beirut, Syria. Mem. I.A.G., etc. Clubs: Chicago (Chicago), Denver, Mile High (Denver). Operates the Haystack Gulch Ranch, 600 acres in Rocky Mountains, Clear Creek Co., Colo. Residence: 3238 R St., Washington, D.C.

1–**DODGE, Regina Lunt (Mrs. Clarence Phelps),** *b* Evanston, Ill., Oct. 1, 1879.
12–Francis **Cooke** (qv);
11–John, *m* Sarah Warren;
10–Sarah, *m* Arthur **Hathaway**;
9–Hannah (*d* ca. 1718), *m* George **Cadman**;
8–Elizabeth, *m* William **White**;
7–Sarah, *m* 1726, John **Brown**;
6–Mary, *m* Pardon **Gray**;
5–Job, *m* Judith Briggs;
4–Samuel (1785-1859), *m* 1812, Susan Felton;
3–Cornelia (*b* 1819), *m* Orrington **Lunt** (1815-97);
2–Horace Gray (*b* 1847), *m* 1874, Caroline Kirby Isaacs; for issue and other lineages see Horace Fletcher Lunt, Vol. I, p. 701.
1–*m* Jan. 1, 1900, Clarence Phelps Dodge (qv); issue: 1–Regina Phelps, *b* Colorado Springs, Colo., Nov. 20, 1903; 2–Clarence Phelps, Jr., *b* Colorado Springs, July 10, 1906.
1–Mem. Daughters of the Cincinnati. Residence: 3238 R St., Washington, D.C.

1–**DODSON, Shelby Martineau,** *b* Martinsburg, Mo., Feb. 9, 1873.
6–Jesse **Dodson**;
5–George;
4–Thomas;
3–George (1789-1865), fought under Jackson at New Orleans; *m* Polly Rodgers (*b* 1792);
2–Shelby Martin (2 below).
5–Gen. John **Thomas** (1724-75), Kingston, Mass.; comd. army at Roxbury at beginning of Am. Rev.; officer in expdn. against Canada;
4–Jane (*b* 1769), *m* 1791, George **Procter** (*b* 1760), of Fayette Co., Ky.; LaFayette's aide in Am. Rev.;
3–Rowland Thomas (*b* 1800), *m* Diana D. Chapman (*b* 1806);
2–Susan Eleanor (*b* 1838), *m* 1864, Dr. Shelby Martin **Dodson** (1839-1906), physician; issue: I–Dr. George Rowland (*b* 1865; *m* Nellie E. Wheeler); II–James Berry (*b* and *d* 1867); III–Jesse Clay (1869-1900); IV–Julia Proctor (*b* 1871); V–Shelby Martineau (1 above); VI–Minnie May (*b* 1875; *m* 1912, James A. Harliss); VII–Susan Eleanor (*b* 1877; *m* 1901, Newell O. Morse).
1–*m* June 11, 1913, Elizabeth Emma Brown, *b* Camptonville, Yuba Co., Calif., Oct. 28, 1882; dau. of Richard M. Brown, of Utica, N.Y.; issue: 1–Elizabeth Alice, *b* San Jose, Calif., Aug. 6, 1915.
1–Stanford U., class of '95 (President Hoover's class). Lawyer and realtor. Summer place: "Tiana," Boulder Creek, Calif. Residence: 198 S. 16th St., San Jose, Calif.

1–**FENNESSY, Florence Pamela,** *b* Avon, Ill., Jan. 17, 1877.
8–John **Woods** (1610-78), original grantee of Sudbury, Mass., 1638; a founder Marlboro, 1656; selectman, 1664-65; *m* Mary Parmenter (*d* 1690, aet. 80);
7–James (1646-1718), dea. 1st ch., 1716; *m* 1678, Hopestill Ward (1645-1718; William[8], grantee of Sudbury, 1638, a founder of Marlboro, rep. Gen. Ct., 1644,66, chmn. of selectman, 1661-65,71, *m* Elizabeth–);
6–James (1685-1772), dea., town clk., rep. Gen. Ct., assessor; *m* 1718, Dorothy Barnes (1697-1734; John[7], *m* Hannah–; Thomas[8]);

5–David (1720-1807), *m* 1744, Martha Wheeler;
4–Samuel (1757-1813), soldier Am. Rev.; minute man at Lexington Alarm, 1775; *m* 2d, 1778, Phoebe Holton (1755-1845; Israel[5], *m* Sibilla–);
3–Jonas (1780-1841), from Madison Co., N.Y., to Ill., 1837, helped establish village of Woodstock (later called Avon); *m* 1810, Ethelinda Grow;
2–Cornelia (2 below).
9–George **Wheeler,** at Concord, Mass., 1638; *m* Katherine–;
8–Thomas (*d* 1686), tithing man, 1680; *m* 1657, Hannah Harwood (George[9], *m* Hannah–);
7–John (1661-1712), *m* 1686, Elizabeth Wells;
6–John (*b* 1695), assessor, constable, parish clk., moderator in town meetings, 1746, etc.; *m* 1717, Mary Hapgood (1694-1759; Thomas[7]; Shadrach[8]);
5–Martha (1726-1819), *m* David **Woods** (5 above).
9–William **Meade** (qv);
8–John (1634-99), Hempstead, L.I.; *m* 1657, Hannah Potter;
7–Jonathan (1665-1727), of Greenwich, Conn.; *m* 1688, Martha Finch;
6–Jonathan (*b* 1689), Nine Partners, Dutchess Co., N.Y.; *m* 1726, Sarah Husted;
5–Jonathan (1727-1804), 1st lt., Dutchess Co. militia, 1775; signer of the Articles of Assn., 1775; *m* 1758, Sarah Guernsey (1736-1800);
4–Sarah (1768-post 1816), *m* 1788, Jacob **Grow** (1765-1816; John[5], *m* Mary, dau. of Edward Farrington);
3–Ethelinda (1789-1851), *m* Jonas **Woods** (3 above);
2–Cornelia (1832-81), of Avon, Ill.; *m* 1854, William Thomas Richard **Fennessy** (1830-1904), civil engineer, from Ireland, 1852, settled at Avon, Fulton Co., Ill.; issue: I–William Barton (*b* 1857; *m* Belle Harry); II–Ernest Julian (1859-1919; *m* Minnie Bliss); III–Edward Clinton (1861-1913; *m* Evelyn Washburn); IV–Maurice Richard (1866-1927; *m* Augusta Myers; *m* 2d, Ida Volkman); V–Effie Dorothea (*b* 1873); VI–Florence Pamela (1 above).
1–Residence: Avon, Ill.

ADMIRAL FRANK F. FLETCHER, U.S.N. (1855-1928).

1–**FLETCHER, Frank Friday** (Nov. 23, 1855-Nov. 28, 1928).
7–John **Fletcher** (*b* Eng. ca. 1680), went from Wales to Ireland;
6–John (*b* 1707), from Ireland to Adams (now Lancaster) Co., Pa., 1728;
5–John;
4–Archibald (1742-1824), ens. Bedford Co. militia, Am. Rev.; *m* Rebecca Bracken;
3–John (*b* Adams Co., Pa.), moved to Westmoreland Co., Pa.; *m* his 2d cousin, Rachael Fletcher (*d* 1796);
2–James Duncan (2 below).
5–James **Jack** (*d* 1776), *m* Jane Carneband;
4–John (1748-1815), *m* Nancy McCoy (1766-1858);
3–Thomas (1787-1875), *m* Isabella Miller (1798-1876);
2–Nancy Powers (1826-73), *m* 1845, James Duncan **Fletcher** (1810-63), saddle and harness mfr.; issue: I–Thomas Jack (*d* 1929; *m* Alice Glick); II–James Carlyle (*d* 1923; *m* Carrie Seeven); III–Emma B. (*d* 1914); IV–Frank Friday (1 above); V–May (*m* I. K. Richards).
1–*m* Feb. 26, 1895, Susan Hunt Stetson, *b* E. Braintree, Mass., July 3, 1867; dau. of George Rochford Stetson, of Boston; issue: 1–Sybil Avery, *b* Washington, Dec. 30, 1897; ed. Vassar, '20; *m* June 1923, Lt. Reginald Worth Hubbell, U.S.A.; grad. U.S.M.A.; commd. 2d lt. Inf., Nov. 1, 1918, with 57th Inf., 1919, 33d Inf., July 16, 1919; commd. 1st lt., Nov. 11, 1919; with Tank Corps (issue: Frank Fletcher); 2–Alice S., *b* Washington, Sept. 17, 1901; ed. Vassar, '23.
1–Grad. U.S.N.A., '75. Commd. ens., 1876, and promoted thru the grades to rank of rear adm., 1911. Aide to Sec. Navy for div. of material, 1910; comdg. 3d div. Atlantic Fleet, 1913, 2d div., then 1st div.; seized and occupied Vera Cruz, 1914; cdr.-in-chief, Atlantic Fleet, 1914; adm. 1915 (see Who's Who in America). Mem. War Industries Bd. of Council of Nat. Defense, 1917; Gen. Bd. of Navy; Joint Army and Navy Bd.; Presidents Air Craft Bd., 1925. Invented Fletcher breech mechanism and gun mounts. Awarded medal of honor for distinguished conduct during battle of Vera Cruz; D.S.M. for service in World War. Mem. S.A.R. Former residence: 404 E. 59th St., New York, N.Y.

1–**FREEMAN, Elmer Burkitt,** *b* Mattoon, Ill., Feb. 5, 1875.
5–Moses **Freeman** (*b* 1738), from Eng., 1760, settled on Eastern Shore of Md. near the present town of Snow Hill; *m* ca. 1760, Nancy Knight (*b* 1740);
4–Joseph, pioneer settler of Northwest Ty., 1799; *m* ca. 1795, Elizabeth Higgins;
3–William (*b* 1805), *m* Tamar Beach;
2–Joseph Biglow (2 below).
4–Hosea **Moore** (1763-1832; probably son of Aaron, of Uniontown, Pa., will probated 1781, *m* Mary–); *m* Isabelle Hannah (1766-1851);
3–Newton (1806-90), *m* 1827, Rebecca Burkitt (1811-1901; Thomas[4] [1763-1836], *m* Polly Wheeler, 1766-1820);
2–Mary Jane (1838-1913), *m* Joseph Biglow **Freeman** (1830-1901); issue: I–Alice A. (*b* 1859; *m* Harry Ashworth); II–Newton W. (*b* 1861; *m* Janet Eleanor Matheson); III–Agnes (*b* 1866; *m* —Rhine); IV–Wheeler C. (*b* 1870; *m* Mary Gustin, 1872-1926); V–Thomas Oscar (*b* 1872; *m* Nellie Voight); VI–Elmer Burkitt (1 above).
1–*m* Aug. 29, 1903, Rosa May Weeks, *b* Baltimore, Md., Sept. 5, 1874; dau. of Alfred Weeks, of Baltimore.
1–B.S., Austin Coll., '96 (Phi Chi); M.D., Baltimore Med. Coll., 1900. Resident physician, Md. Gen. Hosp., 1900-01; instr. clinical medicine, Baltimore Med. Coll., 1901-04, asso. prof. same, 1904-10, and prof. therapeutics, 1910-14; asso. prof. clinical medicine, U.Md., 1913-14; asst. in clinical medicine, Johns Hopkins U., 1916-22, instr. 1922-29, asso. in same since 1929; asst. visiting physician, John Hopkins Hosp., since 1929; physician-in-chief, Md. Gen. Hosp., since 1917; gastro-enterologist, St. Agnes' Hosp., since 1910; attending physician, Bon Secours Hosp., since 1917; attending physician, Church Home and Infirmary, since 1929. Mem. Advisory Bd. No. 4, State of Md. Sec., section on gastro-enterology Southern Med. Assn.; trustee Md. Tuberculosis Assn.; mem. Am. Coll. Physicians, Am. Gastro-Enterol. Assn., A.M.A., Southern Med. Assn., Am. Radiol. Assn., Baltimore City Med. Soc., Md. Hist. Soc., etc.; hon. mem. State Med. Soc. of Minnesota. Episcopalian. Republican. Clubs: University, Baltimore, Gibson Island, Maryland Jockey. Summer place: Gibson Island, P.O. Pasadena, Md. Residence: 807 Cathedral St., Baltimore, Md.

1-**JOHNSON, Sylvia Jessamine Spear (Mrs. William V.),** *b* Big Horn, Wyo., Sept. 11, 1886.
7-David **Spear** (1676-1760), from Ireland, 1720; settled on the Kennebec River in Me.; at Windsor, Conn., 1725, and Palmer, Mass., 1727; commr., deacon, mem. Assembly, selectman, del. to Congress; *m* 1703 (?), Jean (Jane) Fulton? (*d* probably 1726/27);
6-William (1720-1804), of Ellington, Conn.; served at Lexington Alarm; *m* 2d, 1763, Elizabeth Murdock (1742-89);
5-David (1763-1813), Melrose, Conn.; said to have enlisted in Am. Rev. aet. 15, and served thruout the war; *m* 1787, Mary Clarke (1765-1859; Ebenezer[6], *m* Anna Dimmock);
4-John (1788-1886), fifer War 1812; *m* 1813, Mary Osborn (1797-1840; Moses[5], *m* Mary Shaw; Daniel[6]);
3-Willis Bradford (1824-1912), Mexican War; crossed plains to Calif., 1849; *m* 1853, Jane (Ferguson) Wood;
2-Willis Moses (2 below).
5-George **Ferguson,** from Scotland, settled in Pa.; supposed to have served in Am. Rev.;
4-Jonathan, of Warsaw, Ind.; *m* 1823, Catherine Ritchie, or Richards;
3-Jane (1826-1905), as Widow Wood, *m* 2d, Willis B. **Spear** (3 above).
10-Edward **Benton** (*d* 1680), from Eng., 1640, settled at Guilford, Conn.; freeman, 1651; *m* Anne- (*d* 1671);
9-Andrew (1639-1714), *m* 1664, Elizabeth Relf (*d* 1713; Thomas[10]);
8-James (1665-1733), weaver; *m* 1694, Hannah Bushnell (1670-1756; John[9], of Saybrook, *m* Sarah Scranton);
7-James (1700-85), *m* 1719, Experience Stocker (Edward[8], of Lyme);
6-James (1720-1810), *m* 1st, 1739, Margaret Naughty (*d* 1763);
5-Capt. Zebulon (ca. 1758-60-1842), of Rowe, Mass.; capt. militia; gunner in Am. Rev., pensioned; *m* 3d, 1795, Abigail (Burt) Dinsmore (1767-1831; Ebenezer Burt[6], *m* Abigail Bartlett);
4-Horace (1796-1886), Kewanee, Ill.; *m* 1816, Anna Case (1796-1888; Nathan[5], *m* Hannah Rhodes);
3-Dr. George Washington, M.D., D.D. (1824-95), of Mass., Ill., Wis., Kan., and Wyo.; *m* 1849, Hannah Torrey;
2-Virginia Belle (2 below).
9-Capt. William **Torrey** (qv);
8-Dea. Micajah (1640-1710), Weymouth, Mass.; *m* Susanna-;
7-Samuel (1688-1782), Taunton; *m* 1732, Constant Lincoln;
6-Daniel (*d* 1795), Sutton; Am. Rev.; *m* 1761, Keziah Stockbridge (*b* 1741);
5-Samuel (1762-1819), Am. Rev.; *m* 1787, Hannah Carpenter (1763-1845; Nathaniel[6], *m* Mary Leffingwell);
4-Lewis (1788-1880), *m* 1812, Betsey Titus (1794-1878; John[5], *m* Mercy Axtell; John[6]);
3-Hannah (1823-98), *m* George W. **Benton** (3 above);
2-Virginia Belle (*b* 1863), Wyo. state regent D.A.R.; *m* 1885, Willis Moses **Spear** (*b* 1862), state senator, Sheridan Co., Wyo.; cattle and sheep stockman; issue: I-Sylvia Jessamine (1 above); II-Willis Benton (*b* 1888; *m* 1914, Ruth Henderson); III-Phillip Torrey (*b* 1892; *m* 1915, Jessie Mather); IV-Elsie Hannah (*b* 1896; *m* 1916, Harold Charles Edwards).
1-*m* June 6, 1906, William Victor Johnson, *b* Oakland, Neb., May 6, 1870; son of Samuel William Johnson, of Oakland; issue: 1-Jessamine Annabelle, *b* Sheridan, Wyo., Apr. 12, 1907; *m* Dec. 10, 1925, Jackson Davis, son of Willis Edward Moody; 2-Phyllis Vie, *b* Sheridan, Sept. 26, 1908; *m* July 3, 1929, Leon Noel, son of Miles Chalfant, of Story, Wyo.; 3-William Spear, *b* Spear Ranch, Big Horn, Wyo., Jan. 23, 1912; 4-Elsa Eileen, *b* Ucross, Wyo., June 8, 1915; 5-Torrey Benton, *b* Ucross, Dec. 6, 1916; 6-Victor Elarth, *b* Sheridan, May 11, 1922; 7-Homer Bradford, *b* Sheridan, May 15, 1925.
1-Manager Spear Wigwam Camp, a "dude ranch." Mem. S.M.D., D.A.R., I.A.G., Neb. Geneal. Soc. Baptist. Republican. Club: Woman's. Summer place: Spear Wigwam Camp, Big Horn, Wyo. Residence: Rosebud X4 Ranch, Kirby, Mont.

COWDREY

Arms: *Gules, ten billets or, four, three, two, one.*
Crest: *Out of a ducal coronet or, a dexter arm embowed in armour proper, garnished of the first, holding in the gauntlet an anchor gules, stock sable, to the ring a piece of cable of the last entwined around the arm.*

1-**GUY, Austa Jane Applegate (Mrs. William S.),** *b* Liberty Tp., nr. Youngstown, O., Sept. 17, 1877.
10-William **Cowdrey** (1602-87), from Eng., 1630, settled at Lynn, Mass.; deacon; clk. of units, town clk., selectman; rep. Gen. Assembly of the Colonies; *m* 1638, Joanna- (*d* 1666);
9-Nathaniel (1639-90), of Redding; *m* 1654, Elizabeth- (*d* 1659);
8-Samuel (*b* 1657), *m* 1685, Elizabeth Parker;
7-Nathaniel (1691-1751), Hadley; *m* 1718, Mehitabel Damon (1699-1763);
6-William (1737-1832), Woodstock, Vt.; *m* 1760, Hannah Emmons;
5-William (1765-1847), E. Haddam, Conn.; *m* Rebecca Fuller (1768-1809);
4-Erastus (1796-1833), of Youngstown, O.; *m* Rebecca McCormick (1783-1862; Robert[5], *m* Nancy Gibson, of Center Co., Pa.);
3-Sarah Jane (1820-1902), *m* 1834, Calvin **Applegate** (1809-91);
2-John (1844-1907), served in Co. C, 171st Ohio Vol. Inf., Civil War; hon. dicharged at close of war; *m* 1876, Orpha Jane Campbell (1851-79); issue: I-Austa Jane (1 above); II-Orpha (*b* and *d* 1879).
1-*m* June 17, 1903, William Sampson Guy, *b* Churchill, O., May 8, 1879; son of Thomas Guy, of Churchill; issue: 1-Harriet Elizabeth, *b* Churchill, O., June 28, 1904; B.A., Lake Erie Coll., '26.
1-Taught in public schools 9 yrs. Mem. N.E.-H.G.S. Methodist. Republican. Residence: Churchill, O.

1-**McNEIL, Tom H.,** *b* Burdette, Mo., Feb. 29, 1860.
5-Abraham **McNeil,** from Scotland to Ireland, thence to Derryfield (now Manchester), N.H., 1750, with wife Jane, and son, William;
4-William, *m* 1774, Rachael Patterson;
3-Peter (1786-1847), *m* Mary Stiles (1796-1882; Cyrus[4], fought at Battle of Lexington, 1775);
2-James (1827-97), *m* 1852, Jane C. Wilson (*d* 1919); issue: I-Frank E. (1853-54); II-Abbie J. (*b* 1855; *m* 1875, L. W. Rosier); III-John W. (*b* 1857; *m* 1880, Eda Shorb); IV-Tom H. (1 above); V-Alice L. (*b* 1862; *m* 1881, William S. Mudd); VI-Lilly B. (1865-73); VII-George D. (*b* 1867; *m* Alice L. Mudd, *d* 1924); VIII-Fred M. (*b* 1871; *m* Ella Burns); IX-Annie E. (*b* 1873; *m* Dudley Chambers); X-Milo C. (1876-77), and XI-Merritt C., twins (*m* Grace Wolford); XII-Infant (*b* and *d* 1879).
1-*m* Feb. 28, 1906, Willie M. Black, *b* Cameron, Mo., Jan. 31, 1876; dau. of Samuel H. Black; issue (all *b* Kansas City, Mo.): 1-Jane W., *b* Dec. 25, 1906; 2-Ollie F., *b* Sept. 9, 1908; *m* Aug. 27, 1929, Louis Lee Leininger; 3-Anna, *b* Aug. 10, 1910; *m* Apr. 21, 1928, Lyle W. Bryan; 4-Martha L., *b* Nov. 28, 1911; *m* Oct. 11, 1930,

Charles V. Dean; 5–Tom H., Jr., *b* Dec. 20, 1916.
1–Ed. Keystone Acad., Factoryville, Pa., 1880; A.B., U. of Mich., '85, LL.B., 1886. Lawyer and deputy coroner; with Kansas City Public Service Co., and predecessors, since 1901. Mem. I.A.G.; scout master Boy Scouts of America. Past Grand Chancellor of Mo. K. of P.; Past Master A.F. and A.M.; life mem. B.P.O.E. Residence: 2810 Harrison St., Kansas City, Mo.

1–**MATHISON, Flora Annette,** *b* Ansonia, Conn., Dec. 24, 1898.
9–Nathaniel **Colburn,** from Eng., settled at Dedham, Mass., ca. 1637; *m* Priscilla Clark;
8–John (*b* 1648), *m* 1672, Experience Leland;
7–Daniel (*b* 1689), of Stafford, Conn.;
6–Daniel;
5–Daniel, of Stafford; *m* Elizabeth Moulton;
4–Sylvester (1806-70), of Ansonia, Conn.; *m* 1831, Elizabeth Hull (1810-1900);
3–Frederick E. (1832-1919), *m* 1859, Flora Ann Smith (1837-1904);
2–Elizabeth Hull (*b* 1866), *m* 1898, Rev. Edward Thompson **Mathison** (1870-1930), Episcopal clergyman; issue: I–Flora Annette (1 above); II–Catharine (*b* 1900); III–Elizabeth (*b* 1901); IV–Robert Edward (*b* 1903; *m* Elizabeth R. Wurthman); V–Frederic Huntington (1907-27).
1–M.A., Teachers College, N.Y. Dietitian. Mem. I.A.G. Episcopalian. Residence: 139 N. Arlington Av., E. Orange, N.J.

1–**NEEDHAM, Henry Chapman,** *b* Brooklyn, N.Y., Nov. 8, 1866.
8–Anthony **Needham** (qv);
7–Anthony (1663-1758), of Salem, Mass.; *m* 1695, Mary Swinnerton (*b* 1670; Joseph[8]; Job[9]; Job[10]; Widow Elisabeth[11]);
6–Anthony (1696-1763), *m* 1722, Mary Moulton (1702-90; Robert[7], *m* 1698, Hannah Graves; Robert[8], *m* 1672, Mary Cook);
5–Nehemiah (1734-83), of Brimfield (now Wales), Mass.; served on expdn. to Crown Point during French and Indian War, in company of Uncle, Capt. Moulton, attached to Col. Pomeroy's regt.; served in Am. Rev., under Capt. Stone, of Lenox, at Ticonderoga; selectman, S. Brimfield, 1778; moved to Marlboro, Vt.; *m* 1st, 1758, Eunice Fuller (*d* 1778);
4–Jonathan (1764-1811), in Am. Rev., 1780, re-enlisted, 1782, 4th Mass. Regt.; *m* 1786, Eunice Fisk (1768-97; Capt. Asa[5], *m* Elizabeth–);
3–Jonathan (1793-1862); pvt. Capt. Ephraim Scott's co., War 1812; enlisted Sept. 13-Nov. 1, 1814; *m* 1816, Lodisa Pratt (1799-1873);
2–Henry M. (1829-90), of Wales, Mass.; lawyer; *m* 1864, Helen Elizabeth Chapman (1840-1903; Henry Thomas[3] [1809-97], from Eng., settled in N.Y., *m* 1835, Clarissa Charlotte Curtis, 1817-94); issue: I–Helen P. (1865-1926; *m* George C. Flynt); II–Henry C. (1 above); III–George A. (*b* 1868).
1–Not married. LL.B., Columbia Law Sch., 1888. Mem. L.I. Hist. Soc. Republican. Summer place: Wales, Mass. Residence: 89 Hancock St., Brooklyn, N.Y.

1–**RENKIN, William Oran,** *b* Allegheny (now N.S., Pittsburgh), Pa., Feb. 6, 1875.
8–Alexander (Rankin) **Renkin,** escaped from Scotland to Ireland, 1688, with son William;
7–William, whose three sons Adam, John and Hugh, settled in Chester Co., Pa., 1721;
6–Adam (1688-1750), *m* Mary Steele;
5–William (1713-92), *m* Mary Huston;
4–William Jackson (1770-1850), *m* Abigail McGinley;
3–William Johnson (*b* 1804), *m* Nancy Johnson Anthony;
2–William Wilson (2 below).
9–John **Anthony** (qv);
8–Abraham (1650-1727), of Portsmouth, R.I.; *m* 1671, Alice Wodell (1650-1734; William[9], *m* Mary–);
7–Jacob (1693-1727), *m* 1714;
6–Thomas (*b* 1722);
5–Jacob (1759-1810), of Phila., and Indiana Co., Pa.; pvt., Capt. George Forpaugh's 8th Co., 2d Bn., Phila. Militia, 1781; *m* 1777, Ann (Nancy) Johnson;
4–David (1793-1852), of Indiana Co.; *m* 1814, Florana Campbell Armstrong;
3–Nancy Johnson (1815-70), *m* 1835, William Johnson (Rankin) **Renkin** (3 above).
6–William **Armstrong,** from Dublin, Ireland, settled in Franklin Co., Pa., 1742?; *m* Flora Campbell;
5–Alexander, *m* Lena Hindman;
4–Florana Campbell (1796-1868), *m* David **Anthony** (4 above);
3–Nancy Johnson, *m* William **Renkin** (3 above);
2–William Wilson (1842-1922), Signal Corps, U.S.A. in Civil War; owner W. W. Renkin Machine & Pattern Making Shop, Pittsburgh, 50 yrs.; *m* 1869, Sarah Hefron Hunter (1848-1921); issue: I–Minnie Hunter (1869-70); II–Anna Ewing (1871-98); III–Thomas Hunter (*b* 1873; *m* 1899, Anna Wilson); IV–William Oran (1 above); V–Martha Hefron (1877-78); VI–David Anthony (*b* and *d* 1879); VII–Samuel McCauley (*b* 1881; *m* 1904, Ora Wyatt; *m* 2d, 1929, Marie Glick); VIII–Nannetta (1883-94); IX–Ulysses Grant (1885-94); X–Sarah Jane (*b* 1887; *m* 1913, Albert Danber); XI–James (1888-89).
1–*m* May 22, 1901, Jane Fulton Stewart, *b* N.S., Pittsburgh, Pa., Oct. 19, 1878; grad. Slippery Rock Coll. for Teachers, 1897; taught in public school of Pittsburgh, 1897-1901; dau. of James Porter Stewart (1838-1901), corpl. in Civil War, city official, Pittsburgh, 25 years, *m* 1870, Jane Johnson Fulton (1841-1917), from North of Ireland, 1849; issue: 1–William Stewart, *b* N.S., Pittsburgh, June 16, 1913; ed. Allentown Prep., '29, Bordentown Mil. Inst., 1930, Lehigh U. Adopted dau. Louise Eunice Stewart (a niece now known as Louise Stewart Renkin), *b* N.S., Pittsburgh; Cedar Crest Coll., '28.
1–Student engring., Cornell U. Under father Renkin Mfg. Co., Pittsburgh, 1893-95; collaborated with George F. Myers, developing wing surfaces, carrying Prof. Langley's work further in heavier than air machines, 1896-97; in charge of construction, Pittsburgh & Kittaning Plate Glass Co., 1898-1901; engr. in charge of works, U.S. Plate Glass Co. and town, Valley Park, Mo., 1902-07; resident engr. Sakchi, Bengal, India, for Tata Iron & Steel Co., 1908-11; chief engr. Curtis Machine Co., St. Louis, 1912-15; chief engr., A.M. Byers, Pittsburgh, 1915-17; managing engr., v.p. and dir., Quigley Fuel Systems, New York, 1917-27, pioneer in field pulverization, adding improvements and inventions to that industry; mgr. Dry Quenching Equipment & Industrial Furnace Dept., Internat. Combustion Engring. Corpn., New York, since 1928. Hon. Magistrate, Indian Civil Service, under dept. commissioner, of Chota Nagpur, Bengal, India; acting hon. lt. of foot, Chota Nagpur Mounted Rifles, Bengal, India, 1908-11; some active service in the Bastar State Insurrection, 1910; pvt. Co. D, 1st Bergen Co. Bn. Inf., N.J. Militia Reserve, 1917-19. Mem. S.A.R., I.A.G., Am. Soc. M.E., Engrs. of Western Pa., New York Professional Engrs., Soc. Mining and Metall. Engrs., Market Research Inst. of Nat. Coal Assn. (see Who's Who in Engineering, etc.). Presbyterian. Republican. Residence: "Green Gables," Oradell, N.J.

1–**ROBINSON, Horace Eddy,** *b* Portland, Me., Jan. 16, 1887.
9–George **Robinson,** from Scotland, was at Rehoboth, 1646; *m* 1651, Joanna Ingraham (*d* 1699);
8–George (*b* 1656), *m* 1680, Elizabeth Guild;
7–Nathaniel (1692-1771), of Attleboro, *m* 1721, Zelpha Daggett (*d* 1792);
6–Gen. George (1726-1812), officer Am. Rev.; *m* 1st, 1748, Abigail Everett (1727-62);
5–Rev. George (*b* bet. 1750-54-*d* 1847), *m* 1st, 1777, Asenath Carpenter (1751-1827);
4–George (1786-1861), W. Bridgewater, Mass.; *m* 1808, Annis Willard (1788-1866);
3–Jacob Winchell (1824-1914), Portland, Me.; *m* 1849, Martha Allen (1830-1902);
2–George William (1856-1927), of Revere, Mass., and Portland, Me.; *m* 1883, Mary M. Maney (1864-1918); issue: I–Henrietta (*b* May 1884; *m* Talbot Case, Fayetteville, N.Y.); II–Martha A. (1885-86); III–Horace Eddy (1 above); IV–Margarett E. (*b* 1888; *m* Carlton H. Holmes), V–George William (*b* 1890; *m* Ida Geiger); VI–Harriet (*b* and *d* 1891); VII–Ruth (*b* 1892; *m* Frank Cahill); VIII–Gertrude (*b* 1894; *m* Clarence O. Dodge).

1–*m* June 17, 1912, Louise Gulick (qv for issue).
1–M.D., Tufts Med. Coll. Pediatrician, Babies' (N.Y. City), Grasslands, Mt. Kisco hospitals (Westchester Co.). Mem. A.M.A., N.Y. Acad. Medicine, S.A.R. Club: Columbia. Residence: 370 Bedford Rd., Pleasantville, N.Y.

1–**ROBINSON, Louise Gulick (Mrs. Horace E.),** *b* New York, N.Y., Dec. 31, 1888.
9–Hendrick **Gulick** (*d* 1653), from Holland, settled at Gravesend, L.I., 1653; *m* Geertruy, dau. of Jochem Willekins;
8–Jochem (1652-1712), of N.J.; *m* 1676, Jacomyntie Van Pelt (*d* 1723; Teunis[9]);
7–Peter (bap. 1689-1774), of N.J.; *m* Eve Van Sicklen (Fernandus[8]; Fernandus[9]);
6–Peter (1733-98), of nr. Cranberry, N.J.; *m* Willemptje – (1736-95);
5–John (*b* 1764), lived at Jamesburg, Middlesex Co., later moved to Englishtown, Monmouth Co., N.J.; *m* Lydia Combs (1767-1835);
4–Peter Johnson (1797-1877), of Freehold, N.J.; missionary in Hawaii; *m* 1827, Fanny Hinckley Thomas (1798-1883);
3–Luther Halsey, D.D. (1828-91), missionary, in Hawaii; *m* 1851, Louisa Lewis (1830-94; Junius Sidney[4], *m* Sarah Wardell);
2–Luther Halsey, M.D. (1865-1918), of Springfield, Mass., and New York; educator; *m* 1886, Lottie Emily Vetter (1865-1928); issue: I–Louise (1 above); II–Francis Jewett (*b* 1891); III–Charlotte (*b* 1892); IV–Katharine (*b* 1895; *m* A. E. Hamilton, divorced; *m* 2d, Alan B. Curtis); V–Luther (*b* and *d* 1897); VI–John Halsey (*b* 1899; *m* Gretchen Messer, divorced).
1–*m* June 17, 1912, Horace Eddy Robinson (qv); issue: 1–Charlotte, *b* Mt. Kisco, N.Y., June 27, 1919; 2–Louise, *b* Pleasantville, N.Y., Aug. 9, 1921.
1–Grad. Sargent Normal School for Physical Edn. Mem. I.A.G., N.Y.G.B.S. Presbyterian. Republican. Residence: 370 Bedford Rd., Pleasantville, N.Y.

1–**SANDERS, Natalie Rood (Mrs. Louis P.),** *b* New York, N.Y., Jan. 17, 1884.
9–Thomas **Rood** (*d* 1672), from Eng., settled at Norwich, Conn., 1649; *m* Sarah– (*d* 1668);
8–John (1658-1706), *m* 1687, Mary Ede; and thru his g.son:
6–Moses (*b* 1743) of Torrington, Conn.; *m* 1768, Sarah Loomis (*b* 1743/44; Isaac[7]; Isaac[8]; Sgt. Daniel[9]; Dea. John[10]; Joseph[11], qv);
5–Moses;
4–Simeon, *m* Margaret Smith;
3–Ira (*d* 1910), *m* 1845, Maria Melissa Deyo;
2–Ira Daniel (2 below).
10–Christian **Deyo** (1620-86), Huguenot from France to the Palatinate, thence to Kingston, N.Y., 1676; received deed for 144 sq. miles in Ulster Co., N.Y., 1677; called the "Grandpere of New Paltz"; *m* 1643:
9–Pierre (*b* ca. 1646), came with his father; *m* 1672, Agatha Nickols (*b* ca. 1650);
8–Christian (*b* 1674), *m* 1702, Martje de Graff;
7–Jacobus, *m* 1724, Janatje Freer;
6–Peter (1738-1812), Am. Rev.; *m* 1765, Charity Maria Cramer (*b* 1745);
5–James;
4–James (*b* 1800), *m* Caroline Deyo;
3–Maria Melissa (1821-99), *m* Ira **Rood** (3 above).
9–William **Hill**, from Eng. in the "William and Francis," 1632, settled at Dorchester; *m* Sarah–;
8–Nathan (*b* 1658), *m* Elizabeth Jones;
7–John, *m* Esther Bulkeley;
6–Nathan (*b* 1731), *m* 1753, Eunice Wakeman (1735-65);
5–Aaron (*b* 1755), *m* 1777, Hannah Fiske (1762-1823);
4–Jonathan (1796-1886), *m* 1818, Sally Wright (1801-80; Joseph[5]; Gilbert[6]; Capt. Caleb[7], Am. Rev.; Capt. Noah[8]; Ebenezer[9]; Sgt. Samuel[10]; Samuel[11]);
3–Joseph Wright (1829-1901), *m* 1852, Mary Jane Randall (*d* 1902);
2–Ada Mary (1855-1918), *m* 1876, Ira Daniel **Rood** (1850-98), attorney; issue: I–Chester Harold (*m* Marie MacMann); II–Natalie (1 above); III–Marie Hill (*m* Frank Cecil Bunker); IV–Ira Daniel, Jr. (*m* Jasmine Schoonover).
1–*m* Louis Justin Brown (Sept. 17, 1880-July 11, 1916); son William Watrous Brown; issue (all *b* N.Y. city): 1–Helen, *b* June 12, 1904; ed. Mills Coll. and U. of Mont.; *m* Oct. 23, 1925, George, son of George Nelson (issue: Helen; George, Jr.); 2–Wilbur, *b* Dec. 15, 1906; ed. U. of Mont.; 3–Louise Merris, *b* June 30, 1909; ed. U. of Mont.; 4–Jean Edgerton, *b* May 12, 1911; ed. U. of Mont.
1–*m* 2d, Sept. 16, 1920, Louis Peck Sanders.
1–Mem. D.A.R., I.A.G., N.E.H.G.S., N.Y. State Hist. Assn. Presbyterian. Republican. Summer place: "Endokare" on Flathead Lake, Montana. Residence: Butte, Mont.

CAPT. JOSEPH BUTCHER ROGERS (b 1842), from a daguerreotype taken at the age of 17.

1–**ROGERS, Weaver Henry,** *b* Pittsburgh, Pa., Nov. 9, 1876.
8–John **Rogers** (*d* 1697), Quaker, from London and Yorkshire, Eng., with Friends Colony; settled in N.J. on Rancocas River nr. Burlington, 1678; *m* 1685, Mary Groome, of Abington, Pa.;
7–John (*b* 1687), purchased 150 acres in Evesham Tp., Burlington Co., N.J.; *m* 1712, Martha Middleton;
6–William (*b* 1731);
5–Abraham (1755-1814), *b* on Rancocas River, buried at Haleyville Cemetery, nr. Mauricetown, N.J.; served in N.J. Cont. Army, Am. Rev.; *m* 1780, Mary Hovey (1763-1832; desc. Daniel Hovey, from Eng. to Mass. in the "Griffin," 1633, settled at Ipswich, 1639);
4–William (1788-1849), *m* 1808, Mary Wheaton (1781-1813; desc. Robert Wheaton, qv);
3–Henry (1809-88), *m* 1832, Keziah Weaver;
2–Capt. Joseph Butcher (2 below).
6–Thomas **Weaver** (*d* 1708), of Eng. and N.Y.; *m* Catherine Weaver;
5–Joseph (*d* 1821), of Cumberland Co.; *m* 1770, Rachel Robinson;
4–Jacob H. (*d* 1847), of Cape May Co., N.J.;
3–Keziah (1813-91), *m* Henry **Rogers** (3 above);
2–Capt. Joseph Butcher (*b* 1842), retired (see portrait); *m* 1871, Margaret Thompson Matthews (1845-1916; desc. George Matthews [*d* 1882], *m* Amanda [1841-73], dau. of Edward Carr, of Brownesville, Pa.).
1–*m* May 22, 1901, Analdean Friebertshauser, *b* Pittsburgh, Pa., Jan. 10, 1877; dau. of William Friebertshauser; issue: 1–Dorothy Analdean, *b* Pittsburgh, Pa., Apr. 24, 1905; Mt. Holyoke, '25; *m* Oct. 28, 1926, Lloyd Hornbostel, Lehigh, '24, son of Henry Hornbostel, *m* Martha Armitage; 2–Virginia Emily, *b* Pittsburgh, Pa., Jan. 18, 1907; Mt. Holyoke, '27; *m* Nov. 9, 1929, Nathan Hofer White, Yale, '24, son of Nathan S. White, *m* Katherine Hofer.
1–Grad. U. of Pittsburgh, 1896. Pres. Weaver H.

Rogers & Co., Inc., investments (see Who's Who in America). Maj. and lt. col., Ordnance Dept., U.S.A., chief of fuel and pwr. and steel sections and with A.E.F., 1917-19. Trustee Clergy Life Ins. Fund, Episcopal Church Home of Western Pa.; pres. Church Club of Western Pa.; pres. 14th Ward School Bd., etc. Mem. S.A.R. (v.p. Pa. Soc.; pres. Pittsburgh Chapter). Mason (33°, Shrine); Royal Order Scotland. Clubs: Metropolitan, Columbia, Chevy Chase (Washington), Duquesne, Pittsburgh Athletic, Church, Pittsburgh Country. Residence: 5815 Northumberland Av., Pittsburgh, Pa.

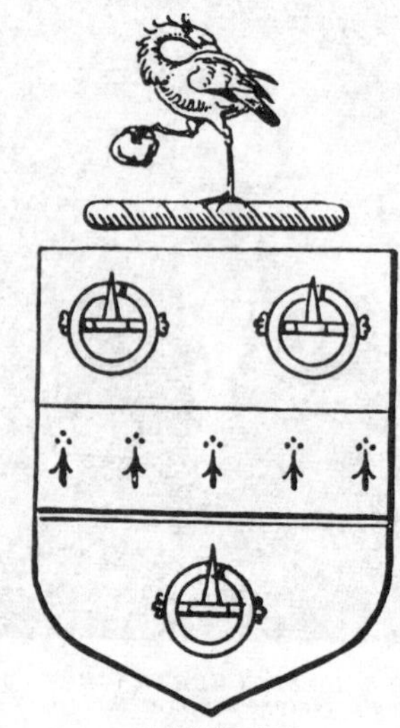

SATTERLEE

Arms: Gules, a fess ermine, between three round buckles or.
Crest: A stork resting, holding in the dexter claw a stone proper.
Motto: Semper fidelis.

1–**SATTERLEE, Joseph,** *b* Tolland, Conn., Sept. 22, 1858.
7–Benedict **Satterlee** (1655-ca. 1689), from Eng., 1682, settled at New London, Conn.; *m* 1682, Rebecca–, widow of John Dymond;
6–William (*b* 1683/84), *m* 1711, Ann Avery;
5–William (1712-52), *m* 1736, Mary Powers; *m* 2d, 1738, Eliza Crary; *m* 3d, Rachel Parks;
4–Jonas (*d* 1777), Am. Rev.; *m* 1764, Lydia Geer;
3–Elisha (1772-1859), *m* 1795, Polly Avery;
2–Dwight Alden (1814-1901), *m* 1851, Charity Hibbard Stoddard; issue: I–Charity Emma (1852-1930; *m* 1877, Austin L. Edgerton); II–Mary Hester (*b* 1854); III–Joseph (1 above).
1–*m* Jan. 30, 1895, Mary I. Crawford, *b* Stafford, Conn., June 22, 1861; dau. of Lawrens Crawford; issue (all *b* Needham, Mass.): 1–Dwight Crawford (June 6, 1896-Mar. 27, 1903); 2–Dorothy, *b* Sept. 24, 1904; Simmons Coll.; 3–Howard Avery, *b* May 12, 1906; Wentworth Inst.; *m* Aug. 18, 1928, Ruth E., dau. of Ernest T. Cushman, of Needham.
1–Mem. I.A.G. Residence: 16 Mark Lee Rd., Needham Heights, Mass.

1–**SCUDDER, Henry Darcy, Jr.,** *b* Trenton, N.J., Nov. 26, 1884.
11–Thomas **Scudder** (qv);
10–John (1619-90), *m* 1642, Dorothy King;
9–John (1645-1732), *m* 1669, Joanna Betts;
8–Capt. Richard (1671-1754), of Newtown, L.I.; *m* Hannah Reeder (1671-1734);
7–John (1701-48), of Newtown; *m* 1734, Phoebe Howell (1707-87; Daniel[8], *m* Mary–; Richard[9]; Edward[10], qv);
6–Daniel (1736-1811), of Scudder Falls, N.J.; mem. Com. of Safety in Am. Rev.; *m* Mary Snowden (1738-98);
5–Elias (1769-1811), *m* Sarah Smith (1770-1858);
4–Jasper Smith (1797-1877), *m* 1821, Mary Stillwell Reeder (1797-1883; Amos[5], *m* Mary, dau. of Joseph Stillwell, capt. in Am. Rev.);
3–Edward Wallace (1822-93), of Trenton, N.J.; A.B., Princeton, '41, A.M., 1844, LL.D., 1880; pres. N.J. Senate, 1865; justice Supreme Ct. of N.J., 1869-93; *m* 1847, Mary Louise Drake;
2–Henry Darcy (2 below).
9–Capt. Francis **Drake** (will dated 1687), *m* Mary Walker;
8–Rev. John (*d* 1739), *m* Rebecca Trotter;
7–Abraham (1685-1763), *m* Deliverance Wooden;
6–Abraham (*d* before father), *m* Anne Young;
5–Col. Jacob (1732-1823), mem. Com. Corr. and officer Am. Rev.; mem. N.J. Legislature; *m* Esther Dickerson;
4–George King (1788-1837), A.B., Princeton, 1808, A.M., 1811; speaker N.J. Assembly, 1825-26; justice Supreme Ct. of N.J., 1826-34; *m* Mary Alling Halsey (Jacob[5], *m* Jemima Cook);
3–Mary Louisa (1824-90), *m* Edward Wallace **Scudder** (3 above).
9–Philemon **Dickerson** (1598-1672), *m* Mary Paine;
8–Peter (1648-1721), *m* Naomi Mapes;
7–Thomas (ca. 1677-1725), *m* Abigail Reeve;
6–Peter (1725-80), capt. in Am. Rev.; mem. 1st Provincial Congress of N.J.; mem. Soc. Cincinnati; *m* Ruth Coe (Joseph[7]);
5–Esther (1757-1819), *m* Col. Jacob **Drake** (5 above);
4–George King, *m* Mary Alling Halsey (4 above);
3–Mary Louisa, *m* Edward Wallace **Scudder** (3 above);
2–Henry Darcy (1851-1930), banker, Belmar, N.J.; *m* 1879, Marvina James Davis (*b* 1856); issue: I–Mary Louisa; II–James Davis; III–Henry Darcy (1 above).
1–*m* June 20, 1917, Bessie Osborn, *b* Newark, N.J., Nov. 9, 1886; dau. of Joseph Kelsey Osborn (John[3]); issue: 1–Henry Huston, *b* New York, N.Y., Mar. 3, 1918; 2–Joseph Osborn, *b* Wanamassa, N.J., Feb. 23, 1921; 3–Miss Darcy, *b* Wanamassa, Mar. 21, 1924.
1–Architect. Served in N.J.N.G., 1906-17; Mexican border service, 1916; 1st lt. in World War. Mem. Am. Soc. of C.E., N.J. Soc. of Architects. Episcopalian. Republican. Club: Essex (Newark). Residence: Riverside Drive, Red Bank, N.J.

1–**SHAW, J(ohn) Bruce,** *b* St. Louis, Mo., Feb. 18, 1884.
6–William **Shaw,** *m* Mary McKeag;
5–Thomas, *m* Margaret Calvert;
4–John, *m* Nancy Gown;
3–John (1812-57), from Ireland, *d* in Jackson Co., Ill.; *m* 1842, Margaret Ann Baldridge;
2–Dr. Alexander B. (2 below).
8–Sir James **Holmes** (*d* 1727), *m* Jane Jennings;
7–Janet (1694-1768), *m* 1714, William **Baldridge** (1689-1772; Richard[8], of Ireland);
6–Alexander (1717-1805), pvt. Am. Rev.; *m* 1745, Jane Ramsey;
5–Rev. William (1773-1830), *m* 1792, Rebecca Agnew (1771-1817; Lt. Col. James[6], lt. col. 7th Bn., Asso. Bn. of York, Pa., 1778, *m* 1768, Mary Ramsey; Capt. James[7], from Ireland 1717, with father; James[8], from Ireland, landowner in Lancaster Co., Pa., 1717);
4–Alexander Holmes, M.D. (1795-1874), *m* 1817, Evalina Bradford (1801-45; William[5], *m* Margaret Parkison);
3–Margaret Ann (1823-1907), *m* John **Shaw** (3 above).
5–Samuel **Allen,** *m* Nancy Anderson;
4–James (1775-1862), *m* Sarah Boyd (John[5], *m* Elizabeth Duff);
3–Rev. Henry (1817-67), *b* in Ireland, *d* at Jersey City, N.J.; *m* 1847, Elizabeth Ann Richardson;
2–Favola (2 below).
11–Samuel **Richardson** (*d* 1719), from Eng. via Jamaica, 1686, settled at Phila.; mem. Provincial Council, 1688; justice, 1688; judge Co. Ct.; mem. Assembly, 1691-1709; Quaker; *m* 1st, Taliner– (*d* 1703);
10–Joseph (*d* 1752), *m* Elizabeth Bevan;
9–Edward, *m* Ann Jones;
8–Joseph (*d* 1772), of Bucks Co.;
7–Joshua (*d* 1800);

6–Capt. Joseph (*d* 1808), served in Pa. Regt., 1758,59;
5–Clement (*d* 1827), pvt. Am. Rev.; *m* Catherine Baker;
4–Malachi (1802-88), *m* 1823, Sarah Annah Ewalt Patterson (1804-48; Capt. James[5], *m* Annah Elizabeth, dau. of Peter Hull; Capt. James[6]);
3–Elizabeth Ann (1824-1900), *m* Rev. Henry **Allen** (3 above);
2–Favola (1848-98), *m* 1871, Dr. Alexander Baldridge **Shaw** (1847-96); issue: I–Edna (1873-1921; *m* Warren M. Chandler); II–Guy A. (1875-1924); III–Roy Adolos (*b* 1882; *m* Hannah Irwin Nevin); IV–John Bruce (1 above).
1–*m* Sept. 11, 1917, Ruth Clarinda Duncan (Apr. 14, 1892-Apr. 23, 1922); dau. Jackson H. Duncan (Capt. John[3], resigned commn. in British army and came to U.S., *m* Clarinda, dau. of Col. Dingwell, who was the last honorary keeper of the Scottish crown jewels); issue: 1–Duncan Bruce, *b* Cincinnati, O., Jan. 9, 1919; 2–Ruth Joan Duncan, *b* Cincinnati, June 7, 1921.
1–*m* 2d, Aug. 3, 1926, Cameron Edson, *b* New York, N.Y., Apr. 1, 1900; dau. of R. Stewart Edson, of New York; issue: 1–John Bruce, 2d, *b* Cincinnati, June 9, 1927.
1–Sec. and treas. The Duncan & Ohio Co., mfr. paper products. Mem. S.C.W., S.A.R., I.A.G., Cincinnati Geneal. Soc. Presbyterian. Republican. Club: Camargo Hunt and Country. Residence: "Greenock Farms," Brill Rd., Indian Hill, Cincinnati, O.

1–**SLOSSON, Preston William,** *b* Laramie, Wyo., Sept. 2, 1892.
7–Nathaniel **Slosson** (ca. 1696-1787), of Deerfield, Mass.; bought land at Captain's Plain, Norwalk, Conn., and probably settled there 1720/21, in King Parish, 1738; constable, 1739; lister, 1744; *m* Margaret Belden (ca. 1700-1780; William[8], of Norwalk);
6–Daniel (*d* 1805), built "Caswell House," Norwalk; removed to Richmond, Mass.; *m* 2d, Keziah Benton;
5–Nathaniel (1754-1822), Kent; *m* 1st, Eunice Sisson (*d* ante 1805);
4–Anson Seymour (1796-1861), Maine, N.Y.; *m* 1827, Mary Steele (1795-1867; Samuel[5], *m* Nancy McKeen; James[6]; Thomas[7]);
3–William Butler (1835-1907), Sabetha, Kan.; mem. Slosson Brothers & Co.; *m* 1860, Achsah Louise Lilly;
2–Edwin Emery (2 below).
10–John **Lilly** (desc. Sir Robert de Lisle, of Castle Lille, Normandy, France, who entered Eng. with William the Conqueror, 1066); from Scotland, 1640; settled at Wethersfield, Conn., and Reading, Mass.; *m* Ruth–;
9–George (*b* 1636), Reading; *m* Hannah Smith; *m* 2d, Jane–;
8–Dea. Samuel (*b* 1665), *m* Hannah–;
7–Samuel (*b* 1695), weaver, Woodstock, Conn.; *m* 2d, 1727, Mehitabel Bacon;
6–Jonathan (1739-1828), *m* 1761, Sarah Foster;
5–Foster (1772-1857), *m* 1796, Deborah Hall;
4–Orsamus (1800-57), *m* 1st, 1826, Louisa Lilly (1800-42; Silas[5], *m* Lucy Bachelor, or Batcheller; Silas[6]; Reuben[7]; George[8]; George[9]);
3–Achsah Louise (1836-1906), *m* William B. **Slosson** (3 above).
10–Myles **Standish,** Mayflower Pilgrim (qv);
9–Josiah (1634-90), *m* 1654, Mary Dingley; *m* 2d, Sarah Allen;
8–Dea. Josiah (*d* 1753), *m* Sarah– (*d* 1742);
7–Hannah (*b* 1706), *m* 1724, Nathan **Foster** (1700-53);
6–Sarah (1742-1828), *m* Jonathan **Lilly** (6 above).
11–William **Brewster,** Mayflower Pilgrim (qv);
10–Patience (ca. 1600-1624), *m* Gov. Thomas **Prence** (qv);
9–Sarah (*b* 1624), *m* 1660, Jeremiah **Howe** (*b* 1637);
8–Ebenezer (*b* 1675), *m* 1699, Sarah Gorham (1676?-1705; Capt. John[9], *m* Mary Otis; Capt. John[10], qv, *m* Desire, dau. of John Howland, qv);
7–Thomas (*b* 1699), *m* Deborah Sears;
6–Sarah (1749-1817), *m* 1775, Reuben **Hall** (1747-1821), Ashfield, Me. (David[7]; Daniel[8]; Joseph[9]; John[10]; John[11]);
5–Deborah (1779-1863), *m* Foster **Lilly** (5 above);
4–Orsamus, *m* Louisa Lilly (4 above);
3–Achsah Louise, *m* William B. **Slosson** (3 above);
2–Edwin Emery (1865-1929), editor Science Service; *m* 1891, May Genevieve Preston (Levi C.[3], *m* Mary Gorsline); issue: I–Preston William (1 above); II–Raymond Alfred (1894-1900).
1–*m* June 21, 1927, Lucy Chase (Denny) Wright, (see Vol. II, p. 237); issue: 1–Flora May, *b* Richmond, Va., June 21, 1928.
1–B.S., Columbia, 1912 (P.B.K.), M.A., 1913, Ph.D., 1916. Asso. prof. history, U.Mich., since 1927. Author (see Who's Who in America). Asst. librarian, Am. Peace Commn., 1917-19. Conglist. Residence: 2101 Devonshire Rd., Ann Arbor, Mich.

1–**SMITH, Madeleine Crozer (Mrs. Arthur Whitmore),** *b* Trenton Junction, N.J., Apr. 13, 1893.
9–Duncan **Williamson,** *m* Wallery–;
8–William, *m* Elizabeth–;
7–Peter, *m* 1731, Leah–;
6–Peter, *m* 1764, Sarah Satcher (Robert[7], *m* 1731, a dau. of George Brown; John[8], *m* 1701, Mary Loftie);
5–Mercy (1766-1830), *m* 1790, William **Crozer** (1764-1835), Penn's Manor, Pa. (Andrew[6], came to N.J., 1723, to Pa., 1758, *m* Mary, dau. of John Richardson, of Burlington Co., N.J.);
4–Peter (1791-1877), Trenton, N.J.; *m* 1815, Elizabeth Hance;
3–Peter Williamson (1831-1924), banker, Trenton; *m* 1864, Mary Larzelere McKee (1835-92; William[4], *m* Elizabeth Larzelere);
2–Edward Hance (2 below).
9–John **Hance,** *m* 1669, Elizabeth Hanson (Thomas, or Tobias[10]);
8–Isaac, *m* 1710, Rachel White;
7–Timothy, *m* 1736, Rebecca Allen;
6–David, *m* 1762, Hannah Cook;
5–Timothy (*b* 1765), *m* 1789, Sarah Thompson (*d* 1800; Thomas[6], Falls Tp., Pa., *m* Rachel–);
4–Elizabeth (1795-1873), *m* 1815, Peter **Crozer** (4 above).
7–James **Cubberley** (*d* 1754), came to N.J. ca. 1720; *m* Mary– (1690-1772);
6–John, *m* Mary Rulon (*b* 1730; David[7], *m* Exercise, dau. of Henry Allen);
5–Exercise (*b* 1763), *m* Benjamin **Stelle** (1757-1812);
4–Peter Wilson (1806-78), Hamilton Tp., N.J.; *m* Mary Dubbs (1809-78; Michael[5], of Phila., *m* Mary Fagans);
3–S. Martin Dubbs (1833-1914), White Horse, N.J.; *m* 1862, Mary Elizabeth Nutt;
2–Lillie D. (2 below).
11–Steven Coerte (Van Voorhees) **Voorhees** (qv);
10–Coerte Stevense (1637-post 1702), dea. Dutch Ch. of Flatlands, 1677; magistrate, 1664,73; took oath of allegiance, 1687; capt. of militia, 1689; *m* ante 1664, Marretje Gerritse Van Couwenhoven (Gerrit Wolfertse[11], *m* Aeltie Lambertse Cool);
9–Cornelis Coerte (bap. 1678), ens. of militia, 1700; *m* Antie Remsen (*b* 1681);
8–Coert, the elder (ca. 1698-ca. 1775), began to write name Voorhees; moved to Windsor Tp., Middlesex Co., N.J.; trustee of ch. at Cranbury, N.J., 1739; *m* Peternelletje–;
7–Coert (1735-1817), of Dutch Neck, Mercer Co., N.J.; *m* Catherine Van Pelt; *m* 2d, Helena (Hoagland) Bergen;
6–Coert (1756-1821), pvt. Am. Rev.; *m* 1779, Ann Updike (1760-1845);
5–Cornelius (*b* 1786), *m* Mary Cubberley (William[6], *m* Elizabeth Tindall; Thomas[7]; James[8]);
4–Ann Elizabeth (1808-67), *m* Nathan **Nutt** (1806-67; Samuel[5]);
3–Mary Elizabeth (1833-1907), of Allentown, N.J.; *m* S. Martin Dubbs **Stelle** (3 above);
2–Lillie D. (1866-1927), *m* 1888, Edward Hance **Crozer** (*b* 1866), Trenton and Hamilton Sq., N.J.; fire ins.; issue: I–Ethel Mary (*b* 1890; *m* Houghton Currier Smith, M.D., see Vol. III, p. 423); II–Madeleine (1 above); III–Peter Williamson (*b* 1895; *m* 1925, Mrs. Anne Allen Eldridge); IV–Elizabeth (*b* 1908).
1–*m* Feb. 16, 1918, Harold LeRoy Dennis (1893-1927), of Hamilton Square, N.J.; son of Henry Calvin Dennis (Joseph B.[3] *m* Cornelia Blackwell Snook); issue: 1–Ethel Crozer, *b* Jan. 31, 1919; 2–Lillian Crozer, *b* Sept. 7, 1923.
1–*m* 2d, Feb. 1, 1928, Arthur Whitmore Smith, Ph.D. (see Vol. II, p. 206); issue: 1–Marcia Houghton, *b* Ann Arbor, Mich., June 3, 1929.
1–Teacher of piano, Naylor Coll. of Music, Trenton, N.J., 1914-23; organist and choir dir.,

Baptist Ch., Hamilton Square, N.J., 1924-28. Residence: 1008 Oakland Av., Ann Arbor, Mich.

1-**STEVENSON, George Urie,** *b* Sandusky, O., July 28, 1874.
5-James **Stevenson** (*d* 1749), from North of Ireland ca. 1738, settled at Manor of the Maske, nr. Gettysburg, Pa.; *m* in Ireland, Margaret-;
4-James (ca. 1725-1817), of York Co., Pa., and Frederick Co., Md.; overseer of poor, Strabane Tp., Pa., 1750; mentioned in log of Mason & Dixon's survey as living north of line, 1765; pvt., Cont. Flying Camp, at Head of Elk, Md., 1776, attached to Capt. John Ogilvie's Co.; *m* 2d, 1770, Jane Buchanan (*d* 1829);
3-Dr. Matthew (1777-1849), of Md., Pa., and Ohio; was one of the pioneer "saddle-bags" physicians and surgeons of Sandusky Co., O.; Methodist lay preacher; founder of the first M.E. church in Western Pa., at Homestead, 1830; *m* 1810, Jane Gilson;
2-Matthew Asbury (2 below).
7-Rev. Thomas **Craighead** (*d* 1739; son of Rev. Robert, a native of Scotland, who went to Ireland and was pastor of the Presbyn. ch. of Donoughmore, 1657-87, later pastor at Londonderry, escaping during the siege by the forces of James II, and fleeing to Glasgow, later returned to Londonderry, where he died 1711); ed. in Scotland as a physician; returned to Ireland, where he was pastor for several yrs. in Donegal; came to N.E., 1715, with Rev. William Homes; removed to Lancaster Co., Pa., 1733; *m* a dau. of a Scotch Laird;
6-John (*b* in Ireland ante 1715-*d* after Am. Rev.), tailor, Phila.; bought a large tract of land on the Yellow Breeches Creek, nr. Carlisle, Pa., 1742; mem. Stony Ridge Conv., 1775; *m* ca. 1736, Rachel Montgomery; their son, Rev. John, Princeton U., 1763, officer in Cont. Army;
5-Elizabeth, *m* ca. 1764, William **Gilson** (*d* 1806), of Cumberland Co., Pa., and Ft. Barr, New Derry, Westmoreland Co., Pa.; pvt., Capt. James Laird's Co., 3d Bn., 3d Class, Cumberland Co. (Pa.) Militia, 1777; companion-in-arms of David Boyd, qv (Richard[6] [*d* 1783], settled nr. E. Pennsboro, Lancaster Co., Pa., *m* Margaret-);
4-Thomas (1765-1813), drowned in Tuscarora Creek; soldier War 1812; *m* 1786, Nancy Boyd;
3-Jane (1789-1877), *m* Dr. Matthew **Stevenson** (3 above).
6-John **Boyd** (ca. 1722-ca. 1788), from North of Ireland, 1740, and settled in that part of Cumberland Co., Pa., which is now Northumberland Co.; ranger for protection of the frontier, 1755; fought in a co. of militia under Gen. Broadhead at destruction of Indian town of Kittanning, Pa., 1756; paymaster, 8th Pa. State Line, 1776; *m* 1st, ca. 1742, Nancy Urie (ca. 1725-1756);
5-David (1743-1831), was a renowned marksman, having learned to shoot during his youth, while a captive of the Delaware Indians during French and Indian War; enlisted in Capt. James Chambers' Co., Col. William Thompson's Bn., expert riflemen, known as 1st Regt., Pa. Line, Cont. Army, 1775; re-enlisted in Capt. James Grier's Co., same regt., 1776, in Capt. James Laird's Co., 3d Bn., 3d Class, 1777; *m* 1771, Elizabeth Henderson (ca. 1753-ca. 1825);
4-Nancy (1772-1846), *m* 1st, Thomas **Gilson** (4 above);
3-Jane, *m* Dr. Matthew **Stevenson** (4 above);
2-Matthew Asbury (1827-95), one of the earliest daguerreotypists in America, in which art he made a fortune; camp-photographer at Camp Dennison, O., during Civil War; *m* 1858, Sophia Ellen Thompson (1837-1911); issue: I-Irene Louise (*b* 1858; *m* W. Clinton Arnold); II-Joseph Asbury (*d* 1910, aet. 50); III-Edward Franklin (1863-74); IV-Eugenie Victoria (*b* 1865; *m* Frederick Raine); V-Adelaide Israella (*b* 1867; *m* Harry Hopkins; *m* 2d, James W. Wilson); VI-Bertha Jennie (*b* 1869); VII-Mabel Josephine (*b* 1871; *m* Clarence Holton Upson); VIII-George Urie (1 above); IX-Evangeline V. R. (*b* 1877; *m* Thomas E. Kirk); X-Pearl (*b* and *d* 1877), twin; XI-Byron G. (*b* 1879); XII-Helene Lucile (Mrs. Frederic Dalrymple, qv).
1-Not married. Reporter, Record and Inter-Ocean, Chicago, 1894-96; helped found Chicago Weekly Amusement Guide, 1897, owner and publisher, 1901-09; author and compiler History of Chicago for German Press Club, 1900; mgr. New York and Chicago offices, respectively, of The Billboard, 1910-12; publicity and advertising mgr. Universal Film Co., N.Y. City, 1913-14; publicity and advertising mgr. Trans-Atlantic Film Co., Ltd., London, Eng., 1914-15; mgr. ednl. dept., Universal Pictures Corpn., N.Y. City, 1916-17; wrote, directed and edited 8-reel educational motion-picture, A visit to Battle Creek Sanitarium, for Dr. John Harvey Kellogg, Apr.-Nov., 1922; scenarist for Atlas Ednl. Film Co., Chicago, 1923-24; editor 1926 edition of Who's Who in Chicago; advertising, N.Y. City, 1926-28; sec. for affiliations, Institute of Am. Genealogy, 1929-30. Compiler of geneal. data of Stevenson, Urie, Thompson and Beaver families. Motion-picture survey of A.E.F. camps in Eng. and France for Fosdick Commn., Sept.-Dec. 1917; capt. in A.R.C., France, May 1918-May 1919, in charge of A.R.C. photographic personnel, and with co-operation of Signal Corps of Army, secured official pictures of Red Cross front post activities in Argonne and Chateau-Thierry sectors. Mem. S.A.R., Md. Hist. Soc. Summer place: "Marais du Cygne," Port Clinton, O. Residence: 4704 Drexel Boul., Chicago, Ill.

1-**DALRYMPLE, Helene Lucile Stevenson (Mrs. Frederic),** *b* Sandusky, O., Oct. 29, 1882.
4-William (Thomson) **Thompson** (1763-1814 or 15), owner of Alexandria Hotel, Frenchtown, N.J.; *m* 1790, Sophia Vail (1776-1847);
3-Henry (1802-68), *m* 1823, Helen Permelia Frees;
2-Sophia Ellen (2 below).
6-John (Bever, Bevier) **Bevers,** the first of record in America, living in Bethlehem Tp., Hunterdon Co., N.J., 1753;
5-Col. Joseph (*d* 1816), of Hunterdon Co., N.J.; wrote name Beavers; dep. N.J. Provincial Congress at Trenton, 1775; commd. col. of 2d Hunterdon Co. Militia, 1775, and served thru 1781; *m* ca. 1757, Mary White (*d* post 1817; Alexander[6] [*d* 1776], from Scotland to N.J., settled in Sussex Co., nr. Greenwich, ca. 1756, bought a tract of land, 1762, bet. Roxburg and Belvidere, upon which he built "Whitehall");
4-Naomi (ca. 1780-ca. 1838), *m* 1800, James **Frees** (1771-1822), soldier in N.J. Militia in St. Clair's and Wayne's expdns. against the Indians in Ohio;
3-Helen Permelia (1808-48), *m* 1823, Henry **Thompson** (3 above);
2-Sophia Ellen (1837-1911), *m* 1858, Matthew Asbury **Stevenson** (1827-95), one of the earliest daguerreotypists in America, in which art he made a fortune; camp-photographer at Camp Dennison, O., during Civil War; for issue and other lineages see George Urie Stevenson.
1-*m* Aug. 4, 1915, Frederic Dalrymple, *b* Galesburg, Ill., Apr. 10, 1889; son of Charles Robert Dalrymple, *m* Belle Gould; issue: 1-Dorothy Diane, *b* Sandusky, O., Dec. 23, 1916.
1-Pupil, Art Inst. of Chicago; J. Francis Smith Acad., Chicago. Painter of miniatures on ivory, and portraits in oil, since 1910. Pres. Chicago Soc. of Miniature Painters, 1930-31. Mem. D.A.R., Am. Federation of Arts, Ill. Acad. of Fine Arts, South Side Art Assn., Cordon Club. Summer place: "Marais du Cygne," Port Clinton, O. Residence: 4704 Drexel Boul., Chicago, Ill.

1-**STOKES, Lula Walker (Mrs. James S.),** *b* Daviess Co., Mo., Jan. 16, 1864.
5-Robert **Lemon,** *m* Mary McCown;
4-Martha, *m* Robert **Nelson**;
3-Joseph Lemon (1807-89), *m* Sallie Ann Rowland (William[4], *m* Nancy Copeland; John[5], *m* Nancy-);
2-Mary Ellen (1845-1923), *m* 1862, Motier Lafayette **Walker** (1839-93; Dr. John[3], of Tenn., later of Mo., *m* Artemisia Quinn, of Mt. Vernon, Ky.); issue I-Lula (1 above); II-Laura May; III-George Lemon (*m* Martha

Rusch); IV–Ernest L. (*m* Annie Walker); V–Joseph Orvis (*m* Jeannette Griffin; *m* 2d, Octavia Redmond); VI–Nell; VII–Mary Estelle (*d* 1927; *m* Frank Jerome Durham, *d* 1927); VIII–Jo (*m* Ira Hale Humphrey, *d* ca. 1913).
1–*m* Dec. 26, 1888, James Stephen Stokes, *b* May 28, 1860; son of Henry B. Stokes; issue: 1–Stanley Walker, *m* Gladys Chance; 2–Robert Rowland, *m* Genevieve Crain; 3–Laura Marian, *m* C. M. Browning.
1–Mem. D.A.R., I.A.G. Residence: 1220 E. Normal Av., Kirksville, Mo.

1–**ALLEN, Virgil Douglas,** *b* Cardington, O., Sept. 7, 1869.
8–Edward **Allen,** of Ipswich, Mass., and Suffield, Conn.; *m* Sarah Kimball;
7–Samuel (1679-1728), to Hanover, N.J., 1711; *m* at Concord, Mass., 1706, Anna Hayward;
6–Job (1709-67), of Rockaway, N.J.; capt. co. of foot, Hanover, N.J.; *m* Christian–;
5–Job (1750-98), pioneer iron maker at Rockaway; capt. eastern and western bn. of Morris Co., N.J., Am. Rev.; *m* 1774, Mary Minturn (1757-1826; Jacob[6]);
4–Job (1780-1855), of Knox Co., O.; capt. of militia at time of War 1812; prob. served, as he was always called capt.; *m* 1800, Elizabeth Jackson;
3–James Madison (1810-97), of Newark, N.J.; 1st lt. and q.m., 1st Ohio Vol. Cav., 1861-62; *m* 1832, Harriet Brown (1816-71; Peter Post[4]; Martin[5]);
2–James Madison (2 below).
10–Richard **Jackson** (1582-1672), from Eng.; settled at Cambridge, Mass., 1636; removed to L.I., 1640; later at Southold; *m* Isabelle Maltby (*d* 1661; John[11]);
9–Robert (1620-84), of Eng.; settled at Stamford, Conn.; removed to Hempstead, L.I., 1640; magistrate many yrs.; dep., 1665; constable; overseer; Indian commr.; *m* ca. 1644, Agnes Washburn (ca. 1624-1683);
8–Col. John (1645-1725), patentee of Hempstead, L.I.; commr., 1683; judge, 1685; high sheriff, 1691-95; mem. Assembly; dep., 23 yrs.; col. 1699; *m* 1671, Elizabeth Seaman (Capt. John[9], *m* Elizabeth–);
7–James, *m* Rebecca Hallet;
6–Joseph;
5–Benjamin, *m* Abigail Mitchell;
4–Elizabeth (1782-1862), *m* Job **Allen** (4 above);
3–James Madison, *m* Harriet Brown (3 above);
2–James Madison (1840-91), manufacturer and farmer, Columbus, O.; capt. and commissary, 10th Ohio Vol. Cav., 1863-64; *m* Mifflin Tp., Franklin Co., O., 1865, Roxana Moore (1845-1921); issue: I–Virgil Douglas (1 above); II–Hosmer Copeland (1870-1908); III–Charles Leavitt (*b* 1876); IV–Julia Moore (*b* 1883; *m* 1925 Clement C. Wheeler).
1–*m* Dec. 15, 1897, Gertrude S. Burgess, *b* Toledo, O., Aug. 27, 1873; dau. of Oscar Seth Burgess; issue: 1–Virgil Douglas, Jr., *b* Columbus, O., Sept. 17, 1898; A.B., Western Reserve, '21; *m* Sept. 17, 1921, Margaret Rachel, dau. of Elmer B. Wight, of Cleveland (issue: John Wight; Elizabeth Alice); 2–Annabel Elizabeth (Nov. 28, 1902-June 25, 1926); A.B., Western Reserve, '26; 3–Edward Madison (Feb. 4, 1906-Nov. 5, 1909).
1–Ed. Ohio State U. Engineering and architectural business since 1891. Served as civilian in construction div., Q.M. Dept., Washington, 1917-18. Mem. I.A.G., Cleveland Geneal. Soc. (trustee). Unitarian. Residence: 10830 Pasadena Av., Cleveland, O.

1–**ANABLE, Anna Maria,** *b* Westerlo, N.Y.
9–Roger **Williams** (qv);
8–Mary (1636-87), *m* 1650, John **Sayles** (qv);
7–Eleanor (1671-1714), *m* Richard **Greene** (1660-1711; Maj. John[8]; "Surgeon John"[9], qv);
6–Audrey (1692-1763), *m* 1719, Thomas **Stafford** (1682-1765), dep. Gen. Ct. from Warwick, to Colonial Assembly, 1720,22,25,28; rep. Colonial Assembly, from Coventry, 1747 (Samuel[7]; Thomas[8], qv);
5–Alma (1728-99), *m* 1760, Capt. Samuel **Low,** Am. Rev.;
4–Isabel (1766-1847), *m* 1784, Asa **Sheldon** (1761-1848);
3–Alma (1785-1875), *m* 1814, Joseph **Anable** (1773-1831);
2–Samuel Low (2 below).
9–Dea. Samuel **Chapin** (qv);
8–Henry (*d* 1718), of Springfield; rep. Gen. Ct., 1689; *m* 1664, Bethia Cooley (1643-1711; Benjamin[9], qv);
7–Benjamin (1682-1756), *m* 1704, Hannah Colton (*d* 1739; Isaac[8], of Longmeadow, *m* Mary–);
6–Benjamin (1708-62), *m* 1735, Anna Howard;
5–Charles (*b* 1742), *m* 1st, 1766, Silence Kellog;
4–William (1767-1847), *m* 1796, Sally Brayton (1767-1815);
3–Lorinda (1806-72), *m* 1st, 1824, Josiah Hubbell **Babcock** (1801-36);
2–Sarah Roxcina (1826-1916), *m* 1844, Samuel Low **Anable** (1821-1913), maj. 7th N.Y. Heavy Arty., Civil War; took part in all battles of the Potomac; apptd. by Gen. Grant, U.S. pension agt. for Va.; moved to Chicago, 1883, and engaged in real estate (for issue and other lineages see Vol. III, p. 29).
1–Grad. Miss Anable's School, Phila.; student of Anglo-Saxon, French, Northwestern U.; Spanish, mathematics, U. of Chicago. Mem. Magna Charta Dames, C.D.A., D.C.W., S.D.P., Women Descs. of A. and H.A. Co. of Mass. (organizer and first pres. N.Y. State), D.A.R., Tarrytown Hist. Soc., Anable Alumnae Assn. Residence: Philipse Manor-on-the-Hudson, N.Y.

1–**BOYCE, John Kirkpatrick,** *b* Covington, Tipton Co., Tenn., Dec. 31, 1893.
5–James (Boyes, Boyse) **Boyce** (*d* 1795), from Ireland, settled in Mecklenburg Co., N.C., ca. 1750; *m* in Ireland, Margaret Morehead (*d* post 1795);
4–John (1777-1845), of Mecklenburg Co.; grad. Jefferson Coll., Canonsburg, Pa.; *m* 1801, Isabella Kirkpatrick (*b* 1783; John[5], Am. Rev., *m* Margaret–);
3–Rev. John Kirkpatrick (1815-81), began to write name Boyce; ed. Jefferson Coll.; located in Tenn., 1845; Presbyn. minister; *m* 1845, Martha Rebekah Bowen;
2–William Christopher (2 below).
7–Moses **Bowen** (desc. from Evan ap Owen, of Pentoc, Wales, and was the first to assume the name Bowen); came from Wales, settled in Pa. ca. 1698; *m* Rebecca Reese;
6–John, from Pa. to Augusta Co., Va., ca. 1710; *m* Lily McIlheny (Henry[7], of Ireland, *m* Jane–)
5–Robert (1749-1817), capt. Am. Rev.; *m* 1770, Mary Gillespie;
4–Reese (1788-1844), *m* Sarah Strong (1784-1827; Christopher[5], Am. Rev., *m* 1st, 1782, Frances Elizabeth Dunn; Charles[6], who, with brothers, John, James and Robert, was banished from Ireland for religious reasons);
3–Martha Rebekah (1821-89), *m* 1845, Rev. John Kirkpatrick **Boyce** (3 above).
8–William **Hooker** (*d* 1717), settled in Anne Arundel Co., Md.; removed to Chowan Co., N.C.; large landowner;
7–Godfrey (*d* 1729), of Bertie Co., N.C.; *m* Elizabeth–;
6–Benjamin (*d* 1774), *m* Ann Freeman;
5–Benjamin (1764-1834), of Tenn.; *m* 1791, Annie Frizzelle (1769-1862);
4–Nancy (1792-1844), Fayette Co., Tenn.; *m* 1815, John **Eddins** (*b* 1792), pvt. and sgt. in War 1812 (William[5] [*d* 1847], from Eng., settled at Charleston, S.C., 1785, removed to middle Tenn., 1800, *m* in Eng., 1785, Rebecca, dau. of Robert Chandler);
3–Thomas Partlow (1833-1921), served in S.C. forces; *m* 1859, Alla Amanda Tucker (1838-1918; William Barrow[4], *m* Elizabeth, dau. of William Murphy; Wright[5], *m* Miss Barrow);
2–Victoria Eddins (*b* 1862), *m* 1886, William Christopher **Boyce** (1858-1929), ed. in Tenn.; removed to Amarillo, Potter Co., Tex., 1908; issue: I–Rebekah Bowen (*b* 1887; *m* Frank Kennedy); II–Alla Tucker (*b* 1890; *m* William Woods Ellison); III–Joe Eddins (*b* and *d* 1892); IV–John Kirkpatrick (1 above); V–William Carl (*b* 1897; *m* Julia Enochs).
1–*m* Jan. 10, 1922, Margaret Owen Curtis (see Vol. III, p. 81); issue: 1–Margaret Cannon, *b* Amarillo, Tex., Dec. 13, 1922; 2–John Kirkpatrick, Jr., *b* Amarillo, Sept. 24, 1924.
1–Mem. firm of Williams-Boyce, ins. agents. Served pvt. to capt., 142d Inf., 36th Div., A.E.F., July 18, 1917-Sept. 17, 1919; awarded Croix

du Guerre, 1919, for gallantry in action in the Champagne-Marne offensive; cited in War Dept. Gen. Orders, Feb. 20, 1930, and awarded silver star for gallantry in action, 1918, at St. Etienne (France), during the Champagne offensive; served as bn. adj., 2d Bn., 142d Inf., Sept. 5, 1918-Oct. 28, 1918; capt., Oct. 28, 1918, and assigned to 142d Inf. as regtl. adj.; transferred to Insp. Gen.'s Dept. May 15-Aug. 17, 1919. Capt., Tex. N.G., 1922, maj., 1925. Mem. V.F.W., A.L., "40 and 8" Soc., Kiwanis Club. Mason. Elk. Presbyterian. Residence: 106 Crestway, Amarillo, Texas.

1–**BRADBURY, Bertha Augusta Scofield (Mrs. Walter O.),** *b* Portland, Mich., Feb. 24, 1875.
8–Daniel **Scofield** (1595-1670), from Eng., 1639, settled at Ipswich, Mass.; a founder of Stamford, Conn., 1640, and received land grant there; *m* Mary Youngs (*d* 1696);
7–John (1647-98), of Stamford, *m* 1677, Hannah Mead (*b* 1661; John[8], *m* Hannah, dau. of William Potter; William[9]);
6–Nathaniel (1688-1768), *m* 1713, Elizabeth Pettit (*b* 1690; David[7]; John[8]);
5–Abraham (1736-1812), Am. Rev.; *m* 1764, Sarah Lockwood (*b* 1745; John[6], *m* Sarah, dau. of Daniel Scofield);
4–David (1782-1832), War 1812; *m* Mary Peck (1779-1844; Rev. David[6], *m* Amy Rundall);
3–David Lockwood (1800-60), farmer, Painted Post, N.Y.; *m* 1824, Unis Blodgett;
2–Judge Thomas Donaldson (2 below).
10–Capt. James **Parker** (1617-1701; son of Abraham, *m* Rose–); came from Eng.; petitioner, large propr. and early settler of Groton, Mass.; petitioner and propr. of Dunstable; selectman, 1662; moderator; town clk.; rep. Gen. Ct., 1693; *m* 1st, 1643, Elizabeth Long (*b* 1623; Robert[11], qv);
9–Anna (1647-1728), *m* 1670, Nathaniel **Blood** (*b* 1650; Richard[10], from Eng., an original petitioner for Groton, and a propr., *m* Isabel–; James[11], from Eng. ca. 1638);
8–Anna (1671-1704), *m* Dea. James **Blanchard** (1666-1704; Dea. John[9], *m* Hannah, dau. Capt. Richard Brackett, qv; Widow Ann Blanchard[10]);
7–Anna (*b* 1701), *m* 1719, Moses **Bennett** (*d* 1759), of Groton;
6–Eunice (1731-94), *m* 1749, Jerameel (Jeraphiel) **Powers** (1718-1805), French and Indian War; moved to Springfield, Vt., 1772; town officer and patriot during Am. Rev. (Daniel[7], *m* 2d, Martha Bates; Walter[8], qv);
5–Eunice (*b* 1757), *m* 1772, John **Nott** (*d* 1815), first settler at Springfield, Vt.; owned Nott's Ferry; large property owner; soldier in Am. Rev.; town officer;
4–Mehettable (1774-1841), *m* Asa **Blodgett** (*b* 1765), Gorham, N.Y. (Asa[5], *m* Irene, dau. of Joseph Owen; Samuel[6]; Samuel[7]; Samuel[8]; Thomas[9], qv);
3–Unis (1802-59), *m* David Lockwood **Scofield** (3 above).
9–John **Hoyt** (qv);
8–Thomas (*b* 1641), of Salisbury; *m* Mary Brown (*b* 1647; William[9], *m* Elizabeth Murford; Widow Christian Brown[10], qv);
7–Benjamin (1680-1748), Newbury, Mass.; tanner; *m* 1704, Hannah Pillsbury (*b* 1686; Moses[8], *m* Susanna, dau. of Lionel Worth; William[9]);
6–Joseph (1717-88), Exeter, N.H.; soldier in Indian wars under Braddock; physician, school teacher, seaman; dea. Congl. Ch., Boscawen; *m* 2d, 1746, Susanna French (*b* 1720);
5–Oliver (1747-1827), Concord, N.H.; patriot during Am. Rev.; mem. Com. of Safety; signer Assn. Test of N.H.; dea. Bapt. Ch.; *m* 1765, Rebecca Fitzgerald (1748-1808);
4–Moses (*b* 1768), Green Springs, O.; *m* 1797, his cousin, Abanezar Fitzgerald (*b* 1777; Lt. Edward[5], *m* Abanezar, dau. of John Corser; Edward[6], from Ireland, *m* Mehettable, dau. of Richard Urann);
3–Ruth (1798-1862), as Widow Van Horn, *m* 2d, 1838, Lawrence Daily **Way** (1776-1858; Francis, Jr.[4]; Francis[5]; James[6]; Francis[7]; James[8]);
2–Frances Mary (2 below).
10–Dea. John **Whipple** (qv);
9–Susanna (*b* 1622), *m* Lionel **Worth** (*d* 1667; from Eng., at Newbury, Mass., as early as 1655);
8–Sarah (*b* 1656), *m* 1678, Samuel **Gill** (*b* 1652; John[9], planter, Salisbury, *m* Phebe, dau. of Isaac Buswell);
7–Phebe (*b* 1693), *m* 1717, James **French** (*b* 1692; Simon[8], *m* Joanna Jackman; Joseph[9], *m* Susanna Stacy; Edward[10], immigrant);
6–Susanna (*b* 1720), *m* Joseph **Hoyt** (6 above).
2–Judge Thomas Donaldson **Scofield** (1833-97), atty. at law, Montesano, Wash.; pros. atty., Adams Co., Neb.; held many town offices at Montesano; mayor three times; dea. Meth. Ch.; gave a large tract of land to establish a Meth. Sch., at Montesano; lt. in Civil War from Portland, Mich., raised a co. and took it to Washington, D.C., was captured before Richmond, and was in Richmond prison until liberated by Sherman; went to Mich., 1859, to Neb., 1875, Washington, 1882; *m* 1861, Frances Mary Way (1840-1907); issue: I–Ruth Ann (*b* 1862; *m* Lewis Durley Dent; *m* 2d, John Fensley Soule); II–Judge George Daily (*b* 1864; *m* Zilpha Mace; *m* 2d, Sara Ellen Amidon); III–Susie Arville (1866-1906; *m* Luther Glick); IV–James Adelbert (1867-68); V–Francis Herbert (1872-1929; *m* Millie Miller; *m* 2d, Charlotte Alvis); VI–Bertha Augusta (1 above); VII–Clara Elnora (*b* 1876; *m* Harry Bellamy Martin); VIII–Christie Rosetta (*b* 1878; *m* Loren Hines Brewer).
1–*m* Dec. 25, 1893, Walter Osborne Bradbury, *b* Watertown, Wis., July 10, 1868; son of Daniel Osborne Bradbury; issue: 1–Eugene Daniel, *b* Gladstone, Mich., July 12, 1895; U.Mich., '17; 1st lt., World War; 2–Evelyn Mary, *b* Gladstone, Oct. 26, 1897; Wash. State Coll., '20; *m* June 11, 1924, Marion E. McAninch, of Waitsburg, Wash.; 3–Hazel Mae, *b* Gladstone, Nov. 27, 1898; Wash. State Coll., '20; *m* June 13, 1921, Fred L. Prescott (issue: Walter Bradbury); 4–Walter Osborne, *b* Gladstone, Oct. 2, 1905; Coll. of Puget Sound; *m* Sept. 3, 1927, Mildred, dau. of Solomon Conatser, of Parker, Wash.; 5–Loren Hines, *b* Yakima, Wash., Oct. 1, 1907; 6–Eleanor Scofield, *b* Yakima, Feb. 3, 1910; *m* Jan. 2, 1929, Alfred Vincent Henry.
1–Ed. Coll. of the Pacific, San Jose, Calif. Mem. D.A.R. (state librarian, state historian, Wash. state chmn., registrar, regent), I.A.G., N.E.H.G.S., Wash. State Hist. Soc., Calif. Geneal. Soc. Clubs: Yakima Country, etc. Residence: East Parker, Wash.

1–**BURTON, Lewis William,** *b* Cleveland, O., Nov. 9, 1852.
8–William **Judson** (qv);
7–Sgt. Jeremiah (1621/2-1700/1), from Eng., admitted freeman at Stratford, 1658; mem. com. on fortifications; constable; justice; *m* 1st, 1652, Sarah Foote (ca. 1632-1672/73; Nathaniel[8], qv);
6–Mercy (1665-1736), *m* Solomon **Burton** (ca. 1660-1720), Stratford, Conn.; *m* 1687, Mercy Judson;
5–Judson (1699-1774), *m* 1721/22, Eunice Lewis (1700-1789; Benjamin[6], *m* 2d, Hannah [1654-1728], dau. of Sgt. John Curtis, of Stratford, Conn., *m* Elizabeth Welles);
4–Silas (ca. 1737-1767), *m* Mary Welles (see Vol. III, p. 44, for Welles lineage);
3–John (1766-1848), removed from Conn. to Erie County, Pa., 1811; *m* 2d, 1807, Hannah Miller (see Vol. III, p. 44, for Miller lineage);
2–Lewis (2 below).
9–John **Benjamin** (qv);
8–Caleb (*d* 1684) removed to Wethersfield, Conn., before 1670; *m* Mary (Hale?);
7–John (1677-1753), Hartford, Conn.; *m* 1st, 1699, Ann Latimer;
6–John (1700-73), lived at Stratford from before 1727, *m* Mary Smith (1699-after 1774; Philip[7], of East Hartford);
5–Mary, *m* William **Welles** (1716-45);
4–Mary (1742/43-1782), *m* Silas **Burton** (4 above).
4–James **Wallace** (1723-1806), of County Down, Ireland, resided at Moydaligan, in that county; *m* Elizabeth Singer of the same county;
3–James 1787-1855), *m* 1808, Margaret Hanna Chambers (1789-1873; Alexander[4], *m* Mrs. Margaret [Hanna] Lemmon, from Ireland to Ohio, 1812);
2–Agnes Jane (1821-1901), *m* 1841, Lewis **Burton,** D.D. (1815-94), A.B., Allegheny, '37; D.D., Kenyon, 1868; rector St. John's Ch., Cleveland, O. (succeeding his brother William); for issue see Vol. III, p. 44.

1–*m* Jan. 15, 1883, George Cornelia Paine Hendree Ball (qv for issue).
1–A.B., Kenyon, '73, A.M., 1886; grad. Phila. Div. Sch., 1877; (D.D., Kenyon, and U.South; LL.D., St. John's, and Transylvania). Consecrated 1st P.E. bishop, Diocese of Lexington, Ky., 1896, retired 1928 (see Who's Who in America). Mem. I.A.G., etc. Residence: 644 N. Broadway, Lexington, Ky.

1–**BURTON, George Cornelia Paine Hendree Ball (Mrs. Lewis W.),** *b* Tuskegee, Ala., Jan. 31, 1857 (was named "George" from her father, George Rieley Hendree; was adopted by her paternal aunt, Sarah Austin Tinsley Hendree, *m* Col. James M. Ball, of Atlanta, Ga., and her surname was changed to Ball by act of the Ga. Legislature).
7–John Jacob **Diefendorf** (*b* 1677, in German Palatinate; *d* 1781, in Montgomery Co., N.Y.), came to America, 1730, with two sons John and Jacob, and their families, and settled in Montgomery Co., N.Y.;
6–John (*b* 1700, Zurich, Switzerland; *d* 1791, Montgomery Co., N.Y.);
5–George (*b* Zurich, 1725-*d* Montgomery Co., N.Y., 1815), *m* Catherine Hendree;
4–John Diefendorf **Hendree** (1745-1802), whose espousing England's side in Am. Rev. caused such bitter estrangement in his family, that he took for his surname that of his mother, **Hendree**; *m* 2d, Anna Maria Esler (*b* 1761);
3–George Diefendorf Hendree (*b* Portsmouth, Va., 1792-*d* 1834), *m* Sarah Austin Tinsley;
2–George Rieley (2 below).
8–Thomas **Tinsley** (*b* Yorkshire, Eng., *d* Hanover Co., Va., 1700), came with his wife to Va. before 1650, in which year there is record of a land grant to him on Totopatomoys Creek, then in New Kent, now in Hanover Co., called "Totomoi"; this original grant is still in the Tinsley family; *m* Elizabeth (Randolph?);
7–Thomas (*d* 1745), *m* Martha Ragland;
6–Thomas (*d* 1761), *m* Mary–;
5–Thomas (1731-74), *m* Agnes (Garland?);
4–John (*b* 1759), lived at Tinsley Hall, Goochland Co., Va.; *m* Sarah Chapman Austin (Thomas[5], *m* Constance Chapman; William[6]; William[7], [*b* ca. 1600], capt. British Army, came to America before 1650);
3–Sarah Austin (1790-1875), *m* 1814, George Diefendorf **Hendree** (3 above).
5–Thomas W. **Paine** (*d* 1781), from Ireland bet. 1738-43; lived in Chester and Berks Cos., Pa.; *m* 1744, Hannah Pim (1723-56; William[6], from Ireland to Chester Co., Pa.);
4–William (1745-1827), removed to Baltimore, Md.; capt. Am. Rev.; col. U.S.A.; *m* 1767, Elizabeth Drury (1743-1832; Edward[5] [1708-63], Berks Co., Pa.; *m* 1742, Sarah, dau. William Maugridge [1696-1766], co. judge Berks Co.);
3–Edward Courtenay (1769-1842), Clarke Co., Ga.; lawyer; mem. original bd. trustees U.Ga.; *m* 1807, Caroline Matilda Brinton (1790-1838; Henry[4], *m* Jane Ware, dau. of Robert Hunter, of Va.);
2–Cornelia Jane (1822-1906), *m* 1843, George Rieley **Hendree,** M.D. (1819-56); for issue see Vol. III, p. 44.
1–*m* Jan. 15, 1883, Lewis William Burton (qv); issue (all *b* Richmond, Va.): 1–Lewis James Hendree (June 10, 1885-June 4, 1887); 2–Sarah Louise, *b* Sept. 22, 1887; *m* June 29, 1910, Henry Kavanaugh Milward, of Lexington, Ky. (issue, all *b* Lexington: 1–Lewis William Burton, *b* Oct. 15, 1911; 2–Henry Kavanaugh, Jr., Jan. 4-Jan. 30, 1915; 3–Hendree Paine Brinton, *b* Feb. 12, 1917; 4–Sarah Louise Burton, *b* Jan. 13, 1924); 3–Cornelia Paine Wallace, *b* June 8, 1890; *m* Dec. 30, 1913, Thomas Gresham Machen, of Baltimore, Md. (issue: 1–Thomas Gresham, Jr., *b* Washington, D.C., Nov. 25, 1914; 2–Louise Brantly, *b* Baltimore, Md., Feb. 14, 1916; 3–Cornelia Paine Burton, *b* Baltimore, July 2, 1923).
1–Mem. C.D.A., U.D.C., Women's Club of Central Kentucky. Residence: 644 North Broadway, Lexington, Ky.

1–**CARPENTER, Sarah Alliene Mercer (Mrs. Horace R.),** *b* Chariton, Lucas Co., Ia., Apr. 19, 1870.
8–Thomas **Mercer** (*d* 1734), from Scotland to Ireland, thence to America ante 1670, settled in Cecil Co., Md.; *m* Elizabeth Savory (*d* post 1734);
7–Robert (1703-69), of Cecil Co.; *m* 1723, Ann Mounce (1704-post 1769; Christopher[8], *m* Martha–);
6–Robert (1728-67), of Cecil and Kent cos., Md.; *m* 1748, Mary Walmsley? (1730-post 1767);
5–Robert (1750-93), of New Castle, Del.; midshipman on the frigate "Delaware," 1778; prisoner on board the prison ship "Old Jersey"; *m* 1771, Sarah Beeson, or Beaston (1752-96);
4–Simon (1773-1832), of Del., Va., and Ohio; War 1812; *m* 1794, Elizabeth LaForge (1775-1812);
3–Jeremiah (1809-83), of Highland Co., O.; *m* Elizabeth Cochran;
2–John Cochran (2 below).
6–William **Cochran** (*d* 1772), *m* Sarah Cochran (*d* 1782);
5–John (1742-83), *m* Sarah Miller (*d* 1813);
4–Andrew (1769-1814), War 1812; *m* Jane Barker (1774-1863; John[5], sea capt., *m* Mary Curry);
3–Elizabeth (1812-62), *m* Jeremiah **Mercer** (3 above).
7–Robert **Murphin,** came in the "Shield," 1678, to N.J.; *m* Ann–;
6–William, *m* Sarah Bunting;
5–William, *m* Elizabeth Brooks;
4–William (1775-1846), War 1812; *m* 1806, Mary Anne West;
3–Eli (1806-76), of Ohio, Ia., and Kan.; *m* 1832, Mary Anne Art (1811-52; William[4], War 1812, *m* Mary Anne, dau. of James Stockdale);
2–Mary Anne (2 below).
9–George **Maris** (qv);
8–George (1652-1753), mem. Pa. Assembly, 1717; *m* 1690, Jane Maddox (1668-1705);
7–Hannah (1698-1752), *m* 1719, John **Owen** (1692-1752), high sheriff, Chester Co., several yrs.; mem. Provincial Assembly of Pa., 1738-48; collector of excise (Robert[8], from Wales, 1690, with the planters of the Great Welsh Barony and founders of Merion, Haverford and Radnor tps.; settled at Merioneth, Phila. Co., Pa.; prominent minister among Friends; founder Merion Meeting; colonial justice, 1695; mem. Colonial Assembly, 1695,97; *m* 1678/79, Rebecca Owen, dau. of Owen Humphrey, Esq., Gent., of Wales);
6–Jane (1720-91), of Phila., Pa., Fairfax and Pittsylvania cos., Va.; *m* 1740, Joseph **West** (1716-1802; John[7], *m* Sarah, dau. of Thomas Pearson, from Eng. in the "Welcome"; Maj. Thomas[8]);
5–Joseph (1757-1845), Highland Co., O.; *m* 1784, Judith Ballinger (1759-1834);
4–Mary Anne (1785-1845), *m* William **Murphin** (4 above);
3–Eli, *m* Mary Anne Art (3 above);
2–Mary Anne (1848-80), of Ohio, and Lucas Co., Ia.; *m* 1865, John Cochran **Mercer** (1840-1921), farmer; issue: I–David Newton (*b* 1868; *m* Katherine Smith); II–Sarah Alliene (1 above); III–Mary Ellen (*b* 1873; *m* Oliver Leon Leekliter); IV–Emma Maude (*b* 1875; *m* E. Perry Brightwell); V–William Wilson (*b* 1876; *m* Stella Purcell); VI–Ida May (*b* 1879; *m* Charles Albert Baker).
1–*m* Sept. 14, 1898, Horace Raymond Carpenter, *b* Afton, N.Y., Oct. 7, 1860; son of Daniel A. Carpenter, of Afton, *m* Sarah Maria Williams.
1–Instructor in schools of Ia., Neb., and Colo.; genealogist. Mem. D.A.C. (genealogist), D.A.R. (registrar and genealogist Cornelia Green Chapter), U.S.D. 1812 (state pres., v.p. and state treas.), I.A.G., Md. Hist. Soc. Episcopalian. State treas. Colo. Federation of Women's Clubs, 1902-03. Residence: Route 1, Box 72, La Junta, Colo.

1–**COOK, Jane James,** *b* Davids Island (now Fort Slocum), N.Y., July 15, 1885.
9–Walter **Cook** (qv);
8–Nicholas (1659-1730), of Mendon and Bellingham, Mass.; husbandman and farmer; possessed "Military Arms"; *m* 1684, Joanna Rockwood;
7–Nicholas (1687-1779), 1st Bapt. deacon at Mendon; *m* Elizabeth–; *m* 2d, Mehitable Staples;
6–Nathaniel (1718-73), pastor Elder Ballou Meeting House, formerly known as Elder Cook Meeting House, Cumberland Hill, R.I.;

m 1741/42, Martha Ballou (1720-1803; James[7], *m* Catherine Arnold);
5–Nathaniel (1748-1846), pvt. and sgt., R.I. militia, and landsman in Cont. Navy, 1776, under Lt. John Paul Jones, on flag ship "Alfred"; *m* 1768, Amey Whipple (*b* 1742; Daniel[6], *m* Anne–);
4–Amasa (1772-1843), *m* 1816, Mary Wilkinson (1776-1861; Israel[5], *m* Silence Ballou);
3–Elliott Wilkinson (1818-77), Lockport, N.Y.; capt., maj., lt. col., 28th N.Y. Vols., 1861-63; accredited agent of State of N.Y. to recruit vols. in Tenn. and Miss., 1864; in command of his regt. at Battle of Chancellorsville; captured twice; died Riverside, Calif., 1877; *m* 1842, Malvina Louisa Littlefield (1820-93; Joseph[4], *m* Mary Wright);
2–George Hamilton (2 below).
6–William **James** (*d* post 1776), ironmaster and part owner of Antietam Furnace in Frederick Co. (now Washington Co.), Md., 1761-69; invested in iron mines, in Berkeley and Bedford cos., Va., 1765-76; *m* bet. 1748-50, Margaret (Clark) Williams (Matthew Clark[7], *m* Elizabeth Ford-Barnes);
5–Thomas (*b* ca. 1750-*d* 1784-86), ironmaster and inventor of a steam wagon, ante 1784; invested in iron and lead cos. in Baltimore Co., Md., Berkeley and Bedford cos., Va.; Cont. commissary of mil. stores at Accokeek Furnace in Stafford Co., Va., 1779-81; mgr. Frederick Forge in Md., 1783; *m* bet. 1772-75, Esther Cooke (Giles[6], *m* Margaret Savage);
4–Thomas (1776-1856), ironmaster, Ross Co., O.; owner of Rapid Forge, Buckhorn Furnace, Marble Iron Works, etc., and Maramec Iron Works, Mo., 1826; *m* 2d, 1819, Jane Byrne Claypoole (Capt. Abraham G.[5], *m* Elizabeth Steele);
3–William (1823-1912), mgr. Maramec Iron Works, Phelps Co., Mo., 1843-ca. 1879; *m* 1846, Lucy Ann Dun (1822-1908; Robert[4], *m* Lucy Angus);
2–Jane (*b* 1851), of Baltimore; *m* 1881, Capt. George Hamilton **Cook** (1846-89), 1st lt. vols., 1864; capt. and bvt. lt. col., 1865; present at fall of Richmond, 1865; recommd. regular army, 1867; lt. and capt. 19th U.S. Inf.; capt. and asst. q.m., 1882-89; issue: I–Lucy James (*b* 1882; *m* Francis Nash Iglehart); II–Elizabeth Graham (1884-1902); III–Jane James (1 above); IV–Frances Swayne (*b* 1887; *m* Rev. Harold Noel Arrowsmith).
1–Ed. Southern Home School, Baltimore, and the Misses Masters,' Dobbs Ferry, N.Y. Served overseas as sec. doing canteen service, Woman's Section, Y.M.C.A., Dec. 1918-June 1919. Mem. C.D.A., I.A.G., N.E.G.H.S., Md. Hist. Soc. Episcopalian. Republican. Residence: 103 Stratford Rd, Guilford, Baltimore, Md.

1–**ANDERSON, Anne Page Wilder (Mrs. Jefferson Randolph),** *b* Apr. 15, 1873.
8–Thomas **Lord** (qv);
7–William (1623-78), removed to Saybrook, ca. 1645; *m* 2d, Lydia Brown;
6–Lt. Richard (*d* 1727), settled at Lyme, Conn., ca. 1680; justice of peace and quorum, 1705; commd. by Gov. Saltonstall lt. of Foot Co., Hampshire Co.; *m* 1682, Elizabeth Hyde (1660-1736), first English child born in Norwich, Conn. (Samuel[7], *m* Jane Lee);
5–John (1703-76), of North Lyme; *m* 1st, 1734, Hannah Rogers (1712-62; Lt. Joseph[6], *m* Sarah–);
4–Hannah (*b* 1747), *m* 1780, Lt. Daniel **King** (1749-1815); see Vol. III, p. 611;
3–Thomas Butler (1797-1864), reared by uncle, Gen. Zebulon Butler, of Wilkes-Barre, Pa.; removed to Ga., 1823; mem. Ga. Senate, 1832-36 and 59; mem. Congress, 1836-50; sent by President Taylor to investigate conditions in Calif., 1849; apptd. 1st collector Port of San Francisco by President Fillmore, 1850-52; returned to Ga.; spl. del. of Confed. Govt. to Europe, 1862; *m* 1824, Anne Matilda Page;
2–Georgia Page (2 below).
5–Thomas **Page** (1719-80), of Page's Point, Prince William Parish, S.C.; *m* 2d, 1756, Eleanor Holden (*d* 1780);
4–Maj. William (1764-1827), removed to Ga. and bought "Retreat" plantation at south end of St. Simons Island, ca. 1796; commd. maj. in Am. forces, War 1812; *m* 1781, his 1st cousin, Hannah Timmonds (*d* 1826);
3–Anne Matilda (1798-1859), *m* Thomas Butler **King** (3 above);
2–Georgia Page (1833-1914), v.regent for Ga. of Mount Vernon Ladies Assn., 1891-1914; pres. Ga. Soc. C.D.A.; *m* Gen. William Duncan Smith, C.S.A. (*d* Oct. 4, 1862); *m* 2d, June 9, 1870, Joseph John **Wilder** (1844-1900), mcht. and ship broker, Savannah, Ga.
1–*m* Nov. 27, 1895, Jefferson Randolph Anderson (see Vol. III, p. 610); issue: 1–Page Randolph (Mrs. Henry Norris Platt, see Vol. III, p. 611); 2–Jefferson Randolph (Sept. 3, 1902-Nov. 30, 1903); 3–Joseph Randolph (qv).
1–Pres. Telfair Hosp., Savannah. Mem. C.D.A.; vice regent for Ga. of Mount Vernon Ladies Assn. Residence: 119 E. Charlton St., Savannah, Ga.

1–**ANDERSON, Joseph Randolph,** *b* Savannah, Ga., Mar. 22, 1905.
6–Capt. George **Anderson,** "Mariner" from Scotland, settled in N.Y.; removed to Savannah, Ga., 1763; *m* 1761, Deborah Grant (1736-1812);
5–George (1767-1847), mcht. and exporter, Savannah; mem. City Council, 1798; *m* 1794, Elizabeth Clifford Wayne (Richard[6], *m* Elizabeth Clifford);
4–George Wayne (1796-1872), pres. Planters Bank of State of Ga.; *m* 1820, his 1st cousin, Eliza Clifford Stites (1805-65); see Vol. III, p. 610;
3–Edward Clifford (1839-76), maj., 24th Bn. Ga. Cav., 1862; lt. col. and col., 7th Ga. Cav., C.S.A., 1863-65; banker; planter; chmn. Chatham Co. Commrs.; *m* 1860, Jane Margaret Randolph;
2–Jefferson Randolph (2 below).
10–Thomas **Jefferson** (*d* 1697), of Henrico Co., Va., 1677; *m* Martha Branch (William[11]; Christopher[12], qv);
9–Capt. Thomas (1679-1725), of "Osborne," Chesterfield Co., Va.; justice, 1706; *m* 1697, Mary Field (Peter[10], *m* Judith Soane);
8–Col. Peter (1708-57), of "Shadwell," Albemarle Co., Va.; col. of militia; justice; surveyor; burgess, 1755; *m* 1739, Jane Randolph (1720-76; Isham[9], *m* Jane Rogers, of Eng.);
7–Thomas (1743-1826), author of the Declaration of Independence; Sec. of State under President Washington, 1790-94; V.P. of the U.S., 1797-1801; 3d President of U.S., 1801-09; founder of the U. of Va.; *m* Jan. 1, 1772, Martha (Wayles) Skelton (1748-82; John Wayles[8]);
6–Martha (1772-1836), *m* 1790, Thomas Mann **Randolph** (1768-1828), of "Edgehill," Albemarle Co., Va.; gov. of Va.;
5–Thomas Jefferson (1792-1875), mem. Va. Legislature, 1832-34, Va. Constl. Conv., 1851-52; rector U. of Va.; pres. Dem. Nat. Conv., Baltimore, 1872; *m* 1814, Jane Hollins Nicholas (1798-1871; Col. Wilson C.[6], *m* Margaret, dau. Hon. John Smith, *m* Mary Buchanan);
4–Margaret Smith (1816-43), *m* 1836, her 2d cousin, William Mann **Randolph** (*d* 1850); see Vol. III, p. 610;
3–Jane Margaret (1840-1914), *m* Edward Clifford **Anderson** (3 above);
2–Jefferson Randolph (see Vol. III, p. 610), *m* 1895, Anne Page Wilder (qv).
1–Residence: 119 E. Charlton St., Savannah, Ga.

1–**COOLIDGE, John Gardner,** *b* Boston, Mass., July 4, 1863.
9–John **Coolidge** (qv);
8–Jonathan (1646/47-1723/24), *m* Martha Rice (1662-95);
7–John (*b* 1690/91), *m* Hannah Ingram;
6–Joseph (1718/19-1771), *m* Marguerite Olivier (1726-1816);
5–Joseph (1747-1820), see portrait; *m* Elizabeth Boyer (1754-86);
4–Joseph (1773-1840), *m* Elizabeth Bulfinch (1777-1837);
3–Joseph (1798-1879), A.B., Harvard, 1817; *m* 1825, Eleonora Wayles Randolph;
2–Joseph Randolph (2 below).
9–John **Jefferson,** from Wales with father; part-founder of Yorktown, Va.; burgess, 1619; and probably thru;
8–Thomas (*d* 1697), owned a plantation in Henrico Co., Va., 1677; *m* Martha Branch

JOSEPH COOLIDGE, 2d (1747-1820).

(William[9], of Henrico Co.; Christopher[10], qv);
7–Capt. Thomas (1679-1725), of "Osborne," on the James River, Chesterfield Co.; justice, 1706; *m* 1697, Mary Field (Peter[8], *m* Judith Soane);
6–Peter (1707/08-1757), of "Shadwell"; adj. gen. of Va.; *m* 1739, Jane Randolph (Isham[7], of "Dungeness");
5–Thomas (1743-1826), author of the Declaration of Independence and 3d President of the U.S.; *m* Martha Wayles;
4–Martha, *m* 1790, Thomas Mann **Randolph** (1768-1828); see Vol. I, p. 352, for Randolph lineage;
3–Eleonora W. (*d* 1876), *m* Joseph **Coolidge** (3 above).
10–Thomas **Gardner** (qv);
9–Lt. George (ca. 1620-1679), from Eng. to Salem, Mass.; *m* ca. 1647, Elizabeth (Horne) Orne (*d* 1658);
8–Samuel (1643-1724), merchant, Salem; rep. Mass. Gen. Ct.; *m* Elizabeth Brown (1644-83; widow of Joseph Grafton);
7–Capt. John (1681-1721), at the defense of Haverhill against the Indians; capt. provincial militia; rep. Gen. Ct.; *m* Elizabeth Weld (*b* 1681);
6–John (1707-84), *m* Elizabeth Putnam (1700-64);
5–John (1731-1805), *m* 2d, Elizabeth Pickering (1737-1823);
4–Samuel Pickering (1767-1843), *m* Rebecca Russell Lowell (1779-1853);
3–John Lowell (1804-84), *m* Catherine Elizabeth Peabody (1808-83);
2–Julia (1841-1921), *m* Joseph Randolph **Coolidge** (1828-1925), lawyer (for issue see Vol. I, p. 351).
1–*m* Apr. 29, 1909, Helen Granger Stevens, *b* Boston, Apr. 3, 1876; dau. of Henry James Stevens, of N. Andover, Mass. (desc. John Stevens, qv).
1–A.B., Harvard, '84. Diplomatic service; acted as U.S. vice consul at Pretoria, S. Africa, 1900 (1st yr. of Boer War); sec. legation and charge d'affaires, Peking, 1902-06; sec. embassy and charge d'affaires, City of Mexico, 1907-08; apptd. E.E. and M.P. to Nicaragua, July 1, 1908, resigned Nov. 26, 1908; spl. agt. of Dept. of State to assist the Am. ambassador at Paris, Nov. 27, 1914-Aug. 1917; spl. asst. in Dept. of State, July 1918-Aug. 1919. Author: Random Letters from many countries. Summer place: "Ashdale Farm," North Andover, Mass. Residence: 171 Commonwealth Av., Boston, Mass.

1–**ANTHONY, John William, Jr.,** *b* 1886.
7–Sir Charles **Anthony,** of Eng., who, for services rendered the crown, was knighted and given land in Va.;
6–Mark, early Va. settler; lived in New Kent Co.; *m* Isabella Hart;
5–John (1715-60), lived at the Fall's Plantation (later Manchester, now South Richmond), opposite Richmond, and removing thence, built a fort on Walnut Hill, overlooking the Otter River in Campbell Co., Va.; capt. of the rangers by particular order of the gov.; *m* ca. 1740, Elizabeth Banks (*d* 1801);
4–Rev. John (1749-1822), in Am. Rev.; *m* 1771, Susannah Austin (bet. 1752-55-ante 1825), of Bedford Co., Va.;
3–Charles (1795-1884), *m* Martha Davis Haden (1806-70);
2–John William (2 below).
7–Thomas **Arnold** (qv);
6–William (will proved 1774), *m* Elizabeth–;
5–Moses (will proved 1811), *m* Elizabeth–;
4–Wyatt (*b* 1776), *m* 1803, Keziah Penick (*b* 1781; William[5]);
3–Dulaney Reid (1821-1908), *m* Ann Brown (1823-88; James[4], *m* Catherine, dau. of Col. Thomas Leftwich);
2–Emma Reid (1851-1914), *m* 1874, John William **Anthony** (1841-1920), fought in War Between the States; issue: I–Martha Davis (*b* 1876); II–Bernard (1878-97); III–Annie (*b* 1880); IV–Miss Charles (*b* 1883); V–John William, Jr. (1 above); VI–Reid Arnold (*b* 1889; *m* Elizabeth Miles); VII–Callie (*d* infancy); VIII–son (*d* infancy).
1–*m* Julia Brooks Moses; issue: 1–Ann Kathryn; 2–Billy Moses; 3–John William.
1–Ed. Washington and Lee U. Residence: 2123 Grove Av., Richmond, Va.

1–**BUSH, Mattie Hinds (Mrs. William T.),** *b* Red Hill, Ala., Sept. 25, 1869.
4–Levi **Hinds** (ca. 1762-1826; probably son of Joseph), *m* 1787, Huldah Byram (1766-1829; Peter[5] [1740-1807], pvt. in Am. Rev., of Henrico Co., Va., *m* 1763, Lydia Lindsey, 1744-1810);
3–Byram (1792-1870), farmer; 2d lt. in War 1812; *m* 1813, Elizabeth Childress (1798-1870; John[4], Am. Rev.);
2–Dr. Byram Wilborn, M.D. (2 below).
6–Stephen **Bedford** (*d* 1758), of Cumberland Co., Va.; *m* Elizabeth Mosley;
5–Thomas, of Charlotte Co., Va.; *m* 2d, Drusilla Williamson;
4–Margaret, *m* John **Fennell,** of Charlotte Co. (Isham[5], Greenville Co., Va.);
3–Martha Ann (*d* ca. 1857), *m* 1842, as his 1st wife, Rev. James Jefferson **Pickett** (John[4], *m* Miss Collier);
2–Margaret Rebecca (1843-1904), *m* 1860, Dr. Byram Wilborn **Hinds,** M.D. (1837-1906), lt., Co. B, 48th Ala. Regt., C.S.A., discharged at Richmond, Va., 1862, for physical disability, he rejoined the army the same year with the 3d Ala. Regt., and was on detached service thruout the war, serving with Gen. Joseph E. Johnson's escort, and surrendering with him at Greensboro, N.C., 1865; issue: I–Ernest (*b* 1864; maj. gen. U.S.A.; *m* Minnie Hatton Miller); II–Ida (*b* 1867; *m* Harry R. Johnson); III–Mattie (1 above); IV–Elizabeth (*b* 1871; *m* Charles E. Stevens); V–Alfred Walton (*b* 1874; *m* Mary Beardsley); VI–Willie (1876-77); VII–Clifton (1878-82); VIII–Harry Lee (1880-1906); IX–Mary Bertie (*b* 1885; *m* Joseph T. Lowry).
1–*m* Oct. 19, 1893, William Thomas Bush, *b* New Hope, Ala., July 1, 1871; son of William Thomas Bush; issue: 1–Fennell Hinds (Dec. 8, 1894-Mar. 10, 1897); 2–Margaret Genevieve, *b* New Hope, Ala.; grad. Tex. Woman's Coll., Ft. Worth, '19; *m* Nov. 15, 1917, Marvin Houston, son of John Houston Cunningham (issue: Marvin Houston, Jr.; William Thomas; Margaret Elizabeth; Vernon Hinds); 3–Mary Elizabeth, *b* Texarkana, Ark., Aug. 10, 1904; U. of Tex., '28.
1–Grad. Huntsville Female Coll., '89. Methodist. Democrat. Residence: 3523 Tularosa St., El Paso, Tex.

1–**CALL, Alice Emma Spear (Mrs. George C.),** *b* Algona, Ia., Apr. 29, 1873.
10–John **Howland,** Mayflower Pilgrim (qv);
9–Desire (*d* 1683), *m* 1643, Capt. John **Gorham** (qv);

8–James (1650-1707), of Marshfield, Mass.; *m* 1673, Hannah Huckins (1653-1727; Thomas[9], ens. A. and H.A. Co., 1639, dep. Plymouth Gen. Ct., Council of War, commissary gen.);
7–Ebenezer (1695-1776), Barnstable, Mass.; *m* 1727, Temperance Hawes;
6–Thankful (1739-1824), of Gorham, Me.; *m* 1759, Josiah **Davis** (1733-1824), of Barnstable;
5–John (*b* 1763), of Barnstable; *m* 1789, Patience Irish (1770-1854), of Gorham, Me. (James[6], Am. Rev.);
4–Rebecca (1795-1861), of Buxton, Me.; *m* 1817, Rev. George **Thomes** (1795-1871), of Gorham;
3–Emeline Foster (1817-1910), of Gorham; *m* 1837, Charles William **Strout** (1814-79);
2–Emeline Charletina (2 below).
10–Thomas **Hawes** (*d* 1665), of the Norfolk family Hawes, of "Morningthorpe"; from Eng. to Yarmouth, Cape Cod, Mass., being one of the 3 grantees of the town; dep. Gen. Ct.; *m* Mary Burr (who *m* 2d, Gov. Thomas Prence);
9–Jeremiah (1637-1706), Dennis, Mass.; *m* Sarah Prence (Gov. Thomas[10], qv, *m* Patience, dau. William Brewster, qv);
8–Mary, *m* Joseph **Hawes** (John[9]; Edmond[10]);
7–Temperance (1705-67), *m* Ebenezer **Gorham** (7 above).
2–Emeline Charletina Strout (*b* 1849), of Portland, Me.; *m* 1870, Simon Cameron **Spear** (1843-1927), of Portsmouth, N.H.; in Civil War.
1–*m* 1894, George Caspar Call, *b* Algona, Ia., Sept. 24, 1860; son of Asa Cyrus Call, of Cleveland, O.; issue: 1–George Richard, *b* Algona, Ia., May 22, 1898; *m* Sept. 8, 1923, Alice Hawthorne; 2–Helen Emeline, *b* Sioux City, Ia., Mar. 19, 1903; *m* Nov. 25, 1926, Mark Cord.
1–Ed. Bradford (Mass.) Acad. Mem. S.M.D., Pilgrim John Howland Soc., D.A.R. Residence: 1529 Grandview Boul., Sioux City, Ia.

1–**CAREY, Charles Henry,** *b* Cincinnati, O., Oct. 27, 1857.
4–Dennis M. **Carey,** from Donegal, Ireland, to Hawkins Co., Tenn.; deed dated Sept. 24, 1806;
3–Patrick (*d* ca. 1849), from Tenn. to Yorkville, S.C.; postmaster, publisher and editor; *m* 1818, Esther Montgomery Lowry;
2–Samuel Doak (2 below).
6–Samuel **Doak** (*d* 1771-72), from N. of Ireland; settled in Chester Co., Pa., ante 1741; removed to Augusta Co., Va.; *m* Jane Mitchell;
5–Samuel, D.D. (1749-1830), A.B., Princeton, 1775; Presbyn. minister, 1777; ens. Va. militia Am. Rev.; founder, 1785, and 1st pres. Martin Acad. (incorporated as Washington Coll., 1795), 1795-1818; removed to Bethel, Green Co., Tenn., 1818; established Tusculum Coll.; mem. Constl. Conv. forming State of Franklin, 1784; *m* 1st, 1776 or 77, Esther Houston Montgomery (*d* 1807; John[6], of Pa. and Va., *m* Esther, dau. of John Houston, from Ireland to Phila., 1735, moved to Va., *m* Margaret Cunningham);
4–Julia (*b* 1777), *m* 1794, Adam **Lowry,** removed to Ripley, O.;
3–Esther M. (*b* 1798), *m* Patrick **Carey** (3 above).
8–Robert **Fenton** (*d* post 1712), from Eng.; at Woburn, Mass., 1688; later at Windham and Mansfield, Conn.; patentee, Mansfield, 1703; *m* Dorothy–;
7–Jacob (1698-1763), Norwich, Vt.; *m* 1730, Mary Pierce (Nathaniel[8]);
6–Jacob (1731-56), of Mansfield, Conn.; *m* 1754, Rebecca Cross (Wade[7]);
5–Roswell (1755-1806), removed to Ohio, 1806, and was buried at Twelve Mile Island, nr. Louisville, Ky.; his family arrived after his death and settled in Green Tp., O.; *m* 1773, Deborah Freeman (1753-1846; Stephen[6]);
4–Roswell (1786-1830), removed to Hamilton Co., O., ca. 1807; *m* Anna McFannan;
3–Alfred (*b* ca. 1808-*d* aet. 27), Madison, Ind.; *m* 1832, Mary Ann Cooper, from England;
2–Martha Louisa (1832-88), *m* 1852, Samuel Doak **Carey** (1830-1925), lt., Ohio regt. and q.m.c., Civil War; business man, Cincinnati, officer Legion of Honor and G.A.R.; founder of Symphony Orchestra, Los Angeles; issue: I–Eva Montgomery (*b* 1853; *m* 1884, George Clifford Horton); II–Charles Henry (1 above); III–Frank Niles (1859-72); IV–Howard Fenton (1862-93; *m* Nettie Wilder); V–Forrest Woodnut (*b* 1868; *m* Pauline Wymond; *m* 1929, Mrs. Edith May Harding **Lane**).
1–*m* Sept. 25, 1884, Mary Noble Bidwell (May 17, 1858-Jan. 29, 1928); dau. of Capt. Lawson Bidwell, of Madison Co., O.; issue (all *b* Portland, Ore.): 1–Louise Harrington (Oct. 19, 1885-July 30, 1911); 2–Alice, *b* May 16, 1890; *m* 1914, Dr. Eugene Watson Rockey, of Portland (issue: Mary Alice, *b* June 23, 1915; Jane, *b* Aug. 22, 1916; Evelyn Joy, *b* July 22, 1918; Louise Carey, *b* Nov. 10, 1921); 3–Evelyn, *b* July 2, 1892; *m* 1918, Charles Tenney Donworth, of Seattle (issue: Charles Carey, *b* Oct. 8, 1924; Mary Evelyn, *b* Oct. 14, 1926).
1–Ph.B., Denison U., '81; LL.B., Cincinnati Coll., 1883; (hon. M.A., Ore. State U., 1928). Engaged in law practice at Portland since 1883; sr. mem. firm of Carey, Hart, Spencer & McCulloch; Ore. counsel for various rys. and public service corpns., etc. Author and historian. Dir. U.S. Spruce Production Corpn. and chmn. Ore. War Industries, World War. Mem. Rep. Nat. Com., 1904-08; chmn. Rep. Congressional Com., 1894-98; Am. del. to Inst. of Pacific Relations, Kyoto, Japan, 1929; presidential elector, 1928. Founder and pres., Multnomah Law Library; trustee Portland Art Assn. (pres., 1927–), etc. (see Who's Who in America). Mason (32°). Clubs: Arlington (ex-pres.), Century, University (New York). Residence: "Avalon," Riverdale, Portland, Ore.

1–**CLAIBORNE, Charles Ferdinand,** *b* New Orleans, La., Feb. 2, 1848.
8–William (Clayborne) **Claiborne** (qv);
7–Lt. Col. Thomas (1647-83), of "Romancoke," Va.; *m* Sarah–;
6–Capt. Thomas (1680-1732), of "Sweet Hall," King William Co.; *m* 3d, Ann Fox;
5–Col. Nathaniel, of "Sweet Hall"; *m* Jane Cole (William[6], of Warwick Co., Va.);
4–William (*d* 1809), of Manchester, Va.; *m* Mary Leigh (Ferdinand[5], of King William Co., Va.);
3–William Charles Cole (1775-1817), gov. of Miss., 1801, La. Ty., 1803, and State of La., 1812-16; U.S. senator from La., 1816; *m* Eliza Lewis, of Nashville, Tenn.; *m* 2d, Clarisse Duralde; *m* 3d, Suzette Booque;
2–William C. C. (1808-78), *m* 1834, Louise de Balathier; issue: I–Clarisse (*b* 1835); II–William C. C. (1837-1925; *m* Jeanne Robelot); III–Henry de Balathier (1838-73), IV–George Washington (1840-killed in Battle of Mansfield, Apr. 7, 1864); V–Arthur (*b* 1841); VI–Marie (1842-49); VII–Lucy (1845-1915); VIII–John Randolph (*b* 1846); IX–Charles Ferdinand (1 above); X–Ferdinand (1853-1928; *m* Louise Villeré).
1–*m* Dec. 23, 1875, Amelie Soniat du Fossat (Jan. 27, 1855-Aug. 14, 1914); dau. of Meloney Soniat du Fossat; issue (all *b* New Orleans, La.): 1–Marie Louise, *b* Dec. 26, 1876; *m* Dec. 9, 1902, Louis Perrilliat (issue: William Cole, *b* Oct. 3, 1903; Howard Auguste Kelley, *b* Dec. 5, 1904); 2–Charles de Balathier, *b* Jan. 11, 1879; *m* Dec. 21, 1903, Virginia, dau. Felix Couturie (issue: Virginia, *b* Oct. 1904; Martha, *b* July 1907; Charles de Balathier, Jr., *b* Sept. 1910); 3–Amelie, *b* Sept. 9, 1883; *m* Martin L. Matthews; 4–Lucy M. (June 17, 1888-Jan. 9, 1919); *m* Samuel C. Coleman; 5–Duralde, *b* Mar. 10, 1895.
1–Ed. U.La. and Christian Brothers. Admitted to bar, 1869; chmn. finance com., City Council of New Orleans, 1888-92, chmn. budget com., 1896-1900; pres. New Orleans City Park Assn., and of Isaac Delgado Museum of Art, and New Orleans Public Library; apptd. by Gov. Hall, as one of three judges of Ct. of Appeals, for Parish of New Orleans and six other parishes, 1913; elected judge same ct., 1920 for 8 yrs.; del. Constl. Conv., 1921. Mem. I.A.G., New Orleans Geneal. and Hist. Soc. (trustee), etc. Warden St. Louis Cathedral. Residence: 905 Esplanade Av., New Orleans, La.

1–**COCKE, Sarah Cobb Johnson (Mrs. Lucian H.),** *b* Selma, Ala., Feb. 7, 1865.
7–Thomas **Johnson** (qv);
6–Thomas (1701/02-1779), of Calvert Co., Md.; later in Frederick Co.; *m* 1725, Dorcas Sedgewick (1702-71; Joshua[7], of Conn., *m* Elizabeth–); their son, Thomas, was gov. of Md., 1777-79;

5–Benjamin, adopted by his bro. Roger Johnson;
4–James (*b* 1750);
3–James (*b* 1782), *m* Jane Leeper;
2–Dr. John Milton (2 below).
9–Col. William **Bernard** (qv);
8–Lucy (*d* 1675), *m* Dr. Edward **Gwyn,** of Ware Parish, Va. (Rev. John[9], rector Abington Parish, Gloucester Co., Va.);
7–Lucy, *m* 1670, Thomas **Reade** (*b* ca. 1645), of Gloucester Co. (George[8], qv, *m* Elizabeth, dau. of Nicholas Martian, qv);
6–Mildred, *m* Maj. Philip **Rootes** (*b* ca. 1696), justice, vestryman, King and Queen Co., Va.;
5–Thomas Reade, *m* 1763, Martha Jacquelin Smith;
4–Thomas Reade (1763-1824), *m* Sarah Ryng Battaille (1766-1811);
3–Sarah Robinson (1792-1867), *m* John Addison **Cobb** (1783-1855), see Vol. I, p. 557 for Cobb lineage;
2–Mary Willis (2 below).
10–George **Reade** (same as 8 above);
9–Mildred, *m* "Speaker" Augustine **Warner,** II (1642-81; Capt. Augustine[10], qv);
8–Mary, *m* 1680, Maj. John **Smith** (*d* 1698), of "Purton," Gloucester Co.; mem. Colonial Council, 1657; speaker, House of Burgesses, 1657; burgess, 1691 (John[9], *m* Anne Bernard);
7–Augustine (*b* 1689), "Shooter's Hill," Middlesex Co.; *m* 1711, Sarah Carver (*d* 1736; John[8]);
6–Maj. John, of "Shooters Hill"; *m* Mary Jacquelin (Edward[7], *m* Martha Cary);
5–Martha J., *m* Thomas R. **Rootes** (5 above).
2–Mary Willis Cobb, *m* 2d, 1864, Dr. John Milton **Johnson** (1812-86), physician, Atlanta, Ga.; issue: I–Sarah C. (1 above); II–James Lovic.
1–*m* Oct. 26, 1887, Dr. Hugh Hagan (*d* 1898); son Hugh Hagan, *m* Sarah Copeland McMinn, Richmond, Va.; issue: 1–Hugh Johnson, *b* Atlanta, Ga., Dec. 11, 1888; B.A., Washington and Lee, '10; M.D., Johns Hopkins, 1914; capt., M.C., U.S.A., World War; *m* 1917, Barbara Fowle, dau. William Campbell (issue: Hugh Campbell); 2–Willis Cobb, *b* Atlanta, Dec. 3, 1894; B. A., Washington and Lee, '17; 2d and 1st lt., Co. F, 60th Inf., A.E.F.; *m* 1918, Elizabeth Allen, dau. Joseph Nancred Guerard (issue: Sarah Elizabeth).
1–*m* 2d, Oct. 28, 1903, Lucian Howard Cocke (see Vol. I, p. 557 for genealogy).
1–Ed. Lucy Cobb Inst., Ga., and Waverly Sem., Washington, D.C. Writer, contributor to Century Magazine and Saturday Evening Post. Author: Master of the Hills; Mammy Stories of the South. Mem. C.D.A., O.C., D.A.R., U.D.C. Clubs: Colonial Dames (Washington), Nat. Arts (New York), Woman's (Richmond, Va.). Residence: "Cockspur," 818 Orchard Hill, Roanoke, Va.

Arms: Azure, guttee argent, on a fess between three leopards' heads erased or, three cross crosslets gules.
Crests: (1) A leopard's head erased; (2) a winged pillar surmounted by a globe.

1–**DARLINGTON** (See issue of Thomas Darlington below).
5–Henry **Darlington** (desc. William d'Arlington, of West Riding, Yorkshire, Eng.), of West Riding, Eng.; *m* Mary Walker;
4–William, of Darlington, Co. Durham, Eng.; removed to Broomhouse, Scotland; *m* 1788, Alice Brown;
3–Peter (Oct. 7, 1792-Jan. 21, 1851), from Broomhouse, Scotland, to New York, first of family in America, settled at Pleasant Valley, N.Y.; a pioneer paper mfr.; see portrait; *m* June 17, 1819, Maria Wilde (see 3 below);

PETER DARLINGTON (1792-1851).

2–Thomas (*b* Aug. 29, 1826-May 18, 1903), see below.
9–Richard **Wilde,** (*d* bet. 1688-89), from Eng. to Charlestown, Mass., 1639; first of family in America; removed to Flushing, N.Y., where he was a patentee, 1669; *m* Edith– (*d* 1688);
8–Thomas, soldier in the company of Capt. Jonathan Wright, Flushing, L.I., 1715; *m* Elizabeth–;

MARIA (WILDE) DARLINGTON (1800-1900).

7–Richard, also soldier in the company of Capt. Jonathan Wright; *m* Patience Tatum;
6–Thomas (1718-76), in French and Indian War, 1755; also in Cont. Army, Am. Rev., killed in the Battle of White Plains, Oct. 28, 1776; a large landowner at Tarrytown, N.Y.; *m* 1st, Sarah Griffin;
5–Griffin (1738-1817), of Princetown, Schenectady Co., and Kinderhook, and Tarrytown, N.Y.; soldier 5th Regt. Dutchess Co. Militia, Am. Rev.; *m* Anna Bishop (*b* Bolton, Conn., 1738);
4–James (*b* Feb. 1770-*d* at Manchester Bridge, Dutchess Co., N.Y. June 27, 1816), of Pleasant Valley, N.Y.; *m* Feb. 15, 1792, Phoebe Rainous;
3–Maria (*b* Pleasant Valley, N.Y., June 29, 1800-*d* N.Y. City, Aug. 20, 1900), see portrait; *m* June 17, 1819, Peter **Darlington** (3 above).
9–Edward **Griffen** (*b* ca. 1602), sailed from London, Eng., Oct. 24, 1635, in the "Abraham"; first of family in America; settled at Kent Island, Va.; taken prisoner by Lord Baltimore, held in Md., 1638-40, escaped to New Amsterdam, 1640; settled at Flushing, 1653; Indian interpreter, 1661; overseer, Flushing, 1680; *m* Mary–;
8–John, soldier in the company of Capt. Jonathan Wright, Flushing, 1715; *m* Elizabeth–;
7–Jacob, also soldier in the company of Capt. Jonathan Wright, 1715; *m* Sarah Wright (Capt. Jonathan[8], *m* Winnifred–; Jonathan[9] [*b* 1620, Essex Co., Eng.], came in the "Safety," landed in Mass. Colony, 1635; first at Saugus, 1635, at Flushing, N.Y., 1664);
6–Sarah, *m* Thomas **Wilde** (6 above).

"In Sleepy Hollow Cemetery, erected in 1894, stands the Tarrytown Memorial Monument and there, near by, in the Wilde Family plot, Thomas Wilde, his sons (except Griffin), and daughters and his sons-in-law Capt. George Combs and Col. James Hammond, are buried."

8–James **Bishop** (*d* June 22, 1691), sec. of New Haven Colony, 1661-65; dep.gov., 1683-7, 1689-91; *m* Mary (probably Lewin, *d* Nov. 26, 1664);
7–John (*b* 1662), of New Haven, removed to Hartford; *m* Abigail Willet (*b* and *d* Hartford, Conn.);
6–John (*b* 1693), removed to Coventry, Conn.; *m* Susannah–, who removed to Philipse Manor, N.Y., and *d* Aug. 1763;
5–Anna, *m* Griffin **Wilde** (5 above).
8–Daniel (Reynaud) **Rainous** (*b* 1643; son of a Protestant minister at Chenac, France); fled to Eng. after revocation of Edict of Nantes, 1685; sailed from Bristol, Apr. 6, 1693; first of family in America; settled at New Rochelle, N.Y.; surveyor; *m* Judith– (*b* 1653);
7–John, *m* Susannah–;
6–John;
5–James (ca. 1743-1810), of Pleasant Valley, N.Y.; *m* Sally, or Susie Milliken (Lt. James[6], of 8th Co., 2d Ulster Co. Militia, Col. Ellison, French and Indian War, was captain of 3d Regt., Ulster Co. Militia, Am. Rev., slain in action, Oct. 6, 1777, at Fort Clinton; Alexander[7], first of family in America, soldier in Wallkill militia, Ulster Co., Capt. John Byard, Col. A. Gassbeek Chambers, 1738);
4–Phoebe, *m* Feb. 15, 1792, James **Wilde** (4 above);
3–Maria, m June 17, 1819, Peter **Darlington** (3 above);

THOMAS DARLINGTON (b Salisbury Mills, N.Y., Aug. 29, 1826-d New York City, May 18, 1903); Hannah Anne Goodliffe, his wife (b Brampton, Eng., April 1, 1830-d New York City, Feb. 22, 1900).

2–Thomas **Darlington** (*b* Salisbury Mills, N.Y., Aug. 29, 1826-*d* May 18, 1903), lawyer, N.Y.; *m* Aug. 1, 1850, Hannah Anne Goodliffe (*b* Apr. 1, 1830-*d* Feb. 22, 1900; dau. of James Yarrow Goodliffe[3], from Bedford, Eng., to N.Y., 1831); issue:–
I–Alice (May 5, 1851-May 5, 1853).
II–Alfred Ernest (Dec. 6, 1853-May 22, 1857).
III–James Henry (Brooklyn, N.Y., June 9, 1856-Aug. 14, 1930); graduated A.B., New York University, '77, A.M., 1880; Princeton Theol. Sem., 1880; Ph.D., Princeton, 1884; (D.D., New York U.; LL.D., St. John's, Dickinson, Lafayette colls.). Consecrated 1st Episcopal bishop of Harrisburg, Pa., 1905. Chaplain with rank of capt., 47th Regt., N.G.N.Y., 8 yrs.; lt. col. on staff of gov. of Pa.; vol. chaplain, Ft. Totten, L.I., 1918. In 1920 as chairman of the commission to confer with the Eastern Orthodox Churches and the Old Catholics visited with two secretaries Athens, Constantinople, Bucharest, Berne and having signed the concordat between eastern and western churches visited Egypt and Holy Land for same in 1923. Officier de l'Legion d'Honneur (France), Grand Cdr. Order George 1st (Greece), Order St. Sava (Serbia), Order Leopold (Belgium), Knight of the Holy Sepulchre (Jerusalem), Order Queen Isabella the Catholic (Spain), Royal Order Victor Emanuel (Italy), Mason (33°). *M* July 26, 1888, Ella Louise Bearns, *b* Brooklyn, N.Y., June 2, 1859; dau. of James Sterling Bearns, banker, Brooklyn; issue: 1–Rev. Henry Vane Bearns (see Vol. II, p. 29, for Bearns lineage); 2–Alfred William Bearns (Dec. 12, 1890-Aug. 10, 1891); 3–Gilbert Sterling Bancroft, *b* Brooklyn, Jan. 8, 1892; Columbia, '12; P.E. clergyman; lt. U.S.N. in World War; *m* Apr. 30, 1919, Elizabeth Remsen, dau. Joseph Todhunter Thompson (issue: Jane); 4–Eleanor Townsend, *b* Brooklyn, Sept. 8, 1893;

m Feb. 1, 1919, Joel Ellis Fisher; 5–Rev. Elliott Christopher Bearns, *b* Brooklyn, Apr. 3, 1895; A.B., Columbia, '17, LL.B., 1920; was attached to Am. Embassy, Copenhagen, during World War; 6–Kate Brampton, b Brooklyn, Nov. 18, 1900.

BISHOP JAMES H. DARLINGTON (1856-1930).

IV–Thomas, *b* Brooklyn, Sept. 24, 1858; Ph.B., New York U., '78; M.D., Columbia, 1880; C.E., New York U., 1914; (Litt. D., Juniatta, 1924). Physician; commr. and pres. N.Y. Bd. of Health, 1904-10); compensation commr. State of N.Y., 1914-15; prof. anatomy, New York Coll. of Dentistry and New York U., etc. Maj. M.C., 1917-19. Asst. pres. Am. Iron and Steel Institute; physician, N.Y. Chamber of Commerce; father of the Council of Sachems, Tammany Soc. or Columbian Order; Deacon First Presbyn. Ch. Author: Health and Efficiency and many med. monographs (see Who's Who in America). Mem. S.N.S., H.S., S.R., etc. Clubs: Church, National Democratic. Residence: 27 Washington Sq., New York, N.Y. *M* June 9, 1886, Josephine Alice Sergeant (Nov. 9, 1864-June 16, 1890); dau. of the late Joseph A. Sergeant, Spuyten Duyvil, N.Y.; issue: 1–Clinton Pelham, *b* Kings Bridge, New York City, Mar. 10, 1887; 2–Dorothea, *b* Kings Bridge, Oct. 26, 1888.

V–Charles Francis, *b* Brooklyn, Nov. 1, 1860; A.B., Princeton, '82, A.M., 1884, LL.B., Columbia, 1884. Lawyer, N.Y. Mem. The Pilgrims, H.S.A., S.N.S., S.C.W., S.R., S.W. 1812. Clubs: Down Town, Bankers, Mt. Kisco Golf, Manursing Island. Summer home: Mt. Kisco, N.Y. Residence: 944 5th Av., N.Y. City. *M* Jan. 28, 1903, Letitia Craig O'Neill, *b* N.Y.C. Nov. 10, 1871; dau. of Hugh O'Neill, N.Y.C.; issue: 1–Charles Francis, *b* N.Y. City, Sept. 13, 1904; A.B., Harvard '26, and Oxon, '27; mem. S.R.; attache secretariat, League of Nations, Geneva; 2–Caroline Craig, *b* Mt. Kisco, N.Y., June 13, 1910; mem. D.A.R., D.C., H.S.A., C.D.A., Junior League.

VI–Gustavus Cornelius, *b* Brooklyn, Oct. 16, 1862; attended Princeton, 1883; in business and engineering; M.D., Long Island Med. Coll., 1901; World War; regtl. surgeon, 1st Motor Mechanics, and overseas post surgeon, "Caserne Pitié" Nevers, France; mem. A.M.A., N.Y. State and co. med. socs. *M* Apr. 29, 1884, Kate Annabel Bearns (July 13, 1865-Dec. 28, 1898); issue: 1–Marguerite Bearns, *b* Aug. 26, 1886; 2–Charles Goodliffe, *b* Jan. 28, 1892. *M* 2d, Jan. 1, 1928, Lilyan M. Kuenemann Stokes.

VII–Marion Goodliffe, *b* Kingston, N.J., Dec. 9, 1865; mem. H.S.A.

VIII–Marguerite, *b* Newark, N.J., July 5, 1873; *m* June 14, 1897, Rev. Arthur Wilson Wilde (*d* Dec. 1912); issue: 1–Katharine Darlington, *b* Mar. 23, 1898; 2–Dorothy Goodliffe, *b* Sept. 26, 1900; 3–Charles Francis Darlington, *b* Mar. 21, 1902. *M* 2d, Dr. Joseph T. Lippincott.

1–**DEVINE, Olive Ann French (Mrs. Joseph Philip),** *b* San Antonio, Tex., Feb. 25, 1860.

10–Christopher **Webb,** settled at Braintree, Mass., ante 1645;

9–Christopher (*b* 1630), *m* 1655, Hannah Scott (Benjamin[10]);

8–Samuel, *m* 1686, Mary Adams (1664-1744; Capt. Samuel[9], *m* Rebecca, dau. of Thomas Graves; Henry[10], qv);

7–Samuel (*b* 1690), *m* Hannah Ripley (1685-1751; Joshua[8], *m* Hannah, dau. of Maj. William Bradford, son of Gov. William Bradford, Mayflower Pilgrim, qv);

6–Ebenezer (1719-1803), pvt. Am. Rev.; *m* 1740, Ruth Crane (1718-96; Isaac[7], *m* Ruth Waldo);

5–Christopher (*b* 1755), Cazenovia, N.Y.; pvt. Am. Rev.; *m* 1st, 1778, Olive Brown (1757-86);

4–Maj. Adin (1780-1865), maj. War 1812; noted educator, Ithaca, N.Y.; *m* 1800, Deborah Carter;

3–Henry (1802-36), *m* 1832, Olive Ann Selkrigg (1812-48);

2–Sarah Lorinilla (1836-1915), C.D.A., D.A.R., U.D.C., U.S.D. 1812; *m* 1856, Capt. James Henry **French,** C.S.A. (*b* "Fenton," Fauquier Co., Va., 1835-*d* San Antonio, Tex., 1893); issue: I–Junius Butler, D.D. (1858-1918; *m* Annie Dial); II–Olive Ann (1 above); III–James Vassar (1864-1926; *m* Augusta Hirschfield); IV–Sarah Lorinilla (1867-1914; *m* William Logan French); V–Franklina Gray (*b* 1872; *m* Francis G. Yates).

1–*m* Sept. 2, 1879, Joseph Philip Devine (July 17, 1856-May 28, 1902); son of Judge Thomas Jefferson Devine, of San Antonio; issue (all *b* San Antonio, Tex.): 1–Sarah Lorinilla (see Vol. III, p. 524), *b* June 9, 1880; *m* Dec. 30, 1903, James Francis Clarkson, *b* Refugio, Tex., Nov. 17, 1880 (issue: Lorrie, *b* San Antonio [Nov. 14, 1904-Mar. 15, 1914]; Olive, *b* Austin, Tex., Oct. 30, 1906, *m* June 12, 1929, James Oswald Williams; Helen Frances, *b* San Antonio, Oct. 23, 1911; Palmer Blair, *b* San Diego, Tex., Oct. 31, 1916); 2–Joseph Philip, *b* Oct. 29, 1881; *m* 1905, Bell Throop (issue: Olive K., *b* Feb. 20, 1906; Virginia, *b* Jan. 3, 1908); *m* 2d, June 12, 1915, Elizabeth, dau. of Thomas Fitzgibbon, of Cleveland, O. (issue: Joseph P., *b* Mar. 29, 1917; Thomas Franklin, *b* Sept. 8, 1921); 3–Helen Olive (Nov. 30, 1882-Apr. 18, 1920); grad. U. of Tex., '03 (P.B.K., Kappa Kappa Gamma); 4–James Henry (June 24, 1884-May 19, 1886); 5–Thomas Jefferson, *b* Feb. 26, 1887; U. of Tex., '11 (Sigma Chi); served as 2d lt. Co. B, 358th Inf., 179th Brig., 90th Div., 1917-19; with A.E.F. in France, June 19, 1918-Aug. 15, 1919; wounded in Preny demonstration, Sept. 26, 1918; cited for gallantry in action; *m* Sept. 27, 1924, Helen Frances, dau. of Rev. Crawford McKibbin, D.D., of St. Paul, Minn. (issue: Sarah Angier, *b* Nov. 15, 1925-*d*; Thomas Jefferson, Jr., *b* Aug. 23, 1927); 6–William Webb, *b* Mar. 15, 1890; U. of Tex., '11 (Sigma Chi); *m* June 11, 1916, Isabel, dau. of Lavoisier L. Lamar, of Macon, Ga. (issue: William W., Jr., *b* June 1, 1917; Lamar French, *b* July 6, 1919; Mary Frances, *b* July 3, 1921; Lanier Henry, *b* Aug. 1, 1923); 7–Franklin French, *b* Oct. 10, 1892; cadet in flying corps, Rich Field, Waco, Tex., May 11-Dec. 13, 1918; *m* Nov. 14, 1927, Elizabeth Johnson, dau. of Neil Masterson, of Houston, Tex. (issue: Franklin French, Jr., *b* Sept. 14, 1928).

1–Ed. Vassar Coll. Mem. F.F.V., U.D.C. Residence: 3518 Broadway, San Antonio, Tex.

1–**DIXON, John Wesley,** *b* Charlotte Co., Va., Aug. 26, 1875.

5–John **Dixon** (*d* 1790), of Prince Edward Co., Va.; soldier in Am. Rev.; *m* Sarah– (*d* 1838);

4–John;

3–William T. (*d* 1870), of Prince Edward Co.; *m* 1835, Martha Bell Bagby (*d* 1888);

2–John Thomas (2 below).

7–John **Ragland** (qv);

6–Evan (*d* 1795), vestryman, Antrim Parish,

Halifax Co., 1767-95; *m* Susannah Lipscomb;
5–Lipscomb (*d* 1813), *m* Martha–;
4–Thomas (*d* 1815); *m* 1788, Frances Glass (*d* 1846);
3–Mary (*d* 1844), *m* 2d, 1827, William **Barbour** (Shadrack[4]);
2–Mary Ragland (1833-1911), of Lunenburg Co., Va.; *m* 1866, John Thomas **Dixon** (1835-1917), of Hickory Hill, Charlotte Co., Va.; tobacco planter; in 56th Va. Inf., Pickett's Div., Longstreet's Corps, wounded in charge at Gettysburg; issue: I–Charles Henry (*b* 1867; *m* Minnie Gertrude Carter); II–Roberta Susan (1868-1913; *m* John Allen); III–Nannie Bell (*b* 1870; *m* Herbert M. Shelton); IV–William Floyd (1873-1918; *m* Annie Shelton); V–John Wesley (1 above); VI–Mary Frances (1877-1906; *m* Davis Perkins).
1–*m* Apr. 5, 1905, Margaret Collins Denny (see Vol. I, p. 544 for genealogy); issue (all *b* Richmond, Va.): 1–Elizabeth Denny, *b* Mar. 2, 1910; Randolph-Macon Woman's Coll. 3 yrs.; U. of Mich., 1931 (Delta Zeta); 2–John Wesley, Jr. (Aug. 19, 1912-May 12, 1913); 3–Mary Barbour, *b* Mar. 2, 1915; 4–John Wesley, Jr. II, *b* Aug. 18, 1919; 5–William Denny, *b* Nov. 24, 1921.
1–B.A., Hampden-Sidney College, '00; B.D., Vanderbilt U., 1903. Pastor Brookneal circuit, 1904-07, Fountain Heights M.E. Ch., Birmingham, Ala., 1907-08; supt. Methodist Inst., Richmond, 1908-21, Va. Conference Evangelist, 1921-25; pastor Crewe M.E. Ch., 1925-29; pastor Rocky Mt., Va. since 1929. Mason. Democrat. Clubs: Kiwanis, Lions. Residence: Rocky Mount, Va.

1–**FAILING, Henrietta Ellison,** *b* Portland, Ore., Sept. 27, 1859.
7–Robert **Corbett,** from Eng. after the death of Cromwell, 1658; settled in N.E., and took up residence in Woodstock, Conn.; soldier in King Philip's War; *m* 1682, Priscilla Rockwood, of Mendon, Mass.;
6–Dr. John (1686-1729), liberally educated; large landowner; physician; *m* 1703, Mehetable Rockwood (*b* 1686; Josiah[7], *m* Mary Twitchell);
5–Dr. John (1704-94), physician; *m* 1727, Hopestill Chapin (*b* 1705; Capt. Seth[6], *m* Bethiah Thurston);
4–Elijah (*b* 1736), of Mass.; *m* Polly Freeland;
3–Elijah (1791-1848), selectman; mfr. of edged tools; removed to White Creek, Washington Co., N.Y., and was also a resident of Cambridge, N.Y.; *m* 1816, Melinda Forbush;
2–Emily Phelps (2 below).
8–Daniel (Pfarrabas) **Forbush** (*d* 1687), from Scotland, prob. with other Scotch soldiers, by order of Cromwell; of Cambridge, Mass., 1660; received land grant, 1665; later at Marlborough; *m* 1st, 1660, Rebecca Perriman (*d* 1677);
7–Samuel (ca. 1674-ca. 1766), with his father and bro. Thomas; a first settler of Westborough; his house was used as a garrison; apptd. fence viewer at 1st town meeting, 1718; selectman, 1723; lt., 1730; capt., 1737, Westborough Co.; *m* 1699, Abigail Rice (*b* 1672);
6–Capt. Samuel (ca. 1705-67), *m* Sarah– (*d* 1776);
5–Samuel (1733-1818), selectman; *m* 1756, Abigail Forbush (*d* 1788);
4–Jonah (1775-98), killed by fall from a horse; *m* 1794, Martha Wood (1771-living 1806);
3–Melinda (1795-1842), *m* 1816, Elijah **Corbett** (3 above);
2–Emily Phelps (1836-70), of Little White Creek, Vt.; *m* 1858, Henry **Failing** (1834-98), pres. First Nat. Bank of Portland, Ore.; mayor, 1856,66; issue: I–Henrietta Ellison (1 above); II–Mary Forbush (qv for other lineages); III–Emily Corbett (*b* 1867; *m* 1904, Col. Henry C. Cabell, of Richmond, Va.); IV–Martha Fox (1869-70).
1–Mem. C.D.A., Portland Art Assn. Clubs: Colony (New York), Town. Residence: 443 Montgomery Pl., Portland, Ore.

1–**FAILING, Mary Forbush,** *b* Portland, Ore., Apr. 25, 1862.
6–Nicholas **Failing** (1720-87), of Failing family which came to America from the Palatinate, 1708, and settled in Mohawk Valley; Nicholas removed from Livingston Manor to Canajoharie, Montgomery Co., prior to Am. Rev.; pvt. Am. Rev.; *m* Elizabeth Schnell;
5–Henry Nicholas (1740-1831), pvt. Am. Rev. with his father;
4–Henry Jacob (1770-1826), farmer and had trading post in Mohawk Valley; *m* 1804, Mary Chapman (*d* aet. 86), of Bradford, Eng.;
3–Josiah (*b* 1806), city supt. of carts, Albany; dea. Bapt. Ch.; sailed Apr. 15, 1851, from N.Y. City with his sons, Henry and John, to Portland, Ore.; arrived, June 9; while waiting for stock of store goods to arrive, they built a store on s.w. corner of Front and Oak Sts.; *m* 1828, Henrietta Legge Ellison (1801-83; Henry[4], of S.C.);
2–Henry (1834-98), *m* 1858, Emily Phelps Corbett (1836-70); for issue and other lineages see Henrietta E. Failing.
1–Mem. C.D.A., Mt. Vernon Ladies Assn. of the Union. Residence: 443 Montgomery Pl., Portland, Ore.

1–**FELDHAUSER, Goode Wiles King (Mrs. Edward),** *b* Paducah, Ky.
11–Capt. William **King,** mem. Va. London Co., cdr. of "Diamond" to Va., 1609; *m* Blanche Mainwaring;
10–Capt. John, capt. of "Falcon" to Barbados, 1636, which carried loyalists to the Stuart cause; settled in Charles City Co., Va., 1642; buried in Bruton Churchyard, 1669; *m* in Chester, Eng., Ann Daniel;
9–Francis, came to Va. with Giles Brent, 1653; *m* Dorothy Aston;
8–Robert (*d* post 1680), col. colonial militia; justice, 1660; *m* his 2d cousin, Hannah Scarborough;
7–William (ca. 1659-1702), Middlesex Co.; capt. colonial militia, 1687; justice, Stafford Co., 1700-02; *m* Judith Peyton (Col. Valentine[8], *m* Frances, dau. of Dr. Thomas Gerard);
6–William Alfred (*b* ca. 1685), lived at "Brooke," King estate in Stafford Co.; *m* Sophia Burgess (Col. William[7], *m* Sophia Ewell, widow of Maj. Richard Ewen);
5–William Valentine (1711-1777-78), clk., Stafford Co. Ct., 1748; justice, 1752-54; capt. colonial militia; was at Valley Forge; *m* 1738, Elizabeth Edwards;
4–John Edwards (1757-1828), gen. in War 1812 from Ky.; fought at King's Mountain; clk. of co. and circuit cts., Cumberland Co., Ky.; presdl. elector for Pres. Monroe; *m* Versailles, Ky., 1791, Sarah Clifton;
3–Milton (1799-1874), clk., Cumberland Co. Ct., 1828-50; *m* Susan Wiles, of Norfolk, Va.;
2–John Quincy Adams (2 below).
9–Andrew **Monroe** (qv);
8–Andrew (*d* 1714), capt. colonial militia, Westmoreland Co.; justice; *m* Eleanor Spence (Patrick[9], *m* Dorcas, dau. of Capt. Thomas Ewell);
7–Elizabeth, *m* Thomas **Arrington** (*d* 1715; Gerard[8]);
6–Jane, *m* John **Edwards,** capt. colonial militia, Prince William Co., in French and Indian War (William[7], *m* Ann Harrison);
5–Elizabeth (1717-92), *m* William V. **King** (5 above).
9–Charles **Ashton** (1625-72), justice and capt. Northumberland Co.; colonial militia; *m* Isabel Clare (Capt. Richard[10]);
8–John (*d* 1677), capt. colonial militia, Northumberland Co.; *m* Grace Smith (William[9]; Humphry[10]);
7–Sarah (*d* 1749), *m* 2d, 1707, Thomas **Clifton** (*b* 1660; James[8], *m* Ann, dau. of George Brent);
6–Burdette (1708-61), justice, Prince George Co., 1756-58; *m* Frances Hill (g.dau. of Col. Edward Hill, of "Shirley," gov. of Md., 1649);
5–Burdette (1736-96), ens. colonial militia, 1761; pvt. Fauquier Co. troops Am. Rev.; received bounty land grant in Ky.; *m* Rebecca Kenner;
4–Sarah (1759-1815), *m* John E. **King** (4 above).
12–Col. Richard **Lee** (qv);
11–Charles (*b* 1656), *m* Elizabeth Medstand (Thomas[12]);
10–Elizabeth, *m* Capt. John **Howson,** colonial militia (Robert[11]);
9–Elizabeth, *m* Mathew **Rodham**;
8–Elizabeth, *m* Capt. Richard **Kenner** (*d* 1692), burgess, Northumberland Co., 1688-91;
7–Francis (1675-1728), *m* Elizabeth Turberville (George[8], *m* Frances Ashton);
6–Howson (1711-78), midshipman in Am. Rev.;

m 1735, Margaret Eskridge (George[7], Eng. to Va., 1667);
5–Rebecca, *m* Burdette **Clifton,** Jr. (5 above).
10–Col. George **Reade** (qv);
9–Mildred (*d* 1694), *m* Col. Augustine **Warner,** 2d;
8–Mildred, *m* 1690, Lawrence **Washington** (1661-97; John[9], qv);
7–Mildred (*b* 1695), *m* 2d, 1733, Col. Henry **Willis,** founder of Fredericksburg, Va.;
6–Ann (*b* 1735), *m* William **Grymes** (Col. Charles[7], *m* Frances, dau. of Gov. Edmund Jennings; John[8], of Middlesex Co.; Gen. Thomas[9]; Sir Thomas[10]);
5–William, "first capt. to enlist in Am. Rev. under George Washington, who was his cousin"; maj. Cont. Line; *m* Sarah Nicholas (Nathaniel[6]);
4–Ann Nancy (1778-1845), *m* 1st, 1792, Dr. William Willis **Wiles,** of Norfolk, Va.;
3–Susan (1801-39), "the Norfolk Beauty"; *m* Milton **King** (3 above);
2–John Quincy Adams (1828-80), ed. Transylvania Coll.; state senator; speaker; acting gov. of Ky., 1858; mem. law firm King & Bennett, Denver, Colo., at time of death; *m* 1854, Leanna Sophia King (Col. Alfred[3] [1806-72], Mexican War); issue: I–Mary E. (*m* Dr. James Gaunt Brooks); II–Nancy S. (*m* Robert Bagnell); III–Ellen H. (*m* Robiou White); IV–Leann Q. (*m* R. A. Gurley); V–Goode W. (1 above).
1–*m* in Denver, Colo., 1882, Charles Fred Robinson Hayward, *b* Fitchburg, Mass.; author; editor Denver Republican at time of death, 1889.
1–*m* 2d, Denver, Aug. 30, 1892, Edward Feldhauser, *b* St. Paul, Minn.; ed. Berea (O.) Coll.; son of Philip Feldhauser.
1–Ed. Wolf Hall Coll., Denver. Mem. C.D.A., D.F.P.A., D.A.R., U.S.D. 1812. Residence: Commodore Hotel, St. Paul, Minn.

1–**FREEMAN, J(ohn) Douglas,** *b* Augusta, Ga., Feb. 11, 1882.
10–Rev. William **Wilkinson** (ca. 1612-1663), from Eng.; was in Va., 1635; in Md., 1650; clergyman of Anglican Ch.; *m* 1st, Naomi–;
9–Rebecca (*d* 1726), *m* ante 1660, Thomas **Dent** (ca. 1635-1676), from Eng.; justice, high sheriff, St. Mary's Co., Md.; mem. Md. Assembly;
8–Margaret, *m* 1681, Edmund **Howard** (ca. 1650-1713), from Eng.; justice, Somerset Co., 1684; clk., Charles Co., ante 1703;
7–John (ca. 1688-1743), "styled captain"; *m* ca. 1725, Rebecca Brooke;
6–Eleanor, *m* ante 1740, John **Douglas** (1709-80), of Charles Co., Md.;
5–Ann (1740-1800), *m* ca. 1760, Nathaniel **Freeman** (1733-1807);
4–James (1763-1807), justice, Charles Co.; *m* 1785, Eleanor Douglas (1761-1830); see Vol. I, p. 920;
3–John Douglas (1800-91), of Charles and St. Mary's cos., Md.; mem. Md. Legislature; *m* ca. 1821, Eleanor Ann Semmes (*b* 1803); see Vol. I, p. 920;
2–Bernard (2 below).
10–Robert **Brooke** (qv);
9–Thomas (1632-76), justice, high sheriff, Calvert Co.; mem. Md. Assembly; *m* ca. 1658, Eleanor Hatton (1642-1724; Richard[10]);
8–Thomas (1659/60-1730/31), *m* 2d, 1696, Barbara Dent (1676-1754; Thomas[9], 9 above);
7–Rebecca (1709-63), *m* John **Howard** (7 above).
2–Bernard **Freeman** (*b* 1842), served in Co. A, 2d Md. Bn., C.S.A.; *m* 1879, Georgia Randall (1851-1924); for issue see Vol. I, p. 920.
1–*m* Nov. 3, 1909, Eleanor Washington Perine, *b* Baltimore, Md., Apr. 21, 1888; dau. E. Glenn Perine, of Baltimore; issue (all *b* Baltimore): 1–Eleanor Ann Washington, *b* July 15, 1910; 2–Douglas Semmes (girl), *b* July 14, 1911; 3–John Douglas, 3d (Aug. 23, 1912-Feb. 10, 1915); 4–Coleman Randall, *b* Dec. 14, 1914; 5–Stanley Hart (girl), *b* Sept. 21, 1916.
1–Insurance broker, Baltimore. Mem. Fifth Veteran Corps, Md. Hist. Soc., Southern Md. Soc. Hobby: Americana. Residence: 203 Woodlawn Rd., Roland Park, Md.

1–**FULLER, Clara Cornelia,** *b* Steuben, Oneida Co., N.Y., Aug. 26, 1852.
10–Edward **Fuller,** Mayflower Pilgrim (qv);
9–Samuel (ca. 1612-1683), *m* by Capt. Miles Standish, 1635, Jane Lathrop;
8–Samuel (1637/38-ante Dec. 28, 1691), *m* Anna Fuller;
7–Barnabas (ca. 1659-1738), of Barnstable; *m* 1680/81, Elizabeth Young;
6–Samuel (1681-1758), *m* ca. 1718, Ruth Crocker;
5–Lot (1733-1811), *m* Rachel–, of Colchester, Conn.;
4–Simeon (1762-1852), Steuben, N.Y.; capt. Am. Rev.; *m* 1790, Wealthy Woodward;
3–Russell (1795-1856), of Steuben, N.Y.; *m* 1821, Lydia Potter;
2–Simeon Russell (2 below).
6–Hugh **White** (1691-1770), *m* 1717, Mary Stone;
5–Aaron (1723-1814), *m* 1749, Sarah Olmsted;
4–Samuel (1762-1833), to Holland Patent, N.Y.; *m* Anna Merrow;
3–Aaron (*b* 1788), *m* Rhoda Bagg, of Lanesboro, Mass.;
2–Martha (*b* 1823), *m* 1851, Simeon Russell **Fuller** (1821-1902), of Steuben, N.Y.; issue: I–Clara C. (1 above); II–Frank Russell (*b* 1856).
1–Ed. Holland Patent H.S., and Utica Female Sem. Prin. The Ossining Sch. for Girls, 1889–. Mem. S.M.D., D.A.R. Sorosis, Ossining Women's Club, etc. Residence: Ossining-on-Hudson, N.Y.

Gardiner

Arms: Or, on a chevron gules, between three griffins' heads erased azure, two lions counterpassant of the field.
Crest: On a wreath, a saracen's head couped at the shoulders full faced proper, bearded sable, on the head a cap turned up gules and azure.
Motto: Praesto pro patria.

1–**GARDINER, Asa Bird,** *b* Glencoe, Md., July 31, 1866.
10–George **Gardiner** (ca. 1600-ca. 1677), from Eng. ante 1638; settled at Newport, 1640; *m* 1st, 1640, Herodias (Long) Hicks (1622-1705), separated ca. 1660;
9–Benoni (1643-1731), of Portsmouth, R.I.; *m* 1666, Mary Sherman (1645-1730; Philip[10], qv);
8–Isaac (1687-1762), of Kingston, R.I.; *m* 1709, Elizabeth Davis (*d* 1759);
7–Benoni (1720-65), of N. Kingston, R.I.; *m* 1741, Elizabeth Hall (Zuriel[8]);
6–Othniel (1743-77), of Exeter, R.I.; 2d lt., 14th Regt. Militia, Am. Rev.; *m* 1764, Lydia Reynolds (1747-80; George[7]);
5–George (1766-1843), of Exeter, R.I., and Troy, N.Y.; *m* 1st, Hannah Dawley (*d* 1786);
4–George (1786-1826), of Hoosic, N.Y.; *m* 1807, Christina Rosenberg;
3–Asa (1814-61), of Troy, and N.Y. City; *m* 1838, Rebeckah Bentley (1822-82; John[4], of Lorraine, N.Y.);
2–Asa Bird (2 below).
5–John **Austen,** from Eng. with son John, to Baltimore, 1795; settled at Deer Creek, nr. Darlington, Harford Co., Md.;
4–John, *m* 1792, Martha Colgate (1766-1825; John[5], 1727-1801);
3–George (1798-1877), of "Filston," Glencoe, Md.; *m* Caroline Millemon (1803-61), of Baltimore;

AUSTEN

Arms: Or, a chevron gules, between three lion's gambs erect and erased sable.
Crest: On a mural coronet or, a buck sejant argent, attires of the first.
Motto: Pax nostra corona.

ASA BIRD GARDINER (Sept. 30, 1839-Apr. 24, 1919), A.B., N.Y. City Coll., '59, A.M., 1862; LL.B., New York U., 1860; (A.M., Dartmouth, 1864, Columbia, 1869; LL.D., New York U., 1875; L.H.D., Hobart, 1896); admitted to New York bar, 1860. First lt., 31st N.Y. Vol. Inf., 1861; capt., 22d N.Y. State Vol. Inf., 1862; 1st lt. and adj., U.S. Vet. Reserve Corps, 1865; bvtd. capt. and maj., U.S. Vols. for "Gallant and meritorius services during the War"; mustered out of vol. service, 1866; 2d lt., 9th U.S. Inf., 1866; 1st lt., 1868; transferred to 1st Arty., 1869; maj. judge adv., U.S.A., 1873; awarded Medal of Honor, 1872, for services in Gettysburg Campaign, where he was wounded; prof. law, U.S.M.A., 1874-78; judge adv., Military Div. of the South, 1871-73, Div. of the Atlantic, 1878-87; actg. Sec. of War, 1887-88; retired as lt. col. U.S.A., Dec. 8, 1888. Dist. atty., New York Co., 1897-1900; counsel for Generals Grant and Sheridan in the G. K. Warren Court of Inquiry.

2-Mary (1842-1900), *m* 1865, Asa Bird **Gardiner** (1839-1919), see portrait and biography; *m* 2d, 1902, Harriet Isabella Lindsay; issue (1st marriage): I-Asa Bird (1 above); II-Norman Bentley (*b* 1874; *m* Minnie Lawrence; issue: Norman Bentley, *b* 1907; Asa B., *b* 1911; Lawrence, *b* 1915); III-Philip Parkhurst (*b* 1877; *m* Evelyn Terry Poor; *m* 2d, Helen Ramsay Turnbull); IV-George Austen (1868-1909); V-Williard (*b* and *d* 1872); issue (2d marriage): I-John Doane (*b* 1903); II-William (*b* 1908).
1-*m* Jan. 6, 1897, Mary Norcum Campbell, *b* New York, N.Y., Feb. 26, 1872; dau. of Howard Campbell, of New York.
1-A.B., Columbia, '87 (D.K.E.). Importer, New York City, 1888-94; mgr. Filston Farm, Baltimore Co., Md., 1894-1903; pres. Gardiner Dairy, Baltimore, 1903-13, City Dairy, Baltimore, 1913-22, Western Md. Dairy, Baltimore, 1922-26; retired. Dir. Commonwealth Bank, Baltimore. Mem. Soc. Cincinnati. Episcopalian. Republican. Clubs: Baltimore Country, Elkridge, Rolling Road Golf, Rodgers Forge Golf. Residence: Cockeysville, Baltimore Co., Md.

1-**GARFIELD, Charles Fowler,** *b* at Holley, N.Y., Oct. 10, 1872.
9-Edward **Garfield** (qv);
8-Edward (*b* ca. 1605), *m* Rebecca-;
7-Benjamin (1643-1717), *m* 1678, Elizabeth Bridge;
6-Samuel (*b* 1690), *m* 1714, Mary Bowman;
5-Eliakim (*b* 1732), *m* Lucy Chase;
4-Nathaniel (1760-1839), *m* 1788, Eunice Woodward;
3-Nathaniel (1793-1853), *m* 1825, Charlotte Harwood;
2-George (1840-88), grain buyer and shipper, of Holley, N.Y., *m* Sarah Purdy Fowler (1844-1908; Richard R.[3] [1803-86], *m* Martha Purdy); issue: I-Charles Fowler (1 above); II-Harry Harwood (*b* 1878; *m* Lillian F., dau. John Jenks).
1-*m* Aug. 24, 1894, Myra Avalene Shipley (July 20, 1871-Apr. 28, 1925); dau. of William Watters Shipley, of Williamson, N.Y.
1-Investor; pres. several corpns. (see Who's Who in America). Mem. S.A.R., Rochester Hist. Soc. Club: Genesee Valley, Lake Placid. Summer place: Williamson, N.Y. Winter place: Beverly Hills, Calif.

1-**GRAY, Alfred Leftwich,** *b* Palmyra, Va., Oct. 2, 1873.
6-Garrit **Gray** (probably desc. Thomas Graye who came from Eng. to Va., 1624, *m* Margaret-); was in N.J. ante 1803; *m* Hannah-;
5-John, lived in Va., 1803; *m* Susanna Watkins;
4-William, col. in War 1812; *m* Jane Guerrant (Maj. Peter[5], *m* Magdalen Trabue);
3-William Alfred (1806-88), M.D., U.Pa., 1830; *m* 1831, Mary Ann Brooks (1812-91);
2-Alphonso Alexander (2 below).
9-Ralph **Leftwich,** of Leftwich Hall, Eng.; patented lands in New Kent Co., Va., 1658; *m* Elizabeth Mainwaring;
8-Thomas (ca. 1660-ca. 1730), *m* 2d, ca. 1706, Mary North (Augustine[9], *m* Dorothy-);
7-Augustine (ca. 1712-1795), of Bedford Co., Va.; *m* twice;
6-Col. William (1737-1829), of Caroline and Bedford cos., Va.; capt. in colonial and Indian wars; capt. militia, 1772; maj., 1778; lt. col., 1780; *m* ca. 1757, Elizabeth Haynes (William[7], *m* Elizabeth-);
5-Capt. John, *m* 1783, Susanna Smith;
4-Rev. William, *m* Frances Otey (Col. John A.[5], officer Am. Rev.);
3-Rev. James, *m* Ann Bilbro.
2-Alphonso Alexander **Gray** (1835-1908), atty. at law, Palmyra, Va.; *m* 1860, Sallie Terrill Shepherd (1842-65); *m* 2d, 1870, Bettie Ann Leftwich (1842-1924); issue (1st marriage): 1-Willie Blanche (*b* 1865; *m* Frank Terry Shepherd); issue (2d marriage): I-Alfred Leftwich (1 above); II-Ernest Alphonso (*b* 1878; *m* Manella Susan Cochran).
1-*m* Dec. 23, 1903, Alice Lear Clark, *b* Petersburg, Va., Aug. 27, 1879; dau. of Lyman Emery Clark, formerly asst. treas. and auditor, A.C.L. R.R.; issue (all *b* Richmond, Va.): 1-Alfred Leftwich, Jr., *b* July 11, 1907; U. of Va., '29; 2-Ernest Emery, *b* July 2, 1909; U. of Va.; 3-John Newton, *b* Oct. 1, 1917.
1-M.D., U. of Va., 1897 (Phi Kappa Sigma, Pi Mu, Phi Chi, Theta Nu Epsilon, Phi Beta

Kappa, etc.). Physician and roentgenologist; prof. roentgenology, Med. Coll., of Va., since 1916. Author (see Who's Who in America). Served as maj. M.O.R.C., 1917, in charge Richmond Sch. of Mil. Roentgenology, training x-ray specialists for army service. Mem. Am. Roentgen Ray Soc. (pres. 1915), A.M.A., Med. Soc. of Va. (pres. 1920-21), Tri-State Med. Assn. of Carolinas and Va. (v.p. 1913), Richmond Acad. Medicine and Surgery (pres. 1914); fellow Am. Coll. Physicians, Am. Coll. of Radiology (pres. 1928-29), etc. Clubs: Farmington Country, Commonwealth, University, Country, of Va. Residence: 2006 Monument Av., Richmond, Va.

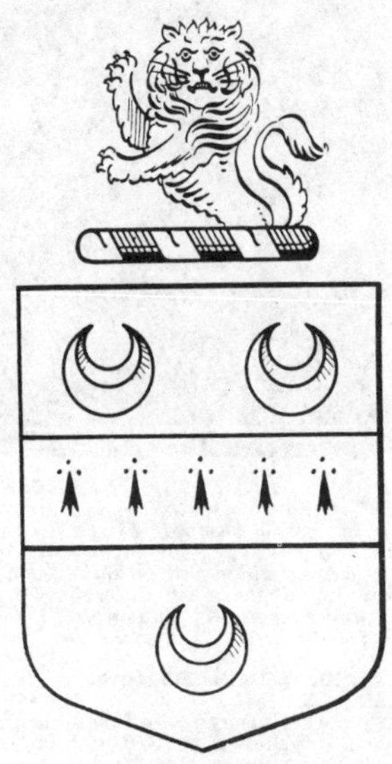

HOLLOWAY

Arms: Gules, a fess ermine, between three crescents argent (mantled gules doubled argent).
Crest: A demi-lion rampant guardant purpure.

1–**HOLLOWAY, Harry Cyrus,** *b* Webster Groves, Mo., Nov. 29, 1874.
9–William **Holloway,** from Eng., settled at Boston and Taunton, Mass.; *m* Elizabeth– (*d* 1679/80);
8–Malachi (bap. 1650), *m* Elizabeth Shove (George[9], of Taunton);
7–William, of Taunton; *m* 1702, Elizabeth Holyday;
6–William (1706-78), Dighton, Mass.; *m* 1739, Sarah Walker (Peter[7], of Taunton);
5–Peter (1751-1832), York, N.Y.; Am. Rev.; *m* 1775, Abigail Gooding;
4–Cyrus (1786-1842), Sylvania, O.; *m* 1812, Permelia Tobey (1789-1850; Prince[5], of Dartmouth and Conway, Mass.);
3–Frederick Madison (1815-91), Hillsdale, Mich.; *m* 1837, Sybil Bacon Bassett;
2–George Allen (2 below).
11–Thomas **Rogers** (*d* 1621), Mayflower Pilgrim (qv);
10–John (*d* 1691/92), rep. Duxbury, Mass., 1657; *m* 1639, Ann Churchman;
9–Abigail (1641/42-1727), *m* John **Richmond** (1627-1715);
8–Lt. Joseph (*b* 1663), *m* 1685, Mary Andrews (Henry[9], of Taunton);
7–Abigail, *m* Matthew **Gooding** (1695-1756; George[8]);
6–George (*b* 1723), settled at Dighton; *m* 1746, Sarah Reed;
5–Abigail, *m* Peter **Holloway** (5 above).
10–James **Leonard,** desc. Charlemagne, Alfred the Great and Magna Charta Barons (qv);
9–Maj. Thomas (1641-1713), Taunton; ens., 1665; capt., 1690; maj. in comd. of Bristol Co. troops; dep., 1680-90; *m* 1662, Mary Watson;
8–Mary (*b* 1663), *m* Joseph **Tisdale** (John[9]);
7–Sarah, *m* Thomas **Reed,** of Dighton;
6–Sarah (1727-98), *m* George **Gooding** (6 above).
10–John **Howland,** Mayflower Pilgrim (qv);
9–Hope (ca. 1629-1683), *m* 1646, John **Chipman**;
8–Hope (1652-78), *m* 1670, John **Huckens,** of Barnstable;
7–Mary (1673-1743), *m* ca. 1690, Nathan **Bassett**;
6–William (1702-82), *m* Anna Mayhew (1710-80; Matthew[7]);
5–Fortunatus (1741-79), French and Indian War, 1761-62; lt. sea coast defense, 1775-77; officer Cont. Army, 1777-78; *m* 1769, Sarah Bassett (1747-91; Cornelius[6]);
4–Fortunatus (1775-1815), Gorham, N.Y.; *m* ante 1815, Sybil Bacon (1784-1815; Timothy[5], Hillsdale, N.Y.);
3–Sybil Bacon (1815-95), *m* Frederick Madison **Holloway** (3 above);
2–George Allen (1839-1910), of Hillsdale, Mich., and Chicago, Ill.; *m* 1865, Olive Melissa Tibbits (1839-1920; George[3], of Adams, Mass., and Farmington, Mich.); issue: I–George Frederick; *m* Aura Howes); II–Frank Leroy (*d* 1883, aet. 15); III–Bertha; IV–Harry Cyrus (1 above); V–Olive (*d* infancy 1880).
1–*m* Jan. 27, 1904, Nema Marie Whitcomb (qv).
1–Grad. Cornell U., 1896 (D.K.E.). Draftsman and estimator, Ill. Car & Equipment Co., 1897-98; Western Electric Co., 1898-1902; Weber Ry. Joint Mfg. Co. and its succesesor, The Rail Joint Co., 1902-14; Maintenance Equipment Co., 1914-29; v.p. Poor & Co. since 1929; also treas. P. & M. Co., Canton Forge & Axle Co., Vermilion Malleable Iron Co., Maintenance Equipment Co. Mem. Am. Iron and Steel Inst., Western Soc. of Engrs., S.R., Chicago Art Inst. (life), Field Museum. Clubs: University, Engineers (Chicago), Skokie (Ill.) Country, Stockbridge (Mass.) Golf, Berkshires Hunt and Country (Lenox, Mass.). Residence: 589 Sheridan Rd., Glencoe, Ill.

WHITCOMB

Arms: Paly of six or and sable, three eagles displayed counter-changed, mantled sable, doubled or.
Crest: Out of a ducal coronet argent, a demi-eagle per pale sable and argent, wings counter-changed.

1–**HOLLOWAY, Nema Marie Whitcomb (Mrs. Harry C.),** *b* Clinton, Ind., May 24, 1875.
9–John **Whitcomb** (1588-1662), from Eng., 1633, settled at Dorchester, Scituate and Lancaster, Mass.; *m* Frances– (*d* 1671);
8–Robert, *m* 1660, Mary Cudworth (*b* 1637; Gen. James[9], from Eng., settled at Scituate);
7–James (1668-1728), Rochester, Mass.; *m* 1694, Mary Parker (1667-1729);
6–Nathaniel (1697-1771), Hardwick, Mass.; *m* 1722, Rosilla Coombs (*d* 1737);
5–Asa (1735-1812), Barnard, Vt.; enlisted in "Old French War," 1756-57, in Capt. Joseph Warner's co.; selectman, justice, 1778; rep., 1797; *m* 1759, Joanna Raymond;
4–Anthony (*b* 1766), in Capt. Nehemiah Lovewell's co. of Vt., 1781; *m* Lucy Wright (*b* 1774);

3–Benjamin Raymond (1798-1861), Clinton, Ind.; *m* 1819, Anna Sutton (1804-60);
2–John (2 below).
9–James **Leonard** (qv);
8–Rebecca (1657-1736), *m* 1678, Isaac **Chapman** (1647-1737);
7–James (*b* ca. 1685), *m* 1711, Mercy– (1690-1715);
6–Mercy (*b* 1712), of Rochester, Mass.; *m* 1737, Benjamin **Raymond** (1714-79);
5–Joanna (1740-1809), *m* 1759, Asa **Whitcomb** (5 above).
10–Robert **Parke** (qv);
9–Thomas (*d* 1709), from Eng., settled at Stonington, Conn.; soldier in King Philip's War; *m* Dorothy Thompson (*b* 1624);
8–Nathaniel (*d* 1718), of Groton, Conn.; *m* Sarah Geer (*b* 1659);
7–Joseph, of Groton; *m* 1709, Mary Smith;
6–Daniel (*b* 1719), Sharon, Conn.; *m* 1741, Ann Chapman (*b* 1726);
5–Daniel (1742-1818), Am. Rev.; *m* Lydia–;
4–Solomon (1765-1843), Moreau, N.Y.; Am. Rev. and War 1812; *m* 1789, Susannah Burnham (1771-1859);
3–Barzilla (1791-1866), *m* 1824, Susan Marie Budd Burghardt (1804-84);
2–Lydia Amelia (1840-1924), of Sandy Hill, N.Y.; *m* 1870, John **Whitcomb** (1821-91), merchant; issue: I–Larz Augustus (*b* 1871); II–William Arthur (*b* 1873); III–Nema Marie (1 above).
1–*m* Jan. 27, 1904, Harry Cyrus Holloway (qv).
1–Mem. Soc. of Knights of the Garter, Magna Charta Dames, Colony of N.E. Women, D.F.P.A., S.D.P., Women Desc. of A. and H.A. Co., D.C.W., D.A.C., D.A.R., U.S.D. 1812, N.E.H.G.S., Chicago Hist. Soc., Scituate Hist. Soc. Clubs: Chicago Woman's, Woman's City, Woman's Athletic, Arts, Woman's Nat. Republican (dir.), Ill. Republican (v.p.), Woman's Nat. Country (Washington, D.C.); Berkshires Hunt and Country (Lenox, Mass.), Stockbridge (Mass.) Golf, Skokie Country, Woman's Dundee Country. Summer residence: "Tamarack," Tyringham, Mass. (Berkshire Hills). Residence: 589 Sheridan Rd., Glencoe, Ill.

1–**HUBBARD, Thomas Foy,** *b* Baltimore, Md., Sept., 14, 1898.
10–Tristram **Coffin** (qv);
9–James (1640-1720), of Nantucket, Mass.; *m* 1663, Mary Severance (1645-1720; John[10], qv);
8–John (1672-1741), *m* 1692, Hope Gardner (1669-1750; Richard[9]; Thomas[10], *m* Sarah Shattuck);
7–Elias (1702-73), *m* 1729, his cousin, Love Coffin (1705-82; Ebenezer[8]; James[9] as above);
6–John (1748-1813), of Nantucket; *m* Elizabeth Gardner (1758-1839; George[7], *m* Elizabeth, dau. of James Chase; Jeremiah[8]; John[9]; John[10]; Thomas[11]);
5–George (1787-1867), of Nantucket; *m* 1809, Nancy Stubbs (1790-1814; James[6]; Benjamin[7]; William[8]; Richard[9]; Richard[10]);
4–Obed Mayo (1811-65), of Nantucket; *m* 1844, Caroline Marshall (1820-1909; Greenbury[5]; Meredith[6]);
3–Georgeanna (1844-1913), of St. Michael's, Md.; *m* 1863, John Thomas **Hubbard** (1843-97; Thomas H.[4], *m* Elizabeth, dau. of Mark Sewell; Hugh[5]);
2–Thomas Matthew (2 below).
7–James **Gould** (1673-1737), settled in Queen Ann's Co., Md.;
6–Richard, *m* 1739, Mary Woodland;
5–William (1753-1817), *m* Julia Ann–;
4–Susan (1809-36), *m* 1832, Samuel **Plummer** (1802-68);
3–William James (1832-1901), of Baltimore; *m* 1859, Elizabeth Foy (1835-1926; James H.[4], *m* Henrietta, dau. of Henry Cruser, War 1812; John [Fiyea] Foy[5]);
2–Mary Ann (*b* 1866), *m* 1892, Thomas Matthew **Hubbard** (*b* 1869), of St. Michael's, Md.; claim adjuster for textile mills; issue: I–Ruth (*b* 1893; *m* Stanley Baer Kessler); II–Elsie (*b* 1896; *m* Walter Leroy Glanville); III–Thomas Foy (1 above).
1–*m* Nov. 26, 1924, Rose Elizabeth Hicks, *b* Baltimore, Dec. 5, 1901; dau. of John Frederick Hicks (John[3], of Cambridge, Eng.), *m* Rose Bell (John Archer[3]; Abraham[4]); issue: 1–Thomas Hicks, *b* Baltimore, May 8, 1929.
1–B.E., Johns Hopkins, '21 (Omicron Delta Kappa, Tau Beta Pi, Alpha Mu Tau, Scabbard and Blade). Field engr., Baltimore, 1922-23; structural engr., 1924; instr. civil engring., Johns Hopkins U., since 1925; structural engr. since 1929. Sec. Johns Hopkins Alumni Assn. since 1926. Mem. Am. Soc. C.E., Md. Hist. Soc., Nantucket Hist. Soc. Mason. Methodist. Republican. Residence: 3324 Ellerslie Av., Baltimore, Md.

CAPT. EDWIN BEDFORD JEFFRESS (1823-91), founder of South Boston, Va.; largely instrumental in establishment of public schools in Halifax Co., Va.; superintendent of schools several years; aided in establishment of State Hospital for negroes at Petersburg; successful planter and merchant; known for his friendship and hospitality.

1–**JEFFRESS, Edwin Bedford,** *b* nr. Canton, N.C., May 29, 1887.
7–John Fitz (Geoffreys) **Jeffress,** from Ireland with two brothers, ca. 1700, settled in "Hell's Corner," Lunenburg Co., Va.;
6–John (*b* 1730), of Lunenburg Co.; began to write name Jeffress; *m* Mary Jennings;
5–Coleman (1765-1834), *m* 1788, Mary E. Fowlkes;
4–Coleman (1799-1870), *m* 1st, 1819, Narcissa Hamlette;
3–Edwin Bedford (1823-91), see portrait; *m* 1846, Mary Harwood Harvey;
2–Charles James (2 below).
9–Benjamin **Poindexter,** of New Kent Co., Va.;
8–Mary, *m* Benjamin **Mosby,** came to Va. at the end of the 17th Century;
7–Elizabeth (*d* post 1758), *m* Stephen **Bedford** (will probated Aug. 28, 1758, at Cumberland C.H., Va.), of Southampton Parish, Cumberland Co.; vestryman; capt. of militia in Colonial wars of Va.; to Gloucester Co., Va., 1745, bought up large areas of land; justice Goochland Co., 1741; sheriff Cumberland Co., 1749; patented 329 acres of land on Twitty's Creek, Brunswick Co., 1745; patentee of 1688 acres in Lunenburg Co., 1750;
6–Thomas (1725-85), *b* in Goochland Co., Va.; justice Cumberland Co., 1749; mem. Com. of Safety, Charlotte Co., 1775-76; justice Charlotte Co., 1765-78, being presiding judge of ct. part of time; trustee Halifax Co. and different towns of Halifax and Lunenburg cos.; *m* 1st, 1750, Mary (Ligon) Coleman (*b* 1731; John[7], *m* Mary–);
5–Mary (1753-1812), *m* 1772, James **Hamlette** (1751-1819), served in Va. cav. in Am. Rev.;
4–Narcissa, *m* Coleman **Jeffress** (4 above).
9–Miles **Cary** (qv);
8–Capt. William (1657-1713), burgess, 1710; *m* Martha Scarborough, or Scarbrooke (Maj. John[9], *m* Mary Martain);
7–Harwood;
6–William, sold Skiff Creek and other lands and slaves in Warwick Co., 1764, and moved to Buckingham Co., Va., 1765; *m* Elizabeth Haynes (Thomas[7], of Warwick Co., Va.);

5-Harwood (*b* 1742), *m* Mary Cardwell (*d* ca. 1845?);
4-Elizabeth Haynes, *m* 1823, Thomas **Harvey** (1803-73), of Charlotte Co.; large land and slave owner and used many of his slaves in construction work on the Richmond and Danville R.R.;
3-Mary Harwood (1825-1917), *m* Edwin Bedford **Jeffress** (3 above).
6-Christopher **Osborne** (will probated 1789), from Eng. to Pa., to Cecil Co., Md., thence to Mecklenburg Co., N.C.; *m* Sarah MacGruder (Dr. Archibald[7], of Va.);
5-Jonathan (1771-1826), moved to western N.C. and purchased 600 acres at Clyde, Haywood Co., 1807; *m* Martha Roland (1773-1845);
4-Ephraim (1799-1864), large landowner along Pigeon River; *m* 1822, Mary Gooch (1808-58; John[5], of Va., went to Greene Co., N.C., ca. 1785, granted 50 acres on Pigeon River, Haywood Co., 1790, on which he built a homesite, and where the Osborne homesite "Garden Creek" now is);
3-Adoniram Judson (1841-1917), served in Commissary Dept., Asheville, during Civil War; *m* 1865, Mary Plott;
2-Maria Love (2 below).
5-Henry **Plott** (1770-1839), from Germany, settled in Haywood Co., N.C., nr. Waynesville; *m* Lydia Osborne (sister of Jonathan, above);
4-John (1813-76), *m* 1838, Louisa Avaline Reeves (1820-1901; Andrew Jackson[5], served in Mexican War, 1845, *m* Rachel Radcliffe, 1785-1880);
3-Mary (1841-1913), *m* Adoniram Judson **Osborne** (3 above);
2-Maria Love (*b* 1866), *m* 1884, Charles James **Jeffress** (*b* 1860), started work on old Richmond and Danville R.R.; merchant at South Boston, Va., Salisbury, N.C., Asheville, N.C.; later realtor and farmer; issue: I-Edwin Bedford (1 above); II-Mary Elizabeth (*b* 1889; *m* Winfred William Whaley); III-Ernest Judson (*b* 1890; *m* Elizabeth Kersey); IV-Florence (*b* 1892; *m* Dr. John Homer Hamilton); V-Horace Lenoir (*b* 1893; *m* Mrs. Stella Martin King); VI-Charles Osborne (*d* infancy); VII-Cary (*b* 1899; *m* Josephine Burgin).
1-*m* July 17, 1913, Louise Bond Adams (qv); issue (all *b* Greensboro, N.C.): 1-Rebecca Bond, *b* June 15, 1914; 2-Edwin Bedford, Jr., and 3-Carl Osborne (twins), *b* July 8, 1915; 4-Mary Louise, *b* July 20, 1916; 5-Sarah Clark Tate, *b* Aug. 21, 1924.
1-A.B., U. of N.C., '07 (P.B.K.). Teacher, Bingham School, Asheville, 1907-09; reporter Asheville Gazette News, 1909-11, Raleigh corr., Asheville Gazette News and Greensboro News, 1911; business manager Greensboro News, 1911-; sec. treas., Greensboro News Co., 1911-18, pres. since 1918; purchased Greensboro Record, 1930, becoming pres., and consolidating publication of both newspapers under same management; pres. North State Engraving Co.; dir. N.C. Bank & Trust Co. Mayor of Greensboro, 1925-29; acting city manager, 1927-28. Pres. Greensboro Chamber of Commerce, 1921-23, Greensboro Community Chest, 1930. Awarded loving cup, 1923, for greatest civic service, Greensboro. Mem. S.A.R., I.A.G., etc. Mason (K.T., Shriner), Elk, K.P., Moose. Episcopalian. Democrat. Clubs: National Press (Washington), Merchants and Manufacturers, Greensboro Country, Sedgfield Country, Kiwanis. Residence: 208 Country Club Place, Greensboro, N.C.

1-**JEFFRESS, Louise Bond Adams (Mrs. Edwin B.),** *b* Augusta, Ga., Feb. 14, 1884.
6-David **Adams** (1682?-1720), mariner of N.E.; *m* Elizabeth Capers (Richard[7], *m* Mary Barnet?), she *m* 2d, 1727, John Jenkins, Sr., of Edisto Island;
5-David (1718-86), of the Beaufort or Edisto Island section of S.C.; *m* 2d, 1753, Catherine Grimball;
4-David (1753-1828), officer Am. Rev.; dea. 1st Bapt. Ch., Charleston; *m* 2d, 1791, Mary Lawrence (Etsell[5]);
3-David Lawrence (1793-1873), see portrait; *m* 1811, Mary Byers Milligan (1793-1863); their son, David, was lt. in Palmetto Regt. in Mexican War, and fell in battle at Churubusco, 1847, awarded medal for bravery;

DAVID LAWRENCE ADAMS (1793-1873), important cotton factor at Augusta, Ga., and Charleston, S.C.; Sea Island cotton planter and exporter.

2-Lawrence Augustus (2 below).
8-Paul **Grimball** (*d* 1696), English mcht. to S.C.; Lord Shaftesbury and two other Lords Proprs. addressed a communication to the Gov. and Council containing among other things, a commn. to grant 3,000 acres of land to "Mr. Paul Grimball, merchant, bound for Ashley River to settle there," Apr. 10, 1681; granted other lands on Cooper River; propr.'s dep., 1683; settled on Edisto Island where his house with that of Gov. Morton was sacked by the Spaniards, 1686; sec. province, 1683; apptd. receiver gen. and escheator, 1688; mem. com. to consider modification of the Fundamental Constn., 1687; disqualified by Seth Sothell from holding office, 1690; new commn. granted by proprs., 1691; given power to appt. and remove sheriffs or judges of the cos. at pleasure, 1693; *m* Madam Mary Grimball (*d* bet. 1711-20);
7-Thomas (*d* 1724), *m* 1st, ante 1700, Elizabeth Adams (William[8], of Charleston);
6-Paul (ca. 1700-1749/50), planter of Edisto; *m* at least 3 times; *m* 2d, Mary Barnwell (*b* ca. 1708; John[7], qv);
5-Catherine (*b* 1737 or earlier), *m* David **Adams** (5 above).
6-Rev. John **MacKenzie** (*d* 1754), from Scotland to Surry Co., Va.; bought lands in Bertie Co., N.C.; *m* 1744, Janet Gray (John[7], *m* Anne Bryan);
5-Janet Gray (*b* 1750), *m* 1771, Collin **Clark** (*b* 1750), from Scotland to Plymouth, N.C., 1770;
4-David (1772-1829), *m* 1806, Louisa Norfleet;
3-Sarah Hill (1816-61), *m* 1836, Henry Francis **Bond** (1814-81; Southey[4], of Raleigh, N.C., *m* Anne Cannon);
2-Rebecca Branch (2 below).
7-Marmaduke **Norfleet** (1700-74), from Nansemond Co., Va., to Perquimans Co., N.C., *d* in Northampton Co., N.C.; *m* 1728, Eliza Gordon;
6-Reuben (1730-1801), *m* 1st, 1765, Lucy (Smith) Langley (Capt. James[7], a "signer");
5-Marmaduke (1766-1818), *m* 1786, Hannah Ruffin;
4-Louisa (1789-1828), *m* David **Clark** (4 above).
7-Robert **Ruffin** (*d* 1767), from Va. to N.C., 1735, settled in Northampton Co.; *m* Anne Bennett (*d* 1758; William[8]);
6-William (*d* 1781), *m* 1762, Sallie Hill (*d* 1774; Richard[7], of Va.);
5-Hannah (1763-1847), *m* 1st, Marmaduke **Norfleet** (5 above).
2-Rebecca Branch Bond (*b* 1847), *m* 1883, as his 2d wife, Lawrence Augustus **Adams** (1833-94), cotton factor, Augusta, Ga., many yrs., retired to Morganton, N.C.; vestryman St. Paul's Episcopal Ch., Augusta, 1860-66; mem. Co. C, 1st S.C. Cav., C.S.A.; he *m* 1st, 1855,

Mary Josephine Tate, of Morganton, N.C.; issue (1st marriage): I–David (*d* young); II–Samuel Caldwell (1858-1908; *m* Harriett Hammond Randall); III–Elizabeth Leath (1860-98; *m* Hamilton Erwin); IV–Mary Milligan (*b* 1862; *m* James Marion Baker, sec. U.S. Senate, during President Wilson's administration); V–Laura Alexander (*d* young); issue (2d marriage): I–Louise B. (1 above); II–Lawrence Augustus (*b* 1885; *m* 1916, Etta Sloan Brand).
1–*m* July 17, 1913, Edwin Bedford Jeffress (qv for issue).
1–Residence: 208 Country Club Place, Greensboro, N.C.

1–**JOHNSON, (Mamie) Mary Jane Perry (Mrs. Rudolph C.),** *b* Sibley, Ia., Jan. 28, 1887.
8–Edward **Perry** (qv);
7–Benjamin (ca. 1677-1748), of R.I.; *m* 1727, Susannah Barber;
6–Freeman (1733-1813), pvt. Am. Rev.; *m* 1755, Mercy Hazard (Oliver[7]);
5–George Hazard (1767-1825), of R.I. and N.Y.; *m* 1786, Abigail Chesebrough;
4–Freeman (1795-1852), of N.Y.; *m* Hannah Peckham (*b* 1795);
3–George Hazard (1819-91), of N.Y. and Ia.; 1st lt., Co. F, 146th N.Y. Vol. Inf.; *m* 1842, Mary L. Hawley (*d* 1885);
2–Harry Chesebro (2 below).
10–John **Alden** (qv);
9–David (*b* 1646), *m* Mary Southworth;
8–Priscilla, *m* 1699/1700, Samuel **Chesebrough** (*b* 1674; Nathaniel[9]; William[10]);
7–Amos (1709-70), of Stonington, Conn.; lt.-col., 8th Regt., Horse and Foot, Colony of Conn.; *m* 1729, Desire Williams (*b* 1712);
6–Amos (*b* 1730), of Conn.; *m* 1755, Mary Christopher (1734-73);
5–Abigail (*b* 1761), of Conn.; *m* George Hazard **Perry** (5 above).
2–Harry Chesebro **Perry** (*b* 1860), of N.Y., and Wash.; rancher; *m* 1885, Elizabeth Belle Conrad (*b* 1867); issue: I–(Mamie) Mary Jane (1 above); II–Vera Belle (*b* 1888; *m* Claude Stewart Councilman); III–Hattie Genevra (*b* 1890; *m* Victor Leonard Freeman); IV–George Husted (*b* 1893; *m* Alice Elizabeth Briere); V–Mildred Elizabeth (1899-1901).
1–*m* Oct. 16, 1915, Rudolph Carl Johnson, *b* Black River Falls, Wis., Mar. 29, 1878; son of Elias Johnson; issue: 1–Eline Mary, *b* Newport, Wash., Apr. 24, 1923; 2–Conrad Perry, *b* Newport, Nov. 22, 1924.
1–Grad. State Normal, Mankato, Minn., State Normal, Bellingham, Wash. Teacher in Minn. and Wash.; county supt. of schools, Pend Oreille Co., Wash.; mem. Co. Bd. of Edn. Mem. D.A.R. O.E.S. Conglist. Democrat. Residence: Newport, Wash.

1–**JOHNSTON, Allen Wheelock,** *b* Palatine Bridge, N.Y., Oct. 9, 1847.
6–George **Johnston** (*d* 1714), from Scotland in the "Henry and Francis," 1685, landed at Perth Amboy, N.J.; went to Stratford, Conn., 1686; *m* 1694/95, Hannah Dorman (Edmund[7], *m* Hannah Hull);
5–Joseph (*b* 1708/09), of N. Stratford, Conn.; *m* 1732, Rachel Mead;
4–Joseph (*b* 1740), removed to Moose Hill, Huntington, Conn., 1767; *m* Margaret–;
3–George Whitfield (1770-1830), resided between Charlton and Glenville; supervisor; *m* 1792, Nancy Wright (Medad[4], *m* Ruth Tooker);
2–George Granville (*b* 1794), removed to Palatine Bridge, N.Y., ca. 1813; foundryman and contractor; justice of peace 18 years; trustee of Union Free School; *m* 1817, Gertrude Van Slyck (*d* 1826); *m* 2d, 1827, Mary Ann Ruby (*d* 1833); *m* 3d, 1834, Atlanta Boutelle Allen (*d* 1892); issue (1st marriage): I–Charles Theodore (1819-21); II–Henry Whitfield (*b* 1821); III–George Alonzo (*b* 1823); IV–Emily Gertrude (*b* 1826); issue (2d marriage): I–Helen Augusta (1828-45); II–Charles Granville (*b* 1830); III–Mary Ann (*b* 1833); issue (3d marriage): I–Agnes Atlanta (*b* 1835; *m* George A. Cheney); II–Sarah Anna (*b* 1837); III–Albert Jacob (*b* 1840; *m* Eliza Campbell); IV–William Nevins (*b* 1842; *m* Elizabeth Dolson); V–Allen Wheelock (1 above); VI–Sarah Henrietta (1849-51).
1–Not married. Ed. Canajoharie (N.Y.) Acad. Ticket agent and telegraph operator N.Y. Central R.R.; teller Nat. Spraker Bank; teller and bookkeeper Canajoharie Nat. Bank; dep. co. clk., Montgomery Co., N.Y.; clk. Farmers & Mechanics Bank, Albany; now exec. v.p., Schenectady (N.Y.) Savings Bank. N.Y. State Banking Dept. examiner, 1893-94. Enlisted in 192d Regt. U.S. Vols., April 1865, age 17. Trustee Y.M.C.A. Mem. I.A.G., N.Y. State Hist. Soc. Democrat. Residence: 500 State St., Schenectady, N.Y.

1–**JONES, William Macfarlane,** *b* Richmond, Va., Dec. 2, 1868.
10–Capt. Francis **Epes**;
9–Lt. Col. Francis, *m* Mrs. Elizabeth Worsham;
8–Lt. Col. Littleberry, *m* —Llewellyn;
7–Llewellyn, *m* Martha Epes;
6–Llewellyn;
5–Peter (*d* 1773), of Charles City Co., Va.; *m* Anne Hardyman (John[6], *m* Henrietta Maria, dau. of John Taylor; John[7]);
4–Peter (1759-1828), of Charles City Co., and Richmond, Va.; *m* Lucy Ballard (1764-1844; Thomas[5], *m* Sarah–);
3–Angelica (1813-36), *m* 1829, Sampson **Jones** (1804-63; Herbert[4], of Isle of Wight Co., *m* Catherine Jones);
2–Sampson (2 below).
9–Robert **Taliaferro** (ca. 1635-ca. 1693), from Eng. to Va., ca. 1656; *m* Sarah Grymes (Rev. Charles[10]);
8–John (ca. 1672-1720), lt. of rangers; justice and sheriff of Essex Co., Va.; burgess; *m* Sarah Smith (Maj. Laurence[9], to Va. ante 1650);
7–Laurence, sheriff of Essex Co., 1720; *m* Sarah Thornton (*b* 1690; Francis[8], settled in Va. ante 1700);
6–Ann Hay, *m* Richard **Brooke** (1732-92), of "Smithfield" (Robert[7], *m* Phoebe–; Robert[8]);
5–Dr. Lawrence (1758-1803), of Stafford Co.; surgeon, "Bon Homme Richard," Am. Rev.; *m* Frances Alexander (*b* 1762; John[6], *m* Lucy Thornton; Philip[7]; Philip[8]);
4–Ann Hay, *m* 1809, Stephen **Macfarlane**;
3–William (1810-73), *m* 1835, Elizabeth Elba Day;
2–Susanna Day (2 below).
7–Maj. Robert **Harris** (1635-1701), of "The Forks"; *m* Mary (Claiborne) Rice (William Claiborne[8], qv);
6–Col. William (*d* 1695), burgess, Henrico and Hanover cos.; *m* Temperance Overton (*d* 1699; William[7], *m* Peggy Garland; William[8]);
5–Anne, *m* William **Day** (John[6], *m* Esom Day);
4–William, *m* 1790, Susannah Chiles (1772-1854; Walter[5], *m* Phoebe, dau. of Capt. William Carr; Henry[6]; John[7]; Lt. Col. Walter[8]; Walter[9], qv);
3–Elizabeth Elba (1814-91), of Richmond, Spotsylvania Co., Va.; *m* William **Macfarlane** (3 above);
2–Susanna Day (1836-1926), *m* Sampson **Jones** (1836-84), lt. C.S.A.; mercantile business; issue: I–Lizzie Deane (*m* Chapman W. Morriss); II–Lulie F.; III–L. S. (*m* Sadie H. Chalkley); IV–M. Carrington; V–William Macfarlane (1 above).
1–*m* Sept. 18, 1912, Amy Allen (Nov. 19, 1884-July 16, 1913); dau. of William F. Allen (1830-89), of Allen, Md., *m* Nora Disharoon (1848-1927); issue: 1–Carl Macfarlane, *b* Atlanta, Ga., July 10, 1913.
1–Stenographer C.&O. Ry.; commercial traveler; newspaper reporter and cartoonist; sec. to pres. S.A.L. Ry.; with advertising agency; treas. mining co.; entertainer on Lyceum course; genealogist, conducts Geneal. Bureau of Va. Mem. S.A.R. (genealogist gen.), I.A.G., S.C.V. (life), Va. Hist. Soc., A.P.V.A. Democrat. Club: Chess and Whist. Residence: 311 S. 4th St., Richmond, Va.

1–**JOSLYN, Marcellus Lindsey,** *b* Woodstock, Ill., Feb. 6, 1873.
9–Thomas **Joslyn** (qv);
8–Abraham (*d* ante 1670), came to America after his father, and was at Hingham, 1647; removed to Lancaster before 1663; *m* Beatrice–;
7–Henry (1652-1730), settled at Scituate, Mass., 1669; at Hanover Center, Mass., 78 yrs. old; *m* 1676, Abigail Stockbridge (*d* 1743; Charles[8] [*d* 1683], *m* Abigail–; John[9], came in the "Blessing," 1635, *m* Anne–);

6–Jabez (1690/91-1734), part owner of "Josselyn's Forge," later known as the "Old Forge," Scituate, Mass.; *m* 1722, Sarah Turner (*d* 1756);
5–Jabez (*b* 1723), Manchester, Mass., thence to Poultney, Vt.; *m* 1742, Mary Lindsey;
4–Lindsey (1749-1826), soldier Am. Rev.; removed from Sheffield, Mass., to Poultney, Vt., where he erected an iron forge; thence to Mt. Morris, Geneseo Co., N.Y.; *m* 1st, 1773, Susan Welsh (*d* 1794);
3–Lindsey (1786-1863, aet. 77), from Geneseo Co., N.Y., thence to Crystal Lake, McHenry Co., Ill.; *m* 1809, Polly (Mary) Wait (*b* 1787; Benjamin[4], of Granville, N.Y.);
2–Merritt Lindsey (2 below).
9–William **Robinson** (qv);
8–Increase (2d son; bap. 1642-1699), of Taunton, Mass.; *m* 1663, Sarah Penniman (*b* 1641; James[9], *m* Lydia Eliot, of Braintree; Lydia was a sister of John Eliot, "Apostle to the Indians");
7–Increase (*d* 1738), of Pembroke and Plympton, Mass.; *m* Mehitabel Williams, of Taunton;
6–George, of Taunton, Mass.; *m* Elizabeth Cobb (Thomas[7]; Morgan[8]; Augustine[9]);
5–Capt. Nathaniel (1752-1841), pvt. and musician in Am. Rev.; *m* 1775, Hannah (Eunice) Woodcock (*d* 1845, aet. 93; Jonathan[6], of Taunton, Mass.);
4–David (1780-1828), *m* Mary French;
3–David Wilmarth (1807-90), settled at Woodstock, Ill., 1865; *m* 1834, Maria N. Clapp (*b* 1817);
2–Mary Augusta Robinson (1837-1923), *m* 1862, Merritt Lindsey **Joslyn** (1825-1904), lawyer of Woodstock, Ill.; capt. Co. H, 36th Ill. Vols. in Civil War; many yrs. mem. Ill. House and Senate; first asst. secretary of the interior under President Garfield (for issue see Vol. II, p. 306).
1–*m* Oct. 22, 1899, Alice Cecilia Newell, *b* Faribault, Minn.; dau. of George Washington Newell, of Faribault; issue: 1–Marcellus Newell, *b* Woodstock, Ill., Feb. 28, 1901; B.S., Dartmouth, '24; LL.B., Harvard, 1927; *m* June 30, 1925, Beth Le Fèvre, of Santa Monica, Calif. (issue: Marcellus Le Fevre, *b* July 8, 1928; Audry and Roland R., *b* Nov. 21, 1929); 2–George Robinson, *b* Woodstock, Nov. 22, 1902, B.S., Dartmouth, '25; *m* Aug. 25, 1928, Charlotte Case, of LaGrange, Ill. (issue: Joy Louise, *b* June 25, 1930); 3–Merritt Lindsey, *b* Woodstock, July 12, 1905; Dartmouth, '27; 4–Mary Cecilia, *b* LaGrange, Ill., Nov. 15, 1909; Emma Willard Sch., '27; U. of Calif. at Los Angeles.
1–B.S., Notre Dame, '93; LL.B., Harvard, 1896. Pres. Citizens Telephone Co., Woodstock, Ill., 1895-1905; pres. Citizens Electric Light & Mfg. Co., Crystal Lake, Ill., 1897-1903; pres. Independent Arm & Pin Co., Chicago, 1902-10; pres. Joslyn Mfg. & Supply Co., Chicago, since 1910; also pres. Jobbers Supply Co. (St. Paul), Joslyn Co. of Calif. (Los Angeles and San Francisco), Joslyn Co. (New York), Southern Joslyn Co. (New Orleans), Southeast Joslyn Co. (Cincinnati and Atlanta), Joslyn Co. Southwest (Dallas), Joslyn Investment Co. (Chicago). Vice chmn. Independent Religious Soc. (Chicago). Mem. I.A.G. Clubs: Suburban, LaGrange Country, Hinsdale Golf, Edgewood Valley Golf. Winter place: "Violet Cottage," Santa Monica, Calif. Residence: "The Manor," Hinsdale, Ill.

1–**LAKIN, James Sansome,** *b* Moundsville, W.Va., Mar. 1, 1864.
6–Abraham **Lakin** (*d* 1744), of Prince George's Co., Md.; received patent for land, 1717, called "Abraham's Fancie"; *m* 1717, Martha Lee (*b* 1699; William[7], *m* Ann–);
5–Benjamin (1739-1776), of Montgomery Co., Md; according to tradition, was sea capt. and shipped a cargo of tobacco in his own vessel at beginning of Am. Rev.; *m* 1760, Rachel Fee (1739-1811; George[6], *m* Parnell–);
4–Thomas (1763-1835), of Bedford Co., Pa.; mem. of the first M.E. ch. in America, in the home of Robert Strawbridge, Sam's Creek, Md.; ordained by Bishop Asbery; itinerant preacher with William Shaw and John J. Jacobs, known as "the three bishops," in Md. and Pa.; owned land at Bean's Cove, Bedford Co., Pa.; was mem. of first M.E. ch. to be built in Cumberland, Md.; *m* 1782, Priscilla Sullivan (1757-1833; Daniel[5], prob. killed Braddock's War, *m* Mary Lovejoy);
3–William (1791-1855), of Harrison Co., O.; *m* 1836, Lewessa Packer (*b* 1814; Wiliam L.[4], of Chester Co., Pa., *m* Anna Elizabeth Cooper, Quakers);
2–Rev. Calvin Harris (2 below).
6–James **Finney** (*d* 1770), Lancaster Co., Pa.;
5–James (1726-1802), *m* Martha Mayes;
4–John Wesley Finney (1760-1839), of Tuscarawas Co., O.; *m* Oct. 23, 1808, Mary Taylor (1785-1848);
3–James (1809-65), *m* 1836, Sarah Adair (*b* 1816; Andrew[4], owned property in Columbus, O., which was later sold to city of Columbus, *m* Sarah–);
2–Catherine (1843-1910), of Huntington, W.Va.; *m* 1863, Rev. Calvin Harris **Lakin** (1838-1918), M.E. minister, 60 yrs.; active ministry in W.Va., 50 yrs.; presiding elder, 12 yrs.; issue: I–James Sansome (1 above); II–Sarah Lewessa (1866-1900; *m* Jennings M. King, M.D., *d* 1929; issue: Jennings M., M.D., Lessie Lois, *m* Harold R. Tipton); III–Anna Belle (*b* 1869; *m* Jacob Sheets, *d* 1914; issue: Lessie, *m* Sterrett O. Neal; Calvin; David Finney); IV–Joseph William (*b* 1875; *m* Maude Rinard; issue: Calvin Rinard; Hubert); V–Finney Lee (*b* 1886; *m* Charlotte Beverly Tyler).
1–*m* Nov. 14, 1889, Lura Olivia Lakin (qv); issue (all *b* Terra Alta, W.Va.): 1–James Offutt, *b* Apr. 14, 1896; A.B., U. of W.Va., '22 (Phi Kappa Psi); 2d lt. inf., Mexican border, 1916-17; overseas, 1st lt., 113th Inf.; asst. adj., A.E.F.; mem. W.Va. House of Dels., 1928-30; *m* Dec. 21, 1921, Marguerite, dau. of George Coleman Baker, of Morgantown, W.Va. (issue: Barbara Ann; Marguerite Baker); 2–Marion Elizabeth, *b* Oct. 1, 1898; A.B., Smith Coll., '22; *m* Nov. 7, 1922, John Vickers Ray, A.B., U. of Va., '13, B.L., 1920; Rhodes Scholar, 1919, A.B., Oxford U.; served in World War, capt. regular army, 1919; son of Dr. Charles A. Ray, of Charleston, W.Va. (issue: John Lakin; Olivia Lakin); 3–Florence Katherine, *b* June 24, 1903; A.B., U. of W.Va., '25; *m* June 1, 1929, Thomas Augustus Deveny, Jr., of W. Fairmont, W.Va., A.B., U. of W.Va., '25.
1–Ed. Fairmont (W.Va.) State Normal Sch., and Ohio Wesleyan U. Pres. First Nat. Bank, Terra Alta, W.Va., Mem. State Bd. of Control of W.Va., 1909– (pres. 1909-17, 1921–); chmn. Pub. Service Commn., 1913. Mem. W.Va. "Big Four," Rep. Nat. Conv., 1920. First lt., Co. M, 1st W.Va. Inf., 1899-1908 (see Who's Who in America). Mem. Md. Hist. Soc., Civil Legion. Mason (32°, K.T.), Elk, K.P., Rotarian. Club: Edgewood Country. Methodist. Residence: 1575 Virginia St., Charleston, W.Va.

1–**LAKIN, Lura Olivia Lakin (Mrs. James S.),** *b* Columbus, O., Dec. 3, 1865.
6–Abraham **Lakin** (*d* 1744), of Prince George's Co., Md.; *m* 1717, Martha Lee (*b* 1699; William[7], *m* Ann–);
5–Abraham (1722-96), of Frederick Co., Md.; *m* 1744(?), Sarah– (1724-95);
4–Daniel (1759-1829), of Frederick Co.; *m* 1787, Ann Sheckels (1766-1822);
3–Daniel (1803-72), of Franklin Co., O.; *m* 1833, Dorcas Flenniken (1808-86; Samuel G.[4] [1774-1846], of N.C., *m* Elizabeth Morehead, of Georgetown, Ky.);
2–George Washington (2 below).
4–Thomas **Johnston** (*b* 1777), *m* 1808, Elizabeth Stewart (*b* 1782; John[5], of Pa.);
3–Edmund, *m* Martha Wright (1818-1900; Thomas[4], of Pa., *m* Elizabeth Watt);
2–Mary Elizabeth (1842-1919), *m* 1864, George Washington **Lakin** (1836-1914), 1st lt., 133d Ohio Vol. Inf., Civil War; issue: I–Lura Olivia (1 above); II–Edmund Bedell (*b* 1867; *m* Mary Clarinda Barnard; issue: Mary Elizabeth, *b* 1905; Edmund B., Jr., *b* 1909); III–Florence (*b* 1870); IV–Herbert Hays (1871-1921; *m* Anna Phenegar; issue: George, 1910-28; Daniel, *b* 1918).
1–Nov. 14, 1889, James Sansome Lakin (qv for issue).
1–Ed. Ohio Wesleyan U. Mem. D.A.R., Methodist. Republican. Residence: 1575 Virginia St., Charleston, W.Va.

1–**LANDIS, Robert Edward,** *b* Nashville, Tenn., May 18, 1895.
Amending and correcting Landis lineage in Vol. II, p. 370.
7–Felix **Landis** (will dated Apr. 29, 1737, probated Dec. 29, 1739, Lancaster Co., Pa.); from Alsace, Germany, settled in Conestoga Dist., old Chester (now Lancaster) Co., on four 200 acre tracts bought from the London Company, 1718; *m* Rosina–;
6–Felix, Jr., only son (ca. 1708, in Germany-will [in German] dated Jan. 25, 1770, Lancaster Co. records); removed to Lebanon Tp., 1747, thence to Derry Tp., 1757, which became part of Dauphin Co. on erection, 1785; many of his descendants became early settlers of the south and west; *m* 2d, Mary–, who survived him;
5–Christopher (1759-ante July 26, 1814), freeman of Derry Tp., 1780; pvt. Lancaster Co. militia, 1777-82; to N.C. ante 1790, thence to Warren Co., Ky., on a land grant south of Green River surveyed Aug. 8, 1799; thence to Bedford Co., Tenn., on Thompson's Creek; *m* Phoebe Lee (Feb. 28, 1774-1841), of Rutherford Co., N.C. (Robert[6]);
4–John (Apr. 19, 1795 in N.C.-July 4, 1854, in Tenn.), from Ky. to Bedford Co., Tenn.; planter, leather tannery; *m* Nov. 18, 1820, Mary Lowe (Oct. 14, 1796-Dec. 14, 1868; Abraham[5], Am. Rev.);
3–Absalom Lowe (Aug. 31, 1823, in Bedford Co., Tenn.-June 6, 1896, in Nashville); see portrait and biography in Vol. II, p. 370; *m* June 27, 1843, Nancy Carter (Mar. 20, 1826-Feb. 5, 1901, at "Riverside" nr. Shelbyville); of royal descent thru the line of her father, William Carter, of Culpeper Co., Va., for whose genealogy see Vol. II, p. 370-371;
2–John Tannahill (2 below).
11–Richard **Bowen** (qv);
10–Obadiah (1627-99), of Rehoboth and Swansea, Mass.; freeman, 1658; dep. 1681; removed to Warren, R.I.; *m* 1646/47, Mary Clifford (Thomas[11]);
9–Obadiah (1652-1710), of Swansea; *m* Abigail Bullock (Richard[10], qv);
8–James, *m* May 6, 1703, Elizabeth Guernsey (*b* Apr. 23, 1682; John[9]);
7–Obadiah (*b* Sept. 27, 1708), *m* Jan. 23, 1730, Barbara Martin (*b* Mar. 13, 1713; John[8]; John[9]);
6–Elizabeth (*b* May 25, 1732), *m* Dec. 7, 1751, Solomon **Guernsey** (Garney or Gufernsey), (Oct. 15, 1727-1802); removed to Ballston, Albany Co., N.Y., ante 1790 (John, Jr.[7], of Rehoboth, *m* Elizabeth Titus [John[8], of Rehoboth, *m* Sarah Miller; John[9], *m* Abigail–]; John[8]);
5–James (1757-1810), of Ballston, N.Y.; *m* Sarah Roe (1758-1840; Peter[6], *m* Elizabeth Lee);
4–Melinda (1802-86), *m* Nov. 15, 1822, Cyrus **Bacon** (1796-1873), of Edwardsburg, Mich.;
3–Sarah Hannah (Aug. 3, 1841-Nov. 7, 1921; desc. Rhodri Mawr, King of Wales, thru Richard Bowen, 11 above); *m* Oct. 9, 1866, Rev. John **Boone** (Nov. 9, 1825-Aug. 31, 1904, Berrien Springs, Mich.);
2–Melinda Bacon (*b* Mar. 9, 1870), for whose genealogy, and for comparison for correction of certain inaccuracies in the pedigrees of Landis, and of Guernsey an allied line of Bacon, that appeared therein, see Vols. I and II; *m* Dec. 17, 1890, John Tannahill **Landis** (*b* Aug. 4, 1866, at "Beech Hall Plantation," Bedford Co., Tenn.).
1–*m* June 1, 1916, at Nashville, Tenn., Pauline Acklen (qv); issue: 1–Robert Livingston, *b* Nashville, Apr. 9, 1917; 2–Pauline Acklen, *b* Nashville, Nov. 4, 1920.
1–Ed. Severy Mil. Sch., Fogg-Hume Nashville High Sch. Enlisted U.S.A., July 1, 1918; sgt., instr., U.Tenn. motor corps unit; named for O.T.S., Camp Hancock, M.G. Div.; 2d lt. Inf., U.S.R.C.; hon. disch., Nov. 26, 1918. Real estate business at Nashville; moved to Detroit, 1924; asso. mem. Detroit Real Estate Bd. Mem. B.O.R. Residence: 3741 Waverly Av., Detroit, Mich.

1–**LANDIS, Pauline Acklen (Mrs. Robert E.),** *b* Nashville, Tenn., Jan. 28, 1897.
5–Capt. John **Hunt**, soldier Am. Rev. from Va.; founder of Huntsville, Ala., first known as "Hunt's Big Spring," erecting there the 1st log house, 1806;
4–Elizabeth, *m* Samuel Black (Acalen, Acland) **Acklen,** from Abingdon, Va., to Huntsville, Ala.;
3–Col. Joseph Alexander Smith (*b* Huntsville, Ala., July 6, 1816-*d* "Angola," West Feliciana, La., Sept. 11, 1863), U.S. atty. for Ala. under Presidents Van Buren, Tyler and Polk; col. Mexican War, promoted for bravery; owner of "Belmont," estate nr. Nashville, Tenn., now site of Ward-Belmont Coll.; *m* May 9, 1849, Adelicia (Hayes) Franklin (1817-87);
2–Joseph Hayes (2 below).
5–Dr. Thomas **Tillotson** (1757-1832), of Md.; surgeon gen. of northern dept. of Cont. Army; *m* 1779, Margaret Beekman Livingston (1749-1823; Robert R.[6], 7 below);
4–Maj. John C. (1791-1867), from Rhinebeck, N.Y., to N.Y. City; 2d lt., N.Y. Light Dragoons, 1812; maj. and asst. insp. gen., 1813; *m* 1816, Maria Livingston;
3–Richard Montgomery (1818-74), from N.Y., to Leavenworth, Kan.; *m* 1871, Mary Agnes Parke (1831-1915);
2–Jeannette (2 below).
9–Robert **Livingston** (qv);
8–Robert (1688-1775), 1st propr. of Clermont; *m* 1717, Margaret Howarden (1693-1775), of N.Y.;
7–Robert R. (1718-75), judge Admiralty Ct., 1760; justice, Supreme Ct. N.Y., 1763; mem. Stamp Act Congress; *m* 1742, Margaret Beekman (1724-1800; Col. Henry[8], *m* Janet Livingston; Col. Henry[9]; Wilhelmus[10], qv);
6–Robert R. (1746-1813), chancellor, administered oath of office to President George Washington; U.S. minister to France; one of five men to draft the Declaration of Independence; *m* 1770, Mary Stevens (1752-1814; John[7], *m* Elizabeth, dau. of James Alexander; John[8], from Eng.);
5–Margaret Maria (1783-1823), *m* 1799, Robert L. **Livingston** (*d* 1843);
4–Maria (1800-30), *m* John C. **Tillotson** (4 above).
2–Col. Joseph Hayes **Acklen** (*b* 1850), *m* 2d, 1890, Jeannette Tillotson (*b* 1871); for issue and other lineages see Mrs. Oscar French Noel.
1–*m* June 1, 1916, Robert Edward Landis (qv for issue).
1–Ed. Gunston Hall, Washington, and Duncan Prep. Sch., Nashville, Tenn. Mem. C.D.A., D.B.R., D.A.R., U.S.D. 1812; Pres. John Paul Jones Chapter C.A.R. Residence: 3741 Waverly Av., Detroit, Mich.

1–**NOEL, Jeannette Tillotson Acklen (Mrs. Oscar F.),** *b* Nashville, Tenn., May 7, 1891.
11–Robert (Dibel, Deble, Deeble) **Dibble** (*d* ca. 1640), from Eng., 1635, settled at Dorchester, Mass., and Windsor, Conn., 1635;
10–Thomas (*b* 1613), freeman, Dorchester, 1637, Windsor, 1640; *m* 1st, — (*d* 1681);
9–Samuel (bap. Mar. 24, 1643-June 5, 1709);
8–Abigail (1666-post 1725), *m* George **Hayes** (qv);
7–Daniel (1686-1756), Indian captive in Canada, 1708-13; freeman, 1717; *m* 1721, Sarah Lee (1692-1738; John[8], *m* Elizabeth Crampton; Dennis[9]);
6–Joel (1728-1800), collector and constable, 1761-62; selectman, 1770-72; lt. Am. Rev.; *m* 1751, Rebecca Post (1736-1817; Thomas[7], *m* Rebecca Bruen);
5–Rev. Joel (1753-1827), A.M., Yale, 1773; Congl. pastor 45 yrs., *d* while preaching to his people; one of the "Boston Tea Party," 1773; *m* 1782, Mary Bliss;
4–Oliver Bliss (1783-1858), to Nashville, Tenn., 1808; *m* 1811, Sarah Clements Hightower (1796-1871; Dr. Richard[5], *m* a dau. of Reuben Smith, of James River, Va.);
3–Adelicia (1817-87), grad. Nashville Female Coll.; as widow of Isaac Franklin, *m* 2d, 1849, Col. Joseph A. S. **Acklen** (1816-63); she *m* 3d, 1867, Dr. William Archer Cheatham (*b* 1820);
2–Joseph Hayes (2 below).
10–Thomas **Bliss** (qv);
9–Samuel (1624-1720), from Eng. to Springfield, Mass.; *m* 1664, Mary Leonard;
8–Thomas (1668-1738), *m* Hannah Cadwell;
7–Capt. Abdiel (*b* 1706), Am. Rev.;
6–Oliver, *m* Catherine Brewer;
5–Mary (1762-1825), *m* Joel **Hayes** (5 above).
10–Daniel **Brewer** (qv);
9–Daniel (ca. 1624-1708), *m* Hannah Morrill (1636-1717; Isaac[10], of Roxbury, Mass.);

8–Rev. Daniel (1667-1733), of Springfield, Mass.; grad. Harvard, 1687; *m* 1699, Catherine Chauncey (1675-1754; Rev. Nathaniel[9], Harvard, 1661, *m* 1673, Abigail, dau. of Elder John Strong, qv; Charles[10], qv);
7–Isaac, of Wilbraham, Mass.;
6–Catherine (*b* 1732), *m* Oliver **Bliss** (6 above).
2–Col. Joseph Hayes **Acklen** (*b* May 20, 1850), of Nashville, Tenn.; grad. Burlington Coll., and Lebanon Law Sch.; lawyer; Dem. mem. 45th and 46th Congresses from La.; col. La. militia, 1876; pres. Tenn. Bar Assn., 1901-02; pres. Nat. Assn. Game and Fish Commrs., 1912-29; chief game warden U.S., 1913-28; *m* July 11, 1871, Hattie Leonora Bethell (*d* June 1873); *m* 2d, Jan. 30, 1890, Jeannette Tillotson (*b* Nov. 11, 1871); issue (2d marriage; all *b* Nashville, Tenn.); I–Jeannette T. (1 above); II–Joseph Hayes (*d* yng.); III–Catherine Parke (Mrs. Thomas Hartwell Brown, qv for other lineages); IV–Pauline (Mrs. Robert E. Landis, qv for other lineages); V–William Hayes (*d* yng.); VI–Claudia Maria Livingston (*d* yng.); VII–Richard Montgomery (*b* June 21, 1908); VIII–Robert Livingston (*b* Dec. 19, 1915).
1–*m* June 5, 1913, Oscar French Noel, *b* Nashville, Tenn., Dec. 5, 1887; B.A., Yale, '10; son of Edwin Thomas Noel; issue (all *b* Nashville, Tenn.): 1–Oscar French, *b* Feb. 28, 1914; 2–Hayes Acklen, *b* July 10, 1915; 3–Sarah Catherine, *b* Dec. 5, 1916.
1–Grad. Price's Coll. for Young Ladies, Nashville. Mem. D.A.R., Polk Memorial Assn., Junior League. Residence: Nashville, Tenn.

1–**BROWN, Catherine Parke Acklen (Mrs. Thomas H.),** *b* Nashville, Tenn., Nov. 17, 1894.
7–Arthur **Parke** (qv);
6–John (1706-87), of Chester Co., Pa.; *m* Elizabeth McKnight (1712-94);
5–Joseph (1737-1823), lt. col. Am. Rev.; justice; mem. Gen. Assembly; *m* 2d, ante 1776, Mary Ann Maxwell (1754-1821; Robert[6], *m* Harriet, dau. of Gen. John Steel, of Lancaster Co., Pa.);
4–David (1785-1846), *m* 2d, Catherine Maxwell (1800-60; Robert[5], from Scotland, ca. 1750, to Lancaster, Pa., mem. Pa. Legislature, *m* Mary Smith);
3–Mary Agnes (Ann), (1831-1915), *m* 1871, Richard Montgomery **Tillotson** (1818-74).
2–Col. Joseph Hayes **Acklen** (*b* 1850), *m* 2d, 1890, Jeannette Tillotson (*b* 1871); for issue and other lineages see Mrs. Oscar French Noel.
1–*m* Dec. 25, 1917, Thomas Hartwell Brown, M.D., *b* Gallatin, Tenn., July 2, 1890; 1st lt., M.C.-U.S.A., World War; issue (all *b* Toledo, O.): 1–Catherine Acklen, *b* May 21, 1919; 2–Thomas Hartwell, Jr., *b* Aug. 22, 1921; 3–Janet Tillotson, *b* Sept. 13, 1924; 4–Ann Hunt, *b* Apr. 28, 1928.
1–B.S., Vanderbilt U., '15; M.D., U.Mich., 1919. Mem. D.A.R., U.S.D. 1812, A.A.U.W., Delta Delta Delta, Alpha Epsilon Iota. Residence: 3865 Beechway Boul., Beverly Pl., Toledo, O.

1–**LEWIS, Bruce Lochman,** *b* Germantown, Phila., Pa., Dec. 31, 1903.
10–John **Lewis** (*d* 1690), of Westerly, R.I.;
9–John (*d* 1735), *m* 1682, Ann–;
8–Joseph (1683-1764), *m* Mary Wilcox (1688-1762; Edward[9], *m* Mary, dau. of Robert Hazzard; Stephen[10]; Edward[11], *d* 1638);
7–Amos (*b* ca. 1715), *m* 1736, Eleanor Greene (*b* 1718);
6–Thankful (*d* 1819), *m* Eleazer **Lewis** (see Vol. III, p. 302);
5–Benjamin (1774-1843), N. Java, N.Y.; War 1812, Staten Island, N.Y.; *m* 1798, Zintha Merritt;
4–Merritt Bradford (1812-97), Lockport, N.Y.; *m* 1835, Elvira Mann (1817-88);
3–Seth Clark (1837-1926), farmer; sheriff, Niagara Co., N.Y.; *m* 2d, 1871, Esther Josephine Langdon;
2–Robert Bruce (2 below).
10–Thomas (Joslyn) **Josselyn** (qv);
9–Rebecca, *m* Thomas **Nichols**;
8–Thomas, *m* 1663, Sarah Whiston;
7–Joseph, *m* Bathsheba Pincon (Thomas[8], *m* Elizabeth, dau. of Gowan White);
6–Jane (*d* ante 1803), *m* 1749, Thomas **Merritt** (1721-1804);
5–Zintha (1769-1835), *m* Benjamin **Lewis** (5 above).
9–Henry **Doud** (qv);
8–John, *m* Mary Bartlett (John[9]; Edmund[10], from Eng., 1634);
7–David (1695-1740), *m* 1718, Mary Cornwall (*b* 1700; John[8], *m* Mary, dau. of John Hilton; John[9]; William[10]);
6–Giles B. (1735-76), capt. Am. Rev., *d* at Crown Point; *m* Esther Bacon;
5–Ann (1763-1824), *m* Seth **Langdon** (1759-1851), corpl. Mass. militia, 1777-81;
4–Seth (1799-1881), New Haven, Vt.; *m* 1821, Laura Squier (1802-77; Waite[5], *m* Hannah, dau. of Col. Miles Powell; Lt. Andrew[6], Am. Rev.);
3–Esther Josephine (1839-91), *m* 1871, as his 2d wife, Seth Clark **Lewis** (3 above).
12–John **Gregory**;
11–Elizabeth (*d* 1680), *m* 1655, Richard **Webb** (*d* 1665), founder of Hartford;
10–John (*d* 1720), Hartford;
9–Mary, *m* John **Earle** (1639-63);
8–Mary (1663-1732), *m* 1682, Nathaniel **Hubbard** (1652-1738; George[9]);
7–Esther (1702-42), *m* 1727, Nathaniel **Bacon** (1706-92), Am. Rev. (Nathaniel[8], *m* Hannah Wetmore; Nathaniel[9]);
6–Esther, *m* 1757, Giles B. **Doud** (6 above).
2–Robert Bruce **Lewis** (*b* 1873), see Vol. III, p. 302, for other lineages; *m* 1900, Alberta Anne Lochman (*b* 1876).
1–Not married. M.E., Cornell, '27 (Zodiac). Mechanical engineer. Mem. O.F.P.A., B.O.R., Am. Soc. for Steel Treating. Residence: "Langdon Lodge," 51 E. Penn St., Germantown, Phila., Pa.

1–**LEWIS, Esther Langdon,** *b* Germantown, Philadelphia, Pa., Nov. 13, 1907.
10–Benjamin **Congdon** (1650-1718), from Wales; *m* Elizabeth Albro (*d* 1720; Maj. John[11], from Eng. in the "Francis," 1634);
9–Benjamin (*d* 1756), *m* 1701, in North Kingston, R.I., Frances Stafford (1679-1774; Joseph[10], *m* Sarah, dau. of Hon. Randal Holden; Thomas[11], qv);
8–William (1711-55), *m* 1732, Ann Gifford (1715-95; Yelverton[9], *m* Ann Northup);
7–Anna, *m* Samuel **Sherman** (*b* 1723; Stephen[8], *m* Sarah–; Eber[9]; Hon. Philip[10]);
6–Stephen (*b* 1768), *m* 1789, Asa Ann Congdon;
5–Lucy (*b* 1797), *m* 1815, James **Mann** (1794-1878);
4–Elvira (1817-88), *m* 1835, Merritt Bradford **Lewis** (1812-97);
3–Seth Clark (1837-1926), *m* 2d, 1871, Esther Josephine Langdon;
2–Robert Bruce (2 below).
8–Adam **Heilman** (1727-70), from Germany, settled at Lebanon (then in Lancaster Co.), Pa.; capt. colonial wars; *m* Anna Maria–;
7–John (1745-1827), capt. Am. Rev. and War 1812; *m* 1771, Catherine Schmidt;
6–John Adams (1771-1833), lt. War 1812; *m* Eva Margaret Shuey;
5–Catherine (1803-58), *m* Peter **Myers,** War 1812 (Jacob[6], *m* Anna Maria–; Frederick[7]);
4–Mary (1820-63), Pidgeon Hills, Pa.; *m* 1839, David **Weaver** (*b* 1817);
3–Mary Alice (*b* 1846), *m* as his 2d wife, Dr. Charles Leitheiser **Lochman** (1821-1900), U.Pa., 1857; physician; author of medical and botanical works;
2–Alberta Anne (2 below).
10–Jacob (Lewengut) **Livingood** (*d* 1758), came to America 1709; murdered by Indians, Tulpehocken Tp., Berks Co., 1758; *m* Margaret–;
9–Jacob (*d* 1782), capt., 1781, to raise riflemen for frontier service; *d* in uniform; *m* 1750, Catherine Derr (Ludwig[10], founded Lewisburg, then Derrtown, Pa., ante 1756);
8–Barbara, *m* Peter **Schmidt**;
7–Catherine, *m* John **Heilman** (7 above).
9–Daniel (Shue) **Shuey,** from Germany, 1732, to Bethel, Pa.; *m* Mary Martha–;
8–Ludwig (1726-92), of Lancaster, Pa.;
7–Henry (1748-1804), *m* 1770, Barbara Rice (Thiess);
6–Eva Margaret (*b* 1782), *m* John Adams **Heilman** (6 above);
5–Catherine, *m* Peter **Myers** (5 above);
4–Mary, *m* David **Weaver** (4 above);
3–Mary Alice, *m* Dr. Charles L. **Lochman** (3 above);
2–Alberta Anne (*b* 1876), *m* 1900, Robert Bruce **Lewis** (*b* 1873); see Vol. III, p. 302.
1–A.B., Bucknell, '30 (Phi Mu); post-grad. Bryn Mawr Coll., 1930. Mem. D.C.G. Resi-

dence: "Langdon Lodge," 51 E. Penn St., Germantown, Philadelphia, Pa.

1-**LINSLEY, Ray Keyes,** *b* Central City, Colo., Nov. 3, 1875.
9-John (Lindley, Lindsley) **Linsley** (*d* ca. 1698), from Eng., settled at Guilford, Conn., 1639-40; removed to Branford; *m* Ellen- (*d* 1654); *m* twice after her death;
8-John (1650-ca. 1684), of Branford; *m* Hannah (Griffin) Pond (*d* 1736);
7-John (1671-1748), of Branford; began to write name Linsley; *m* 1699, Mary Harrison (1668-1738; Thomas[8]);
6-Joseph (1707-86), *m* 1731, Lydia Wilford (*d* 1780; Dr. Richard[7]);
5-Dan (1734-73), of Northford, Conn.; ens.; *m* 1758, Anne Lucretia Tyler (1737-1817; Peter[6], *m* Hannah-);
4-James (1763-1828), Am. Rev.; *m* 1786, Sarah Maltby (1763-1848; Dea. Benjamin[5], *m* Elizabeth Fowler);
3-John Stephen (1806-76), farmer; Baptist; Republican; *m* 1834, Eliza Ann Halsey (Simon[4], *m* Prudence Corwin);
2-Rev. Harvey (1843-1920), of Northford; Bapt. minister; *m* 1873, Rachel Keyes (1844-1920), teacher (Joseph[8], *m* Eunice Jewett); issue: I-Grace Jennie (1873-77); II-Ray Keyes (1 above); III-Vivian Halsey (1878-1928; *m* Jennie Green; *m* 2d, Bessie Samuels); IV-Edna Eunice (*b* 1879; *m* James Fullerton Gressitt); V-Earl Garfield (*b* 1882; *m* Marguerite Gorton Vesper); VI-Paul Judson (*b* 1882; *m* Alice Williams).
1-*m* June 6, 1900, Flora Madeline Ladd, *b* S. Manchester, Conn., Oct. 9, 1878; dau. of Frank H. Ladd; issue: 1-Frank Harvey, *b* Bristol, Conn., Mar. 28, 1901; B.S., Worcester Poly. Inst., '25; *m* June 25, 1927, Grace E., dau. of Anson C. Griffen, of Pittsfield, Mass.; 2-Ralph Halsey, *b* Bristol, Feb. 3, 1903; U.S.-N.A., '26; *m* June 1, 1929, Bernice Rockwell, dau. of George Burwell Ward; 3-Ray Keyes, Jr., *b* Hartford, Conn., Jan. 13, 1917.
1-Ed. Vt. Acad., 1894. Gen. auditor, Conn. Electric Service Co. and affiliated cos. Assessor, Borough of Bristol. Served in Spanish-Am. War, 1898 for 6 mos.; Conn. N.G., 1898-1918, retired with rank of maj. Sec. and mem. Nat. Council Boy Scouts America, and pres. Bristol Council. Director Bristol Bldg. & Loan Assn. Mem. U.S.W.V., 1st Conn. Vol. Inf. War Vets, Maltby Family Assn., Jewett Family Assn. Baptist. Republican. Clubs: City (Hartford), Chipanee Country. Residence: Bristol, Conn.

1-**LOVEJOY, Clarence Earle,** *b* Waterville, Me., June 26, 1894.
9-John **Lovejoy** (1622-90), from Eng., 1635, settled at Andover, Mass.; in King Philip's War, 1675-76; *m* 1st, 1651, Mary Osgood (1633-75; Christopher[10], *m* 1st, Mary Everett);
8-Christopher (1661-1736), of Andover; *m* 1685, Sarah Russ (1668-1737; John[9], first rep. to Mass. Gen. Ct., 1651, *m* Deborah Osgood);
7-Hezekiah (1701-51), of Andover and Haverhill; *m* 1722, Hannah Austin (1704-1805, *d* aet. 101);
6-Capt. Abiel (1731-1811), of Sidney, Me.; rep. to Mass. Great and Gen. Ct. from Lincoln Co. (then Mass., now Me.); sgt. and capt. colonial wars; *m* 1758, Mary Brown (1734-1812);
5-Francis (1768-1841), *m* 1798, Betsy Smith (1778-1860);
4-Nahum (1814-85), of Sidney and Belgrade; *m* 1832, Phebe Miller (*d* 1866);
3-John Elbridge (1837-1913), of Saxonville, Mass.; *m* 1863, Annie Margaret Evans (*b* 1821);
2-Arthur Evans (1865-96), Waterville, Me.; *m* 1893, Florence Mary Early (*b* 1870), from Eng., 1888, settled at Lowell, Mass., *m* 2d, 1899, Charles Wells Sloper.
1-*m* Dec. 10, 1919, Ethel Clifford Hill, *b* Brooklyn, N.Y., Sept. 2, 1894 (divorced, Reno, Nev., Jan. 4, 1928); dau. of Spencer Hill, of New York; issue: 1-Catharine Florence (Sept. 22-23, 1922).
1-A.B., Columbia, '17 (Phi Kappa Sigma); certificate, Sorbonne, 1919. Reporter and editor of newspapers, 1910-17, 1919-20, 1925-, including 5 yrs. on the New York Times; resigned commn. in Regular Army, Apr. 1925 to establish Bronxville (N.Y.) Press as editor and publisher; Alumni sec., Columbia U., New York, and managing editor Columbia Alumni News since 1927. Second lt., 1st lt. and capt., U.S.A. (regular), 1917-19, 1920-25; served in 38th Inf., 3d Div. with A.E.F. in France; cited for gallantry at Moulins, on Marne River, near Chateau Thierry, July 19, 1918; maj. R.C., 1925-30. Author: Story of the Thirty-Eighth, 1919; Lovejoy Genealogy, 1930. Mem. S.C.W., S.R., N.E.H.G.S., N.Y. State Hist. Assn., M.O.F.W., S.A.W., A.L., V.F.W., Sojourners. Mason. Clubs: Columbia University, Briarcliff Sports. Address: Alumni Office, 110 Library, Columbia University, Broadway at 116th St., New York, N.Y.

LUCAS

Arms: *Argent, a fess between six annulets gules, three and three.*
Crest: *Out of a ducal coronet or, a wyvern's head gules.*
Motto: *Veritas vincit.*

1-**LUCAS, Alexander Hume,** *b* Santee, S.C., Feb. 18, 1878.
4-Jonathan **Lucas** (*b* 1754; son of John, *m* Ann Noble); came from Eng., settled at Charleston, S.C., 1790; rice planter; invented rice pounding mill; *m* 2d, 1788, Anne Ashburne (1752-1838);
3-William (1790-1878), rice planter; *m* 1819, Charlotte Hume (John[4], *m* Mary Mazyck);
2-Alexander Hume (1838-1914), rice planter; capt. C.S.A.; *m* 1869, Elizabeth Anne Doar (1845-1921); issue: I-Stephen Doar (*b* 1870; *m* Emily Fudge); II-Anne Ashburne (*b* 1871; *m* John D. Cheshire); III-Mary Mazyck (*b* 1876; *m* Rev. Alexander Robert Mitchell); IV-Alexander Hume (1 above); V-Harriett Gadsden (*b* 1880; *m* John Marion Lofton); VI-Charlotte (*b* 1882); VII-Alice (*b* 1884); VIII-Camilla Cordes (*b* 1888).
1-*m* June 30, 1915, Lillian Hauser Farmer, *b* Florence, S.C., Oct. 28, 1886; dau. of Johnston Luke Farmer; issue: 1-Alexander Hume, Jr., *b* Wilmington, N.C., Apr. 5, 1916.
1-Ed. Porter Mil. Acad., Charleston, S.C. Mem. I.A.G., Huguenot Soc. of S.C. Episcopalian. Democrat. Residence: McClellanville, S.C.

1-**McDONALD, Hunter,** *b* Winchester, Va., June 12, 1860.
4-Angus **McDonald** (1727-78), from Scotland to Falmouth, Va., 1746, to Winchester ca. 1760; served in French and Indian War, 1754-63; maj. militia, 1765; vestryman old Frederick

Parish, 1768; a founder of Hiram Lodge No. 12, A.F. and A.M., at Winchester; agent for Lord Fairfax; built first fort at Wheeling, 1774; lt. col. of Va. Militia, 1774; in command of Wappatomica expdn., Dunmore's war; sheriff, 1775; justice and dep. sheriff, 1776; mem. Com. Safety, Frederick Co.; *m* Anna Thompson;
3–Angus (1769-1814), p.m. Swearinger's regt., Va. militia in "Whiskey Rebellion," 1795; 1st lt., 12th U.S. Inf., War 1812; maj. U.S.A., 1814; *m* Mary McGuire (Edward[4]);
2–Angus William (2 below).
4–Humphrey **Peake,** *m* Mary Stonestreet;
3–Dr. Humphrey, collector Port of Alexandria, Va.; nearest neighbor to, and was present at death of George Washington; *m* Anne Linton Lane (Capt. William[4], officer Am. Rev.);
2–Cornelia (1822-1909), *m* 1847, Col. Angus William **McDonald** (1799-1864), U.S.M.A., 1817; col., C.S.A.; issue: I–Harry Peake (1848-1904; *m* Alice Keats Speed); II–Allan Lane (1849-1913; *m* Fannie B. Snead); III–Humphrey (1850-51); IV–Kenneth (*b* 1852; *m* America R. Moore); V–Ellen (*b* 1854; *m* James Henry Lyne); VI–Roy (1856-1921; *m* Nellie Cain; *m* 2d, Jean Martin); VII–Donald (1858-1924; *m* Betsey Breckenridge Carr); VIII–Hunter (1 above); IX–Elizabeth (1861-62).
1–*m* Feb. 8, 1893, Mary Eloise Gordon, *b* Aug. 18, 1867; dau. of Richard Cross Gordon, of Cross Bridges, Maury Co., Tenn.; issue: 1–Hunter, Jr., *b* Nashville, Tenn., July 12, 1896; Vanderbilt, '21; 1st lt., 5th F.A. Brig., 135th Aero Squadron, service with latter in France.
1–Washington and Lee U., ex-'79. Chief engr., N.,C.&St.L. Ry. (see Who's Who in America). Mem. S.A.R. Clubs: Cosmos (Washington), Bellemeade Country, Old Oak, Rotary. Residence: 1915 West End Av., Nashville, Tenn.

1–**MacPIKE, Eugene Fairfield,** *b* Alton, Ill., July 18, 1870.
4–James **MacPike** (ca. 1751-1825), from Scotland, settled in Western Md., 1772; later at Newport, Ky.; soldier in Am. Rev.; *m* ca. 1782, Martha Mountain;
3–John Mountain (1795-1876), of Alton, Ill.; commd. lt. 55th Regt. Light Inf., Ind. Militia, 1826; asso. judge, Dearborn Co., Ind., 1830-35; probate judge, 1837; *m* 1820, Lydia Jane Guest (*b* 1803: Capt Moses[4], *m* Lydia Dumont);
2–Henry Guest (2 below).
9–William **Lyon** (qv);
8–John (*b* 1647), of Roxbury, Mass.; *m* 1670, Abigail Polley;
7–William (1675-1741);
6–Aaron (1706/07-1746), killed by Indians at Charlestown, N.H.; *m* Elizabeth Allen;
5–Isaiah (1743-1813), of S. Woodstock, Conn.;
4–Luther Wells (*d* ca. 1851);
3–Luther Wells (1802-85).
2–Henry Guest **MacPike** (1825-1910), mayor of Alton, Ill., 1887-91; *m* 1st, 1854, Mary Burns (1833-67); *m* 2d, 1869, Nannie Louise Lyon (1844-1923); *m* 3d, Eleanor Moreland; issue (1st marriage): I–James Henry (1855-80; *m* Jennie Wilkinson); II–Jane (*b* 1856; *m* William Robert Wilkinson); III–John Haley (*b* 1861; *m* Josephine Meier; *m* 2d, Elizabeth Drummond); issue (2d marriage): I–Eugene Fairfield (1 above); issue (3d marriage): I–Moreland.
1–*m* Sept. 2, 1895, Ada Florence Denton, *b* nr. London, Eng., Feb. 8, 1870; dau. of John Denton, of Yorkshire, Eng.; issue: 1–Elizabeth, *b* Chicago, Ill., June 11, 1897; Ph.B., U. of Chicago, '18, M.A., 1919, Ph.D., 1923; *m* June 18, 1924, Leslie Parker, son of Francis T. Brown, of Waterbury, Conn. (issue: Richard MacPike); 2–Helen, *b* Chicago, Oct. 19, 1903; Ph.B., U. of Chicago, '24; *m* Aug. 16, 1930, Willard Wilson, son of John William Strahl, of Dayton, O., now of Princeton, N.J.
1–With Ill. Central System since 1894. Editor of Correspondence and papers of Dr. Edmond Halley. Genealogist. Author: Tales of Our Forefathers, 1898. Mem. S.A.R., I.A.G., A.H.A.; Ill. State Hist. Soc., Oxford Hist. Soc., Soc. of Genealogists (London), Ky. Hist. Soc., Geneal. Soc. of Pa., A.L.A., World Assn. for Adult Edn. (London), A.A.A.S., Inst. of Transport (London), L'Institut International du Froid (Paris), etc. Republican. Residence: 5418 Woodlawn Av., Chicago, Ill.

1–**ALBEE, Ada Fredericka Strong (Mrs. George E.),** *b* Kent Co., Md., Nov. 13, 1878.
8–George **Strong,** from Eng., 1650; settled in "Middle Neck," Kent Co., Md., ante 1655; *m* Hannah–;
7–George;
6–Thomas, *m* 1711, Jane Phillips;
5–John (1743-1804), of Kent Co., Md.; Am. Rev.; *m* 1786, Susan– (1768-1840);
4–William (1788-1824), of "The Home Farm," Kent Co.; *m* 1806, Susannah Miller;
3–Thomas (1813-96), *m* 1834, Catherine Tilden Eagle (1813-56; desc. Charles Tilden, of Pentridge, Kent Co., from Eng., 1677);
2–Charles Cornell (2 below).
9–Michael **Miller** (1643-98), from Eng., 1670; *m* ante 1673, Alice Stevens (*d* ante 1680), of "Hinchingham" and "Arcadia," Kent Co.;
8–Michael (1675-1738), *m* ante 1698, Martha Weeks, or Wickes (*d* 1746; Maj. Joseph[9], of Wichliffe, Kent Co.);
7–Michael (1698-1746), *m* 1732, Elizabeth Tolly, or Tully;
6–Michael (1732-83), pvt. Am. Rev.; *m* Martha Glanville;
5–Nathaniel (bap. 1758-1802), pvt. Am. Rev.; *m* Sarah–;
4–Susannah (ca. 1791-1842), *m* William **Strong** (4 above);
3–Thomas, *m* Catherine Tilden Eagle (3 above);
2–Charles Cornell (1838-1913), *m* 1876, Julia Anne Webb (*b* 1845); issue: I–Ada Fredericka (1 above); II–Roy Thomas (*b* 1880); III–Charles Cornell (b 1884; *m* Winifred Brevoort Tucker).
1–*m* June 20, 1910, Capt. George Emerson Albee, U.S.A. (Jan. 27, 1845-Mar. 27, 1918); son of Otis A. Albee, *m* Maria Gould.
1–Grad. normal dept. of Washington Coll., 1901. Mem. D.A.R., Md. Hist. Soc., Soc. of Valor U.S.A. Episcopalian. Democrat. Club: Woman's. Residence: Laurel, Md.

1–**ANDERSON, Lydia Stauffer (Mrs. Edward Earl),** *b* Joplin, Mo., Jan. 12, 1885.
7–Hans **Stauffer** (*b* 1650 or 55; son of Daniel, a desc. of the ancient House of Hohenstaufen in Suabia); from Switzerland, 1709, arrived at London, Eng., 1710, thence to America; settled in Chester Co., Pa.; *m* Kinget (Hiestand) Risser;
6–Jacob (1696-1780), moved to Hereford (now Washington) Tp., Berks Co., Pa.; Mennonite; *m* Barbara– (*d* 1785);
5–John (*b* 1737), Am. Rev.;
4–Jacob (1785-1829), *m* Miss Kendig;
3–William K. (1809-78), *m* Lydia S. Moyer;
2–Levi M. (2 below).
6–Rev. Peter (Meyer) **Moyer** (*b* 1723), from Switzerland; settled in Springfield Tp., Bucks Co., Pa., nr. Pleasant Valley; minister Mennonite Ch., Springfield; Am. Rev.;
5–Christian (*d* 1826), Am. Rev.; *m* Anna L. Bauer;
4–Peter B. (1781-1848), *m* 1809, Eva Shelly (1787-1869);
3–Lydia S. (1812-93), *m* William K. **Stauffer** (3 above).
7–Hans **Bauer,** fled from Switzerland with a company of Mennonites to America, bet. 1708-17; settled in Colebrookdale Tp., Berks Co. (then Phila. Co.), Pa.;
6–Michael (*d* 1784), *m* Fronica Landis (Johannes[7]);
5–Anna L., *m* Christian **Moyer** (5 above);
4–Peter B., *m* Eva Shelly (4 above);
3–Lydia S., *m* William K. **Stauffer** (3 above);
2–Levi M. (1834-91), Lutheran; served in Co. K, 15th N.J. Vol. Inf., 1st N.J. Brig., 1st Div., 6th A.C., Civil War; mem. G.A.R.; *m* 1877, Jennie (1861-1912), dau. of John Wesley Councill (Rev. Benjamin[3], of N.C.); issue: I–William (*d* infancy); II–Guy (*d* infancy); III–Elsie (1885-86); IV–Lydia (1 above).
1–*m* 1902, Charles L. Bishop (1877-1912); son of Samuel Bishop; issue: 1–Stauffer C., *b* Mt. Vernon, Ill., Oct. 5, 1903.
1–*m* 2d, Edward Earl Anderson, *b* Mt. Vernon, Ill.; Mar. 5, 1887; ordnance sgt., acting chief buglar, with A.E.F. in France, World War; son of Edward T. Anderson (Col. William B.[3], of 60th Ill. Vol. Inf., Civil War; bvtd.

brig. gen. for gallant and meritorious service during the war, 1865; mem. Constl. Conv. which framed the present constn. of Ill.; mem. 44th Congress).
1–Mem. D.A.R., D.U.V. Residence: 3751 Pine Grove Av., Chicago, Ill.

1–**BOYLE, Jessie Anne Boyle (Mrs. Peter A.)**, *b* Shelby Co., Ala., Feb. 14, 1866.
8–Col. Richard **Lee** (qv);
7–Hancock (1653-1709), of "Ditchley"; burgess, Northumberland Co., 1688; naval officer; justice; collector of Va.; *m* 1st, 1675, Mary Kendall (Col. William[8], burgess, Northampton Co., speaker, 1684-85);
6–Richard (1691-1740), of "Ditchley"; *m* 1720, Judith Steptoe;
5–Capt. Thomas (1729-1816), surveyor; lt. in N.C. colonial militia under Col. Needham Bryan, 1774; in Am. Rev. under John Sevier; had land grants in Greene Co., Tenn., for service in Am. Rev.; finally settled in Hawkins Co., Tenn., first record of him there is 1783; *m* 2d, 1761, Mary Bryan (*b* 1745; William[6], of Johnston Co., N.C., *m* Elizabeth Smith; Needham[7], *m* Annie Rambeau; William[8], qv);
4–Needham (1770-1820), moved to Ala.; *m* Susan Bailey;
3–Needham (1808-96), *m* 1829, Nancy Wharton (1809-69; Stephen[4], *m* Sarah Griffin; Col. Samuel[5], capt. S.C. Line, and col. of militia, *m* Madeline, dau. of Owen O'Sullivan, of Caroline Co., Va.);
2–Helen (*b* 1847), *m* 1862, Bartholomew **Boyle** (1827-75), of an old Anglo-Irish family long seated at Castle Comer, Co. Kilkenny, Ireland; issue: I–Jessie Anne (1 above); II–Mary Lee (*b* 1870; *m* Edward Averett); III–Robert Edmund (1873-1905).
1–*m* June 5, 1884, her cousin, Peter Alexander Boyle, *b* nr. New Haven, Conn., Oct. 1847; son of John Robert Boyle; issue: 1–Mary Lee (June 20, 1885-Sept. 1, 1898); 2–John Robert, *b* Davenport, Ia., Sept. 21, 1893; *m* Apr. 14, 1925, Elizabeth Bowie Crawford.
1–Residence: 2801 Rhodes Circle, Birmingham, Ala.

1–**CISSEL, Georgia Estelle Hobbs (Mrs. Sebastian B.)**, *b* Marriottsville, Md., Mar. 28, 1877.
9–John **Hammond** (qv);
8–Maj. Charles (*d* 1713), of Anne Arundel Co.; military officer, 1696; county commr., 1702-10; mem. Assembly, 1710-13; maj. colonial forces ante 1705; *m* 1691, his first cousin, Hanna Howard (Capt. Philip[9], *m* Ruth Baldwin);
7–Philip (1696-1760), of Annapolis, Md.; speaker Assembly 11 times; merchant; *m* 1727, Rachel Brice (1711-86; Capt. John[8], *m* Sarah, dau. of Matthew Howard);
6–Col. Charles (1729-77), of Anne Arundel Co.; large landowner; *m* Rebecca Wright;
5–Charles (will probated 1827), of Anne Arundel Co.; inherited 1500 acres from his father; *m* 1785, Providence Smith;
4–Ruth, *m* Lenox I. **Martin** (Thomas[5]);
3–Rebecca (1812-88), of Marriottsville (now Howard) Co., Md.; *m* 1836, Wilson Lee **Hobbs** (1805-83; Larkin[4], *m* Elizabeth Norwood);
2–John Wesley (2 below).
8–Robert **Ridgely** (qv);
7–Charles (*d* 1705), of Prince George Co., Md.; *m* Deborah Dorsey (Hon. John[8], mem. Provincial Congress, *m* Pleasance Ely; Edward[9], qv);
6–William (*d* 1755), of Baltimore Co.; *m* his cousin, Elizabeth Duvall (Lewis[7]; Mareen[8], qv);
5–Charles "Blackhead" (1749-1810), of Anne Arundel Co.; mem. Legislature 27 yrs., speaker of the House, 13 yrs.; presidential elector when Washington was made president; *m* 1773, Ruth Norwood (1754-1806; Samuel[6]);
4–Dr. Charles (1785-1861), of Howard Co.; *m* Elizabeth Dorsey (Amos[5], *m* Mary, dau. of Nicholas Dorsey; Ely[6]; Capt. John[7]; Edward[8], qv);
3–George Washington (1812-92), of Howard Co.; *m* Margaret Ann Turner (1827-1889).
2–John Wesley **Hobbs** (1838-1916), of Howard Co., Md.; farmer; justice; *m* 1860, Martha Cornell (*d* 1867); *m* 2d, 1875, Elizabeth Dorsey Ridgely (1857-1922); issue (1st marriage): I–Mary Rebecca (*b* and *d* 1863); II–Albert Wilson (*b* 1866; *m* Elizabeth Gorman); issue (2d marriage): I–Georgia Estelle (1 above); II–Jessie Eudora (*b* 1880; *m* Edmund Walter Scott); III–Charles Wesley (*b* 1883; *m* Sophia Eleanor Cissel).
1–*m* Dec. 26, 1906, Sebastian Brown Cissel, *b* Highland, Md., July 8, 1884; son of Wilbur Fisk Cissel; issue: 1–Eleanor Elizabeth, *b* Marriottsville, Md., Sept. 27, 1908; Md. State Normal Sch.; *m* Sept. 17, 1930, John George, son of George W. Hurt, *m* Ida Sarah Bailey; 2–Sebastian Brown, Jr., *b* Marriottsville, Feb. 5, 1911.
1–Grad. Md. State Normal School. Teacher in public schools of Howard Co., Md., 1897-1907. Mem. Md. Hist. Soc. Methodist. Democrat. Residence: "Alpha," Marriottsville P.O., Howard Co., Md.

1–**FRY, John Walker**, *b* Richmond, Va., June 13, 1854.
6–Col. Joshua **Fry** (*d* 1754), prof. William and Mary Coll., Williamsburg, Va., 1728-32; living in Goochland Co. when Albemarle Co. was cut off from Goochland, 1744; commr. Albemarle Co.; justice of the peace; co. lt., Albemarle Co.; presided at the first ct. of the co., 1744; apptd. col. of Va. Regt., 1754, by Gov. Dinwiddie, while on way to Ft. Duquesne (now Pittsburgh, Pa.), he fell from his horse at Millis Creek, now Cumberland, Md., where he died; at his death, Lt. Col. George Washington then about 21, succeeded to the command; *m* Mary (Micou) Hill;
5–Henry (1738-1823), of Madison Co., Va.; *m* Susanna Walker (Dr. Thomas[6], of Castle Hill, *m* Mildred [Thornton] Meriwether, a widow; Capt. Thomas[7], of Gloucester Co., Va., 1650);
4–Joshua (1769-1838), of Madison Co.; *m* Catherine Walker;
3–Hugh Walker (1796-1872), of Richmond; *m* Maria White;
2–John James (2 below).
10–Robert **Lewis** (qv);
9–Maj. John (*b* 1635), of "Warner Hall," Va.; *m* Isabella Warner (Augustine[10], qv);
8–Col. John (1669-1725), mem. Royal Council; co. lt.; judge Supreme Ct.; *m* his cousin, Elizabeth Warner ("Speaker" Augustine, II[9], *m* Mildred, dau. Capt. George Reade, qv; Col. Augustine[10]);
7–John, *m* Frances Fielding;
6–Col. Robert, *m* Jane Meriwether;
5–Col. Charles, *m* Mary Lewis (Howell[6], *m* Mary Randolph [Isham[7], *m* Jane Rogers; Col. William[8], qv]; Col. Charles[7], *m* Mary Howell; John[8], 7 above);
4–Howell, *m* Mary Carr;
3–James Howell, *m* Sarah Stanford;
2–Mary Carr (1831-1901), *m* John James **Fry** (1824-88), mcht., Richmond, Va.; supt. gas works; farmer; issue: I–Howell Lewis (*b* 1850; *m* Mollie Pepper); II–John Walker (1 above); III–Samuel Gordon (1856-1928; *m* Mary Banks); IV–Sadie (*b* 1863; *m* Aylett L. Everett).
1–*m* Feb. 16, 1881, Annie Morehead Gray (Sept. 21, 1860-May 1895); dau. of Julius A. Gray, of Greensboro, N.C.; issue (all *b* Greensboro): 1–Emma Morehead, *m* Bradford M. Adams (issue: Jennie Morehead); 2–Mary Lewis, *m* Pierce C. Rucker (issue: Pierce C., Jr.; Mary Lewis; Walker Fry); 3–Annie Gray, *m* Frederick Isler Sutton (issue: Frederick Isler, Jr.).
1–*m* 2d, Oct. 25, 1897, Nannie Walter Caldwell (Jan. 27, 1867-May 22, 1916); daughter of Walter Caldwell, of Greensboro.
1–*m* 3d, June 14, 1919, Alice Harrison Everett, *b* Keswick, Va., Oct. 14, 1871; dau. of Dr. Charles Everett, of Albemarle Co., Va.
1–Civil engineer, C. & O. Ry., and Carolina Central Ry.; city engring., Manchester, Va.; rd. master, Richmond & Danville R.R.; supt. Greenville & Columbia R.R., East Tenn., Va. & Ga. R.R., M.&O. R.R.; gen. mgr. Cape Fear & Yadkin Valley Ry.; pres. Greensboro Bank & Trust Co. since 1899; Mem. S.C.W., S.R., S.C., I.A.G. Presbyterian. Democrat. Residence: Greensboro, N.C.

1–**GARDNER, Josephine Eggleston (Mrs. A. Ferdinand)**, *b* July 7, 1864-*d* June 20, 1930.
8–Richard **Eggleston**, from Eng., 1635, settled at "Powhatan," James City Co., Va.; was in

battle of Bloody Run against Indians, 1656;
7–Richard;
6–Joseph (1678-1730), of "Powhatan"; burgess, James City Co., Va., 1728-30; *m* 2d, 1720, Anne Pettus (1702-36; John[7], *m* Anne, dau. Samuel Overton; Thomas[8]; Col. Thomas[9], of Gov.'s Council, *m* Mrs. Elizabeth Durant; Sir James[10], of Eng.);
5–Joseph (1721-92), of Amelia Co., Va.; *m* 1753, Judith Segar (*b* 1729; Oliver[6], *m* Jane–);
4–Joseph (1754-1811), grad. Coll. of William and Mary; mem. Congress and Va. Assembly; *m* 1788, Sallie Meade (1769-92; Everard[5], *m* 1st Mary, dau. of John Thornton, of N.C.; David[6], *m* Susannah, dau. of Sir Richard Everard; Andrew[7], qv);
3–William (1794-1845), *m* 1821, Frances Peyton Archer (John R.[4], *m* Frances Cook, dau. of John Tabb, *m* Frances Peyton);
2–Stephen Archer (2 below).
9–Humphrey **Tabb** (qv);
8–Thomas (1647-95), *m* 1674, Martha–;
7–John (*b* 1676), *m* 1701, Martha Hand;
6–Col. Thomas, of "Clay Hill," Amelia Co., Va.; burgess; *m* Rebecca Booker (Col. Edward[7]; Capt. Richard[8]);
5–Mary Marshall, *m* Robert **Bolling**, IV (Robert[6], *m* Anne Cocke; Robert[7]);
4–Thomas T., *m* Seignora Peyton (Sir John[5], *m* Frances Cooke; Thomas[6]; Sir Robert[7]);
3–Harriet Elizabeth (1800-68), *m* Charles Seager **Eggleston** (1792-1847), of Va., Md., and Miss. (Joseph[4], above);
2–Frances (1833-1902), *m* 1855, Stephen Archer **Eggleston** (1829-77), ed. for the law at U. of Va.; planter; issue: I–Robert Bolling (1856-1914; *m* 1890, Mary Nunnally); II–Sallie Meade (1858-62); III–William Francis (1860-90); IV–John Randolph (*b* 1862-1904); V–Josephine (1 above); VI–Yelverton Tabb (1866-1929; *m* Daisye Bryan); VII–Marianna Barksdale (1867-75); VIII–Fanny Peyton (1870-88); IX–Stephen Archer (1871-1930; *m* 1898, Hallie Sims); X–Delia Sessions (*b* 1876; *m* John J. North).
1–*m* Feb. 14, 1888, A. Ferdinand Gardner, *b* Houston, Tex., June 26, 1860; son of Frank Bowen Gardner, of Columbus, Miss.; issue (all *b* Greenwood, Miss.): 1–A. Frank, *b* Dec. 31, 1888; U. of Miss., 1914; *m* June 24, 1915, Edna Earl, dau. of Rufus Calhoun King, of Greenwood (issue: Margaret King, *b* Apr. 9, 1916; Joseph Eggleston, *b* May 15, 1918; Edna Earl, *b* Nov. 9, 1920; Rufus King, *b* June 7, 1926); 2–Robert Eggleston, *b* Aug. 21, 1890; U. of Miss.; *m* Dec. 13, 1913, Lillian Price, dau. of Thomas W. Yates, of Oxford, Miss. (issue: Robert Eggleston, *b* Dec. 31, 1915; Thomas Yates, *b* Aug. 15, 1919; Samuel Parker, *b* Oct. 25, 1926); 3–Stephen, (Apr. 24, 1892-Nov. 9, 1896); 4–Fanny Tabb, *b* Sept. 4, 1896; *m* June 6, 1917, Samuel Ferguson, son of Alexander Keach Parker, of Greenville; 5–Delia Eggleston, *b* July 26, 1898; A.B., Agnes Scott; U.Chicago; U.Tenn.; 6–Josephine Peyton, *b* Sept. 13, 1900; Agnes Scott; U.Chicago; *m* Nov. 4, 1926, Charles Jeptah, son of William Jefferson Stratton, of Greenwood (issue: Josephine Eggleston, *b* Apr. 7, 1928); 7–Mary Pitts, *b* Jan. 1904; Columbia Inst., Tenn.; Randolph-Macon Inst.; *m* Jan. 14, 1926, Earlwood Brady, son of Joel Sims Kelly, of Greenwood (issue: Ferdinand Gardner, *b* Apr. 24, 1930); 8–Roberta Bolling, *b* Greenwood, Nov. 12, 1905; Stephens Coll., Mo.; *m* Feb. 1, 1928, Robert Tully, son of Robert Tully Wade, of Sunnyside, Miss.

1–**HOUGH, Elizabeth Trigg Thornton (Mrs. Charles P.),** *b* Platte Co., Mo., Feb. 9, 1865.
8–Daniel **Trigg** (1650-1716), of Va.; *m* Susan– (*d* 1687);
7–Abraham (1684-1718), *m* 2d, 1710, Judith Clarke (*b* 1687);
6–Judge William (1716-73), judge, Bedford Co.; *m* Mary Johns;
5–Col. John (1748-1804), comd. a co. of militia of Bedford Co., Va., 1775; capt., 1778; was at the siege of Yorktown and surrender of Cornwallis; justice; maj. of a regt., and later lt. col., militia; mem. Va. House of Dels., 1784-92; rep. Bedford Dist. in 5th, 6th, 7th and 8th Congresses, 1797-1804; mem. Va. Conv. which ratified the Constn. of the U.S., 1788; *m* 1767, Dinah Ayres;
4–Gen. Stephen (1768-1834), *m* 1790, Elizabeth Clark;
3–Elizabeth (*d* 1858), *m* 1820, Col. John **Thornton** (1786-1847);
2–Col. John C. Calhoun (2 below).
7–Capt. Christopher **Clark** (*b* in Eng., ca. 1700-*d* 1754), *m* Penelope Massie Bolling (g.dau. of Earl of Shaftsbury);
6–Micajah (1718-1801), Am. Rev.; *m* 1736, Judith Adams (*b* 1716; Robert[7], *m* Mourning Adams);
5–Robert (*b* 1738), Am. Rev.; *m* 1764, Susannah Henderson;
4–Elizabeth (1772-1822), *m* Gen. Stephen **Trigg** (4 above);
3–Elizabeth, *m* Col. John **Thornton** (3 above);
2–Col. John C. Calhoun, C.S.A. (1834-87), *m* 1864, Louisa Archer (1841-1916).
1–*m* Sept. 22, 1891, Dr. Charles Pinckney Hough (Apr. 14, 1846-Mar. 12, 1926); son of George Washington Hough; issue: 1–Charles P., Jr., *b* Butte, Mont., Nov. 4, 1892; *m* Christine Hall, *b* Framingham, Mass., Jan. 27, 1896.
1–Ed. Hardin Coll., Mo. Mem. C.D.A., D.A.R., U.S.D. 1812, U.D.C., I.A.G., etc. Residence: 1015 W. 61st St. Terrace, Kansas City, Mo.

JENISON

Arms: Azure, on a bend wavy or, between two swans argent, three roses gules.
Crest: A dragon's head couped armed azure and or.

1–**JENISON, Orien Austin,** *b* Lansing, Mich., Oct. 2, 1865.
8–Robert **Jenison** (*d* 1690), from Eng., 1630; settled at Watertown, Mass., 1636; freeman, 1638; *m* Elizabeth–; *m* 2d, Grace– (*d* 1686);
7–Robert (1645-1701), *m* 1666, Judith Macomber (*d* 1722);
6–Robert (*b* 1684), Watertown; *m* Dorothy Rebecca (Maverick) Whittemore (Elias[7]; Rev. John[8]; Rev. Peter[9], of Eng.);
5–Joseph (1720-1813), Cambridge; *m* 1745, Martha Twiss (*d* 1806, aet. 87);
4–Peter (1750-1821), Am. Rev.; *m* 1764, Mehitable Singleterry;
3–Luther (1779-1823), *m* 1806, Lovina Polly;
2–Orien Austin (2 below).
8–Richard **Singletary** (*d* 1687), of Salem, 1637; freeman, Newbury, 1638; at Haverhill, 1652; *m* Susanne Cook (*d* 1682);
7–Nathaniel (*b* 1644), of Haverhill; *m* 1673, Sarah Belknap;
6–John (*b* 1675), Sutton, Mass.; *m* Mary Greele;
5–Amos (1721-1806), Topsfield; rep. 2d Provincial Congress of Mass., 1775; *m* Mary Curtis;
4–Mehitable (*d* 1812), *m* Peter **Jenison** (4 above);
3–Luther, *m* Lovina Polly (3 above);

2–Orien Austin (1823-95), of Watertown, N.Y.; *m* 1851, Helen Maria Butler-Pompeii (1830-79); issue: I–Helen A. (*b* and *d* 1853); II–Frank H. (*b* 1859; *m* 1904, Adelaide Ashbrooke); III–Fred H. (*b* and *d* 1859); IV–Orien A. (1 above).
1–*m* June 2, 1892, Mary Monell Hawley, *b* Detroit, Mich., July 6, 1868; dau. of Sen. Thos. deReimer Hawley; issue: 1–Austin Hawley, *b* Lansing Michigan, May 9, 1893; *m* Jan. 2, 1917, Margaret Daniell (issue: Judith, *b* Oct. 3, 1917; Barbara, *b* June 2, 1919; Daniell, *b* July 9, 1921; Lucetta Lenore, *b* July 12, 1929).
1–Ed. pub. grammar and high schools. Messenger and clerk in state office, 1880-86; manufacturing, 1886-96; book store, 1896-98; general insurance, 1898–; pres. The Dyer-Jenison-Barry Co. Mem. I.A.G., etc. Residence: 915 Townsend St., Lansing, Mich.

1–**JOHNSON, Frances Howe (Mrs. Jacob C.),** *b* Audrain Co., Mo., Nov. 26, 1878.
10–Edward **Howe** (qv);
9–William (1629-76), of Concord, Mass.; *m* ca. 1653, Mary–;
8–Samuel (1654-1724), Plainfield, Conn.; *m* 2d, 1678, Mary Nutting (1655/56-1727; John[9]);
7–John (1688-1727), *m* 1709, Phoebe Butterfield (1684-1758; Samuel[8]);
6–Samuel (1716-90), Canaan, Conn.; *m* 1st, 1740, Martha Spaulding (1723-58; Josiah[7]);
5–Stephen (1748-1829), Poultney, Vt.; *m* 1774, Lois Barden (1756-1842);
4–Stephen (1784-1866), *m* ca. 1809, Chloe Norton (1788-1851);
3–James (1810-1900), Mexico, Mo.; *m* 1837, Harriet Angevine;
2–George (2 below).
9–Jehu **Burr** (qv);
8–Jehu (ca. 1625-ca. 1692), of Fairfield; dep. Gen. Ct., 1670,73; given 200 acres land for his services; lt. Fairfield Train Band, 1673-75; dep. Gen. Ct., mem. Standing Council, re-apptd., 1676; commr., 1678-89; *m* 1st, Mary Ward (Andrew[9]);
7–Daniel (*d* 1722), of Fairfield; called Lt.; *m* 3d, ca. 1695, Elizabeth Pinckney (Capt. Philip[8]);
6–Stephen (1697/98-ca. 1778), of Redding, Conn.; lt., 1749; *m* 1721, Elizabeth Hull (*b* 1699; Cornelius[7]);
5–Esther (1743-1829), *m* 1761, Anthony **Angevine** (1730-1828), of Stratfield; served in French and Indian War (Zacherie[6], *m* Joanna, dau. of John Mallet);
4–Oliver Lawrence (1780-1870), of Poultney, Vt.; in War 1812; *m* 1806, Sally Whitney;
3–Harriet (1810-99), *m* James **Howe** (3 above).
9–John **Whitney** (qv);
8–Joshua (*b* 1635), of Groton, Mass.; deacon; in King Philip's War; *m* 3d, 1672, Abigail Tarball (Thomas[9]);
7–Col. David (1682-1769), Plainfield, Conn.; rep. Gen. Ct., 1757-64,66; 2d lt. French and Indian War, 1755; lt. col., 1757; col. of militia; *m* 1712, Elizabeth Warren (1698-1767; Jacob[8]);
6–Solomon (1735-72), Canaan, Conn.; *m* 1755, Sarah Roberts (1738-1812; Lt. Samuel[7]);
5–Solomon (1766-1854), Poultney, Vt.; pvt. Am. Rev.; *m* ca. 1785, Mary (Polly) Marshall;
4–Sally (1788-1880), *m* Oliver Lawrence **Angevine** (4 above).
10–Edmund **Marshall** (1598-ante 1676), from Ireland, settled at Salem, Mass.; later at Ipswich; *m* Millicent– (1601-post 1666);
9–Joseph (*b* ca. 1650), of Ipswich;
8–Thomas (1692-1766), Holliston, Mass.; *m* 1st, 1715, Esther Larned (1690-1761; Isaac[9]);
7–Joseph (*b* 1717), *m* 1736, Mary Leland (1720-79);
6–Ichabod (1740-42-1792), Poultney, Vt.; sgt. in Am. Rev.; *m* 1760, Lydia Stearns (1744-1836; Jonathan[7]);
5–Mary (1768-1837), *m* Solomon **Whitney** (5 above);
4–Sally, *m* Oliver Lawrence **Angevine** (4 above);
3–Harriet, *m* James **Howe** (3 above);
2–George (1844-90), Audrain Co., Mo.; stock farmer; *m* 1874, Charlotte Ralph (1843-99; Mathias[8], *m* Comfort Townsend).
1–*m* Feb. 6, 1899, Lt. (now Col.) Jacob Calvin Johnson, U.S.A., *b* Marietta, O., Nov. 17, 1872; son of William Johnson; issue: 1–Marion Rolfe, *b* Everett, Mass., Apr. 27, 1903; B.A., Devon Manor, '21; *m* June 21, 1922, Caroll H. Dietrick, of Watsontown, Pa.
1–B.A., Hardin Coll., '93. Mem. C.D.A., D.A.R., I.A.G., Huguenot Soc. Residence: Ft. Hancock, N.J.

1–**KEPLER, Sarah Estelle Smith (Mrs. Irvin T.),** *b* Elkton, Md., Feb. 9, 1882.
5–George **Batten** (1758-1818), from Eng., settled at Batten's Mills, Del.; *m* Rachel E. Batten (1755-1826);
4–William (*b* 1792), of Del.; *m* 1817, Mary McCombs (1797-1832; Samuel[5] [1765-1825], *m* Margaret–);
3–Sarah Jane (1818-92), of Del.; *m* Samuel **Smith** (1802-62);
2–William James (2 below).
10–Thomas (Bouldin, Boulding) **Boulden** (1580-1655), from Eng., settled at Elizabeth City, Va., 1610; *m* Mary–;
9–William (ca. 1620-1691), of Va., and Kent Island, Md.; *m* Ann–;
8–William (1650-1717), *m* Elizabeth–;
7–William, of Cecil Co., Md.; *m* Thomasin–;
6–Richard (1697-1740), *m* 1716, Mary Hewes (*b* 1691; Owen[7], *m* Mary–);
5–Thomas (1728-83), 1st lt., Sassafras Bn., Md.; capt. Bohemia Bn., 1778; *m* Augustina Boulding (James[6], *m* Elizabeth–);
4–John (1765-1826), *m* 1807, Ann Faries (1784-1809);
3–Sarah Ann (1809-90), of Elkton, Md.; *m* 1844, Joseph Miles **Ash** (1819-63);
2–Mary Anna (*b* 1852), *m* 1876, William James **Smith** (1850-1906), postmaster at Elkton; issue: I–Gertrude A. (1879-1928); II–Sarah Estelle (1 above); III–Julian Constable (*b* 1886; maj. U.S. Marine Corps; *m* Harriott Wanamaker Byrd); IV–Mary Beatrice (*b* 1888; *m* E. Roy James).
1–*m* Sept. 15, 1917, Irvin Talmage Kepler, *b* Port Royal, Pa., Aug. 19, 1891; son of George B. M. Kepler, *m* Annie E. Leyder.
1–Mem. Md. Hist. Soc.; organizing regent "Head of Elk" Chapter D.A.R. Residence: 240 E. Main St., Elkton, Md.

1–**KNIGHT, Martha Morton Hogeman (Mrs. Harold W.),** *b* Charleston, W.Va., Jan. 18, 1874.
9–Dr. John **Woodson** (qv);
8–Robert (1634-1707), of Henrico Co., Va.; *m* ca. 1656, Elizabeth Ferris;
7–Richard (1662-1730), *m* Anne Smith (*d* 1746);
6–Obadiah (*b* 1712), capt. and cdr. of militia, 1755; *m* 1735, Constance Watkins;
5–Judith (*b* 1743), of Prince Edward Co., Va.; *m* Moses **Fuqua** (*b* 1738);
4–Nancy (1766-1842), of Campbell Co., Va.; removed to nr. Greenup, Ky.; *m* 1790, Josiah **Morton** (1763-1838), Am. Rev. (Capt. John[5], an original incorporator of Hampden-Sidney Coll., capt. 4th Va. Cont. Line);
3–Martha Anderson (1805-65), of Kanawha C.H., Charleston, W.Va.; *m* 1832, James **Ruffner** (1807-68);
2–Anastine Woodson (*b* 1846), of Charleston; *m* 1871, William Henry **Hogeman** (1845-85), lawyer, New York, N.Y.; removed to Charleston, 1865 (Henry[3], from Germany, settled in New York, ante 1840, *m* Mary Moore); issue: I–Henry James (1872-73); II–Martha Morton (1 above); III–Andrew Lewis (1875-1909; *m* Mary Elizabeth Dunlap); and IV–Meredith Ruffner, twins (*b* and *d* 1875).
1–*m* Apr. 4, 1903, Harold Warren Knight (July 3, 1868-Mar. 28, 1915); son of Edward Boardman Knight; issue (all *b* Charleston, W.Va.): 1–Annie Hogeman, *b* Feb. 22, 1904; A.B., Wellesley, '26; 2–William Henry, *b* Oct. 20, 1905; Dartmouth, '31; 3–Harold Warren, II, *b* Jan. 25, 1907; Dartmouth, '30; *m* Oct. 24, 1928, Elizabeth Godfrey, dau. of Edward G. Miller (issue: Harold Warren, III); 4–Martha Morton, *b* July 29, 1908; Wellesley, '30.
1–Elmira Coll., '96. Mem. I.A.G. Episcopalian. Residence: 1319 Quarrier St., Charleston, W.Va.

1–**KYSER, William Dennis,** *b* Richmond, Ala., July 17, 1882.
4–George **Kyser,** of Ala.; *m* Emily–;
3–Malachi (1811-61), of Ackerville, Ala.; *m* 1837, Amanda Dennis (*d* 1884);
2–Dr. George W. (1841-1911), physician; of Richmond, Ala.; *m* 1868, Sallie Patton (1846-1924); issue: I–John Patton (1870-86); II–James Henry (1872-1904); III–George Herbert (1874-1920; *m* Ada Belle Moore); IV–Mary Amanda

(1876-79); V–Samuel Joseph (*b* 1879; *m* Halsa Alison); VI–Georgia (*b* 1880; *m* B. L. Youngblood); VII–William Dennis (1 above).
1–*m* June 9, 1917, Tempe D. Swoope, *b* Memphis, Tenn., Apr. 22, 1893; dau. of William C. Swoope, of Courtland, Ala.; issue: 1–William Dennis, Jr. (Apr. 29, 1918-July 25, 1921); 2–Tempe Darrow Swoope, *b* Memphis, Tenn., Apr. 29, 1925.
1–B.A., U.Ala., '03 (Kappa Alpha, Southern); LL.B., Cumberland U., 1906. Atty.-at-law; mem. McKellar & Kyser, 1909-17, McKellar, Kyser & Allen, 1917-20, mem. Kyser & Allen, 1920-30; U.S. atty., 1917-21 (see Who's Who in America). Dir. Bank of Commerce & Trust Co.; pres. and gen. counsel Memphis Power & Light Co., Memphis St. Ry. Co. Clubs: Memphis Country, Tennessee, Rotary. Residence: 2225 S. Parkway E., Memphis, Tenn.

1–**LINDSAY, Edwin Blair,** *b* Davenport, Ia., Oct. 12, 1897.
7–Donald **Lindsay** (ca. 1670-post 1765), from Scotland, 1739, settled in Argyle, Washington Co., N.Y.; *m* 2d, in Scotland, Mary McQuarrie;
6–Duncan (*d* ca. 1785), of Argyle, N.Y.; *m* Anna McDougal; *m* 2d, Agnes (McIntyre) McCoy;
5–Daniel (1773-1840), *m* Eleanor McIntyre; *m* 2d, Martha McDowall (*d* 1862);
4–Robert D. (1804-73), of Northumberland, Schroon, Essex Co., and Crown Point, N.Y.; maj. N.Y. militia; *m* ca. 1824, Elizabeth Churchill;
3–James Edwin (1826-1915), of Schroon, N.Y., and Davenport, Ia.; maj. N.Y. militia; vol. in Mexican War; *m* 1858, Mary Helen Phelps;
2–Ralph Edwin (2 below).
10–Josiah **Churchill** (qv);
9–Joseph (1649-99), of Wethersfield; *m* 1674, Mary Edwards ("Widow Mary"), who lived to a great age;
8–Nathaniel (1677-1715), *m* 1701, Mary Hurlbut (1679-1738; John[9], of Middletown, Conn.);
7–Nathaniel (*b* 1703), *m* Rebecca Griswold;
6–Nathaniel (*b* 1731), *m* 1755, Elizabeth Sage; *m* 2d, Jane Bushnell;
5–Sage (1763-1813), Elizabethtown, N.Y.; *m* Elizabeth Mather;
4–Elizabeth (1809-75), *m* Robert D. **Lindsay** (4 above).
9–George **Phelps** (qv);
8–Jacob (1649-89), of Westfield, Mass.; *m* 1672, Dorothy Ingersoll (*b* 1654);
7–Israel (*b* 1681), Enfield, Conn.; *m* 2d, 1714, Rachel Jones, a widow;
6–David (1716-1803), *m* 1737, Margaret Colton (1714-1810);
5–John (1756-1840), of Colebrook, Conn.; in Am. Rev.; *m* 1st, 1779, Anna Baker (*d* 1797);
4–Elihu (1782-1856), of Schroon, N.Y.; *m* 1816, Margaret Cruikshank;
3–Mary Helen (1832-1912), Davenport, Ia.; *m* James Edwin **Lindsay** (3 above);
2–Ralph Edwin (1861-1913), of Davenport, Ia.; *m* 1891, Margaret Idelle Blair (*b* 1865; Andrew[3], from Ireland to Galena, Ill., and later at Princeton, Ia.).
1–*m* 1930, Elizabeth Montgomery (*b* 1903), dau. of William McLean Stewart, *m* Elizabeth Montgomery.
1–A.B., Dartmouth, '20 (P.B.K., Chi Phi); M.B.A., Harvard, 1922 (Staplers Club). Second lt., U.S.A., 1918. Mem. firm Lindsay & Phelps Co., Davenport, Ia.; trustee Public Library; dir. U. of Dubuque; mem. bd. Christian edn. of Presbyn. Ch. U.S.A. (Phila.). Mem. I.A.G., etc. Residence: 310 Forest Rd., Davenport, Ia.

1–**LUSCHER, Julia Adaline Gile (Mrs. Gustav S.),** *b* Wautoma, Wis., June 10, 1855.
8–Samuel (Guild, Guile) **Gile** (1620-83), from Scotland, 1636, to Dedham, Mass.; one of 12 founders of Haverhill; propr.; *m* Judith Davis (*d* 1667; James[9], from Eng.);
7–John (1652-1726), wrote name Guile; *m* Widow Sarah Sutton;
6–Joseph (*b* 1695), Providence, R.I.;
5–Joseph (*d* 1785), S. Scituate, R.I.; Am. Rev.; *m* 1st, 1758, Elethan Harris;
4–John (1759-89), *m* Mary–;
3–William (1787-1873), began to write name Gile; Oxford, N.Y.; dea. Presbyn. Ch. 40 yrs.; *m* 1810, Ann Stephens (1790-1864; Capt. Abram[4], of Preston, N.Y.);
2–Gordon Hall (2 below).
7–Rev. Malichi **Jones** (1651-1729), from Wales; settled at Abington, Pa., 1714; pastor of Presbyn. Ch.; *m* 1681, Mary–;
6–Malichi, II (1694-1754), Downington, Pa.; *m* 1729, Mary Parry (James[7], from Wales to Fredyffrin, Pa., *m* Ann–);
5–William (*b* 1741), *m* 1762, Elizabeth Hunter (John[6], *m* Margrate–);
4–George (1765-1835), Batavia, N.Y.; Am. Rev.; *m* 1799, Caty Howe (*d* 1810);
3–Benjamin H. (1802-55), Newark, N.Y.; *m* 1826, Betsey (Wheeler) Garlick (1799-1880).
2–Gordon Hall **Gile** (1828-1902), Oshkosh, Wis.; *m* 1851, Julia Jones (1829-63); *m* 2d, 1867, Sarah Willson (1831-1913); issue (1st marriage): I–Julia Adaline (1 above); II–Jennie C. (*b* 1858).
1–*m* June 1, 1886, Gustav S. Luscher, *b* Oshkosh, Wis., Feb. 12, 1856; son of William Luscher, of Oshkosh; issue: 1–Julia Gordon (June 14, 1887-June 25, 1917); Smith Coll.; 2–Margaret Mae Rose, *b* Oshkosh, July 3, 1895; ed. Downer Sem.; *m* July 26, 1927, J. Stafford, son of James F. Trottman.
1–Ed. private schools and Oshkosh Normal Sch. Mem. Twentieth Century Club, D.A.R., D.F.P.A., etc. Residence: 47 Church St., Oshkosh, Wis.

1–**MARBLE, Annie Maria Russell (Mrs. Charles F.),** *b* Worcester, Mass., Aug. 10, 1864.
8–Henry **Dunster** (qv);
7–Jonathan (1653-1725), Cambridge, Mass.; *m* 1st, 1678, Abigail Eliot;
6–Henry (1680-1753), Cambridge; *m* 1707/08, Martha Russell (1691-1771; Jason[7], *m* Mary Hubbard);
5–Jason (1725/26-1806), Mason, N.H.; surveyor of highways, 1773; constable, 1774; *m* 1749, Rebecca Cutler (1731 or 33-1806; Samuel[6], *m* Anne Harrington);
4–Jason (1763-1828), pvt. Am. Rev.; *m* 1793, Mary Meriam (1768-1858; Joseph[5], Concord, Mass., *m* Mary Brooks);
3–Betsey (*b* 1801), *m* 1819, Moses **Russell** (*b* 1793; Hubbard[4], *m* Sarah Warren);
2–Isaiah Dunster (2 below).
5–Maj. Jonathan **Wentworth** (*b* Dover, N.H., 1741-*d* Somersworth, N.H., 1790), comd. co., Bunker Hill; served at Ticonderoga and campaign in R.I., 1778; served in Legislature, 1779-82; *m* Betsey Philpot;
4–Richard Philpot, *m* Deborah Burley;
3–Jonathan, *m* Nancy Fiske;
2–Nancy Maria (*b* 1825), *m* 1846, Isaiah Dunster **Russell** (*b* 1820), mcht.; issue: I–Addison Charles (1847-51); II–Charles Addison (*b* 1852; *m* Ella Sayles); III–Annie Maria (1 above).
1–*m* Nov. 18, 1890, Charles Francis Marble, *b* Worcester, Mass.; son of Edwin T. Marble, of Worcester; issue: 1–Anna Bell, *b* Apr. 12, 1905; grad. Smith Coll., '27; 2–Paul Francis, *b* Dec. 11, 1906; grad. Brown U., '30.
1–A.B., Smith, '86, A.M., 1895. Taught school, 1887-90; author (see Who's Who in America). Mem. D.A.R., Worcester Hist. Soc., A.A.U.W. Conglist. Republican. Clubs: Women's University, Boston College, Boston Authors. Residence: 16 Marble St., Worcester, Mass.

1–**MARKLE, Augustus Robert,** *b* Bowling Green, Ind., Nov. 24, 1869.
4–Abraham **Markle** (1770-1826), of Ulster Co., N.Y.; maj. Canadian vols., War 1812; 1st clk. of Ulysses, now Ithaca, N.Y.; propr. of town of Terre Haute, Ind., 1816; *m* Catharine– (1772-1846);
3–Nelson (1807-78), of Ancaster, Ont.; *m* 1830, Matilda Annon Bennett (1811-81; William Plunkett[4], *m* Elizabeth Harris);
2–Theodore (2 below).
9–Ralph **Keeler** (qv);
8–Samuel (1656-1713), of Norwalk, Conn.; *m* 1682, Sarah St. John (1659-1714; Mark[9], *m* Elizabeth, dau. of Timothy Stanley; Matthias[10]);
7–Joseph (1683-1757), of Norwalk; *m* Elizabeth Whitney (*d* 1763; John[8], *m* Elizabeth, dau. of Richard Smith; Henry[9]);
6–Lot (*b* 1719), of Ridgefield, Conn.; *m* Elizabeth Goodenough;
5–David (*d* 1826), of South Salem, N.Y.; *m* Amy Ingersol (*b* ca. 1798; John[6]; John[7]; John[8]);
4–David (1771-1846), *m* Abigail Skeele (1777-1840);
3–Julia Ann (1811-77), *m* 1834, Cyrus **Kilgore** (1813-92; David[4], *m* Margaret Baird);
2–Lorenda Elizabeth (1839-82), *m* 1868, Theodore

Markle (1842-1922), accountant, Rob Roy, Ind.; 1st lt. Ind. Heavy Arty.; issue: I-Augustus Robert (1 above); II-Grace (*b* 1871; *m* George Starr); III-Florence (*b* 1873); IV-Paul (*b* 1876; *m* Mabel Lancaster).
1-*m* Mar. 31, 1894, Lena Elizabeth Blue, *b* Aledo, Ill., Sept. 14, 1866; dau. of Daniel Blue (1837-66); issue: 1-John (Aug. 26, 1895-Feb. 8, 1915); 2-Margaret Mary, *b* Brazil, Ind., Aug. 3, 1900; *m* Feb. 24, 1925, Arthur, son of Thomas Woodcock, *m* Jane Lythgoe (issue: Elizabeth Jane; Julia Ann); 3-Richard Theodore, *b* Terre Haute, Sept. 1, 1906.
1-Carriage blacksmith, 1887-91; electrical contractor, 1892-1910; consulting electrical engr. since 1910. Mem. S.C.W. (genealogist Ind. Soc.), S.A.R. (genealogist Ind. Soc.), S.W. 1812 (historian Ind. Soc., v.p. gen., 1930), I.A.G., Soc. Ind. Pioneers, Ind. Hist. Soc., Vigo Co. Hist. Soc. (sec.), Hist. Soc. Berks Co., Pa. Residence: Terre Haute, Ind.

1 **MARVEL, John Everett,** *b* nr. Waynesville, Ill., Jan. 2, 1883.
8-John **Marvel** (1630-1709), from Eng., settled in Accomac Co., Va., 1649; removed to Worcester Co., Md.; *m* 1651, Ann- (1632-1710);
7-Thomas (1674-1757), of Sussex Co., Del.; *m* 1702, Elizabeth Huggins (1684-1755);
6-David (1721-96), of Sussex Co.; *m* 1744, Sarah Prettyman (1725-1801);
5-Prettyman (1763-1856), removed to Greene Co., Ga., 1796, to Gibson Co., Ind., 1808, to Waynesville, DeWitt Co., Ill., 1854; *m* 1793, Lovina Rogers (1765-1848; John[6], *m* Comfort Prettyman);
4-Prettyman (1801-42), of DeWitt Co., Ill.; *m* 1823, Rebecca Barr (1806-93; John[5], *m* Nancy Agnes, dau. of William Hamilton, Am. Rev., of S.C.);
3-John Shrader (1824-61), *m* 1847, Jane Roberts (1829-90; Elisha[4], *m* Elizabeth Montgomery; John[5]);
2-William Thomas (2 below).
8-William **Jones** (ca. 1675-1754), from Wales, settled in Phila. Co., Pa., 1694; *m* 1701, Mary Roberts;
7-Cadwallader (1704-49), *m* 1732, Sybil Herrien (*b* 1706);
6-Cadwallader (1734-1826), to Forsyth Co., N.C., 1758; served in Am. Rev. as maker of guns; cousin of John Paul Jones; *m* 1758, Sarah Jones (1737-1805);
5-Cadwallader (1760-1801), to Madison Co., Ky., 1786, to Christian Co., 1800; *m* 1785, Martha Pitts (1762-1854);
4-Charles (1791-1864), Gibson Co., Ind.; col. in War 1812; *m* 1819, Eleanor Warwick (1799-1869; Capt. Jacob[5], *m* Jane Montgomery; John[6], Am. Rev., *m* Mary, dau. of Samuel Powell, Am. Rev.; Lt. William[7], *m* Elizabeth Dunlap);
3-John (1825-1902), of Midland City, Ill.; *m* 1856, Permelia Montgomery;
2-Eleanor Jane (2 below).
8-Robert **Montgomery,** from Co. Down, Ireland, settled on James River, Va., 1666; granted 850 acres of land, 1679;
7-Hugh (ca. 1705-1785), *m* Caroline Anderson (had 7 sons in Am. Rev., all lived to return home);
6-Lt. Thomas (1745-1818), to Gibson Co., Ind., 1806; in Am. Rev.; *m* 1767, Martha Crockett (1747-1805; Joseph Louis, Jr.[7], *m* Jeanne de Vigné);
5-Walter Crockett (1784-1856), War 1812; *m* Nancy Roberts (1790-1845; John[6], *m* Mary Johnson);
4-Jacob Warrick (1811-92), *m* Jane McFadin (1815-1904; John[5], *m* Lucinda Davis);
3-Permelia (1836-1929), *m* John **Jones** (3 above);
2-Eleanor Jane (1860-1922), *m* 1881, William Thomas **Marvel** (1850-1928), of DeWitt Co., Ill.; farm owner and live stock producer; issue: I-John Everett (1 above); II-Eva May (1885-1902); III-Ethel Fern (*b* 1892; *m* Rev. Albert E. Blomberg); IV-Opal Irene (*b* 1896).
1-Not married. A.B., U. of Ill., '07; M.D., Rush Med. Coll., 1909. Passavant Memorial Hosp., Chicago, 1909-11; post-grad. work in surgery and Bd. of Health med. inspector for Chicago, 1911-12; pvt. practice, Waynesville, Ill., since 1912. Mem. Bd. of Supervisors, DeWitt Co., 1914-16, City Council, 1920-28. First lt. U.S.A., World War, 1918. Mem. A.M.A., Ill. State and DeWitt Co. med. socs. I.A.G., Ill. State Hist. Soc., Marvel Family Assn., A.L. Mason. Odd Fellow. Residence: Waynesville, Ill.

1-**MASON, Elizabeth Venable (Mrs. Frank T.),** *b* Atlanta, Ga., Oct. 29, 1873.
7-Abraham **Venable** (qv);
6-Capt. Abraham (1700-68), great landowner; burgess 20 yrs.; justice, Hanover and Louisa cos.; vestryman, Fredericksville Parish, 1742-61, Trinity Parish, 1762-68; capt. colonial militia; friend of Patrick Henry; *m* 1723, Martha Davis; and thru his g.son:
4-John (1740-1811), capt. Am. Rev.; removed to Jackson Co., Ga., 1791; *m* Agnes Moorman (Charles[5], a Quaker);
3-Nathaniel (1781-1832), *m* Sarah Montgomery;
2-William Richard (2 below).
9-Simon **Hoyt** (qv);
8-Walter (ca. 1618-1698), dep. Gen. Ct., Norwalk, Conn., 1658, et seq.;
7-John (1644-1711), one of the 8 original settlers of Danbury, Conn.; *m* 1666, Mary Lindall; *m* 2d, Hanna-;
6-Thomas (1674-1749), *m* Anna-;
5-Comfort (1723-1812), capt. of the Alarm, and a minuteman 1st Co., 16th Conn. Regt., Am. Rev.; prudential commr., 1755-83; *m* 1750, Anna Beach;
4-Ard (1776-1828), Danbury, missionary to Cherokee Indians; *m* Esther Booth (*b* 1774);
3-Rev. Darius (1804-37), prof. theology, Maryville Coll., Tenn.; *m* Lucy Mariah Bogle (1809-88);
2-Sarah Cornelia (2 below).
6-Robert **Nelson** (*b* Ordsall, Lancastershire, Eng., 1725-*d* Bowling Green, Ky., 1804), from Lancastershire, Eng., settled in Va.; later settled nr. Anderson's Ferry on the Susquehanna River, Juniata Co., Pa.; his home was a rendezvous for patriots during Am. Rev.; he paid soldiers from his own resources; later in Ky.; *m* Martha Patterson (ca. 1731-1794);
5-Nancy (1761-1828), *m* 1782, James **Bogle** (*d* 1786);
4-Robert (*b* 1782), *m* Anne Reed;
3-Lucy Mariah, *m* 1827, Rev. Darius **Hoyt** (3 above);
2-Sarah Cornelia (1834-1916), *m* 1850, William Richard **Venable** (1826-73), clk. Superior Ct. of Ga. 20 yrs.; for issue see Samuel Hoyt Venable, Vol. I, p. 871.
1-*m* Aug. 29, 1906, Frank Tucker Mason, *b* Chicago, Ill., Apr. 26, 1880; B.A., Yale, '02; pres. Pine Mountain Granite Co., Atlanta, Ga.; son of William Mason (1849-1920), silk mfg., Paterson, N.J.; issue: 1-Leila Elizabeth, *b* Atlanta, Ga., Jan. 19, 1909; 2-Samuel Venable, *b* Atlanta, Nov. 27, 1911.
1-Mem. D.F.P.A. (Ga. state v.p., 1929), C.D.A., D.B.R., O.C., D.A.R. Summer place: Stone Mountain, Ga. Residence: "Stonehenge," 1410 Ponce de Leon Av., Druid Hills, Atlanta, Ga.

1-**MILLS, Charles Fremont,** *b* Burlington, Conn., Nov. 6, 1858.
5-Ebenezer **Mills,** from Eng.;
4-Ebenezer;
3-Daniel (1773-1835), of Weston, Conn.; capt. 2d Light Inf. Co., 26th Regt., Conn. militia, 1806, maj., 1810, lt. col., 1813; *m* 1796, Mary Potter Dunbar;
2-Leavet Dunbar (2 below).
8-William **Potter** (1607-43), from Eng. in the "Abigail," 1635, with son Joseph, settled at E. Haven, Conn.; *m* Frances- (*b* 1609);
7-Nathaniel (*b* 1642), of E. Haven;
6-Daniel (1685-1765), E. Haven;
5-Daniel (1718-73), of New Haven; *m* 1741, Martha Ives (1716-70);
4-Mary Ives (1751-1827), *m* 1773, Aaron **Dunbar** (1748-1820; 5 below);
3-Mary Potter (1776-1857), of Plymouth, Conn.; *m* 1796, Daniel **Mills** (3 above).
9-Robert **Dunbar** (*d* 1693), from Scotland 1635, settled at Hingham, Mass.; *m* Rose- (*d* 1700);
8-John (*b* 1657), of Hingham; *m* 1679, Mathiole Aldridge;
7-John (*d* 1746), New Haven, Conn.; *m* 1716, Elizabeth Fenn;
6-John (*b* 1724), apptd. 1777, one of a com. of 15 to collect clothing, etc. for soldiers; *m* 1743, Temperance Hall (1727-70);

5–Aaron (1748-1820), of Plymouth, Conn.; Am. Rev.; *m* 1773, Mary Ives Potter (1751-1827);
4–Aaron (1779-1852), of Sharon, Conn.; *m* 1798, Mary Dummer (1771-1847);
3–Henrietta (1802-37), *m* 1827, Seth Barstow **St. John** (1798-1884; Silas[4] [1772-1848], *m* 1795, Olive Barstow, 1771-1854);
2–Melissa (1828-1901), *m* 1854, Leavet Dunbar **Mills** (1817-66), sgt., Inf. Co. 7, 14th Regt. of Conn., 1837, lt., 1843; farmer; issue: I–Seth Barstow (*b* 1855; *m* 1875, Emerett Louisa Russell, 1856-1900); II–Mary Henrietta (1856-75); III–Charles Fremont (1 above); IV–Dwight Elmore (1860-1914; *m* 1885, Abby Cornelia Beach, *b* 1867); V–Harriette Melissa (1861-1929; see Who's Who in America); VI–Samuel John (1863-1909).
1–*m* Feb. 25, 1886, Sadie Minnie Pratt, *b* Narrowsburg, N.Y., Apr. 27, 1861; dau. of George Washington Pratt, of Burlington, Conn.
1–Farmer to age of 20; shipping clk. P. & F. Corbin factory 9 yrs.; salesman, 25 yrs., New York manager, 10 yrs., retired, March 1926; manager emeritus P. & F. Corbin, Div. of Am. Hardware Corpn. of New York. Republican. Residence: 50 Sound View St., Port Chester, N.Y.

1–**MORSE, Theoda Mears (Mrs. Edward H.),** *b* Morrill, Me., Feb. 15, 1876.
9–Robert (Meares, Meers) **Mears** (1592-1666/67), from Eng. in the "Abigail," 1635, settled at Boston; propr. Boston and Braintree; *m* Elizabeth Johnson (ca. 1605-post 1674);
8–Samuel (1641-76), in King Philip's War; wrote name Meares; *m* Mary Stace, or Stacy, of Ipswich;
7–Samuel (1671-1727), wrote name Meers; served in Capt. Ebenezer Hunt's co., 1690, in the expdn. to Can.; keeper of the St. George Tavern, Roxbury, 1708-26; Sun Tavern, Dock Square, Boston, 1726-27; *m* 1st, 1697, Mariah Katharina (Smith?) Gross (*d* 1706);
6–James (1703/04-1771), of Roxbury; *m* 1st, 1726, Mehitable Davenport (*b* 1705; John[7], *m* Naomi Foster?; Thomas[8], of Dorchester);
5–James (1731-1804), of Roxbury; wrote name Mears; Am. Rev.; *m* 1757, Ann Greaton (1737-1805; John[6], *m* Catherine Sharrard, widow of Joseph Linton of Boston);
4–John (1764-1854), Belmont, Me.; War 1812; *m* 1789, Mary Parker;
3–James (1809-86), treas. Belmont and Morrill, Me.; first selectman nearly every year from 1856-73; *m* 1836, Sarah Cross;
2–Horatio (2 below).
9–Dea. Thomas **Parker** (1605-83), from Eng., 1635, settled at Lynn and Reading, Mass.; *m* Amy– (*d* 1689/90);
8–Ens. Nathaniel (1651-1737), of Reading; *m* 1677, Bethiah Polly (1659-1748; John[9], *m* 1st, Susanna Bacon);
7–Timothy (1695/96-ca. 1737), inn holder; *m* 1718, Mary Scarborough (Dea. Samuel[8], *m* 3d, Bethiah–);
6–Jeremiah (1719-78), patriot Am. Rev.; *m* 1st, 1743, Mary Williams (1722/23-1749; Lt. John[7], *m* Sarah Weld; Lt. Samuel[8]; Dea. Samuel[9]; Robert[10], qv);
5–Lt. Jeremiah (1744-80), Am. Rev.; *m* 1766, Abigail Peele (1745-1825; Jonathan[6], *m* 3d, Bethia Allen; George[7]; George[8]);
4–Mary (1769-1855), *m* John **Mears** (4 above).
7–Robert **Cross** (*d* 1738), of Ipswich; *m* 1719, Elizabeth Graves;
6–Robert (bap. 1721-1804), *m* 1744, Anstress Ellery (1726-1808; Dependance[7], *m* Sarah Warner; William[8], *m* 2d, Mary, dau. of John Coit, Jr.);
5–Nathaniel (*d* 1801), *m* Martha Woodman (1751-1840; Joshua[6]);
4–Dea. Joseph Warren (1782-1862), *m* 1804, Lucy Jackson;
3–Sarah (1818-97), *m* James **Mears** (3 above).
11–John **Howland,** Mayflower Pilgrim (qv);
10–Hope, *m* Elder John **Chipman** (qv);
9–Samuel (1661/62-1723), *m* Sarah Cobb (*d* 1742; Elder Henry[10], *m* 2d, Sarah Hinckley);
8–Abigail (*b* 1692), *m* 1713, Nathaniel **Jackson** (Nathaniel[9], *m* Ruth Jenney; Abraham[10], *m* Remember Morton [Nathaniel[11], *m* Lydia Cooper; George[12], *m* Julianna Carpenter]);
7–Nathaniel (1716-68), *m* 1734, Patience Cole (John, Jr.[8], *m* Patience Barber);
6–Lemuel (ca. 1735/36-ca. 1818), Am. Rev.; *m* 1757, Jemima (Sampson) Bennett (Seth Sampson[7], *m* Ruth Barrows; George[8]; Abraham[9]);
5–Isaac (1758-1845), Am. Rev.; *m* Submit Scott (*d* 1800);
4–Lucy (1785-1868), *m* Dea. Joseph W. **Cross** (4 above).
8–John **Gay** (qv);
7–Eliezer (1647-1726), of Wrentham; *m* Lydia Hawes (1649-1717; Edward[8], *m* Eliony Lumber);
6–Eleazer (*b* 1677), Wrentham; *m* 1706, Mary Nutting (*d* 1750);
5–Jonah (1721-78), of Attleboro, Mass., and Medumcook, Me.; *m* 1745/46, Sarah Wellington (*b* 1719; Ebenezer[6], *m* Deliverance Bond; Benjamin[7]; Roger[8]);
4–Jonah (ca. 1765-1802), of Union, Me.; patriot Am. Rev.; *m* 1788, Mary Thomas (1762-1843);
3–Richard (1800-89), of Waldo, Me.; *m* 3d, 1849-50, Sarah (Vickery) Neal (1813-97; David Vickery[4], *m* Betsey Simmons; Mathias[5]; David[6]; Dea. Jonathan[7]; Rev. Jonathan[8]; George[9]);
2–Mary Frances (1854-97), *m* 1873, Horatio **Mears** (1849-1925), of Belfast, Me., and Pasadena, Calif.; cabinet maker, piano and furniture manufacturer.
1–*m* Apr. 20, 1908, Edward Hayes Morse, *b* Johnson, Vt., Feb. 5, 1877; son of Charles Clinton Morse, *m* Ida Lucinda Barber, of Hyde Park and Swanton, Vt., Atlanta, Ga., New Orleans, La., and Pasadena, Calif.; issue: 1–Ida Frances (*b* Sept. 9, 1915-*d* young).
1–Ed. private schools, with special work in history and astronomy; studied music. Genealogist; compiler of about 4,000 pages of manuscript records of The Mears Family and Allied Lines, including the spellings of Mears, Meares, Meers, Meres, etc., in the United States, England, and Ireland, and probably has the most extensive collection of records on the Mears family in America; compiled the manuscript records of the Cross family of Exeter, N.H., and Belmont, Me.; Gay family of Union, and Waldo, Me.; Jackson family of Paris, and Belmont, Me.; Barber family of Richmond, Vt.; Niles family of Haverhill, N.H.; Vickery family of Waldo, and Morrill, Me.; descendants of Stephen and Sarah (Kay) Morse of Haverhill, N.H., and the ancestral records of Edward H. Morse, Horatio Mears, and Mary Frances Gay. Author of many articles on genealogy which have been published in newspapers, magazines, and the bulletins of patriotic societies. Mem. D.A.R. (chapter registrar 4 yrs.), I.A.G., Los Angeles Geneal. Soc., Pasadena Hist. Soc., Nat. Soc. N.E. Women (historian), Society of Genealogists (London), etc. Unitarian. Republican. Residence: 2401 Mar Vista Av., Altadena, Calif.

1–**OLTROGGE, Marie Sylvia Estelle Trichelle (Mrs. Henry C.),** *b* Notchitoches Parish, La., Dec. 13, 1854.
7–John **Walker,** from Derry, Ireland, 1720, settled in Del. where he died;
6–Col. John (1728-96), settled on south branch of Potomac River, Hampshire Co., Va. (now W.Va.); vol. under Col. George Washington, and shared in Braddock's defeat, 1755; moved to Lee Creek, Lincoln Co., N.C.; served against the Cherokee Indians, 1761; moved to Crowder's Creek, nr. King's Mountain, 1763; purchased 400 acres in Rutherford Co., moved there, 1768; col.-commandant of Tryon militia; justice, judge; apptd. by Legislature, 1774, as one of the commrs. to "select a site and build thereon the court house, prison and stocks" for Tryon Co.; chmn. Tryon Co. Com. of Safety; del. 3d Provincial Congress, held in Hillsboro; capt. and maj., 1st Regt., N.C. Cont. troops, 1775-77; *m* 1751, Elizabeth Watson;
5–Felix (1753-ca. 1828), a founder of Boonesboro, Ky., 1775; clk. Washington Dist. Ct., and Washington Co. Ct.; in Am. Rev. and Indian wars; clk. Ct. of Pleas and Quarter Sessions of Rutherford Co., 1779-87; mem. State House of Commons, 1792, et seq.; removed to Haywood Co., 1808; rep. U.S. Congress from the western dist., 1817-23; *m* 1780, Isabella Henry (William[6], of York Dist., N.C.);
4–Isabella Henry, *m* James **Baird** (desc. John Baird, from Scotland 1683);
3–Felix Walker, *m* Harriet Pucket (John[4], *m*

Nancy, dau. of William Johnston, *m* Mary Ford);
2–Narcissa (1835-1924), *m* 1st, Feb. 22, 1854, Sylvain (Trichel, Trichell) **Trichelle** (Feb. 17, 1824-June 11, 1854), served in Mexican War; *m* 2d, 1870, Francis M. Grant; issue (mother's 1st marriage): I–Marie Sylvia Estelle (1 above); issue (2d marriage): I–Belle (*b* 1871; *m* J. B. Sawyer, *d* 1902; *m* 2d, Stuart Douglas Rollins, *d* 1930); II–Mary (*d* in childhood).
1–*m* July 4, 1871, George M. Hayden (May 25, 1844-1883); issue: 1–Estelle Trichelle, *b* Clinton, La., Nov. 1873.
1–*m* 2d, May 17, 1884, Henry C. Oltrogge, *b* N.Y. City, Oct. 5, 1859; issue: 1–Annie Frederica, *b* Jacksonville, Fla., Mar. 13, 1885; *m* Nov. 2, 1904, Elton Winslow Baker (issue: Laurence; girl, *d* in a few days; Ellen Winslow [*m* Jan. 18, 1930, Frederick Bertels]; Harriette Marie; Elton W.; Carl Francis); 2–Henry Carl, *b* Jacksonville, Jan. 26, 1889; *m* Oct. 7, 1922, Margaret Winstead Worsham (issue: Frances Estelle, *b* Jan. 21, 1926).
1–Private schools. Contbr. to newspapers and periodicals; musical composer. Mem. D.A.R., I.A.G., U.D.C. (poet laureate Fla. div.), W.C.-T.U., Internat. Writers' League, Daughters of the King. Episcopalian. Residence: 2224 Ernest St., Jacksonville, Fla.

1–**PERKINS, George Gilpin,** *b* Burlington, Ky., July 10, 1839.
12–William **Perkins,** of Warwickshire, 1495;
11–Thomas (*d* 1528), Hillmorton; *m* Alys– (*d* 1538);
10–Henry (*d* 1546 or 47);
9–Thomas (*d* 1592), *m* Alice Kebble (*d* 1613?);
8–Henry (*d* 1608/09), *m* 1579, Elizabeth–;
7–John (qv);
6–Isaac (*b* ca. 1612), settled at Hampton, N.H., ca. 1638; was among the first grantees when the plantation was laid out, and resided in that part of the town called Seabrooke; took freeman's oath at Boston, 1642; *m* Susanna Wise (Humphrey[7], of Ipswich);
5–Joseph (*b* 1661), removed to Del., 1693; *m* ca. 1687, Martha–;
4–Joseph (*d* ante 1790), *m* Mary Hilton;
3–William (1776-1849), *m* 1804, Nancy Gilpin;
2–John Hilton (2 below).
6–Joseph **Gilpin** (qv);
5–Joseph (1703/04-1792), removed from Brandywine to Wilmington, 1761; *m* 1729, Mary Caldwell;
4–Israel (1740-1834), col. Am. Rev.; *m* 1765, Elizabeth Hannum;
3–Nancy (1778-1843), *m* William **Perkins** (3 above).
6–John **Hannum,** from Eng.; *m* Margery Southery (Robert[7]);
5–Robert, settled at Birmingham, as early as 1717; at Wilmington, 1732; burgess;
4–Elizabeth (*d* 1802), *m* Israel **Gilpin** (4 above).
4–John **Robinson,** from Pa. to Ky.; *m* Sallie Brown;
3–Maria (1796-1878), *m* Abram **Stansifer** (1788-1866; John[4], from Holland, settled in Campbell Co., Ky., *m* Jemima Clore);
2–Maria Robinson (*b* 1816), *m* 1835, John Hilton **Perkins** (1808-94), mfr. and farmer; issue: I–Henry Abram (*b* 1836; *m* 1865, Harriet Moores); II–George Gilpin (1 above); III–Laura (*b* 1841; *m* 1864, Xerxes W. Culbertson); IV–John Edgar (*b* 1844; *m* 1870, Laura Alice Senour); V–Charles Lewis (*b* 1846; *m* 1891, Bessie E. Calkins); VI–William Stansifer (1850-1921; *m* 1880, Emma Sophia Clendenning); VII–Mary Nancy (*b* 1854; *m* 1875, W. W. Riggs); VIII–Anna Maria (1857-60); IX–Robert Trimble (1859-83); X–Frank Hilton (*b* 1861; equipped and was in charge of Belgian mfg. plants in France; later capt. and maj., Q.M.C., U.S.A. in charge of salvage depot in France; head of animal and leather transportation, Paris; lt. col., Q.M. sect. of O.R.C.; *m* 1885, Blanche Mayberry).
1–*m* June 7, 1864, Lavinia Jane Smith (Feb. 26, 1844-Mar. 14, 1930); grad. Ohio Female Coll., dau. of Irby Smith, *m* Ann Maria Todd (Robert W.[3], 1st lt., 6th Ind. Cav., asso. judge, Ripley Co. Ct.); issue: 1–Anna Todd, *b* Covington, Ky., Mar. 18, 1865; *m* Dec. 10, 1902, Henry Clay Stewart, lawyer, of Washington, D.C.; 2–Gilbert Brooke, *b* Covington, May 27, 1871; commd. 1st lt., M.T.C., assigned to Camp Meigs, adj. of hdqrs., motor command No. 33; transferred to Camp Benning, Columbus, Ga., as actg. capt.; hon. discharged, May 1919; *m* Apr. 30, 1902, Clara Leonora (*b* Feb. 2, 1878), dau. of Henry Edwards Huntington (see Vol. I, p. 384; issue: Huntington Todd, *b* Nov. 29, 1910; Jane, *b* May 15, 1912; Mary, *b* Feb. 22, 1915); *m* 2d, Feb. 14, 1928, Alice Esther, dau. of Albert Upson Smith (*b* 1859; desc. Nicholas Sever Smith, from Holland, settled at Milford, Conn., 1660), *m* 1882, Lizzie Maria Prichard (*b* 1859; g.g.g.dau. Lt. Jabez Prichard, Am. Rev.).
1–Ed. Shelby (Ky.) Coll.; Belmont (O.) Coll.; studied law and admitted to bar, 1863. Mem. Ky. Gen. Assembly, 1867-69; pres. Dem. State Conv., 1869; del. Dem. Nat. Conv., 1872; apptd. Ky. commr. to N.O. World's Cotton Exposition, 1883-84; judge Kenton Co. Ct. to fill a vacancy, 1869, Criminal and Circuit Ct., Covington and Newport dist., 1871-89. Author: The Kentucky Gilpins. Mem. I.A.G. Residence: The Wyoming Apt., Washington, D.C.

1–**ROGERS, Eliza Burk (Mrs. William),** *b* Doniphan Co., Kan., Aug. 30, 1857.
5–Thomas **Burk** (*d* 1775), settled in Albemarle Co., Va.; soldier French and Indian War; *m* Clara–; *m* 2d, Mary–;
4–Capt. John (*b* 1756-57-*d* 1832-35), of Va.; in Am. Rev.; *m* 1778, Mary Porter (1760-ca. 1825);
3–George (1779-1867), in War 1812; *m* 1813, Ann Grey Stoops (Philip[4], *m* Mary Ferguson);
2–Philip (2 below).
9–John **Andrews** (*d* 1681), from Eng., 1640, settled at Farmington, Conn.; *m* ca. 1643, Mary–;
8–Joseph (1651-1706);
7–Dr. Joseph;
6–Joshua;
5–Jeremiah, of Farmington, Conn.; in Am. Rev.;
4–Elijah;
3–Amos (1803-67), *m* 1826, Roxy Cordelia Taylor;
2–Eliza M. (2 below).
9–Richard **Taylor,** from Eng.; was at Yarmouth, Mass., ante 1664; *m* Ruth–;
8–Elisha (*b* Yarmouth, 1663/64), *m* Rebecca–;
7–Elisha (*b* 1694), *m* 1718, Sarah Davis (Josiah[8], *m* Anne Taylor);
6–Stephen (1721-1813), *m* 1746, Deliverance Rust (*d* 1813; Noah[7], *m* Keziah Strong);
5–Elisha (1748-1822), Am. Rev.; *m* 1773, Jerusha Hutchins (1752-1829; John[6], *m* Ann Howard);
4–Dr. Elijah (1776-ca. 1817), *m* 1805 or 06, Roxy Roberts;
3–Roxy Cordelia (1807-68), *m* Amos **Andrews** (3 above).
11–George **Steele** (qv);
10–James (ca. 1623-1681), of Hartford; served in Pequot and King Philip's wars; *m* 1st, ante 1654, Ann Bishop (*d* 1676; John[11], of Guilford, Conn., *m* Ann–);
9–James (1654 or 58-post 1712), lt. at Hartford; *m* Sarah Barnard (1658-1732; Bartholomew[10], *m* Sarah, dau. Thomas Birchard, qv);
8–Sarah, *m* 1707/08, John **Watson** (*d* 1724; John[9]; John[10]);
7–Mary (*b* 1710/11), of Hartford; *m* 1731, William **Webster,** sgt. in militia (William[8]; Robert[9]; Gov. John[10], qv);
6–Susannah (1743-1820), *m* 1764, Amos **Gillette** (bap. 1743-1829), Am. Rev. (Jonathan[7]; Cornelius[8]; Cornelius[9]; Jonathan[10], qv);
5–Roxy (1769-1826-27), *m* 1786, Lemuel **Roberts** (1766-1829; Capt. Lemuel[6]; Lemuel[7]; John[8]);
4–Roxy (1787-1822), *m* Dr. Elijah **Taylor** (4 above);
3–Roxy Cordelia, *m* Amos **Andrews** (3 above);
2–Eliza M. (1830-1915), of Canaan, N.Y.; *m* as his 2d wife, 1856, Philip **Burk** (1819-69), served with 13th Kan. Inf. troops, in Civil War; issue: I–Eliza (1 above); II–Cynthia Caroline (1861-1907; *m* 1878, W. R. Keefover); III–Philip Taylor (*b* 1864; *m* 1886, Clara Spealman).
1–*m* Apr. 29, 1883, William Rogers (Mar. 24, 1844-Feb. 14, 1919); son of John Rogers, from Eng., settled at Rockford, Ill.; issue: 1–Clarence John, *b* Marysville, Kan., Jan. 25, 1884; M.D., Bennett Med. Coll., 1907; 2–Grace Darling, *b* Barnes, Kan.; studied violin, Neb. Wesleyan, 3 yrs.; *m* June 16, 1921, Charles H., son of John H. Best, of Studley, Kan.
1–Former sch. teacher. Now compiling Burk

Family History and Genealogy. Mem. D.F.P.-A., D.A.C., D.A.R., Neb. Hist. Soc. (an organizer, pres., mem. editorial bd.). Unitarian. Democrat. Residence: Studley, Kan.

1-**VAN BLARCOM, Sara Streit Riker (Mrs. Andrew),** *b* Newark, N.J., Feb. 6, 1882.
9-Gysbert or Guisbert (Rycken, Rycker) **Riker,** from Holland, 1630; received large land grants, New Amsterdam and Newtown, L.I.;
8-Abraham (1619-89), received grant from W. Indies Co., 1638; received patent, 1664, for L.I. property and Ricker's Island; *m* Grietje, or Margaret, Hendrikse (Hendrick[9]);
7-Jan (*b* 1651), wrote name Rycker; Flushing, L.I.; *m* 1691, Sara Schouten (Jan[8], *m* Sara [Jansen] Vanderbeck);
6-Abraham (bap. 1695), removed to Essex Co., N.J., 1728; *m* Anneke Oliver;
5-Isaac (*b* 1728), began to write name Riker; of Verona, N.J.; *m* thrice;
4-Samuel (1784-1849), of W. Bloomfield (now Montclair), N.J.; *m* Dorcas Jacobus (Henry Isaacse[5]);
3-William (1822-97), head of jewelry business, Riker & Goble; Presbyn.; *m* 1848, Sarah M. Hunter;
2-Joseph Marsh (*b* Jan. 8, 1852), ed. pvt. schs.; pres. Merchants' Nat. Bank; *m* 1881, Sara Ellen Streit (Samuel[3], *m* Martha Smith); issue: I-Sara S. (1 above); II-Marian Berrien (*b* 1884; *m* Franklin Conklin, Jr.); III-Joseph Marsh (*b* 1889); IV-Marguerite Streit (*b* 1891).
1-*m* May 9, 1906, Andrew Van Blarcom (see Vol. III, p. 285); issue (all *b* Newark, N.J.): 1-Andrew, Jr., *b* Apr. 19, 1907; 2-Sarah Hunter, *b* Sept. 24, 1909; *m* Ralph H. Inslee, of Newton (issue: Thomas Edsall, *b* Apr. 9, 1930); 3-Mary Thomson, *b* Apr. 25, 1913; 4-Joseph Riker, *b* Aug. 19, 1916; 5-Anne Brackenridge, *b* May 7, 1921.
1-Residence: 530 Ridge St., Newark, N.J.

1-**WINSLOW, Randolph,** *b* Hertford, N.C., Oct. 23, 1852.
6-Thomas **Winslow** (*d* ca. 1745), supposed to have emigrated from New England to Perquimans Co., N.C.; *m* Elizabeth Clear (*b* 1686);
5-Timothy (*d* 1752), *m* Rachel Wilson (*d* 1777);
4-Caleb (1749-1811), *m* 1st, Ann Perry (1755-96);
3-Nathan (1795-1873), *m* 1819, Margaret Fitz Randolph (1781-1848);
2-Dr. Caleb (2 below).
6-Thomas **Parry** (1680-1751), from Wales, settled in Montgomery Co., Pa.; *m* 1715, Jane Morris (*d* 1741);
5-John (1721-89), of Moorland Manor, Pa.; *m* Margaret Tyson (*d* 1807);
4-Benjamin (1757-1839), of New Hope, Bucks Co., Pa.; *m* 1787, Jane Paxson (1757-1826);
3-Oliver (1794-1874), of Phila.; *m* 1827, Rachel Randolph (1804-66; Edward Fitz Randolph[4]);
2-Jane Paxson (1829-1910), of Phila.; *m* 1852, Dr. Caleb **Winslow** (1824-95), from Perquimans Co., N.C., to Baltimore, Md., 1866; physician; issue: I-Randolph (1 above); II-Oliver Parry (1855-60); III-John Randolph (1856-60); IV-Nathan (1857-58); V-Edward R. Parry (1859-62); VI-Margaret Fitz Randolph (*b* and *d* 1863); VII-Julianna Randolph (1861-1928); VIII-John Randolph (*b* 1866; *m* Elizabeth Lewis Redd).
1-*m* Dec. 12, 1877, Rebecca Fayssoux Leiper, *b* Delaware Co., Pa., May 29, 1856; dau. of John Chew Leiper, of Chester, Pa.; issue (all *b* Baltimore, Md.): 1-Nathan, *b* Nov. 17, 1878; A.B., Johns Hopkins, '00; M.D., U.Md., 1901; A.M., St. John's Coll., 1912; 1st lt., Med. Corps, July 1916, then maj., served in Mexico and World War, 3 yrs. 5 mos.; *m* Oct. 5, 1904, Margaret Kable, dau. of J. Lewellyn Massey; 2-John Leiper, *b* Mar. 7, 1880; A.B., Haverford, '01; LL.B., U.Md., 1903; *m* June 27, 1906, Anna Stuart, dau. of William G. D. Tonge (issue: John Leiper, Jr.; Rebecca Fayssoux); 3-Fitz Randolph, *b* July 2, 1881; A. B., Haverford, '03; M.D., U.Md., 1906; *m* Oct. 1, 1913, Florence I. Reese; 4-Edwards Fayssoux, *b* Nov. 23, 1883; A.B., Haverford, '13; Phar. D., U.Md., 1907; *m* June 6, 1905, Emma W., dau. of Samuel M. Garrigues (issue: Randolph, II; Sally G.); 5-Mary Fayssoux, *b* July 7, 1885; *m* Sept. 9, 1911, J. Merriwether Shellman (issue: Josephine Keith; Randolph Winslow); 6-Jane Parry, *b* Nov. 7, 1886; A.B., Wellesley, '10; *m* Nov. 23, 1910, Herbert Fuller, son of Judson Carroll (issue: Herbert Fuller, Jr.); 7-Caleb, *b* July 1, 1889; A.B., Haverford, '11; A.M., 1912; *m* June 21, 1916, Lena Rebecca, dau. of Col. Robert J. W. Garey (issue: Caleb, Jr.; Robert Garey; Vashti Louise; Elizabeth Reed); 8-Eliza Leiper, *b* Feb. 10, 1891; *m* Oct. 23, 1915, Dr. John S. B., son of John Steven Brohawn Woolford (issue: Eliza Leiper; Helen Randolph); 9-George Leiper, *b* Mar. 4, 1893; A.B., St. John's, '12; Sc.B., Haverford, 1913; B.S., Johns Hopkins, 1916; 1st lt., 117th Engrs., 42d (Rainbow) Div., 2 yrs., served in France, participated in Argonne and Chateau Thierry; *m* May 5, 1917, Dorothy H., dau. of Dr. G. Betton Massey (issue: Fitz Randolph, II); 10-Oliver Parry, *b* Feb. 9, 1895; Sc.B., St. John's, '15; B.S., Haverford, 1916; B.S., Johns Hopkins, 1918; 2d lt., U.S.A. during World War; *m* July 19, 1919, Harriet A., dau. of Harrison Christian (issue: Nathan, II; Oliver Parry, Jr.); 11-Richard Randolph Parry, *b* May 8, 1897; St. John's Coll., 3 yrs.; 2d lt. M.G. Co., 1918-19; now 1st lt., U.S.A.; *m* Apr. 24, 1919, Anne, dau. of Foster William Sherlock; 12-Saint Clair Spruill (Apr. 13, 1899-Aug. 18, 1899); 13-Callender Fayssoux, *b* Dec. 12, 1901; A.B., St. John's, '22; M.F., Yale; *m* Dec. 14, 1927, Lucy Buchannan (issue: Lucy Buchannan).
1-A.B., Haverford, '71, A.M., 1874; M.D., U.Md., 1873; post-grad. work U. of Pa., 1873, Vienna, 1883; (LL.D., St. John's, 1909, U.Md., 1924). Prof. anatomy, 1891-1902, prof. surgery, 1902-20, now emeritus, U. of Md.; surgeon to Univ. Hosp. (see Who's Who in America). Formerly 1st lt. Med. R.C., U.S.A. Mem. Md. Hist. Soc. Republican. Residence: 1900 Mt. Royal Terrace, Baltimore, Md.

1-**McCULLOUGH, George Seymour,** *b* San Francisco, Calif., Apr. 9, 1892.
9-Richard **Seymour** (qv);
8-John (1641-1713), of Hartford, Conn.; *m* Mary Watson (John[9], of Hartford);
7-John (1666-1748), *m* 1693, Elizabeth Webster (*d* 1754; Robert[8]; Gov. John[9]);
6-Moses (1711-95), *m* 1738, Rachael Goodwin (*d* 1763; Nathaniel[7], *m* Sarah Easton);
5-Aaron (1749-1820), soldier in Am. Rev., was at Saratoga Springs at the surrender of Burgoyne; *m* 1775, Anna Phelps (1754-1823; Edward, Jr.[6], of Litchfield);
4-Israel (1784-1852), *m* 2d, 1824, Lucinda Pierce (1796-1874; William[5], *m* Lucinda Brintnall);
3-George Ruthven (1829-84), of Troy, N.Y.; *m* 1862, Elizabeth Hall Howland;
2-Elizabeth Townsend (2 below).
9-Henry **Howland** (qv);
8-Samuel, *m* Mary Merrihew;
7-Joshua, of Fall River; *m* Elizabeth Halloway; *m* 2d, Dorothy Lee;
6-Malichi, of Fall River; *m* Hope Dwella;
5-Consider (1752-1834), of Middleborough, Mass.; *m* Elizabeth Hull (Abraham[6], of N.J.);
4-Abraham (1789-1846), *m* 1826, Sally Margaret Townsend (1805-51; Henry[5], *m* Sally Rice);
3-Elizabeth Hall (1840-1915), *m* George Ruthven **Seymour** (3 above).
2-Ernest **McCullough** (*b* 1867), in engineering practice since 1887, in N.Y. City, since 1923; editor and author; maj. engrs. O.R.C., promoted lt. col. C.W.S. in World War; wounded nr. Cambrai, Nov. 1917; chief engr. Am. Red Cross, France, June-Oct. 1917; served as chief gas officer, 1st Corps; chief gas officer, Army Arty., 1st Army; asst. chief and later chief, arty. sect. C.W.S.; lt. col. C.W.S., O.R.C. (see Who's Who in America); *m* 1891, Elizabeth Townsend Seymour (1866-1919); *m* 2d, 1919, Therese Claquin; issue (1st marriage): I-George Seymour (1 above); II-Caroline McBlain (*b* 1897; *m* Col. Paul C. Galleher); III-Elizabeth Howland (1901-02); IV-James David (*b* 1904; *m* Katharine Tuttle).
1-*m* Sept. 1, 1921, Olivia Sophia Nelson, *b* Stillwater, Minn., Jan. 9, 1892; dau. of Hon. John G. Nelson, of Stillwater.
1-Northwestern U., 3 yrs., 1913 (Delta U.). Railroad civil engr., 1912-16. Capt. U.S.A. Episcopalian. Address: C/o Adjutant General's Office, Washington, D.C.

BOSTON

Arms: *Vert, a lion rampant argent, crowned or.*
Crest: *A horse's head in armour proper.*

1–**BOSTON, L(eonard) Napoleon,** *b* Town Hill, Pa., Mar. 18, 1872.
8–William **Jayne** (*b* 1618), from Eng. to Setauket, L.I., 1640; *m* 1675, Anna Briggs:
7–William, II (1678-1730); *m* 1710, Elizabeth Woodhill;
6–William, III (1712-98), signed Pledge of Loyalty, 1777; *m* 1733, Tabitha Horton (1713-1808); they had 5 sons in Am. Rev.: William, Capt. Timothy, Isaac, John and David;
5–Isaac (1746-1806), pvt., Capt. Timothy Jayne's (his brother) Co., Am. Rev.; *m* 1769, Ann Lauterman (1744-1809);
4–Sarah (1778-1864), *m* 1798, George **Labar** (1771-1852);
3–Margaret (1803-94); *m* 1818, Rev. Septimus **Bacon** (1794-1861), pvt. War 1812;
2–Bethiah (1833-1910), *m* 1858, Alfred Harvey **Boston** (1835-1902); farmer; (for issue see Vol. III, p. 78).
1–*m* Oct. 28, 1905, Caroline Crandall, *b* Westerly, R.I., July 21, 1872; issue: 1–Barbara (qv for Crandall lineage).
1–M.D., Medico-Chirurg. Coll., 1896; hon. A.M., Ursinus Coll., 1902 (Phi Rho Sigma). Prof. physical diagnosis, U. of Pa.; prof. medicine, Woman's Med. Coll. of Pa. Author (see Who's Who in America). Mem. S.A.R. (chapter pres.), S.W. 1812, Eilenberger-Bacon Geneal. Soc. Clubs: University, Rotary. Residence: 2423 S. 21st St., Phila., Pa.

1–**BOSTON, Barbara Crandall,** *b* Phila., Pa., Aug. 13, 1906.
10–Elder John **Crandall** (*d* 1676), from Eng., to Boston, 1634/35; moved to Westerly, R.I.;
9–Rev. Joseph, *m* Deborah Burdick;
8–Joseph, *m* Anne Langworthy;
7–Joseph (1716-92), of Westerly, R.I.; served Am. Rev.; town clk., Westerly, 1760-90; *m* 1738, Elizabeth Crandall;
6–Phineas (*b* 1743), *m* Ruth Rogers;
5–Ezekiel (1784-1855), *m* 1808, Susan Wells;
4–Ezekiel Rogers (1820-1915), *m* 1843, Nancy Celestia Burdick;
3–Ira Burdick (*b* 1846), *m* 1870, Sardinia E. Hall;
2–Caroline (*b* 1872), *m* 1905, L. Napoleon **Boston** (qv).
1–A.B., Ursinus Coll., '27. Residence: 2423 S. 21st St., Phila., Pa.

1–**BUCHANAN, Thomas Gittings,** *b* Baltimore, Md., Feb. 14, 1877.
5–Dr. George **Buchanan** (1698-1750; son of Mungo [*d* 1710], of Hiltoun and Auchintorlie, Scotland, *m* 1687, Anna Barclay); came from Scotland, settled at Baltimore, Md., 1723; *m* Eleanor Rogers (1705-58; Nicholas[6]);
4–William (1748-1824), of Baltimore; *m* 2d, Hepzibah (Brown) Perine;
3–Charles Adams (1808-91), of Baltimore; *m* Ann Lux Cockey (1803-83);
2–James Hollis (2 below).
4–John Sterrett **Gittings**:
3–Lambert (1806-87), *m* 1827, Henrietta Tenant (1810-39; Thomas[4]);
2–Henrietta (1838-1918), *m* 1864, James Hollis **Buchanan** (1834-1911), lawyer, Baltimore, Md.; issue: I–Ann S. (*b* 1865; *m* Oswald T. Shreve, *d*); II–Henrietta (1867-1918; *m* George L. Gale, *d*); III–Mary (*b* 1868; *m* J. Taylor Albert); IV–Harriet G. (1871-1908); V–Louisa (*b* 1873; *m* Eugene G. de Bullet); VI–Thomas Gittings (1 above); VII–Eliza S. (1878-1921; *m* William S. Thomas).
1–*m* Nov. 16, 1911, Ellen Gilmor, *b* Baltimore, Md., May 7, 1883; dau. of Robert Gilmor, *m* Josephine Albert; issue: 1–Thomas Gittings, Jr., *b* Baltimore, Mar. 14, 1919.
1–Insurance business. Served in Spanish War. Mem. Md. Hist. Soc. Residence: Charles St. Av., Towson P.O., Baltimore Co., Md.

1–**GREEN, Mary Wolcott,** *b* Athens, Pa., Dec. 14, 1872.
5–Capt. John **Green** (1736-96), of Phila. and Bristol, Pa.; capt. Pa. Navy, 1776; capt. Cont. Navy, 1778; captured 1779; comd. the "Duc du Lausan," 20 guns; took first Am. flag to China; *m* 1765, Alice Kollock (1743-1832; Jacob[6], of Lewes, Del.);
4–John (1766-1831), Phila.; *m* 1792, Hester Craig (1765-1818; Capt. James[5], of Phila.);
3–John Sims (1794-1872), Laporte, Pa.; War 1812; *m* 1821, Elizabeth Henley (1804-72; William[4], of Ga.);
2–Walter Kerr (2 below).
8–Henry **Wolcott** (qv);
7–George (*d* 1657), *m* Elizabeth Treat;
6–George (1652-1726), *m* Elizabeth Curtis;
5–Josiah (1713-84), *m* 1740, Lucy (White) French;
4–Silas (1755-1834), pvt. Am. Rev.; *m* Margaret Rowan (1756-1844);
3–Elijah (1781-1840), of Litchfield, Pa.; *m* 1802, Elizabeth Park (1786-1872);
2–Marion (1831-1917), *m* 1857, Walter Kerr **Green** (1830-1911), Staten Island, N.Y.; issue: I–Harry Clinton (*b* 1858; *m* Elizabeth Hayward); II–Craig Walter (*b* 1866; *m* Ella O'Haughey); III–Marion Euphemia (*b* 1868); IV–Mary W. (1 above); V–Virginia Louisa (*b* 1880; *m* Elmer Freese).
1–Grad. Chemist, Cooper Institute, New York; A.B., Syracuse U. '95 (Litt.D., 1914). Retired school teacher, City of New York; now postmaster, Englewood, Fla. Mem. Soc. of Descs. of Henry Wolcott (sec.), D.A.R., U.S.D. 1812, I.A.G., etc. Residence: Englewood, Fla.

DR. R. N. MAYFIELD

1–**MAYFIELD, Reuben Newton,** *b* nr. Bedford, Ind., June 13, 1859.
5–James (Nevil) **Neville** (*b* Prince William, now Fauquier, Co., Va., 1741), served Am. Rev.; removed to Lincoln Co., Ky., 1779; *m* Sarah–;
4–Joyce (*d* 1861, aet. 93), *m* 1787, Jeremiah **Boone** (1760-1832), served with his cousin, Daniel Boone, and Gen. George R. Clarke at the ending of the northwest Indian war; moved to Lawrence Co., Ind., 1817 (see Vol. III, p. 326);

3–Charlotte (1794-1883), *m* Reuben **Mayfield** (1792-1861); see Vol. III, p. 326;
2–Alexander Campbell (1831-85), farmer; *m* 1854, Winnie Tate Short (1836-1919); for issue see Vol. II, p. 122.
1–*m* Feb. 27, 1908, Patti Ayres (Eng., June 8, 1876-Jan. 14, 1921); concert singer; dau. of John Ayres, from Eng., 1884, *m* Alice Boyd O'Neil (desc. Earl of Tyrone).
1–M.D., L.I. Coll. Hosp., 1880, and Rush Med. Coll., Chicago, 1883. Physician and surgeon; surgeon, U.P. Ry., 1886-91; pres. Colo. State Bd. of Med. Examiners, 1891-97. Served 2d lt. to maj., surgeon, Colo. N.G., 1886-1912. Mem. I.A.G. Address: 705 1st Av., Seattle, Wash.

1–**McCLINTIC, Mary Ethel Knight (Mrs. George W.),** *b* Charleston, W.Va., Jan. 21, 1870.
8–Philip **Knight** (*d* 1665), settled at Charletown, Mass., ante 1637; *m* Margerie–;
7–Philip (1645-96), Topsfield, Mass.; *m* Margerie, or Margaret–;
6–Benjamin (1692-1781), Middletown, Mass.; *m* 1719, Ruth Fuller (1697-1771);
5–Enos (1729-1804), New Ipswich, N.H.; minute man at Lexington Alarm; *m* 1750, Lois (Gould) Hawke (1726-88);
4–Lt. Ebenezer (1751-1815), Hancock, N.H.; *m* 1774, Margaret Peabody (1753-1813);
3–Asa (1791-1871), New London, N.H.; *m* 1817, Melinda Adams (1790-1868);
2–Edward Boardman (2 below).
5–Enoch **White** (probably son of Isaac, of Smithfield, R.I.); of Smithfield, R.I., and Newport, N.H.; *m* 1755, Lydia Sprague (*b* 1726);
4–Enoch (1771-1853), *m* Betsy Tandy (1781-1867);
3–Nathan (1800-75), *m* Diploma Wheeler (1802-77).
2–Edward Boardman **Knight** (1834-97), lawyer; *m* 1864, Hannah Elizabeth White (1833-78); *m* 2d, 1882, Mary Elizabeth White (1858-1916); issue (1st marriage): I–Edward Wallace (*b* 1866; *m* Mary Catherine Dana); II–Harold Warren (1868-1915; *m* Martha Morton Hogeman, qv); III–Mary Ethel (1 above).
1–*m* Oct. 17, 1907, George Warwick McClintic, *b* Mill Point, W.Va., Jan. 14, 1866; son of William Hunter McClintic, of Pocahontas Co., W.Va.; issue: 1–Elizabeth Knight, *b* Charleston, W.Va., Feb. 19, 1913.
1–Attended Buchtel Coll. (now Akron U.), (Delta Gamma). Mem. I.A.G., N.E.H.G.S., Ipswich (Mass.) Hist. Soc. Presbyterian. Republican. Residence: 1598 Kanawha St., Charleston, W.Va.

1–**McLENDON, Martha Virginia,** *b* Kansas City, Mo., Sept. 18, 1901.
7–Thomas **Waring** (ante 1680-1754), from Eng., 1680, settled in Essex Co., Va.; burgess, 1736; justice and vestryman for St. Anne's Parish; *m* Elizabeth Gouldman;
6–Thomas (*b* 1719), of Va.; *m* Betty Payne;
5–Robert Payne, Am. Rev.; *m* Ann Lowry;
4–William Lowry (1783-1841), capt. War 1812; *m* Mary Banks (*d* 1841);
3–Robert Payne (ca. 1813-ca. 1890), dea. Ephesus Baptist Ch., Dunnsville, Va., from his 21st birthday until death; *m* Martha Ann Campbell;
2–Harriet Susan (*b* 1860), *m* 1886, John Bradford **McLendon** (*b* 1856), wholesale grocer; issue: I–James Waring (*b* 1887); II–Elizabeth Campbell (1889-1900); III–Ellen Eugenia (*b* 1892; *m* John Willard Anderson); IV–Martha Virginia (1 above).
1–LL.B., Kansas City School of Law, 1924 (Kappa Beta Pi); Ph.B., U. of Chicago, 1926, J.D., 1927; attended U.Mo., 1919,20. Licensed to practice law, 1923; began active practice of law in office of the late Hon. Oliver H. Dean, 1927; continued the practice of law alone since decease of Mr. Dean, 1928; served as divorce proctor 2 terms, 1929. Dir. Citizens' League of Kansas City, Mo.; mem. I.A.G. Baptist. Democrat. Clubs: Milburn Golf and Country, Rockhill Tennis, Woman's City, Women's Chamber of Commerce, Business and Professional Women's, Lincolnshire Golf and Country. Residence: 3440 College Av., Kansas City, Mo.

1–**MENGE, Jessica Belle Crofoot (Mrs. Edward John von Komorowski),** *b* Fond du Lac, Wis.
9–Joseph **Crofoot** (*d* 1678, in Northampton, Mass.), from Eng.; was in "The Falls Fight," in King Philip's War;
8–Joseph, *m* 1658, Mary Hillier;
7–Joseph (*b* 1660), *m* 1686, Margaret– (*d* 1733);
6–Ephraim (*b* 1704), of Weathersfield, Conn.; *m* Mary Williams, a widow (*d* 1795);
5–Elisha (1754-1813), of Berlin, Conn.; *m* Rachel Higby (*d* 1813);
4–Judge Isaac (1784-1868), Fond du Lac, Wis.; *m* 1st, Sally– (1783-1814);
3–Lewis (1804-73), *m* Levina Wilcox (*d* 1883);
2–Isaac Daniel (1836-95), of Turin, Lewis Co., N.Y., and Fond du Lac, Wis.; farmer; *m* 1871, Cornelia Louisa Ruth (*b* 1852); issue: I–Allie Ruth (*m* Dr. C. D. Eshleman); II–Jessica Belle (1 above); III–Samuel Level; IV–Lt. Frank Lewis (1882-1918).
1–*m* Sept. 16, 1903, Dr. Edward John von Komorowski Menge, *b* Fond du Lac, June 25, 1882; B.A., U. of Dallas, '14, M.A., 1915, Ph.D., 1916, M.Sc., 1917; (Sc.D., De Paul U., 1926); dir. of dept. of animal biology, Marquette U. (see Who's Who in America); son of Theodore Edward von Komorowski Menge, *m* Josephine Wurzburger.
1–Special student, U. of Ariz. and Marquette U. (Sigma Alpha Iota). Episcopalian. Address: Marquette University, Milwaukee, Wis.

1–**MERONEY, Hubert Harold,** *b* Rockwood, Tenn., July 31, 1882.
6–Philip De Lancey (O'Meroney, O'Maroney, O'Moroney) **Meroney** (*b* bet. 1730-34-*d* 1830), from Ireland, settled in Charleston, S.C.; capt. in Am. Rev.; *m* 1st, 1768, Sarah Nelson (*d* 1776);
5–Philip De Lancey (1775-1869), of Md.; *m* 1799, Martha Davis;
4–Philip Nelson (1800-70), of S.C.; *m* 1819, Elizabeth Ragon (*b* 1799);
3–William Denton (*b* 1823), served in C.S.A.; *m* 1844, Mary Jane Lane (1824-1905);
2–Samuel Nelson (*b* 1846), soldier in Federal army; coal and iron business; *m* 1st ca. 1872, Matilda Adams (1854-79); *m* 2d, 1880, Mattie Bell Scaggs (*b* 1864); issue (1st marriage): I–Thomas Jefferson (*b* 1874; *m* Nellie Lee); issue (2d marriage): I–Hubert H. (1 above); II–Walter H. (*b* 1884); III–Fannie D. (*b* 1888; *m* Paul Plaisir); IV–Clarence E. (*b* 1891; *m* Lucile Royce).
1–*m* Aug. 9, 1908, Mary E. Faulkner, *b* Harrison, Tenn., Apr. 22, 1885; dau. of John E. Faulkner; issue: 1–Lucile Mae, *b* Hixson, Tenn., May 21, 1910; 2–Addie Bell, *b* Chattanooga, Tenn., Nov. 12, 1911; 3–Mary Elizabeth, *b* Chattanooga, Dec. 15, 1915; 4–Carrie Evelyn, *b* Chattanooga, July 13, 1918.
1–B.L., Knoxville Coll. of Law, 1924. With U.S. Gov. 19 yrs.; supt. of Post Office, 1922. Served in Spanish-Am. War and Philippine Insurrection, July 11, 1898-Sept. 24, 1902. Mem. U.S.W.V., V.F.W. Mason (32°), K.P. Methodist. Republican. Club: Chattanooga Rod and Gun. Residence: 901 Meroney St., Chattanooga, Tenn.

1–**PARSONS, Ella,** *b* in Burlington Co., N.J., Nov. 8, 1866.
8–John **Parsons** (*b* in Somersetshire, Eng., ca. 1630), Quaker; *m* Florence– (both witnessed a marriage at The Friends Meeting House, Burlington, N.J., Apr. 8, 1686);
7–Thomas (ca. 1663-1721), from Eng.; settled at Phila.; he and his brother John are said to have been the first Englishmen to own and operate a mill in Phila., located on the Delaware River at Cedar St.; in partnership with Cadwalader Lewis, purchased a mill and 50 acres of land at Frankford on the Tacony Creek, Phila. Co., 1690; owned 800 acres on Dutch Creek, Kent Co., Del., and 500 acres in Salem Co., N.J.; subsequently be became resident on a grant of land which he possessed in Bucks Co.; settled at Frankford, Phila. Co., and successfully conducted a mill, about 1704-1720; *m* 1st, 1685, Jean (Jane) Culling (John[8], of Eng.);
6–Thomas (*b* 1688), removed to Va.;
5–Abraham (bap. 1720/21-1768), farmer, Lower Duplin Tp., Phila. Co.; *m* Joanna Ayres (*d* 1779; James[6], of Lower Duplin Tp., *m* Margaret–);
4–Isaac (1748-1818), removed from Bristol Tp.,

PARSONS

Arms: Azure, a chevron ermine, between three herons proper.

Crest: A dove, wings addorsed holding in the beak an olive branch vert.

Bucks Co., to Falls Tp., Bucks Co.; Episcopalian; *m* 2d, ca. 1791, Elizabeth Brodnax;
3–Isaac (1794-1857), of Falls Tp.; *m* 1821, Lydia Ann Anderson;
2–Ellwood (2 below).
8–John **Brodnax** (bap. 1608-1657), from Eng.; settled in York Co., Va.; he was the goldsmith (or banker) of Jamestown; *m* Dorothy–;
7–Robert (bap. 1641-1688), *m* Ann–;
6–John (ca. 1664-66-1719), removed to Va., 1694; goldsmith of Williamsburg, Va.; *m* ca. 1698, Mary Skerme (William[7], of Henrico Co., *m* Mary–);
5–Robert (*b* ca. 1700), of Pa.; *m* 1734, Christiana Keen, of Pa.;
4–Elizabeth (1755-1827), *m* Isaac **Parsons** (4 above).
9–Andries Jochemsen (*b* ca. 1610-20), believed to have been of the Frisian family in Holland, and a native of the place called Albada; at New Amsterdam 1650, when, with Hilegond

ELLWOOD PARSONS (b Falls Tp., Bucks Co., Pa., Apr. 5, 1822-d Oct. 13, 1891), large landowner, lumberman and banker; director First Nat. Bank of Trenton from 1868, and shortly before his death was unanimously elected president; dir. Trenton City Bridge Co. and of Bucks County Contributorship for Insuring Homes and Other Buildings from Loss by Fire, etc.

Megapolensis, he was a sponsor for Adriaen, son of Thomas Fredricksz, in the Dutch Reformed Ch. there; *m* Seletje, or Celetie Arens;
8–Jochem (Andries) **Anderson** (*b* ca. 1630-40), founder of Elizabethtown, N.J.;
7–Enoch (ca. 1663-1741), founder of Trenton, N.J., and settled nr. Assumpink Creek; mem. Grand Jury, 1699; trustee of two acres for a meeting house, the site of the Presbyn. Ch. at Ewing, N.J., 1709; *m* Tryntie Opdyck (g.dau. of Jansen Op Dyke, of Newtown);
6–Jeremiah (ca. 1705-1790), *m* Sarah Hoff;
5–Josiah, *m* his cousin, Sarah Anderson (Eliakim[6] [ca. 1702-1781 or 82], *m* 1743, Rebecca Ely; Enoch[7], above);
4–Joseph, *m* Sarah Norton;
3–Lydia Ann (1801-1901), *m* Isaac **Parsons** (3 above);
2–Ellwood (1822-91), see portrait and biography; *m* 1851, Mercy Ann Taylor (1824-90; William[3], *m* Mary, dau. of William Crozer, *m* Mercy–); issue: I–William Taylor (1852-75); II–Annie Crozer (1853-95; *m* 1891, Edward C. Williamson); III–Mary Taylor (1856-1909); IV–Lydia Anderson (1858-1914; *m* 1891, Henry W. Comfort); V–George Taylor (1861-69); VI–Rose (*b* and *d* 1864); VII–Ella (1 above).
1–Mem. Pa. Soc. of Colonial Dames of America, Scions of Colonial Cavaliers (Order of Palatine and Lady of the Golden Horseshoe), Swedish Colonial Soc., Geneal. Soc. of Pa. Residence: Philadelphia, Pa.

1–**PATTON, Sarah Ellen Glasgow (Mrs. William A.),** *b* Peoria Co., Ill., Aug. 1, 1855.
4–Robert **Glasgow** (1749-1834), of Scotch ancestry, came from North Ireland with his brothers Joseph and Arthur, 1765, settled in Nottingham Co., Va.; moved to Rockbridge Co., Va., 1769; soldier in Am. Rev.; moved to Adams Co., O., 1806; *m* Rosannah Uster;
3–Robert Uster (1791-1861), *m* 1809, Rosanna Finley (1789-1865; Robert[4], *m* Martha, dau. of Samuel Steele; William[5], moved from Oxford, Pa., to Staunton, Va.);
2–Stewart (2 below).
5–Samuel **Wiley** (*b* Cecil Co., Md., 1757), of Scotch ancestry, whose father came from North Ireland; settled with his father in Cumberland Co., Pa., 1772; served in Am. Rev.; removed to Miami Co., O., 1812;
4–John, of Hagerstown, Md.; maj. War 1812;
3–Samuel (1810-77), *m* 1832, Sarah McCullough;
2–Haddassah Jane (2 below).
6–Robert **Carruthers,** of Va.;
5–Ester, of Sidney, O.; *m* Henry **McClung,** of Va.;
4–Ester (1778-1850), *m* John **McCullough** (1777-1840);
3–Sarah (1809-88), of Adams Co., O.; *m* Samuel **Wiley** (3 above);
2–Haddassah Jane (1833-93), of Miami Co., O.; *m* 1854, as his 2d wife, Stewart **Glasgow** (1823-1904), of Adams Co., O.; issue: I–Sarah Ellen (1 above); II–Rosa Bell (1856-1917; *m* John Turner Patton, 1854-1928); III–Samuel Finley (*b* 1858; *m* Harriet Gardner); IV–William Ellsworth (1860-1923; *m* Edith McCullough, 1867-1923); V–John Wiley (*b* 1865; *m* Fannie Davis; *m* 2d, Mrs. Olive Shultz); VI–Harry J. (1872-1922; *m* Jennie Bates).
1–*m* Jan. 1, 1874, William Andrew Patton (Jan. 22, 1852-Dec. 9, 1915); son of Thomas Elder Patton (1822-1902; Thomas[3], *m* 1809, Jane Glasgow, *b* 1785; John[4], of Scotch descent, pvt. Am. Rev., *m* Martha Sharpe), *m* 1844, Martha Ann Finley (1823-1906); issue (all *b* Peoria Co., Ill.): 1–Maud Patton, *b* Nov. 5, 1874; *m* Sept. 23, 1897, Arlo Richard (issue: William Gail; Berneice); 2–Grace, *b* Jan. 7, 1877; *m* Oct. 27, 1909, Oliver Joseph, son of Charles Howard, of Fresno, Calif. (issue: Charles Patton; Oliver Joseph); 3–Chester Andrew, *b* Jan. 7, 1883; *m* June 14, 1911, Nellie, dau. of Claudius Banks (issue: Claudius Banks; Jean); 4–Jessie (June 15, 1888-*d* 1929), *m* July 19, 1913, Robert N., son of Alexander Peterson, of Chicago, Ill. (issue: Sarah Louise).
1–Mem. D.A.R. Presbyterian. Republican. Summer place: Alder Springs, Calif. Residence: 3263 Huntington Av., Fresno, Calif.

1–**PURCELL, Margaret,** *b* Greenville, Miss., Dec. 12, 1888.
4–Charles **Purcell** (*b* 1790), from Ireland, 1813 or 14, settled at Richmond, Va.; *m* Sarah Elizabeth Brouggy (1794-1856);
3–Charles William (1818-87), of Richmond; *m* Margaret Adams Freeman (1825-75);
2–Samuel Harwood (2 below).

6–William **Garrett**, Louisa Co., Va.;
5–Henry, went to Ky., 1810;
4–Alexander (1778-1860), *m* Evalina Bolling;
3–John Bolling (1809-55), *m* Nannie Harrison;
2–Elizabeth Ashton (2 below).
9–Col. Robert **Bolling** (qv);
8–Col. John (1676-1729), *m* Mary Kennon (Richard[9]);
7–Maj. John (1700-57), burgess nearly 30 yrs.; *m* 2d, Elizabeth Blair (Dr. Archibald[8]);
6–John;
5–John;
4–Evalina (1789-1862), *m* Alexander **Garrett** (4 above).
9–Benjamin **Harrison** (qv);
8–Benjamin (1645-1712), of "Wakefield-Surrey"; burgess, commr. to Eng., 1702; councillor; *m* Hannah (Churchill?), (1654-99);
7–Benjamin (1673-1710), of "Berkeley," atty. gen. and treas. of Va.; speaker House of Burgesses; *m* Elizabeth Burwell (1677-1734; Lewis[8]; Lewis[9]);
6–Col. Benjamin (1693-1745), sheriff Charles City Co., Va.; burgess; *m* Anne Carter (Robert[7]); among their sons was Benjamin, a "signer," and Gen. Charles;
5–Carter Henry (1726-99), of Clifton, Cumberland Co., Va.; capt., 1755-56; Ho. of Delegates; chmn. Com. Safety Cumberland Co., drafted first resolutions adopted in any of the Colonies demanding freedom of Colonies from British control, Apr. 23, 1776; *m* Susanna Randolph (Col. Isham[6]);
4–Randolph (1769-1839), of "Clifton"; *m* his cousin, Mary Randolph (Thomas Isham[5]);
3–Nannie (1819-92), *m* John B. **Garrett** (3 above);
2–Elizabeth Ashton (1853-1922), *m* 1882, Samuel Harwood **Purcell** (1851-1926), grad. V.M.I.; civil engr. and ry. supt., Richmond, Va.; issue: I–John Bolling (*b* 1883; *m* Helena Gertrude Keister); II–Charles William (1885-1927; *m* Margaret McComas); III–Samuel (1887-90); IV–Margaret (1 above); and V–Nannie (twins; 1888-92); VI–McDaniel (*b* 1892; *m* Dorothy Hockaday); VII–Evelyn Garrett (*b* 1894; *m* Staige Davis); VIII–Philip Sutton (*b* 1896).
1–Teacher 9 yrs. in grade schools in Va. Mem. U.D.C., I.A.G. (life), A.P.V.A. Episcopalian. Democrat. Residence: "Clifton," Greenwood, Va.

1–**RALPH, Elizabeth Spotswood Dodge (Mrs. Stuart H.)**, *b* Bolivar, Miss., July 16, 1897.
11–Gen. Robert **Lewis** (qv);
10–John (*b* 1635), "Warner Hall," *m* Isabella Warner;
9–Col. John (1669-1725), mem. Royal Council; co. lt.; judge Supreme Ct.; *m* his cousin, Elizabeth Warner (Augustine[10], qv);
8–Robert, of "Belvoir," Albemarle Co., Va.; *m* Jane Meriwether;
7–Col. Fielding (1725-81), of "Kenmore," Fredericksburg, Va.; *m* 2d, 1750, Betty Washington (*b* 1733; Augustine[8]);
6–Gen. Fielding, *m* Nancy Ann Alexander;
5–Elizabeth A., *m* Alexander Eliot **Spotswood** (1769-1851); see Vol. III, p. 388;
4–Elizabeth Washington (1796-1873), *m* Rev. Jerial **Dodge** (1788-1843); see Vol. III, p. 388;
3–Jerial (1821-91), plow mfr., Louisville, Ky.; *m* 1843, Mary E. Goodall (Peter C.[4], atty., *m* Adaline B., dau. of Alexander E. Spotswood, 5 above);
2–Dr. John Lewis (1859-1904), physician; *m* 1892, Frances Richardson (1872-1902); see Vol. III, p. 388 for issue.
1–*m* Feb. 16, 1918, Stuart Harrison Ralph, *b* Oil City, Pa., May 27, 1893; son William Bates Ralph, of Oil City; issue: 1–Elizabeth Spotswood Dodge, *b* Memphis, Tenn., June 19, 1919; 2–Virginia Bates Washington, *b* Cambridge, Mass., Apr. 29, 1921.
1–Ed. Conservatory of Music, Cincinnati, O. Mem. Magna Charta Dames, D.A.R., N.E.H.-G.S., F.F.V. Summer place: Falmouth Heights, Mass. Residence: 59 Stultz Rd., Belmont, Mass.

1–**RANNEY, Clifford Horace**, *b* Hillsdale, Mich., Sept. 4, 1888.
9–Thomas **Ranney** (qv);
8–Thomas (1660-1726), *m* 1691, Rebecca Willett;
7–George (1695-1725), *m* Mary Hale (*d* 1749);
6–George (1723-1804), *m* 1745, Hanna Sage (1724-97);

ACHSAH (SEARS) RANNEY (1789-1869).

5–George (1746-1822), *m* 1771, Esther Hall (1751-1807);
4–George (1789-1842), *m* 1811, Achsah Sears (see portrait);
3–Alonzo Franklin (1812-1901), *m* 1st, 1837, Damaris A. Peck (1815-47; Horace[4], *m* Sebe Chapman);
2–Horace Peck (2 below).
11–William **Brewster** (qv);
10–Patience (ca. 1600-1634), *m* Gov. Thomas **Prence** (qv);
9–Mercy (1631-1711), *m* 1649/50, Maj. John **Freeman** (1621-1719; Edmund[10], qv);
8–Thomas (1653-1715), selectman, clk., coroner; *m* 1673, Rebecca Sparrow (1655-1740; John[9]);
7–Mercy (1674-1747), *m* 1693, Paul **Sears** (1669-1739/40; Paul[8]; Richard[9], from Eng., first appears on tax list, Plymouth, Mass., 1633);
6–Daniel (*b* 1710), *m* 1736, Mercy Snow;
5–Paul (1750-1808), sea capt.; corpl. in Am. Rev.; *m* 1782, Elenor Smith;
4–Achsah (1789-1869), *m* 1811, George **Ranney** (4 above).
7–Philip **Short** (1679-1763), from Eng., settled at Rehoboth, Mass.; *m* Joanna– (1683-1756);
6–Philip (1714-1805), *m* Lydia– (1725-98);
5–Daniel (*b* 1741); soldier in Am. Rev.; *m* 1764, Hopestill Wheeler (*b* 1746);
4–Daniel (1766-1822), *m* 1788, Ruth Reed;
3–Shobal (1803-69), *m* 2d, Mahetabel Ann Judd;
2–Harriet Newell (1845-93), *m* 1871, Horace Peck **Ranney** (*b* 1840), farmer of Hillsdale, Mich.; issue: I–Phylana Bell (*b* 1871; *m* Albert Kennan; missionary in India, 1899-1917); II–Josephine (*b* 1873; artist); III–Hattie Minerva (*b* 1875; *m* Will C. Osius); IV–May Elizabeth (*b* 1883); V–Clifford Horace (1 above).
1–*m* 1914, Bess Kempf; issue: 1–Beth Louise, *b* June 11, 1915.
1–Mgr. J. S. Bache & Co., brokers. Address: 137 Penobscot Bldg., Detroit, Mich.

1–**READ, J(ay) Marion**, *b* Helena, Mont., Apr. 14, 1889.
6–John **Read** (*d* 1765), from Eng. ante 1730; settled at Culpeper, Va.; *m* Winifred Favour (Theophilus[7]);
5–Hankerson, capt. Culpeper Co. militia, 1776; *m* Mary Slaughter;
4–Francis Slaughter (*b* Culpeper, 1773-*d* Ky., 1852), of Danville, Ky.; *m* 1804, Hannah McKinley;
3–Alexander Pope (1808-82), St. Joseph, Mo.; served in C.S.A.; *m* 1831, Harriet Perrin;
2–John McKinley (2 below).
6–James **Lane** (1718-90), of Loudoun Co., Va.; *m* Lydia Hardage (1723-93);
5–Lydia (1751-1804), *m* 1775, Temple **Smith** (*b* 1745);
4–Jane (1779-1857), *m* 1801, Achilles **Perrin** (1778-1868);

3–Harriet (*b* 1809), *m* 1831, Alexander Pope **Read** (3 above).
9–John **Baldwin** (qv);
8–Ens. Thomas (1672-1747); *m* Sarah–;
7–Jacob (*b* 1704);
6–Isaac, of Jaffrey, N.H.; *m* Elizabeth Shaddock;
5–Isaac, *m* at Pomfret, Chautauqua Co., N.Y., 1785, Parthena Harris;
4–Levi, *m* Eliza Ann Putnam;
3–Oliver Taylor (*b* 1834), Dunkirk, N.Y.; *m* 1858, Nancy Jane Wright;
2–Kate Barstow (*b* 1862), *m* 1888, John McKinley **Read** (1856-1929), of Helena, Mont.; physician; issue: I–J. Marion (1 above); II–Harriet Baldwin (1892-1930; *m* George Wesley Middleton).
1–*m* Aug. 18, 1917, Louise Mae Schussler, *b* San Diego, Calif., May 30, 1889; dau. of John Schussler, of Chula Vista, Calif.; issue: 1–John Marion, *b* San Francisco, Calif., June 13, 1918; 2–Jane, *b* San Francisco, Nov. 17, 1919.
1–B.S., U.Calif., '12 (Pi Kappa Alpha, Nu Sigma Nu, Sigma Xi), M.S., 1913, M.D., Stanford Med. School, 1915. Interne, St. Luke's Hosp., San Francisco, 1915-16; asso. clinical prof. of medicine, Stanford U. Med. School, since 1919. First lt., M.R.C., 1918, capt. Med. Corps U.S.A. 1918-19. Mem. S.A.R., Reade Soc. Mason. Residence: 1461 17th Av., San Francisco, Calif.

1–**REINHARDT, David Jones,** *b* Norristown, Pa., Nov. 6, 1867.
5–Ulric **Reinhardt,** from Germany, 1733, settled in Chester Co., Pa.;
4–John;
3–Isaac (*b* Marietta, Pa., 1785-*d* 1850), *m* Lydia Ludwick;
2–William Dell (2 below).
6–Benjamin **Hawley** (1703-82; son of Thomas, *m* Frances Malin, of Eng.); came from Eng., settled in Chester Co., Pa., 1722; *m* 1st, Dinah Gabiter;
5–Benjamin (1730-1815), *m* 1756, Mary Johnson;
4–Joseph (1760-1856), *m* 1798, Rebecca Meredith;
3–Jesse (1806-87), of Chester Co.; *m* his first cousin, 1829, Esther Meredith;
2–Rebecca (2 below).
7–Simon **Meredith** (*d* 1745), from Eng., settled in Chester Co., Pa., 1708;
6–John (*b* 1699), *m* Grace Williams;
5–Simon, *m* Dinah Pugh;
4–Rebecca (1766-1851), *m* Joseph **Hawley** (4 above).
7–Benjamin **Mendenhall,** Quaker, from Village of Mildenhall, Eng., to Concord, Pa., ca. 1684, settled on a tract of land deeded to him by William Penn, which is still owned by a member of the family; *m* 1689, Ann Pennell;
6–Robert (*b* 1713), of Pa.; *m* 1st, 1734, Phoebe Taylor;
5–Stephen, of Pa.; *m* Margaret Farlow;
4–Ann (1776-1871), *m* John **Meredith;**
3–Esther (1807-1900), *m* her first cousin, Jesse **Hawley** (3 above);
2–Rebecca (1841-1915), of Pughtown, Pa.; *m* 1867, William Dell **Reinhardt** (1830-80), of Marietta, Pa.; U. of Pa., 1852; physician; issue: I–David Jones (1 above); II–Jesse Hawley (*b* 1869); III–Mary B. (*b* 1870); IV–Esther Meredith (*b* 1872); V–Lydia Ludwig (*b* 1875); VI–Elizabeth C. (*b* 1877).
1–*m* June 30, 1896, Anna Margaret Hewes, *b* Salem, N.J., Jan. 2, 1867; mem. I.A.G.; dau. of Thomas Hewes, *m* Elizabeth Andrews Miller; issue (all *b* Wilmington, Del.): 1–Rebecca, *b* Nov. 14, 1897; B.A., Bryn Mawr, '19; *m* Dec. 28, 1923, Maurice Langhorne, son of George Peyton Craighill, Lynchburg, Va. (issue: Maurice L., Jr., *b* July 28, 1925; Margaret Hewes, *b* Apr. 28, 1930); 2–Louise, *b* Oct. 21, 1899; B.A., Bryn Mawr, '21; *m* May 30, 1930, Charles Francis, son of Rev. Albert E. Francis, of Eng.; 3–David Jones, Jr., *b* Jan. 31, 1903; Haverford, ex-'25; *m* Sept., 1923, Elizabeth Bunting, dau. of David Bunting Andrews (issue: David Jones, III, *b* Mar. 4, 1925); 4–Joseph (*b* and *d* July 14, 1906); 5–Margaret, *b* June 29, 1910; Bryn Mawr, '31.
1–B.S., Haverford, '89; law student, Col. Benjamin Nield's office, 1892-96. Teacher Friends' Sch., Wilmington, Del., 1889-94; admitted to bar, June 1896. City solicitor, Wilmington, 1901-03; mem. Del. Senate, 1913-14; atty. gen. of Del., 1917-21; U.S. dist. atty. for Del., 1924-27. Republican. Clubs: Wilmington, Tuscarora, Little Bushkill Rod and Gun (Pa.). Residence: 1107 Franklin St., Wilmington, Del.

1–**ROBINSON, Eleanor Johnson Waite (Mrs. Drew King),** *b* West Newton, Mass., Sept. 25, 1879.
9–Richard **Waite** (qv);
8–Thomas (1641-1722), of Watertown, Mass.; soldier in Indian war, 1675; *m* 1673, Sarah Cutler;
7–Joseph (1682-1753), of Sudbury, Mass.; soldier in Queen Anne's War, 1702; *m* 1705, Mrs. Sarah Stone, of Lexington;
6–John (1708-61), soldier in French and Indian War, 1745; *m* 1727, Anna Wellington (seven sons were soldiers in Am. Rev.);
5–John (1730-1815), of Brookfield, Mass.; capt. in French and Indian War; capt. at Lexington Alarm; mem. Com. of Safety and Corr.; *m* 1752, Martha Wolcott (1728-1807), of Brookfield;
4–Nathaniel (1761-1834), q.-m. sgt., Am. Rev.; *m* 1782, Mercy Jenks (1762-1848), of Providence, R.I.;
3–Otis (1790-1869), of N. Brookfield; War 1812; *m* 1825, Polly Johnson (1802-87);
2–Henry Edward (1845-1912), of N. Brookfield and Boston; inventor and genealogist; treas. Ala. & Chattanooga R.R. Co., 1869; *m* 1867, Ellen Ingersoll Broughton (1844-1924), of Marblehead; issue: I–Henry Ingersoll (1868-1920); II–Edward Broughton (1871-1928; *m* Cora H. Harvey); III–Amory Hooper (*b* 1873; *m* Alice F. Wade); IV–Robert Nicholson (1874-88); V–Elise Otis (*b* and *d* 1877); VI–Eleanor Johnson (1 above).
1–*m* Oct. 15, 1902, Drew King Robinson, *b* N.Y. City, Dec. 10, 1871; son of Andrew J. Robinson, of New York *m* Harriett E. King (William G[3]; William W.[4]; William[5]; Johannes[6]); issue: 1–Eleanor (Sept. 2, 1903-May 18, 1907); 2–Harriett King, *b* Brooklyn, Jan. 18, 1906; ed. N.Y. Sch. of Applied Design for Women; 3–Marjorie Waite, *b* Brooklyn, Oct. 27, 1907; ed. Elmira (N.Y.) Coll. for Women; 4–Lillian Edith, *b* Brooklyn, Nov. 1, 1909; ed. Elmira Coll. for Women; 5–Beatrice, *b* New York, Oct. 17, 1912; ed. Elmira Coll. for Women.
1–Ed. Lasell Sem. for Young Women. Mgr. M. E. Home for Aged, N.J. Mem. S.M.D., C.D.A., D.F.P.A., Descendants A. and H.A. Co., D.A.R. (organizing regent, 1925, regent, 1926-29, Richard Stockton Chapter, N.J.), Marblehead Hist. Soc., Geneal. Soc. of N.J. Methodist. Residence: 21 Ocean Av., Ocean Grove, N.J.

1–**ROGERS, Arthur Carpenter,** *b* Maysville, Ky., Jan. 26, 1864.
7–Capt. John **Rogers,** who located land in Montgomery Co., Md. (formerly in Prince George's Co.), 1721; *m* Joan–;
6–Samuel (ca. 1717-1763);
5–John (*d* 1792), *m* Susannah Gassaway (*d* 1792); see Vol. III, p. 402;
4–Charles (*d* 1813), *m* 2d, 1803, Susannah Smith (1785-1850; Weathers[5] [*b* 1740] *m* Jane Lane [1748-1825; James[6]; William[7]]; Nathaniel[6], *m* Elizabeth–, *d* 1752);
3–George Washington (1810-47), *m* 1833, Charlotte Carrell (1809-63; Sanford[4] [*b* 1772], *m* 1801, Jane [*b* 1782], dau. of William Byers; Dempsey[5] [1740-1806], *m* 1761, Mary Hall, 1742-1806; Dempsey[6], will proved 1776 in Loudoun Co., Va.);
2–John Gassaway (2 below).
10–Matthew **Howard,** patented land, 1650; *m* Ann–;
9–Matthew, *m* Sarah Dorsey (Edward[10], qv);
8–Sarah, *m* Capt. John **Worthington** (1650-1701);
7–Thomas (1691-1753), burgess, 1753; *m* 1711, Elizabeth Ridgely (*d* 1754; Henry[8], *m* Katherine, dau. of Col. Nicholas Greenberry; Col. Henry[9], qv);
6–Catherine (1720-88), *m* Maj. Nicholas **Gassaway** (*d* 1775; Capt. Thomas[7]; Col. Nicholas[8], qv);
5–Susannah (*d* 1792), *m* John **Rogers** (5 above).
4–Robert **Arthur;**
3–George Wiles, *m* Lydia Hunt (Charles[4], *m* Lydia Ball, 1784-1847);
2–Sarah (1842-80), *m* 1863, Lt. Col. John Gassaway **Rogers** (1836-65), 10th Ky. Cav. and 54th Ky. Mtd. Inf., U.S.V.

1–*m* Feb. 3, 1886, Lauretta Raymond Plumer (see Vol. III, p. 402).
1–Production mgr., "Time." Served in War with Spain as capt. and adj. 1st Ohio Vol. Cav.; actg. asst. adj. gen. 2d Provisional Cav. Brig., 4th Corps; in World War, maj. ordnance (U.S.R.), Aug. 30, 1917; active service, Sept. 25, 1917; lt. col. (U.S.A.), Mar. 5, 1919; overseas, Nov. 6, 1917-June 12, 1919; cited for "Especially meritorious and conspicuous services" as div. ord. officer, 2d Div. by cdr.-in-chief A.E.F. and by comdg. gen. 2d Div.; discharged Oct. 15, 1919; lt. col., Ord.-Res., June 7, 1920; col. A.G.-Res., Feb. 5, 1923; col., Aux.-Res., Feb. 5, 1928. Mason. Mem. S.C.W., M.O.L.L., M.O.F.W., U.S.W.V., A.L., I.A.G. Clubs: Olympia Fields Country; hon. mem. Hermit Club (Cleveland). Residence: 5208 Dorchester Av., Chicago, Ill.

MARY EDITH (COFFIN) SISSON

1–**SISSON, Mary Edith Coffin (Mrs. Rufus L.),** *b* Lisbon, N.Y., Mar. 27, 1862.
12–Tristram **Coffin** (desc. of Sir Richard Coffin, knight, accompanied William the Conqueror from Normandy to Eng., 1066); of Brixton, Co. Devon, Eng.;
11–Nicholas (*d* 1603), of Butler's Parish, Devonshire; *m* Joan–;
10–Peter (ca. 1580-1627/28), *m* Joan or Joanna Thember (*d* 1661, aet. 77);
9–Tristram, came to America (qv);
8–Hon. Peter (1631-1715), chief justice Superior Ct., of N.H.; counsellor of the province; moved to Exeter, N.H., 1690; *m* Abigail Starbuck (Edward[9]);
7–Jethro (1663-1726), of Nantucket; *m* Mary Gardner (1670-1767; John[8], *m* Priscilla Grafton);
6–John (1694-1768), *m* Lydia Gardner (*b* 1687; Richard[7], *m* Mary Austin);
5–John (*b* ca. 1720), to Fishkill, N.Y., 1740; *m* Mary Davis;
4–Edward (1762-1824), settled in Montgomery Co., N.Y., ante 1790; *m* Sibyl– (*d* 1838, aet. 76);
3–Isaac (ca. 1784-1858), of Herkimer Co., and DePeyster, N.Y.; *m* Margaret Patten (1782-1841);
2–Julius Augustus (2 below).
8–John **Partridge** (ca. 1620-1706), from Eng. with brother William and sister Margery, 1650; *m* 1655, Magdalen Bullard (*d* 1677; John[9], *m* Magdalen–);
7–John (1656-1743), *m* 1st, 1678, Elizabeth Rockwood (1657-88; Nicholas[8], *m* Margaret Holbrook);
6–Benoni (1687-1769), *m* 1708, Mehetabel Wheelock (1689-1761; Samuel[7], *m* Sarah Kendrick; Rev. Ralph[8], founder of Medfield);
5–Eli (1729-ca. 1800), was in Colonial service 1745; *m* Rachel Sheffield (*b* 1732; Nathaniel[6], *m* Mary–);
4–Amos (1758-1844), served in Am. Rev., from Mendon, Mass., and Chesterfield, N.H.; participated in battles of Ticonderoga and Bennington; *m* 1783, Sarah Harvey (1764-1849; Capt. Ebenezer[5], *m* Sarah James);
3–Amos (1794-1886), *m* 1823, Abigail Lewis (1800-85; Capt. David[4], *m* Mary Chambers);
2–Jane Ann (1826-96), *m* 1845, Julius Augustus **Coffin** (1816-68), farmer at DePeyster and Lisbon, St. Lawrence Co., N.Y.; removed to Pa. where he engaged in lumber and milk business; issue: I–Josephine (*b* 1848; *m* Herbert T. Morian); II–Annette Emogene (*b* 1851); III–Lewis Augustus, M.D. (*b* 1856; *m* 1889, Grace Geer); IV–Julia Ann (*b* 1858; *m* Frank Wallace Jennings); V–Mary (1 above); VI–(*d* infancy).
1–*m* Sept. 1, 1886, Rufus Lasher Sisson (see Vol. III, p. 419); issue: 1–Lewis H., *b* 1887; Dartmouth Coll.; *m* 1914, Margaret Parker; 2–Rufus L., Jr., *b* 1890; Dartmouth Coll.; *m* 1916, Dorothy I. Castle; 3–Ruth C., *b* 1892; grad. Welles Coll.; *m* 1921, Jefferson C. Bynum; 4–Walter C., *b* 1894; Dartmouth Coll.; capt. U.S.A., with A.E.F. in France during World War; *m* 1924, Ruth A. Griffith.
1–Mem. D.A.R. (organizing regent Nihanawate Chapter); active in Fed. of Women's Clubs. Residence: 53 Elm St., Potsdam, N.Y.

1–**SLATE, Jannie Ragland (Mrs. William Clem),** *b* Hyco, Halifax Co., Va., Jan. 1, 1872.
6–John **Ragland** (qv);
5–Evan (*d* 1795), vestryman, Antrim Parish, Halifax Co., Va., 1767-95; *m* Susanna Lipscomb;
4–John, *m* his cousin, Elizabeth Pettus;
3–Dabney (*b* 1792-*d* 1871), of Hyco, Va.; War 1812; *m* 1822, Harriet Byron Faulkner (1802-81);
2–Joseph Edward (2 below).
4–John **Lawson,** of N.C.;
3–David.
2–Joseph Edward **Ragland** (1838-1929), of Hyco, Va.; pvt. in Southern Confed. Army, 4 yrs.; courier for Gen. Robert E. Lee at different times; *m* 1868, Mary Bailey (1840-69); *m* 2d, 1870, Lucy Anne Lawson (*b* 1842; David[3]; John[4], of N.C.); issue (1st marriage: I–Charles Dabney (*b* 1869; *m* Fisher Luckett); issue (2d marriage): I–Jannie (1 above); II–David Lawson (*b* 1873; *m* Mary Will Stovall).
1–*m* Sept. 6, 1900, William Clem Slate, *b* Cluster Springs, Va., Jan. 2, 1865; son of Rev. William Slate; issue (all *b* Hyco, Halifax Co., Va.): 1–Lucile, *b* July 13, 1901; 2–Mary Elizabeth, *b* Dec. 24, 1903; *m* Aug. 9, 1921, Edwin William Wessman (issue: Mary Jane); 3–Joseph Edward, *b* Sept. 21, 1908; Pa. State Coll., 1½ yrs.; 4–Martha Jane, *b* Dec. 25, 1910; 5–Kathryn Elise, *b* Nov. 14, 1912.
1–Grad. Danville (Va.) Coll. for Young Ladies (now Stratford Coll.). Mem. U.D.C. Methodist. Democrat. Residence: 600 Logan St., South Boston, Va.

1–**SMITH, Denta Watson (Mrs. Herschel W.),** *b* Athens, Ga., Feb. 15, 1892.
5–Samuel **Watson** (1731-1810), Am. Rev.; *m* Elizabeth McDowell (1738-1807);
4–James (1785-1865), *m* 1804, Polly Mary Walker (1783-1862);
3–Marion Francis (1823-1903), *m* 1848, Emily Ann Norton;
2–James William (2 below).
9–William **Norton** (qv);
8–John (*d* 1716), of Hingham; *m* 1674, Mary Mason;
7–Capt. John, *m* Elizabeth Thaxter;
6–William (*d* 1751), of Bladen Co., N.C.;
5–Thomas (1736-1802), Am. Rev.; of DeKalb Co.; *m* 1757, Mary– (1740-1807);
4–William (1765-1843), of Oglethorpe Co., Ga.; *m* 1810, Mary Landrum (1791-1862);
3–Emily Ann (1823-1902), of Clarke Co., Ga.; *m* Marion Francis **Watson** (3 above).
6–William **England,** settled in Chatham Co., N.C.; *m* Elizabeth Wilcox;
5–Daniel (*b* 1750), *m* 1772, Margaret Lovick (*d* 1840);
4–Elisha (1793-1863), of Burke Co., N.C.; *m* 1818, Mary S. Erwin (1800-57);
3–Alphonzo (1831-1900), of White Co., Ga.; *m* 1856, Martha England (1832-1905; Martin[4]);

2–Georgia (1858-1930), *m* 1874, James William **Watson** (1850-1919); issue: I–James Dala (*b* 1875; *m* Daisy Threasher); II–Daisy (*b* 1877; *m* J. O. Chandler); III–Doma A. (*b* 1880; *m* Maude Cook, *d* 1929); IV–Marion Damon (*b* 1885; *m* Mary Andrews); V–DeWitte (*b* 1887; *m* Mae Masters); VI–Della (*b* 1888; *m* C. A. Bone); VII–Denta (1 above); VIII–Darice (*b* 1893; *m* M. N. Bodenbach); IX–Dorothy (*b* 1903; *m* Norris Ford).
1–*m* June 22, 1916, Herschel Willoughby Smith, *b* Watkinsville, Ga., July 23, 1887; son of George Blakely Smith, of Watkinsville; issue: 1–George Watson, *b* Athens, Ga., Dec. 31, 1918; 2–Joan, *b* Winder, Ga., Feb. 8, 1923; 3–Dala, *b* Winder, Apr. 22, 1928.
1–Mem. S.D.P. (state historian), D.A.R. Residence: 111 Church St., Winder, Ga.

1–**SMITHY, Rosalie McCormick (Mrs. Horace G.),** *b* Berryville, Va., July 5, 1877.
6–Dr. John **McCormick,** from Ireland, 1730, settled in Jefferson Co., Va.; grad. in medicine at Dublin Inst.;
5–Francis (*b* 1734), *m* Miss Provin;
4–William, *m* Elizabeth Rice;
3–Province (*b* 1800), of Berryville, Va.; *m* Margaretta Moss;
2–James Marshall (2 below).
10–William **Powell,** from Eng., to Chesapeake Bay, with Capt. Smith, 1607; settled at Jamestown, Va.; burgess, 1619;
9–Cuthbert;
8–William (*d* 1715), planter, Somerset Co., Md.;
7–William (1705-87), *m* 1735, Eleanor Peyton (Valentine[8] [1687-1751], burgess; *m* Frances, dau. of Capt. Thomas Harrison, of Chapawamsic);
6–Col. Levin (1737-1810), lt. col. in Am. Rev.; *m* 1763, Sarah Harrison (*b* 1739; Burr[7]);
5–Maj. Burr (1768-1838), "The Hills," Middleburg, Va.; *m* 1792, Catherine Brooke (Humphrey[6]; Humphrey[7], *m* Elizabeth, dau. of Col. George Braxton, *m* Elizabeth Parlin);
4–Dr. William Levin (1797-1853), of Alexandria, Va.; *m* his cousin, Ann Maria Powell (1800-85; Hon. Cuthbert[5] [1775-1849], *m* Catherine, dau. of Col. Charles Simms (1755-1819), *m* Nancy, dau. of Col. William Douglas, *m* Catherine, dau. of Laurens Andriessen Van Buskirk, qv);
3–Virginia C. (1821-87), *m* Laurence Berry **Taylor** (1818-73);
2–Rosalie Allen (1852-1918), *m* James Marshall **McCormick** (1849-1918), lawyer; issue: I–Virginia Taylor (*b* 1873; *m* J. Jett McCormick); II–Margaretta Holmes (*b* 1874; *m* Charles F. McGuire); III–Hugh Holmes (*b* 1875; *m* Edith Allen); IV–Rosalie (1 above); V–Ann Broun (*b* 1879; *m* Walter Cox; *m* 2d, John F. Williams, Jr.); VI–Province (1880-1903); VII–Gertrude Marshall (*b* 1883; *m* Thomas M. Reynolds); VIII–Marshall (1889-1929; *m* Hazel Becker); IX–Harriet Taylor (*b* 1895; *m* Thomas B. Stillman).
1–*m* June 14, 1911, Horace Gilbert Smithy, *b* Marion, S.C., Jan. 25, 1880; son of J. W. G. Smithy; issue: 1–Horace G., Jr., *b* July 19, 1914.
1–Ed. private schools. Mem. C.D.A., D.A.R. Residence: 2132 Wyoming Av. N.W., Washington, D.C.

1–**STREET, Ralph Wood,** *b* St. Joseph, Mo., Dec. 25, 1882.
6–Peter **Street**;
5–Zadok;
4–Aaron;
3–Isaac;
2–James Mather (2 below).
10–Richard **Warren,** Mayflower Pilgrim (qv);
9–Elizabeth (*d* 1670), *m* 1632, Richard **Church** (qv);
8–Joseph (1638-1711), *m* 1658, Mary Tucker (1641-1711; John[9]);
7–Deborah (*b* 1672), *m* 1699, Samuel **Gray** (*d* 1712);
6–Samuel (1700-64), *m* Hannah Kent (1703-96);
5–Desire (1735-1822), *m* 1762, George **Wood** (1730-1820), lt., Capt. Gideon Simmons' Co., Col. Cook's Regt., R.I. Militia, 1778;
4–John (1773-1864), *m* 1798, Lydia Woodman (*b* 1773);
3–John Woodman (1814-1900), *m* 1844, Sarah J. Lake (1826-1915);
2–Susan E. (1847-97), *m* 1879, James Mather **Street** (1836-96), pres. life ins. co.
1–*m* June 8, 1915, Alice Victoria Brown, *b* Sedalia, Mo., Nov. 14, 1886; dau. of Owen Brown, of Sedalia.
1–LL.B., U.Mich., 1905 (Phi Gamma Delta). Began practicing law at St. Joseph, Mo., 1905, moved to Kansas City, Mo., 1909; pres. Street & Co., investment bankers, 1919; v.p. and active head Mo. Hydro Electric Power Co., 1924. Conceived, planned and promoted the Osage River Hydro Electric project ($30,-000,000, building in 1930), now owned by the Union Electric Light & Power Company of St. Louis. Mem. S.R. (state registrar, 1907-09; pres. Kansas City Chapter, 1930), I.A.G. Presbyterian. Republican. Club: Kansas City. Residence: 1408 W. 51st St., Kansas City, Mo.

1–**THOMPSON, Joseph,** *b* Mays Landing, N.J., Sept. 21, 1853.
10–Cornelis Lambertsen **Cool,** freeholder Gowanus, 1639; patentee Breuckelen, 1642; one of the "Eight men," 1643; *m* Altien Brickhonge;
9–Altie Cornelis, *m* Gerrit Wolfertse **Covwenhoven** (1610-45); freeholder of Amersfoort, 1638; one of the "Eight men," 1643; magistrate of Flatlands, 1644 (Wolfert G.[10], qv);
8–Judge Willem Gerritse (1637-post 1727), *m* Jannetje Monfoort (bap. 1646; Peter[9] [*d* 1661], magistrate, Breuckelen, 1658, *m* Sarah de Plancken);
7–Peter Willemse (1671-ca. 1755), *m* Patience Davis (*b* 1674);
6–Peter (1712-64), *m* Leah Schenck (1714-69; Jan Roelefse[7] [1670-1753], *m* Sarah Willemse Covenhoven [1674-1761]; Roelof Martense[8], qv);
5–Sarah (1744-1821), *m* Joseph **Thompson** (1743-1808); see Vol. II, p. 67 for Thompson lineage;
4–Elias (1771-1847), *m* Rachel Wills (1773-1851; Carvel[5]);
3–Joseph (1802-81), *m* 1826, Eliza Scott;
2–William Wright (2 below).
9–Richard **Lippincott** (qv);
8–Restore (1653-1741), of Burlington Co., N.J.; mem. West Jersey Gen. Assembly, 1701, and N.J. Assembly, 1703-04; *m* 1674, Hannah Shattuck (*b* 1654; William[9]);
7–Abigail (*b* 1677), *m* James **Shinn** (1678-1751; John[8] [1623-will proved 1711], one of the Bd. of Proprs. who purchased, surveyed and distributed land among the members of the Soc. of Friends who followed him to America, freeholder, Burlington Co., N.J., 1680, *m* Jane–);
6–Hannah, *m* Jonathan **Eldridge** (*d* 1769);
5–Noah (*d* 1793), *m* Margaret Haines;
4–Hannah (1780-1854), *m* John **Scott** (see Vol. III, p. 577);
3–Eliza (1799-1888), *m* Joseph **Thompson** (3 above).
10–George **Hull** (qv);
9–Elizabeth (*d* 1682), *m* Samuel **Gaylord** (1620-89; William[10], qv);
8–Abigail (*b* 1653), *m* Daniel **Westcott** (*d* 1702; Col. Richard[9], Pequot War);
7–Daniel (*d* 1742), *m* Elizabeth–;
6–Daniel (1707-91), *m* Deborah Smith (1709-91);
5–Col. Richard (1733-1825), *m* Margaret Brazure (1736-1830);
4–Margaret, *m* 2d, Nathan **Pennington** (see Vol. III, p. 577);
3–John, *m* Elizabeth Taylor;
2–Hester Taylor (1825-1910), *m* William Wright **Thompson** (1830-65).
1–*m* May 10, 1877, Isabella Louisa Phillips (see Vol. II, p. 67 for genealogy).
1–Lawyer; pres. Atlantic Safe Dep. & Trust Co. and Atlantic Guaranty & Title Ins. Co.; dir. 2d Nat. Bank. Solicitor for Atlantic Co., N.J., 1880-1905; co. collector, 1881-83; prosecutor of pleas, 1881-91; judge Co. Ct., 1892-98; mayor of Atlantic City, 1898; mem. bd. mgrs. State Hosp. for Insane, 1898; mem. State Bd. Taxation, 1898-1914; chmn. legal advisory bd., Atlantic City, World War. Mem. S.D.P., S.A.R., etc. Club: Seaview Golf. Residence: 19 N. Dorset Av., Ventnor, N.J.

1–**VAN DEREN, Henry Spurgeon,** *b* Cynthiana, Ky., May 16, 1876.
8–Christian Barendtse **Van Horn** (qv);
7–Barendt (*d* 1726), *m* Geertje Dirckse (*b* 1662);

6–Christian (1681-1751), *m* ca. 1708, Williamtje Van Dyck (1681-1760);
5–Charity (1723-post 1760), *m* ante 1748, Godfrey (Van Dueren) **Van Deren** (ca. 1720-1792), soldier French and Indian War; pvt. Am. Rev.; trustee Lutheran Ch., Bucks Co., Pa.;
4–Barnard (ca. 1748-1800), moved to Loudoun Co., Va., to Bourbon Co., Ky., 1788, to Harrison Co., Ky., 1790, where he purchased land and built his log house; *m* ca. 1773, Sarah Murray (*b* 1755);
3–James (1780-1867), *m* 1808, Sarah Journey (1790-1882; Capt. Joseph[4], *m* Margaret Magee);
2–John (2 below).
9–Jacob **Barney** (qv);
8–Jacob, of Salem, Mass.; *m* 1660, Ann Witt (Jonathan[9], of Lynn, Mass., *m* Elizabeth–);
7–John (1665-1728), *m* 1686, Mary Throop (1667-post 1728; William[8], *m* Mary Chapman; Col. Adrian[9]);
6–Joseph (*d* 1745), of Rehoboth, Mass.; *m* 1726, Joanna Martin (*d* ca. 1764);
5–Joanna (1745-1819), *m* Daniel **Sanders** (1738-1819), Am. Rev. (Jacob[6], of Rehoboth, Mass.);
4–Ezra (1777-1859), of Grafton, N.H.; *m* ca. 1798, Betsey Carr (1780-1861);
3–James Riddle (1799-1871), of Millersburg, Ky.; *m* 1830, Martha Woodson Smith (1814-64; Capt. Alexander[4], of Bourbon Co., Ky.; Alexander[5], of Fayette Co., Ky.);
2–Martha Clay (1844-1927), *m* 1864, John **Van Deren** (1828-1914), farmer and landowner; issue: I–James Woodson (*b* 1866; *m* 1891, Lutie Virginia Poage); II–Allie Varden (*b* 1869; *m* 1890, Harry Rhodes Wiglesworth); III–John Harlan (1871-1915; *m* 1901, Daisy Jouett); IV–Henry Spurgeon (1 above); V–Joseph Journey (*b* 1877; *m* 1902, Dawson Lake); VI–Frank Alexander (*b* 1879; *m* 1905, Willie Ball); VII–William W. (*b* 1881; *m* 1911, Anna Mai Shropshire).
1–*m* Mar. 24, 1914, Willie Josephine Lively, *b* McMinnville, Tenn., Mar. 17, 1894; dau. of Joseph Lively, of McMinnville; issue (all *b* Nashville, Tenn.): 1–Henry Spurgeon, Jr., *b* June 17, 1915; 2–Catherine Lively, *b* Mar. 11, 1917; 3–Frances McKeon, *b* Mar. 29, 1920; 4–Martha Ellen, *b* Oct. 9, 1925.
1–Business manager, city public schools, of Nashville, since 1898. Mem. S.A.R. (registrar Tenn. Soc.), I.A.G. Mason, Scottish Rite. Baptist. Club: Belle Meade Country. Address: Hume-Fogg Bldg., Nashville, Tenn.

1–**WILKINSON, Laura May Simpson (Mrs. Samuel A.),** *b* Tibbee, Miss., May 19, 1871.
4–Dr. William **Simpson,** surgeon War 1812;
3–John;
2–Alexander Heath (2 below).
10–Capt. Francis **Eppes** (qv);
9–Col. Francis (1628-78), mem. Colonial Council, 1652;
8–Col. Francis (1659-1718), burgess sheriff, justice, Henrico Co., Va.; *m* 1685, Anne Isham (Maj. Henry[9], qv);
7–Col. Francis (*d* 1734), justice, trustee; burgess; *m* Sarah Hamlin;
6–Ann (*d* 1787), *m* Benjamin **Harris** (*d* 1759), of Goochland Co.;
5–Francis Eppes (1750-1834), *m* Mary Macon (*d* aet. 74);
4–Rebecca Macon (1780-1858), Huntsville, Ala.; *m* John Perratt **Steger** (*b* 1769);
3–Kennon Harris (1806-92), of Powhatan Co., Va., and Huntsville, Ala.; *m* 1838, Mary Elizabeth Wall (1821-97);
2–Helen Grey (1843-98), *m* 1868, Alexander Heath **Simpson** (*b* 1841), planter and mcht., of Tibbee, Miss.; issue: I–Laura May (1 above); II–Mary Kennon (*b* 1876; *m* Josiah Charles Trent); III–Helen Grey (*b* 1878; *m* Barney Edwards Eaton); IV–John Russel (*m* Susan A. Strother).
1–*m* Dec. 20, 1893, Samuel Allen Wilkinson, *b* Raleigh, Miss., Feb. 11, 1862; son of Duncan Allen Wilkinson, of Raleigh, Miss.; issue: 1–Samuel A., Jr., *b* McAlester, Okla., May 24, 1898; A.B., Harvard, '19; entered Signal Corps, U.S.A.; at Camp Devens, Mass., 1917-18; corpl. Co. A, 301st Field Signal Bn., 76th Div.; attached to 6th Army Corps, A.E.F.; sgt. 1919; participated in defense of Marbache, Toul and Metz sectors; with Army of Occupation in Luxemburg, 1918-19; *m* Aug. 20, 1925, Margaret Jones (issue: Samuel Allen, III); 2–Russel, *b* Birmingham, Ala., Mar. 21, 1901; U.S.N.A., '22; ens. U.S.N.R.; 3–Laura **Steger,** *b* Memphis, Tenn.; Gulf Park Coll., 1924.
1–A.B., Huntsville Female Coll., '87. Dir. Camp Kinnikinnik for Girls, Manitou, Colo. Mem. O.C., C.D.A., D.A.R., U.S.D. 1812, U.D.C. Summer place: Manitou, Colo. Residence: 220 E. Pear St., Wewoka, Okla.

1–**WINSLOW, John Randolph,** *b* Baltimore, Md., June 10, 1866.
6–Thomas **Winslow** (*d* ca. 1745), from New England, settled in Perquimans Co., N.C.; *m* Elizabeth Clear (*b* 1686);
5–Timothy (*d* 1752), of Perquimans Co.; *m* Rachel Wilson (*d* 1777);
4–Caleb (1749-1811), of Perquimans Co.; *m* 1st, 1769, Ann Perry (1755-96);
3–Nathan (1795-1873), of Perquimans Co.; *m* 1819, Margaret Fitz Randolph (1781-1848);
2–Dr. Caleb (2 below).
6–Thomas **Parry** (1680-1751), from Wales, settled in Montgomery Co., Pa.; *m* 1715, Jane Morris (*d* 1741);
5–John (1721-89), of Moorland Manor, Pa.; *m* Margaret Tyson (*d* 1807);
4–Benjamin (1757-1839), of New Hope, Bucks Co., Pa.; *m* 1787, Jane Paxson (1757-1826);
3–Oliver (1794-1874), of Phila., Pa.; *m* 1827, Rachel Randolph (1804-66; Edward Fitz Randolph[4]);
2–Jane Paxson (1829-1910), of Phila.; *m* 1852, Dr. Caleb **Winslow** (1824-95), of Perquimans Co., N.C.; removed to Baltimore, Md., 1866; physician (for issue see Randolph Winslow).
1–*m* Feb. 6, 1894, Elizabeth Lewis Read, *b* Phila., Pa., June 28, 1870; dau. of Dr. Thomas B. Read.
1–B.A., Johns Hopkins U., '86 (Beta Theta Pi); M.D., U.Md., 1888; post-grad. work, U. of Vienna, 1890, U. of Munich, 1895, Berlin, 1905. Lecturer on chemistry, 1888-89, prof. physiology, 1889-94, Woman's Med. Coll., Baltimore; clin. prof. nose and throat diseases, 1903-13, and professor, 1913-21, Univ. of Md., now emeritus. Throat surgeon, Presbyterian Eye, Ear and Throat Hosp., 1891-1908; surgeon Baltimore Eye, Ear and Throat Hosp., since 1909 (see Who's Who in America). Residence: 3101 St. Paul St., Baltimore, Md.

CHARLES BRADLEY WOOD (1843-1907).

1–**WOOD, Elizabeth C.,** *b* Sewickley, Pa., Nov. 15, 1867.
4–William **Wood** (1780-1849), of Middle Rasen, Eng.; *m* 1805, Mary Bradley (1784-1866; Francis[5], of Lincolnshire, Eng., *m* his cousin, Mary Wood);
3–Bradley (1815-1850), from Eng., settled at Delta, O., and Maumee, O.; *m* Anne Hancock (1822-81; Morris[4], of Ashford, Kent, Eng.);
2–Charles Bradley (2 below).

9-Roger **Haskell** (qv);
8-Mark (ca. 1647-post 1698), Rochester, Mass.; *m* 1678, Mary Smith;
7-Mark (*b* 1683), probably of Rochester;
6-Mark (*b* ca. 1705), *m* 1730, Mary Spooner;
5-Samuel (1733-1820), called "Deacon Haskell"; served in the English army; adj. in Sir William Johnson's fight at Lake George, 1755, French and Indian War; chmn. com. of 5 to recruit the quota of 33 men assigned to Brookfield in Am. Rev.; *m* 1765, Elizabeth Macomber;
4-Silas (1772-1831), Perry, O., 1822; *m* 1799, Sarah Bond;
3-Ferdinand (*b* 1804), *m* Mary Crosby (1809-89);
2-Mary Adaline (2 below).
9-John **Macomber** (*d* 1687), of Scotch ancestry, belonging to the clan of Campbell; settled at Taunton, 1643; admitted freeman; enrolled in militia at Taunton, 1643; permitted to build a mill, 1659; *m* 1646, Mary Babcock;
8-John (*d* 1724), was in military cos., 1680-1700, and served in King Philip's War; *m* 1678, Anna Evans;
7-John (1681-1747), served in Queen Anne's War, 1701-11; *m* 1707, Elizabeth Rogers Williams (*b* 1686; Nathaniel[8], *m* Elizabeth, dau. of John Rogers and g.dau. of Thomas Rogers, qv);
6-Josiah (1711-1801), lt. militia, Taunton, 1762; *m* 1736, Ruth Paul (Benjamin[7], *m* Ruth-);
5-Elizabeth (1737-1825), *m* Samuel **Haskell** (5 above).
9-William **Bond** (qv);
8-Thomas (1654-1704), served in King Philip's War, 1676; *m* Sarah Woolson;
7-Thomas (1683-1737), *m* 1st, 1706, Lydia Spring;
6-Jonathan (1710-89), of Waltham, Mendon and Westboro; deacon; served in the capture of Louisburg, 1745; *m* 1732, Mary Harrington;
5-Thomas (*b* 1739), of Westboro, N. Brookfield and Brookfield; 1st lt., Capt. Edmund Brigham's Co. of Minute Men at the Lexington Alarm, 1775; m 1765, Lydia Newton (*b* 1743; Dea. Josiah[6], *m* Rheuhama-);
4-Sarah (1775-1852), *m* 1799, Silas **Haskell** (4 above);
3-Ferdinand, *m* Mary Crosby (3 above);
2-Mary Adaline (1847-1930), *m* 1867, Charles Bradley **Wood** (1843-1907), see portrait; issue: I-Elizabeth C. (1 above); II-Harrison (*b* 1869; *m* Annie Kennedy); III-Mary (1880-1912; *m* George Warner); IV-Agnes A. (*b* 1890).
1-A.B., Alleghany Coll.; A.M., Columbia. Chmn. dept. of history and civics, Wadleigh High School, New York, 1897-1930. Mem. Phi Beta Kappa, D.F.P.A., D.A.R., I.A.G. Clubs: Women's University, Women's City (New York). Residence: 412 Terrace Av., Sea Girt, N.J. Address: Women's University Club, New York.

1-**YOUNG, Grace Whiting Mason (Mrs. Percy S.)**, *b* Brookline, Mass., Oct. 17, 1879.
8-Sampson **Mason** (qv);
7-Benjamin (1670-1740), of Rehoboth, Mass.; *m* Ruth Rounds (*d* 1740);
6-Charles (*b* 1713), *m* Keziah Miller;
5-Noble (1747-1827), of Swansea, Mass.; *m* 1769, Lydia Thurber (*d* 1802);
4-Aaron Thurber (1778-1848), *m* 1803, Mary Bullock (*d* 1818);
3-Albert Thompson (1806-68), of Providence, R.I.; *m* 1829, Arlina Orcutt (1804-79);
2-Albert (2 below).
9-James (Whiton) **Whiting**, in Hingham, 1647; *m* 1647, Mary Beal (*d* 1696);
8-James (1651-1721), *m* Abigail- (*d* 1740);
7-James (*b* 1680), *m* Mercy Whiton;
6-Elisha, *m* 1728, Joanna Dunham;
5-Elisha (*b* 1729), of Plymouth; *m* Betsy Holmes;
4-Nathan, of Plymouth; began to write name Whiting; *m* 1795, Rebecca Doten;
3-Nathan (*b* 1797), of Plymouth; *m* Experience Finney;
2-Lydia Finney (1835-1907), *m* 1857, Albert **Mason** (1836-1905), judge of the Superior Ct. of Mass.; issue: I-Anne Bullock (*b* and *d* 1860); II-John Whiting (*b* 1861); III-Mary Arlina (*b* 1866); IV-Alice (1868-96); V-Charles Noble (*b* 1869; *m* Emily Elizabeth Reed); VI-Martha (*b* 1872); VII-Richard Bullock, and VIII-Robert Sampson, twins (both 1874-75); IX-Grace Whiting (1 above).
1-*m* Dec. 7, 1904, Percy Sacret Young, *b* London, Eng., Dec. 19, 1870; son of Richard Young; issue: 1-Albert Mason, (Nov. 19, 1905-July 21, 1908); 2-Percy Sacret, *b* Newark, N.J., Apr. 12, 1907; 3-Dorothy, *b* Newark, Sept. 15, 1908; 4-George Wooldridge, *b* Newark, May 20, 1910; 5-William Clements, *b* Newark, Sept. 6, 1911; 6-Thomas Rumsey, *b* Newark, Feb. 21, 1914; 7-Margaret (*b* and *d* Aug. 27, 1915); 8-Gertrude Mary, *b* Plymouth, Mass., Aug. 24, 1916; 9-Katharine, *b* Plymouth, Aug. 7, 1918; 10-Sarah Sacret, *b* Newark, Mar. 29, 1920.
1-A.B., Smith College, '02. Residence: 97 Warren Place, Montclair, N.J.

SAMUEL COPP WORTHEN

1-**WORTHEN, Samuel Copp**, *b* Corinna, Me., Apr. 10, 1871.
9-George **Worthen** (*d* 1642), from Eng., ante 1638, to Salem, Mass.; *m* Margery- (*d* 1644);
8-Ezekiel (1636-1716), *m* 1661, Hannah Martin (1644-1730; George[9], *m* 1st, Hannah- [mother of Hannah above], *m* 2d, Susanna North, executed as a witch at Salem, 1692, see Whittier's poem, "Mabel Martin" in which Hannah Martin is called "Mabel" and Ezekiel Worthen "Esek Harden");
7-Samuel (1676-1760), *m* 1701, Deliverance Heath (1680-1714);
6-Samuel (1708-56), *m* 1733, Mehitable Heath (1710-89);
5-Samuel (1739-1815), pvt. French and Indian War and Am. Rev.; mem. Com. Safety; *m* 1764, Deborah Johnson (1743-1825);
4-Dea. Moses (1773-1845), *m* 1797, Bethiah Meacham (Samuel[5], of Canaan, N.H., Am. Rev.; Samuel[6]; Jeremiah[7]; Jeremiah[8]; Jeremiah[9], *d* 1695, Salem, Mass.);
3-Dea. Joseph (1812-95), *m* 1838, Eliza A. Gilman (1817-81); see Vol. III, p. 494;
2-Joseph Henry (2 below).
10-Ralph **Blaisdell** (qv);
9-Henry (1632?-1709), *m* 1st, ca. 1656, Mary Haddon (*d* 1691; Jarrett[10], came to Cambridge, Mass., 1632, *m* Margaret-);
8-Ebenezer (1657-1710), *m* 1680, Sarah Colby (John[9], *m* Frances, dau. of John Hoyt, qv; Anthony[10], came with Gov. Winthrop);
7-Ebenezer (*b* 1686), *m* Sarah Chase; *m* 2d, Abigail Ingersoll;
6-Ephraim (1717-1802), *m* ca. 1742, Thankful Webber;
5-Rev. John, Am. Rev., *m* Abigail Legro (formerly Le Gros, a name derived from the Isle of Jersey, Channel Islands);
4-Abigail (1786-1853), *m* as his 2d wife, 1810, Rev. Roger **Copp** (1781-1860); see Vol. III, p. 494;
3-Samuel (1816-98), *m* 1838, Betsey Mills;
2-Amanda (2 below).

9–Capt. Thomas **Webber** (*d* 1687), sea capt.; *m* 1655, Mary Parker (*b* 1639; John[10], propr. Parker's Island, Kennebec River);
8–Samuel (1656-1716), *m* Deborah Littlefield (Capt. John[9], of Wells, Me.);
7–John, *m* Mrs. Elizabeth (Boothby) Gypson;
6–Lydia (*b* 1729), *m* John **McLucas**;
5–Lucy (1749-1832), *m* Capt. Eligood **Mills** (1744-1832); see Vol. III, p. 494;
4–Luke (1778-1856), *m* 1804, Betsey Goodwin (1782-1880);
3–Betsey (1813-76), *m* Samuel **Copp** (3 above).
2–Joseph Henry **Worthen** (1839-1924), *m* 1863, Amanda Copp (1839-88); *m* 2d, 1891, Mrs. Mary Kemp (Maddocks) Gould (*b* 1870); for issue see Vol. III, p. 494.
1–*m* Aug. 28, 1909, Julia Regina McSwyny, *b* New York, N.Y. (June 23, 1883-Oct. 31, 1918); dau. of Cornelius George McSwyny, *m* Elizabeth Boyce Henderson.
1–Ed. Corinna (Me.) Acad., Me. Central Inst.; A.B., Columbia, 1898 (P.B.K., class pres. and salutatorian, 1898, sr. honors in rhetoric and English), A.M., LL.B., 1900. Attorney at law, 165 Broadway, New York, N.Y.; specialist in wills and and surrogate's practice. Mem. S.A.R. (sec. Orange Chapter, 1918-20, historian, 1924-27, genealogist, N.J. State Soc., 1920-29), S.R. (N.Y. Soc.), I.A.G. (life), N.J. Hist. Soc., N.Y.G.B.S., Geneal. Soc. of N.J. (life; pres. 1926–, asso. editor mag., 1925–); Assn. of the Alumni of Columbia Coll., Alumni Assn. of Columbia Law School, Met. Museum of Art. Author of numerous articles on hist. and geneal. subjects, also a History and Genealogy of the Worthen-Worthing Family in America, and a Copp Genealogy (mss.). Residence: 125 Park St., E. Orange, N.J.

1–**BROWDER, Sara Eleanor Bridges (Mrs. John C.),** *b* Clark Co., Ala., Dec. 16, 1855.
5–George **Bridges,** first cousin of Sir George Bridges Rodney;
4–John, of New Port; *m* Mindiville Whipple (sister of Abraham Whipple [1733-1819], one of the first captains in 1st Cont. Navy, desc. of John Whipple);
3–John Whipple (179–-1863), *m* ca. 1820, Eleanor Brooke Jones;
2–Dr. William Henry (2 below).
9–Cecil **Calvert** (1603-75), 2d Lord Baltimore;
8–Lady Calvert, *m* —**Sewall** (tradition says the Sewalls came to America with the "Ark of Avalon" and the "Dove" expdn., 1634);
7–Robert, *m* Lady Mary Carroll (Charles[8], of Carrollton, a "signer");
6–Charles, *m* —Fenwick (desc. Sir Robert de Fenwick, of Fenwick, Northumberland Co., Eng.);
5–Robert, *m* Lady Mary Darnley, of Eng.;
4–Anne (*b* ca. 1775; sister of Lewis Sewall [*b* 1760], *m* Elizabeth Howard Wailes); *m* 1st, 179–, Basil **Jones**; *m* 2d, Francis Farrar (1st cousin of Thomas Jefferson);
3–Eleanor Brooke (1800-75), *m* John Whipple **Bridges** (3 above);
2–Dr. William Henry (1825-66), studied medicine under his cousin, Dr. Francis L. Sewall; physician, farmer and ranchman, Bosque Co., Tex.; *m* 1850, Harriet Maria English (1833-65; David[3], *m* 1832, Sarah Anne Singleton, she *m* 2d, 1838, Dr. Francis L. Sewall); issue: I–Lewis Sewall (*d* infancy); II–Ann Howard (1853-1901; *m* 1872, Alex. Delgado); III–Sara Eleanor (1 above); IV–Reuben McDonald (1857-1903; *m* Sallie Davis Wooldridge); V–William H.
1–*m* June 2, 1875, John Cunningham Browder (1853-1917); son of Dr. George W. Browder (*b* in Va., 1822), *m* 1851, Rebecca Cunningham, of Laurens, S.C.; issue (all *b* Waverly, Tex.): 1–Rebbe Lewers (July 17, 1876-1911); *m* C. T. Hill, Jr. (issue: Nellie Sewall, *b* 1906, *m* 1923, William E. Walker [issue: Rebbe, *b* 1924, Louise Bridges, *b* 1926, Jeane, *b* 1928]; Minnie Browder, *b* 1909, *m* 1929, Bailey White); 2–Frank Grimke, *b* Sept. 1878; Southwestern U., Georgetown, Tex.; *m* 1907, Rosa, dau. of J. C. Hill (issue: John Grimke, *b* 1908; Cally Hill, *b* 1915; Reuben McDonald Bridges, *b* 1917); 3–Sewall Singleton (1880-1901); 4–John Craig, *b* Feb. 11, 1883; U. of Tex.; *m* Adeline, dau. of Dana Pond, of Austin, Tex. (issue: Rebbe Lewers, 1912-14; John Dana, *b* 1915); 5–William Bridges, *b* Feb. 11, 1883, twin; U. of Tex.; *m* 1908, Anna (*b* 1887), dau. of William Yancy Barr, of Huntsville (issue: William Bridges, *b* 1909-*d* infancy; Will Barr, *b* 1910; John Sewall, *b* 1913); 6–George W., *b* 1888; Southwestern U.; *m* 1917, Katrena (*b* 1895), dau. of William Stark, of Houston (issue: Mary Josephine, *b* 1920; Eleanor Anne, *b* 1921); 7–James Daniel, *b* 1891; *m* 1918, Mildred, dau. of Dr. Frank Lesley, of Willis, Tex. (issue: James Leslie, *b* 1920; Kenneth Fielding, 1922-27; John Craig, *b* 1924; Sallie Bouyer, *b* 1926); 8–Fielding S., *b* 1894; U. of Tex.; *m* Robbie, dau. of John Hart Hardy, of Hawthorne, Tex. (issue: John Fielding, *b* 1926; Robert James, *b* 1930); 9–Julien Montague, *b* 1897; left school to go to France; *m* 1921, Kathryn, dau. of Sam McMurrey, of Cold Springs, Tex. (issue: Kathryn Lewers, *b* 1923).
1–Presbyterian. Democrat. Residence: Route 1, Box 27, New Waverly, Walker Co., Tex.

1–**COLES, Stricker,** *b* "Estouteville," Albemarle Co., Va., Mar. 13, 1867.
5–John **Coles** (qv);
4–John (1745-1808), of "Enniscorthy," Albemarle Co., Va.; col. Am. Rev.; *m* Rebecca E. Tucker (their son Edward, was pvt. sec. to President Madison, later 1st gov. Ill. Ty., and 2d gov. of the state; their son Isaac, was pvt. sec. to President Jefferson, 1805-09);
3–John (1774-1848), *m* 1822, Selina Skipwith;
2–Peyton Skipwith (2 below).
7–Sir Grey **Skipwith** (qv);
6–Sir William, of "Prestwould," Va.; *m* Sarah Peyton (John[7]);
5–Sir William (1707-64), of "Prestwould"; *m* 1733, Elizabeth Smith (John[6]);
4–Sir Peyton (*b* 1743), *m* 2d, Jean Miller (Hugh[5]);
3–Selina (1793-1870), *m* John **Coles** (3 above);
2–Peyton Skipwith (1826-87), of "Estouteville," Albemarle Co., Va.; *m* 1852, his cousin, Julia Isaetta Coles (Isaac A.[3], *m* 2d, Julia Stricker); issue: I–Peyton Skipwith; II–Selina; III–Isaac A. (*m* Erna Balch); IV–Julia Stricker (*m* Edmund L. Mackenzie); V–John E.; VI–Robert (*m* Mary Minor); VII–Edward; VIII–William B.; IX–Stricker (1 above); X–Henry Aylett (*b* 1870; *m* Mary Norris); XI–Arthur N.
1–*m* Sept. 16, 1908, Bertha H. Lippincott (qv for issue).
1–Ed. Roanoke, U. of Va., Jefferson Med. Coll. Physician. Residence: "Alscot," Bryn Mawr, Pa.

1–**COLES, Bertha H. Lippincott (Mrs. Stricker),** *b* Phila., Pa., July 19, 1880.
9–Richard **Lippincott** (qv);
8–Restore (1653-1741), of Mt. Holly, N.J.; *m* Hannah Shattuck (*b* 1654);
7–James (1687-1760), of Shrewsbury; *m* Anna Eves (*b* 1689);
6–Jonathan (*d* 1759), of Evesham, N.J.; *m* his cousin, 1746, Anna Eves;
5–Levi (1749-1818), of Evesham; *m* 1773, Lettice Wills;
4–Jacob (1783-1834), *m* 1812, Sarah Ballinger;
3–Joshua Ballinger (1813-86), of Phila.; founder J.B. Lippincott Co., publishers, Phila.; *m* 1845, Josephine Craige;
2–Walter (2 below).
8–Hugh **Craige,** from Scotland, 1700, settled in Kent Co., Del.;
7–James (will dated Apr. 14, 1766);
6–Thomas (*d* Kent Co., Del., Jan. 20, 1768);
5–Seth (*d* 1831), *m* Margaret Wright (William[6], *m* Ann McCrait);
4–Seth (1799-1859), *m* 1821, Angelina Shaw;
3–Josephine (1823-99), *m* Joshua B. **Lippincott** (3 above).
11–Gov. William **Bradford** (qv);
10–Maj. William (1624-1703), *m* Alice Richards (1627-89);
9–Maj. John (1653-1736), *m* 1674, Mercy Warren (1653-1747; Richard[10], qv);
8–Lt. Samuel (1683-1740), *m* 1714, Sarah Gray (*b* 1697);
7–Abigail (*b* 1732), *m* Caleb **Stetson,** Jr.;
6–Mary (1759-1843), *m* 1776, Isaac **Lobdell,** minute man at Lexington;
5–Mary Gray (1784-1833), *m* 1803, Joshua **Shaw,** of Phila.;
4–Angelina (1804-40), *m* Seth **Craige** (4 above);
3–Josephine, *m* Joshua B. **Lippincott** (3 above);
2–Walter (1849-1927), of Phila., Pa.; dir. J. B.

Lippincott Co.; *m* 1879, Elizabeth Trotter Horstmann (1854-1917; Sigmund[3], *m* Elizabeth C. West).
1–*m* Sept. 16, 1908, Stricker Coles (qv); issue (all *b* Bryn Mawr, Pa.): 1–Elizabeth Lippincott, *b* Oct. 11, 1909; Vassar, 1 yr.; 2–Walter Lippincott, *b* Sept. 11, 1911; U. of Va., '33; 3–Bertha Stricker, *b* May 14, 1919.
1–Pres. United Service Club (for enlisted men in U.S. service) since 1923; chmn. social service com., Lying-in-Hosp. Mem. S.M.D., C.D.A., I.A.G. Episcopalian. Republican. Residence: "Alscot" Bryn Mawr, Pa.

1–**CRALLE, Ruth,** *b* Louisville, Ky., July 29, 1901.
6–Peter **Martin** (*b* 1741), of Prussia; *m* 1761, Sarah Redding, of Eng.;
5–Elizabeth (*b* 1762), of Va.; *m* 1782, as his 1st wife, Samuel **Jacobs** (1752-1840), Am. Rev.;
4–Elizabeth (1790-1869), of Va. and Ky.; *m* 1810, William Kenner **Cralle** (1789-1859), of Va. and Ky. (Rodham K.[5], *m* Nancy–);
3–Isaac Shelby (1828-1903), of Louisville, Ky.; *m* 1852, his 1st cousin, Martha Ellen Jacobs (1830-1906; Martin[4] [1792-1877], of Shelby Co., Ky., *m* 1st, 1813, Nancy, or Juliet, dau. of Presley Doggett; Samuel[5], above);
2–George Claybourne Thompson (2 below).
8–Thomas **Ford** (*d* 1776), of Fairfax Co., Va.; *m* Jane Milstead, of Wales;
7–John (1728?-1803), of Va., Spartanburg, S.C., and Shelby Co., Ky.; *m* 1st, ca. 1750, Rachel Spencer;
6–William (1753-1835), surveyor; *m* 1777, Cassandra Ford (1760-1835), of Md.;
5–Ann (1787-1844), *m* 1805, Thomas **King** (1778-1851; John[6], of Va., *m* Mary Hampton);
4–John Ford (1813-64), of Ky.; *m* 1836, Evaline Bright;
3–Edwin Franklin (1843-1913), of Eminence, Ky.; *m* 1867, Mary Esom Brown;
2–Carrie Eva (2 below).
11–John **Nuthall** (son of John, of London), of Cross Manor, Va., and Md.; a signer of the Submission to Parliament; *m* Elizabeth (Bacon) Holloway (widow of John Holloway);
10–Eleanor (*d* ante 1704), *m* as his 2d wife, ante Sept. 1668, Col. Thomas **Sprigg** (1630-1704), from Kethering, Northamptonshire, Eng., appeared in Northampton Co., Va., 1650, and earlier; removed to Calvert Co., Md., 1660-61, and later received a grant of 1000 acres from Lord Baltimore in Prince George Co., Md., which became "Northampton," the ancestral seat of the Sprigg family; the colonial mansion built at this time is still standing; commr., Calvert Co.; high sheriff; signed the Submission to Parliament;
9–Lt. Col. Thomas (1669-1726), civil officer, Calvert and Prince George cos., Md.; *m* Margaret Mariarte (*d* 1739; Prof. Edward[10], *m* Honore–, of Anne Arundel Co., Md.);
8–Priscilla (1700-post 1734), *m* 1716, Ralph **Crabb** (1694-1734; Henry[9], immigrant);
7–Edward (posthumous son), *m* 1759, Ursula Sprigg;
6–Priscilla Sprigg (1765-1831), *m* 1793, Stephen **Drane** (1768-1844), of Md., moved to Shelby Co., Ky., 1801;
5–Eleanor Crabb (1802-81), *m* 1818, William (Brite) **Bright** (1795-1859), lived in Va., the Carolinas, and Shelby Co., Ky. (Tobias[6], *m* Jane, dau. of John Ford, 7 above; Albertus[7], *m* Patience Hopkins);
4–Evaline (1820-78), *m* John Ford **King** (4 above).
6–Swanson **Brown** (1728-1833), from Scotland, settled in Va., later in Clark and Bracken cos., Ky.; *m* Polly Woodsides, of Scotland;
5–William Woodsides (1779-1855), *m* ca. 1800, Sarah Staples (1780-1829);
4–Lawson Esom (1818-91), of Clark Co., and Eminence, Ky.; *m* 1841, Mary Cracraft Watson (1824-47; Cain[5], *m* Rebecca, dau. of Samuel Cracraft);
3–Mary Esom (1847-1900), *m* Edwin F. **King** (3 above);
2–Carrie Eva (*b* 1868), *m* 1898, George Claybourne Thompson **Cralle** (1868-1903), of Louisville, Ky.; issue: I–Margaret Elma (*b* 1898; *m* 1923, her 2d cousin, Robert Elza Cralle); II–Ruth (1 above); III–Georgia Catherine (*b* 1903; *m* 1924, George Gibson Harrison).
1–U.Calif., ex-'26. Mem. Ky. State Hist. Soc., I.A.G. Residence: 2113 Rose St., Berkeley, Calif.

1–**CROCKER, Annie Glenn Michaux (Mrs. Thomas H.),** *b* Greensboro, N.C., Oct. 13, 1875.
8–Dr. John **Woodson** (qv);
7–Col. Robert, *m* Elizabeth Ferris (Richard[8], of "Curles," Henrico Co., Va.);
6–Benjamin, *m* Sarah Porter;
5–John, *m* 1731, Mary Miller, of Lancaster Co.;
4–Judith (1747-1803), *m* 1761, Capt. Joseph **Michaux** (1739-1807), Am. Rev.;
3–Joseph (1771-1837), *m* 2d, 1822, Anne Meade Randolph;
2–John LaFayette (2 below).
7–Sir Richard **Everard,** Bt. (11th from Edward, III, King of Eng.); gov. of N.C., 1724-32; returned to Eng.; *m* Susanna Kidder (Richard[8], bishop of Bath and Wells);
6–Susanna, *m* David **Meade,** of Va. (Andrew[7], qv);
5–Nancy, *m* Richard **Randolph,** Jr., of "Curles" (Col. Richard[6]; Col. William[7], qv);
4–Ann, *m* Brett **Randolph** (Brett[5], *m* Mary Scott);
3–Anne Meade (1787-1836), *m* Joseph **Michaux** (3 above);
2–John LaFayette (1824-98), editor and publisher (see portrait p. 365), *m* 1855, Sarah McLemore Macon (1831-94); for issue and other lineages see Mrs. Thomas M. McConnell, p. 365.
1–*m* Oct. 2, 1906, Thomas Henly Crocker, *b* Warren Co., N.C., Oct. 20, 1868; son of Luther Rice Crocker, of Middleburg, N.C.; issue: 1–Michaux Henly, *b* Greensboro, N.C., Apr. 13, 1908; U. of N.C., ex-'29; 2–Macon Rice, *b* Middleburg, N.C., Jan. 30, 1910; Washington and Lee U., '32; 3–Lucy McConnell, *b* Middleburg, Sept. 5, 1911; N.C. Coll. for Women, '33.
1–N.C. Coll. for Women, 1896. Mem. D.A.R., U.D.C. Methodist. Democrat. Residence: 836 W. Market St., Greensboro, N.C.

1–**DeMOTT, John Jacques,** *b* Somerset Co., N.J., Nov. 24, 1881.
8–Michael **DeMott,** from Holland 1665 or earlier, settled at Esopus (Kingston), Ulster Co., N.Y.; *m* 1682 or earlier, Anna Westbrook (Anthony Jans[9], of Albany, N.Y.);
7–Dirck, or English form Richard (bap. 1684), settled in Raritan Valley, N.J.;
6–Johannes (1716-77), of Neshanic, N.J.; *m* 1739, Elizabeth Davis (*d* ante 1764);
5–John (1746-1834), *m* 1773, Catherine Vroom (1750-1836; Hendrick[6]);
4–Henry Vroom (1786-1875), farmer, butcher, New Brunswick, N.J.; q.m. in military co. under the mil. estab. of 1815; *m* 1809, Ida Van Liew (1787-1874; Cornelius[5], *m* Mary Hegeman);
3–John (1812-96), of Middlebush, N.J.; grad. Rutgers Coll., 1833; mem. N.J. Legislature; in lumber business at New Brunswick; *m* 1839, Matilda Voorhees (1817-93; Jaques[4], *m* Anne Van Liew);
2–Jacques Voorhees (2 below).
9–Jaques **Cortelyou** (*d* ca. 1693), from Holland ca. 1652, settled at New Utrecht, L.I., N.Y.; studied at U. of Utrecht; surveyor gen. of New Netherland; leader in the settlement of New Utrecht; *m* Neeltje Van Duyn, from Holland;
8–Jaques (ca. 1662-1726), of New Utrecht; took Oath of Allegiance, 1687; capt. of militia, 1693; *m* 2d, 1706, Altie I. Boerman;
7–Hendrick (*b* 1711), of Ten-Mile-Run, on line bet. Somerset and Middlesex cos., N.J.; *m* 1st, 1731, Antie Albertse Van Voorhees (*d* ante 1742);
6–Hendrick (1736-1800), *m* Johanna Stoothoff (1742-1809);
5–Hendrick (1761-1841), served 9 mos. with Somerset Co. troops in Am. Rev.; at battles of Monmouth and Springfield; pensioned; *m* 2d, 1795, Elizabeth Nevius (1762-1848; Peter[6], *m* Maria Van Doren), widow of Lucas Voorhees;
4–Peter (1796-1879), *m* 1st, 1820, Mary Ann Gulick (1800-31; Cornelius[5], *m* Elizabeth Pumyea);
3–Henry P. (1823-1910), of Franklin Park; *m* 1850, Margaret Hageman (1830-1900; Peter A.[4], *m* Sarah DeHart);
2–Sarah Frances (1853-1922), *m* 1880, Jacques Voorhees **DeMott** (1852-89), grad. Rutgers

Coll., 1874; counsellor-at-law, New Brunswick; issue: I–John Jacques (1 above); II–Henry Vroom (*b* 1887).
1–*m* Aug. 27, 1914, Grace Stedman, *b* Castleton, N.Y., Apr. 5, 1881; dau. of Byron Stedman, of Mechanicville, N.Y.; issue: 1–John Jacques, *b* Arlington, N.J., Apr. 19, 1920; 2–Lawrence Lynch, *b* Arlington, Jan. 16, 1922.
1–Sec., Missionary Edn. Movement of the U.S. and Can., 1913-17; purchasing agent for Near East Relief, 1920-22; magazine circulation manager, The Plumbers and Heating Contractors Trade Journal, New York, since 1930. Mem. Bd. of Publn. and deacon, Reformed Ch. in America. Second lt., A.M. Corps, U.S.A., 1917-18, 1st lt., 1918, capt., 1918-19. Fellow Am. Geog. Soc.; mem. I.A.G., N.J. Hist. Soc., N.Y. State Hist. Assn., Kings Co. (N.Y.) Hist. Soc., L.I. Hist. Soc. Ruling elder Presbyn. Ch. Republican. Summer place: Elm Cottage, Stockbridge, Mass. Residence: 28 New Lawn Av., Arlington, N.J.

1–**LAING, George Irving**, *b* Tranquility, N.J., Dec. 12, 1862.
7–John **Laing** (*d* 1699), from Scotland, settled at Plainfield, N.J., 1685; *m* Margaret–;
6–John (1680-1731), of Plainfield; *m* 1705, Elizabeth Shotwell (John[7]; Abraham[8]);
5–John (1709-88), of Johnsonburg, N.J.; *m* Hannah Webster (*d* 1815);
4–Samuel (1767-1834), *m* 1792, Edith Lundy (Judge Samuel[5]; Richard[6]; Richard[7]; Richard[8]; Sylvester[9]);
3–Joseph Chapman (1804-54), *m* Phebe Bunting (Abner[4] [1787-1851], *m* Ann Coursen);
2–Watson Bunting (2 below).
6–Rev. Samuel **Kennedy**, M.D. (1720-87), from Scotland; Presbyn. minister, Basking Ridge, N.J., 1751-87; *m* Sarah– (1723-87);
5–Samuel (1745-1804), physician and co. judge, Johnsonburg, N.J.; *m* 1768, Elizabeth Beavers; *m* 2d, Ann Schaffer;
4–Moses Washington (*b* 1776), settled in Ohio:
3–Amos Hart (1799-1870), Tranquility, N.J.; *m* 1820, Catharine Stillwell (*d* 1872; Tobias[4] [*b* 1774]; Capt. Richard[5] [1742-1826]; Col. Nicholas[6] [1705-80]; Jeremiah[7]; Nicholas[8], qv);
2–Sarah Reading (1842-1914), *m* 1861, Watson Bunting **Laing** (1834-63), farmer, Johnsonburg, N.J.
1–*m* Nov. 20, 1920, Edna Florence Bachman, *b* Stony Run, Pa., July 16, 1892; dau. of Jacob Bachman (1847-1902; Adam[3] [1816-95]; John Jacob[4], 1779-1831); issue: 1–Edna Caroline, *b* Phila., Pa., Feb. 16, 1922.
1–D.D.S., U. of Pa., 1902. Teacher, merchant, salesman, dentist. Mem. I.A.G., Pa. Hist. Soc., Pa. Geneal. Soc., Colonial Soc. Pa. Episcopalian. Residence: 5922 Cobbs Creek Pkwy., Phila., Pa.

1–**LOUCKS, Annie**, *b* Pacheco, Calif., July 14, 1858.
6–John D. (Laux) **Loucks**, of French Huguenot parentage who moved to Germany; came from Germany, 1709, settled at Stone Arabia, N.Y.; one of the patroons and was given 2,000 acres; *m* Maria Starig;
5–Adam (1715-90), mem. 2d Regt., Tyron Co., N.Y., militia; the first and second meetings of the Tyron Co. Com. of Safety were held at his home at Stone Arabia, 1774-75; justice; *m* 1746, Catherine Elizabeth Snell, or Schnell (1719-97; George[6], Am. Rev.);
4–George (1759-1835), of New York; pvt. 2d Regt., Tyron Co. militia; *m* 1781, Catherine Elizabeth Bellinger (1760-1825);
3–Peter G. (1792-1870), New York; War 1812; *m* 1815, Nancy Gray (1794-1861; Lt. Col. Andrew[4], served in Am. Rev. and War 1812);
2–George P. (2 below).
4–Anthony **Lieber**, from Germany, settled at New York;
3–John (1789-1843), of New York; interested in milling business; justice of peace; *m* 1817, Catherine Lyke (1798-1830; John[4], pvt. Am. Rev.);
2–Ann (1821-1912), New York; *m* 1841, Col. George P. **Loucks** (1819-1903), served in N.Y. Vols., 1838-48; capt., maj. and col.; a.-d.-c. to Maj. Gen. Averill; general merchandise, grain and forwarding business, Canajoharie, N.Y., until 1848; brokerage and commn. bus., New York, until 1851; sailed for Isthmus of Panama, 1851, thence to San Francisco; commn. and shipstore business until 1857; mem. Vigilantes Com., San Francisco, Calif.; co. clk., and supervisor several yrs., Contra Costa Co.; sec. and dir. Granger's Warehouse Assn., Contra Costa Co.; pres. and dir. Contra Costa Co. Agrl. Soc.; school trustee 20 yrs.; issue: I–Catherine (1842-43); II–Peter G. (1844-1917; *m* Clarissa Elizabeth Standish); III–Frank Lieber (1855-1917; *m* Jane Davis Bunnell); IV–Annie (1 above); V–Sara Belle (*b* 1863; *m* William Allison Sears).
1–Ed. San Jose State Teachers' Coll., 1878. Taught school, 1878-1912; retired; mem. Bd. Edn., Contra Costa Co., Calif., 14 yrs.; trustee Mt. Diablo Union High School, 9 yrs.; managed ranch, since 1912. Mem. D.A.R. Episcopalian. Republican. Residence: Pacheco, Contra Costa Co., Calif.

1–**MacKENZIE, Luella Wood (Mrs. Gilbert A.)**, *b* Hunnewell, Mo., Apr. 2, 1868.
9–Abraham Isaacson **Ver Planck** (qv);
8–Susannah, *m* John **Garland**;
7–Sylvester (*d* 1719), of Newcastle, Pa.; licensed by William Penn as an Indian trader;
6–Sudt (1694-1736), *m* Rev. James **Anderson** (1678-1740), ordained Presbyn. minister, 1705; pastor First Donegal Presbyn. Ch., Susquehanna, Pa.;
5–Susannah (*b* 1725), *m* Col. John **Wood** (1712-91), from Scotland; of "Blair Park," Va.; signed Albemarle Co. Declaration of Independence (Michael[6], qv);
4–James (1748-1823), capt. Va. militia in Am. Rev.; *m* Mary Garland (James[5], of Va., Am. Rev.);
3–William (1784-1854), served in Ohio militia in War 1812; *m* Mary Ann (Jane) Wilson;
2–Daniel (2 below).
6–James **Johnston**, of Pa.; Am. Rev.;
5–Jane, *m* Capt. John **Foster**, Am. Rev.;
4–Nancy (Agnes), *m* John **Wilson** (Peter[5], Am. Rev., *m* Jean Galbraith);
3–Mary Ann (Jane), *m* William **Wood** (3 above);
2–Daniel (May 30, 1830-Nov. 3, 1893), breeder of thoroughbred stock; U.S.A. in Civil War; *m* Apr. 13, 1861, Mary Elizabeth Johnson (Mar. 8, 1836-Aug. 4, 1916); for issue and other lineages see Vol. III, p. 559.
1–*m* Feb. 28, 1892, Gilbert A. MacKenzie, *b* Browning, Mo., Jan. 5, 1870; mcht. and banker; son of Donald MacKenzie (Alexander[3], of N.S., Can., *m* Margaret Frazier), *m* Agnes Anderson, of Can.
1–Mem. Knights of the Golden Horseshoe, S. D.P., D.A.C., D.A.R., U.S.D. 1812, I.A.G., Taylor Family Assn. of Ky., Huguenot Soc. of Pa., hist. socs. of Ky., Mo., N.Y., Va.; O.E.S. (White Shrine of Jerusalem), Pythian Sister. Mem. Ia. State Chess Assn. (state champion, 1905; won medal, 1912, in Rice Gambit Tournament, Iowa vs. N.Y. Chess League). Residence: Moulton, Ia.

1–**MURPHY, Mary Moore Colvin (Mrs. W. B.)**, *b* Pender Co., N.C., Sept. 2, 1888.
6–Alexander **Colvin**, from Scotland; *m* Margaret Robinson;
5–John, mem. Wilmington Com. of Safety; *m* Anne De Rossett;
4–Col. John (1763-1839), col. War 1812; *m* 1792, Flora McAllister (1769-1807; Col. Alexander[5] [1715-1800], from Scotland, 1735, settled at Wilmington, N.C.; col. Cumberland Co. militia; mem. Provincial Congress at Hillsboro, N.C., 1775, at Halifax, N.C., 1776; mem. Com. of Safety for Wilmington Dist.; mem. com. to interview the Highlanders and explain to them the nature of the controversy with Great Britain, 1775; mem. N.C. Senate, 1787,88,-89; *m* 1763, Jean Colvin, *b* 1740);
3–William B. (1804-36), *m* 1827, Flora Ann Shaw;
2–James William (2 below).
5–William **Shaw** (*d* 1777), from Scotland; *m* Mary McCurdy;
4–Allen (*b* 1760), *m* 1806, Mary McAllister;
3–Flora Ann (1807-90), *m* William B. **Colvin** (3 above).
5–William **Robinson**, from Scotland; *m* Catharine Sellors;
4–Duncan (*b* 1771), *m* Mary Sellors (William[5], *m* Betsey, dau. of John Torrey, from Scotland, via Pa., to N.C. ca. 1765);
3–Mary Maria (*b* 1822), *m* Charles Peyton **Moore**;

2–Annie B. (*b* 1856), *m* 1886, James William **Colvin** (1835-1924), large landowner and farmer; issue: I–Mary Moore (1 above); II–Flora Shaw (1889-1907).

1–*m* June 12, 1912, Dr. W. B. Murphy, *b* Wilmington, N.C., Sept. 18, 1877; v.p. N.C. Med. Soc., 1929-30; son of Dr. W. B. Murphy, of Tomahawk, N.C.; issue: 1–Mary Colvin, *b* Garland, N.C., Apr. 27, 1927.

1–Ed. Peace Inst., Raleigh, N.C. Trustee East Carolina Teachers Coll., since 1927; historian Greene Co.; v.chmn. Greene Co. Dem. exec. com., 1924-30; mem. state Dem. exec. com., 1930; state pres. Woman's Auxiliary of N.C. Med. Soc., 1930-31. V.chmn. Co. Council Nat. Defense, World War; sec. co. Red Cross, 1917-18. Mem. D.A.R. (regent, 1924-30), U.D.C. (pres. Green Co. Chapter, 1924-26; dist. dir., 1924-26), N.C. Hist. Soc., Peace Alumnae Assn. (state pres., 1928-29). Presbyterian. Democrat. Clubs: Woman's (pres. 1926-27), Kinston Country. Residence: Snow Hill, N.C.

1–**PATTON, Mary Weatherby Cole (Mrs. James Hull),** *b* Baltimore, Md., Sept. 10, 1863.

7–Whitehead **Weatherby,** of Eng.; *m* 1716;

6–Benjamin (1720-90), *m* 1741, Miss Foucks;

5–David (1747-1812), capt. 2d Bn., Gloucester Co., N.J., Militia, Am. Rev.; *m* 1772, Mary Cavalier;

4–Benjamin (*b* 1780), *m* 1801, Rachael Smith (*b* 1782);

3–Jeremiah (1804-94), *m* 1829, Ann Budd Sexton;

2–Tamzon (2 below).

8–George **Sexton** (1630-90), settled at Windsor, Conn., later at Westfield, Mass.; *m* Catharine–;

7–Daniel (1660-1710), to Queens Co., L.I., N.Y., 1687; *m* Sarah Bancroft (John[8], of Westfield, Mass.; John[9], from Eng. in the "James," 1632, settled at Lynn, Mass.);

6–William (1686-1732), Monmouth Co., N.J.; *m* Ann Stringham (Peter[7], Queens Co., L.I.);

5–James (1718-84), of Upper Freehold, N.J.; *m* Rebecca–;

4–James, pvt. N.J. militia, Am. Rev.; *m* Deborah Budd (Samuel[5], of Burlington Co., N.J.);

3–Ann Budd (*d* 1886), *m* Jeremiah **Weatherby** (3 above);

2–Tamzon (1832-1921), *m* 1860, as his 2d wife, Lewis Hiram **Cole** (1833-87; Hiram[3] [1806-80], *m* Elizabeth Andrew, dau. of Augustus Taylor, *m* Hester Saunders); issue: I–Elizabeth Tasker (1860-1928); II–Mary Weatherby (1 above); III–Florence Belle (*b* 1866; *m* Joseph S. Shefloe); IV–Rachael Smith (1868-70); V–Anna Lewis (*b* 1870).

1–*m* Nov. 19, 1884, James Hull Patton, *b* Baltimore, Md., May 8, 1862; v.p.-treas., Md. Casualty Co.; son of Robert Patton (1827-96; James Hull[3] [1792-1849], *m* Rebekah Joiner [1792-1847; William[4] (*b* 1758), pvt. Phila. Militia, 1777, *m* 1791, Margaretta George]), *m* 1857, Isabella Norrie Taylor (1834-1905; Robert[3], from Scotland to Columbia, S.C., 1828, thence to Baltimore, *m* Isabella Train); issue (all *b* Baltimore, Md.): 1–Helen Marguerite (Apr. 3, 1886-1893); 2–Elizabeth Cole, *b* Nov. 10, 1889; D.A.R.; *m* May 10, 1924, Albert Austin May; 3–James Hull, Jr., *b* Jan. 7, 1900; Baltimore City Coll.; U.Pa. (Sigma Alpha Epsilon); S.A.R.; *m* Sept. 22, 1920, Elizabeth Whiting Bates (issue: Mary Elizabeth, mem. C.A.R.); 4–Mary Anna, *b* Mar. 7, 1902; D.A.R.; *m* Jan. 1921, John Lampkin Robertson, Jr. (issue: John Lampkin, 3d; James Patton; William Lewis, mem. C.A.R.); 5–Robert Lewis, *b* Feb. 28, 1904; St. John's Coll., Annapolis, Md. (Kappa Alpha), S.A.R.

1–Ed. private and public schools of Baltimore; Peabody Conservatory of Music and private music masters of Baltimore. Musician, soloist, contralto, pianist and organist. Organized John Eager Howard Chapter D.A.R., 1911, regent until 1914; organized Commodore Joshua Barney Chapter, 1916. Mem. Md. Hist. Soc., Auxiliary Aid Soc. for Relief of Widows and Orphans of Seamen, Woman's Auxiliary Bd. of the Hosp. of U.Md. Clubs: Woman's (Roland Park), Arundel, Goucher College Glee (organizer), Treble Clef, Old Wednesday, Oratorio Soc. Residence: 622 W. University Parkway, Baltimore, Md.

1–**PORTER, Olive Linn Anthony (Mrs. Robert Lynn),** *b* Hernando, Miss., Apr. 13, 1879.

9–Col. Richard **Lee** (qv);

8–Richard (1647-1714), councillor, burgess; *m* Letitia Corbin (1657-1706; Henry[9], qv);

7–Philip, *m* Elizabeth Sewall;

6–John, *m* Susannah Smith (Philip[7], *m* Mary Mathews);

5–Col. Philip, of "Nomini," Westmoreland Co., Va.; *m* Mary Jaquelin Smith;

4–Mary Smith (1788-1866), *m* 1808, James C. **Anthony,** of Richmond, Va. (Rev. John[5], *m* Susan Austin);

3–William Austin (1813-84), *m* 1st, 1837, Malinda Dyson (1817-57; Aquilla[4]);

2–Josephine Leola (2 below).

10–Col. John **Smith,** speaker House of Burgesses, 1657; *m* Anne Bernard;

9–Capt. John (*d* 1698), of "Purton," Gloucester Co., Va.; mem. Colonial Council, 1657; speaker House of Burgesses, 1657; burgess, 1691; *m* 1680, Mary Warner (Augustine[10], speaker Va. House of Burgesses, mem. Royal Council, Va., *m* Mildred, dau. of George Reade, qv);

8–Augustine (*b* 1689), of "Shooter's Hill," Middlesex Co.; *m* 1711, Sarah Carver (*d* 1736; John[9]);

7–Maj. John (*d* 1771, aet. 56), of "Shooter's Hill"; *m* 1737, Mary Jaquelin;

6–Mary (*d* 1791), *m* 1765, Rev. Thomas **Smith** (*d* 1789, aet. 50), last colonial rector of Cople Parish, Westmoreland Co.;

5–Mary Jaquelin (1769-1854), *m* Col. Philip **Lee** (5 above).

10–Miles **Cary** (qv);

9–Capt. William (1657-1713), *m* Martha Scarbrooke (Maj. John[10], *m* Mary Martian);

8–Martha, *m* 1706, as his 2d wife, Edward **Jaquelin** (1668-1730), came to Va., 1697 (John[9], *m* Elizabeth Craddock);

7–Mary (1714-54), *m* John **Smith** (7 above).

2–Rev. William Linn **Anthony** (*b* 1843), soldier C.S.A.; Baptist minister over 45 yrs.; *m* 1873, Josephine Leola Anthony (*b* 1848); issue: I–Alcea Agusta (*b* 1874); II–Antoinette (*b* 1876); III–Olive Linn (1 above); IV–Josephine Leola (*b* and *d* 1882); V–Irine Hope (*b* and *d* 1885).

1–*m* Mar. 27, 1912, Robert Lynn Porter, *b* Ripley, Tenn., June 10, 1877; son of Robert Scott Porter, of Ripley, *m* Phalicea Anthony.

1–Ed. Clinton (Ky.) Coll.; Union U., Jackson, Tenn. Mem. U.D.C. Baptist. Residence: Marked Tree, Ark.

1–**POTEAT, William Louis,** *b* Caswell Co., N.C., Oct. 20, 1856.

3–Miles **Poteat,** of Caswell Co., N.C.;

2–James (2 below).

4–John **McNeill**;

3–Hosea, *m* Mar. 18, 1807, Isabella Graves (Mar. 16, 1788-Dec. 26, 1861; Rev. Barzillai[4], *m* Ursula Wright).

2–James **Poteat** (1809-89), planter; *m* Isabella Roberts; *m* 2d, 1855, Julia Annise McNeill (1833-1910); issue (1st marriage): I–Lindsay (*d* 1864); II–John Miles (*d* 1867); III–Elizabeth Bettie (*d* 1873; *m* George R. Lindsay); IV–Virginia; V–James Preston (*d* 1907; *m* Emma Moore); issue (2d marriage): I–William Louis (1 above); II–Ida Isabella (*b* 1858); III–Edwin McNeill (*b* 1860; *m* Haley Gordon; *m* 2d, Harriet Brittingham); IV–Emma Lindsay (1862-82).

1–*m* June 24, 1881, Emma James Purefoy, *b* Wake Forest, N.C., Oct. 13, 1859; dau. of Addison F. Purefoy, of Wake Forest; issue (all *b* Wake Forest, N.C.): 1–Hubert McNeill, *b* Dec. 12, 1886; B.A., Wake Forest Coll., '06, M.A., 1908; Ph.D., Columbia, 1912; *m* June 26, 1912, Essie, dau. of J. L. Morgan, of Marion, N.C. (issue: Hubert McN., Jr.; William Morgan); 2–Louie, *b* Feb. 12, 1889; B.A., Meredith Coll., '08; *m* Aug. 28, 1912, Wheeler Martin, Jr. (issue: Wheeler, Jr.); 3–Helen Purefoy, *b* Apr. 6, 1896; Meredith Coll., 1912-16; *m* Mar. 6, 1919, Laurence T. Stallings, Jr. (issue: Sylvia, *b* Apr. 22, 1926).

1–B.A., Wake Forest Coll., '77, M.A., 1889; post-grad. studies Marine Biol. Lab. and short time in Zool. Inst., U. of Berlin; (LL.D., Baylor U., 1905, U. of N.C., 1906, Brown U., 1927). Teacher in Wake Forest Coll., since 1878, prof. biology, since 1883, pres., 1905-27. Author and lecturer (see Who's Who in America). Residence: Wake Forest, N.C.

1–**POWERS, Pauline Watkins (Mrs. Edwin B.),** *b* Tehuacana, Tex., Nov. 7, 1890.

8–Henry **Watkins** (*b* 1637), Henrico Co., Varina Parish, "Malborn Hills," Va.;
7–Henry (*b* 1660), *m* Mary–;
6–John (will 1744), the "tray maker"; *m* Elizabeth–;
5–William E. (?), (1742-1820), of Halifax Co., Va.; Am. Rev.; *m* Elizabeth Jearnigan, of Va.;
4–Jesse J. (1776-1838), of Va.; removed to Henderson Co., Tenn., 1830, to Red River Co., Tex., 1833; killed by Indians while serving the Republic; personal friend of Sam Houston; *m* 1809, Mary White McCorkle (kinswoman of Gen. James White, the founder of Knoxville, Tenn.);
3–John Marr (1814-76), of Nacogdoches, Tex.; *m* 1842, Malvina Kemp Noble (1823-63; Levi[4], *m* Jane Stean, of Miss.; the town of Kemp, Tex., is named for her;
2–Archibald Seborn (2 below).
8–Duncan **Campbell,** from the west coast of Scotland thru Ireland to Pa., 1742; Lancaster Co., S.C., 1756; *m* Mary McCoy;
7–Mary, *m* Moses **White**;
6–Joseph, of S.C.; *m* Elizabeth Russell;
5–Joanna, *m* Archibald **McCorkle,** soldier Am. Rev.; pensioned; fought at Guilford C.H., Eaton Springs, and Ninety-Six;
4–Mary (1791-1860), *m* in Lancaster Dist., S.C., Jesse J. **Watkins** (4 above).
4–Ephriam **Cox,** *m* Charlotte–;
3–Moses (1819-73), of Ala., moved to East Texas, 1859; *m* Martha Bennett (1829-94; Rev. Mitchell[4], of Darlington Dist., S.C., *m* Martha Turner);
2–Martha (*b* 1862), *m* 1879, Archibald Seborn **Watkins** (1852-1914), physician, Limestone Co., Tex.; issue: I–Mabel (1881-1927; *m* Rev. Gordon Lang); II–Malvina Kemp; III–John Bennett (*m* Lutie McKee); IV–Archibald Flint (*m* Grace Chapin); V–Pauline (1 above); VI–Noble (1893-1905); VII–Mary Kate (*m* Harrison McGill); VIII–Olive; IX–Texas (*d* childhood); X–Jessie (*d* childhood).
1–*m* June 9, 1918, Edwin Booth Powers, *b* Ovilla, Tex., Aug. 6, 1880; A.B., Trinity U., '06; M.S., U.Chicago, 1913; Ph.D., U.Ill., 1918; prof. and head of dept. of zoology, U. of Tenn., 1924 (see Am. Men of Science, Who's Who in Am. Education); son of William Wilson Powers (1837-1919; David[3], *m* Louisa, dau. of Blake Wilson), *m* Eveline Crocia Wood (1841-1909; Joshua[3], *m* Crocia Walsh Chewning; Benjamin[4], *m* Elizabeth Winters); issue: 1–Edwine Watkins, *b* Lincoln, Neb., Nov. 11, 1920; 2–Wilson Watkins, *b* Knoxville, Tenn., Sept. 1, 1924.
1–A.B., Westminster Coll., '09; A.B., Trinity U., '14; student Columbia U., 1917; travelled and studied abroad, 1920-21; M.A., U.Tenn., 1926. Teacher of French, Thackston Private School, since 1926. Mem. East Tenn. Hist. Soc. Clubs: Knoxville Art Center, Ossoli Circle (pres., 1930-31), Flower Lovers, Tenn. Federation of Women's (chmn. div. of literature, 1929-31). Residence: 133 E. Hillvale Dr., Knoxville, Tenn.

1–**PRICE, Susan Hill Jones (Mrs. John R.),** *b* Lauderdale Co., Ala., Feb. 24, 1858.
9–Garrard **Spencer** (qv);
8–Samuel (*d* 1705), *m* 1673, Hannah Willey Blachford;
7–Isaac (1678-1751), dep. from E. Haddam to Gen. Ct. of Conn., 1734-41; justice; *m* 1707, Mary Selden;
6–Samuel (1708-58), *m* 1732, Jerusha Brainerd;
5–Judge Samuel (1738-94), grad. Princeton, 1759; settled at Wadesboro, N.C.; mem. Assembly from Anson Co., N.C., 1766-68; mem. Council of War at Hillsboro, N.C., 1768; mem. Provincial Congress at Newbern, 1774, at Hillsboro, 1775, at Halifax, 1776; mem. Provincial Council of Safety, 1775-76; one of three judges first elected under the Constn., 1777; *m* ca. 1766, Sybil Pegues;
4–Mary (*b* 1770), *m* 1782, Isaac **Jackson** (1762-1828); see portrait;
3–Philippa Augusta (*b* 1800), *m* 1817, Frederick **Jones** (*b* 1794);
2–Albert Hampden (2 below).
10–Richard **Church** (qv);
9–Edward, of Hatfield, Mass.;
8–Rebecca, *m* Joseph **Selden** (1651-1724; Thomas[9]);

SPENCER

Arms: Quarterly, argent and gules, in two and three a fret or, over all on a bend sable three escallops of the first.
Crest: Out of a ducal coronet or, a griffin's head argent, gorged with a bar gemella gules, between two wings expanded of the second.

7–Mary, *m* Isaac **Spencer** (7 above).
8–Daniel **Brainerd** (qv);
7–Hon. Hezekiah (1681-1727), mem. Gen. Assembly of Conn. 16 yrs.; clk. House of Deps., 1720; speaker, 1721-22; mem. Council, 1723-25; auditor, justice, asst.; *m* Dorothy (Hobart) Mason;

ISAAC JACKSON (1762-1828), and his wife, MARY SPENCER (b 1770).

6–Jerusha (*d* 1747), *m* Samuel **Spencer** (6 above).
8–William **Boddie** (qv);
7–John (1664-1720), of Isle of Wight Co., Va.; planter; *m* Elizabeth Thomas;
6–William (1710-72), officer in colonial militia 20 yrs.; lt. in Northampton Foot, in Spanish Alarm, 1748; *m* Mary Bennett:
5–Nathaniel (1732-97), owned 9,400 acres of land in Wake Co., N.C.; rep. Edgecombe Co. in Provincial Congress, at Halifax, 1776; rep. Gen. Assembly, N.C., 1771; mem. House of Commons; *m* 1760, Chloe Crudup (1745-81);
4–George (*b* 1769), *m* 1st, 1790, Susan Hill;
3–Nathan (1795-1861), *m* 1820, Mary Thomas Smith;
2–Rebecca Ann (1832-87), *m* 1855, Albert Hampden **Jones** (1822-84); issue: I–Frederick Fearn (1856-68); II–Susan Hill (1 above); III–Mary Philippa (*b* 1860); IV–Percy Rivers (1862-

1927; *m* Mary Ford); V–Emmett Lee (*b* 1865; *m* Annie Ford); VI–Louisa (1868-1923); VII–Minnie (*b* and *d* 1871).
1–*m* Aug. 23, 1883, John Robert Price, *b* Moulton, Ala., Sept. 13, 1842; midshipman U.S.N. and lt. C.S.N.; son of William Price, *m* Elizabeth Dixon; issue: 1–John Robert (Dec. 22, 1884-Jan. 16, 1897); 2–Marjorie, *b* Feb. 21, 1887; *m* Dec. 9, 1917, Lt. Harry Morton Trafford (issue: Harry, *b* Aug. 14, 1918; Marjorie, *b* Sept. 11, 1920; John Robert Price, *b* Aug. 14, 1923; Bert Fearn, *b* Aug. 28, 1927; Donald Hampden, *b* Mar. 1928).
1–Grad. Florence Synodical Coll.; State Teachers Coll., Florence, Ala.; U. of Chicago. Mem. C.D.A., U.D.C., I.A.G., A.A.U.W., Firenze Club. Residence: 714 N. Wood Av., Florence, Ala.

1–**PROCTOR, Lucy Boardman Chapman (Mrs. John P.),** *b* Brooklyn, N.Y., June 7, 1873.
9–Edward **Chapman** (qv);
8–Samuel (*b* 1655), *m* Ruth Ingalls (Samuel[9]; Edmund[10], qv);
7–Samuel (1679-1742), *m* 1702, Phebe Balch (1684-1738; Samuel[8]; Benjamin[9]);
6–Samuel (1706-*d* aet. 90), Newmarket and Stratham, N.H.; *m* —York;
5–David (1752-1819), *m* Elizabeth Clark (1754-1823; Caleb[6], Am. Rev., *m* Mary, dau. of Giles Barley; Richard[7]; Richard[8]);
4–Edmund, *m* Susanna Lord;
3–Eben Lord, *m* Martha Hilton;
2–Frank Hilton (*b* 1848), druggist; *m* 1872, Ella Frances James (*b* 1853; Thomas William[3], Deerfield, N.H., *m* Julia Bean); issue: I–Lucy Boardman (1 above); II–Eben Lord (*m* Edith Rice); III–Frank William (*m* Ethel Dixon); IV–Charles Edward (see Vol. III, p. 120); V–John Hilton (1883-1917; *m* Helen Healey).
1–*m* Oct. 11, 1893, John Patten Proctor, *b* Franklin, N.H., Nov. 9, 1865; son of Alexis Proctor; issue (all *b* Franklin, N.H.): 1–Alexis Chapman, *b* Mar. 27, 1897; ed. Phillips Exeter and Dartmouth; 2–Dorothy Bradstreet, *b* Nov. 19, 1899; ed. Miss Capen's School, Northampton, Mass., and U. of Calif.; 3–John Winthrop, *b* Apr. 10, 1901; ed. Phillips Exeter and Dartmouth; *m* Aug. 16, 1930, Charlotte Roy.
1–Ed. Miss Gilman's School, Boston. Mem. D.A.R. Residence: Franklin, N.H.

1–**SMITH, George Henry, Jr.,** *b* St. Louis, Mo., Sept. 27, 1861.
8–John **Randall** (1629-84), from Eng., 1667, to Westerly, R.I.; *m* Elizabeth Morton (*d* 1685);
7–John (1666-post 1720), early settler of Westerly, and Stonington, Conn.; *m* 1695, Abigail Billing (1677-1705; William[8], qv);
6–John (1701-61), lt. of Train Band, Stonington; *m* Mary (Holmes) Palmer;
5–Joshua (1743-1808), a mariner, died in shipwreck on No Man's Land; commd. to buy provisions for families of enlisted men in Cont. Army, 1777; *m* 1767, Rhoda Chesebrough (*b* 1748; Zebulon[6]; Elisha[7]; Samuel[8]);
4–Chesebrough (1776-1825), Norwich, N.Y.; *m* 1799, Prudence Miner (1778-1862; Daniel[5], Am. Rev.; Charles[6]; James[7]; Ephraim[8]; Thomas[9], qv);
3–Prudence (1800-37), *m* Squire **Smith** (1799-1855);
2–Maj. George Henry (2 below).
10–Robert **Holmes** (*d* 1670), settled at Stonington, Conn.; served in King Philip's War;
9–Joshua (ante 1656-1694), *m* Abigail (Ingraham) Chesebro;
8–Joshua (1678-1729), *m* 1698, Fear Sturgis (*d* 1753);
7–Abigail (1703-32), *m* 1728, Jedediah **Brown** (1709-32; John[8], of Stonington, *m* Elizabeth Miner; Thomas[9]);
6–Lucy (1730-65), *m* 1750, Capt. John **Randall** (1730-1802), Am. Rev. (John[7]; John[8]; John[9], 8 above);
5–Lucy (1751-1831), *m* 1768, Amos **Breed** (1744-85);
4–Elias (1782-1849), *m* 2d, 1807, Betsey Randall (1784-1868; Thomas[5]; John[6]; John[7]; John, 8 above);
3–Mary Elizabeth (1811-87), *m* 1830, Henry Villiers **Brown** (1808-62; Hezekiah[4]; Jesse[5]; Richard[6]; Richard[7]; Henry[8], of Providence);
2–Mary Frances (*b* 1835), *m* 1855, Maj. George Henry **Smith** (1833-1905), organizer and cdr., U.S. Mil. Telegraph Corps, Civil War, hdqrs. St. Louis; for issue and other lineages see Henry V. B. Smith, page 468.
1–*m* Oct. 25, 1887, Hallie E. Getchell, *b* St. Cloud, Minn., Dec. 1, 1862; dau. Jesse Benton Getchell, of St. Cloud; issue: 1–Olive Van Rensselaer, *b* St. Paul, Minn., Sept. 27, 1888; A.B., U. of Calif., '16; *m* Dec. 25, 1917, Roy Almon Wiley, of Santa Rosa, N.M. (issue: George Carter; Charles Getchell; Roy Oliver); 2–Herbert Getchell, *b* St. Paul, Mar. 11, 1890; grad. N.M. Coll. of Agr. and Mech. Arts, '13; post-grad. work, U. of Ore., 1925; *m* Dec. 29, 1915, Florence Reed Davis, of Malvern, Pa. (issue: Hugh Davis; Florence Sylvia).
1–Merchant. Was with G.N. Ry., N.P. Ry., A., T.&S.F. Ry., 22 yrs. Mayor of Santa Rosa, N.M., 1917-18; mem. sch. bd.; trustee. M.E. Ch., Santa Rosa, 1902-29. Mason (32°). Republican. Residence: Santa Rosa, N.M.

1–**SMITH, Bertha Grace Lane (Mrs. William R.),** *b* Sandy Hook, Newtown, Conn., Aug. 11, 1869.
5–Richard **Lane** (1743-1838), *m* 1765, Elizabeth Cahoone (1748-1820);
4–John (1766-1849), *m* 1790, Sarah– (1768-1838);
3–Daniel Page (1792-93-1865), *m* 2d, 1837, Polly Betsey Sherman, widow of Charles Sherwood;
2–John Sherman (1840-1913), *m* 1864, Emma Shepard Plumb (1844-1928); issue: I–Arthur Sherman (*b* 1865); II–Bertha Grace (1 above); III–Ernest LeRoy (*b* 1875; *m* 1898, Harriet Estelle Puffer, *b* 1875); IV–Harry Clifford (*b* 1879); V–Edna Carolyn (*m* Oliver E. Yale).
1–*m* Jan. 23, 1895, William Rice Smith, *b* N. Haven, Conn., Oct. 17, 1867; son of J. Boardman Smith; issue: 1–Sally Lane, *b* Meriden, Conn., Mar. 15, 1903; *m* June 9, 1925, John Burgis Kirby, Jr. (issue: Sibyl Smith, *b* June 3, 1927); 2–Helen Lane, *b* Meriden, June 14, 1906.
1–Grad. State Normal School. Ex-regent, Susan Carrington Clarke Chapter D.A.R. Residence: 189 E. Main St., Meriden, Conn.

1–**TILLMAN, James David, III,** *b* Carrollton, Miss., Apr. 3, 1912.
7–Robert **Hamilton** (son of Ninian, Presbyn., who went from Scotland to Ireland ca. 1680-90, on account of religious persecution; g.son of John, of Scotland); came from Ireland, settled in Rockbridge Co., Va.; *m* Margaret McKee;
6–Capt. William (*b* ca. 1754), removed to Fayette Co., Ky.; capt. Am. Rev.; *m* Mary McClung (John[7], from Ireland to Rockbridge Co., 1747, *m* Elizabeth Alexander; Archibald[8], from Scotland to New Providence, Pa., 1736, to Rockbridge Co., 1747, *m* Margaret Parks);
5–Joseph Daviess (1782-1827), of Nashville, Tenn.; *m* 1813, Sally Bedinger Morgan (1793-1853; Col. Abraham[6], officer Am. Rev., *m* Mary, dau. of Henry Bedinger; Capt. William[7], Am. Rev.; Col. Richard[8], came to Va., 1732);
4–Dr. Oscar (1815-61), of Hinds Co., Miss.; *m* 1844, Sigismunda Mary Taylor;
3–John Moore (1853-1928), U. of Nashville; civil engr.; co. surveyor; *m* 1876, Sara Elizabeth Collins (*b* 1853; Rev. Jeptha Sylvester[4] [1817-71], of Hinds Co., Miss., *m* 1839, Margaret Anne, dau. of James Birmingham Baird);
2–Anne Sigismunda (2 below).
9–James **Taylor** (qv);
8–James (1665-1730), of Orange Co., Va.; *m* 1699, Martha Thompson (1679-1762; Col. William[9], from Eng. to Va.);
7–Erasmus (1715-94), "Greenfield," Orange Co., Va.; *m* 1749, Jane Moore (1728-1812; John[8], *m* Rebecca [Catlett] Conway, dau. Col. John Catlett, of King George Co., Va.);
6–Capt. John (1760-1826), capt. Am. Rev.; *m* 1786, Anna Gilbert (1769-1823);
5–John Moore (1788-1856); judge Supreme Ct. of Ala., 1825-34; removed to Clinton, Miss.; on staff of Gen. Zachary Taylor during Mexican War; *m* 1811, Anne Foote (1788-1847; William[6], *m* Sara, dau. of William Alexander; George[7]; Richard[8]; Richard[9]);
4–Sigismunda Mary (1827-81), *m* Dr. Oscar **Hamilton** (4 above);
3–John M., *m* Sara E. Collins (3 above);
2–Anne Sigismunda (Sept. 18, 1886-Apr. 20, 1920), *m* 1911, James David **Tillman,** Jr. (*b* Feb. 6, 1882); see Vol. III, p. 449.
1–Not married. Student Ga. School of Tech.,

1930 (Kappa Sigma). Mem. C.A.R., Taylor Family Assn. Residence: 1924 34th Av., Meridian, Miss.

1-**WAITE, Julia Alston (Mrs. Frederick D.),** *b* Orrville, nr. Selma, Ala., Feb. 9, 1868.
8-Rt. Hon. John **Alston** (qv);
7-John (*d* 1704), *m* Anne Wallis (b ca. 1645; John[8]);
6-Col. John (1673-1758), asso. justice Supreme Ct. of N.C., 1725; *m* Mary Clarke (g.dau. of John Palin, chief justice of N.C., 1731);
5-Soloman, of Granville Co., N.C.; *m* Sarah Ann Hinton;
4-Lemuel James (1760-1836), mem. 10th and 11th Congresses from S.C., 1807-11; moved to Clark Co., Ala., 1816; *m* 1st, Elisabeth Williams;
3-William Williams (1799-1860), *m* 1820, Mary Haywood Burges (1803-41);
2-Dr. Alfred Augustus (1839-92), *m* 1867, Margaret Ulmer (1840-1902); for issue see Vol. III, p. 127.
1-*m* Frederick Daniel Waite, *b* Apr. 10, 1858; issue: 1-Margaret (*b* and *d* Sept. 4, 1889); 2-Edith, *b* Belleview, Fla., Mar. 16, 1892; Shorter Coll., Rome, Ga.; *m* Apr. 18, 1912, Hatton B. Rogers, pres. Bank of Commerce, Tampa, Fla. (issue: Hatton B., Jr.; Dorothy Waite); 3-Ethel Alston, *b* Belleview, Nov. 12, 1897; Brenau Coll., Gainesville, Ga., and Belcourt Sem., Washington; *m* Feb. 11, 1920, Harold Van Voorhees, of Indianapolis, Ind.; *m* 2d, June 13, 1929, Ralph Ellwood Brown, of Buffalo, N.Y.
1-Mem. C.D.A., U.D.C. Clubs: Woman's (past pres.), Golf and Country. Residence: 1404 Riverside St., Palmetto, Fla.

HARRY F. BARRELL

1-**BARRELL, Harry Ferdinand,** *b* Warwick, N.Y., Dec. 6, 1858.
8-George **Barrell** (qv);
7-John (ca. 1618-1658), *m* Mary Colburn (Elder William[8], one of the 12 original founders of the colony);
6-John (1656-1742), mariner; *m* 4th, Abiah (Ardell) Beards;
5-John (1707-81), shipping mcht.; *m* Ruth Green;
4-Joseph (1740-1804), with others fitted out the "Columbia," the 1st Am. ship to circumnavigate the globe, which, in 1792, entered Columbia River, and her captain claimed for the govt. the ty. now Wash., Ida. and Ore.; *m* 3d, Sarah (Webb) Simpson (1752-1832); among their sons were Charles and Henry, see portraits; Vol. III, p. 612.
3-George (1788-1870), one of the first brokers in Wall St., New York (see portrait); *m* Eliza Leaycraft;
2-Henry Ferdinand (2 below).
8-Capt. Christopher **Leaycraft,** British mariner of Bermuda, sometimes named gov. of Bermuda; and thru his g.son:

GEORGE BARRELL (1788-1870).

Residence of George Barrell, built by him in 1859, in Harrison Street, East Orange, N.J. (was the residence of Harry F. Barrell, 1860-83).

6-Richard;
5-Capt. Viner, mariner and cdr. of privateer; *m* Elizabeth Codwise (Capt. Christopher[6], of Brooklyn, cdr. privateer against French, lt. col. and pay master Kings Co. militia);
4-Capt. George, of N.Y.; *m* 2d, Elizabeth (Winset) Heymer, of Hackensack;
3-Eliza (1799-1867), *m* George **Barrell** (3 above).
8-Johannes (Weesner) **Wisner** (1676-1744), officer of Queen Anne's Swiss contingent; came to America, 1713; *m* Elizabeth Dumbaugh;
7-Hendrick (1698-1767), *m* Mary Shaw;
6-John (1722-78), capt. French and Indian War and Am. Rev.; *m* Anne–;
5-Henry (1742-1812), lt. col. Am. Rev.; mem. N. Y. Assembly; *m* Susannah Goldsmith;
4-Gabriel (1784-1836), *m* Elizabeth Board;
3-Henry Board (1815-44), *m* his cousin, Mary Ann Wood (3 below);
2-Elizabeth (2 below).
9-Philip Pieterson (van) **Schuyler** (qv);
8-Capt. Arent (1662-1730), capt. French and Indian War; employed by govt. to negotiate with Minnesink Indians; had estates at Pompton Plains, Belleville, Burlington and Elizabethtown, N.J.; *m* 1684, Janneke Teller (William[9], soldier at Albany Ft.);
7-Phillipus (1687-1709), in expdn. against Can.; *m* Hester Kingsland (Capt. Isaac[8], lord of Kingsland Manor, Bergen Co., N.J., mem. Council);
6-Anne (1728-1816), *m* James **Board,** a Welchman;
5-Cornelius (1762-1830), *m* his cousin, Annis Board (5 below);
4-Elizabeth (1791-1830), *m* Gabriel **Wisner** (4 above).
9-Thomas **Beach** (qv);
8-Zopher (*b* 1662), removed to N.J., 1683, still living there 1728; *m* Martha Pratt (Dea. John[9], of Milford, Conn.);
7-Josiah (ca. 1705-1777), of Newark, N.J.; his house was plundered by the British, 1777;

SCHUYLER

Arms: Vert, an arm clothed or, issuing from the dexter side holding in the hand a falcon proper, hooded of the second.
Crest: A falcon as in the arms.

killed at Battle of Scotch Plains, N.J.; *m* 1726, Anna Day (ca. 1710-1782);
6–Phoebe, *m* 1762, Joseph **Board**;
5–Annis, *m* her cousin, Cornelius **Board** (5 above);
4–Phoebe, *m* Capt. John Durland **Wood** (1788-1834), officer War 1812;
3–Mary Ann (1813-1910), *m* Henry Board **Wisner** (3 above);

Florida residence of Harry F. Barrell, Tangerine Av., St. Petersburg, Fla.

Summer residence of Harry F. Barrell, at Shandelee, Sullivan Co., N.Y., in the western Catskills.

2–Elizabeth (1838-1926), *m* 1858, Henry Ferdinand **Barrell** (1833-95); for issue see Vol. I, p. 209.
1–*m* June 1904, Pearl Foster Slayback, *b* Boone Co., Ky., Dec. 1875; dau. of George M. Slayback, Boone Co., Ky.; 1 adopted son: Charles, *b* Newark, N.J., Oct. 1, 1892; *m* June 29, 1921, Blanch B. Wirt, *b* Swains, N.Y., 1889 (issue: Robert Lee, *b* Feb. 20, 1922).
1–A.B., Columbia, '82 (P.B.K.), Ph.B., 1883, A.M., 1884, LL.B., Ph.D., 1885. Lawyer, retired. Mem. O.F.P.A., S.C.W., H.S.A., S.A.R., S.W. 1812. Extensive traveler. Hobby: Bibliophile; owner of a private library of over 6,000 volumes. Summer place: Shandelee, Sullivan Co., N.Y. Residence: 1905 W. Cass St., Tampa, Fla.

1–**SAGENDORPH, Ethel May Abbott (Mrs. William K.),** *b* Omaha, Neb., Nov. 20, 1872.
9–George (Abbot) **Abbott** (qv);
8–William (1657-1712), Andover; *m* 1682, Elizabeth Gray (*d* 1712);
7–James (1695-1787), *m* 1714, Abigail Farnum (*b* 1692);
6–James (1717-1803), town clk., selectman, mem. Com. of Safety of Haverhill; *m* 1742, Sarah Bancroft (*b* 1722);
5–Bancroft (1757-1829), of Newbury, Vt.; mathematician and surveyor; held town offices; pvt. Am. Rev.; *m* 1787, Lydia White (1763-1853; Ebenezer[6], pvt. Am. Rev.);
4–Thomas (*b* 1788), *m* 1812, Anna Powers (1792-1841);
3–William (1815-85), *m* 1838, Maranda Dye (1820-87);
2–Samuel Clarence (2 below).
7–Dea. Nathaniel **Wales** (1694-1782), of Windsor, Conn.; mem. Com. of Safety, 1775-77; mem. Council of War; *m* 1726, Prudence Denison (*d* 1792);
6–Jonathan (1738-1802), *m* 1757, Zibiah Abbe (*b* 1737);
5–William (1762-1813), *m* 1779, Sarah Tinker (1763-1851; Nehemiah[6], settled at Mansfield, Conn., *m* 1760, Mary Huntington);
4–Laura (1792-1880), of Mexico, N.Y.; *m* Cyrus **Smith** (1792-1857);
3–Lucy (1818-1908), of London, O.; *m* 1842, James **McLain** (1806-69);
2–Laura Wales (1846-1929), of Bloomington, Ill.; *m* 1869, Samuel Clarence **Abbott** (1842-1916), merchant, Middletown, O.; issue: I–James McLain (1869-1918; *m* 1902, Emily Neil); II–Mabel Clara (1870-71); III–Ethel May (1 above); IV–Louise Estelle (1878-1910; *m* Francis M. Ball).
1–*m* June 13, 1900, William Kent Sagendorph, *b* Charlotte, Mich., June 1, 1871; son of Daniel Perry Sagendorph, of Jackson, Mich.; issue (all *b* Jackson, Mich.): 1–Kent Huntington, *b* Apr. 23, 1902; 2–Ethel Margaret, *b* Dec. 5, 1904; U.Mich., 1926; *m* June 16, 1926, L. Wallace Hoffman, of Richmond Hill, N.Y.; 3–Theodore Abbott, *b* May 1, 1906; 4–Perry Munson, *b* Nov. 22, 1907.
1–Studied German at Berlin 2 yrs.; studied French in Convent Notre Dame de Sion, Paris, 2 yrs. Taught French and German 6 yrs. Mem. D.F.P.A., D.A.R., I.A.G. Conglist. Republican. Clubs: Jackson Country, Jackson Woman's. Residence: 415 W. Franklin St., Jackson, Mich.

1–**ABRAMS, John Davison,** *b* E. Rockaway, L.I., May 28, 1871.
5–John **Abrams** (1736-1800; prob. desc. of Charles, of Hempstead, L.I., 1684); of Hempstead; *m* 1756, Hanna Shaw;
4–Capt. John (1792-1855), of Pearsall Corner, L.I.; soldier in War 1812; *m* 1812, Margaret Watts (1792-1886);
3–Sgt. John (1829-80), Rockville Centre, L.I.; *m* 1849, Marinda Abrams;
2–Clayton (2 below).
6–Jerome **Abrams** (ca. 1740-ca. 1812), of Pearsall Corner, L.I.; *m* Lucy Doxey;
5–Elijah (1765-1818), *m* 1785, Hanna Cornell (*d* 1818);
4–Zacharia (1799-1876), *m* 1822, Amelia Pearsall (1799-1880);
3–Miranda (1829-1903), *m* John **Abrams** (3 above).
6–Alexander **Davison** (1698-1764), from Scotland or Eng. to Norwich, Conn., ante 1750; *m* Margaret–;

5–Robert (1756-1823), Am. Rev.; *m* 1776, Nancy (Anne) De Mott (1750-1836);
4–Thomas (1787-1844), E. Rockaway, L.I.; *m* 1805, Fannie Valentine (1783-1858);
3–William (1811-88), *m* 1832, Martha Ann Poole (1815-92);
2–Caroline (1846-79), *m* 1870, Clayton **Abrams** (1849-80), of Rockville Centre, L.I.; issue: I–John Davison (1 above); II–Martha C. (1878-1918; *m* 1898, William Hicks, issue: Vera G., *m* Marvin Pellit).
1–*m* 1892, Mabel Scott, *b* Merrick, L.I., Aug. 26, 1872; issue: 1–Myrtle (1892-Apr. 3, 1918); *m* 1915, Clifford Cornell (issue: Clifford John, 1916-18); 2–Hazel, *b* Apr. 7, 1894; 3–Aubrey Scott, *b* Nov. 27, 1895; pvt., 77th M.P. Co. in World War (on U.S. pension list for life); 4–Norman John, *b* Aug. 25, 1898; World War service; *m* 1923, Grace West (issue: David John, *b* 1927); 5–Ronald Scott, *b* Aug. 2, 1910; *m* Loronia Carrington Cross Welsh.
1–Mason (32°, K.T.), I.O.O.F. Mem. I.A.G., etc. Residence: 320 Franklin St., Hempstead, N.Y.

L. ESTELLE APPLETON

1–**APPLETON, L(illa) Estelle,** *b* Victory, Vt., Nov. 9, 1858.
9–Samuel **Appleton** (qv);
8–Maj. Samuel (1625-96), judge Essex Co. Quarterly Ct., 15 yrs.; selectman, 1662; dep. Gen. Ct., 10 yrs.; capt. of Ipswich mil. co., 1673; cdr.-in-chief in King Philip's War; asst. gov.'s council, 1681-86; sgt.-maj. of S. Regt., Essex Co., 1682; in command of army forces at Cocheco, War of William and Mary, 1689; named in new charter of William and Mary as "one of the councillors of our said province," 1692; judge Inferior Ct. of Common Pleas, 1692-96; *m* 2d, 1656, Mary Oliver (1640-98; John[9], *m* Joanna, dau. Percival Lowle);
7–Maj. Isaac (1664-1747), maj. Essex Co. Regt., 1700; lt. under Col. John March, cdr.-in-chief of land forces in expdn. against Port Royal, Queen Anne's War, 1707; *m* prob. 1696, Priscilla Baker (1674-1731; Maj. Thomas[8], *m* Priscilla, dau. of Dep. Gov. Samuel Symonds);
6–Isaac (1704-94), yeoman; one of original grantees of New Ipswich, N.H., but probably never lived there; lt. provincial militia, 1771; *m* 1st, 1730, Elizabeth Sawyer (1709-85; Francis[7], mcht., Wells, Me.; William[8]);
5–Francis (bap. 1733-1816), removed to New Ipswich, N.H., 1771; pvt. French and Indian War, in expdn. to Lake George, 1755; present at surrender of Burgoyne, 1777; one of 32 founders of New Ipswich Acad., 1789; *m* 1758, Elizabeth Hubbard;
4–Francis (1759-1849), removed to Dublin, N.H., 1786 (?); dea. of Dublin Ch., 36 yrs.; pvt. Am. Rev.; *m* 1789, Mary (Polly) Ripley;
3–Ashley (1796-1876), to Granby, Vt., probably 1823; dea. first organized ch. of Granby, 1843; justice 16 yrs.; *m* 1823, Nancy Metcalf;
2–George Ashley (2 below).
8–William **Hubbard** (qv);
7–Richard (1631-81), settled at "Ipswich Farms," Hamlet Parish, Ipswich, where he lived until his death; A.B., Harvard, 1653; dep. Gen. Ct., 1660; feoffee of Ipswich Coll., 1664-81; selectman, 1665; tithingman, surveyor, etc.; *m* ca. 1658, Sarah Bradstreet (Gov. Simon[8], qv, *m* Anne, dau. of Gov. Thomas Dudley, qv);
6–John (1676-1750), surveyor of highways, 1720-35; named in list of "New Commoners belonging to Hamblett"; *m* 1710, Mary Brown (1688-1766);
5–Elizabeth (1729/30-1815), *m* Francis **Appleton** (5 above).
9–William **Ripley** (qv);
8–John (*d* 1683/84), received land grant, 1655; on list of freemen, 1657; *m* Elizabeth Hobart (1632-92; Rev. Peter[9]);
7–Peter (1668-1742), constable, 1708; selectman, 1725; *m* 1693, Sarah Lasell (1666-1736; John[8], *m* Elizabeth Gates);
6–Peter (1695-1765), constable, 1735; selectman, 1738,41; *m* 1st, 1720, Silence Lincoln (1692-1760; Caleb[7], *m* Rachel Bate);
5–Noah (1721-88), removed to Woodstock, 1747, to Rutland Dist. (now Barre), Mass., 1762; *m* 1743, Lydia Kent (1725-1816; Ebenezer[6], *m* Hannah Gannett);
4–Mary (bap. 1766-1840), *m* Francis **Appleton** (4 above).
10–Michael **Metcalf** (qv);
9–Michael (1620-54), came with parents to Boston, 1637; settled at Dedham, Mass.; admitted to the church, 1640; freeman, 1642; *m* 1644, Mary Fairbanks (John[10]);
8–Michael (bap. 1644-1693), *m* 1672, Elizabeth Fuller (1648-1732; Thomas[9], *m* Hannah Flower);
7–Michael (*b* 1674), *m* 1705, Lydia–;
6–Michael (1707-1768?), removed to Keene, probably 1749; *m* 1728, Meletia Hamart;
5–Michael (1730-77), signed Assn. Test, 1776; killed in Battle of Bennington; *m* 1751, Sarah Allen;
4–Capt. Thaddeus (1758-1823), *m* ca. 1782, Hepzibah Baker (1763-1851; Thomas[5], *m* Sarah Hale);
3–Nancy (1793-1889), *m* 1823, Ashley **Appleton** (3 above).
8–Edward **Wooster** (1622-89), called "Goodman Worster"; probably came from Eng.; settled at Milford, Conn.; bought land in Pagasset, 1655; constable, Hartford, 1669; selectman, 1680; surveyor, 1685; *m* 2d, probably 1669, Tabitha Tomlinson (*d* 1690);
7–Thomas (ca. 1656-1712/13), selectman; fence viewer; lt. Train Band, Darby, 1706; took oath of freeman, 1707/08; *m* sister of his stepmother, Phebe Tomlinson (1656 or 59-1739/40; Henry[8], *m* Alice–);
6–Thomas (1691/92-1777), selectman; *m* 1718, Sarah Hawkins (1695-1785; Joseph[7], *m* Elizabeth Gunn);
5–David (1734/35-1812), *m* 2d, 1762, Ann Doolittle (1739/40-1819; Thomas[6], *m* Hannah Fenn);
4–David (*b* 1762), *m* Roxanna Willey;
3–Rev. John (1798-1873), ordained minister, 1832; preached in Vt. and N.H. chs., 1830-72; first settled minister of Granby, Vt., 1843-58; rep. Granby in Legislature; first postmaster of mail route established between E. Burke, Vt., and Northumberland, N.H., running thru and back once a week, 1849-54; at Littleton, N.H., 1858-72; *m* 2d, 1832, Fanny Reed Stebbins (1804-88; Brainard[4]);
2–Fanny Reed (1833-1918), *m* 1851, George Ashley **Appleton** (1823-1913), removed to Victory, Vt., probably 1866; held many important town offices; town rep. for Victory (see Vol. III, p. 34 for issue).
1–Grad. State Normal Sch., Randolph, Vt., '79; B.L., Oberlin, '86, Ph.B., 1890; grad. State Normal Sch., Oswego, N.Y., 1897 and 1898; Ph.-D., U. of Chicago, 1909; research student Clark U., 1908-09, Columbia U., 1910-11. Head dept. psychology and edn., Oxford (O.) Coll. for Women, 1919-29. Author (see Who's Who in America). Mem. Institut Solvay-Institut de Sociologie (Brussels, Belgium), I.A.G.; fel-

low A.A.A.S. Address: 5704 Kenwood Av., Chicago, Ill.

1-**CLARKSON, Hattie Peck (Mrs. John W.),** *b* Ironton, Mo., Mar. 21, 1869.
9-Joseph **Peck** (qv);
8-Nathaniel (bap. 1641-1676), Barrington, R.I.; *m* Deliverance- (*d* 1675);
7-Nathaniel (1670-1751), of Swansea, Mass.; was called lt., and dea.; *m* 1st, 1695/96, Christian Allen (*d* 1702);
6-Nathaniel (1699-1756), of Rehoboth; in service at Ft. Edward; *m* Alice Fish, of Portsmouth, R.I.;
5-Thomas (*b* 1726 or 27), of Providence and Scituate, R.I.; *m* 2d, Dorothy-, of Scituate;
4-Peleg (1760-1849), Richfield, N.Y.; *m* 1779, Betsey Sweet (*d* 1838; Jeremiah[5]);
3-Dr. Dorastus (1803-68), of Ironton, Mo.; physician and surgeon more than 40 yrs.; surgeon in Civil War; del. to Mo. Constl. Conv., 1865; *m* 1st, 1825, Rosella Park;
2-Capt. Carroll Romeyn (2 below).
10-Robert **Park** (qv);
9-Thomas (1620-1709), of New London, Preston, and Wethersfield, Conn.; *m* Dorothy Thompson;
8-Robert (1651-1707), Norwich, Conn.; *m* 1681, Mary Rose;
7-Hezekiah (ca. 1695-1752), of Preston, Conn.; *m* ca. 1716, Margery Dyke (ca. 1693-1776);
6-Silas (bap. ca. 1726), *m* 1746, Sarah Ayers (*d* 1778);
5-Elijah (1755-93), *m* 1778, Lucy Starkweather (1758-1809);
4-Silas (1778-81), Lafayette, N.Y.; *m* 1802, Dolly Clapp (1781-1865);
3-Rosella (1809-ca. 1848), *m* Dorastus **Peck** (3 above).
5-Charles Alfred Caleb **Lindsay** (1732-1829), of Orange Co., Va.; *m* Sarah Stevens (*d* 1852), of Cadiz, Ky.;
4-Landon (1789-living 1838), *m* 1810, Celia Mills (1790-1834);
3-Col. James (1814-98), *m* 1st, 1836 or 37, Caroline Frier (1818-1851 or 52), of Fredericktown, Mo.;
2-Emily (1840-83), *m* 1858, Carroll Romeyn **Peck** (1831-96), of Batavia, N.Y.; removed to Iron Co., Mo., where he was an early settler; mem. Union League; apptd. by President Lincoln, receiver of the Land Office when it was moved from Jackson to Ironton; made adj. 68th militia regt., and participated in many engagements; provost marshal at Pilot Knob and Ironton; made capt.; dist. provost marshal under the draft law; postmaster at Ironton many yrs.; rep. Iron Co. in the Legislature; issue: I-James Carroll (*b* 1859; *m* May McFarlane; *m* 2d, Claudia Webster); II-Emily (*b* 1862; *m* Thomas Arnold Davis); III-Harry Lindsay (*b* 1866; *m* Alla McCool); IV-Hattie (1 above); V-Roy Romeyn (*b* 1879; *m* Mary Emma Drane); VI-Ralph Park (*b* 1881; *m* Ethel Hackett).
1-*m* Jan. 3, 1895, John Walter Clarkson, *b* Washington Co., Mo., Oct. 25, 1867; son of Joseph Clarkson; issue: 1-Jeannette, *b* Pawnee City, Neb., Aug. 9, 1900; B.A., Lindenwood Coll., '23.
1-Mem. D.A.R., O.E.S. Congregationalist. Republican. Residence: Clarks, La.

1-**BOND, Octavia Louise Zollicoffer (Mrs. John B.),** *b* "Gordon's Ferry," Hickman Co., Tenn., Apr. 18, 1846.
5-Jacob Christopher **Zollicoffer** (1686-1779), Baron Zollikofer von Altonklingen, of St. Gallen, Switzerland; to Spotsylvania Co., Va., 1719; empowered by English Soc. for Propagating the Gospel in Foreign Parts, to go to Europe and obtain from prosperous Christians, subscriptions for building a ch. in Spotsylvania Co.; brought numbers of German, Slavic and Palatinate colonists to America, 1749; removed to New Bern, N.C.; *m* 2d, 1735, Avarilla Dudley (Maj. Robert[6], in the West Indies, *m* Elizabeth-);
4-Capt. George (1738-1815), of Halifax Co., N.C.; succeeded to title of Baron; capt. N.C. Militia prior to Am. Rev.; served in Am. Rev.; *m* 1774, Anna Lindsay;
3-John Jacob (1775-1840), of Halifax Co., N.C.; removed to Tenn., and was one of earliest settlers of Maury Co.; *m* 1st, 1803, Martha Kirk (*d* 1815; Isaac[4], of Halifax Co., N.C., *m* Patience-);

ZOLLICOFFER

Arms: Quarterly, first and fourth, or, with a canton azure; second and third, sable, semée of billets or, over all a lion rampant crowned or.
Crests: (1) A demi-man, habited or, the face azure; (2) the head and neck of a lion argent, crowned or, four peacock feathers natural in the mane.

2-Felix Kirk (2 below).
8-James **Lindsay,** from Scotland ca. 1635; landowner Gloucester Co., Va., 1636; farmer;
7-Caleb (ca. 1664-1717), of Caroline Co., Va.; homestead 12 miles from Pt. Royal, Va.; *m* —Claire;
6-James (1700-82), lived nr. Pt. Royal; vestryman, St. Mary's Parish, Va.; *m* Sarah Daniel (William[7], of Caroline Co.);
5-Col. John, soldier in French and Indian War; removed from Va. to N.C.; *m* Mary Masterson (Edward[6]; Sir Thomas[7], of Ireland);
4-Anna (*b* 1753), *m* Baron George **Zollicoffer** (4 above).
7-Rev. James **Clack** (*d* 1723), from Eng., 1679; settled Ware Parish, Gloucester Co., Va.; minister Established Ch., Ware Parish, 44 yrs. (William[8], of Eng., *m* Mary, prob. Spencer);
6-James (1690-1757), of Brunswick Co., Va.; surveyor; called capt.; patrolled Va. shores; *m* post 1711, Mary Sterling (*d* 1763);
5-Sarah (*d* post 1803), of Brunswick Co., Va.; *d* Davidson Co., Tenn.; *m* 1754, William **Maclin** (ca. 1732-1803), of Surry and Brunswick cos., Va.; served in Am. Rev.; removed to N.C.

BRIG. GEN. FELIX KIRK ZOLLICOFFER, C.S.A. (1812-62).

land granted to him for services and became pioneer in Davidson Co., Tenn. (then N.C.), 1783 (William[6] [will filed 1762], Surry Co. Ct.; Capt. William[7]);
4–Anna (ca. 1755-ca. 1785), *m* 1770, Richard **Cross** (ca. 1750-1802), of Amelia and Nottoway cos., Va.; removed to Nashville ca. 1790; served in Am. Rev.; apptd. by state of N.C. one of "additional trustees" of Nashville, empowered to organize Superior Ct. of Pleas and Quarter Sessions; received land grants for mil. service;
3–Dorothy or Dolly (1779-1859), of Hickman Co., Tenn.; *m* 1794, Capt. John **Gordon** (1763-1819), pioneer of Tenn.; border soldier; commd. capt. by Gov. Blount; capt. of co. in Creek Campaign, War 1812; lived at Gordon's Ferry, Hickman Co.;
2–Louisa Pocahontas (1819-57), of Hickman Co., Tenn.; *m* 1835, Felix Kirk **Zollicoffer** (1812-62), of Maury Co., Tenn.; to Nashville to take editorial charge of the Republican Banner under Whig party; mem. Tenn. Congress, 1861; commd. brig. gen. of Provisional Army of Tenn. and later of C.S.A.; assigned to command all troops in East Tenn.; adj. gen. of Tenn. under Gov. James C. Jones, 1841-44; issue: I–Virginia Pocahontas (1837-1912; *m* 1858, James H. Wilson, *d*); II–Anne Maria (1844-1902); III–Octavia L. (1 above); IV–Mary Dorothy (1850-72; *m* 1869, Nat Gaither); V–Felicia Kirk (*b* 1854; *m* 1876, James Martin Metcalfe, 1843-1921); VI–Louisa Gordon (*m* Richard Henry Sansom, 1854-1923).
1–*m* June 10, 1869, John Bryan Bond (Apr. 23, 1845-Mar. 16, 1920); son of John Bond, of Williamson Co., Tenn., *m* Sarah Dabney Warren.
1–Ed. privately and Miss Nicholl's Sch., Nashville, Tenn. Author, poet, genealogist. Mem. bd. of lady mgrs. of Tenn. Centennial Exposition, 1897. Mem. U.D.C., D.A.R., U.S.D. 1812. Episcopalian. Democrat. Residence: Magnolia Plantation, Terrebonne Parish, La.

1–**DAILEY, Marguerite Frances Fuller (Mrs. Clarke G.),** *b* Jersey City, N.J., Nov. 7, 1883.
9–John **Fuller** (*d* 1666), of Ipswich, Mass., 1634; *m* 1648, Elizabeth Emerson;
8–Joseph (*b* 1660), *m* 1685, Mary–;
7–John (*b* 1701), *m* 2d, Hannah Lord;
6–John (*b* 1731), *m* 1755, Hannah Kimball;
5–Benjamin (*b* 1758), of Hampton, Conn.; *m* 1st, 1780, Joanna Trobridge (*d* 1822);
4–James (1788-1884), *m* 1808, Pamela Warner (*d* 1866);
3–John B. (*b* 1826) *m* 1858, Frances Evaline Root;
2–Eugene Frederick (*b* 1859), grad. U.Tenn.; civil and hydraulic engr.; *m* 1882, Jean Emslie Lockett (sister of Mrs. Joseph E. Lopez, see p. 352), issue I–Marguerite Frances (1 above); II–Frederick Lockett (*b* 1886; *m* Agnes Jennings).
1–*m* Sept. 1, 1906, Clarke Gibson Dailey, *b* Dayton, Ky., Jan. 13, 1879; son of John Alexander Dailey, of Topeka, Kan.; issue: 1–Gibson Fuller, *b* New York, N.Y., May 8, 1910; U. of Pa., '33.
1–Residence: 4508 Livingston Av., Riverdale, New York, N.Y.

1–**DAMUTH, Ida Stroud (Mrs. Louis),** *b* Des Moines, Ia., Sept. 14, 1874.
9–John **Sherburne** (1615-93), from Eng., 1632, settled at Portsmouth, N.H.; assessor, selectman, commissioner, large landowner, held many offices of the town; sgt. of Portsmouth militia, 1675; *m* 1645, Elizabeth Tucke (Robert[10], one of the historic founders of N.H.);
8–Capt. John (1650-1730), selectman of Portsmouth; lt. of militia 1715, then capt.; landholder in Portsmouth, Greenland, Barrington, and Louden, N.H.; *m* 1671, Mary Jackson (Thomas[9], of Portsmouth, *m* Hannah Johnson);
7–Dea. James (1688-1760), of Portsmouth; surveyor many yrs., large landowner; *m* 1709, Margaret Roe or Rowe;
6–Thomas (1724-1791-93), yeoman of Greenland, Canterbury, Northfield; *m* 1749, Sarah Johnson;
5–James (1751-1813), husbandman, Canterbury, N.H., 1775; pvt. and corpl. in Am. Rev.; *m* 1781, Betsey Gibson;
4–Henry (*b* 1785), *m* 1810, Hannah Dunbar;

SHERBURNE

Arms: Argent, a lion rampant vert, charged on the shoulder with a cross potent or.
Crest: A unicorn's head argent, crined and armed or.

3–Hannah (1814-92), *m* 1845, William **Stroud** (1794-1857);
2–Alfred (1846-1909), ry. engr., grocer, postmaster; *m* 1872, Cordelia Frances Vernon (1852-80; William or Daniel[3], *m* Elizabeth Throckmorton, *b* Columbus, O.); issue: I–Ida (1 above); II–Effie Pearl (*b* 1876; *m* U. S. Appel); III–Erma Grace (*b* 1879; *m* Charles Labatte); IV–Paul Alfred (*b* 1885).
1–*m* Apr. 11, 1911, Louis Damuth, *b* Ft. Atkinson, Wis., Nov. 3, 1882 (Sheldon[2] [*b* Oneida Co., N.Y., 1834] of Ft. Atkinson, *m* Cynthia, dau. of Ephraim Bingham [*b* Scranton, Pa., 1806], *m* Laura Lattin [*b* Vt., 1818]; Daniel[3], of Conn., *m* Phoebe Root).
1–Matron of Walworth Co. Home since 1915. Congregational. Republican. O.E.S. Mem. D.A.R., I.A.G. Residence: County Home, Elkhorn, Wis.

1–**DANCE, Frances Lee Pyron (Mrs. John E.),** *b* Acworth, Ga., Aug. 22, 1876.
8–Thomas **Cox** (qv);
7–James (1672-1750), held 275 acres in Upper Freehold, N.J., 1731; mem. Middletown Bapt. Ch.; *m* Ann– (1672-1747); *m* 2d, apparently, Rebecca (Stillwell) Saltar (John[8], *m* Rebecca Throckmorton);
6–John (*b* 1727), Am. Rev.; from Trenton, N.J., to Lincoln Co., N.C.; *m* ca. 1750, Margaret Morris (1732-92);
5–Elisha (1771-1824), capt. War 1812; *m* 1792, Margaret Holland (1774-1825; Isaac[6] [1745-1810], Am. Rev., *m* 1770, Hannah [Wiley] Liggett [1747-1818]; William[7], from Eng. to Pa., 1726, *m* Mary Harrison);
4–John Morris (1797-1851), moved to McDonough, Henry Co., Ga.; *m* 1st, ca. 1820 or 21, Mary Blanton Hawkins (1805-49; Joseph[5], *m* Elizabeth Blanton);
3–Elizabeth Ann (1823-1910), *m* 1842, James **Pyron** (1816-67), guarded prisoners at Andersonville during Civil War (James[4] [1776-1820], *m* Lucy [1782-1822], dau. of Stephen Johnson);
2–Thomas Jefferson (1846-1906), served in Co. A, 18th Ga. Regt., 1861-65; *m* 1868, Sarah Martha Buchanan (1850-1918; Thomas Jones[3], *m* Elizabeth S. Mize); issue: I–Emma Ryals (1869-1910; *m* N. J. Pugh); II–Sue Elizabeth (*b* 1872-*d* infancy); III–Mamie Lou (*b* 1874-*d* in-

fancy); IV–Frances Lee (1 above); V–Cora Beatrice (1879-86); VI–James Thomas (*b* 1883; *m* Annie B. Huggins); VII–Leonard McCall (*b* 1888; *m* Read Dillard).
1–*m* Feb. 17, 1910, John Edwards Dance, *b* Eatonton, Ga., May 22, 1880; son of John Lewis Dance (1840-1914), of Putnam Co., Ga., *m* Maria Louisa Edwards (1846-1908).
1–Mem. D.A.R., U.D.C., U.S.D. 1812, Mid-West Edwards Heirs Assn. (pres.). Baptist. Residence: 509 Langhorne St., Atlanta, Ga.

1–**GROSVENOR, Elsie May Bell (Mrs. Gilbert H.),** *b* London, Eng., May 8, 1878.
10–Lion **Gardiner** (qv);
9–David (*d* 1689), *m* 1657, Mary Teringman;
8–John (1661-1738), *m* Sarah Chandler (1675-1711);
7–Hanna (*d* 1738/39), *m* 1716, John **Chandler** (*b* 1693);
6–Mary (1717-56), *m* 1736, Benjamin **Greene** (1712-76; Nathaniel[7], *m* Anne Gold, or Gould; Thomas[8]; John[9]);
5–Gardiner (1753-1832), *m* 1788, Elizabeth Hubbard (1760-97);
4–Mary Ann (1790-1827), *m* Samuel **Hubbard,** LL.D (1785-1847);
3–Gardiner Greene, LL.D. (1822-97), *m* 1846, Gertrude Mercer McCurdy;
2–Mabel Gardiner (2 below).
6–John **McCurdy** (1724-85), from Ireland to Lyme, Conn., 1745; *m* Anne Lord;
5–Richard (1769-1857), *m* Ursula Griswold (their son Charles J., was minister to Austria and justice Supreme Court of Conn.);
4–Robert Henry (1800-80), dry goods commn. mcht., New York; *m* Gertrude Mercer Lee;
3–Gertrude Mercer (1827-1909), *m* Gardiner G. **Hubbard** (3 above).
8–Peter **Murdock** (1679-1753; son of John, *m* Mary Munson); came from Ireland ca. 1696; settled at Phila.; trader in N.J. and L.I.; settled at Easthampton, L.I.; *m* ca. 1705, Mary Fithian (*d* 1753);
7–John (ca. 1706-1778), of Saybrook, Conn.; dea. Congl. Ch.; mem. Assembly; judge Ct. Common Pleas; maj. of militia; *m* 2d, 1732, Frances Conkling (*d* 1799);
6–Abigail (*b* 1742), *m* 1761, Lt. Elisha **Lee** (*b* 1740), of E. Lyme, Conn.; Am. Rev. (Elisha[7] [1714-47], *m* his cousin, Hepzibah Lee);
5–Dr. James, *m* Gertrude Mercer;
4–Gertrude Mercer (*d* 1876), *m* 1826, Robert Henry **McCurdy** (4 above);
3–Gertrude Mercer, *m* Gardiner G. **Hubbard** (3 above);
2–Mabel Gardiner (1858-1923), *m* 1877, Alexander Graham **Bell,** Ph.D., M.D., LL.D. (*b* Scotland, 1847-*d* 1922), famous as the inventor of the telephone; issue: I–Elsie May (1 above); II–Marian Hubbard Graham (Mrs. David G. Fairchild, qv for other lineages); III–Edward (*d* infancy); IV–Robert (*d* infancy).
1–*m* Oct. 23, 1900, Gilbert Hovey Grosvenor (see Vol. I, p. 30); issue: 1–Melville Bell, *b* Washington, D.C., Nov. 26, 1901; U.S.N.A., '23; 2–Gertrude Hubbard, *b* Baddeck, Can., July 28, 1903; 3–Mabel Harlakendon, *b* Baddeck, July 28, 1905; 4–Lilian Waters, *b* Washington, Apr. 8, 1907; 5–Alexander Graham Bell (1909-15); 6–Elsie Alexandra Carolyn, *b* Washington, Mar. 3, 1911; 7–Gloria, *b* Bethesda, Md., Sept. 17, 1918.
1–Residence: Wild Acres, Bethesda, Md.

1–**FAIRCHILD, Marian Hubbard Graham Bell (Mrs. David G.),** *b* Washington, D.C., Feb. 15, 1880.
10–William **Hubbard** (qv);
9–Rev. William (1621/22-1704), A.B., Harvard, 1st class, 1642; historian, wrote "King Philip's War," and "History of New England"; Congl. minister, Ipswich; *m* 1646, Mary Rogers (1628-85; Rev. Nathaniel[10], *m* Martha Crane, of Ipswich);
8–John (1648-1709/10), Boston mcht.; *m* 1671, Anne Leverett (1652-1717; Gov. John[9] [1616-79], *m* Sarah [*b* 1629], dau. of Maj. Gen. Robert Sedgwick, qv);
7–Rev. John (1677-1705), A.B., Harvard, 1695; Presbyn. pastor, Jamaica, L.I.; *m* 1701, Mabel Russell;
6–Daniel (1706-41, posthumous son), A.B., Yale, 1727; lawyer; sheriff, 1735; *m* 1730, Martha Coit (1706-82; John[7], of New London);
5–William, *m* Joanna Perkins;
4–Samuel, LL.D. (1785-1847), justice Supreme Jud. Ct. of Mass.; *m* 1st, Mary Ann Greene (Gardiner[5], *m* Elizabeth Hubbard);
3–Gardiner Greene, LL.D. (1822-97), A.B., Dartmouth, '41; pioneer promoter of the telephone; capitalist, philanthropist; *m* Gertrude Mercer McCurdy;
2–Mabel Gardiner (2 below).
10–John **Haynes** (qv);
9–Ruth (1638-88), *m* 1655, Samuel **Wyllis** (1632-1709; Gov. George[10], qv);
8–Mehitabel (1658-97), *m* 1st or 2d (?), 1676, Rev. Daniel **Russell** (1642-1731);
7–Mabel (1677-1730), *m* Rev. John **Hubbard** (7 above).
2–Mabel Gardiner Hubbard (1858-1923), *m* 1877, Alexander Graham **Bell,** Ph.D., M.D., LL.D. (*b* Scotland, 1847-*d* 1922), famous as the inventor of the telephone (for issue and other lineages see Mrs. Gilbert H. Grosvenor).
1–*m* Apr. 25, 1905, David Grandison Fairchild (see Vol. I, p. 596); issue (all *b* Washington, D.C.): 1–Alexander Graham Bell, *b* Aug. 17, 1906; 2–Barbara Lathrop, *b* Mar. 18, 1909; *m* May 29, 1930, Leonard R. Muller; 3–Nancy Bell, *b* Nov. 6, 1912.
Summer residence: Beinn Bhreagh, Baddeck, N.S., Can. Winter residence: Coconut Grove, Fla.

CAPT. CHARLES GUILLE WARNER (1844-1911), capt., 31st and 32d Mo. Vols., 1865; was v.p. Mo. Pacific Ry. Co., St. Louis.

1–**KOOSER, Clara Anne Warner (Mrs. Herman B.),** *b* St. Louis, Mo., Jan. 2, 1873.
11–William **Warner,** from Norfolk, Eng., 1637, settled at Ipswich, Mass.; *m* Esther–;
10–John (*b* 1616), *m* 1655, Priscilla Symonds;
9–Andrew (*d* 1684), a founder of Hartford, Conn.; surveyor; selectman; *m* Mary–; *m* 2d, Esther Wakeman Seldon;
8–Daniel (*d* 1692), of Hatfield, Mass.; ens. in foot co. of Hadley; lt. in French and Indian War; *m* Mary– (*d* 1673); *m* 2d, Martha Boltwood (*d* 1710);
7–Daniel (1666-1754), of Hardwick, Mass.; *m* Mary Hubbard; *m* 2d, Thankful Billings (*d* 1716);
6–Jonathan (1704-63), selectman 5 yrs.; treas. 19 yrs.; innkeeper; *m* 1733, Batsheba Allis (*b* 1710);
5–Capt. Daniel (1734-1823), pvt. in French and Indian War; capt. Mass. militia; com. of corr. in Am. Rev.; selectman and assessor; *m* 1758, Mary Wright (*b* 1738);
4–Col. Alpha (1770-1854), Chillicothe, O.; comd. regt. of Vt. militia; *m* 1st, 1796, Lydia Cobb;
3–Daniel (1811-69), of E. Hardwick, Vt.; *m* 1844, Juliet Hester Buckmaster (1825-88);
2–Capt. Charles G. (2 below).
8–Samuel **Rider** (1630-1715), of Plymouth, Mass.; *m* 2d, 1656, Lydia Tilden;

7–Lydia (*b* 1686), *m* 1703, Elisha **Cobb** (*b* 1678), of Plymouth;
6–Col. Elisha (*b* 1704), *m* 1733, Priscilla Merrick;
5–Lemuel (*b* 1735), of Hardwick, Vt.; soldier in Am. Rev.; in Crown Point Expdn.; *m* 1765, Lydia Allen (1744-76);
4–Lydia (1769-1816), *m* Col. Alpha **Warner** (4 above);
3–Daniel, *m* Juliet H. Buckmaster (3 above);
2–Capt. Charles Guille (1844-1911), see portrait; *m* 1871, Anne Cecilia Roden (1845-1914); issue: I–Clara Anne (1 above); II–Juliet Sara (*b* 1876; *m* William Marvin Armstrong); III–Elizabeth Roden (*b* 1879; *m* Archibald Grey Douglass).
1–*m* Apr. 12, 1899, Herman Benjamin Kooser, *b* Somerset, Pa., July 14, 1860; son of Curtis Kooser (Jacob[3], *m* Eleanor, dau. of Zebulon Parke; Jacob[4], of Bucks Co., Pa.); issue: 1–Clara Bond, *b* Salt Lake City, Utah, Feb. 11, 1900; A.B., Wellesley Coll., '22; *m* June 28, 1924, Arthur Wayne, son of James F. Green (issue: Arthur Wayne, Jr.); 2–Parke Herman, *b* Denver, Colo., Mar. 2, 1905; attended Princeton U., Washington U. Law School; 3–Juliet Warner, *b* Dallas, Tex., Mar. 24, 1907.
1–Ed. Lindenwood Coll., St. Charles, Mo., '93. Chmn. production dept., A.R.C., since 1917. Mem. C.D.A., D.A.R. (treas.), I.A.G., Mo. Hist. Soc., M.O.L.L.U.S. (by inheritance). Episcopalian. Clubs: Monday, Lindenwood College, and Beta Mothers Club of Washington University. Residence: 210 Rosemont Av., Webster Groves, Mo.

1–**LEWIS, William Ely,** *b* Pentwater, Mich., Aug. 22, 1882.
10–George **Lewis** (qv);
9–Edward (1641-1703), of Barnstable, Mass.; *m* 1661, Hannah Cobb;
8–John (1666-1738), *m* 1695, Elizabeth Huckins;
7–John L. (*b* 1700), *m* 1726, Mary Hopkins (*b* 1709);
6–Timothy (1727-1818), of Harwich, Mass.; *m* Sarah– (*d* 1808);
5–Timothy (1764-1858), of Ashfield, Mass.; *m* Molly Bradley;
4–Stillman (1787-1871), of Sunderland, Vt., and Belvidere, Ill.; *m* Elizabeth Smith;
3–Charles Emerson (1813-1900), of Bennington Co., Vt., and Lyons, Mich.; *m* 1837, Ann E. Tufts (1818-1910);
2–Charles Fremont (*b* 1856), of Pentwater, Mich.; mem. Mich. Legislature, 1922-30; *m* 1881, Lizzie L. Webb (1859-1926); issue: I–William Ely (1 above); II–F. Esther (*b* 1886; *m* Albert D. Pearce); III–Ermine G. (*b* 1894; *m* Williard M. Cannon).
1–*m* May 6, 1908, Ethel W. Sibley, *b* Pentwater, Mich., Apr. 13, 1885; dau. of John O. Sibley; issue: 1–Geraldine M., *b* Hart, Mich., June 13, 1922.
1–Ed. Ferris Inst. Hardware mcht., Pentwater, 1901-13, at Hart, Mich., 1925-30; postmaster, Hart, Mich., since 1929. Register of deeds, Oceana Co., Mich., 1913-25. First lt., Co. 55, Mich. N.G., 1918-19. Mason. Episcopalian. Republican. Residence: Hart, Mich.

1–**MERRELL, Lewis Charles,** *b* Syracuse, N.Y., Oct. 25, 1877.
10–Nathaniel **Merrell** (qv);
9–John, *m* Sarah Watson;
8–John, *m* Sarah Marsh;
7–Nathaniel, *m* Ester Warner;
6–Caleb, *m* Susannah Tompkins;
5–Nathaniel (1756-1823), *m* Honor Doud (*d* 1796);
4–Caleb (1783-1864), of Waterbury, Conn.; *m* Sally Packard (1790-1871);
3–Oliver Dunbar (1811-99), of Greene, N.Y.; *m* Polly Lewis;
2–Gaius Lewis (1843-1909), mfr. food products, Syracuse; *m* 1874, Mary Antoinette Seward (1846-1911); for issue and Lewis lineage see Irving Seward Merrell, p. 390.
1–*m* June 1906, Henrietta Irene Hoes (divorced); issue: 1–Esther Hill, *b* Syracuse, N.Y., Apr. 6, 1909; 2–Gaius Lewis, II, *b* Syracuse, Oct. 15, 1912.
1–*m* 2d, June 17, 1914, Margaretta Delphine Marie Michael, *b* Syracuse, N.Y., Mar. 31, 1890; dau. of Nicholas C. Michael; issue: 1–Dorothy Margaretta, *b* Boise, Ida., Mar. 11, 1915; 2–Lewis Charles, Jr., *b* Boise, May 1, 1920.
1–B.A., Amherst, '99 (D.K.E.). Asst. sec. Merrell-Soule Co., and dir. Syracuse Trust Co., 1910-13; sec.-treas. Boise Stone Co., 1915-18; v.p. Overland Nat. Bank, Boise, 1917-19; pres. El Paseo Co., since 1927. Pres. Syracuse, N.Y. City Council, and mem. bd. of estimate, 1910-12. Catholic. Republican. Clubs: Amherst, Delta Kappa Epsilon, Cypress Point Golf and Country. Residence: Pebble Beach, Calif.

MAGRUDER (MacGREGOR)

Arms: Argent, a fir tree on a mount vert, surmounted of a sword bendways, on its point an imperial crown proper; a canton azure.
Crest: A lion's head erased proper crowned with an antique crown.
Motto: Srioghail mo dhream; E'en do bot spair nocht.

1–**MAGRUDER, Kenneth Dann,** *b* Springfield, O., Apr. 22, 1899.
9–Alexander **Magruder** (1610-77), *b* in Scotland; captured at Battle of Worcester in army of Charles, II; sent via Barbados to Va., 1652; settled in Calvert (now Prince George's) Co., Md.; *m* Margaret Braithwaite (William[10], Gent., mem. 1st Gen. Assembly, cdr. of Kent Island, collector and receiver, deputy gov., etc.);
8–Samuel (1654-1711), of Prince George's Co.; vestryman, St. Paul's P.E. Ch.; burgess; mil. and civil officer, Prince George's Co.; justice; *m* Sarah Beall (*d* 1734; Col. Ninian[9], qv);
7–Ninian (1686-1751), warden St. Barnabas' P.E. Ch.; planter; *m* Elizabeth Brewer;
6–Samuel, 3d (1708-86), Montgomery Co., Md.; vestryman St. Paul's P.E. Ch.; capt. of militia, Prince George's Co.; a commr. to establish Georgetown; mem. Com. of Observation for Frederick Co., 1775; took "Patriot's Oath," 1778; justice, Montgomery Co.; *m* Margaret Jackson;
5–Lt. Samuel Brewer (1744-1818), pvt., 4th Co., 29th Bn., Montgomery County, 1777, commd. ens. of same; supported Washington in 1777, 78 campaigns; 1st lt., Lower Bn., 2d Co., 1780; *m* Rebecca Magruder (1746-1806);
4–Ninian (1772-1830), of Magruder's Mills, Ashby's Gap (now Clark Co.), Va.; *m* 1814, Elizabeth Lyons (1797-1868; James[5], *m* Mary Newhouse);
3–Thomas Jefferson (1826-1901), see portrait; *m* 1855, Elizabeth Fribley (1831-1906; Jacob[4], *m* Elizabeth Woods, pioneers in Old Town Valley, Tuscarawas Co., O.; Christopher Friebeley[5], *m* Margaret–);
2–James William (2 below).
11–William **Harris,** London merchant; copatentee in Charles City Co., Va.; settled

THOMAS JEFFERSON MAGRUDER (1826-1901), of Marion, O.; of Magruder's Saddlery Works; was township and corporation treasurer, mem. City Council and School Board, Marion. Mem. finance committee of the People's Temperance Reform Convention, 1881; delegate to the first Ohio M.E. Sunday School Convention, etc.; Odd Fellow.

finally on South River, Anne Arundel Co., Md.; *m* Elizabeth Lee, Quakeress;
10–Elizabeth, of Bound Bay, Severn River, at "Warner's Neck," Md.; *m* James **Warner** (*d* 1673), warden, Elizabeth River Ch., Sewell's Point, Va., 1649;
9–Sarah, of Annapolis, Md.; *m* Hon. Henry **Ridgely** (qv);
8–Sarah, *m* John **Brewer** (*d* 1690; Hon. John[9], said to have been born in Wales, mem. Nansemond Co. Puritans in Va. and Md., founder Annapolis, etc.);
7–Elizabeth (*b* 1690), of Prince George's Co.; *m* Ninian **Magruder** (7 above).
10–Col. Ninian **Beall** (qv);
9–John (ca. 1647-1725), of Prince George's Co.; *m* Sarah Gibson; *m* 2d, Joan (*d* 1675), widow of Robert Tyler and George Reid;
8–Alexander (ca. 1667-1744), civil officer and magistrate; trustee and elder Presbyn. meeting house, founded by Col. Ninian Beall in Prince George's Co.; *m* 1687, Elizabeth Dick;
7–Ruth, of Frederick Co.; *m* John **Jackson** (*d* 1761);
6–Margaret (1711-1801), of Montgomery Co.; *m* Capt. Samuel **Magruder,** 3d (6 above).
11–William **Goodwin** (qv);
10–Elizabeth, *m* John **Crow** (1606-86), from Eng., 1634; a founder of Hartford; surveyor of highways; selectman of Hadley, 1675; his home at E. Hartford was used as a garrison against the Podunk Indians;
9–Mehitable (ca. 1652-1730), *m* 1668, Col. Samuel **Partridge** (1645-1740), recorder Northampton cts., Mass., 1676; asso. judge from Hadley, 1685; chief justice, Hampshire Co.; clk. of ct., Hampshire Co., 1689; judge Ct. Common Pleas; judge Probate Ct., 1702-29; selectman of Hadley and later of Hatfield; dep. from Hadley at Gen. Ct., later from Hatfield; cdr.-in-chief of western Province; councillor (William[10], qv);
8–Mehitable (1675-1756), of Northampton, Mass.; *m* 1693, Nathaniel **Dwight** (1666-1711; Capt. Timothy[9], *m* Anna, dau. of Rev. Henry Flynt; John[10], a founder of Dedham, Mass.);
7–Abiah (1704-48), *m* 1721/22, Capt. Samuel **Kent** (1698-1772; John[8], *m* Abigail, dau. William Dudley, Jr.; Sgt. Samuel[9]; Thomas[10]);
6–Abiah (1727-82), *m* 1745, Capt. John **Leavitt** (1724-98), minute man in Am. Rev. (Lt. Joshua[7], *m* Hannah, dau. of John Devotion; Josiah[8], *m* Margaret, dau. Sgt. Humphrey Johnson; Sgt. John[9], *m* Sarah, dau. of Edward Gilman, qv);

REV. LYMAN MUMFORD (1810-83), and his family.

JESSE DANN (1837-93), and his wife, CHARLOTTE ANN MUMFORD (1839-1909), from photograph taken in 1859.

5–Charlotte (1769-1868), *m* 1794, Capt. William **Mumford** (*b* 1766);
4–Rev. Lyman (1810-83), of Utica, N.Y.; *m* Margaret Reed Rice (see portrait);
3–Charlotte Ann (1839-1909), of Columbus, O.; *m* 1859, Jesse **Dann** (1837-93; John[4], *m* Mary, dau. of John Alexander MacPherson); see portrait;
2–Mary Estelle (2 below).
11–Stephen **Hopkins,** Mayflower Pilgrim (qv);
10–Damaris, *m* 1646, Jacob **Cooke** (1618-63), to America 1623 (Francis[11], Mayflower Pilgrim, qv);
9–Jacob (1653-1747), *m* Lydia Miller;
8–William (*b* 1683), *m* Tabitha–;
7–Elisha (1717-94);
6–Levi;
5–Sarah, *m* Rev. Jacob **Rice**;
4–Margaret Reed (1808-79), *m* Rev. Lyman **Mumford** (4 above);
3–Charlotte Ann, *m* Jesse **Dann** (3 above);
2–Mary Estelle (*b* 1867), studied at Ohio Wesleyan U., 1883-84; *m* 1887, Rev. James William **Magruder,** see portrait and biography; issue: I–Marguerite (*b* 1892; A.B. Goucher, '15; Johns Hopkins, 1915-17; teacher, Women's Christian Coll., Tokyo, Japan, since 1927; *m* 1924, Masahito Iwamoto, grad. Waseda Coll., Japan, and grad. student Harvard U.); II–Kenneth Dann (1 above).
1–Not married. A.B., Harvard, '22. Agent, Mass. Soc. for the Prevention of Cruelty to Children, 1922-25; dir. Social Service Exchange, Wilkes-Barre, Pa., 1925-28; publicity dir., Luzerne Co. Child Health Com., Pa., 1926, for Luzerne Co. Public Health Assn., 1926-28; chmn., Luzerne Co. Child Health Council, 1927,28; sec., Wyo. Valley Toxin Antitoxin Com., 1927-28; exec. sec., Welfare Council of Wyo. Valley, Wilkes-Barre, 1927-28; field agent, Pa. Crime Commn., 1928; field sec., Pa. Com. on Penal Affairs, 1928-29; exec. sec.,

REV. JAMES WILLIAM MAGRUDER (1864-1918), A.B., Ohio Wesleyan U., '85 (Phi Beta Kappa, Delta Tau Delta); grad. Drew Theol. Sem., 1887; Greek scholar, Div. Sch., U. of Cambridge, Eng., 1887-88; D.D., Ohio Wesleyan U., 1905; held Methodist pastorates in Geauga Co., O., Madrid, N.Y., Camp Washington and Wesley Chapel, Cincinnati, O., St. Paul's Church, Springfield, O., Chestnut St. Church, Portland, Me.; mem. Baltimore Conf.; first prof. sociology and economics, Ohio Wesleyan U., 1899; organized the military dept. there, and was capt. of 1st co.; pres. Associated Charities, Portland, Me.; gen. sec., Federated Charities, Baltimore, Md., 1907-18; in charge of Red Cross flood relief work, Hamilton, O., 1913; asst. dir. civilian relief, Am. Red Cross, 1917; dir. civilian relief Potomac division, Red Cross, 1917-18; southern division mgr., War Camp Community Service, 1918; lecturer on philanthropy, Goucher Coll., 1910-18.

Pa. Com. on Penal Affairs, western branch, 1929-30. Mem. Rep. City Com., Cambridge, Mass., 1922-25; del. Rep. State Conv., 1922,24. Mem. S.C.W., S.A.R., I.A.G., Am. Clan Gregor Soc. Methodist. Residence: 5562 Hobart St., Squirrel Hill, Pittsburgh, Pa.

1–**METCALF, Ralph,** *b* Providence, R.I., Nov. 2, 1861.
9–Michael **Metcalf** (qv);
8–Michael (1620-54), *m* 1644, Mary Fairbanks (*d* 1654; Jonathan[9]);
7–Jonathan (1648-1727), *m* 1674, Hannah Kenric (1639-1731; John[8]);
6–Nathaniel (1691-1752), *m* 1712, Mary Gay (John[7]; Samuel[8]; John[9]);
5–Nathaniel (1718-81), *m* 1739, Ruth Whiting (1721-96; Jeremiah[6]);
4–Joel (1755-1834), removed to Providence, 1780; mem. Providence school com. for 22 yrs., and town council many yrs.; judge Ct. Common Pleas; *m* 1779, Lucy Gay;
3–Joseph Gay (1796-1854), *m* 1820, Evelina Houghton (1798-1868);
2–Alfred (2 below).
10–John **Alden,** Mayflower Pilgrim (qv);
9–Elizabeth, *m* William **Peabodie**;
8–Elizabeth (1647-79), *m* John **Rogers**;
7–Hannah (1668-1733), *m* Capt. Samuel **Bradford** (1667-1714; Maj. William[8]; Gov. William[9], qv);
6–Perez (1694-1746), *m* 1720, Abigail Belcher (1695-1746);
5–Hannah (*b* 1723), *m* 1747, Jabez **Gay,** Am. Rev.;
4–Lucy (1759-1822), *m* Joel **Metcalf** (4 above);
3–Joseph Gay, *m* Evelina Houghton (3 above);
2–Alfred (1828-1904), woolen mfr.; *m* 1860, Rosa Clinton Maloy (1828-1917); issue: I–Ralph (1 above); II–Frederick (1865-1923; *m* Alice Butts); III–Guy (*m* Clare Burt); IV–Clinton (*d* childhood); V–Alfred (*d* childhood).
1–*m* Apr. 20, 1887, Edith Olena Simpson, *b* Winona, Minn., Sept. 28, 1864; dau. of Verazano Simpson (Dr. Benjamin Franklin[3]), of Lowell, Mass.; issue: 1–Alfred (*b* Winona, Minn., 1888-*d* infancy); 2–Elizabeth, *b* Tacoma, Wash., June 21, 1890; *m* G. E. Ledbetter.
1–Ed. Brown U.; A.B., U.Mich., '83; (LL.D., Puget Sound Coll., conferred for long public service, and studies and writings upon internat. economics). Editor, mfr., retired (see Who's Who in America). Mem. Wash. State Senate, 1907-34 (pres. pro tem., 1927-29). Episcopalian. Republican. Mason (K.T., Shriner), Elk, Woodman. Clubs: Union, University, Commercial, Country and Golf. Residence: 918 N. Yakima Av., Tacoma, Wash.

1–**RANDOLPH, Howard Stelle Fitz,** *b* New York, N.Y., Aug. 29, 1883.
8–Rev. Joseph **Hull** (qv);
7–Samuel (*b* ca. 1650), of Piscataway, N.J.; *m* 1677, Mary Manning (Jeffrey[8]);
6–Mercy (1683-1746), *m* 1700, Thomas Piatt (1681-ca. 1707); *m* 2d, ca. 1709, Rev. Benjamin **Stelle** (1684-1759; Poncet[7]);
5–Rachel (1720-91), *m* 1752, Ephraim Fitz **Randolph** (1724-93), pvt. Am. Rev. (see Vol. II, p. 21 for Randolph lineage);
4–Stelle (1761-1822), pvt. Am. Rev.; *m* 1791, Anna Dunn (1768-1854; Benjamin[5]; Hugh[6]; Hugh[7]);
3–Ambrose (1798-1883), of New Brunswick, N.J.; *m* 1821, Deborah Runyon (1799-1873; Richard Elias[4]; Elias[5]; Richard[6]; Peter[7]; Vincent[8]);
2–Howard (2 below).
9–William **Bassett** (qv);
8–Nathaniel (1628-1710), of Yarmouth, Mass.; *m* Mary, or Dorcas Joyce; *m* 2d, Hannah–;
7–Nathan (*d* 1728), of Yarmouth and Chatham; *m* 1709, Mary Crowell (1688-1742; Thomas[8]);
6–Samuel, of Barnstable; *m* 1st, 1743, Susannah Lombard (1723-55; Jedidiah[7]; Thomas[8]; Jedidiah[9]; Thomas[10]);
5–Nehemiah (*b* 1743), of Chatham, Mass., and Flatlands, N.Y.; Am. Rev.; *m* 1st, 1763, Dorcas Cole; *m* 2d, —?;
4–Ebenezer (1781-1815), of New York, N.Y.; *m* 1801, Catherine (Newkirk) Baldwin (1775-1814); see Vol. II, p. 21;
3–Rebecca (1811-81), *m* 1831, John Clasback **Howser** (1804-72; Matthias[4]);
2–Sophia Topping (1842-1911), *m* 1866, Howard Fitz **Randolph** (1842-94), woolen merchant (see Vol. II, p. 21, for issue and other lineages).
1–*m* N.Y. City, Oct. 7, 1914, Mary Leland Bloomer (see Vol. III, p. 390); issue: 1–Mary Fitz, *b* Bronxville, N.Y., Sept. 6, 1922.
1–Columbia, '05. Asst. librarian, New York Geneal. and Biographical Soc. and asst. editor of its Record. With A.R.C., service in France, World War. Mem. S.C.W., O.F.P.A. (registrar gen.), S.N.S., I.A.G., H.S., S.R., N.Y.G.B.S., N.J. Hist. Soc., Westchester Co. Hist. Soc. Residence: 231 Pondfield Rd., Bronxville, N.Y.

1–**MONEY, Mary Elizabeth Young (Mrs. George P.),** *b* Winona, Miss., Feb. 21, 1869.
5–Hugh **Young** (son of Andrew Lamont, and

g.son of the murdered chief Sir James Lamont of the Clan Lamont, of Little Cumbrae Islands, Scotland; when the Duke of Argyle murdered the chief and plundered the castles, Andrew fled to Ireland and assumed his mother's maiden name Young, and *m* Mary Adair, *b* Ballyclare, Co. Antrim, Ireland); came from Ireland 1741, settled nr. Staunton, Augusta Co., Va.; *m* his 2d cousin, Agnes Sitlington;
4–John (1737-1824), capt. in Am. Rev.; *m* 1st, 1763, Mary White (1744-79; Isaac[5], *m* Jean Gordon);
3–Capt. David (1774-1829), Augusta Co., Va.; capt. in War 1812; *m* 1809, Mary Hart;
2–David Lucian (2 below).
7–William **Leake,** from Eng. to Va. ca. 1685; settled in Henrico (now Goochland) Co.; *m* ca. 1687, Mary Bostick;
6–Walter (ca. 1704-1756), lived and *d* in the old homestead in Goochland Co.; vestryman, King William Parish; *m* Judith Mask;
5–Rev. Samuel, grad. Princeton; Presbyn. minister; chaplain in Am. Rev.; *m* Elizabeth Morice;
4–Elizabeth (1752-92), *m* 1786, Rev. Andrew **Hart** (1754-1832), from Scotland to Albemarle Co., Va., 1772; settled in South Garden, Va., as the valley of the south fork of Hardware River is called, and built "Sunny Bank," ca. 1790; elder in the "Cove," Presbyn. Ch.;
3–Mary (1787-1825), *m* David **Young** (3 above).
5–Alexander **Marr** (*b* in Scotland), settled in Stafford (now Fauquier) Co., Va.;
4–John Miller, Am. Rev.; *m* Susannah (Prior) Perkins;
3–Constant Hardin Perkins, *m* Elizabeth Stewart White (*b* in N.C.).
2–David Lucian **Young** (1823-1905), farmer, Albemarle Co., Va.; served 4 yrs. in War Between the States; *m* 1847, Mary Ann Marr (1830-74); *m* 2d, 1882, Elizabeth (Marshall) Coleman (*d* 1891); issue (1st marriage): I–Sarah Robertson (1851-95; *m* Albert West Campbell); II–Hardin Marr (1853-95; *m* Martha J. Arnold); III–Margaret Jane (1855-58); IV–Duncan Lucien (1858-92); V–William Hart (1860-99; *m* Mary Merrin); VI–Catherine Eleanor (*b* 1865; *m* William Brown Whitehead); VII–Mary Elizabeth (1 above).

MONEY OF WALTHAMSTOW.

MONEY

Arms: *Or, on a pile azure, ten bezants four, three, two, one, a chief ermine, charged with a lion passant, langued gules, of the second.*
Crest: *A bezant between two wings azure.*
Motto: *Factis non verbis.*

1–*m* Nov. 23, 1893, George Pierson Money, *b* "Ellersby," nr. Clinton, Miss., Nov. 16, 1867; son of Senator Hernando De Soto Money, *m* Claudia Jane Boddie (see Vol. I, p. 730); issue: 1–Dorothy Marr, *b* Santa Fe, N.M., July 25, 1896; *m* May 3, 1918, Victor Hubert Gramount (issue: Hardin Stewart Marr; George Pierson Money; Victor Hubert); 2–Hernando De Soto, *b* Las Vegas, N.M., May 20, 1900; ed. Gulf Coast Mil. Acad.
1–Grad. Winona Female Coll., 1885. Mem. D.A.R., U.S.D. 1812, U.D.C. Presbyterian. Democrat. Residence: Gulfport, Miss.

1–**ROWLEY, Howard Cortland,** *b* Cortland, N.Y., Mar. 28, 1876.
8–Henry **Rowley** (*d* 1673), came to Mass. ca. 1630 or 1632; *m* 1st, Sarah Palmer (William[9], qv);
7–Moses (ante 1632-1705), *m* 1652, Elizabeth Fuller (*d* post 1714; Matthew[8]; Edward[9], Mayflower Pilgrim, qv);
6–Nathan (ca. 1664-post 1742), *m* Mercy Hatch (*b* 1667; Jonathan[7], *m* Sarah Rowley);
5–Matthew (1720-1801), *m* 1745, Christiana Weeks (1716-1808);
4–Nathan C. (1756-1830), pvt. Mass. militia in Am. Rev.; *m* Lucy Lament (or Lamen, LaMan, LaMont; Cornelius[5], pvt. Mass. militia in Am. Rev.);
3–Nathan Weeks (1802-51), *m* 1830, Caroline Billger (1812-82);
2–Nathan Brainard (1848-1903), also known as Brainard Nathan; editor and pub. Calif. Fruit Grower (now the Calif. Fruit News, San Francisco); *m* 1874, Mary Eleanor Gallagher (1851-1920); see Vol. II, p. 199, for issue.
1–*m* Sept. 25, 1901, Belle Gardner, *b* Santa Cruz, Calif., Aug. 27, 1877; dau. of Alonzo Gardner, *m* Eunice Wardwell.
1–Editor and pub. Calif. Fruit News (established by father, 1888). Mem. S.C.W., S.A.R. (pres. Calif. Soc., 1925-26; president general Nat. Soc., 1929-30). Clubs: Bohemian, Commercial, Commonwealth. Residence: 1100 Sacramento St., San Francisco, Calif.

1–**STEVENS, Mary Morris,** *b* New York, N.Y.
8–John **Stevens** (qv);
7–Erasmus (*d* 1690), ensign First Co. of Foot, Marblehead, Mass.; *m* Elizabeth Clarke (Capt. Thomas[8]);
6–Erasmus (1686-1750), lt. A. and H.A. Co.; *m* 1707, Persis Bridge (*b* 1683; Samuel[7], of Boston);
5–Ebenezer (1726-63), *m* 1750, Elizabeth Weld (*b* 1727; Edmund[6], below);
4–Ebenezer (1751-1823), mem. "Boston Tea Party;" lt. col. Cont. Army; maj. gen. militia War 1812; a founder Soc. Cin.; *m* 2d, 1784, Lucretia (Ledyard) Sands (1756-1846); see Vol. I, p. 746, for Ledyard lineage;
3–John Austin (1795-1874), Yale, 1813; mcht., banker, financier; sec. Chamber of Commerce, N.Y., 1827-32; 1st pres. Merchants Exchange; pres. Bank of Commerce, N.Y., 1839-66, of the associate banks of Phila. and Boston; chmn. of the treasury note com. which managed the $150,000,000 loan to the govt. during the Civil War; *m* 1824, Abby Weld;
2–John Austin (2 below).
9–Rev. Thomas **Weld** (qv);
8–Thomas (1620-82), freeman, 1654; rep., 1676,77; *m* 1650, Dorothy Whiting (1628-94; Rev. Samuel[9]);
7–Edmund (*b* 1659), gent.; *m* 1687, Elizabeth White (1667-1721);
6–Edmund (*b* 1695), *m* 1725, Clemence Dove (*b* 1700);
5–Edward (1734-1809), *m* 1757, Hannah D. Church;
4–Benjamin (1758-1839), gent.; Brunswick, Me.; pvt. Lexington Alarm; commissary Cont. Army; *m* 1792, Abby Perkins (1773-1840; Col. William[5], *m* Abigail Case);
3–Abby (1799-1886), *m* John A. **Stevens** (3 above).
10–Richard **Warren,** Mayflower Pilgrim (qv);
9–Elizabeth (1583-1673), *m* 1636, Sgt. Richard **Church** (qv);
8–Col. Benjamin (1639-1717/18), cdr. of troops of Mass. Bay and Plymouth Colonies in King Philip's War; *m* 1671, Alice Southworth (Constant[9], qv);
7–Capt. Edward (*b* 1680), commd. capt. and served with his father against the French and Indians; *m* Martha Burton (1677-1750; Stephen[8], *m* Abigail Denton);
6–Dea. Benjamin (1704-81), grad. Harvard, 1727; *m* 2d, 1731, Hannah Dyer (*d* 1794; Col. Giles[7], mem. A. and H.A. Co., *m* Mary Bannister);
5–Hannah D., *m* Edward **Weld** (5 above);
4–Benjamin, *m* Abby Perkins (4 above);
3–Abby, *m* John A. **Stevens** (3 above);
2–John Austin (1827-1910), B.A., Harvard, '46; recruited and maintained 51st Regt., N.Y. Vols., 1861-65; organizer and sec. Nat. War Com., 1862-63; confidential sec., treas. Note Com., 1862-63, of which his father was chmn., which mgd. the $150,000,000 loan to the govt. during

Civil War; founder Loyal Nat. League, 1863; sec. Chamber of Commerce, New York, 1862-68; librarian N.Y. Hist. Soc., 1876-78; founder and editor Mag. of Am. Hist., 1877-81; organized S.C.W. in R.I., 1899, historian until death; hon. mem., founder, 1876, and 1st pres., 1883, S.R.; author; financier; *m* 1855, Margaret Antoinette Morris (1830-1911), for issue see Vol. I, p. 746.

1-Ter-Centenary mem. in perpetuity N.E.H.G.S. and Mass. S.M.D.; mem. Newport Hist. Soc., Soc. for Preservation N.E. Antiquities, Sulgrave Instn. (founder). Residence: "Pleasaunce," 73 Rhode Island Av., Newport, R.I.

WOODWARD

Arms: Argent, two bars azure, over all three bucks' heads cabossed or.
Crest: On a ducal coronet a boar's head couped argent.
Motto: Virtus semper viret.

1-**SMITH, Mellcene Thurman (Mrs. Edward T.),** *b* Buchanan Co., Mo., Nov. 13, 1872.
10-Nathaniel **Woodward** (qv);
9-Nathaniel (*d* 1694), freeman, 1637; *m* 2d, Katherine–;
8-John (*d* 1688), of Taunton and Plymouth; soldier King Philip's War, 1675; *m* 1675, Sarah Crossman (*b* 1652; Robert[9], "The drum maker of N.E.," fitted out with guns and drums Capt. Gallop's company for Phipps' expdn. against Can., 1690);
7-Israel (1681-1776), in Queen Anne's War; *m* Elizabeth– (*d* 1765);
6-Benajah (*d* 1792), *m* 1742, Abigail Harvey (*d* 1792);
5-Elisha (1754-1841), of Taunton; in Capt. Ichabod Leonard's co. from Taunton, on the R.I. alarm, 1776; *m* 1778, Lucy Manson (*d* 1791);
4-David (1781-1832), of Petersham, Mass.; *m* 1814, Diedema Hare (1796-1845);
3-Manson Jesse (1821-98), of Boston; *m* 1849, Fanny B. Abell (1826-1903), of Williamstown, Vt.;
2-Cecelia Marion (1851-1918), of St. Joseph, Mo.; *m* 1869, John William **Thurman** (*b* 1850), farmer and stockman; issue: I-Mellcene (1 above); II-Fanny L. (*b* 1875; *m* 1897, Edgar Louis Gratigny); III-Jessymin (*b* 1877; *m* 1903, Arthur Stuart Lewis, 1877-1918); IV-Cecelia Mabel (*b* 1879; *m* 1910, Lloyd A. Bechtel, *d* 1920); V-John William (*b* 1886; *m* 1907, Effie Cisco); VI-Claud Manson (*b* 1894; *m* 1919, Sadie Moon).
1-*m* Jan. 1, 1893, Edward T. Smith, *b* Westport, Mo., Jan. 12, 1872.

MELLCENE (THURMAN) SMITH

1-Ed. public and private schools; extension courses, Washington U.; studied music under Italian and French masters. Sec. and treas., St. Louis Law Printing Co. First woman to take the oath of office as mem. Mo. Gen. Assembly, 1923-24. Mem. D.A.C., D.A.R., U.D.C., I.A.G., Mo. Hist. Soc., St. Louis Woman's Club, Twentieth Century Art Club, Town Club, St. Louis Art Club, L.A.P.W., Chamber of Commerce. Winter place: San Diego, Calif. Residence: 7171 Kingsbury Boul., St. Louis, Mo.

1-**WILLIAMS, E(dward) Victor,** *b* Richmond, Va., Feb. 6, 1864.
4-John **Williams,** of New Kent Co., Va.; in Capt. W.H. Richardson's co. of riflemen, 1st Corps d'Elite (Randolph's), Va. Militia in War 1812;
3-James (1780-1872), War 1812;
2-John Henry (2 below).
10-Robert **Tower,** *m* Dorothe Damon;
9-John (qv), *m* 1638/39, Margaret Ibrook;
8-Ibrook (*b* 1643/44), *m* 1668, Margaret Hardin (*b* 1647; John[9], of Braintree, Mass.);
7-Daniel (*b* 1692), *m* Susan Lincoln (*b* 1694; Mordecai[8], of Cohasset, *m* Sarah Jones);
6-Daniel (*b* 1720), *m* 1741/42, Bethiah Nichols (Roger[7], *m* Bethiah Winslow);
5-Isaac (*b* 1752), *m* 1777, Betsey Stoddard (*b* 1759; Stephen[6], *m* Rachel Stoddard);
4-Elizabeth (*b* 1785), *m* 1803, Hugh **Smith** (1769-1858), to Springfield, Vt. (Sylvanus[5] [1746-1830], Shirley, Mass., lt. and capt. Am. Rev., at Lexington Alarm, siege of Boston, etc., *m* 1765, Agnes Moore [1747-1830], of Boylston);
3-Hiram Moore (1809-99), to Richmond, Va.; *m* 1837, Elizabeth Ames (1819-99; Amos[4], Am. Rev., *m* Abigail, dau. Col. Bulkley; Amos[5]; William[6]);
2-Elizabeth Victoria (1838-1917), *m* John Henry **Williams** (1827-1913), made fortune during "gold rush," in Calif., 1849; among those who captured John Brown at Harper's Ferry; issue: I-Coleman Cooke (1859-1916); II-Henry Ames (*m* Elizabeth Selden Dimrock); III-Edward Victor (1 above); IV-Louise; V-Adele.
1-*m* Apr. 23, 1907, Kate Burwell Williams (qv for issue).
1-Ed. McGuire's Sch., Richmond, Va. Entered employ of Allen & Ginter, formerly the John F. Allen Co., now part of the Liggett & Myers Tobacco Co., as office boy; served through various positions to that of mgr., 1880-1919, retired. Dir. Standard Paper Mfg. Co., Richmond Trust Co., The Spotless Co. Mem. 1st Regt. Va. Militia, 8 yrs. Mem. S.R., Va. Hist. Soc. Episcopalian. Democrat. Clubs: Commonwealth, The Country, Princess Anne

Country, Swannanoa Country. Residence: Cary Street Rd., Richmond, Va.

1–**WILLIAMS, Kate Burwell Williams (Mrs. E. Victor),** *b* "Wood Park," Orange Co., Va., Jan. 11, 1877.
7–William **Williams** (*d* 1712), justice, Stafford Co., Va., 1699; *m* 1702, Jael Harrison (*d* 1733; James[8], of Essex Co.); she *m* 2d, Richard Johnson;
6–James (1703-35), lt. of militia, Spotsylvania Co., 1729; *m* 1724, Ann– (she *m* 2d, Samuel Wharton);
5–William (1725-78), justice, Culpeper Co., resigned, 1765, in protest against the Stamp Act; mem. Com. Safety, 1775-78; *m* 1750, Lucy Clayton;
4–William Clayton (1768-1817), lawyer, Richmond, Va.; dep. clk. of Shenandoah Co. for his brother, Maj. John Williams; *m* Alice Grymes Burwell (Lewis[5], *m* Judith Page; Lewis[6]; Nathaniel[7], *m* Elizabeth, dau. of Robert, "King," Carter; Lewis[8]; Lewis[9], qv);
3–Lewis Burwell (1802-80), grad. Princeton, aet. 18; lawyer; mem. Ho. of Dels., 1830; commonwealth's atty., Orange Co., 47 yrs.; mem. Va. Legislature from Orange, 1833-34; *m* 1st, Mary Williams Catlett;
2–John Green (2 below).
10–Col. John **Catlett** (1630-70), from Eng. to Va. ca. 1650; resided in Essex Co.; col. of militia; magistrate; justice, commr. to settle boundary line between Md. and Va.; accompanied John Lederer on his 3d exploration of the country west of the Blue Ridge;
9–Nicholas, came with parents; *m* Susannah Meriwether;
8–David;
7–William (*d* 1775), moved to Shenandoah Valley, Frederick Co., ca. 1745;
6–James (*d* ca. 1797), Frederick Co.; *m* Jane–;
5–John (*d* 1816), *m* 1779, Rachel Rosett;
4–Robert, *m* Ann Clayton Tutt (Benjamin[5], of "The Retreat," Culpeper Co., *m* Elizabeth C., dau. of Nathaniel Pendleton; Capt. James[6]; Col. Richard[7]; Richard[8]);
3–Mary W. (*d* 1850), *m* Lewis Burwell **Williams** (3 above).
8–William **Byrd** (qv);
7–William (1674-1744), ed. in Eng. and Holland; studied at the Inner Temple; receiver gen. of the colony; pres. Council; founder of Richmond, Va.; *m* 2d, Mary Taylor;
6–Anne (1725-57), *m* as his 2d wife, Charles **Carter,** of Cleve, King George Co.; burgess; col. of King George Co. militia (Robert[7], of "Corotoman"; *m* 2d, Betty Landon);
5–Anne, as Widow Champe, *m* as his 3d wife, Col. Lewis **Willis** (1734-1813), of Willis Hill, Fredericksburg; lt. col. 10th Va. Cont. troops, 1776-78 (Col. Henry[6], burgess from Gloucester, 1718-28, an original trustee of Fredericksburg, *m* 1733, Mildred Washington, Widow Gregory);
4–Byrd Charles (1781-1846), adj., Col. Lewis' regt., stationed on the Canadian frontier in Vt., War 1812; *m* Mary Willis Lewis (their dau. Catherine D., *m* 2d, Achille, son of Joachim Murat);
3–George (1809-61), ed. West Point; surveyor of public lands; collector and inspector of Charlotte Harbor; lived for many years in Fla.; *m* 2d, 1841, Sallie Innes Smith (1820-81; George[4], *m* Delia, dau. of Dr. David Forbes, *m* 1774, in Edinburgh, Margaret Sterling, and emigrated to Va. and settled at Dumfries about the time of the Am. Rev.);
2–Kate Murat (2 below).
11–Nicholas **Martian** (qv);
10–Elizabeth, *m* George **Reade** (qv);
9–Mildred, *m* Augustine **Warner,** II (1642-81), of Warner Hall, Gloucester, Va.; ed. Merchant Taylor's School, London; burgess; speaker of the House; mem. gov.'s Council;
8–Mildred, *m* Lawrence **Washington,** of Westmoreland Co., Va.;
7–Augustine (1694-1745), of Wakefield, Westmoreland Co.; *m* 2d, Mary Ball (1707/08-1789);
6–Elizabeth or Betty (*b* 1733), *m* as his 2d wife, Fielding **Lewis** (1725-82), of Kenmore, Fredericksburg, Va.; burgess for Spotsylvania, 1760-68; patriot of Am. Rev. gave large sums towards the mfr. of arms at Fredericksburg;
5–Maj. George Washington (1757-1821), of Marmion, King George Co., Va.; 1st lt., Gen. Washington's Guard, 1776; capt. 3d Regt. Cont. Dragoons, 1777; promoted to maj., 1778, and served to the end of Am. Rev.; *m* 1779, Catherine Daingerfield (1764-1820; Col. William[6], *m* Mary Willis; William[7]; William[8]; John[9]; William[10]);
4–Mary Willis (1782-1834), *m* Byrd Charles **Willis** (4 above);
3–George, *m* Sallie I. Smith (3 above);
2–Kate Murat (1845-1917), *m* 1871, John Green **Williams** (1843-1911), see portrait and biography Vol. III, p. 484.
1–*m* Apr. 23, 1907, Edward Victor Williams, (qv); issue: 1–Catherine Murat, *b* Richmond, Va., May 19, 1908; ed. Collegiate Sch. for Girls, Richmond, Va.; mem. Junior League, Woman's Club, Country Club of Va.
1–Ed. Powell's Sch., Richmond, Va. Mem. C.D.A. Clubs: Woman's, Country. Residence: Cary Street Rd., Richmond, Va.

1–**WILLIAMSON, Mary Cornelius Thompson (Mrs. Warren P.),** *b* Caldwell Co., Mo., Apr. 16, 1867.
5–James (or William) **Thompson,** from near Hagerstown, Md., to Pa.; *m* —Turner;
4–James Lawrence (1801-76), of Center Co., Pa.; *m* 1821, Catherine Gearhart (1803-50; John[5] [1754-1840], came to Half Moon Valley, Pa., 1788, ens. Lancaster Co. militia, *m* 1784, Catherine [1767-1846], dau. of Peter Gray; probably Mordecai[6], from Alsace-Lorraine to Frederick Co., Md. about middle of 17th Century);
3–Rev. John Gearhart (1823-1905), of Center Co.; ed. Meadville (Pa.) Coll.; pastor Erie M.E. Conf. 20 yrs.; *m* 1843, Catherine Gearhart;
2–Dallas Jeremiah (2 below).
7–Eberhardt, or Everhard **Ream** (*b* 1692), of Lancaster Co., Pa., 1723; received a patent for 400 acres of land from Thomas Penn, 1725; his father or g.father fled from the Palatinate to Eng., thence to America with William Penn, 1682, settled at Phila. or "New Germany" Pa.;
6–John (*b* 1718), Lancaster Co.;
5–John Frederick (1754-1837), Am. Rev.; assisted in building Fort Lee on the Hudson River; served in campaigns of 1776 and 1777, in N.J., and wintered at Valley Forge; moved to Center Co., Pa.; *m* twice;
4–Mary Magdalena (1799-1858), *m* ca. 1820, Isaac Elias **Gearhart** (1797-1860; John[5], above);
3–Catherine (1821-97), *m* Rev. John G. **Thompson** (3 above);
2–Dallas Jeremiah (1844-1915), ed. Meadville Coll.; served in Co. H, 78th Pa. Vol. Inf., 1861-64; served in Hancock's 1st Army Corps until end of war; wounded at Stone River; moved to Mo., 1866, returned to Pa., 1867; oil operator; moved to Ohio 1883; in U.S. postal service, 1887-1915; *m* 1866, Mary Anderson Cornelius (1847-1920; Maxwell[3], *m* Margaret Winters, 1779-1862); issue: I–Mary Cornelius (1 above); II–Frank Dallas (*b* 1869; *m* 1903, Sara Barclay); III–Frederick M. (1874-75); IV–Royal Eugene (1884-99).
1–*m* Dec. 31, 1890, Warren Pyatt Williamson, *b* Youngstown, O., Nov. 4, 1858; son of Joseph Williamson, of Youngstown; issue: 1–Joseph Dallas, *b* Youngstown, May 17, 1897; Culver Mil. Acad.; B.S. in M.E. and C.E., Tri-State Coll., Angola, Ind., '22; Mercersburg Acad.; U. of Mich.; served in 68th Anti-aircraft Bn., enlisted Sept. 6, 1918-discharged, Dec. 20, 1918, Camp Sherman, O.; licensed aviator; Mason (32°, K.T.), Elk; 2–Warren Pyatt, II (qv).
1–Ed. supplementary courses at Harvard and Boston univs. Taught in public schools, 1881-1921; church choir and public singer. Apptd. community song dir. for Ohio of Nat. Council of Women; chmn. Woman's Mahoning Co. Rep. Com. Mem. D.A.R., A.L. Auxiliary (1st v.p. for Ohio), Monday Musical Club (past pres.), Wimodaughsis Club (pres.), Youngstown Fed. of Women's Clubs (1st pres.), Ohio Fed. of Music Clubs (1st v.p.; chmn. of music 5 yrs.), O.E.S., White Shrine of Jerusalem, etc. Residence: 18 W. Warren Av., Youngstown, O.

1–**WILLIAMSON, Warren Pyatt, II,** *b* Youngstown, O., May 10, 1900.
5–Joseph **Williamson** (1765-1827), from N.J. to Washington Co., Pa.; to the Western Re-

serve, 1800; Am. Rev.; Methodist; *m* 1789, Margaret Dustman (1766-1848);
4–Piatt (1801-77), *m* 1826, Annie Knox (1804-79; Hugh[5], served in English navy 4 yrs., from Ireland to Dauphin Co., Pa., to Youngstown, O., 1822, *m* 1803, as her 1st husband, Martha Ellenbarger, *b* in Germany, 1784);
3–Joseph (1827-1912), *m* 1856, Belinda Detchon (1835-1924; Elijah[4], *m* 1828, Elizabeth [*b* 1810], dau. of Andrew Kentner, *m* as her 1st husband, Rebecca Hall [*b* 1795], whose father was a soldier in Am. Rev.);
2–Warren Pyatt (*b* 1858), grad. Iron City Coll., Pittsburgh, Pa.; banker, realtor; Mason (32°, K.T.), Odd Fellow, Elk; mem. Bd. Edn.; *m* 1890, Mary Cornelius Thompson (qv).
1–*m* Feb. 6, 1924, Isabell Seymour De Nio, *b* Boston, Mass., Dec. 14, 1903; dau. of James Franklin De Nio; issue: 1–Barbara Marie, *b* Youngstown, O., May 9, 1925; 2–Warren Pyatt, III, *b* Youngstown, May 14, 1930.
1–Ed. U.Mich.; U.Wis., 1923. Wireless operator; owns and operates Radio Station WKBN, Youngstown, O. Master signal electrician, 7th Signal Bn., Southern Dept., U.S.A.; enlisted at Columbus, O., Aug. 7, 1918-discharged at Ft. Bliss, Tex., Aug. 30, 1919; apptd. corpl., sgt. (sgt. 1st class), non-commd. officer when discharged. Mason (32°, K.T.). Residence: 26 Auburndale St., Youngstown, O.

1–**WILSON, Benjamin Franklin, III,** *b* Surry C.H., Va., Jan. 3, 1867.
6–George **Wilson** (1715-85), from Co. Armagh, near Charlemont, Ireland, 1740, settled in Chester Co. (later Delaware), Pa.; removed to Adams Co., Pa., 1747 (later called Wilsonville, now Bendersville); *m* 1738, Ruth (Buler) Douglas (1709-84), from Co. Tyrone, Ireland;
5–Benjamin (1743-1813), *b* in Chester Co., and moved to Adams Co., Pa., 1747; *m* 1774, Sarah Bowen (1745-1815; Thomas[6], *m* Jane Edwards);
4–George (1778-1859), of Adams Co.; *m* 1798, Sarah Wright (1774-1831; John, II[5], *m* Elizabeth Hammond);
3–Benjamin Franklin (1801-34), of Adams Co.; *m* 1830, Susan Wierman (1808-84; Nicholas[4], *m* Jane Underwood);
2–Benjamin Franklin, II (1834-1909), farmer; *m* 1865, Maria Frances Edwards (1845-73); issue: I–Benjamin Franklin, III (1 above); II–Albert Edwards (qv for Edwards Lineage); III–Nicholas George, (qv for Tyler lineage); IV–Thornton Seawell (1878-99); V–Maria Mildred (*b* 1880; *m* John G. Wallace); VI–Franklin Davis, M.D. (*b* 1882; *m* Ruth Pendleton, dau. of Robert Lucius Harrison, *m* Lilian Elsom, of Richmond, Va.; issue: Ruth Harrison; Anne Elizabeth; Franklin Davis, II); VII–Charles Bonner (*b* 1884; *m* Marion Mercier Earle).
1–*m* Oct. 4, 1895, Myra Stewart, *b* Cowan, Tenn., Mar. 20, 1876; dau. of J. M. Stewart; issue: 1–Benjamin Franklin, IV, *b* Cowan, Tenn., Aug. 17, 1896; *m* Aug. 16, 1928, Lyra Summers; 2–Elizabeth Virginia, *b* S. Pittsburg, Tenn., Sept. 16, 1899; 3–Albert Stewart, *b* S. Pittsburg, May 12, 1902; *m* Nov. 6, 1924, Nannie Mae Adcox (issue: Albert S., Jr., *b* Apr. 18, 1927); 4–Myra Frances, *b* Dayton, Tenn., Aug. 12, 1905; *m* June 30, 1927, E. Herbert Qualls (issue: E. Herbert, Jr., *b* Dec. 5, 1929); 5–Howard Thurman, *b* Oxmoor, Ala., July 8, 1908.
1–M.I.T., '89. Asst. chemist, chemist, asst. supt. and supt., Tenn. Coal, Iron & Ry. Co., 1889-1908; v.p. and gen. mgr. Williamson Furnace Co., 1908-10; sec. and gen. mgr. Jefferson Brown Ore Co., 1910-12; gen. supt. Shelby (Ala.) Iron Co., 1912-19; gen. supt. Bon Air Coal & Iron Co., Wrigley, Tenn., 1919-22; pres. and gen. mgr. Tenn. Motor Transportation Co., Nashville, 1922-23; insurance, 1923-26; sales mgr. Nashville Auto Club, 1926-30; gen. insurance, 1930–. Residence: B-6 Washington Apts., Nashville, Tenn.

1–**WILSON, Albert Edwards,** *b* "Chippokes" on James River, Surry Co., Va., June 23, 1868.
10–William **Edwards** (*d* 1623), from Eng., settled at Jamestown, Va.;
9–William (1615-73), of Jamestown and Surry Co., Va.; importing merchant and planter; he and Rice Davis obtained patent for 1080 acres on the Sunken Marsh, James City Co., 1648; granted 491 acres opposite to Jamestown, 1657, later granted 720 acres in Sunken Marsh; burgess, 1652,53; justice of the peace; *m* Dorothy–;
8–William (*d* 1698), of Jamestown and Surry Co.; clk. Gen. Ct., 1688; clk. of Surry Ct., and of the Council of the Colony, 1694; *m* Ann Manfeild;
7–William (*d* 1721), of Surry Co.; burgess, 1706; *m* 2d, a dau. of Micajah Lowe;
6–Micajah (1716-70), *m* Elizabeth Blow (Richard[7], of Sussex Co., Va.);
5–William (*d* 1797), of Southampton Co., Va.; lt. and capt. in Am. Rev.; *m* Susannah Edmunds, of Sussex Co., Va. (John[6]);
4–William (1780-1827), of Surry Co.; *m* 1804, Frances Green Seawell (*d* 1857; John[5], *m* Fannie Hobday, of Gloucester Co.);
3–Albert Sterling, M.D. (1810-73), of Surry Co.; M.D., U.Pa., 1837; *m* 1842, Maria Louisa Seawell;
2–Maria Frances (1845-73), *m* 1865, Benjamin Franklin **Wilson,** II (1834-1909), farmer; for issue and other lineages see Benjamin F. Wilson, III.
1–*m* June 27, 1899, Grace Hammersley, *b* Baltimore, Md., Nov. 29, 1872; dau. of William N. Hammersley, of Baltimore, *m* Esther Virginia Magers; issue: 1–Albert Edwards, II, *b* Norfolk, Va., Feb. 15, 1913; William and Mary Coll.
1–M.D., U. of Md., 1896; post-grad., Presbyn. Eye, Ear, Nose and Throat Hosp., Baltimore, 1897. Specialist in eye, ear, nose and throat, Norfolk, Va., since 1897. Mem. 7th Ward Local Bd. of Improvement, Norfolk, 1906-17. Mem. Vol. Med. Service Corps, World War; mem. Med. Advisory Bd. No. 3, 1917-19. Trustee Park Place M.E. Church, mem. bd. of stewards and chmn. of building com. Mem. A.P.V.A., I.A.G. (charter), Va. Med. Soc., A.M.A., Norfolk Co. Med. Soc., Seaboard Med. Assn. of Va. and N.C., Norfolk and Portsmouth Chamber of Commerce. Democrat. Club: Lions. Residence: 1019 Westover Av., Norfolk, Va.

1–**WILSON, Nicholas George,** *b* Norfolk Co., Va., Sept. 13, 1871.
9–Henry **Tyler** (1604-72), from Eng. to Middle Plantation (now Williamsburg), Va., ca. 1645; justice for York Co.; *m* 2d, Ann Orchard (widow of John Orchard);
8–Henry (1661-1729), justice; coroner; high sheriff of York Co.; *m* Elizabeth Chiles (g.dau. Col. Walter Chiles, mem. Council of State, 1652);
7–John (1686-1727), student William and Mary Coll.; justice of James City; *m* Elizabeth Jarrett (John[8]);
6–John (ca. 1710-1773), marshal to Vice Admiralty Ct. of Va.; *m* Anne Contesse (Dr. Lewis[7], Huguenot, from France to Williamsburg, Va., ca. 1715);
5–John (1747-1813), capt. Va. vols.; mem. House of Delegates; judge Admiralty Ct.; v.p. Va. Constl. Conv. of 1788; judge Gen. Ct., 1788-1808; gov. Va., 1808-11, resigned to become judge U.S. Dist. Ct. of Va.; *m* Mary Armistead (Robert[6]; Ellyson[7]; Robert[8]; Anthony[9]; William[10], from Eng. to Va., 1635, a patentee in Elizabeth City Co., 1636); their son, John, was 10th President of the U.S.;
4–Maria Henry, *m* John B. **Seawell,** of Gloucester Co.;
3–Maria Louisa (1814-86), *m* Albert Sterling **Edwards;**
2–Maria Frances (1845-73), *m* 1865, Benjamin Franklin **Wilson,** II (1834-1909), farmer; for issue and other lineages see Benjamin F. Wilson, III.
1–*m* Nov. 28, 1895, Beulah Murray Halstead, *b* Moyock, N.C., Sept. 13, 1872; dau. of George N. Halstead, M.D., *m* Margaret Courtney Jane Wilson, of Norfolk Co., Va.; issue (all *b* South Norfolk, Va.): 1–Beulah Margaret, *b* Sept. 8, 1896; 2–Nicholas George, II, *b* Feb. 12, 1898; *m* May 29, 1928, Elizabeth Douthat Tyler; 3–Mildred Tyler, *b* Apr. 6, 1906.
1–M.D., U. of Md., 1895. Mem. Norfolk Co. Med. Soc. (past pres.), Med. Soc. of Va., A.M.A. Mem. official bd. of Ghent M.E. Church, South. Residence: 1201 Matoaka St., Norfolk, Va.

1–**MATLACK, Cora Tebbs (Mrs.),** *b* Covington, Ky., Sept. 3, 18–.
5–Daniel **Tebbs** (*b* Va.), *m* at least twice;
4–Daniel Heath (*b* 1755), of Va.; *m* Sarah Heath;
3–William Travis (*b* at sea during Am. Rev., on his father's ship, 1778-*d* 1848), of Va., and

Fleming Co., Ky.; *m* Nancy Miller; *m* 2d, 1807, Margaret Robertson (1777-1845; George[4] [1749-ca. 1806], Am. Rev., *m* Susan Simpson, 1749-1811);
2-Willoughby Heath (2 below).
6-Isaac **Clemons,** aet. 9, landed at Salem, Mass., early in 1700, with bro. Jacob, aet. 7, "they became separated never to meet again, Jacob settled in Canada";
5-John (*b* Danvers, Mass.-*d* 1790), colonial soldier, 1755; founder of Hiram, Me.; settled there 1780; *m* 1757, Abigail Southwick (1730-1834; desc. Lawrence and Cassandra Southwick, landed at Salem, 1630, Quaker exiles who *d* at Shelter Island, 1660);
4-John (1763-1845), soldier Am. Rev., aet. 16; settled at Hiram, Me., 1790; *m* 1789, Mary McLellan (both buried on farm, at Hiram);
3-Cary (1790-1844), pioneer resident of Covington, Ky.; *m* 1813, Mary Merrill (*b* Cazenovia, N.Y., 1792-*d* 1882);
2-Martha (1831-88), *m* 1847, Samuel Cloon (1824-61); *m* 2d, in Covington, Ky., 1864, as his 2d wife, Willoughby Heath **Tebbs** (1815-83), capt. in Seminole War, 1838, a.-d.-c. to Brig. Gen. Rodgers; mayor of Covington, Ky., 1870; issue (mother's 1st marriage, surname Cloon): I-George B.; II-Will Wilshire; III-Sallie Clifford (*m* Richard Bacon Jones, see their son Clifford Cloon Jones); issue (2d marriage): I-Grace (1865-1914; *m* William Klappert, see their dau. Mrs. Earl William Wagner); II-Cora (1 above).
1-*m* Jan. 4, 1893, Dr. Harry Crout Matlack; issue: 1-Elizabeth Tebbs, *b* Covington, Ky., June 1, 189–; *m* 1916, Enos William Abare (issue: William Tebbs); 2-Harry Clemons, *b* Home City, Hamilton Co., O., May 6, 1900; U.S.N.R., served in World War, submarine-chaser fleet at Corfu, Greece; on S-C. 215 at Battle of Durazzo, Oct. 2, 1918, wounded at Durazzo, spent 3 weeks in hosp. in Montenegro; on surrendered Austrian battleship "Zrinyi"; served on Am. Food Commn. in Austria, 1919; *m* 1925, Catherine Gaughn (issue: Harry Clemons, II).
1-Mem. C.D. 17th C., Colonial Daughters (registrar gen.), D.A.R. Mem. Christian Ch. Residence: 123 W. Parkwood Dr., Dayton, O.

McLELLAN

Arms: *Azure, three doves rising paleways between two mullets or.*
Crest: *A dove rising, in its beak a sprig.*

1-**WAGNER, Ruth Tebbs Klappert (Mrs. Earl William),** *b* Cincinnati, O., Nov. 27, 1892.
4-Henry **Klappert** (*b* Zurich, Switzerland-*d* 1881), enlisted at Cincinnati, O., in Co. C, 47th Ohio Inf., discharged 1862; re-enlisted 1864, Co. I, 108th Ohio Inf., pvt., Capt. Heintz' co., hon. disch., 1865;
3-John Jacob (1826-1904), in Civil War, 1861-65; *m* Mary Elizabeth Dohrman (1823-1907);
2-William (2 below).
7-Hugh **McLellan** (1710-87), from Antrim, Ulster, Ireland, 1735, settled at Gorham, Me.; patriot in Colonial and Rev. wars; selectman, 1768; frontier protection, 1746-47; scout, 1748; provided for soldiers' families during Am. Rev.; mem. com. on new constn., 1778; ruling elder; *m* Elizabeth McLellan (1708-1804), saved Ft. Narragansett, Gorham, Me., 1750; both lineal desc. of Sir Hugh McLellan, Clan Argyl-Campbell, Scotland, knighted 1515;
6-Lt. Cary (1745-1805), of Gorham; colonial constable, 1774; lt. of minute-men, 1775; marched to Lexington Alarm; ens., Hart Williams' Co.; recommended by council to be commd. by Gen. Washington, 1775; made daring escape from prison ship "Jersey"; *m* 1st, 1767, Eunice Elder (1745-84; Samuel[7], will probated York Co., 1753, came to America, 1720, *m* Mary Huston);

The old HUGH McLELLAN HOUSE, Gorham, Me., erected 1773, the first brick house in Cumberland Co., Me.

5-Mary (1767-1832), *m* 1789, John **Clemons** (1763-1845), soldier Am. Rev., aet. 16; settled at Hiram, Me., 1790; both buried on farm, at Hiram;
4-Cary (1790-1844), pioneer resident of Covington, Ky.; *m* 1813, Mary Merrill (*b* Cazenovia, N.Y., 1792-*d* 1882);
3-Martha (1831-88), *m* 2d, Willoughby Heath **Tebbs** (see their dau. Mrs. Cora Tebbs Matlack for Tebbs lineage);
2-Grace Tebbs (1855-1914), of Covington, Ky.; *m* 1885, William **Klappert** (1856-1929), founder William Klappert Ins. Agency, Cincinnati; issue: I-Cora Tebbs (1886-96); II-Grace (*d* infancy); III-Martha E. (*m* William J. Whitacre); IV-Henrietta V. (*m* Alfred E. Meyer); V-Ruth Tebbs (1 above); VI-William L.; VII-Hugh McLellan; VIII-Tebbs R.; IX-John S.; X-Charles E.
1-*m* Mar. 14, 1914, Earl William Wagner, *b* San Diego, Calif., Oct. 18, 1889; son of Rev. Edwin R. Wagner, of Dayton, O., *m* Dora Hawker; issue: 1-Grace Tebbs, *b* Buffalo, N.Y., Dec. 1, 1914; 2-Ruth Clemons, *b* Cincinnati, O., June 6, 1920; 3-Janet McLellan, *b* Cincinnati, Sept. 16, 1923.
1-Attended U.Cincinnati, 2 yrs. Mem. C.D. 17th C. (asst. nat. sec.), Colonial Daughters (sec. Cincinnati Chapter), D.A.R. (chapter registrar). Cincinnati Colony N.E. Women, Dames of Court of Honor. Presbyterian. Clubs: Hyde Park Garden, Riverside Culture (sec.). Residence: 3588 Mooney Av., Hyde Park, Cincinnati, O.

1-**WILSON, Benjamin Franklin,** *b* Mannington, W.Va., Nov. 18, 1883.
6-Benjamin **Wilson** (ca. 1745-1833), of Monongalia Co., Va.; *m* ca. 1773, Eleanor Tomlinson (*d* ca. 1833);
5-George P. (1779-1873), capt. War 1812; *m* 1802, Rebecca Kennedy (1779-1886; Jacob[6], *m* Betty Kennedy);
4-Benjamin S. (1803-58), *m* Susanna Raler (1804-90; Christopher[5], *m* Sarah Fluharty; Christopher[6], from Holland, *m* Catherine–);
3-George R. (1828-93), of McCurdysville, W.Va.;

in Co. B, 20th Va. Cav., C.S.A., 1863-65; *m* 1849, Susanna Statler;
2–Christopher Columbus (2 below).
6–Jacob **Statler,** killed and scalped by Indians while defending Ft. Statler, Monongalia Co., Va. (now W.Va.), summer of 1778;
5–John (ca. 1767-*d* 1826);
4–Jacob (1805-73), *m* 1826, Elizabeth Walker (1802-74);
3–Susanna (1830-88), *m* George R. **Wilson** (3 above).
6–Peter **Mock** (1742-1817), from Germany to Bedford Co., Pa.; *m* E– (1747-1813);
5–David (1777-1853), *m* Elizabeth Bowser (1770-1863; Jacob[6]);
4–Sarah (1799-1892), *m* John **Mittank,** or Mittong;
3–Jacob M. (1821-97), *m* 1st, Louisa Clark (1829-61; Zadock[4], *m* Nancy Entler);
2–Mandilla (1854-1924), wrote name Mittong; *m* 1879, Christopher Columbus **Wilson** (*b* 1853), farmer, Mannington, W.Va.; issue: I–James Elmer (*b* 1880; *m* Doris Helen Edwards); II–Mary Jennet (*b* 1881; *m* Andrew Cutlip); III–Benjamin Franklin (1 above); IV–Henry Lee (*b* 1886; *m* Elah Myrtle Shanks); V–Luther Jackson (*b* 1888; *m* Bertha Lee Pixler); VI–Lawrence Early (*b* 1890; *m* Mabel Clayton); VII–Charles Lonnel (*b* 1893; *m* Allie Hall).
1–*m* Jan. 27, 1909, Zella Elizabeth Hall (qv); issue: 1–Robert Franklin, *b* Mannington, W.Va., Dec. 10, 1911; Mt. Union Coll., 1933.
1–Telegraph operator, Wheeling, W.Va. Mason (32°, Shriner), Odd Fellow. Methodist. Republican. Residence: 127 Center Av., Elm Grove, W.Va.

1–**WILSON, Zella Elizabeth Hall (Mrs. Benjamin F.),** *b* Mannington, W.Va., Sept. 22, 1888.
6–John **Jarvis** (1720-95), served in Am. Rev.; *m* Hannah– (1725-1800);
5–Solomon (1753-1835), sgt. Am. Rev., 1776; *m* 1774, Margaret Haythorn (1758-1810);
4–Joseph (1795-1833), *m* 1817, Lucy Beall (1800-52; Thomas[5]);
3–Mary Jane (1818-77), *m* John **Hall** (1791-1851);
2–William McCombs (2 below).
9–John **Kendall** (*b* 1637), from Eng., settled in Norfolk Co., Va.; *m* 1667, Susanna Savage;
8–Thomas (*b* 1672);
7–William (1695-1777), of Va.; *m* 1716, Sarah–;
6–William (1717-90), of Fauquier Co., Va.; *m* Jamima Kirk (1718-77);
5–Samuel (1749-1821), of Va.; *m* Mary Smith (1750-1809);
4–William (1781-1855), of nr. Winchester, Va.; *m* Elizabeth Simons (1781-1822);
3–Stephen (1819-93), of Va.; *m* 1837, Mary Ann Watson (1817-62; David[4] [1780-1808], *m* Mary Ann, dau. of James Barker; George[5]);
2–Elizabeth (1857-99), of Marion Co., W.Va.; *m* 1874, William McCombs **Hall** (1848-1900).
1–*m* Jan. 27, 1909, Benjamin Franklin Wilson (qv for issue).
Residence: 127 Center Av., Elm Grove, W.Va.

1–**CHARTERS, Madeleine Searcy Smith (Mrs. Harold F.),** *b* Huntsville, Ala., Sept. 16, 1883.
7–Jacob **Showalter,** from Holland in the "Brotherhood," 1750, settled at Phila.; *m* Mariah–;
6–Ulrich, of Phila.; Am. Rev.; *m* Susannah Watterson (*d* 1815);
5–Joseph (*d* 1859), *m* 1799, Anna Burkholder (*d* 1865);
4–Barbara (*d* 1827), *m* 1818, Peter **Smith** (1792-1862);
3–Joseph Showalter (1824-84), of Portland, Ore.; practiced law at Salem, Ore., several yrs.; pros. atty. in Wash. Ty.; speaker Wash. Ty. Legislature, 1855; U.S. dist. atty. for Wash. Ty.; returned to Ore., 1858; nominated asso. justice of Supreme Ct., 1862, declined; mem. Congress, 1868; as congressman he secured the passage of the N.P.R.R. Bill; brother-in-law and one time law partner of LaFayette Grover, who was gov. of Ore., and senator from Ore.; *m* 1849, Julia Ann Carter;
2–Preston Carter (2 below).
6–Joseph **Lyons** (1755-post 1832), of Halifax, Vt.; pvt. in Am. Rev.; *m* 1778 or 79, Mary Montgomery;
5–Elizabeth (*b* 1790), *m* 1807, Joel **Felch;**
4–Minerva Lyons (1808-95), *m* 1826, Thomas **Carter** (1804-87; George[5], *m* Anne Montgomery Johnston);

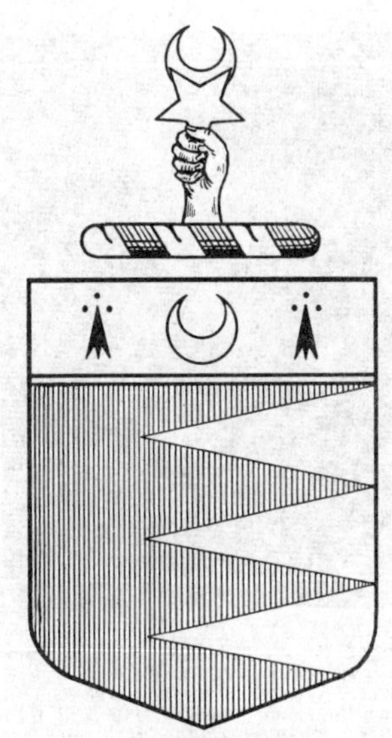

HENDERSON

Arms: *Gules, three piles issuing out of the sinister side argent, on a chief of the last a crescent azure, between two ermine spots.*
Crest: *A cubit arm proper, the hand holding a star or, ensigned with a crescent azure.*
Motto: *Sola virtus nobilitat.*

3–Julia Ann (1827-86), *m* Joseph Showalter **Smith** (3 above).
6–John **Williamson,** *m* 1755, Magdalen Pastell;
5–John Garnier, *m* 1776, Jane Parmenter;
4–John Pastell (1778-1842), rice planter; *m* 2d, 1820, Madeleine Juliet Dennis;
3–William Henry (1827-58), *m* 1854, Susan Searcy Turner;
2–Jeannie Read (2 below).
10–Thomas **Dennis,** from Eng. or Ireland in the "Jewell," with Winthrop's fleet, 1630; an early settler of Cape Cod; lived at Boston, and later was a propr. of Woodbridge, N.J., and its rep., 1668;
9–John (1638-89), of Woodbridge; *m* 1668, Sarah Bloomfield;
8–John (1669-1703), *m* 1694, Rachel Hull;
7–John (*b* 1700), *m* Mary Cozzens;
6–John (1726-1806), gov. of N.J., 1775; del. from Middlesex Co., N.J., to Provincial Congress, 1776; confined in provost jail, N.Y. City, by the British, 1 yr.; *m* 1753, Mary Jaques;
5–Richard (1771-1845), *m* Harriet Elizabeth Duffield (1783-1805);
4–Madeleine Juliet (1803-95), *m* John Pastell **Williamson** (4 above).
9–Thomas **Henderson** (desc. of Sir James Henderson, of Fordell); from Dumfries, Scotland, to Jamestown, 1607; later located at Blue or Yellow Springs, nr. Jamestown;
8–Richard, of Hanover Co., Va.; *m* Margaret Washer, dau. of Ens. Washer, burgess, 1619, rep. Capt. Lawne's Plantation, later known as Isle of Wight Plantation;
7–Samuel (1700-83), high sheriff of Granville Co., N.C., 1754; moved to Edgecombe Co., N.C., ca. 1760; *m* 1732, Elizabeth Williams (*b* 1714; Judge John H.[8], of Wales, *m* Mary, dau. of Lord George Kelynge);
6–Susan (*b* Apr. 23, 1743), *m* Reuben **Searcy,** high sheriff, Granville Co., 1764; clk. of ct., 1777 (John[7], Granville Co., *m* 1727, Phoebe–);
5–Col. Robert (1765-1820), treas., Mero Dist. of Tenn., 1797-1803; clk. of ct., Nashville; dir. Nashville Branch, Bank of U.S.A., 1817, later pres.; trustee of Davidson Acad., 1806; founder Nashville Female Acad., 1816; Grand Master of the grand Masonic Lodge of Tenn., 1815-16; officer War 1812; *m* Elizabeth Wendell (David[6], *m* Susanna, dau. of Dr. David Deaderick, from

COL. ROBERT SEARCY (1765-1820), treas. Mero District of Tenn., 1797-1803; clerk of court, Nashville; dir. Nashville Branch Bank of U.S.A., 1817, later pres.; trustee Davidson Acad., 1806; founder Nashville Female Acad., 1816; 2d Grand Master, Grand Masonic Lodge of Tenn., 1815,16; officer in War of 1812.

Germany, 1747, settled at Winchester, Va., *m* Margarette Baker; Samuel[7]);
4-Susanna Deaderick (1805-58), *m* 1822, Capt. Daniel Burrus **Turner** (*b* 1801), sheriff, Madison Co., Ala.; mem. Ala. Senate 3 yrs.; postmaster Huntsville; served in Paymaster's Dept. in Civil War (John[5], capt. Am. Rev., moved to Caroline Co., Va., *m* 1st, Elizabeth Burrus; George[6], from Eng., 1740, settled in Prince William Co., Va.);
3-Susan Searcy (1835-94), *m* 1st, 1854, William Henry **Williamson** (3 above); she *m* 2d, 1865, Capt. David Humphrey Todd, C.S.A., half brother of Mrs. Abraham Lincoln.
2-Preston Carter **Smith** (1857-97), grad. Dickinson Coll.; organizer and incorporator Ainsworth Nat. Bank; organizer Portland Cable R.R.; organizer and pres. Arlington Club; was tendered the nomination for gov. of Ore., but declined because of ill health; *m* 1880, Jeannie Read Williamson (1857-85); *m* 2d, 1889, Susan Williamson (1855-1919), sister of 1st wife; issue (1st marriage): I-Preston Williamson (*b* 1881; *m* Lacey Stuart Johnston; issue Lacey Stuart, *b* 1915); II-Madeleine Searcy (1 above); issue (2d marriage): I-Susie Aubrey (*b* 1890); II-Henry Anderson (*b* 1891).
1-*m* July 10, 1907, Harold Fessenden Charters, *b* Sussex, N.B., Can., Oct. 20, 1877; son of Edmund Asa Charters, of Sussex; issue: 1-Harold Fessenden, II, *b* Eureka, Calif., Nov. 30, 1915.
1-Grad. Portland Acad., 1902, New Haven Normal School of Gymnastics, 1904. Chmn. Belgium Relief Com. during World War. Mem. D.A.R. (regent), U.D.C. Western Woman's Club (San Francisco). Summer place: Redway, Humboldt Co., Calif. Residence: 2635 H St., Eureka, Calif.

1-**GREGORY, William Benjamin,** *b* Penn Yan, N.Y., Mar. 13, 1871.
10-Henry **Gregory** (qv);
9-John (*d* 1690), settled at Norwalk, Conn.; dep. Provincial Council, 1662-63; *m* Sarah Burt, or Burr (*d* 1689);
8-Judah (1643-1753, aet. 110), settled at Danbury, Conn., 1684; *m* 1664, Hannah Hoyt (Walter[9]);
7-John (1668-1758), justice, Danbury, 1735;
6-Rev. Elnathan (1734-1816), A.B., Princeton, 1757; revolutionary patriot and preacher at Carmel, N.Y., 20 yrs.;
5-Daniel, served in Am. Rev.; *m* distant cousin, Elizabeth Gregory (Elnathan[6]);
4-Ezra (1776-1846), *m* Martha Hoyt (1774-1857);
3-Lewis (1805-83), *m* Martha Gage (1805-59);
2-Ezra Eugene (1845-1922), farmer, Penn Yan, N.Y.; *m* Mary Elizabeth Bush (1848-1922); for issue and Bush lineage see Vol. I, p. 305.
1-*m* June 21, 1898, Selina Elizabeth Bres, *b* Jan. 1, 1870, dau. of late John B. Bres, of New Orleans, La.; issue (all *b* New Orleans): 1-Elizabeth, *b* 1899; Newcomb Coll., '20; *m* June 5, 1923, Henry Stark Ferriss (issue: Gregory Stark); 2-William Bres, *b* 1901; Tulane, '21, Cornell '23; 3-Angela, *b* 1903; Newcomb, '25.
1-M.E., Cornell, '94 (Sigma Xi), M.M.E., 1908. Prof. exptl. engring., Tulane U. of La. (see Who's Who in America). Maj. of engrs. in France, Nov. 1917-Jan. 1919. Mem. S.A.R. Club: Round Table. Residence: 630 Pine St., New Orleans, La.

1-**DUNLAP, Robert Finley,** *b* Giles Co., Va., July 25, 1872.
6-Capt. Alexander **Dunlap** (qv);
5-Ens. Robert (1740-81), "Aspen Grove," Rockbridge Co., Va.; furnished money to found McConnell's Sta. (located in what is now Lexington, Ky.), for which he was to receive 500 acres of present site of Lexington, which estate was lost to grandchildren by decision of Ct. of Appeals of Ky., 1805; ensign at Battle of Guilford Ct. House, in which he was lost or killed, because he refused to obey orders of his half brother, Capt. (later Maj.) James Bratton, to retreat; *m* Mary Gay (William[6], of Ireland, of Gay's Run [now] Rockbridge Co., Va., *m* Mary Walkup, *b* nr. Belfast, Ireland [sister Capt. James Walkup, a cdr. at Battle of Walkup's Plantation, N.C., Am. Rev., *m* Margaret Pickens, aunt of Gov. Israel Pickens, of Ala., and of Lt. John Walkup, cdr. Warm Springs Ft., Va., Am. Rev., whose g.son was Joseph Walkup, lt. gov. Calif., 1858]);
4-Hon. Alexander (1768-1841), mem. Va. Legislature, 1823-27, 1829; *m* Jane Alexander (aunt of Gen. Augustus A. Chapman, M.C., Va., and aunt of Delilah B. Alexander, *m* Hugh Caperton, M.C., Va., and whose stepson was Allen T. Caperton, Conf. States Senator of Va., and U.S. Senator of W.Va.);
3-Alexander (1812-53), lawyer, owner Red Sulphur Springs, (now) W.Va., famous ante-bellum Southern resort; *m* Mary Ann Shanklin (Robert[4], desc. Shanklins of Rockingham Co., Va., *m* Polly Shirkey, desc. Shirkeys of Botetourt Co., Va.);
2-Henry (*b* 1848), of Monroe Co., W.Va., and "Bellevue Farm," Pulaski Co., Va.; merchant and farmer; *m* 1870, Amelia Margret Humphreys (1851-84); *m* 2d, 1896, Margaret E. Nicholson; issue (1st marriage): I-Robert Finley (1 above); II-Mary Elizabeth (*b* 1877; *m* 1903, Andrew Hogeman); III-Ida Bittinger (Mrs. John S. Draper, Jr., qv for Finley lineage); issue (2d marriage): I-McClure; II-Louis A.
1-*m* Nov. 17, 1904, Emma May Wysor, *b* Newbern, Va., Aug. 16, 1880; dau. of Hon. J. C. Wysor, of Pulaski; issue: 1-May Lucile, *b* Hinton, W.Va., Mar. 2, 1906; 2-Emma, *b* Hinton, Aug. 4, 1910.
1-A.B., B.S., Hampden-Sidney Coll., '94 (Sigma Chi). Lawyer, and pres. or dir. various corpns. Pros. atty., Summers Co., W.Va., 1905-09; chmn. W.Va. Dem. State Exec. Com., since 1920; apptd. atty. for spl. State Tax Commn. by the gov. During World War, atty. for local draft bd., local counsel for food and fuel administration, and chmn. of bond sales and Red Cross drives. Clubs: Kanawha Country (Charleston, W.Va.), White Oak Country (White Oak, W.Va.), Willow-wood Country (Hinton, W.Va.), Cheat Mtn. and Allegheny Sportsmen's Assn., Black Knight Country (Beckley, W.Va.). Residence: Hinton, W.Va.

1-**DRAPER, Ida Bittinger Dunlap (Mrs. John S., Jr.),** *b* Dec. 14, 1878.
7-Michael **Finley** (1683-1750; son of Robert, of Balchrystie, Fifeshire, Scotland, *m* Margaret Lauder); came from Ireland to Phila., Pa., 1734; first settled on Neshaminey Creek, Bucks Co., Pa.; removed to Salem Co., N.J., thence to Sadsbury Tp., Pa.; *m* 1712, Ann, dau. of Samuel O'Neill, of Co. Armagh, Ireland (among their sons was Rev. Samuel Finley, pres. Coll. of N.J., now Princeton U.);

6–William (1717-1800), *m* 3d, 1748, Ann Cowan (*d* 1763; David[7]);
5–Margaret (1751-1848), *m* 1770, David Carlisle **Humphreys** (1741-1826), from Co. Armagh, Ireland, ca. 1763, settled in Chester Co., Pa.; merchant; served in Am. Rev.; moved to nr. Greenville, Augusta Co., Va.; elder Bethel Presbyn. Ch. (John[6], of Co. Armagh, Ireland);
4–Samuel (1785-1860), farmed the old homestead, Greenville, Va.; elder Bethel Presbyn. Ch.; *m* 1812, Margaret Moore (1789-1856; John[5], of Lexington, Va.);
3–Rev. James Moore (1816-90), grad. Washington and Lee U., 1841; Presbyn. minister; *m* 1850, Margaret Elizabeth Faris (*b* 1824);
2–Amelia Margret (1851-84), *m* 1870, Henry **Dunlap** (*b* 1848), he *m* 2d, 1896, Margaret E. Nicholson; for issue and Dunlap lineage see Robert Finley Dunlap.
1–*m* June 25, 1903, John S. Draper, Jr., *b* Apr. 13, 1872; issue: 1–Margaret Finley, *b* June 16, 1904; 2–Mary Dunlap, *b* May 29, 1907.
1–Residence: Pulaski, Va.

TABER

Arms: *Azure, on a chevron engrailed argent, between three lions' heads erased or, as many tigers passant collard.*
Crest: *A lion's head erased or, pierced with an arrow.*

1–**TABER, William Brock,** *b* Summerville, S.C., Mar. 2, 1888.
11–Sir John **Taber,** Knighted by King Charles III, at Whitehall;
10–Philip (qv);
9–Joseph (1637-93);
8–Joseph (1663-1738);
7–Pardon (1691-1761);
6–Samuel (1715-91);
5–John (1758-1820), *m* 1789, Sarah Robinson;
4–William Robinson (1792-1866), sympathized with south and broke off relations with northern relatives; banker, Charleston, S.C.; *m* 1824, Emma Smith (1803-67; James[5], below);
3–William Robinson, II (1828-56), killed in duel with Magrath; editor and half owner of Charleston Mercury; buried in Magnolia Gardens, Charleston, S.C.; *m* 1850, Margaret Ellen Thomson (1823-68; Charles Robert[4] [*d* ca. 1867], *m* 1820, Eleanor Sabb [*b* 1800], dau. of John Samuel Hrabowski, Polish nobleman, who left Poland during a revolution, *m* Margaret Ann, dau. of Robert Swainston, *m* Deborah Sabb; Lt. William Russell[5], *m* Elizabeth Sabb);
2–Edmund Rhett (2 below).
8–Rowland **Robinson** (1654-1716), from Eng. to America, 1675; *m* 1676, Mary Allen (1656-1706; John[9], *m* Mary Bacon);

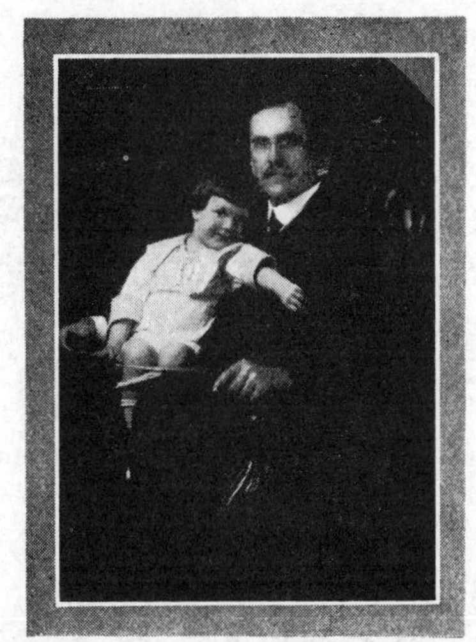

EDMUND RHETT TABER (July 23, 1854-Mar. 21, 1926), and his grandson, WILLIAM RHETT TABER. Ed. The Citadel, Charleston, S.C.; member of the "S.C. Rifles" during the time of the "carpet-baggers." Was pres. Bigbee Fertilizer Co., Flaketown Graphite Co., Kreiss Process Products Co. (Jacksonville, Fla.); sec.-treas. Ala. Machinery & Supply Co.; treas. Montgomery Street Car Co.; influential in the organization of the Am. Agrl. Chemical Co., of which he was district mgr. at Montgomery. Twice declined nomination for mayor of Montgomery; vestryman St. John's Episcopal Church 35 years.

7–Hon. William (1693-1751), of Narragansett, Mass.; dep.gov. of R.I.; *m* 2d, 1727, Abigail (Gardiner) Hazard (1697-1773; William Gardiner[8]);
6–John (1742-1801), of Narragansett; *m* 1761, Sarah Peckham (*d* 1775; probably dau. of William G.[7]; Daniel?[8]);
5–Sarah (1764-1837), *m* John **Taber** (5 above).
22–Ralfe **Morthemer,** Erle of Gloucester; *m* Joane, dau. of King Edward I, desc. William the Conqueror;
21–Thomas (1272-1307);
20–Margaret, *m* John **Montague,** Knight;
19–Robert;
18–John, *m* Agnes, dau. of More;
17–Willm, of Sutton Montague;
16–William, of Slow of Com. Somers; *m* dau. of Peverell, de Com. Devon;
15–Elianor, *m* John **Bevin;**
14–Katherin, *m* Alexander **Muttleberry,** of Jordan's, Co. Somersetshire;
13–Alice, *m* John **Smith,** of Holditch in Thornecombe, Co. Dorset, formerly in Co. Devon, ob. 1560 (26 Mellerche), erroneously called in Visitation, "of Burridge";
12–Sir George, of Madworthy or Mount Radford, ob. 1619; *m* Joan, dau. of James Walker, of Exeter, desc. of the Mathewes of Wales, who were desc. of Flewillins and Herberts;
11–Sir Nicholas (*d* 1622), of Larkbeare; knight; *m* Dorothea, dau. of Sir Raphe Horsey, de Com. Dorset;
10–John, cassique of Carolina, Exeter, Eng., 1611;
9–Rt. Hon. Thomas (1648-94), from Eng.; first landgrave and gov. of Carolina, 1690; *m* Barbara (Schencking) D'Arsens, dau. of Baron Bernard Schencking;
8–Thomas (1669-1738), 2d landgrave; *m* Sarah Blake (*d* 1708; Col. and Gov. Joseph[9] [*b* Eng., 1600], landgrave, Charleston, S.C., *m* Annett, dau. of Landgrave Daniel Axtell, of S.C., *b* Eng.);
7–Sabina (*b* 1699), *m* 1714, Thomas **Smith,** III (1691-1723), planter, of Carolina (Thomas, II[8] [*b* 1665], of Boston, Mass., later Carolina, *m* Elizabeth, dau. of Col. Benjamin Schencking,

m Elizabeth, dau. of Gov. James Moore; Thomas, I[9], of Boston, *m* Sarah, dau. of Dr. Thomas Boylston, of London);
6–Thomas, IV (1719-90), of Charleston, S.C.; *m* 1744, Sarah Moore;
5–James (1761-1835), of Middle Temple and Charleston, S.C.; *m* 1791, Marianna Gough (Capt. Richard[6], *m* Elizabeth, dau. of Nathaniel Barnwell [son of Col. John, *m* Anne Bevners; desc. of Barons of Trimlestown, Ireland], *m* Mary, dau. of John Gibbs [son of Gov. Robert], *m* Mary Woodward);
4–Benjamin Smith **Rhett** (1798-1868), of Charleston, S.C.; by act of Legislature of S.C., 1837, took the name of Rhett; *m* 1827, Mary Pauline Haskell (1808-51; Maj. Elnathan[5] [*b* 1755], *m* 1791, Charlotte [1769-1850], dau. of Col. William Thomson, "Old Danger," picture in Gibbes Art Gallery, Charleston, S.C.);
3–Benjamin Smith (1832-93), served in Co. K, 4th S.C. Cav., C.S.A.; awarded Southern Cross of Honor; *m* 1860, Pauline Brock (1835-87; William[4], of nr. New Orleans, *m* Mathilde, dau. of Pierre Sauve, I [1749-1822], of New Orleans, La., French nobleman, picture hangs in the Library of Congress, No. 321, chosen commr. by French at sale of Louisiana to U.S.A., *m* Miss Second, of Marseilles, France);
2–Marie Mathilde (2 below).

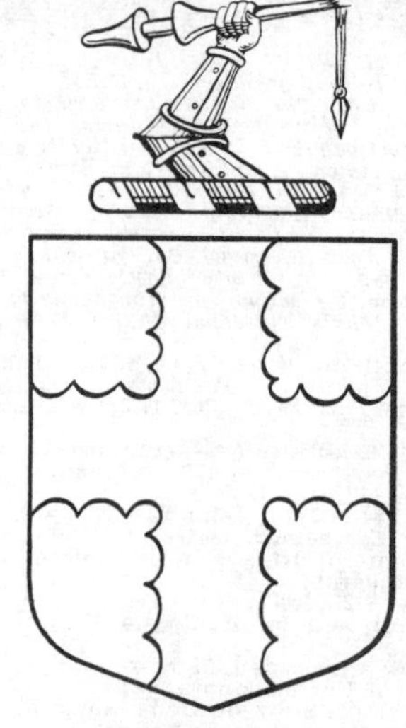

RHETT

Arms: Or, a cross engrailed sable.
Crest: An arm in armour embowed, the hand grasping a broken tilting spear, its head to the sinister and hanging from the staff.
Motto: Aut faciam, aut periam.

9–Sir Walter **Rhett,** originally Gaulter De Raedt, from Hague with Charles II; knighted, June 30, 1660;
8–Col. William (1666-1722), from Eng.; resided in Province of Carolina, 1694-1722; lt. col. militia; receiver gen. and comptroller of customs; lt. gen. militia and vice admiral; dispatched on an expdn. against the notorious pirate Steed Bonnett, whom he defeated and captured, Bonnett and his crew were brought to Charleston and hanged, this put a stop to piracy and rid the colony of a horde of desperadoes; placed in command of a small fleet, 1706, when the French appeared off Charleston and demanded the surrender of the town, he put the French to flight, a few days after he attacked a large vessel which had arrived and so determined was his onslaught that she struck her colors without firing a shot; apptd. gov. of the Bahamas by the crown in acknowledgment of his many services, but died before his commn. reached him; *m* Sarah Amy (Thomas[9], a lord propr. and landgrave of Carolina);
7–Catherine (1705-45), *m* 1721, Roger **Moore** (1694-1759; Gov. James[8] [1640-1706], *m* Margaret or Elizabeth, dau. of Sir John Yeamans, Baronet [*d* 1674; son of Sir Robert, defender of Bristol, beheaded by Sir Nathaniel Fiennes], from Eng., settled in Carolina, gov. and landgrave, *m* Margaret, dau. of Rev. John Foster, of Barbados; Roger[9], Irish patriot, to Hague from Ireland, desc. of the earls and viscounts of Drogheda in Ireland);
6–Sarah (1728-74), *m* Thomas **Smith,** IV (6 above).

MARIE MATHILDE (RHETT) TABER (1861-1920).

2–Edmund Rhett **Taber** (1854-1926), see portrait and biography; *m* 1881, Marie Mathilde Rhett (1861-1920); issue: I–Edmund Rhett, Jr. (*b* July 4, 1883); II–William Brock (1 above); III–Eugene Francis (*b* Nov. 17, 1889); IV–Alfred Haskell (*b* Oct. 4, 1894).
1–*m* 1911, Marye Goodwyn Ashley (qv); issue: 1–William Rhett, *b* St. Louis, Mo., July 29, 1912; student Starkes Univ. Sch., Montgomery; winner Holtzclaw medal, 1929, and U.D.C. scholarship; 2–Marion Mathilde, *b* Montgomery, Ala., Sept. 11, 1922.

WILLIAM BROCK TABER

1–M.E., Ala. Poly. Inst. (A.T.O.). Asst. supt., Bigbee Fertilizer Co., 1910-12; Ala. auditor Flaketown Graphite Co., 1914-18; mgr. Flaketown Graphite Co., Montgomery, Ala., 1918-20; v.p. (now dir.) Kreiss Process Products

Co., Jacksonville, Fla., 1920-22. Industrial engr., Johns-Manville Co., Ltd., Asbestos, P.Q., Can., since 1929. Under U.S. Dept. Justice, Bureau of Investigation, Am. Protective League, during World War. Mason (32°). Episcopalian. Democrat. Residence: Montgomery, Ala. Address: Iroquois Hotel, Asbestos, P.Q., Can.

Ashley

Arms: Argent, three bulls passant sable, armed and unguled or.
Crest: On a chapeau gules, turned up ermine, a bull statant sable, armed, unguled and ducally gorged or.
Supporters: A bull sable, armed, unguled, ducally gorged and line reflexed over the back or.

1–**TABER, Marye Goodwyn Ashley (Mrs. William Brock),** *b* Montgomery, Ala., Feb. 17, 1895.
5–William **Ashley** (1729-1800; desc. Lord Ashley, Earl of Shaftsbury); came from Eng., 1748, settled at Charleston, S.C.;
4–William Pinckney (*d* 1826; maternally desc. from the Pinckneys of S.C.); financed and was capt. of a company under Gen. Francis Marion ("The Swamp Fox"); large plantation owner, Lumberton, N.C.; *m* 1780, Mary Griffin (1764-1816), of S.C., of Scotch descent;
3–Col. Felix Leonard (June 20, 1807-Apr. 17, 1883), referred to as "The Chesterfield of Montgomery"; one of the largest plantation and slave owners in Ala.; *m* 2d, Martha Ellen Rush (Charles George[4]);
2–Robert Augustus (*b* June 13, 1857), ed. private school and U. of Ala.; one of the most extensive plantation owners in Ala.; inherited several large plantations in Montgomery Co., which have been in the family over 150 years, and acquired others; *m* 1882, Marion Motte Myrick (1855-1920), noted Georgia belle, of Milledgeville (Dr. John Wesley[3], one of the most distinguished surgeons in C.S.A., *m* Marye Goodwyn, of Va.); issue: I–Mittie Ellen (*b* 1884; *m* John Savage Whiteman, of Nashville, Tenn.); II–John Myrick (*b* 1886; *m* Ethel Ross, of Opelika, Ala.; issue: Marion Ross, John Myrick, Jr., Wyley Ross, William, Albert Sydney); III–Robert Augustus, Jr. (*b* 1889; *m* Thelma Ford; issue: Mary Ellen); IV–Albert Sidney (*b* 1891); V–Marye Goodwyn (1 above).
1–*m* 1911, William Brock Taber (qv for issue).
1–Ed. Miss Rutson Hatchett's select school for young ladies, and Wesleyan Female Coll., Macon, Ga. Mem. D.A.R., U.D.C., etc. Episcopalian. Residence: Montgomery, Ala.

1–**NEWTON, Josephine,** *b* Pooler, Ga., June 28, 1893.
6–Robert **Southerland** (1722-89), *m* 1745, Joyce Woodstock (1727-84);
5–Robert (1747-1835), Am. Rev.; *m* 1777, Patience Touille (1756-1833);
4–David (1789-1878), *m* 1811, Sarah Brown (1788-1824; Isaac[5]);
3–Alsa (1819-94), *m* 2d, 1855, Lucy Iona Carr (1836-1901; David[4] [1788-1836], *m* 1833, Lavina Carr);
2–Lavina (Ina), (*b* 1865), *m* 1885, Joseph Boney **Newton** (1853-1926); issue: I–Lucy Catherine (*b* 1886; *m* James S. Jussely); II–Robert Melvin (*b* 1889; *m* Pearl Henderson); III–Josephine (1 above); IV–James Gordon (*b* 1895; *m* Thelma Hyde); V–Ina May (*b* 1897; *m* William Ernest Batty); VI–Clarence S. (*b* 1900); VII–Mary Lilly (*b* 1903; *m* C. C. Precott).
1–Mem. D.A.R. (chapter sec. and regent), U.D.C. (chapter pres., sec. and treas.), I.A.G., Huguenot Soc. of S.C., O.E.S. (worthy matron, sec.). Presbyterian. Democrat. Address: Box 73, Long Beach, Miss.

1–**ROGERS, Elvinah Elizabeth Tannehill (Mrs. Robert B.),** *b* Moberly, Mo., Oct. 23, 1872.
8–John **White** (1624-85), from Eng., ca. 1644, settled in Somerset Co., Md.; justice; mem. Assembly and Council of Md.; sheriff, Somerset Co.; burgess; *m* 1652, Sarah Stevens (*d* 1687; Col. William[9], *m* Magdalen–);
7–William (1654-1708), of Md.; *m* Catherine–;
6–John (*d* 1761), *m* Elizabeth White;
5–William, of Md.; *m* Elizabeth Smith (*d* 1763; Nathan[6], *m* Elizabeth Cole);
4–Benjamin (1756-1822), Am. Rev.; *m* 1786, Rebecca O'Dell Chiswell (Stephen[5], *m* Sarah Newton);
3–Elizabeth S., *m* Carlton **Tannehill**;
2–Carlton Jack (2 below).
8–John **Woods** (*b* 1654), from Eng., settled in Lancaster Co., Pa., 1724; removed to Albemarle, Va., 1734; *m* 1681, Elizabeth Worsop (*b* 1656; Thomas[9], *m* Elizabeth, dau. Richard Parsons);
7–Michael (1684-1762), *m* 1705, Mary Campbell (1690-1765);
6–John (1712-91), *m* 1742, Susanna Anderson (1725-80; Rev. James[7]);
5–James (1748-1822), of Albemarle Co., Va.; *m* 1779, Mary Garland (1760-1835; James[6], *m* Nancy Rice);
4–Frances (1800-36), of Albemarle Co.; *m* 1817, William **Slavin** (1793-1848; John[5], *m* Nancy Graham);
3–Elvinah Frances (1828-82), of Boone Co., Mo.; *m* 1846, William Tandy **O'Rear** (1818-83; Daniel[4], *m* Elizabeth Bush);
2–Luella (1854-1911), *m* 1872, Dr. Carlton Jack **Tannehill** (1836-91), of Frederick Co., Md.; doctor and druggist; issue: I–Elvinah Elizabeth (1 above); II–Ruth (*m* E. C. McQueen); III–Hattie Gee; IV–Mattie Locke (*m* C. H. Kelly); V–N. O.
1–*m* Dec. 6, 1892, Robert Baker Rogers, *b* Mayfield, Ky., Mar. 12, 1864; son of John H. Rogers, issue: 1–Ruth Elizabeth, *b* Brownwood, Tex., Aug. 10, 1896; U. of Tex.; *m* June 1927, Tony James Bettes.
1–Grad. in music Hardin Coll. Mem. C.D.A., D.A.R., U.D.C., U.S.D. 1812, I.A.G., Country Club, etc. Presbyterian. Democrat. Residence: 707 Center Av., Brownwood, Tex.

1–**SLOAN, Helen Cornwell Hill (Mrs. Clarence R.),** *b* Lower Newport, O., Aug. 15, 1883.
9–Luke **Hill** (living in Simsburg Conn., 1694), *m* 1651, Mary Hart;
8–Luke (*b* 1661), *m* Hannah–;
7–Ebinezer (1687-1758), *m* 1716, Martha Dibble (*b* 1697);
6–Zenas (*b* 1730), soldier in Am. Rev.; *m* 1752, Kezia Hill (1733-1801; Luke[7], and Sarah Frederick);
5–Capt. Ira (1755-1841), capt. Am. Rev.; Lower Salem, O.; *m* 1786, Esther Post;
4–Dea. Ira (1787-1866), maj. militia; a founder of Denison U.; *m* 1816, Welthea Little;
3–Hervey Dale (1828-67), of Lower Newport, O.; merchant and lumberman; *m* 1855, Angeline Dye (1833-1910; Daniel[4]; Daniel[5]; Daniel[6]);
2–Willis Edgar (2 below).
10–Stephen **Post** (*d* 1659), from Eng. ante 1634; settled at Newton, Mass., 1634; removed to Hartford, 1636; at Saybrook ante 1659;
9–John (1627-1711), an original propr. of Norwich, Conn.; *m* 1652, Hester Hyde (*d* 1703; William[10], of Eng.);
8–Samuel (1668-1735), *m* 1697/98, Ruth Lathrop (*d* 1750; John[9]; Samuel[10]; Rev. John[11], qv);
7–Nathaniel (*b* 1702), *m* 1st, 1725, Abigail Birchard (*d* 1733; James[8]; John[9]; Thomas[10], qv);
6–John (*b* 1726), of Norwich, Conn.; *m* 2d, 1757, Abigail Leffingwell;
5–Esther (1759-1851), of Norwich; *m* Capt. Ira **Hill** (5 above).
10–Gov. William **Bradford** (qv);
9–William (1624-1703), of Plymouth; maj. in Indian war; cdr.-in-chief of Plymouth forces in King Philip's War; mem. Council of Mass.; *m* Alice Richards (ca. 1627-1671);
8–Samuel (1668-1714), of Duxbury, Mass.; lt.; selectman, juryman; *m* 1689, Hannah Rogers (*b* 1668);
7–Gamaliel (1704-78), judge county ct.; mem.

Mass. Council; *m* 1728, Abigail Bartlett (1703-76);
6–Paybody (1735-82), of Kingston, Mass.; *m* 1760, Welthea Delano (1741-83);
5–Pamela (1764-1823), *m* 1792, Nathaniel **Little** (1759-1808), served in Am. Rev.; a first settler of Newport, O.;
4–Welthea (1793-1870), *m* Dea. Ira **Hill** (4 above).
7–James **Oglevee** (*d* ca. 1751-53), *m* Sarah– (*d* 1753);
6–John (*d* Jan. 1797), *m*–, had 6 ch.;
5–John (ante 1765-1815), *m* Mrs. Agnes (Passmore) Patterson (1771-1853);
4–William (1808-84), *m* 1830, Susannah Price (1811-1879);
3–John (1831-1907), *m* 1858, Rachel Anne Cornwell (1832-1865);
2–Emma Elizabeth (1859-88), teacher; writer; *m* 1882, Willis Edgar **Hill** (1857-1918), of Marietta, O.; city recorder; farmer; mcht.; issue: I–Helen Cornwell (1 above); II–Harold Bruce (1884-88); III–Charles Edgar (*m* Margaret Elizabeth Patterson).
1–*m* Nov. 5, 1908, Dr. Clarence Reuben Sloan, *b* Williamstown, Va., July 2, 1878; son of Dr. Elias Sloan, *m* Sarah Elizabeth Cline; issue (all *b* Marietta, O.): 1–Richard Hill, *b* Sept. 10, 1910; Marietta Coll., '31 (Alpha Tau Omega); 2–Marion Bradford, *b* Nov. 9, 1911; 3–David Edgar, *b* Apr. 4, 1913.
1–Ed. Denison U., 1907. Mem. S.M.D., C.D.A. (pres. Marietta Circle), D.A.R. (past regent), I.A.G., Ohio State Archael. and Hist. Soc. (life), Washington Co. Pioneer Assn., Fed. of Women's Clubs, Woman's Centennial Assn., etc. Baptist. Republican. Clubs: Washington Co. Country, Betsey Gates Mills. Residence: 215 4th St., Marietta, O.

EDWARD PAYSON BIGELOW (1843-1925).

1–**BILLINGSLEY, Harriet Bigelow (Mrs. Paul),** *b* New York, N.Y., Sept. 7, 1889.
9–John **Bigelow** (qv);
8–Joshua (1655-1745), of Westminster, R.I.; served in King Philip's War; *m* Elizabeth Flagg;
7–Lt. John (1681-1777), *m* Hannah–;
6–David (1706-99), *m* Edith Day;
5–David (1732-1820), *m* 1762, Patience Foote (*d* 1791);
4–Asa (1779-1850), *m* 1802, Lucy Isham (1780-1853);
3–Edward (1810-89), of Malden, N.Y.; *m* 1st, 1841, Carolyn Boies (1814-52);
2–Edward Payson (2 below).
5–Benjamin **Doolittle** (1764-1854), of Winchester, N.H., and Northfield, Mass.; *m* 1784, Editha Field (*b* 1763);
4–Lucius (1792-1875), *m* 1818, Seraph Ashley;
3–Ossian (1821-1904), changed his name to Ossian Doolittle **Ashley,** Mar. 12, 1842; cdr. -regt. "Boston Tigers," and col. during Civil War; *m* 1845, Harriet Amelia Nash;
2–Mary Frances (2 below).
10–Robert **Ashley** (*d* 1682), *m* Mary– (*d* 1683);
9–David (1642-1718), *m* 1663, Hannah Glover (1646-1722);
8–Samuel (1664-1722), *m* 1686, Sarah Kellogg (1666-1729; Joseph[9], qv);
7–Daniel (1691-1726), *m* 1718, Thankful Hawkes (*b* 1690);
6–Samuel (1720-92), one of grantees of Claremont, N.H.; Cape Breton and French and Indian wars; del. Provincial convs., 1774-75; del. 1st Provincial Congress of N.H.; col. 13th N.H. Regt. in Am. Rev.; asso. justice Ct. Common Pleas, 1776-91; mem. Com. of Safety; *m* 1742, Eunice Doolittle (1724-1807);
5–Daniel (1754-1810), lt. in Am. Rev.; *m* 1777, Mercy Pratt;
4–Seraph (*b* 1791), *m* Lucius **Doolittle** (4 above).
10–Robert **Pierce** (qv);
9–Thomas (1635-1706), of Dorchester; *m* Mary Proctor (1642-1704);
8–John (1668-1744), *m* 1693, Abigail Thompson (1667-1744);
7–Samuel (1702-68), *m* 1732, Abigail Mosely (1711-66);
6–Samuel (1739-1815), col. in Cont. Army, Am. Rev.; *m* Elizabeth Howe (1743-97);
5–Abraham (1769-1822), *m* 1791, Lois Davenport (*d* 1842);
4–Harriet (1799-1854), *m* 1819, Joseph **Nash**;
3–Harriet Amelia (1823-1914), *m* 1845, Ossian Doolittle **Ashley** (3 above);
2–Mary Frances (1847-1930), of New York; *m* 1872, Edward Payson **Bigelow** (1843-1925), U.S.M.A. '63; 1st lt., U.S. cav., 1863; twice wounded in battle (see portrait); Am. Steel Foundries; issue: I–Lois (*d* 1901); II–Ashley; III–Richard (*m* Irma Frederica Himely); IV–Bushnell (*m* Sophie Louise Himely); V–Ruth (*m* William L. Sweet, Jr.); VI–Harriet (1 above).
1–*m* May 18, 1912, Paul Billingsley, *b* New York, N.Y., Nov. 30, 1887; 2d lt. in World War; son of Rev. John Alva Billingsley; issue (all *b* Butte, Mont.): 1–Lucy Ann, *b* Aug. 16, 1913; 2–Harriet Joy, *b* Aug. 4, 1915; 3–Paul, Jr., *b* Oct. 5, 1916.
1–Mem. D.A.R. Residence: Portage, Wash.

1–**WELLS, T(homas) Tileston,** *b* New York, N.Y., Sept. 12, 1865.
6–John **Wells** (*d* 1777), from Ireland, settled in New York; capt. French and Indian War; maj. in 3d Regt.; justice of the peace of Tryon Co.;
5–Robert (*d* 1775), of Cherry Valley, N.Y.; maj. Tryon Co. militia; judge of Tryon Co.; *m* Mary Dunlop;
4–John (1770-1823), lawyer, New York City; *m* 1796, Eliza Lawrence (1775-1812);
3–Thomas Lawrence (1799-1886), lawyer; *m* Julia Beach Lawrence;
2–John (2 below).
8–Maj. Thomas **Lawrence** (qv);
7–Capt. John (1659-1729), high sheriff; *m* Deborah Woodhull (Richard[8]);
6–John (1695-1765), magistrate of Queens; *m* Patience Sackett (1701-74; Capt. Joseph[7]);
5–William, *m* Anne Brinckerhoff;
4–Isaac (1768-1841), *m* Cornelia Beach (*d* 1857);
3–Julia Beach (1811-70), *m* 1831, Thomas Lawrence **Wells** (3 above).
9–Thomas **Tileston** (1611-94), was at Dorchester, Mass., 1636; *m* Elizabeth–;
8–Timothy (1636-97), dep. Gen. Ct., 1689,92,94; *m* Sarah Bridgman (1643-1712);
7–Timothy (1664-1736), *m* Hannah Stetson;
6–Timothy (1699-1755), *m* Prudence Leeds;
5–Ezekiel (1731-99), Am. Rev.; *m* Sarah Belcher;
4–Lemuel (1763-1835), *m* 2d, 1789, Mary Minns (1771-1826);
3–Thomas (1793-1869), *m* 1820, Mary Porter (1799-1879);
2–Grace (1841-1928), *m* 1864, John **Wells** (1834-71).
1–*m* Apr. 18, 1894, Georgina Betts, *b* New York, N.Y., Nov. 13, 1868 (sister of Samuel Rossiter Betts, see Vol. II, p. 268); issue: 1–John (qv); 2–Rossiter Betts (Oct. 18, 1900-June 12, 1902); 3–Georgina Lawrence, *b* Oct. 5, 1902; *m* Courtland S. Van Rensselaer.
1–Student Columbia, 1883-87, LL.B., 1888 (Delta

Psi); Harvard, 1888-89; (Litt.D., Rutgers, 1912). Admitted to bar, 1890, and since in practice at N.Y. City; now sr. member law firm of Wells & Moran (see Who's Who in America). Clubs: Down Town, Union. Residence: 52 E. 76th St., New York, N.Y.

1-**WELLS, John,** *b* New Rochelle, N.Y., May 10, 1895.
9-Thomas **Betts** (1618-88), from Eng. ca. 1639; was a founder of Guilford, Conn.; *m* Mary-;
8-Daniel (1657-1758), *m* 1692, Deborah Taylor (1671-1751; Thomas[9]);
7-Daniel (1699-1783), *m* 1724 or 25, Sarah Comstock (1707-81; Capt. Samuel[8]);
6-Samuel Comstock (1732-1823), Am. Rev.; *m* 1754, Mary Taylor (1731-1807; Reuben[7]);
5-Uriah (1761-1841), Am. Rev.; *m* 1st 1783, Sarah Rossiter (1763-96; Hon. Nathan[6]);
4-Samuel Rossiter, LL.D. (1786-1868), officer War 1812; mem. Congress, 1815-17; judge Circuit Ct. of N.Y., 1823-27; U.S. district judge, southern dist. of N.Y., 1827-67; *m* 1816, Caroline A. Dewey (1798-1882; Hon. Daniel[5]);
3-George Frederic (1827-98), A.B., Williams, '44; lt. col. 9th N.Y. Vols. in Civil War; lawyer; *m* 1851, Ellen Porter;
2-Georgina (2 below).
10-John **Porter** (qv);
9-John (1620-88), *m* Mary Stanley;
8-John (*b* 1651), *m* Joanna Gaylord;
7-David (*b* 1685), *m* Anna Phelps;
6-Increase (*b* 1722), *m* Abigail Kellogg;
5-David (1763-1851), Am. Rev.; *m* Sarah Collins;
4-William Augustus (1798-1830), prof. Williams Coll.; *m* Mary A. Noble;
3-Ellen (1829-99), *m* 1851, George Frederic **Betts** (3 above);
2-Georgina (*b* 1868), *m* 1894, Thomas Tileston **Wells** (qv).
1-*m* Nov. 11, 1917, Emily Rita Norrie, *b* Southampton, L.I., N.Y., Aug. 28, 1898; dau. of Lanfear Norrie; issue: 1-Jacqueline Barbey, *b* New Rochelle, N.Y., Aug. 21, 1918; 2-Rita Norrie, *b* New York, Apr. 21, 1922.
1-Insurance broker, New York City. Enlisted Nov. 19, 1915, Co. K, 7th Inf., N.G.N.Y., discharged, May 3, 1917, federal service, June 26-Dec. 2, 1916, and on Mexican border service, July 2-Nov. 22, 1916; commd. 2d lt., Co. K, 12th Inf., N.G.N.Y., May 2, 1917; 1st lt., inf., U.S.A., Mar. 1, 1919; discharged, Apr. 12, 1919; participated in St. Mihiel, Meuse Argonne, etc. Awarded Conspicuous Service Cross (N.Y.), Knight Order of the Crown of Roumania; 5th Class Order St. Sava of Serbia, etc. Life mem. B.O.R., S.C.W., S.R., S.N.S., S.W. 1812, N.O.U.S., M.O.L.L., M.O.F.W., A.L., etc. Mason (32°, K.T.). Clubs: Badminton, Union, Am. Yacht. Residence: 52 E. 76th St., New York, N.Y.

1-**STICKNEY, Louis R.,** *b* Newark, N.J., Feb. 26, 1879.
10-William **Stickney** (qv);
9-Amos (1635-78), from Eng. with parents ca. 1638; removed from Rowley to Newbury after marriage; *m* 1663, Sarah Morse (1641-1711; Anthony[10], qv);
8-Benjamin (1673-1756), to Rowley, ante 1694; *m* 1700/01, Mary Palmer (1674-1747; Dea. Samuel[9], *m* Mary, dau. of Dea. John Pearson, from Eng., among first settlers of Rowley; Thomas[10], from Eng., a founder of Rowley, 1638);
7-Joseph (1705-56), dep. sheriff of Essex Co., 1737; *m* 2d, 1737, Hannah Goodridge (1712/13-1806; Samuel[8], *m* Hannah, dau. of Colin Frazer; Benjamin[9], removed to Rowley, 1685, killed by Indians with wife and two children at evening prayers; William[10], from Eng., at Watertown, Mass., 1636);
6-Samuel (1741-1802), of Beverly, Mass.; *m* 1766, Rebecca Raymond (1742-1825);
5-Samuel (1771-1859), of Boxford; *m* 1794, Edith Wallis (1774-1855);
4-Luther Wallis (1798-1849), Beverly; *m* 1817, Ruth Glover (*b* 1799);
3-Jonathan Gage (1819-89), of Hartford, Conn.; *m* Mary Leonard;
2-George R. (*b* 1851), of Hartford; *m* 1876, Sylvia E. De Wulf (*b* 1852); issue: I-George G. (*b* 1877; *m* May Prue); II-Louis R. (1 above); III-Claire V. (*b* 1881); IV-Sylvia E. (*b* 1882; *m* Albert Martel); V-Maurice (1887-88); VI-Thomas M. (*b* 1892; *m* Ruth Maynard); VII-Hilda L. (*b* 1895; *m* Thomas F. O'Brien, M.D.).
1-A.B., St. Charles Coll., Ellicott City, Md., '96; S.T.L., North Am. Coll., Rome, 1902. Ordained priest R.C. Ch., 1902; pastor Shrine of the Sacred Heart, Mount Washington, Baltimore, since 1928. Awarded medal Pro Ecclesia et Pontifice, by Pope Pius X, 1908; Chevalier Order of the Crown, Belgium, 1920; created domestic prelate by Pope Pius XI, 1922 (see Who's Who in America). Mem. Md. Hist. Soc. Residence: 1701 Regent Rd., Mt. Washington, Baltimore, Md.

1-**THOMPSON, Lucy Pritchard Sawyer (Mrs. William A., Jr.),** *b* Indianapolis, Ind., Oct. 4, 1873.
11-Tristram **Coffin** (qv);
10-Tristram (1632-1704), *m* 1652/53, Judith (Greenleaf) Somerby (1625-1705);
9-Lydia (*b* 1662), *m* 1st, Moses **Little** (1657-91; George[10], qv);
8-Moses (1691-1780), *m* 1716, Sarah Jaques (1697-1763; Sgt. Stephen[9], *m* Deborah Plumor);
7-Dea. Stephen (1719-93), *m* 1743, Judith Bailey (1724-64; Joshua[8], *m* Sarah Coffin);
6-Dr. Stephen (1745-1800), *m* Sarah Jackson (Dr. Clement[7], *m* Sarah Leavitt);
5-Stephen (1774-1852), *m* 1797, Rebecca (Dodge) Caldwell (*d* 1847; William[6], *m* Rebecca Appleton);
4-Harriet (1798-1881), *m* 1st, 1816, Nathan **Sawyer** (Reuben[5], *m* 1789, Deborah Small);
3-Stephen Little (1817-61), *m* 1st, Annie Maria Pritchard;
2-Russell (2 below).
10-Zaccheus **Gould** (qv);
9-John (*b* 1635), *m* 1660, Sarah Baker (*d* 1709/10; John[10]);
8-John (*b* 1662), *m* 1684, Phebe French (*d* 1724; John[9]);
7-John (*b* 1687), *m* 1708/09, Hannah Curtis (*d* 1712);
6-Martha (1709-71), *m* 1st, 1729, John **Pritchard** (1706-53); she *m* 2d, 1761, Samuel Perkins;
5-John (1744-75), of Rindge, N.H.; *m* Lucy Wood (*b* 1746; Solomon[6], *m* Hannah Jewett, John[7], *m* Ruth, dau. of Capt. John Peabody);
4-Capt. John (1771-1823), of Portland, Me.; War 1812; *m* 1795, Margaret Hammond (1764-1846);
3-Annie M. (*d* 1856), *m* Stephen L. **Sawyer** (3 above).
6-Charles (Stuart) **Stewart,** *m* Mary-;
5-Jacob, *m* Edith Dunn; *m* 2d, Rachel Fisher;
4-Silas (1796-1871), *m* 1st, 1823, Mary Hendricks;
3-John House (1826-93), *m* 1st, 1847, Lucinda Nevitt (1830-66);
2-Eliza Thayer (2 below).
9-Hendrick **Hendricks,** *m* 2d, Helena, dau. of Cortelyou Van Brunt;
8-William, *m* 1677, Wilhelmintje Van Pelt (Gysbrecht T. L.[9]);
7-Daniel, *m* Mary-;
6-Col. Abraham (1749-1819), Am. Rev.; *m* Ann Jameson (1753-1834);
5-Col. Thomas (1773-1835), War 1812; *m* 1st, 1799, Elizabeth Trimble (*d* ante 1827);
4-Mary (1803-33), *m* Silas **Stewart** (4 above);
7-John **Crow,** *m* Elizabeth-;
6-Elizabeth, *m* Thomas **Trimble**;
5-Elizabeth, *m* 1799, Col. Thomas **Hendricks** (5 above);
4-Mary, *m* Silas **Stewart** (4 above);
3-John House, *m* Lucinda Nevitt (3 above);
2-Eliza Thayer (*b* 1854), *m* 1870, Russell **Sawyer** (1847-1902); issue: I-Anne (*m* Charles Jacob Giezendanner); II-Lucy Pritchard (1 above).
1-*m* Sept. 4, 1894, William Andrew Thompson, Jr. (May 22, 1872-July 24, 1922); son of W. A. Thompson; issue: 1-Sawyer, *b* (West) Superior, Wis., June 12, 1896; A.B., Cornell, '18; Harvard Law Sch., 1922; *m* Jan. 26, 1921, Thora Lund (issue: William Andrew, *b* July 1, 1924; Sawyer, Jr., July 28, 1926); 2-William A., 3d, *b* New Orleans, La., Oct. 16, 1902.
1-Mem. C.D.XVIIC., Colonial Descs. of America (v.p.), D.A.R., D.R., U.S.D. 1812 (regent), Brooklyn Colony N.E. Women, Soc. of Indiana Pioneers, Ind. Hist. Soc., Kings Co. Hist. Soc., Sons and Daus. of the First Settlers of Newbury, Mass., I.A.G. Club: Priscilla Study (Brooklyn). Residence: 54 W. 74th St., New York, N.Y.

1-**WHEELER, Louisa M. Coe (Mrs. Frank W.),** *b* Sterling, Ill., June 28, 1858.
9-Robert **Coe** (qv);

8–Robert (1626-59), *m* 1650, Hannah Butterfield Mitchel (1631-1702);
7–Capt. John (1658-1741), of Stratford, Conn.; served in French and Indian War; *m* 1682, Mary Birdsey Hawley (1663-1731);
6–John (1693-1751), of Durham, Conn.; *m* 1715, Hannah Taylor Parsons (1698-1760);
5–Ens. Simeon (1721-82), took oath of fidelity at Durham, 1777; *m* 1745/46, Anna Moulthrop Morris (1728-1813);
4–Dea. Simeon (1755-1838), *m* 1774, Eunice Seward Strong (1752-1828);
3–Simeon Maltby (1784-1848), of Rush, Monroe Co., N.Y.; *m* 1807, Mary Cady Miles (1785-1856);
2–Marcus Lafayette (2 below).
7–Alphonsus **Kirk** (1659-1745), from Ireland, 1688, settled in New Castle Co., Pa.; *m* 1692, Abagail Sharpley (*d* 1748);
6–William (1708-87), *m* Mary Buckingham;
5–Caleb (1734-87), *m* 1756, Elizabeth– (Widow Coats);
4–Caleb (1759-1836), of York, Pa.; pvt., Capt. Ephraim Pennington's 7th Co., 1st Bn., York Co. Militia, Am. Rev.; *m* 1785, Lydia Updegraff (1767-1837);
3–Aquila (1794-1860), *m* 1818, Sarah Berry Needles;
2–Sarah (2 below).
8–Lt. John **Needles,** from Eng. in the "Pink Rebecca," 1679; settled on the Pianketank River in Va.; *m* Frances–;
7–John (*d* 1704), *m* 1682, Elizabeth Mann (1663-1717; Edward[8], *m* Anne Clavering);
6–Edward (1695-1752), *m* 1723, Elizabeth Thomas (*d* 1775; William[7], *m* Jane–);
5–Edward (1729-72), *m* 1752, Elizabeth Stevens (*d* 1766; Walter[6]);
4–Edward (1756-98), *m* 1789, Sarah Berry (*d* 1796; Joseph[5], *m* Sarah–);
3–Sarah Berry (1794-1860), *m* Aquila **Kirk** (3 above);
2–Sarah (1826-1906), *m* 1855, Marcus Lafayette **Coe** (1824-81), farmer; issue: I–D. Octavius (*b* 1857; *m* Emma Parks, *b* 1865); II–Louisa M. (1 above); III–Cora Belle (*b* 1860); IV–Elizabeth Needles (*b* 1863); V–Edward Kirk (1868-1928; *m* Emma Witmer, *b* 1868).
1–*m* Feb. 2, 1881, Frank Wellington Wheeler (Sept. 15, 1850-Sept. 27, 1919); son of Almon Wheeler, *m* Eliza Wellington, of Sterling, Ill.; issue: 1–Arthur Wellington, *b* Rock Falls, Ill., Mar. 17, 1889; U.Chicago, 1911; *m* Oct. 12, 1911, Mildred, dau. of John Howard Lawrence, of Sterling (issue: Lawrence Wellington); 2–LeRoy Coe, *b* Rock Falls, Nov. 18, 1893; B.S., U.Chicago, '17; *m* Apr. 17, 1922, Gladys, dau. of Edwin Field Lawrence, of Sterling (issue: Thomas Lawrence; Mary Wellington).
1–Mem. D.A.R. Conglist. Republican. Clubs: Woman's, Country, Mendelssohn. Residence: 501 W. 3d St., Sterling, Ill.

1–**BLAKE, Anson Stiles,** *b* San Francisco, Calif., Aug. 6, 1870.
9–William **Blake** (qv);
8–Edward (*b* Eng. ca. 1625-*d* 1692), settled at Milton, Mass.; *m* ca. 1653, Patience Pope (*d* 1690);
7–Jonathan (1672-1727), Wrentham, Mass.; *m* 1698, Elizabeth Caudage;
6–Ebenezer (1709-94), *m* 1st, 1729, Petronella Peck (*d* 1757);
5–Ebenezer (1730-1819), French and Indian War; *m* 1756, Tamar Thompson (*d* 1775);
4–Elihu (1764-1849), of Westboro, Mass.; *m* Elizabeth Whitney (Nathaniel[5], whose son, Eli, was inventor of the cotton gin);
3–Eli Whitney, LL.D. (1795-1886), of New Haven, Conn.; B.A. Yale, 1816; inventor, mfr., scientist; *m* 1822, Eliza Maria O'Brien;
2–Charles Thompson (2 below).
9–James (Pierrepont) **Pierpont** (qv);
8–John (1617-82), Ipswich, 1640, Roxbury, 1656; rep. Gen. Ct.; *m* Thankful Snow (*d* 1668; John[9]);
7–Rev. James (1659/60-1714), B.A., Harvard, 1681; pastor First Congl. Ch., New Haven; a founder of Yale Coll.; *m* 3d, 1698, Mary Hooker (1673-1740; Samuel[8]; Rev. Thomas[9], qv);
6–Hezekiah (1712-41), *m* 1736/37, Lydia Hemingway (*d* 1779);
5–John (1740-1805), *m* 1767, Sarah Beers (1744-1835);
4–Mary (1778-1852), *m* 1st, 1796, Edward J. **O'Brien** (*b* 1779), of New Haven;
3–Eliza Maria (1800-76), *m* 1822, Eli Whitney **Blake** (3 above);
2–Charles Thompson (1826-97), of San Francisco, Calif.; grad. Yale, 1847; miner, express agent, banker, contractor; *m* 1868, Harriet Waters Stiles (1840-1928); issue: I–Anson Stiles (1 above); II–Eliza Seely (*m* Sherman Day Thacher, see Vol. I, p. 439); III–Edwin Tyler (*m* Harriet Whitney Carson); IV–Robert Pierpont (*m* Nadjesda Kryzanofsky); also three *d* infancy.
1–*m* May 17, 1894, Anita Day Symmes, *b* San Francisco, Calif., Mar. 9, 1872; dau. of Frank Jameson Symmes.
1–A.B., U. of Calif., '91 (D.K.E.). Sec. Bay Rock Co., 1891; with Oakland Paving Co., 1894; sec., 1897, pres., 1900-13; cashier Central Bank, Oakland, Calif., 1905-07; pres. Blake Bros. Co. since 1913. Mem. I.A.G., Soc. Calif. Pioneers (dir.), Calif. Hist. Soc. (dir). Republican. Clubs: University, Engineers, Claremont Country, Berkeley Country. Residence: Arlington Av. and Rincon Road, Berkeley, Calif.

1–**McBRIDE, Glen C.,** *b* Mattoon, Ill., May 28, 1903.
5–John **McBride** (1767-Mar. 14, 1838), of Lough Neigh, N. Ireland; came to N.J.; settled on farm nr. Lamington; became mem. Presbyn. Ch., 1787; *m* Mary McClinton (1763-Mar. 14, 1847); they had issue: Robert (below); Hannah, *m* Oct. 6, 1811, Matthew Gray, and went to Va. or the Carolinas; William (1797-May 1860), *m* Nov. 18, 1818, Esther McClinick; infant (*d*);
4–Robert (Oct. 7, 1795-Aug. 5, 1855), farmer, Lamington; *m* Feb. 2, 1822, Mary Whitehead (Sept. 18, 1797-Nov. 5, 1865), *b* prob. in Eng., *d* while on visit to Ill.; they had issue: Sarah (Dec. 4, 1822-Nov. 5, 1865), *m* Sept. 4, 1850, Dan Doty, and had issue; Hannah Marie (Oct. 6, 1824-Nov. 3, 1855), *m* Nov. 7, 1849, David Huffman, and had issue; Elizabeth (Jan 30, 1827-May 25, 1910), *m* Nov. 1, 1852, John Whitenack, and had issue; Margaret Anne (Feb. 24, 1829-Apr. 12, 1865), *m* Dec. 19, 1852, Morris Cramer, and had issue; Robert Whitehead (Mar. 14, 1831-Apr. 9, 1891), removed to Mattoon, Ill.; *m* Jan. 25, 1865, Catharine V. Ames or Amos (*d*); *m* 2d, Rachel Horning, and had issue; Henrietta (July 9, 1833-Oct. 1898), *m* Jan. 2, 1861, John L. Lane (Sept. 15, 1836-Nov. 9, 1869), and had issue; Catherine (Aug. 30, 1835-Nov. 1, 1859); Jane (Dec. 6, 1837-Nov. 29, 1858); John R. (below); William (Aug. 15, 1842-Apr. 1910), *m* Apr. 3, 1862, Hannah Harmer, and had issue;
3–John R. (Jan. 10, 1840-Oct. 18, 1922), removed to Ill.; settled in N. Okaw Tp., Coles Co., 1867; removed to Humboldt Tp., 1874; collector, Humboldt Tp., 1 term; owned 320 acres; *m* in N.J., Dec. 1, 1864, Anna Paulson Krymer (Dec. 1, 1847 or 48-1923); they had issue: Minnie (*b* 1866), *m* William T. Avery; Morris Krymer (below);
2–Morris Krymer (*b* 1879), real estate broker, Tulsa, Okla.; *m* 1900, Minnie Newby (*b* 1881; Joseph[3], lt., Ohio vol. cav., removed to nr. Mattoon, Ill., *m* Caroline Davis); issue: I–Glen C. (1 above); II–Paul (*b* 1905; *m* Juanita–); III–Lloyd (*b* 1907); IV–Dale (*b* 1911).
1–*m* Dec. 23, 1926, Winifred Spates, *b* Taylorville, Ill., June 30, 1904; dau. of George W. Spates, of Taylorville; issue: 1–Robert Dana, *b* Decatur, Ill., Nov. 5, 1927; 2–Harriett Carolyn, *b* Glen Ellyn, Ill., July 8, 1930.
1–B.A., U.Ill., '25 (Tau Kappa Epsilon, Scabbard and Blade). Asst. engr., Ill. Highway Commn., 1926-29. Asso. with Chicago Title & Trust Co. since 1929. Mason. Residence: Glen Ellyn, Ill.

1–**WALTON, Kenneth Betts,** *b* Phila., Pa., Jan. 8, 1901.
4–Hiram **Walton** (1765-post 1815), of Phila.; *m* 1793, Elizabeth Dougherty (*b* 1771);
3–William (1800-80), *m* 1842, Ann McKeen Budd (1819-96), widow;
2–John Gardener (2 below).
9–Richard **Betts** (qv);
8–Thomas (*b* 1660), *m* 1683, Mercy Whitehead (Maj. Daniel[10], *m* Abigail Stevenson);
7–Thomas (*b* 1689), magistrate; *m* 2d, 1724, Susannah Field (*b* 1704; Nathaniel[8], *m* Patience Bull);
6–Zachariah (1736-1808), *m* 2d, 1770, Bethula Cary (*d* 1777; Samuel[7], *m* Sarah Stackhouse);

5–Samuel Cary (1776-1861), *m* 1798, Grace Biles (1776-1848; William[6], *m* Hannah Kirkbride);
4–Richard Kinsey (*b* 1807), of Phila.; *m* 2d, 1835, Anna Brooks (1807-50; John[5], *m* Elizabeth Baker);
3–John Brooks (*b* 1836), of Phila.; *m* 1863, Jeanette Shivers Carter (1844-1921; James Tilton[4], *m* Sarah Ann Dauphin);
2–Clara Rowena Gray (*b* 1868), *m* 1900, John Gardener **Walton** (1865-1924); issue: I–Kenneth Betts (1 above); II–William Wyclif (*b* 1902); III–Helen (*b* 1903; *m* Irving Bell Smith, Jr.); IV–Jeanette Desire Betts (*b* 1904).
1–*m* Apr. 26, 1930, Jessie Sellers, *b* Overbrook, Pa., June 25, 1906; dau. of Horace Wells Sellers, of "Millbank," Ardmore, Pa., *m* Cora Wells.
1–B.S., Haverford Coll., '22; M.I.T., 1922-23. (Sigma Alpha Epsilon, Theta Tau). Joined Medway Oil & Storage Co., Isle of Grain, Kent, Eng., 1923, supt. of refining, 1924; pres. Kent's Restaurant & Baking Co., retail stores, Atlantic City, N.J., since 1927; pres. Kent's Orderphone Co., Atlantic City, since 1929. Past pres. Atlantic City Restaurant Assn.; chmn. Aviation Com., Atlantic City Chamber of Commerce. Mem. S.D.P. Mason. Quaker. Republican. Clubs: Merion Cricket (Haverford), Haverford (Phila.). Summer residence: "Sand Dune Shanty," Brigantine, N.J.

1–**MILLER, Mary Catharine Buck (Mrs. Charles Robert),** *b* Warrensburg, Mo., Apr. 10, 1869.
5–Robert **Buck** (desc. old Scottish families of the Clan Campbell, of which the Duke of Argyle was chief); came from Belfast, Ireland, 1772-74, settled later in Hampshire Co., Va. (now W.Va.); later in Morgan Co., W.Va., where he received land grant on Sleepy Creek nr. Berkeley Springs;
4–Robert (1768-1847), of Berkeley Springs, W.Va.; *m* Margret Maxwell (Robert[5], of Hampshire Co., W.Va.);
3–Hon. Isaiah (1797-1892), *m* 1819, Catherine Waugh (Singleton[4], received land grant in Kan. for services in War 1812);
2–James Harvey (2 below).
7–William **Frost** (*b* Devonshire, Eng.), came to N.J. ca. 1750; located in N.C.;
6–Ebenezer (1746-1824), *m* Sarah Fairchild; *m* 2d, Elizabeth Wilson;
5–Capt. John (*b* 1770), *m* Rebecca Boone; *m* 2d, Mrs. Elizabeth Hunt;
4–Ebenezer (1794 or 95-1836), *m* Elizabeth Gaither; *m* 2d, Nancy W. Clary;
3–Nimrod Bailey (1817-1907), *m* Mary Frances Atkinson;
2–Sarah B. (1852-1923), *m* 1868, James Harvey **Buck** (1841-1920), agriculturist and stock raiser; ed. Moorfield Mil. Acad. and studied medicine under Dr. Yaggie; sgt. Co. G, 17th Va. Cav., Laurel Brig., Gen. "Stonewall" Jackson's Corps, enlisted, June 17, 1861; captured, May 28, 1864, prisoner at Point Lookout, paroled, Feb. 15, 1865; slightly wounded on chin; hon. discharged from C.S.A.; issue: I–Mary Catharine (1 above); II–John Lee (*b* 1871; *m* 1906, Bessie Belle Franklin; *m* 2d, 1918, Viadia Naomia Page); III–Anna (*b* 1873); IV–Rose Maria (1874-80); V–Minnie (1876-1929); VI–James N. (1878-1917); VII–Edmund Isaiah (*b* 1880; *m* 1909, Nannie Mann); VIII–Singleton Ebenezer (*b* 1882; *m* 1919, Erma Palmer); IX–Eleanor Gertrude (1884-99); X–Ruth M. (*b* 1887; *m* Ernest T. Wolf); XI–Davie Francis (*b* 1892; *m* Henry A. Ray).
1–*m* Oct. 30, 1888, Charles Robert Miller, *b* Carlisle, Ky., Jan. 22, 1859; son of George Washington Miller; issue: 1–David Raymond, *b* Shannon Belmont Farm, Atchison Co., Kan., Aug. 26, 1889; 2–Ethel Virginia Lee, *b* Bellmount Acres, Atchison, Kan., July 27, 1893; *m* Mar. 29, 1919, Glenn M., son of Francis Whitfield Shaeffer, of Omaha, Neb.
1–Ed. Mt. St. Scholastica Convent Acad., 1887. Red Cross worker during World War. Mem. D.A.R. (treas. Atchison chapter), U.S.D. 1812, I.A.G., Boone Family Assn., etc. Residence: Bellmount Acres, R. 3, Atchison, Kan.

1–**HOVER, William Adgate,** *b* Mazomanie, Dane Co., Wis., Mar. 9, 1856.
5–Hendricks **Hover,** from Holland, ante 1738, settled in Sussex Co., N.J.; mem. of Com. of Safety, 1775;
4–Emanuel (1748-1824), *m* Mary Schoonover (*d* 1827);
3–Ezekiel (1771-1851), *m* 1807, Sally Adgate (*d* 1841);
2–William Ulysses (2 below).
8–Thomas **Adgate** (1620-1707), of Saybrook, Conn., 1651; *m* widow of Richard Bushnell;
7–Thomas (1669/70-1760), *m* 1692, Ruth Brewster;
6–Thomas (1702/03-1736), *m* 1733, Anne Huntington (1715-59);
5–Thomas (1734-77), *m* 1753, Ruth Leffingwell (*b* 1736);
4–John Hart (1759-1809), *m* 1782, Sarah Fitch (1764-1814);
3–Sally (1784-1841), *m* 1807, Ezekiel **Hover** (3 above).
10–William **Brewster,** Mayflower Pilgrim (qv);
9–Jonathan, *m* Lucretia Oldham;
8–Benjamin (1633-1710), *m* Ann Darte (*d* 1708 or 09);
7–Ruth (1671-1734), *m* 1692, Thomas **Adgate** (7 above).
2–William Ulysses **Hover** (1830-1910), Sparta, Tenn.; *m* 1855, Harriet Harbaugh (1831-1915; Joseph[3] [*d* 1868], of Pa., *m* Merianne Howard, *d* 1865); issue: I–William Adgate (1 above); II–Harriet (*b* 1858; *m* 1885, Charles Ford Harding); III–Charles L. (*b* 1867; *m* 1898, Katherine Stuart Avey); IV–Lilly (*b* and *d* 1870).
1–*m* Sept. 1, 1886, Marianna Vought, *b* Milwaukee, Wis., Mar. 1, 1860; dau. of James Throckmorton Vought; issue: 1–William Tracy, *b* Pittsford, N.Y., June 17, 1887; B.A., U. of Wis., '11; *m* Oct. 15, 1912, Dorothy Byrd, dau. of Judge Robert E. Lewis (issue: William Adgate, *b* May 24, 1916; Robert Lewis, *b* Feb. 27, 1920); 2–Mary Throckmorton, *b* Denver, Colo., Nov. 19, 1888; Wolcott School, Denver, and Mary Baldwin Sem.; *m* Dec. 10, 1918, Thomas Arnold, son of Judge Thomas A. Dickson, of Leadville, Colo. (issue: George Richard, *b* June 20, 1926); 3–Ruth Grandin, *b* Denver, Apr. 15, 1891; Wolcott Sch., and Rye (N.Y.) Sem.; *m* Nov. 14, 1923, Norman M. Ives (issue: Norman, Jr., *b* July 5, 1929); 4–Dorothy Adgate, *b* Denver, Aug. 11, 1893; Bishop's Sch., La Jolla, Calif., and St. Mary's Hall, Burlington, N.J.; *m* Jan. 15, 1930, Bruce Ellsworth, son of Melville O. Stratton; 5–Harriet Harbaugh, *b* Denver, Jan. 6, 1895; Wolcott Sch., Washington Coll., and Sweetbrier; *m* Sept. 30, 1921, Joseph Adolph, son of Henry Lentz (issue: Hover Throckmorton, *b* Sept. 30, 1923); 6–Anne Vought, *b* Denver, Mar. 9, 1897; *m* Oct. 12, 1925, Walter Marshall (issue: Nancy); 7–James Throckmorton, *b* Denver, Apr. 15, 1898; U. of Mich., '21; served in World War, 1918-19; *m* Aug. 22, 1918, Blanche, dau. of Thomas J. Shelton (issue: Beverly Ann, *b* Aug. 22, 1922; James Throckmorton, Jr., *b* Jan. 5, 1927); 8–Charles Stedman, *b* Denver, June 14, 1900; B.A., U. of Mich., '24; *m* Apr. 20, 1927, Cornelia, dau. of Albert R. Sampliner (issue: Charles Stedman, Jr., *b* May 28, 1929); 9–Lloyd de Barbarie, *b* Denver, Mar. 27, 1902.
1–B.M.E., U. of Wis., '77 (Phi Kappa Psi), spl. student School of Mines (Columbia), 1877,78. Senior partner, W. A. Hover & Co., wholesale druggists, Denver, since 1882; pres. U.S. Nat. Bank, 1904-08 and 1917-23, chmn. bd. same, 1908-17, and since 1923; dir. Mountain States Telephone & Telegraph Co. (see Who's Who in America). Mem. S.R. (pres. Colo. Soc., 1909-10), S.M.D. Episcopalian. Republican. Clubs: Chemists, Drug and Chemical (New York), Denver Univ., Denver Athletic, Denver Motor, Denver Country. Residence: 1507 Lafayette St., Denver, Colo.

1–**PETERS, Flora Davidson,** *b* nr. Royalton, Fairfield Co., O., Jan. 22, 1887.
5–Jacob **Peters** (1749-1828), of Manchester, Md.; *m*—— (*d* 1812);
4–Samuel (*b* 1772), of Manchester; *m* 1796, Mary Stevenson (1773-1861);
3–Andrew (1809-94), *m* 1841, Ann H. Reber (1821-97);
2–Milton (2 below).
6–Samuel T. **Davidson;**
5–William T.;
4–William T.;
3–John Smith (Mar. 31, 1828-Jan. 31, 1905);
2–Anna (1860-1912), *m* 1885, Milton **Peters** (1849-1924), farmer; issue: I–Flora Davidson (1

above); II–Horace Milton (*m* Ruth Robinson).
1–Ohio Wesleyan U., 1904-06. Mem. I.A.G. Methodist. Republican. Residence: East Main St., Ashville, O.

1–**MEAD, David Irving**, *b* Brooklyn, N.Y., Feb. 9, 1875.
9–William **Mead** (qv);
8–John (1634-99), *m* Hannah Potter;
7–Ebenezer (1663-1728), of Greenwich, Conn.; *m* 1691, Sarah Knapp;
6–Ebenezer (1697-1775), *m* 1717, Hannah Brown;
5–Ebenezer (1718-58), *m* 1747, Amy Knapp;
4–Enoch (1756-1807), of Lake Waccabuc, N.Y.; pvt. Am. Rev.; adj. Westchester Co. militia, Associated Exempts; *m* 1776, Jemima Mead (1756-1837);
3–Alphred (1781-1855), *m* 1814, Polly Brundage (1791-1878);
2–George W. (2 below).
8–Thomas **Studwell** (1620?-1670), from Eng. ca. 1641, settled at Rye, Conn., later at Greenwich;
7–Thomas (1650?-ante 1734), of Rye; *m* Martha–;
6–Thomas (1709-83), *m* Jemima–;
5–Joseph (*d* 1784), *m* Deborah Lockwood;
4–Joseph (1777-1865), of Bedford, N.Y.; *m* 2d, 1807, Rebecca Mead (1780-1852; Caleb[5]);
3–John J. (1813-84), of Brooklyn, N.Y.; *m* 1838, Elizabeth LaForge Moore (1813-93);
2–Sarah Frances (1838-1919), *m* 1858, George W. **Mead** (1827-99), Yale, '51; practiced law, Brooklyn; issue: I–Frances Studwell (*b* 1861); II–Elizabeth Brundage (1862-1929; *m* Richards M. Cahoone); III–Loretta Josephine (1865-1925; *m* Herbert A. Smith); IV–Florence Church (1867-1929; *m* Horace I. Brightman); V–George Washington (*b* 1869); VI–John Studwell (twin, 1871-1907; *m* Ruth Parker); VII–Joseph (twin, 1871-1927; *m* Louise Griswold); VIII–Martin Rockwell (*b* 1872; *m* Marie Andrews); IX–David Irving (1 above); X–Alice LaForge (*b* 1877; *m* Charles F. Neergaard); XI–Coralie Hutchinson (*b* 1882; *m* Robert Brooke).
1–*m* June 25, 1920, Elizabeth Young, *b* Brooklyn, N.Y., Mar. 3, 1890; dau. of Charles T. Young, of Brooklyn; issue: 1–David Irving, Jr., *b* Brooklyn, Apr. 3, 1921; 2–Charles Young, *b* Brooklyn, Oct. 20, 1922; 3–Jane Willits, *b* Brooklyn, Sept. 20, 1926; 4–Elizabeth, *b* White Plains, Feb. 17, 1930.
1–B.A., Yale, '97; Columbia Law School; New York Law School. Practiced law at Brooklyn, 1900-11; v.p. Nat. City Bank, Brooklyn, 1911-19, and of its successor, Irving Trust Co. of New York, 1919-22; pres. South Brooklyn Savings Instn., since 1922 (trustee since 1913); treas. and dir. Beaver Hills Co., Kings & Westchester Land Co. Trustee Polhemus Clinic, Brooklyn Hosp., Northern Westchester Hosp.; mem. advisory bds. Brooklyn Home for Consumptives, Brooklyn Home for Aged Men. Chmn. Brooklyn War Savings Stamp Com., 1918-19; mem. exec. com. Brooklyn Chapter A.R.C., since 1923. Mem. N.Y. State Bankers Assn. (pres. 1919-20), Am. Bankers Assn. (exec. council), S.R., I.A.G., L.I. Hist. Soc., Westchester Hist. Soc., Kings Co. Hist. Soc., Brooklyn Inst. of Arts and Sciences, N.Y. State Hist. Soc., St. Nicholas Soc. of Nassau Co. Presbyterian. Republican. Clubs: Hamilton (Brooklyn), University (New York), Waccabuc Country, Scarsdale Golf, Boulder Brook Riding. Residence: Lake Waccabuc, N.Y.

1–**TAPPAN, Jennie Bertha Stevens (Mrs. Walter H.)**, *b* Vergennes, Vt., Apr. 8, 1865.
7–Henry **Stevens** (qv);
6–Thomas (1678-1750), from Westerly, R.I., to Plainfield, Conn.; *m* Mary Hall (1677-1719; Stephen[7], *m* Ruth–);
5–Zebulon (*b* 1717), moved to Canaan, Conn.; *m* Miriam Fellows (*b* 1726);
4–Zebulon, *m* 1779, Sarah Herrick;
3–Thomas (*b* 1794), *m* 1816, Sally Ann Tappan;
2–Herrick (2 below).
8–Henerie **Herrick** (qv);
7–Joseph (1645-1717/18), *m* Mary Endicott;
6–Rufus, *m* Sarah Phillips;
5–Rufus, *m* Mary Conant, of Salem;
4–Sarah (*b* 1756), *m* Zebulon **Stevens** (4 above).
9–Abraham (Toppan) **Tappan** (qv);
8–Isaac, *m* Mary March;
7–Abraham, *m* Mary Stone;
6–Abraham, *m* Sarah Reynolds;
5–Jacob, wrote name Tappan; *m* Sarah Ogden;
4–Silas, *m* Anna Stagg;
3–Sally Ann (*b* 1797), *m* Thomas **Stevens** (3 above).
9–Maj. Simon **Willard** (qv);
8–Henry (1655-1701), *m* 1st, 1674, Mary Lakin (*d* 1688);
7–Henry (1675-ca. 1747), *m* 1st, Abigail Temple;
6–Henry, *m* Abigail Fairbanks;
5–Oliver, *m* Lucy Haskell;
4–Oliver, *m* Abigail Keith;
3–Hosea, *m* Betsy Electa Benton;
2–Electa Jane (1834-89), *m* 1855, Herrick **Stevens** (1820-95); issue: I–Mary Electa (*b* 1858; *m* 1879, Charles Lyman Hammond); II–Helen Doane (*b* 1861; *m* 1886, Horace Josiah Parker); III–Jennie Bertha (1 above); IV–Herrika Mariette (*b* 1871; *m* 1898, William Henry Button).
1–*m* Apr. 15, 1896, Walter House Tappan, *b* Troy, N.Y., July 19, 1864; son of Shepard Tappan; issue: 1–Herrick Ogden, *b* New York, N.Y., Nov. 23, 1899; *m* June 13, 1925, Eugenie Stafford Brown, *b* May 1, 1896 (issue: Eugenie Stafford, *b* Feb. 19, 1927); 2–Eleanor House, *b* New York, Mar. 4, 1903; *m* May 11, 1929, John Sherwood Foley, *b* Feb. 18, 1897 (issue: Robert Tappan, *b* Mar. 20, 1930).
1–Mem. I.A.G. Summer place: Tree Tops, North Hero, Vt. Residence: 154 Riverway, Boston, Mass.

1–**FAIRCHILD, Agnes Doll**, *b* Monticello, N.Y., July 17, 1871.
8–Thomas **Fairchild** (qv);
7–Samuel (1640-ca. 1704), *m* Mary Wheeler (Moses[8], qv);
6–Jonathan (1692-1772), *m* Eleanor Whitney;
5–Abraham, Redding, Conn.; *m* 1742, Rachel Scribner (six of their sons were soldiers in Am. Rev. at the same time);
4–John (1764-1846), *m* 1st, 1793, Abigail Wakeman (*d* 1820);
3–Eli (1795-1885), settled at Monticello, N.Y.; mfr. and mill owner; *m* 1822, Clarrissa Wheeler (1800-88; Amos[4], of Hartford, Conn., *m* Lucy Baxter);
2–Eli Wheeler (1824-1909), of Monticello, N.Y.; *m* 1869, Mary Christina Doll (*b* 1843); issue: I–Mary Cady (*b* 1870; *m* 1898, Frederick A. Torsch); II–Agnes Doll (1 above); III–Abbie Eloise (*b* 1873; *m* 1903, John Wilbur Morrison); IV–Eli Francis (1879-80); V–John Gifford (*b* 1882; *m* 1907, Marie Helen Beatty).
1–Ed. Monticello Acad., Miss Fulton's Private School (Monticello), Golden Hill Sem. (Bridgeport, Conn.); grad. Salisbury School (New York), '91. Mem. D.R., O.E.S., I.A.G., Sullivan Co. (N.Y.) Hist. Soc. Residence: St. John St., Monticello, N.Y.

BAUMAN

1–**FAIRCHILD, Mary Christina Doll (Mrs. Eli Wheeler)**, *b* Purvis, Livingston Manor, N.Y., July 31, 1843.
4–George Jacob Leonard **Doll**, D.D. (1739-1811), came from Germany and Amsterdam, Holland, 1770; called as pastor to the First Dutch

DR. WILLIAM HENRY DOLL (1775-1829).

GEORGE JACOB LEONARD DOLL (1803-72), of Purvis (Livingston Manor) N.Y.

Reformed Ch. at Fort Orange (Albany), N.Y.; pastor of the First Dutch Reformed Ch., Kingston, N.Y., 1775-1805; the last minister to preach in Dutch; *m* 1760, Christina Ebtkin (1742-1805);

3–William Henry, M.D. (1775-1829), *m* 1796, Sophia Christina Beauman (1773-1848; Sebastian[4] [1739-1803], from Germany; original mem. Society of Cincinnati from New York City; *m* 1766, Anna [1751-86], dau. of John Wetzell, *m* 1748, Christina Ernest, dau. of Dr. Ernest, of Mannheim, Germany, a martyr of the Reformed religion at the stake);

2–George Jacob Leonard (1803-72), *m* 1829, Nancy Overton (1809-98).

1–*m* Ellenville, N.Y., Feb. 21, 1869, Eli Wheeler Fairchild (1824-1909), A.B., Union Coll., 1846

Residence of MRS. ELI WHEELER FAIRCHILD, Monticello, N.Y.

MARY CHRISTINA (DOLL) FAIRCHILD

(Phi Beta Kappa, Sigma Phi), A.M., 1849; studied law; admitted to bar at Albany, N.Y., 1848; founder and trustee of Monticello Acad., 1855; promoter and dir. Port Jervis & Monticello R.R., 1870; acting postmaster of Monticello during Civil War; town clk.; justice of the peace; issue: 1–Mary Cady, *b* Apr. 15, 1870; *m* Sept. 29, 1898, Frederick A. Torsch, *b* Jan. 1, 1858 (issue: a–Frederick Fairchild, *b* Aug. 7, 1899, *m* Apr. 29, 1922, Katharine Husted Smith, *b* Aug. 14, 1902, issue: a–Mary Imogene, *b* May 31, 1925; b–John Bauman, *b* Aug. 26, 1901; c–Margaret Fairchild, *b* Apr. 18, 1906; d–Charles Edward, *b* July 10, 1914); 2–Agnes Doll (qv for Fairchild lineage); 3–Abbie Eloise, *b* Jan. 23, 1873; *m* Nov. 2, 1903, John Wilbur Morrison, *b* Oct. 12, 1866 (issue: Marjorie Doll, *b* Sept. 15, 1904); 4–Eli Francis (Feb. 16, 1879-Feb. 14, 1880); 5–John Gifford, *b* May 28, 1882; *m* Apr. 7, 1907, Helen Marie Beatty, *b* Jan. 6, 1886 (issue: Helen Christina, *b* Nov. 4, 1910).

1–Attended Sem. of Louise Beauman Saulpaugh. Editor: Memoirs of Colonel Sebastian Beauman and His Descendants, 1900. Residence: St. John St., Monticello, N.Y.

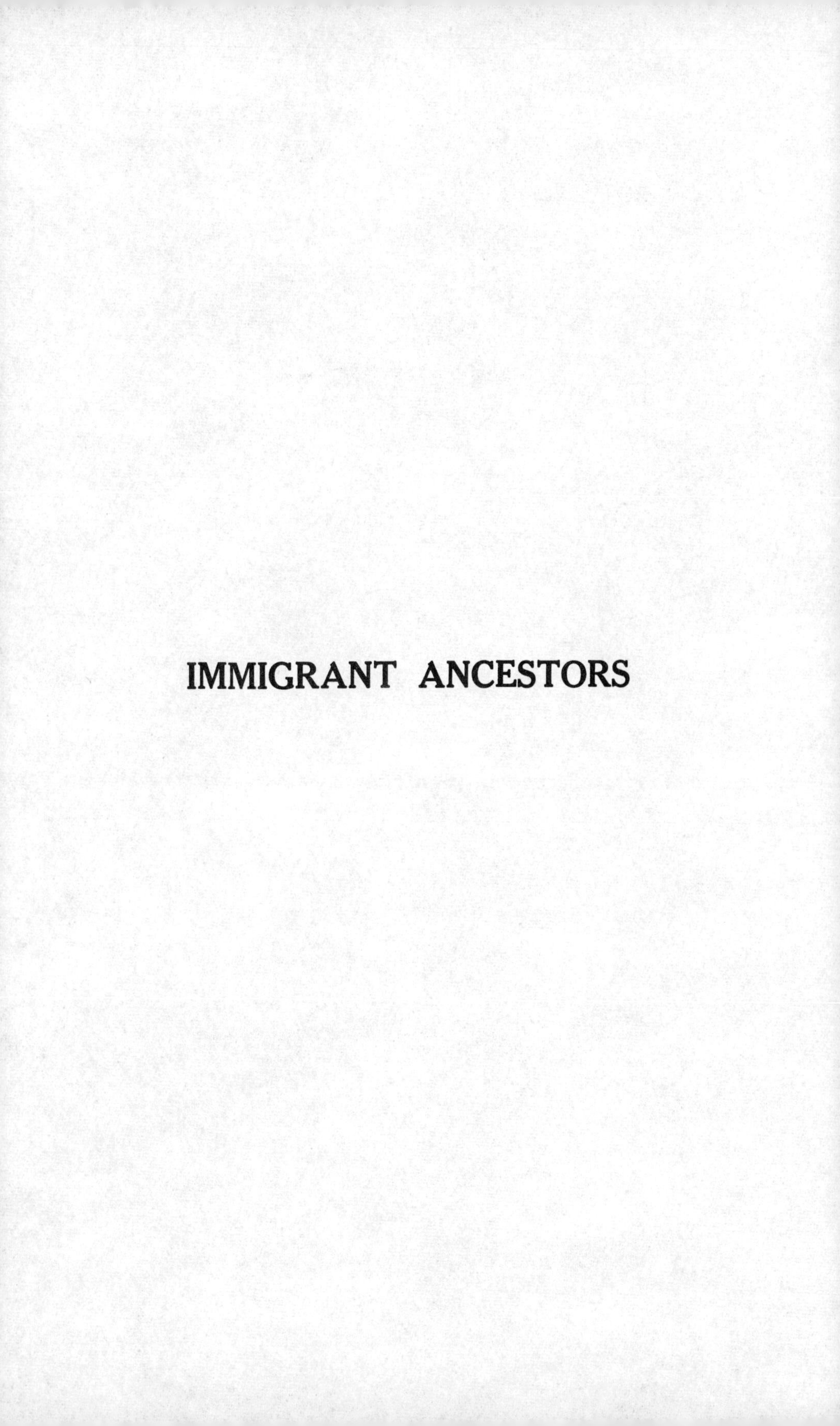

IMMIGRANT ANCESTORS

IMMIGRANT ANCESTORS

Following is a list of about 1,800 of the Immigrant Ancestors whose names appear so frequently in the published lineage records of this work that repetition of the identical data would be burdensome, and superfluous. Hence, where the following names appear in the lineage records, the cross-reference (qv) is employed to refer the reader to this particular section of this volume where all the authentic data available, pertaining to these names, may be found.

It should be understood, however, that this is not a list of all the Immigrant Ancestors mentioned in the lineage records in this work. The largest number by far do not appear in this list because their names have appeared only once, or only occasionally, and the data pertaining to them will be found in those records.

For the most complete list of immigrants to all the early settlements in America the reader is referred to The Magazine of American Genealogy, which includes as one of its sections an alphabetical list entitled "Immigrants to America Before 1750."

ABBE (Abbey), John (1613-abt. 1690), from London, Eng., in the "Bonadventure," 1634 or 35; granted land at Salem, Mass., 1637/38; an early settler at Wenham, 1646; *d* at Salem; *m* Mary – (*b* Eng., abt. 1615-20-*d* Wenham, Sept. 9, 1672); *m* 2d, Nov. 25, 1674, Mrs. Mary Goldsmith (widow of Richard).

ABBOTT (Abbot), George, "of Andover" (Yorkshire, Eng., 1615/16-Andover, Mass., Dec. 24, 1681/82); came with Rev. Ezekiel Rogers, in same ship with future wife, about 1638; first settler at Andover, Mass., 1643; house he built still in possession of descendants; *m* at Andover, about 1647, Hannah (*b* Eng., abt. 1629-*d* June 11, 1711), dau. William Chandler (qv); she *m* 2d, Francis Dane.

ABBOTT, George, "of Rowley" (prob. *b* in Eng.-*d* Rowley, Essex co., Mass., 1647); came from Eng., 1642; settled at Rowley, where his name heads the list of 54 inhabitants to whom house lots were registered in 1643; *m* in Eng.

ABBOTT (Abbitt), Robert (*d* Branford Conn., Sept. 31, 1658); came from Eng. and settled at Watertown, Mass., 1634; later at Wethersfield, Conn., 1636-40, at New Haven, 1642; mem. ct., 1642; granted land at Totoket (now Branford), removed there, 1645; *m* prob. as 2d wife, Mary – (who *m* 2d, 1659, John Robins).

ABELL (Abel), Robert (*b* prob. in Eng.-*d* Rehoboth, Mass., June 20, 1663; s. of George Abell, who *m* Frances –, of Hemington, Leicestershire, Eng.); first record at Weymouth, Mass., where he desired to be made freeman, Oct. 19, 1630; later at Rehoboth; *m* Joanna –, who survived him (she *m* 2d, at Rehoboth, Mass., June 4, 1667, William Hyde of Norwich, Conn.);

ADAMS, George (*d* Oct. 10, 1696); first record of him is his marriage at Watertown, Mass., 1645; at Cambridge Farms (now Lexington), 1664; soldier in King Philip's War; *m* at Watertown, 1645, Frances – (*b* 1604).

ADAMS, Henry, "of Braintree" (*b* Barton Saint David, Somersetshire, Eng., abt. 1583, where at least 4 generations of his ancestors had lived; *d* at Braintree, Mass., Oct. 6, 1646; son of John Adams of Barton St. David); came from Eng. 1638, and settled at Braintree, Mass., where he was granted 40 acres of land, Feb. 24, 1639/40; was maltster and yeoman; *m* in Eng., Oct. 19, 1609, Edith (1587-1673), dau. of Henry Squire (1563-after 1649); she *m* 2d, 1651, John Fussell of Weymouth and Medfield.

ADAMS, Jeremy (*b* in Eng.-*d* Hartford, Conn., Aug. 11, 1683); came to N.E. with Rev. Thomas Hooker's co., 1632 and settled at Cambridge; freeman, 1635, and possessed a town-lot; went with Hooker to Hartford, Conn., 1636, being an original propr. of that town; sent by Gen. Ct., 1638, with Capt. Mason and 4 others, to treat with the Indians; land grants of 30 acres, 1639, and 340 acres, 1661/62, at what later became Colchester; was constable and custom-master; kept the inn, at which the General Court held its meetings for many yrs.; *m* abt. 1637, Rebecca – (*d* 1678), widow of Samuel Greenhill, from Staplehurst, Kent, Eng.; *m* 2d, 1678, Rebecca (1638-1715), dau. of John Fletcher, and widow of Andrew Warner, Jr.; issue (all by 1st marriage).

ADAMS, John (*d* 1633), came in the "Fortune," Nov. 9, 1621; settled at Plymouth, Mass.; *m* at Plymouth, after 1623, Ellen Newton, who came in the "Ann," 1623 (she *m* 2d, 1634, Kenelm Winslow, qv).

ADAMS, John, "of Cambridge" (*b* Kingweston, Eng., 1622-*d* Menotomy, now Arlington, Mass., 1706; son of Henry Adams, qv); came with his parents, 1638; was millwright at Cambridge; returned to Eng. to administer property, returning to N.E., 1651; *m* Ann – (*d* after 1714).

ADAMS, Robert (*b* Ottery St. Mary, Eng., Oct. 10, 1602-*d* Newbury, Mass., Oct. 12, 1682; son of Peter, of Ottery St. Mary, Devonshire); from Eng., 1635, and settled at Ipswich, Mass.; at Newbury, 1640-1680; tailor; *m* Eleanor Wilmott (*d* June 12, 1677); *m* 2d, Feb. 1678, Sarah Glover (*d* Oct. 24, 1697), widow of Henry Short.

ALDEN, John (ca. 1599-1687), 7th and last surviving signer of the Mayflower Compact; in Capt. Myles Standish's Duxbury Co., 1643; gov.'s asst., 1632-40, 50, 86; dep. Gen. Ct., 1641, 42, 44, 49; mem. Council of War, 1646 et seq.; actg. dep. gov., 1664-77; *m* at Plymouth, Mass., before 1624, Priscilla (*d* after 1650), dau. William Mullins (qv).

ALDRICH (Aldridge, Eldridge), George (*d* 1683), from Eng. to Dorchester, Mass., 1631; freeman 1636; was at Braintree 1644; one of the first settlers at Mendon, 1663; *m* 1629, Catherine Seald (1610-91).

ALEXANDER, Archibald (*b* Manor Cunninghame, Ire., Feb. 4, 1708-*d* Augusta [now Rockbridge] Co., Va., after 1773, eldest son of William Alexander of Co. Donegal, Ire., and descended from the house of Mac Alexander of Tarbet, Kintyre, Scotland); came from N. of Ire. with his bro. Robert, 1736, and settled at New Providence, Pa.; removed to Augusta (now Rockbridge) Co., Va., 1747; *m* in Ireland, Dec. 31, 1734, his cousin, Margaret (*d* July 1755), dau. of Joseph Parks of Donegal; *m* 2d, Augusta Co., Va., 1757, Margaret (or Jane) M'Clure of Augusta Co.

ALEXANDER, James (*b* Scotland, 1691 or 93-*d* 1756; second son of David, of the Ward of Muthill, Scotland, and a descendant of the 1st

Earl of Stirling); was officer of engineers in the army of the Pretender, and was forced to flee from Scotland shortly after the uprising of 1715, coming to New Jersey, where he was made surveyor-general of East and West Jersey, 1716; was successively receiver-gen. of quit rents, advocate-gen., mem. King's Council, and attorney-gen.; *m* 1720/21, Mary (1693-1760), widow of David Provoost, and dau. of John Spratt, of Scotland.

ALGER, Thomas (prob. *b* Eng.-prob. *d* Bridgewater, Mass.), from Eng. abt. 1665, and settled at Taunton, Mass., where he was granted land; later at Bridgewater; *m* at Taunton, Nov. 14, 1665, Elizabeth, dau. of Samuel Packard (qv).

ALLEN, see also Allyn.

ALLEN, Edmund (also called Edward), from Scotland to N.E., 1636, settled at Ipswich, Mass., was at Suffield, Conn., before 1683, later at Northfield, Mass.; *m* Sarah Kimball (*d* June 12, 1696).

ALLEN, George (1568-1648), from Weymouth, Eng., settled nr. Lynn, Mass., 1635; was at Weymouth, Mass.; in company with others obtained a grant, 1637, and founded Sandwich, Mass., settled there, 1638; 1st dep. Gen. Ct., constable, freeman; the house erected by George Allen, 1646, was in good repair, 1860, but was taken down, 1880, situated at Sandwich, Mass., about a quarter of a mile from the Friends Meeting house on the main road to the cape; *m* Katherine Collins (*b* 1605).

ALLEN, James (*d* Medfield, Mass., Sept. 27, 1673), prob. came from Colby, Norfolk, Eng., with his uncle Rev. John Allin (Savage says bro., the will says "cousin"), 1635; settled at Dedham, Mass., 1637; lands granted, 1638; one of the first 13 settlers of Medfield; *m* Anna Guild (1616-73).

ALLEN, Ralph (*d* 1698; apparently was son or bro. of George Allen, qv); Quaker, reported in vicinity of Boston, 1628; at Newport, R.I., 1638, Weymouth, Mass., 1639, Rehoboth, 1643; Sandwich, 1645; *m* 2d, 1645, Easter, or Esther, dau. of William Swift (qv).

ALLEN (Allyn), Samuel (*b* Eng., 1596-*d* Braintree, Mass., 1665; prob. son of George Allen, qv); came in the "Mary and John," to Newton, Mass., 1630; freeman at Braintree, Mass., 1635; at Windsor, Conn., 1644; *m* Ann – (*d* Sept. 29, 1641); *m* 2d, Margaret, widow of Edward Lamb.

ALLEN, Samuel (*b* Braintree, Essex Co., Eng., abt. 1588-*d* Windsor, Conn., buried, Apr. 28, 1648), from Eng. with the Dorchester Co. in the "Mary and John," 1630; settled at Windsor, Conn., 1640; juryman, 1644; *m* Ann, or Amy – (died 1687); his widow and family removed to Northampton, Mass.; she *m* 2d, William Hulburd (qv).

ALLEN, William (*b* Eng. abt. 1602-*d* Manchester, Mass., 1678), from Eng. as one of the Dorchester co., 1624, and settled at Gloucester; at Salem, 1626, freeman, 1630; later settled at Manchester; *m* 1629, to Elizabeth Bradley (1603-Mar. 1632).

ALLERTON, Isaac (ca. 1586-1659), 5th signer of the Mayflower Compact; dep. gov. Plymouth Colony, 1621-24, asst., 1624, 31, 33; removed to New Amsterdam ca. 1639; one of the Eight Men of New Netherland, 1643; purchased a tract of land, and built a warehouse and residence, 1647, where Peck Slip now is; lived at New Haven, Conn.; *m* 1st, at Leyden, Holland, 1611, Mary Norris (*d* in 1621); *m* 2d, at Plymouth, Mass., bet. 1623-27, Fear (*d* 1634), dau. Elder William Brewster (qv); *m* 3d, before 1644, Joanna – (*d* 1682).

ALLING (now Allen), Roger (*d* New Haven, Conn., Sept. 27, 1674), settled at New Haven at beginning of settlement, 1639; a signer of the compact; deacon; treas. of colony, 1661 and later; *m* Mary (*d* Aug. 16, 1683), dau. of Thomas Nash (qv).

ALLIS, William (*b* prob. in Essex, Eng., bet. 1613 and 1616-*d* Hatfield, Conn., Sept. 6, 1678); came with Winthrop's fleet, 1630, settled at Braintree; had grant from Boston of 12 acres for 3 heads; freeman, 1640; removed to Hadley 1661; selectman, 1662; lt. of cavalry; dea.; *m* 1641, Mary – (*d* 1677), *m* 2d, June 25, 1678, Widow Mary Graves, nee Brownson (her 1st husband was John Wyatt; she *m* 4th, 1682, Samuel Gaylord).

ALLYN, Hon. Matthew (1604/05-1670/71; son of Richard, will proved 1652, *m* Margaret –); from Eng. to Charlestown, Mass., 1632; freeman, Cambridge, 1635; settled at Hartford, Conn., 1637, later at Windsor; rep. Mass. Gen. Ct., 1636; dep. from Windsor, Conn., 1648, 57; asst., 1658-67; commr. to United Colonies, 1660-64; *m* 1627, Margaret Wyatt, from Eng., of royal descent.

ALLYN, Robert (*b* Eng., 1608-*d* New Haven, Conn., 1683), bro. of William Allen of Manchester (qv); from Eng., 1637, and settled at Salem; admitted to ch., 1642; removed to New London, Conn., 1657, and to Norwich, at its first settlement, 1659; constable 1669; returned to New London, where Allyn's Point perpetuates his memory; sec. Gen. Ct. of Conn., 1637; *m* at Salem.

ALMY (Almey or Almond), William (*b* prob. at Dunton-Bassett or South Kilworth, Leicestershire, Eng., 1600-*d* Portsmouth, R.I., abt. Apr. 1677; only son of Christopher Almey of South Kilworth; executor of father's estate, 1624); came to N.E., 1631; went home and returned with wife and 2 children in 1635, and settled at Lynn (Saugus); one of the founders of Sandwich, 1637; sold his lands there and removed to Portsmouth, R.I., land grant, 1644; freeman, 1655, later juryman and commnr.; *m* at Lutterworth, Eng., abt. 1626, Audrey Barlowe (1603-living 1676).

ALSOP, Richard (1660-1718), from Eng. to Newtown, L.I., post 1665; commissioned capt. Newtown troop of horse; inherited the estate of his uncle, Thomas Wardell; *m* 1686, Hannah – (1667-1757).

ALSTON, John (1610-87), of the Inner Temple and Parvenham, Eng., was granted tract embracing most of Fairfax Co., N.C.; *m* 1634, Lady Dorothy (*d* 1668), dau. of Sir John Temple.

ALSTON (Allston), John (bap. Felmersham, Bedfordshire, Eng., Dec. 5, 1673-*d* Chowan Co., N.C., 1758; s. of John, qv); came to Carolina colony, prob. in 1710; settled on Bennett's creek, where Gatesville, N.C., now stands, 1711; land-grants to sons in 1713; juror, 1715, grand-juror, 1721-24; justice of the peace and associate justice, 1724-29; held military rank of capt., major and col. after 1725; was sheriff of Chowan Co., several terms; vestryman, St. Paul's parish; *m* abt. 1700, Mary (*b* abt. 1687-*d* after 1758), dau. of John Clark, *m* Mary Palin, of Pasquotank, N.C.

ALVORD, Alexander (ca. 1620-87), from Eng., bet. 1636-40, settled at Windsor, Conn., 1645, at Northampton, Mass., 1661; *m* Oct. 29, 1646, Mary (*b* July 6, 1617-*d* before 1683), dau. Richard Vore (or Voar).

AMBLER, Richard (ca. 1611-1699; son of Richard [1587-1637]; g.son of Thomas, of Kiddington-in-Lindsay, nr. Yorkshire, Eng.); came to Watertown, Mass., ca. 1638; at Weymouth, 1640, Boston, 1643, Stamford, Conn., 1649; freeman, 1669; with his son, Abraham (Abram), and others bought from the Indians "the hopp-ground" (now called Bedford), Westchester Co., N.Y., 1699; a leader of the little company which founded the 1st church at Bedford, of which his son Abraham was minister, 1689 et seq.; *m* 1st, Sarah – (mother of all his children, all *b* Watertown); *m* 2d, Elizabeth – (*d* Mar. 27, 1685).

AMES, Thomas, see Eames.

AMES, William (*b* Bruton, Somersetshire, Eng., Oct. 6, 1605-*d* Braintree, Mass., Jan. 1, 1653/54), John, from Eng. to Duxbury, Mass., as early as 1640; later at Braintree; freeman, 1647; *m* 1639/40, Hannah –.

AMORY, Jonathan (*b* Bristol, Eng., Mar. 14, 1654-*d* Charleston, S.C., 1699; son of Thomas Amory, *m* Ann Elliott); from Eng. via Jamaica, to S.C., Aug. 29, 1682; mcht.; apptd. by the crown as advocate gen. in S.C. admiralty courts, 1697; speaker of House of Commons, S.C., at time of his death from the "plague"; extensive landholder thru grant and purchase; also receiver for the public treasury, 1699; *m* abt. 1679, Rebecca (*d* abt. 1685), widow of David Houston, of Ireland; *m* 2d, Martha –.

ANDERSON, Richard, (*b* 1585), from London in the "Merchant's Hope," to Va., 1635; was of Gloucester Co.

ANDERSON, Robert (ca. 1733-1825), from Ireland to Phila., Pa., 1755, thence before 1764, to Delaware; to Botetourt Co., Va., 1769; *m* 1764, Margaret Neely (1738-1810).

ANDREWS, William (prob. *b* in Hampsworth, Eng.-*d* East Haven, Conn., Mar. 4, 1675/76; Savage says *d* Jan. 3, 1664); carpenter came to Boston, in the "James" of London,

1635; freeman, 1635; removed to New Haven, Conn., where he signed the compact, 1639; built first meetinghouse there, 1644; lt. of arty. co., May 22, 1648; kept the inn under direction of Gen. Ct. for many yrs.; *m* in Eng., Mary – (*d* 1639/40); *m* 2d, 1665, Anna Gibauds.

ANGELL, Thomas (*b* Eng. abt. 1618-*d* Providence, R.I., 1694); came in the "Lyon," Dec. 1630, arrived in Boston, Feb. 5, 1631, going soon after to Salem; winter of 1635 at Seekonk, and made the settlement at Providence before July 1636; signed the compact, Aug. 20, 1637; signed agreement for a form of govt. for colony, 1640; successively commr., juryman, constable; freeman 1655; *m* Alice Ashton (*d* 1695).

ANTHONY, John (*b* Hempstead, Eng., 1607-*d* Portsmouth, R.I., July 28, 1675; son of John Anthony, physician of London); came in the "Hercules," 1634; settled at Portsmouth, R.I.; freeman, 1641; corpl., 1644; received land grant at Wadding River, Nov. 14, 1644; apptd. to "keep a house of entertainer," May 25, 1655; commr., 1661; purchased house and 3 acres at Portsmouth, Dec. 3, 1663; sold this and other land, Nov. 7, 1666; dep. Gen. Ct., 1666-72; *m* Susanna Potter (*d* 1675).

APPLETON, Samuel (*b* Little Waldingfield, Suffolk, Eng., 1586-*d* Rowley, Mass., June 1670; son of Thomas, *m* Mary Isaack); gent., armiger; came from Eng. to Ipswich, Mass., with 2d wife and family, 1635; freeman, May 25, 1636; granted 460 acres of land on the Hamilton town line bet. Ipswich River and Mile Brook; dep. Gen. Ct. 1637; mem. grand jury, 1641; resided at Rowley, Mass.; *m* 1st, Preston, Eng., Jan. 24, 1616, Judith Evarard (*d* ca. 1630); *m* 2d, ca. 1633, Martha –.

ARMISTEAD, John (1635-98), Gloucester Co., Va.; was justice before 1675; high sheriff, 1675; burgess, 1685; lt. col. of horse, 1680; col. and county lt., 1685; mem. Council, 1688-98; *m* Judith Robinson.

ARMISTEAD, William (bap. 1610-ante 1660; son of Anthony, of Deighton Park, in the West Riding of Yorkshire, Eng., *m* Frances Thompson), came to Va., 1635; a patentee of Elizabeth City Co., 1636; *m* 1651, Anne –;

ARMOUR, James, from Ireland, settled at Unionville, Conn.; *m* 1751, Margaret Anderson.

ARMS, William (supposed to have been *b* on Isle of Jersey, 1654-*d* Deerfield, Mass., Aug. 25, 1731), came from either the Isle of Jersey or Guernsey, presumed to have assumed the name of Arms, as no one of the name is found on the island from which he came; knitter of stockings; first known as soldier under Capt. William Turner at Hadley, Mass., Apr. 6, 1676; in Indian fight at Great Falls, May 17, 1676; at Hatfield, Mass., 1677; at Deerfield, abt. 1684; constable, 1699; tithing man, 1700; at Sunderland, Mass., 1714-22; returned to Deerfield abt. 1722; *m* Nov. 21, 1677, Joanna (*b* abt. 1653-*d* Nov. 22, 1729), dau. of John Hawks, of Hadley, Mass.

ARNOLD, Thomas (bap. Eng., Apr. 18, 1599-*d* Smithfield, R.I., Sept., 1674; son of Thomas, of Cheselbourne, Dorsetshire, Eng.); came in the "Plaine Joan," 1635, ship's record says "age 30 yrs."; settled at Watertown, Mass.; freeman; May 13, 1640; moved before 1661, to Providence, R.I.; sold rest of his Watertown holdings in 1661 and 1662; dep. Gen. Assembly, R.I., 1666, 67, 70-72; *m* in Eng., –; *m* 2d, 1640, Phebe (bap. 1612-*d* ca. 1688), dau. of George Parkhurst, Sr.

ARNOLD, William (*b* Eng., June 24, 1587-*d* 1676; son of Thomas, *m* Alice Cully of Cheselbourne, Eng., and half-bro. of Thomas, qv); brought his family to N.E., May 1, 1635, and was at Hingham for awhile; removed with Roger Williams to Pawtuxet, 1638, and was one of the 13 original proprs. of Providence Plantations; signed agreement for the first form of govt., 1640; commr. from Providence to Gen. Ct. of R.I., 1661; *m* Christian (*b* 1583), dau. of Thomas Peake.

ASPINWALL, Peter (*b* Eng. ca. 1612-*d* Brookline, Mass., 1687), came to Dorchester ca. 1630; freeman, 1645; settled at Muddy River (Brookline), ante 1650; *m* ca. 1645, Alice Sharp; *m* 2d, Feb. 12, 1662, Remember (1638-1701), dau. of Peter Palfrey (qv).

ASTON, Lt. Col. Walter (1606/07-Apr. 6, 1656; son of Walter, of Longden, Stafford Co., Eng.; g.g.son of Sir Walter, knighted 1560); from Staffordshire, Eng., to Va., ca. 1628; burgess, Shirley Hundred, 1629-30, 31-32, 32-33, Charles City Co., 1642-43; justice of the peace; named lt. col. militia, Charles City Co., Sept. 17, 1655; patented 590 acres, July 26, 1638, on Kimage's Creek, of which land 200 acres, known as "Cawsey's Care," were purchased by a deed dated Feb. 7, 1634, from John Causey, as heir of Nathaniel Causey (the rest of this land was due Aston for the transportation into Va. of ten persons); patented an additional 250 acres, Charles City, Apr. 10, 1643; buried at Westover, on James River; permission to probate his will was granted in Charles City, Jan. 25, 1656/57; *m* Miss Narbow (or Warbow); *m* 2d, Hannah Jordan (*d* post 1656).

ASTOR, John Jacob (*b* Waldorf, Duchy of Baden, July 17, 1763-*d* New York City, Mar. 29, 1848; son of Johann Jacob Astor, a bailiff of Waldorf); went to London, 1780, and engaged in manufacture of musical instruments as employee of bro. George's firm; came to Baltimore, Md., Mar. 1784, as agent of firm with consignment of goods; during voyage to America, his conversations with officers of the Hudson Bay Co. had interested him in the fur trade and having disposed of his goods he entered the employ of a fur dealer; established his own fur business and amassed a fortune of $250,000 in six years, which he invested mainly in N.Y. City real estate; continued in fur trade and real estate investments until he was reputed to be the richest man in America; *m* 1786, Sarah, dau. of Adam Todd, *m* Sarah Cox.

ATHERTON, Humphrey, (*b* Lancashire, Eng., 1609-*d* Sept. 16, 1661; prob. son of Edmund Atherton, of Lancashire); came in the "James," 1635; settled at Dorchester, Mass., 1636; freeman, May 2, 1638; dep. Gen. Ct., 1638, et seq.; speaker of the house, 1653; mem. council of war for United Colonies, 1645; capt. Dorchester company, May 16, 1646; capt. of A. and H. A. Co., 1650, 1658; commr. of United Colonies, 1653; asst., 1645-1661; supt. of Indian affairs, 1658; maj. gen. of Mass. Colony, 1661; died from fall from his horse which stumbled over a cow lying in the road; *m* in England, Mary Wales (*d* 1672).

ATKINSON (Adkinson, Atkeson), John (*b* ca. 1640), from Boston, Mass., to Newbury ca. 1663, *m* 1664, Sarah Myrick.

ATLEE (At Lee) William (*b* Fordhook House, Brentford, Eng., abt. 1700-*d* Phila., Apr. 27, 1744, son of Samuel Atlee of Brentford, Eng.); was first of the name to reach America; came 1734 as private sec. to Lord Howe, Gov. of Barbados; *m* June 1, 1734, Jane Alcock (*d* Lancaster, Pa., Jan. 18, 1777), dau. of an English clergyman and cousin of William Pitt, first Earl of Chatham (it is said she was maid of honor to the queen).

ATWATER, David (*b* Royton Manor in Lenham, Co. of Kent, Eng., bap. Oct. 8, 1615-*d* New Haven, Conn., Oct. 5, 1692; son of John, *m* Susan –); settled at New Haven, Conn., 1638, with bro. Joshua and sister Ann; signed plantation covenant, June 4, 1639; large landowner; freeman, 1665; *m* bet. 1643-1646, Demaris (*d* Apr. 1, 1691), dau. of Thomas Sayre (qv).

ATWOOD, John, from Eng., 1636; propr. Plymouth, Mass., 1636; *m* Sarah Masterson.

AUSTIN, Richard (*b* ca. 1598), from Eng. in the "Bevis," to Charlestown, Mass., 1638; tailor; brought wife and two children.

AVERILL (Averell), William (*b* Ash, nr. Farmingham, Kent, Eng., bet. 1611 and 1613-*d* 1653, will proved Mar. 29, 1653), settled at Ipswich, Mass., before Mar. 2, 1637, when he received his first grant of land from that town; *m* in Eng. ca. 1631 or 32, Abigail Hynton, or Hinton (*d* 1655).

AVERY, Christopher (*b* Eng. abt. 1590-*d* New London, Conn., buried Mar. 12, 1679; son of Christopher, of Newton Abbott, Co. Devon, Eng.); came in the "Arbella," 1630; settled at Gloucester, Mass.; weaver; selectman, 1646, 52, 54; took freeman's oath, Salem, June 29, 1652; sold land in Gloucester and removed to Boston, where he purchased home, Mar. 18, 1658; removed to New London, Conn.; freeman, Colony of Conn., Oct., 1669; *m* 1616, Margery Stevens (or Stephens), who did not come to America.

AVERY, Capt. James (1620-1700; son of Christopher, qv), of New London, Conn., 1650; acquired large tracts of land at Groton, Conn., and built the homestead "Hive of the Averys,"

1656; selectman, 1660-80; commr., 1663-78; lt., Train Band, New London, 1665; ens., lt. and capt. in King Philip's War, cdr. of soldiers from Stonington, New London and Lyme thruout the war; rep. Gen. Ct., 1656-80; asst. judge Prerogative Ct.; *m* 1643, Joanna Greenslade (1622-bet. 1693-98); *m* 2d, Abigail (Ingraham) Chesebrough.

AVERY, William (1622-1686/87), from Eng. with his wife and three children to Dedham, Mass., 1650; dep. Gen. Ct., lt. of Dedham Co., 1673; mem. A. and H. A. Co.; earliest physician of Dedham; dep. Gen. Ct., 1669; lt., Dedham Co., 1673; removed to Boston, 1680; *m* Margaret (*d* Sept. 28, 1678), dau. of William Allright, of Eng., *m* Jone –; *m* 2d, 1679, Maria (Woodmansey) Tappin (ca. 1629-May 21, 1707), dau. of Robert Woodmansey, and widow of John Tappin, of Boston.

AYER (Eyer, Eyers, Ayres), John (*b* Eng., 1590 or 92-*d* Haverhill, Mass., Mar. 31, 1657; son of Thomas, *m* Elizabeth Rogers); came in the "James," 1635, settled at Newbury, Mass.; received land in the "first division," at Salisbury, 1640; removed to Ipswich, 1646, to Haverhill, 1647; *m* Hannah – (1598-July 13, 1686).

BABCOCK (Badcock), James (*b* in Eng., 1612-*d* Westerly R.I., June 12, 1679); came from Eng., bet. 1630 and 1640; settled at Portsmouth, R.I., by 1642; blacksmith; admitted inhabitant, Feb. 25, 1642; ordered by town, with Richard Morris, to repair all arms, 1643 and 1650; 10 acres were ordered "laide out" to him; freeman, July 10, 1648; mem. of com. for "tryall of the general officers"; assessor, 1650; mem. Gen. Ct. for Portsmouth, 1657, 8, 9; removed to Westerly, R.I., Mar. 1662; *m* 1st, Sarah – (*d* 1665, or later); *m* 2d, 1669 (?), Elizabeth – (she *m* 2d, Sept. 22, 1679, William Johnson.

BACHE, Richard (*b* Settle, Yorkshire, Eng., Feb. 23 or Sept. 12, 1737-*d* July 29, 1811; son of William, *m* Mary Blyckenden); was settled at Phila. as a merchant, 1760; sec. of Province of Pa., 1775-76; register-general, 1775-76; was postmaster general under the crown, 1776-82; mem. Board of War, 1777; a protestant against the Stamp Act, and held with the Revolutionists; *m* Phila., Oct. 3 or 29, 1767, Sarah (*b* Sept. 11 or 22, 1743 or 44-*d* Oct. 5, 1808), only dau. of Benjamin Franklin, of Phila.

BACHILER, see Batchelder.

BACKUS, William (*d* 1664), from Eng. with his two sons, William and Stephen, in the "Rainbow," 1637, to Saybrook, Conn.; a founder of Norwich, 1659; *m* Sarah, dau. of Rev. John Charles, of Branford, Conn.; *m* 2d, ca. 1660, Anne (Stenton) Bingham (*d* 1670), widow of Thomas Bingham.

BACON, Michael (bap. Winston, Co. Suffolk, Eng., Dec. 6, 1579-*d* Apr. 18, 1648; son of Michael, *m* Elizabeth Wylie; descended from Roger Bacon, who aided the barons against King John; the Bacon estates were confiscated by Henry, III, but were restored in 1216); came from Eng. and signed the Dedham, Mass., agreement, 1633; returned to Eng.; apparently went to Ire., 1633, thence returned to Dedham, 1640, with wife, 3 sons and 3 daus.; made one of proprietors, 1640; signed church covenant of Dedham; granted land to town for a highway, 1644; *m* Eng., Sept. 20, 1607, Grace Blowerses; *m* 2d, Eng., Alice – (*d* Apr. 2, 1647/48).

BACON, Nathaniel (*d* Oct. 1673), perhaps came from Stratton, Co. Rutland, Eng.; settled at Barnstable, Mass., 1640; tanner and currier; proposed as freeman, 1645; constable, 1650; rep., 1652-1665; asst. of Plymouth Colony, 1667-1673; mem. council of war, 1658 and 1667; large landowner; *m* Dec. 4, 1642, Hannah (living 1691), dau. of Rev. John Mayo, of Barnstable.

BACON, Nathaniel (*b* Stretton Parish, Co. Rutland, Eng., 1630-*d* Jan. 27, 1705; son of William); came abt. 1649; settled at Mettabesett (now Middletown), Conn., 1650; received large legacies from his "Unkell" Andrew Bacon, who had no children; *m* Anne (*d* July 6, 1680), dau. of Thomas Miller of Stretton Parish; *m* 2d, Apr. 17, 1682, Elizabeth Pierpont.

BACOT, Pierre (*b* Tours, France, abt. 1670-*d* 1702; son of Pierre Bacot, *m* Jacqueline Menissier, and g.son of Pierre, *m* Jeanne Moreau); came from France, 1694, settled at Goose Creek, abt. 19 miles from Charleston, S.C.; planter (one account seems to show that Pierre, who was *b* 1638 and *d* near Charles-town, 1702, was the father of Pierre, the immigrant above; that he came from the vicinity of Tours, France, to Charles Town, Carolina, 1685, with wife Jacquine Menessier, who *d* 1709, and sons Daniel and Pierre; that in 1699 and 1700 grants of land were made to Pierre, Sr., in St. Andrew's Parish, lands which are now part of the well known Middleton Place, near Charleston, and that the sons Daniel and Pierre removed to Goose Creek); *m* Jacquine (*d* 1709), dau. of Abraham Mercier, *m* Jacquine Selipeaux.

BADGER, Giles or Gyles (*b* Eng.-*d* Newbury, Mass., July 10 or 17, 1647), settled at Newbury, by 1635; farmer; *m* 1st, abt. 1642, Elizabeth (bap. Jan. 16, 1622), dau. of Capt. Edmond Greenleaf (qv); she *m* 2d, Richard Brown, of Newbury.

BAILEY, John (1590-1651), from Eng. in the "Angel Gabriel," 1635; settled at Salisbury, Mass.; weaver; yeoman at Newbury, 1651; *m* Eleanor Knight (*d* in Eng.).

BAILEY (Baily, Bayly, Bailie), Richard (1619-1647), from Eng. in the "Bevis," to Lynn, Mass., 1638; later at Rowley; one of a company to set up the first cloth mill in America; selectman and overseer of the poor several yrs.; *m* Edna (Lambert) Holstead (?).

BAIRD, John (*b* Scotland, abt. 1730-kld. at Grant's Fort, near Pittsburgh, Pa., Sept. 14, 1758), prob. came from Ayr, Scotland, before 1747; first settled in Chester Co., Pa., where he is on assessment list of 1747; is called the ancester of the Baird family of Washington Co., Pa.; came as an English officer in Braddock's army; served against Fort Duquesne, and shared in "Braddock's Defeat" of July 9, 1755; also said to have served in Gen. Forbes' expdn., 1758; supposed to have *d* in service; *m* Phila., abt. 1755, Catharine McLean or McClean (July 19, 1733-Nov. 28, 1802).

BAIRD (Beard), Thomas (1608-78), from Scotland with Gov. John Endicott, to Naumkeag (Salem), Mass., 1628.

BAKER, Alexander (*b* London, Eng., 1607 or 1611-*d* Boston, 1685), came in the "Elizabeth and Ann," 1635, with his wife Elizabeth, and daus. Elizabeth and Christiana; was a proprietor of Gloucester, before 1642; removed to Boston, where he was a rope and collar maker; admitted to Boston church with wife, Oct. 4, 1645, when his first 7 children were bap.; freeman, May 6, 1646; *m* abt. 1632, Elizabeth Farrar? (*b* abt. 1612).

BAKER, Francis (*b* Great St. Albans, Hertfordshire, Eng., 1611-*d* Yarmouth, Mass., July 23, 1696), came in the "Planter," 1635; tailor; settled at Yarmouth; admitted inhabitant, June 1, 1641; became a cooper; settled near Tollen's Pond, at the head of Bass River; surveyor of highways, 1648; freeman, 1657; was in Eastham, Mass., 1659; *m* June 21, 1641, Isabel (*d* Yarmouth, May 16, 1706), dau. of William Twining.

BAKER, Col. Henry (1640-42-1712), from Eng. to Isle of Wight Co., Va., ca. 1665; burgess, 1692-93; justice of Orphans' Court; styled maj. and col.; *m* Mary (1666-1734), dau. of Edward Bennett of London, mem. Va. company of colonizers.

BAKER (Backer), Thomas (*b* Eng., Sept. 29, 1618-*d* Easthampton, L.I., N.Y., Apr. 30, 1700), came to America, 1639; settled at Milford, Conn., and enrolled as a "free planter," Nov. 29, 1639, and as a mem. of the church; removed to Easthampton, L.I., 1650; received several allotments as a proprietor; chosen a "townsman," 1650-62; with John Hand apptd. "to go vnto keniticut for to bring vs vnder their government," Mar. 19, 1657/58; compact bet. Easthampton and Conn. Colony, May 3, 1658, by John Hand and Thomas Baker, and Thomas was elected by the Gen. Ct. of Conn., one of the magistrates to that ct., 1658-63; went to Huntingdon as agent of town to confer with agents of the other towns to consider their grievances against the English government, Sept. 24, 1681; foreman of grant jury, 1665; overseer, 1666; constable, 1667; apptd. justice of ct. of assizes in N.Y., Southampton and Southold, L.I., 1675-85; *m* June 20, 1643, Alice (*b* Eng., May 22, 1620-*d* Amagansett, L.I., Feb. 4, 1708/09), dau. of Ralph Dayton, of New Haven, Conn. and East Hampton, L.I.

BALCH, John (*b* Eng., 1579-*d* Salem, Mass.,

1648), from Eng. to Weymouth, Mass., 1623; a founder of Salem, 1626; freeman, 1631; received grants of land, 1635/36, now in Beverly; *m* Margary Lovett; *m* 2d, Agnes, or Annis Patch (*d* 1657).

BALDWIN, John (buried Milford, Conn., June 21, 1681), came from Eng., in the "Martin"; settled at Milford, Conn., 1639; joined church, Mar. 19, 1648; removed to Newark, N.J., about 1668, but returned to Milford; sgt. Conn. militia, 1658; *m* 1st, Mary –; *m* 2d, 1653, Mary (*d* Sept. 2, 1670), dau. of John Bruen, of Eng.

BALDWIN, John (*b* Eng.-*d* Dec. 25, 1687), from Eng., abt. 1640; settled at Billerica, Mass., as early as 1655; farmer; had grant of land, 1657; petitioner for land in Chelmsford, 1653; freeman, 1670; mem. garrison No. 6 at James Patterson's, 1675; *m* May 15, 1655, Mary (bap. Nov. 17, 1638), dau. of Thomas Richardson (qv).

BALDWIN, Joseph (*b* Cholesbury, Eng., abt. 1609-*d* Hadley, Mass., Nov. 2, 1684; son of Richard Baldwin, of Cholesbury); settled at Milford, Conn., 1639; free planter, Nov. 20, 1639; his wife Hannah joined the church June 23, 1644; removed to Hadley, abt. 1663; freeman, 1666; *m* Hannah –; *m* 2d, Isabel (Ward?), widow of James Northam; *m* 3d, Elizabeth (Hitchcock) Warriner (*d* Apr. 25, 1696), widow of William Warriner.

BALDWIN, Richard (1622-65), from Eng. in the "Martin," to Milford, Conn., ca. 1636; town clk., 1648; rep. Gen. Court, 1660-65; *m* Elizabeth Alsop, of New Haven.

BALL, Col. William (*b* London, Eng., ca. 1615-*d* "Millenbeck," Lancaster Co., Va., Nov. 1680); settled at the mouth of the Corotoman River, Lancaster Co., Va., Apr. 1650, where he built "Millenbeck"; merchant and planter; burgess, 1670-80; *m* London, July 2, 1638 (or 1644), Hannah (*d* 1695), dau. of Thomas Atherold, of Eng.

BALLARD, William (*b* Eng., ca. 1617-*d* Andover, Mass., July 10, 1689), probably came in the "Mary and John," 1634; settled at Andover ca. 1644; farmer; in King Philip's War, 1675-76; lived at Salem; mem. A. and H. A. Co.; *m* Grace – (*d* Andover, Apr. 27, 1694).

BALLOU, Maturin (*b* Eng. bet. 1610-20-*d* 1661-63), was at Providence, R.I., ante 1645/46, when he subscribed to agreement for grant of 25 acres from the town; freeman at Warwick, 1658; *m* ca. 1646-49, Hannah (ca. 1627-ca. 1715), dau. of Robert Pike, of Providence.

BANCROFT, Thomas (*b* Eng., 1622-*d* Aug. 19, 1691), from Eng. to Dedham, Mass., ca. 1645; settled at Reading ca. 1652; styled lt.; *m* Jan. 31, 1647, Alice (*d* Jan. 29, 1648), dau. of Michael Bacon (qv); *m* 2d, Sept. 15, 1648, Elizabeth (Oct. 4, 1626-May 11, 1711), dau. of Michael Metcalf (qv).

BANGS, Edward (*b* Eng., 1591/92-*d* Eastham, Mass., 1678), came in the "Ann" to Plymouth, Mass., 1623; freeman, 1633; assessor, 1634-36; removed to Eastham, 1644; capt. of the guard against Indians; dep. Gen. Ct., 1650, 52, 63; town treas., 1646-65; *m* ca. 1633, Lydia (*d* ca. 1635), dau. of Robert Hicks (qv); *m* 2d, ca. 1636, Rebecca (Hobart or Tracy?).

BARBER (Barbour), George (1615-83), from Eng., was at Dedham, Mass., 1635; an original propr. of Medfield, 1656; capt. A. and H. A. Co.; sgt. Medfield foot, 1646, and chief mil. officer of Medfield after 1649; served in King Philip's War.

BARBER, Dr. Luke (*d* 1671), from Eng. in the "Golden Fortune," 1654; settled in St. Mary's Co., Md.; received land grant of 1,000 acres for services rendered in Battle of the Severn; of "Wickham Hall"; dep.; lt. gov., Md.; mem. Gov.'s Council; dep. gov.; *m* in Eng., Elizabeth Younge.

BARBER (Barbour), Thomas (1614-62), from Eng. in the "Christian," 1634; settled at Windsor, Conn., 1635; soldier in Pequot War; *m* 1640, Joan – (*d* 1662).

BARCLAY, John (1659-1731), from England to Perth Amboy, N.J., 1682; dep. gov. of East Jersey under his brother, Robert; *m* Cornelia Van Schaick.

BARCROFT, Ambrose (1681-1724; eldest son of Thomas, gentleman, of Barcroft Hall and Noyna, Colne, Lancashire); from Eng. to Talbot Co., Md., post 1716; removed ante 1722, to Bucks Co., Pa.; drowned nr. Easton, Pa.; *m* 1702, Maria Walshman (*d* Eng., 1705).

BARNARD, John (1604-46), from Eng. in the "Elizabeth," 1634, and settled at Watertown, Mass.; selectman, 1644; *m* Phoebe – (*d* 1685).

BARNARD, Thomas (ca. 1612-1677), from Eng. to Salisbury, Mass., ca. 1634; killed by Indians; *m* Helen –.

BARNES, Thomas (1636-79), from Eng. in the "Speedwell," to Boston, Mass., 1656; was at Marlborough, 1666, where he bought land, 1663; house and goods burned in King Philip's War; *m* Abigail, dau. Thomas Goodnow, of Sudbury.

BARNEY (Berney), Jacob (1601-73; son of Sir Edward Berney, of Reedham, Norfolk, Eng., *m* Isbell Rooles); came from Eng. to Salem, Mass., ca. 1630; tailor; freeman, 1634; dep. Gen. Ct., 1635, 38, 47, 53; selectman; mem. 1st grand jury; *m* Elizabeth –.

BARNWELL, "Tuscarora" John (1671-1724), from Ireland to Charleston, S.C., 1701, later at Beaufort; cdr. first expdn. against the Tuscaroras, 1712; col. in Yemansee War, 1715; agt. in Eng. for the colony; *m* Elizabeth Anne Berners.

BARRELL, George (*d* 1643), from Eng. to Boston, 1637; freeman, 1643; *m* Ann –.

BARRETT, James (1615-72), from Eng., 1635, settled at Charlestown, Mass.; townsman, 1639; surveyor, 1656; removed to Malden; *m* Hannah (1615-81), dau. of Stephen Fosdick (qv).

BARRINGER (Baringer, Beringer), John Paul (1721-1807), from Ger. to Pa., 1743, settled at Mt. Pleasant, N.C., ca. 1750, where he built the family home, "Poplar Grove"; magistrate of the crown; capt. colonial militia in Am. Rev., suffered long imprisonment at Camden, S.C.; mem. N.C. Legislature; *m* 1750, Ann Eliza Iseman; *m* 2d, 1777, Catharine Blackwelder.

BARROWS (Barrow, Barrus), John (*d* 1692), from Eng. to Salem, Mass., 1637; at Plymouth, 1665; *m* Deborah –.

BARSTOW, William (*d* 1669), from Eng. in the "Truelove," 1635, and settled at Dedham; freeman at Scituate, 1649; first settler at Hanover, Mass.; *m* Anne Hubbard.

BARTHOLOMEW, William (1602/03-1681), from Eng. in ship with Ann Hutchinson, 1634, and settled at Ipswich; freeman, 1635; rep. Gen. Ct., 1635, and later; removed to Boston, 1660; was a witness against Ann Hutchinson; *m* Anna Lord.

BARTLETT (Bartlet, Barttelot) Richard (*b* bet. 1580-90-1647), from Eng. in the "Mary and John," to Newbury, 1635.

BARTLETT, Robert (1603-76), from Eng. in the "Ann," to Plymouth Colony, 1623; a cooper; mem. grand jury; surveyor; *m* 1628, Mary (*d* 1678), dau. Richard Warren (qv).

BARTON, Thomas (1730-80), from Ireland to Lancaster, Pa., ca. 1751; pastor St. James Ch. nearly 20 yrs., *m* 1753, Esther Rittenhouse (g. dau. William Rittenhouse, from Holland to Germantown, Pa., built the first paper mill in America, 1690).

BARTOW, Rev. John (*d* 1727), grad. Cambridge, 1692; came to America, 1702, sent over by the Society for the Propagation of the Gospel; in charge of Westchester, Yonkers and Pelham congregations; *m* 1705, Helena (*b* 1681), dau. of John Reid, from Scotland to America in charge of a party of settlers sent by Scotch Presbyns. to East N.J. in 1683; dep. surveyor, 1685, surveyor-gen., 1703, *m* 1678, Margaret Miller.

BASCOM (Bascome), Thomas (*d* 1682), from Eng. in the "Mary and John," to Dorchester, Mass., 1634; settled at Windsor, Conn., 1639, later at Northampton, Mass.; *m* Avis – (*d* 1676).

BASS, Samuel (1600-94), from Eng. ca. 1630, at Roxbury, Mass., 1632; freeman, 1634; removed to Braintree, 1640; dep. Gen. Ct.; *m* Ann – (*d* 1663).

BASSETT, John (*d* 1656), from Eng. to Mass. Colony, 1638; moved to New Haven, Conn., 1642; *m* Margery –.

BASSETT, William (*d* 1667), from Eng. in the "Good Fortune," to Plymouth, Mass., 1621; an original propr. of Bridgewater; later at Sandwich and Duxbury, Mass.; served in Pequot War; mem. Capt. Myles Standish's mil. co., 1643; dep. Gen. Ct., 1640, 1643-46, 1648; large landowner; had large library; *m* Elisabeth Tilden (*d* 1667).

BATCHELDER, Rev. Stephen (*b* 1560-1-*d* Hackney, near London, Eng., 1660, aged nearly 100), a noted English divine of Hampshire; B.A., Oxford U., 1586; came in the "William and Francis" arriving at Boston, Thursday, June 5, 1632; went to Lynn, where his dau., Theodate, lived; ordered by the Ct. at Boston "to forbeare exercising his giftes as a pastor or teacher," Oct. 3, 1632, which restriction was removed, Mar. 4, 1633; freeman, 1635, removed to Ipswich, Mass., 1636; to Winnicunnet, N.H., 1638, which was named Hampton at his request; removed to Casco, Me., 1647; returned to Eng., 1654, where he *d*; *m* 1st wife in Eng., where she *d*; *m* 2d, Eng., Helen – (1583-1642 or 44); *m* 3d, 1648, Mary –.

BATES (Bate), Clement (1589-1671; son of James, *m* Mary Martin; g.son of John, *m* Mildred Ward); from Eng. in the "Elizabeth," to Hingham, Mass., 1635; freeman, 1636; *m* Ann – (*d* 1669, aet. 74);

BATES (Bate) James (1582-1655; son of James, *m* Mary Martin, of Lydd, Kent Co., Eng.; desc. John Bate, 1415, legendary soldier in battle of Agincourt), from Eng. in the "Elizabeth," to Dorchester, Mass., 1635; freeman, 1636; elder; selectman, 1636; rep. Gen. Ct., 1641; *m* 1603, Alice Glover (*d* 1657);

BATTLE, John (*d* 1690), from Eng., 1654, landowner, 1654, on Nansemond River, Colony of Va., also on Paspetank River, N.C., 1663, *m* Elizabeth –.

BAXTER, Gregory, from Eng. with Winthrop's fleet, 1630, and settled at Roxbury, Mass.; removed to Braintree, 1631; *m* Margaret Paddy.

BAXTER, Lt. Thomas, of Yarmouth, Mass.; *m* 1679, Temperance, dau. Capt. John Gorham (qv).

BAYARD, Petrus (son of Samuel Bayard, *m* Anna Stuyvesant, sister of Peter), from Holland in the "Princess," to New Amsterdam, 1647.

BAYLESS (Baylis, Baylies, Bayliss, Bayles), John (1617-82), from Eng. to Bermuda, 1635; to America in the "Truelove"; settled at New Haven, Conn., 1654; at Southold, L.I., 1658; purchased from the Indians, 1664, with some associates, about 200,000 acres, where Newark, Paterson, and Passaic now stand; and same was deeded by John Bayles and associates to Philip Carteret, then gov. of N.J., 1665, both deeds are recorded at Trenton, N.J.; *m* Rebecca –.

BAYNTON, Peter (*b* Bedminster, Eng.), came to Phila., ca. 1720; *m* 1st, a dau. of Col. Paris, of Charleston; *m* 2d, Mary Budd; *m* 3d, – Wheeler.

BEACH, John (1623-77; son of Rev. John, of Derbyshire, Eng.); came to New Haven, Conn., 1640 or 43; removed to Stratford, purchased house and lot, 1660; freeman, 1669; town crier, 1671; King Philip's War; *m* Mary –.

BEACH, Richard (*b* ca. 1620), from Eng. to Watertown, Mass., 1635, thence to New Haven Colony, and signer of the Compact of 1639; removed to New London, 1667; *m* ca. 1640, Catherine (Cook) Hull (*b* 1620), (widow of Andrew Hull, of New Haven).

BEACH, Thomas (*d* 1662), from Eng. to Quinnipiack (New Haven), Conn., ca. 1638; took oath of allegiance, 1654; at Milford, 1658; *m* 1652, Sarah (1635-70), dau. of Richard Platt.

BEAL (Beale, Beall, Beals), John (1588-1688), from Eng. in the "Diligente," to Hingham, Mass., 1638; freeman, 1639; dep. Gen. Ct., 1649-59; *m* Nazareth Hobart (*d* 1658); *m* 2d, 1659, Mary, widow of Nicholas Jacob.

BEALE, Thomas (1626-ante 1700), from Eng., 1640; settled at York River, Va., 1645; mem. Royal Council, 1674; *m* Alice –.

BEALL (Beal, Beale), Col. Ninian (1625-1717), from Scotland, 1652, settled in Prince George Co., Md.; later at Calvert Co., Md.; lt., 1668, 76; dep. surveyor, Charles Co., 1684; chief mil. officer, Calvert Co., 1688; maj. Calvert Co. militia, 1689; high sheriff, 1692; col. of militia, 1694; mem. Gen. Assembly, 1697-1701; Gen. Assembly (Md.) passed "Act of Gratitude" for distinguished Indian services, 1699; ruling elder, and "Father of Presbyterianism in Md."; *m* Elizabeth Gordon; *m* 2d, ca. 1670, Ruth, dau. Richard Moore.

BEARDSLEY (Beardslee, Berdsley, Bersley), William (1605-61), from Eng. in the "Planter," to Mass., 1635; extensive land owner; founder of Stratford, Conn., 1639; dep. Gen. Ct., 1645-51; *m* Mary –.

BEATTY, Charles (ca. 1712-1772, son of John Beatty, officer British Army, *m* Christiana Clinton, who came to America, 1729, with her brother, Col. Charles Clinton, of N.Y.), came from Ireland, 1729, to Forks of Neshaminy, Pa., 1743; chaplain in French and Indian War; hon. A.M., Princeton, 1762, and trustee same, 1763-72; missionary to Indians, commr. to the Barbados to collect funds for Princeton Coll., *m* Ann, dau. John Reading, pres. Provincial Council of N.J.

BECKWITH, Matthew (1610-80), from Eng. to Saybrook Point, Conn., 1636; later at Branford, at Hartford, 1645, and later at Lyme and New London; a founder of the Ch. at Lyme; *m* Elizabeth –.

BEECHER, John (1623-59), from Eng. with his widowed mother, Hannah – (1600-58), arriving at Boston, Apr. 26, 1637; settled at Quinnipiack, Conn.

BEEKMAN, Wilhelmus (1623-1707; son of Hendrick), from Holland, in the "Princess," to New Amsterdam with Peter Stuyvesant, 1647; vice dir. of the colony on South River, 1658-64; lt. Burgher Corps of New Amsterdam, 1652-58, of New Orange, 1673-74; schout and commissary at Esopus, 1664; lt. militia, 1673; dep. mayor of N. Y., 1681-83; *m* 1649, Catalina (*d* 1700), dau. Hendrick de Boogh, of Albany.

BEERS, James (*d* 1694; son of James, of Gravesend, Co. Kent, Eng., where the family originated in Antony Bere, 1486); came to America with his uncle, Richard Beers (qv), 1635, thence to Watertown, Mass., thence Fairfield, Conn.; *m* Martha, dau. of John Barlow.

BEERS, Richard (*d* 1675), from Eng. to Watertown, Mass., 1635; capt. in King Philip's War, and killed at Northfield, Mass.

BELDEN (Bayldon, Belding), Richard (1591-1655), from Eng., an original settler at Wethersfield, Conn., 1640.

BELKNAP, Abraham (1589-1643), from Eng. with two brothers, Joseph and Thomas, 1637, settled at Lynn, Mass.

BELL, Thomas (1618-78), from Eng. to Jamestown, Va., 1635; *m* Mary, dau. Capt. John Neal.

BELLINGER, Capt. Sir Edmund (desc. Walter Bellinger, of Northumberland, who was granted coat-of-arms, 1475), from Westmoreland Co., Eng., 1674, settled on James Island, S.C.; landgrave, 1698; surveyor gen.; receiver of public moneys, 1700; *m* ca. 1680, Sarah Cartwright; issue: Edmund, 2d landgrave.

BEMIS (Bemiss, Beamis), Joseph (1619-1684) from Eng. to Watertown, Mass., 1640; soldier King Philip's War; was often selectman; *m* Sarah –.

BENEDICT, Thomas (1617-90), from Eng. to Mass., 1638; at Southold, L.I.; mem. Colonial Assembly from Hempstead; finally at Norwalk, Conn., where was deacon, selectman, town clk. and dep. to Gen. Ct.; *m* Mary Bridgum, or Bridgham (*d* aet. 100).

BENJAMIN, John (1598-1645), from Eng. in the "Lion," to Boston, 1632, large landed propr. at Watertown, freeman, 1632; constable, 1633; *m* 1619, Abigail (1600-87), dau. Rev. William Eddy.

BENNETT (Bennet), James, from Eng., 1639; freeman at Concord, Mass., same yr.; *m* Hannah, dau. Thomas Wheeler.

BENNETT (Bennet), Richard (*d* 1675), came to Va. ca. 1626, and settled in Nansemond Co.; burgess, 1629, 31; mem. Council, 1639-49, 1658, et seq.; removed to Md., 1649; apptd. by Parliament one of the three commrs. to reduce Va. and Md., Dec. 1651; gov. of Va., 1652-55; went to Eng. 1655, as agent for the colony; maj. gen. militia, 1665; *m* Mary Ann Utie.

BENSON (Bensen), Dirck (*d* Albany, 1659), removed from Gröningen to Amsterdam, Holland; came with wife to New York, ca. 1648; granted land at Fort Orange (Albany), 1653, resided there the following year; as a carpenter, helped construct the new church at Albany, 1656, and loaned the deacons 100 guilders, 1658; *m* Catalina Berck (1625-post 1663); she *m* 2d, Harmen Thomase Hun.

BENT, John (1596-1672), from Eng. to Sudbury, Mass., 1638; in expdn. against Ninigret, 1654.

BENTON, Andrew (1620-83; son of Edward); from Eng. to Watertown, Mass., ca. 1630; first settler of Milford, Conn., 1639; fence viewer, 1663-64; juror, 1664; freeman, 1665; collector of minister's fees, 1667; *m* 1649, Hannah (*d* 1670), dau. of George Stocking; *m* 2d Ann (*d* 1686), dau. of John Cole (the "bewitched man" for whom Nathaniel Greene and his wife were hanged, 1663).

BERGEN (van Bergen), Hans Hansen (*d* in

1653/54), native of Norway, came from Holland in the "Salt Mountain," to New Amsterdam, 1633; owned large plantation on Manhattan Island; *m* 1st, 1639, Sarah (1625-85), dau. Joris Jansen de Rapalje (qv).

BERNARD, Col. William (1598-1665), from Eng. in the "America," to Va., 1625, settled in Isle of Wight Co.; mem. Council, 1642-60; *m* Lucy (Higginson) Burwell, dau. of Capt. Robert Higginson, and widow of Lewis Burwell, of Carter's Creek, Gloucester Co.

BERNON, Gabriel (1644-1736; son of Andre, *m* Suzane –), a Huguenot, from Rochelle, France; imprisoned 2 yrs. because of religious faith; fled to Eng.; came to America, June 1688; founder of first three P.E. churches in R.I.; *m* 2d, 1714, Mary Harris.

BERRIEN, Cornelius Janse (*d* 1689), Huguenot; fled from France to Holland, thence came to New Amsterdam, 1669, settled at Flatbush, L.I.; removed to Newtown, L.I., 1685; was deacon and tax commr.; *m* Jannetje, dau. of Jan Stryker (qv).

BETTS, Richard (1613-1713), from Eng. to Ipswich, Mass., 1648; removed to Newtown, L.I., 1656; capt., 1663; mem. Provincial Assembly of N.Y., 1665; high sheriff of Yorkshire, L.I., 1678-81.

BICKNELL, Zachary (1590-1636), from Eng. with Rev. Joseph Hull, to Weymouth, Mass., 1635, of which he was a propr.; *m* at Weymouth, Eng., Agnes Lovell (*d* 1643).

BIDDLE, William (1630-1712), from Eng. to New Jersey, 1681, becoming one of the proprietors of West Jersey; was pres. bd. of trustees and Council Proprietary of West Jersey, Gov.'s Council, Gen. Assembly, and was justice; *m* 1665, Sarah Kemp (1634-1709).

BIGELOW (Baguley, Biglo, Biglow), John (1616/17-1703), from Eng., ca. 1630, settled at Watertown, Mass., 1642; soldier Pequot and King Philip's wars; *m* 1642, Mary (1628-91), dau. John Warren; *m* 2d, 1694, Sarah, dau. Joseph Bemis.

BILES (Byles), William (*d* 1710), an "Eminent Friend"; from Dorchester, Eng., in the "Eliza and Sarah," to Del., 1679; large landowner in Bucks Co., Pa.; mem. pro-provincial govt., Jan. 4, 1681, before arrival of William Penn; justice Uplands Ct.; signer of Penn's Great Charter; mem. first Council, Phila., Mar. 10, 1683, "William Penn presiding in person"; judge Ct. of Inquiry, 1700; the first known meeting of Friends in Pa. was held in his house, just below the Falls of Neshaminy, May 2, 1683; *m* 2d, Joan, or Jane Atkinson.

BILLINGS (Billing), William (ca. 1629-1713), from Eng. to Dorchester, Mass., ante 1649; settled at Stonington, Conn., 1658; *m* Feb. 12, 1657/58, Mary – (*d* 1718).

BILLINGTON, John (*d* 1630), 26th signer of the Mayflower Compact; *m* before 1605, Eleanor – (*d* 1643).

BINGHAM, Thomas (1642-1730), from Eng. to Saybrook, Conn., 1659, later a founder of Norwich, and at Windham, 1693; *m* 1666, Mary (1648-1726), dau. Jonathan Rudd, of New Haven, Conn.

BIRCHARD, Thomas (*d* 1684), came in the "Truelove," 1635; an original propr. of Hartford, 1636; rep., 1650-51; *m* Mary – (*d* 1655).

BISSELL, John (1591-1677), from Eng. to Plymouth, Mass., 1628, settled at Windsor, Conn., before 1640; established "Bissell's Ferry" across Connecticut River, under charter from King Charles, still operated by his descendants; dep. 1648; soldier King Philip's War; capt. of Windsor Troop, 1676; q.m. troop of horse, 1677; *m* Mary Drake (*d* 1641).

BIXBY, Joseph (bap. 1621-1700), from Eng. to Ipswich, Mass., ca. 1640, where held public offices; *m* widow of Luke Hearde.

BLACK, John (1768-1849), Presbyn. minister, ed. U. Glasgow; came from Ireland to Phila., ca. 1797; prof. Western U. Pa.; *m* Elizabeth, dau. Andrew Watters, from Scotland, 1773, soldier in Am. Rev. (*m* Margaret, dau. Alexander Thomson, from Scotland to Pittsburgh, 1784).

BLACKSHAW, Randall (son of Capt. Ralph [?], of Hollongee, Cheshire, who commanded a company under Charles I, and lost in the civil war most of the fortune and estates inherited from his father); came in the "Welcome" with William Penn, 1682; present when Penn signed the Shackawaxon treaty with the Delaware Indians; helped build the first Quaker meeting house in Pa., 1692; *m* Mary Burgess.

BLAINE, James (*d* 1792), from Ireland with his first wife, ca. 1745, settled in Toboyne Tp., Cumberland Co., Pa.; *m* Elizabeth –; *m* 2d, Elizabeth Carskaden.

BLAIR, John (1720-71), from Scotland to Cumberland Co., Pa., ca. 1740; v.p., trustee and first prof. of theology of Coll. of N.J. (Princeton), 1767-71.

BLAISDELL, Ralph (*d* 1650), from Scotland in the "Angel Gabriel," to York, Me., 1635; settled at Salisbury, Mass.; *m* Elizabeth – (*d* 1667).

BLAKE, William (abt. 1594-1663), from Eng. in the "Mary and John," 1630; settled at Dorchester, Mass.; freeman, 1639; selectman, town clk., etc.; a founder of Agawam, Mass.; mem. A. and H. A. Co.; *m* 1617, Agnes (Thorne) Band (1594-1678).

BLAKEMAN, Rev. Adam, D.D. (1598-1665), ed. Christ Coll., Eng.; established 1st ch. at Stratford, and was one of the first settlers there, 1640.

BLAKESLEY (Blakeslee, Blakeslie), Samuel (*d* May 17, 1672), from Eng. with his brother Thomas, in the "Hopewell," ca. 1635; brought their blacksmithing equipment; settled first at Boston Neck; thence New Haven, Conn.; later Thomas went to Woodbury and settled, while Samuel remained at New Haven; *m* Dec. 3, 1650, Hannah, dau. of John Potter, of New Haven, *m* Elizabeth –.

BLANCHARD, Thomas (*d* 1654; desc. of Alain Blanchard, of Rouen, France, 1418, patriot executed by British after surrender at Rouen); came from Lorraine, France, to Eng.; from Eng. in the "Jonathan," to Charlestown, Mass., 1639; was at Braintree, 1646-50; Charlestown, 1651, et seq.; *m* 2d, 1637, Agnes (Bent) Barnes (*d* on voyage); *m* 3d, Mary –, of "Noodle's Island," Boston Harbor.

BLAND, Theodoric (1629-Apr. 23, 1671; son of John [1573-1632], an eminent merchant of London and a member of the Virginia Company); came to Va., 1654, and settled at "Westover," Charles City Co.; speaker House of Burgesses, 1659 and 61, and mem. Council, 1665-71; *m* Ann (*d* 1687), dau. of Richard Bennett (qv).

BLEECKER, Jan Jansen (1642-1732), from Holland to New York at 16 yrs. of age, and settled at Fort Orange (Albany), 1658; Indian commr.; mem. Assembly, 1698-1701; mayor of Albany, 1700-1701; capt. in Indian war, 1684; *m* 1667, Grietjen, dau. Rutger Jacobsen Van Schoenderwoert.

BLISS, Thomas (ca. 1580-1650), from Eng. to Braintree, Mass., 1635; settled at Hartford, Conn., 1639, where he was a propr.; *m* in Eng., ca. 1610, Margaret Lawrence (1594-1684), she removed to Springfield, Mass., after husband's death.

BLODGETT (Blogget), Thomas (1605-42), from Eng. in the "Increase," to Cambridge, Mass., 1635; freeman, 1636; *m* in Eng., Susanna –.

BLOODGOOD (Bloetgoet), Frans Jansen (1635-1676), from Holland to New Amsterdam, 1659; chief officer of Dutch militia, privy councillor to governor for surrender of colony to British, 1675; magistrate, 1673; dep. to New Orange, 1674; *m* in Holland, Lysbeth Jans.

BLOSSOM, Thomas (*d* 1633), from Eng., in 2d voyage of the "Mayflower," 1629 (a passenger in the "Speedwell" which returned to British port, 1620); settled at Plymouth; removed later to Barnstable; a deacon; *m* Ann –.

BOARDMAN (Boreman), Samuel (*b* Banbury, Eng., ca. 1615-*d* Wethersfield, Conn., Apr. 1675), arrived at Boston, 1638; settled at Ipswich, Mass.; at Wethersfield, Conn., 1641; first customs master, 1659; dep. Gen. Ct., 1657, and for 18 yrs.; gov.'s asst., 1676; *m* 1641, Mary (ca. 1623-Aug. 1684), dau. of John Betts.

BODDIE, William (ca. 1635-1717), from Eng. to Isle of Wight Co., Va., 1655; Quaker; received grant of 6,700 acres land from Gov. Berkeley for transporting 134 emigrants; *m* Anne –; *m* 2d, 1679(?), Elizabeth – (1650-99); *m* 3d, Mrs. Mary Edwards.

BOGARDUS, Dominie Everardus (*d* 1637-38), from Holland to New Amsterdam, ca. 1630; 1st pastor of Dutch Reformed Ch. at New Amsterdam; *m* as her 2d husband, Anneke (Webber) Jans (*b* 1605), dau. of Wolfert Webber (*b* 1565), of Holland, said to have been son of William, 9th prince of Orange and later King of Holland.

BOGERT (Bogaert), Jan Laurensz, commonly referred to as Jan Louwe (Lowesen) (born 1630/40), from Holland in the "Bonte Coe," to Bedford, L.I., 1663, settled at Bogert's Point, Harlem, 1672, at New York, 1707; magistrate 1675-76; *m* Cornelia Everts.

BOLLES, Joseph (1608-78), from Eng. to Winter Harbor, Me., ante 1640; removed to Wells, Me.; town clk., 1654-64; *m* Mary – (supposed to have been dau. of Morgan Howell, who bequeathed her all his property, will probated, 1679).

BOLLING, Robert (Dec. 26, 1646-July 17, 1709; son of John, *m* Mary Clarke); from Eng. at 14 yrs. of age, 1660, settled at Kippax, Prince George's Co., Va.; col., Prince George's Co.; burgess; justice of Charles City Co. before 1698; high sheriff, 1699; surveyor, 1702; col. and county lt., 1705-09; *m* 1st, 1675, Jane (*d* 1678), dau. Lt. Thomas Rolfe (son of John, *m* Princess Pocahontas); *m* 2d, 1681, Anne, dau. Maj. John Stith, and widow Jane Parsons.

BOLTWOOD, Robert (*d* 1684), from Eng. to Hartford, Conn., 1648, settled at Hadley, 1659; freeman, 1661; sgt. of militia; operated a corn mill, 1677; *m* Mary Gernon Rice (*d* 1687).

BOND, John (bap. 1624-1674/75), from Eng. ca. 1639; was at Newbury, Mass., 1642; removed to Rowley, 1660, thence to Haverhill; *m* 1649, Esther Blakely (or Hester Blakely).

BOND, Robert (1599-1677), from Kent Co., Eng., to Lynn, Mass., 1635; a founder of Elizabeth, N.J., 1664; *m* Hannah Ogden.

BOND, William (1625-95; son of Thomas; g.son of Jonas); from Eng. with his brothers, John and Thomas; settled at Watertown, Mass.; *m* Sarah, dau. of Nathaniel Biscoe.

BOOGHER, Nicholas (*b* 1690; desc. of Peter Bucher, granted coat of arms, 1450, for mil. service), from Germany in the "Friendship," to Pa., 1727; *m* Katherine –.

BOONE, George (1666-July 27, 1744; son of George, of Bradnich, nr. Exeter, Eng., *m* Sarah Uppey); landed at Phila., Pa., Sept. 29, 1717; settled in Berks Co., 1718; founded and named Exeter Tp.; mem. Gwynedd Monthly Meeting, later of Exeter meeting; landowner; *d* Exeter, Pa.; *m* 1689, in Eng., Mary Milton (1669-Berks Co., Pa., Feb. 2, 1740), dau. of John Maugridge, of Eng., *m* Mary Milton; they were g.parents of Daniel Boone, the pioneer.

BOORAEM (Van Boerum), Hendrick Wilhelmse (*b* 1642), from Holland to Newtown, L.I., 1666; *m* Marie Adrians.

BOOTHE, Richard (1606/07-1688), from Eng., an original settler at Stratford, Conn., 1639; *m* 1640, Elizabeth Hawley (sister of Richard Hawley, qv).

BORDEN, Richard (1595/96-1671), from Eng. with his wife and two sons to Portsmouth, R.I., 1635; surveyor; owned large tracts in R.I. and in Monmouth Co., East Jersey; freeman, Portsmouth, 1641; gov.'s asst., 1653, 54; commr., 1654-57; treas., 1654-55; dep. Gen. Ct., 1667, 70; resident of Gravesend, L.I., 1665; *m* 1625, Joan Fowle (*d* 1688).

BOSTWICK (Bostock), Arthur (Dec. 22, 1603-post Dec. 10, 1680), from Tarporley, Cheshire Co., Eng., to Stratford, Conn., ca. 1640; *m* Jan. 8, 1627, Jane, dau. of Rev. Robert Whittel.

BOSWORTH, Edward, from Eng. in the "Elizabeth Dorcas," 1634; *d* as the ship was entering Boston harbor; his widow and children settled at Hingham, where she *d* 1648.

BOURNE, Richard (*d* 1682), from Eng. to Lynn, Mass., 1637; one of the early settlers at Sandwich, Mass.; dep. General Court; mem. Council of War, 1675; *m* Martha Hallett; *m* 2d, Ruth (Sargent) Winslow.

BOURNE, Thomas (1581-1664), was at Plymouth, Mass., 1637; one of the early settlers at Marshfield, Mass.; dep. Gen. Ct., 1642-45.

BOUTON (Boughton), John, or Jean (1615-1704/05; son of Count Nicholas, Huguenot); from Gravesend, Eng., in the "Assurance," to Boston, Dec. 1635; moved to Danbury, Conn., where he *d*; *m* Joan Turney; *m* 2d, 1656, Abigail (1640-72), dau. of Matthew Marvin (qv); *m* 3d, ca. 1673, Mary –, widow of Jonathan Stevenson.

BOUTWELL, James (ca. 1625-ca. 1651), from Eng., was at Salem, Mass., 1638, *m* Alice –.

BOWDITCH, William (1640-81), from Eng. to Salem, Mass., 1671; collector of the port; *m* Sarah –.

BOWDOIN (Baudouin), Pierre, Huguenot refugee, settled in Mass.; *m* Elizabeth –.

BOWEN, Griffith (*d* bet. 1671-76), from Wales to Boston, ca. 1638; freeman, 1639; later at Roxbury; returned to Eng., and was living at London, 1670; *m* Margaret, dau. Henry Fleming, of Wales.

BOWEN, Richard (1600-75), from Wales to Weymouth, Mass., 1640, with his wife and children, settled at Rehoboth, 1642; dep. Plymouth Gen. Ct., 1651; *m* Ann (or Anna) –; *m* 2d, Elizabeth – (*d* 1675).

BOWIE, John (1688-1759), from Scotland to Md., ca. 1705 or 06; settled nr. Nottingham, Prince George's Co., Md.; *m* 1707, Mary (*d* 1750), dau. of James Mullikin.

BOWIE, John (*d* 1789), from Scotland to Va. ca. 1742, settled on the Rappahannock; *m* 1745, Judith Catlett (*d* 1798).

BOWLES, John (*d* 1680), from Eng. in the "Hopewell," to Roxbury, Mass., 1636; admitted to the church, 1640; mem. A. and H. A. Co., 1645; *m* Elizabeth Heath.

BOWNE, John (1626/27-1695; son of Thomas), from Eng. to Flushing, L.I., 1649; built the old Bowne house there, 1661; *m* 1656, Hannah (ca. 1637-1677), dau. Lt. Robert Feake; *m* 2d, 1679/80, Hannah Bickerstaffe (*d* 1690); *m* 3d, 1693, Mary, dau. James Cock.

BOWNE, John (ca. 1630-1684; son of William), of Salem, Mass,, 1637, Gravesend, L.I., 1645; removed to Monmouth Co., N.J., 1665; one of 12 original patentees of Monmouth Co., 1665; patentee of Middletown, N.J., 1672; commd. as pres. of the ct., to hold a ct. at Middletown and Shrewsbury, N.J., 1677; judge, 1679; justice of the peace, 1679; maj. of militia, 1683; mem. of Assembly, and speaker, 1668, 75, 80, 81, 83; *m* Lydia (bap. 1646), dau. Rev. Obadiah Holmes (qv).

BOWNE (De La Bowne), William (*d* 1677), Huguenot, from Yorkshire to Salem, 1629, to Boston, 1631, to L.I., 1646; patentee of Gravesend and its magistrate 7 yrs.; associate in Monmouth Patent, 1665; mem. Assembly of Patentees and Deputies of N.J., 1669; *m* Anne –.

BOYDEN, Thomas (*b* 1613), from Eng. in the "Francis," 1634, settled at Scituate, Mass.; freeman, 1647; removed to Boston, 1650, and later at Medfield, Watertown and Groton; *m* Frances – (*d* 1658); *m* 2d, Hannah (Phillips) Morse.

BRACKETT, Richard (1611/12-91), was at Boston, Mass., 1632; removed to present site of Quincy, 1639; cdr. militia of Braintree; mem. A. and H. A. Co.; dep. Gen. Ct., 1655-80.

BRADBURY, Thomas (1610-95), was at York, Me., 1634; later at Ipswich, Mass.; an original propr. of Salisbury; ensign and capt. Salisbury Train Band; dep. Gen. Ct., 1651-57; *m* 1636, Mary Perkins (*d* 1700).

BRADFORD, William (bap. 1590-1657), 2d signer of the Mayflower Compact; gov. of the Colony 31 years; asst. 1634 et seq.; *m* 1st, at Leyden, Holland, 1613, Dorothy (1597-1620), dau. John May; *m* 2d, Plymouth, Mass., 1623, Alice (Carpenter) Southworth (1590-1670), widow of Edward Southworth.

BRADLEY, William (1619-91), soldier in Cromwell's army; came to New Haven with Theophilus Eaton, 1637; admitted freeman, 1644; started settlements at Wallingford and North Haven; on standing committee to manage affairs of Wallingford; rep. Gen. Ct. 6 terms; *m* Alice, dau. of Roger Pritchard.

BRADSTREET, Simon (1603-97), from Eng. with Gov. Winthrop, 1630; settled at Andover; first sec. of Colony of Mass. Bay, 1630-36, asst., 1630-78, commr. United Colonies, 1643, 1663-66, dep. gov., 1672-76, gov., 1676-86 and 1689; *m* 1628, Anne (*d* 1672), dau. Gov. Thomas Dudley; *m* 2d, Anna (Gardner) Downing.

BRAINERD (Brainard), Daniel (1641-1715), brought from Eng. to Hartford, Conn., at 8 yrs. of age, 1649; a propr. and settler of Haddam, Conn., ca. 1662; justice of the peace; deacon; dep. Gen. Ct.; *m* 1st, 1663 or 64, Hannah (1641-91), dau. of Gerard Spencer; *m* 2d, Hannah Saxton, widow.

BRANCH, Christopher (1595-1682), Henrico Co., Va.; justice many yrs.; burgess, 1639-41; *m* Mary Adie.

BRANCH, Peter (1601-38), from Eng. in the

"Castle," 1638, but *d* on shipboard; his will was the first recorded at Boston; *m* Elizabeth Gillame.

BRATTON, Capt. Robert (1712-85), from Ireland to Orange (now Augusta) Co., Va., 1733; capt. French and Indian War, 1756-58; mem. council of war for protection of Va. frontier, 1756; owner of 2,284 acres in Augusta Co., and other lands (uncle of Col. William Bratton, comd. at Battle of Huck's Depot, in Am. Rev., whose g.son was Brig. Gen. John Bratton, C.S.A.); *m* Ann (McFarland) Dunlap, desc. of chief of Clan MacFarlane, and widow of Capt. Alexander Dunlap (qv).

BRECKENRIDGE, Alexander (*d* 1744), a Scottish Covenanter, from Scotland via Ireland, 1728, to Phila., Pa., settled in Orange Co., Va., ca. 1739; *m* Jane –.

BREED (Bread, Braid), Allen (1601-92), a Quaker, from Eng., 1630, with Gov. Winthrop, settled at Lynn, Mass.; freeman, 1681; a grantee from the Indians of Southampton, L.I., but did not remain there; *m* 2d, 1656, Elizabeth Knight (*d* 1695).

BRENT, Giles (*b* 1600), treas. Province of Md.; cdr. Kent Island; dep. gov. and lt. gen., 1643-44; lord of Ft. Kent Manor.

BRERETON, Thomas (1720-87, desc. Sir William Bereton, lord high marshal and chief justice of Ireland, under Henry VIII), came from Ireland in command of the privateer "Betty," 1761, settled at Baltimore; *m* 1781, Sarah, dau. Thomas John Marshall, Northampton Co., Va.

BREWER, Daniel (*d* 1646), from Eng. in the "Lion," to Boston, 1632; freeman, 1634; settled at Roxbury; *m* Joanna – (1602-88).

BREWSTER, William (1566/67-1644), 4th signer of the Mayflower Compact; a ruling elder of the church, 1620-44; dep. 1636; chaplain of military co.; *m* before 1593, Mary – (*d* 1627).

BRIDGE, John (1576-1665), was admitted freeman at Cambridge, Mass., 1635; dep. Gen. Ct., 1637, 39, 41.

BRIDGMAN, James (*d* 1676), from Eng. before 1640, to Hartford, Conn., settled at Agawam (Springfield), Mass., 1645; a first settler of Northampton, 1654; *m* Sarah – (*d* 1668).

BRIGGS, Clement (1595-1650), from Eng. in the "Fortune," settled at Plymouth, Mass., 1621; *m* 1631, Joan Allen.

BRIGGS, John (1609-90), was admitted inhabitant of Newport, R.I., 1638; later at Portsmouth and Kingston, R.I.; dep. Gen. Ct., 1664, et seq.; gov.'s asst., 1648; R.I. commr., 1654, et seq.

BRIGGS, Richard, one of the grantors of the town of Taunton, Mass., 1772; *m* 1772, Rebekah Hoskin.

BRIGHAM, Thomas (1603-53), from Eng. in the "Susan and Ellen," 1635; freeman at Cambridge, Mass., 1636; *m* 1637, Mercy Hurd (*b* 1615).

BRINSMADE, John (1617-73), from Eng. 1637, settled at Charlestown, Mass., at Stratford, Conn., 1650, rep. Conn. Gen. Assembly; *m* Mary Carter.

BRINTON, William (1630-1700), from Eng. to Delaware Co., Pa., 1684; mem. and founder of Concord Meeting, Delaware Co., Pa.; *m* ca. 1659, Ann (1635-99), dau. of Edward Bagley.

BRISCOE, John (*b* ca. 1590), from Eng. in the "Ark" and "Dove" expdn., to Md., 1634; *m* Elizabeth Du Bois.

BRODHEAD, Daniel (*d* 1667), from Eng. with his family; officer in army of King Charles, II; on expdn. under Col. Richard Nicholls to take New Netherland, 1664; cdr. garrison at Esopus (Kingston), N.Y., 1665-67; *m* 1660, Anne (*d* 1714), dau. of Francis Tye, *m* Lettos Salmon.

BROKAW (Broucard), Bourgon (*b* 1645), Huguenot, fled from France to Holland, thence to New York, settled at Newtown, L.I., 1675; *m* Catherine Le Febre.

BRONSON (Brownson, Brounson), John (1600-1680), from Eng. to Hartford, Conn., 1636; an original propr. of Farmington, 1641, and dep., 1651; settled at Waterbury, Conn.; soldier in Pequot War.

BROOKE, John (*d* 1699), from Eng. in the "Britannia," 1699, landed in New Jersey, where he and his wife *d* shortly after; *m* Frances –.

BROOKE, Robert (1602-55), of royal descent; B.A., Wadham Coll., Oxford, 1620, M.A., 1624; from Eng. in his own ship with his family and 28 servants, June 30, 1634; settled at de la Brooke Manor, on the Patuxent River, Charles Co., Md.; cdr., 1650; pres. Provincial Council, 1652; acting gov. 1652; *m* Feb. 25, 1627, Mary Baker (*d* 1634; dau. of Thomas Baker, of Battle, Co. Sussex, desc. John Baker, granted arms by Edward III, 1327-77, *m* Mary Engham, desc. Allen Engham, of Parish of Woodchurch, Co. Kent, under King John, 1204-16); *m* 2d, 1635, Mary Mainwaring (*d* Nov. 29, 1663; dau. of Roger Mainwaring, D.D., dean of Worcester, bishop of St. David's, 1636).

BROOKS (Brookes, Brooke), Thomas (ca. 1613-1667), from Eng. in the "Susan and Ellen," to Watertown, Mass., where he was assigned land, 1631; admitted freeman, 1636; removed to Concord, Mass., 1636, where he became a large landowner, 1638, dep. Gen. Ct., 1642-62; capt. 1643; *m* Grace – (*d* 1664).

BROWN, Abraham (1590-1650), from Eng. to Watertown, Mass., ca. 1631; freeman, 1632; *m* Lydia – (*d* 1686).

BROWN (Browne), Chad (*d* ca. 1665), from Eng. in the "Martin," to Boston, 1638; signer of the Providence Plantations Compact; settled at Bapt. Ch., Providence, after Roger Williams, 1642; *m* (before 1638), Elizabeth Sharparrowe.

BROWN, John (1584-1662), from Eng. to Salem, Mass., 1629; lawyer, on of the purchasers of the patent from Sir Henry Roswell; commr. United Colonies, 1644-56; asst., mem. Council of War; with Edward Winslow was patentee of Rehoboth, Mass.

BROWN (Browne), John (1601-1636/37); from Hawkden, Eng., in the "Lion," to Boston, Mass., Sept., 1632; *m* Dorothy –.

BROWN, John (1631-97), from Eng. to Boston, 1632; removed to Falmouth, 1678, later at Watertown; *m* 1655, Esther, dau. Thomas Makepeace.

BROWN, Peter (*d* 1633), 33d signer of the Mayflower Compact; *m* 1st, at Plymouth, Mass., 1624/25, Mrs. Martha Ford (*d* bet. 1627-31); *m* 2d, bet. 1627-31, Mary – (*d* 1634).

BROWNE, Mrs. Christian (*d* 1641), from Eng. 1640, with her three sons, George, William and Henry, to Salisbury, Mass., with its first company of settlers and received grants of land there.

BROWNELL, Thomas (1619-65), from Eng., 1639, to Little Compton, R.I., commr., 1655, 61, 63; dep., 1664; *m* 1638, Ann Bourne.

BROWNING, Nathaniel, from Eng., 1636; settled at Warwick, R.I., 1645; *m* Sarah, dau. of William Freeborn.

BROYLL, John (*d* 1733/34), from Germany to Culpeper Co., Va., 1717; *m* ante 1717, Ursley –.

BRUSH, Thomas (*b* probably ca. 1610-ca. 1675), from Eng., was at Southold, L.I., before 1653, removed to Huntington, L.I., 1656; admitted freeman, 1664; *m* Rebecca, dau. John Conclyne.

BRYAN, Alexander (1602-79), from Eng. to Milford, Conn., 1639; gov.'s asst., 1668-79; *m* Ann – (*d* 1661); *m* 2d, widow of Samuel Fitch.

BRYAN, George (1730-91; son of Samuel, of Dublin, Ireland), came from Ireland to Phila., Pa., 1751; mem. Stamp Act Congress, 1765; a founder of the British Colony, Pictou, in Acadian N.S.; father of the Pa. Constn. of 1776, chief lawmaker of Pa. during Am. Rev.; author of the First General Emancipation of Negro Slaves in History, the Pa. Abolition Act of 1780; pres. Exec. Council; justice Supreme Ct. and High Ct. of Errors and Appeals of Pa.; *m* 1757, Elizabeth Smith.

BRYAN, William, Marquis of Thomond (1655-1742), from Ireland to Isle of Wight Co., Va., 1689; settled on Albemarle Sound, N.C., 1722; high sheriff, and justice of peace, Bertie Co.; mem. Assembly for Pasquotank Co.; *m* 1689, in Eng., Lady Alice (1656-1729), dau. of Lord Needham, Viscount of Killorey.

BRYANT, Stephen, from Eng. to Plymouth, Mass., 1632; constable, 1633; *m* Abigail Shaw.

BUCKINGHAM, Thomas (*d* 1657), from Eng. to Boston, 1637; settled at Quinnipiack (New Haven), Conn., 1638; dep. Gen. Ct., *m* Hannah –.

BUCKLAND, William (*d* 1679), from Eng. in Capt. Barker's ship, 1635; settled at Hingham, Mass., and had land grant, 1636; later removed to Rehoboth where he took the oath of fidelity as freeman, 1658; donated funds for King Philip's War.

BUCKNER, John (ca. 1631-1701), came from Eng. to Gloucester Co., Va., ca. 1667, at which time he acquired a land patent there; vestryman Petsworth Parish, Gloucester, 1671; burgess, 1683; clk. of Gloucester Co.; was instrumental in bringing to Va. the first printing press; collector High Ct. of Admiralty, 1680; clk. of House of Burgesses; *m* 1661, Deborah Ferrers, of Eng.

BUDD, Lt. John (*d* 1678), from Eng. to Hampton, Mass., in the "Swallow," 1633; planter at New Haven, 1639; moved to Southold, L.I.; dep. Gen. Ct., New Haven, 1653; rep. town of Rye, Westchester Co., N.Y., 1666, 68; *m* Kathrine Brown.

BUDD, Thomas (*b* 1646; son of Rev. Thomas, of Somersetshire, Eng.); a Quaker; a propr. Province of Jersey, 1668; author of "Good Order Established in Pa. and N.J. in America," 1683; also of a proposal to create vocational education in the public school and the appropriation of public lands for educational purposes; mem. Assembly, 1682-85; Gov.'s Council, 1682-83; treas., 1683; *m* 1667, Susanna, dau. of William Robinson.

BUDD, William (1649-1722; son of Rev. Thomas [1615-70], of Somersetshire, Eng., matriculated at Merton College, Oxford, 1633, B.A., 1633, M.A., 1636; vicar of Montacute, 1639; became interested in the teachings of George Fox the Quaker; sequestered to the vicarage of Kingsbury, 1646; 4 of his 5 sons came to this country, 1668-84, settling in W. Jersey and Phila.); William settled in Province of West Jersey, 1684-85; mem. N.J. Assembly from Burlington Co., 1685; justice of the peace, 1703, 05, 06; judge of the Supreme Ct., 1705; commd. judge Superior Ct. Common Pleas, Burlington Co., 1705, 06, 14; *m* Ann Claypoole (1652-1722).

BUFFUM, Robert (*d* 1669), from Eng. to Salem, Mass., 1634; mem. Train Band of Salem; *m* 1638, Widow Tamasine Thompson.

BUFORD (Beauford), Richard (*b* 1617), from Eng. in the "Elizabeth," 1635, settled in Christ Ch. Parish, Lancaster Co., Va. (now Middlesex Co.); *m* 1635, a dau. of John Vaulx (or Vause).

BUIST, Rev. George (*b* 1770; son of Arthur, Laird of Pittuncarthy Abernathy, Co. Fife, Scotland), from Scotland to Charleston, S.C., 1793; *m* Mary Somers.

BULKELEY (Bulkley, Buckley), Peter (1583-1659), grad. St. John's Coll., Cambridge, Eng., 1608; came in the "Susan and Ellen," to Cambridge, Mass., 1635, first settler and minister at Concord, and founder of the 12th church in the colony; his library formed the nucleus of Harvard Coll. library; *m* Jane (*d* 1626), dau. Thomas Allen; *m* 2d, 1634, Grace (*d* 1669), dau. Sir Richard Chetwode (or Chitwood).

BULL, Henry (1610-94), from Eng. to Roxbury, Mass., 1635; removed to Boston, 1637, to Portsmouth, R.I., 1638; corp. and sgt., 1638-39; gov.'s asst. 1674-75; gov. of R.I., 1685-86 and 1689-90.

BULL, Thomas (ca. 1606-1684), from Eng. to Boston, 1635; settled at Hartford, Conn., 1636; lt. Pequot War, 1637; capt. of Hartford company in defense of Saybrook, 1675; dep. Gen. Ct., 1648-49.

BULLITT, Joseph (ca. 1653-1692; son of Benjamin Bullett, a Huguenot, who left France after the revocation of the Edict of Nantes, 1685); was settled in Charles Co., Md., before 1676, *m* ca. 1685, Elizabeth, dau. Capt. Randolph Brandt.

BULLOCK, Richard (1622-67), from Eng., 1643/44, settled at Rehoboth, Mass.; freeman, 1646; town clk., 1659-67; excise collector; one of two men appointed to regulate trade with the Indians; *m* 1647, Elizabeth Ingraham (*d* 1659), *m* 2d, Elizabeth Billington.

BUMSTEAD, Thomas (1611-77), from Eng. to Roxbury, Mass., 1640; removed to Boston, 1642; mem. A. and H. A. Co.; *m* Susanna –.

BUNCE, Thomas (1612-83), of Scotch ancestry: a propr. of Hartford, Conn., 1636; soldier in Pequot War, 1637.

BUNKER, George (*d* 1658; son of William, a Huguenot, who went from France to Eng.); came from Eng., 1634; settled at Ipswich, Mass.; original settler at Topsfield, Mass.; *m* Jane Godfrey.

BUNNELL, William (*b* 1617), from Eng., 1638; an early settler at Wallingford, Conn., *m* Annie, dau. of Benjamin Wilmot.

BUNYAN, James (son of William, and g.son of John, author of "Pilgrim's Progress"); of Kingston, Jamaica; was in New York, 1748; merchant; *m* Margaret Grant, of Kingston.

BURCHARD, Thomas (1595-1657), from Eng. in the "Truelove," to Boston, 1635; removed to Saybrook, Conn., 1639, later to Hartford; dep. Gen. Ct.; *m* Mary Andrews (1597-1655).

BURDICK, Robert, from Eng. to Newport, R.I., 1651; freeman, 1655; a founder of Westerly, R.I.; dep. Colonial Assembly; *m* 1655, Ruth (first white child *b* at Agawam), dau. Samuel Hubbard.

BURGAMY, William (1739-1819), from France to Ga. and S.C.; soldier in Am. Rev.; captured by British at Augusta, 1780, but escaped; *m* 1759, Susan Hawkins (1742-1846).

BURGESS, Thomas (1603-85), from Eng. to Salem, Mass., ca. 1630; settled at Sandwich, 1637; was an original mem. of the church there, and dep. Gen. Ct., 1646, et seq.; *m* Dorothy –.

BURGESS, Col. William (1622-86), from Wales, settled in Anne Arundel Co., Md.; mem. Assembly and Council of Md.; col. of foot; justice High Provincial Ct.; cdr.-in-chief Provincial forces; *m* 1st, Elizabeth, dau. of Edward Robins.

BURLINGAME, Roger (ca. 1620-1718), from Eng., was at Stonington, Conn., 1654, settled finally at Meshanticut, R.I., ca. 1660; mem. Town Council; *m* ca. 1663, Mary, dau. John Lippitt.

BURNHAM, John (1618-94), from Eng. in the "Angel Gabriel," 1635, to Ipswich, Mass., soldier in Pequot War.

BURNHAM, Thomas (1623-94; son of Robert, *m* Mary Andrews); came in the "Angel Gabriel," to Cape Cod, Mass., 1635; settled at Ipswich, Mass.; carpenter; surveyor, 1646; propr., 1647; freeman, 1653; corpl., 1662, ens. mil. co., 1675; lt., 1683; signer Ipswich petition, 1681-82; dep. Gen. Ct. from Ipswich, 1683, 84, 85; selectman; *m* 1645, Marie (1624/25-1715), dau. of Thomas Lawrence, of St. Albans, Eng., *m* Joan Antrobus; *m* 2d, Mary, dau. of John Tuttle.

BURR, Jehu (1600-72), from Eng. with Gov. Winthrop, to Roxbury, Mass., 1630; freeman, 1631; a founder of Springfield, 1636; settled at Fairfield, Conn.; rep. Gen. Ct., 1641, 5, 6; commr. United Colonies; *m* – Stedman.

BURR, Jonathan (1604-41), from Eng. to Dorchester, Mass., 1639; died of smallpox; *m* Frances – (1612-82).

BURRAGE, John (1616-85), from England to Charlestown, Mass., ca. 1636; freeman, 1637; *m* 1654/55, Joanna Stowers.

BURRELL, John (bap. 1597-1649), from Eng. to Wethersfield, Conn., ca. 1637-39, later at Milford; *m* 1622, Hester Winchester.

BURSLEY, John (*d* 1660), from Eng. to Weymouth, Mass., 1629; freeman, 1630; removed to W. Barnstable, 1639; *m* Nov. 28, 1639, Joanna Hull, dau. of Rev. Joseph Hull (qv).

BURT, Henry (1615-62), from Eng. to Roxbury, Mass., 1638; settled at Springfield, 1640; mem. first mil. company at Springfield; mem. 1st board of selectmen, 1644; *m* Eulalia – (*d* 1690).

BURT, James (1622-80), from Eng., 1635, settled at Taunton, Mass.; *m* Anna – (d 1665).

BURTON, Boniface (*d* 1730), from Eng. to Lynn, Mass., ca. 1632.

BURWELL, Maj. Lewis (1621-58), from Eng. ca. 1640; settled at Fairfield, on Carter's Creek, Gloucester Co., Va., ca. 1640; *m* Lucy, dau. of Capt. Robert Higginson.

BUSHNELL, Francis (*b* 1576-1646), from Eng. to New Haven Colony, 1638; settled at Guilford, Conn., 1639; *m* Rebecca Holme(?).

BUTLER, Richard (*d* 1684), from Eng. to Cambridge, Mass., 1632; freeman, 1634; a founder of Hartford, Conn., 1636; rep. Gen. Ct., 1656-60; deacon; *m* 2d, Elizabeth –.

BUTLER, Thomas (*b* 1720; 3d son of Edmund, 8th baron of Dunboyne); settled nr. Lancaster, Pa., 1748, where he purchased large tracts of land and founded the first Episcopal Church (St. John's) in that section; *m* Eleanor Parker (their 5 sons were officers Cont. Army).

BUTT (Butts), Robert (*d* 1676; son of Joshua, of Warrington Hall, Kent, Eng.), came from Eng., 1640, settled in Lower Norfolk Co., Va.; *m* Ann Riddlehurst.

BUTTERFIELD, Benjamin (*d* 1688), was at Charlestown, Mass., 1638, at Woburn, 1640; an original propr., at Chelmsford, 1654; *m* Anne – (*d* 1661); *m* 2d, Hannah Whittemore, widow.

BUTTOLF, Thomas (1603-67), from Eng. in the "Abigail," to Boston, 1635; *m* Ann – (ca. 1610-1680).

BUTTON, Matthias (*d* 1672), from Eng. to Salem, Mass., 1628, with Gov. Endicott (qv); at Ipswich, Mass., 1641, *d* Haverhill, Mass.; *m* Lettice – (*d* 1662).

BYLES, William, see William Biles.

BYRD, William (1652-1704; son of John Byrd, of London, *m* Grace, dau. of Capt. Thomas Stegg [*d* 1651], speaker Va. House of Burgesses), came from Eng., 1674; settled nr. the Falls of the James River, Va.; established "Westover"; was burgess, councillor, auditor and receiver-general; *m* 1673, Mary (1652-99), dau. of Col. Warham St. Leger Horsmanden, from Eng., to Charles City Co., Va., was burgess and councillor.

CABANISS, Henri, a Huguenot, from France in the "Mary and Ann," 1687, to Nottaway Co., Va., *m* Marie –, *m* 2d, Magdalene –.

CABELL, William (1699 or 1700-1774), grad. London Coll. of Surgery and Medicine; surgeon in British Navy; settled in Henrico (now Nelson) Co., Va., 1724/25, established "Warminster," 1742, capt. militia, under sheriff, co. coroner, justice, burgess several yrs.; *m* 1726, Elizabeth (1705-56), dau. Samuel Burks, of Hanover Co., Va.; *m* 2d, 1762, Margaret Meredith.

CADWALADER, John (1677/78-1734), from N. Wales to Pa., 1697; freeman, 1705; settled at Merion, Pa.; mem. Common Council and Provincial Assembly; *m* 1699, Martha Jones (*d* 1747).

CALHOUN (Colhoon, Colquhoun), James (1694-ca. 1772), from Ireland with his wife, four sons and one daughter, to Pa., 1733, removed to Wythe Co., Va., to Abbeville Co., S.C., 1756, *m* Catherine Montgomery.

CALKINS (Calkin, Caulkin), Hugh (1600-90), from Wales to New London, Conn., 1638, arrived at Plymouth, Mass., 1640; mem. Conn. Assembly, 1672-83; dep. Mass. Gen. Ct., from Gloucester, New London and Norwich, Conn.; a founder of Gloucester, 1644; *m* Ann –.

CALVERT, Leonard (1606-47; son of George, first Lord Baltimore, and brother of Cecil, second Lord Baltimore), sent as first gov. of Md. by his brother, who had obtained a charter for the colony, 1632; arrived, 1634, with the "Ark of Avalan" and the "Dove"; gov. Palatine of Md., 1633-47; founded St. Mary's, the first capital, 1634; *m* Anne Brent.

CAMP, Nicholas (*b* 1597), from Eng. to Salem, Mass., 1630; a founder of Milford, Conn.; *m* 1st, Sarah Beard (*d* 1645).

CANBY, Thomas (1668-1742; son of Benjamin Canby, *m* Mary Baker), from Eng. in the "Vine," 1683, to Bucks Co., Pa.; mem. Pa. Assembly and justice several yrs.; *m* 1693, Sarah Jerves; *m* 2d, 1709, Mary Oliver, she came from Wales in the "Welcome," with William Penn, 1682.

CANDLER, Daniel, from Ireland to Bedford Court House, Va., ca. 1735; *m* Elizabeth Antony.

CANFIELD, Thomas (*d* 1689), is supposed to have come from France via Eng. to America ca. 1634; with bros., Timothy and Matthew, settled at Milford, Conn., 1639; rep. Gen. Ct., 1674-76; sgt. Milford Train Band, 1669; *m* 1646, Phoebe Crane.

CAPEN, Bernard (1552-1638), from Eng., 1632; original grantee of Dorchester, Mass., propr., 1633; freeman, 1636; his was the first tombstone of the Mass. Bay Colony, and is now preserved by the N.E.H.G.S., Boston; *m* 1596, Joan (*d* 1653, aet. 75), dau. of Oliver Purchase.

CARHART, Thomas (1650-1695/96; son of Anthony, gent., of Co. Cornwall, Eng.); arrived at New York, 1683, as private sec. to Col. Thomas Dongan, gov. Province of N.Y.; removed to Staten Island; apptd. clerk of Richmond Co., 1691; *m* 1691, Mary (*b* 1668), dau. of Robert Lord, *m* Rebecca Stanley.

CARLETON, Edward (1605-51; 5th son of John, of Brightwell Park, Oxon, lord of the Manor of E. Clandon, and desc. Baldwin de Carleton, of Carleton Hall, Cumberland), came from Eng. to Rowley, Mass., 1638; freeman, 1642; rep. Gen. Ct., 1644, 47; returned to Eng., 1651; *m* Eleanor, dau. Sir Thomas Denton.

CARMAN, John, from Eng. with John Eliot (qv), arrived Mass. Bay, Nov. 3, 1631; mem. Mass. Gen. Ct., 1634; one of 12 grand jurors of Essex Co., Mass., July 27, 1636; a founder of Hempstead, L.I.; with Rev. Robert Fordham he purchased land from the natives; received patent, Nov. 16, 1644, from Gov. William Kieft, covering 120,000 acres of land from river to sea, with full powers, civil and political, to organize towns, build forts, establish courts of justice, and to use and exercise the Reformed religion which they professed; freeholder; *m* Florence Fordham.

CARPENTER, Alexander, of Wrentham, Eng.; removed to Leyden (?) because of being a Dissenter; thought to have stopped at Yarmouth for a time.

CARPENTER, William (1576-1659/60), from Eng. in the "Bevis," to Weymouth, Mass., 1638, but returned to Eng. in the same ship, leaving his son William (*b* 1605), who settled at Rehoboth, Mass.; *m* Abigail –.

CARPENTER, William (1605-85), from Eng. to Boston, 1635; an original settler at Providence Plantations; a founder of the 1st Bapt. Ch. in America; *m* Elizabeth, dau. of William Arnold.

CARR, Caleb (1616-95), from Eng. to Newport, R.I., 1638; commr. for Newport, 1654, et seq.; gen. treas. of the colony, 1661; dep., 1664, et seq.; gov.'s asst., 1679, et seq.; justice, 1687-88; gov., 1695.

CARR, George (1599-1682), from London, Eng., 1633, to Ipswich, Mass.; a founder of Salisbury, Mass., 1640; *m* 2d, Elizabeth (*d* 1691), dau. of Rev. Thomas Oliver (qv).

CARRINGTON, George (1711-89; son of Dr. Paul Carrington, from Eng. to the Barbados), came from Bermuda to Goochland Co., Va., abt. 1723; *m* 1732, Anne, dau. Col. William Mayo, who laid out the city of Richmond, Va.

CARROLL, Charles (1660-1720), from Ireland to Md., 1688, as atty. gen. of Md. for Lord Baltimore, *m* 1689, Martha Underwood (*d* 1690); *m* 2d, 1693, Mary (*d* 1742), dau. Henry Darnall.

CARTER, John (~~1620-69~~), from Eng. to Va., 1649, settled at "Corotoman," Lancaster Co., Va.; burgess from Nansemond, 1649, from Lancaster, 1654, 1657-60; mem. Council, 1657-58; col. comdg. expdn. against Rappahannock Indians, 1654; *m* Jane Glyn; *m* 2d, Eleanor Brocas; *m* 3d, Anne, dau. Cleave Carter; *m* 4th, Sarah, dau. Gabriel Ludlow.

CARTER, Thomas (1610-84), grad. St. John's Coll., Cambridge, 1629, from Eng. in the "Planter," to Dedham, Mass., 1635, freeman, 1637, first minister at Woburn, Mass., 1642, *m* 1638, Mary (*d* 1687), dau. George Parkhurst.

CARTER, Capt. Thomas (1630/31-1700), from London, Eng., to Nansemond Co., Va., 1650; later of "Barford," Lancaster Co., Va.; purchased a large plantation on the Rappahannock River; commr. Lancaster Co. Ct., 1663; dep., 1663-65; burgess, 1667; vestryman Christ Ch. and St. Mary's; capt. Lancaster militia, 1667; *m* 2d, 1670, Katherine (1652-1703), dau. of Edward Dale (qv).

CARVER, John (*d* 1621), 1st signer of the Mayflower Compact; 1st gov. Plymouth Colony, 1620-21; *m* Katharine – (*d* 1621).

CARY (Carew), John (*b* 1609 or 10), from Eng. to Plymouth, Mass., 1634, later at Duxbury, and Bridgewater, Mass., where was town clerk; *m* 1644, Elizabeth (*d* 1680), dau. Francis Godfrey.

CARY, Miles (*b* Bristol, Eng., 1620-*d* Warwick Co., Va., June 10, 1667; son of John, of Bristol, *m* Alice Hobson, and nephew of James Cary, of N.E.; desc. Henry Cary, Lord Hunsdon, and was, at time of his death, the heir apparent of the barony); settled in Warwick Co., Va., ca. 1645; royal naval officer for James River; col. and county lt., 1659-67; burgess, 1659-63; mem. Council, 1663-67; lived on an estate known as "Magpie Swamps," obtained from his father-in-law; owned two houses in Bristol, Eng., 2,000 acres in Va., numerous slaves, a mill and a store; *m* ante 1646, Anne, dau. of Capt. Thomas Taylor, burgess, of Warwick Co.

CASSEL, Johannes (1639-91), from Germany with his wife, Mary –, in the "Jefries," 1686; mem. committee of the first Council of Germantown.

CATLETT, Col. John (1630-70), from Kent Co., Eng. to Va. ca. 1650; resided in Essex Co.; col. of militia; magistrate; justice of the peace; commr. to settle boundary line between Md. and Va.; accompanied John Lederer on his 3d exploration of the country west of the Blue Ridge; *m* 1654, Elizabeth W. Slaughter.

CATLIN, Thomas (1612-90), from Eng. to

Hartford, Conn., ca. 1645; settled at New Haven; constable, 1662; often selectman.

CHACE (Chase), William (1595-1659), from Eng. with Gov. Winthrop to Roxbury, Mass., 1630; freeman, 1634; at Scituate, 1645, thence to Yarmouth; *m* in Eng., Mary – (*d* 1659).

CHAMBERLAIN, Edmund, from Eng. to Woburn, Mass., before 1647; removed to Chelmsford, 1655; freeman, 1665; *m* 1647, at Roxbury, Mary Turner (*d* 1669); *m* 2d, at Malden, 1670, Hannah Burden.

CHAMBERLAIN (Chamberlin), William (ca. 1620-1706), from Eng., settled at Woburn, 1648; removed to Billerica, 1654; *m* 2d, Rebecca – (*d* in prison on charge of witchcraft, 1692).

CHAMPLIN, Geoffrey (*d* before 1695), admitted inhabitant of R.I., 1638, freeman 1640, was at Portsmouth, Newport and Westerly.

CHANDLER, William (*d* 1642), from Eng. to Roxbury, Mass., 1637; freeman, 1640; one of original proprietors of Andover; *m* Annis (or Hannah) Alcock (*d* 1683).

CHANNING, John (1684-1731), from Eng. to Boston, ca. 1715; settled at Newport, R.I.; *m* Mary (Antram) Antrim.

CHAPIN, Samuel (Oct. 8, 1598-Nov. 11, 1675; son of John, of Paignton, Devonshire, Eng., *m* Philippa Easton); settled at Roxbury, Mass., 1635; freeman, 1641; removed to Agawam (Springfield), Mass., 1642; deacon; constable, 1645; selectman, 1644-51; commr., 1652; apptd. by Gen. Court of Colony of Mass. Bay to govern there; *m* Feb. 9, 1623/24, Cicely (bap. Feb. 21, 1601/02-Feb. 8, 1682/83), dau. of Henry Penney.

CHAPLINE, Isaac (*b* ca. 1584), ens. Royal Navy; from Eng. in the "Starr," as King's Council under Lord Delaware, 1610; settled in "Chaplaine's Choyce," south side of James River, 1622; *m* ca. 1606, Mary Calvert (*b* ca. 1586), to America, 1622, in the "James" with son John and 4 servants.

CHAPMAN, Edward (*d* ca. 1678), from Eng. to Boston, 1639; grantee of Ipswich, 1642, later at Rowley; *m* Mary (*d* 1658), dau. Mark Symonds; *m* 2d, Dorothy, dau. Richard Swann, and widow of Thomas Abbot, of Rowley, Mass.

CHAPMAN, Robert (1616-85), from Eng. to Boston, 1635; removed to Saybrook, Conn.; served in Pequot and King Philip's wars; dep. Gen. Ct. 43 sessions; gov.'s asst., 1681-85; *m* 1642, Ann (*d* 1685), dau. Thomas Bliss, of Hartford.

CHASE, Aquila (ca. 1618-1670), from Eng. to Mass. before 1640; settled at Hampton, N.H.; at Newbury, Mass., 1646; *m* Ann (1620-87), dau. John Wheeler.

CHASE, William, see William Chace.

CHAUNCY, Charles (bap. 1592-1672), B.A. Trinity Coll., Cambridge U., 1613; from Eng. to Plymouth, Mass., 1637; pastor at Scituate, 1641-53; 2d pres. Harvard Coll., 1654-1671/72; *m* 1630, Catharine, dau. Robert Eyre, of Salisbury, Eng.

CHENEY, John, from Eng. to Roxbury, Mass., ca. 1635; settled at Newbury, 1636; freeman, 1637; selectman; shoemaker; was drowned at Roxbury; *m* in Eng., Martha –.

CHESEBROUGH, William (1594-1667), from Eng. in the "Arbella," with Winthrop's fleet to Boston, Mass., 1630, founder and first white settler of Stonington, Conn.; dep. Colony of Mass. Bay and Gen. Assembly of Conn.; *m* Anne Stevenson.

CHESTER, Leonard (1609-48), from Eng. to Watertown, Mass., 1633; removed to Wethersfield, Conn., 1636; *m* Mary (Sharpe) Wade (or [Wade] Sharpe).

CHEVALIER, Peter (ca. Dec. 1, 1695-1769; son of Jean, Huguenot exile, from Normandy, after the revocation of the Edict of Nantes, 1685, to Flanders, later to Eng. where he, with wife and children, were naturalized, Apr. 1687, *m* Jeanne de Creguy); settled in America, 1715 or 20; *m* Mary Wood.

CHEW, John (1590-1655), from England in the "Charitie," to Jamestown, Va., 1622; was col., burgess from Hog Island and from York Co., and justice from York Co.; removed to Md. ca. 1653; *m* Sarah –.

CHEW, Col. Samuel (1634-77; son of John, qv); col. provincial forces of Md., 1675; mem. Council; burgess, chancellor; sec. Province of Md.; *m* 1658/59, Ann (*d* 1695), dau. of William Ayers, of Nansemond Co., Va.

CHICKERING, Francis (*d* 1658), from Eng., in 1637; freeman at Dedham, Mass., 1640; mem. A. and H. A. Co.; dep. Gen. Ct., 1644-53.

CHILES, Lt. Col. Walter (*d* 1653), from Eng. in his own ship, 1637/38; settled in Charles City Co., Va.; burgess, 1643-46, 49-52; speaker Va. House of Burgesses; mem. Council, 1651; *m* Elizabeth –.

CHILTON, James (*d* 1620), 24th signer of the Mayflower Compact; *m* Susanna – (*d* 1621).

CHIPMAN, John (*b* ca. 1614), from Eng. in the "Friendship," to Boston, 1631; settled at Barnstable, Cape Cod, where he was ruling elder of the church, 1670; *m* 1646, Hope (1629-83), dau. of John Howland (qv).

CHITTENDEN, William (1593-1660/61), from Eng. to New Haven, Conn., 1639; removed to Guilford, and founder of the church there, 1639; trustee of land purchased from the Indians; lt. of Colonial forces; magistrate; rep. Gen. Ct.; *m* Joanna (*d* 1668), dau. Dr. Jacob Sheaffe.

CHOATE, John (1624-95), from Eng. to Ipswich, Mass., 1643; admitted freeman, 1667; *m* Anne – (*d* 1727).

CHOUTEAU, Rene Auguste (1698-1776), from France to New Orleans, La., 1718; formed the firm of Maxent, Laclede & Co., to develop the trade of Upper Louisiana; *m* 1739, Marie Therese Bourgeois.

CHURCH, Richard (1608-68), carpenter, from Eng. in Winthrop's fleet, 1630; settled at Plymouth, 1633, at Charlestown, 1653, Hingham, 1657, Sandwich, 1664; freeman, 1632; soldier in Pequot War; *m* 1636/37, Elizabeth, dau. Richard Warren.

CHURCH, Richard (1610-67; son of Richard, of Braintree, Co. Essex, Eng.); settled at Hartford, Conn., probably ca. 1636, where his name appears on Founder's Monument; drew 12 acres in first land divided, 1639; freeman, 1658; one of sixty persons who founded South Hadley, Mass., 1650; *m* in Eng., 1627, Anne, dau. of Edward Marsh.

CHURCHILL, John (*d* Jan. 1, 1662/63), from Eng. to Plymouth, 1643; *m* Dec. 18, 1644, Hannah (1623 in Eng.-Dec. 22, 1690), dau. of William Pontus, at Plymouth, 1633; she *m* 2d, Giles Ricard, whom she survived.

CHURCHILL, Josiah (ca. 1615-ca. 1686), from Eng., ca. 1636; settled at Wethersfield, Conn., ca. 1641; soldier Pequot War, constable, town surveyor; *m* ca. 1638, Elizabeth (ca. 1616-1700), dau. Nathaniel Foote (qv).

CHURCHILL, William (1649-1710), from Eng., 1669, settled in "Bushy Park," Middlesex Co., Va., on the Rappahannock River; burgess, 1691-92; mem. Assembly, 1704; mem. Va. Council, 1705; warden and vestryman of Christ Ch., Middlesex Co.; *m* 1703, Elizabeth (Armistead) Wormley, dau. of Col. John Armistead (*d* ante 1703), mem. Va. Council, from 1688.

CILLEY, Robert, see Seeley.

CLAFLIN (MackClaflin, MackClaphlan, Macklathlan, MacClaflin), Robert (*d* 1690), from Scotland to Wenham, Mass., 1661; soldier in French and Indian War; *m* 1664, Joanna Warner.

CLAIBORNE (Clayborne), William (1587-1676; son of Edmund Cleborne, of "Cliburn Hall," lord of the manor of Cliburn and Killerby), from Eng. to Va. with Governor Wyatt, 1621; sec. of state of Va., 1625, et seq.; mem Council, 1625-60; made treas. for life, 1642; dep. gov., 1653; comd. against Indians, 1629 and 1644; had one grant of 24,000 acres of land in King William Co., Va.; one of three commrs. apptd. to rule Va. under Cromwell; *m* Elizabeth Butler.

CLAPP (Clap), Roger (1609-92), from Eng. to Dorchester, Mass., 1630; lt. Dorchester mil. company, 1644; 2d sgt., A. and H. A. Co., 1646, lt. 1655; capt. at the Castle, 1665-86; dep. Gen. Ct., 1652-73; *m* 1633, Joanna (1617-95), dau. of Thomas Ford.

CLARK, Daniel (1623-1710), from Eng. ca. 1639, a first settler at Windsor, Conn., 1639; settled at Hartford, 1644; sec. Colony of Conn., 1658-66; asst., 1662, 64, 67; dep. 1657-61; magistrate, 1662-64; named asst. in charter of Charles II; *m* 1644, Mary, dau. Thomas Newberry (qv); *m* 2d., Mrs. Martha Pitkin Wolcott.

CLARK, John (1614-74), from Eng., 1632; admitted freeman, at Newton, Mass., 1632; an original settler at Hartford, Conn., 1636, soldier Pequot War; dep. for Hartford, 1641-44, for Saybrook, 1649-60, for Milford, 1666-68; *m* Mary, dau. John Coley (Cooley); *m* 2d, Mary, dau. of Joyce Ward, and widow of John Fletcher.

CLARK (Clarke) Nathaniel, from Eng. to Newbury, Mass., before 1663; freeman, 1668; *d* on board schooner "Six Friends," in expdn. against Quebec; *m* 1663, Elizabeth, dau. Henry Somerly.

CLARK, Thomas (1599-1697), carpenter, from Eng. in the "Ann," 1623, to Plymouth, Mass.; at Harwich, 1670; rep. Gen. Ct., 1651-55; soldier in Pequot war; *m* Susannah Ring; *m* 2d, Alice Nichols (widow), dau. Richard Hallett; *m* 3d, Elizabeth Crow.

CLARK, William (1609-90), from Eng. in the "Mary and John," 1630, with Matthew Grant, to Nantasket, Mass.; at Dorchester, Mass., before 1635; selectman, 1646, 47; removed to Northampton, 1659; rep. Gen. Ct., 1663 and 13 yrs. more; lt. King Philip's War; co. judge 14 yrs.; one of the incorporators of the First Ch. (Congl.) at Northampton; *m* Sarah Strong (*d* 1675); *m* 2d, 1676, Sarah, widow Thomas Cooper, of Springfield, Mass.

CLARKE, Charles (1721-85), from Eng., was settled in Cumberland (now Powhatan) Co., Va., 1745; *m* Marianne, dau. Abraham Salle.

CLARKE, Hugh (1613-93), from Eng. to Watertown, Mass., 1638; removed to Roxbury, 1657; freeman, 1660; mem. A. and H. A. Co.; *m* Elizabeth – (*d* 1692).

CLARKE, Jeremiah, or Jeremy (1605-52), from Eng. to R.I. ca. 1638; at Portsmouth, 1640; settled at Newport; 1st constable of Newport; was asst. pres., regent and actg. gov., and treas. of R.I. Colony, 1648; *m* Frances (Latham) Dungan (1611-77), dau. of Lewis Latham.

CLARKE, John (1609-76), from Eng. to Boston, 1637; driven from Mass. as a follower of Mrs. Hutchinson, 1638, and was a founder of Newport, R.I.; made treas. of Colony, 1649, and sent to Eng., 1651, to prevail on Council of State to revoke extra powers given to Coddington; dep. gov. R.I. and Providence Plantations, 1669, 70; again agt. in London; wrote book entitled "Ill News from New England"; twice married.

CLARKE (Clark), Joseph (1618/19-ca. 1694), from Eng., 1637; settled at Boston, 1638; removed to Newport, R.I., one of founders of Baptist Church there; gov.'s asst., dep. Gen. Assembly; finally settled at Westerly, R.I.; *m* 2d, Margaret – (*d* 1694).

CLARKSON, Matthew (*b* in Eng., 1666-*d* New York, July 20, 1702); settled in New York, 1685; sec. of Province of New York, 1689-1702; clk. of Council; register and examiner of the Ct. of Chancery; clk. of Supreme Ct. of Judicature and register of the Prerogative Ct.; *m* 1692, Catharine, dau. of Gerrit Van Schaick, of Albany, N.Y.

CLAY (Claye), John (son of Sir John Clay, of Wales); called "The Grenadier"; from Eng. in the "Treasurer," 1613; in Powhatan Co., Va.; resided in Charles City Co., 1624; settled finally nr. Jamestown, Va.; *m* Anne –, who came in the "Ann," 1623.

CLAYTON, John (1665-1737; son of Sir John); from Eng. to Va., 1705; was atty. gen., recorder, burgess, etc.; *m* Anne Page.

CLAYTON, William (son of Thomas); from Chichester, Eng., in the "Kent," to N.J., 1677, settled at Burlington; one of several commrs. from London sent out by proprs. of N.J. to purchase land from the Indians; moved to Pa. nr. Chester; mem. Provincial Council, presided at 1st meeting under govt. of William Penn; actg. gov. of Pa., 1684-85; mem. Gov.'s Council during drafting of Great Charter; he and Daniel Francis Pastorious were first two judges of Phila.; *m* Prudence –.

CLEEVE, George (ca. 1575-ca. 1667), from Eng.; first settler at Casco (now Portland), Me.; gov. Province of Lygonia, Me., 15 yrs.; *m* Joan –.

CLEMENT (Clemens, Clements, Clemence), Robert (bap. Dec. 14, 1595-*d* Sept. 29, 1658), from Eng., 1642, with three sons and two daughters, settled at Haverhill, Mass., where he was justice and asso. judge for Norfolk Co.; *m* 1st, ante 1615, Lydia – (*d* 1642); *m* 2d, ante 1657, Judith – (*d* 1669).

CLEVELAND, Moses (1624-1701/02), from Eng., 1635; settled at Woburn, Mass., 1641; freeman, 1643; served in King Philip's War; *m* 1648, Ann Winn (ca. 1626-ante 1682).

CLINTON, Charles (1690-1773), from Ireland to Mass., 1729; settled at New Britain, N.Y., ca. 1732, *m* Elizabeth Denniston.

CLOPTON, William, immigrant; from Eng., settled in York Co., Va., 1655, later in St. Peter's Parish, New Kent Co., constable of Hampton Parish; mem. Council; *m* Ann (Booth) Dennett (1647-1716), dau. of Robert Booth.

COALE, William (*b* Bristol, Eng., 1592-*d* 1669), Quaker minister, from Eng., 1618, settled in Va., later in Anne Arundel Co., Md.; *m* Hester –; *m* 2d, Hannah – (*d* 1669); *m* 3d, Elizabeth, dau. Philip Thomas.

COATES, Thomas (1659-1719), from Eng. to Phila., Pa., 1683; *m* 1696, Beulah Jacques.

COBB, Henry (1596-1679), from Eng. to Plymouth, Mass., ca. 1629; at Scituate, 1633; a founder of Barnstable, 1639; a deacon; rep. Gen. Ct., 1645-51; *m* 1631, Patience Hurst (*d* 1648); *m* 2d, 1649, Sarah, dau. Samuel Hinckley.

COBURN (Colborne), Edward (1618-1700), came in the "Defense," 1635; settled at Ipswich, Mass., over 30 years; removed to Dracut; settled on North side of Merrimac River; *m* Hannah –.

COCKE (Cox) Richard (1600-65), from Eng. to Henrico Co., Va., ca. 1627; lt. col., Henrico Co., 1632; sheriff; burgess from Weyanoke, 1632, from Henrico Co., 1644-54; patented 3,000 acres on James River, Henrico Co., 1636; *m* 1st, an English lady; *m* 2d, ca. 1647, Mary, dau. of Walter Aston (qv).

CODD, Col. St. Leger (g.son of Sir Warham, of royal descent); mem. Va. Company; came to Va., thence to Md.; *m* Anna, dau. of Richard Bennett, colonial gov. of Md., and widow of Governor Bland.

CODDINGTON, William (1601-78), from Eng. with Winthrop's fleet, 1630; returned to Eng. but came again to Boston, 1633; removed to Newport, R.I., 1636; asst. Mass. Bay Colony, 1630-37; treas., 1634-36; dep. from Boston, 1636-37; chief exec. of Adquidneck, 1638, of Newport, 1639-40; gov. of Portsmouth and Newport, 1640-47; gov.'s asst., 1647; pres. of four united towns, 1648-49; commr., 1656-63; dep., 1666; gov.'s asst., 1666-67; dep. gov., 1673-74; gov., 1674-76, 78.

CODMAN, Robert (*d* 1678), from England to Charlestown, Mass., 1630.

CODRINGTON, Simon, mem. Va. Company, 1615; said to have been the "First individual Englishman to own in his own right a foot of land in America"; his grant from the Va. Co., according to memorandum now preserved in the British museum, was for 100 acres of land, and bore the date Mar. 6, 1615; *m* Agnes, dau. of Richard Seacole, of Didmarton.

COE, Robert (1596-1672), from Eng. to Watertown, Mass., 1634; moved to Wethersfield, Conn., 1635; a founder of Stamford, Conn., 1640; removed to Hempstead, L.I., 1652, later to Newtown, and a founder of Jamaica, L.I., 1658; dep. Gen. Ct., 1653; magistrate, Jamaica, 1662; *m* Mary –.

COFFIN, Tristram (1605 or 09-1681; son of Peter Coffin, *d* 1628; son Nicholas Coffin, *d* 1613), came from Eng., 1642; at Salisbury, and Haverhill, Mass., 1642, removed to Newbury, ca. 1648; returned to Salisbury, 1654/55; a founder of Nantucket, 1660, where he was chief magistrate, 1671, commissioner, 1655; *m* ca. 1630, Dionis Stevens (*d* after 1682).

COGGESHALL, John (ca. 1581-1647), from Eng. with his wife and three children, to Roxbury, Mass., 1632; freeman, 1632, removed to Boston, 1634, where he was selectman and dep. Gen. Ct.; settled at Providence Plantations, 1637; pres. Colony and Providence Plantations, 1647; gov.'s asst., 1640-44; moderator, 1647; *m* Mary – (1604-84).

COGSWELL (Coggeswell), John (1592-1669; son of Edward, *m* Alice –); from Westbury Leigh, Eng., in the "Angel Gabriel," to Ipswich, Mass., 1635; *m* 1615, Elizabeth (*d* 1676), dau. of Rev. William Thompson, first minister at Braintree, *m* Phyllis –.

COIT (Coyte), John (*d* 1659), shipwright, from Wales to Mass. ca. 1634; granted land at Salem, Mass., 1638; removed to Gloucester, 1644, to New London, Conn., 1650; selectman, 1648; *m* Mary Jenners (1596-1676).

COLBURN, Edward, see Coburn.

COLDEN, Cadwallader (1687-1776; son of Rev. Alexander, of Berwickshire, Scotland), grad. U. Edinburgh, 1705; came to Phila., Pa., where he practiced medicine until 1718, when he removed to N.Y. City; lt. gov. and acting gov.; *m* Nov. 11, 1715, Alice Christy, of Scotland.

COLEMAN, Thomas (1598-1674), from Eng.,

1630; an original propr. of Hadley; *m* 2d, Mrs. Frances Wells (*d* 1674).

COLES, John (1677-1747), from Ireland to Va., 1710, with his bro. William; reputed to have built first house where Richmond now stands; father-in-law of President Madison and of John Payne; *m* Mary Ann, dau. of Isaac Winston of Va., *m* Mary Dabney.

COLES, Robert (1598-before 1655), from Eng. to Roxbury, Mass., 1630; removed to Ipswich, 1633; a founder of Providence, R.I.; dep. Gen. Ct.; *m* Mary Hawkhurst.

COLEY (Cooley), Samuel (*d* 1684), from Eng. to Mass. Bay Colony, 1631; an original settler at Milford, Conn., 1639; joined church, 1640; *m* Ann, dau. of James Prudden.

COLGATE, Robert (1758-1826), from Eng. to Harford Co., Md., 1795; settled in Delaware Co., N.Y.; *m* Mary Bowles.

COLLINS, Edward (1603-89), from Eng., settled at Cambridge, Mass., 1638; freeman, 1640; dep. Gen. Ct., 1654-70; mem. A. and H. A. Co.; deacon; *m* in Eng., Martha –.

COLLINS, Henry (1606-87), from Eng. in the "Abigail," with his family and servants to Lynn, Mass., 1635; mem. Salem Ct.; selectman, etc.; *m* Ann – (*b* 1605).

COLT (Coult), John (*d* 1730), from Eng. to Dorchester, Mass., 1625; removed to Hartford, Conn., 1638, thence to Windsor, *m* Mary Fitch.

COLTON, George (*d* 1699), from Eng. to Springfield, Mass., 1644; later at Longmeadow; q.m. Hampshire Co. troop, 1663; served in King Philip's War; dep. Gen. Ct., 1669, 71, 77; *m* 1644, Deborah Gardner (*d* 1689).

COMBES (Combs, Coombs, Combe, Coomes), Richard, from Eng. before 1690, settled at Hempstead, N.Y.; *m* Elizabeth –.

COMSTOCK, William (1595-1683), from Eng. to Wethersfield, Conn., 1637, later at New London; soldier in Pequot War; *m* 1625, Elizabeth – (1608-post 1665).

CONANT, Roger (bap. 1592-1679), from Eng. in the "Ann," to Plymouth, Mass., 1623, with his wife and son Caleb; removed to Nantasket (Hull), to Gloucester, 1625, to Salem, where he built the first house, 1626; freeman, 1630; gov. Colony of Cape Ann, 1625-26, Salem, 1627-29; rep. Gen. Ct., of Mass., 1634; *m* 1618, Sarah Horton.

CONDIT (Cunditt), John (*d* 1713), from Eng. or Wales with his son Peter, 1678; settled at Newark, N.J.

CONKLIN (Conkling, Conklyne), Ananias (ca. 1600-1684), from Eng. to Salem, Mass., 1638; removed to Southhold, L.I., 1650, to Huntington, L.I., 1653; established first window-glass works in America.

CONOVER, Wolfert Gerretse, see Couwenhoven.

CONVERSE (Conyers, Convers), Edward (1590-1663; son of Christopher, *m* Mary Halford); from Eng. to Mass., 1630, with Gov. Winthrop; settled at Salem; granted land at Charlestown, 1631; a founder of Woburn; granted first ferry to Boston, 1631; selectman at Salem, 1635-40; deacon; dep. Gen. Ct., 1660; *m* Jane Clark (*d* ante 1617); *m* 2d, in Eng., 1617, Sarah – (*d* Jan. 14, 1662).

CONWAY, Edwin (ca. 1610-1675), from Eng., 1640; settled in Lancaster Co., Va., where he was a large landed proprietor; *m* 1st, Martha, dau. of Richard Eltonhead.

COOK (Cooke), Aaron (1610-90), from Eng. to Dorchester, Mass., 1634; removed to Windsor, Conn., 1636, to Northampton, Mass., 1661; a propr. of Westfield, 1667; mem. of Windsor Troop of Horse, 1658; maj. Hartford Troop, 1658; capt. in King Philip's War; dep. Gen. Ct., 1668; *m* 1637, Joanna Ford.

COOK (Cooke), Ellis (ca. 1618-79), went from Lynn, Mass., abt. 1644, and settled at Southampton, L.I., ca. 1644; *m* Martha (1630-after 1690), dau. John Cooper (*b* 1594), from Eng. in the "Hopewell," 1635.

COOK (Cooke), Walter (*d* 1694/95), from Eng. ante 1643, settled at Weymouth, Mass.; freeman, 1653; a founder of Mendon, Mass., 1663; propr. and selectman; *m* Experience –; *m* 2d, Catherine –.

COOKE, Francis (ca. 1583-1663), 17th signer of the Mayflower Compact; *m* at Leyden, Holland, 1603, Hester Mahieu, a Walloon and Huguenot (*d* bet. 1666-75).

COOLEY (Coley), Benjamin (1620-84), from Eng. to Mass., ca. 1630; settled at Longmeadow; selectman, 1646; ensign Hampshire regt.; *m* 1642, Sarah –.

COOLEY, Samuel, see Coley.

COOLIDGE, John (1604-91; son of William, of Cottenham, Cambridge, Eng.), came from Eng. to Watertown, Mass., ca. 1630; freeman, 1636; selectman, 1639, and later; dep. Gen. Ct., 1658; *m* Mary (Wellington) Maddock.

COOPER, William (1649-1709), Quaker, from Snapt, Yorkshire, Eng., to Bucks Co., Pa., 1699; at his house was held the first Quaker meeting in Bucks Co. 1700; *m* ca. 1672, Thomasin –.

COPE, Oliver (ca. 1647-97), from Eng., with William Penn on his 2d voyage, and settled at "Backington," on Naaman's Creek, New Castle Co., Pa., now in Del., 1683; *m* Rebecca – (*d* 1728).

CORBIN (Corbyn), Clement (1626-Aug. 1, 1696, aet. 70), from Eng. to Roxbury, Mass., 1638; settled at Muddy River before 1655; at Woodstock, Conn., 1687; *m* Dorcas Bookmaster (1629-1722).

CORBIN, Henry (1629-Jan. 8, 1676), of London; draper; came to Md. in the "Charity," 1654; settled in Lancaster Co., Va.; established "Buckingham Lodge," on South side of Rappahannock River, also owned "Pickatone" in Westmoreland and "Corbin Hall," in Middlesex; justice of Lancaster Co., 1657; vestryman, Christ Ch., Middlesex; burgess Lancaster Co., 1658-60; mem. Council, 1663; justice Middlesex, 1673; *m* ca. 1655, Alice (*d* ca. 1684), widow of Rowland Burnham, and dau. of Richard Eltonhead, of "Eltonhead," Lancaster Co., Va.

CORLISS, George (1617-86; son of Thomas), from Eng., settled at Newbury, Mass., ca. 1639; moved to Haverhill, built a loghouse in "West Parish," 1647, the farm was later known as "Poplar Lawn"; *m* 1645, Joanna Davis (their dau. Mary [1646-1722], *m* 1663, William Neff [*d* 1689, aet. 47], captured, 1697, with Mrs. Hannah Emerson Dustin, by a party of 12 Indians and carried off toward Can., they, Mrs. Dustin, Mrs. Neff, and Samuel Leonardson, a youth captured previously, rose in the night, Mar. 30, and killed 10 out of the 12 Indians, with the scalps they returned to Haverhill and later went to Boston; they were rewarded by the Gen. Ct. of Mass. with money and grants of land; two monuments were erected to their memory, one in Haverhill and the other, a duplicate, on Dustin's Island, see Vol. II, p. 135).

CORNELL (Cornil), Thomas (ca. 1595-ca. 1655/56), from Eng. with the 2d Winthrop expdn. to Boston, 1636; removed to Portsmouth, R.I., 1654, and was freeman there; settled at Flushing, L.I., 1643; ensign Portsmouth militia, and served under Gov. Kieft against Indians; *m* Rebecca Briggs (1600-73).

CORNING, Samuel (*d* 1694), from Eng., was at Salem, Mass., 1638; later at Beverly, Mass., where he founded a church, 1667; *m* Elizabeth –.

COTTON, John (1585-1652), grad. Cambridge U., 1606; from Eng. in the "Griffin," to Boston, 1633; teacher of first Ch. in Boston; freeman, 1634; author of nearly 50 books; *m* 2d, in Eng., Sarah (Hankredge) Story.

COURSEN, Peter (ca. 1577-1648), a Huguenot refugee to New Amsterdam, N.Y., progenitor of the Corson-Coursen family in America.

COUWENHOVEN (Van Couwenhoven, or Conover), Wolfert Gerretse, from Holland, 1630; as overseer of farms for the Patroon Van Rensselaer; freeholder in Midwout, 1637, 41; commr. from the colony to Holland, 1653; schepen of New Amsterdam, 1654; great burgher, 1657; *m* Neeltje –.

COWLES (Cole), John (1598-1675), from Wales to Mass., 1635; settled at Hartford, Conn., 1636, at Farmington, 1640, at Hadley, Mass., 1664; dep. Gen. Ct., 1653-54; *m* Hannah – (*d* 1684).

COX, Richard (1600-65), see Richard Cocke.

COX, Thomas (*d* 1681), from Eng., was at Marshpath Kills, at head of Newtown Creek, L.I., 1665; a patentee of Monmouth tract, East Jersey; settled at Middletown, N.J., 1665; founder Bapt. Ch., Middletown; overseer, deputy, town agent; with three others, was chosen to make prudential laws for the newly formed settlement of Middletown, 1668; received 240 acres, 1675, 269 acres, 1676; juryman; dep. to meet gov. and council at Woodbridge, 1676; *m* 1665, Elizabeth Blashford.

CRANE, Henry (1621-1709), from Eng. to Dorchester, Mass., 1654; *m* Tabitha Kinsley; *m* 2d,

1655, Elizabeth, dau. of Stephen Kinsley, of Milton, Mass.

CRANE, Henry (1635-1711), settled at Wethersfield, Conn., 1655; at Guilford, 1664, later at Killingworth; one of the first settlers of what is now Clinton, Conn.; gov.'s asst. and dep. Gen. Ct.; *m* Concurrence Meigs.

CRANE, Jasper (1590-1680), from Eng. to Mass. about 1635, an original propr. of New Haven, Conn., 1639; a first settler of Newark, N.J., 1666; magistrate; rep. Gen. Ct., 1653-58; gov.'s asst., 1662-67; dep. Provincial Assembly of East Jersey, 1667-73; *m* Alice –.

CRANSTON, John (1626-80), arrived in Newport ante 1644; capt. and maj. of militia; capt. of all forces of the Colony in King Philip's War; atty. gen.; gov. 1678; licensed and recorded Doctor of Physic and Chirurgery; *m* 1658, Mary (1641-1711), dau. of Jeremy Clarke (qv).

CRESAP, Thomas (1702-88), from Yorkshire, Eng. to Md., 1715; col. Cont. Army, founder of "Sons of Liberty," first patriotic society in U.S.; surveyor; noted Indian fighter; burgess; col. of the Provincials, 1730-70; *m* 1726, Hannah Johnson; *m* 2d, Mrs. Milburn (*d* Old Town, Md., 1788).

CROCKER, William (1612-92), from Eng. to Scituate, Mass., ca. 1634; removed to Barnstable, 1639; rep. Gen. Ct., 1670, 71, 74; *m* Alice –.

CROSBY, Thomas (ca. 1575-1661), from Eng. to Cambridge, Mass., 1640, settled at Rowley, 1641; *m* 1600, Jane (bap. 1581-1662), dau. William Sotheron.

CROSMAN, Robert (*d* 1692), from Eng. before 1642, settled Dedham, Mass.; mem. A. and H. A. Co.; *m* 1652, Sarah Kingsbury, of Dedham, Mass.; *m* 2d, 1687, Martha Eaton, of Bristol, Mass.

CROSS, Robert (1612-93), from Eng. in the "Mary and John," 1635, settled at Ipswich, Mass., 1639; soldier in Pequot War; *m* – (*d* 1677).

CROW, John (1606-85; son of John), came in the "Lion"; a first settler of Hartford, Conn.; moved to Hadley, Mass., but later returned to Hartford; *m* Elizabeth, dau. of Elder Goodwin, who also came in the "Lion."

CROWNINSHIELD (von Kronsheldt), Johannes Caspar Richter (*d* 1711), came to Lynn, Mass., ca. 1670; *m* Elizabeth, dau. of Jacob Allen.

CULVER, Edward (1600-85), a Puritan, from Eng., 1635, a founder of Dedham, Mass., 1636, later at New London, Conn.; served in Pequot, Narragansett and King Philip's wars; *m* 1638, Anne, dau. of John Ellis.

CUMMINGS (Cummins), Isaac (1600-77), from Scotland to Topsfield, Mass., ca. 1630; removed to Watertown, Mass., 1636; propr. at Ipswich, Mass., 1639.

CUNNINGHAM, Andrew (1654-1735), from Scotland to Boston, ca. 1680; glazier; *m*, at Boston, 1685, Sarah, dau. William Gibson.

CURTIS (Cuttris), Henry (*d* 1678), from Eng. to Watertown, Mass., 1635; an original propr. of Watertown, 1636, of Sudbury, 1639; *m* 1640, Mary, dau. of Nicholas Guy.

CURTIS, John (1577-1640), from Eng. in the "Lion," to Boston, 1632, thence to Roxbury, Mass.; *m* 1610, Elizabeth Hutchins (*d* 1658).

CURTIS (Curtiss), William (*d* 1702), from Eng. to Roxbury, Mass., 1632, settled at Stratford, Conn., 1649; capt. Stratford Train Band, also Fairfield forces; mem. Com. of Safety, 1673; dep. Gen. Ct.; *m* Mary Morris; *m* 2d, Sarah, widow of William Goodrich.

CURTIS, William (1592-1672), from Eng. in the "Lion" to Roxbury, Mass., 1632; freeman, 1633; settled at Stratford, Conn.; *m* Sarah Eliot (1600-73), sister of Apostle John Eliot.

CUSHING, Matthew (1588-1660), from Eng. in the "Diligent," to Hingham, Mass., 1638; *m* in Eng., 1613, Nazareth (1586-1681), dau. Henry Pitcher.

CUSHMAN, Robert (1580-1625), a leader and financial agt. at Leyden of the Mayflower Pilgrims, was a passenger in the "Speedwell," which was compelled to return to Eng., but came in the "Fortune," 1621, but returned to Eng. one month later; *m* 1606, Sarah Rider; *m* 2d, at Leyden, 1617, Mary Singleton, who came to Plymouth with her family after 1625.

CUTLER, James (1606-94), from Eng. to Watertown, Mass., 1634; removed to Cambridge; at Lexington, 1651; soldier King Philip's War; *m* Anna – (*d* 1644); *m* 2d, 1645, Mary, widow of Thomas King; *m* 3d, Phebe, dau. John Page.

CUTLER, John (1600-38), from Sprauston (Norwich), Eng.; a founder of Hingham, Mass., 1635, and settled there permanently, 1637; *m* 1625, Mary – (*d* 1681).

CUTLER, Richard (1621-93), from Eng. with his mother, Elizabeth; was freeman at Cambridge, 1641; mem. A. and H. A. Co.; officer Cambridge militia.

CUTTING, Leonard (1724-94), from Eng. to New York, 1750; pastor at New Brunswick, N.J., Hempstead and Oyster Bay, L.I.; prof. King's Coll.; *m* a dau. of John Pintard, alderman of New York.

DABNEY (d'Aubigné, Daubeny), Corneille (1667-1700), Huguenot, from France to Wales after the revocation of Edict of Nantes, thence to New Kent Co., Va., ca. 1722; *m* 2d, 1721, Sarah Jennens (or Jennings).

DAGGETT (Dogget, Doggett, Dogett), Thomas (1607-Aug. 18, 1692), from Eng. in the "Mary Anne," of Yarmouth, Eng., to Salem (or Concord), Mass., May 1637; resided at Weymouth for a time; settled in Marshfield, Mass., 1652; farmer, selectman, juryman, constable, surveyor; *m* 1st, – (*d* June 23, 1642 at Concord, Mass.); *m* 2d, 1643, at Weymouth, Elizabeth (Humphrey) Fry (*b* Eng.-*d* Weymouth, Mass., 1652; widow of William Fry; dau. of Jonas Humphrey, of Dorchester, Mass., *m* Frances –); *m* 3d, at Marshfield, Aug. 17, 1654, Joane Chillingsworth (*b* prob. Eng.-*d* Marshfield, Sept. 4, 1684; widow of Thomas Chillingsworth).

DAINGERFIELD, William (desc. Sir Philip, of Co. Worcester, Eng.); English gentleman, came to Essex Co., Va., before 1660; established "Greenfield"; *m* Frances –;

DALE, Maj. Edward (*d* Feb. 2, 1695), from Eng. to Lancaster Co., Va., among the royalists who sought refuge in Va., after the death of Charles I, 1649/50; justice; 1st clk. Westmoreland Co., Va., 1653; clk. Lancaster Co., Va., 1665-74; maj. of militia; high sheriff, 1670-80; burgess, 1677, 82-83; *m* Lady Diana (*b* Prestwould, ca. 1625), dau. of Sir Henry Skipwith (*b* 1589), knight and baronet of Prestwould, Leicestershire, Eng., *m* Amy Kempe.

DANA, Richard (1612-90), from Eng. to Cambridge, Mass., ca. 1640; propr. 1644; extensive landholder; progenitor of the Dana family in N.E.; *m* Ann, dau. of Robert Bullard, landowner, Watertown, Mass.

DANFORTH, Nicholas (ca. 1585-1638), from Eng. to Cambridge, Mass., 1634; rep. Gen. Ct., 1636-37; *m* Elizabeth Symmes (*d* 1629).

DANIEL, Col. William (ca. 1640-*d* 1698), of Wiggan Co., Lancastershire, Eng.; col. of a regt. of foot in Scotland, and gov. of the garrison and citadel of Ayre, Scotland; to Portugal, served in battle of Evora against Don John of Austria; came to Va. with Maj. Gen. Robert Smith, 1663; received land grant, Middlesex Co., 1669, in Lancaster, 1672; justice, Middlesex Co., 1684; vestryman, Christ Ch., 1669; capt. in Middlesex militia, 1689; *m* Dorothy, dau. and heiress of Hugh Forth, of Wiggan Co., Lancastershire, Eng.; *m* 2d, Jochebid –; all children *b* by first wife.

DARCY, Edward, see Dorsey.

DARNALL, Col. Henry (*d* 1711; son of Philip), came to Province of Md., 1672; held estate "The Woodyard"; was collector port of St. Mary's; col. of horse; dep. gov. of Md.; *m* Elinor, dau. of Richard Hatton, and widow of Thomas Brooke.

DAVENPORT, John (1597-1670), grad. Magdalen Coll.; as a non-conformist fled to Holland, 1633, thence to Boston, in the "Hector," 1637; a founder of New Haven, Conn., 1638; pastor First Ch., Boston, 1668-70; *m* Elizabeth Wolley (1603-76).

DAVENPORT, Thomas (ca. 1589/90-1685), from Eng. to Dorchester, Mass., 1638; joined church, 1640; freeman 1642; constable; *m* ca. 1610, Mary Forth (bap. 1589/90-1691).

DAVIS (Davies), David, from Wales to Newcastle, Del., 1760, brought by his father, who purchased 30,000 acres from William Penn; one of the founders of the Welsh Tract, Pa.

DAVIS, Dolor (1593-1673), master builder, from Eng. to Cambridge, Mass., 1634, settled at Duxbury, 1635, Barnstable, 1643, and again in 1666; Concord, 1655-66; petitioner for the grant of the Town of Groton, 1656; one of the twenty of the Plymouth Colony who had lands granted to them at Concord, Mass., 1658; sec. to 1st colonial gov. of Mass. Bay Colony; *m* Margery Willard (sister of Lt. Simon Willard, of Kent, Eng.); *m* 2d, 1671, Mrs. Joanna Bursley.

DAVIS, Samuel, Presbyn. minister, came under auspices of Soc. for Propagation of the Gospel in Foreign Parts, 1692, settled at Lewes, Sussex Co., Del.; *m* Mary Simpson.

DAVIS, William (1617-83), from Eng. ca. 1635, was at Roxbury, Mass.; freeman, 1673; *m* Elizabeth – (*d* 1658); *m* 2d, Alice Thorp (*d* 1667); *m* 3d, Jane – (*d* 1714).

DAWES, William (1620-69; son of William, who came to America, 1628, but later returned to Eng.); bricklayer; came in the "Planter," to Braintree, Mass., 1635; freeman, 1646; settled at Boston, 1652; *m* Susanna, dau. of John Mills.

DAY, Anthony (1617-1707), from Eng. in the "Paule," 1635; an original settler at Leominster, Mass.; later at Salem and Ipswich.

DAY, Robert (1604-48), from Eng. in the "Elizabeth," 1634, to Cambridge, Mass.; freeman, 1635; an original settler of Hartford, Conn., 1636; *m* in Eng., Mary –; *m* 2d, Editha, sister of Dea. Edward Stebbins.

DEANE (Dean), Walter (ca. 1615-1693), from Eng. to Dorchester, Mass., 1636; freeman at Taunton, 1637; rep. Gen. Ct.; selectman; *m* in Eng., Eleanor, dau. of William Cogan.

DE COURCY, Col. Henry (1620-95), from Eng. with Leonard Calvert, to Md., 1634; sec. of Md., 1660-61; chief justice of provincial cts.; col. comdg. forts of Cecil and Kent cos., 1670, 76, 81; burgess, Talbot Co., Md., 1694-95; mem. Gov.'s Council, 1660, 70, 76, 84; *m* Elizabeth (Smith) Carpenter.

DeFOREST (DeFrees), Jesse (ca. 1575-1624), Walloon leader of the Huguenots, from France, recruited the first band of colonists for New Amsterdam; led another expdn. to South America, 1623; *m* 1601, Marie du Cloux.

de GRAFFENRIED, Christopher (*b* Switzerland-*d* Oct. 27, 1742; son of Landgrave, Baron Christopher V, who visited America, founded New Bern, S.C., *m* Regina Tscharner); "brought over a colony of Swiss Palatines to North Carolina in 1709"; after marriage "moved first to Phila., to Maryland, and lastly to Va.," settled permanently in Prince Edward Co., Va., maintaining a town house in Williamsburg; *d* on his plantation on the James River; *m* Feb. 22, 1714, at Charleston, S.C., Barbara (Needham) Tempest (1688-June 26, 1744), dau. of Sir Arthur Needham of Wymondsley, Hertfordshire, Eng.

DeKAY, Willem (1606-68; son of Guillaume de Kay, director in Dutch West India Co.); came from Holland to New Amsterdam before Gov. Kieft, was fiscal or treas. of the colony, 1641.

DELAFIELD (de la ffelde), John (1748-1824?), from Eng. in the "Vigilant," to New York, 1783; was a founder and pres. Mutual Ins. Co., and of United Ins. Co., large landowner; established "Sunswyck" on the East River opposite Blackwell's Island; was created count of the Holy Roman Empire; *m* 1784, Ann (1766-1839), dau. Joseph Hallett.

De la MONTAGNE, Dr. Johannes, Huguenot physician, from Holland to New Amsterdam, 1637; *m* Rachel Monjour.

DELANO (de la Noye, de Lannoye), Philippe (bap. Leyden, Holland, Dec. 7, 1603-*d* Bridgewater, Mass., 1681); from Holland in the "Fortune," to Duxbury, Mass., 1621; soldier Pequot War; *m* Hester Dewsbury; *m* 2d, 1657, at Duxbury, Mary (Pontus) Glass (*b* Leyden, ca. 1625-*d* Feb. 2, 1690), widow of James Glass.

DEMING, John (ca. 1615-ca. 1705), from Eng. to Wethersfield, Conn., 1635; rep. Gen. Ct. 50 sessions; one of the patentees named in the Royal Charter of Conn., 1662; *m* 1637, Honour, dau. Richard Treat (qv).

DENISON (Denyson), William (1586-1653/54; son of John Denyson [*d* 1582], of Bishops Stortford, Eng., *m* Agnes –); came in the "Lyon," 1631, bringing his three sons, Daniel, Edward and George, and their tutor, Rev. John Eliot (qv); settled at Roxbury, Mass.; freeman, 1632; dep. Gen. Ct., 1635; mem. Roxbury militia, 1636; *m* in Eng., Nov. 7, 1602, Margaret (Chandler) Monck (*b* Eng., 1586-*d* Roxbury, Feb. 23, 1645), who came in 1632.

DENNIS, John (1612-79), from Eng. in "Ye Merchants Hope," to Va., 1635, settled in Northumberland Co., ca. 1651.

DENT, Thomas (1628-76), from Eng. to St. Mary's Co., Md., 1650; was high sheriff and justice county ct.; *m* Rebecca, dau. of Rev. William Wilkinson.

DENTON, Richard (1586-1662/63), grad. Cambridge U., 1623; from Eng., 1630; was at Watertown, Mass., 1634, at Wethersfield, Conn., 1635, at Stamford, 1641-44, later at Hempstead, L.I.; founded Congl. church at Stamford and said to have been the founder of Presbyterianism in America.

DE PEYSTER, Johannes (1620-85), a Huguenot, from Holland to New Amsterdam, 1645; cadet of Burgher Corps at New Amsterdam; burgomaster, dep. mayor of New Amsterdam and New York, and commissioner; *m* Cornelia Lubberts.

DERBY, Roger (1643-89), from Eng. to Boston, 1671; removed to Ipswich; settled at Salem, Mass., 1681; was a chandler; *m* in 1668, Lucretia Hillman (*d* 1689); *m* 2d, Elizabeth (Hasket) Dynn, dau. Stephen Hasket, and widow of William Dynn.

DEVEREUX, John (ca. 1615-ca. 1695), from Eng. to Salem, Mass., bet. 1630-36; at Marblehead, 1637; freeman, 1683; owned the Devereux Farm, celebrated in Longfellow's poem, "Driftwood"; *m* Ann – (*d* 1708, aet. 88).

DEWEY, Thomas (*d* 1648), from Eng. to Boston, 1631; settled at Dorchester; freeman, 1634; settled at Windsor, Conn., 1635; cornet of the troop; *m* 1638/39, Frances –, widow of Joseph Clark.

DE WOLF, Balthasar (1623-96), was at Hartford, Conn., 1654, settled at Lyme, Conn., 1664; mem. militia; *m* Alice –.

DEXTER, Gregory (1610-1700), from Eng., 1644, settled at Providence, later at Warwick, R.I.; clergyman; commr., 1651-54; pres. of the colony, 1653-54; dep. Gen. Ct., 1654-55; *m* Abigail Fullerton.

DEXTER, Thomas (*d* 1677), from Eng., was at Sudbury, Mass., ca. 1638; admitted freeman, 1640; was the first white settler at Marlborough, Mass., ca. 1657; soldier King Philip's War; *m* Mary –.

DICKINSON, Nathaniel (1600-76), from Eng. to Watertown, Mass., 1634; removed to Wethersfield, Conn., ca. 1636; town clk., 1645; to Hadley, Mass., 1659; served in Hampshire Guard; a founder of Hopkins Acad.; deacon; dep. Gen. Ct., 1642; *m* in Eng., 1630, Anna –, widow of William Gull.

DIMMOCK (Dimmick, Dymoke), Elder Thomas (*d* 1658 or 59), from Eng., settled at Dorchester, Mass., 1635, at Hingham, 1638, Scituate, 1639, Barnstable, 1640; *m* Ann (*d* 1683), dau. of Wm. Hammond, and g.dau. of Sir William Penn (father of William Penn, of Pa.).

DINGLEY, John (1608-58), from Eng. to Lynn, Mass., 1637; removed to Sandwich, 1637, to Marshfield, 1644; *m* Sarah –.

DOANE, John (1591-1686), from Eng. to Plymouth, Mass., 1630; removed to Eastham, 1644; gov.'s asst., 1632, 33, 39; mem. Plymouth mil. company, 1643; dep. Gen. Ct., 1639-42 and 1649, et seq.; *m* Abigail –.

DODGE, Richard (ca. 1602-1672), from Eng., 1629, and settled at Salem, Mass.; donated large sum to Harvard Coll., 1653; a founder of Beverly, Mass., 1667; *m* Edith – (1603-78).

DODGE, William (1605-90), from Eng. in the "Lyon's Whelp," 1629, to Salem, Mass.; freeman, 1637; a founder of church at Beverly.

DOGGETT, Thomas, see Thomas Daggett.

DOLE, Richard (1622-1705), from Eng. to Parker River, old Newberry, Mass., 1639; dep. 1673; *m* in 1647, Hannah Rolfe (*d* 1678); *m* 2d, 1679, Hannah, widow of Capt. Samuel Brocklebank.

DOOLITTLE, Abraham (1619/20-1690), from Eng., was at Boston, 1640; removed to New Haven, Conn., 1644, to Wallingford, Conn., 1670; dep. Gen. Ct. from New Haven and Wallingford; mem. Vigilance Com. in King Philip's War; *m* Joane Allen (1625-61); *m* 2d, 1663, Abigail Moss.

DORR, Edward (1647/48-1733/34), from Eng. to Rowley, Mass., 1674; selectman; *m* 1st, 1679, Elizabeth (1656-1719), dau. Thomas Hawley.

DORSEY (Darcy), Edward (*d* 1681, from Eng. to Anne Arundel Co., Md., 1650; *m* Ann –.

DOTY, Edward (*d* 1655), 40th signer of the

Mayflower Compact; in the "First Encounter," 1620; *m* 2d, at Plymouth, Mass., 1635, Faith (*d* 1675), dau. Tristram Clark.

DOUGLAS, William (1610-82), came with his wife and two children to Gloucester, Mass., 1640; freeman at Boston, 1640; settled at New London, Conn., 1659, rep. Gen. Ct.; *m* Ann (*d* 1685), dau. of Thomas Mattle.

DOW, Henry (1608-ante 1661), from Eng. to Watertown, Mass., ca. 1638; dep. Gen. Ct., 1655-56; *m* Joan Hudd.

DOWD (Doude, Dowde, Dowdy), Henry (*d* in 1668), from Eng. to Guilford, Conn., 1639; *m* Elizabeth – (*d* 1683).

DOWS (Dowse), Lawrence (1613-92), from Eng. to Charlestown, Mass., 1640; *m* 1st, Martha – (*d* in 1644); *m* 2d, Margery Rand.

DRAKE, John (1600-59; son of William); from Devon Co., Eng., to Boston, 1630; settled at Windsor, Conn., ca. 1639; *m* Elizabeth Rogers (*d* 1681).

DRAKE, Thomas (bap. 1635-1691), from Eng. to Weymouth, Mass., 1653/54, served in King Philip's War; *m* Jane, dau. Thomas Holbrook, of Weymouth; *m* 2d, 1681, Mellicent (Ford) Carver, dau. William Ford.

DRAKE, William, of Weymouth and Marshfield, Mass.; *m* 1620, Margaret Westover.

DRAPER, James (1618-94; son of Thomas Draper); a Puritan, came from Eng. bet. 1647-50, settled at Roxbury, Mass.; *m* 1646, Miriam Stansfield (1625-97).

DRAYTON, Thomas, from Eng. to the Barbados, thence to Cape Fear River, N.C., 1671; settled at Drayton Hall, on Ashley River, nr. Charleston, S.C., ca. 1680.

DRINKER, Philip (1596-1647), from Eng. in the "Abigail," to Charlestown, Mass., 1635; freeman, 1637; kept the first ferry over the Mistick River, 1640; *m* Elizabeth – (*b* 1603).

DRURY, Hugh (1616-July 6, 1689), from Eng. to Boston, Mass.; lt. colonial wars; *m* ca. 1645, at Sudbury, Mass., Lydia (*b* Barkhamstead, Co. Herts., Eng., 1627/28-*d* Boston, Apr. 5, 1675), dau. of Edmund Rice (qv).

DU BOIS, Louis (1626-95; son of Christien, Huguenot, of Lille, France); came in the "St. Jean Baptiste," to New Amsterdam, 1661; a patentee of New Paltz, N.Y., 1664; mem. first Ct. of Sessions; led expdn. against Indians, 1663; *m* at Mannheim, Germany, 1655, Catherine Blanshan.

DU BOSE (Du Boce), Isaac, a Huguenot, from France to Jamestown, on south side of Santee River, nr. Charleston, S.C., ca. 1689, after the revocation of the Edict of Nantes; *m* Suzanne Couillaudeau.

DUDLEY, Francis (1640-living 1702), settled at Concord, Mass.; *m* 1665, Sarah (1640-1713), dau. of George Wheeler, of Concord.

DUDLEY, Thomas (bap. Yardley, Hastings, Northants, Eng., Oct. 12, 1576-buried Roxbury, Mass., July 31, 1653), came in the "Arbella"; dep. gov. Colony of Mass. Bay 13 yrs., gov.'s asst. 7 yrs., and gov., 1634, 40, 45, 50; commr. United Colonies, 1643, 47, 49; lt. col., Suffolk Co., Mass., 1636; commr. of mil. affairs, 1636; founder of Harvard Coll., 1637; name on new charter of Harvard Coll., 1650; pres. of the Confederacy, 1643, 47, 49; *m* in Eng., Apr. 25, 1603, Dorothy Yorke (*b* Eng., 1582-buried Roxbury, Dec. 27, 1643); *m* 2d, 1644, Catherine –, widow of Samuel Hackburne.

DUER, William (1747-99; son of John, one of his majesty's council for Antigua, *m* Frances, dau. Gen. Frederick Frye, of Brit. Army), served with Lord Clive in India, came to New York, ca. 1768; del. Cont. Congress. asst. sec. of the treas.; *m* Lady Catharine, dau. Maj. Gen. William Alexander, Earl of Stirling (*m* Sarah, dau. Philip Livingston, 2d lord of the manor).

DUNHAM, Hon. and Dea. John (1588/89-1668), in Plymouth Colony ante 1631; was elected dep. Gen. Ct., Plymouth, 1639-64; mem. Council of War; dea. of ch. at Plymouth under Elder Brewster; was a widower with 3 children when *m* at Leyden, Holland, Pilgrim Colony, 1622, to Abigail, dau. of Thomas Bailliou, *m* Anne –, probably Huguenot refugees as the name occurs frequently in publications of the Huguenot Soc. of London, and is identified with Baliol, Scotch King, and with Bella Aqua, of ancient Eng. Abigail Bailliou, was still resident at Leyden, witness at marriage of a sister, June 1624.

DUNLAP, Capt. Alexander (1716-44), from Ireland to Augusta (now Rockridge) Co., Va., and also came to Augusta Co., Va., Capt. James and William Dunlap (these three leaving many distinguished descendants), and to Knoxville, Tenn., came Hugh Dunlap (Knoxville's first mcht., and among whose sons were Gen. Richard Gilliam Dunlap, Sec. of War of the Republic of Texas, and William Claiborne Dunlap, M.C., Tenn.), all four immigrants being related; was capt. of horse, 1743; first settler in the Pastures region of the Valley of Va.; grantee by orders of council of lands (unpatented) on Greenbrier river, (now) W.Va.; *m* Ann McFarland (*b* Scotland), said to have been desc. of a chief of Clan MacFarlane (she *m* 2d, Capt. Robert Bratton).

DUNSTER, Rev. Henry (bap. 1609-*d* 1659/60), grad. Magdalen Coll., Cambridge, Eng., B.A., 1630, M.A., 1634; came to Boston, 1640; first pres., Harvard Coll., 1640-54, and for several yrs. its sole teacher; settled at Scituate, 1654; *m* 1641, Elizabeth (ca. 1627-1690), probably dau. of Hugh Atkinson, of Eng.

DU PONT de Nemours, Pierre Samuel (1739-1817), ex-pres. Constituent Assembly and of the Counceil des Anciens, of France; sec. Provisional French Govt., 1814, statesman and author, arrived at Newport, R.I., with his sons, Jan. 1, 1800; *m* Nicole-Charlotte-Marie-Louise Le Dee de Rencourt (or Roccourt) (1743-1874).

DU PUY, Barthelemy (1653-1743), captain of Household Guards, of Louis XIV; in battles in Flanders; escaped to Germany, 1685, at revocation of Edict of Nantes; to England, 1699, to Virginia 1700; *m* Countesse Susanne La Villian.

DURAND, John (1667-1727), Huguenot, from France to New York, 1694; settled at Milford, Conn., 1696; surgeon in expdn. to Can., 1709; *m* ca. 1698, Elizabeth, dau. of Richard Bryan.

DURANT, George (*b* Eng., Oct. 1, 1632), in Mar. 1661, Kelcokomer, great Indian chief of Yeopims deeded to him for a "valuable consideration" a tract of land bearing the name of Wecameke (a peninsula now called Durant's Neck), this is the earliest recorded deed in history of N.C.; with Samuel Pricklove, established 1st permanent settlement in N.C. at Durant's Neck, 1661; atty. gen., Grand Council, Albemarle Co., 1679; resided at Durant's Neck, 1691; an acknowledged leader in public affairs; with Culpeper led the Culpeper rebellion against unjust restriction of trade; *m* Jan. 4, 1658, Ann Marwood, of North Cumberland Co., Va.

DURYEA (Durje), Joost (*d* 1727), a Huguenot, from France to New York, ca. 1675; *m* Magdalena Le Febvre.

DUVAL (Duvall, Du Val), Mareen (*d* 1694), a Huguenot refugee, settled in Anne Arundel Co., Md., on land patented to him by Lord Baltimore ca. 1655; commr. for laying out towns, 1683; *m* 2d, Susanna –; *m* 3d, Mary Stanton.

DWIGHT, John (*d* 1660), from Eng. to Watertown, Mass., 1634, settled at Dedham, 1635, and founded the Church of Christ; was one of the five trustees of the first free school in America supported by a town tax, 1644; *m* Hannah – (*d* in 1656); *m* 2d, 1658, Elizabeth (*d* 1660), widow of William Ripley.

DYER (Dyar, Dyre), William (*d* 1667), from Eng. to Boston, 1635; disarmed as a supporter of Wheelwright, 1637, disfranchised and driven from the colony, 1638; one of 18 original proprs. of R.I.; sec. Providence Plantations, 1639; col. of R.I., 1640-42; gen. recorder, 1647-48; commr. at Newport to act against the Dutch, 1648; commr. to the Assembly from Providence, 1655, from Warwick, 1661, from Newport, 1662; *m* Mary – (executed, 1660, on Boston commons, for preaching Quakerism).

EAMES, Anthony (1595/96-1686), from Eng., was a propr. of Charlestown, Mass., 1634; removed to Hingham, 1636, to Marshfield, 1650; dep. Gen. Ct., 1637-38, 43; capt., Hingham mil. company, 1644-45.

EAMES (Ames), Thomas (1618-80), from Eng. ca. 1634; settled at Dedham, 1640, finally on Mount Wayte, Framingham, Mass.; *m* Margaret –; *m* 2d, Mary, dau. of John Blamford, and widow of Jonathan Paddlefoot; she and five children killed by Indians and four other children captured in King Philip's War, of whom Samuel escaped.

EARLE, Sir John (1614-60; son of Sir Richard, of Dorset Co., Eng.), from Eng., ca. 1649-52, with his wife and three children, and for paying the passage of 34 persons received land grants aggregating 1700 acres located on Earle's Creek and Yeocomico River, now Westmoreland Co., Va., which, exclusive of other patents subsequently granted by the lords proprietors of the Northern Neck, descended in a single male representative for 100 yrs.; *m* Mary Symons (1619-59).

EARLE (Earl), Ralph (*b* Aug. 25, 1605-*d* 1678; son of Ralph, *m* Margaret Browne); came to Boston, 1634; at Newport, R.I., 1638; at Portsmouth, R.I., 1649, later a townsman of Dartmouth, Mass.; was one of the petitioners for a charter, 1638; capt. of troops, 1667; *m* in Eng., Apr. 22, 1632, Joan (bap. 1609), dau. of Richard Savage.

EASTMAN, Roger (bap. Charleton, Eng., Apr. 4, 1610-*d* Salisbury, Mass., Dec. 16, 1694; son of Nicholas, of Charleton, *m* Barbara –); came in the "Confidence," 1638, settled at Salisbury; *m* Sarah (Smith?) (1621-97).

EASTON, Nicholas (1593-1675), *b* Wales; came to N.E. with his two sons, Peter and John, 1634; was at Ipswich, Mass., 1634; removed to Newbury, 1635; built the first house at Hampton, 1638; settled in R.I., 1638, and built the first house at Newport, 1639; pres. of R.I., 1650-51 and 1654; dep. gov., 1670-71; gov. under royal charter, 1672-1674.

EATON, Francis (*d* 1633), 23rd signer of the Mayflower Compact; *m* 1st, Sarah – (*d* 1621); *m* 2d, probably Governor Carver's maid servant; *m* 3d, at Plymouth, Mass., 1624 or 25, Christian Penn (*d* ca. 1684), she *m* 2d, Francis Billington.

EATON, John (1611-58), from Eng. in the "Elizabeth and Ann," 1635; freeman at Watertown, Mass., 1636; surveyor of boundaries; built bridge across St. Charles River; removed to Dedham, 1637; *m* 1630, Abigail Darmont.

EATON, Theophilus (1590-1657; son of Rev. Richard, vicar of Great Budworth, Cheshire, Eng.); with Rev. John Davenport to Boston, 1637; a founder of Quinnipiack (New Haven), Conn.; gov., 1639-57; *m* 2d, in Eng., 1619, Ann, widow of David Yale and dau. Thomas Morton, bishop of Chester.

EATON, Col. William (1680-1749), from Leicester, Eng., to nr. Petersburg, Va.; settled in Edgecombe Co., N.C., ca. 1739; high sheriff; mem. N.C. Colonial Assembly; *m* Mary Rives.

EDDY, Samuel (1608-88; son of Rev. William Eddy, ca. 1550-1616, vicar of St. Dunstans, Cranbrook, Eng., *m* Mary Fosten), came from Eng. in the "Handmaid," with his brother, John, to Plymouth Colony, 1631; settled finally at Swansea, Mass.; *m* Elizabeth – (1601-82).

EDES, John (Mar. 31, 1651-1693; son of John, of Essex Co., Eng.; g.son John [*d* Apr. 12, 1658], A.B., St. John's Coll., Cambridge, 1610, M. A., 1614, rector, 41 yrs.; g.g.son Henry of Bocking, Co. Essex, Eng.); came from Lawford, Co. Essex, Eng., to Charlestown, Mass., 1655; King Philip's War; *d* Middlesex, Mass.; *m* 1674, Mary, dau. of Peter Tufts (qv).

EDSALL, Samuel (1630-1706), from Eng. in the "Triall," to Boston, 1648; settled at New Amsterdam, 1655-68; founder of Bergen, N.J.; mem. Council, Province of East Jersey, 1668, and Province of N.Y., 1689-91; Indian interpreter, New Castle on the Delaware, 1675-76; *m* 3d, Ruth, dau. of Richard Woodhull (1620-90), of Setauket, L.I., from Eng. ante 1648, *m* Debora –).

EDSON, Samuel (bap. Fillongley, Warwickshire, Eng., Sept. 5, 1613-*d* July 19, 1692; son of Thomas, *m* Elizabeth Copson); came to Salem, Mass., ca. 1639; removed to Bridgewater, 1650; *m* in Eng., 1638, Susanna Orcutt (1618-Feb. 20, 1699, aet. 81);

EDWARDS, William (1620-85), from Eng., with his mother and step-father, Cole, to Hartford, Conn., 1639; freeman, 1658; *m* Agnes, widow of William Spencer.

EELLS (Ells, Eels, Eales), John (1575-1653), from Eng. to Dorchester, Mass., 1629; freeman, 1634; removed to Hingham, and in 1645 to Newbury; called the "beehive maker."

EGGLESTON, Begat (1590-1674), from Eng. in the "Mary and John," to Dorchester, Mass.; removed to Windsor, Conn., 1635; an original member of Warehams Church (second Congl. church organized).

ELDERKIN, John (ca. 1612-1687), from Eng., 1637; built first merchant vessel ever owned in New England; went to Lynn, Dedham, Reading, Providence, New London, building churches, mills and other buildings; finally settling in Norwich, Conn., where he died; *m* Abigail –.

ELIOT (Elliot, Elliott), Andrew (1627-1704), from Eng. to Beverly, Mass., 1670; dep. Gen. Ct.; served in expdn. against Canada; *m* Grace Woodier.

ELIOT, Rev. John (1604-90), grad. Jesus Coll., Cambridge U., 1622; came from Eng. in the "Lyon," to Boston, 1631; teacher of the church at Roxbury, 1632; known as the "Apostle to the Indians"; *m* 1632, Hanna Munford (or Mountford).

ELIOT, Philip (1602-57; brother of Rev. John), from Eng., was admitted freeman at Roxbury, Mass., 1636; mem. A. and H. A. Co.; col., Mass. militia; dep. Gen. Ct., 1654-57; commr. for Roxbury.

ELLERY, William (1643-96), from Eng., settled at Gloucester, Mass.; *m* Hannah Vinson.

ELLICOTT, Andrew (*d* 1766), from Eng., 1730/31 to Bucks Co., Pa., inventor, clock and astronomical instrument maker; *m* Mary Fox.

ELLIS, Richard (bap. 1600-1694), from Eng. in the "Lion," to Boston, 1632; an original propr. of Dedham, 1636; ensign and lt.; dep., 1692-93; *m* Elizabeth French.

ELLSWORTH, Josiah (1629-89), from Eng., 1645, settled at Windsor, Conn.; *m* 1654, Elizabeth, dau. Thomas Holcomb.

ELLYSON, Hon. Robert, M.D. (*b* in Eng.), established in Md. ante 1643; sheriff, St. Mary's Co., 1643; removed to James City Co., Va.; burgess from that co., 1656, 1659-61, 63; magistrate; militia officer.

ELTINGE, Jan (*b* 1632; son of Roelof), from Holland to New Amsterdam; was settled on L.I., 1663; apptd. judge Court of Sessions of Ulster Co., N.Y., 1675; *m* 1677, Jacomyntje, dau. of Cornelis Barentse Slecht, who was at Esopus, N.Y., 1655.

ELY, Nathaniel (1605-75), from Eng. to Cambridge, Mass., 1632; freeman, 1635; an original propr. of Hartford, Conn.; constable, 1639; a settler of Norwalk, 1651; rep. Gen. Ct., 1657; finally settled at Springfield, Mass., 1659; *m* Martha – (*d* 1688).

ELY, Richard (1610-84), from Eng. to Boston, ca. 1660; a merchant; settled at Lyme, Conn.; *m* Joane Phipps (*d* 1660); *m* 2d, 1664, Elizabeth, widow of John Cullick, and sister of Col. George Fenwick.

EMERSON, Michael (1627-1715), from Eng. to Haverhill, Mass., 1656; *m* Hannah, dau. of John Webster, *m* Mary Shatswell.

EMERSON, Thomas (1584-1666), from Eng. in the "Elizabeth Ann," ca. 1635; settled at Ipswich, Mass., 1638; *m* Elizabeth Brewster.

EMERY (Emmerie, Emory), Anthony (1600-90), from Eng. in the "James," to Boston, 1635; removed to Newbury, Mass., thence to Dover, N.H., 1644, to Kittery, Me., 1648; freeman, 1652; selectman, 1652-59; constable, 1658; resident of Portsmouth, 1662; dep. Gen. Ct., 1672; rep. Gen. Assembly, 1680; *m* Frances –.

EMERY, John (1598-1683; son of John, *m* Agnes –); came in the "James," 1635; settled at Newbury, Mass.; freeman, 1641; selectman, 1661; surveyor of highways, 1668, 80; presented by grand jury for entertaining Quakers, the deposition alleging that "two mennequakers wr entertained very kindlie to bed and table & John Emmerie shok ym by ye hand and bid ym welcome"; *m* in Eng., Mary – (*d* 1649); *m* 2d, 1650, Mary (Shatswell) Webster.

EMLEY, William (*b* in Eng., 1648-1704), arrived in the "Kent," 1677; one of commrs. to buy West Jersey land from Indians; returned to America with family in the "Shield," 1678, and settled nr. present site of Trenton; mem. West Jersey Gen. Assembly; justice; land commr.; mem. Council; surveyor; boundary commr., boundary between N.Y. and N.J., 1687; *m* Ruth (Stacy?).

EMMONS (Emons), Thomas (*d* 1664), from Eng. to Newport, R.I., ca. 1638; freeman at Boston, 1652; *m* Martha –.

ENDICOTT, John (1589-1665), from Eng. in the "Abigail," to Salem, Mass., 1628; one of the 6 original purchasers of Mass. Bay from the Plymouth Council; named in the Royal Charter as one of the eighteen, and was named by his associates at London as head of 1st settlement at Salem; col. 3d Regt. Mass. Militia in first expdn. against the Pequot Indians, 1636; gen. in command of Block Island expdn., 1636; maj. gen., 1645-49; dep. gov., 1641, and gov. most of time, 1644-65; pres. United Colonies, 1658; *m* in Eng., Ann Gower; *m* 2d, 1630, Elizabeth Gibson.

EPPES, Francis (*d* 1655), from Eng. to Prince George Co., Va., 1635; settled on lands at the junction of the James and the Appomattox rivers, still owned by the family; lt. col. Va. troops; burgess, 1625-32; justice for Charles City Co., 1639-45; mem. Royal Council, 1652.

ERSKINE, Christopher (1701-75; desc. John Erskine, Earl of Mar, of Scotland), came from Scotland to Abingdon (Bridgewater), Mass., 1725; *m* Susannah Robinson (1714-89).

ERWIN (Irwin), Nathaniel (1713-94), from North Ireland to Phila., Pa., 1740; moved to Bucks Co., Pa., finally settled in York Co., S.C.; *m* 1733, Leah Julian.

EUSTIS, William (*d* 1694); whose name first appeared on the tax list of Romey Marsh (now Chelsea), Mass., 1674; was at Charlestown, later at Malden, and at Boston; *m* Sarah – (1639-1713).

EVANS, Thomas (1651-1738; son of Evan ap Evan of Wales, and desc. Conan Tyndaethy, king of Wales, who died 818); came to Gwynedd, Delaware Co., Pa., 1698; *m* Ann –.

EVERETT, Richard (*d* 1682), with his first wife, from Essex Co., Eng., to Cambridge, Mass., ca. 1634-35; with William Pynchon in settlement among the Indians on the Conn. River, 1636; settled at Dedham; freeman, 1646; constable and selectman; *m* 1st, Mary – (issue: six children); *m* 2d, 1643, Mary Winch (issue: five children).

EWEN, Col. Richard (*b* Eng.-*d* post 1674), to Md., 1649, probably Anne Arundel Co.; one of Cromwell's commrs.; mem. Severn's Provincial Council; speaker lower house; justice Anne Arundel Co.; sheriff; asst. cdr., regt.; *m* Sophia –.

EWING, Nathaniel (ca. 1692-1748), from Ireland to Cecil Co., Md., 1725; *m* his cousin, Rachel Porter.

EWING, Robert (*d* 1787), from Ireland with his brother Charles, to Bedford Co., Va., bet. 1735-47; in Lord Dunmore's war; *m* Mary (*b* 1730), dau. of Caleb Baker, *m* Catherine Hodwill; *m* Mary Baker.

EWING, Thomas (1695-1748), from Londonderry, Ireland, emigrated to Long Island, 1718; settled at Greenwich, West Jersey; *m* Mary Maskell.

FAIRBANKS (Fairbank), Jonathan (*d* 1668), from Eng. with four sons in the "Speedwell," to Boston, 1633; settled at Dedham, 1636, and built there the house, still standing, said to be the oldest dwelling in America; *m* 1617, Grace Smith.

FAIRCHILD, Thomas (ca. 1610-1670), from Eng., a founder of Stratford, Conn., 1639, and was first magistrate of the town; dep. Gen. Ct. of Conn., 1646, served 11 sessions; apptd. by the Gen. Ct. to press men for the Narragansett expdn.; *m* Emma, dau. of Robert Seabrook; *m* 2d, 1662, Catharine Craig, a widow.

FAIRFAX, William (1691-1757), from Eng. to the Bahamas, 1718, came to Salem, Mass., 1725; was Va. agt. for his cousin, 6th Lord Fairfax, 1733, established "Belvoir," Fairfax Co., Va., 1735; was burgess and pres. Colonial Council; *m* 1723, Sarah, dau. Thomas Walker; *m* 2d, 1731, Deborah (1708-44), dau. Francis Clarke.

FARNSWORTH, Matthias (1612-89; son of Joseph, *d* 1660); of Lynn, later of Groton, Mass.; *m* Mary (*d* 1717), dau. of George Farr, *m* Elizabeth Stower.

FARNUM, Ralph (1603-93), from Eng., in the "James," 1635, settled at Ipswich, Mass.; *m* Alice–.

FARWELL, Henry (*d* 1670), from Eng., one of original settlers of Concord, Mass., 1639; freeman, 1639; removed to Chelmsford; *m* 1629, Olive Welbie.

FAUNTLEROY, Col. Moore (1610-63; 2d son of John [bap. 1588], of Crondall, Hampshire, Eng., *m* 1609, Phoebe Wilkinson; and g.g.g.son of Tristram Fauntleroy [*d* 1538], of Michels Mersh, Hampshire, *m* Joan, dau. John Holt, of Crondall, and widow of Thomas Villiers, of Leicestershire, Eng.); came to Va., 1641; patented land, Upper Norfolk Co., called "Royes-Rest," 1643; removed to Northern Neck, Va.; purchased land from Rappahannock Indians, 1651; settled finally at "Crondall," Naylor's Hole, Lancaster (now Richmond), Co., Va.; *m* in Eng., Dorothy Castle; *m* 2d, 1648, Mary Hill (dau. Capt. Thomas of Warwick Co., later of York Co., Va., *m* Mary, dau. Hon. Abraham Piersey, *m* Elizabeth Draper, of Weyaneke, Va.).

FAY, John (1648-90), Huguenot, refugee from France to Wales, thence in the "Speedwell," to Mass., 1656; lived at Watertown, later at Sudbury, and at Marlboro, 1675; *m* 1668, Mary (*d* ca. 1677), dau. of Thomas Brigham (qv); *m* 2d, 1678, Susanna, widow of Joseph Morse and dau. William Shattuck.

FEAKE, Robert (1610-63), from Eng. in Winthrop's fleet, 1630, settled at Watertown, Mass.; freeman, 1631; lt., colonial forces, 1632-36; dep. Gen. Ct., Colony of Mass. Bay, 1635-36; *m* Elizabeth Fones.

FEARING, John (*d* 1665), from Eng. in the "Diligent," to Hingham, Mass., 1638; selectman, 1648; constable, 1650; freeman, 1652; a deacon; *m* Margaret –.

FELLOWES (Fellows), William (1609-77), from Eng. in the "Planter," 1635; settled at Ipswich, Mass., 1643.

FELTON, Nathaniel (1615-1705), from Eng. to Salem, Mass., 1633; *m* Mary Skelton.

FENNER, Arthur (1622-1703), was at Providence, R.I., 1650, or before; commr. for United Colonies, 1653, et seq.; gov.'s asst., 1657-90; dep. Gen. Ct., 1664-1700; cdr. Providence forces in King Philip's War; *m* Mehitable (*d* 1684), dau. of Richard Waterman.

FERNALD, Reginald, or Renald (ca. 1595-1656), surgeon, from Eng. to Kittery, Me., 1626-30; settled at Portsmouth, N.H., 1631; was surgeon of a company of colonists sent by Mason and Gorges; was town clerk; clk. of ct., 1640; recorder, 1654; etc.; his lands included "Lady Claim" or "Doctor's" Island (since 1806 U.S. Navy Yard); *m* Johanna Warburton.

FERREE, Mme. Mary (Maria Warenbur) Warrenbuer (1650-1716; widow of Daniel [*d* in exile ante 1708], desc. Jean [Fuehre] LaVerree, a French Protestant, of Picardy who removed to Flanders at the revocation of the Edict of Nantes); went from Lindau in Bavaria, German Palatinate, to Eng., obtained letters patent for citizenship under the privy seal of Queen Anne, Aug. 30, 1708; visited William Penn in person and he covenanted with her for a grant of land in Pa.; arrived New York, Dec. 31, 1708, with 6 children, as a mem. of a party of French and Palatine refugees headed by Rev. Joshua Kocherthal from Lindau; went from Esopus, on the Hudson River, as a founder of Huguenot colony in the Pequea Valley, Lancaster Co., Pa.

FERRIS, Jeffrey (1610-56), from Eng., ca. 1634; admitted freeman at Boston, 1635; an original settler at Greenwich, 1642; *m* Judy Burns.

FERRY (Ferre), Charles (1637-99), from Eng., ca. 1660/61, to Agawam (Springfield), Mass.; *m* Sarah Harmon (1644-1740).

FIELD, John (*d* 1686), from Eng. to Providence, R.I., 1637; commr. to Gen. Assembly; deputy; was at Bridgewater, Mass., 1655.

FIELD (Feild), Robert (1605-1673?), from Eng., was living at Newport, R.I., 1638, returned to Eng. ca. 1641, but came again, 1644; was patentee of Bayside, L.I.; landed propr. of Newtown, L.I.; *m* Ruth Fairbank; *m* 2d, 1630, Elizabeth Taylor.

FIELD, Robert (1613-75), from Eng. in the "James," 1635; arrived at Boston; went to Providence, R.I., 1638; returned to Boston, 1650; *m* 1650, Mary (ca. 1630-living 1677), dau. Christopher Stanley, from London, 1635.

FIELD, Zechariah (1596-1666), from Eng., 1629; later at Dorchester, Mass., thence to Northampton, 1659, to Hatfield, 1666; settled finally at Hartford, Conn.; soldier Pequot War; *m* 1641, Mary, dau. of Christopher Stanley, of Boston.

FILMER, Maj. Henry (*d* post 1673), from Eng. to Va. ante 1642, settled first at James City and later in Warwick Co.; burgess, James City Co., 1642-43; justice of Warwick, 1647; had land grants as early as 1637; officer British Army of Occupation; *m* Elizabeth –.

FINLEY, Michael (*b* 1683-*d* bet. 1747-50; son of Robert, *m* Margaret Lauder); from Ireland to Phila., Pa., 1734; settled on Neshaminy Creek, Bucks Co., Pa.; later in N.J.; removed to Sadsbury Tp., Chester Co., Pa.; *m* 1712, Ann, dau. of Samuel O'Neill, of Ireland.

FISH, Jonathan (1610-63), from Eng. with his brothers, Nathaniel and John, to Lynn, Mass., ca. 1635; removed to Sandwich, Cape Cod, 1637, to Newtown, L.I., ca. 1659; *m* Mary –.

FISHER, Anthony (bap. 1591-1671; son of Anthony Fisher, *d* 1640, *m* Mary Fiske); came from Eng. in the "Rose," to Boston, 1637, and settled at Dedham same yr.; dep. Gen. Ct.; mem. A. and H. A. Co.; freeman, 1645; selectman, 1664-66; *m* Mary –; *m* 2d, 1647, Joanna, dau. Thomas Faxon.

FISHER, Daniel (1619-83), from Eng. to Boston, 1637, settled at Dedham same yr.; freeman, 1640; selectman, 1650-81; capt. co. of Foot, 1640; mem. A. and H. A. Co., 1640; dep. Gen. Ct., speaker 3 times; gov.'s asst., 1682; *m* 1641, Abigail (*d* 1683), dau. of Thomas Marriott, *m* Susanna –.

FISHER, John, from Eng. in the "Welcome," with William Penn, 1682; settled at Cape Henlopen, Del.; *m* Margaret Hindle.

FISHER, Joshua (1585-1674; brother of Anthony Fisher, qv; son of Anthony, *d* 1640, of "Wignotte," Suffolk, Eng., *m* Mary Fiske); came from Eng., 1640; *m* Elizabeth –.

FISKE, John (ca. 1601-77); A.B., Cambridge U., 1625; from Eng. to Cambridge, Mass., 1637, removed same yr. to Salem; freeman, 1637; teacher; ordained at Wenham, Mass., 1644, later at Chelmsford; *m* in Eng. Ann Gipps (*d* 1672); *m* 2d, 1673, Elizabeth, widow of Edmund Henchman.

FISKE, William (1613-54; desc. Symond Fiske, lord of the manor of Stradbaugh), came from Eng. with his brother, Rev. John, and two sisters, to Salem, Mass., 1637, freeman, 1642; settled at Wenham, Mass., 1640, where he was first town clerk, 1643-60; rep. Gen. Ct., 1646, 49, 50, 52; *m* 1643, Bridget Muskett, of Pelham, Eng.

FITCH, James (1622-1702), from Eng. to Hartford, Conn., 1638; admitted to the ministry at Saybrook, Conn., 1646; removed to Norwich, 1660, to Lebanon, Conn., 1696; chaplain King Philip's War; *m* 1648, Abigail (*d* 1659), dau. Rev. Henry Whitfield; *m* 2d, 1664, Priscilla (*b* 1641), dau. Maj. John Mason.

FITCH, Thomas (1612-1704), from Eng., 1637; settled at Norwalk, Conn., ca. 1651; freeman, 1657; dep. Gen. Ct., 1654-57; one of the wealthiest men in the colony; commr. for Norwalk, 1670-1674; clk. of Train Band, 1656; *m* 1632, Anna Stacie (Stacey); *m* 2d, Ruth Clark.

FITZHUGH, William (1651-1701; son of Hon. Henry, of Bedford Co., Eng.); from Eng., 1670, settled at Bedford, on the Rappahannock, Stafford Co., Va.; lt. col. Westmoreland Co., Va., 1683; burgess, 1678-87; col. Stafford Co., 1690; *m* May 1, 1674, Sarah Tucker (*d* 1701).

FITZRANDOLPH, see Randolph.

FLAGG (Flegg), Thomas (1616-98), from Eng. in the "Rose," to Boston, 1637; a propr. of Watertown, 1641; in Train Band until 1681; *m* Mary –.

FLETCHER, Robert (1592-1677), from England, 1630; a founder of Concord, Mass.; a founder of Chelmsford, later at Middletown, Conn.

FLINT, Thomas (1603-63), from Eng. to Boston, 1636; settled at Concord; freeman, 1638; magistrate; rep. Gen. Ct., 1638-41; gov.'s asst., 1642-51, 1653; *m* Ann –.

FLOOD, John (*d* 1661), from Eng. to Va., in the "Swann," 1610; living at "Jordan's Journey," 1625; rep. Gen. Assembly, 1630, 32, 42, 45; Charles City, 1638; capt.; Indian interpreter, for this was allowed 4,000 lbs. of tobacco yearly; lt. col. Surry Co.; mem. legislature, 1652-55; *m* ante 1625, Widow Margaret Finch, who came in the "Supply," 1620, in which William Tracy brought the immigrants to Berkley Hundred.

FLOYD, Richard (*d* 1700), from Wales to Mass., 1654, later settled at Setauket, L.I.; judge, Suffolk Co.; col. militia; *m* Susanna –.

FOLGER, John (*d* 1660), from Eng., 1635; settled at Watertown, Mass.

FOLSOM (Foulsom, Foulsham), John (1615-81), from Eng. in the "Diligent," to Hingham, Mass., 1638; settled at Exeter, N.H., 1655; constable; *m* 1636, Mary, dau. Edward Gilman.

FOOTE, Nathaniel (1593-1644), from Eng. to Watertown, Mass., 1630; freeman, 1634; settled at Wethersfield, Conn., 1636; rep. Gen. Ct., 1641-44; *m* in Eng., ca. 1615, Elizabeth Deming (sister of John Deming, one of the first settlers of Wethersfield, Conn.), she *m* 2d, ca. 1646, Thomas Welles.

FORD, Thomas (*d* 1676), came in the "Mary and John," 1630; rep., 1640, 41, 43; mem. com. which sat with magistrates, 1638-39, before govt. was organized.

FORD, William (1604-76), from Eng. in the "Fortune," to Plymouth, Mass., 1621; was a miller at Duxbury, Mass.; later removed to Marshfield, Mass.; *m* Anna – (*d* 1684).

FOSDICK, Stephen (1583-1664), from Eng. to Charlestown, Mass., 1636; freeman, 1638; *m* 2d, in Eng., Sarah Wetherell.

FOSTER, Christopher (*b* 1603), from Eng. in the "Abigail," 1635; settled at Lynn, Mass.; a founder and constable; removed to Southampton, 1651; *m* Frances – (*b* 1607).

FOSTER, Reginald (1595-1681; son of Renald, desc. Sir Richard Forester, brother-in-law of William the Conqueror), settled at Ipswich, Mass., 1638; *m* 1st Judith – (*d* 1664); *m* 2d, 1665, Sarah, widow of John Martin.

FOULKE, Edward (1651-1741; son of Foulke Thomas Lloyd; desc. Edward I, of Eng.), scholar and writer; from Merionethshire, Wales, in the "Robert and Elizabeth," to Phila., Pa., 1698, with 9 children; owned 700 acre estate; a founder of Gwynedd, Pa.; *m* Eleanor (Hughes), dau. of Hugh Cadwalader Rhys, *m* Gwenn –;

FOWKE, Gerard (*d* 1700), gent. of the bed chamber of Charles I, col. in Royalist Army; came to Va., 1650; merchant and wealthy planter; mem. House of Burgesses from Westmoreland Co., 1663.

FOWLER, Capt. Richard, (son of Richard, of Northumberland, Eng., *m* Isabel Mather), of British Army; killed at Battle of Harlem Heights; *m* Sarah, dau. of Thomas Hunt, of Hunt's Point, N.Y.

FOWLER (Fowle, Fowlar), William (*d* 1661), from Eng. with Rev. John Davenport, to Boston, 1637; settled at New Haven, Conn., 1638, where he was 1st magistrate, asst., and dep. Gen. Ct.; at Milford, 1661; *m* Sarah –; *m* 2d, Elizabeth Baldwin, widow.

FOX, Thomas (ca. 1620-1658), from Eng. ca. 1640; freeman at Concord, Mass.; *m* Rebecca – (*d* 1647); *m* 2d, 1647, Hannah, dau. of Henry Brooks, of Woburn.

FRANCIS, Richard (1606-87), from Eng. to Dorchester, Mass., 1636, thence to Cambridge; a bricklayer; freeman, 1640; *m* 1638, Alce or Alice Wilcockes (Wilcox).

FREEBORN, William (1594-1670), came to Boston in the "Mary and Francis"; a signer of the Providence Compact, 1636; freeman, 1655; commr., 1657; *m* Mary –.

FREEMAN, Edmund (1590-1682), from Eng. in the "Abigail," with wife and four children; settled at Lynn, Mass., where he presented the colony with 20 corslets (armor) moved to Plymouth, 1637, where he was admitted freeman, 1637; was one of the ten to settle at Sandwich, Mass., 1639, and received the largest land grant; dep. Plymouth Colony, 1641; asst. to Gov. Bradford, 1640-47; mem. Council of War, 1642; presiding officer of a court of three "to hear and determine controversies and cawses," and later selected judge; *m* Elizabeth – (*d* 1675/76).

FREEMAN, Henry (1672-1763; son of Joseph, *b* 1639, *m* 1666, Elizabeth Grosse), came from Eng. to Phila. ca. 1683; settled at Woodbridge, N.J.; judge Ct. Common Pleas; *m* in 1695, Elizabeth Boune.

FREEMAN, Samuel, from Eng., in Winthrop's fleet, to Watertown, Mass., 1630; took oath of allegiance, 1639, and soon after returned to Eng., leaving family in Mass., and *d* soon after; *m* Mary –.

FRENCH, Edward (1598-1674), from Eng., with his wife and children, 1636; a founder of Ipswich, Mass., where he was a large landowner; removed to Salisbury, 1652; *m* Ann –.

FRENCH, John (1612-92), from Eng. to Dorchester, Mass., 1630; removed to Braintree, 1640, the homestead, acquired 1640, or soon after, is still in the family; *m* Grace – (*d* 1681); *m* 2d, Elinor, dau. Rev. William Thompson, widow of William Veazey.

FRENCH, Thomas (1608-80), from Eng. to Boston, 1631; freeman, 1632; removed to Ipswich, in 1639; *m* Alice –.

FRENCH, William (1603-81), from Eng. in the "Defense," to Cambridge, Mass., 1635; an original propr. of Billerica, Mass., 1652; officer King Philip's War; rep. Gen. Ct.; mem. A. and H. A. Co.; *m* in Eng., Elizabeth Godfrey (1605-68); *m* 2d, 1669, Mary, widow of John Stearns and dau. Thomas Lothrop, of Barnstable.

FRICK, Conrad (*b* 1688, in Switzerland-1761; desc. Heinrich Frick, Zurich, Switzerland; of Celtic-Burgundian ancestry, traced to 1113); came from Rotterdam, in the "Pennsylvania," 1732, to Phila., Pa.; settled at Germantown, Pa.; naturalized 1749; *m* Barbara Enten.

FROST, Edmund (ca. 1610-1672; son of John), came from Eng. in the "Great Hope," to Cambridge, Mass., 1635; freeman, 1636; *m* Thomasine –; *m* 2d, Mary –; *m* 3d, widow of Robert Daniels.

FROST, Nicholas (1595-1663), from Eng. to Kittery, Me., 1634; had a garrison house at Kittery.

FROTHINGHAM, William (ca. 1600-1651), from Eng. with Gov. Winthrop, 1630, to Mass.; one of original proprs. of Charlestown; took oath of allegiance, 1632; a deacon; *m* Ann – (1607-74).

FRY, Col. Joshua (*d* 1754), prof. William and Mary Coll., Williamsburg, Va., 1728-32; living in Goochland Co. when Albemarle Co. was cut off from Goochland, 1744; commr. Albemarle Co.; justice of the peace; co. lt., Albemarle Co.; presided at the first ct. of the co., 1744; apptd. col. of Va. regt., 1754, by Gov. Dinwiddie, while on way to Ft. Duquesne (now Pittsburgh, Pa.), he fell from his horse at Millis Creek, now Cumberland, Md., where he died; at his death, Lt. Col. George Washington then about 21, succeeded to the command; *m* Mary (Micou) Hill.

FRYE, John (1601-1693 or 95), from Eng. in the "Bevis," 1638; *m* Ann –.

FULLER, Edward (bap. 1575-1621), 21st signer of the Mayflower, *m* Ann – (*d* 1621).

FULLER, John (1611-99), from Eng. in the "Abigail," 1635, to Mass.; settled at Cambridge, in that part known as Newtown; farmer and maltster; freeman, 1690; *m* Elizabeth – (*d* 1700).

FULLER, Samuel (*d* 1633), 8th signer of the Mayflower Compact; dea. of the church at Leyden and Plymouth; the first physician among the Pilgrims; asst., 1632; *m* 1st, Alice Glascock (*d* before 1613); *m* 2d, at Leyden, Holland, 1613, Agnes (*d* before 1617), dau. Alexander Carpenter; *m* 3d, at Leyden, 1617, Bridget Lee (*d* 1664).

FULLER, Lt. Thomas (1618-98), from Eng., was at Salem, Mass., 1638; settled at Dedham, 1643; later at Middleton and Woburn; selectman, freeman; ensign; rep. Gen. Ct.; *m* 1643, Elizabeth Tidd; *m* 2d, Hannah Flower (*d* 1672).

GAILLARD, Joachim, from France upon the revocation of the Edict of Nantes, 1685; was in S.C. by Oct. 10, 1687, when he received 600 acres in James Town precinct; settled on the Santee River, Craven Co., S.C.; *m* 1694, Ester Paparel.

GALE, Edmond (*d* 1642), from Eng. to Newtown, Mass., ca. 1630.

GALLATIN, Albert (1761-1849), grad. U. of Geneva, 1779; came from Switzerland to Boston, 1780; served in Am. Rev.; purchased land in Fayette Co., Va., 1785, which later was included in boundary of Pa.; mem. Constl. Conv. of Pa., 1789, Ho. of Rep., 1790-92; elected to U.S. Senate, but was not seated; mem. 4th, 5th and 6th Congresses, 1795-1801; Sec. of the Treas., 1802-14, in Cabinets of Presidents Jefferson and Madison; minister to France, 1815-23, to Great Britain, 1826-27; *m* Hannah, dau. Commodore James Nicholson, U.S.N.

GALLUP (Gallop), John (1590-1650), from Eng. in the "Mary and John," arriving at Natascot (changed to Hull, 1646), 1630; admitted freeman at Boston, 1634; *m* Crestabel –, who followed him to America with four children in the "Griffin," 1633.

GANO (Gerneaux), Francis (1620-1723), Huguenot; from the Island of Guernsey, France; was at New Rochelle, N.Y., 1661.

GARDINER, George (*d* 1677), from Eng. in the "Fellowship," to Boston, 1637; settled at Newport, R.I.; dep., 1662; sgt., 1642, ensign, 1644; *m* Sarah Slaughter.

GARDINER, Lion (ca. 1599-1663), officer English army, came from Holland in the "Bachilor" of only 35 tons, to Boston, 1635; settled at Saybrook, Conn.; built and commanded the fort at Saybrook during Pequot War; later at East-hampton, L.I.; 1st lord of the manor of Gardiner's Island, 1640; *m* in Holland, Mary Wilemson Deurcant.

GARDNER, Joseph (1601-79; son of Sir Thomas, Kt.), from Eng. to Newport, R.I., bet. 1635-40.

GARDNER, Thomas (1592-1674 or 77), from Eng. in the "Charity," to Cape Ann, Mass., as head of the Dorchester Co., 1624; removed to Salem, 1626; freeman, 1637; rep. Gen. Ct., 1637; capt. Train Band; *m* Margaret Tryer (or Fryer).

GARFIELD (Gairfield), Edward (ca. 1575-1672), from Wales with Gov. Winthrop, 1630; a propr. Watertown, Mass., 1635; *m* Rebecca – (*d* 1661, aet. ca. 55); *m* 2d, 1661, Johannah Buckmaster.

GARY, Charles, from Va. to S.C., name 1st appears in land grants in Newberry Co., 1767; planter; soldier Am. Rev.; *m* Elizabeth –.

GASSAWAY, Col. Nicholas (1650-91), brought to Md., 1650; was of Anne Arundel Co.; capt. militia, 1678, maj. 1681; justice, 1687; asst. cdr. of the rangers, 1691; *m* Anne, dau. of Capt. Thomas Beeson (will proved, 1679).

GATES, George (ca. 1634-1724), a Puritan, from Eng. to Hartford, Conn., ca. 1651; an original propr. of Haddam, 1661; rep. Gen. Ct., 1668-73; capt. colonial forces; *m* Sarah, dau. Nicholas Olmsted.

GATES, Stephen (*d* 1662), from Eng. in the "Diligent," to Hingham, Mass., 1638; was a founder of Lancaster, Mass., 1654; *m* Anna Hill (*d* 1682/83).

GAY, John (*d* 1688), from Eng. in the "Mary and John," to Watertown, Mass., 1630; freeman, 1635; a founder of Dedham, 1636; selectman; *m* Joanna – (*d* 1691).

GAYLORD, Dea. William (1585-1673), from Eng. in the "Mary and John," with his brother John, to Dorchester, Mass., 1630; freeman, 1630; signed first land grants at Dorchester, his own grant being dated 1633; selectman; rep. Gen. Ct.; removed to Windsor, Conn., which town he represented in the Gen. Assembly nearly 40 sessions; *m* Sara – (*d* 1657).

GEER (Geare, Gears, Gere), Thomas (1623-1722; 6th from Walter Geere, *b* 1450, of Heavitree, Exeter), from Eng. to Boston, 1635; settled at Enfield, Conn., ca. 1682; *m* Deborah Davis.

GERE (Geer, Gear), George (ca. 1621-1726, aet. 105; son of Jonathan, of Hewitree, Co. Devon, Eng.), from Eng. to Boston, 1635; settled at New London, Conn., 1651; soldier Pequot War; later at Preston, Conn.; *m* Feb. 17, 1658/59, Sarah (1642-post 1723), dau. of Robert Allyn (qv).

GERRISH, William (ca. 1617-1687), settled at Newbury, Mass., 1639; removed to Boston, 1678; capt., Newbury mil. company and cdr. of garrison there; capt. in King Philip's War; dep. Gen. Ct., 1650, et seq.; *m* 1645, Joan (*d* 1677), dau. of Percival Lowell (qv), and widow of John Oliver.

GEST, Henry (*b* 1658; desc. John Geste or Ghest, of Handsworth, nr. Birmingham, Eng.), from Eng. in the "Delaware," to Chester, Pa., 1686; *m* Mary –.

GIBSON, John (1601-94), from Eng. to Cambridge ante 1634; Cambridge records show he owned many acres of land; planted linden trees; mentioned in Longfellow's "The Open Window."

GIFFORD, William (*d* Apr. 16, 1687), Quaker; from Eng. ante 1647; believed to have first emigrated to a southern port and afterward went north; before Stamford, Conn., Ct., ca. 1647, sentenced to be whipped, banished; earliest record at Sandwich, Mass., 1650; a propr. Monmouth, N.J., resided there, 1665-70; *m* 2d, July 16, 1683, Mary Miles (*d* Feb. 10, 1734).

GILBERT, Jonathan (1618-82), from Eng. with his brothers, Thomas, Obadiah and Josiah, to Boston, 1635; was at Hartford, Conn., 1640, later at New Haven; innkeeper; was marshal Gen. Assembly; collector of customs; dep. Gen. Ct.; commr. United Colonies; *m* 1646, Mary (*d* 1650), dau. of Elder John White (or Whight); *m* 2d, 1650, Mary (*d* 1700), dau. of Hugh Welles and sister of Thomas Welles, of Hadley.

GILDERSLEEVE, Richard, (1601-80), from Eng., 1635; propr. Wethersfield and Glastonbury, Conn., 1636, New Haven Colony, 1639, Stamford, Conn., 1641, Hempstead, L.I., 1644,

Newtown, L.I., 1652-59; dep. New Haven Ct.; magistrate; colonial commr. for Conn., 1664; constable of Hempstead under the Dukes laws, and surveyor; *m* Joanna Appleton (*b* 1601).

GILLETTE (Gillet, Gillett), Jonathan (*d* 1677), from Eng. in the "Mary and John," with his wife and three children and his brother, Nathan, to Dorchester, Mass., 1630; freeman at Dorchester, 1635; removed to Windsor, Conn., 1636; constable, 1656; *m* Mary –.

GILMAN, Edward (1587-1681), from Eng. in the "Diligent," with his wife, five children and three servants, to Hingham, Mass., 1638; freeman same yr.; removed to Rehoboth, 1643; thence to Ipswich; settled at Exeter, N.H., 1652; *m* 1614, Mary Clark.

GILPIN, Joseph (1664-1741; son of Thomas Gilpin, col. in Cromwell's army and later became a Quaker; desc. Richard de Gaylpyn, 1206), from Eng. to Chester Co., Pa., 1696; *m* 1691/92, Hannah Glover.

GLIDDEN, Charles (ca. 1632-post 1707), from Eng., to Portsmouth, N.H., ca. 1660; took oath of fidelity at Exeter, 1677; granted land at Newmarket, N.H., 1697; *m* 1658, Eunice Shore.

GODDARD (Godard), William (1627-91; son of Gen. Edward, of Norfolkshire), from Eng. to Watertown, Mass., 1665; schoolmaster; soldier King Philip's War; *m* Elizabeth (*d* 1697), dau. Benjamin Miles.

GODFREY, Richard (1631-91), settled at Taunton, Mass., 1652; *m* Jane, dau. of John Turner.

GOFORTH, Aaron (*d* 1736), Quaker; from Eng. to Phila., Pa., 1711; *m* 2d, Tabitha Bethell (*d* 1721/22).

GOLDSBOROUGH, Nicholas (1639-70), from Malcolm Regis, nr. Weymouth, Dorsetshire, Eng., 1670, settled at Kent Island, Md.; *m* ca. 1659, Margaret, dau. Abram Howes, of Eng.

GOODALE, Robert (1604-83), from Eng. in the "Elizabeth," 1634; was at Salem, Mass., 1634; propr., 1636; *m* Katherine – (*b* 1606).

GOODHUE, William (1613-99), from Eng. to Ipswich, Mass., 1635/36; rep. Gen. Ct., 1666-83; selectman; *m* 1st, 1634, Mary Watson (*d* 1668).

GOODRICH, William (*d* 1676; son of William, *m* Margery –); from Eng. ca. 1635; was at Wethersfield, Conn., 1643; ensign; dep. Gen. Ct., 1660-66; *m* 1648, Sarah (1631-1702), dau. of Matthew Marvin (qv).

GOODWIN, Ozias (1596-1683), from Eng. in the "Lion," to Newtown, Mass., 1632; one of first settlers of Hartford, Conn., 1636; *m* in Eng., Mary Woodward.

GOODWIN, William (1598-1673), fled from Eng. to escape religious persecution, 1632; ruling elder of Braintree company at Mount Wollaston, Newtown (now Cambridge), Mass., Hartford, Conn., and Hadley, Mass.; dep. Gen. Ct., 1634; as trustee of Gov. Edward Hopkins' estate, he distributed funds to various ednl. institutions, existing or to be created; founded present Hopkins Grammar School, Hadley, Mass., and built a grist-mill to maintain it; a founder of Hartford and Hadley; *m* 1616, Elizabeth (bap. 1591), dau. of Robert White, *m* Bridget Allgar.

GOODYEAR, Stephen (1600-58), from Eng. to New Haven Colony, 1638; dep. gov., 1643-58; commr. for United Colonies, 1643, 46; lost at sea on return to Eng.; *m* Margaret –, widow of Capt. George Lamberton.

GOOKIN, Daniel (1612-87), from Eng., to Va., thence to Boston, Mass., 1644; resided at Roxbury and Cambridge; capt., 1648; maj. gen. Mass. forces, 1681; dep. Gen. Ct., 1649-51; speaker, 1651; gov.'s asst., 1652-86; commr. to the Indians, 1656; *m* 1639, Mary Dalling.

GORDON, James (ca. 1714-1768), from Ireland, with his brother, John, to Merry Pt., Lancaster Co., Va., before 1738; *m* Mary, dau. Col. Nathaniel Harrison.

GORDON, John (*d* 1780), from Ireland with his brother James, ca. 1738, settled in Lancaster Co., Va., later in Middlesex and Richmond counties; tobacco merchant; justice; *m* 1756, Lucy, dau. Col. Armistead Churchill.

GORE, John (*d* 1657 Roxbury), probably from Waltham Abbey, Essex, Eng., with wife, to Boston, 1635, settling in Roxbury as a freeman; *m* Rhoda –.

GORHAM (Gorum), John (1621-1675/76; son of Ralph, who came from Eng., 1635, but returned to Eng.), was landowner at Yarmouth; resided at Barnstable and Plymouth, Mass.; capt. 2d Barnstable company in Great Swamp Fight, King Philip's War, 1675; *m* 1643, Desire (*d* 1683), dau. of John Howland (qv).

GORTON, Samuel (1592-1677), from Eng. to Boston, 1636; removed to Plymouth, Mass.; to R.I., 1638; settled at Warwick, R.I., 1641; dep. Gen. Ct., 1651, et seq.; commr. to Narraganset Indians.

GOULD, John, from Eng., 1664; landowner, Southampton, L.I., 1686; was at Elizabeth, N.J., 1690; *m* Sarah Axtell.

GOULD (Gold), Nathan (*d* 1694), from Eng. ca. 1643; settled at Milford, Conn., 1647, Fairfield, 1650; asst., 1657, 62, 94; mem. Gov.'s Council; rep. in 1st Colonial Congress in N.Y., 1690; mem. Com. of Defense against the Dutch, 1662; maj. of dragoons, 1675; *m* Martha –, widow of Edmund Harvey.

GOULD, Zaccheus (1589-1668; 6th from Thomas Gould of Boringdon, Co. Bucks, Eng.); early settler of Topsfield, Mass.; *m* Phebe Deacon.

GRAHAM, John (1694-1774), from Scotland to Boston, 1718; settled at Exeter, N.H.; chaplain Crown Point expdn.; *m* Abigail Chauncy.

GRANGER, Lancelot (1624-89), from Eng. to Newberry, Mass., 1640; soldier King Philip's War; *m* 1654, Joanna (1634-1701), dau. of Robert Adams (qv).

GRANT, Matthew (1601-81), from Eng. in the "Mary and John," to Dorchester, Mass., 1630; freeman, 1631; a founder of Windsor, Conn., 1636; where he was town clerk and surveyor many yrs.; *m* 1625, Priscilla Grey (1601-44); *m* 2d, 1645, Susanna (1602-1665/66), dau. William Rockwell.

GRAY, Robert (1634-1718), from Eng., 1658, settled at Andover, Mass., 1659; *m* 1669, Hannah Holt.

GREELEY (Greele, Grele), Andrew (ca. 1617-1697), from Eng., ca. 1638; an original propr. of Salisbury, Mass.; at Haverhill, 1669; *m* Mary, dau. Joseph Moyse.

GREEN, James (ca. 1610-1687), from Eng. ca. 1634; freeman at Charlestown, Mass., 1647; *m* ca. 1638, Elizabeth (*d* 1687), dau. of Robert Newman, of Co. Kent, Eng.

GREEN (Greene), Thomas (1600-67), from Eng. to Lynn, Mass., 1635; later at Ipswich, Mass., and Malden, 1638; *m* Elizabeth (*d* 1658); *m* 2d, 1659, Frances –, widow of Richard Cook.

GREENBERRY, Col. Nicholas (ca. 1627-1697, aet. 70), came to Md. in the "Constant Friendship," 1674; settled at Greenberry's Point, Anne Arundel Co., Md.; mem. Council of Sir Lionel Copley; acting gov. Province of Md., 1693; chancellor and keeper of the great seal, 1692-94; *m* Anne – (1648-98).

GREENE, "Surgeon John" (1597-1658), from Eng. in the "James," to Boston, 1635; a founder with Roger Williams of Providence Plantations where he lived until 1643; with twelve other men purchased Narragansett from the Indians; a founder of Warwick, 1643; magistrate, dep., commr., etc.; *m* in Eng., 1619, Joanna Tattershall; *m* 2d, Alice Daniels; *m* 3d, Philippa – (*d* 1687, aet. 87).

GREENLEAF, Edmond (1573-1671), from Eng., 1635; capt. Indian wars; overseer of "collection of arms"; settled at Newbury, Mass., 1639; removed to Boston, 1650; *m* Sarah Dole (*d* 1663).

GREENOUGH, William (1641-93), from Eng. to Boston, and established a ship yard there; freeman, 1673; ensign A. and H. A. Co.; capt. King Philip's War; *m* Ruth, dau. Thomas Swift, of Dorchester; *m* 2d, Elizabeth (*d* 1688), dau. Elder Edward Rainsford; *m* 3d, 1688, Sarah Shobe, of Chelmsford.

GREGG, James (1678-1735), from Scotland to Ireland, 1690; came to Londonderry, N.H., 1718, a founder of that town; cdr. of company during war with eastern Indians, 1719; mem. N.H. Assembly, 1736; *m* Janet Cargill (?).

GREGORY, Henry (*b* ca. 1570), from Eng. to Boston, 1633; later at Springfield; a founder of Stratford, Conn.

GRESHAM, Edward (son of Sir Thomas Gresham, Kt., seated at Tetsey, *m* Mary, dau. of John Lennard, or Leonard); to Va. ca. 1650, located in New Kent Co.; ancestor of the Va. Greshams; purchased abt. 500 acres of land which had been patented by Robert Joanes, 1658, which patent was renewed by patent direct to Edward Gresham, issued by Sir William Berkeley, Mar. 18, 1662; received grant from Gov. Berkeley of 111 acres in New Kent adjoining above grant, June 10, 1675; was granted 640 acres in New Kent, same locality, 1690.

GRIFFEN, Edward (1602-living at Flushing, L.I., 1698), sailed in the "Abraham," from London, Oct. 24, 1635, and settled on Palmer's Island, Va. (now Md.); thence to New Amsterdam, 1640; overseer of Flushing, 1680; *m* Mary – (living in 1698).

GRIFFIN, Jasper (1648-1718), from Wales to Southold, L.I., ca. 1675; maj. provincial militia; *m* Hannah –.

GRIFFIN, Matthew, from Eng., was at Saybrook, Conn., 1645; fortified same; served in King Philip's War; *m* at Charlestown, Mass., Aug. 29, 1654, Hannah (*b* 1636?-*d* Dec. 2, 1674), dau. of Robert Cutler, landed 1637, *m* Rebecca –.

GRINNELL, Matthew (*b* 1602; desc. Pierre Grinnell, 1480, Duchy of Bourgogne, France), a Huguenot refugee from France ca. 1630; freeman at Newport, R.I., 1638; removed to Portsmouth, 1655; *m* Rose –.

GRISWOLD, Edward (1607-91), from Eng., 1639; a founder of Windsor, Conn.; later settled at Killingsworth; was dep. Gen. Ct., justice, deacon; built "Old Fort," at Springfield; *m* Margaret – (*d* 1670); *m* 2d, 1672, Sarah Bevius, widow, of New London, Conn.

GRISWOLD, Matthew (1620-1698/99), from Eng. to Windsor, Conn., 1639; removed to Saybrook, 1644; a settler of Lyme; magistrate, dep., etc.; *m* 1646, Anne, dau. Henry Wolcott.

GROVER, James, Sr. (*d* 1686), presumed to have gone from N.E. to Gravesend, L.I., 1648; set up the standard of Eng. at Gravesend, which was under Dutch rule, Mar. 9, 1655; sent to Oliver Cromwell, with letters, 1655, returning with a letter from Cromwell to the English inhabitants of L.I., 1657; grantee of Monmouth (N.J.) patent, 1663; lt. of 1st co. of militia in N.J., Dec. 1, 1663; mem. court at Portland Point, July 16, 1670; justice at Shrewsbury and Middletown, 1676; burgess for Middletown in first Assembly, 1668; dep. to treat with admirals and commanders of fleet of the States-General, 1673; *m* Rebecca –.

GUILD, John (1612-82), one of the founders of Dedham, Mass., 1636; freeman, 1640; soldier King Philip's War; *m* 1645, Elizabeth Crooke (*d* 1669).

HACKETT, Capt. William (1635-1713), from Eng., commanded the "Endeavor," from Salisbury, Mass., on voyage to New York, 1671, the first time any ship had been a commercial carrier between the two ports; *m* 1666, Sarah, dau. of Thomas Barnard.

HAINES, see also Haynes.

HAINES, Richard (*d* 1682), from Eng., 1682, *d* on the voyage; his wife, Margaret, settled on Rancocus Creek, nr. Lumberton, Burlington Co., N.J.

HAIRSTON, Peter (1700?-1760?), officer in the army of Charles Edward Stuart, the Pretender; after the disastrous battle of Drummassie Moore (Culloden), where his son Peter was lost, he, then a widower, fled to Va., 1747, with 5 children, a man of means, he purchased large estates in Bedford, and nearby counties, Va.; his sons served in the House of Burgesses and as officers in colonial wars; two g.sons and one g.son-in-law were officers in Am. Rev.; wife was a dau. of an Irish gentleman, name now unknown.

HALE, Robert (*d* 1659), Puritan; from Eng. to Boston, 1630; joined the first church at Charlestown, 1632; mem. A. and H. A. Co.; *m* Jane –.

HALE, Samuel (1610-93), from Eng., was at Hartford, Conn., 1640, removed to Wethersfield; one of first proprs. of Norwalk, 1654; finally at what is now Glastonbury; served in Pequot War, 1637; rep. Gen. Ct., for Norwalk, 1657 and later; *m* Mary Welles.

HALE, Thomas (1604-82), from Eng. to Newbury, Mass., 1634; freeman, 1638; removed to Haverhill, 1649; selectman there; later again at Newbury; resident of Salem, 1659; sgt. of militia; *m* in Eng., Thomasin Dowsett; *m* 2d, Margaret, dau. Sir Henry Tamorin.

HALL, John (1606-76), from Eng. to Boston, 1633, thence to Hartford, Conn.; at New Haven, 1639; a founder of Wallingford; soldier in Pequot War; dep. Gen. Ct., Conn., 1653-61; *m* Jane Wallen (or Woolen).

HALL, Samuel (1648-1725), of New Haven, Conn.; King Philip's War; dep. Gen. Ct., 1698-1700; capt. Train Band, 1704; *m* Hannah Walker (1646-1728).

HALLETT, William (1616-74), from Eng. to Greenwich, Conn., thence to Hallett's Cove, L.I.; dep. Gen. Ct. of Conn.

HALLOWELL, John (*b* 1647), a Quaker, from Eng. to Darby, Pa., 1682; removed to Abington, Pa.; *m* Mary, dau. Thomas Sharpe.

HALSEY, Thomas (1592-1678; son of Robert Halsey, *d* 1618, *m* Dorothy Downes), from Eng., settled at Lynn, Mass., 1637, where he owned 100 acres of land; a founder of Southampton, L.I., 1640; marshal, 1646; dep. Hartford Gen. Ct., 1664; adj. Train Band, 1650; *m* before 1627, Phoebe – (killed by two Pequot Indians, 1649); *m* 2d, 1660, Ann –, widow of Edward Johnes.

HAMLIN, Giles (1622-89), a sea captain for 50 yrs., came from Eng. to Middletown, Conn., 1654; was commr. for the United Colonies, 1666; dep. Gen. Ct., 1666-68, 1670-84; asst., 1685, 87, 89; *m* 1655, Hester, dau. John Crow, of Hartford.

HAMLIN (Hamblen), James (1606-1690), Huguenot from Eng. to Barnstable, Mass., ca. 1639; *m* 1628, Anne –.

HAMMOND, John (1643-1707), from Isle of Wight, to Annapolis, Md., 1685; burgess, 1692; judge High Ct. of Admiralty; col. forces of Anne Arundel Co., 1699; maj. gen. of Western Shore, 1707; *m* Mary Howard.

HAMPTON, William (1586-1652), from London, Eng., to Va. in the "Bona Nova," 1621; settled first nr. old Point Comfort; planter; established "Hampfield," Gloucester Co., Va., 1652; *m* Joan – (*b* 1596), who came with their three children in the "Abigail," to Va., 1621.

HAND, John (1611-63), from Eng. ca. 1636; settled first at Lynn, Mass.; moved to Southampton, L.I., 1644; one of nine founders of East Hampton, 1648; magistrate, 1657-60; *m* Alice Stanborough, sister of Josiah Stanborough.

HANFORD (Handford), Thomas (*d* 1693), from Eng. to Scituate, Mass., 1643; ordained at Norwalk, Conn., 1652; freeman, 1650; *m* Hannah –; *m* 2d, 1661, Mary, widow of Jonathan Miles.

HANSON (Hansen), John (1630-1713; son of John Hanson, *b* London, Eng., 1575, who immigrated to Sweden and was killed in battle, 1632); with three brothers was in care of Gov. John Printz, of New Sweden, and brought to Tinicum Island, in the Delaware, 1642; removed to Kent Co., Md., 1653, shortly after to St. Mary's Co., and settled in Charles Co., ca 1656; officer in colonial wars.

HANSON, Thomas (*d* 1666), from Eng., was at Dover, N.H., before 1643.

HAPGOOD, Shadrach (1642-75), from Eng. in the "Speedwell," to Sudbury, Mass., 1656; killed in King Philip's War; *m* 1664, Elizabeth, dau. Nathaniel Treadway.

HARDENBERGH (Van Hardenbergh), Jan (*d* ca. 1659), from Holland to New Amsterdam ca. 1640, where he was a large land holder.

HARDING, Abraham (1605-55), from Eng. to Plymouth Colony, 1623; was at Dedham, 1638; settled at Braintree, 1642; *m* Elizabeth Harding.

HARDY, George (1633-93), from Eng. to Isle of Wight Co., Va., ca. 1660; burgess, 1642-52; *m* Mary Jackson.

HARLOW, Sgt. William (1624-91), from Eng. to Plymouth, Mass.; built house, 1677, which is still standing, from remnants of Pilgrim's fort; *m* Mary, dau. of John Francis, came in the "Ann," 1623, *m* Patience, dau. of George Morton (qv);

HARMON, John (1617-61), from Eng. to Boston, ca. 1636; a founder of Springfield, 1644; *m* Elizabeth –.

HARRINGTON, Robert (*d* 1707), from Eng.; freeman, 1668; a propr. of Watertown, Mass.; *m* 1649, Susanna George (1632-95).

HARRIS, Thomas (1573-1658), from Wales in the "Prosperous," to Jamestown, Va., 1611; a founder of Manakin Town, Henrico (now Powhatan) Co., Va., received extensive land grants from the crown; burgess, 1623; *m* Adria, dau. Thomas Osborne, who came to Va. with Harris; *m* 2d, Joane –.

HARRIS, Thomas (1600-86), from Eng. to Charlestown, Mass., 1630; signer of Providence

Plantations Compact, 1637; served as dep. Gen. Assembly, gov.'s asst. and commr.; patentee in charter of King Charles, II, to R.I., 1663; *m* Elizabeth –.

HARRISON, Benjamin (ca. 1600-1648/49), from Eng. to Surry Co., Va., 1631; clk. of Council of Va., 1636-40; burgess, 1642; *m* Mary Stringer; *m* 2d, Mary Sidway.

HARRISON, Burr (1636-1706; son of Cuthbert), from Eng. to Va. ante 1670; sent by the House of Burgesses on a dangerous mission to the Piscatoway Indians; *m* Sarah Frances Burdette.

HART, Edward, an Englishman, was one of the 18 incorporators of Flushing, L.I., 1645; as clk. of the town, 1657, he wrote a remonstrance against the persecutions of the Quakers and sent it to Gov. Stuyvesant, for which he was punished by the governor.

HART, Isaac (1628-99), from Eng. to Lynn, Mass., ca. 1637; to Reading, 1647; later at Lynnfield; *m* Elizabeth Hutchinson.

HART, Samuel (*b* 1622), from London, Eng., settled at Lynn, Mass., 1640; *m* 1653, Mary Needham (*d* 1671).

HART, Stephen (1605-1682/83; son of Stephen); from Eng. to Newton, Mass., 1632; freeman, 1634; settled at Hartford, Conn., 1639; one of original proprs. of Farmington; soldier Pequot War; rep. Gen. Ct., 1647 and most of time to 1660; a deacon; *m* 2d, Margaret –, widow of Arthur Smith.

HARTSHORNE, Richard (1641-1722; son of Hugh); came from Eng., 1669, as commr. from the Proprietors of E. Jersey; settled at Shrewsbury, N.J.; speaker of Assembly, 1687-1708; mem. Council; judge Ct. of Common Rights at Perth Amboy, 1698-99; *m* 1670, Margaret, dau. of Robert Carr, from Scotland, granted Connecticut Island, R.I.

HARVEY, John (1639-1702), from Eng., settled at Harvey's Neck, Perquimans Co., N.C.; was pres. of Council and actg. gov. of N.C.; *m* Mary –.

HASBROUCK (Hasbroucq), Abraham (*d* 1717), his family removed to the Palatinate previous to the revocation of Edict of Nantes, migrated to America, 1675; patentee of New Paltz, N.Y., 1677; *m* 1676, Maria Deyo (1653-1741), a fellow passenger in the same ship.

HASKELL, Roger (1613-67), from Eng. with his brothers William and Mark, to Salem (now Beverly), Mass., 1632; *m* a dau. of John Stone; *m* 2d, Elizabeth, dau. John Hardy.

HASTINGS, Thomas (1605-85), from Eng. in the "Elizabeth," to Watertown, Mass., 1634; selectman 5 yrs.; town clk. 3 yrs.; rep. Gen. Ct., 1673; *m* Susanna – (*d* 1650); *m* 2d, 1651, Margaret (1604-67), dau. William Cheney, of Roxbury, Mass.

HATHORNE, William (1607-81), from Eng. in Winthrop's fleet, 1630, to Dorchester, Mass.; removed to Salem, 1636; dep. Gen. Ct., 1635, et seq.; first speaker House of Deputies, 1644, 45, et seq.; commr. United Colonies, 1650, 54, 73; maj., Salem mil. company; gov.'s asst., 1662-79; in charge mil. affairs of Marblehead, 1666; judge, 1667-78; *m* Ann – (*d* post 1681).

HAVEN, Richard (1620-1703), from Eng. to Lynn, Mass., 1640-45; sgt. King Philip's War; freeman, 1691; *m* Susanna Newhall.

HAWLEY, Joseph (1603-90), from Eng., 1629 or 30; was first town recorder of Stratford, Conn.; dep. Gen. Ct., 1665-87; *m* 1646, Katharine Birdsey (*d* 1692).

HAY, John (son of a Scottish soldier), came from the Rhenish Palatinate, ca. 1750, and settled in York Co., Pa.

HAYDEN (Heydon, Heaydon), John (*d* 1682), from Eng. in the "Mary and John," to Boston, 1630; propr. Dorchester, 1632; freeman, 1634; settled at Braintree; *m* Susanna –.

HAYDEN, William (1600-69), from Eng., with his brother John, in the "Mary and John," to Dorchester, Mass., 1630; a founder of Windsor, Conn., 1640; removed to Kennilworth (now Clinton), 1660; *m* 2d, Margaret Wilcoxson.

HAYES, George (1655-1725), from Scotland, 1680, settled at Windsor, Conn., 1682; removed to Simsbury; *m* 1683, Abigail Dibble (1666-post 1725).

HAYHURST, Cuthbert (ca. 1633-1683), Quaker minister, from Eng. to Pa., 1682, accompanying William Penn on his first voyage in the "Welcome"; purchased 500 acres on the Neshaminy Creek, Bucks Co., Pa.; the house still standing (1925), occupied by the Phila. Camp Fire Girls; *m* 1666, Mary (*d* 1686), dau. of Edward Rudd.

HAYNES, see also Haines.

HAYNES, John (1594-1654), from Eng., 1633; gov. Colony of Mass. Bay, 1635; a founder of Hartford, 1636, and gov. Colony of Conn., 1639, and alternate yrs. until his death; pres. 1st Gen. Ct., 1637; commr. United Colonies, 1650; col. of regt. raised against the Indians, 1636; *m* 2d, Mabel (*b* 1614), dau. Richard Harlakenden.

HAYNES, Walter (1583-1664/65), from Wilts., Eng., 1638; dep. from Sudbury, Mass., to Gen. Ct., 1641, 42, 43, 44, 46, 48, 51; *m* bet. 1612-16, Elizabeth – (*d* 1659).

HAYWARD (Haward, Howard) William (1614-59), from Eng., 1635; propr. Charlestown, Mass., 1637; removed to Braintree; dep. Gen. Ct., 1641; *m* Margery (*d* 1676), dau. of Thomas Thayer (bap. 1596-1665), from Eng. to Braintree, Mass., ante 1636, *m* 1618, Majorie (*d* 1672/73), dau. Abiel Wheeler (*d* 1614), *m* 1588, Jane Sheperd (*d* 1629).

HAZARD, Thomas (1610-80), ship-carpenter, surveyor and planter; probably originally from Nottinghamshire, Eng., but came immediately from Lyme Regis, Dorset, on the Channel, to Boston, Mass., 1635, with wife Martha and son Robert, where he was admitted freeman, 1636; thence to Portsmouth, R.I., where he was admitted freeman, 1638, as of Aquidneck; was a signer of the Compact for the settlement of Newport, R.I., 1639; admitted freeman and was apptd. with three others to lay out the town of Newport, 1639; apptd. mem. Gen. Ct. of Elections, 1640; was one of the founders of Newtown, L.I., 1652, where he was a magistrate under the Dutch, 1652-55; mem. Gov.'s Council, 1654; returned to Portsmouth, R.I., 1655, but again appears at Newtown, 1656 and 1665; *m* Martha – (*d* post 1669); *m* 2d, 1675, Martha (*d* 1691), widow of Thomas Sheriff, of Plymouth, Mass., and Portsmouth, R.I., she *m* 3d, Lewis Hues, of Portsmouth.

HAZELTINE, John (1620-90), from Eng., 1637, settled at Salem, Mass.; an original settler at Rowley, 1640; freeman, 1637-40; selectman, 1668; served in King Philip's War; *m* Jane Auter (*d* 1698).

HEBARD (Hibbard, Hibbert, Heberd), Robert (1612-84), from Eng., to Salem, Mass., ca. 1636; *m* Joanne –.

HELM, Thomas (1731-1816), whose family had settled in Va.; was lt. 3d Va. Regt. in Am. Rev., 1776/77; removed to the Falls of Ohio, in Ky., 1779, established "Helm Place," Hardin Co.; *m* ca. 1760, Jean Pope (desc. Nathaniel Pope, from Eng. to Md., ca. 1635, mem. Md. Assembly, later settled in Westmoreland Co., Va.).

HEMENWAY (Hemmenway), Ralph, was a resident of Roxbury, Mass., 1633; was devoted to the interests of Apostle John Eliot; *m* 1634, Elizabeth Hewes (*d* 1686, aet. 82).

HEMPSTEAD, Robert (ca. 1600-1655), from Eng. to New London, Conn., 1643, where he was one of the first nine settlers; *m* 1646, Joanna Wyllie (*d* 1660).

HENRY, Rev. Robert (1720-67; a cousin of Patrick Henry, the statesman), from Scotland, 1740; A.B., Princeton, 1751; Presbyn. minister in Charlotte Co., Va.; *m* Jean (Johnson) Caldwell.

HENRY, Robert, from Scotland, 1722, settled in Chester Co., Pa.; *m* Mary Ann –.

HERNDON, William (1649-1722), from Eng., patented large tracts of land in St. Stephen's Parish, New Kent Co., Va., Feb. 1673/74; *m* 1677, Catherine (1654-1727), dau. of Gov. Edward Digges, of Va.

HERR, Hans (1639-1725), from Switzerland to Lampeter, Lancaster Co., Pa., 1709; *m* 1660, Elizabeth (1644-1730), dau. John Kendig.

HERRESHOFF, Charles Frederick, scientist, linguist and musician; came from Germany and settled at Providence; *m* Sarah, dau. John Brown, banker, Revolutionary patriot; mem. Congress; a founder Brown U.; desc. Chad Brown and Richard Warren (both qv).

HERRICK, (Heyricke), Henry (1600-71; 5th son of Sir William, *m* Lady Joan –); from Eng., settled on "Cape Ann Syde," 1629; freeman, 1630; removed to Wenham, finally to Beverly, was a founder of the first church there; *m* Edith (*b* 1614), dau. Hugh Laskin.

HERSEY (Hersie, Harsie, Hearsey), William (1596-1658), from Eng., 1635; an original settler at

Hingham, Mass.; freeman, 1638; mem. A. and H. A. Co.; *m* Elizabeth Croade.

HEWITT, John (1777-1857), from Eng. to Rockland Co., N.Y., 1796; *m* Ann Garnee (desc. Isaac Garnier, a Huguenot, from Isle de France to N.Y., 1692).

HEYWARD, Daniel, from Eng. to Charleston, S.C., ca. 1672.

HICKS, Robert (*d* 1647), from Eng. in the "Fortune," to Plymouth, Mass., 1621; *m* 1596, Margaret Morgan (*d* 1607); *m* 2d, 1610, Margaret Winslow, who came in the "Ann," 1622.

HIGGINS, Richard, came from England to Plymouth, Mass., 1632; mem. Council of War, 1653; dep., 1647; selectman; a founder of Eastham, Mass., 1644; *m* 1634, Lydia Chandler; *m* 2d, 1651, Mary Yates.

HIGGINSON, Francis (1587/88-1630), A.B., Cambridge, 1609; elected at London mem. council of Colony of Mass. Bay, 1629, and came in the "Talbot," with wife and eight children (one of whom *d* on the passage) to Salem, Mass., 1629; was minister at Leicester, Eng.; ordained at Salem, 1629, and minister of the first church in the Colony; *m* Anne – (*d* 1640).

HIGLEY, Capt. John (July 22, 1649-1714), from Frimley, Surrey, Eng., settled at Windsor, Conn., 1664; *m* 1671, Hannah Drake; *m* 2d, 1696, Sarah Strong Bissell (Mar. 14, 1666-May 27, 1739).

HILL, Clement (*d* 1708), from Eng. with the third Lord Baltimore, 1662/63, settled in Md.; high sheriff St. Mary's Co., 1674-76; mem. Lower House of Md. Assembly, 1677-85; mem. Council, privy councillor, vice regent, probate judge, etc.; *m* Elizabeth (Hatton) Gardiner, widow of Luke Gardiner, of St. Mary's Co., Md.

HILL, Peter (*d* 1667), from Eng. in the "Huntress," 1632/33, settled on Saco River, present site of Biddeford, Me.; mem. Assembly of Lygonia, 1648, and asst. of same.

HILL, Ralph (*d* 1663), from Eng. before 1638, to Plymouth, Mass.; selectman at Woburn, 1649; freeman, 1647; an original grantee of Billerica, Mass., 1653; *m* Margaret Toothaker.

HILL, Robert, to Va., 1642, settled in Isle of Wight Co.; *m* ante 1642, Mary –.

HILLHOUSE, James (ca. 1687-1740, son of John), from Ireland, 1721; was 1st pastor of the first church at Montville, Conn.; *m* Mary, dau. Daniel Fitch; *m* 2d, Mary Sherwood.

HILLS, Joseph (1602-88), from Eng., settled at Charlestown, Mass., 1638; a founder of Malden, Mass.; settled at Newbury, 1664; dep. from Charlestown and speaker of the House, 1647; dep. from Malden, 1650 and 1660-64, from Newbury, 1667, 69; capt. Malden mil. company; *m* 1651, Hannah (Smith) Mallows.

HILLYER, John (*d* 1655), from Eng. to Windsor, Conn., a founder, 1639; *m* Ann –.

HINCKLEY, Samuel (1595-1662), from Eng. in the "Hercules," to Scituate, Mass., 1635; removed to Barnstable, 1639; *m* in Eng., 1617, Sarah Soole (*d* 1656); *m* 2d, Bridget Bodfish.

HINMAN, Sgt. Edward (*d* 1681), from Eng. ante 1650; lived at Stamford, Conn., settled finally at Stratford; served in Indian campaign, 1644; *m* 1651, Hannah (*d* 1677), dau. of Francis Stiles.

HINSDALE, Robert (ca. 1617-1675), from Eng. to Dedham, Mass., ca. 1632; a founder of the church there; with three sons was slain by Indians at Deerfield, Mass., Sept. 18, 1675; *m* Ann Woodward.

HITCHCOCK, Luke (*d* Nov. 1659), from Eng. ca. 1635, an original settler at New Haven, Conn., 1638; freeman, 1644; later at Wethersfield, Conn.; selectman and dep.; capt. early colonial wars; *m* Elizabeth Gibbons.

HITCHCOCK, Matthew, or Matthias (1614-69), from Eng. in the "Susan and Ellen," to Boston and Watertown, Mass., 1635; removed to New Haven; *m* Elizabeth –.

HITE (Hans Jost Heydt), Joist (*d* 1760-61), from Germany, in his own ship, the "Swift," bringing with him 16 families, to Kingston, N. Y., 1710, thence to Germantown, Pa., 1716; was the first white settler in Shenandoah Valley, Va., 1731; obtained grants for 140,000 acres and settled there over 100 families; justice first court of Orange Co.; *m* 1st, Anna Maria, dau. Louis DuBois, a Huguenot.

HOAG, John (1642/43-1728; son of Richard, *m* ante 1637, Joan –), Quaker; from Eng. or Wales with his father's family, 1650, to Boston; the family returned to Eng., he alone remaining; settled at Newbury, Mass.; a judge Salem witchcraft trials and dissented from the other judges by opposing the persecution; *m* 1669, dau. of John Emery (qv).

HOBART (Hobard, Hubbard), Edmund (1570-1646); son of Henry, *m* Dorothy Ball, of Cutwood); from Eng. to Charlestown, Mass., 1633; freeman; 1634; constable; one of the first settlers at Hingham, 1635; dep. Gen. Ct., 1639, 40, 42; *m* Margaret Dewey.

HODGE, Andrew (1711-89), from Ireland, with his brothers William and Hugh, settled at Phila., Pa., 1731; *m* Jane McCulloch.

HODGES, William (*d* 1654), from Eng. to Salem, Mass., before 1643, settled at Taunton; *m* Mary Andrews.

HOFFMAN, Martinus Hermanzen (*b* 1625; son of Herman, a native of Revel on the Gulf of Finland), from Holland to Esopus (Kingston), New Netherland, 1657; removed to New Amsterdam, later to Kingston, Ulster Co.; *m* 1663 Lysbeth Hemans; *m* 2d, Emmerentje Claesen de Witt.

HOGE, William (1660-1745), from Scotland ca. 1680; settled at Perth Amboy, N.J., 1689; founder of Washington Co., Pa.; settled finally at Opequon, Va.; *m* Barbara Hume (1670-1745).

HOLCOMBE, Thomas (*d* 1657), resident of Dorchester, 1634; removed to Windsor, Conn., ante 1639, where he *d*; *m* Elizabeth –.

HOLDEN, Justinian (1611-91), from Eng. in the "Elizabeth" to Watertown, Mass., 1634; served in King Philip's War; *m* 2d, Mary Rutter.

HOLDEN, Randall (1612-92), from Eng., was settled at Portsmouth, R.I., 1638; removed to Warwick; marshal and corp. at Portsmouth, 1638; gov.'s asst., 1647, et seq.; capt., 1664; dep. Gen. Ct. 1666-86; *m* 1648, Frances Dungan (*d* 1697).

HOLDEN, Richard (ca. 1609-1695/96), from Eng. in the "Frances," 1634; an original propr. of Groton, Mass.; *m* 1640/41, Martha (1620-1681), dau. of Stephen Fosdick.

HOLLADAY, John (*d* 1743), from Eng. to Spotsylvania Co., Va., 1702; *m* Elizabeth Brocas.

HOLLINGSWORTH, Valentine (1632-ca. 1711; son of Henry, of Ireland), a Quaker; came to Pa., 1682; mem. first Provincial Assembly of Pa., 1682-1683, et seq.; justice; signer of the Great Charter; *m* 1st, Ann Ree (ca. 1628-1671).

HOLLIS, John, from Eng. to Weymouth, Mass., 1642; removed to Wethersfield, Conn., 1644; *m* Elizabeth Priest.

HOLLISTER, John (ca. 1612-1665), from Eng., 1641, settled at Wethersfield, Conn., 1642; large landowner on east side Conn. River; freeman, 1643; collector, 1660; rep. Gen. Ct., Mass. and Conn.; lt. colonial forces; *m* Joanna (*d* 1694), dau. Richard Treat.

HOLMES, John (*d* 1667), from Eng. to Plymouth, Mass., 1632; 1st messenger Gen. Ct., 1638; *m* Sarah –.

HOLMES, John (*b* 1644), from Eng. to Dorchester, Mass.; an original propr. Woodstock, Conn., 1686.

HOLMES, Rev. Obadiah (1607-82), from Preston, Lancashire Co., Eng.; ed. at Oxford U.; living at Salem, Mass., 1639; Newport, R.I., 1652-82; commr. from Newport to the Gen. Ct. of R.I., 1655, 56, 58; one of the 12 original patentees of Monmouth Co., N.J., 1655, to whom Gov. Richard Nicholls granted nearly the whole of the present county; mem. of special Governor's Council, 1676; lt. in Plymouth militia; pastor Bapt. Ch., Newport, R.I., 1652-84; *m* in Eng., 1630, Catherine Hyde (1608-84).

HOLT, Nicholas (1602-85), from Eng. in the "James," to Newbury, Mass., 1635; a tanner; freeman, 1637; removed to Andover, Mass., 1644; *m* 1st, Elizabeth – (*d* 1656); *m* 2d, 1658, Hannah – (*d* 1665), dau. Humphrey Bradstreet, and widow of Daniel Rolfe; *m* 3d, 1666, – Preston, widow.

HOLTON, Joseph (1621-1705), from Eng., wheelwright; *m* Sarah (Ingersoll) Haynes, dau. of Richard Ingersoll (qv).

HOLTON, William (1611-Aug. 12, 1691), from Eng. in the "Francis," 1634; one of first settlers of Hartford, Conn., and at Northampton, Mass., 1654, where he was justice and the first deacon; rep. Gen. Ct., 1664, 67, 69, 71; introduced the first motion known in American history for the suppression of intemperance; *m* Mary – (*d* Nov. 16, 1691).

HOLYOKE, Hon. Elizur (son of Edward), *m* 1640 Mary, dau. of Col. William Pynchon.

HOOKER, Thomas (1586-1647), A.B., Cambridge, 1608; fled from Eng. to Holland, 1630, thence in the "Griffin" to Boston, 1633; freeman, 1634; elected pastor of the 8th Ch., Newton, Mass., and moved with his congregation and family to Hartford, Conn., 1636, of which he was the founder; *m* Susanna Pym.

HOPKINS, Gerrard (or Jared), (*d* ante 1693/94), from Eng., was settled in Anne Arundel Co., Md., about the middle of the 17th Century; *m* Thomasin –.

HOPKINS, Stephen (1583-1644), 14th signer of the Mayflower Compact; in the "First Encounter," 1620; asst. 1633-36; mem. Council of War for the Colony, 1642-44; volunteer in Pequot War, 1637; *m* 2d, 1617, or earlier, Elizabeth Fisher (*d* bet. 1640-44).

HOPKINSON, Thomas (1709-51), from Eng. to Phila., Pa., 1731; judge of vice admiralty, mem. Provincial Council, etc.; *m* Mary Johnson.

HOPPIN (Hopin), Stephen (1624-78), from Eng., was at Dorchester, Mass., 1653; also lived at Roxbury; *m* Hannah, dau. Thomas Makepeace.

HORTON, Thomas (*d* 1641), from Eng., 1633; settled at Springfield, Mass., 1638; witnessed an Indian deed; *m* Mary Eddy.

HOTCHKISS, Samuel (*d* 1663), from Eng. in the "Hector," with the Davenport colony; one of founders of New Haven, Conn., 1638; *m* 1642, Elizabeth Cleaverly.

HOUGH, Richard (*d* 1705), from Co. Chester, Eng., in the "Endeavor," to Phila., Pa.; settled in Bucks Co., where he owned 2,500 acres; provincial councillor, 1693, 1700; mem. Assembly; justice of the peace Bucks Co. Ct.; drowned in Delaware River; *m* 1683, Margery (*d* 1719-20), dau. of John Clows, Quaker, from Eng. in the "Endeavor," mem. Pa. Assembly, 1683-84, *m* Margery –.

HOUGHTON (Hoghton), John (1624-84; son of John, II, who came in the "Abigail," 1635, but returned to Eng.), from Eng. in the "Abigail," to Mass., 1635; at Concord, and at Lancaster, 1652; *m* Beatrix –.

HOUGHTON, Ralph (1623-1705), from Eng., ca. 1636; settled at Lancaster, Mass., 1652; clk. of writs, 1656-82; rep. Gen. Ct., 1673-89; was constable, collector and town treas.; removed to Milton, Mass.; *m* Jane Stowe (1626-1700/01).

HOUSTOUN, Sir Patrick (1688-1762; son of Sir Patrick, 5th baron), philanthropist; came to America with Gen. Oglethorpe, 1731, to found colony of Ga.; settled at Fredrica, St. Simons Island, Ga., 1732; was pres. of His Majesty's Council, Province of Ga.; *m* Priscilla Dunbar, who came from Eng. in same ship with him (with her brother Capt. Dunbar); their son John was twice colonial governor.

HOWARD, John (1620-1700), from Eng., 1638, settled at Roxbury, Mass.; one of 54 original proprs. of land at Bridgewater; surveyor; ens. in King Philip's War; dep. and rep. Gen. Cts.; commd. lt., 1689; innkeeper and carpenter, Bridgewater; *m* ca. 1651, Martha, dau. of Capt. Thomas Hayward (*d* 1691), came in the "Hercules," 1635, *m* Susanna –.

HOWARD, Joshua (ca. 1665-1738), from Eng. to Baltimore, Md., 1686; *m* Joanna O'Carroll (*d* 1763).

HOWE, Edward (1575-1639), from Hatfield, Broad Oaks, Eng., 1635; settled at Lynn, Mass., Sept. 19, 1635; rep. Gen. Ct.; *m* Elizabeth – (1585-1672).

HOWE, James (ca. 1606-1702), from Eng. to Roxbury, Mass., ca. 1637; freeman; settled at Ipswich before 1648; *m* Elizabeth, dau. of John Dane.

HOWE (How), John (1602-1680; son of John), from Eng., was at Sudbury, Mass., ca. 1635; freeman, 1640; selectman, 1643; first white settler at Marlborough, Mass., ca. 1657, where he commanded a garrison house in King Philip's War; *m* Mary – (*d* ca. 1687).

HOWELL, Edward (1584-1655), from Eng. to Boston, 1639; had land grant of 500 acres at Lynn, Mass., before 1639; founder of Southampton, L.I., 1640; gov.'s asst. Conn. Colony, 1647-53; magistrate; mem. Legislature; *m* Frances – (*d* 1630); *m* 2d, Eleanor –.

HOWELL, William (1645?-1710), of Castle Bigot, provincial councillor, Wales (son of Morgan Howell, *m* Margaret Edwards, *m* 2d, Mary Thomas, widow, dau. of John and Joan Husband); came from Wales to Phila., among the earliest founders of Pa.; a surveyor and man of education he became one of the first magistrates, and the founder of Haverford Town, Pa.; 5 surviving children.

HOWLAND, Henry (*d* 1671), from Eng., 1621-23; early settler of Duxbury, Mass., where he was constable; grantee of Bridgewater, 1645; *m* Mary (*d* 1674), dau. Henry Newland.

HOWLAND, John (ca. 1593-1673), 13th signer of the Mayflower Compact; asst., 1633-35; dep. Gen. Ct., 1641-69; in the "First Encounter," 1620; in command of Kennebec Trading Post, 1634; *m* at Plymouth, Mass., before 1624, Elizabeth (ca. 1607-1687), dau. John Tilley (qv).

HOYT, John (1610-87), from Eng., 1639; an original settler of Salisbury, Mass., 1640; killed by the Indians; *m* 1635, Frances – (*d* 1642); *m* 2d Frances –.

HOYT (Haight, Hoyte), Simon (*b* Somerset, Eng., ca. 1595-*d* 1659), first appeared at Charlestown, Mass., 1629; first settler of Dorchester, 1630; freeman, 1631; at Scituate, 1633-36, where he and his wife joined ch.; removed to Windsor, Conn., 1639, to Fairfield, 1645, at Stamford, 1658, where he died; *m* Deborah Stowers (1593-1625); *m* 2d, Susanna Smith (*d* 1674).

HUBBARD, George (1591-1684), from Eng. to Concord, Mass., 1633, was at Hartford, Conn., 1636, later was Indian agt. at Middletown; dep. Gen. Ct.; *m* Mary Bishop (*d* 1675).

HUBBARD, William (1594-1670), grad. Cambridge U. ca. 1620; came in the "Defense," to Ipswich, Mass., 1635; freeman, 1638; rep. Gen. Ct., 1638 and several yrs. following; settled at Boston, 1662; *m* probably 2d, Judith (*b* 1601), dau. of John Knapp, *m* Martha Blosse.

HUBBELL, Richard (1627-99, son Richard, of Worcestershire, Eng., *m* Sarah, dau. Francis Wakeman); from Eng. to Poquonnock, Conn., bet. 1631-39; settled at New Haven, 1647; sgt. of militia, Fairfield, Conn., 1677-99; dep. Gen. Ct., 1678; *m* 1650, Elizabeth (*d* 1664), dau. of John Meigs, Sr., *m* Thomasine Fry.

HUDSON, Daniel, came to America in first half of 17th Century; settled at Watertown, Mass., then at Lancaster, Mass.; killed by Indians in Lancaster in massacre of Sept. 11, 1697; *m* Joanna –.

HUGER, Daniel (1651-1711), Huguenot; from France, 1685; settled on the Santee River, S.C.; *m* Margaret Perdriau.

HUGHES (Hugh), John (1652-1736; son of Hugh Cadwalader Rhys by his wife Gwenn, dau. of Ellis Williams, Gentleman, of royal descent; descent that of the Hughes of Gwerclas, Wales; desc. Humphrey de Bohun X, Earl of Hereford, Essex and Northampton), came from Wales to Philadelphia in "Robert and Elizabeth," 1698; estate 500 acres at Gwynedd.

HUIDEKOPER, Harm Jan (1776-1854), came from Holland to New York in the "Prudence," 1796; entered employ of The Holland Land Co. at Oldenbarneveld (now Trenton Falls), N.Y., 1799; transferred to its main office at Phila., Pa., 1802; apptd. agt. gen. of its lands in Pa., 1804, moved to Meadville, Pa., Nov. 1804; assumed agency of its possessions east of Allegheny River, 1805; built "Pomona Hall," bought all the holdings of The Holland Land Co. in northwestern Pa., 1836; founded the Meadville Theol. School, 1844; *m* 1806, Rebecca (1779-1839), dau. of Andrew Colhoon.

HULBERT (Hurlbut, Hurlburt), Thomas (ca. 1610-1675), from Eng., probably with Lion Gardiner in the "Bachilor," to Boston, 1635; was at Saybrook, Conn., 1637, later at Wethersfield; granted 160 acres for services under Lion Gardiner in Pequot War; dep. Gen. Ct. and constable, 1644; *m* Sarah –.

HULBURD (Hulbert), William (1611-94), from Eng. to Dorchester, Mass., 1630; freeman, 1632; at Windsor, Conn., 1636, at Hartford, later Northampton, Mass., 1655; *m* 2d, Ann –, widow of Samuel Allen, of Windsor, Conn.

HULL, George (1590-1659), from Eng.; was at Plymouth, Mass., 1629; resided at Boston and Dorchester, Mass., Windsor, Killingworth and Fairfield, Conn.; dep. Gen. Ct. of Conn., 1637; *m* 1614, Thamzen Michell.

HULL, Joseph (1594-1665; son of Thomas, *m* Joane Peson); B.A., St. Mary's Hall, Oxford U.,

1614; from Eng. with a company of 106 persons, to Boston, 1635; founder of Barnstable, Mass.; later at Yarmouth and at York, Me.; clergyman; dep. Gen. Ct., 1638, 39; *m* Joanne –; *m* 2d, Agnes –.

HULL, Richard (*d* 1662), from Eng. to Dorchester, Mass., ca. 1632; freeman, 1634; at New Haven, Conn., abt. 1640; master of the watch, 1649.

HUME, George (1698-1760; son of Sir George, 9th Baron Wedderburn, Scotland, and desc. King Robert Bruce, King Malcolm II, and Edward, the Elder); from Scotland; surveyor for William and Mary Coll., 1727-29; laid out city of Fredericksburg, Va.; *m* 1728, Elizabeth Procter (*b* 1700), of Va.

HUMPHREY (Humphreys), Michael (ca. 1620-post 1697), from Eng. to Windsor, Conn., 1642; freeman, 1657; settled at Simsbury, 1669; dep. Gen. Ct., 1670; *m* 1647, Priscilla (*b* 1626), dau. Matthew Grant (qv).

HUNGERFORD, Thomas (1602-63), from Eng. to Hartford, Conn., 1638; to New London, 1650.

HUNT, Peter (1610-92), one of the first settlers at Rehoboth, Mass.; lt., Rehoboth Train Band, 1654-82, and capt., 1682-92; mem Council of War, 1658, 85; dep. Gen. Ct., 15 yrs.; served in King Philip's War.

HUNT, William (1605-67; son of Robert, of Halifax, Yorkshire, Eng.); from Eng. to Concord, Mass.; freeman, 1641; *m* 1630, Elizabeth Best (*d* 1661).

HUNTINGTON, Simon (1583-1633), Puritan, from Eng., 1633, *d* at sea of smallpox; his wife, Margaret Barrett (dau. Peter or Christopher Barret, mayor of Norwich, Eng.), and three children arrived at Boston, 1633, settled at Roxbury, Mass.; she *m* 2d, 1635, Thomas Stoughton (*d* 1661).

HURD, John (1613-81), one of the earliest settlers at Windsor, Conn.; settled at Stratford, 1639, dep. Gen. Ct., 1657-58.

HURLBUT, Thomas (*d* 1671), *b* Scotland; was at Wethersfield, Conn.; soldier in Pequot War; clk. of Train Band, 1640; dep. Gen. Ct., 1644; lt. at Saybrook Fort.

HUSSEY (Huzzey), Capt. Christopher (1598-1686), from Eng. in the "William and Francis," to Boston, Mass., 1632; lived first in Lynn; propr. of Hampton, N.H., 1638; mem. Mass. Gen. Ct., 1658-60, 72; one of the purchasers of Nantucket Island from Indians, 1659; mem. Royal Council of N.H., 1679-85; capt. of militia; *m* Theodate, dau. of Rev. Stephen Bachiler (qv).

HUTCHINSON, William (1586-1642), from Eng. to Boston, Mass., 1634; freeman, 1635; removed to R.I., 1638; rep. Gen. Ct. of Mass., 1635-38; gov. of Portsmouth, R.I., 1639-40; *m* ca. 1612, Ann Marbury (ca. 1590-1643), distinguished religious teacher; was banished and with her husband and fifteen children went to the Narragansett country where they purchased Aquidneck Island from the Indians and founded the town of Portsmouth, R.I.; after her husband's death, went into the Dutch country west of New Haven, where she and most of her family were murdered by the Indians.

HYDE, Jonathan (1626-1711), from Eng., was at Newtown, Mass., 1647; settled at Cambridge, 1648; served in King Philip's War.

HYDE, William (ca. 1597-1681), from Eng. with Rev. Thomas Hooker, to Newton, Mass., 1633; removed to Hartford, Conn., 1636; an original propr. of Norwich, 1660.

HYNSON, Thomas (*b* 1621), from Eng. to Kent Co., Md., ca. 1650, he and Joseph Wickes were awarded a grant of 800 acres called "Wickcliffe," at the Eastern Neck, nr. the mouth of Chester River; commr. of Kent Island, 1654; high sheriff; burgess, 1659; *m* Grace –.

INGALLS, Edmund (ca. 1598-1648), from Eng. to Salem, Mass., 1628, with Gov. Endicott; a first settler of Lynn, 1629; *m* Ann –.

INGERSOLL, John (1615-84), from Eng., was at Hartford, Conn., 1651; at Northampton, Mass., 1655, at Westfield, Mass., 1665; *m* ca. 1651, Dorothy, dau. Thomas Lord; *m* 2d, 1656, Abigail, dau. Thomas Bascom; *m* 3d, 1668, Mary Hunt (sister of Jonathan Hunt and g.dau. Gov. John Webster, of Conn.).

INGERSOLL, Richard (1600-44), from Eng., with Gov. Higginson, 1629, to Salem, Mass.; *m* Ann Langley (*d* 1677).

INGHAM, Jonas (*d* 1755), from Eng. to New England, ca. 1705, removed to Trenton, N.J., thence to Bucks Co., Pa.; *m* Elizabeth – (*d* 1748).

INMAN, Abednego (1752-1831), from Eng., ca. 1765-67, settled at Limestone, Va., then at Danridge, Tenn.; maj. Am. Rev.; *m* 1778, Mary Ritchie (1757-1836).

IRVING, William (1731-1807), from Shapinsha, one of the Orkney Islands, came to New York, 1763; *m* Sarah Sanders (among their sons was Washington Irving, distinguished author).

ISHAM, Henry (1628-1675), from Eng. to Va., 1654; justice; maj. militia; *m* Catherine Banks (*d* 1686), widow of Joseph Royall (qv).

ISHAM (Isum), John (*d* 1713), was at Newburyport, Mass., 1667; settled at Barnstable, Mass., 1670; *m* 1677, Jane (1664-1719), dau. Robert Parker, of Barnstable.

IVES, William (1607-48), from Eng. to Boston, 1635, an original settler at Quinnipiack (New Haven), Conn., 1638; soldier at New Haven in Indian alarms of 1642, 46; *m* Hannah – (who *m* 2d, William Bassett).

IZARD, Ralph (*d* 1710), from Eng. to Charleston, Carolina, 1682; settled in St. James' Parish, S.C.; mem. Council, 1700; justice; pres. Indian Commn.; *m* Mary –, widow of Arthur Middleton; *m* 2d, Dorothy –, widow of Christopher Smith.

JACKSON, Edward (1602-81), from Eng. to Newtown, Mass., 1643; freeman 1645; purchased farm of 500 acres from Gov. Bradstreet; selectman; dep. Gen. Ct. 18 sessions; aid of Apostle Eliot in evangelization of the Indians; gave 400 acres of land to Harvard Coll.; *m* Frances – (*d* 1648); *m* 2d, 1649, Elizabeth, dau. John Newgate, and widow of John Oliver.

JACOB (Jacobs), Nicholas (*d* 1657), from Eng. with his wife and two children to Watertown, Mass.; removed to Hingham, 1635; freeman, 1636; dep. Gen. Ct., 1648-49; selectman; *m* Mary – (*d* 1681).

JANNEY, Thomas (1633-Feb. 12, 1696), from Styall, Pownall Fee, Parish of Wilmslow, Macclesfield Hundred, Co. Chester, Eng. in the "Endeavor," to Bucks Co., Pa., July 29, 1683; minister Soc. of Friends; provincial councillor, mem. William Penn's Council, 1684, 85, 86, 91; justice of the peace for Bucks Co.; *m* Sept. 24, 1660, in Eng., Margery Heath.

JAY, Augustus (1665-1751), Huguenot, from France, upon the revocation of the Edict of Nantes, 1685, settled at New York; *m* 1697, Anna Maria, dau. Balthazar Bayard.

JEFFERSON, John, from Wales; among the first settlers in Va.; part-founder of Yorktown, Va.; lived in Osborne's on the James; burgess, 1619.

JENKINS, John (1609-ca. 1690), from London, Eng., in the "Defense," to Plymouth, 1635; soldier Pequot War, 1637; soldier Narragansett Expdn., 1645; moved to Barnstable, 1652.

JENKINS, Thomas (1642-ca. 1729), from Wales to Md., ca. 1670; settled in Charles Co.; *m* 1669, Ann Spaulding.

JENKS (Jenckes), Joseph (1602-Mar. 1683), from Eng. to Boston, ca. 1640; established the iron works at Lynn, 1642; was the first patentee in America; built the first fire engine, and cut the dies for the "Pine Tree Shilling"; inventor of the grass scythe; *m* 2d, Elizabeth –.

JENNINGS, Edmund (1659-1727), of "Ripon Hall," York Co., Va.; was atty. gen., sec. of state, pres. of the Council and acting gov.; *m* Frances, dau. of Henry Corbin (qv).

JENNINGS, Joshua (ca. 1620-1674/75), from Eng. to Hartford, Conn., ca. 1645; at Fairfield, 1656; *m* 1647, Mary Williams, of Hartford.

JEWELL, Thomas (*b* 1598-will dated, 1654), from Eng. to Mt. Wollaston, Mass., 1639; lived at Braintree; *m* Grisell –.

JEWETT, Joseph (bap. 1609-1660/61), Puritan, from Eng. in the "John," 1638; admitted freeman at Rowley, Mass., 1639; dep. Gen. Ct., 1651-54 and 1660; *m* 1634, Mary Mallinson (*d* 1652), *m* 2d, Ann Allen.

JEWETT, Maximilian (bap. 1607-1684; son of Edward [1580-1614], of Bradford, West Riding, Yorkshire, Eng., clothier, *m* Mary Taylor); from Eng. in the "John," to Boston, 1638; a founder of Rowley, 1639; deacon 50 yrs.; dep. Gen. Ct., 1641-76; *m* 1st, Ann – (*d* 1667).

JOHNSON, Edward (bap. 1598-1672), from Eng., 1630; freeman at Charlestown, Mass., 1630; was at Merrimac, 1632; a founder of Woburn, 1642; a founder of the A. and H. A. Co., 1637; lt., Middlesex Co. troop, 1643, capt., 1644; surveyor gen. of the mil. stores of the colony, 1659; dep. Gen. Ct., 1643-47, 1649-70, and speaker, 1655, historical author; *m* Susan Munnter (1598-1689).

JOHNSON, Elihu, of Conn., soldier in French and Indian War and Am. Rev.; *m* 1762, Sarah (Webb) Converse (*b* 1741), widow of Joshua Converse, and desc. Christopher Webb, from Eng. before 1645, and Henry Adams.

JOHNSON, John (1630-85), from Eng., to Rowley, Mass.; soldier King Philip's War; *m* 1655, Hannah, dau. Anthony Crosby.

JOHNSON, Thomas (*d* 1714), from Eng. to Md., ca. 1660; settled in Calvert Co., ca. 1690, where he was Indian trader; *m* Mary, dau. Roger Baker, of Liverpool, Eng.

JONES, Capt. Lewis (*d* 1684), from Wales and Eng., 1635, settled at Weston, Roxbury or Belmont, Mass., ca. 1640; *m* Anne (*d* 1680), dau. of Deacon Simeon Stone (qv).

JONES, Capt. Roger (1642-1701), came to Va. with Lord Culpeper, 1680, but returned to London, 1684/85; *m* Dorothy (*b* 1642), dau. of John Walker; *m* 2d, Priscilla Haddock.

JONES, Thomas (1665-1713), from Ireland to R.I., 1692; became ranger gen. of L.I., and maj. of Queens Co. regt.; *m* Freelove, dau. Capt. Thomas Townsend.

JORDAN, Robert (1612-79), from Eng., ca. 1641; clergyman; preacher at Richmond Island, nr. Scarborough, Me., later at Falmouth, Me., and Portsmouth, N.H.; mem. Council of George Cleves, of Lygonia, 1648; apptd. one of four to govern Province of Me., 1665; *m* Sarah, dau. of John Winter.

JORDAN (Jourdan), Samuel (*d* 1623), came from France in the "Sea Voyage," which was wrecked off Bermuda Coast; settled at "Jordan's Journey," on James River, 1610; mem. first legislative assembly in America at Jamestown, 1619; *m* 1618, Cicely – (*b* 1600), came in the "Swan," 1611.

JOSLYN, Thomas (ca. 1591-1660/61) from Eng. in the "Increase" to Sudbury, then Hingham, Mass., 1635; propr.; then Watertown, then removed to Lancaster; *m* ca. 1615, Rebecca –.

JOY, Thomas (1611-78), from Eng. in the "Constance," 1635, was an architect and builder at Boston; supported Dr. Robert Child's petition for extension of the right of suffrage, 1646; settled at Hingham, 1647; mem. A. and H. A. Co., 1658; freeman Mass. Bay Colony, 1665; built Boston Town House, 1657; *m* 1637, Joan Gallup.

JUDD, Thomas (ca. 1608-1688), settled at Cambridge, Mass., 1634; at Hartford, Conn., 1636; one of earliest proprs. of Farmington, Conn., 1644; settled at Northampton, Mass., 1679; dep. Gen. Ct. several yrs.

JUDSON, William (*d* 1660), from Eng. to Concord, Mass., 1634; one of first settlers at Stamford, Conn., 1639; moved to New Haven.

KEASBEY, Edward, from Eng., ca. 1694; joined John Fenwick's colony of Quakers; founder of Salem, N.J., 1675; mem. Gen. Assembly; del. Provincial Congress; *m* 1701, dau. of Andrew Thompson, and widow of Isaac Smart.

KEELER, Ralph (1613-72), from Eng., settled at Hartford, Conn., ca. 1637; a first settler at Norwalk, Conn., 1650; *m* 1653, Sarah Whelpley.

KEEN (Kyn), Jöran (ca. 1620-1693), from Sweden in the "Fama," with his son, Johan Printz, to Christiana, New Sweden (now Wilmington, Del.), 1643, and founded Upland, New Sweden (now Chester, Pa.).

KEITH, James (1696-ca. 1757), from Scotland, settled in Fauquier Co., Va.; rector of Hamilton Parish 40 yrs.; *m* 1733, Mary Isham, dau. of Thomas Randolph, son of William Randolph (qv).

KELLOGG, Joseph (1626-1707), from Eng. to Farmington, Conn., 1651; freeman, 1654; a founder of Hadley, Mass., where the house he built is still standing; commanded Hadley men, in the Falls fight; selectman; *m* 1650, Joanna – (*d* 1666); *m* 2d, 1667, Abigail (*b* 1646), dau. Stephen Terry, of Windsor, Conn.

KENDALL, Francis (1612-1708), from Eng. to Charlestown, Mass., 1640; one of the first settlers at Woburn, 1644; freeman, 1647; selectman 18 yrs.; *m* 1644, Mary (1630-1705), dau. of Sgt. John Tidd.

KENNON, Richard (1650-96), from Eng. to Va., 1670; was of Conjurer's Neck, Henrico Co.; justice and burgess; *m* Elizabeth, dau. of William Worsham.

KENRICK, John (*b* 1604), from Bristol, Eng., with Rev. Richard Mather (qv), in the "James"; was at Boston, 1639; took freeman's oath, 1646; mem. 1st Ch., Boston, 1658; *m* Anna Smith (*d* Nov. 1656); *m* 2d, Judith – (*d* Aug. 23, 1687).

KENT, Daniel (1765-1844), from Ireland to Phila., Pa., 1785; settled in Chester Co., Pa.; *m* Esther Hawley (g.dau. of Benjamin Hawley, from London to Phila., 1723, settled at Goshen, Pa.).

KENT, Thomas (*d* 1656), from Eng., ca. 1640, an original propr. of Gloucester, Mass.

KETCHAM, John (*d* 1697), from Eng., settled at Ipswich, Conn., 1648; later at Setauket, L.I.; removed to Newton, 1668; mem. Huntington militia.

KEY, Philip (1696-1764), from Eng., ca. 1720, settled in St. Mary's Co., Md.; mem. Lower House of Md. Assembly several sessions; high sheriff, 1744-45; mem. Council, 1763-64; *m* Susanna, dau. John Gardiner (desc. Richard Gardiner, of St. Mary's Co., Md.); *m* 2d, Theodosia (Lawrence) Humphries.

KEYSER, Dirck (1635-1714; silk merchant, son of Dirck Gerrits Keyser by his wife Cornelia, dau. of Tobias Govertz Van Den Wyngaert, a writer and a Mennonite preacher); came from Bavaria to Pa., 1685; built the first stone house in Germantown, still standing; *m* Elizabeth, dau. of Peter ter Himpel; *m* 2d, Johanna Harpers Snoeck.

KIDDER, James (1626-76), from Eng. to Cambridge, Mass., 1649; later settled at Billerica; his dwelling used as a garrison house in King Philip's War, in which he was killed; *m* ca. 1649/50, Anna, dau. Elder Francis Moore.

KIERSTEDE, Dr. Hans (*d* 1671), from Magdenburg to New Amsterdam, 1638, with Gov. Kieft; noted physician and surgeon of New Amsterdam; *m* 1642, Sarah Roelofse, eldest dau. of the celebrated Anneke Jans.

KIMBALL, Richard (ca. 1595-1675), of Rattlesden, Suffolk; came in the "Elizabeth," 1634; settled at Watertown, Mass.; freeman, 1635; removed to Ipswich, ca. 1637; selectman, 1645; surveyor of fences, 1653; *m* ca. 1615, Ursula, dau. of Henry Scott, *m* Martha Whatlock, of Rattlesden, the latter coming to Mass. with her son after her husband's death; *m* 2d, 1661, Margaret – (*d* 1675), widow of Henry Dow.

KING, John (1629-1703; son of John, sec. for Ireland under reign of Queen Elizabeth, son of Lord Edward, first archbishop of Ireland after the Reformation), was at Northampton, Mass., 1645, later at Hartford, Conn.; lt. and capt. Northampton forces; dep. Gen. Ct.; *m* Sarah, dau. William Holton; *m* 2d, Sarah, dau. William Whiting, and widow of Jacob Mygatt.

KING, John (*d* 1744), from Eng. to Boston, ca. 1710, later at Watertown, Mass., and Scarboro, Me.; *m* 1714, Sarah Allen; *m* 2d, 1718, Mary, dau. Benjamin Stowell.

KINGSBURY, Joseph (*d* 1676), from Eng. to Dedham, Mass., bet. 1628-30; *m* Millicent Ames.

KIP (Kype), Hendrik Hendriksen (1600-1680), from Holland to New Amsterdam, bet. 1636-42; one of "The Nine Men," 1647, 49, 50; asst. to the director or gov.; mem. Council; schepen, 1656; great burgher, 1657; *m* 1624, Tryntie Lubberts; *m* 2d, ca. 1627, Tryntje Droogle; *m* 3d, Margaret de Marneil.

KIRKBRIDGE (Kirkbride), Joseph (*d* Jan. 1, 1737), to Newcastle, Pa., with William Penn, 1682; *d* Phila.; *m* Phoebe Blackshaw.

KIRKHAM, Thomas (*d* ca. 1677), from Eng. ca. 1646; settled at Wethersfield, Conn., ca. 1648; taxgatherer, 1648-49.

KITCHELL, Robert (*b* Kent, Eng., 1604-*d* 1672), from Eng. with brothers-in-law, Henry Whitfield and William Chittenden, 1639; name stands first on Plantation Covenant, made on board "Confidence"; treas. of Conn.; dep.; a founder of Guilford and New Haven, Conn., and Newark, N.J., 1666; *m* 1632, Margaret, dau. of Rev. Edmund Sheaffe.

KNOWLES, John (*d* 1705), from Eng. to Cambridge, Mass., ca. 1650, later at North Hampton, N.H.; *m* 1660, Jemima Aster.

KYN, Joran, see Keen.

LADD, Daniel, from Eng., in the "Mary and John," to Mass., 1634; was at Salisbury, ca. 1639; *m* Ann –.

LANE, Job (1620-97), from Eng., was at Rehoboth, Mass., 1644; freeman at Malden, 1656; resided at Bedford, Mass.; served in his own garrison houses in King Philip's War; dep. Gen. Ct. from Bedford, 1678-79, from Malden, 1685, 93.

LANGHORNE (Lacharn), John (11th gen. from Richard Lacharn of Pembrokeshire, Wales, *m* Joan, dau. of Sir Peter Russell, Kt.); came from Wales, ca. 1672; mem. Va. House of Burgesses, 1675; patented a large tract on James River in Warwick Co., Va., 1681; established "Gambell" in Warwick Co.

LANIER, John (1633-1719), from Eng. ca. 1670, settled in Prince George's Co., Va.

LANSING, Gerrit Fredericksе (*d* before Oct. 3, 1679) from Holland to New Amsterdam, 1640; settled at Rensselaerwyck.

LATHROP (Laythrop, Lathropp, Lothrop), John (1584-1653), ed. Oxford U.; was pastor First Independent, or Congl. Ch. at London; came to Scituate, Mass., 1634, where he was first minister; removed to Barnstable, Mass., 1639, and was first minister there; *m* 1st, 1610, Hannah Howse (or House).

LAURENS, Andre (*d* post 1715-16; son of Jean), Huguenot; from La Rochelle, France to Eng. with his widowed mother, 1682, soon afterward to Ireland, thence to New Rochelle, N.Y., 1695, and settled at Charleston, S.C., 1715 or 16; *m* in Eng., Feb. 22, 1688, Marie Lucas (*d* 1715).

LAWRENCE, Benjamin (*d* 1685), from Accomac Co., Va., to Somerset Co., Md., thence to Anne Arundel Co., Md.; *m* Ann Ascomb; *m* 2d, 1676, Elizabeth (Talbott) Preston (ca. 1656-ante 1719), dau. of Richard Talbott, *m* Elizabeth, dau. of Richard Ewen.

LAWRENCE, John (bap. at Wissett, Eng., Oct. 8, 1609-*d* July 11, 1667; son of Henry, *m* Mary –); settled at Watertown, Mass., 1635; freeman, 1637; settled at Groton, 1662, where he was an original land proprietor of a 20-acre tract; mem. first Bd. of Selectmen; *m* Elizabeth – (*d* Aug. 29, 1663); *m* 2d, at Charlestown, Susanna (*d* July 8, 1668), dau. William Batchelder.

LAWRENCE, John (1618-99; *e.* son of Thomas [1588-1625], chief burgher of St. Albans, Co. Herts., Eng., *m* 1609, Joan Antrobus, who *m* 2d, Thomas Tuttle, of Ireland, and came in the "Planter" 1635, with her children, John, William [qv], and Marie Lawrence, and her three Tuttle children); he was an incorporator of Hempstead, L.I., 1644, and of Flushing, 1645; removed to Amsterdam, 1658; alderman; twice mayor of N.Y. City; councillor; deposed by Gov. Bellomont, restored and made a justice Supreme Ct. of N.Y.; *m* Susanna –.

LAWRENCE, Maj. Thomas (1625-1703), from Eng. to Flushing, L.I.; bought patent for Hell Gate Neck from Governor Dungan, 1686; maj. Queens Co. forces; *m* Mary –.

LAWRENCE, William (1623-80), from Eng. in the "Planter," 1635, with his brother John; lived at Ipswich, Mass.; was one of the first patentees of Flushing, L.I., 1645; mem. Queens Co. militia, 1665-80; cdr. Flushing company at surrender of New York to the Dutch, 1673; *m* 2d, Elizabeth Smith.

LAWRENCE, William (ante 1638-1704), from Eng. to L.I., to N.J., 1666; mem. Middletown Ct., 1670; mem. Gen. Ct., 1669; burgess, Elizabeth Town, 1671; overseer.

LAY, Robert (1617-89), of Lynn 1638; removed to Saybrook 1647; *m* 1647, Sarah – (1616-76).

LEA (Lygh), John (1661-1726), Quaker, from Eng. in the "Canterbury," with William Penn on his second voyage, 1699, to Upland, nr. Chester, Pa., settled at Concord, Chester Co., Pa.; *m* in Eng., 1698, Hannah (Hopton) Webb (1665-1735).

LEARNED, William (1590-1646), from Eng., ca. 1625; recorded at Charlestown, Mass., 1632; freeman, 1634; settled at Woburn, ca. 1640; selectman, 1644; *m* Goditha –.

LEAVITT, John (1608-91), from Eng. in the "Diligent," to Dorchester, Mass., 1634; later at Hingham; freeman, 1636; dep. Gen. Ct., 1658-64; *m* Sarah –.

LE CONTE, Guillaume (1659-1710/11), a Huguenot, from France to Holland before the revocation of the Edict of Nantes, 1685; came to New York, 1698; *m* Marguerite DeValleau.

LEE (Leigh), John (1600-71), from Eng. to Mass., ca. 1635; settled at Ipswich; *m* Anne Hungerford.

LEE, Col. Richard (1619-84; son of Hon. Henry, Lord Mayor's sec., justice of Highgate Assizes, 1623, *m* Janet Mann; son of Sir Lancelot [1589-1643?], spl. envoy to Holland and ct. rep. to Spain, *m* Lady Aurelia Marbough; *m* 2d, Ellice Brookwalter; son of Sir Thomas [1561-1626], chief justice of Ireland, 1608-12, *m* Lady Mary Huntingdon, of Dell-Manors, Eng.); "The Cavalier," came to Va., 1641; sec. of state to Gov. Sir John Harvy; King's counsellor; large landowner in York and Westmoreland cos.; *m* Lady Minerva Grace, dau. Lord Stethford Grace, King's regent for Oxford U.; *m* 2d, Anna, dau. Christopher Tittsworth, mcht. of Nottingham, Eng.

LEE, Richard (*d* ca. 1663/64), from Eng. to York Co., Va., 1641; said to have been the first white settler in the Northern Neck of Va.; colonial sec. of Va. under Sir William Berkeley; mem. Council and justice; *m* Anne –.

LEE, Thomas (1710-69), *b* Barbados, came to Charleston, S.C.; *m* 1732, Mary Giles (*d* 1751).

LEETE, William (1613-83), clk. of Bishop's Ct., Cambridge, Eng.; Whitfield's company, one of the signers Plantation Covenant, shipboard, June 1, arriving at New Haven, July 10, 1639; one of the founders and first clk. Guilford, Conn.; propr. Leete's Island, Conn.; asst. of colony, dep. gov. and gov. New Haven Colony; asst. and dep. gov. Conn. Colony; succeeding Winthrop as gov. of Conn., 1676, dying in office, 1683; pres. of Congress of Commissioners, United Colonies of N.E.; protector of Goffe and Whalley, judges of Charles I; *m* Anne, dau. Rev. John Payne.

LEFFINGWELL, Thomas (1622-1714), from Eng. to Saybrook, Conn., 1637; a founder of Norwich and its first settler; dep. Gen. Assembly, 1661-1710; lt. King Philip's War; *m* Mary White.

LEGARE, Solomon (1662-1760), Huguenot, who with his mother Janette, fled from France to America after the revocation of the Edict of Nantes, and settled at Charleston, S.C., 1686.

LEGGETT (Legat), Gabriel (1638-98), from Eng. to the Barbados, thence to New Amsterdam, ca. 1640; West Farms (now part of greater New York), 1661; became patentee of a large estate on Hunt's Point, also called Leggett's Point; *m* Elizabeth, dau. John Richardson, an original patentee of West Farms, 1664.

LEIDY (Ludwig, Lydig, Leydig), Carl, (1678-1765), from Alsace-Lorraine, settled in Phila. Co., Pa., 1727; *m* Catherine –.

LEONARD, James (1621-91), from Eng. to Md. after 1628; thence to N.E., and was at Providence, R.I., 1645; with his brother Henry, built the first iron foundry in Plymouth Co., at Taunton, Mass., 1652; defended his garrison house in King Philip's War; *m* Mary Martin; *m* 2d Margaret –.

LEVERETT, John (1616-78; son of Thomas, who came from Eng. to Boston, 1633, and was ruling elder); freeman, 1640; mem. A. and H. A. Co., 1639, sgt., 1642, lt., 1652; agt. of Colony of Mass. Bay in Eng.; maj. gen. Mass. forces, 1663-73; rep. Gen. Ct., 1663, 64, 65, and speaker, 1663, 64; gov.'s asst., 1665-71; gov., 1673-78; *m* Hannah (ca. 1621-1646), dau. of Ralph Hudson (*b* 1593), *m* Marie (*b* 1592), dau. of John Twing, *m* Helen –; *m* 2d, ? Sara Sedgwick (1629-1704).

LEVERING, Wygard (ca. 1648-1745; son of Rosier, a Huguenot, fled from France either to Holland or Germany, *m* Elizabeth Van de Waller, of Germany); Huguenot, came from Germany to Germantown, Pa., 1685; *m* Magdaline Böker.

LEWIS, George (*d* 1662), from East Greenwich, Co. Kent, Eng., to Plymouth, Mass., 1630; one of first makers of cloth at Scituate, 1634; a founder of Barnstable, 1639, where he died; *m* Sarah Jenkins.

LEWIS, Henry (1671-1731), *b* in Wales, came to Pa.; mem. Pa. Assembly, 1700, 08, 09, 15, 18; *m* 1692, Mary Taylor.

LEWIS, "Pioneer" John (*b* Donegal Co., Ireland, 1678-*d* Feb. 1, 1762; son of Andrew, and g.son of William, Huguenot, from France to Wales after the revocation of the Edict of Nantes, 1685, thence to North of Ireland, where he *m* Mary McCollough, or McCleland); John fled from Ireland to Portugal, thence to Pa., ca. 1731; was the first white settler in now Augusta Co., Va., 1732, where he built "Ft. Lewis"; col. militia; justice; high sheriff; had 5 sons in Am. Rev.; *m* 1715/16, Margaret (1693-1775), dau. of the Laird of Loch Lynn, in Scotland.

LEWIS, Robert (1607-45), officer British Army; came from Wales, in the "Blessing," to Gloucester Co., Va., 1635; *m* Elizabeth –.

LEWIS, William (1594-1683), from Eng. in the "Lion," to Boston, 1632; freeman, 1632; an original settler of Hartford, Conn., 1636; at Hadley, 1659; rep. Gen. Ct., 1662, for Northampton, 1664; settled at Farmington, ca. 1675; *m* Felix Collins (*d* 1671).

LEWIS, William (1610-71), from Eng., 1630, was a propr. in Cambridge, Mass. Bay Colony, 1630; returned to Eng. and *m* Amy Wells; was at Roxbury, 1639, where he was land owner and freeman, 1642; an original settler of Lancaster, Mass., 1653, where he died.

LIBBY (Libbey), John (ca. 1602-1682), from Eng. bet. 1630-35; granted land at Scarborough, Me., before 1640; first selectman, 1669; served in Indian wars; *m* Agnes –.

LILLINGTON, Alexander (1643-97), dep. gov., 1693-95, pres. Council and asso. justice Supreme Ct. of N.C.; judge Precinct Ct., 1690-1695; *m* 2d, 1675, Elizabeth Cooper.

LINCOLN, Samuel (1622-ca. 1690), from Eng. to Salem, Mass., 1637; settled at Hingham; *m* Martha Lewis (*d* 1693).

LINDLY, Francis (1600-1704, aet. 104; son of John, from Eng., settled at Branford, Conn.); from Eng. to Colony of New Haven, Conn., 1639; one of first settlers of Newark, N.J., 1666; *m* ca. 1639, Susannah Culpepper.

LIPPINCOTT, Richard (*d* 1683), from Eng. to Dorchester, Mass., ca. 1639; freeman, 1640; removed to Boston, 1644; disagreed with church and was cast out from the community, 1651; returned to Eng.; again came to America and lived in R.I.; removed to N.J. and was a patentee of Shrewsbury, 1669; dep. Gen. Assembly of East Jersey, 1669-77; overseer; *m* Abigail – (*d* 1697).

LIPPITT (Lippett), John (*d* 1669), from Eng. to R.I., 1638, and became a landholder and commr. to form government under a charter, Colony of R.I. and Providence Plantations, 1647; landholder at Warwick, 1648.

LITCHFIELD, Laurence (1620-49), from Kent, Eng., to Scituate, Mass., 1639; mem. A. and H. A. Co.; served in colonial wars; *m* 1640, Judith Denniss (1620-85).

LITTELL (Little), Benjamin, from London, Eng. to Newberry, Mass., 1630.

LITTLE, George, from Eng. to Newbury, Mass., ca. 1640; *m* 1st, Alice Poor (1618-80), came from Eng. in the "Bevis," 1638.

LITTLE, Thomas (*d* 1671/72), from Eng., was at Plymouth, Mass., 1630; purchased 1000 acres at Marshfield, 1650; *d* at Scituate; mem. Plymouth mil. company; *m* 1633, Anne, dau. Richard Warren (qv).

LITTLETON, Col. Nathaniel, in Va., 1622; gov. of Accomac, 1652; burgess; *m* Anne, dau. of Henry Southey, *m* Elizabeth –.

LIVERMORE, John (1606-84 son of Peter), from Eng. in the "Francis," 1634, freeman, 1635; at Wethersfield, Conn., to 1640; at New Haven to 1647; corpl. New Haven company, 1647; settled at Watertown, Mass.; *m* Grace (1615-90), dau. Edmund Sherman (qv).

LIVINGSTON, Robert (1654-1728; desc. William, 4th Lord Livingston, of Callendar), from Scotland to Charlestown, Mass., 1673; settled at Albany, N.Y., 1674; large landowner, patented from Gov. Dungan, 1686, and confirmed by royal charter, 1715, erecting the manor and lordship of Livingston; mem. Council Province of N.Y., 1698-1701; mem. Assembly, 1709-11; *m* 1679, Alida (Schuyler) Van Rensselaer, dau. Philip Pieterse Schuyler, and widow of Rev. Nicholas Van Rensselaer.

LLOYD, John, from Wales, settled at Camptown, N.J.; *m* 1765, Rebecca Ball (cousin of Mary Ball, mother of George Washington).

LLOYD, Thomas (1640-94), from Wales in the "Fortune," with William Penn, in 1682, to Pa.; mem. and pres. of the Council, and dep. gov. Province of Pa., during William Penn's absence; chief magistrate, 1684-93; first master of rolls and keeper of the great seal; *m* 1665, Mary (*d* 1680), dau. of Roger Jones, of Wales.

LOBDELL, Simon (*d* 1717; desc. Count Nicholas Lobdell), from Eng. ca. 1645; settled at Milford, Conn., 1646; *m* Persis, dau. of Thomas Pierce, *m* Elizabeth –, of Charlestown, Mass.

LOCKWOOD, Robert (*d* 1658), from Eng. in the "Mary and John," with Winthrop's fleet, to Watertown, Mass., 1630; freeman, 1637; settled at Fairfield, Conn.; sgt. Fairfield regt.; *m* Susannah St. John.

LOGAN, James (1674-1751), came with William Penn, 1699, as his secretary, established "Stenton," in Phila. Co., Pa.; eminent educationalist; sec. of the province and clk. of the Council, 1701; commr. of property; justice Ct. Common Pleas, 1715-23, presiding judge, 1723; mayor of Phila., 1723; chief justice Supreme Ct., 1731-39; pres. Provincial Council and actg. gov., 1736-38; *m* 2d, Amy Child.

LOMBARD, Thomas (*b* ca. 1610-1662), from Eng. in the "Mary and John," 1630, settled at Dorchester, Mass., later at Scituate and Barnstable where he died; *m* Joyce –.

LONG (Longe), Robert (*b* Eng. 1590-*d* Charlestown, Mass., Jan. 9, 1663), came in the "Defense," to Boston, 1635, with 2d wife, 10 children and one servant; purchased the "Great House," Charlestown, 1636, for an inn; freeman, 1636; selectman; mem. A. and H. A. Co.; *m* Oct. 8, 1614, Sarah (1595-1631), dau. of John Taylor, of Eng.; *m* 2d, Elizabeth – (*b* 1605).

LONGSTRETH, Bartholomew (1679-1749), from Eng. to Edgehill, nr. Phila., Pa., 1699; *m* Ann Dawson.

LOOMIS, Joseph (1590-1658; son of John, *m* Agnes –); came to Boston in the "Susan and Ellen," 1638; woolendraper; settled on "The Island," at Windsor, Conn., 1639; dep. Gen. Ct., 1643-44; *m* 1614, in Eng., Mary (bap. 1590-1652), dau. of Robert White, of Eng., *m* 1585, Bridget Allgar.

LORD, Thomas (1585/86-1667), from Eng. in the "Elizabeth and Ann," to Cambridge, Mass., 1635; joined Rev. Thomas Hooker's party in founding of Hartford, Conn., 1636; an original propr. of Hartford; *m* Dorothy (*b* 1589), dau. of Robert Bird; *m* 2d, Dorothy (1589-1675), dau. of Rev. Bulkley, prebend, of Litchfield, Eng.

LORILLARD, Peter (1746-76), Huguenot, from Holland; settled at Hackensack, N.J.; killed during Am. Rev.; *m* Catherine Moore.

LORING, Thomas (*d* 1661), from Eng. to Dorchester, Mass., 1634, with his wife and sons, Thomas and John; removed to Hingham, where he was one of the first deacons of the church established there, 1635; freeman, 1635; settled at Hull, 1641; constable, 1646; *m* in Eng., Jane Newton.

LOTHROP, see Lathrop.

LOW (Louw) Peter Cornelissen, from Holstein, 1659, settled at Esopus, N.Y.; *m* 1668, Elizabeth, dau. of Mattheus Blanchan, *m* Maddelen Jorisse, from Artois, France, 1660.

LOWELL (Lowle), Percival (1571-1665; son of Richard), merchant, from Eng. with his wife and sons, John and Richard, and daughter, Joan, in the "Jonathan," to Newbury, Mass., 1639; *m* Rebecca –.

LOWNDES, Christopher (1713-85), from Eng. ca. 1738; settled in Prince George's Co., Md., where he was justice and judge; *m* 1747, Elizabeth (*d* 1789), dau. Benjamin Tasker, pres. Council and dep. gov. of Md.

LOWTHER, William (*d* 1750), a Quaker, came from Ireland with his wife, Martha, to Abingdon, Pa., ca. 1727, settled finally in Bucks Co., Pa.

LUDLOW, Roger (1590-1665), from Eng. to Dorchester, Mass., 1630; removed to Windsor, Conn., 1635, to Fairfield, 1639; to Va., 1654; gov.'s asst., 1630; dep. gov., Colony of Mass. Bay, 1634, of Conn., 1639; served in Pequot War.

LUDWELL, Philip, came to Va., ca. 1660; mem. Council; dep. sec. of Va.; gov. of North and South Carolina, 1693; returned to Eng. where he *d* post 1704, was buried at Bow Ch., nr. Stratford in Middlesex; *m* Lucy Higginson.

LUKENS (Lucken, Luckens), Jan (*d* 1744), he and his wife, Mary, together with twelve other families came from Crefeld, Germany, sailed from Rotterdam, Holland, in the "Concord," July 17, 1682, arrived at Phila., Oct. 8, 1682; an original settler of Germantown, Pa.; was constable, burgess, sheriff and bailiff; *m* Mary – (*d* 1742).

LUSK, John (1702-88), from Scotland with his father, Stephen, to Wethersfield, Conn.; *m* Janet – (*d* 1742); *m* 2d, Jane Trumbell (*d* 1788).

LYFORD, Francis (1645-1723), from Eng., was at Boston, 1667; later at Exeter, N.H.; served in King William's War; *m* 1681, Rebecca, dau. Rev. Samuel Dudley (son of Gov. Thomas Dudley, qv).

LYMAN, Richard (1580-1640), from Eng. in the "Lion," with his wife and children, to Boston, 1631; freeman, 1633; an original propr. of Hartford, Conn., 1636; *m* in Eng., Sarah, dau. Roger Osborne.

LYNDE, Simon (bap. 1624-*d* 1687; 3d son of Enoch, *m* Elizabeth Digby); came to Boston, Mass., 1650; clk. and sgt. A. and H. A. Co.; gov.'s asst., 1668-1679; served in King Philip's War; *m* 1652, Hannah (1635-84), dau. of John Newgate, emigrant.

LYNDE, Thomas (1593/94-1671), from Eng., settled at Charlestown, Mass., 1634; dep. Gen. Ct., 1636-37, 1645-52.

LYON, Henry (ca. 1625-1703), from Scotland to New Milford, Conn., 1648; one of the first settlers at Newark, N.J., 1666, where was dep., mem. Council and first treas.; removed to Elizabeth Town, N.J., but returned to Newark; *m* 1652, Elizabeth Bateman.

LYON, William (1620-92), from Eng. in the "Hopewell," Sept. 11, 1635, aet. 14; settled at Roxbury, Mass. (home still standing on Belleview Av., nr. Atwood St., Roxbury); mem. A. and H. A. Co., 1645; *m* 1646, Sarah (*b* 1627/28), dau. of John Ruggles, of Eng., *m* Mary Curtis.

McCOOK, George (Scotch descent), from Ireland, 1780, settled at Canonsburg, Pa.; founder of Jefferson Coll.; *m* Mary McCormick (parents of "The Fighting McCooks," 2 sons and 14 g. sons in army or navy in Civil War).

McCORMICK, Thomas (1702-1762), from Ireland, settled in Lancaster Co., Pa., ca. 1734; moved to E. Pennsboro Tp., Cumberland Co., Pa., ca. 1745; *m* 1728, Elizabeth (1705-66), dau. Adam Carruth.

McCULLOCH, Roderick (*d* 1745; of the Clan McCulloch, Ardwall, Galloway, Scotland), came to Va., with Gov. Gooch and Commissary Blair, 1727; rector Washington Parish, Westmoreland Co., Va.; *m* Elizabeth Weedon.

McDONALD, Angus (1727-78), from Scotland to Falmouth, Va., 1746, to Winchester ca. 1760; served in French and Indian War, 1754-63; maj. militia, 1765; vestryman old Frederick Parish (Episcopal), 1768; one of the founders of Hiram Lodge No. 12, A. F. & A. M., at Winchester; agent for Lord Fairfax; built first fort at Wheeling, 1774; lt. col. of Va. militia, 1774; sheriff, 1775; justice and dep. sheriff, 1776; *m* Anna Thompson.

McDOWELL, Ephraim (ca. 1683-1774), soldier in siege of Londonderry and battle of Boyne; Scotch descent; came from Ireland, with two sons John and James to Pa., 1729-35; settled in Burden's Grant (now Rockbridge) Co., Va., 1737; *m* Margaret, dau. of James Irvine, *m* Mary Wylie.

McINTOSH, John Mohr (1700-61), from Scotland with Gov. Oglethorpe, to Darien, Ga., 1734; capt., Highland Light Inf., under Spaniards, 1740; wounded and captured at Ft. Moosa, Fla.; *m* Jean Gordon.

MACK, John (1652/53-1721), from Scotland to Salisbury, Conn., 1680; later at Lynn; *m* 1681, Sarah (*b* 1663), dau. of Orlando Bagley, *m* Mary Colby.

MACKALL, James (1630-*d* ca. 1693), from Scotland before 1666, settled at "The Clifts," Calvert Co., Md.; *m* Mary Grahame.

McKIM, Thomas (1710-84-86; son of Sir John, knighted by King William III), from Ireland, 1734; settled at Phila., Pa., later at Brandywine, Del.; was justice of quarter sessions and judge Ct. Common Pleas; lt. of militia, 1756.

McLANE (MacLean), Allan (1719-76), from Scotland to Phila., Pa., 1740; *m* Jane, dau. Samuel Erwin, of Falls of Schuylkill.

McLEAN, Allan (1715-86), received grant of land from King for services as lt. in British Army during French and Indian War; came from Scotland to Boston, 1740; moved to Hartford, Conn., finally settled at North Bolton (now Vernon), Conn.; *m* 2d, 1744, Mary Loomis.

MacNUTT, Alexander (1656-1746, of the family MacNaught, of Scotland), from Scotland to Palmer, Mass., ca. 1720 (others of the family settled in Augusta Co., Va., and in Nova Scotia, 1760); *m* Sarah – (*d* 1744, aet. 84).

MACY, Thomas (1608-82), from Eng. to Newbury, Mass., bet. 1635-39; a founder of Salisbury, Mass., 1639; dep. from Salisbury to Gen. Ct. of Elections, Boston, 1654; was one of ten men to purchase island of Nantucket, 1659; chief magistrate of Nantucket, 1675, and first recorder of deeds; *m* 1639, Sarah Hopcott (or Hopcut, or Hopeat; 1612-1706).

MAGRUDER, Alexander (1610-77), officer in Army of Charles II, sent as prisoner of war to Va., 1651, ransomed himself and received land grant of 500 acres in Calvert Co., Md.; *m* Margaret, dau. William Braithwaite, mem. first Gen. Assembly and actg. gov. of Md.; *m* 2d, Sarah –; *m* 3d, Elizabeth Hawkins.

MAINDORT, Doodes, see Minor, Doodes.

MAKEPEACE, Thomas (*d* 1666), of Dorchester, Mass., 1636, Boston, 1639; in Narragansett War; mem. A. and H. A. Co.

MANIERRE, Louis (1757-94), Huguenot, from France; soldier Am. Rev.; settled at New London, Conn., 1785; *m* Rebecca Miner.

MANIGAULT, Pierre, or Peter (*d* 1729), from France to S.C., ca. 1691; *m* ca. 1699, Judith (Gitton) Rover, a widow, who left France, 1685.

MANN, Richard (drowned 1655), to Plymouth at age 14 with Elder Brewster's family, in "Mayflower"; served in King Philip's war; took oath of fidelity; lived on Mann's Hill; *m* Rebecca –.

MANN, William (1607-62), came to Cambridge, Mass., 1636; *m* Mary Jerauld (or Gerald).

MANNING, Thomas (ca. 1594-1668), from Eng. to Salem, Mass.; was at Ipswich, 1636; *m* Mary Giddings.

MAPES, Thomas (1628-86), from Eng. to Southold, L.I., before 1640; ensign, Suffolk Co. militia, 1686; *m* Sarah, dau. Capt. William Purrier, of Southold.

MARCH, Hugh (1620-93), from Eng. in the "Confidence," 1638; settled at Newbury, Mass.; *m* Judith – (*d* 1675); *m* 2d, 1676, Dorcas Blackleach; *m* 3d, 1685, Sarah Healy.

MARIS, George (1630-1705), from Eng., 1683, to Darby, Chester Co., Pa.; Provincial Councillor and colonial justice of Pa.; settled at "The Home House," Springfield Tp., Chester Co.; *m* Alice – (1623-99).

MARSHALL, John (1596-1660; 9th in descent from Gilbert, *d* 1150); capt. of cav. in army of Charles I, came from Eng. to Jamestown, Va., ca. 1650; settled in Westmoreland Co., served in Indian wars in Va.

MARTIAN, Nicholas (1591-1657), a Frenchman who was naturalized in England and came to America in the "Francis Bonadventure," 1620; resided in the Colony of Va.; justice of York for Kiskyache, 1622-57; burgess, 1623, 31, 33; owned the site of Yorktown; *m* 1627, Jane –, widow of Edward Berkeley; *m* 3d, Isabella Beach.

MARTIN, Lt. Samuel (*d* 1683), from England to Wethersfield, Conn., ca. 1640 or 45; soldier in King Philip's War; was in Great Swamp Fight; *m* 1646, Phebe (Bisby) Bracey, dau. of William Bisby.

MARVIN, Matthew (bap. 1600-1679/80), was sr. warden St. Mary's, Great Bentley, Essex, Eng.; came in the "Increase," 1635, with wife Elizabeth and five children; his name is on monument in honor of the first settlers of Hartford, Conn.; surveyor of highways, 1639, 47; to Norwalk, Conn., 1650; deputy, 1654; *m* ca. 1622, Elizabeth – (ca. 1604-1640); *m* 2d, ca. 1647, Alice – (ca. 1610-1680/81), widow of John Bouton.

MARVIN, Reynold (or Reinold), (ante 1594-1662), from Eng., was at Hartford, Conn., 1638; later at Farmington, thence to Saybrook; *d* Lyme, Conn.; *m* Marie –.

MASON, George (1629-86), from Eng. to Norfolk, Va., ca. 1651; county lt., Stafford Co., 1675; mem. Bacon's Assembly, 1676; in Indian wars, 1675-84.

MASON, Hugh (1605/06-1678), from Eng. in the "Frances," 1634; settled at Watertown, Mass.; tanner; freeman, 1635; lt., 1645; capt., 1652-78; dep. Gen. Ct., 1635, et seq.; mem. Council of War, 1676; cdr. of volunteers against Manhattoes, 1664; cdr. company in King Philip's War; *m* 1632/33, Hester, dau. of Thomas Wells.

MASON, John (ca. 1600-1672), from Eng. to Dorchester, Mass., 1630 or 1632; freeman, 1635; settled at Windsor, Conn.; a leader in mil. and civil affairs; in chief command of forces at close of Pequot War, 1637; at Saybrook, 1647, Norwich, 1659; rep. Gen. Ct., 1637-41; asst., 1641-59; commr. United Colonies, 1647-61; dep. gov., 1659-69; dep. gov. under charter of Charles II, 1662; maj. and cdr.-in-chief of Conn. militia; organized the first troop of horse in the colony, 1657-58; *m* 2d, 1640, Anna, dau. Rev. Robert Peck, from Eng., 1637.

MASON, Sampson (*d* 1676), from Eng. to Dorchester, Mass., 1651; at Rehoboth, 1657; Swansea, 1667; shoemaker; *m* Mary Butterworth (*d* 1714).

MATHER, Richard (1596-1669; son of Thomas), non-conformist; from Eng. in the "James," to Boston, 1635; settled as teacher over the church at Dorchester, 1636; regarded as one of the most useful men in the colony; eminent theologian and author; *m* 1st, 1624, Catharine, dau. Edmund Holt (or Hoult); *m* 2d, 1656, Sarah Story, widow of John Cotton.

MATTHEWS (Mathews), James (*d* 1686), from Eng. to Charlestown, Mass., ca. 1634; was at Yarmouth, 1639; mem. Yarmouth mil. company, 1643; dep. Gen. Ct. of Plymouth Colony, 1644, from Yarmouth, 1664.

MAULE, D. Patrick (*d* Apr. 1736, Bath Beaufort Precinct, Bath Co., N.C.), from Scotland, to N.C., 1714; trustee, Bath Pub. Library; vestryman St. Thomas's Parish, 1715; dep. surveyor; dep. surveyor gen.; mem. grand jury, 1721; mem. Gen. Assembly; justice of peace; dep. admiralty judge, 1733; *m* Elizabeth –.

MAULE (Mauld), Thomas (ca. 1643-1701; nephew of Sir Patrick Maule, Earl of Panmure, Baron Maule of Brechin and Navarre), from Eng. to the Barbados ca. 1655, at age of 12, thence to Salem, Mass.; joined the Quakers; twice whipped for "ill words"; shopkeeper; *m* 2d, 1670, Naomi –; *m* 3d, Mary –.

MAUPIN, Gabriel (*b* in bas Pyrennes, France, 1651 or 75?-will proved in 1720; son of Amos), Huguenot; officer army of Navarre; fled from France to Eng., ca. 1699; arrived at Yorktown, Va., in the "Nassau," Mar. 1700, with about 191 refugee Huguenots; comdt. royal arsenal at Williamsburg; a founder of Manakin Town, Va.; *m* Marie, dau. of Earl Spencer, of Eng.

MAURY, Matthew (*d* 1752), fled from France to Eng. after the revocation of the Edict of Nantes, 1685; came to Va., 1717; *m* 1716, at Dublin, Ireland, Mary Anne (1690-1755), dau. Rev. James de la Fontaine.

MAY (Maies, Mayes, Mays), John (1590-1670), from Eng. to Roxbury, Mass., ca. 1640; freeman, 1641; in Roxbury mil. company, 1647; *m* Sarah –.

MAYHEW, Thomas (1592-1681), from Eng. to Mass. with his son Thomas, 1631; settled at Edgartown, 1642; Indian teacher; dep. Gen. Ct. from Watertown, Mass., 1636-37; gov. and cdr. of Martha's Vineyard, Province of N.Y., 1647-81, under commissions from Governors Lovelace and Nichols; *m* Jane Gallion; *m* 2d, Martha Parkhurst, of Eng.

MAYNARD, John (*d* 1672), from Eng. to Mass.; an original propr. of Sudbury, 1640; freeman, 1644; a petitioner for grant for Marlborough, 1656; *m* Mary, widow of Thomas Axtell.

MAYO, John (1629-88; son of Thomas), from Eng. in the "William and Francis," to Roxbury, Mass.; *m* Hannah, dau. John Graves.

MAYO, William (1684-1744; son of Joseph [1656-91], of Co. Wilts., Eng., *m* Elizabeth Hooper; g.son of William [*d* 1707], *m* Jane –; g.g.son of William [*d* 1640], *m* Margaret –); went from Eng. to the Barbados, which island he surveyed; came to Va. ca. 1723; was at Richmond, 1729; col. Goochland Co. troop, provincial forces of Va., 1740; *m* Frances, dau. Enoch Gold, of Barbados; *m* 2d, ca. 1732, Ann Perratt, of Barbados.

MEAD, Gabriel (1588-1666), from Eng. to Dorchester, Mass.; admitted freeman, 1638; *m* 2d, Joanna –.

MEAD (Meade, Meades, Mede), William (1600-63), from Eng. in the "Elizabeth," to Mass., 1635; removed to Hempstead, L.I., later to Wethersfield, Conn., and to Stamford, 1641.

MEADE, Andrew (*d* 1745), from Ireland to Eng., thence to N.Y., ca. 1685; settled in Nansemond Co., Va.; burgess, co. judge, col. militia; *m* Mary, dau. of Daniel Latham, of Flushing, L.I.

MEANS, Robert (1742-1823; son of Thomas), from Ireland, 1766; settled at Merrimac, N. H., later at Amherst, N. H., where he was a weaver; later a merchant; rep. Gen. Ct. of N.H. several sessions; state senator 2 yrs.; treas. Hillsborough Co., N.H., long period; *m* 1774, Mary, dau. Rev. David McGregor, of Londonderry, N. H.

MEEKER (Mecar, Meaker), Robert, from Eng. to Quinnipiack (New Haven), Conn., before 1651; removed to Fairfield before 1670; *m* 1651, Susan Tuberfeeld.

MEEKES, Thomas, see Mix.

MEIGS (Meggs), Vincent (ca. 1583-1658), from Eng. with his sons John and Mark, to Weymouth, Mass., ca. 1639; was at New Haven, Conn., 1646, later at Milford, Guilford and what is now Killingworth; *m* 1606, – Churchill.

MELYN (Meleyn), Cornelius (1602-74), from Holland to New Netherlands, 1638; went to Holland, 1640, for his wife and children, and returned to New Amsterdam, 1641, with an order granting him nearly the whole of Staten Island; planted a colony, 1641, dispersed by Indian War, 1643; pres. "Council of Eight," under Dir. Gen. Kieft, 1643-47; removed to New Amsterdam, returned again to Holland when banished by Peter Stuyvesant for espousing popular side in politics; returned to Staten Island, 1649; after Indian massacre of 1655, removed to New Haven, Conn.; *m* at Amsterdam, 1627, Jannetje Adriaens (1604-81).

MERCER, Gen. Hugh (1720-77; son of William, *m* Anne, dau. of Sir Robert Munro, of Scotland); came from Scotland to Pa., 1747; removed to Fredericksburg, Va.; brig. gen. Cont. Army; physician; capt. in army at Braddock's defeat, 1755; capt. Military Assn. of Western Pa., 1756; capt. in command of a garrison, Shippensburg, 1757; maj. in command of forces in Pa., 1757; maj. in command of expdn. of Gen. Forbes against Ft. Duquesne, Jan. 12, 1777; brig. gen. U.S.A., wounded at battle of Princeton and died of these wounds; *m* Isabella, dau. of John Gordon.

MERIWETHER, Nicholas (*b* in Wales, Oct. 26, 1647-*d* at Charlottesville, Va., Dec. 1744; son of Nicholas [*d* 1678], *m* Elizabeth Wodenhouse); came to America, with two brothers, during the reign of Charles II, 1681, to accept a large grant of land in the Dominion of Va., in settlement of a large loan made by his father to the crown; vestryman of St. Peter's Ch., 1685-98; burgess of Va. from New Kent Co., 1702-14, from Hanover, 1723; *m* 1688/89, Elizabeth, dau. of David Crawford, of Assasquin, New Kent Co., Va.

MERRICK, Thomas (*b* 1620), from Wales, settled at Roxbury, 1636; settled at Springfield ca. 1638; *m* Elizabeth Tilley.

MERRILL (Merrell), Nathaniel (1610-55; desc. de Merle family, French Huguenots, name changed to Merrill in Eng.), from Eng. to Ipswich, Mass., 1633; settled at Newbury, 1635; *m* Sussanah Wilterton, or Walterton (she *m* 2d Stephen Jordan).

MERRITT, Thomas (ca. 1634-ca. 1725), from Eng. to Wethersfield, Conn., 1662; dep. Conn. Gen. Assembly, 1699; settled at Rye, N. Y., 1673; vestryman, trustee, etc; *m* 1656, Jane (1636-85), dau. of Thomas Sherwood; *m* 2d, ante 1688, Abigail (1660-ca. 1721), dau. Robert Francis, of Wethersfield, Conn.

METCALF (Metcalfe), Michael (*b* Tatterford, Norfolk Co., Eng., June 17, 1587-*d* 1664; son of Rev. Leonard, rector of Tatterford); to Boston, 1637; settled at Dedham; freeman, 1640 or 1642; *m* Oct. 13, 1616, Sarah (June 17, 1593-1644), dau. of Thomas Elwyn; *m* 2d, 1645, Martha –, widow of Thomas Piggs, or Pidge.

MICOU, Dr. Paul (1658-1736), Huguenot, from France after the revocation of the Edict of Nantes, 1685; settled in Essex Co., Va., ante 1695; justice 1700-20; physician; lawyer; *m* Margaret LeRoy.

MIDDLETON, Edward (*d* 1685), from Eng. to the Barbados, thence to S.C., 1678, where he received large tracts of land; was lord proprietor's dep., and asst. justice; mem. Grand Council, 1678-84, Province of S.C.; *m* 2d, 1680, Sarah – (widow of Richard Towell, of the Barbados).

MILES (Myles), John (1603-93), from Eng. to Concord, Mass., ante 1637; freeman, 1638; large landowner; *m* 2d, 1679, Susannah (1647-post 1698), dau. of Thomas Goodnow.

MILLARD, John, was one of three brothers who came from Eng., 1643, and settled at Rehoboth; *m* Elizabeth – (*d* 1680).

MILLER, Joseph (1617-97; 13th child, 9th son of "Maister" Thomas Miller, M.A., of Bishop's Stortford, Co. Herts., Eng., *d* 1627, *m* Agnes –; and g.son of John Myllar [*d* 1584], *m* Joan Thorowgood, also of Stortford); came in the "Hopewell," 1635, settled at Cambridge, Mass.; *m* Mary, dau. of Walter Pope, of Charlestown.

MINER (Minor), Thomas (1608-90), from Eng. in the "Arbella," 1630; settled at Salem and later at Charlestown, Mass., 1632; a founder of the church at Charlestown; founder of Pequot (New London), Conn., 1645, and of Stonington, Conn., 1653-54; lt. and capt. King Philip's War; dep. Gen. Ct. for New London, 1650-51, for Stonington, bet. 1665-89; chief mil. officer at Mystic, 1665; *m* 1634, Grace, dau. of Walter Palmer.

MINOR (Maindort), Doodes (*d* 1687), from Holland to Middlesex Co., Va., 1640; *m* Mary Johnson.

MINOT, George (1594-1671; son of Thomas); from Eng. to Dorchester, Mass., 1630; freeman, 1634; rep. Gen. Ct., 1635; ruling elder 30 yrs.; *m* Martha – (1597-1657).

MITCHELL, John (1763-1840), from Eng. to Pendleton Co., Va., later in Harrison Co.; pioneer minister and a founder of Meth. Church; pensioner Am. Rev.; *m* Margaret Teter.

MITCHELL, Matthew (1590-1645), from Eng. with Rev. Richard Mather in the "James," to Mass., 1635; was at Concord, later at Springfield, and signed compact there, 1636; removed to Saybrook, Conn.; one of his sons was roasted alive by the Indians; dep. Gen. Ct., 1637, which voted war against the Pequot Indians, and served in garrison at Saybrook Fort; *m* 1616, Susan Butterfield.

MIX (Meekes), Thomas, from Eng. to New Haven, Conn., 1643; one of the first grantees there; *m* 1649, Rebecca, dau. of Capt. Nathaniel Turner.

MONCURE, John (1709-64), from Eng. to Stafford Co., Va., 1733; *m* Frances (*b* 1713), dau. Dr. Gustavus Brown (*m* Frances, dau. Col. Gerrard Fowke, Jr.).

MONROE, Andrew (*d* 1668), from Scotland, was in Md., 1644, when he "took sides with Parliament against" Lord Baltimore; patented land at mouth of Appomattox Creek, Westmoreland Co., Va., 1652; *m* Elizabeth Alexander.

MONTAGUE, Peter (1603-59; 2d son of Peter, *m* Eleanor Allen; desc. Droge de Monteacute, from Normandy to Eng. with William the Conqueror); came in the "Charles" to Jamestown, Va., 1621; was burgess from Nansemond, 1652, from Lancaster Co., 1651, 58; *m* Cicely, dau. Gov. Mathews, of Va. Colony.

MONTAGUE (Montaque), Richard (ca. 1614-81; 3d son of Peter *m* Eleanor Allen); came in the "Speedwell," 1634; resided at Welles, Me., 1646; removed to Boston, Mass.; to Wethersfield, Conn., 1651, and later to Hadley, Mass.; *m* ca. 1637, Abigail (*d* 1691), dau. of Rev. Dr. Downing, of Norwich, Eng.

MOODY, John (1593-1655), from Eng., admitted freeman at Roxbury, Mass., 1633; *m* Sarah Fox (1598-1671).

MOORE, John (1620-57), from Eng. to Southampton, L.I., 1641, to Newtown, L.I.; was dep. and commr.; *m* Margaret Howell.

MOORE, John (*d* 1677), from Eng. in the "Mary and John," to Dorchester, Mass.; freeman, 1631; went to Windsor, 1635 or 1636, rep. Gen. Ct.

MOORE, John (1658-1732), from Eng. to Charleston, S.C., 1680; sec. of the Province, 1682; receiver gen., 1683; mem. Gov.'s Council, 1684; moved to Phila., bet. 1687-90, where he was crown advocate and dep. judge, 1695; atty. gen. of the Province, 1698-1700; registrar gen. of Pa., 1693-1703; registrar of wills, 1701-04; founder and vestryman of Christ's Church, Phila.; *m* 1685, Lady Rebecca, dau. Daniel Axtell (son of Lt. Col. Daniel Axtell, gov. of Kilkenny, Ireland).

MORE, Richard (1613/14-bet. 1694-96), lived at Salem, Mass., where his gravestone still stands; mariner and known as captain; *m* 1st, 1636, Christian Hunt (*d* 1677, aet. 60); *m* 2d, Jane Hollingsworth (*d* 1686).

MOREHEAD, Charles (1609-1705; son of David, of London); came from Scotland to look after his father's interest which was partial ownership of the Isle of Kent project with William Claiborne, 1630; settled in the Northern Neck of Va.; *m* twice.

MORGAN, David, Quaker; from Wales, settled in America, ca. 1700; probably came by way of Jamaica.

MORGAN, James (1607-85; son of William); from Wales in the "Mary," to Sandy Bay, nr. Gloucester, Mass., 1636; freeman at Roxbury, 1643; settled at New London, Conn., ca. 1650; mem. 1st Colonial Assembly of Conn.; soldier Pequot War; *m* Aug. 6, 1640, Margery Hill, of Roxbury.

MORGAN, Capt. Miles (1616-99; son of William); from Eng., 1636; a founder of Springfield, Mass., ca. 1640; built a block house which he defended against the Indians in the sacking of Springfield, 1675; *m* Prudence Gilbert (*d* 1660); *m* 2d, 1669, Elizabeth Bliss (*d* 1683).

MORRILL, (Morrell), Abraham (1586-1662), from Eng. in the "Lion," to Cambridge, Mass., 1632; settled at Salisbury, 1634; he and Henry Sawood built a corn mill on the Powow, 1642; commoner, and taxed in 1650; signed petition of 1658; *m* June 10, 1645, Sarah Clement (she *m* 2d, 1665, Thomas Mudgett).

MORRIS, Anthony, 2d (1654-1721), Quaker, from Eng. to Burlington, N.J., 1682; removed to Phila., Pa., 1685; was presiding justice Ct. of Common Pleas of Phila.; justice Supreme Ct. of Pa., 1693-98; mayor of Phila., 1703-04; provincial councillor, 1696; rep. Assembly of Province, 1698-1704; *m* 1676, Mary Jones (*d* 1688); *m* 2d, 1689, Agnes – (*d* 1692), widow of Cornelius Barr; *m* 3d, Mary – (*d* 1699), widow of Thomas Coddington; *m* 4th, 1700, Elizabeth, dau. Luke Watson.

MORRIS, Richard (*d* ca. 1673), capt. English army, from Eng. to the Barbados, 1654, thence to New York; obtained a land grant, 1668, with manorial privileges, 3000 acres nr. Harlem, which became known as Morrisania; *m* Sarah Pole.

MORRIS, Thomas (*d* 1673), from Eng. in the "Hector," to Boston, 1637; at Quinnipiack (New Haven), 1638; signer of the Plantation Covenant, 1639; *m* Elizabeth –.

MORSE, Anthony (1606-86), from Eng. in the "James," to Newbury, Mass., 1635; freeman, 1636; lt. of militia; shoemaker; treas. Colony of Mass.; *m* Mary –; *m* 2d, Ann –.

MORSE, Joseph (1619-91), from Eng. in the "Elizabeth," 1634, freeman, 1635, an early propr. of Watertown, Mass.; *m* Hester, dau. of John Peirce (qv).

MORSE, Samuel (1587-1654), from Eng. in the "Increase," to Watertown, Mass., 1635; a founder and first treas. of Dedham, 1637; freeman, 1640; settled at Medfield, 1649; *m* Elizabeth –.

MORTON (Mourt), George (1585-1624), financial agent at London of the Mayflower Pilgrims; came in the "Ann" to Plymouth, Mass., 1623, with his wife and five children; settled at Middleboro, Mass.; *m* at Leyden, 1612, Juliana (1584-1665), dau. Alexander Carpenter.

MOSELEY (Maudesley), John (*d* Aug. 29, 1661; son of Sir John, of Lancashire, Eng.); came in the "Mary and John," 1630; settled at Dorchester, Mass., 1631; buried at Dorchester, a few feet north of Rev. Richard Mather (qv); signature is on document establishing the first free school; *m* Cecily, or Cecilia – (*d* Dec. 1661).

MOTT, Adam (1620-86), *b* Eng.; came to New Amsterdam ca. 1640; purchased, 1660, a tract of land at Great Neck, L.I., part of which is still occupied by some of his descendants; lt. provincial forces; commr. to settle dispute between Dutch and English residents of L.I., 1666; *m* 1643, Jane Hulet; *m* 2d, 1667, Elizabeth Redman, step-dau. of John Richbell, first patentee of Mamaroneck.

MOTT, James (*d* 1707), from Eng. before 1670, settled at Mamaroneck, Westchester Co., N.Y.; capt. of a company of foot; justice; vestryman; *m* 1670, Mary (*d* ca. 1685), dau. John Richbell; *m* 2d, 1690, Elizabeth Bloomer.

MOULTON, Robert (*b* Norfolk Co., Eng. – *d* Feb. 20, 1655), from Eng. to Salem, Mass., 1629; ship builder and owner; mem. Colonial Legislature; rep. Gen. Ct., 1634; built house at Moulton's Pt. (present site of Charlestown Navy Yard), 1630, where British landed before battle of Bunker Hill; *m* Deborrah – (*d* 1656).

MOULTON, William (1617-64), from Eng. to Newburyport, Mass., 1637; one of the first settlers of Hampton, N.H., ca. 1639; *m* Margaret, dau. of Robert Page.

MUDGE (Mugge), Thomas (*b* ca. 1624), from Eng., 1654 or earlier; settled at Malden, Mass.; in garrison at Wading River, 1675; *m* Mary –.

MULLINS, William (*d* 1621), 10th signer of the Mayflower Compact; m Alice – (*d* 1621).

MUMFORD, Thomas (1625-92), from Eng. to Portsmouth, R.I., ca. 1650; purchased land and settled at S. Kingston, nr. Point Judith, R.I., 1655; *m* Sarah, dau. Philip Sherman, 1st sec. of Providence Plantations.

MUNROE (Monroe), William (1625-1717), from Eng. to Mass., ca. 1652; settled at Lexington; freeman, 1690; *m* 1st, 1665, Martha George.

MUNSON, Thomas (1612-85), from Eng. to Hartford, Conn., 1637; received a grant of land in recognition of his services in the Pequot War; granted land at New Haven; rep. Colonial Assembly 27 sessions; capt. New Haven Co. forces King Philip's War; *m* Joanna –.

MURDOCK, Robert (*b* 1667), from Scotland to Roxbury, Mass., before 1692; *m* Hannah Stedman.

MYGATT, Joseph (1596-1680), from Eng. to Newton, Mass., 1633; a founder of Hartford, Conn., 1636; *m* Ann – (their dau. Sarah, *m* John Webster, the father of Daniel, also ancestor of Noah Webster).

NAPIER, Dr. Patrick (1610-69; son of Robert, of Edinburgh, Scotland, and desc. of Sir John Napier, of Merchistown, who *m* Lady Elizabeth Monteith); came to Va., 1655; *m* Elizabeth (1645-1672), dau. of Robert Booth (1619-64), from Eng. to York Co., Va., clerk, 1639, justice, 1652, burgess, 1653-64.

NASH, Thomas (1587-May 12, 1658), from Eng. with wife and five children; was at Guilford, Conn., 1639; signed Guilford Covenant; at New Haven, 1643, or earlier; signed Fundamental Agreement of New Haven; *m* Margery (*d* bet. Feb. 11, 1655-Aug. 1657), dau. of Nicholas Baker (son of John, *m* Margery Madistard), of Hertsfordshire, Herts Co., Eng., *m* Mary Hodgetts.

NEEDHAM, Anthony (1628-1705; son of Anthony); from Eng., 1653; settled at Salem, Mass.; corpl. Salem Old Troop, 1665; lt. in King Philip's War, 1675; lt., Troop of Horse, 1678; *m* 1655, Ann (*d* 1695), dau. of Humphrey Potter, of Coventry, Eng., killed in Irish massacre at Dublin, 1641; g.dau. of Thomas Potter, mayor of Coventry, 1622.

NELSON, Thomas, "Scotch Tom" (1677-1745), from Scotland to Va., ca. 1690; founded and laid out the town of York, 1705; built the first custom house in the colonies; founded "Nelson House," which was rebuilt by his son Gov. William, 1740; *m* Margaret, dau. of Robert Reade (son of Col. George Reade, qv); *m* 2d, Mrs. Tucker.

NEWBERRY, Thomas (1594-1636), from Eng. to Dorchester, Mass., ca. 1630; freeman, 1634; rep. Gen. Ct., 1635; by his will left large property; *m* in Eng., 1619, Joan Dabinott; *m* 2d, Jane (probably Jane Dabinott, a cousin of his first wife), she *m* 2d, Rev. John Warham.

NEWCOMB (Newcome), Andrew (1618-86), master mariner, from Eng. to Va., where he married; thence to Mass., ca. 1640, where he died; *m* Grace –, widow of William Rix.

NEWCOMB, Francis (ca. 1605-1692), from Eng. to Boston, 1635; settled at Braintree ca. 1639; *m* Rachel –.

NEWELL, Abraham (1581-1672), from Eng., 1634, settled at Roxbury, Mass.; *m* Frances – (*b* 1594).

NEWHALL, Thomas (*d* 1674), from Eng. to Salem, Mass., 1630; settled at Lynn; mem. Train Band at Lynn, released, 1649; *m* Mary – (*d* 1665).

NEWLIN, Nicholas (1620-99), from Eng. to Concord, Chester Co., Pa., 1683; justice County Ct.; mem. Provincial Council; *m* Elizabeth Paggott.

NEWTON, Richard (*b* ca. 1601-1609-*d* 1701), was a founder of Sudbury, Mass.; *m* Ann, sister of Henrie Loker, *d* Bures St. Mary, Essex, Eng., 1630.

NEWTON, Roger (*d* 1687), from Eng., settled in Mass. before 1645, later moved to Conn.; *m* 1645, Mary (*b* 1616), dau. Rev. Thomas Hooker (qv).

NICHOLS (Nicholl), Francis (1600-50), from Eng. to Stratford, Conn., 1639; training sgt. for Stratford, 1639; *m* 2d, Anna Wines.

NICHOLS, Thomas (*d* 1710), from Eng. to Amesbury, Mass., before 1665; owned lands on Merrimac River.

NICOLL, Matthias (1626-87), from Eng. to New York, 1664; sec. Province of N.Y., 1664-80; mem. King's Council, 1667-80; speaker Provincial Assembly, 1683; judge Ct. of Admiralty, 1686; mayor of New York, 1672; *m* Abigail Johns.

NIGHTINGALE, William (1637-1714), settled at Braintree, Mass., before 1690; *m* Bethia (*b* 1649), dau. Samuel Deering.

NOBLE, Thomas (*b* ca. 1632-Jan. 20, 1704), an early settler at Springfield, Mass., 1653; removed to Westfield, Mass., Jan. 16, 1669; constable; took oath of allegiance to King, Jan. 23, 1678; freeman, Oct. 12, 1682; co. surveyor, Mar. 2, 1696; *m* Nov. 1, 1660, Hannah (Aug. 17, 1643-ante May 12, 1721), dau. of William Warriner, *m* Joanna Scant.

NORRIS (Norrice), Isaac (1671-1735; son of Thomas, who settled in Jamaica, B.W.I., 1678), came to Phila., Pa., 1693; established "Fairhill"; was mem. Gov.'s Council over 30 yrs.; speaker Assembly; presiding judge Ct. Common Pleas; mayor of Phila., 1724; trustee under William Penn's will and atty. for Hannah Penn; *m* 1694, Mary, dau. Thomas Lloyd, 1st dep. gov. and pres. Council of Pa.

NORRIS, Nicholas (ca. 1640-ca. 1725), resided at Hampton and Exeter, N.H.; soldier King Philip's War; *m* 1664, Sarah, dau. Moses Coxe, of Hampton, N.H.

NORTH, John (1615-91), from Eng. in the "Susan and Ellen," 1635; an original landowner of Farmington, Conn., and an early settler of Hartford; *m* Hannah Bird.

NORTHRUP, Joseph (*d* 1669), from Eng. to Boston, Mass., 1637; a first settler at Milford, Conn.; *m* 1648, Mary (*d* 1683), dau. of Francis Norton.

NORTON, William (*d* 1694), from Eng. in the "Hopewell," to Ipswich, Mass., 1635; freeman, 1636; *m* Lucy, dau. Emmanuel Downing.

NOYES, James (1608-56; son of Rev. William), ed. Brasenose Coll., Oxford U.; from Eng. in the "Mary and John," to Mass., 1634; preached at Medford; freeman, 1634; settled at Newbury, 1635, where he was teacher of the church for more than 20 yrs.; *m* in Eng., 1634, Sarah, eld. dau. Joseph Brown, of Southampton.

NOYES, Nicholas (1614-1701; brother of Rev. James; son of Rev. William, *m* Ann Stephens); came in the "Mary and John," to Mass., 1634; freeman, 1637; rep. Gen. Ct., 1660 and later; deacon; *m* 1640, Mary (*d* 1689), dau. Capt. John Cutting.

NYE, Benjamin (1620-1704), from Eng. in the "Abigail," to Sandwich, Mass., 1629; settled at Lynn, Mass., 1635; *m* 1640, Katharine Tupper, of Sandwich, Mass.

OAKES, Edward (*b* Eng. 1604-*d* Concord, Mass., Oct. 13, 1689), came to Cambridge, Mass., 1640; q.m. Middlesex Co. troop, 1656; dep. Gen. Ct., 1659-61 and 1668-81; to Concord, 1683; *m* Jane – (*d* post 1691).

OFFLEY, David, of Boston; mem. A. and H. A. Co., 1638; removed to Plymouth, 1643, but on account of complaints of Indians against him it is declared he returned to Boston.

OGDEN, David (1655-1705), from Eng. in the "Welcome," with William Penn; settled at Phila., Pa., 1682; *m* 1686, Martha, dau. of John Houlston.

OGDEN, John (1610-81/82), from Eng. ca. 1641, settled at Stamford, Conn., where he was a magistrate; removed to Hempstead and Southampton, L.I.; was a founder of Elizabethtown, N.J.; magistrate, 1656; mem. Upper House of Gen. Ct., 1660-61; mem. King's Council, 1665; schout and actg. gov. of English Colony in East Jersey, 1673; a patentee in the Royal Charter for Conn., 1662; *m* 1637, Jane, dau. Jonathan Bond.

OLDS (Ould) Robert (1645-1728), from Eng., was at Windsor, Conn., 1667; *m* Susannah Hanford (*d* 1688).

OLIVER, Thomas (*d* 1657), from Eng. in the "William and Francis," to Boston, 1632; *m* Anne –.

OLMSTED, James (1580-1640), from Great Leighs, Essex, Eng., in the "Lyon," 1632, settled 1st at Mt. Wollaston (now Quincy), Mass., later at Newton (Cambridge), one of the 12 men, apptd. by Rev. Thomas Hooker (qv), who selected the site of Hartford, Conn., and lead the migration thither, 1635; *m* 1605, Joyce Cornish (*d* Fairsted, Essex, Eng., 1621).

OLMSTED (Olmstead), Richard (1612-86), from Eng. in the "Lyon," to Cambridge, Mass., 1632; an original settler at Hartford, Conn.; removed to Norwalk, 1650; rep. Gen. Ct. many yrs.; commr. for Norwalk, 1668; was sgt., lt., muster master, and capt.; *m* twice.

OLNEY, Thomas (1600-82), from Eng. named in R.I. charter given by Charles II, 1663; 1st treas., 1638; commnr., 1647; asst., 1648-63; judge Justices Ct., 1655; commr., 1657-63; dep. 1665-71; mem. town councils, 1665-81; mem. Gen Assembly; *m* 1631, Marie Small.

ORCUTT, William (*d* 1693), from Eng. to Weymouth, Mass., 1660; settled at Hingham; *m* 2d, Martha –.

ORTON, Thomas (1613-88), from Eng. to Mass., 1636; of record at Windsor, Conn., 1641, at Farmington, 1655; dep. Gen. Ct.; *m* 1641, Margaret Pratt.

ORVIS, George (*d* 1664), referred to as "the emigrant"; from Eng., 1629; one of the first settlers and original proprs. of Farmington, Conn., ante 1639; *m* 1652, Elizabeth – (*d* 1694), widow of David Carpenter.

OSBORN, John (1604-86), from Eng. in the "Hector," 1638; settled at East Windsor, Conn., 1644; *m* 1645, Ann, dau. of Richard Oldage.

OSBORN (Osborne), Richard (1612-86), from Eng.; at Hingham, Mass., 1635; served in Pequot War, 1637; at New Haven, 1639, Fairfield, 1653.

OSGOOD, Christopher (*d* 1650), from Eng. in the "Mary and John," to Ipswich, Mass., 1634; *m* 1632, Mary Everatt (*d* 1633); *m* 2d, 1633, Margery (bap. 1615), dau. of Philip Fowler, who also came in the "Mary and John," *m* Mary Windey or Window.

OSGOOD, John (1595-1651), from Eng. to Ipswich, Mass., 1638; settled finally at Andover, 1645; dep. Gen. Ct., 1651; *m* ca. 1627, Sarah Booth.

OTIS (Ottis), John (ca. 1581-1657), from Eng. to Hingham, Mass., 1635; freeman, 1636; selectman; removed to Weymouth after 1653; *m* in Eng., Margaret – (*d* 1653/54); *m* 2d, Elizabeth Streame, widow.

OVERTON, William (*b* Dec. 3, 1638; son of Col. Robert [*b* ca. 1609], who was a distinguished soldier of the Parliamentary wars, *m* 1630, Anne Gardiner); came to Va., 1669; received grant of 4,600 acres for bringing over 92 persons, grant dated Apr. 23, 1681, the land on the south side of the Pamunkey River in New Kent (now Hanover) Co.; granted land in St. Peter's Parish, New Kent Co., 1690; *m* Nov. 24, 1670, Mary Elizabeth Waters, of St. Sepulchre's Parish, London.

PACKARD, Samuel (*d* 1684), from Eng. in the "Diligence," 1638; settled at West Bridgewater, Mass.

PADDOCK, Robert (*d* 1650), from Eng. to Duxbury, Mass., 1634; mem. military co., Plymouth, 1643; *m* Mary – (*d* 1650).

PAGE, John (1586-1676), from Eng. with Gov. Winthrop, to Boston, Mass., 1630; at Dedham, 1636; freeman, 1640; *m* Phebe –; *m* 2d, Mary Paine.

PAGE, John (1627-Jan. 23, 1691), from Eng. to Va. ca. 1650; civil and military officer for York Co., Va.; justice before 1655; burgess, 1655-56; mem. Colonial Council of Va., 1681-91; gave the ground and aided in the erection of Bruton Parish Church, at Williamsburg, Va.; maj. 1676; col. and county lt., 1680-85; *m* ca. 1656, Alice Luckin (ca. 1625-ca. 1698).

PAIGE, Nathaniel (*d* 1692), from Eng. with his wife and three children ca. 1685, and settled at Roxbury, Mass.; marshal of Suffolk Co., 1686; purchased land and lived at Billerica for a brief time; one of the eight purchasers of Hardwick, 1686; *m* Joanna –.

PAINE, Moses (1581-1643; son of Nicholas), from Eng. to Cambridge, Mass., 1638; *m* 1st, Mary Benison; *m* 2d, ca. 1618, Elizabeth – (*d* in Eng., 1632); *m* 3d, Judith – (*d* 1654), widow of Edmund Quincy.

PAINE, Stephen (*d* 1679), from Eng. in the "Diligent," with his wife, three children and four servants, to Hingham, Mass., 1638; freeman, 1639; a founder and early propr. of Rehoboth, 1643; rep. Gen. Ct. of Mass., until his death; *m* Rose (also called Neele) – (*d* 1660); *m* 2d, 1662, Alice – (*d* 1682), widow of William Parker, of Taunton.

PAINE (Payne), Thomas (1587-1639), from Eng. in his own ship, the "Mary Anne," to Salem, Mass., 1637; weaver; *m* 1610, Elizabeth –.

PAINE (Payne) Thomas (1586-1650), from Eng., with his son Thomas, to Plymouth, Mass., 1621; settled at Yarmouth; freeman, 1639; 1st dep. Gen. Ct.; *m* Margaret, dau. Sir Thomas Pultney.

PAINE, William (1598-1660; son of William, of Nowton, Co. Suffolk, Eng.); came to Ipswich and Boston, Mass.; *m* Hannah –.

PALFREY (Palfery, Palfry, Palfray), Peter (*d* 1663), from Eng., was at Salem, Mass., 1626; freeman, 1630; rep. Gen. Ct., 1635; removed to Reading; *m* Edith –; *m* 2d, Elizabeth –, widow of John Fairchild; *m* 3d, Alice –.

PALMER, Walter (1585-1661/62), from Eng. to Salem, Mass., 1628; at Charlestown, 1629-43; freeman, 1634; constable, 1633; removed to Rehoboth; 1st rep. Gen. Ct. from that town, 1646, 47; a founder of Stonington, Conn., 1653; *m* Ann (Elizabeth) –; *m* 2d, Rebecca Short; *m* 3d, Esther –.

PALMER, William, from Eng., was at Watertown, Mass., 1636-37, at Newbury, 1637, and one of the original settlers and patentees of the town of Hampton, N.H., 1638; *m* 2d, Ann –.

PALMER, William (ca. 1585-1638), from Eng. in the "Fortune," to Plymouth, Mass., 1621; later at Duxbury; *m* Frances –, who came in the "Anne," 1623.

PANCOAST, John (*d* 1694), from Northamptonshire, Eng., 1675; brought his children in the "Paradice," Oct. 1680; a framer of the first constitution of lower N.J., the "Concessions and Agreements of the Proprietors, Freeholders and Inhabitants of West N.J. in America," signed in Eng., Mar. 3, 1676 (William Penn also a signer); regulator of weights and measures, Burlington Co., 1681; constable of Yorkshire Tenth, 1682; mem. Assembly of West Jersey at Burlington, 1685; signer of the memorial address to the Quakers, in the Keithian controversy, 1692; *m* in Eng., Elizabeth – (*d* in Eng.).

PARDEE, George (bap. Feb. 19, 1624-Apr. 1700; son of Rev. Anthony; from Pitsminster and Tauxton, Somerset, Eng., to New Haven, Conn., 1644; rector Hopkins Grammar Sch.; *m* Oct. 20, 1650, Martha, dau. of Richard Miles (*d* Jan. 7, 1667), from Eng., to New Haven.

PARK, Arthur (*d* Jan. 1739), of Scotch-Irish descent; from Ireland with his wife and son, Joseph, to Westchester Co., Pa.; settled in Union Co., S.C.; *m* Mary – (*d* ca. 1760).

PARK, Richard (ca. 1602-1665), from Eng. in the "Defense," 1635; a propr. at Cambridge, Mass., 1636; *m* 1st, Margery –.

PARK (Parke), Sir Robert (1580-1664), English baronet, coat of arms recorded in College of Heraldry; came from Eng. in the "Arbella," 1630, as sec. to John Winthrop; removed to Wethersfield, Conn., 1639; to Pequot (now New London), 1649; later to Mystic (now Stonington); was dep. Gen. Ct. and selectman; served in Colonial forces; *m* 1st, Martha Chaplin.

PARKER, Elisha (*d* after July 24, 1701), from Eng. to Barnstable, Mass.; *m* 1657, Elizabeth Hinckley (*b* 1635; sister of Gov. Thomas).

PARKER, Thomas (1609-83), from Eng. in the "Susan and Ellen," 1635; freeman at Lynn, Mass., 1637; one of the first settlers at Reading ca. 1638; selectman, 1661; *m* ca. 1635, Amy – (*d* 1690).

PARKER, William (1660-1736), from Eng. to Portsmouth, N.H., 1703; *m* 1703, Zerviah Stanley (1665-1718; dau. Earl of Derby).

PARMELEE (Palmerley, Permerly, Permerlee, Parmele), John (*d* New Haven, Conn., Nov. 1659; will probated Jan. 3, 1659/60); from Eng. in the "Elizabeth and Ann," 1635, and settled at Guilford, Conn.; signer of the Plantation Covenant, 1639; *m* 1st, in Eng., Hannah –; *m* 2d, as her first husband, Elizabeth Bradley (she *m* 2d, 1663, John Evarts).

PARROTT, Richard (*d* 1686), from Barbados, an early settler in Lancaster Co., Va., 1649; sr. justice, 1673-86; commr., 1650; high sheriff, 1657; *m* Margaret – (*d* 1687).

PARSONS, Joseph (1618-83), from Eng. to Springfield, Mass., 1634; mem. A. and H. A. Co.; grantee in Indian deed to Springfield, 1636; a founder of Northampton; freeman, 1669; cornet of the horse; again settled at Springfield, 1679, and was one of the richest men there; *m* 1646, Mary (1620-1711), dau. Thomas Bliss; she was charged with witchcraft, sent to Boston, tried and acquitted.

PARTRIDGE (Partrigg), William (*d* 1668), from Eng. to Hartford, Conn., 1640; removed to Hadley, Mass., 1659; cooper; *m* Mary Smith (1625-1680), of Hartford.

PATTEN, William (*d* 1668), from Eng. to Cambridge, Mass., ca. 1635; served in Pequot War; original propr. of Billerica; mem. A. and H. A. Co.; *m* in Eng. Mary – (*d* 1673).

PATTERSON, James (1633-1701), arrived at Charlestown, in the "John and Sarah," 1652; an adherent of Charles II, taken captive by Cromwell's army and transported to America, 1652; soldier in King Philip's War and Canadian expdn.; settled at Billerica; *m* 1662, Rebecca, dau. of Andrew Stevenson, of Cambridge, Mass.

PATTON, Robert (1755-1814), from Ireland to Phila., Pa., 1762; maj. Pa. Line; a founder of Soc. Cincinnati; was the first postmaster of Phila., under the new constitution, nearly 20 yrs.; *m* Cornelia Bridges.

PAUL, Joseph (1657-1717), from Eng., 1685; mem. Provincial Assembly of Pa., 1687; *m* 1680, Margaret Roberts.

PAYNE, Sir John, came to America, 1620; he and his brother, Sir William Payne, were both knighted by King James II, and were especially mentioned in the first land charter granted May 23, 1609; they received from the King a grant of land 12 miles square nr. Alexandria, Va., called "Payne Manor"; Sir John settled in the manorial estate in (then) Fairfax Co.

PAYSON, Edward (1613-91), from Eng. to Roxbury, Mass., ca. 1633; freeman 1640; removed to Dorchester; *m* 1640, Ann Park (*d* 1641); *m* 2d, 1642, Mary, dau. Philip Eliot, and sister of Apostle John Eliot.

PEABODY, Francis (1614-97; son of John, qv); from Eng. in the "Planter," to Ipswich, Mass., 1635; an original settler at Hampton, N.H., 1639; freeman, 1642; removed to Topsfield before 1657; selectman at Hampton and Topsfield; town clk.; lt. local mil. company; *m* Lydia –; *m* 2d, Mary (Foster) Wood (1618-1705), dau. of Reginald Foster (qv).

PEABODY (Pabody, Paybodie, Pabodie, Peabodie), John (ca. 1590-ca. 1667), from Eng. to Plymouth, Mass., 1640; an original propr. of Bridgewater, Mass., 1645; *m* Isabel –.

PEARSON, John (1615-79), from Eng., settled at Lynn, Mass., 1637; *m* Maudlin –.

PEASE, Robert (1607-44; son of Robert, *m* Margaret –), from Eng. in the "Francis," to Boston, ca. 1634; later at Salem; *m* Marie –, a Huguenot.

PECK, Henry (*d* 1651), from Eng. in the "Hector," to Boston, 1637; moved to New Haven, Conn., 1638; *m* Joan –.

PECK, Joseph (ca. 1587-1663/64), from Eng. in the "Diligent," to Hingham, Mass., 1638; freeman, 1639; rep. Gen. Ct., 1639-42; removed to Rehoboth, 1645; commr. for Hingham, 1639; served in Indian wars; *m* 1617, Rebecca Clark.

PECKHAM, John (1595-1681), from Eng., settled at Aquidneck (Newport), R.I.; *m* Mary (1607-48), dau. of Thomas Clarke, of Bedfordshire, Eng.; *m* 2d, Eleanor –.

PEGRAM, Edward, from Eng. with Col. Daniel Baker, 1699; was Queen's surveyor in the colonies; *m* Mary Scott, dau. of Col. Daniel Baker.

PEIRCE, George (*d* 1734), from Eng. with his wife and three children, 1684, settled in what is now Thornbury Tp., Chester Co., Pa.; mem. Provincial Assembly, 1706; removed to East Marlborough, Pa.; Quaker; *m* 1679, Ann Gainer.

PELL, John (1643-drowned 1702; son of Rev. John, 1609/10-1685, distinguished clergyman and mathematician, whose brother Thomas, 1608-69, surgeon in Pequot War, dep., etc., established "Pelham Manor," Westchester Co., N.Y., and willed all his property to his nephew, John), came from Eng. to Boston, 1670, as the 2d lord of Pelham Manor, N.Y.; capt. of horse, 1684, maj., 1692; first judge Ct. of Common Pleas, Westchester Co., 1688; mem. Provincial Assembly, 1691-95; mem. Com. for Defense of the Frontier and chmn. of the Grand Com.; *m* Rachel, dau. Philip Pinckney.

PENDLETON, Brian (1599-1681), from Eng., was at Watertown, Mass., 1634; settled at Sudbury, 1638, later at Ipswich, Mass., Portsmouth, N.H., and Saco, Me.; capt. of Portsmouth mil. company, 1664; maj. at Saco, 1668; dep. Mass. Gen. Ct. from Watertown, 1635, et. seq.; from Sudbury, 1638-39; from Portsmouth, 1652-54; dep. gov. Province of Me.; *m* Eleanor –.

PENDLETON, Philip (1654-1721), from Eng. to Caroline Co., Va., 1674; *m* 1682, Isabella Hurt.

PENNEBACKER (Pennebecker), Hendrick (1674-1754; son of Johannes, of Crefelt, Germany, and g.g.g.son of Herr J. Pfannebecker of Holland); came from Germany to Germantown, Pa., ante 1699; of fine education, he became surveyor for the Penns; purchased Bebber's Tp., and became one of the three Dutch patroons of Pa.; *m* Eve (*b* 1676), dau. of Nicholas Umstadt, who arrived in Pa., 1685.

PENNIMAN, James (ca. 1600-will proved 1664/65), from Eng. in the "Lion," 1631, with John Winthrop, Jr.; admitted to the church, Boston, 1631; removed to Braintree, 1639; *m* Lydia Eliot (sister of Apostle John Eliot).

PENROSE, Bartholomew (bap. 1674-1711), from Eng. to Phila., Pa., ca. 1700; shipbuilder; *m* 1703, Esther, dau. Tobias Leech.

PEPPER, Robert (*d* 1684), from Eng., settled at Roxbury, Mass.; freeman, 1643; *m* 1643, Elizabeth Johnson (*d* 1684).

PEPPERRELL, William (1647-1733), *b* in Wales, apprenticed to the captain of a fishing schooner on the coast of N.E.; settled at Isle of Shoals, later at Kittery, Me.; capt. provincial militia, 1714; cdr. of fort at Kittery Point, 1714; later lt. col. of militia of York Co.; justice Ct. Common Pleas, 1715-30; dep. Gen. Ct. of Mass., 1696, et seq.; *m* Margery (*d* 1741), dau. of John Bray, of Kittery, Me.

PERKINS, Abraham (1613-83), from Eng. to Hampton, N.H., 1639; *m* Mary – (1618-1706).

PERKINS, Edmund (*d* 1693), from Eng. with his widowed mother, to Salem, Mass., ca. 1650; *m* Susannah, dau. of Francis Hudson, and widow of John Howlett.

PERKINS, John (1583-1654), from Eng. in the "Lion," with Roger Williams, to Mass., 1631; freeman, 1631; went to Ipswich with John Winthrop, the younger, 1633; rep. Gen. Court, 1636; sgt. in war with the Tarratines, 1631; *m* 1608, Judith, dau. Michael Gater.

PERRINE (Perrin, Perine), Daniel (*d* 1719), from France, 1665, settled at Elizabethtown, N.J.; *m* 1666, Maria Thorel (*d* 1719).

PERRY (Pury), Edward (1630-95), Quaker, from Eng. to Sandwich, Mass., 1653; *m* Mary, dau. Lt. Gov. Edward Freeman.

PERRY, John (1604-74), from Eng. to Watertown, Mass., 1666; *m* Johannah Holland.

PERRY, Richard, from Eng. to New Haven Colony, 1640; at Fairfield, Conn., 1650; *m* Grace –, widow of John Nichols.

PERS, see Pierce.

PERSHING (Pfershing), Frederick (1724-94), from Alsace, in the "Jacob," to Phila., Pa., 1749, lived in York Co., Pa., where he was naturalized, 1765; removed to Westmoreland (then Cumberland) Co., nr. Youngstown, 1769, *m* 1751, Maria Elizabeth Weygandt (1738-1824).

PETERS, Andrew (1634/35-1713), from Eng. to Boston, 1659; removed to Ipswich, 1665, thence to Andover; distiller; two sons killed by Indians, 1689; soldier in Narragansett campaign, King Philip's War; *m* Mercy, dau. William Beamsley.

PETERS, William (1702-89), from England to Phila., Pa., ca. 1735, where he erected Belmont Mansion (still standing in Fairmount Park, Phila.); was register of the admiralty; judge common pleas, quarter sessions and orphans cts., Phila.; mem. Assembly and sec. of the Land Office; *m* 1741, Mary, dau. John Brientnall.

PETTINGELL, Richard (ca. 1620-ca. 1695), was settled at Salem, Mass., before 1641, when he was admitted freeman; removed to Wenham, 1649, to Newbury, 1651, where he bought land; *m* ca. 1643, Joanna (ca. 1625-1692/93), dau. Richard Ingersoll.

PHELPS, George (1605 or 06-1687), from Tewksbury, Eng., in the "Mary and John," to Dorchester, Mass., May 30, 1630; founded Windsor, Conn., 1635; finally settled at Westfield, Mass., 1670; mem. Council of Ten; *m* 1637, Phillury Randall; *m* 2d, 1648, Frances Dewey.

PHELPS, William (1599-1672; son of William, bailiff of Tewksbury, Eng.), from Eng. in the "Mary and John," to Dorchester, Mass., 1630; freeman, 1631; rep. 1st Gen. Court of Mass., 1634; selectman, 1634, 35; removed to Windsor, Conn., 1636; one of 8 commissioners apptd. by Colony of Mass. Bay to govern Colony of Conn., in 1636; gov.'s asst., 1636-42, 1658-62; rep. Gen. Court, 1645-57; mem. Council, 1637; magistrate; *m* Elizabeth –; *m* 2d, Mary Dover.

PHILBRICK, Thomas (*d* 1667), from Eng. with Gov. Winthrop, Sir Richard Saltonstall and others, arrived in Mass. Bay, 1630; settled at Watertown, Mass.; removed to Hampton, N.H., 1645; *m* Elizabeth – (*d* 1663).

PHILLIPS, George (1593-1644), A.B., Cambridge, 1613; from Eng. in the "Arbella," to Salem, Mass., 1630; a founder of Watertown, where he founded the first Congl. Ch. in America; *m* 1st, 1631, – Sergeant; *m* 2d, Mrs. Elizabeth Welden.

PHIPPS, James (son of Sir Wiliam); gunsmith; founded Phippsburg, Me., nr. mouth of Kennebec River before 1649.

PICKERING, John (1615-ca. 1657), from Eng. to Ipswich, Mass., 1634; removed to Salem, 1637; *m* Elizabeth –.

PICKETT (Pigot, Picquette), Capt. William (*d* 1640), mem. Va. Company, but did not come to America; *m* Sarah Stonor (*d* 1663).

PIERCE (Pers), John (1588-1661), from Eng. in either "Rose of Yarmouth" or "John and Dorothy," 1637; was one of the early proprietors of Watertown, Mass.; projected settlement of Sudbury and Lancaster, Mass.; dep. Gen. Ct., 1638-39; *m* Elizabeth – (1591 or 1601-1666).

PIERCE, Robert (*d* 1664), from Eng. in the "Mary and John," to Dorchester, Mass., 1630; built home on land which is still in possession of his descendants; *m* Ann (1591-1695, aet. 104), dau. of John Greenway, from Eng. in the "Mary and John."

PIERCE (Pers), Thomas (1583/84-1666), from Eng., 1633/34, settled at Charlestown; freeman, 1635; one of 21 commrs. apptd. by Gen. Ct. "to see that Saltpetre heapes were made by all the farmers of the Colony," 1642; *m* Elizabeth – (*b* 1595/96).

PIERPONT (Pierrepont), James (*d* ante 1664), from Eng., settled at Ipswich, Mass.; *m* Margaret – (*d* 1664).

PIERSON, Rev. Abraham (*b* Yorkshire, Eng., 1613-*d* Aug. 9, 1678), grad. Trinity Coll., Cambridge, 1632, and ordained; came to Boston, 1639, but soon removed to Lynn, Mass.; established a settlement at Southampton, L.I., 1640-1641; removed to Branford, Conn., with many of his congregation; Indian interpreter and translated the catechism into the Indian dialect; later at Newark, N.J., where he died; *m* Abigail, dau. of Rev. John Wheelwright, of Lincolnshire, Eng. (his son, Abraham Pierson [1641-1707], was first pres. of Yale Coll., 1701-07).

PIERSON (Pearson, Parsune, Person), Henry (1618-ca. 1680), from Eng. to Boston, 1639; to Southampton, L.I., 1640; clerk of Suffolk Co. Ct., 1669; founder of the public school system; *m* Mary, dau. of John Cooper, of Lynn, Mass., from Eng. in the "Hopewell," to Southampton, 1635.

PILLSBURY, William (1615-86), from Eng. to Dorchester, Mass., 1641; removed to Newbury, 1651; freeman, 1668; *m* Dorothy Crosby.

PITKIN, William (1635-94), from Eng., 1659; settled at Hartford, Conn.; prosecutor for Conn. Colony; atty. gen. for the King; rep. Hartford, 1675-90; treas. Com. to United Colonies; *m* 1661, Hannah (1637-1724), dau. of Ozias Goodwin, an original settler of Hartford.

PITNEY, James (1583/84-1663), from Eng. to New Brunswick, N.J., ante 1622; settled at Basking Ridge; *m* Sarah Smythe (1612/13-1658).

PLATER, George (*d* 1707), from Eng., resided in Md., 1685-1707; atty. for the king, 1691; collector of customs, Patuxent Dist., 1692; *m* Ann –.

PLATT, Richard (ca. 1603-1684), from Eng. with his wife and four children, to New Haven Colony, 1638; a founder of Milford, Conn., 1639; deacon; *m* Mary –.

PLEASANTS, John (1644-98), from Eng. to Va., 1665; settled at Curles Neck, Henrico Co.; *m* 1670, Jane Larcome (*d* 1708), widow of Samuel Tucker.

PLIMPTON (Plympton), John (ca. 1620-1677), from Eng. ca. 1630; was at Dedham, Mass., before he settled at Deerfield, ca. 1673; sgt. mil. company; captured and burned at the stake by Indians, 1677; *m* 1644, Jane Dammant.

PLUMB, John (July 28, 1594-July 1648), came from Spaynes Hall, Great Yeldham, Essex Co., Eng., in his own ship, 1635; an early settler and propr. of Wethersfield, Conn.; shipowner; traded with Indians; mem. Wethersfield Ct.; probably with Capt. Mason in Pequot War, 1637; removed to Branford, 1644; town clk., 1645; *m* ca. 1616, Dorothy – (*d* post 1669).

PLUMMER (Plumer), Francis (ca. 1595-1672/1673), from Wales in the "Elizabeth Dorcas," to Newbury, Mass., 1633; admitted freeman, Ipswich, 1634; Newbury, Mass., 1634; *m* 1st, Ruth –.

POLK, Capt. Robert (*d* bet. May 6, 1699, date of his will, and June 5, 1704, when it was proved), from Ireland to Somerset Co., Md., bet. 1672-80; received from the Lords Baltimore grants of land in the Eastern Shore, "Polk's Lott," May 7, 1687, and "Polk's Folly," 1700; *m* in Ireland, Magdalen (Tasker) Porter (*d* "White Hall," Eastern Shore, 1726), dau. of Colonel Tasker, of Broomfield Castle, nr. Londonderry, a chancellor of Ireland, and widow of Colonel Porter in whose regt., a part of the Parliamentary forces under Cromwell, Robert Polk served as captain.

POMEROY (Pomroy, Pummery, Pumry), Eltweed (1585-1673), from Eng. in the "Mary and John," to Nantasket, Mass., 1630; settled at Dorchester; freeman, 1632; selectman, 1633; removed to Windsor, where he received a grant of 1,000 acres, 1636; to Northampton, 1672; *m* 1617, Johannah Keech (*d* 1620); *m* 2d, 1629, Margery (christened Mary, but called Margery) Rockett (1605-55); *m* 3d, 1661, Lydia Brown, widow of Thomas Parsons.

POND, Samuel (*d* 1654), from Eng. with Winthrop's fleet, 1630; *m* 1642, Sarah Ware.

POOLE (Poal, Pole), Edward (1609-64), from Eng. to Boston, Mass., 1635; settled at Weymouth, the same year; capt. militia; propr. of a sawmill, and a large amount of land; *m* bet. 1641-45, Sarah, dau. John Pynney.

POOR (Poore), John (1615-84), from Eng. to Newbury, Mass., 1635; *m* Sarah –.

POPE, Col. Nathaniel (ca. 1610-Apr. 1660), from Eng. to Va., 1634; resided in Md., 1637-50; mem. Md. Assembly, 1637, 1641-42; removed to Va., 1650; settled at "The Cliffs," Pope's Creek Westmoreland Co., Va., upon a grant from Charles I; lt. col. Westmoreland Co., 1655; *m* Lucy –.

POPE, Thomas (1608-83), from Eng. in the "Mary and John," settled at Dorchester, Mass., 1630, at Dartmouth, ca. 1674; *m* 1637, Ann, dau. Gabriel Fallowell; *m* 2d, 1646, Sarah, dau. John Jenney.

PORTER, John (1590-1648), from Eng. probably 1638; received large land grant and was constable at Windsor, Conn., 1639; dep. Gen. Ct., 1639, et seq.; *m* Ann or Rosanna White.

POSEY, Francis (ca. 1610-1657), mem. Lower House of Burgesses, from St. Mary's Co., Md., 1640-50; one of first settlers in St. Mary's Co.

POST, Richard (1617-ca. 1689), from Eng., at Southampton, L.I., 1640; one of first settlers of New London, Conn., 1646 or 47; blacksmith; *m* ca. 1640, Dorothy Johnson (1625-ca. 1689).

POTTER, Robert (1610-55), from Eng. to Lynn, Mass., 1630; freeman, 1634; removed to Newport, R.I., 1638; a founder of Warwick, 1641; taken prisoner to Boston on account of preaching a "monstrous doctrine," was banished and went to Eng. and secured restoration of his estate; kept an inn at Warwick and *d* there; *m* Isabel –; *m* 2d, Sarah –.

POWELL, Capt. William, from Wales to Va., 1607, with Capt. John Smith; rep. from James City in first House of Burgesses, 1619; *m* Elizabeth, dau. of Joseph Welles.

POWERS, Walter (1639-1708), from Eng. to Concord Village, Mass., 1660; bought town of Nashoba from Indians; *m* 1661, Trial, dau. of Ralph Shepherd (qv);

POYTHRESS, Capt. Francis, from Eng. to Va., 1633; burgess for Charles City 1645, 47; commanded against the Indians, 1645; burgess for Northumberland, 1649.

PRATT, John (*d* 1655), from Eng. 1632; a founder of Hartford, Conn., 1636; dep. Gen. Ct., 1639, et seq.; *m* Elizabeth –.

PRATT, Matthew (1600-72), from Eng., settled at Weymouth, Mass.; freeman, 1640; removed to Rehoboth; *m* Elizabeth Bate.

PRATT, Richard (1615-91), from Eng. to Charlestown, Mass., ca. 1640; removed to Malden, Mass.; *m* 1643, Mary – (*d* ca. 1691).

PRATT, William (1622-78; son of Rev. William Pratt), from Eng. with Rev. Thomas Hooker; an original settler at Hartford, Conn., 1636; dep. Gen. Ct., 1666, et seq.; mem. Council of War, 1642; removed to Saybrook, 1645; lt. of Saybrook forces in Pequot War; *m* Elizabeth, dau. John Clark, one of the 19 patentees named in the Royal Charter from Charles, II.

PREBLE, Abraham (1603-63), from Eng. to Scituate, Mass., 1637, removed to York, Me., 1642, magistrate 1650; freeman, 1652; treas. of Me. Company, 1659; commr. for York, 1655-57, 1659-60; held first mil. appointment with rank of major; *m* Judith, dau. Nathaniel Tilden.

PRENCE (Prince), Thomas (1600-73), from Eng. to Plymouth, Mass., 1621; asst. Plymouth Colony, 1635; gov., 1634-38, 57, 72; mem. Council of War, and served in Pequot War; commr. United Colonies, 1645; removed to Duxbury, 1635, to Eastham, Mass., 1645; *m* Patience, dau. Elder William Brewster.

PRENTICE (Prentis), Capt. Thomas (1621-1710), from Eng. to Cambridge, Mass., ante 1652; freeman, 1652; lt. horse troop, 1656; laid out Worcester, 1667; rep. Gen. Ct., 1672-74; capt. Indian war, 1675, in Pequot and Narragansett wars; commr. to rebuild Lancaster, Mass., 1689; overseer of Indians, 1691; *m* ca. 1643, Grace –.

PRESCOTT, James (1642-1728; g.g.son James, lord of the manor of Driby, Lincolnshire, *m* Alice, dau. Sir Richard Mollyneux, of Sefton); from Eng. to Hampton, N.H., 1655; took oath of allegiance, 1678; *m* Mary, dau. Nathaniel Boulter.

PRESCOTT, John (ca. 1604-1683), from Eng. to the Barbados, 1638, thence to Watertown, Mass., 1640; with others bought from Indians a large tract of land and became a founder of Lancaster, Mass., 1645 or 46; took oath of allegiance, 1652; admitted freeman, 1669; blacksmith and miller; *m* in Eng., 1629, Mary Platts (*d* 1674).

PRESTON, John (1699-1747), from Ireland to Augusta Co., Va., 1740; grantee with Breckenridge and Patton of 12,000 acres; *m* 1725, Elizabeth Patton (1700-76).

PRESTON, Roger (*d* 1666), from Eng. in the "Elizabeth," 1635; settled at Ipswich, Mass., 1639, at Salem, 1659-60; *m* 1642, Martha –.

PRICE, John (1584-1628), from Wales in the "Starr," to Jamestown, Va., 1621; mem. Provincial Council; *m* Anne Mathews (*b* 1597).

PRICE, Thomas, from Eng. in the "Ark" and "Dove" expdn. to St. Mary's Co., Md., 1633; mem. Council; *m* Elizabeth, dau. Robert Phillips, of Calvert Co., Md.

PRIEST, Degory (ca. 1579-1621), 29th signer of the Mayflower Compact; *m* at Leyden, Holland, 1611, Sarah (Allerton) Vincent, widow of John Vincent.

PRINCE, John (1610-76), from Eng. to Mass., 1633, freeman at Watertown, 1635; removed to Hull; ruling elder; *m* Alice Honour (*d* 1668); *m* 2d, 1670, Ann –, widow of William Barstow.

PROVOOST, David (1608-85; 3d from Guillaume Prevost [*b* 1545], of Paris, *m* Margaretta Ten Waert); came to N.Y., 1624; cdr., Ft. Good Hope for Dutch West India Co.; head of the "Nine Men," New Amsterdam schepen 1645, of Breucklen, Midwout and Amersfoort until death; mem. Gov.'s Council.

PRUDDEN, Rev. Peter (1600-56), from Hertfordshire, Eng., settled at New Haven and Milford; pastor of the first ch. at Milford, Conn., 1640-56; *m* Joanna Boyse, from Eng.

PRUYN, Franz Janse (*d* 1712), from Holland to Albany, N.Y., ca. 1661; *m* Aeltje –.

PUGH, Francis, I (son of a Welsh squire of Glendower Hall, Carnavon, Wales); came to America, 1665, with his brothers, Thomas and Daniel, and settled in Upper Nansemond, Surry Co., Va., where they built a manor house of English brick upon an estate called "Jericho."

PUREFOY, Capt. Thomas (ca. 1578-ca. 1652-55; son of Humphrie, g.son of Sir Nicholas Purefoy, of royal descent); came to America in "The George," 1621; settled in Elizabeth City Co., Va.; commr.; justice and principal cdr. Elizabeth City Co., 1628; mem. Council, 1631; burgess; settled on "Drayton," a tract of 1,000 acres; *m* 1620, Lucy Ransom (1598-1657-60).

PUTNAM, John (bap. 1579-1662), from Eng., to Salem, Mass., 1640, when he received a land grant of 100 acres in Salem Village (now Danvers), Mass., became principal landowner there; *m* 1611/12, Priscilla Deacon.

PYNCHON (Pincheon), William (1590-1662), from Eng. with Winthrop's fleet to Roxbury, Mass., 1630, a founder of Springfield, Mass., 1636; governing magistrate of Conn., 1637-38; governor's asst., treas., 1632-34; gov. of Springfield, 1641-50; returned to Eng., 1652, and devoted himself to theological writing; *m* Anna, dau. William Andrew; *m* 2d, Frances Sanford.

QUINCY, Edmund (1602-35), from Eng. to Mass., 1628; returned to Eng., but came again with John Cotton, 1633, to Quincy, Mass.; freeman, 1634; rep. Gen. Ct., 1634; a founder of Braintree, 1635; *m* Judith Pares.

RAGLAND, John, from Wales to Eng., thence to Va. ca. 1720, with his wife and 10 children; settled in Henrico Co.; was granted 15,000 acres in Hanover Co.; his home "Ripping Hall," on the Chickahominy was burned in 1825; *m* Ann Beaufort, his kinswoman.

RAMBO, Peter Gunnarsson (*b* in Sweden, 1605-*d* in Pa., 1698), from Rambo, in northeastern Sweden, 1638, settled at New Sweden (later called Upper Merion, now Phila.); a founder of the Swedish colony in America; deputy under Gov. Rising, 1665; councilman under Dutch regime; magistrate, 1658; commr. under Duke of York, 1664; *m* ca. 1648, Bretta – (*d* 1684).

RANDALL, Thomas (1688 or 90-1759), from Eng. to King George Co., Va., ca. 1717-20; provincial judge; was of "Tuckahoe," and Henrico and Goochland cos., Va.; burgess, 1720-22; col. and county lt. of Goochland, 1727; *m* 1728, Jane Davis.

RANDOLPH (Fitz Randolph), Edward (ca. 1614-1675), from Eng. to Scituate, Mass., 1630; *m* 1637, Elizabeth (1620-1713), dau. Thomas Blossom, came in the 2d "Mayflower," to Salem, Mass., 1629.

RANDOLPH, William (*b* Yorkshire, Eng., 1651-*d* Turkey Island, Henrico Co., Va., Apr. 10, 1711); from Eng. to Jamestown, Va., 1674; settled on Turkey Island, James River, Henrico Co., Va., 1674; clk. of Henrico Co., 1683-1711; burgess, 1685-99, 1703-05, and 1710; atty. gen. and mem. Royal Council; capt. Henrico Co. forces, 1680; lt. col., 1699; a founder of William and Mary College; *m* 1680, Mary (*d* 1742), dau. Henry Isham, of Bermuda Hundred, Henrico Co., Va., *m* Catherine Royall.

RANNEY, Thomas (1616-1713), from Scotland to Middletown, Conn., ca. 1657; *m* 1659, Mary, dau. George Hubbard.

RAPELJE (de Rapalie), Joris Janssen (ca. 1600-ca. 1663; desc. noble family of Brittany), Huguenot, fled from France to Holland, thence in the "Unity" to New Amsterdam, 1623; at Albany, 1623-37; resided at Wallabout; magistrate; one of the "Twelve Men," Brooklyn; *m* Catalyntie (1605-89), dau. of Joris Trico, of Paris.

RAVENEL (de Ravenal), Rene (*b* 1656; sieur de la Haute, Massais), Huguenot, from France, 1682, before the revocation of the Edict of Nantes, to Charleston, S.C.; mem. Assembly; *m* 1687, Charlotte, dau. Pierre de St. Julien (sieur de Malacare, Brittany).

RAWSON, Edward (1615-93), from Eng. to Newbury, Mass., 1637; removed to Boston, 1650; sec. Colony of Mass. Bay, 1650-81; commr. at Boston, 1658; officer to enforce English naval laws, 1663.

RAYMOND, Capt. Richard (ca. 1602-1692), was at Salem, Mass., ante 1634; founder of Norwalk, Conn., 1662; called "Honored fore-father of Saybrook"; *m* Judith –.

READE, Col. George (1600-71), from Eng. to Va., 1637; sec. Colony of Va., 1637; acting gov., 1638; burgess, 1649, 56; mem. King's Council, 1657-71; *m* Elizabeth (1627-87), dau. of Nicholas Martian (qv).

READING, Col. John (*d* 1717), from Eng. to Gloucester Co., N.J., 1684; mem. Assembly, 1685; co. clk., 1688-1702; removed to Burlington (later Amwell Tp., Hunterdon) Co., 1709; capt. N.J., Militia, 1713; lt. col., 1715; *m* Elizabeth –.

REDMAN, see Rodman.

REED, William (*b* 1605), from Eng. in the "Assurance," to Boston, 1635; rep. Gen. Ct., 1636, 38; townsman, 1651; *m* Avis (Deacon or Chapman).

REMINGTON (Rimmington), John (1617-67), from Eng. to Rowley, Mass., 1637; removed to Newbury; freeman, 1639; later at Greenwich,

R.I.; lt. mil. company; soldier Pequot War; *m* Elizabeth – (*d* 1657), *m* 2d, Rhoda –, widow of John Gore.

REMSEN (Rem Jensen Vanderbeeck), Rem (*d* 1681), probably from Westphalia, to New Netherland, 1642; resided at Albany, later at Wallabout, L.I.; *m* Jannette de Rapalje.

REVERE (Rivoire), Apollos (1702-54), from France to Guernsey, thence to Boston, 1715; *m* Deborah Hichborne (1704-77).

REYNOLDS, James (ca. 1620-1700), from Eng. to Plymouth, Mass., ca. 1645; settled at Potowomut Neck, nr. E. Greenwich, North Kingstown, R.I., ca. 1665; *m* ca. 1648 Deborah – (ca. 1620-ante 1692).

REYNOLDS, John (*b* ca. 1612), first recorded mention is in Watertown, Mass., where he was made a freeman, 1635; *m* Sarah – (*b* ca. 1614).

REYNOLDS, Robert (*d* 1659), from Eng., was at Boston, 1632; freeman, 1634; *m* Mary –.

RHETT (Lwirete-Rhett, from Lwirte), George, from Eng. to Carolina, 1671, later to Charlestown, Mass.; *m* Sarah Boyleston.

RHINELANDER, Philip Jacob (*d* 1737), a Huguenot, from France after the revocation of the Edict of Nantes, settled at New Rochelle, N.Y., 1686.

RICE, Edmund (1594-1663), from Eng., 1638; a founder of Sudbury, Mass.; freeman, 1640; rep. Gen. Ct.; magistrate; an early settler of Marlborough; selectman; *m* Tamazine Hosmer (*d* 1654); *m* 2d, 1655, Mercy, widow of Thomas Brigham.

RICHARDS, Edward (ca. 1610-84), from Eng. in the "Lion" with Roger Williams, 1631; at Dedham, Mass., 1632; freeman, 1641; *m* 1638, Susanna Hunting.

RICHARDSON (Richeson), Ezekiel (1602-47), from Eng. in the "Arbella," with Gov. Winthrop, to Charlestown, Mass., 1630; freeman, 1631; constable, 1633; rep. Gen. Ct., 1635; selectman; a founder of Woburn; *m* in Eng., Susanna –.

RICHARDSON, Samuel (ca. 1610-1658), from Eng. with two brothers, Ezekiel and Thomas, in the "Arbella," with Gov. Winthrop, 1630, settled at Charlestown, Mass., 1636; founder and largest landowner of Woburn, Mass., *m* Joanna –.

RICHARDSON, Thomas (*d* 1651), from Eng. in the "Arbella," with Gov. Winthrop, 1630, to Charlestown, Mass.; freeman, 1638; a founder of Woburn, 1642; *m* Mary –.

RICHMOND, John (1594-1664), from Eng. to Mass., ca. 1635; one of the first purchasers of land at Taunton, 1637; in R.I., 1655, but returned to Taunton; mem. R.I. Ct. of Commissioners, 1656.

RICKARD, Giles (1597-1684), from Wales, settled at Plymouth, Mass., 1635; freeman, 1640; surveyor and constable; *m* 1st, 1622, Judith – (*d* 1661); *m* 2d, 1662, Joan Tilson.

RIDGELY, Henry (1625-1710), from Devonshire, Eng., settled on the Patuxent River, Prince George's Co., Md., 1659; justice for Anne Arundel Co., 1686-92; mem. Gov.'s Council and Assembly; col. militia; *m* Elizabeth Howard; *m* 2d, Sarah Warner; *m* 3d, Mary DuVall.

RIDGELY, Robert (*d* 1682), from Eng. in the "Assurance," to St. Mary's Co., Md., 1634/35; one of the principal attorneys for the province and clk. House of Assembly many yrs.; principal sec., 1671; examiner High Ct. of Chancery; probate judge; keeper of lesser seals; *m* Martha –.

RIPLEY, William (1600-56), from Eng. in the "Diligent," ca. 1638, settled at Hingham, Mass.; admitted freeman, 1642; *m* 2d, 1654, Elizabeth – (*d* 1660), widow of Thomas Thaxter, of Hingham; she *m* 3d, 1657/58, John Dwight, of Dedham.

ROBBINS, Richard (*d* after 1683), from Eng. to Charlestown, Mass., 1639; removed to Boston, thence to Cambridge; *m* Rebecca –.

ROBERTS, Hugh (*d* 1702), from Eng. with his widowed mother (*d* 1699), to Pa., 1683; settled in Merion Tp.; Quaker; mem. Provincial Council of Pa.; *m* Jane, dau. Owen ap Evan; *m* 2d, Elizabeth John.

ROBERTS, John, from Wales to Montgomery Co., Pa., 1683; *m* Gainor Hugh.

ROBERTSON, William, from Scotland to Charles City, Va., was receiver of York River and sec. of Council of State, 1719, under Gov. Spottswood; *m* Christian Ferguson.

ROBESON, Andrew (1654-1719/20), from Scotland to Gloucester Co., N.J., ca. 1676; moved to Philadelphia Co., Pa., 1702; purchased, 1690, "Shoomac Park," now known as Fairmont Park; chief justice of Pa., 1693-98; *m* 1685, Mary Spencer (1666-1716), of Stuart descent.

ROBINSON, Alexander (1750-1845), from Ireland to Baltimore, Md.; *m* Priscilla (Lyles) Booth (1760-90), widow of Robert Booth; *m* 2d, a dau. of Charles Wilson Peale.

ROBINSON, Isaac (1610-1704; son of Rev. John), from Eng. in the "Lion," 1631; was at Duxbury, Mass., 1635, at Scituate, 1636, at Barnstable, 1639; mem. Grand Inquest for the colony, 1639, 48; dep. Gen. Ct. from Barnstable, 1645, 51; receiver of excise; recorder at Tisbury; *m* 1636, Margaret Hanford.

ROBINSON, John (ca. 1576-1625), M.A., Cambridge, 1599; from Eng. to Holland, and settled at Leyden, 1609; pastor at Leyden of the Pilgrims; regarded as "the most learned, polished and modest spirit that ever separated from the Church of England"; active in promoting emigration to America; *m* Bridget White.

ROBINSON, William (*d* 1668), from Eng.; at Dorchester, Mass., ca. 1636; name first appears as member of the church there, 1639; freeman, 1642; mem. A. and H. A. Co., 1643; *m* 1st, Margaret –.

ROCKEFELLER (Rockenfeller), Johan Peter (*b* 1682), from Germany to Amwell, N.J., 1723; *m* Anna Maria Remagen (1684-1719); *m* 2d, 1720, Elizabeth Christina Runkel.

ROCKWELL, William (bap. 1591-1640), from Eng. to Dorchester, Mass., 1630; freeman, 1631; removed to Windsor, Conn., ca. 1636; *m* 1624, Susan Capen (1602-66); she *m* 2d, 1645, Matthew Grant.

RODMAN (Redman), John (1653-1731; son of John, who settled in the Barbados), from Eng. to Barbados, thence to Newport, R.I., ca. 1682; freeman, 1684; removed to Block Island, ca. 1688, to Flushing, L.I., 1691; freeman, New York City, 1698; physician; Quaker; *m* Mary Scammon (1663-1748).

RODMAN, Dr. Thomas (1640-1728; son of John [*d* 1686], from Eng. to Ireland, 1654, planter in the Barbados, *m* ca. 1638, Elizabeth –); a Quaker; came to Newport, R.I., 1675; eminent physician and surgeon; large landowner in N.J. and Pa.; *m* 2d, 1682, Patience Easton (1655-90), dau. of Peter Easton, *m* Ann, dau. of John Coggeshall (qv).

ROGERS, Giles (1643 or 45-1730; desc. John Rogers, the martyr, burned at the stake, 1555; nephew of Thomas Rogers, Mayflower pilgrim), came to Va., 1670, returned 2d time, 1680; *m* in Eng., Rachel Eastham.

ROGERS, Nathaniel (1598-1655), A.B., Cambridge, 1617; from Eng. to Boston, Mass., 1636; pastor at Ipswich, 1638-55; *m* Margaret, dau. Robert Crane.

ROGERS, Thomas (*d* 1621), 18th signer of the Mayflower Compact.

ROGERS, William, from Eng. to Conn., 1635; with two others bought from the Indians what was called the Eastern land purchase, on which the town of Huntington, L.I., was founded.

ROLFE, John (*b* Beacham Hall, May 6, 1585-*d* 1622; son of John, of Beacham Hall, Co. Suffolk, Eng., *m* Dorothea Mason); capt. English army; came to Va., 1607; was mem. Council and the first sec. and recorder general of Colony of Va.; *m* 1613, Pocahontas (Rebecca Matoaka), (1595-1617), dau. of Powhatan, Indian chieftain of Va.

ROLLINS (Rawlins), James, from Eng. to Ipswich, Mass., 1632; settled at Dover, N.H., ca. 1641; *m* Hannah –.

ROOSEVELT (Van Rosevelt), Claes Martenszen (*d* ca. 1658), from Holland, seems to have first appeared in New Netherland 1638; *m* Jannetje Samuels, or Hamel, or Thomas (*d* 1660).

ROOT (Roote), John (*d* 1684), from Eng. to Farmington, Conn., 1640; freeman, 1657; *m* Mary (*d* 1697), dau. Thomas Kilbourne.

ROOT (Roote), Thomas (1605-94; son of John, of Badby, Eng., *m* Ann Russell); came to Salem, Mass., 1637; an early settler at Hartford, Conn.; soldier in Pequot War.

ROSE, Robert (1594-1664), from Eng. in the "Francis," to Mass., 1634; thence to Wethersfield, Conn.; constable, 1640; rep. Gen. Ct. 3 terms; removed to Stratford before 1648; served in Pequot War; *m* Margery –.

ROSSITER, Edward (*d* 1630), from Eng. in the "Mary and John," to Dorchester, Mass., 1630, with son Brian; was gov.'s asst., Mass. Bay Colony.

ROYALL, Joseph (1600-58), from Eng. in the "Charitie" to Jamestown, Va., 1622; settled on James River above Shirley Hundred; large landowner, fought in the Indian wars; *m* 3d, ca. 1645, Katharine Banks of Canterbury, Eng., who *m* 2d, Henry Isham (qv).

RUMSEY (Rumsie), Robert, from Wales to Fairfield, Conn., ca. 1664; *m* Rachel –.

RUNK (Runck), Jacob (ca. 1716-ca. 1771), from the Palatinate in the "Winter Galley," to Phila., Pa., 1738; purchased farm and settled in Amwell Tp., Hunterdon Co., N.J.; *m* Ann (bap. 1724-ca. 1771), dau. Johann Peter Rockefeller.

RUSH, John (1620-99), from Eng., 1683, settled at Byberry, Pa.; cdr. of horse in Cromwell's Army, also his personal friend; *m* 1648, Susanna Lucas, of Hornton.

RUSSELL, John (1597-1680), from Wales ca. 1632; freeman at Cambridge, Mass., 1636; removed to Wethersfield, Conn., 1649, to Hadley, Mass., 1659.

RUSSELL, John (1608-95), an original propr. and settler at Dartmouth, Mass.; freeman, 1670; took oath of fidelity, 1684; rep. Gen. Ct., 1665-83, except two yrs.; in expedn. against Narragansett Indians, 1645; *m* Dorothy – (*d* 1687).

RUSSELL, Richard (1611 in Eng.-1676; son of Paul), to Charlestown, Mass., 1640; mem. A. and H. A. Co.; dep. Gen. Ct., 7 times; speaker; treas. of colony; gov.'s asst.; *m* in Eng., 1640, Maud (*d* 1642), dau. of William Pitt.

RUTHERFORD, Thomas (*b* 1766), from Scotland, settled at Richmond, Va., 1784; *m* 1790, Sallie Winston.

RYERSON (Reyerszen), Marten (*d* ca. 1687), from Holland to Wallabout, L.I. (present site of Brooklyn Navy Yard), ca. 1647; settled in Bergen Co., N.J.; *m* 1663, Annetje Joris, dau. Joris Jansen de Rapelje, from France in the first ship sent out by West India Co.

SAGE, David (1639-Mar. 31, 1703), from Wales, 1650; one of first settlers at Middletown, Conn., 1652; freeman, 1667; *m* Elizabeth (1646-72), dau. John Kirby; *m* 2d, 1673, Mary Wilcox (*d* Dec. 7, 1711).

ST. JOHN (Sention, Sension), Matthias (1603-99; son of Sir Oliver, of London, Eng., *m* Sarah Buckley, *b* Cayshoe, Bedfordshire, Eng.); to Dorchester, Mass., 1631/32, settled at Norwalk, 1634, Windsor, Conn., 1640, Hartford, 1650; freeman, 1699; *m* Elizabeth –.

SALTAR, Richard (*d* ca. 1724), settled in Monmouth Co., N.J., ca. 1687; mem. House of Deps. to Gen. Assembly 1695, 1704; mem. Gen. Assembly, 1706, 11; justice of the peace, 1704, 05, 08; captain; supported claims for supremacy of the Nicolls Patent, 1700-01; judge Monmouth Co., N.J. until 1724; *m* 1693, Sarah (*b* 1669), dau. of John Bowne (qv).

SALTONSTALL, Sir Richard (bap. 1586-ca. 1660), from Eng. in the "Arbella" with Gov. Winthrop, to Watertown, Mass., 1630; gov.'s asst.; returned to Eng., 1631; active friend of the colonists; *m* in Eng., Grace, dau. Robert Kaye; *m* 2d, Elizabeth West (sister of Sir Thomas West, 3d Lord De la Warr); *m* 3d, Martha Wilfred.

SAMSON (Sampson), Abraham, from Eng., settled at Plymouth, Mass., ca. 1629-30; his name appears on the list of persons in Plymouth "able to bear arms," 1643; one of the original 54 grantees of Bridgewater, 1645; surveyor of highways, 1648; constable, 1653; admitted freeman, 1654; *m* the dau. of Lt. Samuel Nash, of the Duxbury Co.

SAMSON (Sampson), Henry (*d* 1685), Mayflower Pilgrim, 1620; freeman, Duxbury, Mass., 1635; *m* at Plymouth, Mass., 1636, Ann Plummer (*d* bet. 1669-85).

SANBORN (Samborne), John (1620-92), from Eng. with his grandfather, Rev. Stephen Bachiler, to Boston, 1632; settled at Hampton, N.H., 1638; ensign and lt., Hampton mil. company; rep. Gen. Ct.; served in King William's War; *m* Mary (*d* 1668), dau. Robert Tuck; *m* 2d, Margaret, dau. Robert Page, and widow of William Moulton.

SANBORN (Samborne), William (1622-92), from Eng. with his grandfather, Rev. Stephen Bachiler, to Boston, 1632; at Hampton, Mass. (now N.H.), 1638; served in King Philip's War, selectman 4 yrs., etc.; *m* Mary Moulton.

SANDS (Sandes, Sandys), James (1622-95), from Eng., 1638, settled at Portsmouth, R.I., 1640; later at Block Island; dep. Gen. Ct. for New Shoreham Co., 1665; asst. warden, 1676; cdr. militia co. in King Philip's War; *m* Sarah, dau. John Walker.

SANFORD, Thomas (1607/08-1681), from Eng. in the "Arbella," with Gov. John Winthrop, 1630; settled at Milford, Conn., 1637; *m* 1636/37, Sarah – (*d* 1681).

SANGER, Richard (*d* 1661), from Eng. in the "Confidence," to Hingham, Mass., 1638; settled at Sudbury, 1646; at Watertown, 1649; blacksmith.

SARGENT, James (*d* 1795), from Eng. to Frederick Co., Md., before 1735; *m* Eleanor Taylor.

SARGENT, William (1602-75), from Eng. to Ipswich, Mass., 1633; later at Newbury, Hampton, Salisbury, and an original settler at Amesbury; *m* 1633, Elizabeth (*b* 1611), dau. John Perkins; *m* 2d, 1670, Joanna (Pindor) Rowell.

SARGENT, William (bap. 1602-82; son of Roger), from Eng. to Charlestown, Mass., 1638; mem. of the ch., 1639; freeman the same year; resident of Malden, where he was a lay preacher, 1648-50; removed to Barnstable, 1656; freeman Plymouth Colony, 1658; *m* Hannah – (*d* 1632); *m* 2d, Marie – (*d* 1637); *m* 3d, Sarah – (*d* 1688/89), widow of William Minshall.

SATTERLEE, Benedict (desc. Sir Edmund de Sotterley, 1223; and son of Rev. William, vicar of St. Ide, Devonshire, Eng.); settled at New London, Conn., ca. 1688; *m* Rebecca, dau. of James Bemis.

SAVAGE, Thomas (1592 or 94-1627), from Eng. to Jamestown, Va., 1607; at 13, was exchanged as hostage for "Namontock," an Indian from Powhatan's tribe; ens. in Indian war, 1624; given 9,000 acres, known as Savage's Neck, by Indians; *m* 1621, Hannah –.

SAVAGE, Thomas (1607-82; son of William, of Taunton, Eng.); to Boston, 1635; went to Providence, 1638, but returned to Boston the following yr.; later at Hingham and Andover, Mass.; tailor; lt. and capt. A. and H. A. Co.; capt. Suffolk regt. before 1655; maj. comdg. Mass. forces in Mt. Hope campaign, King Philip's War, 1675; dep. Gen. Ct., 1654, et seq.; and speaker, 1659, et seq.; gov.'s asst., 1680-81; *m* 1637, Faith, dau. William Hutchinson.

SAWYER, Thomas (1616-1706; son of John); from Eng. to Rowley, Mass., 1636; an original settler at Lancaster, 1647; *m* 1648, Mary, dau. of John Prescott (qv).

SAYLES, John (1633-81), from Eng. 1645; was at Providence, R.I., 1654; was commr., assistant, treas., warden, mem. Gen. Council, and dep. Gen. Ct.; *m* ca. 1650, Mary (1633-81), eldest dau. of Roger Williams (qv).

SAYRE (Sayer, Sayres), Thomas (1590-1670; son of Francis); from Eng., 1630; first recorded at Lynn, Mass., 1638; a founder of Southampton, L.I., 1640; where he built a house still standing; served as a scout against the Indians at Southampton.

SCARBOROUGH (Scarburgh), Capt. Edmund (1584-1635/36; son of Henry [1565-1619], *m* Mary, dau. of John Humberstone); from Eng., 1620, settled in Accomac Co., Va.; burgess, Va., 1629-35; first cdr. Plantation of Accomac, 1631; *m* Hannah, dau. of Robert Butler.

SCATTERGOOD, Thomas (*d* 1697), from Eng. to Burlington, N.J., ca. 1676; *m* 1667, Elizabeth Jarvis.

SCHENCK (Shenk), Johannes (1656-1747/48), from Holland to New Netherland, was first at New Amsterdam, 1684-85; at Esopus, 1685-89, at Flatbush, L.I., 1691-ca. 1712; town clk., 1691-94; schoolmaster, 1700-12; supervisor at Bushwick, 1719.

SCHENCK, Roelof Martense (1619-1704), from Holland to New Amsterdam, 1650; removed to Flatlands, L.I.; capt. of horse, Kings Co., 1690.

SCHERMERHORN (van Schermerhooren), Jacob Jansen (1622-88), from Holland to Beverwycke (Albany), N.Y., ca. 1636 or 1643; magistrate several yrs.; removed to Schenectady, 1686; *m* ca. 1650, Jannetje Segers (1632-1700), dau. Cornelis Segerse Van Voorhoudt.

SCHIEFFELIN, Jacob (*d* 1769), from Germany to Phila., Pa., ca. 1734; *m* 1756, Regina Margarette Ritschausin.

SCHLEY, John Thomas (1712-89), from the

Palatinate to Phila., Pa., 1737; settled in the Catochin Valley, Frederick Co., Md., 1745, at the head of about 100 families, and founded Frederick City, Md.; educator; *m* 1735, Margaret Winz von Winz.

SCHOFF, Jacob (bet. 1725-30-after 1806), from Germany to Braintree, Mass., 1752; at Ashburnham, 1757, later at Maidstone, Vt.; *m* Mary –.

SCHOONMAKER, Lt. Hendrick Jochense (*d* 1681), from Hamburg, Germany; lt. in mil. service of Holland, settled at Ft. Orange (Albany), ante 1654; later at Esopus, N.Y.; leader against the Indians; *m* Elsie Janse Van Breestede.

SCHUYLER, Philip Pieterse, van (ca. 1628-83), from Holland to Rensselaerwyck, N.Y., 1650; settled at Beverwyck (Albany); general merchant and trader and a dealer in land; commissionary at Ft. Orange, 1655, a magistrate there for many terms; commr. of Albany, 1678; del. to Mohawk Indians, 1655; vice-dir. or dep. under Govs. Stuyvesant and Nicolls; he had the first commn. of captain at Albany, 1667, at Schenectady, 1669; in 1662 he, with others, laid out "New Village," at Esopus (Kingston); *m* 1650, Margarita (1628-1711), dau. Brant Arentse Van Slichtenhorst, first resident director of Rensselaerwyck, 1646.

SCRANTON, John (1609-71), from Eng. to Boston, 1637; an original settler at Guilford, Conn., and at New haven, 1638; dep. Gen. Ct.; *m* 1666, Adaline Hill.

SCRIBNER (Scrivener), Benjamin (*d* 1704), from Eng., was at Norwalk, Conn., before 1680; *m* 1679, Hannah (*b* 1662), dau. of John Crampton.

SCUDDER, Thomas (*d* 1658), from Eng. to Salem, Mass., ca. 1635; awarded grant of land, 1648; *m* Elizabeth Somers (*d* 1666).

SEABURY, John, from Eng. to Barbados, 1638, thence to Boston, Mass., 1639.

SEARS (Sares), Richard (ca. 1590-1676), from Eng. ca. 1630; first appears on tax list at Plymouth, Mass.; awarded grant of land at Salem, 1638; a founder of Yarmouth; dep. Plymouth Colony, 1662; *m* 1632, Dorothy Thacher.

SEDGWICK, Robert (1611-56), from Eng. in the "Truelove," to Mass., 1635; settled at Charlestown, 1636; freeman, 1637; rep. Gen. Ct. 17 terms; cdr. at the Castle, 1641; a founder and capt. A. and H. A. Co.; sgt. maj. Middlesex regt., 1643-44; cdr.-in-chief, 1652; with Capt. Leverett organized an expdn. against the Dutch in Manhattan, 1654; cdr. fleet of four vessels against Acadia, 1654; cdr. regt. to occupy Jamaica, 1655, and apptd. commr. to govern the island; maj. gen., 1656; *m* Joanna –.

SEELEY (Cilley), Robert (*d* 1667), and wife Mary landed at Salem, Mass., with Governor Winthrop, 1630; lt. in Pequot War, 1637; a founder of Watertown, Mass., 1630, Wethersfield, 1635, New Haven, 1638, Fairfield and Stamford, Conn.; of Huntington, L.I., and Elizabethtown, N.J.; marshal of New Haven Colony and cdr. of its militia.

SELDEN, Thomas (*b* Ticehurst, Co. Sussex, Eng., bap. Mar. 17, 1616/17-*d* 1655; son of John, *m* Mary Baldock; desc. ancient yeoman family located in Sussex Co., 1210); an original settler at Hartford, Conn., 1636; constable, 1650; *m* Hester (bap. 1617), dau. of Francis Wakeman, of Bewdley, Eng.

SELLERS, Samuel (1655-1732), from Eng. with William Penn, to Chester Co., Pa., 1682; *m* Anna Gibbons.

SERGEANT, Jonathan (*d* 1667), came from Eng. to Branford, Conn., ca. 1644; founder of Newark, N.J., 1667.

SEVERANCE (Severns, Severans), John (*d* 1682), from Eng. to Ipswich, Mass., 1634; an original propr. of Salisbury; freeman, 1637, before the town was settled; mem. A. and H. A. Co.; *m* Abigail Kimball (*d* 1658); *m* 2d, Susanna –, widow of Henry Ambrose.

SEWALL, Henry (bap. 1576-1657), from Eng. and settled at Newbury, Mass., 1635; removed to Rowley; *m* Ellen –.

SEWALL (Sewell, Seawell), Henry (1614-1700), from Eng., in the "Elizabeth and Dorcas," to Newbury, Mass., 1634; wintered at Ipswich and helped begin that plantation, furnishing English with meat, cattle and provisions; dep. Gen. Ct., 1661; *m* 1646, Jane Dummer.

SEWARD, William (1627-89), from Eng., settled at Taunton, Mass.; moved to Guilford, Conn., ca. 1654; lt. in colonial wars; *m* 1651, Grace Norton.

SEYMOUR (Seimor, Seamor, Seamer), Richard (1596-1655), from Eng. abt. 1635; removed to Hartford, Conn., 1639-46; to Farmington, 1652, thence to Norwalk, 1653-54; selectman, 1655; *m* Mary (or Mercy) Rashleigh (*d* 1656).

SHAPLEIGH (Shapley, Sharpley), Alexander (1585-ca. 1650), from Eng., ca. 1635, in his own ship "Benediction," to Kittery, Me., where he built the first house; he returned to England and died there.

SHARPLESS (Sharples), John (1624-85), from Eng. with William Penn, to nr. Chester, Pa., 1682; *m* 1662, Jane Moore.

SHATTUCK (Shathock), William (1614-72), from Eng. ca. 1630; was at Watertown, Mass., 1642; *m* Susanna –.

SHAW, Abraham (1585-1638), from Eng., settled at Dedham and Watertown, Mass., 1636-1638; *m* 1616, Elizabeth (Bridget) Best (*b* 1592).

SHEARMAN, see Sherman.

SHEDD (Shed), Daniel (1620-1708), from Eng., and was an original settler at Braintree, Mass.; at Shed's Neck, Germantown, 1639/40; land owner at Billerica, 1659; assigned to garrison house, Billerica, 1667; corpl. in King Philip's War, 1675; *m* 1st, Mary – (1628-1658/59).

SHEFFIELD, Edward (1615-1705), from Eng.; *m* Mary Woods.

SHELBY, Evan (ca. 1694-1750/51), came from Wales to Pa., 1735; purchased and patented land; removed to Prince George's Co., Md., 1739; became a large landowner; *m* Catherine Davies.

SHELDON, Isaac (1629-1708), from Eng. to Mass.; at Windsor, Conn., 1640; settled at Northampton, Mass., ca. 1655; *m* 1653, Mary (*d* 1684), dau. Thomas Woodford, of Hartford, Conn., *m* Mary Blott; *m* 2d, 1685, Mehitable, dau. Thomas Gunn, and divorced wife of David Ensign.

SHELDON, John (1630-1708; nephew of Gilbert Sheldon, bishop of London, archbishop of Canterbury, primate of all England), came to America and joined Roger Williams' Colony at Providence, R.I.; *m* 1660, Joan Vincent.

SHEPARD (Shepherd), Edward (*d* 1679/80), from Eng. to Cambridge, Mass., 1639; freeman, 1643; *m* Violet – (*d* 1649); *m* 2d, Mary –, widow of Robert Pond, of Dorchester.

SHEPARD, John (1599-1650), from Eng. in the "Defense," 1635, with his wife (age 35), and his son Thomas; settled at Braintree, Mass.; admitted freeman, 1643; one of the 30 petitioners for the R.I. grant before Roger Williams secured it; *m* Margaret –.

SHEPARD (Shepherd, Shepheard), Ralph (1606-93), from Eng. in the "Abigail," to Charlestown, Mass., 1635; lived at Dedham, Rehoboth, Weymouth, Concord and Malden, Mass.; *m* Thank Lord.

SHEPARD, Thomas (1632-1719), from Eng. to Malden, Mass., 1658; *m* Hannah Ensign (*d* 1698), of Scituate, Mass.

SHERMAN, Edmund (1595-1641), from Eng. in the "Elizabeth," to Boston, Mass., 1634; an original propr. of Wethersfield, Conn., 1636; freeman at New Haven, Conn., 1640; *m* Judith Angier.

SHERMAN (Shearman), John (ca. 1613-ca. 1691), from Eng. to Watertown, Mass., 1634; freeman, 1637; selectman many yrs.; town clk.; rep. Gen. Ct., 1651, 53, 63; ensign, 1654; capt., 1680; *m* Martha –.

SHERMAN (Shearman) Philip (1610-87), from Eng. to Roxbury, Mass., 1633; freeman, 1634; banished, 1637, on account of religious differences; settled in R.I.; first sec. or recorder; mem. Ct. of Commrs., 1656; dep. Gen. Ct., 1665-1667; mem. Council, King Philip's War; *m* Sarah Odding.

SHERMAN, Samuel (1618-1700), from Eng. to Mass., ca. 1634; at Wethersfield and Stratford, Conn., and among the first residents of Stamford; dep. Gen. Ct. of Conn., 1637, which declared war against the Pequots; asst., 1663-1668; active in settlement of Woodbury, 1672; *m* ~~Sarah~~ Mitchell (Cr—),

SHERWOOD, Thomas (1586-1655), from Eng. in the "Francis," 1634; land records of Conn. show his name in many transactions; moved from Wethersfield to Fairfield, ante 1648; built 1st grist mill on Mill Plain; original will with signature still at Fairfield, Conn., Town Hall; *m* ca. 1612, Alice Seabrook (*b* 1587); *m* 2d, Mary Fitch (*d* 1693/94).

SHIPMAN, Edward (*d* 1697), from Eng. to Saybrook, Conn., ca. 1650; freeman, 1667; given 3,000 acres of land "within sight of Hartford," in will of Indian Sachem Uncas, 1676; *m* 1st, 1651, Elizabeth Comstock.

SHIPPEN, Edward (1639-1712; son of William [ca. 1600-1681], of Mathley, Yorkshire, Eng., *m* 1626, Mary [1592-1672], dau. of John Nunes, *m* 1584, Effam Crosfeld); from Eng. to Boston, 1668, where he was mem. A. and H. A. Co., 1669; removed to Phila., Pa., 1693/94; speaker Pa. Assembly, 1695; mem. Provincial Council, 1696-1712, and pres., 1702-04; dep. gov., 1703; first mayor of Phila., 1701; presiding justice Common Pleas and Quarter Sessions courts; treas. of Phila., 1705; *m* 1671, Elizabeth Lybrand (*d* 1688); *m* 2d, 1689, Rebecca (Howard) Richardson (*d* 1704/05), dau. John Howard and widow of Francis Richardson; *m* 3d, Esther (Wilcox) James (1673-1724), dau. Barnabas Wilcox, and widow of Philip James.

SHOEMAKER (Schumacher), Thomas, arrived at New York, 1710; settled at Little Falls, later at Mohawk, N.Y.; lt. colonial forces; *m* Anna Dorothea, dau. of Rudolph Curring.

SHRIVER (Schreiber), Andreas (ca. 1673-ca. 1723), from Germany to Phila., Pa., 1721; settled on the Schuylkill; *m* 1706, Anna Margaretta (Hess) Jung, dau. Hans Theobold Hess, and widow of John Jung.

SIBLEY (Sebley, Sybley), John (*d* 1661), from Eng. to Charlestown, Mass., ca. 1629-30; later at Salem; freeman, 1634; selectman, 1636; at Manchester, 1637; dep. Gen. Ct.; *m* 2d, Rachel, dau. John Pickworth.

SILLIMAN, Daniel (*d* 1690), from Holland, ca. 1630, settled at Fairfield, Conn., where he received a land grant and established "Holland Hill"; *m* Peaceable –, widow of John Eggleton.

SILSBEE (Sillsbey), Henry (*b* before 1618), from Eng. to Naumkeag (Salem), Mass., 1639; removed to Ipswich, and to Lynn, 1651; shoemaker; *m* Dorothy – (*d* 1676); *m* 2d, 1680, Grace –, widow of Jonas Eaton, of Reading, Mass.

SIMMONS, Moses (*d* 1697), from Eng. in the "Fortune," to Plymouth, Mass., 1621; settled at Duxbury, 1637; *m* Sarah –.

SINGLETON, Col. Matthew (*b* Isle of Wight, 1730-*d* 1787), came to Va., thence to S.C., 1752; received land grant from George II, 1756, which has since remained in the family; mem. Gen. Assembly, 1772, 76; vestryman St. Mark's Parish, 1770; capt., later col. troop of horse during Am. Rev. under Gen. Francis Marion; *m* 1750, Mary, dau. of Sherwood James, *m* Ann –.

SISSON, Richard (1608-84), from Wales; freeman, Portsmouth, R.I., 1653; mem. grand jury, Dartmouth; large landowner; surveyor; *m* Mary – (*d* 1692).

SKIFF, James (*d* 1688), from Eng., settled at Sandwich, Mass., 1637; *m* Mary Reeves (*d* 1673).

SKINNER, John (*d* 1650), from Eng.; an original propr. of Hartford, Conn.; *m* 1638, Mary (ca. 1620-1680), dau. Joseph Loomis (qv).

SKIPWITH, Sir Grey (*d* 1680), from Eng. to Va., established "Prestwould"; *m* Elizabeth –.

SLECHT, Cornelis Barentse (*d* 1671), from Holland, was at Esopus, N.Y., 1655; sgt. of mil. company which built the stockade at Esopus; mem. first Bd. of Schepens, 1661; mem. Ct. of Sessions, 1676; *m* Tryntje Tysse Bos.

SMALLEY, John, from Eng. in the "Francis and James," to Boston, Mass.; thence to N.J., 1688; *m* 1638, Ann Walden.

SMEDLEY, Baptiste (*d* 1675), probably from Parish Odell, Bedfordshire, to Concord, Mass., ante 1639, *m* 1645, Katherine Shorthouse (*d* 1679).

SMITH, George, from Eng. in the "James," 1635; settled at Dover, N.H.; tailor; town clk., 1646; at the head of the tax list, 1648; lt. of mil. company, 1645; asso. justice of the county.

SMITH, Sir Henry (son of Sir Hugh Smith, of Ashton, Somerset, Eng.); with his wife, Elizabeth Gorges, came to N.E., 1630, as chaplain in charge of fleet with Gov. Winthrop.

SMITH, John (ca. 1698-1776), officer British army, from Ireland to Augusta Co., Va., ca. 1730; capt. Va., militia, 1742-60; served in Col. George Washington's regt. in French and Indian War; cdr. Ft. Vause, which was captured by French, 1756, and sent to France as a prisoner of war, 1756-58; *m* in Ireland, Margaret –.

SMITH, Rev. Nehemiah (1605-86), from Eng.; at Plymouth, 1637/38; removed to Conn.; an original propr., Norwich; *m* 1639/40, Sarah Anne (ca. 1615-post 1684), dau. of Thomas Bourne (qv).

SMITH, Samuel (1602-80), from Eng. in the "Elizabeth," with his wife and four children, to Watertown, Mass., 1634; freeman, 1634; a founder of Wethersfield, Conn., where he was "antient serjeant"; dep. Gen. Ct., 1640-61; founder of Hadley, 1659; dep. Mass. Bay Colony, 1661-73; lt. Hadley troop, 1661-78; commr. to the Mohawks, 1667, magistrate; *m* Elizabeth Chileah (1602-1685).

SMITH, Thomas (1648-94), came from Eng. to Carolina, 1684; settled at Charles Town, S. C.; 1st landgrave and gov. of S.C.; *m* 1st, 1668, Barbara, dau. of Bernard Sheneking, of Eng.

SNOW, Nicholas (*d* 1676), from Eng. in the "Ann," to Plymouth, Mass., 1623; a founder of Eastham, 1645; first town clerk 17 yrs. and selectman 7 yrs.; dep. Gen. Ct.; *m* 1623/24, Constance, dau. Stephen Hopkins (qv).

SNOWDEN, Richard (*d* 1711), from Wales to South River, Md., ca. 1652; large landowner; capt. provincial forces of Md., 1700-03.

SOHIER, Edward, III (*b* 1724), from Eng. to Boston, ca. 1750; *m* Susanne Brimmer.

SOMERVELL (Somerville), James (1694-1754), from Eng. to Md., 1719; physician; justice and high sheriff for Calvert Co.; *m* 1722, Sarah, dau. Thomas Howe, of Calvert Co., Md.

SOULE, George (*d* 1680), 35th signer of the Mayflower Compact; dep. Gen. Ct., from Duxbury, 1645-54; volunteer in Pequot War, 1637; *m* at Plymouth, Mass., before 1627, Mary Becket, or Bucket (*d* 1676), came in the "Anne," 1621.

SOUTHGATE, Richard (bap. 1670/71-1758), from Eng. to Boston, 1715; settled at Leicester, Mass., where he was the first town treas.; *m* 1700, Elizabeth, dau. William Steward.

SOUTHWICK, Lawrence (*d* 1660), from Eng., settled at Salem, Mass., 1639; with wife, was fined, whipped and banished for being Quakers; on L.I., 1659; *m* Cassandra – (*d* 1660).

SOUTHWORTH (Southard), Constant (1615-1679; son of Edward, whose widow, Alice [Carpenter] Southworth, came in the "William and Mary," to Plymouth, Mass., 1623, and *m* 2d, Gov. William Bradford), came from Eng. at 13 (1628); freeman at Plymouth 1637; soldier Pequot War; dep. 22 yrs.; dep. treas. Plymouth Colony; mem. Council of War, 1658, commr. for United Colonies, 1668; commissary gen. King Philip's War; *m* Elizabeth, dau. William Collier.

SPAULDING (Spalding), Edward (*d* 1670), who came to Jamestown, Va., with Sir George Yeardley, 1619, later removed to Braintree, Mass., 1630; freeman, 1640; removed to Wenham, 1645; was an original incorporator of Chelmsford, Mass., 1653, where he died; mem. 1st Bd. of Selectmen; *m* Margaret – (*d* 1640); *m* 2d, Rachel –.

SPENCER, Gerard or Jared (1614-85), from Eng. to Newton, Mass., 1633; a founder of Hartford, Conn., 1636; ensign mil. cos., Lynn, Mass. 1656, and Haddam, 1662; rep. Gen. Ct., 1674, et seq.; *m* perhaps ca. 1637, Hannah –.

SPENCER, Thomas (1607-87), from Eng. to Cambridge, Mass., 1633; settled at Hartford, Conn., ca. 1637; received land grants; soldier in Pequot War; constable, 1657; surveyor, 1672; *m* Sarah, dau. Nathaniel Bearding.

SPENCER, Hon. William (1601-40), came to America, 1633; a founder A. and H. A. Co. of Boston; rep. Mass. Bay Gen. Ct., 1634, 1639-40; *m* Agnes –.

SPOTTSWOOD (Spottiswoode, Spotswode), Sir Alexander (1676-1740), officer British Army; apptd. gov. of Va., 1710, and brought from the king the right of habeas corpus, hitherto denied to Virginians; gov., 1710-22; dep. postmaster gen. of the colonies, 1730-39, and postmaster of Pa.; maj. gen., 1740; formed the "Knights of the Golden Horseshoe," for exploration; *m* Anne Butler, dau. Edward Brayne.

SPRAGUE, Ralph (1603-50; brother of William), came from Eng. to Salem, Mass., ca. 1626; removed to Charlestown, 1629; constable, 1631; dep. Gen. Ct., 1635, et seq.; ensign for Charlestown, 1646; lt., 1637-41, 1647-49; mem. A. and H. A. Co., 1637; *m* 1623, Joan, dau. Richard Warren (qv).

SPRAGUE, William (1609-75; brother of

Ralph), came from Eng. to Charlestown, Mass., 1629; removed to Hingham, Mass., 1636; *m* 1635, Millicent, dau. of Anthony Eames (qv).

SPRIGG, Thomas (1630-1704), from Eng. to Va., and resided in Northampton Co.; removed to Md.; served against Nanticoke Indians before 1678; commr. for Calvert Co., 1661; justice, 1667-1674; presiding justice, 1674; high sheriff, 1663-64; *m* Katherine –; *m* 2d, before 1668, Eleanor, dau. John Nuthall.

SPRING, John (*b* Eng., 1589), came in the "Elizabeth," 1634, with his wife Elinor, age 46, and children Mary, 11, Henry 6, John 4, and William, 9 mos.; settled at Watertown, 1636; took oath of fidelity, 1652; *m* 2d, Grace –, widow of Thomas Hatch, at Scituate.

STACY, Mahlon (1638-1704), from Eng. in the "Shield," with his family, to Burlington, West Jersey, 1678; settled under a proprietary land grant of several thousand acres, at the Falls of the Delaware, 1679 (now Trenton, N.J.); signer of the Constitution of West New Jersey, 1676; mem. Assembly, 1681, et seq.; House of Reps., 1697-1701; Gov.'s Council, 1682-83; Council of Proprietors, 1688; *m* 1668, Rebecca (*d* 1711), dau. Richard Ely.

STAFFORD, Thomas (1605-77), from Eng. to Plymouth, Mass., ca. 1626, and is said to have built there the first grist mill operated by water power in America; removed to Newport, R.I.; later to Warwick; dep. Gen. Assembly; *m* Elizabeth – (*d* 1677).

STANDISH, Myles (*d* 1656), 6th signer of the Mayflower Compact; captain and military leader of Plymouth Colony, 1621; asst. 1631-50; six years treas.; general-in-chief of all the companies in the colony, 1649; *m* 1st, Rose – (*d* 1621); *m* 2d, at Plymouth, Mass., 1623/24, Barbara Allen (*d* 1659).

STANLEY, John (*d* 1698), from Eng. to Md., 1683; surveyor gen.; mem. Lower House of Assembly, 1689; capt. of troop, Talbot Co., Md., 1689; maj., 1692.

STANLEY, Thomas (*d* 1663), from Eng. to Cambridge, Mass., later settled at Hartford, Conn.; juryman, 1639-43; constable, 1644-53; *m* Benett (1609-64), dau. of John Shepherd, *m* Rebecca Waller.

STANTON, Robert (1599-1672), from Eng.; signed compact, Portsmouth, R.I., 1638; freeman, 1641; sgt., 1644; dep., 1670; *d* Newport, R.I.; *m* Avis –.

STANTON, Thomas (1616-1677/78), from Eng., 1635; to Hartford, Conn., 1637; noted as Indian interpreter; Indian interpreter to the Gen. Ct. of Conn. in all controversies; dep. Gen. Ct. 1666; settled at Stonington, Conn., 1658; *m* 1637, Ann (1621-88), dau. Dr. Thomas Lord, of Hartford.

STARR, Comfort (1584-1659), from Eng. in the "Hercules," to Boston, 1635; later at Cambridge, Duxbury and Dedham, Mass.; dep. Gen. Ct., 1642; charter fellow of Harvard Coll., 1650; *m* Elizabeth – (1595-1658).

STEARNS (Stearne, Sterne), Isaac (*d* 1671), from Eng. in the "Arbella," to Salem, 1630; freeman, 1631; selectman; *m* Mary (*d* 1677), dau. of John Barker, *m* Margaret –.

STEBBINS (Stebbing), Rowland (*b* 1594-1671), from Eng. to Boston, Mass., 1634; later at Agawam, Mass., settled at Northampton, Mass., 1649, where he died.

STEDMAN, Isaac (1605-78), from Eng. in the "Elizabeth," to Scituate, Mass., 1635, where he built the old stone mill, still standing; removed to Boston, 1650; an organizer of Brookline; *m* in Eng., Elizabeth –.

STEELE, George (*d* 1663), from Eng. to Cambridge, 1631/32; to Hartford, 1635; commr. United Colonies; rep., 1637-60; in Pequot War; *m* Rachel – (*d* 1653).

STEELE, John (prob. 1591-1665), from Eng. to Newton, Mass., 1631; freeman, 1634; rep. Gen. Ct., 1634; to Hartford, 1635, one of eight commrs. to govern Colony of Conn., 1636-37; sec. of the colony, 1636-1639; dep. Com. Gen. Assembly, 1637, 39, 1640-43, 1645-48; town clk; removed to Farmington, Conn., 1645; *m* Rachel (*d* 1653), dau. John Talcott; *m* 2d, 1655, Mary –.

STETSON, Robert (1613-1703), from Eng. to Scituate, Mass., 1634; dep. Gen. Ct., 1655, et seq.; mem. Council of War, 1661, 71, 81; cornet, first body of Plymouth Horse; press master, 1675; commr. for settling boundary with colonies of Mass. and Plymouth; *m* 1st, Honor –; *m* 2d, Mary Hiland, widow of John Bryant.

STEVENS, Henry (ca. 1653-1726), from Eng. ca. 1660; was at Narragansett, later at Stonington, Conn.; selectman, 1696-99, 1702-04, '07; rep. Gen. Ct., 1699-1707; received land grant at Voluntown, Conn., for services in King Philip's War; *m* Elizabeth, dau. Capt. John Gallup.

STEVENS, John (1605-62), from Caversham, Oxford Co., Eng., in the "Confidence," 1638; a founder of Andover, Mass., 1640; freeman, 1642; *m* Elizabeth –.

STEVENS, William (1617-53), from Eng. in the "Confidence"; became landowner and propr., Newbury, Mass.; *m* 1645, Elizabeth Bitfield (*d* 1652/53).

STICKNEY, William (bap. 1592-1664/65; son of William, of Trampton, Lincs., Eng., *m* Margaret Penson); from Eng. with wife and 3 children ca. 1638; among first settlers of Rowley, Mass.; freeman, 1640; selectman, 1652, 57, 60, 62; *m* Elizabeth –.

STILES, John (1595-1662), from Eng. to Windsor, Conn., 1635; *m* Rachel – (*d* 1674).

STILLMAN, George (1654-1728), from Eng. to Hadley, Mass., 1683; later at Wethersfield, Conn.; *m* Rebecca, dau. Philip Smith.

STILLWELL, Nichols (*d* 1671), from Eng. to New York, 1638; settled on Staten Island, 1664; lt. French and Indian War; *m* Anne Baxter.

STIMSON (Stimpson), George (*b* 1641), settled at Ipswich, 1668; soldier King Philip's War; *m* 1676, Alice Philips.

STIRLING, James (1752-1820), from Scotland to Baltimore, Md., ca. 1774; soldier Am. Rev.; *m* Elizabeth, dau. Judge Andrew Gibson, of Pa.

STITES, John, M.D. (1595-1717, aet. 122), surgeon in Col. John Hampden's Regt. in revolution of 1640, and was said to have been one of the physicians designated to certify to the death of Charles I; was excepted from the amnesty proclamation of Charles II, and had to flee for his life to Holland; came to Plymouth, Mass., 1633; later at Hempstead, L.I.; surgeon and physician to the colonists.

STOCKBRIDGE, John (1608-57), from Eng. in the "Blessing," to Scituate, Mass., 1635; wheelwright; removed to Boston, where he died; *m* Ann –; *m* 2d, 1643, Elizabeth Sloane.

STOCKTON, Richard (ca. 1630-1707; son of John, Lord of Stockton Manor, Walpos Parish, Cheshire, Eng.); from Eng. ante 1656; settled at Flushing, L.I.; lt. of Flushing Troop of Horse, 1665; converted to Quaker faith; moved to Burlington, N.J., 1660; *m* 1652, Abigail –.

STODDARD (Stodder), Anthony (*d* 1687), from Eng. to Boston, Mass., 1639; freeman, 1640; constable; rep. Gen. Ct. 23 yrs.; clk., 1642, et seq. and 3d sgt., 1650, A. and H. A. Co.; linen draper; *m* Mary Downing (*d* 1647; sister of Sir George Downing, celebrated English politician), dau. of Emand Downing, *m* Lucy Winthrop, sister of Gov. Winthrop; *m* 2d, 1647, Barbara – (*d* 1655), widow of Capt. Joseph Weld, of Roxbury; *m* 3d, Christian –; *m* 4th, Mary, dau. Rev. Zachariah Symmes, and a widow of Maj. Thomas Savage.

STODDARD (Stodder), John (*b* 1612-*d* ca. 1676), from Eng. in the "Diligent" to Hingham, Mass., 1638; later a founder of New London, Conn.; *m* Catherine –; *m* 2d, Hannah – (*d* 1675).

STONE, Gregory (1590-1672), from Eng. ca. 1635; admitted freeman at Watertown, Mass., 1636; settled at Cambridge, 1638, where he was extensive landowner; deacon; dep. Gen. Ct.; *m* Margaret Garrard; *m* 2d, Mrs. Lydia Cooper.

STONE, John, from Eng. in the "Increase," to Watertown, Mass., 1635; with his brother, Rev. Simon, was one of the early settlers of Guilford, Conn., 1639; *m* Sarah –.

STONE, Simon (1585-1665), from Eng. in the "Increase," to Watertown, Mass., 1635; freeman, 1636; early settler of Guilford, Conn.; mem. "Committee of Four" presenting the petition of 1664; dep. Gen. Ct., 1636-56; *m* Joan, dau. William Clark; *m* 2d, 1654, Sarah –, widow of Richard Lumpkin, of Ipswich.

STORM, Dirck, from Holland with his wife and three children, to New Amsterdam, 1662; was sec. at Brooklyn, 1670, and town clk. of Flatbush, L.I.; lived in Orange Co., and later in Westchester Co., N.Y.; *m* Maria Pieters.

STORRS, Samuel (1640-1719), from Eng. to Barnstable, Mass., 1663; at Mansfield (now

Storrs), Conn., 1698; *m* 1st, 1666, Mary Huckins.

STOUGHTON, Thomas (*d* 1661), from Eng., to Dorchester, Mass., 1630; freeman, 1631; constable; an original settler of Windsor, Conn., 1635; made lt., 1640; *m* Mary, dau. William Wadsworth (1610-75), an original settler of Hartford, Conn., 1636; *m* 2d, Margaret –, widow of Simon Huntington.

STOUT, Richard (1604-1703; son of John, of Eng.), first English settler in East Jersey; *m* 1644, Penelope von Princis (or von Princin), a widow who came from Holland with her first husband, 1640, when the vessel was wrecked at Sandy Hook; all passengers escaping from the ship were killed by the Indians except Penelope, who was left for dead, but was finally brought to New Amsterdam by friendly Indians.

STOWELL, Samuel (*d* 1683), from Eng., settled at Hingham, Mass.; *m* 1649, Mary, dau. John Farrow.

STREET, Nicholas (1603-74), from Eng., was minister at Taunton, Mass., 1637-59, and New Haven, Conn., 1659-74; *m* Ann (Pole) Waldron, sister of Elizabeth Pole, foundress of Taunton, 1637, and dau. of Sir William Pole (1561-1635), of Colyton Devon, *m* Marie, dau. of Sir Wm. Periam, lord chief baron of the exchequer, 1597-1604; *m* 2d, Mary –, widow of Gov. Francis Newman.

STREETER, Stephen (*d* 1652) shoemaker; resident of Gloucester, 1642; later removed to Charlestown, Mass.; he and his wife doubtless arrived with the settlers as early as 1635 or before; will probated July 24, 1652; *m* Ursula Adams (1600-73; said to have been dau. of Henry Adams, of Braintree).

STRONG, "Elder" John (ca. 1610-1699), Puritan; to N.E., 1630-36; said to have been at Dorchester, 1630, but first found at Hingham, 1635-36, Taunton, 1638, Windsor, 1646, Northampton, 1659; dep. Gen. Ct., Plymouth, 1641-45; first ruling elder Northampton ch.; *m* 1st, in Eng., Margery, dau. of William Deane; *m* 2d, 1635/36, Abigail (bap. 1619-1688), dau. of Thomas Ford, *m* 2d, 1616, Elizabeth Cooke.

STROTHER, William (ca. 1630-1702), from Eng. to Va., ca. 1650; settled nr. present site of Port Conway; *m* ca. 1651, Dorothy – (*d* 1716).

STRYCKER, Jan (1615-97), from Holland to New Amsterdam, 1652; chief magistrate and rep. in great landtag; schepen; *m* Lambertje Seubering.

STURGIS, Edward (1613-95; son of Philip, of Hannington, Eng.); from Eng. to Charlestown, Mass., ca. 1634; at Sandwich; removed to Yarmouth, 1639; dep. Gen. Ct.; *m* Elizabeth Hinckley.

STURTEVANT, Samuel (1622-69), from Eng., to Plymouth, Mass., ca. 1643; mem. Plymouth mil. company; soldier colonial wars; *m* 1643, Ann –.

STUYVESANT, Peter (1591-1671), entered mil. service of Holland at an early age; fought in the West Indies and became gov. of Island of Curacoa; lost a leg in expdn. against the Island of St. Martin; apptd., 1646, by the West India Co., dir.-gen. of the New Netherlands, in which office he remained until 1664, when New Amsterdam passed into the hands of the English; *m* Judith, dau. of Samuel Bayard.

SULLIVAN, John (Owen O'Sullivan, "Master John, of Berwick," 1690-1795, aet. 105), came from Ireland, settled at York, Mass. (now Me.), ca. 1720; *m* ca. 1735, Margery Brown (1714-1801).

SUMNER, William (1604/05-ca. 1688), from Eng. to Dorchester, Mass., 1636; admitted freeman, 1637; dep. Gen. Ct., 1658, et seq.; clk. of the Train Band, 1663; *m* 1625, Mary West (*d* 1676).

SUTPHEN (van Zutphen), Derick Janse (1645-1706), from Holland to New Utrecht, L.I., 1676; *m* Lysbett Van Nuyse.

SUYDAM (van Zuyt Dam), Hendrick Rycken (*d* 1701), from Holland to New Amsterdam, 1663 a patentee of Flatbush, L.I., ca. 1679; *m* 1666, Ida Jacobs.

SWAN, Richard (1600-78), from Eng. to Boston, Mass., ca. 1634; removed to Rowley, 1639; freeman, 1635; rep. Gen. Ct., 1666-77; in King Philip's War and in expdn. to Canada; *m* Ann –.

SWEARINGEN, Garret (Gerett), van (1636-1698), from Holland to New Amstel (New Castle), Del., 1655; councillor at Amstel on the Delaware, 1659; schout, 1660; commr. to Holland, 1661-62; removed to Md., 1664; commr. to Holland, 1661-62; sheriff of St. Mary's Co., 1686-87; mem. Council, 1694; commissary gen.; *m* 1st, 1659, Barbara de Barrette (*d* 1670), Huguenot.

SWEET, John, from Wales to Salem, Mass., ca. 1630; later at Warwick or Kingston, R.I.; *m* at Newport, R.I., Elizabeth – (*d* 1688).

SWIFT (Swyft), William (*d* 1644), from Eng. ca. 1630; a propr. of Watertown, Mass., 1636; removed to Sudbury, and to Sandwich ca. 1637; served in Lt. John Blackmer's company, 1643; *m* Joan –.

SYLVESTER, Richard (*d* 1663), from Eng., settled at Weymouth, Mass.; freeman, 1633; removed to Scituate, 1663; *m* ca. 1632, Naomi Torrey.

TABB, Humphrey (1608-58), from Eng., settled in Elizabeth City Co., Va., 1637; burgess, 1652; *m* 1646, Joanna –.

TABOR (Taber), Philip (1605-69), from Eng. to Watertown, Mass., 1634; freeman, 1634; one of first settlers of Yarmouth; mem. earliest Assembly of Plymouth Colony, 1639, 40; was at Vineyard, New London, Conn., 1651, Portsmouth, Providence and Tiverton; rep. Gen. Court, from Providence, 1661.

TAFT (Taffe), Robert (ca. 1640-1725), from Eng., was at Braintree, Mass., and an original settler at Mendon, when it was set off from Braintree, 1667; mem. first Bd. of Selectmen, 1680; *m* Sarah – (*d* 1725).

TAINTER (Tayntor, Taintor), Joseph (1613-90), from Eng. in the "Confidence," to Watertown, Mass., 1638; served in King Philip's War, as did three of his sons; *m* Mary, dau. Nicholas Guy.

TAINTOR, Charles (*d* 1654), from Wales, ca. 1640, settled at Wethersfield, Conn., 1643; later at Branford and Fairfield; dep. Gen. Ct., 1643-1646; dep. from Fairfield, Conn., 1647-48.

TALBOT, Peter (1652-1704), from Lancashire, Eng., supposed to have been victim of a press-gang that carried him to an American-bound ship from which he escaped and swam ashore to coast of R.I.; settled at Dorchester, Mass., 1675; at Milton, and Chelmsford, 1684; *m* last, Dec. 29, 1687, Hannah (Clark) Frizell (*b* Feb. 13, 1646), dau. of William Clark (1595-Mar. 15, 1682), *m* Margaret – (1599-Nov. 11, 1694).

TALBOTT (Talbot), Richard (*d* 1666), was in Md., 1652; purchased "Poplar Knowle" plantation, on West River, Anne Arundel Co., Md., 1656; *m* 1656, Elizabeth, dau. Maj. Richard Ewen, speaker of Maryland Assembly.

TALCOTT (Tailecoat, Taylcoat), John, "The Worshipful" (ante 1604-1660), from Eng. in the "Lion," with Rev. Thomas Hooker's company, to Boston, 1632; freeman, 1632; removed with Hooker to Hartford, 1636; rep. first Gen. Ct., 1637-54; gov.'s asst., 1654-60; treas. of colony, 1652-60; commr., 1656-58; *m* Dorothy (*d* 1670), dau. of Mark Mott, Esq., *m* Frances Gutter, of Braintree, Essex Co., Eng.

TALLMADGE (Talmadge, Talmage, Talmash), Thomas (*d* 1690; son of Sir Lionel Tolleemach, high sheriff, *m* Lady Catherine Cromwell, dau. Lord Cromwell), from Eng. to Boston, Mass., 1631; freeman, 1634; removed to Lynn, 1637; to Southampton, L.I.; lt., 1665; dep. Gen. Ct.; recorder, 1650.

TAPPAN (Toppan), Abraham (bap. 1606-1689), from Eng. to Essex Co., Mass., 1637; *m* Susanna Taylor.

TARBELL, Thomas (*d* ca. 1678 or 81), from Eng., was at Watertown, Mass., ca. 1644; removed to Groton, 1663, thence to Charlestown; soldier King Philip's War; *m* Mary – (1620-74); *m* 2d, 1676, Susanna –, widow of John Lawrence.

TATNALL, Edward (1704-90), from Eng. with his mother and 4 brothers, to Pa., 1725; was at Wilmington, Del., ca. 1735; *m* Elizabeth Pennock.

TAYLOR, Edward (1642-1729), from Eng. to Westfield, Mass., ca. 1669; A.B., Harvard, 1671, A.M., 1720; clergyman; *m* 1674, Elizabeth (*d* 1689), dau. James Fitch; *m* 2d, Ruth, dau. Samuel Wyllys, mem. Colonial Congress (and g.dau. of Gov. John Haynes).

TAYLOR, James (1615-80; desc. Earls of Hare, Carlisle, Eng.), from Eng. ca. 1635; established "Hare Forest," in Va.; *m* 1st, Frances –; *m* 2d, Mary Gregory.

TAYLOR, John (*d* 1647), from Eng. in the "Arbella," to Mass. with Gov. Winthrop, 1630; settled at Windsor, Conn., 1639; sailed for Eng.

in the "Phantom Ship," 1647, and was lost at sea; *m* 1640, Rhoda –, a widow.

TAYLOR, Samuel (*d* 1723), a Quaker, came from Eng. to Chesterfield, Burlington Co., N.J., 1677; a propr. of West Jersey; his house and farm are still in possession of the family; *m* Susanna Horsman.

TAYLOR (Taylour, Tailer), William (*b* 1609), from Eng. to Barbados, 1635; came to Wethersfield, Conn., 1647; *m* Mary –.

TEN BROECK, Dirck Wesselse (1638-1717; son of Wessel, who was supposed to have come from Holland with Peter Minuit, 1626), appeared at Albany as early as 1662; was magistrate, commissary, alderman and recorder, and mayor of Albany, 1696-98; mem. 1st to 5th Provincial Assemblies; commr. of Indian affairs many yrs.; political agent to Canada four times; *m* 1663, Christyna Van Buren (1644-1729).

TEN BROECK, Wessel W. (1635-1704; eldest son of Wessel, who was supposed to have come from Holland with Peter Minuit in 1626); came from Munster, Westphalia, in the "Faith," 1659; removed to Kingston (then Esopus), N.Y., 1670; received grant of land there, 1676; erected a stone house now known as the "Senate House of the State of N.Y." in which 1st constn. of the State was adopted, 1777; *m* Dec. 17, 1670, Maria (*d* 1694), dau. of Conraedt Ten Eyck; *m* 2d, Laurentia Kellenaer, widow of both Dominie Van Gaasbeek and Maj. Thomas Chambers, lord of the Manor of Foshall, Kingston, N.Y.

TENNEY (Tenny), Thomas (1614-1699/1700, from Eng. to Salem, Mass., 1638; at Rowley, 1640; later at Bradford, Mass.; sgt. and ensign of Rowley foot company, 1677; *m* Ann Parratt (*d* 1657).

TERHUNE (Terheun), Albert Albertse (*d* in 1685), Huguenot, went from France to Holland and thence to New Utrecht, L.I., 1641; settled at Gravesend, L.I., 1642; *m* Geertje De Nyce.

TERRY, Sgt. Samuel (1633-1730), from Eng. to Boston, 1650; granted land at Agawam, 1650; an original settler at Enfield, Conn.; *m* 1660, Anna Lobdell (*d* 1684, aet. ca. 50), of Springfield.

TERRY, Thomas (1607-72), from Eng. in the "James," 1635; resided at Braintree, Mass., and New Haven, Conn.; a founder of Southold, L.I.; freeman of Conn., 1662; *m* Marie – (*d* 1659).

THACHER (Thatcher), Thomas (1620-78; son of Rev. Peter, rector Parish of St. Edmonds, Salisbury, Eng.), from Eng. to Boston, 1635; prepared for the ministry under Rev. Charles Chauncey, of Scituate; ordained at Weymouth, 1644/45; was first minister of Old South Ch. at Boston; *m* Elizabeth (*d* 1664), dau. Rev. Ralph Partridge, of Duxbury; *m* 2d, Margaret, dau. of Rev. Henry Webb, of Boston, and widow of Jacob Sheaffe.

THATCHER (Thacher) Anthony (1588/89-1667), from Eng. to Mass., 1635; was taxpayer at Marblehead, Mass., 1637; removed to Yarmouth; clergyman; rep. Gen. Ct., 1643, et seq.; mem. militia and of Council of War, 1642; *m* 1635, Elizabeth Jones.

THAYER, Richard (1621-1705; son of Richard, qv), from Eng., admitted freeman at Braintree, Mass., 1640; was at Boston, 1641; *m* 1654, Dorothy Pray.

THAYER, Richard (bap. 1601-68), from Eng. to Mass., with his brother, Thomas, 1630; admitted freeman at Braintree, 1630; later settled at Boston; *m* Dorothy Mortimore.

THEBALD (Theobald), Clement (*d* 1675), from Eng., was in Lower Norfolk Co., Va., 1641, in Md., 1654; *m* 2d, Mary –.

THOMAS, James, from Wales to Kent Co., Md., 1702; *m* 2d, Elizabeth Hackett.

THOMAS, John (1629-71), from Eng. in the "Hopewell," to Marshfield, Mass., 1635; *m* 1648, Sarah, dau. James Pitney, of Marshfield.

THOMAS, Peter (1640-1722), from Wales to Westtown, Pa., 1683; *m* Elizabeth Morris.

THOMAS, Philip (1600-1674/75), from Eng., 1651, settled in West River, Md.; lt. provincial forces before 1655; high commr. governing Md., 1656-58, and one of those effecting the surrender of the province to Lord Baltimore, 1658; *m* Sarah Harrison (*d* 1687).

THOMAS, Thomas (will proved 1671), from Eng. with his wife, son James and servants, to St. Mary's Co., Md., ca. 1639; received land warrant on Patuxent River, near Buzzard Island; high commr. of Provincial Ct.; *m* Elizabeth, dau. William Barton.

THOMAS, William (1573-1651), from Eng. to Marblehead, Mass., 1637; later at Marshfield, Mass.; freeman, 1642; governor's asst., 1642, 43, 44, 47, 51; mem. Council of War; dep. Gen. Ct., 1640, 44.

THOMPSON (Tomson, Thomson, Tompson), Anthony (1612-47), from Eng. in the "Hector," 1637; a founder of Quinnipiack (New Haven), 1638, and a signer of the Compact; soldier in Indian troubles, 1642; *m* Katherine –.

THOMPSON, James (1593-1682), from Eng. in Winthrop's fleet, to Charlestown, Mass., 1630; freeman, 1634; original settler at Woburn, 1640; *m* in Eng., Elizabeth – (*d* 1643); *m* 2d, 1644, Susanna –, widow of Thomas Blodget, of Cambridge.

THOMPSON, John (1616-96), dep. Gen. Ct. from Barnstable, Mass., 1671-72, from Middleboro, 1674, et seq.; sgt. mil. company, 1673; lt., 1675; cdr. garrison in King Philip's War, 1675; *m* 1645, Mary (1626-1714), dau. of Francis Cooke (qv).

THOMPSON, John (1730-78), from Scotland to Hunterdon Co., N.J., moved to Shamokin on West Susquehanna, 1776; soldier Cont. Army; killed by Tories and Indians, nr. Cherry Valley; *m* Judith Bodine (1735-96; g.dau. Jean Bodin, *d* 1695, a Huguenot, naturalized at London, 1681).

THOMPSON, John Lewis (1640-1726), from Wales with a brother, to Va., ca. 1650; *m* Elizabeth McGrath.

THOMSON, Alexander (1722-1800), from Scotland to Chambersburg, Cumberland Valley, Pa., 1772; soldier Am. Rev.; *m* 1748, Elizabeth Edmundstone.

THORN (Thorne), William, supposed to have landed at Boston, 1629; admitted freeman at Lynn, Mass., 1638; later one of the patentees of Flushing, L.I., 1645; a propr. of Jamaica, L.I., 1657; *m* Sarah –.

THORNDIKE, John (ca. 1603-1668-70), from Eng. to Boston, Mass., 1632; a founder of Ipswich, 1633; returned to Eng., 1668, leaving his son Paul at Beverly; *m* Elizabeth Stratton; *m* 2d, Alice Coleman.

THORNTON, William, Gent., of the "Hills," Yorkshire, Eng. (son of William [*d* 1600], of noble ancestry); came to Va., ante 1641; settled in Petsworth Parish, now Gloucester Co.; moved to Stafford Co.

THOROGOOD (Thoroughgood, Thorowgood), Capt. Adam (1602-40; son of William of Norfolk Co., Eng.); came to Va. in the "Charles," 1621; later settled at Lynnhaven, Princess Ann Co., Va.; commr. and burgess for Elizabeth City; mem. Council; presiding justice Co. Ct. of lower Norfolk, 1637; *m* 1627, Sarah (1609-57), dau. of Robert Offley, *m* Anne, dau. of Sir Edward Osborne, Kt., lord mayor of London, 1583.

THRALL, William (1606-79), from Eng. in the "Mary and John," 1630; settled at Windsor, Conn., 1633; served in Pequot War; *m* Miss Goode (*d* 1676).

THROCKMORTON, John (*d* 1687), from Eng. in the "Lion," to Boston, 1631; moved to Providence, R.I., 1638; one of the 13 original proprs. with Roger Williams of R.I.; lands conveyed to him by Roger Williams, 1637; obtained a grant of land for himself and 35 associates, from Governor Kieft, in New York, July 6, 1640, which was called Throgg's Neck, an abbreviation of Throckmorton; dep. to R.I. Gen. Assembly, 1664-68, 1670-75; treas., 1667; mem. Gen. Assembly at Newport, R.I., 1664-65; moved to Monmouth Co., N.J., 1673; *m* Mary –.

THROCKMORTON, Robert, lord of the Manor of Ellington, Huntingdonshire, Eng. (bap. Aug. 15, 1609-*d* Sept. 1657); received a grant of 300 acres in Charles River (now Gloucester) Co., Aug. 24, 1637, for transporting five persons into the Colony of Va., and a grant of 650 acres in Upper Norfolk Co., Sept. 16, 1644; subsequently returned to Eng. where he died.

THRUSTON, Edward (1638/39-1717), from Eng., settled first in Lower Norfolk Co., Va., 1663; returned to Eng., 1670, but again came to Va., 1717, to join son; *m* 2d, Susannah Perry.

TICKNOR (Tickner, Tickenor), William, from Eng. to Scituate, Mass., ca. 1646; soldier King Philip's War; *m* Hannah (*d* 1665), dau. John Stockbridge; *m* 2d, 1666, Deborah, dau. Thomas Hyland.

TIFFANY, Humphrey (*d* 1685), from Eng. to

Mass., ca. 1660; settled at Rehoboth, Mass., 1663; later at Swansea; killed by lightning; *m* Elizabeth –.

TILDEN, Nathaniel (1583-1641), from Tenderden, Co. Kent, Eng., in the "Hercules," 1635, with his wife, Lydia, and seven children and seven servants; settled at Scituate, Mass., where he was ruling elder; *m* Lydia, dau. of Stephen Huckstep, of Tenderden, Eng.

TILGHMAN, Richard (1626-76), English surgeon, came in the "Elizabeth and Mary," 1661, settled at "The Hermitage," Talbot Co., Md.; high sheriff, 1669-71; *m* Mary Foxley.

TILLEY, John (1586-1621), 16th signer of the Mayflower Compact.

TILLINGHAST, Pardon (1622-1718), from Eng. to Providence, R.I., ca. 1643, where built at own expense, 1st Bapt. church in America, and gave it to the society; pastor 40 years; dep. Gen. Ct., 1672, 80, 94, 97, 1700; *m* 2d, Lydia Taber.

TILLMAN, Roger, from Eng. to Va., ante 1689; landgrant, south side of Appomatox River, Charles City Co., nr. Bristol; *m* 1680, Mrs. Susanna Parham (Parram) (1647-*d* Prince George Co., 1717).

TILTON, John (*d* 1688), from Eng. bet. 1630-1640; settled at Saugus (Lynn) Mass.; a founder of Gravesend, L.I., 1643, where he was town clk. 20 yrs.; an original purchaser of land from the Carnasie Indians, and purchased Barren Island, L.I., from the Indians, 1664; an explorer and interpreter in the purchase of lands in Monmouth Co., N.J., from the Indians, 1664/65, on behalf of himself and eleven associates known as "John Tilton and Co."; *m* Mary – (*d* 1683).

TILTON, William (ante 1618-ca. 1653), from Eng. to Lynn, Mass., 1640; freeman; *m* Susanna –.

TINKER, John (*d* 1662; son of Henry, of Eng., and nr. kinsman Thomas of the Mayflower); came to Boston, 1635; a founder of Lancaster, Mass.; asst. gov. of Conn.; *m* 2d, 1651, Alice (1629-1714), dau. of John Smith.

TITUS, Robert (*b* 1600), from Eng. in the "Hopewell" to Boston, 1635; settled at Weymouth, Mass.

TODD, Christopher (1617-86; son of William, of York, Eng., *m* Katherine Ward); came in the "Hector," to Boston, 1637; a founder of New Haven Colony, 1638, and a signer of the covenant; owned the present site of Yale U.; *m* Grace, dau. of Michael Middlebrook.

TODD, John (*b* 1621), from Eng. to Charlestown, Mass., 1637; an early settler of Rowley, 1648; rep. Gen. Ct., 1664, 86; *m* Susanna –.

TODD, Thomas (1619-76), from Eng. to Gloucester Co., Va., 1640; built original "Toddsbury," for which two other homes were named, 1654; built second home nr. Baltimore, Md., 1664; mem. Assembly, 1675; *m* 1657, Anne (1638-95), dau. of Rev. John Gorsuch, of Eng., *m* Anne, dau. of Sir William Lovelace.

TOMPKINS, Nathaniel (1650-1724), from Eng. to Newport, R.I., 1671; temporarily resided at Boston; later at Little Compton, R.I.; merchant; *m* 1671, Elizabeth (1651-1714), dau. John Allen.

TORREY, William (1608-abt. 1690), from Eng. to Weymouth, Mass., ca. 1640; freeman, 1642; rep Gen. Ct., 1642, et seq.; lt. and capt.; clk. Ho. of Deputies, 1648, et seq.; *m* Agnes Combe (*d* 1640); *m* 2d, Elizabeth, dau. of George Frye.

TOWER (Towers), John (1609-1702; son of Robert, *m* Dorithe Damon); from Eng. to Hingham, Mass., 1637; freeman, 1639; removed to Lancaster, 1654; served in garrison house in King Philip's War; *m* 1639, Margaret (1617-1700), dau. of Richard Ibrook.

TOWNSEND, John (1578[?]-1668/69), from Eng. with brothers Henry and Richard, to Lynn, Mass., 1643; removed to Providence, R.I., 1644, and to Oyster Bay, L.I., 1645; *m* Elizabeth Montgomery.

TOWNSEND, Thomas (bap. 1594-1677), from Eng. to Lynn, Mass., 1637; freeman, 1639; *m* Mary Newgate.

TRACEY (Tracy), Stephen (1596-1655; son of Stephen, *m* Agnes Erdley); from Eng. in the "Ann," to Plymouth, 1623; settled at Duxbury, Mass., 1633; returned to Eng., 1654, and *d* there; *m* 1621, Tryphosa Lee.

TRACY, Thomas (1610-85), from Eng. to Watertown, Mass., 1636; to Salem, Mass., 1637; removed soon to Saybrook, Conn., to Wethersfield and finally settled at Norwich, of which he was an original propr., 1659; rep. Gen. Ct., 1662 and for many yrs.; ensign and lt.; commissary and q.m. in King Philip's War; *m* 1641, widow of Edward Mason; *m* 2d, 1679, Martha, dau. Thomas Bourne, and widow of John Bradford.

TRAIN (Traine), John (ca. 1610-1681), from Eng. in the "Susan and Ellen," to Watertown, Mass., 1635; mem. Watertown Train Band, 1652; *m* Margaret Dix (*d* 1660); *m* 2d, 1675, Abigail Bent.

TREAT, Richard (1584-1669), from Eng. to Watertown, Mass., 1635; at Wethersfield, Conn., 1637; dep. Gen. Ct., 1637-44; gov.'s asst., 1657-65; patentee of Conn. under royal charter of Charles II, 1662; mem. Gov. John Winthrop's Council, 1663-65; *m* Alice Gaylord.

TREDWELL (Treadwell), Edward (*d* ca. 1660-1661), from Eng. to Ipswich, Mass., 1637; settled at Hempstead, L.I., 1660; *m* Sarah –.

TRIPP, Hon. John (1610/11-1678), from Eng.; first record of him in America, when he became an original founder and propr. of Portsmouth, R.I., 1638; in 1660 he deposed in court and stated his age as about 49; dep. R.I. Gen. Assembly, 1648, 1654-58, 1661-64, 1666-69, 72; commr. Ct. of Commissioners, 1655; asst. or mem. Gov.'s Council, 1670, 1673-75; *m* 1639, Mary (*d* 1687), dau. of Anthony Paine, *m* Rose Potter.

TRIPPE, Henry (1632-1697/98); from Eng. to Dorchester Co., Md., 1663, where he took up land; mem. Lower House of Assembly, 1671-81; maj. of horse, 1689; lt. col. of field officers, 1694; *m* 1665, Frances –, widow of Michael Brooke, of Calvert Co., Md.; *m* 2d, Elizabeth –.

TROWBRIDGE, Thomas (*d* 1672/73), from Eng. to Dorchester, Mass., 1634; settled at New Haven, Conn., 1639; returned to England leaving his sons; of their direct male descendants 56 fought in Am. Rev.; 41 in War of 1812; 152 in Civil War; *m* 1627, Elizabeth (1602/03-1641/42), dau. of John Marshall.

TRUAX (du Trieux), Philip (ca. 1586-88-*d* bet. 1649-53), a Walloon, from Holland to New Amsterdam, in the "New Netherlands," ante 1624; marshal of New Netherland; *m* 1621, Susanna de Chesne (living in 1654).

TRUESDELL, Samuel, from Eng. to Boston ca. 1630, with brothers Richard and John.

TRUMBULL, John, from Eng. to Roxbury, Mass., 1639; freeman, 1640; later at Rowley; *m* Ann –.

TUCK (Tucke, Tewk), Robert (*d* 1664), from Eng. to Watertown, Mass., 1636; removed to Hampton, N.H., 1638; obtained license for first inn at Hampton; *m* Joanna –.

TUCKER, St. George, LL.D. (1752-1827), from the Bermudas to Williamsburg, Va., 1771; lt. col. Am. Rev.; mem. Council of State, 1781; county lt. and del. to the Annapolis conv., 1786, for amendment of the Articles of Confederation; judge Gen. Ct. of Va., 1788-1804; prof. law, Coll. of William and Mary, 1790-1804; judge Ct. of Appeals of Va., 1804-13; U.S. dist. judge, 1813-25; eminent legal author; *m* 1778, Frances (Bland) Randolph (mother of John Randolph, of Roanoke), dau. of Theodoric Bland, and widow of John Randolph, of "Matoax"; *m* 2d, 1791, Lelia (Skipwith) Carter, dau. of Sir Peyton Skipwith, of "Prestwould," and widow of George Carter, of "Corotoman."

TUCKER, Robert (1604-82), from Eng. to Weymouth, Mass., 1635; removed to Dorchester, later to Milton, Mass.; rep. Gen. Ct., 1669, 80, 81; *m* Elizabeth Allen.

TUCKERMAN, John (1624-98), from Eng. to Boston, Mass., 1649; *m* Sarah –.

TUFTS, Peter (*b* 1617), from Eng., founder of Malden, Mass., 1638; *m* 1640, Mary Pierce (*d* 1701).

TUPPER, Thomas (1578-1676), from Eng. to Sandwich, Mass., ca. 1635, where the house built by him, 1637, still stands, and is owned by the family; was deputy Gen. Ct.; *m* Anne –.

TURNER (de Tourneur), Daniel (1626-73), fled from France to Leyden, Holland, ca. 1648, thence, with his wife and son Daniel, to New Netherland, 1652; corp. mil. company at Midwout for defense against English, 1654, against Indians, 1660; magistrate, 1660-63; patentee of Harlem; *m* 1650, Jacqueline de Parisis (*d* 1700).

TURNER, Humphrey (ca. 1593-1673), from Eng. to Plymouth, Mass., 1628; removed to Scituate,

1633; a founder of the ch. there, 1635, constable; rep. Gen. Ct., 1640, 52, 53; pvt. in mil. company; *m* Lydia Gamer.

TUTHILL, Henry (1612-1648-50), from Eng. in the "Planter," 1635; settled at Hingham, Mass.; freeman, 1638; constable, 1640; removed to Southold, L.I., with Rev. Young's company, 1644; *m* Bridget –.

TUTTLE, William (1609-73), from Eng. in the "Planter," to Boston, 1635; had a mill on Tower Hill, 1635; a propr. of Charlestown, 1636; removed to New Haven after 1639; served in the night watch at New Haven, 1646; *m* Elizabeth – (1612-84).

TWOMBLY, Ralph (*d* 1656), from Eng. ca. 1656, settled at Dover, N.H.; *m* Elizabeth –.

TYLER, Job (ca. 1619-1700), from Eng., was at Portsmouth or Newport, R.I., 1638; removed to Andover, Mass., 1640; to Roxbury, 1665, to Mendon, 1669; later to Rowley; *m* Mary –.

TYLER, Robert (1637/38-1674), from Eng., 1663; settled in Anne Arundel Co., Md., where he had several grants of land; also a grant of about 750 acres called "Brough," on west side of north fork of Patuxent River, Calvert Co., which remained in the Tyler family until 1866; *m* at Deptford, Kent, Eng., June 29, 1663, Joanna Ravens.

TYLER, Thomas (*d* 1703), from Eng. to Boston, Mass., ca. 1680; *m* Miriam Simpkins (1663-1730).

TYSON, Rhiner, or Reynier (1659-1745), from Germany, with his brother Derrick, and Daniel Pastorius, in the "Concord," to Phila., Pa., 1683; an original incorporator of Germantown, Pa.; burgess, 1692, 93, 94, 96; purchased land and settled at Abington, Pa.; *m* Margaret Kunders.

UNDERHILL, John (1597-1672), from Eng. with Winthrop, as capt. of mil. forces; freeman, 1630; officer A. and H. A. Co.; dep. Gen. Ct. several times; selectman; officer in Pequot War; driven out of the colony for "heresy" and went to New Hampshire; gov. of Exeter and Dover, N.H.; soon left for New Amsterdam and settled on L.I.; led the Dutch troops against the Simaroy Indians, 1644; mem. Council of New Netherland; *m* Helena Kruger (*d* 1658); *m* 2d, 1658/59, Elizabeth (1633-1674/75), dau. Lt. Robert Feake.

UPDEGRAFF (Op-den-Graeff), Abraham (*d* 1731), from Crefeld, Germany, via Eng., with William Penn, in the "Concord," 1683; moved from Germantown, Pa. to Perkiomen, nr. Phila.; mem. Pa. Assembly; *m* Trintje –.

UPHAM, John (1598-1682), from Eng., with the Hull colony to Mass.; settled at Weymouth, 1635; freeman, 1638; removed to Malden, 1648; rep. Gen. Ct., 1636-42; mem. Provincial Assembly; *m* in Eng. Elizabeth Slade (or Webb; *d* 1671); *m* 2d, 1671, Catharine –, widow of Angel Hollard, of Boston.

USHER, Robert (*d* 1669), from Eng. to Newtown, Mass., ca. 1637; settled at New Haven, Conn.; admitted freeman, 1644; removed to Stamford, 1647; constable, 1665, 1667; selectman, 1668; rep. Gen. Ct., 1665-67; *m* 1659, Elizabeth –, widow of Jeremy Jagger.

VAIL (Vayle), Thomas (*b* bet. 1620-30-*d* 1687), from Eng. with his wife, Sarah, to Salem, Mass., 1640; moved to Southampton, L.I., 1649; with Thomas Pell and others bought a tract of land from the Indians (for which they received a grant from Conn. Colony, 1654), on which they founded Westchester, now in the boundaries of N.Y. City, where he was magistrate.

VAN BUSKIRK, Laurens Andriessen (*d* 1694), from Holland, first appeared in records in America, 1654, on the occasion of the baptism of a child; removed to west shore of Hudson River, 1662; mem. Gov. Carteret's council; first coroner of Bergen Co.; justice; pres. English Ct. of Bergen; magistrate; mem. Ct. of Common Right; *m* 1658, Jannetje Jans (*d* 1694).

VAN CORTLANDT, Oloff Stevensen (1610-84), from Holland to New Amsterdam, ca. 1638; one of the eight men to adopt measures against the Indians, 1645; col. Burgher Corps, 1649, 1655-64; burgomaster, 1655, 56, 58, 60, 62, 63; schepen, 1654; commr. to settle boundaries bet. New Netherland and New England; commr. to surrender New Netherland to the English, 1664; *m* 1642, Annetje Loockermans.

VAN COUWENHOVEN, Wolfert Gerretse, see Couwenhoven.

VAN DE WATER, Jacobus (1626-1712), from Holland to New Amsterdam, 1660; town mayor, 1674; settled at Bedford, L.I., 1677; county clerk of Kings Co., L.I.; *m* Engeltje Juriaans.

VAN DYKE (Van Dyk, Van Dyck), Jan Thomasen (1605-73), from Holland to New Utrecht, L.I., 1652; was 1st magistrate there; *m* Teuntje Hagen.

VAN DYKE, Thomasse Janse (ca. 1580-ca. 1665), from Holland to New Amsterdam, 1652; *m* Lytie Dirks.

VAN HORN, Christian Barentsen (*d* 1658), from Holland, settled in New Amsterdam ante 1653; prominent officer of New Amsterdam; *m* Jannetje (*d* 1694), dau. of Tyman Jansen Jans, *m* Martije Webber.

VAN PETTEN, Claas Fredericksе (1641-1728: son of Frederick), from Holland to Schenectady, N.Y., 1664; moved to Papsne, nr. Albany, 1683; mem. Dutch Reformed Ch.; justice of peace, 1690; *m* Aifie, dau. of Arentse Bradt, from Holland to Albany, then to Schenectady where he was an original propr., killed in massacre of 1690, *m* Catalina, dau. of Andrew de Vos, Huguenot, dep. dir. of Rensselaerwyck.

VAN RENSSELAER, Jeremias (1632-74; son of Kiliaen), from Holland to Rensselaerwyck, 1642, of which he was 3d patroon; col. of militia; mem. Colonial Assembly and speaker, 1664; *m* Maria, dau. of Oloff Stevensen Van Cortlandt (qv).

VAN RENSSELAER, Kiliaen (1595-1644), was one of the lords directors of the Dutch West India Co., purchased from the Indians a very large tract of land now including part of Albany and Van Rensselaer counties, New Netherland, which he named Rensselaerwyck; title of "patroon" conferred on him, 1624; the grant was divided into two manors, 1704, and title changed to "lord of the manor"; the patroonship vested in Rensselaerwyck; never came to America.

VAN SANT, Garret, from Holland to New Utrecht, N. Y., 1651; *m* Lysbeth Gerritse.

VAN SANTVOORD, Cornelius (1686-1752), grad. U. of Leyden; from Holland to Staten Island, N.Y., ca. 1717, where he was preacher; removed to Schenectady, N.Y., 1742, and was pastor Old Dutch Church there; scholar and writer; *m* Anna Staats.

VAN SCHAICK, Gozen Geritse (1630-76), from Holland to Rensselaerwyck, 1652; lt. at Albany, Rensselaerwyck, and Schenectady, 1672; capt., 1673; *m* 1st, Geertje Barents Peelen.

VAN SCHOONHOVEN, Guert Hendrikse (*d* 1702), from Holland to Albany Co., N.Y., before 1681; *m* Maritie Cornelie.

VAN VOAST (Van Vorst), Gerrit Janszen (1618-42), from Holland ante 1639, settled at Corlear's Hook, New Amsterdam, New Netherlands; *m* Geertryud–.

VAN ZANDT, Gerret Stoffelse (son of Christoffle, of the Netherlands, among the early settlers in Kings Co.); came from Holland, ca. 1651; settled at New Utrecht; patentee, 1668; supervisor Richmond Co. records; magistrate, 1681; rep., 1712, 14, 19; *m* Lisbeth (*d* ante 1706), dau. of Cornelus Gerrets, of New Utrecht, L.I.

VEDDER, Harmen Albertse (*d* 1715?), from Holland, 1630; first mentioned in Albany records, 1657; one of the three commissioners of Schenectady.

VEEDER, Simon Volkertse (1624-96), sailed between Amsterdam and New Amsterdam, 1644-1652; settled at New Amsterdam, 1652; removed to Beaverwyck, 1654, to Schenectady, 1662; soldier French and Indian War; *m* Engeltie –.

VENABLE, Abraham, from Eng. in the "Friend's Adventure," to New Kent Co., Va., ca. 1685; *m* Sara – (*d* 1687), *m* 2d, Elizabeth (Lewis) Hicks, dau. of Capt. Hugh ap Lewis.

VER PLANCK, Abraham Isaacsen (*d* ca. 1680), from Holland to New Amsterdam, 1636; one of the "Twelve Men," 1641; *m* 1630, Maria (Vinge) Roos, dau. Geyeyn Vinge.

VILAS, Peter (1704-56), believed to have come from Eng., ca. 1720, settled at or nr. Dedham, Mass.; *m* Mercy, dau. John Gay.

VOORHEES (Van Voor Hees), Steven Coerte (1600-84), from Holland in the "Bonte Koe," with his family to New Amsterdam, 1660; settled at Flatlands, L.I.; magistrate; *m* 2d, Willempie (1619-90), dau. Roelof Seubering.

WADE, (Armigall) Armiger (*d* 1676; desc. of

Armigall, of Bellsize, nr. Hampstead, Eng.); to Va. ante 1655; burgess for York Co., Va., 1655-56.

WADHAMS (Wadham), John, from Eng. to Wethersfield, Conn., ca. 1645.

WADLEIGH, John (ca. 1600-1671), from Eng. with Richard Vines' Company, 1630; settled at Biddeford, Saco, Wells and Kittery, Me.; *m* Mary –.

WADSWORTH, William (1610-75), from Eng. in the "Lion," to Cambridge, Mass., 1632; freeman, 1632; at Hartford, Conn., with Rev. Thomas Hooker, 1636; rep. Gen. Ct. many times bet. 1656-75; *m* 2d, Elizabeth Stone.

WAIT (Waite, Waight), Richard (1608-1668/69), from Eng. to Watertown, Mass., 1630, where he had land grants; commissary in Pequot War; special commissary to the Narragansets, 1664; *m* Mary – (1606-78).

WAIT (Waite, Wayte), Thomas (1601-77), from Eng.; went to Portsmouth, R.I., 1638, with Ann Hutchinson and her associates.

WAKEFIELD, John (ca. 1614-1667), from Eng., landing either in Va. or Md., was at Martha's Vineyard, Mass., before 1647; at Boston, ca. 1650; *m* Ann –.

WAKEMAN, Capt. John (1598/99-1661), from Eng. to New Haven Colony, 1638; a signer of the New Haven Compact, 1639; dep. Gen. Ct., 1641-44, 1646-48, 56, 61; treas. of the Colony, 1655-1660; capt. of colonial forces; *m* 1628, Elizabeth Hopkins (bap. 1610-*d* 1658).

WALDO, Cornelius (*b* 1624), from Eng., settled at Ipswich, *m* Hannah, dau. of John Cogswell (qv).

WALDRON, Resolved (1610-90), from Holland, 1654, settled at New Amsterdam; dep. sheriff; one of five patentees named in Nicolls' patent; constable, 1665; overseer, 1668; assessor, 1683; elder of the church; *m* 1st, 1645, Rebecca Hendricks;

WALDRON (Walderne), Maj. Richard (1614-89), from Eng. to Dover, Mass., 1635; at Dover Neck until 1655; capt. of a militia co., 1652, maj., 1674; cdr.-in-chief (colonel) of Eastern military forces in King Philip's War; dep. for Dover in Mass. Gen. Ct., 1654-79; speaker of the House several sessions; royal councillor and dep. gov. of the Province of N.H., when it was organized, 1680; chief justice Superior Ct. of the Province, 1683; his garrison was captured and burned by the Indians, June 28, 1689, and he was killed; *m* in Eng., 1637, – (ca. 1617-1680).

WALES, Nathaniel (bap. 1586-*d* 1661), shipwright; from Eng. in the "James," to Mass., 1635; freeman, 1637; *m* Susanna Greenway.

WALKER, James (1619-91), from Eng. to Taunton, Mass., ca. 1633; freeman, 1650; dep. Gen. Ct. 16 yrs.; mem. and chmn. Council of War, 1667, 75, 78; mem. Plymouth Council of War, 1658, 61, 71, 81; constable, selectman; *m* Elizabeth Phillips (1620-78).

WALLER, John (*b* 1617), from Eng. to Va., 1635; settled in North Kent Co., Va., later at "Enfield," King William Co., Va.; *m* Mary Key, or Kay.

WALLER, Col. John (1673-1754), from England, ca. 1686; settled in King and Queen Co. and established "Newport"; sheriff, 1702; justice King William Co., 1705; burgess, 1710-14, 1720-22; first clk. of Spotsylvania Co., 1722; lt. col. of militia; *m* Dorothy King (1675-1759).

WALN, Nicholas (ca. 1650-1721), from Eng. in the "Welcome," with William Penn, 1682; purchased 1000 acres; settled in Middletown Tp., Pa., on the Neshaminy River, 1682/83-96; removed to Phila. Co., 1696; mem. first Assembly many yrs.; sheriff of Bucks Co., 1685; director of public schools, etc.; *m* 1673, Jane Turner.

WALTON, Rev. William (ca. 1598-1668), Puritan; M.A., Emanuel Coll., Cambridge, 1625; D.D., 1625; came to Mass., 1635; settled at Marblehead where he was pastor over 30 yrs.; *m* Elizabeth –.

WARD, Andrew (ca. 1600-1659), from Eng. to Mass., 1630; freeman at Watertown, Mass., 1634; removed to Wethersfield, Conn., 1635, to Stamford, 1641, later to Fairfield, where he died; one of commrs. apptd. by Colony of Mass. Bay to govern Colony of Conn., 1635-36; magistrate, 1636, 37; dep. Gen. Ct., 1638, 39, 1653-56, 1658; mem. com. to press men for the expdn. against the Dutch, 1653, and against the Narragansets, 1654; *m* Hester Sherman.

WARD, William (1603-87), from Eng. to Sudbury, Mass., 1639; freeman, 1643; selectman; rep. Gen. Ct., 1644; a founder of Marlborough, 1660; again rep., 1666; in garrison at Marlborough in King Philip's War; *m* 2d, Elizabeth – (1613-1700).

WARE (Weares) Robert (*d* 1699), from Eng. to Dedham, Mass., 1642; *m* 1644/45, Margaret Huntinge.

WARFIELD, Richard (*d* ca. 1703/04), from Eng., settled nr. Annapolis, Anne Arundel Co., Md.; mil. officer of the county, 1696; large landowner; vestryman; *m* 1670, Elinor, dau. Capt. John Browne.

WARHAM, Rev. John (*d* 1670), had been minister at Exeter, Devon Co., Eng.; came in the "Mary and John," 1630; died at Windsor, Conn.; *m* thrice.

WARING, Benjamin (*d* 1713), from Lea, nr. Wolverhampton, Staffordshire, Eng., in the "Loyal Jamaica," settled at Pine Hill, S.C.; mem. House of Commons, 1685; mem. Assembly from Berkeley Co., 1693; maj. of militia in Indian wars; commr. of taxes, 1703-11; *m* Elizabeth Beamer.

WARING, Sampson (1618-68), from Eng. to Lower Norfolk Co., Va., ca. 1643; removed to "The Clifts," Calvert Co., Md., ca. 1646; lawyer; mem. Council, 1655-59; *m* 1648, Sarah Leigh.

WARNER, Andrew (ca. 1595-1684), from Eng. to Cambridge, Mass., 1632; freeman, 1634; a founder of Hartford, Conn., 1636, and of Hadley, Mass., 1659; deacon; *m* 1st, Mary –; *m* 2d, Esther, or Hester, dau. of Thomas Selden.

WARNER, Augustine (1610-74), from Eng. to York Co., Va., 1628; burgess, 1652, 1658, 59; councillor, 1669; *m* Mary – (1614-62).

WARNER, John (1615-79), from Eng. to Hartford, Conn., 1635, to Farmington, 1644; soldier Pequot War, and received land grant for his services; *m* Ann, dau. of Thomas Norton.

WARNER, Capt. William (1627-1706), from Eng. to Salem, N.J., 1675; settled at "Blockley," Phila., 1677; mem. first Council of Province of Pa.; *m* Anne Dide (or Dyde).

WARREN, John (1585-1667), from Eng. in the "Arbella," to Salem, Mass., 1630; settled at Watertown; freeman, 1631; selectman, 1636-40; *m* Margaret – (*d* 1662).

WARREN, Richard (*d* 1628), 12th signer of the Mayflower Compact; in the "First Encounter," 1620; *m* before 1611, Elizabeth (Jouatt) Marsh (ca. 1583-1673), came with five children, 1623.

WARREN (Waren, Warin, Waring), Richard (*b* 1616), from Eng. in the "Endeavor," to Boston, 1664; removed to Oyster Bay, L.I., ca. 1670.

WARREN, William (*d* 1746), from Eng. with his wife and son William, in the "Expectation," to Boston, 1715; purchased land and settled at Leicester, 1717; *m* Dorothea –.

WASHBURN (Washburne), John (bap. 1597-*d* 1670; son of John), sec. in Eng. of the Governor and Company of Mass. Bay in N.E.; from Eng., was at Duxbury, Mass., 1631 where he was made freeman; purchased land from Massasoit, the Indian, and founded Bridgewater, to which place he removed, 1645; served in expdn. against the Narragansets, 1645; *m* in Eng., 1618, Margery (*b* 1586), dau. Robert Moore.

WASHINGTON, John (1627-78; brother of Lawrence), from Eng. 1656, settled at "Wakefield," Westmoreland Co., Va.; justice of the peace, 1662; burgess, 1666, 75, 77; col. of Va. troops in Indian war, 1675; *m* 1659, Anne, widow of Walter Brodhurst and dau. Nathaniel Pope, *m* Frances, dau. Thomas Gerard, and widow of Valentine Peyton.

WASHINGTON, Lawrence (bap. 1635-1676; brother of John), from Eng. to Va., 1677, settled in Stafford Co.; *m* 1660, Mary, dau. of Edmund Jones; *m* 2d, Jane (or Joyce) –, widow of Alexander Fleming.

WATERMAN, Robert (*d* 1652; son of Thomas, of Norwich, Eng.), from Eng., was at Salem, Mass., 1636; at Plymouth, 1638; settled finally at Marshfield; rep. Gen. Ct., 1644-49; *m* 1638, Elizabeth, dau. of Thomas Bourne (qv).

WATERS, Lt. Edward, Gent. (1568-1630), mem. London Co. organized for the purpose of colonizing Va.; from Eng. in the "Sea Venture," returned to Eng., ship-wrecked on the Bermudas, returned to Va. ca. 1618 and settled on South bank of the James River; commr.; mem. Co. Ct.; burgess; lt., capt. Va. militia; *m* 1618, Grace O'Neil (*b* 1603).

WATSON, Josiah (1748-1828), from Pa. to Alexandria, Va., ca. 1771, landowner in Tenn., Ky., and Va.; *m* Jane Taylor (1752-1830).

WEAVER, Clement (*d* 1683; son of Clement, *m* Rebecca Holbrook); from Eng. to Newport, R.I., ca. 1630; admitted freeman, 1655; mem. Colonial Assembly, 1678; *m* Mary (*b* 1627), dau. of William Freeborn, of R.I.

WEBB, Richard (*d* 1665), from Eng. to Cambridge, Mass., 1632; freeman, 1632; a founder of Hartford, Conn., 1636; mem. grand jury, 1643; one of first settlers of Norwalk, Conn.; was at Stamford, 1655; *m* Elizabeth (*d* 1680), dau. John Gregory.

WEBSTER, John (1590-1661), from England to Mass.; one of original settlers at Hartford, Conn., 1636; dep. Gen. Ct., 1637; gov.'s asst., 1639-55; commr. for United Colonies, 1654; dep. gov., 1655, and gov., 1656, Colony of Conn.; first magistrate, 1657-59; a founder of Hadley, Mass., 1659; *m* in Eng., Agnes – (*d* 1667).

WEBSTER, Thomas (1631-1715), from Eng. to Watertown, Mass., with his mother, Margary –, and his stepfather, William Godfrey; removed to Hampton, N.H.; *m* 1657, Sarah, dau. of Thomas Brewer, of Roxbury, Mass.; *m* 2d (?), Susannah Batchelder.

WEEKS (Weekes), George, from Devonshire, Eng., in the same ship with Richard Mather, to Dorchester, Mass., 1635; freeman, 1640; *m* in Eng., Jane, sister of Roger Clap.

WELD, Joseph (ca. 1595-1646), from Eng. to Roxbury, Mass., ca. 1632; mem. A. and H. A. Co.; dep. Gen. Ct., 1637; freeman, 1639; capt. and first comdg. officer in service of colony; *m* Elizabeth –; *m* 2d, Barbara Clapp.

WELD, Rev. Thomas (1590-1661), ed. Trinity Coll., Cambridge; excommunicated from Ch. of Eng. by the Archbishop of London; came in the "William and Francis," to Boston, 1632, with his wife, Margaret, and three children; was pastor of the first church at Roxbury.

WELLES (Wells), Thomas (1598-1660), from Eng. to Boston, Mass., 1635; removed to Saybrook, Conn., 1636, to Hartford, 1637; magistrate, 1637-60; treas., 1639-51; sec., 1640-48; gov. pro tem., 1651; dep. gov., 1654, et seq.; gov. Colony of Conn., 1655-58; commr. for United Colonies, 1649; *m* 1st, Alice, dau. of John Tomes; *m* 2d, Elizabeth Hunt, widow of Nathaniel Foote, of Wethersfield, Conn.

WELLS (Welles), Thomas (1605-66), from Eng. in the "Susan and Ellen," to Boston, 1635; freeman, 1637; an original settler of Ipswich, Mass.; mem. A. and H. A. Co.; ensign "Mil. Co. of the Massachusetts"; *m* Abigail Warner.

WENDELL, Evert Jansen (1615-1709), from Holland to New Amsterdam, 1642; settled at Fort Orange (Albany), 1651, where he was ruling elder and magistrate; *m* 1644, Susanna du Trieux (*d* 1660), *m* 2d, 1663, Maritje, dau. Abraham Pieter Vosburgh, and widow of Thomas Mingael.

WENTWORTH, William (1615/16-1696/97), from Eng. to Boston, 1636; a founder of Exeter, N.H., 1639; removed to Wells, Me., 1642, to Dover, N.H., 1649; *m* Elizabeth Kenney.

WEST, Francis (1606-92), carpenter; came from Salsbury, Eng.; *m* 1639, Margery Reeves.

WEST, John (1590-1659; son of Sir Thomas West, 2d Lord Delaware [new creation], *m* Anne, dau. of Sir Francis Knollys, K.G.), B.A., Magdalen Coll., 1613; came to Va.; mem. Council of Va. 29 yrs.; gov. and capt.-gen., 1635-37; *m* Anne –, dau. of Francis Knollys.

WEST, Mathew (*d* post 1677), was at Lynn, Mass., 1636; removed to Newport, R.I., ca. 1646; mem. Ct. of Commrs., for Providence, R.I.

WEST, Sir Thomas (son of Sir Thomas West, 2d Lord Delaware [new creation], and brother of John), arrived in Va., 1610, and was first gov. and capt.-gen.

WESTCOTT (Wescott, Westcoatt), Stukeley (1592-1677), from Eng., settled at Salem, Mass., 1636; a founder of Providence Plantations; removed to Warwick, R.I., 1648; dep. Gen. Ct., 1650; commr., 1651, et seq.; gov.'s asst., 1656, et seq.

WHARTON, Thomas (1664-1718; son of Richard, of Kellorth, Westmorelandshire, Eng.), settled at Phila., Pa., ca. 1683; mem. Phila Council; *m* Rachel Thomas.

WHEATON, Robert (1605-96), from Wales to Salem, Mass., 1636; removed to Rehoboth, Mass., 1645; one of founders, 1st Bapt. Ch. in Mass.; *m* Alice Bowen (*d* 1696).

WHEELER, Moses (1598-ca. 1690), from Eng. to New Haven, Conn., 1638; removed to Stratford, 1648; charter from Conn. Gen. Court for ferry on Housatonic River; freeman, 1669; shipwright; *m* Miriam Hawley.

WHEELOCK, Ralph (1600-83), A.B., A.M., Cambridge U.; from Eng. with his wife and daughter to Watertown, Mass., 1637; removed to Dedham, 1638; founded town of Medfield, 1650; dep. Gen. Ct. from Dedham and Medfield several yrs.; *m* Rebecca – (*d* before 1651); *m* 2d, Hannah – (*d* 1682).

WHIPPLE, Dea. John (*d* 1669), from Eng., settled at Ipswich, Mass., 1638; freeman, 1640; dep. Gen. Ct., 1640-42, 46, 50, 54; deacon, ruling elder, 1658; agent for "The Worshipful Mr. Saltonstall" in his business affairs; selectman; the "Whipple House" is now the home of the Ipswich Hist. Soc.; *m* Sarah Hawkins (*d* 1659).

WHITAKER, Jabez (*b* 1596; posthumous son of Rev. William [1548-95], noted Puritan preacher in the Ch. of Eng. and distinguished scholar, master of St. John's Coll., Cambridge, 1586-95); came to Va.; commended by name in the records of the Va. Co., 1620, and at other times for his service to the colony; mem. House of Burgesses which met, 1623/24, from "Elizabeth City beyond Hampton River"; councillor, 1626, 28; referred to as capt., 1622, and later; *m* Mary, dau. of Sir John Bourchier, of the Parish of Lambert, Surrey Co., Eng.

WHITE, John (1595-1683; son of Robert, *m* Bridget, dau. of William Algar); came in the "Lion," to Newton, Mass., 1632; freeman, 1633; an original propr. of Hartford, 1636, and elder of the Hooker colony; removed to Hadley, 1659; rep. Gen. Ct., 1664, 69; returned to Hartford before 1675; *m* Mary Levit (*d* post 1666).

WHITE, Nicholas (*d* 1697), from Eng., freeman at Dorchester, Mass., 1643; moved to Taunton bet. 1652-55; *m* ca. 1643, Susanna, dau. of Jonas Humphrey, *m* Frances –.

WHITE, Peregrine (*b* in the Mayflower, Cape Cod Harbor, bet. Dec. 7 and 10, 1620-*d* 1704; son of William), capt. Mass troops; mem. Council of War, 1675; *m* 1649, Sarah (1630-1711), dau. William Bassett.

WHITE, Capt. Thomas (1599-1679), from Eng., a founder of Weymouth, Mass., ante 1635; freeman, 1635; lawyer; capt. of a military company; selectman; rep. Gen. Ct.; rep. Colonial Legislature, 1636-37.

WHITE, William (*d* 1621), 11th signer of the Mayflower Compact; *m* at Leyden, Holland, 1612, Susanna Fuller, who *m* 2d, Edward Winslow.

WHITE, William (1610-90), from Eng. in the "Mary and John," to Ipswich, Mass., 1634; freeman at Newbury, 1642; one of the first settlers at Haverhill, where he died; capt. of first mil. company at Haverhill; *m* 1st, Mary – (*d* 1681, aet. 75).

WHITELEY, Arthur (1652-1732), from Eng. to Dorchester Co., Md., 1676; *m* 1705, Elizabeth –, widow of William Rich, of Md.; *m* 2d, 1719, Joan –.

WHITFIELD, William (1688-ca. 1770), from Eng. in his own ship, "The Providence," in early part of the 18th Century, and settled at Nansemond, Va., finally in Lenoir Co., N.C.; *m* 1713, Elizabeth Goodman (ca. 1697-1773), of Gates Co., N.C.

WHITING, Nathaniel (ca. 1609-1682), from Eng. to Dedham, Mass., ca. 1635; granted land at Lynn; *m* Hannah, dau. John Dwight.

WHITING, Samuel (1597-1679; son of John, mayor of Boston, Lincolnshire, Eng.), from Eng. to Boston, Mass., 1636, settled at Lynn, where he was freeman, 1636; clergyman; *m* 2d, Elizabeth St. John.

WHITING, William (*d* 1647), from Eng. to Cambridge, Mass., 1633; an original settler at Hartford, 1636; dep. Gen. Ct., 1637; 2d colonial treas. of Conn., 1641-47; maj. in colonial forces; *m* Susanna –.

WHITMAN (Whiteman), John (ca. 1603-1692), from Eng. to Dorchester, Mass., 1635; freeman, 1639; removed to Weymouth, ca. 1641; ensign, mil. company, 1645; apptd. by Gen. Ct. "to end small causes"; *m* Ruth Reed.

WHITNEY, John (ca. 1589-1673; son of Thomas and g.son of Sir Robert, knighted by Queen Mary, 1553), from Eng., in the "Elizabeth and Ann," to Watertown, Mass., 1635; freeman, 1636; constable, 1641; selectman and town clk.; garrison duty during King Philip's War; *m* Elinor – (1599-ca. 1670); *m* 2d, Judah Clement.

WHITRIDGE (Whitred, Whitteredd, Whittredge, Whittridge, Whitrig), William (1599-1668), from Eng. in the "Elizabeth," with his wife and son Thomas, 1635; settled at Ipswich, Mass., 1637; *m* Elizabeth –; *m* 2d, Susanna –, widow of Anthony Colby.

WHITSETT, William (1709-98), came from Ireland to Pa., 1740; with his two brothers, John and Joseph; *m* in Ireland, Elizabeth Dawson, and had two sons also born in Ireland, Henry (*b* 1730), and William (*b* 1731).

WHITTINGHAM, John (*d* 1649; son of Baruch, of Southerton, Eng.), from Eng. to Ipswich, Mass.; *m* Martha, dau. of William Hubbard (qv).

WICKES, John (1609-75), from Eng., 1634; a signer of the Aquidneck Compact; dep. Gen. Ct.; gov.'s asst., 1650-55; killed by Indians in King Philip's War; *m* Mary –.

WICKHAM, Thomas (1624-1688/89), from Eng., was at Wethersfield, Conn., 1648; freeman, 1658; *m* Sarah Churchill (1630-1700).

WICKLIFFE, David (*b* Yorkshire, Eng.-*d* 1643), came in the "Evelyn" expedition to Md., 1635; mem. Md. Assembly from St. George's Hundred, 1636-43.

WILBUR (Wilboare, Wilbur, Wilbor, Willbore, Wildbore), Samuel (*d* 1656), from Eng. to Boston, 1633; admitted to the church at Boston, 1633; banished on account of religious differences and was an original propr. of Aquidneck, R.I., 1638; returned to Boston after a number of yrs.; *m* in Eng., Ann (*d* Sept. 24, 1656), dau. Thomas Bradford; *m* 2d, Elizabeth Letchford.

WILCOX (Willcocks), "John of Hartford" (*d* 1651), from Eng. with his wife and family to Boston before 1636; an original propr. of Hartford, Conn., 1636; resided on site now occupied by state capitol; surveyor; selectman; *m* Mary –.

WILCOCKSON (Wilcocks, Wilcox, Wilcoxson), William (1601-1652/53), from Eng. in the "Planter," to Concord, Mass., 1635; freeman at Cambridge, 1636; removed to Stratford, Conn., 1639, later to Hartford and Windsor; rep. Gen. Ct., 1647; *m* Margaret –.

WILDER, Thomas (ca. 1618-1667), from Eng., was at Charlestown, Mass., 1638; freeman, 1641; settled at Lancaster, 1659; selectman; *m* 1641, Anna Eames (*d* 1692).

WILKINSON, Lawrence (*d* 1692), cavalier, officer in army of Charles I; came to Providence, R.I., 1645; dep. R.I. Assembly; *m* ca. 1649, Susannah (*d* 1692), dau. of Christopher Smith, of R.I.

WILLARD, Simon (1605-76), from Eng. to Cambridge, Mass., 1634; removed to Concord, 1635, thence to Lancaster, 1657; dep. Gen. Ct., 1636-54; gov.'s asst., 1654-76; lt., 1637; capt., 1646; maj., 1655; cdr.-in-chief of expdn. against Minigret, 1655; mayor of Middlesex, 1655-76; cdr. Middlesex regt. in King Philip's War; was given 1,000 acres of land by the govt.; *m* in Eng., Mary (bap. 1614-ca. 1650), dau. Henry Sharpe; *m* 2d, Elizabeth Dunster; *m* 3d, Mary Dunster.

WILLET (Willett), Thomas (1610/11-1674), from Eng. to Plymouth, Mass., 1632; settled at Swansea, Mass.; capt. Plymouth colonial militia, 1648; mem. Council of War, 1653; Gen. Council, 1672; served in expdn. which captured New Amsterdam from the Dutch, 1664, and became the first English mayor of New York; returned to Swansea, where he died.

WILLETT, Thomas (1621-1646/47), from Bristol, Eng., to L.I.; *m* 1643, in New Amsterdam, Sara, dau. of Thomas Cornell (qv).

WILLIAMS, Gov. Francis (1602-48), from Eng. or Wales, settled at Laconia, now N.H., 1631; first colonial gov. of N.H.; *m* Mary –.

WILLIAMS, George, from Wales to Phila., Pa., ca. 1690; shortly after removed to Prince George's Co., Md.

WILLIAMS, James (*d* 1735), from England to Fredericksburg, Va., ca. 1726; *m* Ann Johnson.

WILLIAMS, Richard (*b* 1599), *b* in Wales; came to Salem, Mass., 1633; a founder of Taunton, Mass., 1637; rep. Gen. Ct., 1646-48, 50.

WILLIAMS, Richard (1606-93), from Eng. 1636; settled at Dorchester; founder of Taunton, Mass., called "Father of Taunton"; freeman, 1639; mem. Gen. Ct., 1640-60; one of original purchasers of "North Purchase"; *m* 1632, Frances (1611-1706), dau. John Dighton, *m* Jane Bassett.

WILLIAMS, Robert (1607-93; son of Stephen of Great Yarmouth); was freeman and alderman of Norwich, Eng.; came to Roxbury, Mass., June, 1637; freeman, 1638; selectman; trustee Roxbury school; mem. A. and H. A. Co.; *m* in Eng., Elisabeth (1597-1674), dau. of John Stalham, jurat, *m* Alice Gibson; *m* 2d, 1675, Margaret (*d* 1690), widow of John Fearing (qv).

WILLIAMS, Roger (1599-1683), grad. Oxford or Cambridge Univ.; ordained a minister of the Church of Eng.; came from Eng. in the "Lyon," to Boston, Mass., 1631; teacher of the church at Salem, 1631; asst. at Plymouth, 1631-33; again at Salem, 1633-35; banished from the colony and founded R.I. and Providence Plantations, 1636; secured a charter for the colony in Eng., 1644; gov. of the Plantations, 1654-56, later gov.'s asst. and dep.; *m* Mary Barnard.

WILLISTON, Joseph (1667-1747); was at Westfield, and Springfield, Mass.; *m* Mary (*d* 1711), dau. of Joseph Parsons and widow of Joseph Ashley; *m* 2d, 1714, Sarah –, widow of Thomas Stebbins.

WINCHESTER, John (1616-94), from Eng. in the "Elizabeth," to Boston, Mass., 1635; removed to Hingham, 1636; freeman, 1637; removed to Boston after 1650; mem. A. and H. A. Co.; *m* 1638, Hannah, dau. Dea. Richard Sealis, of Scituate.

WING, Daniel (will dated May 3, 1659, *d* 1664; son of Rev. John, qv); from Eng. with his mother, in the "William and Francis," 1632; *d* at Sandwich, Mass.; *m* 1641, Hannah, dau. of William or John Swift.

WING, Rev. John (1584-1630; son of Mathew, of Banbury, Oxford); entered Oxford Coll., 1599; grad. Queen's Coll., 1604; preached at Flushing and Middlebury, Holland; *d* at London; *m* 1609/10, Deborah Batchellor (*b* ca. 1592; dau. of Rev. Stephen Batchelder, qv), who with four sons came in the "William and Francis," to Lynn, Mass., 1632, settled at Sandwich, 1637.

WINSHIP (Winshope, Windship), Edward (1612/13-1688), from Eng. in the "Defense," to Newtown, Mass., 1634; freeman, 1635; selectman many yrs.; rep. Gen. Ct., 1663, et seq.; mem. A. and H. A. Co.; *m* Jane –; *m* 2d, Elizabeth –.

WINSLOW, Edward (1595-1655), 3d signer of the Mayflower Compact; 3d gov. of the Colony, 1633, 36, 44; commr. United Colonies, 1643; *m* 1st, at Leyden, Holland, 1618, Elizabeth Barker (*d* in 1621); *m* 2d, at Plymouth, Mass., 1621, Susanna (Fuller) White, widow of William White.

WINSLOW, John (1597-1674; brother of Gov. Edward, qv); from Eng. to Plymouth, Mass., 1623; mem. Council of War, 1646; rep. Gen. Court, 1653-55; removed to Boston, 1657, and was a mcht. there; freeman, 1672; *m* 1627, Mary (Mayflower Pilgrim), dau. James Chilton.

WINSLOW, Kenelm (bap. 1599-1672; brother of Gov. Edward, qv), from England to Plymouth, Mass., 1629; admitted freeman, 1632; surveyor, town of Plymouth; original propr. of Assonet (Freetown), 1659; rep. Gen. Ct., 1642, et seq.; engaged in settlement of Yarmouth and other towns; mem. Marshfield mil. company; *m* 1634, Ellen (Newton) Adams (1598-1681), widow of John Adams (qv).

WINSOR (Windsor), Joshua, from Eng., was at Providence, R.I., 1638; an original purchaser of that town, with Roger Williams.

WINTHROP, John (1588-1649), elected gov. of the Mass. Company, 1629; leader of a fleet which arrived at Salem, Mass., 1630; served as gov. 1630-34, 1637-40, 1642, 1646-49, first pres. United Colonies of N.E., 1643; *m* at 17, in Eng., Mary Forth (*d* 1616); *m* 2d, Thomasine Clopton (*d* shortly); *m* 3d, 1618, Margaret (*d* 1647), dau. Sir John Tyndal; *m* 4th, 1648, Martha (Norwell) Coytmore, widow of Thomas Coytmore.

WISNER, Johannes (1676-1744), from Eng., 1714, settled on the Wawayanda Patent, Orange Co., N.Y.; *m* 1697, Elizabeth Dumbaugh.

WITHINGTON, Henry (1589/90-1666/67), from Eng., probably in the "James," to Dorchester, Mass., ca. 1636; one of the 6 founders of the ch. there; selectman, 1636; never a freeman; *m* 1st, Anne Leech (*d* 1621); *m* in Eng., Elizabeth Smith (*d* 1661); *m* 2d, 1662, Margaret, wid. of Richard Paul.

WITTER, William (ca. 1584-1659), from Eng., 1629, settled at Lynn, Mass.; later purchased for two pestle stones, from Poquonnum, the Indian Sagamore, all the land now occupied by Swampscott, Sagamore Hill and Nahant, Mass.; active religious worker; *m* Annis –.

WOLCOTT, Henry (1578-1655), from Eng. in the "Mary and John," to Dorchester, Mass., 1630; brought with him a commn. from the crown as justice; freeman, 1634; a founder of Dorchester, and of Windsor, Conn., 1635; constable, 1636; dep. Gen. Ct., 1639; gov.'s asst., 1643-55; *m* in Eng., 1606, Elizabeth (*d* 1655), dau. Thomas Saunders.

WOOD, Henry (1594-1670), from Eng. to Plymouth, Mass.; was with Pilgrims in Leyden, Holland; at Falmouth and Middleboro, Mass.; *m* 1644, Abigail (1619 in Leyden, Holland-1690), dau. of John Jenney (*d* 1644), gov.'s asst., 1637, 1640, dep., 1641-43; *m* Sarah Carey (*d* 1655).

WOODBRIDGE, John (1613-95), from Eng. in the "Mary and John," 1635, settled at Newbury, Mass.; a founder of Andover; returned to Eng., 1647, but came again, 1663, settling at Boston; gov.'s asst., 1683, 84; mem. A. and H. A. Co.; *m* 1639, Mercy, dau. of Gov. Thomas Dudley (qv).

WOODFORD, Thomas (*d* 1667), from Eng. in the "Francis and Mary," to Cambridge and Roxbury, Mass., 1632; settled at Hartford, Conn.; *m* Mary, dau. of Robert Blott.

WOODRUFF, John (1604-70; son of John, of Fordwich, Eng., *m* Elizabeth Cartwright; g.son of Robert; g.g.son of William; g.g.g.son of Thomas Woodrove); came to Lynn, Mass., with his mother and stepfather, John Gosmer; thence to Southampton, L.I., 1640-41, where he was church warden; *m* Anne –.

WOODRUFF (Woodrove, Woodroffe), Matthew (1612-82; son of Sir David), from England, ca. 1640; settled at Hartford, Conn.; at Farmington, Conn., 1640/41; freeman, 1657; *m* Hannah –.

WOODS, Michael (*b* Ulster, Ireland, 1684-*d* 1762; son of John Woods, *b* Scotland, 1654, *m* Elizabeth Warsup, and desc. Adam Loftus [*b* 1534], archbishop of Dublin and lord chancellor of Ireland); migrated to Pa., 1725, then to Va., 1732, settled in Albemarle Co., 1734; founded the estate in after years known as "Blair Park"; *m* Lady Mary Campbell (*d* 1762).

WOODS (Wood), Samuel (1686-1763), from Eng. to Chelmsford, Mass., ca. 1700; *m* 1717, Mary Parker.

WOODSON, Dr. John (1586-1644), grad. St. John's Coll., Oxford, 1604; came in the "George," 1619, as surgeon to a co. of soldiers, and settled at Fleur de Hundred, on the James River; killed in Indian massacre; *m* Sarah Winston.

WOODWARD, Nathaniel (*d* after 1673), from Eng. to Boston, 1630; mathematician and surveyor; ran the line between Plymouth colony and Mass., 1638, also between Mass. and Conn.; was sent to the Merrimac survey; *m* Margaret Jackson.

WOODWARD, Richard (1590-1665), from Eng. in the "Elizabeth," to Watertown, Mass., 1634; freeman, 1635; *m* in Eng., Rose – (*d* 1662); *m* 2d, 1663, Ann –, widow of Stephen Gates, of Cambridge.

WOOLSEY, Joris, or George (1610-98), from Eng. to New Amsterdam, 1623; later at Plymouth, Mass.; at Flushing, L.I., 1647; cadet Burgher Corps; *m* Rebecca, dau. of Thomas Cornell.

WORCESTER, William, from Eng. to Salisbury, Mass., ca. 1639; served in ministry in Eng.; the first minister at Salisbury; freeman, 1640; *m* in Eng., Sarah – (*d* 1650); *m* 2d, 1650, Rebecca Cornell, widow of John Hall (she had also been widow of Henry Byley).

WORTHINGTON, Capt. John (1650-1701; son of John, of Jesus Coll., Cambridge, Eng.); came to America with his brother, Samuel; was in Md., 1670; capt. Anne Arundel Co. militia; burgess; judge Provincial Ct.; mem. Quorum; *m* Sarah, dau. of Matthew Howard.

WURTS (Wirtz), Johannes Conrad (1706-63), from Switzerland, 1735; clergyman in several of the colonies, settled at York, Pa., 1762; *m* Anna Goetchius.

WYATT, Rev. Hawte (1594-1638; brother of Sir Francis, gov. of Va.), came to Va. with wife and children, 1621; returned to Eng., 1625; *m* Elizabeth – (*d* 1626); *m* 2d, Ann – (*d* 1631).

WYCKOFF, Pieter Claessen (1615-95; son of Claes Cornelissen), presumed to have come with his father, from the Netherlands, 1636; had a farm near Albany until about 1649; del. from Flatlands to conv. held at New Amsterdam, 1664; magistrate, Amesfoort, 1655, 1662-63; removed to New Amsterdam where he was magistrate and patentee in charters, 1667 and 1686; adopted the name Wyckoff (derived from Dutch words "refuge" and "city"); *m* 1649, Gretien, dau. of Cornelis Hendrickson van Nes (1600-81), from Holland, 1642, Indian commr., Ft. Orange, 1665-66, capt., *m* 1625, Maykee Burghgraef.

WYLLYS, George (1589/90-1645), from Eng., 1638, settled at Hartford, Conn.; trooper in Pequot War; gov.'s asst., 1639; gov. Colony of Conn., 1641-42; *m* Bridget Young (*d* 1629); *m* 2d, Mary Smith.

WYMAN, Francis (bap. 1619-*d* 1699, aet. 82; son of Francis, of West Mill, Co. Herts., Eng., *m* Elizabeth Richardson), came to Charlestown, Mass., 1635; an original settler of Woburn, 1642; *m* 2d, 1650, Abigail, dau. of William Read, from Eng. in the "Defense," 1635, *m* Mabel –.

WYNNE, Dr. Thomas (ca. 1630-1692), physician to William Penn and came with him in the "Welcome," 1682; leader of the Welsh group which purchased the "Welsh Tract," nr. Phila., Pa.; was speaker of the Assembly; judge Provincial Supreme Ct.; author; *m* ca. 1655, Martha Buttall; *m* 2d, Elizabeth Rowden, widow.

YALE, Capt. Thomas (1616-83; son of Thomas Yale [*d* 1619], *m* Anne, dau. of George Lloyd, bishop of Chester, Eng.), came to Boston, Mass., 1637; settled at New Haven, Conn., 1638; *m* 1645, Mary (*d* 1704), dau. of Capt. Nathaniel Turner, of New Haven (their 3d son, Elihu, founded Yale Coll.).

YARDLEY, Thomas, from Eng. to Pa., 1704; mem. Pa. Assembly, 1715, 22; *m* 1706, Ann (*b* 1685), dau. William Biles.

YEAMANS, Sir John (ca. 1605-1674; son of Robert, high sheriff of Bristow and gov. of Isle of Wight); knighted by King Charles II, 1661; high sheriff of Bristow; gov. Isle of Wight; from Eng., to Barbados, 1655; apptd. gov. of Barbados; founded Clarendon Colony, Carolinas, 1665; apptd. landgrave and gov. of Carolinas, 1672; *m* Margaret Foster.

YEARDLEY, Sir George (1577-1627), dep. gov. of Va., 1616-17; gov. and captain general, 1618-26; *m* 1618, Temperance West.

YORK, James (1614-83), from Eng. in the "Philip," 1635, to Stonington, Conn.; *m* Joannah –.

YOUNG (Yonges), Rev. John (1598-1671; son of Rev. Christopher Yonges, Vicar of Reydon and Southwold, Eng.); came to Salem, Mass., in the "Mary Anne," 1637; founder of Southold, L.I., 1640, and first pastor Presbyn. Ch.; *m* 1622, Joan Herrington (*d* 1630); *m* 2d, Joan Harris; *m* 3d, 1639, Mary Warren Gardner (*d* 1678).

ALPHABETICAL INDEX

ALPHABETICAL INDEX OF NAMES IN VOLUME IV

Since the "heart" of any genealogical work is its alphabetical index of names, and since one of the chief purposes of this work is to index America genealogically, the following alphabetical index of names in this volume refers also to the surnames which appear frequently in Volumes I, II and III of this work. But many additional thousands of surnames, which appear in the earlier volumes only once or only occasionally, are not included in this index; therefore, if the name sought for is not listed in this index it may be found in the earlier volumes, which should also be consulted.

The name of every man mentioned in the lineages in the preceding pages is listed in alphabetical order in this index. Women have been omitted from the index because their inclusion would double the number of names without any appreciable advantage, because it is only in rare instances that a genealogical investigator does not know the name of the father or husband of the woman whose name he is seeking, and the names of the father and husband are listed in the index when known.

However, women who are the subjects of the lineage records are listed in the index in **bold face** type under their maiden names or, if married, under their married names. The husbands and fathers of these women are also listed in proper alphabetical order.

Names in **bold face** *type indicate the subjects of preceding records, and numbers in* **bold face** *type indicate the page on which the record appears.*

The **bold face** type numbers following the names of immigrant ancestors in the index, refer to the pages on which their biographical records appear (pages 727-777); other page numbers refer to lineage records.

A

B

F

H

I

J

K

L

M

N

O

P

Q

R

T

Y